CW00584901

# The Form Book ®

# FLAT ANNUAL FOR 2015

## THE OFFICIAL FORM BOOK

### ALL THE 2014 RETURNS

Complete record of Flat Racing
from 1 January to 31 December 2014

Raceform

## Associated Raceform products

The Form Book is updated weekly. Subscribers receive a binder, together with all the early racing. Weekly sections and a new index are threaded into the binder to keep it up to date.

The data contained in *The Form Book Flat Annual for 2015* is available in paper form or on computer disk. The disk serice, Raceform Interactive, contains the same data as The Flat Form Book, and operates on any PC within a 'Windows' environment. The database is designed to allow access to the information in a number of different ways, and is extremely quick and easy to use.

Published in 2015 by Raceform Ltd
27 Kingfisher Court, Hambridge Road, Newbury, Berkshire RG14 5SJ



A catalogue record for this book is available from the British Library

ISBN 978-1-909471-83-2

Printed in the UK by CPI William Clowes Beccles NR34 7TL

Full details of all Raceform services and publications are available from:

Raceform Ltd, Sanders Road, Wellingborough, Northants NN8 4BX
Tel: 01933 304858 • Fax: 01933 304796
Email: shop@racingpost.com
www.racingpost.com

*Cover picture*: Kingman (James Doyle, right) beats Toronado and Darwin to win the Sussex Stakes at Glorious Goodwood

# CONTENTS

Key to Racereaders' initials ........................................ iii
Weight for Age scale.................................................. iv
Introduction.............................................................. v
Abbreviations and their meanings ........................... vii
Racing Post Ratings .................................................. ix
Course descriptions.................................................... x
2014 Turf and All-Weather racing ................................ 1
Index to Horses ...................................................... 1283
Index to Meetings ................................................... 1397
Statistics (trainers/jockeys/owners/sires) ............. 1398
Raceform Median Times......................................... 1402
Split Second Speed Ratings .................................. 1407

Editor: Graham Dench

# Key to racereaders' initials

| | | |
|---|---|---|
| WG .................... Walter Glynn | JN ............ Jonathan Neesom | JR .................... Joe Rowntree |
| RL............... Richard Lowther | DO ................... Darren Owen | AS.................. Andrew Sheret |
| LM.................... Lee McKenzie | SP...................... Steve Payne | ST...................... Steve Taylor |
| TM ..................... Tim Mitchell | CR ................... Colin Roberts | RY.................. Richard Young |

# The Official Scale of Weight, Age & Distance (Flat)

The following scale should only be used in conjunction with the Official ratings published in this book. Use of any other scale will introduce errors into calculations. The allowances are expressed as the number of pounds that is deemed the average horse in each group falls short of maturity at different dates and distances.

| Dist | | Jan | | Feb | | Mar | | Apr | | May | | Jun | | Jul | | Aug | | Sep | | Oct | | Nov | | Dec | |
|---|---|---|---|---|---|---|---|---|---|---|---|---|---|---|---|---|---|---|---|---|---|---|---|---|---|
| (fur) | Age | 1-15 | 16-31 | 1-14 | 15-28 | 1-15 | 16-31 | 1-15 | 16-30 | 1-15 | 16-31 | 1-15 | 16-30 | 1-15 | 16-31 | 1-15 | 16-31 | 1-15 | 16-30 | 1-15 | 16-31 | 1-15 | 16-30 | 1-15 | 16-31 |
| 5 | 2 | - | - | - | - | - | 47 | 44 | 41 | 38 | 36 | 34 | 32 | 30 | 28 | 26 | 24 | 22 | 20 | 19 | 18 | 17 | 17 | 16 | 16 |
| | 3 | 15 | 15 | 14 | 14 | 13 | 12 | 11 | 10 | 9 | 8 | 7 | 6 | 5 | 4 | 3 | 2 | 1 | 1 | - | - | - | - | - | - |
| 6 | 2 | - | - | - | - | - | - | - | - | 44 | 41 | 38 | 36 | 33 | 31 | 28 | 26 | 24 | 22 | 21 | 20 | 19 | 18 | 17 | 17 |
| | 3 | 16 | 16 | 15 | 15 | 14 | 13 | 12 | 11 | 10 | 9 | 8 | 7 | 6 | 5 | 4 | 3 | 2 | 2 | 1 | 1 | - | - | - | - |
| 7 | 2 | - | - | - | - | - | - | - | - | - | - | - | - | 38 | 35 | 32 | 30 | 27 | 25 | 23 | 22 | 21 | 20 | 19 | 19 |
| | 3 | 18 | 18 | 17 | 17 | 16 | 15 | 14 | 13 | 12 | 11 | 10 | 9 | 8 | 7 | 6 | 5 | 4 | 3 | 2 | 2 | 1 | 1 | - | - |
| 8 | 2 | - | - | - | - | - | - | - | - | - | - | - | - | - | - | 37 | 34 | 31 | 28 | 26 | 24 | 23 | 22 | 21 | 20 |
| | 3 | 20 | 20 | 19 | 19 | 18 | 17 | 15 | 14 | 13 | 12 | 11 | 10 | 9 | 8 | 7 | 6 | 5 | 4 | 3 | 3 | 2 | 2 | 1 | 1 |
| 9 | 3 | 22 | 22 | 21 | 21 | 20 | 19 | 17 | 15 | 14 | 13 | 12 | 11 | 10 | 9 | 8 | 7 | 6 | 5 | 4 | 4 | 3 | 3 | 2 | 2 |
| | 4 | 1 | 1 | - | - | - | - | - | - | - | - | - | - | - | - | - | - | - | - | - | - | - | - | - | - |
| 10 | 3 | 23 | 23 | 22 | 22 | 21 | 20 | 19 | 17 | 15 | 14 | 13 | 12 | 11 | 10 | 9 | 8 | 7 | 6 | 5 | 5 | 4 | 4 | 3 | 3 |
| | 4 | 2 | 2 | 1 | 1 | - | - | - | - | - | - | - | - | - | - | - | - | - | - | - | - | - | - | - | - |
| 11 | 3 | 24 | 24 | 23 | 23 | 22 | 21 | 20 | 19 | 17 | 15 | 14 | 13 | 12 | 11 | 10 | 9 | 8 | 7 | 6 | 6 | 5 | 5 | 4 | 4 |
| | 4 | 3 | 3 | 2 | 2 | 1 | 1 | - | - | - | - | - | - | - | - | - | - | - | - | - | - | - | - | - | - |
| 12 | 3 | 25 | 25 | 24 | 24 | 23 | 22 | 21 | 20 | 19 | 17 | 15 | 14 | 13 | 12 | 11 | 10 | 9 | 8 | 7 | 7 | 6 | 6 | 5 | 5 |
| | 4 | 4 | 4 | 3 | 3 | 2 | 2 | 1 | 1 | - | - | - | - | - | - | - | - | - | - | - | - | - | - | - | - |
| 13 | 3 | 26 | 26 | 25 | 25 | 24 | 23 | 22 | 21 | 20 | 19 | 17 | 15 | 14 | 13 | 12 | 11 | 10 | 9 | 8 | 8 | 7 | 7 | 6 | 6 |
| | 4 | 5 | 5 | 4 | 4 | 3 | 3 | 2 | 1 | - | - | - | - | - | - | - | - | - | - | - | - | - | - | - | - |
| 14 | 3 | 27 | 27 | 26 | 26 | 25 | 24 | 23 | 22 | 21 | 20 | 19 | 17 | 15 | 14 | 13 | 12 | 11 | 10 | 9 | 9 | 8 | 8 | 7 | 7 |
| | 4 | 6 | 6 | 5 | 5 | 4 | 4 | 3 | 2 | 1 | - | - | - | - | - | - | - | - | - | - | - | - | - | - | - |
| 15 | 3 | 28 | 28 | 27 | 27 | 26 | 25 | 24 | 23 | 22 | 21 | 20 | 19 | 17 | 15 | 14 | 13 | 12 | 11 | 10 | 9 | 8 | 8 | 7 | 7 |
| | 4 | 6 | 6 | 5 | 5 | 4 | 4 | 3 | 3 | 2 | 1 | - | - | - | - | - | - | - | - | - | - | - | - | - | - |
| 16 | 3 | 29 | 29 | 28 | 28 | 27 | 26 | 25 | 24 | 23 | 22 | 21 | 20 | 19 | 17 | 15 | 14 | 13 | 12 | 11 | 10 | 9 | 9 | 8 | 8 |
| | 4 | 7 | 7 | 6 | 6 | 5 | 5 | 4 | 4 | 3 | 2 | 1 | - | - | - | - | - | - | - | - | - | - | - | - | - |
| 18 | 3 | 31 | 31 | 30 | 30 | 29 | 28 | 27 | 26 | 25 | 24 | 23 | 22 | 21 | 20 | 18 | 16 | 14 | 13 | 12 | 11 | 10 | 10 | 9 | 9 |
| | 4 | 8 | 8 | 7 | 7 | 6 | 6 | 5 | 5 | 4 | 3 | 2 | 1 | - | - | - | - | - | - | - | - | - | - | - | - |
| 20 | 3 | 33 | 33 | 32 | 32 | 31 | 30 | 29 | 28 | 27 | 26 | 25 | 24 | 23 | 22 | 20 | 18 | 16 | 14 | 13 | 12 | 11 | 11 | 10 | 10 |
| | 4 | 9 | 9 | 8 | 8 | 7 | 7 | 6 | 6 | 5 | 4 | 3 | 2 | 1 | - | - | - | - | - | - | - | - | - | - | - |

# The Form Book

Welcome to the *The Form Book Flat Annual for 2015,* comprising the complete year's Flat results for 2014.

Race details contain Racing Post Ratings assessing the merit of each individual performance, speed figures for every horse that clocks a worthwhile time, weight-for-age allowances, stall positions for every race and the starting price percentage, in addition to the traditional features.

Race Focus comments are printed below most races, along with the results of stewards' enquiries.

# The official record

**THE FORM BOOK** records comprehensive race details of every domestic race, every major European Group race and every foreign event in which a British-trained runner participated.

**MEETING BACK REFERENCE NUMBER** is the Raceform number of the last meeting run at the track and is shown to the left of the course name. Abandoned meetings are signified by a dagger.

**THE GOING**, The Official going, shown at the head of each meeting, is recorded as follows: Turf: Hard; Firm; Good to firm; Good; Good to soft; Soft; Heavy. All-Weather: Fast; Standard to fast; Standard; Standard to slow; Slow. There may be variations for non-British meetings

Where appropriate, a note is included indicating track bias and any differences to the official going indicated by race times.

**THE WEATHER** is shown below the date for selected meetings.

**THE WIND** is given as a strength and direction at the Winning Post, classified as follows:
Strength: gale; v.str; str; fresh; mod; slt; almost nil; nil.
Direction: (half) against; (half) bhd; (half) across from or towards stands.

**VISIBILITY** is good unless otherwise stated.

**RACE NUMBERS** for foreign races carry the suffix 'a' in the race header and in the index.

**RACE TITLE** is the name of the race as shown in the Racing Calendar.

**COMPETITIVE RACING CLASSIFICATIONS** are shown on a scale from Class 1 to Class 7. All Pattern races are Class 1.

**THE RACE DISTANCE** is given for all races, and is accompanied by (s) for races run on straight courses and (r) for courses where there is a round track of comparable distance. On All-Weather courses (F) for Fibresand or (P) for Polytrack indicates the nature of the artificial surface on which the race is run.

**OFFICIAL RACE TIME** as published in the Racing Calendar is followed in parentheses by the time when the race actually started. This is followed by the race class, age restrictions, handicap restrictions and the official rating of the top weight.

**PRIZE MONEY** shows penalty values down to sixth place (where applicable).

**THE POSITION OF THE STARTING STALLS** is shown against each race, in the form of: High (H), Centre (C) or Low (L). In keeping with all other major racing nations, stalls are now numbered from the inside rail. If the stalls are placed adjacent to the inside rail they are described as low, if against the outside rail they are described as high. Otherwise they are central.

**IN THE RACE RESULT**, the figures to the far left of each horse (under FORM) show the most recent form figures. The figure in bold is the finishing position in this race as detailed below.

**1...40** - finishing positions first to fortieth; **b** - brought down; **c** - carried out; **f** - fell; **p** - pulled up; **r** - refused; **ro** - ran out; **s** - slipped up; **u** - unseated rider; **v** - void race.

**THE OFFICIAL DISTANCES** between the horses are shown on the left-hand side immediately after their position at the finish.

**NUMBER OF DAYS SINCE PREVIOUS RUN** is the superscript figure immediately following the horse name and suffix.

**PREVIOUS RACEFORM RACE NUMBER** is the boxed figure to the right of the horse's name.

**THE HORSE'S AGE** is shown immediately before the weight carried.

**WEIGHTS** shown are actual weights carried.

**OFFICIAL RATING** is the figure in bold type directly after the horse's name in the race result. This figure indicates the Official BHA rating, at entry, after the following adjustments had been made:
(i) Overweight carried by the rider.
(ii) The number of pounds out of the handicap (if applicable).
(iii) Penalties incurred after the publication of the weights.
However, no adjustments have been made for:
(i) Weight-for-age.
(ii) Riders' claims.

**HEADGEAR** is shown immediately before the jockey's name and in parentheses and expressed as: **b** (blinkers); **v** (visor); **h** (hood); **e** (eyeshield); **c** (eyecover); **p** (sheepskin cheekpieces); **t** (tongue-tie).

**THE JOCKEY** is shown for every runner followed, in superscript, by apprentice allowances in parentheses.

**APPRENTICE ALLOWANCES** The holders of apprentice jockeys' licences under the provisions of Rule 60(iii) are permitted to claim the following allowances in Flat races:
7lb until they have won 20 Flat races run under the Rules of any recognised Turf Authority; thereafter 5lb until they have won 50 such Flat races; thereafter 3lb until they have won 95 such Flat races. These allowances can be claimed in the Flat races set out below, with the exception of races confined to apprentice jockeys:
(a) All handicaps other than those Rated stakes which are classified as listed races.
(b) All selling and claiming races.
(b) All weight-for-age races classified 3, 4, 5, 6 and 7.

**THE DRAW** for places at the start is shown after each jockey's name.

**RACING POST RATINGS**, which record the level of performance attained in this race for each horse, appear in the end column after each horse. These are the work of handicappers Simon Turner, Sam Walker and Paul Curtis, who head a dedicated team dealing with Flat races for Raceform and sister publication, the *Racing Post*.

**THE TRAINER** is shown for every runner.

**COMMENT-IN-RUNNING** is shown for each horse in an abbreviated form. Details of abbreviations appear later in this section.

**STARTING PRICES** appear below the jockey in the race result. The favourite indicator appears to the right of the Starting Price;
1 for the favourite, 2 for the second-favourite and 3 for third-favourite. Joint favourites share the same number.

**RACE TIMES** in Great Britain are official times which are electronically recorded and shown to 100th of a second. Figures in parentheses following the time show the number of seconds faster or slower than the Raceform Median Time for the course and distance.

**RACEFORM MEDIAN TIMES** are compiled from all races run over the course and distance in the preceding five years. Times equal to the median are shown as (0.00). Times under the median are preceded by minus, for instance, 1.8 seconds under the median would be shown (-1.8). Record times are displayed either referring to the juvenile record (2y crse rec) or to the overall record (course record).

**TRACK VARIANT** appears against each race to allow for changing conditions of the track and ground. It is shown to a hundredth of a second and indicates the adjustment per furlong against the median time. The going based on the going correction is shown in parentheses and is recorded in the following stages:
Turf: HD (Hard); F (Firm); GF (Good to firm); G (Good); GS (Good to soft); S (Soft); HVY (Heavy). All-Weather: FST (Fast); SF (Standard to fast); STD (Standard); SS (Standard to slow); SLW (Slow)

**WEIGHT-FOR-AGE** allowances are given where applicable for mixed-age races.

**STARTING PRICE PERCENTAGE** follows the going correction and weight-for-age details, and gives the total SP percentage of all runners that competed. It precedes the number of runners taking part in the race.

**SELLING DETAILS** (where applicable) and details of any claim are given. Friendly claims are not detailed.

**SPEED RATINGS** appear below the race time and going correction. They are the work of time expert Dave Bellingham and differ from conventional ratings systems in that they are an expression of a horse's ability in terms of lengths-per-mile, as opposed to pounds in weight. They are not directly comparable with BHA and Racing Post Ratings.

The ratings take no account of the effect of weight, either historically or on the day, and this component is left completely to the user's discretion. What is shown is a speed rating represented in its purest form, rather than one that has been altered for weight using a mathematical formula that treats all types of horses as if they were the same.

A comparison of the rating achieved with the 'par' figure for the grade of race - the rating that should be achievable by an average winner in that class of race - will both provide an at-a-glance indication of whether or not a race was truly run and also highlight the value of the form from a time perspective.
In theory, if a horse has a best speed figure five points superior to another and both run to their best form in a race over a mile, the first horse should beat the second by five lengths. In a race run over two miles, the margin should be ten lengths and so on.

Before the speed figures can be calculated, it is necessary to establish a set of standard or median times for every distance at every track, and this is done by averaging the times of all winners over a particular trip going back several years. No speed ratings are produced when insufficient races have been run over a distance for a reliable median time to be calculated.

Once a meeting has taken place, a raw unadjusted speed rating is calculated for each winner by calculating how many lengths per mile the winning time was faster or slower than the median for the trip. A difference of 0.2 of a second equals one length. The raw speed ratings of all winners on the card are then compared with the 'par' figure for the class of race. The difference between the 'raw' speed rating and the 'par' figure for each race is then noted, and both the fastest and slowest races are discarded before the rest are averaged to produce the going allowance or track variant. This figure gives an idea as to how much the elements, of which the going is one, have affected the final times of each race.

The figure representing the going allowance is then used to adjust the raw speed figures and produce the final ratings, which represent how fast the winners would have run on a perfectly good surface with no external influences, including the weather. The ratings for beaten horses are worked out by taking the number of lengths they were behind the winner, adjusting that to take into account the distance of the race, and deducting that figure from the winner's rating. The reader is left with a rating which provides an instant impression of the value of a time performance.

The speed 'pars' below act as benchmark with which to compare the speed figures earned by each horse in each race. A horse that has already exceeded the 'par' for the class he is about to run in is of special interest, especially if he has done it more than once, as are horses that have consistently earned higher figures than their rivals.

| | |
|---|---|
| Class 1 Group One | 117 |
| Class 1 Group Two | 115 |
| Class 1 Group Three | 113 |
| Class 1 Listed | 111 |
| Class 2 | 109 |
| Class 3 | 107 |
| Class 4 | 105 |
| Class 5 | 103 |
| Class 6 | 101 |
| Class 7 | 99 |

Allowances need to be made for younger horses and for fillies. These allowances are as follows.

| MONTH | 2yo | 3yo |
|---|---|---|
| Jan / Feb | n/a | -6 |
| Mar / Apr | -11 | -5 |
| May / Jun | -10 | -4 |
| Jul / Aug | -9 | -3 |
| Sep / Oct | -8 | -2 |
| Nov / Dec | -7 | -1 |
| Races contested by fillies only | | -3 |

Allowances are cumulative. For example, using a combination of the above pars and allowances, the par figure for the Epsom Oaks would be 110. The Group One par is 117, then deduct 4 because the race is confined to three year olds and run in June, then subtract another 3 because the race is confined to fillies.

**TOTE** prices include £1 stake. Exacta dividends are shown in parentheses. The Computer Straight Forecast dividend is preceded by the letters CSF, Computer Tricast is preceded by CT and Trifecta dividend is preceded by the word Trifecta. Jackpot, Placepot and Quadpot details appear at the end of the meeting to which they refer.

**OWNER** is followed by the breeder's name and the trainer's location.

**STEWARDS' ENQUIRIES** are included with the result, and any suspensions and/or fines incurred. Objections by jockeys and officials are included, where relevant.

**HISTORICAL FOCUS** details occasional points of historical significance.

**FOCUS** The Focus section helps readers distinguish good races from bad races and reliable form from unreliable form, by drawing together the opinions of handicapper, time expert and paddock watcher and interpreting their views in a punter-friendly manner.

# Abbreviations and their meanings

## *Paddock comments*

gd sort - well made, above average on looks
attr - attractive, but not as impressive as good sort
gd bodied - good bodied, well put together
h.d.w - has done well, improved in looks
wl grwn - well grown, has filled to its frame
lengthy - longer than average for its height
tall - tall
rangy - lengthy and tall but in proportion.
cl cpld - close coupled
scope - scope for physical development
str - strong, powerful looking
w'like - workmanlike, ordinary in looks
lt-f - light-framed, not much substance
cmpt - compact
neat - smallish, well put together
leggy - long legs compared with body
angular - unfurnished behind the saddle, not filled to frame
unf - unfurnished in the midriff, not filled to frame
narrow - not as wide as side appearance would suggest
small - lacks any physical scope
nt grwn - not grown
lw - looked fit and well
bkwd - backward in condition
t - tubed
swtg - sweating
b (off fore or nr fore) - bandaged in front
b.hind (off or nr) - bandaged behind

## *At the start*

stdd s - jockey purposely reins back the horse
dwlt - missed the break and left for a short time
s.s - slow to start, left longer than a horse that dwelt
s.v.s - started very slowly
s.i.s - started on terms but took time to get going
ref to r - does not jump off, or travels a few yards then stops
rel to r - tries to pull itself up in mid-race
w.r.s - whipped round start

## *Position in the race*

led - in lead on its own
disp ld - upsides the leader
w ldr - almost upsides the leader

w ldrs - in a line of three or more disputing the lead
prom - on the heels of the leaders, in front third of the field
trckd ldr(s) - just in behind the leaders giving impression that it could lead if asked
chsd ldr - horse in second place
chsd clr ldrs - horse heads main body of field behind two clear leaders
chsd ldrs - horse is in the first four or five but making more of an effort to stay close to the pace than if it were tracking the leaders.
clsd - closed
in tch - close enough to have a chance
hdwy - making ground on the leader
gd hdwy - making ground quickly on the leader, could be a deliberate move
sme hdwy - making some ground but no real impact on the race
w.w - waited with
stdy hdwy - gradually making ground
ev ch - upsides the leaders when the race starts in earnest
rr - at the back of main group but not detached
bhd - detached from the main body of runners
hld up - restrained as a deliberate tactical move
nt rcvr - lost all chance after interference, mistake etc.
wknd - stride shortened as it began to tire
lost tch - had been in the main body but a gap appeared as it tired
lost pl - remains in main body of runners but lost several positions quickly

## Riding

effrt - short-lived effort
pushed along - received urgings with hands only, jockey not using legs
rdn - received urgings from saddle, including use of whip
hrd rdn - received maximum assistance from the saddle including use of whip
drvn - received forceful urgings, jockey putting in a lot of effort and using whip
hrd drvn - jockey very animated, plenty of kicking, pushing and reminders

## Finishing comments

jst failed - closing rapidly on the winner and probably would have led a stride after the line
r.o - jockey's efforts usually involved to produce an increase in pace without finding an appreciable turn of speed
r.o wl - jockey's efforts usually involved to produce an obvious increase in pace without finding an appreciable turn of speed
unable qckn - not visibly tiring but does not possess a sufficient change of pace
one pce - not tiring but does not find a turn of speed, from a position further out than unable qckn
nt r.o. - did not consent to respond to pressure
styd on - going on well towards the end, utilising stamina
nvr able to chal - unable to produce sufficient to reach a challenging position
nvr nr to chal - in the opinion of the racereader, the horse was never in a suitable position to challenge.
nrst fin - nearer to the winner in distance beaten than at any time since the race had begun in earnest
nvr nrr - nearer to the winner position-wise than at any time since the race had begun in earnest
rallied - responded to pressure to come back with a chance having lost its place
no ex - unable to sustain its run
bttr for r - likely to improve for the run and experience
rn green - inclined to wander and falter through inexperience
too much to do - left with too much leeway to make up

## Winning comments

v.easily - a great deal in hand
easily - plenty in hand
comf - something in hand, always holding the others
pushed out - kept up to its work with hands and heels without jockey resorting to whip or kicking along and wins fairly comfortably
rdn out - pushed and kicked out to the line, with the whip employed
drvn out - pushed and kicked out to the line, with considerable effort and the whip employed
all out - nothing to spare, could not have found any more
jst hld on - holding on to a rapidly diminishing lead, could not have found any more if passed
unchal - must either make all or a majority of the running and not be challenged from an early stage

# Complete list of abbreviations

a - always
abt - about
a.p - always prominent
appr - approaching
awrdd - awarded
b.b.v - broke blood-vessel
b.d - brought down
bdly - badly
bef - before
bhd - behind
bk - back
blkd - baulked
blnd - blundered
bmpd - bumped
bnd - bend
btn- beaten
bttr - better
c - came
ch - chance
chal - challenged
chse - chase
chsd - chased
chsng - chasing
circ - circuit
cl - close
clr - clear
clsd - closed
comf - comfortably
cpld - coupled
crse - course
ct - caught
def - definite
dismntd - dismounted
disp - disputed
dist - distance
div - division
drvn - driven
dwlt - dwelt
edgd - edged
effrt - effort

ent - entering
ev ch - every chance
ex - extra
f - furlong
fin - finished
fnd - found
fnl - final
fr - from
gd - good
gng - going
gp - group
grad - gradually
grnd - ground
hd - head
hdd - headed
hdwy - headway
hld - held
hmpd - hampered
imp - impression
ins - inside
j.b - jumped badly
j.w - jumped well
jnd - joined
jst - just
kpt - kept
l - length
ld - lead
ldr - leader
lft - left
mod - moderate
m - mile
m.n.s - made no show
mde - made
mid div - mid division
mstke - mistake
n.d - never dangerous
n.g.t - not go through
n.m.r - not much room
nk - neck
no ex - no extra
nr - near
nrr - nearer
nrst fin - nearest finish
nt - not
nvr - never
one pce - one pace
out - from finish
outpcd - outpaced
p.u - pulled up
pce - pace
pckd - pecked
pl - place
plcd - placed
plld - pulled
press - pressure
prog - progress
prom - prominent
qckly - quickly
qckn - quicken
r - race
racd - raced
rch - reach
rcvr - recover
rdn - ridden
rdr - rider
reard - reared
ref - refused
rn - ran
rnd - round
r.o - ran on
rr - rear
rspnse - response
rt - right
s - start
sddle - saddle
shkn - shaken
slt - slight
sme - some
sn - soon
spd- speed
st - straight
stmbld - stumbled
stdd - steadied
stdy - steady
strly - strongly
styd - stayed
styng - staying
s. u - slipped up
swtchd - switched
swvd - swerved
tk - took
t.k.h - took keen hold
t.o - tailed off
tch - touch
thrght - throughout
trbld - troubled
trckd - tracked
u.p - under pressure
u.str.p- under strong pressure
w - with
w.r.s - whipped round start
wd - wide
whn - when
wknd - weakened
wl - well
wnr - winner
wnt - went
1/2-wy - halfway

# Racing Post Ratings

**Racing Post Ratings for each horse are shown in the right hand column, headed RPR, and indicate the actual level of performance attained in that race. The figure in the back index represents the BEST public form that Raceform's Handicappers still believe the horse capable of reproducing.**

To use the ratings constructively in determining those horses best-in in future events, the following procedure should be followed:

(i) In races where all runners are the same age and are set to carry the same weight, no calculations are necessary. The horse with the highest rating is best-in.

(ii) In races where all runners are the same age but are set to carry different weights, add one point to the Racing Post Rating for every pound less than 10 stone to be carried; deduct one point for every pound more than 10 stone.

For example,

| Horse | Age & wt | Adjustment from 10st | Base rating | Adjusted rating |
|---|---|---|---|---|
| Treclare | 3-10-1 | -1 | 78 | 77 |
| Buchan | 3-9-13 | +1 | 80 | 81 |
| Paper Money | 3-9-7 | +7 | 71 | 78 |
| Archaic | 3-8-11 | +17 | 60 | 77 |

**Therefore Buchan is top-rated (best-in)**

(iii) In races concerning horses of different ages the procedure in (ii) should again be followed, but reference must also be made to the Official Scale of Weight-For-Age.

For example,

12 furlongs, July 20th

| Horse | Age & wt | Adjustment from 10st | Base rating | Adjusted rating | W-F-A deduct | Final rating |
|---|---|---|---|---|---|---|
| Archaic | 5-10-0 | 0 | 90 | 90 | Nil | 90 |
| Orpheus | 4-9-9 | +5 | 88 | 93 | Nil | 93 |
| Lemonora | 3-9-4 | +10 | 85 | 95 | -12 | 83 |
| Tamar | 4-8-7 | +21 | 73 | 94 | Nil | 94 |

**Therefore Tamar is top-rated (best-in)**

(A 3-y-o is deemed 12lb less mature than a 4-y-o or older horse on 20th July over 12f. Therefore, the deduction of 12 points is necessary.)

The following symbols are used in conjunction with the ratings:

++: almost certain to prove better

+: likely to prove better

d: disappointing (has run well below best recently)

?: form hard to evaluate

t: tentative rating based on race-time rating may prove unreliable

**Weight adjusted ratings for every race are published daily in Raceform Private Handicap.**

**For subscription terms please contact the Subscription Department on 01933 304858.**

# Course descriptions

**(R.H.) denotes right-hand and (L.H.) left-hand courses.**

**ASCOT (R.H)**

Right-handed triangular track just under 1m 6f in length. The Round course descends from the 1m 4f start into Swinley Bottom, the lowest part of the track. It then turns right-handed and joins the Old Mile Course, which starts on a separate chute. The course then rises to the right-handed home turn over a new underpass to join the straight mile course. The run-in is about 3f, rising slightly to the winning post. The whole course is of a galloping nature with easy turns.

**AYR (L.H)**

A left-handed, galloping, flat oval track of 1m 4f with a 4f run-in. The straight 6f is essentially flat.

**BATH (L.H)**

Galloping, left-handed, level oval of 1m 4f 25y, with long, stiff run-in of about 4f which bends to the left. An extended chute provides for races over 5f 11y and 5f 161y.

**BEVERLEY (R.H)**

A right-handed oval of 1m 3f, generally galloping, with an uphill run-in of two and a half furlongs. The 5f course is very stiff.

**BRIGHTON (L.H)**

Left-handed, 1m 4f horseshoe with easy turns and a run-in of three and a half furlongs. Undulating and sharp, the track suits handy types.

**CARLISLE (R.H)**

Right-handed, 1m 4f pear-shaped track. Galloping and undulating with easy turns and a stiff uphill run-in of three and a half furlongs. 6f course begins on an extended chute.

**CATTERICK (L.H)**

A sharp, left-handed, undulating oval of 1m 180y with a downhill run-in of 3f.

**CHEPSTOW (L.H)**

A left-handed, undulating oval of about 2m, with easy turns, and a straight run-in of 5f. There is a straight track of 1m 14y.

**CHESTER (L.H)**

A level, sharp, left-handed, circular course of 1m 73y, with a short run-in of 230y. Chester is a specialists' track which generally suits the sharp-actioned horse.

**DONCASTER (L.H)**

A left-handed, flat, galloping course of 1m 7f 110y, with a long run-in which extends to a straight mile.

**EPSOM (L.H)**

Left-handed and undulating with easy turns, and a run-in of just under 4f. The straight 5f course is also undulating and downhill all the way, making it the fastest 5f in the world.

**FFOS LAS (L.H)**

The track is a 60m wide, basically flat, 1m4f oval with sweeping bends.

**GOODWOOD (R.H)**

A sharp, undulating, essentially right-handed track with a long run-in. There is also a straight 6f course.

**HAMILTON PARK (R.H)**

Sharp, undulating, right-handed course of 1m 5f with a five and a half furlong, uphill run-in. There is a straight track of 6f.

**HAYDOCK PARK (L.H)**

A galloping, almost flat, oval track, 1m 5f round, with a run-in of four and a half furlongs and a straight 6f course.

**KEMPTON PARK (R.H)**

A floodlit Polytrack circuit opened in March 2006. A 1m 2f outer track accommodates races over 6f, 7f, 1m, 1m 3f, 1m 4f and 2m. The 1m inner track caters for races over 5f and 1m 2f.

**LEICESTER (R.H)**

Stiff, galloping, right-handed oval of 1m 5f, with a 5f run-in. There is a straight course of 7f.

**LINGFIELD PARK (L.H)**

**Turf Course**: A sharp, undulating left-handed circuit, with a 7f 140y straight course.

**Polytrack course**: left-handed all-weather is 1m 2f round. It is a sharp, level track with a short run-in.

**MUSSELBURGH (R.H)**

A sharp, level, right-handed oval of 1m 2f, with a run-in of 4f. There is an additional 5f straight course.

**NEWBURY (L.H)**

Left-handed, oval track of about 1m 7f, with a slightly undulating straight mile. The round course is level and galloping with a four and a half furlong run-in. Races over the round mile and 7f 60y start on the adjoining chute.

**NEWCASTLE (L.H)**

Galloping, easy, left-handed oval of 1m 6f, with an uphill 4f run-in. There is a straight course of 1m 8y.

**NEWMARKET (R.H)**

**Rowley Mile Course**: There is a straight 1m2f course, which is wide and galloping. Races over 1m4f or more are right-handed. The Rowley course has a long run-in and a stiff finish.

**July Course**: Races up to a mile are run on the Bunbury course, which is straight. Races over 1m2f or more are right-handed, with a 7f run-in. Like the Rowley course, the July track is stiff.

**NOTTINGHAM (L.H)**

Left-handed, galloping, oval of about 1m 4f, and a run-in of four and a half furlongs. Flat with easy turns.

**PONTEFRACT (L.H)**

Left-handed oval, undulating course of 2m 133y, with a short run-in of 2f. It is a particularly stiff track with the last 3f uphill.

**REDCAR (L.H)**

Left-handed, level, galloping, oval course of 1m 6f with a straight run-in of 5f. There is also a straight 1m.

**RIPON (R.H)**

A sharp, undulating, right-handed oval of 1m 5f, with a 5f run-in. There is also a 6f straight course.

**SALISBURY (R.H)**

Right-handed and level, with a run-in of 4f. There is a straight 1m track. The last half mile is uphill, providing a stiff test of stamina.

**SANDOWN PARK (R.H)**

An easy right-handed oval course of 1m 5f with a stiff straight uphill run-in of 4f. Separate straight 5f track is also uphill. Galloping.

**SOUTHWELL (L.H)**

Left-handed oval, Fibresand course of 1m 2f with a 3f run-in. There is a straight 5f. Sharp and level, Southwell suits front-runners.

**THIRSK (L.H)**

Left-handed, oval of 1m 2f with sharp turns and an undulating run-in of 4f. There is a straight 6f track.

**WARWICK (L.H)**

Left-handed, sharp, level track of 1m 6f 32y in circumference, with a run-in of two and a half furlongs. There is also a 6f chute.

**WINDSOR (Fig. 8)**

Figure eight track of 1m 4f 110y. The course is level and sharp with a long run-in. The 6f course is essentially straight.

**WOLVERHAMPTON (L.H)**

Left-handed oval, Tapeta course of 1m, with a run-in of 380y. A level track with sharp bends.

**YARMOUTH (L.H)**

Left-handed, level circuit of 1m 4f, with a run-in of 5f. The straight course is 1m long.

**YORK (L.H)**

Left-handed, level, galloping track, with a straight 6f. There is also an adjoining chute of 7f.

# SOUTHWELL (L-H)

Wednesday, January 1

**OFFICIAL GOING: Standard**

Wind: Fresh half against Weather: Heavy cloud and rain

## 1 CORAL MOBILE "JUST THREE CLICKS TO BET" H'CAP 1m 4f (F)

**12:15** (12:17) (Class 5) (0-70,69) 4-Y-O+ **£2,911** (£866; £432; £216) **Stalls** Low

Form RPR

334- **1** **Short Shrift (IRE)**[12] 8372 4-8-12 **61** ........ TonyHamilton 4 70
(Richard Fahey) *trckd ldr: hdwy and cl up over 3f out: led wl over 2f out: rdn wl over 1f out: kpt on wl u.p fnl f* **4/1**[3]

324- **2** 2 1/4 **Royal Marskell**[14] 8337 5-9-5 **64** ........ TomEaves 3 69
(K F Clutterbuck) *trckd ldng pair: pushed along and sltly outpcd wl over 3f out: hdwy on inner wl over 2f out: rdn to chal over 1f out: edgd rt and one pce ins fnl f* **5/2**[1]

060- **3** 1/2 **Bethan**[28] 8160 5-8-13 **58** ........(p) AdamBeschizza 5 62
(Julia Feilden) *trckd ldrs: hdwy on outer over 3f out: rdn and ev ch wl over 1f out: sn drvn and one pce* **7/2**[2]

340- **4** 2 1/2 **Push Me (IRE)**[15] 7876 7-9-10 **69** ........ AdamKirby 6 69
(Iain Jardine) *hld up: hdwy over 3f out: effrt to chal 2f out: sn rdn and wknd ent fnl f* **7/2**[2]

300- **5** 8 **Perivale (USA)**[11] 8388 4-8-6 **58** ........ MichaelJMMurphy(3) 2 45
(Mark Johnston) *led: rdn along wl over 3f out: hdd wl over 2f out and sn wknd* **5/1**

2m 42.39s (1.39) **Going Correction** -0.10s/f (Stan)
**WFA** 4 from 5yo+ 4lb 5 Ran SP% **109.7**
Speed ratings (Par 103): **91,89,89,87,82**
CSF £14.15 TOTE £4.30: £1.60, £1.50; EX 13.10 Trifecta £51.10.
**Owner** R A Fahey **Bred** Floors Farming And Dominic Burke **Trained** Musley Bank, N Yorks

**FOCUS**
The five runners were light on Fibresand experience coming into this 1m4f handicap, run in wet and windy conditions. The winner stepped up on her turf form.

## 2 CORAL.CO.UK BEST ODDS GUARANTEED ON RACING CLAIMING STKS 1m 4f (F)

**12:50** (12:54) (Class 6) 4-Y-O+ **£2,264** (£673; £336; £168) **Stalls** Low

Form RPR

423- **1** **Reve De Nuit (USA)**[137] 5513 8-9-9 **94** ........ RobertWinston 5 99+
(K R Burke) *trckd ldng pair: hdwy on outer and slt ld 1/2-way: rdn clr over 2f out: styd on strly fnl f* **4/11**[1]

111- **2** 7 **Stand Guard**[264] 1513 10-9-9 **87** ........ TomQueally 3 89
(John Butler) *hld up: hdwy 4f out: chsd wnr 3f out: rdn to cl wl over 1f out: drvn and one pce ent fnl f* **11/4**[2]

160- **3** 16 **Goal (IRE)**[5] 8408 6-9-0 **75** ........(t) JackGarritty(7) 1 60
(Charles Smith) *hld up in tch: smooth hdwy on inner and cl up over 4f out: rdn along 3f out: sn outpcd* **10/1**[3]

600- **4** 14 **Inside Knowledge (USA)**[3] 8436 8-8-9 **49** ........ NataliaGemelova(3) 4 29
(Garry Woodward) *led 1 1/2f: cl up: rdn along over 4f out: sn outpcd and bhd fnl 3f* **100/1**

005- **5** 15 **Bix (IRE)**[36] 8056 4-8-10 **46** ow1 ........(b) StevieDonohoe 2
(Alan Berry) *t.k.h: cl up: led after 1 1/2f: hdd 1/2-way: sn rdn along and wknd: bhd fnl 3f* **100/1**

2m 38.01s (-2.99) **Going Correction** -0.10s/f (Stan)
**WFA** 4 from 6yo+ 4lb 5 Ran SP% **111.1**
Speed ratings (Par 101): **105,100,89,80,70**
CSF £1.70 TOTE £1.40: £1.10, £1.30; EX 2.00 Trifecta £2.20.
**Owner** Mrs Z Wentworth **Bred** Ecurie Du Haras De Meautry **Trained** Middleham Moor, N Yorks

**FOCUS**
The front pair set a high standard in this claimer and the winner was the clear form pick.

## 3 CORAL APP DOWNLOAD FROM THE APP STORE H'CAP 1m 3f (F)

**1:25** (1:27) (Class 3) (0-90,88) 4-Y-O+ **£7,762** (£2,310; £1,154; £577) **Stalls** Low

Form RPR

010- **1** **Masterful Act (USA)**[42] 7975 7-9-9 **88** ........ TomQueally 7 100
(Alan McCabe) *prom: cl up 4f out: rdn to ld 2f out: hdd and drvn ent fnl f: rallied wl to ld last 50yds* **7/2**[3]

100- **2** nk **Layl (USA)**[14] 8327 4-9-3 **85** ........ AdamKirby 3 96
(Mark Johnston) *led 1f: cl up: effrt on outer to chal wl over 2f out: rdn wl over 1f out: drvn to ld ent fnl f: sn edgd lft: hdd and no ex last 50yds* **11/4**[2]

021- **3** 1 1/2 **Returntobrecongill**[12] 8366 4-8-12 **80** ........ TomEaves 6 89
(James Given) *led after 1f: pushed along over 3f out: rdn over 2f out and sn hdd: ev ch tl drvn appr fnl f and kpt on same pce* **9/4**[1]

011- **4** 9 **St Ignatius**[13] 8353 7-9-0 **79** ........(v) RobertWinston 1 73
(Alan Bailey) *trckd ldrs: effrt over 3f out and sn rdn along: drvn over 2f out and sn one pce* **11/1**

211- **5** 11 **Magika**[19] 8276 4-8-10 **81** ........(t) RobertTart(3) 2 56
(Marco Botti) *in rr: pushed along after 2f: hdwy to chse ldrs over 4f out: rdn over 3f out: sn wknd* **6/1**

400- **6** 9 **Mica Mika (IRE)**[19] 8276 6-8-8 **80** ........ JoshQuinn(7) 5 40
(Richard Fahey) *in tch: pushed along 1/2-way: rdn over 4f out: sn wknd* **25/1**

024- **7** 10 **Back Burner (IRE)**[13] 8353 6-9-1 **83** ........ SamJames(3) 4 26
(David O'Meara) *in tch: rdn along 1/2-way: outpcd fr 4f out* **16/1**

2m 23.92s (-4.08) **Going Correction** -0.10s/f (Stan)
**WFA** 4 from 6yo+ 3lb 7 Ran SP% **112.0**
Speed ratings (Par 107): **110,109,108,102,94 87,80**
CSF £12.97 TOTE £5.00: £2.40, £2.10; EX 16.70 Trifecta £88.50.
**Owner** Universal Recycling Company **Bred** Fiona Craig & Dermot Cantillon **Trained** Averham Park, Notts

**FOCUS**
A strong handicap in which the front three pulled clear in a good time. Personal bests from the first two,but this is Southwell form.

## 4 COMPARE BOOKMAKERS AT BOOKMAKERS.CO.UK H'CAP 5f (F)

**2:00** (2:03) (Class 3) (0-95,95) 4-Y-O **£7,561** (£2,263; £1,131; £566; £282) **Stalls** High

Form RPR

006- **1** **Even Stevens**[22] 8232 6-8-8 **89** ........(v[1]) MatthewHopkins(7) 3 104
(Scott Dixon) *mde most: rdn clr 2f out: edgd lft fnl f: kpt on strly* **4/1**[1]

034- **2** 3 **Silken Express (IRE)**[22] 8232 5-9-1 **89** ........ AdamKirby 8 93
(Robert Cowell) *trckd ldrs: hdwy over 2f out: rdn to chse wnr wl over 1f out: drvn and no imp fnl f* **4/1**[1]

200- **3** 3 1/2 **Jiroft (ITY)**[28] 8155 7-9-4 **95** ........ RobertTart(3) 11 87
(Robert Cowell) *racd towards stands' side: in tch: rdn to chse ldrs 2f out: sn drvn and kpt on same pce* **16/1**

130- **4** 2 3/4 **Royal Bajan (USA)**[14] 8324 6-8-9 **83** ........(v) TomEaves 6 65
(James Given) *chsd ldrs: rdn along over 2f out: swtchd lft and drvn over 1f out: no imp* **10/1**[3]

312- **5** 1/2 **Powerful Wind (IRE)**[3] 8439 5-8-9 **83** ........ LiamJones 2 63
(Ronald Harris) *dwlt: sn prom: cl up 1/2-way: sn rdn and wknd wl over 1f out* **5/1**[2]

040- **6** nk **Prohibit**[28] 8155 9-9-2 **90** ........(p) PaddyAspell 1 69
(Robert Cowell) *racd wd: in tch: rdn along over 2f out: n.d* **16/1**

120- **7** 1/2 **Equitania**[14] 8334 4-9-5 **93** ........ RobertWinston 4 70
(Alan Bailey) *prom: rdn along over 2f out: sn wknd* **4/1**[1]

000- **8** 1 1/4 **Fratellino**[22] 8231 7-8-10 **91** ow2 ........(t) NatalieHambling-Yates(7) 12 64
(Alan McCabe) *dwlt: a in rr* **20/1**

500- **9** 1 **Khawatim**[22] 8232 6-9-0 **91** ........ BillyCray(3) 9 60
(Richard Guest) *dwlt: a in rr* **66/1**

001- **10** 3 **Rusty Rocket (IRE)**[56] 7777 5-8-11 **85** ........ TonyHamilton 5 43
(Paul Green) *a towards rr* **12/1**

001- **11** 4 **Tax Free (IRE)**[14] 8324 12-8-13 **87** ........ AdrianNicholls 7 31
(David Nicholls) *dwlt: a in rr* **14/1**

59.88s (0.18) **Going Correction** +0.325s/f (Slow) 11 Ran SP% **118.1**
Speed ratings (Par 107): **111,106,100,96,95 94,94,92,90,85 79**
CSF £19.58 CT £236.85 TOTE £6.20: £1.70, £1.10, £8.20; EX 30.80 Trifecta £484.20.
**Owner** Paul J Dixon **Bred** Mrs Yvette Dixon **Trained** Babworth, Notts

**FOCUS**
Course specialists aplenty in this sprint handicap. The winner is rated back to his old C&D best.

## 5 BOOKMAKERS.CO.UK MEDIAN AUCTION MAIDEN STKS 5f (F)

**2:35** (2:37) (Class 6) 3-5-Y-O **£1,940** (£577; £288; £144) **Stalls** High

Form RPR

**1** **Ruby Looker** 3-8-11 **0** ........ FrederikTylicki 2 65+
(J R Jenkins) *trckd ldng pair: hdwy and cl up 2f out: rdn and green over 1f out: carried lft and styd on u.p fnl f to ld nr fin* **4/1**[2]

324- **2** nk **The Dandy Yank (IRE)**[167] 4451 3-8-11 **65** ........ WilliamCarson 6 64
(Jamie Osborne) *prom: led after 2f: rdn wl over 1f out: drvn and edgd lft ins fnl f: hdd and no ex nr fin* **13/8**[1]

40- **3** nk **Jalebi**[175] 4164 3-8-6 **0** ........ NickyMackay 4 58
(Jim Boyle) *chsd ldrs: rdn over 2f out: n.m.r and swtchd rt jst over 1f out: kpt on strly fnl f* **5/1**

**4** 1 1/4 **Apophenia** 3-8-6 **0** ........ BarryMcHugh 1 54+
(Richard Fahey) *in tch: rdn along and outpcd bef 1/2-way: hdwy wl over 1f out: kpt on fnl f: nrst fin* **9/2**[3]

3/3- **5** 1/2 **Moss Quito (IRE)**[19] 8277 4-9-9 **57** ........(v[1]) SamJames(3) 5 63
(David O'Meara) *led 2f: cl up: rdn and wknd wl over 1f out* **6/1**

330- **6** 9 **Highland Princess (IRE)**[105] 6511 3-8-1 **45** ........ ShirleyTeasdale(5) 3 20
(Paul Midgley) *blind removed late and lost several l s: a bhd* **25/1**

1m 1.79s (2.09) **Going Correction** +0.325s/f (Slow)
**WFA** 3 from 4yo 15lb 6 Ran SP% **111.1**
Speed ratings (Par 101): **96,95,95,93,92 77**
CSF £10.72 TOTE £5.30: £3.30, £1.30; EX 12.60 Trifecta £62.60.
**Owner** M K P Turner **Bred** Michael Turner **Trained** Royston, Herts

**FOCUS**
A poor maiden that illustrated that the centre of the track is the place to be on the 5f course. The form is rated around the second and third.

## 6 32RED H'CAP 6f (F)

**3:10** (3:12) (Class 5) (0-70,69) 3-Y-O **£2,911** (£866; £432; £216) **Stalls** Low

Form RPR

431- **1** **Exceeding Power**[23] 8222 3-9-7 **69** ........ TomQueally 2 75
(Michael Bell) *prom on inner: hdwy over 2f out: rdn to chal over 1f out: slt ld appr fnl f: edgd rt wl ins fnl f: kpt on* **11/8**[1]

132- **2** nk **Little Big Man**[12] 8364 3-9-4 **66** ........(b) LiamKeniry 5 71
(Sylvester Kirk) *led: rdn along over 2f out: jnd and drvn over 1f out: sn hdd: rallied u.p ins fnl f and ev ch tl no ex towards fin* **5/2**[2]

044- **3** 4 1/2 **Day Star Lad**[15] 8317 3-8-7 **55** ........(v[1]) LiamJones 6 47
(Derek Shaw) *chsd ldng pair: rdn along wl over 2f out: drvn wl over 1f out and sn one pce* **9/1**

013- **4** 1 1/2 **Trinity Lorraine (IRE)**[19] 8274 3-8-2 **55** oh1 ........(v) TimClark(5) 4 42
(Alan Bailey) *towards rr and sn rdn along: hdwy wl over 2f out: drvn and no imp fr over 1f out* **9/1**

053- **5** 7 **Sandsman's Girl (IRE)**[19] 8273 3-9-1 **63** ........ TomEaves 7 29
(James Given) *chsd ldrs: rdn along 1/2-way: sn outpcd* **13/2**[3]

000- **6** 7 **Sandfield (IRE)**[116] 6206 3-8-2 **55** ........ ShirleyTeasdale(5) 3
(Paul Midgley) *sn rdn along in rr: sme hdwy over 3f out: outpcd and bhd fnl 2f* **14/1**

1m 16.74s (0.24) **Going Correction** -0.10s/f (Stan) 6 Ran SP% **110.7**
Speed ratings (Par 97): **94,93,87,85,76 66**
CSF £4.80 TOTE £2.30: £1.10, £1.70; EX 5.20 Trifecta £20.40.
**Owner** Dr Ali Ridha **Bred** Rabbah Bloodstock Limited **Trained** Newmarket, Suffolk

**FOCUS**
The front two pulled clear in this 6f handicap for 3yos and this might be form to keep an eye on. The runner-up is probably the key to the form.

## 7 LADBROKES MOBILE H'CAP 1m (F)

**3:45** (3:45) (Class 6) (0-55,60) 4-Y-O+ **£2,385** (£704; £352) **Stalls** Low

Form RPR

252- **1** **General Tufto**[6] 8399 9-8-8 **47** ........(b) JoeyHaynes(5) 13 59
(Charles Smith) *dwlt and in rr: hdwy and wd st: rdn to chse ldrs 2f out: styd on wl to ld last 100yds* **9/2**[2]

560- **2** nk **Queen Of Skies (IRE)**[19] 8270 5-9-5 **53** ........ AndrewMullen 3 64
(Michael Appleby) *prom: hdwy 3f out: rdn to ld wl over 1f out: drvn and wknd ins fnl f: hdd and no ex last 75yds* **13/2**

400- **3** 10 **Kielty's Folly**[32] 8118 10-9-3 **51** ........ AdamKirby 11 39
(Brian Baugh) *cl up on outer: led 3f out: rdn over 2f out: hdd wl over 1f out and kpt on same pce* **10/1**

012- **4** 1 3/4 **Frosty Friday**[22] 8233 6-9-5 **53** ........(v) FrederikTylicki 1 37
(J R Jenkins) *chsd ldrs on inner: rdn along 3f out: drvn and plugged on fnl 2f: n.d* **7/2**[1]

063- **5** 1 **Heidi's Delight (IRE)**[22] 8235 5-8-13 **47** ........(p) PJMcDonald 10 29
(Ann Duffield) *chsd ldrs: rdn along 3f out: no imp fnl 2f* **14/1**

002- **6** 1 1/4 **Flying Applause**[5] 8409 9-8-7 **46** oh1 ........(bt) TimClark(5) 9 25
(Roy Bowring) *dwlt and towards rr: hdwy 3f out: rdn and hung lft to inner over 1f out: no imp* **12/1**

030- **7** 2 3/4 **Action Front (USA)**[20] 8065 6-8-12 **46** ........(v) DaleSwift 4 19
(Derek Shaw) *dwlt and a towards rr* **12/1**

526- **8** *1 1/2* **Bapak Pesta (IRE)**[5] 8409 4-9-1 **54**....(b) ShaneGray(5) 6 23
(Kevin Ryan) *sn led: rdn along and hdd 3f out: sn wknd* 12/1

023- **9** *3 3/4* **Marina Ballerina**[32] 8116 6-9-1 **49**.... JimmyQuinn 2 10
(Roy Bowring) *sn rdn along and a in rr* 10/1

051- **10** *4 1/2* **Kept**[12] 8361 5-9-7 **55**.... LiamJones 8 5
(Ronald Harris) *prom: cl up over 3f out: sn rdn along and wknd fnl 2f* 6/1[3]

004- **11** *5* **Armada Bay (IRE)**[100] 6683 4-9-1 **49**....(t[1]) TonyHamilton 5
(Bryan Smart) *a towards rr: bhd fnl 3f* 25/1

/00- **12** *67* **Zoom In**[165] 4544 6-8-12 **46** oh1....(tp) StevieDonohoe 7
(Lee James) *a in rr: wl bhd fnl 3f* 66/1

1m 42.9s (-0.80) **Going Correction** -0.10s/f (Stan) **12** Ran SP% **121.3**
Speed ratings (Par 101): **100,99,89,87,86 85,82,81,77,73 68,1**
CSF £34.85 CT £288.33 TOTE £6.20: £1.70, £2.90, £3.50; EX 57.90 Trifecta £629.00.
**Owner** J R Theaker **Bred** Hascombe And Valiant Studs **Trained** Temple Bruer, Lincs

**FOCUS**
A low-grade handicap to close the card, with the first two clear. The winner's best run for quite a while.

T/Plt: £26.60 to a £1 stake. Pool: £48,351.08 - 1,324.53 winning units T/Qpdt: £11.70 to a £1 stake. Pool: £3,674.90 - 230.90 winning units JR

# [1]SOUTHWELL (L-H)
Thursday, January 2

**OFFICIAL GOING: Standard**
Wind: Moderate across Weather: Fine & dry

## 8 BEST ODDS AT BOOKMAKERS.CO.UK H'CAP — 6f (F)
**12:30** (12:31) (Class 5) (0-70,70) 4-Y-O+ **£2,911** (£866; £432; £216) **Stalls** Low

Form RPR

442- **1** **Maakirr (IRE)**[6] 8407 5-8-10 **62**....(tp) MarkCoumbe(3) 7 75
(Roy Bowring) *chsd ldrs: hdwy 3f out: effrt 2f out and sn chal: rdn over 1f out: drvn ins fnl f: kpt on wl to ld on line* 2/1[1]

322- **2** *nse* **Lexi's Hero (IRE)**[16] 8321 6-9-7 **70**.... JamieSpencer 4 83
(Richard Fahey) *chsd ldr: led 2f out: sn jnd and rdn: drvn ins fnl f: hdd on line* 11/4[2]

020- **3** *6* **Colourbearer (IRE)**[31] 8128 7-9-6 **69**....(t) AdamKirby 1 63
(Milton Bradley) *prom on inner: hdwy and cl up over 2f out: sn rdn and ev ch tl drvn and one pce appr fnl f* 12/1

540- **4** *1* **Guishan**[23] 8235 4-8-8 **57**.... AndrewMullen 9 47
(Michael Appleby) *prom: rdn along over 2f out: sn one pce* 14/1

026- **5** *1 1/4* **Cadeaux Pearl**[14] 8351 6-8-9 **65**....(v) MatthewHopkins(7) 3 51
(Scott Dixon) *in tch: hdwy on inner 1/2-way: cl up over 2f out: sn rdn and one pce* 10/1

006- **6** *1/2* **Majestic Manannan (IRE)**[16] 8319 5-9-7 **70**.... AdrianNicholls 5 55
(David Nicholls) *led: rdn along 3f out: hdd 2f out and sn wknd* 16/1

525- **7** *1* **Amenable (IRE)**[37] 8048 7-8-13 **62**....(p) WilliamCarson 8 44
(Ann Stokell) *a towards rr* 16/1

024- **8** *3/4* **Burnhope**[16] 8321 5-9-5 **68**....(p) TomQueally 6 47
(Scott Dixon) *dwlt: chsd ldrs: rdn along over 2f out and sn btn* 4/1[3]

060- **9** *12* **Oil Strike**[16] 8321 7-8-13 **69**.... DanielleMooney(7) 10 10
(Michael Easterby) *a in rr* 33/1

1m 15.47s (-1.03) **Going Correction** -0.05s/f (Stan) **9** Ran SP% **118.2**
Speed ratings (Par 103): **104,103,95,94,92 92,90,89,73**
CSF £7.74 CT £52.10 TOTE £2.90: £1.10, £1.60, £2.40; EX 8.80 Trifecta £69.60.
**Owner** K Nicholls **Bred** Darley **Trained** Edwinstowe, Notts

**FOCUS**
There was a tight finish between the two market leaders in this handicap and the pair pulled clear. The winner was well in on his C&D latest.

## 9 COMPARE BOOKMAKERS AT BOOKMAKERS.CO.UK H'CAP — 5f (F)
**1:00** (1:00) (Class 6) (0-65,65) 4-Y-O+ **£2,385** (£704; £352) **Stalls** High

Form RPR

213- **1** **Sir Geoffrey (IRE)**[4] 8439 8-8-9 **60**....(p) MatthewHopkins(7) 7 71
(Scott Dixon) *slt ld: rdn along 2f out: hdd narrowly ent fnl f: rallied u.p to ld nr fin* 3/1[1]

600- **2** *nk* **Only Ten Per Cent (IRE)**[44] 7953 6-9-7 **65**....(v) StephenCraine 1 75
(J R Jenkins) *trckd ldrs: smooth hdwy on wd outside 1/2-way: sn cl up: rdn to take slt ld ent fnl f: sn drvn: hdd and no ex towards fin* 10/1

203- **3** *2* **Master Of Disguise**[14] 8351 8-9-7 **65**.... AdamKirby 2 68
(Brian Baugh) *cl up: rdn wl over 1f out: drvn and kpt on same pce fnl f* 5/1[3]

304- **4** *shd* **Confidential Creek**[14] 8351 4-8-12 **61**....(p) JacobButterfield(5) 9 63
(Ollie Pears) *trckd ldrs: hdwy 2f out: rdn to chse ldng pair over 1f out: drvn and one pce fnl f* 8/1

344- **5** *hd* **Amis Reunis**[6] 8413 5-8-10 **54**....(p) RobertHavlin 3 56
(Alan Berry) *prom: rdn along 2f out: drvn over 1f out: kpt on same pce* 12/1

326- **6** *hd* **Monnoyer**[4] 8439 5-9-5 **63**....(b) TomQueally 8 64+
(Scott Dixon) *dwlt and in rr: hdwy 2f out: styd on fnl f: nrst fin* 7/2[2]

604- **7** *1 3/4* **Captain Scooby**[6] 8411 8-8-12 **59**....(e) BillyCray(3) 5 54
(Richard Guest) *dwlt and in rr: swtchd lft and rdn over 2f out: kpt on fnl f: nrst fin* 14/1

200- **8** *nse* **Imperial Spirit**[57] 7772 4-8-3 **54**....(v) HarryBurns(7) 10 48
(Jo Hughes) *racd towards stands' rail: in tch: rdn along 2f out: sn edgd lft and no imp* 25/1

502- **9** *2 1/4* **Max The Machine**[14] 8351 4-9-3 **61**....(v) DaleSwift 6 47
(Derek Shaw) *chsd ldrs: rdn along over 2f out: sn wknd* 5/1[3]

050- **10** *6* **We Have A Dream**[51] 7848 9-9-1 **59**....(p) WilliamCarson 11 24
(Ann Stokell) *a in rr* 50/1

410- **11** *1 1/2* **Edith Anne**[104] 6604 4-9-2 **60**.... PJMcDonald 4 19
(Paul Midgley) *prom: rdn along 1/2-way: sn wknd* 20/1

59.68s (-0.02) **Going Correction** +0.025s/f (Slow) **11** Ran SP% **125.7**
Speed ratings (Par 101): **101,100,97,97,96 96,93,93,90,80 78**
CSF £36.17 CT £156.99 TOTE £4.90: £2.00, £3.20, £2.20; EX 45.50 Trifecta £407.40.
**Owner** General Sir Geoffrey Howlett **Bred** P Rabbitte **Trained** Babworth, Notts

**FOCUS**
The first three were always prominent in this minor handicap and the hold-up runners couldn't get involved. The winner will still be on a good mark on his old form.

## 10 DOWNLOAD THE LADBROKES APP CLAIMING STKS — 1m (F)
**1:30** (1:30) (Class 6) 4-Y-O+ **£2,385** (£704; £352) **Stalls** Low

Form RPR

203- **1** **Silly Billy (IRE)**[14] 8350 6-8-11 **67**....(p) DaleSwift 7 75
(Brian Ellison) *chsd ldrs: pushed along over 2f out: rdn to chse ldr over 1f out: styd on u.p ent fnl f: led last 75yds* 9/4[2]

404- **2** *3/4* **Khajaaly (IRE)**[38] 8038 7-8-11 **64**....(bt) AndrewMullen 5 73
(Michael Appleby) *t.k.h: trckd ldrs: cl up 1/2-way: led wl over 2f out: rdn and edgd lft ent fnl f: sn drvn and carried hd high: hdd and no ex last 75yds* 8/1[3]

6U4- **3** *6* **Jullundar (IRE)**[129] 5839 4-8-4 **66**.... HarryBurns(7) 6 59
(Jo Hughes) *in rr: hdwy over 2f out: sn rdn along and kpt on fnl f* 20/1

004- **4** *hd* **Sofias Number One (USA)**[20] 8269 6-8-12 **77**....(b) MarkCoumbe(3) 3 63
(Roy Bowring) *cl up: led 1/2-way: rdn along and hdd wl over 2f out: drvn and wknd over 1f out* 10/11[1]

062- **5** *5* **Miami Gator (IRE)**[19] 8294 7-8-6 **55**....(v) BTTreanor(7) 8 50
(K R Burke) *led over 3f: cl up tl rdn along 3f out and sn wknd* 25/1

331- **6** *21* **Misleading Promise (IRE)**[295] 988 4-9-3 **70**....(tp) LiamKeniry 2 5
(John Butler) *trckd ldrs on inner: rdn along 3f out: sn wknd* 14/1

1m 43.19s (-0.51) **Going Correction** -0.05s/f (Stan) **6** Ran SP% **109.5**
Speed ratings (Par 101): **100,99,93,93,88 67**
CSF £18.77 TOTE £3.40: £1.40, £3.70; EX 17.50 Trifecta £118.80.Silly Billy was claimed by Mr R L Crowe for £6,000.
**Owner** Koo's Racing Club & Brian Ellison **Bred** Sir E J Loder **Trained** Norton, N Yorks

**FOCUS**
The first two pulled clear in this claimer and the favourite was disappointing. The race is rated around the winner to his C&D form.

## 11 LADBROKES H'CAP — 7f (F)
**2:00** (2:02) (Class 4) (0-80,79) 4-Y-O+ **£5,175** (£1,540; £769; £384) **Stalls** Low

Form RPR

005- **1** **Tellovoi (IRE)**[23] 8231 6-9-6 **78**....(v) AdamKirby 5 91
(Ian Williams) *prom: cl up 1/2-way: chal over 2f out: rdn to ld 1 1/2f out: drvn and edgd lft ins fnl f: styd on* 13/8[1]

020- **2** *1 1/4* **Piceno (IRE)**[6] 8408 6-8-8 **73**....(b) MatthewHopkins(7) 7 83
(Scott Dixon) *dwlt and towards rr: hdwy to chse ldrs 1/2-way: rdn 2f out: styd on to chal ent fnl f: ev ch tl drvn and no ex last 75yds* 14/1

231- **3** *1 3/4* **Maggie Pink**[31] 8134 5-9-2 **74**.... AndrewMullen 3 79
(Michael Appleby) *cl up: led over 4f out: jnd and rdn over 2f out: hdd 1 1/2f out and sn drvn: hld whn n.m.r ins fnl f: kpt on same pce* 6/1[3]

333- **4** *2 1/4* **Hellbender (IRE)**[7] 8401 8-8-11 **69**....(t) JimmyQuinn 8 68
(Shaun Harris) *in tch: hdwy to chse ldrs 3f out: rdn over 2f out: drvn and one pce appr fnl f* 7/1

234- **5** *3 1/4* **Masai Moon**[301] 912 10-8-7 **70**.... ShelleyBirkett(5) 10 61
(Rod Millman) *in tch on wd outside: rdn along and hdwy to chse ldrs over 2f out: drvn wl over 1f out and sn no imp* 20/1

403- **6** *shd* **Unex Michelangelo (IRE)**[17] 8308 5-8-8 **66**.... BarryMcHugh 2 57
(Michael Easterby) *sn rdn along and outpcd in rr: swtchd wd after 1f and bhd 1/2-way: swtchd lft to inner over 2f out: kpt on wl fnl f: nrst fin* 14/1

550- **7** *2 1/4* **Smalljohn**[19] 8304 8-8-10 **68**....(v) FergusSweeney 1 53
(Bryan Smart) *led over 2f: cl up on inner tl rdn along over 3f out and sn wknd* 33/1

260- **8** *nk* **Caldercruix (USA)**[20] 8269 7-8-11 **76**....(v) DanielCremin(7) 4 60
(James Evans) *chsd ldrs: rdn along 3f out: sn wknd* 14/1

114- **9** *3* **Two No Bids (IRE)**[7] 8401 4-9-7 **79**....(be) PaddyAspell 9 55
(Phil McEntee) *dwlt: sn in tch on wd outside: rdn along 1/2-way: sn btn: b.b.v* 7/2[2]

065- **10** *16* **Gabrial's Gift (IRE)**[13] 8365 5-9-1 **73**....(b[1]) TomQueally 6 8
(Scott Dixon) *dwlt: a in rr* 25/1

1m 28.84s (-1.46) **Going Correction** -0.05s/f (Stan) **10** Ran SP% **118.7**
Speed ratings (Par 105): **106,104,102,100,96 96,93,93,89,71**
CSF £27.35 CT £116.50 TOTE £2.30: £1.10, £5.50, £2.30; EX 33.70 Trifecta £209.80.
**Owner** Miss Magdalena Gut **Bred** Whisperview Trading Ltd **Trained** Portway, Worcs

**FOCUS**
The hot favourite delivered in decent style in this fair handicap. The winner is rated back to last year's turf best.

## 12 LADBROKES MOBILE H'CAP — 7f (F)
**2:30** (2:32) (Class 6) (0-55,60) 4-Y-O+ **£2,385** (£704; £352) **Stalls** Low

Form RPR

/50- **1** **De Lesseps (USA)**[119] 6130 6-8-8 **48**.... VictorSantos(7) 4 55
(James Moffatt) *chsd ldrs: hdwy over 2f out: rdn to chse ldr and edgd lft over 1f out: styd on to ld ins fnl f* 12/1

404- **2** *1 1/2* **Partner's Gold (IRE)**[4] 8438 4-8-13 **46**....(b) RobertHavlin 9 49
(Alan Berry) *dwlt: sn pushed along and chsd ldrs after 1f: hdwy 1/2-way: cl up on outer 3f out: led over 2f out: rdn and edgd lft ent fnl f: sn drvn: hdd and one pce* 12/1

005- **3** *1 1/4* **Mucky Molly**[19] 8293 6-9-1 **48**....(vt) LiamKeniry 5 48
(Alison Hutchinson) *led 2f: cl up: rdn along over 2f out: drvn over 1f out: kpt on same pce* 8/1[3]

243- **4** *6* **Greek Islands (IRE)**[266] 1497 6-9-4 **54**.... MarkCoumbe(3) 2 38
(Ed de Giles) *in tch: chsd ldrs 3f out: sn rdn and kpt on one pce fnl 2f* 8/1[3]

000- **5** *4* **Satwa Laird**[58] 7752 8-8-9 **47**....(be) AnnStokell(5) 3 21
(Ann Stokell) *a towards rr* 33/1

506- **6** *3* **Elusive Warrior (USA)**[23] 8235 11-8-10 **50**....(p) AaronJones(7) 8 16
(Alan McCabe) *dwlt: sn pushed along and in tch tl rdn and wknd 3f out* 6/1[2]

000- **7** *1* **Ichimoku**[14] 8351 4-9-2 **49**....(t) FergusSweeney 1 12
(Bryan Smart) *a in rr* 20/1

200- **8** *2* **Viking Warrior (IRE)**[14] 8341 7-9-5 **52**....(b) DuranFentiman 7 10
(Shaun Harris) *cl up: led after 2f: hdd 4f out: cl up tl rdn along wl over 2f out and sn wknd* 12/1

501- **9** *12* **Mick Dundee (IRE)**[3] 8446 4-9-13 **60** 6ex....(bt) AdamKirby 6
(John Ryan) *cl up: led 4f out: rdn along over 2f out: sn hdd & wknd* 10/11[1]

1m 30.49s (0.19) **Going Correction** -0.05s/f (Stan) **9** Ran SP% **119.7**
Speed ratings (Par 101): **96,94,92,86,81 78,76,74,60**
CSF £149.92 CT £1245.07 TOTE £16.60: £3.00, £3.30, £2.00; EX 200.40 Trifecta £1202.60.
**Owner** Ms A Hartley **Bred** Darley **Trained** Cartmel, Cumbria
■ A belated first winner for Portuguese rider Victor Santos.

**FOCUS**
Most of the runners had plenty to prove in this low-grade handicap and the odds-on favourite finished tailed off, but the winner scored in decent style and could strike again this winter. No depth to the race and the form is rated slightly negatively.

## 13 32RED MAIDEN FILLIES' STKS — 1m 3f (F)
**3:00** (3:00) (Class 5) 4-Y-O+ **£2,911** (£866; £432; £216) **Stalls** Low

Form RPR

23-0 **1** **Marina Ballerina**[1] 7 6-8-12 **49**.... TimClark(5) 7 62
(Roy Bowring) *hld up: hdwy 4f out: chsd ldng pair 3f out: rdn to chal wl over 1f out: led appr fnl f: edgd lft and kpt on towards fin* 7/2[3]

622- **2** 1 1/4 **Strandfield Bay (IRE)**[21] 8200 8-9-3 72 PaddyAspell 4 60
(Sharon Watt) *cl up: led 5f out: rdn clr 2f out: drvn and hdd appr fnl f: kpt on same pce* **11/4**[2]

42- **3** 9 **Charlotte Rhodes**[22] 8245 4-9-0 0 AdamKirby 6 45
(Marco Botti) *stmbld sltly s: sn pushed along to join ldrs after 1f: cl up 5f out: chal over 3f out: sn rdn along: drvn wl over 1f out and sn btn* **11/10**[1]

600- **4** 4 1/2 **Felice (IRE)**[37] 8046 4-9-0 35 (p) TomQueally 2 37
(Scott Dixon) *led: rdn along and hdd 5f out: drvn over 3f out and plugged on one pce* **50/1**

3- **5** 1 3/4 **Acton Gold**[27] 8185 5-9-3 0 WilliamCarson 3 34
(Brian Baugh) *in tch: hdwy 1/2-way: chsd ldrs over 3f out: sn rdn and outpcd* **14/1**

4- **6** hd **I Am Who I Am**[26] 8200 4-9-0 0 BarryMcHugh 8 34
(Iain Jardine) *a in rr* **20/1**

603- **7** 3 1/2 **Silver Marizah (IRE)**[16] 8318 5-8-10 44 (e) RhiainIngram(7) 5 28
(Roger Ingram) *in tch: hdwy to chse ldrs over 4f out: rdn along over 3f out and sn wknd* **25/1**

66- **P** **Share The Dosh**[21] 8260 6-9-3 0 (t) FergusSweeney 1
(J R Jenkins) *rn wout declared tongue strap: chsd ldrs: rdn along and lost pl 1/2-way: bhd whn lost action and p.u 3f out* **33/1**

2m 26.86s (-1.14) **Going Correction** -0.05s/f (Stan)
**WFA** 4 from 5yo+ 3lb 8 Ran SP% **116.7**
Speed ratings (Par 100): **102,101,94,91,90 89,87,**
CSF £13.33 TOTE £5.10: £1.20, £1.10, £1.40; EX 11.40 Trifecta £29.50.
**Owner** S R Bowring **Bred** S R Bowring **Trained** Edwinstowe, Notts

**FOCUS**
The winner got off the mark on her 21st attempt in this weak maiden for fillies. She is given some credit here.

## 14 32RED.COM AMATEUR RIDERS' H'CAP 2m (F)
3:30 (3:30) (Class 6) (0-65,62) 4-Y-0+ £2,305 (£709; £354) Stalls Low

Form RPR

553- **1** **Flash Crash**[20] 8270 5-10-9 62 (tp) MrGrahamCarson(5) 8 78+
(Anthony Carson) *trckd ldrs: cl up after 6f: led over 3f out: sn rdn clr: unchal* **7/2**[2]

641- **2** 11 **Jawaab (IRE)**[40] 8027 10-10-2 55 (e) PhillipDennis(5) 5 57
(Philip Kirby) *trckd ldrs: hdwy to chse ldng pair 6f out: rdn over 3f out: drvn and styd on to chse wnr wl over 1f out: sn no imp* **5/1**[3]

021- **3** 15 **Rock Of Ages**[23] 8229 5-10-10 61 (b) MrMichaelJMurphy(3) 7 45
(Michael Murphy) *dwlt and in tch: rapid hdwy on outer to ld after 3f: rdn along and hdd over 3f out: sn drvn and wknd fnl 2f* **5/4**[1]

U06- **4** 1/2 **Miss Mohawk (IRE)**[23] 8229 5-9-11 45 (p) MissSBrotherton 2 28
(Alan Brown) *prom: rdn along 5f out: drvn and lost pl 4f out: plugged on u.p fnl 2f* **25/1**

406- **5** 12 **Capitol Gain (IRE)**[17] 8308 5-11-0 62 MrSWalker 3 31
(George Baker) *in tch: hdwy to chse ldrs 6f out: rdn along wl over 3f out: sn outpcd* **5/1**[3]

636- **6** 4 1/2 **Father Shine (IRE)**[18] 7612 11-9-8 49 MissMeganHarris(7) 9 12
(Shaun Harris) *a in rr* **16/1**

650- **7** 33 **Rapid Water**[4] 8436 8-9-4 45 (p) MrDGannon(7) 6
(Pat Eddery) *hld up: a in rr* **25/1**

003- **8** 3 3/4 **Zainda (IRE)**[19] 8298 4-9-2 50 MrAFrench(7) 1
(John Wainwright) *t.k.h: led 3f: chsd ldrs tl lost pl over 7f out: bhd fnl 4f* **20/1**

3m 43.16s (-2.34) **Going Correction** -0.05s/f (Stan)
**WFA** 4 from 5yo+ 7lb 8 Ran SP% **118.3**
Speed ratings (Par 101): **103,97,90,89,83 81,65,63**
CSF £21.49 CT £32.33 TOTE £4.00: £1.10, £1.60, £1.30; EX 27.50 Trifecta £60.80.
**Owner** David J Newman & Ross Bennett **Bred** J R Furlong **Trained** Newmarket, Suffolk

**FOCUS**
There was an emphatic winner of this staying handicap for amateur riders. The level revolves around the winner, who was well on top.
T/Plt: £74.90. Pool: £69,574.92 - 677.60 winning units. T/Qpdt: £26.90. Pool: £6164.34 - 169.23 winning units. JR

# WOLVERHAMPTON (A.W) (L-H)
Thursday, January 2

**OFFICIAL GOING: Standard**
Wind: Fresh behind Weather: Overcast

## 15 32RED.COM H'CAP 5f 20y(P)
3:50 (3:50) (Class 6) (0-55,55) 3-Y-0 £2,264 (£673; £336; £168) Stalls Low

Form RPR

406- **1** **Global Explorer (USA)**[187] 3815 3-9-5 53 AdamBeschizza 9 64+
(Stuart Williams) *chsd ldrs: shkn up to ld over 1f out: pushed out* **9/4**[1]

042- **2** shd **Argent Touch**[20] 8273 3-8-12 46 oh1 DaleSwift 4 56+
(Derek Shaw) *plld hrd and prom: chsd wnr fnl f: sn rdn and ev ch: styd on* **3/1**[2]

330- **3** 3 1/2 **Rebel Code (USA)**[62] 7665 3-9-7 55 TomEaves 3 52
(James Given) *led 1f: chsd ldr: shkn up over 1f out: no ex ins fnl f* **3/1**[2]

430- **4** hd **Countess Lupus (IRE)**[31] 8133 3-8-7 46 oh1 (b) ShirleyTeasdale(5) 7 42
(Lisa Williamson) *led 4f out: rdn and hdd over 1f out: no ex ins fnl f* **33/1**

343- **5** 1 1/2 **Anfield**[4] 8435 3-9-4 55 RobertTart(3) 1 46
(Mick Quinn) *s.i.s: sn prom: hmpd 1/2-way: sn pushed along: styd on same pce fnl f* **9/2**[3]

000- **6** 2 1/2 **Red Oasis**[76] 7352 3-8-12 46 oh1 ChrisCatlin 5 28
(Robert Eddery) *sn outpcd: nvr nrr* **12/1**

005- **7** 1 3/4 **Minnyvinny**[51] 7844 3-8-12 46 oh1 LiamJones 8 22
(James Unett) *s.i.s: sn pushed along in rr: sme hdwy 1/2-way: rdn and wknd over 1f out* **33/1**

200- **8** 1/2 **Red Tiger Lily**[89] 7036 3-8-12 46 AdrianNicholls 6 20
(Nigel Tinkler) *hld up: rdn over 3f out: sn wknd* **20/1**

1m 4.58s (2.28) **Going Correction** +0.275s/f (Slow) 8 Ran SP% **117.3**
Speed ratings (Par 95): **92,91,86,85,83 79,76,75**
CSF £9.32 CT £19.57 TOTE £3.80: £1.20, £1.30, £1.10; EX 11.30 Trifecta £40.30.
**Owner** T W Morley & Mrs J Morley **Bred** James Millar & Janice Millar **Trained** Newmarket, Suffolk

**FOCUS**
A low-grade sprint handicap run at a fair pace. The first three were relatively unexposed and are perhaps better than their current levels.

## 16 32RED H'CAP 2m 119y(P)
4:20 (4:20) (Class 4) (0-85,85) 4-Y-0+ £5,175 (£1,540; £769; £384) Stalls Low

Form RPR

134- **1** **Shelford (IRE)**[43] 7975 5-10-0 85 AndrewMullen 5 95
(Michael Appleby) *chsd ldr after 2f: pushed along to ld over 2f out: rdn over 1f out: styd on gamely* **9/4**[1]

013- **2** nse **Scottish Boogie (IRE)**[11] 8392 7-9-10 81 (t) GeorgeBaker 4 91
(Seamus Durack) *hld up: hdwy over 2f out: chsd wnr over 1f out: rdn and ev ch ins fnl f: styd on* **9/4**[1]

303- **3** 6 **Lexington Bay (IRE)**[20] 8276 6-9-7 78 TonyHamilton 3 81
(Richard Fahey) *chsd ldrs: rdn over 2f out: styd on same pce fnl f* **8/1**

13- **4** nk **Layline (IRE)**[14] 8353 7-9-8 79 RobertWinston 7 81
(Gay Kelleway) *hld up: hdwy on outer over 2f out: rdn over 1f out: styd on same pce fnl f* **6/1**[2]

52- **5** 4 **Eshtyaaq**[35] 8089 7-9-3 74 ChrisCatlin 1 72
(David Evans) *set stdy pce tl qcknd over 4f out: rdn and hdd over 2f out: wknd fnl f* **8/1**

044- **6** 2 1/2 **Rapid Heat Lad (IRE)**[20] 8004 5-9-0 71 (tp) ShaneKelly 6 66
(Andrew Hollinshead) *hld up: n.m.r over 2f out: rdn and wknd over 1f out* **20/1**

125- **7** 1 1/2 **Sherman McCoy**[14] 8353 8-9-4 75 TomEaves 2 68
(Brian Ellison) *chsd ldr 2f: remained handy: rdn over 3f out: wknd over 1f out: b.b.v* **7/1**[3]

3m 45.04s (3.24) **Going Correction** +0.275s/f (Slow) 7 Ran SP% **115.3**
Speed ratings (Par 105): **103,102,100,100,98 96,96**
CSF £7.22 TOTE £3.90: £2.20, £1.50; EX 9.30 Trifecta £40.70.
**Owner** Carl Hodgson **Bred** Brittas & Minch Bloodstock **Trained** Danethorpe, Notts

**FOCUS**
The pace was honest for this competitive staying handicap with the front two fighting out a thrilling finish. The first two are credited with improving.

## 17 LADBROKES H'CAP 1m 141y(P)
4:50 (4:50) (Class 7) (0-50,52) 4-Y-0+ £1,940 (£577; £288; £144) Stalls Low

Form RPR

463- **1** **Katmai River (IRE)**[15] 8329 7-8-11 47 CharlotteJenner(7) 5 58
(Mark Usher) *a.p: chsd ldr 1/2-way: led over 2f out: shkn up over 1f out: pushed out* **10/1**

354- **2** 1 3/4 **Aureolin Gulf**[13] 8371 5-8-11 45 JackDuern(5) 4 52
(Andrew Hollinshead) *a.p: chsd wnr 2f out: rdn 1f out: styd on same pce ins fnl f* **8/1**

005- **3** 7 **Huzzah (IRE)**[13] 8371 9-8-9 45 (t) AlistairRawlinson(7) 12 36
(Michael Appleby) *s.i.s: hld up: hdwy over 2f out: rdn over 1f out: wnt 3rd ins fnl f: nt trble ldrs* **4/1**[1]

000- **4** 2 1/4 **Mr Chocolate Drop (IRE)**[6] 8409 10-9-5 48 (vt) JimmyQuinn 11 34
(Mandy Rowland) *hld up: pushed along over 5f out: hdwy over 2f out: rdn over 1f out: edgd lft and wknd ins fnl f* **20/1**

600- **5** shd **Justcallmehandsome**[7] 8399 12-8-9 45 (be) JosephineGordon(7) 13 30
(Dominic Ffrench Davis) *hld up: hdwy over 3f out: rdn and edgd lft fr over 1f out: wknd ins fnl f* **20/1**

035- **6** 1 **Supa Seeker (USA)**[64] 7636 8-8-12 48 MrAidenBlakemore(7) 9 31
(Tony Carroll) *hld up: rdn over 1f out: nvr on terms* **16/1**

063- **7** 1 **Holli Deya**[37] 8055 4-8-13 46 (v) RobertTart(3) 8 27
(Andi Brown) *prom: rdn over 2f out: nt clr run over 1f out: wknd fnl f* **10/1**

544- **8** hd **Mataajir (USA)**[6] 8409 6-9-7 50 (v) DaleSwift 7 30
(Derek Shaw) *hld up: rdn over 3f out: n.d* **11/2**[3]

006- **9** 5 **Stanlow**[64] 7624 4-9-6 50 StephenCraine 6 19
(Daniel Mark Loughnane) *mid-div: pushed along and lost pl 5f out: n.d after* **4/1**[1]

431- **10** hd **Storey Hill (USA)**[6] 8418 9-9-9 52 6ex TonyHamilton 1 20
(Richard Guest) *chsd ldr to 1/2-way: sn pushed along: rdn and wknd over 1f out* **5/1**[2]

066- **11** 2 1/4 **Thomas Blossom (IRE)**[47] 7932 4-9-1 45 AndrewMullen 3 8
(Nigel Tinkler) *s.i.s: hld up: pushed along over 5f out: a in rr* **16/1**

666- **12** nse **Bertie Blu Boy**[37] 8055 6-9-2 45 (b) TomEaves 2 8
(Lisa Williamson) *led: rdn and hdd over 2f out: wknd over 1f out* **16/1**

060- **13** 1 **Spessartine (IRE)**[29] 8154 4-9-1 45 ChrisCatlin 10 6
(Robert Eddery) *hld up: pushed along 1/2-way: a in rr* **50/1**

1m 51.68s (1.18) **Going Correction** +0.275s/f (Slow)
**WFA** 4 from 5yo+ 1lb 13 Ran SP% **130.5**
Speed ratings (Par 97): **105,103,97,95,95 94,93,93,88,88 86,86,85**
CSF £94.06 CT £401.54 TOTE £13.60: £3.90, £3.70, £1.50; EX 92.30 Trifecta £1592.10.
**Owner** M D I Usher **Bred** Mrs S M Roy **Trained** Upper Lambourn, Berks

**FOCUS**
A modest if open handicap run at a fair gallop. It paid to race handily. The first two finished clear, with both on good marks based on their old form.

## 18 DOWNLOAD THE LADBROKES APP H'CAP 7f 32y(P)
5:20 (5:20) (Class 7) (0-50,48) 4-Y-0+ £1,940 (£577; £288; £144) Stalls High

Form RPR

043- **1** **Interchoice Star**[6] 8413 9-9-3 46 (p) GeorgeBaker 11 55
(Ray Peacock) *w ldr tl over 4f out: wnt 2nd over 2f out: led 1f out: sn rdn: jst hld on* **4/1**[2]

020- **2** hd **Chez Vrony**[58] 7753 8-9-3 46 WilliamCarson 5 54
(Dave Morris) *hld up: hdwy over 1f out: hung lft and rdn ins fnl f: r.o* **7/1**[3]

003- **3** 3 1/2 **Vale Of Clara (IRE)**[23] 8234 6-9-5 48 (be) TomEaves 2 47+
(Peter Niven) *hld up: rdn over 2f out: hdwy over 1f out: rdn and swtchd rt ins fnl f: r.o to go 3rd post: nt rch ldrs* **12/1**

003- **4** shd **Starbotton**[11] 8390 4-8-12 46 ShirleyTeasdale(5) 4 45
(James Bethell) *led: hdd over 4f out: led again 1/2-way: rdn and hdd 1f out: styd on same pce* **8/1**

040- **5** 3 1/4 **Direct Trade**[47] 7931 4-8-9 45 (e) CharlotteJenner(7) 8 36
(Mark Usher) *hld up: nt clr run over 1f out: r.o ins fnl f: nvr nrr* **20/1**

533- **6** hd **Tony Hollis**[6] 8418 6-9-5 48 (tp) AndrewMullen 7 38
(Michael Appleby) *prom: rdn over 2f out: hung rt over 1f out: wknd ins fnl f* **9/4**[1]

/60- **7** 6 **Louis Vee (IRE)**[30] 8142 6-9-2 45 ShaneKelly 3 20
(Roy Brotherton) *prom: rdn 1/2-way: wknd over 1f out* **33/1**

000- **8** 5 **Ellies Image**[36] 8065 7-8-11 45 JoshBaudains(5) 9 7
(Richard Ford) *mid-div: drvn along 1/2-way: wknd over 1f out* **33/1**

260- **9** 1 3/4 **Farmers Dream (IRE)**[181] 4034 7-9-2 45 ChrisCatlin 1 2
(John Spearing) *prom: pushed along 1/2-way: wknd over 1f out* **20/1**

006- **10** *2¼* **Poetic Belle**[13] 8361 4-9-4 **47**..............................(b[1]) JimmyQuinn 10
(Shaun Harris) *trckd ldrs: t.k.h: led over 4f out tl over 3f out: rdn and wknd over 1f out* **16/1**

446- **11** *1½* **Misty Eyes**[4] 8438 5-9-5 **48**..............................(b[1]) PJMcDonald 6
(Geoffrey Harker) *hld up: rdn over 2f out: a in rr* **4/1**[2]

1m 32.41s (2.81) **Going Correction** +0.275s/f (Slow) **11** Ran SP% **123.4**
Speed ratings (Par 97): **94,93,89,89,85 85,78,73,71,68 66**
CSF £32.27 CT £323.53 TOTE £3.00: £1.50, £1.80, £2.80; EX 26.80 Trifecta £466.40.
**Owner** John P Evitt **Bred** M Bishop **Trained** Kyre Park, Worcs

**FOCUS**
A tight handicap with only 3lb covering the field. The time was slow and the winner backed up a better latest run.

## 19 BEST ODDS AT BOOKMAKERS.CO.UK MEDIAN AUCTION MAIDEN STKS 5f 216y(P)
**5:50** (5:53) (Class 5) 3-5-Y-O **£2,587** (£770; £384; £192) **Stalls** Low

Form RPR

32- **1** **Captain Myles (IRE)**[127] 5877 3-8-11 0..............................(t) StevieDonohoe 2 78+
(Tim Pitt) *trckd ldrs: shkn up to ld over 1f out: r.o wl* **10/11**[1]

622- **2** *3¼* **Ain't No Surprise (IRE)**[15] 8325 3-8-6 0.............................. WilliamCarson 4 63
(Jamie Osborne) *sn led: rdn and hdd over 1f out: styd on same pce ins fnl f* **7/2**[3]

023- **3** *1* **Cash Is King**[30] 8140 4-9-13 66..............................(b) GeorgeBaker 1 69
(Nick Littmoden) *hld up in tch: rdn over 1f out: styd on same pce fnl f* **11/4**[2]

046- **4** *4½* **Sunningdale Rose (IRE)**[23] 8228 3-8-6 57..............................(v) ChrisCatlin 3 45
(Gay Kelleway) *led early: prom: pushed along over 2f out: rdn: hung lft and wknd fnl f* **20/1**

**5** *4½* **On And On (IRE)** 4-9-1 0.............................. JoshQuinn(7) 5 35
(Richard Fahey) *s.i.s: hdwy to chse ldr over 4f out: pushed along over 2f out: wknd over 1f out* **14/1**

1m 16.81s (1.81) **Going Correction** +0.275s/f (Slow)
**WFA** 3 from 4yo 16lb **5** Ran SP% **112.7**
Speed ratings (Par 103): **98,93,92,86,80**
CSF £4.64 TOTE £1.60: £1.30, £2.10; EX 4.20 Trifecta £7.00.
**Owner** Paul Wildes **Bred** Burgage Stud And Partners **Trained** Market Drayton, Shropshire

**FOCUS**
This modest maiden was run at a steady pace. The third helps set the standard.

## 20 COMPARE BOOKMAKERS AT BOOKMAKERS.CO.UK CLASSIFIED CLAIMING STKS 5f 216y(P)
**6:20** (6:20) (Class 5) 4-Y-O+ **£3,040** (£904; £452; £113; £113) **Stalls** Low

Form RPR

201- **1** **Powerful Pierre**[7] 8401 7-8-6 70..............................(b) JacobButterfield(5) 5 80
(Ollie Pears) *a.p: pushed along and n.m.r over 2f out: bmpd and led wl ins fnl f: r.o* **9/4**[1]

165- **2** *hd* **George Fenton**[7] 8401 5-8-11 75..............................(p) LiamKeniry 7 79
(Conor Dore) *chsd ldrs: pushed along over 2f out: rdn to ld and edgd lft ins fnl f: sn hdd: r.o* **4/1**[2]

305- **3** *2½* **Bogsnog (IRE)**[24] 8224 4-9-2 74.............................. TomEaves 6 76
(Kristin Stubbs) *sn led: rdn and hdd ins fnl f: styd on same pce* **10/1**

/06- **4** *¾* **Abi Scarlet (IRE)**[185] 3906 5-8-4 74.............................. CharlieBennett(7) 1 69
(Hughie Morrison) *chsd ldr: ev ch fr over 2f out tl rdn and no ex ins fnl f* **33/1**

345- **4** *dht* **Sewn Up**[16] 8319 4-8-13 66..............................(p) ShaneKelly 3 71
(Andrew Hollinshead) *s.i.s: hld up: hdwy over 1f out: rdn and hung lft ins fnl f: nt rch ldrs* **14/1**

633- **6** *3½* **Lastkingofscotland (IRE)**[20] 8278 8-8-5 57..............................(b) ShelleyBirkett(5) 9 57
(Conor Dore) *hld up: rdn over 1f out: nvr nrr* **20/1**

610- **7** *hd* **Haadeeth**[12] 8384 7-8-6 69..............................(t) ChrisCatlin 2 52
(David Evans) *prom: t.k.h: pushed along over 2f out: rdn over 1f out: sn hung lft and wknd* **8/1**

633- **8** *nk* **Electric Qatar**[27] 8177 5-8-9 72.............................. RichardKingscote 10 54
(Tom Dascombe) *led early: sn stdd and lost pl: rdn over 2f out: wknd over 1f out* **9/2**[3]

050- **9** *2¾* **Red Explorer (USA)**[36] 8068 4-8-7 75.............................. FergusSweeney 4 43
(Jamie Osborne) *hld up: rdn and hung lft over 1f out: sn wknd* **7/1**

1m 15.75s (0.75) **Going Correction** +0.275s/f (Slow) **9** Ran SP% **116.0**
Speed ratings (Par 103): **106,105,102,101,101 96,96,96,92**
CSF £11.16 TOTE £3.70: £2.50, £1.50, £3.40; EX 16.00 Trifecta £70.70.No claims.
**Owner** Terence Elsey **Bred** Hedsor Stud **Trained** Norton, N Yorks

**FOCUS**
The pace was solid for this fair claimer in which the first two set the standard.

## 21 CORAL APP DOWNLOAD FROM THE APP STORE H'CAP 1m 4f 50y(P)
**6:50** (6:50) (Class 5) (0-75,75) 4-Y-O+ **£3,040** (£904; £452; £226) **Stalls** Low

Form RPR

023- **1** **Royal Alcor (IRE)**[30] 8139 7-9-5 **75**..............................(t) ShelleyBirkett(5) 6 87+
(Gay Kelleway) *hld up: nt clr run over 2f: hdwy sn after: led 1f out: sn hung lft: r.o wl* **7/4**[1]

530- **2** *4½* **Fly Solo**[41] 8004 5-9-7 **72**.............................. BenCurtis 5 77
(Alan Swinbank) *a.p: chsd ldr over 2f out: led wl over 1f out: sn hung lft: rdn and hdd 1f out: styd on same pce* **5/1**[2]

200- **3** *3* **Blazing Desert**[157] 4838 10-8-11 **62**.............................. AdamBeschizza 1 62
(William Kinsey) *led after 1f: rdn and hdd wl over 1f out: no ex fnl f* **20/1**

15- **4** *3¼* **Doldrums (USA)**[24] 8226 4-9-6 **75**.............................. AdamKirby 2 70
(Mark Johnston) *chsd ldrs: pushed along over 3f out: rdn and wknd over 1f out* **7/4**[1]

306- **5** *¾* **Dazzling Valentine**[14] 8343 6-8-10 **66**..............................(v[1]) TimClark(5) 4 60
(Alan Bailey) *hld up: rdn over 2f out: wknd over 1f out* **16/1**

/02- **6** *9* **A Little Bit Dusty**[17] 8309 6-9-9 **74**..............................(p) GeorgeBaker 3 53
(Conor Dore) *led 1f: chsd ldr tl rdn over 2f out: wknd over 1f out* **7/1**[3]

2m 43.11s (2.01) **Going Correction** +0.275s/f (Slow)
**WFA** 4 from 5yo+ 4lb **6** Ran SP% **112.5**
Speed ratings (Par 103): **104,101,99,96,96 90**
CSF £11.26 TOTE £2.20: £1.40, £3.90; EX 10.70 Trifecta £66.10.
**Owner** A MacLennan, G Kelleway & P Kerridge **Bred** John Hayes **Trained** Exning, Suffolk

**FOCUS**
A tight handicap run at a steady pace. The race lacked depth but this rates a clear best from the winner.

T/Jkpt: Part won. £7,100.00. Pool: £10,000.00 - 0.50 winning units. T/Plt: £34.30. Pool: £130,095.40 - 2761.43 winning units. T/Qpdt: £16.20. Pool: £12,695.10 - 578.57 winning units. CR

22 - 27a (Foreign Racing) - See Raceform Interactive

# [8]SOUTHWELL (L-H)
Friday, January 3

**OFFICIAL GOING: Standard**
Wind: Strong across Weather: Fine and dry

## 28 32RED H'CAP 1m (F)
**12:30** (12:30) (Class 6) (0-55,54) 3-Y-O **£2,045** (£603; £302) **Stalls** Low

Form RPR

035- **1** **It's All A Game**[66] 7604 3-8-13 **49**..............................(b) BillyCray(3) 6 52
(Richard Guest) *led: rdn along wl over 2f out: hdd wl over 1f out: 3 l down whn lft in ld last 100yds: sltly hmpd by loose horse and kpt on* **5/1**[3]

565- **2** *¾* **Royal Bushida**[17] 8317 3-8-12 **45**.............................. TonyHamilton 3 46
(Derek Shaw) *hld up in rr: sn pushed along: hdwy on inner over 3f out and sn in tch: rdn to chse ldrs over 1f out: kpt on fnl f* **14/1**

546- **3** *3¾* **Tortoise**[14] 8363 3-8-12 **45**..............................(b[1]) RobbieFitzpatrick 4 37
(Richard Guest) *prom: rdn along wl over 2f out: drvn and one pce fr over 1f out* **50/1**

000- **4** *shd* **Water For Life**[51] 7855 3-9-2 **54**.............................. JacobButterfield(5) 2 48
(Dave Morris) *prom: cl up 3f out: rdn along over 2f out: sn wknd: hld whn sltly hmpd ins fnl f* **12/1**

001- **5** *6* **Bonnie Fairy**[20] 8296 3-9-2 **49**.............................. AndrewMullen 5 27
(Michael Appleby) *dwlt: sn pushed along to go prom: rdn along wl over 2f out: sn wknd* **7/4**[2]

**6** *61* **Diamond Lucy (IRE)**[149] 5159 3-9-6 **53**.............................. TomQueally 1
(John Butler) *sn rdn along in rr: outpcd after 2f and bhd fr 1/2-way* **20/1**

502- **U** **Columbian Roulette (IRE)**[39] 8040 3-9-1 **48**.............................. MartinDwyer 7 58
(Charles Hills) *trckd ldrs: smooth hdwy on outer and cl up 3f out: led wl over 1f out: 3 l clr whn jinked bdly lft and uns rdr 100yds out* **6/4**[1]

1m 47.51s (3.81) **Going Correction** +0.125s/f (Slow) **7** Ran SP% **114.1**
Speed ratings (Par 95): **85,84,80,80,74 13,**
CSF £67.24 TOTE £5.90: £2.10, £4.30; EX 22.80 Trifecta £585.90.
**Owner** Viscount Environmental Ltd **Bred** Mrs G Sainty **Trained** Wetherby, W Yorks

**FOCUS**
A moderate 0-55 handicap, but a dramatic race as it turned out.

## 29 LADBROKES H'CAP 1m (F)
**1:00** (2:08) (Class 5) (0-75,75) 4-Y-O+ **£2,911** (£866; £432; £216) **Stalls** Low

Form RPR

231- **1** **Tatting**[21] 8269 5-9-0 **73**.............................. ShelleyBirkett(5) 8 88
(Chris Dwyer) *hld up towards rr: smooth hdwy 3f out: trckd ldng pair 2f out: rdn and edgd lft over 1f out: led ent fnl f: rdn out* **7/4**[1]

521- **2** *½* **No Win No Fee**[24] 8233 4-8-7 **61**..............................(p) AndrewMullen 6 75
(Michael Appleby) *trckd ldrs: hdwy and wd st: led wl over 2f out: rdn and edgd lft over 1f out: hdd and drvn ent fnl f: no ex towards fin* **7/2**[2]

315- **3** *2* **Peter's Friend**[45] 7952 5-8-12 **66**.............................. PJMcDonald 7 75
(Michael Herrington) *hld up in tch: hdwy 3f out: cl up 2f out: sn rdn and ev ch tl drvn and one pce ins fnl f* **4/1**[3]

565- **4** *6* **My Single Malt (IRE)**[21] 8269 6-9-2 **70**.............................. BarryMcHugh 9 65
(Julie Camacho) *chsd ldrs: wd st: rdn wl over 2f out: sn drvn and kpt on same pce* **14/1**

201- **5** *5* **Spes Nostra**[95] 6906 6-9-4 **72**..............................(b) BenCurtis 5 56
(David Barron) *chsd ldrs: rdn along wl over 2f out: sn drvn and one pce* **14/1**

123- **6** *3¼* **Raging Bear (USA)**[55] 7824 4-8-12 **73**.............................. DanielCremin(7) 2 49
(James Evans) *dwlt and bhd tl sme late hdwy* **12/1**

60-3 **7** *1* **Goal (IRE)**[2] 2 6-9-0 **75**..............................(t) JackGarritty(7) 12 49
(Charles Smith) *racd wd: cl up: slt ld after 3f: hdd over 3f out and sn wknd* **25/1**

130- **8** *10* **Zaitsev (IRE)**[145] 5304 4-9-6 **74**.............................. RobertWinston 10 25
(Ollie Pears) *led 3f: cl up: rdn along 3f out: wknd over 2f out* **7/1**

000- **9** *hd* **Dancing Maite**[24] 8230 9-8-7 **64** ow1.............................. MarkCoumbe(3) 1 15
(Roy Bowring) *trckd ldrs on inner: hdwy to ld over 3f out and sn rdn: hdd wl over 2f and sn wknd* **50/1**

000- **10** *nk* **Sky Crossing**[21] 8269 5-8-11 **65**.............................. MartinLane 11 15
(Tom Tate) *racd wd: cl up: rdn along over 3f out: sn wknd* **66/1**

1m 42.2s (-1.50) **Going Correction** +0.125s/f (Slow) **10** Ran SP% **119.4**
Speed ratings (Par 103): **112,111,109,103,98 95,94,84,84,83**
CSF £7.92 CT £21.92 TOTE £3.30: £1.40, £1.50, £1.60; EX 11.00 Trifecta £32.70.
**Owner** Mrs K W Sneath **Bred** Darley **Trained** Newmarket, Suffolk

**FOCUS**
This modest handicap was delayed by over an hour to allow for the return of the doctor after Martin Dwyer was taken to hospital following his fall in the opener.

## 30 LADBROKES (S) H'CAP 7f (F)
**1:30** (2:26) (Class 6) (0-60,59) 4-Y-O+ **£2,385** (£704; £352) **Stalls** Low

Form RPR

412- **1** **Munaawib**[20] 8293 6-9-5 **57**..............................(bt) AdamKirby 3 66
(David C Griffiths) *trckd ldrs: hdwy wl over 2f out: rdn over 1f out: styd on fnl f to ld last 75yds* **2/1**[1]

000- **2** *¾* **Lutine Charlie (IRE)**[16] 8329 7-9-1 **53**..............................(p[1]) MartinLane 9 60
(Pat Eddery) *sn led: rdn along wl over 2f out: drvn over 1f out: hdd and no ex last 75yds* **8/1**[3]

162- **3** *1¾* **Bitaphon (IRE)**[20] 8295 5-9-5 **57**..............................(t) AndrewMullen 1 59
(Michael Appleby) *cl up on inner: rdn along 3f out: drvn wl over 1f out: kpt on u.p fnl f* **2/1**[1]

040- **4** *1* **Offbeat Safaris (IRE)**[37] 8073 6-9-0 **52**..............................(p) LiamJones 6 52
(Ronald Harris) *dwlt: sn in tch: hdwy on outer and cl up 3f out: rdn to chal wl over 1f out: sn drvn and ev ch tl wknd ins fnl f* **8/1**[3]

360- **5** *nk* **Exceedexpectations (IRE)**[14] 8360 5-9-7 **59**.............................. TomQueally 5 58
(Conor Dore) *chsd ldrs: rdn along wl over 2f out: drvn over 1f out and kpt on same pce* **6/1**[2]

200- **6** *1¾* **Just A Pound (IRE)**[18] 8308 4-8-11 **56**.............................. JosephineGordon(7) 7 51
(Jo Hughes) *trckd ldrs: rdn along over 2f out: drvn and wknd over 1f out* **10/1**

1m 30.59s (0.29) **Going Correction** +0.125s/f (Slow) **6** Ran SP% **112.3**
Speed ratings (Par 101): **103,102,100,99,98 96**
CSF £18.96 CT £34.40 TOTE £2.70: £2.20, £2.60; EX 15.00 Trifecta £81.00.There was no bid for the winner.
**Owner** Willie McKay **Bred** Shadwell Estate Company Limited **Trained** Bawtry, S Yorks



The Form Book, Raceform Ltd, Newbury, RG14 5SJ

**FOCUS**
A moderate selling handicap.

## 31 LADBROKES MEDIAN AUCTION MAIDEN STKS 1m (F)
2:00 (2:48) (Class 6) 4-6-Y-O £2,385 (£704; £352) Stalls Low

Form RPR
/24- 1 **Roger Thorpe**[20] 8294 5-9-0 61 JackDuern(5) 4 65
(Deborah Sanderson) *dwlt: sn chsng ldrs: chsd ldr after 2f: rdn wl over 2f out: drvn and hdwy over 1f out: led ins fnl f: sn clr* 7/2[2]
/06- 2 3 1/4 **Flying Giant (IRE)**[104] 6630 4-9-5 0 LiamJones 1 58
(Jo Hughes) *led: rdn clr 2f out: drvn over 1f out: hdd and one pce ins fnl f* 6/1[3]
336- 3 11 **Primary Route (IRE)**[131] 5789 4-9-0 57 BenCurtis 2 27
(David Barron) *chsd ldr 1f: rdn along and outpcd wl over 3f out: styd on u.p fnl 2f: tk poor 3rd ins fnl f* 2/1[1]
- 4 1 3/4 **Daring Pursuit** 4-8-7 0 RobJFitzpatrick(7) 6 23
(K R Burke) *racd wd: chsd ldng pair: rdn along over 3f out: sn outpcd* 6/1[3]
366- 5 13 **The Bay Tigress**[27] 8200 4-8-7 45 HarryBurns(7) 3
(Jo Hughes) *in rr and rdn along after 3f: sn bhd* 14/1
56/ 6 9 **Lady Of The Vine (USA)**[448] 7014 4-9-0 0 LiamKeniry 5
(Andrew Balding) *chsd ldrs: rdn along 1/2-way: drvn 3f out and sn wknd* 7/2[2]

1m 45.48s (1.78) **Going Correction** +0.125s/f (Slow) 6 Ran SP% 113.0
Speed ratings: **96,92,81,80,67 58**
CSF £24.29 TOTE £4.80: £3.10, £3.80; EX 20.50 Trifecta £71.30.
**Owner** J M Lacey **Bred** J M Lacey **Trained** Tickhill, S Yorks

**FOCUS**
This moderate maiden didn't make for pretty viewing and the front pair were the only ones in it from before halfway.

## 32 CORAL APP DOWNLOAD FROM THE APP STORE H'CAP 1m 3f (F)
2:30 (3:06) (Class 4) (0-80,78) 4-Y-O+ £5,175 (£1,540; £769; £384) Stalls Low

Form RPR
011- 1 **Luv U Whatever**[14] 8372 4-8-10 70 LiamJones 4 81
(Jo Hughes) *trckd ldr: cl up over 4f out: chal wl over 2f out: rdn to ld over 1f out: drvn and edgd lft ins fnl f: kpt on gamely towards fin* 6/4[1]
112- 2 3/4 **Honoured (IRE)**[15] 8353 7-9-7 78 (t) AndrewMullen 7 88
(Michael Appleby) *trckd ldrs on outer: hdwy 1/2-way and sn cl up: rdn to ld wl over 2f out: sn jnd: drvn and hdd over 1f out: sn edgd lft: rallied u.p ins fnl f and ev ch tl no ex last 50yds* 2/1[2]
256- 3 8 **Mystery Bet (IRE)**[25] 8218 4-9-2 76 TonyHamilton 1 72
(Richard Fahey) *led: rdn along 4f out: hdd wl over 2f out: sn drvn and one pce* 8/1
000- 4 1 **My History (IRE)**[15] 8353 4-8-6 69 MichaelJMMurphy(3) 5 63
(Mark Johnston) *chsd ldrs: swtchd rt and pushed along 5f out: rdn wl over 3f out: drvn and one pce fnl 2f* 10/1
363- 5 2 **Absent Amy (IRE)**[17] 8316 5-9-2 73 RobertHavlin 8 64
(Amy Weaver) *hld up: hdwy 5f out: rdn along over 3f out: chsd ldrs 3f out: drvn and no imp fnl 2f* 7/1[3]
0/5- 6 26 **Fair Trade**[48] 3856 7-9-4 75 TomQueally 3 22
(Alan Swinbank) *in tch: rdn along 5f out: drvn and wknd over 3f out* 12/1

2m 26.21s (-1.79) **Going Correction** +0.125s/f (Slow)
**WFA** 4 from 5yo+ 3lb 6 Ran SP% 113.7
Speed ratings (Par 105): **111,110,104,103,102 83**
CSF £4.85 CT £15.54 TOTE £2.10: £1.40, £1.30; EX 5.60 Trifecta £18.40.
**Owner** 21C Telecom.co.uk **Bred** Richard Hunt **Trained** Lambourn, Berks
■ Stewards' Enquiry : Liam Jones two-day ban: use of whip (17-18 Jan)

**FOCUS**
They finished well spread out in this fair handicap and it produced a thrilling finish between the two market leaders, who pulled well clear of the others.

## 33 CORAL MOBILE JUST THREE CLICKS TO BET H'CAP 1m 4f (F)
3:00 (3:26) (Class 6) (0-62,62) 4-Y-O+ £2,385 (£704; £352) Stalls Low

Form RPR
000- 1 **Grandad Mac**[7] 8410 6-8-11 52 LiamJones 3 61
(Alan Coogan) *in tch on outer: hdwy 1/2-way: cl up over 4f out: slt ld wl over 2f out: drvn over 1f out: kpt on gamely u.p fnl f* 16/1
433- 2 hd **Rancho Montoya (IRE)**[25] 8223 4-8-9 54 (v) LiamKeniry 7 63
(Andrew Balding) *cl up: led 1/2-way: rdn along over 3f out: narrowly hdd wl over 2f out: sn drvn: rallied u.p ent fnl f and ev ch tl edgd lft and no ex towards fin* 5/2[2]
3/3- 3 6 **Think**[35] 7376 7-8-10 51 oh4 (t) BarryMcHugh 4 50
(Clive Mulhall) *hld up: hdwy to chse ldrs over 4f out: drvn to chse ldng pair 2f out: sn no imp* 5/1[3]
10P- 4 1 1/4 **Kyllachykov (IRE)**[246] 1949 6-8-12 56 NeilFarley(3) 1 53
(Robin Bastiman) *led to 1/2-way: rdn along over 4f out: drvn 3f out: sn one pce* 16/1
000- 5 9 **Kai**[34] 8118 5-8-10 51 oh4 (v) AndrewMullen 6 34
(Alan McCabe) *chsd ldrs: rdn along 5f out: sn outpcd* 16/1
360- 6 6 **Everlasting Light**[20] 8299 4-9-3 62 PaddyAspell 5 35
(Tim Walford) *a in rr: bhd fnl 5f* 10/1
625- 7 17 **My Manekineko**[65] 7628 5-9-5 60 TomQueally 2 6
(J R Jenkins) *t.k.h: chsd ldrs on inner: n.m.r and lost pl bnd after 2f: pushed along 1/2-way: rdn 5f out and sn outpcd: bhd and eased fnl 2f* 5/4[1]

2m 42.52s (1.52) **Going Correction** +0.125s/f (Slow)
**WFA** 4 from 5yo+ 4lb 7 Ran SP% 116.4
Speed ratings (Par 101): **99,98,94,94,88 84,72**
CSF £57.82 TOTE £19.20: £7.10, £2.30; EX 89.50 Trifecta £667.00.
**Owner** A B Coogan **Bred** Aiden Murphy **Trained** Soham, Cambs

**FOCUS**
This lot boasted a combined record of 5-96 on the Flat and it developed into a dour battle between the front pair over the last half-mile.

## 34 COMPARE BOOKMAKERS AT BOOKMAKERS.CO.UK H'CAP 6f (F)
3:30 (3:49) (Class 6) (0-55,61) 4-Y-O+ £2,385 (£704; £352) Stalls Low

Form RPR
001- 1 **Pick A Little**[7] 8412 6-9-10 61 6ex RobertTart(3) 4 72
(Michael Blake) *trckd ldrs: hdwy 2f out: swtchd lft to inner and rdn to chal over 1f out: led ins fnl f: styd on* 2/1[1]
246- 2 2 **Divertimenti (IRE)**[14] 8370 10-8-13 52 (p) TimClark(5) 5 57
(Roy Bowring) *mde most: rdn over 1f out: hdd ins fnl f: kpt on same pce* 20/1
564- 3 1/2 **Orwellian**[17] 8315 5-9-1 49 PaddyAspell 8 52
(Bryan Smart) *dwlt: towards rr: hdwy whn n.m.r and sltly hmpd 3f out: rdn and styd on wl down outer appr fnl f: nrst fin* 11/2[3]
250- 4 1/2 **Doctor Hilary**[49] 7905 12-8-13 47 (b) RobertHavlin 9 49
(Mark Hoad) *towards rr: hdwy over 2f out: sn rdn and styd on fnl f: nrst fin* 10/1
2- 5 1 1/4 **Commandable (AUS)**[15] 8352 10-9-7 55 BarryMcHugh 10 53
(Ian Semple) *trckd ldrs: hdwy to chal whn hmpd by loose horse 2f out: rdn and ev ch over 1f out: wknd fnl f* 4/1[2]
005- 6 1/2 **Lexi's Beauty (IRE)**[21] 8277 4-8-12 46 oh1 (p) AndrewMullen 11 42
(Brian Baugh) *chsd ldrs: rdn along and hdd by loose horse wl over 2f out: one pce after* 50/1
103- 7 1 1/2 **Red Shadow**[7] 8412 5-8-13 52 (b) JoshBaudains(5) 1 43
(Alan Brown) *chsd ldrs on inner: rdn along over 2f out: sn drvn and btn* 16/1
000- 8 nk **Night Trade (IRE)**[30] 8152 7-9-2 55 (p[1]) DCByrne(5) 7 45
(Ronald Harris) *a towards rr* 16/1
000- 9 2 3/4 **Novalist**[119] 6180 6-8-11 48 (b) NeilFarley(3) 6 30
(Robin Bastiman) *cl up: rdn along 3f out: hmpd by loose horse 2f out: sn wknd* 12/1
065- 10 2 **Diamond Vine (IRE)**[7] 8412 6-9-4 52 (b) LiamJones 2 27
(Ronald Harris) *a in rr* 16/1
032- U **Ridgeway Hawk**[226] 2582 6-9-5 53 (v) LiamKeniry 3
(Mark Usher) *uns rdr s* 7/1

1m 17.16s (0.66) **Going Correction** +0.125s/f (Slow) 11 Ran SP% 122.4
Speed ratings (Par 101): **100,97,96,96,94 93,91,91,87,84**
CSF £51.31 CT £205.05 TOTE £2.90: £1.10, £3.70, £2.80; EX 29.80 Trifecta £297.70.
**Owner** C Weare and A Pierce **Bred** D R Tucker **Trained** Trowbridge, Wilts
■ Stewards' Enquiry : Tim Clark two-day ban: use of whip (17-18 Jan)

**FOCUS**
A moderate sprint handicap and early drama when Ridgeway Hawk lost his rider after exiting the stalls.
T/Jkpt: Not won. T/Plt: £269.90. Pool: £68,180.31 - 184.37 winning units. T/Qpdt: £28.00. Pool: £7739.19 - 204.10 winning units. JR

# [15] WOLVERHAMPTON (A.W) (L-H)
Friday, January 3

**OFFICIAL GOING: Standard**
Wind: Fresh behind Weather: Raining

## 35 BEST ODDS AT BOOKMAKERS.CO.UK CLAIMING STKS 5f 20y(P)
4:00 (4:02) (Class 5) 4-Y-O+ £2,587 (£770; £384; £192) Stalls Low

Form RPR
540- 1 **Dark Lane**[25] 8216 8-8-7 66 ChrisCatlin 2 69
(David Evans) *chsd ldr tl pushed along 1/2-way: r.o u.p to ld nr fin* 12/1
005- 2 nk **R Woody**[35] 8096 7-8-11 68 (e) ShaneKelly 1 72
(Robert Cowell) *sn led: rdn over 1f out: hdd nr fin* 7/1[3]
203- 3 1 1/4 **Steelcut**[7] 8411 10-8-9 59 (v) JimmyQuinn 6 65
(Mark Buckley) *hld up in tch: shkn up over 1f out: rdn ins fnl f: styd on same pce* 25/1
501- 4 4 1/2 **Hamoody (USA)**[28] 8177 10-9-5 83 AdrianNicholls 5 59
(David Nicholls) *s.s: sn prom: chsd ldr 1/2-way: rdn over 1f out: wknd and eased wl ins fnl f* 11/10[1]
000- 5 5 **Profile Star (IRE)**[16] 8324 5-9-1 80 JamieSpencer 7 37
(David Barron) *prom: drvn along over 3f out: wknd and eased fnl f* 6/4[2]
6 23 **Offherocker** 7-8-7 0 MrAidenBlakemore(7) 4
(Claire Dyson) *dwlt: outpcd* 100/1

1m 2.93s (0.63) **Going Correction** +0.175s/f (Slow) 6 Ran SP% 112.6
Speed ratings (Par 103): **101,100,98,91,83 46**
CSF £88.09 TOTE £12.80: £4.30, £2.80; EX 53.20 Trifecta £189.50.Profile Star was bought by Miss A Stokell for £8000.
**Owner** Mrs E Evans **Bred** David Jamison Bloodstock **Trained** Pandy, Monmouths

**FOCUS**
This was an unremarkable claimer run at an ordinary pace for the trip.

## 36 COMPARE BOOKMAKERS AT BOOKMAKERS.CO.UK H'CAP 5f 216y(P)
4:30 (4:30) (Class 4) (0-85,85) 4-Y-O+ £4,690 (£1,395; £697; £348) Stalls Low

Form RPR
222- 1 **Burren View Lady (IRE)**[45] 7959 4-9-1 79 (e) DuranFentiman 5 90
(Tim Easterby) *prom: lost pl over 4f out: hdwy over 1f out: rdn to ld ins fnl f: jst hld on* 3/1[3]
/00- 2 hd **Angel's Pursuit (IRE)**[173] 4329 7-9-4 82 AdamKirby 8 92
(Robert Cowell) *trckd ldrs: shkn up to ld ins fnl f: sn rdn: edgd lft and hdd: r.o* 5/2[2]
113- 3 3 1/2 **Fat Gary**[28] 8189 4-9-7 85 (p) StephenCraine 7 84
(Tom Dascombe) *sn led: hdd 4f out: led again 2f out: rdn over 1f out: hdd and no ex ins fnl f* 2/1[1]
151- 4 3 **Fortinbrass (IRE)**[14] 8365 4-9-0 78 ShaneKelly 6 68
(John Balding) *chsd ldrs: nt clr run and lost pl 5f out: n.d after* 6/1
600- 5 1 1/4 **Caspian Prince (IRE)**[14] 8369 5-9-4 85 MarkCoumbe(3) 4 71
(Tony Carroll) *plld hrd: sn w ldr: led 4f out: hdd 2f out: sn rdn: wknd fnl f* 25/1
360- 6 6 **Clubland (IRE)**[24] 8232 5-9-0 78 JimmyQuinn 1 44
(Roy Bowring) *s.i.s: hmpd sn after s: hdwy over 4f out: rdn and wknd over 1f out* 8/1
400- 7 12 **Mister Manannan (IRE)**[97] 6848 7-9-1 79 AdrianNicholls 2 7
(David Nicholls) *s.i.s: plld hrd and sn prom: rdn over 2f out: wknd over 1f out* 14/1

1m 15.64s (0.64) **Going Correction** +0.175s/f (Slow) 7 Ran SP% 122.8
Speed ratings (Par 105): **102,101,97,93,91 83,67**
CSF £12.12 CT £18.86 TOTE £4.80: £2.00, £1.80; EX 20.30 Trifecta £41.80.
**Owner** Habton Farms **Bred** L Mulryan **Trained** Great Habton, N Yorks

**FOCUS**
This was a well-contested handicap despite the smallish field, but the pace was nothing special.

## 37 LADBROKES MEDIAN AUCTION MAIDEN STKS 7f 32y(P)
5:00 (5:01) (Class 6) 3-5-Y-O £1,940 (£577; £288; £144) Stalls High

Form RPR
1 **Unscripted (IRE)** 3-8-10 0 SeanLevey 4 91
(Richard Hannon) *hmpd sn after s: hld up: pushed along and hdwy over 2f out: led over 1f out: hung lft and rdn clr fnl f* 2/1[1]
3- 2 10 **Coillte Cailin (IRE)**[20] 8303 4-9-9 0 ShaneKelly 7 64
(Daniel Mark Loughnane) *s.i.s: hdwy to trck ldrs over 5f out: led over 2f out: rdn and hdd over 1f out: hung lft and no ex ins fnl f* 6/1

3 1 3/4 **Hardy Black (IRE)** 3-8-10 0 FergusSweeney 8 60
(Jamie Osborne) *s.i.s: hdwy over 5f out: rdn over 1f out: no ex fnl f* 8/1
2- 4 1 3/4 **Indira**[22] 8259 3-8-5 0 MartinLane 2 51
(John Berry) *prom: lost pl after 1f: pushed along 1/2-way: kpt on ins fnl f* 10/1
6- 5 1 **This Charming Man (IRE)**[15] 8346 3-8-10 0 PJMcDonald 5 53
(Keith Dalgleish) *led: rdn and hdd over 2f out: wknd fnl f* 5/1[3]
626- 6 1/2 **Sakhee'Ssquirrel**[185] 3914 3-8-5 62 FrankieMcDonald 9 47
(Sean Curran) *prom: pushed along over 2f out: nt clr run over 1f out: sn wknd* 25/1
3- 7 3 1/2 **Captain Mo**[14] 8367 3-8-10 0 PaoloSirigu 1 43
(Marco Botti) *prom: lost pl over 5f out: rdn 1/2-way: wknd over 2f out* 4/1[2]
8 2 **Intensive (IRE)** 3-8-5 0 WilliamCarson 6 33
(Jamie Osborne) *s.s: a in rr: pushed along 1/2-way: sn wknd* 16/1
0/6- 9 17 **Highway United (IRE)**[321] 686 4-9-9 30 AdamKirby 10
(Sean Curran) *prom: chsd ldr over 5f out tl rdn over 2f out: hmpd and wknd sn after* 33/1
56- 10 shd **Echologic**[18] 8313 4-10-0 0 ChrisCatlin 3
(Brian Baugh) *sn pushed along in rr: bhd fr 1/2-way* 50/1

1m 31.1s (1.50) **Going Correction** +0.175s/f (Slow)
**WFA** 3 from 4yo 18lb 10 Ran SP% **119.1**
Speed ratings (Par 101): **98,86,84,82,81 80,76,74,55,55**
CSF £14.53 TOTE £2.80: £1.90, £2.10, £3.50; EX 17.90 Trifecta £77.30.
**Owner** Brian Dolan **Bred** Brian Dolan **Trained** East Everleigh, Wilts
■ The first runner and winner for Richard Hannon jnr since he took over from his father on January 1.
**FOCUS**
This was a routine maiden, run at a medium gallop, but the debutant winner scored in style.

## 38 LADBROKES H'CAP 7f 32y(P)
**5:30** (5:31) (Class 3) (0-95,94) 4-Y-0 **£7,246** (£2,168; £1,084; £542; £270) **Stalls** High

Form RPR
002- 1 **Apostle (IRE)**[25] 8217 5-8-12 **85** JamieSpencer 8 95
(David Simcock) *led: hdd over 5f out: chsd ldr tl led again over 2f out: rdn over 1f out: all out* 11/4[1]
406- 2 nse **Georgian Bay (IRE)**[175] 4265 4-8-12 **90** JoeyHaynes(5) 3 100
(K R Burke) *sn prom: chsd wnr over 1f out: sn rdn: r.o: jst failed* 4/1[2]
606- 3 4 1/2 **Sir Reginald**[43] 7991 6-8-12 **90** GeorgeChaloner(5) 7 88
(Richard Fahey) *ldrs: rdn over 2f out: styd on same pce fnl f* 4/1[2]
513- 4 1 3/4 **Fantasy Gladiator**[38] 8053 8-8-7 **80** oh1 JimmyQuinn 2 73
(John Quinn) *pushed along early in rr: hmpd 6f out: hdwy over 1f out: sn rdn: no ex ins fnl f* 8/1
605- 5 1 **Clockmaker (IRE)**[6] 8428 8-9-7 **94** GeorgeBaker 4 84
(Conor Dore) *t.k.h: trckd ldr tl led over 5f out: pushed along and hdd over 2f out: rdn over 1f out: wknd ins fnl f* 9/2[3]
102- 6 6 **Jay Bee Blue**[20] 8305 5-8-7 **80** oh1 (bt) ChrisCatlin 5 54
(Sean Curran) *hld up: rdn over 2f out: wknd wl over 1f out* 12/1
135- 7 8 **Al's Memory (IRE)**[14] 8369 5-8-8 **81** MartinLane 1 33
(David Evans) *s.i.s: sn pushed along: sme hdwy whn hmpd 6f out: rdn and wknd over 2f out* 8/1

1m 28.92s (-0.68) **Going Correction** +0.175s/f (Slow) 7 Ran SP% **114.8**
Speed ratings (Par 107): **110,109,104,102,101 94,85**
CSF £14.02 CT £42.70 TOTE £4.50: £2.40, £1.70; EX 19.70 Trifecta £136.30.
**Owner** Dr Marwan Koukash **Bred** Mrs Eleanor Kent **Trained** Newmarket, Suffolk
■ Star Links was withdrawn. Price at time of withdrawl 8-1. Rule 4 applies to board prices prior to withdrawal, but not to SP bets - deduction 15p in the £. New market formed.
**FOCUS**
Some good handicappers contested this at a generous pace, so the form looks reliable.

## 39 DOWNLOAD THE LADBROKES APP H'CAP 1m 141y(P)
**6:00** (6:00) (Class 6) (0-65,70) 4-Y-0+ **£1,940** (£577; £288; £144) **Stalls** Low

Form RPR
/2- 1 **Disco Dave (IRE)**[14] 8371 6-8-9 **52** ow1 ShaneKelly 6 62
(Daniel Mark Loughnane) *hld up: hdwy over 2f out: chsd ldr over 1f out: shkn up to ld wl ins fnl f: comf* 5/1[3]
531- 2 1/2 **Ellaal**[14] 8371 5-8-13 **56** DaleSwift 3 65
(Ruth Carr) *trckd ldr tl pushed along to ld over 2f out: rdn over 1f out: hdd wl ins fnl f* 3/1[1]
031- 3 4 1/2 **Staff Sergeant**[7] 8410 7-9-6 **70** 6ex AlistairRawlinson(7) 2 69
(Michael Appleby) *trckd ldrs: t.k.h: nt clr run over 2f out: rdn and hung lft 1f out: styd on same pce* 4/1[2]
033- 4 hd **Delightful Sleep**[28] 8183 6-9-4 **61** AdamKirby 1 59
(David Evans) *hld up: hdwy over 1f out: sn rdn: no ex ins fnl f* 3/1[1]
661- 5 5 **Hail Promenader (IRE)**[27] 8199 8-9-4 **61** (tp) WilliamCarson 7 48
(Anthony Carson) *led: t.k.h: pushed along and hdd over 2f out: wkng whn hmpd 1f out* 3/1[1]

1m 51.8s (1.30) **Going Correction** +0.175s/f (Slow) 5 Ran SP% **111.7**
Speed ratings (Par 101): **101,100,96,96,91**
CSF £20.20 TOTE £3.40: £3.20, £2.10; EX 20.00 Trifecta £74.30.
**Owner** Mrs C Loughnane **Bred** B Walsh **Trained** Baldwin's Gate, Staffs
**FOCUS**
The race attracted typical 0-65 types, but the runners were in decent form and their SPs covered a small range from 3-1 to 5-1. The pace was modest until quickening 3f out, making it a test of finishing speed.

## 40 CORAL MOBILE "JUST THREE CLICKS TO BET" H'CAP 1m 1f 103y(P)
**6:30** (6:30) (Class 7) (0-50,50) 4-Y-0+ **£1,940** (£577; £288; £144) **Stalls** Low

Form RPR
064- 1 **Daniel Thomas (IRE)**[45] 7963 12-9-4 **47** (tp) WilliamCarson 10 59
(Ann Stokell) *s.i.s: hld up: hdwy over 2f out: led over 1f out: sn rdn and hung rt: styd on* 4/1[2]
06-0 2 2 **Stanlow**[1] 17 4-9-6 **50** StephenCraine 8 58
(Daniel Mark Loughnane) *trckd ldr over 4f: remained handy: rdn over 2f out: edgd rt over 1f out: styd on* 10/1
256- 3 4 **Kyle Of Bute**[21] 8275 8-9-2 **50** JoshBaudains(5) 9 49
(Richard Ford) *trckd ldrs: wnt 2nd 5f out: rdn over 2f out: no ex ins fnl f* 4/1[2]
244- 4 nk **Windsor Secret**[7] 8418 4-9-2 **46** PJMcDonald 4 45
(Keith Dalgleish) *a.p: rdn over 3f out: styd on same pce fr over 1f out* 7/1[3]
040- 5 1 **Arte Del Calcio**[44] 7981 5-9-0 **46** MarkCoumbe(3) 3 43
(Tony Carroll) *stmbld s: hld up: hdwy u.p over 1f out: nt rch ldrs* 12/1
655- 6 shd **Global Leader (IRE)**[37] 8063 4-9-6 **50** (b) AdamKirby 7 46
(Paul D'Arcy) *sn led: rdn over 2f out: hdd over 1f out: wknd ins fnl f* 2/1[1]
000- 7 2 3/4 **Oriental Cavalier**[45] 7962 8-9-6 **49** (v) MartinLane 1 40
(Mark Buckley) *mid-div: rdn over 3f out: wknd over 1f out* 25/1
060- 8 nse **Zed Candy Girl**[45] 7963 4-9-1 **45** ShaneKelly 2 36
(John Stimpson) *hld up: nt clr run over 3f out: swtchd rt: nvr on terms* 20/1
006- 9 3 **Stamp Duty (IRE)**[8] 8399 6-9-2 **45** StevieDonohoe 6 29
(Suzzanne France) *hld up: rdn over 2f out: n.d* 10/1
550- 10 37 **Queen's Princess**[17] 8320 6-9-2 **45** (p) PaulPickard 5
(John Wainwright) *trckd ldrs: plld hrd: wknd 4f out* 66/1

2m 2.81s (1.11) **Going Correction** +0.175s/f (Slow)
**WFA** 4 from 5yo+ 1lb 10 Ran SP% **121.8**
Speed ratings (Par 97): **102,100,96,96,95 95,92,92,90,57**
CSF £44.74 CT £174.84 TOTE £6.60: £2.50, £3.00, £1.50; EX 75.90 Trifecta £769.40.
**Owner** Pallet And Recycling Sales Ltd **Bred** Lawn Stud **Trained** Southwell, Notts
■ Stewards' Enquiry : Stephen Craine three-day ban: weighed in heavy (17-19 Jan)
**FOCUS**
This was a weak handicap, won by a veteran on a basement mark, but the pace was solid.

## 41 CORAL APP DOWNLOAD FROM THE APP STORE MEDIAN AUCTION MAIDEN STKS 1m 4f 50y(P)
**7:00** (7:00) (Class 6) 4-6-Y-0 **£1,940** (£577; £288; £144) **Stalls** Low

Form RPR
1 **Great Link**[30] 5-9-6 0 (t) MarkCoumbe(3) 1 66
(Tony Carroll) *trckd ldr: pushed along over 3f out: rdn to ld over 1f out: styd on: eased nr fin* 6/4[1]
435- 2 2 1/2 **Sian Gwalia**[255] 1741 4-9-0 56 MartinLane 6 57
(David Simcock) *s.i.s: hld up: hdwy over 2f out: rdn to chse wnr over 1f out: hung lft ins fnl f: no imp* 9/4[2]
005- 3 11 **Willow Island (IRE)**[7] 8417 5-9-9 40 (b[1]) AdamKirby 5 44
(David Evans) *set stdy pce tl qcknd over 3f out: rdn over 2f out: hdd & wknd over 1f out* 4/1[3]
4 3/4 **Alizari (IRE)**[194] 6365 5-9-4 0 JoeyHaynes(5) 3 43
(Barry Brennan) *chsd ldrs: rdn over 2f out: sn wknd* 10/1
5 52 **Taraakum (FR)**[27] 4-8-12 0 (e[1]) MatthewHopkins(7) 4
(Andrew Crook) *s.s: bhd and sn drvn along: tk clsr order over 8f out: wknd over 5f out* 8/1

2m 43.44s (2.34) **Going Correction** +0.175s/f (Slow)
**WFA** 4 from 5yo 4lb 5 Ran SP% **111.0**
Speed ratings: **99,97,90,89,54**
CSF £5.19 TOTE £2.30: £1.20, £1.60; EX 6.60 Trifecta £9.80.
**Owner** Carl Hodgson **Bred** Granham Farm And P Hearson Bloodstock **Trained** Cropthorne, Worcs
**FOCUS**
Lacking in numbers and quality, this was a poor maiden run at an ordinary pace
T/Plt: £341.00. Pool: £113,766.51 - 243.53 winning units. T/Qpdt: £34.40. Pool: £14,978.29 - 321.38 winning units. CR

42 - 48a (Foreign Racing) - See Raceform Interactive

# LINGFIELD (L-H)
Saturday, January 4

**OFFICIAL GOING: Standard**
Wind: Fresh, half behind Weather: Rain clearing

## 49 CORAL MOBILE "JUST THREE CLICKS TO BET" CLASSIFIED CLAIMING STKS 1m 2f (P)
**11:50** (11:50) (Class 6) 4-Y-0+ **£2,045** (£603; £302) **Stalls** Low

Form RPR
431- 1 **Ocean Applause**[4] 8450 4-8-1 70 (t) JoeDoyle(7) 7 79
(John Ryan) *hld up in midfield: rdn and hdwy to chse ldrs 1f out: str run to ld wl ins fnl f: r.o wl* 3/1[1]
415- 2 3/4 **Copperwood**[4] 8450 9-8-3 68 JimmyQuinn 12 71
(Lee Carter) *hld up in midfield: rdn and hdwy to chse ldr wl over 1f out: r.o u.p to ld wl ins fnl f: sn hdd and no ex* 5/1[3]
435- 3 1 1/2 **Paddy's Saltantes (IRE)**[14] 8388 4-8-6 65 (b) LukeMorris 4 73
(J S Moore) *chsd ldrs: rdn to ld and wnt clr ent fnl 2f: hdd ins fnl f: no ex and outpcd fnl 75yds* 8/1
125- 4 1 1/4 **Exclusive Waters (IRE)**[16] 8339 4-8-6 69 (b) AndreaAtzeni 3 70
(Gary Moore) *restless in stalls: s.i.s: sn rcvrd and in tch in midfield: rdn and hdwy over 1f out: kpt on wl ins fnl f* 7/2[2]
226- 5 2 1/2 **Honey Of A Kitten (USA)**[4] 8450 6-8-4 70 (b) NickyMackay 5 61
(David Evans) *in tch in midfield: effrt u.p to chse ldrs wl over 1f out: wknd ins fnl f* 7/1
34- 6 2 1/2 **Tempuran**[44] 3865 5-9-2 67 (p) StephenCraine 11 68
(David Bridgwater) *stdd and dropped in bhd after s: hld up in last trio: rdn and hdwy over 1f out: edgd rt and styd on same pce fnl f* 20/1
/00- 7 hd **Buzz Law (IRE)**[8] 8416 6-8-3 65 JoeyHaynes(5) 6 60
(K R Burke) *hld up in last trio: rdn and effrt but stl plenty to do 2f out: kpt on ins fnl f: nvr trbld ldrs* 6/1
400- 8 1 1/4 **Gabrial's Hope (FR)**[17] 8335 5-8-4 62 ow1 (t) ChrisCatlin 1 53
(David Simcock) *t.k.h: led tl over 7f out: chsd ldr tl 3f out: wknd u.p over 1f out* 20/1
600- 9 3/4 **Zenarinda**[17] 8335 7-8-6 65 BenCurtis 2 54
(Mark H Tompkins) *in tch in midfield: rdn and struggling over 2f out: wknd over 1f out* 33/1
000- 10 1/2 **Standpoint**[32] 8136 8-8-3 64 LiamJones 9 50
(Conor Dore) *stdd and dropped in bhd after s: hld up in last trio: rdn wl over 1f out: no hdwy* 50/1
600- 11 4 1/2 **Poor Duke (IRE)**[4] 8454 4-8-6 68 (b) FergusSweeney 10 46
(Jamie Osborne) *t.k.h: sn chsng ldr: led over 7f out tl ent fnl 2f: sn btn: bhd fnl f* 16/1

2m 4.96s (-1.64) **Going Correction** -0.10s/f (Stan)
**WFA** 4 from 5yo+ 2lb 11 Ran SP% **122.1**
Speed ratings (Par 101): **102,101,100,99,97 95,95,94,93,93 89**
CSF £18.15 TOTE £5.60: £1.60, £2.70, £2.60; EX 29.40 Trifecta £243.80.
**Owner** W McLuskey **Bred** R G Levin **Trained** Newmarket, Suffolk
**FOCUS**
A modest claimer and a few of these had met each other recently.

## 50 32RED MAIDEN STKS (DIV I) 1m 2f (P)
**12:20** (12:23) (Class 5) 3-Y-0 **£3,067** (£905; £453) **Stalls** Low

Form RPR
6- 1 **Joyful Friend**[17] 8332 3-9-0 0 WilliamBuick 2 79+
(John Gosden) *mde all: dictated stdy gallop tl qcknd and wnt clr 3f out: in n.d over 1f out: rn green and edgd rt ins fnl f: easily* 11/4[1]
62- 2 9 **Artful Rogue (IRE)**[26] 8213 3-9-5 0 JimCrowley 9 67+
(Amanda Perrett) *dwlt: t.k.h: hld up in tch in last trio: swtchd rt and then bk lft over 2f out: rdn 2f out: styd on to go 2nd ins fnl f: no ch w wnr* 3/1[2]


The Form Book, Raceform Ltd, Newbury, RG14 5SJ

50- **3** 2¼ **Tower Power**[33] 8123 3-9-5 0 ..................(t) RobertWinston 7 63
(Ismail Mohammed) *chsd wnr: rdn and outpcd 3f out: no ch w wnr fnl 2f: lost 2nd ins fnl f: wknd towards fin* **12/1**

**4** *nk* **Dark Tsarina (IRE)** 3-9-0 0 .................. AndreaAtzeni 4 57
(Tim Pitt) *v.s.a and rdn along early: clsd on to bk of field and in tch 8f out: rdn and outpcd wl over 2f out: no ch but styd on again ins fnl f* **33/1**

00- **5** *nk* **Izbushka (IRE)**[7] 8425 3-9-5 0 .................. StevieDonohoe 3 62
(Ian Williams) *s.i.s and rdn along early: in tch in last trio: rdn and outpcd wl over 2f out: no ch but styd on again ins fnl f* **100/1**

5- **6** ½ **Cosquillas (IRE)**[29] 8176 3-9-0 0 .................. AdamKirby 8 56
(Mark Johnston) *chsd ldrs: rdn and outpcd wl over 2f out: stl 3rd but no ch w wnr 1f out: wknd wl ins fnl f* **10/1**

03- **7** 7 **Timeless War (USA)**[13] 8389 3-9-5 0 .................. GeorgeBaker 5 48
(William Haggas) *in tch in midfield: rdn over 3f out: drvn and outpcd over 2f out: wl bhd fnl f* **5/1[3]**

00- **8** 4½ **Astrovirtue**[33] 8123 3-9-5 0 .................. BenCurtis 1 39
(Mark H Tompkins) *chsd ldrs: rdn and lost pl over 3f out: wl bhd over 1f out* **100/1**

2m 6.82s (0.22) **Going Correction** -0.10s/f (Stan) **8** Ran SP% **90.0**
Speed ratings (Par 97): **95,87,86,85,85 85,79,75**
CSF £6.65 TOTE £2.90: £1.10, £1.10, £2.60; EX 7.80 Trifecta £34.90.
**Owner** Saeed H Al Tayer **Bred** Rabbah Bloodstock Limited **Trained** Newmarket, Suffolk
■ Rule 4 of 20p in the pound applies to all bets; Withdrawn: Lil Rockerfeller

**FOCUS**
An ordinary maiden, weakened to a degree when Lil Rockerfeller, who had attracted plenty of market support, refused to enter the stalls (deduct 20p in the £ under R4).

## 51 32RED MAIDEN STKS (DIV II) 1m 2f (P)
12:50 (12:50) (Class 5) 3-Y-O £3,067 (£905; £453) Stalls Low

Form RPR

00- **1** **Fractal**[16] 8340 3-9-5 0 .................. MartinLane 7 74
(David Simcock) *hld up in tch in last pair: hdwy on outer over 3f out: rdn and chsd ldr 1f out: chal and bmpd ins fnl f: sn led and r.o wl* **20/1**

3- **2** *nk* **Anglo Irish**[16] 8340 3-9-5 0 .................. WilliamBuick 1 73+
(John Gosden) *led: rdn and qcknd over 2f out: hung rt u.p 1f out: bmpd wnr ins fnl f and sn hdd: rallied and kpt on wl towards fin but a hld* **1/3[1]**

405- **3** 2¼ **Habdab**[45] 7979 3-9-0 65 .................. SeanLevey 5 64
(Richard Hannon) *wnt lft s: in tch in midfield: rdn and effrt 2f out: 3rd and keeping on same pce whn hung rt ins fnl f* **12/1**

524- **4** 3¼ **Alfaayza (IRE)**[21] 8297 3-9-0 73 .................. MartinHarley 2 57
(K R Burke) *chsd ldr: rdn and ev ch over 2f out: no ex 1f out: wknd ins fnl f* **7/1[3]**

0- **5** ¾ **Third Strike**[80] 7302 3-9-5 0 .................. GeorgeBaker 3 61
(Gary Moore) *t.k.h: chsd ldng pair: rdn and effrt on inner over 1f out: no ex 1f out: wknd ins fnl f* **10/1**

05- **6** 1¼ **Confucius Legend (IRE)**[13] 8389 3-9-5 0 .................. StephenCraine 4 58
(Jim Boyle) *bmpd s and s.i.s: in tch in last trio: outpcd and rdn 3f out: n.d but kpt on again ins fnl f* **66/1**

**7** *hd* **Swivel** 3-9-5 0 .................. AdamKirby 8 58
(Mark Johnston) *chsd ldrs: rdn and struggling 3f out: lost pl and wl hld 2f out: plugged on again ins fnl f* **6/1[2]**

00- **8** 10 **Miss Verdoyante**[8] 8415 3-9-0 0 .................. LukeMorris 9 33
(Sir Mark Prescott Bt) *dwlt: sn in tch in midfield: reminders over 4f out: sn lost pl: bhd fnl 2f* **66/1**

0- **9** 22 **Zealand (IRE)**[17] 8328 3-9-5 0 .................. LiamJones 6
(John Best) *pushed along in midfield: rdn and struggling 4f out: sn bhd: t.o fnl 2f* **66/1**

2m 6.43s (-0.17) **Going Correction** -0.10s/f (Stan) **9** Ran SP% **127.8**
Speed ratings (Par 97): **96,95,93,91,90 89,89,81,64**
CSF £30.08 TOTE £28.40: £4.30, £1.10, £2.90; EX 67.00 Trifecta £618.00.
**Owner** The Black Gold Partnership **Bred** Jeremy Green And Sons **Trained** Newmarket, Suffolk

**FOCUS**
The winning time was 0.39sec quicker than the first division. A result that would have left many punters scratching their heads.

## 52 DOWNLOAD THE LADBROKES APP H'CAP 7f 1y(P)
1:25 (1:25) (Class 5) (0-70,70) 4-Y-0+ £3,067 (£905; £453) Stalls Low

Form RPR

600- **1** **Kyllachy Star**[26] 8227 8-8-11 65 .................. (v[1]) GeorgeChaloner(5) 8 76
(Richard Fahey) *in tch in midfield: hmpd bnd 5f out: hdwy u.p to chse ldr 1f out: r.o wl to ld ins fnl f: rdn out* **10/1**

041- **2** 1¾ **Iceblast**[42] 8029 6-9-3 66 .................. (v) MartinHarley 10 72
(Michael Easterby) *hld up towards rr: hdwy u.p over 1f out: styd on wl fnl 100yds to go 2nd last strides: no threat to wnr* **7/1[3]**

320- **3** *hd* **Shaolin (IRE)**[103] 6702 4-9-6 69 .................. (t) GeorgeBaker 5 74+
(Seamus Durack) *led: rdn over 1f out: drvn and hdd ins fnl f: styd on same pce after: lost 2nd last strides* **7/2[1]**

000- **4** ½ **Top Offer**[29] 8178 5-9-5 68 .................. ShaneKelly 3 72
(Peter Crate) *stdd s: hld up in rr: swtchd rt over 2f out: rdn and hdwy over 1f out: drvn and kpt on ins fnl f* **12/1**

400- **5** 2¼ **Golden Desert (IRE)**[31] 8158 10-9-0 63 .................. LukeMorris 11 61
(Simon Dow) *s.i.s: in rr: swtchd rt and pushed along over 2f out: hdwy ent fnl f: kpt on wl fnl 150yds: nvr trbld ldrs* **20/1**

040- **6** ¾ **Lucky Di**[16] 8345 4-9-7 70 .................. JimCrowley 12 66
(Peter Hedger) *hld up towards rr: effrt on outer wl over 1f out: drvn and hdwy 1f out: rdn hands and heels and kpt on ins fnl f: nvr trbld ldrs* **6/1[2]**

1/0- **7** ¾ **Dozy Joe**[31] 8157 6-9-5 68 .................. RobertWinston 1 62
(Joseph Tuite) *hld up in rr: rdn and stl plenty to do over 1f out: clsng and nt clr run jst ins fnl f: kpt on fnl 100yds: nvr trbld ldrs* **20/1**

260- **8** *hd* **Perfect Mission**[33] 8127 6-9-0 70 .................. (b[1]) JackGarritty(7) 6 63
(Andrew Balding) *chsd ldrs: rdn and chsd ldr ent fnl 2f tl 1f out: wknd ins fnl f* **16/1**

602- **9** *hd* **Shifting Star (IRE)**[42] 8019 9-8-13 62 .................. SeanLevey 14 55
(John Bridger) *chsd ldr tl ent fnl 2f: drvn and btn jst over 1f out: wknd ins fnl f* **20/1**

511- **10** 1¾ **The Dancing Lord**[24] 8244 5-8-12 68 .................. DanielCremin(7) 9 56
(Brett Johnson) *in tch in midfield: shkn up over 2f out: rdn and no hdwy over 1f out: wknd ins fnl f* **14/1**

044- **11** 6 **Ewell Place (IRE)**[26] 8227 5-9-4 67 .................. JamieSpencer 4 39
(David Simcock) *rrd as stalls opened: sn in tch in midfield: swtchd rt 5f out: rdn and effrt on inner over 1f out: no imp 1f out: wl hld and eased ins fnl f* **8/1**

005- **12** 2½ **Valdaw**[21] 8304 6-9-3 66 .................. AndreaAtzeni 2 31
(Mike Murphy) *chsd ldrs: short of room and lost pl 5f out: rdn and dropped to rr over 2f out: wknd over 1f out: eased wl ins fnl f* **16/1**

332- **13** 3¾ **The Mongoose**[24] 8244 6-9-4 67 .................. (t) AdamKirby 13 22
(David Evans) *chsd ldrs: rdn and struggling over 2f out: bhd and eased wl ins fnl f* **7/1[3]**

1m 23.51s (-1.29) **Going Correction** -0.10s/f (Stan) **13** Ran SP% **122.1**
Speed ratings (Par 103): **103,101,100,100,97 96,95,95,95,93 86,83,79**
CSF £77.72 CT £293.93 TOTE £16.10: £5.20, £3.10, £2.10; EX 142.80 Trifecta £1396.30.
**Owner** Dr Marwan Koukash **Bred** John James **Trained** Musley Bank, N Yorks
■ Stewards' Enquiry : Sean Levey two-day ban: careless riding (18-19 Jan)

**FOCUS**
An ordinary handicap, but competitive nonetheless.

## 53 BOOKMAKERS.CO.UK SPRINT SERIES ROUND 1 H'CAP (QUALIFIER) 6f 1y(P)
2:00 (2:01) (Class 6) (0-65,65) 4-Y-O+ £3,408 (£1,006; £503) Stalls Low

Form RPR

003- **1** **Chevise (IRE)**[42] 8022 6-9-1 59 .................. (b[1]) AndreaAtzeni 1 67
(Steve Woodman) *chsd ldrs: effrt u.p 2f out: drvn over 1f out: ev ch ins fnl f: styd on wl to ld cl home* **20/1**

603- **2** *shd* **Parisian Pyramid (IRE)**[21] 8306 8-9-5 63 .................. JamieSpencer 9 71
(Richard Fahey) *broke fast and led: rdn and edgd rt wl over 1f out: battled on gamely u.p fnl f tl hdd and no ex cl home* **8/1[3]**

432- **3** ½ **Joyous**[17] 8330 4-9-5 63 .................. RobertWinston 5 69
(Dean Ivory) *stmbld leaving stalls: in tch in midfield: rdn and hdwy over 1f out: pressed wnr ins fnl f: styd on same pce fnl 75yds* **6/4[1]**

256- **4** ½ **Idle Curiosity (IRE)**[107] 6560 4-9-1 59 .................. StephenCraine 2 64
(Jim Boyle) *in tch in midfield: rdn and effrt to press ldrs 1f out: kpt on same pce wl ins fnl f* **50/1**

606- **5** ½ **One Way Or Another (AUS)**[19] 8314 11-9-5 63 .................. (t) AdamKirby 3 66
(David Evans) *stdd s: hld up in last quartet: effrt u.p over 1f out: kpt on wl ins fnl f: nt rch ldrs* **8/1[3]**

231- **6** *hd* **Presumido (IRE)**[52] 7862 4-9-2 65 .................. JackDuern(5) 4 68
(Simon Dow) *stdd s: t.k.h: hld up in last quartet: rdn and gd hdwy on inner over 1f out: chsd ldrs 1f out: no ex ins fnl f: wknd towards fin* **4/1[2]**

005- **7** *nk* **Dishy Guru**[52] 7862 5-8-13 57 .................. LukeMorris 7 59
(Michael Blanshard) *chsd ldr: ev ch and carried rt wl over 1f out: no ex jst ins fnl f: wknd fnl 75yds* **8/1[3]**

065- **8** *hd* **Two In The Pink (IRE)**[17] 8330 4-8-11 62 .................. DanielCremin(7) 10 63
(Ralph J Smith) *in tch in midfield: rdn and effrt over 1f out: swtchd lft and styd on same pce ins fnl f* **25/1**

000- **9** ½ **Bussa**[8] 8411 6-8-13 57 .................. (t) ChrisCatlin 6 56
(David Evans) *chsd ldrs: rdn ent fnl 2f: unable qck ent fnl f: wknd ins fnl f* **12/1**

401- **10** ½ **Spellmaker**[37] 8082 5-8-6 55 .................. EoinWalsh(5) 11 53
(Tony Newcombe) *stdd s: t.k.h: hld up in tch in rr: effrt on outer wl over 1f out: kpt on but nvr trbld ldrs* **14/1**

055- **11** 2½ **Speedyfix**[16] 8351 7-8-10 54 .................. (t) JimmyQuinn 12 44
(Christine Dunnett) *stdd and swtchd lft after s: hld up in tch in last quartet: rdn and effrt over 1f out: no real hdwy: wknd ins fnl f* **50/1**

1m 11.64s (-0.26) **Going Correction** -0.10s/f (Stan) **11** Ran SP% **120.2**
Speed ratings (Par 101): **97,96,96,95,94 94,94,93,93,92 89**
CSF £170.41 CT £401.09 TOTE £15.90: £4.10, £2.80, £1.40; EX 50.50 Trifecta £252.10.
**Owner** The Chevise Partnership **Bred** Paul And Mrs Jenny Green **Trained** East Lavant, W Sussex

**FOCUS**
The first qualifier in this always popular series, albeit a modest event.

## 54 CORAL.CO.UK H'CAP 1m 4f (P)
2:35 (2:35) (Class 2) 4-Y-0+
£28,012 (£8,388; £4,194; £2,097; £1,048; £526) Stalls Low

Form RPR

202- **1** **Castilo Del Diablo (IRE)**[17] 8327 5-8-9 95 .................. (p) JamieSpencer 3 102
(David Simcock) *hld up in tch towards rr: clsd and nt clr run jst over 2f out: rdn and hdwy on inner over 1f out: hung rt fnl f: led fnl 100yds: r.o wl u.p* **9/2[2]**

241- **2** *nk* **Modernstone**[14] 8387 4-8-2 92 ow2 .................. AndreaAtzeni 13 99
(William Knight) *stdd and dropped in bhd after s: hld up in last trio: hdwy over 1f out: str chal fnl 100yds: r.o wl but hld towards fin* **4/1[1]**

324- **3** 1 **Swing Alone (IRE)**[9] 8398 5-8-4 90 .................. LukeMorris 10 95
(Gay Kelleway) *hld up in tch in midfield: rdn and effrt wl over 1f out: ev ch ins fnl f: no ex and outpcd towards fin* **8/1[3]**

022- **4** *hd* **Grendisar (IRE)**[14] 8387 4-8-0 90 oh3 .................. (p) PaoloSirigu 8 95+
(Marco Botti) *stdd s: hld up in tch in rr: clsd over 1f out: chsng ldrs and stl on bit whn gap clsd and swtchd lft ins fnl f: rdn and r.o wl fnl 75yds: nt rch ldrs* **10/1**

144- **5** 1 **Presburg (IRE)**[17] 8327 5-8-0 86 oh5 .................. JimmyQuinn 5 89
(Joseph Tuite) *hld up in tch towards rr: rdn and hdwy on inner over 1f out: chsd ldrs 1f out: styd on same pce fnl 100yds* **20/1**

010- **6** 1½ **Shavansky**[17] 8327 10-7-11 88 .................. ShelleyBirkett(5) 2 89
(Rod Millman) *t.k.h: hld up in midfield: swtchd rt and hdwy on outer over 6f out: jnd ldr over 5f out: led 3f out: rdn over 1f out: hdd fnl 100yds: wknd towards fin* **20/1**

302- **7** ½ **Kashmir Peak (IRE)**[48] 7526 5-8-3 89 .................. (b[1]) MartinLane 6 89
(John Quinn) *t.k.h: hld up wl in tch: rdn and effrt to chse ldng pair 2f out: no ex 1f out: wknd fnl 100yds* **8/1[3]**

632- **8** 1¼ **Teolagi (IRE)**[9] 8398 4-7-9 90 oh5 .................. JoeyHaynes(5) 12 88
(J S Moore) *stdd s: hld up in last trio: hdwy on outer bnd wl over 1f out: kpt on but no threat to ldrs* **10/1**

303- **9** 2 **Kiama Bay (IRE)**[28] 8202 8-7-8 87 .................. JoeDoyle(7) 1 82
(Richard Fahey) *t.k.h: chsd ldr for 3f: styd handy: rdn and effrt ent fnl 2f: no ex 1f out: wknd ins fnl f* **14/1**

/32- **10** 2½ **Uramazin (IRE)**[31] 8156 8-8-13 99 .................. JimCrowley 14 90
(Philip Hide) *t.k.h: hld up in tch in midfield: rdn over 2f out: no ex and outpcd over 1f out: wknd ins fnl f* **8/1[3]**

603- **11** 7 **Persepolis (IRE)**[26] 8218 4-8-0 90 oh4 .................. AndrewMullen 4 69
(Brett Johnson) *chsd ldrs: rdn over 2f out: lost pl u.p wl over 1f out: sn wknd and bhd fnl f* **16/1**

210- **12** 8 **Halfsin (IRE)**[17] 8327 6-8-2 88 .................. (t) NickyMackay 9 55
(Marco Botti) *led tl 3f out: sn rdn: wkng whn hmpd over 1f out: sn dropped out and wl bhd fnl f* **20/1**

**13** 1¼ **Energia Eros (BRZ)**[230] 5-9-12 112 .................. MartinHarley 7 77
(Marco Botti) *hld up in tch towards rr: hdwy on outer 3f out: rdn and btn wl over 1f out: sn btn and fdd ent fnl f* **12/1**

1/0- **14** *16* **Media Hype**[105] 6620 7-9-5 **105**........................................ SeanLevey 11 44
(K R Burke) *t.k.h: chsd ldrs: wnt 2nd 9f out tl 6f out: lost pl qckly 3f out: wl bhd and eased over 1f out: t.o* **12/1**

2m 28.33s (-4.67) **Going Correction** -0.10s/f (Stan)
**WFA** 4 from 5yo+ 4lb **14** Ran SP% **131.9**
Speed ratings (Par 109): **111,110,110,110,109 108,108,107,105,104 99,94,93,82**
CSF £24.51 CT £144.92 TOTE £4.00: £2.10, £2.40, £3.10; EX 23.40 Trifecta £499.80.

**Owner** The Khat Partnership **Bred** Ennistown Stud **Trained** Newmarket, Suffolk

■ Stewards' Enquiry : Jamie Spencer three-day ban: use of whip (18-20 Jan)

**FOCUS**
A red-hot 86-112 handicap, though the early pace looked ordinary.

## 55 COMPARE BOOKMAKERS AT BOOKMAKERS.CO.UK H'CAP 6f 1y(P)

**3:10** (3:12) (Class 2) (0-100,102) 4-Y-0+ **£12,291** (£3,657; £1,827; £913) **Stalls** Low

Form RPR

111- **1** **Perfect Pasture**[52] 7851 4-9-0 **93**........................................(v) AdamKirby 5 105
(Michael Easterby) *w ldr: rdn 2f out: led 1f out: drvn and asserted ins fnl f: r.o wl and gng away at fin* **11/4**[1]

061- **2** *2* **Rivellino**[21] 8305 4-9-1 **94**........................................ MartinHarley 8 100
(K R Burke) *t.k.h: rdn wl over 1f out: hdd 1f out: no ex and outpcd fnl 100yds: hld on for 2nd* **11/4**[1]

000- **3** *½* **Kyllachy Rise**[23] 8264 4-8-11 **90**........................................(b[1]) SeanLevey 4 94
(Richard Hannon) *t.k.h: chsd ldrs: rdn and effrt over 1f out: kpt on same pce u.p ins fnl f* **8/1**[2]

042- **4** *hd* **Diamond Charlie (IRE)**[29] 8189 6-8-8 **87**.................... AndreaAtzeni 12 90
(Simon Dow) *t.k.h: hld up in tch in midfield on outer: rdn and lost pl bnd wl over 1f out: rallied and styd on wl ins fnl f* **10/1**[3]

316- **5** *hd* **Picansort**[31] 8155 7-8-8 **87**........................................(b) JimmyQuinn 10 90
(Peter Crate) *stdd s: hld up in last trio: clsd over 2f out: rdn and hdwy on inner to chse ldrs 1f out: no ex and one pce fnl 100yds* **16/1**

125- **6** *hd* **Noble Deed**[13] 8391 4-8-11 **90**........................................ LiamJones 3 92
(Michael Attwater) *taken down early: chsd ldrs: rdn and swtchd lft jst over 1f out: styd on same pce ins fnl f* **14/1**

631- **7** *¾* **Naabegha**[26] 8217 7-8-10 **89**........................................(p) BenCurtis 1 89
(Alan McCabe) *stdd and rrd as stalls opened: slowly away: t.k.h: hld up in rr: hdwy over 1f out: swtchd lft and styd on wl ins fnl f: nvr trbld ldrs* **12/1**

000- **8** *hd* **Doctor Parkes**[25] 8232 8-8-11 **90**........................................ AdamBeschizza 9 89
(Stuart Williams) *chsd ldrs: rdn and unable qck over 1f out: no ex and wknd fnl 100yds* **20/1**

600- **9** *3 ¼* **Capone (IRE)**[16] 8344 9-9-0 **93**........................................ ShaneKelly 2 82
(Michael Attwater) *stdd s: hld up in last quartet: rdn and effrt over 1f out: no imp: n.d* **33/1**

000- **10** *¾* **Whaileyy (IRE)**[209] 3135 6-9-9 **102**........................................(b) WilliamBuick 7 88
(Marco Botti) *t.k.h: w ldrs tl stdd bk but stl wl in tch in midfield after 1f: rdn and effrt over 1f out: no ex and wknd ins fnl f* **8/1**[2]

000- **11** *nk* **Elusivity (IRE)**[91] 7010 6-9-1 **94**........................................ JamieSpencer 6 79
(Peter Crate) *stdd s: hld up in last quartet: rdn and no hdwy over 1f out: n.d* **10/1**[3]

1m 10.16s (-1.74) **Going Correction** -0.10s/f (Stan) **11** Ran SP% **121.7**
Speed ratings (Par 109): **107,104,103,103,103 102,101,101,97,96 95**
CSF £9.43 CT £55.50 TOTE £3.40: £1.10, £1.50, £3.80; EX 12.20 Trifecta £116.40.

**Owner** Mrs Jean Turpin **Bred** Mrs Jean Turpin **Trained** Sheriff Hutton, N Yorks

**FOCUS**
A decent sprint handicap, though the first two dominated the contest throughout.

## 56 LADBROKES H'CAP 1m 1y(P)

**3:45** (3:47) (Class 4) (0-85,84) 4-Y-0+ **£4,942** (£1,459; £730) **Stalls** High

Form RPR

/30- **1** **Indian Jack (IRE)**[44] 7989 6-9-7 **84**........................................ LukeMorris 5 95
(Ed Walker) *in tch in midfield: rdn and effrt 2f out: hdwy and nt clr run 1f out: drvn and chsd ldr ins fnl f: r.o wl to ld fnl 50yds* **5/1**[3]

055- **2** *½* **Naaz (IRE)**[26] 8218 4-9-3 **80**........................................(b) AdamKirby 2 90
(Ed Dunlop) *hld up in tch in midfield: swtchd lft and effrt over 1f out: led 1f out and sn drvn clr: r.o tl hdd and no ex fnl 50yds* **9/2**[2]

411- **3** *3 ¾* **Scottish Glen**[26] 8219 8-8-6 **83**........................................ GeorgeBaker 8 84
(Patrick Chamings) *hld up in tch in midfield: effrt and rdn over 1f out: wnt 3rd ins fnl f: no imp and wknd towards fin* **3/1**[1]

414- **4** *nse* **The Great Gabrial**[16] 8350 5-9-2 **79**........................................(v) JamieSpencer 4 80
(Alan McCabe) *t.k.h: chsd ldrs: rdn and effrt over 1f out: unable qck and btn ins fnl f: wknd towards fin* **7/1**

003- **5** *½* **My Kingdom (IRE)**[21] 8304 8-8-10 **73**........................................(t) AdamBeschizza 1 73
(Stuart Williams) *hld up in tch towards rr: gd hdwy on inner over 1f out: chsd ldrs 1f out: edgd rt and wknd ins fnl f* **16/1**

254- **6** *3 ¾* **Ishikawa (IRE)**[17] 8336 6-8-9 **79**........................................(p) RobJFitzpatrick(7) 11 70
(K R Burke) *chsd ldr tl led 6f out: rdn and hdd over 1f out: wknd fnl f* **8/1**

251- **7** *½* **Canadian Run (IRE)**[102] 6734 4-9-7 **84**........................................ SeanLevey 9 74
(Robert Mills) *led for 2f: styd chsng ldr: hrd drvn and led over 1f out: hdd and unable qck 1f out: wknd ins fnl f* **6/1**

106- **8** *5* **Camachoice (IRE)**[220] 2776 4-9-0 **77**........................................ MartinHarley 7 56
(Marco Botti) *chsd ldrs tl stdd into midfield but stl wl in tch after 2f: lost pl u.p over 2f out: bhd fnl f* **16/1**

346- **9** *3* **Ancient Greece**[146] 5310 7-8-13 **76**........................................(t) AndrewMullen 10 48
(George Baker) *s.i.s and rdn along: a towards rr: struggling u.p ent fnl 2f: wknd over 1f out* **14/1**

103- **10** *1 ¼* **Soaring Spirits (IRE)**[26] 8219 4-9-3 **80**........................................(b) RobertWinston 6 49
(Dean Ivory) *hld up in tch towards rr: rdn and struggling whn v wd bnd 2f out: sn wknd* **14/1**

1m 35.53s (-2.67) **Going Correction** -0.10s/f (Stan) **10** Ran SP% **122.8**
Speed ratings (Par 105): **109,108,104,104,104 100,99,94,91,90**
CSF £29.47 CT £83.08 TOTE £6.80: £2.30, £1.40, £1.80; EX 33.10 Trifecta £192.50.

**Owner** Forza Azzurri **Bred** Waterford Hall Stud **Trained** Newmarket, Suffolk

**FOCUS**
A fair handicap and a stirring finish.

T/Jkpt: Not won. T/Plt: £13.00. Pool: £161,417.69 - 9,022.73 winning units. T/Qpdt: £5.60. Pool: £12,450.37 - 1,643.05 winning units. SP

# DEAUVILLE (R-H)

Saturday, January 4

**OFFICIAL GOING: Fibresand: standard**

## 57a PRIX DE BEAUFOSSE (CLAIMER) (5YO+) (LADY AMATEUR RIDERS) (FIBRESAND) 7f 110y

**12:45** (12:00) 5-Y-0+ **£6,250** (£2,500; £1,875; £1,250; £625)

RPR

**1** **Morrocoy (IRE)**[64] 6-9-4 0........................................ MlleJessicaMarcialis 2 77
(G Botti, France) **14/5**[2]

**2** *1* **Conry (IRE)**[16] 8350 8-9-8 0........................................ MlleSandrineHagenbach 4 79?
(Ian Williams) *midfield on inner: rdn 2f out: styd on and wnt 2nd wl ins fnl f: nt pce of wnr* **205/10**

**3** *½* **Princess Vati (FR)**[39] 5-9-5 0........................................ MlleAlisonMassin 8 74
(P Monfort, France) **79/10**

**4** *3* **Eastside Gallery** 5-9-1 0........................................ MlleAlexandraRosa 10 63
(S Smrczek, Germany) **31/5**[3]

**5** *hd* **Lavallo (GER)**[91] 7-9-8 0........................................(p) MissSilkeBruggemann 7 69
(Waldemar Hickst, Germany) **13/5**[1]

**6** *½* **Boltcity (FR)**[17] 7-9-8 0........................................ MlleBarbaraGuenet 5 68
(Braem Horse Racing Sprl, Belgium) **124/10**

**7** *shd* **Sugarformyhoney (IRE)**[33] 8134 5-9-10 0.... MllePaulineBoisgontier 12 70
(Brendan Powell) *midfield on outer: rdn over 2f out: outpcd by ldrs ins fnl f: kpt on* **74/10**

**8** *2 ½* **Fergand (FR)**[295] 5-9-4 0........................................ MlleStephanieHusser 11 58
(M Drean, France) **89/1**

**9** *1 ¼* **Thyan (FR)**[16] 7-9-8 0........................................ MmeIrmaBrandt 13 58
(P Capelle, France) **72/1**

**10** *2 ½* **Tiger Cliff (FR)**[12] 9-9-1 0........................................(p) MmeCatherineRieb-Menard 1 45
(J-L Bertin, France) **204/10**

**11** *snk* **Earl Of Fire (GER)**[192] 9-9-4 0........................................ MlleBlancheDeGranvilliers 14 48
(C Boutin, France) **30/1**

**12** *¾* **Babylona (FR)**[793] 7256 7-8-10 0........................................ MlleEmmanuelleBarrier(5) 3 43
(Philippe Le Geay, France) **123/1**

**13** *snk* **Baratom (FR)**[438] 8-9-0 0........................................(p) MlleMarieRollando(4) 9 46
(F-X De Chevigny, France) **29/1**

**14** *¾* **Dernier Chichi (FR)** 5-9-4 0........................................ MmeClaireGerald(4) 6 48
(D Allard, France) **61/1**

1m 30.52s (90.52) **14** Ran SP% **119.4**
WIN (incl. 1 euro stake): 3.80. PLACES: 1.70, 5.00, 2.50. DF: 44.90. SF: 74.60.
**Owner** Angelo Lietti **Bred** Sig Massimo Parri **Trained** France

# [28]SOUTHWELL (L-H)

Sunday, January 5

**OFFICIAL GOING: Standard**
Wind: moderate 1/2 against Weather: overcast, cold, becoming fine and sunny after race 3

## 58 BOOKMAKERS.CO.UK "HANDS AND HEELS" APPRENTICE SERIES H'CAP (RACING EXCELLENCE INITIATIVE) 5f (F)

**12:40** (12:42) (Class 6) (0-55,55) 4-Y-0+ **£2,264** (£673; £336; £168)

Form RPR

504- **1** **Imjin River (IRE)**[5] 8457 7-8-12 **46**........................................(t) LouisSteward 11 61
(William Stone) *hld up towards rr: smooth hdwy 2f out: led jst ins fnl f: pushed clr* **9/2**[3]

221- **2** *2 ¾* **Major Muscari (IRE)**[9] 8413 6-9-0 **53**........................................(p) AlexHopkinson(5) 2 58
(Shaun Harris) *led: hdd jst ins fnl f: kpt on same pce* **3/1**[2]

005- **3** *1 ¼* **Upper Lambourn (IRE)**[9] 8406 6-9-1 **49**........................................(t) RobJFitzpatrick 7 50
(Christopher Kellett) *mid-div: hdwy 2f out: kpt on ins fnl f* **8/1**

622- **4** *3 ¼* **Errigal Lad**[38] 8082 9-9-1 **52**........................................ JackGarritty(3) 6 41
(Garry Woodward) *s.i.s: bhd: hdwy 2f out: kpt on ins fnl f* **10/1**

626- **5** *shd* **Lucky Mark (IRE)**[9] 8413 5-9-1 **52**........................................(p) AlfieWarwick(3) 9 41
(Garry Moss) *mid-div: hdwy 2f out: kpt on ins fnl f* **10/1**

012- **6** *1* **Pearl Noir**[7] 8438 4-9-7 **55**........................................(b) MatthewHopkins 8 40
(Scott Dixon) *w ldr: wknd appr fnl f* **11/4**[1]

355- **7** *3 ½* **Chateau Lola**[16] 8370 5-8-12 **46** oh1........................................(v) AdamMcLean 1 18
(Derek Shaw) *in tch: effrt over 2f out: wknd over 1f out* **14/1**

44-5 **8** *1 ¼* **Amis Reunis**[3] 9 5-9-1 **52**........................................(p) JordanHibberd(3) 10 20
(Alan Berry) *s.i.s: sn outpcd and in rr: nvr a factor* **14/1**

/60- **9** *2 ½* **Lucky Mellor**[23] 8272 7-8-9 **46**........................................(t) PaulBooth(3) 5 5
(Barry Murtagh) *racd towards far side: in tch: lost pl over 1f out* **33/1**

600- **10** *hd* **Lord Buffhead**[31] 8169 5-8-11 **50**........................................(p) MelissaThompson(5) 4 8
(Richard Guest) *s.i.s: a in rr* **20/1**

006- **11** *34* **Mrs Medley**[9] 8407 8-8-9 **46** oh1........................................ AaronJones(3) 3
(Ann Stokell) *swvd lft and reluctant s: rdr briefly lost iron: a t.o* **100/1**

58.6s (-1.10) **Going Correction** -0.175s/f (Stan) **11** Ran SP% **121.2**
Speed ratings (Par 101): **101,96,94,89,89 87,82,80,76,75 21**
CSF £18.73 CT £109.83 TOTE £6.00: £2.60, £1.20, £3.90; EX 23.00 Trifecta £172.40.
**Owner** Miss Caroline Scott **Bred** Glending Bloodstock **Trained** West Wickham, Cambs

**FOCUS**
Malfunctioning starting stalls meant this moderate handicap was started by flag. Only a handful figured in this messy event and the winner came down the centre.

## 59 COMPARE BOOKMAKERS AT BOOKMAKERS.CO.UK H'CAP 6f (F)

**1:10** (1:13) (Class 6) (0-60,60) 4-Y-0+ **£2,587** (£770; £384; £192) **Stalls** Low

Form RPR

300- **1** **Prince Of Passion (CAN)**[26] 8235 6-9-5 **58**........................................(v) TonyHamilton 7 70
(Derek Shaw) *mde virtually all: hld on wl towards fin* **8/1**

224- **2** *¾* **Grace Hull**[26] 8235 4-9-1 **57**........................................ BillyCray(3) 13 67
(Garry Moss) *sn trcking ldrs on outside: chal jst ins fnl f: no ex towards fin* **7/2**[3]

031- **3** *1 ½* **Borough Boy (IRE)**[7] 8438 4-9-5 **58** 6ex........................................(v) DaleSwift 9 63
(Derek Shaw) *hld up in mid-div: hdwy stands' side over 2f out: hung lft over 1f out: kpt on same pce* **9/4**[1]

04-0 **4** *4* **Captain Scooby**[3] 9 8-9-5 **58**........................................(e) RobbieFitzpatrick 4 50
(Richard Guest) *s.i.s: in rr: kpt on fnl 2f: nvr a factor* **10/1**

022- **5** *shd* **Ivestar (IRE)**[32] 8152 9-9-4 **57**........................................(v) AdamKirby 8 49
(Michael Easterby) *chsd ldrs: drvn over 2f out: one pce* **3/1**[2]



The Form Book, Raceform Ltd, Newbury, RG14 5SJ

240- **6** 1 ½ **Molly Jones**[115] 6344 5-8-7 **49**....................(p) RosieJessop(3) 5 36
(Derek Haydn Jones) *rrd s: in rr: sme hdwy 2f out: nvr nr ldrs* **25/1**

003- **7** ¾ **All Right Now**[19] 8315 7-9-0 **53**.................... ChrisCatlin 1 37
(Tony Newcombe) *s.i.s: in rr: sme hdwy 2f out: nvr a factor* **16/1**

530- **8** 1 **Fathom Five (IRE)**[7] 8439 10-9-2 **60**.................... ShirleyTeasdale(5) 3 41
(Shaun Harris) *w wnr: wknd over 1f out* **10/1**

200- **9** 3 ¼ **Madame Kintyre**[17] 8338 6-8-9 **48**.................... MartinLane 10 19
(Rod Millman) *chsd ldrs: lost pl over 1f out* **25/1**

1m 15.46s (-1.04) **Going Correction** -0.15s/f (Stan) **9 Ran SP% 120.9**
Speed ratings (Par 101): **100,99,97,91,91 89,88,87,82**
CSF £37.95 CT £85.62 TOTE £11.00: £3.20, £1.60, £1.30; EX 43.10 Trifecta £204.30.
**Owner** Chris Hamilton **Bred** Majestic Thoroughbred Investments Inc **Trained** Sproxton, Leics

**FOCUS**
Exposed performers in a moderate handicap that saw the starting stalls back in operation. Although the gallop was sound, not many figured and the winner came down the centre.

## 60 BEST ODDS AT BOOKMAKERS.CO.UK H'CAP 6f (F)
**1:40** (1:42) (Class 5) (0-75,75) 4-Y-O+ **£2,911** (£866; £432; £216) **Stalls** Low

Form RPR

143- **1** **Hannahs Turn**[19] 8319 4-9-2 **75**.................... ShelleyBirkett(5) 1 93
(Chris Dwyer) *trckd ldr: led on bit over 2f out: shkn up and wnt clr 1f out: eased towards fin* **5/4**[1]

006- **2** 7 **Kellys Eye (IRE)**[186] 3955 7-9-0 **68**.................... TomQueally 2 64
(Ian Williams) *chsd ldrs: drvn over 2f out: tk modest 2nd 1f out: no ch w wnr* **9/4**[2]

000- **3** 3 ½ **Dorback**[27] 8224 7-9-4 **72**.................... ChrisCatlin 6 56
(Tony Newcombe) *chsd ldrs: outpcd over 3f out: hdwy over 2f out: kpt on to take modest 3rd last 100yds* **14/1**

600- **4** 3 **Climaxfortackle (IRE)**[7] 8439 6-8-12 **66**.................... LiamJones 5 41
(Derek Shaw) *s.i.s: drvn over 3f out: outpcd over 2f out: nvr a factor* **8/1**[3]

204- **5** 1 **Greenhead High**[16] 8365 6-9-5 **73**....................(v) AdrianNicholls 4 45
(David Nicholls) *led: hdd over 2f out: wknd fnl f* **8/1**[3]

600- **6** 11 **Point North (IRE)**[19] 8321 7-9-2 **70**....................(b) LukeMorris 3 17
(John Balding) *s.s: swtchd rt after s and racd wd: hdwy over 3f out: sn chsng ldrs: wknd 2f out: bhd whn eased clsng stages* **9/1**

1m 14.91s (-1.59) **Going Correction** -0.15s/f (Stan) **6 Ran SP% 114.1**
Speed ratings (Par 103): **104,94,90,86,84 70**
CSF £4.38 TOTE £1.70: £1.10, £2.10; EX 5.50 Trifecta £36.60.
**Owner** Mrs K W Sneath **Bred** Wayland Stud **Trained** Newmarket, Suffolk

**FOCUS**
A fair handicap but not many arrived here in top form. The gallop was an ordinary one and the easy winner came down the centre.

## 61 LADBROKES H'CAP 1m (F)
**2:10** (2:10) (Class 3) (0-95,93) 4-Y-O **£7,246** (£2,168; £1,084; £542; £270) **Stalls** Low

Form RPR

220- **1** **Frontier Fighter**[16] 8369 6-9-4 **93**.................... SamJames(3) 1 103
(David O'Meara) *led: qcknd pce over 3f out: shkn up and edgd lft over 1f out: drvn out: readily* **9/4**[2]

664- **2** 1 **The Lock Master (IRE)**[9] 8408 7-8-7 **79** oh2.................... AndrewMullen 2 87
(Michael Appleby) *s.i.s: drvn to sn chse wnr: hrd drvn over 3f out: hung lft over 1f out: kpt on to take 2nd last 100yds: no real imp* **7/2**[3]

051- **3** 1 ¾ **Greyfriarschorista**[9] 8408 7-8-7 **84**.................... ShelleyBirkett(5) 3 88
(Tom Keddy) *trckd ldrs: 2nd and upsides 3f out: rdn and swtchd rt over 1f out: kpt on same pce* **2/1**[1]

155- **4** 5 **First Post (IRE)**[9] 8408 7-8-10 **82**.................... LiamKeniry 4 74
(Derek Haydn Jones) *chsd ldrs on outer: drvn over 3f out: wknd over 1f out* **4/1**

0/0- **5** 15 **Arabian Heights**[164] 4683 6-8-4 **79** oh1.................... MichaelJMMurphy(3) 6 37
(Ian Williams) *dwlt: in rr and sn pushed along: lost pl over 3f out: sn bhd* **20/1**

1m 40.52s (-3.18) **Going Correction** -0.15s/f (Stan) **5 Ran SP% 111.1**
Speed ratings (Par 107): **109,108,106,101,86**
CSF £10.48 TOTE £3.60: £2.60, £2.30; EX 11.10 Trifecta £19.10.
**Owner** Archibald Nichol & Partners **Bred** Darley **Trained** Nawton, N Yorks

**FOCUS**
Not a competitive event given the money on offer but nevertheless a very useful handicap in which the gallop was no more than fair. The winner edged towards the inside rail in the closing stages.

## 62 32RED H'CAP 6f (F)
**2:40** (2:40) (Class 4) (0-85,84) 3-Y-O **£5,175** (£1,540; £769; £384) **Stalls** Low

Form RPR

021- **1** **Captain Secret**[16] 8364 3-9-7 **84**.................... LukeMorris 3 93
(Marco Botti) *chsd ldrs: drvn and edgd lft over 2f out: led wl over 1f out: styd on strly: readily* **5/2**[2]

421- **2** 3 ½ **Queenie's Home**[16] 8368 3-8-10 **73**.................... DaleSwift 4 71
(James Given) *chsd ldrs: drvn and sltly outpcd over 2f out: kpt on to take 2nd last 75yds: no imp* **7/2**

252- **3** ½ **Searchlight**[6] 8442 3-8-12 **75**.................... TonyHamilton 2 71
(Kevin Ryan) *sn led: hdd wl over 1f out: kpt on same pce* **3/1**[3]

31-1 **4** 6 **Exceeding Power**[4] 6 3-8-12 **75** 6ex.................... TomQueally 1 52
(Michael Bell) *led early: chsd ldrs: drvn over 2f out: wknd fnl f* **2/1**[1]

1m 14.77s (-1.73) **Going Correction** -0.15s/f (Stan) **4 Ran SP% 109.1**
Speed ratings (Par 99): **105,100,99,91**
CSF £10.91 TOTE £2.70; EX 10.40 Trifecta £22.00.
**Owner** Scuderia Blueberry **Bred** R G Percival **Trained** Newmarket, Suffolk

**FOCUS**
Only four runners but a very useful effort from the winner. The gallop was reasonable and the winner came down the centre.

## 63 CORAL MOBILE JUST THREE CLICKS TO BET (S) STKS 1m 4f (F)
**3:10** (3:11) (Class 6) 4-Y-O+ **£2,587** (£770; £384; £192) **Stalls** Low

Form RPR

301- **1** **La Estrella (USA)**[19] 8318 11-9-10 87.................... GrahamLee 2 71+
(Don Cantillon) *led 2f: w ldr: led over 4f out: nudged clr over 1f out: v easily* **1/25**[1]

050- **2** 3 ¾ **Loulou Vuitton**[9] 8418 4-8-4 47....................(p[1]) JackDuern(5) 5 46
(Steph Hollinshead) *rrd s: t.k.h and trckd ldrs after 2f: clr 2nd over 2f out: no ch w wnr* **10/1**[2]

05-5 **3** 2 ¼ **Bix (IRE)**[4] 2 4-8-7 46.................... JordanHibberd(7) 4 47
(Alan Berry) *w ldr: led after 2f: hdd over 4f out: one pce fnl 3f* **25/1**[3]

046/ **4** 33 **Kneesy Earsy Nosey**[1371] 1114 8-8-9 35 ow1....................(p) AnnStokell(5) 3
(Ann Stokell) *t.k.h: trckd ldng pair: reminders over 5f out: lost pl 4f out: sn bhd: t.o over 2f out* **40/1**

2m 42.59s (1.59) **Going Correction** -0.15s/f (Stan)
**WFA** 4 from 5yo+ 4lb **4 Ran SP% 111.5**
Speed ratings (Par 101): **88,85,84,62**
CSF £1.53 TOTE £1.10; EX 1.80 Trifecta £2.20.Winner bought in 5,250gns.
**Owner** Don Cantillon **Bred** Five Horses Ltd And Theatrical Syndicate **Trained** Newmarket, Suffolk

**FOCUS**
A very one-sided event. The gallop was on the steady side and the easy winner raced in the centre.

## 64 CORAL.CO.UK BEST ODDS GUARANTEED H'CAP 1m 4f (F)
**3:40** (3:40) (Class 5) (0-70,69) 4-Y-O+ **£2,911** (£866; £432; £216) **Stalls** Low

Form RPR

153- **1** **Afro**[121] 6158 4-9-1 **64**.................... LukeMorris 2 71
(Peter Hedger) *dwlt: sn chsng ldrs: drvn over 4f out: styd on to ld jst ins fnl f: kpt on wl* **5/2**[2]

132- **2** 1 ¼ **Yasir (USA)**[7] 8433 6-9-10 **69**....................(p) LiamKeniry 1 74
(Conor Dore) *dropped in last: effrt over 4f out: reminders over 3f out: hdwy on outside over 2f out: kpt on to take 2nd clsng stages* **5/4**[1]

135- **3** ½ **Atalanta Bay (IRE)**[17] 8343 4-9-1 **64**.................... GrahamLee 4 68
(Marcus Tregoning) *w ldr: kpt on same pce fnl f* **4/1**[3]

023- **4** 1 ½ **Alborz (IRE)**[20] 8310 5-9-8 **67**.................... LeeTopliss 5 69
(Tim Vaughan) *led: increased pce over 4f out: hdd jst ins fnl f: wknd nr fin* **4/1**[3]

2m 39.79s (-1.21) **Going Correction** -0.15s/f (Stan)
**WFA** 4 from 5yo+ 4lb **4 Ran SP% 113.0**
Speed ratings (Par 103): **98,97,96,95**
CSF £6.37 TOTE £2.60; EX 5.20 Trifecta £10.80.
**Owner** P C F Racing Ltd **Bred** The Lavington Stud **Trained** Dogmersfield, Hampshire

**FOCUS**
A modest handicap in which the gallop was on the steady side. The winner came down the centre.
T/Jkpt: £1,307.20 to a £1 stake. Pool: £59,837.73 - 32.50 winning tickets. T/Plt: £22.40 to a £1 stake. Pool: £111,310.33 - 3,617.61 winning tickets. T/Qpdt: £7.20 to a £1 stake. Pool: £5,562.25 - 567.74 winning tickets. WG

# [35]WOLVERHAMPTON (A.W) (L-H)
### Monday, January 6

**OFFICIAL GOING: Standard**
Wind: Strong behind Weather: Overcast

## 65 LADBROKES APPRENTICE H'CAP 7f 32y(P)
**2:10** (2:10) (Class 6) (0-65,64) 4-Y-O+ **£1,940** (£577; £288; £144) **Stalls** High

Form RPR

526- **1** **Dance For Georgie**[20] 8316 5-9-4 **64**.................... GeorgeChaloner(3) 3 76
(Ben Haslam) *chsd ldr tl rdn to ld over 1f out: styd on u.p* **4/1**[2]

505- **2** 1 ¾ **Minimee**[10] 8409 4-8-10 **53**....................(v) RobertTart 5 60
(Phil McEntee) *hld up: hdwy 2f out: rdn and ev ch ins fnl f: styd on same pce* **11/2**

346- **3** 3 **McCool Bannanas**[96] 6943 6-9-2 **62**.................... TimClark(3) 2 61
(James Unett) *s.i.s: hdwy over 5f out: rdn and ev ch over 1f out: styd on same pce ins fnl f* **5/1**[3]

33-6 **4** shd **Lastkingofscotland (IRE)**[4] 20 8-9-0 **57**........(b) MichaelJMMurphy 7 56
(Conor Dore) *sn led: rdn and hdd over 1f out: hung lft and no ex ins fnl f* **7/2**[1]

003- **5** shd **Darnathean**[40] 8059 5-8-13 **63**....................(p) StaceyKidd(7) 4 62
(Paul D'Arcy) *hld up: pushed along over 2f out: r.o ins fnl f: nvr nrr* **8/1**

515- **6** 1 **Ad Vitam (IRE)**[24] 8278 6-8-11 **57**....................(vt) JacobButterfield(3) 1 53
(Mel Brittain) *prom: pushed along 1/2-way: rdn over 2f out: styd on same pce fr over 1f out* **8/1**

326- **7** 1 ¼ **Medam**[7] 8446 5-8-6 **52**.................... ShirleyTeasdale(3) 6 45
(Shaun Harris) *prom: rdn over 1f out: wknd ins fnl f* **11/2**

1m 30.7s (1.10) **Going Correction** +0.225s/f (Slow) **7 Ran SP% 111.9**
Speed ratings (Par 101): **102,100,96,96,96 95,93**
CSF £24.78 TOTE £3.70: £2.80, £4.30; EX 28.40 Trifecta £238.60.
**Owner** Mark James **Bred** West Dereham Abbey Stud **Trained** Middleham Moor, N Yorks

**FOCUS**
A modest handicap for apprentice riders, but they went a solid pace and the front two pulled away. The winner is rated to her turf form.

## 66 LADBROKES (S) STKS 1m 141y(P)
**2:40** (2:40) (Class 6) 4-Y-O+ **£1,940** (£577; £288; £144) **Stalls** Low

Form RPR

630- **1** **Saharia (IRE)**[31] 8179 7-9-4 70....................(b) BenCurtis 4 80
(Jo Hughes) *hld up: hdwy over 2f out: shkn up to ld wl ins fnl f: r.o* **7/2**[3]

032- **2** 1 ½ **Prime Exhibit**[6] 8450 9-9-4 64....................(t) StephenCraine 5 77
(Daniel Mark Loughnane) *trckd ldr tl led over 5f out: shkn up over 1f out: rdn: hdd and unable qck wl ins fnl f* **5/2**[2]

111- **3** 1 ¼ **Matraash (USA)**[21] 8309 8-9-4 78....................(be) ShaneKelly 6 74
(Daniel Mark Loughnane) *a.p: trckd ldr 4f out: shkn up over 1f out: rdn and ev ch ins fnl f: styd on same pce* **11/10**[1]

155/ **4** 12 **I Confess**[433] 7461 9-8-13 72....................(b) PJMcDonald 3 41
(Geoffrey Harker) *led 3f: rdn over 3f out: wknd over 1f out* **10/1**

1m 52.35s (1.85) **Going Correction** +0.225s/f (Slow) **4 Ran SP% 107.5**
Speed ratings (Par 101): **100,98,97,86**
CSF £12.00 TOTE £4.50; EX 11.10 Trifecta £13.60.There was no bid for the winner.
**Owner** Brooklands Racing **Bred** Woodcote Stud Ltd **Trained** Lambourn, Berks

**FOCUS**
An ordinary seller but doubts over the form.

## 67 CORAL MOBILE "JUST THREE CLICKS TO BET" H'CAP 1m 1f 103y(P)
**3:10** (3:10) (Class 6) (0-60,66) 4-Y-O+ **£1,940** (£577; £288; £144) **Stalls** Low

Form RPR

400- **1** **Outlaw Torn (IRE)**[27] 8233 5-9-5 **58**....................(e) RobbieFitzpatrick 9 69
(Richard Guest) *trckd ldr over 3f: remained handy: rdn to ld ins fnl f: r.o* **7/1**[3]

102- **2** 1 ½ **Shirazz**[23] 8302 5-9-2 **55**....................(t) GeorgeBaker 8 63
(Seamus Durack) *hld up: hdwy over 2f out: rdn to chse wnr and hung lft ins fnl f: r.o* **9/2**[1]

025- **3** 3 ¾ **Derfenna Art (IRE)**[24] 8275 5-9-6 **59**....................(t) MartinHarley 11 59
(Seamus Durack) *led: racd keenly: rdn over 1f out: hdd and no ex ins fnl f* **8/1**

313- **4** ¾ **Minstrel Lad**[35] 8121 6-9-4 **57** PaddyAspell 2 55
(Lydia Pearce) *hld up: hdwy over 5f out: rdn and ev ch over 1f out: wknd ins fnl f* **9/2**[1]

150- **5** *hd* **Time Square (FR)**[40] 8060 7-9-7 **60** LukeMorris 4 58
(Tony Carroll) *trckd ldrs: plld hrd: wnt 2nd 6f out: rdn and ev ch over 1f out: wknd ins fnl f* **33/1**

001- **6** 3 ¼ **Auden (USA)**[8] 8436 6-9-13 **66** 6ex (v) FrederikTylicki 7 57
(J R Jenkins) *prom: rdn over 2f out: wknd over 1f out* **6/1**[2]

624- **7** *hd* **Taxiformissbyron**[11] 8399 4-9-6 **60** GrahamLee 3 51
(Michael Herrington) *chsd ldrs: rdn over 2f out: wknd fnl f* **10/1**

000- **8** 2 ¼ **Scamperdale**[11] 8399 12-9-2 **55** (b[1]) TomQueally 6 41
(Brian Baugh) *s.i.s: hld up: rdn over 1f out: nvr on terms* **12/1**

163- **9** 1 **Berkeley Street (USA)**[10] 8410 4-9-3 **57** (v) AdamKirby 1 41
(Jane Chapple-Hyam) *hld up: hdwy u.p over 2f out: wknd over 1f out* **7/1**[3]

052- **10** 13 **Eco Warrior**[34] 8141 4-9-5 **59** MartinLane 5 16
(J W Hills) *s.i.s: hld up and a in rr: rdn and wknd over 2f out* **14/1**

000- **11** 26 **Final Delivery**[51] 7923 5-9-3 **56** (v) StephenCraine 10
(Jim Boyle) *hld up: hdwy over 5f out: rdn and wknd over 2f out* **8/1**

2m 1.77s (0.07) **Going Correction** +0.225s/f (Slow)
**WFA** 4 from 5yo+ 1lb **11 Ran SP% 124.3**
Speed ratings (Par 101): **108,106,103,102,102 99,99,97,96,84 61**
CSF £40.88 CT £267.93 TOTE £10.00: £3.70, £1.10, £4.10; EX 61.80 Trifecta £470.20.
**Owner** James S Kennerley **Bred** Derek Veitch & Rory O'Brien **Trained** Wetherby, W Yorks

**FOCUS**
A modest handicap in which the pace steadied down the back straight. The winner is up slightly on his autumn form.

## 68 CORAL APP DOWNLOAD FROM THE APP STORE H'CAP 1m 4f 50y(P)
3:40 (3:40) (Class 6) (0-52,52) 4-Y-0+ **£1,940** (£577; £288; £144) **Stalls Low**

Form RPR

060- **1** **Primacy (IRE)**[8] 8436 5-9-3 **48** LiamKeniry 4 57
(Neil Mulholland) *a.p: rdn to chse ldr over 1f out: styd on to ld wl ins fnl f* **16/1**

642- **2** *nk* **Ice Tres**[17] 8373 5-9-6 **51** MartinLane 5 59
(Rod Millman) *trckd ldr 1f: wnt 2nd again over 9f out tl led over 2f out: rdn over 1f out: hdd wl ins fnl f* **7/1**

000- **3** 4 **The Yank**[33] 8148 5-9-3 **48** LukeMorris 3 50
(Tony Carroll) *chsd ldrs: rdn over 1f out: styd on same pce fnl f* **4/1**[3]

5RR- **4** ½ **Azabitmour (FR)**[31] 8182 4-9-2 **51** GrahamLee 8 52
(John Best) *s.i.s: hld up: hdwy over 2f out: rdn over 1f out: styd on: nt rch ldrs* **20/1**

300- **5** *hd* **Excellent News (IRE)**[146] 5377 5-8-12 **48** JackDuern[(5)] 6 49
(Tony Forbes) *hld up: hdwy on outer over 2f out: rdn over 1f out: edgd lft and no ex fnl f* **25/1**

564- **6** *nk* **Fair Breeze**[27] 6099 7-8-8 **46** oh1 (b[1]) JoeDoyle[(7)] 7 46
(Richard Phillips) *mid-div: pushed along over 2f out: styd on appr fnl f: nt trble ldrs* **25/1**

630- **7** 7 **Lord Golan**[48] 7951 6-9-6 **51** (b) WilliamCarson 2 40
(Ann Stokell) *mid-div: drvn along over 3f out: hdwy over 2f out: wknd fnl f* **20/1**

00/- **8** 7 **Agapanthus (GER)**[11] 651 9-9-1 **46** (p) TomQueally 11 24
(Neil Mulholland) *s.i.s: hdwy over 10f out: pushed along and wknd over 3f out* **7/2**[2]

502- **9** 3 ¼ **Impeccability**[10] 8417 4-8-11 **46** JimmyQuinn 9 19
(John Mackie) *hld up: hdwy on outer over 3f out: rdn and wknd over 2f out* **7/1**

500- **10** 3 **Midnight Bahia (IRE)**[112] 6479 5-9-4 **49** RobertWinston 1 17
(Dean Ivory) *led: rdn and hdd over 2f out: wknd over 1f out* **14/1**

003- **11** 38 **Layla's Boy**[23] 8302 7-9-7 **52** (bt) AdamKirby 10
(Simon West) *chsd ldr after 1f tl over 9f out: remained handy tl wknd 2f out: eased fnl f* **3/1**[1]

2m 42.49s (1.39) **Going Correction** +0.225s/f (Slow)
**WFA** 4 from 5yo+ 4lb **11 Ran SP% 122.0**
Speed ratings (Par 101): **104,103,101,100,100 100,95,91,88,86 61**
CSF £121.33 CT £544.42 TOTE £32.50: £8.40, £3.70, £2.00; EX 200.10 Trifecta £2017.40.
**Owner** Prime Of Life 2 **Bred** E A M Leatham **Trained** Limpley Stoke, Wilts

**FOCUS**
A weak middle-distance handicap. The runner-up is probably the bset guide.

## 69 32RED.COM FILLIES' H'CAP 5f 216y(P)
4:10 (4:10) (Class 5) (0-70,70) 4-Y-0+ **£3,234** (£962; £481; £240) **Stalls Low**

Form RPR

0- **1** **Lapis Blue (IRE)**[9] 8427 4-9-4 **67** AdamKirby 6 77+
(David Evans) *s.i.s: outpcd: swtchd rt 5f out: hung lft over 2f out: hdwy over 1f out: r.o u.p to ld wl ins fnl f* **14/1**

103- **2** 1 **Barbs Princess**[41] 8052 4-9-7 **70** RobertWinston 3 77
(Charles Hills) *sn prom: shkn up to ld over 1f out: rdn: edgd rt and hdd wl ins fnl f* **6/4**[1]

530- **3** ½ **Dodina (IRE)**[38] 8095 4-9-6 **69** DaleSwift 5 74
(Brian Ellison) *chsd ldrs: rdn and ev ch over 1f out: styd on same pce ins fnl f* **2/1**[2]

233- **4** 3 **Available (IRE)**[55] 7845 5-8-13 **62** (tp) StephenCraine 2 57
(John Mackie) *led 5f out tl over 3f out: led again over 2f out: rdn and hdd over 1f out: no ex wl ins fnl f* **5/1**[3]

425- **5** 5 **Lady Poppy**[84] 7236 4-8-11 **60** PJMcDonald 1 39
(George Moore) *led 1f: led again over 3f out: rdn and hdd over 2f out: wknd fnl f* **8/1**

/00- **6** 1 ½ **Back In The Frame**[8] 8437 4-8-10 **62** SamJames[(3)] 8 37
(David O'Meara) *chsd ldrs: rdn over 3f out: wknd over 2f out* **25/1**

405- **7** 1 **Layla's Oasis**[28] 8216 4-9-5 **68** BarryMcHugh 7 39
(Richard Fahey) *hld up in tch: racd keenly: pushed along over 2f out: rdn and wknd over 1f out* **16/1**

000- **8** 3 ¼ **Mey Blossom**[79] 7381 9-8-8 **62** ow1 GeorgeChaloner[(5)] 9 23
(Richard Whitaker) *chsd ldrs: rdn 1/2-way: wknd over 1f out* **33/1**

1m 16.03s (1.03) **Going Correction** +0.225s/f (Slow) **8 Ran SP% 120.4**
Speed ratings (Par 100): **102,100,100,96,89 87,86,81**
CSF £37.54 CT £65.09 TOTE £12.20: £3.70, £1.10, £1.10; EX 39.70 Trifecta £134.90.
**Owner** Peter O'Callaghan **Bred** Moyglare Stud Farm Ltd **Trained** Pandy, Monmouths

**FOCUS**
A moderate fillies' handicap run at a decent pace. The winner is capable of better.

## 70 32RED MAIDEN STKS 7f 32y(P)
4:40 (4:42) (Class 5) 3-Y-O **£3,234** (£962; £481; £240) **Stalls High**

Form RPR

00- **1** **Secret Suspect**[72] 7532 3-9-0 0 GrahamLee 9 73
(James Tate) *a.p: chsd ldr 5f out: pushed along over 2f out: rdn and edgd rt over 1f out: r.o to ld towards fin* **12/1**

005- **2** ¾ **Excellent Royale (IRE)**[52] 7892 3-9-5 67 RobertWinston 8 76
(Charles Hills) *led at stdy pce 6f out: qcknd over 2f out: hung rt over 1f out: sn rdn: hdd towards fin* **7/4**[1]

2- **3** 7 **Jaeger Train (IRE)**[10] 8414 3-9-5 0 MartinHarley 2 58
(K R Burke) *led 1f: trckd ldrs: rdn over 1f out: no ex fnl f* **2/1**[2]

**4** 1 **Marweena (IRE)** 3-9-0 0 TomQueally 6 50+
(Michael Bell) *s.i.s: hld up: nt clr run over 2f out: swtchd lft and hdwy over 1f out: styd on: nvr nrr* **8/1**[3]

**5** *nse* **Dove Mountain (IRE)**[156] 5018 3-9-5 74 GeorgeBaker 10 55
(Gary Brown) *hld up: hdwy 3f out: rdn over 1f out: styng on same pce whn edgd lft ins fnl f* **12/1**

04- **6** 1 **Blue Oyster**[39] 8083 3-9-0 0 WilliamCarson 1 47
(Philip McBride) *mid-div: drvn along over 2f out: styd on same pce fr over 1f out* **10/1**

0- **7** ½ **Anjin (IRE)**[9] 8425 3-9-5 0 LukeMorris 3 51
(Sir Mark Prescott Bt) *hld up: pushed along over 2f out: nt clr run over 1f out: n.d* **25/1**

0- **8** ½ **Shannon Haven (IRE)**[19] 8333 3-9-5 0 ShaneKelly 4 50
(Daniel Mark Loughnane) *s.i.s: hld up: pushed along over 2f out: n.d* **20/1**

0- **9** *shd* **Up Hill Battle's**[19] 8332 3-9-0 0 StephenCraine 7 45
(Daniel Mark Loughnane) *prom: rdn over 2f out: wknd over 1f out* **66/1**

**10** 5 **Marmande (IRE)** 3-9-0 0 RichardKingscote 11 32
(Daniel Kubler) *s.i.s: hld up: rdn over 2f out: a in rr* **20/1**

55- **11** 5 **Chatsworth Express**[32] 8165 3-9-0 0 GeorgeChaloner[(5)] 5 24
(Richard Whitaker) *prom: racd keenly: rdn over 2f out: wknd over 1f out* **50/1**

1m 32.06s (2.46) **Going Correction** +0.225s/f (Slow) **11 Ran SP% 122.1**
Speed ratings (Par 97): **94,93,85,84,83 82,82,81,81,75 70**
CSF £33.05 TOTE £15.20: £3.30, £1.20, £1.10; EX 52.30 Trifecta £228.60.
**Owner** Saeed Manana **Bred** Patrick Fahey **Trained** Newmarket, Suffolk

**FOCUS**
Not much depth to this maiden and the front two pulled well clear. The time was slow but the form is rated around the race averages.

## 71 32RED CASINO H'CAP 1m 1f 103y(P)
5:10 (5:10) (Class 6) (0-60,60) 3-Y-O **£1,940** (£577; £288; £144) **Stalls Low**

Form RPR

042- **1** **Masterpaver**[17] 8363 3-9-3 **56** (v) RobertWinston 4 63
(Alan Bailey) *a.p: pushed along over 2f out: rdn to ld ins fnl f: hung rt: styd on* **7/4**[1]

060- **2** *hd* **Blossom Lane**[53] 7874 3-9-2 **55** NickyMackay 1 61
(John Gosden) *sn led: hung rt almost thrght: rdn over 2f out: hdd ins fnl f: styd on* **6/1**[2]

454- **3** 2 ¼ **Jayeff Herring (IRE)**[34] 8138 3-9-3 **56** TomQueally 6 57
(Michael Bell) *a.p: trckd ldr over 7f out: rdn and ev ch over 1f out: styd on same pce ins fnl f* **7/4**[1]

254- **4** ¾ **Choice Of Destiny**[30] 8201 3-9-0 **60** LouisSteward[(7)] 2 59
(Philip McBride) *plld hrd: trckd ldr 2f: sn stdd and lost pl: hdwy over 2f out: rdn over 1f out: styd on same pce ins fnl f* **6/1**[2]

066- **5** ½ **Belle Peinture (FR)**[24] 8266 3-8-7 **46** oh1 BarryMcHugh 3 44
(Richard Fahey) *hld up: hdwy 3f out: sn rdn: styd on same pce fr over 1f out* **25/1**

062- **6** ½ **Sarlat**[24] 8274 3-8-8 **47** LukeMorris 5 44
(Mark Brisbourne) *hld up: hdwy 6f out: rdn over 2f out: styd on same pce appr fnl f* **12/1**[3]

2m 5.41s (3.71) **Going Correction** +0.225s/f (Slow) **6 Ran SP% 112.8**
Speed ratings (Par 95): **92,91,89,89,88 88**
CSF £13.30 TOTE £2.90: £1.60, £3.30; EX 13.50 Trifecta £29.60.
**Owner** Mrs A M Riney **Bred** Mrs A M Riney **Trained** Newmarket, Suffolk

**FOCUS**
A small field, but an interesting 3-y-o handicap for the grade featuring a number of potential improvers. The pace however was steady, and the winning time almost four seconds slower than the older horses recorded over the same C&D earlier in the card. The first three may prove better than the bare form.
T/Jkpt: Not won. T/Plt: £131.80 to a £1 stake. Pool: £124077.22 - 686.79 winning tickets T/Qpdt: £9.40 to a £1 stake. Pool: £12446.86 - 976.50 winning tickets CR

# 58 SOUTHWELL (L-H)
### Tuesday, January 7

**OFFICIAL GOING: Standard**
Wind: Strong across Weather: Cloudy with sunny periods

## 72 CORAL APP DOWNLOAD FROM THE APP STORE H'CAP 1m 4f (F)
12:30 (12:31) (Class 5) (0-75,81) 4-Y-0+ **£3,067** (£905; £453) **Stalls Low**

Form RPR

111- **1** **Mr Burbidge**[9] 8433 6-10-2 **81** 6ex (b) LiamKeniry 3 95
(Neil Mulholland) *trckd ldr: cl up over 4f out: pushed along to chal 3f out: rdn and slt ld whn edgd lft 2f out: drvn and styd on gamely fnl f* **1/1**[1]

053- **2** 1 ¼ **Summerfree (USA)**[75] 7488 4-8-11 **66** AdrianNicholls 4 78
(Mark Johnston) *led: pushed along over 3f out and sn jnd: rdn and hdd 2f out: sn carried lft: styd cl up: drvn and ev ch ent fnl f: one pce last 150yds* **5/4**[2]

450- **3** 22 **Phoenix Flight (IRE)**[80] 6490 9-9-10 **75** LukeMorris 1 58
(James Evans) *trckd ldng pair: pushed along over 4f out: rdn over 3f out and sn outpcd* **16/1**

214- **4** 4 ½ **Monzino (USA)**[9] 8433 6-8-12 **70** (b) PaulBooth[(7)] 2 40
(Michael Chapman) *s.i.s: t.k.h and sn trcking ldrs: rdn along over 5f out: sn outpcd* **10/1**[3]

2m 37.09s (-3.91) **Going Correction** -0.10s/f (Stan)
**WFA** 4 from 6yo+ 4lb **4 Ran SP% 109.4**
Speed ratings (Par 103): **109,108,93,90**
CSF £2.58 TOTE £1.70; EX 3.00 Trifecta £8.10.
**Owner** Dajam Ltd **Bred** M Burbidge **Trained** Limpley Stoke, Wilts

**FOCUS**
This modest handicap only involved the two market leaders from a long way out. The winner is rated in line with a best view of his previous form.

## 73 32RED.COM H'CAP 2m (F)
**1:00** (1:02) (Class 6) (0-60,60) 4-Y-0+ £2,385 (£704; £352) **Stalls** Low

Form RPR
323- **1** **Pass The Time**[40] 4713 5-9-0 **48**....(p) LiamKeniry 6 59+
(Neil Mulholland) *trckd ldng pair: hdwy to ld 1/2-way: pushed along 3f out: rdn and edgd lft to ins rail wl over 1f out: drvn and kpt on fnl f* **5/1**[3]

655- **2** 1 1/2 **Opus (IRE)**[48] 7984 5-9-2 **50**.... LukeMorris 1 59
(Lucy Wadham) *in tch: hdwy to trck ldrs after 6f: chsd wnr over 4f out: rdn to chal 3f out: drvn wl over 1f out: kpt on same pce* **8/1**

41-2 **3** 15 **Jawaab (IRE)**[5] 14 10-9-7 **55**....(e) AdamKirby 7 46
(Philip Kirby) *dwlt and reminders s: in rr: hdwy 1/2-way: rdn along to chse ldrs over 4f out: drvn 3f out and plugged on one pce* **7/4**[1]

06-4 **4** 3 **Miss Mohawk (IRE)**[5] 14 5-8-12 **46** oh1....(b) DaleSwift 4 33
(Alan Brown) *dwlt and sn swtchd rt to outer and bhd: hdwy over 5f out: rdn to chse ldrs over 3f out: sn drvn and plugged on fnl 2f* **25/1**

054- **5** 1 3/4 **Celebrian**[19] 8349 7-8-12 **46**....(t) ChrisCatlin 8 31
(Alex Hales) *chsd ldrs: rdn along over 3f out: sn drvn and wknd over 2f out* **8/1**

404- **6** 25 **Shirls Son Sam**[57] 5833 6-9-2 **50**.... DuranFentiman 5
(Chris Fairhurst) *hld up towards rr: hdwy 6f out: rdn along over 3f out: sn outpcd* **14/1**

664- **7** 14 **Una Bella Cosa**[9] 8436 4-8-5 **46** oh1....(be) AndrewMullen 2
(Alan McCabe) *led: pushed along and hdd 1/2-way: rdn along 6f out: sn wknd and bhd fnl 3f* **16/1**

000- **8** 61 **Hartlebury**[34] 8149 4-8-8 **49**.... JimmyQuinn 3
(James Bethell) *chsd ldr: rdn along over 6f out: sn wknd: bhd and virtually p.u over 2f out* **20/1**

056/ **9** 99 **Cape Safari (IRE)**[373] 8297 5-9-7 **60**....(p) HarryPoulton(5) 10
(Tim Vaughan) *chsd ldrs: pushed along and lost pl after 4f: rdn along and bhd fr 1/2-way: sn t.o and virtually p.u fnl 4f* **7/2**[2]

3m 42.25s (-3.25) **Going Correction** -0.10s/f (Stan)
**WFA** 4 from 5yo+ 7lb **9** Ran SP% **118.6**
Speed ratings (Par 101): **104,103,95,94,93 80,73,43,**
CSF £45.81 CT £97.72 TOTE £5.90: £1.60, £2.00, £1.20; EX 33.10 Trifecta £54.30.
**Owner** Dajam Ltd **Bred** M Burbidge **Trained** Limpley Stoke, Wilts

**FOCUS**
This modest staying handicap developed into a war of attrition. Preety weak form with the market 1-2 disappointing.

## 74 32RED H'CAP 1m (F)
**1:35** (1:35) (Class 5) (0-75,72) 3-Y-O £2,911 (£866; £432; £216) **Stalls** Low

Form RPR
141- **1** **Slinky McVelvet**[25] 8265 3-8-13 **70**.... BillyCray(3) 4 74+
(Garry Moss) *trckd ldr: effrt and cl up wl over 2f out: rdn to ld 2f out: clr appr fnl f: pushed out* **9/2**[2]

044- **2** 1 1/2 **Yeah Baby (IRE)**[73] 7533 3-9-4 **72**.... LukeMorris 2 72
(Charles Hills) *chsd ldng pair on outer: pushed along over 3f out: rdn wl over 2f out and sn outpcd: styd on u.p fnl f* **9/2**[2]

031- **3** 6 **Excel Best**[9] 8434 3-9-3 **71** 6ex....(b) PaddyAspell 3 57
(James Tate) *led: pushed and jnd wl over 2f out: sn rdn and hdd 2f out: carried hd high and drvn wl over 1f out: sn wknd* **4/6**[1]

310- **4** 41 **Eddiemaurice (IRE)**[108] 6619 3-9-4 **72**....(e[1]) RobbieFitzpatrick 1
(Richard Guest) *chsd ldrs on inner: rdn along over 3f out: sn outpcd and bhd* **8/1**[3]

1m 43.03s (-0.67) **Going Correction** -0.10s/f (Stan) **4** Ran SP% **107.5**
Speed ratings (Par 97): **99,97,91,50**
CSF £21.47 TOTE £3.80; EX 18.30 Trifecta £40.90.
**Owner** Ron Hull **Bred** Jason Paxton **Trained** Tickhill, S Yorks

**FOCUS**
An ordinary 3yo handicap, but with the favourite disappointing the form may not amount to much. The winner backed up her latest wide-margin CD claimer win.

## 75 LADBROKES H'CAP 7f (F)
**2:10** (2:10) (Class 5) (0-75,74) 4-Y-0+ £2,911 (£866; £432; £216) **Stalls** Low

Form RPR
022- **1** **Kung Hei Fat Choy (USA)**[11] 8408 5-9-6 **73**....(b) GrahamLee 8 83
(James Given) *trckd ldrs: hdwy 3f out: chal wl over 1f out: rdn to ld ins fnl f: kpt on* **6/4**[1]

020- **2** 3/4 **Strong Man**[12] 8401 6-9-1 **68**....(b) JamesSullivan 6 76
(Michael Easterby) *t.k.h early: cl up: led wl over 2f out: rdn wl over 1f out: drvn and hdd ins fnl f: kpt on same pce* **20/1**

020- **3** 1 3/4 **Barbados Bob (USA)**[12] 8401 4-8-12 **70**.... GeorgeChaloner(5) 7 75
(Michael Wigham) *trckd ldrs on outer: hdwy wl over 2f out: rdn and edgd rt wl over 1f out: kpt on u.p fnl f* **4/1**[2]

045- **4** 3/4 **Repetition**[19] 8345 4-9-0 **67**.... TonyHamilton 1 70
(Kristin Stubbs) *chsd ldrs on inner: rdn along over 2f out and sltly outpcd: styd on u.p fnl f* **20/1**

046- **5** 5 **Marciano (IRE)**[29] 8224 4-9-7 **74**....(v) RobertHavlin 5 64
(Alan Brown) *dwlt: sn in tch: hdwy to trck ldrs 3f out: rdn over 2f out and sn one pce* **5/1**[3]

141- **6** nk **Arabian Flight**[21] 8315 5-8-10 **63**.... AndrewMullen 2 52
(Michael Appleby) *prom: rdn along 3f out: wknd 2f out* **5/1**[3]

20-2 **7** 3 3/4 **Piceno (IRE)**[5] 11 6-8-13 **73**....(b) MatthewHopkins(7) 3 52
(Scott Dixon) *slt ld: rdn along 3f out: hdd wl over 2f out: sn wknd* **7/1**

560- **8** 9 **Sam Spade (IRE)**[45] 8030 4-8-6 **66**.... AdamMcLean(7) 4 22
(Derek Shaw) *in rr: rdn along 3f out: sn outpcd* **50/1**

1m 28.45s (-1.85) **Going Correction** -0.10s/f (Stan) **8** Ran SP% **117.3**
Speed ratings (Par 103): **106,105,103,102,97 96,92,82**
CSF £38.44 CT £106.96 TOTE £2.50: £1.10, £3.90, £1.50; EX 36.10 Trifecta £151.00.
**Owner** The Cool Silk Partnership **Bred** Gilgai Farm **Trained** Willoughton, Lincs

**FOCUS**
With a few in here that like to force it, a strong pace was always likely. The form looks sound.

## 76 LADBROKES MAIDEN STKS 1m (F)
**2:40** (2:40) (Class 5) 4-Y-0+ £2,911 (£866; £432; £216) **Stalls** Low

Form RPR
055- **1** **Xclusive**[34] 8149 4-9-5 47.... LukeMorris 3 62
(Ronald Harris) *prom: cl up over 3f out: led wl over 2f out: rdn clr over 1f out: readily* **7/2**[2]

055- **2** 8 **Island Express (IRE)**[9] 8438 7-9-0 51....(t[1]) AnnStokell(5) 6 44
(Ann Stokell) *dwlt: in tch: hdwy 3f out: rdn to chse ldng pair wl over 1f out: kpt on to take 2nd ins fnl f: no ch w wnr* **25/1**

205- **3** nk **Bubbly Bailey**[252] 1903 4-9-5 57.... FrederikTylicki 1 43
(J R Jenkins) *slt ld: rdn along 3f out: sn hdd: drvn and edgd rt over 1f out: sn one pce* **9/2**[3]

000- **4** 6 **Pink Cadillac (IRE)**[60] 7806 4-8-9 40.... GeorgeChaloner(5) 2 24
(Ben Haslam) *cl up: rdn along over 3f out: sn drvn and wknd over 2f out* **14/1**

**5** 8 **Spencers Lad**[17] 4-9-5 0.... JamesSullivan 4 11
(Michael Easterby) *dwlt: sn rdn along and a in rr: outpcd and bhd fr 1/2-way* **8/1**

04- **6** 3/4 **Limon Squeezy**[9] 8437 5-9-0 0.... AdamKirby 7
(Mike Murphy) *prom on wd outside: effrt 3f out: rdn along over 2f out: sn wknd* **5/2**[1]

266- **7** 11 **Abbotsfield (IRE)**[61] 7791 4-9-0 65....(p) GrahamLee 5
(Ben Haslam) *chsd ldrs: rdn along 1/2-way: sn outpcd and bhd fnl 3f* **7/2**[2]

1m 44.99s (1.29) **Going Correction** -0.10s/f (Stan) **7** Ran SP% **112.8**
Speed ratings (Par 103): **89,81,80,74,66 65,54**
CSF £73.93 TOTE £3.80: £1.80, £6.50; EX 75.10 Trifecta £294.50.
**Owner** Monmouthshire Racing Club **Bred** Cheveley Park Stud Ltd **Trained** Earlswood, Monmouths

**FOCUS**
A poor maiden and a couple of major disappointments. The time was slow.

## 77 BET ON YOUR MOBILE WITH LADBROKES H'CAP 7f (F)
**3:15** (3:15) (Class 6) (0-52,52) 4-Y-0+ £2,385 (£704; £352) **Stalls** Low

Form RPR
63-5 **1** **Heidi's Delight (IRE)**[6] 7 5-9-2 **47**....(b) PJMcDonald 7 56
(Ann Duffield) *sn trcking ldrs: hdwy on outer 3f out: chal over 2f out: led wl over 1f out: sn rdn and edgd lft: clr ent fnl f: kpt on* **4/1**[2]

40-4 **2** 2 3/4 **Offbeat Safaris (IRE)**[4] 30 6-9-7 **52**....(p) LukeMorris 2 54
(Ronald Harris) *dwlt and in rr: hdwy wl over 2f out: swtchd rt and rdn over 1f out: styd on to chse wnr ins fnl f: sn no imp* **5/2**[1]

05-3 **3** 1 1/4 **Mucky Molly**[5] 12 6-9-3 **48**....(vt) GrahamLee 3 47
(Alison Hutchinson) *cl up: disp ld 3f out: rdn and ev ch 2f out: sn drvn and kpt on same pce appr fnl f* **5/2**[1]

03-0 **4** 3 **Red Shadow**[4] 34 5-9-7 **52**....(p[1]) DaleSwift 4 43
(Alan Brown) *slt ld: rdn along 3f out: drvn and hdd wl over 1f out: sn swtchd rt and grad wknd* **7/1**[3]

00-0 **5** 3/4 **Viking Warrior (IRE)**[5] 12 7-9-7 **52**....(be) DuranFentiman 5 41
(Shaun Harris) *trckd ldrs: hdwy wl over 2f out: swtchd lft: rdn and ch wl over 1f out: sn drvn and wknd* **14/1**

062- **6** 6 **Moss Hill**[125] 6113 5-9-7 **52**.... FrederikTylicki 1 25
(Jason Ward) *chsd ldrs on inner: pushed along 3f out: rdn and ch wl over 1f out: sn wknd* **7/1**[3]

660- **7** 3 1/2 **Hold The Star**[272] 1474 8-8-10 **46** oh1.... AnnStokell(5) 6 10
(Ann Stokell) *chsd ldrs: rdn along 3f out: sn wknd* **25/1**

1m 30.47s (0.17) **Going Correction** -0.10s/f (Stan) **7** Ran SP% **112.7**
Speed ratings (Par 101): **95,91,90,87,86 79,75**
CSF £13.99 TOTE £4.70: £1.80, £1.90; EX 16.60 Trifecta £30.80.
**Owner** David & Carole McMahon **Bred** Mountarmstrong Stud **Trained** Constable Burton, N Yorks

**FOCUS**
A moderate 46-52 handicap. The winner is rated back to her best.

## 78 LADBROKES MOBILE H'CAP 1m (F)
**3:45** (3:46) (Class 6) (0-52,56) 4-Y-0+ £2,385 (£704; £352) **Stalls** Low

Form RPR
44-0 **1** **Mataajir (USA)**[5] 17 6-9-4 **49**....(v) DaleSwift 4 60
(Derek Shaw) *dwlt and towards rr: wd st: gd hdwy 2f out: rdn wl over 1f out: styd on strly fnl f to ld nr fin* **5/2**[1]

05-3 **2** 1/2 **Huzzah (IRE)**[5] 17 9-9-1 **46** oh1....(t) AndrewMullen 7 56
(Michael Appleby) *prom: led 3f out: rdn wl over 1f out: drvn ins fnl f: hdd and no ex nr fin* **7/2**[2]

52-1 **3** 3 3/4 **General Tufto**[6] 7 9-9-4 **56** 6ex....(b) JordanVaughan(7) 8 57
(Charles Smith) *trckd ldrs: cl up 3f out: chal over 2f out and ev ch tl rdn and one pce ent fnl f* **9/2**

230- **4** 2 1/4 **Bladewood Girl**[42] 8056 6-9-5 **50**.... FrederikTylicki 1 46
(J R Jenkins) *trckd ldrs on inner: effrt 3f out: rdn over 2f out: sn one pce* **4/1**[3]

0/0- **5** 10 **Botanist**[9] 8436 7-9-2 **47**.... PaddyAspell 5 20
(Shaun Harris) *prom: rdn along 3f out: wknd over 2f out* **25/1**

620- **6** 7 **Amber Moon**[272] 1473 9-8-10 **46** oh1....[1] AnnStokell(5) 3 3
(Ann Stokell) *a in rr: bhd fnl 3f* **33/1**

004- **7** 4 **The Troyster**[11] 8407 4-9-1 **46** oh1.... PaulPickard 6
(Brian Ellison) *dwlt: a in rr: bhd fnl 3f* **14/1**

/34- **8** 1/2 **Tijuca (IRE)**[349] 335 5-9-7 **52**.... AdamKirby 2
(Ed de Giles) *led: rdn along and hdd 3f out: sn wknd* **7/1**

1m 43.45s (-0.25) **Going Correction** -0.10s/f (Stan) **8** Ran SP% **114.9**
Speed ratings (Par 101): **97,96,92,90,80 73,69,69**
CSF £11.45 CT £36.61 TOTE £3.50: £1.30, £1.70, £1.50; EX 13.30 Trifecta £48.20.
**Owner** Brian Johnson (Northamptonshire) **Bred** Shadwell Australia Ltd **Trained** Sproxton, Leics

**FOCUS**
Another moderate handicap and the first four pulled a long way clear. All were on good marks based on their old form.
T/Jkpt: £13,512.50 to a £1 stake. Pool: £19,031.77 - 1.00 winning ticket. T/Plt: £433.70 to a £1 stake. Pool: £79,868.38 - 134.42 winning tickets. T/Qpdt: £148.10 to a £1 stake. Pool: £5,346.39 - 26.70 winning tickets. JR

# KEMPTON (A.W) (R-H)
Wednesday, January 8

**OFFICIAL GOING: Standard**
Wind: Light, half behind Weather: Overcast

## 79 BETDAQ - THE SPORTS BETTING EXCHANGE H'CAP 1m 2f (P)
**4:10** (4:11) (Class 5) (0-75,75) 4-Y-0+ £2,587 (£770; £384; £192) **Stalls** Low

Form RPR
315- **1** **Swehan (IRE)**[8] 8453 4-9-5 **75**.... JamieSpencer 2 84
(Kevin Ryan) *mde all: rdn 2f out: kpt on wl fr over 1f out* **7/2**[2]

000- **2** 3/4 **Travelling**[124] 6167 5-9-5 **73**.... WilliamCarson 1 80
(Tony Carroll) *hld up in midfield: prog over 2f out: rdn over 1f out: chsd wnr ins fnl f: styd on but a hld* **50/1**

433- **3** 1/2 **Red Dragon (IRE)**[30] 8226 4-9-3 **73**.... FergusSweeney 7 79
(Michael Blanshard) *hld up wl in rr: pushed along 3f out: stl in rr over 1f out: styd on wl fnl f to snatch 3rd last stride* **8/1**

130- **4** *hd* **Poitin**[18] 8386 4-8-13 **69** .......... TomQueally 11 75+
(Harry Dunlop) *hld up and sn in last pair: pushed along and looking for room fr 2f out: prog over 1f out: swtchd lft ins fnl f: styd on but nvr able to chal* **14/1**

000- **5** *shd* **King Olav (UAE)**[21] 8323 9-8-12 **69** .......... MarkCoumbe(3) 6 74
(Tony Carroll) *cl up on inner: lost pl sltly over 2f out: renewed effrt over 1f out: kpt on but nt pce to chal* **25/1**

302- **6** *nk* **Perfect Cracker**[33] 8179 6-9-5 **73** .......... AdamKirby 10 78
(Clive Cox) *hld up in midfield: prog 2f out: chsd wnr over 1f out: nt qckn and lost 2nd ins fnl f: lost pls nr fin* **11/4**[1]

000- **7** *1 ¼* **Imperator Augustus (IRE)**[21] 8323 6-8-4 **65** .......... JackGarritty(7) 13 67
(Patrick Holmes) *s.s: rcvrd and in tch towards rr: sme prog on outer wl over 1f out: one pce whn short of room nr fin* **66/1**

400- **8** *hd* **Mr Red Clubs (IRE)**[70] 7629 5-9-0 **68** .......... AndrewMullen 9 70
(Michael Appleby) *hld up in rr: sme prog on outer wl over 1f out: one pce fnl f: no ch whn hmpd nr fin* **9/2**[3]

600- **9** *½* **Mountain Range (IRE)**[42] 8059 6-8-12 **66** .......... StevieDonohoe 8 67
(Willie Musson) *hld up and sn in last pair: pushed along over 2f out: no prog tl kpt on after one reminder ins fnl f: nvr involved* **16/1**

623- **10** *½* **Understory (USA)**[21] 8323 7-9-2 **70** .......... GrahamLee 14 70
(Tim McCarthy) *trckd ldrs: rdn over 2f out: tried to cl w others over 1f out: losing pl whn bmpd ins fnl f* **16/1**

112- **11** *1 ½* **Lady Lunchalot (USA)**[21] 8323 4-9-0 **70** ..........(p) LiamJones 12 67
(Laura Mongan) *chsd wnr to over 3f out: sn rdn: wknd wl over 1f out* **14/1**

/60- **12** *6* **Planetoid (IRE)**[49] 7970 6-9-6 **74** .......... AmirQuinn 3 59
(Jim Best) *stdd s: wl in rr: prog on wd outside into midfield 1/2-way: rdn and wknd over 2f out* **14/1**

460- **13** *1 ¾* **Song Light**[63] 7765 4-9-3 **73** .......... ChrisCatlin 4 54
(David Elsworth) *free to post: stdd s: hld up in last pair: t.k.h and rapid prog to press wnr over 3f out: wknd rapidly over 1f out* **25/1**

2m 7.7s (-0.30) **Going Correction** -0.05s/f (Stan)
**WFA** 4 from 5yo+ 2lb **13** Ran SP% **121.1**
Speed ratings (Par 103): **99,98,98,97,97 97,96,96,95,95 94,89,88**
CSF £185.29 CT £1341.88 TOTE £3.80: £1.60, £9.90, £1.90; EX 159.70 Trifecta £1298.60.
**Owner** Mubarak Al Naemi **Bred** Camogue Stud Ltd **Trained** Hambleton, N Yorks
■ Stewards' Enquiry : Tom Queally three-day ban: careless riding (Jan 22-24)

**FOCUS**
This moderate handicap was run at a generous early pace, but slowed up on the far side. The form has been rated at face value.

## 80 £500 FREE BETS AT BETDAQ H'CAP 5f (P)
**4:40** (4:40) (Class 4) (0-85,85) 4-Y-O+ **£4,690** (£1,395; £697; £348) **Stalls** Low

Form RPR

00-5 **1** **Caspian Prince (IRE)**[5] 36 5-9-4 **85** ..........(t[1]) MarkCoumbe(3) 2 95
(Tony Carroll) *mde all and immediately clr w two rivals: rdn over 1f out: hrd pressed fnl f: hld on wl* **7/1**[3]

031- **2** *¾* **Bapak Bangsawan**[37] 8128 4-8-2 **71** .......... ShaneGray(5) 9 78
(Kevin Ryan) *pushed up fr wdst draw and chsd wnr: drvn to chal fnl f: kpt on but a hld* **12/1**

043- **3** *1* **Blessington (IRE)**[11] 8430 4-9-7 **85** ..........(t) RobertHavlin 1 88
(John Gosden) *chsd ldng pair and immediately clr of rest: urged along over 1f out and didn't find much: kpt on but nvr able to chal* **5/4**[1]

624- **4** *1 ¼* **Pabusar**[21] 8324 6-9-5 **83** ..........(p) AdamKirby 5 82
(Jamie Osborne) *chsd ldng trio but nvr on terms: no imp over 1f out: kpt on* **7/1**[3]

000- **5** *nse* **Trader Jack**[18] 8385 5-9-6 **84** .......... StephenCraine 3 83
(David Flood) *hld up and immediately wl off the pce: no ch whn rdn over 1f out: styd on ins fnl f: nvr involved* **25/1**

0/1- **6** *½* **Expose**[18] 8384 6-8-8 **72** .......... AndrewMullen 6 69
(Michael Appleby) *stdd s: hld up and immediately wl off the pce: no ch whn shkn up over 1f out: kpt on: nvr involved* **9/2**[2]

660- **7** *2* **Sandfrankskipsgo**[11] 8430 5-8-13 **77** .......... ShaneKelly 7 67
(Peter Crate) *hld up and immediately wl off the pce: no ch whn shkn up over 1f out: nvr involved* **16/1**

340- **8** *nk* **Sulis Minerva (IRE)**[21] 8324 7-8-7 **78** .......... DavidParkes(7) 4 67
(Jeremy Gask) *hld up and immediately wl off the pce: no ch whn shkn up over 1f out: nvr involved* **25/1**

200- **9** *2 ½* **The Art Of Racing (IRE)**[55] 7887 4-9-4 **82** ..........(tp) MartinHarley 8 62
(Alan McCabe) *blindfold off late and slowly away: immediately wl off the pce in last: rdn over 2f out: no prog* **20/1**

59.05s (-1.45) **Going Correction** -0.05s/f (Stan) **9** Ran SP% **113.7**
Speed ratings (Par 105): **109,107,106,104,104 103,100,99,95**
CSF £81.55 CT £171.30 TOTE £6.50: £2.10, £2.40, £1.10; EX 79.90 Trifecta £348.50.
**Owner** Stephen Louch **Bred** Ballygallon Stud Limited **Trained** Cropthorne, Worcs

**FOCUS**
A modest sprint handicap in which there was no hanging about, but the principals led the breakaway group and it was a decent winning time. The winner is rated close to his French form.

## 81 JUMP RACING HERE ON SATURDAY H'CAP 7f (P)
**5:10** (5:10) (Class 7) (0-50,50) 4-Y-O+ **£1,617** (£481; £240; £120) **Stalls** Low

Form RPR

640- **1** **Mill I Am (USA)**[19] 8371 4-9-6 **49** .......... AdamBeschizza 5 58
(Stuart Williams) *sn chsd clr ldng pair: rdn to take 2nd 2f out: clsd over 1f out: led last 100yds: styd on* **6/1**[2]

500- **2** *1 ¼* **Pastoral Dancer**[8] 8456 5-9-2 **45** .......... ChrisCatlin 6 50
(Richard Rowe) *w.w in 8th: rdn and prog over 2f out: styd on fnl f to take 2nd nr fin: no ch to chal* **33/1**

005- **3** *1 ¼* **Surrey Dream (IRE)**[17] 8393 5-9-2 **45** .......... AdamKirby 14 47+
(John Bridger) *stdd s fr wdst draw: hld up in last trio: rdn over 2f out: prog wl over 1f out: styd on to take 3rd last strides* **10/1**

002- **4** *½* **Seamster**[12] 8418 7-9-5 **48** ..........(bt) GrahamLee 4 49
(Richard Ford) *led and clr w one rival: rdn 3 l clr wl over 1f out: wknd and hdd last 100yds: lost two more pls nr fin* **5/1**[1]

545- **5** *shd* **Wishformore (IRE)**[35] 8151 7-9-7 **50** ..........(p) LiamKeniry 10 50
(Zoe Davison) *chsd ldrs: rdn over 2f out: edgd lft and nt qckn wl over 1f out: kpt on fnl f* **12/1**

440- **6** *shd* **Custom House (IRE)**[246] 2126 6-9-0 **46** .......... NataliaGemelova(3) 7 46
(John E Long) *awkward s: towards rr: rdn over 2f out: kpt on one pce fr over 1f out: n.d* **25/1**

000- **7** *1 ¾* **Chandrayaan**[27] 8258 7-9-6 **49** ..........(v) JimmyQuinn 1 44
(John E Long) *s.s: mostly in last trio: rdn and no prog on inner over 2f out: pushed along and styd on wl fnl f* **25/1**

005- **8** *¾* **Slip Of A Girl (IRE)**[33] 8180 4-9-5 **48** .......... StevieDonohoe 13 41
(Patrick Holmes) *dwlt: towards rr: rdn over 2f out: tried to make prog over 1f out: n.d* **40/1**

000- **9** *1 ¼* **Chiltern Secret**[17] 8393 4-9-2 **45** .......... RobertWinston 3 35
(Dean Ivory) *mostly in last trio: rdn over 2f out: no prog tl plugged on fnl f* **20/1**

643- **10** *hd* **Choral Rhythm (IRE)**[191] 3885 4-9-2 **45** .......... LukeMorris 2 34
(Tony Carroll) *chsd ldrs: rdn over 2f out: disp 3rd jst over 1f out: wknd qckly fnl f* **7/1**[3]

003- **11** *¾* **Blue Noodles**[27] 8258 8-9-5 **48** ..........(v) PaddyAspell 8 35
(John Wainwright) *nvr beyond midfield: rdn and struggling over 2f out: sn btn* **5/1**[1]

0/ **12** *2* **Jjs Pride (IRE)**[390] 8123 5-8-11 **45** ..........(b) TimClark(5) 9 27
(Denis Quinn) *pressed ldr and sn clr of rest: lost 2nd and wknd qckly 2f out* **8/1**

406- **13** *14* **Roxy Lane**[146] 5429 5-9-6 **49** .......... WilliamCarson 11
(Peter Hiatt) *prom to 1/2-way: wknd rapidly over 2f out: t.o* **7/1**[3]

1m 27.02s (1.02) **Going Correction** +0.075s/f (Slow) **13** Ran SP% **118.3**
Speed ratings (Par 97): **97,95,94,93,93 93,91,90,89,88 87,85,69**
CSF £199.82 CT £2009.47 TOTE £5.30: £1.90, £7.20, £5.10; EX 286.50 Trifecta £1611.10.
**Owner** Eclipse Horse Racing **Bred** Horse France & Knighton House **Trained** Newmarket, Suffolk

**FOCUS**
This looked wide open. It was run at a fair pace and once more the pace bias towards prominent racers played out. Ordinary form, with a length personal best from the winner.

## 82 DINE IN THE PANORAMIC MEDIAN AUCTION MAIDEN STKS 6f (P)
**5:40** (5:40) (Class 6) 3-5-Y-O **£1,940** (£577; £288; £144) **Stalls** Low

Form RPR

436- **1** **Costa Filey**[21] 8326 3-8-12 70 .......... JimmyQuinn 2 72
(Ed Vaughan) *hld up bhd ldng pair: chal towards inner 2f out: rdn to ld 1f out: grad asserted last 100yds* **7/2**[3]

635- **2** *½* **Perfect Pursuit**[21] 8326 3-8-7 75 .......... LukeMorris 4 65
(Clive Cox) *trckd ldr: led 2f out: sn hrd pressed and strly drvn: hdd 1f out: styd on but hld nr fin* **6/4**[1]

**3** *7* **Kissed By Fire** 4-9-9 0 .......... StephenCraine 5 47
(Jim Boyle) *s.v.s: in tch after 2f: shkn up over 2f out: wknd over 1f out but tk modest 3rd nr fin* **25/1**

32- **4** *nk* **Rosie Prospects**[21] 8326 3-8-7 0 .......... RobertHavlin 3 42
(Roger Ingram) *led to 2f out: wknd over 1f out: lost modest 3rd nr fin* **5/2**[2]

**5** *shd* **Jenny Sparks** 3-8-7 0 .......... JoeFanning 1 42
(Mick Channon) *s.s: in tch after 2f: pushed along over 2f out: wknd over 1f out but stl chal for 3rd nr fin* **6/1**

1m 13.44s (0.34) **Going Correction** +0.075s/f (Slow)
**WFA** 3 from 4yo 16lb **5** Ran SP% **108.9**
Speed ratings (Par 101): **100,99,90,89,89**
CSF £9.01 TOTE £3.70: £3.10, £1.10; EX 11.20 Trifecta £94.00.
**Owner** A M Pickering **Bred** Alan Pickering CBE **Trained** Newmarket, Suffolk

**FOCUS**
A weak maiden rated around the winner, and run in a slow time.

## 83 BOOK NOW FOR SATURDAY H'CAP 6f (P)
**6:10** (6:10) (Class 6) (0-65,65) 4-Y-O+ **£1,940** (£577; £288; £144) **Stalls** Low

Form RPR

343- **1** **Insolenceofoffice (IRE)**[26] 8271 6-8-13 **57** ..........(p) GrahamLee 4 64
(Richard Ford) *plld hrd early: cl up: pushed along to ld wl over 1f out: rdn and kpt on wl enough fnl f* **5/1**[3]

200- **2** *¾* **Indian Affair**[8] 8456 4-9-7 **65** .......... AdamKirby 5 70
(Milton Bradley) *led to 1/2-way: led again briefly 2f out: pressed wnr after: kpt on but no real imp fnl f* **6/1**

406- **3** *nk* **Divine Call**[25] 8306 7-9-3 **61** .......... LiamJones 2 65+
(Milton Bradley) *hld up in 7th: looking for room 2f out: urged along over 1f out: rdn and r.o fnl f to take 3rd nr fin* **8/1**

003- **4** *nk* **Safwaan**[20] 8341 7-8-13 **57** .......... MartinHarley 3 60
(Michael Squance) *hld up in 6th: rdn and prog to chse ldng pair over 1f out: kpt on u.p but lost 3rd nr fin* **4/1**[2]

601- **5** *1 ¾* **New Rich**[35] 8152 4-9-4 **62** ..........(p) JohnFahy 9 59+
(Eve Johnson Houghton) *stdd s: hld up in detached last: struggling once pce lifted over 2f out: drvn and kpt on into 5th ins fnl f: no ch* **11/4**[1]

046- **6** *¾* **Rutterkin (USA)**[17] 8393 6-8-0 **51** oh5 .......... VictorSantos(7) 8 46
(James Moffatt) *racd wd: sn trckd ldr: led 3f out to 2f out: fdd fnl f* **12/1**

000- **7** *5* **Rose Garnet (IRE)**[224] 2773 6-8-12 **56** .......... LukeMorris 7 35
(Tony Carroll) *t.k.h: hld up in 5th: rdn 2f out: wknd qckly 1f out* **11/1**

100- **8** *7* **Katy Spirit (IRE)**[54] 7897 4-9-4 **62** .......... FergusSweeney 6 18
(Michael Blanshard) *prom: shkn up over 2f out: wknd rapidly over 1f out* **20/1**

03- **9** *nse* **Tingle Tangle (USA)**[126] 6113 4-8-13 **60** .......... MarkCoumbe(3) 1 16
(Tony Carroll) *stdd s: hld up in 8th and detached fr main gp: shkn up and no rspnse jst over 2f out: wknd qckly* **16/1**

1m 13.13s (0.03) **Going Correction** +0.075s/f (Slow) **9** Ran SP% **115.4**
Speed ratings (Par 101): **102,101,100,100,97 96,90,80,80**
CSF £34.99 CT £236.46 TOTE £2.90: £1.20, £2.20, £4.10; EX 33.10 Trifecta £389.60.
**Owner** CCCNLP **Bred** Gerard Kennedy **Trained** Garstang, Lancs

**FOCUS**
An ordinary sprint handicap, run at an average pace. The winner is rated close to last year's form.

## 84 WINNERS ARE WELCOME AT BETDAQ FILLIES' H'CAP 7f (P)
**6:40** (6:40) (Class 5) (0-70,69) 4-Y-O+ **£2,587** (£770; £384; £192) **Stalls** Low

Form RPR

252- **1** **Welsh Sunrise**[11] 8432 4-9-5 **67** .......... GeorgeBaker 1 78+
(Stuart Williams) *hld up disputing 5th: clsd over 2f out: led over 1f out: hung bdly lft fnl f: drvn and hld on* **7/4**[1]

010- **2** *nk* **Ivor's Princess**[22] 8316 5-9-1 **63** ..........(b) LukeMorris 5 70
(Rod Millman) *furiously drvn 1st 2f in last: gng bttr 1/2-way: rdn over 2f out: carried lft sn after: styd on to take 2nd jst ins fnl f: clsd grad on wnr fin* **12/1**

000- **3** *1* **Russian Ice**[35] 8158 6-9-6 **68** ..........(b) RobertWinston 9 72
(Dean Ivory) *hld up and last after 3f: brought wd in st and carried lft 2f out: rdn and styd on to take 3rd nr fin* **9/1**

443- **4** *1* **Funky Cold Medina**[92] 7114 4-9-7 **69** .......... MartinHarley 2 71
(Peter Chapple-Hyam) *hld up disputing 5th: prog over 2f out: carried lft sn after: drvn to go 2nd briefly 1f out: one pce after* **10/1**

034- **5** *3* **Magical Rose (IRE)**[11] 8432 4-9-2 **64** ..........(p) LiamKeniry 7 58
(Paul D'Arcy) *chsd ldr: carried lft 2f out: sn lost 2nd: wknd fnl f* **7/1**[3]

041- **6** *2 ¼* **Perfect Haven**[11] 8432 4-9-5 **67** .......... AdamKirby 8 54
(Clive Cox) *led: hung lft 2f out and set off chain reaction: hdd over 1f out: wknd* **9/2**[2]

500- **7** *3 ½* **Tammuz (IRE)**[37] 8125 4-8-10 **58** .......... WilliamCarson 3 36
(Tony Carroll) *sn in 7th: rdn whn carried lft and impeded 2f out: no imp on ldrs 1f out: wknd* **25/1**

620- **8** *1 3/4* **Pucker Up**[11] 8432 4-9-0 **62**.............................................. KieranO'Neill 6 35
(David Brown) *trckd ldng pair to 2f out: sn wknd* **25/1**

520- **9** *10* **Byroness**[20] 8345 4-9-5 **67**.................................................. LiamJones 4 13
(Heather Main) *racd wd: chsd ldrs: rdn 1/2-way: wknd qckly over 2f out: t.o* **7/1**[3]

1m 25.99s (-0.01) **Going Correction** +0.075s/f (Slow) **9** Ran SP% **114.0**
Speed ratings (Par 100): **103,102,101,100,96 94,90,88,76**
CSF £24.60 CT £146.99 TOTE £1.30: £1.20, £3.00, £2.60; EX 20.30 Trifecta £294.10.
**Owner** Seize The Day Racing Partnership **Bred** Mr & Mrs Sells **Trained** Newmarket, Suffolk

**FOCUS**
This moderate handicap was run at a routine pace. The winner gave the impression she was better than the bare form.

## 85 BETDAQ 1ST UK COMMISSION FREE H'CAP (FOR AMATEUR RIDERS) 1m 4f (P)
**7:10** (7:12) (Class 4) (0-85,84) 4-Y-0+ **£4,523** (£1,402; £701; £350) **Stalls** Centre

Form RPR

231- **1** **Echo Brava**[21] 8337 4-9-11 **71**.............................. MissSBrotherton 4 83
(Luke Dace) *hld up towards rr: prog over 3f out: clsd on outer to ld wl over 1f out: rdn clr* **4/1**[3]

**2** *2 1/2* **Silsol (GER)**[28] 5-9-8 **71**..................................... MissMeganNicholls(7) 5 79
(Paul Nicholls) *disp ld after 3f tl def advantage over 3f out: shkn up and hdd wl over 1f out: kpt on but no ch w wnr* **15/2**

063- **3** *1 3/4* **Mawaakef (IRE)**[18] 8387 6-10-10 **83**.................. MrMichaelJMurphy(3) 8 88
(J R Jenkins) *hld up in rr: prog 3f out: rdn over 2f out: hanging and nt qckn over 1f out: tk 3rd fnl f: one pce* **9/4**[1]

3/1- **4** *1 1/2* **Fujin Dancer (FR)**[23] 8308 9-10-9 **79**.............................. MissHBethell 2 82
(Brian Ellison) *hld up in rr: stdy prog on inner fr 3f out: stl gng easily 2f out: urged along frntically and one pce over 1f out* **10/1**

311- **5** *3/4* **Odin (IRE)**[13] 8400 6-11-0 **84**.............................................. MrSWalker 7 86
(Don Cantillon) *trckd ldrs: clsd 5f out: rdn to dispute 2nd briefly over 2f out: wknd over 1f out* **5/2**[2]

444- **6** *8* **No Such Number**[36] 7506 6-10-0 **70** oh3.............................. MrRBirkett 1 59
(Julia Feilden) *trckd ldrs: rdn over 2f out: no imp wl over 1f out: sn wknd and eased* **12/1**

333- **7** *15* **Star Of Namibia (IRE)**[19] 8373 4-9-7 **70** oh6..(be) MissMMullineaux(3) 6 35
(Michael Mullineaux) *disp ld after 3f tl rdn and wknd over 3f out: t.o* **25/1**

000/ **8** *13* **Cygnet**[23] 3627 8-10-0 **75**................................................ SeanBowen(5) 10 19
(Peter Bowen) *struggling in last after 4f: t.o* **50/1**

134- **9** *3/4* **Foxhaven**[74] 7539 12-10-3 **73**.....................................(v) FreddieMitchell 9 16
(Patrick Chamings) *chsd ldrs on outer: rdn and wknd 4f out: t.o* **25/1**

020- **10** *27* **Flag Of Glory**[23] 8308 7-9-10 **71** oh4 ow1.................. MrGeorgeCrate(5) 3
(Peter Hiatt) *reluctant to go to post: led or disp ld to 1/2-way: wknd rapidly over 3f out: wl t.o* **40/1**

2m 34.87s (0.37) **Going Correction** +0.075s/f (Slow)
**WFA** 4 from 5yo+ 4lb **10** Ran SP% **120.0**
Speed ratings (Par 105): **101,99,98,97,96 91,81,72,72,54**
CSF £33.74 CT £84.61 TOTE £4.20: £2.00, £2.80, £1.10; EX 31.70 Trifecta £189.90.
**Owner** Mark Benton **Bred** Adweb Ltd **Trained** Five Oaks, W Sussex

**FOCUS**
Not a bad handicap, confined to amateur riders. There wasn't much pace on early and plenty were in with a chance 2f out, but once again on the night it paid to race handy. The unexposed winner built on his Lingfield win.
T/Plt: £128.20. Pool: £90,757.60 - 516.54 winning units. T/Qpdt: £33.50. Pool: £10,011.05 - 220.69 winning units. JN

# 49 LINGFIELD (L-H)
## Wednesday, January 8

**OFFICIAL GOING: Standard**
Wind: medium, half behind Weather: dry

## 86 32RED H'CAP 6f 1y(P)
**12:30** (12:31) (Class 6) (0-60,60) 3-Y-0 **£2,045** (£603; £302) **Stalls** Low

Form RPR

146- **1** **Dandys Perier (IRE)**[22] 8317 3-9-3 **56**.............................. LukeMorris 5 61
(Ronald Harris) *chsd ldrs: rdn to ld over 1f out: drvn and hld on wl fnl f: drvn out* **8/1**[3]

6U2- **2** *nk* **Shamardyh (IRE)**[13] 8396 3-9-6 **59**.............................. AdamKirby 2 63
(David Evans) *nt best away but sn rcvrd to chse ldrs after 1f out: rdn and effrt on inner wl over 1f out: ev ch fnl f: hrd drvn and r.o but a hld* **11/4**[1]

003- **3** *3* **Alumina (IRE)**[46] 8017 3-9-2 **55**.............................. MartinHarley 9 49
(Andrew Balding) *chsd ldrs: rdn and effrt 2f out: styd on same pce u.p fnl f* **4/1**[2]

534- **4** *1 3/4* **Armelle (FR)**[10] 8434 3-8-10 **56**..........................(p) MatthewHopkins(7) 7 45
(Scott Dixon) *hld up wl in tch in midfield: rdn and effrt over 1f out: edgd lft 1f out: styd on same pce fnl f* **10/1**

154- **5** *hd* **Biscuiteer**[12] 8404 3-9-7 **60**.....................................(p) TomQueally 4 48
(Scott Dixon) *taken down early: led: rdn and hdd over 1f out: wknd ins fnl f* **14/1**

245- **6** *1 1/4* **Vodka Chaser (IRE)**[18] 8383 3-9-3 **56**.............................(b) JohnFahy 6 40
(J S Moore) *hld up in tch in midfield: hdwy u.p over 1f out: btn ins fnl f: wknd fnl 100yds* **16/1**

000- **7** *nse* **Wiki Tiki**[21] 8322 3-9-6 **59**.....................................(t) AdamBeschizza 3 43
(Stuart Williams) *restless in stalls: rrd as stalls opened and dwlt: hld up in tch towards rr: sme hdwy ent fnl f: nvr trbld ldrs* **10/1**

666- **8** *1* **Dont Have It Then**[34] 8166 3-9-5 **58**.............................. RobertWinston 1 39
(Willie Musson) *hld up in tch in midfield: nt clr run ent fnl 2f: pushed along and effrt ent fnl f: no imp* **4/1**[2]

000- **9** *3 3/4* **Dawnfromthepast (IRE)**[126] 6111 3-8-7 **46** oh1.......... JimmyQuinn 11 15
(Luke Dace) *swtchd lft after s: hld up in rr: n.d* **100/1**

000- **10** *4* **Birikyno**[19] 8364 3-9-7 **60**.............................................. LiamKeniry 8 16
(Mark Usher) *hld up in tch in last trio: rdn and struggling over 2f out: bhd fnl f* **16/1**

060- **11** *3/4* **Caroline's Beach (IRE)**[11] 8425 3-9-0 **53**.......................... LiamJones 10 7
(J S Moore) *in tch in midfield: rdn and lost pl 1/2-way: bhd fnl f* **33/1**

1m 12.38s (0.48) **Going Correction** -0.10s/f (Stan) **11** Ran SP% **118.3**
Speed ratings (Par 95): **92,91,87,85,85 83,83,81,76,71 70**
CSF £30.40 CT £105.69 TOTE £7.50: £2.00, £1.40, £1.70; EX 23.60 Trifecta £37.80.
**Owner** Farley, Mares & Ridge House Stables **Bred** John Doyle **Trained** Earlswood, Monmouths

**FOCUS**
This was a modest sprint handicap run at a steady pace and it paid to race handy. The form is rated as standard.

## 87 COMPARE BOOKMAKERS AT BOOKMAKERS.CO.UK H'CAP 5f 6y(P)
**1:00** (1:00) (Class 5) (0-70,70) 4-Y-0+ **£2,726** (£805; £402) **Stalls** High

Form RPR

450- **1** **Desert Strike**[11] 8431 8-9-6 **69**.....................................(p) LiamKeniry 4 78
(Conor Dore) *led tl over 3f out: chsd ldr tl rdn to ld again wl over 1f out: drvn 1f out: styd on wl fnl f: rdn out* **14/1**

602- **2** *nk* **Drawnfromthepast (IRE)**[18] 8384 9-9-5 **68**.............. FergusSweeney 1 76
(Luke Dace) *hld up wl in tch: hdwy on inner over 1f out: rdn and ev ch ins fnl f: no ex and hld fnl 50yds* **4/1**[2]

00-2 **3** *1/2* **Only Ten Per Cent (IRE)**[6] 9 6-9-2 **65**..................(v) FrederikTylicki 5 71
(J R Jenkins) *s.i.s: hld up in tch towards rr: rdn and hdwy 1f out: styd on wl to go 3rd wl ins fnl f* **7/2**[1]

222- **4** *1* **Mossgo (IRE)**[8] 8457 4-8-13 **62**.....................................(t) GrahamLee 8 65
(John Best) *t.k.h: hld up trcking ldrs: nt clr run and shuffled bk wl over 1f out: swtchd rt and hdwy 1f out: kpt on but no threat to ldrs* **6/1**

010- **5** *1/2* **Pull The Pin (IRE)**[11] 8431 5-9-3 **66**..........................(bt) WilliamCarson 3 67
(Ann Stokell) *chsd ldrs on inner: effrt but wanting to hang rt over 1f out: continued to hang and btn whn nt clr run towards fin* **16/1**

620- **6** *1/2* **Different**[22] 8319 4-9-3 **66**.............................................. JoeFanning 2 65
(Bryan Smart) *dwlt: sn rcvrd and wl in tch in midfield: rdn and effrt to chal jst over 1f out: no ex and btn whn nt clr run towards fin* **9/2**[3]

/12- **7** *3* **Secret Millionaire (IRE)**[342] 448 7-9-1 **64**.......................... LukeMorris 7 52
(Tony Carroll) *awkward leaving stalls and jostling w rival: s.i.s: sn bustled along and hdwy to ld over 3f out: rdn and hdd wl over 1f out: wknd ins fnl f* **8/1**

000- **8** *2 1/2* **Decision By One**[11] 8431 5-9-7 **70**.....................................[1] AdamKirby 6 49
(David Evans) *awkward leaving stalls and jostling w rival: s.i.s: a bhd* **5/1**

58.28s (-0.52) **Going Correction** -0.10s/f (Stan) **8** Ran SP% **115.0**
Speed ratings (Par 103): **100,99,98,97,96 95,90,86**
CSF £69.58 CT £245.80 TOTE £16.30: £4.10, £1.60, £1.80; EX 82.90 Trifecta £573.60.
**Owner** Andrew Page **Bred** Mrs Mary Rowlands **Trained** Hubbert's Bridge, Lincs

**FOCUS**
They went a decent gallop for this contest with plenty keen to lead. The form is rated around the runner-up.

## 88 CORAL.CO.UK BEST ODDS GUARANTEED ON RACING (S) H'CAP 1m 2f (P)
**1:30** (1:30) (Class 6) (0-60,60) 4-Y-0+ **£2,045** (£603; £302) **Stalls** Low

Form RPR

220- **1** **Sutton Sid**[37] 8121 4-9-4 **59**.....................................(v[1]) AdamKirby 9 71
(Chris Gordon) *hld up towards rr: rdn and gd hdwy on outer to chse ldng pair over 2f out: drvn to ld ins fnl f: sn clr and r.o strly* **6/1**[2]

013- **2** *3 1/2* **Archelao (IRE)**[9] 8448 6-9-2 **55**.............................................. AmirQuinn 8 60
(Lee Carter) *hld up in midfield: rdn and effrt to chse ldng trio 2f out: swtchd rt over 1f out: styd on u.p to go 2nd towards fin: no threat to wnr* **5/2**[1]

046/ **3** *1/2* **Hail Tiberius**[13] 634 7-9-7 **60**.....................................(t[1]) GrahamLee 12 64
(Martin Keighley) *hld up in midfield: rdn and outpcd in 5th 2f out: rallied u.p and styd on wl ins fnl f: wnt 3rd cl home* **8/1**

240- **4** *3/4* **Mojo Bear**[13] 8399 4-9-2 **57**.....................................(b[1]) MartinHarley 6 60
(Sylvester Kirk) *in tch in midfield: rdn and qcknd to ld over 2f out: drvn and hdd ins fnl f: sn outpcd and btn: lost 2 pls towards fin* **12/1**

64-1 **5** *1/2* **Daniel Thomas (IRE)**[5] 40 12-9-0 **53** 6ex............(tp) WilliamCarson 4 55+
(Ann Stokell) *bustled along early: hld up in midfield: shuffled bk and stuck bhd rivals over 2f out: hdwy and swtchd rt over 1f out: styd on strly fnl f: nt rch ldrs* **7/1**[3]

004- **6** *1 3/4* **Cabal**[20] 8341 7-8-10 **56**..........................................(b) MatthewHopkins(7) 10 54
(Andrew Crook) *hld up in rr: stdy hdwy on outer 5f out: rdn to chse ldr and clr in ldng trio over 2f out: btn 1f out: wknd ins fnl f* **16/1**

503- **7** *9* **Rigid**[34] 3736 7-8-0 **46** oh1.............................................. JoeDoyle(7) 13 26
(Tony Carroll) *stdd s: hld up in last trio: rdn and effrt ent fnl f: no ch but kpt on fnl f* **66/1**

560- **8** *3/4* **The Wonga Coup (IRE)**[9] 8448 7-9-2 **55**.................. FergusSweeney 5 34
(Pat Phelan) *in tch in midfield: rdn and outpcd over 2f out: wl hld whn nt clr run over 1f out: wknd* **8/1**

05-3 **9** *1 1/2* **Willow Island (IRE)**[5] 41 5-8-7 **46** oh1...........................(b) ChrisCatlin 3 22
(David Evans) *chsd ldrs: rdn and struggling over 2f out: losing pl whn short of room wl over 1f out: no ch after* **25/1**

/00- **10** *2 3/4* **What's Up Doc (IRE)**[37] 8129 13-8-7 **46** oh1.................. LiamJones 2 16
(Lawney Hill) *pressed ldr tl rdn to ld wl over 3f out: hdd and struggling over 2f out: bhd over 1f out* **66/1**

303- **11** *2 1/2* **Herbalist**[21] 8335 4-9-5 **60**..............................................(b) JohnFahy 11 25
(Ben Pauling) *rdn along early to chse ldrs: 4th and outpcd over 2f out: wknd over 1f out* **10/1**

200- **12** *8* **Appyjack**[26] 8279 6-8-7 **46** oh1...........................................(t) LukeMorris 7
(Tony Carroll) *s.i.s: nvr gng wl and a in rr* **16/1**

300- **13** *19* **Pastoral Jet**[37] 8125 6-9-1 **57**.............................. RossAtkinson(3) 1
(Richard Rowe) *led tl rdn and hdd wl over 3f out: sn dropped out: t.o fnl f* **25/1**

2m 4.03s (-2.57) **Going Correction** -0.10s/f (Stan)
**WFA** 4 from 5yo+ 2lb **13** Ran SP% **116.8**
Speed ratings (Par 101): **106,103,102,102,101 100,93,92,91,89 87,80,65**
CSF £20.15 CT £121.34 TOTE £6.70: £2.10, £1.50, £2.70; EX 21.20 Trifecta £111.50.There was no bid for the winner.
**Owner** Mrs Kate Digweed **Bred** Peter Hunt & Mrs Sally Hunt **Trained** Morestead, Hants
■ Stewards' Enquiry : William Carson caution: careless riding.

**FOCUS**
The pace was sound for this open selling handicap. The winner stepped up on even his early form.

## 89 CORAL.CO.UK H'CAP 1m 2f (P)
**2:00** (2:01) (Class 4) (0-85,85) 4-Y-0+ **£6,469** (£1,925; £962; £481) **Stalls** Low

Form RPR

510- **1** **Cayuga**[67] 7696 5-9-4 **82**.............................................. TomQueally 7 90
(Brett Johnson) *hld up in last pair: hdwy on outer over 2f out: rdn to chse ldrs over 1f out: led ins fnl f: edgd rt but styd on wl: rdn out* **10/1**

321- **2** *3/4* **Miguel Grau (USA)**[21] 8323 4-8-11 **77**..........................(b) MartinHarley 2 83+
(Roger Varian) *t.k.h early: hld up in tch in midfield: nt clr run ent fnl 2f: effrt to chse ldrs 1f out: swtchd rt and drvn ins fnl f: styd on to chse wnr and carried rt cl home* **5/2**[1]

020- **3** *1/2* **Chapter And Verse (IRE)**[39] 8117 8-9-6 **84**.................. ShaneKelly 8 89
(Mike Murphy) *t.k.h: hdwy to chse ldr 9f out: led over 7f out and sn clr: 4 l clr 2f out: drvn 1f out: hdd and styd on same pce ins fnl f* **25/1**

062- **4** *nse* **Munsarim (IRE)**[8] 8454 7-8-7 **71** oh1..............................(b) JimmyQuinn 1 76+
(Lee Carter) *stdd s: hld up in tch in last quartet: nt clr run 2f out: rdn and effrt over 1f out: pressed ldrs ins fnl f: styd on same pce fnl 100yds* **12/1**

315- **5** *nk* **Rakaan (IRE)**[9] 8445 7-9-7 **85**.......................................FergusSweeney 4 89
(Jamie Osborne) *hld up in tch in last quartet: rdn and effrt to chse ldr wl over 1f out: ev ch ins fnl f: no ex towards fin* **14/1**

110- **6** *3¼* **Modernism**[25] 8301 5-9-2 **80**.................................... JamieSpencer 9 78
(David Simcock) *led tl over 7f out: chsd ldr tl wl over 1f out: unable qck u.p whn nt clr run jst ins fnl f: sn btn and eased* **4/1**[2]

210- **7** *4* **Maria's Choice (IRE)**[26] 8269 5-8-12 **76**.......................(p) LukeMorris 10 66
(Alan McCabe) *hld up in tch in midfield: hemmed in and nt clr run over 2f out: rdn and no hdwy over 1f out: wknd fnl f* **16/1**

421- **8** *4* **Karam Albaari (IRE)**[30] 8218 6-9-7 **85**.......................... FrederikTylicki 6 67
(J R Jenkins) *t.k.h early: chsd ldrs: rdn and unable qck ent fnl 2f: btn over 1f out: wknd fnl f* **5/1**[3]

613- **9** *32* **Syncopate**[21] 8336 5-8-10 **74**............................................. LiamKeniry 3
(Pam Sly) *chsd ldrs: rdn and lost pl 3f out: t.o and eased ins fnl f* **8/1**

/00- **10** *86* **Franco Is My Name**[48] 7990 8-9-2 **80**..............................(p[1]) KierenFox 5
(Peter Hedger) *short of room leaving stalls: in tch in last pair: rdn and lost tch 3f out: t.o and virtually p.u fnl 2f: lame* **14/1**

2m 3.31s (-3.29) **Going Correction** -0.10s/f (Stan)
**WFA** 4 from 5yo+ 2lb **10** Ran SP% **116.2**
Speed ratings (Par 105): **109,108,108,107,107 105,101,98,73,4**
CSF £35.11 CT £622.16 TOTE £10.00: £3.40, £1.40, £9.80; EX 40.50 Trifecta £1273.00.
**Owner** J Daniels **Bred** Juddmonte Farms Ltd **Trained** Epsom, Surrey

**FOCUS**
A fair contest run at a sound gallop. The third sets the standard.

## 90 CORAL MOBILE "JUST THREE CLICKS TO BET" MEDIAN AUCTION MAIDEN STKS 1m 2f (P)
**2:35** (2:36) (Class 6) 4-6-Y-O **£2,045** (£603; £302) **Stalls** Low

Form RPR
004- **1** **Fearless Lad (IRE)**[9] 8443 4-9-5 62..............................(t) GeorgeBaker 5 67
(John Best) *chsd ldrs: rdn to chse ldr 2f out: drvn and kpt on ins fnl f to ld cl home* **4/1**[3]

535- **2** *nk* **Secret Song**[13] 8399 4-9-5 56........................................... LukeMorris 2 66
(Sir Mark Prescott Bt) *sn led: rdn 2 l clr 2f out: drvn ins fnl f: hdd and no ex cl home* **3/1**[2]

/24- **3** *3¾* **Pearl Ransom (IRE)**[37] 8125 4-9-5 58....................(v[1]) RobertWinston 3 59
(Lady Herries) *in tch in last pair: clsd to chse ldrs over 2f out: effrt in 3rd and hung lft ent fnl f: outpcd fnl 150yds* **6/1**

422- **4** *6* **Up Tipp**[20] 8341 4-9-5 57................................................ AdamKirby 4 47
(Mike Murphy) *chsd ldr: hung rt bnd after 1f: rdn and nt qckn over 2f out: 4th and btn over 1f out: wknd fnl f* **5/4**[1]

204- **5** *8* **Caerwyn**[33] 8185 4-9-5 62.............................................. GrahamLee 1 31
(Tony Carroll) *s.i.s: in tch in last pair: rdn and struggling jst over 2f out: wknd over 1f out* **14/1**

050- **6** *2½* **Maygo's Joy**[11] 8427 4-9-5 44..........................................[1] JoeFanning 6 26
(Ralph J Smith) *chsd ldrs: n.m.r over 2f out: rdn and outpcd 2f out: sn wknd* **33/1**

2m 5.02s (-1.58) **Going Correction** -0.10s/f (Stan) **6** Ran SP% **113.3**
Speed ratings: **102,101,98,93,87 85**
CSF £16.62 TOTE £4.70: £2.50, £1.60; EX 17.00 Trifecta £90.20.
**Owner** Mrs Jackie Jones **Bred** Brittas House Stud & Lynch Bages & Samac **Trained** Hucking, Kent

**FOCUS**
A sensible pace for this modest maiden. The form is rated around the winner.

## 91 BOOKMAKERS.CO.UK H'CAP 6f 1y(P)
**3:10** (3:10) (Class 5) (0-75,73) 4-Y-O+ **£2,726** (£805; £402) **Stalls** Low

Form RPR
250- **1** **Valmina**[42] 8069 7-9-6 **72**..........................................(t) JoeFanning 3 81
(Tony Carroll) *hld up in tch towards rr: rdn and hdwy over 1f out: qcknd to ld ins fnl f: r.o wl* **16/1**

624- **2** *¾* **Seek The Fair Land**[25] 8304 8-9-6 **72**..........................(b) AmirQuinn 5 79
(Lee Carter) *stdd s: t.k.h: sn in tch in midfield: rdn and effrt over 1f out: styd on wl ins fnl f to go 2nd wl ins fnl f* **9/2**[2]

545- **3** *1* **Rigolleto (IRE)**[37] 8128 6-9-2 **68**................................... GeorgeBaker 6 71
(Anabel K Murphy) *chsd ldr tl over 4f out: styd chsng ldrs: rdn and chal over 1f out: no ex and outpcd fnl 100yds* **16/1**

043- **4** *nse* **Bajan Bear**[11] 8431 6-9-3 **69**........................................ MartinHarley 7 72+
(Michael Blanshard) *hld up in tch in last pair: effrt and nt clr run over 1f out: hdwy 1f out: kpt on wl ins fnl f* **5/1**[3]

632- **5** *½* **Smokethatthunders (IRE)**[11] 8431 4-9-7 **73**.................. LukeMorris 9 75+
(James Toller) *taken down early: stdd s: hld up in tch in midfield: effrt on outer bnd 2f out: styd on u.p fnl f: nvr gng pce to chal* **7/4**[1]

540- **6** *¾* **Alnoomaas (IRE)**[78] 7444 5-9-2 **68**............................. JimmyQuinn 4 67
(Luke Dace) *chsd ldrs tl wnt 2nd over 4f out: led over 2f out: drvn and hrd pressed over 1f out: hdd ins fnl f: sn wknd* **14/1**

435- **7** *½* **Senator Bong**[46] 8021 4-9-6 **72**....................................... LiamKeniry 1 70
(David Elsworth) *chsd ldrs: rdn and effrt 2f out: unable qck ent fnl f: wknd fnl 100yds* **8/1**

000- **8** *2¼* **El Mirage (IRE)**[104] 6777 4-9-5 **71**............................. RobertWinston 10 61
(Dean Ivory) *led tl over 2f out: rdn and btn over 1f out: wknd ins fnl f* **33/1**

300- **9** *1¼* **Panther Patrol (IRE)**[11] 8430 4-9-6 **72**........................ JohnFahy 8 58
(Eve Johnson Houghton) *chsd ldrs: rdn and unable qck ent fnl 2f: lost pl and btn jst over 1f out: wknd fnl f* **6/1**

010- **10** *5* **Billy Red**[42] 8069 10-9-6 **72**.................................(b) FrederikTylicki 2 42
(J R Jenkins) *dwlt: a last: struggling 1/2-way: sn bhd* **33/1**

1m 11.06s (-0.84) **Going Correction** -0.10s/f (Stan) **10** Ran SP% **120.9**
Speed ratings (Par 103): **101,100,98,98,97 96,96,93,91,84**
CSF £89.87 CT £1195.88 TOTE £22.80: £5.40, £1.70, £4.70; EX 83.90 Trifecta £4043.80 Part won..
**Owner** Mayden Stud **Bred** Mayden Stud, J A And D S Dewhurst **Trained** Cropthorne, Worcs

**FOCUS**
A tight handicap with only 5lb covering the field, run at a fair gallop. Ordinary form with the winner rated pretty much to his best.

## 92 LADBROKES APPRENTICE H'CAP 1m 1y(P)
**3:40** (3:40) (Class 6) (0-60,61) 4-Y-O+ **£2,045** (£603; £302) **Stalls** High

Form RPR
650- **1** **Nubar Boy**[8] 8456 7-9-2 **59**...............................(p) CharlotteJenner(5) 5 66
(Ian Williams) *chsd ldrs: allowed ldng pair to go clr after 2f: rdn and clsd over 1f out: kpt on u.p to ld wl ins fnl f: hld on cl home* **10/1**

66-0 **2** *hd* **Bertie Blu Boy**[6] 17 6-8-7 **45**.................................(b) EoinWalsh 7 52
(Lisa Williamson) *t.k.h: chsd ldr tl led 5f out: sn clr: 7 l clr 2f out: rdn over 1f out: hdd wl ins fnl f: kpt on but hld cl home* **10/1**

132- **3** *nk* **Olivers Mount**[42] 8065 4-9-1 **53**.............................(t) LouisSteward 10 59
(Ed Vaughan) *racd off the pce in midfield: rdn and clsd over 1f out: 4th 1f out: styd on wl u.p fnl 100yds: nt quite rch ldrs* **9/4**[1]

600- **4** *½* **Cataria Girl (USA)**[11] 8427 5-8-13 **54**..................(t) JordanVaughan(3) 12 59
(Marcus Tregoning) *racd off the pce in midfield: rdn and clsd jst over 1f out: r.o wl ins fnl f: swtchd lft towards fin: nt quite rch ldrs* **14/1**

400- **5** *¾* **Annes Rocket (IRE)**[41] 8087 9-9-1 **58**.........................(p) GaryMahon(5) 6 61
(Jimmy Fox) *racd off the pce in last quartet: rdn and effrt on outer over 1f out: styd on wl ins fnl f: nt rch ldrs* **14/1**

600- **6** *hd* **Dreaming Again**[125] 6133 4-8-7 **50**................................ CamHardie(5) 8 53
(Jimmy Fox) *racd off the pce in last pair: rdn and hdwy over 1f out: styd on wl ins fnl f: nt rch ldrs* **50/1**

200- **7** *hd* **Claude Greenwood**[166] 4722 4-9-7 **59**.......................... JoshBaudains 9 62
(Roger Curtis) *racd off the pce in last trio: rdn and effrt over 2f out: no imp tl styd on wl ins fnl f: nt rch ldrs* **33/1**

021- **8** *hd* **Fonterutoli (IRE)**[9] 8449 7-9-2 **61** 6ex........................(e) RhiainIngram(7) 2 64+
(Roger Ingram) *hld up off the pce in last: stl last whn nt clr run and hmpd 2f out: swtchd rt and hdwy over 1f out: styd on wl ins fnl f: clsng whn nt clr run and eased fnl 50yds* **6/1**[3]

132- **9** *hd* **One Last Dream**[35] 8151 5-9-7 **59**................................(b) RyanWhile 3 61
(Ron Hodges) *broke fast and led for 3f: chsd clr ldr after but stl clr of field: rdn and effrt over 1f out: kpt on tl lost 2nd ins fnl f: kpt on same pce and lost many pls fnl 100yds* **6/1**[3]

415- **10** *¾* **Skidby Mill (IRE)**[37] 8125 4-9-1 **56**.............................. JoeDoyle(3) 1 56
(Laura Mongan) *racd off the pce in midfield: effrt u.p on inner over 1f out: drvn and kpt on ins fnl f: nvr able to chal* **5/1**[2]

600- **11** *8* **Icanboogie**[12] 8417 4-8-7 **45**........................................ DanielCremin 11 26
(Anthony Middleton) *prom in main gp but nvr on terms w ldrs: rdn and struggling over 2f out: wknd over 1f out* **66/1**

460- **12** *shd* **Daneside (IRE)**[20] 8351 7-8-9 **47**..........................(t) MatthewHopkins 4 28
(P J O'Gorman) *racd off the pce in midfield: rdn and no hdwy over 2f out: wknd over 1f out* **16/1**

1m 37.69s (-0.51) **Going Correction** -0.10s/f (Stan) **12** Ran SP% **119.8**
Speed ratings (Par 101): **98,97,97,97,96 96,95,95,95,94 86,86**
CSF £106.29 CT £311.38 TOTE £16.70: £4.40, £2.40, £1.90; EX 214.00 Trifecta £1100.60.
**Owner** Phil Slater **Bred** Low Ground Stud **Trained** Portway, Worcs

**FOCUS**
This open yet modest handicap, confined to apprentice riders, was run at a fierce pace. They finished in a bunch and the form does not look strong. The winner's best run since early 2012.
T/Plt: £67.20. Pool: £85,000.92 - 922.43 winning units. T/Qpdt: £28.20. Pool: £5103.59 - 133.70 winning units. SP

# [72]SOUTHWELL (L-H)
### Thursday, January 9

**OFFICIAL GOING: Standard**
Wind: Fresh half behind Weather: Cloudy with sunny periods

## 93 BOOKMAKERS.CO.UK APPRENTICE CLASSIFIED CLAIMING STKS 5f (F)
**12:50** (12:50) (Class 6) 4-Y-O+ **£2,385** (£704; £352) **Stalls** High

Form RPR
101- **1** **Shawkantango**[13] 8406 7-8-9 69..............................(v) AdamMcLean(5) 8 79
(Derek Shaw) *racd wd: in tch: rdn along 2f out: hdwy wl over 1f out: styd on to ld ins fnl f: sn clr* **3/1**[1]

000- **2** *2½* **Miako (USA)**[21] 8351 4-8-5 62....................................[1] LouisSteward(5) 4 66
(Michael Appleby) *led: pushed along wl over 1f out: rdn and edgd lft 1f out: drvn and hdd ins fnl f: one pce* **6/1**

05-2 **3** *1* **R Woody**[6] 35 7-8-11 68......................................(e) MichaelJMMurphy 1 63
(Robert Cowell) *dwlt and towards rr: pushed along and hdwy on outer to chse ldrs over 2f out: rdn wl over 1f out: kpt on same pce fnl f* **3/1**[1]

613- **4** *shd* **Quality Art (USA)**[13] 8406 6-8-11 63.............................. BillyCray 2 63
(Richard Guest) *cl up: effrt 2f out and sn rdn: drvn wl over 1f out and ev ch tl edgd lft ins fnl f: n.m.r and one pce towards fin* **4/1**[3]

224- **5** *1* **Take The Lead**[86] 7262 4-8-8 65..................................... JoeDoyle(5) 6 61
(David Nicholls) *chsd ldrs: effrt 2f out: sn rdn and wknd appr fnl f* **14/1**

200- **6** *hd* **Where's Reiley (USA)**[19] 8384 8-8-11 68..........................(b) RobertTart 3 59
(Michael Attwater) *sn pushed along and towards rr: rdn 2f out: kpt on u.p fnl f: n.d* **7/2**[2]

000- **7** *3¾* **Midnight Dream (FR)**[41] 8096 4-8-9 70.................. GeorginaBaxter(7) 5 50
(Kristin Stubbs) *cl up: rdn along 1/2-way: sn wknd* **25/1**

600- **8** *16* **Vogarth**[99] 6952 10-8-0 36........................................(b) PaulBooth(7) 7
(Michael Chapman) *sn rdn along and outpcd in rr: bhd fr 1/2-way* **100/1**

57.84s (-1.86) **Going Correction** -0.20s/f (Stan) **8** Ran SP% **118.0**
Speed ratings (Par 101): **106,102,100,100,98 98,92,66**
CSF £22.46 TOTE £3.40: £1.40, £2.50, £1.10; EX 25.80 Trifecta £110.30.
**Owner** Shawthing Racing Partnership **Bred** Derek Shaw **Trained** Sproxton, Leics

**FOCUS**
A competitive race for the grade, featuring a couple of multiple C&D winners. A length personal best from the winner.

## 94 COMPARE BOOKMAKERS AT BOOKMAKERS.CO.UK MAIDEN STKS 5f (F)
**1:20** (1:20) (Class 5) 3-Y-O+ **£3,067** (£905; £453) **Stalls** High

Form RPR
304- **1** **Sweet Angelica**[13] 8405 3-8-7 53..............................(v[1]) JamesSullivan 2 60
(James Given) *prom: cl up 1/2-way: sn rdn along: drvn over 1f out: styd on to chal ent fnl f: edgd rt and kpt on gamely to ld last 50yds* **25/1**

0- **2** *hd* **Precariously Good**[160] 4963 3-8-7 0................................. JamieSpencer 3 59
(David Barron) *led: rdn along over 1f out: drvn ins fnl f: hdd and no ex last 50yds* **5/2**[2]

2- **3** *1¾* **Meebo (IRE)**[13] 8405 3-8-2 58..............................(v[1]) ShelleyBirkett(5) 8 53
(J R Jenkins) *cl up: effrt 2f out: sn rdn and ev ch tl drvn and one pce ins fnl f* **9/4**[1]

**4** *1¾* **Chatalong (IRE)** 3-8-7 0.................................................. BarryMcHugh 5 47
(Richard Fahey) *chsd ldrs: rdn along and outpcd over 2f out: styd on fnl f* **8/1**

2- **5** *shd* **Twilight Angel**[54] 7929 6-9-8 0......................................... RobertHavlin 4 52
(Pat Eddery) *dwlt: sn trcking ldrs: rdn along 2f out: drvn over 1f out and sn one pce* **5/1**

40-3 **6** *nk* **Jalebi**[8] 5 3-8-0 0.............................................. DanielCremin(7) 1 45
(Jim Boyle) *prom on outer: cl up 1/2-way: rdn and ev ch wl over 1f out: wknd appr fnl f* **4/1**[3]

06-0 **7** *12* **Mrs Medley**[4] 58 8-9-3 20.............................................[1] AnnStokell(5) 6 8
(Ann Stokell) *in rr whn n.m.r and swtchd lft after 1f: sn rdn along and outpcd: bhd fr 1/2-way* **200/1**

00- 8 *10* **Silent Sam**[24] 8313 6-9-13 0............................ AndrewMullen 7
(Michael Appleby) *sn rdn along in rr: outpcd and bhd fr 1/2-way* **25/1**
58.96s (-0.74) **Going Correction** -0.20s/f (Stan)
**WFA** 3 from 6yo+ 15lb **8** Ran SP% **115.3**
Speed ratings (Par 103): **97,96,93,91,90 90,71,55**
CSF £87.19 TOTE £18.60: £3.90, £1.30, £1.10; EX 96.40 Trifecta £293.80.
**Owner** The Cool Silk Partnership **Bred** G Doyle & Lord Margadale **Trained** Willoughton, Lincs
**FOCUS**
A weak-looking maiden and with little market confidence shown in the two unexposed, well-bred fillies, it just emphasised the weakness of the form.

## 95 BEST ODDS AT BOOKMAKERS.CO.UK H'CAP 6f (F)
**1:50** (1:50) (Class 6) (0-65,71) 4-Y-0+ **£2,385** (£704; £352) **Stalls** Low

Form RPR
42-1 **1** **Maakirr (IRE)**[7] 8 5-9-8 **69** 6ex............................(tp) MarkCoumbe[(3)] 1 79
(Roy Bowring) *hld up towards rr: hdwy on inner 1/2-way: chsd clr ldr 2f out: sn rdn: styd on to ld ins fnl f: jnd and drvn last 100yds: sn edgd rt: kpt on gamely towards fin* **2/1**[1]
24-2 **2** *nk* **Grace Hull**[4] 59 4-8-10 **57**.............................................. BillyCray[(3)] 6 66
(Garry Moss) *dwlt and towards rr: wd st: hdwy over 2f out: rdn over 1f out: styd on wl to chal ins fnl f: ev ch tl drvn: edgd lft and no ex towards fin* **7/2**[3]
12-6 **3** *3 1/2* **Pearl Noir**[4] 58 4-8-4 **55**.................................(b) MatthewHopkins[(7)] 7 53
(Scott Dixon) *led: rdn clr wl over 2f out: drvn over 1f out: hdd ins fnl f: wkng whn n.m.r last 100yds* **8/1**
000- **4** *1 1/4* **Ferdy (IRE)**[41] 8095 5-9-4 **62**............................................ JoeFanning 4 56
(Paul Green) *dwlt: sn in tch: hdwy on inner 1/2-way: chsd ldrs 2f out: sn rdn and no imp appr fnl f* **25/1**
140- **5** *8* **Caramelita**[12] 8432 7-8-13 **62**................................(v) ShelleyBirkett[(5)] 5 30
(J R Jenkins) *prom: rdn along over 2f out: drvn wl over 1f out and sn wknd* **12/1**
211- **6** *1/2* **Thorpe Bay**[11] 8439 5-9-6 **71** 6ex........................... AlistairRawlinson[(7)] 2 38+
(Michael Appleby) *plld hrd: trckd ldrs: sddle slipped after 2f: wknd 1/2-way* **3/1**[2]
60- **7** *1/2* **Mambo Spirit (IRE)**[31] 8224 10-9-4 **62**............................ MartinHarley 8 27
(Tony Newcombe) *racd wd: a in rr* **25/1**
005- **8** *3 1/4* **Baltic Prince (IRE)**[134] 5886 4-9-7 **65**........................... TonyHamilton 3 20
(Paul Green) *chsd ldng pair: pushed along bef 1/2-way: sn wknd* **12/1**
1m 14.89s (-1.61) **Going Correction** -0.325s/f (Stan) **8** Ran SP% **114.7**
Speed ratings (Par 101): **97,96,91,90,79 78,78,73**
CSF £9.21 CT £43.22 TOTE £3.30: £1.50, £1.60, £2.60; EX 9.80 Trifecta £53.90.
**Owner** K Nicholls **Bred** Darley **Trained** Edwinstowe, Notts
■ Stewards' Enquiry : Billy Cray two-day ban: used whip above permitted level (Jan 23-24)
**FOCUS**
A modest handicap contested by three in-form horse, but little depth to the contest below the three market leaders. Another step up from the winner.

## 96 LADBROKES H'CAP 1m (F)
**2:20** (2:20) (Class 5) (0-70,70) 4-Y-0+ **£2,911** (£866; £432; £216) **Stalls** Low

Form RPR
15-3 **1** **Peter's Friend**[6] 29 5-9-3 **66**.......................................... PJMcDonald 2 74
(Michael Herrington) *dwlt and bhd: hdwy 3f out: wd st and rdn over 2f out: styd on strly u.p fr over 1f out: drvn and edgd lft towards fin: led on line* **15/8**[1]
314- **2** *nse* **Royal Holiday (IRE)**[61] 7824 7-9-7 **70**......................(p) DanielTudhope 6 78
(Marjorie Fife) *led: rdn along and jnd 3f out: drvn over 1f out: kpt on gamely u.p ins fnl f: hdd on line* **5/1**[3]
651- **3** *1* **Dandarrell**[13] 8409 7-9-0 **63**..........................................(p) BarryMcHugh 3 69
(Julie Camacho) *hld up: hdwy 3f out: effrt 2f out: chal wl over 1f out: rdn ins fnl f and ev ch tl no ex last 75yds* **3/1**[2]
053- **4** *2 1/4* **Waverunner**[20] 8366 4-9-5 **68**..........................................(b) JoeFanning 4 68
(Mark Johnston) *trckd ldrs: hdwy on inner to chal 3f out: sn disputing ld and ev ch: rdn wl over 1f out: wknd fnl f* **10/1**
152- **5** *11* **On The Cusp (IRE)**[11] 8436 7-8-7 **56** oh1.....................(p) WilliamCarson 7 31
(Ann Stokell) *cl up on outer: rdn along 3f out and sn wknd* **7/1**
005- **6** *2* **Red Art (IRE)**[23] 8321 5-9-7 **70**........................................ MartinHarley 8 41
(Tony Newcombe) *racd wd: a in rr* **8/1**
560- **7** *1/2* **Mcmonagle (USA)**[9] 8454 6-9-0 **68**.......................(p[1]) JacobButterfield[(5)] 5 37
(Alan Brown) *chsd ldrs: rdn along wl over 3f out: sn wknd* **33/1**
000- **8** *9* **Lieutenant Dan (IRE)**[36] 8157 7-9-4 **67**..................(v) AndrewMullen 1 16
(Michael Appleby) *cl up on inner: rdn along wl over 3f out: sn wknd* **14/1**
1m 41.42s (-2.28) **Going Correction** -0.325s/f (Stan) **8** Ran SP% **118.8**
Speed ratings (Par 103): **98,97,96,94,83 81,81,72**
CSF £12.28 CT £27.77 TOTE £2.50: £1.20, £1.50, £1.50; EX 11.80 Trifecta £23.60.
**Owner** Stuart Herrington **Bred** Norton Grove Stud Ltd **Trained** Cold Kirby, N Yorks
**FOCUS**
Another modest handicap that revolved around a couple of runners with good recent local form. The winner may have a bit more to offer on this surface.

## 97 CORAL.CO.UK BEST ODDS GUARANTEED ON RACING MEDIAN AUCTION MAIDEN STKS 1m 3f (F)
**2:50** (2:50) (Class 5) 4-6-Y-0 **£2,911** (£866; £432; £216) **Stalls** Low

Form RPR
622- **1** **Persian Patriot**[21] 8343 4-9-0 66.......................................... RobertHavlin 3 68+
(William Jarvis) *sn led: pushed clr 3f out: rdn wl over 1f out: kpt on* **2/5**[1]
6- **2** *2 1/2* **Sheila's Heart**[202] 3539 4-9-0 0.................................. ShelleyBirkett[(5)] 4 69
(Julia Feilden) *dwlt: sn trcking ldng pair: hdwy to chse wnr 3f out: rdn wl over 1f out: sn no imp* **4/1**[2]
03-0 **3** *9* **Zainda (IRE)**[7] 14 4-9-0 50................................................ PaddyAspell 2 48
(John Wainwright) *chsd wnr: rdn along over 3f out: sn drvn and one pce* **16/1**
303- **4** *32* **Taming The Tweet**[52] 1343 4-9-0 50......................................... JoeFanning 1
(J R Jenkins) *chsd ldng pair: rdn along over 4f out: sn wknd* **8/1**[3]
2m 24.92s (-3.08) **Going Correction** -0.325s/f (Stan) **4** Ran SP% **108.4**
Speed ratings: **98,96,89,66**
CSF £2.33 TOTE £1.20; EX 2.50 Trifecta £10.60.
**Owner** Miss J Margossian **Bred** Dr J Ahmadzadeh **Trained** Newmarket, Suffolk
**FOCUS**
A weak and uncompetitive maiden, and a shaky level to the form.

## 98 32RED.COM H'CAP 5f (F)
**3:20** (3:20) (Class 6) (0-65,64) 3-Y-0 **£2,385** (£704; £352) **Stalls** High

Form RPR
42-2 **1** **Argent Touch**[7] 15 3-8-0 **50** oh5................................ AdamMcLean[(7)] 3 60
(Derek Shaw) *t.k.h: cl up: slt ld ent fnl f: sn shkn up and kpt on: readily* **7/4**[1]
23- **2** *1 1/2* **Ealain Aibrean (IRE)**[26] 8300 3-9-2 **64**........................... EoinWalsh[(5)] 1 68
(David Evans) *cl up: led 2f out: sn rdn: hdd and drvn ent fnl f: kpt on same pce* **3/1**[3]
605- **3** *4* **Bold Max**[218] 2978 3-8-7 **53**........................................ RossAtkinson[(3)] 2 43
(Zoe Davison) *prom: rdn along and outpcd after 1 1/2f: styd on fr over 1f out: n.d* **16/1**
354- **4** *4 1/2* **Douneedahand**[22] 8322 3-9-0 **64**.............................. JordanVaughan[(7)] 5 38
(Seamus Mullins) *slt ld: rdn along 1/2-way: hdd 2f out: drvn and wknd over 1f out* **9/4**[2]
050- **5** *2 3/4* **Previous Acclaim (IRE)**[19] 8383 3-8-6 **54**..............(p) ShelleyBirkett[(5)] 4 18
(Julia Feilden) *sn rdn along in rr: outpcd and bhd fr 1/2-way* **7/1**
59.56s (-0.14) **Going Correction** -0.20s/f (Stan) **5** Ran SP% **110.5**
Speed ratings (Par 95): **93,90,84,77,72**
CSF £7.36 TOTE £2.50: £1.60, £1.10; EX 3.50 Trifecta £25.00.
**Owner** Brian Johnson (Northamptonshire) **Bred** Reid & Shriver **Trained** Sproxton, Leics
**FOCUS**
A truly run handicap, contested by five runners having their first run on Fibresand. The time was relatively slow and the level of the form is fluid.

## 99 32RED H'CAP 1m 3f (F)
**3:50** (3:50) (Class 5) (0-75,75) 3-Y-0 **£2,911** (£866; £432; £216) **Stalls** Low

Form RPR
411- **1** **Groovejet**[35] 8164 3-9-7 **75**.............................................. MartinHarley 3 84
(Peter Chapple-Hyam) *trckd ldr: cl up 1/2-way: led over 2f out: rdn wl over 1f out: styd on* **6/1**
113- **2** *2 3/4* **Big Kenny**[11] 8434 3-8-3 **62**........................................ EoinWalsh[(5)] 5 66
(David Evans) *trckd ldrs: hdwy on outer and cl up over 4f out: effrt to chal 2f out: sn rdn and ev ch tl edgd lft ent fnl f and kpt on same pce* **7/2**[3]
421- **3** *1/2* **Power Up**[24] 8312 3-9-0 **68**................................................ JoeFanning 1 71
(Mark Johnston) *led: jnd and pushed along over 3f out: hdd over 2f out and sn rdn: edgd rt jst over 1f out and kpt on one pce* **11/4**[2]
201- **4** *1 1/2* **Lesha (IRE)**[26] 8297 3-9-2 **70**........................................ JamieSpencer 2 70
(Kevin Ryan) *trckd ldrs: effrt over 2f out: rdn and n.m.r over 1f out: swtchd rt ent fnl f: sn no imp* **2/1**[1]
364- **5** *2* **Wealth (IRE)**[35] 8164 3-8-11 **65**.................................... TonyHamilton 4 62
(Richard Fahey) *trckd ldrs: cl up 1/2-way: rdn along over 3f out: wknd over 2f out* **6/1**
2m 25.01s (-2.99) **Going Correction** -0.325s/f (Stan) **5** Ran SP% **110.8**
Speed ratings (Par 97): **97,95,94,93,92**
CSF £26.46 TOTE £5.00: £2.20, £2.10; EX 19.40 Trifecta £62.00.
**Owner** Phil Cunningham **Bred** P M Cunningham **Trained** Newmarket, Suffolk
**FOCUS**
A competitive handicap despite the small field and the form is rated slightly positively. The gallop was no more than reasonable and the field were tightly grouped until the straight.
T/Plt: £7.20 to a £1 stake. Pool of £90880.0 - 9191.98 winning tickets. T/Qpdt: £2.10 to a £1 stake. Pool of £7220.05 - 2437.84 winning tickets. JR

# 65 WOLVERHAMPTON (A.W) (L-H)
Thursday, January 9

**OFFICIAL GOING: Standard**
Wind: Fresh behind Weather: Cloudy with sunny spells

## 100 COMPARE BOOKMAKERS AT BOOKMAKERS.CO.UK H'CAP 5f 216y(P)
**4:10** (4:10) (Class 7) (0-50,52) 4-Y-0+ **£1,940** (£577; £288; £144) **Stalls** Low

Form RPR
43-1 **1** **Interchoice Star**[7] 18 9-9-9 **52** 6ex.......................(p) GeorgeBaker 5 62+
(Ray Peacock) *mde all: shkn up over 1f out: rdn out* **7/4**[1]
053- **2** *2 3/4* **Red Star Lady (IRE)**[11] 8438 4-9-2 **45**............................ JimmyQuinn 3 46
(Shaun Harris) *chsd ldrs: rdn over 1f out: styd on u.p to go 2nd wl ins fnl f: no ch w wnr* **20/1**
006- **3** *1/2* **Scommettitrice (IRE)**[13] 8412 6-9-4 **47**.....................(v[1]) KieranO'Neill 10 47
(Nigel Twiston-Davies) *sn pushed along to chse wnr: rdn over 2f out: styd on same pce ins fnl f* **7/1**[3]
460- **4** *1 3/4* **Play The Blues (IRE)**[18] 8393 7-8-12 **46**..............(bt[1]) JoshBaudains[(5)] 2 40
(Dominic Ffrench Davis) *a.p: racd keenly: rdn over 1f out: no ex ins fnl f* **8/1**
00-0 **5** *1* **Lord Buffhead**[4] 58 5-9-7 **50**................................(v) RobbieFitzpatrick 8 41
(Richard Guest) *hld up: rdn over 2f out: hdwy over 1f out: styd on same pce fnl f* **8/1**
034- **6** *1* **Vhujon (IRE)**[35] 8169 9-8-13 **45**.......................................... SladeO'Hara[(3)] 1 33
(Peter Grayson) *hld up: hdwy over 1f out: sn rdn: nt trble ldrs* **16/1**
000- **7** *1* **Rightcar**[35] 8168 7-9-2 **45**............................................. StephenCraine 13 29
(Peter Grayson) *chsd ldrs: rdn over 2f out: styd on same pce fr over 1f out* **16/1**
250- **8** *6* **Chester Deelyte (IRE)**[28] 8258 6-9-1 **47**...................(v) MarkCoumbe[(3)] 9 12
(Lisa Williamson) *s.i.s: hld up: rdn 1/2-way: sn wknd* **7/1**[3]
052- **9** *1/2* **Christopher Chua (IRE)**[18] 8393 5-8-12 **46**..............(v) DavidKenny[(5)] 7 10
(Michael Scudamore) *hld up: rdn over 2f out: wknd fnl f* **6/1**[2]
000- **10** *9* **Bridge Valley**[217] 3026 7-9-3 **46**..................................(b) ChrisCatlin 6
(Jason Ward) *s.i.s: outpcd* **20/1**
1m 16.13s (1.13) **Going Correction** +0.25s/f (Slow) **10** Ran SP% **119.2**
Speed ratings (Par 97): **102,98,97,95,94 92,91,83,82,70**
CSF £44.28 CT £205.81 TOTE £2.50: £1.40, £4.00, £2.20; EX 42.40 Trifecta £463.20.
**Owner** John P Evitt **Bred** M Bishop **Trained** Kyre Park, Worcs
**FOCUS**
An inauspicious beginning to a seven-race card made up entirely by handicaps.

## 101 LADBROKES H'CAP 1m 141y(P)
**4:40** (4:40) (Class 4) (0-80,80) 4-Y-0+ **£5,175** (£1,540; £769; £384) **Stalls** Low

Form RPR
1- **1** **Big Baz (IRE)**[12] 8427 4-9-6 **80**........................................ GrahamLee 1 92+
(William Muir) *trckd ldr 1f: remained handy and a gng wl: wnt 2nd again 2f out: shkn up to ld wl ins fnl f: r.o: readily* **4/7**[1]
103- **2** *1* **Canon Law (IRE)**[107] 6735 4-8-10 **73**............................ SamJames[(3)] 2 81
(David O'Meara) *led: rdn over 1f out: hdd wl ins fnl f: kpt on* **8/1**
061- **3** *4 1/2* **Tartan Trip**[27] 8278 7-8-12 **71**.................................(v) AndrewMullen 4 69
(Michael Appleby) *hld up: pushed along over 2f out: hdwy over 1f out: sn rdn: styd on same pce fnl f* **9/2**[2]
300- **4** *13* **Hilali (IRE)**[94] 7075 5-9-3 **76**........................................(t) GeorgeBaker 5 44
(Gary Brown) *trckd ldr over 7f out tl pushed along 2f out: wknd over 1f out* **11/2**[3]
1m 54.21s (3.71) **Going Correction** +0.25s/f (Slow)
**WFA** 4 from 5yo+ 1lb **4** Ran SP% **108.3**
Speed ratings (Par 105): **93,92,88,76**
CSF £5.56 TOTE £1.30; EX 4.80 Trifecta £8.80.

**Owner** The Big Baz Partnership **Bred** Haras De La Perelle **Trained** Lambourn, Berks
**FOCUS**
A fair small-field handicap, and the feature race on the card in which they went a steady gallop until the tempo increased just after halfway.

## 102 DOWNLOAD THE LADBROKES APP H'CAP 7f 32y(P)
5:10 (5:10) (Class 5) (0-70,70) 4-Y-O+ £2,911 (£866; £432; £216) Stalls High

Form RPR
04-2 1 **Khajaaly (IRE)**[7] 10 7-9-1 64 (bt) AndrewMullen 6 73
(Michael Appleby) *hld up: pushed along over 2f out: hdwy over 1f out: sn rdn: edgd lft and r.o to ld post* 7/2[1]
33-4 2 hd **Hellbender (IRE)**[7] 11 8-9-2 70 (t) AdamCarter(5) 2 78
(Shaun Harris) *chsd ldr tl led over 5f out: rdn over 1f out: edgd rt wl ins fnl f: hdd post* 9/2[3]
563- 3 1 1/4 **Fame Again**[24] 8314 6-9-4 67 JamesSullivan 7 72
(Michael Easterby) *led: hdd over 5f out: chsd ldr: pushed along over 2f out: rdn over 1f out: styng on whn hmpd towards fin* 4/1[2]
113- 4 hd **Izzy Boy (USA)**[13] 8409 4-8-10 59 LiamJones 1 63
(Mark Johnston) *sn pushed along and prom: shkn up over 2f out: rdn over 1f out: r.o* 8/1
44-0 5 hd **Ewell Place (IRE)**[5] 52 5-8-11 67 (p) LewisWalsh(7) 4 71
(David Simcock) *hld up: swtchd lft and hdwy over 1f out: r.o* 10/1
45-4 6 2 3/4 **Sewn Up**[7] 20 4-9-3 66 (v[1]) RobertHavlin 3 62
(Andrew Hollinshead) *prom: rdn over 1f out: styd on same pce ins fnl f* 10/1
120- 7 2 3/4 **Daring Dragon**[36] 8158 4-9-7 70 (p[1]) GeorgeBaker 8 59
(Ed Walker) *hld up: racd keenly: shkn up over 2f out: nvr nrr* 7/2[1]
006- 8 1/2 **Crown Choice**[101] 6905 9-9-2 65 GrahamLee 9 52
(Jedd O'Keeffe) *dwlt: hld up: shkn up over 1f out: a in rr* 33/1
231- 9 1/2 **For Shia And Lula (IRE)**[154] 5166 5-9-5 68 (p) ShaneKelly 5 54
(Daniel Mark Loughnane) *trckd ldrs: racd keenly: rdn over 1f out: wknd fnl f* 14/1

1m 31.37s (1.77) **Going Correction** +0.25s/f (Slow) 9 Ran SP% **121.5**
Speed ratings (Par 103): **99,98,97,97,96 93,90,90,89**
CSF £20.64 CT £67.82 TOTE £4.50: £1.90, £2.10, £1.60; EX 30.40 Trifecta £156.80.
**Owner** New Kids On The Trot **Bred** Barry Noonan And Denis Noonan **Trained** Danethorpe, Notts
■ Stewards' Enquiry : Adam Carter two-day ban: careless riding (Jan 23-24)
Andrew Mullen one-day ban: careless riding (Jan 23)
**FOCUS**
A modest handicap in which they went a stop-start, muddling gallop.

## 103 32RED H'CAP 7f 32y(P)
5:40 (5:40) (Class 5) (0-75,69) 3-Y-O £2,911 (£866; £432; £216) Stalls High

Form RPR
014- 1 **First Experience**[19] 8382 3-9-6 68 ChrisCatlin 3 72
(Rae Guest) *sn trcking ldrs: shkn up over 1f out: r.o u.p to ld towards fin* 4/1[3]
61- 2 nk **Bint Malyana (IRE)**[40] 8114 3-9-4 66 GrahamLee 4 69
(James Tate) *w ldr: shkn up over 2f out: rdn to ld ins fnl f: hdd towards fin* 5/4[1]
521- 3 3/4 **Bon Port**[20] 8367 3-9-1 63 RobertHavlin 1 64
(Hughie Morrison) *led: pushed along 2f out: rdn over 1f out: hdd and unable qck ins fnl f* 5/2[2]
313- 4 1 1/4 **Howz The Family (IRE)**[24] 8311 3-9-6 68 JohnFahy 2 66
(John Spearing) *hld up: pushed along over 2f out: r.o ins fnl f: nt rch ldrs* 14/1
323- 5 2 **Kodafine (IRE)**[10] 8442 3-9-4 69 RossAtkinson(3) 5 61
(David Evans) *chsd ldrs: pushed along 1/2-way: rdn over 1f out: styd on same pce ins fnl f* 8/1

1m 32.16s (2.56) **Going Correction** +0.25s/f (Slow) 5 Ran SP% **110.8**
Speed ratings (Par 97): **95,94,93,92,90**
CSF £9.59 TOTE £5.90: £1.70, £2.70; EX 9.70 Trifecta £29.00.
**Owner** Fitorfat Racing & Guy Carstairs **Bred** Northmore Stud **Trained** Newmarket, Suffolk
**FOCUS**
A modest small-field 3yo handicap.

## 104 32RED.COM H'CAP 2m 119y(P)
6:10 (6:10) (Class 6) (0-65,68) 4-Y-O+ £2,264 (£673; £336; £168) Stalls Low

Form RPR
53-1 1 **Flash Crash**[7] 14 5-9-13 68 6ex (tp) LouisSteward(7) 2 78
(Anthony Carson) *trckd ldrs: pushed along and hmpd over 3f out: nt clr run over 2f out: shkn up to ld ins fnl f: styd on wl* 5/6[1]
506- 2 3 3/4 **Easydoesit (IRE)**[40] 8115 6-10-0 62 GrahamLee 1 68
(Tony Carroll) *led: rdn over 1f out: hdd and unable qck ins fnl f* 7/1
106- 3 1 3/4 **Honest Strike (USA)**[22] 8331 7-9-13 61 (b) ShaneKelly 3 64
(Daniel Mark Loughnane) *s.i.s: hdwy and hmpd over 3f out: sn swtchd rt: rdn over 1f out: no ex ins fnl f* 5/1[3]
125- 4 8 **Luckster**[22] 7668 4-9-2 57 GeorgeBaker 5 51
(David Evans) *chsd ldr: shkn up over 7f out: reminder over 5f out: pushed along and edgd lft over 3f out: sn rdn: wknd fnl f* 3/1[2]

3m 44.71s (2.91) **Going Correction** +0.25s/f (Slow)
**WFA** 4 from 5yo+ 7lb 4 Ran SP% **108.7**
Speed ratings (Par 101): **103,101,100,96**
CSF £6.90 TOTE £1.50; EX 7.10 Trifecta £5.90.
**Owner** David J Newman & Ross Bennett **Bred** J R Furlong **Trained** Newmarket, Suffolk
■ Stewards' Enquiry : George Baker two-day ban: careless riding (Jan 23-24)
**FOCUS**
An ordinary staying handicap in which they went an even gallop.

## 105 CORAL MOBILE "JUST THREE CLICKS TO BET" H'CAP 1m 1f 103y(P)
6:40 (6:40) (Class 6) (0-65,65) 4-Y-O+ £2,264 (£673; £336; £168) Stalls Low

Form RPR
000- 1 **Tiger Reigns**[56] 7880 8-9-7 65 GeorgeBaker 1 77
(John Butler) *mde all: shkn up over 1f out: rdn clr and hung lft ins fnl f: eased nr fin* 5/1[3]
020- 2 4 1/2 **Yourinthewill (USA)**[214] 3138 6-9-7 65 StephenCraine 4 68
(Daniel Mark Loughnane) *hld up: hdwy over 2f out: rdn to chse wnr fnl f: styd on same pce* 8/1
100- 3 2 1/4 **Pim Street (USA)**[20] 8372 4-8-12 60 (v[1]) JulieBurke(3) 8 58
(David O'Meara) *a.p: rdn over 1f out: no ex fnl f* 10/1
026- 4 1 **Cane Cat (IRE)**[42] 6851 7-8-9 56 (t) MarkCoumbe(3) 7 52
(Tony Carroll) *s.i.s: hld up: rdn over 1f out: hung lft and styd on ins fnl f: nvr nrr* 16/1
012- 5 nk **Mosman**[27] 8275 4-9-3 62 (tp) FergusSweeney 5 57
(Dean Ivory) *prom: chsd wnr over 2f out tl rdn over 1f out: wknd ins fnl f* 11/4[2]
624- 6 3 **Polar Forest**[69] 7666 4-8-9 57 (e) BillyCray(3) 3 46
(Richard Guest) *hld up: nvr on terms* 8/1
31-2 7 4 **Ellaal**[6] 39 5-8-12 56 (p) DaleSwift 2 36
(Ruth Carr) *prom: pushed along over 3f out: rdn and n.m.r over 2f out: wknd fnl f* 2/1[1]
000- 8 11 **Striking Echo**[14] 8401 4-9-1 60 (p) GrahamLee 6 17
(Andrew Hollinshead) *chsd wnr tl pushed along over 2f out: rdn and wknd over 1f out* 20/1

2m 2.34s (0.64) **Going Correction** +0.25s/f (Slow)
**WFA** 4 from 5yo+ 1lb 8 Ran SP% **118.6**
Speed ratings (Par 101): **107,103,101,100,99 97,93,83**
CSF £45.85 CT £390.37 TOTE £6.60: £1.70, £4.20, £4.90; EX 64.50 Trifecta £642.40.
**Owner** Wildcard Racing Syndicate **Bred** Richard Green And New England Stud **Trained** Newmarket, Suffolk
■ Stewards' Enquiry : Dale Swift three-day ban: used whip without giving gelding time to respond (Jan 23-25)
**FOCUS**
Another modest handicap in which they went an honest gallop.

## 106 CORAL APP DOWNLOAD FROM THE APP STORE H'CAP 1m 4f 50y(P)
7:10 (7:10) (Class 6) (0-60,60) 4-Y-O+ £2,264 (£673; £336; £168) Stalls Low

Form RPR
/66- 1 **Reality Show (IRE)**[10] 8449 7-9-5 55 DuranFentiman 5 64
(Shaun Harris) *trckd ldr tl rdn to ld over 2f out: edgd rt ins fnl f: styd on u.p* 8/1
343- 2 1/2 **Geeaitch**[13] 8417 5-9-3 53 WilliamCarson 4 61
(Peter Hiatt) *hld up: hdwy over 5f out: rdn to chse wnr over 1f out: styd on u.p* 5/2[2]
/66- 3 2 **Lac Sacre (FR)**[25] 6853 5-8-7 46 oh1 (tp) MarkCoumbe(3) 3 51
(Tony Carroll) *a.p: pushed along over 3f out: rdn over 1f out: styd on same pce ins fnl f* 6/1
00-5 4 2 1/4 **Excellent News (IRE)**[3] 68 5-8-5 48 JackGarritty(7) 1 49
(Tony Forbes) *led: rdn and hdd over 2f out: no ex ins fnl f* 10/1
413- 5 1 1/4 **Rainford Glory (IRE)**[19] 8388 4-9-6 60 LiamKeniry 2 59
(David Simcock) *trckd ldrs: pushed along over 2f out: rdn over 1f out: no ex fnl f* 7/4[1]
540- 6 15 **Blackstone Vegas**[84] 5560 8-9-4 54 DaleSwift 7 29
(Derek Shaw) *hld up: rdn and wknd over 2f out* 9/2[3]

2m 43.97s (2.87) **Going Correction** +0.25s/f (Slow)
**WFA** 4 from 5yo+ 4lb 6 Ran SP% **117.6**
Speed ratings (Par 101): **100,99,98,96,96 86**
CSF £29.84 TOTE £10.40: £4.90, £1.50; EX 35.60 Trifecta £234.00.
**Owner** Miss H Ward **Bred** Highfort Stud **Trained** Carburton, Notts
**FOCUS**
The concluding contest was a moderate middle-distance handicap which turned into something of a sprint off a steady gallop.
T/Jkpt: £4,733.30 to a £1 stake. Pool of £10000.00 - 1.50 winning tickets T/Plt: £179.60 to a £1 stake. Pool of £105103.87 - 427.19 winning tickets. T/Qpdt: £53.00 to a £1 stake. Pool of £10679.41 - 149.0 winning tickets. CR

# [22]MEYDAN (L-H)
Thursday, January 9
**OFFICIAL GOING: Turf - good to soft; tapeta - standard**

## 107a LONGINES MASTER COLLECTION (H'CAP) (TURF) 5f
3:05 (3:05) (100-110,106) 3-Y-O+
£43,373 (£14,457; £7,228; £3,614; £2,168; £1,445)

RPR
1 **Ahtoug**[152] 5257 6-9-2 101 MickaelBarzalona 7 105
(Charlie Appleby) *mid-div: rdn 2 1/2f out: r.o wl fnl 1 1/2f out: led cl home* 6/1[2]
2 1/2 **Hototo**[317] 4-9-4 104 (v) LukeMorris 4 105
(Fawzi Abdulla Nass, Bahrain) *sn led: rdn 2f out: r.o wl: hdd cl home* 20/1
3 1 1/4 **Desert Law (IRE)**[313] 868 6-9-1 100 SilvestreDeSousa 11 98
(Saeed bin Suroor) *trckd ldrs: ev ch 1 1/2f out: one pce fnl 110yds* 20/1
4 nk **Roicead (USA)**[21] 8357 7-9-1 100 (t) JamesDoyle 9 96+
(D Selvaratnam, UAE) *chsd ldrs: r.o same pce fnl 1 1/2f* 16/1
5 hd **Take Ten**[13] 8422 7-9-4 104 RichardMullen 10 99
(S Seemar, UAE) *chsd ldrs: ev ch 2f out: one pce fnl f* 20/1
6 2 **Monsieur Joe (IRE)**[76] 7521 7-9-3 102 WilliamBuick 3 91
(Paul Midgley) *mid-div: kpt on same pce fnl 2f* 12/1
7 nse **Rafeej**[21] 8357 5-9-5 105 PaulHanagan 12 92
(M Al Muhairi, UAE) *trckd ldrs: ev ch 2f out: nt qckn fnl f* 7/2[1]
8 nse **Racy**[82] 7364 7-9-2 101 FrederikTylicki 14 89
(Brian Ellison) *mid-div: kpt on same pce fnl 1 1/2f* 10/1
9 3 **Fityaan**[364] 150 6-9-6 106 RoystonFfrench 2 82
(M Al Muhairi, UAE) *chsd ldrs tl outpcd 2f out* 16/1
10 1 3/4 **Seachantach (USA)**[159] 4981 8-8-11 102 (bt) MarcMonaghan(6) 8 73
(S Seemar, UAE) *nvr bttr than mid-div* 25/1
11 shd **My Propeller (IRE)**[138] 5772 5-9-3 102 AndreaAtzeni 15 73
(Peter Chapple-Hyam) *nvr bttr than mid-div* 7/1[3]
12 3 **Alhebayeb (IRE)**[156] 5120 4-9-3 102 DaneO'Neill 5 62
(M F De Kock, South Africa) *s.i.s: a in rr* 14/1
13 2 **Red Dubawi (IRE)**[67] 7719 6-9-2 101 PatDobbs 13 53
(David Marnane, Ire) *nvr bttr than mid-div* 25/1
14 hd **Bungle Inthejungle**[120] 6305 4-9-3 102 WilliamTwiston-Davies 6 55
(Mick Channon) *nvr nr to chal* 16/1
P **Nero Emperor (IRE)**[102] 6883 5-9-3 102 WayneLordan 1
(T Stack, Ire) *s.i.s: nvr nr to chal: p.u* 6/1[2]

57.62s (57.62) 15 Ran SP% **126.4**
CSF: 130.66; EX 124.10; TRIFECTA: 2308.90; TRICAST: 2277.22 WIN: 8.30; PL: 2.70, 3.70, 6.00..
**Owner** Saeed H Al Tayer **Bred** Darley **Trained** Newmarket, Suffolk

**FOCUS**
The rail was out four metres on the turf course. There had been a lot of rain around earlier in the week, but the ground dries out quickly in Dubai and the time of this opener suggested conditions were on the fast side. The action unfolded middle to far side in what was a competitive sprint handicap.

## 108a LONGINES SAINT IMIER (H'CAP) (TAPETA) 1m 1f 110y
**3:40** (3:40) (95-105,105) 3-Y-0+

**£39,759** (£13,253; £6,626; £3,313; £1,987; £1,325)

RPR

1 **Busker (USA)**[49] 7998 6-8-10 **95**.....................(t) AdriedeVries 6 100+
(A bin Harmash, UAE) *slowly away: smooth prog 3f out: led 1 1 1/2f out: r.o wl: comf* **12/1**

2 1 1/4 **Layali Al Andalus**[313] 871 7-8-7 **97** ow2............ MarcMonaghan(5) 9 97
(S Seemar, UAE) *settled in rr: rdn 3f out: r.o fnl 1 1/2f: nrst fin* **16/1**

3 nk **Ottoman Empire (FR)**[105] 6772 8-9-2 **100**............ RichardMullen 5 102
(S Seemar, UAE) *settled in rr: rdn 3f out: kpt on fnl 1 1/2f but nvr able to chal* **10/1**

4 1 1/4 **Transparent (USA)**[110] 4-9-2 **102**...............(v) SilvestreDeSousa 3 102
(Saeed bin Suroor) *mid-div: led 4 1/2f out: hdd 1 1/2f out: kpt on same pce* **5/1[3]**

5 1 1/4 **El Estruendoso (ARG)**[336] 553 5-9-3 **101**......... ChristopheSoumillon 4 98
(M F De Kock, South Africa) *mid-div: shuffled bk 3 1/2f out: kpt on fnl 2f but n.d* **5/2[1]**

6 1 **Clon Brulee (IRE)**[110] 6620 5-9-1 **99**............ MickaelBarzalona 7 94
(Saeed bin Suroor) *mid-div: chsd ldrs 3f out: nt qckn fnl f* **10/3[2]**

7 1 1/4 **Izaaj (USA)**[21] 8358 7-9-2 **100**............................ JamesDoyle 2 93
(A bin Harmash, UAE) *sn led: hdd 4 1/2f out: one pce fnl 2 1/2f* **11/1**

8 shd **Specific Gravity (FR)**[322] 742 6-9-1 **99**................. PatDobbs 1 91
(M F De Kock, South Africa) *trckd ldng pair tl outpcd 3f out* **8/1**

9 2 1/4 **Submariner (USA)**[293] 1133 8-9-6 **105**...............(p) DaneO'Neill 10 92
(A bin Huzaim, UAE) *nvr bttr than mid-div* **28/1**

10 1 1/2 **Sweet Lightning**[26] 8301 9-9-4 **102**...............(t) WilliamBuick 8 87
(David O'Meara) *trckd ldrs: ev ch 3 1/2f out: wknd fnl 2f* **16/1**

2m 0.63s (1.63) **Going Correction** +0.075s/f (Slow)
**WFA** 4 from 5yo+ 1lb **10** Ran SP% **119.8**
Speed ratings: **96,95,94,93,92 91,90,90,89,87**
CSF: 191.38; EX 180.80; TRIFECTA: 4123.40; TRICAST: 1997.43 WIN: 11.40; PL: 2.90, 8.70, 3.10..
**Owner** Sheikh Ahmed bin Mohammed Al Maktoum **Bred** Darley **Trained** United Arab Emirates

**FOCUS**
A really muddling race and the bare form is misleading. They went desperately slow early before the pace gradually increased: 28.68 (400m, from standing start), 26.78 (800m), 25.00 (1200m), 23.35 (1600m). To emphasise the point, the Trakus par time for the final 300m is 18.18sec and all ten runners went quicker.

## 109a LONGINES DOLCE VITA (H'CAP) (TAPETA) 7f
**4:15** (4:15) (95-105,105) 3-Y-0+

**£39,759** (£13,253; £6,626; £3,313; £1,987; £1,325)

RPR

1 **Fulbright**[64] 7775 5-9-4 **102**.......................... MickaelBarzalona 9 105+
(Charlie Appleby) *in rr of mid-div: smooth prog 2 1/2f out: r.o wl: led fnl 55yds* **6/1[3]**

2 1/2 **Modern History (IRE)**[315] 836 6-9-4 **102**............. AhmedAjtebi 3 103
(Charlie Appleby) *sn led: rdn clr 2 1/2f out: hdd cl home* **20/1**

3 3/4 **Bertiewhittle**[50] 7974 6-9-4 **102**........................ HarryBentley 7 101
(David Barron) *mid-div: rdn 3f out: r.o fnl 2f: nrst fin* **13/2**

4 1 3/4 **Mont Ras (IRE)**[21] 8344 7-9-4 **102**....................... WilliamBuick 4 96
(David O'Meara) *trckd ldrs: ev ch 3f out: one pce fnl 110yds* **11/2[2]**

5 1/2 **Maraheb**[35] 8173 6-9-2 **100**...............................(t) DaneO'Neill 8 93
(A Al Raihe, UAE) *mid-div: kpt on same pce fnl 1 1/2f out* **25/1**

6 nk **My Freedom (IRE)**[75] 7540 6-9-4 **102**.............. SilvestreDeSousa 2 94
(Saeed bin Suroor) *nvr bttr than mid-div* **11/4[1]**

7 nk **Jamesie (IRE)**[76] 7519 6-9-2 **100**.......................... FergalLynch 12 91
(David Marnane, Ire) *trckd ldng pair: ev ch 2f out: nt qckn fnl f* **12/1**

8 1/2 **Lui Rei (ITY)**[307] 940 8-9-3 **101**...........................(v) LukeMorris 6 91
(Fawzi Abdulla Nass, Bahrain) *mid-div: chsd ldrs 3f out: ev ch 1 1/2f out: wknd fnl 110yds* **20/1**

9 1 1/2 **Tennessee Wildcat (IRE)**[97] 7004 4-9-5 **104**............... GaryCarroll 10 89
(G M Lyons, Ire) *nvr nr to chal: r.o one pce fnl 1 1/2f out* **12/1**

10 hd **Mutin (FR)**[172] 4573 4-9-2 **100**.......................... PaulHanagan 13 85
(M F De Kock, South Africa) *settled in rr: nvr nr to chal* **10/1**

11 1 1/4 **Ocean Tempest**[103] 6826 5-9-6 **105**...................(p) BrettDoyle 14 86
(John Ryan) *trckd ldrs tl outpcd 2 1/2f out* **12/1**

12 1 3/4 **Proud Possibility (USA)**[105] 4-9-2 **100**...............(t) AdriedeVries 1 77
(Niels Petersen, Norway) *slowly away: trckd ldng trio tl outpcd 2f out* **20/1**

13 3/4 **Rochdale**[21] 8356 11-9-2 **100**.........................(t) RoystonFfrench 5 75
(R Bouresly, Kuwait) *nvr nr to chal* **40/1**

14 5 3/4 **Muraweg (IRE)**[316] 8-9-6 **105**...............................(v) HMaki 11 63
(Fawzi Abdulla Nass, Bahrain) *nvr bttr than mid-div* **25/1**

1m 23.9s (-1.30) **Going Correction** +0.075s/f (Slow) **14** Ran SP% **126.3**
Speed ratings: **110,109,108,106,106 105,105,104,103,102 101,99,98,91**
CSF: 130.67; EX 111.70; TRIFECTA: 1131.80; TRICAST: 827.02 WIN: 8.00; PL: 2.50, 4.40, 2.30..
**Owner** Sheikh Hamdan bin Mohammed Al Maktoum **Bred** Rf & Sd Knipe **Trained** Newmarket, Suffolk

**FOCUS**
A competitive handicap in which Modern History set a good gallop, each sectional a bit quicker than the Trakus par times: 25.28 (400m), 23.17 (800m), 23.29 (1200m). The runner-up sets the standard.

## 110a SINGSPIEL STKS PRESENTED BY LONGINES PRIMA LUNA (LISTED RACE) (TURF) 1m 1f (T)
**4:50** (4:50) 3-Y-0+

**£54,216** (£18,072; £9,036; £4,518; £2,710; £1,807)

RPR

1 **Mushreq (AUS)**[285] 1267 6-9-0 117.......................... PaulHanagan 5 111+
(M F De Kock, South Africa) *mid-div: smooth prog 2 1/2f out: led 1 1/2f out: r.o wl: comf* **7/2[1]**

2 1 1/4 **Gabrial (IRE)**[89] 7196 5-9-0 106........................ HayleyTurner 10 107+
(Richard Fahey) *s.i.s: settled in rr: smooth prog 3f out: n.m.r 1 1/2f out: r.o fnl f: nrst fin* **10/1**

3 1/2 **Artigiano (USA)**[432] 7568 4-8-13 105............... MickaelBarzalona 3 106+
(Charlie Appleby) *sn led: hdd 2f out but kpt on same pce fnl 1 1/2f* **11/2[3]**

4 1 1/4 **Tales Of Grimm (USA)**[19] 8386 5-9-0 107.................. JamesDoyle 4 104+
(Richard Fahey) *settled in rr: chsd ldrs 2 1/2f out: nt qckn fnl f* **8/1**

5 3/4 **Tarbawi (IRE)**[21] 8355 4-8-13 98.......................... AdriedeVries 6 102
(A bin Harmash, UAE) *in rr of mid-div: nvr able to chal but r.o fnl 2f* **40/1**

6 1 1/4 **Do It All (USA)**[322] 745 7-9-0 105....................(v) SilvestreDeSousa 7 100
(Saeed bin Suroor) *trckd ldrs: led 2f out: hdd 1 1/2f out: one pce fnl 110yds* **14/1**

7 1/2 **Dux Scholar**[95] 7059 6-9-0 115.................................... PatDobbs 1 98
(Doug Watson, UAE) *mid-div: chsd ldrs 2 1/2f out: one pce fnl 1 1/2f* **11/2[3]**

8 hd **Rasmy**[4] 7-9-0 97.................................. WilliamTwiston-Davies 9 98
(M Al Muhairi, UAE) *slowly away: settled in rr: nvr able to chal but r.o fnl 2f* **40/1**

9 3/4 **Derbaas (USA)**[21] 8356 8-9-0 105.........................(t) DaneO'Neill 12 96
(A Al Raihe, UAE) *chsd ldrs: ev ch 1 1/2f out: nt qckn fnl f* **14/1**

10 1 1/4 **Burano (IRE)**[257] 1846 5-9-0 102.............................. KierenFallon 11 94
(Brian Meehan) *nvr nr to chal* **16/1**

11 1 1/4 **Fervent Prince**[740] 7947 9-9-0 96.................................. JRosales 8 91
(A bin Huzaim, UAE) *nvr bttr than mid-div* **40/1**

12 16 **David Livingston (IRE)**[123] 6253 5-9-2 113....... ChristopheSoumillon 2 60
(M F De Kock, South Africa) *trckd ldrs tl rdn and wknd 3f out* **4/1[2]**

1m 50.32s (-0.38) **Going Correction** +0.30s/f (Good)
**WFA** 4 from 5yo+ 1lb **12** Ran SP% **119.7**
Speed ratings: **113,111,111,110,109 108,108,107,107,106 105,90**
CSF: 39.40; EX 66.70; TRIFECTA: 322.70 WIN: 5.10; PL: 1.80, 4.40, 2.40..
**Owner** Hamdan Al Maktoum **Bred** Shadwell Stud Australasia Ltd **Trained** South Africa

**FOCUS**
Upgraded to Listed status since last year, but not form to get excited about. Sectionals showed the early gallop was ordinary: 26.41 (400m), 24.50 (800m), 24.36 (1200m), 23.11 (1600m). The fifth and eighth limit the standard.

## 111a AL MAKTOUM CHALLENGE ROUND 1 PRESENTED BY LONGINES (GROUP 2) (TAPETA) 1m
**5:25** (5:25) 3-Y-0+

**£90,361** (£30,120; £15,060; £7,530; £4,518; £3,012)

RPR

1 **Shuruq (USA)**[113] 6536 4-8-9 109.....................(p) SilvestreDeSousa 6 105+
(Saeed bin Suroor) *mid-div: rdn 3f out: r.o wl fnl 2f: led fnl 55yds* **11/2[3]**

2 3/4 **Empire Storm (GER)**[81] 7-9-0 107.........................(t) KierenFallon 8 108
(Michael Attwater) *sn led: kicked clr 2 1/2f out: hdd cl home* **25/1**

3 shd **Brendan Brackan (IRE)**[82] 7388 5-9-0 115...................... ColinKeane 2 108
(G M Lyons, Ire) *s.i.s: settled in rr: smooth prog 2 1/2f out: ev ch 110yds out: nt qckn cl home* **6/1**

4 1 1/4 **Steeler (IRE)**[439] 7398 4-9-0 109........................ MickaelBarzalona 5 105+
(Charlie Appleby) *settled in rr: t.k.h: rdn 4f out: nvr able to chal but kpt on fnl 2f* **3/1[1]**

5 1 1/4 **Samurai Sword**[21] 8356 6-9-0 104.......................(t) AdriedeVries 3 102+
(A bin Harmash, UAE) *s.i.s: nvr able to chal but kpt on fnl 2f* **25/1**

6 shd **Daddy Long Legs (USA)**[68] 7698 5-9-0 112...... ChristopheSoumillon 1 102
(M F De Kock, South Africa) *trckd ldrs tl outpcd 2f out: kpt on same pce* **8/1**

7 hd **Rerouted (USA)**[285] 1262 6-9-0 113.............................. ANienaber 9 102
(M F De Kock, South Africa) *mid-div: chsd ldrs 2 1/2f out: one pce fnl 2f* **12/1**

8 2 **Mufarrh (IRE)**[21] 8356 7-9-0 112............................ PaulHanagan 7 97
(A Al Raihe, UAE) *trckd ldrs: ev ch 2 1/2f out: one pce fnl f* **7/2[2]**

9 4 3/4 **Barbecue Eddie (USA)**[21] 8356 10-9-0 111...............(b) DaneO'Neill 10 86
(Doug Watson, UAE) *trckd ldrs tl outpcd 2f out* **20/1**

10 1 1/2 **Capital Attraction (USA)**[285] 1262 7-9-0 113................ JamesDoyle 4 83
(Ernst Oertel, UAE) *mid-div: rdn 3f out: one pce fnl 1 1/2f out* **12/1**

1m 35.84s (-1.66) **Going Correction** +0.075s/f (Slow) **10** Ran SP% **115.8**
Speed ratings: **111,110,110,108,107 107,107,105,100,99**
CSF: 135.10; EX 121.70; TRIFECTA: 1601.30; WIN: 6.50; PL: 1.60, 6.70, 2.60..
**Owner** Godolphin **Bred** Darley **Trained** Newmarket, Suffolk

**FOCUS**
A rank ordinary running of this Group 2 contest, but they went a good gallop with each of the sectionals comfortably under the Trakus pars: 25.66 (400m), 22.71 (800m), 23.66 (1200m) before the winner came home in 23.35. The second and fifth help with the form.

## 112a LONGINES CONQUEST CLASSIC (H'CAP) (TURF) 7f
**6:00** (6:00) (100-110,110) 3-Y-0+

**£43,373** (£14,457; £7,228; £3,614; £2,168; £1,445)

RPR

1 **Anaerobio (ARG)**[315] 838 7-9-2 **106**...............(t) ChristopheSoumillon 3 109+
(M F De Kock, South Africa) *mid-div: smooth prog 2 1/2f out: led 1f out: comf* **6/1[3]**

2 1 3/4 **Iguazu Falls (USA)**[293] 1134 9-9-6 **110**...............(t) AdriedeVries 9 108+
(A bin Harmash, UAE) *nvr able to chal but r.o fnl 2f* **16/1**

3 3/4 **Dafeef**[364] 154 7-9-1 **105**..........................................(e) PatDobbs 11 101
(Doug Watson, UAE) *s.i.s: nvr nr to chal but r.o fnl 2f* **40/1**

4 1/2 **Roi De Vitesse (IRE)**[317] 7-9-1 **105**.......................(b) HarryBentley 7 100
(Ali Jan, Qatar) *trckd ldrs: led 2f out: hdd 1f out: one pce fnl 110yds* **20/1**

5 1 **Royal Ridge (SAF)**[306] 957 6-9-3 **107**.......................... DaneO'Neill 5 99
(M F De Kock, South Africa) *mid-div: kpt on same pce fnl 2f but n.d* **12/1**

6 3/4 **Free Wheeling (AUS)**[75] 7530 6-9-1 **105**...........(t) MickaelBarzalona 14 95
(Saeed bin Suroor) *nvr bttr than mid-div* **14/1**

7 nk **Dormello (IRE)**[13] 8421 6-9-0 **104**.............................. JamesDoyle 8 93
(D Selvaratnam, UAE) *settled in rr: nvr nr to chal* **22/1**

8 1/2 **Complicate (AUS)**[85] 5-9-2 **106**......................... SilvestreDeSousa 13 94
(Saeed bin Suroor) *trckd ldrs tl outpcd 2 1/2f out* **3/1[1]**

9 3/4 **Disa Leader (SAF)**[306] 957 9-9-2 **106**........................ JGeroudis 10 92
(M F De Kock, South Africa) *settled in rr: nvr able to chal* **18/1**

10 1 1/4 **Nawwaar (USA)**[32] 8207 5-9-4 **108**........................... PaulHanagan 16 90
(A Al Raihe, UAE) *sn led: hdd & wknd 2f out* **20/1**

11 1 1/4 **The Gold Cheongsam (IRE)**[96] 7021 4-8-13 **102**.......(t) WilliamBuick 1 82
(Jeremy Noseda) *chsd ldrs tl 3f out* **5/1[2]**

12 shd **Gold City (IRE)**[13] 8422 5-8-7 **102**.....................(t) MarcMonaghan(6) 6 82
(S Seemar, UAE) *a in rr* **33/1**

13 1 1/4 **Arnold Lane (IRE)**[61] 7821 5-9-1 **105**............. WilliamTwiston-Davies 2 80
(Mick Channon) *trckd ldrs tl 2 1/2f out* **12/1**

14 3 1/4 **Across The Rhine (USA)**[32] 8207 8-8-13 **102**............. RichardMullen 4 70
(S Seemar, UAE) *chsd ldrs tl fnl 2 1/2f* **14/1**

15 3/4 **McCartney (GER)**[32] 8207 9-8-4 **103** ow1.......(t) AhmadAlSubousi(10) 12 68
(S Seemar, UAE) *slowly away: settled in rr: n.d* **33/1**

16 6 ¼ **Now Spun (USA)**[116] 6427 4-8-13 **102**...................... RoystonFfrench 15 51
(A Al Raihe, UAE) *trckd ldrs tl outpcd 2 1/2f out* **20/1**
1m 23.09s (83.09) **16** Ran SP% **125.7**
PLACEPOT: Part won. £5421.90 to a £1 stake. Pool of £7427.38 - 0.60 winning tickets..QUADPOT: £166.10 to a £1 stake. Pool of £897.99 - 4.00 winning tickets..
**Owner** Mohd Khaleel Ahmed **Bred** Haras La Madrugada **Trained** South Africa
**FOCUS**
There were a distinct lack of unexposed types for this big-field handicap, so not form to get carried away with. They went a fair gallop, quicker than the Trakus par times through each split: 24.76 (400m), 23.72 (800m), 23.16 (1200m) before the winner clocked 11.43 to the line.

## [86]LINGFIELD (L-H)
Friday, January 10
**OFFICIAL GOING: Standard**
Wind: medium, behind Weather: dry, rain races 6 and 7.

### 113 LADBROKES (S) STKS 7f 1y(P)
**12:00** (12:00) (Class 6) 4-Y-O+ **£2,045** (£603; £302) **Stalls** Low

Form RPR
243- **1** **Hillbilly Boy (IRE)**[10] 8450 4-8-3 70.............................(p) RyanWhile(7) 2 78
(Bill Turner) *led for 1f: chsd ldr after: rdn and ev ch whn rdr dropped whip wl over 1f out: sustained duel w ldr after: styd on wl to ld last strides* **14/1**
114- **2** *hd* **Kuanyao (IRE)**[13] 8430 8-9-1 73.................................(v) AdrianNicholls 3 82
(David Nicholls) *w ldr tl led after 1f: rdn ent fnl 2f: sustained duel w wnr after: styd on wl tl hdd and no ex last strides* **9/4**[2]
662- **3** *2 ¾* **Ocean Legend (IRE)**[39] 8122 9-8-10 77............................ LukeMorris 5 70
(Tony Carroll) *chsd ldng pair thrght: rdn and effrt 2f out: drvn and styd on same pce fr over 1f out* **5/4**[1]
550- **4** *1 ¼* **Greensward**[15] 8401 8-8-10 70.........................................(b) LiamKeniry 4 67
(Conor Dore) *hld up in last pair: rdn and effrt 2f out: one pce and no imp fr over 1f out* **8/1**
664- **5** *8* **Polar Kite (IRE)**[32] 8217 6-8-7 78.................... RossAtkinson(3) 6 45
(Paul Morgan) *stdd and dropped in bhd after s: hld up in rr: wknd wl over 1f out* **9/2**[3]
1m 23.24s (-1.56) **Going Correction** -0.10s/f (Stan) **5** Ran SP% **111.2**
Speed ratings (Par 101): **104,103,100,99,90**
CSF £45.62 TOTE £11.90: £2.90, £1.60; EX 25.80 Trifecta £37.70.The winner was bought by Martin Smith for 8,800gns. Kuanyao was claimed by LA Carter for £6,000. Polar Kite was claimed by Mr J M Curran for £6,000.
**Owner** P Moore **Bred** Tipper House Stud **Trained** Sigwells, Somerset
**FOCUS**
A race hit by three non-runners, but a fair seller with all five contenders rated in the 70s. The order barely changed during the contest. The winner's best effort since he was a 2yo.

### 114 COMPARE BOOKMAKERS AT BOOKMAKERS.CO.UK H'CAP 5f 6y(P)
**12:30** (12:30) (Class 6) (0-60,63) 4-Y-O+ **£2,385** (£704; £352) **Stalls** High

Form RPR
232- **1** **Random Success (IRE)**[10] 8456 4-9-5 58.................. GeorgeBaker 10 68+
(Roger Charlton) *t.k.h: hld up in rr: gd hdwy and swtchd lft ent fnl f: qckned to ld fnl 50yds: in command and eased nr fin* **2/1**[1]
653- **2** *¾* **Roy's Legacy**[10] 8457 5-9-5 58.......................................(t) AdamKirby 6 65
(Shaun Harris) *led: rdn 2f out: fnd ex u.p over 1f out: hdd and no ex fnl 50yds* **9/4**[2]
201- **3** *½* **Pharoh Jake**[10] 8457 6-9-3 63 6ex.......................... RyanWhile(7) 5 68
(John Bridger) *hld up off the pce in midfield: hdwy over 1f out: rdn and styd on wl ins fnl f* **10/1**
614- **4** *½* **College Doll**[21] 8370 5-9-1 54..............................(t) AdamBeschizza 8 57
(Christine Dunnett) *chsd clr ldng trio: rdn ent fnl 2f: kpt on u.p ins fnl f* **20/1**
000- **5** *1* **Above The Stars**[14] 8411 6-9-5 58..................................(p) LiamKeniry 2 58
(Conor Dore) *chsd ldr: rdn and unable qck over 1f out: wknd fnl 100yds* **25/1**
000- **6** *1 ¼* **Ghostwing**[80] 7437 7-9-4 57........................................ LukeMorris 4 52
(Tony Carroll) *dwlt: hld up in rr: nt clr run ent fnl 2f: effrt on inner whn hmpd 1f out: styd on but no threat to ldrs* **7/1**[3]
252- **7** *½* **Metropolitan Chief**[48] 8022 10-9-1 54..............................(p) JimmyQuinn 9 48
(Paul Burgoyne) *hld up in last trio: rdn and effrt over 1f out: kpt on ins fnl f: nvr trbld ldrs* **20/1**
004- **8** *½* **Sherjawy (IRE)**[22] 8338 10-8-7 49.......................... RossAtkinson(3) 1 41
(Zoe Davison) *racd off the pce in midfield: rdn over 2f out: keeping on but stl plenty to do whn hmpd 1f out: one pce after* **33/1**
450- **9** *½* **Mrs Warren**[23] 8330 4-9-7 60.........................................(b1) RobertHavlin 3 50
(George Baker) *chsd ldrs and clr in ldng trio: rdn and btn over 1f out: wknd fnl f* **12/1**
600- **10** *1* **Balatina**[21] 8370 4-8-5 51........................................ ThomasHemsley(7) 7 37
(Chris Dwyer) *racd off the pce in midfield: rdn and lost pl wl over 1f out: wknd fnl f* **20/1**
58.05s (-0.75) **Going Correction** -0.10s/f (Stan) **10** Ran SP% **114.5**
Speed ratings (Par 101): **102,100,100,99,97 95,94,94,93,91**
CSF £5.77 CT £34.40 TOTE £3.30: £1.50, £1.10, £2.30; EX 7.70 Trifecta £27.70.
**Owner** Beckhampton 2 **Bred** M Smith & Grennanstown Stud **Trained** Beckhampton, Wilts
**FOCUS**
A moderate sprint handicap, but a dramatic performance by the winner. Sound form, and the winner can do better.

### 115 CORAL.CO.UK BEST ODDS GUARANTEED ON RACING MAIDEN STKS 1m 4f (P)
**1:00** (1:00) (Class 5) 4-Y-O+ **£3,067** (£905; £453) **Stalls** Low

Form RPR
203- **1** **Candyman Can (IRE)**[13] 7396 4-9-5 68........................ AdamKirby 5 67
(Dominic Ffrench Davis) *t.k.h: chsd ldr tl rdn to ld 2f out: drvn over 1f out: kpt on ins fnl f: drvn out* **7/4**[1]
6/5- **2** *nk* **After The Storm**[55] 7422 5-9-9 65.......................... LukeMorris 3 66
(John O'Shea) *t.k.h: hld up wl in tch: rdn and effrt to chal wl over 1f out: styd on same pce ins fnl f* **8/1**
6- **3** *½* **Shalianzi (IRE)**[15] 7298 4-9-5 73..................................(b) GeorgeBaker 2 65
(Gary Moore) *chsd ldrs: rdn and edgd lft jst over 1f out: styd on same pce u.p ins fnl f* **5/2**[2]
35-2 **4** *nk* **Sian Gwalia**[7] 41 4-9-0 56.......................................... MartinLane 1 60
(David Simcock) *hld up in midfield: effrt u.p to chse ldrs over 1f out: styd on same pce ins fnl f* **12/1**
066- **5** *10* **Revise (IRE)**[37] 8154 4-9-5 70.................................. LiamKeniry 4 49
(David Elsworth) *t.k.h: led tl rdn and hdd 2f: btn over 1f out: wknd fnl f* **7/2**[3]

06- **6** *4 ½* **Tammis**[198] 3674 4-9-0 0.............................................. KieranO'Neill 7 37
(Ron Hodges) *stdd s: hld up in last pair: clsd 6f out: rdn and outpcd 2f out: sn wknd* **66/1**
46- **7** *3 ½* **Ninepointsixthree**[15] 6486 4-9-5 0.......................... FergusSweeney 6 36
(John O'Shea) *stdd s: hld up in rr: rdn over 2f out: sn btn and bhd* **33/1**
2m 33.0s **Going Correction** -0.10s/f (Stan)
**WFA** 4 from 5yo 4lb **7** Ran SP% **110.4**
Speed ratings (Par 103): **96,95,95,95,88 85,83**
CSF £15.44 TOTE £2.30: £1.30, £3.30; EX 16.20 Trifecta £51.10.
**Owner** Miss A Jones **Bred** Jim McCormack **Trained** Lambourn, Berks
**FOCUS**
A modest middle-distance maiden in which they went no pace early and the first four, who pulled clear, finished in a heap. Over half the field were returning to the Flat after running over hurdles. Unconvincing form.

### 116 CORAL.CO.UK H'CAP (DIV I) 1m 2f (P)
**1:30** (1:30) (Class 6) (0-55,57) 4-Y-O+ **£2,385** (£704; £352) **Stalls** Low

Form RPR
060- **1** **Night's Watch**[39] 8125 4-9-4 54........................................ RobertHavlin 9 64
(William Jarvis) *dwlt: hld up in tch: rdn and hdwy over 1f out: styd on to ld wl ins fnl f: r.o wl: rdn out* **9/2**[2]
/2-1 **2** *½* **Disco Dave (IRE)**[7] 39 6-9-2 57 6ex.................. LouisSteward(7) 3 66
(Daniel Mark Loughnane) *wl in tch in midfield: rdn and effrt to chal jst over 1f out: led ins fnl f: hdd and one pce wl ins fnl f* **11/4**[1]
042- **3** *1 ¾* **Polydamos**[19] 8390 5-9-0 48........................................ LukeMorris 8 53
(Tony Carroll) *in tch in midfield: effrt on outer bnd 2f out: chsd ldrs and styd on same pce u.p ins fnl f* **5/1**[3]
422- **4** *¾* **Attain**[11] 8448 5-9-2 55..............................................(p) ShelleyBirkett(5) 1 59
(Julia Feilden) *led: rdn ent fnl 2f: hdd ins fnl f: wknd towards fin* **9/2**[2]
334- **5** *hd* **Petersboden**[11] 8448 5-9-3 51.................................... FergusSweeney 7 54
(Michael Blanshard) *chsd ldrs: rdn and effrt to chse ldrs wl over 1f out: no ex and btn ins fnl f: wknd towards fin* **10/1**
/00- **6** *2 ¼* **Poste Restante**[119] 6361 4-9-3 53.......................................(p) MartinLane 4 52
(David Simcock) *rn in snatches: in tch in midfield: drvn 3f out: outpcd and btn 1f out: one pce after* **20/1**
500- **7** *nk* **Dolly Colman (IRE)**[11] 8448 6-8-12 46 oh1........................(p) JohnFahy 6 44
(Zoe Davison) *hld up in tch in rr: effrt u.p and edgd rt 1f out: kpt on but nvr threatened ldrs* **33/1**
404- **8** *1 ¼* **Royal Etiquette (IRE)**[11] 8449 7-9-7 55............................(vt) GeorgeBaker 2 51
(Lawney Hill) *chsd ldr tl over 1f out: sn drvn and no ex: wknd ins fnl f* **5/1**[3]
000- **9** *5* **Red Willow**[11] 8449 8-8-12 46........................................ JimmyQuinn 10 32
(John E Long) *chsd ldrs: rdn and unable qck jst over 2f out: wknd and pushed rt 1f out: b.b.v* **66/1**
/00- **10** *75* **Tuxedo**[23] 8335 9-9-7 55..................................................(b) ChrisCatlin 5
(Peter Hiatt) *nvr gng wl: a towards rr: rdn and dropped to last 7f out: t.o fnl 4f* **50/1**
2m 4.65s (-1.95) **Going Correction** -0.10s/f (Stan)
**WFA** 4 from 5yo+ 2lb **10** Ran SP% **116.6**
Speed ratings (Par 101): **103,102,101,100,100 98,98,97,93,33**
CSF £16.80 CT £64.27 TOTE £7.90: £3.60, £1.70, £1.30; EX 22.20 Trifecta £116.70.
**Owner** William Jarvis **Bred** Hofgut Heymann Kg **Trained** Newmarket, Suffolk
**FOCUS**
They went no pace early in this moderate handicap, but the winner still came from well back. The faster division, and the form's not too bad for the grade.

### 117 CORAL.CO.UK H'CAP (DIV II) 1m 2f (P)
**2:00** (2:00) (Class 6) (0-55,55) 4-Y-O+ **£2,385** (£704; £352) **Stalls** Low

Form RPR
6-02 **1** **Stanlow**[7] 40 4-9-0 50..................................................(v1) StephenCraine 7 58
(Daniel Mark Loughnane) *wl in tch in midfield: effrt u.p to chse ldrs 2f out: ev ch 1f out: led fnl 100yds: r.o wl: drvn out* **6/1**
303- **2** *nk* **Kindlelight Storm (USA)**[11] 8449 4-9-4 54................(b) GeorgeBaker 1 61
(Nick Littmoden) *hld up in tch in midfield: n.m.r over 2f out: clsd to chse ldrs 2f out: effrt and ev ch ins fnl f: unable qck towards fin* **5/2**[1]
32-3 **3** *nk* **Olivers Mount**[2] 92 4-9-3 53..........................................(t) JimmyQuinn 8 60
(Ed Vaughan) *in tch in midfield: rdn and effrt 2f out: styd on u.p ins fnl f: wnt 3rd cl home* **11/4**[2]
00-1 **4** *nk* **Grandad Mac**[7] 33 6-9-3 51 6ex................................ AdamKirby 3 57
(Alan Coogan) *led: rdn 3f out: drvn over 1f out: hdd fnl 100yds: no ex towards fin* **5/1**[3]
500- **5** *1 ½* **Standing Strong (IRE)**[39] 8125 6-9-7 55....................(p) RobertHavlin 10 58
(Zoe Davison) *s.i.s: hld up in tch in last trio: clsd and n.m.r 2f out: rdn and hdwy on inner to chse ldrs 1f out: no ex fnl 100yds: wknd towards fin* **20/1**
560- **6** *3 ¼* **Fairy Mist (IRE)**[10] 8450 7-8-5 46 oh1........................ RyanWhile(7) 2 43
(John Bridger) *chsd ldrs: effrt u.p but unable qck 2f out: wknd ins fnl f* **50/1**
500- **7** *1 ½* **White Diamond**[24] 7081 7-9-7 55.................................. LukeMorris 6 49
(Nigel Twiston-Davies) *chsd ldr tl over 3f out: sn u.p: lost pl over 1f out: wknd fnl f* **10/1**
40-5 **8** *1 ½* **Arte Del Calcio**[7] 40 5-8-9 46.............................. MarkCoumbe(3) 4 37
(Tony Carroll) *s.i.s: hld up in tch in last trio: rdn and no hdwy over 1f out: nvr trbld ldrs* **25/1**
002- **9** *½* **Salient**[11] 8449 10-9-1 49................................................ KierenFox 9 39
(Michael Attwater) *chsd ldrs: rdn to chse ldr over 3f out tl 2f out: lost pl u.p jst over 1f out: wknd fnl f* **16/1**
500- **10** *18* **Edgware Road**[25] 8314 6-9-7 55........................................ JohnFahy 5 9
(Paul Morgan) *s.i.s: a bhd: lost tch 2f out* **50/1**
2m 5.85s (-0.75) **Going Correction** -0.10s/f (Stan)
**WFA** 4 from 5yo+ 2lb **10** Ran SP% **113.7**
Speed ratings (Par 101): **99,98,98,98,97 94,93,92,91,77**
CSF £20.07 CT £49.48 TOTE £5.90: £1.60, £1.60, £1.80; EX 27.60 Trifecta £107.80.
**Owner** Ms A Quinn **Bred** Ed's Stud Ltd **Trained** Baldwin's Gate, Staffs
**FOCUS**
The second division of this moderate handicap was run in a time 1.2sec slower than the first and there wasn't much covering the front four at the line. The first three were all relatively unexposed.

### 118 32RED FILLIES' H'CAP 1m 1y(P)
**2:30** (2:30) (Class 5) (0-75,75) 4-Y-O+ **£3,067** (£905; £453) **Stalls** High

Form RPR
1- **1** **Conversational (IRE)**[38] 8140 4-9-4 72.......................... GeorgeBaker 7 80+
(Mick Channon) *broke wl but sn stdd and hld up in last pair: effrt and hdwy 2f out: drvn and r.o ins fnl f to ld fnl 75yds: sn in command and eased cl home* **7/4**[1]

353- **2** *1* **Flamborough Breeze**[35] 8178 5-9-1 **74**......................(t) DavidKenny(5) 5 79
(Ed Vaughan) *in tch in midfield: hdwy to chse clr ldng pair over 2f out: swtchd out and drvn over 1f out: styd on and ev ch fnl 100yds: unable qck towards fin* **7/1**

200- **3** *1/2* **Bowstar**[39] 8127 5-9-5 **73**..........................................(p) RobertHavlin 1 77
(Michael Attwater) *chsd ldr: rdn and ev ch 2f out: drvn to ld 1f out: hdd fnl 75yds: no ex* **8/1**

336- **4** *2 3/4* **Serenity Spa**[137] 5825 4-9-2 **75**.............................. GeorgeDowning(5) 3 73
(Tony Carroll) *led: rdn and hrd pressed 2f out: hdd 1f out: no ex and wknd wl ins fnl f* **10/1**

133- **5** *3* **Chrissycross (IRE)**[14] 8408 5-9-3 **74**..............(v) MichaelJMMurphy(3) 4 65
(Roger Teal) *sn rdn along: in tch in last pair: rdn 4f out: outpcd and btn 2f out: plugged on but wl hld fnl f* **6/1**[3]

011- **6** *3 1/4* **Shaunas Spirit (IRE)**[37] 8157 6-9-5 **73**...............................(p) AdamKirby 6 56
(Dean Ivory) *t.k.h: hld up in tch in midfield: rdn and unable qck 2f out: wknd fnl f* **3/1**[2]

154/ **7** *19* **Devote Myself (IRE)**[564] 3432 5-8-9 **63**................................ LukeMorris 2
(Tony Carroll) *chsd ldrs: rdn 4f out: lost pl and last over 2f out: lost tch 2f out* **14/1**

1m 36.66s (-1.54) **Going Correction** -0.10s/f (Stan) **7** Ran SP% **115.0**
Speed ratings (Par 100): **103,102,101,98,95 92,73**
CSF £14.95 TOTE £2.30: £1.20, £3.40; EX 12.30 Trifecta £65.80.
**Owner** Mrs T Burns **Bred** South House Stud **Trained** West Ilsley, Berks

**FOCUS**
Just a fair fillies' handicap and rather muddling form.

## 119 LADBROKES MAIDEN STKS 7f 1y(P)
**3:00** (3:00) (Class 5) 3-Y-O+ **£3,067** (£905; £453) **Stalls** Low

Form RPR

443- **1** **Ostralegus**[37] 8146 4-9-10 58.............................. MichaelJMMurphy(3) 5 66
(John Gallagher) *mde all: set stdy gallop tl rdn and qcknd ent fnl 2f: drvn and edgd lft fnl f: a holding on* **33/1**

0- **2** *hd* **Secret Pursuit (IRE)**[23] 8332 3-7-11 0.............................. JoeDoyle(7) 4 56
(Marcus Tregoning) *t.k.h: hld up in tch: hdwy to chse ldr 5f out: rdn 2f out: styd on and clsng on wnr fnl 100yds: nvr quite getting up* **16/1**

02- **3** *1 1/4* **Clear Spell (IRE)**[23] 8333 3-8-9 0.............................. LukeMorris 3 58
(Ed Walker) *dwlt: t.k.h and sn wl in tch: rdn over 2f out: rn green and wanting to hang lft fr over 1f out: kpt on ins fnl f* **4/5**[1]

46- **4** *1/2* **Aldeburgh**[13] 8427 5-9-13 0.............................. GeorgeBaker 2 61
(Jim Old) *broke wl: trckd wnr tl 5f out: styd trcking ldrs: rdn and effrt over 1f out: no ex and outpcd wl ins fnl f* **6/1**[3]

5- **5** *1 1/4* **Ganymede**[13] 8425 3-8-9 0.............................. JohnFahy 1 53
(Eve Johnson Houghton) *hld up wl in tch in last: effrt u.p over 1f out: no ex and outpcd ins fnl f* **9/4**[2]

1m 25.87s (1.07) **Going Correction** -0.10s/f (Stan)
**WFA** 3 from 4yo+ 18lb **5** Ran SP% **109.4**
Speed ratings (Par 103): **89,88,87,86,85**
CSF £346.34 TOTE £15.40: £4.80, £6.30; EX 112.30 Trifecta £308.20.
**Owner** The Oystercatcher Racing Syndicate **Bred** B Brookfield **Trained** Chastleton, Oxon

**FOCUS**
A moderate maiden and a nightmare for punters with the two complete outsiders filling the first two places having held those positions throughout. The form is rated around the surprise winner.

## 120 CORAL MOBILE "JUST THREE CLICKS TO BET" APPRENTICE H'CAP 1m 4f (P)
**3:30** (3:30) (Class 5) (0-70,68) 4-Y-O+ **£3,067** (£905; £453) **Stalls** Low

Form RPR

002- **1** **The Blue Dog (IRE)**[11] 8447 7-9-5 **62**.............................. JoeDoyle 6 78
(Phil McEntee) *hld up in midfield: hdwy to trck ldr on bit 2f out: led 1f out: shkn and sn drew clr: v esily* **4/1**[3]

213- **2** *7* **Keene**[23] 8337 4-9-7 **68**.............................. RobJFitzpatrick 7 73
(Philip McBride) *t.k.h: chsd ldr tl led 3f out: rdn ent 2f out: hdd 1f out and sn brushed aside: kpt on for 2nd* **7/4**[1]

003- **3** *2 3/4* **Living Leader**[11] 8447 5-9-10 **67**..............................(v) JordanVaughan 5 67
(Nick Littmoden) *hld up in last trio: rdn and effrt on outer over 1f out: styd on to go 3rd wl ins fnl f: no ch w wnr* **9/4**[2]

255/ **4** *shd* **Rowan Ridge**[387] 8175 6-9-3 **67**..............................(v) MrJamieCoates(7) 1 67
(William Knight) *hld up in last pair: nt clr run over 2f out: wl bhd whn swtchd v wd bnd wl over 1f out: r.o wl fnl f: no ch w wnr* **25/1**

052- **5** *1 1/2* **Special Mix**[23] 8337 6-9-6 **68**.............................. BradleyBosley(5) 2 66
(Martin Smith) *rrd as stalls opened and lost many l: rcvrd and wl in tch after 3f: rdn and effrt to chse ldrs over 2f out: outpcd and wl hld over 1f out: wknd ins fnl f* **8/1**

635- **6** *1/2* **Celtic Charlie (FR)**[23] 8337 9-8-11 **54** oh1..................(t) GeorgeBuckell 8 51
(Pat Phelan) *in tch in midfield: effrt to chse ldr over 2f out tl 2f out: sn outpcd and btn: wknd ins fnl f* **10/1**

560- **7** *1 3/4* **Elegant Ophelia**[241] 2348 5-9-2 **62**.............................. PaulBooth(3) 3 56
(Dean Ivory) *chsd ldrs tl rdn and lost pl wl over 2f out: wknd over 1f out* **33/1**

534- **8** *17* **Mazij**[211] 3244 6-9-2 **64**.............................. JoshQuinn(5) 4 31
(Peter Hiatt) *led tl 3f out: lost pl ent fnl 2f: sn bhd* **20/1**

2m 28.88s (-4.12) **Going Correction** -0.10s/f (Stan)
**WFA** 4 from 5yo+ 4lb **8** Ran SP% **118.9**
Speed ratings (Par 103): **109,104,102,102,101 101,99,88**
CSF £11.70 CT £19.55 TOTE £5.60: £1.70, £1.10, £1.30; EX 11.30 Trifecta £42.90.
**Owner** R Carson **Bred** Mervyn Stewkesbury **Trained** Newmarket, Suffolk

**FOCUS**
An ordinary apprentice handicap and one-way traffic. The winner was back to her best at least.
T/Jkpt: Not won. T/Plt: £18.10 to a £1 stake. Pool: £77583.28 - 3123.55 winning tickets T/Qpdt: £5.60 to a £1 stake. Pool: £7512.83 - 983.70 winning tickets SP

# 100 WOLVERHAMPTON (A.W) (L-H)
Friday, January 10

**OFFICIAL GOING: Standard**
Wind: Moderate, behind Weather: Mainly clear

## 121 BEST ODDS AT BOOKMAKERS.CO.UK H'CAP 5f 216y(P)
**4:00** (4:00) (Class 6) (0-55,58) 4-Y-O+ **£1,940** (£577; £288; £144) **Stalls** Low

Form RPR

051- **1** **Kasbhom**[19] 8393 4-9-6 **54**..............................(tp) WilliamCarson 9 69+
(Anthony Carson) *chsd ldrs: hrd rdn 2f out: r.o to ld ins fnl f* **3/1**[1]

31-3 **2** *3/4* **Borough Boy (IRE)**[5] 59 4-9-10 **58** 6ex..................(v) DaleSwift 5 67
(Derek Shaw) *s.i.s: sn in midfield: rdn and r.o fr over 1f out: tk 2nd nr fin* **7/1**[3]

652- **3** *3/4* **Hamis Al Bin (IRE)**[14] 8413 5-9-6 **54**..................(t) RichardKingscote 12 61
(Milton Bradley) *towards rr: hdwy and rdn over 1f out: styd on* **4/1**[2]

245- **4** *nk* **Consistant**[27] 8306 6-9-7 **55**.............................. AndrewMullen 10 61
(Brian Baugh) *prom: led over 2f out: hdd and one pce ins fnl f* **8/1**

26-5 **5** *1 1/2* **Lucky Mark (IRE)**[5] 58 5-9-1 **52**..............................(p) BillyCray(3) 4 53
(Garry Moss) *led: rdn and hdd ent st: wknd fnl f* **14/1**

21-2 **6** *nse* **Major Muscari (IRE)**[5] 58 6-9-0 **53**..................(p) AdamCarter(5) 3 54
(Shaun Harris) *cl up on rail: pressed ldrs wl over 1f out: wknd fnl f* **3/1**[1]

423- **7** *1 1/4* **Mid Yorkshire Golf**[22] 8338 5-8-11 **48**.............................. SladeO'Hara(3) 2 45
(Peter Grayson) *s.s: towards rr: rdn 2f out: nt rch ldrs* **25/1**

326- **8** *2* **Glennten**[330] 655 5-9-4 **52**..............................(p) TomQueally 8 42
(Sylvester Kirk) *chsd ldr tl 1/2-way: wknd wl over 1f out* **12/1**

032- **9** *nk* **Celestial Dawn**[14] 8412 5-9-7 **55**..............................(b) MartinHarley 1 44
(John Weymes) *s.s: bhd: hrd rdn 2f out: nvr trbld ldrs* **14/1**

00-0 **10** *7* **Night Trade (IRE)**[7] 34 7-9-7 **55**..............................(b) LiamJones 7 22
(Ronald Harris) *s.i.s: sn chsng ldrs on outer: rdn and outpcd 3f out: wknd wl over 1f out* **16/1**

1m 15.56s (0.56) **Going Correction** +0.15s/f (Slow) **10** Ran SP% **124.4**
Speed ratings (Par 101): **102,101,100,99,97 97,95,93,92,83**
CSF £26.66 CT £90.89 TOTE £6.30: £2.80, £2.50, £1.50; EX 45.90 Trifecta £182.30.
**Owner** Macattack, William Lea Screed & Form IT **Bred** Darley **Trained** Newmarket, Suffolk

**FOCUS**
Plenty of these had been running creditably at a similar lowly level of late, and the form looks solid for the grade.

## 122 COMPARE BOOKMAKERS AT BOOKMAKERS.CO.UK H'CAP 5f 216y(P)
**4:30** (4:31) (Class 4) (0-85,85) 4-Y-O+ **£4,690** (£1,395; £697; £348) **Stalls** Low

Form RPR

22-2 **1** **Lexi's Hero (IRE)**[8] 8 6-8-7 **71** oh1..............................(p) BarryMcHugh 8 81
(Richard Fahey) *led after 1f: drvn along and hld on wl fnl 2f* **3/1**[1]

246- **2** *hd* **Light From Mars**[22] 8350 9-8-13 **77**..............................(p) LiamJones 3 86
(Ronald Harris) *cl up: chsd wnr after 2f: kpt on u.p fnl f* **10/1**

001- **3** *3/4* **Mappin Time (IRE)**[24] 8321 6-8-7 **76**..................(be) AdamCarter(5) 5 83+
(Tim Easterby) *lft stalls awkwardly and lost 8 l: wl bhd tl hdwy and in tch on outer over 3f out: r.o fnl f* **4/1**[3]

044- **4** *nk* **Muhdiq (USA)**[100] 6948 5-9-2 **80**.............................. ShaneKelly 4 86
(Mike Murphy) *plld hrd: in tch: effrt and rn wd bnd over 2f out: kpt on fnl f* **7/2**[2]

13-3 **5** *1/2* **Fat Gary**[7] 36 4-9-4 **85**..............................(p) RossAtkinson(3) 6 89
(Tom Dascombe) *led 1f: prom: struggling to hold pl 3f out: styd on same pce* **3/1**[1]

65-2 **6** *shd* **George Fenton**[8] 20 5-8-11 **75**..............................(p) LiamKeniry 1 79
(Conor Dore) *prom: n.m.r and lost pl after 2f: rallied and hrd rdn over 1f out: one pce* **10/1**

310- **7** *7* **Steel Rain**[65] 7776 6-8-9 **76**.............................. MatthewCosham(3) 2 58
(Nikki Evans) *in rr: rdn 1/2-way: n.d fnl 2f* **25/1**

1m 15.52s (0.52) **Going Correction** +0.15s/f (Slow) **7** Ran SP% **114.3**
Speed ratings (Par 105): **102,101,100,100,99 99,90**
CSF £32.96 CT £120.54 TOTE £3.60: £2.10, £4.50; EX 34.70 Trifecta £136.30.
**Owner** Dr Marwan Koukash **Bred** T J Pabst **Trained** Musley Bank, N Yorks

**FOCUS**
There were some useful AW sprinters in this line-up but, with little in the way of early pace on offer, it remains to be seen how well the form holds up but all the first six had something to recommend them going into the race. The runner-up is the key to the level.

## 123 32RED H'CAP 1m 5f 194y(P)
**5:00** (5:00) (Class 6) (0-65,64) 4-Y-O+ **£2,264** (£673; £336; £168) **Stalls** Low

Form RPR

02- **1** **Fire In Babylon (IRE)**[32] 8223 6-8-8 **46**..................(b) AdamBeschizza 3 52
(Noel Quinlan) *led after 1f tl 7f out: led 3f out: kicked clr 2f out: hrd rdn ins fnl f: coasting in nr fin* **7/1**

420- **2** *3/4* **Sommersturm (GER)**[23] 8331 10-9-6 **58**..................(t) MartinHarley 4 63
(David Evans) *hld up in tch: drvn and outpcd 3f out: rallied and r.o to take 2nd nr fin* **7/4**[1]

/12- **3** *1/2* **Stormy Morning**[318] 430 8-9-5 **64**..............................(p) EvaMoscrop(7) 2 68
(Philip Kirby) *hld up in rr: rdn 4f out: hdwy 2f out: chsd wnr ins fnl f: lost 2nd nr fin: hmpd and uns rdr after line* **7/2**[3]

411- **4** *3/4* **Funky Munky**[12] 8302 9-8-12 **50**..............................(p) PJMcDonald 1 53
(Alistair Whillans) *t.k.h: led 1f: chsd ldrs tl outpcd and struggling over 3f out: styd on fnl f* **5/1**

13-5 **5** *1 1/2* **Rainford Glory (IRE)**[1] 106 4-8-9 **60**.............................. LewisWalsh(7) 6 60
(David Simcock) *sn chsng wnr: led 7f out tl 3f out: hrd rdn and wknd 1f out* **11/4**[2]

3m 7.83s (1.83) **Going Correction** +0.15s/f (Slow)
**WFA** 4 from 6yo+ 6lb **5** Ran SP% **114.4**
Speed ratings (Par 101): **100,99,99,98,98**
CSF £20.53 TOTE £9.20: £4.10, £1.30; EX 21.80 Trifecta £61.90.
**Owner** Ms Fiona Donald **Bred** The Goldsmith Bloodstock Partnership **Trained** Newmarket, Suffolk

**FOCUS**
A competitive betting heat despite the small field, but the form is rated slightly negatively.

## 124 CORAL MOBILE 'JUST THREE CLICKS TO BET' CLAIMING STKS 1m 4f 50y(P)
**5:30** (5:30) (Class 5) 4-Y-O+ **£2,587** (£770; £384) **Stalls** Low

Form RPR

11-2 **1** **Stand Guard**[9] 2 10-9-11 87.............................. TomQueally 2 90
(John Butler) *chsd ldr: led ent st: rdn and a jst holding runner-up: pushed out fnl 100yds* **6/4**[2]

03-0 **2** *hd* **Kiama Bay (IRE)**[6] 54 8-9-8 87.............................. GeorgeChaloner(3) 4 90
(Richard Fahey) *led at modest pce: qcknd tempo 2f out: sn hdd: kpt on u.p: a jst hld* **4/7**[1]

6 **3** *32* **Offherocker**[7] 35 7-8-9 0.............................. MrAidenBlakemore(7) 3 29
(Claire Dyson) *hld up in tch in 3rd: rdn and outpcd over 2f out: no ch after* **66/1**[3]

2m 46.77s (5.67) **Going Correction** +0.15s/f (Slow) **3** Ran SP% **105.1**
Speed ratings (Par 103): **87,86,65**
CSF £2.71 TOTE £2.30; EX 2.50 Trifecta £2.20. Kiama Bay was claimed by Jim Best for £12,000.
**Owner** Maxilead Limited **Bred** Juddmonte Farms Ltd **Trained** Newmarket, Suffolk

**FOCUS**
Nothing more than a match and a thoroughly professional performance from the admirable Stand Guard, who recorded his 23rd win on the AW. The first two are rated close to their marks.

## 125 CORAL APP DOWNLOAD FROM THE APP STORE H'CAP 1m 4f 50y(P)
**6:00** (6:00) (Class 3) (0-95,89) 4-Y-O-**£7,561** (£2,263; £1,131; £566; £282) **Stalls** Low

Form RPR
11-5 **1** **Magika**[9] 3 4-8-12 **81**..............................(t) MartinHarley 3 92
(Marco Botti) *chsd ldrs: rdn over 2f out: led over 1f out: sn clr: edgd lft: comf* **7/2**[3]
02-0 **2** 1 ¾ **Kashmir Peak (IRE)**[6] 54 5-9-10 **89**..............................(b) TomEaves 4 97
(John Quinn) *sn chsng ldr: led over 2f out tl over 1f out: unable qck* **11/4**[1]
245- **3** 7 **All The Winds (GER)**[28] 8276 9-8-12 **77**..............................(t) ChrisCatlin 6 74
(Shaun Lycett) *dwlt: in rr: rdn 3f out: styd on to take mod 3rd fnl 100yds* **16/1**
23-1 **4** ¾ **Royal Alcor (IRE)**[8] 21 7-8-11 **81** 6ex..............................(t) ShelleyBirkett[(5)] 7 77
(Gay Kelleway) *hld up in 5th: nt clr run 3f out: hdwy on inner 2f out: wknd over 1f out* **3/1**[2]
444- **5** 3 ¾ **Super Say (IRE)**[20] 8387 8-9-2 **81**..............................(t) AndrewMullen 1 71
(Michael Appleby) *led tl over 2f out: wknd wl over 1f out* **7/1**
123- **6** 3 **Gabrial's King (IRE)**[13] 8429 5-9-8 **87**..............................(p) LiamKeniry 2 72
(David Simcock) *prom tl wknd 3f out* **3/1**[2]
2m 39.87s (-1.23) **Going Correction** +0.15s/f (Slow)
**WFA** 4 from 5yo+ 4lb **6** Ran SP% **117.3**
Speed ratings (Par 107): **110,108,104,103,101 99**
CSF £14.32 TOTE £3.50: £2.00, £1.70; EX 11.90 Trifecta £169.00.
**Owner** Marco & Sara Moretti & Partner **Bred** Immobiliare Casa Paola SRL **Trained** Newmarket, Suffolk

**FOCUS**
It's debatable as to how strong a race this was. The pace was ordinary and, while there's a chance the form could be a bit better than rated, it doesn't look strong for the grade.

## 126 LADBROKES H'CAP 7f 32y(P)
**6:30** (6:31) (Class 6) (0-60,63) 4-Y-O+ **£1,940** (£577; £288; £144) **Stalls** High

Form RPR
021/ **1** **Blackthorn Stick (IRE)**[145] 5571 5-9-4 **57**.............................. TomQueally 7 65
(John Butler) *mid-div: hdwy on inner over 1f out: drvn to ld fnl 100yds* **9/2**[2]
142- **2** ¾ **Sweet Vintage (IRE)**[28] 8278 4-9-3 **56**.............................. LukeMorris 5 62
(Mark Brisbourne) *prom: wnt 2nd over 2f out: drvn to ld over 1f out: hdd fnl 100yds: kpt on* **8/1**
12-1 **3** 1 **Munaawib**[7] 30 6-9-10 **63** 6ex..............................(bt) AdamKirby 6 66
(David C Griffiths) *chsd ldrs: clsd and hrd rdn over 1f out: one pce fnl f* **5/2**[1]
560- **4** ¾ **Boom To Bust (IRE)**[46] 8038 6-9-7 **60**..............................(b) WilliamCarson 3 61
(Barry Brennan) *outpcd and bhd: c wd and hdwy over 1f out: edgd lft: nrest at fin* **20/1**
3-64 **5** *hd* **Lastkingofscotland (IRE)**[4] 65 8-9-4 **57**..............................(b) LiamJones 8 58
(Conor Dore) *in tch: rdn 3f out: styd on fnl f* **8/1**
600- **6** 1 ¾ **David's Secret**[28] 8275 4-9-2 **55**.............................. ShaneKelly 11 51
(Roy Brotherton) *dwlt: towards rr: rdn 3f out: sme hdwy over 1f out: edgd lft: no imp* **33/1**
425- **7** 6 **Nifty Kier**[23] 8329 5-9-5 **58**.............................. MartinHarley 2 38
(Martin Bosley) *led tl over 1f out: sn wknd* **6/1**
000- **8** 2 **Giorgio's Dragon (IRE)**[137] 5816 5-9-5 **58**.............................. AdamBeschizza 4 32
(Robert Stephens) *towards rr: rdn 3f out: n.d fnl 2f* **50/1**
60-5 **9** *nse* **Exceedexpectations (IRE)**[7] 30 5-9-6 **59**.............................. LiamKeniry 9 33
(Conor Dore) *chsd ldr tl over 2f out: wknd over 1f out* **11/2**[3]
460- **10** 1 **Boy The Bell**[45] 8042 7-8-10 **54**..............................(be) JacobButterfield[(5)] 1 26
(Ollie Pears) *in tch tl wknd over 2f out* **14/1**
056- **11** ½ **Art Dzeko**[24] 8315 5-9-4 **57**.............................. TomEaves 10 27
(Brian Baugh) *prom 5f: midfield and wkng whn squeezed over 1f out* **25/1**
600- **11** *dht* **Ptolemy**[116] 6464 5-9-3 **56**.............................. AndrewMullen 12 26
(David Barron) *s.s and swtchd lft: a bhd* **16/1**
1m 30.26s (0.66) **Going Correction** +0.15s/f (Slow) **12** Ran SP% **124.7**
Speed ratings (Par 101): **102,101,100,99,98 96,90,87,87,86 86,86**
CSF £41.09 CT £113.18 TOTE £6.40: £2.90, £1.80, £1.60; EX 62.00 Trifecta £203.70.
**Owner** W J Dunphy **Bred** F Prendergast **Trained** Newmarket, Suffolk

**FOCUS**
They went plenty quick enough in this moderate handicap. The winner is rated close to his November C&D mark.

## 127 LADBROKES MEDIAN AUCTION MAIDEN STKS 1m 141y(P)
**7:00** (7:01) (Class 6) 3-4-Y-O **£1,940** (£577; £288; £144) **Stalls** Low

Form RPR
2- **1** **Like A Diamond (IRE)**[37] 7932 4-10-0 **78**.............................. AdamKirby 4 82
(Evan Williams) *prom and gng wl: rdn to ld 1f out: sn clr: comf* **10/11**[1]
5- **2** 3 ¾ **God's Speed (IRE)**[34] 8201 3-8-7 .............................. ChrisCatlin 7 69
(Rae Guest) *wd: chsd ldrs: rdn over 3f out: wnt 2nd and edgd lft ins fnl f: styd on* **3/1**[2]
2-4 **3** 1 ¾ **Indira**[7] 37 3-8-2 .............................. JimmyQuinn 5 60
(John Berry) *led: rdn 2f out: hdd 1f out: one pce* **12/1**
3-2 **4** ½ **Coillte Cailin (IRE)**[7] 37 4-9-9 .............................. TomQueally 3 63
(Daniel Mark Loughnane) *stdd s: hld up in rr: hdwy and c wd ent st: hrd rdn over 1f out: one pce* **10/1**
**5** ¾ **Zamra (IRE)** 3-8-2 .............................. LukeMorris 2 57
(James Tate) *in tch: rdn over 2f out: one pce* **6/1**[3]
**6** 7 **Parkhill Star** 3-8-2 .............................. KieranO'Neill 6 41
(Tom Dascombe) *chsd ldr: stmbld after 2f: wknd over 1f out* **20/1**
00- **7** 14 **Application**[104] 6829 3-8-7 .............................. DuranFentiman 1 14
(Bryan Smart) *towards rr: drvn along 3f out: sn bhd* **33/1**
1m 51.89s (1.39) **Going Correction** +0.15s/f (Slow)
**WFA** 3 from 4yo 22lb **7** Ran SP% **116.2**
Speed ratings (Par 101): **99,95,94,93,93 86,74**
CSF £3.95 TOTE £1.80: £1.10, £2.40; EX 4.30 Trifecta £23.50.
**Owner** R E R Williams **Bred** J Costello **Trained** Llancarfan, Vale Of Glamorgan

**FOCUS**
A weak maiden. The third and fourth have been rated close to their initial maiden efforts.
T/Plt: £107.00 to a £1 stake. Pool: £114435.21 - 780.14 winning tickets T/Qpdt: £14.90 to a £1 stake. Pool: £11073.30 - 549.45 winning tickets LM

# [42] DUNDALK (A.W) (L-H)
Friday, January 10

**OFFICIAL GOING: Standard**

## 128a WINTER SERIES AT DUNDALK H'CAP 5f (P)
**6:15** (6:16) (47-65,65) 4-Y-O+ **£4,025** (£933; £408; £233)

RPR
**1** **Catwilldo (IRE)**[28] 8284 4-8-11 **55**..............................(b) GaryPhillips[(7)] 8 63
(Garvan Donnelly, Ire) *racd in mid-div: hdwy on outer fr 2f out: clsd u.p to ld narrowly ins fnl 100yds: kpt on wl* **9/1**
**2** ½ **Strategic Heights (IRE)**[188] 4088 5-8-7 **47**.............................. ShaneBKelly[(3)] 4 53
(John James Feane, Ire) *disp early: narrow advantage bef 1/2-way: rdn 2f out and sn strly pressed: edgd sltly rt u.p ins fnl f and hdd ins fnl 100yds: kpt on wl wout matching wnr* **6/1**[3]
**3** ½ **Times In Anatefka (IRE)**[35] 8192 4-9-3 **54**..............................(tp) FergalLynch 7 58
(Adrian Brendan Joyce, Ire) *chsd ldrs: hdwy in 4th into st to chal 1 1/2f out: sn rdn almost on terms tl no ex in 3rd between horses ins fnl 100yds* **9/2**[2]
**4** ½ **Breezolini**[7] 45 6-9-11 **65**.............................. AndrewPThornton[(3)] 3 67
(Muredach Kelly, Ire) *in rr of mid-div: pushed along into st and sn clsd u.p to chse ldrs in 5th ins fnl f: kpt on towards fin wout threatening principals* **16/1**
**5** ½ **Never A Quarrel (IRE)**[10] 8457 4-9-13 **64**.............................. JosephO'Brien 1 65
(Jeremy Gask) *chsd ldrs: niggled along in 5th into st: rdn into 3rd over 1f out and sn no ex u.p: kpt on one pce* **6/1**[3]
**6** ¾ **Gallena**[28] 8284 4-9-10 **61**.............................. RoryCleary 5 59
(James M Barrett, Ire) *dwlt sltly: settled in mid-div: tk clsr order 2f out: rdn in 5th and no imp on ldrs ent fnl f: kpt on one pce* **7/1**
**7** ½ **Affinia Fifty (IRE)**[35] 8192 4-8-10 **47**..............................(t) NGMcCullagh 12 43
(Patrick Martin, Ire) *dwlt sltly and racd towards rr: pushed along bef 1/2-way and no imp: sme late hdwy fr 1 1/2f out: nvr nrr* **50/1**
**8** *nk* **The Hamptons (IRE)**[28] 8281 9-8-3 **47**..............................(p) TomMadden[(7)] 2 42
(Niall Madden, Ire) *slowly away and racd in rr: pushed along bef 1/2-way: sme hdwy far side 1 1/2f out: kpt on towards fin* **25/1**
**9** 1 ¾ **Above The Law (IRE)**[30] 8251 5-9-11 **65**.............................. ConorHoban[(3)] 6 54
(A Oliver, Ire) *in rr of mid-div: rdn and no imp fr 2f out: one pce fnl f* **5/2**[1]
**10** ½ **Inishmot Duchess (IRE)**[28] 8284 6-9-6 **60**..............................(v) ColinKeane[(3)] 11 47
(T G McCourt, Ire) *trckd ldrs: cl 3rd bef 1/2-way: rdn and no ex fr 2f out: one pce fnl f* **10/1**
**11** 7 **La Canaada (IRE)**[83] 7386 6-8-5 **49**..............................(t) RossCoakley[(7)] 10 11
(Gerard Joseph Martin, Ire) *disp early: cl 2nd bef 1/2-way: pushed along into st and sn lost pl: rdn and wknd fr 2f out: eased ins fnl f* **25/1**
59.43s (59.43) **11** Ran SP% **122.5**
CSF £63.73 CT £283.12 TOTE £9.70: £2.60, £2.70, £1.70; DF 84.40 Trifecta £658.20.
**Owner** Catshipper Partnership **Bred** G Clarke **Trained** Garristown, Co Dublin

**FOCUS**
The winner continues on an upward curve. The runner-up helps set the standard.

129 - 139a (Foreign Racing) - See Raceform Interactive

# [113] LINGFIELD (L-H)
Saturday, January 11

**OFFICIAL GOING: Standard**
Wind: medium, across Weather: dry and bright

## 140 32RED.COM MAIDEN STKS 6f 1y(P)
**12:20** (12:20) (Class 5) 3-Y-O **£3,067** (£905; £453) **Stalls** Low

Form RPR
22- **1** **Outbacker (IRE)**[11] 8451 3-9-0 0.............................. JoeFanning 8 76+
(Mark Johnston) *chsd ldr and sn clr of field: rdn and ev ch over 1f out: led and hung lft 1f out: continued to hang to inner rail and hmpd runner-up wl ins fnl f: lft clr and r.o* **9/4**[2]
5- **2** 2 ¾ **Three D Alexander (IRE)**[140] 5771 3-9-0 **89**.............................. MartinHarley 1 73+
(David Evans) *led and sn clr w wnr: rdn 2f out: hdd 1f out: stl ev ch but one pce and looking btn whn hmpd and snatched up wl ins fnl f: nt rcvr* **11/10**[1]
00- **3** ½ **Fruit Pastille**[24] 8326 3-9-0 0.............................. NickyMackay 4 65
(Hughie Morrison) *racd off the pce in last pair: rdn and hdwy over 3f out: wnt modest 3rd 2f out: kpt on but no threat to ldrs* **50/1**
**4** 2 ¼ **Voyageofdiscovery (USA)** 3-9-5 0.............................. AdamKirby 7 63+
(Clive Cox) *s.i.s: sn rdn along and wl off the pce in rr: sme hdwy and modest 5th wl over 1f out: styd on fnl f: nvr trbld ldrs* **3/1**[3]
0- **5** 7 **Dansante**[23] 8342 3-9-0 0.............................. KieranO'Neill 2 36
(Richard Hannon) *chsd clr ldng pair tl 2f out: sn wknd* **20/1**
00- **6** 3 **She's A Lucky Lady**[208] 3414 3-8-7 0.............................. RyanWhile[(7)] 5 26
(Bill Turner) *racd off the pce in midfield: rdn and lost pl 1/2-way: no ch after* **66/1**
00- **7** 2 **Mistress And Maid**[185] 4175 3-9-0 0.............................. LiamKeniry 3 20
(Joseph Tuite) *racd off the pce in midfield: rdn and lost pl over 2f out: sn bhd* **66/1**
1m 11.38s (-0.52) **Going Correction** -0.175s/f (Stan) **7** Ran SP% **113.1**
Speed ratings (Par 97): **96,92,91,88,79 75,72**
CSF £4.99 TOTE £2.60: £2.20, £1.10; EX 5.50 Trifecta £59.10.
**Owner** Mrs Christine E Budden **Bred** Christine E Budden & Partners **Trained** Middleham Moor, N Yorks

**FOCUS**
While sprint maidens are often pretty weak, in this case it might be worth being positive about the front four, even with the runner-up below her official mark. The third is the key, short-term.

## 141 COMPARE BOOKMAKERS AT BOOKMAKERS.CO.UK SPRINT SERIES (ROUND 2) H'CAP (QUALIFIER) 6f 1y(P)
**12:55** (12:56) (Class 5) (0-70,70) 4-Y-O+ **£3,408** (£1,006; £503) **Stalls** Low

Form RPR
065- **1** **Lujeanie**[21] 8384 8-9-6 **69**..............................(p) ShaneKelly 7 78
(Peter Crate) *hld up off the pce in midfield: clsd on ldrs 2f out: rdn to chse ldr jst ins fnl f: led fnl 100yds: drvn and kpt on wl* **7/1**[3]
311- **2** *nk* **Welease Bwian (IRE)**[24] 8330 5-9-4 **67**.............................. AdamBeschizza 8 75
(Stuart Williams) *hld up off the pce in midfield: swtchd sharply lft and hdwy over 1f out: str chal on inner fnl 100yds: r.o but hld towards fin* **5/1**[2]
101- **3** 2 **Run It Twice (IRE)**[12] 8443 4-9-7 **70**..............................(b) AdamKirby 10 72
(David Evans) *hld up off the pce in last trio: hdwy on inner and hmpd over 1f out: styd on wl ins fnl f* **4/1**[1]

40-1 **4** *1* **Dark Lane**[8] 35 8-9-3 **66** ChrisCatlin 5 64
(David Evans) *sn rdn along and chsd clr ldng pair: clsd wl over 1f out: kpt on same pce ins fnl f* **14/1**

010- **5** *3/4* **Monsieur Royale**[21] 8384 4-9-1 **67** (b) RobertTart(3) 6 63
(Geoffrey Oldroyd) *racd off the pce in midfield: rdn 1/2-way: kpt on ins fnl f but nvr gng pce to threaten ldrs* **4/1**[1]

400- **6** *nse* **Catflap (IRE)**[49] 8023 5-8-5 **57** RosieJessop(3) 3 53
(Derek Haydn Jones) *mounted on crse and taken down early: chsd clr ldng pair: rdn and clsd over 1f out: no ex ins fnl f: wknd towards fin* **33/1**

10-0 **7** *1/2* **Haadeeth**[9] 20 7-9-5 **68** (t) GeorgeBaker 1 62
(David Evans) *led tl rdn and hdd 2f out: battled on u.p and led again 1f out: hdd fnl 100yds: wknd towards fin* **10/1**

150- **8** *1/2* **Sister Guru**[68] 2588 5-9-4 **67** JohnFahy 2 63
(Peter Hedger) *s.i.s: hld up off the pce in rr: clsd over 1f out: styng on but stl plenty to do whn nt clr run and eased wl ins fnl f* **20/1**

06-5 **9** *shd* **One Way Or Another (AUS)**[7] 53 11-9-0 **63** (t) MartinHarley 4 58
(David Evans) *stdd s: hld up off the pce in rr: clsd over 1f out: styng on but stl plenty to do whn nt clr run and swtchd rt ins fnl f: no threat and eased after* **5/1**[2]

555- **10** *7* **Rise To Glory (IRE)**[11] 8456 6-9-0 **63** (b) DuranFentiman 9 33
(Shaun Harris) *chsd ldr and clr of field: rdn to ld 2f out: drvn and hdd 1f out: wknd qckly jst ins fnl f: bhd and eased towards fin* **16/1**

1m 10.64s (-1.26) **Going Correction** -0.175s/f (Stan) 10 Ran SP% 115.2
Speed ratings (Par 103): **101,100,97,96,95 95,94,94,94,84**
CSF £41.39 CT £144.12 TOTE £9.70: £3.80, £1.50, £2.20; EX 67.50 Trifecta £205.90.
**Owner** Peter Crate & Gallagher Equine Ltd **Bred** K T Ivory **Trained** Newdigate, Surrey

**FOCUS**
A strong gallop with Haadeeth returned to front-running tactics, closely pursued by Rise To Glory. The winner has been rated close to his spring form/best for this yard.

## 142 32RED CASINO MEDIAN AUCTION MAIDEN STKS 1m 1y(P)
1:30 (1:32) (Class 6) 3-Y-O £2,385 (£704; £352) Stalls High

Form RPR

0 **1** **Swivel**[7] 51 3-9-5 0 JoeFanning 6 70+
(Mark Johnston) *mde all: rdn and qcknd 2f out: in command and r.o wl fnl f: comf* **7/2**[2]

\- **2** *2 1/4* **La Napoule** 3-9-0 0 KieranO'Neill 1 60+
(Richard Hannon) *dwlt: sn rcvrd and in tch in midfield: rdn and hdwy on inner over 1f out: chsd clr wnr ent fnl f: styd on but no imp* **7/2**[2]

0- **3** *3 1/4* **Bishan Bedi (IRE)**[40] 8124 3-9-5 0 RobertHavlin 7 57+
(William Jarvis) *s.i.s: t.k.h: hld up in tch in rr of main gp: hdwy ent fnl 2f: rdn and chsd ldng pair 1f out: sn outpcd: plugged on* **3/1**[1]

0- **4** *2* **Jessy Mae**[119] 6409 3-8-11 0 RosieJessop(3) 8 47
(Derek Haydn Jones) *chsd wnr: rdn and unable qck over 1f out: lost pl and btn ent fnl f: wknd fnl 150yds* **50/1**

0- **5** *3/4* **Appellez Baileys (FR)**[23] 8342 3-9-5 0 LukeMorris 5 50?
(Chris Dwyer) *chsd ldrs: rdn over 4f out: struggling and edgd lft over 1f out: sn wknd* **20/1**

3- **6** *3 1/4* **Deano's Devil (IRE)**[35] 8201 3-9-0 0 JamieSpencer 4 37
(Richard Fahey) *chsd ldrs: drvn and unable qck wl over 1f out: sn btn: fdd fnl f* **9/2**[3]

**7** *2 3/4* **Needs The Run** 3-9-5 0 AdamKirby 3 36
(David Evans) *stdd s: hld up in last pair: swtchd rt and wd after 2f out: clsd and in tch 5f out: rdn and wknd over 2f out* **14/1**

00- **8** *3 1/2* **Redy To Rumble**[185] 4175 3-9-5 0 KierenFox 2 27
(Michael Attwater) *in tch in midfield: rdn and struggling over 2f out: wknd over 1f out: bhd fnl f* **100/1**

**9** *24* **In Seine** 3-9-5 0 GeorgeBaker 9
(John Best) *slowly away: sn wl bhd: t.o 1/2-way* **8/1**

1m 38.09s (-0.11) **Going Correction** -0.175s/f (Stan) 9 Ran SP% 113.1
Speed ratings (Par 95): **93,90,87,85,84 81,78,75,51**
CSF £15.59 TOTE £5.00: £1.50, £1.90, £1.40; EX 16.30 Trifecta £65.30.
**Owner** Sheikh Hamdan bin Mohammed Al Maktoum **Bred** Stratford Place Stud And Watership Down **Trained** Middleham Moor, N Yorks

**FOCUS**
A modest-looking maiden. It was slowly run and the form is muddling.

## 143 32RED H'CAP 1m 1y(P)
2:05 (2:05) (Class 4) (0-85,78) 3-Y-O £4,690 (£1,395; £697; £348) Stalls High

Form RPR

412- **1** **Examiner (IRE)**[21] 8382 3-9-7 **78** LiamJones 3 85+
(William Haggas) *chsd ldng pair: clsd 3f out and nt clr run ent fnl 2f: rdn and hdwy to ld over 1f out: sn edgd rt u.p: r.o wl fnl f* **6/4**[1]

021- **2** *1 1/2* **Jalingo (IRE)**[14] 8425 3-9-4 **75** JoeFanning 4 79
(Mark Johnston) *chsd ldrs: clsd over 3f out: rdn and ev ch 2f out: stl ev ch whn carried rt over 1f out: outpcd and swtchd lft ins fnl f: one pce after* **2/1**[2]

315- **3** *1 3/4* **Truancy (IRE)**[14] 8426 3-8-12 **69** RobertWinston 2 69
(K R Burke) *sn detached in last: rdn over 4f out: clsd u.p and chsd ldrs bnd 2f out: styd on same pce ins fnl f* **3/1**[3]

003- **4** *1 3/4* **Galaxy (IRE)**[21] 8382 3-9-1 **72** (v) MartinHarley 1 68
(Alan McCabe) *rdn leaving stalls: led: clr 5f out: rdn and hdd over 1f out: wknd ins fnl f* **8/1**

1m 36.12s (-2.08) **Going Correction** -0.175s/f (Stan) 4 Ran SP% 109.4
Speed ratings (Par 99): **103,101,99,98**
CSF £4.85 TOTE £2.10; EX 6.00 Trifecta £5.50.
**Owner** Ian and Christine Beard **Bred** River Downs Stud **Trained** Newmarket, Suffolk

**FOCUS**
Only four runners and the top weight was rated 7lb below the race ceiling, but still a fair little race. The pace was better than expected thanks to Galaxy. The front-running fourth has been rated a length off his best.

## 144 LADBROKES CONDITIONS STKS 1m 1y(P)
2:35 (2:35) (Class 2) 4-Y-O+ £12,291 (£3,657; £1,827; £913) Stalls High

Form RPR

312- **1** **Grey Mirage**[23] 8344 5-9-0 **96** (p) MartinHarley 1 105
(Marco Botti) *mde all: rdn and qcknd wl over 1f out: drvn ins fnl f: kpt on and a jst holding on* **7/4**[1]

222- **2** *hd* **Chookie Royale**[65] 7793 6-9-0 **98** (p) TomEaves 4 104
(Keith Dalgleish) *hld up wl in tch: hdwy to join ldr 5f out: rdn 2f out: sltly outpcd over 1f out: rallied ins fnl f: r.o wl fnl 100yds: nvr quite getting to wnr* **12/1**

011- **3** *2 1/4* **Alfred Hutchinson**[12] 8445 6-9-0 **97** RobertTart 3 99
(Geoffrey Oldroyd) *t.k.h: hld up wl in tch: rdn and effrt 2f out: 3rd and styd on same pce ins fnl f* **6/1**

002- **4** *1 1/4* **Emerald Wilderness (IRE)**[21] 8385 10-9-0 **92** AdamKirby 7 96?
(Mark Rimmer) *stdd s: hld up wl in tch in rr: rdn and effrt on outer bnd 2f out: no imp tl kpt on ins fnl f: no threat to ldrs* **16/1**

331- **5** *1 3/4* **Galician**[14] 8428 5-8-9 **102** JoeFanning 2 87
(Mark Johnston) *chsd ldr for 3f: rdn and lost pl jst over 2f out: one pce and wl hld fnl f* **2/1**[2]

106- **6** *1/2* **Robin Hoods Bay**[126] 6198 6-9-0 **100** LukeMorris 6 91
(Ed Vaughan) *wl in tch in midfield: rdn and effrt to chse ldrs ent fnl 2f: no imp over 1f out: wknd fnl f* **4/1**[3]

1m 34.87s (-3.33) **Going Correction** -0.175s/f (Stan) 6 Ran SP% 117.6
Speed ratings (Par 109): **109,108,106,105,103 103**
CSF £23.95 TOTE £3.10: £1.10, £5.30; EX 28.60 Trifecta £59.00.
**Owner** Giuliano Manfredini **Bred** Grundy Bloodstock Srl **Trained** Newmarket, Suffolk

**FOCUS**
A reasonable enough conditions event and, while the front two dominated from an early stage, the time was only 0.10secs outside the track record. The winner has been rated as running a small personal best, with the third and fourth close to their marks.

## 145 CORAL.CO.UK H'CAP 1m 2f (P)
3:10 (3:10) (Class 3) (0-95,93) 4-Y-O+ £7,439 (£2,213; £1,106; £553) Stalls Low

Form RPR

24-3 **1** **Swing Alone (IRE)**[7] 54 5-9-4 **90** LukeMorris 8 98
(Gay Kelleway) *dwlt: in tch in last pair: rdn over 3f out: hdwy u.p 1f out: styd on wl u.p fnl 100yds: led last strides* **5/2**[1]

655- **2** *nk* **Tinshu (IRE)**[21] 8386 8-9-7 **93** (p) AdamKirby 5 100
(Derek Haydn Jones) *dwlt and pushed along leaving stalls: in tch in midfield: effrt to chal 2f out: rdn to ld over 1f out: drvn and kpt on ins fnl f tl hdd and no ex last strides* **6/1**[3]

602- **3** *3/4* **Well Painted (IRE)**[12] 8445 5-8-13 **85** JamieSpencer 1 91
(William Haggas) *hld up in tch in midfield: nt clr run 2f out: chsng ldrs but forced to switch rt 1f out: kpt on ins fnl f* **3/1**[2]

430- **4** *3/4* **Sound Advice**[15] 8416 5-8-8 **80** TomEaves 7 84
(Keith Dalgleish) *led: rdn ent fnl 2f: hdd over 1f out: styd on same pce u.p ins fnl f* **16/1**

034- **5** *hd* **Mia's Boy**[21] 8385 10-9-4 **90** GeorgeBaker 3 94
(Chris Dwyer) *chsd ldrs: effrt on inner over 1f out: styd on same pce ins fnl f* **8/1**

040- **6** *nk* **True To Form (IRE)**[21] 8386 7-9-7 **93** (p) MartinHarley 2 96
(Alan McCabe) *taken down early: hld up in tch in rr: nt clr run jst over 2f out: rdn and hdwy over 1f out: no imp ins fnl f* **8/1**

045- **7** *1 1/4* **Crius (IRE)**[21] 8385 5-9-0 **86** RichardKingscote 4 87
(Daniel Kubler) *taken down early: chsd ldrs tl lost pl over 2f out: drvn and plugged on same pce fr over 1f out* **7/1**

/06- **8** *6* **Deia Sunrise (IRE)**[14] 8428 5-9-6 **92** (t) RobertHavlin 6 81
(Paul Webber) *taken down early: chsd ldr tl jst over 1f out: lost pl over 1f out: wknd fnl f* **25/1**

2m 3.1s (-3.50) **Going Correction** -0.175s/f (Stan) 8 Ran SP% 112.3
Speed ratings (Par 107): **107,106,106,105,105 105,104,99**
CSF £17.22 CT £45.18 TOTE £3.60: £1.50, £1.90, £1.10; EX 11.30 Trifecta £33.30.
**Owner** Whatley, Stanbrook, Brown & Kelleway **Bred** M Sinanan **Trained** Exning, Suffolk

**FOCUS**
A decent handicap, but a bunched finish. The runner-up sets the standard.

## 146 CORAL MOBILE "JUST THREE CLICKS TO BET" H'CAP 1m 2f (P)
3:45 (3:45) (Class 5) (0-75,75) 4-Y-O+ £3,067 (£905; £453) Stalls Low

Form RPR

635- **1** **Archie Rice (USA)**[36] 8179 8-9-0 **71** RobertTart(3) 5 78
(Tom Keddy) *wl in tch in midfield: rdn and chal ent fnl f: drvn and led wl ins fnl f: hld on gamely cl home: all out* **9/2**[3]

000- **2** *shd* **Apache Glory (USA)**[36] 8179 6-9-5 **73** (p) LukeMorris 9 80
(John Stimpson) *taken down early: hld up in tch in midfield: hdwy u.p over 1f out: pressed ldrs fnl f: styd on and str chal towards fin: jst failed* **25/1**

214- **3** *1/2* **Havelovewilltravel (IRE)**[58] 7876 4-9-4 **74** GrahamLee 3 80
(Jeremy Noseda) *led for over 2f: chsd ldr after: swtchd lft and effrt to chal over 1f out: ev ch fnl f: unable qck towards fin* **2/1**[1]

240- **4** *hd* **Red Shuttle**[103] 6898 7-9-4 **72** AdamKirby 10 77
(Andi Brown) *taken down early and led rdrless to s: stdd s: t.k.h: hld up in last trio: rdn and hdwy over 1f out: drvn and kpt on wl ins fnl f* **7/1**

12-0 **5** *nk* **Lady Lunchalot (USA)**[3] 79 4-9-0 **70** (p) LiamJones 7 75
(Laura Mongan) *chsd ldrs tl hdwy to ld over 7f out: rdn wl over 1f out: hdd wl ins fnl f: no ex* **8/1**

000- **6** *2 1/2* **Unmoothaj**[45] 8059 4-8-11 **67** LiamKeniry 2 67
(Pam Sly) *chsd ldrs: nt clr run ent fnl 2f: rdn and effrt over 1f out: styd on same pce ins fnl f* **25/1**

31-1 **7** *3/4* **Ocean Applause**[7] 49 4-8-9 **72** (t) JoeDoyle(7) 11 70
(John Ryan) *hld up in tch in last trio: rdn and effrt over 1f out: kpt on ins fnl f but nvr gng pce to threaten ldrs* **7/2**[2]

205- **8** *1* **Shirataki (IRE)**[45] 8060 6-8-13 **67** ChrisCatlin 1 63
(Peter Hiatt) *hld up in tch in midfield: rdn and unable qck over 1f out: styd on same pce fnl f* **14/1**

60-0 **9** *7* **Planetoid (IRE)**[3] 79 6-9-6 **74** (p) AmirQuinn 8 56
(Jim Best) *stdd s: hld up in tch in last trio: rdn and no hdwy 2f out: wknd over 1f out* **25/1**

001- **10** *4* **Dame Nellie Melba**[28] 8299 4-9-5 **75** JoeFanning 4 49
(Mark Johnston) *chsd ldr tl over 7f out: styd chsng ldrs tl rdn and btn over 1f out: fdd and eased ins fnl f* **5/1**

2m 4.8s (-1.80) **Going Correction** -0.175s/f (Stan)
**WFA** 4 from 6yo+ 2lb 10 Ran SP% 132.2
Speed ratings (Par 103): **100,99,99,99,99 97,96,95,90,86**
CSF £123.88 CT £301.24 TOTE £7.50: £2.10, £4.10, £1.10; EX 107.20 Trifecta £128.00.
**Owner** Mrs H Keddy **Bred** Baltusrol Thoughbreds Llc Et Al **Trained** Newmarket, Suffolk

**FOCUS**
A bunch finish to this modest handicap.

T/Plt: £16.40 to a £1 stake. Pool: £88255.79 - 3917.90 winning tickets T/Qpdt: £7.30 to a £1 stake. Pool: £5095.53 - 512.84 winning tickets SP

# [121]WOLVERHAMPTON (A.W) (L-H)

Sunday, January 12

**OFFICIAL GOING: Standard**

Wind: Light behind Weather: Overcast

## 147 COMPARE BOOKMAKERS AT BOOKMAKERS.CO.UK APPRENTICE H'CAP 5f 216y(P)

**1:00** (1:00) (Class 6) (0-65,65) 4-Y-O+ **£2,264** (£673; £336; £168) **Stalls** Low

Form RPR

500- **1** **Caramack**[34] 8227 4-9-2 **65** .......... EoinWalsh(5) 2 74
(Richard Lee) *s.i.s: hdwy over 4f out: pushed along over 2f out: r.o to ld nr fin* **5/1**[3]

03-2 **2** ½ **Parisian Pyramid (IRE)**[8] 53 8-9-6 **64** ..........(p) GeorgeChaloner 3 71
(Richard Fahey) *led: rdn and hdd over 1f out: rallied to ld ins fnl f: hdd nr fin* **3/1**[1]

26-0 **3** *hd* **Medam**[6] 65 5-8-8 **52** ..........(b[1]) NeilFarley 5 58
(Shaun Harris) *a.p: rdn over 1f out: r.o* **10/1**

43-1 **4** *1* **Insolenceofoffice (IRE)**[4] 83 6-9-0 **63** 6ex..........(p) JoshBaudains(5) 7 66
(Richard Ford) *trckd ldr tl led over 1f out: rdn and hdd ins fnl f: styd on same pce* **3/1**[1]

540- **5** *shd* **Invigilator**[15] 8432 6-9-1 **64** ..........(t) AdamMcLean(5) 8 67
(Derek Shaw) *hld up: hdwy over 1f out: r.o* **9/2**[2]

26-5 **6** *7* **Cadeaux Pearl**[10] 8 6-9-0 **63** ..........(v) MatthewHopkins(5) 1 43
(Scott Dixon) *chsd ldrs: rdn over 2f out: wknd over 1f out* **7/1**

060- **7** *9* **Whisky Bravo**[26] 8315 5-8-11 **60** .......... GeorgeBuckell(5) 4 12
(David C Griffiths) *prom: drvn along 1/2-way: wknd over 2f out* **25/1**

041- **8** *8* **My Time**[23] 8370 5-8-10 **54** .......... RobertTart 6
(Michael Mullineaux) *sn pushed along in rr: rdn and wknd 1/2-way* **14/1**

1m 16.02s (1.02) **Going Correction** +0.25s/f (Slow) **8** Ran SP% **117.0**

Speed ratings (Par 101): **103,102,102,100,100 91,79,68**

CSF £20.93 CT £145.66 TOTE £7.20: £2.90, £1.20, £4.10; EX 24.90 Trifecta £171.10.

**Owner** D E Edwards **Bred** Wellsummers Stud **Trained** Byton, H'fords

■ Stewards' Enquiry : Neil Farley two-day ban: used whip in incorrect place (Jan 27-28)

**FOCUS**

A moderate sprint handicap.

## 148 COMPARE BOOKMAKERS AT BOOKMAKERS.CO.UK H'CAP 5f 20y(P)

**1:30** (1:30) (Class 3) (0-95,97) 4-Y-O **£7,246** (£2,168; £1,084; £542; £270) **Stalls** Low

Form RPR

0-51 **1** **Caspian Prince (IRE)**[4] 80 5-8-12 **89** 7ex..........(t) MarkCoumbe(3) 4 98
(Tony Carroll) *mde virtually all: rdn and hung lft ins fnl f: all out* **5/1**[3]

211- **2** *hd* **Trinityelitedotcom (IRE)**[23] 8369 4-9-1 **89** .......... RichardKingscote 3 97
(Tom Dascombe) *a.p: chsd wnr 1/2-way: shkn up over 1f out: rdn and edgd lft ins fnl f: sn ev ch: r.o* **11/10**[1]

42-4 **3** *1* **Diamond Charlie (IRE)**[8] 55 6-8-13 **87** .......... GrahamLee 7 92
(Simon Dow) *hld up: nt clr run 1/2-way: hdwy over 1f out: running on whn nt clr run wl ins fnl f: nt rch ldrs* **9/4**[2]

06-1 **4** 1½ **Even Stevens**[11] 4 6-9-2 **97** ..........(v) MatthewHopkins(7) 2 96
(Scott Dixon) *chsd wnr to 1/2-way: rdn over 1f out: styd on same pce ins fnl f* **12/1**

01-0 **5** *5* **Tax Free (IRE)**[11] 4 12-8-13 **87** .......... AdrianNicholls 5 68
(David Nicholls) *prom: drvn along 3f out: edgd lft over 1f out: wknd fnl f* **25/1**

432- **6** *11* **Nafa (IRE)**[25] 8324 6-8-11 **85** .......... ShaneKelly 6 27
(Daniel Mark Loughnane) *hld up: pushed along 1/2-way: wknd over 1f out* **16/1**

1m 2.37s (0.07) **Going Correction** +0.25s/f (Slow) **6** Ran SP% **112.5**

Speed ratings (Par 107): **109,108,107,104,96 79**

CSF £11.05 CT £14.94 TOTE £8.30: £4.20, £1.20; EX 13.50 Trifecta £31.80.

**Owner** Stephen Louch **Bred** Ballygallon Stud Limited **Trained** Cropthorne, Worcs

■ Stewards' Enquiry : Mark Coumbe two-day ban: used whip in incorrect place (Jan 27-28)

**FOCUS**

Not many runners, but decent form.

## 149 32RED H'CAP 5f 20y(P)

**2:00** (2:00) (Class 4) (0-85,82) 3-Y-O **£4,690** (£1,395; £697; £348) **Stalls** Low

Form RPR

521- **1** **Thataboy (IRE)**[13] 8442 3-8-6 **72** .......... EoinWalsh(5) 1 81
(Tom Dascombe) *a.p: rdn to chse wnr fnl f: sn hung lft: r.o to ld nr fin* **5/4**[1]

104- **2** *nk* **Expect**[31] 8261 3-9-3 **78** .......... MartinHarley 3 86
(Jeremy Noseda) *w ldr tl led and edgd lft wl over 3f out: rdn over 1f out: hdd nr fin* **3/1**[2]

U2-2 **3** 3¾ **Shamardyh (IRE)**[4] 86 3-7-9 **63** oh4.......... JoeDoyle(7) 5 58
(David Evans) *s.i.s and hmpd s: hld up: hdwy 2f out: rdn over 1f out: edgd lft and styd on to go 3rd wl ins fnl f: nt trble ldrs* **7/1**[3]

231- **4** 1¾ **Three Pips**[16] 8414 3-8-9 **70** .......... ChrisCatlin 8 58
(Ed McMahon) *prom: racd keenly: chsd wnr 1/2-way: sn pushed along: lost 2nd 1f out: no ex* **8/1**

416- **5** 1¾ **Debt Settler (IRE)**[25] 8322 3-8-6 **74** ow2.......... JoshQuinn(7) 4 54
(Luke Dace) *s.i.s and edgd rt s: hld up: nt clr run 1/2-way: nvr nrr* **14/1**

236- **6** *4* **Corncockle**[13] 8442 3-9-7 **82** .......... DanielTudhope 2 50
(David O'Meara) *led: hdd and hmpd wl over 3f out: lost 2nd 1/2-way: rdn over 1f out: wknd fnl f* **8/1**

534- **7** *9* **Song Of Rowland (IRE)**[113] 6654 3-8-4 **65** .......... WilliamCarson 6
(Alan Jones) *sn pushed along towards rr: rdn 1/2-way: sn wknd* **33/1**

1m 2.98s (0.68) **Going Correction** +0.25s/f (Slow) **7** Ran SP% **113.8**

Speed ratings (Par 99): **104,103,97,94,91 85,71**

CSF £5.03 CT £17.09 TOTE £2.40: £1.50, £1.50; EX 5.10 Trifecta £26.00.

**Owner** David Lowe & Laurence Bellman **Bred** Mrs Brid Cosgrove **Trained** Malpas, Cheshire

■ Stewards' Enquiry : Josh Quinn two-day ban: weighed in 2lb heavy (Jan 27-28)

Martin Harley two-day ban: careless riding (Jan 27-28)

**FOCUS**

The front two are both quite useful.

## 150 CORAL APP DOWNLOAD FROM THE APP STORE MAIDEN STKS 2m 4f 50y(P)

**2:30** (2:30) (Class 5) 4-Y-O+ **£2,587** (£770; £384; £192) **Stalls** Low

Form RPR

**1** **Kettlewell**[89] 5-9-9 0..........(t) LiamKeniry 5 74+
(Warren Greatrex) *s.s: hld up: hdwy 5f out: led 2f out: sn clr: eased nr fin* **7/4**[2]

**2** *5* **Teenage Dream (IRE)**[6] 6-9-2 0..........(vt) AdamMcLean(7) 4 61
(Derek Shaw) *s.s: outpcd: hdwy over 3f out: rdn over 1f out: styd on to go 2nd wl ins fnl f: no ch w wnr* **10/1**

22-2 **3** 1½ **Strandfield Bay (IRE)**[10] 13 8-9-4 **69** .......... PaddyAspell 1 54
(Sharon Watt) *chsd ldrs: wnt 2nd over 5f out: led wl over 2f out: rdn and hdd 2f out: styd on same pce: lost 2nd wl ins fnl f* **7/2**[3]

325- **4** *16* **Lookbeforeyouleap**[43] 8115 4-8-11 **69** .......... SamJames(3) 2 28
(David O'Meara) *led: clr 10f out: rdn: hdd & wknd wl over 2f out* **11/10**[1]

40- **5** *50* **Another Journey**[31] 8260 5-9-6 0.......... MarkCoumbe(3) 3
(Lisa Williamson) *chsd clr ldr tl rdn over 5f out: wknd over 4f out* **40/1**

2m 45.03s (3.93) **Going Correction** +0.25s/f (Slow)

**WFA** 4 from 5yo+ 4lb **5** Ran SP% **117.7**

Speed ratings (Par 103): **96,92,91,81,47**

CSF £18.99 TOTE £3.70: £1.30, £7.00; EX 26.40 Trifecta £66.70.

**Owner** Mark Duthie Partnership **Bred** Giles W Pritchard-Gordon (farming) Ltd **Trained** Upper Lambourn, Berks

**FOCUS**

An uncompetitive maiden and the front two were making their Flat debuts after running over jumps.

## 151 CORAL MOBILE "JUST THREE CLICKS TO BET" H'CAP 1m 1f 103y(P)

**3:00** (3:00) (Class 5) (0-70,70) 4-Y-O+ **£2,587** (£770; £384; £192) **Stalls** Low

Form RPR

216- **1** **Frost Fire (USA)**[16] 8408 4-9-6 **70** .......... JoeFanning 6 78+
(Mark Johnston) *mde all: racd keenly: shkn up over 1f out: rdn out* **11/10**[1]

153- **2** ¾ **Spanish Plume**[120] 6377 6-9-4 **67** ..........(p) RobertWinston 2 73
(Andrew Hollinshead) *trckd wnr 4f: remained handy: pushed along to go 2nd again over 2f out: rdn ins fnl f: styd on* **3/1**[2]

26-5 **3** *4* **Honey Of A Kitten (USA)**[8] 49 6-9-0 **68** ..........(v) EoinWalsh(5) 1 66
(David Evans) *chsd ldrs: lost pl over 5f out: sn bhd and rdn: r.o ins fnl f* **3/1**[2]

551- **4** ½ **Diletta Tommasa (IRE)**[127] 6218 4-9-3 **67** .......... ShaneKelly 4 64
(John Stimpson) *hld up: pushed along and hdwy to trck wnr over 5f out tl rdn over 2f out: styd on same pce fr over 1f out* **6/1**[3]

2m 3.6s (1.90) **Going Correction** +0.25s/f (Slow)

**WFA** 4 from 5yo+ 1lb **4** Ran SP% **111.9**

Speed ratings (Par 103): **101,100,96,96**

CSF £4.89 TOTE £1.80; EX 5.10 Trifecta £13.20.

**Owner** Sheikh Hamdan bin Mohammed Al Maktoum **Bred** Woodford Thoroughbreds LLC **Trained** Middleham Moor, N Yorks

**FOCUS**

Not much of a race.

## 152 DOWNLOAD THE LADBROKES APP H'CAP 1m 141y(P)

**3:30** (3:30) (Class 6) (0-65,67) 4-Y-O+ **£2,264** (£673; £336; £168) **Stalls** Low

Form RPR

32-2 **1** **Prime Exhibit**[6] 66 9-9-9 **67** ..........(t) StephenCraine 1 77+
(Daniel Mark Loughnane) *hld up: hdwy over 2f out: shkn up to ld 1f out: rdn out* **7/4**[1]

000- **2** ½ **Benandonner (USA)**[47] 8055 11-8-7 **51** oh1.......... LukeMorris 5 60
(Mike Murphy) *hld up: racd keenly: hdwy over 2f out: pushed along and nt clr run over 1f out: rdn: edgd rt and r.o wl ins fnl f* **8/1**

026- **3** 4½ **Classy Trick (USA)**[23] 8371 4-8-8 **53** .......... JoeFanning 2 52
(Patrick Morris) *led: rdn and hdd 1f out: no ex ins fnl f* **6/1**

004- **4** ½ **Violent Velocity (IRE)**[90] 7238 11-8-13 **64** .......... JoeDoyle(7) 4 61
(John Quinn) *chsd ldrs: rdn over 1f out: styd on same pce fnl f* **7/1**

120- **5** 1¾ **Dansili Dutch (IRE)**[29] 8295 5-8-10 **61** .......... JoshDoyle(7) 3 54
(David O'Meara) *chsd ldr tl rdn over 1f out: wknd fnl f* **4/1**[2]

00- **6** *3* **Brown Pete (IRE)**[13] 8448 6-8-9 **53** .......... WilliamCarson 6 39
(Ann Stokell) *sn pushed along to chse ldrs: rdn over 3f out: hmpd and wknd over 2f out* **5/1**[3]

1m 52.47s (1.97) **Going Correction** +0.25s/f (Slow)

**WFA** 4 from 5yo+ 1lb **6** Ran SP% **110.9**

Speed ratings (Par 101): **101,100,96,96,94 91**

CSF £15.91 TOTE £2.70: £1.70, £4.30; EX 13.30 Trifecta £77.90.

**Owner** R M Brilley **Bred** Matthews Breeding And Racing Ltd **Trained** Baldwin's Gate, Staffs

**FOCUS**

A moderate handicap.

## 153 LADBROKES H'CAP 7f 32y(P)

**4:00** (4:01) (Class 4) (0-85,82) 4-Y-O+ **£4,690** (£1,395; £697; £348) **Stalls** High

Form RPR

426- **1** **Forceful Appeal (USA)**[157] 5190 6-9-4 **79** .......... GrahamLee 5 86+
(Simon Dow) *hld up: nt clr run over 2f out: hdwy over 1f out: shkn up to ld wl ins fnl f: comf* **8/1**

35-0 **2** ½ **Al's Memory (IRE)**[9] 38 5-9-5 **80** .......... MartinHarley 7 86
(David Evans) *led: rdn over 1f out: hdd wl ins fnl f* **14/1**

00-1 **3** *nk* **Kyllachy Star**[8] 52 8-8-9 **70** ..........(v) JoeFanning 3 75
(Richard Fahey) *chsd ldrs: rdn over 1f out: r.o* **7/2**[2]

500- **4** *1* **Trojan Rocket (IRE)**[149] 5489 6-9-3 **78** .......... DanielTudhope 2 81
(Michael Wigham) *a.p: rdn over 1f out: styd on same pce ins fnl f* **12/1**

002- **5** *nk* **Pearl Nation (USA)**[17] 8401 5-9-2 **77** .......... WilliamCarson 6 79
(Brian Baugh) *hld up: hdwy 1/2-way: rdn to chse wnr over 1f out tl styd on same pce ins fnl f* **7/2**[2]

130- **6** 1¼ **Ruwaiyan (USA)**[43] 8117 5-9-7 **82** ..........(p) LukeMorris 4 81
(James Tate) *hld up: hdwy on outer 2f out: sn rdn and edgd lft: styd on same pce fnl f* **2/1**[1]

01-1 **7** ¾ **Powerful Pierre**[10] 20 7-8-9 **75** ..........(b) JacobButterfield(5) 1 72
(Ollie Pears) *hld up in tch: pushed along over 2f out: styd on same pce fr over 1f out* **6/1**[3]

13-4 **8** 1¼ **Fantasy Gladiator**[9] 38 8-9-3 **78** .......... RobertWinston 8 71
(John Quinn) *sn pushed along and prom: chsd ldr over 5f out tl rdn over 1f out: no ex ins fnl f* **12/1**

1m 30.7s (1.10) **Going Correction** +0.25s/f (Slow) **8** Ran SP% **125.2**

Speed ratings (Par 105): **103,102,102,100,100 99,98,96**

CSF £119.30 CT £478.04 TOTE £12.00: £2.90, £3.90, £1.70; EX 127.20 Trifecta £760.70.

**Owner** Simon Caunce **Bred** Juddmonte Farms Inc **Trained** Epsom, Surrey

**FOCUS**

A fair handicap.

T/Plt: £41.10 to a £1 stake. Pool: £140,833.98 - 2,500.93 winning tickets. T/Qpdt: £14.00 to a £1 stake. Pool: £8,323.03 - 437.75 winning tickets. CR

# [140]LINGFIELD (L-H)

Monday, January 13

**OFFICIAL GOING: Standard**

Wind: Moderate, behind Weather: Fine but cloudy, raining by final race

## 154 LADBROKES MOBILE H'CAP (DIV I) 1m 1y(P)

**12:15** (12:18) (Class 6) (0-65,65) 4-Y-0+ **£2,045** (£603; £302) **Stalls High**

Form RPR

224- **1** **Tee It Up Tommo (IRE)**[46] 8087 5-9-5 **63**.................. RobertWinston 1 77
(Michael Wigham) *trckd ldrs: cl 3rd 2f out: pushed into ld jst over 1f out: hanging sltly lft but bounded clr: easily* **6/4**[1]

060- **2** 4 1/2 **Timothy T**[26] 8336 6-9-6 **64**..........................(b[1]) TonyHamilton 7 68
(Philip Hide) *led: pressed over 2f out: drvn over 1f out: sn hdd and outpcd: kpt on* **8/1**

113- **3** 3 1/4 **Little Indian**[63] 7841 4-9-4 **62**.................. FergusSweeney 6 59
(J R Jenkins) *hld up in last trio: prog wl over 1f out: shkn up to take 3rd fnl f: no ch* **5/1**[3]

000- **4** hd **Bold Ring**[16] 8432 8-8-12 **63**.................. JenniferFerguson(7) 5 59
(Edward Creighton) *trckd ldrs: shkn up and nt qckn 2f out: kpt on same pce fnl f* **20/1**

346- **5** hd **Schottische**[30] 8295 4-8-11 **58**..................(v) RosieJessop(3) 9 54
(Derek Haydn Jones) *hld up in tch on outer: shkn up over 2f out: no prog and btn over 1f out: kpt on nr fin* **16/1**

400- **6** 1 1/4 **Midnight Feast**[40] 8158 6-9-4 **65**..................(v) MarkCoumbe(3) 3 58
(Lee Carter) *mistimed s and lost 5 l: detached in last: rdn over 1f out: kpt on same pce fnl f: no ch* **8/1**

00-5 **7** 1/2 **Perivale (USA)**[12] 1 4-8-9 **53**.................. JoeFanning 10 45
(Mark Johnston) *mostly chsd ldr: chal over 2f out: lost 2nd and wknd wl over 1f out* **16/1**

600- **8** 1 3/4 **Mafi (IRE)**[13] 8453 6-9-4 **62**..................(t) WilliamCarson 4 50
(Mark Hoad) *hld up in rr: effrt on inner over 2f out: wknd jst over 1f out* **20/1**

344- **9** 2 **Santadelacruze**[47] 8072 5-9-5 **63**..................(b) GeorgeBaker 8 46
(Gary Moore) *trckd ldrs towards outer: rdn over 2f out: wknd qckly over 1f out* **4/1**[2]

1m 37.05s (-1.15) **Going Correction** -0.075s/f (Stan) **9 Ran SP% 120.2**

Speed ratings (Par 101): **102,97,94,94,93 92,92,90,88**

CSF £15.39 CT £49.36 TOTE £2.30: £1.02, £6.80, £3.50; EX 17.40 Trifecta £80.60.

**Owner** Palatinate Thoroughbred Racing Limited **Bred** Oghill House Stud **Trained** Newmarket, Suffolk

**FOCUS**

A moderate handicap and pretty weak form with the favourite disappointing.

## 155 LADBROKES MOBILE H'CAP (DIV II) 1m 1y(P)

**12:45** (12:45) (Class 6) (0-65,65) 4-Y-0+ **£2,045** (£603; £302) **Stalls High**

Form RPR

15-0 **1** **Skidby Mill (IRE)**[5] 92 4-8-12 **56**.................. LiamJones 7 63
(Laura Mongan) *trckd ldng trio: nipped through on rail to ld over 1f out: drvn fnl f: hld on wl* **16/1**

411- **2** hd **Pretty Bubbles**[42] 8125 5-9-7 **65**.................. JoeFanning 5 72
(J R Jenkins) *t.k.h early: trckd ldrs: chalng whn wd bnd 2f out: pressed wnr fnl f: styd on but jst hld* **5/2**[1]

203- **3** 3/4 **Club House (IRE)**[14] 8443 4-8-11 **62**.................. GeorgeBuckell(7) 1 67
(Robert Mills) *dwlt: hld up in 7th: prog wl over 1f out: pressed ldng pair ins fnl f: styd on but nvr quite able to chal* **10/1**

03-6 **4** 1 **Unex Michelangelo (IRE)**[11] 11 5-9-7 **65**.................. JamesSullivan 6 68
(Michael Easterby) *led 3f: pressed ldr: led 2f out: edgd lft and hdd over 1f out: nt qckn* **11/4**[2]

230- **5** 1/2 **Teen Ager (FR)**[187] 4163 10-9-6 **64**..................(p) JimmyQuinn 2 65
(Paul Burgoyne) *t.k.h early: hld up in 5th: pushed along and quite wd bnd 2f out: n.d after: kpt on* **25/1**

401- **6** 1 **Spirit Of Gondree (IRE)**[25] 8341 6-9-2 **60**..................(b) RobertWinston 9 59
(Milton Bradley) *hld up in last: cajoled along fr 2f out: hanging over 1f out: styd on nr fin: nvr involved* **8/1**

000- **7** 1/2 **Sea Soldier (IRE)**[103] 6937 6-8-12 **63**.................. RobHornby(7) 3 61
(Andrew Balding) *sltly awkward s: t.k.h and sn pressed ldr: led 5f out to 2f out: steadily lost pl* **12/1**

054- **8** shd **Sweet Marwell (IRE)**[16] 8427 4-9-5 **63**.................. JohnFahy 4 61
(Jo Crowley) *hld up in 6th: rdn 2f out: no prog and wl hld fnl f* **9/2**[3]

1m 37.71s (-0.49) **Going Correction** -0.075s/f (Stan) **8 Ran SP% 111.0**

Speed ratings (Par 101): **99,98,98,97,96 95,95,94**

CSF £52.96 CT £421.04 TOTE £16.70: £3.70, £1.40, £2.50; EX 88.00 Trifecta £820.70.

**Owner** Ronnie Coates **Bred** Michael O'Mahony **Trained** Epsom, Surrey

**FOCUS**

This looked more competitive than the first division. The winner has been rated back to her 2yo best, with the runner-up close to her Kempton win.

## 156 DOWNLOAD THE LADBROKES APP (S) H'CAP 1m 1y(P)

**1:15** (1:15) (Class 6) (0-60,60) 4-Y-0+ **£2,045** (£603; £302) **Stalls High**

Form RPR

43-4 **1** **Greek Islands (IRE)**[11] 12 6-9-1 **54**.................. ChrisCatlin 8 62
(Ed de Giles) *hld up in 5th: prog over 1f out: rdn to ld ins fnl f: hrd drvn and jst hld on* **8/1**

100- **2** nk **Penbryn (USA)**[13] 8456 7-9-5 **58**.................. GeorgeBaker 9 65
(Nick Littmoden) *stdd s: hld up in last: plld out and prog over 1f out: r.o to take 2nd last 75yds: clsd on wnr but jst too much to do* **5/1**[3]

62-5 **3** 2 **Miami Gator (IRE)**[11] 10 7-8-13 **52**..................(v) WilliamCarson 1 55
(K R Burke) *trckd ldr: clsd to ld wl over 2f out: sn rdn: hdd and one pce u.p ins fnl f* **6/1**

40-4 **4** shd **Mojo Bear**[5] 88 4-8-13 **57**..................(b) JoshBaudains(5) 4 59
(Sylvester Kirk) *chsd ldng pair: rdn over 2f out: cl enough 1f out: edgd lft and fnd little after* **11/4**[2]

33-4 **5** 3 1/2 **Delightful Sleep**[10] 39 6-9-7 **60**..................(v[1]) AdamKirby 5 54
(David Evans) *chsd ldng trio: rdn over 2f out: tried to cl over 1f out: wknd fnl f* **5/2**[1]

600- **6** 1 **Kilburn**[67] 7784 10-9-2 **55**..................(b) FergusSweeney 3 47
(Alastair Lidderdale) *racd freely: led at str pce: hdd wl over 2f out: wknd over 1f out* **8/1**

065- **7** 1/2 **Total Obsession**[202] 3655 7-8-5 **51**..................(v) LouisSteward(7) 6 42
(Mark Hoad) *a in last trio: rdn fr 1/2-way: struggling over 2f out* **20/1**

1m 37.35s (-0.85) **Going Correction** -0.075s/f (Stan) **7 Ran SP% 113.2**

Speed ratings (Par 101): **101,100,98,98,95 94,93**

CSF £46.04 CT £256.99 TOTE £11.20: £3.90, £2.30; EX 43.20 Trifecta £184.90.Greek Islands was bought by Eddie Creighton for 3,000gns.

**Owner** E B De Giles **Bred** Petra Bloodstock Agency Ltd **Trained** Ledbury, H'fords

**FOCUS**

A depleted field but still quite a competitive selling handicap. The runner-up helps set the standard.

## 157 32RED.COM H'CAP 1m 1y(P)

**1:45** (1:46) (Class 5) (0-70,70) 3-Y-O **£2,726** (£805; £402) **Stalls High**

Form RPR

240- **1** **Starlight Princess (IRE)**[16] 8426 3-8-13 **62**..................(b) JohnFahy 6 67+
(J S Moore) *slowly away: swtchd to inner and hld up in last: stl there and plenty to do 2f out: plld out wd and rapid prog jst over 1f out: r.o wl to ld post* **10/1**

566- **2** shd **Crowdmania**[106] 6865 3-9-6 **69**.................. JoeFanning 9 74
(Mark Johnston) *wl plcd: chsd ldng pair 3f out: rdn over 2f out: clsd to ld jst ins fnl f: sn over a l clr: kpt on but hdd post* **7/4**[1]

044- **3** 1 1/2 **Sweetness Lady**[13] 8451 3-9-0 **63**.................. RobertWinston 2 64
(Olly Stevens) *t.k.h: trckd ldr: chal fr over 2f out: stl upsides 1f out: nt qckn* **8/1**

046- **4** 1 1/4 **Amontillado (IRE)**[13] 8452 3-8-4 **60**..................(b[1]) CamHardie(7) 7 58
(Richard Hannon) *in tch towards rr: rdn 3f out: outpcd over 2f out: kpt on fr over 1f out: no ch* **25/1**

042- **5** 3/4 **Evacusafe Lady**[15] 8434 3-9-2 **65**..................(tp) AdamKirby 1 62
(John Ryan) *led: drvn and hrd pressed fr over 2f out: hdd & wknd jst ins fnl f* **8/1**

423- **6** 1 1/2 **Plough Boy (IRE)**[32] 8262 3-8-8 **57**.................. ChrisCatlin 4 50
(Willie Musson) *hld up in last trio: gng bttr than many but only 8th 2f out: jst bmpd along after and nvr remotely involved* **7/1**[3]

100- **7** nk **Sweet Alibi (IRE)**[13] 8452 3-9-1 **67**.................. MichaelJMMurphy(3) 8 60
(J S Moore) *racd wd: chsd ldrs: rdn 3f out: wknd 2f out* **33/1**

404- **8** 3 **Warbrook (IRE)**[16] 8425 3-9-7 **70**.................. NickyMackay 5 56
(John Gosden) *in tch: pushed along 1/2-way: struggling and outpcd wl over 2f out: sn btn* **7/2**[2]

634- **9** 3 1/2 **Ronya (IRE)**[86] 7371 3-9-2 **65**.................. WilliamCarson 3 43
(K R Burke) *chsd ldng pair to 3f out: sn rdn and wknd* **16/1**

1m 38.91s (0.71) **Going Correction** -0.075s/f (Stan) **9 Ran SP% 115.1**

Speed ratings (Par 97): **93,92,91,90,89 87,87,84,81**

CSF £27.80 CT £152.63 TOTE £13.60: £3.00, £1.10, £2.60; EX 37.90 Trifecta £338.10.

**Owner** J S Moore **Bred** Coleman Bloodstock Limited **Trained** Upper Lambourn, Berks

**FOCUS**

The last of the races to be run over 1m was a handicap for 3yos, and it saw a thrilling finish. The fourth and fifth have been rated close to their marks.

## 158 32RED H'CAP 1m 5f (P)

**2:20** (2:20) (Class 5) (0-75,74) 4-Y-0+ **£3,238** (£956; £478) **Stalls Low**

Form RPR

02-1 **1** **The Blue Dog (IRE)**[3] 120 7-8-6 **63**.................. JoeDoyle(7) 6 79
(Phil McEntee) *hld up in 4th: prog to trck ldr over 3f out: rdn and clsd to ld jst ins fnl f: forged clr nr fin* **7/4**[2]

53-2 **2** 2 1/2 **Summerfree (USA)**[6] 72 4-8-11 **66**.................. JoeFanning 4 78
(Mark Johnston) *led at gd pce: breather 1/2-way: kicked on again 3f out: hdd jst ins fnl f: wl clr of rest but no match for wnr nr fin* **5/4**[1]

005- **3** 8 **Nave (USA)**[22] 8392 7-9-3 **74**..................(p) GeorgeBuckell(7) 3 74
(David Simcock) *trckd ldng pair to over 3f out: nt clr run and wl outpcd over 2f out: kpt on to take 3rd 1f out: no ch w ldng pair* **8/1**

421- **4** 2 **Admirable Duque (IRE)**[25] 8139 8-9-4 **73**..................(be) JoshBaudains(5) 2 70
(Dominic Ffrench Davis) *hld up in last pair: rdn over 3f out: outpcd but wnt 3rd over 2f out to 1f out: no ch* **25/1**

554- **5** 1 1/2 **Peachez**[26] 8331 6-8-11 **66**..................(p) AmyScott(5) 1 61
(Seamus Durack) *hld up in last: outpcd fr 3f out: no ch after* **33/1**

146- **6** 13 **The Holyman (IRE)**[158] 5168 6-9-9 **73**.................. AdamKirby 5 49
(Jo Crowley) *chsd ldr: rdn 4f out: sn lost 2nd and wknd: t.o* **9/2**[3]

2m 42.46s (-3.54) **Going Correction** -0.075s/f (Stan)

**WFA** 4 from 6yo+ 5lb **6 Ran SP% 116.9**

Speed ratings (Par 103): **107,105,100,99,98 90**

CSF £4.58 TOTE £2.60: £2.40, £1.10; EX 5.60 Trifecta £18.40.

**Owner** R Carson **Bred** Mervyn Stewkesbury **Trained** Newmarket, Suffolk

■ Stewards' Enquiry : Joe Doyle one-day ban: careless riding (Jan 27)

**FOCUS**

Straightforward form. The runner-up has been rated up to his revised Southwell figure.

## 159 BEST ODDS AT BOOKMAKERS.CO.UK MAIDEN STKS 6f 1y(P)

**2:50** (2:51) (Class 5) 3-Y-O+ **£2,726** (£805; £402) **Stalls Low**

Form RPR

322- **1** **Ex Ex**[30] 8303 4-9-13 65.................. GeorgeBaker 1 72
(Nick Littmoden) *trckd ldr to 1/2-way: styd cl up: shkn up to ld on inner over 1f out: pressed fnl f: rdn out* **6/4**[2]

042- **2** 3/4 **Bretherton**[44] 8114 3-8-11 70.................. TonyHamilton 7 66
(Richard Fahey) *cl up: trckd ldr on outer 1/2-way: rdn and nt qckn wl over 1f out: kpt on to press wnr fnl f: a readily hld* **8/13**[1]

**3** 3 3/4 **Avondream** 5-9-13 0.................. JimmyQuinn 3 58
(Milton Bradley) *hld up in tch: pushed along and outpcd jst over 2f out: reminder and kpt on to take 3rd ins fnl f* **33/1**

60- **4** 1 **Vermuyden**[40] 8146 5-9-13 0..................(t) AdamKirby 8 54
(Pam Sly) *spd fr wdst draw and led: rdn 2f out: hdd over 1f out: fdd* **14/1**[3]

/6-0 **5** 8 **Highway United (IRE)**[10] 37 4-9-5 30..................(t) RossAtkinson(3) 2 24
(Sean Curran) *in tch: outpcd over 2f out: wknd qckly jst over 1f out* **66/1**

00- **6** 9 **Miss Glorioso**[47] 8068 5-9-1 0.................. LouisSteward(7) 6
(Alexandra Dunn) *a in rr: wknd over 2f out: t.o* **50/1**

0- **7** 10 **Minnie Miracle**[26] 8326 3-8-7 0 ow1.................. JohnFahy 4
(Mark Usher) *s.i.s: sn outpcd: wl t.o* **33/1**

1m 11.81s (-0.09) **Going Correction** -0.075s/f (Stan)

**WFA** 3 from 4yo+ 16lb **7 Ran SP% 117.9**

Speed ratings (Par 103): **97,96,91,89,79 67,53**

CSF £2.84 TOTE £3.40: £1.50, £1.10; EX 3.50 Trifecta £16.80.

**Owner** Nick Littmoden **Bred** Mr & Mrs A E Pakenham **Trained** Newmarket, Suffolk

**FOCUS**

A very weak maiden. It's been rated around the winner for now but the third and fourth are possibly the key longer-term.

## 160 CORAL.CO.UK H'CAP 1m 4f (P)

**3:20** (3:20) (Class 4) (0-85,85) 4-Y-0+ **£4,884** (£1,453; £726; £363) **Stalls Low**

Form RPR

000- **1** **Blue Wave (IRE)**[75] 7635 4-8-11 **79**.................. JoeFanning 5 92
(Mark Johnston) *w.w in 5th: prog over 2f out: clsd on outer over 1f out: led jst ins fnl f: pushed clr and r.o wl* **11/4**[2]

31-1 **2** 3 ¼ **Echo Brava**[5] 85 4-8-6 77 6ex.................................. RossAtkinson(3) 7 85
(Luke Dace) *hld up in 6th: quick move on outer fr 3f out to go 2nd over 2f out: rdn to ld over 1f out: didn't fnd much in front: hdd and easily outpcd jst ins fnl f* **9/4**[1]

206- **3** ½ **Scottish Star**[26] 8336 6-8-6 77.................................. LouisSteward(7) 3 84
(James Eustace) *trckd ldr after 2f: led after 4f: hdd wl over 1f out: stl nrly upsides tl wnr swept by jst ins fnl f* **6/1**[3]

615- **4** 4 **Oratorio's Joy (IRE)**[26] 8336 4-8-9 77.................. FergusSweeney 1 78
(Jamie Osborne) *cl up: chsd ldr 3f out to over 2f out: steadily fdd* **12/1**

133- **5** nk **Slip Of The Tongue**[91] 7242 4-8-12 80.................. RobertWinston 6 80
(Derek Haydn Jones) *racd freely early: led 4f: chsd ldr to 3f out: steadily wknd* **6/1**[3]

000- **6** ¾ **Cry Fury**[156] 5259 6-9-7 85.................................. GeorgeBaker 4 84
(Gary Moore) *stdd s: hld up in last: stl there jst over 2f out: shuffled along and no real prog: nvr involved* **6/1**[3]

00-6 **7** 4 ½ **Mica Mika (IRE)**[12] 3 6-9-0 78.................................. TonyHamilton 2 70
(Richard Fahey) *trckd ldr 2f: styd prom: rdn 3f out: wknd 2f out* **16/1**

2m 29.43s (-3.57) **Going Correction** -0.075s/f (Stan)
**WFA** 4 from 6yo 4lb **7** Ran SP% **113.9**
Speed ratings (Par 105): **108,105,105,102,102 102,99**
CSF £9.30 TOTE £4.20: £1.70, £1.30; EX 10.80 Trifecta £41.80.
**Owner** Sheikh Hamdan bin Mohammed Al Maktoum **Bred** Tom Darcy And Vincent McCarthy **Trained** Middleham Moor, N Yorks

**FOCUS**
A modest little handicap. The third has been rated in line with most of his form since last February.

## 161 LADBROKES H'CAP 7f 1y(P)
**3:50** (3:50) (Class 5) (0-75,75) 4-Y-0+ **£2,726** (£805; £402) **Stalls** Low

Form RPR

600- **1** **Compton**[89] 7313 5-9-7 75.................................. (t) GeorgeBaker 6 87+
(Stuart Williams) *hld up in last: quick prog on inner 2f out: led jst over 1f out: pushed along and sn clr: readily* **5/2**[1]

056- **2** 2 ¼ **Intomist (IRE)**[13] 8455 5-8-12 71.................. (p) NathanAlison(5) 1 77
(Jim Boyle) *trckd ldng pair: wnt 2nd 2f out and sn upsides: chsd wnr fnl f but readily outpcd* **12/1**

331- **3** nk **Go Far**[17] 8407 4-9-0 68.................................. (v) RobertWinston 4 73
(Alan Bailey) *trckd ldng trio: rdn 2f out: edgd lft 1f out: kpt on to take 3rd ins fnl f* **9/2**[3]

41-2 **4** ¾ **Iceblast**[9] 52 6-8-13 67.................................. (v) AdamKirby 3 72+
(Michael Easterby) *hld up in tch: rdn 2f out: hld whn nt clr run 1f out: kpt on to take 4th nr fin* **11/4**[2]

60-0 **5** ½ **Perfect Mission**[9] 52 6-8-7 68.................. KieranShoemark(7) 2 70
(Andrew Balding) *led but pressed: hdd against ins rail jst over 1f out: fdd last 100yds* **20/1**

044- **6** nk **Comrade Bond**[42] 8122 6-9-4 72.................................. BenCurtis 8 73
(Mark H Tompkins) *pressed ldr: upsides 4f out to 2f out: fdd over 1f out* **16/1**

505- **7** ½ **Mister Musicmaster**[13] 8454 5-9-7 75.................. WilliamCarson 5 75
(Ron Hodges) *hld up in tch: effrt on outer and v wd bnd 2f out: no ch after* **5/1**

/0-0 **8** 2 **Dozy Joe**[9] 52 6-8-9 66.................................. (v) MichaelJMMurphy(3) 7 61
(Joseph Tuite) *hld up in tch: effrt on outer 3f out: wdst of all bnd 2f out: lost all ch* **16/1**

1m 23.62s (-1.18) **Going Correction** -0.075s/f (Stan) **8** Ran SP% **114.3**
Speed ratings (Par 103): **103,100,100,99,98 98,97,95**
CSF £33.03 CT £129.22 TOTE £3.00: £1.10, £4.40, £1.70; EX 37.50 Trifecta £260.70.
**Owner** The Morley Family **Bred** Lawn Stud **Trained** Newmarket, Suffolk
■ Stewards' Enquiry : Robert Winston one-day ban: careless riding (Jan 27)

**FOCUS**
An ordinary handicap and a back-to-form winner. The runner-up has been rated in line with his recent form.
T/Plt: £17.30. Pool: £65,838.18 - 2773.37 winning units. T/Qpdt: £11.20. Pool: £5507.68 - 363.00 winning units. JN

# [147] WOLVERHAMPTON (A.W) (L-H)
Monday, January 13

**OFFICIAL GOING: Standard**
Wind: Light behind Weather: Fine, turning to rain after the 3-40

## 162 LADBROKES CLAIMING STKS 7f 32y(P)
**2:10** (2:10) (Class 6) 4-Y-0+ **£2,264** (£673; £336) **Stalls** High

Form RPR

05-1 **1** **Tellovoi (IRE)**[11] 11 6-9-5 83.................................. (v) GrahamLee 1 89
(Ian Williams) *mde virtually all: shkn up and edgd rt over 1f out: reminder ins fnl f: r.o: cosily* **5/4**[1]

100- **2** 1 **Capaill Liath (IRE)**[13] 8455 6-9-4 81.................. (p) JamieSpencer 4 85
(Kevin Ryan) *trckd ldrs: drvn along 1/2-way: chsd wnr over 1f out: rdn and ev ch ins fnl f: unable qck towards fin* **7/2**[3]

331- **3** 10 **Mr David (USA)**[22] 8391 7-9-4 85.................................. (b) DavidProbert 2 59
(Jamie Osborne) *chsd wnr: shkn up over 2f out: rdn and lost 2nd over 1f out: wknd ins fnl f* **7/4**[2]

1m 30.39s (0.79) **Going Correction** +0.15s/f (Slow) **3** Ran SP% **103.0**
Speed ratings (Par 101): **101,99,88**
CSF £4.91 TOTE £2.60; EX 5.20 Trifecta £5.30.
**Owner** Miss Magdalena Gut **Bred** Whisperview Trading Ltd **Trained** Portway, Worcs

**FOCUS**
Only three runners but all are useful at best and all were recent winners. Not surprisingly the gallop was just a modest one, and the winner came down the centre. The runner-up has been rated a length off his recent best.

## 163 LADBROKES H'CAP 1m 141y(P)
**2:40** (2:42) (Class 3) (0-95,99) 4-Y-0+ **£7,439** (£2,213; £1,106; £553) **Stalls** Low

Form RPR

15- **1** **Star Links (USA)**[30] 8301 8-8-12 84.................................. (b) LukeMorris 6 96
(S Donohoe, Ire) *trckd ldr tl rdn to ld over 1f out: styd on u.p* **3/1**[1]

135- **2** ½ **Silverware (USA)**[17] 8416 6-8-10 82.................................. TomEaves 5 93
(Kristin Stubbs) *led: rdn and hdd over 1f out: styd on gamely* **14/1**

000- **3** 1 ½ **Stasio (USA)**[32] 8263 4-8-13 86..................................[1] LiamKeniry 1 93
(David Simcock) *hld up: nt clr run over 2f out: hdwy over 1f out: rdn and edgd rt wl ins fnl f: r.o: nt rch ldrs* **10/1**

210- **4** 1 **Dixie's Dream (IRE)**[32] 8263 5-9-0 86..................................[1] GrahamLee 9 91
(William Jarvis) *hld up: pushed along over 3f out: hdwy over 2f out: rdn and edgd lft ins fnl f: styd on* **4/1**[3]

110- **5** 1 **Yojojo (IRE)**[15] 8440 5-9-2 88.................................. DavidProbert 4 91
(Gay Kelleway) *a.p: rdn over 2f out: styng on same pce whn hmpd wl ins fnl f* **8/1**

20-1 **6** 1 **Frontier Fighter**[8] 61 6-9-10 99 6ex.................................. SamJames(3) 7 100
(David O'Meara) *trckd ldrs: rdn over 1f out: no ex ins fnl f* **5/1**

063- **7** 7 **Lions Arch (IRE)**[13] 8455 4-8-11 84.................................. KieranO'Neill 3 68
(Richard Hannon) *chsd ldrs: rdn over 2f out: wknd fnl f* **7/2**[2]

0/5- **8** 5 **Cockney Class (USA)**[197] 2976 7-9-2 88.................................. PaddyAspell 2 61
(Dave Roberts) *s.i.s: hld up: pushed along over 2f out: a in rr* **33/1**

112- **9** ½ **Brigadoon**[149] 5520 7-8-12 84.................................. JamieSpencer 8 56
(Philip Kirby) *hld up: rdn over 2f out: a in rr* **10/1**

1m 49.23s (-1.27) **Going Correction** +0.15s/f (Slow)
**WFA** 4 from 5yo+ 1lb **9** Ran SP% **122.8**
Speed ratings (Par 107): **111,110,109,108,107 106,100,95,95**
CSF £49.65 CT £391.55 TOTE £4.50: £1.40, £3.70, £4.30; EX 48.30 Trifecta £572.80.
**Owner** Gerry Dolan & Mrs Marie E Dolan **Bred** Shell Bloodstock **Trained** Cootehill Road, Co Cavan
■ Stewards' Enquiry : Liam Keniry two-day ban: careless riding (Jan 27-28)

**FOCUS**
A useful handicap in which a steady gallop saw those held up at a disadvantage. The winner edged towards the far side in the closing stages. The first two have been rated as running small personal bests.

## 164 BEST ODDS AT BOOKMAKERS.CO.UK H'CAP 5f 20y(P)
**3:10** (3:10) (Class 6) (0-52,52) 4-Y-0+ **£1,940** (£577; £288; £144) **Stalls** Low

Form RPR

235- **1** **Volcanic Dust (IRE)**[59] 7903 6-9-7 52.................. (t) RichardKingscote 6 59
(Milton Bradley) *trckd ldr tl led on bit 2f out: rdn out* **5/1**

431- **2** ½ **Daneglow (IRE)**[31] 8277 4-9-4 49.................................. (e) LukeMorris 8 54
(Mike Murphy) *hld up: hdwy over 1f out: sn rdn: r.o* **4/1**[3]

560- **3** shd **Ishetoo**[39] 8169 10-8-12 46 oh1.................................. SladeO'Hara(3) 2 51
(Peter Grayson) *chsd ldrs: pushed along 1/2-way: rdn over 1f out: r.o* **40/1**

00-0 **4** 1 **Rightcar**[4] 100 7-9-1 46 oh1..................................[1] StephenCraine 7 47
(Peter Grayson) *s.i.s: hld up: hdwy over 1f out: r.o: nt rch ldrs* **12/1**

55-0 **5** 1 ¼ **Speedyfix**[9] 53 7-9-2 52.................................. (t) EoinWalsh(5) 4 49
(Christine Dunnett) *s.i.s: hld up: hdwy over 1f out: rdn and nt clr run ins fnl f: nt rch ldrs* **7/2**[2]

002- **6** 2 **Marmot Bay (IRE)**[52] 8002 4-8-9 47.................................. EvaMoscrop(7) 5 36
(Philip Kirby) *led 3f: rdn: edgd lft and no ex ins fnl f* **5/2**[1]

046- **7** ¾ **Robyn**[17] 8406 4-8-9 47.................................. MatthewHopkins(7) 1 34
(Scott Dixon) *sn pushed along and prom: rdn over 1f out: no ex* **7/1**

55-0 **8** 6 **Chateau Lola**[8] 58 5-9-1 46 oh1.................................. (v) TomEaves 3 11
(Derek Shaw) *chsd ldrs: pushed along 1/2-way: rdn and wknd over 1f out* **14/1**

1m 3.65s (1.35) **Going Correction** +0.15s/f (Slow) **8** Ran SP% **116.8**
Speed ratings (Par 101): **95,94,94,92,90 87,86,76**
CSF £25.90 CT £729.65 TOTE £6.70: £2.00, £1.30, £6.80; EX 21.00 Trifecta £440.60.
**Owner** Miss Diane Hill **Bred** Top Of The Form Syndicate **Trained** Sedbury, Gloucs

**FOCUS**
A low-grade handicap in which the gallop was sound. The winner raced centre-to-far side in the straight. Shaky form with the third and fourth showing their first form for some time.

## 165 32RED CASINO H'CAP 5f 216y(P)
**3:40** (3:40) (Class 6) (0-55,55) 3-Y-0 **£2,264** (£673; £336; £168) **Stalls** Low

Form RPR

023- **1** **Spreadable (IRE)**[42] 8133 3-9-4 52.................................. (v[1]) LukeMorris 3 66
(Nick Littmoden) *t.k.h: trckd ldrs: n.m.r over 3f out: shkn up to ld 1f out: sn clr: easily* **1/1**[1]

466- **2** 5 **My My My Diliza**[23] 8383 3-9-5 53.................................. (b) GrahamLee 4 51
(J S Moore) *prom: n.m.r over 3f out: lost pl over 2f out: hdwy over 1f out: edgd lft and wnt 2nd wl ins fnl f: no ch w wnr* **8/1**[3]

30-4 **3** 1 ¼ **Countess Lupus (IRE)**[11] 15 3-8-7 46 oh1......(b) ShirleyTeasdale(5) 9 40
(Lisa Williamson) *led: rdn and hdd over 1f out: no ex ins fnl f* **25/1**

530- **4** 1 ½ **El Duque**[39] 8166 3-8-12 53.................................. (p) RyanWhile(7) 8 42
(Bill Turner) *sn pushed along towards rr: hdwy and edgd lft over 3f out: rdn over 1f out: hung lft and wknd ins fnl f* **14/1**

600- **5** shd **Frankthetank (IRE)**[39] 8165 3-9-2 50.................................. TomEaves 7 39+
(Keith Dalgleish) *broke wl enough but sn pushed along: hmpd and lost pl after 100yds: drvn along 1/2-way: r.o ins fnl f: nrst fin* **16/1**

050- **6** ¾ **Copper Cavalier**[88] 7327 3-8-12 46 oh1.................. (v[1]) AdamBeschizza 6 32
(Robert Cowell) *slowly ins stride: sn pushed along in rr: rdn over 2f out: styd on ins fnl f: nvr nrr* **8/1**[3]

056- **7** 1 ¾ **Keep To The Beat**[24] 8362 3-9-7 55.................................. JamieSpencer 2 39
(Kevin Ryan) *sn pushed along to chse ldrs: rdn over 1f out: wknd and eased fnl f* **9/2**[2]

600- **8** nk **Krackerjill (IRE)**[146] 5610 3-8-11 52.................. CharlotteJenner(7) 1 32
(Mark Usher) *mid-div: rdn over 2f out: wknd over 1f out* **10/1**

205- **9** 6 **Elualla (IRE)**[136] 5970 3-9-7 55.................................. AndrewMullen 10 16
(Nigel Tinkler) *chsd ldr: rdn over 2f out: wknd fnl f* **25/1**

1m 16.71s (1.71) **Going Correction** +0.15s/f (Slow) **9** Ran SP% **119.7**
Speed ratings (Par 95): **94,87,85,83,83 82,80,79,71**
CSF £10.46 CT £126.51 TOTE £2.00: £1.10, £2.70, £4.70; EX 10.30 Trifecta £143.30.
**Owner** G F Chesneaux **Bred** Patsy Myers & Edward Myers **Trained** Newmarket, Suffolk

**FOCUS**
A couple of unexposed sorts in a moderate handicap. The gallop was sound and the winner hung towards the far rail in the closing stages. The third has been rated close to her latest 5f effort.

## 166 32RED H'CAP 1m 141y(P)
**4:10** (4:10) (Class 5) (0-75,73) 3-Y-0 **£3,234** (£962; £481; £240) **Stalls** Low

Form RPR

423- **1** **Our Gabrial (IRE)**[31] 8267 3-9-7 73.................................. (b[1]) JamieSpencer 2 83+
(Richard Fahey) *hld up: hdwy over 2f out: led on bit over 1f out: edgd lft and sn clr: easily* **4/5**[1]

204- **2** 5 **Bonjour Steve**[42] 8126 3-8-11 63.................................. (b[1]) LukeMorris 3 60
(J S Moore) *trckd ldr after 1f: pushed along 3f out: rdn to ld and hung lft wl over 1f out: sn hdd and outpcd* **5/1**[3]

24-4 **3** 3 ¾ **Alfaayza (IRE)**[9] 51 3-9-3 69.................................. (p) MartinHarley 4 57
(K R Burke) *led: rdn and hdd wl over 1f out: wknd fnl f* **3/1**[2]

302- **4** 7 **Lady Knight (IRE)**[30] 8296 3-9-1 67.................................. LiamKeniry 1 39
(J S Moore) *chsd ldr 1f: remained handy: rdn over 2f out: wknd wl over 1f out* **7/1**

1m 51.88s (1.38) **Going Correction** +0.15s/f (Slow) **4** Ran SP% **109.7**
Speed ratings (Par 97): **99,94,91,85**
CSF £5.22 TOTE £1.50; EX 4.70 Trifecta £7.20.
**Owner** Dr Marwan Koukash **Bred** Michael Woodlock & Seamus Kennedy **Trained** Musley Bank, N Yorks

**FOCUS**
A modest handicap in which the gallop was on the steady side. The easy winner drifted towards the far rail in the closing stages. Not form to be too positive about.

## 167 32RED.COM MAIDEN STKS 1m 1f 103y(P)
4:40 (4:40) (Class 5) 3-Y-O £2,911 (£866; £432; £216) Stalls Low

Form RPR
02- 1 **Captain Morley**[17] 8415 3-9-5 0 JamieSpencer 6 81+
(David Simcock) *a.p: reminder over 2f out: led over 1f out: edgd lft: rdn out* 6/4[1]
2- 2 2 1/4 **L'Avenue (IRE)**[28] 8312 3-9-0 0 GrahamLee 2 71+
(James Tate) *a.p: chsd ldr over 5f out: rdn and hung lft over 1f out: styd on* 6/4[1]
00- 3 1 1/4 **Notebook**[16] 8425 3-9-5 0 DanielTudhope 4 74
(William Haggas) *led: rdn over 2f out: hdd over 1f out: styd on same pce ins fnl f* 20/1
30- 4 hd **Special Miss**[35] 8213 3-9-0 0 MartinHarley 7 68
(Marco Botti) *hld up: hdwy over 2f out: rdn over 1f out: styd on* 5/1[2]
5 5 **Wildes (IRE)** 3-9-5 0 StevieDonohoe 5 63
(Tim Pitt) *s.i.s: sn pushed along in rr: nvr nrr* 25/1
05-3 6 2 **Habdab**[9] 51 3-9-0 64 KieranO'Neill 3 54
(Richard Hannon) *chsd ldrs: lost pl over 3f out: hdwy over 2f out: rdn and wknd over 1f out* 14/1[3]
5- 7 39 **Rio Ranger (IRE)**[31] 8266 3-9-0 0 LukeMorris 8
(Bryan Smart) *hld up: hdwy over 5f out: rdn over 3f out: sn wknd* 33/1
0- 8 12 **Antioch (IRE)**[55] 7955 3-9-5 0 StephenCraine 1
(Jennie Candlish) *chsd ldr tl over 5f out: rdn and wknd 3f out* 50/1

2m 2.93s (1.23) **Going Correction** +0.15s/f (Slow) 8 Ran SP% 116.8
Speed ratings (Par 97): **100,98,96,96,92 90,55,45**
CSF £3.68 TOTE £2.60: £1.10, £1.10, £4.90; EX 4.10 Trifecta £35.60.
**Owner** Dr Marwan Koukash **Bred** Miss K Rausing **Trained** Newmarket, Suffolk

**FOCUS**
No more than a fair maiden. The gallop was soon steadied and the winner edged towards the far rail in the closing stages. The first two set an okay standard.

## 168 CORAL APP DOWNLOAD FROM THE APP STORE H'CAP 1m 4f 50y(P)
5:10 (5:11) (Class 5) (0-75,73) 4-Y-O+ £2,911 (£866; £432; £216) Stalls Low

Form RPR
500- 1 **My Lord**[95] 6787 6-9-2 65 LukeMorris 5 72
(Tony Carroll) *s.i.s: hld up: hdwy over 4f out: rdn to ld over 1f out: styd on u.p: jst hld on* 16/1
234- 2 shd **Gioia Di Vita**[41] 8139 4-8-13 73 RobJFitzpatrick(7) 2 80
(David Thompson) *a.p: rdn to chse ldr over 3f out: led over 2f out: hdd over 1f out: r.o* 5/2[2]
32-2 3 1 **Yasir (USA)**[8] 64 6-9-6 69 (p) LiamKeniry 4 74
(Conor Dore) *s.i.s: hdwy to ld after 1f: rdn and hdd over 2f out: styd on u.p* 3/1
06-2 4 3 1/2 **Easydoesit (IRE)**[4] 104 6-8-13 62 GrahamLee 8 62
(Tony Carroll) *led 1f: chsd ldr to 1/2-way: outpcd over 2f out: styd on ins fnl f* 9/4[1]
5 24 **Hejaz (IRE)**[209] 3453 4-9-3 70 StevieDonohoe 1 31
(Tim Pitt) *plld hrd and prom: trckd ldr 1/2-way tl rdn over 3f out: wknd over 2f out* 11/4[3]

2m 43.98s (2.88) **Going Correction** +0.15s/f (Slow)
**WFA** 4 from 5yo+ 4lb 5 Ran SP% 116.9
Speed ratings (Par 103): **96,95,95,92,76**
CSF £58.08 TOTE £15.40: £6.30, £2.00; EX 40.70 Trifecta £110.30.
**Owner** Robert E Lee Syndicate **Bred** Mrs Monica Teversham **Trained** Cropthorne, Worcs

**FOCUS**
An ordinary handicap in which Tony Carroll withdrew three of his five runners. The gallop was steady and the winner raced centre-to-far side in the straight. The runner-up and third have been rated to form.
T/Jkpt: £2057.50. Pool: £52,163.84 - 18.00 winning units. T/Plt: £65.70. Pool: £97,518.28 - 1083.26 winning units. T/Qpdt: £5.20. Pool: £6385.83 - 906.40 winning units. CR

# 57 DEAUVILLE (R-H)
Monday, January 13

**OFFICIAL GOING: Fibresand: standard**

## 169a PRIX DU MERLERAULT (MAIDEN) (3YO COLTS & GELDINGS) (FIBRESAND) 7f 110y
11:30 (12:00) 3-Y-O £10,000 (£4,000; £3,000; £2,000; £1,000)

RPR
1 **Got Fly (FR)** 3-9-2 0 JulienAuge 2 80
(C Ferland, France) 9/5[1]
2 nse **Blacktype (FR)**[32] 3-9-2 0 AntoineHamelin 9 80
(J-P Gauvin, France) 10/1
3 3 1/2 **Sabi Sand (FR)** 3-8-11 0 TheoBachelot 1 66
(S Wattel, France) 24/1
4 snk **Treasure Cay (IRE)**[16] 8425 3-9-2 0 IoritzMendizabal 8 71
(Paul Cole) *trckd ldr: rdn to chal 2f out: nt qckn and readily outpcd by front pair ins fnl f: kpt on but dropped to 4th fnl strides* 48/10[3]
5 1 **Cash In Mind (FR)**[9] 3-9-2 0 FabienLefebvre 5 68
(E J O'Neill, France) 50/1
6 shd **Dernier Empereur (FR)** 3-8-10 0 EnzoCorallo(6) 10 68
(C Ferland, France) 53/10
7 nk **Diamant De Vati (FR)** 3-8-11 0 JeromeCabre 7 62
(S Wattel, France) 42/1
8 1 1/4 **Grey Frost (FR)**[26] 3-8-8 0 EmmanuelEtienne(8) 3 64
(S Wattel, France) 28/1
9 3 **Bombelli (USA)**[15] 3-9-2 0 (b) Pierre-CharlesBoudot 11 57
(Mme A Fabre, France) 7/2[2]
10 2 **Rasuan (FR)**[118] 3-9-2 0 EddyHardouin 4 52
(Yannick Fouin, France) 66/1
11 1 1/2 **Kirikkale (FR)**[15] 3-9-2 0 AnthonyCrastus 13 48
(P Demercastel, France) 33/1
12 2 1/2 **Espoir En Tete (FR)**[156] 5296 3-9-2 0 RonanThomas 12 42
(P Adda, France) 42/1
13 1 **Riversou (FR)** 3-8-6 0 NicolasLarenaudie(5) 6 34
(J-M Lefebvre, France) 103/1

1m 31.58s (91.58) 13 Ran SP% 119.6
WIN (incl. 1 euro stake): 2.80. PLACES: 1.50, 2.70, 4.90. DF: 21.80. SF: 34.30.
**Owner** Brian Yeardley **Bred** Earl Haras De Magouet **Trained** France

# 93 SOUTHWELL (L-H)
Tuesday, January 14

**OFFICIAL GOING: Standard**
Wind: Moderate across Weather: Sunny

## 170 LADBROKES MOBILE H'CAP 7f (F)
12:40 (12:40) (Class 6) (0-65,64) 4-Y-O+ £1,940 (£577; £288; £144) Stalls Low

Form RPR
/60- 1 **Basingstoke (IRE)**[274] 1568 5-9-7 64 TomEaves 1 79
(Keith Dalgleish) *trckd ldrs: hdwy on inner 3f out: rdn to chal wl over 1f out: styd on to ld ins fnl f* 25/1
U53- 2 2 **Victorian Number (FR)**[17] 8432 6-9-7 64 GeorgeBaker 2 74
(Geoffrey Deacon) *led: pushed along wl over 2f: rdn and edgd lft 2f out: drvn and hdd ins fnl f: kpt on same pce* 5/1[3]
021- 3 1 3/4 **George Benjamin**[31] 8293 7-9-1 58 (t) AndrewMullen 4 63
(Michael Appleby) *dwlt: sn pushed along and bhd: hdwy on outer and wd st: rdn over 2f out: kpt on u.p appr fnl f: nrst fin* 11/10[1]
2-13 4 3/4 **Munaawib**[4] 126 6-9-4 61 (bt) BenCurtis 7 65
(David C Griffiths) *trckd ldrs: hdwy on outer 3f out: rdn over 2f out: drvn and no imp fr over 1f out* 3/1[2]
006- 5 1 **Star Up In The Sky (USA)**[123] 6367 4-9-0 57 (b[1]) GrahamLee 3 58
(Kevin Ryan) *cl up: rdn over 2f out: drvn and wknd over 1f out* 10/1
00-2 6 4 **Lutine Charlie (IRE)**[11] 30 7-8-12 55 (p) LukeMorris 5 46
(Pat Eddery) *chsd ldng pair: pushed along 3f out: rdn over 2f out and sn wknd* 7/1
300- 7 6 **Fairy Wing (IRE)**[16] 8439 7-9-6 63 (b) WilliamCarson 6 38
(Ann Stokell) *chsd ldrs: rdn along wl over 2f out: sn wknd* 25/1

1m 27.09s (-3.21) **Going Correction** -0.20s/f (Stan) 7 Ran SP% 118.6
Speed ratings (Par 101): **110,107,105,104,103 99,92**
CSF £149.40 CT £259.85 TOTE £19.60: £9.10, £2.80; EX 116.10 Trifecta £590.70.
**Owner** Straightline Construction Ltd **Bred** Mrs M Togher **Trained** Carluke, S Lanarks

**FOCUS**
An ordinary handicap. The best time on the card and it's been rated positively.

## 171 DOWNLOAD THE LADBROKES APP H'CAP 1m (F)
1:10 (1:10) (Class 6) (0-60,64) 4-Y-O+ £1,940 (£577; £288; £144) Stalls Low

Form RPR
60-2 1 **Queen Of Skies (IRE)**[13] 7 5-9-7 59 AndrewMullen 5 67
(Michael Appleby) *in tch: hdwy wl over 2f out: rdn to chal wl over 1f out: led appr fnl f: drvn and edgd rt ins fnl f: kpt on* 11/4[1]
4-01 2 1/2 **Mataajir (USA)**[7] 78 6-9-2 54 6ex (v) DaleSwift 6 61
(Derek Shaw) *towards rr: wd st: hdwy 2f out: sn rdn: styd on wl u.p fnl f* 6/1[3]
236- 3 3/4 **Quadriga (IRE)**[15] 8448 4-9-1 53 JimmyQuinn 13 58
(Robert Eddery) *trckd ldrs: hdwy 3f out: led over 2f out: rdn and hdd wl over 1f out: sn drvn and kpt on same pce fnl f* 12/1
00-1 4 nk **Outlaw Torn (IRE)**[8] 67 5-9-12 64 6ex (e) RobbieFitzpatrick 9 68
(Richard Guest) *in tch: hdwy to chse ldrs over 2f out: rdn wl over 1f out: kpt on same pce fnl f* 8/1
030- 5 shd **Xpres Maite**[18] 8409 11-8-13 56 (b) TimClark(5) 11 60
(Roy Bowring) *s.i.s and bhd: hdwy wl over 2f out: sn swtchd lft to inner: styd on fnl f: nrst fin* 16/1
26-0 6 2 **Bapak Pesta (IRE)**[13] 7 4-9-0 52 (p) GrahamLee 3 52
(Kevin Ryan) *chsd ldrs on inner: rdn along over 2f out: one pce* 25/1
2-13 7 5 **General Tufto**[7] 78 9-8-9 54 (b) JackGarritty(7) 1 42
(Charles Smith) *towards rr: rdn along and sme hdwy on inner over 2f out: nvr nr ldrs* 12/1
00-0 8 2 1/4 **Sky Crossing**[11] 29 5-9-6 58 JamesSullivan 7 41
(Tom Tate) *nvr bttr than midfield* 33/1
006- 9 3 1/2 **Chief Executive (IRE)**[15] 8443 4-9-5 57 (v[1]) JoeFanning 2 32
(Jo Hughes) *slt ld: rdn along 3f out: hdd over 2f out: sn drvn and wknd* 10/1
00-5 10 1 1/4 **Kai**[11] 33 5-8-7 45 (b) BenCurtis 8 17
(Alan McCabe) *prom: rdn along and wkng whn hmpd wl over 2f out: sn in rr* 50/1
55-1 11 nk **Xclusive**[7] 76 4-9-1 53 6ex LukeMorris 4 24
(Ronald Harris) *trckd ldrs: effrt whn bdly hmpd wl over 2f out: nt rcvr* 3/1[2]
04-2 12 1 **Partner's Gold (IRE)**[12] 12 4-8-6 47 ow1 (b) MarkCoumbe(3) 10 16
(Alan Berry) *dwlt: a in rr* 20/1
00-3 P **Kielty's Folly**[13] 7 10-8-13 51 TomEaves 12
(Brian Baugh) *cl up: effrt to chal whn lost action and p.u wl over 2f out: fatally injured* 33/1

1m 42.57s (-1.13) **Going Correction** -0.20s/f (Stan) 13 Ran SP% 123.9
Speed ratings (Par 101): **97,96,95,95,95 93,88,86,82,81 81,80,**
CSF £19.16 CT £184.16 TOTE £3.40: £1.20, £2.90, £4.00; EX 18.70 Trifecta £308.00.
**Owner** Ferrybank Properties Limited **Bred** Sheikh Sultan Bin Khalifa Al Nayhan **Trained** Danethorpe, Notts

**FOCUS**
A moderate handicap. Sound enough form rated through the winner to a small personal best, the runner-up to his latest C&D win and the fourth to his Polytrack best.

## 172 LADBROKES APPRENTICE H'CAP 1m (F)
1:45 (1:45) (Class 4) (0-80,80) 4-Y-O+ £4,690 (£1,395; £697; £348) Stalls Low

Form RPR
200- 1 **Noble Citizen (USA)**[54] 7988 9-9-2 80 (be) GeorgeBuckell(5) 5 92
(David Simcock) *dwlt and in rr: gd hdwy on inner 3f out: cl up 2f out: sn rdn: styd on to ld appr fnl f: drvn out* 8/1
422- 2 nk **Aqua Ardens (GER)**[14] 8453 6-8-12 74 (t) LouisSteward(3) 1 85
(George Baker) *trckd ldrs on inner: swtchd rt and smooth hdwy over 2f out: chal wl over 1f out: rdn and hung lft jst ins fnl f: ev ch whn edgd lft and no ex last 75yds* 5/1[3]
31-1 3 2 3/4 **Tatting**[11] 29 5-9-6 79 ShelleyBirkett 6 84+
(Chris Dwyer) *hld up towards rr: hdwy over 2f out: rdn over 1f out: styng on inner whn n.m.r ins fnl f: kpt on* 9/4[1]
/00- 4 nk **Warfare**[255] 2028 5-8-13 75 KevinStott(3) 7 79
(Kevin Ryan) *trckd ldng pair: hdwy 3f out: rdn and ch 2f out: drvn and hld whn n.m.r and hmpd ins fnl f* 12/1
04-4 5 3/4 **Sofias Number One (USA)**[12] 10 6-9-2 75 (b) TimClark 9 78
(Roy Bowring) *sn cl up: led 3f out: rdn over 2f out: drvn and hdd over 1f out: hld whn n.m.r and hmpd ins fnl f* 8/1
21-2 6 1 1/2 **No Win No Fee**[11] 29 4-8-7 66 oh1 (p) ShirleyTeasdale 3 65
(Michael Appleby) *trckd ldrs on inner: rdn along wl over 2f out: drvn and wknd over 1f out* 3/1[2]

211- **7** 3¾ **Pravda Street**[31] 8294 9-8-8 72 RobJFitzpatrick(5) 8 62
(Christopher Kellett) *chsd ldrs: rdn along over 2f out: sn wknd* **20/1**
122- **8** 16 **Our Ivor**[222] 3027 5-9-2 80 AlistairRawlinson(5) 4 34
(Michael Appleby) *led: rdn along and hdd 3f out: sn wknd and eased over 1f out* **8/1**
1m 40.67s (-3.03) **Going Correction** -0.20s/f (Stan) 8 Ran SP% **118.2**
Speed ratings (Par 105): **107,106,103,103,102 101,97,81**
CSF £49.19 CT £122.74 TOTE £14.40: £4.10, £1.90, £1.10; EX 43.60 Trifecta £221.90.
**Owner** Khalifa Dasmal **Bred** Don M Robinson **Trained** Newmarket, Suffolk
**FOCUS**
No a bad handicap for the class. The runner-up has been rated as running a small personal best.

## 173 32RED.COM H'CAP 7f (F)
**2:20** (2:20) (Class 6) (0-60,60) 3-Y-O **£1,940** (£577; £288; £144) **Stalls** Low

Form RPR
00-5 **1** **Frankthetank (IRE)**[1] 165 3-8-11 50 TomEaves 6 59
(Keith Dalgleish) *led 1 1/2f: cl up: pushed along 2f out: rdn over 1f out: styd on to ld ins fnl f: kpt on strly* **10/1**
310- **2** 2¼ **Witchy Woman**[105] 6914 3-9-5 58 DanielTudhope 10 61
(K R Burke) *prom: hdwy 3f out: led over 2f out: rdn over 1f out: hdd ins fnl f: kpt on same pce* **16/1**
44-3 **3** ½ **Day Star Lad**[13] 6 3-8-13 52 DaleSwift 4 54
(Derek Shaw) *trckd ldrs: hdwy over 2f out: rdn along wl over 1f out: kpt on u.p fnl f* **7/1**
005- **4** 1 **Illegal Action (USA)**[14] 8452 3-9-3 56 LiamKeniry 2 55
(Olly Stevens) *trckd ldrs on inner gng wl: effrt over 2f out: rdn wl over 1f out: ev ch tl one pce appr fnl f* **3/1**[1]
343- **5** ½ **Definite Secret**[28] 8317 3-9-5 58 GrahamLee 5 56
(James Tate) *trckd ldrs: n.m.r and lost pl bnd after 3f: wd st: hdwy over 2f out: sn rdn and kpt on appr fnl f* **9/2**[2]
030- **6** nk **Volodina (IRE)**[16] 8434 3-9-7 60 (b) BenCurtis 3 57
(Alan McCabe) *prom: led after 1 1/2f: rdn along 3f out: hdd over 2f out: sn drvn and grad wknd* **25/1**
053- **7** 5 **Solent Lad (USA)**[25] 8363 3-8-9 48 (p) JimmyQuinn 1 32
(Robert Eddery) *towards rr: effrt on inner 3f out: rdn along over 2f out: n.d* **8/1**
305- **8** ½ **Clapperboard**[32] 8273 3-9-6 59 [1] GeorgeBaker 8 42
(Paul Fitzsimons) *dwlt: a towards rr* **16/1**
000- **9** 8 **Trigger Park (IRE)**[33] 8262 3-8-13 52 LukeMorris 9 14
(Ronald Harris) *chsd ldrs: rdn along 3f out: sn wknd* **10/1**
006- **10** 3¼ **Tinchy Ryder**[85] 7419 3-8-13 52 JoeFanning 11
(Bryan Smart) *chsd ldrs on outer: rdn along 3f out: wknd over 2f out* **5/1**[3]
605- **11** 6 **Casper Lee (IRE)**[25] 8364 3-9-7 60 RussKennemore 7
(Alan Berry) *a in rr* **25/1**
1m 29.3s (-1.00) **Going Correction** -0.20s/f (Stan) 11 Ran SP% **121.1**
Speed ratings (Par 95): **97,94,93,92,92 91,86,85,76,72 65**
CSF £163.11 CT £1216.76 TOTE £16.90: £4.90, £5.80, £2.80; EX 227.80 Trifecta £1579.40.
**Owner** Straightline Construction Ltd **Bred** Burgage Stud **Trained** Carluke, S Lanarks
**FOCUS**
The pace was honest for this modest handicap. The fourth and sixth have been rated close to their marks.

## 174 32RED MAIDEN FILLIES' STKS 6f (F)
**2:50** (2:50) (Class 5) 3-Y-O+ **£2,587** (£770; £384; £192) **Stalls** Low

Form RPR
40-4 **1** **Guishan**[12] 8 4-9-10 55 (p) AndrewMullen 4 63
(Michael Appleby) *mde all: rdn clr wl over 1f out: drvn out* **10/1**[3]
562- **2** 1¾ **Diamondsinthesky (IRE)**[16] 8435 3-8-1 57 AdamMcLean(7) 6 48
(Derek Shaw) *chsd wnr: rdn along over 2f out: drvn over 1f out: kpt on one pce* **12/1**
623- **3** nk **Ishisoba**[16] 8437 4-9-10 50 LukeMorris 1 51
(Ronald Harris) *prom: rdn along 3f out: drvn 2f out and kpt on one pce* **7/1**[2]
5- **4** 1½ **Cocoa's Princess**[25] 8368 3-8-7 0 ow2 GeorgeChaloner(3) 5 44
(Richard Fahey) *trckd ldrs: effrt wl over 2f out: sn rdn and no imp* **20/1**
30- **5** ½ **La Paiva (FR)**[32] 8266 3-8-8 0 AdamBeschizza 7 40
(Scott Dixon) *chsd ldrs on outer: wd st: rdn over 2f out: grad wknd* **16/1**
06- **6** 2 **Whispering Star (USA)**[41] 8145 3-8-8 0 ChrisCatlin 2 34
(David Simcock) *dwlt: a in rr* **10/1**[3]
-4 **7** 7 **Daring Pursuit**[11] 31 4-9-3 0 RobJFitzpatrick(7) 8 16
(K R Burke) *racd wd: a in rr: bhd fr 1/2-way* **20/1**
23- **D** 1¾ **Billowing (IRE)**[69] 7764 3-8-8 0 (t) NickyMackay 3 53
(John Gosden) *towards rr: pushed along after 1f: hdwy on inner wl over 2f out: rdn wl over 1f out: drvn to chse wnr ins fnl f: no imp towards fin* **4/9**[1]
1m 15.6s (-0.90) **Going Correction** -0.20s/f (Stan)
**WFA** 3 from 4yo 16lb 8 Ran SP% **123.0**
Speed ratings (Par 100): **98,93,92,90,90 87,78,95**
CSF £16.11 TOTE £14.60: £2.20, £1.10, £2.50; EX 29.20 Trifecta £134.30.
**Owner** Brian D Cantle **Bred** B D Cantle **Trained** Danethorpe, Notts
**FOCUS**
A desperately weak fillies' maiden. The winner has been rated back to her best and the third and fourth give the form a chance to be a bit better.

## 175 COMPARE BOOKMAKERS AT BOOKMAKERS.CO.UK H'CAP 5f (F)
**3:25** (3:26) (Class 4) (0-85,83) 4-Y-O+ **£4,690** (£1,395; £697; £348) **Stalls** High

Form RPR
300- **1** **Sleepy Blue Ocean**[35] 8232 8-9-2 78 (p) RobertWinston 1 88
(John Balding) *cl up: effrt wl over 1f out: rdn to ld ent fnl f: hdd ins fnl 100yds: kpt on wl to ld again nr fin* **10/1**
43-1 **2** hd **Hannahs Turn**[9] 60 4-9-0 81 6ex ShelleyBirkett(5) 2 91
(Chris Dwyer) *trckd ldrs: hdwy on wd outside and cl up 1/2-way: rdn to chal over 1f out: slt ld wl ins fnl f: edgd rt and hdd nr fin* **7/4**[1]
31-2 **3** ½ **Bapak Bangsawan**[6] 80 4-8-4 71 ShaneGray(5) 5 79
(Kevin Ryan) *t.k.h: cl up: effrt wl over 1f out: sn rdn and ev ch tl drvn ins fnl f: no ex last 100yds* **5/1**[3]
12-5 **4** ¾ **Powerful Wind (IRE)**[13] 4 5-9-7 83 LukeMorris 8 88
(Ronald Harris) *led: rdn along 2f out: drvn and hdd ent fnl f: one pce* **10/1**
030- **5** 1½ **Moorhouse Lad**[40] 8167 11-9-3 79 GrahamLee 6 79
(Garry Moss) *cl up: rdn along 2f out: drvn and one pce appr fnl f* **10/1**
00-0 **6** 1½ **The Art Of Racing (IRE)**[6] 80 4-9-6 82 (b[1]) BenCurtis 3 76
(Alan McCabe) *chsd ldrs: rdn along 2f out: grad wknd* **25/1**
525- **7** 1¼ **Monsieur Jamie**[35] 8232 6-9-2 78 (v) JoeFanning 9 68
(J R Jenkins) *chsd ldrs: rdn along 2f out: grad wknd* **9/2**[2]
60-6 **8** 1½ **Clubland (IRE)**[11] 36 5-8-13 75 JimmyQuinn 4 59
(Roy Bowring) *dwlt: a towards rr* **8/1**

201- **9** hd **Beacon Tarn**[26] 8352 4-8-7 72 NeilFarley(3) 10 56
(Eric Alston) *chsd ldrs: rdn along 2f out: sn wknd* **14/1**
00-5 **10** ½ **Profile Star (IRE)**[11] 35 5-8-13 75 WilliamCarson 7 57
(Ann Stokell) *dwlt: a in rr* **50/1**
58.29s (-1.41) **Going Correction** -0.15s/f (Stan) 10 Ran SP% **122.1**
Speed ratings (Par 105): **105,104,103,102,100 97,95,93,93,92**
CSF £29.20 CT £105.40 TOTE £12.60: £4.30, £1.10, £1.90; EX 38.80 Trifecta £219.00.
**Owner** Tykes And Terriers Racing Club **Bred** Exors Of The Late N Ahamad & P C Scott **Trained** Scrooby, Notts
**FOCUS**
A modest sprint handicap. The runner-up has been rated close to her latest 6f effort, with the fourth also close to form.

## 176 CORAL APP DOWNLOAD FROM THE APP STORE H'CAP 1m 4f (F)
**3:55** (3:55) (Class 6) (0-60,60) 4-Y-O+ **£1,940** (£577; £288; £144) **Stalls** Low

Form RPR
0-14 **1** **Grandad Mac**[4] 117 6-9-3 54 LiamJones 6 63
(Alan Coogan) *cl up: led 5f out: rdn clr 3f out: drvn wl over 1f out: kpt on gamely fnl f* **11/4**[1]
33-2 **2** 1 **Rancho Montoya (IRE)**[11] 33 4-9-0 55 (v) LiamKeniry 8 62
(Andrew Balding) *trckd ldng pair: hdwy to chse wnr 3f out: rdn 2f out: drvn over 1f out: kpt on* **3/1**[2]
345- **3** 1¼ **Omega Omega**[26] 8349 5-8-9 46 (b) AdamBeschizza 3 51
(Julia Feilden) *hld up towards rr: hdwy 4f out: rdn to chse ldng pair over 2f out: drvn over 1f out: kpt on same pce fnl f* **5/1**[3]
364- **4** 6 **West End Lad**[18] 8410 11-9-4 60 (p) TimClark(5) 4 55
(Roy Bowring) *chsd ldrs: rdn along and outpcd 1/2-way: drvn 3f out: plugged on fnl 2f* **10/1**
50-2 **5** 1¼ **Loulou Vuitton**[9] 63 4-8-1 47 (p) ShelleyBirkett(5) 5 40
(Steph Hollinshead) *trckd ldrs: hdwy over 4f out: chsd ldng pair 3f out: sn rdn: drvn and one pce fnl 2f* **16/1**
251- **6** 3¾ **Goodlukin Lucy**[26] 8349 7-9-2 53 TomEaves 7 40
(Keith Dalgleish) *chsd ldrs: rdn along over 5f out and sn lost pl: plugged on u.p fnl 2f* **3/1**[2]
300- **7** 19 **Dontpaytheferryman (USA)**[26] 8349 9-9-4 55 (v) DaleSwift 1 12
(Peter Hiatt) *led: rdn along 1/2-way: hdd 5f out and sn wknd* **12/1**
04-0 **8** 34 **The Troyster**[7] 78 4-8-5 46 oh1 (b[1]) BenCurtis 2
(Brian Ellison) *a in rr: rdn along over 5f out: sn outpcd and bhd* **20/1**
2m 39.31s (-1.69) **Going Correction** -0.20s/f (Stan)
**WFA** 4 from 5yo+ 4lb 8 Ran SP% **120.8**
Speed ratings (Par 101): **97,96,95,91,90 88,75,52**
CSF £12.07 CT £40.12 TOTE £3.80: £1.60, £1.30, £2.00; EX 13.60 Trifecta £71.30.
**Owner** A B Coogan **Bred** Aiden Murphy **Trained** Soham, Cambs
**FOCUS**
A weak handicap, the winner confirming C&D form with the runner-up.
T/Plt: £210.10 to a £1 stake. Pool of £106101.18 - 368.49 winning tickets. T/Qpdt: £11.20 to a £1 stake. Pool of £12621.96 - 833.69 winning tickets. JR

# CAGNES-SUR-MER
Tuesday, January 14
**OFFICIAL GOING: Polytrack: standard**

## 177a PRIX DU DOCTEUR GAZAGNAIRE (CONDITIONS) (4YO+) (POLYTRACK) 1m 2f (D)
**12:30** (12:32) 4-Y-O+ **£11,666** (£4,666; £3,500; £2,333; £1,166)

RPR
**1** **Pump Pump Boy (FR)**[65] 7833 6-9-0 0 Pierre-CharlesBoudot 8 93
(M Pimbonnet, France) **13/2**
**2** nk **Faraway Run (IRE)**[46] 5-9-4 0 FranckBlondel 5 96
(P Khozian, France) **33/10**[2]
**3** ½ **Zack Hope**[65] 7833 6-9-4 0 TonyPiccone 9 95
(N Caullery, France) **97/10**
**4** nse **A Ready Dream (FR)**[42] 8144 5-9-6 0 StephanePasquier 1 97
(Rod Collet, France) **94/10**
**5** nse **Zagros (FR)**[60] 7921 5-9-0 0 RomainAuray 10 91
(J Heloury, France) **173/10**
**6** 2½ **Fundao (SWI)**[471] 5-9-6 0 (p) MickaelForest 7 92
(Carmen Bocskai, Switzerland) **40/1**
**7** 14 **Tepmokea (IRE)**[144] 5723 8-9-0 0 ThomasMessina 2 58
(Andrew Hollinshead) *t.k.h: trckd ldrs: scrubbed along over 2 1/2f out: shortlived effrt 2f out: sn rdn and wknd fr over 1 1/2f out* **38/1**
**8** ½ **Rock Of Nassau (FR)**[31] 8307 8-9-6 0 NicolasPerret 6 63
(X Nakkachdji, France) **23/10**[1]
**9** 2½ **Theo Danon (GER)**[42] 8144 6-9-6 0 EddyHardouin 3 58
(Mario Hofer, Germany) **10/1**
**10** 7 **Varadero (IRE)**[11] 6-9-6 0 IoritzMendizabal 4 44
(L Baudron, France) **58/10**[3]
2m 1.23s (121.23) 10 Ran SP% **120.1**
WIN (incl. 1 euro stake): 7.50. PLACES: 2.10, 1.50, 2.50. DF: 13.00. SF: 35.90.
**Owner** Benoit Bouret **Bred** J-C Bouret **Trained** France

## 178a PRIX DES BOUCHES DU LOUP (CLAIMER) (4YO+) (POLYTRACK) 1m 4f
**1:05** (1:10) 4-Y-O+ **£7,083** (£2,833; £2,125; £1,416; £708)

RPR
**1** **Destin Blue (FR)**[260] 6-9-2 0 EddyHardouin 13 80
(P Marion, Germany) **47/10**[3]
**2** nse **Street Lair (USA)**[11] 7-9-2 0 ThomasMessina 9 80
(L Baudron, France) **13/2**
**3** 1 **Diodoros (FR)**[109] 8-9-2 0 IoritzMendizabal 7 78
(F Chappet, France) **11/5**[1]
**4** shd **Uphold**[67] 7805 7-9-6 0 (b) Pierre-CharlesBoudot 4 82
(Gay Kelleway) *t.k.h: hld up in tch: effrt on outside over 2f out: cl 3rd and rdn 1 1/2f out: nt qckn: kpt on u.p fnl 75yds* **41/10**[2]
**5** 4½ **Reelside (FR)**[140] 5-8-13 0 (p) Francois-XavierBertras 12 68
(Y Fertillet, France) **197/10**
**6** nse **Fair Boss (IRE)**[56] 6-8-8 0 (p) BenjaminPinard(8) 1 71
(F Chappet, France) **116/10**
**7** 4½ **Ace Chop (FR)**[138] 5-9-2 0 NicolasPerret 6 64
(P Marion, Germany) **78/1**
**8** ½ **Always True (GER)**[13] 4-8-3 0 (p) ValentinGambart(5) 5 59
(N Milliere, France) **26/1**

9 1 **Eskadi (FR)**[31] 6-8-10 0....................(b) JimmyTastayre(6) 8 61
(C Boutin, France) **194/10**
10 2½ **Dynamoon (FR)**[32] 4-8-8 0....................(b) FabriceVeron 11 53
(H-A Pantall, France) **113/10**
0 **Passion Du Tango (FR)**[655] 5-9-3 0.......... StephaneRichardot 2
(T Larriviere, France) **70/1**
0 **Ash Cloud (FR)**[238] 5-8-13 0....................(p) AlexisBadel 3
(P Azzopardi, France) **77/1**
0 **Vespero (ITY)** 4-9-2 0.................... CFiocchi 10
(Stefano Botti, Italy) **217/10**

2m 31.04s (151.04)
**WFA** 4 from 5yo+ 4lb **13** Ran SP% **119.6**
WIN (incl. 1 euro stake): 5.70. PLACES: 1.70, 2.30, 1.70. DF: 19.30. SF: 42.60.
**Owner** Christian Faure **Bred** M Debeusscher **Trained** Germany

# [79]KEMPTON (A.W) (R-H)
Wednesday, January 15

**OFFICIAL GOING: Standard**
Wind: Moderate, across Weather: Changeable with showers

## 179 DINE IN THE PANORAMIC H'CAP 1m (P)
**4:25** (4:28) (Class 7) (0-50,50) 4-Y-O+ **£1,617** (£481; £240; £120) **Stalls** Low

Form RPR
00-4 **1** **Mr Chocolate Drop (IRE)**[13] 17 10-9-2 **45**..........(t) MartinHarley 2 54
(Mandy Rowland) *in tch in midfield: prog on inner jst over 2f out: sn rdn: clsd to ld and stl on inner 1f out: drvn out* **8/1**[3]
35-6 **2** *nk* **Supa Seeker (USA)**[13] 17 8-8-11 **47**.......(b[1]) MrAidenBlakemore(7) 11 55
(Tony Carroll) *t.k.h early: hld up and sn in last: prog over 2f out: threaded way through over 1f out: tk 2nd last 100yds: urged along and clsd on wnr nr fin* **10/1**
00-0 **3** 1¼ **Chandrayaan**[7] 81 7-9-6 **49**..........(v) JimmyQuinn 14 54
(John E Long) *rousted along early in midfield: racd on outer: drvn over 2f out: prog over 1f out: styd on to take 3rd nr fin* **25/1**
30-4 **4** ¾ **Bladewood Girl**[8] 78 6-9-7 **50**.......... JoeFanning 8 53
(J R Jenkins) *chsd ldrs on outer: drvn 2f out: disp 2nd over 1f out: kpt on same pce* **6/1**[2]
0/0- **5** *hd* **Prohibition (IRE)**[316] 884 8-9-7 **50**.......... LiamKeniry 12 53
(John Butler) *dropped in fr wd draw and last early: prog over 2f out: encouraged along over 1f out: rdn and kpt on one pce fnl f* **3/1**[1]
5-32 **6** *nk* **Huzzah (IRE)**[8] 78 9-9-2 **45**..........(t) AndrewMullen 4 47
(Michael Appleby) *plld hrd early: hld up in rr: rdn over 2f out: no prog tl styd on fnl f: nrst fin* **3/1**[1]
60-6 **7** ½ **Fairy Mist (IRE)**[5] 117 7-8-9 **45**..........(p) RyanWhile(7) 9 46
(John Bridger) *chsd ldr after 2f tl over 1f out: fdd* **20/1**
450- **8** ½ **Ryedale Lass**[26] 8371 6-9-4 **47**..........(b[1]) JamieSpencer 13 47
(Geoffrey Deacon) *led: hld together fr over 2f out tl rdn jst over 1f out: fnd nil: sn hdd & wknd* **12/1**
600- **9** 1¼ **Ermyntrude**[28] 8329 7-9-6 **49**..........(v) RobertWinston 10 46
(Pat Phelan) *nvr beyond midfield: u.p over 2f out: no prog over 1f out: fdd* **9/1**
/00- **10** 2 **Marvo**[142] 5816 10-9-7 **50**..........(b) DavidProbert 1 42
(Bernard Llewellyn) *chsd ldrs: drvn over 2f out: steadily wknd over 1f out* **25/1**
100- **11** 2½ **Ficelle (IRE)**[19] 8418 5-8-13 **45**.......... MatthewCosham(3) 3 32
(Nikki Evans) *t.k.h early: hld up in rr: pushed along over 3f out: struggling over 2f out* **66/1**
050- **12** 4 **Sally Bruce**[24] 8393 4-8-11 **47**..........(b) JenniferFerguson(7) 5 25
(Edward Creighton) *t.k.h early: hld up wl in rr on outer: no prog over 2f out: wl btn after* **33/1**
050- **13** 4 **Mistress Shy**[110] 6804 7-9-0 **48**..........(t) ShirleyTeasdale(5) 7 16
(Peter Hiatt) *chsd ldr 2f: u.p and losing pl over 3f out: sn no ch* **66/1**
50-6 **14** ½ **Maygo's Joy**[7] 90 4-9-2 **45**..........(b[1]) JimCrowley 6 12
(Ralph J Smith) *prom tl wknd rapidly wl over 1f out: heavily eased* **10/1**

1m 41.15s (1.35) **Going Correction** +0.25s/f (Slow) **14** Ran SP% **129.7**
Speed ratings (Par 97): **103,102,101,100,100 100,99,99,97,95 93,89,85,84**
CSF £86.38 CT £2003.71 TOTE £11.00: £2.10, £3.30, £9.30; EX 120.30 Trifecta £3752.10.
**Owner** Miss M E Rowland **Bred** P J Munnelly **Trained** Lower Blidworth, Notts
■ Stewards' Enquiry : Jimmy Quinn two-day ban: used whip above permitted level (Jan 29-30)

**FOCUS**
A low-grade handicap run at an even pace. Standard form.

## 180 BOOK NOW FOR JUMP RACING 22.02.14 CLAIMING STKS 1m (P)
**4:55** (4:55) (Class 6) 4-Y-O+ **£1,940** (£577; £288; £144) **Stalls** Low

Form RPR
402- **1** **Gabrial The Boss (USA)**[27] 8339 4-8-5 69..........(t) LukeMorris 5 65
(David Simcock) *trckd ldng trio: urged along and prog 2f out: led over 1f out: vigorously cajoled and kpt on fnl f* **11/8**[1]
100- **2** 1 **Mahadee (IRE)**[15] 8450 9-8-5 73..........(b) ChrisCatlin 3 63
(Ed de Giles) *dwlt: mostly in last: rdn and no prog 2f out: stl no hdwy 1f out: fnlly r.o ins fnl f: tk 2nd nr fin* **10/1**
62-4 **3** *nk* **Munsarim (IRE)**[7] 89 7-9-2 72..........(b) LouisSteward(7) 2 80
(Lee Carter) *trckd ldng pair: chal on inner 2f out: hanging and nt qckn fnl f* **5/1**[3]
051- **4** *nk* **Wakeup Little Suzy (IRE)**[27] 8339 4-9-0 73..........(t) MartinHarley 4 70
(Marco Botti) *chsd ldr: chal 2f out: upsides over 1f out: one pce fnl f* **9/4**[2]
15-2 **5** 2¼ **Copperwood**[11] 49 9-8-7 67.......... JimmyQuinn 1 58
(Lee Carter) *led: rdn and hdd over 1f out: wknd fnl f* **8/1**

1m 42.85s (3.05) **Going Correction** +0.25s/f (Slow) **5** Ran SP% **109.7**
Speed ratings (Par 101): **94,93,92,92,90**
CSF £14.86 TOTE £1.70: £1.10, £5.30; EX 14.40 Trifecta £70.80.
**Owner** Dr Marwan Koukash **Bred** Hunter Valley Farm Et Al **Trained** Newmarket, Suffolk

**FOCUS**
A fair claimer. The winner didn't have to match his best to score.

## 181 £500 FREE BETS AT BETDAQ H'CAP (LONDON MILE SERIES QUALIFIER) 1m (P)
**5:25** (5:26) (Class 5) (0-75,75) 4-Y-O+ **£2,587** (£770; £384; £192) **Stalls** Low

Form RPR
112- **1** **Diplomatic (IRE)**[65] 7836 9-9-3 **71**..........(p) AdamKirby 10 78+
(Michael Squance) *hld up in last trio: plenty to do once pce lifted over 2f out: clsd on inner fr over 1f out: sustained effrt u.p to ld last strides: did wl to win* **3/1**[2]
50-4 **2** *nk* **Greensward**[5] 113 8-9-2 **70**..........(b) LiamKeniry 3 76
(Conor Dore) *t.k.h: trckd ldng pair: chal fr 2f out: led ins fnl f: kpt on but hdd last strides* **20/1**
06-0 **3** 1 **Camachoice (IRE)**[11] 56 4-9-7 **75**..........(p) MartinHarley 5 79
(Marco Botti) *led at mod pce: kicked on wl over 2f out: sn hrd pressed: hdd ins fnl f: one pce* **11/2**
/10- **4** *hd* **Captain Starlight (IRE)**[183] 4383 4-9-5 **73**.......... FergusSweeney 9 76
(Jo Crowley) *trckd ldng trio: nt clr run 2f out and over 1f out: swtchd lft fnl f: nt qckn but styd on* **10/1**
0/0- **5** ¾ **Cathedral**[346] 511 5-9-0 **68**.......... SeanLevey 1 70
(Michael Wigham) *t.k.h: hld up in midfield: urged along once pce lifted over 2f out: didn't look v determined but styd on fnl f* **11/4**[1]
030- **6** *hd* **Zaeem**[40] 8179 5-9-1 **69**.......... RobertWinston 6 70
(Dean Ivory) *nt that wl away but rcvrd to chse ldr: chal and upsides 2f out: nt qckn over 1f out: fdd fnl f* **8/1**
00-2 **7** 2 **Conry (IRE)**[11] 57 8-8-11 **65**.......... StevieDonohoe 4 61
(Ian Williams) *hld up in midfield: rdn whn pce lifted over 2f out: nvr able to make any real inroads* **5/1**[3]
413- **8** 2 **Admirable Art (IRE)**[86] 7430 4-8-7 **61**.......... LukeMorris 11 53
(Tony Carroll) *racd wd in last trio: shkn up once pce lifted over 2f out: struggling after* **16/1**
600- **9** 1¼ **Hill Of Dreams (IRE)**[30] 8314 5-9-1 **69**..........(p) JimCrowley 8 58
(Dean Ivory) *hld up in last trio: struggling once pce lifted over 2f out: shkn up and no prog* **12/1**

1m 42.82s (3.02) **Going Correction** +0.25s/f (Slow) **9** Ran SP% **122.3**
Speed ratings (Par 103): **94,93,92,92,91 91,89,87,86**
CSF £64.07 CT £329.62 TOTE £3.10: £1.10, £6.90, £1.80; EX 59.70 Trifecta £268.40.
**Owner** Miss K Squance **Bred** Darley **Trained** Newmarket, Suffolk

**FOCUS**
A fair handicap run at a steady gallop, the pace only quickening on the turn into the home straight. Muddling form.

## 182 BETDAQ - THE SPORTS BETTING EXCHANGE H'CAP 2m (P)
**5:55** (5:55) (Class 4) (0-85,85) 4-Y-O+ **£4,690** (£1,395; £697; £348) **Stalls** Low

Form RPR
214- **1** **Norfolk Sky**[24] 8392 5-9-2 **73**.......... FergusSweeney 3 83
(Laura Mongan) *hld up in 4th: only one of chsng pce gng wl 3f out: wnt 2nd over 2f out: clsd and nudged into ld 1f out: comf* **4/1**[3]
335- **2** 3½ **Icebuster**[18] 8429 6-9-7 **85**.......... PatMillman(7) 5 91
(Rod Millman) *stdd s: tk fierce hold in last: plld way through to ld 1/2-way: sn clr: 6 l up 4f out: rdn 2f out: hdd and no ex 1f out* **7/4**[1]
13-4 **3** 4 **Layline (IRE)**[13] 16 7-9-7 **78**.......... DavidProbert 1 79
(Gay Kelleway) *t.k.h: cl up 6f then pce qcknd: rdn over 3f out: one pce and n.d after: kpt on* **6/1**
021- **4** 3¼ **First Warning**[97] 7158 4-9-0 **78**.......... StevieDonohoe 2 75
(Tim Pitt) *led at modest pce: hdd 1/2-way but clr of rest: chsd ldr to over 2f out: fdd* **5/2**[2]
210- **5** 43 **Honourable Knight (IRE)**[122] 6424 6-9-1 **72**.......... JimCrowley 4 18
(Mark Usher) *chsd ldr over 6f: sn lost pl once pce qckned: rdn and wknd over 3f out: t.o and eased* **8/1**

3m 34.8s (4.70) **Going Correction** +0.25s/f (Slow)
**WFA** 4 from 5yo+ 7lb **5** Ran SP% **110.3**
Speed ratings (Par 105): **98,96,94,92,71**
CSF £11.49 TOTE £4.00: £2.50, £1.10; EX 11.80 Trifecta £29.60.
**Owner** Condover Racing **Bred** Farmers Hill Stud **Trained** Epsom, Surrey

**FOCUS**
A fair staying handicap but the pace was muddling and the form should be treated with caution. The runner-up has been rated to form.

## 183 WINNERS ARE WELCOME AT BETDAQ CONDITIONS STKS (FAST TRACK QUALIFIER) 6f (P)
**6:25** (6:25) (Class 2) 3-Y-O
**£11,827** (£3,541; £1,770; £885; £442; £222) **Stalls** Low

Form RPR
540- **1** **Alutiq (IRE)**[109] 6836 3-8-11 95.......... JamieSpencer 6 89
(Eve Johnson Houghton) *hld up in 4th: prog to chse ldr over 1f out: sn drvn: clsd fnl f to ld last strides: readily* **5/4**[1]
211- **2** ½ **Oriental Relation (IRE)**[19] 8404 3-9-2 81..........(b) GrahamLee 2 92
(James Given) *led: wnt for home jst over 2f out: stl 2 l up 1f out: collared last strides* **5/1**[3]
246- **3** 2¼ **Scruffy Tramp (IRE)**[39] 8203 3-9-2 90.......... RobertWinston 3 85
(Alan Bailey) *hld up in 5th: tried to cl 2f out: one pce after: kpt on to take 3rd nr fin* **12/1**
4 ½ **Golden Amber (IRE)**[84] 7473 3-8-11 90.......... JimCrowley 1 78
(Dean Ivory) *trckd ldng pair: wnt 2nd 2f out to over 1f out: fdd fnl f* **7/1**
32-1 **5** 2½ **Captain Myles (IRE)**[13] 19 3-9-2 81..........(t) StevieDonohoe 5 75
(Tim Pitt) *hld up in last: hung lft briefly bnd 3f out: lft w lot to do after ldng wnt for home 2f out: shkn up over 1f out: nvr involved* **25/1**
223- **6** 2½ **Ticking Katie (IRE)**[109] 6839 3-8-11 89.......... MartinHarley 4 62
(K R Burke) *chsd ldr to 2f out: wknd over 1f out* **11/4**[2]

1m 12.29s (-0.81) **Going Correction** +0.25s/f (Slow) **6** Ran SP% **111.8**
Speed ratings (Par 103): **115,114,111,110,107 104**
CSF £7.93 TOTE £2.10: £1.50, £2.00; EX 8.30 Trifecta £36.20.
**Owner** Qatar Racing Limited **Bred** Wardstown Stud Ltd **Trained** Blewbury, Oxon

**FOCUS**
An interesting conditions event despite the small field and the form should work out. The level is a bit fluid but literal/positive view taken for the time being.

## 184 BETDAQ 1ST UK RACE COMMISSION FREE H'CAP 7f (P)
**6:55** (6:55) (Class 6) (0-55,55) 4-Y-O+ **£1,940** (£577; £288; £144) **Stalls** Low

Form RPR
05-2 **1** **Minimee**[9] 65 4-9-5 **53**..........(v) PaddyAspell 2 61
(Phil McEntee) *prom: trckd ldr over 2f out: pushed into ld over 1f out: hrd pressed fnl f: drvn and hld on wl* **5/1**[2]
34-0 **2** *nk* **Tijuca (IRE)**[8] 78 5-9-4 **52**.......... AdamKirby 3 59
(Ed de Giles) *hld up towards rr: prog jst over 2f out: rdn to press wnr fnl f: styd on but jst hld* **10/1**
500- **3** 1½ **Buaiteoir (FR)**[16] 8448 8-8-13 **50**.......... MatthewCosham(3) 1 53
(Nikki Evans) *in tch in midfield: rdn over 2f out: styd on fr over 1f out to take 3rd last stride* **20/1**
520- **4** *shd* **Welsh Inlet (IRE)**[76] 7643 6-9-5 **53**.......... KieranO'Neill 10 56
(John Bridger) *plld hrd early: hld up in last pair: rdn and prog on inner 2f out: chsd ldng pair fnl f: no imp: lost 3rd last stride* **8/1**[3]

05-3 **5** ¾ **Surrey Dream (IRE)**[7] 81 5-8-12 **46** oh1 ........................ SeanLevey 8 47
(John Bridger) *settled towards rr: pushed along and dropped to last jst over 2f out: rdn over 1f out: styd on: unable to rch ldrs* **12/1**

000- **6** ¾ **Ryan Style (IRE)**[42] 8151 8-9-2 **53** ..................(p) MarkCoumbe(3) 4 52
(Lisa Williamson) *t.k.h: hld up in last pair: rdn 2f out: kpt on same pce after: n.d* **20/1**

40-6 **7** 1 ¼ **Custom House (IRE)**[7] 81 6-8-9 **46** .................. NataliaGemelova(3) 5 41
(John E Long) *in tch in midfield: rdn 3f out: struggling 2f out: no imp after* **16/1**

000- **8** nse **Strategic Action (IRE)**[32] 8293 5-9-3 **51** ......................(p) LiamKeniry 12 46
(Linda Jewell) *led: rdn and hdd over 1f out: wknd fnl f* **14/1**

645- **9** ¾ **Torres Del Paine**[16] 8446 7-9-5 **53** .................................. DavidProbert 9 46
(Brett Johnson) *hld up towards rr on outer: sme prog and wdst of all 2f out: no hdwy 1f out: fdd* **5/1**[2]

235- **10** 2 ¾ **Pour La Victoire (IRE)**[102] 7034 4-9-4 **52** ........................ LukeMorris 6 38
(Tony Carroll) *prom: rdn over 2f out: steadily wknd over 1f out* **9/4**[1]

40-5 **11** nk **Direct Trade**[13] 18 4-8-5 **46** oh1 ......................(e) CharlotteJenner(7) 11 31
(Mark Usher) *pressed ldr to over 2f out: wknd qckly* **25/1**

1m 27.28s (1.28) **Going Correction** +0.25s/f (Slow) **11** Ran SP% **117.9**
Speed ratings (Par 101): **102,101,99,99,98 98,96,96,95,92 92**
CSF £52.61 CT £675.12 TOTE £3.10: £1.20, £3.50, £6.40; EX 35.70 Trifecta £1219.90.
**Owner** Eventmaker Racehorses **Bred** M A Jarvis **Trained** Newmarket, Suffolk

**FOCUS**
A moderate but competitive handicap. The runner-up has been rated as running a small personal best.

## 185 KEMPTON FOR WEDDINGS H'CAP — 1m 4f (P)
**7:25** (7:27) (Class 7) (0-50,52) 4-Y-0+ — **£1,617** (£481; £240; £120) **Stalls** Centre

Form — RPR

000- **1** **Midnight Sequel**[100] 7081 5-9-4 **47** ............................(p) JamieSpencer 9 60+
(Neil Mulholland) *hld up in midfield: smooth prog 3f out: led over 2f out: sn drvn wl clr: in n.d after* **9/4**[1]

0/0- **2** 3 **Graylyn Ruby (FR)**[47] 7159 9-9-4 **47** ........................ WilliamCarson 1 53
(Robin Dickin) *hld up in midfield: prog on inner over 2f out: rdn to chse wnr over 1f out: styd on but no ch* **16/1**

143- **3** 1 **Ice Apple**[33] 8268 6-9-4 **47** ............................................ JimmyQuinn 10 51
(John E Long) *towards rr: shoved along 4f out: trying to make prog whn nowhere to go and swtchd lft over 2f out: styd on fnl 2f to take 3rd ins fnl f* **8/1**[3]

00- **4** 1 ½ **Illegale (IRE)**[58] 7636 8-9-2 **48** ..........................(t) MatthewCosham(3) 11 50
(Nikki Evans) *racd on outer towards rr: rdn and struggling 3f out: kpt on u.p fr 2f out to take 4th ins fnl f* **66/1**

/56- **5** 2 ¾ **Zelos Diktator**[10] 704 8-9-4 **47** ........................................ JohnFahy 4 44
(Sean Curran) *slowly away and reminders: mostly in last pair tl rdn and sme prog over 2f out: kpt on to take 5th nr fin: no ch* **33/1**

500- **6** ¾ **Beggers Belief**[30] 8121 6-9-7 **50** ......................(p) FergusSweeney 8 46
(Zoe Davison) *wl plcd: rdn to dispute 2nd 2f out to over 1f out: wknd fnl f* **20/1**

000- **7** ½ **Mohair**[85] 7440 5-9-5 **48** ................................................. LukeMorris 2 43
(Tony Carroll) *prom: rdn to dispute 2nd 2f out to over 1f out: wknd fnl f* **9/2**[2]

500- **8** hd **Kindia (IRE)**[42] 8149 6-9-6 **49** ..............................(p) JoeFanning 5 44
(Michael Attwater) *t.k.h: prom: rdn over 2f out: steadily wknd* **16/1**

240- **9** 3 ½ **Like Clockwork**[47] 7951 5-9-7 **50** .................................. BenCurtis 7 39
(Mark H Tompkins) *mde most to over 2f out: sn lost pl and btn* **8/1**[3]

005- **10** 4 ½ **Parsons Green**[34] 8260 5-9-2 **45** .................................. LiamJones 6 27
(Michael Attwater) *a in rr: rdn and no prog on inner over 2f out: wknd over 1f out* **66/1**

00-0 **11** 3 ¾ **Midnight Bahia (IRE)**[9] 68 5-9-6 **49** ..........................(t[1]) AdamKirby 13 25
(Dean Ivory) *sn pressed ldr: rdn over 3f out: wknd over 2f out* **16/1**

540- **12** 1 ¾ **Kaylee**[24] 8393 5-9-5 **48** ............................................ ChrisCatlin 3 21
(Brett Johnson) *stdd s: t.k.h in last pair: shkn up 3f out: no prog* **50/1**

60-1 **13** 1 **Primacy (IRE)**[9] 68 5-9-9 **52** 6ex ................................ LiamKeniry 14 24
(Neil Mulholland) *racd wd: trckd ldrs: rdn over 3f out: wknd over 2f out* **9/2**[2]

2m 36.19s (1.69) **Going Correction** +0.25s/f (Slow)
**WFA** 4 from 5yo+ 4lb **13** Ran SP% **119.7**
Speed ratings (Par 97): **104,102,101,100,98 98,97,97,95,92 89,88,87**
CSF £41.82 CT £253.46 TOTE £3.80: £1.50, £6.80, £2.80; EX 49.40 Trifecta £534.90.
**Owner** Dajam Ltd **Bred** M Burbidge **Trained** Limpley Stoke, Wilts

**FOCUS**
A moderate handicap, the winner won unchallenged. Some dubious types in the line-up leaves the level a bit fluid.
T/Jkpt: £6,124.50 to a £1 stake. Pool: £12939.16 - 1.50 winning tickets T/Plt: £434.20 to a £1 stake. Pool: £97810.02 - 164.42 winning tickets T/Qpdt: £15.30 to a £1 stake. Pool: £12617.40 - 608.63 winning tickets JN

# 154 LINGFIELD (L-H)
## Wednesday, January 15

**OFFICIAL GOING: Standard**
Wind: medium, half behind Weather: drizzle

## 186 32RED ON THE APP STORE CLAIMING STKS — 1m 7f 169y(P)
**12:30** (12:30) (Class 6) 4-Y-0+ — £2,385 (£704; £352) **Stalls** Low

Form — RPR

01-1 **1** **La Estrella (USA)**[10] 63 11-9-10 87 ................................ GrahamLee 3 80+
(Don Cantillon) *led and sn clr: rdn over 2f out: edgd rt u.p and hdd fnl 150yds: battled bk and led again fnl 50yds: styd on wl: rdn out* **4/7**[1]

200- **2** nk **While You Wait (IRE)**[55] 7840 5-9-7 72 ............................ SeanLevey 6 77
(Gary Moore) *hld up in tch in last pair: chsd clr ldr wl over 2f out: rdn and chal 1f out: led fnl 150yds: hdd and no ex fnl 50yds* **3/1**[2]

0/0- **3** 21 **Bollin Judith**[41] 5168 8-8-11 80 ..............................(t) JamieSpencer 5 48
(Jim Best) *s.i.s: sn rcvrd and chsd wnr: rdn over 3f out: lost 2nd wl over 2f out and sn btn: eased fnl f* **5/1**[3]

534/ **4** 96 **Tirol Livit (IRE)**[910] 821 11-9-0 36 ................................ WilliamCarson 2
(Mark Hoad) *in tch in last pair: rdn 5f out: sn lost tch: t.o and eased over 2f out* **100/1**

3m 24.83s (-0.87) **Going Correction** -0.025s/f (Stan) **4** Ran SP% **106.3**
Speed ratings (Par 101): **101,100,90,42**
CSF £2.46 TOTE £1.30; EX 2.00 Trifecta £2.80.
**Owner** Don Cantillon **Bred** Five Horses Ltd And Theatrical Syndicate **Trained** Newmarket, Suffolk
■ Stewards' Enquiry : Graham Lee one-day ban: careless riding (Jan 29)

**FOCUS**
A decent claimer on official figures. Shaky form with the runner-up having been below his best since the summer.

## 187 32RED CASINO CLAIMING STKS — 7f 1y(P)
**1:00** (1:01) (Class 6) 3-Y-0 — **£2,385** (£704; £352) **Stalls** Low

Form — RPR

331- **1** **Kantara Castle (IRE)**[30] 8311 3-9-1 72 ............................ SeanLevey 1 67
(Richard Hannon) *broke wl: stdd and chsd ldng pair: swtchd out rt and effrt to chse ldr over 1f out: drvn to ld fnl 150yds: styd on wl u.p* **3/1**[1]

22-2 **2** 1 **Ain't No Surprise (IRE)**[13] 19 3-8-10 62 ........................ WilliamCarson 5 59
(Jamie Osborne) *s.i.s: bhd and pushed along early: hdwy into midfield 4f out: effrt to chse ldrs and swtchd out rt wl over 1f out: kpt on u.p ins fnl f: wnt 2nd towards fin* **5/1**[3]

04-2 **3** ¾ **Bonjour Steve**[2] 166 3-8-13 63 ........................................(b) LiamKeniry 7 60
(J S Moore) *sn led: rdn over 2f out: hdd and edgd rt fnl 150yds: styd on same pce after: lost 2nd towards fin* **4/1**[2]

355- **4** ¾ **Rose Buck**[25] 8382 3-8-7 61 ........................................ MarkCoumbe(3) 9 56
(Lee Carter) *sn pressing ldr: rdn and unable qck wl over 1f out: kpt on same pce u.p ins fnl f* **12/1**

223- **5** nk **Dancing Sal (IRE)**[19] 8414 3-8-2 64 ................................ EoinWalsh(5) 8 52
(David Evans) *hld up in tch in midfield: rdn and unable qck whn swtchd lft over 1f out: swtchd bk rt ins fnl f: styd on u.p fnl 100yds* **6/1**

255- **6** 2 **Conflicting**[46] 8113 3-9-3 68 ........................................ JamieSpencer 4 57
(Richard Hannon) *stdd s: hld up in tch in rr: rdn and effrt over 1f out: kpt on fnl f: nvr trbld ldrs* **4/1**[2]

006- **7** 1 **Mighty Force (IRE)**[28] 8333 3-9-1 62 ................................ LukeMorris 10 52
(Nick Littmoden) *stdd and dropped in bhd after s: rdn and hdwy over 1f out: no imp ins fnl f* **14/1**

00- **8** 2 ¼ **Emerald Gg (IRE)**[85] 7568 3-8-13 0 .................................. LiamJones 3 44
(J S Moore) *rn green and rdn along early: in tch in midfield: rdn and struggling over 2f out: wknd over 1f out* **33/1**

0- **U** **Marti's Boy**[15] 8451 3-8-6 0 ........................................ KristyFrench(7) 2
(J S Moore) *in tch in midfield on inner: shuffled bk to rr 3f out: pushed along and hung rt jst over 1f out: stl bhd whn uns rdr fnl 75yds* **100/1**

1m 25.23s (0.43) **Going Correction** -0.025s/f (Stan) **9** Ran SP% **114.2**
Speed ratings (Par 95): **96,94,94,93,92 90,89,86,**
CSF £18.01 TOTE £3.50: £1.30, £2.10, £2.10; EX 17.00 Trifecta £60.30.Bonjour Steve was claimed by Mr R. J. Price for £6,000. Dancing Sal was claimed by Mr Paul Naughton for £5,000.
**Owner** Middleham Park Racing XXV **Bred** Tally-Ho Stud **Trained** East Everleigh, Wilts

**FOCUS**
A weak claimer and a chance could have been given to a few of these. Muddling form and rated slightly cautiously.

## 188 32RED ON THE APP STORE MEDIAN AUCTION MAIDEN STKS — 7f 1y(P)
**1:30** (2:47) (Class 6) 3-Y-0 — **£2,385** (£704; £352) **Stalls** Low

Form — RPR

05-2 **1** **Excellent Royale (IRE)**[9] 70 3-9-5 67 ........................ RobertWinston 5 73
(Charles Hills) *mde all: rdn and wnt clr wl over 1f out: hung rt and in command fnl f: comf* **2/1**[2]

3- **2** 2 ¼ **Bowie Boy (IRE)**[28] 8333 3-9-5 0 .................................. JimCrowley 3 67
(Ralph Beckett) *chsd ldrs: rdn and effrt ent fnl 2f: hung lft u.p but hdwy to chse clr wnr 1f out: kpt on but no imp* **6/4**[1]

**3** 1 ½ **Silent Pursuit** 3-9-0 0 ................................................ TomEaves 1 58
(Philip Hide) *hld up in tch in midfield: 5th and rdn wl over 1f out: no imp tl styd on steadily ins fnl f: snatched 3rd on post* **33/1**

542- **4** nse **Sebs Sensei (IRE)**[15] 8452 3-9-5 73 ............................ WilliamCarson 2 63
(Mark Hoad) *chsd ldrs: rdn and chsd wnr 2f out: drvn and edgd out rt wl over 1f out: unable qck and 3rd 1f out: kpt on same pce: lost 3rd on post* **7/1**[3]

0- **5** 1 ¼ **Sand Stormer (IRE)**[15] 8451 3-9-5 0 .................................. GrahamLee 6 60
(William Muir) *t.k.h: hld up in tch in midfield: hdwy to chse wnr 5f out tl 2f out: sn drvn and outpcd: wknd ins fnl f* **8/1**

06- **6** 1 ¾ **Harry's Summer (USA)**[15] 8451 3-8-12 0 .................... JordanVaughan(7) 7 55
(Nick Littmoden) *t.k.h: hld up in tch in midfield: rdn and unable qck ent fnl 2f: styd on same pce fr over 1f out* **25/1**

**7** 1 ½ **Jammy Moment** 3-9-0 0 ................................................ LukeMorris 9 46
(William Muir) *in tch in midfield: rdn and unable qck over 2f out: wknd over 1f out* **20/1**

0 **8** 2 ½ **Needs The Run**[4] 142 3-9-5 0 ........................................ AdamKirby 4 45
(David Evans) *stdd s: t.k.h: hld up in tch in rr: rdn and no hdwy 2f out: nvr trbld ldrs* **25/1**

0- **9** hd **French Accent**[28] 8328 3-8-11 0 .................................. RobertTart(3) 8 39
(John Best) *s.i.s: rdn over 2f out: no imp over 1f out: nvr trbld ldrs* **100/1**

**10** 1 **Feisty Dragon (IRE)** 3-9-0 0 ........................................ FergusSweeney 10 37
(Jamie Osborne) *wnt rt s: s.i.s: a in rr: n.d* **50/1**

1m 26.09s (1.29) **Going Correction** -0.025s/f (Stan) **10** Ran SP% **115.3**
Speed ratings (Par 95): **91,88,86,86,85 83,81,78,78,77**
CSF £4.85 TOTE £3.00: £1.30, £1.10, £6.10; EX 7.20 Trifecta £165.10.
**Owner** Jim & Susan Hill **Bred** P Kelly **Trained** Lambourn, Berks

**FOCUS**
There was no depth beyond the market leaders but with a 73-rated runner back in fourth this looked a fair enough maiden. The fourth has been rated below form on his first start for his new yard, while the sixth has been rated close to his initial efforts.

## 189 32RED.COM MAIDEN FILLIES' STKS — 1m 1y(P)
**2:00** (3:09) (Class 5) 3-Y-0+ — **£3,067** (£905; £453) **Stalls** High

Form — RPR

024- **1** **Just One Kiss**[15] 8454 4-9-13 75 .................................... JimCrowley 5 78
(Lady Cecil) *travelled strly: pressed ldr tl led 2f out: rdn and wnt clr over 1f out: in n.d and r.o wl fnl f: comf* **5/4**[1]

6- **2** 5 **Speechday (IRE)**[27] 8342 3-8-7 0 .................................... LukeMorris 2 63
(Marco Botti) *restless stalls: chsd ldrs: rdn 2f out: 3rd and no ch w wnr over 1f out: wnt 2nd ins fnl f: kpt on* **10/1**

4- **3** 2 ¾ **Windlass (IRE)**[62] 7875 3-8-7 0 .................................... NickyMackay 1 56
(John Gosden) *led tl 2f out: sn rdn and outpcd by wnr: lost 2nd and wknd ins fnl f* **9/4**[2]

/ **4** ½ **Against The Tide (IRE)** 4-9-13 0 .................................. SeanLevey 9 59
(Richard Hannon) *hld up in tch in last trio: hdwy 1/2-way: midfield and rdn over 2f out: chsd clr ldng trio over 1f out: styd on steadily but no threat to wnr: b.b.v* **8/1**[3]

4- **5** 1 **Marphilly (IRE)**[28] 8328 3-8-7 0 .................................... JohnFahy 10 53
(John Best) *stdd s: hld up in tch in last trio: hdwy over 2f out: rdn and no imp over 1f out: kpt on but n.d* **12/1**

0 **6** *1 1/2* **Intensive (IRE)**[12] 37 3-8-1 0 ow1 ............................ JohnLawson(7) 6 50?
(Jamie Osborne) *chsd ldrs: outpcd and lost pl on outer bnd 2f out: edging lft ent fnl f: swtchd rt and styd on same pce after* **100/1**

4- **7** *4 1/2* **Windshield**[26] 8362 3-8-7 0 ............................ LiamJones 4 39
(Sir Mark Prescott Bt) *in tch in midfield: rdn over 4f out: outpcd and btn over 2f out: wknd over 1f out* **16/1**

**8** *nk* **Laguna Belle** 4-9-13 0 ............................ FergusSweeney 8 42
(Pat Phelan) *hld up in tch in midfield: hmpd and dropped to last trio 5f out: rdn and struggling over 2f out: wl hld after* **100/1**

**9** *2 3/4* **Pembroke Pride** 4-9-13 0 ............................ TomEaves 7 36
(Philip Hide) *stdd s: hld up in tch in last trio: rdn over 3f out: outpcd over 2f out: wl hld after* **100/1**

**10** *9* **Concoct (IRE)** 3-8-7 0 ............................ RichardKingscote 3 11
(Tom Dascombe) *in tch in midfield: rdn and lost pl wl over 3f out: flashed tail u.p and sn struggling: wl bhd over 1f out* **16/1**

1m 38.34s (0.14) **Going Correction** -0.025s/f (Stan)
**WFA** 3 from 4yo 20lb **10** Ran SP% **117.8**
Speed ratings (Par 100): **98,93,90,89,88 87,82,82,79,70**
CSF £15.98 TOTE £2.10: £1.30, £1.90, £1.40; EX 21.80 Trifecta £38.20.
**Owner** Lordship Stud **Bred** Lordship Stud **Trained** Newmarket, Suffolk

**FOCUS**
Some big stables represented in this fillies' maiden but the hot favourite turned it into a one horse race. The winner has been rated to form for now, with the runner-up improving on her debut effort.

## 190 32RED H'CAP — 1m 2f (P)
**2:35** (3:29) (Class 5) (0-75,70) 3-Y-O **£3,316** (£979; £489) **Stalls** Low

Form RPR

224- **1** **Jazzy Lady (IRE)**[20] 8397 3-9-7 **70** ............................ AdamKirby 1 75
(David Evans) *hld up wl in tch: rdn and swtchd lft ent fnl 2f: drvn and chal over 1f out: led and edgd rt ins fnl f: r.o wl* **3/1**[2]

634- **2** *nk* **Samtu (IRE)**[74] 7694 3-9-4 **67** ............................ LukeMorris 6 71
(Clive Brittain) *led: rdn ent fnl 2f: drvn and hrd pressed over 1f out: hdd ins fnl f: keeping on but looked hld whn bmpd wl ins fnl f: kpt on* **1/1**[1]

00-0 **3** *7* **Sweet Alibi (IRE)**[2] 157 3-9-1 **67** ............................ MichaelJMMurphy(3) 4 57
(J S Moore) *dwlt: in tch in last pair: hdwy to chse ldr 6f out tl 2f out: 4th and btn over 1f out: fdd fnl f* **10/1**

00-5 **4** *2 1/2* **Izbushka (IRE)**[11] 50 3-9-2 **65** ............................ (v[1]) StevieDonohoe 5 50
(Ian Williams) *s.i.s and rdn along leaving stalls: nvr travelling in last: drvn and no hdwy over 2f out: n.d but styd on past btn horses ins fnl f* **8/1**

105- **5** *1 1/2* **Cascadia (IRE)**[17] 8434 3-8-9 **58** ............................ RichardKingscote 3 40
(K R Burke) *chsd ldr tl 6f out: rdn and lost pl over 2f out: wknd over 1f out* **16/1**

02-4 **6** *1 3/4* **Lady Knight (IRE)**[2] 166 3-9-4 **67** ............................ LiamJones 2 46
(J S Moore) *chsd ldrs: rdn and hdwy to press ldr 2f out tl wl over 1f out: 3rd and btn 1f out: wknd ins fnl f* **7/1**[3]

2m 6.5s (-0.10) **Going Correction** -0.025s/f (Stan) **6** Ran SP% **113.6**
Speed ratings (Par 97): **99,98,93,91,89 88**
CSF £6.54 TOTE £2.20: £1.90, £1.10; EX 4.60 Trifecta £31.80.
**Owner** Will Dawson **Bred** Limestone And Tara Studs **Trained** Pandy, Monmouths

**FOCUS**
Just the six for this modest handicap but an interesting affair nonetheless with the gambled on Samtu just being touched off. The runner-up shapes as though he wants a trip and has been rated as running a personal best.

## 191 COMPARE BOOKMAKERS AT BOOKMAKERS.CO.UK H'CAP — 5f 6y(P)
**3:10** (3:48) (Class 5) (0-75,75) 4-Y-O+ **£3,067** (£905; £453) **Stalls** Low

Form RPR

402- **1** **Song Of Parkes**[50] 8052 7-8-11 **68** ............................ SladeO'Hara(3) 1 78
(Peter Grayson) *in tch towards rr: pushed along and hdwy on inner to chse ldng pair and swtchd rt jst over 1f out: r.o wl to ld wl ins fnl f: gng away at fin* **12/1**

005- **2** *1 3/4* **Island Legend (IRE)**[28] 8324 8-9-6 **74** ............................ (p) LiamJones 4 78
(Milton Bradley) *led: hrd pressed and rdn 2f out: drvn and forged ahd ins fnl f: hdd wl ins fnl f: no ex and outpcd towards fin* **8/1**[3]

114- **3** *2* **Gregori (IRE)**[18] 8431 4-9-7 **75** ............................ (t) SeanLevey 2 72
(Brian Meehan) *chsd ldr: rdn to chal 2f out: hrd drvn and unable qck ent fnl f: btn fnl 100yds: wknd towards fin* **8/13**[1]

000- **4** *3/4* **Flash City (ITY)**[29] 8319 6-9-4 **72** ............................ (vt) GrahamLee 3 66
(Bryan Smart) *restless in stalls: rdn and outpcd 2f out: no imp and styd on same pce after* **8/1**[3]

10-0 **5** *2 1/2* **Billy Red**[7] 91 10-9-4 **72** ............................ (b) FergusSweeney 5 57
(J R Jenkins) *dwlt: a in rr: rdn and struggling 1/2-way: wknd over 1f out* **16/1**

500- **6** *3/4* **West Coast Dream**[70] 7776 7-9-4 **72** ............................ (b[1]) TomEaves 7 54
(Roy Brotherton) *hld up in tch: rdn and effrt ent fnl 2f: no hdwy and outpcd wl over 1f out: sn wknd* **5/1**[2]

58.02s (-0.78) **Going Correction** -0.025s/f (Stan) **6** Ran SP% **114.4**
Speed ratings (Par 103): **105,102,99,97,93 92**
CSF £98.81 TOTE £9.50: £2.90, £3.00; EX 37.90 Trifecta £61.60.
**Owner** E Grayson **Bred** Joseph Heler **Trained** Formby, Lancs

**FOCUS**
Mainly out-of-form sprinters took to the post for this sprint. The winner was on a good mark and the race has been rated around her.

## 192 BEST ODDS AT BOOKMAKERS.CO.UK APPRENTICE H'CAP — 6f 1y(P)
**3:45** (4:04) (Class 6) (0-60,60) 4-Y-O+ **£2,385** (£704; £352) **Stalls** Low

Form RPR

550- **1** **Reginald Claude**[42] 8152 6-8-12 **56** ............................ CharlotteJenner(5) 11 64
(Mark Usher) *hld up off the pce in midfield: rdn and clsd on ldrs over 1f out: r.o strly to ld fnl 50yds: styd on* **8/1**[3]

60-0 **2** *1/2* **Daneside (IRE)**[7] 92 7-8-5 **47** ............................ GeorgeBuckell(3) 10 53
(P J O'Gorman) *hld up off the pce in last quartet: rdn and gd hdwy over 1f out: r.o strly ins fnl f to go 2nd cl home* **10/1**

322- **3** *hd* **Volito**[99] 7086 8-8-12 **56** ............................ JackGarritty(5) 6 62
(Anabel K Murphy) *dwlt: sn in midfield but off the pce: rdn and clsd 2f out: kpt on u.p ins fnl f* **8/1**[3]

104- **4** *3/4* **Compton Prince**[51] 8035 5-9-3 **59** ............................ (b) JordanVaughan(3) 1 62+
(Milton Bradley) *chsd ldr and clr in ldng trio: rdn to ld 1f out: kpt on tl hdd fnl 50yds: no ex and lost 3 pls towards fin* **14/1**

000- **5** *1 1/4* **Catalinas Diamond (IRE)**[37] 8220 6-9-4 **60** ............................ (t) JoeDoyle(3) 12 59
(Pat Murphy) *stdd and dropped in bhd after s: hld up off the pce in last quartet: rdn and hdwy over 1f out: kpt on fnl f: nt rch ldrs* **8/1**[3]

060- **6** *3/4* **Green Millionaire**[113] 6732 4-8-13 **57** ............................ DavidParkes(5) 2 54
(Jeremy Gask) *chsd clr ldng trio: rdn and effrt ent fnl 2f: kpt on same pce ins fnl f* **33/1**

300- **7** *nk* **Proper Charlie**[32] 8306 6-8-12 **58** ............................ (v) PaigeBolton(7) 3 54+
(Lee Carter) *chsd ldng pair and clr of field: rdn and chal on inner over 1f out: no ex ins fnl f: wknd towards fin* **6/1**[2]

430- **8** *3/4* **Johnny Splash (IRE)**[55] 7985 5-9-0 **58** ............................ (v) SineadAlderman(5) 9 52
(Roger Teal) *racd off the pce in last quartet: pushed along and hdwy jst over 1f out: kpt on fnl f: nvr trbld ldrs* **8/1**[3]

030- **9** *2 1/4* **Brandywell Boy (IRE)**[107] 6901 11-8-2 **46** oh1 ............................ JohnLawson(5) 5 32
(Dominic Ffrench Davis) *racd off the pce in midfield: effrt u.p 2f out: no imp fnl f* **14/1**

300- **10** *nk* **Waterloo Dock**[16] 8446 9-8-13 **52** ............................ (v) PatMillman 8 37
(Mick Quinn) *sn bustled along: racd off the pce in midfield: reminder 4f out: lost pl u.p wl over 1f out: plugged on but n.d after* **25/1**

143- **11** *hd* **Fleetwoodsands (IRE)**[306] 1021 7-8-12 **51** ............................ EoinWalsh 7 36
(David Evans) *stdd s: hld up off the pce in last quartet: effrt u.p over 1f out: kpt on but nvr a threat* **4/1**[1]

00-0 **12** *2* **Imperial Spirit**[13] 9 4-8-9 **53** ............................ (b[1]) JosephineGordon(5) 4 31+
(Jo Hughes) *rrd as stalls opened: sn led and clr w 2 rivals: rdn and hdd 1f out: sn fdd* **10/1**

1m 11.98s (0.08) **Going Correction** -0.025s/f (Stan) **12** Ran SP% **117.0**
Speed ratings (Par 101): **98,97,97,96,94 93,93,92,89,88 88,85**
CSF £84.47 CT £674.75 TOTE £14.20: £4.10, £6.00, £2.60; EX 162.10 Trifecta £1274.90 Part won..
**Owner** High Five Racing **Bred** Whitsbury Manor Stud **Trained** Upper Lambourn, Berks
■ Stewards' Enquiry : Paige Bolton two-day ban: careless riding (Jan 29-30)

**FOCUS**
A weak race to close the card and once again they went a good pace. The third helps set the level.
T/Plt: £23.20 to a £1 stake. Pool: £66837.91 - 2097.21 winning tickets T/Qpdt: £10.10 to a £1 stake. Pool: £6930.10 - 503.05 winning tickets SP

# [177]CAGNES-SUR-MER
Wednesday, January 15

**OFFICIAL GOING: Polytrack: standard**

## 193a PRIX LOUIS GAUTIER VIGNAL (CONDITIONS) (3YO) (POLYTRACK) — 1m (F)
**1:20** (12:00) 3-Y-O **£12,083** (£4,833; £3,625; £2,416; £1,208)

RPR

**1** **Baby Foot (IRE)**[101] 7056 3-9-4 0 ............................ FranckBlondel 8 88
(F Rossi, France) **3/5**[1]

**2** *1* **Flamboyant (FR)**[69] 3-9-0 0 ............................ IoritzMendizabal 7 82
(J-C Rouget, France) **33/10**[2]

**3** *1* **Mr Pommeroy (FR)**[57] 3-9-0 0 ............................ FabriceVeron 2 80
(H-A Pantall, France) **12/1**[3]

**4** *1 1/2* **Twombly (SPA)**[11] 3-9-0 0 ............................ (p) AntoineHamelin 4 76
(C Boutin, France) **12/1**[3]

**5** *1* **Flying Cape (IRE)**[125] 6340 3-8-10 0 ............................ ThomasMessina 6 70
(Andrew Hollinshead) *t.k.h: hld up in midfield: rdn over 2f out to chse ldng gp: kpt on at same pce u.p fnl f: nvr able to chal* **48/1**

**6** *1* **Skiperia (FR)**[42] 3-8-10 0 ............................ AnthonyCrastus 3 68
(E Lellouche, France) **25/1**

**7** *snk* **Denusa (IRE)**[74] 3-8-10 0 ............................ FBossa 5 67
(Laura Grizzetti, Italy) **65/1**

**8** *nk* **Zhayrem (FR)** 3-8-10 0 ............................ TonyPiccone 1 67
(J Heloury, France) **31/1**

**9** *2 1/2* **Mokka (FR)**[34] 3-8-10 0 ............................ (p) FranckForesi 9 61
(F Foresi, France) **49/1**

**10** *3* **Ascot Memory (IRE)**[84] 7571 3-8-10 0 ............................ TheoBachelot 10 54
(S Wattel, France) **16/1**

1m 39.13s (99.13) **10** Ran SP% **119.5**
WIN (incl. 1 euro stake): 1.60. Places: 1.10, 1.20, 1.50. DF: 2.60. SF: 3.50..
**Owner** Jean-Claude Seroul **Bred** J-C Seroul **Trained** France

## 194a PRIX DE FABRON (MAIDEN) (UNRACED 3YO) (POLYTRACK) — 1m (F)
**1:50** (12:00) 3-Y-O **£10,000** (£4,000; £3,000; £2,000; £1,000)

RPR

**1** **Verdura (USA)** 3-8-13 0 ............................ IoritzMendizabal 15
(J-C Rouget, France) **13/5**[1]

**2** *1/2* **Saint Pois (FR)** 3-8-13 0 ............................ MatthiasLauron(3) 5
(J-C Rouget, France) **31/5**[3]

**3** *nk* **See You Soon (FR)** 3-9-2 0 ............................ FabriceVeron 7
(H-A Pantall, France) **59/10**[2]

**4** *nse* **Poudlard Express (FR)** 3-9-2 0 ............................ Francois-XavierBertras 9
(D De Watrigant, France) **13/1**

**5** *nse* **Sealed (USA)** 3-9-2 0 ............................ Pierre-CharlesBoudot 17
(Gay Kelleway) *trckd ldrs on outer: cl 3rd and ev ch 2f out: rdn 1 1/2f out: sltly hmpd ins fnl f: kpt on u.p* **21/1**

**6** *1* **Ar Poulgwenn (IRE)** 3-9-2 0 ............................ (b[1]) ThomasHenderson 4
(J-C Rouget, France) **87/10**

**7** *shd* **Bhaktapur (FR)** 3-8-13 0 ............................ StephanePasquier 10
(F Rohaut, France) **87/10**

**8** *nk* **Osmior (IRE)** 3-9-2 0 ............................ DavidBreux 13
(G Botti, France) **20/1**

**9** *4* **Lovable (CAN)** 3-8-5 0 ............................ SoufianeSaadi(8) 1
(J-C Rouget, France) **13/1**

**10** *shd* **Best Love Royal (FR)** 3-9-2 0 ............................ TheoBachelot 3
(F-X De Chevigny, France) **31/1**

**11** *4* **Belle Miss (FR)** 3-8-13 0 ............................ SebastienMaillot 6
(E Caroux, France) **34/1**

**12** *nk* **Ave Cesare** 3-9-2 0 ............................ AlexisBadel 12
(M Delcher Sanchez, France) **18/1**

**13** *6* **Sainte Glace (IRE)** 3-8-13 0 ............................ MarcLerner 14
(Robert Collet, France) **38/1**

**14** *2* **Bolero D'Azur (FR)** 3-8-13 0 ............................ PaulineProd'homme 2
(D Prod'Homme, France) **18/1**

**15** *7 1/2* **Katsumi (FR)** 3-8-13 0 ............................ MickaelForest 11
(E Caroux, France) **56/1**

1m 39.05s (99.05) **15** Ran SP% **121.2**
WIN (incl. 1 euro stake): 3.60. Places: 1.60, 2.10, 1.90. DF: 10.60. SF: 13.00..
**Owner** Joseph Allen **Bred** J Allen **Trained** Pau, France

# 162 WOLVERHAMPTON (A.W) (L-H)

Thursday, January 16

**OFFICIAL GOING: Standard**

Wind: Virtually nil Weather: cold

## 195 BEST ODDS AT BOOKMAKERS.CO.UK MEDIAN AUCTION MAIDEN STKS 5f 216y(P)

**4:30** (4:30) (Class 5) 3-5-Y-O **£2,911** (£866; £432; £216) **Stalls** Low

Form RPR

1 **Crisis Averted (IRE)** 3-8-10 0 LeeTopliss 5 68+
(Richard Fahey) *bmpd s: t.k.h: trckd ldrs: wnt 2nd over 3f out: led ins fnl 2f: drvn clr: green and hung lft appr fnl f: pushed out* **1/1**[1]

20- 2 *1* **Winterwell (USA)**[28] 8348 4-9-4 67 (v[1]) SamJames(3) 3 61
(David O'Meara) *s.i.s: sn chsng: rdn and outpcd in last pl 1/2-way: styd on again fnl f to take 2nd fnl 110yds: no ch w wnr* **7/1**

24-2 3 *2 1/4* **The Dandy Yank (IRE)**[15] 5 3-8-10 64 WilliamCarson 6 55
(Jamie Osborne) *t.k.h and sn led: hdd and rdn ins fnl 2f: no ch w wnr over 1f out: one pce into 3rd fnl 110yds* **11/4**[2]

234- 4 *1/2* **Coiste Bodhar (IRE)**[18] 8435 3-8-10 60 LukeMorris 4 53
(Joseph Tuite) *bmpd s: chsd ldrs: rdn half way: outpcd u.p 2f out: styd on for wl-hld 4th clsng stages* **4/1**[3]

446- 5 *1 1/4* **Busy Bimbo (IRE)**[18] 8437 5-9-4 45 MarkCoumbe(3) 1 48
(Alan Berry) *chsd ldr to 1/2-way: sn rdn and one pce: no ch fr over 1f out* **33/1**

1m 16.61s (1.61) **Going Correction** +0.175s/f (Slow)
**WFA** 3 from 4yo+ 16lb 5 Ran SP% **112.1**
Speed ratings (Par 103): **96,94,91,91,89**
CSF £8.93 TOTE £3.00: £1.20, £2.90; EX 13.80 Trifecta £29.10.
**Owner** D O'Callaghan **Bred** Sean Gorman **Trained** Musley Bank, N Yorks

**FOCUS**
A modest maiden lacking in strength. The gallop was no more than fair and the winner edged to the far rail in the straight. The form is anchored by the fifth.

## 196 32RED FILLIES' H'CAP 5f 216y(P)

**5:00** (5:00) (Class 5) (0-70,73) 4-Y-O+ **£2,911** (£866; £432; £216) **Stalls** Low

Form RPR

05-0 1 **Layla's Oasis**[10] 69 4-9-2 68 (p) GeorgeChaloner(3) 2 76
(Richard Fahey) *t.k.h: trckd ldrs: drvn to ld over 1f out: hld on wl u.p fnl 110yds* **25/1**

03-2 2 *hd* **Barbs Princess**[10] 69 4-9-7 70 RobertWinston 7 77
(Charles Hills) *in rr: hdwy on outer over 2f out: styd on u.p to chse wnr fnl 110yds: nt quite get up* **7/4**[1]

403- 3 *1 1/4* **Spray Tan**[108] 6901 4-9-0 63 LukeMorris 6 66
(Tony Carroll) *in rr but in tch: hdwy over 1f out: styd on to take 3rd u.p fnl 150yds: no imp on ldng duo sn after* **20/1**

30-3 4 *1 1/2* **Dodina (IRE)**[10] 69 4-9-6 69 DaleSwift 4 67
(Brian Ellison) *sn chsng ldr: chal fr 2f out tl 1f out: one pce fnl 110yds* **3/1**[3]

0-1 5 *3 1/4* **Lapis Blue (IRE)**[10] 69 4-9-10 73 6ex AdamKirby 5 61
(David Evans) *swtchd lft to rail sn after s and in rr: shkn up 2f out: a outpcd* **11/4**[2]

4-50 6 *3/4* **Amis Reunis**[11] 58 5-8-0 56 oh3 (p) JordanHibberd(7) 3 41
(Alan Berry) *t.k.h: chsd ldrs tl wknd ins fnl 2f* **33/1**

543- 7 *1 1/2* **Laughing Rock (IRE)**[149] 5611 4-8-13 62 AndrewMullen 1 43
(Michael Appleby) *sn led: hrd pressed fr over 3f out tl hdd over 1f out: wknd qckly* **7/1**

1m 16.04s (1.04) **Going Correction** +0.175s/f (Slow) 7 Ran SP% **112.1**
Speed ratings (Par 100): **100,99,98,96,91 90,88**
CSF £66.64 TOTE £22.20: £10.90, £1.60; EX 73.00 Trifecta £591.90.
**Owner** Dr Marwan Koukash **Bred** P T Tellwright **Trained** Musley Bank, N Yorks

**FOCUS**
A modest fillies' handicap in which the pace was no more than fair. The winner raced towards the far rail in the straight. The winner has been rated as running a small personal best and the runner-up to her latest C&D effort.

## 197 32RED CASINO CLAIMING STKS 1m 5f 194y(P)

**5:30** (5:30) (Class 6) 4-Y-O+ **£2,264** (£673; £336; £168) **Stalls** Low

Form RPR

51/- 1 **Bute Hall**[527] 4910 5-8-13 77 RobJFitzpatrick(7) 1 81
(David Thompson) *t.k.h early: trckd ldrs: n.m.r and wnt 2nd ins fnl 2f: chal 1f out: sn led and rdn: hld on wl under hand driving in clsng stages* **11/4**[3]

325- 2 *shd* **Scribe (IRE)**[18] 8433 6-9-2 69 (vt) AdamKirby 2 77
(David Evans) *trckd ldr: led 3f out: rdn 2f out: jnd 1f out and sn hdd: rallied u.p and styng on again in clsng stages: nt quite get up* **6/4**[1]

3- 3 *23* **Wild Desert (FR)**[110] 3744 9-9-4 80 LukeMorris 6 47
(Tony Carroll) *led tl hdd 3f out: edgd lft 2f out: wknd qckly over 1f out* **5/2**[2]

000- 4 *3 3/4* **Wildomar**[25] 8392 5-9-6 82 MarkCoumbe(3) 3 47
(Tony Carroll) *in 4th pl most of way and in tch w ldng trio 4f out: rdn and wknd 3f out* **6/1**

6- 5 *26* **Terntheothercheek**[16] 641 5-8-13 0 StephenCraine 5
(Jennie Candlish) *s.i.s: a in rr: t.o fnl 6f* **50/1**

63 6 *43* **Offherocker**[6] 124 7-8-7 0 MrAidenBlakemore(7) 4
(Claire Dyson) *in tch tl dropped in rr over 6f out: sn t.o* **100/1**

3m 6.6s (0.60) **Going Correction** +0.175s/f (Slow) 6 Ran SP% **112.5**
Speed ratings (Par 101): **105,104,91,89,74 50**
CSF £7.33 TOTE £2.50: £1.30, £1.10; EX 8.30 Trifecta £21.10.
**Owner** Seneca Racing **Bred** Southcourt Stud **Trained** Bolam, Co Durham

**FOCUS**
Question marks over the majority in this uncompetitive claimer. The gallop was on the steady side and the winner raced against the far rail in the straight. The runner-up has been rated to form for now.

## 198 32RED.COM H'CAP 1m 4f 50y(P)

**6:00** (6:01) (Class 6) (0-65,65) 3-Y-O **£2,264** (£673; £336; £168) **Stalls** Low

Form RPR

000- 1 **Right Of Appeal**[68] 7817 3-8-10 54 JoeFanning 7 67+
(Mark Johnston) *trckd ldr: led 3f out: pushed clr ins fnl 2f: v easily* **5/6**[1]

66-5 2 *6* **Belle Peinture (FR)**[10] 71 3-8-2 46 oh1 JimmyQuinn 3 47
(Richard Fahey) *in rr: hdwy on outer fr 2f out: drvn to take 2nd 1f out and kpt on but no ch w v easy wnr* **20/1**

13-2 3 *2* **Big Kenny**[7] 99 3-9-4 62 AdamKirby 5 59
(David Evans) *in rr but in tch: shkn up and outpcd 3f out: no clr run u.p fr over 2f out tl over 1f out: styd on to take one pce 3rd in clsng stages but no ch w v easy wnr and wl hld by 2nd* **7/4**[2]

0-54 4 *hd* **Izbushka (IRE)**[1] 190 3-9-7 65 (p) StevieDonohoe 2 62
(Ian Williams) *chsd ldrs: drvn along 4f out: wnt 2nd u.p ins fnl 2f but nvr nr v easy wnr: dropped to 3rd 1f out and one pce into 4th in clsng stages* **20/1**

00-0 5 *6* **Miss Verdoyante**[12] 51 3-8-2 46 oh1 (b[1]) LukeMorris 4 33
(Sir Mark Prescott Bt) *led tl hdd 3f out: wknd wl over 1f out* **12/1**[3]

00-4 6 *7* **Water For Life**[13] 28 3-8-7 51 WilliamCarson 6 27
(Dave Morris) *chsd ldrs: rdn 3f out: wknd ins fnl 2f* **25/1**

62-6 7 *2 1/4* **Sarlat**[10] 71 3-8-3 47 KieranO'Neill 1 20
(Mark Brisbourne) *unruly ent stalls: t.k.h: in rr: rdn over 3f out: sn btn* **33/1**

2m 43.86s (2.76) **Going Correction** +0.175s/f (Slow) 7 Ran SP% **114.9**
Speed ratings (Par 95): **97,93,91,91,87 82,81**
CSF £22.89 TOTE £2.10: £1.30, £11.30; EX 21.10 Trifecta £46.30.
**Owner** Sheikh Hamdan bin Mohammed Al Maktoum **Bred** Lordship Stud **Trained** Middleham Moor, N Yorks

**FOCUS**
A modest handicap in which none of the runners were proven over the trip. The gallop was no more than fair and the ready winner raced centre-to-far side in the straight. The winner made a mockery of his opening mark, the runner-up had shaped like a stayer and has been rated as running a small personal best, while the fourth has been rated in line with the better view of his maiden form.

## 199 CORAL MOBILE "JUST THREE CLICKS TO BET" (S) STKS 1m 1f 103y(P)

**6:30** (6:30) (Class 6) 4-Y-O+ **£2,264** (£673; £336; £168) **Stalls** Low

Form RPR

11-3 1 **Matraash (USA)**[10] 66 8-9-5 78 (be) ShaneKelly 1 71+
(Daniel Mark Loughnane) *t.k.h in rr and stl keen 4f out: hdwy 3f out: tk 3rd 2f out: c wd bnd over 1f out: shkn up to chal ins fnl f: led fnl 140yds: comf* **1/2**[1]

31-6 2 *2 1/4* **Misleading Promise (IRE)**[14] 10 4-8-13 67 (vt[1]) LiamKeniry 2 61
(John Butler) *sn trcking ldr: led 2f out and sn rdn: jnd jst ins fnl f: hdd fnl 140yds: sn outpcd and wl hld in clsng stages* **3/1**[2]

035- 3 *6* **Lucy Bee**[27] 8372 4-8-8 55 AndrewMullen 5 43
(Michael Appleby) *led: rdn and hdd 2f out: wknd fnl f* **5/1**[3]

5-53 4 *3/4* **Bix (IRE)**[11] 63 4-8-13 44 GrahamLee 3 47
(Alan Berry) *t.k.h towards rr but in tch: drvn and sme hdwy to cl on ldrs 3f out: nvr on terms and wknd wl over 1f out* **25/1**

46/4 5 *11* **Kneesy Earsy Nosey**[11] 63 8-8-6 36 ow2 (p) AnnStokell(5) 4 21
(Ann Stokell) *chsd ldrs: wknd ins fnl 3f* **100/1**

2m 3.85s (2.15) **Going Correction** +0.175s/f (Slow)
**WFA** 4 from 8yo 1lb 5 Ran SP% **113.2**
Speed ratings (Par 101): **97,95,89,89,79**
CSF £2.47 TOTE £1.20: £1.10, £1.20; EX 2.90 Trifecta £3.90.
**Owner** Over The Moon Racing **Bred** Shadwell Farm LLC **Trained** Baldwin's Gate, Staffs

**FOCUS**
A mixed bag of ability on show and a steady gallop but the two market leaders, who raced centre-to-far side, pulled clear in the straight. The poor fourth limits the form.

## 200 CORAL APP DOWNLOAD FROM THE APP STORE H'CAP 1m 1f 103y(P)

**7:00** (7:00) (Class 4) (0-85,85) 4-Y-O+ **£5,175** (£1,540; £769; £384) **Stalls** Low

Form RPR

10-6 1 **Modernism**[8] 89 5-9-2 80 LiamKeniry 5 92
(David Simcock) *chsd ldrs: wnt 2nd 6f out: drvn to chal 1f out: led fnl 150yds: hld on wl* **6/1**[3]

042- 2 *3/4* **Legendary**[38] 8219 5-9-5 83 JimmyQuinn 2 93
(Ed Vaughan) *sn led: rdn over 1f out and sn jnd: hdd fnl 150yds: kpt on u.p but no imp in clsng stages* **7/1**

332- 3 *1 3/4* **Excellent Puck (IRE)**[20] 8416 4-8-11 79 RobertTart(3) 9 86+
(Shaun Lycett) *in rr: hrd drvn 3f out: hdwy ins fnl 2f: styd on to take 3rd ins fnl f but no imp on ldng duo* **11/4**[1]

214- 4 *2 1/4* **Off The Pulse**[20] 8416 4-9-3 82 StephenCraine 8 84
(John Mackie) *chsd ldrs: rdn to take 3rd 2f out: no imp on ldng duo and dropped to 4th ins fnl f* **12/1**

245- 5 *2* **High Time Too (IRE)**[38] 8219 4-8-12 77 GrahamLee 10 75
(Hugo Palmer) *chsd ldrs: pushed along 3f out: wknd appr fnl f* **8/1**

15-5 6 *1 1/2* **Rakaan (IRE)**[8] 89 7-9-7 85 AdamKirby 6 80
(Jamie Osborne) *s.i.s: in rr: pushed along and hdwy over 2f out: styd on to dispute one pce 3rd 1f out: sn btn* **9/2**[2]

15-4 7 *1/2* **Doldrums (USA)**[14] 21 4-8-7 72 JoeFanning 11 66
(Mark Johnston) *in rr: drvn and sme hdwy fr 3f out: nvr rchd ldrs and wknd ins fnl 2f* **7/1**

5/2- 8 *3 1/4* **Palus San Marco (IRE)**[48] 2418 5-9-0 78 (t) LukeMorris 7 65
(Tony Carroll) *in rr: pushed along and sme prog 3f out: nvr beyond mid-div: wknd 2f out* **33/1**

014- 9 *nse* **Aglaophonos**[29] 7307 4-8-9 74 (p) StevieDonohoe 3 61
(Ian Williams) *nvr really travelling: sn u.p: a bhd* **20/1**

521- 10 *1/2* **Berlusca (IRE)**[20] 8416 5-9-1 82 SamJames(3) 1 68
(David O'Meara) *chsd ldrs tl wknd appr fnl 2f* **8/1**

2m 1.17s (-0.53) **Going Correction** +0.175s/f (Slow)
**WFA** 4 from 5yo+ 1lb 10 Ran SP% **121.8**
Speed ratings (Par 105): **109,108,106,104,103 101,101,98,98,97**
CSF £49.90 CT £144.51 TOTE £6.20: £1.90, £2.30, £1.10; EX 60.20 Trifecta £384.10.
**Owner** Dr Marwan Koukash **Bred** Darley **Trained** Newmarket, Suffolk

**FOCUS**
A useful handicap in which an ordinary gallop saw those held up at a disadvantage. The winner came down the centre in the straight. The winner has been rated back to his 3yo best, with the runner-up to his best.

## 201 LADBROKES H'CAP 7f 32y(P)

**7:30** (7:30) (Class 7) (0-50,50) 4-Y-O+ **£2,264** (£673; £336; £168) **Stalls** High

Form RPR

044- 1 **Medecis Mountain**[51] 8054 5-8-9 45 JoeDoyle(7) 6 55
(John Wainwright) *s.i.s: in rr: hdwy on outside over 2f out: styng on whn bmpd over 1f out: kpt on again to ld fnl 120yds: pushed out* **7/1**

20-2 2 *1* **Chez Vrony**[14] 18 8-9-6 49 WilliamCarson 5 56
(Dave Morris) *bmpd sn after s: towards rr but in tch: n.m.r 2f out: hdwy sn after and drvn to ld ins fnl f: hdd fnl 120yds: one pce* **9/2**[2]

4-20 3 *1 1/2* **Partner's Gold (IRE)**[2] 171 4-9-3 46 (b) GrahamLee 7 49
(Alan Berry) *bmpd sn after s: chsd ldrs: edgd rt over 1f out: styd on to chal whn pushed lft ins fnl f: one pce* **6/1**[3]

/0-5 **4** 1 3/4 **Prohibition (IRE)**[1] 179 8-9-7 50 AdamKirby 2 48+
(John Butler) *s.i.s: in rr: effrt on inner and n.m.r 2f out: sn rdn: sme hdwy over 1f out but no imp on ldrs and kpt on same pce* **6/4**[1]

00-5 **5** *hd* **Satwa Laird**[14] 12 8-8-11 45 (be) AnnStokell(5) 10 43
(Ann Stokell) *s.i.s: in rr: hdwy to chse ldrs over 2f out: styng on whn bmpd on outer over 1f out: outpcd fnl f* **33/1**

60-0 **6** *nk* **Louis Vee (IRE)**[14] 18 6-9-2 45 (t) ShaneKelly 4 42
(Roy Brotherton) *sn led: hdd after 2f: styd pressing ldr tl led again over 2f out: hdd ins fnl f: sn btn* **100/1**

03-3 **7** 4 **Vale Of Clara (IRE)**[14] 18 6-9-5 48 (b) TomEaves 8 34
(Peter Niven) *chsd ldrs: rdn to go 2nd 2f out: wknd 1f out* **9/2**[2]

03-0 **8** *shd* **Blue Noodles**[8] 81 8-9-5 48 (p) PaddyAspell 9 34
(John Wainwright) *led after 2f: hdd over 2f out: wknd wl over 1f out* **12/1**

305- **9** 3/4 **Michael's Nook**[282] 1452 7-9-6 49 LukeMorris 1 33
(Alastair Lidderdale) *chsd ldrs: rdn over 2f out: wknd wl over 1f out* **14/1**

06-3 **10** *shd* **Scommettitrice (IRE)**[7] 100 6-9-4 47 (p) KieranO'Neill 3 31
(Nigel Twiston-Davies) *s.i.s: rdn 3f out: a outpcd* **20/1**

1m 31.44s (1.84) **Going Correction** +0.175s/f (Slow) **10 Ran SP% 126.2**
Speed ratings (Par 97): **96,94,93,91,90 90,86,85,85,84**
CSF £41.39 CT £209.85 TOTE £15.50: £4.90, £1.40, £3.20; EX 43.00 Trifecta £433.30.
**Owner** J S Wainwright **Bred** J S Wainwright **Trained** Kennythorpe, N Yorks

**FOCUS**
A very moderate handicap in which the gallop was reasonable. The winner came down the centre in the straight. The runner-up has been in good form and has been rated close to his C&D latest.
T/Plt: 14.80 to a £1 stake. Pool of £88235.64 - 4323.66 winning tickets. T/Qpdt: £5.60 to a £1 stake. Pool of £11513.16 - 1520.68 winning tickets. ST

## 107 MEYDAN (L-H)
### Thursday, January 16
**OFFICIAL GOING: Tapeta - standard; turf - good**

### 202a DUBAI DUTY FREE TENNIS CHAMPIONSHIPS (H'CAP) (TAPETA) 1m 3f
**2:30** (2:30) (95-105,105) 3-Y-O+
**£39,759** (£13,253; £6,626; £3,313; £1,987; £1,325)

RPR

**1** **Cat O'Mountain (USA)**[113] 6751 4-9-0 100 MickaelBarzalona 3 114+
(Charlie Appleby) *in rr of mid-div: smooth prog 3f out: led 2f out: easily* **6/4**[1]

**2** 2 **Haafaguinea**[117] 6638 4-9-2 102 WilliamBuick 7 107
(Saeed bin Suroor) *s.i.s: settled in rr: nvr nr to chal but r.o fnl 2f: no ch w wnr* **9/1**

**3** *nk* **Energia Davos (BRZ)**[26] 8386 6-9-3 101 MartinHarley 9 104
(Marco Botti) *mid-div: chsd ldrs 2 1/2f out: kpt on same pce fnl 1 1/2f: lost 2nd cl home* **11/2**[3]

**4** 6 **Abdel (FR)**[53] 6-9-6 105 JulienAuge 2 97
(J-M Osorio, Spain) *trckd ldrs: ev ch whn outpcd 2 1/2f out: kpt on same pce fnl 2f* **20/1**

**5** 1 1/4 **Balladry (USA)**[320] 870 6-9-6 105 (tp) RichardMullen 6 94
(S Seemar, UAE) *s.i.s: nvr nr to chal but r.o fnl 2f* **33/1**

**6** 1/2 **Saxo Jack (FR)**[117] 6638 4-9-0 100 (p) SilvestreDeSousa 8 91
(Saeed bin Suroor) *mid-div: led 3 1/2f out: hdd 2 1/2f out: kpt on same pce* **4/1**[2]

**7** 8 1/2 **Ralston Road (IRE)**[28] 8358 4-9-2 102 (bt) TadhgO'Shea 11 77
(S Seemar, UAE) *trckd ldng pair: ev ch tl outpcd 2 1/2f out* **14/1**

**8** 3/4 **Sadeek's Song (USA)**[364] 246 6-9-1 99 MartinLane 1 72
(Charlie Appleby) *sn led: hdd & wknd 2 1/2f out* **25/1**

**9** 2 3/4 **Great Hall**[71] 7768 4-8-13 99 (b) KierenFallon 12 68
(Brian Meehan) *nvr bttr than mid-div* **16/1**

**10** 2 **Burano (IRE)**[7] 110 5-9-4 102 (b) JamieSpencer 5 66
(Brian Meehan) *settled last: nvr able to chal* **20/1**

**11** *shd* **Mutin (FR)**[7] 109 4-9-0 100 PaulHanagan 10 65
(M F De Kock, South Africa) *in rr of mid-div: nvr able to chal* **8/1**

**12** 7 1/4 **Jardim (BRZ)**[28] 8358 8-8-13 97 (tp) JamesDoyle 4 48
(M Kettle, UAE) *trckd ldrs tl wknd 5f out* **66/1**

2m 17.6s (-0.80) **Going Correction** +0.20s/f (Slow)
**WFA** 4 from 5yo+ 3lb **12 Ran SP% 126.8**
Speed ratings: **110,108,108,103,103 102,96,95,93,92 92,87**
CSF: 16.65; EX 11.50; TRIFECTA: 91.80; TRICAST: 67.39 WIN: 1.90; PL: 1.00, 2.20, 2.70..
**Owner** Godolphin **Bred** Darley **Trained** Newmarket, Suffolk

**FOCUS**
Strong Carnival form.

### 203a UAE 1000 GUINEAS TRIAL SPONSORED BY DUBAI DUTY FREE MILLENNIUM MILLIONAIRE (FILLIES) (TAPETA) 7f
**3:05** (3:05) 3-Y-O
**£27,108** (£9,036; £4,518; £2,259; £1,355; £903)

RPR

**1** **Wedding Ring (IRE)**[103] 7016 3-8-8 96 MickaelBarzalona 9 93+
(Charlie Appleby) *in rr of mid-div: smooth prog 2 1/2f out: led fnl 50yds: comf* **5/4**[1]

**2** 1 1/4 **Magrooma (AUS)**[194] 4-9-4 98 ChristopheSoumillon 7 93
(M F De Kock, South Africa) *mid-div: smooth prog 2 1/2f out: led 1 1/2f out: hdd fnl 50yds* **6/1**

**3** 1 3/4 **Letterfromamerica (USA)**[192] 4128 3-8-8 82 (bt) TadhgO'Shea 10 85
(S Seemar, UAE) *sn led: hdd 1 1/2f out but kpt on gamely* **25/1**

**4** 3/4 **More Aspen (USA)**[77] 7640 3-8-8 77 RichardMullen 2 83
(S Seemar, UAE) *trckd ldrs: ev ch 2 1/2f out: kpt on same pce fnl 1 1/2f* **25/1**

**5** *nk* **Autumn Lily (USA)**[110] 6839 3-8-8 99 SilvestreDeSousa 4 82
(Charlie Appleby) *trckd ldrs: ev ch 2 1/2f out: wknd fnl 1 1/2f* **11/4**[2]

**6** 1/2 **Magroora (AUS)**[222] 4-9-4 90 ThierryThulliez 1 84
(M F De Kock, South Africa) *trckd ldrs: ev ch 2f out: one pce fnl f* **16/1**

**7** 1 **Oxsana**[82] 7537 3-8-8 93 WilliamBuick 3 78
(William Haggas) *nvr bttr than mid-div* **11/2**[3]

**8** 1/2 **Max Beauty (FR)**[14] 22 3-8-8 RoystonFfrench 6 77
(A Al Raihe, UAE) *nvr bttr than mid-div* **33/1**

**9** 2 3/4 **Wish Me Luck (FR)** 3-8-2 SaeedAlMazrooei(6) 5 69
(A Al Raihe, UAE) *a in rr* **50/1**

**10** 10 1/2 **Anwar Dubai** 3-8-9 ow1 DaneO'Neill 8 42+
(M Al Muhairi, UAE) *v.s.a: a in rr* **40/1**

1m 25.67s (0.47) **Going Correction** +0.20s/f (Slow)
**WFA** 3 from 4yo 18lb **10 Ran SP% 121.7**
Speed ratings: **105,103,101,100,100 99,98,98,94,82**
CSF: 9.50; EX 11.00; TRIFECTA: 160.40; WIN: 1.90; PL: 1.00, 1.90, 4.90..
**Owner** Godolphin **Bred** Swettenham Stud **Trained** Newmarket, Suffolk

**FOCUS**
These fillies don't look a great bunch.

### 204a UAE 2000 GUINEAS TRIAL SPONSORED BY DUBAI DUTY FREE AND JUMEIRAH CREEKSIDE HOTEL (TAPETA) 7f
**3:40** (3:40) 3-Y-O
**£27,108** (£9,036; £4,518; £2,259; £1,355; £903)

RPR

**1** **Emirates Flyer**[103] 7026 3-8-8 104 SilvestreDeSousa 7 101
(Saeed bin Suroor) *trckd ldrs: led 1f out: r.o wl* **5/2**[1]

**2** 1/2 **Safety Check (IRE)**[87] 7421 3-8-8 98 MickaelBarzalona 5 100
(Charlie Appleby) *chsd ldrs: n.m.r 2f out: r.o fnl 1 1/2f: nrst fin* **4/1**[2]

**3** *hd* **My Catch (IRE)**[145] 5765 3-8-10 102 PatDobbs 11 101
(Doug Watson, UAE) *sn led: hdd 1f out but r.o gamely* **12/1**

**4** 2 **Najm Suhail**[14] 25 3-8-8 93 RoystonFfrench 8 94
(A Al Raihe, UAE) *trckd ldrs: ev ch 1f out: one pce fnl 50yds* **20/1**

**5** *nk* **Full Combat (SAF)**[194] 4-9-4 100 PaulHanagan 4 96
(M F De Kock, South Africa) *in rr of mid-div: rdn 3f out: kpt on fnl 2f: nrst fin* **9/1**

**6** *shd* **Figure Of Speech (IRE)**[96] 7207 3-8-8 105 (p) AhmedAjtebi 14 93
(Charlie Appleby) *in rr of mid-div: kpt on same pce fnl 1 1/2f* **8/1**

**7** 1 1/4 **Vigor (IRE)**[54] 8032 3-8-8 85 HayleyTurner 9 89
(Ernst Oertel, UAE) *nvr bttr than mid-div* **33/1**

**8** 3/4 **Dolce N Karama (IRE)**[82] 7528 3-8-8 105 TadhgO'Shea 10 87
(John Patrick Shanahan, Ire) *mid-div: rdn 3f out: one pce fnl 2f* **10/1**

**9** 1/2 **Journeyman (SAF)**[263] 4-9-4 98 ChristopheSoumillon 13 89
(M F De Kock, South Africa) *settled in rr: nvr bttr than mid-div* **15/2**[3]

**10** *nk* **Chord Chart (IRE)**[92] 7300 3-8-8 78 RichardMullen 3 85
(S Seemar, UAE) *nvr nr to chal* **40/1**

**11** 1 1/2 **Nezar (IRE)**[96] 7195 3-8-8 96 (b) WilliamBuick 2 81
(William Haggas) *nvr bttr than mid-div* **10/1**

**12** 3 **Man Amongst Men (IRE)**[64] 7859 3-8-8 85 (bt) JamieSpencer 1 73
(Brian Meehan) *settled in rr: n.d* **33/1**

**13** 1/2 **Make It Reel (FR)**[128] 6293 3-8-8 98 SamHitchcott 6 71
(Doug Watson, UAE) *nvr bttr than mid-div* **20/1**

**14** 3 3/4 **Dubawi Fun**[173] 4747 3-8-8 89 KierenFallon 12 61
(Ismail Mohammed) *trckd ldrs tl wknd 2f out* **16/1**

1m 24.62s (-0.58) **Going Correction** +0.20s/f (Slow)
**WFA** 3 from 4yo 18lb **14 Ran SP% 131.0**
Speed ratings: **111,110,110,107,107 107,106,105,104,104 102,99,98,94**
CSF: 12.17; EX 12.50; TRIFECTA: 265.00; WIN: 3.10; PL: 1.40, 1.90, 6.20..
**Owner** Godolphin **Bred** Carmel Stud **Trained** Newmarket, Suffolk

**FOCUS**
Modest form due to an ordinary pace.

### 205a DUBAI DUTY FREE GOLD WORLD CUP (H'CAP) (TURF) 1m 2f
**4:15** (4:15) (100-110,109) 3-Y-O+
**£43,373** (£14,457; £7,228; £3,614; £2,168; £1,445)

RPR

**1** **Sheikhzayedroad**[145] 5766 5-9-3 106 MartinLane 12 109
(David Simcock) *settled in rr: smooth prog 2f out: led 110yds out: comf* **7/1**

**2** 1 1/4 **Aussie Reigns (IRE)**[50] 8062 4-8-13 102 (v) AndreaAtzeni 10 104
(William Knight) *in rr of mid-div: smooth prog 2 1/2f out: ev ch 110yds out: nt qckn fnl 50yds* **14/1**

**3** *hd* **Star Empire (SAF)**[292] 1263 8-9-6 109 ChristopheSoumillon 11 109
(M F De Kock, South Africa) *settled in rr: nvr nr to chal but r.o fnl 2f: nrst fin* **11/1**

**4** *hd* **Tha'ir (IRE)**[110] 6838 4-8-13 102 SilvestreDeSousa 1 103
(Saeed bin Suroor) *led main gp: chsd ldrs 2 1/2f out: led 1f out: hdd fnl 50yds* **5/1**[2]

**5** 1 1/4 **Dabadiyan (IRE)**[111] 6818 4-9-2 106 ShaneFoley 8 104
(M Halford, Ire) *settled in rr: kpt on same pce fnl 2f but nvr able to chal* **11/1**

**6** *nk* **Energizer (GER)**[512] 5489 5-9-2 105 MickaelBarzalona 6 101
(Charlie Appleby) *sn led: clr 7f out: rdn 3 1/2f out: hdd 1f out: kpt on same pce* **6/1**[3]

**7** 2 3/4 **Code Of Honor**[110] 6838 4-9-2 106 KierenFallon 5 98
(Saeed bin Suroor) *s.i.s: mid-div: rdn 2 1/2f out: one pce fnl 1 1/2f* **3/1**[1]

**8** 2 1/2 **Chapter Seven**[75] 7697 5-9-2 105 JamieSpencer 2 91
(G M Lyons, Ire) *nvr bttr than mid-div* **16/1**

**9** *nse* **Sahawar (FR)**[102] 7058 4-9-2 106 ThierryThulliez 9 93
(C Ferland, France) *settled in rr: nvr nr to chal* **14/1**

**10** 3/4 **Pisco Sour (USA)**[322] 833 6-8-11 100 RichardMullen 4 84
(S Seemar, UAE) *nvr bttr than mid-div* **25/1**

**11** 4 1/4 **Sefri (USA)**[172] 4-9-2 106 DaneO'Neill 3 83
(E Charpy, UAE) *nvr bttr than mid-div* **25/1**

**12** 11 **So Beautiful (FR)**[313] 959 5-9-5 108 PaulHanagan 7 62
(Doug Watson, UAE) *nvr bttr than mid-div* **12/1**

2m 1.56s (121.56)
**WFA** 4 from 5yo+ 2lb **12 Ran SP% 119.7**
CSF: 102.02; EX 330.80; TRIFECTA: 1745.00; TRICAST: 1067.11; WIN: 12.30; PL: 4.10, 6.50, 2.40..
**Owner** Mohammed Jaber **Bred** Rabbah Bloodstock Limited **Trained** Newmarket, Suffolk

**FOCUS**
A bit of depth to this handicap.

### 206a DUBAWI STKS SPONSORED BY DUBAI DUTY FREE FULL OF SURPRISES (LISTED RACE) (TAPETA) 6f
**4:50** (4:50) 3-Y-O+
**£54,216** (£18,072; £9,036; £4,518; £2,710; £1,807)

RPR

**1** **United Color (USA)**[20] 8422 5-9-0 112 (t) JamesDoyle 9 109
(D Selvaratnam, UAE) *trckd ldrs: led 1 1/2f out: r.o wl: hld on gamely* **9/2**[2]

**2** *nk* **Russian Soul (IRE)**[124] 6414 6-9-2 109 (p) ShaneFoley 6 110
(M Halford, Ire) *settled in rr: smooth prog 2 1/2f out: ev ch 1f out: r.o wl: nrst fin* **12/1**

3 1 1/4 **Rafeej**[7] 107 5-9-0 105 PaulHanagan 4 104
(M Al Muhairi, UAE) *trckd ldng pair: ev ch 1f out: nt qckn fnl 50yds* **7/1**

4 1/2 **Balmont Mast (IRE)**[89] 7364 6-9-0 115 WilliamBuick 7 102
(Edward Lynam, Ire) *mid-div: r.o fnl 1 1/2f: nrst fin* **11/2**

5 3/4 **Kavanagh (SAF)**[103] 7013 7-9-0 112 (t) ChristopheSoumillon 5 100
(M F De Kock, South Africa) *mid-div: kpt on same pce fnl 2f* **10/1**

6 1 **Krypton Factor**[170] 4856 6-9-0 115 KierenFallon 2 97
(Fawzi Abdulla Nass, Bahrain) *slowly away: settled in rr: n.d: r.o fnl 2f* **5/1**[3]

7 2 **Reynaldothewizard (USA)**[292] 1266 8-9-0 118 (bt) RichardMullen 3 90
(S Seemar, UAE) *mid-div: n.m.r after 2f: nt rcvr* **11/4**[1]

8 nk **Farmleigh House (IRE)**[124] 6414 7-9-0 108 NGMcCullagh 8 89
(W J Martin, Ire) *sn led: hdd & wknd 1 1/2f out* **14/1**

9 4 **Hitchens (IRE)**[61] 7928 9-9-0 108 SilvestreDeSousa 1 77
(David Barron) *nvr bttr than mid-div* **16/1**

1m 11.75s (0.15) **Going Correction** +0.20s/f (Slow) **9** Ran SP% **118.7**
Speed ratings: **107,106,104,104,103 101,99,98,93**
CSF: 58.47; EX 76.70; TRIFECTA: 537.80; WIN: 6.20; PL: 1.40, 4.50, 2.10..
**Owner** Sheikh Ahmed Al Maktoum **Bred** Adena Springs **Trained** United Arab Emirates

**FOCUS**
This was a slowly run Listed sprint.

## 207a DUBAI DUTY FREE FINEST SURPRISE (H'CAP) (TAPETA) 1m
**5:25** (5:25) (95-105,105) 3-Y-0+
**£39,759** (£13,253; £6,626; £3,313; £1,987; £1,325)

RPR

1 **Zain Shamardal (IRE)**[14] 6-9-6 **105** (t) RoystonFfrench 15 105
(A Al Raihe, UAE) *mid-div: chsd ldrs 3f out: led 2f out: kpt on wl: jst hld on* **20/1**

2 shd **Alnashmy (FR)**[42] 8173 6-9-0 **98** (tp) DaneO'Neill 6 99
(J Peromingo, UAE) *mid-div: smooth prog 2f out: r.o wl fnl f: jst failed* **14/1**

3 3/4 **Intrigo**[89] 7368 4-9-1 **99** MartinLane 14 98
(Charlie Appleby) *mid-div: r.o fnl 2f: nrst fin* **10/1**

4 nk **Lehaaf (ARG)**[194] 5-9-0 **98** (t) ChristopheSoumillon 4 97
(M F De Kock, South Africa) *in rr of mid-div: r.o fnl 2f but nvr able to chal* **5/1**[2]

5 1/2 **Derbaas (USA)**[7] 110 8-9-6 **105** (t) PaulHanagan 16 101
(A Al Raihe, UAE) *in rr of mid-div: r.o fnl 2f: nrst fin* **16/1**

6 nse **Van Rooney (USA)**[265] 5-9-4 **102** (t) WilliamBuick 10 99
(Ali Jan, Qatar) *s.i.s: settled in rr: r.o fnl 1 1/2f: nrst fin* **16/1**

7 nk **Risby (IRE)**[46] 6-9-2 **100** JulienAuge 9 97
(J-M Osorio, Spain) *slowly away: settled in rr: nvr nr to chal* **20/1**

8 1 **Chilworth Icon**[104] 6990 4-8-13 **97** WilliamTwiston-Davies 2 91
(Mick Channon) *nvr bttr than mid-div* **25/1**

9 nse **Regulation (IRE)**[48] 8101 5-9-2 **100** ShaneFoley 3 94+
(M Halford, Ire) *mid-div: chsd ldrs 2f out: one pce fnl f* **8/1**

10 3/4 **Start Right**[350] 462 7-8-13 **97** (b) RichardMullen 5 89+
(S Seemar, UAE) *s.i.s: trckd ldrs: ev ch 2 1/2f out: wknd fnl 1 1/2f* **11/1**

11 3/4 **Counterglow (IRE)**[357] 363 5-9-2 **100** MickaelBarzalona 12 91
(Charlie Appleby) *nvr bttr than mid-div* **13/2**[3]

12 3/4 **Robert The Painter (IRE)**[97] 7172 6-8-13 **97** (v) JamieSpencer 11 86+
(David O'Meara) *sn led: hdd after 2f: wknd fnl 3f* **16/1**

13 1 **Validus**[103] 7018 5-9-4 **102** (p) SilvestreDeSousa 8 89+
(Saeed bin Suroor) *trckd ldrs: ev ch 1 1/2f out: wknd fnl f* **4/1**[1]

14 6 1/4 **Famous Warrior (IRE)**[300] 1135 7-9-1 **99** (t) PatDobbs 7 71+
(Doug Watson, UAE) *trckd ldrs tl outpcd 1 1/2 out* **25/1**

15 3/4 **Nine Realms**[110] 6838 5-8-11 **96** AhmedAjtebi 1 66
(Charlie Appleby) *nvr bttr than mid-div* **12/1**

16 3/4 **Storm Ultralight (ARG)**[322] 834 8-8-7 **97** ow2 (t) MarcMonaghan(5) 13 63+
(S Seemar, UAE) *led after 2f: hdd & wknd 2 1/2f out* **50/1**

1m 37.05s (-0.45) **Going Correction** +0.20s/f (Slow) **16** Ran SP% **129.7**
Speed ratings: **110,109,109,108,108 108,108,107,106,106 105,104,103,97,96 95**
.
**Owner** Royal Cavalry Oman **Bred** Kevin & Meta Cullen **Trained** UAE

**FOCUS**
They went hard up front in this fair handicap.

# [186]LINGFIELD (L-H)
Friday, January 17

**OFFICIAL GOING: Standard**
Wind: Fresh, half behind Weather: Changeable with showers; course surrounds flooded

## 208 BEST ODDS AT BOOKMAKERS.CO.UK CLAIMING STKS 6f 1y(P)
**1:00** (1:00) (Class 6) 4-Y-0+ **£2,045** (£603; £302) **Stalls** Low

Form RPR

14-2 1 **Kuanyao (IRE)**[7] 113 8-8-11 73 (v) LouisSteward(7) 1 84
(Lee Carter) *mde all: drew clr 1/2-way: hrd rdn over 1f out: kpt on: unchal* **7/4**[1]

000- 2 2 1/2 **Mac's Power (IRE)**[88] 7427 8-9-3 83 RobertWinston 4 75
(Willie Musson) *hld up towards rr: outpcd 1/2-way: prog 2f out: chsd wnr 1f out: styd on but no ch of threatening* **7/2**[2]

320- 3 1 3/4 **Angelo Poliziano**[21] 8406 8-8-9 69 (b) BenCurtis 2 61
(Jo Hughes) *dwlt: hld up in last: prog on inner 2f out: styd on to take 3rd last 100yds* **33/1**

340- 4 1 1/4 **Homeboy (IRE)**[37] 8244 6-8-0 56 (b) JordanVaughan(7) 3 55
(Marcus Tregoning) *prom on inner: chsd wnr after 2f: no imp over 2f out: lost 2nd and wknd 1f out* **25/1**

0-14 5 hd **Dark Lane**[6] 141 8-8-10 66 ChrisCatlin 8 58
(David Evans) *racd wd: chsd ldrs: outpcd 1/2-way: lost grnd bnd 2f out: no ch after: kpt on* **14/1**

35-0 6 3/4 **Senator Bong**[9] 91 4-9-5 72 (b[1]) LiamKeniry 6 64
(David Elsworth) *hld up in rr: bandage c loose 1/2-way: nt clr run and outpcd sn after: nvr on terms* **12/1**

01-4 7 nse **Hamoody (USA)**[14] 35 10-8-12 80 AdrianNicholls 7 57
(David Nicholls) *dwlt: racd wd: in tch: rdn over 2f out: lost grnd bnd sn after: no ch but kpt on last 150yds* **7/2**[2]

02-2 8 1/2 **Drawnfromthepast (IRE)**[9] 87 9-8-6 68 JackGarritty(7) 5 57
(Luke Dace) *chsd wnr 2f: rdn over 2f out: wknd over 1f out* **6/1**[3]

1m 10.29s (-1.61) **Going Correction** -0.125s/f (Stan) **8** Ran SP% **116.2**
Speed ratings (Par 101): **105,101,99,97,97 96,96,95**
CSF £8.15 TOTE £2.80: £1.40, £1.40, £5.40; EX 13.20 Trifecta £216.90.Homeboy was claimed by David Evans for £3,000.
**Owner** John Joseph Smith **Bred** Newlands House Stud **Trained** Epsom, Surrey

**FOCUS**
Some fair sorts in this claimer, many of them well into the veteran stages of their careers.

## 209 CORAL MOBILE "JUST THREE CLICKS TO BET" (S) STKS 1m 4f (P)
**1:30** (1:33) (Class 6) 4-6-Y-O **£2,045** (£603; £302) **Stalls** Low

Form RPR

02-6 1 **A Little Bit Dusty**[15] 21 6-9-3 72 (p) LiamKeniry 3 63
(Conor Dore) *hld up in 4th: prog to join ldr 1/2-way: led 3f out: drvn over 2f out: kpt on u.p* **5/4**[1]

00-0 2 2 1/2 **Gabrial's Hope (FR)**[13] 49 5-9-3 58 AdamKirby 2 59
(David Simcock) *chsd ldr to 1/2-way: sharp reminders over 3f out: chsd wnr wl over 2f out: cl enough but hanging and nt qckn over 1f out: one pce after* **9/4**[2]

/35- 3 13 **Lascaux**[105] 809 5-8-12 63 LukeMorris 5 33
(Luke Dace) *v reluctant to enter stalls: chsd ldng pair to 1/2-way: rdn and no rspnse over 4f out: n.d fnl 3f: tk modest 3rd last stride* **6/1**

5/3- 4 shd **Ballyheigue (IRE)**[32] 8309 5-9-3 68 (b) GeorgeBaker 1 38
(Gary Moore) *rousted along to ld then t.k.h: hdd 3f out: sn btn: lost modest 3rd last stride* **3/1**[3]

600- 5 17 **East Texas Red (IRE)**[29] 8339 4-8-13 41 (p) LiamJones 4
(Mick Quinn) *t.k.h: hld up in last: rdn 5f out: sn lost tch: t.o* **33/1**

2m 31.27s (-1.73) **Going Correction** -0.125s/f (Stan)
**WFA** 4 from 5yo+ 4lb **5** Ran SP% **117.4**
Speed ratings: **100,98,89,89,78**
CSF £4.81 TOTE £2.40: £1.20, £2.40; EX 5.60 Trifecta £15.60.The winner was bought in for 4,800gns.
**Owner** David Baldwin & Chris Marsh **Bred** T O C S Limited **Trained** Hubbert's Bridge, Lincs

**FOCUS**
As poor a race as you're likely to see. The runner-up has been rated in line with his recent runs.

## 210 CORAL.CO.UK BEST ODDS GUARANTEED ON RACING H'CAP 1m 2f (P)
**2:00** (2:02) (Class 6) (0-65,71) 4-Y-0+ **£2,385** (£704; £352) **Stalls** Low

Form RPR

450- 1 **Whitby Jet (IRE)**[30] 8323 6-9-6 **64** LiamKeniry 2 74
(Ed Vaughan) *hld up in midfield on inner: waiting for room fr 3f out tl prog over 1f out: r.o to ld last 100yds: sn clr* **8/1**

011- 2 2 **Brave Decision**[46] 8121 7-9-2 **60** AdamKirby 11 66
(Suzy Smith) *chsd ldrs but trapped out wd: rdn and prog to go 3rd over 2f out: kpt on fnl f to take 2nd post* **6/1**[3]

00-1 3 hd **Tiger Reigns**[8] 105 8-9-13 **71** 6ex GeorgeBaker 1 77
(John Butler) *led: pushed along and pressed over 2f out: kpt on but hdd and outpcd last 100yds: lost 2nd post* **7/4**[1]

00-0 4 nk **Final Delivery**[11] 67 5-8-7 **56** NathanAlison(5) 6 61
(Jim Boyle) *hld up in last pair: sme prog on outer 3f out: v wd bnd 2f out: cajoled along and styd on wl fnl f* **50/1**

35-2 5 nse **Secret Song**[9] 90 4-8-10 **56** (p) LukeMorris 5 61
(Sir Mark Prescott Bt) *trckd ldr: chal over 2f out: nrly upsides 1f out: outpcd last 10yds: lost pls nr fin* **4/1**[2]

42-3 6 1 1/4 **Charlotte Rhodes**[15] 13 4-9-0 **60** AndreaAtzeni 8 62
(Marco Botti) *chsd ldrs: pushed along over 3f out: tried to cl over 1f out: one pce fnl f* **20/1**

21-0 7 1/2 **Fonterutoli (IRE)**[9] 92 7-9-0 **58** (e) RobertWinston 10 59
(Roger Ingram) *hld up in last: prog wl over 1f out: rdn and kpt on: no ch* **8/1**

600- 8 3/4 **Ogaritmo**[51] 8072 5-9-2 **60** (bt[1]) JimCrowley 3 60
(Seamus Durack) *early reminder and shoved along in rr: gng bttr after 3f: nt clr run in last pair over 2f out: shkn up and sme prog over 1f out: no hdwy fnl f* **20/1**

02-0 9 3/4 **Salient**[7] 117 10-8-7 **51** oh2 LiamJones 4 49
(Michael Attwater) *rousted along early and sn chsd ldng pair: lost 3rd over 2f out: sn wknd* **33/1**

42-2 10 1 **Ice Tres**[11] 68 5-8-7 **51** DavidProbert 7 47
(Rod Millman) *trckd ldrs tl lost pl and btn over 2f out* **12/1**

000- 11 3 3/4 **Claude Monet (BRZ)**[62] 7931 5-8-10 **54** SeanLevey 9 43
(Simon Dow) *t.k.h: hld up towards rr: rdn and no rspnse 2f out: sn wknd* **25/1**

2m 4.71s (-1.89) **Going Correction** -0.125s/f (Stan)
**WFA** 4 from 5yo+ 2lb **11** Ran SP% **118.8**
Speed ratings (Par 101): **102,100,100,100,99 98,98,97,97,96 93**
CSF £52.02 CT £123.44 TOTE £11.40: £3.00, £2.00, £1.30; EX 78.50 Trifecta £356.60.
**Owner** A M Pickering **Bred** Rathasker Stud **Trained** Newmarket, Suffolk

**FOCUS**
A fair handicap for the grade but muddling form. The third and fourth were both well in after their recent runs.

## 211 LADBROKES H'CAP 1m 1y(P)
**2:30** (2:33) (Class 6) (0-65,69) 4-Y-0+ **£2,385** (£704; £352) **Stalls** High

Form RPR

24-1 1 **Tee It Up Tommo (IRE)**[4] 154 5-9-11 **69** 6ex RobertWinston 1 76
(Michael Wigham) *hld up in 6th: eased to outer and prog over 2f out: clsd on ldrs over 1f out: cajoled along to chal fnl f: hanging and threatened nt to respond: put hd in front on line* **4/6**[1]

506- 2 shd **Carrera**[95] 7249 4-8-10 **54** DavidProbert 6 61
(Michael Blanshard) *trckd ldng pair: wnt 2nd 2f out: rdn to ld narrowly jst over 1f out: hrd pressed after: hdd post* **33/1**

165- 3 nk **Prince Of Burma (IRE)**[20] 8432 6-9-7 **65** (v) AdamKirby 4 71
(David Evans) *hld up in 8th: prog 2f out: rdn to chal ins fnl f: upsides nr fin: jst denied* **3/1**[2]

50-1 4 3 1/2 **Nubar Boy**[9] 92 7-8-6 **57** (p) CharlotteJenner(7) 11 55
(Ian Williams) *racd freely: led: rdn and hdd jst over 1f out: fdd fnl f* **10/1**[3]

043- 5 1 **Indian Violet (IRE)**[216] 3329 8-8-10 **54** (p) LiamKeniry 3 50
(Zoe Davison) *hld up in last trio: prog towards inner 2f out: tried to cl on ldrs over 1f out: wknd fnl f* **33/1**

246- 6 nk **South Cape**[123] 6459 11-8-12 **63** HectorCrouch(7) 2 58
(Gary Moore) *hld up in last pair: pushed along and sme prog on inner over 1f out: no hdwy fnl f* **20/1**

323- 7 1 **Warbond**[46] 8125 6-9-0 **58** (p) JohnFahy 10 51
(Michael Madgwick) *hld up in last pair: sme prog on inner and rdn over 1f out: no hdwy and wl hld whn short of room nr fin* **25/1**

61-5 **8** *10* **Hail Promenader (IRE)**[14] 39 8-8-12 **61**..............(tp) PhilipPrince(5) 8 31
(Anthony Carson) *sn rdn to chse ldrs on outer: styd in tch tl wknd qckly 2f out* **20/1**

000- **9** *3/4* **Cuthbert (IRE)**[26] 8390 7-8-7 **51** oh6..............................(b) LiamJones 7 19
(Michael Attwater) *chsd ldr to 2f out: wknd qckly* **100/1**

640- **10** *13* **Gunning For Glory**[206] 3665 4-9-1 **59**.............................. JimCrowley 5
(Dean Ivory) *trckd ldrs in 5th: gng wl enough whn bdly hmpd over 2f out: nt rcvr and eased* **25/1**

1m 36.92s (-1.28) **Going Correction** -0.125s/f (Stan) **10** Ran SP% **118.2**
Speed ratings (Par 101): **101,100,100,97,96 95,94,84,84,71**
CSF £38.28 CT £53.39 TOTE £1.80: £1.10, £6.90, £1.10; EX 50.80 Trifecta £228.50.
**Owner** Palatinate Thoroughbred Racing Limited **Bred** Oghill House Stud **Trained** Newmarket, Suffolk

**FOCUS**
This was much more competitive than the market suggested and it served up a thrilling finish. The runner-up has been rated pretty much to his best, with the third in line with his 7f win here in November.

## 212 CORAL.CO.UK CONDITIONS STKS 1m 4f (P)
3:00 (3:00) (Class 3) 4-Y-O+ £7,439 (£2,213; £1,106) Stalls Low

Form RPR

41-2 **1** **Modernstone**[13] 54 4-8-10 **94**...................................... AndreaAtzeni 3 99
(William Knight) *trckd ldr: clsd to take narrow ld jst over 3f out: rdn over 2f out: steadily asserted fnl f* **11/10**[2]

02-1 **2** *1 1/4* **Castilo Del Diablo (IRE)**[13] 54 5-9-2 **98**...................... AdamKirby 4 99
(David Simcock) *led at modest pce: tried to qckn over 3f out but sn narrowly hdd: pressed wnr tl nt qckn and hld fnl f* **4/5**[1]

3-14 **3** *8* **Royal Alcor (IRE)**[7] 125 7-8-9 **80**..............(t) TomasHarrigan(7) 2 86
(Gay Kelleway) *s.s: t.k.h in last: moved up to chal on outer 4f out: upsides over 2f out: wknd over 1f out* **25/1**[3]

2m 38.33s (5.33) **Going Correction** -0.125s/f (Stan)
**WFA** 4 from 5yo+ 4lb **3** Ran SP% **107.0**
Speed ratings (Par 107): **77,76,70**
CSF £2.34 TOTE £2.60; EX 2.10 Trifecta £3.10.
**Owner** Biddestone Racing Club **Bred** Oscar Stud **Trained** Patching, W Sussex

**FOCUS**
A disappointing turn out for this conditions event, in which tactics played a big part in deciding the outcome. The winner has been rated close to form and the runner-up a bit off it.

## 213 32RED MAIDEN STKS 5f 6y(P)
3:35 (3:35) (Class 5) 3-Y-O £3,067 (£905; £453) Stalls High

Form RPR

52-3 **1** **Searchlight**[12] 62 3-9-5 **78**..............................(t) JimCrowley 3 72
(Kevin Ryan) *trckd ldng pair: hanging rt but nipped through on inner bnd 2f out: sn led: hrd pressed and rdn 1f out: fnd enough and pushed out nr fin* **5/4**[2]

5-2 **2** *1* **Three D Alexander (IRE)**[6] 140 3-9-0 **89**................... AdamKirby 2 63
(David Evans) *pressed ldr: upsides whn carried rt bnd 2f out: pressed wnr and upsides 1f out: nt qckn* **10/11**[1]

605- **3** *4* **Cheeky Peta'S**[19] 8435 3-8-11 **47**.................(v) GeorgeChaloner(3) 6 49
(James Given) *chsd ldrs: carried rt bnd 2f out: sn outpcd: tk 3rd ins fnl f* **100/1**

5- **4** *3/4* **Sylvan Spirit (IRE)**[73] 7737 3-9-0 0.............................. RobertWinston 5 46
(Roger Teal) *mostly in 5th: pushed along to try to cl 2f out: one pce over 1f out* **50/1**

5 **5** *2 1/4* **Dove Mountain (IRE)**[11] 70 3-9-5 **74**.......................... GeorgeBaker 4 43
(Gary Brown) *c out of the stalls slowly: detached in last: jst pushed along and kpt on to take modest 5th nr fin* **20/1**[3]

43-5 **6** *shd* **Anfield**[15] 15 3-9-0 **55**...................................... AndreaAtzeni 1 38
(Mick Quinn) *led: hung rt bnd 2f out: sn hdd & wknd* **33/1**

58.18s (-0.62) **Going Correction** -0.125s/f (Stan) **6** Ran SP% **107.5**
Speed ratings (Par 97): **99,97,91,89,86 86**
CSF £2.41 TOTE £2.50: £1.30, £1.10; EX 3.50 Trifecta £43.60.
**Owner** Elite Racing Club **Bred** Elite Racing Club **Trained** Hambleton, N Yorks

**FOCUS**
A straight match on paper was played out in the race itself. The level is a bit fluid with a doubt over what the runner-up retains.

## 214 32RED.COM H'CAP 1m 7f 169y(P)
4:05 (4:06) (Class 6) (0-65,65) 4-Y-O+ £2,385 (£704; £352) Stalls Low

Form RPR

533- **1** **Keep Kicking (IRE)**[30] 8331 7-9-6 **57**........................ JimCrowley 1 63
(Simon Dow) *hld up towards rr: wl in tch 3f out: shkn up and prog 2f out: wnt 2nd 1f out: styd on wl to ld post* **5/1**[3]

0- **2** *shd* **Shadarpour (IRE)**[36] 7863 5-9-9 **60**..............(b) GeorgeBaker 9 66
(Gary Moore) *a in ldng trio: narrow ld over 4f out: wnt for home over 2f out: 3 l clr 1f out: collared last stride* **7/1**

21- **3** *1/2* **Echua (IRE)**[22] 8257 8-9-10 **61**.............................. JohnFahy 10 66
(Emmet Michael Butterly, Ire) *hld up in rr: wl in tch 3f out: prog and rdn 2f out: styd on wl fnl f: nrst fin* **3/1**[1]

06-3 **4** *3/4* **Honest Strike (USA)**[8] 104 7-9-10 **61**..............(b) ShaneKelly 2 65
(Daniel Mark Loughnane) *stdd s: hld up in last: brought wdst of all bnd 2f out: rdn over 1f out: styd on wl fnl f: no ch to chal* **4/1**[2]

654- **5** *3* **Dr Finley (IRE)**[44] 8160 7-9-5 **56**.....................(v) PaddyAspell 5 56
(Lydia Pearce) *trckd ldrs: n.m.r over 5f out: rdn 2f out: nt pce to threaten fr over 1f out* **20/1**

563- **6** *1/2* **Where's Susie**[29] 8343 9-10-0 **65**.......................... AndreaAtzeni 8 65
(Michael Madgwick) *hld up in midfield: lost pl over 3f out: rdn over 2f out: kpt on one pce after: no ch* **6/1**

415- **7** *2* **Epsom Salts**[30] 8331 9-9-8 **62**..................(p) JemmaMarshall(3) 7 59
(Pat Phelan) *s.s: prog fr rr 1/2-way: n.m.r over 5f out: chsd ldrs over 2f out: wknd over 1f out* **10/1**

20-2 **8** *1/2* **Sommersturm (GER)**[7] 123 10-9-2 **58**................(t) EoinWalsh(5) 3 55
(David Evans) *hld up: prog on wd outside to chal 6f out: w ldr over 4f out to 3f out: wknd jst over 1f out* **8/1**

445- **9** *14* **Royal Defence (IRE)**[59] 7612 8-8-9 **46**.......................... LiamJones 4 26
(Mick Quinn) *led to over 10f out: rdn and lost pl qckly 5f out: sn bhd: t.o* **33/1**

040- **10** *3 1/4* **Balady (IRE)**[20] 6325 5-9-12 **63**.............................. RobertWinston 6 39
(Dominic Ffrench Davis) *t.k.h: trckd ldrs tl plld way through to ld over 10f out: hdd over 4f out: wknd rapidly over 2f out: t.o* **25/1**

3m 24.5s (-1.20) **Going Correction** -0.125s/f (Stan) **10** Ran SP% **120.2**
Speed ratings (Par 101): **98,97,97,97,95 95,94,94,87,85**
CSF £40.18 CT £125.20 TOTE £5.10: £1.60, £3.20, £1.30; EX 65.30 Trifecta £424.60.
**Owner** P McCarthy **Bred** Sunny Days Ltd **Trained** Epsom, Surrey

**FOCUS**
A steadily run finale and little convincing about the form.

T/Plt: £6.50 to a £1 stake. Pool: £87275.06 - 9746.14 winning tickets T/Qpdt: £3.50 to a £1 stake. Pool: £6968.08 - 1444.88 winning tickets JN

# [195]WOLVERHAMPTON (A.W) (L-H)
Friday, January 17

**OFFICIAL GOING: Standard**
Wind: Light behind Weather: Overcast

## 215 COMPARE BOOKMAKERS AT BOOKMAKERS.CO.UK H'CAP 5f 216y(P)
4:30 (4:31) (Class 7) (0-50,49) 4-Y-O+ £2,102 (£625; £312; £156) Stalls Low

Form RPR

5/0- **1** **Catalyze**[345] 537 6-9-2 **45**..............................(t) WilliamCarson 7 56
(Ann Stokell) *hld up in tch: plld hrd: shkn up to chse ldr over 1f out: rdn to ld ins fnl f: styd on u.p* **6/4**[1]

064- **2** *nk* **Flow Chart (IRE)**[43] 8168 7-8-13 **45**.................. SladeO'Hara(3) 5 55
(Peter Grayson) *sn led: rdn and hdd ins fnl f: styd on* **4/1**[2]

53-2 **3** *6* **Red Star Lady (IRE)**[8] 100 4-9-2 **45**.......................... JimmyQuinn 8 36
(Shaun Harris) *prom: chsd ldr 1/2-way tl shkn up over 1f out: no ex ins fnl f* **9/2**[3]

200- **4** *1 3/4* **Cheyenne Red (IRE)**[35] 8271 8-9-4 **47**........................ PJMcDonald 4 32
(Michael Herrington) *w ldr tl pushed along over 3f out: rdn over 1f out: styd on same pce* **8/1**

045- **5** *nk* **Very First Blade**[112] 6808 5-9-6 **49**......................(p) TomEaves 9 33
(Michael Mullineaux) *mid-div: sn pushed along: rdn over 2f out: nt trble ldrs* **8/1**

0/0 **6** *2 3/4* **Jjs Pride (IRE)**[9] 81 5-9-2 **45**......................(tp) AdamBeschizza 6 20
(Denis Quinn) *sn outpcd* **8/1**

004- **7** *1 1/4* **Princess Bounty**[56] 8003 4-8-9 **45**......................(t) JoeDoyle(7) 3 16
(Phil McEntee) *s.s: sme hdwy over 2f out: rdn and wknd over 1f out* **8/1**

000/ **8** *43* **Bowmans Well (IRE)**[725] 273 9-8-11 **45**..............(e) ShelleyBirkett(5) 1
(Peter Purdy) *chsd ldrs: pushed along over 3f out: sn wknd* **100/1**

1m 15.9s (0.90) **Going Correction** +0.15s/f (Slow) **8** Ran SP% **123.6**
Speed ratings (Par 97): **100,99,91,89,88 85,83,26**
CSF £8.54 CT £23.93 TOTE £2.90: £1.10, £1.40, £1.40; EX 13.00 Trifecta £47.10.
**Owner** Pallet And Recycling Sales Ltd **Bred** The Hon Robert Hanson **Trained** Southwell, Notts

**FOCUS**
A massive gamble was narrowly landed in this modest handicap and the first two pulled clear.

## 216 32RED.COM H'CAP 5f 20y(P)
5:00 (5:00) (Class 6) (0-55,57) 3-Y-O £2,425 (£721; £360; £180) Stalls Low

Form RPR

66-2 **1** **My My My Diliza**[4] 165 3-9-5 **53**......................(b) GrahamLee 6 57
(J S Moore) *chsd ldrs: rdn to ld ins fnl f: r.o* **11/4**[2]

2-21 **2** *1* **Argent Touch**[8] 98 3-9-2 **57** 6ex...................... AdamMcLean(7) 2 57
(Derek Shaw) *plld hrd: trckd ldr 4f out tl led over 1f out: rdn: edgd rt and hdd ins fnl f: styd on same pce* **5/4**[1]

036- **3** *3* **Mahon Falls**[28] 8368 3-8-12 **53**.............................. JoeDoyle(7) 4 43
(David Evans) *led over 3f: sn rdn: no ex ins fnl f* **8/1**[3]

0-43 **4** *1* **Countess Lupus (IRE)**[4] 165 3-8-7 **46** oh1......(b) ShirleyTeasdale(5) 1 32
(Lisa Williamson) *chsd ldrs: pushed along and lost pl over 3f out: rdn 1/2-way: hdwy over 1f out: no ex ins fnl f* **12/1**

440- **5** *2 1/4* **Back On Baileys**[30] 8322 3-9-1 **54**.................. ShelleyBirkett(5) 3 32
(Chris Dwyer) *prom: rdn over 1f out: rdr dropped whip sn after: hung rt and wknd fnl f* **8/1**[3]

400- **6** *2 1/2* **Loma Mor**[122] 6493 3-9-7 **55**..........................(p) WilliamCarson 5 24
(Alan McCabe) *dwlt: hdwy 1/2-way: rdn over 1f out: sn hung lft and wknd* **20/1**

46-4 **7** *2 1/4* **Sunningdale Rose (IRE)**[15] 19 3-9-5 **53**..............(v) TomEaves 7 14
(Gay Kelleway) *hld up: rdn and wknd 1/2-way* **14/1**

1m 3.52s (1.22) **Going Correction** +0.15s/f (Slow) **7** Ran SP% **112.5**
Speed ratings (Par 95): **96,94,89,88,84 80,76**
CSF £6.32 TOTE £3.40: £1.60, £1.20; EX 6.60 Trifecta £30.60.
**Owner** R Styles, P Grimes & J S Moore **Bred** M C Humby **Trained** Upper Lambourn, Berks

**FOCUS**
The strong favourite was overhauled by his main market rival in this low-grade handicap.

## 217 32RED H'CAP 7f 32y(P)
5:30 (5:31) (Class 4) (0-85,79) 3-Y-O £5,175 (£1,540; £769; £384) Stalls High

Form RPR

66-2 **1** **Crowdmania**[4] 157 3-8-11 **69**.............................. JoeFanning 5 74
(Mark Johnston) *chsd ldrs: shkn up to ld 2f out: rdn and hung lft ent fnl f: styd on* **8/13**[1]

351- **2** *nk* **Mersad (IRE)**[17] 8452 3-8-13 **71**......................(b[1]) JimmyQuinn 4 75
(James Tate) *hld up: hdwy over 1f out: rdn to chse wnr fnl f: sn hung lft: styd on* **7/1**[3]

21-2 **3** *2 1/4* **Queenie's Home**[12] 62 3-9-1 **73**.............................. GrahamLee 6 71
(James Given) *set stdy pce tl pushed along and hdd 2f out: styd on same pce fnl f* **5/1**[2]

443- **4** *3 3/4* **Intense Feeling (IRE)**[30] 8325 3-8-0 **65**.................. JoeDoyle(7) 2 53
(David Evans) *w ldr to 1/2-way: pushed along and lost 2nd 2f out: no ex fnl f* **25/1**

1m 32.43s (2.83) **Going Correction** +0.15s/f (Slow) **4** Ran SP% **94.9**
Speed ratings (Par 99): **89,88,86,81**
CSF £3.49 TOTE £1.20; EX 4.50 Trifecta £4.80.
**Owner** Sheikh Hamdan bin Mohammed Al Maktoum **Bred** Car Colston Hall Stud **Trained** Middleham Moor, N Yorks
■ Rule 4 of 10p in the pound applies to all bets; Withdrawn: Spiritual Flame

**FOCUS**
They went a steady pace in this small-field handicap and hot favourite showed a good attitude to score. Spiritual Flame got agitated in the stalls and was withdrawn.

## 218 LADBROKES MAIDEN STKS 7f 32y(P)
6:00 (6:01) (Class 5) 3-Y-O+ £2,911 (£866; £432; £216) Stalls High

Form RPR

3 **1** **Hardy Black (IRE)**[14] 37 3-8-10 0.......................... FergusSweeney 7 72
(Jamie Osborne) *chsd ldr: rdn to ld ins fnl f: r.o* **7/2**[2]

0- **2** *3/4* **Royal Encounter**[20] 8425 3-8-10 0.......................... JimmyQuinn 8 70
(Ed Vaughan) *sn led: shkn up over 1f out: rdn and hdd ins fnl f: styd on* **11/4**[1]

**3** *3 3/4* **Jaahiez (USA)** 3-8-7 0.............................. RossAtkinson(3) 3 60
(Roger Varian) *chsd ldrs: pushed along over 2f out: styd on same pce fnl f* **7/2**[2]

03- 4 1 **Female Strategy (IRE)**[43] 8165 3-8-5 0 ChrisCatlin 5 52
(Peter Chapple-Hyam) *chsd ldrs: rdn over 1f out: styd on same pce fnl f* 7/2[2]

5 7 **Lockedoutaheaven (IRE)** 3-8-10 0 PaoloSirigu 4 38
(Marco Botti) *s.i.s: hld up: pushed along 1/2-way: nvr on terms* 6/1[3]

00 6 ¾ **Needs The Run**[2] 188 3-8-7 0 MarkCoumbe(3) 2 36
(David Evans) *s.i.s: pushed along 1/2-way: a in rr* 25/1

1m 30.76s (1.16) **Going Correction** +0.15s/f (Slow) 6 Ran SP% **111.5**
Speed ratings (Par 103): **99,98,93,92,84 83**
CSF £13.31 TOTE £2.80: £1.30, £1.60; EX 19.80 Trifecta £39.20.

**Owner** Patrick Gage & Tony Taylor **Bred** A M V Nicoll **Trained** Upper Lambourn, Berks

**FOCUS**
There was an open market for this ordinary maiden. The pace was not strong but the first two pulled clear.

## 219 LADBROKES H'CAP 7f 32y(P)
**6:30** (6:31) (Class 6) (0-60,63) 4-Y-0+ **£2,425** (£721; £360; £180) **Stalls** High

Form RPR

405- 1 **True Spirit**[101] 7109 4-9-2 **55** SeanLevey 3 61
(Paul D'Arcy) *a.p: chsd ldr 1/2-way: rdn over 2f out: r.o u.p to ld nr fin* **8/1**

65-0 2 *nk* **Two In The Pink (IRE)**[13] 53 4-9-7 **60** JoeFanning 4 65
(Ralph J Smith) *hld up in tch: shkn up over 1f out: rdn and r.o ins fnl f* **4/1**

20U- 3 *hd* **Layla's Hero (IRE)**[99] 7148 7-9-6 **59** (v) TomEaves 7 63
(David Nicholls) *led at stdy pce over 5f out: qcknd over 2f out: rdn over 1f out: hdd nr fin* **20/1**

21/1 4 *hd* **Blackthorn Stick (IRE)**[7] 126 5-9-10 **63** 6ex LiamKeniry 6 67+
(John Butler) *s.i.s: hld up: rdn over 1f out: r.o wl ins fnl f* **9/4**[1]

5-21 5 *nse* **Minimee**[2] 184 4-8-13 **59** 6ex (v) JoeDoyle(7) 1 63
(Phil McEntee) *chsd ldrs: rdn over 2f out: ev ch ins fnl f: r.o* **11/4**[2]

624- 6 2¼ **Harvest Mist (IRE)**[35] 8278 6-9-5 **58** GrahamLee 2 56
(Shaun Lycett) *set stdy pce tl hdd over 5f out: chsd ldr to 1/2-way: rdn over 1f out: no ex wl ins fnl f* **16/1**

642- 7 4½ **Coastal Passage**[48] 8118 6-8-11 **50** (tp) LukeMorris 5 36
(Gordon Elliott, Ire) *broke wl: sn lost pl: in rr and rdn 1/2-way: n.d* **7/2**[3]

1m 30.22s (0.62) **Going Correction** +0.15s/f (Slow) 7 Ran SP% **121.4**
Speed ratings (Par 101): **102,101,101,101,101 98,93**
CSF £42.78 CT £636.79 TOTE £9.50: £7.00, £4.50; EX 45.80 Trifecta £1629.30.

**Owner** Paul D'Arcy **Bred** D E And Mrs J Cash **Trained** Newmarket, Suffolk

**FOCUS**
There was a tight five-way finish in this steadily-run handicap.

## 220 CORAL MOBILE "JUST THREE CLICKS TO BET" CONDITIONS STKS 1m 1f 103y(P)
**7:00** (7:00) (Class 2) 4-Y-0+ **£11,827** (£3,541; £1,770; £885) **Stalls** Low

Form RPR

0/1- 1 **Jakkalberry (IRE)**[314] 956 8-9-11 115 (t) AdamKirby 3 101
(Marco Botti) *trckd ldrs: shkn up to ld over 1f out: styd on: comf* **1/6**[1]

32-3 2 3 **Excellent Puck (IRE)**[1] 200 4-9-3 79 RobertTart 2 88
(Shaun Lycett) *led: pushed along over 2f out: rdn and hdd over 1f out: styd on same pce fnl f* **12/1**[3]

661- 3 4 **Come On Blue Chip (IRE)**[63] 7906 5-9-4 90 (p) SeanLevey 4 80
(Paul D'Arcy) *trckd ldr tl shkn up over 2f out: sn rdn: no ex fnl f* **6/1**[2]

-534 4 36 **Bix (IRE)**[1] 199 4-9-3 44 JordanHibberd 1 4
(Alan Berry) *s.v.s: tk clsr order over 6f out: lost tch fnl 5f* **100/1**

2m 0.3s (-1.40) **Going Correction** +0.15s/f (Slow)
**WFA** 4 from 5yo+ 1lb 4 Ran SP% **108.7**
Speed ratings (Par 109): **112,109,105,73**
CSF £3.22 TOTE £1.10; EX 3.20 Trifecta £6.00.

**Owner** Australian Thoroughbred Bloodstock **Bred** Azienda Agricola Allevamento Deni **Trained** Newmarket, Suffolk

**FOCUS**
The high-class favourite had to work to land the odds in this conditions event but was well on top in the closing stages.

## 221 CORAL APP DOWNLOAD FROM THE APP STORE H'CAP 1m 4f 50y(P)
**7:30** (7:30) (Class 6) (0-65,71) 4-Y-0+ **£2,425** (£721; £360; £180) **Stalls** Low

Form RPR

2-11 1 **The Blue Dog (IRE)**[4] 158 7-9-7 **69** 6ex JoeDoyle(7) 3 78+
(Phil McEntee) *trckd ldr 2f: remained handy: led on bit over 1f out: shkn up wl ins fnl f: jst hld on* **6/4**[2]

410- 2 *shd* **Jamaica Grande**[21] 8410 6-9-4 **59** GrahamLee 7 68
(Dave Morris) *hld up: hdwy and hung lft over 1f out: rdn and r.o wl: jst failed* **5/1**[3]

300- 3 3 **Penny Stock (IRE)**[119] 6611 4-8-7 **52** JoeFanning 1 56
(Mark Johnston) *plld hrd: led: rdn and hdd over 1f out: styd on same pce ins fnl f* **10/1**

00-3 4 1¼ **Blazing Desert**[15] 21 10-9-5 **60** AdamBeschizza 5 62
(William Kinsey) *trckd ldr after 2f: rdn over 1f out: no ex ins fnl f* **10/1**

050- 5 1 **Uncle Bernie (IRE)**[48] 8116 4-8-6 **51** oh4 (p) JimmyQuinn 6 51
(Andrew Hollinshead) *hld up: hdwy over 3f out: rdn over 1f out: no ex ins fnl f* **33/1**

6 6 **Seismic (IRE)**[14] 46 4-8-6 **51** oh6 (p) ChrisCatlin 8 42
(Gordon Elliott, Ire) *prom: pushed along over 5f out: rdn and wknd over 2f out* **11/10**[1]

U4-3 7 4 **Jullundar (IRE)**[15] 10 4-9-6 **65** (v) BenCurtis 4 49
(Jo Hughes) *hld up: rdn over 2f out: wknd over 1f out* **33/1**

2m 42.74s (1.64) **Going Correction** +0.15s/f (Slow)
**WFA** 4 from 6yo+ 4lb 7 Ran SP% **128.3**
Speed ratings (Par 101): **100,99,97,97,96 92,89**
CSF £11.48 CT £61.58 TOTE £2.40: £1.60, £2.20; EX 11.20 Trifecta £44.80.

**Owner** R Carson **Bred** Mervyn Stewkesbury **Trained** Newmarket, Suffolk

**FOCUS**
The winner completed a quickfire hat-trick in this handicap.

T/Plt: £21.50 to a £1 stake. Pool: £101089.74 - 3425.83 winning tickets T/Qpdt: £14.30 to a £1 stake. Pool: £7216.25 - 372.04 winning tickets CR

# [208]LINGFIELD (L-H)
Saturday, January 18

**OFFICIAL GOING: Standard**
Wind: light, half behind Weather: dry, overcast

## 229 CORAL.CO.UK (S) STKS 1m 2f (P)
**12:15** (12:15) (Class 6) 4-6-Y-0 **£2,045** (£603; £302) **Stalls** Low

Form RPR

35-3 1 **Paddy's Saltantes (IRE)**[14] 49 4-8-12 66 (b) LukeMorris 4 66
(J S Moore) *mde all: set stdy gallop tl pushed along and qcknd over 2f out: clr and in command over 1f out: styd on wl* **6/4**[2]

20-2 2 2½ **Yourinthewill (USA)**[9] 105 6-9-0 66 ShaneKelly 6 61
(Daniel Mark Loughnane) *t.k.h: hld up wl in tch in midfield: n.m.r jst over 2f out: rdn and effrt over 1f out: chsd clr wnr fnl 75yds: kpt on but n.d* **5/1**[3]

20-1 3 1¼ **Sutton Sid**[10] 88 4-9-4 66 (v) AdamKirby 5 65
(Chris Gordon) *chsd wnr: rdn as wnr qcknd over 2f out: drvn and outpcd wl over 1f out: kpt on same pce after* **5/4**[1]

00-5 4 *nse* **Standing Strong (IRE)**[8] 117 6-9-0 53 (p) LiamKeniry 7 58
(Zoe Davison) *stdd s: hld up wl in tch in last pair: rdn and effrt over 1f out: kpt on ins fnl f: no threat to wnr* **14/1**

050- 5 2 **Blue Deer (IRE)**[27] 8390 6-8-7 49 (p) LouisSteward(7) 1 54
(Lee Carter) *t.k.h: chsd ldng pair: rdn and unable qck 2f out: outpcd and btn 1f out: wknd ins fnl f* **50/1**

04-5 6 3¼ **Caerwyn**[10] 90 4-8-9 58 (b[1]) MarkCoumbe(3) 3 48
(Tony Carroll) *hld up wl in tch in last pair: rdn and outpcd over 1f out: wknd fnl f* **20/1**

2m 9.64s (3.04) **Going Correction** -0.075s/f (Stan)
**WFA** 4 from 6yo 2lb 6 Ran SP% **114.5**
Speed ratings: **84,82,81,80,79 76**
CSF £9.82 TOTE £1.90: £1.80, £2.60; EX 9.50 Trifecta £20.00.There was no bid for the winner.

**Owner** Wall To Wall Partnership **Bred** Tom And Hazel Russell **Trained** Upper Lambourn, Berks

**FOCUS**
A modest seller in which the gallop was on the steady side. The winner raced towards the far rail in the straight.

## 230 32RED MAIDEN STKS (DIV I) 1m 1y(P)
**12:50** (12:50) (Class 5) 3-Y-0 **£3,067** (£905; £453) **Stalls** High

Form RPR

6- 1 **War Of Art (IRE)**[21] 8425 3-9-5 0 (t[1]) RichardKingscote 9 77+
(Tom Dascombe) *chsd ldrs: rdn along briefly over 4f out: hdwy to join ldr jst over 2f out: rdn to ld over 1f out: styd on wl and drew clr ins fnl f* **3/1**[2]

5- 2 2¾ **Mbhali (IRE)**[22] 8415 3-9-5 0 JoeFanning 4 71
(Mark Johnston) *dwlt: sn rcvrd to join ldr after 1f: rdn ent fnl f: hdd over 1f out: outpcd and btn 1f out: one pce after* **5/4**[1]

62- 3 2¼ **Final Countdown**[29] 8367 3-9-5 0 WilliamCarson 2 66
(Anthony Carson) *chsd ldrs: rdn and effrt 2f out: 3rd and swtchd rt wl over 1f out: outpcd and btn 1f out: plugged on* **12/1**

0-0 4 1½ **Anjin (IRE)**[12] 70 3-9-5 0 LukeMorris 5 62
(Sir Mark Prescott Bt) *wl in tch in midfield: rdn and chsd ldng trio ent fnl 2f: outpcd and btn over 1f out: wl hld and one pce fnl f* **33/1**

46- 5 7 **Here For Good (IRE)**[22] 8415 3-9-5 0 SeanLevey 7 46
(Richard Hannon) *sn pushed along and outpcd in last trio: drvn wl over 2f out: 5th and wl btn over 1f out* **6/1**

6 5 **Bobby Benton (IRE)** 3-9-5 0 FergusSweeney 6 35
(Luke Dace) *s.i.s: detached in last: rdn over 2f out: 6th and no ch over 1f out* **33/1**

0-5 7 4½ **Third Strike**[14] 51 3-9-5 0 GeorgeBaker 8 24
(Gary Moore) *led tl 4f out: styd upsides ldr tl lost pl qckly jst over 2f out: dropped out qckly and wl btn over 1f out: fdd* **5/1**[3]

00- 8 17 **Foxie Girl**[72] 7780 3-9-0 0 AdamKirby 1
(John Best) *sn pushed along and outpcd in last trio: dropped to last and toiling wl over 2f out: t.o fnl f* **66/1**

1m 37.51s (-0.69) **Going Correction** -0.075s/f (Stan) 8 Ran SP% **115.5**
Speed ratings (Par 97): **100,97,95,93,86 81,77,60**
CSF £7.14 TOTE £4.20: £1.30, £1.10, £3.20; EX 8.70 Trifecta £44.70.

**Owner** N A Jackson **Bred** Mrs Cherry Faeste **Trained** Malpas, Cheshire

**FOCUS**
A fair maiden in which the gallop was just an ordinary one. The winner came down the centre.

## 231 32RED MAIDEN STKS (DIV II) 1m 1y(P)
**1:25** (1:25) (Class 5) 3-Y-0 **£3,067** (£905; £453) **Stalls** High

Form RPR

4- 1 **Can't Change It (IRE)**[85] 7513 3-9-5 0 MartinLane 9 78
(David Simcock) *mde all: rdn and qcknd 3 l clr 2f out: kpt on and a holding runner-up ins fnl f: m green and edgd rt cl home* **3/1**[2]

00- 2 1¼ **Sir Charlie Kunz**[148] 5727 3-9-5 0 JoeFanning 3 75
(Mark Johnston) *chsd ldr tl shuffled bk and hmpd over 6f out: in tch in midfield after: rdn and effrt to chse clr ldr wl over 1f out: kpt on wl ins fnl f: nvr gng to rch wnr* **10/11**[1]

03-0 3 3½ **Timeless War (USA)**[14] 50 3-9-5 68 (b[1]) AndreaAtzeni 4 67
(William Haggas) *in tch in last trio: n.m.r and swtchd rt over 6f out: rdn over 2f out: no ch w wnr but kpt on to go 3rd ins fnl f* **7/1**[3]

35- 4 3¼ **Duly Acclaimed (IRE)**[126] 6409 3-9-0 0 LukeMorris 8 55
(J S Moore) *chsd ldr over 6f out: rdn and outpcd by wnr ent fnl 2f: 3rd and btn over 1f out: wknd fnl f* **12/1**

0- 5 1¼ **Witch From Rome**[30] 8340 3-8-12 0 PatrickO'Donnell(7) 1 57
(Ralph Beckett) *awkward leaving stalls: wl in tch in midfield: 4th and struggling u.p 2f out: wknd over 1f out* **8/1**

0-5 6 3 **Dansante**[7] 140 3-9-0 0 KieranO'Neill 7 45
(Richard Hannon) *in tch in last trio: rdn and outpcd over 2f out: n.d after* **33/1**

7 8 **Bongo Beat** 3-9-5 0 JimmyQuinn 2 31
(Michael Attwater) *s.i.s: t.k.h: hld up in rr: rdn and btn wl over 2f out: sn bhd* **66/1**

- 8 31 **Literally On Fire (IRE)** 3-8-12 0 JackGarritty(7) 5
(Brendan Powell) *t.k.h: hdwy to chse ldrs over 6f out: lost pl qckly and bhd over 2f out: t.o fnl f* **66/1**

1m 37.34s (-0.86) **Going Correction** -0.075s/f (Stan) 8 Ran SP% **114.6**
Speed ratings (Par 97): **101,99,96,93,91 88,80,49**
CSF £6.06 TOTE £4.10: £1.10, £1.40, £2.10; EX 7.50 Trifecta £16.90.

**Owner** Mrs Fitri Hay **Bred** Peter & Hugh McCutcheon **Trained** Newmarket, Suffolk

**FOCUS**
Division two of this ordinary maiden but it's worth viewing the form of the first two, who pulled clear, in a positive light. The gallop was an ordinary one and the winner raced centre-to-far side.

## 232 32RED CASINO (S) STKS 6f 1y(P)
2:00 (2:00) (Class 6) 3-Y-O £2,045 (£603; £302) Stalls Low

Form RPR
322- 1 **Skinny Love**[39] 8228 3-8-12 66.....(p) AdamBeschizza 5 67
(Robert Cowell) *sn led and mde rest: drvn and qcknd over 1f out: sustained duel w runner-up ins fnl f: r.o wl to assert towards fin* **3/1**[2]
110- 2 ¾ **Aspirant**[19] 8442 3-8-10 78..... RyanWhile(7) 3 70
(Bill Turner) *chsd ldrs: drvn and effrt over 1f out: ev ch ins fnl f: kpt on tl no ex and btn fnl 50yds* **10/11**[1]
23-2 3 1 ¾ **Ealain Aibrean (IRE)**[9] 98 3-8-7 67..... ChrisCatlin 4 54
(David Evans) *chsd ldr: rdn and ev ch 2f out: unable qck u.p over 1f out: styd on same pce fnl f* **4/1**[3]
53-5 4 1 **Sandsman's Girl (IRE)**[17] 6 3-8-12 60.....(b) JoeFanning 6 56
(James Given) *in tch in midfield: rdn and unable qck over 1f out: styd on same pce ins fnl f* **8/1**
5 5 nk **Jenny Sparks**[10] 82 3-8-2 0..... KatiaScallan(5) 7 50
(Mick Channon) *dwlt: in tch in last pair: rdn and unable qck wl over 1f out: styd on same pce after* **33/1**
500- 6 12 **Bearing Kisses (IRE)**[147] 5773 3-8-7 0.....(t) DuranFentiman 8 11
(Shaun Harris) *in tch in last pair: rdn over 2f out: wknd wl over 1f out* **66/1**
1m 12.14s (0.24) **Going Correction** -0.075s/f (Stan) **6** Ran SP% **112.9**
Speed ratings (Par 95): **95,94,91,90,89 73**
CSF £6.20 TOTE £3.90: £3.10, £1.10; EX 9.50 Trifecta £22.00.Skinny Love was bought by Zoe Davison for £6000. Aspirant was bought by B Ellison for £6000.
**Owner** T W Morley & J Barton **Bred** Raffles Dancers **Trained** Six Mile Bottom, Cambs

**FOCUS**
An ordinary seller in which the gallop was reasonable. The winner came down the centre.

## 233 BEST ODDS AT BOOKMAKERS.CO.UK SPRINT SERIES ROUND 3 H'CAP (QUALIFIER) 6f 1y(P)
2:35 (2:35) (Class 5) (0-75,77) 4-Y-O+ £3,408 (£1,006; £503) Stalls Low

Form RPR
50-1 1 **Valmina**[10] 91 7-9-9 77.....(t) JoeFanning 5 85
(Tony Carroll) *hld up in tch in last quartet: clsd and travelling strly over 1f out: swtchd lft and rdn ins fnl f: r.o wl to ld towards fin: hld on cl home* **8/1**
230- 2 shd **Glastonberry**[21] 8430 6-9-7 75..... GeorgeBaker 12 83
(Geoffrey Deacon) *stdd and swtchd lft after s: hld up in tch in last trio: swtchd rt and hdwy over 1f out: r.o wl and str chal towards fin: jst hld* **10/1**
11-2 3 ¾ **Welease Bwian (IRE)**[7] 141 5-9-2 70..... AdamBeschizza 4 76
(Stuart Williams) *hld up in tch in midfield: hdwy on inner to join ldrs travelling strly over 1f out: drvn to ld wl ins fnl f: sn hdd and styd on same pce* **4/1**[1]
200- 4 nk **Tagula Night (IRE)**[18] 8455 8-9-7 75.....(tp) RobertWinston 9 80
(Dean Ivory) *in tch in midfield: rdn and chal over 1f out: led ent fnl f: hdd and one pce wl ins fnl f* **7/1**[3]
24-2 5 1 **Seek The Fair Land**[10] 91 8-8-13 74.....(b) LouisSteward(7) 8 75
(Lee Carter) *in tch in midfield on outer: wdst and rdn bnd 2f out: kpt on same pce u.p ins fnl f* **5/1**[2]
65-1 6 1 ¼ **Lujeanie**[7] 141 8-9-5 73.....(p) ShaneKelly 11 70
(Peter Crate) *stdd and dropped in bhd after s: clsd and n.m.r jst over 1f out: drvn and styd on ins fnl f: nvr trbld ldrs* **14/1**
450- 7 ¾ **Queen Aggie (IRE)**[18] 8454 4-9-2 70..... MartinLane 10 65
(David Evans) *stdd s: hld up in tch in last trio: hdwy on inner and nt mich room over 1f out: kpt on ins fnl f: nvr trbld ldrs* **16/1**
50-1 8 hd **Desert Strike**[10] 87 8-9-5 73.....(p) LiamKeniry 3 67
(Conor Dore) *taken down early: chsd ldr: ev ch and carried rt bnd wl over 1f out: unable qck 1f out: wknd ins fnl f* **25/1**
00-0 9 2 ¼ **Decision By One**[10] 87 5-8-13 67..... ChrisCatlin 2 54
(David Evans) *led: hung rt bnd wl over 1f out: hdd jst over 1f out: stl hanging and wknd ins fnl f* **50/1**
0-00 10 ¾ **Haadeeth**[7] 141 7-9-0 68 ow1..... AdamKirby 6 53
(David Evans) *chsd ldrs: rdn and unable qck whn short of room over 1f out: wknd ins fnl f* **14/1**
250- 11 ¾ **Bapak Muda (USA)**[30] 8345 4-9-4 72..... JimCrowley 7 54
(Kevin Ryan) *in tch in midfield: rdn over 1f out: keeping on same pce on inner whn sltly impeded jst ins fnl f: n.d after* **7/1**[3]
406- 12 ½ **Temple Road (IRE)**[254] 2196 6-9-5 73..... RichardKingscote 1 54
(Milton Bradley) *t.k.h: chsd ldrs: rdn and edgd lft over 1f out: wknd ins fnl f* **7/1**[3]
1m 10.77s (-1.13) **Going Correction** -0.075s/f (Stan) **12** Ran SP% **119.4**
Speed ratings (Par 103): **104,103,102,102,101 99,98,98,95,94 93,92**
CSF £86.24 CT £377.89 TOTE £10.40: £2.70, £2.80, £1.90; EX 107.40 Trifecta £940.60.
**Owner** Mayden Stud **Bred** Mayden Stud, J A And D S Dewhurst **Trained** Cropthorne, Worcs

**FOCUS**
A competitive event in which the strong gallop suited those held up. The winner came down the centre.

## 234 COMPARE BOOKMAKERS AT BOOKMAKERS.CO.UK H'CAP 6f 1y(P)
3:10 (3:10) (Class 3) (0-95,90) 4-Y-O+ £7,439 (£2,213; £1,106; £553) Stalls Low

Form RPR
11-2 1 **Trinityelitedotcom (IRE)**[6] 148 4-9-6 89..... RichardKingscote 8 101
(Tom Dascombe) *mde all: hung rt fr over 1f out: r.o strly fnl f: rdn out* **9/4**[2]
521- 2 1 ½ **Agerzam**[21] 8431 4-9-7 90..... AndreaAtzeni 2 97
(Roger Varian) *chsd ldrs: styd on inner rail and chsd wnr over 1f out: kpt on same pce fnl 100yds* **2/1**[1]
25-6 3 ¾ **Noble Deed**[14] 55 4-9-5 88..... AdamKirby 3 93+
(Michael Attwater) *taken down early: in tch in midfield: hmpd and dropped to rr after 1f: rdn and effrt wdst bnd 2f out: styd on wl u.p ins fnl f* **10/1**
326- 4 ½ **Corporal Maddox**[30] 8344 7-9-3 86.....(p) LukeMorris 1 89
(Ronald Harris) *s.i.s: hld up in tch in last trio: effrt u.p on inner over 1f out: kpt on u.p ins fnl f* **16/1**
211- 5 shd **Novellen Lad (IRE)**[43] 8181 9-9-0 83..... RobertWinston 4 86
(Willie Musson) *hld up in tch in last trio: nt clr run 2f out: rdn and hdwy ent fnl f: styd on fnl 100yds: nt rch ldrs* **8/1**[3]
000- 6 ½ **Taajub (IRE)**[117] 6699 7-9-6 89..... ShaneKelly 9 90
(Peter Crate) *chsd ldrs: hdwy to chse wnr 2f out tl drvn and unable qck over 1f out: 3rd and btn ins fnl f: wknd towards fin* **25/1**
5-02 7 1 ¼ **Al's Memory (IRE)**[6] 153 5-8-11 80..... ChrisCatlin 7 77
(David Evans) *chsd wnr tl 2f out: lost pl u.p over 1f out: wknd ins fnl f* **14/1**
31-0 8 ¾ **Naabegha**[14] 55 7-9-4 87.....(p) DavidProbert 6 82
(Alan McCabe) *taken down early: stdd s: t.k.h: hld up in tch in last trio: no imp and stl bhd whn nt clr run 1f out: one pce after* **8/1**[3]
1m 10.49s (-1.41) **Going Correction** -0.075s/f (Stan) **8** Ran SP% **111.8**
Speed ratings (Par 107): **106,104,103,102,102 101,99,98**
CSF £6.79 CT £33.21 TOTE £3.10: £1.40, £1.10, £2.80; EX 7.80 Trifecta £51.50.
**Owner** Manor House Racing Club **Bred** Natasha Newsome **Trained** Malpas, Cheshire

**FOCUS**
A useful handicap but the gallop was only a reasonable one and very few figured. The winner came down the centre in the straight.

## 235 LADBROKES H'CAP 1m 1y(P)
3:45 (3:47) (Class 2) (0-100,100) 4-Y-O+ £12,291 (£3,657; £1,827; £913) Stalls High

Form RPR
04U- 1 **Birdman (IRE)**[21] 8428 4-8-10 89.....(be[1]) MartinLane 10 99
(David Simcock) *taken down early: s.i.s: hld up in tch in last pair: effrt on outer bnd wl over 1f out: str run u.p ins fnl f to ld fnl 50yds* **25/1**
305- 2 ¾ **Luhaif**[198] 3987 4-8-11 95.....(p) ShelleyBirkett(5) 11 103
(Julia Feilden) *chsd ldrs tl led over 6f out: rdn and 3 l clr 2f out: hung rt and hdd fnl 50yds: no ex* **14/1**
606- 3 1 ¼ **Dance And Dance (IRE)**[35] 8301 8-8-11 90..... AndreaAtzeni 1 95
(Ed Vaughan) *hld up in last trio: hdwy jst over 2f out: swtchd lft and styd on wl u.p fnl 100yds* **9/2**[3]
40-6 4 nk **True To Form (IRE)**[7] 145 7-8-12 91.....(p) DavidProbert 2 95
(Alan McCabe) *hld up in tch in midfield: swtchd rt over 2f out: kpt on wl u.p fnl 100yds* **20/1**
333- 5 nk **George Guru**[37] 8263 7-9-0 93 ow1..... AdamKirby 4 97
(Michael Attwater) *in tch in midfield: effrt to chse clr ldr 2f out: hung lft u.p over 1f out: pressing ldr and keeping on same pce whn hmpd and snatched up fnl 50yds* **4/1**[2]
34-5 6 ¾ **Mia's Boy**[7] 145 10-8-10 89..... LukeMorris 6 91
(Chris Dwyer) *in tch in midfield: rdn along briefly over 4f out: effrt u.p to chse ldrs over 1f out: keeping on same pce whn short of room fnl 50yds* **20/1**
200- 7 1 ¾ **Favourite Treat (USA)**[19] 8445 4-8-9 88..... JoeFanning 8 86
(Mark Johnston) *led for over 1f: styd chsng ldrs: rdn and outpcd ent fnl 2f: kpt on same pce u.p fnl f* **20/1**
522- 8 nk **Loyalty**[21] 8428 7-8-4 90.....(v) AdamMcLean(7) 7 87
(Derek Shaw) *hld up in last pair: rdn and effrt bnd wl over 1f out: styd on u.p ins fnl f: nvr trbld ldrs* **12/1**
02-4 9 2 **Emerald Wilderness (IRE)**[7] 144 10-8-13 92..... NickyMackay 9 85
(Mark Rimmer) *in tch in midfield: rdn and effrt 2f out: drvn and unable qck ent fnl f: wknd wl ins fnl f* **20/1**
036- 10 ½ **Strictly Silver (IRE)**[72] 7793 5-9-7 100..... RobertWinston 5 92
(Alan Bailey) *chsd ldrs tl 5f out: rdn and unable qck ent fnl 2f: wknd ent fnl f* **5/1**
016- 11 ½ **Upavon**[37] 8264 4-8-8 87..... LiamKeniry 3 77
(David Elsworth) *broke wl but stdd and hld up in midfield: nt clr run and shuffled bk to rr ent fnl 2f: rdn and no hdwy over 1f out* **33/1**
013- 12 2 ¼ **Haaf A Sixpence**[49] 8117 5-9-2 95..... JimCrowley 12 80
(Ralph Beckett) *chsd ldrs: wnt 2nd 5f out tl 2f out: outpcd u.p over 1f out: fdd ins fnl f* **11/4**[1]
1m 35.06s (-3.14) **Going Correction** -0.075s/f (Stan) **12** Ran SP% **121.7**
Speed ratings (Par 109): **112,111,110,109,109 108,106,106,104,104 103,101**
CSF £312.65 CT £1903.98 TOTE £35.60: £6.80, £3.90, £2.50; EX 484.30 Trifecta £3422.40.
**Owner** Anthony Hogarth **Bred** Lynchbages Edgeridge Ltd & Glenvale Stud **Trained** Newmarket, Suffolk
■ Stewards' Enquiry : Shelley Birkett two-day ban: careless riding (Feb 1-2)
Martin Lane two-day ban: careless riding (Feb 1-2)

**FOCUS**
A good-quality handicap in which a fair pace increased around halfway. The winner came down the centre in the straight.

## 236 32RED.COM H'CAP 1m 2f (P)
4:15 (4:15) (Class 6) (0-65,64) 3-Y-O £2,385 (£704; £352) Stalls Low

Form RPR
42-1 1 **Masterpaver**[12] 71 3-9-3 60.....(v) RobertWinston 9 63+
(Alan Bailey) *s.i.s: in tch in last trio: hdwy to press ldrs ent fnl 2f: led wl over 1f out: rdr dropped rein and edgd rt briefly ins fnl f: kpt on wl u.p fnl 100yds* **6/1**[3]
035- 2 nk **Bountiful Sin**[66] 7853 3-9-5 62..... AdamKirby 4 64
(George Margarson) *t.k.h: chsd ldr: rdn and ev ch 2f out: kpt on wl u.p but hld towards fin* **4/1**[2]
604- 3 hd **Frederic Chopin**[66] 7855 3-8-13 56..... SeanLevey 3 58+
(Stuart Williams) *chsd ldrs early: grad stdd and in last trio 7f out: rdn and effrt over 1f out: swtchd rt 1f out: str run fnl 100yds: nt quite rch ldrs* **4/1**[2]
004- 4 ½ **Mary Le Bow**[40] 8213 3-9-6 63..... LukeMorris 5 64
(Lucy Wadham) *in tch in midfield: rdn and effrt on outer bnd 2f out: kpt on wl u.p fnl 100yds* **8/1**
401- 5 shd **Dutchartcollector**[37] 8262 3-9-7 64..... GeorgeBaker 6 65+
(Gary Moore) *s.i.s: hld up in last trio: stl travelling but nt clr run over 2f out: hdwy on inner over 1f out: chsd ldrs 1f out: kpt on same pce fnl 100yds* **5/2**[1]
46-4 6 ½ **Amontillado (IRE)**[5] 157 3-8-10 60.....(b) CamHardie(7) 8 60
(Richard Hannon) *chsd ldrs: rdn 2f out: drvn and edgd rt 1f out: kpt on ins fnl f* **20/1**
60-2 7 ½ **Blossom Lane**[12] 71 3-9-1 58..... NickyMackay 7 57
(John Gosden) *s.i.s: hdwy into midfield after 2f: rdn and unable qck wl over 1f out: kpt on same pce ins fnl f: n.m.r nr fin* **8/1**
055- 8 1 ¾ **Ede's The Business**[31] 8328 3-9-1 58..... FergusSweeney 2 53
(Pat Phelan) *chsd ldrs tl lost pl and bhd ent 2f out: wknd ins fnl f* **33/1**
656- 9 1 ½ **Three Heart's**[20] 8434 3-9-1 58..... JoeFanning 1 50
(Hugo Palmer) *led: rdn and hdd wl over 1f out: wknd ins fnl f* **33/1**
2m 9.27s (2.67) **Going Correction** -0.075s/f (Stan) **9** Ran SP% **115.7**
Speed ratings (Par 95): **86,85,85,85,85 84,84,82,81**
CSF £29.63 CT £106.34 TOTE £6.40: £3.20, £1.80, £2.10; EX 53.90 Trifecta £185.60.
**Owner** Mrs A M Riney **Bred** Mrs A M Riney **Trained** Newmarket, Suffolk

**FOCUS**
A modest handicap run at an ordinary gallop but, although the first seven finished in a heap, this race could throw up a few winners. The winner came down the centre.
T/Plt: £12.00 to a £1 stake. Pool: £68636.25 - 4161.74 winning tickets. T/Qpdt: £4.00 to a £1 stake. Pool: £5883.62 - 1080.92 winning tickets. SP

## [193]CAGNES-SUR-MER
Saturday, January 18

**OFFICIAL GOING: Polytrack: standard**

### 237a PRIX JOSEPH COLLIGNON (CONDITIONS) (3YO) (POLYTRACK) 1m (F)
1:15 (12:00) 3-Y-O £15,416 (£6,166; £4,625; £3,083; £1,541)

RPR

1 **Zvarov (IRE)**[46] 8143 3-8-11 0 IoritzMendizabal 4 90
(J-C Rouget, France) **17/10**[1]

2 1/2 **Cockney Bob**[46] 3-9-1 0 FabriceVeron 3 93
(J Parize, France) **78/10**

3 snk **Aldabra (FR)**[140] 3-8-8 0 Pierre-CharlesBoudot 1 85
(D Prod'Homme, France) **213/10**

4 nk **En Civil (IRE)** 3-8-11 0 AlexandreGavilan 8 87
(D Guillemin, France) **67/10**[3]

5 3/4 **Charay (FR)** 3-8-11 0 FranckBlondel 12 86
(F Rossi, France) **4/1**[2]

6 1 **Ice Love (FR)**[36] 3-8-8 0 RaphaelMarchelli 10 80
(T Castanheira, France) **16/1**

7 2 1/2 **Whitby High Light**[112] 6829 3-8-11 0 ThomasMessina 11 78
(Andrew Hollinshead) *stdd fr wd draw and hld up in last pair: rdn over 2f out: stl in rr ent fnl f: kpt on and wnt 7th fnl strides but n.d* **70/1**

8 nk **Singapore Spur (FR)**[14] 3-8-11 0 (p) AlexisBadel 7 77
(D De Waele, France) **12/1**

9 1 1/2 **Jonh Jonh (FR)**[64] 3-8-11 0 MickaelForest 5 74
(W Walton, France) **107/10**

10 2 **Louarn (IRE)**[63] 7939 3-8-8 0 ThomasHenderson 6 66
(J Heloury, France) **26/1**

11 5 1/2 **Greatolo (FR)** 3-8-11 0 NicolasRomeo 9 56
(T Larriviere, France) **28/1**

12 3 1/2 **Tout En Cardoun (FR)**[75] 3-8-8 0 (p) AntoineHamelin 2 45
(Mme P Butel, France) **34/1**

1m 38.35s (98.35) **12** Ran SP% **119.4**

WIN (incl. 1 euro stake): 2.70. PLACES: 1.40, 2.40, 3.90. DF: 12.30. SF: 15.20.

**Owner** Cuadra Montalban Srl **Bred** Oceanic Bloodstock & Mme A Gravereaux **Trained** Pau, France

## [202]MEYDAN (L-H)
Saturday, January 18

**OFFICIAL GOING: Tapeta: standard; turf: good**

### 238a HAYAT 95.6 (MAIDEN) (TAPETA) 1m 1f 110y
2:50 (2:50) 3-Y-O+ £6,414 (£2,138; £1,175; £641; £320)

RPR

1 **Exploratory (USA)**[149] 5678 4-8-13 (t) AdriedeVries 7 63
(A bin Harmash, UAE) *trckd ldrs: rdn 2f out: led 1f out: r.o wl* **5/1**

2 3/4 **Fa'lz (IRE)**[16] 27 5-8-7 70 (p) NoelGarbutt(7) 5 61
(E Charpy, UAE) *mid-div: smooth prog 2 1/2f out: ev ch 100yds out: one pce fnl 25yds* **14/1**

3 1 1/4 **Covert Desire**[16] 27 6-9-0 80 (t) HarryBentley 3 59
(Ismail Mohammed) *mid-div: chsd ldrs 3f out: r.o fnl 1 1/2f* **7/2**[2]

4 1 1/4 **Lake Hawk (IRE)**[30] 8355 5-8-7 63 SaeedAlMazrooei(7) 9 56
(A Al Raihe, UAE) *trckd ldrs: led 2 1/2f out: hdd 1f out: kpt on same pce* **33/1**

5 hd **Sooth Al Ssalam (USA)**[30] 8355 4-8-13 70 (b) RichardMullen 4 57+
(S Seemar, UAE) *mid-div: rdn 2 1/2f out: no room 1 1/2f out: kpt on same pce fnl 1f* **3/1**[1]

6 1 **White City (USA)**[16] 27 5-8-8 65 (bt) MarcMonaghan(6) 12 54
(S Seemar, UAE) *mid-div: r.o fnl 2f but nvr able to chal* **25/1**

7 1/2 **Tailoring (IRE)**[58] 7996 5-9-0 (p) TadhgO'Shea 16 53
(E Charpy, UAE) *sn led: hdd 2 1/2f out and r.o same pce fnl 2f* **16/1**

8 nk **Extroverted**[36] 8290 6-9-0 60 PatDobbs 1 52
(Doug Watson, UAE) *nvr bttr than mid-div* **25/1**

9 3/4 **Oakham**[30] 8355 4-8-13 70 (b) DaneO'Neill 13 50
(A bin Huzaim, UAE) *slowly away: a in rr* **16/1**

10 nk **Dress Down (USA)**[16] 22 4-8-13 JamesDoyle 10 50
(M Al Muhairi, UAE) *mid-div: r.o same pce fnl 2f* **4/1**[3]

11 1 1/4 **Albayan (IRE)**[16] 24 5-9-0 72 (t) RoystonFfrench 8 47
(A Al Raihe, UAE) *nvr nr to chal* **14/1**

12 shd **Mutarjim (USA)**[530] 4882 5-9-0 WilliamTwiston-Davies 11 47
(M Al Muhairi, UAE) *nvr nr to chal* **12/1**

13 1 **Mr Churchill (IRE)**[30] 8355 5-9-0 60 (b) MChaves 2 45
(Ismail Mohammed) *a in rr* **40/1**

14 16 1/2 **Admirals Braid (SAF)**[16] 22 6-8-5 AhmadAlSubousi(9) 14 13
(Ismail Mohammed) *trckd ldrs tl wknd 3f out* **33/1**

15 10 3/4 **Polyphemus (USA)**[386] 8284 7-9-0 55 SamHitchcott 15
(S Deeb, UAE) *s.i.s: a in rr* **66/1**

16 4 3/4 **Vermeer (SAF)**[22] 8424 6-9-0 58 KierenFallon 6
(Doug Watson, UAE) *nvr nr to chal* **40/1**

1m 59.04s (0.04)

**WFA** 4 from 5yo+ 1lb **16** Ran SP% **136.6**

CSF: 78.35; EX 122.70; TRIFECTA: 617.60; WIN: 6.20; PL: 2.60, 5.40, 1.00..

**Owner** Sheikh Majid bin Mohammed Al Maktoum **Bred** Darley **Trained** United Arab Emirates

### 239a WHEELS (H'CAP) (TAPETA) 1m
3:25 (3:25) (60-75,79) 3-Y-O+ £6,414 (£2,138; £1,175; £641; £320)

RPR

1 **Touch Gold (IRE)**[8] 137 5-8-13 74 DanielMuscutt(6) 5 77
(Ernst Oertel, UAE) *sn led: rdn 2f out: r.o wl* **10/1**

2 3/4 **Bravo Ragazzo (IRE)**[16] 27 4-9-0 68 (t) RoystonFfrench 13 70
(A Al Raihe, UAE) *trckd ldng pair: ev ch 1f out: nt qckn fnl 100yds* **16/1**

3 1 1/4 **Centrifugal (IRE)**[16] 24 5-9-2 70 PatDobbs 11 69+
(Doug Watson, UAE) *in rr of mid-div: r.o fnl 2f: nrst fin* **20/1**

4 hd **Kahruman (USA)**[16] 24 5-9-3 72 PaulHanagan 6 70
(E Charpy, UAE) *s.i.s: settled in rr: smooth prog 3f out: chsd ldrs 2f out: one pce fnl 1f* **20/1**

5 1 1/4 **Furnace (IRE)**[310] 1003 10-8-10 72 (tp) NoelGarbutt(7) 7 67
(E Charpy, UAE) *s.i.s: nvr able to chal but r.o fnl 2 1/2f* **20/1**

6 1 1/4 **Canary Wharf (IRE)**[16] 27 5-9-3 72 (vt) JamesDoyle 8 64
(M Al Muhairi, UAE) *mid-div: r.o one pce fnl 1 1/2f but nvr able to chal* **20/1**

7 3/4 **Mutual Force (USA)**[16] 27 6-8-13 74 (t) SaeedAlMazrooei(6) 1 64
(A Al Raihe, UAE) *mid-div: chsd ldrs 2 1/2f out: n.m.r 1 1/2f out: r.o same pce fnl 1f* **12/1**

8 hd **Mountain Lion (IRE)**[68] 7834 3-8-5 75 (v) HayleyTurner 2 65
(Saeed bin Suroor) *trckd ldrs: ev ch 2f out: wknd fnl 1 1/2f* **13/2**[3]

9 3 1/2 **Karma Chameleon**[16] 27 5-9-1 75 MarcMonaghan(5) 3 58
(Doug Watson, UAE) *nvr nr to chal* **16/1**

10 4 1/2 **Tahadee (IRE)**[115] 6740 3-8-7 79 ThierryThulliez 9 48
(M F De Kock, South Africa) *settled in rr: n.d* **3/1**[1]

11 3/4 **Petty Officer (IRE)**[16] 24 6-9-3 72 (b) AdriedeVries 14 41
(A bin Harmash, UAE) *nvr bttr than mid-div* **20/1**

12 shd **Daar Rashid (USA)**[22] 8424 4-9-0 68 (v) SilvestreDeSousa 12 38
(M Al Muhairi, UAE) *trckd ldrs tl wknd 2 1/2f out* **12/1**

13 5 1/2 **Janna's Jingle (IRE)**[16] 27 4-9-6 75 TadhgO'Shea 4 32
(S Seemar, UAE) *nvr bttr than mid-div* **20/1**

14 8 **Count Paris (USA)**[16] 23 8-9-4 73 JRosales 10 11
(A bin Huzaim, UAE) *nvr bttr than mid-div* **10/1**

15 3 1/4 **Istikshaf (IRE)**[81] 7606 3-8-5 78 ow9 AhmadAlSubousi(10) 15 25
(Saeed bin Suroor) *a in rr* **6/1**[2]

1m 37.2s (-0.30)

**WFA** 3 from 4yo+ 20lb **15** Ran SP% **126.5**

CSF: 131.90; EX 404.70; TRIFECTA: 5891.10; TRICAST: 2251.57; WIN: 7.50.

**Owner** H E Sheikh Sultan Bin Khalifa Al Nahyan **Bred** Runnymede Farm Inc **Trained** United Arab Emirates

■ Tamarrud was withdrawn. Rule 4 applies to all bets - deduct 10p in the pound.

### 240a GULFNEWS.COM (HANDICAP (TURF) 6f
4:00 (4:00) (85-99,99) 3-Y-O+ £10,361 (£3,453; £1,899; £1,036; £518)

RPR

1 **Roicead (USA)**[9] 107 7-9-6 99 (t) JamesDoyle 11 107
(D Selvaratnam, UAE) *led in centre: rdn clr 1 1/2f out: r.o wl: comf* **7/2**[1]

2 2 1/4 **Hattaash**[16] 25 5-8-7 86 PaulHanagan 8 87
(M Al Muhairi, UAE) *chsd ldrs: ev ch 1 1/2f out: r.o but no ch w wnr* **4/1**[2]

3 1 1/2 **Chasing Halos (USA)**[8] 139 7-9-5 98 DaneO'Neill 2 94
(M Al Muhairi, UAE) *led for side: ev ch 1 1/2f out: r.o same pce fnl 1f* **6/1**

4 1 1/4 **Kilt Rock (IRE)**[8] 139 7-9-4 97 (b) PatDobbs 5 89
(Doug Watson, UAE) *mid-div: r.o fnl 2f but nvr nr to chal* **20/1**

5 nk **Brazen**[30] 8357 4-8-13 91 TadhgO'Shea 7 82
(Ernst Oertel, UAE) *mid-div: r.o same pce fnl 2f* **7/1**

6 1 1/4 **Pied A Terre (AUS)**[105] 7014 6-9-2 95 (t) AhmedAjtebi 9 82
(Saeed bin Suroor) *s.i.s: settled rr: kpt on one pce fnl 1 1/2f but n.d* **10/1**

7 nk **Global City (IRE)**[30] 8357 8-8-6 85 (t) RichardMullen 13 71
(S Seemar, UAE) *chsd ldrs tl outpcd 2f out* **25/1**

8 1/2 **Vocational (USA)**[36] 8288 5-8-4 89 (t) SaeedAlMazrooei(6) 4 74
(A Al Raihe, UAE) *mid-div: kpt on same pce fnl 31 1/2f* **20/1**

9 3/4 **Red Duke (USA)**[224] 3101 5-9-5 98 JGeroudis 14 80
(M F De Kock, South Africa) *broke awkwardly: settled rr: nvr nr to chal* **8/1**

10 nk **Warsaw (IRE)**[16] 26 9-8-7 91 (b) MarcMonaghan(6) 1 73
(S Seemar, UAE) *nvr bttr than mid-div* **33/1**

11 1 1/4 **Hajoum (IRE)**[36] 8288 8-8-11 90 (t) RoystonFfrench 6 67
(A Al Raihe, UAE) *nvr bttr than mid-div* **25/1**

12 1/2 **I'm Back (IRE)**[96] 7247 4-9-3 96 (t) SilvestreDeSousa 3 72
(Saeed bin Suroor) *nvr bttr than mid-div* **5/1**[3]

13 3 1/4 **Burj Alzain (IRE)**[322] 869 6-9-4 97 (vt) KierenFallon 15 62
(Fawzi Abdulla Nass, Bahrain) *nvr able to chal* **20/1**

14 4 1/2 **Mon Cadeaux**[336] 696 7-8-11 90 (b) CSandoval 12 41
(A bin Huzaim, UAE) *nvr able to chal* **33/1**

1m 9.66s (-0.94) **14** Ran SP% **133.7**

CSF: 17.61; EX 29.50; TRIFECTA: 72.80; TRICAST: 88.51; WIN: 4.60; PL: 2.10, 2.00, 1.70..

**Owner** Michael Gerard Daly **Bred** Michael Daly **Trained** United Arab Emirates

### 241a AQUARIUS (H'CAP) (TAPETA) 7f
4:35 (4:35) (75-90,90) 3-Y-O+ £8,388 (£2,796; £1,537; £838; £419)

RPR

1 **Mundahesh (IRE)**[16] 26 4-9-2 86 PaulHanagan 10 91
(A Al Raihe, UAE) *trckd ldrs: led 1 1/2f out: r.o wl* **14/1**

2 1/2 **Musaddas**[72] 7787 4-8-13 83 SilvestreDeSousa 1 86+
(Saeed bin Suroor) *slowly away: in rr of mid-div: r.o wl fnl 2f: nrst fin* **7/2**[2]

3 3/4 **Jamhoori**[16] 24 6-9-1 85 ThomasBrown 8 87+
(M Al Muhairi, UAE) *settled in rr: nvr nr to chal but r.o wl fnl 1 1/2f: nrst fin* **20/1**

4 1/2 **Forevertheoptimist (IRE)**[16] 25 5-8-13 83 PatDobbs 9 83
(Doug Watson, UAE) *mid-div: smooth prog 2f out: ev ch 1f out: one pce fnl 100yds* **14/1**

5 1 **Toolain (IRE)**[364] 289 6-8-9 85 MarcMonaghan(6) 13 83
(S Seemar, UAE) *mid-div: r.o fnl 1 1/2f but nvr able to chal* **40/1**

6 nse **Light Burst (USA)**[120] 6609 5-9-2 86 HarryBentley 4 84
(Ismail Mohammed) *mid-div: chsd ldrs 2f out: ev ch 1f out: wknd fnl 100yds* **10/1**[3]

7 nk **Discoverer (IRE)**[41] 8207 5-9-6 90 JamesDoyle 2 87
(M Al Muhairi, UAE) *mid-div: r.o fnl 1 1/2f but nvr able to chal* **33/1**

8 1 1/4 **Colour Guard**[16] 26 6-9-0 84 (v) WilliamTwiston-Davies 14 78
(M Al Muhairi, UAE) *mid-div: r.o same pce fnl 2f* **20/1**

9 nk **Darkening (IRE)**[8] 137 4-9-1 85 AdriedeVries 3 78
(Ismail Mohammed) *settled in rr: n.d* **33/1**

10 3/4 **Scotland Forever (IRE)**[22] 8423 4-8-13 83 TadhgO'Shea 7 73
(S Seemar, UAE) *nvr bttr than mid-div* **16/1**

11 1 1/2 **Glenleven (USA)**[50] 8105 6-8-10 80 (t) RichardMullen 11 67
(S Seemar, UAE) *sn led: hdd & wknd 1 1/2f out* **33/1**

12 1 1/2 **Desert Wings (IRE)**[100] 7154 4-8-11 82 MickaelBarzalona 5 64
(Charlie Appleby) *trckd ldng pair: t.k.h: rdn 2f out: wknd 1 1/2f* **4/6**[1]

13 3/4 **Al Farahidi (USA)**[58] 7997 7-8-13 83 (t) DaneO'Neill 12 63
(A bin Huzaim, UAE) *trckd ldrs: rdn 3f out: wknd 2 1/2f out* **25/1**

14 13 **Black Snowflake (USA)**[16] 26 7-8-7 84 (bt) SaeedAlMazrooei(7) 6 30
(S Seemar, UAE) *s.i.s: a in rr* **50/1**

1m 24.24s (-0.96) **14** Ran SP% **137.1**

CSF: 66.23; EX 134.60; TRIFECTA: 1004.70; TRICAST: 1058.63; WIN: 18.00; PL: 3.20, 2.50, 3.00..

**Owner** Hamdan Al Maktoum **Bred** Shadwell Estate Co Ltd **Trained** UAE

## 242a GULF NEWS (H'CAP) (TURF) 1m

5:10 (5:10) (85-99,99) 3-Y-O+ **£10,361** (£3,453; £1,899; £1,036; £518)

RPR

1 **Jawhar (IRE)**[72] 7798 6-9-2 **95** ................ PaulHanagan 8 99
(Doug Watson, UAE) *led main gp: rdn 2 1/2f out: led 1 1/2f out: r.o wl: jst hld on* **12/1**

2 *shd* **Oasis Dancer**[36] 8289 7-8-13 **91** ................ PatDobbs 3 95+
(Doug Watson, UAE) *mid-div: smooth prog 2 1/2f out: n.m.r 1 1/2f out: r.o fnl 100yds: jst failed* **14/1**

3 *nk* **Antinori (IRE)**[44] 8174 8-8-13 **91** ................(b) RichardMullen 11 94+
(S Seemar, UAE) *in rr of mid-div: r.o fnl 2f: nrst fin* **12/1**

4 *1* **Entifaadha**[16] 26 5-8-13 **91** ................(v) DaneO'Neill 13 92
(M Al Muhairi, UAE) *mid-div: r.o fnl 2f but nvr nr to chal* **16/1**

5 *3/4* **Ghaamer (USA)**[16] 26 4-8-9 **88** ................(t) RoystonFfrench 16 87
(A Al Raihe, UAE) *sn led: hdd 1 1/2f out: r.o gamely* **9/1**

6 *hd* **Georgetown**[122] 4-8-10 **89** ow1 ................(v) AdriedeVries 7 89
(A bin Harmash, UAE) *settled in rr: nvr nr to chal: r.o wl fnl 2f: nrst fin* **10/1**

7 *shd* **Specific Gravity (FR)**[9] 108 6-9-6 **99** ................ ThierryThulliez 15 97
(M F De Kock, South Africa) *nvr bttr than mid-div* **7/1**[3]

8 *shd* **Tesslam**[50] 8108 7-9-0 **93** ................ ThomasBrown 10 91
(D Selvaratnam, UAE) *nvr bttr than mid-div* **33/1**

9 *nk* **Dream Tune**[8] 138 5-9-2 **95** ................ TadhgO'Shea 14 92
(Ernst Oertel, UAE) *trckd ldrs: ev ch 2 1/2f out: wknd fnl 1 1/2f* **6/1**[2]

10 *1 1/4* **Marching Time**[22] 8423 8-9-3 **96** ................ SamHitchcott 4 91
(Doug Watson, UAE) *settled in rr: nvr able to chal* **33/1**

11 *3/4* **Fervent Prince**[9] 110 9-9-3 **96** ................ HarryBentley 2 89
(A bin Huzaim, UAE) *nvr nr to chal* **25/1**

12 *nk* **Canwinn (IRE)**[16] 26 8-9-2 **95** ................ JamesDoyle 9 87
(D Selvaratnam, UAE) *settled in rr: n.d* **8/1**

13 *hd* **Famous Poet (IRE)**[161] 5255 5-9-3 **96** ................ SilvestreDeSousa 12 88
(Saeed bin Suroor) *nvr bttr than mid-div* **5/1**[1]

14 *1* **Final Button (SAF)**[322] 869 6-9-5 **98** ................ JGeroudis 6 87
(M F De Kock, South Africa) *slowly away: settled in rr: nvr nr to chal* **14/1**

15 *7 1/2* **Kidnapped (AUS)**[345] 555 8-8-10 **95** ................(b) MarcMonaghan(6) 1 67
(S Seemar, UAE) *nvr nr to chal* **33/1**

16 *1 1/4* **Musaafer (IRE)**[16] 24 7-8-10 **89** ................(p) ANienaber 5 58
(M Al Muhairi, UAE) *nvr able to chal* **25/1**

1m 36.0s (-1.80) **16** Ran SP% **136.7**
CSF: 181.00; EX 303.50; TRIFECTA: 9070.20; TRICAST: 2099.73; WIN: 24.80..
**Owner** Hamdan Al Maktoum **Bred** Shadwell Estate Co Ltd **Trained** United Arab Emirates

## 243a FRIDAY (H'CAP) (TAPETA) 1m 1f 110y

5:45 (5:45) (75-90,95) 3-Y-O+ **£8,388** (£2,796; £1,537; £838; £419)

RPR

1 **Ducab (IRE)**[27] 4-8-9 **80** ................(t) MickaelBarzalona 7 89
(A bin Harmash, UAE) *settled in rr: smooth prog 3f out: led 1 1/2f out: comf* **16/1**

2 *2* **Representation (USA)**[16] 24 5-8-13 **83** ................ KierenFallon 3 86
(A bin Huzaim, UAE) *mid-div: r.o fnl 2f but nvr nr to chal* **12/1**

3 *1/2* **Paschendale**[16] 27 7-9-4 **88** ................(e) ANienaber 8 91+
(M Al Muhairi, UAE) *mid-div: r.o fnl 2f: nrst fin* **8/1**

4 *1 1/2* **Blue Tiger's Eye (IRE)**[16] 27 6-8-10 **80** ................(v) AdriedeVries 4 80
(A bin Harmash, UAE) *s.i.s: settled in rr: nvr able to chal but r.o fnl 2f* **7/1**[3]

5 *1 3/4* **Almoonqith (USA)**[131] 4-9-3 **88** ................ PaulHanagan 6 85
(M F De Kock, South Africa) *mid-div: r.o fnl 2f but nvr able to chal* **4/1**[1]

6 *1* **Dr Faustus (IRE)**[13] 9-9-6 **90** ................(t) PatDobbs 11 84+
(Doug Watson, UAE) *s.i.s: stl in rr: nvr nr to chal but r.o fnl 2f* **20/1**

7 *nk* **Fadhaa (IRE)**[27] 6-8-10 **80** ................(p) WilliamTwiston-Davies 2 74
(M Al Muhairi, UAE) *settled in rr: r.o fnl 2f but n.d* **20/1**

8 *3/4* **Mawhub**[336] 699 5-9-3 **87** ................(b) RichardMullen 13 79
(S Seemar, UAE) *mid-div: r.o same pce fnl 2f* **10/1**

9 *3 1/4* **Blue Sea (IRE)**[8] 135 5-8-11 **82** ................(t) RoystonFfrench 16 66
(A Al Raihe, UAE) *mid-div: r.o one pce fnl 2f* **14/1**

10 *1 1/2* **Mushaakis (IRE)**[8] 137 4-8-9 **80** ................ DaneO'Neill 5 63
(A Al Raihe, UAE) *nvr bttr than mid-div* **16/1**

11 *1* **Somalian (IRE)**[16] 26 5-9-0 **84** ................ HarryBentley 9 64
(Ismail Mohammed) *trckd ldng pair: led briefly 3f out: wknd fnl 2f* **9/2**[2]

12 *1/2* **Induna (AUS)**[324] 833 6-9-6 **90** ................ SilvestreDeSousa 10 69
(Saeed bin Suroor) *nvr bttr than mid-div* **12/1**

13 *11 1/2* **Mantoba**[13] 6-9-6 **90** ................(t) SamHitchcott 1 46
(Doug Watson, UAE) *nvr able to chal* **33/1**

14 *13 1/2* **Hold The Line (IRE)**[30] 8356 4-9-2 **87** ................(t) TadhgO'Shea 12 16
(S Seemar, UAE) *trckd ldrs: rdn 3f out: wknd 2 1/2f out* **20/1**

15 *hd* **Watheeq (USA)**[27] 5-8-8 **95** ................ SaeedAlMazrooei(7) 15 13
(A Al Raihe, UAE) *sn led: hdd & wknd 3f out* **20/1**

16 *2 1/4* **Fehaydi**[22] 8423 4-9-3 **88** ................ JamesDoyle 14 12
(D Selvaratnam, UAE) *trckd ldng pair tl wknd 3f out* **12/1**

1m 56.73s (-2.27)
**WFA** 4 from 5yo+ 1lb **16** Ran SP% **134.4**
CSF: 199.65; EX 238.40; TRICAST: 1693.92; TRIFECTA: 8056.10; WIN: 27.90.
**Owner** Sultan Ali **Bred** Watership Down Stud **Trained** United Arab Emirates

# 179 KEMPTON (A.W) (R-H)

Sunday, January 19

**OFFICIAL GOING: Standard**
Wind: Light; half behind Weather: Dry and bright

## 244 RACING POST CELEBRATES 100,000 TWITTER FOLLOWERS H'CAP 6f (P)

1:30 (1:32) (Class 6) (0-55,55) 4-Y-O+ **£1,940** (£577; £288; £144) **Stalls** Low

Form RPR

01-0 1 **Spellmaker**[15] 53 5-8-13 **54** ................ EoinWalsh(5) 8 63
(Tony Newcombe) *hld up in last quartet: plld wd over 2f out: rdn and gd hdwy over 1f out: led ins fnl f: r.o wl: rdn out* **11/2**[3]

52-3 2 *nk* **Hamis Al Bin (IRE)**[9] 121 5-9-4 **54** ................(t) AdamKirby 9 62+
(Milton Bradley) *hld up in last trio: stl 11th and nt clr run over 2f out: gd hdwy and weaving through ins fnl f: chsd wnr wl ins fnl f: r.o but nvr quite getting to wnr* **7/2**[1]

622- 3 *1* **Birdie Queen**[20] 8446 4-9-5 **55** ................ GeorgeBaker 2 60
(Gary Moore) *chsd ldr tl led over 1f out: sn drvn: hdd and styd on same pce ins fnl f* **9/2**[2]

020- 4 *shd* **My Sweet Lord**[23] 8412 4-9-4 **54** ................ DavidProbert 5 59
(Mark Usher) *in tch in midfield: pushed along 1/2-way: effrt and hdwy on inner 2f out: chsd ldrs fnl f: kpt on* **12/1**

05-0 5 *3/4* **Dishy Guru**[15] 53 5-9-5 **55** ................ LiamKeniry 3 57
(Michael Blanshard) *stdd s: in tch in midfield: hdwy u.p over 1f out: chsd ldrs fnl f: n.m.r and styd on same pce fnl 100yds* **11/2**[3]

32-0 6 *nk* **Celestial Dawn**[9] 121 5-9-5 **55** ................(b) LukeMorris 11 56
(John Weymes) *in tch in midfield: rdn and effrt to chse ldrs 1f out: drvn and styd on same pce ins fnl f* **20/1**

20-4 7 *1/2* **Welsh Inlet (IRE)**[4] 184 6-8-10 **53** ................ RyanWhile(7) 12 53
(John Bridger) *in tch in midfield: rdn 2f out: no imp whn sltly hmpd over 1f out: hdwy and kpt on ins fnl f: no threat to ldrs* **16/1**

020- 8 *2 1/4* **Sweet Talking Guy (IRE)**[103] 7109 4-9-5 **55** ................(t) PaddyAspell 10 47
(Lydia Pearce) *chsd ldrs: effrt u.p 2f out: unable qck and btn 1f out: wknd ins fnl f* **9/1**

526- 9 *hd* **Renoir's Lady**[140] 6017 6-9-5 **55** ................ MartinLane 6 47
(Joseph Tuite) *stdd s: hld up towards rr: shkn up and n.m.r ent fnl f: pushed along and styd on same pce after* **16/1**

604- 10 *1 3/4* **Outbid**[95] 7292 4-9-1 **54** ................ MarkCoumbe(3) 1 40
(Tony Carroll) *t.k.h: chsd ldrs: rdn and short-lived effrt jst over 1f out: wknd ins fnl f* **33/1**

500- 11 *1* **Thrasos (IRE)**[116] 6753 5-9-2 **52** ................ FergusSweeney 7 35
(Jo Crowley) *stdd s: hld up in rr: swtchd lft and effrt over 1f out: no real imp: n.d* **16/1**

330- 12 *3 3/4* **Dixie Gwalia**[57] 8023 6-8-12 **55** ................(v) LouisSteward(7) 4 26
(Michael Attwater) *led: rdn 2f out: hdd over 1f out: fdd fnl f* **20/1**

1m 13.24s (0.14) **Going Correction** +0.05s/f (Slow) **12** Ran SP% **119.0**
Speed ratings (Par 101): **101,100,99,99,98 97,97,94,93,91 90,85**
CSF £24.42 CT £96.99 TOTE £7.90: £2.10, £1.20, £2.00; EX 33.70 Trifecta £100.10.
**Owner** Joli Racing **Bred** Dxb Bloodstock Ltd **Trained** Yarnscombe, Devon

**FOCUS**
A modest contest which was soundly run.

## 245 RACING POST CELEBRATES 100,000 FACEBOOK LIKES H'CAP 7f (P)

2:00 (2:04) (Class 5) (0-70,70) 4-Y-O+ **£2,749** (£818; £408; £204) **Stalls** Low

Form RPR

20-3 1 **Shaolin (IRE)**[15] 52 4-9-6 **69** ................(t) GeorgeBaker 14 79
(Seamus Durack) *stdd and dropped in bhd after s: swtchd lft and effrt 2f out: hdwy and edgd rt over 1f out: str run ins fnl f to ld fnl 50yds: pushed out* **5/1**[2]

310- 2 *nk* **Fab Lolly (IRE)**[48] 8134 4-9-2 **65** ................ AdamKirby 11 74
(James Bethell) *hld up in last trio: clsd and nt clr run over 2f out: swtchd rt and hdwy 2f out: chal ent fnl f: drvn to ld fnl 100yds: hdd and no ex fnl 50yds* **20/1**

460- 3 *1/2* **Afkar (IRE)**[120] 6648 6-9-6 **69** ................ LukeMorris 5 77
(Clive Brittain) *chsd ldng pair: drvn and ev ch over 1f out: led ins fnl f: hdd and one pce fnl 100yds* **12/1**

00-4 4 *1* **Top Offer**[15] 52 5-9-4 **67** ................ ShaneKelly 3 72
(Peter Crate) *in tch in midfield: clsd and nt clr run 2f out: swtchd rt and hdwy to chse ldrs over 1f out: hung lft and one pce ins fnl f* **6/1**[3]

20-2 5 *nse* **Strong Man**[12] 75 6-9-6 **69** ................(b) JamesSullivan 12 74
(Michael Easterby) *chsd ldr: rdn and ev ch 2f out: led and edgd lft over 1f out: hdd ins fnl f: no ex and outpcd fnl 100yds* **14/1**

00- 6 *1/2* **The Happy Hammer (IRE)**[66] 7880 8-8-13 **65** ................(b[1]) RobertTart(3) 6 69
(Eugene Stanford) *t.k.h: hld up in tch in midfield: rdn and effrt 2f out: styd on same pce ins fnl f* **10/1**

330- 7 *1* **First Class**[46] 8158 6-9-1 **64** ................(p) DavidProbert 4 65
(Rae Guest) *in tch in midfield: swtchd rt and effrt 2f out: styd on same pce ins fnl f* **7/1**

030- 8 *3/4* **Sheikh The Reins (IRE)**[19] 8453 5-9-7 **70** ................(v) JohnFahy 9 69
(John Best) *hld up in last quartet: rdn and sme hdwy wl over 1f out: kpt on but no real imp fnl f* **11/1**

05-6 9 *hd* **Red Art (IRE)**[10] 96 5-9-3 **66** ................ WilliamCarson 2 65
(Tony Newcombe) *dwlt and rdn along leaving stalls: in tch in last trio: rdn over 2f out: styd on ins fnl f: nvr trbld ldrs* **20/1**

34-5 10 *2 1/2* **Masai Moon**[17] 11 10-8-12 **68** ................(v[1]) PatMillman(7) 13 60
(Rod Millman) *chsd ldrs on outer: rdn ent fnl 2f: unable qck and btn 1f out: wknd ins fnl f* **33/1**

300- 11 *1 1/4* **Al Aqabah (IRE)**[22] 8432 9-8-13 **62** ................(b) MartinLane 1 50
(Brian Gubby) *in tch in midfield: swtchd rt and effrt on inner 2f out: no real imp: and no threat to ldrs fnl f* **33/1**

004- 12 *1 3/4* **Kakapuka**[46] 8157 7-9-6 **69** ................ LiamKeniry 10 53
(Anabel K Murphy) *led: rdn ent fnl 2f: hdd over 1f out: sn btn: wknd fnl f* **20/1**

542- 13 *1 3/4* **Tarquin (IRE)**[53] 8063 5-9-1 **64** ................ TomEaves 8 43
(Kristin Stubbs) *t.k.h: chsd ldrs: drvn and btn over 1f out: wknd fnl f* **25/1**

121- 14 *5* **Sakash**[40] 8234 4-9-4 **67** ................ FergusSweeney 7 32
(J R Jenkins) *in tch in midfield: swtchd lft and effrt u.p jst over 2f out: no imp and struggling whn hmpd over 1f out: wl btn after and bhd fnl f* **9/2**[1]

1m 25.48s (-0.52) **Going Correction** +0.05s/f (Slow) **14** Ran SP% **117.4**
Speed ratings (Par 103): **104,103,103,101,101 101,100,99,99,96 94,92,90,85**
CSF £107.57 CT £1162.88 TOTE £6.20: £2.20, £6.10, £3.90; EX 114.30 Trifecta £2652.80 Part won..
**Owner** P A Deal **Bred** Joe Fogarty **Trained** Baydon, Wilts

**FOCUS**
A fair handicap. The leading pair both came from off the pace, but that's not to say the gallop looked particularly strong.

## 246 BET THROUGH THE RACING POST MOBILE APP H'CAP (DIV I) 1m 4f (P)

2:30 (2:31) (Class 6) (0-55,58) 4-Y-O+ **£1,940** (£577; £288; £144) **Stalls** Centre

Form RPR

66-1 1 **Reality Show (IRE)**[10] 106 7-9-10 **58** ................ DuranFentiman 6 66
(Shaun Harris) *t.k.h: chsd ldr for 2f: styd chsng ldrs: drvn to ld ent fnl f: battled on gamely and hld on wl fnl 100yds* **9/2**[2]

000- 2 *1/2* **Thane Of Cawdor (IRE)**[20] 8447 5-9-6 **54** ................ GeorgeBaker 4 61
(Joseph Tuite) *stdd s: hld up in tch in midfield: swtchd lft and smooth hdwy 2f out: rdn to chse wnr 1f out: drvn and ev ch ins fnl f: unable qck and hld fnl 100yds* **3/1**[1]

004- 3 *4* **Rowlestone Lass**[38] 8260 4-8-12 **50** ................ ShaneKelly 3 51
(Richard Price) *in tch in midfield: hdwy u.p over 1f out: drvn and chsd clr ldng pair ins fnl f: kpt on but no imp* **16/1**

040- **4** *2* **Rhinestone Rebel (IRE)**[46] 8149 8-9-3 **51**.................. WilliamCarson 11 49
(Peter Hiatt) *t.k.h: chsd ldrs: chse ldr over 2f out: chalng and wandered u.p 2f out: unable qck and btn 1f out: wknd ins fnl f* **33/1**

02-1 **5** *1* **Fire In Babylon (IRE)**[9] 123 6-9-1 **49**....................(b) AdamBeschizza 5 45
(Noel Quinlan) *led: rdn jst over 2f out: drvn and hdd over 1f out: wknd ins fnl f* **3/1**[1]

00-6 **6** *nk* **Poste Restante**[9] 116 4-8-11 **49**..................................(p) MartinLane 7 45
(David Simcock) *racd in last trio and niggled along: rdn wl over 2f out: no hdwy tl styd on wl ins fnl f: nvr trbld ldrs* **7/1**[3]

000- **7** *½* **Last Chance Ranch**[12] 7666 4-8-1 **46** oh1................ AdamMcLean(7) 8 41
(Derek Shaw) *stdd and awkward leaving stalls: hld up in rr: stl plenty to do and rdn wl over 1f out: styd on wl ins fnl f: nvr trbld ldrs* **100/1**

404- **8** *1 ¼* **Fair Comment**[29] 8388 4-9-3 **55**.................................. FergusSweeney 2 48
(Michael Blanshard) *chsd ldrs: rdn 2f out: outpcd and btn over 1f out: wknd fnl f* **10/1**

046- **9** *3 ¼* **Mayan Flight (IRE)**[173] 3168 6-8-9 **46** oh1.............. MarkCoumbe(3) 10 34
(Tony Carroll) *hld up in tch: rdn and no rspnse wl over 1f out: sn wknd* **25/1**

005- **10** *1* **Ctappers**[46] 8160 5-9-0 **48**.................................................. LukeMorris 9 34
(Michael Madgwick) *s.i.s: sn drvn and reminders early: hdwy to join ldr after 2f: rdn and lost pl over 2f out: wknd over 1f out* **8/1**

00-0 **11** *½* **Dolly Colman (IRE)**[9] 116 6-8-12 **46** oh1.........................(p) JohnFahy 1 31
(Zoe Davison) *hld up in rr: swtchd rt and effrt on inner 2f out: sn no imp and wknd over 1f out* **20/1**

2m 36.16s (1.66) **Going Correction** +0.05s/f (Slow)
**WFA** 4 from 5yo+ 4lb **11** Ran SP% **119.3**
Speed ratings (Par 101): **96,95,93,91,91 90,90,89,87,86 86**
CSF £18.03 CT £202.12 TOTE £6.40: £2.40, £1.40, £5.90; EX 20.20 Trifecta £310.90.
**Owner** Miss H Ward **Bred** Highfort Stud **Trained** Carburton, Notts

**FOCUS**
Run-of-the-mill stuff, but worth viewing the leading pair, who pulled clear off an ordinary gallop, in a positive light.

## 247 BET THROUGH THE RACING POST MOBILE APP H'CAP (DIV II) 1m 4f (P)
**3:00** (3:01) (Class 6) (0-55,55) 4-Y-0+ **£1,940** (£577; £288; £144) **Stalls** Centre

Form RPR

001- **1** **The Ginger Berry**[20] 8448 4-8-10 **51**........................... RobertTart(3) 11 62
(Dr Jon Scargill) *in tch in midfield: hdwy to join ldr wl over 2f out: rdn to ld wl over 1f out: styd on wl and drew wl clr fnl f: readily* **3/1**[1]

000- **2** *6* **Dance**[45] 3272 5-8-12 **46** oh1.............................................. DavidProbert 4 48
(Rod Millman) *in tch in midfield: effrt but outpcd by ldrs 2f out: wnt modest 3rd and over 1f out: plugged on to go 2nd wl ins fnl f: no ch w wnr* **25/1**

005- **3** *½* **Lisahane Bog**[20] 8448 7-9-3 **51**..................................(v) LiamKeniry 3 52
(Peter Hedger) *in tch in midfield: rdn 3f out: outpcd and no ch w ldng pair wl over 1f out: plugged on to go 3rd wl ins fnl f* **7/1**[2]

00-6 **4** *¾* **Beggers Belief**[4] 185 6-9-2 **50**....................................(v) JohnFahy 7 50
(Zoe Davison) *s.i.s: detached in last pair but in tch: rdn and outpcd over 2f out: 6th and wl btn over 1f out: plugged on to go 4th towards fin: nvr trbld ldrs* **7/1**[2]

200- **5** *1* **Ocean Power (IRE)**[29] 8388 4-8-1 **46**.............................. JoeDoyle(7) 5 44
(Richard Phillips) *in tch in midfield: rdn and outpcd by ldng pair wl over 1f out: no ch and plugged on same pce fnl f* **9/1**[3]

540- **6** *½* **Bennelong**[20] 8449 8-9-4 **52**.........................................(b) AmirQuinn 9 49
(Lee Carter) *in tch in midfield: hdwy to chse ldrs 8f out tl led wl over 2f out: rdn and hdd wl over 1f out: btn over 1f out: fdd and lost 4 pls wl ins fnl f: eased cl home* **7/1**[2]

050- **7** *20* **Yes Chef**[20] 8447 7-9-7 **55**.......................................(p) AdamKirby 6 20
(Chris Gordon) *chsd ldr for 2f: chsd ldrs after: rdn 4f out: wknd u.p over 2f out: eased over 1f out* **3/1**[1]

554- **8** *3* **Reach The Beach**[24] 7612 5-9-0 **48**............................ StevieDonohoe 1 9
(Brendan Powell) *led tl after 4f out: sn lost pl u.p: wl bhd over 1f out* **10/1**

000- **9** *5* **Jeer (IRE)**[57] 8031 10-8-12 **46** oh1..............................(b) JamesSullivan 8
(Michael Easterby) *short of room leaving stalls and s.i.s: hdwy to chse ldr after 2f tl led 4f out: hdd and rdn wl over 1f out: sn btn: wl bhd over 1f out* **16/1**

630/ **10** *75* **Gainsborough's Art (IRE)**[69] 2361 9-8-12 **46** oh1............ ChrisCatlin 2
(Harry Chisman) *dropped to rr after 2f: lost tch 1/2-way: t.o and virtually p.u over 2f out* **100/1**

2m 35.48s (0.98) **Going Correction** +0.05s/f (Slow)
**WFA** 4 from 5yo+ 4lb **10** Ran SP% **117.3**
Speed ratings (Par 101): **98,94,93,93,92 92,78,76,73,23**
CSF £92.93 CT £492.78 TOTE £4.70: £1.70, £5.50, £2.30; EX 49.70 Trifecta £763.40.
**Owner** Strawberry Fields Stud & Stuart Howard **Bred** Strawberry Fields Stud **Trained** Newmarket, Suffolk

**FOCUS**
The second division of this low-grade handicap was won in clear-cut fashion.

## 248 FOLLOW @RACINGPOST ON TWITTER H'CAP 6f (P)
**3:30** (3:30) (Class 5) (0-70,69) 4-Y-0+ **£2,749** (£818; £408; £204) **Stalls** Low

Form RPR

45-3 **1** **Rigolleto (IRE)**[11] 91 6-9-6 **68**........................................ GeorgeBaker 1 76
(Anabel K Murphy) *broke fast: mde all: rdn over 1f out: r.o wl fnl f: rdn out* **9/2**[3]

030- **2** *1* **Ray Of Joy**[33] 8321 8-9-5 **67**....................................(v) FergusSweeney 3 72
(J R Jenkins) *dwlt: sn rcvrd and chsd ldrs: rdn and effrt to chse wnr jst over 1f out: styd in same pce ins fnl f* **8/1**

43-4 **3** *shd* **Bajan Bear**[11] 91 6-9-7 **69**.............................................. DavidProbert 8 73
(Michael Blanshard) *t.k.h early: hld up in midfield: jostled after 1f out: rdn and effrt over 1f out: chsd ldng pair jst ins fnl f: kpt on* **7/2**[2]

1-24 **4** *1* **Iceblast**[6] 161 6-9-5 **67**...........................................(b) JamesSullivan 5 68
(Michael Easterby) *wnt lft s: in tch in midfield: effrt u.p 2f out: kpt on ins fnl f but nvr gng pce to threaten ldrs* **3/1**[1]

40-5 **5** *¾* **Invigilator**[7] 147 6-9-2 **64**.............................................(t) DaleSwift 10 63
(Derek Shaw) *taken down early: stdd and dropped in bhd after s: hld up in last trio: hdwy 2f out: lft and effrt wl over 1f out: edging rt over 1f out: swtchd lft and styd on ins fnl f* **11/1**

-645 **6** *¾* **Lastkingofscotland (IRE)**[9] 126 8-8-8 **56**.....................(b) LiamJones 4 52
(Conor Dore) *chsd wnr: ev ch and drvn 2f out: lost 2nd ent fnl f: wknd fnl 150yds* **10/1**

003- **7** *2* **Avonmore Star**[19] 8456 6-9-0 **62**.....................................(e) ShaneKelly 7 52
(Mike Murphy) *chsd ldrs: rdn and unable qck 2f out: wknd ins fnl f* **10/1**

20-3 **8** *2* **Colourbearer (IRE)**[17] 8 7-9-5 **67**......................(t) RichardKingscote 9 51
(Milton Bradley) *stdd and awkward leaving stalls: in tch in last trio: rdn and no hdwy over 1f out: n.d* **14/1**

60-0 **9** *1* **Mambo Spirit (IRE)**[10] 95 10-8-11 **59**................................ ChrisCatlin 6 39
(Tony Newcombe) *stdd s: hld up in tch in rr: rdn and no hdwy over 1f out: n.d* **20/1**

1m 12.45s (-0.65) **Going Correction** +0.05s/f (Slow) **9** Ran SP% **114.5**
Speed ratings (Par 103): **106,104,104,103,102 101,98,95,94**
CSF £39.80 CT £140.19 TOTE £5.70: £1.80, £3.00, £1.80; EX 42.90 Trifecta £159.70.
**Owner** All The Kings Horses **Bred** Michael O'Mahony **Trained** Wilmcote, Warwicks

**FOCUS**
A fair handicap. There wasn't much competition for the lead, the winner making all.

## 249 RACING POST CELEBRATES 200,000 SOCIAL FOLLOWERS CONDITIONS STKS 6f (P)
**4:00** (4:03) (Class 2) 4-Y-0+
**£12,294** (£3,681; £1,840; £920; £460; £231) **Stalls** Low

Form RPR

164- **1** **Forest Edge (IRE)**[24] 8395 5-9-2 **104**..............................(b) AdamKirby 6 108
(David Evans) *rdn leaving stalls to ld: mde all: stdd gallop after 2f: rdn and qcknd 2f out: drvn clr 1f out: in n.d after: comf* **7/1**[2]

**2** *2 ½* **Rummaging (IRE)**[30] 8377 6-9-2 **99**................................ ConorHoban 3 100
(M Halford, Ire) *chsd ldrs: rdn 2f out: chsd clr wnr over 1f out: kpt on but no imp* **7/2**[1]

001- **3** *hd* **Ballista (IRE)**[24] 8395 6-9-2 **104**............................... RichardKingscote 7 99
(Tom Dascombe) *t.k.h: hld up in midfield: rdn and effrt wl over 1f out: no threat to wnr but kpt on ins fnl f* **7/2**[1]

540- **4** *2 ½* **Stonefield Flyer**[60] 7982 5-9-2 **87**.......................................... TomEaves 2 91
(Keith Dalgleish) *chsd wnr: rdn and outpcd by wnr 2f out: lost 2nd over 1f out: wknd ins fnl f* **16/1**[3]

20-0 **5** *1 ¼* **Daring Dragon**[10] 102 4-9-2 **70**....................................(b) LukeMorris 5 87?
(Ed Walker) *hld up in tch in last pair: rdn and outpcd 2f out: drvn and no hdwy fnl f* **100/1**

00-0 **6** *11* **Capone (IRE)**[15] 55 9-9-2 **90**.............................................. ShaneKelly 1 52
(Michael Attwater) *hld up in tch in rr: rdn and outpcd wl over 1f out: wknd 1f out: wl bhd and eased towards fin* **33/1**

1m 11.64s (-1.46) **Going Correction** +0.05s/f (Slow) **6** Ran SP% **66.8**
Speed ratings (Par 109): **111,107,107,104,102 87**
CSF £10.39 TOTE £3.10: £1.70, £1.40; EX 8.80 Trifecta £20.30.
**Owner** P & K Swinnerton **Bred** Alberto Panetta **Trained** Pandy, Monmouths
■ Hoof It was withdrawn. Price at time of withdrawal was EvensF. Rule 4 applies to all bets - deduction of 45p in the pound.

**FOCUS**
A useful conditions event, although weakened by the non-participation of Hoof It, who was withdrawn after proving troublesome at the start. The winner was able to dictate a modest tempo.

## 250 LIKE RACING POST ON FACEBOOK H'CAP 1m 3f (P)
**4:30** (4:31) (Class 5) (0-75,75) 4-Y-0+ **£2,749** (£818; £408; £204) **Stalls** Low

Form RPR

015- **1** **Artistical (IRE)**[34] 8310 4-9-3 **71**........................................... LiamJones 1 78
(Lee Carter) *t.k.h: in tch in midfield: hdwy to chse ldrs and swtchd lft 3f out: drvn and ev ch over 2f out: led wl over 1f out: kpt on wl ins fnl f: drvn out* **16/1**

244- **2** *½* **Incendo**[43] 8202 8-9-10 **75**....................................(p) StevieDonohoe 6 81
(Ian Williams) *in tch in midfield: hdwy on inner to chse ldrs 2f out: rdn and chal 1f out: ev ch after: unable qck and hld cl home* **8/1**

230- **3** *nk* **Leitrim Pass (USA)**[19] 8453 4-9-6 **74**................................. ShaneKelly 4 80
(William Haggas) *led: rdn and hrd pressed ent fnl 2f: hdd wl over 1f out: kpt on wl and ev ch after: no ex fnl 100yds* **7/2**[2]

33-3 **4** *nse* **Red Dragon (IRE)**[11] 79 4-9-5 **73**................................ FergusSweeney 2 78
(Michael Blanshard) *hld up in tch: effrt and swtchd lft 2f out: drvn and chsd ldrs fnl f: kpt on* **6/1**[3]

000- **5** *¾* **Reflect (IRE)**[46] 8159 6-9-7 **72**.......................................(vt) DaleSwift 8 76
(Derek Shaw) *stdd s: t.k.h: hld up in rr: hdwy on inner 2f out: kpt on same pce u.p fnl f* **16/1**

00-2 **6** *2 ¼* **Travelling**[11] 79 5-9-9 **74**............................................ WilliamCarson 9 74
(Tony Carroll) *in tch in midfield: rdn and effrt over 1f out: no imp and kpt on same pce fnl f* **16/1**

020- **7** *2* **Top Diktat**[54] 8047 6-8-9 **67**.......................................... HectorCrouch(7) 7 63
(Gary Moore) *stdd after s: hld up in last pair: stl bhd 2f out: hdwy and shkn up v briefly jst over 1f out: clsng on bit whn rn up bhd rival and swtchd rt ins fnl f: stl nt asked for effrt but kpt on fnl 100yds* **25/1**

212- **8** *½* **Bobs Her Uncle**[53] 8059 5-9-3 **68**.......................................... AdamKirby 3 64
(James Bethell) *t.k.h: chsd ldr for 2f: chsd ldrs after: rdn over 2f out: drvn and outpcd over 1f out: wknd fnl f* **3/1**[1]

35-1 **9** *hd* **Archie Rice (USA)**[8] 146 8-9-5 **73**.............................. RobertTart(3) 12 68
(Tom Keddy) *s.i.s: rcvrd and in midfield after 2f out: swtchd lft and effrt on outer over 2f out: styd on but no threat to ldrs* **11/1**

055- **10** *2 ¾* **Magnolia Ridge (IRE)**[24] 8400 4-9-5 **73**...........................(b) TomEaves 5 63
(Kristin Stubbs) *chsd ldrs: rdn and unable qck over 2f out: drvn and wknd over 1f out* **20/1**

13-2 **11** *10* **Keene**[9] 120 4-8-7 **68**........................................... LouisSteward(7) 13 40
(Philip McBride) *chsd ldrs: rdn and no rspnse over 2f out: wl btn over 1f out: wknd fnl f* **7/2**[2]

2/0- **12** *1 ¾* **Sugar Hiccup (IRE)**[20] 8447 6-8-10 **68**..................... AprilKitchener(7) 11 37
(Jim Best) *hld up in last trio: wknd 2f out: bhd fnl f* **100/1**

20-0 **13** *21* **Flag Of Glory**[11] 85 7-8-13 **64**........................................ ChrisCatlin 10
(Peter Hiatt) *t.k.h: chsd ldrs on outer: wnt 2nd after 2f tl over 2f out: sn wknd: wl bhd and eased ins fnl f: t.o* **66/1**

2m 20.68s (-1.22) **Going Correction** +0.05s/f (Slow)
**WFA** 4 from 5yo+ 3lb **13** Ran SP% **131.9**
Speed ratings (Par 103): **106,105,105,105,104 103,101,101,101,99 91,90,75**
CSF £149.20 CT £571.54 TOTE £18.80: £7.00, £2.70, £2.10; EX 260.20 Trifecta £3889.70.
**Owner** John Joseph Smith **Bred** D I Scott **Trained** Epsom, Surrey
■ Stewards' Enquiry : Hector Crouch 10-day ban: failed to ride out to obtain best possible position (Feb 2-11)

**FOCUS**
A fair handicap. The gallop looked sedate, not quickening to any great extent until around 3f out.

## 251 DOWNLOAD THE RACING POST IPAD APP H'CAP 7f (P)
**5:00** (5:00) (Class 6) (0-52,52) 4-Y-0+ **£1,940** (£577; £288; £144) **Stalls** Low

Form RPR

6-03 **1** **Medam**[7] 147 5-9-2 **50**........................................ NeilFarley(3) 3 59
(Shaun Harris) *in tch in midfield: rdn and hdwy over 1f out: led ins fnl f: r.o wl: rdn out* **3/1**[2]

5-33 **2** *¾* **Mucky Molly**[12] 77 6-9-1 **46**.....................................(vt) TomEaves 11 53
(Alison Hutchinson) *led and set stdy gallop: rdn and qcknd jst over 2f out: hdd and styd on same pce ins fnl f* **10/1**

006- **3** 1 3/4 **Salford Prince (IRE)**[80] 7644 6-9-1 **46** oh1................(b[1]) LiamKeniry 13 48
(David Elsworth) *t.k.h: chsd ldr: rdn ent fnl 2f: no ex and styd on same pce fnl 150yds* **12/1**

26-0 **4** 1/2 **Glennten**[9] 121 5-9-5 **50**..............................(b) RenatoSouza 7 51
(Sylvester Kirk) *chsd ldrs: rdn ent fnl 2f: hung rt over 1f out: outpcd and btn fnl 150yds: kpt on* **12/1**

43-0 **5** 1 1/4 **Choral Rhythm (IRE)**[11] 81 4-9-1 **46** oh1..................... LukeMorris 8 44
(Tony Carroll) *chsd ldrs: rdn ent fnl 2f: drvn and unable qck over 1f out: kpt on same pce fnl f* **20/1**

5-35 **6** nk **Surrey Dream (IRE)**[4] 184 5-9-1 **46** oh1.......................... AdamKirby 2 43
(John Bridger) *in tch in midfield: rdn and effrt ent fnl 2f: keeping on whn hmpd over 1f out: no imp and one pce fnl f* **5/2**[1]

420- **7** 3/4 **My Scat Daddy (USA)**[350] 510 5-9-6 **51**........................... JohnFahy 10 46
(Zoe Davison) *stdd and dropped in bhd after s: rdn and effrt over 1f out: styd on ins fnl f: nvr trbld ldrs* **16/1**

34-6 **8** hd **Vhujon (IRE)**[10] 100 9-8-12 **46** oh1............................ SladeO'Hara[(3)] 6 40
(Peter Grayson) *hld up in tch in midfield: rdn and outpcd 2f out: rallied and kpt on again ins fnl f: no threat to ldrs* **14/1**

660- **9** hd **My Learned Friend (IRE)**[20] 8446 10-9-0 **52**.........(p) JackGarritty[(7)] 12 46
(Andrew Balding) *chsd ldrs: rdn and outpcd wl over 1f out: kpt on same pce fnl f* **9/1**[3]

/60- **10** nk **Little Red Nell (IRE)**[47] 8140 5-9-7 **52**.......................(p) GeorgeBaker 5 45
(Martin Bosley) *stdd after s: rdn and effrt over 1f out: kpt on ins fnl f: nvr trbld ldrs* **20/1**

00-0 **11** 1 1/2 **Chiltern Secret**[11] 81 4-9-1 **46** oh1.......................... FergusSweeney 1 35
(Dean Ivory) *t.k.h: hld up in tch in midfield: effrt u.p 2f out: outpcd over 1f out: wknd fnl f* **33/1**

060- **12** 1 **Gold Weight**[31] 8339 4-9-1 **46** oh1....................................(v) ChrisCatlin 9 32
(Michael Madgwick) *in tch in midfield on outer: rdn and unable qck 2f out: outpcd and btn over 1f out: wknd fnl f* **100/1**

304- **13** 3 1/4 **Jackie Love (IRE)**[86] 7511 6-8-8 **46** oh1..................(v) RhiainIngram[(7)] 4 23
(Roger Ingram) *t.k.h: hld up in rr: swtchd to outer 3f out: rdn and no hdwy over 2f out: n.d* **16/1**

1m 28.67s (2.67) **Going Correction** +0.05s/f (Slow) 13 Ran SP% **119.9**
Speed ratings (Par 101): **86,85,83,82,81 80,79,79,79,79 77,76,72**
CSF £32.02 CT £333.09 TOTE £3.60: £1.40, £3.10, £4.30; EX 28.40 Trifecta £345.20.
**Owner** Burton Agnes Bloodstock **Bred** Burton Agnes Stud Co Ltd **Trained** Carburton, Notts
■ Stewards' Enquiry : Renato Souza two-day ban: careless riding (2-3 Jan)

**FOCUS**
Another contest in which they dawdled, the winner arguably deserving of a little extra credit for getting there from mid-division, the next three home all having been prominent from the off.
T/Jkpt: Not won. T/Plt: £178.00 to a £1 stake. Pool: £114,112.59 - 467.82 winning units T/Qpdt: £35.20 to a £1 stake. Pool: £7,310.57 - 153.50 winning units SP

# 170 SOUTHWELL (L-H)
## Monday, January 20

**OFFICIAL GOING: Standard**
Wind: Virtually nil Weather: Fine and dry

### 252 CORAL MOBILE "JUST THREE CLICKS TO BET" H'CAP — 1m 3f (F)
**1:05** (1:05) (Class 6) (0-60,60) 4-Y-0+ — £1,940 (£577; £288; £144) Stalls Low

Form RPR

-141 **1** **Grandad Mac**[6] 176 6-9-9 **60** 6ex.................................... LiamJones 6 68
(Alan Coogan) *sn disputing ld: slt ld 1/2-way: rdn clr over 3f out: jnd 2f out and sn drvn: kpt on gamely u.p fnl f* **5/2**[1]

0P-4 **2** hd **Kyllachykov (IRE)**[17] 33 6-8-13 **53**.................................... NeilFarley[(3)] 10 61
(Robin Bastiman) *chsd ldrs: rdn along 4f out: hdwy to chse wnr over 2f out: sn chal: drvn over 1f out and ev ch tl no ex towards fin* **12/1**

3-01 **3** 3 **Marina Ballerina**[18] 13 6-8-13 **55**.................................... TimClark[(5)] 7 58
(Roy Bowring) *sn outpcd in rr: reminders 1/2-way: hdwy over 3f out: rdn wl over 2f out: drvn to chse ldng pair ent fnl f: no imp* **5/1**[3]

00-0 **4** 3 1/4 **Dontpaytheferryman (USA)**[6] 176 9-9-4 **55**.........(b) WilliamCarson 5 53
(Peter Hiatt) *cl up: chsd ldng pair fr 7f out: rdn along over 3f out: drvn over 2f out: kpt on same pce* **20/1**

410- **5** 2 3/4 **Entrapping**[49] 8121 4-9-2 **56**.......................................... JimmyQuinn 3 50
(John E Long) *chsd ldrs: rdn along 5f out: drvn over 3f out: sn btn* **10/1**

440- **6** shd **Booktheband (IRE)**[187] 4405 4-8-13 **53**.......................... RobertWinston 1 46
(Clive Brittain) *trckd ldrs: hdwy 1/2-way: rdn along to chse wnr 3f out: drvn over 2f out and grad wknd* **6/1**

-012 **7** 4 **Mataajir (USA)**[6] 171 6-9-2 **53**.......................................(v) DaleSwift 11 40
(Derek Shaw) *dwlt and in rr: racd wd and bhd 1/2-way: rdn along and wd st: n.d* **11/4**[2]

00-0 **8** 9 **Oriental Cavalier**[17] 40 8-8-8 **45**.................................(v) MartinLane 4 18
(Mark Buckley) *sn pushed along: a in rr* **25/1**

010- **9** 3 3/4 **Kheskianto (IRE)**[51] 8116 8-8-1 **45**..............................(bt) PaulBooth[(7)] 9 12
(Michael Chapman) *dwlt: hdwy to chse ldrs after 2f: rdn along and lost pl 1/2-way: sn in rr* **50/1**

/35- **10** 55 **Wrecking Ball (IRE)**[19] 7877 4-9-0 **59**...................(be[1]) DavidKenny[(5)] 2
(Amy Weaver) *slt ld and set str pce: hdd 1/2-way: cl up tl rdn along wl over 3f out: sn drvn and wknd* **16/1**

2m 29.46s (1.46) **Going Correction** +0.05s/f (Slow)
**WFA** 4 from 6yo+ 3lb 10 Ran SP% **119.4**
Speed ratings (Par 101): **96,95,93,91,89 89,86,79,77,37**
CSF £33.80 CT £144.55 TOTE £3.90: £2.20, £3.80, £1.80; EX 40.20 Trifecta £150.30.
**Owner** A B Coogan **Bred** Aiden Murphy **Trained** Soham, Cambs

**FOCUS**
A modest middle-distance handicap run at a decent pace. The winner got closer to his old form.

### 253 CORAL APP DOWNLOAD FROM THE APP STORE H'CAP — 1m 4f (F)
**1:35** (1:37) (Class 5) (0-70,70) 4-Y-0+ — £2,587 (£770; £384; £192) Stalls Low

Form RPR

31-3 **1** **Staff Sergeant**[17] 39 7-9-10 **70**.................................... AndrewMullen 2 86
(Michael Appleby) *trckd ldrs: smooth hdwy 4f out: led wl over 2f out and sn clr: edgd lft over 1f out: kpt on strly* **7/2**[2]

53-1 **2** 9 **Afro**[15] 64 4-9-2 **66**.......................................................... RobertHavlin 4 68
(Peter Hedger) *chsd ldrs: reminders and hdwy 4f out: rdn wl over 2f out: kpt on u.p to chse wnr appr fnl f: sn no imp* **3/1**[1]

300- **3** 7 **Blades Lad**[25] 6346 5-9-10 **70**.......................................... TomEaves 5 60
(Peter Niven) *cl up: led after 4f: rdn along and jnd 4f out: drvn and hdd wl over 2f out: sn one pce* **7/1**

2-23 **4** 1/2 **Yasir (USA)**[7] 168 6-9-9 **69**.........................................(p) LiamKeniry 1 59
(Conor Dore) *slt ld on inner: hdd after 4f: cl up tl rdn along and lost pl over 4f out: plugged on one pce u.p fnl 2f: tk modest 4th nr fin* **5/1**[3]

34-1 **5** 1 1/2 **Short Shrift (IRE)**[19] 1 4-8-12 **65**.......................... GeorgeChaloner[(3)] 8 52
(Richard Fahey) *cl up: chal over 4f out: rdn along over 3f out: drvn and edgd lft 2f out: sn wknd* **3/1**[1]

14-4 **6** 5 **Monzino (USA)**[13] 72 6-9-0 **67**..................................(v[1]) PaulBooth[(7)] 3 46
(Michael Chapman) *a towards rr: outpcd and bhd fr over 3f out* **16/1**

050- **7** hd **Arashi**[35] 8308 8-9-5 **65**................................................... DaleSwift 7 44
(Derek Shaw) *racd wd: a towards rr: bhd fnl 3f* **25/1**

000- **8** 2 3/4 **Persian Peril**[23] 7342 10-9-5 **65**.................................... BenCurtis 6 39
(Alan Swinbank) *a in rr: bhd fnl 4f* **25/1**

2m 40.17s (-0.83) **Going Correction** +0.05s/f (Slow)
**WFA** 4 from 5yo+ 4lb 8 Ran SP% **115.0**
Speed ratings (Par 103): **104,98,93,93,92 88,88,86**
CSF £14.55 CT £66.75 TOTE £4.90: £1.50, £1.40, £1.90; EX 15.70 Trifecta £119.00.
**Owner** Andrew Gargan **Bred** Darley **Trained** Danethorpe, Notts

**FOCUS**
They finished well strung out in this moderate middle-distance handicap. The winner is rated back to his best with the second close to form.

### 254 LADBROKES MOBILE MEDIAN AUCTION MAIDEN STKS — 7f (F)
**2:05** (2:06) (Class 6) 3-5-Y-0 — £1,940 (£577; £288; £144) Stalls Low

Form RPR

305- **1** **Nick The Odds (IRE)**[33] 8325 3-8-10 61..........................(t) BenCurtis 2 65
(Jo Hughes) *cl up on inner: effrt to chal 2f out: rdn to ld appr fnl f: kpt on wl* **12/1**

3- **2** 2 3/4 **Playtothewhistle**[32] 8346 3-8-10 0.................................... JimmyQuinn 6 58
(Bryan Smart) *dwlt: sn in tch on outer: pushed along over 3f out: hdwy on outer to chse ldng pair wl over 1f out: sn rdn and edgd lft: kpt on u.p fnl f: tk 2nd nr fin* **5/4**[1]

0-4 **3** nk **Jessy Mae**[9] 142 3-8-2 0.............................................. RosieJessop[(3)] 7 52
(Derek Haydn Jones) *slt ld: pushed along wl over 2f out: jnd and rdn wl over 1f out: hdd appr fnl f: kpt on same pce: lost 2nd nr fin* **5/1**[2]

3- **4** 5 **Nixyba**[35] 8312 3-7-12 0.............................................. ChloeIngram[(7)] 3 39
(Tim Vaughan) *in rr: pushed along 1/2-way: rdn over 2f out: kpt on fnl f: n.d* **20/1**

6-5 **5** 2 **This Charming Man (IRE)**[17] 37 3-8-10 0........................ TomEaves 1 39
(Keith Dalgleish) *trckd ldrs on inner: pushed along over 3f out: rdn wl over 2f out and sn btn* **6/1**[3]

00- **6** 3/4 **Beastfromtheeast**[32] 8342 3-8-10 0.............................. RobertHavlin 4 37
(Ed Walker) *chsd ldrs: rdn along 3f out: wknd over 2f out* **20/1**

0-5 **7** 5 **Appellez Baileys (FR)**[9] 142 3-8-10 0........................... LiamKeniry 8 24
(Chris Dwyer) *prom: rdn along 1/2-way: drvn 3f out and sn wknd* **5/1**[2]

**P** **Smart Life** 3-8-10 0........................................................ LiamJones 5
(Jo Hughes) *dwlt: in rr and pushed along after 2f: sn lost pl and bhd whn lost action 1/2-way: p.u wl over 2f out: dismntd* **12/1**

1m 30.06s (-0.24) **Going Correction** +0.05s/f (Slow) 8 Ran SP% **117.0**
Speed ratings (Par 101): **103,99,99,93,91 90,84,**
CSF £28.24 TOTE £9.80: £3.30, £1.10, £2.10; EX 22.60 Trifecta £61.90.
**Owner** James Henderson & Jo Hughes **Bred** Patrick J Corbet **Trained** Lambourn, Berks

**FOCUS**
A weak maiden rated around the winner's best turf run.

### 255 DOWNLOAD THE LADBROKES APP H'CAP — 7f (F)
**2:40** (2:40) (Class 5) (0-75,75) 4-Y-0+ — £2,587 (£770; £384; £192) Stalls Low

Form RPR

203- **1** **Ace Master**[34] 8321 6-9-4 **75**.....................................(b) MarkCoumbe[(3)] 6 86
(Roy Bowring) *mde all: pushed clr 3f out: rdn wl over 1f out: drvn and kpt on strly fnl f* **5/1**

03-1 **2** 1 1/2 **Silly Billy (IRE)**[18] 10 6-8-13 **67**.............................(p) RobertWinston 3 74
(John Balding) *trckd ldrs: hdwy over 3f out: rdn to chse wnr wl over 1f out: drvn ins fnl f: no imp towards fin* **4/1**[2]

0-13 **3** 1 1/2 **Kyllachy Star**[8] 153 8-8-13 **70**.........................(v) GeorgeChaloner[(3)] 4 73
(Richard Fahey) *in rr: hdwy over 2f out: rdn to chse ldrs over 1f out: kpt on fnl f: nrst fin* **11/4**[1]

5-26 **4** 3 **George Fenton**[10] 122 5-9-6 **74**.....................................(p) LiamKeniry 5 69
(Conor Dore) *dwlt and towards rr: hdwy on outer 1/2-way: reminders 3f out: rdn to chse ldng pair over 2f out: drvn over 1f out and sn one pce* **10/1**

000- **5** 3 3/4 **Gabrial's Wawa**[20] 8453 4-8-13 **67**................................ RobertHavlin 7 53
(Roger Ingram) *cl up: rdn along over 3f out: drvn over 2f out and sn btn* **5/1**

43-1 **6** 3/4 **Ostralegus**[10] 119 4-8-12 **69**................................ MichaelJMMurphy[(3)] 1 53
(John Gallagher) *prom on inner: effrt 3f out: rdn along over 2f out: wknd wl over 1f out* **16/1**

334- **7** 4 1/2 **Cape Of Hope (IRE)**[42] 8224 4-9-6 **74**............................ DanielTudhope 2 46
(David O'Meara) *trckd ldrs: hdwy to chse wnr over 3f out: rdn wl over 2f out: sn wknd: bhd and eased appr fnl f* **9/2**[3]

1m 29.8s (-0.50) **Going Correction** +0.05s/f (Slow) 7 Ran SP% **113.2**
Speed ratings (Par 103): **104,102,100,97,92 92,86**
CSF £24.61 TOTE £5.90: £2.20, £1.80; EX 18.90 Trifecta £72.00.
**Owner** S R Bowring **Bred** S R Bowring **Trained** Edwinstowe, Notts

**FOCUS**
A moderate handicap in which the winner made all. He rated a length personal best.

### 256 LADBROKES H'CAP — 1m (F)
**3:10** (3:10) (Class 4) (0-80,80) 4-Y-0+ — £4,690 (£1,395; £697; £348) Stalls Low

Form RPR

00-1 **1** **Noble Citizen (USA)**[6] 172 9-9-0 **80**..................(be) GeorgeBuckell[(7)] 6 96
(David Simcock) *dwlt: sn trcking ldr: effrt 2f out: sn led and qcknd clr over 1f out: readily* **2/1**[1]

64-2 **2** 4 **The Lock Master (IRE)**[15] 61 7-9-6 **79**........................ AndrewMullen 5 86
(Michael Appleby) *set stdy pce pushed along and qcknd 3f out: rdn over 2f out: hdd wl over 1f out: drvn and kpt on fnl f: no ch w wnr* **11/4**[2]

560- **3** 1 **Rebellious Guest**[93] 7368 5-9-7 **80**................................ MartinLane 2 85
(George Margarson) *hld up in rr: hdwy on outer over 2f out: rdn wl over 1f out: kpt on same pce fnl f* **9/2**[3]

1-13 **4** 1 **Tatting**[6] 172 5-9-1 **79**................................................ ShelleyBirkett[(5)] 1 81
(Chris Dwyer) *hld up in rr: sme hdwy to chse ldrs 2f out: sn rdn and one pce* **2/1**[1]

/0-5 **5** 8 **Arabian Heights**[15] 61 6-8-8 **70**........................ MichaelJMMurphy[(3)] 4 54
(Ian Williams) *t.k.h: trckd ldng pair: rdn along 3f out: outpcd fnl 2f* **50/1**

1m 43.72s (0.02) **Going Correction** +0.05s/f (Slow) 5 Ran SP% **113.5**
Speed ratings (Par 105): **101,97,96,95,87**
CSF £8.16 TOTE £3.20: £1.30, £2.40; EX 7.00 Trifecta £23.10.
**Owner** Khalifa Dasmal **Bred** Don M Robinson **Trained** Newmarket, Suffolk

**FOCUS**
A fair handicap, but the pace was steady and it turned into a dash for the line in the straight. The winner's is rated to his best form in the last two years.

## 257 COMPARE BOOKMAKERS AT BOOKMAKERS.CO.UK H'CAP 6f (F)
3:40 (3:40) (Class 4) (0-80,78) 4-Y-0+ £4,690 (£1,395; £697; £348) Stalls Low

Form RPR
01-3 1 **Mappin Time (IRE)**[10] 122 6-9-0 76....(be) AdamCarter(5) 7 86
(Tim Easterby) *hld up: pushed along 3f out: hdwy on outer over 2f out: rdn to chal over 1f out: edgd lft and drvn to take slt ld ins fnl f: jst hld on* 11/4[2]
10-5 2 shd **Pull The Pin (IRE)**[12] 87 5-8-9 66....(bt) WilliamCarson 4 76
(Ann Stokell) *led: rdn 2f out: drvn over 1f out: hdd narrowly ins fnl f: rallied gamely towards fin: jst hld* 9/1
00-4 3 1 ½ **Trojan Rocket (IRE)**[8] 153 6-9-7 78.... RobertWinston 2 83
(Michael Wigham) *hld up: hdwy over 2f out: rdn wl over 1f out: ev ch appr fnl f: kpt on same pce* 5/1[3]
51-4 4 1 ½ **Fortinbrass (IRE)**[17] 36 4-9-3 77.... BillyCray(3) 5 77
(John Balding) *chsd ldr: cl up 3f out: rdn 2f out and evc ch tl hld whn n.m.r ent fnl f: one pce after* 8/1
11-6 5 1 ½ **Thorpe Bay**[11] 95 5-8-13 70.... AndrewMullen 3 65
(Michael Appleby) *trckd ldrs: hdwy 3f out: rdn 2f out: wknd over 1f out* 6/1
06-2 U **Kellys Eye (IRE)**[15] 60 7-8-7 67.... MichaelJMMurphy(3) 1
(Ian Williams) *unruly in stalls: anticipated s, hit hd and fell as stalls opened: fatally injured* 10/1
2-11 P **Maakirr (IRE)**[11] 95 5-8-13 73....(tp) MarkCoumbe(3) 6
(Roy Bowring) *trckd ldng pair: smooth hdwy to chal over 2f out: ev ch whn lost action and p.u 2f out: fatally injured* 5/2[1]

1m 15.72s (-0.78) **Going Correction** +0.05s/f (Slow) 7 Ran SP% **116.4**
Speed ratings (Par 105): **107,106,104,102,100** ,
CSF £28.01 TOTE £2.90: £2.80, £6.40; EX 35.20 Trifecta £207.00.
**Owner** P Baillie **Bred** J Jamgotchian **Trained** Great Habton, N Yorks

**FOCUS**
This looked pretty competitive beforehand, but fatal injuries to Kellys Eye and Maakirr made it less so and ensured a sombre note.

## 258 BEST ODDS AT BOOKMAKERS.CO.UK H'CAP 5f (F)
4:10 (4:14) (Class 6) (0-60,60) 4-Y-0+ £1,940 (£577; £288; £144) Stalls High

Form RPR
04-1 1 **Imjin River (IRE)**[15] 58 7-8-7 53....(t) LouisSteward(7) 4 64
(William Stone) *in tch: hdwy 2f out: rdn to chal over 1f out: led ent fnl f: kpt on wl towards fin* 3/1[1]
2-5 2 ½ **Commandable (AUS)**[17] 34 10-9-0 53.... DanielTudhope 6 62
(Ian Semple) *cl up: effrt wl over 1f out: rdn ent fnl f and ev ch tl edgd lft and one pce towards fin* 8/1
00-6 3 1 ¼ **Ghostwing**[10] 114 7-9-1 57....(vt) MarkCoumbe(3) 12 62
(Tony Carroll) *in tch: effrt wl over 1f out: swtchd rt and rdn appr fnl f: kpt on* 7/2[2]
300- 4 ½ **Jiminy**[24] 8406 4-8-3 49.... MatthewHopkins(7) 2 52
(Scott Dixon) *cl up: rdn to ld wl over 1f out: drvn and hdd ent fnl f: kpt on same pce* 14/1
05-3 5 1 ¼ **Upper Lambourn (IRE)**[15] 58 6-8-3 49....(t) RobJFitzpatrick(7) 3 48
(Christopher Kellett) *dwlt and towards rr: rdn along 1/2-way: hdwy over 1f out: swtchd rt ent fnl f: kpt on: nrst fin* 8/1
00-0 6 ½ **Novalist**[17] 34 6-8-4 46....(b) NeilFarley(3) 5 43
(Robin Bastiman) *cl up: rdn 2f out and ev ch tl wknd appr fnl f* 20/1
22-5 7 ¾ **Ivestar (IRE)**[15] 59 9-8-11 57....(v) DanielleMooney(7) 14 51
(Michael Easterby) *racd nr stands' rail: midfield: rdn along over 2f out: kpt on fnl f* 25/1
40-6 8 1 ½ **Molly Jones**[15] 59 5-8-6 48....(p) RosieJessop(3) 11 37
(Derek Haydn Jones) *dwlt and in rr: hdwy to chse ldrs 1/2-way: rdn along 2f out: grad wknd* 50/1
25-0 9 shd **Amenable (IRE)**[18] 8 7-9-7 60....(p) WilliamCarson 1 48
(Ann Stokell) *dwlt: a towards rr* 10/1
00-5 10 ½ **Above The Stars**[10] 114 6-9-3 56....(p) LiamKeniry 9 42
(Conor Dore) *led: rdn along 1/2-way: hdd wl over 1f out and sn wknd* 16/1
4-04 11 ½ **Captain Scooby**[15] 59 8-9-3 56....(e) RobbieFitzpatrick 8 41
(Richard Guest) *dwlt: a in rr* 16/1
336- 12 1 **Two Turtle Doves (IRE)**[222] 3197 8-9-0 60.... LewisStones(7) 10 41
(Michael Mullineaux) *chsd ldrs: rdn along 1/2-way: sn wknd* 33/1
04-4 13 2 ¾ **Confidential Creek**[18] 9 4-9-7 60....(b[1]) RobertWinston 13 31
(Ollie Pears) *cl up: disp ld 2f out: sn rdn and wknd over 1f out* 6/1[3]

1m 0.81s (1.11) **Going Correction** +0.25s/f (Slow) 13 Ran SP% **124.8**
Speed ratings (Par 101): **101,100,98,97,95 94,93,91,90,90 89,87,83**
CSF £27.74 CT £94.67 TOTE £5.30: £1.80, £3.10, £2.20; EX 34.40 Trifecta £173.80.
**Owner** Miss Caroline Scott **Bred** Glending Bloodstock **Trained** West Wickham, Cambs

**FOCUS**
A modest sprint handicap. The winner confirmed his C&D latest.
T/Plt: £37.50 to a £1 stake. Pool of £116,449.53 - 2,262.23 winning tickets. T/Qpdt: £9.60 to a £1 stake. Pool of £8,390.68 - 641.84 winning tickets. JR

# 215 WOLVERHAMPTON (A.W) (L-H)
Monday, January 20

**OFFICIAL GOING: Standard**
Wind: Light; behind Weather: Cloudy with sunny spells

## 259 COMPARE BOOKMAKERS AT BOOKMAKERS.CO.UK H'CAP 5f 20y(P)
2:30 (2:30) (Class 5) (0-70,70) 4-Y-0+ £2,911 (£866; £432; £216) Stalls Low

Form RPR
325- 1 **I'll Be Good**[22] 8439 5-8-9 58.... LukeMorris 9 72
(Alan Berry) *mde all: rdn clr over 1f out: eased nr fin* 4/1[1]
054- 2 3 ½ **Bilash**[58] 8030 7-9-4 67.... ShaneKelly 11 68
(Andrew Hollinshead) *hld up: hdwy over 1f out: styd on to go 2nd wl ins fnl f: no ch w wnr* 14/1
03-3 3 nk **Master Of Disguise**[18] 9 8-9-1 64.... DuranFentiman 3 64
(Brian Baugh) *chsd ldrs: rdn over 1f out: styd on* 14/1
402- 4 ¾ **Your Gifted (IRE)**[31] 8370 7-8-2 56 oh1....(v) ShirleyTeasdale(5) 8 54
(Lisa Williamson) *hld up: r.o ins fnl f: nt rch ldrs* 33/1
211- 5 1 ¼ **Give Us A Belle (IRE)**[24] 8411 5-9-2 65....(vt) AdamBeschizza 1 58
(Christine Dunnett) *prom: pushed along 1/2-way: styd on same pce fnl f* 5/1[3]

320- 6 1 **Solemn**[22] 8439 9-9-6 69....(v) RichardKingscote 5 59
(Milton Bradley) *chsd wnr tl over 3f out: pushed along 1/2-way: rdn over 1f out: no ex fnl f* 11/2
00-4 7 nse **Climaxfortackle (IRE)**[15] 60 6-8-7 63.... AdamMcLean(7) 2 52
(Derek Shaw) *s.i.s: hld up: rdn over 1f out: r.o towards fin: nvr nrr* 20/1
410- 8 nse **Passionada**[49] 8135 5-9-2 65.... GrahamLee 4 54
(Ed McMahon) *hld up: effrt over 1f out: nvr on terms* 7/1
25-5 9 1 **Lady Poppy**[14] 69 4-8-9 58.... PJMcDonald 12 44
(George Moore) *prom: rdn 1/2-way: wknd over 1f out* 20/1
00-3 10 nk **Dorback**[15] 60 7-9-7 70....(t) ChrisCatlin 7 54
(Tony Newcombe) *sn outpcd* 7/1
561- 11 1 **New Decade**[37] 8306 5-9-4 67.... AdamKirby 6 48
(Milton Bradley) *prom: chsd wnr over 3f out: rdn over 1f out: hung lft and wknd fnl f* 9/2[2]

1m 2.2s (-0.10) **Going Correction** +0.10s/f (Slow) 11 Ran SP% **121.0**
Speed ratings (Par 103): **104,98,97,96,94 93,93,92,91,90 89**
CSF £61.17 CT £744.24 TOTE £6.60: £3.10, £4.90, £3.50; EX 64.00 Trifecta £1844.30.
**Owner** Do Well Racing **Bred** Cobhall Court Stud **Trained** Cockerham, Lancs

**FOCUS**
Exposed sorts in a modest handicap and, although the gallop was reasonable, not many figured. The winner raced close to the inside rail in the straight. His best form since he was a 3yo.

## 260 32RED H'CAP 1m 5f 194y(P)
3:00 (3:00) (Class 5) (0-75,72) 4-Y-0+ £3,234 (£962; £481; £240) Stalls Low

Form RPR
21-3 1 **Echua (IRE)**[3] 214 8-9-1 61.... LukeMorris 6 76
(Emmet Michael Butterly, Ire) *chsd ldrs: wnt 2nd over 4f out: rdn to ld wl over 2f out: sn clr: eased ins fnl f* 4/1[2]
25-2 2 10 **Scribe (IRE)**[4] 197 6-9-9 69....(vt) AdamKirby 1 70
(David Evans) *chsd ldrs: pushed along 8f out: drvn along over 3f out: sn outpcd: wnt mod 2nd over 1f out* 4/1[2]
3 ½ **Old Way (IRE)**[14] 8-9-6 66.... GrahamLee 5 66
(Venetia Williams) *s.i.s: in rr and drvn along 7f out: outpcd 5f out: styd on to go 3rd wl ins fnl f* 25/1
3-22 4 3 ½ **Summerfree (USA)**[7] 158 4-9-3 69.... JoeFanning 4 64
(Mark Johnston) *led: rdn and hdd wl over 2f out: sn wknd* 4/5[1]
224- 5 15 **Montjess (IRE)**[35] 8310 4-9-6 72....(v) RichardKingscote 2 46
(Tom Dascombe) *chsd ldr: rdn over 5f out: lost 2nd over 4f out: sn wknd* 8/1[3]
030- 6 60 **Iktiview**[25] 7372 6-9-4 64....(bt) RussKennemore 3
(Philip Kirby) *s.i.s: sn pushed along in rr: rdn and lost tch fnl 7f* 66/1

3m 5.31s (-0.69) **Going Correction** +0.10s/f (Slow)
**WFA** 4 from 6yo+ 6lb 6 Ran SP% **112.0**
Speed ratings (Par 103): **105,99,99,97,88 54**
CSF £19.97 TOTE £4.90: £1.90, £2.10; EX 20.10 Trifecta £95.70.
**Owner** D J Dolan **Bred** Newberry Stud Company **Trained** Letterkenny, Co Donegal

**FOCUS**
A modest handicap which took less winning than had seemed likely with the market leader disappointing. The gallop was an ordinary one and the winner raced towards the inside rail in the straight. The winner's best Flat effort.

## 261 32RED.COM H'CAP 7f 32y(P)
3:30 (3:31) (Class 6) (0-55,58) 3-Y-0 £2,264 (£673; £336; £168) Stalls High

Form RPR
23-1 1 **Spreadable (IRE)**[7] 165 3-9-10 58 6ex....(v) LukeMorris 3 69+
(Nick Littmoden) *hld up: racd keenly: hdwy 1/2-way: chsd ldr over 1f out: shkn up to ld and edgd lft wl ins fnl f: comf* 4/9[1]
56-0 2 1 **Keep To The Beat**[7] 165 3-9-2 55.... ShaneGray(5) 7 63
(Kevin Ryan) *chsd ldr tl pushed along to ld over 2f out: rdn: edgd lft and hdd wl ins fnl f* 16/1
13-4 3 5 **Trinity Lorraine (IRE)**[19] 6 3-9-2 53....(v) RobertTart(3) 2 48
(Alan Bailey) *s.i.s: hld up: r.o u.p ins fnl f to go 3rd nr fin* 6/1[3]
30-4 4 nk **El Duque**[7] 165 3-8-12 53....(p) RyanWhile(7) 8 47
(Bill Turner) *prom: rdn over 1f out: edgd lft and wknd ins fnl f* 16/1
5 2 **The Moat Field (IRE)**[120] 6671 3-8-5 46 oh1.... JoeDoyle(7) 4 35
(Michael J Browne, Ire) *s.i.s: hdwy u.p over 1f out: no ex fnl f* 20/1
000- 6 1 **Mavree (IRE)**[34] 8317 3-8-12 46 oh1....(be) DuranFentiman 5 32
(Tim Easterby) *led: rdn and hdd over 2f out: wknd fnl f* 33/1
400- 7 2 ½ **Aussie Sky (IRE)**[52] 8090 3-8-12 46 oh1.... ShaneKelly 1 26
(Daniel Mark Loughnane) *hld up: rdn over 2f out: wknd wl over 1f out* 20/1
30-3 8 8 **Rebel Code (USA)**[18] 15 3-9-5 53.... GrahamLee 6 12
(James Given) *chsd ldrs: pushed along over 2f out: wknd wl over 1f out* 9/2[2]

1m 31.47s (1.87) **Going Correction** +0.10s/f (Slow) 8 Ran SP% **125.9**
Speed ratings (Par 95): **93,91,86,85,83 82,79,70**
CSF £11.99 TOTE £1.40: £1.02, £4.40, £1.90; EX 11.80 Trifecta £67.90.
**Owner** G F Chesneaux **Bred** Patsy Myers & Edward Myers **Trained** Newmarket, Suffolk
■ Stewards' Enquiry : Shane Kelly one-day ban: careless riding (3 Feb)

**FOCUS**
A moderate handicap run at just an ordinary gallop. The first two - both unexposed sorts - pulled clear down the centre in the closing stages. The winner was well in after his previous win here.

## 262 LADBROKES (S) STKS 1m 141y(P)
4:00 (4:01) (Class 6) 4-Y-0+ £1,940 (£577; £288) Stalls Low

Form RPR
30-1 1 **Saharia (IRE)**[14] 66 7-9-5 71....(b) ShaneKelly 5 69+
(Daniel Mark Loughnane) *hld up: pushed along over 3f out: hdwy over 1f out: shkn up to ld ins fnl f: styd on* 4/6[1]
60-4 2 1 ½ **Boom To Bust (IRE)**[10] 126 6-9-0 59....(b) LukeMorris 1 61
(Barry Brennan) *chsd ldr: pushed along over 2f out: rdn over 1f out: styd on same pce fnl f* 8/1[3]
530- 3 1 ¾ **Elusive Hawk (IRE)**[128] 6403 10-9-1 80 ow1....(v) AdamKirby 4 58
(David Evans) *led and sn clr: pushed along 2f out: hdd and no ex ins fnl f* 7/4[2]

1m 51.05s (0.55) **Going Correction** +0.10s/f (Slow) 3 Ran SP% **107.5**
Speed ratings (Par 101): **101,99,98**
CSF £5.23 TOTE £1.90; EX 3.30 Trifecta £5.40.The winner was bought in for 4750gns.
**Owner** Over The Moon Racing **Bred** Woodcote Stud Ltd **Trained** Baldwin's Gate, Staffs


The Form Book, Raceform Ltd, Newbury, RG14 5SJ

**FOCUS**
An uncompetitive claimer in which the gallop was only fair. The winner came down the centre in the straight. Inconclusive form.

## 263 LADBROKES H'CAP 1m 141y(P)
4:30 (4:30) (Class 6) (0-55,53) 4-Y-0+ £2,264 (£673; £336; £168) Stalls Low

Form RPR
023- **1** **Reggie Bond**[48] [8142] 4-9-3 **53**.......................(b[1]) RobertTart(3) 2 64
(Geoffrey Oldroyd) *hld up: hdwy over 3f out: shkn up to ld ins fnl f: r.o wl* **2/1**[2]
000- **2** *2 3/4* **John Potts**[189] [4357] 9-9-6 **52**....................... AdamKirby 6 57
(Brian Baugh) *hld up: hdwy over 2f out: rdn and ev ch ins fnl f: styd on same pce* **8/1**
000- **3** *1 1/2* **Compton Silver**[21] [8446] 4-9-1 **48**.......................(b) LukeMorris 9 49
(Paul Fitzsimons) *led: rdn over 1f out: hdd and unable qck ins fnl f* **16/1**
413- **4** *nk* **Tukitinyasok (IRE)**[25] [8399] 7-9-7 **53**....................... BarryMcHugh 10 54
(Clive Mulhall) *chsd ldrs: rdn over 2f out: styd on same pce ins fnl f* **7/1**[3]
64-0 **5** *1 1/2* **Una Bella Cosa**[13] [73] 4-8-12 **45**.......................(p) JoeFanning 12 42
(Alan McCabe) *chsd ldr: rdn over 1f out: no ex ins fnl f* **16/1**
000- **6** *nk* **My Renaissance**[173] [4885] 4-9-5 **52**....................... GrahamLee 3 48
(Ben Case) *sn pushed along in rr: hdwy over 2f out: styd on same pce fr over 1f out* **16/1**
63-1 **7** *hd* **Katmai River (IRE)**[18] [17] 7-8-13 **52**....................... CharlotteJenner(7) 5 51
(Mark Usher) *hld up in tch: effrt and nt clr run fr over 1f out tl styd on same pce ins fnl f* **7/4**[1]
00-5 **8** *5* **Justcallmehandsome**[18] [17] 12-8-8 **45**.......................(p) JoshBaudains(5) 4 29
(Dominic Ffrench Davis) *hld up: pushed along 3 out: nvr on terms* **20/1**
00-0 **9** *3/4* **Ellies Image**[18] [18] 7-8-13 **45**....................... PJMcDonald 1 28
(Richard Ford) *chsd ldrs: pushed along over 2f out: rdn over 1f out: wknd fnl f* **66/1**
00-6 **10** *13* **David's Secret**[10] [126] 4-9-5 **52**.......................[1] TomEaves 7
(Roy Brotherton) *mid-div: drvn along 1/2-way: wknd 3f out* **20/1**
000/ **11** *19* **Sir Lexington (IRE)**[471] [6885] 5-8-6 **45**....................... DanielCremin(7) 11
(Brian Forsey) *s.i.s: a in rr: pushed along 1/2-way: sn wknd* **50/1**

1m 51.0s (0.50) **Going Correction** +0.10s/f (Slow)
**WFA** 4 from 5yo+ 1lb 11 Ran SP% **123.9**
Speed ratings (Par 101): **101,98,97,96,95 95,95,90,90,78 61**
CSF £19.19 CT £219.45 TOTE £3.20: £1.20, £2.20, £6.10; EX 20.20 Trifecta £232.50.
**Owner** R C Bond **Bred** R C Bond **Trained** Brawby, N Yorks

**FOCUS**
A moderate handicap in which the strong gallop suited those held up. The winner drifted from the centre towards the stands' side in the straight. The winner found a bit for the blinkers.

## 264 CORAL MOBILE "JUST THREE CLICKS TO BET" MAIDEN STKS 1m 1f 103y(P)
5:00 (5:04) (Class 5) 4-Y-0+ £2,587 (£770; £384) Stalls Low

Form RPR
320- **1** **Ruffled**[74] [7786] 4-9-0 **70**....................... ChrisCatlin 4 61
(Rae Guest) *trckd ldr: shkn up over 2f out: rdn to ld 1f out: edgd lft: drvn out* **8/11**[1]
/54- **2** *1 1/2* **Colour My World**[116] [6781] 4-9-5 **60**....................... GrahamLee 1 63
(Ed McMahon) *led: reminder 3f out: rdn and hdd 1f out: unable qck towards fin* **2/1**[2]
4- **3** *36* **Just Poppy (IRE)**[101] [3774] 5-9-1 **0**....................... TomEaves 2
(Iain Jardine) *hld up: pushed along over 3f out: sn wknd* **8/1**[3]

2m 2.31s (0.61) **Going Correction** +0.10s/f (Slow)
**WFA** 4 from 5yo 1lb 3 Ran SP% **102.3**
Speed ratings (Par 103): **101,99,67**
CSF £2.11 TOTE £1.60; EX 2.00 Trifecta £2.10.
**Owner** C J Murfitt **Bred** Juddmonte Farms Ltd **Trained** Newmarket, Suffolk
■ Acton Gold was withdrawn. Price at time of withdrawal 11/2. Rule 4 applies to all bets - deduct 15p in the pound.

**FOCUS**
A most uncompetitive maiden in which the gallop was only fair. The winner came down the centre in the straight. The level of the form revolves around the runner-up.

## 265 CORAL APP DOWNLOAD FROM THE APP STORE H'CAP 1m 1f 103y(P)
5:30 (5:30) (Class 5) (0-75,75) 4-Y-0+ £3,234 (£962; £481; £240) Stalls Low

Form RPR
/23- **1** **Secular Society**[23] [8427] 4-9-5 **74**....................... SeanLevey 4 85
(Brian Meehan) *mde all: rdn over 1f out: styd on wl* **6/4**[1]
055- **2** *2 1/2* **Arlecchino (IRE)**[88] [7491] 4-9-1 **70**.......................(b) GrahamLee 3 76
(Ed McMahon) *trckd wnr: shkn up over 2f out: rdn over 1f out: styd on same pce ins fnl f* **5/1**[3]
164- **3** *4* **Lean On Pete (IRE)**[42] [8226] 5-9-2 **75**....................... JacobButterfield(5) 1 73
(Ollie Pears) *trckd ldrs: racd keenly: pushed along over 2f out: styd on same pce fr over 1f out* **7/4**[2]
110- **4** *3/4* **Eastern Dragon (IRE)**[32] [8345] 4-8-13 **73**....................... DavidKenny(5) 2 69
(Michael Scudamore) *hld up: plld hrd: rdn over 2f out: styd on same pce appr fnl f* **12/1**
63-5 **5** *4 1/2* **Absent Amy (IRE)**[17] [32] 5-9-4 **72**....................... RobertHavlin 5 59
(Amy Weaver) *hld up: rdn over 2f out: wknd over 1f out* **8/1**

2m 3.37s (1.67) **Going Correction** +0.10s/f (Slow)
**WFA** 4 from 5yo 1lb 5 Ran SP% **111.8**
Speed ratings (Par 103): **96,93,90,89,85**
CSF £9.50 TOTE £2.50: £1.50, £2.60; EX 8.40 Trifecta £28.30.
**Owner** Orwell Partnership **Bred** Aston Mullins Stud **Trained** Manton, Wilts

**FOCUS**
A fair handicap but a steady gallop means this bare form isn't reliable, although it's been taken at face value for now. The winner edged towards the far rail in the straight.
T/Jkpt: £1,219.00 to £1 stake. Pool of £183,648.92 - 106.96 winning tickets. T/Plt: £134.80 to a £1 stake. Pool of £133,435.09 - 722.10 winning tickets. T/Qpdt: £6.40 to a £1 stake. Pool of £10,557.00 - 1,212.29 winning tickets. CR

# [237]CAGNES-SUR-MER
Monday, January 20

**OFFICIAL GOING: Polytrack: standard**

## 266a PRIX DES OLIVIERS (CLAIMER) (4YO) (POLYTRACK) 1m (F)
3:25 (12:00) 4-Y-0 £6,250 (£2,500; £1,875; £1,250; £625)

RPR
**1** **Holly Filly (IRE)**[60] [7993] 4-8-11 **0**....................... StephaneRichardot 11 66
(T Larriviere, France) **14/5**[1]
**2** *2* **Bomber (ITY)** 4-9-2 **0**....................... CFiocchi 2 67
(Stefano Botti, Italy) **3/1**[2]
**3** *3/4* **Knight Charm**[22] [8441] 4-8-11 **0**....................... Pierre-CharlesBoudot 3 60
(Gay Kelleway) *broke wl: trckd ldr: rdn to chal 2f out: sn ev ch: one pce u.p fr 1f out: lost 2nd fnl 50yds* **63/10**
**4** *nse* **Number Winner (FR)**[94] 4-9-2 **0**.......................(b) TonyPiccone 12 65
(M Gentile, France) **11/2**[3]
**5** *snk* **Tiolache (FR)**[300] 4-8-11 **0**.......................(p) SylvainRuis 4 60
(J-M Capitte, France) **47/1**
**6** *nk* **Adjudant Chef (FR)**[230] 4-9-1 **0**.......................(p) XavierBergeron(3) 6 66
(D Rabhi, France) **11/2**[3]
**7** *1 1/2* **Alhavolle (IRE)**[33] 4-8-4 **0**....................... AllanMonnier(7) 9 55
(J-M Capitte, France) **14/1**
**8** *nse* **Jack Muscolo (USA)**[48] 4-8-11 **0**.......................(p) AnthonyCrastus 5 55
(C Cardaioli, Italy) **15/1**
**9** *1/2* **Ryedale Valley**[22] [8441] 4-8-8 **0**....................... AntoineWerle(3) 1 54
(Mlle M Henry, France) **69/1**
**10** *nk* **Starki (FR)**[9] 4-8-6 **0**.......................(b) JimmyTastayre(5) 8 53
(C Boutin, France) **43/1**
**11** *nk* **Special Dream (FR)**[196] 4-8-11 **0**....................... SebastienMartino(4) 10 57
(H-A Namur, France) **81/1**
**12** *hd* **Il Penna (FR)**[225] 4-9-4 **0**....................... TheoBachelot 7 59
(Laura Grizzetti, Italy) **23/1**

1m 33.12s (93.12) **12** Ran SP% **119.9**
WIN (incl. 1 euro stake): 3.80. PLACES: 1.50, 1.60, 1.90. DF: 9.60. SF: 17.80.
**Owner** Ecurie Kura & Haras De Bernesq **Bred** Ecurie Kura **Trained** France

# [252]SOUTHWELL (L-H)
Tuesday, January 21

**OFFICIAL GOING: Standard**
Wind: Light; across Weather: Fine, dry

## 267 32RED H'CAP 1m (F)
1:00 (1:00) (Class 6) (0-60,56) 3-Y-0 £2,385 (£704; £352) Stalls Low

Form RPR
500- **1** **Pacquita**[105] [7096] 3-9-2 **50**....................... JoeFanning 6 60+
(Mark Johnston) *trckd ldr: cl up 3f out: led 2f out: sn rdn clr: kpt on wl u.p fnl f* **7/2**[2]
02-U **2** *1* **Columbian Roulette (IRE)**[18] [28] 3-9-7 **55**.......................(b[1]) LukeMorris 3 61
(Charles Hills) *dwlt: sn swtchd wd: rdn along and outpcd in rr: sme hdwy and rdn over 2f out: drvn over 1f out: styd on fnl f: nt rch wnr* **5/4**[1]
4-33 **3** *nk* **Day Star Lad**[7] [173] 3-9-4 **52**.......................(v) DaleSwift 7 57
(Derek Shaw) *dwlt: sn trcking ldrs: hdwy 3f out: rdn wl over 1f out: styng on whn rdr dropped whip ins fnl f: kpt on same pce* **8/1**
35-1 **4** *1/2* **It's All A Game**[18] [28] 3-8-13 **50**.......................(b) BillyCray(3) 5 54
(Richard Guest) *led: rdn along and hdd 2f out: drvn over 1f out: one pce fnl f* **12/1**
0-51 **5** *hd* **Frankthetank (IRE)**[7] [173] 3-9-8 **56** 6ex....................... TomEaves 1 59
(Keith Dalgleish) *trckd ldrs on inner: pushed along and outpcd 3f out: rdn 2f out: styng on whn swtchd rt appr fnl f: sn drvn and kpt on same pce* **4/1**[3]
00-0 **6** *7* **Application**[11] [127] 3-8-13 **47**....................... DuranFentiman 2 34
(Bryan Smart) *in rr: rdn along 3f out: outpcd fnl 2f* **50/1**
015- **7** *8* **Marlismamma (FR)**[105] [7096] 3-9-6 **54**....................... DanielTudhope 4 23
(David O'Meara) *trckd ldrs: rdn along wl over 2f out: sn drvn and wknd* **20/1**

1m 44.21s (0.51) **Going Correction** -0.025s/f (Stan) **7** Ran SP% **112.2**
Speed ratings (Par 95): **96,95,94,94,94 87,79**
CSF £7.94 TOTE £4.60: £1.70, £1.60; EX 11.90 Trifecta £49.70.
**Owner** Sheikh Hamdan bin Mohammed Al Maktoum **Bred** Darley **Trained** Middleham Moor, N Yorks

**FOCUS**
A crisp and bright afternoon. The ground had dried out, although was officially described as standard and they went a decent pace for this ordinary handicap. The time was modest and the form seems ordinary.

## 268 LADBROKES MOBILE (S) STKS 7f (F)
1:30 (1:30) (Class 6) 4-Y-0+ £2,385 (£704; £352) Stalls Low

Form RPR
60-1 **1** **Basingstoke (IRE)**[7] [170] 5-9-5 **64**....................... TomEaves 5 79+
(Keith Dalgleish) *trckd ldr: hdwy to ld 1/2-way: jnd and rdn over 2f out: drvn over 1f out: kpt on strly fnl f* **1/2**[1]
61-3 **2** *4* **Tartan Trip**[12] [101] 7-9-5 **70**.......................(v) AndrewMullen 1 67
(Michael Appleby) *trckd ldng pair: hdwy to chse wnr 3f out: chal 2f out: sn rdn and ev ch tl drvn and one pce fnl f* **2/1**[2]
20-6 **3** *16* **Amber Moon**[14] [78] 9-8-6 **42** ow2....................... AnnStokell(5) 3 17
(Ann Stokell) *chsd ldng pair on inner: rdn along 3f out: outpcd fnl 2f* **100/1**
000- **4** *1* **Ishiamiracle**[38] [8293] 5-8-9 **43**.......................(p) PaddyAspell 4 12
(Phil McEntee) *led: hdd 1/2-way and sn rdn along: drvn over 2f out and sn wknd* **16/1**[3]
500- **5** *10* **Lenderking (IRE)**[118] [6756] 6-8-7 **27**....................... PaulBooth(7) 2
(Michael Chapman) *s.i.s: a outpcd and bhd* **100/1**

1m 28.58s (-1.72) **Going Correction** -0.025s/f (Stan) **5** Ran SP% **107.9**
Speed ratings (Par 101): **108,103,85,84,72**
CSF £1.62 TOTE £1.30: £1.10, £1.10; EX 1.70 Trifecta £7.10.The winner was bought by Simon Hodgson for 9,500gns
**Owner** Straightline Construction Ltd **Bred** Mrs M Togher **Trained** Carluke, S Lanarks

**FOCUS**
The pace was fair for this uncompetitive, poorly-contested seller. The winner is possibly capable of better again.

## 269 LADBROKES H'CAP 1m (F)
2:05 (2:06) (Class 6) (0-60,60) 4-Y-0+ £2,385 (£704; £352) Stalls Low

Form RPR
422- **1** **Ivy Port**[35] [8316] 4-9-7 **60**.......................(p) AndrewMullen 7 73
(Michael Appleby) *t.k.h early: cl up: led after 2f: pushed clr 2f out: rdn and edgd lft over 1f out: hung bdly rt ent fnl f: kpt on strly* **7/4**[1]
602- **2** *4* **Amtired**[26] [8360] 8-9-6 **59**.......................(p) DanielTudhope 6 63
(Marjorie Fife) *towards rr: hdwy 1/2-way: wd st: rdn to chse wnr wl over 1f out and sn hung bdly lft: drvn and no imp fnl f* **9/4**[2]

31-0 **3** *8* **Storey Hill (USA)**19 17 9-8-13 **52** JoeFanning 9 38
(Richard Guest) *in tch: hdwy to chse ldrs over 3f out: rdn wl over 2f out: sn one pce* **6/1**3

30-5 **4** *nk* **Xpres Maite**7 171 11-8-12 **56** (b) TimClark(5) 2 41
(Roy Bowring) *s.i.s and bhd: hdwy on inner 2f out: sn rdn and styd on appr fnl f* **10/1**

600- **5** *nse* **Lucky Mountain**77 7752 4-8-7 **46** oh1 (b1) LukeMorris 10 31
(Scott Dixon) *prom: rdn along 3f out: drvn 2f out: sn one pce* **50/1**

1-20 **6** *5* **Ellaal**12 105 5-9-5 **58** DaleSwift 3 31
(Ruth Carr) *trckd ldrs: pushed along 3f out: rdn over 2f out and sn wknd* **16/1**

435- **7** *3* **Baile Atha Cliath (IRE)**25 8038 5-8-8 **50** NeilFarley(3) 5 16
(Declan Carroll) *a in rr* **12/1**

06-2 **8** *3 3/4* **Flying Giant (IRE)**18 31 4-9-7 **60** (t) BenCurtis 1 18
(Jo Hughes) *led 2f: cl up on inner: rdn along wl over 2f out: sn wknd* **8/1**

0-50 **9** *5* **Kai**7 171 5-8-7 **46** oh1 (b) MartinLane 4
(Alan McCabe) *a in rr* **50/1**

55-2 **10** *14* **Island Express (IRE)**14 76 7-8-6 **50** ow2 (t) AnnStokell(5) 8
(Ann Stokell) *chsd ldrs on outer to 1/2-way: sn wknd* **50/1**

1m 43.14s (-0.56) **Going Correction** -0.025s/f (Stan) **10 Ran SP% 121.1**
Speed ratings (Par 101): **101,97,89,88,88 83,80,76,71,57**
CSF £6.00 CT £18.42 TOTE £3.00: £1.30, £1.20, £2.10; EX 5.90 Trifecta £38.90.
**Owner** Goldform Racing **Bred** John Branson **Trained** Danethorpe, Notts

**FOCUS**
A modest handicapper with the winner rated up to her recent runs.

## 270 CORAL APP DOWNLOAD FROM THE APP STORE H'CAP 1m 4f (F)
**2:40** (2:40) (Class 4) (0-85,85) 4-Y-0+ **£5,175** (£1,540; £769; £384) **Stalls** Low

Form RPR

00-1 **1** **Blue Wave (IRE)**8 160 4-9-6 **85** 6ex JoeFanning 6 100+
(Mark Johnston) *trckd ldrs: smooth hdwy over 3f out: led wl over 1f out: sn pushed clr: readily* **6/4**1

050- **2** *4* **Dewala**23 7342 5-9-3 **78** AndrewMullen 8 84
(Michael Appleby) *cl up: led wl over 2f out: sn rdn: hdd wl over 1f out: sn drvn and kpt on same pce fnl f* **6/1**3

03-3 **3** *1 1/2* **Lexington Bay (IRE)**19 16 6-9-2 **77** (p) LeeTopliss 3 81
(Richard Fahey) *trckd ldng pair on inner: pushed along 3f out: effrt and rdn 2f out: drvn and one pce appr fnl f* **7/1**

13-2 **4** *6* **Scottish Boogie (IRE)**19 16 7-9-10 **85** (t) GeorgeBaker 7 79
(Seamus Durack) *hld up in tch: hdwy on outer over 3f out: effrt to chse ldrs over 2f out: sn rdn and no imp* **7/1**

**5** *4 1/2* **Ruzeiz (USA)**264 5-9-10 **85** GrahamLee 5 72
(Peter Hedger) *hld up in tch: pushed along 4f out: rdn 3f out: one pce fnl 2f* **16/1**

11-1 **6** *10* **Luv U Whatever**18 32 4-8-11 **76** LiamJones 4 47
(Jo Hughes) *led: pushed along and jnd 4f out: rdn and hdd wl over 2f out: sn drvn and wknd* **5/2**2

2m 39.74s (-1.26) **Going Correction** -0.025s/f (Stan)
**WFA** 4 from 5yo+ 4lb **6 Ran SP% 113.7**
Speed ratings (Par 105): **103,100,99,95,92 85**
CSF £11.36 CT £47.44 TOTE £2.20: £1.30, £2.10; EX 10.10 Trifecta £44.90.
**Owner** Sheikh Hamdan bin Mohammed Al Maktoum **Bred** Tom Darcy And Vincent McCarthy **Trained** Middleham Moor, N Yorks

**FOCUS**
Despite the small field this competitive race, run at a fair pace, was turned into a procession. The placed form looks ordinary.

## 271 COMPARE BOOKMAKERS AT BOOKMAKERS.CO.UK H'CAP 5f (F)
**3:15** (3:17) (Class 2) (0-100,99) 4-Y-0+ **£12,291** (£3,657; £1,827; £913) **Stalls** High

Form RPR

34-2 **1** **Silken Express (IRE)**20 4 5-8-11 **89** SeanLevey 1 102
(Robert Cowell) *cl up: rdn to ld wl over 1f out: drvn out* **9/2**3

6-14 **2** *1 1/4* **Even Stevens**9 148 6-8-12 **97** (v) MatthewHopkins(7) 2 105
(Scott Dixon) *slt ld: rdn 2f out: sn hdd: drvn and kpt on same pce ins fnl f* **4/1**2

000- **3** *1 1/2* **Woolfall Sovereign (IRE)**74 7803 8-9-5 **97** BarryMcHugh 11 100
(George Margarson) *towards rr: hdwy over 2f out: rdn wl over 1f out: styd on appr fnl f: nrst fin* **16/1**

01- **4** *1 1/2* **Bedloe's Island (IRE)**42 8232 9-8-9 **87** LiamJones 10 84
(Alan McCabe) *in rr and sn rdn along: hdwy 2f out: styd on fnl f: nrst fin* **8/1**

00-0 **5** *2 3/4* **Doctor Parkes**17 55 8-8-10 **88** AdamBeschizza 3 75
(Stuart Williams) *chsd ldrs: rdn along over 2f out: drvn and wknd over 1f out* **10/1**

00-0 **6** *1/2* **Fratellino**20 4 7-8-9 **87** (t) BenCurtis 9 73
(Alan McCabe) *sn rdn along and outpcd in rr tl styd on fr wl over 1f out: n.d* **33/1**

00-0 **7** *shd* **Whaileyy (IRE)**17 55 6-9-7 **99** (b) LukeMorris 5 84
(Marco Botti) *chsd ldrs: rdn along 1/2-way: sn wknd* **14/1**

543- **8** *1* **Alben Star (IRE)**32 8369 6-8-12 **93** GeorgeChaloner(3) 4 75
(Richard Fahey) *towards rr: rdn along 1/2-way: n.d* **5/2**1

40-6 **9** *3/4* **Prohibit**20 4 9-8-10 **88** (p) MartinLane 8 67
(Robert Cowell) *in tch: rdn along over 2f out: sn wknd* **33/1**

00-3 **10** *7* **Jiroft (ITY)**20 4 7-8-13 **94** RobertTart(3) 6 48
(Robert Cowell) *dwlt: sn chsng ldrs: rdn along 1/2-way: sn wknd* **10/1**

20-0 **U** **Equitania**20 4 4-8-9 **92** TimClark(5) 7
(Alan Bailey) *stmbld and uns rdr as stalls opened: rn loose and collided w stalls: fatally injured* **14/1**

1m 0.19s (0.49) **Going Correction** +0.325s/f (Slow) **11 Ran SP% 121.1**
Speed ratings (Par 109): **109,107,104,102,97 97,96,95,94,82**
CSF £23.65 CT £271.48 TOTE £4.60: £2.00, £1.40, £8.20; EX 19.30 Trifecta £228.00.
**Owner** Malih Lahej Al Basti **Bred** Redpender Stud Ltd **Trained** Six Mile Bottom, Cambs

**FOCUS**
A decent sprint handicap but the form's relevance elsewhere is questionable.

## 272 BOOKMAKERS.CO.UK (S) STKS 5f (F)
**3:45** (3:45) (Class 6) 4-Y-0+ **£2,385** (£704; £352) **Stalls** High

Form RPR

0-23 **1** **Only Ten Per Cent (IRE)**13 87 6-9-0 **69** (v) StephenCraine 8 82
(J R Jenkins) *cl up: led on bit 1/2-way: pushed clr over 1f out: readily* **1/1**1

060- **2** *4* **Heartsong (IRE)**92 7432 5-8-6 **67** 1 MichaelJMMurphy(3) 3 63
(John Gallagher) *prom: chsd wnr fr wl over 1f out: drvn and one pce fnl f* **14/1**

20-3 **3** *nk* **Angelo Poliziano**4 208 8-8-7 **69** (p) JosephineGordon(7) 10 67
(Jo Hughes) *chsd ldrs: edgd lft after 1f: rdn along over 2f out: styd on u.p fnl f* **8/1**

003/ **4** *1 1/2* **Dissent (IRE)**480 6641 5-9-0 **65** GrahamLee 1 61
(James Given) *cl up on outer: effrt 2f out: sn rdn and one pce* **7/1**

04-5 **5** *1 1/2* **Greenhead High**16 60 6-9-0 **70** AdrianNicholls 2 56
(David Nicholls) *slt ld: rdn along and hdd 1/2-way: grad wknd* **6/1**3

600- **6** *4 1/2* **Spic 'n Span**25 8411 9-9-0 **57** (b) LukeMorris 5 40
(Ronald Harris) *chsd ldrs: rdn along 1/2-way: sn outpcd* **33/1**

00-2 **7** *1 1/2* **Miako (USA)**12 93 4-8-7 **63** AlistairRawlinson(7) 9 34
(Michael Appleby) *in tch whn n.m.r and hmpd after 1f: sn swtchd lft to stands' rail and in rr after* **4/1**2

13-4 **8** *5* **Quality Art (USA)**12 93 6-8-12 **62** JackGarritty(7) 6 21
(Richard Guest) *v s.i.s and a bhd* **10/1**

/40- **9** *nk* **Gypsy Jazz (IRE)**88 7508 7-8-6 **45** ow2 1 AnnStokell(5) 4 12
(Ann Stokell) *a in rr: outpcd and bhd fr 1/2-way* **100/1**

1m 1.15s (1.45) **Going Correction** +0.325s/f (Slow) **9 Ran SP% 127.6**
Speed ratings (Par 101): **101,94,94,91,89 82,79,71,71**
CSF £21.39 TOTE £2.10: £1.20, £3.30, £2.80; EX 16.60 Trifecta £111.80.The winner was bought in for 8,250 gns
**Owner** B Silkman **Bred** Sandro Garavelli **Trained** Royston, Herts

**FOCUS**
A weak race but an impressive winner in a relatively good time. He's rated back to his best.

## 273 BEST ODDS AT BOOKMAKERS.CO.UK H'CAP 6f (F)
**4:15** (4:16) (Class 6) (0-60,61) 4-Y-0+ **£2,385** (£704; £352) **Stalls** Low

Form RPR

0U-3 **1** **Layla's Hero (IRE)**4 219 7-9-6 **59** (v) AdrianNicholls 1 69
(David Nicholls) *trckd ldrs on inner: hdwy wl over 2f out: rdn to chal over 1f out: led ins fnl f: drvn out* **8/1**

4-22 **2** *1 1/2* **Grace Hull**12 95 4-9-7 **60** GrahamLee 8 65
(Garry Moss) *towards rr: pushed along 1/2-way: hdwy over 2f out: chsd ldrs over 1f out: rdn to chse wnr ins fnl f: no imp* **3/1**1

0-41 **3** *1 3/4* **Guishan**7 174 4-9-8 **61** 6ex (p) AndrewMullen 5 60
(Michael Appleby) *slt ld: hdd over 3f out: cl up and rdn over 2f out: ev ch tl drvn and one pce ent fnl f* **5/1**3

552- **4** *3/4* **Beachwood Bay**35 8315 6-9-7 **60** (p) BenCurtis 3 57
(Jo Hughes) *cl up on inner: slt ld over 3f out: rdn 2f out: drvn and hdd ent fnl f: one pce* **7/2**2

004- **5** *1 1/2* **Solarmaite**25 8406 5-8-13 **55** (b) MarkCoumbe(3) 9 47
(Roy Bowring) *chsd ldrs: rdn along over 2f out: sn drvn and one pce* **5/1**3

64-3 **6** *1* **Orwellian**18 34 5-8-10 **49** PaddyAspell 4 38
(Bryan Smart) *in rr: hdwy wl over 2f out: sn rdn along and n.d* **10/1**

60- **7** *2 3/4* **Belle Bayardo (IRE)**34 8330 6-9-6 **59** (p) LukeMorris 6 39
(Ronald Harris) *towards rr: rdn along wl over 2f out: n.d* **10/1**

00-0 **8** *1/2* **Dancing Maite**18 29 9-9-2 **60** (b) TimClark(5) 10 39
(Roy Bowring) *s.i.s and bhd: hdwy and in tch 1/2-way: sn rdn along over 2f out and n.d* **14/1**

32-U **9** *1* **Ridgeway Hawk**18 34 6-9-0 **53** (v) RobertHavlin 2 28
(Mark Usher) *sn rdn along and bhd: swtchd to outer and wd st: nvr a factor* **16/1**

05-6 **10** *1 3/4* **Lexi's Beauty (IRE)**18 34 4-8-9 **48** oh1 ow2 (p) TomEaves 7 18
(Brian Baugh) *chsd ldng pair on outer: rdn along 1/2-way: wknd over 2f out* **50/1**

1m 16.47s (-0.03) **Going Correction** -0.025s/f (Stan) **10 Ran SP% 124.4**
Speed ratings (Par 101): **99,97,94,93,91 90,86,86,84,82**
CSF £34.52 CT £142.40 TOTE £12.60: £3.70, £1.20, £2.30; EX 48.40 Trifecta £319.20.
**Owner** Hart Inn I **Bred** Epona Bloodstock Ltd **Trained** Sessay, N Yorks

**FOCUS**
They spread out across the track in this run-of-the-mill sprint handicap. Straightforward form.
T/Plt: £7.60 to a £1 stake. Pool: £86,175.06 - 8,176.69 winning units T/Qpdt: £6.10 to a £1 stake. Pool: £7,222.16 - 872.28 winning units JR

# 244 KEMPTON (A.W) (R-H)
Wednesday, January 22

**OFFICIAL GOING: Standard**
Wind: Light, across Weather: Cloudy

## 274 KEMPTON.CO.UK H'CAP 6f (P)
**4:25** (4:31) (Class 7) (0-50,51) 4-Y-0+ **£1,617** (£481; £240; £120) **Stalls** Low

Form RPR

000/ **1** **Indus Valley (IRE)**700 651 7-9-2 **45** ShaneKelly 3 59
(Des Donovan) *mostly chsd ldr: rdn jst over 2f out: grad clsd fr over 1f out: drvn to ld last 75yds* **4/6**1

02-4 **2** *1/2* **Seamster**14 81 7-9-5 **48** (bt) GrahamLee 9 60
(Richard Ford) *led: more than 2 l clr 2f out: rdn over 1f out: worn down last 75yds* **7/2**2

/0-1 **3** *4* **Catalyze**5 215 6-9-8 **51** 6ex (t) WilliamCarson 6 50
(Ann Stokell) *hld up in midfield: prog over 2f out: shkn up to chse clr ldng pair over 1f out: no imp* **9/2**3

003- **4** *1 1/4* **Microlight**31 8393 6-9-3 **46** (b) JimmyQuinn 4 41
(John E Long) *chsd ldrs: rdn to dispute 3rd 2f out to 1f out: one pce* **25/1**

04-0 **5** *1/2* **Sherjawy (IRE)**12 114 10-9-1 **47** RossAtkinson(3) 7 41
(Zoe Davison) *disp 2nd pl to over 2f out: outpcd u.p after* **40/1**

46-6 **6** *1 1/2* **Rutterkin (USA)**14 83 6-8-10 **46** VictorSantos(7) 8 35
(James Moffatt) *s.s: mostly in last pair: urged along and sme prog jst over 2f out: no imp on ldrs over 1f out* **16/1**

356- **7** *1/2* **Twist And Twirl**40 8277 4-9-4 **47** DaleSwift 2 34
(Derek Shaw) *hmpd on inner after 1f and dropped to rr: nvr on terms after* **25/1**

6-04 **8** *1 1/4* **Glennten**3 251 5-9-7 **50** (b) RenatoSouza 5 33
(Sylvester Kirk) *hld up in last pair: urged along over 2f out: rn into trble over 1f out: nvr a factor* **12/1**

50-4 **9** *1 1/2* **Doctor Hilary**19 34 12-9-4 **47** (v) PaddyAspell 10 25
(Mark Hoad) *a in rr: rdn and no prog over 2f out* **33/1**

6-30 **10** *1/2* **Scommettitrice (IRE)**6 201 6-8-10 **46** (v) LouisSteward(7) 11 23
(Nigel Twiston-Davies) *disp 2nd pl to over 2f out: sn wknd* **25/1**

0-05 **11** *hd* **Lord Buffhead**13 100 5-9-5 **48** (v) AndrewMullen 1 24
(Richard Guest) *prom: hmpd on inner and lost pl after 1f: rdn over 2f out: wknd over 1f out* **25/1**

1m 12.52s (-0.58) **Going Correction** +0.15s/f (Slow) **11 Ran SP% 134.7**
Speed ratings (Par 97): **109,108,103,101,100 98,98,96,94,93 93**
CSF £3.67 CT £9.05 TOTE £2.20: £1.10, £1.40, £1.50; EX 6.50 Trifecta £22.10.
**Owner** River Racing **Bred** P Morris & B McKenna **Trained** Exning, Suffolk



The Form Book, Raceform Ltd, Newbury, RG14 5SJ

**FOCUS**
A basement-level handicap livened up by a big gamble on the winner. His first form since September 2011, but he used to be a stone+ better than this.

## 275 £500 FREE BETS AT BETDAQ MAIDEN FILLIES' STKS 7f (P)
4:55 (4:57) (Class 5) 3-Y-O+ £2,587 (£770; £384; £192) Stalls Low

Form RPR
0- 1 **Platinum Pearl**[35] 8332 3-8-10 0 AndreaAtzeni 3 72
(Peter Chapple-Hyam) *cl up: led jst over 2f out: sn rdn and pressed: hdd u.p 1f out then edgd rt and bmpd rival: kpt on to ld again last strides* **5/2**[2]
605- 2 *hd* **Arabian Music (IRE)**[22] 8451 3-8-10 65 LiamKeniry 5 72
(David Simcock) *trckd ldrs: prog to chal 2f out: pushed into ld 1f out and bmpd sn after: stl pushed along to hold narrow advantage fnl f: rdn 50yds out: hdd last strides* **9/4**[1]
3 *3* **Ishiamber** 4-10-0 0 LukeMorris 2 68
(George Baker) *s.s: hld up in last pair: shkn up and prog 2f out: tk 3rd jst ins fnl f: kpt on but no imp* **14/1**
064- 4 *¾* **River Goddess (IRE)**[160] 5435 3-8-10 67 JimCrowley 4 61
(Charles Hills) *t.k.h: pressed ldr to over 2f out: sn nt qckn u.p: one pce* **11/4**[3]
4- 5 *1 ¼* **Lady Kathian (IRE)**[41] 8259 3-8-10 0 JimmyQuinn 6 58
(Joseph Tuite) *in tch in midfield: rdn over 2f out: sn outpcd: no imp after* **12/1**
56- 6 *nk* **Aeolian Blue**[47] 8180 4-10-0 0 AdamKirby 8 62
(William Knight) *plld hrd early: hld up in last trio: effrt over 2f out but outpcd: fdd fnl f* **12/1**
060- 7 *4 ½* **The Cat**[51] 8123 3-8-10 0 KieranO'Neill 1 45
(Nigel Twiston-Davies) *racd freely and lugged lft: led: hdd jst over 2f out: sn btn* **66/1**
8 *3 ¼* **Kristal Hart** 5-10-0 0 PaddyAspell 7 41
(Neil Mulholland) *s.s: mostly detached in last: nvr a factor* **50/1**

1m 26.81s (0.81) **Going Correction** +0.15s/f (Slow)
**WFA** 3 from 4yo+ 18lb 8 Ran SP% 111.5
Speed ratings (Par 100): **101,100,97,96,95 94,89,85**
CSF £8.07 TOTE £3.30: £1.80, £1.20, £3.70; EX 9.00 Trifecta £70.10.
**Owner** Ziad A Galadari **Bred** Galadari Sons Stud Company Limited **Trained** Newmarket, Suffolk

**FOCUS**
Modest maiden form and a steadily run race. The first two improved to pull clear.

## 276 BETDAQ - THE SPORTS BETTING EXCHANGE MAIDEN STKS 1m 3f (P)
5:25 (5:25) (Class 5) 4-Y-O+ £2,587 (£770; £384; £192) Stalls Low

Form RPR
4- 1 **Sagesse**[170] 5071 4-9-0 0 LukeMorris 4 72
(Sir Mark Prescott Bt) *mde virtually all: set slow pce tl past 1/2-way: wound it up 3f out: hrd pressed and drvn 2f out: fnd enough and on top last 100yds* **5/2**[2]
543- 2 *1 ¼* **Conserve (IRE)**[23] 8444 4-8-9 72 (b[1]) DavidKenny(5) 5 70
(Amy Weaver) *trckd ldr after 2f tl 5f out: styd cl up: rdn to take 2nd again and chal over 1f out: nt qckn last 150yds* **7/2**[3]
2- 3 *1* **Avidly**[23] 8444 4-8-9 73 ShelleyBirkett(5) 3 68
(Julia Feilden) *t.k.h: hld up in 4th: prog to trck wnr 5f out: chal over 2f out: sn rdn and fnd little: lost 2nd over 1f out* **11/10**[1]
2 4 *5* **Teenage Dream (IRE)**[10] 150 6-9-1 0 (vt) AdamMcLean(7) 2 64?
(Derek Shaw) *t.k.h: hld up in last pair: wknd u.p over 2f out* **14/1**
5 *11* **Fleetwood Nix** 4-8-11 0 JemmaMarshall(3) 1 39
(Pat Phelan) *trckd ldr 2f: styd cl up tl wknd over 2f out* **33/1**
0- 6 *11* **Comfort And Joy (IRE)**[76] 7781 4-9-0 0 LiamJones 6 19
(Lee Carter) *hld up in last pair: rousted along over 3f out: sn wknd: t.o* **50/1**

2m 30.2s (8.30) **Going Correction** +0.15s/f (Slow)
**WFA** 4 from 6yo 3lb 6 Ran SP% 110.0
Speed ratings (Par 103): **75,74,73,69,61 53**
CSF £11.11 TOTE £2.90: £1.10, £2.60; EX 8.80 Trifecta £13.00.
**Owner** Miss K Rausing **Bred** Miss K Rausing **Trained** Newmarket, Suffolk
■ Stewards' Enquiry : David Kenny two-day ban: careless riding (Feb 5-6)

**FOCUS**
This was handed on a plate to Sagesse, who was left alone in front to set her own gallop. She stepped up from her debut but the second and third are not entirely convincing.

## 277 KEMPTON FOR WEDDINGS H'CAP (DIV I) 1m 4f (P)
5:55 (5:55) (Class 6) (0-60,60) 4-Y-O+ £1,940 (£577; £288; £144) Stalls Centre

Form RPR
405- 1 **Obboorr**[96] 7346 5-9-10 60 TomEaves 7 67
(John Wainwright) *wl in tch: trckd ldrs 4f: rdn to go 2nd wl over 1f out: clsd to ld 150yds out: jst hld on* **11/4**[2]
10-2 2 *nk* **Jamaica Grande**[5] 221 6-9-9 59 GrahamLee 9 66
(Dave Morris) *stdd s: hld up in last pair: prog on outer wl over 1f out: rdn and r.o fnl f: clsd on wnr fin: jst failed* **13/8**[1]
006- 3 *2 ½* **Waving**[26] 8417 5-8-11 50 (t) MarkCoumbe(3) 1 54+
(Tony Carroll) *trckd ldr 2f: steadily lost pl fr 1/2-way and last 3f out: rdn and trying to make prog whn nt clr run over 1f out: r.o to take 3rd last strides* **16/1**
25-0 4 *shd* **My Manekineko**[19] 33 5-9-9 59 JoeFanning 8 62
(J R Jenkins) *stdd s: hld up in last pair: rapid prog to ld 6f out: rdn over 2f out: hdd 150yds out: sn lost 2nd: fdd and lost 3rd last strides* **10/1**
660- 5 *½* **Rocky Rebel**[153] 5672 6-9-10 60 SeanLevey 3 62
(Michael Blake) *trckd ldrs: lost pl and pushed along in rr 5f out: u.p and no prog over 2f out: plugged on fr over 1f out* **11/1**
000- 6 *hd* **Superstición**[48] 1953 5-8-10 46 oh1 JohnFahy 6 48?
(Michael Madgwick) *sn led at modest pce: hdd 7f out: sn lost pl and pushed along towards rr 5f out: drvn 3f out: kpt on one pce fr over 1f out* **100/1**
00-1 7 *1 ¼* **Midnight Sequel**[7] 185 5-9-3 53 6ex (p) LiamKeniry 2 53
(Neil Mulholland) *trckd ldrs: prog to go 2nd 5f out to wl over 1f out: steadily wknd* **7/2**[3]
342- 8 *2* **Princess Willow**[49] 8148 6-9-7 57 JimmyQuinn 4 54
(John E Long) *trckd ldr after 2f: led 7f out to 6f out: rdn wl over 2f out: steadily wknd* **14/1**
553- 9 *1 ½* **James Pollard (IRE)**[55] 6068 9-9-2 59 (p) LouisSteward(7) 5 53
(Bernard Llewellyn) *hld up: prog to trck ldrs 4f out: rdn over 2f out: wknd over 1f out* **50/1**

2m 38.11s (3.61) **Going Correction** +0.15s/f (Slow) 9 Ran SP% 119.9
Speed ratings (Par 101): **93,92,91,91,90 90,89,88,87**
CSF £7.95 CT £59.84 TOTE £5.90: £1.70, £1.10, £6.20; EX 10.10 Trifecta £120.30.
**Owner** J S Wainwright **Bred** Darley **Trained** Kennythorpe, N Yorks

**FOCUS**
The early pace was ordinary but they quickened for home a lot sooner than in the previous maiden, and, while he didn't quite get there, the runner-up came from last place. The bare form is ordinary at best.

## 278 KEMPTON FOR WEDDINGS H'CAP (DIV II) 1m 4f (P)
6:25 (6:25) (Class 6) (0-60,60) 4-Y-O+ £1,940 (£577; £288; £144) Stalls Centre

Form RPR
/00- 1 **Low Key (IRE)**[350] 542 7-9-10 60 (v[1]) LiamKeniry 6 68+
(John Butler) *hld up disputing 5th: prog 3f out: rdn to ld wl over 1f out: drvn out fnl f* **4/7**[1]
345- 2 *1* **Our Golden Girl**[33] 8373 4-8-6 53 (b) DavidParkes(7) 1 58
(Shaun Lycett) *hld up in last pair: rdn 3f out: no prog tl over 1f out on outer: styd on to take 2nd last 100yds: unable to chal* **25/1**
246- 3 *1* **Stag Hill (IRE)**[33] 6700 5-9-2 59 (p) LouisSteward(7) 8 62
(Bernard Llewellyn) *stdd s: hld up in last pair: rdn 3f out: styd on fr wl over 1f out to dispute 2nd briefly 100yds out: kpt on* **12/1**[3]
60-0 4 *1* **Elegant Ophelia**[12] 120 5-9-8 58 (t) AdamKirby 4 59
(Dean Ivory) *hld up disputing 5th: no prog 3f out but gng wl enough: hdwy and reminder over 1f out: carried rt briefly sn after: disp 2nd and light reminder ins fnl f: pushed along and dropped to 4th nr fin* **14/1**
50-5 5 *1 ½* **Time Square (FR)**[16] 67 7-9-9 59 LukeMorris 5 58
(Tony Carroll) *chsd ldng pair: rdn over 3f out: kpt on to press for a pl 1f out: wknd last 150yds* **5/1**[2]
34-0 6 *4 ½* **Mazij**[12] 120 6-9-10 60 WilliamCarson 7 52
(Peter Hiatt) *pressed ldr: led over 3f out and kicked on: hdd wl over 1f out: edgd rt sn after: wknd qckly fnl f* **25/1**
23-1 7 *1 ¾* **Pass The Time**[15] 73 5-9-5 55 (p) JimCrowley 2 44
(Neil Mulholland) *t.k.h: trckd ldng pair: shkn up and wknd 2f out* **5/1**[2]
00-0 8 *7* **White Diamond**[12] 117 7-9-2 52 AndrewMullen 3 30
(Nigel Twiston-Davies) *led: hdd and rdn over 3f out: sn wknd* **25/1**

2m 33.24s (-1.26) **Going Correction** +0.15s/f (Slow)
**WFA** 4 from 5yo+ 4lb 8 Ran SP% 122.9
Speed ratings (Par 101): **110,109,108,108,107 104,102,98**
CSF £25.51 CT £98.40 TOTE £1.50: £1.10, £5.70, £3.00; EX 34.50 Trifecta £243.60.
**Owner** J Butler **Bred** Christoph Berglar **Trained** Newmarket, Suffolk

**FOCUS**
The second division of an ordinary handicap, but more significantly, and to the cost of at least some bookmakers, the race in which the final leg of a substantial four-timer coup was landed. Modest form, rated around the second and third.

## 279 WINNERS ARE WELCOME AT BETDAQ H'CAP 6f (P)
6:55 (6:55) (Class 4) (0-85,83) 3-Y-O £5,498 (£1,636; £817; £408) Stalls Low

Form RPR
11-2 1 **Oriental Relation (IRE)**[7] 183 3-9-5 81 (b) GrahamLee 3 91+
(James Given) *t.k.h early: hld up in 4th: nt clr run briefly 2f out: prog over 1f out: shkn up to ld last 150yds: won w smething in hand* **4/6**[1]
014- 2 *¾* **Harwoods Volante (IRE)**[23] 8442 3-9-7 83 RobertHavlin 7 90
(Amanda Perrett) *led: rdn over 1f out: hdd last 150yds: styd on but readily hld* **7/2**[2]
111- 3 *1 ¼* **Drive On (IRE)**[25] 8426 3-9-1 77 (p) JohnFahy 5 80+
(Eve Johnson Houghton) *dwlt: hld up in last: rdn and prog over 1f out: tk 3rd ins fnl f: one pce after* **8/1**[3]
1-14 4 *¾* **Exceeding Power**[17] 62 3-8-5 74 LouisSteward(7) 1 75
(Michael Bell) *trckd ldng pair: rdn to go 2nd 2f out to jst over 1f out: one pce u.p* **16/1**
110- 5 *1 ¾* **Nova Princesse (GER)**[41] 8261 3-9-1 77 (t) LukeMorris 2 72
(Marco Botti) *hld up in 5th: tried to make prog on inner over 1f out: rdn and wknd fnl f* **16/1**
512- 6 *6* **Zain Zone (IRE)**[177] 4833 3-9-1 77 (p) AdamKirby 9 53
(Robert Cowell) *dwlt: rcvrd to chse ldr to 2f out: wknd qckly: eased* **16/1**

1m 11.82s (-1.28) **Going Correction** +0.15s/f (Slow) 6 Ran SP% 111.0
Speed ratings (Par 99): **114,113,111,110,108 100**
CSF £3.13 CT £7.82 TOTE £1.30: £1.50, £2.10; EX 3.70 Trifecta £10.60.
**Owner** The Cool Silk Partnership **Bred** Brendan Laffan & Michael McCormick **Trained** Willoughton, Lincs

**FOCUS**
Not a bad handicap. The winner was well in and the runner-up improved to beat the rest.

## 280 BETDAQ 1ST UK COMMISSION FREE H'CAP 1m (P)
7:25 (7:25) (Class 6) (0-55,56) 3-Y-O £1,940 (£577; £288; £144) Stalls Low

Form RPR
65-2 1 **Royal Bushida**[19] 28 3-8-12 46 oh1 DaleSwift 4 42
(Derek Shaw) *t.k.h: hld up bhd ldrs: pushed along to chal 2f out: rdn to ld 1f out: drvn and hld on* **6/4**[2]
46-3 2 *hd* **Tortoise**[19] 28 3-8-12 46 oh1 (b) WilliamCarson 7 41
(Richard Guest) *led: set sedate pce tl kicked on 3f out: hdd over 2f out and drvn: rallied 1f out: kpt on and pressed wnr nr fin* **16/1**
005- 3 *shd* **Flying Kyte**[142] 6035 3-8-9 46 JemmaMarshall(3) 3 41
(Pat Phelan) *trckd ldr: nipped through on inner bnd 3f out: led over 2f out: wandered and idling in front: hdd 1f out: kpt on last 100yds: jst hld* **10/1**
50-6 4 *2* **Copper Cavalier**[9] 165 3-8-12 46 oh1 (v) AdamBeschizza 5 36
(Robert Cowell) *t.k.h: hld up bhd ldrs: rdn to chal 2f out: nt qckn over 1f out: fdd fnl f* **13/2**[3]
444- 5 *1 ¼* **Libra Romana (IRE)**[33] 8368 3-9-5 53 LukeMorris 8 40
(Sir Mark Prescott Bt) *t.k.h: hld up in last pair: tapped for spd once dash sed over 2f out: swtchd to inner and briefly tried to cl over 1f out: sn no prog* **11/8**[1]
00-0 6 *1 ½* **Dawnfromthepast (IRE)**[14] 86 3-8-9 46 oh1 RossAtkinson(3) 1 30
(Luke Dace) *t.k.h: hld up in last pair: rdn over 2f out once pce lifted: no imp over 1f out: fdd* **33/1**

1m 46.18s (6.38) **Going Correction** +0.15s/f (Slow) 6 Ran SP% 113.4
Speed ratings (Par 95): **74,73,73,71,70 68**
CSF £24.28 CT £179.98 TOTE £3.10: £1.80, £4.30; EX 18.40 Trifecta £112.00.
**Owner** Brian Johnson (Northamptonshire) **Bred** D D & Mrs J P Clee **Trained** Sproxton, Leics

**FOCUS**
All but two of these ran from out of the handicap, there was no pace early, it developed into a sprint up the straight and concluded with a bunched finish. Not a race to take seriously.

## 281 DINE IN THE PANORAMIC H'CAP 1m (P)
7:55 (7:55) (Class 6) (0-55,60) 4-Y-O+ £1,940 (£577; £288; £144) Stalls Low

Form RPR
006/ 1 **Callisto Light**[821] 7069 7-9-6 54 AdamKirby 3 62+
(Michael Squance) *led 1f: trckd ldng pair after: wnt 2nd over 2f out: pushed into ld over 1f out: rdn out* **7/4**[1]

2-33 **2** *1* **Olivers Mount**[12] 117 4-9-6 **54**....................(tp) JimmyQuinn 5 60
(Ed Vaughan) *trckd ldrs: rdn 2f out: prog to chse wnr fnl f: styd on but hld last 75yds* **9/4**[2]

000- **3** *2 1/4* **Byrd In Hand (IRE)**[23] 8449 7-8-12 **46** oh1....................(b[1]) LiamKeniry 7 47
(John Bridger) *led after 1f: rdn and hdd over 1f out: grad outpcd* **50/1**

3-41 **4** *shd* **Greek Islands (IRE)**[9] 156 6-9-12 **60** 6ex.................... ChrisCatlin 1 61+
(Edward Creighton) *t.k.h and hld up in rr: prog over 2f out: rdn and kpt on fr over 1f out: nrst fin* **12/1**

00-0 **5** *1 1/2* **Marvo**[7] 179 10-9-2 **50**....................(b) DavidProbert 4 47
(Bernard Llewellyn) *hld up in midfield: gng wl 3f out: lost grnd on ldrs over 2f out: rdn over 1f out: kpt on same pce after* **33/1**

60-0 **6** *3/4* **The Wonga Coup (IRE)**[14] 88 7-9-3 **51**.................... FergusSweeney 6 46
(Pat Phelan) *hld up and sn in last: pushed along and prog over 2f out: rdn and kpt on fr over 1f out: no ch of being involved* **16/1**

4-15 **7** *2* **Daniel Thomas (IRE)**[14] 88 12-9-4 **52**....................(tp) WilliamCarson 10 43
(Ann Stokell) *awkward s: wl in rr: drvn on wd outside over 2f out: modest late prog* **12/1**

05-3 **8** *2* **Bubbly Bailey**[15] 76 4-9-6 **54**....................(v) JoeFanning 13 40
(J R Jenkins) *trckd ldr after 1f: hanging and lost 2nd over 2f out: wknd jst over 1f out* **16/1**

0-22 **9** *3 1/4* **Chez Vrony**[6] 201 8-9-1 **49**.................... GrahamLee 8 28
(Dave Morris) *broke w ldrs but sn restrained into rr: rdn and no prog over 2f out* **9/2**[3]

00-0 **10** *3/4* **Kindia (IRE)**[7] 185 6-9-1 **49**....................(v) LiamJones 12 26
(Michael Attwater) *s.i.s: a wl in rr: struggling over 2f out* **25/1**

00-6 **11** *nse* **Kilburn**[9] 156 10-9-2 **55**.................... EoinWalsh(5) 9 32
(Alastair Lidderdale) *hld up in rr: prog on outer 5f out: rdn and wknd over 2f out* **20/1**

350- **12** *6* **Coach Montana (IRE)**[97] 7323 5-8-12 **46** oh1.......... AdamBeschizza 2 9
(Christine Dunnett) *chsd ldrs: rdn and wknd 3f out* **40/1**

1m 39.31s (-0.49) **Going Correction** +0.15s/f (Slow) **12 Ran SP% 128.4**
Speed ratings (Par 101): **108,107,104,104,103 102,100,98,95,94 94,88**
CSF £5.95 CT £155.85 TOTE £3.60: £1.10, £1.30, £14.50; EX 10.80 Trifecta £567.80.
**Owner** G D J Linder **Bred** Hermes Services Ltd **Trained** Newmarket, Suffolk
■ Stewards' Enquiry : Adam Kirby eight-day ban, plus six deferred: used whip in incorrect place (Feb 5-15,17-19)

**FOCUS**
On a day of gambles another significant punt was landed here. It's hard to be positive about the overall form.
T/Jkpt: £591.60. Pool: £10,000.00 - 12.00 winning units. T/Plt: £7.60 Pool: £100,339.89 - 9534.29 winning units. T/Qpdt: £6.20. Pool: £7471.14 - 879.36 winning units. JN

# 229 LINGFIELD (L-H)
## Wednesday, January 22

**OFFICIAL GOING: Standard**
Wind: medium, across Weather: overcast, dry

## 282 CORAL.CO.UK MEDIAN AUCTION MAIDEN STKS — 1m 4f (P)
**1:00** (1:00) (Class 6) 4-6-Y-O — **£2,385** (£704; £352) **Stalls** Low

Form RPR

52-0 **1** **Eco Warrior**[16] 67 4-9-5 57....................(b[1]) FrankieDettori 6 73
(J W Hills) *mde all: rdn and qcknd clr w runner-up over 2f out: sustained duel after: kpt on wl and asserted towards fin* **8/1**

234- **2** *nk* **Wilhana (IRE)**[23] 8444 4-9-0 70.................... LiamKeniry 4 68
(Pam Sly) *chsd wnr: upsides 3f out: rdn and qcknd clr w wnr over 2f out: sustained duel w wnr after: kpt on tl no ex and hld towards fin* **10/11**[1]

/25- **3** *7* **Experimentalist**[27] 378 6-9-9 64....................(t) DavidProbert 3 62
(Tim Vaughan) *chsd ldng pair for 4f: wl in tch in midfield after: rdn and effrt to go 3rd wl over 2f out: outpcd and btn 2f out: plugged on* **9/4**[2]

**4** *1 3/4* **Candesta (USA)**[217] 4-9-0 0.................... ShelleyBirkett(5) 7 59
(Julia Feilden) *in tch in midfield: rdn and effrt wl over 2f out: outpcd and btn over 2f out: modest 4th and plugged on same pce fnl 2f* **7/1**[3]

**5** *8* **Celtic Sunlight** 4-9-5 0.................... FergusSweeney 1 46
(Pat Phelan) *in tch in last pair: rdn over 3f out: outpcd and btn over 2f out: wknd wl over 1f out: bhd fnl f* **50/1**

00- **6** *1* **Be A Rebel**[68] 7894 4-9-0 0.................... JimmyQuinn 5 40
(John E Long) *rn in snatches: in tch in rr: reminder 4f out: drvn and outpcd 3f out: sn wknd: bhd fnl f* **100/1**

05-0 **7** *1 1/4* **Parsons Green**[7] 185 5-9-4 45.................... LiamJones 2 38
(Michael Attwater) *in tch in midfield: chsd ldng pair 8f out tl wl over 2f out: sn lost pl and wknd 2f out: bhd fnl f* **100/1**

2m 31.57s (-1.43) **Going Correction** -0.15s/f (Stan)
**WFA** 4 from 5yo+ 4lb **7 Ran SP% 110.7**
Speed ratings: **98,97,93,91,86 85,85**
CSF £14.91 TOTE £6.00: £2.90, £1.10; EX 26.60 Trifecta £43.40.
**Owner** D J Deer **Bred** D J And Mrs Deer **Trained** Upper Lambourn, Berks
■ A winner for Frankie Dettori on his first ride since breaking an ankle in October.

**FOCUS**
The going was standard. This was an u weak, uncompetitive maiden run at a steady pace. The form is rated a bit cautiously.

## 283 32RED CASINO H'CAP — 1m 5f (P)
**1:30** (1:30) (Class 6) (0-60,63) 4-Y-O+ — **£2,385** (£704; £352) **Stalls** Low

Form RPR

00/- **1** **Eye Of The Tiger (GER)**[481] 6626 9-9-9 **56**.................... ShaneKelly 9 77
(Des Donovan) *a travelling wl: chsd ldr tl led 3f out: sn pushed along and readily qcknd clr: in n.d fnl 2f: v easily* **1/1**[1]

360- **2** *9* **Cabuchon (GER)**[35] 8337 7-9-8 **55**.................... SeanLevey 4 62
(David Evans) *hld up in tch in rr of main gp: hdwy on inner 3f out: rdn to chse clr wnr 2f out: plugged on for clr 2nd but no imp* **20/1**

43-2 **3** *3* **Geeaitch**[13] 106 5-9-8 **55**.................... WilliamCarson 3 58
(Peter Hiatt) *chsd ldrs: drvn over 3f out: 3rd and no ch w wnr whn edgd rt over 1f out: plugged on* **12/1**

6/0- **4** *5* **Magicalmysterytour (IRE)**[23] 8447 11-9-9 **56**.......... RobertWinston 7 51
(Willie Musson) *hld up detached in last pair: clsd and in tch 5f out: outpcd over 2f out: no ch w wnr but styd on past btn horses fnl f* **66/1**

03-2 **5** *1 1/2* **Kindlelight Storm (USA)**[12] 117 4-9-4 **56**..............(b) GeorgeBaker 6 49
(Nick Littmoden) *hld up in tch in midfield: effrt but outpcd by wnr over 2f out: 4th and wl hld over 1f out: wknd fnl f* **9/2**[2]

RR-4 **6** *3 1/2* **Azabitmour (FR)**[16] 68 4-8-11 **49**.................... ChrisCatlin 1 37
(John Best) *v.s.a: detached in last: steadily clsd but stl 10 l last 5f out: lost tch over 3f out* **33/1**

33-1 **7** *7* **Keep Kicking (IRE)**[5] 214 7-10-2 **63** 6ex.................... JimCrowley 2 40
(Simon Dow) *wl in tch in midfield: chsd ldrs over 4f out: struggling u.p over 3f out: fdd wl over 1f out: wl bhd fnl f* **5/1**[3]

000- **8** *3/4* **Highly Likely (IRE)**[146] 5934 5-9-10 **57**.................... AdamKirby 8 33
(Steve Woodman) *led tl 3f out: sn rdn and lost pl: wknd 2f out: wl bhd fnl f* **8/1**

260- **9** *12* **El Libertador (USA)**[49] 8148 8-9-5 **52**....................(b) LukeMorris 5 10
(Eric Wheeler) *chsd ldrs: rdn and lost pl over 4f out: bhd 2f out: t.o fnl f* **25/1**

2m 41.15s (-4.85) **Going Correction** -0.15s/f (Stan)
**WFA** 4 from 5yo+ 5lb **9 Ran SP% 116.7**
Speed ratings (Par 101): **108,102,100,97,96 94,90,89,82**
CSF £28.81 CT £165.54 TOTE £2.40: £1.60, £4.80, £2.90; EX 41.30 Trifecta £462.30.
**Owner** River Racing **Bred** Baron G Von Ullmann **Trained** Exning, Suffolk

**FOCUS**
The pace was honest for this moderate handicap. There was a major plunge on the winner. He had smart form in Germany but it was hard to know what he might retain.

## 284 32RED.COM MAIDEN STKS — 6f 1y(P)
**2:00** (2:00) (Class 5) 3-Y-O — **£3,067** (£905; £453) **Stalls** Low

Form RPR

5- **1** **Gone With The Wind (GER)**[63] 7972 3-9-5 0.................... FrankieDettori 7 74
(Jeremy Noseda) *chsd ldrs tl trckd ldr over 4f out: rdn to ld wl over 1f out: hrd drvn 1f out: kpt on and outbattled runner-up ins fnl f* **7/4**[1]

5- **2** *nk* **Android (IRE)**[151] 5757 3-9-5 0.................... AdamKirby 6 73
(Clive Cox) *chsd ldr for 2f: hung lft and swtchd rt over 3f out: effrt and hung lft 2f out: stl hanging but chsd wnr over 1f out: ev ch but nt qckning ins fnl f: drvn and hld fnl 75yds* **5/2**[2]

-2 **3** *1* **La Napoule**[11] 142 3-9-0 0.................... SeanLevey 5 65
(Richard Hannon) *hld up wl in tch: rdn and effrt 2f out: chsd ldng pair 1f out: styd on same pce u.p fnl 150yds* **3/1**[3]

200- **4** *1/2* **Misty Sparkler**[91] 7463 3-9-0 71.................... FergusSweeney 3 63
(Jamie Osborne) *led tl rdn and hdd wl over 1f out: styd on same pce fnl f: n.m.r towards fin* **16/1**

050- **5** *5* **Beatabout The Bush (IRE)**[124] 6590 3-9-5 58.............. AndreaAtzeni 2 52
(Charles Hills) *wl in tch: drvn and unable qck 2f out: wknd u.p ent fnl f* **20/1**

0- **6** *50* **Mercury Magic**[35] 8326 3-9-5 0.................... JimCrowley 4
(Ralph Beckett) *rrd as stalls opened and slowly away: sn detached: rdr looking down after 1f: allowed to come home in own time: t.o* **6/1**

1m 12.25s (0.35) **Going Correction** -0.15s/f (Stan) **6 Ran SP% 114.9**
Speed ratings (Par 97): **91,90,89,88,81 15**
CSF £6.65 TOTE £2.40: £1.60, £2.10; EX 7.80 Trifecta £21.90.
**Owner** Mrs Susan Roy **Bred** Graf And Grafin Von Stauffenberg **Trained** Newmarket, Suffolk

**FOCUS**
Some powerful stables in opposition for this maiden which was run at a steady pace. The front four finished in a bunch but the form might be a bit better than the average sprint maiden.

## 285 32RED CONDITIONS STKS (FAST TRACK QUALIFIER) — 1m 7f 169y(P)
**2:30** (2:30) (Class 2) 4-Y-O+ — **£12,291** (£3,657; £1,827; £913) **Stalls** Low

Form RPR

414- **1** **Arch Villain (IRE)**[25] 8429 5-9-2 94....................(b) JimCrowley 3 99
(Amanda Perrett) *chsd ldrs: rdn and effrt over 1f out: ev ch ent fnl f: r.o wl u.p to ld towards fin: hld on wl: all out* **11/4**[1]

045- **2** *hd* **Communicator**[35] 7823 6-9-2 90.................... DavidProbert 5 98
(Andrew Balding) *short of room sn after s and bustled along briefly: hld up in tch in rr: hdwy over 3f out: rdn to chal ent fnl f: drvn and ev ch fnl f: r.o but hld cl home* **5/1**

046/ **3** *nse* **Ted Spread**[39] 6519 7-9-2 0....................(t) LukeMorris 8 98
(Suzy Smith) *wl in tch in midfield: swtchd rt and pressed ldrs 3f out: rdn and led wl over 1f out: hrd pressed and drvn over 1f out: battled on gamely u.p tl hdd and no ex towards fin* **16/1**

/00- **4** *12* **Two Days In Paris (FR)**[69] 7891 5-8-11 0.................... SeanLevey 6 79
(Stuart Williams) *chsd ldr: rdn to ld 2f out: sn hdd: no ex and btn ent fnl f: wknd* **25/1**

22-4 **5** *1* **Grendisar (IRE)**[18] 54 4-8-9 90....................(p) AndreaAtzeni 4 82
(Marco Botti) *hld up wl in tch in last quartet: rdn and effrt over 2f out: 6th and outpcd 2f out: wknd over 1f out* **4/1**[3]

021- **6** *3 3/4* **Theology**[25] 8429 7-9-2 93.................... GeorgeBaker 1 78
(Steve Gollings) *led: rdn and hdd 2f out: btn over 1f out: fdd fnl f* **3/1**[2]

131/ **7** *10* **Exemplary**[27] 577 7-9-2 90.................... FrankieDettori 10 66
(Alexandra Dunn) *hld up wl in tch in last quartet: rdn 3f out: sn outpcd and btn: bhd over 1f out* **10/1**

11-1 **8** *1 1/4* **Mr Burbidge**[15] 72 6-9-2 87....................(b) LiamKeniry 7 64
(Neil Mulholland) *s.i.s: sn rcvrd and hld up wl in tch in last quartet: hdwy on outer 6f out: rdn 5f out: wknd over 2f out: bhd over 1f out* **6/1**

21-3 **9** *31* **Returntobrecongill**[21] 3 4-8-9 80.................... TomEaves 9 27
(James Given) *chsd ldrs tl lost pl qckly over 2f out: t.o over 2f out* **50/1**

3m 16.73s (-8.97) **Going Correction** -0.15s/f (Stan) course record
**WFA** 4 from 5yo+ 7lb **9 Ran SP% 123.4**
Speed ratings (Par 109): **116,115,115,109,109 107,102,101,86**
CSF £18.42 TOTE £3.10: £1.30, £1.70, £4.90; EX 22.50 Trifecta £347.30.
**Owner** Mr & Mrs F Cotton, Mr & Mrs P Conway **Bred** Summerhill Bloodstock **Trained** Pulborough, W Sussex
■ Stewards' Enquiry : Jim Crowley two-day ban: used whip above permitted level (Feb 5-6)

**FOCUS**
This decent contest, a fast track qualifier for the AW Championships on Good Friday, was run at a sound pace. The first four home broke the track record. The third is perhaps the key to the form.

## 286 DOWNLOAD THE LADBROKES APP H'CAP — 1m 1y(P)
**3:05** (3:05) (Class 5) (0-75,75) 4-Y-O+ — **£3,067** (£905; £453) **Stalls** High

Form RPR

253- **1** **Wilfred Pickles (IRE)**[22] 8453 8-9-2 **70**....................(p) AdamKirby 5 77
(Jo Crowley) *hld up in tch in midfield: swtchd rt and effrt to chse ldrs jst over 1f out: ev ch over 1f out: drvn to ld ins fnl f: r.o: drvn out* **4/1**[1]

0-42 **2** *hd* **Greensward**[7] 181 8-8-13 **67**....................(b) LiamKeniry 4 74
(Conor Dore) *chsd ldng trio: hemmed in and nt clr run jst over 2f out: swtchd rt over 1f out: hdwy u.p ins fnl f: r.o wl to snatch 2nd last stride: nt quite rch wnr* **12/1**

006- **3** *shd* **Gracious George (IRE)**[34] 8345 4-9-6 **74**.............. KieranO'Neill 7 80
(Jimmy Fox) *chsd ldr tl rdn to ld 2f out: hrd pressed and drvn over 1f out: hdd ins fnl f: battled on wl and ev ch after: no ex last strides* **14/1**

03-3 **4** *nk* **Club House (IRE)**[9] 155 4-8-8 **62**.................... TomEaves 9 68
(Robert Mills) *stdd s: hld up in tch in last quartet: clsd and nt clr run 2f out: swtchd lft and hdd 1f out: r.o u.p fnl 150yds* **20/1**

2-43 **5** *1 1/4* **Munsarim (IRE)**[7] 180 7-9-4 **72**.......................(b) LiamJones 8 75
(Lee Carter) *t.k.h: hld up in tch in last quartet: effrt and edgd rt u.p over 1f out: styd on u.p ins fnl f: no threat to ldrs* **6/1**

31-3 **6** *1/2* **Go Far**[9] 161 4-9-0 **68**.......................(v) RobertWinston 3 71
(Alan Bailey) *chsd ldrs: nt clr run 2f out: swtchd lft and drvn 1f out: nvr enough room fnl 150yds and eased towards fin* **9/2**[2]

404- **7** *3/4* **Swift Cedar (IRE)**[34] 8339 4-9-1 **72**....................... RobertTart(3) 6 72
(Jeremy Gask) *stdd after s: hld up in tch in last pair: hdwy u.p jst over 1f out: sltly hmpd jst ins fnl f: kpt on but no imp after* **6/1**

104- **8** *3/4* **Bloodsweatandtears**[22] 8453 6-8-12 **66**....................... AndreaAtzeni 10 64
(William Knight) *stdd s: t.k.h: hld up in tch in last pair: c wd and effrt u.p wl over 1f out: kpt on but no threat to ldrs* **5/1**[3]

006- **9** *2* **Storm Runner (IRE)**[35] 8323 6-8-11 **68**....................... RyanPowell(3) 1 62
(George Margarson) *hld up wl in tch in midfield: rdn over 2f out: drvn and no hdwy on inner over 1f out: wknd ins fnl f* **10/1**

0/1- **10** *6* **Toymaker**[362] 376 7-9-7 **75**....................... PaddyAspell 2 55
(Phil McEntee) *led tl 2f out: drvn and btn over 1f out: wknd fnl f* **14/1**

1m 36.8s (-1.40) **Going Correction** -0.15s/f (Stan) **10** Ran SP% **118.3**
Speed ratings (Par 103): **101,100,100,100,99 98,97,97,95,89**
CSF £53.48 CT £618.90 TOTE £3.60: £2.00, £3.00, £4.30; EX 31.90 Trifecta £261.70.
**Owner** Kilstone Limited **Bred** Eurostrait Ltd **Trained** Whitcombe, Dorset
■ Stewards' Enquiry : Robert Winston caution: failed to take all reasonable and permissable measures to obtain best possible placing.

**FOCUS**
An open handicap run at a steady pace. A bunch finish and ordinary form.

## 287 LADBROKES H'CAP — 7f 1y(P)
**3:35** (3:35) (Class 4) (0-85,85) 4-Y-0+ **£4,690** (£1,395; £697; £348) **Stalls** Low

Form RPR

500- **1** **Nassau Storm**[22] 8455 5-9-3 **81**....................... AndreaAtzeni 2 90
(William Knight) *hld up in tch in midfield: rdn and effrt to chse ldrs over 1f out: qcknd to ld fnl 100yds: r.o wl* **7/1**[2]

32-5 **2** *1/2* **Smokethatthunders (IRE)**[14] 91 4-8-9 **73**....................... LukeMorris 7 81
(James Toller) *taken down early: stdd after s: hld up in last trio: hdwy u.p ent fnl f: swtchd rt and r.o wl ins fnl f: chsd wnr and clsng fnl 50yds* **10/1**[3]

00-1 **3** *hd* **Compton**[9] 161 5-9-3 **81** 6ex.......................(t) SeanLevey 8 88
(Stuart Williams) *hld up in midfield: nt clr run wl over 1f out: swtchd rt over 1f out: r.o wl u.p ins fnl f* **5/4**[1]

31-3 **4** *3/4* **Mr David (USA)**[9] 162 7-9-7 **85**.......................(b) DavidProbert 1 90
(Jamie Osborne) *hld up in tch in midfield: nt clr run and shuffled bk 2f out: hdwy jst ins fnl f: styd on wl u.p fnl 100yds* **16/1**

4-25 **5** *hd* **Seek The Fair Land**[4] 233 8-8-10 **74**.......................(b) LiamJones 10 78
(Lee Carter) *t.k.h: chsd ldrs tl wnt 2nd wl over 3f out: rdn and ev ch over 1f out: led 1f out: hdd and no ex fnl 100yds: lost 3 pls fnl 50yds* **16/1**

606- **6** *1 1/4* **Silverheels (IRE)**[32] 8385 5-9-4 **82**.......................(b[1]) MartinLane 3 83
(Paul Cole) *chsd ldr tl wl over 3f out: rdn and unable qck jst over 2f out: btn jst ins fnl f: wknd fnl 100yds* **12/1**

324- **7** *1 1/4* **Living The Life (IRE)**[57] 8053 4-9-0 **78**.......................(b) JimCrowley 11 76
(Jamie Osborne) *led: grad crossed to inner rail: rdn and hdd 1f out: fdd ins fnl f* **16/1**

00-3 **8** *hd* **Bowstar**[12] 118 5-8-9 **73**.......................(p) RobertHavlin 9 70
(Michael Attwater) *chsd ldrs: drvn and unable qck over 1f out: wknd ins fnl f* **25/1**

14-4 **9** *nk* **The Great Gabrial**[18] 56 5-9-1 **79**.......................(v) AdamKirby 5 75
(Alan McCabe) *hld up in tch in midfield: rdn and unable qck over 1f out: btn 1f out: wknd ins fnl f* **10/1**[3]

650- **10** *nk* **Toga Tiger (IRE)**[156] 5580 7-9-0 **78**....................... RobertWinston 6 74
(Jeremy Gask) *s.i.s: bhd: stl plenty to do and pushed wd bnd wl over 1f out: kpt on but nvr trbld ldrs* **12/1**

300- **11** *nk* **Kickingthelilly**[115] 6875 5-9-2 **80**....................... ChrisCatlin 4 75
(Rae Guest) *dwlt: pushed along early: a towards rr: rdn 3f out: swtchd out rt bnd wl over 1f out: kpt on: nvr trbld ldrs* **14/1**

1m 22.4s (-2.40) **Going Correction** -0.15s/f (Stan) **11** Ran SP% **118.7**
Speed ratings (Par 105): **107,106,106,105,105 103,102,102,101,101 101**
CSF £75.81 CT £147.12 TOTE £7.00: £2.00, £2.30, £1.30; EX 91.30 Trifecta £263.70.
**Owner** The Oil Men Partnership **Bred** Glebe Stud & J F Dean **Trained** Patching, W Sussex

**FOCUS**
A fair contest run at a sound pace. The form is rated around the fourth and fifth.

## 288 LADBROKES MOBILE APPRENTICE H'CAP — 7f 1y(P)
**4:05** (4:05) (Class 6) (0-60,60) 4-Y-0+ **£2,385** (£704; £352) **Stalls** Low

Form RPR

6-02 **1** **Bertie Blu Boy**[14] 92 6-8-2 **46** oh1.......................(b) KevinLundie(5) 9 54
(Lisa Williamson) *mde all: sn clr and swtchd to inner 6f out: 8 l clr and rdn over 1f out: a holding on: rdn out* **7/1**

143- **2** *1 1/2* **Resonare**[92] 7454 5-9-2 **58**....................... JackGarritty(3) 5 62
(Stuart Williams) *stdd s but chsd clr ldr: 8 l down and rdn wl over 1f out: styd on ins fnl f: nvr getting to wnr* **11/4**[1]

146- **3** *hd* **Perfect Pastime**[22] 8456 6-9-0 **58**.......................(b) CamHardie(5) 4 62
(Jim Boyle) *prom in main gp: rdn and effrt on inner over 1f out: styd on u.p fnl f: nvr getting to wnr* **8/1**

00-5 **4** *hd* **Annes Rocket (IRE)**[14] 92 9-9-2 **58**.......................(p) GaryMahon(3) 2 61
(Jimmy Fox) *hld up towards rr: hdwy wl over 1f out: styd on u.p fnl f: nvr getting to wnr* **12/1**

640- **5** *1 1/4* **Cyflymder (IRE)**[160] 5427 8-9-4 **60**.......................(b[1]) CharlotteJenner(3) 6 60
(David C Griffiths) *hld up in last quartet: rdn and hdwy over 1f out: kpt on fnl f: nvr a threat to wnr* **4/1**[2]

-215 **6** *1* **Minimee**[5] 219 4-9-4 **60** 6ex.......................(v) DavidParkes(3) 7 57
(Phil McEntee) *prom in main gp: rdn and effrt over 1f out: plugged on but nvr a threat to wnr* **5/1**[3]

000- **7** *3/4* **Dear Maurice**[39] 8295 10-9-2 **60**.......................(tp) AlfieWarwick(5) 10 55
(Tobias B P Coles) *rdn along leaving stalls: sn in midfield but stuck wd: rdn and lost pl 2f out: styd on again fnl f: nvr a threat to wnr* **25/1**

00-2 **8** *1/2* **Penbryn (USA)**[9] 156 7-9-5 **58**....................... JordanVaughan 3 52
(Nick Littmoden) *hld up in rr: swtchd rt and effrt over 1f out: kpt on fnl f: nvr a threat to wnr* **6/1**

-500 **9** *1* **Kai**[1] 269 5-8-4 **46** oh1.......................(b) AaronJones(3) 1 37
(Alan McCabe) *rrd as stalls opened: a in rr: kpt on u.p fnl f: n.d* **50/1**

00-0 **10** *5* **Cuthbert (IRE)**[5] 211 7-8-0 **46** oh1.......................(e[1]) RhiainIngram(7) 8 24
(Michael Attwater) *midfield: rdn and dropped to rr 3f out: no ch fnl 2f* **50/1**

1m 24.77s (-0.03) **Going Correction** -0.15s/f (Stan) **10** Ran SP% **116.7**
Speed ratings (Par 101): **94,92,92,91,90 89,88,87,86,80**
CSF £26.30 CT £163.18 TOTE £11.20: £3.30, £1.20, £3.00; EX 35.80 Trifecta £230.80.
**Owner** B & B Hygiene Limited **Bred** H Bourchier **Trained** Saighton, Cheshire

**FOCUS**
A modest handicap, confined to apprentice riders, run at a solid gallop. The form is best rated around the second.

T/Plt: £21.40. Pool: £73,924.56 - 2512.07 winning units. T/Qpdt: £11.00. Pool: £4778.05 - 320.45 winning units. SP

# [274]KEMPTON (A.W) (R-H)
### Thursday, January 23

**OFFICIAL GOING: Standard**
Wind: across, light to medium Weather: dry

## 289 BOOK TICKETS FOR JUMPING 22.02.14 H'CAP — 1m (P)
**4:30** (4:30) (Class 6) (0-60,60) 4-Y-0+ **£1,940** (£577; £288; £144) **Stalls** Low

Form RPR

502- **1** **Icy Blue**[49] 8162 6-9-3 **60**.......................(p) GeorgeChaloner(3) 4 68
(Richard Whitaker) *chsd ldrs: rdn and effrt between horses to ld over 1f out: battled on gamely u.p ins fnl f: all out* **7/1**[3]

162- **2** *3/4* **Multitask**[24] 8443 4-9-6 **60**....................... JimCrowley 2 66
(Michael Madgwick) *hld up in midfield: rdn and effrt 2f out: drvn and chal ins fnl f: no ex and styd on same pce fnl 100yds* **4/1**[1]

366- **3** *hd* **Divine Rule (IRE)**[197] 4169 6-8-11 **58**....................... CharlotteJenner(7) 12 64
(Laura Mongan) *hld up in last pair: swtchd rt over 2f out: gd hdwy on inner over 1f out: chsd ldrs ins fnl f: kpt on wl towards fin* **14/1**

03-4 **4** *shd* **Safwaan**[15] 83 7-9-0 **57**....................... RobertTart(3) 6 63
(Michael Squance) *in tch in midfield: rdn and effrt wl over 1f out: pressed ldng pair ins fnl f: kpt on* **8/1**

01-6 **5** *hd* **Spirit Of Gondree (IRE)**[10] 155 6-9-6 **60**.......................(b) AdamKirby 3 66+
(Milton Bradley) *hld up in last pair: hmpd over 2f out: stl plenty to do and drvn over 1f out: str run and swtchd rt ins fnl f: gng on strly at fin: nt rch ldrs* **6/1**[2]

04-1 **6** *nk* **Fearless Lad (IRE)**[15] 90 4-9-6 **60**.......................(t) MartinLane 11 64+
(John Best) *hld up in last quartet: rdn and effrt on outer over 2f out: no real imp tl styd on wl u.p ins fnl f: nt rch ldrs* **12/1**

340- **7** *1/2* **Great Conquest (USA)**[26] 8427 4-9-4 **58**....................... FergusSweeney 10 61
(Jamie Osborne) *in tch in midfield: rdn and effrt 2f out: no imp tl kpt on ins fnl f: nvr gng pce to threaten ldrs* **11/1**

13-2 **8** *2* **Archelao (IRE)**[15] 88 6-8-12 **59**....................... LouisSteward(7) 13 58
(Lee Carter) *wl in tch in midfield: rdn and effrt to chse ldrs 2f out: no ex jst ins fnl f: wknd towards fin* **7/1**[3]

32-0 **9** *1 1/4* **One Last Dream**[15] 92 5-9-5 **59**.......................(b) DavidProbert 9 55
(Ron Hodges) *led: rdn ent fnl 2f: hdd over 1f out: wknd ins fnl f* **14/1**

24-0 **10** *nse* **Taxiformissbyron**[17] 67 4-8-13 **58**.......................(b[1]) JacobButterfield(5) 7 54
(Michael Herrington) *chsd ldr: rdn and ev ch 2f out: no ex ent fnl f: wknd fnl 150yds* **8/1**

00-0 **11** *1* **Tammuz (IRE)**[15] 84 4-9-2 **56**....................... WilliamCarson 1 49
(Tony Carroll) *in tch in midfield: rdn and no hdwy ent fnl 2f: wknd ent fnl f* **20/1**

54/0 **12** *12* **Devote Myself (IRE)**[13] 118 5-9-3 **60**....................... MarkCoumbe(3) 5 26
(Tony Carroll) *chsd ldrs: rdn and struggling over 2f out: wknd qckly over 1f out: bhd fnl f* **50/1**

500- **13** *3 1/2* **Studfarmer**[77] 7783 4-9-1 **60**....................... EoinWalsh(5) 8 18
(John Panvert) *hld up in last quartet: rdn and no hdwy over 2f out: wknd 2f out: sn bhd* **66/1**

1m 38.76s (-1.04) **Going Correction** +0.025s/f (Slow) **13** Ran SP% **119.1**
Speed ratings (Par 101): **106,105,105,104,104 104,103,101,100,100 99,87,84**
CSF £34.43 CT £401.83 TOTE £6.30: £2.30, £2.20, £4.40; EX 37.10 Trifecta £1709.60.
**Owner** Country Lane Partnership **Bred** Cheveley Park Stud Ltd **Trained** Scarcroft, W Yorks
■ Stewards' Enquiry : Charlotte Jenner one-day ban: careless riding (Feb 6)

**FOCUS**
This was competitive enough for the class and there was no hanging about early on. Ordinary form.

## 290 TRY OUR HOSPITALITY H'CAP — 7f (P)
**5:00** (5:01) (Class 7) (0-50,51) 4-Y-0+ **£1,617** (£481; £240; £120) **Stalls** Low

Form RPR

0-54 **1** **Prohibition (IRE)**[7] 201 8-9-4 **50**....................... RossAtkinson(3) 11 60
(Mandy Rowland) *s.i.s and rdn along early: racd in last trio: rdn and gd hdwy over 1f out: led wl ins fnl f: r.o strly and gng away at fin* **16/1**

50-0 **2** *2* **Ryedale Lass**[8] 179 6-9-4 **47**.......................(b) RichardKingscote 2 52
(Geoffrey Deacon) *led for 1f: chsd ldr after tl rdn to ld over 1f out: drvn 1f out: hdd wl ins fnl f: sn outpcd by wnr but hung on for 2nd* **14/1**

0-04 **3** *nk* **Rightcar**[10] 164 7-8-13 **45**....................... SladeO'Hara(3) 10 49
(Peter Grayson) *s.i.s: bhd: rdn and hdwy over 1f out: running on wl and swtchd rt ins fnl f: gng on wl at fin: no threat to wnr* **33/1**

4-60 **4** *nk* **Vhujon (IRE)**[4] 251 9-9-2 **45**....................... FergusSweeney 6 48
(Peter Grayson) *racd in last trio: rdn and hdwy on inner 2f out: chsd ldrs and swtchd lft jst ins fnl f: styd on wl but no threat to wnr* **20/1**

6-66 **5** *nk* **Rutterkin (USA)**[1] 274 6-8-10 **46**....................... VictorSantos(7) 8 49
(James Moffatt) *hld up in midfield: rdn and hdwy over 1f out: styng on whn swtchd rt and rdr unbalanced ins fnl f: kpt on wl towards fin: nvr trbld ldrs* **20/1**

06-3 **6** *1* **Salford Prince (IRE)**[4] 251 6-9-2 **45**.......................(b) DavidProbert 13 45
(David Elsworth) *in tch in midfield: rdn and unable qck 2f out: kpt on again u.p ins fnl f* **13/2**[3]

000- **7** *hd* **Pipers Piping (IRE)**[352] 523 8-9-7 **50**....................... ChrisCatlin 4 50
(Mandy Rowland) *wl in tch in midfield: swtchd lft and effrt u.p to chse ldrs over 1f out: drvn and unable qck 1f out: plugged on same pce fnl f* **6/4**[1]

054- **8** *3/4* **Lichen Angel**[93] 7443 4-9-3 **49**....................... GeorgeChaloner(3) 7 47
(Richard Whitaker) *racd in midfield: rdn and effrt 2f out: unable qck and plugged on same pce fnl f* **33/1**

0-60 **9** *1* **Custom House (IRE)**[8] 184 6-9-2 **45**.......................(v[1]) JimmyQuinn 3 40
(John E Long) *chsd ldrs: unable qck u.p wl over 1f out: wknd ins fnl f* **25/1**

046/ **10** *2 1/4* **Cavalry Guard (USA)**[700] 662 10-8-13 **45**.......................(b) RobertTart(3) 12 34
(Tim McCarthy) *chsd ldrs tl led after 1f: rdn and hdd over 1f out: wknd ins fnl f* **66/1**

00-3 **11** *hd* **Bualteoir (FR)**[8] 184 8-9-4 **50**....................... MatthewCosham(3) 5 39
(Nikki Evans) *in tch in midfield: rdn and no hdwy 2f out: wknd ent fnl f* **10/1**

00-2 **12** *hd* **Pastoral Dancer**[15] 81 5-9-4 **47**....................... JimCrowley 14 35
(Richard Rowe) *hld up in tch towards rr: rdn and no hdwy 2f out: wknd ent fnl f* **16/1**

4-02 **13** *3* **Tijuca (IRE)**[8] [184] 5-9-7 **50** ........ AdamKirby 9 30
(Ed de Giles) *chsd ldrs: rdn: unable qck and edgd lft 2f out: sn btn: fdd fnl f* **5/2**[2]

1m 26.75s (0.75) **Going Correction** +0.025s/f (Slow) **13** Ran SP% **130.2**
Speed ratings (Par 97): **96,93,93,93,92 91,91,90,89,86 86,86,82**
CSF £219.98 CT £7396.17 TOTE £26.80: £6.00, £5.40, £13.20; EX 228.30 Trifecta £2903.70 Part won..
**Owner** Miss M E Rowland **Bred** Kevin Buckley **Trained** Lower Blidworth, Notts

**FOCUS**
The pace was good and most of the principals came from the rear. Limited form, but sound for the grade.

## 291 DOWNLOAD THE BETVICTOR APP NOW MEDIAN AUCTION MAIDEN STKS 7f (P)
**5:30** (5:32) (Class 6) 3-5-Y-0 **£1,940** (£577; £288; £144) **Stalls** Low

Form RPR
0- **1** **Pactolus (IRE)**[35] [8342] 3-8-10 0 ........ AdamBeschizza 7 75+
(Stuart Williams) *chsd ldr and travelled strly: led on bit 2f out: rdn and qcknd clr ent fnl f: r.o wl: readily* **4/1**[2]

**2** *2 ¾* **Sleipnir** 3-8-10 0 ........ JimCrowley 2 68
(Philip Hide) *in tch in midfield: rdn and effrt 2f out: battling for 2nd ent fnl f: chsd clr wnr ins fnl f: kpt on but no imp* **4/1**[2]

053- **3** *hd* **What A Dandy (IRE)**[23] [8451] 3-8-10 66 ........ WilliamCarson 11 67
(Jim Boyle) *chsd ldrs: effrt u.p 2f out: battling for 2nd but nt pce of wnr jst over 1f out: kpt on but no imp fnl f* **7/4**[1]

35- **4** *nk* **Tax Reform (IRE)**[26] [8427] 4-9-7 68 ........(p) LouisSteward[(7)] 4 71
(Mark Hoad) *led tl 2f out: rdn and unable qck w wnr over 1f out: kpt on same pce and lost 2 pls ins fnl f* **5/1**[3]

3 **5** *5* **Avondream**[10] [159] 5-10-0 0 ........(t) RichardKingscote 1 58
(Milton Bradley) *chsd ldrs: rdn and outpcd wl over 1f out: wknd fnl f* **8/1**

5 **6** *nk* **On And On (IRE)**[21] [19] 4-9-6 0 ........ GeorgeChaloner[(3)] 9 52
(Richard Fahey) *hld up in tch in last trio: rdn and effrt jst over 2f out: sn outpcd and 6th over 1f out: plugged on* **25/1**

3-6 **7** *6* **Deano's Devil (IRE)**[12] [142] 3-8-5 0 ........ BarryMcHugh 5 31
(Richard Fahey) *in tch in midfield: rdn and effrt over 2f out: outpcd and btn 2f out: sn wknd* **20/1**

**8** *hd* **Premier Jack's** 3-8-7 0 ........ MatthewCosham[(3)] 6 35
(Nikki Evans) *awkward leaving stalls and s.i.s: reminder sn after s: rn green in rr: rdn and hung rt over 2f out: sn wknd* **66/1**

**9** *9* **Jazz Bay** 3-8-7 0 ........ MichaelJMMurphy[(3)] 3 11
(John Bridger) *s.i.s: a in last pair: rdn and btn over 2f out: wknd 2f out* **66/1**

1m 26.93s (0.93) **Going Correction** +0.025s/f (Slow)
**WFA** 3 from 4yo+ 18lb **9** Ran SP% **115.7**
Speed ratings (Par 101): **95,91,91,91,85 85,78,78,67**
CSF £19.73 TOTE £5.30: £1.60, £1.60, £1.10; EX 24.10 Trifecta £68.30.
**Owner** T W Morley & Mrs J Morley **Bred** Tom McDonald **Trained** Newmarket, Suffolk

**FOCUS**
A steadily run maiden but the form makes sense at face value.

## 292 BACK OF THE NET AT BETVICTOR.COM H'CAP 2m (P)
**6:00** (6:00) (Class 5) (0-70,70) 4-Y-0+ **£2,749** (£818; £408; £204) **Stalls** Low

Form RPR
5/1- **1** **Coup De Grace (IRE)**[33] [12] 5-9-7 63 ........ ShaneKelly 1 70+
(Pat Phelan) *hld up in tch in midfield: rdn 3f out: drvn and chal jst over 1f out: led ins fnl f: styd on wl: rdn out* **11/4**[1]

00-5 **2** *1 ¾* **King Olav (UAE)**[15] [79] 9-9-10 69 ........ MarkCoumbe[(3)] 5 74
(Tony Carroll) *t.k.h: chsd ldrs: rdn over 2f out: hdwy u.p to chse ldrs ins fnl f: kpt on: wnt 2nd last stride* **9/2**[2]

602- **3** *shd* **Arty Campbell (IRE)**[26] [7279] 4-9-7 70 ........ MartinLane 2 75
(Bernard Llewellyn) *t.k.h: chsd ldrs tl led 12f out: drvn ent fnl 2f: kpt on gamely tl hdd and one pce ins fnl f: lost 2nd last stride* **11/1**

405- **4** *¾* **Daring Indian**[247] [2552] 6-9-13 69 ........ RichardKingscote 7 73
(Tom Dascombe) *t.k.h early: hld up in tch in last trio: rdn and effrt ent fnl 2f: styd on to chse ldrs ins fnl f: one pce fnl 100yds* **5/1**[3]

50-3 **5** *1* **Phoenix Flight (IRE)**[16] [72] 9-10-0 70 ........ FergusSweeney 3 73
(James Evans) *hld up in last trio: clsd and swtchd rt ent fnl 2f: drvn to chse ldrs over 1f out: styd on same pce ins fnl f* **20/1**

25-4 **6** *nse* **Luckster**[14] [104] 4-8-0 56 ........(v[1]) JoeDoyle[(7)] 9 59
(David Evans) *chsd ldr tl 3f out: stl ev ch and rdn over 2f out: no ex and btn ent fnl f: plugged on same pce after* **8/1**

366- **7** *1 ¾* **Taste The Wine (IRE)**[175] [4915] 8-8-13 62 ........ LouisSteward[(7)] 6 63
(Bernard Llewellyn) *hld up in tch in last trio: rdn wl over 2f out: no imp tl kpt on steadily ins fnl f: nvr gng pce to trble ldrs* **33/1**

63-6 **8** *4* **Where's Susie**[6] [214] 9-9-9 65 ........ AdamKirby 8 61
(Michael Madgwick) *in tch in midfield: hdwy to chse ldrs 7f out: drvn to chal 3f out: no ex and btn jst over 1f out: wknd ins fnl f* **8/1**

003- **9** *18* **Valid Reason**[34] [7210] 7-9-11 67 ........ JimCrowley 4 41
(Dean Ivory) *led for 4f: chsd ldrs: drvn 5f out: lost pl and bhd over 3f out: lost tch over 2f out* **9/2**[2]

3m 32.98s (2.88) **Going Correction** +0.025s/f (Slow)
**WFA** 4 from 5yo+ 7lb **9** Ran SP% **118.0**
Speed ratings (Par 103): **93,92,92,91,91 91,90,88,79**
CSF £15.45 CT £118.67 TOTE £2.90: £1.10, £2.50, £3.90; EX 24.20 Trifecta £326.20.
**Owner** Hugh J F Lang **Bred** Oliver Donlon **Trained** Epsom, Surrey

**FOCUS**
A competitive staying handicap in which the field were tightly bunched a furlong out due to the ordinary fractions.

## 293 BETVICTOR NON-RUNNER FREE BET CHELTENHAM 2014 H'CAP 1m 4f (P)
**6:30** (6:32) (Class 5) (0-75,75) 4-Y-0+ **£2,587** (£770; £384; £192) **Stalls** Centre

Form RPR
265- **1** **Java Rose**[37] [6405] 5-9-6 71 ........ AdamKirby 1 83
(Charlie Longsdon) *chsd ldrs: rdn to ld 2f out: styd on wl u.p to assert wl ins fnl f: rdn out* **7/1**[3]

30-4 **2** *¾* **Poitin**[15] [79] 4-9-0 69 ........ RichardKingscote 10 80
(Harry Dunlop) *chsd ldrs: effrt u.p to chal wl over 1f out: ev ch after: no ex u.p and btn fnl 75yds* **5/1**[2]

60-0 **3** *6* **Song Light**[15] [79] 4-9-1 70 ........ DavidProbert 5 71
(David Elsworth) *stdd s: hld up in rr: nt clr run wl over 2f out: rdn 2f out: drvn and styd on fr over 1f out: wnt 3rd ins fnl f: no threat to ldng pair* **25/1**

30-3 **4** *1 ¾* **Leitrim Pass (USA)**[4] [250] 4-9-5 74 ........(p) ShaneKelly 9 73
(William Haggas) *led: rdn and hdd 2f out: drvn and unable qck over 1f out: wknd fnl f* **11/8**[1]

03-3 **5** *1 ¾* **Living Leader**[13] [120] 5-9-0 68 ........(b) MichaelJMMurphy[(3)] 3 64
(Nick Littmoden) *in tch in midfield: rdn and effrt ent fnl 2f: drvn and no ex over 1f out: wknd fnl f* **7/1**[3]

000/ **6** *¾* **Acer Diamonds (IRE)**[549] [4411] 5-8-12 63 ........ JimCrowley 2 58
(Luke Dace) *hld up in tch towards rr: rdn and hdwy 2f out: drvn and no imp over 1f out: wknd fnl f* **16/1**

000- **7** *½* **Shalambar (IRE)**[36] [8323] 8-8-9 63 ........ MarkCoumbe[(3)] 7 57
(Tony Carroll) *dwlt and bustled along early: hdwy to chse ldrs after 2f: rdn 4f out: drvn and outpcd ent fnl 2f: wknd over 1f out* **20/1**

236- **8** *1* **Langham Lily (USA)**[68] [4172] 5-8-10 61 ........ RobertHavlin 4 53
(Sarah Humphrey) *in tch in midfield: rdn wl over 3f out: struggling u.p ent fnl 2f: sn outpcd and btn over 1f out* **33/1**

45-3 **9** *1 ¼* **All The Winds (GER)**[13] [125] 9-9-3 75 ........(t) CamHardie[(7)] 6 65
(Shaun Lycett) *stdd s: hld up in rr: rdn and effrt on outer wl over 2f out: no hdwy and outpcd 2f out: n.d after* **9/1**

5- **10** *7* **Innoko (FR)**[46] [4349] 4-9-6 75 ........(t) WilliamCarson 11 54
(Tony Carroll) *in tch in last quartet: dropped to rr 3f out: losing tch and rdn 2f out: sn bhd* **50/1**

05-0 **11** *3 ¼* **Shirataki (IRE)**[12] [146] 6-9-0 65 ........ ChrisCatlin 8 39
(Peter Hiatt) *t.k.h: chsd ldr tl wl over 2f out: sn dropped out: bhd 1f out* **16/1**

2m 33.9s (-0.60) **Going Correction** +0.025s/f (Slow)
**WFA** 4 from 5yo+ 4lb **11** Ran SP% **119.0**
Speed ratings (Par 103): **103,102,98,97,96 95,95,94,93,89 87**
CSF £40.80 CT £840.25 TOTE £8.10: £2.10, £2.00, £8.40; EX 27.60 Trifecta £418.20.
**Owner** Mildmay Racing & Mark E Smith **Bred** Mrs David Low **Trained** Over Norton, Oxon

**FOCUS**
This modest handicap was run at a fair pace, but still it paid to race handily and the first pair came nicely clear late on.

## 294 CHELTENHAM 2014 NRFB AT BETVICTOR.COM H'CAP 6f (P)
**7:00** (7:01) (Class 4) (0-85,85) 4-Y-0+ **£5,175** (£1,540; £769; £384) **Stalls** Low

Form RPR
211- **1** **Discussiontofollow (IRE)**[45] [8224] 4-8-12 76 ........ ShaneKelly 6 92+
(Mike Murphy) *t.k.h: hld up off the pce in midfield: clsd and travelling strly over 2f out: smooth hdwy to cruise upsides ldr ins fnl f: led wl ins fnl f: rdr barely moved: impressive* **7/2**[2]

1/1- **2** *nk* **Absolutely So (IRE)**[26] [8430] 4-9-5 83 ........ DavidProbert 8 94+
(Andrew Balding) *chsd ldrs: clsd to chse ldr and travelled strly 1/2-way: rdn to ld over 1f out: drvn and wnt clr w cruising wnr ins fnl f: hdd and one pce wl ins fnl f* **11/8**[1]

002- **3** *1 ½* **Palace Moon**[26] [8430] 9-9-4 82 ........(t) JimCrowley 11 88
(William Knight) *stdd s: hld up in rr: clsd on inner over 2f out: drvn and effrt over 1f out: r.o to go 3rd ins fnl f: no imp on ldrs fnl 75yds* **8/1**

3-35 **4** *2* **Fat Gary**[13] [122] 4-9-6 84 ........(p) RichardKingscote 1 84
(Tom Dascombe) *chsd ldr tl 1/2-way: sn rdn but styd chsng ldrs: drvn over 1f out: outpcd and btn jst ins fnl f: wknd fnl 100yds* **7/1**

00-2 **5** *¾* **Angel's Pursuit (IRE)**[20] [36] 7-9-7 85 ........ AdamKirby 3 82
(Robert Cowell) *racd in midfield: clsd and wl in tch over 2f out: drvn and effrt over 1f out: no ex fnl 150yds: wknd fnl 100yds* **11/2**[3]

005- **6** *1 ¼* **Top Cop**[133] [6337] 5-8-8 77 ........ DCByrne[(5)] 2 70
(Ronald Harris) *led: rdn ent fnl 2f: drvn and hdd over 1f out: wknd ins fnl f* **33/1**

02-6 **7** *hd* **Jay Bee Blue**[20] [38] 5-9-1 79 ........(bt) JohnFahy 5 72
(Sean Curran) *dwlt and swtchd rt s: racd off the pce in midfield: clsd over 2f out: drvn and effrt on inner over 1f out: no ex 1f out: wl hld whn forced to switch rt ins fnl f* **33/1**

055- **8** *2 ½* **Captain Kendall (IRE)**[35] [8344] 5-8-8 72 ........ ChrisCatlin 4 57
(Harry Chisman) *racd off the pce in midfield: clsd and rdn 1/2-way: lost pl and outpcd u.p 2f out: n.d after* **33/1**

400- **9** *3 ¾* **Secret Beau**[23] [8455] 4-8-9 78 ........(b[1]) EoinWalsh[(5)] 9 51
(David Evans) *chsd ldrs: effrt u.p and edgd lft ent fnl 2f: wknd over 1f out* **16/1**

**10** *2 ¼* **Bainne (IRE)**[169] [5160] 4-9-6 84 ........ SeanLevey 7 49
(Jeremy Gask) *hld up off the pce in rr: clsd 1/2-way: pushed along and effrt 2f out: sn btn and wknd over 1f out* **33/1**

1m 11.42s (-1.68) **Going Correction** +0.025s/f (Slow) **10** Ran SP% **121.0**
Speed ratings (Par 105): **112,111,109,106,105 104,104,100,95,92**
CSF £8.79 CT £32.89 TOTE £4.50: £1.70, £1.60, £3.00; EX 11.50 Trifecta £71.80.
**Owner** David Spratt **Bred** Jerry O'Sullivan **Trained** Westoning, Beds

**FOCUS**
A fair sprint. It was run at a solid pace and the form is strong. The winner scored with something in hand.

## 295 BETVICTOR.COM NON-RUNNER FREE BET CHELTENHAM 2014 H'CAP (DIV I) 6f (P)
**7:30** (7:30) (Class 6) (0-65,65) 4-Y-0+ **£1,940** (£577; £288; £144) **Stalls** Low

Form RPR
06-3 **1** **Divine Call**[15] [83] 7-9-3 61 ........ RichardKingscote 12 70
(Milton Bradley) *stdd and swtchd sharply rt after s: hld up in rr: gd hdwy over 1f out: chal 1f out: led ins fnl f: pushed out hands and heels and r.o wl* **6/1**[3]

600- **2** *½* **West Leake (IRE)**[23] [8456] 8-8-13 57 ........(p) JimmyQuinn 2 64
(Paul Burgoyne) *hld up in midfield: effrt u.p to chal over 1f out: ev ch fnl f: kpt on same pce fnl 75yds* **15/2**

3-14 **3** *nk* **Insolenceofoffice (IRE)**[11] [147] 6-8-11 60 ........(p) JoshBaudains[(5)] 8 66
(Richard Ford) *chsd ldrs: rdn and chal over 1f out: led 1f out: hdd ins fnl f: styd on same pce towards fin* **9/2**[2]

200- **4** *nk* **Ghost Train (IRE)**[36] [8330] 5-8-10 57 ........(p) RobertTart[(3)] 6 62
(Tim McCarthy) *hld up towards rr: rdn and effrt 2f out: hdwy jst over 1f out: chsd ldrs ins fnl f: kpt on wl but nvr quite rching ldrs* **20/1**

00-2 **5** *1 ¼* **Indian Affair**[15] [83] 4-9-7 65 ........ AdamKirby 4 66
(Milton Bradley) *broke fast: led: rdn and hdd 2f out: drvn and led again over 1f out: hdd 1f out: wknd fnl 100yds* **3/1**[1]

22-3 **6** *1* **Volito**[8] [192] 8-8-12 56 ........ MartinLane 5 54
(Anabel K Murphy) *dwlt: sn rcvrd and in tch in midfield: hmpd over 4f out: rdn and effrt over 1f out: styd on same pce ins fnl f* **14/1**

260- **7** *¾* **Last Minute Lisa (IRE)**[52] [8134] 4-8-13 64 ........ LouisSteward[(7)] 9 59
(Sylvester Kirk) *chsd ldr: rdn to ld but racing awkwardly 2f out: hdd over 1f out: wknd ins fnl f* **20/1**

03-5 **8** *nk* **Darnathean**[17] [65] 5-8-11 62 ........(b) StaceyKidd[(7)] 7 57
(Paul D'Arcy) *taken down early: stuck wd: in tch in midfield: hdwy on outer to chse ldrs 3f out: rdn and no ex over 1f out: wknd ins fnl f* **10/1**

100- **9** *2 ¾* **My Gigi**[36] [8330] 4-9-2 60 ........(be) WilliamCarson 1 46
(Gary Moore) *hld up in tch in last trio: rdn and sme hdwy on inner 2f out: no imp over 1f out: wknd fnl f* **12/1**

00-0 **10** 2 3/4 **Midnight Dream (FR)**[14] 93 4-9-7 **65**......................(tp) ShaneKelly 11 42
(Kristin Stubbs) *t.k.h: in tch in midfield: rdn and btn wl over 1f out: wknd ent fnl f* **25/1**

03-3 **11** 1 1/2 **Spray Tan**[7] 196 4-9-5 **63**........................................ DavidProbert 3 35
(Tony Carroll) *t.k.h: hld up in midfield: swtchd lft over 4f out: rdn and no hdwy 2f out: wknd over 1f out* **8/1**

03-0 **12** 13 **Tingle Tangle (USA)**[15] 83 4-8-10 **57**.................. MarkCoumbe(3) 10
(Tony Carroll) *in tch in midfield: lost pl and dropped to rr over 2f out: bhd over 1f out* **50/1**

1m 13.05s (-0.05) **Going Correction** +0.025s/f (Slow) **12** Ran SP% **119.1**
Speed ratings (Par 101): **101,100,99,99,97 96,95,95,91,87 85,68**
CSF £48.24 CT £227.84 TOTE £4.90: £1.80, £3.20, £2.10; EX 58.40 Trifecta £423.10.
**Owner** E A Hayward **Bred** Cheveley Park Stud Ltd **Trained** Sedbury, Gloucs

**FOCUS**
There was a strong pace on in this moderate handicap. Straightforward form.

## 296 BETVICTOR.COM NON-RUNNER FREE BET CHELTENHAM 2014 H'CAP (DIV II) 6f (P)
**8:00** (8:00) (Class 6) (0-65,65) 4-Y-0+ **£1,940** (£577; £288; £144) **Stalls** Low

Form RPR

524- **1** **Street Power (USA)**[23] 8456 9-9-7 **65**...................... SeanLevey 5 73
(Jeremy Gask) *hld up in midfield: rdn and hdwy over 1f out: chal jst ins fnl f: led fnl 100yds: r.o wl and hld on wl towards fin* **7/4**[1]

465- **2** nk **Littlecote Lady**[27] 8413 5-8-1 **52**...................... CharlotteJenner(7) 2 59
(Mark Usher) *hld up in last trio: rdn and hdwy over 1f out: styd on wl and ev ch wl ins fnl f: wnt 2nd towards fin* **12/1**

661- **3** nk **Assertive Agent**[57] 8070 4-8-13 **57**......................... DavidProbert 11 63
(Tony Carroll) *t.k.h: hld up in tch in midfield: nt clr run 2f out: swtchd lft and effrt over 1f out: kpt on wl u.p ins fnl f: snatched 3rd last stride* **9/1**

3-22 **4** shd **Parisian Pyramid (IRE)**[11] 147 8-9-6 **64**.................(p) BarryMcHugh 6 70
(Richard Fahey) *wnt lft s: sn led: rdn over 1f out: hdd fnl 100yds: kpt on but no ex and lost 2 pls last strides* **7/2**[2]

12-0 **5** 1 **Secret Millionaire (IRE)**[15] 87 7-9-1 **62**................ MarkCoumbe(3) 8 65
(Tony Carroll) *pushed lft and bmpd s: t.k.h: hld up in tch in rr: clsd and pushed along over 1f out: rdn and chsd ldrs ins fnl f: gap clsng in front and one pce whn nudged along fnl 75yds* **20/1**

00-0 **6** 1 1/4 **Mey Blossom**[17] 69 9-8-12 **59**........................(p) GeorgeChaloner(3) 10 58
(Richard Whitaker) *taken down early: chsd ldrs: rdn over 2f out: drvn and unable qck ent fnl f: one pce fnl 150yds* **50/1**

05-0 **7** shd **Valdaw**[19] 52 6-9-5 **63**............................................... ShaneKelly 9 61
(Mike Murphy) *dwlt and short of room s: hld up in last trio: hdwy u.p ent fnl f: kpt on but nvr gng pce to chal* **5/1**[3]

500- **8** 1 1/2 **Loyal Royal (IRE)**[198] 4148 11-8-12 **56**...............(bt) RichardKingscote 1 49
(Milton Bradley) *chsd ldrs: drvn and effrt on inner 2f out: hrd drvn and unable qck over 1f out: wknd ins fnl f: eased towards fin* **33/1**

00-0 **9** 6 **Katy Spirit (IRE)**[15] 83 4-9-2 **60**............................. FergusSweeney 3 34
(Michael Blanshard) *chsd ldr tl 2f out: sn struggling and wknd over 1f out* **33/1**

000- **10** 1 3/4 **Belinsky (IRE)**[69] 7896 7-8-13 **57**.................................. JimCrowley 12 26
(Dean Ivory) *in tch in midfield: lost pl 2f out: sn rdn and btn: bhd whn edgd rt and eased wl ins fnl f* **5/1**[3]

1m 13.15s (0.05) **Going Correction** +0.025s/f (Slow) **10** Ran SP% **122.2**
Speed ratings (Par 101): **100,99,99,99,97 96,95,93,85,83**
CSF £25.93 CT £164.03 TOTE £3.40: £1.10, £2.90, £2.00; EX 28.60 Trifecta £217.50.
**Owner** Horses First Racing & Ownaracehorse **Bred** John Hawkins **Trained** Sutton Veny, Wilts
■ Stewards' Enquiry : Sean Levey three-day ban: used whip without giving gelding time to respond (Feb 6-8)

**FOCUS**
The second division of the moderate sprint handicap. Similar form.
T/Jkpt: Not won. T/Plt: £324.20. Pool: £96,298.26 - 216.83 winning units. T/Qpdt: £6.30. Pool: £12,961.33 - 1518.10 winning units. SP

# 267 SOUTHWELL (L-H)
## Thursday, January 23

**OFFICIAL GOING: Standard**
Wind: Strong behind Weather: Fine & dry

## 297 BOOKMAKERS.CO.UK (S) STKS 6f (F)
**1:10** (1:10) (Class 6) 4-Y-0+ **£2,264** (£673; £336; £168) **Stalls** Low

Form RPR

06-4 **1** **Abi Scarlet (IRE)**[21] 20 5-8-2 70............................ CharlieBennett(7) 6 75
(Hughie Morrison) *trckd ldr: led over 2f out: rdn clr over 1f out: readily* **11/4**[2]

00-1 **2** 5 **Prince Of Passion (CAN)**[18] 59 6-9-6 63...................(v) TomEaves 4 70
(Derek Shaw) *trckd ldng pair: hdwy over 2f out: sn rdn: chsd wnr over 1f out: sn no imp* **12/1**

212- **3** 1 1/2 **Spitfire**[44] 8230 9-9-6 70................................................(t) JoeFanning 5 65
(J R Jenkins) *in tch: swtchd rt and effrt 2f out: sn rdn and one pce* **6/4**[1]

4-55 **4** 1 1/2 **Greenhead High**[2] 272 6-9-0 70................................. AdrianNicholls 1 54
(David Nicholls) *led: rdn along and hdd over 2f out: grad wknd* **6/1**[3]

26-6 **5** 3/4 **Monnoyer**[21] 9 5-8-7 62...........................................(b) MatthewHopkins(7) 3 52
(Scott Dixon) *in tch: rdn along wl over 2f out: n.d* **8/1**

004- **6** 9 **Tarrsille (IRE)**[138] 6209 8-9-0 72...........................................(v[1]) GrahamLee 2 23
(Paul Midgley) *sn outpcd and a in rr* **7/1**

1m 14.45s (-2.05) **Going Correction** -0.15s/f (Stan) **6** Ran SP% **112.3**
Speed ratings (Par 101): **107,100,98,96,95 83**
CSF £32.59 TOTE £3.70: £3.40, £5.00; EX 36.10 Trifecta £105.30.No bid for winner
**Owner** H Morrison **Bred** Henry O'Callaghan **Trained** East Ilsley, Berks

**FOCUS**
A fair effort from the winner, who scored easily in the pick of the round course times. The runner-up sets the standard.

## 298 BEST ODDS AT BOOKMAKERS.CO.UK MAIDEN STKS 5f (F)
**1:40** (1:40) (Class 5) 3-Y-0+ **£3,067** (£905; £453) **Stalls** High

Form RPR

0/0- **1** **Ysper (FR)**[53] 4-9-7 57.............................................. DanielTudhope 1 69+
(David O'Meara) *trckd ldrs: smooth hdwy on outer and cl up 2f out: shkn up to ld over 1f out: sn pushed clr: readily* **4/1**[2]

0-2 **2** 2 1/4 **Precariously Good**[14] 94 3-8-6 0............................... JoeFanning 7 49
(David Barron) *cl up: effrt 2f out and ev ch: rdn over 1f out and sn one pce* **4/5**[1]

00-4 **3** 3/4 **Jiminy**[3] 258 4-9-5 49...........................................(p) MatthewHopkins(7) 5 57
(Scott Dixon) *led: rdn along 2f out: hdd and drvn appr fnl f: one pce* **8/1**[3]

434- **4** 2 **The Doyle Machine (IRE)**[27] 8414 3-8-11 60.......(b[1]) AdamBeschizza 8 44
(Noel Quinlan) *in tch: hdwy to chse ldrs 2f out: sn rdn and no imp* **10/1**

6- **5** 1 3/4 **River Dreamer (IRE)**[48] 8188 3-8-6 0................................. LiamJones 2 33
(Robert Stephens) *racd wd: rdn along and outpcd in rr bef 1/2-way: sme late hdwy* **33/1**

250- **6** 2 3/4 **Prisca**[133] 6320 3-8-6 68........................................... WilliamCarson 6 23
(Jamie Osborne) *a towards rr* **8/1**[3]

4 **7** 2 3/4 **Chatalong (IRE)**[14] 94 3-8-6 0.................................. JamesSullivan 9 13
(Richard Fahey) *dwlt and towards rr: rdn along 1/2-way: sn outpcd* **14/1**

6-00 **8** 2 **Mrs Medley**[14] 94 8-9-2 20..........................................(v[1]) AnnStokell(5) 3 12
(Ann Stokell) *chsd ldrs: rdn along bef 1/2-way: sn lost pl and bhd* **250/1**

58.95s (-0.75) **Going Correction** -0.15s/f (Stan)
**WFA** 3 from 4yo+ 15lb **8** Ran SP% **116.9**
Speed ratings (Par 103): **100,96,95,92,89 84,80,77**
CSF £7.73 TOTE £5.00: £1.40, £1.20, £1.60; EX 9.20 Trifecta £61.60.
**Owner** Middleham Park Racing XL **Bred** Edy S R L **Trained** Nawton, N Yorks

**FOCUS**
A weak maiden with the favourite disappointing, but the winner did it readily. The form is rated around the third.

## 299 COMPARE BOOKMAKERS AT BOOKMAKERS.CO.UK H'CAP 5f (F)
**2:10** (2:10) (Class 5) (0-75,75) 4-Y-0+ **£2,911** (£866; £432; £216) **Stalls** High

Form RPR

024- **1** **Rambo Will**[37] 8319 6-9-0 **71**.................................. NataliaGemelova(3) 1 80
(J R Jenkins) *cl up: slt ld 1/2-way: rdn over 1f out: drvn and edgd rt ins fnl f: jst hld on* **6/1**[2]

460- **2** nse **Rowe Park**[57] 8069 11-9-4 **72**....................................(p) LiamKeniry 4 80
(Linda Jewell) *trckd ldrs: swtchd rt and hdwy 2f out: rdn over 1f out: styd on strly fnl f: jst failed* **7/1**[3]

01-0 **3** 1 1/2 **Beacon Tarn**[9] 175 4-9-1 **72**.......................................... NeilFarley(3) 2 75
(Eric Alston) *cl up: effrt 2f out: sn rdn and ev ch tl drvn appr fnl f and kpt on same pce* **7/1**[3]

1-23 **4** nk **Bapak Bangsawan**[9] 175 4-9-0 **73**............................. ShaneGray(5) 5 75
(Kevin Ryan) *slt ld: hdd 1/2-way: cl up: rdn along wl over 1f out: drvn and one pce fnl f* **6/4**[1]

5-01 **5** hd **Layla's Oasis**[7] 196 4-9-3 **71** 6ex.........................................(p) TomEaves 3 72
(Richard Fahey) *racd wd: trckd ldrs: effrt and ch wl over 1f out: sn rdn and kpt on same pce fnl f* **20/1**

0-60 **6** 3 1/4 **Clubland (IRE)**[9] 175 5-9-2 **75**.......................................... TimClark(5) 8 65
(Roy Bowring) *awkward s: racd nr stands' rail: in tch: rdn along over 2f out: n.d* **8/1**

13-1 **7** 3/4 **Sir Geoffrey (IRE)**[21] 9 8-8-4 **65**.....................(p) MatthewHopkins(7) 6 52
(Scott Dixon) *chsd ldrs: rdn along bef 1/2-way: sn lost pl and in rr* **6/1**[2]

00-0 **8** 21 **Mister Manannan (IRE)**[20] 36 7-9-7 **75**.................(b[1]) AdrianNicholls 7
(David Nicholls) *t.k.h: chsd ldrs: hanging lft bef 1/2-way: lost pl wl over 2f out: sn bhd and eased* **12/1**

58.13s (-1.57) **Going Correction** -0.15s/f (Stan) **8** Ran SP% **117.1**
Speed ratings (Par 103): **106,105,103,103,102 97,96,62**
CSF £48.29 CT £303.05 TOTE £9.20: £1.70, £2.10, £2.70; EX 49.80 Trifecta £524.10.
**Owner** Mrs S Bambridge **Bred** T H Bambridge **Trained** Royston, Herts
■ Stewards' Enquiry : Natalia Gemelova seven-day ban: used whip above permitted level (Feb 6-12)

**FOCUS**
A fair sprint and the form rates as standard.

## 300 LADBROKES H'CAP 1m (F)
**2:40** (2:41) (Class 5) (0-75,75) 4-Y-0+ **£2,911** (£866; £432; £216) **Stalls** Low

Form RPR

45-4 **1** **Repetition**[16] 75 4-8-11 **65**.............................................. TomEaves 1 75
(Kristin Stubbs) *mde all: rdn clr 2f out: drvn and edgd rt ins fnl f: kpt on wl towards fin* **16/1**

414- **2** 1 **Mishrif (USA)**[34] 8360 8-9-3 **71**..........................................(v) JoeFanning 4 79
(J R Jenkins) *trckd ldrs: effrt over 2f out: n.m.r and swtchd lft over 1f out: styd on u.p to chse wnr ins fnl f: no imp towards fin* **7/1**

22-2 **3** 1 1/4 **Aqua Ardens (GER)**[9] 172 6-9-6 **74**.......................(tp) StephenCraine 6 79
(George Baker) *hld up in tch: smooth hdwy on outer over 3f out: wd st: rdn to chse ldng pair 2f out: drvn and edgd lft over 1f out: kpt on same pce* **5/4**[1]

6-03 **4** 1 1/4 **Camachoice (IRE)**[8] 181 4-9-7 **75**...............................(p) PaddyAspell 3 77
(Marco Botti) *chsd wnr: rdn along 2f out: drvn wl over 1f out: grad wknd* **16/1**

00-4 **5** 1 **Warfare**[9] 172 5-9-7 **75**................................................ GrahamLee 7 75
(Kevin Ryan) *trckd ldrs: smooth hdwy 3f out: rdn 2f out: edgd rt and wknd over 1f out* **9/2**[2]

21-3 **6** 2 1/2 **George Benjamin**[9] 170 7-8-7 **61** oh3.................(bt) AndrewMullen 2 55
(Michael Appleby) *chsd ldrs on inner: rdn along 3f out: drvn and wknd over 2f out* **8/1**

33-5 **7** 2 **Chrissycross (IRE)**[13] 118 5-9-6 **74**.......................(v) RobertWinston 5 63
(Roger Teal) *s.i.s and bhd: hdwy and in tch over 3f out: sn rdn along and wknd over 2f out* **5/1**[3]

1m 42.24s (-1.46) **Going Correction** -0.15s/f (Stan) **7** Ran SP% **114.7**
Speed ratings (Par 103): **101,100,98,97,96 94,92**
CSF £120.07 TOTE £27.50: £7.30, £3.70; EX 147.80 Trifecta £510.70.
**Owner** The B P J Partnership **Bred** G Reed **Trained** Norton, N Yorks

**FOCUS**
A competitive enough race for the level and no reason why the form won't hold up, despite the slow time.

## 301 32RED H'CAP 1m (F)
**3:10** (3:10) (Class 4) (0-80,79) 3-Y-O **£5,175** (£1,540; £769; £384) **Stalls** Low

Form RPR

01 **1** **Swivel**[12] 142 3-9-0 **72**............................................... JoeFanning 4 84+
(Mark Johnston) *trckd ldrs: hdwy wl over 2f out: rdn to ld wl over 1f out: drvn: green and edgd lft ins fnl f: kpt on strly* **11/4**[2]

23-1 **2** 2 1/4 **Our Gabrial (IRE)**[10] 166 3-9-7 **79** 6ex.............................(b) TomEaves 3 85
(Richard Fahey) *trckd ldrs on inner: effrt 3f out: rdn along 2f out: styd on to chse wnr appr fnl f: sn drvn and one pce* **10/1**

212- **3** shd **Resolute**[28] 8397 3-9-7 **79**.............................................. LiamJones 5 85
(William Haggas) *trckd ldrs: hdwy over 3f out: cl up over 2f out: sn rdn and ev ch tl drvn and one pce appr fnl f* **8/13**[1]

41-1 **4** 12 **Slinky McVelvet**[16] 74 3-9-0 **75**.................................. BillyCray(3) 2 53
(Garry Moss) *cl up: led after 2f: rdn along 3f out: hdd wl over 1f out: sn drvn and wknd* **8/1**[3]

10-4 **5** *26* **Eddiemaurice (IRE)**[16] [74] 3-8-12 **70**........................ AndrewMullen 1
(Richard Guest) *led 2f: cl up: rdn along wl over 3f out: sn lost pl and bhd fnl 2f* **50/1**

1m 42.04s (-1.66) **Going Correction** -0.15s/f (Stan) **5** Ran SP% **110.7**
Speed ratings (Par 99): **102,99,99,87,61**
CSF £26.35 TOTE £2.80: £1.70, £2.30; EX 15.80 Trifecta £26.80.
**Owner** Sheikh Hamdan bin Mohammed Al Maktoum **Bred** Stratford Place Stud And Watership Down **Trained** Middleham Moor, N Yorks

**FOCUS**
A promising performance from the winner and the form is rated on the positive side. The second is the key.

## 302 32RED.COM H'CAP 6f (F)
**3:40** (3:40) (Class 6) (0-60,58) 3-Y-O **£2,264** (£673; £336; £168) **Stalls** Low

Form RPR

213- **1** **Razin' Hell**[27] [8404] 3-9-5 **56**........................................(v) RobertWinston 5 65+
(Alan McCabe) *mde all: rdn clr 2f out: styd on* **4/7**[1]

05-3 **2** *1 1/4* **Bold Max**[14] [98] 3-8-13 **50**.......................................... LiamJones 3 46
(Zoe Davison) *in tch: pushed along 3f out: rdn and hdwy on inner 2f out: drvn and kpt on fnl f* **16/1**

62-3 **3** *nk* **Diamondsinthesky (IRE)**[9] [174] 3-8-13 **57**............. AdamMcLean(7) 7 52
(Derek Shaw) *trckd ldng pair: effrt to chse wnr 3f out: rdn over 2f out: drvn over 1f out: kpt on one pce: lost 2nd nr fin* **7/1**[3]

2-3 **4** *3 3/4* **Meebo (IRE)**[14] [94] 3-9-2 **58**................................... ShelleyBirkett(5) 8 41
(J R Jenkins) *chsd ldrs on outer: hdwy over 2f out: sn rdn and no imp* **3/1**[2]

00-0 **5** *1 1/4* **Red Tiger Lily**[21] [15] 3-8-8 **45**.................................... AdrianNicholls 1 24
(Nigel Tinkler) *in rr: rdn along on inner 1/2-way: sme late hdwy* **25/1**

30-6 **6** *2 1/2* **Highland Princess (IRE)**[22] [5] 3-8-3 **45**........... ShirleyTeasdale(5) 6 16
(Paul Midgley) *dwlt and in rr: hdwy and in tch 3f out: rdn wl over 2f out and sn btn* **33/1**

55-0 **7** *9* **Chatsworth Express**[17] [70] 3-9-1 **52**................................ TomEaves 2
(Richard Whitaker) *cl up on inner: rdn along 3f out: wknd over 2f out* **33/1**

1m 16.77s (0.27) **Going Correction** -0.15s/f (Stan) **7** Ran SP% **116.8**
Speed ratings (Par 95): **92,90,89,84,83 79,67**
CSF £12.59 CT £36.66 TOTE £1.50: £1.30, £4.00; EX 19.40 Trifecta £57.60.
**Owner** Timms, Timms, McCabe & Warke **Bred** Alan J McCabe **Trained** Averham Park, Notts

**FOCUS**
A one-sided handicap. The second and third were close to their recent marks.

## 303 CORAL MOBILE "JUST THREE CLICKS TO BET" H'CAP 1m 4f (F)
**4:10** (4:10) (Class 6) (0-60,66) 4-Y-O+ **£2,264** (£673; £336; £168) **Stalls** Low

Form RPR

2-15 **1** **Fire In Babylon (IRE)**[4] [246] 6-9-1 **49**...........................(b) PaddyAspell 7 59+
(Noel Quinlan) *prom: trckd ldr after 4f: cl up 1/2-way: led over 4f out: rdn clr wl over 2f out: drvn and kpt on fnl f* **16/1**

02-2 **2** *2 1/4* **Shirazz**[17] [67] 5-9-10 **58**...............................................(t) DanielTudhope 5 64
(Seamus Durack) *hld up in tch: hdwy over 4f out: chsd ldrs and rdn along wl over 2f out: drvn to chse wnr over 1f out: one pce u.p fnl f* **7/1**

3-22 **3** *1 1/4* **Rancho Montoya (IRE)**[9] [176] 4-9-3 **55**......................(v) LiamKeniry 3 59
(Andrew Balding) *trckd ldrs: hdwy 4f out: effrt to chse wnr 3f out: rdn over 2f out: drvn and no imp fr wl over 1f out* **7/2**[1]

0-04 **4** *1 1/4* **Dontpaytheferryman (USA)**[3] [252] 9-9-7 **55**..........(b) RobertWinston 6 57
(Peter Hiatt) *towards rr: hdwy 4f out: rdn along to chse ldrs 3f out: drvn and kpt on one pce fnl 2f* **12/1**

006- **5** *1 3/4* **Goldmadchen (GER)**[27] [8410] 6-9-4 **52**............................ GrahamLee 2 52
(James Given) *chsd ldrs on inner 2f: sn lost pl and towards rr over 7f out: sn swtchd rt to outer: rdn along over 3f out: wd st: drvn and kpt on fnl 2f: nrst fin* **10/1**

002- **6** *4* **Bavarian Nordic (USA)**[27] [8410] 9-9-10 **58**.......................(b) TomEaves 9 51
(Richard Whitaker) *chsd ldrs: rdn along 4f out: drvn wl over 2f out: sn btn* **9/2**[3]

1411 **7** *5* **Grandad Mac**[3] [252] 6-10-4 **66** 12ex................................. LiamJones 8 51
(Alan Coogan) *sn led: rdn along over 5f out: hdd over 4f out: sn drvn and wknd over 3f out* **4/1**[2]

45-3 **8** *28* **Omega Omega**[9] [176] 5-8-7 **46**..................................(b) ShelleyBirkett(5) 1
(Julia Feilden) *a in rr: bhd fnl 4f* **8/1**

00-3 **9** *33* **Penny Stock (IRE)**[6] [221] 4-9-0 **52**...................................... JoeFanning 4
(Mark Johnston) *racd freely: chsd ldng pair: pushed along bef 1/2-way and sn lost pl: rdn and bhd over 4f out: t.o and eased fnl 3f* **7/1**

2m 40.15s (-0.85) **Going Correction** -0.15s/f (Stan)
**WFA** 4 from 5yo+ 4lb **9** Ran SP% **119.2**
Speed ratings (Par 101): **96,94,93,92,91 89,85,67,45**
CSF £126.71 CT £491.11 TOTE £17.50: £4.70, £3.10, £1.70; EX 148.90 Trifecta £949.50.
**Owner** Ms Fiona Donald **Bred** The Goldsmith Bloodstock Partnership **Trained** Newmarket, Suffolk

**FOCUS**
The second and third are both solid enough yardsticks and there's no reason to question the return to form from the winner.
T/Plt: £543.30. Pool: £61,050.74 - 82.02 winning units. T/Qpdt: £107.00. Pool: £4663.93 - 32.25 winning units. JR

# 238MEYDAN (L-H)
Thursday, January 23

**OFFICIAL GOING: Tapeta - standard; turf - good**

## 304a GULF NEWS TABLOID (H'CAP) (TAPETA) 6f
**2:30** (2:30) (95-105,105) 3-Y-O+
**£39,759** (£13,253; £6,626; £3,313; £1,987; £1,325)

RPR

**1** **Jamesie (IRE)**[14] [109] 6-9-2 100.................................. FergalLynch 3 105
(David Marnane, Ire) *s.i.s: settled in rr: smooth prog 2 1/2f out: rdn to ld fnl 55yds* **15/2**

**2** *1* **Merhee (AUS)**[201] 6-9-6 105............................ ChristopheSoumillon 2 106
(M F De Kock, South Africa) *sn led: kicked clr 2f out: r.o but hdd fnl 55yds* **4/1**[1]

**3** *nk* **Masamah (IRE)**[28] [8395] 8-9-4 102.................................(p) MartinHarley 9 103+
(Marco Botti) *trckd ldng pair: ev ch 1 1/2f out: r.o same pce fnl f* **14/1**

**4** *1* **Mujaazef**[13] [139] 7-9-2 100.........................................(t) PaulHanagan 8 98+
(A Al Raihe, UAE) *trckd ldrs: ev ch 1 1/2f out: one pce fnl 110yds* **20/1**

**5** *hd* **Spirit Of Battle (USA)**[307] [1135] 6-9-2 100.................(b) TadhgO'Shea 1 97
(A bin Huzaim, UAE) *in rr of mid-div: r.o same pce fnl 1 1/2f* **7/1**[3]

**6** *3/4* **Racy**[14] [107] 7-9-3 101...................................................... FrederikTylicki 11 96+
(Brian Ellison) *slowly away: nvr nr to chal* **14/1**

**7** *nk* **Proud Possibility (USA)**[14] [109] 4-9-2 100.................(t) WilliamBuick 4 94
(Niels Petersen, Norway) *trckd ldng pair tl outpcd fnl 1 1/2f* **6/1**[2]

**8** *3/4* **Lui Rei (ITY)**[14] [109] 8-9-2 100........................................(v) LukeMorris 10 91+
(Fawzi Abdulla Nass, Bahrain) *s.i.s: nvr able to chal* **8/1**

**9** *nk* **Alraihjan (KSA)**[33] 4-9-2 100................................... MickaelBarzalona 12 90+
(B Al Shaibani, Saudi Arabia) *s.i.s: settled in rr: r.o fnl 1 1/2f but n.d* **12/1**

**10** *1/2* **Arnold Lane (IRE)**[14] [112] 5-9-5 104.............. WilliamTwiston-Davies 6 92+
(Mick Channon) *nvr bttr than mid-div* **14/1**

**11** *3/4* **Intransigent**[110] [7013] 5-9-6 105.................................... JamieSpencer 13 90+
(Andrew Balding) *nvr bttr than mid-div* **10/1**

**12** *2* **Red Dubawi (IRE)**[14] [107] 6-9-2 100.................................(p) PatDobbs 7 80+
(David Marnane, Ire) *nvr bttr than mid-div* **33/1**

**13** *nk* **Master Of War**[111] [6990] 4-9-2 100................................. JamesDoyle 5 79+
(D Selvaratnam, UAE) *mid-div: nvr able to chal but r.o fnl 2f: nrst fin* **33/1**

**14** *5 1/2* **Tennessee Wildcat (IRE)**[14] [109] 4-9-5 104................. GaryCarroll 14 64+
(G M Lyons, Ire) *nvr nr to chal* **12/1**

1m 11.77s (0.17) **Going Correction** +0.25s/f (Slow) **14** Ran SP% **124.8**
Speed ratings: **108,106,106,104,104 103,103,102,101,101 100,97,97,89**
CSF: 40.60; EX 43.90; TRIFECTA: 191.30; TRICAST: 243.40 WIN: 8.20; PL: 2.30, 1.60, 3.20..
**Owner** Damian Lavelle **Bred** John R Jeffers **Trained** Bansha, Co Tipperary

**FOCUS**
Running rail out 12m on turf track. A sensible enough pace for this decent, competitive sprint handicap. Here are the splits with the Trakus par times in brackets: 24.76 (24.48), 47.81 (47.44) with the clock stopped in 1:11.77 (1:11.57). The first two and the fifth were well drawn.

## 305a GN FOCUS (H'CAP) (TURF) 1m 4f 38y
**3:05** (3:05) (95-105,105) 3-Y-O+
**£39,759** (£13,253; £6,626; £3,313; £1,987; £1,325)

RPR

**1** **Certerach (IRE)**[81] [7723] 6-9-4 **102**................................... ShaneFoley 7 105
(M Halford, Ire) *in rr of mid-div: smooth prog 2 1/2f out: led fnl f: comf* **10/1**

**2** *1/2* **Topclas (FR)**[312] 8-9-4 **102**.........................................(v) AdriedeVries 12 104
(A bin Harmash, UAE) *settled in rr: rdn 3f out: r.o fnl 2f nrst fin* **16/1**

**3** *3/4* **Tanfeeth**[13] [136] 6-9-2 **100**..............................................(t) PaulHanagan 4 101
(M Al Muhairi, UAE) *mid-div: chsd ldrs 2f out: nt qckn fnl 110yds* **14/1**

**4** *3/4* **Excellent Result (IRE)**[103] [7206] 4-8-11 **99**............ SilvestreDeSousa 14 100+
(Saeed bin Suroor) *settled in rr: nvr nr to chal but r.o fnl 2f* **10/3**[1]

**5** *hd* **Jutland**[13] [136] 7-9-6 **105**.................................................. PatDobbs 6 103
(Doug Watson, UAE) *trckd ldng pair: ev ch 1 1/2f out: one pce fnl f* **12/1**

**6** *3/4* **Bank Of Burden (USA)**[119] [6784] 7-9-6 **105**.......(t) Per-AndersGraberg 3 102
(Niels Petersen, Norway) *mid-div: r.o fnl 1 1/2f: nrst fin* **25/1**

**7** *nse* **Inthar (USA)**[18] 5-8-10 **95**.......................................... RichardMullen 2 92
(S Seemar, UAE) *trckd ldng pair: ev ch 1 1/2f out: one pce fnl f* **12/1**

**8** *2 1/4* **Dormello (IRE)**[14] [112] 6-9-5 **104**.................................. JamesDoyle 10 98
(D Selvaratnam, UAE) *mid-div: chsd ldrs 3f out: led briefly 2 1/2f out* **10/1**

**9** *hd* **Handsome Man (IRE)**[145] [5993] 5-8-13 **97**.................(p) KierenFallon 1 91
(Saeed bin Suroor) *trckd ldrs: ev ch 1 1/2f out: wknd fnl 110yds* **6/1**[3]

**10** *2* **Restraint Of Trade (IRE)**[446] [7554] 4-8-7 **95**......... MickaelBarzalona 13 86
(Charlie Appleby) *settled in rr: n.m.r 2 1/2 out: nvr able to chal* **4/1**[2]

**11** *2* **Jedi**[714] [486] 8-8-10 **95**................................................. TadhgO'Shea 5 82
(A bin Huzaim, UAE) *slowly away: settled in rr: nvr nr to chal* **33/1**

**12** *nse* **Genius Beast (USA)**[866] [5928] 6-9-2 100........................ AhmedAjtebi 11 88
(Charlie Appleby) *settled in rr: nvr able to chal* **14/1**

**13** *14* **Thecornishcockney**[329] [823] 5-9-4 **102**............................(p) BrettDoyle 8 67
(John Ryan) *in rr of mid-div: wknd fnl 2f* **16/1**

**14** *3* **Submariner (USA)**[14] [108] 8-9-3 **101**.............................. DaneO'Neill 9 62
(A bin Huzaim, UAE) *sn led: hdd & wknd 2 1/2 out* **33/1**

2m 31.91s (151.91)
**WFA** 4 from 5yo+ 4lb **14** Ran SP% **125.8**
CSF: 164.52; EX 222.80; TRIFECTA: 2218.60; TRICAST: 2254.69 WIN: 14.50; PL: 3.20, 4.00, 4.50.
**Owner** Paul Rooney **Bred** Newberry Stud Company **Trained** Doneany, Co Kildare

**FOCUS**
The rail was out 12 metres on the turf course. They went a reasonable gallop in this tight handicap. The winner is rated close to his best.

## 306a GULF NEWS CLASSIFIEDS (H'CAP) (TAPETA) 1m
**3:40** (3:40) (100-110,110) 3-Y-O+
**£43,373** (£14,457; £7,228; £3,614; £2,168; £1,445)

RPR

**1** **Alexandra Palace (SAF)**[299] 5-9-0 **104** ow3.... ChristopheSoumillon 15 105+
(M F De Kock, South Africa) *in rr of mid-div: smooth prog 2 1/2f out: rdn to ld cl home* **7/1**[2]

**2** *1/2* **Free Wheeling (AUS)**[14] [112] 6-9-1 **105**...............(t) SilvestreDeSousa 5 105
(Saeed bin Suroor) *trckd ldrs: ev ch 110yds out: nt qckn cl home* **7/1**[2]

**3** *nk* **Capital Attraction (USA)**[14] [111] 7-9-6 **110**.................... TadhgO'Shea 8 109
(Ernst Oertel, UAE) *trckd ldrs: ev ch 1f out: one pce fnl 55yds* **25/1**

**4** *nse* **Disa Leader (SAF)**[14] [112] 9-9-0 **104**.............................. JGeroudis 7 103
(M F De Kock, South Africa) *in rr of mid-div: chsd ldrs 2f out: ev ch 55yds out: one pce fnl stride* **16/1**

**5** *nse* **Solar Deity (IRE)**[40] [8301] 5-9-4 **108**.............................. MartinHarley 4 107
(Marco Botti) *mid-div: chsd ldrs 1 1/2f out: r.o fnl f: nrst fin* **5/1**[1]

**6** *1/2* **Captain Joy (IRE)**[111] [7005] 5-9-2 **106**............................ GaryCarroll 14 104
(Tracey Collins, Ire) *mid-div: chsd ldrs 1 1/2f out: nt qckn fnl 110yds* **14/1**

**7** *3/4* **Spoil The Fun (FR)**[104] [7186] 5-9-4 **108**.............................(t) JulienAuge 6 104
(C Ferland, France) *mid-div: r.o fnl 1 1/2f: nrst fin* **22/1**

**8** *3/4* **Derbaas (USA)**[7] [207] 8-9-1 **105**..........................................(t) DaneO'Neill 10 99
(A Al Raihe, UAE) *trckd ldrs: rdn 3f out: ev ch 110yds out: wknd fnl 55yds* **16/1**

**9** *nk* **Mont Ras (IRE)**[14] [109] 7-8-13 **102**................................ WilliamBuick 2 97
(David O'Meara) *trckd ldrs: ev ch 2f out: one pce fnl 110yds* **7/1**[2]

**10** *hd* **Ocean Tempest**[14] [109] 5-9-1 **105**.................................... BrettDoyle 12 98+
(John Ryan) *nvr nr to chal* **20/1**

**11** *1 1/4* **Bertiewhittle**[14] [109] 6-8-13 **102**.................................... JamieSpencer 1 93
(David Barron) *nvr bttr than mid-div* **7/1**[2]

**12** *1 1/2* **Chil The Kite**[104] [7186] 5-9-4 **108**................................... GeorgeBaker 3 95
(Hughie Morrison) *s.i.s: a in rr* **12/1**[3]

**13** *nk* **Barbecue Eddie (USA)**[14] [111] 10-9-2 **106**.................(b) PaulHanagan 9 92
(Doug Watson, UAE) *nvr bttr than mid-div* **20/1**

**14** *4 3/4* **Not A Given (USA)**[336] [742] 5-8-10 **100**................ MickaelBarzalona 11 75
(Charlie Appleby) *sn led: hdd 4 1/2f out: chsd ldrs 2f out: one pce fnl 110yds* **12/1**[3]

15 3 ¾ **Silver Ocean (USA)**[130] 6-9-2 **106**.............................. FrankieDettori 13 73
(Niels Petersen, Norway) *trckd ldrs: led 4 1/2f out: hdd & wknd 2f out* **20/1**

16 3 ¾ **Sommerabend**[40] 8307 7-9-6 **110**.............................. AdriedeVries 16 68
(M Rulec, Germany) *trckd ldrs tl outpcd 2 1/2f out* **14/1**

1m 37.69s (0.19) **Going Correction** +0.25s/f (Slow) **16** Ran SP% **129.6**
Speed ratings: **109,108,108,108,108 107,106,106,105,105 104,102,102,97,94 90**
CSF: 54.00; EX 237.30; TRIFECTA: 3880.10; TRICAST: 1206.20 WIN: 25.90;.
**Owner** Tmen Stable **Bred** Varsfontein Stud **Trained** South Africa

**FOCUS**
A decent handicap and a winner to follow. The pace was good early but slowed. The runner-up sets the standard.

## 307a XPRESS (H'CAP) (TAPETA) 1m 2f
**4:15** (4:15) (95-112,112) 3-Y-0+
**£54,216** (£18,072; £9,036; £4,518; £2,710; £1,807)

RPR

1 **Windhoek**[145] 5986 4-8-10 **104**.............................. SilvestreDeSousa 8 104
(Saeed bin Suroor) *settled in rr: rdn 3f out: r.o wl: led cl home* **3/1**[1]

2 hd **Layali Al Andalus**[14] 108 7-8-5 **97**.............................. RichardMullen 9 97
(S Seemar, UAE) *slowly away: settled in rr: smooth prog 2 1/2f out: r.o fnl 1 1/2f: jst failed* **10/1**

3 nse **Mutajare (IRE)**[13] 136 6-9-3 **109**..............................(t) PaulHanagan 1 109
(A Al Raihe, UAE) *trckd ldrs: led briefly 55yds out: hdd nr line* **16/1**

4 1 **Plantagenet (SPA)**[102] 7-8-6 **98**.............................. Per-AndersGraberg 10 96
(Niels Petersen, Norway) *settled in rr: chsd ldrs 3f out: led 2 1/2f out: clr 2f out: hdd cl home* **14/1**

5 shd **Manalapan (IRE)**[97] 7361 4-9-1 **108**.............................. TedDurcan 5 107
(P J Prendergast, Ire) *mid-div: chsd ldrs 1 1/2f out: r.o same pce fnl f* **8/1**

6 nk **Banoffee (IRE)**[57] 8062 4-8-8 **101** ow1.............................. KierenFallon 3 99
(Hughie Morrison) *mid-div on rail: nvr able to chal but r.o fnl 2f* **7/1**[3]

7 4 ¼ **Sweet Lightning**[14] 108 9-8-8 **100**.............................. JamieSpencer 7 89
(David O'Meara) *settled in rr: rdn 2f out: r.o same pce* **25/1**

8 3 ¾ **Zip Top (IRE)**[824] 7020 5-9-4 **110**.............................. MickaelBarzalona 2 91
(Charlie Appleby) *mid-div: rdn 3 1/2f out: sn struggling* **3/1**[1]

9 2 ¾ **Izaaj (USA)**[14] 108 7-8-5 **96**.............................. TadhgO'Shea 6 73
(A bin Harmash, UAE) *sn led: hdd & wknd 2 1/2f out* **20/1**

10 12 **Daddy Long Legs (USA)**[14] 111 5-9-6 **112**...... ChristopheSoumillon 4 64
(M F De Kock, South Africa) *trckd ldrs tl outpcd 2 1/2f out* **11/2**[2]

2m 4.26s (-0.44) **Going Correction** +0.25s/f (Slow)
**WFA** 4 from 5yo+ 2lb **10** Ran SP% **119.2**
Speed ratings: **111,110,110,110,109 109,106,103,101,91**
CSF: 35.95; EX 29.80 ; TRIFECTA: 274.50; TRICAST:421.46 WIN: 2.50; PL: 1.30, 1.90, 4.60.
**Owner** Godolphin **Bred** Horizon Bloodstock Limited **Trained** Newmarket, Suffolk

**FOCUS**
They went a decent gallop, but there was still a bunch finish and this might not have been much a race. The second and third help with the standard.

## 308a AL FAHIDI FORT SPONSORED BY GULF NEWS (GROUP 2) (TURF) 7f
**4:50** (4:50) 3-Y-0+
**£90,361** (£30,120; £15,060; £7,530; £4,518; £3,012)

RPR

1 **Anaerobio (ARG)**[14] 112 7-9-0 111..................(t) ChristopheSoumillon 1 113
(M F De Kock, South Africa) *trckd ldrs: led 1f out: comf* **5/1**[1]

2 ¾ **Mshawish (USA)**[110] 7047 4-9-0 113.............................. FrankieDettori 3 111+
(M Delzangles, France) *trckd ldrs: rdn 2f out: r.o fnl 1 1/2f: nrst fin* **5/1**[1]

3 ¾ **Pearl Flute (IRE)**[82] 7706 4-9-0 112.............................. JamieSpencer 5 109
(F-H Graffard, France) *sn led: rdn clr 2f out: hdd 1f out: r.o same pce* **12/1**

4 3 ¼ **Iguazu Falls (USA)**[14] 112 9-9-0 110..............................(t) AdriedeVries 9 100+
(A bin Harmash, UAE) *mid-div: r.o fnl 2f: nvr nr to chal* **10/1**

5 ½ **Kavanagh (SAF)**[7] 206 7-9-0 112..............................(t) ThierryThulliez 6 99+
(M F De Kock, South Africa) *trckd ldrs: ev ch 2 1/2f out: r.o same pce fnl 1 1/2f* **16/1**

6 ½ **Fulbright**[14] 109 5-9-0 109.............................. MickaelBarzalona 2 98+
(Charlie Appleby) *s.i.s: nvr nr to chal but r.o fnl 2f* **6/1**[2]

7 hd **Dux Scholar**[14] 110 6-9-0 113.............................. PatDobbs 10 97+
(Doug Watson, UAE) *nvr bttr than mid-div* **11/1**

8 ½ **Mustaheel (IRE)**[63] 7998 5-9-0 106..............................(t) RoystonFfrench 4 96+
(A Al Raihe, UAE) *trckd ldrs tl outpcd 2f out* **33/1**

9 ¾ **Tamaathul**[35] 8357 7-9-0 113..............................(t) PaulHanagan 8 94+
(A Al Raihe, UAE) *nvr bttr than mid-div* **7/1**[3]

10 hd **Heavy Metal (SAF)**[201] 6-9-5 118.............................. JGeroudis 7 98+
(S G Tarry, South Africa) *nvr nr to chal* **9/1**

11 ½ **Roi De Vitesse (IRE)**[14] 112 7-9-0 104..............................(v) HarryBentley 12 92+
(Ali Jan, Qatar) *nvr nr to chal* **33/1**

12 ½ **Dafeef**[14] 112 7-9-0 105..............................(e) DaneO'Neill 11 90+
(Doug Watson, UAE) *nvr bttr than mid-div* **33/1**

13 shd **Gale Force Ten**[130] 6450 4-9-0 113..............................(b) PatCosgrave 13 90+
(M F De Kock, South Africa) *nvr nr to chal* **8/1**

14 2 ½ **Le Drakkar (AUS)**[327] 872 9-9-0 108..............................(t) TadhgO'Shea 14 83+
(A bin Huzaim, UAE) *slowly away: a in rr* **28/1**

1m 23.36s (83.36) **14** Ran SP% **124.5**
CSF: 28.89; EX 26.00; TRIFECTA: 299.00; WIN:4.10; PL: 2.00, 2.30, 3.90.
**Owner** Mohd Khaleel Ahmed **Bred** Haras La Madrugada **Trained** South Africa

**FOCUS**
This Group 2 contest was formerly run over 1m in February. There was a reasonable line-up for this year's race, but a slow-fast pace meant it paid to be handy. A person best from the progressive winner.

## 309a PROPERTY WEEKLY (H'CAP) (TURF) 1m 1f
**5:25** (5:25) (100-110,108) 3-Y-0+
**£43,373** (£14,457; £7,228; £3,614; £2,168; £1,445)

RPR

1 **Gabrial (IRE)**[14] 110 5-9-4 **106**.............................. JamieSpencer 3 110
(Richard Fahey) *slowly away: settled in rr: smooth prog 2f out: rdn to ld fnl 55yds* **4/1**[2]

2 hd **El Estruendoso (ARG)**[14] 108 5-9-0 **101**.............................. PatCosgrave 2 106
(M F De Kock, South Africa) *mid-div: smooth prog 2 1/2f out: led 1f out: hdd cl home* **6/1**[3]

3 ¾ **Tarbawi (IRE)**[14] 110 4-9-0 **102**.............................. AdriedeVries 1 105
(A bin Harmash, UAE) *mid-div: chsd ldrs 2 1/2f out: ev ch 110yds out: nt qckn fnl 55yds* **16/1**

4 ¾ **Sanshaawes (SAF)**[355] 5-9-0 **101** ow1.............................. ChristopheSoumillon 5 102
(M F De Kock, South Africa) *in rr of mid-div: rdn 2 1/2f out: r.o fnl 1 1/2f nrst fin* **11/4**[1]

5 1 ½ **Vasily**[145] 6001 6-9-1 **102**.............................. AndreaAtzeni 6 100
(M F De Kock, South Africa) *trckd ldng pair: ev ch 2 1/2f out: r.o same pce fnl 1 1/2f* **9/1**

6 nk **Elleval (IRE)**[130] 6440 4-9-4 **107**.............................. FergalLynch 4 104
(David Marnane, Ire) *settled in rr: nvr nr to chal but r.o fnl 2f* **10/1**

7 1 ¾ **Auditor (USA)**[107] 7116 4-8-13 **101**..............................(t) JulienAuge 12 95
(C Ferland, France) *nvr bttr than mid-div* **20/1**

8 1 ½ **Starboard**[115] 5-9-2 **104**.............................. WilliamBuick 7 94
(David Simcock) *settled in rr: nvr nr to chal* **10/1**

9 hd **War Monger (USA)**[46] 8207 10-8-13 **100**.............................. PaulHanagan 8 90
(Doug Watson, UAE) *trckd ldrs: led 4 1/2f out: kicked clr 2 1/2f out: hdd & wknd f out* **25/1**

10 7 ¾ **Fantastic Moon**[196] 4216 4-8-11 **100**.............................. KierenFallon 9 73
(Jeremy Noseda) *settled in rr: nvr nr to chal* **14/1**

11 3 ¾ **Do It All (USA)**[14] 110 7-9-2 **104**..............................(v) SilvestreDeSousa 10 69
(Saeed bin Suroor) *trckd ldng pair tl outpcd 2f out* **14/1**

12 2 ¾ **Without Fear (FR)**[119] 6784 6-9-6 **108**.............................. Per-AndersGraberg 11 67
(Niels Petersen, Norway) *sn led: hdd & wknd 4 1/2f out* **25/1**

1m 48.75s (108.75)
**WFA** 4 from 5yo+ 1lb **12** Ran SP% **120.8**
CSF: 28.13; EX 20.50; TRICAST: 348.19, TRIFECTA: 251.60; WIN:3.00; PL: 1.70, 2.60, 3.90.
Placepot: £1146.70. Pool: £7383.35 - 4.70 winning units. Quadpot: £103.60. Pool: £532.00 - 3.80 winning units..
**Owner** Dr Marwan Koukash **Bred** B Kennedy **Trained** Musley Bank, N Yorks

**FOCUS**
The strong gallop helped set things up for the grade-dropping winner. He and the third are rated in line with their C&D latest.

# 282 LINGFIELD (L-H)
## Friday, January 24

**OFFICIAL GOING: Standard**
Wind: Light, behind Weather: Thick cloud, damp

## 310 LADBROKES CLASSIFIED CLAIMING STKS 7f 1y(P)
**1:00** (1:00) (Class 5) 4-Y-0+ **£2,726** (£805; £402) **Stalls** Low

Form RPR

3-42 1 **Hellbender (IRE)**[15] 102 8-8-10 70.............................. DavidProbert 6 73
(Shaun Harris) *pressed ldr: led ins fnl f: rdn out* **5/1**

62-3 2 1 **Ocean Legend (IRE)**[14] 113 9-8-3 75.............................. JoeDoyle(7) 1 70
(Tony Carroll) *led: shkn up over 1f out: hdd ins fnl f: unable qck* **4/1**[3]

03-5 3 ¾ **My Kingdom (IRE)**[20] 56 8-8-10 72..............................(t) AdamBeschizza 5 68
(Stuart Williams) *chsd ldrs: effrt over 1f out: kpt on u.p fnl f* **3/1**[1]

40-5 4 ¾ **Cyflymder (IRE)**[2] 288 8-7-13 60..............................(b) ShelleyBirkett(5) 3 60
(David C Griffiths) *prom: hrd rdn over 1f out: no ex fnl f* **16/1**

65-3 5 ¾ **Prince Of Burma (IRE)**[7] 211 6-8-0 65..............................(v) NickyMackay 8 54
(David Evans) *in tch: effrt on outer over 2f out: one pce* **7/2**[2]

00-5 6 2 **Golden Desert (IRE)**[20] 52 10-8-8 61.............................. LukeMorris 4 57
(Simon Dow) *dwlt: a towards rr: rdn and no imp fnl 2f* **25/1**

100- 7 2 ½ **Menelik (IRE)**[24] 8453 5-8-8 66..............................(p) RichardKingscote 7 50
(Tom Dascombe) *s.s: hld up in rr: n.d fnl 2f* **5/1**

1m 24.38s (-0.42) **Going Correction** -0.075s/f (Stan) **7** Ran SP% **110.3**
Speed ratings (Par 103): **99,97,97,96,95 93,90**
CSF £23.31 TOTE £5.10: £1.60, £2.10; EX 18.10 Trifecta £43.40.
**Owner** Southwell Racecourse Owners Group **Bred** James Lombard **Trained** Carburton, Notts

**FOCUS**
A trappy little claimer to kick-off proceedings, but Ocean Legend was allowed to dictate at just a steady pace and it proved difficult for the hold-up horses to get in a blow. The fourth is the key to the form.

## 311 32RED.COM H'CAP 7f 1y(P)
**1:30** (1:32) (Class 6) (0-65,65) 3-Y-0 **£2,385** (£704; £352) **Stalls** Low

Form RPR

003- 1 **Basil Berry**[24] 8452 3-9-3 **64**.............................. RobertTart(3) 7 70
(Chris Dwyer) *mid-div on outer: gd hdwy to ld 1f out: rdn out* **9/2**[2]

2-22 2 1 **Ain't No Surprise (IRE)**[9] 187 3-9-4 **62**.............................. AdamKirby 1 65
(Jamie Osborne) *in tch on rail: lost pl and short of room 2f out: gd hdwy over 1f out: chsd wnr fnl f: a hld* **8/1**[3]

55-4 3 1 ¾ **Rose Buck**[9] 187 3-9-3 **61**.............................. LiamJones 10 59
(Lee Carter) *chsd ldr: led 3f out tl 1f out: one pce* **33/1**

3-11 4 hd **Spreadable (IRE)**[4] 261 3-9-6 **64** 12ex..............................(v) LukeMorris 6 67+
(Nick Littmoden) *mid-div: hdwy and nt clr run over 1f out: swtchd lft: styd on fnl f* **10/11**[1]

524- 5 nk **Hot Stock (FR)**[35] 8363 3-9-4 **62**.............................. JimmyQuinn 4 59
(Jo Hughes) *chsd ldrs: rdn and one pce fnl 2f* **16/1**

00-3 6 ¾ **Fruit Pastille**[13] 140 3-9-7 **65**.............................. NickyMackay 9 62+
(Hughie Morrison) *in tch: effrt over 2f out: hmpd and swtchd wd over 1f out: nt rcvr* **12/1**

062- 7 ¾ **Tanojin (IRE)**[104] 7198 3-8-10 **61**.............................. DanielCremin(7) 8 54+
(Mick Channon) *hld up in rr: shkn up and styd on fnl 2f: nt rch ldrs* **25/1**

5-36 8 ½ **Habdab**[11] 167 3-9-6 **64**.............................. SeanLevey 3 56
(Richard Hannon) *hld up towards rr: sme hdwy on inner over 1f out: nt trble ldrs* **25/1**

23-5 9 ¾ **Dancing Sal (IRE)**[9] 187 3-9-6 **64**.............................. GrahamLee 13 54
(Brett Johnson) *towards rr: rdn 2f out: styng on at fin* **33/1**

600- 10 nk **Charlies Mate**[57] 8085 3-8-11 **55**.............................. MartinLane 14 44
(John Best) *prom tl wknd over 1f out* **50/1**

000- 11 1 ½ **Desert Colours**[121] 6755 3-8-11 **55**.............................. JamieSpencer 11 40
(Kevin Ryan) *led tl 3f out: wknd over 1f out* **20/1**

030- 12 2 **Rush**[57] 8083 3-8-9 **60**.............................. LouisSteward(7) 2 39
(Paul Cole) *prom on rail tl wknd 2f out* **20/1**

063- 13 11 **Pieman's Girl**[29] 8396 3-9-7 **65**.............................. WilliamCarson 5 15
(Anthony Carson) *dwlt: towards rr: n.d fnl 2f* **66/1**

1m 24.83s (0.03) **Going Correction** -0.075s/f (Stan) **13** Ran SP% **121.8**
Speed ratings (Par 95): **96,94,92,92,92 91,90,90,89,88 87,84,72**
CSF £36.65 CT £1130.69 TOTE £5.10: £1.60, £2.40, £7.90; EX 44.10 Trifecta £1023.40.
**Owner** Strawberry Fields Stud **Bred** Strawberry Fields Stud **Trained** Newmarket, Suffolk

**FOCUS**
Quite a few unexposed horses in here, as you would expect given they've only just turned three-years-old and, perhaps unsurprisingly for a 14-runner race around here, it got a bit messy for some, not least the favourite, around the home turn. The second and third help with the standard.

## 312 COMPARE BOOKMAKERS AT BOOKMAKERS.CO.UK H'CAP 6f 1y(P)
**2:00** (2:00) (Class 5) (0-75,80) 4-Y-0+ **£3,234** (£962; £481; £240) **Stalls** Low

Form RPR
2-21 **1** **Lexi's Hero (IRE)**[14] 122 6-9-7 **75**...........................(v[1]) JamieSpencer 4 91
(Richard Fahey) *mde all: dominated at decent pce: rdn 6 l clr over 1f out: unchal* **11/4**[2]
40-6 **2** 4 ½ **Alnoomaas (IRE)**[16] 91 5-8-12 **66**.................................. LukeMorris 7 68
(Luke Dace) *bhd: hdwy over 1f out: r.o to shade 2nd on line: no ch w wnr* **10/1**
-255 **3** nk **Seek The Fair Land**[2] 287 8-9-6 **74**..............................(b) LiamJones 3 75
(Lee Carter) *towards rr: hdwy over 1f out: disp 2nd ins fnl f: no ch w wnr* **4/1**[3]
0-10 **4** ¾ **Desert Strike**[6] 233 8-9-5 **73**..........................................(p) LiamKeniry 6 71
(Conor Dore) *chsd wnr tl no ex ins fnl f* **25/1**
300- **5** 1 ¾ **Liberty Jack (IRE)**[33] 8391 4-9-6 **74**............................ StephenCraine 1 67
(Jim Boyle) *chsd ldrs tl rdn and btn over 1f out* **4/1**[3]
00-6 **6** 2 ¾ **Where's Reiley (USA)**[15] 93 8-8-11 **65**..................(v) RobertWinston 2 49
(Michael Attwater) *chsd ldrs: rdn 3f out: wknd over 1f out* **33/1**
4-21 **7** ½ **Kuanyao (IRE)**[7] 208 8-9-5 **80** 6ex.........................(v) LouisSteward(7) 5 62
(Lee Carter) *s.i.s: nvr gng wl towards rr: in last and struggling over 2f out* **5/2**[1]
1m 9.69s (-2.21) **Going Correction** -0.075s/f (Stan) 7 Ran SP% **111.1**
Speed ratings (Par 103): **111,105,104,103,101 97,96**
CSF £27.72 TOTE £3.40: £1.80, £3.40; EX 27.50 Trifecta £75.20.
**Owner** Dr Marwan Koukash **Bred** T J Pabst **Trained** Musley Bank, N Yorks

**FOCUS**
There looked to be plenty of pace on here and the time was fast. A useful effort from the winner.

## 313 BEST ODDS AT BOOKMAKERS.CO.UK H'CAP 5f 6y(P)
**2:30** (2:30) (Class 6) (0-60,60) 4-Y-0+ **£2,385** (£704; £352) **Stalls** High

Form RPR
53-2 **1** **Roy's Legacy**[14] 114 5-9-7 **60**........................................ AdamKirby 8 68
(Shaun Harris) *mde all: sn swtchd to ins rail fr wdst stall: rdn clr over 1f out: jst hld on* **6/5**[1]
160- **2** ½ **Imaginary Diva**[24] 8457 8-8-13 **59**........................ JordanVaughan(7) 6 65
(George Margarson) *in tch: hdwy over 1f out: chsd wnr ins fnl f: clsng at fin* **25/1**
02-4 **3** 1 **Your Gifted (IRE)**[4] 259 7-8-13 **55**.........................(v) MarkCoumbe(3) 4 58
(Lisa Williamson) *dwlt: hld up and bhd: shkn up over 1f out: fin wl* **6/1**[3]
5-05 **4** hd **Speedyfix**[11] 164 7-8-13 **52**..........................................(t) JimmyQuinn 7 54
(Christine Dunnett) *s.i.s: towards rr: rdn and hdwy 1f out: r.o* **14/1**
30-0 **5** 1 ¼ **Johnny Splash (IRE)**[9] 192 5-9-5 **58**.....................(v) RobertWinston 2 55
(Roger Teal) *chsd ldrs: rdn over 2f out: one pce fnl f* **4/1**[2]
260- **6** 2 ¼ **Falasteen (IRE)**[24] 8457 7-9-7 **60**.......................................... LiamJones 5 49
(Milton Bradley) *chsd wnr tl wknd ins fnl f* **6/1**[3]
30-0 **7** ½ **Brandywell Boy (IRE)**[9] 192 11-8-7 **46** oh1............ AdamBeschizza 1 33
(Dominic Ffrench Davis) *sn pushed along in 6th: n.d fnl 2f* **33/1**
000- **8** 1 ¼ **Sarah Berry**[24] 8457 5-9-2 **55**.........................................(b[1]) LukeMorris 3 38
(Chris Dwyer) *chsd ldrs over 3f* **25/1**
58.95s (0.15) **Going Correction** -0.075s/f (Stan) 8 Ran SP% **111.3**
Speed ratings (Par 101): **95,94,92,92,90 86,85,83**
CSF £37.72 CT £130.63 TOTE £2.30: £1.20, £4.20, £1.70; EX 29.80 Trifecta £83.20.
**Owner** K Blackwell Steve Mohammed & Stew Rowley **Bred** A Christou **Trained** Carburton, Notts

**FOCUS**
A weak race with most of these coming here out of form. The winner is possibly a bit better than the bare form.

## 314 DOWNLOAD THE LADBROKES APP H'CAP 7f 1y(P)
**3:05** (3:05) (Class 2) 4-Y-0+
**£28,012** (£8,388; £4,194; £2,097; £1,048; £526) **Stalls** Low

Form RPR
11-3 **1** **Alfred Hutchinson**[13] 144 6-9-1 **97**........................... RobertTart(3) 3 107
(Geoffrey Oldroyd) *prom on rail: led jst over 1f out: drvn clr* **8/1**
100- **2** 1 **Brocklebank (IRE)**[112] 6988 5-8-3 **82**............................ NickyMackay 7 89
(Simon Dow) *hld up in rr: rdn over 1f out: fin strly to snatch 2nd* **50/1**
346- **3** ½ **Verse Of Love**[25] 8445 5-8-1 **87**................................ JoeDoyle(7) 6 93
(David Evans) *led after 1f tl jst over 1f out: one pce* **20/1**
242- **4** hd **Hawkeyethenoo (IRE)**[37] 8334 8-9-10 **103**................ GrahamLee 5 108
(Jim Goldie) *stdd s: hld up in rr: hdwy and weaved through over 1f out: r.o wl fnl f* **11/4**[1]
33-5 **5** nk **George Guru**[6] 235 7-8-13 **92**.......................................... AdamKirby 12 96
(Michael Attwater) *hld up in rr: swtchd wd and rdn ent st: fin wl* **5/1**[3]
0-16 **6** ½ **Frontier Fighter**[11] 163 6-9-3 **96**............................. DanielTudhope 11 99
(David O'Meara) *prom: hrd rdn 1f out: no ex fnl f* **16/1**
60-3 **7** 1 ¼ **Afkar (IRE)**[5] 245 6-8-0 **79** oh10.................................... JimmyQuinn 8 79
(Clive Brittain) *chsd ldrs tl wknd 1f out* **66/1**
26-1 **8** nk **Forceful Appeal (USA)**[12] 153 6-8-6 **85** 6ex................ LukeMorris 13 84
(Simon Dow) *towards rr: rdn 2f out: nt trble ldrs* **20/1**
360- **9** nk **Burning Blaze**[176] 4922 4-8-9 **88**.................................. JamieSpencer 2 86
(Kevin Ryan) *dwlt: sn in tch on rail: rdn to chse ldrs over 1f out: wknd fnl f* **9/2**[2]
1-00 **10** ¾ **Naabegha**[6] 234 7-8-8 **87**................................................(p) LiamJones 4 83
(Alan McCabe) *s.i.s: plld hrd in midfield: rdn over 1f out: unable to chal* **16/1**
06-2 **11** ½ **Georgian Bay (IRE)**[21] 38 4-9-1 **94**.............................. JimCrowley 1 89
(K R Burke) *dwlt: mid-div on inner: rdn 2f out: no imp over 1f out* **5/1**[3]
034- **12** hd **Bravo Echo**[36] 8344 8-9-0 **93**.......................................... RobertHavlin 9 87
(Michael Attwater) *led 1f: chsd ldr after tl wknd jst over 1f out* **33/1**
05-5 **13** ¾ **Clockmaker (IRE)**[21] 38 8-8-13 **92**................................ LiamKeniry 10 84
(Conor Dore) *plld hrd: in tch on outer tl outpcd and btn 2f out* **33/1**
1m 22.09s (-2.71) **Going Correction** -0.075s/f (Stan) 13 Ran SP% **119.9**
Speed ratings (Par 109): **112,110,110,110,109 109,107,107,107,106 105,105,104**
CSF £374.09 CT £7494.43 TOTE £7.40: £2.40, £11.90, £8.30; EX 386.30 Trifecta £2605.00 Part won..
**Owner** R C Bond **Bred** R C Bond **Trained** Brawby, N Yorks

**FOCUS**
A very strong handicap for the track and they broke the course record. There were several strong finishers in the closing stages, but the bird had already flown. The form appears sound.

## 315 32RED CASINO H'CAP 5f 6y(P)
**3:40** (3:40) (Class 6) (0-65,64) 3-Y-O **£2,385** (£704; £352) **Stalls** High

Form RPR
4-23 **1** **The Dandy Yank (IRE)**[8] 195 3-9-7 **64**...................... WilliamCarson 7 69
(Jamie Osborne) *led 1f: pressed ldr after tl regained ld 1f out: drvn out* **10/1**
350- **2** ¾ **Saffire Song**[56] 8090 3-8-9 **55**.......................................... RobertTart(3) 10 57
(Alan Bailey) *prom on outer: drvn to chse wnr 1f out: r.o* **14/1**
06-1 **3** ½ **Global Explorer (USA)**[22] 15 3-9-4 **61**................(t) AdamBeschizza 8 61+
(Stuart Williams) *bhd: hdwy and hung lft over 1f out: fin wl* **11/4**[1]
2-23 **4** nk **Shamardyh (IRE)**[12] 149 3-9-6 **63**...................................[1] AdamKirby 5 62
(David Evans) *mid-div: rdn and hdwy over 1f out: r.o* **3/1**[2]
060- **5** hd **Wedgewood Estates**[57] 8083 3-8-10 **56**...................... MarkCoumbe(3) 4 54+
(Tony Carroll) *towards rr: rdn and hdwy over 1f out: r.o wl fnl f* **33/1**
54-4 **6** 1 ½ **Douneedahand**[15] 98 3-8-13 **63**................................ GaryMahon(7) 3 56
(Seamus Mullins) *prom tl no ex ins fnl f* **14/1**
40-5 **7** ¾ **Back On Baileys**[7] 216 3-8-9 **52**............................................ LiamJones 1 42
(Chris Dwyer) *led after 1f tl wknd 1f out* **25/1**
00-6 **8** hd **Loma Mor**[7] 216 3-8-12 **55**............................................. RobertWinston 9 45
(Alan McCabe) *rrd s and missed break: bhd tl sme late hdwy* **66/1**
6-21 **9** 1 ¼ **My My My Diliza**[7] 216 3-9-2 **59** 6ex..............................(b) GrahamLee 2 44
(J S Moore) *n.m.r early: in tch on rail: outpcd 2f out: sn btn* **9/2**[3]
524- **10** ¾ **Red House**[210] 3766 3-9-3 **60**.........................................(p) DavidProbert 6 42
(David C Griffiths) *in tch tl wknd wl over 1f out* **6/1**
59.05s (0.25) **Going Correction** -0.075s/f (Stan) 10 Ran SP% **114.8**
Speed ratings (Par 95): **95,93,93,92,92 89,88,88,86,85**
CSF £134.76 CT £413.09 TOTE £11.80: £3.10, £5.40, £1.60; EX 197.00 Trifecta £2121.90.
**Owner** Chris Watkins And David N Reynolds **Bred** Martyn J McEnery **Trained** Upper Lambourn, Berks

**FOCUS**
A run-of-the-mill heat and once again it paid to be close to the pace on the home turn. The winner is rated back to his earlier form.

## 316 32RED MAIDEN STKS 1m 2f (P)
**4:10** (4:11) (Class 5) 3-Y-O **£3,067** (£905; £453) **Stalls** Low

Form RPR
3-2 **1** **Anglo Irish**[20] 51 3-9-5 ............................................. NickyMackay 12 77+
(John Gosden) *chsd ldrs: rdn 3f out: bmpd over 2f out: str chal fnl f: drvn to ld nr fin* **6/5**[1]
00- **2** nk **Dynamic Ranger (USA)**[72] 7854 3-9-5 ................... AdamBeschizza 10 73
(Gary Moore) *in tch: led over 2f out and easily qcknd 2 l clr: hrd rdn fnl f: jst ct* **66/1**
**3** 2 **Miss Crystal (IRE)** 3-9-0 ................................................ JimCrowley 9 64
(Charles Hills) *plld hrd: hld up in midfield: gd hdwy on inner ent st: unable qck ins fnl f* **20/1**
34-2 **4** ¾ **Samtu (IRE)**[9] 190 3-9-5 67............................................... AdamKirby 2 69+
(Clive Brittain) *prom and gng wl tl rdn and outpcd 2f out: kpt on fnl f* **9/4**[2]
**5** 2 ¼ **Barye** 3-9-5 ................................................................... MartinLane 1 63+
(David Simcock) *mid-div: dropped to last and struggling 5f out: hdwy on inner over 1f out: styd on same pce* **20/1**
4 **6** nk **Dark Tsarina (IRE)**[20] 50 3-9-0 ................................ StevieDonohoe 6 57
(Tim Pitt) *in tch: effrt over 2f out: one pce appr fnl f* **33/1**
**7** hd **Mymatechris (IRE)** 3-9-5 .............................................. DavidProbert 7 62+
(Andrew Balding) *green and rdn early: bhd tl styd on fnl 2f: nvr nrr* **14/1**
04-6 **8** ½ **Blue Oyster**[18] 70 3-9-0 67.......................................... WilliamCarson 11 56
(Philip McBride) *bhd: rdn 2f out: sme late hdwy* **25/1**
265- **9** 1 ¼ **Officer Drivel (IRE)**[132] 6401 3-9-2 71........................ MarkCoumbe(3) 4 58+
(Luke Dace) *plld hrd: trckd ldr tl squeezed and bmpd over 2f out: lost pl and nt rcvr* **10/1**[3]
63- **10** 1 ¾ **Outback Warrior (IRE)**[42] 8266 3-9-5 ........................ DanielTudhope 8 55
(Kevin Ryan) *chsd ldrs tl wknd over 2f out* **12/1**
0- **11** nse **St Paul'S (IRE)**[36] 8346 3-9-5 .....................................(p) RobertHavlin 14 54?
(David C Griffiths) *led fr wdst stall: awkward on 1st bnd: hdd over 2f out: wknd over 1f out* **100/1**
06 **12** 1 ¾ **Intensive (IRE)**[9] 189 3-8-7 ........................................ JohnLawson(7) 5 46
(Jamie Osborne) *hld up towards rr: pushed along 2f out: n.d* **66/1**
60- **13** 2 ¼ **Swale Star**[37] 8328 3-8-7 ............................................... GaryMahon(7) 13 41
(Seamus Mullins) *mid-div on outer: bhd fnl 2f* **100/1**
0-0 **14** 4 **Zealand (IRE)**[20] 51 3-9-5 .................................................. LiamJones 3 38
(John Best) *a bhd* **100/1**
2m 7.56s (0.96) **Going Correction** -0.075s/f (Stan) 14 Ran SP% **121.9**
Speed ratings (Par 97): **93,92,91,90,88 88,88,87,86,85 85,84,82,79**
CSF £133.15 TOTE £2.30: £1.30, £12.60, £3.30; EX 83.30 Trifecta £598.40.
**Owner** George Strawbridge **Bred** George Strawbridge **Trained** Newmarket, Suffolk
■ Stewards' Enquiry : Adam Beschizza three-day ban: careless riding (Feb 7-9)

**FOCUS**
The betting suggested there wasn't much depth to this maiden and although he had to work very hard for his victory, the market-leader got the job done. Middling form, rated around the race averages and the winner.
T/Plt: £634.70 to a £1 stake. Pool: £80462.54 - 92.53 winning tickets T/Qpdt: £68.10 to a £1 stake. Pool: £7796.02 - 84.60 winning tickets LM

# 259 WOLVERHAMPTON (A.W) (L-H)
Friday, January 24

**OFFICIAL GOING: Standard**
Wind: medium, half behind Weather: light rain, heavy rain last 4 races

## 317 CORAL APP DOWNLOAD FROM THE APP STORE APPRENTICE H'CAP 1m 1f 103y(P)
**4:30** (4:34) (Class 6) (0-55,54) 4-Y-0+ **£2,264** (£673; £336; £168) **Stalls** Low

Form RPR
56-3 **1** **Kyle Of Bute**[21] 40 8-8-13 **49**.................................. JoshBaudains(3) 7 58
(Richard Ford) *chsd ldr: wnt clr w ldr 7f out: led and rdn 2f out: clr 1f out: kpt on and a doing enough fnl f: rdn out* **3/1**[1]
6-06 **2** ¾ **Bapak Pesta (IRE)**[10] 171 4-9-1 **52**..........................(p) KevinStott(3) 2 59
(Kevin Ryan) *hld up in midfield: clsd on inner 3f out: rdn and chsd clr wnr over 1f out: kpt on and steadily clsd fnl f* **10/1**
401- **3** 3 ½ **Do More Business (IRE)**[29] 8399 7-9-7 **54**.................(vt) PhilipPrince 9 54
(Liam Corcoran) *in tch in midfield: hdwy to chse clr ldng pair over 3f out: drvn and clsd over 2f out: 3rd and plugged on same pce fnl f* **6/1**[3]

26-4 **4** 3¾ **Cane Cat (IRE)**[15] 105 7-9-5 **52** (t) GeorgeDowning 11 44
(Tony Carroll) *hld up in midfield: effrt u.p 2f out: plugged on to go 4th wl ins fnl f: no ch w wnr* **8/1**

254- **5** 1 **Monsieur Pontaven**[94] 7455 7-9-5 **52** (b) ShaneGray 6 42
(Robin Bastiman) *stdd s: hld up in last trio: rdn and effrt on inner 2f out: kpt on fnl f: nvr trbld ldrs* **10/1**

604- **6** nk **Hispania (IRE)**[111] 7034 4-9-2 **53** EoinWalsh(3) 3 42
(John Mackie) *t.k.h: led: qcknd gallop and wnt clr w wnr 7f out: rdn and hdd 2f out: 4th and btn over 1f out: wknd fnl f* **8/1**

36-3 **7** 4½ **Quadriga (IRE)**[10] 171 4-9-0 **53** JoshQuinn(5) 10 33
(Robert Eddery) *stdd s: hld up in last trio: hung rt and wnt wd off bnd over 5f out: rdn and no hdwy over 2f out: sn wknd* **7/2**[2]

00-0 **8** 1½ **Edgware Road**[14] 117 6-9-6 **53** TimClark 12 30
(Paul Morgan) *styd wd and t.k.h early: hld up in midfield tl stdd bk to rr after 2f out: rdn over 3f out: wknd over 2f out* **25/1**

-130 **9** 2 **General Tufto**[10] 171 9-9-2 **54** (b) JackGarritty(5) 1 27
(Charles Smith) *t.k.h: chsd ldrs: rdn and lost pl over 2f out: wknd 2f out* **12/1**

06-0 **10** nse **Stamp Duty (IRE)**[21] 40 6-8-12 **45** JacobButterfield 5 18
(Suzzanne France) *in tch in midfield: rdn and lost pl over 2f out: wknd 2f out* **18/1**

2m 5.2s (3.50) **Going Correction** +0.30s/f (Slow)
**WFA** 4 from 5yo+ 1lb **10** Ran SP% **118.7**
Speed ratings (Par 101): **96,95,92,88,88 87,83,82,80,80**
CSF £34.63 CT £173.21 TOTE £3.70: £1.30, £3.10, £2.10; EX 40.00 Trifecta £138.00.
**Owner** J H Chrimes And Mr & Mrs G W Hannam **Bred** Chippenham Lodge Stud Ltd **Trained** Garstang, Lancs

**FOCUS**
A modest handicap run at a fair pace. It paid to race handy. The winner is rated back to his autumn form.

## 318 COMPARE BOOKMAKERS AT BOOKMAKERS.CO.UK CLAIMING STKS 5f 20y(P)
**5:00** (5:00) (Class 6) 4-Y-0+ **£2,264** (£673; £336; £168) **Stalls** Low

Form RPR

5-23 **1** **R Woody**[15] 93 7-8-11 **65** (e) ShaneKelly 1 72
(Robert Cowell) *chsd ldng pair: swtchd rt and effrt over 1f out: drvn to ld fnl 75yds: hld on cl home* **5/2**[1]

33-0 **2** shd **Electric Qatar**[22] 20 5-8-12 **69** (p) RichardKingscote 4 73
(Tom Dascombe) *taken down early: led but sn pestered: hdd over 3f out: styd upsides ldr tl rdn to ld jst over 1f out: hdd fnl 75yds: rallied gamely u.p towards fin* **11/4**[2]

01-1 **3** 1¾ **Shawkantango**[15] 93 7-8-10 **74** (v) AdamMcLean(7) 2 71
(Derek Shaw) *taken down early: awkward leaving stalls: sn outpcd in rr and rdn along: clsd on inner over 1f out: kpt on to go 3rd wl ins fnl f: nvr gng pce to rch ldrs* **3/1**[3]

0-06 **4** ½ **The Art Of Racing (IRE)**[10] 175 4-9-0 **77** (tp) SeanLevey 6 67
(Alan McCabe) *dwlt: sn reovered and upsides ldr: led over 3f out tl rdn and hdd jst over 1f out: no ex and btn fnl 100yds: wknd towards fin* **7/2**

250- **5** 3¼ **Amelia Jay**[55] 8118 4-8-3 **50** JoeFanning 3 44
(Danielle McCormick) *broke wl: sn stdd bk into 4th: rdn 2f out: wknd 1f out* **25/1**

1m 3.48s (1.18) **Going Correction** +0.30s/f (Slow) **5** Ran SP% **106.3**
Speed ratings (Par 101): **102,101,99,98,93**
CSF £8.93 TOTE £2.90: £1.50, £2.10; EX 9.00 Trifecta £19.70.R Woody was claimed by Mr George Baker for £6,000.
**Owner** Quintessential Thoroughbreds & Partner **Bred** R, D And M Close **Trained** Six Mile Bottom, Cambs
■ Stewards' Enquiry : Sean Levey 21-day ban. of which seven days will be deferred until Apr 21: used whip without giving gelding time to respond (5th suspension within 6mths) (Feb 7 - 21)

**FOCUS**
The pace was solid for this open sprint claimer. The form is rated a bit cautiously.

## 319 BET ON YOUR MOBILE WITH LADBROKES H'CAP 7f 32y(P)
**5:30** (5:32) (Class 6) (0-65,65) 4-Y-0+ **£2,264** (£673; £336; £168) **Stalls** High

Form RPR

00-1 **1** **Caramack**[12] 147 4-9-2 **65** EoinWalsh(5) 8 78+
(Richard Lee) *in tch in midfield but stuck wd: stdd and dropped in towards rr over 5f out: rdn and effrt wd over 1f out: r.o to ld and edgd lft fnl 75yds: r.o wl: comf* **7/2**[2]

50-0 **2** ¾ **Smalljohn**[22] 11 8-9-4 **65** (v) GeorgeChaloner(3) 9 76
(Bryan Smart) *w ldr tl led over 4f out: drvn 2f out: kpt on wl tl hdd and no ex fnl 75yds* **3/1**[1]

332- **3** 1½ **Severiano (USA)**[26] 8437 4-9-7 **65** JoeFanning 1 72
(Roger Varian) *t.k.h early: chsd ldrs: rdn to chse ldr over 1f out tl ins fnl f: no ex fnl 75yds: wknd towards fin* **7/2**[2]

34-5 **4** ¾ **Magical Rose (IRE)**[16] 84 4-9-5 **63** (p) SeanLevey 7 68
(Paul D'Arcy) *in tch in midfield: rdn and effrt to chse ldrs 2f out: keeping on same pce and btn whn carried sltly lft wl ins fnl f* **10/1**

1/14 **5** ½ **Blackthorn Stick (IRE)**[7] 219 5-9-3 **61** TomEaves 3 65
(John Butler) *taken down early: dwlt: sn in tch in midfield: hdwy u.p on inner over 1f out: kpt on same pce ins fnl f* **7/1**[3]

00-0 **6** 1½ **Lieutenant Dan (IRE)**[15] 96 7-9-5 **63** (v) AndrewMullen 4 63
(Michael Appleby) *chsd ldrs tl rdn to chse ldr 3f out tl over 1f out: no ex and btn whn pushed lft wl ins fnl f* **16/1**

5-46 **7** 3¾ **Sewn Up**[15] 102 4-9-6 **64** (v) ShaneKelly 11 53
(Andrew Hollinshead) *taken down early: dwlt: hld up in rr of main gp: nt clr run over 2f out: rdn and no hdwy over 1f out: wknd fnl f* **16/1**

05-0 **8** 7 **Baltic Prince (IRE)**[15] 95 4-8-13 **62** PhilipPrince(5) 2 32
(Paul Green) *led tl over 4f out: chsd ldr tl 3f out: drvn and lost pl over 2f out: bhd fnl f* **33/1**

06-0 **9** 2¾ **Crown Choice**[15] 102 9-9-2 **60** PJMcDonald 5 23
(Jedd O'Keeffe) *taken down early: hld up in tch in midfield: rdn and lost pl over 2f out: wknd 2f out* **20/1**

46-3 **10** 3 **McCool Bannanas**[18] 65 6-8-12 **61** TimClark(5) 6 16
(James Unett) *dwlt: sn in tch in midfield but stuck wd: rdn and lost pl over 2f out: wknd and bhd fnl f* **20/1**

520- **11** 2 **Clear Loch**[64] 7987 4-8-9 **53** (b[1]) ChrisCatlin 10
(John Spearing) *s.i.s: sn rdn and a outpcd in last: moved wd over 5f out: wl bhd fnl 3f* **50/1**

1m 31.02s (1.42) **Going Correction** +0.30s/f (Slow) **11** Ran SP% **117.2**
Speed ratings (Par 101): **103,102,100,99,99 97,93,85,81,78 76**
CSF £13.67 CT £39.76 TOTE £6.20: £2.00, £1.50, £1.30; EX 19.60 Trifecta £86.50.
**Owner** D E Edwards **Bred** Wellsummers Stud **Trained** Byton, H'fords

**FOCUS**
They went a decent gallop for this open handicap. The form is good for the grade.

## 320 LADBROKES CLASSIFIED CLAIMING STKS 1m 141y(P)
**6:00** (6:01) (Class 5) 4-Y-0+ **£2,911** (£866; £432; £216) **Stalls** Low

Form RPR

2-21 **1** **Prime Exhibit**[12] 152 9-8-8 **68** (t) ShaneKelly 5 77
(Daniel Mark Loughnane) *stdd s: hld up in rr: clsd on outer 3f out: chal and rdn jst over 1f out: edgd lft u.p but led fnl 100yds: styd on wl: in command and pushed out cl home* **6/5**[1]

41-6 **2** ¾ **Arabian Flight**[17] 75 5-8-3 **63** AndrewMullen 3 70
(Michael Appleby) *mounted on crse and taken down early: led: rdn ent fnl 2f: edgd lft u.p 1f out: hdd and styd on same pce fnl 100yds* **3/1**[2]

1-62 **3** 5 **Misleading Promise (IRE)**[8] 199 4-8-9 **67** (vt) TomEaves 7 66
(John Butler) *t.k.h: hld up in tch: clsd and chsd ldr jst over 2f out: rdn 2f out: 3rd and btn 1f out: wknd ins fnl f* **7/1**[3]

220- **4** 1 **Cantor**[35] 8360 6-8-5 **62** ow2 (t) RossAtkinson(3) 6 61
(Paul Morgan) *drvn early: hdwy to chse ldr after 1f: rdn and lost pl jst over 2f out: wknd u.p ent fnl f* **8/1**

4-05 **5** 2¾ **Ewell Place (IRE)**[15] 102 5-8-5 **65** (p) JoeFanning 4 52
(Patrick Morris) *hld up in tch: rdn and effrt on inner to chse ldrs 2f out: no ex and btn over 1f out: wknd fnl f* **7/1**[3]

030- **6** 21 **Hidden Talent**[87] 7608 4-8-11 **66** [1] FergusSweeney 2 11
(Steph Hollinshead) *chsd ldr for 1f: in tch in midfield after: lost pl u.p over 2f out: lost tch wl over 1f out: t.o* **50/1**

0/0- **7** 24 **Costa Del Fortune (IRE)**[39] 8308 5-8-6 **65** (p) FrankieMcDonald 1
(Paul Morgan) *t.k.h early: chsd ldrs tl drvn and dropped to rr 4f out: t.o fnl 2f* **66/1**

1m 52.77s (2.27) **Going Correction** +0.30s/f (Slow)
**WFA** 4 from 5yo+ 1lb **7** Ran SP% **110.0**
Speed ratings (Par 103): **101,100,95,95,92 73,52**
CSF £4.46 TOTE £1.70: £1.80, £1.70; EX 5.70 Trifecta £19.00.
**Owner** R M Brilley **Bred** Matthews Breeding And Racing Ltd **Trained** Baldwin's Gate, Staffs

**FOCUS**
A tight claimer with only 6lb covering the field run at a sound gallop. They came home at long intervals. The second sets the standard.

## 321 DOWNLOAD THE LADBROKES APP H'CAP 1m 141y(P)
**6:30** (6:30) (Class 7) (0-50,50) 4-Y-0+ **£1,940** (£577; £288; £144) **Stalls** Low

Form RPR

00-2 **1** **Benandonner (USA)**[12] 152 11-9-7 **50** ShaneKelly 2 60
(Mike Murphy) *chsd ldr: rdn over 2f out: styd on and grad clsd on ldr 1f out: led ins fnl f: sn in command and eased cl home* **7/4**[1]

00-3 **2** ½ **Compton Silver**[4] 263 4-9-4 **48** (b) LukeMorris 3 57
(Paul Fitzsimons) *racd keenly: led: rdn and 2 l clr 2f out: hrd drvn 1f out: hdd ins fnl f: no ex and sn btn* **11/4**[2]

000- **3** 4½ **Refuse Colette (IRE)**[109] 7083 5-9-2 **45** JoeFanning 10 44
(Paul Green) *hld up in last pair early: rdn and effrt over 2f out: styd on u.p fnl f to go 3rd towards fin: no threat to ldng pair* **25/1**

54-2 **4** ¾ **Aureolin Gulf**[22] 17 5-9-4 **47** ChrisCatlin 9 44
(Andrew Hollinshead) *t.k.h: hld up in 4th: rdn and effrt 2f out: chsd clr ldng pair over 1f out: no imp: wknd ins fnl f and lost 3rd towards fin* **7/2**[3]

0-00 **5** 2½ **Ellies Image**[4] 263 7-8-11 **45** JoshBaudains(5) 6 36
(Richard Ford) *hld up in last pair: pushed along and short-lived effrt over 2f out: no hdwy 2f out: wknd over 1f out* **33/1**

60-0 **6** 3¾ **Hold The Star**[17] 77 8-8-11 **45** AnnStokell(5) 7 27
(Ann Stokell) *in tch in midfield: hdwy to chse ldng pair over 3f out: rdn and outpcd 2f out: wknd over 1f out* **50/1**

400- **7** shd **Troy Boy**[115] 6919 4-8-12 **45** NeilFarley(3) 12 27
(Robin Bastiman) *hld up in tch towards rr: hdwy over 3f out: rdn and no hdwy over 2f out wknd 2f out* **14/1**

500/ **8** 7 **Italian Lady (USA)**[442] 7643 5-9-2 **50** JacobButterfield(5) 8 16
(Ollie Pears) *sn rdn along in midfield: dropped to rr 4f out: wl bhd fnl 2f* **8/1**

00/0 **9** 1½ **Sir Lexington (IRE)**[4] 263 5-8-9 **45** DanielCremin(7) 4 8
(Brian Forsey) *sn bustled along: chsd ldrs: reminders over 6f out: lost pl u.p 3f out: bhd over 1f out* **50/1**

000- **10** 1½ **Gifted Heir (IRE)**[55] 8116 10-8-11 **45** EoinWalsh(5) 11 4
(Ray Peacock) *hld up in tch in midfield: rdn and btn over 2f out: sn wknd: bhd fnl f* **40/1**

1m 53.0s (2.50) **Going Correction** +0.30s/f (Slow)
**WFA** 4 from 5yo+ 1lb **10** Ran SP% **116.2**
Speed ratings (Par 97): **100,99,95,94,92 89,89,83,81,80**
CSF £6.29 CT £83.56 TOTE £2.80: £1.40, £1.40, £4.80; EX 6.00.
**Owner** M Murphy **Bred** Gainsborough Farm Llc **Trained** Westoning, Beds

**FOCUS**
They went a messy pace for this weak handicap. The winner is rated to his latest form.

## 322 32RED H'CAP 2m 119y(P)
**7:00** (7:00) (Class 4) (0-85,84) 4-Y-0+ **£5,175** (£1,540; £769; £384) **Stalls** Low

Form RPR

030- **1** **Hunting Ground (USA)**[104] 7211 4-9-7 **84** JoeFanning 5 101+
(Mark Johnston) *chsd ldr tl led 4f out: readily wnt clr over 2f out: in n.d fnl 2f: eased towards fin: v easily* **5/6**[1]

3-11 **2** 8 **Flash Crash**[15] 104 5-8-11 **74** (tp) LouisSteward(7) 3 79
(Anthony Carson) *in tch in midfield: rdn to chse wnr 3f out: outpcd and btn 2f out: wl hld but plugged on to hold 2nd fnl f* **5/2**[2]

3-43 **3** 2¼ **Layline (IRE)**[9] 182 7-9-8 **78** LukeMorris 7 80
(Gay Kelleway) *stdd s: hld up in rr: hdwy into midfield 7f out: 3rd and drvn over 2f out: sn outpcd and btn: wl hld but plugged on fnl f* **15/2**[3]

3 **4** 1½ **Old Way (IRE)**[4] 260 8-8-10 **66** PJMcDonald 1 67
(Venetia Williams) *chsd ldrs tl drvn and outpcd over 3f out: wnt 4th but no ch w wnr 2f out: plugged on* **20/1**

465- **5** 6 **Murcar**[60] 8041 9-9-2 **77** (b) PhilipPrince(5) 2 70
(Liam Corcoran) *s.i.s: in tch towards rr: rdn and struggling 4f out: sn outpcd and btn 3f out: sn wknd* **16/1**

045/ **6** 19 **Good Of Luck**[42] 5442 5-9-0 **70** LiamKeniry 6 41
(Warren Greatrex) *led tl 4f out: sn drvn: lost pl and btn over 2f out: sn wknd: t.o fnl f* **25/1**

**7** 77 **Darroun (IRE)**[48] 3359 6-9-12 **82** ChrisCatlin 4
(Shaun Lycett) *dwlt: in tch in rr: rdn and dropped to last 8f out: lost tch 5f out: wl t.o fnl 3f* **66/1**

3m 43.54s (1.74) **Going Correction** +0.30s/f (Slow)
**WFA** 4 from 5yo+ 7lb **7** Ran SP% **110.9**
Speed ratings (Par 105): **107,103,102,101,98 89,53**
CSF £2.76 TOTE £2.00: £1.30, £1.30; EX 3.40 Trifecta £10.50.

**Owner** Sheikh Hamdan bin Mohammed Al Maktoum **Bred** Darley **Trained** Middleham Moor, N Yorks
■ Stewards' Enquiry : Joe Fanning caution: careless riding.
**FOCUS**
A fair staying handicap run at a stop/start gallop and turned into a procession by the heavily backed favourite. The form is taken at face value around the second and third.

## 323 32RED.COM MAIDEN FILLIES' STKS 1m 141y(P)
7:30 (7:31) (Class 5) 3-Y-O+ £2,911 (£866; £432; £216) Stalls Low

Form RPR
22- 1 **Fashion Line (IRE)**$^{221}$ [3398] 4-9-12 0............................ JamieSpencer 7 82
(Michael Bell) *t.k.h: hld up wl in tch in midfield: trckd ldng pair over 2f out: upsides ldr gng best over 1f out: led and pushed clr jst ins fnl f: easily* 13/8$^{1}$
24/ 2 2¾ **Nasijah**$^{478}$ [6791] 4-9-12 0............................ GrahamLee 3 76
(James Tate) *t.k.h: led and set stdy gallop tl hdd over 5f out: rdn to ld again wl over 1f out: hdd and brushed aside by wnr jst ins fnl f: kpt on* 9/4$^{2}$
3 ¾ **Rohesia** 3-8-5 0............................ LukeMorris 4 69
(Sir Mark Prescott Bt) *wl in tch in midfield: rdn over 3f out: 4th and rn green over 1f out: wnt 3rd and kpt on steadily ins fnl f: no threat to wnr* 8/1$^{3}$
226- 4 4½ **Marble Statuette (USA)**$^{25}$ [8444] 4-9-12 69............................ LeeTopliss 6 64
(Richard Fahey) *chsd ldr tl led over 5f out: hdd and rdn wl over 1f out: 3rd and btn 1f out: wknd ins fnl f* 20/1
5 2¼ **Rose Kazan (IRE)** 3-8-5 0............................ JoeFanning 1 53
(Marco Botti) *s.i.s: in tch in rr: rdn 3f out: sn outpcd and wl hld 2f out: plugged on fnl f* 8/1$^{3}$
05- 6 nk **Al Shoogh**$^{49}$ [8175] 3-8-5 0............................ ChrisCatlin 2 53
(David Simcock) *chsd ldrs: rdn over 2f out: outpcd and btn 5th over 1f out: wknd fnl f* 10/1
2- 7 1½ **Wildcat Lass (USA)**$^{35}$ [8362] 3-8-2 0............................ JulieBurke$^{(3)}$ 8 49
(David O'Meara) *wl in tch in midfield: rdn and lost pl over 3f out: outpcd and wknd 2f out* 10/1
8 1 **Mary's Prayer** 3-8-0 0............................ TimClark$^{(5)}$ 5 47?
(John Holt) *s.i.s: rn green in rr: rdn and outpcd over 2f out: sn wknd and bhd fnl f* 80/1

1m 53.18s (2.68) **Going Correction** +0.30s/f (Slow)
**WFA** 3 from 4yo 22lb 8 Ran SP% **115.3**
Speed ratings (Par 100): **100,97,96,92,90 90,89,88**
CSF £5.44 TOTE £1.50: £1.10, £1.60, £2.40; EX 5.80 Trifecta £22.10.
**Owner** Sheikh Marwan Al Maktoum **Bred** Darley **Trained** Newmarket, Suffolk
**FOCUS**
Not a bad fillies' maiden run at a steady pace.
T/Plt: £8.30 to a £1 stake. Pool: £100811.31 - 8850.44 winning tickets T/Qpdt: £2.30 to a £1 stake. Pool: £10758.67 - 3329.37 winning tickets SP

324 - 337a (Foreign Racing) - See Raceform Interactive

# 310 LINGFIELD (L-H)
Saturday, January 25

**OFFICIAL GOING: Standard**
Wind: light, half behind Weather: dry

## 338 32RED H'CAP 6f 1y(P)
12:15 (12:15) (Class 5) (0-70,70) 3-Y-O £3,067 (£905; £453) Stalls Low

Form RPR
103- 1 **Tautira (IRE)**$^{46}$ [8228] 3-8-11 67............................ LouisSteward$^{(7)}$ 7 70
(Michael Bell) *wl in tch in midfield: rdn and effrt to chal over 1f out: drvn to ld jst ins fnl f: hld on gamely: all out* 12/1
31-4 2 ½ **Three Pips**$^{13}$ [149] 3-9-5 68............................ ChrisCatlin 6 69
(Ed McMahon) *t.k.h: led: hung rt bnd wl over 1f out: hrd pressed and drvn over 1f out: hdd jst ins fnl f: kpt on wl but no ex towards fin* 8/1
461- 3 hd **Dazza**$^{96}$ [7426] 3-9-7 70............................ GeorgeBaker 4 71
(Gary Moore) *chsd ldr for 2f: styd chsng ldrs: rdn and ev ch over 1f out: kpt on wl but unable qck cl home* 12/1
052- 4 shd **Drinkuptrig (IRE)**$^{66}$ [7973] 3-9-1 64............................(t) SeanLevey 10 64
(Stuart Williams) *wl in tch in midfield: rdn and effrt 2f out: swtchd lft 1f out: kpt on wl u.p fnl 100yds: nt quite rch ldrs* 6/4$^{1}$
030- 5 hd **Alfie Lunete (IRE)**$^{49}$ [8203] 3-9-2 65............................ LiamJones 9 65
(J S Moore) *in tch in last trio: rdn and effrt towards inner over 1f out: styd on wl ins fnl f: nt quite rch ldrs* 16/1
32-2 6 hd **Little Big Man**$^{24}$ [6] 3-9-7 70............................(b) FrankieDettori 8 69
(Sylvester Kirk) *chsd ldrs tl wnt 2nd 4f out: ev ch and carried rt bnd wl over 1f out: kpt on same pce ins fnl f* 6/1$^{3}$
06-0 7 1 **Mighty Force (IRE)**$^{10}$ [187] 3-8-11 60............................(b$^{1}$) LukeMorris 2 56
(Nick Littmoden) *in tch in last trio: rdn and effrt to chse ldrs on inner over 1f out: no ex ins fnl f: wknd towards fin* 20/1
065- 8 9 **Exceed And Exceed**$^{54}$ [8126] 3-8-13 62............................ JamieSpencer 5 29
(George Margarson) *stdd s: hld up in last: pushed along and clsd 4f out: rdn and no hdwy over 1f out: sn wknd* 4/1$^{2}$

1m 11.8s (-0.10) **Going Correction** -0.125s/f (Stan) 8 Ran SP% **111.4**
Speed ratings (Par 97): **95,94,94,93,93 93,92,80**
CSF £97.48 CT £1153.32 TOTE £18.70: £4.10, £3.70, £3.50; EX 108.30 Trifecta £1217.80.
**Owner** Sheikh Marwan Al Maktoum **Bred** Darley **Trained** Newmarket, Suffolk
**FOCUS**
An ordinary 3yo sprint handicap and, with the front six finishing in a heap, the form may not amount to much. It makes sense though.

## 339 COMPARE BOOKMAKERS AT BOOKMAKERS.CO.UK SPRINT SERIES ROUND 4 H'CAP (QUALIFIER) (DIV I) 6f 1y(P)
12:50 (12:52) (Class 6) (0-65,65) 4-Y-O+ £3,408 (£1,006; £503) Stalls Low

Form RPR
240- 1 **Putin (IRE)**$^{42}$ [8295] 6-9-0 58............................(bt) PaddyAspell 6 68
(Phil McEntee) *mde all: drvn and wnt clr over 1f out: styd on wl fnl f: rdn out* 5/1$^{2}$
01-3 2 1½ **Pharoh Jake**$^{15}$ [114] 6-8-12 63............................ RyanWhile$^{(7)}$ 7 68
(John Bridger) *hld up in midfield: effrt u.p to chse ldng pair 1f out: kpt on wl u.p to snatch 2nd on post: no threat to wnr* 8/1$^{3}$
03-1 3 nse **Chevise (IRE)**$^{21}$ [53] 6-9-3 61............................(b) LukeMorris 8 66
(Steve Woodman) *chsd ldrs: rdn to chse clr wnr over 1f out: kpt on but no imp fnl f: lost 2nd on post* 8/1$^{3}$
411- 4 2¾ **Foie Gras**$^{37}$ [8338] 4-8-11 60............................ ShelleyBirkett$^{(5)}$ 4 56
(Chris Dwyer) *racd in midfield: hmpd bnd after 1f: rdn and effrt over 1f out: kpt on fnl f: no threat to wnr* 5/1$^{2}$
00-5 5 shd **Catalinas Diamond (IRE)**$^{10}$ [192] 6-9-0 58............................(t) FergusSweeney 5 54
(Pat Murphy) *hld up in last trio: rdn and effrt wdst bnd 2f out: kpt on fnl f: nvr trbld ldrs* 10/1
-145 6 ½ **Dark Lane**$^{8}$ [208] 8-9-6 64............................ AdamKirby 9 58
(David Evans) *broke fast and bustled up to press ldr: rdn and unable qck over 1f out: 4th and btn 1f out: wknd ins fnl f* 4/1$^{1}$
0-02 7 nk **Daneside (IRE)**$^{10}$ [192] 7-8-2 53 oh4 ow2............................ GeorgeBuckell$^{(7)}$ 3 46
(P J O'Gorman) *hld up off the pce in last trio: effrt on inner over 1f out: styd on but nvr any threat to ldrs* 16/1
100- 8 1½ **Artful Lady (IRE)**$^{99}$ [7347] 5-9-1 62............................ RyanPowell$^{(3)}$ 1 51
(George Margarson) *dwlt: sn outpcd in rr: rdn 1/2-way: kpt on fnl f but n.d* 25/1
40-4 9 nk **Homeboy (IRE)**$^{8}$ [208] 6-8-11 55............................ ChrisCatlin 2 43
(David Evans) *chsd ldrs: rdn and struggling 2f out: drvn and btn over 1f out: wknd fnl f* 8/1$^{3}$

1m 10.65s (-1.25) **Going Correction** -0.125s/f (Stan) 9 Ran SP% **105.5**
Speed ratings (Par 101): **103,101,100,97,97 96,96,94,93**
CSF £36.79 CT £229.39 TOTE £5.70: £2.40, £2.90, £1.60; EX 44.50 Trifecta £657.20.
**Owner** Steve Jakes **Bred** D Llewelyn & J Runeckles **Trained** Newmarket, Suffolk
■ Sister Guru was withdrawn. Price at time of withdrawal 8-1. Rule 4 applies to all bets - deduction of 10p in the pound all bets.
**FOCUS**
The latest qualifier of the series, but it took place without last year's winner Sister Guru, who refused to enter the stalls despite being given special dispensation to be reversed into them. The pace looked strong and the form is sound.

## 340 COMPARE BOOKMAKERS AT BOOKMAKERS.CO.UK SPRINT SERIES ROUND 4 H'CAP (QUALIFIER) (DIV II) 6f 1y(P)
1:25 (1:25) (Class 6) (0-65,65) 4-Y-O+ £3,408 (£1,006; £503) Stalls Low

Form RPR
32-1 1 **Random Success (IRE)**$^{15}$ [114] 4-9-5 63............................ GeorgeBaker 2 79+
(Roger Charlton) *stdd s: t.k.h: hld up in tch in last quartet: smooth hdwy on inner over 1f out: led fnl 100yds: r.o wl: eased cl home: easily* 1/1$^{1}$
00-0 2 1¾ **Waterloo Dock**$^{10}$ [192] 9-8-7 51 oh2............................(v) LukeMorris 7 58
(Mick Quinn) *led: drvn over 1f out: hdd fnl 100yds: sn brushed aside by wnr but hld on for 2nd* 66/1
013- 3 ¾ **Clock Opera (IRE)**$^{47}$ [8220] 4-8-12 63............................ LouisSteward$^{(7)}$ 4 68
(William Stone) *t.k.h: chsd ldr: rdn and unable qck over 1f out: 3rd and styd on same pce ins fnl f* 6/1$^{3}$
31-6 4 ½ **Presumido (IRE)**$^{21}$ [53] 4-9-7 65............................ JamieSpencer 8 68
(Simon Dow) *stdd s: hld up in last pair: rdn and hdwy on inner 1f out: r.o u.p ins fnl f: no threat to wnr* 3/1$^{2}$
2156 5 ½ **Minimee**$^{3}$ [288] 4-9-0 58............................(v) PaddyAspell 3 59
(Phil McEntee) *in tch in midfield: effrt u.p over 1f out: kpt on same pce u.p ins fnl f* 16/1
6-50 6 nse **One Way Or Another (AUS)**$^{14}$ [141] 11-9-4 62............................(t) AdamKirby 6 63
(David Evans) *stdd s: hld up in last trio: hdwy ent fnl f: rdn and styd on fnl 150yds: nvr trbld ldrs* 8/1
56-4 7 ½ **Idle Curiosity (IRE)**$^{21}$ [53] 4-9-1 59............................ StephenCraine 1 59
(Jim Boyle) *chsd ldrs: rdn and unable qck over 1f out: outpcd and btn 1f out: kpt on same pce after* 25/1
00-0 8 nk **Dear Maurice**$^{3}$ [288] 10-9-2 60............................(t) MartinLane 5 59
(Tobias B P Coles) *racd in last quartet: rdn and reminder over 4f out: no imp tl styd on ins fnl f: swtchd rt fnl 50yds: nvr trbld ldrs* 25/1
0-05 9 2 **Johnny Splash (IRE)**$^{1}$ [313] 5-8-11 55............................(v) RobertWinston 9 47
(Roger Teal) *in tch in midfield: rdn and unable qck bnd 2f out: outpcd over 1f out: wknd ins fnl f* 25/1

1m 11.17s (-0.73) **Going Correction** -0.125s/f (Stan) 9 Ran SP% **119.3**
Speed ratings (Par 101): **99,96,95,95,94 94,93,93,90**
CSF £114.53 CT £310.73 TOTE £1.90: £1.10, £5.90, £2.00; EX 72.10 Trifecta £655.20.
**Owner** Beckhampton 2 **Bred** M Smith & Grennanstown Stud **Trained** Beckhampton, Wilts
**FOCUS**
The winning time was just over half a second slower than the first division. The winner is progressing well.

## 341 DOWNLOAD THE LADBROKES APP MAIDEN STKS 1m 1y(P)
2:00 (2:01) (Class 5) 3-Y-O+ £3,067 (£905; £453) Stalls High

Form RPR
0-2 1 **Secret Pursuit (IRE)**$^{15}$ [119] 3-7-9 0............................ JoeDoyle$^{(7)}$ 9 74+
(Marcus Tregoning) *hld up in tch in midfield: hdwy to chse ldrs and rdn 2f out: chsd wnr 1f out: r.o wl to ld fnl 75yds: gng away at fin* 7/1
02-3 2 2 **Clear Spell (IRE)**$^{15}$ [119] 3-8-7 75............................ RobertHavlin 2 73
(Ed Walker) *led: rdn 2f out: forged clr 1f out: drvn and hdd fnl 75yds: sn outpcd but kpt on for clr 2nd* 4/1$^{3}$
3 2 **Dubawi Light** 3-8-7 0............................ LukeMorris 6 68+
(James Tate) *chsd ldr: rdn: rn green and hung lft over 1f out: 3rd and unable qck 1f out: outpcd but hld on for 3rd fnl f* 11/4$^{2}$
5 4 nk **Zamra (IRE)**$^{15}$ [127] 3-8-2 0............................ JimmyQuinn 10 63
(James Tate) *in tch towards rr: rdn and hdwy jst over 2f out: no imp over 1f out: rallied and kpt on fnl 100yds* 10/1
5 ¾ **Late Night Mark (IRE)** 3-8-8 0 ow1............................ JamieSpencer 11 67+
(Charles Hills) *dwlt and niggled along early: effrt and rn green bnd 2f out: 5th and stl plenty to do 1f out: kpt on but nvr trbld ldrs* 9/4$^{1}$
6 6 **No Refund (IRE)** 3-8-7 0............................ MartinLane 4 52+
(David Simcock) *dwlt: sn rcvrd and in tch in midfield: rdn and unable qck 2f out: outpcd and btn over 1f out: wknd fnl f* 8/1
0 7 2¾ **Marmande (IRE)**$^{19}$ [70] 3-8-2 0............................ KieranO'Neill 3 41
(Daniel Kubler) *chsd ldrs: hmpd bnd 5f out and rdn briefly over 4f out: rdn and unable qck ent fnl 2f: wknd over 1f out* 66/1
8 3¼ **Beggers Luck** 4-9-3 0............................ JoeyHaynes$^{(5)}$ 5 38
(Eric Wheeler) *hld up in tch in last quartet: rdn and struggling over 2f out: bhd 2f out: sn wknd* 100/1
0- 9 1¾ **Haaffa Sovereign**$^{25}$ [8451] 3-8-4 0............................ RyanPowell$^{(3)}$ 1 34
(George Margarson) *chsd ldrs: hmpd bnd 5f out: rdn and struggling ent fnl 2f: sn btn and wknd over 1f out* 100/1
10 17 **Madrinas Prince (IRE)** 5-9-6 0............................ RyanWhile$^{(7)}$ 8
(Paddy Butler) *s.i.s and rn green leaving stalls: a last: clsd and in tch 1/2-way: wknd 3f out: t.o* 100/1

1m 37.04s (-1.16) **Going Correction** -0.125s/f (Stan)
**WFA** 3 from 4yo+ 20lb 10 Ran SP% **114.6**
Speed ratings (Par 103): **100,98,96,95,94 88,86,82,81,64**
CSF £34.61 TOTE £7.30: £2.30, £1.70, £1.60; EX 18.20 Trifecta £130.20.
**Owner** Guy Brook **Bred** Petra Bloodstock Agency Ltd **Trained** Whitsbury, Hants

**FOCUS**
The pair with previous form on the board had looked vulnerable in this maiden, so the fact they filled the first two places suggests this wasn't a strong race. It's rated around the runner-up.

## 342 LADBROKES H'CAP 1m 1y(P)
2:35 (2:36) (Class 4) (0-85,85) 4-Y-O+ £4,690 (£1,395; £697; £348) Stalls High

Form RPR

60-3 **1** **Rebellious Guest**[5] 256 5-9-2 **80** JamieSpencer 5 90
(George Margarson) *stdd s: hld up in last trio: hdwy ent fnl 2f: rdn to chse ldr jst over 1f out: r.o wl to ld ins fnl f: sn clr: readily* **3/1**[1]

364- **2** *2 ¼* **Emkanaat**[25] 8455 6-9-1 **79** (b) GeorgeBaker 1 84
(Amy Weaver) *stdd s: hld up in last trio: rdn and effrt over 1f out: r.o wl ins fnl f to snatch 2nd last stride: no threat to wnr* **8/1**

51-0 **3** *shd* **Canadian Run (IRE)**[21] 56 4-8-12 **83** GeorgeBuckell(7) 3 88
(Robert Mills) *led: rdn ent fnl 2f: hdd ins fnl f: sn brushed aside by wnr and one pce after: lost 2nd last stride* **5/1**[3]

033- **4** *1* **Veeraya**[26] 8445 4-9-7 **85** (p) AdamBeschizza 2 87
(Julia Feilden) *in tch in midfield: rdn and effrt to chse ldrs on inner wl over 1f out: no ex 1f out: one pce after* **9/2**[2]

200- **5** *2* **Patriotic (IRE)**[139] 6236 6-9-2 **80** (p) LukeMorris 6 78
(Chris Dwyer) *t.k.h: chsd ldrs: rdn to chse ldr ent fnl 2f: lost pl and btn ent fnl f: wknd fnl 150yds* **16/1**

006- **6** *2 ¾* **Lionheart**[124] 6692 4-9-3 **81** ShaneKelly 7 73
(Peter Crate) *stdd s: hld up in rr: rdn and effrt over 1f out: no imp: nvr trbld ldrs* **33/1**

55-4 **7** *nk* **First Post (IRE)**[20] 61 7-9-2 **80** AdamKirby 8 71
(Derek Haydn Jones) *chsd ldr tl ent fnl 2f: sn outpcd and btn: wknd fnl f* **10/1**

461- **8** *5* **The Tichborne (IRE)**[25] 8453 6-9-0 **78** (v) RobertWinston 4 62
(Roger Teal) *in tch in midfield: effrt u.p on outer bnd 2f: btn over 1f out: wknd 1f out: bhd and eased towards fin* **3/1**[1]

1m 36.32s (-1.88) **Going Correction** -0.125s/f (Stan) **8 Ran SP% 113.9**
Speed ratings (Par 105): **104,101,101,100,98 95,95,90**
CSF £27.68 CT £116.47 TOTE £4.80: £1.40, £1.80, £2.60; EX 23.90 Trifecta £140.20.
**Owner** John Guest Racing **Bred** Equity Bloodstock & Newsells Park Stud **Trained** Newmarket, Suffolk
**FOCUS**
A fair handicap, but the early pace didn't look that strong. The winner may build again on this form.

## 343 CORAL MOBILE "JUST THREE CLICKS TO BET" MAIDEN STKS 1m 4f (P)
3:10 (3:11) (Class 5) 4-Y-O+ £3,067 (£905; £453) Stalls Low

Form RPR

050- **1** **Gentlemax (FR)**[26] 8443 4-9-5 62 StephenCraine 1 69
(Jim Boyle) *chsd ldrs: rdn and outpcd 3f out: drvn and rallied 2f out: chal ins fnl f: kpt on wl to ld cl home* **25/1**

/5-2 **2** *hd* **After The Storm**[15] 115 5-9-9 65 FrankieDettori 7 69
(John O'Shea) *chsd ldr: upsides ldr 8f out: rdn 3f out: drvn and ld ins fnl f: kpt on tl hdd and no ex cl home* **5/4**[1]

30/ **3** *1 ¾* **Rocky Elsom (USA)**[39] 119 7-9-9 63 JimCrowley 3 66
(David Arbuthnot) *led: rdn ent fnl 2f: drvn over 1f out: hdd ins fnl f: no ex and btn fnl 100yds: wknd towards fin* **7/1**[2]

**4** *5* **Ceevee**[34] 4-9-5 0 (t) DavidProbert 6 58
(Tim Vaughan) *chsd ldrs: rdn and outpcd 3f out: last and no imp 2f out: plugged on same pce and hld after* **16/1**[3]

/4 **5** *2 ¾* **Against The Tide (IRE)**[10] 189 4-9-0 0 SeanLevey 4 51
(Richard Hannon) *stdd s: t.k.h: hld up in tch in rr: rdn and effrt 3f out: sn outpcd: 4th and wl hld over 1f out: wl btn and eased wl ins fnl f: b.b.v* **5/4**[1]

2m 32.27s (-0.73) **Going Correction** -0.125s/f (Stan)
**WFA** 4 from 5yo+ 4lb **5 Ran SP% 111.1**
Speed ratings (Par 103): **97,96,95,92,90**
CSF £58.11 TOTE £22.00: £7.10, £1.10; EX 73.60 Trifecta £261.30.
**Owner** Allen B Pope **Bred** Bernard Leclere & Mme Raymonde Leclere **Trained** Epsom, Surrey
■ Stewards' Enquiry : Stephen Craine four-day ban: used whip above permitted level (Feb 8-11)
**FOCUS**
A weak older-horse maiden, especially with the favourite running so poorly, but the first three were officially rated within 3lb of each other so appeared to run close to their marks.

## 344 CORAL.CO.UK H'CAP 1m 2f (P)
3:45 (3:56) (Class 2) (0-100,100) 4-Y-O+ £12,291 (£3,657; £1,827; £913) Stalls Low

Form RPR

06-6 **1** **Robin Hoods Bay**[14] 144 6-9-7 **100** LukeMorris 4 109
(Ed Vaughan) *hld up in midfield: switchng out rt and effrt 2f out: drvn and hdwy to chal ins fnl f: pushed rt and bmpd towards fin: r.o wl to ld cl home* **4/1**[2]

012- **2** *hd* **Captain Cat (IRE)**[44] 8263 5-9-4 **97** GeorgeBaker 2 105
(Roger Charlton) *hld up in tch in midfield: n.m.r jst over 2f out: rdn and hdwy to chse ldr jst over 1f out: drvn and styd on to ld fnl 50yds: hung rt and bmpd wnr towards fin: hdd cl home* **11/10**[1]

55-2 **3** *¾* **Tinshu (IRE)**[14] 145 8-9-1 **94** (p) AdamKirby 11 100
(Derek Haydn Jones) *chsd ldng trio: rdn to ld over 1f out: drvn and hdd fnl 50yds: no ex* **8/1**[3]

10-6 **4** *½* **Shavansky**[21] 54 10-8-3 **87** ShelleyBirkett(5) 3 92
(Rod Millman) *hld up in tch in last trio: n.m.r and swtchd rt wl over 1f out: rdn and hdwy over 1f out: r.o wl ins fnl f: nt rch ldrs* **8/1**[3]

36-0 **5** *½* **Strictly Silver (IRE)**[7] 235 5-9-7 **100** (p) RobertWinston 8 104
(Alan Bailey) *in tch in midfield: effrt u.p 2f out: no imp over 1f out: styd on u.p fnl 100yds: nvr gng pce to chal* **10/1**

401- **6** *¾* **Stepping Ahead (FR)**[92] 7497 4-9-1 **96** DanielTudhope 6 99
(K R Burke) *chsd ldrs: effrt u.p on inner wl over 1f out: no ex 1f out: styd on same pce fnl f* **12/1**

22-0 **7** *nk* **Loyalty**[7] 235 7-8-4 **90** (v) AdamMcLean(7) 9 92
(Derek Shaw) *hld up in last trio: rdn and effrt over 1f out: kpt on ins fnl f: nvr gng pce to chal* **25/1**

206- **8** *shd* **Lowther**[35] 8387 9-8-4 **90** (v) LouisSteward(7) 5 92
(Lee Carter) *rdr v slow removing hood and slowly away: bhd: swtchd lft and hdwy u.p over 1f out: kpt on same pce fnl 100yds* **20/1**

162- **9** *4 ½* **Stevie Thunder**[52] 8150 9-8-4 **86** oh5 (v) MichaelJMMurphy(3) 7 79
(Ian Williams) *chsd ldr: rdn over 3f out: lost 2nd over 1f out and sn btn: wknd fnl f* **50/1**

10-0 **10** *3 ½* **Halfsin (IRE)**[21] 54 6-8-8 **87** (tp) JamieSpencer 1 73
(Marco Botti) *led: reminder 4f out: drvn and 3 l clr 3f out: drvn and hdd over 1f out: sn btn: fdd ins fnl f* **25/1**

2m 1.73s (-4.87) **Going Correction** -0.125s/f (Stan)
**WFA** 4 from 5yo+ 2lb **10 Ran SP% 121.0**
Speed ratings (Par 109): **114,113,113,112,112 111,111,111,107,105**
CSF £8.75 CT £34.81 TOTE £5.30: £1.50, £1.30, £2.30; EX 12.40 Trifecta £65.00.
**Owner** A M Pickering **Bred** Palm Tree Thoroughbreds **Trained** Newmarket, Suffolk
**FOCUS**
They went a good pace in this hot handicap and it may be no coincidence that the pair who filled the first two places early ultimately ended up last and last-but-one. The third is a fair guide.

## 345 CORAL.CO.UK BEST ODDS GUARANTEED ON RACING H'CAP 1m 2f (P)
4:20 (4:22) (Class 5) (0-70,70) 4-Y-O+ £3,067 (£905; £453) Stalls Low

Form RPR

3-20 **1** **Keene**[6] 250 4-8-10 **68** LouisSteward(7) 1 79
(Philip McBride) *sn pushed into ld: hdd 5f out: rdn to ld again over 2f out and kicked clr 2f out: kpt on wl fnl f: rdn out* **9/2**[2]

2-05 **2** *1 ¼* **Lady Lunchalot (USA)**[14] 146 4-9-4 **69** (p) LiamJones 2 78
(Laura Mongan) *wl in tch in midfield: n.m.r over 2f out: rdn to chse ldrs wl over 1f out: sn chsng clr ldr: kpt on and steadily clsd tl no imp fnl 50yds* **10/1**

60-1 **3** *3 ¼* **Night's Watch**[15] 116 4-8-7 **58** RobertHavlin 11 60+
(William Jarvis) *stdd and dropped in bhd after s: hld up in tch towards rr: nt clr run over 2f out: rdn and hdwy but stl plenty to do over 1f out: wnt 3rd ins fnl f: no real imp* **7/4**[1]

30-6 **4** *nk* **Zaeem**[10] 181 5-9-4 **67** AdamKirby 8 68+
(Dean Ivory) *s.i.s: hld up in tch in rr: bhd and nt clr run over 2f out: hdwy but stl plenty to do over 1f out: styd on: nvr trbld ldrs* **12/1**

00-6 **5** *2* **Unmoothaj**[14] 146 4-9-0 65 LiamKeniry 5 62
(Pam Sly) *stdd s: hld up in last trio: nt clr run and switching rt over 2f out: styd on u.p fr over 1f out: nvr trbld ldrs* **10/1**

23-0 **6** *1 ¾* **Understory (USA)**[17] 79 7-9-2 **68** RobertTart(3) 10 62
(Tim McCarthy) *chsd ldrs but stuck wd: rdn to chse ldr over 2f out: 3rd and btn 1f out: wknd ins fnl f* **6/1**[3]

5-31 **7** *3 ¼* **Paddy's Saltantes (IRE)**[7] 229 4-9-3 **68** (b) LukeMorris 3 55
(J S Moore) *chsd ldr for 2f: stdd and wl in tch in midfield after: rdn and unable qck 2f out: wknd over 1f out* **8/1**

006- **8** *6* **Raamz (IRE)**[58] 8087 7-8-10 **59** JimmyQuinn 6 34
(Kevin Morgan) *hld up in tch in midfield: nt clr run and hmpd jst over 2f out: rdn and no rspnse wl over 1f out: sn wknd: bhd fnl f* **33/1**

000- **9** *1 ¼* **Rezwaan**[50] 8178 7-9-7 **70** (b) ShaneKelly 7 43
(Murty McGrath) *hld up in tch towards rr: hdwy on outer and rdn 3f out: drvn and lost pl 2f out: sn wknd: bhd fnl f* **66/1**

22-4 **10** *nk* **Attain**[15] 116 5-8-2 **56** (p) ShelleyBirkett(5) 9 28
(Julia Feilden) *chsd ldr after 2f tl led 5f out: rdn and hdd over 2f out: lost pl 2f out: sn wknd: bhd fnl f* **16/1**

51-4 **11** *hd* **Diletta Tommasa (IRE)**[13] 151 4-9-2 **67** (p) StephenCraine 4 39
(John Stimpson) *t.k.h: hld up wl in tch in midfield: stl cl enough whn bdly hmpd jst over 2f out: nt rcvr: bhd fnl f* **25/1**

2m 3.69s (-2.91) **Going Correction** -0.125s/f (Stan)
**WFA** 4 from 5yo+ 2lb **11 Ran SP% 120.0**
Speed ratings (Par 103): **106,105,102,102,100 99,96,91,90,90 90**
CSF £49.32 CT £109.04 TOTE £7.90: £2.50, £3.50, £1.10; EX 54.60 Trifecta £394.10.
**Owner** Four Winds Racing Partnership **Bred** Wood Farm Stud (Waresley) **Trained** Newmarket, Suffolk
**FOCUS**
A modest handicap run in a time nearly two seconds slower than the preceding 86-100 handicap.
T/Plt: £105.60. Pool: £90,962.38 - 628.74 winning units. T/Qpdt: £7.90. Pool: £7751.61 - 719.37 winning units. SP

# 317 WOLVERHAMPTON (A.W) (L-H)
Sunday, January 26

**OFFICIAL GOING: Standard**
Wind: mild breeze across Weather: showers

## 346 BOOKMAKERS.CO.UK MEDIAN AUCTION MAIDEN STKS 5f 20y(P)
1:50 (1:50) (Class 6) 3-5-Y-O £1,940 (£577; £288; £144) Stalls Low

Form RPR

00-4 **1** **Misty Sparkler**[4] 284 3-8-6 71 FergusSweeney 7 54
(Jamie Osborne) *chsd ldrs: rdn wl over 1f out: r.o ins fnl f: led fnl 30yds* **5/4**[1]

455- **2** *½* **Chuckamental**[124] 6718 3-8-11 62 (t) JoeFanning 6 57
(Bryan Smart) *trckd ldr tl rdn 2f out: kpt on w wnr ins fnl f: wnt 2nd nring fin* **7/1**

36-3 **3** *nk* **Mahon Falls**[9] 216 3-8-6 50 ChrisCatlin 3 51
(David Evans) *led: rdn 2f out: kpt on gamely: no ex whn hdd fnl 30yds* **20/1**

34-4 **4** *¾* **The Doyle Machine (IRE)**[3] 298 3-8-4 60 (b) JoeDoyle(7) 5 53
(Noel Quinlan) *t.k.h: trckd ldrs: rdn to chal over 1f out: ev ch tl no ex fnl 50yds* **3/1**[2]

35 **5** *1* **Avondream**[3] 291 5-9-12 0 AdamKirby 8 56
(Milton Bradley) *in tch: sn pushed along: rdn over 2f out: kpt on but nvr gng pce to get involved* **4/1**[3]

46-5 **6** *4 ½* **Busy Bimbo (IRE)**[10] 195 5-9-4 45 MarkCoumbe(3) 2 35
(Alan Berry) *chsd ldrs: rdn 2f out: wknd ins fnl f* **50/1**

05-3 **7** *hd* **Cheeky Peta'S**[9] 213 3-8-6 53 (v) JamesSullivan 1 28
(James Given) *hld up in tch: rdn over 2f out: wknd fnl f* **20/1**

- **8** *2* **Oriental Maid** 3-8-0 0 ow1 KevinLundie(7) 4 22
(Brian Ellison) *dwlt: sn outpcd: a last* **20/1**

1m 3.16s (0.86) **Going Correction** +0.175s/f (Slow)
**WFA** 3 from 5yo 15lb **8 Ran SP% 118.2**
Speed ratings (Par 101): **100,99,98,97,95 88,88,85**
CSF £10.71 TOTE £2.50: £1.70, £1.70, £2.40; EX 9.70 Trifecta £118.80.
**Owner** J A Osborne **Bred** Newsells Park Stud **Trained** Upper Lambourn, Berks
**FOCUS**
There was a good pace on here.

## 347 BEST ODDS AT BOOKMAKERS.CO.UK H'CAP 5f 216y(P)
2:20 (2:20) (Class 5) (0-70,70) 4-Y-O+ £2,587 (£770; £384; £192) Stalls Low

Form RPR

0-30 **1** **Colourbearer (IRE)**[7] 248 7-9-4 67 (t) RichardKingscote 6 76
(Milton Bradley) *chsd ldr: rdn to chal wl over 1f out: led ent fnl f: hld on wl towards fin: all out* **8/1**[3]

-000 **2** *nse* **Haadeeth**[8] 233 7-9-2 65 (t) AdamKirby 5 74
(David Evans) *in tch: rdn 2f out: r.o wl to chal ins fnl f: jst hld* **8/1**[3]

-460 **3** *3 ½* **Sewn Up**[2] 319 4-9-1 64 (v) ShaneKelly 4 62
(Andrew Hollinshead) *hld up but in tch: rdn over 2f out: no imp tl r.o ent fnl f wnt 3rd towards fin* **5/1**[2]

25-1 **4** *2 ¼* **I'll Be Good**[6] 259 5-9-1 64 6ex LukeMorris 1 54
(Alan Berry) *sn led: rdn 2f out: hdd ent fnl f: fdd fnl 120yds* **5/4**[1]

-224 **5** 3 3/4 **Parisian Pyramid (IRE)**[3] 296 8-9-1 64........................(p) TomEaves 7 42
(Richard Fahey) *chsd ldrs: pushed along 3f out: sn rdn: one pce fnl 2f* **5/1**[2]

616- **6** 2 1/2 **Alpha Tauri (USA)**[43] 8294 8-9-6 69.......................... WilliamCarson 2 39
(Richard Guest) *chsd ldrs: rdn 2f out: wknd fnl f* **10/1**

00-4 **7** 3/4 **Flash City (ITY)**[11] 191 6-9-7 70........................................(v) GrahamLee 3 38
(Bryan Smart) *in tch: rdn 2f out: nvr finding pce to get involved* **16/1**

1m 14.71s (-0.29) **Going Correction** +0.175s/f (Slow) 7 Ran SP% **115.0**
Speed ratings (Par 103): **108,107,103,100,95 91,90**
CSF £68.59 TOTE £11.40: £3.60, £3.10; EX 82.90 Trifecta £211.70.
**Owner** E A Hayward **Bred** Corduff Stud & J Corcorcan **Trained** Sedbury, Gloucs
**FOCUS**
Modest sprint form.

## 348 COMPARE BOOKMAKERS AT BOOKMAKERS.CO.UK H'CAP 5f 216y(P)
2:55 (2:55) (Class 3) (0-95,93) 4-Y-0+ £7,439 (£2,213; £1,106; £553) Stalls Low

Form RPR
43-0 **1** **Alben Star (IRE)**[5] 271 6-9-4 93............................ GeorgeChaloner(3) 8 106
(Richard Fahey) *chsd ldrs: rdn to chse ldr wl over 1f out: sn chalng: tk narrow advantage ins fnl f: kpt on wl: drvn out* **7/4**[2]

1-21 **2** 1/2 **Trinityelitedotcom (IRE)**[8] 234 4-9-7 93.............. RichardKingscote 1 104
(Tom Dascombe) *led: rdn whn pressed over 1f out: edgd rt and narrowly hdd ins fnl f: kpt on: hld towards fin* **5/4**[1]

00-0 **3** 3 1/4 **Elusivity (IRE)**[22] 55 6-9-4 90......................................... ShaneKelly 6 91
(Peter Crate) *hld up last but wl in tch: rdn to chal for 3rd over 1f out: kpt on but no threat to ldng pair* **16/1**

40-4 **4** nse **Stonefield Flyer**[7] 249 5-9-1 87.......................................... TomEaves 7 88
(Keith Dalgleish) *trckd ldr tl rdn 2f out: sn hld: kpt on same pce* **10/1**

22-1 **5** 3/4 **Burren View Lady (IRE)**[23] 36 4-8-11 83...........(e) DuranFentiman 5 81
(Tim Easterby) *chsd ldrs: rdn 2f out: kpt on same pce* **6/1**[3]

46-2 **6** 12 **Light From Mars**[16] 122 9-8-7 79.......................................(p) LukeMorris 2 39
(Ronald Harris) *chsd ldrs: struggling to hold pl 3f out: wknd 1f out* **16/1**

1m 14.12s (-0.88) **Going Correction** +0.175s/f (Slow) 6 Ran SP% **115.9**
Speed ratings (Par 107): **112,111,107,106,105 89**
CSF £4.53 CT £21.88 TOTE £3.00: £1.60, £1.80; EX 6.80 Trifecta £66.70.
**Owner** J K Shannon & M A Scaife **Bred** Rathasker Stud **Trained** Musley Bank, N Yorks
**FOCUS**
A good handicap but not many got into it.

## 349 32RED H'CAP 1m 5f 194y(P)
3:30 (3:30) (Class 6) (0-60,60) 4-Y-0+ £1,940 (£577; £288; £144) Stalls Low

Form RPR
-151 **1** **Fire In Babylon (IRE)**[3] 303 6-9-5 55 6ex..............(b) AdamBeschizza 2 64
(Noel Quinlan) *trckd ldrs: rdn to ld over 1f out: styd on wl fnl f: rdn out* **9/2**[2]

50-5 **2** 1/2 **Uncle Bernie (IRE)**[9] 221 4-8-6 48...............................(p) JimmyQuinn 3 56
(Andrew Hollinshead) *slowly away: bhd: hdwy fr 3f out: rdn over 1f out: str chal ent fnl f: styd on: hld nring fin* **20/1**

60-5 **3** 2 **Rocky Rebel**[4] 277 6-9-10 60.......................................... RichardKingscote 5 65
(Michael Blake) *in tch: nt clrest of runs on rails 2f out: swtchd rt: sn rdn: styd on wl to go 3rd towards fin* **9/2**[2]

0-34 **4** 3/4 **Blazing Desert**[9] 221 10-9-3 58.................................. ShelleyBirkett(5) 6 62
(William Kinsey) *trckd ldrs: led over 2f out: rdn and hdd over 1f out: styd on same pce fnl f* **8/1**[3]

5-25 **5** 7 **Secret Song**[9] 210 4-9-2 58................................................ LukeMorris 1 50
(Sir Mark Prescott Bt) *trckd ldrs: pushed along 3f out: rdn 2f out: wknd ins fnl f* **5/2**[1]

0-20 **6** 1/2 **Sommersturm (GER)**[9] 214 10-9-8 58............................ AdamKirby 8 50
(David Evans) *hld up in last pair: rdn 2f out: nvr any imp* **9/2**[2]

/41- **7** 5 **Annaluna (IRE)**[209] 3884 5-9-1 56.................................. EoinWalsh(5) 7 40
(David Evans) *disp ld tl rdn over 2f out: sn hld: wknd fnl f* **14/1**

0-50 **8** 16 **Perivale (USA)**[13] 154 4-8-6 48........................................ JoeFanning 4 6
(Mark Johnston) *disp ld tl rdn over 2f out: wknd over 1f out* **10/1**

3m 7.13s (1.13) **Going Correction** +0.175s/f (Slow)
**WFA** 4 from 5yo+ 6lb 8 Ran SP% **114.7**
Speed ratings (Par 101): **103,102,101,101,97 96,94,84**
CSF £85.33 CT £427.03 TOTE £5.10: £2.40, £4.40, £1.80; EX 62.20 Trifecta £402.80.
**Owner** Ms Fiona Donald **Bred** The Goldsmith Bloodstock Partnership **Trained** Newmarket, Suffolk
**FOCUS**
A modest handicap.

## 350 CORAL APP DOWNLOAD FROM THE APP STORE H'CAP 1m 4f 50y(P)
4:00 (4:00) (Class 4) (0-80,80) 4-Y-0+ £4,851 (£1,443; £721; £360) Stalls Low

Form RPR
606- **1** **Lilac Tree**[75] 7849 4-9-1 75.............................................. JoeFanning 3 84+
(Mark Johnston) *trckd ldrs: travelling strly but nt clr run 2f out: shkn up whn swtchd rt over 1f out: str run to ld fnl 40yds: pushed out* **9/4**[1]

15-4 **2** 1/2 **Oratorio's Joy (IRE)**[13] 160 4-9-2 76........................ FergusSweeney 7 82
(Jamie Osborne) *hld up: tk clsr order over 6f out: led over 1f out: sn rdn: kpt on but no ex whn hdd fnl 40yds* **8/1**

11-4 **3** 2 1/4 **St Ignatius**[25] 3 7-9-4 79...................................(v) NatashaEaton(5) 6 81
(Alan Bailey) *led: rdn and hdd over 1f out: styd on same pce fnl f* **7/1**

3-33 **4** 1/2 **Lexington Bay (IRE)**[5] 270 6-9-4 77.................(v[1]) GeorgeChaloner(3) 2 79
(Richard Fahey) *trckd ldrs: rdn wl over 2f out: styd on same pce fr over 1f out* **3/1**[2]

220- **5** 1 1/4 **Arr' Kid (USA)**[93] 7510 4-8-10 70...................................... TomEaves 4 70
(Keith Dalgleish) *trckd ldrs: pushed along 3f out: rdn and ev ch over 1f out: no ex ins fnl f* **8/1**

120- **6** 8 **Noguchi (IRE)**[224] 3370 9-9-9 79................................(b) AdamKirby 8 66
(George Margarson) *awkward leaving stalls: last: rdn wl over 2f out: nvr threatened: wknd ins fnl f* **6/1**[3]

126- **P** **Dunhoy (IRE)**[205] 4029 6-9-10 80...................................... GrahamLee 5
(Tony Newcombe) *hld up: pushed along 3f out: styng on whn lost action ent fnl f: immediately eased and p.u: lame* **8/1**

2m 42.67s (1.57) **Going Correction** +0.175s/f (Slow)
**WFA** 4 from 5yo+ 4lb 7 Ran SP% **115.9**
Speed ratings (Par 105): **101,100,99,98,98 92,**
CSF £21.48 CT £109.72 TOTE £4.00: £2.20, £2.80; EX 20.20 Trifecta £189.20.
**Owner** Sheikh Hamdan bin Mohammed Al Maktoum **Bred** Biddestone Stud Ltd **Trained** Middleham Moor, N Yorks

**FOCUS**
This was a fair race and it produced a taking winner.

## 351 LADBROKES H'CAP 7f 32y(P)
4:30 (4:30) (Class 6) (0-55,58) 4-Y-0+ £1,940 (£577; £288; £144) Stalls High

Form RPR
-031 **1** **Medam**[7] 251 5-9-10 58 6ex.............................................. NeilFarley(3) 4 66
(Shaun Harris) *hld up: rdn and hdwy 2f out: led ins fnl f: r.o wl: rdn out* **3/1**[2]

3-30 **2** 1 1/2 **Vale Of Clara (IRE)**[10] 201 6-9-1 46..............................(b) TomEaves 1 50
(Peter Niven) *chsd ldrs: rdn over 2f out: chalng for 2nd whn bmpd ins fnl f: kpt on to snatch 2nd fnl stride* **14/1**

-203 **3** nse **Partner's Gold (IRE)**[10] 201 4-9-0 45..............................(b) RobertHavlin 2 49
(Alan Berry) *led tl over 3f out: sn rdn: led again over 1f out: hdd ins fnl f: sn hld: lost 2nd fnl stride* **4/1**[3]

26-3 **4** nk **Classy Trick (USA)**[14] 152 4-9-6 51...............................(p) GrahamLee 3 54
(Patrick Morris) *prom: led over 3f out: sn pushed along: rdn 2f out: hdd over 1f out: bmpd ins fnl f: kpt on same pce* **11/4**[1]

0-55 **5** 2 1/2 **Satwa Laird**[10] 201 8-8-9 45..................................(be) AnnStokell(5) 6 41
(Ann Stokell) *chsd ldrs: rdn over 2f out: kpt on same pce fr over 1f out* **16/1**

150- **6** 1 **Auntie Mildred (IRE)**[44] 8271 4-9-6 51......................... DanielTudhope 5 45
(David O'Meara) *hld up: rdn over 2f out: nvr any imp* **10/1**

00-6 **7** 3/4 **Ryan Style (IRE)**[11] 184 8-9-5 50.....................................(p) AdamKirby 8 42
(Lisa Williamson) *hld up in tch: rdn over 2f out: rdr sn lost whip: fdd ins fnl f* **4/1**[3]

000/ **8** 5 **Poker Hospital**[418] 7982 5-8-11 47.................................. PhilipPrince(5) 7 25
(John Stimpson) *awkward leaving stalls: sn trcking ldrs: rdn over 2f out: wknd over 1f out* **33/1**

1m 31.53s (1.93) **Going Correction** +0.175s/f (Slow) 8 Ran SP% **116.2**
Speed ratings (Par 101): **95,93,93,92,90 88,88,82**
CSF £44.23 CT £171.24 TOTE £3.40: £1.70, £2.90, £1.40; EX 48.80 Trifecta £151.20.
**Owner** Burton Agnes Bloodstock **Bred** Burton Agnes Stud Co Ltd **Trained** Carburton, Notts
■ Stewards' Enquiry : Robert Havlin one-day ban: careless riding (Feb 9)
**FOCUS**
Just an ordinary handicap, but there was a good gallop.

## 352 DOWNLOAD THE LADBROKES APP H'CAP 1m 141y(P)
5:00 (5:00) (Class 6) (0-55,49) 4-Y-0+ £1,940 (£577; £288; £144) Stalls Low

Form RPR
60-0 **1** **Zed Candy Girl**[23] 40 4-9-2 45.......................................... LukeMorris 7 48
(John Stimpson) *racd in disp 4th: pushed along and hdwy fr 3f out: led over 1f out: kpt on wl: drvn out* **7/1**[3]

0-63 **2** 3/4 **Amber Moon**[5] 268 9-8-12 45.......................................... AnnStokell(5) 1 46
(Ann Stokell) *t.k.h: trckd ldr: led over 3f out: rdn and hdd over 1f out: kpt on* **25/1**

5-62 **3** 1 **Supa Seeker (USA)**[11] 179 8-9-0 49..............(b) MrAidenBlakemore(7) 2 48
(Tony Carroll) *racd in disp 4th: rdn over 1f out: kpt on but nt pce to chal* **10/11**[1]

4-05 **4** 3/4 **Una Bella Cosa**[6] 263 4-9-2 45........................................(v) ShaneKelly 4 42
(Alan McCabe) *hld up: rdn over 2f out: styd on wl ent fnl f: wnt 4th fnl 120yds: no further imp on ldrs* **3/1**[2]

40-5 **5** 3 1/4 **Another Journey**[14] 150 5-9-0 45.............................(e[1]) MarkCoumbe(3) 3 35
(Lisa Williamson) *trckd ldrs: rdn over 2f out: fdd ins fnl f* **14/1**

503- **6** 9 **Zafaraban (IRE)**[36] 4173 7-9-5 47.................................. WilliamCarson 5 16
(Aytach Sadik) *hld up: rdn 3f out: sn wknd* **10/1**

/0-5 **P** **Botanist**[19] 78 7-9-3 45............................................................ PaddyAspell 6
(Shaun Harris) *led tl over 3f out: sn wknd: t.o whn p.u fnl f* **7/1**[3]

1m 52.77s (2.27) **Going Correction** +0.175s/f (Slow)
**WFA** 4 from 5yo+ 1lb 7 Ran SP% **122.0**
Speed ratings (Par 101): **96,95,94,93,90 82,**
CSF £152.40 TOTE £6.90: £3.40, £2.90; EX 67.60 Trifecta £294.90.
**Owner** J T S (International) Ltd **Bred** H H L Bloodstock **Trained** Butterton, Staffs
■ Stewards' Enquiry : Ann Stokell two-day ban: used whip above permitted level (Feb 9-10)
**FOCUS**
A poor race, the topweight coming in 6lb below the ceiling and all but two of the runners racing from out of the handicap.
T/Plt: £225.30. Pool: £76,338.86 - 247.26 winning units. T/Qpdt: £12.90. Pool: £8857.16 - 505.70 winning units. TM

# 346 WOLVERHAMPTON (A.W) (L-H)
Monday, January 27

**OFFICIAL GOING: Standard**
Wind: light, behind Weather: dry, overcast

## 353 COMPARE BOOKMAKERS AT BOOKMAKERS.CO.UK AMATEUR RIDERS' H'CAP 5f 216y(P)
2:40 (2:40) (Class 6) (0-55,55) 4-Y-0+ £2,183 (£677; £338; £169) Stalls Low

Form RPR
45-4 **1** **Consistant**[17] 121 6-11-0 **55**...................................... MissSBrotherton 4 64
(Brian Baugh) *chsd clr ldng pair: chsd clr ldr wl over 1f out: effrt and steadily clsd fr over 1f out: rdn and r.o wl to ld wl ins fnl f* **11/4**[1]

2-36 **2** 1/2 **Volito**[4] 295 8-10-11 **55**.....................................[1] MissJoannaMason(3) 12 62
(Anabel K Murphy) *hld up off the pce in last quartet: hdwy u.p and swtchd rt over 1f out: r.o wl u.p to go 2nd cl home* **7/1**

400- **3** 1/2 **Masked Dance (IRE)**[48] 8234 7-10-6 **52**...............(b) MrKLocking(5) 9 57
(Scott Dixon) *led and clr w rival tl wnt clr 1/2-way: rdn over 1f out: drvn and hdd wl ins fnl f: no ex and lost 2nd cl home* **14/1**

0-26 **4** 1/2 **Lutine Charlie (IRE)**[13] 170 7-10-13 **54**............................ MrSWalker 10 58
(Pat Eddery) *racd off the pce in midfield: rdn 3f out: hdwy u.p over 1f out: styd on u.p ins fnl f* **4/1**[2]

634- **5** 1 3/4 **Methaaly (IRE)**[31] 8412 11-10-8 **52**.................(be) MissMMullineaux(3) 3 50
(Michael Mullineaux) *rrd as stalls opened: rdr removed hood late: v.s.a: bhd: tagged on bk of main gp 1/2-way: rdn over 1f out: kpt on wl ins fnl f: nt rch ldrs* **10/1**

00-0 **6** 1 **Rose Garnet (IRE)**[19] 83 6-10-10 **54**....................... MrChrisMartin(3) 13 49
(Tony Carroll) *t.k.h: hld up off the pce in midfield: rdn and effrt over 2f out: hdwy u.p over 1f out: styd on same pce ins fnl f* **18/1**

6-56 **7** 1 1/4 **Busy Bimbo (IRE)**[1] 346 5-9-12 **46** oh1........................ JasonNuttall(7) 2 37
(Alan Berry) *prom in main gp: rdn and no imp 2f out: outpcd and btn over 1f out: wknd ins fnl f* **50/1**

0-40 **8** 1 **Homeboy (IRE)**[2] 339 6-10-9 **55**.................................. HollieDoyle(5) 7 43
(David Evans) *pressed ldr and clr tl 1/2-way: sn rdn and struggling over 2f out: lost pl and btn wl over 1f out: wknd fnl f* **8/1**

500- **9** *nse* **True That (IRE)**[120] 6878 4-10-0 **46** oh1 MrJohnWilley(5) 8 34
(Brian Ellison) *racd off the pce in midfield: rdn and no imp 2f out: plugged on: nvr trbld ldrs* **9/2**[3]

-506 **10** *¾* **Amis Reunis**[11] 196 5-10-6 **52** (p) MrJamesHughes(5) 5 37
(Alan Berry) *racd wl off the pce: towards rr 1/2-way: v wd and no hdwy bnd 2f out: nvr trbld ldrs* **40/1**

3-23 **11** *6* **Red Star Lady (IRE)**[10] 215 4-10-0 **46** oh1 MrGrahamCarson(5) 11 12
(Shaun Harris) *racd off the pce in midfield: rdn and no hdwy over 2f out: wknd wl over 1f out* **14/1**

6/45 **12** *3¾* **Kneesy Earsy Nosey**[11] 199 8-9-12 **46** oh1(p) MissCharlotteCooper(7) 6
(Ann Stokell) *sn pushed along in last pair: swtchd rt to outer after 1f: a bhd* **150/1**

000/ **13** *7* **Saktoon (USA)**[517] 5720 6-9-12 **46** oh1 (v) MrJMorris(7) 1
(Derek Shaw) *s.i.s: a bhd* **150/1**

1m 16.56s (1.56) **Going Correction** +0.05s/f (Slow) **13** Ran SP% **121.9**
Speed ratings (Par 101): **91,90,89,89,86 85,83,82,82,81 73,68,58**
CSF £22.89 CT £244.91 TOTE £3.40: £1.20, £3.50, £3.90; EX 26.70 Trifecta £345.50.
**Owner** Miss J A Price **Bred** Bearstone Stud **Trained** Audley, Staffs

**FOCUS**
Few came into the opening amateur contest in form. It was run at a strong pace and the form is pretty straightforward.

## 354 £32 FREE AT 32RED.COM CLAIMING STKS 5f 216y(P)
**3:10** (3:12) (Class 6) 3-Y-O £2,264 (£673; £336; £168) **Stalls** Low

Form RPR

2-26 **1** **Little Big Man**[2] 338 3-8-7 70 (b) LukeMorris 3 68
(Sylvester Kirk) *chsd ldng pair: swtchd rt and effrt to chse ldr wl over 1f out: drvn and led ins fnl f: styd on strly and gng away at fin* **4/5**[1]

43-4 **2** *2½* **Intense Feeling (IRE)**[10] 217 3-7-7 61 (v[1]) JoeDoyle(7) 1 53
(David Evans) *led: rdn and edgd lft over 1f out: hdd and no ex ins fnl f: kpt on for clr 2nd* **3/1**[2]

05-0 **3** *1¾* **Clapperboard**[13] 173 3-7-11 57 (b[1]) KieranShoemark(7) 4 51
(Paul Fitzsimons) *v.s.a: in tch in last: rdn wl over 1f out: styd on ins fnl f to go 3rd towards fin: no threat to wnr* **33/1**

065- **4** *1¼* **Danfazi (IRE)**[28] 8442 3-9-6 72 JacobButterfield(5) 2 68
(Kristin Stubbs) *chsd ldr: rdn: unable qck whn edgd rt bnd 2f out: 3rd and btn 1f out: wknd and lost 3rd towards fin* **7/1**

4- **5** *1¼* **Our Red Devil (IRE)**[144] 6127 3-8-5 0 MartinLane 5 44
(David Simcock) *t.k.h: hld up in tch in last pair: rdn over 3f out: no imp and wl hld 1f out* **11/2**[3]

1m 15.66s (0.66) **Going Correction** +0.05s/f (Slow) **5** Ran SP% **111.4**
Speed ratings (Par 95): **97,93,91,89,88**
CSF £3.54 TOTE £1.70: £1.10, £2.00; EX 3.70 Trifecta £16.00.Little Big Man was the subject of a friendly claim.
**Owner** N Simpson & S Kirk **Bred** Paul Merritt **Trained** Upper Lambourn, Berks

**FOCUS**
A weak claimer for 3yos. The winner looks the best guide.

## 355 32RED.COM MAIDEN STKS 7f 32y(P)
**3:40** (3:42) (Class 5) 3-Y-O £2,911 (£866; £432; £216) **Stalls** High

Form RPR

5-6 **1** **Cosquillas (IRE)**[23] 50 3-9-0 0 JoeFanning 12 65
(Mark Johnston) *hld up in midfield: hdwy 5f out: chsd ldrs 3f out: rdn to ld over 1f out: hld on wl cl home: all out* **10/1**

04-0 **2** *hd* **Warbrook (IRE)**[14] 157 3-9-5 66 (b[1]) RobertHavlin 2 69
(John Gosden) *chsd ldrs: nt clr run 2f out: swtchd lft and effrt on inner wl over 1f out: hrd drvn and chal fnl 100yds: kpt on but a jst hld* **7/1**[3]

345- **3** *½* **Upholland**[79] 7819 3-9-5 70 BarryMcHugh 3 68
(Richard Fahey) *in tch in midfield: rdn and effrt over 2f out: hdwy to chse ldng pair and hung lft jst ins fnl f: pressing ldrs fnl 50yds: kpt on but hld cl home* **6/4**[2]

6 **4** *5* **Parkhill Star**[17] 127 3-9-0 0 RichardKingscote 4 50
(Tom Dascombe) *chsd ldr tl led 3f out: sn rdn: hdd and no ex over 1f out: wknd fnl 150yds* **22/1**

**5** *1¼* **Fitzgerald (IRE)** 3-9-5 0 AdamKirby 9 51
(Marco Botti) *dwlt: racd in midfield: rdn and effrt over 2f out: 6th and no imp 1f out: wknd fnl f* **6/5**[1]

0-0 **6** *3* **Shannon Haven (IRE)**[21] 70 3-9-5 0 (b[1]) ShaneKelly 7 43
(Daniel Mark Loughnane) *t.k.h: chsd ldrs: wnt 2nd 3f out: rdn and ev ch 2f out: no ex and btn over 1f out: hung lft and fdd fnl f* **25/1**

00- **7** *1¾* **Oly'Roccs (IRE)**[75] 7853 3-8-12 0 EvaMoscrop(7) 8 38
(Philip Kirby) *in tch in midfield: rdn and outpcd jst over 2f out: btn and hung lft 1f out: fdd fnl f* **150/1**

0-0 **8** *2¼* **Up Hill Battle's**[21] 70 3-9-0 0 StephenCraine 10 27
(Daniel Mark Loughnane) *hld up in midfield: swtchd rt and rdn over 3f out: no prog and wknd 2f out* **100/1**

**9** *6* **Aboody** 3-9-5 0 LukeMorris 11 16
(Sir Mark Prescott Bt) *s.i.s: rn green and a off the pce in rr* **18/1**

**10** *1* **Shades Of Silk** 3-9-0 0 JamesSullivan 5 8
(James Given) *sn rdn along and outpcd in last trio: n.d* **40/1**

000- **11** *2¼* **Spirit O Goodchild**[178] 4964 3-9-5 0 BenCurtis 6 7
(Alan McCabe) *s.i.s: a off the pce in last trio: n.d* **125/1**

**12** *hd* **Maro** 3-8-12 0 AdamMcLean(7) 1 7
(Derek Shaw) *led tl 3f out: sn lost pl u.p: fdd over 1f out and bhd fnl f* **150/1**

1m 30.4s (0.80) **Going Correction** +0.05s/f (Slow) **12** Ran SP% **126.0**
Speed ratings (Par 97): **97,96,96,90,89 85,83,81,74,73 70,70**
CSF £80.60 TOTE £10.50: £2.80, £1.90, £1.10; EX 46.20 Trifecta £158.70.
**Owner** Haras D'Etreham Stud **Bred** Ballygallon Stud Limited **Trained** Middleham Moor, N Yorks

**FOCUS**
A trio with previous experience fought out this 3yo maiden, clear of the rest. Mixed messages from the form.

## 356 32RED ON THE APP STORE (S) STKS 1m 141y(P)
**4:10** (4:10) (Class 6) 3-Y-O £2,264 (£673) **Stalls** Low

Form RPR

516- **1** **Boogangoo (IRE)**[53] 8164 3-8-13 73 TomEaves 4 74
(Keith Dalgleish) *mde all: 3 l clr over 2f out: rdn and kpt on fr over 1f out: eased nr fin* **11/8**[2]

31-1 **2** *3¾* **Kantara Castle (IRE)**[12] 187 3-9-4 72 SeanLevey 1 70
(Richard Hannon) *chsd wnr: rdn over 3f out: drvn and 3 l down wl over 2f out: no imp* **8/13**[1]

1m 51.25s (0.75) **Going Correction** +0.05s/f (Slow) **2** Ran SP% **104.0**
Speed ratings (Par 95): **98,94**
TOTE £1.80.The winner was bought in for 4,750gns; Kantara Castle was claimed by David Penman for £6,000.
**Owner** Middleham Park Racing II **Bred** Marie & Mossy Fahy **Trained** Carluke, S Lanarks

**FOCUS**
With the two likely outsiders non-runners this claimer was left with just the two runners, both of whom raced under the Middleham Park Racing banner. Such a scenario does raise the question as to why this race was scheduled on a card that had a 6f seller for 3yos and a 0-75 handicap over the extended 1m1f also for 3yos. The winner was the form choice.

## 357 32RED CASINO H'CAP 1m 1f 103y(P)
**4:40** (4:40) (Class 5) (0-75,75) 3-Y-O £2,911 (£866; £432; £216) **Stalls** Low

Form RPR

00-2 **1** **Sir Charlie Kunz**[9] 231 3-9-6 **74** JoeFanning 6 81+
(Mark Johnston) *chsd ldng pair: effrt and lft w ev ch wl over 1f out: rdn hands and heels to ld 1f out: drvn and asserted fnl 50yds* **1/2**[1]

041- **2** *½* **Aramadyh**[115] 6999 3-9-0 **68** (p) LukeMorris 1 74
(James Tate) *led: rdn 3f out: hung rt bnd wl over 1f out: drvn and hdd 1f out: battled on wl u.p: no ex and btn fnl 50yds* **11/1**

01-4 **3** *2½* **Lesha (IRE)**[18] 99 3-9-2 **70** JamieSpencer 3 71
(Kevin Ryan) *w ldr: drvn over 3f out: stl ev ch whn carried rt bnd wl over 1f out: 3rd and unable qck 1f out: one pce fnl 150yds* **7/1**[2]

24-1 **4** *2* **Jazzy Lady (IRE)**[12] 190 3-9-7 **75** AdamKirby 4 72
(David Evans) *chsd ldng trio: effrt u.p but unable qck over 1f out: one pce and no imp fnl f* **10/1**

62-3 **5** *8* **Final Countdown**[9] 230 3-8-12 **66** WilliamCarson 5 46
(Anthony Carson) *stdd and dropped in bhd after s: a off the pce in 5th: rdn and no hdwy 3f out: wl bhd fnl f* **8/1**[3]

13-4 **6** *¾* **Howz The Family (IRE)**[18] 103 3-8-12 **66** JohnFahy 2 44
(John Spearing) *stdd s: a off the pce in last: rdn and no hdwy 3f out: wl bhd fnl f* **33/1**

2m 1.48s (-0.22) **Going Correction** +0.05s/f (Slow) **6** Ran SP% **110.6**
Speed ratings (Par 97): **102,101,99,97,90 89**
CSF £6.86 TOTE £1.50: £1.10, £4.40; EX 8.10 Trifecta £38.50.
**Owner** Paul Dean **Bred** Rabbah Bloodstock Limited **Trained** Middleham Moor, N Yorks

**FOCUS**
A decent 3yo handicap and the front pair are both horses to follow. The form is sound enough.

## 358 32RED FILLIES' H'CAP 1m 4f 50y(P)
**5:10** (5:10) (Class 5) (0-75,74) 4-Y-O+ £2,911 (£866; £432; £216) **Stalls** Low

Form RPR

5-40 **1** **Doldrums (USA)**[11] 200 4-9-1 **69** JoeFanning 6 81
(Mark Johnston) *sn pressing ldr: led 3f out: rdn over 1f out: styd on strly and drew clr fnl f: readily* **2/1**[2]

22-1 **2** *3* **Persian Patriot**[18] 97 4-8-12 **66** RobertHavlin 7 73
(William Jarvis) *t.k.h: hld up in tch in midfield: lft chsng wnr over 2f out: rdn and effrt 2f out: no ex and btn ins fnl f: kpt on same pce after* **13/8**[1]

406- **3** *6* **Remix (IRE)**[75] 7865 5-9-1 **65** StevieDonohoe 3 63
(Ian Williams) *hld up in tch in last pair: effrt and lft chsng clr ldng pair jst over 2f out: styd on same pce and no imp fr over 1f out* **16/1**[3]

-111 **4** *1¼* **The Blue Dog (IRE)**[10] 221 7-9-3 **74** JoeDoyle(7) 2 70+
(Phil McEntee) *t.k.h: hld up wl in tch in midfield: nt clr run: rn into rival and bdly hmpd over 2f out: nt rcvr: wnt 4th over 1f out but no threat to ldrs after* **2/1**[2]

0-06 **5** *10* **Hold The Star**[3] 321 8-8-7 **62** oh15 ow2 AnnStokell(5) 5 42
(Ann Stokell) *hld up in last pair: rdn 3f out: sn struggling: wknd 2f out* **100/1**

500- **5** *dht* **Witch Way Went**[69] 7952 4-7-13 **60** oh1 KevinLundie(7) 1 40
(Brian Ellison) *led: rdn over 3f out: hdd 3f out: stl 2nd but struggling whn bmpd and bdly hmpd over 2f out: no ch after: wknd 2f out* **25/1**

2m 43.97s (2.87) **Going Correction** +0.05s/f (Slow)
**WFA** 4 from 5yo+ 4lb **6** Ran SP% **115.5**
Speed ratings (Par 100): **92,90,86,85,78 78**
CSF £5.91 TOTE £3.40: £1.80, £1.40; EX 6.40 Trifecta £36.70.
**Owner** Sheikh Hamdan bin Mohammed Al Maktoum **Bred** Lothenbach Stables Inc **Trained** Middleham Moor, N Yorks
■ Stewards' Enquiry : Kevin Lundie five-day ban: careless riding (Feb 10-14)

**FOCUS**
Three dominated the market in this fillies' handicap. The winner is rated back to her debut form.

## 359 LADBROKES H'CAP 7f 32y(P)
**5:40** (5:41) (Class 5) (0-70,70) 4-Y-O+ £2,911 (£866; £432; £216) **Stalls** High

Form RPR

0-02 **1** **Smalljohn**[3] 319 8-9-2 **65** (v) JoeFanning 5 76
(Bryan Smart) *chsd ldr tl rdn to ld over 1f out: kpt on wl fnl f: rdn out* **5/2**[1]

43-4 **2** *1* **Funky Cold Medina**[19] 84 4-9-5 **68** (v[1]) JamieSpencer 6 76
(Peter Chapple-Hyam) *chsd ldr: rdn and effrt to chse wnr jst over 1f out: drvn and kpt on same pce fnl 150yds* **8/1**

01-3 **3** *1¼* **Run It Twice (IRE)**[16] 141 4-9-7 **70** (b) AdamKirby 11 75
(David Evans) *hld up in tch in rr: clsd over 2f out: rdn and effrt over 1f out: flashed tail u.p but styd on to go 3rd ins fnl f: kpt on* **10/3**[2]

00-0 **4** *2¼* **Menelik (IRE)**[3] 310 5-9-3 **66** (v) RichardKingscote 1 65
(Tom Dascombe) *sn led: rdn and hdd over 1f out: nt qckn u.p and 3rd 1f out: wknd fnl 75yds* **9/1**

/45- **5** *shd* **Tumbledown (USA)**[54] 8154 4-8-12 **61** LukeMorris 10 60
(Ed Walker) *bustled along in midfield early: rdn again 4f out: hrd drvn and unable qck over 2f out: no threat to ldrs but kpt on again towards fin* **14/1**

6-1 **6** *1* **Dance For Georgie**[21] 65 5-9-3 **69** GeorgeChaloner(3) 3 65
(Ben Haslam) *chsd ldrs: rdn over 1f out: stl chsng ldrs but unable qck over 1f out: wknd ins fnl f* **7/1**[3]

104- **7** *5* **Dimitar (USA)**[95] 7487 5-9-5 **68** StevieDonohoe 9 50
(Johnny Farrelly) *dwlt: hld up in rr: pushed along over 1f out: rdn and no hdwy fnl f: n.d* **8/1**

11-0 **8** *4* **Pravda Street**[13] 172 9-9-0 **70** RobJFitzpatrick(7) 4 42
(Christopher Kellett) *in tch in last trio: rdn and struggling 1/2-way: wknd 2f out* **20/1**

50-0 **9** *6* **Bapak Muda (USA)**[9] 233 4-9-2 **70** KevinStott(5) 12 25
(Kevin Ryan) *in tch in midfield: rdn 4f out: lost pl u.p over 2f out: wknd 2f out: bhd and eased wl ins fnl f* **20/1**

1m 28.91s (-0.69) **Going Correction** +0.05s/f (Slow) **9** Ran SP% **112.6**
Speed ratings (Par 103): **105,103,102,99,99 98,92,88,81**
CSF £22.36 CT £66.16 TOTE £2.90: £1.40, £2.60, £1.50; EX 23.10 Trifecta £95.90.
**Owner** B Smart **Bred** W H R John And Partners **Trained** Hambleton, N Yorks

**FOCUS**
The closing handicap saw a tough performance from the winner who was recording his 12th win. Pretty solid form.
T/Jkpt: £1086.60 to a £1 stake. Pool: £11,478.50 - 7.50 winning units. T/Plt: £20.30 to a £1 stake. Pool: £125,057.90 - 4493.10 winning units. T/Qpdt: £5.90 to a £1 stake. Pool: £8,332.05 - 1039.70 winning units. SP

## 266 CAGNES-SUR-MER
Monday, January 27
**OFFICIAL GOING: Polytrack: standard**

### 360a PRIX DE GRIMAUD (MAIDEN) (3YO COLTS & GELDINGS) (POLYTRACK) 1m 2f (D)
1:05 (12:00) 3-Y-O £10,000 (£4,000; £3,000; £2,000; £1,000)

RPR
1 **Le Prelat (FR)** 3-9-2 0 SylvainRuis 7 77
(J-M Capitte, France) 166/10
2 nk **Whitby High Light**[9] 237 3-9-2 0 ThomasMessina 10 76
(Andrew Hollinshead) *hld up in rr: last 1/2-way: swtchd to outer and rdn over 2f out: styd on and chal ins fnl f: wnt 2nd cl home: nt quite pce of wnr* 18/1
3 ½ **Sealed (USA)**[12] 194 3-9-2 0 Pierre-CharlesBoudot 9 75
(Gay Kelleway) *midfield in tch on outer: rdn to chal over 2f out: led narrowly ent fnl f: strly pressed and hdd 100yds out: kpt on but dropped to 3rd cl home* 33/10[1]
4 1 **Take The Crown (FR)** 3-9-2 0 (b[1]) IoritzMendizabal 1 73
(J-C Rouget, France) 48/10[3]
5 1 **Riquet Enfin (FR)** 3-9-2 0 AnthonyCrastus 6 71
(E Lellouche, France) 14/1
6 ½ **General (FR)**[115] 3-9-2 0 AurelienLemaitre 4 70
(S Kobayashi, France) 17/1
7 1 **Sailor (FR)** 3-9-2 0 TonyPiccone 12 68
(J Heloury, France) 6/1
8 ¾ **In For Dinner (FR)**[29] 3-9-2 0 TheoBachelot 8 67
(P Monfort, France) 11/1
9 2 **Docteur Vigousse (FR)** 3-9-2 0 (p) FranckForesi 11 63
(J Parize, France) 34/1
10 1 ½ **Folklo (FR)** 3-9-2 0 Francois-XavierBertras 5 60
(M Mace, France) 4/1[2]
11 2 **Sixcentdixneuf (FR)**[23] 3-8-8 0 ValentinGambart(8) 13 56
(M Boutin, France) 11/1
12 4 **Falbo (IRE)**[86] 3-9-2 0 FredericSpanu 3 48
(Laura Grizzetti, Italy) 67/1
13 4 ½ **Turtle Boson (IRE)**[44] 3-8-10 0 NicolasLarenaudie(6) 2 39
(G Martin, Austria) 102/1
2m 4.24s (124.24) 13 Ran SP% 119.9
WIN (incl. 1 euro stake): 17.60. PLACES: 4.20, 4.40, 2.00. DF: 124.50. SF: 263.60.
**Owner** Herve Coulomb **Bred** T De La Heronniere & Pontchartrain Stud **Trained** France

## 297 SOUTHWELL (L-H)
Tuesday, January 28
**OFFICIAL GOING: Standard**
Wind: moderated across Weather: heavy cloud and rain showers

### 361 32RED.COM AMATEUR RIDERS' H'CAP 1m 6f (F)
1:20 (1:25) (Class 5) (0-70,70) 4-Y-0+ £3,119 (£967; £483; £242) Stalls Low

Form RPR
0/0- 1 **Luctor Emergo (IRE)**[50] 2540 5-10-7 **63** (p) MrSWalker 4 71
(Keith Dalgleish) *trckd ldrs: smooth hdwy and cl up over 5f out: led 4f out: jnd and rdn 2f out: drvn over 1f out: kpt on wl towards fin* 5/1[3]
6-34 2 ½ **Honest Strike (USA)**[11] 214 7-10-5 **61** (b) FreddieMitchell 3 68
(Daniel Mark Loughnane) *trckd ldrs: hdwy 4f out: effrt to chal 2f out: rdn wl over 1f out: ev ch tl drvn and edgd rt ins fnl f: no ex towards fin* 4/1[2]
626- 3 3 ¾ **Brunello**[33] 7081 6-9-12 **59** (p) PhillipDennis(5) 6 61
(Philip Kirby) *trckd ldrs: hdwy 5f out: cl up over 3f out: chal on outer 2f out: sn rdn and ev ch tl drvn and one pce fnl f* 14/1
303- 4 1 ½ **Mediterranean Sea (IRE)**[30] 8433 8-11-0 **70** MissSBrotherton 1 70
(J R Jenkins) *hld up in tch: hdwy to trck ldrs over 5f out: rdn along 3f out: sn one pce* 11/4[1]
005- 5 1 ¾ **Adili (IRE)**[7] 7423 5-10-0 **56** MissHBethell 7 54
(Brian Ellison) *prom: cl up after 5f: rdn along over 3f out: drvn wl over 2f out and sn wknd* 14/1
5-46 6 6 **Luckster**[5] 292 4-9-3 **56** (v) HollieDoyle(5) 5 45
(David Evans) *led: pushed along over 5f out: rdn along over 4f out: sn hdd & wknd fr 3f out* 5/1[3]
001- 7 12 **Royal Trooper (IRE)**[57] 8129 8-10-2 **61** BeckyBrisbourne(3) 8 33
(Mark Brisbourne) *hld up in rr: sme hdwy on outer 5f out: rdn along wl over 3f out: nvr a factor* 4/1[2]
000- 8 26 **Diamond Pro (IRE)**[39] 8373 5-9-4 **51** oh1 BenFfrenchDavis(5) 2
(Christopher Kellett) *prom on inner: reminders after 4f: rdn along and lost pl bef 1/2-way: bhd fnl 4f* 50/1
3m 9.02s (0.72) **Going Correction** -0.075s/f (Stan)
**WFA** 4 from 5yo+ 6lb 8 Ran SP% 115.3
Speed ratings (Par 103): **94,93,91,90,89 86,79,64**
CSF £25.53 CT £262.28 TOTE £5.40: £1.60, £1.50, £3.40; EX 24.70 Trifecta £191.00.
**Owner** Straightline Construction Ltd **Bred** Kilnamoragh Stud **Trained** Carluke, S Lanarks
**FOCUS**
This was run at a leisurely early pace and saw a return to form on the Flat for the winner.

### 362 32RED FILLIES' H'CAP 6f (F)
1:50 (1:55) (Class 5) (0-75,72) 4-Y-0+ £3,234 (£962; £481; £240) Stalls Low

Form RPR
24-5 1 **Take The Lead**[19] 93 4-8-13 **64** AdrianNicholls 2 70
(David Nicholls) *mde all: jnd and rdn 3f out: edgd lft jst over 1f out: sn drvn and edgd rt ins fnl f: kpt on gamely towards fin* 7/2
100- 2 nk **Amosite**[31] 8431 8-9-7 **72** (v) FrederikTylicki 3 77
(J R Jenkins) *cl up: chal wl over 2f out: sn rdn and ev ch: drvn ent fnl f: no ex last 100yds* 3/1[3]
40-5 3 1 ½ **Caramelita**[19] 95 7-8-10 **61** (v) JoeFanning 4 61
(J R Jenkins) *trckd ldrs: effrt wl over 2f out: sn rdn: drvn and one pce fnl f* 11/4[2]
43-0 4 2 ½ **Laughing Rock (IRE)**[12] 196 4-8-8 **59** AndrewMullen 6 51
(Michael Appleby) *chsd ldng pair: hdwy on outer 1/2-way: rdn over 2f out: drvn and one pce fr over 1f out* 7/4[1]
40-0 5 23 **Gypsy Jazz (IRE)**[7] 272 7-8-7 **58** oh13 WilliamCarson 1
(Ann Stokell) *chsd ldrs: rdn along and outpcd bef 1/2-way: sn bhd* 50/1
1m 16.11s (-0.39) **Going Correction** -0.075s/f (Stan) 5 Ran SP% 112.2
Speed ratings (Par 100): **99,98,96,93,62**
CSF £14.45 TOTE £2.90: £2.40, £2.00; EX 15.30 Trifecta £35.30.
**Owner** David Nicholls Racing Club **Bred** Lady Whent **Trained** Sessay, N Yorks
■ Stewards' Enquiry : Adrian Nicholls four-day ban: use of whip (11-14 Feb)
**FOCUS**
Only a weak fillies' handicap, but hard to fault the performance of the winner who basically ran to form.

### 363 CORAL APP DOWNLOAD FROM THE APP STORE (S) STKS 1m 4f (F)
2:20 (2:25) (Class 6) 4-Y-0+ £2,264 (£673) Stalls Low

Form RPR
1-21 1 **Stand Guard**[18] 124 10-9-5 87 TomQueally 3 69+
(John Butler) *trckd ldr: cl up 4f out: led on bit 2f out: canter* 1/80[1]
5344 2 1 **Bix (IRE)**[11] 220 4-8-3 44 JordanHibberd(7) 4 47
(Alan Berry) *dwlt: sn led: rdn along 4f out: hdd 2f out: sn drvn: no ch w wnr* 20/1[2]
2m 46.9s (5.90) **Going Correction** -0.075s/f (Stan)
**WFA** 4 from 6yo+ 4lb 2 Ran SP% 103.6
Speed ratings (Par 101): **77,76**
TOTE £1.02.There was no bid for the winner.
**Owner** Maxilead Limited **Bred** Juddmonte Farms Ltd **Trained** Newmarket, Suffolk
**FOCUS**
An unfortunate injury picked by La Estrella in the saddling boxes robbed us of the much touted clash between Don Cantillon's prolific 11yo and Stand Guard, who cruised home.

### 364 BET ON YOUR MOBILE WITH LADBROKES CLAIMING STKS 1m (F)
2:50 (2:55) (Class 6) 4-Y-0+ £2,264 (£673; £336; £168) Stalls Low

Form RPR
5-11 1 **Tellovoi (IRE)**[15] 162 6-9-6 83 (v) AdamKirby 4 92
(Ian Williams) *mde all: rdn clr wl over 1f out: readily* 1/2[1]
204- 2 7 **Pelmanism**[61] 7608 7-9-1 75 TomEaves 6 71
(Brian Ellison) *chsd ldng pair: rdn along over 2f out: kpt on to chse wnr appr fnl f: sn no imp* 10/1[3]
345- 3 2 ¾ **Alice's Dancer (IRE)**[165] 5493 5-9-0 79 GrahamLee 5 64
(William Muir) *cl up: rdn along over 2f out: drvn and one pce fr wl over 1f out* 16/1
4-45 4 hd **Sofias Number One (USA)**[14] 172 6-8-9 73 (b) MarkCoumbe(3) 1 61
(Roy Bowring) *sn outpcd and detached in rr: rdn along and sme hdwy over 3f out: n.d* 5/2[2]
1m 40.41s (-3.29) **Going Correction** -0.075s/f (Stan) 4 Ran SP% 110.2
Speed ratings (Par 101): **113,106,103,103**
CSF £6.36 TOTE £1.30; EX 4.60 Trifecta £8.50.Tellovoi was claimed by Miss A Stokell for £16,000.
**Owner** Miss Magdalena Gut **Bred** Whisperview Trading Ltd **Trained** Portway, Worcs
**FOCUS**
This uncompetitive claimer was won as the market suggested.

### 365 LADBROKES MAIDEN STKS 1m (F)
3:20 (3:25) (Class 5) 4-5-Y-0 £3,234 (£962; £481; £240) Stalls Low

Form RPR
230- 1 **Thatchmaster (USA)**[99] 7425 4-9-5 80 JoeFanning 2 82+
(Mark Johnston) *mde all: shkn up and clr wl over 1f out: edgd rt to stands' rail ins fnl f: readily* 2/5[1]
346- 2 2 ½ **Waveguide (IRE)**[75] 7876 5-8-7 66 LewisWalsh(7) 4 69
(David Simcock) *hld up: swtchd rt to outer and hdwy 3f out: rdn over 2f out: chsd wnr ent fnl f: no imp* 11/4[2]
360- 3 1 **Vastly (USA)**[125] 6748 5-9-5 68 AdamBeschizza 1 72
(Julia Feilden) *chsd ldng pair: effrt on inner 3f out: rdn over 2f out: drvn and one pce appr fnl f* 10/1[3]
055- 4 11 **Mobley Chaos**[30] 8437 4-9-0 40 DCByrne(5) 5 46?
(Ronald Harris) *t.k.h: chsd wnr: rdn along over 2f out: sn edgd lft and wknd* 100/1
1m 42.7s (-1.00) **Going Correction** -0.075s/f (Stan) 4 Ran SP% 108.2
Speed ratings: **102,99,98,87**
CSF £1.77 TOTE £1.40; EX 1.80 Trifecta £2.50.
**Owner** Sheikh Hamdan bin Mohammed Al Maktoum **Bred** Darley **Trained** Middleham Moor, N Yorks
**FOCUS**
Another winning favourite on the card. The winner was the form choice and didn't need to improve.

### 366 DOWNLOAD THE LADBROKES APP H'CAP 1m (F)
3:50 (3:55) (Class 6) (0-65,65) 4-Y-0+ £2,587 (£770; £384; £192) Stalls Low

Form RPR
100- 1 **Hot Right Now**[229] 3232 4-8-11 **62** RobJFitzpatrick(7) 8 74
(K R Burke) *mde all: rdn along 2f out: edgd lft appr fnl f: kpt on wl towards fin* 33/1
0-21 2 1 ¼ **Queen Of Skies (IRE)**[14] 171 5-9-4 **62** AndrewMullen 3 71
(Michael Appleby) *trckd ldrs: hdwy over 2f out: rdn whn n.m.r and swtchd rt over 1f out: drvn and kpt on fnl f* 6/1
53-2 3 nk **Victorian Number (FR)**[14] 170 6-9-6 **64** (p) GeorgeBaker 5 73
(Geoffrey Deacon) *cl up on inner: effrt over 2f out and sn ev ch: rdn and edgd lft to ins rail ent fnl f: sn one pce* 3/1[2]
-134 4 2 ½ **Munaawib**[14] 170 6-9-5 **63** (bt) AdamKirby 11 66
(David C Griffiths) *chsd ldrs on outer: wd st: rdn 2f out: kpt on same pce* 14/1
6-30 5 nk **Quadriga (IRE)**[4] 317 4-8-6 **53** GeorgeChaloner(3) 4 55
(Robert Eddery) *dwlt and in rr: hdwy over 3f out: rdn to chse ldrs wl over 1f out: kpt on same pce fnl f* 14/1
01-6 6 1 ¼ **Auden (USA)**[22] 67 6-9-7 **65** (v) FrederikTylicki 2 64
(J R Jenkins) *in tch on inner: rdn along 3f out: drvn and kpt on same pce fnl 2f* 10/1
02-2 7 nse **Amtired**[7] 269 8-9-1 **59** (b) DanielTudhope 12 58
(Marjorie Fife) *midfield: hdwy over 3f out: rdn to chse ldrs over 2f out: sn drvn and no imp* 5/2[1]
51-3 8 ½ **Dandarrell**[19] 96 7-9-5 **63** (p) BarryMcHugh 1 61
(Julie Camacho) *sn outpcd in rr: pushed along 1/2-way: hdwy and rdn over 2f out: edgd lft wl over 1f out: sn no imp* 9/2[3]
0120 9 4 ½ **Mataajir (USA)**[8] 252 6-8-12 **56** (v) TomEaves 10 44
(Derek Shaw) *dwlt: a towards rr* 16/1
1P5- 10 3 ¾ **Better Value (IRE)**[39] 8360 4-9-0 **58** (p) AdamBeschizza 9 37
(Noel Quinlan) *chsd ldng pair: rdn along wl over 2f out: sn drvn and grad wknd* 16/1

60-0 **11** *nk* **Sam Spade (IRE)**[21] [75] 4-8-11 **62**.......................... AdamMcLean(7) 6 41
(Derek Shaw) *midfield: rdn along 1/2-way: sn wknd* **50/1**
0-00 **12** *7* **Sky Crossing**[14] [171] 5-8-8 **52**...................................... JamesSullivan 7 14
(Tom Tate) *midfield: pushed along after 3f: sn lost pl: wd st and sn bhd* **50/1**

1m 41.14s (-2.56) **Going Correction** -0.075s/f (Stan) **12** Ran SP% **127.1**
Speed ratings (Par 101): **109,107,107,104,104 103,103,102,98,94 94,87**
CSF £234.85 CT £807.67 TOTE £44.10: £10.70, £2.70, £1.50; EX 576.40 Trifecta £1008.30.
**Owner** Mrs Elaine M Burke **Bred** Hillwood Bloodstock **Trained** Middleham Moor, N Yorks

**FOCUS**
This competitive, if low-grade handicap, saw something of an upset. The form is rated slightly positive.

## 367 BET ON YOUR MOBILE WITH LADBROKES H'CAP 7f (F)
4:20 (4:26) (Class 6) (0-60,60) 4-Y-O+ £2,587 (£770; £384; £192) Stalls Low

Form RPR
1-36 **1** **George Benjamin**[5] [300] 7-8-12 **58**..................(tp) AlistairRawlinson(7) 8 69
(Michael Appleby) *dwlt: hdwy and in tch 1/2-way: wd st: rdn to chse ldrs 2f out: styd on u.p appr fnl f: led last 100yds* **7/2**[2]
04-5 **2** *1* **Solarmaite**[7] [273] 5-8-13 **55**......................................(b) MarkCoumbe(3) 6 63
(Roy Bowring) *led: rdn 2f out: drvn ent fnl f: hdd and no ex last 100yds* **14/1**
31- **3** *2 1/4* **Stun Gun**[30] [8437] 4-9-7 **60**........................................................ TomEaves 9 62
(Derek Shaw) *prom: hdwy to chal over 2f out: sn rdn: drvn and one pce appr fnl f* **7/4**[1]
50-1 **4** *nk* **De Lesseps (USA)**[26] [12] 6-8-5 **51**............................ VictorSantos(7) 1 52
(James Moffatt) *rdn along and outpcd in rr: bhd over 3f out: hdwy 2f out: styd on fnl f: nrst fin* **4/1**[3]
5-02 **5** *1 1/4* **Two In The Pink (IRE)**[11] [219] 4-9-0 **60**................... LouisSteward(7) 4 58
(Ralph J Smith) *cl up on inner: rdn wl over 1f out: styd on inner rail and grad wknd* **10/1**
2033 **6** *1/2* **Partner's Gold (IRE)**[2] [351] 4-8-7 **46** oh1.................(b) BarryMcHugh 5 43
(Alan Berry) *trckd ldrs: hdwy 1/2-way: chsd ldr 3f out: rdn over 2f out: sn drvn and grad wknd* **10/1**
0-42 **7** *2 1/2* **Boom To Bust (IRE)**[8] [262] 6-9-6 **59**.........................(b) WilliamCarson 3 49
(Barry Brennan) *sn rdn along and a towards rr* **20/1**
00-4 **8** *17* **Ferdy (IRE)**[19] [95] 5-9-7 **60**.................................................. JoeFanning 2
(Paul Green) *midfield: rdn along wl over 3f out: sn wknd* **12/1**

1m 29.01s (-1.29) **Going Correction** -0.075s/f (Stan) **8** Ran SP% **115.9**
Speed ratings (Par 101): **104,102,100,99,98 97,95,75**
CSF £50.85 CT £112.60 TOTE £4.70: £1.30, £3.20, £1.20; EX 65.00 Trifecta £279.50.
**Owner** Mick Appleby Racing **Bred** Mascalls Stud **Trained** Danethorpe, Notts

**FOCUS**
A race that revolved heavily around handicap debutant Stun Gun, who disappointed. The first two were both potentially well treated.
T/Plt: £25.70 to a £1 stake. Pool: £102,802.96 - 2910.30 winning units. T/Qpdt: £4.30 to a £1 stake. Pool: £7023.57 - 1183.70 winning units. JR

# 289 KEMPTON (A.W) (R-H)
Wednesday, January 29

**OFFICIAL GOING: Standard**
Wind: Fresh, across Weather: Cold, raining until race 5.

## 368 KEMPTON.CO.UK H'CAP 1m 2f (P)
4:50 (4:52) (Class 7) (0-50,50) 4-Y-O+ £1,617 (£481; £240; £120) Stalls Low

Form RPR
-062 **1** **Bapak Pesta (IRE)**[5] [317] 4-9-4 **49**..............................(p) JamieSpencer 13 59
(Kevin Ryan) *prog to ld after 1f: mde rest: kicked on 2f out: drvn out: unchal* **11/4**[2]
6-31 **2** *1 3/4* **Kyle Of Bute**[5] [317] 8-9-1 **49**........................................ JoshBaudains(5) 2 56
(Richard Ford) *t.k.h in midfield: prog over 2f out: rdn to chse wnr over 1f out: one pce and nvr able to chal* **5/2**[1]
06-3 **3** *3/4* **Waving**[7] [277] 5-9-4 **50**...............................................(t) MarkCoumbe(3) 14 55+
(Tony Carroll) *stdd s fr wdst draw and hld up in last trio: prog over 3f out but only midfield 2f out: rdn and styd on to take 3rd last strides* **11/4**[2]
/50- **4** *nk* **Beauchamp Sunset**[40] [8371] 4-9-2 **47**..................... RichardKingscote 6 51
(Paul Fitzsimons) *led 1f: chsd wnr to 6f out: styd prom: wnt 2nd again 2f out to over 1f out: one pce* **25/1**
404- **5** *2* **Vergality Ridge (IRE)**[117] [4353] 4-8-12 **48**......................... DCByrne(5) 3 48
(Ronald Harris) *towards rr: prog on inner 2f out: rdn and kpt on one pce after: n.d* **50/1**
65-0 **6** *1 3/4* **Total Obsession**[16] [156] 7-9-2 **50**.............................(v) LouisSteward(5) 4 47
(Mark Hoad) *towards rr: rdn 3f out: plugged on fnl 2f: no ch* **33/1**
001/ **7** *nk* **Catching Zeds**[850] [4846] 7-9-7 **50**................................... StevieDonohoe 12 46
(Kevin Frost) *mostly in last trio: rdn over 3f out: v modest prog over 1f out: no ch* **25/1**
30- **8** *nk* **Novel Dancer**[175] [5126] 6-8-12 **46**.............................. ShelleyBirkett(5) 10 42
(Lydia Richards) *in tch: prog on outer 1/2-way: hdwy to chse wnr over 3f out: wd bnd 2f out and wknd qckly* **25/1**
600- **9** *1 1/4* **Guardi (IRE)**[42] [3909] 5-9-5 **48**.............................................. AdamKirby 7 41
(Dean Ivory) *t.k.h: hld up bhd ldrs: cl enough over 2f out: carried wd bnd sn after: fnd nil and wknd* **7/1**[3]
06-6 **10** *11* **Tammis**[19] [115] 4-9-4 **49**.................................................... DavidProbert 8 20
(Ron Hodges) *a in last trio: struggling 3f out: sn bhd* **40/1**
000- **11** *59* **Finlodex**[86] [7321] 7-9-7 **50**.................................................(b[1]) ShaneKelly 11
(Murty McGrath) *sn prom: chsd wnr 6f out to over 3f out: wknd v rapidly: t.o and eased* **10/1**

2m 8.59s (0.59) **Going Correction** -0.025s/f (Stan)
**WFA** 4 from 5yo+ 2lb **11** Ran SP% **122.4**
Speed ratings (Par 97): **96,94,94,93,92 90,90,90,89,80 33**
CSF £9.78 CT £21.12 TOTE £3.60: £1.50, £1.40, £1.90; EX 9.60 Trifecta £20.80.
**Owner** T A Rahman **Bred** Theo Waddington And Mrs Theo Waddington **Trained** Hambleton, N Yorks

**FOCUS**
Little got into what was a moderate handicap, run at a fairly steady pace in driving rain. The first two ran similar to their latest Wolverhampton marks.

## 369 £500 FREE BETS AT BETDAQ H'CAP 1m 2f (P)
5:20 (5:21) (Class 5) (0-75,75) 4-Y-O+ £2,587 (£770; £384; £192) Stalls Low

Form RPR
1-10 **1** **Ocean Applause**[18] [146] 4-9-1 **71**......................................(t) AdamKirby 5 81
(John Ryan) *hld up in 5th: pushed along 3f out: prog 2f out: drvn to go 2nd jst over 1f out: clsd to ld last 100yds: pushed out after* **7/1**
060- **2** *3/4* **Steelriver (IRE)**[116] [7024] 4-9-3 **73**.................................... JamieSpencer 2 81
(James Bethell) *trckd ldng pair: rdn to go 2nd wl over 2f out: led wl over 1f out: hdd and one pce last 100yds* **13/8**[1]
0-42 **3** *2 1/4* **Poitin**[6] [293] 4-8-13 **69**........................................................ TomQueally 3 73
(Harry Dunlop) *trckd ldng trio: effrt over 2f out: rdn to dispute 2nd briefly over 1f out: nt qckn and sn wl hld* **9/4**[2]
00-2 **4** *4* **Apache Glory (USA)**[18] [146] 6-9-6 **74**.............................(p) LukeMorris 6 70
(John Stimpson) *hld up in last: rdn over 3f out: sn lost tch: kpt on again fr over 1f out to take 4th nr fin* **12/1**
36-4 **5** *1 1/2* **Serenity Spa**[19] [118] 4-9-0 **75**.................................... GeorgeDowning(5) 4 69
(Tony Carroll) *led: kicked on over 3f out: hdd wl over 1f out: wknd qckly fnl f* **14/1**
403- **6** *2 1/4* **Kelpie Blitz (IRE)**[54] [8179] 5-9-4 **72**..............................(t) GeorgeBaker 7 61
(Seamus Durack) *chsd ldr to wl over 2f out: wknd qckly* **4/1**[3]

2m 6.68s (-1.32) **Going Correction** -0.025s/f (Stan)
**WFA** 4 from 5yo+ 2lb **6** Ran SP% **115.7**
Speed ratings (Par 103): **104,103,101,98,97 95**
CSF £19.68 TOTE £8.50: £4.30, £1.10; EX 26.10 Trifecta £84.60.
**Owner** W McLuskey **Bred** R G Levin **Trained** Newmarket, Suffolk

**FOCUS**
Although run at just a steady pace, the form looks fair for the level. The winner rates close to his autumn form.

## 370 VISIT AND DINE IN THE PANORAMIC H'CAP 7f (P)
5:50 (5:52) (Class 7) (0-50,50) 4-Y-O+ £1,617 (£481; £240; £120) Stalls Low

Form RPR
03-4 **1** **Starbotton**[27] [18] 4-9-2 **45**............................................... JamieSpencer 3 58
(James Bethell) *wl away: mde all: kicked clr jst over 2f out: rdn and in n.d fr over 1f out* **11/2**[3]
400- **2** *2 1/4* **Six Silver Lane**[34] [8399] 6-9-6 **49**.................................(v) GeorgeBaker 9 56
(Derek Shaw) *trckd ldng trio on inner: rdn and prog to chse clr wnr over 1f out: styd on but no imp* **3/1**[1]
43-0 **3** *3 1/4* **Fleetwoodsands (IRE)**[14] [192] 7-9-5 **48**......................(bt) SeanLevey 13 47
(David Evans) *plld hrd in midfield: rdn and prog 2f out: kpt on to take 3rd nr fin* **6/1**
6-36 **4** *3/4* **Salford Prince (IRE)**[6] [290] 6-9-2 **45**...............................(b) LiamKeniry 1 42
(David Elsworth) *chsd wnr: rdn and nt qckn 2f out: outpcd after* **8/1**
0-02 **5** *1/2* **Ryedale Lass**[6] [290] 6-9-2 **45**................................(b) RichardKingscote 4 40
(Geoffrey Deacon) *chsd wnr: nt qckn 2f out: lost 2nd and fdd over 1f out* **6/1**
-040 **6** *1 3/4* **Glennten**[7] [274] 5-9-2 **50**............................................(b) JoshBaudains(5) 5 41
(Sylvester Kirk) *pushed along fr s to rch midfield: drvn and tried to cl 2f out: one pce* **20/1**
00-0 **7** *nse* **Strategic Action (IRE)**[14] [184] 5-9-6 **49**............................. RobertHavlin 2 40
(Linda Jewell) *chsd ldng trio: rdn over 2f out: no prog over 1f out: wknd fnl f* **10/1**
-356 **8** *1 1/4* **Surrey Dream (IRE)**[10] [251] 5-9-2 **45**............................................ AdamKirby 8 32
(John Bridger) *a in rr: rdn and no prog over 2f out: plugged on fnl f* **8/1**
64-2 **9** *hd* **Flow Chart (IRE)**[12] [215] 7-9-4 **50**............................ SladeO'Hara(3) 12 37
(Peter Grayson) *dropped in fr wd draw and hld up last: urged along furiously over 1f out: kpt on but no ch* **20/1**
50-0 **10** *1/2* **Chester Deelyte (IRE)**[20] [100] 6-8-13 **45**.............(v) MarkCoumbe(3) 10 31
(Lisa Williamson) *towards rr: rdn whn hmpd and swtchd lft over 2f out: no prog after* **33/1**
-332 **11** *1 3/4* **Mucky Molly**[10] [251] 6-9-3 **46**.............................................(vt) TomEaves 7 27
(Alison Hutchinson) *dwlt: a in rr: rdn and no prog over 2f out* **9/2**[2]
50-0 **12** *1 1/2* **Coach Montana (IRE)**[7] [281] 5-9-2 **45**........................(p[1]) AdamBeschizza 11 22
(Christine Dunnett) *chsd ldng trio on outer: rdn: edgd lft and wknd over 2f out* **50/1**
40-0 **13** *1/2* **Kaylee**[14] [185] 5-9-5 **48**...........................................................(v[1]) ChrisCatlin 6 24
(Brett Johnson) *hld up in rr: gng bttr than most over 2f out: shkn up and no rspnse wl over 1f out* **50/1**
05-0 **14** *1* **Michael's Nook**[13] [201] 7-9-5 **48**....................................(p) LukeMorris 14 21
(Alastair Lidderdale) *plld hrd: hld up in rr: rdn and no prog over 2f out* **25/1**

1m 25.36s (-0.64) **Going Correction** -0.025s/f (Stan) **14** Ran SP% **138.7**
Speed ratings (Par 97): **102,99,95,94,94 92,92,90,90,90 88,86,85,84**
CSF £24.37 CT £116.74 TOTE £7.90: £2.70, £1.90, £3.10; EX 34.40 Trifecta £241.10.
**Owner** Clarendon Thoroughbred Racing **Bred** Miss H Budgett & Kirtlington Stud Ltd **Trained** Middleham Moor, N Yorks

**FOCUS**
The winner made all in the best relative time obn the card, stepping up on recent form.

## 371 BETDAQ - THE SPORTS BETTING EXCHANGE MEDIAN AUCTION MAIDEN STKS 6f (P)
6:20 (6:20) (Class 5) 3-5-Y-O £2,587 (£770; £384; £192) Stalls Low

Form RPR
222- **1** **Pool House**[75] [7893] 3-8-12 76.............................................. DavidProbert 7 79+
(Andrew Balding) *trckd ldng trio: shkn up 2f out: wnt 2nd over 1f out: no imp on ldr tl r.o last 100yds to ld post* **4/9**[1]
222- **2** *nse* **Taquka (IRE)**[198] [4346] 3-8-12 76........................................ JimCrowley 3 79
(Ralph Beckett) *led at mod pce: kicked on jst over 2f out: 2 l clr fnl f: styd on but hdd post5* **5/2**[2]
40- **3** *4* **Why Not Now**[29] [8451] 3-8-2 0........................................... JoeyHaynes(5) 1 61
(Roger Charlton) *restless stalls: in tch in 5th: urged along and prog fr 2f out: tk 3rd ins fnl f but nt pce to threaten* **25/1**
050- **4** *1* **Katja**[118] [6972] 3-8-7 59..................................................... JoeFanning 6 58
(J W Hills) *t.k.h: trckd ldr: nt qckn 2f out: lost 2nd over 1f out: fdd* **33/1**
**5** *2* **Harboured (USA)** 3-8-7 0............................................... LukeMorris 4 52
(Sir Mark Prescott Bt) *dwlt: rn v green in last and shoved along: nvr a factor: plugged on fnl f* **20/1**[3]
23-4 **6** *1 3/4* **Ishisoba**[15] [174] 4-9-9 50............................................... LiamJones 5 50
(Ronald Harris) *chsd ldng pair to wl over 1f out: wknd fnl f* **50/1**

1m 13.38s (0.28) **Going Correction** -0.025s/f (Stan)
**WFA** 3 from 4yo 16lb **6** Ran SP% **111.3**
Speed ratings (Par 103): **97,96,91,90,87 85**
CSF £1.64 TOTE £1.40: £1.10, £1.60; EX 2.00 Trifecta £8.80.
**Owner** David Brownlow **Bred** R, J D & M R Bromley Gardner **Trained** Kingsclere, Hants

**FOCUS**
As expected, the two 76-rated runners pulled clear late on in this maiden. The runner-up sets the standard.

## 372 WINNERS ARE WELCOME AT BETDAQ H'CAP 7f (P)
6:50 (6:50) (Class 4) (0-85,87) 4-Y-O+ £4,690 (£1,395; £697; £348) Stalls Low

Form RPR
0-30 1 **Bowstar**[7] 287 5-8-9 73 ....................(b[1]) RobertHavlin 5 83
(Michael Attwater) *trckd ldng pair: rdn 2f out: led over 1f out: drvn and asserted fnl f* 20/1
301- 2 1 1/2 **Firmdecisions (IRE)**[41] 8345 4-9-3 81 .................... JimCrowley 3 87
(Brett Johnson) *trckd ldng pair: rdn to chal and upsides over 1f out: chsd wnr after: nt qckn fnl f* 4/1[1]
2-52 3 nk **Smokethatthunders (IRE)**[7] 287 4-8-9 73 .................... LukeMorris 6 78
(James Toller) *in tch disputing 5th: rdn wl over 2f out: styd on fr over 1f out to take 3rd nr fin* 4/1[1]
64-2 4 nk **Emkanaat**[4] 342 6-8-10 79 ....................(b) DavidKenny(5) 1 84
(Amy Weaver) *wl in tch disputing 5th: rdn 2f out: styd against far rail after: kpt on but nvr able to chal* 7/1
31-3 5 1 1/4 **Maggie Pink**[27] 11 5-8-9 73 .................... AndrewMullen 7 74
(Michael Appleby) *disp ld at solid pce: led 2f out to over 1f out: wknd fnl f* 10/1
605- 6 nk **Glanely (IRE)**[29] 8455 4-8-13 77 .................... ShaneKelly 2 78
(Martyn Meade) *dwlt: hld up in 7th: rdn and nt qckn over 2f out: no ch after: plugged on* 7/1
26-4 7 1 3/4 **Corporal Maddox**[11] 234 7-9-7 85 ....................(p) GeorgeBaker 4 81
(Ronald Harris) *stdd s: hld up in last and off the pce: shuffled along over 2f out: no prog and no ch whn reminders 1f out* 11/2[3]
210- 8 3/4 **Tasrih (USA)**[39] 8385 5-9-5 83 .................... TomQueally 8 77
(Alan McCabe) *disp ld at solid pce to 2f out: wknd u.p sn after* 9/2[2]

1m 24.42s (-1.58) **Going Correction** -0.025s/f (Stan) 8 Ran SP% **112.4**
Speed ratings (Par 105): **108,106,105,105,104 103,101,100**
CSF £94.90 CT £391.50 TOTE £21.10: £5.10, £1.60, £1.50; EX 119.60 Trifecta £865.40.
**Owner** Canisbay Bloodstock **Bred** Juddmonte Farms Ltd **Trained** Epsom, Surrey

**FOCUS**
They appeared to go a sound gallop, but the race produced a surprise winner. The second and third were close to their recent marks.

## 373 MIX BUSINESS WITH PLEASURE AT KEMPTON H'CAP (DIV I) 6f (P)
7:20 (7:20) (Class 6) (0-55,55) 3-Y-O £1,940 (£577; £288; £144) Stalls Low

Form RPR
000- 1 **Artemis (IRE)**[42] 8328 3-9-4 52 ....................[1] JoeFanning 3 63
(Conrad Allen) *hld up in 6th: smooth prog 2f out: led over 1f out and sn dashed clr: easily* 4/1[3]
50-2 2 2 1/2 **Saffire Song**[5] 315 3-9-4 55 .................... RobertTart(3) 5 60+
(Alan Bailey) *plld hrd early: wl in tch: rdn over 2f out: prog whn nt clr run briefly 1f out: styd on to take 2nd last 100yds: no ch w wnr* 2/1[1]
6-33 3 1 3/4 **Mahon Falls**[3] 346 3-9-2 50 .................... AdamKirby 9 47
(David Evans) *chsd ldr: rdn to ld narrowly 2f out to over 1f out: no ch w wnr after and fdd ins fnl f* 5/1
03-4 4 3/4 **Female Strategy (IRE)**[12] 218 3-9-7 55 .................... JamieSpencer 6 50
(Peter Chapple-Hyam) *wnt lft s: racd wd: chsd ldrs: rdn and hung bdly lft 2f out: no ch after: plugged on fnl f* 5/2[2]
406- 5 1 1/4 **Shirley Vanessa (IRE)**[109] 7199 3-8-13 47 .................... LukeMorris 7 38
(Luke Dace) *led: rdn and narrowly hdd 2f out: wknd over 1f out* 10/1
00-0 6 2 1/2 **Mistress And Maid**[18] 140 3-8-12 46 oh1 ....................(v[1]) LiamKeniry 1 29
(Joseph Tuite) *chsd ldrs: drvn to try to cl over 2f out: wknd qckly over 1f out* 25/1
00-6 7 8 **She's A Lucky Lady**[18] 140 3-8-5 46 oh1 .................... RyanWhile(7) 10
(Bill Turner) *sltly impeded s: a last and nvr gng wl: t.o* 66/1

1m 14.39s (1.29) **Going Correction** -0.025s/f (Stan) 7 Ran SP% **113.0**
Speed ratings (Par 95): **90,86,84,83,81 78,67**
CSF £12.14 CT £39.11 TOTE £3.90: £2.30, £2.80; EX 12.80 Trifecta £53.50.
**Owner** sportsdays.co.uk **Bred** Shane Doyle **Trained** Newmarket, Suffolk

**FOCUS**
Low-grade form, and a slower time than division II. The winner may have more to offer.

## 374 MIX BUSINESS WITH PLEASURE AT KEMPTON H'CAP (DIV II) 6f (P)
7:50 (7:51) (Class 6) (0-55,55) 3-Y-O £1,940 (£577; £288; £144) Stalls Low

Form RPR
03-3 1 **Alumina (IRE)**[21] 86 3-9-4 52 .................... DavidProbert 5 58+
(Andrew Balding) *chsd ldr: shkn up over 2f out: drvn and clsd over 1f out: led ins fnl f: styd on wl* 7/4[1]
0-44 2 1 1/4 **El Duque**[9] 261 3-8-10 51 ....................(v) RyanWhile(7) 3 53
(Bill Turner) *trckd ldng pair: hrd rdn and tried to chal on inner over 1f out: wnt 2nd ins fnl f: styd on but nt pce of wnr* 20/1
00-0 3 1 **Wiki Tiki**[21] 86 3-9-7 55 ....................(t) AdamBeschizza 1 54+
(Stuart Williams) *rrd s: t.k.h early and hld up towards rr: rdn over 2f out: prog wl over 1f out: styd on to take 3rd last strides* 6/1[3]
54-5 4 nse **Biscuiteer**[21] 86 3-9-7 55 ....................(b[1]) LukeMorris 2 54
(Scott Dixon) *racd freely: led: kicked on over 2f out: 2 l clr over 1f out: hdd and fdd ins fnl f* 7/1
004- 5 3 1/4 **Charleys Angel**[70] 7973 3-8-9 46 oh1 .................... JemmaMarshall(3) 10 34
(Pat Phelan) *racd on outer: chsd ldrs: wl outpcd fr 2f out: modest 5th and no imp fnl f* 14/1
-434 6 1 1/4 **Countess Lupus (IRE)**[12] 216 3-8-7 46 oh1 ....(b) ShirleyTeasdale(5) 4 30
(Lisa Williamson) *dwlt: hld up in last pair: shkn up and no prog over 2f out: modest late hdwy* 33/1
5-32 7 shd **Bold Max**[6] 302 3-9-2 50 .................... LiamJones 9 34
(Zoe Davison) *hld up in rr: rdn and struggling over 2f out: nvr on terms* 14/1
600- 8 1 3/4 **Limegrove**[89] 7665 3-9-7 55 .................... AdamKirby 7 33
(David Evans) *stdd s: hld up in last and detached after 2f: pushed along over 2f out: reminder and modest prog over 1f out: nvr involved* 10/1
00-0 9 3/4 **Krackerjill (IRE)**[16] 165 3-8-8 49 .................... CharlotteJenner(7) 8 25
(Mark Usher) *t.k.h early: chsd ldrs: lost pl over 2f out: steadily wknd* 14/1
006- 10 6 **Pay The Greek**[165] 5539 3-8-13 47 .................... SeanLevey 6
(Noel Quinlan) *nvr beyond midfield: wknd qckly 2f out* 11/4[2]

1m 13.35s (0.25) **Going Correction** -0.025s/f (Stan) 10 Ran SP% **126.6**
Speed ratings (Par 95): **97,95,94,93,89 87,87,85,84,76**
CSF £46.42 CT £194.42 TOTE £3.40: £1.90, £3.10, £1.60; EX 43.50 Trifecta £654.50.
**Owner** Shapoor Mistry **Bred** Eimear Mulhern & Abbeville Stud **Trained** Kingsclere, Hants

**FOCUS**
As in the first division, this went to a filly with the potential to rate higher. It was the faster division and slightly faster form.

## 375 BETDAQ 1ST UK RACE COMMISSION FREE H'CAP 1m (P)
8:20 (8:20) (Class 3) (0-95,90) 3-Y-O £7,158 (£2,143; £1,071; £535) Stalls Low

Form RPR
12-1 1 **Examiner (IRE)**[18] 143 3-9-0 83 .................... LiamJones 5 89+
(William Haggas) *settled in 3rd: pushed along over 2f out: prog to ld wl over 1f out: rdn and kpt on wl enough fnl f* 1/1[1]
15-3 2 1 1/2 **Truancy (IRE)**[18] 143 3-7-11 71 oh3 .................... JoeyHaynes(5) 2 72
(K R Burke) *led: set stdy pce for 3f: rdn over 2f out: hdd wl over 1f out: kpt on to win battle for 2nd but safely hld by wnr* 15/2
21-2 3 hd **Jalingo (IRE)**[18] 143 3-8-8 77 .................... JoeFanning 1 77
(Mark Johnston) *pressed ldr: chal 2f out: nt qckn as wnr wnt past: styd on same pce after* 2/1[2]
46-3 4 1/2 **Scruffy Tramp (IRE)**[14] 183 3-9-4 90 .................... RobertTart(3) 3 89
(Alan Bailey) *dwlt: t.k.h early: hld up in last: swtchd lft and rdn 2f out: clsd on plcd horses 1f out: effrt flattened out* 5/1[3]

1m 39.75s (-0.05) **Going Correction** -0.025s/f (Stan) 4 Ran SP% **111.8**
Speed ratings (Par 101): **99,97,97,96**
CSF £8.71 TOTE £1.40; EX 6.90 Trifecta £19.90.
**Owner** Ian and Christine Beard **Bred** River Downs Stud **Trained** Newmarket, Suffolk

**FOCUS**
The first three had met in a handicap over the same trip at Lingfield last time. The winner confirmed that form in a muddling race.
T/Jkpt: Not won T/Plt: £13.80 to £1 stake. Pool: £204,567.98. 10,787.39 winning units. T/Qpdt: £5.70 to £1 stake. Pool: £12,214.24. 1,581.51 winning units. JN

# [368]KEMPTON (A.W) (R-H)
Thursday, January 30

**OFFICIAL GOING: Standard**
Wind: Virtually nil Weather: cold

## 376 BETVICTOR NONRUNNER NO BET CHELTENHAM 2014 APPRENTICE H'CAP 1m (P)
4:50 (4:50) (Class 5) (0-75,75) 4-Y-O+ £2,749 (£818; £408; £204) Stalls Low

Form RPR
24-1 1 **Just One Kiss**[15] 189 4-9-7 75 .................... LouisSteward 8 84+
(Lady Cecil) *trckd ldr: led over 2f out: drvn clr fnl f* 11/10[1]
000- 2 2 3/4 **Emman Bee (IRE)**[77] 7876 5-8-2 63 .................... KieranShoemark(7) 1 66
(Luke Dace) *in rr: hdwy 2f out: styd on wl fnl f to take 2nd in clsng stages but no ch w wnr* 50/1
016- 3 nk **Collodi (GER)**[93] 7608 5-9-7 75 .................... NedCurtis 2 77
(Roger Curtis) *chsd ldrs: rdn to chse wnr appr fnl f but no imp: dropped to 3rd in clsng stages* 10/1
06-3 4 nk **Gracious George (IRE)**[8] 286 4-9-1 74 .................... GaryMahon(5) 7 75
(Jimmy Fox) *in tch: wd and lost position over 3f out: hdwy again fnl f: kpt on wl in clsng stages* 6/1[2]
014- 5 1 1/2 **Hierarch (IRE)**[54] 8198 7-8-5 66 .................... PaigeRanger(7) 10 64
(David Simcock) *in rr: hdwy over 1f out: kpt on in clsng stages* 25/1
-422 6 hd **Greensward**[8] 286 8-9-4 72 ....................(b) RyanWhile 5 69
(Conor Dore) *s.i.s: in rr: rdn over 2f out: styd on in clsng stages* 12/1
46-0 7 hd **Ancient Greece**[26] 56 7-9-3 74 .................... JordanVaughan(3) 4 71
(George Baker) *slowly away: in rr: hdwy 2f out: kpt on fnl f: nt rch ldrs* 12/1
50-0 8 6 **Queen Aggie (IRE)**[12] 233 4-8-9 68 .................... RobHornby(5) 3 51
(David Evans) *in tch: rdn over 2f out and sn btn* 8/1[3]
266- 9 3/4 **Jewelled**[122] 6898 8-9-4 72 .................... DanielCremin 11 53
(Ralph J Smith) *outpcd most of way* 25/1
11-6 10 1 **Shaunas Spirit (IRE)**[20] 118 6-9-0 73 ....................(p) PaulBooth(5) 6 52
(Dean Ivory) *t.k.h: led tl hdd over 2f out: sn btn* 20/1
500- 11 15 **Vanvitelli**[181] 4961 4-8-6 65 .................... JackGarritty(5) 9 10
(Pat Murphy) *chsd ldrs 4f* 33/1

1m 38.18s (-1.62) **Going Correction** +0.025s/f (Slow) 11 Ran SP% **114.8**
Speed ratings (Par 103): **109,106,105,105,104 103,103,97,97,96 81**
CSF £90.57 CT £398.01 TOTE £1.90: £1.20, £9.70, £3.50; EX 61.30 Trifecta £1190.70.
**Owner** Lordship Stud **Bred** Lordship Stud **Trained** Newmarket, Suffolk

**FOCUS**
Little depth to the race, and straightforward for the winner.

## 377 BOOK NOW FOR JUMP RACING 07.02.14 H'CAP 1m (P)
5:20 (5:20) (Class 7) (0-50,50) 4-Y-O+ £1,617 (£481; £240; £120) Stalls Low

Form RPR
2-53 1 **Miami Gator (IRE)**[17] 156 7-9-2 50 ....................(v) JoeyHaynes(5) 14 58
(K R Burke) *mde all: hrd drvn fr over 2f out and sn hrd pressed: styd on gamely u.p thrght fnl f* 10/1
42-3 2 nk **Polydamos**[20] 116 5-9-5 48 .................... LukeMorris 2 55
(Tony Carroll) *chsd ldrs: drvn to chal appr fnl f: kpt on fnl f but a jst hld by wnr* 3/1[1]
45-5 3 3/4 **Wishformore (IRE)**[22] 81 7-9-6 49 ....................(p) JimCrowley 6 54
(Ian Williams) *chsd ldr: drvn to chal appr fnl f: no ex and one pce into 3rd fnl 120yds* 5/1[2]
0-44 4 nk **Bladewood Girl**[15] 179 6-9-5 48 ....................(v[1]) FrederikTylicki 7 53
(J R Jenkins) *chsd ldrs: rdn over 2f out: styd on fnl f to press for 3rd in clsng stages: no imp on wnr* 8/1
3-03 5 hd **Fleetwoodsands (IRE)**[1] 370 7-9-5 48 ....................(bt) SeanLevey 1 52
(David Evans) *plld hrd: chsd ldrs: rdn over 2f out: styd on same pce ins fnl f* 6/1[3]
0-41 6 1 **Mr Chocolate Drop (IRE)**[15] 179 10-9-5 48 ....................(t) AdamKirby 12 50
(Mandy Rowland) *in rr: hdwy 2f out: styd on fnl f: nt rch ldrs* 8/1
00-0 7 1/2 **Appyjack**[22] 88 6-9-2 45 ....................(b) LiamKeniry 8 46
(Tony Carroll) *s.i.s: in rr: rdn over 2f out: styd on ins fnl f* 20/1
00-6 8 1/2 **Dreaming Again**[22] 92 4-9-0 50 .................... CamHardie(7) 9 50
(Jimmy Fox) *in rr: hmpd after 1f: sn in tch: hdwy 2f out: styd on same pce fnl f* 12/1
006- 9 1 1/2 **Man In The Arena**[107] 7266 4-8-13 45 .................... RobertTart(3) 11 41
(Dr Jon Scargill) *in tch: rdn and one pce over 2f out: no imp fnl f* 20/1
0-03 10 nk **Chandrayaan**[15] 179 7-9-6 49 ....................(v) JohnFahy 13 44
(John E Long) *chsd ldrs: rdn over 2f out: btn sn after* 20/1
0-60 11 3/4 **Fairy Mist (IRE)**[15] 179 7-8-9 45 ....................[1] RyanWhile(7) 4 39
(John Bridger) *in tch: rdn over 2f out: btn sn after* 25/1
50-5 12 1 **Blue Deer (IRE)**[12] 229 6-9-1 49 ....................(tp) LouisSteward(5) 5 40
(Lee Carter) *hmpd after 1f: sme hdwy 2f out: sn btn* 20/1


The Form Book, Raceform Ltd, Newbury, RG14 5SJ

505- **13** *2 ½* **Querido (GER)**[59] 2747 10-8-13 **45**......................(tp) JemmaMarshall(3) 3 31
(Paddy Butler) *s.i.s: towards rr most of way* **66/1**
050- **14** *4* **Telamon (IRE)**[205] 4153 4-8-9 **45**.......................... JordanVaughan(7) 10 21
(Milton Bradley) *in tch whn hmpd after 1f: sn towards rr* **66/1**
1m 41.21s (1.41) **Going Correction** +0.025s/f (Slow) **14** Ran SP% **120.8**
Speed ratings (Par 97): **93,92,91,91,91 90,89,89,87,87 86,85,83,79**
CSF £36.64 CT £178.75 TOTE £13.80: £3.70, £1.50, £1.70; EX 43.30 Trifecta £403.50.
**Owner** Ontoawinner & Mrs E Burke **Bred** Newlands House Stud **Trained** Middleham Moor, N Yorks
**FOCUS**
A weak race run at a steady gallop, and it paid to race handily. The winner didn't need to find much on his latest form.

## 378 TURFTV H'CAP 1m (P)
**5:50** (5:50) (Class 6) (0-60,60) 3-Y-O **£1,940** (£577; £288; £144) **Stalls** Low

Form RPR
005- **1** **Like A Prayer**[64] 8061 3-9-6 **59**..................................... JimCrowley 6 68+
(Ralph Beckett) *hld up in tch: hdwy and nt clr run appr fnl 2f tl edgd lft and qcknd wl over 1f out: led ins fnl f: readily* **1/1**[1]
34-4 **2** *2 ¼* **Armelle (FR)**[22] 86 3-9-0 **53**........................................ LukeMorris 2 55
(Scott Dixon) *chsd ldrs: drvn to ld ins fnl 2f: hdd and outpcd ins fnl f: hld on wl for 2nd* **10/1**
23-6 **3** *hd* **Plough Boy (IRE)**[17] 157 3-9-5 **58**................................. ChrisCatlin 9 59
(Willie Musson) *chsd ldrs: led appr fnl f: hdd sn after: kpt on fnl f to press for 2nd but no ch w wnr* **5/1**[3]
05-3 **4** *6* **Flying Kyte**[8] 280 3-8-4 **46**............................... JemmaMarshall(3) 3 34
(Pat Phelan) *in rr: pushed along over 2f out: styd on fnl f but nvr any ch* **20/1**
441- **5** *¾* **Jazri**[155] 5893 3-9-7 **60**........................................... AdamKirby 1 46
(Milton Bradley) *in rr: drvn and hdwy over 2f out: wknd appr fnl f* **9/2**[2]
34-0 **6** *3 ½* **Ronya (IRE)**[17] 157 3-9-2 **60**............................ JoeyHaynes(5) 7 38
(K R Burke) *rdn over 2f out: nvr gng pce to get into contention* **20/1**
000- **7** *hd* **Henry Grace (IRE)**[42] 8342 3-8-12 **58**...................... GaryMahon(7) 11 35
(Jimmy Fox) *chsd ldrs: ev ch appr fnl 2f: wknd wl over 1f out* **20/1**
006- **8** *1 ¾* **Touche De Rouge (IRE)**[48] 8274 3-8-7 **46** oh1.................... LiamJones 4 19
(Peter Makin) *led 1f: styd chsng ldrs: wknd over 1f out* **33/1**
00-0 **9** *8* **Redy To Rumble**[19] 142 3-8-0 **46** oh1........................ RhiainIngram(7) 8 1
(Michael Attwater) *towards rr most of way* **66/1**
0-06 **10** *2 ¾* **Dawnfromthepast (IRE)**[8] 280 3-8-7 **46** oh1.................. MarcHalford 10
(Luke Dace) *led after 1f: hdd over 2f out and wknd qckly* **66/1**
040- **11** *20* **Sakuramachi**[66] 8039 3-8-13 **55**............................ MatthewCosham(3) 5
(Nikki Evans) *s.i.s: wl bhd fnl fr 1/2-way* **66/1**
1m 40.09s (0.29) **Going Correction** +0.025s/f (Slow) **11** Ran SP% **115.6**
Speed ratings (Par 95): **99,96,96,90,89 86,86,84,76,73 53**
CSF £10.80 CT £35.72 TOTE £2.00: £1.40, £2.80, £1.40; EX 13.50 Trifecta £52.70.
**Owner** The Rat Pack Partnership **Bred** Kirtlington Stud Ltd **Trained** Kimpton, Hants
**FOCUS**
A moderate race, but it went the way of a handicap debutant who probably has more to offer. The first three were clear and the winner was value for a bit extra.

## 379 CHELTENHAM 2014 NRNB AT BETVICTOR.COM CLASSIFIED CLAIMING STKS 1m 3f (P)
**6:20** (6:21) (Class 5) 4-Y-O+ **£2,749** (£818; £408; £204) **Stalls** Low

Form RPR
20-0 **1** **Top Diktat**[11] 250 6-9-7 67................................................ GeorgeBaker 3 78+
(Gary Moore) *hld up in tch: pushed along and hdwy over 1f out: led fnl 110yds: readily* **15/8**[1]
0-02 **2** *1* **Gabrial's Hope (FR)**[13] 209 5-8-7 58...........................(p) MartinLane 4 62
(David Simcock) *trckd ldr: rdn and styd on u.p fnl 2f: bmpd 1f out: styd on for 2nd in clsng stages but no ch w wnr* **4/1**[2]
03-0 **3** *hd* **Herbalist**[22] 88 4-8-5 59 ow1...........................(v[1]) ChrisCatlin 1 63?
(Ben Pauling) *led at modest pce: pushed along and qcknd ins fnl 3f: kpt on fnl f: hdd and outpcd fnl 110yds: lost 2nd in clsng stages* **25/1**
0-13 **4** *2 ¼* **Sutton Sid**[12] 229 4-8-10 66............................................(v) SeanLevey 2 64
(Chris Gordon) *chsd ldrs: rdn over 2f out: styd on one pce and edgd lft u.p 1f out: sn wknd* **6/1**
064- **5** *1 ¼* **Tartan Gigha (IRE)**[43] 8335 9-8-4 69...................(v[1]) JackGarritty(7) 5 60
(Geoffrey Harker) *in rr: pushed along and sme hdwy fr 2f out: no prog fnl f* **8/1**
00-1 **6** *¾* **My Lord**[17] 168 6-9-7 67.................................................. LukeMorris 7 68
(Tony Carroll) *in rr: drvn over 2f out: styd on same pce* **11/2**[3]
/0-3 **7** *6* **Bollin Judith**[15] 186 8-8-0 70.........................(vt) AprilKitchener(7) 8 44
(Jim Best) *chsd ldrs 1/2-way: wknd over 2f out* **25/1**
5-25 **8** *¾* **Copperwood**[15] 180 9-8-4 64........................................ LouisSteward(5) 6 44
(Lee Carter) *in rr: hdwy 4f out: wknd over 2f out* **8/1**
2m 21.77s (-0.13) **Going Correction** +0.025s/f (Slow)
**WFA** 4 from 5yo+ 3lb **8** Ran SP% **114.4**
Speed ratings (Par 103): **101,100,100,98,97 97,92,92**
.Gabrial's Hope was claimed by D Tate for £3000. Sutton Sid was claimed by M Elvin for £6000.\n\x\x
**Owner** Miss T R Hale **Bred** Wretham Stud **Trained** Lower Beeding, W Sussex
**FOCUS**
The pace slowed a lot down the back before the race developed into a sprint up the straight. The form revolves around the third.

## 380 BETVICTOR NONRUNNER FREE BET CHELTENHAM 2014 H'CAP 2m (P)
**6:50** (6:50) (Class 6) (0-60,60) 4-Y-O+ **£1,940** (£577; £288; £144) **Stalls** Low

Form RPR
004- **1** **Newtown Cross (IRE)**[108] 7248 4-8-2 **50**...................... CamHardie(7) 1 54
(Jimmy Fox) *in rr but in tch: hdwy 2f out: styd on wl fnl f: pushed out to ld cl home* **14/1**
R-46 **2** *nk* **Azabitmour (FR)**[8] 283 4-8-8 **49**............................... MartinLane 8 53
(John Best) *t.k.h towards rr: hdwy on outside and rdn 2f out: sn edging rt: styd on wl to chal fnl 110yds: no ex cl home* **13/2**
00-5 **3** *¾* **Ocean Power (IRE)**[11] 247 4-8-5 **46**........................... LukeMorris 7 49
(Richard Phillips) *sn in tch: hdwy 2f out to take slt ld appr fnl f: hdd fnl 110yds: styd on same pce in clsng stages* **8/1**
340- **4** *½* **Boston Blue**[22] 7767 7-9-8 **56**...................................... JimCrowley 6 58
(Tony Carroll) *chsd ldrs: rdn 2f out: chal u.p ins fnl f: no ex in clsng stages* **3/1**[1]
154- **5** *1* **Bold Adventure**[35] 3688 10-9-10 **58**........................... JamieMackay 5 59
(Willie Musson) *hld up in rr: stl plenty to do 3f out: hdwy on ins 2f out: sn chsng ldrs: no imp ins fnl f* **8/1**
04-3 **6** *½* **Rowlestone Lass**[11] 246 4-8-9 **50**............................ ShaneKelly 2 51
(Richard Price) *led: rdn over 2f out: hdd appr fnl f wknd fnl 110yds* **9/2**[2]
160- **7** *4 ½* **Superciliary**[24] 7539 5-9-12 **60**.................................. AdamKirby 3 55
(Chris Gordon) *chsd ldr: rdn over 2f out: wknd fnl f* **5/1**[3]
006- **8** *5* **Isdaal**[49] 7278 7-9-12 **60**.............................................. JimmyQuinn 4 49
(Kevin Morgan) *chsd ldrs: rdn 2f out: wknd over 1f out* **10/1**
3m 38.86s (8.76) **Going Correction** +0.025s/f (Slow)
**WFA** 4 from 5yo+ 7lb **8** Ran SP% **111.2**
Speed ratings (Par 101): **79,78,78,78,77 77,75,72**
CSF £95.40 CT £760.80 TOTE £19.40: £6.50, £3.20, £2.90; EX 143.50 Trifecta £1022.90.
**Owner** Mutton & Lamb **Bred** Mrs Anne Coughlan **Trained** Collingbourne Ducis, Wilts
**FOCUS**
They pottered around for most of this weak race and it came down to which horse had the best turn of foot. They finished in a bunch.

## 381 DOWNLOAD THE BETVICTOR APP NOW H'CAP 6f (P)
**7:20** (7:21) (Class 4) (0-85,85) 4-Y-O+ **£5,175** (£1,540; £769; £384) **Stalls** Low

Form RPR
0-43 **1** **Trojan Rocket (IRE)**[10] 257 6-8-13 **77**...............(p) RichardKingscote 3 86
(Michael Wigham) *mde all: pushed along 2f out: styd on strly thrght fnl f* **5/2**[2]
6-26 **2** *¾* **Light From Mars**[4] 348 9-9-1 **79**.................................(p) LiamJones 2 86
(Ronald Harris) *chsd ldrs: rdn to chse wnr jst ins fnl 2f: kpt on but a readily hld* **12/1**
65-0 **3** *4 ½* **Gabrial's Gift (IRE)**[28] 11 5-8-7 **71** oh1.......................(p) LukeMorris 1 64
(Scott Dixon) *chsd wnr: rdn and dropped to 3rd jst ins fnl 2f: sn outpcd* **8/1**
426- **4** *¾* **Foxtrot Jubilee (IRE)**[33] 8430 4-9-5 **83**...................... JimCrowley 6 73
(Ralph Beckett) *in tch: rdn and hdwy 2f out: nvr gng pce to rch ldrs* **6/4**[1]
24-4 **5** *3 ¼* **Pabusar**[22] 80 6-9-4 **82**.................................................. AdamKirby 5 62
(Jamie Osborne) *in rr but in tch tl rdn and btn over 2f out* **7/2**[3]
1m 12.07s (-1.03) **Going Correction** +0.025s/f (Slow) **5** Ran SP% **109.6**
Speed ratings (Par 105): **107,106,100,99,94**
CSF £27.02 TOTE £3.40: £1.70, £2.50; EX 10.50 Trifecta £34.80.
**Owner** G Linder, D Hassan, R Warner **Bred** J G F Fox **Trained** Newmarket, Suffolk
**FOCUS**
On paper a fairly competitive little race, but as it happens the first two had it between them from over a furlong out. The winner basically ran to last year's turf form.

## 382 BACK OF THE NET AT BETVICTOR.COM H'CAP 1m 4f (P)
**7:50** (7:50) (Class 6) (0-65,65) 4-Y-O+ **£1,940** (£577; £288; £144) **Stalls** Centre

Form RPR
01-1 **1** **The Ginger Berry**[11] 247 4-8-9 **57** 6ex........................... RobertTart(3) 2 68+
(Dr Jon Scargill) *in tch: hdwy 3f out: led ins fnl 2f: drvn fnl f: hld on wl* **6/4**[1]
60-2 **2** *¾* **Cabuchon (GER)**[8] 283 7-9-0 **55**................................... SeanLevey 3 64
(David Evans) *in rr: swtchd lft and hdwy wl over 1f out: styd on wl u.p to chse wnr ins fnl f but a hld* **9/1**
2-01 **3** *2 ¼* **Eco Warrior**[8] 282 4-9-4 **63** 6ex.................................(b) MartinLane 1 68
(J W Hills) *led: rdn and hdd ins fnl 2f: outpcd by ldng duo ins fnl f* **9/1**
544- **4** *½* **India's Song**[34] 8417 4-8-7 **59**...............................(t) GeorgeBuckell(7) 4 63
(David Simcock) *in rr: drvn and hdwy fr 2f out: styd on fnl f: nt rch ldrs* **20/1**
560- **5** *¾* **If I Were A Boy (IRE)**[31] 8447 7-9-6 **61**........................(p) AdamKirby 10 64
(Dominic Ffrench Davis) *chsd ldrs: drvn to dispute 2nd over 2f out: wknd ins fnl f* **9/1**
00-2 **6** *nk* **Thane Of Cawdor (IRE)**[11] 246 5-8-13 **54**.................... LukeMorris 6 57
(Joseph Tuite) *in tch: rdn to chse ldrs over 2f out: styd on same pce fr over 1f out* **4/1**[2]
6-11 **7** *½* **Reality Show (IRE)**[11] 246 7-9-4 **64** 6ex.................. AdamCarter(5) 12 66
(Shaun Harris) *in tch: rdn and sme hdwy ins fnl 2f: styd on same pce fr over 1f out* **5/1**[3]
/04- **8** *4 ½* **Ashkalara**[318] 1059 7-9-3 **58**......................................... LiamKeniry 5 53
(Stuart Howe) *in rr: hdwy 2f out: wknd over 1f out* **40/1**
15-0 **9** *4 ½* **Epsom Salts**[13] 214 9-9-2 **60**.........................(p) JemmaMarshall(3) 9 48
(Pat Phelan) *in rr: rdn and sme hdwy over 2f out: sn btn* **16/1**
34-6 **10** *1 ¼* **Tempuran**[19] 49 5-9-10 **65**.....................................(p) StephenCraine 7 51
(David Bridgwater) *chsd ldrs: rdn ins fnl 3f: sn btn* **33/1**
/00- **11** *11* **Reillys Daughter**[56] 7767 6-8-12 **53**.............................(b) JimCrowley 11 21
(Richard Mitchell) *chsd ldr: rdn ins fnl 3f: sn btn* **50/1**
2m 34.61s (0.11) **Going Correction** +0.025s/f (Slow)
**WFA** 4 from 5yo+ 4lb **11** Ran SP% **124.7**
Speed ratings (Par 101): **100,99,98,97,97 96,96,93,90,89 82**
CSF £17.23 CT £101.64 TOTE £2.90: £1.30, £3.90, £2.60; EX 24.60 Trifecta £170.80.
**Owner** Strawberry Fields Stud & Stuart Howard **Bred** Strawberry Fields Stud **Trained** Newmarket, Suffolk
**FOCUS**
An ordinary handicap but one featuring a few improving sorts, so fair form for the grade.
T/Jkpt: £16,116.80 to a £1 stake. Pool of £45399.55 - 2.0 winning tickets. T/Plt: £234.00 to a £1 stake. Pool of £111875.99 - 348.99 winning tickets. T/Qpdt: £127.50 to a £1 stake. Pool of £10608.21 - 61.55 winning tickets ST

# 361 SOUTHWELL (L-H)
### Thursday, January 30

**OFFICIAL GOING: Standard**
Wind: Moderate across Weather: Heavy cloud and wintry showers

## 383 BEST ODDS AT BOOKMAKERS.CO.UK H'CAP 5f (F)
**1:30** (1:31) (Class 6) (0-65,65) 4-Y-O+ **£2,264** (£673; £336; £168) **Stalls** High

Form RPR
3-10 **1** **Sir Geoffrey (IRE)**[7] 299 8-9-0 **65**...............(p) MatthewHopkins(7) 4 74
(Scott Dixon) *mde most: rdn wl over 1f out: kpt on strly* **8/1**
112- **2** *1* **Iffranesia (FR)**[34] 8411 4-9-6 **64**................................(p) GrahamLee 7 69
(Robert Cowell) *in tch: hdwy to chse ldrs 2f out: swtchd rt and rdn over 1f out: kpt on wl fnl f* **10/1**
000- **3** *½* **Flirtinaskirt**[44] 8319 4-9-4 **62**.................................(b[1]) ChrisCatlin 8 66
(Ed McMahon) *prom: cl up 2f out: sn rdn and ev ch tl drvn and one pce ins fnl f* **20/1**
063- **4** *1 ¼* **Dancing Freddy (IRE)**[362] 494 7-9-2 **60**...............(tp) WilliamCarson 2 59
(Ann Stokell) *cl up: rdn wl over 1f out and ev ch tl wknd ent fnl f* **20/1**
4-11 **5** *1 ¾* **Imjin River (IRE)**[10] 258 7-8-10 **59** 6ex.................(t) LouisSteward(5) 3 52
(William Stone) *chsd ldrs: rdn along 2f out: drvn over 1f out and sn one pce* **5/1**[2]
00-6 **6** *nk* **Catflap (IRE)**[19] 141 5-8-11 **55**...................................... LiamKeniry 6 47
(Derek Haydn Jones) *towards rr: hdwy to chse ldrs 1/2-way: rdn along wl over 1f out: kpt on same pce* **16/1**

-413 7 3/4 **Guishan**[9] 273 4-9-2 **60**..........(p) AndrewMullen 1 49
(Michael Appleby) *dwlt: chsd ldrs on outer: rdn along over 2f out: sn one pce* **6/1**[3]
6-56 8 2 3/4 **Cadeaux Pearl**[18] 147 6-9-2 **60**..........(v) TomQueally 10 39
(Scott Dixon) *chsd ldrs: rdn along 1/2-way: sn btn* **6/1**[3]
/0-1 9 shd **Ysper (FR)**[7] 298 4-9-5 **63** 6ex.......... DanielTudhope 5 42
(David O'Meara) *chsd ldrs: rdn along over 2f out: sn wknd* **7/4**[1]
00-0 10 4 **Fairy Wing (IRE)**[16] 170 7-9-3 **61**..........(b) BenCurtis 9 25
(Ann Stokell) *sn outpcd and a in rr* **50/1**
59.19s (-0.51) **Going Correction** -0.075s/f (Stan) **10** Ran SP% **119.2**
Speed ratings (Par 101): **101,99,98,96,93 93,92,87,87,81**
CSF £84.40 CT £1554.12 TOTE £12.20: £3.20, £3.10, £3.70; EX 85.30 Trifecta £638.00.
**Owner** General Sir Geoffrey Howlett **Bred** P Rabbitte **Trained** Babworth, Notts
**FOCUS**
The early speed came from those drawn low. Straightforward, ordinary form.

## 384 COMPARE BOOKMAKERS AT BOOKMAKERS.CO.UK H'CAP 6f (F)
**2:00** (2:00) (Class 6) (0-60,65) 4-Y-0+ **£2,264** (£673; £336; £168) **Stalls** Low

Form RPR
06-5 1 **Star Up In The Sky (USA)**[16] 170 4-9-1 **53**..........(b) GrahamLee 2 69
(Kevin Ryan) *mde all: rdn clr over 1f out: readily* **11/4**[2]
4-36 2 4 1/2 **Orwellian**[9] 273 5-8-11 **49**.......... PaddyAspell 7 52
(Bryan Smart) *chsd ldng pair on outer: wd st: hdwy over 2f out: sn rdn and ev ch: drvn over 1f out: sn edgd lft and one pce* **10/1**
U-31 3 3/4 **Layla's Hero (IRE)**[9] 273 7-9-13 **65** 6ex..........(v) AdrianNicholls 5 65
(David Nicholls) *dwlt and hld up in rr: hdwy and wd st: rdn to chse ldrs wl over 1f out: sn drvn and edgd lft: kpt on same pce* **2/1**[1]
5-35 4 2 1/2 **Upper Lambourn (IRE)**[10] 258 6-8-11 **49**..........(t) JoeFanning 4 42
(Christopher Kellett) *chsd ldrs: rdn along and outpcd 1/2-way: kpt on u.p appr fnl f* **4/1**[3]
000- 5 1 1/4 **Gebayl**[91] 7652 4-9-2 **57**..........(t) MarkCoumbe(3) 8 46
(Roger Ingram) *trckd wnr: cl up 1/2-way: rdn and ev ch 2f out: sn drvn and wknd* **16/1**
0-60 6 hd **Molly Jones**[10] 258 5-8-10 **48**.......... LiamKeniry 3 36
(Derek Haydn Jones) *chsd ldrs on inner: hdwy and cl up over 2f out: sn rdn and wknd* **50/1**
255- 7 1 1/4 **Triple Aitch (USA)**[64] 8073 4-9-0 **57**.......... HarryPoulton(5) 6 42
(Giles Bravery) *chsd ldrs: rdn along over 2f out: sn wknd* **5/1**
1m 14.84s (-1.66) **Going Correction** -0.30s/f (Stan) **7** Ran SP% **113.6**
Speed ratings (Par 101): **99,93,92,88,87 86,85**
CSF £29.08 CT £64.88 TOTE £4.00: £2.50, £2.90; EX 36.40 Trifecta £118.70.
**Owner** Matt & Lauren Morgan **Bred** Dixiana Stables Inc **Trained** Hambleton, N Yorks
**FOCUS**
As in the first race, the winner made all. The form is rated around the runner-up.

## 385 CORAL APP DOWNLOAD FROM THE APP STORE H'CAP 1m 3f (F)
**2:30** (2:30) (Class 5) (0-75,76) 4-Y-0+ **£2,911** (£866; £432; £216) **Stalls** Low

Form RPR
0/3- 1 **Gogeo (IRE)**[47] 8299 7-9-8 **72**.......... BenCurtis 3 84
(Alan Swinbank) *t.k.h: trckd ldrs: hdwy over 3f out: rdn 2f out: styd on u.p to ld last 50yds* **9/2**[3]
-224 2 1 **Summerfree (USA)**[10] 260 4-9-5 **72**.......... JoeFanning 2 82
(Mark Johnston) *led: jnd 4f out: rdn along 3f out: drvn over 1f out: hdd and no ex last 50yds* **11/4**[2]
1-31 3 1 3/4 **Staff Sergeant**[10] 253 7-9-12 **76** 6ex.......... AndrewMullen 5 83
(Michael Appleby) *trckd ldr: cl up 4f out: chal 3f out: rdn and ev ch wl over 1f out: drvn: edgd lft and one pce fnl f* **8/11**[1]
06-5 4 7 **Dazzling Valentine**[28] 21 6-8-9 **64**..........(v) NatashaEaton(5) 6 58
(Alan Bailey) *dwlt: hld up in rr: hdwy over 3f out: rdn along wl over 2f out: n.d* **33/1**
4-46 5 8 **Monzino (USA)**[10] 253 6-9-3 **67**..........(b) RussKennemore 4 47
(Michael Chapman) *dwlt: sn chsng ldrs: rdn along over 3f out: sn wknd* **33/1**
053/ 6 19 **Air Chief**[35] 4459 9-9-0 **71**..........(e[1]) LukeLeadbitter(7) 1 17
(Andrew Crook) *a in rr: rdn along 1/2-way: sn outpcd and bhd* **50/1**
2m 24.62s (-3.38) **Going Correction** -0.30s/f (Stan)
**WFA** 4 from 6yo+ 3lb **6** Ran SP% **110.6**
Speed ratings (Par 103): **100,99,98,92,87 73**
CSF £16.47 TOTE £6.50: £1.90, £1.10; EX 16.10 Trifecta £24.70.
**Owner** Mrs J Porter **Bred** Peter Nolan **Trained** Melsonby, N Yorks
**FOCUS**
Fair form for the level, with the first three clear.

## 386 CORAL MOBILE JUST THREE CLICKS TO BET H'CAP 1m 4f (F)
**3:00** (3:00) (Class 2) (0-105,91) 4-Y-0+ **£12,938** (£3,850; £1,924; £962) **Stalls** Low

Form RPR
10-1 1 **Masterful Act (USA)**[29] 3 7-9-12 **91**.......... TomQueally 2 106
(Alan McCabe) *cl up: slt ld over 2f out: rdn wl over 1f out: drvn ent fnl f: kpt on gamely towards fin* **5/2**[2]
30-1 2 nk **Hunting Ground (USA)**[6] 322 4-9-7 **90** 6ex.......... JoeFanning 4 105
(Mark Johnston) *trckd ldrs: hdwy 4f out and sn cl up: chal 2f out: sn rdn and ev ch tl drvn wl ins fnl f and no ex towards fin* **4/6**[1]
50-2 3 15 **Dewala**[9] 270 5-8-13 **78**.......... AndrewMullen 3 69
(Michael Appleby) *slt ld: pushed along 4f out: rdn over 3f out: hdd over 2f out and sn one pce* **20/1**
44-5 4 2 1/4 **Presburg (IRE)**[26] 54 5-9-6 **85**.......... JimmyQuinn 6 72
(Joseph Tuite) *hld up in tch: hdwy 4f out: rdn along to chse ldrs 3f out: outpcd fnl 2f* **16/1**
35-2 5 8 **Icebuster**[15] 182 6-9-6 **85**.......... DavidProbert 1 60
(Rod Millman) *hld up in tch: hdwy 4f out: rdn along over 3f out: sn outpcd* **14/1**[3]
340- 6 16 **Flying Power**[144] 6239 6-9-11 **90**.......... PaddyAspell 7 39
(John Norton) *chsd ldrs: rdn along 4f out: sn lost pl and bhd* **50/1**
003- P **Hanoverian Baron**[111] 7174 9-9-9 **88**.......... GrahamLee 5
(Tony Newcombe) *trckd ldr: pushed along after 5f: reminders, lost pl qckly and p.u over 5f out: collapsed and fatally injured* **16/1**
2m 34.39s (-6.61) **Going Correction** -0.30s/f (Stan)
**WFA** 4 from 5yo+ 4lb **7** Ran SP% **113.7**
Speed ratings (Par 109): **110,109,99,98,92 82,**
CSF £4.41 TOTE £4.20: £1.30, £1.70; EX 6.00 Trifecta £26.50.
**Owner** Universal Recycling Company **Bred** Fiona Craig & Dermot Cantillon **Trained** Averham Park, Notts

**FOCUS**
The front pair in the market drew clear in a race run at a decent gallop, and in a fast time. Smart form.

## 387 BET ON YOUR MOBILE WITH LADBROKES (S) STKS 7f (F)
**3:30** (3:30) (Class 6) 4-Y-0+ **£2,264** (£673; £336) **Stalls** Low

Form RPR
1-62 1 **Arabian Flight**[6] 320 5-8-10 **63**.......... AndrewMullen 2 70
(Michael Appleby) *mde all: rdn and jnd wl over 1f out: drvn ins fnl f: hld on wl towards fin* **8/15**[1]
12-3 2 nk **Spitfire**[7] 297 9-9-1 **70**..........(t) JoeFanning 3 74
(J R Jenkins) *trckd ldng poair: hdwy on inner over 2f out: chal wl over 1f out: sn rdn: drvn and ev ch ins fnl f tl no ex nr fin* **13/8**[2]
06-6 3 6 **Elusive Warrior (USA)**[28] 12 11-8-10 **48**.......... BenCurtis 1 53?
(Alan McCabe) *cl up: pushed along 3f out: rdn over 2f out and sn one pce* **20/1**[3]
1m 28.28s (-2.02) **Going Correction** -0.30s/f (Stan) **3** Ran SP% **108.1**
Speed ratings (Par 101): **99,98,91**
CSF £1.71 TOTE £1.60; EX 2.00 Trifecta £1.80.There was no bid for the winner.
**Owner** Dallas Racing **Bred** Mr & Mrs A E Pakenham **Trained** Danethorpe, Notts
**FOCUS**
A modest seller.

## 388 LADBROKES H'CAP 1m (F)
**4:00** (4:00) (Class 5) (0-70,71) 4-Y-0+ **£2,911** (£866; £432; £216) **Stalls** Low

Form RPR
3-12 1 **Silly Billy (IRE)**[10] 255 6-9-4 **67**..........(p) DanielTudhope 3 75
(John Balding) *trckd ldrs: hdwy over 2f out: rdn over 1f out: led jst ins fnl f: styd on* **5/1**[3]
46-5 2 3/4 **Schottische**[17] 154 4-8-7 **56**..........(v) JoeFanning 4 62
(Derek Haydn Jones) *sn pushed along in rr: hdwy on inner whn n.m.r over 3f out: effrt to chse ldrs over 2f out: rdn over 1f out: ev ch ent fnl f: kpt on* **20/1**
5-41 3 nk **Repetition**[7] 300 4-9-8 **71** 6ex.......... TomEaves 2 77
(Kristin Stubbs) *led: rdn 2f out: drvn over 1f out: hdd jst ins fnl f: kpt on same pce* **7/1**
241- 4 1 **Emperatriz**[41] 8360 4-9-7 **70**.......... RobertHavlin 5 73
(John Holt) *in tch: hdwy wl over 2f out: rdn to chse ldrs wl over 1f out: sn drvn and kpt on same pce* **7/1**
5-31 5 2 **Peter's Friend**[21] 96 5-9-6 **69**.......... PJMcDonald 7 68
(Michael Herrington) *trckd ldrs on outer: effrt wl over 2f out sn rdn: edgd lft and wknd wl over 1f out* **7/4**[1]
22-1 6 2 1/2 **Ivy Port**[9] 269 4-9-3 **66** 6ex..........(p) AndrewMullen 1 59
(Michael Appleby) *trckd ldrs on inner: hdwy 3f out: cl up over 2f out: sn rdn and wknd over 1f out* **4/1**[2]
00-5 7 4 **Gabrial's Wawa**[10] 255 4-9-4 **67**..........(b[1]) GrahamLee 6 51
(Roger Ingram) *cl up: rdn wl over 2f out: drvn wl over 1f out: sn wknd* **14/1**
24-1 8 7 **Roger Thorpe**[27] 31 5-9-1 **67**.......... BillyCray(3) 8 35
(Deborah Sanderson) *dwlt and bhd: hdwy and in tch over 3f out: sn rdn along and wknd* **14/1**
1m 41.54s (-2.16) **Going Correction** -0.30s/f (Stan) **8** Ran SP% **116.1**
Speed ratings (Par 103): **98,97,96,95,93 91,87,80**
CSF £95.23 CT £701.99 TOTE £4.20: £1.50, £5.20, £1.70; EX 67.00 Trifecta £956.30.
**Owner** R L Crowe **Bred** Sir E J Loder **Trained** Scrooby, Notts
**FOCUS**
Moderate form, but sound enough.

## 389 DOWNLOAD THE LADBROKES APP APPRENTICE H'CAP 7f (F)
**4:30** (4:30) (Class 5) (0-75,75) 4-Y-0+ **£2,911** (£866; £432; £216) **Stalls** Low

Form RPR
1-32 1 **Tartan Trip**[9] 268 7-8-9 **70**..........(v) AlistairRawlinson(7) 4 79
(Michael Appleby) *trckd ldr: cl up 3f out: sn led: rdn clr wl over 1f out: drvn and edgd lft ins fnl f: kpt on* **5/2**[2]
1-36 2 nk **Go Far**[8] 286 4-8-11 **68**..........(v) TimClark(3) 2 76
(Alan Bailey) *hld up in tch: pushed along wl over 2f out: rdn and hdwy on outer wl over 1f out: drvn to chse wnr whn edgd lft ent fnl f: kpt on towards fin* **11/10**[1]
-264 3 5 **George Fenton**[10] 255 5-9-6 **74**..........(p) RossAtkinson 5 69
(Conor Dore) *led: jnd and rdn along 3f out: sn hdd: drvn and edgd lft to far rail wl over 1f out: sn wknd* **7/1**
020- 4 3/4 **Great Expectations**[89] 7699 6-9-4 **75**.......... DCByrne(3) 1 68
(J R Jenkins) *trckd ldng pair on inner: effrt over 2f out: rdn along wl over 1f out: sn one pce* **4/1**[3]
1m 27.83s (-2.47) **Going Correction** -0.30s/f (Stan) **4** Ran SP% **108.7**
Speed ratings (Par 103): **102,101,95,95**
CSF £5.72 TOTE £4.00; EX 4.90 Trifecta £11.40.
**Owner** M Andrews **Bred** Kingsclere Stud **Trained** Danethorpe, Notts
■ Stewards' Enquiry : Tim Clark four-day ban: used whip above permitted level (Feb 13-15,17)
**FOCUS**
The front pair in the market pulled clear late on, but the form doesn't look up to much.
T/Plt: £383.40 to a £1 stake. Pool of £75368.23 - 143.48 winning tickets. T/Qpdt: £16.40 to a £1 stake. Pool of £8066.31 - 363.26 winning tickets. JR

# 360 CAGNES-SUR-MER
Thursday, January 30
**OFFICIAL GOING: Polytrack: standard**

## 390a PRIX DE L'ILE SAINT-HONORAT (MAIDEN) (3YO COLTS & GELDINGS) (POLYTRACK) 1m (F)
**11:55** (12:00) 3-Y-0 **£10,000** (£4,000; £3,000; £2,000; £1,000)

RPR
1 **Saint Pois (FR)**[15] 194 3-9-2 0.......... IoritzMendizabal 10 89
(J-C Rouget, France) **11/5**[2]
2 2 1/2 **Lotus Garden (FR)**[98] 3-9-2 0.......... FredericSpanu 7 83
(F Chappet, France) **13/1**
3 snk **Poudlard Express (FR)**[15] 194 3-9-2 0.......... ThomasHenderson 4 83
(D De Watrigant, France) **16/1**
4 2 **Handasy** 3-9-2 0.......... Francois-XavierBertras 6 78
(F Rohaut, France) **6/4**[1]
5 snk **Silver March (FR)**[162] 3-9-2 0..........(b[1]) Roberto-CarlosMontenegro 3 78
(P Sogorb, France) **9/1**


The Form Book, Raceform Ltd, Newbury, RG14 5SJ

6 ½ **He Loves Me (FR)** 3-9-2 0........ AnthonyCrastus 5 77
(E Lellouche, France) **4/1[3]**
7 shd **Flying Cape (IRE)**[15] 193 3-9-2 0........ ThomasMessina 9 77
(Andrew Hollinshead) *stdd and hld up in last pair on inner: rdn 2f out: kpt on same pce and nvr threatened* **28/1**
8 3 **Soldat Bleu (FR)** 3-9-2 0........ Pierre-CharlesBoudot 8 70
(D Prod'Homme, France) **39/1**
9 nse **Osmior (IRE)**[15] 194 3-9-2 0........(p) DavidBreux 2 70
(G Botti, France) **32/1**
1m 39.12s (99.12) **9** Ran SP% **123.3**
WIN (incl. 1 euro stake): 3.20. PLACES: 2.00, 5.20, 3.90. DF: 36.10. SF: 67.70.
**Owner** Gerard Augustin-Normand **Bred** Franklin Finance S.A. **Trained** Pau, France

## 391a PRIX DE L'ILE SAINTE-MARGUERITE (MAIDEN) (3YO FILLIES) (POLYTRACK) 1m (F)
**12:30** (12:00) 3-Y-O **£10,000** (£4,000; £3,000; £2,000; £1,000)

RPR
1 **Stosur (IRE)**[89] 7695 3-9-2 0........ Pierre-CharlesBoudot 9 78
(Gay Kelleway) *prom on outer: pressed ldr fr bef 1/2-way: rdn to ld over 1f out: r.o strly and asserted ins fnl f: readily* **49/10[3]**
2 3 **Galesburg (FR)**[83] 3-9-2 0........ TheoBachelot 10 71
(P Decouz, France) **8/1**
3 1 **Heureuse (FR)**[26] 3-9-2 0........ IoritzMendizabal 3 69
(D Prod'Homme, France) **5/2[1]**
4 2½ **Misti River (FR)** 3-9-2 0........ EddyHardouin 6 63
(J C Napoli, France) **17/1**
5 1 **Balouba (FR)** 3-9-2 0........ AlexisBadel 2 61
(C Scandella, France) **4/1[2]**
6 3 **Peut Etre (IRE)**[47] 3-9-2 0........ MarcLerner 4 54
(Robert Collet, France) **7/1**
7 nse **Wilona (IRE)**[135] 3-8-8 0........ MedhiChouit[(8)] 1 54
(J Heloury, France) **85/1**
8 nse **Zarazalay (FR)** 3-8-8 0........ AllanMonnier[(8)] 8 54
(J-M Capitte, France) **11/1**
9 nse **Pretty Pearl (FR)**[91] 7653 3-9-2 0........ TonyPiccone 12 54
(N Caullery, France) **10/1**
10 nse **Roseberry Hill (FR)** 3-9-2 0........(b[1]) RomainAuray 7 54
(J-M Capitte, France) **43/1**
11 2 **Bolero D'Azur (FR)**[15] 194 3-9-2 0........ PaulineProd'homme 5 49
(D Prod'Homme, France) **23/1**
1m 41.52s (101.52) **11** Ran SP% **119.7**
WIN (incl. 1 euro stake): 5.90. PLACES: 1.80, 2.20, 1.70. DF: 30.00. SF: 44.80.
**Owner** Brian C Oakley **Bred** Mervyn Stewkesbury **Trained** Exning, Suffolk

## 392a PRIX DU COL DE BRAUS (CLAIMER) (4YO+) (POLYTRACK) 6f 110y
**2:50** (12:00) 4-Y-O+ **£6,250** (£2,500; £1,875; £1,250; £625)

RPR
1 **Tirion (USA)**[114] 6-8-10 0........ ValentinGambart[(8)] 5 83
(M Boutin, France) **5/2[1]**
2 nse **Mister Chop (FR)**[57] 9-9-2 0........ ThomasMessina 4 81
(W Walton, France) **15/1**
3 nse **Calrissian (GER)**[99] 10-9-0 0........ MlleSarahCallac[(5)] 9 84
(F Foresi, France) **83/10**
4 nk **Cat Melody (FR)**[22] 6-8-13 0........(b) Roberto-CarlosMontenegro 16 77
(P Marion, Germany) **53/10[2]**
5 2½ **Dawn Salute (FR)**[47] 4-9-1 0........ FabriceVeron 12 72
(H-A Pantall, France) **8/1[3]**
6 hd **Touch Of Luck (FR)**[235] 5-8-11 0........(b) FredericSpanu 13 67
(Laura Grizzetti, Italy) **14/1**
7 1 **Star Seed (FR)**[57] 5-8-13 0........(b) AntoineCoutier 15 66
(R Chotard, France) **56/1**
8 ½ **Caratterina (IRE)** 6-9-3 0........(b[1]) LManiezzi 8 69
(C De Ferrari & N Ferrucci, Italy) **13/1**
9 1 **Principe Uromonte (IRE)**[522] 8-9-1 0........ Francois-XavierBertras 14 64
(J-M Capitte, France) **21/1**
10 snk **Little Garcon (USA)**[42] 7-8-11 0........(p) SebastienMaillot 3 59
(S Cerulis, France) **40/1**
11 snk **Divine Davis (FR)**[34] 4-8-11 0........ AlexisBadel 2 59
(L A Urbano-Grajales, France) **60/1**
12 ¾ **Doggy Tail (IRE)** 4-9-10 0........ CFiocchi 11 70
(Stefano Botti, Italy) **24/1**
13 ¾ **Laura Green** 8-8-8 0........ AntonioFresu 10 52
(F Trappolini, Italy) **21/1**
14 shd **Knight Charm**[10] 266 4-8-13 0 ow2........ Pierre-CharlesBoudot 1 56
(Gay Kelleway) *sn prom on inner: rdn and ev ch 2f out: no ex ent fnl f: fdd: eased towards fin* **16/1**
15 1 **Salinas Road (FR)**[58] 4-9-4 0........ TheoBachelot 6 58
(M Figge, Germany) **16/1**
16 4 **Wise Boy (GER)**[112] 7-9-4 0........ MarcLerner 7 47
(J-P Perruchot, France) **36/1**
1m 18.41s (78.41) **16** Ran SP% **119.8**
WIN (incl. 1 euro stake): 3.50. PLACES: 1.70, 3.90, 2.40. DF: 32.40. SF: 51.00.
**Owner** Mme Marie-Carmen Boutin **Bred** Lady O De North Cliff **Trained** France

# [304]MEYDAN (L-H)
Thursday, January 30
**OFFICIAL GOING: Turf: good; tapeta: standard**

## 393a DUBAL EXCELLENCE TROPHY (H'CAP) (TURF) 5f
**2:40** (2:42) (100-110,109) 3-Y-O+
**£63,253** (£21,084; £10,542; £5,271; £3,162; £2,108)

RPR
1 **Alsaaeqah (KSA)**[34] 7-9-2 **105**........ WilliamBuick 1 107
(B Al Shaibani, Saudi Arabia) *mid-div: r.o wl fnl 1 1/2f: led on line* **25/1**
2 shd **Beat Baby (IRE)**[126] 7-9-6 **109**........(t) Per-AndersGraberg 5 111
(Niels Petersen, Norway) *wl away: sn led: hdd fnl stride* **33/1**
3 nk **Medicean Man**[117] 7010 8-9-3 **106**........(tp) HarryBentley 13 107+
(Jeremy Gask) *mid-div: kpt on fnl 1 1/2f: nrst fin* **6/1[3]**
4 nk **Abstraction (IRE)**[159] 5772 4-9-3 **106**........ FergalLynch 2 106+
(Sarah Dawson, Ire) *chsd ldng pair: ev ch 1f out: nt qckn fnl 110yds* **9/1**
5 ½ **Racy**[7] 304 7-8-11 **100**........ JamieSpencer 8 98
(Brian Ellison) *chsd ldrs: kpt on same pce fnl 2f* **14/1**
6 shd **Masamah (IRE)**[7] 304 8-9-1 **104**........(p) MartinHarley 6 102
(Marco Botti) *wl away: trckd ldrs: ev ch 1 1/2f out: one pce fnl 110yds* **8/1**
7 hd **Monsieur Joe (IRE)**[21] 107 7-9-0 **102**........ KierenFallon 3 100
(Paul Midgley) *nvr bttr than mid-div* **16/1**
8 1 **Ahtoug**[21] 107 6-9-4 **107**........ MickaelBarzalona 14 100
(Charlie Appleby) *settled in rr: rdn 3f out: nvr able to chal* **9/2[2]**
9 nk **Take Ten**[21] 107 7-9-0 **102**........ RichardMullen 12 95
(S Seemar, UAE) *nvr able to chal* **20/1**
10 ½ **Roicead (USA)**[12] 240 7-9-5 **108**........(t) JamesDoyle 9 98
(D Selvaratnam, UAE) *nvr able to chal* **9/1**
11 1 **Dungannon**[96] 7527 7-8-13 **101**........ ThomasBrown 4 89
(Andrew Balding) *nvr able to chal* **14/1**
12 1¾ **Merhee (AUS)**[7] 304 6-9-4 **107**........ ChristopheSoumillon 10 88
(M F De Kock, South Africa) *nvr nr to chal but r.o fnl 1 1/2f* **7/2[1]**
13 shd **Seachantach (USA)**[21] 107 8-8-8 **102**........(bt) MarcMonaghan[(6)] 7 83
(S Seemar, UAE) *nvr nr to chal* **40/1**
14 hd **Fityaan**[21] 107 6-9-2 **105**........ DaneO'Neill 15 85
(M Al Muhairi, UAE) *nvr able to chal* **33/1**
15 1¼ **My Propeller (IRE)**[21] 107 5-9-0 **102**........ FrankieDettori 11 78
(Peter Chapple-Hyam) *nvr bttr than mid-div* **16/1**
16 2¼ **Hitchens (IRE)**[14] 206 9-9-5 **108**........ RichardHughes 16 75
(David Barron) *a in rr* **25/1**
57.61s (57.61) **16** Ran SP% **131.7**
CSF: 699.83; EX 701.70; TRIFECTA: 6,865.00; TRICAST: 5,523.56 WIN: 43.70;.
**Owner** King Abdullah Bin Abdulaziz & Sons **Bred** King Abdullah Bin Abdulaziz Sons **Trained** Saudi Arabia

**FOCUS**
They went a good pace (each split fractionally under the Trakus par times), but the main action unfolded middle to far side and the low-drawn runners might have had a slight edge.

## 394a DUBAL BILLET TROPHY (H'CAP) (TAPETA) 1m 1f 110y
**3:15** (3:17) (95-105,105) 3-Y-O+
**£39,759** (£13,253; £6,626; £3,313; £1,987; £1,325)

RPR
1 **Ottoman Empire (FR)**[21] 108 8-9-2 **100**........ RichardMullen 1 105
(S Seemar, UAE) *trckd ldrs: led 2f out: r.o wl* **9/2[2]**
2 1 **String Theory (IRE)**[35] 8398 4-9-3 **102**........ FrankieDettori 4 106
(Marco Botti) *trckd ldrs: ev ch 1f out: nt qckn fnl 110yds* **11/4[1]**
3 nk **Start Right**[14] 207 7-8-7 **97**........(p) MarcMonaghan[(6)] 10 99
(S Seemar, UAE) *s.i.s: settled in rr: r.o fnl 2f: nrst fin* **16/1**
4 1 **Clon Brulee (IRE)**[21] 108 5-9-1 **99**........ SilvestreDeSousa 9 99
(Saeed bin Suroor) *mid-div: rdn 4f out: r.o fnl 1 1/2f but nvr able to chal* **9/2[2]**
5 ½ **Intrigo**[14] 207 4-9-0 **99**........ MickaelBarzalona 6 99
(Charlie Appleby) *settled in rr: a mid-div and wd* **5/1[3]**
6 nk **Sahawar (FR)**[14] 205 4-9-4 **104**........(t) ThierryThulliez 7 103
(C Ferland, France) *settled in rr: nvr nr to chal* **25/1**
7 1¼ **Abdel (FR)**[14] 202 6-9-6 **105**........ JulienAuge 5 100
(J-M Osorio, Spain) *nvr bttr than mid-div* **14/1**
8 1¾ **Rebel Song (IRE)**[56] 8174 5-8-10 **95**........(t) AdriedeVries 3 86
(A bin Harmash, UAE) *sn led: kicked clr 3 1/2f out: hdd 2 1/2f out: wknd fnl f* **8/1**
9 2¾ **Regulation (IRE)**[14] 207 5-9-2 **100**........ ShaneFoley 11 87
(M Halford, Ire) *settled in rr: nvr able to chal* **25/1**
10 3 **Agent Allison**[82] 7822 4-8-9 **95**........ JamieSpencer 2 76
(Peter Chapple-Hyam) *slowly away: mid-div tl wknd fnl 1 1/2f* **14/1**
11 5¼ **Robert The Painter (IRE)**[14] 207 6-8-13 **97**........(v) TadhgO'Shea 8 67
(David O'Meara) *trckd ldrs tl outpcd 3f out* **25/1**
1m 58.85s (-0.15)
**WFA** 4 from 5yo+ 1lb **11** Ran SP% **121.6**
CSF: 17.48; EX 34.00; TRIFECTA: 378.30; TRICAST: 178.49 WIN: 7.20; PL: 2.10, 1.20, 3.80..
**Owner** Abdulla Ahmad Al Shaikh **Bred** Scea Haras De La Perelle **Trained** United Arab Emirates

**FOCUS**
A fair gallop (splits compared to the Trakus pars: 26.13 (26.94), 50.17 (51.59), 1:15.10 (1:16.31), 1:39.41 (1:40.69), 1:58.85 (1:58.87)), but the closers struggled to get into it. The form is set around the third and fifth.

## 395a CAPE VERDI SPONSORED BY DUBAL (GROUP 2) (F&M) (TURF) 1m
**3:50** (3:50) 3-Y-O+
**£72,289** (£24,096; £12,048; £6,024; £3,614; £2,409)

RPR
1 **Certify (USA)**[489] 6635 4-9-3 108........ MickaelBarzalona 5 113+
(Charlie Appleby) *racd in rr: t.k.h: smooth prog 2f out: led 1f out: easily* **2/1[2]**
2 ¾ **L'Amour De Ma Vie (USA)**[32] 8440 5-9-3 100........ MaximeGuyon 2 109
(Mme Pia Brandt, France) *mid-div: led 2f out: hdd fnl f* **33/1**
3 4¾ **Pearl Of Africa (IRE)**[90] 7673 4-9-3 105........ JamieSpencer 6 98
(Edward Lynam, Ire) *slowly away: settled in rr: nvr nr to chal* **11/1**
4 1¼ **Flotilla (FR)**[137] 6450 4-9-3 116........ Christophe-PatriceLemaire 4 95
(M Delzangles, France) *trckd ldrs tl outpcd 2f out* **6/4[1]**
5 1¼ **Mensoora (SAF)**[208] 4-8-10 100 ow1........ ChristopheSoumillon 1 85
(M F De Kock, South Africa) *trckd ldng pair: rdn 4f out: sn btn* **8/1**
6 nk **Shuruq (USA)**[21] 111 4-9-6 109........(p) SilvestreDeSousa 3 95
(Saeed bin Suroor) *sn led: t.k.h: hdd 2f out: wknd fnl 1 1/2f* **5/1[3]**
1m 36.09s (96.09) **6** Ran SP% **112.4**
CSF: 51.17; EX 43.80; TRIFECTA: 158.10; WIN: 2.40;.
**Owner** Godolphin **Bred** Hurstland Farm Inc Et Al **Trained** Newmarket, Suffolk

**FOCUS**
The pace was slow for the first couple of furlongs but quickly picked up to a good gallop. Here are the splits along with Trakus pars: 27.30 (26.41), 50.07 (50.36), 1:12.95 (1:14.09), 1:36.09 (1.37.93). The form fits the race averages.

## 396a DUBAL CASTHOUSE TROPHY (H'CAP) (TAPETA) 7f
**4:25** (4:26) (100-110,110) 3-Y-O+
**£43,373** (£14,457; £7,228; £3,614; £2,168; £1,445)

RPR
1 **Zahee (NZ)**[306] 1264 5-9-1 105........ ChristopheSoumillon 6 112+
(M F De Kock, South Africa) *in rr of mid-div: smooth prog 2f out: led 1/2f out: comf* **7/2[2]**
2 1 **Gold City (IRE)**[21] 112 5-8-11 101........(bt) RichardMullen 8 105
(S Seemar, UAE) *trckd ldrs: led 2f out: hdd fnl 1/2f* **33/1**
3 shd **Eastern Rules (IRE)**[168] 5454 6-8-10 100........ ShaneFoley 9 104
(M Halford, Ire) *sn led: hdd 2f out: r.o same pce* **11/2[3]**

4 1 1/2 **Mufarrh (IRE)**[21] 111 7-9-6 110 ................ RoystonFfrench 7 110
(A Al Raihe, UAE) *chsd ldrs: led 1 1/2f out: hdd fnl 1f* 7/1

5 1 **Tamarkuz (USA)**[112] 7157 4-9-1 105 ................ DaneO'Neill 3 102+
(M Al Muhairi, UAE) *slowly away: nvr nr to chal but r.o fnl 1 1/2f* 9/4[1]

6 1 **Dafeef**[7] 308 7-9-1 105 ................ (e) SamHitchcott 5 99+
(Doug Watson, UAE) *nvr bttr than mid-div* 20/1

7 2 **Risby (IRE)**[14] 207 6-8-10 100 ................ (t) JulienAuge 10 89+
(J-M Osorio, Spain) *settled in rr: r.o fnl 1 1/2f out: nrst fin* 14/1

8 nk **The Gold Cheongsam (IRE)**[21] 112 4-8-13 102 ....... (t) WilliamBuick 4 91+
(Jeremy Noseda) *trckd ldng trio tl outpcd 3 1/2f out* 10/1

9 1/2 **Alhebayeb (IRE)**[21] 107 4-8-13 102 ................ RichardHughes 2 90+
(M F De Kock, South Africa) *trckd ldrs tl outpcd 2 1/2f out* 14/1

10 2 1/4 **Tennessee Wildcat (IRE)**[7] 304 4-8-11 101 ............ (p) GaryCarroll 11 82+
(G M Lyons, Ire) *nvr bttr than mid-div* 28/1

11 1 3/4 **Santefisio**[187] 4744 8-8-13 102 ................ (b) JamieSpencer 1 79+
(Keith Dalgleish) *slowly away: settled in rr: nvr nr to chal* 14/1

1m 24.77s (-0.43) **11 Ran SP% 121.1**
CSF: 121.93; EX 163.20; TRIFECTA: 1,033.90; TRICAST: 641.66 WIN: 2.90; PL: 1.30, 8.30, 2.00..

**Owner** Sheikh Mohammed Bin Khalifa Al Maktoum **Bred** Sh Mohd Bin Khalifa Al Maktoum **Trained** South Africa

**FOCUS**
The splits compared to the Trakus par times show the pace was pretty modest: 26.24 (25.42), 49.85 (48.75), 1:12.99 (1:12.52), 1:24.77 (1:24.89). The runner-up helps the standard.

## 397a AL RASHIDIYA SPONSORED BY DUBAL (GROUP 2) (TURF) 1m 1f
**5:00** (5:06) 3-Y-0+
**£72,289** (£24,096; £12,048; £6,024; £3,614; £2,409)

RPR

1 **Mujaarib (AUS)**[253] 6-9-0 108 ................ ChristopheSoumillon 10 117+
(M F De Kock, South Africa) *settled in rr: smooth prog 2f out: led a f out: jst hld on* 25/1

2 nk **Mushreq (AUS)**[21] 110 6-9-0 117 ................ DaneO'Neill 1 116+
(M F De Kock, South Africa) *mid-div: smooth prog 1 1/2f out: r.o wl: jst failed* 3/1[1]

3 2 **Maputo**[117] 7049 4-8-13 113 ................ MickaelBarzalona 8 112
(Charlie Appleby) *sn led: t.k.h: hdd 1f out: r.o same pce* 7/1[3]

4 nk **Dastarhon (IRE)**[47] 8307 4-8-13 113 ................ (t) MaximeGuyon 9 111
(Mme Pia Brandt, France) *mid-div: r.o fnl 2f: nrst fin* 33/1

5 hd **Steeler (IRE)**[21] 111 4-8-13 109 ................ KierenFallon 5 111
(Charlie Appleby) *trckd ldrs: ev ch 1f out: one pce fnl 110yds* 3/1[1]

6 1 **Educate**[124] 6838 5-9-0 112 ................ WilliamBuick 2 109
(Ismail Mohammed) *mid-div: r.o fnl 2f: nrst fin* 14/1

7 1 **Tales Of Grimm (USA)**[21] 110 5-9-0 107 ................ (b) FrankieDettori 11 107
(Richard Fahey) *slowly away: settled in rr: nvr nr to chal* 14/1

8 1 1/4 **Van Rooney (USA)**[14] 207 5-9-0 102 ................ (t) AdriedeVries 7 104
(Ali Jan, Qatar) *settled in rr: nvr able to chal* 40/1

9 3/4 **Tasaday (USA)**[116] 7057 4-8-11 113 ................ SilvestreDeSousa 4 100
(Saeed bin Suroor) *mid-div: chsd ldrs: n.m.r 1 1/2f out: nt rcvr* 4/1[2]

10 4 **Trade Storm**[137] 6456 6-9-0 115 ................ JamieSpencer 3 94
(David Simcock) *s.i.s: settled in rr: nvr able to chal* 8/1

11 3/4 **Zambucca (SAF)**[235] 6-9-0 106 ................ RichardMullen 6 92
(S Seemar, UAE) *in rr of mid-div: chsd ldrs 2f out: wknd fnl f* 40/1

12 3 3/4 **Brendan Brackan (IRE)**[21] 111 5-9-0 115 ................ ColinKeane 12 85
(G M Lyons, Ire) *trckd ldrs tl outpcd 3f out* 14/1

1m 48.36s (108.36)
**WFA** 4 from 5yo+ 1lb **12 Ran SP% 125.3**
CSF: 102.37; EX 39.00; TRIFECTA: 431.00; WIN: 6.50; PL: 3.50, 1.50, 2.70..

**Owner** Hamdan Al Maktoum **Bred** Shadwell Stud Australasia Ltd **Trained** South Africa

**FOCUS**
There was a false start ahead of this Group 2 after the stalls opened at different times, but none of the runners looked to do too much unnecessary running and they got away at the second attempt. A competitive contest and each split was comfortably under the Trakus par: 26.04 (26.61), 49.67 (50.51), 1:13.89 (1:14.84), 1:36.77 (1:38.35), 1:48.36 (1:50.44). Mike De Kock was winning the Al Rashidiya for the sixth time, and he also had the second.

## 398a DUBAL POTLINES TROPHY (H'CAP) (TURF) 1m 2f
**5:35** (5:40) (95-113,113) 3-Y-0+
**£54,216** (£18,072; £9,036; £4,518; £2,710; £1,807)

RPR

1 **Saxo Jack (FR)**[14] 202 4-8-6 **100** ................ MickaelBarzalona 13 107
(Saeed bin Suroor) *in rr of mid-div: smooth prog 2 1/2f out: led 1f out: r.o wl* 5/1[2]

2 1/2 **Haafaguinea**[14] 202 4-8-8 **102** ................ SilvestreDeSousa 4 108
(Saeed bin Suroor) *mid-div: chsd ldrs 2f out: nt qckn fnl f* 5/2[1]

3 1 1/4 **Burano (IRE)**[14] 202 5-8-7 **100** ................ (b) HarryBentley 8 102
(Brian Meehan) *mid-div: chsd ldrs 2f out: led 1 1/2f out: hdd 1f out: r.o same pce* 25/1

4 shd **Busker (USA)**[21] 108 6-8-9 **102** ow2 ................ (t) AdriedeVries 10 104+
(A bin Harmash, UAE) *settled in rr: r.o fnl 1 1/2f: nrst fin* 10/1

5 1 1/2 **Aussie Reigns (IRE)**[14] 205 4-8-8 **102** ................ (v) AndreaAtzeni 14 102
(William Knight) *in rr of mid-div: chsd ldrs 2f out: nt qckn fnl f* 5/1[2]

6 3/4 **Master Plan (SAF)**[208] 6-9-6 **113** ................ JGeroudis 12 110
(M F De Kock, South Africa) *settled in rr: nvr able to chal but r.o fnl 2f* 14/1

7 3/4 **Izaaj (USA)**[7] 307 7-8-5 **95** ................ XZiani 11 94
(A bin Harmash, UAE) *trckd ldrs tl outpcd 2f out* 40/1

8 nse **Sefri (USA)**[14] 205 4-8-2 **102** ................ NoelGarbutt[(6)] 3 99
(E Charpy, UAE) *nvr bttr than mid-div* 33/1

9 nk **Chapter Seven**[14] 205 5-8-11 **105** ................ JamieSpencer 5 99
(G M Lyons, Ire) *settled in rr: nvr nr to chal* 16/1

10 shd **Jawhar (IRE)**[12] 242 6-8-7 **100** ................ DaneO'Neill 9 95
(Doug Watson, UAE) *mid-div: hdd 1f out: one pce fnl 110yds* 8/1[3]

11 1 1/2 **Moonlight Dash**[11] 6-8-5 **98** ................ RichardMullen 7 90
(S Seemar, UAE) *led main gp: ev ch 2 1/2f out: wknd fnl f* 14/1

12 5 3/4 **Daddy Long Legs (USA)**[7] 307 5-9-2 **109** ................ PatCosgrave 1 89
(M F De Kock, South Africa) *a in rr* 14/1

13 14 1/2 **Expense Claim (IRE)**[348] 698 5-8-5 **97** ................ (p) TadhgO'Shea 6 49
(S Seemar, UAE) *sn led: hdd & wknd 2f out* 20/1

14 15 **Energia Eros (BRZ)**[26] 54 5-9-2 **109** ................ (p) MartinHarley 2 30
(Marco Botti) *mid-div tl outpcd 3f out* 20/1

2m 1.91s (121.91)
**WFA** 4 from 5yo+ 2lb **14 Ran SP% 126.7**
CSF: 17.56; EX 22.10; TRIFECTA: 516.60; TRICAST: 304.58 WIN: 6.90; PL: 2.40, 1.40, 7.30..

**Owner** Sheikh Juma Dalmook Al Maktoum **Bred** Bloomsbury Stud **Trained** Newmarket, Suffolk

**FOCUS**
The split times compared to Trakus pars: 26.01 (26.48), 50.22 (50.42), 1:14.23 (1:14.81), 1:38.50 (1:39.12), 2:01.91 (2:03.34). The sixth and seventh help with the standard.

# 338 LINGFIELD (L-H)
Friday, January 31

**OFFICIAL GOING: Standard**
Wind: Strong, behind Weather: Very overcast, raining from race 4 onwards

## 399 LADBROKES CLAIMING STKS 7f 1y(P)
**1:00** (1:02) (Class 6) 4-Y-0+ **£2,045** (£603; £302) **Stalls Low**

Form RPR

1-34 1 **Mr David (USA)**[9] 287 7-9-7 85 ................ (b) DavidProbert 7 91
(Jamie Osborne) *settled in 6th: prog and wdst of all bnd 2f out: r.o fr over 1f out to ld ins fnl f: sn in command* 7/4[1]

260- 2 1 1/2 **Jubilee Brig**[31] 8455 4-9-3 75 ................ (v) GeorgeBaker 4 83
(Gary Moore) *trckd ldng pair: gng easily fr 3f out: wnt 2nd over 2f out: edgd rt bnd sn after: shkn up to ld over 1f out: hdd and nt qckn ins fnl f* 7/2[2]

2553 3 1 3/4 **Seek The Fair Land**[7] 312 8-8-12 74 ................ (b) LouisSteward[(5)] 8 78
(Lee Carter) *chsd ldrs: effrt whn carried wd bnd 2f out: kpt on fr over 1f out to take 3rd ins fnl f* 7/1

00-2 4 nk **Capaill Liath (IRE)**[18] 162 6-9-2 80 ................ (p) KevinStott[(5)] 5 81
(Kevin Ryan) *trckd ldng trio: rdn and cl up 2f out: tried to chal but hd at unattractive angle and nt qckn over 1f out* 7/1

5-35 5 2 1/4 **Prince Of Burma (IRE)**[7] 310 6-8-7 67 ................ (b) ChrisCatlin 3 61
(David Evans) *dwlt: mostly in 8th: struggling to stay in tch over 4f out: nvr on terms but plugged on fnl f* 20/1

-210 6 1 3/4 **Kuanyao (IRE)**[7] 312 8-9-3 77 ................ (v) LiamJones 6 67
(Lee Carter) *pressed ldr: led over 3f out: hdd & wknd over 1f out* 5/1[3]

030- 7 3/4 **Bay Knight (IRE)**[49] 8269 8-8-13 75 ................ JoeFanning 9 61
(Sean Curran) *pushed along in rr after 3f: nt on terms after: hanging sltly over 1f out: no real prog and one light reminder fnl f* 20/1

32-0 8 11 **The Mongoose**[27] 52 6-8-2 64 ................ (t) JoeyHaynes[(5)] 1 25
(David Evans) *led to over 3f out: wknd over 2f out: t.o* 20/1

210/ P **Niger (IRE)**[541] 4949 5-8-11 75 ................ LukeMorris 2
(Ronald Harris) *restless stalls: rrd bdly as they opened and lft 20 l: t.o tl p.u and dismntd 3f out* 20/1

1m 23.17s (-1.63) **Going Correction** 0.0s/f (Stan) **9 Ran SP% 119.3**
Speed ratings (Par 101): **109,107,105,104,102 100,99,86,**
CSF £7.57 TOTE £2.50: £1.10, £2.00, £2.30; EX 8.40 Trifecta £59.60.Bay Knight was claimed by A Stokell for £8,000. Mr David was claimed by C Bjorling for £12,000.

**Owner** Steve Jakes & S J Piper Partnership **Bred** Mr & Mrs R David Randal **Trained** Upper Lambourn, Berks

**FOCUS**
A fair claimer and run at a good pace thanks to a contested lead. The form is rated around the runner-up.

## 400 32RED.COM (S) H'CAP 1m 7f 169y(P)
**1:30** (1:32) (Class 6) (0-60,60) 4-Y-0+ **£2,045** (£603; £302) **Stalls Low**

Form RPR

300- 1 **Bert The Alert**[79] 7857 6-8-12 **55** ................ CharlotteJenner[(7)] 5 66
(Laura Mongan) *s.i.s: hld up in last pair: prog over 3f out: wnt 2nd wl over 1f out: pushed along firmly and clsd to ld ins fnl f: styd on* 8/1

46/3 2 3/4 **Hail Tiberius**[23] 88 7-9-10 **60** ................ (t) GrahamLee 2 70
(Martin Keighley) *led: shkn up over 2f out: pressed and rdn over 1f out: hdd and one pce ins fnl f* 2/1[1]

040- 3 5 **Galiotto (IRE)**[46] 8160 8-9-3 **53** ................ (v) GeorgeBaker 4 57
(Gary Moore) *hld up in 5th: prog over 3f out: chsd ldr over 2f out to wl over 1f out: fdd* 3/1[2]

-206 4 6 **Sommersturm (GER)**[5] 349 10-9-8 **58** ................ (bt[1]) SeanLevey 6 55
(David Evans) *slowly away: hld up in last: quick prog on outer to chse ldr over 4f out: rdn over 3f out: lost 2nd over 2f out: wknd over 1f out* 5/1

66-3 5 9 **Lac Sacre (FR)**[14] 106 5-8-10 **46** oh1 ................ (tp) LukeMorris 7 32
(Tony Carroll) *cl up: disp 2nd briefly 5f out: drvn and wknd over 3f out* 9/2[3]

/46- 6 10 **Aureate**[33] 8436 10-8-4 **47** ................ (v[1]) DanielCremin[(7)] 1 21
(Brian Forsey) *prom: chsd ldr after 4f to over 4f out: wknd over 3f out: t.o* 25/1

000- 7 44 **Sings Poet**[49] 8268 4-8-5 **48** oh1 ow2 ................ ChrisCatlin 8
(Peter Hiatt) *rn in snatches: chsd ldr 4f: wknd qckly 4f out: wl t.o* 50/1

3m 23.95s (-1.75) **Going Correction** 0.0s/f (Stan)
**WFA** 4 from 5yo+ 7lb **7 Ran SP% 110.1**
Speed ratings (Par 101): **104,103,101,98,93 88,66**
CSF £22.63 CT £55.00 TOTE £9.40: £3.30, £1.80; EX 34.60 Trifecta £124.80.There was no bid for the winner.

**Owner** Condover Racing **Bred** Pleasure Palace Racing **Trained** Epsom, Surrey

**FOCUS**
A moderate selling handicap, run at just a fair pace. The form is rated cautiously although the field have all slipped to good marks.

## 401 32RED ON THE APP STORE H'CAP 6f 1y(P)
**2:00** (2:01) (Class 6) (0-65,70) 3-Y-O **£2,385** (£704; £352) **Stalls Low**

Form RPR

66-0 1 **Dont Have It Then**[23] 86 3-8-12 **56** ................ ChrisCatlin 8 61
(Willie Musson) *racd on outer in rr: prog after 1/2-way: more hdwy over 1f out to ld jst ins fnl f: hrd pressed after: hld on wl* 8/1

03-1 2 1/2 **Basil Berry**[7] 311 3-9-9 **70** 6ex ................ RobertTart[(3)] 2 73
(Chris Dwyer) *hld up in midfield: looking for room on inner 2f out: prog over 1f out: wnt 2nd ins fnl f and str chal: jst hld nr fin* 5/2[1]

6-13 3 1/2 **Global Explorer (USA)**[7] 315 3-9-3 **61** ................ (t) AdamBeschizza 10 62+
(Stuart Williams) *nt pce to grab gd position fr wd draw and hld up last: stl there 2f out: gd prog over 1f out: styd on to take 3rd nr fin* 3/1[2]

30-5 4 nk **Alfie Lunete (IRE)**[6] 338 3-9-7 **65** ................ LiamJones 5 65
(J S Moore) *t.k.h bhd ldng trio: pushed along over 2f out: rdn to chal jst over 1f out: one pce* 8/1

46-1 5 1 **Dandys Perier (IRE)**[23] 86 3-9-2 **60** ................ LukeMorris 7 57
(Ronald Harris) *mostly in midfield: rdn over 2f out: styd on fnl f: nvr able to threaten* 7/1[3]

002- 6 2 1/4 **Soul Instinct**[78] 7882 3-9-2 **65** ................ KevinStott[(5)] 11 55
(Kevin Ryan) *gd spd fr wdst draw to ld and t.k.h: hdd jst ins fnl f: wknd qckly* 10/1

066- **7** *shd* **Crystalized (IRE)**[140] 6354 3-9-1 **59** FergusSweeney 9 48
(Dean Ivory) *mostly in last trio: wd bnd 2f out in 10th pl: no ch whn reminders 1f out: kpt on* **66/1**

3-54 **8** *½* **Sandsman's Girl (IRE)**[13] 232 3-9-2 **60** (b) GrahamLee 6 48
(James Given) *chsd ldrs: cl up and rdn over 1f out: nt qckn and sn btn* **25/1**

34-4 **9** *nk* **Coiste Bodhar (IRE)**[15] 195 3-8-13 **60** (p) GeorgeChaloner(3) 3 47
(Joseph Tuite) *t.k.h: pressed ldr: lost pl over 1f out: wknd fnl f* **20/1**

44-3 **10** *nse* **Sweetness Lady**[18] 157 3-9-0 **63** LouisSteward(5) 4 50
(Olly Stevens) *dwlt: a in rr: rdn and no prog over 1f out* **10/1**

42-5 **11** *2¾* **Evacusafe Lady**[18] 157 3-9-3 **64** (tp) RyanPowell(3) 1 42
(John Ryan) *pressed ldr: sing to lose pl whn n.m.r on inner 2f out: wknd qckly* **16/1**

1m 12.54s (0.64) **Going Correction** 0.0s/f (Stan) **11** Ran SP% **122.5**
Speed ratings (Par 95): **95,94,93,93,91 88,88,88,87,87 84**
CSF £29.00 CT £78.59 TOTE £12.30: £3.60, £1.60, £1.40; EX 56.70 Trifecta £329.40.
**Owner** Laurence Mann **Bred** Charley Knoll Partnership **Trained** Newmarket, Suffolk

**FOCUS**
A moderate 3yo sprint handicap run at a fair pace with a few keen to get on with it. The winner's best since his standout 2yo run.

## 402 COMPARE BOOKMAKERS AT BOOKMAKERS.CO.UK H'CAP 6f 1y(P)
**2:35** (2:35) (Class 6) (0-52,52) 4-Y-0+ **£2,385** (£704; £352) **Stalls** Low

Form RPR

2-42 **1** **Seamster**[9] 274 7-9-3 **48** (bt) GrahamLee 12 62
(Richard Ford) *gd spd fr wdst draw: led after 1f: mde rest: drew clr fr 2f out: shkn up and in n.d fnl f* **6/4**[1]

05/- **2** *3½* **Chapellerie (IRE)**[557] 4394 5-9-7 **52** (b) WilliamCarson 4 55
(Richard Guest) *hld up in midfield: prog over 2f out gng wl: rdn fnl f: styd on to take 2nd nr fin but wnr long gone* **7/2**[2]

52-0 **3** *hd* **Metropolitan Chief**[21] 114 10-9-7 **52** (p) JimmyQuinn 3 54
(Paul Burgoyne) *prom: chsd wnr wl over 2f out: lft bhd fr wl over 1f out: kpt on but lost 2nd nr fin* **6/1**[3]

4-05 **4** *3½* **Sherjawy (IRE)**[9] 274 10-8-13 **47** (p) RossAtkinson(3) 8 38
(Zoe Davison) *chsd ldrs on outer: rdn 2f out: wl outpcd sn after: n.d after* **25/1**

304- **5** *½* **Demoiselle Bond**[40] 8393 6-8-10 **48** NedCurtis(7) 7 37
(Lydia Richards) *chsd ldng pair: disp 2nd briefly over 2f out: pushed along and fdd over 1f out* **14/1**

000- **6** *hd* **Bint Alzain (IRE)**[43] 8341 5-9-4 **52** JemmaMarshall(3) 5 41
(Pat Phelan) *hld up towards rr: rdn and sme prog over 1f out: nvr on terms and no hdwy fnl f* **12/1**

52-0 **7** *nk* **Christopher Chua (IRE)**[22] 100 5-8-10 **46** (v) DavidKenny(5) 6 34
(Michael Scudamore) *hld up in last pair: shkn up 2f out: no great prog* **16/1**

646- **8** *2* **Fantasy Invader (IRE)**[99] 7485 4-9-3 **48** GeorgeBaker 1 29
(Gary Moore) *restless stalls: dwlt: a in last pair: shkn up and no prog 2f out* **6/1**[3]

060/ **9** *74* **Dashing Storm**[484] 6822 4-9-5 **50** (b[1]) FergusSweeney 2
(Jeremy Gask) *led 1f: chsd wnr to wl over 2f out: wknd rapidly: t.o and virtually p.u over 1f out* **66/1**

1m 10.92s (-0.98) **Going Correction** 0.0s/f (Stan) **9** Ran SP% **116.4**
Speed ratings (Par 101): **106,101,101,96,95 95,95,92,**
CSF £6.71 CT £24.18 TOTE £1.90: £1.10, £1.80, £2.60; EX 8.10 Trifecta £35.00.
**Owner** P Bamford **Bred** D G Hardisty Bloodstock **Trained** Garstang, Lancs

**FOCUS**
Not many got into this moderate handicap, which was run in a good time for the grade. The winner was close to last winter's Southwell best.

## 403 CORAL.CO.UK BEST ODDS GUARANTEED ON RACING MAIDEN STKS 1m 2f (P)
**3:10** (3:12) (Class 5) 3-Y-0+ **£3,067** (£905; £453) **Stalls** Low

Form RPR

**1** **Hill Fort**[222] 4-9-7 75 DCByrne(5) 4 78
(Ronald Harris) *mde virtually all: rdn and more than 2 l clr fr 2f out: tied up last 100yds: jst hld on* **16/1**

5-2 **2** *hd* **Mbhali (IRE)**[13] 230 3-8-5 0 JoeFanning 3 74+
(Mark Johnston) *trckd wnr 2f: cl up in 3rd after: rdn 3f out: no imp after tl fnlly styd on fnl f: tk 2nd and clsd qckly on wnr fin* **1/2**[1]

44-2 **3** *nk* **Yeah Baby (IRE)**[24] 74 3-8-0 72 LukeMorris 2 68
(Charles Hills) *chsd wnr after 2f: rdn over 2f out: nt qckn wl over 1f out: clsd ins fnl f but lost 2nd nr fin* **7/2**[2]

0- **4** *5* **Lil Rockerfeller (USA)**[81] 7835 3-8-5 0 KieranO'Neill 6 63
(Richard Hannon) *chsd ldng trio: rdn over 3f out: sn outpcd: hrd drvn and no imp over 1f out* **5/1**[3]

**5** *1¼* **New Tarabela** 3-8-5 0 JimmyQuinn 8 61
(James Tate) *s.i.s and early reminder: in tch in rr but rn green: outpcd over 3f out: nvr on terms after: plugged on* **14/1**

0 **6** *6* **Pembroke Pride**[16] 189 4-9-7 0 JohnFahy 5 48
(Philip Hide) *hld up in last: lft bhd fr over 3f out: no ch whn nt clr run twice over 2f out: nvr in it* **50/1**

5 **7** *1¼* **Celtic Sunlight**[9] 282 4-9-12 0 FergusSweeney 1 50
(Pat Phelan) *settled in rr: pushed along and lft bhd fr over 3f out: nvr on terms after* **50/1**

5 **8** *26* **Fleetwood Nix**[9] 276 4-9-4 0 JemmaMarshall(3) 7
(Pat Phelan) *racd wd: in tch in rr: shkn up and wknd over 3f out: t.o* **50/1**

2m 7.41s (0.81) **Going Correction** 0.0s/f (Stan) **8** Ran SP% **124.0**
**WFA** 3 from 4yo 23lb
Speed ratings (Par 103): **96,95,95,91,90 85,84,64**
CSF £26.96 TOTE £26.60: £3.60, £1.02, £1.90; EX 51.20 Trifecta £159.30.
**Owner** Ridge House Stables Ltd **Bred** Darley **Trained** Earlswood, Monmouths

**FOCUS**
A muddling maiden lacking strength in depth, but rather a surprise result. The winner is rated in line with his French form.

## 404 32RED H'CAP 1m 2f (P)
**3:45** (3:45) (Class 4) (0-85,78) 3-Y-O **£4,942** (£1,459; £730) **Stalls** Low

Form RPR

011 **1** **Swivel**[8] 301 3-9-7 **78** 6ex JoeFanning 6 86+
(Mark Johnston) *trckd ldr: shkn up to ld wl over 1f out and sn dashed 3 l clr: rdn out fnl 100yds as rivals clsd* **5/6**[1]

4-14 **2** *1* **Jazzy Lady (IRE)**[4] 357 3-9-4 **75** SeanLevey 1 78
(David Evans) *hld up: in 5th pl as ldng pair drew clr fr 3f out: swtchd rt over 2f out: prog to chse wnr jst over 1f out: styd on but a too much to do: bmpd nr fin* **16/1**

40-1 **3** *nse* **Starlight Princess (IRE)**[18] 157 3-8-9 **66** (b) JohnFahy 5 69
(J S Moore) *s.s: hld up in last: stl there over 2f out w ldng pair wl away: rdn and prog over 1f out: disp 2nd fnl f: styd on but too much to do: hung rt nr fin* **12/1**[3]

014- **4** *6* **Aristocracy**[115] 7107 3-8-5 **69** DanielCremin(7) 4 60
(Mick Channon) *wnt bdly rt s: hld up: outpcd fr 3f out: no imp on ldrs after* **33/1**

4-1 **5** *10* **Can't Change It (IRE)**[13] 231 3-9-7 **78** MartinLane 3 59+
(David Simcock) *racd keenly: led: drew clr w wnr fr 3f out: hdd wl over 1f out: wknd rapidly and heavily eased* **7/4**[2]

205- **6** *1* **Ultimate Warrior (IRE)**[121] 6946 3-8-12 **69** StephenCraine 2 38
(Jim Boyle) *chsd ldng pair: pushed along 1/2-way: wknd qckly 3f out* **25/1**

2m 7.32s (0.72) **Going Correction** 0.0s/f (Stan) **6** Ran SP% **111.3**
Speed ratings (Par 99): **97,96,96,91,83 82**
CSF £15.79 TOTE £1.40: £1.10, £4.30; EX 9.50 Trifecta £29.30.
**Owner** Sheikh Hamdan bin Mohammed Al Maktoum **Bred** Stratford Place Stud And Watership Down **Trained** Middleham Moor, N Yorks
■ Stewards' Enquiry : John Fahy one-day ban; careless riding (14th Feb)

**FOCUS**
What had looked a fascinating clash between two progressive 3yos became anything but when one of the pair ran too badly to be true. The pace was modest and the form is rated around the runner-up.

## 405 CORAL.CO.UK AMATEUR RIDERS' H'CAP 1m 4f (P)
**4:15** (4:15) (Class 5) (0-70,70) 4-Y-0+ **£2,963** (£911; £455) **Stalls** Low

Form RPR

301- **1** **Swift Blade (IRE)**[32] 8447 6-11-0 **70** MrSWalker 3 77
(Lady Herries) *hld up in last trio: stdy prog on outer fr 4f out: wnt 3rd over 2f out: clsd over 1f out: rdn to ld ins fnl f: styd on* **2/1**[1]

24-2 **2** *½* **Royal Marskell**[30] 1 5-10-8 **64** MrPCollington 5 70
(K F Clutterbuck) *t.k.h: hld up towards rr: prog over 4f out: wnt 2nd 3f out: rdn to ld narrowly wl over 1f out: hdd and one pce ins fnl f* **10/1**

001- **3** *1* **Linkable**[72] 7984 5-10-5 **66** (tp) JennyPowell(5) 4 71
(Brendan Powell) *wl in tch: pushed along 3f out: clsd on ldrs over 1f out: kpt on to take 3rd last stride* **10/1**

05-1 **4** *nse* **Obboorr**[9] 277 5-10-3 **66** 6ex MrKWood(7) 8 71
(John Wainwright) *hld up towards rr: prog on outer over 2f out: rdn and clsd on ldrs jst over 1f out: kpt on same pce after* **9/4**[2]

605- **5** *shd* **Teide Peak (IRE)**[46] 8308 5-9-12 **59** MrsRWilson(5) 7 63
(Paul D'Arcy) *t.k.h: hld up in last pair: plld way through to ld over 5f out: narrowly hdd wl over 1f out: upsides jst ins fnl f: nudged along and no ex* **20/1**

016- **6** *1½* **Dellbuoy**[32] 8447 5-10-6 **67** MissLDempster(5) 11 69
(Pat Phelan) *hld up in midfield: shkn up and effrt over 2f out: tried to cl on ldrs over 1f out: kpt on same pce* **10/1**

035- **7** *3½* **Whinging Willie (IRE)**[65] 8059 5-10-9 **68** MissHayleyMoore(3) 2 64
(Gary Moore) *plld hrd and hld up: dropped to last pair 4f out: tried to make prog 2f out but no ch* **8/1**[3]

0-00 **8** *2* **Flag Of Glory**[12] 250 7-10-3 **64** MissMEdden(5) 6 57
(Peter Hiatt) *led to over 5f out: styd cl up: pushed along and wknd wl over 1f out* **50/1**

36-0 **9** *16* **Langham Lily (USA)**[8] 293 5-9-12 **61** (b[1]) MrWDegnan(7) 10 29
(Sarah Humphrey) *t.k.h: prom: rdn and wknd over 3f out: t.o* **25/1**

000/ **10** *19* **Osgood**[285] 6131 7-10-1 **62** GeorgeGorman(5) 1
(Gary Moore) *t.k.h: prom: lost pl over 4f out: sn bhd: wl t.o* **33/1**

306- **U** **Baan (USA)**[58] 8160 11-9-8 **57** MrDeanSmith(7) 9
(James Eustace) *hld up in rr: no real prog over 2f out: tack problems after: 9th whn uns rdr nr fin* **50/1**

2m 33.64s (0.64) **Going Correction** 0.0s/f (Stan) **11** Ran SP% **118.0**
Speed ratings (Par 103): **97,96,96,95,95 94,92,91,80,67**
CSF £21.62 CT £163.99 TOTE £2.70: £1.10, £3.40, £3.40; EX 21.10 Trifecta £101.00.
**Owner** Angmering Park **Bred** Messrs Mark Hanly & James Hanly **Trained** Patching, W Sussex

**FOCUS**
An ordinary amateur riders' handicap with a tight finish. The first two got the best rides.
T/Plt: £5.40 to a £1 stake. Pool: £91380.97 - 12179.48 winning tickets T/Qpdt: £2.20 to a £1 stake. Pool: £6539.91 - 2126.56 winning tickets JN

# [353]WOLVERHAMPTON (A.W) (L-H)
Friday, January 31

**OFFICIAL GOING: Standard**
Wind: medium to strong, behind Weather: dry after heavy rain earlier

## 406 CORAL MOBILE "JUST THREE CLICKS TO BET" APPRENTICE H'CAP 1m 1f 103y(P)
**4:50** (4:51) (Class 6) (0-65,65) 4-Y-0+ **£2,264** (£673; £336; £168) **Stalls** Low

Form RPR

3-25 **1** **Kindlelight Storm (USA)**[9] 283 4-8-12 **56** (b) JordanVaughan 7 66
(Nick Littmoden) *hld up in midfield: hdwy 4f out: swtchd rt and effrt over 2f out: chsd ldr over 1f out: led 1f out: idling but in command fnl 100yds: rdn out* **5/1**[2]

125- **2** *1¾* **Dubai Celebration**[35] 8410 6-9-5 **65** JackGarritty(3) 2 71
(Julie Camacho) *hld up in midfield: hdwy 4f out: rdn to chse ldr ent fnl 2f tl over 1f out: chsd wnr fnl 100yds: kpt on but no imp* **8/1**

13-4 **3** *1¾* **Minstrel Lad**[25] 67 6-8-9 **57** JackGilligan(5) 10 59
(Lydia Pearce) *stdd and wnt rt s: hld up off the pce in last trio: hdwy whn nt clr run and swtchd rt over 2f out: r.o wl ins fnl f to snatch 3rd last strides: no threat to wnr* **6/1**[3]

12-5 **4** *hd* **Mosman**[22] 105 4-9-1 **62** (tp) PaulBooth(3) 8 64
(Dean Ivory) *chsd ldrs: rdn and clsd 4f out: drvn to ld over 2f out: hdd and no ex 1f out: wknd and lost 2 pls fnl 100yds* **16/1**

0-22 **5** *1½* **Yourinthewill (USA)**[13] 229 6-9-8 **65** RobJFitzpatrick 5 64
(Daniel Mark Loughnane) *stdd s: t.k.h: hld up in last trio: rdn and hdwy over 2f out: styd on same pce and no imp fr over 1f out* **6/1**[3]

1-26 **6** *3¾* **No Win No Fee**[17] 172 4-9-4 **65** (p) AlistairRawlinson(3) 3 56
(Michael Appleby) *hld up in midfield: rdn and no rspnse over 2f out: drvn over 1f out: no hdwy: nvr trbld ldrs* **11/4**[1]

215- **7** *2¾* **Camerooney**[48] 8295 11-9-3 **65** (p) KevinLundie(5) 9 50
(Marjorie Fife) *led and sn crossed to rail: clr w rival after 2f tl rdn and hdd over 2f out: wknd wl over 1f out* **9/1**

0-14 **8** *1¼* **Outlaw Torn (IRE)**[17] 171 5-9-0 **64** (e) MelissaThompson(7) 4 46
(Richard Guest) *taken down early: t.k.h: w ldr and clr of field after 2f out tl wl over 2f out: sn wknd* **10/1**

620- **9** *13* **Sixties Queen**[129] 6730 4-8-10 **57**.................................. DavidParkes(3) 6 12
(Alan Bailey) *chsd ldrs tl lost pl over 3f out: lost tch 2f out* **22/1**

040- **10** *15* **Jumbo Prado (USA)**[221] 3642 5-9-0 **62**.......................... JoshQuinn(5) 1
(John Stimpson) *a bhd: lost tch 5f out: t.o* **50/1**

2m 3.89s (2.19) **Going Correction** +0.325s/f (Slow)
**WFA** 4 from 5yo+ 1lb **10** Ran SP% **114.3**
Speed ratings (Par 101): **103,101,99,99,98 95,92,91,79,66**
CSF £43.73 CT £244.20 TOTE £5.70: £1.90, £2.50, £2.30; EX 45.20 Trifecta £391.40.
**Owner** Kindlelight Ltd, N Shields & N Littmoden **Bred** Kirsten Rausing **Trained** Newmarket, Suffolk
■ Stewards' Enquiry : Kevin Lundie three-day ban; careless riding (15th,17th,18th Feb). one-day ban; did not keep straight leaving stalls (19th Feb). £290.00 fine; used mobile phone outside designated area.
Rob J Fitzpatrick two-day ban; used whip above permitted level (14th-15th Feb)

**FOCUS**
They went a generous early pace in this modest apprentices' handicap, run in cold, damp and breezy conditions. The first three came from the rear, with a step up from the winner.

## 407 CORAL.CO.UK BEST ODDS GUARANTEED ON RACING CLAIMING STKS — 1m 1f 103y(P)
**5:20** (5:21) (Class 5) 4-Y-0+ **£2,911** (£866; £432; £216) **Stalls** Low

Form RPR

24-0 **1** **Back Burner (IRE)**[30] 3 6-9-6 **81**............................ DanielTudhope 7 82
(David O'Meara) *chsd ldr tl led 3f out: rdn and qcknd clr 2f out: stl clr and drvn ins fnl f: kpt on and a doing enough: rdn out* **5/2**[2]

61- **2** *2* **Officer In Command (USA)**[63] 8093 8-9-4 **73**.............(p) LiamKeniry 1 76
(John Butler) *chsd ldrs: rdn over 1f out: drvn and chsd clr wnr over 1f out: kpt on u.p fnl 100yds but nvr gng pce to rch wnr* **16/1**

5-56 **3** *1 ¼* **Rakaan (IRE)**[15] 200 7-9-6 **84**............................................. AdamKirby 2 75
(Jamie Osborne) *s.i.s: hld up in rr: clsd but bhd a wall of horses 2f out: edgd lft and hdwy u.p 1f out: kpt on fnl f: nvr trbld wnr* **1/1**[1]

1-31 **4** *shd* **Matraash (USA)**[15] 199 8-9-3 **78**..................................(be) ShaneKelly 5 72
(Daniel Mark Loughnane) *hld up in last pair: rdn over 2f out: no imp and wd bnd wl over 1f out: kpt on ins fnl f: nvr trbld ldrs* **6/1**[3]

00-4 **5** *4 ½* **Wildomar**[15] 197 5-9-3 **75**............................................ MarkCoumbe(3) 6 66
(Tony Carroll) *in tch in midfield: rdn and effrt over 2f out: no imp over 1f out: wknd fnl f* **33/1**

515- **6** *7* **Plunder**[124] 6877 4-8-13 **73**............................................ RobertHavlin 4 45
(Alan Berry) *led: jnd and rdn over 3f out: hdd 3f out: drvn and outpcd 2f out: dropped to rr over 1f out: sn wknd* **12/1**

2m 4.41s (2.71) **Going Correction** +0.325s/f (Slow)
**WFA** 4 from 5yo+ 1lb **6** Ran SP% **109.4**
Speed ratings (Par 103): **100,98,97,97,93 86**
CSF £35.22 TOTE £3.80: £3.60, £3.30; EX 29.70 Trifecta £65.80.
**Owner** Middleham Park Racing LXXV **Bred** Anamoine Ltd **Trained** Nawton, N Yorks

**FOCUS**
They went a sensible pace for this uncompetitive claimer and the market signalled it was between just two - and both had questions to answer. The winner didn't need to match his recent form.

## 408 CORAL APP DOWNLOAD FROM THE APP STORE H'CAP — 1m 1f 103y(P)
**5:55** (5:55) (Class 4) (0-85,85) 4-Y-0+ **£5,175** (£1,540; £769; £384) **Stalls** Low

Form RPR

0-61 **1** **Modernism**[15] 200 5-9-6 **84**........................................... JamieSpencer 3 95
(David Simcock) *hld up wl in tch in midfield: hdwy to join ldrs 2f out: rdn and ev ch over 1f out: led ins fnl f: drvn and asserted fnl 100yds: pushed out towards fin* **6/4**[1]

2-1 **2** *1 ¼* **Like A Diamond (IRE)**[21] 127 4-8-13 **78**......................... AdamKirby 7 86
(Evan Williams) *t.k.h: chsd ldr tl rdn to ld 2f out: drvn over 1f out: hdd ins fnl f: no ex and btn fnl 100yds* **5/2**[2]

0-60 **3** *½* **Mica Mika (IRE)**[18] 160 6-8-7 **74**.......................(v[1]) GeorgeChaloner(3) 2 81
(Richard Fahey) *t.k.h: chsd ldng pair: rdn 2f out: drvn and kpt on same pce ins fnl f* **12/1**

14-2 **4** *2 ¾* **Royal Holiday (IRE)**[22] 96 7-8-8 **72**............................(p) LiamKeniry 5 73
(Marjorie Fife) *led and set stdy gallop: rdn 3f out: hdd and unable qck 2f out: outpcd and btn 1f out: plugged on same pce after* **16/1**

02-3 **5** *shd* **Well Painted (IRE)**[20] 145 5-9-2 **85**......................(e[1]) NathanAlison(5) 4 86
(William Haggas) *hld up wl in tch in midfield: rdn and effrt on inner wl over 1f out: no imp and btn 1f out: one pce after* **3/1**[3]

/5-0 **6** *6* **Cockney Class (USA)**[18] 163 7-9-7 **85**.............................. PaddyAspell 1 73
(Dave Roberts) *stdd s: hld up in tch in rr: rdn and ent fnl 2f: sn outpcd and btn: wknd fnl f* **50/1**

2m 3.63s (1.93) **Going Correction** +0.325s/f (Slow)
**WFA** 4 from 5yo+ 1lb **6** Ran SP% **109.1**
Speed ratings (Par 105): **104,102,102,100,99 94**
CSF £5.13 TOTE £2.30: £1.20, £1.60; EX 5.50 Trifecta £25.70.
**Owner** Dr Marwan Koukash **Bred** Darley **Trained** Newmarket, Suffolk

**FOCUS**
The early pace was modest for this fair handicap and while it turned into something of a sprint, the form looks fairly solid.

## 409 LADBROKES MEDIAN AUCTION MAIDEN STKS — 1m 141y(P)
**6:30** (6:32) (Class 5) 3-5-Y-0 **£2,587** (£770; £384; £192) **Stalls** Low

Form RPR

436- **1** **Rock 'N' Roll Star**[98] 7492 3-8-6 75.................................... LukeMorris 4 74
(Peter Chapple-Hyam) *s.i.s: hld up in tch in rr: rdn and swtchd to outer over 2f out: hdwy to ld 1f out: sn in command: styd on* **6/4**[1]

64- **2** *2 ¼* **Old Town Boy**[53] 8214 3-8-6 0......................................... AndrewMullen 2 69
(Philip McBride) *wl in tch in midfield: rdn and effrt over 2f out: chsd clr wnr jst ins fnl f: kpt on but no imp* **4/1**[3]

220- **3** *2 ¼* **Irish Tears**[31] 8452 3-8-7 72 ow1......................................(t) RobertHavlin 6 65
(John Gosden) *t.k.h: led and set stdy gallop: rdn and hdd 2f out: stl ev ch but nt qckn over 1f out: wknd fnl 100yds* **9/4**[2]

60- **4** *nk* **Honiton Lace**[31] 8451 3-7-12 0 ow2.............................. ShelleyBirkett(5) 3 60?
(J W Hills) *chsd ldr: rdn to ld 2f out: edgd lft and hdd 1f out: sn outpcd and btn: wknd fnl 100yds* **50/1**

**5** *15* **Mount Glenn** 3-8-3 0.......................................... MichaelJMMurphy(3) 1 29
(Mark Johnston) *chsd ldrs: rdn and unable qck ent fnl 2f: sn outpcd and btn: fdd over 1f out* **6/1**

**6** *27* **Clarence Beeks (IRE)**[22] 4-9-6 0.................................... KevinLundie(7) 5
(Brian Ellison) *wl in tch in midfield on outer: rdn 1/2-way: sn dropped to rr: lost tch 3f out: t.o* **20/1**

1m 53.24s (2.74) **Going Correction** +0.325s/f (Slow)
**WFA** 3 from 4yo 22lb **6** Ran SP% **111.8**
Speed ratings (Par 103): **100,98,96,95,82 58**
CSF £7.89 TOTE £2.20: £1.10, £2.80; EX 7.80 Trifecta £18.50.
**Owner** Phil Cunningham **Bred** P M Cunningham **Trained** Newmarket, Suffolk

**FOCUS**
An ordinary maiden won in good style by the well-backed favourite. He's rated to form, but there are doubts.

## 410 LADBROKES H'CAP — 1m 141y(P)
**7:00** (7:01) (Class 5) (0-70,69) 4-Y-0+ **£2,911** (£866; £432; £216) **Stalls** Low

Form RPR

00-0 **1** **Mr Red Clubs (IRE)**[23] 79 5-9-4 **66**.........................(p) AndrewMullen 6 73
(Michael Appleby) *dwlt: sn rcvrd to chse ldrs and t.k.h: rdn to chal 2f out: led ent fnl f: styd on wl u.p: rdn out* **15/8**[1]

142- **2** *1* **Candy Kitten**[67] 8038 4-9-4 **67**.......................................(p) LukeMorris 7 72
(Alastair Lidderdale) *jnd ldr over 6f out: rdn and ev ch 2f out: led wl over 1f out tl ent fnl f: nt quite pce of wnr and kpt on same pce u.p fnl 100yds* **7/1**

264- **3** *shd* **Green Special (ITY)**[13] 3621 4-9-4 **67**................................ PaddyAspell 3 72
(Dave Roberts) *hld up in last pair: rdn and effrt on inner over 1f out: drvn and styd on wl ins fnl f* **50/1**

2-12 **4** *nse* **Disco Dave (IRE)**[21] 116 6-8-12 **60**................................... ShaneKelly 9 65
(Daniel Mark Loughnane) *wl in tch in midfield: rdn and effrt to chse ldrs 2f out: edgd lft and styd on same pce ins fnl f* **7/2**[2]

406- **5** *hd* **Dakota Canyon (IRE)**[202] 4294 5-9-5 **67**.........................(v) LeeTopliss 4 71
(Richard Fahey) *led: rdn over 2f out: drvn and hdd wl over 1f out: styd on same pce u.p ins fnl f* **17/2**

02-1 **6** *½* **Gabrial The Boss (USA)**[16] 180 4-9-6 **69**...................(tp) TomEaves 2 72
(Michael Mullineaux) *chsd ldrs: rdn and effrt wl over 1f out: drvn and styd on same pce ins fnl f* **20/1**

65-4 **7** *½* **My Single Malt (IRE)**[28] 29 6-9-6 **68**.........................(v) BarryMcHugh 8 70
(Julie Camacho) *stdd and swtchd lft after s: t.k.h: hld up wl in tch in midfield: rdn and chsng ldrs but nvr much room thrght fnl f: one pce* **8/1**

3-35 **8** *5* **Living Leader**[8] 293 5-9-3 **68**..........................(v) MichaelJMMurphy(3) 5 58
(Nick Littmoden) *in tch towards rr: rdn and struggling 3f out: sn outpcd: wknd over 1f out* **13/2**[3]

5 **9** *3 ¾* **Hejaz (IRE)**[18] 168 4-9-3 **66**.......................................... StevieDonohoe 1 48
(Tim Pitt) *stdd s: t.k.h: hld up in rr: rdn and outpcd ent fnl 2f: wknd over 1f out* **25/1**

1m 53.17s (2.67) **Going Correction** +0.325s/f (Slow)
**WFA** 4 from 5yo+ 1lb **9** Ran SP% **115.0**
Speed ratings (Par 103): **101,100,100,99,99 98,98,94,91**
CSF £15.21 CT £485.40 TOTE £2.60: £1.30, £3.20, £4.30; EX 16.10 Trifecta £318.50.
**Owner** Ferrybank Properties Limited **Bred** Tally-Ho Stud **Trained** Danethorpe, Notts

**FOCUS**
An honest pace for this ordinary handicap, which saw a bunched finish. Standard form, but with doubts.

## 411 32RED H'CAP — 7f 32y(P)
**7:30** (7:31) (Class 6) (0-60,59) 3-Y-O **£2,264** (£673; £336; £168) **Stalls** High

Form RPR

0-64 **1** **Copper Cavalier**[9] 280 3-8-7 **45**..............................(v) AdamBeschizza 6 50+
(Robert Cowell) *s.i.s and rdn along: in tch in rr: hdwy on outer to join ldrs 1/2-way: led wl over 2f out: rdn clr 2f out: drvn ins fnl f: all out but a lasting home* **14/1**

10-2 **2** *nk* **Witchy Woman**[17] 173 3-9-7 **59**................................ DanielTudhope 3 63
(K R Burke) *w ldr tl led 6f out: hdd and rdn wl over 2f out: 2 l down and drvn over 1f out: rallied gamely u.p fnl f: pressing wnr cl home: jst hld* **7/2**[2]

655- **3** *1 ¾* **Gee Sharp**[43] 8346 3-9-5 **57**..........................................(p) BarryMcHugh 5 56
(Julie Camacho) *wl in tch in midfield: rdn 1/2-way: effrt to chse ldng pair 2f out: kpt on u.p but gng pce to chal* **5/1**[3]

00-0 **4** *3 ¼* **Aussie Sky (IRE)**[11] 261 3-8-7 **45**........................................ LukeMorris 2 36
(Daniel Mark Loughnane) *t.k.h: chsd ldng trio: drvn and outpcd ent fnl 2f: wknd over 1f out* **25/1**

3-43 **5** *nk* **Trinity Lorraine (IRE)**[11] 261 3-8-10 **53**......................(v) TimClark(5) 4 43
(Alan Bailey) *s.i.s and rdn along: in tch in last pair: rdn and outpcd 1/2-way: wl hld but kpt on fnl f* **11/2**

6-02 **6** *½* **Keep To The Beat**[11] 261 3-8-12 **55**.............................. ShaneGray(5) 1 43
(Kevin Ryan) *led for 1f: styd w ldrs tl rdn and outpcd ent 3f out: wknd wl over 1f out* **6/4**[1]

00-0 **7** *21* **Birikyno**[23] 86 3-9-5 **57**.........................................................(p) LiamKeniry 7
(Mark Usher) *w ldrs tl rdn and outpcd 3f out: sn drvn and lost pl: wl bhd and eased ins fnl f* **12/1**

1m 31.89s (2.29) **Going Correction** +0.325s/f (Slow) **7** Ran SP% **112.5**
Speed ratings (Par 95): **99,98,96,92,92 92,68**
CSF £60.20 TOTE £13.90: £6.20, £2.10; EX 81.00 Trifecta £295.50.
**Owner** Mrs D Rix, J Partridge & Partner **Bred** Shadwell Estate Company Limited **Trained** Six Mile Bottom, Cambs

**FOCUS**
A weak handicap which few got in to and they finished well strung out. The level is set around the second and third.

## 412 BEST ODDS AT BOOKMAKERS.CO.UK H'CAP — 5f 20y(P)
**8:00** (8:00) (Class 5) (0-75,81) 4-Y-0+ **£2,911** (£866; £432; £216) **Stalls** Low

Form RPR

/1-6 **1** **Expose**[23] 80 6-8-11 **72**........................................ AlistairRawlinson(7) 7 85
(Michael Appleby) *hld up in midfield: clsd to trck ldrs 1/2-way: rdn to ld 1f out: r.o wl: rdn out* **9/2**[2]

-211 **2** *1 ½* **Lexi's Hero (IRE)**[7] 312 6-9-13 **81** 6ex.......................(v) JamieSpencer 4 89
(Richard Fahey) *drvn early: chsd ldrs: edgd lft and effrt over 1f out: chsd wnr jst ins fnl f: kpt on but no imp fnl 100yds* **10/11**[1]

06-0 **3** *3 ½* **Temple Road (IRE)**[13] 233 6-9-2 **70**......................... RichardKingscote 6 65
(Milton Bradley) *taken down early: dwlt and sn outpcd in last pair: hdwy over 1f out: wnt 3rd ins fnl f: no imp* **7/1**[3]

5-14 **4** *3 ¾* **I'll Be Good**[5] 347 5-8-10 **64** 6ex...................................... LukeMorris 3 46
(Alan Berry) *led for 1f: pressed ldr tl led again 2f out: sn rdn: hdd 1f out: fdd ins fnl f* **7/1**[3]

00-6 **5** *1 ¼* **West Coast Dream**[16] 191 7-9-1 **69**..................................(b) TomEaves 8 46
(Roy Brotherton) *chsd ldng trio: clsd 1/2-way: rdn and btn over 1f out: fdd fnl f* **33/1**

06-6 **6** *1 ¼* **Majestic Manannan (IRE)**[29] 8 5-8-13 **67**............. AdrianNicholls 1 40
(David Nicholls) *s.i.s: sn rdn and a outpcd in rr: n.d* **16/1**

05-2 **7** *16* **Island Legend (IRE)**[16] 191 8-9-6 **74**............................(p) AdamKirby 2
(Milton Bradley) *taken down early: pressed ldr tl led after 1f out: hdd 2f out: struggling whn hmpd over 1f out: sn bhd and heavily eased ins fnl f* **14/1**

1m 2.25s (-0.05) **Going Correction** +0.325s/f (Slow) **7** Ran SP% **111.1**
Speed ratings (Par 103): **113,110,105,99,97 95,69**
CSF £8.44 CT £24.97 TOTE £6.80: £3.30, £1.60; EX 17.20 Trifecta £52.30.
**Owner** The Giggle Factor Partnership **Bred** John And Susan Davis **Trained** Danethorpe, Notts

**FOCUS**
They went a decent pace for this ordinary handicap. The first pair were on good marks based on their old form.
T/Plt: £228.50 to a £1 stake. Pool: £106898.78 - 341.46 winning tickets T/Qpdt: £23.90 to a £1 stake. Pool: £11520.29 - 356.25 winning tickets SP

413 - 415a (Foreign Racing) - See Raceform Interactive

## 324 DUNDALK (A.W) (L-H)
Friday, January 31

**OFFICIAL GOING: Standard**

### 416a FOLLOW DUNDALK ON FACEBOOK H'CAP 1m (P)
7:15 (7:17) 3-Y-O £4,600 (£1,066; £466; £266)

RPR
1 **Master Of Time (IRE)**42 8376 3-9-8 **64**................(p) ColmO'Donoghue 3 76+
(P D Deegan, Ire) *t.k.h and sn led: rdn along and pushed clr ent fnl f: styd on strly* **11/4**2
2 2 3/4 **Political Policy (IRE)**14 223 3-9-6 **62**..........................(t) ShaneFoley 6 68
(M Halford, Ire) *hld up in rr towards inner tl prog under 2f out: wnt 4th 1f out: kpt on wl into 2nd clsng stages* **7/4**1
3 nk **Fix It (IRE)**14 223 3-9-1 **57**.................................. NGMcCullagh 5 62
(J P Murtagh, Ire) *hld up towards rr tl prog under 2f out: 3rd appr fnl f: no imp on wnr ins fnl f* **13/2**
4 2 1/4 **Breenainthemycra (IRE)**14 224 3-8-13 **55**.................. DannyGrant 8 55
(Eoin Doyle, Ire) *chsd ldrs on outer: prog into 2nd 2f out: no imp 1f out and dropped to 4th* **12/1**
5 2 1/4 **Fine Cut (IRE)**131 6671 3-9-10 **66**..............................1 WayneLordan 7 61
(T Stack, Ire) *w.w: pushed along 3f out: no imp under 2f out: kpt on same pce fnl f* **9/2**3
6 4 1/2 **Too Many Diamonds (IRE)**181 5018 3-9-1 **57**................ RoryCleary 4 42
(Damian Joseph English, Ire) *trckd ldr in 2nd tl nt qckn 2f out: sn no ex* **20/1**
7 hd **Ava's Secret (IRE)**42 8376 3-7-13 **48**................(t) TomMadden(7) 2 32
(David Peter Nagle, Ire) *chsd ldrs tl nt qckn under 2f out: sn one pce* **25/1**
8 1 **High Stand**56 8190 3-8-11 **60**.............................. LukeDempsey(7) 1 42
(J P Murtagh, Ire) *chsd ldrs on inner tl over 2f out: no imp whn sltly hmpd sn after: wknd* **12/1**

1m 39.29s (99.29) 8 Ran SP% **118.5**
CSF £8.33 CT £28.07 TOTE £4.30: £1.60, £1.02, £1.50; DF 13.70 Trifecta £74.60.
**Owner** Paolo Zambelli **Bred** Allevamento Degli Aletti Srl **Trained** The Curragh, Co Kildare
■ Stewards' Enquiry : N G McCullagh caution: careless riding.

**FOCUS**
An intriguing race with two leading Flat yards represented by a lightly raced 3yo taking on a typical Halford improver.

417 - 420a (Foreign Racing) - See Raceform Interactive

## 399 LINGFIELD (L-H)
Saturday, February 1

**OFFICIAL GOING: Standard**
Wind: Strong; behind Weather: Changeable with showers

### 421 BET ON YOUR MOBILE WITH LADBROKES (S) STKS 1m 1y(P)
12:10 (12:10) (Class 6) 4-Y-O+ £2,045 (£603; £302) Stalls High

Form RPR
140- 1 **Gaelic Silver (FR)**47 8308 8-9-5 **71**........................ GeorgeBaker 2 66
(Gary Moore) *trckd ldng pair: shkn up to ld over 1f out: wl in command and pushed out last 100yds* **5/2**2
-414 2 1 1/2 **Greek Islands (IRE)**10 281 6-9-5 **56**........................ ChrisCatlin 4 63
(Edward Creighton) *t.k.h: hld up in last: rdn and prog over 1f out: kpt on to take 2nd ins fnl f: no threat to wnr* **50/1**
0-14 3 3/4 **Nubar Boy**15 211 7-8-6 **60**........................(v) CharlotteJenner(7) 1 55
(Ian Williams) *led: rdn over 2f out: wd bnd sn after: hdd and one pce over 1f out* **12/1**3
-211 4 2 1/4 **Prime Exhibit**8 320 9-9-5 **71**........................(t) ShaneKelly 5 56
(Daniel Mark Loughnane) *stdd s: hld up in 4th: rdn and nt qckn over 1f out: no imp after* **4/7**1
0-54 5 2 1/2 **Cyflymder (IRE)**8 310 8-8-13 **59**........................(b) AdrianNicholls 6 44
(David C Griffiths) *pressed ldr: rdn over 2f out: carried wd bnd sn after: wknd* **20/1**

1m 37.87s (-0.33) **Going Correction** -0.125s/f (Stan) 5 Ran SP% **106.6**
Speed ratings (Par 101): **96,94,93,91,89**
CSF £57.28 TOTE £2.90: £1.10, £6.50; EX 34.90 Trifecta £88.40.There was no bid for the winner.
**Owner** The Winning Hand **Bred** Earl Haras Du Camp Bernard Et Al **Trained** Lower Beeding, W Sussex

**FOCUS**
A modest seller run at an ordinary pace. The runner-up is the key to the form.

### 422 LADBROKES MOBILE MEDIAN AUCTION MAIDEN STKS 1m 1y(P)
12:40 (12:41) (Class 6) 3-5-Y-O £2,385 (£704; £352) Stalls High

Form RPR
1 **Glace (IRE)**234 3224 3-8-4 **0**........................ JoeFanning 11 69
(Mark Johnston) *mde all: rdn over 1f out: sltly intimidated by loose horse but hld on wl whn strly pressed nr fin* **5/1**3
54 2 nk **Zamra (IRE)**7 341 3-8-4 **0**........................(p) LukeMorris 5 68
(James Tate) *chsd ldng trio: pushed along fr 1/2-way: rdn over 2f out: wnt 2nd jst over 1f out: chal ins fnl f: jst hld* **11/4**1
3-0 3 5 **Captain Mo**29 37 3-8-9 **0**........................ AndreaAtzeni 8 61
(Marco Botti) *mostly chsd wnr: rdn over 2f out: no imp and lost 2nd jst over 1f out: fdd but clung on to 3rd* **7/1**
0- 4 nse **Last Echo (IRE)**213 3958 3-8-4 **0**........................ ChrisCatlin 1 56+
(Ralph Beckett) *in tch: outpcd and shkn up fr 3f out: styd on fr over 1f out: nrly snatched 3rd* **7/1**
226- 5 1/2 **Awattan**119 7033 4-9-9 **66**........................(b1) JimmyQuinn 6 60
(Ed Vaughan) *t.k.h: trckd ldng pair: rdn to dispute 2nd pl over 2f out to jst over 1f out: fdd* **12/1**
42-4 6 4 **Sebs Sensei (IRE)**17 188 3-8-9 **73**........................ RobertHavlin 4 51
(Mark Hoad) *chsd ldrs: pushed along fr 1/2-way: rdn and no prog over 2f out: no ch after* **7/1**
7 2 1/4 **Pouncing Tiger** 3-8-4 **0**........................ DavidProbert 10 41
(Stuart Williams) *dwlt: in tch in rr to 3f out: outpcd after* **25/1**
8 14 **Amelia George** 4-9-9 **0**........................ AdamBeschizza 3 13
(Julia Feilden) *a in rr: wknd 3f out: t.o* **50/1**
9 19 **Norman's Star** 3-8-9 **0**........................(b1) LiamKeniry 2
(Chris Dwyer) *sn wl bhd: t.o* **100/1**
0-5 U **Sand Stormer (IRE)**17 188 3-8-9 **0**........................ JamieSpencer 7
(William Muir) *rring bef stalls opened: rrd bdly and uns rdr s* **9/2**2

1m 37.44s (-0.76) **Going Correction** -0.125s/f (Stan)
**WFA** 3 from 4yo 19lb 10 Ran SP% **113.5**
Speed ratings (Par 101): **98,97,92,92,92 88,85,71,52,**
CSF £18.39 TOTE £5.50: £2.20, £1.40, £3.80; EX 20.90 Trifecta £227.60.
**Owner** Lady O'Reilly **Bred** Mrs Alice Blake **Trained** Middleham Moor, N Yorks

**FOCUS**
A modest median auction maiden, reduced by one when Sand Stormer reared as the stalls opened and emerged without his rider. It paid to be handy. The form is rated a bit cautiously.

### 423 LADBROKES MAIDEN STKS 7f 1y(P)
1:10 (1:10) (Class 5) 3-Y-O+ £3,067 (£905; £453) Stalls Low

Form RPR
1 **Mr Bossy Boots (IRE)** 3-8-10 **0**........................ JimCrowley 3 81
(Ralph Beckett) *in tch: trckd ldng trio over 3f out gng wl: wdst of all bnd 2f out: r.o to chal ins fnl f: sltly green but drvn to ld last stride* **4/1**3
4 2 nse **Voyageofdiscovery (USA)**21 140 3-8-10 **0**........................ LukeMorris 1 81
(Clive Cox) *trckd ldng pair: shkn up and clsd to ld jst ins fnl f: drvn and styd on but hdd last stride* **2/1**1
3 3 3 1/4 **Jaahiez (USA)**15 218 3-8-10 **0**........................ AndreaAtzeni 10 72
(Roger Varian) *t.k.h: w ldr: rdn to chal 2f out: upsides 1f out: sn outpcd* **3/1**2
2-32 4 nk **Clear Spell (IRE)**7 341 3-8-10 **70**........................ RobertHavlin 4 71
(Ed Walker) *led: rdn and pressed 2f out: hdd and outpcd jst ins fnl f* **3/1**2
5 13 **Spinning Cobblers** 3-8-10 **0**........................ AdamBeschizza 7 36
(Stuart Williams) *settled in rr: wnt modest 5th over 2f out but already wl outpcd: pushed along and lost further grnd: t.o* **33/1**
6 2 1/4 **Radebe (USA)** 3-8-10 **0**........................ TomQueally 2 30
(Kevin Ryan) *rn green and sn pushed along in midfield: wknd 3f out: t.o* **12/1**
306- 7 3 1/2 **Hannah Louise (IRE)**70 8016 3-8-5 **40**........................(t) JimmyQuinn 5 15
(Roger Ingram) *slowly away: t.k.h early in last: lost tch 3f out: t.o* **100/1**
-0 8 1/2 **Literally On Fire (IRE)**14 231 3-8-10 **0**........................ StevieDonohoe 6 19
(Brendan Powell) *prom to 1/2-way: sn wknd u.p: t.o* **100/1**
9 4 **Spin For A Harp (IRE)** 3-8-10 **0**........................ ChrisCatlin 8 8
(David Dennis) *t.k.h early but shoved along and struggling by 1/2-way: sn wknd: t.o* **66/1**

1m 24.2s (-0.60) **Going Correction** -0.125s/f (Stan) 9 Ran SP% **117.4**
Speed ratings (Par 103): **98,97,94,93,79 76,72,71,67**
CSF £12.65 TOTE £4.00: £1.70, £1.40, £1.80; EX 17.10 Trifecta £52.30.
**Owner** Merriebelle Stables LLC **Bred** Kilfrush Stud **Trained** Kimpton, Hants

**FOCUS**
Very few got into this ordinary maiden and the four who dominated the market pulled miles clear of the others. The form is rated around the fourth.

### 424 BOOKMAKERS.CO.UK SPRINT SERIES ROUND 5 H'CAP (QUALIFIER) (DIV I) 6f 1y(P)
1:45 (1:46) (Class 6) (0-65,65) 4-Y-O+ £3,234 (£962; £481; £240) Stalls Low

Form RPR
04-4 1 **Compton Prince**17 192 5-8-11 **58**........................(b) RobertTart(3) 3 69
(Milton Bradley) *trckd ldrs: clsd over 1f out: rdn to ld last 150yds: styd on wl* **6/1**2
0-66 2 2 **Where's Reiley (USA)**8 312 8-9-4 **62**........................(v) GeorgeBaker 7 67
(Michael Attwater) *led: rdn 2f out: hdd and one pce last 150yds* **10/1**
1-32 3 1 1/4 **Pharoh Jake**7 339 6-8-12 **63**........................ RyanWhile(7) 9 64
(John Bridger) *pressed ldr: hrd rdn to chal 2f out: nt qckn over 1f out: sn lost 2nd and one pce* **6/1**2
0002 4 3/4 **Haadeeth**6 347 7-9-7 **65**........................(t) AdamKirby 4 64
(David Evans) *chsd ldrs: rdn and nt qckn 2f out: no imp after: kpt on last 100yds* **6/4**1
-506 5 1 **One Way Or Another (AUS)**7 340 11-8-12 **61**........(t) EoinWalsh(5) 2 56
(David Evans) *stdd s: hld up in last: sme prog over 2f out: rdn over 1f out: kpt on but nvr really in it* **8/1**3
0-02 6 2 1/4 **Waterloo Dock**7 340 9-8-8 **52**........................(v) LukeMorris 1 40
(Mick Quinn) *prom but sn pushed along: lost pl u.p over 3f out: nt on term after* **10/1**
1565 7 4 **Minimee**7 340 4-8-13 **57**........................(v) DavidProbert 6 32
(Phil McEntee) *a towards rr: bmpd 4f out: no prog over 2f out* **8/1**3
00-0 8 4 **Belinsky (IRE)**9 296 7-8-10 **54**........................ JimCrowley 5 17
(Dean Ivory) *hld up in rr: bmpd 4f out: stl wl in rr whn hung bdly rt bnd 2f out: bhd after* **16/1**
004- 9 1 1/4 **Girl At The Sands (IRE)**57 8177 4-8-8 **59**........... JenniferFerguson(7) 8 18
(Edward Creighton) *nvr bttr than midfield: struggling whn carried v wd bnd 2f out: bhd after* **33/1**

1m 10.7s (-1.20) **Going Correction** -0.125s/f (Stan) 9 Ran SP% **117.8**
Speed ratings (Par 101): **103,100,98,97,96 93,88,82,81**
CSF £65.30 CT £382.11 TOTE £7.50: £2.20, £3.80, £1.60; EX 88.20 Trifecta £286.40.
**Owner** E A Hayward **Bred** Whitsbury Manor Stud **Trained** Sedbury, Gloucs

**FOCUS**
The latest qualifier in the series and a moderate sprint handicap to boot. The winner's best form since he was a 3yo.

### 425 BOOKMAKERS.CO.UK SPRINT SERIES ROUND 5 H'CAP (QUALIFIER) (DIV II) 6f 1y(P)
2:20 (2:20) (Class 6) (0-65,65) 4-Y-O+ £3,234 (£962; £481; £240) Stalls Low

Form RPR
62-2 1 **Multitask**9 289 4-9-2 **60**........................ GeorgeBaker 6 74
(Michael Madgwick) *hld up in last pair and sat off furious pce: prog whn nt clr run briefly on inner 2f out: cruised through over 1f out to ld last 150yds: easily* **9/4**1
0-40 2 1 1/2 **Welsh Inlet (IRE)**13 244 6-8-8 **52**........................ LukeMorris 7 60
(John Bridger) *in tch in chsng gp: prog 2f out: rdn to chal and upsides whn wnr cruised by ins fnl f: kpt on* **16/1**
51-1 3 nk **Kasbhom**22 121 4-9-1 **59**........................(tp) WilliamCarson 2 66
(Anthony Carson) *mostly chsd clr ldr: clsd to ld wl over 1f out: hdd and no ex last 150yds* **3/1**3
11-0 4 4 **The Dancing Lord**28 52 5-9-0 **65**........................ DavidParkes(7) 9 59
(Brett Johnson) *in tch in chsng gp: rdn over 2f out: no prog over 1f out* **16/1**
2-43 5 2 1/2 **Your Gifted (IRE)**8 313 7-8-8 **55**........................(v) MarkCoumbe(3) 1 41
(Lisa Williamson) *s.i.s: in last pair tl rapid prog on outer 4f out to dispute 2nd pl over 2f out: fdd over 1f out* **20/1**

43-2 **6** ½ **Resonare**[10] 288 5-9-0 **58** ........ DavidProbert 5 43
(Stuart Williams) *in tch in chsng gp: rdn over 2f out: no prog and wl btn over 1f out* **5/2**[2]

-020 **7** *shd* **Daneside (IRE)**[7] 339 7-8-3 **54** oh4 ow3........ GeorgeBuckell(7) 3 39
(P J O'Gorman) *prom in chsng gp: rdn over 2f out: wknd over 1f out* **16/1**

0-00 **8** 4½ **Decision By One**[14] 233 5-9-6 **64**........(v) ChrisCatlin 4 34
(David Evans) *blasted off in ld and sn 5 l clr: hdd & wknd rapidly wl over 1f out* **16/1**

550- **9** 2½ **Gaelic Wizard (IRE)**[49] 8306 6-8-12 **61**........(p) JoshBaudains(5) 10 23
(Dominic Ffrench Davis) *racd on outer in chsng gp: rdn and struggling whn m v wd bnd 2f out: bhd after* **33/1**

1m 10.45s (-1.45) **Going Correction** -0.125s/f (Stan) **9** Ran SP% **115.6**
Speed ratings (Par 101): **104,102,101,96,92 92,92,86,82**
CSF £39.80 CT £111.75 TOTE £3.30: £1.40, £2.80, £1.20; EX 40.90 Trifecta £243.70.

**Owner** Mrs L N Harmes **Bred** Mrs L N Harmes **Trained** Denmead, Hants

**FOCUS**
Only three counted according to the market in this division and they went a serious pace. The winning time was 0.25sec quicker than the first leg. A length personal best from the winner.

## 426 LADBROKES H'CAP 1m 1y(P)
**2:55** (2:57) (Class 3) (0-95,91) 4-Y-0+ **£7,439** (£2,213; £1,106; £553) **Stalls** High

Form RPR

0-31 **1** **Rebellious Guest**[7] 342 5-9-2 **86**........ TomQueally 8 98
(George Margarson) *hld up in 8th: prog and wdst of all bnd 2f out: clsd on ldrs jst over 1f out: drvn to ld last 120yds: styd on wl* **3/1**[1]

/06- **2** 1¼ **Moonday Sun (USA)**[51] 8263 5-9-7 **91**........ AndreaAtzeni 11 100
(Amanda Perrett) *trckd ldr after 1f: rdn to chal 2f out: led jst over 1f out: edgd rt after: hdd and outpcd last 120yds* **8/1**

02-1 **3** *nk* **Apostle (IRE)**[29] 38 5-9-5 **89**........ LiamKeniry 7 97
(David Simcock) *prom: gng strly over 2f out: rdn and nt qckn over 1f out: styd on again to take 3rd ins fnl f* **7/1**[3]

4-56 **4** 1 **Mia's Boy**[14] 235 10-9-1 **88**........ RobertTart(3) 3 94
(Chris Dwyer) *hld up in last trio: rdn over 2f out: prog over 1f out: styd on to take 4th last strides: n.d* **16/1**

620- **5** *shd* **Royal Prize**[127] 6801 4-9-4 **88**........ JimCrowley 5 93
(Ralph Beckett) *in tch in midfield: rdn and prog fr 2f out: drvn to chal 1f out: one pce after* **3/1**[1]

46-3 **6** ¾ **Verse Of Love**[8] 314 5-9-3 **87**........ GeorgeBaker 6 91
(David Evans) *mde most: rdn 2f out: hdd jst over 1f out: wknd ins fnl f* **16/1**

10- **7** ½ **Shamdarley (IRE)**[175] 5285 6-9-5 **89**........(p) AdamKirby 4 92
(Marco Botti) *broke wl but sn restrained bhd ldng pair: rdn 2f out: chal over 1f out: fdd fnl f* **6/1**[2]

0-64 **8** ¾ **True To Form (IRE)**[14] 235 7-9-6 **90**........(p) DavidProbert 1 91
(Alan McCabe) *dwlt: hld up in last trio: pushed along and sme prog over 1f out: rdn and no hdwy fnl f* **12/1**

0- **9** 1 **Odyssee (FR)**[78] 4-9-2 **86**........ LukeMorris 2 85
(Marco Botti) *in tch in midfield: rdn on inner over 2f out: no real prog over 1f out* **16/1**

2-40 **10** 2½ **Emerald Wilderness (IRE)**[14] 235 10-9-6 **90**........ FrederikTylicki 9 83
(Mark Rimmer) *in tch: trckd ldrs 3f out: lost pl and rdn wl over 1f out: wknd* **16/1**

/00- **11** 2½ **Snow King (USA)**[33] 8445 4-8-12 **87**........ EoinWalsh(5) 10 74
(Ted Powell) *a in rr: rdn and no prog over 2f out: wknd over 1f out* **33/1**

1m 35.76s (-2.44) **Going Correction** -0.125s/f (Stan) **11** Ran SP% **122.1**
Speed ratings (Par 107): **107,105,105,104,104 103,103,102,101,98 96**
CSF £29.17 CT £161.16 TOTE £4.10: £1.60, £3.40, £2.30; EX 43.50 Trifecta £380.70.

**Owner** John Guest Racing **Bred** Equity Bloodstock & Newsells Park Stud **Trained** Newmarket, Suffolk

■ Stewards' Enquiry : Andrea Atzeni one-day ban: careless riding (15 feb)

**FOCUS**
A decent handicap and a typical Lingfield finish, with several holding a chance entering the last furlong. The winner is rated close to his old best.

## 427 CORAL.CO.UK H'CAP 1m 4f (P)
**3:30** (3:32) (Class 3) (0-95,95) 4-Y-0+ **£7,439** (£2,213; £1,106; £553) **Stalls** Low

Form RPR

2-45 **1** **Grendisar (IRE)**[10] 285 4-8-13 **90**........(p) AdamKirby 8 100
(Marco Botti) *hld up in 7th: prog on outer wl over 2f out: clsd over 1f out: produced to ld ins fnl f: styd on wl* **9/4**[1]

4-31 **2** 1¼ **Swing Alone (IRE)**[21] 145 5-9-5 **93**........ LukeMorris 6 101
(Gay Kelleway) *hld up in 6th: prog on outer over 3f out: chsd ldr over 2f out: rdn to ld over 1f out: hdd ins fnl f: styd on but outpcd* **4/1**[3]

0-11 **3** 3¼ **Blue Wave (IRE)**[11] 270 4-9-4 **95**........ JoeFanning 3 98
(Mark Johnston) *trckd ldng pair: wnt 2nd over 3f out: led over 2f out: hdd and outpcd over 1f out* **5/2**[2]

63-3 **4** 1¾ **Mawaakef (IRE)**[24] 85 6-8-9 **83**........ AndreaAtzeni 5 83
(J R Jenkins) *trckd ldrs: cl up 2f out: tried to chal over 1f out: sn wl outpcd* **5/1**

300- **5** 1¼ **Roman Flight (IRE)**[58] 4060 6-8-11 **85**........ ChrisCatlin 7 83
(David Dennis) *hld up in last: stl there and pushed along over 2f out: sme prog on inner and pushed along over 1f out: one reminder ins fnl f: nvr involved* **16/1**

62-0 **6** *nk* **Stevie Thunder**[7] 344 9-8-7 **81** oh1........(p) LiamJones 4 79
(Ian Williams) *wl in tch: clsd over 2f out and n.m.r briefly: no hdwy and btn over 1f out* **16/1**

220/ **7** 11 **Benbecula**[35] 6676 5-8-7 **81** oh4........(b) WilliamCarson 2 61
(Richard Mitchell) *led after 1f to 1/2-way: rdn over 3f out: sn wknd* **50/1**

143 **8** 8 **Royal Alcor (IRE)**[15] 212 7-8-7 **81** oh1........(t) DavidProbert 1 48
(Gay Kelleway) *led 1f: led again 1/2-way: hdd over 2f out: wknd rapidly wl over 1f out: t.o* **16/1**

2m 28.6s (-4.40) **Going Correction** -0.125s/f (Stan)
**WFA** 4 from 5yo+ 3lb **8** Ran SP% **115.6**
Speed ratings (Par 107): **109,108,106,104,104 103,96,91**
CSF £11.84 CT £23.41 TOTE £5.00: £1.60, £2.30, £1.10; EX 14.20 Trifecta £39.90.

**Owner** Mohamed Albousi Alghufli **Bred** Old Carhue & Graeng Bloodstock **Trained** Newmarket, Suffolk

**FOCUS**
A good-quality middle-distance handicap and the key piece of form was the race won by Castilo Del Diablo over C&D last month, in which the first two here finished fourth and third respectively. The winner is generally progressive.

## 428 DOWNLOAD THE LADBROKES APP APPRENTICE H'CAP 7f 1y(P)
**4:05** (4:07) (Class 6) (0-60,60) 4-Y-0+ **£2,385** (£704; £352) **Stalls** Low

Form RPR

-021 **1** **Bertie Blu Boy**[10] 288 6-8-10 **49**........(b) EoinWalsh 8 60
(Lisa Williamson) *racd freely: mde all: spreadeagled field wl over 2f out: rdn over 1f out: kpt on wl: unchal* **3/1**[1]

2-00 **2** 2¾ **One Last Dream**[9] 289 5-9-1 **57**........(b) RyanWhile(3) 6 61
(Ron Hodges) *chsd wnr: outpcd over 2f out: kpt on after but nvr able to land a blow* **12/1**

00-0 **3** 1½ **Sea Soldier (IRE)**[19] 155 6-9-0 **58**........ RobHornby(5) 5 58
(Andrew Balding) *hld up towards rr: no ch once wnr had kicked on over 2f out: prog on inner wl over 1f out: styd on to take 3rd nr fin* **8/1**

304- **4** ½ **Black Truffle (FR)**[124] 6902 4-9-1 **59**........(v) CharlotteJenner(5) 9 58
(Mark Usher) *chsd ldng trio: wl ahd of rest but outpcd over 2f out: kpt on to chse ldng pair over 1f out: nvr able to cl and lost 3rd nr fin* **7/1**[3]

336- **5** 1½ **Gypsy Rider**[44] 8341 5-8-12 **54**........ NedCurtis(3) 4 49
(Roger Curtis) *hld up towards rr: no ch once wnr had kicked on over 2f out: prog over 1f out: styd on nr fin* **14/1**

053- **6** ½ **Alfresco**[33] 8446 10-9-0 **53**........(v) GeorgeDowning 7 46
(Martin Bosley) *dwlt: t.k.h: hld up in rr: no ch once wnr had kicked on over 2f out: kpt on fr over 1f out* **20/1**

00-4 **7** 1¼ **Bold Ring**[19] 154 8-9-7 **60**........ TimClark 13 50
(Edward Creighton) *hld up towards rr: no ch once wnr had kicked on over 2f out: kpt on one pce after* **16/1**

44-1 **8** ¾ **Medecis Mountain**[16] 201 5-8-6 **48**........ LauraBarry(3) 1 36
(John Wainwright) *hld up in last: hmpd 1/2-way: stl last and no ch over 2f out: styd on fnl f* **4/1**[2]

20-0 **9** ½ **My Scat Daddy (USA)**[13] 251 5-8-9 **51**........ LouisSteward(3) 12 37
(Zoe Davison) *hld up towards rr: reminder on outer 1/2-way: sn wl outpcd: no ch after* **10/1**

11-4 **10** *shd* **Foie Gras**[7] 339 4-9-2 **60**........ ThomasHemsley(5) 10 46
(Chris Dwyer) *awkward s: hld up towards rr: no ch once wnr had kicked on over 2f out: wd bnd sn after: rdn and kpt on one pce* **14/1**

46-3 **11** 1¼ **Perfect Pastime**[10] 288 6-9-2 **58**........(b) DanielCremin(3) 14 41
(Jim Boyle) *chsd ldng pair: rdn over 2f out: wknd rapidly over 1f out* **8/1**

40-0 **12** 16 **Gunning For Glory**[15] 211 4-8-13 **57**........(p) PaulBooth(5) 11
(Dean Ivory) *chsd ldrs 2f: sn struggling: wknd 1/2-way: hit rail over 2f out: t.o* **33/1**

1m 23.7s (-1.10) **Going Correction** -0.125s/f (Stan) **12** Ran SP% **123.4**
Speed ratings (Par 101): **101,97,96,95,93 93,91,91,90,90 88,70**
CSF £42.64 CT £274.05 TOTE £3.60: £1.30, £5.60, £2.40; EX 71.00 Trifecta £559.60.
**Owner** B & B Hygiene Limited **Bred** H Bourchier **Trained** Saighton, Cheshire
■ Stewards' Enquiry : Laura Barry nine-day ban: failed to take all reasonable and permissable measures (Feb 28, Mar 1,3-8, 11)

**FOCUS**
Despite the size of the field nothing got into it from off the pace in this moderate apprentice handicap. The winner's best form since last winter.
T/Jkpt: £17,750.00 to a £1 stake. Pool: £25,000.00 - 1.00 winning unit T/Plt: £123.30 to a £1 stake. Pool: £90,844.23 - 537.63 winning units T/Qpdt: £17.60 to a £1 take. Pool: £7,806.34 - 327.32 winning units JN

# [406]WOLVERHAMPTON (A.W) (L-H)
Saturday, February 1

**OFFICIAL GOING: Standard**
Wind: Fresh; behind Weather: Showers

## 429 32RED H'CAP 5f 20y(P)
**2:15** (2:18) (Class 4) (0-85,77) 3-Y-0 **£4,851** (£1,443; £721; £360) **Stalls** Low

Form RPR

-114 **1** **Spreadable (IRE)**[8] 311 3-8-7 66........(v) MichaelJMMurphy(3) 4 75
(Nick Littmoden) *hld up: hdwy 2f out: edgd lft over 1f out: shkn up ins fnl f: r.o to ld nr fin* **7/2**[3]

-133 **2** *nk* **Global Explorer (USA)**[1] 401 3-8-0 61........(t) NathanAlison(5) 3 69
(Stuart Williams) *trckd ldr tl led over 1f out: rdn ins fnl f: hdd nr fin* **3/1**[2]

041- **3** 4 **Under Approval**[34] 8435 3-8-6 65........ SamJames(3) 1 59
(David O'Meara) *led: rdn and hdd over 1f out: no ex ins fnl f* **33/1**

0-54 **4** 1¼ **Alfie Lunete (IRE)**[1] 401 3-8-3 64........ PhilipPrince(5) 5 53
(J S Moore) *prom: pushed along 3f out: rdn over 1f out: edgd lft and no ex fnl f* **11/1**

6-00 **5** 1 **Mighty Force (IRE)**[7] 338 3-8-2 58........(b) KieranO'Neill 2 44
(Nick Littmoden) *chsd ldrs: drvn along 1/2-way: no ex fnl f* **28/1**

21-1 **6** 1¼ **Thataboy (IRE)**[20] 149 3-9-7 77........ StephenCraine 6 58
(Tom Dascombe) *hld up: hdwy 2f out: sn rdn and edgd lft: wknd fnl f* **10/11**[1]

1m 2.93s (0.63) **Going Correction** +0.225s/f (Slow) **6** Ran SP% **114.3**
Speed ratings (Par 99): **103,102,96,94,92 90**
CSF £14.77 TOTE £4.10: £1.30, £3.20; EX 15.80 Trifecta £101.90.
**Owner** G F Chesneaux **Bred** Patsy Myers & Edward Myers **Trained** Newmarket, Suffolk

**FOCUS**
An additional fixture hastily arranged due to the spate of recent abandonments. Only six runners but this sprint handicap for 3yos featured a couple of improving, in-form competitors. The first two were clear and the form is rated slightly positively.

## 430 32RED.COM H'CAP 2m 119y(P)
**2:50** (2:50) (Class 5) (0-70,69) 4-Y-0+ **£2,587** (£770; £384; £192) **Stalls** Low

Form RPR

0-52 **1** **Uncle Bernie (IRE)**[6] 349 4-8-1 50 oh2........(p) JamesSullivan 1 58
(Andrew Hollinshead) *hld up: racd keenly: hdwy 4f out: led on bit over 1f out: edgd rt and c clr ins fnl f* **9/4**[2]

00-0 **2** 5 **Shalambar (IRE)**[9] 293 8-9-3 60........(v) TomEaves 2 62
(Tony Carroll) *a.p: chsd ldr 6f out: rdn over 2f out: styd on same pce fr over 1f out* **5/1**[3]

05-4 **3** 4½ **Daring Indian**[9] 292 6-9-12 69........ StephenCraine 3 66
(Tom Dascombe) *chsd ldr tl led 12f out: rdn and hdd over 1f out: wknd ins fnl f* **5/6**[1]

044- **4** *21* **Moaning Butcher**[41] 5846 4-8-9 58 ow1........................(v) PaddyAspell 4 29
(Dave Roberts) *led at stdy pce tl hdd 12f out: chsd ldr tl 6f out: sn pushed along: wknd over 3f out* **16/1**

3m 51.73s (9.93) **Going Correction** +0.225s/f (Slow)
**WFA** 4 from 6yo+ 6lb **4** Ran SP% **107.9**
Speed ratings (Par 103): **85,82,80,70**
CSF £12.22 TOTE £2.50; EX 16.80 Trifecta £15.90.
**Owner** Graham Brothers Racing Partnership **Bred** Roundhill Stud & Gleadhill House Stud Ltd **Trained** Upper Longdon, Staffs

**FOCUS**
A poor staying handicap featuring maidens and infrequent winners. It was slowly run and the form is shaky.

## 431 COMPARE BOOKMAKERS AT BOOKMAKERS.CO.UK H'CAP 5f 20y(P)
**3:25** (3:30) (Class 3) (0-95,95) 4-Y-O-**£7,246** (£2,168; £1,084; £542; £270) **Stalls** Low

Form RPR
456- **1** **Swiss Cross**[272] 2046 7-9-6 94........................(t) PaddyAspell 3 103
(Phil McEntee) *a.p: led over 1f out: rdn out* **10/1**
44-4 **2** *1 ½* **Muhdiq (USA)**[22] 122 5-8-4 81 oh1........................ MichaelJMMurphy(3) 4 85
(Mike Murphy) *chsd ldrs: wnt 2nd 2f out: sn rdn and ev ch: styd on same pce ins fnl f* **7/2**[2]
4-21 **3** *½* **Silken Express (IRE)**[11] 271 5-9-7 95........................ ShaneKelly 6 97
(Robert Cowell) *hld up: hdwy over 1f out: sn rdn: r.o* **2/1**[1]
-354 **4** *½* **Fat Gary**[9] 294 4-8-9 83........................(p) HayleyTurner 2 83
(Tom Dascombe) *sn pushed along to chse ldr: lost 2nd 2f out: styd on same pce fnl f* **2/1**[1]
0-30 **5** *shd* **Jiroft (ITY)**[11] 271 7-9-4 92........................(p) PJMcDonald 1 92
(Robert Cowell) *led: rdn and hdd over 1f out: styd on same pce fnl f* **12/1**
563- **6** *3* **My Son Max**[45] 8324 6-8-10 84........................ TomEaves 5 73
(Michael Blake) *s.i.s: outpcd* **7/1**[3]

1m 1.88s (-0.42) **Going Correction** +0.225s/f (Slow) **6** Ran SP% **118.2**
Speed ratings (Par 107): **112,109,108,108,107 103**
CSF £46.88 TOTE £8.90: £3.90, £2.90; EX 40.50 Trifecta £108.90.
**Owner** Steve Jakes **Bred** Lordship Stud **Trained** Newmarket, Suffolk

**FOCUS**
The feature on the card. The first two are rated to form.

## 432 BEST ODDS AT BOOKMAKERS.CO.UK H'CAP 5f 216y(P)
**4:00** (4:04) (Class 5) (0-75,75) 4-Y-O+ **£2,911** (£866; £432; £216) **Stalls** Low

Form RPR
1-10 **1** **Powerful Pierre**[20] 153 7-9-2 75........................(b) JacobButterfield(5) 2 85
(Ollie Pears) *a.p: shkn up to ld over 1f out: rdn out* **11/2**
00-6 **2** *¾* **Point North (IRE)**[27] 60 7-8-13 67........................ DanielTudhope 6 75+
(John Balding) *hld up in tch: gng wl and nt clr run over 1f out: sn rdn: r.o* **9/4**[1]
4603 **3** *3* **Sewn Up**[6] 347 4-8-7 61........................(v) JimmyQuinn 4 59
(Andrew Hollinshead) *hld up: hdwy 2f out: rdn over 1f out: styd on same pce ins fnl f* **5/1**[3]
-104 **4** *1* **Desert Strike**[8] 312 8-9-4 72........................(p) HayleyTurner 7 67
(Conor Dore) *chsd ldrs: rdn over 1f out: styd on same pce fnl f* **12/1**
-234 **5** *3 ½* **Bapak Bangsawan**[9] 299 4-9-0 73........................ ShaneGray(5) 1 57
(Kevin Ryan) *sn led: rdn and hdd over 1f out: wknd ins fnl f* **5/2**[2]
356- **6** *1 ½* **Decent Fella (IRE)**[107] 7319 8-9-4 72........................(p) BenCurtis 3 51
(Ann Stokell) *s.i.s: hld up: sme hdwy over 1f out: rdr looked down ins fnl f: eased* **33/1**
450- **7** *5* **Lucky Dan (IRE)**[94] 7633 8-9-7 75........................ TomEaves 8 38
(Paul Green) *hld up: pushed along 1/2-way: wknd over 2f out* **25/1**
4-51 **8** *10* **Take The Lead**[4] 362 4-9-2 70 6ex........................ AdrianNicholls 5
(David Nicholls) *sn chsng ldr: rdn over 2f out: wknd over 1f out* **10/1**

1m 15.59s (0.59) **Going Correction** +0.225s/f (Slow) **8** Ran SP% **115.0**
Speed ratings (Par 103): **105,104,100,98,94 92,85,72**
CSF £18.42 CT £66.14 TOTE £9.20: £2.90, £1.10, £2.90; EX 26.90 Trifecta £75.10.
**Owner** Terence Elsey **Bred** Hedsor Stud **Trained** Norton, N Yorks

**FOCUS**
A competitive handicap in which the front two pulled clear. It was the scene of a big gamble that was just thwarted. The winner confirmed himself better than ever.

## 433 CORAL APP DOWNLOAD FROM THE APP STORE H'CAP 1m 4f 50y(P)
**4:35** (4:38) (Class 6) (0-60,62) 4-Y-O+ **£2,264** (£673; £336; £168) **Stalls** Low

Form RPR
445- **1** **Helmsley Flyer (IRE)**[43] 8366 4-9-0 53........................(v1) DanielTudhope 4 61
(David O'Meara) *racd keenly: trckd ldr 4f remained handy: shkn up over 1f out: rdn to ld wl ins fnl f: styd on* **7/2**[3]
11-4 **2** *¾* **Funky Munky**[22] 123 9-9-0 50........................(p) PJMcDonald 6 57
(Alistair Whillans) *set stdy pce tl pushed along and qcknd over 3f out: rdn and hdd over 1f out: rallied to ld ins fnl f: sn hdd: no ex nr fin* **13/2**
-124 **3** *2 ¼* **Disco Dave (IRE)**[1] 410 6-9-5 60........................ PhilipPrince(5) 1 63
(Daniel Mark Loughnane) *hld up: hdwy 7f out: led over 1f out: rdn and hdd ins fnl f: no ex* **6/4**[1]
206- **4** *6* **Grandiloquent**[70] 8027 5-9-7 57........................ BenCurtis 3 51
(Brian Ellison) *chsd ldrs: wnt 2nd 8f out: rdn and ev ch wl over 1f out: wknd fnl f* **5/2**[2]
-044 **5** *2 ½* **Dontpaytheferryman (USA)**[9] 303 9-9-3 53........(b) StevieDonohoe 2 43
(Peter Hiatt) *plld hrd and prom: dropped last 7f out: rdn over 2f out: wknd over 1f out* **16/1**

2m 45.47s (4.37) **Going Correction** +0.225s/f (Slow)
**WFA** 4 from 5yo+ 3lb **5** Ran SP% **110.0**
Speed ratings (Par 101): **94,93,92,88,86**
CSF £24.13 TOTE £3.60: £1.70, £4.70; EX 23.30 Trifecta £69.80.
**Owner** Direct Racing Partnership **Bred** Skeaghmore Hill **Trained** Nawton, N Yorks

**FOCUS**
A weak middle-distance handicap, which was notable for a winning gamble on the David O'Meara-trained runner. The winner had had fewer chances than the rest.

## 434 CORAL MOBILE "JUST THREE CLICKS TO BET" MEDIAN AUCTION MAIDEN FILLIES' STKS 1m 1f 103y(P)
**5:05** (5:07) (Class 6) 3-5-Y-O **£2,045** (£603; £302) **Stalls** Low

Form RPR
4-60 **1** **Blue Oyster**[8] 316 3-8-7 65........................ BenCurtis 5 65
(Philip McBride) *chsd ldr over 7f out tl led over 3f out: rdn over 1f out: styd on* **6/1**[2]
3 **2** *2* **Rohesia**[8] 323 3-8-7 0........................ JamieSpencer 4 61
(Sir Mark Prescott Bt) *chsd ldrs: wnt 2nd over 3f out: sn pushed along: rdn over 1f out: styd on same pce* **2/7**[1]
2-43 **3** *1 ¼* **Indira**[22] 127 3-8-7 62........................ JimmyQuinn 1 58
(John Berry) *chsd ldrs: rdn and ev ch 1f out: no ex ins fnl f* **6/1**[2]

5- **4** *46* **Au Renoir**[372] 377 4-10-0 0........................[1] StephenCraine 2
(Kevin Ryan) *sn led: rdn and hdd over 3f out: wknd wl over 2f out* **12/1**[3]
4-6 **5** *11* **I Am Who I Am**[30] 13 4-10-0 0........................ TomEaves 3
(Iain Jardine) *in rr: pushed aong over 6f out: rdn and wknd over 5f out* **40/1**

2m 3.6s (1.90) **Going Correction** +0.225s/f (Slow)
**WFA** 3 from 4yo 21lb **5** Ran SP% **116.5**
Speed ratings (Par 98): **100,98,97,56,46**
CSF £8.87 TOTE £7.20: £2.30, £1.10; EX 14.50 Trifecta £33.20.
**Owner** C M Budgett **Bred** Kirtlington Stud Ltd **Trained** Newmarket, Suffolk

**FOCUS**
This maiden was the scene of an upset. but the winner and third are rated close to their marks.

## 435 CORAL MOBILE "JUST THREE CLICKS TO BET" H'CAP 1m 1f 103y(P)
**5:35** (5:35) (Class 6) (0-55,55) 4-Y-O+ **£1,940** (£577; £288; £144) **Stalls** Low

Form RPR
-021 **1** **Stanlow**[22] 117 4-9-5 53........................(v) StephenCraine 5 62
(Daniel Mark Loughnane) *plld hrd and prom: trckd ldr over 7f out: led over 2f out: rdn over 1f out: edgd lft: styd on u.p* **1/1**[1]
01-3 **2** *nk* **Do More Business (IRE)**[8] 317 7-9-1 54........................(vt) PhilipPrince(5) 8 62
(Liam Corcoran) *hld up: hdwy over 3f out: sn pushed along: rdn and ev ch wl ins fnl f: styd on* **7/2**[2]
-150 **3** *1 ¼* **Daniel Thomas (IRE)**[10] 281 12-9-3 51........................(tp) BenCurtis 1 56
(Ann Stokell) *a.p: swtchd rt over 2f out: rdn over 1f out: styd on same pce ins fnl f* **9/2**[3]
454- **4** *3* **Star Request**[162] 5714 4-8-12 51........................ JacobButterfield(5) 7 50
(Ollie Pears) *s.i.s: hld up: rdn over 1f out: r.o ins fnl f: nvr nrr* **14/1**
405- **5** *shd* **Silver Fawn (IRE)**[57] 8186 4-8-12 46 oh1........................(be) JimmyQuinn 3 45
(John Weymes) *plld hrd and prom: stdd and lost pl over 7f out: hdwy over 2f out: rdn over 1f out: edgd lft and no ex ins fnl f* **16/1**
00-3 **6** *1 ¼* **Refuse Colette (IRE)**[8] 321 5-8-12 46 oh1........................ TomEaves 4 42
(Paul Green) *racd keenly: trckd ldr 2f: remained handy: lost pl over 3f out: n.d after* **16/1**
04-0 **7** *6* **Armada Bay (IRE)**[31] 7 4-8-12 46........................(t) PaddyAspell 2 30
(Bryan Smart) *led: rdn and hdd over 2f out: wknd fnl f* **16/1**
4/00 **8** *5* **Devote Myself (IRE)**[9] 289 5-9-4 55........................ MarkCoumbe(3) 6 28
(Tony Carroll) *trckd ldrs: racd keenly: rdn over 3f out: wknd over 2f out* **20/1**

2m 3.95s (2.25) **Going Correction** +0.225s/f (Slow) **8** Ran SP% **119.5**
Speed ratings (Par 101): **99,98,97,94,94 93,88,83**
CSF £4.95 CT £11.39 TOTE £2.50: £1.90, £1.20, £1.50; EX 6.20 Trifecta £15.80.
**Owner** Ms A Quinn **Bred** Ed's Stud Ltd **Trained** Baldwin's Gate, Staffs

**FOCUS**
A poor affair run at a modest pace. The winner built on his Lingfield win.
T/Plt: £347.30 to a £1 stake. Pool: £52,155.30 - 109.62 winning units T/Qpdt: £36.90 to a £1 stake. Pool: £3,768.00 - 75.51 winning units CR

# 390 CAGNES-SUR-MER
Saturday, February 1
**OFFICIAL GOING: Polytrack: standard**

## 436a PRIX DE LA VILLE DE CAGNES-SUR-MER (CONDITIONS) (3YO) (POLYTRACK) 1m 2f (D)
**1:15** (12:00) 3-Y-0 **£15,416** (£6,166; £4,625; £3,083; £1,541)

RPR
**1** **Mr Pommeroy (FR)**[17] 193 3-8-11 0........................ FabriceVeron 1 96
(H-A Pantall, France) **16/5**[3]
**2** *2* **Cockney Bob**[14] 237 3-9-1 0........................ ThomasMessina 4 96
(J Parize, France) **6/4**[1]
**3** *2* **Act Of Charity (IRE)**[37] 8397 3-8-11 0.............. Pierre-CharlesBoudot 5 88
(Gay Kelleway) *trckd ldrs: 4th and scrubbed along over 2 1/2f out: hrd rdn and styd on to chse ldr over 1f out: one pce ins fnl f* **3/1**[2]
**4** *1* **Initial (FR)**[5] 3-8-11 0........................(p) TheoBachelot 2 86
(C Boutin, France) **53/10**
**5** *½* **Uta (FR)**[153] 3-8-8 0........................ RomainAuray 7 82
(J Parize, France) **49/1**
**6** *3 ½* **Monika Jem (FR)**[34] 3-8-8 0........................ FabienLefebvre 6 75
(S Jesus, France) **13/1**
**7** *6* **Lingreville (FR)**[82] 7842 3-8-8 0........................ IoritzMendizabal 3 63
(J-M Lefebvre, France) **12/1**

2m 2.81s (122.81) **7** Ran SP% **121.5**
WIN (incl. 1 euro stake): 4.20. PLACES: 1.90, 1.50. SF: 10.40.
**Owner** Plersch Breeding Sarl **Bred** Rupert Plersch **Trained** France

## 437a PRIX DU HAUT DE CAGNES (CLAIMER) (4YO+) (POLYTRACK) 1m 4f
**4:10** (12:00) 4-Y-0+ **£7,083** (£2,833; £2,125; £1,416; £708)

RPR
**1** **Thomaraz (FR)**[29] 7-9-5 0........................(b) Roberto-CarlosMontenegro 4 84
(P Sogorb, France) **21/10**[1]
**2** *2* **Ketchikan (IRE)**[29] 4-9-2 0........................ TheoBachelot 2 81
(S Cerulis, France) **5/1**[3]
**3** *nse* **Le Bosphore (FR)**[278] 7-9-1 0........................(b) FranckBlondel 7 77
(M Pimbonnet, France) **13/1**
**4** *1* **Uphold**[18] 178 7-9-1 0........................(v) Pierre-CharlesBoudot 1 75
(Gay Kelleway) *broke wl: trckd ldr: rdn to chal over 1 1/2f out: nt qckn w ldrs over 1f out: kpt on at same pce u.p fnl f* **5/1**[3]
**5** *shd* **Street Lair (USA)**[18] 178 7-9-1 0........................ ThomasMessina 3 75
(L Baudron, France) **13/2**
**6** *nk* **Varadero (IRE)**[18] 177 6-9-5 0........................ IoritzMendizabal 5 79
(L Baudron, France) **43/10**[2]
**7** *3* **Tepmokea (IRE)**[18] 177 8-9-5 0........................ MickaelForest 8 74
(Andrew Hollinshead) *led: hdd ent fnl 1 1/2f: wknd fnl f* **12/1**
**8** *3* **Barbancourt (FR)**[636] 8-8-11 0........................(p) DimitriIbouth(8) 6 69
(J-L Dubord, France) **11/1**

2m 30.51s (150.51)
**WFA** 4 from 6yo+ 3lb **8** Ran SP% **121.0**
WIN (incl. 1 euro stake): 3.10. PLACES: 1.40, 1.70, 2.90. DF: 7.80. SF: 12.00.
**Owner** S Kinast & G Sevin **Bred** Michel Berlato **Trained** France

438 - 443a (Foreign Racing) - See Raceform Interactive

# [376]KEMPTON (A.W) (R-H)

Sunday, February 2

**OFFICIAL GOING: Standard**

Wind: medium to fresh, half behind Weather: dry

## 444 DINE IN THE PANORAMIC RESTAURANT H'CAP 5f (P)

**1:50** (1:50) (Class 4) (0-85,85) 4-Y-0+ **£5,175** (£1,540; £769; £384) **Stalls** Low

Form RPR

224- **1** **Triple Dream**[59] 8167 9-9-3 **81**..............(tp) RichardKingscote 6 88
(Milton Bradley) *chsd ldr tl led over 1f out: drvn ins fnl f: hrd pressed fnl 75yds: jst hld on: all out* **7/2**[1]

111- **2** *shd* **Dangerous Age**[117] 7112 4-9-0 **78**.............. JoeFanning 8 87+
(J W Hills) *stdd and swtchd rt after s: t.k.h: hld up in tch in midfield: clsd to trck ldrs and nt clr run over 1f out: chsd ldng pair and swtchd rt jst ins fnl f: str chal fnl 75yds: jst hld* **11/2**[3]

30-5 **3** *¾* **Moorhouse Lad**[19] 175 11-8-13 **77**.............. JimCrowley 7 81
(Garry Moss) *taken down early: wl in tch in midfield: rdn and chal 1f out: drvn and styd on same pce ins fnl f* **6/1**

200- **4** *1 ½* **Clear Praise (USA)**[118] 7080 7-9-5 **83**.............. HayleyTurner 1 82
(Simon Dow) *taken down early: stdd s: t.k.h: hld up in rr: hdwy u.p 1f out: kpt on but nvr gng pce to chal* **7/1**

1-05 **5** *1 ½* **Tax Free (IRE)**[21] 148 12-9-7 **85**.............. AdrianNicholls 2 78+
(David Nicholls) *chsd ldng pair: gng wl but stuck bhd wkng rival: hmpd and shuffled bk over 1f out: swtchd lft jst jst ins fnl f: nt rcvr and styd on same pce after* **7/2**[1]

0-50 **6** *hd* **Profile Star (IRE)**[19] 175 5-8-7 **71** oh1.............. WilliamCarson 3 63
(Ann Stokell) *in touch in last pair: nt clr run on inner over 1f out: last and forced to switch lft and hmpd jst ins fnl f: kpt on but no threat to ldrs: b.b.v* **25/1**

2-54 **7** *7* **Powerful Wind (IRE)**[19] 175 5-9-5 **83**.............. LukeMorris 4 50
(Ronald Harris) *led: rdn and hdd over 1f out: sn struggling: fdd fnl f* **4/1**[2]

59.87s (-0.63) **Going Correction** -0.05s/f (Stan) **7** Ran SP% **110.5**
Speed ratings (Par 105): **103,102,101,99,96 96,85**
CSF £21.26 CT £103.46 TOTE £4.40: £1.90, £1.70; EX 15.50 Trifecta £77.40.
**Owner** J M Bradley **Bred** Hesmonds Stud Ltd **Trained** Sedbury, Gloucs

**FOCUS**
A decent sprint handicap and the only race around the inner bend at the meeting. A couple of these didn't enjoy the smoothest of trips. The winner helps set the standard.

## 445 KEMPTON.CO.UK CLASSIFIED CLAIMING STKS 1m (P)

**2:20** (2:20) (Class 6) 4-Y-0+ **£1,940** (£577; £288; £144) **Stalls** Low

Form RPR

00-2 **1** **Mahadee (IRE)**[18] 180 9-8-4 70..............(b) ChrisCatlin 8 63
(Ed de Giles) *s.i.s: in tch in last pair: rdn and hdwy over 1f out: str chal ins fnl f: r.o wl u.p to ld cl home* **13/2**[3]

0-00 **2** *hd* **Dozy Joe**[20] 161 6-8-8 62..............(v) JimmyQuinn 6 67
(Joseph Tuite) *in tch in midfield: nt clr run over 2f out: swtchd rt and hdwy u.p wl over 1f out: chal ins fnl f: led fnl 100yds: hdd and no ex cl home* **16/1**

25-4 **3** *¾* **Exclusive Waters (IRE)**[29] 49 4-8-9 68..............(b) AndreaAtzeni 4 66
(Gary Moore) *led: rdn wl over 1f out: edgd lft u.p ent fnl f: hdd and styd on same pce fnl 100yds* **11/10**[1]

55/4 **4** *1 ¾* **I Confess**[27] 66 9-8-6 69..............(b) JoeFanning 7 59
(Geoffrey Harker) *in tch in midfield: rdn and unable qck 2f out: outpcd and looked wl hld 1f out: rallied and styd on wl ins fnl f: no threat to ldrs* **20/1**

216- **5** *1 ½* **Larghetto (USA)**[36] 8432 6-8-9 63.............. ShaneKelly 3 59
(Daniel Mark Loughnane) *in tch in midfield: drvn and effrt to chse ldr over 1f out: no ex 1f out: wknd ins fnl f* **9/2**[2]

300- **6** *1* **Lady Who**[34] 8443 4-8-6 60.............. DavidProbert 5 54
(William Muir) *pressed ldr tl drvn and unable qck over 1f out: wknd fnl f* **33/1**

66-3 **7** *3 ¼* **Divine Rule (IRE)**[10] 289 6-8-0 58.............. CharlotteJenner[(7)] 2 47
(Laura Mongan) *stdd s: hld up wl in rr: swtchd rt and effrt 2f out: no imp* **8/1**

365- **8** *2 ½* **Alhaban (IRE)**[277] 1925 8-8-6 64..............(p) LukeMorris 1 40
(Ronald Harris) *chsd ldrs: drvn and unable qck 2f out: btn over 1f out: sn wknd* **10/1**

1m 39.72s (-0.08) **Going Correction** -0.05s/f (Stan) **8** Ran SP% **112.9**
Speed ratings (Par 101): **98,97,97,95,93 92,89,87**
CSF £97.72 TOTE £5.20: £2.10, £4.40, £1.10; EX 92.90 Trifecta £473.50.Larghetto was claimed by Mr Ian Williams for £8,000. Mahadee was claimed by Mr L. A. Carter for £3,000.
**Owner** 2 1/2 - 3 1/2 Club **Bred** Darley **Trained** Ledbury, H'fords

**FOCUS**
A moderate classified claimer run in a slow time and rated cautiously.

## 446 RASHER FRITH H'CAP 1m (P)

**2:50** (2:52) (Class 6) (0-55,55) 4-Y-0+ **£1,940** (£577; £288; £144) **Stalls** Low

Form RPR

5-53 **1** **Wishformore (IRE)**[3] 377 7-9-1 **49**..............(p) TomQueally 7 58
(Ian Williams) *hld up in tch in midfield: hdwy 2f out: rdn and qckd between ldrs to ld ent fnl f: in command but doing little in front after: pushed out: comf* **9/2**[2]

00-3 **2** *1 ¼* **Byrd In Hand (IRE)**[11] 281 7-8-12 **46** oh1..............(b) LiamKeniry 9 52
(John Bridger) *led: rdn ent fnl 2f: hdd ent fnl f: kpt on gamely but a hld by wnr* **33/1**

00-0 **3** *1* **Claude Monet (BRZ)**[16] 210 5-9-2 **50**..............[1] JimCrowley 5 54
(Simon Dow) *in tch in midfield: rdn and effrt on outer 2f out: no imp tl hdwy 1f out: styd on fnl f to go 3rd towards fin* **7/1**

-332 **4** *¾* **Olivers Mount**[11] 281 4-9-7 **55**..............(tp) JimmyQuinn 10 57
(Ed Vaughan) *chsd ldrs: effrt and rdn to chse ldr wl over 1f out: drvn and unable qck 1f out: styd on same pce fnl f* **11/4**[1]

-416 **5** *½* **Mr Chocolate Drop (IRE)**[3] 377 10-9-0 **48**..............(t) AdamKirby 4 49
(Mandy Rowland) *hld up in last quartet: rdn and hdwy 2f out: kpt on ins fnl f: nvr threatened ldrs* **13/2**[3]

-264 **6** *nk* **Lutine Charlie (IRE)**[6] 353 7-9-6 **54**.............. JoeFanning 12 54
(Pat Eddery) *chsd ldrs: effrt u.p ent fnl 2f: drvn and styd on same pce fr over 1f out* **12/1**

-020 **7** *½* **Tijuca (IRE)**[10] 290 5-9-6 **54**.............. AndreaAtzeni 11 53+
(Ed de Giles) *hld up in last quartet: stl plenty to do and rdn ent fnl f: styd on wl ins fnl f: nvr trbld ldrs* **20/1**

40-1 **8** *4 ½* **Mill I Am (USA)**[25] 81 4-9-6 **54**.............. AdamBeschizza 13 43
(Stuart Williams) *chsd ldrs: rdn and effrt ent fnl 2f: drvn and btn over 1f out: wknd fnl f* **12/1**

0-42 **9** *6* **Offbeat Safaris (IRE)**[26] 77 6-9-4 **52**..............(p) LukeMorris 3 27
(Ronald Harris) *s.i.s: hld up in last quartet: rdn and no hdwy over 2f out: wknd over 1f out* **11/1**

000- **10** *3 ¼* **Gung Ho (FR)**[38] 8399 5-9-5 **53**.............. ChrisCatlin 1 20
(Tony Newcombe) *sn outpcd in rr: n.d* **33/1**

060/ **11** *½* **Kassiodor (GER)**[824] 7202 7-9-0 **48**.............. ShaneKelly 2 14
(Sophie Leech) *hld up in midfield: rdn and no rspnse jst over 2f out: sn lost pl and btn: bhd fnl f* **10/1**

0/00 **12** *10* **Sir Lexington (IRE)**[9] 321 5-8-5 **46** oh1.............. DanielCremin[(7)] 8
(Brian Forsey) *chsd ldrs early: steadily lost pl: bhd wl over 2f out* **100/1**

1m 39.82s (0.02) **Going Correction** -0.05s/f (Stan) **12** Ran SP% **115.1**
Speed ratings (Par 101): **97,95,94,94,93 93,92,88,82,78 78,68**
CSF £150.11 CT £1024.31 TOTE £5.50: £2.00, £6.90, £2.80; EX 116.10 Trifecta £2372.50.
**Owner** Paul Mannion **Bred** Tally-Ho Stud **Trained** Portway, Worcs

**FOCUS**
A moderate handicap, but run at a good pace and the field were soon well spread out. The winner ran pretty much to last year's form.

## 447 VISIT AND DINE IN THE PANORAMIC MAIDEN FILLIES' STKS 6f (P)

**3:20** (3:28) (Class 5) 3-Y-0+ **£2,911** (£866; £432; £216) **Stalls** Low

Form RPR

**1** **Divine (IRE)** 3-8-13 0.............. AndreaAtzeni 2 74
(Mick Channon) *trckd ldng pair: smooth hdwy and led on bit over 1f out: pushed along and qcknd clr fnl f: easily* **5/2**[1]

**2** *3 ½* **Blacke Forest** 3-8-13 0.............. LukeMorris 5 62
(William Muir) *chsd ldr: rdn wl over 2f out: drvn and led over 1f out: sn hdd: no ch w wnr but kpt on for clr 2nd* **7/1**[2]

32-4 **3** *7* **Rosie Prospects**[25] 82 3-8-13 63..............(p) JimCrowley 6 40
(Roger Ingram) *led: rdn ent fnl 2f: drvn and hdd over 1f out: sn btn and wknd fnl f* **14/1**[3]

\- **4** *9* **Harlequin Jinks** 3-8-13 0.............. DavidProbert 1 11
(Mark Usher) *sn rdn along and outpcd in 4th: nvr on terms* **33/1**

0- **5** *33* **Lena Player (SWE)**[81] 7860 3-8-13 0..............(p) FrankieMcDonald 3
(Linda Jewell) *s.i.s: racd awkwardly and sn lost tch: t.o fr 1/2-way* **100/1**

1m 13.44s (0.34) **Going Correction** -0.05s/f (Stan) **5** Ran SP% **51.7**
Speed ratings (Par 100): **95,90,81,69,25**
CSF £3.06 TOTE £1.80: £1.20, £1.50; EX 4.30 Trifecta £11.50.
**Owner** M Al-Qatami & K M Al-Mudhaf **Bred** Yeomanstown Stud **Trained** West Ilsley, Berks
■ Garraun was withdrawn. Price at time of withdrawal 4-6F. Rule 4 applies to all bets - deduction 55p in the pound.

**FOCUS**
An uncompetitive maiden and a couple of these fillies behaved badly beforehand, not least the odds-on favourite Garraun who was withdrawn after rearing and unseating Jamie Spencer three times while trying to be loaded. Weak form.

## 448 FAMILY FUN AT KEMPTON 19.04.14 H'CAP (DIV I) 6f (P)

**3:50** (3:54) (Class 6) (0-55,59) 4-Y-0+ **£1,940** (£577; £288; £144) **Stalls** Low

Form RPR

20-0 **1** **Sweet Talking Guy (IRE)**[14] 244 4-9-6 **54**..............(t) JimCrowley 9 71+
(Lydia Pearce) *in tch in midfield: rdn and chsd clr ldr over 1f out: led jst ins fnl f: sn clr: r.o strly* **5/1**[3]

20-4 **2** *4* **My Sweet Lord**[14] 244 4-9-6 **54**.............. DavidProbert 5 58
(Mark Usher) *sn pushed along in midfield: hdwy u.p over 1f out: r.o wl to go 2nd wl ins fnl f: no threat to wnr* **8/1**

2-32 **3** *nk* **Hamis Al Bin (IRE)**[14] 244 5-9-9 **57**..............(t) AdamKirby 12 60+
(Milton Bradley) *stdd and dropped in bhd: rdn and effrt 2f out: nt clr run briefly over 1f out: swtchd lft jst over 1f out: r.o wl fnl f: wnt 3rd towards fin: no ch w wnr* **9/2**[2]

-043 **4** *nk* **Rightcar**[10] 290 7-8-10 **47** oh1 ow1.............. SladeO'Hara[(3)] 10 49
(Peter Grayson) *stdd after: hld up in rr: rdn and nlt clr run over 1f out: sn swtchd lft and r.o strly fnl f: wnt 4th towards fin: no ch w wnr* **25/1**

60-4 **5** *1* **Play The Blues (IRE)**[24] 100 7-8-12 **46** oh1..............(bt) JoeFanning 7 45
(Dominic Ffrench Davis) *led and sn clr: stl clr and rdn over 1f out: hdd jst ins fnl f: sn brushed aside by wnr: wknd and lost* **25/1**

22-3 **6** *2 ¼* **Birdie Queen**[14] 244 4-9-7 **55**.............. GeorgeBaker 3 47
(Gary Moore) *chsd ldr tl over 3f out: rdn and unable qck 2f out: btn over 1f out: wknd fnl f* **11/2**

26-0 **6** *dht* **Renoir's Lady**[14] 244 6-9-6 **54**.............. HayleyTurner 6 46
(Joseph Tuite) *hld up in last trio: rdn ent fnl 2f: plugged on but nvr a threat to ldrs* **33/1**

03-4 **8** *¾* **Microlight**[11] 274 6-8-12 **46**..............(b) JimmyQuinn 2 35
(John E Long) *bustled along leaving stalls: chsd ldrs: rdn and effrt on inner 2f out: no prog: wknd fnl f* **25/1**

6-51 **9** *2* **Star Up In The Sky (USA)**[3] 384 4-9-6 **59** 6ex..........(b) KevinStott[(5)] 11 42
(Kevin Ryan) *taken down early: dwlt: racd freely and sn rcvrd to chse ldrs: wnt 2nd over 3f out: hung rt 2f out: sn btn: wknd over 1f out* **9/4**[1]

04-0 **10** *2* **Outbid**[14] 244 4-9-1 **52**.............. MarkCoumbe[(3)] 8 28
(Tony Carroll) *in tch in midfield: rdn and no hdwy ent fnl 2f: wknd over 1f out* **100/1**

3-46 **11** *8* **Ishisoba**[4] 371 4-9-2 **50**.............. LukeMorris 4
(Ronald Harris) *chsd ldrs: struggling u.p over 2f out: wknd and bhd 1f out* **12/1**

1m 12.32s (-0.78) **Going Correction** -0.05s/f (Stan) **11** Ran SP% **115.3**
Speed ratings (Par 101): **103,97,97,96,95 92,92,91,88,86 75**
CSF £40.81 CT £195.14 TOTE £8.10: £2.30, £2.80, £1.80; EX 40.10 Trifecta £254.90.
**Owner** Killarney Glen **Bred** Churchtown House Stud **Trained** Newmarket, Suffolk

**FOCUS**
A very moderate sprint handicap and the first three all ran in the same race here 14 days earlier. The pace was decent, though.

## 449 FAMILY FUN AT KEMPTON 19.04.14 H'CAP (DIV II) 6f (P)

**4:20** (4:22) (Class 6) (0-55,58) 4-Y-0+ **£1,940** (£577; £288; £144) **Stalls** Low

Form RPR

1-01 **1** **Spellmaker**[14] 244 5-9-5 **58**.............. EoinWalsh[(5)] 4 73+
(Tony Newcombe) *t.k.h: hld up in tch in midfield: hdwy to chse ldr 2f out: qcknd to ld over 1f out: clr ins fnl f: a doing enough: r.o* **4/1**[2]

-362 **2** *¾* **Volito**[6] 353 8-9-7 **55**.............. GeorgeBaker 1 66
(Anabel K Murphy) *hld up in midfield: hdwy on inner 2f out: wnt 4th and swtchd lft over 1f out: chsd clr wnr ins fnl f: r.o wl but nvr quite getting to wnr* **5/1**[3]

-604 **3** *2 ¼* **Vhujon (IRE)**[10] 290 9-8-10 **47** oh1 ow1.............. SladeO'Hara[(3)] 6 51
(Peter Grayson) *hld up in rr: pushed along 2f out: rdn and hdwy over 1f out: r.o strly ins fnl f: nvr trbld ldrs* **12/1**

5-05 **4** ½ **Dishy Guru**[14] 244 5-9-6 **54**.................................(b) LiamKeniry 3 56
(Michael Blanshard) *in tch in midfield: hdwy on inner to chse ldrs over 1f out: styd on same pce ins fnl f* **7/1**

6-55 **5** 1½ **Lucky Mark (IRE)**[23] 121 5-8-13 **50**.................................(v[1]) BillyCray[(3)] 5 47
(Garry Moss) *led: rdn and hdd over 1f out: sn outpcd by wnr: wknd ins fnl f* **10/1**

00/1 **6** 3¾ **Indus Valley (IRE)**[11] 274 7-9-2 **50**................................. ShaneKelly 9 35
(Des Donovan) *stdd s: racd in midfield: hung lft bnd 3f out: effrt u.p but no rspnse 2f out: drvn and one pce fr over 1f out* **5/2**[1]

604- **7** 3¼ **Hinton Admiral**[34] 8446 10-9-6 **54**................................. JoeFanning 12 29
(Pat Eddery) *off the pce in last pair: rdn over 2f out: no hdwy: n.d* **16/1**

060- **8** hd **Bahama Bay**[37] 8418 4-8-12 **46** oh1..............................[1] AdamBeschizza 10 20
(Stuart Williams) *s.i.s: rdn and effrt over 2f out: no real imp: wknd over 1f out* **20/1**

600- **9** 2½ **Athwaab**[206] 4197 7-9-4 **52**................................. WilliamCarson 7 18
(Simon Hodgson) *chsd ldrs: rdn and struggling ent fnl 2f: wknd over 1f out: fdd fnl f* **66/1**

60-6 **10** 2¼ **Green Millionaire**[18] 192 4-9-0 **55**.........................(b[1]) DavidParkes[(7)] 2 14
(Jeremy Gask) *chsd ldr tl jst over 2f out: sn lost pl u.p and wknd: fdd fnl f* **16/1**

1m 12.31s (-0.79) **Going Correction** -0.05s/f (Stan) **10** Ran SP% **112.5**
Speed ratings (Par 101): **103,102,99,98,96 91,87,86,83,80**
CSF £22.47 CT £193.61 TOTE £3.60: £1.50, £1.20, £2.60; EX 18.60 Trifecta £257.80.
**Owner** Joli Racing **Bred** Dxb Bloodstock Ltd **Trained** Yarnscombe, Devon
■ Littlecote Lady was withdrawn. Price at time of withdrawal 10-1. Rule 4 applies to all bets - deduction 5p in the pound.

**FOCUS**
This division was also truly run and the winning time was virtually the same as the first leg. The form seems sound with the winner progressing again.

## 450 KEMPTON PARK CHASE DAY 22.02.14 H'CAP 1m 4f (P)
4:50 (4:54) (Class 5) (0-75,77) 4-Y-0+ £2,749 (£818; £408; £204) Stalls Centre

Form RPR

011- **1** **Asia Minor (IRE)**[45] 8343 5-9-0 **71**.................................(t) RobertTart[(3)] 5 81+
(Dr Jon Scargill) *s.i.s: hld up in last pair: stdy hdwy 3f out: rdn and hdwy to chal over 1f out: led 1f out: styd on strly to assert fnl 100yds* **2/1**[1]

-052 **2** 1¼ **Lady Lunchalot (USA)**[8] 345 4-9-1 **72**.................................(p) LiamJones 11 80
(Laura Mongan) *hld up in midfield: rdn and hdwy over 2f out: pressed ldrs and drvn 1f out: kpt on but outpcd by wnr fnl 150yds* **20/1**

021- **3** 1½ **Modem**[43] 8388 4-8-12 **69**.................................(b) AndreaAtzeni 3 75
(Rod Millman) *t.k.h: chsd ldr for 3f: styd prom: rdn and ev ch 2f out: led over 1f out tl 1f out: outpcd ins fnl f* **5/1**[3]

0-03 **4** hd **Song Light**[10] 293 4-8-13 **70**................................. DavidProbert 8 75
(David Elsworth) *s.i.s: hld up in last pair: hdwy 3f out: rdn over 1f out: styd on wl u.p ins fnl f* **20/1**

05-3 **5** 1½ **Nave (USA)**[20] 158 7-8-10 **71**.................................(p) GeorgeBuckell[(7)] 1 74
(David Simcock) *in tch in midfield: hdwy 4f out: led over 2f out: drvn and hdd over 1f out: wknd ins fnl f* **6/1**

44-2 **6** 1¼ **Incendo**[14] 250 8-9-9 **77**.................................(b) StevieDonohoe 10 78
(Ian Williams) *t.k.h early: hld up in tch in midfield: swtchd rt and effrt on inner 2f out: styd on same pce and no imp fnl f* **12/1**

3-34 **7** nk **Red Dragon (IRE)**[14] 250 4-9-3 **74**................................. FergusSweeney 6 74
(Michael Blanshard) *hld up in tch in midfield: rdn and effrt ent fnl 2f: no hdwy over 1f out: plugged on same pce after* **7/1**

65-1 **8** hd **Java Rose**[10] 293 5-9-8 **76**................................. AdamKirby 2 76
(Charlie Longsdon) *chsd ldrs: rdn and unable qck over 2f out: lost pl 2f out: wknd u.p over 1f out* **4/1**[2]

-3 **9** 7 **Wild Desert (FR)**[17] 197 9-9-3 **74**................................. MarkCoumbe[(3)] 9 63
(Tony Carroll) *led: hdd and rdn over 2f out: drvn and wknd over 1f out: fdd fnl f* **66/1**

/2-0 **10** 2½ **Palus San Marco (IRE)**[17] 200 5-9-7 **75**.................................(t) LukeMorris 4 60
(Tony Carroll) *dwlt and bustled along early: in tch towards rr: rdn wl over 2f out: sn struggling: wknd 2f out* **25/1**

00/ **11** 2 **Swampfire (IRE)**[50] 4379 6-9-7 **75**.................................(v) GeorgeBaker 7 57
(Gary Moore) *hld up in last quartet: hdwy to chse ldr 9f out tl 3f out: wknd ent fnl 2f: hung rt over 1f out and bhd fnl f* **25/1**

2m 32.49s (-2.01) **Going Correction** -0.05s/f (Stan)
**WFA** 4 from 5yo+ 3lb **11** Ran SP% **123.2**
Speed ratings (Par 103): **104,103,102,102,101 100,100,99,95,93 92**
CSF £53.20 CT £190.33 TOTE £3.70: £1.70, £4.40, £2.10; EX 65.40 Trifecta £305.10.
**Owner** Strawberry Fields Stud **Bred** Darley **Trained** Newmarket, Suffolk

**FOCUS**
A fair handicap, but the pace was steady which wouldn't have suited a few. The winner continues to progress.

## 451 MIX BUSINESS WITH PLEASURE AT KEMPTON H'CAP 7f (P)
5:20 (5:23) (Class 5) (0-70,71) 4-Y-0+ £2,749 (£818; £408; £204) Stalls Low

Form RPR

04-0 **1** **Kakapuka**[14] 245 7-9-3 **66**................................. GeorgeBaker 1 76
(Anabel K Murphy) *mde all: squeezed along and fnd ex to go clr 2f out: in command and edgd lft ins fnl f: rdn out* **10/1**

00-3 **2** 1½ **Russian Ice**[25] 84 6-9-5 **68**.................................(b) JimCrowley 3 74
(Dean Ivory) *hld up in tch in midfield: swtchd lft and effrt wl over 1f out: styd on wl u.p fnl f: wnt 2nd last strides* **11/2**[2]

020- **3** hd **Lady Sylvia**[80] 7876 5-9-7 **70**................................. LukeMorris 4 75
(Joseph Tuite) *chsd ldrs: drvn and effrt 2f out: battling for 2nd 1f out: r.o u.p.: chsd clr wnr fnl 75yds' kpt on but no threat to wnr: lost 2nd last strides* **12/1**

3-44 **4** ¾ **Safwaan**[10] 289 7-7-8 **57**................................. LiamJones 11 60
(Michael Squance) *hld up in last pair: hdwy on inner over 1f out: styd on wl u.p ins fnl f: wnt 4th cl home* **16/1**

3-43 **5** nk **Bajan Bear**[14] 248 6-9-6 **69**................................. AdamKirby 8 72
(Michael Blanshard) *stdd s: hld up towards rr: rdn and hdwy wl over 1f out: chsd clr wnr ins fnl f: no real imp: lost 2nd fnl 75yds: wknd towards fin* **5/1**[1]

0-56 **6** ¾ **Golden Desert (IRE)**[9] 310 10-8-11 **60**......................... AndreaAtzeni 13 61
(Simon Dow) *stdd and dropped in bhd after s: hld up in rr: rdn and hdwy on inner over 1f out: r.o wl ins fnl f: nt rch ldrs* **25/1**

30-0 **7** ½ **First Class**[14] 245 6-9-0 **63**.................................(p) DavidProbert 10 62
(Rae Guest) *in tch in midfield: rdn jst over 2f out: outpcd and lost pl over 1f out: rallied and kpt on u.p fnl f: no threat to wnr* **8/1**

000/ **8** hd **Treadwell (IRE)**[480] 6979 7-9-7 **70**................................. FergusSweeney 7 69
(Jamie Osborne) *hld up towards rr: rdn and hdwy over 1f out: midfield and keeping on same pce whn n.m.r and eased wl ins fnl f* **6/1**[3]

5-06 **9** hd **Senator Bong**[16] 208 4-9-5 **68**................................. LiamKeniry 2 66
(David Elsworth) *chsd ldrs: drvn and chsd clr ldr wl over 1f out tl ins fnl f: wknd fnl 100yds* **16/1**

02-0 **10** ½ **Shifting Star (IRE)**[29] 52 9-8-13 **62**................................. WilliamCarson 6 59
(John Bridger) *chsd ldrs: drvn and unable qck 2f out: outpcd and btn over 1f out: plugged on same pce after* **33/1**

0-05 **11** shd **Perfect Mission**[20] 161 6-8-10 **66**.......................(p) JonathanWilletts[(7)] 5 63
(Andrew Balding) *chsd ldrs: rdn and unable qck 2f out: bmpd and lost pl wl over 1f out: kpt on same pce and wl hld after* **16/1**

-421 **12** 1 **Hellbender (IRE)**[9] 310 8-9-8 **71**................................. TomQueally 12 65
(Shaun Harris) *in tch in midfield on outer: effrt u.p but no hdwy 2f out: bmpd wl over 1f out: wknd fnl f* **8/1**

540- **13** ¾ **Keene's Pointe**[148] 6214 4-9-7 **70**.................................(b[1]) JoeFanning 14 62
(J W Hills) *t.k.h: hld up in tch towards rr: bhd and swtchd lft over 1f out: no imp fnl f: n.d* **9/1**

1m 24.9s (-1.10) **Going Correction** -0.05s/f (Stan) **13** Ran SP% **119.8**
Speed ratings (Par 103): **104,102,102,101,100 100,99,99,98,98 98,97,96**
CSF £64.28 CT £499.33 TOTE £15.40: £4.10, £2.20, £4.00; EX 89.20 Trifecta £1788.50.
**Owner** Aiden Murphy & All The Kings Horses **Bred** Paradime Ltd **Trained** Wilmcote, Warwicks

**FOCUS**
This ordinary handicap looked competitive enough beforehand, but it proved to be a one-horse race. The winner is rated to the balance of last year's form.
T/Jkpt: Not won. T/Plt: £81.50 to a £1 stake. Pool: £113083.02 - 1012.76 winning tickets T/Qpdt: £17.60 to a £1 stake. Pool: £7879.15 - 330.60 winning tickets SP

# 444 KEMPTON (A.W) (R-H)
## Monday, February 3

**OFFICIAL GOING: Standard**
Wind: medium, half behind Weather: dry

## 452 DOWNLOAD THE BETVICTOR APP NOW CLAIMING STKS 6f (P)
1:30 (1:30) (Class 5) 3-Y-0+ £2,587 (£770; £384; £192) Stalls Low

Form RPR

60-2 **1** **Jubilee Brig**[3] 399 4-10-0 75.................................(v) GeorgeBaker 1 72+
(Gary Moore) *chsd ldr: tl pushed along to ld over 1f out: rdn clr 1f out: pushed out: comf* **1/2**[1]

4-45 **2** 2¾ **Pabusar**[4] 381 6-10-0 82.................................(p) AdamKirby 4 63
(Jamie Osborne) *stdd s: t.k.h: hld up off the pce in last pair: rdn and effrt 2f out: styd on u.p to chse clr wnr ins fnl f: no imp* **5/1**[3]

60-0 **3** nk **Belle Bayardo (IRE)**[13] 273 6-9-9 57................................. LukeMorris 2 57
(Ronald Harris) *chsd ldng pair: effrt u.p 2f out: no threat to wnr and styd on same pce fnl f* **40/1**

0-06 **4** 2 **Capone (IRE)**[15] 249 9-10-0 85.................................(p) ShaneKelly 5 56
(Michael Attwater) *stdd s: hld up in rr: rdn 2f out: sme hdwy and drvn over 1f out: kpt on fnl f: n.d* **4/1**[2]

0/0- **5** ½ **Jambobo**[16] 3957 5-9-6 25................................. JohnFahy 3 46?
(Chris Down) *racd in midfield: rdn over 2f out: outpcd and wl hld in last over 1f out: n.d but kpt on fnl 100yds* **100/1**

30-0 **6** nk **Dixie Gwalia**[15] 244 6-9-1 52.................................(v) RobertWinston 6 40
(Michael Attwater) *led: rdn and hdd over 1f out: drvn and outpcd 1f out: lost 2nd and wknd fnl 150yds* **50/1**

1m 12.3s (-0.80) **Going Correction** +0.025s/f (Slow) **6** Ran SP% **108.7**
Speed ratings (Par 103): **106,102,101,99,98 98**
CSF £3.16 TOTE £1.60: £1.10, £1.60; EX 3.20 Trifecta £19.10.Jubilee Brig was Mr J. M. Curran for £10,000. Pabusar was claimed by for Miss A. Stokell £10,000.
**Owner** Lookout Partnership **Bred** Sir Eric Parker **Trained** Lower Beeding, W Sussex

**FOCUS**
Overcast, cold conditions and a three-horse market for this uncompetitive claimer, which was run at no more than a fair pace and they finished in a heap. It's been rated around the winner.

## 453 BACK OF THE NET AT BETVICTOR.COM FILLIES' H'CAP 6f (P)
2:00 (2:01) (Class 5) (0-75,72) 4-Y-0+ £2,749 (£818; £408; £204) Stalls Low

Form RPR

52-1 **1** **Welsh Sunrise**[26] 84 4-9-5 **70**................................. GeorgeBaker 3 77+
(Stuart Williams) *trckd ldng pair: smooth hdwy to join ldr and wnt clr over 1f out: pushed into ld and reminder fnl 100yds: in command after: pushed out: comf* **11/10**[1]

24-6 **2** ½ **Harvest Mist (IRE)**[17] 219 6-8-7 **58** oh2......................... LukeMorris 1 63
(Shaun Lycett) *led: rdn 2f out: clr w cruising wnr and hrd drvn over 1f out: hdd fnl 100yds: styd on same pce after* **8/1**

3-22 **3** 2¾ **Barbs Princess**[18] 196 4-9-7 **72**.................................(p) JimCrowley 4 68
(Charles Hills) *stdd s: t.k.h: hld up in last pair: rdn and effrt wl over 1f out: outpcd by ldng pair over 1f out: wnt 3rd ins fnl f: no imp* **11/4**[2]

30-2 **4** 2¼ **Ray Of Joy**[15] 248 8-9-2 **67**.................................(v) FergusSweeney 6 56
(J R Jenkins) *chsd ldr: rdn and unable qck 2f out: 3rd and outpcd over 1f out: lost 3rd and wknd ins fnl f* **7/1**[3]

13-3 **5** 4½ **Clock Opera (IRE)**[9] 340 4-8-5 **63**................................. MatthewHopkins[(7)] 5 38
(William Stone) *dwlt: sn rcvrd and in tch: rdn and struggling over 2f out: wknd over 1f out* **10/1**

/00- **6** ½ **Time For Lambrini (IRE)**[224] 3638 4-8-10 **64**............ MarkCoumbe[(3)] 2 37
(Lisa Williamson) *dwlt: a in rr: rdn and btn 2f out: sn wknd* **66/1**

1m 12.09s (-1.01) **Going Correction** +0.025s/f (Slow) **6** Ran SP% **108.5**
Speed ratings (Par 100): **107,106,102,99,93 93**
CSF £9.94 TOTE £2.10: £1.30, £4.30; EX 10.40 Trifecta £27.10.
**Owner** Seize The Day Racing Partnership **Bred** Mr & Mrs Sells **Trained** Newmarket, Suffolk

**FOCUS**
An ordinary fillies' handicap run at a decent pace. The runner-up is the key to the form.

## 454 BOOK HOSPITALITY AT KEMPTON PARK H'CAP (DIV I) 2m (P)
2:30 (2:31) (Class 6) (0-55,55) 4-Y-0+ £1,940 (£577; £288; £144) Stalls Low

Form RPR

40-3 **1** **Galiotto (IRE)**[3] 400 8-9-5 **53**.................................(v) GeorgeBaker 7 62
(Gary Moore) *hld up in rr of main gp: hdwy on inner over 2f out: rdn to ld 1f out: sn clr and styd on wl: rdn out* **7/2**[2]

54-5 **2** 3¼ **Dr Finley (IRE)**[17] 214 7-9-6 **54**.................................(v) AdamKirby 3 59
(Lydia Pearce) *led for 3f: chsd ldr tl led again over 3f out: rdn and wnt clr wl over 2f out: drvn and hdd 1f out: sn outpcd and btn: plugged on for clr 2nd* **7/2**[2]

00-2 **3** 5 **Dance**[15] 247 5-8-12 **46**................................. FrederikTylicki 2 45
(Rod Millman) *chsd ldrs: wnt 2nd over 6f out: drvn and outpcd and 3rd 2f out: plugged on but wl hld after* **6/1**[3]

442- **4** 1 **Descaro (USA)**[114] 6492 8-9-7 **55**.................................(p) LukeMorris 5 53
(John O'Shea) *in tch in midfield: drvn and outpcd over 2f out: 4th and wl hld over 1f out: plugged on u.p* **10/1**

000- **5** *2* **Maccabees**[21] 2801 5-8-7 **46** oh1.............................. JoshBaudains(5) 9 41
(Roger Curtis) *hld up wl off the pce in rr of main gp: clsd and in tch 12f out: rdn and wknd 3f out: 5th and wl btn 2f out: plugged on* **50/1**

462- **6** *16* **Bell'Arte (IRE)**[109] 7331 4-9-0 **54**.................................(p) FergusSweeney 8 30
(Laura Mongan) *hld up off the pce in rr of main gp: clsd and in tch 1/2-way: rdn and no rspnse over 2f out: sn wknd* **14/1**

40-6 **7** *nk* **Blackstone Vegas**[25] 106 8-9-2 **50**..............................(v) JoeFanning 4 26
(Derek Shaw) *hld up in midfield: rdn and no hdwy over 2f out: sn wknd* **8/1**

00-4 **8** *8* **Illegale (IRE)**[19] 185 8-8-10 **47**..........................(t) MatthewCosham(3) 10 13
(Nikki Evans) *chsd ldrs tl hdwy to ld after 3f: rdn and hdd over 3f out: wknd u.p wl over 1f out: wl bhd and eased ins fnl f: t.o* **33/1**

-462 **9** *99* **Azabitmour (FR)**[4] 380 4-8-7 **47**.................................... HayleyTurner 1
(John Best) *virtually ref to r: set off a f bhd rivals: a wl t.o: virtually p.u fnl 2f* **3/1**[1]

0/0- **10** *25* **Veronica's Pursuit**[35] 8444 4-8-6 **49**....................(p[1]) CharlesBishop(3) 6
(Peter Hedger) *chsd ldr for 3f: chsd ldrs tl lost pl rapidly over 6f out: t.o fnl 5f: virtually p.u fnl 2f* **66/1**

3m 29.64s (-0.46) **Going Correction** +0.025s/f (Slow)
**WFA** 4 from 5yo+ 6lb **10** Ran SP% **117.0**
Speed ratings (Par 101): **102,100,97,97,96 88,88,84,34,22**
CSF £16.13 CT £71.19 TOTE £4.10: £1.20, £2.00, £2.60; EX 18.20 Trifecta £128.50.
**Owner** Andrew Bradmore **Bred** Ballintaggart Syndicate **Trained** Lower Beeding, W Sussex

**FOCUS**
This opening division of the weak staying handicap was run at a reasonable gallop and they finished strung out. The runner-up has been rated to his recent best.

## 455 BOOK HOSPITALITY AT KEMPTON PARK H'CAP (DIV II) 2m (P)

**3:00** (3:00) (Class 6) (0-55,54) 4-Y-0+ **£1,940** (£577; £288; £144) **Stalls** Low

Form RPR

0/1- **1** **The Young Master**[24] 8268 5-9-4 **51**..............................(p) LiamKeniry 6 57+
(Neil Mulholland) *taken down early: mde all: stdd gallop 10f out: rdn and qcknd jst over 3f out: clr and edgd lft u.p over 1f out: styd on wl: rdn out* **3/1**[1]

/0-4 **2** *2* **Magicalmysterytour (IRE)**[12] 283 11-9-6 **53**........... RobertWinston 8 57
(Willie Musson) *hld up off the pce in last pair: clsd and in tch 10f out: swtchd lft and rdn over 2f out: hdwy over 1f out: styd on to chse wnr ins fnl f: no imp fnl 75yds* **6/1**[3]

43-3 **3** *nk* **Ice Apple**[19] 185 6-9-1 **48**............................................. JimmyQuinn 3 52
(John E Long) *chsd ldrs: rdn over 3f out: hdwy u.p to chse wnr over 1f out: styd on same pce and lost 2nd ins fnl f* **3/1**[1]

56-5 **4** *3/4* **Zelos Diktator**[19] 185 8-8-13 **46**........................................ JohnFahy 7 49
(Sean Curran) *in tch in midfield: rdn and effrt on inner 2f out: kpt on same pce u.p fr over 1f out* **14/1**

0-66 **5** *1 1/4* **Poste Restante**[15] 246 4-8-9 **48**...............................(p) FergusSweeney 4 49
(David Simcock) *chsd ldrs: wnt 2nd and rdn 3f out: no imp: drvn and lost 2nd over 1f out: plugged on same pce fnl f* **9/2**[2]

00-6 **6** *1* **Superstición**[12] 277 5-8-12 **45**........................................ HayleyTurner 2 45
(Michael Madgwick) *chsd wnr tl 3f out: rdn and unable qck over 2f out: drvn and btn over 1f out: wknd ins fnl f* **12/1**

/04- **7** *2 1/4* **Go Amwell**[48] 4173 11-8-12 **45**.....................................(v) FrederikTylicki 5 42
(J R Jenkins) *s.i.s: hld up in rr: clsd and in tch 10f out: rdn and outpcd 3f out: wl hld and plugged on same pce fnl 2f* **20/1**

40-4 **8** *7* **Rhinestone Rebel (IRE)**[15] 246 8-9-3 **50**.................. WilliamCarson 9 39
(Peter Hiatt) *taken down early: in tch in midfield: rdn and outpcd over 2f out: wknd over 1f out* **7/1**

3m 31.74s (1.64) **Going Correction** +0.025s/f (Slow)
**WFA** 4 from 5yo+ 6lb **8** Ran SP% **114.1**
Speed ratings (Par 101): **96,95,94,94,93 93,92,88**
CSF £21.32 CT £57.33 TOTE £3.20: £1.20, £1.50, £1.20; EX 20.40 Trifecta £94.30.
**Owner** Dajam Ltd **Bred** Brendan Boyle **Trained** Limpley Stoke, Wilts
■ Stewards' Enquiry : John Fahy three-day ban: used whip without giving gelding time to respond (Feb 19)

**FOCUS**
Run two seconds slower than the first division, they finished in a heap in this weak staying handicap. The third and fourth have been rated to form.

## 456 BETVICTOR NONRUNNER NO BET CHELTENHAM 2014 MAIDEN FILLIES' STKS 1m (P)

**3:30** (3:30) (Class 5) 3-Y-0+ **£2,749** (£818; £408; £204) **Stalls** Low

Form RPR

**1** **Bridie ffrench** 3-8-6 0.............................. WilliamTwiston-Davies(3) 5 70+
(Mick Channon) *chsd ldrs: rdn and hdwy over 1f out: led and flashed tail u.p fnl 75yds: rn green in front but styd on: rdn out* **10/1**

6-2 **2** *3/4* **Speechday (IRE)**[19] 189 3-8-9 0.................................. LukeMorris 10 68
(Marco Botti) *chsd ldrs: rdn to chse ldr 2f out: hrd drvn over 1f out: kpt on u.p ins fnl f: wnt 2nd towards fin* **7/4**[1]

**3** *nk* **Beylerbey (USA)** 4-10-0 0............................................. JoeFanning 11 72
(Mark Johnston) *led: rdn and clr ent fnl 2f: drvn ins fnl f: hdd and styd on same pce fnl 100yds: lost 2nd towards fin* **5/2**[2]

0- **4** *3 1/2* **Joyful Risk (IRE)**[37] 8427 4-10-0 0............................... GeorgeBaker 8 64
(Martin Bosley) *w ldr tl jst over 2f out: sn rdn and unable qck: 4th and btn over 1f out: wknd ins fnl f: edgd lft cl home* **66/1**

03- **5** *1 1/4* **Confiture**[47] 8328 3-8-9 0......................................... FergusSweeney 6 56
(Michael Blanshard) *t.k.h: hld up wl in tch in midfield: rdn and effrt jst over 2f out: 5th and no imp over 1f out: wknd ins fnl f* **6/1**[3]

**6** *3/4* **Ambella (IRE)** 4-9-9 0............................................ GeorgeDowning(5) 7 59
(Ian Williams) *s.i.s: in tch in last trio: rdn and rn green over 1f out: sme hdwy over 1f out: no threat to ldrs but kpt on ins fnl f* **66/1**

0- **7** *hd* **Red Wifey (IRE)**[138] 6512 3-8-9 0..................................... SeanLevey 2 54
(Alan McCabe) *dwlt: in tch in last trio: rdn 3f out: no imp tl sme hdwy over 1f out: n.d and kpt on same pce fnl f* **66/1**

5- **8** *2 1/4* **Alpine Mist**[35] 8444 4-10-0 0...................................... RobertWinston 1 53
(Pat Murphy) *s.i.s: t.k.h: hld up in last trio: rdn and no hdwy over 2f out: wknd over 1f out* **14/1**

0/5- **9** *4 1/2* **Mists Of Time (IRE)**[304] 1364 4-10-0 0............................. AdamKirby 9 42
(Pat Eddery) *in tch in midfield: rdn and unable qck over 2f out: sn struggling and lost pl: bhd fnl f* **8/1**

4-0 **10** *1 1/2* **Windshield**[19] 189 3-8-9 0........................................... LiamJones 3 34
(Sir Mark Prescott Bt) *sn bustled along in midfield: rdn over 3f out: dropped to rr jst over 2f out: wknd and bhd 1f out* **33/1**

1m 42.05s (2.25) **Going Correction** +0.025s/f (Slow)
**WFA** 3 from 4yo 19lb **10** Ran SP% **113.5**
Speed ratings (Par 100): **89,88,87,84,83 82,82,80,75,74**
CSF £26.97 TOTE £17.10: £3.50, £1.10, £2.50; EX 40.20 Trifecta £129.90.
**Owner** Anne & Steve Fisher **Bred** Wansdyke Farms Limited **Trained** West Ilsley, Berks

**FOCUS**
The pace was inconsistent for this fillies' maiden, which resulted in changing fortunes in the last 1f, and the time, 5secs slower than standard, reflected this. The front three finished in a bunch and the form has been rated around the runner-up to her debut effort.

## 457 CHELTENHAM 2014 NRNB AT BETVICTOR.COM H'CAP (LONDON MILE SERIES QUALIFIER) 1m (P)

**4:00** (4:05) (Class 4) (0-85,85) 4-Y-0+ **£4,690** (£1,395; £697; £348) **Stalls** Low

Form RPR

10-4 **1** **Dixie's Dream (IRE)**[21] 163 5-9-7 **85**............................ GeorgeBaker 6 96
(William Jarvis) *sn led and dictated stdy gallop: pushed along and qcknd over 1f out: clr and in command fnl f: comf* **5/1**[2]

2/0- **2** *2 1/4* **Ansaab**[316] 1168 6-9-7 **85**................................................ SeanLevey 2 91
(Alan McCabe) *in tch in midfield: effrt u.p 2f out: styd on to chse wnr ins fnl f: kpt on but no imp* **7/1**

42-2 **3** *1/2* **Legendary**[18] 200 5-9-7 **85**........................................... JimmyQuinn 12 90
(Ed Vaughan) *led briefly early: chsd wnr after: drvn to press ldr 2f out: unable qck over 1f out: styd on same pce and lost 2nd ins fnl f* **9/1**

06-6 **4** *nk* **Silverheels (IRE)**[12] 287 5-9-2 **80**................................. JimCrowley 4 84
(Paul Cole) *t.k.h: chsd ldng trio: rdn and effrt wl over 1f out: kpt on same pce and edgd rt ins fnl f* **6/1**[3]

5-40 **5** *1 1/4* **First Post (IRE)**[9] 342 7-9-0 **78**..................................... AdamKirby 7 79
(Derek Haydn Jones) *in tch in midfield: rdn and effrt ent fnl 2f: outpcd over 1f out: no threat to wnr but kpt on again ins fnl f* **20/1**

3-40 **6** *nk* **Fantasy Gladiator**[22] 153 8-8-12 **76**............................... LukeMorris 3 76
(John Quinn) *in tch in midfield: rdn ent fnl 2f: drvn and unable qck over 1f out: no threat to wnr and one pce fnl f* **16/1**

12-1 **7** *hd* **Diplomatic (IRE)**[19] 181 9-8-10 **74**............................(p) LiamJones 11 74
(Michael Squance) *stdd s: hld up in tch in rr: effrt u.p on inner wl over 1f out: kpt on same pce ins fnl f: nvr trbld ldrs* **14/1**

1-1 **8** *3/4* **Conversational (IRE)**[24] 118 4-8-9 **76**....... WilliamTwiston-Davies(3) 5 74
(Mick Channon) *chsd ldrs: rdn and effrt ent fnl 2f: drvn and outpcd over 1f out: wknd ins fnl f* **3/1**[1]

10-1 **9** *1* **Cayuga**[26] 89 5-9-7 **85**.................................................. TomQueally 9 81
(Brett Johnson) *hld up in last trio: effrt u.p and wd over 2f out: no imp: nvr trbld ldrs* **6/1**[3]

23-6 **10** *1 1/4* **Raging Bear (USA)**[31] 29 4-8-9 **73** ow1...................... StevieDonohoe 1 66
(James Evans) *stdd after s: hld up in tch in last trio: rdn and effrt jst over 2f out: no hdwy: n.d* **33/1**

1m 39.46s (-0.34) **Going Correction** +0.025s/f (Slow) **10** Ran SP% **113.0**
Speed ratings (Par 105): **102,99,99,98,97 97,97,96,95,94**
CSF £36.91 CT £273.10 TOTE £6.40: £2.50, £2.90, £2.40; EX 41.40 Trifecta £376.10.
**Owner** The Dream Team Partnership **Bred** Miss Joan Murphy **Trained** Newmarket, Suffolk
■ Franco Is My Name and Triple Chocolate were withdrawn. Prices at time of withdrawal 50-1 and 12-1 respectively. Rule 4 applies to all bets - deduction 5p in the pound.

**FOCUS**
An ordinary handicap, run at a modest pace. The first three in the early stages filled three of the first four places. The winner has been rated as running a personal best.

## 458 BETVICTOR NONRUNNER FREE BET AT CHELTENHAM 2014 H'CAP 1m 3f (P)

**4:30** (4:34) (Class 5) (0-70,69) 4-Y-0+ **£2,749** (£818; £408; £204) **Stalls** Low

Form RPR

4-16 **1** **Fearless Lad (IRE)**[11] 289 4-8-10 **60**........................(t) HayleyTurner 2 69
(John Best) *hld up in midfield: rdn and effrt on inner wl over 1f out: str chal 1f out: led wl ins fnl f: hld on wl: drvn out* **3/1**[2]

55/4 **2** *hd* **Rowan Ridge**[24] 120 6-9-5 **67**......................................... JimCrowley 1 76
(William Knight) *chsd ldrs: rdn and chal over 1f out: led 1f out: kpt on u.p: hdd wl ins fnl f: battled on wl but a jst hld* **8/1**

00-0 **3** *1 1/4* **Mountain Range (IRE)**[26] 79 6-9-3 **65**...................... StevieDonohoe 7 71
(Willie Musson) *hld up in last pair: rdn and hdwy over 1f out: chsd clr ldng pair 1f out: clsng and edgd rt ins fnl f: kpt on but nvr able to chal* **2/1**[1]

5-0 **4** *2* **Innoko (FR)**[11] 293 4-9-2 **69**..................................(t) MarkCoumbe(3) 6 72
(Tony Carroll) *hld up in last pair: weaved through and gd hdwy over 1f out: rdn along mainly hands and heels and styd on same pce ins fnl f* **100/1**

0-13 **5** *2* **Night's Watch**[9] 345 4-8-8 **58**........................................ RobertHavlin 8 57
(William Jarvis) *hld up in midfield: effrt u.p 2f out: drvn and chsd ldrs 1f out: no ex and wknd ins fnl f* **7/2**[3]

5-10 **6** *7* **Xclusive**[20] 171 4-8-10 **60**............................................. LukeMorris 3 47
(Ronald Harris) *t.k.h: hld up in midfield: clsd to chse ldrs 3f out: drvn and unable qck over 2f out: wknd over 1f out* **14/1**

322/ **7** *1/2* **Mighty Mambo**[34] 6775 7-8-12 **60**.................................(tp) TomQueally 5 46
(Lawney Hill) *in tch in last trio: dropped to rr and drvn over 2f out: wknd 2f out* **33/1**

4-06 **8** *1/2* **Mazij**[12] 278 6-8-9 **57**.................................................. WilliamCarson 9 42
(Peter Hiatt) *chsd ldr tl rdn to ld wl over 1f out: sn hdd and no ex u.p: fdd ins fnl f* **25/1**

1-66 **9** *2* **Auden (USA)**[6] 366 6-9-3 **65**....................................(v) FrederikTylicki 10 46
(J R Jenkins) *t.k.h: chsd ldrs: rdn 3f out: lost pl over 2f out: wknd and bhd over 1f out* **9/1**

0-65 **10** *5* **Unmoothaj**[9] 345 4-8-13 **63**............................................ LiamKeniry 4 35
(Pam Sly) *led: rdn ent fnl 2f: hdd wl over 1f out: sn btn: fdd 1f out* **10/1**

2m 20.41s (-1.49) **Going Correction** +0.025s/f (Slow)
**WFA** 4 from 6yo+ 2lb **10** Ran SP% **125.2**
Speed ratings (Par 103): **106,105,104,103,102 96,96,96,94,91**
CSF £29.41 CT £61.49 TOTE £6.00: £3.80, £2.00, £2.00; EX 25.30 Trifecta £149.90.
**Owner** Mrs Jackie Jones **Bred** Brittas House Stud & Lynch Bages & Samac **Trained** Hucking, Kent
■ Stewards' Enquiry : Mark Coumbe caution: entered wrong stall.

**FOCUS**
The pace was true for this ordinary handicap. The runner-up has been rated as running as well as ever on his second start back off a break.

## 459 TURFTV H'CAP 1m 4f (P)

**5:00** (5:01) (Class 6) (0-55,55) 4-Y-0+ **£1,940** (£577; £288; £144) **Stalls** Centre

Form RPR

/0-2 **1** **Graylyn Ruby (FR)**[19] 185 9-9-1 **49**................................. LukeMorris 8 56
(Robin Dickin) *in tch in midfield: rdn and effrt to chse ldrs over 2f out: chsd ldr over 1f out: styd on wl to ld ins fnl f: drvn out* **8/1**

05-3 **2** *3/4* **Lisahane Bog**[15] 247 7-9-2 **50**......................................(v) AdamKirby 9 56
(Peter Hedger) *hld up in midfield: rdn over 3f out: no real rspnse tl swtchd lft and hdwy ent fnl f: styd on to chse ldrs fnl 100yds: wnt 2nd towards fin* **5/1**[2]

04-0 **3** 3/4 **Royal Etiquette (IRE)**[24] 116 7-9-7 **55**.......................(t) TomQueally 11 60
(Lawney Hill) *chsd ldrs: hdwy to chse ldr and rdn wl over 2f out: drvn to ld wl over 1f out: hdd ins fnl f: stdy on same pce after* **10/1**

10-5 **4** *shd* **Entrapping**[14] 252 4-9-4 **55**........................................ JimmyQuinn 5 60
(John E Long) *wl in tch in midfield: rdn and hdwy switching rt over 1f out: chsd ldrs ins fnl f: kpt on same pce fnl 100yds* **14/1**

34-5 **5** 1 1/4 **Petersboden**[24] 116 5-9-3 **51**................................ FergusSweeney 7 54
(Michael Blanshard) *hld up towards rr: swtchd rt and hdwy wl over 1f out: styd on same pce ins fnl f* **10/1**

153- **6** *nk* **Sudden Wish (IRE)**[48] 7090 5-9-7 **55**............................ GeorgeBaker 13 57
(Gary Moore) *stdd s: hld up in last trio: effrt u.p 2f out: kpt on but no real imp fnl f* **7/2**[1]

305- **7** 1/2 **Mariet**[49] 7090 5-8-9 **46** oh1............................ WilliamTwiston-Davies(3) 4 48
(Suzy Smith) *hld up towards rr: rdn and effrt over 2f out: hdwy u.p over 1f out: kpt on but nvr gng pce to threaten ldrs* **25/1**

0-10 **8** 3 **Midnight Sequel**[12] 277 5-9-7 **55**..................................(p) LiamKeniry 2 52
(Neil Mulholland) *chsd ldr after 2f tl led 3f out: drvn and hdd wl over 1f out: no ex u.p and btn 1f out: wknd ins fnl f* **8/1**

46-0 **9** 2 1/4 **Mayan Flight (IRE)**[15] 246 6-8-9 **46** oh1................(p) MarkCoumbe(3) 3 39
(Tony Carroll) *chsd ldr after 2f tl wl over 3f out: drvn and struggling ent fnl 2f: wknd over 1f out* **50/1**

0/4- **10** 10 **Sovento (GER)**[371] 418 10-9-5 **53**............................ WilliamCarson 12 30
(Thomas McLaughlin, Ire) *stdd s: hld up in last trio: rdn and no hdwy ent fnl 2f: wknd over 1f out* **6/1**[3]

00-0 **11** 8 **Last Chance Ranch**[15] 246 4-8-9 **46** oh1........................ JohnFahy 10 10
(Derek Shaw) *stdd s: hld up off the pce in rr: nvr on terms: lost tch 2f out* **50/1**

0-30 **12** 17 **Penny Stock (IRE)**[11] 303 4-9-1 **52**.................................... JoeFanning 1
(Mark Johnston) *led tl 3f out: sn rdn and dropped out: bhd 2f out: t.o fnl f* **7/1**

2m 34.96s (0.46) **Going Correction** +0.025s/f (Slow)
**WFA** 4 from 5yo+ 3lb **12** Ran SP% **120.5**
Speed ratings (Par 101): **99,98,98,97,97 96,96,94,93,86 81,69**
CSF £48.02 CT £411.50 TOTE £9.10: £3.50, £1.80, £3.90; EX 47.70 Trifecta £1126.90.
**Owner** Graham & Lynn Knight **Bred** Jonathan Jay **Trained** Alcester, Warwicks

**FOCUS**
A poor handicap and a muddling affair, run in a time over 4secs below average. It turned into something of a sprint finish. The third and fifth suggest this is ordinary/straightforward form.
T/Plt: £24.10 to a £1 stake. Pool: £69618.01 - 2105.88 winning tickets T/Qpdt: £6.60 to a £1 stake. Pool: £7321.57 - 813.10 winning tickets SP

## 429 WOLVERHAMPTON (A.W) (L-H)
### Monday, February 3

**OFFICIAL GOING: Standard**
Wind: Fresh half-behind Weather: Overcast

### 460 32RED.COM ALL WEATHER "HANDS AND HEELS" APPRENTICE SERIES H'CAP (RACING EXCELLENCE INITIATIVE) 1m 5f 194y(P)
**2:40** (2:40) (Class 6) (0-60,59) 4-Y-0+ **£1,940** (£577; £288; £144) **Stalls** Low

6-33 **1** **Waving**[5] 368 5-9-3 **50**..................................................(t) AlistairRawlinson 2 57+
(Tony Carroll) *s.i.s: hld up: hdwy 4f out: led 2f out: shkn up over 1f out: eased nr fin* **5/4**[1]

64-6 **2** 1 **Fair Breeze**[28] 68 7-8-12 **45**......................................(b) JordanVaughan 1 51
(Richard Phillips) *chsd ldrs: lost pl 4f out: hdwy over 1f out: chsd wnr fnl f: styd on* **18/1**

545- **3** 6 **Well Owd Mon**[56] 8225 4-8-5 **46**...................................(p) RobHornby(3) 4 44
(Andrew Hollinshead) *s.s: hld up: r.o ins fnl f: wnt 3rd nr fin: nt trble ldrs* **6/1**[3]

66-0 **4** 1/2 **Taste The Wine (IRE)**[11] 292 8-9-12 **59**......................(p) LouisSteward 6 56
(Bernard Llewellyn) *hld up: hdwy to join ldrs 5f out: pushed along and ev ch 2f out: edgd lft and no ex fnl f* **6/1**[3]

0-54 **5** 2 1/4 **Excellent News (IRE)**[25] 106 5-8-9 **45**........................ JackGarritty(3) 7 39
(Tony Forbes) *chsd ldr 4f: remained handy: led 5f out: pushed along and hdd 2f out: ev ch 2f out: wknd fnl f* **11/1**

P-42 **6** 1 1/2 **Kyllachykov (IRE)**[14] 252 6-9-10 **57**............................ LukeLeadbitter 5 49
(Robin Bastiman) *led 9f: sn pushed along: led again 3f out: hdd 2f out: wknd fnl f* **11/2**[2]

234- **7** 1 1/2 **Jebulani**[24] 6629 4-8-12 **53**........................................ PaulBooth(3) 3 43
(Barry Murtagh) *prom: outpcd over 3f out: rallied over 1f out: wknd fnl f* **10/1**

000- **8** 16 **Polvere D'Oro**[128] 6824 4-8-4 **45**................................ GaryMahon(3) 8 12
(Michael Mullineaux) *trckd ldrs: racd keenly: wnt 2nd 10f out tl 5f out: wknd over 3f out* **50/1**

3m 9.23s (3.23) **Going Correction** +0.125s/f (Slow)
**WFA** 4 from 5yo+ 5lb **8** Ran SP% **113.0**
Speed ratings (Par 101): **95,94,91,90,89 88,87,78**
CSF £26.75 CT £101.73 TOTE £2.10: £1.20, £4.30, £2.00; EX 23.60 Trifecta £121.30.
**Owner** Carl Hodgson **Bred** Theakston Stud **Trained** Cropthorne, Worcs

**FOCUS**
A low-grade staying handicap for apprentices to kick-off a card that was to later to be lit up by a Class 2 handicap and a Class 2 conditions race. They went a steady gallop early, however the three to dispute the lead got into a kicked for home with 5f left to run and were a spent force turning into the straight. The runner-up has been rated as running her best race since her 4yo season.

### 461 32RED FILLIES' H'CAP 7f 32y(P)
**3:10** (3:10) (Class 5) (0-75,73) 4-Y-0+ **£2,587** (£770; £384; £192) **Stalls** High

Form RPR
1-35 **1** **Maggie Pink**[5] 372 5-9-7 **73**....................................... AndrewMullen 1 85
(Michael Appleby) *mde all: set stdy pce tl qcknd over 2f out: shkn up over 1f out: comf* **7/4**[1]

065- **2** 2 3/4 **Imaginary World (IRE)**[48] 8316 6-8-11 **66**......................(e) BillyCray(3) 6 71
(John Balding) *a.p: pushed along 1/2-way: rdn over 1f out: hung lft and chsd wnr ins fnl f: no imp* **16/1**

0-00 **3** 1 3/4 **Queen Aggie (IRE)**[4] 376 4-9-2 **68**........................ RichardKingscote 4 68
(David Evans) *hld up: pushed along over 2f out: hdwy over 1f out: r.o to go 3rd nr fin: nt trble ldrs* **4/1**[3]

51-4 **4** *hd* **Wakeup Little Suzy (IRE)**[19] 180 4-9-6 **72**................(t) AndreaAtzeni 2 71
(Marco Botti) *hld up: pushed along over 2f out: hdwy over 1f out: styd on* **6/1**

6-16 **5** 2 1/4 **Dance For Georgie**[7] 359 5-9-0 **69**......................... GeorgeChaloner(3) 3 62
(Ben Haslam) *chsd ldrs: rdn over 2f out: nt clr run over 1f out: wknd fnl f* **9/1**

3-42 **6** *hd* **Funky Cold Medina**[7] 359 4-9-2 **68**.................................(v) ChrisCatlin 7 61
(Peter Chapple-Hyam) *dwlt: in rr: rdn over 2f out: nvr on terms* **3/1**[2]

430- **7** 3/4 **Meddling**[138] 6535 4-8-6 **63**........................................ ShelleyBirkett(5) 5 54
(Julia Feilden) *chsd wnr: rdn over 2f out: hung lft over 1f out: wknd ins fnl f* **25/1**

1m 29.14s (-0.46) **Going Correction** +0.125s/f (Slow) **7** Ran SP% **115.4**
Speed ratings (Par 100): **107,103,101,101,99 98,97**
CSF £32.15 TOTE £3.30: £1.30, £4.00; EX 34.80 Trifecta £237.30.
**Owner** A W Bult **Bred** Harcourt Stud **Trained** Danethorpe, Notts

**FOCUS**
A competitive fillies' handicap which saw a pair of gambles, one of which was successful. The winner had an easy time of it in front and has been rated in line with the best view of her form, with the runner-up and third close to their recent marks.

### 462 32RED H'CAP 2m 119y(P)
**3:40** (3:40) (Class 2) (0-105,90) 4-Y-0+ **£11,971** (£3,583; £1,791; £896; £446) **Stalls** Low

Form RPR
622- **1** **Be Perfect (USA)**[37] 8429 5-9-4 **88**.............................. AdrianNicholls 1 97
(David Nicholls) *mde all: set stdy pce tl qcknd 6f out: rdn clr fnl 2f* **15/2**

2-02 **2** 6 **Kashmir Peak (IRE)**[24] 125 5-9-6 **90**............................... TomEaves 5 92
(John Quinn) *hld up: racd keenly: hdwy 3f out: rdn over 2f out: styd on same pce fr over 1f out: wnt 2nd wl ins fnl f* **9/2**[2]

45-2 **3** 2 **Communicator**[12] 285 6-9-6 **90**.................................... DavidProbert 3 89
(Andrew Balding) *prom: chsd wnr 3f out: rdn 2f out: no ex fnl f* **4/5**[1]

34-1 **4** 2 1/4 **Shelford (IRE)**[32] 16 5-9-6 **90**..................................... AndrewMullen 2 87
(Michael Appleby) *chsd wnr: pushed along 6f out: rdn and lost 2nd 3f out: wkng whn hung lft over 1f out* **5/1**[3]

31/0 **5** 9 **Exemplary**[12] 285 7-8-11 **86**....................................... LouisSteward(5) 4 72
(Alexandra Dunn) *prom tl rdn and wknd over 2f out* **22/1**

**6** 32 **Vedani (IRE)**[27] 4974 5-9-2 **86**.................................(t) AndreaAtzeni 6 34
(Tony Carroll) *hld up: pushed along 6f out: sn bhd* **20/1**

3m 43.67s (1.87) **Going Correction** +0.125s/f (Slow) **6** Ran SP% **111.3**
Speed ratings (Par 109): **100,97,96,95,90 75**
CSF £39.39 TOTE £5.30: £1.70, £3.10; EX 33.50 Trifecta £81.90.
**Owner** Lady O'Reilly **Bred** Joseph Allen **Trained** Sessay, N Yorks

**FOCUS**
The feature handicap saw a blowout from the gamble of the day. The winner had the run of things and has been rated close to her early British form.

### 463 CORAL APP DOWNLOAD FROM THE APP STORE MAIDEN STKS 1m 4f 50y(P)
**4:10** (4:10) (Class 5) 4-Y-0+ **£2,587** (£770; £384; £192) **Stalls** Low

Form RPR
34-2 **1** **Wilhana (IRE)**[12] 282 4-8-11 70.................................. RossAtkinson(3) 8 73
(Pam Sly) *trckd ldr tl led 3f out: rdn over 1f out: styd on wl* **5/2**[2]

**2** 1 **Puzzle Time**[33] 4-9-0 0................................................ DavidProbert 6 71
(Giles Bravery) *a.p: chsd wnr over 1f out: rdn and hung lft ins fnl f: styd on* **3/1**[3]

33-0 **3** 8 **Star Of Namibia (IRE)**[26] 85 4-9-5 64..........................(b) TomEaves 3 64
(Michael Mullineaux) *prom: pushed along 5f out: rdn over 3f out: wknd over 1f out* **7/1**

0- **4** 2 1/4 **Angelot Du Berlais (FR)**[137] 6557 5-9-8 69........................ ChrisCatlin 5 60
(Dr Richard Newland) *led: pushed along and hdd 3f out: rdn and wknd over 1f out* **9/4**[1]

24 **5** 4 **Teenage Dream (IRE)**[12] 276 6-9-1 0..................(vt) AdamMcLean(7) 1 54
(Derek Shaw) *hld up: racd keenly: rdn over 3f out: wknd over 2f out* **10/1**

**6** 3 **Kastela Stari**[30] 7-9-3 0........................................... JamesSullivan 4 44
(Tim Fitzgerald) *s.s: hld up: rdn over 3f out: wknd over 2f out* **50/1**

**7** 11 **Miss Bella Rose**[62] 7-9-0 0.......................................... BillyCray(3) 7 26
(Richard Guest) *s.s: a in rr: wknd over 4f out* **100/1**

**8** 36 **Linden Rose**[32] 5-9-3 0............................................ RussKennemore 2
(Steph Hollinshead) *dwlt: a in rr: rdn and wknd over 4f out* **100/1**

2m 43.81s (2.71) **Going Correction** +0.125s/f (Slow)
**WFA** 4 from 5yo+ 3lb **8** Ran SP% **109.9**
Speed ratings (Par 103): **95,94,89,87,84 82,75,51**
CSF £9.54 TOTE £2.30: £1.10, £2.50, £1.30; EX 10.50 Trifecta £28.40.
**Owner** David L Bayliss **Bred** Darley **Trained** Thorney, Cambs

**FOCUS**
This maiden for older horses was a victory for perseverance. The winner has been rated to form, with the third also helping.

### 464 LADBROKES (S) STKS 7f 32y(P)
**4:40** (4:40) (Class 6) 3-Y-0+ **£1,940** (£577; £288; £144) **Stalls** High

Form RPR
-222 **1** **Ain't No Surprise (IRE)**[10] 311 3-8-2 65....................... AndrewMullen 5 67
(Jamie Osborne) *chsd ldrs: rdn to go 2nd and hung lft over 1f out: styd on to ld nr fin* **3/1**[2]

2-32 **2** *hd* **Ocean Legend (IRE)**[10] 310 9-9-10 73.......................... AndreaAtzeni 6 76
(Tony Carroll) *led: rdn over 1f out: hdd nr fin* **11/8**[1]

15-6 **3** 3 1/2 **Plunder**[3] 407 4-9-10 73.........................................(b) DavidProbert 8 67
(Alan Berry) *plld hrd: trckd ldr 6f out tl hung rt over 5f out: remained handy: rdn over 1f out: styd on to go 3rd nr fin* **15/2**[3]

31-0 **4** 1/2 **For Shia And Lula (IRE)**[25] 102 5-9-10 65....................(p) ShaneKelly 4 66
(Daniel Mark Loughnane) *hld up: hdwy over 2f out: rdn over 1f out: styd on same pce ins fnl f* **11/1**

300- **5** 3 **Bond Club**[35] 8443 4-9-7 60......................................(b) RobertTart(3) 7 58
(Geoffrey Oldroyd) *sn prom: chsd ldr over 5f out: rdn and ev ch 2f out: wknd ins fnl f* **16/1**

131- **6** 17 **Stoney Quine (IRE)**[46] 8347 3-8-8 65 ow2........................ TomEaves 2 8
(Keith Dalgleish) *sn pushed along to chse ldr for 1f: remained handy tl lost pl over 4f out: bhd fr 1/2-way* **8/1**

0-20 **7** 8 **Penbryn (USA)**[12] 288 7-9-3 59.................................... JordanVaughan(7) 3
(Nick Littmoden) *hld up: wknd over 2f out* **20/1**

1m 29.58s (-0.02) **Going Correction** +0.125s/f (Slow)
**WFA** 3 from 4yo+ 17lb **7** Ran SP% **109.0**
Speed ratings (Par 101): **105,104,100,100,96 77,68**
CSF £6.75 TOTE £5.30: £2.30, £1.30; EX 9.90 Trifecta £33.30.The winner was bought in for 8,000gns.
**Owner** Chris Watkins And David N Reynolds **Bred** Mrs C Regalado-Gonzalez **Trained** Upper Lambourn, Berks

**FOCUS**
A tight finish to this seller. The form is a little doubtful, with the third, fourth and fifth not having shown much recently, but it's been rated around the winner to her latest Lingfield effort and the runner-up to his latest run.

## 465 LADBROKES CONDITIONS STKS 1m 141y(P)
**5:10** (5:11) (Class 2) 4-Y-O+ **£11,971** (£3,583; £1,791; £896; £446) **Stalls** Low

Form RPR
22-2 **1** **Chookie Royale**[23] 144 6-9-0 99 (p) TomEaves 7 108+
(Keith Dalgleish) *plld hrd: w ldr tl led over 7f out: pushed clr fr over 2f out: eased nr fin* **7/4**[1]
15-1 **2** *7* **Star Links (USA)**[21] 163 8-9-0 87 (b) ShaneKelly 1 90
(S Donohoe, Ire) *chsd ldrs: rdn over 2f out: styd on same pce: wnt 2nd nr fin* **8/1**
05-2 **3** *nse* **Luhaif**[16] 235 4-9-0 97 (p) AdamBeschizza 5 90
(Julia Feilden) *led 1f: trckd wnr: rdn over 2f out: sn outpcd: lost 2nd nr fin* **11/2**
460- **4** *6* **Don't Call Me (IRE)**[149] 6183 7-9-0 104 (t) AdrianNicholls 2 76
(David Nicholls) *hld up: pushed along over 1/2-way: rdn and wknd over 2f out* **4/1**[3]
4U-1 **5** *3 ¾* **Birdman (IRE)**[16] 235 4-9-0 93 (be) AndreaAtzeni 3 67
(David Simcock) *hld up: rdn over 3f out: wknd over 2f out* **11/4**[2]
1m 47.81s (-2.69) **Going Correction** +0.125s/f (Slow) **5 Ran SP% 109.5**
Speed ratings (Par 109): **116,109,109,104,101**
CSF £15.30 TOTE £2.40: £1.10, £2.30; EX 8.60 Trifecta £28.80.
**Owner** Raeburn Brick Limited **Bred** D And J Raeburn **Trained** Carluke, S Lanarks

**FOCUS**
This conditions event was the scene of a demolition job. He was always in command and the runner-up loosely helps rate the form.

## 466 COMPARE BOOKMAKERS AT BOOKMAKERS.CO.UK H'CAP 5f 20y(P)
**5:40** (5:40) (Class 6) (0-60,60) 4-Y-O+ **£1,940** (£577; £288; £144) **Stalls** Low

Form RPR
055- **1** **Megaleka**[46] 8352 4-8-11 55 TimClark(5) 6 70
(Alan Bailey) *chsd ldr tl led 1/2-way: rdn clr over 1f out: eased nr fin* **11/2**[3]
-435 **2** *3 ¾* **Your Gifted (IRE)**[2] 425 7-8-11 55 (v) ShirleyTeasdale(5) 2 56
(Lisa Williamson) *hld up: nt clr run fr over 2f out tl hdwy over 1f out: hmpd sn after: wnt 2nd ins fnl f: r.o: no ch w wnr* **13/2**
31-2 **3** *1 ½* **Daneglow (IRE)**[21] 164 4-8-10 49 (e) AndreaAtzeni 9 45
(Mike Murphy) *hld up: hdwy over 1f out: r.o to go 3rd nr fin: nt rch ldrs* **9/2**[2]
00-0 **4** *nk* **Loyal Royal (IRE)**[11] 296 11-8-7 53 (bt) RyanWhile(7) 10 48
(Milton Bradley) *chsd ldrs: rdn 1/2-way: styd on same pce fnl f* **33/1**
34-5 **5** *¾* **Methaaly (IRE)**[7] 353 11-8-10 52 (be) RobertTart(3) 8 44
(Michael Mullineaux) *hood removed sltly late and hmpd s: hld up: r.o ins fnl f: n.m.r towards fin: nvr nrr* **11/2**[3]
60-2 **6** *nk* **Imaginary Diva**[10] 313 8-9-0 60 JordanVaughan(7) 4 51
(George Margarson) *prom: rdn over 1f out: styd on same pce* **6/1**
60-0 **7** *¾* **Lucky Mellor**[29] 58 7-8-0 46 oh1 (p) PaulBooth(7) 1 34
(Barry Murtagh) *chsd ldrs: rdn 1/2-way: hung lft over 1f out: wknd fnl f* **100/1**
60-6 **8** *¾* **Falasteen (IRE)**[10] 313 7-9-4 57 DavidProbert 5 42
(Milton Bradley) *led to 1/2-way: sn rdn: wknd ins fnl f* **4/1**[1]
5060 **9** *½* **Amis Reunis**[7] 353 5-8-6 52 (p) JordanHibberd(7) 7 36
(Alan Berry) *hld up: rdn 1/2-way: nvr on terms* **28/1**
36-0 **10** *3* **Two Turtle Doves (IRE)**[14] 258 8-8-11 57 LewisStones(7) 11 30
(Michael Mullineaux) *hld up: rdn and edgd lft over 1f out: n.d* **33/1**
35-1 **11** *6* **Volcanic Dust (IRE)**[21] 164 6-9-1 54 (t) RichardKingscote 3 5
(Milton Bradley) *gates sprung bk and stopped horse fr breaking on terms: a bhd* **7/1**
1m 2.26s (-0.04) **Going Correction** +0.125s/f (Slow) **11 Ran SP% 119.4**
Speed ratings (Par 101): **105,99,96,96,94 94,93,92,91,86 76**
CSF £40.69 CT £180.54 TOTE £5.80: £1.50, £1.70, £1.60; EX 47.10 Trifecta £387.10.
**Owner** North Cheshire Trading & Storage Ltd **Bred** North Cheshire Trading And Storage Ltd **Trained** Newmarket, Suffolk

**FOCUS**
A competitive, low-grade sprint handicap. The runner-up has been rated close to her recent form.
T/Plt: £41.90 to a £1 stake. Pool: £85834.33 - 1493.17 winning tickets T/Qpdt: £13.20 to a £1 stake. Pool: £6502.94 - 361.96 winning tickets CR

# [421]LINGFIELD (L-H)
Tuesday, February 4

**OFFICIAL GOING: Standard**
Wind: Strong, behind Weather: Fine but cloudy

## 467 LADBROKES MOBILE H'CAP 1m 1y(P)
**1:30** (1:30) (Class 6) (0-58,58) 4-Y-O+ **£2,045** (£603; £302) **Stalls** High

Form RPR
24-3 **1** **Pearl Ransom (IRE)**[27] 90 4-9-3 56 (v) GeorgeBaker 8 67
(Lady Herries) *led after 1f: mde rest: stretched on 3f out and only one rival sn after: rdn and hdd briefly jst ins fnl f: asserted nr fin* **7/2**[1]
5-01 **2** *nk* **Skidby Mill (IRE)**[22] 155 4-9-5 58 LiamJones 4 68
(Laura Mongan) *t.k.h early: trckd ldng pair: wnt 2nd 3f out: only danger to wnr sn after: chal on inner over 1f out: led briefly jst ins fnl f: styd on but hld last 75yds* **10/1**
23-0 **3** *4 ½* **Warbond**[18] 211 6-9-3 56 (v) LukeMorris 6 56
(Michael Madgwick) *in tch: outpcd and rdn 3f out: kpt on u.p over 1f out to take 3rd last stride* **10/1**
06-2 **4** *nse* **Carrera**[18] 211 4-9-3 56 DavidProbert 11 56
(Michael Blanshard) *prom: outpcd and rdn over 2f out: chsd clr ldng pair over 1f out: no imp and lost 3rd last stride* **5/1**[2]
00-0 **5** *1 ¾* **Claude Greenwood**[27] 92 4-8-12 58 NedCurtis(7) 2 54
(Roger Curtis) *trckd ldrs: outpcd and rdn over 2f out: no imp after* **33/1**
364- **6** *½* **Abigails Angel**[35] 8450 7-8-12 58 (p) DavidParkes(7) 10 53
(Brett Johnson) *s.s: hld up in rr: outpcd and rdn over 2f out: kpt on u.p fr over 1f out* **10/1**
25-0 **7** *2 ¾* **Nifty Kier**[25] 126 5-9-2 55 JohnFahy 1 43
(Martin Bosley) *hld up and sn in last: lft bhd fr 3f out: no ch whn rdn over 1f out: plugged on* **25/1**
4142 **8** *¾* **Greek Islands (IRE)**[3] 421 6-9-3 56 ChrisCatlin 9 43
(Edward Creighton) *hld up in rr and racd wd: outpcd over 2f out: no ch after* **5/1**[2]
05-1 **9** *1 ¼* **True Spirit**[18] 219 4-9-3 56 SeanLevey 3 40
(Paul D'Arcy) *t.k.h: led 1f: chsd wnr to 3f out: sn rdn: wknd over 1f out* **6/1**[3]
0-54 **10** *1 ½* **Annes Rocket (IRE)**[13] 288 9-8-12 58 (p) GaryMahon(7) 5 38
(Jimmy Fox) *awkward and stdd s: plld hrd early in rr: outpcd over 2f out: no prog after* **20/1**
3-45 **11** *2 ¼* **Delightful Sleep**[22] 156 6-9-5 58 AdamKirby 7 33
(David Evans) *hld up towards rr: outpcd and pushed along over 2f out: wknd over 1f out* **10/1**
1m 37.77s (-0.43) **Going Correction** 0.0s/f (Stan) **11 Ran SP% 117.8**
Speed ratings (Par 101): **102,101,97,97,95 94,92,91,90,88 86**
CSF £38.59 CT £323.87 TOTE £3.90: £1.70, £2.80, £4.10; EX 36.40 Trifecta £369.60.
**Owner** Seymour Bloodstock (uk) Ltd **Bred** J Erhardt **Trained** Patching, W Sussex

**FOCUS**
A competitive low-grade handicap, but nothing got involved from off the pace. The first two were always well placed.

## 468 DOWNLOAD THE LADBROKES APP MAIDEN STKS 1m 1y(P)
**2:00** (2:02) (Class 5) 3-Y-O+ **£2,726** (£805; £402) **Stalls** High

Form RPR
3 **1** **Dubawi Light**[10] 341 3-8-9 0 LukeMorris 6 72+
(James Tate) *chsd ldng pair: wnt 2nd 3f out: drvn to ld over 1f out: kpt on* **7/4**[1]
6 **2** *1* **Bobby Benton (IRE)**[17] 230 3-8-9 0 MarcHalford 12 69
(Luke Dace) *in tch: prog 3f out: shkn up 2f out: styd on to take 2nd ins fnl f: unable to chal* **100/1**
4-02 **3** *1* **Warbrook (IRE)**[8] 355 3-8-9 66 (b) RobertHavlin 11 67
(John Gosden) *led: rdn and hdd over 1f out: fnd nil: lost 2nd ins fnl f* **11/4**[2]
**4** *hd* **Lawsong (IRE)** 3-8-9 0 FergusSweeney 8 67
(Jamie Osborne) *in tch towards rr: prog over 2f out: shkn up over 1f out: styd on to press for a pl ins fnl f: fair debut* **25/1**
0- **5** *1* **Hurricane Harry**[164] 5744 3-8-9 0 AndreaAtzeni 4 64
(William Knight) *in tch: pushed along 3f out: kpt on fr 2f out but nvr gng pce to threaten* **10/1**[3]
6 **6** *3* **No Refund (IRE)**[10] 341 3-8-9 0 LiamKeniry 3 57+
(David Simcock) *towards rr: jst in tch at rr of main gp 3f out and gng wl enough: rdn on inner over 1f out and outpcd: nvr on terms after* **20/1**
60-4 **7** *¾* **Vermuyden**[22] 159 5-10-0 54 (t) AdamKirby 9 61?
(Pam Sly) *chsd ldr to 3f out: lost 2nd and wknd over 1f out: eased last 75yds* **33/1**
5- **8** *3 ½* **Raging Bob (IRE)**[47] 8340 3-8-9 0 JimCrowley 7 47
(Ralph Beckett) *chsd ldng trio to 3f out: shoved along and steaidly lost pl: wknd fnl f* **11/4**[2]
**9** *shd* **Abdication** 3-8-9 0 PaoloSirigu 2 46
(Marco Botti) *difficult to load into stalls: rn green and sn detached in last trio: virtually t.o over 2f out: reminder 1f out: fin w a flourish* **25/1**
**10** *8* **Jalusive (IRE)** 5-9-9 0 EoinWalsh(5) 5 32
(Christine Dunnett) *in tch towards rr to 3f out: wkng whn hit rail over 1f out* **100/1**
60- **11** *11* **Sleeping Angel**[291] 1659 3-8-4 0 ChrisCatlin 1
(David Evans) *a in last trio: t.o* **100/1**
**12** *½* **Proper Job**[17] 6-10-0 0 (p) JohnFahy 10
(Polly Gundry) *s.s: mostly in last and sn struggling: t.o* **100/1**
1m 38.42s (0.22) **Going Correction** 0.0s/f (Stan)
**WFA** 3 from 5yo+ 19lb **12 Ran SP% 118.1**
Speed ratings (Par 103): **98,97,96,95,94 91,91,87,87,79 68,67**
CSF £243.36 TOTE £2.30: £1.10, £13.60, £1.30; EX 126.70 Trifecta £997.30.
**Owner** Saeed Manana **Bred** S A R L Srl **Trained** Newmarket, Suffolk

**FOCUS**
Not a huge amount of strength in depth in this maiden, but a few had shown ability beforehand. The form isn't entirely convincing with the runner-up a big price and the seventh seemingly overperforming as well.

## 469 CORAL.CO.UK (S) H'CAP 1m 2f (P)
**2:30** (2:30) (Class 6) (0-60,59) 4-Y-O+ **£2,045** (£603; £302) **Stalls** Low

Form RPR
415- **1** **Litmus (USA)**[47] 8341 5-9-3 54 (b) LukeMorris 5 61
(Simon Dow) *t.k.h: trckd ldr: rdn to ld narrowly jst over 2f out: idled and hdd ins fnl f: hrd drvn and led again last 75yds* **7/1**
00-0 **2** *¾* **Ogaritmo**[18] 210 5-9-7 58 (t) AdamKirby 1 64
(Seamus Durack) *trckd ldng pair: nt qckn 3f out and 2 l to make up after: drvn over 1f out: styd on ins fnl f to take 2nd post* **6/1**
25-3 **3** *hd* **Derfenna Art (IRE)**[29] 67 5-9-7 58 (t) GeorgeBaker 8 63
(Seamus Durack) *broke wl: led at mod pce: pressed and kicked on 3f out: narrowly hdd jst over 2f out: kpt on to ld again ins fnl f: hdd and no ex last 75yds: lost 2nd post* **9/4**[1]
250- **4** *¾* **Legal Legacy**[69] 8072 8-8-10 52 (p) LouisSteward(5) 4 56
(Lee Carter) *hld up in 4th: nt qckn whn pce lifted 3f out: rdn over 1f out: styd on ins fnl f: gaining at fin* **5/1**[3]
00-0 **5** *2 ½* **Mohair**[20] 185 5-8-8 45 HayleyTurner 3 44
(Tony Carroll) *hld up and sn in last: outpcd fr 3f out: rdn over 1f out: one pce and no prog* **10/1**
40-0 **6** *¾* **Great Conquest (USA)**[12] 289 4-8-12 57 JohnLawson(7) 7 54
(Jamie Osborne) *s.s: in tch on outer: clsd up 4f out: outpcd fr 3f out: sn btn* **3/1**[2]
2m 8.0s (1.40) **Going Correction** 0.0s/f (Stan)
**WFA** 4 from 5yo+ 1lb **6 Ran SP% 108.3**
Speed ratings (Par 101): **94,93,93,92,90 90**
CSF £43.24 CT £109.57 TOTE £5.00: £2.70, £3.10; EX 20.00 Trifecta £35.10.There was no bid for the winner.
**Owner** T G Parker **Bred** Millsec Ltd **Trained** Epsom, Surrey

**FOCUS**
A weak selling handicap in which the pace steadied at about halfway. The winner has been rated as running a small personal best.

## 470 COMPARE BOOKMAKERS AT BOOKMAKERS.CO.UK H'CAP 5f 6y(P)
**3:00** (3:02) (Class 5) (0-70,70) 4-Y-O+ **£2,726** (£805; £402) **Stalls** High

Form RPR
3-21 **1** **Roy's Legacy**[11] 313 5-8-11 63 MichaelJMMurphy(3) 8 77
(Shaun Harris) *fast away fr wd draw: mde all: drvn over 1f out: styd on wl* **10/1**
2-05 **2** *1 ¾* **Secret Millionaire (IRE)**[12] 296 7-8-13 62 LukeMorris 5 69
(Tony Carroll) *chsd ldrs: hrd rdn to go 2nd over 1f out: styd on but nvr able to chal* **11/4**[1]

0-62 **3** 1 1/2 **Alnoomaas (IRE)**[11] 312 5-8-12 **66**........................ GeorgeDowning(5) 2 68
(Luke Dace) *sltly awkward s: hld up in last trio: shuffled along over 1f out: kpt on to take 3rd ins fnl f: nrst fin* **3/1**[2]

004- **4** 1 1/4 **Ask The Guru**[89] 7783 4-9-6 **69**........................(v) JimCrowley 7 67
(Michael Attwater) *trapped out wd: chsd wnr over 3f out to over 1f out: fdd* **8/1**

-231 **5** 1/2 **Only Ten Per Cent (IRE)**[14] 272 6-9-6 **69**..............(v) FrederikTylicki 1 65
(J R Jenkins) *hld up in last trio: shkn up and no prog over 1f out: one pce after* **3/1**[2]

22-4 **6** 1 1/4 **Mossgo (IRE)**[27] 87 4-8-13 **62**........................(t) HayleyTurner 3 53
(John Best) *chsd wnr to over 3f out: shkn up 2f out: wknd on inner over 1f out* **9/2**[3]

0-05 **7** 3 1/4 **Billy Red**[20] 191 10-9-7 **70**........................(b) JoeFanning 6 50
(J R Jenkins) *sltly awkward s: a in last trio: shkn up and no prog 2f out: wknd 1f out* **33/1**

57.94s (-0.86) **Going Correction** 0.0s/f (Stan) **7** Ran SP% **118.0**
Speed ratings (Par 103): **106,103,100,98,98 96,90**
CSF £39.42 CT £106.10 TOTE £6.80: £2.10, £2.60; EX 33.80 Trifecta £198.50.
**Owner** K Blackwell Steve Mohammed & Stew Rowley **Bred** A Christou **Trained** Carburton, Notts

**FOCUS**
A competitive sprint handicap. The form has been rated slightly positively, the winner being rated close to his old best, the runner-up close to last January's form and the third in line with his recent 6f form.

## 471 32RED H'CAP 1m 7f 169y(P)
**3:30** (3:30) (Class 5) (0-75,75) 4-Y-0+ **£2,726** (£805; £402) **Stalls Low**

Form RPR

605- **1** **King's Request (IRE)**[36] 8447 4-8-10 **63**........................ LiamJones 7 72
(Laura Mongan) *trckd ldrs: rdn and prog to ld wl over 2f out: drvn for home sn after: styd on wl fnl f* **11/4**[2]

115- **2** 3 1/2 **Bramshill Lass**[68] 8089 5-9-10 **71**........................ JimCrowley 8 76
(Amanda Perrett) *wl in tch: reminder and prog 3f out: chsd wnr 2f out: tried to cl over 1f out: styd on but no imp* **6/1**

00-2 **3** 2 3/4 **While You Wait (IRE)**[20] 186 5-9-11 **72**..................(v[1]) GeorgeBaker 5 74
(Gary Moore) *hld up in last: stl only 7th over 2f out: prog on outer after: drvn to take 3rd 1f out: no ch to threaten ldng pair* **2/1**[1]

1 **4** 1 1/4 **Kettlewell**[4] 150 5-10-0 **75**........................(t) LiamKeniry 1 75
(Warren Greatrex) *hld up in rr: rdn and struggling over 3f out: kpt on one pce fnl 2f: no ch* **10/1**

00/- **5** *hd* **Princely Hero (IRE)**[40] 7077 10-8-9 **56** oh1..................(p) LukeMorris 4 56
(Chris Gordon) *trckd ldrs: rdn fr over 6f out: outpcd over 2f out: kpt on same pce after* **66/1**

52-5 **6** 1 1/2 **Eshtyaaq**[33] 16 7-9-12 **73**........................ AdamKirby 6 71
(David Evans) *led at mod pce: rdn and hdd over 4f out: styd pressing tl outpcd 2f out: fdd fnl f* **9/2**[3]

2-61 **7** 7 **A Little Bit Dusty**[18] 209 6-9-11 **72**........................(p) HayleyTurner 3 62
(Conor Dore) *trckd ldr: led over 4f out gng wl: hdd wl over 2f out: wknd rapidly over 1f out* **20/1**

10-5 **8** 45 **Honourable Knight (IRE)**[20] 182 6-9-9 **70**........................ DavidProbert 2
(Mark Usher) *a in rr: wknd wl over 3f out: t.o* **20/1**

3m 24.67s (-1.03) **Going Correction** 0.0s/f (Stan)
**WFA** 4 from 5yo+ 6lb **8** Ran SP% **112.6**
Speed ratings (Par 103): **102,100,98,98,98 97,93,71**
CSF £18.64 CT £38.23 TOTE £5.10: £1.60, £2.80, £1.10; EX 31.40 Trifecta £83.50.
**Owner** Mrs P J Sheen **Bred** Runnymede Farm Inc And Catesby W Clay **Trained** Epsom, Surrey

**FOCUS**
The front two pulled clear in this moderate staying handicap. The winner has been rated slightly above his previous best, with the runner-up close to form.

## 472 LADBROKES H'CAP 7f 1y(P)
**4:00** (4:00) (Class 4) (0-85,85) 4-Y-0+ **£5,369** (£1,597; £798; £399) **Stalls High**

Form RPR

6-40 **1** **Corporal Maddox**[6] 372 7-9-7 **85**........................(p) LukeMorris 3 93
(Ronald Harris) *trckd ldrs: cl up 2f out: rdn to ld over 1f out: drvn and styd on wl fnl f* **10/1**

00-1 **2** 1 1/4 **Nassau Storm**[13] 287 5-9-6 **84**........................ AndreaAtzeni 7 89+
(William Knight) *hld up in last: stl there over 1f out: prog fnl f: r.o to take 2nd last strides: too much to do* **6/4**[1]

423- **3** *hd* **Malaysian Boleh**[104] 7462 4-8-10 **74**........................ HayleyTurner 4 78
(Simon Dow) *stdd s: t.k.h: hld up in 5th: prog towards inner over 1f out gng strly: wnt 2nd ins fnl f: cajoled along and nt qckn: lost 2nd last strides* **12/1**

56-2 **4** 1 1/2 **Intomist (IRE)**[22] 161 5-8-2 **71**........................(p) NathanAlison(5) 2 71
(Jim Boyle) *chsd ldr 1f: struggling fr 3f out and lost pl: kpt on same pce over 1f out* **10/1**

00-0 **5** 2 3/4 **Favourite Treat (USA)**[17] 235 4-9-7 **85**........................ JoeFanning 1 78
(Mark Johnston) *mde most to over 1f out: wknd fnl f* **9/4**[2]

-020 **6** 1 3/4 **Al's Memory (IRE)**[17] 234 5-9-2 **80**........................ AdamKirby 5 68
(David Evans) *chsd ldr after 1f: shkn up over 2f out: drvn and wknd jst over 1f out* **6/1**[3]

1m 23.78s (-1.02) **Going Correction** 0.0s/f (Stan) **6** Ran SP% **110.9**
Speed ratings (Par 105): **105,103,103,101,98 96**
CSF £25.04 TOTE £9.60: £3.40, £1.70; EX 32.10 Trifecta £148.20.
**Owner** Robert & Nina Bailey **Bred** Theobalds Stud **Trained** Earlswood, Monmouths

**FOCUS**
A fair handicap although the pace was only modest. The winner was always well placed and has been rated slightly up on his autumn form, while the runner-up has been rated a length off his summer turf form.

## 473 32RED.COM H'CAP 1m 2f (P)
**4:30** (4:30) (Class 5) (0-70,70) 3-Y-0 **£2,726** (£805; £402) **Stalls High**

Form RPR

0-13 **1** **Starlight Princess (IRE)**[4] 404 3-9-3 **66**..................(b) JohnFahy 7 71
(J S Moore) *dwlt: hld up in last while rest battled it out up front: stl last 2f out: prog on outer over 1f out: led jst ins fnl f: drvn and styd on* **7/1**

04-3 **2** 1 **Frederic Chopin**[17] 236 3-8-8 **57**........................ SeanLevey 5 60
(Stuart Williams) *j. off promly but sn settled in rr: prog on outer over 2f out gng wl: drvn to chal and upsides 1f out: styd on but jst outpcd* **7/4**[1]

3-23 **3** 3/4 **Big Kenny**[19] 198 3-9-0 **63**........................ AdamKirby 2 65
(David Evans) *sn settled towards rr: rdn over 2f out: prog on inner over 1f out: styd on but nvr gng pce to chal* **6/1**[3]

65-0 **4** 1/2 **Officer Drivel (IRE)**[11] 316 3-9-2 **70**........................ GeorgeDowning(5) 4 71
(Luke Dace) *hld up in 6th: rapid prog on outer to ld 6f out: drvn over 2f out: hdd and one pce jst ins fnl f* **20/1**

41-2 **5** 2 1/2 **Aramadyh**[8] 357 3-9-5 **68**........................(p) LukeMorris 3 64
(James Tate) *bustled up to go prom: drvn 4f out: struggling over 2f out: plugged on one pce after* **5/2**[2]

00-1 **6** 11 **Pacquita**[14] 267 3-8-5 **54**........................ JoeFanning 6 28
(Mark Johnston) *led after 1f tl 6f out: pressed ldr tl wknd rapidly over 1f out* **7/1**

0-50 **7** 1/2 **Appellez Baileys (FR)**[15] 254 3-8-5 **54**........................(p) LiamJones 1 27
(Chris Dwyer) *set out to ld but hdd after 1f: nvr gng wl after: wknd qckly 2f out* **33/1**

2m 6.24s (-0.36) **Going Correction** 0.0s/f (Stan) **7** Ran SP% **111.9**
Speed ratings (Par 97): **101,100,99,99,97 88,88**
CSF £18.88 CT £76.90 TOTE £8.10: £3.30, £1.50; EX 25.20 Trifecta £83.00.
**Owner** J S Moore **Bred** Coleman Bloodstock Limited **Trained** Upper Lambourn, Berks

**FOCUS**
An interesting 3yo handicap in which the first three all came from the rear. The fourth has been rated to form and the third to his Southwell form.
T/Jkpt: Not won. T/Plt: £59.70 to a £1 stake. Pool of £103801.47 - 1267.92 winning tickets. T/Qpdt: £31.20 to a £1 stake. Pool of £5406.99 - 127.90 winning tickets. JN

# 383 SOUTHWELL (L-H)
Tuesday, February 4

**OFFICIAL GOING: Standard**
Wind: Fresh across Weather: Fine and dry

## 474 CORAL MOBILE "JUST THREE CLICKS TO BET" AMATEUR RIDERS' H'CAP (DIV I) 1m 3f (F)
**1:10** (1:10) (Class 6) (0-52,52) 4-Y-0+ **£1,975** (£607; £303) **Stalls Low**

Form RPR

406- **1** **Light The City (IRE)**[40] 7151 7-10-8 **46** oh1.............. MissSBrotherton 6 62
(Ruth Carr) *trckd ldrs: hdwy over 5f out: cl up 4f out: led 3f out: sn pushed clr: readily* **3/1**[2]

406- **2** 9 **Mister Frosty (IRE)**[53] 8270 8-11-0 **52**........................ MrPCollington 4 53
(Michael Squance) *dwlt and in rr: hdwy 1/2-way: chsd ldrs 4f out: rdn along 3f out: styd on to chse wnr wl over 1f out: sn no imp* **6/4**[1]

06-5 **3** 8 **Goldmadchen (GER)**[12] 303 6-10-12 **50**........................ MrJHamilton 5 37
(James Given) *led: rdn along 4f out: hdd 3f out: sn drvn and grad wknd* **5/1**[3]

0/0- **4** 13 **Kozmina Bay**[46] 2828 5-10-7 **50**........................(b) SeanBowen(5) 8 15
(Bernard Llewellyn) *towards rr: rdn along and outpcd after 4f: hdwy over 3f out: plugged on fnl 2f: nvr a factor* **12/1**

0/0- **5** 1 **Mister Fantastic**[48] 6102 8-10-1 **46**........................ MissSLewis(7) 7 9
(Dai Burchell) *midfield: rdn along 1/2-way: sn outpcd* **50/1**

0-05 **6** 1/2 **Marvo**[13] 281 10-10-9 **47**........................(b) MrSWalker 9 9
(Bernard Llewellyn) *hld up towards rr: hdwy over 6f out: chsd ldng pair 4f out: rdn along 3f out: sn swtchd wd and drvn: sn outpcd* **8/1**

335- **7** 11 **Naughtybychoice**[37] 8436 4-10-6 **51**........................(v) MissHDukes(5) 2
(Ollie Pears) *chsd ldng pair: pushed along 1/2-way: sn lost pl and bhd fnl 3f* **7/1**

/450 **8** 17 **Kneesy Earsy Nosey**[8] 353 8-10-1 **46** oh1(p) MissCharlotteCooper(7) 3
(Ann Stokell) *chsd ldrs: rdn along 1/2-way: sn outpcd and bhd fnl 3f* **100/1**

000/ **9** 66 **Ellies Girl (IRE)**[598] 3143 6-10-3 **46** oh1........................ MrPJohn(5) 1
(Ronald Harris) *cl up: rdn along bef 1/2-way: sn lost pl and bhd: t.o fnl 3f* **50/1**

2m 30.08s (2.08) **Going Correction** +0.15s/f (Slow)
**WFA** 4 from 5yo+ 2lb **9** Ran SP% **117.9**
Speed ratings (Par 101): **98,91,85,76,75 75,67,54,6**
CSF £8.06 CT £21.21 TOTE £3.00: £1.60, £1.10, £2.00; EX 13.20 Trifecta £31.30.
**Owner** Mrs Ruth A Carr **Bred** Rabbah Bloodstock Limited **Trained** Huby, N Yorks

**FOCUS**
A desperately weak opener. The winner has been in good form over jumps though and the runner-up had been given a chance by the handicapper.

## 475 CORAL MOBILE "JUST THREE CLICKS TO BET" AMATEUR RIDERS' H'CAP (DIV II) 1m 3f (F)
**1:40** (1:40) (Class 6) (0-52,52) 4-Y-0+ **£1,975** (£607; £303) **Stalls Low**

Form RPR

050- **1** **Samoset**[53] 8270 4-10-13 **52**........................ MrSWalker 2 61
(Alan Swinbank) *hld up in tch: hdwy over 4f out: cl up 3f out: led 2f out: sn rdn and wandered over 1f out: edgd lft ent fnl f: kpt on* **6/4**[1]

54-0 **2** 2 1/4 **Reach The Beach**[16] 247 5-10-4 **46**..................(v[1]) JennyPowell(5) 5 51
(Brendan Powell) *trckd ldrs: hdwy over 3f out: rdn to chse ldng pair over 2f out: kpt on fnl f: tk 2nd nr fin* **5/1**[3]

600- **3** 1/2 **Josie's Dream (IRE)**[76] 7984 6-10-9 **51**.............. MrJamesHughes(5) 7 55
(Jo Hughes) *prom: cl up 4f out: led 3f out: sn rdn and hdd 2f out: edgd lft over 1f out: drvn and hld whn n.m.r ent fnl f: one pce* **7/1**

000- **4** 14 **Kingaroo (IRE)**[53] 8270 8-10-10 **47**........................ MissSBrotherton 6 28
(Garry Woodward) *led: pushed along over 4f out: rdn and hdd 3f out: sn drvn and wknd* **9/2**[2]

063- **5** 2 1/4 **Drummond**[36] 6457 5-10-8 **50**........................(tp) SeanBowen(5) 4 27
(Bernard Llewellyn) *prom: rdn along over 3f out: drvn and outpcd fr over 2f out* **8/1**

0-25 **6** 3 3/4 **Loulou Vuitton**[21] 176 4-10-6 **45**........................(p) FreddieMitchell 1 15
(Steph Hollinshead) *in tch: pushed along 5f out: rdn over 3f out: sn outpcd* **8/1**

056- **7** 2 1/2 **Heading To First**[92] 3637 7-10-3 **45**........................(p) MissMBryant(5) 9 11
(Paddy Butler) *towards rr: pushed along over 4f out: rdn over 3f out and sn outpcd* **25/1**

505/ **8** 15 **Converti**[569] 6051 10-10-4 **48**........................ MissHHeal(7) 3
(Carroll Gray) *sn rdn along in rr: outpcd and bhd fr 1/2-way* **33/1**

2m 32.63s (4.63) **Going Correction** +0.15s/f (Slow)
**WFA** 4 from 5yo+ 2lb **8** Ran SP% **116.4**
Speed ratings (Par 101): **89,87,87,76,75 72,70,59**
CSF £9.47 CT £40.39 TOTE £2.40: £1.20, £2.60, £1.60; EX 12.10 Trifecta £67.10.
**Owner** Arnold Headdock & Mrs Kath Headdock **Bred** Arnold Headdock & Mrs Kath Headdock **Trained** Melsonby, N Yorks

**FOCUS**
Hard to envisage a weaker handicap. The third has been rated close to form.

## 476 CORAL APP DOWNLOAD FROM THE APP STORE H'CAP 1m 4f (F)
2:10 (2:11) (Class 5) (0-70,69) 4-Y-0+ £2,911 (£866; £432; £216) Stalls Low

Form RPR
00-3 **1** **Blades Lad**[15] 253 5-9-7 **68**........................ GrahamLee 7 76
(Peter Niven) *trckd ldng pair: hdwy over 3f out: effrt over 2f out: rdn and edgd lft over 1f out: drvn and styd on to ld ins fnl f: r.o* **11/4**[1]
03-1 **2** *2* **Candyman Can (IRE)**[25] 115 4-9-4 **68**........................ PaddyAspell 3 73
(Dominic Ffrench Davis) *chsd ldr: hdwy over 3f out: rdn to chal 2f out: drvn over 1f out and ev ch tl kpt on same pce ins fnl f* **7/2**[2]
4110 **3** *3/4* **Grandad Mac**[12] 303 6-9-4 **65**........................ RussKennemore 4 69
(Alan Coogan) *pushed along s and sn led: rdn clr over 3f out: jnd 2f out: sn drvn and edgd rt over 1f out: hdd ins fnl f: kpt on same pce* **5/1**
/0-1 **4** *10* **Luctor Emergo (IRE)**[7] 361 5-9-8 **69** 6ex........................(p) TomEaves 2 57
(Keith Dalgleish) *trckd ldrs: pushed along 4f out: rdn along 3f out: sn drvn and outpcd* **7/2**[2]
316- **5** *1 3/4* **Bold And Free**[39] 7881 4-8-5 **62**........................ RobJFitzpatrick(7) 6 47
(David Thompson) *hld up in tch: pushed along over 4f out: rdn along and outpcd over 3f out* **9/2**[3]
50-0 **6** *20* **Arashi**[15] 253 8-9-1 **62**........................(v) DaleSwift 8 15
(Derek Shaw) *help in rr: pushed along over 4f out: rdn along over 3f out and sn bhd* **16/1**

2m 42.32s (1.32) **Going Correction** +0.15s/f (Slow)
**WFA** 4 from 5yo+ 3lb **6 Ran SP% 111.8**
Speed ratings (Par 103): **101,99,99,92,91 78**
CSF £12.50 CT £43.21 TOTE £3.30: £1.40, £1.80; EX 14.00 Trifecta £95.00.
**Owner** Crown Select **Bred** David Holgate **Trained** Barton-le-Street, N Yorks

**FOCUS**
This competitive, if very moderate affair saw a gritty performance from the winner. Straightforward form with the winner back to his best, the runner-up close to his turf best, and the third to his recent form.

## 477 BEST ODDS AT BOOKMAKERS.CO.UK MAIDEN STKS 6f (F)
2:40 (2:42) (Class 5) 3-Y-0+ £3,067 (£905; £453) Stalls Low

Form RPR
42-2 **1** **Bretherton**[22] 159 3-8-12 70........................(b1) GrahamLee 9 87+
(Richard Fahey) *trckd ldrs: smooth hdwy 3f out: cl up 2f out: led wl over 1f out: sn clr: easily* **5/4**[1]
2-3 **2** *9* **Jaeger Train (IRE)**[29] 70 3-8-7 0........................(v1) JoeyHaynes(5) 4 60
(K R Burke) *cl up: rdn to ld 2f out: drvn and hdd wl over 1f out: kpt on same pce* **9/2**[3]
0-2 **3** *1/2* **Royal Encounter**[18] 218 3-8-12 0........................ JimmyQuinn 1 59
(Ed Vaughan) *cl up on inner: led after 2f: rdn along and hdd 2f out: sn drvn and kpt on same pce* **7/2**[2]
00/ **4** *3 1/2* **Spowarticus**[483] 6965 5-9-6 0........................ MatthewHopkins(7) 8 52
(Scott Dixon) *slt ld 2f: cl up: rdn along 3f out: drvn over 2f out and grad wknd* **100/1**
24-5 **5** *5* **Hot Stock (FR)**[11] 311 3-8-12 62........................ BenCurtis 10 33
(Jo Hughes) *cl up: rdn along wl over 2f out: sn wknd* **6/1**
40- **6** *3 1/4* **Ventura Reef (IRE)**[35] 8451 3-8-5 0........................ JoshQuinn(7) 11 23
(Richard Fahey) *a in rr* **33/1**
00- **7** *1* **Trefnant (IRE)**[112] 7261 3-8-2 0........................ ShelleyBirkett(5) 3 15
(Chris Dwyer) *in tch: rdn along over 3f out: sn wknd* **100/1**
50-5 **8** *1/2* **Beatabout The Bush (IRE)**[13] 284 3-8-12 57........................ TomQueally 2 19
(Charles Hills) *towards rr rdn along 1/2-way: sn outpcd* **14/1**
**9** *2* **Incurs Four Faults** 3-8-12 0........................ TomEaves 7 13
(Keith Dalgleish) *s.i.s: a bhd* **12/1**
00/0 **10** *1/2* **Saktoon (USA)**[8] 353 6-9-8 45........................(v) DaleSwift 5
(Derek Shaw) *a in rr* **100/1**
**11** *7* **Robbian** 3-8-12 0........................ AndrewMullen 6
(Charles Smith) *dwlt: a bhd* **100/1**

1m 16.37s (-0.13) **Going Correction** +0.15s/f (Slow)
**WFA** 3 from 5yo+ 15lb **11 Ran SP% 120.4**
Speed ratings (Par 103): **106,94,93,88,82 77,76,75,73,72 63**
CSF £7.39 TOTE £2.30: £1.20, £1.30, £1.40; EX 8.40 Trifecta £16.90.
**Owner** David W Armstrong **Bred** J & Mrs S Davis **Trained** Musley Bank, N Yorks

**FOCUS**
This moderate maiden was turned into a procession. The time was good and the winner has improved, although it's hard to know by how much, with the form far from solid in behind.

## 478 BOOKMAKERS.CO.UK (S) STKS 5f (F)
3:10 (3:11) (Class 6) 4-Y-0+ £2,264 (£673; £336; £168) Stalls High

Form RPR
3-02 **1** **Electric Qatar**[11] 318 5-8-12 69........................(p) StephenCraine 5 72
(Tom Dascombe) *qckly away and mde all: jnd and rdn wl over 1f out: drvn ent fnl f: kpt on wl towards fin* **11/4**[1]
0-33 **2** *1 1/4* **Angelo Poliziano**[14] 272 8-8-12 62........................(bt) BenCurtis 1 68
(Jo Hughes) *trckd ldrs: hdwy and cl up 2f out: rdn to chal over 1f out: ev ch tl drvn and no ex wl ins fnl f* **7/2**[3]
60-2 **3** *2* **Heartsong (IRE)**[14] 272 5-8-2 60........................ JoeyHaynes(5) 4 55+
(John Gallagher) *dwlt: sn pushed along towards rr: hdwy over 2f out: sn rdn and kpt on appr fnl f* **3/1**[2]
0-43 **4** *8* **Jiminy**[12] 298 4-8-5 49........................(p) MatthewHopkins(7) 8 32
(Scott Dixon) *prom: rdn 2f out: drvn and wknd over 1f out* **16/1**
03/4 **5** *1 1/4* **Dissent (IRE)**[14] 272 5-8-12 60........................ GrahamLee 2 27
(James Given) *prom: rdn along 2f out: sn drvn and wknd* **6/1**
30-0 **6** *1* **Fathom Five (IRE)**[30] 59 10-8-10 58........................ AlexHopkinson(7) 7 28
(Shaun Harris) *chsd ldrs: rdn along 2f out: sn wknd and wl hld whn n.m.r ent fnl f* **20/1**
0-00 **7** *1 3/4* **Imperial Spirit**[20] 192 4-8-5 50........................(b) JosephineGordon(7) 9 17
(Jo Hughes) *prom: rdn along 1/2-way: sn wknd* **33/1**
00-6 **8** *shd* **Spic 'n Span**[14] 272 9-8-12 54........................(b) WilliamCarson 3 17
(Ronald Harris) *slowly away and sn swtchd lft: a bhd* **33/1**
3-40 **9** *3 3/4* **Quality Art (USA)**[14] 272 6-9-0 62........................ BillyCray(3) 6 8
(Richard Guest) *dwlt: a in rr* **8/1**

1m 1.32s (1.62) **Going Correction** +0.35s/f (Slow) **9 Ran SP% 115.8**
Speed ratings (Par 101): **101,99,95,83,81 79,76,76,70**
CSF £12.38 TOTE £3.00: £1.10, £1.80, £1.90; EX 10.60 Trifecta £27.90.The winner was bought in for 5,250gns.
**Owner** A Black & Owen Promotions Limited **Bred** Miss Nicola Kent **Trained** Malpas, Cheshire

**FOCUS**
A strongly run seller, dominated by those towards the head of the market. The runner-up has been rated close to his latest C&D form.

## 479 COMPARE BOOKMAKERS AT BOOKMAKERS.CO.UK H'CAP 6f (F)
3:40 (3:40) (Class 4) (0-85,85) 4-Y-0+ £5,175 (£1,540; £769; £384) Stalls Low

Form RPR
6-41 **1** **Abi Scarlet (IRE)**[12] 297 5-8-4 **71** oh1........................ RyanPowell(3) 7 85
(Hughie Morrison) *trckd ldng pair on outer: hdwy 2f out: rdn over 1f out: led last 100yds: styd on wl* **8/1**
02-5 **2** *2 1/4* **Pearl Nation (USA)**[23] 153 5-8-12 **76**........................ GrahamLee 2 83
(Brian Baugh) *chsd ldrs on inner: hdwy 2f out: rdn over 1f out: drvn and ev ch ins fnl f: kpt on same pce* **9/4**[1]
3-12 **3** *nk* **Hannahs Turn**[21] 175 4-9-2 **85**........................ ShelleyBirkett(5) 3 91
(Chris Dwyer) *led: rdn clr over 2f out: drvn appr fnl f: hdd & wknd last 100yds* **11/4**[3]
1-31 **4** *nk* **Mappin Time (IRE)**[15] 257 6-8-10 **79**........................(be) AdamCarter(5) 4 84
(Tim Easterby) *hld up: hdwy 2f out: rdn over 1f out: styng on wl whn n.m.r and hmpd ins fnl f: swtchd rt and kpt on wl towards fin* **5/2**[2]
1-44 **5** *6* **Fortinbrass (IRE)**[15] 257 4-8-8 **75**........................ BillyCray(3) 5 61
(John Balding) *in tch and sn pushed along: rdn wl over 2f out: no hdwy* **7/1**
500- **6** *3/4* **Tyfos**[189] 4852 9-9-4 **82**........................ AndrewMullen 6 65
(Brian Baugh) *chsd ldr: rdn over 2f out: sn drvn and wknd* **50/1**
0-06 **7** *4 1/2* **Fratellino**[14] 271 7-8-13 **84**........................(t) NatalieHambling-Yates(7) 8 53
(Alan McCabe) *s.i.s: a bhd* **20/1**

1m 16.2s (-0.30) **Going Correction** +0.15s/f (Slow) **7 Ran SP% 116.3**
Speed ratings (Par 105): **108,105,104,104,96 95,89**
CSF £27.26 CT £63.49 TOTE £9.50: £3.30, £1.90; EX 38.70 Trifecta £158.90.
**Owner** H Morrison **Bred** Henry O'Callaghan **Trained** East Ilsley, Berks

**FOCUS**
A hotly contested feature. The runner-up, who was well backed, has been rated to form, with the third to her latest 5f effort.

## 480 32RED MAIDEN H'CAP 1m (F)
4:10 (4:11) (Class 6) (0-55,52) 3-Y-0 £2,264 (£673; £336; £168) Stalls Low

Form RPR
-333 **1** **Day Star Lad**[14] 267 3-9-7 **52**........................(v) DaleSwift 7 61
(Derek Shaw) *trckd ldrs: cl up 3f out: led 2f out: rdn and hung bdly rt over 1f out: drvn out* **5/2**[1]
00-6 **2** *3/4* **Beastfromtheeast**[15] 254 3-9-0 **45**........................(b1) GrahamLee 2 52
(Ed Walker) *hld up: hdwy 3f out: rdn wl over 1f out: styd on to chse wnr ins fnl f: kpt on* **5/1**[2]
000- **3** *3 1/2* **Emerald Breeze (IRE)**[176] 5352 3-9-0 **45**........................(p) StevieDonohoe 12 44
(Tim Pitt) *cl up: swtchd lft and led after 2f: rdn along 3f out: hdd 2f out: sn drvn and kpt on one pce appr fnl f* **20/1**
50-5 **4** *1/2* **Previous Acclaim (IRE)**[26] 98 3-9-5 **50**........................ AdamBeschizza 6 48
(Julia Feilden) *chsd ldrs: rdn along over 2f out: drvn over 1f out: kpt on fnl f* **25/1**
000- **5** *2 3/4* **Streethowlingmama (USA)**[136] 6654 3-8-11 **45**........ CharlesBishop(3) 5 37
(Olly Stevens) *chsd ldrs: effrt on inner over 2f out: sn rdn and no imp appr fnl f* **8/1**
00-6 **6** *3/4* **Mavree (IRE)**[15] 261 3-9-0 **45**........................(be) DuranFentiman 4 35
(Tim Easterby) *chsd ldrs: rdn along over 2f out: drvn wl over 1f out: sn one pce* **50/1**
53-0 **7** *nk* **Solent Lad (USA)**[21] 173 3-9-3 **48**........................(p) JimmyQuinn 11 37
(Robert Eddery) *s.i.s and bhd: hdwy over 3f out: rdn over 2f out: kpt on: nrst fin* **6/1**[3]
6-40 **8** *2 3/4* **Sunningdale Rose (IRE)**[18] 216 3-9-0 **50**........................ ShelleyBirkett(5) 13 33
(Gay Kelleway) *prom on wd outside: rdn along wl over 2f out: sn wknd* **20/1**
0-06 **9** *1 1/2* **Application**[14] 267 3-9-0 **45**........................(p) PaddyAspell 8 25
(Bryan Smart) *racd wd: led 2f: cl up: rdn along 3f out: wknd over 2f out* **16/1**
3-60 **10** *5* **Deano's Devil (IRE)**[12] 291 3-9-5 **50**........................ BarryMcHugh 3 18
(Richard Fahey) *a in rr* **8/1**
6-32 **11** *16* **Tortoise**[13] 280 3-8-12 **46**........................(be) BillyCray(3) 9
(Richard Guest) *dwlt: wd and bhd st* **10/1**
5 **12** *54* **The Moat Field (IRE)**[15] 261 3-9-0 **45**........................(b1) TomQueally 1
(Michael J Browne, Ire) *sn outpcd and wl bhd fr 1/2-way* **8/1**

1m 46.02s (2.32) **Going Correction** +0.15s/f (Slow) **12 Ran SP% 123.2**
Speed ratings (Par 95): **94,93,89,89,86 85,85,82,81,76 60,6**
CSF £14.26 CT £217.22 TOTE £2.50: £1.30, £2.30, £8.70; EX 17.40 Trifecta £472.50.
**Owner** Brian Johnson (Northamptonshire) **Bred** Mrs S J Somner **Trained** Sproxton, Leics

**FOCUS**
A race littered with frustrating and mainly disappointing types. Little solid, although the winner has been going okay of late and the runner-up had blinkers on for the first time.

## 481 32RED.COM H'CAP 5f (F)
4:40 (4:40) (Class 6) (0-60,60) 3-Y-0 £2,264 (£673; £336; £168) Stalls High

Form RPR
0-03 **1** **Wiki Tiki**[6] 374 3-9-2 **55**........................(t) AdamBeschizza 3 68
(Stuart Williams) *trckd ldrs: pushed along and sltly outpcd 1/2-way: hdwy wl over 1f out: swtchd lft and rdn to chal ent fnl f: sn led and kpt on strly* **3/1**[2]
-212 **2** *2 1/2* **Argent Touch**[18] 216 3-9-7 **60**........................ DaleSwift 2 64
(Derek Shaw) *trckd ldrs: hdwy on outer 1/2-way: rdn to chal wl over 1f out: led jst over 1f out: sn drvn and edgd rt: hdd ins fnl f: one pce* **2/1**[1]
140- **3** *1/2* **Fuel Injection**[141] 6467 3-9-7 **60**........................(p) TomQueally 8 62
(Paul Midgley) *racd nr stands' rail: cl up: rdn wl over 1f out and ev ch tl drvn and one pce ins fnl f* **16/1**
3-56 **4** *4 1/2* **Anfield**[18] 213 3-8-13 **52**........................ WilliamCarson 1 38
(Mick Quinn) *led: rdn along over 2f out: drvn and hdd wl over 1f out: hld whn nt mch room and swtchd lft ent fnl f* **14/1**
0-50 **5** *1/2* **Back On Baileys**[11] 315 3-8-9 **48**........................ BenCurtis 5 32
(Chris Dwyer) *prom: rdn along 1/2-way: sn outpcd* **25/1**
004- **6** *3/4* **The Boss Of Me**[150] 6213 3-9-2 **55**........................ TomEaves 7 37
(Kevin Ryan) *chsd ldr: cl up 1/2-way: sn rdn and wknd over 1f out: btn whn n.m.r ent fnl f* **5/1**
661- **7** *1 1/2* **Kinkohyo**[60] 8188 3-9-0 **56**........................ GeorgeChaloner(3) 4 32
(Bryan Smart) *awkward s: sn rdn along and a in rr* **16/1**
0-30 **8** *8* **Rebel Code (USA)**[15] 261 3-9-0 **53**........................(b1) GrahamLee 6
(James Given) *awkward and hung lft ins first f: sn rdn along in rr: bhd and eased fr 1/2-way* **4/1**[3]

1m 2.06s (2.36) **Going Correction** +0.35s/f (Slow) **8 Ran SP% 117.3**
Speed ratings (Par 95): **95,91,90,83,82 81,78,65**
CSF £9.72 CT £80.96 TOTE £4.70: £1.50, £1.10, £3.50; EX 10.80 Trifecta £111.10.


The Form Book, Raceform Ltd, Newbury, RG14 5SJ

**Owner** J W Parry **Bred** Newsells Park Stud **Trained** Newmarket, Suffolk
**FOCUS**
A fair race for the grade. The winner built on her latest promise and has been rated back to her 2yo best.
T/Plt: £11.20 to a £1 stake. Pool of £66243.24 - 4300.42 winning tickets. T/Qpdt: £6.00 to a £1 stake. Pool of £4663.39 - 567.0 winning tickets. JR

## 436 CAGNES-SUR-MER
Tuesday, February 4
**OFFICIAL GOING: Polytrack: standard**

### 482a PRIX DU BORD DE MER (MAIDEN) (3YO) (POLYTRACK) 1m 2f (D)
**2:50** (12:00) 3-Y-O **£10,000** (£4,000; £3,000; £2,000; £1,000)

RPR
1 **Dye Fore (USA)**[81] 3-9-2 0 ....................(b) IoritzMendizabal 6 77
(J-C Rouget, France) **9/10**[1]
2 2 **Flying Cape (IRE)**[5] 390 3-9-2 0 .................... ThomasMessina 12 73
(Andrew Hollinshead) *hld up towards rr on outer: rdn and hdwy fr 2f out: styd on and wnt 2nd ins fnl f: fin strly but no ch w easy wnr* **101/10**
3 1 ½ **General (FR)**[8] 360 3-9-2 0 .................... BriceRaballand 11 70
(S Kobayashi, France) **8/1**[3]
4 1 **Dragonstone (FR)** 3-8-11 0 .................... Francois-XavierBertras 9 63
(D De Watrigant, France) **10/1**
5 ¾ **Docteur Vigousse (FR)**[8] 360 3-8-10 0 ..........(p) StephaneLaurent(6) 5 67
(J Parize, France) **52/1**
6 nk **Peintre Setois (FR)** 3-9-2 0 .................... FranckForesi 2 66
(F Foresi, France) **15/1**
7 3 ½ **La Mer (FR)** 3-8-13 0 .................... FabienLefebvre 13 56
(Mme G Rarick, France) **57/1**
8 1 **Spaliburg Rosetgri (FR)** 3-8-8 0 .................... ValentinGambart(8) 7 57
(M Boutin, France) **161/10**
9 ½ **Virtual Money (FR)** 3-9-2 0 .................... DavidBreux 3 56
(G Botti, France) **63/1**
10 3 **Portulan (FR)** 3-9-2 0 .................... TonyPiccone 10 50
(Y Fertillet, France) **31/1**
11 2 ½ **Zeminenza (FR)** 3-8-8 0 .................... SylvainRuis 4 37
(J-M Capitte, France) **42/1**
12 5 **Lehena (FR)** 3-8-13 0 ....................(b) AntoineHamelin 1 32
(Matthieu Palussiere, France) **61/10**[2]
13 2 **Blanche Des Clos (FR)** 3-8-5 0 .................... MedhiChouit(8) 14 28
(J Heloury, France) **83/1**
2m 4.46s (124.46) **13 Ran SP% 119.8**
WIN (incl. 1 euro stake): 1.90. PLACES: 1.20, 2.20, 2.00. DF: 8.50. SF: 11.00.
**Owner** Joseph Allen **Bred** Joseph Allen **Trained** Pau, France

## 452 KEMPTON (A.W) (R-H)
Wednesday, February 5
**OFFICIAL GOING: Standard**
Wind: fresh to strong, behind Weather: dry after heavy blustery showers

### 483 BOOK NOW FOR JUMP RACING 22.02.14 H'CAP 5f (P)
**5:00** (5:02) (Class 7) (0-50,49) 4-Y-O+ **£1,617** (£481; £240; £120) **Stalls** Low

Form RPR
60-3 1 **Ishetoo**[23] 164 10-9-0 46 .................... SladeO'Hara(3) 4 53
(Peter Grayson) *hld up towards rr: clsng whn nt clr run over 1f out: gap opened 1f out and str run to ld fnl 75yds: r.o wl* **8/1**[3]
6043 2 nk **Vhujon (IRE)**[3] 449 9-9-2 45 .................... FergusSweeney 6 51
(Peter Grayson) *s.i.s: hld up in tch in rr: swtchd lft and effrt wl over 1f out: swtchd lft 1f out: hdwy w wnr and ev ch fnl 75yds: nvr looked like gng past wnr and a hld* **3/1**[1]
0-00 3 2 **Brandywell Boy (IRE)**[12] 313 11-8-11 45 ..........(b) JoshBaudains(5) 3 44
(Dominic Ffrench Davis) *sn rdn along: chsd ldrs: swtchd ins 1f out and sn chsng wnr: outpcd by ldng pair fnl 75yds* **14/1**
00-0 4 1 **Balatina**[26] 114 4-9-5 48 ....................[1] LiamKeniry 2 43
(Chris Dwyer) *led: drvn over 1f out: hdd fnl 75yds: sn outpcd and btn: wknd towards fin* **7/2**[2]
000- 5 1 ¾ **Jemimaville (IRE)**[40] 8413 7-8-13 45 ..........(v) RyanPowell(3) 7 34
(Giles Bravery) *chsd ldr tl unable qck u.p over 1f out: btn 1f out: wknd ins fnl f* **40/1**
0-00 6 2 ½ **Kaylee**[7] 370 5-8-12 48 ..........(bt[1]) DavidParkes(7) 8 28
(Brett Johnson) *t.k.h: hld up in midfield: hdwy to chse ldrs 1/2-way: rdn and hung rt into rival over 1f out: sn wknd* **20/1**
506- 7 2 ½ **Lady Rain**[153] 6145 5-9-2 45 .................... RichardKingscote 5 16
(Milton Bradley) *chsd ldrs: hung lft bnd after 1f and lost pl: bhd over 1f out* **10/1**
1m 1.36s (0.86) **Going Correction** +0.15s/f (Slow) **7 Ran SP% 81.3**
Speed ratings (Par 97): **99,98,95,93,90 86,82**
CSF £15.89 CT £89.45 TOTE £4.20: £2.60, £1.40; EX 8.10 Trifecta £40.90.
**Owner** Richard Teatum **Bred** Longdon Stud Ltd **Trained** Formby, Lancs
■ Fantasy Invader was withdrawn. Price at time of withdrawal 7/4F. Rule 4 applies to all bets - deduction of 35p in the pound
**FOCUS**
The late withdrawal of favourite Fantasy Invader, who was unruly in the stalls, changed the make-up of this race. In-form horses were thin on the ground in this weak handicap. The first two have been rated slightly up on recent figures.

### 484 MIX BUSINESS WITH PLEASURE AT KEMPTON H'CAP 1m 2f (P)
**5:30** (5:30) (Class 7) (0-50,50) 4-Y-O+ **£1,617** (£481; £240; £120) **Stalls** Low

Form RPR
000- 1 **Addikt (IRE)**[78] 7962 9-9-5 48 .................... TomEaves 4 57
(John Spearing) *hld up in tch in midfield: hdwy to trck ldrs and gng wl over 2f out: led over 1f out: sn rdn and qcknd clr w rival: hdd ins fnl f: r.o to ld again last stride* **9/2**[3]
2-32 2 shd **Polydamos**[6] 377 5-9-5 48 ....................(v[1]) LukeMorris 5 57
(Tony Carroll) *t.k.h: chsd ldrs: nt clr run and travelling strly over 2f out: gap opened and qcknd clr w wnr over 1f out: hrd drvn to ld ins fnl f: r.o but hdd last stride* **2/1**[1]
0-00 3 2 ¾ **Kindia (IRE)**[14] 281 6-9-2 45 ....................(v) AndreaAtzeni 10 49
(Michael Attwater) *stdd s: hld up in rr: swtchd lft and effrt wl over 1f out: hdwy on outer to chse clr ldng pair 1f out: r.o but nvr a threat* **25/1**
0-00 4 2 **Appyjack**[6] 377 6-9-2 45 ....................(b) LiamKeniry 8 45
(Tony Carroll) *stdd s: hld up in last trio: rdn over 2f out: no threat to ldng pair but styng on whn nt clr run over 1f out: hdwy to go 4th ins fnl f: kpt on but no threat to ldrs* **8/1**
0-06 5 4 **The Wonga Coup (IRE)**[14] 281 7-9-5 48 .................... FergusSweeney 3 40
(Pat Phelan) *hld up in tch in midfield: swtchd lft and effrt u.p over 1f out: sn outpcd by ldng pair and btn: wknd ins fnl f* **3/1**[2]
05-5 6 5 **Silver Fawn (IRE)**[4] 435 4-9-1 45 ....................(be) JimmyQuinn 7 27
(John Weymes) *t.k.h: hld up in tch in midfield: rdn and effrt 2f out: outpcd and btn over 1f out: wknd ins fnl f* **12/1**
5-06 7 ¾ **Total Obsession**[7] 368 7-9-7 50 ....................(v) RobertHavlin 9 30
(Mark Hoad) *chsd ldr: upsides and rdn over 2f out: drvn and outpcd over 1f out: sn wknd: no ch and eased wl ins fnl f: dismntd after fin* **33/1**
00-0 8 3 ½ **Guardi (IRE)**[7] 368 5-9-5 48 .................... JimCrowley 2 21
(Dean Ivory) *led: rdn 2f out: hdd over 1f out: sn btn and dropped out: wl btn and eased wl ins fnl f* **10/1**
/66- 9 9 **Somerton Star**[123] 7037 4-9-1 45 .................... JoeFanning 6
(Pat Eddery) *stdd s: sn in tch in midfield: rdn and struggling 3f out: lost pl and bhd 2f out: lost tch over 1f out* **20/1**
04-5 P **Vergality Ridge (IRE)**[7] 368 4-8-13 48 .................... DCByrne(5) 1
(Ronald Harris) *chsd ldrs tl rdn and lost pl qckly 5f out: bhd whn eased and p.u 4f out: dismntd* **25/1**
2m 8.16s (0.16) **Going Correction** +0.15s/f (Slow)
**WFA** 4 from 5yo+ 1lb **10 Ran SP% 119.8**
Speed ratings (Par 97): **105,104,102,101,97 93,93,90,83,**
CSF £13.66 CT £207.28 TOTE £8.10: £2.10, £1.10, £5.20; EX 18.00 Trifecta £463.20.
**Owner** Good Breed Limited **Bred** Deerpark Stud **Trained** Kinnersley, Worcs
**FOCUS**
A very moderate handicap. The runner-up is consistent and has been rated up slightly on his recent form, with the third in line with her autumn figures.

### 485 £500 FREE BETS AT BETDAQ H'CAP 5f (P)
**6:00** (6:00) (Class 5) (0-75,75) 3-Y-O **£2,749** (£818; £408) **Stalls** Low

Form RPR
-231 1 **The Dandy Yank (IRE)**[12] 315 3-9-0 68 .................... WilliamCarson 3 71
(Jamie Osborne) *led: rdn and qcknd wl over 1f out: drvn and hdd ins fnl f: battled bk gamely u.p to ld again last strides* **9/1**[3]
1- 2 hd **National Service (USA)**[70] 8058 3-9-2 70 .................... SeanLevey 4 72
(Stuart Williams) *stdd s: t.k.h: chsd wnr: rdn and effrt to chal 1f out: drvn to ld fnl 100yds: sn hdd: r.o wl after: jst hld cl home* **4/9**[1]
00-1 3 nse **Artemis (IRE)**[7] 373 3-8-4 58 6ex .................... JoeFanning 5 60
(Conrad Allen) *taken down early: stdd s: t.k.h: hld up in 3rd: swtchd ins and qcknd to chal 1f out: drvn to ld wl ins fnl f: hdd and lost 2 pls last strides* **2/1**[2]
1m 3.03s (2.53) **Going Correction** +0.15s/f (Slow) **3 Ran SP% 112.6**
Speed ratings (Par 97): **85,84,84**
CSF £14.66 TOTE £3.60; EX 10.60 Trifecta £6.40.
**Owner** Chris Watkins And David N Reynolds **Bred** Martyn J McEnery **Trained** Upper Lambourn, Berks
**FOCUS**
Just the three runners, but a thriller. The runner-up has been rated in line with his maiden win.

### 486 BETDAQ - THE SPORTS BETTING EXCHANGE MAIDEN FILLIES' STKS 7f (P)
**6:30** (6:31) (Class 5) 3-Y-O+ **£2,749** (£818; £408; £204) **Stalls** Low

Form RPR
1 **Khatiba (IRE)** 3-8-11 0 .................... AndreaAtzeni 4 72+
(Roger Varian) *awkward leaving stalls: sn in tch in midfield: rdn and qcknd to ld 1f out: r.o wl and a holding rivals: rdn out* **11/2**
2 ¾ **Joie De Reve (IRE)** 3-8-11 0 .................... JoeFanning 11 70+
(David Simcock) *hld up in tch in midfield: swtchd lft and effrt 2f out: carried lft over 1f out: hdwy ent fnl f: r.o to chse wnr wl ins fnl f: clsng on wnr at fin* **10/1**
3 nk **Labise (IRE)** 3-8-11 0 .................... JimCrowley 6 69+
(Ralph Beckett) *chsd ldr: rdn to ld 2f out: rn green and wnt lft over 1f out: hdd and outpcd by wnr 1f out: kpt on but lost 2nd wl ins fnl f* **9/4**[1]
3 4 2 ¼ **Ishiamber**[14] 275 4-10-0 0 .................... LukeMorris 9 68
(George Baker) *wl in tch in midfield: hdwy to chse ldrs 3f out: rdn and pressed ldrs 2f out: outpcd ent fnl f: kpt on same pce after* **8/1**
-23 5 2 **La Napoule**[14] 284 3-8-11 0 .................... SeanLevey 2 58
(Richard Hannon) *chsd ldrs: drvn and effrt to press ldrs 2f out: drvn and unable qck over 1f out: wknd ins fnl f* **9/2**[3]
4-3 6 ¾ **Windlass (IRE)**[21] 189 3-8-11 0 .................... RobertHavlin 5 56
(John Gosden) *t.k.h: chsd ldrs: trying to switch out lft over 2f out: drvn and nt qckning whn sltly hmpd over 1f out: wknd ins fnl f* **7/2**[2]
0- 7 shd **Madame Mime Artist**[49] 8332 3-8-11 0 .................... KieranO'Neill 13 55
(Alastair Lidderdale) *hld up in tch in midfield: rdn and outpcd 2f out: no threat to ldrs but rallied and swtchd rt ins fnl f: styd on* **50/1**
00 8 hd **Marmande (IRE)**[11] 341 3-8-11 0 .................... RichardKingscote 1 55
(Daniel Kubler) *led: rdn and hdd 2f out: outpcd and btn ent fnl f: wknd ins fnl f* **66/1**
3 9 5 **Kissed By Fire**[28] 82 4-10-0 0 .................... StephenCraine 3 46
(Jim Boyle) *in tch in midfield: rdn and unable qck ent 2f out: outpcd and btn over 1f out: sn wknd* **50/1**
0 10 2 **Laguna Belle**[21] 189 4-10-0 0 .................... FergusSweeney 8 41
(Pat Phelan) *hld up in tch in last quartet: rdn and effrt ent fnl 2f: sn outpcd and btn: wknd over 1f out* **100/1**
0 11 7 **Kristal Hart**[14] 275 5-10-0 0 .................... PaddyAspell 12 22
(Neil Mulholland) *t.k.h: hld up in last trio: rdn and outpcd jst over 2f out: sn btn: wknd over 1f out: bhd fnl f* **100/1**
12 1 ¾ **Her Red Devil (IRE)** 3-8-11 0 .................... TomEaves 7 12
(Richard Fahey) *s.i.s and wnt rt after s: in tch in rr: rdn jst over 2f out: sn btn: wknd wl over 1f out: bhd fnl f* **16/1**
13 ½ **Mrs Burbidge** 4-10-0 0 .................... LiamKeniry 10 16
(Neil Mulholland) *hld up in last pair: rdn jst over 2f out: sn outpcd and btn: wknd wl over 1f out: bhd fnl f* **100/1**
1m 27.35s (1.35) **Going Correction** +0.15s/f (Slow)
**WFA** 3 from 4yo+ 17lb **13 Ran SP% 121.0**
Speed ratings (Par 100): **98,97,96,94,91 91,90,90,85,82 74,72,72**
CSF £59.38 TOTE £6.80: £2.60, £2.70, £1.80; EX 55.10 Trifecta £225.50.
**Owner** Sheikh Ahmed Al Maktoum **Bred** Darley **Trained** Newmarket, Suffolk

**FOCUS**
One or two of these had shown some form beforehand, but newcomers dominated and this was probably not a bad maiden for the time of year. The fifth and sixth have been rated a bit below their latest efforts, and the level is ultimately set by the seventh, eighth and ninth.

## 487 WINNERS ARE WELCOME AT BETDAQ H'CAP 7f (P)
**7:00** (7:00) (Class 4) (0-85,82) 3-Y-O **£4,690** (£1,395; £697; £348) **Stalls** Low

Form RPR
22-1 **1** **Pool House**[7] 371 3-9-13 **82** 6ex DavidProbert 2 92
(Andrew Balding) *mde all: rdn and qcknd ent fnl 2f: hrd pressed 1f out: battled on gamely and hld on wl fnl f: drvn out* **6/4**[1]
01- **2** *nk* **Amahoro**[126] 6947 3-9-3 **75** WilliamTwiston-Davies(3) 3 84+
(Mick Channon) *wnt lft s: t.k.h: chsd wnr: last off the bridle and rdn to chal 1f out: drvn and r.o ins fnl f: a jst hld* **3/1**[3]
14-1 **3** *4* **First Experience**[27] 103 3-9-2 **71** ChrisCatlin 1 69
(Rae Guest) *t.k.h: chsd ldng pair: rdn and effrt ent fnl 2f: drvn and outpcd by ldng pair over 1f out: one pce after* **11/2**
61-2 **4** *½* **Bint Malyana (IRE)**[27] 103 3-8-13 **68** (p) LukeMorris 4 65
(James Tate) *pushed lft s: hld up in last: rdn and effrt on inner ent fnl 2f: outpcd by ldng pair and btn over 1f out: one pce after* **11/4**[2]
1m 28.64s (2.64) **Going Correction** +0.15s/f (Slow) **4** Ran SP% **107.1**
Speed ratings (Par 99): **90,89,85,84**
CSF £6.06 TOTE £1.40; EX 7.40 Trifecta £15.90.
**Owner** David Brownlow **Bred** R, J D & M R Bromley Gardner **Trained** Kingsclere, Hants
**FOCUS**
Only the four runners, but a tight race. They finished in the order they raced and the winner has been rated as stepping up a bit.

## 488 KEMPTON FOR WEDDINGS H'CAP 1m 4f (P)
**7:30** (7:31) (Class 6) (0-65,63) 3-Y-O **£1,940** (£577; £288; £144) **Stalls** Centre

Form RPR
2-11 **1** **Masterpaver**[18] 236 3-9-6 **62** (v) RobertWinston 10 69
(Alan Bailey) *hld up in tch in rr: clsd and travelling wl 3f out: rdn and effrt 2f out: drvn to chal 1f out: sustained chal to ld fnl 50yds: styd on wl: rdn out* **9/4**[1]
04-4 **2** *hd* **Mary Le Bow**[18] 236 3-9-7 **63** (p) LukeMorris 4 69
(Lucy Wadham) *travelled wl: chsd ldng trio: rdn and effrt 2f out: led over 1f out: pressed and hrd drvn 1f out: kpt on wl tl hdd and no ex fnl 5oyds* **7/2**[2]
-544 **3** *2½* **Izbushka (IRE)**[20] 198 3-9-7 **63** (v) StevieDonohoe 2 65
(Ian Williams) *chsd ldng pair tl wnt 2nd 8f out: rdn to ld ent fnl 2f: drvn and hdd over 1f out: 3rd and styd on same pce u.p fnl f* **20/1**
35-2 **4** *6* **Bountiful Sin**[18] 236 3-9-7 **63** TomQueally 8 55
(George Margarson) *hld up in tch in midfield: rdn and effrt jst over 2f out: 4th and outpcd over 1f out: wknd 1f out* **5/1**[3]
05-6 **5** *7* **Confucius Legend (IRE)**[32] 51 3-9-4 **60** StephenCraine 7 41
(Jim Boyle) *hld up in tch in last trio: hdwy 4f out: chsd ldrs and rdn over 2f out: unable qck and outpcd 2f out: sn wknd* **15/2**
004- **6** *1¾* **Flying Author (IRE)**[54] 8274 3-8-7 **49** (v) DavidProbert 3 27
(Phil McEntee) *led tl rdn and hdd ent fnl 2f: sn struggling and btn: fdd ent fnl f* **12/1**
600- **7** *1* **M'Lady Ermyn**[36] 8452 3-8-9 **51** FrankieMcDonald 9 28
(Pat Phelan) *hld up in tch in last pair: rdn and short-lived effrt over 2f out: sn wknd* **16/1**
0-20 **8** *3* **Blossom Lane**[18] 236 3-9-2 **58** RobertHavlin 1 30
(John Gosden) *chsd ldrs: rdn 3f out: nt qckning and short of room over 2f out: sn wknd* **8/1**
006- **9** *14* **Wulfthryth**[83] 7874 3-8-11 **60** (t) AlfieWarwick(7) 6 10
(Tobias B P Coles) *in tch in midfield: dropped to rr and rdn 4f out: lost tch ent fnl 2f: wl bhd fnl f* **16/1**
2m 34.57s (0.07) **Going Correction** +0.15s/f (Slow) **9** Ran SP% **116.8**
Speed ratings (Par 95): **105,104,103,99,94 93,92,90,81**
CSF £10.12 CT £123.48 TOTE £3.10: £1.60, £1.10, £3.90; EX 9.10 Trifecta £105.20.
**Owner** Mrs A M Riney **Bred** Mrs A M Riney **Trained** Newmarket, Suffolk
**FOCUS**
A modest handicap. The third has been rated as running as well as ever.

## 489 BETDAQ 1ST UK RACE COMMISSION FREE H'CAP 6f (P)
**8:00** (8:02) (Class 5) (0-70,70) 4-Y-O+ **£2,749** (£818; £408; £204) **Stalls** Low

Form RPR
22-1 **1** **Ex Ex**[23] 159 4-9-7 **70** GeorgeBaker 3 87+
(Nick Littmoden) *chsd ldrs and a travelling wl: rdn and effrt to ld on inner over 1f out: in command and r.o wl fnl f: comf* **11/10**[1]
0-05 **2** *2½* **Daring Dragon**[17] 249 4-9-7 **70** (b) TomQueally 7 79
(Ed Walker) *hld up in tch in midfield: rdn and effrt to chse ldrs over 1f out: chse wnr ins fnl f: r.o but no threat to wnr* **11/2**[2]
01-5 **3** *1½* **New Rich**[28] 83 4-8-12 **61** (p) JohnFahy 9 65+
(Eve Johnson Houghton) *stdd s and dropped in bhd: rdn and effrt on inner but stl plenty to do over 1f out: styd on to go 3rd wl ins fnl f: nvr trbld ldrs* **10/1**
0-12 **4** *1* **Prince Of Passion (CAN)**[13] 297 6-9-0 **63** (v) JoeFanning 1 64
(Derek Shaw) *awkward leaving stalls: sn rcvrd to ld: drvn and hdd over 1f out: wknd ins fnl f* **12/1**
030- **5** *½* **Nelson Quay (IRE)**[175] 5391 4-9-6 **69** RobertWinston 5 68
(Jeremy Gask) *hld up in midfield: rdn and effrt ent fnl 2f: outpcd and btn 1f out: kpt on same pce after* **8/1**[3]
24-0 **6** *½* **Burnhope**[34] 8 5-8-11 **67** (p) MatthewHopkins(7) 8 65
(Scott Dixon) *dwlt: racd keenly and sn rcvrd to chse ldrs: wnt 2nd 4f out tl wl over 1f out: sn outpcd: btn and one pce fnl f* **8/1**[3]
00-0 **7** *nk* **El Mirage (IRE)**[28] 91 4-9-6 **69** JimCrowley 10 66
(Dean Ivory) *stdd after s: t.k.h: hld up in tch in last trio: rdn and effrt ent fnl 2f: plugged on but no threat to ldrs* **25/1**
0-30 **8** *hd* **Dorback**[16] 259 7-9-4 **67** ChrisCatlin 2 63
(Tony Newcombe) *stdd s: hld up in last trio: rdn and effrt on outer over 2f out: plugged on but nvr trbld ldrs* **33/1**
0-63 **9** *hd* **Ghostwing**[16] 258 7-8-8 **57** LukeMorris 4 53
(Tony Carroll) *hld up in tch in midfield: rdn and unable qck on inner ent 2f out: outpcd and btn over 1f out: wknd fnl f* **12/1**
00- **10** *2¼* **Welliesinthewater (IRE)**[39] 8430 4-9-2 **65** DaleSwift 6 53
(Derek Shaw) *chsd ldr for 2f: steadily lost pl: rdn wl over 2f out: bhd and wl hld 1f out* **50/1**
1m 13.03s (-0.07) **Going Correction** +0.15s/f (Slow) **10** Ran SP% **118.4**
Speed ratings (Par 103): **106,102,100,99,98 98,97,97,97,94**
CSF £7.26 CT £42.81 TOTE £1.70: £1.10, £2.20, £2.70; EX 8.40 Trifecta £34.40.
**Owner** Nick Littmoden **Bred** Mr & Mrs A E Pakenham **Trained** Newmarket, Suffolk
■ Stewards' Enquiry : Matthew Hopkins six-day ban: used whip above shoulder height (Feb 19-22,24-25)

**FOCUS**
This proved straightforward for the winner. There's a chance this form is a bit better than it looks, with the winner progressive, the runner-up still looking on a fair mark and the third having a good record over the C&D.
T/Jkpt: Part won. £49,849.30 to a £1 stake. Pool: £70,210.29 - 0.50 winning tickets. T/Plt: £229.20 to a £1 stake. Pool: £113946.68 - 362.90 winning tickets T/Qpdt: £96.30 to a £1 stake. Pool: £5729.74 - 44.00 winning tickets SP

# 467 LINGFIELD (L-H)
### Wednesday, February 5

**OFFICIAL GOING: Standard**
Wind: Very Strong, behind Weather: Raining 1st 3 races

## 490 CORAL.CO.UK H'CAP 1m 4f (P)
**1:30** (1:30) (Class 6) (0-60,59) 4-Y-O+ **£1,940** (£577; £288; £144) **Stalls** Low

Form RPR
0-22 **1** **Cabuchon (GER)**[6] 382 7-9-5 **57** SeanLevey 3 63
(David Evans) *hld up in last: prog on outer 3f out: wdst of all bnd 2f out: r.o fr over 1f out to ld last 100yds: drvn out* **6/4**[1]
0-54 **2** *½* **Standing Strong (IRE)**[18] 229 6-9-1 **53** (p) LiamKeniry 6 58
(Zoe Davison) *t.k.h: hld up in 6th: prog on outer over 3f out: narrow ld wl over 2f out: hanging lft over 1f out: hdd last 100yds: kpt on* **14/1**
000/ **3** *1* **Red Skipper (IRE)**[283] 5723 9-8-7 **45** LukeMorris 7 49
(John O'Shea) *trckd ldng pair: rdn over 3f out: struggling to hold pl 2f out: styd on again ins fnl f* **12/1**
2-00 **4** *nse* **Salient**[19] 210 10-8-10 **48** JoeFanning 5 52
(Michael Attwater) *led: narrowly hdd wl over 2f out: kpt pressing and upsides jst ins fnl f: one pce* **10/1**
0-04 **5** *shd* **Elegant Ophelia**[14] 278 5-9-6 **58** (t) JimCrowley 8 61
(Dean Ivory) *trckd ldr: chal 3f out: one of three battling for ld fr over 2f out tl no ex ins fnl f* **9/2**[2]
40-6 **6** *nk* **Bennelong**[17] 247 8-8-12 **50** (b) ShaneKelly 1 53
(Lee Carter) *hld up in 7th: stl there but cl enough 2f out: nt qckn over 1f out: kpt on nr fin* **7/1**[3]
46-3 **7** *nk* **Stag Hill (IRE)**[14] 278 5-9-7 **59** (tp) TomQueally 2 61
(Bernard Llewellyn) *dwlt: sn rcovered to trck ldng trio: rdn 3f out: lost pl wl over 1f out: kpt on again nr fin* **9/2**[2]
53-0 **8** *2¾* **James Pollard (IRE)**[14] 277 9-8-13 **56** (tp) LouisSteward(5) 4 54
(Bernard Llewellyn) *hld up in 5th: lost pl sltly 3f out: cl enough 2f out: wknd fnl f* **25/1**
2m 34.74s (1.74) **Going Correction** +0.10s/f (Slow) **8** Ran SP% **116.2**
Speed ratings (Par 101): **98,97,97,96,96 96,96,94**
CSF £26.00 CT £191.11 TOTE £2.10: £1.40, £3.90, £1.50; EX 29.40 Trifecta £109.90.
**Owner** Mrs E Evans **Bred** Gestut Schlenderhan **Trained** Pandy, Monmouths
**FOCUS**
A moderate handicap run at a steady pace. The winner is perhaps a little better than bare form, but he's been rated as not quite matching his recent best.

## 491 32RED.COM FILLIES' H'CAP 1m 2f (P)
**2:00** (2:00) (Class 5) (0-70,66) 4-Y-O+ **£2,726** (£805; £402) **Stalls** Low

Form RPR
46-2 **1** **Waveguide (IRE)**[8] 365 5-9-0 **66** LewisWalsh(7) 5 73
(David Simcock) *slowest away but led after 1f: maintained mod pce: kicked on whn pressed over 2f out: fnd enough to hold on nr fin* **9/2**[2]
620- **2** *nk* **Princess Icicle**[189] 4898 6-9-7 **66** FergusSweeney 6 72
(Jo Crowley) *t.k.h: hld up in slowly run r: rdn wl over 1f out: no imp tl styd on ins fnl f: tk 2nd last strides: nt rch wnr* **8/1**[3]
11-2 **3** *¾* **Pretty Bubbles**[23] 155 5-9-7 **66** FrederikTylicki 1 71
(J R Jenkins) *hld up in slowly run r: last after 3f: rdn and prog on inner wl over 1f out: tk 2nd fnl f and chal: nt qckn and lost 2nd last strides* **7/4**[1]
005- **4** *¾* **Countess Lovelace**[37] 8443 4-8-11 **57** JoeFanning 3 60
(Pat Phelan) *led 1f: styd cl up: rdn 2f out: tried to chal jst over 1f out: nt qckn fnl f* **12/1**
00-2 **5** *¾* **Emman Bee (IRE)**[6] 376 5-9-4 **63** JimCrowley 4 65
(Luke Dace) *trckd ldr after 1f: rdn to chal over 2f out: nt qckn wl over 1f out: lost 2nd and hanging fnl f* **7/4**[1]
000- **6** *6* **Rugosa**[41] 8401 5-8-12 **64** JamesMerrett(7) 2 54
(Charles Hills) *hld up: racd wd after 3f and t.k.h: prom fr 1/2-way tl wknd over 1f out* **25/1**
2m 9.05s (2.45) **Going Correction** +0.10s/f (Slow)
**WFA** 4 from 5yo+ 1lb **6** Ran SP% **113.6**
Speed ratings (Par 100): **94,93,93,92,91 87**
CSF £38.52 TOTE £5.40: £4.10, £2.80; EX 41.50 Trifecta £56.40.
**Owner** Tick Tock Partnership **Bred** T Darcy & Vincent McCarthy **Trained** Newmarket, Suffolk
**FOCUS**
The pace was modest for this fillies' handicap. The winner has been rated to form.

## 492 32RED CASINO H'CAP 1m 1y(P)
**2:30** (2:30) (Class 5) (0-75,71) 3-Y-O **£2,726** (£805; £402) **Stalls** High

Form RPR
05-1 **1** **Like A Prayer**[6] 378 3-9-2 **65** 6ex JimCrowley 2 74+
(Ralph Beckett) *hld up in last: clsd on outer 2f out: chal jst over 1f out: reminder to ld ins fnl f: narrow but decisive advantage after* **1/4**[1]
45-3 **2** *½* **Upholland**[9] 355 3-9-7 **70** (p) ShaneKelly 3 77
(Richard Fahey) *trckd ldr 2f: shkn up over 2f out: nipped through on inner to ld over 1f out: edgd rt u.p: hdd ins fnl f: styd on but readily hld nr fin* **8/1**[3]
21-3 **3** *8* **Power Up**[27] 99 3-9-5 **68** JoeFanning 7 57
(Mark Johnston) *led at mod pce: hdd and lft bhd over 1f out* **6/1**[2]
62-0 **4** *3¾* **Tanojin (IRE)**[12] 311 3-8-9 **61** WilliamTwiston-Davies(3) 5 41
(Mick Channon) *trckd ldr after 2f: chal over 2f out: wknd over 1f out* **20/1**
1m 39.82s (1.62) **Going Correction** +0.10s/f (Slow) **4** Ran SP% **110.2**
Speed ratings (Par 97): **95,94,86,82**
CSF £3.06 TOTE £1.40; EX 2.50 Trifecta £5.80.
**Owner** The Rat Pack Partnership **Bred** Kirtlington Stud Ltd **Trained** Kimpton, Hants

**FOCUS**
An uncompetitive looking handicap run at a steady pace. The level is a bit fluid but, given the lack of depth, the race has been rated cautiously.

## 493 LADBROKES H'CAP 1m 1y(P)
3:05 (3:05) (Class 5) (0-75,75) 4-Y-O+ £2,726 (£805; £402) Stalls High

Form RPR
3-34 **1** **Club House (IRE)**[14] [286] 4-8-8 **62** ............ TomEaves 9 72
(Robert Mills) *dropped in fr wdst draw and hld up: last to 1/2-way: prog to trck ldng trio 3f out: clsd over 1f out: wl-timed run to ld last 100yds: readily* **10/1**
0-31 **2** *1* **Shaolin (IRE)**[17] [245] 4-9-5 **73** ............(t) GeorgeBaker 3 81
(Seamus Durack) *trckd ldng pair: clsd on them bnd 2f out: drvn to ld briefly ins fnl f: outpcd last 75yds* **7/2**[2]
4-11 **3** *1* **Just One Kiss**[6] [376] 4-9-2 **75** ............ LouisSteward(5) 2 81
(Lady Cecil) *pressed ldr at str pce: carried sltly wd bnd 2f out: rdn to ld over 1f out: hdd and no ex ins fnl f* **4/5**[1]
00-5 **4** *2* **Liberty Jack (IRE)**[12] [312] 4-9-4 **72** ............ StephenCraine 5 73
(Jim Boyle) *hld up: in last pair 3f out: prog to go 5th 2f out but nt on terms: shkn up over 1f out: styd on to take 4th nr fin: nvr involved* **20/1**
45-5 **5** *nk* **High Time Too (IRE)**[20] [200] 4-9-7 **75** ............ AndreaAtzeni 1 75
(Hugo Palmer) *led at str pce but jnd: drifted sltly wd bnd 2f out: hdd over 1f out: wknd fnl f* **8/1**[3]
562- **6** *7* **Fiducia**[162] [5853] 4-8-10 **67** ............[1] RobertTart(3) 4 51
(Simon Dow) *chsd ldrs: shkn up and outpcd over 3f out: wknd 2f out: bhd after* **16/1**
53-2 **7** *1 3/4* **Flamborough Breeze**[26] [118] 5-9-6 **74** ............(t) LukeMorris 6 54
(Ed Vaughan) *chsd ldrs: wd bnd 4f out: struggling sn after: wd bnd 2f out: eased and wl bhd* **10/1**
110- **8** *3 1/2* **Peak Storm**[49] [6720] 5-9-5 **73** ............ WilliamCarson 8 45
(John O'Shea) *t.k.h: hld up in tch: outpcd over 3f out: wknd over 2f out: wl bhd after* **50/1**

1m 37.32s (-0.88) **Going Correction** +0.10s/f (Slow) 8 Ran SP% **119.7**
Speed ratings (Par 103): **108,107,106,104,103 96,94,91**
CSF £47.14 CT £61.30 TOTE £10.50: £2.50, £1.80, £1.10; EX 44.40 Trifecta £130.60.
**Owner** Mrs B B Mills A Foreman **Bred** Val & Angela Leeson **Trained** Headley, Surrey

**FOCUS**
Not a bad contest for the grade, run at a steady pace. The fourth has been rated pretty much to form.

## 494 32RED H'CAP 1m 5f (P)
3:40 (3:40) (Class 4) (0-80,80) 4-Y-O+ £4,722 (£1,405; £702; £351) Stalls Low

Form RPR
06-3 **1** **Scottish Star**[23] [160] 6-9-4 **76** ............ LukeMorris 6 85
(James Eustace) *trckd ldrs: clsd to chal on outer over 2f out: hrd rdn to ld last 150yds: styd on wl whn pressed sn after* **4/1**[3]
1-12 **2** *1/2* **Echo Brava**[23] [160] 4-9-2 **78** ............ JimCrowley 7 86
(Luke Dace) *hld up in last: prog jst over 2f out: clsd over 1f out but had to chal against rail: pressed wnr last 100yds: hld nr fin* **7/4**[1]
1114 **3** *1 1/2* **The Blue Dog (IRE)**[9] [358] 7-8-13 **74** ............ RobertTart(3) 3 80
(Phil McEntee) *trckd ldrs: clsd on inner to ld over 2f out: drvn and pressed after: hdd and one pce last 150yds* **6/1**
-433 **4** *4 1/2* **Layline (IRE)**[12] [322] 7-9-5 **77** ............ DavidProbert 1 76
(Gay Kelleway) *hld up in 5th: rdn 3f out: sn lft bhd: no ch fnl 2f: plugged on* **10/1**
33-5 **5** *3 1/2* **Slip Of The Tongue**[23] [160] 4-9-1 **77** ............ LiamKeniry 8 71
(Derek Haydn Jones) *led at decent pce: breather after 6f: urged along 4f out: hdd over 2f out: steadily wknd* **8/1**
-401 **6** *7* **Doldrums (USA)**[9] [358] 4-8-13 **75** 6ex............ JoeFanning 2 59
(Mark Johnston) *trckd ldr to wl over 2f out: sn btn* **3/1**[2]

2m 43.66s (-2.34) **Going Correction** +0.10s/f (Slow)
**WFA** 4 from 6yo+ 4lb 6 Ran SP% **115.9**
Speed ratings (Par 105): **111,110,109,107,104 100**
CSF £11.98 CT £40.89 TOTE £5.90: £3.20, £1.30; EX 11.20 Trifecta £68.30.
**Owner** Ian Rushby **Bred** Mrs J McCreery **Trained** Newmarket, Suffolk

**FOCUS**
A fair handicap, run at a steady pace. The winner has been rated back to his old best, while the runner-up has been rated as running as well as ever.

## 495 COMPARE BOOKMAKERS AT BOOKMAKERS.CO.UK MAIDEN STKS 6f 1y(P)
4:10 (4:10) (Class 5) 3-Y-O+ £2,726 (£805; £402) Stalls Low

Form RPR
5-43 **1** **Rose Buck**[12] [311] 3-8-3 60............ LouisSteward(5) 3 64
(Lee Carter) *mde all: set mod pce tl kicked on over 2f out: rdn out and a holding on* **6/1**[2]
2- **2** *3/4* **Chunghua (USA)**[47] [8368] 3-8-13 0............ JimCrowley 6 67
(Ed Walker) *racd wd: hld up: trckd ldng pair 1/2-way: 3 l to make up after pce lifted over 2f out: rdn over 1f out: styd on to take 2nd last 75yds: a too much to do* **1/4**[1]
**3** *1/2* **Role Reversal** 3-8-8 0............ LukeMorris 4 60
(James Tate) *chsd wnr: shkn up over 2f out: kpt on but hld 1f out: lost 2nd last 75yds* **6/1**[2]
5-20 **4** *5* **Island Express (IRE)**[15] [269] 7-9-9 45............(t) AnnStokell(5) 2 53?
(Ann Stokell) *wl in tch: edgd lft over 2f out: steadily outpcd* **66/1**[3]
00/- **5** *9* **Sweet Piccolo**[433] [7926] 4-9-9 39............(b[1]) DavidKenny(5) 1 24
(Paddy Butler) *in tch: rdn and sing to be outpcd whn hmpd over 2f out: bhd after* **66/1**[3]

1m 12.24s (0.34) **Going Correction** +0.10s/f (Slow)
**WFA** 3 from 4yo+ 15lb 5 Ran SP% **111.6**
Speed ratings (Par 103): **101,100,99,92,80**
CSF £8.23 TOTE £6.60: £1.70, £1.10; EX 12.50 Trifecta £20.00.
**Owner** Miss Victoria Baalham **Bred** Mrs A Brudenell **Trained** Epsom, Surrey
■ Stewards' Enquiry : Ann Stokell three-day ban: careless riding (Feb 19-21)

**FOCUS**
The gallop was fair for this weak maiden. The winner has been rated in line with the best view of her recent form.

## 496 DOWNLOAD THE LADBROKES APP H'CAP 7f 1y(P)
4:40 (4:41) (Class 5) (0-70,70) 4-Y-O+ £2,726 (£805; £402) Stalls Low

Form RPR
00-6 **1** **The Happy Hammer (IRE)**[17] [245] 8-8-12 **64**............(b) RobertTart(3) 7 71
(Eugene Stanford) *t.k.h: sn pressed ldr: led 3f out: sent for home jst over 2f out: drvn fnl f: jst lasted* **10/1**
2-00 **2** *nk* **Shifting Star (IRE)**[3] [451] 9-8-13 **62**............(b) WilliamCarson 4 68
(John Bridger) *t.k.h: cl up: nt qckn jst over 2f out: styd on to take 2nd fnl f: clsd on wnr at fin* **20/1**
1-64 **3** *1* **Presumido (IRE)**[11] [340] 4-9-1 **64**............[1] HayleyTurner 5 68
(Simon Dow) *stdd s: t.k.h: hld up in last: prog wl over 1f out: drvn to take 3rd jst ins fnl f: kpt on same pce after* **7/1**
1-33 **4** *nk* **Run It Twice (IRE)**[9] [359] 4-9-2 **70**............(b) EoinWalsh(5) 9 73+
(David Evans) *hld up in rr: rdn and outpcd jst over 2f out: styd on wl fnl f: gaining at fin* **6/1**[3]
-362 **5** *1* **Go Far**[6] [389] 4-9-5 **68**............(v) RobertWinston 6 68
(Alan Bailey) *mde most at muddling pce: hdd 3f out: hrd rdn and nt qckn 2f out: lost 2nd and fdd fnl f* **7/2**[1]
0-44 **6** *nk* **Top Offer**[17] [245] 5-9-4 **67**............ ShaneKelly 1 66
(Peter Crate) *t.k.h: hld up in tch: outpcd jst over 2f out: drvn and no prog over 1f out: kpt on last 100yds* **5/1**[2]
-133 **7** *1/2* **Kyllachy Star**[16] [255] 8-9-7 **70**............(v) BarryMcHugh 3 68
(Richard Fahey) *hld up: gd passage through on inner 3f out to trck ldrs 2f out: nt qckn sn after: fdd fnl f* **7/2**[1]
0-03 **8** *2 1/4* **Sea Soldier (IRE)**[4] [428] 6-8-2 **58**............ RobHornby(7) 2 50
(Andrew Balding) *wl in tch: outpcd and shkn up jst over 2f out: quite wd bnd sn after: fdd* **10/1**
4-54 **9** *3/4* **Magical Rose (IRE)**[12] [319] 4-8-10 **62**...(p) WilliamTwiston-Davies(3) 10 52
(Paul D'Arcy) *t.k.h: hld up in rr: outpcd and rdn jst over 2f out: wd bnd sn after: fdd* **14/1**

1m 24.94s (0.14) **Going Correction** +0.10s/f (Slow) 9 Ran SP% **117.5**
Speed ratings (Par 103): **103,102,101,101,100 99,99,96,95**
CSF £188.41 CT £1493.79 TOTE £13.60: £4.20, £4.80, £1.40; EX 172.90 Trifecta £2332.90.
**Owner** newmarketracingclub.co.uk **Bred** Rathbarry Stud **Trained** Newmarket, Suffolk

**FOCUS**
An open contest run at a steady pace. The third and fourth have been rated a shade off their marks.
T/Plt: £23.20 to a £1 stake. Pool: £91725.24 - 2877.85 winning tickets T/Qpdt: £3.00 to a £1 stake. Pool: £4782.85 - 1171.55 winning tickets JN

# 460 WOLVERHAMPTON (A.W) (L-H)
Thursday, February 6

**OFFICIAL GOING: Standard**
Wind: Light behind Weather: Raining

## 497 CORAL MOBILE "JUST THREE CLICKS TO BET" APPRENTICE H'CAP 1m 1f 103y(P)
5:00 (5:00) (Class 6) (0-60,60) 4-Y-O+ £2,264 (£673; £336; £168) Stalls Low

Form RPR
20-5 **1** **Dansili Dutch (IRE)**[25] [152] 5-9-2 **60**............ JackGarritty(5) 8 68
(David O'Meara) *hld up: pushed along over 3f out: hdwy 2f out: rdn to ld wl ins fnl f: r.o* **14/1**
3-10 **2** *1 1/4* **Katmai River (IRE)**[17] [263] 7-8-7 **51**............ CharlotteJenner(5) 10 56
(Mark Usher) *hld up: hdwy 2f out: shkn up over 1f out: styd on to go 2nd post* **13/2**[3]
24-6 **3** *hd* **Polar Forest**[28] [105] 4-9-3 **56**............(e) JacobButterfield 6 61
(Richard Guest) *a.p: led ins fnl f: sn rdn and hdd: kpt on* **8/1**
525- **4** *3 1/2* **Ground Ginger**[64] [7923] 4-8-7 **46**............(p) ShirleyTeasdale 7 44
(James Bethell) *chsd ldrs: rdn over 3f out: n.m.r 1f out: styd on same pce ins fnl f* **8/1**
0-50 **5** *3/4* **Exceedexpectations (IRE)**[27] [126] 5-8-13 **55**........(t) LouisSteward(3) 9 51
(John Butler) *hld up: hdwy 2f out: rdn over 1f out: no ex ins fnl f* **6/4**[1]
1243 **6** *3/4* **Disco Dave (IRE)**[5] [433] 6-9-7 **60**............ PhilipPrince 11 54
(Daniel Mark Loughnane) *hld up: hdwy over 3f out: rdn to ld 2f out: sn edgd lft: hdd and no ex ins fnl f* **11/4**[2]
20-0 **7** *4* **Sixties Queen**[6] [406] 4-9-4 **57**............ TimClark 1 43
(Alan Bailey) *led over 8f out: pushed along over 3f out: rdn and hdd 2f out: wknd fnl f* **22/1**
3-55 **8** *4* **Rainford Glory (IRE)**[27] [123] 4-9-0 **58**............ AlistairRawlinson(5) 2 36
(Patrick Morris) *led 1f: trckd ldr: ev ch 2f out: sn rdn: wknd fnl f* **20/1**
00-5 **9** *7* **Witch Way Went**[10] [358] 4-9-1 **59**............(p) KevinLundie(5) 3 22
(Brian Ellison) *mid-div: sn pushed along: wknd 4f out* **40/1**
000- **10** *5* **Moissanite**[138] [6630] 5-8-4 **46** oh1............[1] JordanVaughan(3) 4
(Sean Regan) *chsd ldrs tl rdn and wknd over 3f out* **100/1**

2m 4.07s (2.37) **Going Correction** +0.20s/f (Slow) 10 Ran SP% **121.4**
Speed ratings (Par 101): **97,95,95,92,91 91,87,84,77,73**
CSF £102.11 CT £796.43 TOTE £12.20: £2.70, £1.10, £2.90; EX 65.60 Trifecta £529.80.
**Owner** Direct Racing Partnership **Bred** Castlefarm Stud **Trained** Nawton, N Yorks
■ Stewards' Enquiry : Jordan Vaughan caution: careless riding.

**FOCUS**
A modest but fascinating opener. The winner has been rated back to his December C&D form and the runner-up helps set the standard.

## 498 CORAL APP DOWNLOAD FROM THE APP STORE H'CAP 1m 1f 103y(P)
5:30 (5:30) (Class 5) (0-75,74) 4-Y-O+ £2,911 (£866; £432; £216) Stalls Low

Form RPR
40-4 **1** **Red Shuttle**[26] [146] 7-9-5 **72**............ ChrisCatlin 5 81
(Andi Brown) *s.i.s: hdwy over 2f out: shkn up to ld ins fnl f: pushed out* **8/1**
55-2 **2** *1 1/2* **Arlecchino (IRE)**[17] [265] 4-9-3 **70**............(b) GeorgeBaker 3 76
(Ed McMahon) *a.p: chsd ldr over 4f out: shkn up to ld over 1f out: sn rdn and hung lft: hdd ins fnl f: nt qckn* **15/8**[1]
64-3 **3** *2 1/2* **Lean On Pete (IRE)**[17] [265] 5-9-2 **74**............ JacobButterfield(5) 4 75
(Ollie Pears) *hld up: hdwy over 3f out: rdn over 1f out: styd on same pce ins fnl f* **11/4**[2]
0-13 **4** *3 1/4* **Tiger Reigns**[20] [210] 8-9-0 **74**............ CamHardie(7) 2 68
(John Butler) *plld hrd: disp ld tl led over 6f out: shkn up and hdd over 1f out: wknd fnl f* **9/2**
013- **5** *19* **Elspeth's Boy (USA)**[86] [7849] 7-8-11 **71**............ EvaMoscrop(7) 6 25
(Philip Kirby) *trckd ldrs: plld hrd: rdn over 2f out: wknd wl over 1f out* **7/2**[3]
60-0 **6** *42* **Boy The Bell**[27] [126] 7-8-7 **60** oh9............ JamesSullivan 1
(Ollie Pears) *pushed along to dispute ld tl over 6f out: chsd ldr tl over 4f out: wknd over 3f out* **66/1**

2m 2.92s (1.22) **Going Correction** +0.20s/f (Slow) 6 Ran SP% **114.5**
Speed ratings (Par 103): **102,100,98,95,78 41**
CSF £24.15 TOTE £11.90: £4.60, £1.40; EX 21.30 Trifecta £63.10.
**Owner** Miss Linsey Knocker **Bred** Cheveley Park Stud Ltd **Trained** Newmarket, Suffolk
■ Andi Brown's first winner.

**FOCUS**
A generously run affair. It's been rated around the first two.

## 499 32RED CASINO CLAIMING STKS 1m 141y(P)
6:00 (6:00) (Class 5) 3-Y-O £2,587 (£770; £384) Stalls Low

Form RPR
16-1 1 **Boogangoo (IRE)**[10] 356 3-8-8 73 JoeFanning 3 71
(Keith Dalgleish) *mde all: qcknd 2f out: shkn up over 1f out: rdn out* **8/11**[1]
-142 2 2½ **Jazzy Lady (IRE)**[6] 404 3-8-9 75 EoinWalsh(5) 5 72
(David Evans) *chsd wnr: shkn up over 2f out: rdn over 1f out: styd on same pce ins fnl f* **2/1**[2]
2221 3 nse **Ain't No Surprise (IRE)**[3] 464 3-8-3 65 JohnLawson(7) 2 68
(Jamie Osborne) *s.i.s: sn prom: rdn over 1f out: styd on same pce ins fnl f* **7/1**[3]
1m 54.74s (4.24) **Going Correction** +0.20s/f (Slow) 3 Ran SP% **103.7**
Speed ratings (Par 97): **89,86,86**
.Boogangoo was claimed by Colleen Ford-Ellis for £6,000\n\x\x Jazzy Lady was claimed by Mr Jim Best for £12,000
**Owner** Middleham Park Racing II **Bred** Marie & Mossy Fahy **Trained** Carluke, S Lanarks
**FOCUS**
A disappointing turnout for this claimer. They finished in betting order and have been rated within lengths of their marks.

## 500 32RED.COM MAIDEN STKS 5f 20y(P)
6:30 (6:30) (Class 5) 3-Y-O £2,911 (£866; £432; £216) Stalls Low

Form RPR
5-22 1 **Three D Alexander (IRE)**[20] 213 3-9-0 80 ChrisCatlin 4 74
(David Evans) *mde all: shkn up and c clr fr over 1f out: kpt up to work tl eased towards fin* **1/4**[1]
2 9 **Eva Clare (IRE)** 3-9-0 0 DanielTudhope 1 42
(K R Burke) *sn prom: chsd wnr 3f out: shkn up 1/2-way: wknd ins fnl f* **4/1**[2]
6-5 3 3¼ **River Dreamer (IRE)**[14] 298 3-9-0 0 AdamBeschizza 3 30
(Robert Stephens) *prom: chsd wnr briefly over 3f out: rdn and wknd over 1f out* **9/1**[3]
- 4 9 **Captain T** 3-8-12 0 VictorSantos(7) 2 3
(Richard Ford) *sn outpcd* **66/1**
0 5 2 **Maro**[10] 355 3-8-12 0 AdamMcLean(7) 5
(Derek Shaw) *sn pushed along to chse wnr tl over 3f out: rdn and wknd 1/2-way* **66/1**
1m 2.99s (0.69) **Going Correction** +0.20s/f (Slow) 5 Ran SP% **113.0**
Speed ratings (Par 97): **102,87,82,68,64**
CSF £1.79 TOTE £1.80: £1.10, £2.00; EX 1.80 Trifecta £2.80.
**Owner** Noel O'Callaghan **Bred** Corduff Stud Ltd **Trained** Pandy, Monmouths
**FOCUS**
A weak maiden rated around the winner to the best of her form in Britain.

## 501 32RED H'CAP 5f 216y(P)
7:00 (7:00) (Class 4) (0-85,85) 3-Y-O £5,175 (£1,540; £769; £384) Stalls Low

Form RPR
124- 1 **Lady Frances**[40] 8426 3-9-7 85 JoeFanning 2 93
(Mark Johnston) *mde all: shkn up over 1f out: rdn ins fnl f: r.o* **5/2**[3]
1141 2 1¼ **Spreadable (IRE)**[5] 429 3-8-5 72 6ex (v) MichaelJMMurphy(3) 3 76
(Nick Littmoden) *trckd wnr: plld hrd: rdn over 1f out: styd on* **11/8**[1]
1 3 2¼ **Crisis Averted (IRE)**[21] 195 3-8-11 75 LeeTopliss 4 72
(Richard Fahey) *chsd ldrs: rdn over 1f out: styd on same pce ins fnl f* **9/4**[2]
012- 4 1 **Poetic Choice**[84] 7879 3-8-3 74 JordanVaughan(7) 1 68
(Nick Littmoden) *s.i.s: sn prom: rdn over 2f out: no ex fnl f* **11/1**
241- 5 14 **Vodka Time (IRE)**[295] 1619 3-9-2 80 ChrisCatlin 5 29
(David Evans) *sn nudged along in rr: bhd fr 1/2-way* **8/1**
1m 15.75s (0.75) **Going Correction** +0.20s/f (Slow) 5 Ran SP% **120.9**
Speed ratings (Par 99): **103,101,98,97,78**
CSF £7.16 TOTE £3.60: £2.00, £1.10; EX 5.80 Trifecta £13.10.
**Owner** Sheikh Hamdan bin Mohammed Al Maktoum **Bred** Darley **Trained** Middleham Moor, N Yorks
**FOCUS**
A competitive feature, despite the small field. The runner-up has been rated as running as well as ever.

## 502 COMPARE BOOKMAKERS AT BOOKMAKERS.CO.UK H'CAP 5f 216y(P)
7:30 (7:30) (Class 7) (0-50,50) 4-Y-O+ £1,940 (£577; £288; £144) Stalls Low

Form RPR
0-06 1 **Louis Vee (IRE)**[21] 201 6-9-2 45 (t) ChrisCatlin 6 54
(Roy Brotherton) *mde all: rdn over 1f out: styd on wl* **33/1**
633- 2 1¼ **Knockamany Bends (IRE)**[41] 8407 4-9-7 50 PaddyAspell 8 55
(John Wainwright) *a.p: chsd wnr 4f out: rdn over 1f out: styd on* **7/2**[1]
3-04 3 nk **Red Shadow**[30] 77 5-9-7 50 (p) DaleSwift 7 54
(Alan Brown) *a.p: rdn over 2f out: styd on u.p* **5/1**[2]
4-20 4 ¾ **Flow Chart (IRE)**[8] 370 7-9-4 50 SladeO'Hara(3) 2 52
(Peter Grayson) *hld up: hdwy over 1f out: sn rdn: r.o: nt rch ldrs* **5/1**[2]
0-06 5 ½ **Novalist**[17] 258 6-8-13 45 (b) NeilFarley(3) 4 45
(Robin Bastiman) *prom: rdn over 2f out: sn outpcd: styd on u.p ins fnl f* **11/1**
45-5 6 hd **Very First Blade**[20] 215 5-9-4 47 (be) JoeFanning 10 46
(Michael Mullineaux) *hld up: pushed along and hdwy over 2f out: rdn over 1f out: styd on* **7/2**[1]
-230 7 ½ **Red Star Lady (IRE)**[10] 353 4-9-2 45 JimmyQuinn 5 43
(Shaun Harris) *s.i.s: hld up: swtchd lft and hdwy over 1f out: hrd rdn ins fnl f: nt rch ldrs* **33/1**
-354 8 1¼ **Upper Lambourn (IRE)**[7] 384 6-8-12 48 (t) RobJFitzpatrick(7) 12 42
(Christopher Kellett) *s.i.s: sn pushed along in rr: styd on u.p ins fnl f: nvr on terms* **9/1**
00-0 9 3¼ **True That (IRE)**[10] 353 4-9-2 45 (t) BenCurtis 1 28
(Brian Ellison) *prom: rdn over 2f out: wknd over 1f out* **16/1**
35/ 10 1¼ **Denbigh Raur (IRE)**[71] 8074 4-9-2 45 JohnFahy 9 24
(T G McCourt, Ire) *chsd ldrs: rdn over 2f out: wknd fnl f* **8/1**[3]
02-6 11 hd **Marmot Bay (IRE)**[24] 164 4-8-11 47 (p) EvaMoscrop(7) 11 26
(Philip Kirby) *slowly into strde: rdn over 2f out: a in rr* **12/1**
1m 16.62s (1.62) **Going Correction** +0.20s/f (Slow) 11 Ran SP% **126.7**
Speed ratings (Par 97): **97,95,94,93,93 93,92,90,86,84 84**
CSF £156.90 CT £711.85 TOTE £28.70: £4.70, £2.00, £2.70; EX 229.20 Trifecta £1232.80.
**Owner** Mrs P A Wallis & M A Geobey **Bred** Rev James Browne **Trained** Elmley Castle, Worcs
**FOCUS**
This low grade and devilishly tricky sprint handicap saw something of an upset. The third has been rated to her recent best.

## 503 LADBROKES H'CAP 7f 32y(P)
8:00 (8:01) (Class 6) (0-65,65) 4-Y-O+ £2,264 (£673; £336; £168) Stalls High

Form RPR
1344 1 **Munaawib**[9] 366 6-8-12 63 (bt) RyanWhile(7) 8 72
(David C Griffiths) *led 6f out: rdn over 1f out: r.o u.p* **8/1**
5-00 2 3¼ **Baltic Prince (IRE)**[13] 319 4-9-1 59 JoeFanning 7 59
(Paul Green) *a.p: shkn up to chse wnr over 1f out: styd on same pce ins fnl f* **9/1**
200- 3 nk **Mr Lando**[71] 8060 5-9-6 64 JimmyQuinn 4 63
(Richard Lee) *hld up: pushed along over 2f out: hdwy over 1f out: r.o: nt rch ldrs* **13/8**[1]
0/6- 4 hd **Copper Dock (IRE)**[27] 131 10-8-11 55 BenCurtis 1 54
(T G McCourt, Ire) *hld up: rdn and r.o ins fnl f: nt rch ldrs* **8/1**
1-04 5 ½ **For Shia And Lula (IRE)**[3] 464 5-9-7 65 (p) StephenCraine 5 63
(Daniel Mark Loughnane) *prom: chsd wnr 3f out tl rdn over 1f out: styd on same pce ins fnl f* **15/2**
20-2 6 4½ **Winterwell (USA)**[21] 195 4-9-7 65 (v) DanielTudhope 2 50
(David O'Meara) *prom: rdn over 2f out: wknd fnl f* **2/1**[2]
001- 7 ¾ **Rafaaf (IRE)**[68] 8118 6-9-1 62 MarkCoumbe(3) 3 45
(Richard Phillips) *led 1f: chsd wnr tl rdn 3f out: wknd fnl f* **11/2**[3]
1m 30.58s (0.98) **Going Correction** +0.20s/f (Slow) 7 Ran SP% **130.8**
Speed ratings (Par 101): **102,98,97,97,97 92,91**
CSF £85.71 CT £181.17 TOTE £3.40: £5.10, £10.20; EX 63.00 Trifecta £191.30.
**Owner** Willie McKay **Bred** Shadwell Estate Company Limited **Trained** Bawtry, S Yorks
**FOCUS**
Four of the previous six races on this card had produced all-the-way winners and that trend was to continue here. The winner has been rated as recording a personal best, but their have to be reservations given the uncontested lead.
T/Plt: £87.90 to a £1 stake. Pool: £107,882.51 - 895.60 winning units. T/Qpdt: £3.80 to a £1 stake. Pool: £10,662.21 - 2026.00 winning units. CR

# 438 MEYDAN (L-H)
Thursday, February 6
**OFFICIAL GOING: Turf: good; tapeta: standard**

## 504a IPIC TROPHY (H'CAP) (TAPETA) 7f
3:15 (3:15) (95-105,105) 3-Y-O+
£39,759 (£13,253; £6,626; £3,313; £1,987; £1,325)

RPR
1 **Eastern Rules (IRE)**[7] 396 6-9-4 102 ShaneFoley 5 104
(M Halford, Ire) *trckd ldng pair: led 2f out: r.o wl* **7/2**[2]
2 nk **Mustaheel (IRE)**[14] 308 5-9-5 104 (t) PaulHanagan 6 104+
(A Al Raihe, UAE) *hdwy ent st: r.o wl fnl 110yds: jst failed* **16/1**
3 nk **My Freedom (IRE)**[28] 109 6-9-4 102 SilvestreDeSousa 3 102
(Saeed bin Suroor) *trckd ldrs: led 2f out: hdd 1f out: r.o same pce* **3/1**[1]
4 ½ **Master Of War**[14] 304 4-9-2 100 JamesDoyle 8 99+
(D Selvaratnam, UAE) *mid-div: r.o fnl 2f: nrst fin* **25/1**
5 1¼ **Alnashmy (FR)**[21] 207 6-9-2 100 (tp) PatCosgrave 1 95
(J Peromingo, UAE) *trckd ldng pair: ev ch 1f out: one pce fnl 110yds* **7/1**
6 nk **Dragon Falls (IRE)**[165] 5808 5-9-3 101 MickaelBarzalona 9 96+
(Charlie Appleby) *settled in rr: nvr nr to chal but r.o fnl 1 1/2f* **7/1**
7 shd **Spirit Of Battle (USA)**[14] 304 6-9-2 100 (b) TadhgO'Shea 2 94+
(A bin Huzaim, UAE) *mid-div: chsd ldrs 2f out: nt qckn fnl f* **13/2**[3]
8 shd **Maraheb**[28] 109 6-9-2 100 (vt) DaneO'Neill 4 94
(A Al Raihe, UAE) *sn led: rdn 2 1/2f out: hdd 2f out: wknd fnl 110yds* **12/1**
9 4 **Silver Ocean (USA)**[14] 306 6-9-6 105 FrankieDettori 10 87
(Niels Petersen, Norway) *settled in rr: nvr nr to chal* **33/1**
10 nk **Santefisio**[7] 396 8-9-4 102 (b) TomEaves 12 85
(Keith Dalgleish) *slowly away: a in rr* **20/1**
11 1¼ **Encipher (USA)**[13] 335 5-9-5 104 (t) RoystonFfrench 14 82
(A Al Raihe, UAE) *nvr bttr than mid-div* **14/1**
12 2¾ **Russian Rock (IRE)**[41] 8422 7-9-5 104 WayneSmith 11 75
(M Al Muhairi, UAE) *a in rr* **14/1**
13 1½ **Alraihjan (KSA)**[14] 304 4-9-2 100 WilliamBuick 13 68
(B Al Shaibani, Saudi Arabia) *slowly away: trckd ldng pair tl wknd fnl 1 1/2f* **8/1**
14 4½ **Now Spun (USA)**[28] 112 4-8-8 102 (t) AhmadAlSubousi(10) 7 58
(A Al Raihe, UAE) *mid-div tl outpcd 3f out* **33/1**
1m 24.1s (-1.10) 14 Ran SP% **138.1**
CSF: 66.09; EX 60.80; TRIFECTA: 401.30; TRICAST: 202.33 WIN: 5.10; PL: 1.80, 5.40, 1.10.
**Owner** S Hales **Bred** Michael Woodlock & Seamus Kennedy **Trained** Doneany, Co Kildare
**FOCUS**
The pace was modest early before increasing - here are the splits compared to the Trakus pars: 25.87 (25.42), 49.31 (48.75), 1:12.53 (1:12.52), 1:24.10 (1:24.89). The first, third and fifth were well placed throughout.

## 505a MEYDAN CLASSIC TRIAL SPONSORED BY CEPSA, AN IPIC EMPOWERED COMPANY (CONDITIONS RACE) (TURF) 7f
3:50 (3:50) 3-Y-O
£27,108 (£9,036; £4,518; £2,259; £1,355; £903)

RPR
1 **He's No Saint**[118] 7180 3-8-9 90 FergalLynch 2 101
(David Marnane, Ire) *mid-div on rail: smooth prog 2f out: n.m.r 1 1/2f: led 1f out: comf* **14/1**
2 2 **Make It Reel (FR)**[21] 204 3-8-9 95 PatDobbs 5 96
(Doug Watson, UAE) *sn led: hdd 1f out but r.o gamely* **33/1**
3 nk **Najm Suhail**[5] 441 3-8-9 95 RoystonFfrench 12 95
(A Al Raihe, UAE) *trckd ldng pair: ev ch 1f out: nt qckn fnl 110yds* **10/1**
4 shd **Eye In The Sky (IRE)**[116] 3-8-9 93 (t) Per-AndersGraberg 7 95
(Niels Petersen, Norway) *settled in rr: nvr nr to chal but r.o fnl 2f: nrst fin* **16/1**
5 ¾ **Journeyman (SAF)**[21] 204 4-9-4 98 (e) ChristopheSoumillon 6 95
(M F De Kock, South Africa) *trckd ldng trio: rdn and outpcd 3f out: kpt on again fnl 1 1/2f* **6/1**[3]
6 nk **Figure Of Speech (IRE)**[21] 204 3-8-9 105 (p) AhmedAjtebi 11 92
(Charlie Appleby) *mid-div: r.o same pce fnl 1 1/2f* **13/2**
7 nk **Pretend (IRE)**[92] 7766 3-8-9 98 MickaelBarzalona 3 91
(Charlie Appleby) *trckd ldng trio: ev ch 1f out* **1/1**[1]

8 ½ **Autumn Lily (USA)**21 203 3-8-5 99 SilvestreDeSousa 8 86
(Charlie Appleby) *settled in rr: nvr nr to chal* 5/1²

9 ½ **Salvadori (IRE)** 3-8-10 ow1 AdriedeVries 1 89
(A bin Harmash, UAE) *v.s.a: a in rr* 20/1

10 ½ **Dubawi Fun**21 204 3-8-9 89 WilliamBuick 10 87
(Ismail Mohammed) *nvr nr to chal* 33/1

11 4½ **Man Amongst Men (IRE)**21 204 3-8-9 85 (bt) PaulHanagan 9 75
(Brian Meehan) *trckd ldrs tl outpcd 1/12f out* 33/1

1m 24.16s (84.16)
**WFA** 3 from 4yo 17lb **11** Ran SP% **129.5**
CSF: 427.49; EX 278.10; TRIFECTA: 3454.80; WIN: 13.20; PL: 2.90, 9.10, 4.20.
**Owner** Damian Lavelle **Bred** Follow The Flag Partnership **Trained** Bansha, Co Tipperary

**FOCUS**
A trial for a Listed race to be run over C&D on February 27, but not form to get excited about as the better horses from this age group tend to be aimed at the Tapeta Classics, and the heavily backed favourite disappointed. They did, though, go a good gallop, with each split under the Trakus par, and here are the sectionals: 25.28 (400m), 22.86 (800m), 23.60 (1200m), 12.42 (finish). The second and third have been rated to their marks.

## 506a UAE 1000 GUINEAS SPONSORED BY NOVA, AN IPIC EMPOWERED COMPANY (LISTED RACE) (FILLIES) (TAPETA) 1m
**4:25** (4:25) 3-Y-O

**£90,361** (£30,120; £15,060; £7,530; £4,518; £3,012)

RPR

1 **Ihtimal (IRE)**132 6798 3-8-9 105 SilvestreDeSousa 1 106+
(Saeed bin Suroor) *mid-div: smooth prog 2f out: led 1f out: comf* 5/4¹

2 3¼ **Mensoora (SAF)**7 395 4-9-5 100 ChristopheSoumillon 9 102
(M F De Kock, South Africa) *trckd ldng pair: rdn 3f out: led briefly 1 1/2f out: hdd 1f out: r.o same pce* 6/1³

3 1¾ **Feedyah (USA)**152 6185 3-8-9 91 MartinLane 3 95
(Charlie Appleby) *mid-div: chsd ldrs 2 1/2f out: r.o same* 12/1

4 hd **Wedding Ring (IRE)**21 203 3-8-9 97 MickaelBarzalona 8 94
(Charlie Appleby) *settled in rr: nvr nr to chal but r.o fnl 1 1/2f: nrst fin* 5/1²

5 ¾ **Magrooma (AUS)**21 203 4-9-5 98 RichardHughes 7 95
(M F De Kock, South Africa) *settled in rr: nvr nr to chal but r.o fnl 1 1/2f* 5/1²

6 ¾ **Oxsana**21 203 3-8-9 93 WilliamBuick 4 91
(William Haggas) *slowly away: settled in rr: nvr nr to chal but r.o fnl 1 1/2f* 20/1

7 nse **Magroora (AUS)**21 203 4-9-5 90 ThierryThulliez 2 93
(M F De Kock, South Africa) *sn led: hdd & wknd 1 1/2f out* 25/1

8 2 **More Aspen (USA)**21 203 3-8-9 86 RichardMullen 6 86
(S Seemar, UAE) *nvr nr to chal* 33/1

9 3¾ **Letterfromamerica (USA)**21 203 3-8-9 88 (bt) TadhgO'Shea 10 77
(S Seemar, UAE) *trckd ldng trio tl outpcd 2f out* 25/1

10 1¼ **Illuminating Dream (IRE)**140 6545 3-8-9 84 PaulHanagan 5 74
(David Brown) *nvr bttr than mid-div* 33/1

11 4½ **Sign Of Lucky (USA)**110 3-8-9 85 PatDobbs 11 64
(Doug Watson, UAE) *trckd ldrs tl outpcd 2 1/2f out* 16/1

1m 36.64s (-0.86)
**WFA** 3 from 4yo 19lb **11** Ran SP% **124.0**
CSF: 9.00; EX 18.90; TRIFECTA: 249.20; WIN: 2.50; PL: 1.40, 3.30, 5.10.
**Owner** Godolphin **Bred** Darley **Trained** Newmarket, Suffolk

**FOCUS**
Each split was under the Trakus par: 25.33 (25.91), 48.80 (49.09), 1:13.04 (1:13.06), 1:36.64 (1:37.34). The local trial from January 16, the form of which had already let down by Autumn Lily in the preceding race, failed to produce a top-three finisher from six representatives. The eighth potentially limits the form.

## 507a NOVA STKS (H'CAP) (TURF) 1m 6f 11y
**5:05** (5:05) (95-109,109) 3-Y-O+

**£54,216** (£18,072; £9,036; £4,518; £2,710; £1,807)

RPR

1 **Excellent Result (IRE)**14 305 4-8-6 **99** SilvestreDeSousa 2 102+
(Saeed bin Suroor) *mid-div: rdn 3f out: led fnl 110yds* 7/2²

2 ¾ **Star Empire (SAF)**21 205 8-9-6 **109** ChristopheSoumillon 10 110
(M F De Kock, South Africa) *settled in rr: rdn 4f out: r.o fnl 1 1/2f: nrst fin* 9/4¹

3 nse **Certerach (IRE)**14 305 6-9-2 **105** ShaneFoley 4 106
(M Halford, Ire) *in rr of mid-div: rdn 3f out: chsd ldrs 2f out: led briefly 1f out: hdd fnl 110yds* 4/1³

4 1¾ **Ralston Road (IRE)**21 202 4-8-8 **101** TadhgO'Shea 9 100+
(S Seemar, UAE) *settled in rr: r.o fnl 2f: nrst fin* 20/1

5 ¾ **Great Hall**21 202 4-8-6 **99** (b) MartinLane 11 97
(Brian Meehan) *trckd ldrs: led 10f out: rdn and hdd 3f out: r.o same pce* 25/1

6 shd **Tenenbaum**146 6348 5-9-2 **105** MickaelBarzalona 14 102
(Charlie Appleby) *slowly away: settled in rr: chsd ldrs 1 1/2f out: one pce fnl f* 14/1

7 nk **Manalapan (IRE)**14 307 4-9-1 **108** FrankieDettori 8 106
(P J Prendergast, Ire) *sn led: hdd 10f out: rdn and wknd 3f out* 10/1

8 nk **Jutland**14 305 7-9-2 **105** PatDobbs 5 101
(Doug Watson, UAE) *in rr of mid-div: nvr able to chal* 16/1

9 ¾ **Without Fear (FR)**14 309 6-9-5 **108** Per-AndersGraberg 1 103
(Niels Petersen, Norway) *nvr bttr than mid-div* 33/1

10 1¼ **Statutory (IRE)**122 7064 4-8-10 **104** WilliamBuick 12 98
(Saeed bin Suroor) *trckd ldrs: led 3f out: hdd & wknd 1 1/2f out* 8/1

11 3 **Thecornishcockney**14 305 5-9-0 **102** (p) BrettDoyle 13 92
(John Ryan) *s.i.s: nvr nr to chal* 33/1

12 3¼ **Balladry (USA)**21 202 6-9-1 **104** (tp) RichardMullen 6 89
(S Seemar, UAE) *trckd ldrs: ev ch tl outpcd 3f out* 25/1

13 shd **Tanfeeth**14 305 6-8-11 **100** (t) PaulHanagan 7 85
(M Al Muhairi, UAE) *nvr bttr than mid-div* 10/1

14 5¾ **Jedi**14 305 8-8-6 **95** JRosales 3 72
(A bin Huzaim, UAE) *settled in rr: n.d* 50/1

2m 59.74s (179.74)
**WFA** 4 from 5yo+ 5lb **14** Ran SP% **135.1**
CSF: 12.46; EX 18.00; TRIFECTA: 66.00; TRICAST: 37.14 WIN: 4.80; PL: 1.90, 1.10, 2.30.
**Owner** Godolphin **Bred** Tom & Geraldine Molan **Trained** Newmarket, Suffolk

**FOCUS**
They went an okay gallop and the form seems fair.

## 508a AL MAKTOUM CHALLENGE R2 EMPOWERED BY IPIC (GROUP 2) (TAPETA) 1m 1f 110y
**5:40** (5:40) 3-Y-O+

**£90,361** (£30,120; £15,060; £7,530; £4,518; £3,012)

RPR

1 **Prince Bishop (IRE)**103 7535 7-9-0 110 (v) KierenFallon 7 118
(Saeed bin Suroor) *mid-div: led 3 1/2f out: r.o wl: comf* 14/1

2 1¼ **African Story**313 1269 7-9-0 119 SilvestreDeSousa 12 115+
(Saeed bin Suroor) *settled in rr: rdn 2 1/2f out: r.o fnl 2f: nrst fin* 3/1¹

3 4 **Zambucca (SAF)**7 397 6-9-0 106 PatCosgrave 6 107
(S Seemar, UAE) *mid-div: r.o fnl 2f but no ch w wnr* 50/1

4 1¼ **Hunter's Light (IRE)**110 7367 6-9-0 117 (v) WilliamBuick 8 105
(Saeed bin Suroor) *trckd ldng trio: ev ch 2f out: one pce fnl f* 4/1²

5 shd **Zahee (NZ)**7 396 5-9-0 111 ChristopheSoumillon 1 104
(M F De Kock, South Africa) *mid-div: r.o same pce fnl 2f* 10/1

6 1 **Dunaden (FR)**60 8208 8-9-0 117 HarryBentley 2 102
(M Delzangles, France) *settled in rr: nvr nr to chal but r.o fnl 1 1/2f* 12/1

7 nk **Samurai Sword**28 111 6-9-0 104 (t) AdriedeVries 10 102
(A bin Harmash, UAE) *in rr of mid-div: r.o fnl 2f but nvr able to chal* 50/1

8 nk **Surfer (USA)**49 8356 5-9-0 113 (t) RichardMullen 15 101
(S Seemar, UAE) *trckd ldrs tl outpcd 3f out* 12/1

9 1½ **Zain Shamardal (IRE)**21 207 6-9-0 108 (t) RoystonFfrench 5 98
(A Al Raihe, UAE) *nvr bttr than mid-div* 20/1

10 1¼ **Heavy Metal (SAF)**14 308 6-9-0 118 RichardHughes 9 96
(S G Tarry, South Africa) *settled in rr: nvr able to chal but r.o wl fnl 2f* 8/1³

11 2 **Empire Storm (GER)**28 111 7-9-0 109 (t) DaneO'Neill 4 91
(Michael Attwater) *trckd ldrs: ev ch 1 1/2f out: nt qckn fnl 110yds* 25/1

12 1½ **Mutajare (IRE)**14 307 6-9-0 111 (t) PaulHanagan 14 88
(A Al Raihe, UAE) *nvr bttr than mid-div* 28/1

13 2½ **Prince Alzain (USA)**82 7927 5-9-0 110 (p) OisinMurphy 16 83
(Fawzi Abdulla Nass, Bahrain) *s.i.s: nvr nr to chal* 14/1

14 2¼ **Interpret (USA)**27 136 6-9-0 110 (v) JamesDoyle 3 79
(M Al Muhairi, UAE) *slowly away: nvr nr to chal* 33/1

15 13 **Artigiano (USA)**28 110 4-8-13 105 MickaelBarzalona 13 52
(Charlie Appleby) *sn led: hdd & wknd 3 1/2f out* 10/1

16 5 **Battle Of Marengo (IRE)**208 4325 4-8-13 117 FrankieDettori 11 42
(Ernst Oertel, UAE) *a in rr* 11/1

1m 55.67s (-3.33) **16** Ran SP% **130.3**
CSF: 55.88; EX 133.80; TRIFECTA: 47277.0; WIN: 18.80; PL: 4.20, 2.00, 18.80.
**Owner** Sheikh Hamdan bin Mohammed Al Maktoum **Bred** Thurso Ltd **Trained** Newmarket, Suffolk

**FOCUS**
This was a race that had promised much, but ended up going to the exposed Prince Bishop, thanks in no small part to an outstanding ride from Kieren Fallon. Never worse than fifth off a relatively even early pace (26.21 from standing start, followed by 24.10 at 800m and 24.65 at 1200m), the winner then put in a 23sec furlong to lead at the 1600m point, before coming home in 17.64 compared to 16.88 for the held-up African Story. In the process, Prince Bishop covered eight metres less than the runner-up. The form is rated around the winner, third, fifth and seventh.

## 509a CEPSA MILE (H'CAP) (TURF) 1m
**6:15** (6:15) (100-110,110) 3-Y-O+

**£43,373** (£14,457; £7,228; £3,614; £2,168; £1,445)

RPR

1 **Mont Ras (IRE)**14 306 7-8-11 101 WilliamBuick 4 104
(David O'Meara) *trckd ldrs: rdn 2f out: led 1f out: r.o wl* 6/1³

2 ½ **El Estruendoso (ARG)**14 309 5-9-0 104 ChristopheSoumillon 1 106+
(M F De Kock, South Africa) *mid-div on rail: smooth prog 2 1/2f out: r.o fnl 1 1/2f: nrst fin* 2/1¹

3 1 **Disa Leader (SAF)**14 306 9-9-1 105 ow1 JGeroudis 16 105
(M F De Kock, South Africa) *sn led: rdn 3f out: hdd 1 1/2f out: kpt on same pce fnl 110yds* 11/1

4 nk **Avon Pearl**109 5-8-10 100 (vt) AdriedeVries 5 99+
(Rune Haugen, Norway) *in rr of mid-div: r.o fnl 2f: nrst fin* 33/1

5 shd **Le Drakkar (AUS)**14 308 9-9-3 107 (t) TadhgO'Shea 16 106+
(A bin Huzaim, UAE) *slowly away: nvr nr to chal but r.o fnl 2f* 50/1

6 ½ **Derbaas (USA)**14 306 8-9-0 104 (t) DaneO'Neill 3 101
(A Al Raihe, UAE) *trckd ldng pair: ev ch 2f out: one pce fnl f* 16/1

7 nk **Edu Querido (BRZ)**263 5-9-5 109 MartinHarley 11 106
(Marco Botti) *trckd ldng pair: led briefly 1 1/2f out: hdd 1f out: r.o same pce fnl 110yds* 5/1²

8 1 **Chil The Kite**14 306 5-9-4 108 RichardHughes 7 102
(Hughie Morrison) *settled in rr: nvr able to chal* 5/1²

9 shd **Banna Boirche (IRE)**172 5572 8-8-10 100 ShaneFoley 9 94
(M Halford, Ire) *settled in rr: nvr nr to chal* 12/1

10 nk **Alhebayeb (IRE)**7 396 4-8-10 100 (b) PatCosgrave 10 94
(M F De Kock, South Africa) *nvr able to chal* 25/1

11 shd **Ocean Tempest**14 306 5-9-0 104 BrettDoyle 2 97
(John Ryan) *nvr bttr than mid-div* 20/1

12 1¾ **Spoil The Fun (FR)**14 306 5-9-3 107 (t) JulienAuge 15 96
(C Ferland, France) *nvr bttr than mid-div* 14/1

13 nk **Mufarrh (IRE)**7 396 7-9-5 109 (t) PaulHanagan 12 98
(A Al Raihe, UAE) *nvr bttr than mid-div* 12/1

14 3 **Dux Scholar**14 308 6-9-6 110 PatDobbs 6 92
(Doug Watson, UAE) *nvr bttr than mid-div* 10/1

15 4¼ **Muraweg (IRE)**28 109 8-8-11 105 (v) OisinMurphy(4) 8 77
(Fawzi Abdulla Nass, Bahrain) *nvr bttr than mid-div* 40/1

16 4½ **Gold Pearl (USA)**13 334 6-8-10 100 (t) RichardMullen 13 62
(S Seemar, UAE) *midfield in tch on outer: rdn 2f out: sn no ex and btn: fdd and eased* 20/1

1m 36.55s (96.55) **16** Ran SP% **147.0**
CSF: 20.90; EX 43.00; TRICAST: £153.72, TRIFECTA: 891.70; WIN: 11.30. Placepot: £487.60 to a £1 stake. Pool: £10,488.45 - 15.70 winning units. Quadpot: £330.90 to a £1 stake. Pool: £984.00 - 2.20 winning units..
**Owner** Colne Valley Racing **Bred** Patrick M Ryan **Trained** Nawton, N Yorks

**FOCUS**
It paid to be handy. The second, third and fourth help set the standard.

# [497]WOLVERHAMPTON (A.W) (L-H)

Friday, February 7

**OFFICIAL GOING: Standard**

Wind: Light behind Weather: Cloudy with sunny spells

## 510 BEST ODDS AT BOOKMAKERS.CO.UK H'CAP 5f 20y(P)

**5:00** (5:00) (Class 6) (0-65,71) 4-Y-O+ **£2,264** (£673; £336; £168) **Stalls** Low

Form RPR

12-2 **1** **Iffranesia (FR)**[8] 383 4-9-6 **64** (p) TomQueally 3 72
(Robert Cowell) *s.i.s: hld up: hdwy over 1f out: rdn to ld ins fnl f: r.o readily* **4/5**[1]

3-33 **2** ¾ **Master Of Disguise**[18] 259 8-9-5 **63** DuranFentiman 5 68
(Brian Baugh) *chsd ldrs: rdn over 1f out: r.o* **11/2**[3]

55-0 **3** 1 ½ **Rise To Glory (IRE)**[27] 141 6-9-1 **62** NeilFarley(3) 4 62
(Shaun Harris) *sn led: rdn over 1f out: hdd and unable qck ins fnl f* **3/1**[2]

-101 **4** *nk* **Sir Geoffrey (IRE)**[8] 383 8-9-6 **71** 6ex (p) MatthewHopkins(7) 1 70
(Scott Dixon) *w ldr: rdn and ev ch ins fnl f: styd on same pce* **15/2**

150- **5** *18* **Little Choosey**[111] 7381 4-9-2 **60** GeorgeBaker 2
(Anabel K Murphy) *prom: pushed along 1/2-way: sn wknd* **10/1**

1m 2.03s (-0.27) **Going Correction** +0.05s/f (Slow) **5** Ran SP% **116.8**
Speed ratings (Par 101): **104,102,100,99,71**
CSF £6.38 TOTE £1.50: £1.10, £4.00; EX 8.80 Trifecta £15.30.
**Owner** Cyril Humphris **Bred** Cyril Humphris **Trained** Six Mile Bottom, Cambs

**FOCUS**
There was a disputed lead here.

## 511 COMPARE BOOKMAKERS AT BOOKMAKERS.CO.UK H'CAP 5f 216y(P)

**5:30** (5:30) (Class 6) (0-60,61) 4-Y-O+ **£2,264** (£673; £336; £168) **Stalls** Low

Form RPR

-222 **1** **Grace Hull**[17] 273 4-9-7 **60** (p) TomQueally 11 70
(Garry Moss) *sn pushed along in rr: hdwy over 1f out: rdn to ld wl ins fnl f: r.o* **13/2**[2]

0-40 **2** ¾ **Climaxfortackle (IRE)**[18] 259 6-9-7 **60** JoeFanning 8 68+
(Derek Shaw) *s.i.s: hld up: nt clr run over 2f out: hdwy over 1f out: nt clr run and swtchd lft ins fnl f: sn rdn and edgd rt: r.o* **10/1**

5-41 **3** *2* **Consistant**[11] 353 6-9-3 **61** 6ex EoinWalsh(5) 7 62+
(Brian Baugh) *chsd ldrs: led over 1f out: rdn and hdd wl ins fnl f* **14/1**

2-50 **4** 1 ½ **Ivestar (IRE)**[18] 258 9-9-2 **55** (v) JamesSullivan 2 51
(Michael Easterby) *chsd ldrs: rdn over 2f out: edgd lft and styd on same pce fnl f* **7/1**[3]

3-11 **5** ½ **Interchoice Star**[29] 100 9-9-5 **58** (p) GeorgeBaker 10 53
(Ray Peacock) *chsd ldr tl led 1/2-way: rdn and hdd over 1f out: no ex ins fnl f* **7/1**[3]

50-1 **6** *nk* **Reginald Claude**[23] 192 6-8-12 **58** CharlotteJenner(7) 5 52
(Mark Usher) *hld up: hdwy and nt clr run over 1f out: nt trble ldrs* **12/1**

0-03 **7** *nk* **Belle Bayardo (IRE)**[4] 452 6-9-4 **57** LukeMorris 12 50
(Ronald Harris) *hld up: pushed along 1/2-way: styd on ins fnl f: nvr nrr* **10/1**

/6-4 **8** *nse* **Copper Dock (IRE)**[1] 503 10-9-2 **55** BenCurtis 1 48
(T G McCourt, Ire) *hld up in tch: nt clr run over 2f out: rdn over 1f out: no ex fnl f* **10/1**

2-60 **9** *12* **Marmot Bay (IRE)**[1] 502 4-8-8 **47** (p) JimmyQuinn 9
(Philip Kirby) *led to 1/2-way: wknd fnl f* **33/1**

5-00 **10** 1 ¼ **Valdaw**[15] 296 6-9-7 **60** ShaneKelly 6
(Mike Murphy) *chsd ldrs: rdn over 2f out: wknd over 1f out* **7/2**[1]

446- **11** 3 ½ **Hot Sugar (USA)**[48] 8384 5-9-7 **60** (p) AndrewMullen 13
(Michael Appleby) *mid-div: forced to r wd thrght: wknd 2f out* **8/1**

565- **12** *4* **Admirals Walk (IRE)**[76] 8023 4-9-4 **57** (b) DaleSwift 4
(Barry Brennan) *mid-div: sn pushed along: wknd over 2f out* **20/1**

1m 15.36s (0.36) **Going Correction** +0.05s/f (Slow) **12** Ran SP% **121.0**
Speed ratings (Par 101): **99,98,95,93,92 92,91,91,75,74 69,64**
CSF £71.61 CT £893.39 TOTE £6.60: £2.40, £4.80, £3.50; EX 80.40 Trifecta £294.60.
**Owner** Ron Hull **Bred** Whitsbury Manor Stud & Pigeon House Stud **Trained** Tickhill, S Yorks

**FOCUS**
This looked pretty competitive and there was competition for the lead, resulting in the race being set up for a couple of patiently ridden horses.

## 512 BOOKMAKERS.CO.UK MEDIAN AUCTION MAIDEN STKS 5f 216y(P)

**6:00** (6:02) (Class 6) 3-5-Y-O **£2,264** (£673; £336; £168) **Stalls** Low

Form RPR

3-23 **1** **Ealain Aibrean (IRE)**[20] 232 3-8-7 67 ChrisCatlin 3 65
(David Evans) *mde all: rdn over 1f out: edgd lft ins fnl f: styd on gamely* **7/2**[2]

624- **2** ¾ **Jolly Red Jeanz (IRE)**[92] 7790 3-8-7 63 JoeFanning 1 63
(J W Hills) *chsd ldrs: pushed along 1/2-way: rdn over 1f out: styd on* **4/1**[3]

2 **3** *nk* **Blacke Forest**[5] 447 3-8-7 0 DavidProbert 4 62
(William Muir) *chsd wnr: rdn and ev ch over 1f out: kpt on* **6/5**[1]

64 **4** ½ **Parkhill Star**[11] 355 3-8-7 0 RichardKingscote 2 60
(Tom Dascombe) *sn pushed along and prom: shkn up over 1f out: nt clr run ins fnl f: kpt on* **9/1**

5 **5** 3 ¼ **Harboured (USA)**[9] 371 3-8-7 0 LukeMorris 5 50+
(Sir Mark Prescott Bt) *sn pushed along in rr: hdwy over 3f out: rdn over 2f out: no ex fnl f* **9/1**

1m 16.19s (1.19) **Going Correction** +0.05s/f (Slow) **5** Ran SP% **107.7**
Speed ratings (Par 101): **94,93,92,91,87**
CSF £16.42 TOTE £4.90: £2.20, £3.30; EX 11.20 Trifecta £22.10.
**Owner** Mrs E Evans & C W Racing **Bred** Mrs C L Weld **Trained** Pandy, Monmouths

**FOCUS**
Technically this was not a fillies' maiden, but no colts or geldings were in the line-up.

## 513 32RED H'CAP 1m 5f 194y(P)

**6:30** (6:30) (Class 5) (0-75,75) 4-Y-O+ **£3,234** (£962; £481; £240) **Stalls** Low

Form RPR

422- **1** **Singzak**[43] 8400 6-9-10 **73** GrahamGibbons 4 81
(Michael Easterby) *mde all: rdn over 1f out: hung lft ins fnl f: styd on* **9/4**[1]

0/0- **2** *1* **Pinotage**[16] 7100 6-8-7 **56** oh1 (p) JamesSullivan 6 63
(Peter Niven) *a.p: chsd wnr over 2f out: rdn over 1f out: nt clr run ins fnl f: styd on same pce* **20/1**

310- **3** *5* **Lacey**[51] 8331 5-8-8 **64** RobHornby(7) 2 64
(Andrew Hollinshead) *mid-div: outpcd over 3f out: styd on to go 3rd wl ins fnl f: nt rch ldrs* **11/2**[3]

26-3 **4** *nk* **Brunello**[10] 361 6-8-10 **59** (p) LukeMorris 3 58
(Philip Kirby) *s.i.s: in rr: drvn along over 4f out: hdwy u.p over 2f out: kpt on: nt trble ldrs* **16/1**

5-22 **5** ¾ **Scribe (IRE)**[18] 260 6-9-6 **69** (vt) LiamKeniry 8 67
(David Evans) *chsd wnr tl rdn over 2f out: no ex fnl f* **5/2**[2]

600- **6** 3 ½ **Kayalar (IRE)**[54] 6435 6-9-2 **65** (v[1]) TomQueally 5 58
(Evan Williams) *hld up: rdn over 2f out: n.d* **16/1**

12-3 **7** ¾ **Stormy Morning**[28] 123 8-8-7 **63** (p) EvaMoscrop(7) 7 55
(Philip Kirby) *hld up: sme hdwy over 1f out: nt clr run and wknd ins fnl f* **12/1**

601- **8** *8* **Calaf**[15] 7596 6-9-12 **75** GeorgeBaker 1 56
(Jonjo O'Neill) *trckd ldrs: pushed along over 2f out: rdn and wknd over 1f out* **11/2**[3]

3m 3.61s (-2.39) **Going Correction** +0.05s/f (Slow) **8** Ran SP% **114.3**
Speed ratings (Par 103): **108,107,104,104,103 101,101,96**
CSF £47.11 CT £223.31 TOTE £3.50: £2.00, £5.60, £1.10; EX 68.20 Trifecta £408.60.
**Owner** Clark Industrial Services Partnership **Bred** Clark Industrial Services Partnership **Trained** Sheriff Hutton, N Yorks

**FOCUS**
This was dominated from the front.

## 514 CORAL APP DOWNLOAD FROM THE APP STORE H'CAP 1m 4f 50y(P)

**7:00** (7:00) (Class 4) (0-85,83) 4-Y-O+ **£5,175** (£1,540; £769; £384) **Stalls** Low

Form RPR

2-12 **1** **Like A Diamond (IRE)**[7] 408 4-8-13 **78** TomQueally 6 87+
(Evan Williams) *hld up in tch: led over 1f out: sn rdn: r.o* **3/1**[2]

4-1 **2** ¾ **Sagesse**[16] 276 4-8-11 **76** LukeMorris 9 83+
(Sir Mark Prescott Bt) *trckd ldrs: pushed along and n.m.r over 1f out: rdn: edgd lft and r.o wl ins fnl f* **2/1**[1]

1/-1 **3** *nse* **Bute Hall**[22] 197 5-8-8 **77** RobJFitzpatrick(7) 5 84
(David Thompson) *hld up: hdwy over 1f out: sn hung lft: rdn ins fnl f: r.o* **8/1**

1-30 **4** *shd* **Returntobrecongill**[16] 285 4-9-1 **80** JamesSullivan 8 87
(James Given) *led: rdn and hdd over 1f out: styd on* **15/2**

30-2 **5** 1 ¼ **Fly Solo**[36] 21 5-8-8 **70** BenCurtis 1 75
(Alan Swinbank) *a.p: rdn over 1f out: styd on same pce ins fnl f* **6/1**

3/0- **6** ¾ **Pertemps Networks**[34] 4995 10-9-1 **77** GrahamGibbons 10 80
(Michael Easterby) *chsd ldr: pushed along over 2f out: rdn ins fnl f: eased whn hld towards fin* **25/1**

5-42 **7** *1* **Oratorio's Joy (IRE)**[12] 350 4-8-11 **76** FergusSweeney 3 78
(Jamie Osborne) *hld up: rdn over 1f out: nt trble ldrs* **5/1**[3]

000/ **8** *7* **Coin Of The Realm (IRE)**[285] 3156 9-8-13 **80** EoinWalsh(5) 4 71
(Miss Imogen Pickard) *s.i.s: hld up: rdn over 2f out: a in rr* **50/1**

12-0 **9** *nk* **Brigadoon**[25] 163 7-9-7 **83** GeorgeBaker 7 73
(Philip Kirby) *hld up: a in rr* **8/1**

53-2 **10** 1 ½ **Spanish Plume**[26] 151 6-8-7 **69** oh2 (p) JimmyQuinn 2 57
(Andrew Hollinshead) *trckd ldrs: racd keenly: rdn over 1f out: wknd fnl f* **20/1**

2m 40.48s (-0.62) **Going Correction** +0.05s/f (Slow)
**WFA** 4 from 5yo+ 3lb **10** Ran SP% **133.8**
Speed ratings (Par 105): **104,103,103,103,102 102,101,96,96,95**
CSF £10.92 CT £49.54 TOTE £3.80: £1.50, £2.20, £2.90; EX 13.10 Trifecta £101.10.
**Owner** R E R Williams **Bred** J Costello **Trained** Llancarfan, Vale Of Glamorgan

**FOCUS**
There were several unexposed AW performers in this line-up and the form should work out okay.

## 515 CORAL MOBILE "JUST THREE CLICKS TO BET" MEDIAN AUCTION MAIDEN STKS 1m 1f 103y(P)

**7:30** (7:30) (Class 6) 3-5-Y-O **£2,264** (£673; £336; £168) **Stalls** Low

Form RPR

5-2 **1** **God's Speed (IRE)**[28] 127 3-8-7 0 ChrisCatlin 2 76
(Rae Guest) *led: hdd 8f out: trckd ldr tl led again over 3f out: pushed clr fnl 2f* **4/9**[1]

6- **2** *10* **Hallouella**[105] 7513 3-8-2 0 LukeMorris 3 57
(James Tate) *chsd ldr tl 8f out: pushed along over 5f out: wnt 2nd again 3f out: sn drvn along: outpcd fnl 2f: eased ins fnl f* **15/8**[2]

0-55 **3** *14* **Another Journey**[12] 352 5-9-9 41 (e) EoinWalsh(5) 5 31
(Lisa Williamson) *prom: racd keenly: hmpd after 1f: sn stdd and dropped to rr: hdwy and rdn over 2f out: sn wknd* **50/1**

006- **4** 3 ¾ **Rocky Hill Ridge**[134] 6773 3-8-7 0 (bp) BenCurtis 1 18
(Alan McCabe) *prom: rdn over 3f out: wknd over 2f out* **40/1**

**5** *2* **Blacksmiths Arms**[12] 4-9-7 0 DanielleMooney(7) 4 19
(Michael Easterby) *s.i.s: plld hrd: hdwy to ld 8f out: hdd over 3f out: wknd over 2f out* **33/1**[3]

2m 3.21s (1.51) **Going Correction** +0.05s/f (Slow)
**WFA** 3 from 4yo+ 21lb **5** Ran SP% **111.4**
Speed ratings (Par 101): **95,86,73,70,68**
CSF £1.54 TOTE £1.40: £1.10, £1.30; EX 1.90 Trifecta £6.40.
**Owner** The Hornets **Bred** The Hornets **Trained** Newmarket, Suffolk

**FOCUS**
This proved straightforward for the favourite.

## 516 LADBROKES H'CAP 7f 32y(P)

**8:00** (8:00) (Class 7) (0-50,51) 4-Y-O+ **£2,264** (£673; £336; £168) **Stalls** High

Form RPR

-326 **1** **Huzzah (IRE)**[23] 179 9-8-11 **48** AlistairRawlinson(7) 12 63
(Michael Appleby) *hld up in tch: rdn to ld over 1f out: edgd lft ins fnl f: r.o* **4/1**[2]

00-0 **2** 1 ½ **Pipers Piping (IRE)**[15] 290 8-9-1 **48** RossAtkinson(5) 10 59
(Mandy Rowland) *a.p: chsd ldr 1/2-way: rdn and ev ch 1f out: styd on* **11/1**

3-41 **3** ½ **Starbotton**[9] 370 4-9-2 **51** 6ex ShirleyTeasdale(5) 2 61
(James Bethell) *led: rdn and hdd over 1f out: styd on same pce ins fnl f* **9/4**[1]

-302 **4** *3* **Vale Of Clara (IRE)**[12] 351 6-9-2 **46** (b) PaulMulrennan 9 48+
(Peter Niven) *hld up: rdn over 1f out: r.o ins fnl f: nt rch ldrs* **11/2**[3]

54-0 **5** 3 ¾ **Lichen Angel**[15] 290 4-9-0 **47** (p[1]) GeorgeChaloner(3) 3 38
(Richard Whitaker) *chsd ldr to 1/2-way: rdn over 2f out: wknd fnl f* **40/1**

0-60 **6** 1 ¾ **David's Secret**[18] 263 4-9-5 **49** (v[1]) ShaneKelly 8 36
(Roy Brotherton) *hld up: rdn over 1f out: nvr nrr* **16/1**

**7** *nse* **Ghost Of A Girl (IRE)**[14] 326 4-9-3 **47** (v[1]) BenCurtis 11 34
(T G McCourt, Ire) *s.i.s: hld up: rdn over 1f out: nvr on terms* **16/1**

54-5 **8** *nk* **Monsieur Pontaven**[14] 317 7-9-3 **50** (b) NeilFarley(3) 4 36
(Robin Bastiman) *s.i.s: hld up: hmpd over 2f out: nvr nrr* **8/1**

5-00 **9** ¾ **Michael's Nook**[9] 370 7-9-4 **48** (p) LukeMorris 7 32
(Alastair Lidderdale) *hld up: rdn over 2f out: n.d* **33/1**

000- **10** *3* **High On The Hog (IRE)**[112] 7354 6-9-6 **50**...................(p) GeorgeBaker 5 26
(Mark Brisbourne) *prom: racd keenly: rdn and wknd over 1f out* **8/1**

04-6 **11** *16* **Hispania (IRE)**[14] 317 4-9-1 **50**.......................................... EoinWalsh(5) 1
(John Mackie) *chsd ldrs: rdn and wkng whn hmpd over 2f out* **14/1**

1m 29.76s (0.16) **Going Correction** +0.05s/f (Slow) **11** Ran SP% **120.5**
Speed ratings (Par 97): **101,99,98,95,91 89,88,87,84 66**
CSF £49.08 CT £126.07 TOTE £6.80: £2.30, £4.30, £1.10; EX 48.20 Trifecta £110.80.
**Owner** Richard Popplewell **Bred** S And S Hubbard Rodwell **Trained** Danethorpe, Notts

**FOCUS**
The early gallop wasn't strong and not many got into the race.
T/Plt: £22.50 to a £1 stake. Pool: £133,420.05 - 4,318.05 winning tickets T/Qpdt: £5.30 to a £1 stake. Pool: £10,970.84 - 1,528.95 winning tickets CR

517 - 529a (Foreign Racing) - See Raceform Interactive

# 490 LINGFIELD (L-H)
## Saturday, February 8

**OFFICIAL GOING: Standard**
Wind: strong, half behind Weather: bright spells, heavy showers

## 530 CORAL.CO.UK BEST ODDS GUARANTEED ON RACING H'CAP 1m 4f (P)
**1:30** (1:30) (Class 6) (0-52,52) 4-Y-0+ **£2,385** (£704; £352) **Stalls** Low

Form RPR

331 **1** **Waving**[5] 460 5-9-6 **51**...........................................(t) LukeMorris 3 58+
(Tony Carroll) *in tch in midfield: rdn and effrt to press ldrs 3f out: led wl over 1f out: drew clr 1f out: styd on wl: comf* **4/7**[1]

6/0- **2** *2 1/2* **Miles Of Sunshine**[21] 7668 9-9-3 **48**............................ DavidProbert 7 51
(Ron Hodges) *led: rdn and hdd ent fnl 2f: 3rd and outpcd ent fnl f: no ch w wnr but kpt on to go 2nd cl home* **33/1**

5-32 **3** *shd* **Lisahane Bog**[5] 459 7-9-2 **50**...............(v) WilliamTwiston-Davies(3) 6 53
(Peter Hedger) *chsd ldr: rdn to ld ent fnl 2f: hdd wl over 1f out: outpcd 1f out: styd on same pce fnl f: lost 2nd cl home* **9/4**[2]

0-0 **4** *1/2* **Novel Dancer**[10] 368 6-8-8 **46** oh1...............................(v[1]) NedCurtis(7) 4 48
(Lydia Richards) *chsd ldrs: 4th and outpcd u.p 2f out: no ch w wnr but kpt on u.p fnl f* **16/1**[3]

-632 **5** *6* **Amber Moon**[13] 352 9-8-10 **46** oh1.................................. AnnStokell(5) 1 38
(Ann Stokell) *stdd after s: t.k.h: hld up in last pair: rdn and outpcd over 2f out: wknd 2f out* **33/1**

/4-0 **6** *1/2* **Sovento (GER)**[5] 459 10-9-7 **52**.................................. WilliamCarson 2 44
(Thomas McLaughlin, Ire) *s.i.s: hld up in rr: rdn and outpcd over 2f out: sn btn and wknd 2f out* **16/1**[3]

2m 37.28s (4.28) **Going Correction** -0.075s/f (Stan) **6** Ran SP% **112.1**
Speed ratings (Par 101): **82,80,80,79,75 75**
CSF £23.88 TOTE £1.40: £1.10, £7.40; EX 20.70 Trifecta £48.80.
**Owner** Carl Hodgson **Bred** Theakston Stud **Trained** Cropthorne, Worcs

**FOCUS**
A very weak handicap and it proved straightforward for the winner.

## 531 BOOKMAKERS.CO.UK MAIDEN STKS 5f 6y(P)
**2:00** (2:00) (Class 5) 3-Y-0+ **£3,067** (£905; £453) **Stalls** High

Form RPR

22-2 **1** **Taquka (IRE)**[10] 371 3-8-13 75.......................................... JimCrowley 2 85+
(Ralph Beckett) *mde all: hung rt and wd bnd wl over 1f out: rdn and hands and heels and drew wl clr fnl f: readily* **2/11**[1]

-234 **2** *5* **Shamardyh (IRE)**[15] 315 3-8-8 62...................................... ChrisCatlin 5 62
(David Evans) *w wnr: ev ch and carried rt bnd wl over 1f out: drvn and btn 1f out: wknd ins fnl f* **9/2**[2]

-204 **3** *6* **Island Express (IRE)**[3] 495 7-9-8 45..........................(t) AnnStokell(5) 3 51
(Ann Stokell) *s.i.s: sn wl outpcd in last and bustled along: nvr on terms: wnt modest 3rd 1f out* **100/1**

06-5 **4** *2 1/4* **Shirley Vanessa (IRE)**[10] 373 3-8-6 45 ow1........(b[1]) MarkCoumbe(3) 1 33
(Luke Dace) *s.i.s: sn rdn along and outpcd in 3rd: wknd wl over 1f out and lost 3rd 1f out* **33/1**[3]

58.21s (-0.59) **Going Correction** -0.075s/f (Stan)
**WFA** 3 from 7yo 14lb **4** Ran SP% **106.7**
Speed ratings (Par 103): **101,93,83,79**
CSF £1.29 TOTE £1.20; EX 1.50 Trifecta £3.90.
**Owner** The Pickford Hill Partnership **Bred** Tally-Ho Stud **Trained** Kimpton, Hants

**FOCUS**
A desperately uncompetitive maiden. The time was 0.49 seconds slower than the following Class 4 handicap for 4yos-plus.

## 532 BEST ODDS AT BOOKMAKERS.CO.UK H'CAP 5f 6y(P)
**2:35** (2:35) (Class 4) (0-85,85) 4-Y-0+ **£4,690** (£1,395; £697; £348) **Stalls** High

Form RPR

14-3 **1** **Gregori (IRE)**[24] 191 4-8-7 **74**...............(tp) WilliamTwiston-Davies(3) 4 82
(Brian Meehan) *sn led and mde rest: rdn 2f out: pressed and looked vulnerable fnl 100yds: fnd ex and hld on wl u.p towards fin* **11/4**[2]

04-4 **2** *1/2* **Ask The Guru**[4] 470 4-8-7 **71** oh2...............................(v) KierenFox 6 77
(Michael Attwater) *chsd ldrs: rdn to chse wnr 2f out: styd on u.p and pressed wnr fnl 100yds: kpt on but hld towards fin* **12/1**

440- **3** *1/2* **Fair Value (IRE)**[80] 7982 6-9-6 **84**.............................. FrankieDettori 5 88
(Simon Dow) *stdd s: hld up in tch in last pair: rdn and hdwy over 1f out: pressed ldng pair fnl 100yds: kpt on same pce towards fin* **4/1**[3]

16-5 **4** *1/2* **Picansort**[35] 55 7-9-7 **85**...........................................(b) ShaneKelly 1 91+
(Peter Crate) *stdd after s: hld up in rr: rdn and hdwy 1f out: clsng whn edgd lft and hmpd jst ins fnl f: sn swtchd rt: edgd lft u.p after: kpt on* **9/4**[1]

036- **5** *1* **Sir Pedro**[52] 8324 5-9-1 **79**........................................ JamieSpencer 2 78
(Robert Cowell) *chsd ldr tl 2f out: drvn and unable qck ent fnl f: wknd fnl 100yds* **5/1**

02-1 **6** *1 1/2* **Song Of Parkes**[24] 191 7-8-8 **75** ow2.............................. SladeO'Hara(3) 3 69
(Peter Grayson) *in tch in midfield: effrt on inner but no hdwy over 1f out: wknd ins fnl f* **10/1**

57.72s (-1.08) **Going Correction** -0.075s/f (Stan) **6** Ran SP% **110.9**
Speed ratings (Par 105): **105,104,103,102,101 98**
CSF £31.77 TOTE £2.70: £1.40, £4.30; EX 37.80 Trifecta £171.60.
**Owner** Stephen Tucker **Bred** Mrs James Wigan **Trained** Manton, Wilts

**FOCUS**
A fair sprint handicap.

## 533 CORAL MOBILE "JUST THREE CLICKS TO BET" H'CAP 1m 2f (P)
**3:10** (3:10) (Class 3) (0-95,93) 4-Y-0+ **£7,439** (£2,213; £1,106; £553) **Stalls** Low

Form RPR

30-1 **1** **Indian Jack (IRE)**[35] 56 6-9-4 **90**.................................... LukeMorris 7 98
(Ed Walker) *hld up in midfield: rdn and effrt 2f out: drvn to chal 1f out: led ins fnl f: r.o wl: drvn out* **11/4**[1]

0-64 **2** *3/4* **Shavansky**[14] 344 10-8-10 **87**...................................... ShelleyBirkett(5) 6 94
(Rod Millman) *stdd s: hld up in rr: hdwy on inner 2f out: nt clr run over 1f out tl swtchd rt jst ins fnl f: r.o wl fnl 100yds to snatch 2nd on post* **6/1**

06-2 **3** *nse* **Moonday Sun (USA)**[7] 426 5-9-7 **93**.............................. AndreaAtzeni 2 100
(Amanda Perrett) *led for 1f: chsd ldr tl 5f out: rdn to chse ldr again ent fnl 2f: drvn to ld jst over 1f out: hdd and one pce ins fnl f: lost 2nd on post* **7/2**[2]

-611 **4** *3 1/4* **Modernism**[8] 408 5-9-3 **89**........................................ JamieSpencer 1 90
(David Simcock) *hld up in midfield: rdn and effrt on inner over 1f out: drvn and pressed ldr 1f out: no ex and wknd fnl 100yds* **4/1**[3]

20-3 **5** *1 3/4* **Chapter And Verse (IRE)**[31] 89 8-8-12 **84**.................. ShaneKelly 4 81
(Mike Murphy) *led after 1f out and sn clr: rdn ent fnl 2f: hdd jst over 1f out: wknd ins fnl f* **10/1**

21-0 **6** *nk* **Karam Albaari (IRE)**[31] 89 6-8-13 **85**....................... FrederikTylicki 8 82
(J R Jenkins) *stdd after s: hld up in last trio: rdn 4f out: outpcd u.p wl over 1f out: no threat to ldrs and one pce after* **12/1**

00-5 **7** *2 3/4* **Patriotic (IRE)**[14] 342 6-8-7 **79** oh1.......................(p) HayleyTurner 3 71
(Chris Dwyer) *hld up in last trio: rdn ent fnl 2f: outpcd and btn over 1f out: bhd fnl f* **33/1**

06-0 **8** *8* **Lowther**[14] 344 9-9-3 **89**..........................................(v) KierenFox 5 65
(Lee Carter) *chsd ldrs: wnt 2nd 5f out tl ent fnl 2f: sn u.p and nt qckning: lost pl over 1f out: bhd and eased ins fnl f* **7/1**

2m 3.48s (-3.12) **Going Correction** -0.075s/f (Stan) **8** Ran SP% **115.4**
Speed ratings (Par 107): **109,108,108,105,104 104,101,95**
CSF £19.94 CT £58.59 TOTE £3.60: £1.60, £2.50, £1.30; EX 22.50 Trifecta £129.40.
**Owner** Forza Azzurri **Bred** Waterford Hall Stud **Trained** Newmarket, Suffolk

**FOCUS**
A decent handicap.

## 534 COMPARE BOOKMAKERS AT BOOKMAKERS.CO.UK H'CAP 6f 1y(P)
**3:45** (3:45) (Class 2) (0-100,100) 4-Y-0+ **£12,291** (£3,657; £1,827; £913) **Stalls** Low

Form RPR

61-2 **1** **Rivellino**[35] 55 4-9-1 **94**........................................... DanielTudhope 5 107
(K R Burke) *in tch in midfield: hdwy u.p over 1f out: r.o wl ins fnl f to ld cl home* **8/1**

3-01 **2** *nk* **Alben Star (IRE)**[13] 348 6-9-1 **97**............................ GeorgeChaloner(3) 7 109
(Richard Fahey) *taken down early: pressed ldng pair: upsides ldr 1/2-way: rdn 2f out: drvn to ld over 1f out: styd on wl tl hdd and no ex cl home* **10/1**

/1-2 **3** *nk* **Absolutely So (IRE)**[16] 294 4-8-8 **87**............................ DavidProbert 9 98+
(Andrew Balding) *stdd and trying to drop in after s: fnlly managed to drop into midfield after 1f: hdwy u.p over 1f out: pressed ldrs wl ins fnl f: r.o wl* **5/2**[1]

11-1 **4** *2 1/4* **Perfect Pasture**[35] 55 4-9-7 **100**...........................(v) GrahamGibbons 1 104
(Michael Easterby) *chsd ldng trio: drvn and pressed ldrs over 1f out: no ex and outpcd fnl 75yds* **4/1**[2]

242- **5** *shd* **Iptisam**[50] 8369 5-8-12 **91**.......................................(p) LukeMorris 3 95
(James Tate) *led: rdn ent fnl 2f: drvn and hdd over 1f out: kpt on gamely tl no ex and outpcd fnl 75yds* **5/1**[3]

5-63 **6** *1* **Noble Deed**[21] 234 4-8-9 **88**........................................ LiamJones 2 89
(Michael Attwater) *in tch in midfield: effrt u.p on inner and chsd ldrs 1f out: no ex ins fnl f: wknd fnl 75yds* **20/1**

00-6 **7** *nk* **Taajub (IRE)**[21] 234 7-8-9 **88**...................................... ShaneKelly 8 88
(Peter Crate) *hld up in tch in midfield: rdn and no imp over 1f out: wknd ins fnl f* **33/1**

000- **8** *1/2* **Piscean (USA)**[105] 7540 9-9-2 **95**................................ GeorgeBaker 11 94+
(Tom Keddy) *stdd and dropped in bhd after s: hld up in last trio: stl plenty to do and rdn over 1f out: styd on fnl f: nvr trbld ldrs* **33/1**

200- **9** *1 1/2* **Nocturn**[140] 6623 5-9-7 **100**.................................(p) FrankieDettori 6 94
(Jeremy Noseda) *pressed ldr tl 1/2-way: rdn and unable qck over 1f out: btn 1f out: wknd ins fnl f* **6/1**

5-50 **10** *3/4* **Clockmaker (IRE)**[15] 314 8-8-11 **90**............................. HayleyTurner 12 82
(Conor Dore) *taken down early: stdd s: hld up off the pce in last trio: effrt u.p but stl plenty to do 2f out: kpt on fnl f: n.d* **50/1**

00-3 **11** *1* **Woolfall Sovereign (IRE)**[18] 271 8-9-4 **97**................. BarryMcHugh 4 86
(George Margarson) *racd in midfield: rdn and outpcd ent fnl 2f: wknd over 1f out* **20/1**

2-43 **12** *1/2* **Diamond Charlie (IRE)**[27] 148 6-8-8 **87**...................... JamieSpencer 10 74
(Simon Dow) *stdd s: hld up in last trio: wd and u.p bnd 2f out: no imp: n.d* **14/1**

1m 9.7s (-2.20) **Going Correction** -0.075s/f (Stan) **12** Ran SP% **123.8**
Speed ratings (Par 109): **111,110,110,107,107 105,105,104,102,101 100,99**
CSF £83.26 CT £263.65 TOTE £8.90: £1.90, £3.50, £1.30; EX 92.20 Trifecta £478.00.
**Owner** Mrs Melba Bryce **Bred** Castlemartin Sky & Skymarc Farm **Trained** Middleham Moor, N Yorks

**FOCUS**
A good, competitive sprint handicap.

## 535 BOOKMAKERS.CO.UK SPRINT SERIES ROUND 6 H'CAP (QUALIFIER) 6f 1y(P)
**4:20** (4:22) (Class 5) (0-75,75) 4-Y-0+ **£3,234** (£962; £481; £120; £120) **Stalls** Low

Form RPR

3-53 **1** **My Kingdom (IRE)**[15] 310 8-9-2 **70**..........................(vt[1]) AndreaAtzeni 6 80
(Stuart Williams) *pressed ldr: drvn to ld over 1f out: hrd pressed and r.o wl fnl 100yds: drvn out* **5/2**[1]

00-2 **2** *nk* **Mac's Power (IRE)**[22] 208 8-9-7 **75**............................ RobertWinston 9 84
(Willie Musson) *t.k.h: hld up in tch in midfield: hdwy ent fnl f: chal and drew clr w wnr ins fnl f: nt qckn and hld towards fin* **7/2**[2]

0024 **3** *2 3/4* **Haadeeth**[7] 424 7-8-13 **67**....................................(t) ChrisCatlin 4 68
(David Evans) *t.k.h: chsd ldng pair: drvn and effrt over 1f out: unable qck jst ins fnl f: styd on same pce after* **16/1**

5-16 **4** *1/2* **Lujeanie**[21] 233 8-9-5 **73**..........................................(p) ShaneKelly 8 72
(Peter Crate) *t.k.h: hld up in last pair: swtchd rt and effrt u.p over 1f out: no imp and outpcd fnl 100yds* **12/1**

05-6 **4** *dht* **Top Cop**[16] 294 5-9-2 **75**.......................................(p) DCByrne(5) 5 74
(Ronald Harris) *led: rdn ent fnl 2f: drvn and hdd over 1f out: outpcd by ldng pair and btn ins fnl f* **4/1**[3]

2245 **6** *10* **Parisian Pyramid (IRE)**[13] 347 8-8-10 **64**..............(v) JamieSpencer 7 41
(Richard Fahey) *dwlt and pushed along leaving stalls: bdly hmpd and snatched up after 1f: swtchd to outer over 4f out: rdn and sme hdwy 3f out: lost pl and wd bnd 2f out: sn wknd* **12/1**

1m 11.21s (-0.69) **Going Correction** -0.075s/f (Stan) **6** Ran SP% **92.1**
Speed ratings (Par 103): **101,100,96,96,96 82**
CSF £7.40 CT £46.70 TOTE £2.20: £1.10, £2.90; EX 10.20 Trifecta £48.70.
**Owner** My Kingdom For A Horse **Bred** Irish National Stud **Trained** Newmarket, Suffolk
■ Rule 4 of 20p in the pound applies to all bets; Withdrawn: Rigolleto

**FOCUS**
A weak race.

## 536 32RED MAIDEN STKS 1m 1y(P)
4:50 (4:50) (Class 5) 3-Y-O £3,067 (£905; £453) Stalls High

Form RPR
1 **Sloane Avenue (USA)** 3-9-5 0 FrankieDettori 3 91+
(Jeremy Noseda) *s.i.s: rn green: bhd: clsd on ldrs over 4f out: rdn to chse ldr 2f out: led jst over 1f out and sn clr: r.o strly: eased cl home: v easily* 1/2[1]
5-22 2 9 **Mbhali (IRE)**[8] 403 3-9-5 75 JoeFanning 4 64
(Mark Johnston) *sn pressing ldr: rdn to ld over 2f out: drvn and hdd jst over 1f out: sn brushed aside: wl btn but hld on for 2nd ins fnl f* 7/4[2]
55 3 1 **Dove Mountain (IRE)**[22] 213 3-9-5 68 GeorgeBaker 2 62
(Gary Brown) *chsd ldng pair: clsd on ldrs over 4f out: rdn and effrt 2f out: 3rd and outpcd over 1f out: pressing for 2nd whn edgd lft and one pce fnl 100yds* 33/1[3]
0-5 4 11 **Witch From Rome**[21] 231 3-8-12 0 PatrickO'Donnell(7) 1 36
(Ralph Beckett) *led: rdn 3f out: sn hdd: wknd and dropped to last over 1f out: fdd fnl f* 33/1[3]
1m 37.16s (-1.04) **Going Correction** -0.075s/f (Stan) 4 Ran SP% **108.9**
Speed ratings (Par 97): **102,93,92,81**
CSF £1.64 TOTE £1.50; EX 2.10 Trifecta £3.80.
**Owner** Mrs Susan Roy **Bred** Claiborne Farm & Adele B Dilschneider **Trained** Newmarket, Suffolk
**FOCUS**
While it's hard to say exactly what this form is worth - the runner-up had previously shown fair form, and so had the third, but not since leaving Aidan O'Brien - this was a very taking debut from the winner.
T/Plt: £24.40 to a £1 stake. Pool: £90,578.06 - 2702.24 winning units. T/Qpdt: £12.60 to a £1 stake. Pool: £6436.06 - 377.43 winning units. SP

# 510 WOLVERHAMPTON (A.W) (L-H)
Saturday, February 8

**OFFICIAL GOING: Standard**
Wind: strong half behind Weather: heavy rain

## 537 LADBROKES AMATEUR RIDERS' H'CAP (DIV I) 1m 141y(P)
5:50 (5:50) (Class 6) (0-60,60) 4-Y-O+ £2,183 (£677; £338; £169) Stalls Low

Form RPR
2-40 1 **Attain**[14] 345 5-10-8 54 MrRBirkett 4 64
(Julia Feilden) *trckd ldrs: chal 2f out: led 1f out: pushed clr: readily* 9/4[1]
1-50 2 6 **Hail Promenader (IRE)**[22] 211 8-10-9 60 (tp) MrGrahamCarson(5) 6 57
(Anthony Carson) *disp ld tl clr ldr wl over 3f out: rdn over 1f out: hdd ent fnl f: sn no ex* 7/2[3]
1300 3 7 **General Tufto**[15] 317 9-10-6 52 (b) MissEJJones 9 35
(Charles Smith) *hld up: rdn into 3rd 2f out: kpt on but nvr gng pce to threaten ldng pair* 14/1
-545 4 2 1/4 **Cyflymder (IRE)**[7] 421 8-10-8 57 MissJoannaMason(3) 2 35
(David C Griffiths) *trckd ldrs: rdn over 3f out: one pce fnl 2f* 11/2
20-4 5 1 1/4 **Cantor**[15] 320 6-10-7 60 (bt) MissBHampson(7) 7 35
(Paul Morgan) *pushed along to dispute ld: rdn 4f out: hdd 3f out: sn hld: fading whn swtchd and edgd rt over 1f out* 11/4[2]
-054 6 2 1/2 **Una Bella Cosa**[13] 352 4-9-9 46 oh1 (b) HollieDoyle(5) 5 16
(Alan McCabe) *dwlt: reminders: passed 2 horses after 3f: rdn over 3f out: nvr trbld ldrs* 15/2
05/0 7 4 1/2 **Converti**[4] 475 10-9-9 48 MissHHeal(7) 8 9
(Carroll Gray) *hld up: struggling 4f out: nvr any danger* 66/1
1m 52.68s (2.18) **Going Correction** +0.225s/f (Slow) 7 Ran SP% **115.0**
Speed ratings (Par 101): **99,93,87,85,84 82,78**
CSF £10.62 CT £86.59 TOTE £3.80: £1.60, £2.60; EX 15.30 Trifecta £113.90.
**Owner** Miss J Feilden **Bred** Millsec Limited **Trained** Exning, Suffolk
**FOCUS**
Mostly unreliable sorts and this is not form to dwell on for too long. The pace was quite strong

## 538 LADBROKES AMATEUR RIDERS' H'CAP (DIV II) 1m 141y(P)
6:20 (6:20) (Class 6) (0-60,60) 4-Y-O+ £2,183 (£677; £338; £169) Stalls Low

Form RPR
00-2 1 **John Potts**[19] 263 9-10-7 53 MissSBrotherton 3 65
(Brian Baugh) *t.k.h: trckd ldrs: led 3f out: rdn clr over 1f out: comf* 7/4[1]
566- 2 4 1/2 **Super Duplex**[80] 7984 7-10-4 57 (t) MissLWilliams(7) 5 60
(Roger Teal) *hld up in last trio but in tch: hdwy 3f out: styd on fnl f: wnt 2nd nring fin: no ch w wnr* 11/2[3]
1-32 3 1/2 **Do More Business (IRE)**[7] 435 7-10-3 56 (vt) MrTSquire(7) 8 58
(Liam Corcoran) *trckd ldrs: rdn to chse wnr 2f out: a being hld: no ex whn lost 2nd nring fin* 11/2[3]
05-5 4 1 1/2 **Teide Peak (IRE)**[8] 405 5-10-8 59 MrsRWilson(5) 7 57
(Paul D'Arcy) *slowly away: in last pair: styd on fr over 1f out: wnt 4th ent fnl f: nvr threatened ldrs* 3/1[2]
6-00 5 3 1/4 **Stamp Duty (IRE)**[15] 317 6-9-9 46 oh1 (p) MrAaronJames(5) 1 38
(Suzzanne France) *steadily away: bhd: sme prog on outer to dispute 4th wl over 1f out: fdd fnl f* 33/1
00-6 6 9 **Just A Pound (IRE)**[36] 30 4-10-3 54 MrJamesHughes(5) 2 27
(Jo Hughes) *in tch: rdn 3f out: wknd 2f out* 10/1
460- 7 14 **Shomberg**[184] 5172 5-9-8 47 MissSLewis(7) 9
(Dai Burchell) *chsd ldr: rdn over 2f out: wknd over 1f out* 22/1
01-0 8 3 1/4 **Mick Dundee (IRE)**[37] 12 4-10-7 60 (tp) MissRPLeyshon(7) 4
(Paul Morgan) *led at gd pce tl hdd 3f out: sn wknd* 14/1
1m 52.78s (2.28) **Going Correction** +0.225s/f (Slow) 8 Ran SP% **115.2**
Speed ratings (Par 101): **98,94,93,92,89 81,68,66**
CSF £12.02 CT £44.03 TOTE £2.40: £1.10, £1.30, £1.90; EX 15.40 Trifecta £60.70.
**Owner** Miss S M Potts **Bred** Miss S M Potts **Trained** Audley, Staffs
**FOCUS**
They went quite hard, so much so that the pace-setters dropped right away.

## 539 DOWNLOAD THE LADBROKES APP H'CAP 1m 141y(P)
6:50 (6:51) (Class 5) (0-75,74) 4-Y-O+ £3,234 (£962; £481; £240) Stalls Low

Form RPR
/1-0 1 **Toymaker**[17] 286 7-9-5 72 PaddyAspell 5 82
(Phil McEntee) *trckd ldr: led 2f out sn rdn: edgd rt ent fnl f: kpt on wl* 6/1
5-40 2 2 1/4 **My Single Malt (IRE)**[8] 410 6-8-13 66 (p) PaulMulrennan 1 71
(Julie Camacho) *cl up: rdn 2f out: chsd wnr ent fnl f: kpt on but a being hld* 17/2
03-2 3 2 **Canon Law (IRE)**[30] 101 4-9-7 74 DanielTudhope 3 75
(David O'Meara) *trckd ldr tl pushed along wl over 3f out: rdn over 2f out: kpt on same pce fr over 1f out* 6/4[1]
624- 4 3/4 **One Scoop Or Two**[54] 8314 8-9-4 71 (v) GrahamGibbons 4 71
(Andrew Hollinshead) *led: rdn and hdd 2f out: lost 2nd ent fnl f: kpt on same pce* 3/1[3]
00- 5 1 **Kay Gee Be (IRE)**[185] 5149 10-8-12 70 EoinWalsh(5) 2 67
(Alan Berry) *hld up last but in tch: pushed along over 4f out: rdn 3f out: nvr finding pce to get on terms* 25/1
00-3 6 1 1/2 **Mr Lando**[2] 503 5-8-11 64 JimmyQuinn 8 58
(Richard Lee) *cl up: rdn wl over 2f out: nt pce to get on terms* 11/4[2]
1m 50.38s (-0.12) **Going Correction** +0.225s/f (Slow) 6 Ran SP% **120.3**
Speed ratings (Par 103): **109,107,105,104,103 102**
CSF £55.90 CT £116.26 TOTE £9.80: £4.50, £5.80; EX 61.60 Trifecta £688.40.
**Owner** Eventmaker Racehorses **Bred** A G Antoniades **Trained** Newmarket, Suffolk
**FOCUS**
They appeared to go a reasonable gallop here but very few could land a blow at the business end.

## 540 LADBROKES H'CAP 7f 32y(P)
7:20 (7:20) (Class 5) (0-75,80) 4-Y-O+ £3,234 (£962; £481; £240) Stalls High

Form RPR
0-11 1 **Caramack**[15] 319 4-8-11 70 EoinWalsh(5) 1 79+
(Richard Lee) *in tch: nt best of runs 3f out tl 2f out: sn rdn and hdwy: kpt on wl to ld ins fnl f: rdn out* 9/4[1]
43-1 2 3/4 **Hillbilly Boy (IRE)**[29] 113 4-8-12 73 (p) RyanWhile(7) 6 80
(Martin Smith) *led: rdn 2f out: sn drifted rt: hdd ins fnl f: kpt on gamely: jst hld on for 2nd* 13/2
4-21 3 shd **Khajaaly (IRE)**[30] 102 7-8-11 65 (bt) AndrewMullen 7 72
(Michael Appleby) *in tch: rdn and hdwy to chse wnr over 1f out: ev ch ins fnl f: kpt on but hld towards fin* 7/2[2]
10-4 4 3 1/2 **Eastern Dragon (IRE)**[19] 265 4-9-1 72 WilliamTwiston-Davies(3) 3 70
(Michael Scudamore) *hld up in tch: lost pl sltly over 2f out: rdn and hdwy over 1f out: styd on fnl f* 9/1
-101 5 1 1/4 **Powerful Pierre**[7] 432 7-9-7 80 (b) JacobButterfield(5) 2 75
(Ollie Pears) *trckd ldr: rdn over 2f out: kpt on same pce* 4/1[3]
041- 6 3 **Illustrious Prince (IRE)**[82] 7948 7-9-7 75 PaulMulrennan 5 63
(Julie Camacho) *trckd ldrs: rdn over 2f out: kpt on tl fdd fnl 120yds* 8/1
04-0 7 2 3/4 **Dimitar (USA)**[12] 359 5-8-12 66 StevieDonohoe 8 47
(Johnny Farrelly) *hld up: struggling over 2f out: nvr threatened* 14/1
03-0 8 8 **Avonmore Star**[20] 248 6-8-7 61 BenCurtis 4 23
(Alan McCabe) *hld up: effrt over 2f out: wknd over 1f out* 25/1
1m 29.93s (0.33) **Going Correction** +0.225s/f (Slow) 8 Ran SP% **117.9**
Speed ratings (Par 103): **107,106,106,102,100 97,94,84**
CSF £18.25 CT £50.95 TOTE £1.70: £1.02, £3.20, £1.60; EX 16.80 Trifecta £72.70.
**Owner** D E Edwards **Bred** Wellsummers Stud **Trained** Byton, H'fords
**FOCUS**
A strongly run race.

## 541 32RED ON THE APP STORE (S) STKS 7f 32y(P)
7:50 (7:50) (Class 6) 3-Y-O £2,264 (£673; £336; £168) Stalls High

Form RPR
-442 1 **El Duque**[10] 374 3-8-11 52 (v) RyanWhile(7) 6 62
(Bill Turner) *broke wl: prom: led over 4f out: rdn 2f out: kpt on wl fnl f* 15/2[3]
300- 2 1 **Romantic Bliss (IRE)**[123] 7094 3-8-0 45 (b) RobJFitzpatrick(7) 3 48
(K R Burke) *in last trio but in tch: rdn over 2f out: edgd sltly rt over 1f out: r.o to chse wnr ins fnl f: clsng at fin but a being hld* 20/1
2213 3 1 1/2 **Ain't No Surprise (IRE)**[2] 499 3-8-13 65 WilliamCarson 2 51
(Jamie Osborne) *trckd ldrs: rdn in clly disp 2nd over 2f out: kpt on same pce fnl f* 4/7[1]
5-03 4 nse **Clapperboard**[12] 354 3-8-0 57 (b) CamHardie(7) 5 44
(Paul Fitzsimons) *trckd ldrs: rdn on clly disp 2nd over 2f out: kpt on same pce fnl f* 12/1
516- 5 3 1/2 **Black Vale (IRE)**[50] 8364 3-9-4 67 (bt) PaddyAspell 1 46
(Phil McEntee) *s.i.s: in last trio but in tch: rdn into 4th 2f out: wknd ins fnl f* 6/1[2]
55 6 1 3/4 **Jenny Sparks**[21] 232 3-8-2 0 KatiaScallan(5) 7 31
(Mick Channon) *hld up in last: rdn over 3f out: nvr any imp* 10/1
0-U 7 4 1/2 **Marti's Boy**[24] 187 3-8-7 0 PhilipPrince(5) 4 24
(J S Moore) *led tl over 4f out: rdn over 2f out: wknd over 1f out* 66/1
1m 31.49s (1.89) **Going Correction** +0.225s/f (Slow) 7 Ran SP% **112.7**
Speed ratings (Par 95): **98,96,95,95,91 89,83**
CSF £126.17 TOTE £9.30: £3.20, £6.80; EX 128.80 Trifecta £125.70.Ain't No Surprise was claimed by Mrs Jennie Candlish for £6,000.
**Owner** Ansells Of Watford **Bred** John James **Trained** Sigwells, Somerset
**FOCUS**
Slightly slower than the previous 7f contest but that was a better race and once again they went a sound gallop.

## 542 32RED.COM MAIDEN FILLIES' STKS 1m 141y(P)
8:20 (8:21) (Class 5) 3-Y-O+ £2,911 (£866; £432; £216) Stalls Low

Form RPR
1 **Nellie The Elegant** 3-8-5 0 DavidProbert 2 67+
(Tim Vaughan) *led for 3f: trckd ldrs: nudged along w nt clrest of runs on inner over 2f out: rdn over 1f out: led jst ins fnl f: kpt on gamely* 16/1
5 2 1/2 **Rose Kazan (IRE)**[15] 323 3-8-5 0 LukeMorris 5 66
(Marco Botti) *trckd ldrs: rdn to chal 2f out: ev ch ent fnl f: kpt on towards fin* 2/1[1]
3-24 3 hd **Coillte Cailin (IRE)**[29] 127 4-9-9 67 WilliamTwiston-Davies(3) 4 71
(Daniel Mark Loughnane) *trckd ldrs tl dropped to last pair after 3f out: hdwy over 2f out: sn rdn: narrow ld jst over 1f out: hdd jst ins fnl f: edgd sltly rt: kpt on* 5/2[2]
26-4 4 3 1/4 **Marble Statuette (USA)**[15] 323 4-9-12 67 TonyHamilton 6 64
(Richard Fahey) *t.k.h: prom: led after 3f: rdn and hdd jst over 1f out: kpt on same pce* 7/1
5 1 **Patronella (IRE)** 3-8-5 0 ChrisCatlin 7 57
(David Simcock) *dwlt: bhd: hdwy and wl in tch after 3f: rdn over 2f out: hung lft over 1f out: kpt on same pce* 4/1[3]
6 12 **Montjen (IRE)**[28] 4-9-12 0 PaulMulrennan 1 37
(Karen Tutty) *hld up in last pair: hdwy over 4f out: rdn over 2f out: sn wknd* 10/1

2-0 **7** *85* **Wildcat Lass (USA)**[15] 323 3-8-2 0................................JulieBurke(3) 3
(David O'Meara) *prom for 3f: grad lost pl: bhd fr over 2f out: sn eased: t.o* **12/1**

1m 52.47s (1.97) **Going Correction** +0.225s/f (Slow)
**WFA** 3 from 4yo 21lb **7** Ran SP% **117.1**
Speed ratings (Par 100): **100,99,99,96,95 84,9**
CSF £50.25 TOTE £13.20: £8.00, £1.10; EX 29.80 Trifecta £221.70.
**Owner** W R B Racing 53 **Bred** The Lavington Stud **Trained** Aberthin, Vale of Glamorgan

**FOCUS**
Not a strong maiden by any means and those that had form looked vulnerable to anything with some potential.

## 543 32RED BURNING DESIRE SLOT (S) STKS 1m 1f 103y(P)
8:50 (8:50) (Class 6) 3-Y-O £2,264 (£673; £336; £168) Stalls Low

Form RPR
05-1 **1** **Nick The Odds (IRE)**[19] 254 3-9-4 65................................(t) BenCurtis 2 68
(Jo Hughes) *disp for 1f: trckd ldr: chal over 2f out: sn led: drifted rt but in command ins fnl f: pushed out* **6/5**[1]

05-5 **2** *7* **Cascadia (IRE)**[24] 190 3-8-0 55................................ RobJFitzpatrick(7) 6 53+
(K R Burke) *trcking ldrs whn basically taken clean out of r after 2f: plenty to do: rcvrd to sit on heels of ldrs over 4f out: rdn over 2f out: chsd wnr ent fnl f: no ex fnl 120yds: game effrt* **9/2**

424- **3** *7* **Maupiti Express (FR)**[51] 8347 3-8-9 57................................(v) SamJames(3) 1 36
(David O'Meara) *stmbld baldy leaving stalls: led at stdy pce after 1f: rdn and hdd 2f out: sn hld: wknd ins fnl f* **3/1**[2]

606- **4** *32* **L'Es Fremantle (FR)**[57] 8265 3-8-5 0................................PaulBooth(7) 5
(Michael Chapman) *disp for 1f: trcking ldrs whn bdly hmpd after 2f: chsng ldrs and pushed along over 4f out: wknd wl over 2f out: t.o* **66/1**

30-6 **P** **Volodina (IRE)**[25] 173 3-8-7 57................................(b) AndrewMullen 3
(Alan McCabe) *trcking ldrs: t.k.h whn cocked jaw and rn towards paddock entrnce after 2f: nt rcvr and sn p.u* **7/2**[3]

2m 4.41s (2.71) **Going Correction** +0.225s/f (Slow) **5** Ran SP% **112.4**
Speed ratings (Par 95): **96,89,83,55,**
CSF £7.30 TOTE £2.10: £1.20, £2.90; EX 6.30 Trifecta £26.70.There was no bid for the winner.
**Owner** James Henderson & Jo Hughes **Bred** Patrick J Corbet **Trained** Lambourn. Berks

**FOCUS**
A messy little race.

## 544 CORAL APP DOWNLOAD FROM THE APP STORE H'CAP 1m 4f 50y(P)
9:20 (9:20) (Class 5) (0-75,75) 4-Y-O+ £3,234 (£962; £481; £240) Stalls Low

Form RPR
-603 **1** **Mica Mika (IRE)**[8] 408 6-9-6 74................................(v) TonyHamilton 4 81
(Richard Fahey) *t.k.h: mde all: qcknd pce over 2f out: in command fnl f: styd on wl: pushed out* **15/8**[2]

5-30 **2** *1 1/4* **All The Winds (GER)**[16] 293 9-9-1 72......(t) WilliamTwiston-Davies(3) 5 77
(Shaun Lycett) *hld up last of 5 but in tch: rdn to take clsr order 2f out: styd on ins fnl f: wnt 2nd fnl strides* **9/2**[3]

100- **3** *nk* **Lineman**[106] 7510 4-8-13 70................................ShaneKelly 1 75
(Andrew Hollinshead) *trckd ldng pair: rdn 2f out: chsd wnr ent fnl f: nt pce to get on terms: lost 2nd fnl strides* **8/1**

34-2 **4** *1* **Gioia Di Vita**[26] 168 4-8-10 74................................ RobJFitzpatrick(7) 2 77
(David Thompson) *hld up in 4th: effrt whn nt best of runs over 2f out: swtchd lft sn after: nt pce to threaten* **11/8**[1]

030/ **5** *2 3/4* **Kathleen Frances**[16] 7294 7-9-7 75................................(p) LukeMorris 3 74?
(Ali Stronge) *trckd wnr: rdn 2f out: lost 2nd jst over 1f out: no ex fnl f* **25/1**

2m 46.82s (5.72) **Going Correction** +0.225s/f (Slow)
**WFA** 4 from 6yo+ 3lb **5** Ran SP% **110.0**
Speed ratings (Par 103): **89,88,87,87,85**
CSF £10.44 TOTE £2.40: £1.50, £2.70; EX 7.50 Trifecta £38.90.
**Owner** Mrs Una Towell **Bred** Yeomanstown Stud **Trained** Musley Bank, N Yorks

T/Plt: £1416.10 to a £1 stake. Pool: £110,204.39 - 56.81 winning units. T/Qpdt: £219.60 to a £1 stake. Pool: £9244.32 - 31.15 winning units. TM

# 482 CAGNES-SUR-MER
Saturday, February 8

**OFFICIAL GOING: Polytrack: standard**

## 545a PRIX GRIS DE GRIS (CONDITIONS) (3YO) (POLYTRACK) 1m 2f (D)
1:45 (12:00) 3-Y-O £12,083 (£4,833; £3,625; £2,416; £1,208)

RPR
**1** **Bhaktapur (FR)**[24] 194 3-8-10 0................................ StephanePasquier 7 79
(F Rohaut, France) **21/10**[1]

**2** *nse* **Cajun (FR)** 3-9-0 0................................ FranckBlondel 6 83
(F Rossi, France) **5/2**[2]

**3** *nse* **Whitby High Light**[12] 360 3-8-10 0................................ ThomasMessina 5 79
(Andrew Hollinshead) *t.k.h: hld up in midfield: hdwy on outer over 2f out: hrd rdn 1 1/2f out: r.o wl u.p fnl f: jst failed* **43/10**[3]

**4** *2 1/2* **Tocantins (IRE)**[212] 3-9-0 0................................ Christophe-PatriceLemaire 3 78
(M Boutin, France) **73/10**

**5** *1/2* **Le Prelat (FR)**[12] 360 3-9-0 0................................ SylvainRuis 2 77
(J-M Capitte, France) **78/10**

**6** *1* **Tout En Cardoun (FR)**[21] 237 3-8-10 0................................(p) AntoineHamelin 9 71
(Mme P Butel, France) **19/1**

**7** *1 1/2* **Rajang (FR)**[51] 3-8-6 0................................ BenjaminPinard(8) 4 72
(F Chappet, France) **48/1**

**8** *1 1/2* **Sissi Pompon (IRE)**[129] 3-8-10 0................................ BriceRaballand 1 65
(M Boutin, France) **14/1**

**9** *9* **Turtle Boson (IRE)**[12] 360 3-8-10 0................................(p) FabienLefebvre 8 47
(G Martin, Austria) **59/1**

2m 8.06s (128.06) **9** Ran SP% **118.5**
WIN (incl. 1 euro stake): 3.10. PLACES: 1.30, 1.30, 1.40. DF: 4.00. SF: 8.00.
**Owner** Safsaf Canarias Srl **Bred** Dunmore Stud Ltd **Trained** Sauvagnon, France

# 474 SOUTHWELL (L-H)
Sunday, February 9

**OFFICIAL GOING: Standard**
Wind: Strong across Weather: Cloudy

## 546 CORAL APP DOWNLOAD FROM THE APP STORE (S) H'CAP 1m 4f (F)
1:35 (1:37) (Class 6) (0-60,60) 4-Y-O+ £2,264 (£673; £336; £168) Stalls Low

Form RPR
64-4 **1** **West End Lad**[26] 176 11-8-12 56................................(p) TimClark(5) 4 67
(Roy Bowring) *in tch: hdwy to chse ldng pair 4f out: rdn to ld 2f out: clr appr fnl f: styd on wl* **8/1**

52-5 **2** *4* **On The Cusp (IRE)**[31] 96 7-9-6 59................................(b) WilliamCarson 3 64
(Ann Stokell) *t.k.h: led: rdn along over 3f out: hdd 2f out: sn drvn and kpt on same pce* **5/2**[1]

46-6 **3** *shd* **Aureate**[9] 400 10-8-0 46 oh1................................(p) CharlotteJenner(7) 5 51
(Brian Forsey) *hld up: hdwy over 7f out: chsd ldrs over 3f out: rdn 2f out: styd on wl fnl f: nrst fin* **16/1**

0-54 **4** *6* **Xpres Maite**[19] 269 11-9-0 56................................(b) MarkCoumbe(3) 8 52
(Roy Bowring) *s.i.s and bhd: hdwy 5f out: rdn along over 3f out: styd on to chse ldrs 2f out: swtchd lft over 1f out: sn no imp* **7/1**

0445 **5** *13* **Dontpaytheferryman (USA)**[8] 433 9-8-13 52................................(b) ChrisCatlin 9 28
(Peter Hiatt) *chsd ldr: pushed along over 4f out: rdn along 3f out: sn wknd* **6/1**[3]

250- **6** *4* **Sohcahtoa (IRE)**[54] 6087 8-9-7 60................................(p) LukeMorris 7 30
(Andrew Crook) *towards rr: hdwy on wd outside 1/2-way: rdn along to chse ldrs 4f out: outpcd fnl 3f* **12/1**

303- **7** *1* **Miss Ella Jade**[42] 8436 5-8-6 48 ow1................................(p) GeorgeChaloner(3) 1 17
(Richard Whitaker) *chsd ldng pair: rdn along 4f out: wknd over 3f out* **6/1**[3]

66-5 **8** *8* **The Bay Tigress**[37] 31 4-8-4 46 oh1................................[1] BenCurtis 6 3
(Jo Hughes) *chsd ldrs: rdn along 5f out: wknd over 3f out* **20/1**

6-60 **9** *11* **Tammis**[11] 368 4-8-4 46 oh1................................ DavidProbert 10
(Ron Hodges) *midfield: rdn along 5f over out: sn wknd* **50/1**

03-0 **10** *77* **Layla's Boy**[34] 68 7-8-10 52................................(bt) RobertTart(3) 2
(Simon West) *in tch on inner: pushed along 1/2-way: rdn 5f out: sn lost pl and bhd: t.o and eased fnl 2f* **9/2**[2]

2m 41.4s (0.40) **Going Correction** -0.025s/f (Stan)
**WFA** 4 from 5yo+ 3lb **10** Ran SP% **119.2**
Speed ratings (Par 101): **97,94,94,90,81 78,78,72,65,14**
CSF £28.97 CT £323.60 TOTE £10.20: £3.10, £1.10, £4.10; EX 33.00 Trifecta £555.30.There was no bid for the winner.
**Owner** K Nicholls **Bred** Keith Nicholls **Trained** Edwinstowe, Notts

**FOCUS**
Cool, dry conditions with a strong breeze across the runners in the home straight for this moderate but competitive selling handicap in which few had any sort of form. There was a strong pace, they came up the stands' side entering the straight and finished well strung out.

## 547 32RED.COM H'CAP 6f (F)
2:05 (2:06) (Class 6) (0-60,60) 3-Y-O £2,264 (£673; £336; £168) Stalls Low

Form RPR
3-31 **1** **Alumina (IRE)**[11] 374 3-9-3 56................................ DavidProbert 3 75+
(Andrew Balding) *trckd ldrs: smooth hdwy over 2f out: shkn up to ld and edgd lft wl over 1f out: sn clr: readily* **6/4**[1]

2-34 **2** *6* **Meebo (IRE)**[17] 302 3-8-11 55................................ ShelleyBirkett(5) 1 56
(J R Jenkins) *trckd ldrs on inner: hdwy and cl up 2f out: sn rdn and ev ch tl drvn and kpt on same pce appr fnl f* **12/1**

6-15 **3** *1 1/4* **Dandys Perier (IRE)**[9] 401 3-9-7 60................................ LukeMorris 2 57
(Ronald Harris) *sn pushed along in rr: bhd and rdn over 3f out: drvn over 2f out: styd on u.p appr fnl f: nrst fin* **11/4**[2]

500- **4** *1/2* **Red Biba (IRE)**[96] 7755 3-8-8 47................................ BenCurtis 5 43
(Alan McCabe) *towards rr and sn swtchd rt to outer: hdwy over 2f out: sn rdn to chse ldrs: drvn and edgd lft over 1f out: one pce* **33/1**

06-0 **5** *1 1/4* **Tinchy Ryder**[26] 173 3-8-11 50................................ JoeFanning 6 42
(Bryan Smart) *led: rdn along wl over 2f out: drvn and hdd wl over 1f out: grad wknd* **8/1**

43-5 **6** *1 3/4* **Definite Secret**[26] 173 3-9-3 56................................(p) PaulMulrennan 7 43
(James Tate) *chsd ldrs on outer: rdn along and carried hd high wl over 2f out: sn drvn: edgd lft and sn btn* **5/1**[3]

4-44 **7** *12* **The Doyle Machine (IRE)**[14] 346 3-8-10 56....(b) KieranShoemark(7) 4 7
(Noel Quinlan) *cl up: rdn along over 2f out: sn drvn: edgd lft and wknd wl over 1f out* **8/1**

1m 16.46s (-0.04) **Going Correction** -0.025s/f (Stan) **7** Ran SP% **116.2**
Speed ratings (Par 95): **99,91,89,88,87 84,68**
CSF £21.95 CT £47.11 TOTE £3.90: £2.30, £4.40; EX 17.20 Trifecta £42.90.
**Owner** Shapoor Mistry **Bred** Eimear Mulhern & Abbeville Stud **Trained** Kingsclere, Hants

**FOCUS**
A solid pace for this ordinary 3yo sprint handicap. They spread out across the track turning in.

## 548 32RED FREE £10 BONUS FILLIES' H'CAP 1m (F)
2:35 (2:35) (Class 5) (0-75,70) 4-Y-O+ £3,234 (£962; £481; £240) Stalls Low

Form RPR
65-2 **1** **Imaginary World (IRE)**[6] 461 6-8-13 66................................(e) BillyCray(3) 4 75
(John Balding) *trckd ldrs: smooth hdwy and cl up 3f out: rdn to ld wl over 1f out: edgd lft ent fnl f: drvn out* **5/1**[3]

00-1 **2** *1 1/4* **Hot Right Now**[12] 366 4-8-9 66................................ RobJFitzpatrick(7) 3 72
(K R Burke) *trckd ldng pair on inner: hdwy 3f out: chal 2f out: sn rdn and ev ch: swtchd rt and drvn ent fnl f: kpt on same pce* **1/1**[1]

41-4 **3** *3 3/4* **Emperatriz**[10] 388 4-9-6 70................................ LukeMorris 6 68
(John Holt) *slt ld: narrowly hdd 1/2-way: led again over 3f out: sn rdn: hdd and drvn wl over 1f out: kpt on one pce fnl f* **11/4**[2]

**4** *15* **Carlanda (FR)**[92] 4-9-3 67................................ AndrewMullen 1 30
(Michael Appleby) *trckd ldrs on inner: pushed along 2f out and sn swtchd rt to outer: rdn along wl over 2f out: sn outpcd* **5/1**[3]

640- **5** *2 1/4* **Amethyst Dawn (IRE)**[125] 7076 8-9-3 67................................(p) TomQueally 5 25
(Alan McCabe) *t.k.h: cl up: slt ld 1/2-way: rdn along and hdd 3f out: sn wknd* **25/1**

1m 43.63s (-0.07) **Going Correction** -0.025s/f (Stan) **5** Ran SP% **113.8**
Speed ratings (Par 100): **99,97,94,79,76**
CSF £10.99 TOTE £6.90: £2.60, £1.10; EX 11.10 Trifecta £21.80.
**Owner** Hairy Gorrilaz **Bred** Denis McDonnell **Trained** Scrooby, Notts

**FOCUS**
They went an ordinary pace for this uncompetitive fillies' handicap and finished strung out.

## 549 COMPARE BOOKMAKERS AT BOOKMAKERS.CO.UK CLAIMING STKS 5f (F)
3:05 (3:05) (Class 6) 4-Y-O+ £2,264 (£673; £336; £168) Stalls High

Form RPR
-021 1 **Electric Qatar**[5] 478 5-8-8 69 (p) RossAtkinson(3) 2 75
(Tom Dascombe) *cl up: slt ld after 2f out: rdn wl over 1f out: drvn ins fnl f and kpt on wl towards fin* 3/1[2]
1-13 2 1½ **Shawkantango**[16] 318 7-8-9 74 (v) AdamMcLean(7) 1 75
(Derek Shaw) *dwlt and towards rr: rdn along on outer 1/2-way: hdwy 2f out: drvn to chal jst over 1f out: ev ch tl kpt on same pce ins fnl f* 4/1[3]
25-0 3 ½ **Monsieur Jamie**[26] 175 6-9-5 77 (v) FrederikTylicki 5 76
(J R Jenkins) *cl up: effrt 2f out: sn rdn and ev ch tl drvn ent fnl f and kpt on same pce* 11/10[1]
46-0 4 1¼ **Hot Sugar (USA)**[2] 511 5-8-9 60 (p) AndrewMullen 3 61
(Michael Appleby) *in tch: pushed along 1/2-way: sn rdn: drvn to chse ldrs over 1f out: no imp fnl f* 12/1
-434 5 3¾ **Jiminy**[5] 478 4-8-9 49 (v[1]) LukeMorris 6 48
(Scott Dixon) *led 2f: cl up: rdn 2f out: grad wknd* 33/1
060- 6 3½ **Al Khan (IRE)**[150] 6331 5-9-5 82 WilliamCarson 4 45
(Ann Stokell) *s.i.s: a bhd* 7/1
10-0 7 1½ **Edith Anne**[38] 9 4-8-5 59 JimmyQuinn 7 26
(Paul Midgley) *chsd ldrs: rdn along 1/2-way: sn wknd* 50/1

59.5s (-0.20) **Going Correction** -0.025s/f (Stan) 7 Ran SP% 117.7
Speed ratings (Par 101): **100,97,96,94,88 83,80**
CSF £16.18 TOTE £4.20: £2.10, £3.10; EX 13.70 Trifecta £23.20.Electric Qatar was claimed by Tom Malone for £5000.
**Owner** A Black & Owen Promotions Limited **Bred** Miss Nicola Kent **Trained** Malpas, Cheshire

**FOCUS**
The top three in the market dominated the finish of this modest sprint.

## 550 LADBROKES H'CAP 1m (F)
3:35 (3:35) (Class 3) (0-90,92) 4-Y-O+ £7,439 (£2,213; £1,106; £553) Stalls Low

Form RPR
0-11 1 **Noble Citizen (USA)**[20] 256 9-8-12 88 (be) GeorgeBuckell(7) 7 100
(David Simcock) *hld up in rr: smooth hdwy on outer over 3f out: chal over 2f out: led wl over 1f out: sn clr: rdn out* 5/2[2]
30-4 2 4 **Sound Advice**[29] 145 5-8-10 79 TomEaves 5 82
(Keith Dalgleish) *led: rdn along wl over 2f out: hdd wl over 1f out: sn drvn and kpt on same pce* 10/1
51-3 3 4½ **Greyfriarschorista**[35] 61 7-8-12 84 RobertTart(3) 4 76
(Tom Keddy) *prom: effrt 3f out: sn rdn and ev ch tl drvn wl over 1f out and sn one pce* 5/1[3]
-111 4 4½ **Tellovoi (IRE)**[12] 364 6-9-9 92 (v) WilliamCarson 1 74
(Ann Stokell) *t.k.h: chsd ldrs on inner: rdn along over 2f out: sn wknd* 14/1
30-1 5 10 **Thatchmaster (USA)**[12] 365 4-8-11 80 JoeFanning 2 39
(Mark Johnston) *hld up: pushed along in rr over 3f out: rdn wl over 2f out: swtchd wd and drvn wl over 1f out: n.d* 7/4[1]
22-0 6 12 **Our Ivor**[26] 172 5-8-9 78 (t) AndrewMullen 3 10
(Michael Appleby) *prom: pushed along 1/2-way: sn lost pl and bhd fr wl over 2f out* 14/1
10-0 7 14 **Tasrih (USA)**[11] 372 5-8-13 82 TomQueally 6
(Alan McCabe) *rrd s and s.i.s: t.k.h and rapid hdwy to join ldrs after 2 1/2f: cl up tl rdn over 3f out and sn wknd* 13/2

1m 41.66s (-2.04) **Going Correction** -0.025s/f (Stan) 7 Ran SP% 117.4
Speed ratings (Par 107): **109,105,100,96,86 74,60**
CSF £28.23 TOTE £4.60: £2.40, £6.40; EX 28.20 Trifecta £99.50.
**Owner** Khalifa Dasmal **Bred** Don M Robinson **Trained** Newmarket, Suffolk

**FOCUS**
Despite the paucity of runners for this competitive handicap, the pace was genuine and they finished well strung out behind an impressive winner.

## 551 LADBROKES MAIDEN STKS 7f (F)
4:10 (4:11) (Class 5) 3-Y-O+ £3,234 (£962; £481; £240) Stalls Low

Form RPR
1 **Tigers In Red (USA)** 3-8-10 0 LiamKeniry 1 84
(David Simcock) *trckd ldrs: smooth hdwy over 2f out: rdn to ld wl over 1f out: kpt on strly fnl f* 5/2[2]
2 2½ **Moonlight Venture** 3-8-10 0 TonyHamilton 7 77
(Kevin Ryan) *dwlt: sn trcking ldrs: pushed along on outer 3f out: sn rn green and outpcd wl over 2f out: hdwy wl over 1f out: rdn to chse wnr and edgd lft ins fnl f: sn no imp* 8/1
6- 3 1¼ **On Demand**[157] 6140 3-8-5 0 DavidProbert 3 69
(Andrew Balding) *slt ld 2f: cl up: rdn to ld again briefly 2f out: sn hdd and edgd lft: wknd appr fnl f* 5/4[1]
366- 4 5 **Captain Swift (IRE)**[67] 8147 3-8-7 70 (b[1]) WilliamTwiston-Davies(3) 2 61
(Brian Meehan) *cl up on inner: slt ld after 2f: rdn along 3f out: hdd 2f out and grad wknd* 8/1
5 12 **Nellies Quest** 5-9-1 0 AlistairRawlinson(7) 5 28
(Michael Appleby) *dwlt: green and sn swtchd rt to outer: sn rdn along and a in rr* 20/1
0- 6 3¼ **Sicilian Bay (IRE)**[240] 3298 3-8-0 0 ShirleyTeasdale(5) 6 14
(Paul Midgley) *prom: rdn along over 3f out: sn wknd* 100/1
7 15 **Every Honour** 3-8-10 0 JoeFanning 4
(Mark Johnston) *dwlt: green and sn swtchd rt to outer: sn rdn along: a outpcd and bhd* 5/1[3]

1m 29.5s (-0.80) **Going Correction** -0.025s/f (Stan)
**WFA** 3 from 5yo 17lb 7 Ran SP% 117.7
Speed ratings (Par 103): **103,100,98,93,79 75,58**
CSF £23.61 TOTE £4.10: £1.50, £2.40; EX 23.70 Trifecta £51.70.
**Owner** Al Asayl Bloodstock Ltd **Bred** Fares Farm Llc **Trained** Newmarket, Suffolk

**FOCUS**
A run-of-the-mill maiden run at an honest pace.

## 552 DOWNLOAD THE LADBROKES APP H'CAP 7f (F)
4:40 (4:42) (Class 4) (0-80,80) 4-Y-O+ £5,175 (£1,540; £769; £384) Stalls Low

Form RPR
4-40 1 **The Great Gabrial**[18] 287 5-9-4 77 (p) TomQueally 3 88
(Alan McCabe) *trckd ldrs: hdwy 3f out: cl up wl over 1f out: rdn to chal jst over 1f out: drvn and styd on to ld last 75yds* 16/1
-413 2 ½ **Repetition**[10] 388 4-8-12 71 TomEaves 8 81
(Kristin Stubbs) *cl up: led over 3f out: rdn 2f out: jnd over 1f out: drvn ent fnl f: hdd and no ex last 75yds* 7/1
-411 3 6 **Abi Scarlet (IRE)**[5] 479 5-9-0 76 6ex RyanPowell(3) 6 69
(Hughie Morrison) *in tch: effrt over 2f out: rdn to chse ldng pair whn edgd lft over 1f out: sn drvn and kpt on same pce* 7/2[2]
30-0 4 2¼ **Bay Knight (IRE)**[9] 399 8-9-0 73 WilliamCarson 10 60
(Ann Stokell) *dwlt and in rr tl styd on fnl 2f: nrst fin* 33/1
500- 5 3¼ **Docofthebay (IRE)**[52] 8350 10-8-13 72 (b) LukeMorris 7 51
(Scott Dixon) *dwlt and in rr: rdn along over 2f out and sme late hdwy* 7/1
-321 6 ¾ **Tartan Trip**[10] 389 7-8-12 71 (v) AndrewMullen 1 48
(Michael Appleby) *chsd ldrs: hdwy on outer 3f out: rdn over 2f out and grad wknd* 5/1[3]
-606 7 ¾ **Clubland (IRE)**[17] 299 5-8-13 72 JimmyQuinn 4 47
(Roy Bowring) *in tch: hdwy to chse ldrs wl over 2f out: sn rdn and wknd wl over 1f out* 25/1
03-1 8 2 **Ace Master**[20] 255 6-9-3 79 (b) MarkCoumbe(3) 9 48
(Roy Bowring) *led: rdn along and hdd over 3f out: drvn 2f out and sn wknd* 6/1
30-6 9 4 **Ruwaiyan (USA)**[28] 153 5-9-7 80 (b[1]) PaulMulrennan 5 38
(James Tate) *dwlt and reminders: sn chsng ldrs: rdn 3f out: wknd over 2f out* 5/2[1]

1m 29.34s (-0.96) **Going Correction** -0.025s/f (Stan) 9 Ran SP% 119.4
Speed ratings (Par 105): **104,103,96,94,90 89,88,86,81**
CSF £126.95 CT £495.58 TOTE £12.80: £3.10, £2.10, £1.80; EX 164.20 Trifecta £773.30.
**Owner** Tariq Al Nisf **Bred** Juddmonte Farms Ltd **Trained** Averham Park, Notts

**FOCUS**
A devilishly competitive handicap.
T/Plt: £65.50 to a £1 stake. Pool: £104,707.77 - 1166.97 winning units. T/Qpdt: £17.10 to a £1 stake. Pool: £6807.77 - 294.00 winning units. JR

# 545 CAGNES-SUR-MER
Sunday, February 9
**OFFICIAL GOING: Polytrack: standard**

## 553a PRIX DE LA CALIFORNIE (LISTED RACE) (3YO) (POLYTRACK) 1m (F)
1:45 (12:00) 3-Y-O £25,000 (£10,000; £7,500; £5,000; £2,500)

RPR
1 **Baby Foot (IRE)**[25] 193 3-8-11 0 FranckBlondel 9 103+
(F Rossi, France) 9/10[1]
2 1 **Zvarov (IRE)**[22] 237 3-8-11 0 IoritzMendizabal 5 101+
(J-C Rouget, France) 9/2[3]
3 2 **Passion Blanche**[68] 3-8-8 0 Christophe-PatriceLemaire 1 93
(J-C Rouget, France) 13/1
4 shd **Dancing Sands (IRE)**[23] 3-8-8 0 FabriceVeron 7 93
(H-A Pantall, France) 4/1[2]
5 snk **Cockney Bob**[8] 436 3-8-11 0 ThomasMessina 4 96+
(J Parize, France) 11/1
6 4 **Hatari (FR)**[86] 3-8-11 0 AntoineHamelin 2 86
(Matthieu Palussiere, France) 19/1
7 ½ **Lotus Garden (FR)**[10] 390 3-8-11 0 FredericSpanu 8 85
(F Chappet, France) 61/1
8 6 **Act Of Charity (IRE)**[8] 436 3-8-11 0 (b[1]) Pierre-CharlesBoudot 3 71
(Gay Kelleway) *led: rdn over 1 1/2f out: hdd appr fnl f: sn wknd* 25/1
9 1½ **Letthemusictakeus (IRE)**[207] 4408 3-8-8 0 MatthiasLauron 6 65
(Y Durepaire, France) 18/1

1m 35.89s (95.89) 9 Ran SP% 122.0
WIN (incl. 1 euro stake): 1.90. PLACES: 1.20, 1.50, 2.40. DF: 4.60. SF: 6.20.
**Owner** Jean-Claude Seroul **Bred** J-C Seroul **Trained** France

# ST MORITZ (R-H)
Sunday, February 9
**OFFICIAL GOING: Snow: frozen (abandoned after race 1)**

## 555a GRAND PRIX HANDELS & GEWERBEVEREIN ST MORITZ (CONDITIONS) (4YO+) (SNOW) 4f
11:45 (12:00) 4-Y-O+
£4,256 (£2,128; £1,520; £1,013; £506; £304)

RPR
1 **Lipocco**[85] 10-9-6 0 AndreBest 5 83
(J D Hillis, Germany) 81/10
2 1 **Zarras (GER)**[105] 5-8-9 0 SilviaCasanova(4) 8 72
(P Schaerer, Switzerland) 11/5[1]
3 nk **The Art Of Racing (IRE)**[16] 318 4-9-4 0 APietsch 6 76
(C Von Der Recke, Germany) 11/1
4 ¾ **Boccalino (GER)**[357] 700 6-9-4 0 (p) DanielePorcu 7 73
(P Schaerer, Switzerland) 18/5[2]
5 1½ **R Woody**[16] 318 7-9-0 0 JBojko 4 63
(George Baker) *racd in midfield: styd on ins fnl f: nvr on terms* 11/5[1]
6 ¾ **Sheikh The Reins (IRE)**[21] 245 5-9-0 0 (b) FergusSweeney 1 60
(John Best) *chsd ldng trio: rdn and wknd ins fnl f* 54/10[3]
7 2½ **Niva (IRE)** 5-8-10 0 OlivierPlacais 3 46
(M Weiss, Switzerland) 89/10
8 5 **Cape Town (GER)**[2065] 9-8-11 0 RobertHavlin 2 27
(M Weiss, Switzerland) 58/10

8 Ran SP% 144.0
PARI-MUTUEL (all including 1 chf stakes): WIN 9.10; PLACE 2.90, 1.50, 2.80; SF 4.70.
**Owner** Plersch Breeding Sarl **Bred** C Scott & T Leigh **Trained** Germany

# [537]WOLVERHAMPTON (A.W) (L-H)

Monday, February 10

**OFFICIAL GOING: Standard**

Wind: Light behind Weather: Showery

## 556 COMPARE BOOKMAKERS AT BOOKMAKERS.CO.UK H'CAP 5f 20y(P)

2:30 (2:35) (Class 6) (0-52,52) 4-Y-O+ £2,264 (£673; £336; £168) Stalls Low

Form RPR

050 1 **Lord Buffhead**[19] 274 5-8-12 **46** oh1........(v) BillyCray(3) 3 54
(Richard Guest) *chsd ldrs: drvn along 3f out: r.o u.p to ld post* **14/1**

0-06 2 *hd* **Rose Garnet (IRE)**[14] 353 6-9-4 **52**........ MarkCoumbe(3) 8 59
(Tony Carroll) *w ldr tl led 2f out: rdn over 1f out: hdd post* **4/1[3]**

0434 3 *½* **Rightcar**[8] 448 7-8-12 **46** oh1........ SladeO'Hara(3) 7 51
(Peter Grayson) *s.i.s: outpcd: nt clr run over 1f out: r.o wl ins fnl f: nt rch ldrs* **7/2[2]**

0-45 4 *1* **Play The Blues (IRE)**[8] 448 7-9-1 **46** oh1........(bt) JoeFanning 5 48
(Dominic Ffrench Davis) *led 3f: sn rdn: no ex ins fnl f* **2/1[1]**

5-60 5 *2* **Lexi's Beauty (IRE)**[20] 273 4-9-1 **46** oh1........(p) AndrewMullen 2 40
(Brian Baugh) *hld up: hdwy over 1f out: styd on* **28/1**

50-6 6 *2¼* **Auntie Mildred (IRE)**[15] 351 4-9-1 **49**........(v[1]) SamJames(3) 4 35
(David O'Meara) *s.i.s: hdwy 1/2-way: rdn over 1f out: styd on same pce fnl f* **4/1[3]**

0-06 7 *1* **Dixie Gwalia**[7] 452 6-9-7 **52**........(v) GeorgeBaker 6 35
(Michael Attwater) *chsd ldrs: rdn 1/2-way: edgd rt and styd on same pce appr fnl f* **11/1**

0-00 8 *3* **Lucky Mellor**[7] 466 7-8-8 **46** oh1........(p) PaulBooth(7) 1 18
(Barry Murtagh) *mid-div: drvn along 1/2-way: wknd fnl f* **33/1**

5-00 9 *3¼* **Chateau Lola**[28] 164 5-8-8 **46** oh1........(v) AdamMcLean(7) 9
(Derek Shaw) *s.i.s: hdwy on outer 1/2-way: wknd wl over 1f out* **33/1**

1m 2.52s (0.22) **Going Correction** -0.025s/f (Stan) **9** Ran SP% **119.9**
Speed ratings (Par 101): **97,96,95,94,91 87,85,81,75**
CSF £70.82 CT £247.54 TOTE £16.20: £5.70, £1.70, £1.10; EX 97.00 Trifecta £332.80.
**Owner** Mrs Alison Guest **Bred** T K & Mrs P A Knox **Trained** Wetherby, W Yorks

**FOCUS**
A low-grade handicap in which a pace duel set the race up for the winner.

## 557 BEST ODDS AT BOOKMAKERS.CO.UK (S) STKS 5f 216y(P)

3:00 (3:05) (Class 6) 3-Y-O+ £1,940 (£577; £288) Stalls Low

Form RPR

-662 1 **Where's Reiley (USA)**[9] 424 8-9-8 64........(v) GeorgeBaker 1 65
(Michael Attwater) *mde all: shkn up over 1f out: a doing enough* **9/4[1]**

0243 2 *½* **Haadeeth**[2] 535 7-9-8 67........(t) EoinWalsh(5) 3 68
(David Evans) *trckd wnr: hung rt over 2f out: rdn over 1f out: styd on* **11/4[2]**

6-55 3 *10* **This Charming Man (IRE)**[21] 254 3-8-7 62........(b[1]) TomEaves 4 27
(Keith Dalgleish) *s.i.s: sn pushed along in rr: rdn 1/2-way: outpcd fr over 2f out* **11/2[3]**

1m 15.05s (0.05) **Going Correction** -0.025s/f (Stan)
**WFA** 3 from 5yo+ 15lb **3** Ran SP% **72.8**
Speed ratings (Par 101): **98,97,84**
CSF £3.58 TOTE £1.70; EX 3.00 Trifecta £3.40.The was no bid for the winner.
**Owner** J M Duggan & T P Duggan **Bred** Overbrook Farm **Trained** Epsom, Surrey
■ George Fenton was withdrawn. Price at time of withdrawal 7/4f. Rule 4 applies to all bets - deduct 35p in the pound.

**FOCUS**
The late withdrawal of George Fenton on vet's advice detracted from this already weak seller. The form is rated around the first two.

## 558 CORAL MOBILE "JUST THREE CLICKS TO BET" MAIDEN STKS 1m 4f 50y(P)

3:30 (3:36) (Class 5) 4-Y-O+ £2,587 (£770; £384; £192) Stalls Low

Form RPR

235- 1 **Archive**[178] 5478 4-9-0 76........ ChrisCatlin 5 69+
(Rae Guest) *trckd ldrs: led over 2f out: pushed clr fr over 1f out* **4/9[1]**

0-4 2 *9* **Angelot Du Berlais (FR)**[7] 463 5-9-8 69........ LukeMorris 1 60
(Dr Richard Newland) *led 1f: w ldr tl led again 7f out: rdn and hdd over 2f out: styd on same pce fr over 1f out* **4/1[2]**

3 *1¼* **Gabrial The Terror (IRE)** 4-9-5 0........ LiamKeniry 4 58
(David Simcock) *trckd ldrs: rdn over 1f out: no ex fnl f* **7/1[3]**

6 4 *1¾* **Kastela Stari**[7] 463 7-9-3 0........ JamesSullivan 2 50?
(Tim Fitzgerald) *hld up: effrt and hmpd over 2f out: n.d* **66/1**

5 *¾* **Lucky Leopardsfoot** 4-9-5 0........ JohnFahy 6 54?
(John Spearing) *s.i.s: hld up: pushed along and hdwy over 2f out: wknd fnl f* **100/1**

4 6 *25* **Ceevee**[16] 343 4-8-12 0........(t) ChloeIngram(7) 7 14
(Tim Vaughan) *plld hrd: led after 1f tl 7f out: w ldr tl pushed along over 3f out: wknd 2f out* **20/1**

7 *2¼* **Flamenco Flyer** 5-9-3 0........ EoinWalsh(5) 3 10
(Edward Bevan) *hld up: pushed along 7f out: wknd 5f out* **100/1**

2m 39.86s (-1.24) **Going Correction** -0.025s/f (Stan)
**WFA** 4 from 5yo+ 3lb **7** Ran SP% **110.0**
Speed ratings (Par 103): **103,97,96,95,94 77,76**
CSF £2.22 TOTE £1.30: £1.10, £1.80; EX 3.00 Trifecta £5.00.
**Owner** C J Murfitt **Bred** Juddmonte Farms Ltd **Trained** Newmarket, Suffolk

**FOCUS**
A big odds-on favourite illustrates that there was little strength in depth to this maiden for 4yos and up. The winner did not need to get close to her best.

## 559 CORAL.CO.UK BEST ODDS GUARANTEED ON RACING H'CAP 1m 1f 103y(P)

4:00 (4:06) (Class 2) (0-105,99) 4-Y-O£11,971 (£3,583; £1,791; £896; £446) Stalls Low

Form RPR

5-12 1 **Star Links (USA)**[7] 465 8-8-9 **87**........(b) LukeMorris 1 97
(S Donohoe, Ire) *chsd ldrs: drvn along over 2f out: led over 1f out: r.o u.p* **5/1[3]**

00-3 2 *1¼* **Stasio (USA)**[28] 163 4-8-8 **86**........ LiamKeniry 5 93
(David Simcock) *hld up: hdwy over 1f out: sn rdn: edgd lft ins fnl f: r.o* **13/2**

1-1 3 *2¼* **Big Baz (IRE)**[32] 101 4-8-7 **85**........ DavidProbert 4 87
(William Muir) *hld up: pushed along over 2f out: hdwy over 1f out: sn rdn: styd on same pce ins fnl f* **1/1[1]**

4-22 4 *1* **The Lock Master (IRE)**[21] 256 7-8-2 **80** oh1........ AndrewMullen 6 80
(Michael Appleby) *chsd ldrs: drvn along over 3f out: outpcd over 2f out: styd on ins fnl f* **25/1**

6-05 5 *2* **Strictly Silver (IRE)**[16] 344 5-9-2 **99**........(v[1]) TimClark(5) 8 95
(Alan Bailey) *trckd ldr after 1f tl led over 3f out: rdn and hdd over 1f out: wknd ins fnl f* **4/1[2]**

0-0 6 *½* **Shamdarley (IRE)**[9] 426 6-8-11 **89**........(p) PaddyAspell 7 84
(Marco Botti) *racd keenly: led after 1f tl hdd over 3f out: wknd fnl f* **16/1**

2-35 7 *1¾* **Well Painted (IRE)**[10] 408 5-8-7 **85**........(e) JoeFanning 3 76
(William Haggas) *led 1f: chsd ldrs: nt clr run over 2f out: wknd fnl f* **14/1**

3/0- 8 *12* **Gunner Lindley (IRE)**[14] 7721 7-8-12 **90**........ TomEaves 2 56
(Stuart Coltherd) *hld up: rdn 1/2-way: wknd over 3f out* **80/1**

1m 58.29s (-3.41) **Going Correction** -0.025s/f (Stan) **8** Ran SP% **117.6**
Speed ratings (Par 109): **114,112,110,110,108 107,106,95**
CSF £38.34 CT £57.54 TOTE £4.10: £1.50, £1.60, £1.10; EX 35.80 Trifecta £81.10.
**Owner** Gerry Dolan & Mrs Marie E Dolan **Bred** Shell Bloodstock **Trained** Cootehill Road, Co Cavan

**FOCUS**
A strong handicap even though the favourite was disappointing, in which they didn't get racing until 2f out. The winner rates better than ever.

## 560 CORAL APP DOWNLOAD FROM THE APP STORE H'CAP 1m 1f 103y(P)

4:30 (4:35) (Class 4) (0-85,85) 4-Y-O+ £4,851 (£1,443; £721; £360) Stalls Low

Form RPR

0-00 1 **Halfsin (IRE)**[16] 344 6-9-7 **85**........(t) PaddyAspell 3 93
(Marco Botti) *trckd ldr tl led over 3f out: rdn clr 2f out: hung lft ins fnl f: styd on* **16/1**

143- 2 *¾* **Epic Battle (IRE)**[46] 8398 4-9-6 **84**........ FrankieDettori 1 90
(William Haggas) *chsd ldrs: rdn and nt clr run over 2f out: r.o ins fnl f* **11/8[1]**

/12- 3 *shd* **Appease**[133] 6898 5-8-13 **77**........ TomQueally 8 83
(John Butler) *hld up: hdwy over 2f out: rdn over 1f out: edgd lft ins fnl f: r.o* **11/2[3]**

1/2- 4 *1¾* **Sky Khan**[24] 4437 5-9-0 **81**........(p) BillyCray(3) 5 84
(Richard Guest) *stdd s: hld up: racd keenly: rdn and r.o ins fnl f: nt rch ldrs* **16/1**

11- 5 *shd* **Fleckerl (IRE)**[41] 8454 4-8-12 **76**........ LukeMorris 4 78
(William Muir) *hld up: nt clr run and outpcd over 2f out: r.o ins fnl f: nt trble ldrs* **2/1[2]**

21-0 6 *1* **Berlusca (IRE)**[25] 200 5-9-1 **82**........ SamJames(3) 6 82
(David O'Meara) *prom: chsd wnr over 2f out: rdn over 1f out: edgd lft and no ex ins fnl f* **11/1**

04-2 7 *3¼* **Pelmanism**[13] 364 7-8-11 **75**........ DaleSwift 7 68
(Brian Ellison) *hld up: pushed along over 3f out: rdn over 2f out: n.d* **16/1**

002- 8 *11* **Hydrant**[19] 7424 8-8-7 **78**........ MelissaThompson(7) 2 48
(Richard Guest) *led: hdd over 3f out: sn pushed along: wknd over 2f out* **66/1**

2m 0.56s (-1.14) **Going Correction** -0.025s/f (Stan) **8** Ran SP% **118.3**
Speed ratings (Par 105): **104,103,103,101,101 100,97,88**
CSF £40.03 CT £148.16 TOTE £14.10: £3.40, £1.10, £2.60; EX 39.40 Trifecta £213.20.
**Owner** Dr Marwan Koukash **Bred** Glending Bloodstock **Trained** Newmarket, Suffolk

**FOCUS**
A handicap that was made all the more interesting by a big gamble on the runner-up. The winner is rated back to his Kempton December win.

## 561 32RED PLAY THUNDERSTRUCK WITH £10 FREE H'CAP 1m 141y(P)

5:00 (5:05) (Class 5) (0-70,70) 3-Y-O £2,911 (£866; £432; £216) Stalls Low

Form RPR

035- 1 **Filament Of Gold (USA)**[102] 7640 3-9-4 **67**........ JoeFanning 6 75+
(Mark Johnston) *lost pl over 4f out: hdwy over 2f out: rdn to ld and edgd lft wl ins fnl f: r.o: readily* **11/8[1]**

653- 2 *1½* **Needless Shouting (IRE)**[113] 7393 3-8-12 **64**
WilliamTwiston-Davies(3) 2 67
(Mick Channon) *led: rdn over 1f out: hdd and unable qck wl ins fnl f* **11/2[3]**

-601 3 *3* **Blue Oyster**[9] 434 3-9-4 **67**........ BenCurtis 3 63
(Philip McBride) *s.i.s: hdwy to chse ldr over 5f out: rdn and ev ch over 2f out: styd on same pce fnl f* **14/1**

00-1 4 *½* **Secret Suspect**[35] 70 3-9-7 **70**........ LukeMorris 4 65
(James Tate) *trckd ldrs: rdn over 2f out: styd on same pce fnl f* **15/8[2]**

0-45 5 *¾* **Eddiemaurice (IRE)**[18] 301 3-8-12 **64**........ BillyCray(3) 5 57
(Richard Guest) *hld up: hdwy over 1f out: nt trble ldrs* **20/1**

-233 6 *2¼* **Big Kenny**[6] 473 3-9-0 **63**........ ChrisCatlin 1 51
(David Evans) *chsd ldr tl over 5f out: rdn over 2f out: wknd over 1f out* **8/1**

1m 50.17s (-0.33) **Going Correction** -0.025s/f (Stan) **6** Ran SP% **114.8**
Speed ratings (Par 97): **100,98,96,95,94 92**
CSF £9.94 TOTE £1.90: £1.10, £4.00; EX 10.70 Trifecta £72.80.
**Owner** Sheikh Hamdan bin Mohammed Al Maktoum **Bred** Darley **Trained** Middleham Moor, N Yorks

**FOCUS**
A modest 3yo handicap. The winner was well on top and uis bred to be better.

## 562 LADBROKES H'CAP 7f 32y(P)

5:30 (5:35) (Class 6) (0-60,60) 4-Y-O+ £2,264 (£673; £336; £168) Stalls High

Form RPR

006/ 1 **Amazing Star (IRE)**[24] 226 9-9-7 **60**........(tp) BenCurtis 10 68
(Denis Gerard Hogan, Ire) *hld up: hdwy over 1f out: rdn and edgd lft ins fnl f: r.o to ld post* **9/2[3]**

2646 2 *nse* **Lutine Charlie (IRE)**[8] 446 7-9-0 **53**........(p) TomQueally 3 61
(Pat Eddery) *hld up: hdwy over 2f out: rdn to ld wl ins fnl f: hdd post* **10/1**

0311 3 *1* **Medam**[15] 351 5-9-4 **60**........ NeilFarley(3) 1 65
(Shaun Harris) *chsd ldrs: led over 1f out: rdn and hdd wl ins fnl f* **5/1**

5065 4 *1¼* **One Way Or Another (AUS)**[9] 424 11-9-1 **59**........(t) EoinWalsh(5) 7 61
(David Evans) *hld up: hdwy over 2f out: rdn over 1f out: styd on same pce ins fnl f* **5/1**

42-2 5 *2½* **Sweet Vintage (IRE)**[31] 126 4-9-5 **58**........ LukeMorris 4 53
(Mark Brisbourne) *plld hrd: led: rdn and hdd over 1f out: wknd ins fnl f* **4/1[2]**

360- 6 *3¼* **Piccolo Express**[59] 8278 8-9-3 **56**........ TomEaves 6 42
(Brian Baugh) *s.i.s: hdwy over 5f out: rdn over 2f out: wknd ins fnl f* **14/1**

6-00 7 *nk* **Crown Choice**[17] 319 9-8-11 **55**........(p) JacobButterfield(5) 2 40
(Jedd O'Keeffe) *prom: chsd ldr over 2f out: rdn and ev ch over 1f out: wknd ins fnl f* **66/1**

0-06 8 *3¾* **Lieutenant Dan (IRE)**[17] 319 7-9-7 **60**........(v) AndrewMullen 8 35
(Michael Appleby) *hld up: drvn along 1/2-way: a in rr* **3/1[1]**

005- 9 *1½* **Glenridding**[67] 8163 10-9-7 **60**........(p) DaleSwift 9 31
(James Given) *prom: rdn 1/2-way: wknd over 1f out* **16/1**

-000 10 *9* **Decision By One**[9] 425 5-9-7 **60**........ ChrisCatlin 5 7
(David Evans) *chsd ldr tl rdn 1/2-way: wknd over 2f out* **33/1**

1m 29.29s (-0.31) **Going Correction** -0.025s/f (Stan) **10** Ran SP% **122.6**
Speed ratings (Par 101): **100,99,98,97,94 90,90,86,84,74**
CSF £51.73 CT £243.97 TOTE £9.40: £4.00, £1.80, £2.10; EX 57.00 Trifecta £412.10.

**Owner** M G Hogan **Bred** Glending Bloodstock **Trained** Cloughjordan, Co Tipperary

**FOCUS**

An ultra-competitive 0-60 handicap. The first two came from the rear. The winner is rated towwards last season's best.

T/Jkpt: £11,436.30 to a £1 stake. Pool of £153021.30 - 9.5 winning tickets. T/Plt: £19.10 to a £1 stake. Pool of £131246.19 - 4991.49 winning tickets. T/Qpdt: £4.00 to a £1 stake. Pool of £10387.82 - 1891.98 winning tickets. CR

# 546 SOUTHWELL (L-H)

## Tuesday, February 11

**OFFICIAL GOING: Standard**

Wind: Strong half behind Weather: Heavy rain before racing, dry and fine for racing.

## 563 BEST RACING ODDS AT BOOKMAKERS.CO.UK H'CAP 6f (F)

**1:30** (1:36) (Class 6) (0-55,54) 4-Y-0+ **£2,264** (£673; £336; £168) **Stalls** Low

Form RPR

56-0 **1** **Art Dzeko**[32] [126] 5-9-5 **52**.....(p) TomEaves 6 61
(Brian Baugh) *mde all: rdn wl over 1f out: drvn and edgd rt fnl f: kpt on* **7/2**[1]

0-40 **2** *1* **Doctor Hilary**[20] [274] 12-8-12 **45**.....(v) RobertHavlin 3 51
(Mark Hoad) *trckd ldrs: hdwy over 2f out: rdn to chse wnr over 1f out: ev ch jst ins fnl f: sn drvn and kpt on same pce* **20/1**

3320 **3** *3/4* **Mucky Molly**[13] [370] 6-8-13 **46**.....(vt) LukeMorris 5 50
(Alison Hutchinson) *towards rr and rdn along after 2f: hdwy over 2f out: styd on wl u.p appr fnl f* **6/1**[3]

5-56 **4** *1/2* **Very First Blade**[5] [502] 5-9-0 **47**.....(be) BenCurtis 14 49
(Michael Mullineaux) *in tch on wd outside: rdn along over 2f out: kpt on appr fnl f: nrst fin* **7/1**

-665 **5** *1/2* **Rutterkin (USA)**[19] [290] 6-8-12 **45**..... TomQueally 4 45
(James Moffatt) *trckd ldrs: effrt over 2f out: rdn wl over 1f out: no imp fnl f* **7/2**[1]

00-4 **6** *2 1/2* **Cheyenne Red (IRE)**[25] [215] 8-8-12 **45**..... PaulMulrennan 10 37
(Michael Herrington) *chsd ldng pair: prom: rdn along wl over 2f out: grad wknd* **33/1**

3540 **7** *3/4* **Upper Lambourn (IRE)**[5] [502] 6-9-0 **47**.....(t) JoeFanning 13 37
(Christopher Kellett) *in rr: hdwy over 2f out: sn rdn and no imp* **9/2**[2]

030- **8** *nk* **Durham Express (IRE)**[61] [6761] 7-9-1 **48**.....(p) LeeTopliss 1 37
(Colin Teague) *sn chsd along on inner to chse ldrs: rdn over 2f out and kpt on one pce* **33/1**

-065 **9** *2* **Novalist**[5] [502] 6-8-9 **45**.....(b) NeilFarley(3) 12 28
(Robin Bastiman) *dwlt: hdwy on wd outside 1/2-way: rdn to chse ldrs over 2f out: sn drvn and no further prog* **8/1**

-400 **10** *3 1/4* **Homeboy (IRE)**[15] [353] 6-9-5 **52**.....(b) ChrisCatlin 9 24
(David Evans) *t.k.h: towards rr: rdn along over 2f out: n.d* **20/1**

50-0 **11** *1/2* **Mistress Shy**[27] [179] 7-8-8 **46**.....(t) ShirleyTeasdale(5) 11 17
(Peter Hiatt) *a in rr* **100/1**

00-5 **F** **Gebayl**[12] [384] 4-9-4 **54**.....(t) MarkCoumbe(3) 7
(Roger Ingram) *cl up: rdn along and lost pl over 2f out: sn swvd violently lft and fell: b.b.v* **16/1**

06-0 **B** **Roxy Lane**[34] [81] 5-8-13 **46**..... WilliamCarson 8
(Peter Hiatt) *a towards rr: b.d jst over 2f out* **33/1**

1m 15.89s (-0.61) **Going Correction** -0.25s/f (Stan) 13 Ran SP% **125.7**

Speed ratings (Par 101): **94,92,91,91,90 87,86,85,82,78 77, ,**

CSF £83.59 CT £350.18 TOTE £5.60: £2.30, £8.50, £1.50; EX 116.00 Trifecta £642.80.

**Owner** B Baugh **Bred** Helier Stud **Trained** Audley, Staffs

**FOCUS**

Competitive if modest stuff, but marred by a horrible incident over 2f out where Gebayl swerved across the track and fell, after having apparently bled, and took out Roxy Lane in the process. The winner has a decent record here but didn't need to match his best.

## 564 DOWNLOAD THE LADBROKES APP MAIDEN STKS 1m (F)

**2:00** (3:26) (Class 5) 3-Y-0+ **£3,234** (£962; £481; £240) **Stalls** Low

Form RPR

\- **1** **Mondlicht (USA)** 4-10-0 0..... JoeFanning 5 83+
(Mark Johnston) *trckd ldrs: green and pushed along over 3f out: hdwy 2f out: rdn and led over 1f out: sn clr: styd on* **1/1**[1]

**2** *3 1/4* **Streets Of Newyork**[41] [3801] 7-10-0 0..... TomEaves 2 73
(Brian Ellison) *dwlt and sn pushed along in rr: rdn and hdwy on inner over 2f out: ev ch over 1f out: sn drvn and kpt on same pce fnl f* **16/1**

03- **3** *3* **Lynngale**[84] [7955] 3-7-11 0..... JosephineGordon(7) 8 56
(Jo Hughes) *prom: cl up 3f out: rdn over 2f out: drvn and one pce fr over 1f out* **6/1**

3-2 **4** *nk* **Playtothewhistle**[22] [254] 3-8-9 0..... PaddyAspell 7 60
(Bryan Smart) *led: rdn along over 2f out: drvn and hdd over 1f out: sn one pce* **7/2**[2]

0-0 **5** *9* **St Paul'S (IRE)**[18] [316] 3-8-9 0.....(p) RobertHavlin 4 40
(David C Griffiths) *cl up: rdn along over 2f out: sn drvn and wknd wl over 1f out* **50/1**

405- **6** *nk* **Seaham**[180] [5443] 3-8-9 73..... LukeMorris 3 39
(Rod Millman) *trckd ldrs: effrt and cl up wl over 2f out: sn rdn and wknd* **4/1**[3]

**7** *5* **Bright Acclaim** 3-8-9 0..... BenCurtis 6 27
(Jo Hughes) *towards rr: hdwy on outer 3f out: rdn: green and edgd lft over 2f out: sn outpcd* **20/1**

06-0 **8** *1 1/4* **Hannah Louise (IRE)**[10] [423] 3-8-4 35.....(t) JamesSullivan 1 20
(Roger Ingram) *in tch on inner: n.m.r and lost pl 1/2-way: sn bhd* **100/1**

1m 41.36s (-2.34) **Going Correction** -0.25s/f (Stan)

**WFA** 3 from 4yo+ 19lb 8 Ran SP% **120.1**

Speed ratings (Par 103): **101,97,94,94,85 85,80,78**

CSF £21.83 TOTE £2.10: £1.20, £2.60, £2.20; EX 14.60 Trifecta £101.20.

**Owner** Sheikh Hamdan bin Mohammed Al Maktoum **Bred** Lazy Lane Farms Llc **Trained** Middleham Moor, N Yorks

**FOCUS**

This race was delayed by well over an hour after the doctor accompanied Mark Coumbe to hospital following his fall in the opener. A weak maiden which totally revolved around the winner. The form makes soem sense.

## 565 BET ON YOUR MOBILE WITH LADBROKES (S) STKS 7f (F)

**2:35** (3:48) (Class 6) 4-Y-0+ **£2,264** (£673; £336; £168) **Stalls** Low

Form RPR

-621 **1** **Arabian Flight**[12] [387] 5-8-13 63..... AndrewMullen 6 68
(Michael Appleby) *trckd ldng pair: hdwy to chse ldr 2f out: rdn over 1f out: drvn and styd on wl to ld last 100yds* **5/4**[1]

16-6 **2** *2* **Alpha Tauri (USA)**[16] [347] 8-9-1 67.....(t) BillyCray(3) 4 67
(Richard Guest) *led: rdn clr over 2f out: drvn apprh fnl f: hdd and no ex last 100yds* **7/2**[3]

6-63 **3** *3* **Elusive Warrior (USA)**[12] [387] 11-8-12 48.....(p) BenCurtis 9 53
(Alan McCabe) *in tch and sn rdn along: wd st: hdwy 2f out: drvn and kpt on fnl f: tk 3rd nr fin* **25/1**

5-63 **4** *hd* **Plunder**[8] [464] 4-8-12 70.....(b) RobertWinston 7 52
(Alan Berry) *chsd ldrs: hdwy 3f out: rdn 2f out: drvn to chse ldng pair over 1f out: sn one pce: lost 3rd nr fin* **3/1**[2]

514/ **5** *4 1/2* **Encore Un Fois**[285] [7920] 6-8-12 65..... JamesSullivan 2 41
(Ruth Carr) *pushed along in rr and sn outpcd and bhd: rdn over 2f out: drvn wl over 1f out: kpt on fnl f* **25/1**

000- **6** *1/2* **Mitchum**[119] [7283] 5-8-12 62..... DaleSwift 1 39
(Ron Barr) *chsd ldrs on inner: rdn along over 2f out: sn wknd* **16/1**

-143 **7** *1 1/2* **Nubar Boy**[10] [421] 7-8-5 60.....(p) CharlotteJenner(7) 5 36
(Ian Williams) *chsd wnr: rdn along wl over 2f out: drvn wl over 1f out and sn wknd* **8/1**

000- **8** *hd* **Delicious Patrica**[223] [3954] 5-8-7 40..... ChrisCatlin 3 30
(Ed McMahon) *dwlt: a in rr* **50/1**

1m 29.73s (-0.57) **Going Correction** -0.25s/f (Stan) 8 Ran SP% **118.3**

Speed ratings (Par 101): **93,90,87,87,81 81,79,79**

CSF £6.05 TOTE £2.30: £1.30, £1.70, £3.20; EX 7.50 Trifecta £48.50.There was no bid for the winner.

**Owner** Dallas Racing **Bred** Mr & Mrs A E Pakenham **Trained** Danethorpe, Notts

**FOCUS**

Very few ever got into this uncompetitive seller. The winner is rated close to form.

## 566 LADBROKES H'CAP 7f (F)

**3:05** (4:06) (Class 3) (0-95,95) 4-Y-0+ **£7,439** (£2,213; £1,106; £553) **Stalls** Low

Form RPR

-166 **1** **Frontier Fighter**[18] [314] 6-9-7 **95**..... DanielTudhope 2 104
(David O'Meara) *mde most: rdn wl over 1f out: drvn ent fnl f: kpt on gamely* **5/4**[1]

2-13 **2** *1 1/2* **Apostle (IRE)**[10] [426] 5-9-2 **90**..... LiamKeniry 6 95
(David Simcock) *trckd ldng pair: hdwy 3f out: rdn wl over 1f out: drvn and edgd lft ins fnl f: kpt on u.p towards fin* **7/2**[2]

-123 **3** *1* **Hannahs Turn**[7] [479] 4-8-11 **85**..... LukeMorris 5 88
(Chris Dwyer) *trckd ldrs on inner: hdwy wl over 2f out: rdn to chal over 1f out: ev ch tl drvn and one pce ins fnl f* **6/1**

6-36 **4** *1 3/4* **Verse Of Love**[10] [426] 5-8-13 **87**..... ChrisCatlin 3 85
(David Evans) *cl up: rdn along wl over 2f out: drvn wl over 1f out and sn one pce* **14/1**

000- **5** *nk* **Joe Eile (IRE)**[121] [7227] 6-8-13 **94**..... JoeDoyle(7) 7 91
(John Quinn) *t.k.h early: trckd ldrs on outer: pushed along and outpcd 3f out: rdn and edgd lft wl over 1f out: kpt on one pce fnl f* **5/1**[3]

-000 **6** *9* **Naabegha**[18] [314] 7-8-11 **85** ow1..... TomQueally 4 59
(Alan McCabe) *dwlt: a in rr* **8/1**

1m 27.1s (-3.20) **Going Correction** -0.25s/f (Stan) 6 Ran SP% **115.4**

Speed ratings (Par 107): **108,106,105,103,102 92**

CSF £6.13 CT £18.40 TOTE £2.40: £1.10, £2.60; EX 6.90 Trifecta £19.60.

**Owner** Walker Nicholson **Bred** Darley **Trained** Nawton, N Yorks

**FOCUS**

A decent handicap, run at just a fair pace. Just a minor best from the winner, with the second to form.

## 567 32RED PLAY AVALON II WITH £10 FREE H'CAP 2m (F)

**3:40** (4:25) (Class 5) (0-75,73) 4-Y-0+ **£2,911** (£866; £432; £216) **Stalls** Low

Form RPR

20-5 **1** **Arr' Kid (USA)**[16] [350] 4-9-1 **68**.....(b) TomEaves 2 83+
(Keith Dalgleish) *trckd ldr: cl up 6f out: led 4f out: rdn clr over 2f out: styd on strly* **2/1**[1]

-234 **2** *9* **Yasir (USA)**[22] [253] 6-9-7 **68**.....(p) HayleyTurner 4 72
(Conor Dore) *s.i.s and sn detached in rr: tk clsr order 6f out: chsd ldrs over 3f out: rdn to chse wnr over 2f out: sn drvn wl and kpt on: no ch w wnr* **4/1**[3]

3/1- **3** *4* **Outrageous Request**[55] [8331] 8-9-7 **73**..... LouisSteward(5) 7 72
(William Stone) *hld up: hdwy 4f out: chsd ldrs 3f out: sn one pce* **5/2**[2]

05-5 **4** *4 1/2* **Adili (IRE)**[14] [361] 5-8-7 **54**.....(p) BenCurtis 5 48
(Brian Ellison) *led: pushed along and hdd 4f out: drvn over 3f out and sn wknd* **10/1**

3-03 **5** *4 1/2* **Star Of Namibia (IRE)**[8] [463] 4-8-11 **64**.....(b) TomQueally 6 52
(Michael Mullineaux) *in tch: pushed along 6f out: rdn over 4f out and sn outpcd* **10/1**

435- **6** *30* **Danisa**[192] [5001] 5-9-1 **65**.....(tp) WilliamTwiston-Davies(3) 3 17
(David Bridgwater) *trckd ldrs: hdwy over 4f out: rdn along over 3f out: sn drvn and wknd* **7/1**

4455 **7** *26* **Dontpaytheferryman (USA)**[2] [546] 9-8-7 **54** oh2.....(b) ChrisCatlin 1
(Peter Hiatt) *trckd ldrs: pushed along 6f out: sn rdn and lost pl: wl bhd fnl 3f* **25/1**

3m 37.79s (-7.71) **Going Correction** -0.25s/f (Stan)

**WFA** 4 from 5yo+ 6lb 7 Ran SP% **116.4**

Speed ratings (Par 103): **109,104,102,100,98 83,70**

CSF £10.81 TOTE £2.40: £1.20, £1.90; EX 8.20 Trifecta £36.70.

**Owner** Weldspec Glasgow Limited **Bred** Chestnut Farm **Trained** Carluke, S Lanarks

**FOCUS**

A modest staying event and they finished well spread out. The winner is rated to his turf best.

## 568 32RED.COM H'CAP 7f (F)

**4:10** (4:46) (Class 6) (0-65,71) 3-Y-0 **£2,264** (£673; £336; £168) **Stalls** Low

Form RPR

545- **1** **Beautiful Stranger (IRE)**[96] [7788] 3-9-5 **63**.....(p) TomEaves 3 71+
(Keith Dalgleish) *mde all: rdn over 2f out: drvn ent fnl f: sn edgd rt and kpt on wl towards fin* **6/1**[3]

0-36 **2** *1/2* **Fruit Pastille**[18] [311] 3-9-3 **64**..... WilliamTwiston-Davies(3) 5 70+
(Hughie Morrison) *dwlt: in rr and sn swtchd rt to outer: hdwy 1/2-way: wd st and rdn to chse ldrs over 2f out: chsd wnr over 1f out: swtchd lft and drvn ent fnl f: kpt on* **11/4**[2]

2-50 **3** *2 3/4* **Evacusafe Lady**[11] [401] 3-9-1 **62**.....(tp) RyanPowell(3) 6 61
(John Ryan) *hld up in rr: hdwy whn n.m.r 3f out: chsd ldrs 2f out: sn swtchd lft and rdn wl over 1f out: kpt on* **16/1**

500- **4** *3 3/4* **Kraka Gym (IRE)**[190] [5068] 3-8-13 **57**..... JamesSullivan 4 47
(Michael Easterby) *in rr: hdwy over 2f out: rdn wl over 1f out: kpt on fnl f: nrst fin* **25/1**

5-11 **5** *1 3/4* **Nick The Odds (IRE)**[3] [543] 3-9-13 **71** 6ex.....(bt[1]) BenCurtis 1 56
(Jo Hughes) *awkward s: sn pushed along on inner and prom after 1f: effrt to chse wnr 3f out: rdn 2f out: sn drvn and wknd: hung lft ins fnl f* **5/2**[1]

201- **6** *shd* **Black Geronimo**[89] 7882 3-9-4 **65**....................(b[1]) BillyCray(3) 7 50
(Roy Bowring) *in tch: hdwy to chse ldrs 3f out: rdn and hung lft over 2f out: sn drvn and wknd* **7/1**

3-42 **7** *9* **Intense Feeling (IRE)**[15] 354 3-9-1 **59**....................(b[1]) ChrisCatlin 10 20
(David Evans) *sn chsng wnr: rdn along 3f out: wknd over 2f out* **8/1**

012- **8** *9* **Mornin Mr Norris**[140] 6725 3-8-8 **52**.................... BarryMcHugh 2
(John Quinn) *chsd ldrs: rdn along 1/2-way: sn lost pl and bhd* **14/1**

033- **9** *7* **Sky Ranger (IRE)**[89] 7883 3-9-6 **64**.................... PaulMulrennan 9
(James Tate) *chsd ldrs: rdn along wl over 2f out: sn wknd* **8/1**

1m 29.2s (-1.10) **Going Correction** -0.25s/f (Stan) **9** Ran SP% **120.6**
Speed ratings (Par 95): **96,95,92,88,86 85,75,65,57**
CSF £24.00 CT £259.61 TOTE £7.40: £2.00, £1.80, £4.10; EX 35.90 Trifecta £408.40.
**Owner** Weldspec Glasgow Limited **Bred** D Veitch & B Douglas **Trained** Carluke, S Lanarks
■ Stewards' Enquiry : Billy Cray two-day ban: careless riding (25-26 Feb)

**FOCUS**
A modest 3yo handicap but the time was fair and the form is rated slightly positively.

## 569 CORAL.CO.UK BEST ODDS GUARANTEED ON RACING H'CAP 1m 4f (F)
4:40 (5:06) (Class 6) (0-65,65) 4-Y-0+ £2,264 (£673; £336; £168) Stalls Low

Form RPR

1511 **1** **Fire In Babylon (IRE)**[16] 349 6-9-0 **58**....................(b) AdamBeschizza 3 68+
(Noel Quinlan) *trckd ldng pair: hdwy 4f out: effrt on outer over 2f out and sn led: rdn over 1f out: kpt on wl fnl f* **9/4**[2]

06-1 **2** *1 1/4* **Light The City (IRE)**[7] 474 7-8-7 **51** 6ex.................... JamesSullivan 4 58
(Ruth Carr) *trckd ldr: hdwy 4f out: cl up 3f out: rdn 2f out and chsd wnr: ev ch tl drvn appr fnl f and kpt on same pce* **11/10**[1]

1103 **3** *3 3/4* **Grandad Mac**[7] 476 6-9-7 **65**.................... RussKennemore 5 66
(Alan Coogan) *led: pushed along over 3f out: rdn and hdd 2f out: sn drvn and kpt on same pce* **5/2**[3]

-465 **4** *3 3/4* **Monzino (USA)**[12] 385 6-8-13 **64**....................(b) PaulBooth(7) 6 59
(Michael Chapman) *in tch: pushed along 5f out: rdn and outpcd over 3f out: kpt on u.p fnl 2f: tk modest 4th nr line* **10/1**

5-30 **5** *hd* **Willow Island (IRE)**[34] 88 5-8-7 **51** oh6.................... ChrisCatlin 2 46
(David Evans) *chsd ldrs on inner: pushed along 4f out: rdn along 3f out: drvn and wknd over 2f out: lost modest 4th nr line* **50/1**

2m 37.24s (-3.76) **Going Correction** -0.25s/f (Stan)
**WFA** 4 from 5yo+ 3lb **5** Ran SP% **118.0**
Speed ratings (Par 101): **102,101,98,96,96**
CSF £5.61 TOTE £2.70: £1.50, £1.30; EX 4.80 Trifecta £8.00.
**Owner** Ms Fiona Donald **Bred** The Goldsmith Bloodstock Partnership **Trained** Newmarket, Suffolk

**FOCUS**
A modest handicap, run at an ordinary pace. The form of the first three is sound enough but the next two were close enough.
T/Jkpt: £1092.30 to a £1 stake. Pool: £10,000.00 - 6.50 winning units. T/Plt: £28.40 to a £1 stake. Pool: £129,813.37 - 3332.44 winning units. T/Qpdt: £6.90 to a £1 stake. Pool: £10,435.42 - 1115.19 winning units. JR

# 483 KEMPTON (A.W) (R-H)
## Wednesday, February 12

**OFFICIAL GOING: Standard**
Wind: Strong, across (away from stands) Weather: Fine

## 570 BOOK NOW FOR JUMP RACING 22.02.14 APPRENTICE H'CAP 1m 2f (P)
5:15 (5:16) (Class 7) (0-50,50) 4-Y-0+ £1,617 (£481; £240; £120) Stalls Low

Form RPR

00-6 **1** **My Renaissance**[23] 263 4-9-0 **49**.................... RobJFitzpatrick(5) 8 54
(Ben Case) *hld up off the pce: clsd w others fr over 2f out: drvn to take 2nd 1f out: styd on to ld last 50yds* **4/1**[2]

-322 **2** *1/2* **Polydamos**[7] 484 5-9-7 **50**....................(v) EoinWalsh 10 54
(Tony Carroll) *hld up off the pce: clsd w others fr over 2f out: led over 1f out: urged along fnl f: hdd and nt qckn last 50yds* **4/6**[1]

060- **3** *hd* **Whiskey N Stout (IRE)**[310] 1424 4-9-3 **47**.................... MatthewLawson 7 51
(Sean Curran) *t.k.h: hld up off the pce: drvn 3f out: prog over 1f out: styd on u.str.p fnl f: nrly snatched 2nd* **16/1**

0- **4** *1 1/4* **Hypatia (IRE)**[19] 329 4-9-4 **48**....................(b) DavidKenny 4 50
(John Joseph Murphy, Ire) *chsd clr ldrs: rdn 3f out: sn lost pl: rallied over 1f out: kpt on same pce fnl f* **20/1**

-256 **5** *4 1/2* **Loulou Vuitton**[8] 475 4-9-1 **45**....................(p) ShelleyBirkett 1 38
(Steph Hollinshead) *trckd ldr: clr of rest fr 4f out: rdn over 2f out: lost 2nd and wknd over 1f out* **25/1**

50-4 **6** *1* **Beauchamp Sunset**[14] 368 4-8-10 **47**....................(p) KieranShoemark(7) 6 38
(Paul Fitzsimons) *led at brisk pce: clr w one rival fr 4f out: hdd & wknd over 1f out* **6/1**[3]

0/0- **7** *3/4* **Hardy Plume**[132] 6986 5-9-2 **45**.................... DCByrne 2 34
(Denis Coakley) *t.k.h: chsd ldng pair: dropped off them 4f out: clsd again 2f out: nt clr run on inner over 1f out: wknd* **25/1**

56-0 **8** *2 1/2* **Heading To First**[8] 475 7-8-13 **45**....................(b[1]) RyanWhile(3) 5 29
(Paddy Butler) *s.s: hld up in last and wl off the pce: tried to cl over 2f out: drvn and no hdwy fnl f* **50/1**

005/ **9** *1* **The Right Time**[711] 558 6-8-11 **45**.................... MrAidenBlakemore(5) 9 27
(Tony Carroll) *chsd clr ldrs: rdn and struggling 2f out: wknd* **50/1**

040- **10** *11* **Norphin**[84] 7981 4-9-6 **50**....................[1] PhilipPrince 11 10
(Simon Hodgson) *a wl in rr: no prog over 2f out: wknd rapidly over 1f out: t.o* **20/1**

2m 8.71s (0.71) **Going Correction** 0.0s/f (Stan)
**WFA** 4 from 5yo+ 1lb **10** Ran SP% **121.3**
Speed ratings (Par 97): **97,96,96,95,91 91,90,88,87,78**
CSF £6.80 CT £38.87 TOTE £5.10: £1.50, £1.10, £5.30; EX 11.20.
**Owner** Neil Hutley **Bred** Aston House Stud **Trained** Edgcote, Northants

**FOCUS**
The leaders went quick and fell in a hole, setting it up for those ridden with patience. Weak form.

## 571 BETBRIGHT.COM H'CAP 1m 2f (P)
5:45 (5:48) (Class 6) (0-60,60) 4-Y-0+ £1,940 (£577; £288; £144) Stalls Low

Form RPR

450- **1** **Handsome Stranger (IRE)**[98] 7169 4-9-6 **60**.........(p) RobertWinston 11 68
(Alan Bailey) *settled towards rr: rdn over 2f out: wdst of all bnd sn after: gd prog to ld 1f out: drvn and styd on* **12/1**

4-55 **2** *1 1/4* **Petersboden**[9] 459 5-8-12 **51**.................... RobertHavlin 8 58+
(Michael Blanshard) *hld up: 8th 3f out but gng wl: trying to make prog whn nowhere to go over 1f out: styd on fnl f to take 2nd nr fin* **16/1**

-106 **3** *nk* **Xclusive**[9] 458 4-9-6 **60**.................... LukeMorris 6 65
(Ronald Harris) *trckd ldrs: rdn over 2f out: wd bnd sn after: prog to ld briefly over 1f out: one pce fnl f: lost 2nd nr fin* **14/1**

6-44 **4** *2 1/4* **Cane Cat (IRE)**[19] 317 7-8-11 **50**....................(t) WilliamCarson 2 50
(Tony Carroll) *hld up in last: rdn over 2f out: prog on outer fnl f: styd on: no ch to threaten* **25/1**

3-03 **5** *1* **Herbalist**[13] 379 4-9-4 **58**....................(v) ChrisCatlin 4 56
(Ben Pauling) *led: drvn 3f out: hdd & wknd jst over 1f out* **12/1**

3-43 **6** *3/4* **Minstrel Lad**[12] 406 6-9-4 **57**.................... LiamKeniry 7 54+
(Lydia Pearce) *settled midfield: drvn 3f out: sing to run on whn nowhere to go jst over 1f out: nt rcvr* **7/2**[1]

0-55 **7** *1 3/4* **Time Square (FR)**[21] 278 7-9-5 **58**.................... DavidProbert 12 51
(Tony Carroll) *pressed ldr: drvn and wknd jst over 1f out* **5/1**[2]

0-26 **8** *3/4* **Thane Of Cawdor (IRE)**[13] 382 5-9-4 **57**.................... GeorgeBaker 3 49+
(Joseph Tuite) *trckd ldrs: cl up bhd ldng pair on inner wl over 1f out: trapped bhd them as they wknd and lost all ch: allowed to coast home* **5/1**[2]

06-0 **9** *1/2* **Raamz (IRE)**[18] 345 7-9-2 **58**.................... GeorgeChaloner(3) 10 49
(Kevin Morgan) *a in rr: rdn 3f out: brief effrt on inner wl over 1f out: sn no prog* **10/1**

0-45 **10** *1 1/2* **Cantor**[4] 537 6-9-4 **60**....................(t) RossAtkinson(3) 5 48
(Paul Morgan) *in tch: lost pl rapidly u.p 1/2-way and sn in last: lost no more grnd but no prog fnl 2f* **20/1**

5-04 **11** *2* **My Manekineko**[21] 277 5-9-6 **59**.................... FrederikTylicki 9 43
(J R Jenkins) *stdd s: sn prog fr rr and trckd ldng pair on outer 6f out: losing pl whn bmpd arnd over 1f out: wknd* **7/1**[3]

0-06 **U** **Great Conquest (USA)**[8] 469 4-8-10 **57**.................... JohnLawson(7) 1
(Jamie Osborne) *dwlt: t.k.h: uns rdr in rr after 1f* **20/1**

2m 7.06s (-0.94) **Going Correction** 0.0s/f (Stan)
**WFA** 4 from 5yo+ 1lb **12** Ran SP% **118.5**
Speed ratings (Par 101): **103,102,101,99,99 98,97,96,96,94 93,**
CSF £183.34 CT £2707.99 TOTE £17.00: £3.80, £3.20, £4.60; EX 235.10 Trifecta £2679.40.
**Owner** John Stocker **Bred** Gerrardstown House Stud **Trained** Newmarket, Suffolk

**FOCUS**
The pace picked up some way out and it suited those challenging from the second half of the field. There was a fair bit of trouble and the form is rated around the winner.

## 572 BETBRIGHT MONEYBACK OFFERS H'CAP 5f (P)
6:15 (6:39) (Class 5) (0-75,75) 4-Y-0+ £2,911 (£866; £432; £216) Stalls Low

Form RPR

60-0 **1** **Sandfrankskipsgo**[35] 80 5-9-7 **75**.................... GeorgeBaker 4 87
(Peter Crate) *trckd ldng pair: gng easily whn squeezed through between rivals to ld jst over 1f out: sn clr* **5/4**[1]

1044 **2** *3* **Desert Strike**[11] 432 8-9-2 **70**....................(p) HayleyTurner 5 71+
(Conor Dore) *chsd ldrs: squeezed out 1/2-way and struggling in 6th after: pushed along and styd on fnl f to take 2nd last strides* **15/2**

0-52 **3** *1/2* **Pull The Pin (IRE)**[23] 257 5-9-0 **68**....................(bt) WilliamCarson 1 67
(Ann Stokell) *led: drvn and hdd jst over 1f out: no ch w wnr and lost 2nd last strides* **5/1**[2]

2-46 **4** *1* **Mossgo (IRE)**[8] 470 4-8-8 **62**....................(t) LukeMorris 3 58
(John Best) *chsd ldrs: rdn 2f out: one pce fr over 1f out* **7/1**[3]

5-20 **5** *1/2* **Island Legend (IRE)**[12] 412 8-9-5 **73**....................(p) RichardKingscote 6 67
(Milton Bradley) *pressed ldr: edgd lft u.p over 1f out: fdd fnl f* **10/1**

56-6 **6** *1/2* **Decent Fella (IRE)**[11] 432 8-8-13 **72**....................(t) EoinWalsh(5) 2 64
(Ann Stokell) *awkward s and slowly away: detached in last and nvr able to figure: styd on fnl f* **20/1**

2315 **7** *3/4* **Only Ten Per Cent (IRE)**[8] 470 6-9-1 **69**....................(v) StephenCraine 7 59
(J R Jenkins) *prom but racd wd: rdn 2f out: wknd fnl f* **8/1**

1m 0.14s (-0.36) **Going Correction** 0.0s/f (Stan) **7** Ran SP% **110.3**
Speed ratings (Par 103): **102,97,96,94,94 93,92**
CSF £10.36 CT £32.14 TOTE £1.90: £1.60, £3.30; EX 12.70 Trifecta £45.70.
**Owner** Peter Crate **Bred** Peter Crate **Trained** Newdigate, Surrey

**FOCUS**
This race looked full of pace on paper, and that's how it worked out. The winner is rated to his best.

## 573 BETBRIGHT - LIVE THE MOMENT H'CAP 6f (P)
6:45 (7:15) (Class 5) (0-70,76) 3-Y-0 £2,911 (£866; £432; £216) Stalls Low

Form RPR

6-01 **1** **Dont Have It Then**[12] 401 3-8-11 **60**.................... RobertWinston 11 72
(Willie Musson) *hld up in last trio: gd prog fr 2f out: cajoled along and r.o to ld last 110yds: styd on* **7/1**[3]

1412 **2** *3/4* **Spreadable (IRE)**[6] 501 3-9-7 **70**....................(b) LukeMorris 5 79
(Nick Littmoden) *trckd ldrs: gng wl and prog over 2f out: led wl over 1f out: drvn and styd on but hdd and outpcd last 110yds* **11/4**[2]

2-21 **3** *2 1/4* **Bretherton**[8] 477 3-9-10 **76** 6ex....................(b) GeorgeChaloner(3) 3 78
(Richard Fahey) *cl up: chal on inner and upsides 2f out: drvn to chse wnr to 1f out: one pce* **5/4**[1]

0-13 **4** *3 3/4* **Artemis (IRE)**[7] 485 3-9-2 **65**.................... JoeFanning 8 55
(Conrad Allen) *hld up in 7th: stdy prog over 2f out: clsd on ldrs 1f out: wknd fnl f* **16/1**

-261 **5** *3/4* **Little Big Man**[16] 354 3-9-1 **69**....................(b) LouisSteward(5) 7 57
(Sylvester Kirk) *settled in last trio: rdn and fnd nil jst over 2f out: sn bdly outpcd: pushed along and r.o fnl f* **33/1**

61-3 **6** *1 1/2* **Dazza**[18] 338 3-9-0 **70**.................... HectorCrouch(7) 1 53
(Gary Moore) *led: drvn and hdd wl over 1f out: wknd fnl f* **25/1**

044- **7** *2 1/2* **Lady In Blue (IRE)**[119] 7300 3-9-5 **68**.................... DanielTudhope 4 43
(David O'Meara) *nvr bttr than midfield: rdn over 2f out: outpcd sn after* **12/1**

50-6 **8** *shd* **Prisca**[20] 298 3-9-1 **64**....................(p) WilliamCarson 6 38
(Jamie Osborne) *bdly squeezed out after 1f: dropped to last and nvr able to rcvr* **40/1**

001- **9** *7* **Chookie's Lass**[97] 7789 3-9-3 **66**.................... TomEaves 2 18
(Keith Dalgleish) *chsd ldr to 1/2-way: wknd rapidly 2f out* **20/1**

1-42 **10** *2* **Three Pips**[18] 338 3-9-6 **69**.................... ChrisCatlin 10 15
(Ed McMahon) *chsd ldrs on outer: rdn over 2f out: sn wknd qckly* **14/1**

1m 12.78s (-0.32) **Going Correction** 0.0s/f (Stan) **10** Ran SP% **117.8**
Speed ratings (Par 97): **102,101,98,93,92 90,86,86,77,74**
CSF £25.85 CT £41.25 TOTE £12.50: £2.70, £1.40, £1.30; EX 39.80 Trifecta £109.00.
**Owner** Laurence Mann **Bred** Charley Knoll Partnership **Trained** Newmarket, Suffolk

**FOCUS**
Plenty of in-form horses here, there was a solid gallop on, and the first four saved ground on the rail before being delivered with their challenges in the straight. The form looks a bit better than the grade and should work out.

## 574 BETBRIGHT MOBILE H'CAP — 7f (P)
7:15 (7:45) (Class 4) (0-85,85) 4-Y-0+ £4,851 (£1,443; £721; £360) Stalls Low

| Form | Pos | Dist | Horse / Comment | RPR |
|---|---|---|---|---|
| 0-44 | 1 | | **Stonefield Flyer**[17] [348] 5-9-7 **85**........ TomEaves 5<br>(Keith Dalgleish) *mde all: drvn 2f out: hrd pressed fnl f: battled on wl* **6/1** | 92 |
| 2-60 | 2 | ¾ | **Jay Bee Blue**[20] [294] 5-9-0 **78**........(t) JohnFahy 6<br>(Sean Curran) *dwlt: hld up in 6th: detached 1/2-way: cajoled along and prog 2f out: drvn to take 2nd fnl f and looked a threat: kpt on but nt qckn last 150yds* **16/1** | 83 |
| 50-0 | 3 | 1 ¼ | **Toga Tiger (IRE)**[21] [287] 7-9-0 **78**........ RobertWinston 2<br>(Jeremy Gask) *in tch in 5th: drvn jst over 2f out: nt qckn wl over 1f out: styd on fnl f to take 3rd last strides* **4/1**[2] | 80 |
| -262 | 4 | nk | **Light From Mars**[13] [381] 9-9-3 **81**........(p) LiamJones 7<br>(Ronald Harris) *chsd wnr: drvn 2f out: nt qckn and unable to chal over 1f out: lost 2nd and one pce fnl f* **5/1**[3] | 82 |
| 00-2 | 5 | 1 | **Brocklebank (IRE)**[19] [314] 5-9-5 **83**........ GeorgeBaker 4<br>(Simon Dow) *hld up in last: wl detached 1/2-way: shoved along over 2f out but hanging and no prog: rdn over 1f out: styd on ins fnl f: no ch* **5/2**[1] | 81 |
| -301 | 6 | nk | **Bowstar**[14] [372] 5-8-13 **77**........(b) RobertHavlin 1<br>(Michael Attwater) *dwlt: t.k.h and sn trckd ldng pair: drvn and nt qckn 2f out: stl cl enough 1f out: fdd* **5/1**[3] | 74 |
| 4-24 | 7 | 3 ¼ | **Emkanaat**[14] [372] 6-8-10 **79**........(b) DavidKenny(5) 3<br>(Amy Weaver) *chsd ldng trio: drvn and nt qckn jst over 2f out: wknd fnl f* **7/1** | 68 |

1m 24.64s (-1.36) **Going Correction** 0.0s/f (Stan) 7 Ran SP% **114.6**
Speed ratings (Par 105): **107,106,104,104,103 102,99**
CSF £89.20 TOTE £7.00: £2.00, £6.70; EX 77.40 Trifecta £838.40.
**Owner** G R Leckie **Bred** Ian Crawford And Gordon Leckie **Trained** Carluke, S Lanarks

**FOCUS**
A fair contest rated around the winner.

## 575 BETBRIGHT H'CAP — 1m (P)
7:45 (8:16) (Class 6) (0-55,55) 4-Y-0+ £1,940 (£577; £288; £144) Stalls Low

| Form | Pos | Dist | Horse / Comment | RPR |
|---|---|---|---|---|
| -531 | 1 | | **Wishformore (IRE)**[10] [446] 7-9-8 **55** 6ex........(p) TomQueally 5<br>(Ian Williams) *t.k.h: hld up in midfield: prog jst over 2f out: drvn over 1f out: sustained chal fnl f to ld last strides* **1/1**[1] | 63+ |
| 35-0 | 2 | shd | **Pour La Victoire (IRE)**[28] [184] 4-9-4 **51**........ LukeMorris 6<br>(Tony Carroll) *trckd ldng pair: led over 2f out: hrd pressed and drvn over 1f out: worn down last strides* **5/1**[2] | 59 |
| 0200 | 3 | nk | **Tijuca (IRE)**[10] [446] 5-9-7 **54**........ ChrisCatlin 10<br>(Ed de Giles) *hld up early but sn cl up on outer: prog over 2f out: rdn to chal over 1f out: upsides fnl f: nt qckn nr fin* **12/1** | 61 |
| 060- | 4 | 2 ½ | **Fire King**[210] [4411] 8-9-3 **50**........ JimmyQuinn 7<br>(Paul Burgoyne) *t.k.h: hld up and sn in last pair: jst pushed along fr over 2f out: styd on fr over 1f out to take 4th nr fin: nvr involved* **25/1** | 52 |
| 0-00 | 5 | ½ | **My Scat Daddy (USA)**[11] [428] 5-9-2 **49**........ DavidProbert 1<br>(Zoe Davison) *hld up towards rr: pushed along over 2f out: sme prog and shkn up over 1f out: disp 4th ins fnl f: nvr nr to chal* **14/1** | 49 |
| /46- | 6 | 1 ¾ | **Absolute Bearing (IRE)**[251] [3026] 5-9-0 **47**........ JamesSullivan 3<br>(Tim Etherington) *t.k.h: wl in tch: effrt on inner 2f out: disp 4th briefly 1f out: wknd* **14/1** | 43 |
| 43-5 | 7 | nk | **Indian Violet (IRE)**[26] [211] 8-9-6 **53**........(p) LiamKeniry 12<br>(Zoe Davison) *t.k.h: trckd ldrs: lost pl over 2f out: drvn and tried to rally over 1f out: wknd fnl f* **12/1** | 49 |
| /00- | 8 | 3 | **Beaumont Cooper**[261] [2710] 5-9-7 **54**........ GeorgeBaker 4<br>(Anabel K Murphy) *led: hdd over 2f out: jst pushed along and steadily lost pl* **12/1** | 43 |
| 3-00 | 9 | 4 | **Tingle Tangle (USA)**[20] [295] 4-9-5 **52**........ TomEaves 2<br>(Tony Carroll) *hld up wl in rr: pushed along on inner over 2f out: shkn up and no prog over 1f out* **16/1** | 32 |
| 50-0 | 10 | 1 ¾ | **Rapid Water**[41] [14] 8-8-12 **45**........(b) JoeFanning 11<br>(Pat Eddery) *s.s: in tch in rr: rdn over 2f out: sn struggling* **9/1**[3] | 21 |
| 0/-5 | 11 | 9 | **Sweet Piccolo**[7] [495] 4-8-7 **45**........(b) JoeyHaynes(5) 8<br>(Paddy Butler) *chsd ldr: rdn 3f out: sn wknd: t.o* **66/1** | |

1m 41.2s (1.40) **Going Correction** 0.0s/f (Stan) 11 Ran SP% **124.3**
Speed ratings (Par 101): **93,92,92,90,89 87,87,84,80,78 69**
CSF £6.47 CT £43.23 TOTE £1.70: £1.10, £1.70, £2.50; EX 7.50 Trifecta £26.30.
**Owner** Paul Mannion **Bred** Tally-Ho Stud **Trained** Portway, Worcs

**FOCUS**
With a serious lack of in-form horses in the race this looked at the mercy of the winner. He showed his best form since 2011.

## 576 KEMPTON PARK CHASE DAY 22.02.14 H'CAP — 6f (P)
8:15 (8:45) (Class 6) (0-65,65) 4-Y-0+ £1,940 (£577; £288; £144) Stalls Low

| Form | Pos | Dist | Horse / Comment | RPR |
|---|---|---|---|---|
| 1-53 | 1 | | **New Rich**[7] [489] 4-8-12 **61**........(p) GeorgeDowning(5) 1<br>(Eve Johnson Houghton) *hld up in midfield: swtchd ins and prog 2f out: drvn to ld narrowly jst ins fnl f: jnd rest of way: jst prevailed* **11/2**[3] | 69+ |
| 6-31 | 2 | hd | **Divine Call**[20] [295] 7-9-6 **64**........ RichardKingscote 7<br>(Milton Bradley) *hld up in last pair: gd prog on inner fr 2f out: clsd to chal fnl f: w wnr nr fin: jst pipped* **10/1** | 72+ |
| 0-25 | 3 | hd | **Indian Affair**[20] [295] 4-9-7 **65**........ DavidProbert 4<br>(Milton Bradley) *racd freely: led: rdn and hdd wl over 1f out: kpt on and upsides ins fnl f: no ex nr fin* **12/1** | 72 |
| 0-01 | 4 | shd | **Sweet Talking Guy (IRE)**[10] [448] 4-9-2 **60** 6ex........(t) GeorgeBaker 3<br>(Lydia Pearce) *trckd ldrs: nt clr run briefly and swtchd lft over 1f out: clsd on ldrs fnl f: nvr gng to get there* **11/8**[1] | 67+ |
| 1-40 | 5 | nk | **Foie Gras**[11] [428] 4-8-10 **59**........ ShelleyBirkett(5) 5<br>(Chris Dwyer) *trckd ldr to 2f out: styd chalng: upsides ins fnl f: nt qckn last 50yds* **20/1** | 65 |
| 0-55 | 6 | ¾ | **Invigilator**[24] [248] 6-9-4 **62**........(t) DaleSwift 8<br>(Derek Shaw) *v awkward s: mostly in last pair: rdn in last over 2f out: styd on fr over 1f out: fin best of all* **20/1** | 65 |
| -402 | 7 | ½ | **Climaxfortackle (IRE)**[5] [511] 6-9-2 **60**........ JoeFanning 6<br>(Derek Shaw) *hld up wl in rr: trying to make prog whn nt clr run over 1f out: pushed along and kpt on steadily fnl f: neve rable to land a blow* **5/1**[2] | 62+ |
| 00-2 | 8 | shd | **West Leake (IRE)**[20] [295] 8-9-0 **58**........(p) LiamKeniry 10<br>(Paul Burgoyne) *towards rr: rdn 2f out: kpt on fr over 1f out: nvr gng pce to chal* **25/1** | 59 |
| -052 | 9 | 1 ¼ | **Secret Millionaire (IRE)**[8] [470] 7-9-4 **62**........ LukeMorris 2<br>(Tony Carroll) *trckd ldng pair: clsd to ld wl over 1f out gng strly: hdd jst ins fnl f: fdd tamely* **7/1** | 59 |
| -143 | 10 | 1 | **Insolenceofoffice (IRE)**[20] [295] 6-8-11 **60**........(p) EoinWalsh(5) 9<br>(Richard Ford) *restless stalls: awkward s: sn chsd ldrs: lost pl 2f out: steadily wknd* **12/1** | 54 |
| 1-04 | 11 | 2 ¾ | **The Dancing Lord**[11] [425] 5-8-11 **62**........ DavidParkes(7) 11<br>(Brett Johnson) *plld hrd: hld up in rr: rdn and wknd 2f out* **50/1** | 47 |

1m 13.44s (0.34) **Going Correction** 0.0s/f (Stan) 11 Ran SP% **126.5**
Speed ratings (Par 101): **97,96,96,96,95 94,94,94,92,91 87**
CSF £60.84 CT £667.01 TOTE £8.50: £2.20, £3.20, £2.90; EX 89.30 Trifecta £835.00.
**Owner** Eden Racing Club **Bred** Whitsbury Manor Stud And Mrs M E Slade **Trained** Blewbury, Oxon
■ Stewards' Enquiry : George Downing caution: careless riding.
George Baker caution: careless riding.

**FOCUS**
A fairly competitive heat, and a tight finish. The winner posted a small personal best.
T/Jkpt: Not won. T/Plt: £231.10 to a £1 stake. Pool: £107786.42 - 340.46 winning tickets T/Qpdt: £17.90 to a £1 stake. Pool: £10893.78 - 450.25 winning tickets JN

# 530 LINGFIELD (L-H)
## Wednesday, February 12

**OFFICIAL GOING: Standard**
Wind: strong, half behind Weather: heavy rain, clearing after Race 5, windy

## 577 32RED ON THE APP STORE H'CAP — 1m 2f (P)
1:30 (1:30) (Class 6) (0-60,58) 3-Y-0 £1,545 (£1,545; £352) Stalls Low

| Form | Pos | Dist | Horse / Comment | RPR |
|---|---|---|---|---|
| 3-63 | 1 | | **Plough Boy (IRE)**[13] [378] 3-9-7 **58**........ ChrisCatlin 3<br>(Willie Musson) *chsd ldrs: rdn to chse ldr over 2f out: drvn to ld 2f out: forged ahd ins fnl f: jnd on post* **4/1**[2] | 64 |
| 0-06 | 1 | dht | **Shannon Haven (IRE)**[16] [355] 3-9-2 **53**........ StephenCraine 4<br>(Daniel Mark Loughnane) *squeezed for room leaving stalls: hld up in lasty pair: hdwy 4f out: drvn to chse ldng pair over 1f out: hrd drvn and str chal ins fnl f: styd on to join ldr on post* **14/1**[3] | 59 |
| 4-32 | 3 | 4 ½ | **Frederic Chopin**[8] [473] 3-9-6 **57**........ GeorgeBaker 5<br>(Stuart Williams) *chsd ldr tl led over 2f out: hdd and rdn 2f out: drvn and no ex ins fnl f: wknd towards fin* **1/2**[1] | 54 |
| 04-6 | 4 | 2 | **Flying Author (IRE)**[7] [488] 3-8-12 **49**........(v) PaddyAspell 2<br>(Phil McEntee) *led tl rdn and hdd over 2f out: drvn and btn 1f out: wknd ins fnl f* **25/1** | 42 |
| 60-0 | 5 | 33 | **Swale Star**[19] [316] 3-8-5 **49**........ GaryMahon(7) 1<br>(Seamus Mullins) *in tch in midfield: dropped to rr 7f out: lost tch 5f out: t.o fnl 3f* **50/1** | |
| 0-00 | 6 | 40 | **Redy To Rumble**[13] [378] 3-8-1 **45**........(v[1]) RhiainIngram(7) 6<br>(Michael Attwater) *stdd s: hld up in last pair: rn wd bnd after 1f: hdwy to chse ldrs over 7f out tl over 4f out: sn bhd: t.o fnl 3f* **100/1** | |

2m 7.73s (1.13) **Going Correction** +0.125s/f (Slow) 6 Ran SP% **100.1**
Speed ratings (Par 95): **100,100,96,94,68 36**
WIN: £2.70 Plough Boy, £7.70 Shannon Haven; PL: £1.50 Plough Boy, £4.60 Shannon Haven; EX: PB&SH £15.90, SH&PB £28.30; CSF: PB&SH £18.52, £26.32; TF: PB&SH&FC £27.50, SH&PB&FC £49.00.
**Owner** J McGarry **Bred** J McGarry **Trained** Baldwin's Gate, Staffs
**Owner** K A Cosby & Partners **Bred** J P Keappock **Trained** Newmarket, Suffolk

**FOCUS**
Very blustery conditions confronted the runners in the opener. It was a pretty uncompetitive 3yo handicap, particularly with the favourite below par. The pair of dead-heaters both improved, particularly Shannon Haven.

## 578 CORAL MOBILE "JUST THREE CLICKS TO BET" (S) STKS — 1m 2f (P)
2:00 (2:00) (Class 6) 4-6-Y-0 £2,045 (£603; £302) Stalls Low

| Form | Pos | Dist | Horse / Comment | RPR |
|---|---|---|---|---|
| 44-4 | 1 | | **India's Song**[13] [382] 4-8-7 59........(t) ChrisCatlin 6<br>(David Simcock) *stdd s: hld up in tch in rr: rdn and effrt on outer bnd 2f out: hdwy to chse wnr ins fnl f: styd on wl to ld fnl 50yds* **7/1** | 63 |
| 5-43 | 2 | ½ | **Exclusive Waters (IRE)**[10] [445] 4-8-12 68........(b) TomQueally 1<br>(Gary Moore) *led: rdn and fnd ex to go clr over 1f out: drvn ins fnl f: hdd and no ex fnl 50yds* **1/1**[1] | 67 |
| -225 | 3 | 1 ¾ | **Yourinthewill (USA)**[12] [406] 6-8-13 64........ StephenCraine 3<br>(Daniel Mark Loughnane) *stdd after s: hld up in tch in last pair: rdn and hdwy over 1f out: chsd wnr jst over 1f out tl ins fnl f: 3rd and one pce fnl 150yds* **9/2**[3] | 64 |
| 6-30 | 4 | 1 | **Divine Rule (IRE)**[10] [445] 6-8-13 58........(v) LiamJones 4<br>(Laura Mongan) *in tch in midfield: effrt u.p 2f out: styd on same pce fnl f* **16/1** | 62 |
| -310 | 5 | 5 | **Paddy's Saltantes (IRE)**[18] [345] 4-9-4 67........(b) LukeMorris 2<br>(J S Moore) *sn niggled along: chsd ldrs: drvn 4f out: no ex and btn ent fnl f: wknd fnl 150yds* **4/1**[2] | 58 |
| 2-54 | 6 | 2 ¼ | **Mosman**[12] [406] 4-9-4 62........(tp) FergusSweeney 5<br>(Dean Ivory) *chsd ldr and ev ch 2f out: outpcd and btn over 1f out: lost 2nd jst over 1f out and wknd fnl f* **12/1** | 53 |

2m 6.63s (0.03) **Going Correction** +0.125s/f (Slow)
**WFA** 4 from 6yo 1lb 6 Ran SP% **114.3**
Speed ratings: **104,103,102,101,97 95**
CSF £14.98 TOTE £7.80: £2.30, £2.20; EX 18.60 Trifecta £44.60.The winner was bought in. Exclusive Waters was claimed by Mr C. B. Hills for £6,000.
**Owner** Mrs Julia Annable **Bred** Car Colston Hall Stud **Trained** Newmarket, Suffolk

**FOCUS**
Fair form in this seller but the favourite was below her best. The runner-up dictated what looked no more than a modest gallop for a long way. The form is rated a bit cautiously.

## 579 32RED NEW AVALON II SLOT MAIDEN STKS — 7f 1y(P)
2:30 (2:34) (Class 5) 3-Y-0 £3,067 (£905; £453) Stalls Low

| Form | Pos | Dist | Horse / Comment | RPR |
|---|---|---|---|---|
| | 1 | | **Passing Star** 3-9-5 0........ RobertWinston 1<br>(Charles Hills) *in tch in midfield: rdn and effrt on inner over 1f out: led ins fnl f: rn green and edgd rt fnl 100yds: hld on wl* **6/1** | 76 |
| 62-4 | 2 | nk | **Treasure Cay (IRE)**[30] [169] 3-9-5 70........ TomQueally 2<br>(Paul Cole) *broke fast: chsd ldr: rdn and ev ch 2f out: kpt on but unable qck towards fin* **5/2**[2] | 75 |
| | 3 | hd | **Born In Bombay** 3-9-5 0........ DavidProbert 3<br>(Andrew Balding) *rn green: in tch in midfield: chsd ldrs 3f out: rdn and unable qck over 1f out: rallied and styd on wl fnl 100yds* **3/1**[3] | 74 |

5- **4** *1* **Walk With An Angel**[76] 8084 3-8-9 0 LouisSteward(5) 4 67
(Philip McBride) *hld up in tch in last pair: clsd over 2f out: rdn and hdwy on inner over 1f out: kpt on same pce u.p ins fnl f* **7/1**

2 **5** *1 1/2* **Sleipnir**[20] 291 3-9-5 0 JimCrowley 7 68
(Philip Hide) *sn led: rdn wl over 1f out: hdd ins fnl f: nt qckning and btn whn short of room and hmpd wl ins fnl f: wknd towards fin* **9/4**[1]

**6** *30* **Bikini Club** 3-9-0 0 (e[1]) FrederikTylicki 6
(Paul D'Arcy) *in tch in midfield: pushed rt and hmpd over 5f out: lost pl and nvr traveling in detached last after: lost tch 1/2-way* **25/1**

0- **7** *1 1/2* **Bertie Baby**[121] 7244 3-8-9 0 ShelleyBirkett(5) 5
(Gay Kelleway) *stdd s: plld v hrd: hld up in tch in last pair: hmpd into heels of rivals: swtchd rt and then veered rt over 5f out: chsd ldrs 5f out tl over 3f out: sn dropped out: t.o* **50/1**

1m 25.8s (1.00) **Going Correction** +0.125s/f (Slow) **7** Ran SP% **116.9**
Speed ratings (Par 97): **99,98,98,97,95 61,59**
CSF £22.23 TOTE £8.20: £3.60, £1.40; EX 24.10 Trifecta £98.90.
**Owner** John C Grant **Bred** Whitsbury Manor Stud & A W M Christie-Miller **Trained** Lambourn, Berks

**FOCUS**
A fair maiden, the runner-up a good yardstick to the form, and the winner and the third both made promising starts to their careers. They finished in a bit of a heap.

## 580 32RED PLAY THUNDERSTRUCK WITH £10 FREE H'CAP 1m 7f 169y(P)
**3:05** (3:07) (Class 6) (0-60,60) 4-Y-0+ **£2,385** (£704; £352) **Stalls** Low

Form RPR

3-10 **1** **Keep Kicking (IRE)**[21] 283 7-9-10 **60** JimCrowley 2 71+
(Simon Dow) *hld up in tch in midfield: clsd to trck ldrs over 2f out: pushed along and qcknd to ld ent fnl f: sn in command: easily* **7/4**[1]

006- **2** *2 3/4* **Brave Helios**[56] 5500 4-9-0 **56** RichardKingscote 6 62
(Jonathan Portman) *hld up in tch in midfield: hdwy 4f out: rdn and ev ch 2f out: drvn to ld over 1f out: sn hdd and outpcd by wnr: kpt on for clr 2nd ins fnl f* **11/4**[2]

42-4 **3** *4* **Descaro (USA)**[9] 454 8-9-5 **55** (p) LukeMorris 4 56
(John O'Shea) *t.k.h: chsd ldrs: rdn to ld 3f out: drvn and hdd over 1f out: 3rd and outpcd 1f out: no ch w wnr but hld on for 3rd ins fnl f* **6/1**[3]

-665 **4** *nk* **Poste Restante**[9] 455 4-8-6 **48** ChrisCatlin 1 49
(David Simcock) *hld up in tch in last trio: rdn over 3f out: hdwy u.p over 1f out: no ch w wnr but battling for 3rd fnl f: kpt on* **10/1**

522- **5** *3/4* **Rollin 'n Tumblin**[315] 1325 10-9-1 **51** RobertHavlin 9 51
(Michael Attwater) *stdd and dropped in bhd after s: hld up in rr: hdwy 4f out: effrt and wdst bnd 2f out: outpcd and btn over 1f out: wl hld and plugged on same pce fnl f* **6/1**[3]

62-6 **6** *1/2* **Bell'Arte (IRE)**[9] 454 4-8-12 **54** (p) LiamJones 3 53
(Laura Mongan) *chsd ldrs tl outpcd u.p jst over 2f out: n.d and plugged on same pce fr over 1f out* **16/1**

5-00 **7** *15* **Parsons Green**[21] 282 5-8-10 **46** oh1 KierenFox 8 27
(Michael Attwater) *chsd ldr tl led 5f out: rdn and hdd 3f out: sn struggling and wknd: bhd fnl f* **100/1**

05-0 **8** *1 1/4* **Mariet**[9] 459 5-8-10 **46** oh1 HayleyTurner 7 26
(Suzy Smith) *stdd s: t.k.h: hld up in tch in last trio: lost tch and bhd 3f out* **14/1**

600/ **9** *81* **Muzey's Princess**[183] 7454 8-8-10 **46** oh1 [1] TomEaves 5
(Michael Mullineaux) *led tl 5f out: lost pl and bhd over 3f out: sn t.o and heavily eased fnl f* **100/1**

3m 30.05s (4.35) **Going Correction** +0.125s/f (Slow)
**WFA** 4 from 5yo+ 6lb **9** Ran SP% **115.2**
Speed ratings (Par 101): **94,92,90,90,90 89,82,81,41**
CSF £6.54 CT £22.06 TOTE £2.40: £1.10, £1.30, £2.00; EX 10.00 Trifecta £38.20.
**Owner** P McCarthy **Bred** Sunny Days Ltd **Trained** Epsom, Surrey

**FOCUS**
A one-sided handicap. The pace looked pretty sedate for a long way, but the field still finished well strung out. The winner rates close to his best.

## 581 32RED FREE £10 BONUS MAIDEN STKS 1m 5f (P)
**3:40** (3:41) (Class 5) 4-Y-0+ **£3,067** (£905; £453) **Stalls** Low

Form RPR

6-3 **1** **Shalianzi (IRE)**[33] 115 4-9-5 67 (b) GeorgeBaker 12 71+
(Gary Moore) *t.k.h: chsd ldr for 1f: styd chsng ldrs tl chal ent fnl 2f: led over 1f out: hung lft 1f out: sn clr: eased cl home* **9/4**[2]

43-2 **2** *1 1/2* **Conserve (IRE)**[21] 276 4-9-0 73 (b) HayleyTurner 10 61
(Amy Weaver) *stdd and dropped in bhd after s: hld up in tch in rr: hdwy to trck ldrs over 2f out: effrt on inner over 1f out: chsd clr wnr ins fnl f: kpt on* **6/4**[1]

4 **3** *3/4* **Candesta (USA)**[21] 282 4-9-0 0 ShelleyBirkett(5) 7 65
(Julia Feilden) *chsd ldrs: rdn to ld over 2f out: drvn and hdd over 1f out: 3rd and styd on same pce ins fnl f* **16/1**

5-22 **4** *1 3/4* **After The Storm**[18] 343 5-9-9 65 LukeMorris 3 63
(John O'Shea) *t.k.h: wl in tch in midfield: hdwy to chse ldrs and rdn ent fnl 2f: 4th and styd on same pce fr 1f out* **3/1**[3]

**5** *3 3/4* **Midnight Chorister**[69] 6-9-9 0 (t) ChrisCatlin 6 57
(Alex Hales) *v.s.a: t.k.h: hld up in tch in last pair: hdwy and cl 6th 2f out: rdn and no rspnse ent fnl f: sn wknd* **33/1**

46 **6** *3/4* **Ceevee**[2] 558 4-8-12 0 (t) ChloeIngram(7) 8 56
(Tim Vaughan) *t.k.h: hdwy to chse ldr after 1f: upsides ldr 10f out tl led over 3f out: hdd over 2f out: pushed along and btn over 1f out: wknd ins fnl f: eased towards fin* **50/1**

36- **7** *6* **She's A Honey**[93] 7838 4-8-11 0 GeorgeChaloner(3) 4 42
(Kevin Morgan) *hld up in tch in midfield: rdn over 2f out: outpcd and btn ent fnl 2f: wknd over 1f out* **100/1**

642/ **8** *9* **Sash Of Honour (IRE)**[69] 6839 5-9-9 78 (v) DavidProbert 1 33
(Tim Vaughan) *hld up tch in midfield: rdn and no rspnse over 4f out: dropped to rr 3f out: wknd ent fnl 2f* **5/1**

50 **9** *hd* **Celtic Sunlight**[12] 403 4-9-5 0 FergusSweeney 2 33
(Pat Phelan) *stdd s: t.k.h: hld up in tch in last trio: rdn and no hdwy 3f out: sn wknd* **100/1**

005/ **10** *1 1/4* **Fruity Bun**[32] 7491 4-9-0 40 (t) RobertHavlin 5 26
(Keiran Burke) *led tl rdn and hdd over 3f out: lost pl wl over 2f out: bhd fnl f* **100/1**

2m 49.35s (3.35) **Going Correction** +0.125s/f (Slow)
**WFA** 4 from 5yo+ 4lb **10** Ran SP% **126.2**
Speed ratings (Par 103): **94,93,92,91,89 88,85,79,79,78**
CSF £6.64 TOTE £3.40: £1.20, £1.10, £3.10; EX 7.70 Trifecta £60.10.
**Owner** Ashley Head **Bred** His Highness The Aga Khan's Studs S C **Trained** Lower Beeding, W Sussex

**FOCUS**
A modest maiden with doubts over the field. The pace only picked up 4f out. The winner reversed latest form with the fourth.

## 582 CORAL APP DOWNLOAD FROM THE APP STORE H'CAP 1m 2f (P)
**4:15** (4:16) (Class 5) (0-70,76) 4-Y-0+ **£3,067** (£905; £453) **Stalls** Low

Form RPR

50-1 **1** **Whitby Jet (IRE)**[26] 210 6-9-5 **68** LiamKeniry 9 76
(Ed Vaughan) *hld up in tch in last trio: hdwy over 2f out: rdn and effrt on outer over 1f out: str run to ld wl ins fnl f: r.o wl* **7/2**[1]

46-4 **2** *1 1/4* **Aldeburgh**[33] 119 5-9-2 **65** GeorgeBaker 8 71
(Jim Old) *stdd after s: hld up in tch in last trio: nt clr run 2f out tl hdwy ent fnl f: rdn and gd hdwy to press ldrs fnl 100yds: kpt on to go 2nd towards fin* **9/2**[2]

2-16 **3** *1* **Gabrial The Boss (USA)**[12] 410 4-9-4 **68** (tp) TomQueally 5 72
(Michael Mullineaux) *chsd ldng trio: nt clr run 2f out: rdn and qcknd to ld jst ins fnl f: hdd and outpcd wl ins fnl f* **10/1**

0-64 **4** *2 1/2* **Zaeem**[18] 345 5-9-4 **67** (b[1]) LukeMorris 10 66
(Dean Ivory) *t.k.h: hld up in midfield: hdwy to press ldrs 3f out: sn rdn: edgd rt u.p over 1f out: wknd and edgd lft ins fnl f* **5/1**[3]

/00- **5** *nk* **Seaside Rock (IRE)**[21] 7491 4-9-3 **67** (b[1]) TomEaves 6 65
(Keith Dalgleish) *in tch in midfield: lost pl over 3f out and sn rdn: hdwy u.p and short of room ins fnl f: styd on but no threat to ldrs* **8/1**

0-21 **6** *shd* **Mahadee (IRE)**[10] 445 9-9-13 **76** 6ex (b) AmirQuinn 2 74
(Lee Carter) *wl in tch in midfield: nt clr run ent fnl 2f: rdn and no real imp over 1f out: kpt on same pce fnl f* **25/1**

55-0 **7** *hd* **Magnolia Ridge (IRE)**[24] 250 4-9-6 **70** (p) JamesSullivan 3 67
(Kristin Stubbs) *chsd ldrs: nt clr run 2f out: rdn and effrt on inner over 1f out: no ex 1f out: wknd ins fnl f* **14/1**

54-0 **8** *nse* **Sweet Marwell (IRE)**[30] 155 4-8-12 **62** FergusSweeney 7 59
(Jo Crowley) *chsd ldr tl rdn to ld over 2f out: hdd jst ins fnl f: sn wknd* **14/1**

3-06 **9** *1 1/4* **Understory (USA)**[18] 345 7-9-3 **66** HayleyTurner 4 61
(Tim McCarthy) *led tl rdn and hdd over 2f out: stl pressing ldrs and hrd drvn over 1f out: wknd ins fnl f* **9/2**[2]

0-00 **10** *1/2* **Planetoid (IRE)**[32] 146 6-9-0 **70** AprilKitchener(7) 1 64
(Jim Best) *hld up in tch in rr: shkn up 3f out: sn rdn: hung lft and outpcd: n.d fnl 2f* **20/1**

2m 8.52s (1.92) **Going Correction** +0.125s/f (Slow)
**WFA** 4 from 5yo+ 1lb **10** Ran SP% **117.4**
Speed ratings (Par 103): **97,96,95,93,92 92,92,92,91,91**
CSF £19.16 CT £144.68 TOTE £3.50: £1.40, £2.30, £2.10; EX 23.10 Trifecta £193.20.
**Owner** A M Pickering **Bred** Rathasker Stud **Trained** Newmarket, Suffolk

**FOCUS**
A fair handicap. The gallop looked just a modest one for the most part and there was a congested finish. The winner rates pretty much back to his best.

## 583 LADBROKES APPRENTICE H'CAP 1m 1y(P)
**4:45** (4:46) (Class 5) (0-70,68) 4-Y-0+ **£3,067** (£905; £453) **Stalls** High

Form RPR

-341 **1** **Club House (IRE)**[7] 493 4-9-8 **68** 6ex GeorgeBuckell 1 77
(Robert Mills) *in tch in midfield: swtchd rt and effrt wl over 1f out: rdn to ld jst ins fnl f: r.o strly: readily* **7/4**[1]

00-6 **2** *2* **Midnight Feast**[30] 154 6-9-2 **62** (v) LouisSteward 7 66
(Lee Carter) *chsd ldr tl rdn to ld over 1f out: hdd jst ins fnl f: hung rt and outpcd by wnr ins fnl f: hld on for 2nd* **6/1**[3]

/0-5 **3** *nk* **Cathedral**[28] 181 5-9-4 **67** AlistairRawlinson(3) 6 71
(Ed de Giles) *dwlt: sn rcvrd to chse ldrs: rdn and effrt wl over 1f out: outpcd by wnr and carried rt ins fnl f: kpt on* **4/1**[2]

-002 **4** *3/4* **Dozy Joe**[10] 445 6-9-2 **62** (v) DanielCremin 3 64
(Joseph Tuite) *stdd bk after s: hld up in last trio: 5th and plenty to do 2f out: hdwy u.p 1f out: styd on: no threat to wnr* **12/1**

14-5 **5** *1/2* **Hierarch (IRE)**[13] 376 7-8-12 **65** PaigeRanger(7) 8 66
(David Simcock) *hld up in last trio: stl plenty to do whn pushed along and hdwy on inner over 1f out: styng on whn hmpd and swtchd rt ins fnl f: kpt on: nvr trbld ldrs* **7/1**

644- **6** *3/4* **Enriching (USA)**[56] 8323 6-9-0 **67** JackOsborn(7) 5 66
(Gary Harrison) *dwlt: sn pushed along and racd in midfield: kpt on u.p ins fnl f: nvr trbld ldrs* **6/1**[3]

60-2 **7** *hd* **Timothy T**[30] 154 6-8-13 **62** (b) JackGarritty(3) 2 61
(Philip Hide) *led: rdn over 2f out: hdd over 1f out: edgd lft u.p and btn ins fnl f: wknd fnl 75yds* **4/1**[2]

13-3 **8** *4* **Little Indian**[30] 154 4-9-2 **62** AlexandraVilmar 4 51
(J R Jenkins) *hld up in last trio: last and plenty to whn drvn and effrt over 1f out: no imp: nvr trbld ldrs* **14/1**

1m 36.96s (-1.24) **Going Correction** +0.125s/f (Slow) **8** Ran SP% **131.8**
Speed ratings (Par 103): **111,109,108,107,107 106,106,102**
CSF £15.71 CT £43.03 TOTE £2.40: £1.20, £3.20, £2.20; EX 24.20 Trifecta £145.50.
**Owner** Mrs B B Mills A Foreman **Bred** Val & Angela Leeson **Trained** Headley, Surrey
■ Stewards' Enquiry : Louis Steward three-day ban: careless riding (Feb 26-28)
Jack Garritty one-day ban: careless riding (Feb 26)

**FOCUS**
A modest apprentice event. It appeared to be soundly run. The winner rates back in top form.
T/Plt: £67.20 to a £1 stake. Pool: £89619.02 - 972.62 winning tickets T/Qpdt: £6.90 to a £1 stake. Pool: £10726.90 - 1146.93 winning tickets SP

# 553 CAGNES-SUR-MER
Wednesday, February 12

**OFFICIAL GOING: Polytrack: standard**

## 584a PRIX RADISSON BLU NICE (H'CAP) (5YO+) (POLYTRACK) 1m 4f
**12:50** (12:00) 5-Y-0+
**£20,366** (£8,233; £6,066; £3,900; £2,383; £1,516)

RPR

**1** **Okiel Des Mottes (FR)**[85] 5-9-0 0 AnthonyCrastus 12 86
(E Lellouche, France) **13/1**

**2** *shd* **Special Request (FR)**[60] 7-9-3 **0** AntoineHamelin 9 89
(N Caullery, France) **7/1**[3]

**3** *1* **Uphold**[11] 437 7-9-1 **0** (v) Pierre-CharlesBoudot 10 85
(Gay Kelleway) *t.k.h: prom thrght: rdn to chal and almost upsides ldr 2f out: styd on wl but nt quite pce of wnr and dropped to 3rd towards fin* **14/1**

4 ½ **Divin Leon (FR)**[40] 6-9-2 0 SylvainRuis 11 85
(M Boutin, France) 12/1
5 snk **Destin Blue (FR)**[29] 178 6-8-13 0 EddyHardouin 3 82
(P Marion, Germany) 11/2[1]
6 1 ½ **Palm Frond**[347] 6-9-2 0 GuillaumeMillet 2 83
(Mlle L-L Rohn-Pelvin, France) 22/1
7 ½ **Maintop (FR)**[202] 8-8-8 0 StephanePasquier 13 74
(N Milliere, France) 6/1[2]
8 snk **Tepmokea (IRE)**[11] 437 8-9-6 0 ThomasMessina 6 86
(Andrew Hollinshead) *t.k.h: midfield in tch: rdn over 2f out: styd on same pce in st and nvr able to chal* 43/1
9 2 **Rainbow Knight**[364] 648 6-8-7 0 RaphaelMarchelli 15 69
(J-M Capitte, France) 11/1
10 2 ½ **Lumpaz (FR)**[101] 7668 7-9-3 0 FranckForesi 14 75
(F Foresi, France) 43/1
11 hd **Risquillo (FR)**[32] 8-8-7 0 (p) FabriceVeron 1 65
(M Boutin, France) 20/1
12 hd **Valencin (FR)**[40] 5-9-6 0 FranckBlondel 4 78
(P Decouz, France) 15/1
13 ¾ **Notion (IRE)**[139] 6-9-2 0 AntoineCoutier 5 72
(F Chappet, France) 10/1
14 2 ½ **Ellinis (FR)**[563] 6-8-13 0 AlexisBadel 7 65
(P Marion, Germany) 12/1
15 12 **Sage Riquet (FR)**[125] 7-9-0 0 TonyPiccone 8 47
(E Lellouche, France) 18/1
16 5 ½ **Le Bosphore (FR)**[11] 437 7-8-6 0 (b) IoritzMendizabal 16 30
(M Pimbonnet, France) 13/1

2m 28.99s (148.99) **16** Ran SP% **121.1**
WIN (incl. 1 euro stake): 8.10 (Okiel Des Mottes coupled with Sage Riquet). PLACES: 4.60, 2.60, 4.70. DF: 64.30. SF: 145.40..
**Owner** Elie Lellouche **Bred** Earl Ecurie Des Mottes **Trained** Lamorlaye, France

## 585a PRIX DES CHEVREFEUILLES (MAIDEN) (3YO) (POLYTRACK) 1m 2f (D)
2:20 (12:00) 3-Y-O £10,000 (£4,000; £3,000; £2,000; £1,000)

RPR
1 **Gladstone (FR)**[29] 3-9-2 0 (b[1]) IoritzMendizabal 8 83
(J-C Rouget, France) 11/5[1]
2 snk **Sealed (USA)**[16] 360 3-9-2 0 Pierre-CharlesBoudot 3 83
(Gay Kelleway) *midfield in tch: smooth hdwy to chal on outer 2f out: rdn to dispute ld over 1f out: kpt on wl ins fnl f but hdd and jst hld* 7/2[3]
3 2 **Garlingari (FR)**[39] 3-9-2 0 FredericSpanu 7 79
(Mme C Barande-Barbe, France) 14/5[2]
4 1 **Flying Cape (IRE)**[8] 482 3-9-2 0 ThomasMessina 2 77
(Andrew Hollinshead) *sn midfield: rdn 2f out: nt clr run over 1f out: r.o and wnt 4th ins fnl f: nvr able to chal* 53/10
5 2 **Games Day (FR)** 3-9-2 0 EddyHardouin 6 73
(E Lellouche, France) 44/1
6 shd **Riquet Enfin (FR)**[16] 360 3-9-2 0 AnthonyCrastus 4 73
(E Lellouche, France) 8/1
7 1 **In For Dinner (FR)**[16] 360 3-9-2 0 FabriceVeron 5 71
(P Monfort, France) 21/1
8 3 ½ **Spaliburg Rosetgri (FR)**[8] 482 3-8-8 0 ValentinGambart(8) 9 64
(M Boutin, France) 42/1
9 nk **Docteur Vigousse (FR)**[8] 482 3-8-10 0 (p) StephaneLaurent(6) 10 63
(J Parize, France) 32/1

2m 4.09s (124.09) **9** Ran SP% **118.9**
WIN (incl. 1 euro stake): 3.20. PLACES: 1.30, 1.30, 1.30. DF: 6.50. SF: 12.80..
**Owner** Daniel-Yves Treves **Bred** Snig Elevage **Trained** Pau, France

# 570 KEMPTON (A.W) (R-H)
### Thursday, February 13

**OFFICIAL GOING: Standard**
Wind: Strong, across (away from stands) Weather: Fine

## 586 KEMPTON PARK CHASE 22.02.14 H'CAP 6f (P)
5:10 (5:10) (Class 7) (0-50,50) 4-Y-O+ £1,617 (£481; £240; £60; £60) Stalls Low

Form RPR
45-0 1 **Torres Del Paine**[29] 184 7-9-7 **50** DavidProbert 6 58
(Brett Johnson) *led 1f: trckd ldr: led 2f out and sent for home: looked in command 1f out: rdn and kpt on but ld dwindling nr fin* 5/4[1]
0-00 2 nk **Strategic Action (IRE)**[15] 370 5-9-4 **47** (tp) RobertHavlin 2 54
(Linda Jewell) *chsd ldng pair: rdn 2f out: chsd wnr over 1f out: kpt on and clsd gap nr fin* 7/1[3]
0432 3 ½ **Vhujon (IRE)**[8] 483 9-8-13 **45** SladeO'Hara(3) 12 50
(Peter Grayson) *s.s: hld up in last: urged along fr over 2f out: prog over 1f out: styd on wl to take 3rd nr fin* 8/1
2-00 4 ¾ **Christopher Chua (IRE)**[13] 402 5-8-13 **45** WilliamTwiston-Davies(3) 11 48
(Michael Scudamore) *settled in last trio: rdn 2f out: prog over 1f out: kpt on same pce fnl f* 20/1
65-0 4 dht **Diamond Vine (IRE)**[41] 34 6-9-6 **49** (v) LukeMorris 8 52
(Ronald Harris) *chsd ldrs: rdn wl over 2f out: no prog tl kpt on ins fnl f* 10/1
0-00 6 1 **Chester Deelyte (IRE)**[15] 370 6-8-11 **45** (v) ShirleyTeasdale(5) 4 45
(Lisa Williamson) *dwlt: chsd ldrs: rdn over 2f out: one pce and nvr able to threaten* 20/1
-025 7 ½ **Ryedale Lass**[15] 370 6-9-4 **47** (b) GeorgeBaker 3 45
(Geoffrey Deacon) *hld up towards rr: prog on inner 2f out: chal for 2nd 1f out: wknd last 150yds* 9/2[2]
600- 8 nk **Steel City Boy (IRE)**[112] 7485 11-8-13 **47** AnnStokell(5) 7 44
(Ann Stokell) *racd freely: led after 1f to 2f out: urged along and wknd over 1f out* 33/1
-054 9 1 ¾ **Sherjawy (IRE)**[13] 402 10-9-2 **45** (p) LiamKeniry 10 37
(Zoe Davison) *in tch: rdn over 2f out: wknd over 1f out* 20/1
-003 10 2 ½ **Brandywell Boy (IRE)**[8] 483 11-8-13 **45** (b) BillyCray(3) 1 29
(Dominic Ffrench Davis) *urged along early: a in rr: nvr a factor* 20/1

1m 13.14s (0.04) **Going Correction** +0.025s/f (Slow) **10** Ran SP% **117.3**
Speed ratings (Par 97): **100,99,98,97,97 96,95,95,93,89**
CSF £9.24 CT £53.35 TOTE £2.60: £1.10, £3.40, £1.90; EX 17.10 Trifecta £114.80.
**Owner** Tann Racing **Bred** Deepwood Farm Stud **Trained** Epsom, Surrey
■ Stewards' Enquiry : Robert Havlin two-day ban: used whip above permitted level (Feb 27-28)

**FOCUS**
A moderate sprint handicap in which they went an honest gallop. Straightforward, low-grade form.

## 587 BETVICTOR NONRUNNER NO BET AT CHELTENHAM 2014 H'CAP 7f (P)
5:40 (5:40) (Class 5) (0-75,74) 4-Y-O+ £2,911 (£866; £432; £216) Stalls Low

Form RPR
10-2 1 **Fab Lolly (IRE)**[25] 245 4-9-0 **67** (p) JoeFanning 3 76
(James Bethell) *hld up towards rr: smooth prog towards inner jst over 2f out: led jst over 1f out: rdn fnl f: jst lasted* 8/1
/21- 2 nk **Fanoos**[118] 7343 5-9-6 **73** (p) RichardKingscote 1 81
(Dr Jon Scargill) *t.k.h: hld up in midfield: prog on inner 2f out: chal and upsides jst over 1f out: chsd wnr after: kpt on wl and clsng at fin* 10/1
2-10 3 ¾ **Diplomatic (IRE)**[10] 457 9-9-7 **74** (p) LiamJones 11 80
(Michael Squance) *hld up in last: rdn over 2f out: gd prog on outer over 1f out: r.o to take 3rd last 100yds: nvr quite able to chal* 12/1
0-00 4 ¾ **First Class**[11] 451 6-8-10 **63** (p) DavidProbert 6 67
(Rae Guest) *hld up towards rr: rdn over 2f out: styd on fr over 1f out: tk 4th nr fin* 12/1
350- 5 nk **Al Raqeeb (IRE)**[56] 8345 4-9-4 **71** (t) TomQueally 4 74
(Gary Harrison) *t.k.h: hld up towards rr: prog on inner 2f out: drvn and cl up jst over 1f out: kpt on same pce* 16/1
-623 6 shd **Alnoomaas (IRE)**[9] 470 5-8-13 **66** LukeMorris 12 69
(Luke Dace) *hld up in midfield fr wdst draw: rdn over 2f out: tried to cl on ldrs 1f out: one pce fnl f* 7/1[3]
-213 7 ½ **Khajaaly (IRE)**[5] 540 7-8-5 **65** (bt) AlistairRawlinson(7) 7 67
(Michael Appleby) *hld up in rr: shkn up and no rspnse over 2f out: styd on fr over 1f out: nrst fin* 6/1[2]
1-60 8 shd **Shaunas Spirit (IRE)**[14] 376 6-9-5 **72** (p) RobertWinston 5 73
(Dean Ivory) *trckd ldng pair: clsd to ld 2f out: hdd jst over 1f out: wknd last 150yds* 25/1
-312 9 5 **Shaolin (IRE)**[8] 493 4-9-6 **73** (t) GeorgeBaker 10 61
(Seamus Durack) *trckd ldr to jst over 2f out: shkn up and wknd tamely* 6/4[1]
4-06 10 1 ¾ **Burnhope**[8] 489 5-8-7 **67** (p) MatthewHopkins(7) 9 50
(Scott Dixon) *dwlt: plld hrd on outer and sn prom: wknd 2f out* 25/1
100- 11 ½ **Emperor Julius (IRE)**[56] 8345 4-9-6 **73** FergusSweeney 8 55
(Jo Crowley) *chsd ldrs to over 2f out: sn wknd* 25/1
-630 12 2 **Ghostwing**[8] 489 7-8-7 **60** oh3 WilliamCarson 2 36
(Tony Carroll) *led to 2f out: wknd qckly* 50/1

1m 25.36s (-0.64) **Going Correction** +0.025s/f (Slow) **12** Ran SP% **121.8**
Speed ratings (Par 103): **104,103,102,101,101 101,100,100,95,93 92,90**
CSF £84.20 CT £982.13 TOTE £9.10: £1.80, £3.60, £4.10; EX 60.00 Trifecta £1370.30.
**Owner** James Lambert **Bred** James F Hanly **Trained** Middleham Moor, N Yorks

**FOCUS**
A fair handicap in which they went a strong, contested gallop. The winner improved a bit more.

## 588 BACK OF THE NET AT BETVICTOR.COM MEDIAN AUCTION MAIDEN STKS 1m (P)
6:10 (6:10) (Class 5) 3-5-Y-O £2,911 (£866; £432; £216) Stalls Low

Form RPR
3-2 1 **Bowie Boy (IRE)**[29] 188 3-8-9 0 RichardKingscote 6 81
(Ralph Beckett) *trckd ldr: pushed up to ld wl over 1f out: sn jnd: wandered sltly but r.o wl to assert fnl f* 6/4[2]
3- 2 1 **Bishop Of Ruscombe**[106] 7631 3-8-9 0 DavidProbert 2 79
(Andrew Balding) *cl up in 3rd: pushed up to chal 2f out: w wnr over 1f out: r.o but a outpcd fnl f* 11/10[1]
34 3 5 **Ishiamber**[8] 486 4-9-9 0 LukeMorris 7 67
(George Baker) *trckd ldrs in 4th: pushed along over 2f out: rdn to take 3rd over 1f out: sn wl outpcd by ldng pair* 7/1[3]
4 1 **Dreaming Brave** 3-8-9 0 RobertHavlin 1 65
(Amanda Perrett) *hld up in 5th: pushed along over 2f out: steadily outpcd: nt totally disgracd* 20/1
4-5 5 3 ¾ **Lady Kathian (IRE)**[22] 275 3-8-4 0 JoeFanning 5 51
(Joseph Tuite) *mde most to wl over 1f out: sn wknd* 20/1
4-5 6 1 **Marphilly (IRE)**[29] 189 3-8-4 0 ChrisCatlin 3 49
(John Best) *stdd s: hld up in last: pushed along 3f out: nvr in it but kpt on fnl f* 25/1
0-0 7 3 ¼ **French Accent**[29] 188 3-8-4 0 WilliamCarson 4 42
(John Best) *a in last pair: shkn up 3f out: steadily wknd* 50/1

1m 39.71s (-0.09) **Going Correction** +0.025s/f (Slow)
**WFA** 3 from 4yo 19lb **7** Ran SP% **115.4**
Speed ratings (Par 103): **101,100,95,94,90 89,86**
CSF £3.39 TOTE £2.70: £1.60, £1.10; EX 4.40 Trifecta £10.20.
**Owner** I J Heseltine **Bred** Paul Kavanagh **Trained** Kimpton, Hants

**FOCUS**
A modest maiden. The first two were clear with the winner improving on his Lingfield latest.

## 589 DOWNLOAD THE BETVICTOR APP NOW H'CAP 1m (P)
6:40 (6:41) (Class 6) (0-65,65) 4-Y-O+ £1,940 (£433; £433; £144) Stalls Low

Form RPR
215- 1 **Compton Bird**[119] 7321 5-9-4 **62** RichardKingscote 9 70
(Paul Fitzsimons) *hld up in last quartet and off the pce: gd prog fr 2f out to chse ldng pair 1f out: sustained effrt to ld last 75yds* 16/1
04-0 2 ½ **Bloodsweatandtears**[22] 286 6-9-7 **65** GeorgeBaker 4 72
(William Knight) *trckd ldr: rdn to cl fr 2f out: upsides ins fnl f whn wnr wnt past* 4/1[1]
06/1 2 dht **Callisto Light**[22] 281 7-9-0 **58** LiamJones 5 65
(Michael Squance) *led at gd pce: drvn 2f out: clung on wl but hdd and one pce last 75yds* 6/1[2]
00-0 4 1 ¼ **Hill Of Dreams (IRE)**[29] 181 5-9-7 **65** (b) RobertWinston 14 69
(Dean Ivory) *hld up in last pair and sn wl off the pce: rdn over 2f out: gd prog on outer over 1f out: r.o to take 4th last stride: no ch* 20/1
06-0 5 hd **Storm Runner (IRE)**[22] 286 6-9-4 **65** RyanPowell(3) 10 69
(George Margarson) *chsd ldrs but sn off the bridle: urged along 1/2-way: struggling over 2f out: styd on wl again fnl f: nrst fin* 10/1
000- 6 shd **Angel Cake (IRE)**[83] 8008 5-9-2 **60** AndrewMullen 3 63
(Michael Appleby) *chsd ldng pair: drvn fr 3f out: lost 3rd 1f out: kpt on wl u.p but lost pls last strides* 16/1
00-0 7 nk **Imperator Augustus (IRE)**[36] 79 6-8-12 **63** JackGarritty(7) 11 66
(Patrick Holmes) *wl in tch in midfield: rdn over 2f out: tried to cl on ldrs over 1f out: kpt on one pce fnl f* 8/1[3]
32-3 8 1 ¼ **Severiano (USA)**[20] 319 4-9-6 **64** (p) JoeFanning 13 64
(Roger Varian) *trckd ldrs: rdn over 2f out: nt qckn wl over 1f out: steadily lost pl fnl f* 4/1[1]

4-50 **9** 3/4 **Masai Moon**[25] 245 10-8-13 **64** ow1 ........ PatMillman(7) 8 62
(Rod Millman) *hld up towards rr: dropped to last trio and pushed along over 2f out: nvr involved but styd on quite takingly fnl f* **20/1**

0024 **10** 1 **Dozy Joe**[1] 583 6-9-4 **62** ........ LukeMorris 1 58
(Joseph Tuite) *chsd ldrs: drvn over 2f out: no imp over 1f out: wknd fnl f* **6/1**[2]

13-0 **11** 1 **Admirable Art (IRE)**[29] 181 4-9-2 **60** ........(p) LiamKeniry 12 53
(Tony Carroll) *hld up in last quartet: sme prog jst over 2f out: shkn up and fdd over 1f out* **25/1**

056- **12** 2 1/2 **Not Rigg (USA)**[56] 8339 4-8-12 **63** ........(bt[1]) JackOsborn(7) 6 51
(Gary Harrison) *nvr bttr than midfield: rdn over 3f out: wknd over 1f out* **25/1**

000- **13** 1/2 **Lily Edge**[197] 4894 5-9-4 **62** ........ WilliamCarson 7 48
(John Bridger) *s.i.s: mostly in last pair: swtchd to inner 2f out but then swtchd bk again: pushed along and no prog* **25/1**

1m 39.7s (-0.10) **Going Correction** +0.025s/f (Slow) **13** Ran SP% **121.6**
Speed ratings (Par 101): **101,100,100,99,99 98,98,97,96,95 94,92,91**
WIN: £13.60 Compton Bird; PL: 4.50 Callisto Light £1.60 Bloodsweatandtears £2.80; EX: CB/BS £55.50, CB/CL £35.30; CSF: CB/BS £37.23, CB/CL £51.33; Tricast: CB.BS.CL £217.68, CB/CL/BS £231.79; TF: CB/BS/CL £180.00, CB/CL/BS £149.90.
**Owner** Erik Penser **Bred** Whitsbury Manor Stud **Trained** Upper Lambourn, Berks

**FOCUS**
A modest handicap in which they went a decent gallop. The form seems sound, with the winner better than ever for his new yard.

## 590 BETVICTOR.COM NON-RUNNER FREE BET AT CHELTENHAM H'CAP 1m 4f (P)
**7:10** (7:13) (Class 6) (0-60,60) 4-Y-O+ **£1,940** (£577; £288; £144) **Stalls** Centre

Form RPR

050- **1** **Able Dash**[219] 4151 4-9-1 **57** ........ RichardKingscote 5 69+
(Michael Blake) *wl plcd: pushed along 3f out: prog 2f out: stl green and hanging but drvn to ld ins fnl f: edgd lft: styd on wl* **11/1**

044/ **2** 1 1/4 **Ladies Dancing**[63] 7760 8-8-11 **50** ........ JohnFahy 12 57
(Chris Down) *hld up in midfield: prog 2f out: rdn to ld over 1f out: hdd ins fnl f: r.o but outpcd* **25/1**

0-02 **3** 1 3/4 **Shalambar (IRE)**[12] 430 8-9-3 **59** ........(v) WilliamTwiston-Davies(3) 10 63
(Tony Carroll) *shoved along early to gain prom pl and sn chsd ldng pair: rdn over 3f out: nt qckn w hd to one side 2f out: drvn and styd on to take 3rd again nr fin* **8/1**

0-02 **4** 1/2 **Ogaritmo**[9] 469 5-9-5 **58** ........(t) GeorgeBaker 3 61
(Seamus Durack) *hld up towards rr: prog jst over 2f out: squeezed through on inner over 1f out: shkn up and one pce fnl f* **16/1**

0-21 **5** 1 1/4 **Graylyn Ruby (FR)**[10] 459 9-9-2 **55** 6ex ........ LukeMorris 14 56
(Robin Dickin) *towards rr: rdn 5f out: gng nowhere u.p over 2f out: styd on fr over 1f out: nrst fin* **8/1**

25-4 **6** 3 1/4 **Ground Ginger**[7] 497 4-8-4 **46** ........(p) JoeFanning 7 42
(James Bethell) *pressed ldr: upsides w new ldr over 2f out to over 1f out: wknd fnl f* **6/1**[2]

45-2 **7** 1/2 **Our Golden Girl**[22] 278 4-8-6 **55** ........(b) DavidParkes(7) 9 50
(Shaun Lycett) *hld up in last pair: brought v wd bnd 3f out: nvr on terms but kpt on fr over 1f out* **14/1**

020- **8** 1/2 **Hazzaat (IRE)**[57] 8331 4-9-4 **60** ........ TomQueally 4 54
(Gary Harrison) *v prom: effrt to ld over 2f out: drvn and hdd over 1f out: wknd fnl f* **12/1**

3-23 **9** 3/4 **Geeaitch**[22] 283 5-9-2 **55** ........ WilliamCarson 2 48
(Peter Hiatt) *trckd ldrs on inner: trying to cl whn hmpd over 1f out: nt rcvr and eased* **5/1**[1]

543- **10** 9 **See And Be Seen**[124] 7204 4-9-3 **59** ........(p) RenatoSouza 6 38
(Sylvester Kirk) *hld up in last pair: rdn and detached over 4f out: pass a few late on* **10/1**

42-0 **11** hd **Princess Willow**[22] 277 6-8-13 **55** ........ NataliaGemelova(3) 13 33
(John E Long) *hld up towards rr: prog on outer 5f out: rdn 3f out: sn wknd* **20/1**

0-04 **12** 2 1/4 **Final Delivery**[27] 210 5-9-3 **56** ........ StephenCraine 1 31
(Jim Boyle) *hld up towards rr: rdn and no prog over 2f out: sn wknd and eased* **14/1**

0621 **13** 2 1/4 **Bapak Pesta (IRE)**[15] 368 4-8-8 **55** ........ ShaneGray(5) 8 26
(Kevin Ryan) *led to over 2f out: dropped away qckly* **7/1**[3]

2m 34.22s (-0.28) **Going Correction** +0.025s/f (Slow)
**WFA** 4 from 5yo+ 3lb **13** Ran SP% **118.6**
Speed ratings (Par 101): **101,100,99,98,97 95,95,95,94,88 88,86,85**
CSF £255.90 CT £2316.78 TOTE £11.90: £3.80, £9.70, £2.70; EX 403.30 Trifecta £2353.80 Part won..
**Owner** West Wilts Hockey Lads **Bred** Cheveley Park Stud Ltd **Trained** Trowbridge, Wilts
■ Stewards' Enquiry : Tom Queally one-day ban: careless riding (Feb 27)

**FOCUS**
A moderate middle-distance handicap, although the winner was at least unexposed. The form seems sound enough.

## 591 CHELTENHAM 2014 NRFB AT BETVICTOR.COM H'CAP 2m (P)
**7:40** (7:41) (Class 4) (0-85,85) 4-Y-O+ **£4,851** (£1,443; £721; £360) **Stalls** Low

Form RPR

143- **1** **Rutherglen**[43] 7338 4-8-5 **77** ........ JoeDoyle(7) 4 84
(John Quinn) *trckd ldng pair: wnt 2nd over 2f out: rdn to ld over 1f out: hrd pressed after: kpt on wl and a holding on fnl f* **9/4**[2]

316- **2** 3/4 **Clerk's Choice (IRE)**[47] 8429 8-9-6 **79** ........ GeorgeBaker 5 85
(William Jarvis) *hld up in 5th: clsd on ldrs over 2f out: brought to chal over 1f out: rdn and nt qckn fnl f* **5/4**[1]

505- **3** hd **Softsong (FR)**[36] 5946 6-9-12 **85** ........ LiamTreadwell 1 91
(James Evans) *trckd ldng trio: rdn 2f out: tried to chal fr over 1f out: kpt on but a hld* **6/1**[3]

300/ **4** 1/2 **Rasheed**[13] 6584 6-9-3 **76** ........(b) LukeMorris 3 81
(Lucy Wadham) *trckd ldr: led over 2f out: awkward in front and hdd over 1f out: kpt on again fnl f* **9/1**

440- **5** 6 **First Avenue**[33] 4873 9-9-4 **84** ........ CharlotteJenner(7) 8 82
(Laura Mongan) *hld up in last: detached fr rest 1/2-way: clsd up 4f out: in tch over 2f out: pushed along and sn lft bhd* **12/1**

303- **6** 4 **Kalamill (IRE)**[16] 2087 7-8-6 **68** ow1 ........(t) WilliamTwiston-Davies(3) 2 61
(Shaun Lycett) *rousted along to ld at fair pce: tried to kick on over 3f out: hdd & wknd over 2f out* **20/1**

3m 29.67s (-0.43) **Going Correction** +0.025s/f (Slow)
**WFA** 4 from 6yo+ 6lb **6** Ran SP% **112.0**
Speed ratings (Par 105): **102,101,101,101,98 96**
CSF £5.41 CT £12.17 TOTE £2.90: £1.40, £1.90; EX 5.90 Trifecta £14.90.
**Owner** The Beer Swigging Strangers **Bred** Frank Brady **Trained** Settrington, N Yorks

**FOCUS**
A decent staying handicap in which they went an, at best, even gallop. Hard to have too much confidence in the form, but the winner is progressive.

## 592 VISIT AND DINE IN THE PANORAMIC H'CAP 7f (P)
**8:10** (8:11) (Class 6) (0-55,55) 4-Y-O+ **£1,940** (£577; £288; £144) **Stalls** Low

Form RPR

0-10 **1** **Mill I Am (USA)**[11] 446 4-9-6 **54** ........ AdamBeschizza 8 66
(Stuart Williams) *crowded s: sn in midfield: rdn and prog over 2f out: led over 1f out: drvn clr* **4/1**[2]

-541 **2** 1 3/4 **Prohibition (IRE)**[21] 290 8-9-3 **54** ........ RossAtkinson(3) 6 61
(Mandy Rowland) *dwlt: hld up in last pair: shkn up over 2f out: prog over 1f out: r.o to take 2nd last 100yds: no ch to chal* **7/1**

5-30 **3** 1 1/2 **Bubbly Bailey**[22] 281 4-9-4 **52** ........(v) FrederikTylicki 11 55
(J R Jenkins) *prom: rdn over 2f out: tried to chal over 1f out but hanging and nt qckn: kpt on to take 3rd last stride* **12/1**

5-00 **4** hd **Nifty Kier**[9] 467 5-9-7 **55** ........ RobertHavlin 7 58
(Martin Bosley) *crowded s: sn in midfield: rdn over 2f out: prog over 1f out: got through and tk 2nd briefly ins fnl f: one pce after* **11/2**[3]

-402 **5** 1 3/4 **Welsh Inlet (IRE)**[12] 425 6-9-5 **53** ........ LukeMorris 13 58+
(John Bridger) *hld up in last: effrt over 2f out: hanging but making prog and ch of a pl whn rn into wall of rivals jst ins fnl f: snatched up but styd on again nr fin* **11/2**[3]

00-0 **6** nk **Bussa**[40] 53 6-9-7 **55** ........(t) ChrisCatlin 3 52
(David Evans) *trckd ldng pair: drvn to ld briefly wl over 1f out: wknd ins fnl f* **7/2**[1]

46-0 **7** 1/2 **Misty Eyes**[42] 18 5-8-13 **47** ........(v) JoeFanning 12 43
(Geoffrey Harker) *pressed ldr: rdn to chal wl over 1f out: stl disputing 2nd jst ins fnl f: wknd qckly last 75yds* **10/1**

000- **8** 1 1/4 **Senora Lobo (IRE)**[107] 7598 4-8-7 **46** oh1 ........ ShirleyTeasdale(5) 4 39
(Lisa Williamson) *trckd ldrs: clsd on inner to chal wl over 1f out: wkng whn short of room ins fnl f* **50/1**

0-20 **9** 3/4 **Pastoral Dancer**[21] 290 5-8-10 **47** ........ RyanPowell(3) 2 38
(Richard Rowe) *towards rr: tried to make prog on inner 2f out: no hdwy 1f out: fdd* **10/1**

000- **10** 1 1/4 **Millies Quest**[118] 7346 5-8-13 **54** ........ GeorgeBuckell(7) 5 42
(Martin Smith) *led to wl over 1f out: wknd qckly fnl f* **25/1**

60-0 **11** 1 **Little Red Nell (IRE)**[25] 251 5-9-0 **48** ........(p) PaddyAspell 9 33
(Martin Bosley) *a in rr: rdn and no prog on outer over 2f out: sn btn* **40/1**

600- **12** 3/4 **Iwilsayzisonlyonce**[259] 2791 4-9-3 **54** ........(t) JemmaMarshall(3) 14 37
(Joseph Tuite) *a in rr: rdn and no prog over 2f out* **50/1**

1m 26.43s (0.43) **Going Correction** +0.025s/f (Slow) **12** Ran SP% **121.6**
Speed ratings (Par 101): **98,96,94,94,92 91,91,89,88,87 86,85**
CSF £32.32 CT £314.99 TOTE £4.60: £1.40, £2.20, £4.90; EX 27.40 Trifecta £227.80.
**Owner** Eclipse Horse Racing **Bred** Horse France & Knighton House **Trained** Newmarket, Suffolk
■ Stewards' Enquiry : Chris Catlin two-day ban: careless riding (Feb 27-28)

**FOCUS**
A moderate handicap, but a competitive one and sound form.
T/Jkpt: Not won. T/Plt: £74.30 to a £1 stake. Pool of £101862.67 - 999.71 winning tickets.
T/Qpdt: £10.10 to a £1 stake. Pool of £10381.74 - 755.95 winning tickets. JN

# 504 MEYDAN (L-H)
## Thursday, February 13

**OFFICIAL GOING: Tapeta: standard; turf: good**
Rail moved out 12m on bends.

## 593a FORD F-150 RAPTOR TROPHY (H'CAP) (TAPETA) 1m 2f
**2:45** (2:45) (95-105,102) 3-Y-O+
**£39,759** (£13,253; £6,626; £3,313; £1,987; £1,325)

RPR

**1** **Sanshaawes (SAF)**[21] 309 5-9-4 **100** ........ ChristopheSoumillon 4 106
(M F De Kock, South Africa) *mid-div: smooth prog 2 1/2f out: led 1 1/2f out: r.o wl: comf* **4/1**[2]

**2** 1 1/2 **Storm Belt (USA)**[34] 136 5-9-1 **97** ........ PatDobbs 2 100
(Doug Watson, UAE) *trckd ldrs: ev ch 2f out: r.o same pce fnl 1 1/2f* **33/1**

**3** nse **Energia Davos (BRZ)**[28] 202 6-9-5 **101** ........ MartinHarley 8 104
(Marco Botti) *mid-div: chsd ldrs 2 1/2f out: r.o fnl 1 1/2f* **8/1**[3]

**4** hd **Start Right**[14] 394 7-8-9 **97** ........(p) MarcMonaghan(6) 13 100
(S Seemar, UAE) *slowly away: settled in rr: r.o fnl 2f: nrst fin* **14/1**

**5** 2 **Tha'ir (IRE)**[28] 205 4-9-5 **102** ........ SilvestreDeSousa 15 101
(Saeed bin Suroor) *trckd ldr: led 2 1/2f out: hdd 1 1/2f out: r.o same pce fnl f* **8/1**[3]

**6** nk **Winterlude (IRE)**[120] 7304 4-9-4 **101** ........ MickaelBarzalona 7 99
(Charlie Appleby) *in rr of mid-div: rdn 2 1/2f out: n.m.r 2f out: r.o fnl f* **2/1**[1]

**7** nk **Specific Gravity (FR)**[26] 242 6-9-3 **99** ........ PatCosgrave 6 96
(M F De Kock, South Africa) *sn led: hdd 8f out: ev ch 2 1/2f out: wknd fnl 1 1/2f* **22/1**

**8** 1 1/4 **Pisco Sour (USA)**[28] 205 6-9-2 **98** ........(p) TadhgO'Shea 1 93
(S Seemar, UAE) *nvr nr to chal* **40/1**

**9** nse **Layali Al Andalus**[21] 307 7-9-3 **99** ........ RichardMullen 12 94
(S Seemar, UAE) *nvr nr to chal* **14/1**

**10** 1 3/4 **Busker (USA)**[14] 398 6-9-6 **102** ........(t) MartinLane 10 93
(A bin Harmash, UAE) *nvr nr to chal* **14/1**

**11** shd **Plantagenet (SPA)**[21] 307 7-9-2 **98** ........ WilliamBuick 3 89
(Niels Petersen, Norway) *nvr bttr than mid-div* **8/1**[3]

**12** 4 1/4 **Manchester (FR)**[109] 6-9-4 **100** ........(t) Per-AndersGraberg 16 83
(Niels Petersen, Norway) *settled in rr: nvr nr to chal* **20/1**

**13** 1 3/4 **Red Dubawi (IRE)**[21] 304 6-9-2 **98** ........ GaryCarroll 9 77
(David Marnane, Ire) *trckd ldrs: led 8f out: hdd & wknd 2 1/2f out* **33/1**

**14** shd **Auditor (USA)**[21] 309 4-9-4 **101** ........(t) ThierryThulliez 14 80
(C Ferland, France) *trckd ldrs tl outpcd fnl 2 1/2f* **20/1**

**15** 3 1/2 **Chapter Seven**[14] 398 5-9-6 **102** ........(p) HarryBentley 11 74
(G M Lyons, Ire) *a in rr* **25/1**

2m 4.17s (-0.53)
**WFA** 4 from 5yo+ 1lb **15** Ran SP% **132.7**
CSF: 147.37; EX 187.80; TRIFECTA: 1775.70; TRICAST 1069.11; WIN: 3.80.
**Owner** Sh Ahmed bin Mohd bin Khalifa Al Maktoum **Bred** Oldlands Stud **Trained** South Africa

**FOCUS**
Rail moved out 12m on bends. The field were well bunched for much of the way and it proved hard to make up significant ground. The first two are improving.

## 594a UAE 2000 GUINEAS SPONSORED BY AL TAYER MOTORS (GROUP 3) (TAPETA) 1m

**3:20** (3:20) 3-Y-O

**£90,361** (£30,120; £15,060; £7,530; £4,518; £3,012)

RPR

1 **Long John (AUS)**[110] 7556 4-9-5 113....................(b) MickaelBarzalona 6 115
(Charlie Appleby) *in rr of mid-div: smooth prog 3f out: led 2f out: sn clr* **7/4**[1]

2 *4 1/4* **Emirates Flyer**[28] 204 3-8-9 104.................................. KierenFallon 10 102+
(Saeed bin Suroor) *settled in rr: r.o fnl 2f but no ch w wnr* **10/1**

3 *1 1/4* **Wednaan**[147] 6569 3-8-11 87 ow2.......................... ChristopheSoumillon 5 99
(M F De Kock, South Africa) *mid-div: rdn 2 1/2f out: r.o fnl 1 1/2f but no ch w wnr* **13/2**[3]

4 *1 1/2* **Safety Check (IRE)**[28] 204 3-8-9 102.......................... WilliamBuick 1 96
(Charlie Appleby) *trckd ldr tl outpcd 2 1/2f: kpt on same pce fnl f* **8/1**

5 *3/4* **Asmar (IRE)**[12] 438 3-8-9 86........................................ RichardHughes 9 94
(Fawzi Abdulla Nass, Bahrain) *settled in rr: kpt on same pce fnl 2f but nvr able to chal* **20/1**

6 *1/2* **My Catch (IRE)**[28] 204 3-8-9 102........................................ PatDobbs 7 93
(Doug Watson, UAE) *sn led: hdd & wknd 2f out* **12/1**

7 *nk* **Paximadia (AUS)**[89] 4-9-5 108....................(p) SilvestreDeSousa 3 95
(Saeed bin Suroor) *trckd ldng pair: ev ch 3f out: one pce* **5/1**[2]

8 *shd* **Nezar (IRE)**[28] 204 3-8-9 96.........................................(b) JamesDoyle 8 92
(William Haggas) *settled in rr: nvr nr to chal* **25/1**

9 *3/4* **Jallota**[124] 7191 3-8-9 105........................................ JimCrowley 2 90
(M F De Kock, South Africa) *nvr bttr than mid-div* **12/1**

10 *7 1/2* **Full Combat (SAF)**[28] 204 4-9-5 100.......................(b) PaulHanagan 11 76
(M F De Kock, South Africa) *trckd ldng trio: ev ch 3f out: one pce fnl 2f* **7/1**

11 *5 1/4* **Journeyman (SAF)**[7] 505 4-9-5 95............................(e) AntonMarcus 4 64
(M F De Kock, South Africa) *s.i.s: a in rr* **25/1**

1m 36.23s (-1.27)
**WFA** 3 from 4yo 19lb **11** Ran SP% **126.9**
CSF: 22.43; EX 17.60; TRIFECTA: 78.30; WIN: 2.70; PL 1.00; 1.30; 3.10.
**Owner** Godolphin **Bred** Darley **Trained** Newmarket, Suffolk

**FOCUS**
They went a good gallop early and gradually slowed (winner's splits were 25.69, 22.85, 23.47, 24.22). The form is rated around the second, fourth and eighth.

## 595a FORD TAURIS TROPHY (H'CAP) (TURF) 1m 1f

**3:55** (3:55) (100-113,113) 3-Y-0+

**£63,253** (£21,084; £10,542; £5,271; £3,162; £2,108)

RPR

1 **Vercingetorix (SAF)**[257] 5-9-1 **108**..................... ChristopheSoumillon 5 113
(M F De Kock, South Africa) *trckd ldng trio: led 1 1/2f out: r.o wl* **5/2**[1]

2 *1/2* **Code Of Honor**[28] 205 4-8-13 **106**....................(p) SilvestreDeSousa 6 110+
(Saeed bin Suroor) *settled in rr: r.o wl fnl 2f: nrst fin* **6/1**[2]

3 *nse* **Forjatt (IRE)**[20] 334 6-9-3 **110**........................................ JamesDoyle 2 114
(D Selvaratnam, UAE) *mid-div: rdn 2 1/2f out: ev ch 1f out: one pce fnl 50yds* **12/1**

4 *1 1/4* **Gabrial (IRE)**[21] 309 5-9-2 **109**...................................... KierenFallon 13 110
(Richard Fahey) *settled in rr: nvr nr to chal but r.o fnl 2f* **6/1**[2]

5 *1* **Tarbawi (IRE)**[21] 309 4-8-9 **102**.............................. MickaelBarzalona 8 101
(A bin Harmash, UAE) *nvr nr to chal but r.o fnl 2f* **16/1**

6 *nk* **El Estruendoso (ARG)**[7] 509 5-8-13 **106**....................... PatCosgrave 1 105
(M F De Kock, South Africa) *trckd ldrs: ev ch 2f out: nt qckn fnl f* **17/2**[3]

7 *1/2* **Gale Force Ten**[21] 308 4-9-6 **113**.........................(t) AntonMarcus 12 110
(M F De Kock, South Africa) *trckd ldr: ev ch 2f out: one pce fnl f* **20/1**

8 *nk* **Elleval (IRE)**[21] 309 4-9-0 **107**.......................................(p) FergalLynch 14 104
(David Marnane, Ire) *settled in rr: kpt on same pce fnl 2f* **12/1**

9 *hd* **So Beautiful (FR)**[28] 205 5-8-10 **104**........................ PaulHanagan 11 99
(Doug Watson, UAE) *settled in rr: nvr able to chal* **20/1**

10 *hd* **Mickdaam (IRE)**[521] 2705 5-9-1 **108**............................ AndreaAtzeni 9 104
(M F De Kock, South Africa) *nvr nr to chal* **20/1**

11 *3/4* **Starboard**[21] 309 5-8-9 **102** ow1.................................. WilliamBuick 3 95
(David Simcock) *slowly away: nvr nr to chal* **16/1**

12 *nse* **Regulation (IRE)**[14] 394 5-8-7 **100**................................ ShaneFoley 4 94
(M Halford, Ire) *nvr bttr than mid-div* **25/1**

13 *hd* **Captain Joy (IRE)**[21] 306 5-8-13 **106**............................ GaryCarroll 7 100
(Tracey Collins, Ire) *sn led: hdd & wknd 2f out* **6/1**[2]

14 *1/2* **Al Waab (IRE)**[131] 7049 4-9-2 **109**.................................... PatDobbs 10 102
(Doug Watson, UAE) *nvr bttr than mid-div* **12/1**

1m 51.86s (111.86) **14** Ran SP% **134.9**
CSF: 17.92; EX 21.00; TRICAST: 171.19; TRIFECTA: 364.70; WIN: 1.90; PL 1.10; 3.00; 6.40.
**Owner** Sheikh Mohammed Bin Khalifa Al Maktoum **Bred** Klawervlei Stud **Trained** South Africa

**FOCUS**
A race run at a slow-fast pace. The winner was the least exposed and the second helps with the standard.

## 596a FIREBREAK STKS SPONSORED BY FORD EXPLORER SPORT (GROUP 3) (TAPETA) 1m

**4:30** (4:30) 3-Y-O+

**£72,289** (£24,096; £12,048; £6,024; £3,614; £2,409)

RPR

1 **Variety Club (SAF)**[250] 6-9-0 120.................................. AntonMarcus 5 119
(J Ramsden, South Africa) *sn led: kicked clr 2f out: r.o wl: comf* **1/1**[1]

2 *2* **Haatheq (USA)**[20] 334 7-9-0 113.................................. PaulHanagan 2 114
(A Al Raihe, UAE) *mid-div: chsd ldr 2f out: r.o fnl f but no ch w wnr* **14/1**

3 *3* **Empire Storm (GER)**[7] 508 7-9-0 107...........................(t) KierenFallon 6 107
(Michael Attwater) *mid-div: rdn 3f out: r.o fnl 2f: nrst fin* **20/1**

4 *nk* **Capital Attraction (USA)**[21] 306 7-9-0 110................... TadhgO'Shea 9 106
(Ernst Oertel, UAE) *trckd ldrs: rdn 4f out: r.o same pce fnl 2f* **14/1**

5 *1/2* **Fulbright**[21] 308 5-9-0 109.................................. MickaelBarzalona 7 105
(Charlie Appleby) *s.i.s: settled in rr: r.o fnl 2f but nvr nr to chal* **6/1**[3]

6 *hd* **Mufarrh (IRE)**[7] 509 7-9-0 109................................. RoystonFfrench 8 105
(A Al Raihe, UAE) *settled in rr: nvr nr to chal* **25/1**

7 *shd* **Mars (IRE)**[203] 4696 4-9-0 117.............................. ChristopheSoumillon 3 104
(M F De Kock, South Africa) *trckd ldng trio tl outpcd 2f out* **3/1**[2]

8 *4 1/2* **Snowboarder (USA)**[126] 7157 4-9-0 106................. SilvestreDeSousa 1 94
(Charlie Appleby) *a in rr* **12/1**

9 *3 1/4* **Colmar Kid (IRE)**[20] 334 4-9-0 107...........................(v) RichardHughes 4 87
(M Al Muhairi, UAE) *trckd ldrs tl outpcd 2f out* **20/1**

1m 35.67s (-1.83) **9** Ran SP% **124.7**
CSF: 16.75; EX 18.80; TRIFECTA: 166.40; WIN: 1.60; PL 1.00; 2.70; 4.30.
**Owner** Mrs Ingrid Jooste & Markus Jooste **Bred** Beaumont Stud **Trained** South Africa

**FOCUS**
An impressive performance from South Africa's Horse of the Year for the last two years. The standard is set around the second, third and fifth.

## 597a AL SHINDAGHA SPRINT SPONSORED BY FORD MUSTANG SHELBY (GROUP 3) (TAPETA) 6f

**5:05** (5:05) 3-Y-O

**£72,289** (£24,096; £12,048; £6,024; £3,614; £2,409)

RPR

1 **Russian Soul (IRE)**[28] 206 6-9-2 110..........................(p) ShaneFoley 13 112
(M Halford, Ire) *mid-div: rdn 3f out: led 1f out: r.o wl* **15/2**[3]

2 *1* **Jamesie (IRE)**[21] 304 6-9-0 106..................................... FergalLynch 1 107
(David Marnane, Ire) *in rr of mid-div: chsd ldrs 2f out: ev ch 1f out: nt qckn fnl 50yds* **11/1**

3 *nk* **Complicate (AUS)**[35] 112 5-9-0 106...................... SilvestreDeSousa 10 106+
(Saeed bin Suroor) *settled in rr: r.o wl fnl 2f: nrst fin* **11/1**

4 *1 1/4* **Bello (AUS)**[124] 6-9-0 109...........................(b) MickaelBarzalona 8 102
(Charlie Appleby) *mid-div: chsd ldrs 1 1/2f out: one pce fnl 50yds* **11/1**

5 *shd* **Balmont Mast (IRE)**[28] 206 6-9-0 115........................ WilliamBuick 4 102
(Edward Lynam, Ire) *settled in rr: nvr nr to chal* **11/2**[2]

6 *nk* **Tamaathul**[21] 308 7-9-0 110.....................................(t) PaulHanagan 6 101+
(A Al Raihe, UAE) *slowly away: settled in rr: r.o fnl 1 1/2f: nrst fin* **12/1**

7 *1 1/4* **Krypton Factor**[28] 206 6-9-0 115........................(b) RichardHughes 14 97
(Fawzi Abdulla Nass, Bahrain) *trckd ldrs: ev ch 2f out: one pce fnl 50yds* **9/1**

8 *3/4* **Roi De Vitesse (IRE)**[21] 308 7-9-0 104..................(v) MarcMonaghan 7 94
(Ali Jan, Qatar) *nvr bttr than mid-div* **40/1**

9 *1* **Rafeej**[28] 206 5-9-0 105........................................... WayneSmith 12 91
(M Al Muhairi, UAE) *trckd ldrs tl outpcd 2f out* **11/1**

10 *hd* **United Color (USA)**[28] 206 5-9-0 112..........................(t) JamesDoyle 3 91
(D Selvaratnam, UAE) *mid-div: chsd ldrs whn n.m.r 2f out: nt rcvr* **7/2**[1]

11 *1* **Pearl Flute (IRE)**[21] 308 4-9-0 112............................... HarryBentley 2 87
(F-H Graffard, France) *sn led: hdd & wknd 1 1/2f out* **8/1**

12 *1* **Giant Sandman (IRE)**[89] 7941 7-9-3 113.........................(tp) AStarke 11 87
(Rune Haugen, Norway) *nvr nr to chal* **20/1**

13 *nk* **Farmleigh House (IRE)**[28] 206 7-9-0 108.................... NGMcCullagh 5 83
(W J Martin, Ire) *nvr nr to chal* **22/1**

14 *1/2* **Intransigent**[21] 304 5-9-0 105...................................... KierenFallon 9 82
(Andrew Balding) *trckd ldrs tl outpcd 2f out* **20/1**

1m 10.61s (-0.99) **14** Ran SP% **127.8**
CSF: 88.57; EX 143.10; TRIFECTA: 2370.80; WIN: 8.50; PL 2.10; 6.40; 4.20.
**Owner** Mrs A G Kavanagh **Bred** Societe Civile De L'Ecurie De Meautry **Trained** Doneany, Co Kildare

**FOCUS**
A patient ride was no bad thing, with there being a four-way battle for the lead early on. Small steps up from the first two.

## 598a FORD EDGE SPORT TROPHY (H'CAP) (TURF) 1m 4f 38y

**5:45** (5:45) (100-113,113) 3-Y-O+

**£63,253** (£21,084; £10,542; £5,271; £3,162; £2,108)

RPR

1 **Songcraft (IRE)**[153] 6348 6-8-13 **106**....................(p) SilvestreDeSousa 12 111
(Saeed bin Suroor) *mid-div: smooth prog 2 1/2f out: led 1 1/2f out: r.o wl* **9/1**[3]

2 *1 1/4* **Meandre (FR)**[56] 8358 6-9-6 **113**........................................ PatDobbs 14 116
(Doug Watson, UAE) *trckd ldrs: led 3f out: hdd 1 1/2f out: r.o same pce* **10/1**

3 *1 1/4* **Sheikhzayedroad**[28] 205 5-9-3 **110**................................ MartinLane 7 111+
(David Simcock) *slowly away: settled in rr: r.o fnl 2f: nrst fin* **4/1**[2]

4 *1* **Dabadiyan (IRE)**[28] 205 4-8-10 **106**................................ ShaneFoley 8 105
(M Halford, Ire) *trckd ldng trio: ev ch 2f out: nt qckn fnl f* **3/1**[1]

5 *nk* **Topclas (FR)**[21] 305 8-8-10 **104**........................(v) RichardHughes 10 102
(A bin Harmash, UAE) *settled in rr: r.o fnl 2f but nvr nr to chal* **10/1**

6 *1 3/4* **Buckwheat**[131] 7049 4-9-1 **110**.................................... WilliamBuick 13 107
(Charlie Appleby) *mid-div: r.o same pce fnl 2f* **18/1**

7 *1 1/2* **Aussie Reigns (IRE)**[14] 398 4-8-7 **102**....................(v) HayleyTurner 9 97
(William Knight) *slowly away: settled in rr: n.m.r 2 1/2f out: nt rcvr* **12/1**

8 *1 1/4* **Vasily**[21] 309 6-8-9 **102**.............................................. AndreaAtzeni 5 94
(M F De Kock, South Africa) *sn led: clr 6f out: rdn 3f out: hdd & wknd 1 1/2f out* **9/1**[3]

9 *1 1/4* **Adroitly (AUS)**[350] 833 7-8-7 **100**.................................. AhmedAjtebi 2 90
(Saeed bin Suroor) *settled in rr: nvr nr to chal* **28/1**

10 *3/4* **Dormello (IRE)**[21] 305 6-8-9 **102** ow1.............................. JamesDoyle 4 90
(D Selvaratnam, UAE) *settled in rr: rdn 3f out: nvr nr to chal* **14/1**

11 *1/2* **Tanfeeth**[7] 507 6-8-7 **100**...........................................(t) PaulHanagan 11 88
(M Al Muhairi, UAE) *settled in rr: nvr nr to chal* **25/1**

12 *3/4* **Bank Of Burden (USA)**[21] 305 7-8-11 **105**.......(t) Per-AndersGraberg 3 91
(Niels Petersen, Norway) *nvr bttr than mid-div* **20/1**

13 *2 1/2* **Zip Top (IRE)**[21] 307 5-9-3 **110**................................ MickaelBarzalona 6 93
(Charlie Appleby) *trckd ldrs: ev ch 2 1/2f out: one pce fnl f* **11/1**

2m 33.48s (153.48)
**WFA** 4 from 5yo+ 3lb **13** Ran SP% **123.2**
CSF: 92.06; EX 67.20; TRICAST: 372.91; TRIFECTA: 480.30; WIN: 8.60; PL 2.50; 2.10; 2.00. Placepot: £237.60 to a £1 stake. Pool: £11,099.56 - 34.10 winning units. Quadpot: £40.70 to a £1 stake. Pool: £572.00 - 10.40 winning units..
**Owner** Godolphin **Bred** Darley **Trained** Newmarket, Suffolk

■ Empoli was withdrawn. Price at time of withdrawal 14-1. Rule 4 applies to all bets - deduction 5p in the pound.

**FOCUS**
Vasily gradually opened up a clear lead and had the field strung out. This was the last 1m4f-plus turf handicap of the Carnival. The first five were close to their marks.

# PORNICHET-LA BAULE
Thursday, February 13
**OFFICIAL GOING: Viscoride: standard**

## 599a PRIX DE L'ILE AUX MOINES (MAIDEN) (3YO FILLIES) (VISCORIDE) 1m 2f 110y
5:10 (5:10) 3-Y-O £6,666 (£2,666; £2,000; £1,333; £666)

RPR
1 **Hully Gully (GER)** 3-8-6 0........ EnzoCorallo(5) 10 66
(C Ferland, France) **44/5**
2 1/2 **Abraxa (IRE)** 3-8-11 0........ VincentVion 3 65
(C Ferland, France) **73/10[3]**
3 1 **Iletaitunefois (FR)**[31] 3-9-2 0........(b[1]) MickaelForest 12 68
(G Pannier, France) **39/1**
4 3/4 **Isabella Liberty (FR)**[91] 7875 3-9-2 0........ JimmyQuinn 11 67
(Robert Eddery) *wnt lft s: midfield on outer: rdn over 2f out: styd on and wnt 4th fnl strides: nt quite pce to chal* **2/1[1]**
5 hd **Time Dream (IRE)**[20] 3-9-2 0........ AlexandreRoussel 7 66
(L Baudron, France) **3/1[2]**
6 1 1/2 **Brasilia Sport (FR)**[57] 3-8-10 0........ StephaneLaurent(6) 5 63
(P Chevillard, France) **26/1**
7 3/4 **Wiccalina (FR)** 3-8-11 0........ AntoineHamelin 2 57
(E Leenders, France) **17/1**
8 9 **Antequera (FR)** 3-9-2 0........ MathieuAndrouin 1 44
(C Lecrivain, France) **54/1**
9 2 **Anaphortuna (FR)** 3-8-11 0........ AnthonyClement 4 35
(A Clement, France) **39/1**
10 hd **Picatchu (FR)**[48] 3-8-10 0........(b) SebastienMartino(6) 6 40
(H-A Pantall, France) **20/1**
11 2 **Full In Have (FR)**[40] 3-9-2 0........ ArnaudBourgeais 9 36
(N Leenders, France) **12/1**
12 20 **Birdy Dream (FR)** 3-8-11 0........ AdrienFouassier 8
(Y Durepaire, France) **9/1**
2m 15.94s (135.94) 12 Ran SP% **119.1**
WIN (incl. 1 euro stake: 9.80. PLACES: 2.90, 2.90, 7.90. DF: 20.50. SF: 59.50.
**Owner** Maxime Moczulski **Bred** Haras Du Mezeray & Pierre-Paul Richou **Trained** France

## 600a PRIX EQUIDIA (MAIDEN) (3YO COLTS & GELDINGS) (VISCORIDE) 1m 2f 110y
6:10 (12:00) 3-Y-O £6,666 (£2,666; £2,000; £1,333; £666)

RPR
1 **Rudi Five One (FR)**[98] 7780 3-9-2 0........ JimmyQuinn 3 71
(Robert Eddery) *t.k.h early: midfield in tch on inner: swtchd out and rdn over 1f out: styd on strly ins fnl f: led towards fin and won gng away* **7/5[1]**
2 1 1/2 **Firfol (FR)**[20] 3-9-2 0........(b) AntoineHamelin 7 68
(Mme Pia Brandt, France) **2/1[2]**
3 1 1/2 **Kerdelan (IRE)** 3-8-11 0........ MathieuAndrouin 4 60
(P Monfort, France) **10/1**
4 3/4 **Lead My Way (FR)** 3-8-13 0........ JulienGuillochon(3) 5 64
(J-L Guillochon, France) **10/1**
5 3/4 **Laguna Boy (FR)**[114] 3-9-2 0........ MorganDelalande 1 62
(Y Barberot, France) **10/1**
6 3 **Sistanbul (FR)** 3-8-11 0........ AdrienFouassier 2 51
(E Leenders, France) **25/1**
7 5 **Speedy Glaz (FR)**[186] 5323 3-9-2 0........(p) AnthonyClement 9 47
(A Clement, France) **30/1**
8 3/4 **Saga Man (FR)**[57] 3-9-2 0........ ArnaudBourgeais 8 45
(F Lemercier, France) **81/1**
9 6 **Orage Noir (FR)** 3-8-10 0........(b[1]) SebastienMartino(6) 6 33
(H-A Pantall, France) **9/1[3]**
10 5 **Riversou (FR)**[31] 169 3-9-2 0........ JeromeCabre 10 24
(J-M Lefebvre, France) **67/1**
11 20 **Zagalo (FR)** 3-8-11 0........(p) ChristopherGrosbois 11
(Guy Denuault, France) **78/1**
2m 11.43s (131.43) 11 Ran SP% **123.3**
WIN (incl.1 euro stake): 2.40. PLACES: 1.20, 1.30, 2.20. DF: 3.30. SF: 6.30.
**Owner** Anderson, Mathews & Kerve **Bred** Mme Catherine Niederhauser **Trained** Newmarket, Suffolk

# 577 LINGFIELD (L-H)
Friday, February 14
**OFFICIAL GOING: Standard**
Wind: Strong, behind Weather: Raining

## 601 CORAL APP DOWNLOAD FROM THE APP STORE APPRENTICE (S) STKS 1m 4f (P)
1:30 (1:30) (Class 6) 4-Y-0+ £2,045 (£603; £302) **Stalls** Low

Form RPR
-216 1 **Mahadee (IRE)**[2] 582 9-9-5 70........(b) LouisSteward(5) 3 76
(Lee Carter) *hld up in last and detached early: cl up fr 1/2-way: rdn to chse ldr wl over 1f out: clsd to ld last 100yds: styd on wl* **8/1[2]**
-211 2 2 **Stand Guard**[17] 363 10-9-10 87........ WilliamTwiston-Davies 2 73
(John Butler) *hld up in 3rd: prog and pushed into ld over 2f out: shkn up and hrd pressed 1f out: hdd and nt qckn last 100yds* **1/7[1]**
0-66 3 15 **Bennelong**[9] 490 8-9-5 50........(b) MichaelJMMurphy 6 44
(Lee Carter) *urged along to ld after 100yds and set gd pce: rdn and hdd over 3f out: sn wknd* **100/1**
002- 4 1 **Tight Knit (USA)**[56] 8366 4-8-13 69........(b) JoeyHaynes(3) 5 42
(John Weymes) *led 100yds: chsd ldr: led over 3f out to over 2f out: styd on inner and wknd rapidly over 1f out* **10/1[3]**
2m 30.78s (-2.22) **Going Correction** -0.05s/f (Stan)
**WFA** 4 from 5yo+ 3lb 4 Ran SP% **108.7**
Speed ratings (Par 101): **105,103,93,93**
CSF £10.21 TOTE £11.30; EX 12.70 Trifecta £20.60.Stand Guard was the subject of a friendly claim of £6,000.
**Owner** John Joseph Smith **Bred** Darley **Trained** Epsom, Surrey

**FOCUS**
Strong winds made for unpleasant conditions. A surprise result with the hot favourite disappointing. They didn't dawdle and the winner is rated close to last year's form.

## 602 DOWNLOAD THE LADBROKES APP CLAIMING STKS 7f 1y(P)
2:00 (2:00) (Class 6) 4-Y-0+ £2,045 (£603; £302) **Stalls** Low

Form RPR
5533 1 **Seek The Fair Land**[14] 399 8-9-1 73........(v) WilliamCarson 5 80
(Lee Carter) *hld up in 4th: clsd on ldrs over 2f out: rdn over 1f out: led last 150yds: styd on* **8/1**
0-21 2 nk **Jubilee Brig**[11] 452 4-9-5 76........(v) GeorgeBaker 2 83
(Sean Curran) *trckd ldng pair: wnt 2nd 2f out: rdn to ld briefly 1f out: nt qckn last 100yds* **3/1[1]**
-563 3 2 1/4 **Rakaan (IRE)**[14] 407 7-9-4 82........(p) FergusSweeney 7 76
(Jamie Osborne) *dwlt: hld up in last pair and wl off the pce: pushed along 2f out: rdn and prog 1f out: fin wl: too much to do* **3/1[1]**
0-24 4 hd **Capaill Liath (IRE)**[14] 399 6-9-5 79........ AmyRyan 1 77
(Kevin Ryan) *hld up in 5th and off the pce: pushed along 3f out: rdn and styd on fr over 1f out: nrst fin* **5/1[3]**
2106 5 3 1/4 **Kuanyao (IRE)**[14] 399 8-8-9 76........(b[1]) LouisSteward(5) 6 63
(Lee Carter) *led: kicked on over 2f out: hdd & wknd qckly 1f out* **5/1[3]**
05-0 6 1 3/4 **Mister Musicmaster**[32] 161 5-8-12 73........ DavidProbert 8 57
(Ron Hodges) *chsd ldr to 2f out: wknd qckly* **7/2[2]**
04-0 7 9 **Jackie Love (IRE)**[26] 251 6-7-10 41........(v) RhiainIngram(7) 3 24
(Roger Ingram) *s.s: a last: wl bhd fnl 3f* **66/1**
1m 23.45s (-1.35) **Going Correction** -0.05s/f (Stan) 7 Ran SP% **118.2**
Speed ratings (Par 101): **105,104,102,101,98 96,85**
CSF £33.75 TOTE £12.20: £3.40, £1.50; EX 34.20 Trifecta £109.80.
**Owner** John Joseph Smith **Bred** Raimon Bloodstock **Trained** Epsom, Surrey

**FOCUS**
A fair race for the grade. The winner was up slightly on recent handicap form.

## 603 LADBROKES H'CAP 7f 1y(P)
2:30 (2:31) (Class 6) (0-60,60) 4-Y-0+ £2,385 (£704; £352) **Stalls** Low

Form RPR
0211 1 **Bertie Blu Boy**[13] 428 6-9-3 **56**........(b) RichardKingscote 10 65
(Lisa Williamson) *mde all: drew clr 1/2-way: 6 l up 2f out: drvn over 1f out: ld dwindled but unchal* **5/2[1]**
00-4 2 1 **Ghost Train (IRE)**[22] 295 5-9-4 **57**........(p) HayleyTurner 1 63
(Tim McCarthy) *hld up in 6th: prog on inner over 2f out: chsd clr wnr wl over 1f out: clsd u.p but nvr able to chal* **16/1**
0654 3 1/2 **One Way Or Another (AUS)**[4] 562 11-9-1 **59**........(t) EoinWalsh(5) 3 64
(David Evans) *hld up in midfield: prog over 2f out: swtchd rt and wd bnd wl over 1f out: drvn and styd on to take 3rd fnl f: nrst fin* **8/1[3]**
3-50 4 1 **Darnathean**[22] 295 5-9-7 **60**........(tp) FrederikTylicki 8 63+
(Paul D'Arcy) *chsd ldrs: pushed along wl over 2f out and eased to outside: wd bnd wl over 1f out: styd on u.p after: nrst fin* **10/1**
-566 5 nk **Golden Desert (IRE)**[12] 451 10-9-7 **60**........ GeorgeBaker 9 62
(Simon Dow) *stdd s: hld up in last trio: prog on inner over 2f out: disp 3rd 1f out: one pce after* **11/2[2]**
0-42 6 2 1/4 **My Sweet Lord**[12] 448 4-9-1 **54**........ DavidProbert 12 50
(Mark Usher) *hld up in last trio and swtchd towards inner fr wd draw: sme prog 2f out: rchd 6th 1f out: no hdwy after* **10/1**
-002 7 3 3/4 **One Last Dream**[13] 428 5-9-0 **58**........(b) RyanWhile(5) 14 44
(Ron Hodges) *prom in chsng gp: rdn and wknd 2f out* **16/1**
0-55 8 hd **Catalinas Diamond (IRE)**[20] 339 6-9-3 **56**........(t) JamieSpencer 7 42
(Pat Murphy) *hld up in last trio: effrt and wdst of all bnd wl over 1f out: modest prog after* **8/1[3]**
00-0 9 2 **Artful Lady (IRE)**[20] 339 5-9-4 **60**........ RyanPowell(3) 6 40
(George Margarson) *sn pushed along in midfield: nvr on terms: no prog over 1f out* **33/1**
04-4 10 nk **Black Truffle (FR)**[13] 428 4-9-5 **58**........(v) LiamKeniry 4 38
(Mark Usher) *hld up in midfield: gng wl enough but nt clr run over 2f out: rdn and no prog wl over 1f out* **8/1[3]**
6-40 11 3/4 **Idle Curiosity (IRE)**[20] 340 4-9-5 **58**........ StephenCraine 5 36
(Jim Boyle) *prom: chsd clr wnr 3f out to over 1f out: wknd qckly* **33/1**
434- 12 2 3/4 **Patavium Prince (IRE)**[165] 6039 11-9-5 **58**........ FergusSweeney 13 29
(Jo Crowley) *nvr bttr than midfield: no prog over 2f out: wl btn over 1f out* **20/1**
65-0 13 19 **Admirals Walk (IRE)**[7] 511 4-9-4 **57**........(p) WilliamCarson 11
(Barry Brennan) *chsd wnr 3f: wknd rapidly 3f out: t.o* **66/1**
1m 24.48s (-0.32) **Going Correction** -0.05s/f (Stan) 13 Ran SP% **119.4**
Speed ratings (Par 101): **99,97,97,96,95 93,88,88,86,86 85,82,60**
CSF £45.60 CT £299.34 TOTE £3.20: £1.60, £3.40, £2.40; EX 47.00 Trifecta £267.00.
**Owner** B & B Hygiene Limited **Bred** H Bourchier **Trained** Saighton, Cheshire
■ Stewards' Enquiry : Richard Kingscote one-day ban; did not keep straight leaving stalls (28th Feb)

**FOCUS**
Moderate form. The dominant winner's best run since his early 2011 peak.

## 604 32RED SECRET ADMIRER SLOT H'CAP 1m 1y(P)
3:05 (3:07) (Class 4) (0-85,80) 3-Y-O £4,690 (£1,395; £697; £348) **Stalls** High

Form RPR
6-1 1 **War Of Art (IRE)**[27] 230 3-9-7 **80**........(t) RichardKingscote 3 88+
(Tom Dascombe) *trckd ldng pair: pushed along 3f out: clsd on outer over 1f out: rdn to ld ins fnl f: won shade cosily* **1/1[1]**
3-12 2 3/4 **Basil Berry**[14] 401 3-8-13 **72**........ HayleyTurner 4 78
(Chris Dwyer) *hld up in last: clsd on inner fr 2f out: drvn to ld jst over 1f out to ins fnl f: styd on but readily hld* **4/1[3]**
5-32 3 2 1/2 **Truancy (IRE)**[16] 375 3-8-7 **71**........(p) JoeyHaynes(5) 1 71
(K R Burke) *led after 100yds: shkn up wl over 2f out: hdd over 1f out: outpcd fnl f* **4/1[3]**
1 4 1 **Glace (IRE)**[13] 422 3-8-6 **68**........ MichaelJMMurphy(3) 2 66
(Mark Johnston) *led 100yds: w ldr: drvn to ld briefly over 1f out: wknd fnl f* **7/2[2]**
1m 37.69s (-0.51) **Going Correction** -0.05s/f (Stan) 4 Ran SP% **112.2**
Speed ratings (Par 99): **100,99,96,95**
CSF £5.55 TOTE £1.80; EX 5.10 Trifecta £10.50.
**Owner** N A Jackson **Bred** Mrs Cherry Faeste **Trained** Malpas, Cheshire

**FOCUS**
Only a handful of runners, but they went hard enough in the early stages. The winner was well on top in the end and can do better.

## 605 COMPARE BOOKMAKERS AT BOOKMAKERS.CO.UK MAIDEN STKS 6f 1y(P)
3:40 (3:40) (Class 5) 3-Y-O+ £3,067 (£905; £453) Stalls Low

Form RPR
63- 1 **Castorienta**48 8425 3-8-6 0 HayleyTurner 8 67
(George Baker) *trckd ldr: chal over 1f out: drvn to ld ins fnl f: a jst in command after* **8/1**
5- 2 nk **Touzr**154 6354 3-8-11 0 FrankieDettori 4 71
(Richard Hannon) *led: rdn 2f out: hdd ins fnl f: styd on but hld nr fin* **11/4**3
5-2 3 1½ **Android (IRE)**23 284 3-8-11 0 JohnFahy 2 66
(Clive Cox) *chsd ldng pair: shkn up over 1f out: hanging and nt qckn: kpt on ins fnl f* **9/4**2
0/ 4 2 **Picc Of Burgau**594 3638 4-9-7 0 GeorgeBaker 5 59
(Geoffrey Deacon) *chsd ldrs: pushed along fnl 2f: nvr a threat but kpt on steadily* **33/1**
5 ¾ **Duelling Dragon (USA)** 3-8-11 0 JamieSpencer 9 57+
(David Barron) *chsd ldrs but forced to r wd: shkn up 2f out: nt pce to threaten fr over 1f out* **2/1**1
230/ 6 2 **Tarara**499 6787 4-9-7 70 FergusSweeney 3 50
(Michael Blanshard) *in tch in rr: shuffled along fr 2f out: no prog but nt disgracd* **25/1**
7 shd **Happydoingnothing** 3-8-6 0 EoinWalsh(5) 1 51
(Christine Dunnett) *mostly in last: pushed along fr 1/2-way: nvr on terms reminder and hung rt ins fnl f* **66/1**
8 3½ **Am Fae Govan Tae (IRE)** 3-8-11 0 JimCrowley 7 40
(Seamus Durack) *in tch in rr: shkn up 2f out: wknd fnl f* **14/1**

1m 11.87s (-0.03) **Going Correction** -0.05s/f (Stan)
**WFA** 3 from 4yo 15lb 8 Ran SP% **116.8**
Speed ratings (Par 103): **98,97,95,92,91 89,89,84**
CSF £30.67 TOTE £9.80: £2.30, £1.40, £1.30; EX 29.60 Trifecta £82.40.
**Owner** D P Barrie **Bred** D P Barrie **Trained** Manton, Wilts

**FOCUS**
The pace and time were modest and the market principals all ran below expectations. The form is rated not too positively.

## 606 32RED BURNING DESIRE SLOT H'CAP 1m 5f (P)
4:15 (4:15) (Class 6) (0-65,65) 4-Y-O+ £2,385 (£704; £352) Stalls Low

Form RPR
3311 1 **Waving**6 530 5-8-11 57 6ex (t) JoeyHaynes(5) 2 66+
(Tony Carroll) *slowly away: hld up in last: prog to trck ldng trio wl over 1f out but nt clr run: swtchd arnd them and r.o fnl f: drvn to ld last 50yds* **5/2**1
406- 2 nk **Maison Brillet (IRE)**70 8182 7-9-4 59 (p) RobertHavlin 3 66
(Clive Drew) *trckd ldng pair: wnt 2nd over 2f out: rdn to ld over 1f out but sn jnd: battled it out tl wnr wnt past fnl 50yds* **16/1**
00-1 3 shd **Bert The Alert**14 400 6-8-12 60 CharlotteJenner(7) 1 67
(Laura Mongan) *hld up in last trio: prog on inner over 2f out: chal and w ldr jst over 1f out: battled it out tl wnr wnt past fnl 50yds* **7/1**
6/32 4 5 **Hail Tiberius**14 400 7-9-2 64 (t) AlistairRawlinson(7) 8 63
(Martin Keighley) *racd quite freely: led: tried to kick on 3f out: hdd & wknd over 1f out* **3/1**2
063- 5 5 **Sinbad The Sailor**56 6736 9-9-10 65 (v) JimCrowley 7 57
(George Baker) *trckd ldrs: rdn on outer 3f out: wknd 2f out* **7/2**3
320/ 6 3¾ **Grand Gold**484 7195 5-9-10 65 (t) GeorgeBaker 5 51
(Seamus Durack) *trckd ldr: lost 2nd and shkn up over 2f out: wknd and eased over 1f out* **3/1**2
0-30 7 1 **Bollin Judith**15 379 8-9-10 65 (t) JamieSpencer 4 50
(Jim Best) *hld up in last trio: pushed along 4f out: wknd over 2f out* **33/1**

2m 44.91s (-1.09) **Going Correction** -0.05s/f (Stan) 7 Ran SP% **122.1**
Speed ratings (Par 101): **101,100,100,97,94 92,91**
CSF £45.74 CT £261.50 TOTE £3.20: £2.00, £3.60; EX 55.30 Trifecta £168.80.
**Owner** Carl Hodgson **Bred** Theakston Stud **Trained** Cropthorne, Worcs

**FOCUS**
A warm race for the level and it was sound run. The winner is still on a good mark compared with his form from this time last year.

## 607 32RED IMMORTAL ROMANCE SLOT MEDIAN AUCTION MAIDEN STKS 1m 2f (P)
4:45 (4:47) (Class 6) 3-Y-O £2,385 (£704; £352) Stalls Low

Form RPR
5 1 **Barye**21 316 3-9-5 0 JimCrowley 6 76+
(David Simcock) *trckd ldng pair: trapped on inner over 1f out as ldr wnt for home: in the clr and r.o wl fnl f to ld post* **11/4**2
5 2 shd **Late Night Mark (IRE)**20 341 3-9-5 0 JamieSpencer 7 70
(Charles Hills) *trckd ldng pair: chal on outer 2f out: led over 1f out and sn at least 2 l clr: styd on but hdd post* **1/1**1
045- 3 2¾ **Turnbury**67 8213 3-9-5 68 (t) FrankieDettori 2 66
(Robert Mills) *uns rdr on way to post: led: hung rt bnd after 1f: shkn up 2f out: hdd and eased briefly over 1f out: outpcd but hld on for 3rd* **5/1**3
64-2 4 nk **Old Town Boy**14 409 3-9-5 73 WilliamCarson 3 64
(Philip McBride) *trckd ldr: carried rt bnd after 1f: rdn and lost 2nd 2f out: outpcd after* **5/1**3
0 5 10 **In Seine**34 142 3-9-5 0 FergusSweeney 1 44
(John Best) *dwlt and rousted along early: a in last trio: rdn and wknd 3f out: sn bhd* **100/1**
6 nk **Trafalgar Rock** 3-9-2 0 MichaelJMMurphy(3) 4 43
(Mark Johnston) *rn green and often pushed along in last trio: rdn and wknd 3f out: sn bhd* **25/1**
0-0 7 5 **Haaffa Sovereign**20 341 3-9-2 0 RyanPowell(3) 5 33
(George Margarson) *hld up in last: rdn and wknd over 3f out: sn bhd* **100/1**

2m 8.3s (1.70) **Going Correction** -0.05s/f (Stan) 7 Ran SP% **115.8**
Speed ratings (Par 99): **91,90,88,88,80 80,76**
CSF £6.04 TOTE £4.10: £1.60, £1.60; EX 7.80 Trifecta £27.20.
**Owner** Anthony Hogarth **Bred** Miss K Rausing **Trained** Newmarket, Suffolk

**FOCUS**
A dramatic finale. The winner produced a nice effort in the circumstances, with the form rated around the third.
T/Jkpt: £14,307.20 to a £1 stake. Pool: £40302.12 - 2.00 winning tickets T/Plt: £351.40 to a £1 stake. Pool: £94423.28 - 196.10 winning tickets T/Qpdt: £8.90 to a £1 stake. Pool: £11039.00 - 913.50 winning tickets JN

# 556 WOLVERHAMPTON (A.W) (L-H)
Friday, February 14

**OFFICIAL GOING: Standard**
Wind: Strong behind Weather: Raining

## 608 32RED SECRET ADMIRER SLOT H'CAP 5f 20y(P)
5:05 (5:05) (Class 6) (0-60,60) 3-Y-O £2,264 (£673; £336; £168) Stalls Low

Form RPR
0-22 1 **Saffire Song**16 373 3-9-5 58 MartinHarley 3 69
(Alan Bailey) *led early: settled to trck ldrs: shkn up over 1f out: rdn to ld ins fnl f: r.o* **5/1**3
-031 2 1¾ **Wiki Tiki**10 481 3-9-6 59 6ex (t) AdamBeschizza 2 64+
(Stuart Williams) *hld up: hdwy 1/2-way: rdn over 1f out: r.o to go 2nd post: nt trble wnr* **15/8**1
4-54 3 shd **Biscuiteer**16 374 3-9-0 53 (b) LukeMorris 11 57
(Scott Dixon) *rn w undeclared hood and blinkers: sn led: hdd over 3f out: rdn and ev ch over 1f out: styd on same pce ins fnl f* **9/2**2
100- 4 nk **Notnow Penny**149 6511 3-8-0 46 JordanVaughan(7) 7 49
(Milton Bradley) *chsd ldrs: rdn to ld over 1f out: hdd and unable qck ins fnl f* **66/1**
-005 5 3¼ **Mighty Force (IRE)**13 429 3-9-3 56 (b) TomQueally 6 48
(Nick Littmoden) *s.i.s: outpcd: r.o ins fnl f: nvr nrr* **7/1**
55-2 6 ½ **Chuckamental**19 346 3-9-7 60 (t) JoeFanning 10 50
(Bryan Smart) *prom: rdn over 1f out: no ex fnl f* **8/1**
-333 7 1¼ **Mahon Falls**16 373 3-8-12 51 ChrisCatlin 4 36
(David Evans) *edgd rt s: chsd ldrs: led over 3f out: rdn and hdd over 1f out: wknd ins fnl f* **16/1**
4346 8 nk **Countess Lupus (IRE)**16 374 3-8-2 46 oh1 (b) ShirleyTeasdale(5) 5 30
(Lisa Williamson) *hmpd s: sn pushed along in rr: drvn along and hdwy on outer 1/2-way: wknd fnl f* **66/1**
26-6 9 4½ **Sakhee'Ssquirrel**42 37 3-9-4 57 PaulMulrennan 8 25
(Sean Curran) *mid-div: drvn along 1/2-way: wknd over 1f out* **20/1**
34-0 10 1 **Song Of Rowland (IRE)**33 149 3-9-7 60 PaddyAspell 12 24
(Alan Jones) *hld up: rdn over 1f out: a in rr* **50/1**
00-0 11 1¼ **Limegrove**16 374 3-9-0 53 StevieDonohoe 1 13
(David Evans) *s.i.s: outpcd* **20/1**

1m 5.2s (2.90) **Going Correction** +0.475s/f (Slow) 11 Ran SP% **113.6**
Speed ratings (Par 95): **95,92,92,91,86 85,83,83,75,74 72**
CSF £13.50 CT £44.32 TOTE £5.50: £1.50, £1.20, £1.70; EX 18.00 Trifecta £79.20.
**Owner** Mrs A Shone & P Baker **Bred** Mrs A Shone **Trained** Newmarket, Suffolk

**FOCUS**
A moderate handicap in which the pace was sound. The first four finished clear and the winner came down the centre in the straight.

## 609 32RED BURNING DESIRE SLOT H'CAP 1m 5f 194y(P)
5:35 (5:35) (Class 6) (0-65,62) 4-Y-O+ £1,940 (£577; £288; £144) Stalls Low

Form RPR
520- 1 **Tokyo Brown (USA)**58 8331 5-9-5 55 LukeMorris 3 63
(Heather Main) *hld up: hdwy over 4f out: rdn to ld over 1f out: hld on u.p* **7/2**1
-344 2 nk **Blazing Desert**19 349 10-9-7 57 AdamBeschizza 5 64
(William Kinsey) *a.p: rdn over 1f out: chsd wnr ins fnl f: styd on* **15/2**
-521 3 1¼ **Uncle Bernie (IRE)**13 430 4-9-0 55 (p) JimmyQuinn 6 60+
(Andrew Hollinshead) *s.i.s: hld up: hdwy 2f out: shkn up over 1f out: styd on u.p* **4/1**2
6-12 4 3¼ **Light The City (IRE)**3 569 7-9-1 51 6ex JamesSullivan 11 51
(Ruth Carr) *prom: chsd ldr over 2f out: led over 2f out: rdn and hdd over 1f out: no ex ins fnl f* **13/2**
45-1 5 2½ **Helmsley Flyer (IRE)**13 433 4-8-12 56 (v) SamJames(3) 4 53
(David O'Meara) *hld up: hdwy over 2f out: rdn over 1f out: hung lft and no ex fnl f* **11/2**3
06-4 6 1¾ **Grandiloquent**13 433 5-9-6 56 (v1) BenCurtis 2 50
(Brian Ellison) *prom: lost pl over 5f out: outpcd over 3f out: rdn and hung lft over 1f out: n.d after* **25/1**
-545 7 2¾ **Excellent News (IRE)**11 460 5-8-2 45 (p) JackGarritty(7) 7 35
(Tony Forbes) *hld up: rdn over 2f out: n.d* **66/1**
2-20 8 nse **Ice Tres**28 210 5-9-3 53 MartinHarley 8 43
(Rod Millman) *racd keenly: led 2f: trckd ldr tl led again over 3f out: rdn and hdd over 2f out: wknd fnl f* **11/1**
262- 9 1¼ **Sergeant Pink (IRE)**69 8027 8-9-2 57 EmmaSayer(5) 1 46
(Dianne Sayer) *chsd ldrs: rdn over 3f out: wknd over 2f out* **16/1**
/36- 10 11 **Vexillum (IRE)**50 8223 5-9-12 62 JoeFanning 10 35
(Simon Hodgson) *w ldr tl led at stdy pce 12f out: hdd over 3f out: wknd over 2f out* **66/1**
01-0 11 ½ **Royal Trooper (IRE)**17 361 8-9-11 61 TomQueally 9 34
(Mark Brisbourne) *s.i.s: hld up: a in rr: bhd fnl 3f* **11/1**

3m 15.28s (9.28) **Going Correction** +0.475s/f (Slow)
**WFA** 4 from 5yo+ 5lb 11 Ran SP% **112.1**
Speed ratings (Par 101): **92,91,91,89,87 86,85,85,84,78 77**
CSF £28.08 CT £106.75 TOTE £4.40: £1.50, £2.80, £1.60; EX 37.40 Trifecta £194.30.
**Owner** Wetumpka Racing **Bred** Monticule **Trained** Kingston Lisle, Oxon
■ Stewards' Enquiry : Adam Beschizza two-day ban; used whip above permitted level (28th Feb, 1st Mar)

**FOCUS**
A moderate handicap run at an ordinary gallop. The first three finished clear and the winner edged into the centre late on. The form is rated a bit cautiously.

## 610 COMPARE BOOKMAKERS AT BOOKMAKERS.CO.UK H'CAP 5f 20y(P)
6:05 (6:05) (Class 7) (0-50,52) 4-Y-O+ £1,940 (£577; £288; £144) Stalls Low

Form RPR
-061 1 **Louis Vee (IRE)**8 502 6-9-8 51 6ex (t) ChrisCatlin 8 60
(Roy Brotherton) *s.i.s: rcvrd to ld 4f out: rdn over 1f out: r.o* **11/10**1
0-31 2 1¾ **Ishetoo**9 483 10-9-6 52 6ex SladeO'Hara(3) 4 54
(Peter Grayson) *a.p: rdn over 1f out: r.o u.p to go 2nd towards fin* **8/1**3
-204 3 nk **Flow Chart (IRE)**8 502 7-9-7 50 TomQueally 5 51
(Peter Grayson) *s.i.s: hld up: pushed along 3f out: rdn and hdwy over 1f out: nvr nrr* **9/4**2
-560 4 ½ **Busy Bimbo (IRE)**18 353 5-9-2 45 LukeMorris 3 44
(Alan Berry) *prom: chsd wnr 1/2-way: rdn over 1f out: no ex wl ins fnl f* **12/1**
06-0 5 6 **Lady Rain**9 483 5-9-2 45 BenCurtis 2 23
(Milton Bradley) *hld up: rdn 1/2-way: wknd fnl f* **33/1**


The Form Book, Raceform Ltd, Newbury, RG14 5SJ

-000 **6** *5* **Chateau Lola**[4] [556] 5-9-2 **45**...............(p) JoeFanning 1
(Derek Shaw) *led 1f: chsd wnr tl pushed along 1/2-way: wknd and eased fnl f* **12/1**
1m 5.68s (3.38) **Going Correction** +0.475s/f (Slow) **6 Ran SP% 107.8**
Speed ratings (Par 97): **91,88,87,86,77 69**
CSF £9.75 CT £13.93 TOTE £1.90: £1.70, £1.80; EX 9.60 Trifecta £15.20.
**Owner** Mrs P A Wallis & M A Geobey **Bred** Rev James Browne **Trained** Elmley Castle, Worcs

**FOCUS**
A low-grade handicap in which the gallop was sound throughout. The winner raced centre-to-far side in the straight and the first four pulled clear. Weak form with the second helping with the standard.

## 611 CORAL MOBILE "JUST THREE CLICKS TO BET" H'CAP 1m 4f 50y(P)
6:35 (6:35) (Class 2) (0-105,95) 4-Y-O+ £11,971 (£3,583; £1,791; £896; £446) Stalls Low

Form RPR
-113 **1** **Blue Wave (IRE)**[13] [427] 4-9-7 **95**............... JoeFanning 5 104
(Mark Johnston) *led 1f: chsd ldrs: pushed along over 2f out: r.o to ld wl ins fnl f* **9/2**[3]
-022 **2** *1* **Kashmir Peak (IRE)**[11] [462] 5-9-5 **90**............... RobertWinston 3 97
(John Quinn) *hld up in tch: plld hrd: shkn up to ld over 1f out: sn rdn: hdd and unable qck wl ins fnl f* **9/2**[3]
40-6 **3** *2* **Flying Power**[15] [386] 6-9-0 **85**............... PaddyAspell 6 89
(John Norton) *a.p: chsd ldr 9f out: led over 2f out: rdn and hdd over 1f out: no ex wl ins fnl f* **20/1**
1-51 **4** *nse* **Magika**[35] [125] 4-8-13 **87**...............(t) MartinHarley 4 91
(Marco Botti) *a.p: rdn over 1f out: styd on same pce ins fnl f* **7/4**[1]
6114 **5** *8* **Modernism**[6] [533] 5-9-4 **89**............... LiamKeniry 7 80
(David Simcock) *led after 1f at stdy pce: rdn and hdd over 2f out: wknd fnl f* **6/1**
-121 **6** *2 3/4* **Like A Diamond (IRE)**[7] [514] 4-8-11 **85** 6ex............... TomQueally 1 72
(Evan Williams) *hld up: rdn and wknd over 1f out* **7/2**[2]
2m 44.09s (2.99) **Going Correction** +0.475s/f (Slow)
**WFA** 4 from 5yo+ 3lb **6 Ran SP% 114.0**
Speed ratings (Par 109): **109,108,107,106,101 99**
CSF £25.08 TOTE £5.10: £3.10, £3.20; EX 26.30 Trifecta £196.60.
**Owner** Sheikh Hamdan bin Mohammed Al Maktoum **Bred** Tom Darcy And Vincent McCarthy **Trained** Middleham Moor, N Yorks

**FOCUS**
A very useful handicap in which a couple of the market leaders proved a shade disappointing. The gallop was a steady one to the home turn and the winner raced centre-to-far side in the straight. The winner resumed his progress with the second rated to his penultimate C&D effort.

## 612 32RED IMMORTAL ROMANCE SLOT FILLIES' H'CAP 1m 4f 50y(P)
7:05 (7:06) (Class 5) (0-70,76) 4-Y-O+ £2,911 (£866; £432; £216) Stalls Low

Form RPR
5-24 **1** **Sian Gwalia**[35] [115] 4-8-6 **58**............... ChrisCatlin 7 67
(David Simcock) *hld up: hdwy over 2f out: rdn to ld ins fnl f: hung lft: styd on wl* **11/2**[3]
4-21 **2** *1 3/4* **Wilhana (IRE)**[11] [463] 4-9-7 **76** 6ex............... RossAtkinson(3) 5 83
(Pam Sly) *chsd ldr after 1f tl pushed along to ld over 1f out: rdn and hdd ins fnl f: edgd lft: styd on same pce* **4/1**[2]
/55- **3** *6* **Adiynara (IRE)**[14] [2750] 6-9-6 **69**...............(p) LiamKeniry 2 66
(Neil Mulholland) *chsd ldrs: outpcd 3f out: rallied over 1f out: styd on to go 3rd nr fin* **8/1**
-060 **4** *3/4* **Mazij**[11] [458] 6-8-8 **57**............... LukeMorris 6 53
(Peter Hiatt) *led at stdy pce tl qcknd over 3f out: rdn and hdd over 1f out: wknd ins fnl f* **8/1**
6-54 **5** *5* **Dazzling Valentine**[15] [385] 6-8-13 **62**...............(v) RobertWinston 3 50
(Alan Bailey) *hld up: rdn over 2f out: n.d* **11/2**[3]
06-3 **6** *shd* **Remix (IRE)**[18] [358] 5-8-12 **61**............... StevieDonohoe 1 49
(Ian Williams) *chsd ldr 1f: remained handy: rdn over 2f out: wknd over 1f out* **18/1**
0-51 **7** *1 1/2* **Dansili Dutch (IRE)**[8] [497] 5-8-4 **60**............... JoshDoyle(7) 4 45
(David O'Meara) *s.i.s: hld up and bhd: racd keenly: nvr nr to chal* **7/2**[1]
**8** *23* **Dragon Fei (IRE)**[144] [6709] 4-8-11 **63**...............[1] TomQueally 8 11
(Dermot Anthony McLoughlin, Ire) *prom: rdn over 3f out: wknd over 2f out* **6/1**
2m 46.18s (5.08) **Going Correction** +0.475s/f (Slow)
**WFA** 4 from 5yo+ 3lb **8 Ran SP% 114.8**
Speed ratings (Par 100): **102,100,96,96,93 92,91,76**
CSF £27.86 CT £175.09 TOTE £6.00: £2.10, £1.60, £3.90; EX 25.50 Trifecta £244.40.
**Owner** Mrs Ann Simcock **Bred** Mrs A E Simcock **Trained** Newmarket, Suffolk

**FOCUS**
A modest fillies' handicap in which an ordinary gallop picked up leaving the back straight. The first two pulled clear and the winner edged towards the far rail late on. The first two posted personal bests.

## 613 32RED FREE £10 BONUS H'CAP 7f 32y(P)
7:35 (7:37) (Class 4) (0-85,81) 3-Y-O £5,175 (£1,540; £769; £384) Stalls High

Form RPR
-311 **1** **Alumina (IRE)**[5] [547] 3-8-2 **62** 6ex............... DavidProbert 4 75
(Andrew Balding) *a.p: rdn to chse ldr and edgd lft over 1f out: r.o u.p to ld wl ins fnl f* **15/8**[2]
301- **2** *1 1/4* **Joohaina (IRE)**[69] [8201] 3-9-4 **78**...............(b) MartinHarley 6 88
(Marco Botti) *sn led: rdn over 1f out: edgd lft and hdd wl ins fnl f* **7/1**
5-61 **3** *5* **Cosquillas (IRE)**[18] [355] 3-8-6 **66**............... JoeFanning 1 63
(Mark Johnston) *chsd ldr tl over 5f out: remained handy: rdn over 1f out: no ex fnl f* **13/2**[3]
2-15 **4** *1* **Captain Myles (IRE)**[30] [183] 3-9-7 **81**...............(t) StevieDonohoe 2 75
(Tim Pitt) *hld up: rdn over 1f out: n.d* **7/1**
01-2 **5** *nse* **Amahoro**[9] [487] 3-8-12 **75**............... WilliamTwiston-Davies(3) 5 69
(Mick Channon) *prom: racd keenly: trckd ldr over 5f out tl rdn over 1f out: wknd ins fnl f* **6/4**[1]
416- **6** *3 1/2* **Know Your Name**[97] [7819] 3-9-1 **75**............... ChrisCatlin 3 60
(David Evans) *broke wl enough but sn lost pl and pushed along in rr: rdn and wknd over 1f out* **28/1**
1m 31.3s (1.70) **Going Correction** +0.475s/f (Slow) **6 Ran SP% 116.6**
Speed ratings (Par 99): **109,107,101,100,100 96**
CSF £15.97 TOTE £2.60: £1.40, £3.20; EX 12.00 Trifecta £25.20.
**Owner** Shapoor Mistry **Bred** Eimear Mulhern & Abbeville Stud **Trained** Kingsclere, Hants

**FOCUS**
A fair handicap in which the gallop was an ordinary one. The first two pulled clear and the winner raced against the far rail in the straight. The runner-up seems the key to the form.

## 614 LADBROKES MAIDEN STKS 7f 32y(P)
8:05 (8:06) (Class 5) 3-Y-O+ £2,587 (£770; £384; £192) Stalls High

Form RPR
2342 **1** **Shamardyh (IRE)**[6] [531] 3-8-4 **62**............... ChrisCatlin 1 65
(David Evans) *chsd ldrs: rdn to ld wl ins fnl f: r.o* **8/1**[3]
3-4 **2** *1 1/4* **Nixyba**[25] [254] 3-7-11 **0**............... ChloeIngram(7) 4 62
(Tim Vaughan) *trckd ldr: racd keenly: led 2f out: rdn: hdd and unable qck wl ins fnl f* **25/1**
553- **3** *3 1/4* **Brownsville (USA)**[108] [7592] 3-8-9 **72**............... JoeFanning 8 58
(Mark Johnston) *led: pushed along and hdd 2f out: wknd ins fnl f* **1/1**[1]
**4** *9* **Tashbeeh (IRE)** 3-8-9 **0**............... JamesSullivan 2 34
(Dianne Sayer) *s.s: outpcd: styd on ins fnl f: nvr nrr* **80/1**
0 **5** *1 1/2* **Aboody**[18] [355] 3-8-9 **0**............... LukeMorris 5 30
(Sir Mark Prescott Bt) *in tch but sn pushed along: rdn 1/2-way: wknd over 2f out* **33/1**
0-5U **6** *1/2* **Sand Stormer (IRE)**[13] [422] 3-8-9 **0**...............[1] BenCurtis 6 28
(William Muir) *prom: rdn over 2f out: hung lft and wknd over 1f out* **10/1**
**7** *4 1/2* **Sheriff Of Nawton (IRE)** 3-8-6 **0**............... SamJames(3) 7 16
(David O'Meara) *s.s: a in rr: wknd over 2f out* **28/1**
**U** **Maahir** 3-8-9 **0**............... MartinHarley 3
(Marco Botti) *wnt lft sn after s: hmpd and uns rdr* **6/4**[2]
1m 31.61s (2.01) **Going Correction** +0.475s/f (Slow) **8 Ran SP% 121.7**
Speed ratings (Par 103): **107,105,101,91,89 89,84,**
CSF £167.37 TOTE £6.70: £1.80, £3.70, £1.10; EX 72.00 Trifecta £260.10.
**Owner** Peter O'Callaghan **Bred** Rabbah Bloodstock Limited **Trained** Pandy, Monmouths

**FOCUS**
A race that took little winning with the market leader proving disappointing and with second favourite Maahir failing to complete. The gallop was an ordinary one and the winner raced centre-to-far side in the straight. There are doubts about the form.
T/Plt: £46.00 to a £1 stake. Pool: £126599.99 - 2007.28 winning tickets T/Qpdt: £16.90 to a £1 stake. Pool: £9422.52 - 410.85 winning tickets CR

615 - 621a (Foreign Racing) - See Raceform Interactive

# 601 LINGFIELD (L-H)
Saturday, February 15

**OFFICIAL GOING: Standard**
Wind: strong, half behind Weather: dry and windy

## 622 32RED CASINO MEDIAN AUCTION MAIDEN STKS 5f 6y(P)
1:40 (1:40) (Class 6) 3-Y-O £2,385 (£704; £352) Stalls High

Form RPR
403- **1** **Monsieur Lavene (IRE)**[92] [7893] 3-9-5 **70**............... TomQueally 2 71
(Robert Mills) *sn led and mde rest: rdn over 1f out: drvn and asserted ins fnl f: r.o strly: readily* **5/4**[1]
50-4 **2** *1 3/4* **Katja**[17] [371] 3-9-0 **59**............... JoeFanning 4 60
(J W Hills) *chsd ldrs: rdn and effrt to press wnr jst over 1f out: styd on same pce ins fnl f* **6/1**[3]
4-40 **3** *2 1/2* **Coiste Bodhar (IRE)**[15] [401] 3-9-5 **60**...............(p[1]) LukeMorris 5 56
(Joseph Tuite) *awkward leaving stalls and s.i.s: sn in tch in midfield: rdn 3f out: kpt on u.p to go 3rd ins fnl f: no threat to ldng pair* **12/1**
5-4 **4** *3* **Sylvan Spirit (IRE)**[29] [213] 3-9-0 **0**............... RobertWinston 1 40
(Roger Teal) *t.k.h: wl in tch in midfield: racd awkwardly bnd 2f out: rdn and effrt on inner over 1f out: no ex 1f out: wknd ins fnl f* **20/1**
2-43 **5** *1 1/2* **Rosie Prospects**[13] [447] 3-9-0 **60**...............(p) RobertHavlin 3 35
(Roger Ingram) *chsd wnr: rdn ent fnl 2f: lost pl u.p and btn ent fnl f: wknd ins fnl f* **14/1**
0- **6** *6* **Deavin**[94] [7853] 3-9-5 **0**............... GeorgeBaker 6 18
(Nick Littmoden) *s.i.s: a outpcd in last pair: n.d* **7/2**[2]
4 **7** *3/4* **Apophenia**[45] [5] 3-9-0 **0**............... TonyHamilton 8 10
(Richard Fahey) *sn outpcd in last pair: n.d* **7/1**
57.7s (-1.10) **Going Correction** -0.175s/f (Stan) **7 Ran SP% 112.6**
Speed ratings (Par 95): **101,98,94,89,87 77,76**
CSF £8.97 TOTE £2.00: £2.40, £3.50; EX 11.90 Trifecta £48.20.
**Owner** J Harley Mrs B B Mills R A Mills **Bred** Henry O'Callaghan **Trained** Headley, Surrey

**FOCUS**
There was a very strong wind, mainly behind the runners over this 5f trip, resulting in a pretty rapid time. Over longer distances however, the runners were racing into the wind down the back straight. A moderate sprint maiden but the form makes a fair bit of sense.

## 623 CORAL.CO.UK H'CAP 1m 4f (P)
2:15 (2:15) (Class 4) (0-85,85) 4-Y-O+ £4,690 (£1,395; £697; £348) Stalls Low

Form RPR
6-31 **1** **Scottish Star**[10] [494] 6-8-10 **79**............... RyanTate(5) 5 87
(James Eustace) *wl in tch in midfield: hdwy u.p over 1f out: led ins fnl f: hld on wl towards fin* **6/1**[2]
310- **2** *shd* **Gabrial's Star**[151] [6504] 5-9-4 **82**...............(b) JamieSpencer 7 90
(Richard Fahey) *stdd s: hld up in tch in rr: hdwy over 2f out: styd on u.p and str chal wl ins fnl f: jst hld* **16/1**
-101 **3** *1 1/2* **Ocean Applause**[17] [369] 4-8-9 **76**...............(t) JimmyQuinn 8 81
(John Ryan) *hld up in tch towards rr: clsd but nt clr run 2f out: swtchd ins and hdwy over 1f out: chsd wnr briefly ins fnl f: one pce* **20/1**
41- **4** *1/2* **Music Man (IRE)**[47] [8444] 4-8-13 **80**............... JimCrowley 2 85+
(Jo Crowley) *hld up in tch in midfield: nt clr run 2f out: swtchd lft and hdwy 1f out: styd on wl fnl 100yds: no threat to ldrs* **6/1**[2]
4-12 **5** *1/2* **Sagesse**[8] [514] 4-8-11 **78**............... LukeMorris 6 82
(Sir Mark Prescott Bt) *in tch in midfield: rdn and effrt 3f out: unable qck over 1f out: edgd lft and styd on ins fnl f: no threat to ldrs* **6/1**[2]
06-1 **6** *hd* **Lilac Tree**[20] [350] 4-8-12 **79**............... JoeFanning 4 83
(Mark Johnston) *led for 2f: chsd ldr tl led again over 2f out: rdn 2f out: drvn and hdd ins fnl f: wknd fnl 75yds* **5/2**[1]
124- **7** *1/2* **Knockgraffon Lad (USA)**[64] [8276] 7-8-13 **80**(t) WilliamTwiston-Davies(3) 3 83
(Brendan Powell) *stdd s: hld up in tch in rr: clsd and nt clr run ent fnl 2f: hdwy 1f out: kpt on but no threat to ldrs* **14/1**
4-54 **8** *nk* **Presburg (IRE)**[16] [386] 5-9-2 **85**............... JoeyHaynes(5) 10 88+
(Joseph Tuite) *stdd s: hld up in tch towards rr: clsd and nt clr run ent fnl 2f: nvr much room after tl ins fnl f: styd on wl towards fin: nvr trbld ldrs* **6/1**[2]
3-34 **9** *shd* **Mawaakef (IRE)**[14] [427] 6-9-5 **83**............... FrederikTylicki 11 85
(J R Jenkins) *wl in tch in midfield: rdn and hdwy to chse ldrs over 2f out: no ex 1f out: wknd ins fnl f* **10/1**[3]

606- **10** 4 ½ **Thecornishcowboy**[51] 8400 5-8-4 **71**..........(t) RyanPowell(3) 1 66
(John Ryan) *chsd ldrs: shuffled bk and nt clr run wl over 1f out: wknd ins fnl f* **33/1**

06-0 **11** 7 **Deia Sunrise (IRE)**[35] 145 5-9-7 **85**..........(p) RobertHavlin 12 69
(Paul Webber) *chsd ldrs: styd wd tl led and crossed to inner after 2f: hdd over 2f out: btn u.p ent fnl f: wknd* **50/1**

1-43 **12** 3 ½ **St Ignatius**[20] 350 7-8-13 **77**..........(v) RobertWinston 9 55
(Alan Bailey) *chsd ldrs tl lost pl u.p ent fnl 3f: bhd 1f out* **20/1**

2m 29.86s (-3.14) **Going Correction** -0.175s/f (Stan)
**WFA** 4 from 5yo+ 3lb **12** Ran SP% **121.8**
Speed ratings (Par 105): **103,102,101,101,101 101,100,100,100,97 92,90**
CSF £95.24 CT £1824.28 TOTE £7.10: £2.80, £6.30, £4.90; EX 122.10 Trifecta £1683.40 Part won..
**Owner** Ian Rushby **Bred** Mrs J McCreery **Trained** Newmarket, Suffolk

**FOCUS**
The field were still well bunched turning into the straight and the closing stages were a bit messy. Quite compressed, ordinary form.

## 624 32RED H'CAP 6f 1y(P)
**2:50** (2:51) (Class 3) (0-95,90) 3-Y-O **£7,439** (£2,213; £1,106; £553) **Stalls** Low

Form RPR

14-2 **1** **Harwoods Volante (IRE)**[24] 279 3-9-3 **86**.......... RobertHavlin 9 92
(Amanda Perrett) *wnt lft s: sn rcvrd to chse ldr: rdn to ld over 1f out: drvn and hrd pressed ins fnl f: hld on gamely* **5/1**[3]

11-3 **2** shd **Drive On (IRE)**[24] 279 3-8-8 **77**..........(p) JohnFahy 4 83
(Eve Johnson Houghton) *off the pce in last pair: clsd and hmpd bnd wl over 1f out: swtchd lft and hdwy u.p over 1f out: str chal ins fnl f: r.o: jst hld* **9/2**[2]

4 **3** nk **Golden Amber (IRE)**[31] 183 3-9-5 **88**.......... JimCrowley 1 93
(Dean Ivory) *chsd ldrs and clr in ldng quartet: rdn wl over 1f out: swtchd rt and hdwy 1f out: str chal u.p wl ins fnl f: no ex cl home* **8/1**

1-2 **4** nk **National Service (USA)**[10] 485 3-8-2 **71** oh1.......... AndreaAtzeni 7 75
(Stuart Williams) *wnt rt s: rcvrd into midfield but stl off the pce 4f out: clsd and wl in tch 2f out: drvn and ev ch ins fnl f: unable qck cl home* **2/1**[1]

-221 **5** 4 ½ **Three D Alexander (IRE)**[9] 500 3-8-11 **80**.......... JamieSpencer 2 69
(David Evans) *led: rdn wl over 1f out: hdd over 1f out: no ex jst ins fnl f: wknd fnl 100yds* **16/1**

6-34 **6** 4 **Scruffy Tramp (IRE)**[17] 375 3-9-6 **89**..........(v[1]) RobertWinston 5 71
(Alan Bailey) *chsd ldrs and clr in ldng trio: rdn and unable qck over 1f out: fdd fnl f* **9/2**[2]

535- **7** 3 ¼ **Lone Warrior (IRE)**[136] 6955 3-9-7 **90**.......... MartinHarley 3 56
(David Evans) *racd off the pce in midfield: rdn and struggling over 2f out: bhd over 1f out* **10/1**

334- **8** nk **Intermath (IRE)**[130] 7097 3-8-13 **82**.......... TomQueally 8 47
(David Evans) *racd off the pce in midfield: rdn along 4f out: struggling ent fnl 2f: sn wknd* **33/1**

41-5 **9** nk **Vodka Time (IRE)**[9] 501 3-8-6 **80**.......... EoinWalsh(5) 6 44
(David Evans) *sn outpcd in rr: n.d* **25/1**

1m 10.03s (-1.87) **Going Correction** -0.175s/f (Stan) **9** Ran SP% **119.2**
Speed ratings (Par 101): **105,104,104,104,98 92,88,88,87**
CSF £28.79 CT £181.70 TOTE £6.40: £1.40, £2.80, £3.20; EX 33.30 Trifecta £208.00.
**Owner** Harwoods Racing Club **Bred** Gerry And John Rowley **Trained** Pulborough, W Sussex

**FOCUS**
A decent enough, competitive 3yo sprint. The closely matched 1-2 both found a bit on their Kempton latest.

## 625 LADBROKES H'CAP 1m 1y(P)
**3:25** (3:26) (Class 2) (0-100,97) 4-Y-O+ **£12,291** (£3,657; £1,827; £913) **Stalls** High

Form RPR

3-55 **1** **George Guru**[22] 314 7-9-1 **91**.......... RobertHavlin 5 103
(Michael Attwater) *broke wl: chsd ldrs: clsd to trck ldrs 3f out: gap opened on inner and effrt to chal wl over 1f out: led over 1f out: clr and in command fnl f: r.o wl* **6/1**[3]

1114 **2** 2 ¼ **Tellovoi (IRE)**[6] 550 6-9-2 **92**..........(v) WilliamCarson 8 99
(Ann Stokell) *racd keenly: led and set stdy gallop: drvn and qcknd wl over 1f out: hdd over 1f out: no threat to wnr but hld on for 2nd ins fnl f* **33/1**

210- **3** nk **Spa's Dancer (IRE)**[241] 3458 7-9-1 **91**.......... LukeMorris 2 97
(James Eustace) *in tch in midfield: effrt u.p 2f out: battling for 2nd but no imp on wnr fnl f: kpt on* **16/1**

-311 **4** nk **Rebellious Guest**[14] 426 5-9-2 **92**.......... TomQueally 6 97+
(George Margarson) *hld up in tch towards rr: wd and effrt bnd 2f out: kpt on wl u.p ins fnl f: no threat to wnr* **3/1**[1]

-564 **5** ¾ **Mia's Boy**[14] 426 10-8-12 **88**.......... LiamKeniry 3 92
(Chris Dwyer) *wl in tch in midfield: rdn and unable qck over 1f out: kpt on u.p ins fnl f: no threat to wnr* **33/1**

310- **6** ¾ **Consign**[105] 7696 4-9-5 **95**..........(v) JamieSpencer 7 97
(Jeremy Noseda) *stdd s: t.k.h: hld up in tch in rr: hdwy u.p on inner over 1f out: styd on same pce ins fnl f* **7/2**[2]

5-23 **7** 1 ½ **Luhaif**[12] 465 4-9-2 **97**..........(p) ShelleyBirkett(5) 9 96
(Julia Feilden) *rdn along early: chsd ldrs tl wnt 2nd 6f out tl wl over 1f out: no ex u.p over 1f out: wknd ins fnl f* **7/1**

20-5 **8** 1 ¾ **Royal Prize**[14] 426 4-8-12 **88**.......... JimCrowley 1 83
(Ralph Beckett) *stdd after s: hld up off the pce in rr: rdn and effrt 2f out: no real imp: n.d* **7/1**

124- **9** shd **Talented Kid**[141] 6792 5-9-0 **90**.......... JoeFanning 12 84
(Mark Johnston) *chsd ldr for 2f: chsd ldrs after tl lost pl and on outer bnd 2f out: n.d after: wknd ins fnl f* **8/1**

6-00 **10** 2 ¼ **Lowther**[7] 533 9-8-6 **87**..........(v) LouisSteward(5) 11 76
(Lee Carter) *in tch in midfield on outer: lost pl and bhd whn rdn 2f out: no rspnse: wknd over 1f out* **33/1**

U-15 **11** hd **Birdman (IRE)**[12] 465 4-9-3 **93**..........(b) AndreaAtzeni 4 82
(David Simcock) *stdd s: t.k.h: hld up in tch in rr: rdn and no hdwy 2f out: wknd over 1f out* **10/1**

1m 34.94s (-3.26) **Going Correction** -0.175s/f (Stan) **11** Ran SP% **121.4**
Speed ratings (Par 109): **109,106,106,106,105 104,103,101,101,99 98**
CSF £194.13 CT £3044.61 TOTE £6.40: £2.80, £8.70, £4.60; EX 219.20 Trifecta £2326.80.
**Owner** T M Jones **Bred** T M Jones **Trained** Epsom, Surrey

**FOCUS**
A good handicap but the pace wasn't strong. The winner is rated to his best.

## 626 32RED.COM MAIDEN STKS 1m 1y(P)
**4:00** (4:00) (Class 5) 3-Y-O **£3,067** (£905; £453) **Stalls** High

Form RPR

33 **1** **Jaahiez (USA)**[14] 423 3-9-5 0.......... AndreaAtzeni 3 73
(Roger Varian) *trckd ldrs: rdn wl over 1f out: drvn and keeping on whn nt clr run and swtchd rt ins fnl f: rdn hands and heels and qcknd between horses wl ins fnl f to ld cl home* **3/1**[2]

**2** shd **Watersmeet** 3-9-5 0.......... JoeFanning 2 71
(Mark Johnston) *led: rdn and fnd ex over 1f out: edgd lft u.p ins fnl f: hrd pressed fnl 100yds: edgd rt and hdd cl home* **7/1**[3]

3- **3** ¾ **Premium Pressure (USA)**[126] 7209 3-9-5 0.......... JamieSpencer 4 69
(David Barron) *stdd after s: t.k.h: hld up in tch: rdn and effrt over 1f out: edgd lft but r.o to chal ins fnl f: one pce and hld whn rn green and wnt rt nr fin* **4/6**[1]

**4** 2 ½ **Kiss Of Spring (IRE)** 3-9-0 0.......... TomQueally 5 58
(Charles Hills) *t.k.h: pressed ldr tl rdn and sltly outpcd over 1f out: 4th and wknd ins fnl f* **8/1**

**5** 3 ¼ **Khutze (GER)** 3-9-5 0.......... JohnFahy 6 55
(Eve Johnson Houghton) *s.i.s: rn green: in tch in midfield: rdn and over 2f out: outpcd and btn over 1f out: wknd fnl f* **25/1**

**6** 2 **Diamond Back (IRE)** 3-9-5 0.......... JimmyQuinn 1 50?
(Denis Quinn) *s.i.s: in rr: clsd over 2f out: rdn and outpcd wl over 1f out: wknd ent fnl f* **66/1**

1m 39.66s (1.46) **Going Correction** -0.175s/f (Stan) **6** Ran SP% **113.9**
Speed ratings (Par 97): **85,84,84,81,78 76**
CSF £23.88 TOTE £4.20: £1.90, £2.20; EX 14.80 Trifecta £41.50.
**Owner** Sheikh Ahmed Al Maktoum **Bred** Darley **Trained** Newmarket, Suffolk
■ Stewards' Enquiry : Andrea Atzeni one-day ban; careless riding (1st Mar)

**FOCUS**
Some decent stables were represented. The front four are all entitled to be a bit better than this on paper.

## 627 DOWNLOAD THE LADBROKES APP H'CAP 1m 1y(P)
**4:30** (4:31) (Class 5) (0-75,74) 4-Y-O+ **£3,067** (£905; £453) **Stalls** High

Form RPR

15- **1** **Commissar**[96] 7840 5-9-6 **73**..........(t) TomQueally 11 82
(Ian Williams) *stdd s: hld up in tch in rr: gd hdwy on inner over 1f out: led ins fnl f: pushed out: comf* **8/1**[3]

04-0 **2** ½ **Swift Cedar (IRE)**[24] 286 4-9-3 **70**..........(b[1]) LukeMorris 5 78
(Jeremy Gask) *dwlt: in tch towards rr: hdwy to chse ldrs 2f out: rdn and ev ch over 1f out: drvn to ld 1f out: sn hdd and kpt on same pce ins fnl f* **8/1**[3]

3411 **3** nk **Club House (IRE)**[3] 583 4-8-6 **66**.......... GeorgeBuckell(7) 2 73
(Robert Mills) *hld up wl in tch: rdn and effrt 2f out: kpt on u.p ins fnl f* **2/1**[1]

-334 **4** nse **Run It Twice (IRE)**[10] 496 4-9-2 **69**..........(b) MartinHarley 6 76
(David Evans) *hld up in tch in midfield: swtchd rt and effrt over 1f out: kpt on wl u.p ins fnl f* **8/1**[3]

4-11 **5** 2 ½ **Tee It Up Tommo (IRE)**[29] 211 5-9-5 **72**.......... RobertWinston 9 73
(Michael Wigham) *stdd s: t.k.h: hld up in tch in last pair: swtchd ins and hdwy ent fnl f: styd on: nvr trbld ldrs* **5/2**[2]

45-3 **6** 1 ¼ **Alice's Dancer (IRE)**[18] 364 5-9-7 **74**.......... GeorgeBaker 4 72
(William Muir) *t.k.h: chsd ldrs: rdn and unable qck over 1f out: wknd ins fnl f* **16/1**

6-24 **7** nse **Intomist (IRE)**[11] 472 5-8-12 **70**..........(p) NathanAlison(5) 3 68
(Jim Boyle) *pressed ldr: rdn to ld 2f out: drvn and hdd 1f out: wknd ins fnl f* **20/1**

66-0 **8** 3 ½ **Jewelled**[16] 376 8-8-11 **71**.......... DanielCremin(7) 7 61
(Ralph J Smith) *in tch in midfield: lost pl and u.p in last trio 2f out: no hdwy: wknd ent fnl f* **66/1**

4210 **9** 1 ¼ **Hellbender (IRE)**[13] 451 8-9-3 **70**.......... DavidProbert 1 57
(Shaun Harris) *broke sltly early: led tl rdn and hdd 2f out: no ex u.p over 1f out: wknd fnl f* **20/1**

10-4 **10** 29 **Captain Starlight (IRE)**[31] 181 4-9-6 **73**.......... JimCrowley 8
(Jo Crowley) *in tch: hdwy on outer to chse ldrs 5f out: lost pl qckly and bhd ent fnl 2f: sn lost tch: t.o fnl f* **8/1**[3]

1m 36.26s (-1.94) **Going Correction** -0.175s/f (Stan) **10** Ran SP% **123.2**
Speed ratings (Par 103): **102,101,101,101,98 97,97,93,92,63**
CSF £72.68 CT £184.72 TOTE £14.40: £3.10, £2.70, £1.70; EX 65.90 Trifecta £501.60.
**Owner** S Hassiakos **Bred** R A Instone **Trained** Portway, Worcs

**FOCUS**
A modest but competitive handicap. There's every chance the winner can do better.

## 628 BOOKMAKERS.CO.UK SPRINT SERIES ROUND 7 H'CAP (QUALIFIER) 6f 1y(P)
**5:00** (5:00) (Class 5) (0-70,79) 4-Y-O+ **£3,234** (£962; £481; £240) **Stalls** Low

Form RPR

-011 **1** **Spellmaker**[13] 449 5-8-7 **61**.......... EoinWalsh(5) 1 71+
(Tony Newcombe) *t.k.h: hld up in tch in midfield: switching out rt and hdwy over 1f out: ev ch ins fnl f: led fnl 50yds: r.o wl* **12/1**

-211 **2** ¾ **Roy's Legacy**[11] 470 5-9-3 **69**.......... MichaelJMMurphy(3) 4 77
(Shaun Harris) *led: rdn and fnd ex over 1f out: hrd pressed and edgd rt ins fnl f: hdd and no ex fnl 50yds* **16/1**

6-03 **3** ¾ **Temple Road (IRE)**[15] 412 6-9-6 **69**.......... RichardKingscote 9 75
(Milton Bradley) *in tch towards rr: swtchd lft and hdwy over 1f out: pressed ldrs ins fnl f: kpt on same pce fnl 75yds* **7/1**[3]

-002 **4** ½ **Shifting Star (IRE)**[10] 496 9-8-13 **62**..........(b) WilliamCarson 2 66
(John Bridger) *chsd ldrs: drvn and effrt wl over 1f out: kpt on same pce u.p ins fnl f* **20/1**

005- **5** 1 ¼ **Meridius (IRE)**[116] 7444 4-9-6 **69**..........(b) TomQueally 10 69
(Gary Harrison) *s.i.s: swtchd lft and hld up in rr: hdwy u.p on inner over 1f out: kpt on same pce ins fnl f* **16/1**

2-11 **6** ¾ **Ex Ex**[10] 489 4-10-2 **79**.......... GeorgeBaker 7 77
(Nick Littmoden) *in tch in midfield: rdn and effrt over 1f out: hung rt and no ex 1f out: wknd ins fnl f* **11/10**[1]

2-21 **7** nk **Multitask**[14] 425 4-9-4 **67**.......... LiamKeniry 3 64+
(Michael Madgwick) *stdd s: hld up in tch in rr: clsng but stl plenty to do whn nt clr run and hmpd ins fnl f: nvr trbld ldrs* **4/1**[2]

2432 **8** ¾ **Haadeeth**[5] 557 7-9-3 **66**..........(t) MartinHarley 8 60
(David Evans) *chsd ldr tl over 1f out: btn and wkng whn pushed rt and hmpd ins fnl f* **16/1**

4-41 **9** nk **Compton Prince**[14] 424 5-9-2 **65**..........(b) LukeMorris 12 58
(Milton Bradley) *chsd ldrs on outer: drvn and unable qck over 1f out: btn whn wkng whn pushed rt: hmpd and wknd ins fnl f* **20/1**

0-00 **10** ½ **El Mirage (IRE)**[10] 489 4-9-4 **67**........................ JimCrowley 6 59
(Dean Ivory) *t.k.h: hld up in tch towards rr: rdn and effrt over 1f out: no imp and n.d whn sltly hmpd ins fnl f* **25/1**

1m 10.78s (-1.12) **Going Correction** -0.175s/f (Stan) **10** Ran SP% **118.8**
Speed ratings (Par 103): **100,99,98,97,95 94,94,93,92,92**
CSF £182.39 CT £1500.25 TOTE £14.60: £3.40, £4.20, £2.00; EX 95.90 Trifecta £3256.90.
**Owner** Joli Racing **Bred** Dxb Bloodstock Ltd **Trained** Yarnscombe, Devon

**FOCUS**
Just a moderate handicap. The winner is rated to his latest mark.
T/Plt: £510.00 to a £1 stake. Pool: £98111.40 - 140.41 winning tickets T/Qpdt: £50.70 to a £1 stake. Pool: £6502.26 - 94.85 winning tickets SP

## 584 CAGNES-SUR-MER
Saturday, February 15
**OFFICIAL GOING: Turf: very soft ; polytrack: standard**

### 629a PRIX DES SEMBOULES (CONDITIONS) (3YO) (POLYTRACK) 1m (F)
**12:00** (12:00) 3-Y-O **£12,083** (£4,833; £3,625; £2,416; £1,208)

RPR
**1** **Verdura (USA)**[31] 194 3-8-10 0........................ IoritzMendizabal 5 81
(J-C Rouget, France) **17/10**[2]
**2** *1* **Farmah (USA)** 3-8-10 0........................ Francois-XavierBertras 7 78
(F Rohaut, France) **6/4**[1]
**3** *shd* **Stosur (IRE)**[16] 391 3-8-10 0........................ Pierre-CharlesBoudot 1 78
(Gay Kelleway) *sn led: jnd over 2f out: rdn over 1f out: kpt on but hdd ins fnl f and sn dropped to 3rd* **4/1**[3]
**4** *1 ½* **Falkhair (FR)**[58] 3-9-0 0........................ TheoBachelot 2 79
(C Boutin, France) **14/1**
**5** *shd* **Singapore Spur (FR)**[28] 237 3-9-0 0........................(p) AlexisBadel 4 78
(D De Waele, France) **13/1**
**6** *3 ½* **Il Presuntuoso (FR)**[279] 3-9-4 0........................(b) AurelienLemaitre 3 74
(M Boutin, France) **9/1**
**7** *1 ½* **Pretty Pearl (FR)**[16] 391 3-8-2 0........................ JimmyTastayre(5) 6 60?
(N Caullery, France) **42/1**

1m 38.4s (98.40) **7** Ran SP% **123.2**
WIN (incl. 1 euro stake): 2.70. PLACES: 1.40, 1.40. SF: 4.50.
**Owner** Joseph Allen **Bred** J Allen **Trained** Pau, France

### 630a PRIX DU FORT CARRE (MAIDEN) (3YO COLTS & GELDINGS) (TURF) 7f 110y
**12:30** (12:00) 3-Y-O **£10,000** (£4,000; £3,000; £2,000; £1,000)

RPR
**1** **Ar Poulgwenn (IRE)**[31] 194 3-9-2 0........................ IoritzMendizabal 7 83
(J-C Rouget, France) **6/4**[1]
**2** *3 ½* **He Loves Me (FR)**[16] 390 3-9-2 0........................ AnthonyCrastus 2 74
(E Lellouche, France) **2/1**[2]
**3** *4* **Soul Of Motion**[178] 5635 3-9-2 0........................ Pierre-CharlesBoudot 8 64
(Gay Kelleway) *midfield in tch: rdn and effrt to chal over 2f out: 2nd and ev ch ent fnl f: styd on but sn dropped to 3rd and readily outpcd by front pair* **13/2**[3]
**4** *nk* **Soldat Bleu (FR)**[16] 390 3-9-2 0........................ FranckBlondel 3 63
(D Prod'Homme, France) **13/1**
**5** *3 ½* **Best Love Royal (FR)**[31] 194 3-9-2 0........................ TheoBachelot 9 55
(F-X De Chevigny, France) **31/1**
**6** *5 ½* **The Racer (FR)** 3-8-11 0........................ EdouardLacaille 6 36
(K Borgel, France) **32/1**
**7** *7* **Anoubis (FR)** 3-8-11 0........................ NicolasPerret 4 18
(K Borgel, France) **18/1**
**8** *2 ½* **Soleon (GER)** 3-9-2 0........................ AlexisBadel 1 17
(F-X De Chevigny, France) **8/1**
**9** *6 ½* **Avra (FR)** 3-8-11 0........................ StephaneRichardot 5
(T Larriviere, France) **31/1**

1m 45.14s (105.14) **9** Ran SP% **119.5**
WIN (incl. 1 euro stake) 2.50. PLACES: 1.10, 1.10, 1.30. DF: 2.50. SF: 5.10.
**Owner** J Seche & J-P Vallee-Lambert **Bred** Ecurie Des Monceaux **Trained** Pau, France

631 - 637a (Foreign Racing) - See Raceform Interactive

## 555 ST MORITZ (R-H)
Sunday, February 16
**OFFICIAL GOING: Snow: frozen**

### 638a GRAND PRIX PRESTIGE (CONDITIONS) (4YO+) (SNOW) 1m
**11:45** (12:00) 4-Y-O+
**£4,256** (£2,128; £1,520; £1,013; £506; £304)

RPR
**1** **Zarras (GER)**[7] 555 5-9-4 0........................ EPedroza 8 92
(P Schaerer, Switzerland) **5/1**[3]
**2** *7* **Mont Pelato (USA)**[364] 702 6-9-0 0........................(p) AstridWullschleger(4) 2 76
(M Weiss, Switzerland) **31/5**
**3** *2* **Boccalino (GER)**[7] 555 6-9-6 0........................(b) DanielePorcu 10 73
(P Schaerer, Switzerland) **56/10**
**4** *1 ¾* **Ciocco Sam (GER)**[364] 702 6-9-6 0........................ MissSilkeBruggemann 3 69
(C Von Der Recke, Germany) **103/10**
**5** *1* **Unknown Villain (IRE)**[115] 7487 4-9-0 0........................ TimBurgin(4) 5 65
(A Schennach, Switzerland) **81/10**
**6** *shd* **Exchange**[364] 700 6-8-9 0........................ ClementLheureux(7) 7 63
(Frau M Muller, Switzerland) **94/10**
**7** *dist* **Sunndale** 5-9-8 0........................ OlivierPlacais 6
(M Weiss, Switzerland) **57/10**
**8** *dist* **Sheikh The Reins (IRE)**[7] 555 5-9-4 0........................(b) AndreBest 9
(John Best) *chsd ldng gp: rdn and no imp over 2 1/2f out: bhd fnl 1 1/2f* **37/10**[2]
**9** *dist* **Ishikawa (IRE)**[43] 56 6-9-11 0........................ FredericSpanu 1
(K R Burke) *nvr beyond midfield: wl bhd fr 2f out* **126/10**
**10** *¾* **Ancient Greece**[17] 376 7-9-13 0........................ JBojko 4
(George Baker) *midfield: rdn and no imp 1/2-way: bhd fr over 2f out* **3/1**[1]

1m 43.3s (103.30) **10** Ran SP% **143.7**
PARI-MUTUEL (all including 1 chf stakes): WIN 6.00; PLACE 1.30, 1.80, 1.80; SF 34.30.
**Owner** Scuderia Del Clan **Bred** Gestut Auenquelle **Trained** Switzerland

## 608 WOLVERHAMPTON (A.W) (L-H)
Monday, February 17
**OFFICIAL GOING: Standard**
Wind: Fresh behind Weather: Showery

### 639 CORAL MOBILE "JUST THREE CLICKS TO BET" AMATEUR RIDERS' H'CAP (DIV I) 1m 4f 50y(P)
**2:15** (2:15) (Class 6) (0-52,52) 4-Y-O+ **£2,495** (£774; £386; £193) **Stalls** Low

Form RPR
4-62 **1** **Fair Breeze**[14] 460 7-10-10 **48**........................(b) MrSWalker 7 57+
(Richard Phillips) *s.i.s: hld up: hdwy over 5f out: chsd ldr over 3f out: led over 2f out: rdn over 1f out: styd on* **3/1**[1]
/0-2 **2** *1 ½* **Miles Of Sunshine**[9] 530 9-10-11 **49**........................ MissSBrotherton 12 55
(Ron Hodges) *a.p: chsd ldr over 5f out: led over 3f out: hdd over 2f out: styd on* **12/1**
3-00 **3** *1 ¼* **James Pollard (IRE)**[12] 490 9-10-9 **52**........................(t) SeanBowen(5) 3 56
(Bernard Llewellyn) *hld up: rdn over 2f out: hdwy over 1f out: styd on: nt rch ldrs* **16/1**
/3-3 **4** *½* **Think**[45] 33 7-10-9 **47**........................(t) MrJHamilton 5 50
(Clive Mulhall) *prom: rdn over 3f out: styd on same pce ins fnl f* **3/1**[1]
45-3 **5** *½* **Well Owd Mon**[14] 460 4-10-2 **46**........................(p) MissAliceMills(3) 1 48
(Andrew Hollinshead) *hld up: rdn over 3f out: hdwy over 1f out: r.o: nt rch ldrs* **7/1**[3]
00/3 **6** *1 ¼* **Red Skipper (IRE)**[12] 490 9-10-8 **46** oh1........................ FreddieMitchell 11 46
(John O'Shea) *trckd ldr tl over 5f out: rdn over 3f out: no ex fnl f* **8/1**
606- **7** *2 ¾* **Summerlea (IRE)**[39] 6470 8-10-12 **50**........................ MrWHogg 9 46
(Micky Hammond) *hld up: hdwy over 4f out: rdn over 2f out: wknd fnl f* **13/2**[2]
4550 **8** *7* **Dontpaytheferryman (USA)**[6] 567 9-10-9 **52**.....(b) MissMEdden(5) 10 36
(Peter Hiatt) *led over 8f: rdn and wknd over 1f out* **20/1**
**9** *10* **Tide Runner**[529] 5987 8-10-6 **51**........................(p) MrTSquire(7) 8 19
(Liam Corcoran) *hld up: pushed along over 2f out: sn wknd* **16/1**
060- **10** *37* **Big City Boy (IRE)**[322] 1297 6-10-1 **46** oh1........................ MrJAMcEntee(7) 4
(Phil McEntee) *trckd ldrs: racd keenly: rdn and wknd over 3f out* **50/1**
0/0- **11** *¾* **Rocco Breeze (IRE)**[180] 5650 5-10-3 **46** oh1........................ MrBFurnival(5) 6
(Mark Brisbourne) *prom: rdn over 4f out: sn wknd* **100/1**
000- **12** *3 ¼* **Olynard (IRE)**[52] 8413 8-10-5 **46** oh1........................ MissMMullineaux(3) 2
(Michael Mullineaux) *s.s: a in rr: bhd fr 1/2-way* **66/1**

2m 45.69s (4.59) **Going Correction** +0.275s/f (Slow)
**WFA** 4 from 5yo+ 3lb **12** Ran SP% **115.6**
Speed ratings (Par 101): **95,94,93,92,92 91,89,85,78,53 53,51**
CSF £40.86 CT £495.96 TOTE £3.80: £1.20, £4.80, £6.50; EX 21.00 Trifecta £416.50.
**Owner** The Summer Club **Bred** Richard Phillips **Trained** Adlestrop, Gloucs

**FOCUS**
A weak amateur riders' handicap in which they didn't go particularly quick and two jockeys who excel in this discipline came to the fore. The winner is rated to his old best.

### 640 CORAL MOBILE "JUST THREE CLICKS TO BET" AMATEUR RIDERS' H'CAP (DIV II) 1m 4f 50y(P)
**2:45** (2:45) (Class 6) (0-52,52) 4-Y-O+ **£2,495** (£774; £386; £193) **Stalls** Low

Form RPR
6-53 **1** **Goldmadchen (GER)**[13] 474 6-10-10 **48**........................ MrJHamilton 10 57
(James Given) *a.p: pushed along over 4f out: chsd ldr over 2f out: rdn to ld over 1f out: edgd lft fnl f: styd on* **9/2**[2]
3003 **2** *1* **General Tufto**[9] 537 9-11-0 **52**........................(b) MissEJJones 4 59
(Charles Smith) *hld up: hdwy over 2f out: chsd wnr over 1f out: rdn and edgd lft ins fnl f: styd on* **16/1**
54-5 **3** *3 ¼* **Celebrian**[41] 73 7-10-1 **46** oh1........................(tp) MrNicholasMeek(7) 2 48
(Alex Hales) *hld up: racd wd fr over 3f out tl hdwy over 1f out: r.o ins fnl f: nvr nrr* **14/1**
/0-4 **4** *½* **Kozmina Bay**[13] 474 5-10-5 **48**........................(b) SeanBowen(5) 9 49
(Bernard Llewellyn) *chsd ldr tl led over 4f out: rdn and hdd over 1f out: styd on same pce fnl f* **25/1**
60-3 **5** *½* **Whiskey N Stout (IRE)**[5] 570 4-10-6 **47**........................ FreddieMitchell 11 47
(Sean Curran) *hld up in tch: rdn over 2f out: no ex fnl f* **9/2**[2]
1-42 **6** *3 ¼* **Funky Munky**[16] 433 9-10-13 **51**........................(p) MrSWalker 8 46
(Alistair Whillans) *led over 7f: pushed along over 3f out: wknd fnl f* **7/4**[1]
5/00 **7** *5* **Converti**[9] 537 10-10-1 **46** oh1........................ MissHHeal(7) 7 33
(Carroll Gray) *hld up: wknd over 2f out* **100/1**
0/6- **8** *2* **Windpfeil (IRE)**[37] 2333 8-10-5 **46** oh1........................(p) MissCBoxall(3) 5 30
(Dominic Ffrench Davis) *prom: rdn over 2f out: wknd over 1f out* **16/1**
63-5 **9** *3* **Drummond**[13] 475 5-10-6 **49**........................(bt[1]) MissJodieHughes(5) 6 28
(Bernard Llewellyn) *hld up: rdn over 3f out: sn wknd* **25/1**
00-3 **10** *½* **Josie's Dream (IRE)**[13] 475 6-10-8 **51**...........(b[1]) MrJamesHughes(5) 3 29
(Jo Hughes) *sn pushed along and prom: swtchd rt over 5f out: wknd over 2f out* **7/1**[3]
/0-5 **11** *1 ¼* **Mister Fantastic**[13] 474 8-10-1 **46** oh1........................ MissSLewis(7) 12 22
(Dai Burchell) *hld up: rdn and wknd over 2f out* **50/1**
00-0 **12** *30* **Polvere D'Oro**[14] 460 4-10-2 **46** oh1...........(be[1]) MissMMullineaux(3) 1
(Michael Mullineaux) *hld up: bhd fr 1/2-way* **50/1**

2m 47.84s (6.74) **Going Correction** +0.275s/f (Slow)
**WFA** 4 from 5yo+ 3lb **12** Ran SP% **116.3**
Speed ratings (Par 101): **88,87,85,84,84 82,79,77,75,75 74,54**
CSF £68.36 CT £934.53 TOTE £5.50: £2.00, £3.20, £4.00; EX 77.70 Trifecta £584.10.
**Owner** Andy Clarke **Bred** Gestut Gorlsdorf **Trained** Willoughton, Lincs
■ Stewards' Enquiry : Mr J Hamilton two-day ban: used whip down the shoulder in the forehand (Mar 26,30)

**FOCUS**
Another weak amateur riders' handicap, run in a slower time than division I. The winner didn't need to find much on recent Southwell form.

### 641 CORAL APP DOWNLOAD FROM THE APP STORE H'CAP 1m 4f 50y(P)
**3:15** (3:15) (Class 5) (0-75,75) 4-Y-O+ **£3,557** (£1,058; £529; £264) **Stalls** Low

Form RPR
-610 **1** **A Little Bit Dusty**[13] 471 6-9-3 **71**........................(p) HayleyTurner 8 79
(Conor Dore) *hld up: hdwy over 4f out: rdn to ld and hung lft fr over 1f out: styd on* **20/1**
4016 **2** *1 ½* **Doldrums (USA)**[12] 494 4-9-4 **75**........................ JoeFanning 4 81
(Mark Johnston) *chsd ldrs: nt clr run over 2f out: rdn and ev ch over 1f out: edgd lft ins fnl f: styd on same pce* **4/1**

212- **3** 1 1/4 **Golden Jubilee (USA)**[83] 8047 5-8-13 70(v) WilliamTwiston-Davies(3) 1 76+
(Nigel Twiston-Davies) *prom: nt clr run over 2f out: rdn over 1f out: cl up whn hmpd ins fnl f: kpt on* **9/4**[1]
1143 **4** 2 3/4 **The Blue Dog (IRE)**[12] 494 7-9-6 74 PaddyAspell 7 74
(Phil McEntee) *a.p: rdn over 2f out: edgd lft and styd on same pce fnl f* **3/1**[2]
00-5 **5** 3/4 **Reflect (IRE)**[29] 250 6-9-2 70 (vt) DaleSwift 6 68
(Derek Shaw) *s.s: hld up: hdwy over 2f out: sn rdn: styd on same pce fnl f* **7/2**[3]
00/0 **6** 2 **Coin Of The Realm (IRE)**[10] 514 9-8-13 74 DanielCremin(7) 5 69
(Miss Imogen Pickard) *s.i.s: hld up: rdn over 1f out: nvr on terms* **33/1**
/0-6 **7** 2 3/4 **Pertemps Networks**[10] 514 10-9-7 75 GrahamGibbons 2 71
(Michael Easterby) *trckd ldr tl led 3f out: rdn and hdd over 1f out: wknd fnl f* **8/1**
-30 **8** 9 **Wild Desert (FR)**[15] 450 9-9-3 71 LiamKeniry 3 47
(Tony Carroll) *led 9f: wknd wl over 1f out* **33/1**
2m 42.0s (0.90) **Going Correction** +0.275s/f (Slow)
**WFA** 4 from 5yo+ 3lb 8 Ran SP% **119.7**
Speed ratings (Par 103): **108,107,106,104,103 102,100,94**
CSF £100.92 CT £257.74 TOTE £10.90: £2.60, £1.70, £1.10; EX 70.10 Trifecta £228.60.
**Owner** David Baldwin & Chris Marsh **Bred** T O C S Limited **Trained** Hubbert's Bridge, Lincs
**FOCUS**
A moderate middle-distance handicap, but it got messy in the straight, with the third looking particularly unlucky. The form is rated as standard.

## 642 CORAL APP DOWNLOAD FROM THE APP STORE MAIDEN STKS 1m 1f 103y(P)
3:45 (3:46) (Class 5) 3-Y-O+ £3,234 (£962; £481; £240) Stalls Low

Form RPR
60-3 **1** **Vastly (USA)**[20] 365 5-10-0 68 AdamBeschizza 7 69
(Julia Feilden) *chsd ldr: rdn 3f out: led 2f out: jst hld on* **5/2**[2]
-243 **2** nk **Coillte Cailin (IRE)**[9] 542 4-9-9 67 TomQueally 5 71+
(Daniel Mark Loughnane) *hld up: stl gng wl in last whn n.m.r over 2f out: hdwy to chse ldrs who were clr over 1f out: sn rdn: r.o wl ins fnl f: too much to do* **15/8**[1]
5 **3** 4 1/2 **Mount Glenn**[17] 409 3-8-7 0 JoeFanning 6 53
(Mark Johnston) *led after 1f: rdn and hdd 2f out: no ex ins fnl f* **4/1**[3]
/05- **4** 1 **Many Levels**[172] 4763 4-10-0 41 GeorgeBaker 3 57
(John Quinn) *hld up: hdwy over 1f out: sn rdn and hung lft: styd on: nt trble ldrs* **25/1**
0 **5** 1 **Mary's Prayer**[24] 323 3-7-11 0 JoeyHaynes(5) 4 44
(John Holt) *prom: lost pl 7f out: rdn over 2f out: n.d after* **66/1**
6- **6** 2 1/2 **Cottam Maybel**[22] 4968 5-9-9 0 GrahamGibbons 8 45
(Michael Easterby) *s.i.s: sn prom: rdn and wknd over 1f out* **50/1**
**7** 5 **Abyaat (IRE)** 3-8-7 0 KieranO'Neill 2 33
(Richard Hannon) *s.s: sn pushed along in rr: wkng whn hmpd over 2f out* **5/1**
/ **8** 6 **Beauchamp Bella** 4-9-9 0 [1] RichardKingscote 1 22
(Paul Fitzsimons) *led 1f: chsd ldrs tl rdn over 2f out: sn wknd* **16/1**
2m 4.72s (3.02) **Going Correction** +0.275s/f (Slow)
**WFA** 3 from 4yo+ 21lb 8 Ran SP% **113.2**
Speed ratings (Par 103): **97,96,92,91,90 88,84,78**
CSF £7.40 TOTE £3.70: £1.30, £1.20, £1.50; EX 7.00 Trifecta £24.20.
**Owner** The Sultans of Speed **Bred** Juddmonte Farms Inc **Trained** Exning, Suffolk
**FOCUS**
A weak maiden with two horses rated in the high 60s coming to the fore. The runner-up looked unlucky having been set plenty to do. The slow time and the fourth are doubts over the form.

## 643 CORAL.CO.UK BEST ODDS GUARANTEED ON RACING H'CAP 1m 1f 103y(P)
4:15 (4:15) (Class 6) (0-65,65) 4-Y-O+ £2,587 (£770; £384; £192) Stalls Low

Form RPR
-251 **1** **Kindlelight Storm (USA)**[17] 406 4-9-4 62 (b) GeorgeBaker 2 71+
(Nick Littmoden) *hld up: hdwy 2f out: shkn up and edgd rt over 1f out: rdn to ld and hung lft wl ins fnl f: r.o* **7/4**[1]
6-53 **2** 2 **Honey Of A Kitten (USA)**[36] 151 6-9-7 65 (v) StevieDonohoe 3 70
(David Evans) *chsd ldrs: rdn over 2f out: led over 1f out: hdd and unable qck wl ins fnl f* **14/1**
2253 **3** 1 3/4 **Yourinthewill (USA)**[5] 578 6-9-6 64 LukeMorris 6 65
(Daniel Mark Loughnane) *hld up: hdwy over 2f out: rdn over 1f out: styd on u.p* **9/2**[2]
0-55 **4** nk **Arabian Heights**[28] 256 6-9-3 64 MichaelJMMurphy(3) 8 64
(Ian Williams) *chsd ldr: chal 3f out: rdn and ev ch over 1f out: styd on same pce ins fnl f* **10/1**
-140 **5** 1 1/4 **Outlaw Torn (IRE)**[17] 406 5-8-13 64 (e) MelissaThompson(7) 5 62
(Richard Guest) *chsd ldrs: lost pl over 2f out: hung lft and r.o ins fnl f* **20/1**
54-2 **6** nse **Colour My World**[28] 264 4-9-6 64 GrahamGibbons 4 62
(Ed McMahon) *led: rdn and hdd over 1f out: wknd ins fnl f* **13/2**
-401 **7** 2 1/4 **Attain**[9] 537 5-8-13 62 ShelleyBirkett(5) 7 55
(Julia Feilden) *hld up: rdn over 2f out: nvr on terms* **5/1**[3]
5/44 **8** nk **I Confess**[15] 445 9-9-7 65 (v) JoeFanning 1 57
(Geoffrey Harker) *hld up: rdn over 3f out: n.d* **14/1**
-550 **9** 4 1/2 **Rainford Glory (IRE)**[11] 497 4-8-13 57 LiamKeniry 9 40
(Patrick Morris) *hld up: hdwy over 5f out: rdn and wknd over 1f out* **50/1**
2m 2.62s (0.92) **Going Correction** +0.275s/f (Slow) 9 Ran SP% **113.7**
Speed ratings (Par 101): **106,104,102,102,101 101,99,98,94**
CSF £29.04 CT £95.88 TOTE £2.70: £1.20, £2.50, £1.30; EX 25.50 Trifecta £105.80.
**Owner** Kindlelight Ltd, N Shields & N Littmoden **Bred** Kirsten Rausing **Trained** Newmarket, Suffolk
**FOCUS**
A modest handicap but they went an honest pace and the form looks straightforward enough. Further progress from the winner.

## 644 COMPARE BOOKMAKERS AT BOOKMAKERS.CO.UK H'CAP 5f 20y(P)
4:45 (4:47) (Class 2) 4-Y-O+ £28,354 (£8,487; £4,243; £2,124; £1,057) Stalls Low

Form RPR
-142 **1** **Even Stevens**[27] 271 6-9-4 98 (v) FrederikTylicki 3 107
(Scott Dixon) *mde all: rdn over 1f out: r.o* **20/1**
-213 **2** 1/2 **Silken Express (IRE)**[16] 431 5-9-1 95 TomQueally 8 102
(Robert Cowell) *chsd ldrs: rdn over 1f out: r.o* **11/1**
11-2 **3** 1/2 **Dangerous Age**[15] 444 4-8-1 81 ow1 JoeFanning 12 86+
(J W Hills) *racd on outer but a.p: shkn up over 1f out: rdn and edgd lft ins fnl f: r.o* **5/1**[2]
540- **4** 1/2 **Ubetterbegood (ARG)**[61] 8334 6-8-11 91 (p) JimmyQuinn 10 94
(Robert Cowell) *dwlt: hld up: rdn: swtchd lft and r.o wl ins fnl f: nt rch ldrs* **25/1**
203- **5** 3/4 **Addictive Dream (IRE)**[53] 8395 7-9-5 99 AdrianNicholls 2 100
(David Nicholls) *hld up: rdn over 1f out: r.o ins fnl f: nrst fin* **10/1**
4-42 **6** nk **Muhdiq (USA)**[16] 431 5-7-12 81 JulieBurke(3) 5 81
(Mike Murphy) *a.p: rdn to chse wnr over 1f out tl styd on same pce ins fnl f* **10/1**
64-1 **7** nk **Forest Edge (IRE)**[29] 249 5-9-10 104 (b) GeorgeBaker 9 103
(David Evans) *broke wl enough: lost pl 4f out: sn pushed along: r.o ins fnl f* **7/1**
56-1 **8** 1 **Swiss Cross**[16] 431 7-9-5 99 (t) PaddyAspell 7 94
(Phil McEntee) *prom: rdn over 1f out: styd on* **10/1**
2112 **9** 1/2 **Lexi's Hero (IRE)**[17] 412 6-8-4 84 (v) HayleyTurner 6 77
(Richard Fahey) *prom: shkn up 1/2-way: sn hung lft: styd on same pce fnl f* **9/2**[1]
-511 **10** hd **Caspian Prince (IRE)**[36] 148 5-8-13 93 (t) LukeMorris 11 85
(Tony Carroll) *trckd ldr but forced to r wd: rdn over 1f out: no ex fnl f* **9/1**
0-05 **11** 1 1/2 **Doctor Parkes**[27] 271 8-8-5 85 (e[1]) DavidProbert 1 72
(Stuart Williams) *prom: pushed along and n.m.r 1/2-way: no ex fnl f* **11/2**[3]
-305 **12** 1 1/4 **Jiroft (ITY)**[16] 431 7-8-10 90 (v[1]) GrahamGibbons 4 73
(Robert Cowell) *s.i.s: hld up: rdn over 1f out: n.d* **20/1**
1m 2.2s (-0.10) **Going Correction** +0.275s/f (Slow) 12 Ran SP% **121.7**
Speed ratings (Par 109): **111,110,109,108,107 106,106,104,104,103 101,99**
CSF £224.93 CT £1306.80 TOTE £20.70: £6.20, £3.80, £1.90; EX 273.30 Trifecta £2125.80.
**Owner** Paul J Dixon **Bred** Mrs Yvette Dixon **Trained** Babworth, Notts
■ Stewards' Enquiry : Adrian Nicholls four-day ban: used whip above permitted level (Mar 3-6)
**FOCUS**
A valuable and fiercely competitive handicap featuring a number of in-form horses. The winner set a decent pace and posted a personal best.

## 645 32RED FREE £10 BONUS MAIDEN FILLIES' STKS 7f 32y(P)
5:15 (5:16) (Class 5) 3-Y-O+ £3,234 (£962; £481; £240) Stalls High

Form RPR
05-2 **1** **Arabian Music (IRE)**[26] 275 3-8-7 70 DavidProbert 3 75+
(David Simcock) *chsd ldrs: shkn up to ld over 1f out: pushed clr* **1/1**[1]
64-4 **2** 4 **River Goddess (IRE)**[26] 275 3-8-7 67 RichardKingscote 4 64
(Charles Hills) *trckd ldr tl led wl over 1f out: sn rdn and hdd: no ex ins fnl f* **5/1**[3]
0- **3** 1/2 **Trust The Wind**[109] 7645 3-8-7 0 RobertHavlin 8 63+
(John Gosden) *s.i.s: hld up: hdwy over 1f out: sn rdn and hung lft: styd on same pce fnl f* **13/8**[2]
B0- **4** 4 **Synonym (ITY)**[129] 7162 3-8-7 0 JoeFanning 5 52
(J W Hills) *prom: effrt and hmpd over 1f out: wknd ins fnl f* **25/1**
3-44 **5** 2 **Female Strategy (IRE)**[19] 373 3-8-7 55 LukeMorris 9 46
(Mark Brisbourne) *hld up: rdn over 2f out: hdwy over 1f out: wkng whn hung lft fnl f* **16/1**
56 **6** 5 **On And On (IRE)**[25] 291 4-9-10 0 TonyHamilton 2 45
(Richard Fahey) *mid-div: pushed along over 2f out: hmpd over 1f out: wknd fnl f* **28/1**
-000 **7** 3 1/2 **Mrs Medley**[25] 298 8-9-5 20 (v) AnnStokell(5) 6 30
(Ann Stokell) *plld hrd: led: rdn and hdd wl over 1f out: sn hung lft: wknd fnl f* **100/1**
**8** 6 **Cool Reception** 3-8-7 0 JamesSullivan 1 7
(Ollie Pears) *s.i.s: hld up: wknd over 2f out* **25/1**
1m 31.05s (1.45) **Going Correction** +0.275s/f (Slow)
**WFA** 3 from 4yo+ 17lb 8 Ran SP% **122.8**
Speed ratings (Par 100): **102,97,96,92,90 84,80,73**
CSF £7.27 TOTE £2.00: £1.10, £1.40, £1.10; EX 7.40 Trifecta £19.80.
**Owner** Ahmed Jaber **Bred** Rabbah Bloodstock Limited **Trained** Newmarket, Suffolk
**FOCUS**
An ordinary fillies' maiden lacking much depth. The time was modest but the form still makes sense.

## 646 LADBROKES H'CAP 7f 32y(P)
5:45 (5:45) (Class 5) (0-70,70) 4-Y-O+ £3,557 (£1,058; £529; £264) Stalls High

Form RPR
4-00 **1** **Dimitar (USA)**[9] 540 5-9-1 64 LiamKeniry 9 74
(Johnny Farrelly) *hld up: hdwy over 2f out: rdn to ld and hung lft ins fnl f: r.o* **16/1**
0-20 **2** 1 **Conry (IRE)**[33] 181 8-8-11 65 GeorgeDowning(5) 8 72
(Ian Williams) *hld up: hdwy over 1f out: rdn and edgd lft ins fnl f: r.o* **7/2**[2]
0-25 **3** 2 **Strong Man**[29] 245 6-9-5 68 GrahamGibbons 1 70
(Michael Easterby) *chsd ldrs: rdn over 2f out: ev ch ins fnl f: styd on same pce* **3/1**[1]
3-00 **4** 1 1/4 **Avonmore Star**[9] 540 6-8-10 59 BenCurtis 10 58
(Alan McCabe) *a.p: rdn and ev ch ins fnl f: no ex towards fin* **66/1**
24-4 **5** 1 1/2 **One Scoop Or Two**[9] 539 8-9-7 70 (v) TomQueally 5 64
(Andrew Hollinshead) *hld up: rdn over 2f out: styd on ins fnl f: nt trble ldrs* **7/1**[3]
0-36 **6** 3/4 **Mr Lando**[9] 539 5-9-0 63 RobertHavlin 3 55
(Richard Lee) *hld up: rdn over 1f out: no imp fnl f* **11/1**
3441 **7** hd **Munaawib**[11] 503 6-8-13 67 (bt) RyanWhile(5) 6 59
(David C Griffiths) *prom: rdn over 1f out: wkng whn n.m.r ins fnl f* **9/1**
4-01 **8** 3/4 **Kakapuka**[15] 451 7-9-7 70 GeorgeBaker 12 60
(Anabel K Murphy) *led: hdd 2f out: led again over 1f out: hdd ins fnl f: wknd towards fin* **9/1**
300- **9** 3/4 **See The Storm**[175] 5841 6-9-4 70 NeilFarley(3) 11 58
(Eric Alston) *chsd ldr tl led 2f out: sn rdn and hdd: wknd ins fnl f* **28/1**
000- **10** 1 **Blazeofenchantment (USA)**[80] 8095 4-9-2 68 BillyCray(3) 7 53
(Richard Guest) *s.i.s: hld up: hdwy u.p over 2f out: wknd over 1f out* **33/1**
1330 **11** 2 **Kyllachy Star**[12] 496 8-9-6 69 (v) HayleyTurner 4 49
(Richard Fahey) *hld up: rdn over 1f out: nvr on terms* **7/1**[3]
50 **12** 3 3/4 **Hejaz (IRE)**[17] 410 4-9-0 63 StevieDonohoe 2 33
(Tim Pitt) *s.i.s: hld up: a in rr* **50/1**
1m 30.34s (0.74) **Going Correction** +0.275s/f (Slow) 12 Ran SP% **116.3**
Speed ratings (Par 103): **106,104,102,101,99 98,98,97,96,95 93,88**
CSF £68.68 CT £223.53 TOTE £18.20: £7.70, £1.60, £2.00; EX 99.90 Trifecta £626.20.
**Owner** P Tosh **Bred** Ashbrittle Stud **Trained** Bridgwater, Somerset
**FOCUS**
A modest handicap in which they went a solid gallop and the front two came from off the pace. The winner is rated back to his C&D win in September.

T/Jkpt: Not won. T/Plt: £193.20 to a £1 stake. Pool: £105860.41 - 399.95 winning tickets T/Qpdt: £11.50 to a £1 stake. Pool: £10349.56 - 660.90 winning tickets CR

## 563 SOUTHWELL (L-H)
Tuesday, February 18

**OFFICIAL GOING: Standard**
Wind: Moderate; across Weather: Cloudy with sunny periods

### 647 DOWNLOAD THE LADBROKES APP H'CAP 1m (F)
1:55 (1:55) (Class 5) (0-70,70) 4-Y-O+ £3,234 (£962; £481; £240) Stalls Low

Form RPR
-202 1 **Conry (IRE)**[1] 646 8-8-11 65 GeorgeDowning(5) 6 77+
(Ian Williams) *trckd ldrs: hdwy on outer wl over 3f out: led over 2f out: rdn clr over 1f out: styd on* 9/2[3]
-212 2 1 1/4 **Queen Of Skies (IRE)**[21] 366 5-9-0 63 AndrewMullen 1 70
(Michael Appleby) *in tch: hdwy over 3f out: rdn along wl over 2f out: styd on to chse wnr over 1f out: drvn and kpt on same pce fnl f* 3/1[1]
3-60 3 nk **Raging Bear (USA)**[15] 457 4-9-2 70 (b) RyanTate(5) 9 76
(James Evans) *dwlt and in rr: hdwy on outer 3f out: rdn over 2f out: styd on fnl f: nrst fin* 8/1
1-30 4 5 **Dandarrell**[21] 366 7-8-13 62 (be) PaulMulrennan 8 57
(Julie Camacho) *t.k.h: cl up: pushed along 3f out: rdn over 2f out and grad wknd* 5/1
003- 5 shd **Self Employed**[82] 8087 7-9-2 65 LukeMorris 4 59
(Garry Woodward) *trckd ldng pair: hdwy over 3f out: effrt and ev ch over 2f out: sn rdn and grad wknd* 6/1
-121 6 4 1/2 **Silly Billy (IRE)**[19] 388 6-9-4 70 (p) BillyCray(3) 5 54
(John Balding) *t.k.h: led: pushed along and hdd 3f out: sn rdn and wknd wl over 1f out* 4/1[2]
1-43 7 12 **Emperatriz**[9] 548 4-9-7 70 GrahamGibbons 3 26
(John Holt) *t.k.h: chsd ldng pair on inner: pushed along and lost pl 1/2-way: sn bhd* 9/1

1m 44.34s (0.64) **Going Correction** +0.15s/f (Slow) 7 Ran SP% 115.2
Speed ratings (Par 103): **102,100,100,95,95 90,78**
CSF £18.70 CT £104.24 TOTE £6.10: £3.60, £2.00; EX 27.10 Trifecta £248.80.
**Owner** Ian Williams **Bred** Shay White **Trained** Portway, Worcs

**FOCUS**
A moderate handicap. The pace looked sound. The winner is rated up a length or so on his form the previous day.

### 648 CORAL MOBILE "JUST THREE CLICKS TO BET" H'CAP 1m 4f (F)
2:25 (2:26) (Class 6) (0-60,64) 4-Y-O+ £2,587 (£770; £384; £192) Stalls Low

Form RPR
305- 1 **Kingscombe (USA)**[25] 7847 5-9-3 55 RobertHavlin 5 69
(Linda Jewell) *trckd ldrs: hdwy 4f out: sn cl up: led 2f out and sn rdn: drvn and hdd jst over 1f out: rallied gamely u.p ins fnl f: edgd rt and led again nr fin* 14/1
-013 2 nk **Marina Ballerina**[29] 252 6-8-12 55 TimClark(5) 4 68
(Roy Bowring) *chsd ldrs: pushed along 1/2-way: sn lost pl and in rr: hdwy on outer wl over 3f out: wd st: styd on u.p to chal wl over 1f out: slt ld jst over 1f out: sn drvn: hdd and no ex nr fin* 9/1[3]
405- 3 2 1/4 **Travel (USA)**[122] 7379 4-9-2 57 JoeFanning 9 66
(Mark Johnston) *trckd ldrs: hdwy 4f out: cl up 3f out: rdn 2f out and ev ch tl drvn ent fnl f and kpt on same pce* 2/1[1]
0604 4 12 **Mazij**[4] 612 6-9-3 55 PaddyAspell 2 45
(Peter Hiatt) *set gd pce: pushed along over 3f out: rdn and hdd over 2f out: sn drvn and wknd* 14/1
00-4 5 3/4 **Kingaroo (IRE)**[14] 475 8-8-8 46 LukeMorris 7 35
(Garry Woodward) *cl up: rdn along over 4f out: sn lost pl and bhd: edgd lft and plugged on fr over 1f out* 33/1
50-1 6 7 **Samoset**[14] 475 4-9-3 58 BenCurtis 3 36
(Alan Swinbank) *hld up in tch: hdwy over 3f out: rdn along wl over 2f out: sn btn* 11/4[2]
5111 7 hd **Fire In Babylon (IRE)**[7] 569 6-9-12 64 6ex (b) AdamBeschizza 1 41
(Noel Quinlan) *chsd ldrs on inner: pushed along wl over 3f out: rdn wl over 2f out: sn wknd* 2/1[1]

2m 42.13s (1.13) **Going Correction** +0.15s/f (Slow)
**WFA** 4 from 5yo+ 3lb 7 Ran SP% 119.6
Speed ratings (Par 101): **102,101,100,92,91 87,87**
CSF £134.51 CT £365.24 TOTE £15.40: £4.80, £3.90; EX 150.70 Trifecta £1140.30.
**Owner** Peter Oppenheimer **Bred** Juddmonte Farms Inc **Trained** Sutton Valence, Kent
■ Stewards' Enquiry : Ben Curtis three-day ban: used whip without giving gelding time to respond (Mar 4-6)

**FOCUS**
A weak contest, with only the principals running to form. The second sets the standard.

### 649 CORAL APP DOWNLOAD FROM THE APP STORE MAIDEN STKS 1m 3f (F)
3:00 (3:01) (Class 5) 3-Y-O+ £3,234 (£962; £481; £240) Stalls Low

Form RPR
1 **Turnbuckle** 4-9-12 0 JoeFanning 8 86+
(Mark Johnston) *trckd ldrs: hdwy 4f out: sn chsng ldr: effrt: rn green and edgd lft over 2f out: rdn wl over 1f out: styd on to ld appr fnl f: clr whn broke down nr fin: fatally injured* 11/10[1]
2 2 3 3/4 **Puzzle Time**[15] 463 4-9-7 0 WilliamCarson 6 75
(Giles Bravery) *trckd ldrs: hdwy to ld 4f out: rdn over 2f out: drvn and hdd appr fnl f: kpt on same pce* 4/1[3]
4-23 3 10 **Yeah Baby (IRE)**[18] 403 3-8-0 70 LukeMorris 7 54
(Charles Hills) *sluggish s and remnders early: hdwy to trck ldrs after 3f: effrt 4f out: rdn to chse ldng pair 3f out: sn drvn and one pce* 7/4[2]
4 5 **Crooked Arrow (IRE)**[38] 6-9-9 0 (p) ShirleyTeasdale(5) 9 55
(Marjorie Fife) *dwlt and in rr: hdwy 1/2-way: chsd ldrs over 3f out: sn rdn and no imp* 16/1
64 5 15 **Kastela Stari**[8] 558 7-9-9 0 JamesSullivan 5 24
(Tim Fitzgerald) *in rr: pushed along 1/2-way: sme hdwy fnl 2f: nvr a factor* 25/1
06-4 6 31 **Rocky Hill Ridge**[11] 515 3-8-5 32 (p) BenCurtis 1
(Alan McCabe) *t.k.h: led 3f: cl up tl rdn along and lost pl 5f out: sn bhd* 66/1
0 7 2 1/2 **Norman's Star**[17] 422 3-8-5 0 [1] ChrisCatlin 3
(Chris Dwyer) *midfield: rdn along 5f out: sn outpcd and bhd* 50/1
0 8 shd **Miss Bella Rose**[15] 463 7-9-6 0 (e[1]) BillyCray(3) 2
(Richard Guest) *dwlt and in rr: rdn along 1/2-way: sn outpcd and bhd* 100/1
5-4 9 3/4 **Au Renoir**[17] 434 4-9-7 0 PaulMulrennan 4
(Kevin Ryan) *t.k.h: cl up: led after 3f: pushed along and hdd 4f out: sn rdn and wknd* 14/1

2m 28.48s (0.48) **Going Correction** +0.15s/f (Slow)
**WFA** 3 from 4yo 23lb 4 from 6yo+ 2lb 9 Ran SP% 124.8
Speed ratings (Par 103): **104,101,94,90,79 56,55,55,54**
CSF £6.78 TOTE £2.00: £1.10, £1.40, £1.10; EX 7.50 Trifecta £12.80.
**Owner** Sheikh Hamdan bin Mohammed Al Maktoum **Bred** Darley **Trained** Middleham Moor, N Yorks

**FOCUS**
A race which was marred by the death of the winner. The form is rated around the runner-up.

### 650 32RED FREE £10 BONUS H'CAP 5f (F)
3:35 (3:35) (Class 4) (0-85,82) 3-Y-O £5,822 (£1,732; £865; £432) Stalls High

Form RPR
40-3 1 **Fuel Injection**[14] 481 3-8-2 63 oh4 (p) JamesSullivan 5 65
(Paul Midgley) *cl up: slt ld 1/2-way: rdn and hdd ent fnl f: drvn and rallied wl to ld nr fin* 16/1
2122 2 nk **Argent Touch**[14] 481 3-7-11 65 oh3 ow2 AdamMcLean(7) 4 66
(Derek Shaw) *cl up: effrt 2f out: rdn to ld ent fnl f: drvn and edgd lft last 100yds: hdd and no ex towards fin* 6/1[2]
-231 3 1 1/4 **Ealain Aibrean (IRE)**[11] 512 3-8-6 67 ChrisCatlin 3 63
(David Evans) *led: hdd 1/2-way: cl up and rdn over 2f out: drvn ent fnl f and kpt on same pce* 14/1
2311 4 1 3/4 **The Dandy Yank (IRE)**[13] 485 3-8-8 69 WilliamCarson 8 59
(Jamie Osborne) *cl up: ev ch 2f out: sn rdn and one pce appr fnl f* 8/1[3]
04-2 5 3/4 **Expect**[37] 149 3-9-7 82 MartinHarley 1 69+
(Jeremy Noseda) *s.i.s: in tch on wd outside: rdn along 1/2-way and sn edgd lft to far rail: drvn and one pce fr over 1f out* 1/1[1]
02-6 6 1 3/4 **Soul Instinct**[18] 401 3-8-4 65 JimmyQuinn 2 46
(Kevin Ryan) *cl up: effrt and ev ch over 2f out: sn rdn and grad wknd* 6/1[2]
41-3 7 1 1/2 **Under Approval**[17] 429 3-8-1 65 JulieBurke(3) 6 41
(David O'Meara) *in tch towards stands' rail: rdn along over 3f out and sn outpcd* 8/1[3]

1m 1.08s (1.38) **Going Correction** +0.275s/f (Slow) 7 Ran SP% 113.3
Speed ratings (Par 99): **99,98,96,93,92 89,87**
CSF £104.31 CT £1382.90 TOTE £20.10: £7.50, £2.60; EX 95.50 Trifecta £310.80.
**Owner** Mrs Mandy Verity **Bred** Whitsbury Manor Stud & Pigeon House Stud **Trained** Westow, N Yorks

**FOCUS**
A modest sprint handicap, which was run at a good pace. Not strong form for the grade. The first two were closely matched on their C&D latest.

### 651 COMPARE BOOKMAKERS AT BOOKMAKERS.CO.UK (S) STKS 6f (F)
4:05 (4:07) (Class 6) 3-Y-O+ £2,587 (£770; £384; £192) Stalls Low

Form RPR
30-3 1 **Elusive Hawk (IRE)**[29] 262 10-9-8 80 (v) ChrisCatlin 3 67
(David Evans) *towards rr and pushed along over 3f out: hdwy over 2f out: swtchd rt to outer and chal over 1f out: rdn to ld ent fnl f and sn hung bdly lft: drvn out* 5/4[1]
-342 2 1/2 **Meebo (IRE)**[9] 547 3-7-12 55 ow1 ShelleyBirkett(5) 6 58
(J R Jenkins) *chsd ldrs: hdwy over 2f out: rdn to chal on inner wl over 1f out and ev ch tl drvn: carried lft and one pce last 100yds* 8/1[3]
-554 3 1 1/2 **Greenhead High**[26] 297 6-9-1 65 AnnaHesketh(7) 13 61
(David Nicholls) *qckly away and cl up: led over 3f out: rdn and hdd 2f out: cl up tl hld whn sltly hmpd ins fnl f: one pce after* 10/1
6-62 4 nk **Alpha Tauri (USA)**[7] 565 8-9-10 67 (t) BillyCray(3) 9 65
(Richard Guest) *slt ld: hdd over 3f out and cl up: rdn to ld again 2f out: drvn over 1f out: hdd ent fnl f: hld whn n.m.r and swtchd rt last 100yds: one pce* 4/1[2]
3-04 5 6 **Laughing Rock (IRE)**[21] 362 4-9-3 57 (p) AndrewMullen 5 36
(Michael Appleby) *midfield: pushed along and hdwy on outer 1/2-way: rdn over 2f out: kpt on u.p fr over 1f out* 12/1
00-4 6 1 1/2 **Red Biba (IRE)**[9] 547 3-7-13 47 (p) NataliaGemelova(3) 8 27
(Alan McCabe) *chsd ldrs: rdn along wl over 2f out: drvn and wknd wl over 1f out* 50/1
-124 7 2 1/2 **Prince Of Passion (CAN)**[13] 489 6-9-13 63 (v) JoeFanning 1 33
(Derek Shaw) *a towards rr* 12/1
0-6 8 1/2 **Sicilian Bay (IRE)**[9] 551 3-7-11 0 ShirleyTeasdale(5) 11 17
(Paul Midgley) *dwlt: a towards rr* 66/1
00-6 9 nk **Mitchum**[7] 565 5-9-8 62 DaleSwift 10 25
(Ron Barr) *a towards rr* 20/1
0-06 10 6 **Fathom Five (IRE)**[14] 478 10-9-10 56 NeilFarley(3) 4 11
(Shaun Harris) *cl up on inner: rdn along 1/2-way: sn wknd* 33/1
04-0 11 hd **Girl At The Sands (IRE)**[17] 424 4-9-3 57 (vt[1]) JimmyQuinn 7
(Edward Creighton) *dwlt and a in rr* 20/1
-510 12 9 **Take The Lead**[17] 432 4-9-8 66 AdrianNicholls 2 +
(David Nicholls) *chsd ldrs: rdn wl over 2f out: sn wknd* 12/1

1m 16.94s (0.44) **Going Correction** +0.15s/f (Slow)
**WFA** 3 from 4yo+ 15lb 12 Ran SP% 123.6
Speed ratings (Par 101): **103,102,100,99,91 89,86,85,85,77 77,65**
CSF £11.87 TOTE £2.30: £1.10, £2.20, £3.20; EX 14.40 Trifecta £148.60.There was no bid for the winner.
**Owner** Mrs E Evans **Bred** J Fike **Trained** Pandy, Monmouths

**FOCUS**
A fair effort from the winner in a seller in which the leading quartet came clear, few ever threatening a serious blow. With doubts over most of these the winner did not need to be at his best.

### 652 32RED MEGA MOOLAH MILLIONAIRES CLAIMING STKS 2m (F)
4:40 (4:40) (Class 6) 4-Y-O+ £3,234 (£962; £481; £240) Stalls Low

Form RPR
20-6 1 **Noguchi (IRE)**[23] 350 9-9-4 76 (b) TomQueally 7 72+
(George Margarson) *trckd ldrs: cl up 7f out: led wl over 3f out and sn clr: eased fnl f* 6/4[1]
/324 2 3 3/4 **Hail Tiberius**[4] 606 7-8-8 64 (t) AlistairRawlinson(7) 4 55
(Martin Keighley) *cl up: led after 1f: hdd and pushed along 1/2-way: rdn along over 4f out: chsd wnr over 3f out: drvn and kpt on same pce fnl 2f: no ch w wnr* 7/2[3]
4/0- 3 2 1/2 **Daliance (IRE)**[25] 3960 5-9-4 79 (p) LukeMorris 5 55
(Lucy Wadham) *chsd ldrs: pushed along after 5f: rdn and outpcd over 7 out: drvn along over 3f out: plugged on fnl 2f* 7/4[2]
4 7 **Jaunty Dove**[632] 12-8-2 0 DanielCremin(7) 1 38
(Miss Imogen Pickard) *s.i.s: hdwy to chse ldrs after 2f: rdn along 1/2-way: sn outpcd and bhd: plugged on u.p fnl 3f to take modest 4th towards fin* 50/1

-305 **5** *nk* **Willow Island (IRE)**[7] 569 5-8-13 38 ChrisCatlin 6 41
(David Evans) *chsd ldrs: rdn along over 5f out: wknd 3f out* 25/1

4654 **6** *48* **Monzino (USA)**[7] 569 6-9-8 64 (b) RussKennemore 8
(Michael Chapman) *led 1f: chsd ldrs: rdn along over 7f out: sn lost pl and bhd: t.o fnl 2f* 10/1

00-0 **7** *99* **Sings Poet**[18] 400 4-8-7 33 (b) WilliamCarson 3
(Peter Hiatt) *prom: cl up after 3f: led 1/2-way: rdn along 4f out: hdd over 3f out and wknd qckly: bhd and virtually p.u wl over 1f out* 50/1

3m 48.09s (2.59) **Going Correction** +0.15s/f (Slow)
**WFA** 4 from 5yo+ 6lb 7 Ran SP% **115.4**
Speed ratings (Par 101): **99,97,95,92,92 68,18**
CSF £7.35 TOTE £2.40: £1.10, £3.30; EX 7.40 Trifecta £16.10.
**Owner** Mrs F Shaw **Bred** Cora Srl **Trained** Newmarket, Suffolk

**FOCUS**
A very one-sided claimer with doubts over the whole field. The poor fifth gives perspective.

## 653 32RED.COM H'CAP 1m (F)
**5:10** (5:10) (Class 6) (0-55,55) 3-Y-O £2,587 (£770; £384; £192) **Stalls** Low

Form RPR

-515 **1** **Frankthetank (IRE)**[28] 267 3-9-7 55 (p) JoeFanning 5 68
(Keith Dalgleish) *led: pushed along 3f out: sn hdd and rdn: cl up and drvn wl over 1f out: led again ent fnl f: styd on strly* 11/10[1]

00-5 **2** *5* **Streethowlingmama (USA)**[14] 480 3-8-12 46 oh1 LiamKeniry 7 48
(Olly Stevens) *cl up: chal over 3f out: slt ld wl over 2f out: sn rdn: drvn and edgd lft jst over 1f out: hdd ent fnl f: kpt on same pce* 8/1

5-52 **3** *½* **Cascadia (IRE)**[10] 543 3-9-0 53 JoeyHaynes(5) 6 53
(K R Burke) *trckd ldng pair: hdwy 3f out: rdn over 2f out: swtchd rt and drvn over 1f out: no imp* 9/2[2]

00-2 **4** *2¼* **Romantic Bliss (IRE)**[10] 541 3-8-9 50 (b) RobJFitzpatrick(7) 4 45
(K R Burke) *trckd ldng pair: hdwy 3f out: rdn over 2f out: drvn and one pce fr over 1f out* 14/1

5-21 **5** *1* **Royal Bushida**[27] 280 3-8-13 47 DaleSwift 1 40
(Derek Shaw) *sn outpcd and bhd: pushed along 1/2-way: hdwy over 2f out: styd on appr fnl f: nrst fin* 5/1[3]

0-54 **6** *7* **Previous Acclaim (IRE)**[14] 480 3-8-9 48 ShelleyBirkett(5) 3 25
(Julia Feilden) *chsd ldrs: rdn along wl over 3f out: sn wknd* 16/1

060 **7** *10* **Intensive (IRE)**[25] 316 3-9-4 52 WilliamCarson 2
(Jamie Osborne) *in tch: pushed along after 3f: sn rdn and outpcd fr over 3f out* 10/1

1m 46.28s (2.58) **Going Correction** +0.15s/f (Slow) 7 Ran SP% **115.2**
Speed ratings (Par 95): **93,88,87,85,84 77,67**
CSF £11.11 CT £29.90 TOTE £1.80: £1.50, £4.10; EX 13.60 Trifecta £73.40.
**Owner** Raymond McNeill **Bred** Burgage Stud **Trained** Carluke, S Lanarks

**FOCUS**
A moderate handicap with no depth, but the easy winner is progressive and a slightly positive view has been taken of the form.
T/Jkpt: £19,421.60 to a £1 stake. Pool: £54,708.86 - 2.00 winning units T/Plt: £497.30 to a £1 stake. Pool: £99,502.00 - 146.06 winning units T/Qpdt: £25.30 to a £1 stake. Pool: £8,964.71 - 261.60 winning units JR

# 586 KEMPTON (A.W) (R-H)
## Wednesday, February 19

**OFFICIAL GOING: Standard**
Wind: Almost Nil Weather: Fine

## 654 BETBRIGHT.COM H'CAP 5f (P)
**5:25** (5:25) (Class 5) (0-70,70) 4-Y-O+ £2,587 (£770; £384; £192) **Stalls** Low

Form RPR

2-21 **1** **Iffranesia (FR)**[12] 510 4-9-4 67 (p) TomQueally 1 77
(Robert Cowell) *s.i.s: pushed along in 7th early: gng bttr fr 1/2-way: gd prog over 1f out to ld jst ins fnl f: rdn and styd on wl* 11/4[2]

435- **2** *1¼* **Novabridge**[50] 8457 6-9-1 64 (b) LiamKeniry 8 70
(Neil Mulholland) *dropped in fr wdst draw and hld up last: pushed along 1/2-way: stl last jst over 1f out: rdn and r.o fnl f: tk 2nd last stride* 20/1

2112 **3** *hd* **Roy's Legacy**[4] 628 5-9-3 69 MichaelJMMurphy(3) 7 74+
(Shaun Harris) *chsd ldrs on outer: rdn 1/2-way: prog to chal and upsides 1f out: one pce* 5/2[1]

1014 **4** *¾* **Sir Geoffrey (IRE)**[12] 510 8-9-6 69 (p) FrederikTylicki 2 71
(Scott Dixon) *mde most: drvn over 1f out: hdd and one pce jst ins fnl f* 8/1

0442 **5** *shd* **Desert Strike**[7] 572 8-9-7 70 (p) HayleyTurner 4 72
(Conor Dore) *w ldr: rdn and nt qckn over 1f out: one pce fnl f* 3/1[3]

042- **6** *1* **Dawn Catcher**[91] 7969 4-8-10 59 JimmyQuinn 6 57
(Geoffrey Deacon) *awkward s: trckd ldrs: cl up wl over 1f out: nt clr run after: no prog whn in the clr last 150yds* 20/1

4352 **7** *½* **Your Gifted (IRE)**[16] 466 7-8-2 56 oh1 (v) ShirleyTeasdale(5) 3 56+
(Lisa Williamson) *trckd ldrs: cl up bhd ldng trio fr 2f out but trapped on inner and nowhere to go after: steadily lost pl fnl f* 14/1

-523 **8** *5* **Pull The Pin (IRE)**[7] 572 5-9-5 68 (bt) WilliamCarson 5 46
(Ann Stokell) *racd on outer of ldng trio: rdn over 1f out: wknd qckly fnl f* 10/1

59.55s (-0.95) **Going Correction** 0.0s/f (Stan) 8 Ran SP% **116.6**
Speed ratings (Par 103): **107,105,104,103,103 101,100,92**
CSF £55.20 CT £152.23 TOTE £3.10: £1.40, £4.00, £1.50; EX 44.80 Trifecta £150.50.
**Owner** Cyril Humphris **Bred** Cyril Humphris **Trained** Six Mile Bottom, Cambs

**FOCUS**
Given there was a three-way battle for the lead it's no surprise this was set up for the closers. The winner continues to progress.

## 655 BETBRIGHT MONEYBACK OFFERS H'CAP 1m 2f (P)
**5:55** (5:57) (Class 5) (0-75,79) 4-Y-O+ £2,587 (£770; £384; £192) **Stalls** Low

Form RPR

0-01 **1** **Top Diktat**[20] 379 6-9-6 74 GeorgeBaker 9 83
(Gary Moore) *hld up in last quartet: stdy prog fr wl over 2f out: clsd over 1f out: rdn and styd on to ld last 50yds* 7/1[3]

15-1 **2** *nk* **Commissar**[4] 627 5-9-6 79 6ex (t) GeorgeDowning(5) 8 87+
(Ian Williams) *hld up in midfield: prog wl over 2f out: led over 1f out gng wl: idled once in front: hrd pressed and kpt on fnl f: hdd last 50yds* 2/1[1]

0/0- **3** *1½* **Chain Of Events**[262] 1753 7-9-4 72 HayleyTurner 3 77
(Michael Wigham) *led: set mod pce but untrbld: rdn and hdd over 1f out: kpt on fnl f* 20/1

0-26 **4** *1* **Travelling**[31] 250 5-9-3 74 WilliamTwiston-Davies(3) 1 77+
(Tony Carroll) *trckd ldrs: trapped on inner fr wl over 1f out: styd on fnl f but nvr able to fully rcvr* 10/1

0-54 **5** *½* **Liberty Jack (IRE)**[14] 493 4-9-1 70 WilliamCarson 10 72+
(Jim Boyle) *stdd s: hld up in last: stl there wl over 1f out: taken to outer and jst pushed along after: styd on strly fnl f: too much to do* 12/1

566- **6** *hd* **Gravitate**[76] 7840 5-8-11 65 (t) RobertHavlin 4 67
(Paul Webber) *trckd ldrs: outpcd and lost pl fr 2f out: styd on again ins fnl f: gng on at fin* 14/1

246- **7** *nk* **Mcbirney (USA)**[63] 8337 7-8-8 67 TimClark(5) 11 68
(Paul D'Arcy) *hld up in last quartet: rapid prog on wd outside fr 3f out to press ldrs over 1f out: effrt flattened out fnl f* 14/1

14- **8** *nk* **Triple Chocolate**[62] 8345 4-9-5 74 JimmyQuinn 13 74
(Roger Ingram) *racd on outer: prog to join ldrs 1/2-way: rdn to chal 2f out: nt qckn over 1f out: wknd qckly last 100yds* 5/1[2]

03-6 **9** *1¼* **Kelpie Blitz (IRE)**[21] 369 5-9-3 71 (t) TomQueally 5 69
(Seamus Durack) *t.k.h: hld up and nvr beyond midfield: shkn up and no prog over 1f out* 14/1

001- **10** *½* **Ssafa**[84] 8059 6-9-3 71 (p) FrederikTylicki 6 68
(Alastair Lidderdale) *chsd ldrs: rdn over 2f out: steadily wknd over 1f out* 20/1

5/ **11** *¾* **Treasure The Ridge (IRE)**[116] 7553 5-9-0 75 (b) DavidParkes(7) 2 70
(Brett Johnson) *hld up towards rr: shkn up 2f out: no prog* 33/1

653- **12** *2¼* **Cravat**[268] 2710 5-8-13 67 ChrisCatlin 12 58
(Ed de Giles) *mostly trckd ldr to jst over 2f out: wknd qckly* 10/1

30/5 **13** *1¼* **Kathleen Frances**[11] 544 7-9-1 69 (p) LiamKeniry 7 57
(Ali Stronge) *t.k.h: hld up in last quartet: shkn up and no prog 2f out* 50/1

2m 6.7s (-1.30) **Going Correction** 0.0s/f (Stan)
**WFA** 4 from 5yo+ 1lb 13 Ran SP% **122.8**
Speed ratings (Par 103): **105,104,103,102,102 102,101,101,100,100 99,97,96**
CSF £20.96 CT £283.44 TOTE £8.80: £2.40, £1.10, £9.50; EX 24.10 Trifecta £710.40.
**Owner** Miss T R Hale **Bred** Wretham Stud **Trained** Lower Beeding, W Sussex

**FOCUS**
Two in-form horses came to the fore here. The winner is rated pretty much back to his old best.

## 656 BETBRIGHT CHASE DAY 22.02.14 H'CAP (DIV I) 2m (P)
**6:25** (6:25) (Class 6) (0-60,60) 4-Y-O+ £1,940 (£577; £288; £144) **Stalls** Low

Form RPR

-023 **1** **Shalambar (IRE)**[6] 590 8-9-9 59 (v) JimCrowley 5 71
(Tony Carroll) *hld up in 6th: quick move on outer to ld over 2f out and sn dashed clr: drvn over 1f out: unchal* 9/2[3]

-024 **2** *6* **Ogaritmo**[6] 590 5-9-8 58 (t) GeorgeBaker 2 63
(Seamus Durack) *hld up in last quartet: nt clr run over 2f out as wnr was taking control: gd prog to take 2nd over 1f out: styd on but no ch* 8/1

0-06 **3** *2¼* **Arashi**[15] 476 8-9-10 60 (v) DaleSwift 8 62
(Derek Shaw) *stdd s: hld up in last pair: nt clr run over 2f out as wnr was taking control: prog wl over 1f out: styd on to take 3rd ins fnl f* 13/2

06-2 **4** *2¼* **Brave Helios**[7] 580 4-9-0 56 RichardKingscote 4 56
(Jonathan Portman) *trckd ldng pair: wnt 2nd briefly wl over 2f out: sn drvn and outpcd: kpt on* 11/4[1]

0-42 **5** *hd* **Magicalmysterytour (IRE)**[16] 455 11-9-4 54 RobertWinston 7 53
(Willie Musson) *hld up in 8th: hanging bdly whn asked for effrt wl over 2f out: kpt on fnl f: n.d* 10/1

0-53 **6** *½* **Ocean Power (IRE)**[20] 380 4-8-5 47 JoeFanning 1 46
(Richard Phillips) *hld up in 7th: sme prog jst over 2f out but already outpcd: one pce over 1f out* 14/1

-04 **7** *nk* **Novel Dancer**[11] 530 6-8-10 46 (v) RobertHavlin 11 44
(Lydia Richards) *trckd ldng trio: rdn and outpcd wl over 2f out: n.d after: kpt on fnl f* 33/1

-466 **8** *1* **Luckster**[22] 361 4-8-11 53 (b[1]) StevieDonohoe 9 50
(David Evans) *furiously drvn to ld: tried to kick on over 3f out: hdd over 2f out: wknd fnl f* 12/1

05-0 **9** *7* **Ctappers**[31] 246 5-8-10 46 oh1 LukeMorris 3 35
(Michael Madgwick) *chsd ldrs in 5th: shkn up over 5f out: wknd over 2f out* 16/1

/1-1 **10** *3¾* **The Young Master**[16] 455 5-9-6 56 (p) LiamKeniry 10 40
(Neil Mulholland) *trckd ldr: rdn 4f out: wknd wl over 2f out* 7/2[2]

0/-5 **11** *14* **Princely Hero (IRE)**[15] 471 10-9-3 53 (p) HayleyTurner 6 21
(Chris Gordon) *hld up in last pair: shkn up 5f out: no prog: wl btn 3f out: eased and t.o* 40/1

3m 27.37s (-2.73) **Going Correction** 0.0s/f (Stan)
**WFA** 4 from 5yo+ 6lb 11 Ran SP% **126.2**
Speed ratings (Par 101): **106,103,101,100,100 100,100,99,96,94 87**
CSF £43.86 CT £243.78 TOTE £5.20: £1.90, £2.80, £2.60; EX 43.20 Trifecta £195.50.
**Owner** B J Millen **Bred** His Highness The Aga Khan's Studs S C **Trained** Cropthorne, Worcs

**FOCUS**
They went a solid gallop and the winner stepped up on recent runs.

## 657 BETBRIGHT CHASE DAY 22.02.14 H'CAP (DIV II) 2m (P)
**6:55** (6:56) (Class 6) (0-60,60) 4-Y-O+ £1,940 (£577; £288; £144) **Stalls** Low

Form RPR

22/0 **1** **Mighty Mambo**[16] 458 7-9-5 55 (tp) GeorgeBaker 5 63
(Lawney Hill) *hld up in 8th: smooth prog over 2f out to ld over 1f out: shkn up and asserted fnl f: won gng away* 14/1

0-53 **2** *2* **Rocky Rebel**[24] 349 6-9-10 60 DaleSwift 11 66
(Michael Blake) *trckd ldrs: pushed along 5f out: u.p fr 3f out but responded to chal over 1f out: no ex last 150yds* 5/1[3]

0-31 **3** *1* **Galiotto (IRE)**[16] 454 8-9-8 58 (v) RyanMoore 2 63
(Gary Moore) *hld up in midfield: rdn 3f out: prog to press ldrs over 1f out: one pce after* 2/1[1]

55-2 **4** *nk* **Opus (IRE)**[43] 73 5-9-4 54 LukeMorris 8 58
(Lucy Wadham) *cl up: trckd ldng pair 9f out: rdn over 2f out: clsd to chal over 1f out: fdd fnl f* 4/1[2]

00-0 **5** *2½* **Reillys Daughter**[20] 382 6-8-10 46 oh1 (b) HayleyTurner 9 47
(Richard Mitchell) *t.k.h: trckd ldr: rdn to ld over 2f out: hdd over 1f out: wknd fnl f* 40/1

04-0 **6** *2* **Go Amwell**[16] 455 11-8-3 46 oh1 (v) VictorSantos(7) 1 45
(J R Jenkins) *s.s: hld up in last quartet: bmpd along and tried to make prog on inner over 2f out: fdd over 1f out* 66/1

40-4 **7** *1¾* **Boston Blue**[20] 380 7-9-6 56 JimCrowley 4 53
(Tony Carroll) *hld up in midfield: prog to trck ldrs 1/2-way: cl enough in 5th over 3f out: wknd over 1f out* 8/1

04-1 **8** *hd* **Newtown Cross (IRE)**[20] 380 4-8-4 53 CamHardie(7) 10 50
(Jimmy Fox) *hld up in last quartet: pushed along and no prog 3f out: no ch after: kpt on fnl f* 7/1

2-66 **9** *5* **Bell'Arte (IRE)**[7] 580 4-8-10 52 (v[1]) JoeFanning 7 43
(Laura Mongan) *t.k.h: led at mod pce: rdn and hdd over 2f out: wknd qckly over 1f out* 20/1



The Form Book, Raceform Ltd, Newbury, RG14 5SJ

400- **10** *6* **Pullmen**[36] 1080 6-9-2 **52**................................ RobertWinston 6 36
(Paul Henderson) *stdd s: hld up in 10th: rdn and no prog 3f out: sn no ch*
**33/1**

00-6 **11** *50* **Be A Rebel**[28] 282 4-8-1 **46** oh1.......................... NataliaGemelova(3) 3
(John E Long) *chsd ldng pair: racd awkwardly and appeared to hit rail 9f out: lost pl and last 5f out: t.o*
**50/1**

3m 35.55s (5.45) **Going Correction** 0.0s/f (Stan)
**WFA** 4 from 5yo+ 6lb **11** Ran SP% **113.9**
Speed ratings (Par 101): **86,85,84,84,83 82,81,81,78,75 50**
CSF £76.58 CT £201.99 TOTE £15.10: £3.80, £2.20, £1.20; EX 93.70 Trifecta £178.10.
**Owner** Fortnum Racing **Bred** Norcroft Park Stud **Trained** Aston Rowant, Oxon

**FOCUS**
In contrast to the first division this was run at a dawdling early gallop and wasn't a true test of stamina. The winning time was 8.18 seconds slower than the previous race. The second and third set an ordinary level.

## 658 BETBRIGHT - LIVE THE MOMENT H'CAP — 6f (P)
**7:25** (7:25) (Class 4) (0-85,85) 4-Y-0+ **£4,690** (£1,395; £697; £348) Stalls Low

Form RPR

-431 **1** **Trojan Rocket (IRE)**[20] 381 6-9-4 **82**.................(p) RichardKingscote 3 92
(Michael Wigham) *t.k.h: mde all: mod pce for 2f then stretched field: hrd pressed and drvn jst over 1f out: styd on wl nr fin*
**7/1**[3]

01-2 **2** *½* **Firmdecisions (IRE)**[21] 372 4-9-3 **81**.......................(b[1]) TomQueally 1 89
(Brett Johnson) *t.k.h: trckd ldng pair: rdn over 2f out: wnt 2nd wl over 1f out and sn chalng: nt qckn last 150yds*
**3/1**[2]

02-3 **3** *1 ½* **Palace Moon**[27] 294 9-9-4 **82**....................................(t) JimCrowley 7 86
(William Knight) *hld up in 6th: rdn jst over 2f out: styd on fr over 1f out to take 3rd nr fin*
**5/2**[1]

-602 **4** *nk* **Jay Bee Blue**[7] 574 5-9-0 **78**.......................................(bt) JoeFanning 8 81
(Sean Curran) *patiently rdn in 8th: pushed along towards outer jst over 2f out: stuck bhd 2 rivals after: styd on nr fin: nvr involved*
**7/1**[3]

00-4 **5** *shd* **Clear Praise (USA)**[17] 444 7-9-4 **82**................................ LukeMorris 4 84
(Simon Dow) *t.k.h: hld up in 7th: rdn over 2f out: kpt on same pce after: nvr a threat*
**20/1**

11-5 **6** *½* **Novellen Lad (IRE)**[32] 234 9-9-5 **83**.......................... RobertWinston 5 84
(Willie Musson) *trckd ldng trio: rdn and nt qckn jst over 2f out: one pce after*
**8/1**

40-0 **7** *1 ¼* **Sulis Minerva (IRE)**[42] 80 7-8-11 **75**............................ LiamKeniry 2 72
(Jeremy Gask) *trckd ldrs in 5th: rdn and effrt on inner over 2f out: pressed for a pl over 1f out: fdd fnl f*
**20/1**

-055 **8** *1 ¾* **Tax Free (IRE)**[17] 444 12-9-7 **85**.............................. AdrianNicholls 12 76
(David Nicholls) *t.k.h: trckd wnr: rdn 1/2-way: lost 2nd and wknd wl over 1f out*
**33/1**

-452 **9** *nk* **Pabusar**[16] 452 6-8-11 **75**............................................. WilliamCarson 6 65
(Ann Stokell) *t.k.h: hld up in last trio: shkn up and no prog 2f out* **33/1**

03- **10** *1 ½* **O'Gorman**[154] 6525 5-9-7 **85**............................................ GeorgeBaker 9 70
(Gary Brown) *plld hrd: hld up in last trio: rdn and no prog over 2f out* **12/1**

300- **11** *3* **Langley Vale**[194] 5219 5-8-12 **76**................................... HayleyTurner 11 52
(Roger Teal) *t.k.h: hld up in last trio: lost tch over 2f out*
**25/1**

1m 12.02s (-1.08) **Going Correction** 0.0s/f (Stan) **11** Ran SP% **116.6**
Speed ratings (Par 105): **107,106,104,103,103 103,101,99,98,96 92**
CSF £26.00 CT £68.13 TOTE £4.50: £3.60, £1.20, £1.10; EX 41.40 Trifecta £102.90.
**Owner** G Linder, D Hassan, R Warner **Bred** J G F Fox **Trained** Newmarket, Suffolk

**FOCUS**
This looked competitive on paper, but the winner dominated. He rates a personal best.

## 659 BETBRIGHT MOBILE H'CAP (LONDON MILE SERIES QUALIFIER) — 1m (P)
**7:55** (7:56) (Class 3) (0-95,87) 3-Y-0 **£7,158** (£2,143; £1,071; £535; £267) Stalls Low

Form RPR

-122 **1** **Basil Berry**[5] 604 3-8-6 **72**............................................ HayleyTurner 2 79
(Chris Dwyer) *hld up in 4th: sn tk fierce hold and allowed to circle field to ld over 3f out: mde rest and hld together tl jst over 1f out: kpt on wl whn pressed: rdn out*
**10/1**

001- **2** *¾* **Chinotto (IRE)**[84] 8067 3-8-12 **78**.................................... DavidProbert 1 83
(Andrew Balding) *trckd ldr 3f: rdn to chse wnr over 2f out: clsd over 1f out: kpt on but hld last 150yds*
**7/1**[3]

0111 **3** *½* **Swivel**[19] 404 3-9-2 **82**.................................................. JoeFanning 5 86
(Mark Johnston) *sn led and set modest pce: hdd over 3f out: nt qckn over 2f out and lost pl: kpt on again fnl f*
**11/4**[2]

2-11 **4** *1 ¼* **Examiner (IRE)**[21] 375 3-9-7 **87**...................................... RyanMoore 3 88
(William Haggas) *trckd ldr after 3f to over 3f out: rdn and nt qckn over 2f out: one pce after: fdd ins fnl f*
**10/11**[1]

-131 **5** *½* **Starlight Princess (IRE)**[15] 473 3-8-4 **70**.................(b) LukeMorris 4 70
(J S Moore) *hld up in last: tried to cl on ldrs fr 2f out: no imp 1f out: fdd*
**12/1**

1m 41.03s (1.23) **Going Correction** 0.0s/f (Stan) **5** Ran SP% **108.3**
Speed ratings (Par 101): **93,92,91,90,90**
CSF £66.66 TOTE £14.40: £6.00, £5.20; EX 71.50 Trifecta £167.10.
**Owner** Strawberry Fields Stud **Bred** Strawberry Fields Stud **Trained** Newmarket, Suffolk

**FOCUS**
A 0-95 in name only as the topweight was rated just 87, and it was a messy race with no pace. The winner was well in on his latest form and this rates a personal best.

## 660 BETBRIGHT MAIDEN FILLIES' STKS — 1m (P)
**8:25** (8:26) (Class 5) 3-Y-0+ **£2,587** (£770; £384; £192) Stalls Low

Form RPR

6 **1** *2 ¼* **Ambella (IRE)**[16] 456 4-9-9 0.................................. GeorgeDowning(5) 7 69
(Ian Williams) *in tch in midfield: shkn up over 2f out: prog over 1f out: styd on fnl f to take 2nd last strides*
**20/1**

6-22 **2** *nk* **Speechday (IRE)**[16] 456 3-8-9 71.................................. LukeMorris 4 62
(Marco Botti) *prom: trckd ldr 1/2-way: clsng whn veered lft jst over 2f out: chsd wnr jst over 1f out but sn outpcd: lost 2nd last strides*
**4/1**[3]

0-4 **3** *½* **Joyful Risk (IRE)**[16] 456 4-10-0 0.................................. GeorgeBaker 2 67
(Martin Bosley) *in tch in midfield: pushed along on inner over 2f out: prog wl over 1f out: tk 4th ins fnl f: kpt on*
**25/1**

00- **4** *½* **Her Honour (IRE)**[83] 8083 3-8-9 0.................................. RobertHavlin 3 60+
(John Gosden) *hld up in 9th: pushed along 2f out: prog and nt clr run briefly over 1f out: shkn up and styd on fnl f: nrst fin*
**8/1**

0-4 **5** *1 ¼* **Last Echo (IRE)**[18] 422 3-8-9 0.................................. RichardKingscote 8 57
(Ralph Beckett) *trckd ldrs in 5th: squeezed for room wl over 2f out: kpt on same pce fr over 1f out*
**11/4**[2]

**6** *1 ½* **Purana** 3-8-9 0.......................................................... DavidProbert 14 53+
(Tony Carroll) *awkward s: rn green and wl in rr: styd on quite takingly fr over 1f out*
**33/1**

00 **7** *½* **Kristal Hart**[14] 486 5-10-0 0.......................................... PaddyAspell 10 58?
(Neil Mulholland) *led 2f: styd prom: rdn over 2f out: wknd jst over 1f out*
**100/1**

3 **8** *1 ¾* **Beylerbey (USA)**[16] 456 4-10-0 0.................................. JoeFanning 11 54
(Mark Johnston) *t.k.h: led after 2f: hdd over 1f out: wknd qckly fnl f* **2/1**[1]

**9** *2 ½* **Park Dancer**[305] 7-9-11 0.......................... WilliamTwiston-Davies(3) 9 48
(Martin Bosley) *a towards rr: shkn up and no prog over 2f out* **100/1**

0 **10** *2 ¾* **Mrs Burbidge**[14] 486 4-10-0 0.......................................... LiamKeniry 13 41
(Neil Mulholland) *hld up wl in rr: rdn and no prog over 2f out* **100/1**

06 **11** *shd* **Pembroke Pride**[19] 403 4-10-0 0.................................. RobertWinston 6 41
(Philip Hide) *trckd ldrs: lost pl over 2f out: nudged along and wknd over 1f out*
**100/1**

**12** *¾* **Sound Of Life (IRE)** 3-8-9 0.......................................... ChrisCatlin 5 33
(Rae Guest) *slowly away: rn green and a wl in rr*
**14/1**

6 **13** *6* **Bikini Club**[7] 579 3-8-9 0.......................................(e) HayleyTurner 1 19
(Paul D'Arcy) *a in rr: rdn and wknd wl over 2f out*
**33/1**

0- **D** **The Silver Kebaya (FR)**[126] 7295 3-8-9 0.......................... ShaneKelly 12 70+
(Jeremy Noseda) *wl in tch: prog on outer whn bmpd jst over 2f out: clsd to ld over 1f out: pushed out and readily drew clr*
**5/1**

1m 40.57s (0.77) **Going Correction** 0.0s/f (Stan)
**WFA** 3 from 4yo+ 19lb **14** Ran SP% **132.9**
Speed ratings (Par 100): **93,93,92,92,91 89,89,87,84,82 82,81,75,96**
CSF £110.46 TOTE £5.80: £3.20, £5.70, £1.60; EX 194.30 Trifecta £1502.60.
**Owner** Four Square Blokes Racing Club **Bred** M McGinn **Trained** Portway, Worcs

**FOCUS**
A muddling fillies' maiden but plenty to like about the winner.

## 661 ALL-WEATHER "HANDS AND HEELS" APPRENTICE SERIES H'CAP (PART OF THE RACING EXCELLENCE INITIATIVE) — 1m (P)
**8:55** (8:55) (Class 7) (0-50,50) 4-Y-0+ **£1,617** (£481; £240; £120) Stalls Low

Form RPR

-663 **1** **Bennelong**[5] 601 8-9-1 **49**.......................................(b) PaigeBolton(5) 4 62
(Lee Carter) *hld up in midfield: smooth prog over 2f out: led wl over 1f out: sn drew rt away*
**10/1**

0-01 **2** *9* **Zed Candy Girl**[24] 352 4-9-3 **46**.......................(p) RobJFitzpatrick 3 38
(John Stimpson) *hld up in midfield: prog on inner over 2f out: chal wl over 1f out but wnr sn stormed past: one pce after*
**10/1**

0-32 **3** *2* **Compton Silver**[26] 321 4-9-4 **50**.......................(b) JackGilligan(3) 2 38
(Patrick Gilligan) *led at v fast pce: clr 1/2-way: hdd wl over 1f out: tired after but clung on for 3rd*
**8/1**[3]

-623 **4** *1 ¾* **Supa Seeker (USA)**[24] 352 8-9-3 **49**..........(v) MrAidenBlakemore(3) 1 33
(Tony Carroll) *hld up towards rr: no ch fr over 2f out: prog over 1f out: styd on same pce*
**8/1**[3]

0-03 **5** *1 ¼* **Claude Monet (BRZ)**[17] 446 5-9-7 **50**.......................... JackGarritty 10 31
(Simon Dow) *t.k.h: hld up in rr: no ch fr over 2f out: styd on fr over 1f out: nrst fin*
**3/1**[1]

03-0 **6** *1 ¼* **Rigid**[42] 88 7-9-2 **45**.................................................. JordanVaughan 11 23
(Tony Carroll) *hld up towards rr: no ch fr over 2f out: one pce after* **9/1**

-065 **7** *1 ¼* **The Wonga Coup (IRE)**[14] 484 7-9-3 **46**.......................... DanielCremin 9 21
(Pat Phelan) *hld up in 4th bhd clr ldrs: pushed along over 2f out: wknd over 1f out*
**8/1**[3]

-444 **8** *1 ¼* **Bladewood Girl**[20] 377 6-9-5 **48**.......................(v) GeorgeBuckell 7 20
(J R Jenkins) *t.k.h: hld up in 3rd bhd clr ldng pair: wnt 2nd 3f out: wknd 2f out*
**4/1**[2]

000/ **9** *1* **Magic Beat**[497] 6978 4-8-13 **45**.......................... SophieRalston(3) 8 15
(Pat Phelan) *awkward s: hld up in last and detached: nvr involved: kpt on fnl f*
**40/1**

60-0 **10** *hd* **My Learned Friend (IRE)**[31] 251 10-9-2 **50**....(p) KieranShoemark(5) 5 19
(Andrew Balding) *hld up in midfield on outer: no prog over 2f out: steadily wknd*
**14/1**

00-5 **11** *50* **Lucky Mountain**[29] 269 4-8-13 **45**.......................(b) JonathanWilletts(3) 6
(Scott Dixon) *chsd ldr and clr of rest: wd bnd 3f out and wknd rapidly: t.o*
**25/1**

1m 38.95s (-0.85) **Going Correction** 0.0s/f (Stan) **11** Ran SP% **119.5**
Speed ratings (Par 97): **104,95,93,91,90 88,87,86,85,85 35**
CSF £107.64 CT £609.68 TOTE £12.30: £2.80, £2.90, £3.40; EX 148.90 Trifecta £1890.30 Part won..
**Owner** Miss Victoria Baalham **Bred** The National Stud **Trained** Epsom, Surrey
■ Paige Bolton's first winner.

**FOCUS**
There was a good pace on in this weak race. The winner is rated to last season's form.
T/Jkpt: Not won. T/Plt: £90.90 to a £1 stake. Pool: £99,915.90 - 802.36 winning units. T/Qpdt: £57.60 to a £1 stake. Pool: £9125.75 - 117.10 winning units. JN

# 622 LINGFIELD (L-H)
### Wednesday, February 19

**OFFICIAL GOING: Standard**
Wind: light, half behind Weather: dry

## 662 BEST ODDS AT BOOKMAKERS.CO.UK CLAIMING STKS — 5f 6y(P)
**1:30** (1:30) (Class 6) 4-Y-0+ **£2,385** (£704; £352) Stalls High

Form RPR

1065 **1** **Kuanyao (IRE)**[5] 602 8-8-10 76.......................(b) LouisSteward(5) 2 84
(Lee Carter) *mde all: rdn and wnt clr over 1f out: in command 1f out: eased towards fin: comf*
**2/1**[1]

300- **2** *3 ¼* **Come On Dave (IRE)**[64] 8319 5-8-9 70.......................... AdrianNicholls 6 66
(David Nicholls) *taken down early: pressed wnr tl rdn and nt qckn over 1f out: no ch w wnr but kpt on to hold 2nd fnl f*
**7/2**[3]

0-26 **3** *1* **Imaginary Diva**[16] 466 8-8-1 60.......................... RyanPowell(3) 1 58
(George Margarson) *in tch in midfield: effrt on inner to chse clr ldng pair 2f out: styd on same pce u.p fr over 1f out*
**25/1**

2-20 **4** *1 ¼* **Drawnfromthepast (IRE)**[33] 208 9-8-4 69.......................... KieranShoemark(7) 4 60
(Luke Dace) *squeezed for room and dropped to last pair sn after s: rdn and sme hdwy on inner over 1f out: styd on same pce fnl f*
**3/1**[2]

6621 **5** *¾* **Where's Reiley (USA)**[9] 557 8-8-9 64..........................(v) LukeMorris 3 56
(Michael Attwater) *chsd ldrs: rdn 1/2-way: drvn and btn over 1f out: wknd fnl f*
**6/1**

-006 **6** *½* **Kaylee**[14] 483 5-8-3 46 ow3..........................(v) DavidProbert 7 48
(Kevin Tork) *s.i.s: a in rr: rdn 2f out: no imp*
**100/1**

00-0 **7** *1 ¾* **Proper Charlie**[35] 192 6-8-5 55..........................(b[1]) WilliamCarson 5 43
(Lee Carter) *chsd ldrs on outer: rdn and struggling ent fnl 2f: wknd over 1f out*
**8/1**

57.68s (-1.12) **Going Correction** -0.075s/f (Stan) **7** Ran SP% **110.8**
Speed ratings (Par 101): **106,100,99,97,96 95,92**
CSF £8.64 TOTE £2.60: £1.70, £2.20; EX 12.60 Trifecta £103.10.

**Owner** John Joseph Smith **Bred** Newlands House Stud **Trained** Epsom, Surrey
**FOCUS**
An ordinary claimer in which the pace was reasonable. Not many figured and the winner raced close to the inside rail throughout. He is rated back to last month's win here.

## 663 COMPARE BOOKMAKERS AT BOOKMAKERS.CO.UK H'CAP 6f 1y(P)
**2:00** (2:00) (Class 6) (0-65,65) 4-Y-O+ **£2,726** (£805; £402) **Stalls** Low

Form RPR
3622 **1** **Volito**[17] 449 8-8-4 **55** .................. JackGarritty(7) 8 63
(Anabel K Murphy) *stdd and dropped in after s: hld up in rr: clsd and swtchd rt wl over 1f out: pushed along hands and heels and qckd to ld wl ins fnl f: r.o wl: pushed out* **9/2**[1]

5-03 **2** *1* **Rise To Glory (IRE)**[12] 510 6-8-13 **60** .................. NeilFarley(3) 2 65
(Shaun Harris) *led tl over 3f out: chsd ldr tl rdn to ld again over 1f out: drvn 1f out: hdd wl ins fnl f and one pce after* **6/1**[3]

4-62 **3** *3/4* **Harvest Mist (IRE)**[16] 453 6-8-12 **59** .......... WilliamTwiston-Davies(3) 4 62
(Shaun Lycett) *chsd ldrs: rdn over 1f out: kpt on same pce u.p fnl f* **5/1**[2]

30-5 **4** *nk* **Teen Ager (FR)**[37] 155 10-9-4 **62** .................. (p) JimmyQuinn 1 64
(Paul Burgoyne) *t.k.h: hld up in tch: rdn and effrt to chse ldrs on inner 1f out: no ex and outpcd fnl 75yds* **8/1**

-040 **5** *nk* **The Dancing Lord**[7] 576 5-9-4 **62** .................. DavidProbert 6 63
(Brett Johnson) *in tch towards rr: short of room and shuffled bk over 2f out: nt clr run again wl over 1f out: hdwy u.p 1f out: styd on but no threat to wnr* **12/1**

364- **6** *2 1/2* **Excellent Aim**[72] 8216 7-9-3 **64** .................. RyanPowell(3) 5 57
(George Margarson) *in tch in midfield: effrt and wdst bnd 2f out: unable qck and btn 1f out: wknd fnl f* **9/2**[1]

5543 **7** *1 1/4* **Greenhead High**[1] 651 6-9-7 **65** .................. (b[1]) AdrianNicholls 3 54
(David Nicholls) *t.k.h: hld up in tch in midfield: swtchd rt and hdwy over 4f out: led over 3f out tl rdn and hdd over 1f out: sn btn: wknd ins fnl f* **5/1**[2]

020- **8** *8* **Time Medicean**[112] 7633 8-8-11 **55** .................. RobertWinston 9 18
(Tony Carroll) *chsd ldr tl over 3f out: racing awkwardly downhill over 2f out: lost pl 2f out: sn wknd: bhd and eased wl ins fnl f* **7/1**

1m 10.88s (-1.02) **Going Correction** -0.075s/f (Stan) **8 Ran SP% 115.3**
Speed ratings (Par 101): **103,101,100,100,99 96,94,84**
CSF £31.78 CT £140.90 TOTE £5.20: £2.00, £2.70, £1.80; EX 34.90 Trifecta £147.30.
**Owner** Mrs Anabel K Murphy **Bred** A J And Mrs L Brazier **Trained** Wilmcote, Warwicks
**FOCUS**
A modest handicap in which the gallop was sound. The winner came down the centre in the straight. Straightforward form.

## 664 32RED IMMORTAL ROMANCE SLOT CLAIMING STKS 1m 2f (P)
**2:30** (2:30) (Class 6) 3-Y-O **£2,385** (£704; £352) **Stalls** Low

Form RPR
2336 **1** **Big Kenny**[9] 561 3-9-3 **63** .................. JimCrowley 1 64+
(David Evans) *chsd ldng pair: rdn wl over 2f out: lft in ld over 1f out and sn clr: doing little in front and rdn out fnl f* **5/4**[1]

05-6 **2** *1/2* **Ultimate Warrior (IRE)**[19] 404 3-8-9 **66** .................. (b[1]) WilliamCarson 4 53
(Jim Boyle) *sn bustled along to ld: hdd over 7f out: drvn and ev ch over 2f out: carried rt wl over 1f out: sn swtchd lft and lft chsng clr ldr over 1f out: kpt on ins fnl f* **11/4**[3]

05-0 **3** *4 1/2* **Casper Lee (IRE)**[36] 173 3-8-12 **53** .................. (b[1]) RobertWinston 3 47
(Alan Berry) *t.k.h: hld up in tch in rr: rdn and effrt 2f out: lft 3rd and nt qckn u.p over 1f out: one pce after* **14/1**

0 **4** *3 1/2* **Abdication**[15] 468 3-9-3 **0** .................. LukeMorris 5 59+
(Marco Botti) *t.k.h early: chsd ldr tl led over 7f out: rdn and hung rt bnd 2f out: veered bdly rt: nt run on and hdd over 1f out: last and wl btn after: eased fnl f* **2/1**[2]

2m 7.81s (1.21) **Going Correction** -0.075s/f (Stan) **4 Ran SP% 111.1**
Speed ratings (Par 95): **92,91,88,85**
CSF £5.16 TOTE £1.50; EX 4.40 Trifecta £13.30.Ultimate Warrior was claimed by Richard Ford for £2,000.
**Owner** P D Evans **Bred** O J Williams **Trained** Pandy, Monmouths
**FOCUS**
A modest and uncompetitive claimer in which the gallop was on the steady side. The winner came down the centre and probably only ran to form.

## 665 32RED ON THE APP STORE H'CAP 7f 1y(P)
**3:05** (3:06) (Class 6) (0-65,64) 3-Y-O **£2,726** (£805; £402) **Stalls** Low

Form RPR
004- **1** **Barbary (IRE)**[124] 7352 3-9-0 **57** .................. FrederikTylicki 8 61
(Charlie Fellowes) *chsd ldrs: swtchd lft and drvn to chse ldr jst over 1f out: led fnl 75yds: r.o wl: rdn out* **7/1**[2]

4421 **2** *1* **El Duque**[11] 541 3-9-1 **63** .................. (v) RyanWhile(5) 5 64
(Bill Turner) *chsd ldr tl led 5f out: rdn wl over 5f out: drvn and hrd pressed ins fnl f: hdd and one pce fnl 75yds* **12/1**

040- **3** *nk* **Seven Lucky Seven**[75] 8188 3-8-10 **53** .................. JimmyQuinn 1 54+
(Gary Harrison) *stdd and hmpd sn after s: hld up in last pair: swtchd rt and rdn over 1f out: r.o strly ins fnl f: nvr gng to rch wnr* **33/1**

640- **4** *1 1/4* **Sandy Cove**[152] 6605 3-9-0 **57** .................. LukeMorris 10 54
(James Eustace) *wl in tch in midfield: n.m.r ent fnl 2f: sn drvn and outpcd over 1f out: rallied and kpt on again ins fnl f* **7/1**[2]

35-4 **5** *3/4* **Duly Acclaimed (IRE)**[32] 231 3-8-12 **55** .................. DavidProbert 13 50
(J S Moore) *in tch in midfield: drvn and unable qck over 1f out: kpt on but no threat to ldrs ins fnl f* **8/1**[3]

-433 **6** *hd* **Indira**[18] 434 3-9-2 **62** .................. RossAtkinson(3) 3 57
(John Berry) *in tch in midfield: drvn and unable qck over 1f out: styd on same pce ins fnl f* **16/1**

0-22 **7** *1 1/4* **Witchy Woman**[19] 411 3-9-6 **63** .................. GeorgeBaker 6 55
(Geoffrey Deacon) *led for 2f: chsd ldr after: 3rd and unable qck 1f out: wknd ins fnl f* **12/1**

00-0 **8** *hd* **Henry Grace (IRE)**[20] 378 3-8-13 **56** .................. KieranO'Neill 9 47
(Jimmy Fox) *stdd s: hld up in rr: nt clr run on inner and switching rt ent fnl 2f: rdn and styd on same pce fr over 1f out* **33/1**

60-0 **9** *2 3/4* **Caroline's Beach (IRE)**[42] 86 3-8-2 **50** .................. PhilipPrince(5) 2 34
(J S Moore) *in tch in last quartet: rdn and no prog over 2f out: outpcd and wl hld fr over 1f out* **66/1**

0-00 **10** *4 1/2* **Krackerjill (IRE)**[21] 374 3-7-11 **45** .................. ShirleyTeasdale(5) 11 17
(Mark Usher) *in tch in last quartet: rdn and no hdwy whn wd bnd 2f out: wknd over 1f out* **50/1**

52-4 **P** **Drinkuptrig (IRE)**[25] 338 3-9-7 **64** .................. (t) AndreaAtzeni 7
(Stuart Williams) *chsd ldrs tl lost action after 1f: sn eased and p.u: dismntd: fatally injured* **1/1**[1]

1m 24.61s (-0.19) **Going Correction** -0.075s/f (Stan) **11 Ran SP% 116.7**
Speed ratings (Par 95): **98,96,96,95,94 94,92,92,89,84**
CSF £84.24 CT £2647.44 TOTE £5.00: £2.20, £2.80, £7.00; EX 95.70 Trifecta £4120.10.
**Owner** Graham Mills **Bred** Brinkley Stud, Ficomontanino, Bego Blu **Trained** Newmarket, Suffolk
■ A winner with his first runner for Charlie Fellowes.
**FOCUS**
A modest handicap that took less winning than had seemed likely as well-backed market leader Drinkuptrig broke down badly. The gallop was an ordinary one and the winner raced close to the inside rail. The form looks ordinary but sound.

## 666 BOOKMAKERS.CO.UK MEDIAN AUCTION MAIDEN STKS 6f 1y(P)
**3:35** (3:36) (Class 6) 3-5-Y-O **£2,726** (£805; £402) **Stalls** Low

Form RPR
0- **1** **Monashka Bay (IRE)**[246] 3436 3-8-12 **0** .................. DavidProbert 2 60
(Michael Blanshard) *chsd ldr tl rdn to ld wl over 1f out: drvn and hdd 1f out: led again ins fnl f: kpt on wl* **3/1**[2]

302- **2** *1/2* **Narborough**[154] 6511 3-8-9 **64** .................. WilliamTwiston-Davies(3) 3 58
(Mick Channon) *t.k.h: hld up in last: hdwy on outer to press ldrs on outer bnd 2f out: shkn up to ld but hanging lft 1f out: hdd and continued hanging lft ins fnl f: nt qckn and outbattled fnl 100yds* **1/2**[1]

3460 **3** *2 1/4* **Countess Lupus (IRE)**[5] 608 3-8-2 **44** .................. (b) ShirleyTeasdale(5) 4 46
(Lisa Williamson) *t.k.h: led: rdn and hdd wl over 1f out: 3rd and nt qckn u.p over 1f out: one pce fnl f* **8/1**[3]

064- **4** *3/4* **Purford Green**[154] 6519 5-9-8 **47** .................. (v) RobertHavlin 1 47
(Michael Attwater) *chsd ldng pair: dropped to last but stl wl in tch 2f out: sn rdn and no hdwy: one pce fnl f* **10/1**

1m 12.63s (0.73) **Going Correction** -0.075s/f (Stan)
**WFA** 3 from 5yo 15lb **4 Ran SP% 111.9**
Speed ratings (Par 101): **92,91,88,87**
CSF £5.21 TOTE £7.80; EX 10.60 Trifecta £19.50.
**Owner** W Murdoch **Bred** Pat O'Rourke **Trained** Upper Lambourn, Berks
**FOCUS**
A low-grade and uncompetitive maiden in which the gallop was an ordinary one. The winner edged towards the far rail in the closing stages.

## 667 32RED FREE £10 BONUS H'CAP 6f 1y(P)
**4:05** (4:05) (Class 4) (0-80,79) 3-Y-O **£5,822** (£1,732; £865; £432) **Stalls** Low

Form RPR
040- **1** **Major Crispies**[139] 6972 3-9-2 **79** .................. RyanTate(5) 5 90
(James Eustace) *chsd ldrs on outer: clsd to join ldr ent fnl 2f: rdn to ld over 1f out: qcknd u.p and wnt clr 1f out: r.o wl: readily* **7/2**[2]

1-32 **2** *2 1/4* **Drive On (IRE)**[4] 624 3-9-0 **77** .................. (p) GeorgeDowning(5) 7 81
(Eve Johnson Houghton) *hld up in tch in last pair: swtchd wd and effrt over 1f out: r.o wl fnl f to go 2nd fnl 50yds: no threat to wnr* **11/10**[1]

1332 **3** *1/2* **Global Explorer (USA)**[18] 429 3-8-6 **64** .................. (t) AdamBeschizza 4 66
(Stuart Williams) *wl in tch in midfield: rdn and effrt over 1f out: chsd clr wnr 1f out: styd on same pce and lost 2nd fnl 50yds* **7/1**

4122 **4** *3/4* **Spreadable (IRE)**[7] 573 3-9-2 **74** .................. (b) GeorgeBaker 6 74
(Nick Littmoden) *stdd after s: hld up in tch in last pair: rdn and effrt to chse ldrs on inner over 1f out: no ex and one pce fnl 150yds* **9/2**[3]

10-5 **5** *1* **Nova Princesse (GER)**[28] 279 3-9-3 **75** .................. (bt[1]) LukeMorris 8 72
(Marco Botti) *dwlt and swtchd lft after s: t.k.h: hld up in tch in midfield: rdn and chsd ldrs over 1f out: no ex jst ins fnl f: wknd fnl 100yds* **20/1**

160- **6** *2 3/4* **Minley**[158] 6376 3-8-10 **75** .................. AlfieWarwick(7) 1 63
(Tobias B P Coles) *led: rdn and hdd over 1f out: lost 2nd 1f out and wknd ins fnl f* **50/1**

443- **7** *4 1/2* **Pigeon Pie**[150] 6663 3-8-11 **69** .................. JoeFanning 2 43
(Mark Johnston) *chsd ldr tl jst over 2f out: lost pl and bhd 1f out: wknd fnl f* **20/1**

1m 11.0s (-0.90) **Going Correction** -0.075s/f (Stan) **7 Ran SP% 112.0**
Speed ratings (Par 99): **103,100,99,98,97 93,87**
CSF £7.40 CT £22.81 TOTE £5.20: £2.10, £1.50; EX 13.30 Trifecta £50.50.
**Owner** G Carstairs **Bred** Lowther Racing **Trained** Newmarket, Suffolk
**FOCUS**
A fair handicap in which the gallop was reasonable. The winner came down the centre and showed improved form.

## 668 32RED.COM H'CAP 1m 2f (P)
**4:35** (4:35) (Class 5) (0-75,69) 3-Y-O **£3,408** (£1,006; £503) **Stalls** Low

Form RPR
3-03 **1** **Captain Mo**[18] 422 3-9-0 **62** .................. AndreaAtzeni 1 66
(Marco Botti) *chsd ldrs: swtchd rt and effrt 1f out: str run u.p ins fnl f to chal and pushed rt wl ins fnl f: led last strides* **6/1**

5-04 **2** *hd* **Officer Drivel (IRE)**[15] 473 3-9-0 **69** .................. KieranShoemark(7) 3 73
(Luke Dace) *stdd s: t.k.h: hld up in rr: effrt on outer 1f out: str run to chal wl ins fnl f: carried rt and no ex cl home* **8/1**

-111 **3** *hd* **Masterpaver**[14] 488 3-9-5 **67** .................. (v) RobertWinston 5 71
(Alan Bailey) *hld up in tch in last pair: clsd to press ldrs 2f out: rdn to ld ent fnl f: hrd pressed wl ins fnl f: hung rt and lost 2 pls cl home* **7/4**[1]

2P5- **4** *1 1/4* **Maxie T**[95] 7935 3-9-5 **67** .................. JoeFanning 4 68
(Mark Johnston) *led: rdn ent fnl 2f: hdd wl over 1f out: no ex and outpcd fnl 100yds* **3/1**[3]

4-42 **5** *nse* **Mary Le Bow**[14] 488 3-9-5 **67** .................. (p) LukeMorris 2 68
(Lucy Wadham) *chsd ldr tl drvn to ld wl over 1f out: hdd ent fnl f: no ex and outpcd fnl 100yds* **11/4**[2]

2m 9.25s (2.65) **Going Correction** -0.075s/f (Stan) **5 Ran SP% 113.4**
Speed ratings (Par 97): **86,85,85,84,84**
CSF £47.39 TOTE £5.30: £3.00, £7.50; EX 43.80 Trifecta £110.70.
**Owner** Mohamed Albousi Alghufli **Bred** Mickley Stud **Trained** Newmarket, Suffolk
**FOCUS**
A modest handicap but a steady gallop to the home turn means this bare form isn't entirely reliable. The principals came down the centre. The runner-up sets the standard.
T/Plt: £571.60 to a £1 stake. Pool: £58,713.55 - 74.98 winning units. T/Qpdt: £235.30 to a £1 stake. Pool: £3975.05 - 12.50 winning units. SP

# 629 CAGNES-SUR-MER
Wednesday, February 19
**OFFICIAL GOING: Polytrack: standard**

## 669a PRIX DE MONTE CARLO (CONDITIONS) (4YO+) (POLYTRACK) 1m 2f (D)
**1:20** (12:00) 4-Y-O+ **£10,833** (£4,333; £3,250; £2,166; £1,083)

RPR
**1** **Indomito (GER)**[10] 554 8-9-4 **0** .................. EddyHardouin 8 99
(W Mongil, Germany) **32/5**

2 ½ **Zagros (FR)**[10] 554 5-9-4 0 AlexisBadel 6 98
(J Heloury, France) 131/10
3 shd **Zack Hall (FR)**[163] 6270 7-9-6 0 Francois-XavierBertras 4 100
(F Rohaut, France) 17/10[1]
4 1 **Pump Pump Boy (FR)**[10] 554 6-9-7 0 Pierre-CharlesBoudot 3 99
(M Pimbonnet, France) 13/2
5 snk **Almalyk (FR)**[138] 7009 5-9-2 0 (p) ThomasMessina 7 94
(X Nakkachdji, France) 28/1
6 hd **Zamaam**[23] 4-9-1 0 CesarPasserat(3) 5 96
(F Rohaut, France) 3/1[2]
7 1½ **Tepmokea (IRE)**[7] 584 8-9-2 0 (p) MickaelForest 1 90
(Andrew Hollinshead) *led: rdn and hdd 2f out: rallied u.p: grad outpcd fnl f* 33/1
8 1 **A Ready Dream (FR)**[10] 554 5-9-4 0 StephanePasquier 2 90
(Rod Collet, France) 49/10[3]

2m 1.0s (121.00)
**WFA** 4 from 5yo+ 1lb 8 Ran SP% **119.3**
WIN (incl. 1 euro stake): 7.40. Places: 2.10, 2.70, 1.30. DF: 40.90. SF: 86.90..
**Owner** Stall 5-Stars **Bred** Wilfried Witte U A **Trained** Germany

# 639 WOLVERHAMPTON (A.W) (L-H)

Thursday, February 20

**OFFICIAL GOING: Standard**
Wind: Fresh behind Weather: Cloudy with sunny spells

## 670 32RED FREE £10 BONUS H'CAP 1m 141y(P)
5:30 (5:30) (Class 5) (0-75,73) 3-Y-O £2,911 (£866; £432; £216) Stalls Low

Form RPR
5-32 1 **Upholland**[15] 492 3-9-7 72 (p) AdamKirby 5 78
(Richard Fahey) *pushed along early but in tch: rdn to ld over 1f out: sn hung lft and rt: styd on* 15/8[2]
35-1 2 ¾ **Filament Of Gold (USA)**[10] 561 3-9-8 73 6ex JoeFanning 3 79+
(Mark Johnston) *chsd ldrs: pushed along and nt clr run fr over 2f out tl jst over 1f out: r.o wl: nvr able to chal* 1/1[1]
650- 3 1¼ **Goleador (USA)**[96] 7935 3-8-13 64 (b[1]) AndreaAtzeni 2 65
(Marco Botti) *trckd ldr: t.k.h: rdn and ev ch wl over 1f out: nt clr run sn after: styd on same pce ins fnl f* 12/1
53-2 4 2¼ **Needless Shouting (IRE)**[10] 561 3-8-10 64 WilliamTwiston-Davies(3) 1 60
(Mick Channon) *led: rdn and hdd over 1f out: no ex ins fnl f* 5/1[3]
41-5 5 8 **Jazri**[21] 378 3-8-9 60 DavidProbert 6 37
(Milton Bradley) *prom: rdn over 2f out: wknd over 1f out* 25/1
3-46 6 17 **Howz The Family (IRE)**[24] 357 3-9-0 65 JohnFahy 7
(John Spearing) *a in rr: rdn and wknd over 2f out* 40/1

1m 52.75s (2.25) **Going Correction** +0.275s/f (Slow) 6 Ran SP% **115.4**
Speed ratings (Par 97): **101,100,99,97,90 75**
CSF £4.28 TOTE £2.10: £1.40, £1.30; EX 5.10 Trifecta £31.30.
**Owner** David W Armstrong **Bred** Never Away Partnership **Trained** Musley Bank, N Yorks

**FOCUS**
The winning time confirmed the visual impression that there was little pace on here. It was a case of gamble landed in this opening 3yo handicap. Standard form, rated through the third.

## 671 CORAL APP DOWNLOAD FROM THE APP STORE H'CAP 1m 1f 103y(P)
6:00 (6:00) (Class 6) (0-55,55) 4-Y-O+ £2,264 (£673; £336; £168) Stalls Low

Form RPR
3261 1 **Huzzah (IRE)**[13] 516 9-8-11 52 AlistairRawlinson(7) 4 65
(Michael Appleby) *hld up: t.k.h: hdwy on outer over 3f out: led over 2f out: hung rt and rdn over 1f out: styd on wl* 6/1
13-4 2 4 **Tukitinyasok (IRE)**[31] 263 7-9-5 53 BarryMcHugh 6 58
(Clive Mulhall) *hld up: hdwy over 2f out: rdn over 1f out: styd on same pce fnl f* 5/1[3]
303- 3 ¾ **Shamiana**[63] 8348 4-9-3 51 (b) RichardKingscote 3 54
(Daniel Kubler) *chsd ldrs: rdn over 2f out: styd on same pce fnl f* 9/1
0-00 4 1¾ **Sixties Queen**[14] 497 4-9-1 54 TimClark(5) 9 54
(Alan Bailey) *hld up: rdn over 3f out: styd on u.p fr over 1f out: nt trble ldrs* 14/1
01/0 5 1¾ **Catching Zeds**[22] 368 7-8-13 47 StevieDonohoe 11 43
(Kevin Frost) *s.i.s: hld up: hdwy over 2f out: rdn over 1f out: styd on same pce fnl f* 16/1
-312 6 1¾ **Kyle Of Bute**[22] 368 8-9-5 53 PaulMulrennan 8 45
(Richard Ford) *trckd ldrs: t.k.h: wnt 2nd 5f out: led wl over 2f out: sn rdn and hdd: wknd fnl f* 4/1[1]
-102 7 1½ **Katmai River (IRE)**[14] 497 7-8-10 51 CharlotteJenner(7) 5 40
(Mark Usher) *prom: lost pl 5f out: n.d after* 9/2[2]
5454 8 nk **Cyflymder (IRE)**[12] 537 8-9-7 55 (t) HayleyTurner 7 44
(David C Griffiths) *hld up: rdn over 3f out: n.d* 14/1
35-0 9 5 **Wrecking Ball (IRE)**[31] 252 4-9-2 55 DavidKenny(5) 12 33
(Amy Weaver) *s.i.s: hdwy over 7f out: rdn over 2f out: sn wknd* 14/1
600- 10 12 **Hawaiian Freeze**[52] 8448 5-8-7 46 oh1 (be[1]) PhilipPrince(5) 2
(John Stimpson) *sn led: rdn and hdd wl over 2f out: sn wknd* 33/1
36-3 11 5 **Primary Route (IRE)**[48] 31 4-9-6 54 GrahamGibbons 1
(David Barron) *w ldr tl pushed along 6f out: wknd 3f out* 10/1

2m 3.87s (2.17) **Going Correction** +0.275s/f (Slow) 11 Ran SP% **117.0**
Speed ratings (Par 101): **101,97,96,95,93 92,90,90,86,75 70**
CSF £35.91 CT £270.95 TOTE £8.70: £2.20, £3.10, £4.20; EX 43.80 Trifecta £389.50.
**Owner** Richard Popplewell **Bred** S And S Hubbard Rodwell **Trained** Danethorpe, Notts

**FOCUS**
A low-grade handicap that was taken apart by a reinvigorated performer. The form is rated around the second and third.

## 672 LADBROKES MOBILE H'CAP (DIV I) 1m 141y(P)
6:30 (6:31) (Class 6) (0-55,61) 4-Y-O+ £2,264 (£673; £336; £168) Stalls Low

Form RPR
642- 1 **Bond Artist (IRE)**[86] 8056 5-9-1 52 RobertTart(3) 6 59
(Geoffrey Oldroyd) *mid-div: hdwy and hmpd over 5f out: pushed along over 2f out: rdn to ld over 1f out: styd on* 3/1[2]
0-21 2 ½ **Benandonner (USA)**[27] 321 11-9-6 54 ShaneKelly 2 60
(Mike Murphy) *broke wl and led 1f: settled to trck ldrs: lft 2nd over 5f out: led on bit over 2f out: rdn and hdd over 1f out: swtchd rt sn after: styd on u.p* 5/2[1]
5311 3 ½ **Wishformore (IRE)**[8] 575 7-9-8 61 6ex GeorgeDowning(5) 1 66
(Ian Williams) *mid-div: hdwy over 3f out: rdn over 1f out: styd on* 6/1[3]
00-0 4 hd **Troy Boy**[27] 321 4-8-9 46 oh1 NeilFarley(3) 8 50
(Robin Bastiman) *hld up: hmpd over 5f out: rdn and hdwy over 1f out: r.o* 50/1
006- 5 1¼ **Moves Like Jagger (IRE)**[79] 8140 4-8-12 46 oh1 (v[1]) PaddyAspell 4 47
(Phil McEntee) *mid-div: hdwy over 2f out: rdn and nt clr run over 1f out: kpt on* 17/2
0-36 6 ¾ **Refuse Colette (IRE)**[19] 435 5-8-12 46 oh1 JoeFanning 3 46
(Paul Green) *s.i.s: hld up: nt clr run over 2f out: hdwy over 1f out: styd on same pce ins fnl f* 25/1
5- 7 13 **Eretara (IRE)**[104] 7813 5-8-12 46 oh1 PaulMulrennan 5 16
(S Donohoe, Ire) *chsd ldrs: rdn over 2f out: sn wknd* 6/1[3]
-553 8 6 **Another Journey**[13] 515 5-8-12 46 oh1 GrahamGibbons 9 2
(Lisa Williamson) *led after 1f: rdn and hdd over 2f out: sn wknd* 20/1
1-03 P **Storey Hill (USA)**[30] 269 9-9-3 51 AdamKirby 7
(Richard Guest) *trckd ldr after 1f tl wnt wrong and p.u over 5f out* 7/1

1m 52.83s (2.33) **Going Correction** +0.275s/f (Slow) 9 Ran SP% **115.7**
Speed ratings (Par 101): **100,99,99,98,97 97,85,80,**
CSF £10.72 CT £41.57 TOTE £7.20: £2.60, £1.10, £1.50; EX 14.40 Trifecta £47.40.
**Owner** R C Bond **Bred** Patrick F Kelly **Trained** Brawby, N Yorks
■ Stewards' Enquiry : Shane Kelly one-day ban: careless riding (Mar 6)

**FOCUS**
A bunch finish to the first division of the extended 1m handicap. A fair contest for the grade and slightly the quicker division. The first three were all close to their marks.

## 673 LADBROKES MOBILE H'CAP (DIV II) 1m 141y(P)
7:00 (7:00) (Class 6) (0-55,54) 4-Y-O+ £2,264 (£673; £336; £168) Stalls Low

Form RPR
5412 1 **Prohibition (IRE)**[7] 592 8-9-7 54 AdamKirby 6 62
(Mandy Rowland) *s.i.s: hld up: pushed along and hdwy over 2f out: rdn over 1f out: styd on u.p to ld nr fin* 15/8[2]
-531 2 ½ **Miami Gator (IRE)**[21] 377 7-9-1 53 (v) JoeyHaynes(5) 4 60
(K R Burke) *led: rdn over 2f out: hdd nr fin* 11/10[1]
0- 3 1½ **Erelight (IRE)**[90] 8015 6-8-12 45 (b[1]) GrahamGibbons 1 48
(S Donohoe, Ire) *w ldr tl over 6f out: lost 2nd over 5f out: wnt 2nd again 3f out: rdn and ev ch over 1f out: edgd rt: hung lft ins fnl f: unable qck towards fin* 14/1
-005 4 3¼ **Ellies Image**[27] 321 7-8-12 45 PaulMulrennan 8 41
(Richard Ford) *hld up: hdwy over 3f out: rdn over 1f out: wknd fnl f* 33/1
0546 5 1¾ **Una Bella Cosa**[12] 537 4-8-12 45 (p) BenCurtis 3 37
(Alan McCabe) *s.i.s: hdwy 7f out: chsd ldr over 5f out: rdn 3f out: wknd over 1f out* 16/1
-056 6 7 **Marvo**[16] 474 10-8-12 45 (bt) DavidProbert 7 21
(Bernard Llewellyn) *prom: rdn over 3f out: wknd over 2f out* 10/1[3]
56-0 7 36 **Echologic**[48] 37 4-8-12 45 (t) AndrewMullen 2
(Brian Baugh) *hld up: rdn and wknd 3f out* 14/1

1m 53.4s (2.90) **Going Correction** +0.275s/f (Slow) 7 Ran SP% **113.6**
Speed ratings (Par 101): **98,97,96,93,91 85,53**
CSF £4.21 CT £17.28 TOTE £3.70: £2.20, £1.60; EX 4.60 Trifecta £25.90.
**Owner** Miss M E Rowland **Bred** Kevin Buckley **Trained** Lower Blidworth, Notts

**FOCUS**
A poor handicap, weakened further by the defection of the gamble Ferryview Place. The slightly slower division. The first two are rated to their recent marks.

## 674 LADBROKES H'CAP 1m 141y(P)
7:30 (7:30) (Class 4) (0-85,84) 4-Y-O+ £3,357 (£3,357; £769; £384) Stalls Low

Form RPR
/2-4 1 **Sky Khan**[10] 560 5-9-4 81 (e[1]) GeorgeBaker 6 91+
(Richard Guest) *hld up: rdn: hung lft and r.o wl ins fnl f to join wnr post* 6/1
22-1 1 dht **Fashion Line (IRE)**[27] 323 4-9-0 82 LouisSteward(5) 5 92+
(Michael Bell) *trckd ldr: led on bit over 1f out: sn shkn up: r.o: jnd post* 5/2[1]
35-2 3 2¼ **Silverware (USA)**[38] 163 6-9-6 83 GrahamGibbons 4 88
(Kristin Stubbs) *led: pushed along and qcknd 3f out: rdn and hdd over 1f out: styd on same pce ins fnl f* 11/4[2]
0-01 4 1¾ **Mr Red Clubs (IRE)**[20] 410 5-8-7 70 oh1 (p) AndrewMullen 3 71
(Michael Appleby) *hld up: hdwy 1/2-way: rdn over 2f out: styd on same pce fnl f* 5/1[3]
4-01 5 shd **Back Burner (IRE)**[20] 407 6-9-2 82 SamJames(3) 7 83
(David O'Meara) *prom: outpcd over 3f out: styd on ins fnl f* 10/1
1-01 6 nk **Toymaker**[12] 539 7-9-1 78 PaddyAspell 8 78
(Phil McEntee) *prom: rdn over 2f out: styd on same pce fr over 1f out* 8/1
0-0 7 hd **Odyssee (FR)**[19] 426 4-9-4 84 RobertTart(3) 2 84
(Marco Botti) *chsd ldrs: rdn over 3f out: styd on same pce fr over 1f out* 11/1
1-10 8 3½ **Conversational (IRE)**[17] 457 4-8-10 76 WilliamTwiston-Davies(3) 9 68
(Mick Channon) *hld up: rdn over 3f out: nt trble ldrs* 12/1
00-0 9 5 **Kickingthelilly**[29] 287 5-9-1 78 ChrisCatlin 1 58
(Rae Guest) *hld up: rdn over 3f out: nvr on terms* 20/1

1m 50.88s (0.38) **Going Correction** +0.275s/f (Slow) 9 Ran SP% **127.2**
Speed ratings (Par 105): **109,109,107,105,105 105,104,101,97**
WIN: 8.60 Sky Khan, 2.30 Fashion Line; PL: 1.40 Silverware, 3.60 Sky Khan, 2.30 Fashion Line; EX: FL&SK 13.30, SK&FL 19.00; CSF: FL&SK 10.19, SK&FL 11.89; TC: SK&FL&S 27.03, FL&SK&S 23.61; TF: SK&FL&S 37.40, FL&SK&S 29.30.
**Owner** Sheikh Marwan Al Maktoum **Bred** Darley **Trained** Newmarket, Suffolk
**Owner** The Unique Partnership **Bred** Heather Raw **Trained** Wetherby, W Yorks

**FOCUS**
The feature was a 0-85 handicap over the extended 1m1f and it was a thrilling contest. The form looks sound enough with the dead-heaters likely to do better.

## 675 LADBROKES MEDIAN AUCTION MAIDEN STKS 7f 32y(P)
8:00 (8:02) (Class 6) 3-5-Y-O £2,264 (£673; £336; £168) Stalls High

Form RPR
3- 1 **Mon Petit Secret**[93] 7960 3-8-1 0 ShaneGray(5) 3 67+
(Kevin Ryan) *mde all: clr over 1f out: rdn ins fnl f: jst hld on* 20/1
24-2 2 ½ **Jolly Red Jeanz (IRE)**[13] 512 3-8-6 65 JoeFanning 8 65
(J W Hills) *chsd wnr: pushed along 1/2-way: rdn over 2f out: r.o* 5/1[3]
55 3 ½ **Harboured (USA)**[13] 512 3-8-3 0 RosieJessop(3) 9 64
(Sir Mark Prescott Bt) *hld up: hdwy on outer 1/2-way: rdn and hung lft over 1f out: r.o* 25/1
420- 4 ¾ **Gratzie**[168] 6140 3-8-6 74 ow3 WilliamTwiston-Davies(3) 1 65
(Mick Channon) *chsd ldrs: pushed along 1/2-way: styd on same pce ins fnl f* 5/6[1]
5 1¼ **Tom Mann (IRE)** 3-8-11 0 GrahamGibbons 5 63
(David Barron) *s.i.s: hld up: hdwy over 1f out: nt trble ldrs* 9/2[2]

-4 6 *10* **Harlequin Jinks**[18] 447 3-8-6 0 DavidProbert 7 31
(Mark Usher) *chsd ldrs: lost pl 4f out: rdn 1/2-way: wknd over 2f out* **33/1**

0 7 *3/4* **Premier Jack's**[28] 291 3-8-8 0 MatthewCosham(3) 2 34
(Nikki Evans) *hld up: rdn over 2f out: sn wknd* **66/1**

8 *20* **Erwhons Gift (IRE)**[118] 7520 3-8-6 53 AndrewMullen 10
(S Donohoe, Ire) *prom: rdn 1/2-way: wkng whn hmpd over 2f out* **9/1**

1m 32.75s (3.15) **Going Correction** +0.275s/f (Slow)
**WFA** 3 from 5yo 17lb **8 Ran SP% 112.4**
Speed ratings (Par 101): **93,92,91,91,89 78,77,54**
CSF £97.75 TOTE £22.20: £3.80, £1.30, £2.70; EX 41.80 Trifecta £1237.10.
**Owner** Mrs Sabina Kelly **Bred** Mrs B E Moore **Trained** Hambleton, N Yorks
■ Rule 4 of 10p in the pound applies to all bets; Withdrawn: Mink Coat

**FOCUS**
With the favourite failing to run to her mark, this maiden didn't take much winning. Both Private Jones and Mink Coat were withdrawn after playing up in the stalls. A muddling race, rated around the runner-up.

## 676 BET ON YOUR MOBILE WITH LADBROKES H'CAP 7f 32y(P)
**8:30** (8:31) (Class 7) (0-50,50) 4-Y-0+ **£1,940** (£577; £288; £144) **Stalls** High

Form RPR

0-02 1 **Pipers Piping (IRE)**[13] 516 8-9-6 49 AdamKirby 5 60+
(Mandy Rowland) *hld up: hdwy over 1f out: shkn up to ld wl ins fnl f: comf* **2/1**[1]

2 *1 1/4* **Calling You (IRE)**[76] 8192 5-9-2 45 (b) AndrewMullen 12 53
(S Donohoe, Ire) *plld hrd and prom: chsd ldr 2f out: rdn to ld 1f out: sn hung lft: hdd and unable qck ins fnl f* **7/1**

-564 3 *2* **Very First Blade**[9] 563 5-9-2 45 (be) JoeFanning 7 48
(Michael Mullineaux) *a.p: rdn over 1f out: styd on same pce ins fnl f* **12/1**

00-0 4 *3/4* **High On The Hog (IRE)**[13] 516 6-9-4 47 (p) GeorgeBaker 1 48
(Mark Brisbourne) *sn pushed along to ld: rdn and hdd 1f out: no ex ins fnl f* **20/1**

46-6 5 *6* **Absolute Bearing (IRE)**[8] 575 5-9-4 47 JamesSullivan 4 32
(Tim Etherington) *trckd ldrs: rdn over 1f out: wknd ins fnl f* **20/1**

-035 6 *3/4* **Fleetwoodsands (IRE)**[21] 377 7-9-5 48 LiamKeniry 2 32
(David Evans) *mid-div: rdn over 1f out: n.d* **4/1**[2]

00/0 7 *nk* **Poker Hospital**[25] 351 5-8-11 45 (p) PhilipPrince(5) 9 28
(John Stimpson) *hld up: rdn 1/2-way: nvr on terms* **80/1**

6-34 8 *3/4* **Classy Trick (USA)**[25] 351 4-9-4 50 (p) WilliamTwiston-Davies(3) 3 31
(Patrick Morris) *hld up: rdn over 2f out: n.d* **8/1**

0-66 9 *1 1/2* **Auntie Mildred (IRE)**[10] 556 4-9-3 49 (v) SamJames(3) 10 26
(David O'Meara) *s.i.s: hdwy 1/2-way: rdn over 2f out: wknd fnl f* **50/1**

4-24 10 *3/4* **Aureolin Gulf**[27] 321 5-9-3 46 PaulQuinn 6 21
(Andrew Hollinshead) *hld up: rdn over 2f out: a in rr* **5/1**[3]

0-00 11 *nk* **Coach Montana (IRE)**[22] 370 5-9-2 45 (p) AdamBeschizza 8 19
(Christine Dunnett) *chsd ldr: rdn over 2f out: wknd fnl f* **33/1**

1m 30.36s (0.76) **Going Correction** +0.275s/f (Slow) **11 Ran SP% 117.0**
Speed ratings (Par 97): **106,104,102,101,94 93,93,92,90,89 89**
CSF £15.44 CT £138.78 TOTE £5.60: £1.90, £1.50, £2.00; EX 37.00 Trifecta £251.90.
**Owner** Miss M E Rowland **Bred** Drumhass Stud **Trained** Lower Blidworth, Notts

**FOCUS**
A poor 7f handicap but the best relative time on the card. The winner could find more on this form.

## 677 DOWNLOAD THE LADBROKES APP H'CAP 7f 32y(P)
**9:00** (9:00) (Class 5) (0-75,75) 4-Y-0+ **£2,911** (£866; £432; £216) **Stalls** High

Form RPR

2130 1 **Khajaaly (IRE)**[7] 587 7-8-12 66 (vt[1]) AndrewMullen 9 74
(Michael Appleby) *trckd ldrs: wnt 2nd 1/2-way: led over 1f out: rdn out* **9/2**

64-5 2 *1 1/2* **Polar Kite (IRE)**[41] 113 6-9-7 75 AdamKirby 2 79
(Sean Curran) *a.p: rdn to chse wnr fnl f: styd on* **3/1**[2]

-406 3 *2* **Fantasy Gladiator**[17] 457 8-9-7 75 GeorgeBaker 4 74
(John Quinn) *trckd ldr to 1/2-way: rdn over 1f out: styd on same pce ins fnl f* **7/2**[3]

2114 4 *1 1/2* **Prime Exhibit**[19] 421 9-9-3 71 (t) ShaneKelly 6 66
(Daniel Mark Loughnane) *s.i.s: hld up: rdn over 1f out: r.o u.p ins fnl f: nvr nrr* **13/2**

00-0 5 *1* **See The Storm**[3] 646 6-8-13 70 NeilFarley(3) 11 62
(Eric Alston) *hld up in tch: plld hrd: rdn over 1f out: no ex ins fnl f* **14/1**

23-3 6 *nse* **Malaysian Boleh**[16] 472 4-9-3 74 WilliamTwiston-Davies(3) 1 66
(Simon Dow) *s.s: hld up: hdwy 2f out: sn rdn and edgd lft: no ex fnl f* **5/2**[1]

50-0 7 *nk* **Lucky Dan (IRE)**[19] 432 8-9-4 72 JoeFanning 10 63
(Paul Green) *led: rdn and hdd over 1f out: wknd ins fnl f* **33/1**

00-0 8 *3/4* **Buzz Law (IRE)**[47] 49 6-8-8 62 BenCurtis 8 52
(K R Burke) *hld up: rdn over 1f out: n.d* **20/1**

1m 31.8s (2.20) **Going Correction** +0.275s/f (Slow) **8 Ran SP% 121.7**
Speed ratings (Par 103): **98,96,94,92,91 91,90,89**
CSF £19.78 CT £54.69 TOTE £4.90: £1.90, £2.90, £1.40; EX 21.40 Trifecta £70.20.
**Owner** New Kids On The Trot **Bred** Barry Noonan And Denis Noonan **Trained** Danethorpe, Notts

**FOCUS**
A couple of non-runners resulted in this closing handicap lacking in strength depth. Thr time was relatively slow and the form is rated cautiously.
T/Jkpt: Not won. T/Plt: £19.70 to a £1 stake. Pool: £107,690.43 - 3972.49 winning units. T/Qpdt: £5.00 to a £1 stake. Pool: 10,297.49 - 1496.20 winning units. CR

# 632 MEYDAN (L-H)
Thursday, February 20
**OFFICIAL GOING: Tapeta: standard; turf: good**

## 678a DISTRICT ONE (H'CAP) (TURF) 7f
**3:15** (3:15) (100-113,113) 3-Y-0+
**£63,253** (£21,084; £10,542; £5,271; £3,162; £2,108)

RPR

1 **Eastern Rules (IRE)**[14] 504 6-8-11 105 ShaneFoley 1 108+
(M Halford, Ire) *s.i.s: settled in rr: rdn 2 1/2f out: r.o wl to ld fnl f* **5/1**[3]

2 *1 1/4* **Sommerabend**[28] 306 7-9-2 109 MaximeGuyon 9 110
(M Rulec, Germany) *chsd ldrs: ev ch 1 1/2f out: nt qckn fnl 110yds* **28/1**

3 *shd* **Zahee (NZ)**[14] 508 5-9-4 111 ChristopheSoumillon 7 112
(M F De Kock, South Africa) *sn led: hdd 4 1/2f out: rdn 2 1/2f out: led 2f out: hdd fnl f* **5/2**[2]

4 *3/4* **Regulation (IRE)**[7] 595 5-8-7 100 TadhgO'Shea 2 99+
(M Halford, Ire) *mid-div: r.o same pce fnl 1 1/2f* **25/1**

5 *3/4* **Anaerobio (ARG)**[28] 308 7-9-6 113 (t) PatCosgrave 4 110
(M F De Kock, South Africa) *nvr bttr than mid-div* **9/4**[1]

6 *nk* **Free Wheeling (AUS)**[28] 306 6-8-13 106 (t) SilvestreDeSousa 6 102
(Saeed bin Suroor) *nvr bttr than mid-div* **5/1**[3]

7 *1 1/4* **Intransigent**[7] 597 5-8-11 105 JamieSpencer 3 96
(Andrew Balding) *trckd ldrs: t.k.h: ev ch 3 1/2f out: one pce fnl 2f* **12/1**

8 *1/2* **Kavanagh (SAF)**[28] 308 7-9-3 110 (t) RichardHughes 5 101
(M F De Kock, South Africa) *a in rr* **12/1**

9 *1* **Santefisio**[14] 504 8-8-7 100 (b) TomEaves 8 88
(Keith Dalgleish) *mid-div: led 4f out: hdd & wknd 2f out* **33/1**

1m 23.16s (83.16) **9 Ran SP% 118.3**
CSF: 134.91; EXACTA: 62.80 TRICAST 433.58; WIN: 6.30; PL: 2.00, 2.90, 1.80.
**Owner** S Hales **Bred** Michael Woodlock & Seamus Kennedy **Trained** Doneany, Co Kildare

**FOCUS**
This decent handicap was run at a solid pace.

## 679a MEYDAN SOBHA (H'CAP) (TAPETA) 1m
**3:50** (3:50) (95-105,105) 3-Y-0+
**£39,759** (£13,253; £6,626; £3,313; £1,987; £1,325)

RPR

1 **Avon Pearl**[14] 509 5-9-2 100 (vt) PatDobbs 3 105+
(Rune Haugen, Norway) *mid-div: smooth prog 2f out: led 110yds: comf* **16/1**

2 *2 1/4* **Van Rooney (USA)**[21] 397 5-9-4 102 (t) AdriedeVries 1 101
(Ali Jan, Qatar) *settled in rr: r.o fnl 1 1/2f: nrst fin* **12/1**

3 *1/2* **Ocean Tempest**[14] 509 5-9-4 102 BrettDoyle 2 100
(John Ryan) *trckd ldng trio: led briefly 1f out: hdd fnl 110yds* **33/1**

4 *1 1/4* **Mustaheel (IRE)**[14] 504 5-9-6 105 (t) PaulHanagan 10 99+
(A Al Raihe, UAE) *settled in rr: r.o fnl 2f: nrst fin* **7/1**[3]

5 *nk* **Intrigo**[21] 394 4-9-1 99 SilvestreDeSousa 8 93+
(Charlie Appleby) *settled in rr: r.o fnl 2f: nrst fin* **7/1**[3]

6 *1* **Derbaas (USA)**[4] 8-9-4 102 (t) DaneO'Neill 11 94+
(A Al Raihe, UAE) *mid-div: chsd ldrs 2f out: ev ch 110yds out: nt qckn fnl 55yds* **25/1**

7 *1 1/4* **Qatoomah (KSA)**[26] 5-9-4 102 WilliamBuick 16 91+
(N Bachalard, Saudi Arabia) *trckd ldng trio tl wknd 1 1/2f out* **20/1**

8 *hd* **Disa Leader (SAF)**[14] 509 9-9-5 104 JGeroudis 9 91+
(M F De Kock, South Africa) *trckd ldrs: n.m.r 1 1/2f out: nt rcvr* **10/1**

9 *shd* **Master Of War**[14] 504 4-9-2 100 JamesDoyle 4 88+
(D Selvaratnam, UAE) *nvr bttr than mid-div* **12/1**

10 *1 1/4* **Risby (IRE)**[21] 396 6-9-2 100 (t) ThierryThulliez 6 85+
(J-M Osorio, Spain) *nvr bttr than mid-div* **25/1**

11 *1* **Dragon Falls (IRE)**[14] 504 5-9-3 101 MickaelBarzalona 5 84+
(Charlie Appleby) *slowly away: nvr bttr than mid-div: n.m.r 1 1/2f out* **13/2**[2]

12 *1/2* **Banna Boirche (IRE)**[14] 509 8-9-2 100 ShaneFoley 7 82+
(M Halford, Ire) *settled in rr: kpt on same pce fnl 2f* **16/1**

13 *3 3/4* **String Theory (IRE)**[21] 394 4-9-5 104 MartinHarley 14 76+
(Marco Botti) *trckd ldng pair: ev ch 2f out: wknd fnl f* **6/1**[1]

14 *hd* **Taylor Said (CAN)**[549] 6-9-3 101 (b) AhmedAjtebi 12 74+
(Charlie Appleby) *sn led: hdd 2f out: wknd fnl f* **14/1**

15 *4* **Tales Of Grimm (USA)**[21] 397 5-9-2 100 (b) ChristopheSoumillon 13 64+
(Richard Fahey) *nvr able to chal* **8/1**

16 *3/4* **Mister Big Shuffle (GER)**[140] 4-9-1 99 Per-AndersGraberg 15 61
(Niels Petersen, Norway) *nvr able to chal* **20/1**

1m 37.45s (-0.05) **16 Ran SP% 126.8**
CSF: 189.49; EXACTA: 513.80 TRICAST 6180.24; TRIFECTA: 16134.40 WIN: 39.30.
**Owner** Jostein Jorgensen **Bred** Park Farm Racing **Trained** Norway

**FOCUS**
If proof were still needed that ground loss matters, note the first three home (16-1, 12-1 and 33-1 respectively) came from the bottom three boxes and went the shortest way.

## 680a MEYDAN SOBHA PHASE II (H'CAP) (TURF) 5f
**4:25** (4:25) (100-113,113) 3-Y-0+
**£63,253** (£21,084; £10,542; £5,271; £3,162; £2,108)

RPR

1 **Medicean Man**[21] 393 8-9-1 108 (tp) HarryBentley 7 112
(Jeremy Gask) *mid-div: rdn 3f out: led 1 1/2f out: r.o gamely* **9/2**[2]

2 *nk* **Ahtoug**[21] 393 6-8-13 106 MickaelBarzalona 9 109
(Charlie Appleby) *settled in rr: rdn 3f out: chsd ldrs 1 1/2f out: ev ch 110yds out: nt qckn fnl 55yds* **11/2**[3]

3 *1 3/4* **Hototo**[42] 107 4-8-13 106 (v) LukeMorris 6 103
(Fawzi Abdulla Nass, Bahrain) *trckd ldrs: ev ch 1f out: nt qckn fnl 110yds* **11/2**[3]

4 *shd* **Desert Law (IRE)**[42] 107 6-8-7 100 SilvestreDeSousa 8 96+
(Saeed bin Suroor) *mid-div: rdn 2 1/2f out: r.o fnl f: nrst fin* **9/1**

5 *nk* **Catcall (FR)**[137] 7054 5-9-6 113 Christophe-PatriceLemaire 4 108+
(P Sogorb, France) *broke awkwardly: nvr nr to chal but kpt on fnl 2f* **3/1**[1]

6 *1/2* **Monsieur Joe (IRE)**[21] 393 7-8-9 102 (v) KierenFallon 3 95
(Paul Midgley) *mid-div: chsd ldrs 2f out: nt qckn fnl 1 1/2f* **20/1**

7 *shd* **Racy**[21] 393 7-8-7 100 TomEaves 2 93
(Brian Ellison) *chsd ldrs: ev ch 1f out: wknd fnl 110yds* **8/1**

8 *1 1/2* **Abstraction (IRE)**[21] 393 4-9-0 107 FergalLynch 5 95
(Sarah Dawson, Ire) *sn led: hdd 1 1/2f out: one pce fnl f* **6/1**

9 *2 1/2* **My Propeller (IRE)**[21] 393 5-8-7 100 RichardMullen 10 79
(Peter Chapple-Hyam) *nvr nr to chal* **25/1**

10 *3 1/4* **Dungannon**[21] 393 7-8-8 101 (v) JamieSpencer 1 68
(Andrew Balding) *trckd ldng pair tl outpcd 2f out* **16/1**

57.31s (57.31) **10 Ran SP% 123.8**
CSF: 31.62; EXACTA: 43.70 TRICAST 144.44; TRIFECTA: 256.30 WIN: 6.80; PL: 1.90, 1.80, 2.10.

**Owner** Stuart Dobb & Miss Kate Dobb **Bred** Barry Taylor **Trained** Sutton Veny, Wilts

**FOCUS**
They raced towards the far side, but split into two even groups early and the bunch closest to the middle of the track provided the first four home.

## 681a DISTRICT ONE PHASE I (H'CAP) (TAPETA) 1m 2f
**5:00** (5:00) (95-113,113) 3-Y-0+
**£54,216** (£18,072; £9,036; £4,518; £2,710; £1,807)

RPR

1 **Elleval (IRE)**[7] 595 4-9-0 107 FergalLynch 7 112
(David Marnane, Ire) *mid-div: smooth prog 2 1/2f out: led 110yds out: r.o wl* **16/1**

2 *nk* **Start Right**[7] 593 7-8-5 97 (p) TadhgO'Shea 2 101
(S Seemar, UAE) *mid-div: smooth prog: chsd ldrs 1 1/2f out: ev ch 2 1/2f out: r.o: jst failed* **20/1**

3 *3/4* **Plantagenet (SPA)**[7] 593 7-8-5 97 Per-AndersGraberg 3 100+
(Niels Petersen, Norway) *settled in rr: r.o fnl 2f: nrst fin* **28/1**

**4** *1 3/4* **Clon Brulee (IRE)**[21] 394 5-8-7 **99**........................ SilvestreDeSousa 16 98
(Saeed bin Suroor) *trckd ldrs: ev ch 110yds out: nt qckn fnl 55yds* **14/1**

**5** *nk* **Mutajare (IRE)**[14] 508 6-9-4 **110**....................................(t) DaneO'Neill 13 108
(A Al Raihe, UAE) *nvr nr to chal but r.o fnl 2f: nrst fin* **25/1**

**6** *shd* **Solar Deity (IRE)**[28] 306 5-9-2 **108**................................. MartinHarley 8 106
(Marco Botti) *mid-div: r.o fnl 1 1/2f: nrst fin* **15/2**

**7** *3/4* **Sweet Lightning**[28] 307 9-8-7 **99** ow1.............................. TomEaves 14 96
(David O'Meara) *nvr nr to chal* **40/1**

**8** *nk* **Alexandra Palace (SAF)**[28] 306 5-9-1 **107**........................ JGeroudis 6 103
(M F De Kock, South Africa) *mid-div: n.m.r 1 1/2f out: r.o same pce fnl 110yds* **6/1**[2]

**9** *nk* **Specific Gravity (FR)**[7] 593 6-8-6 **98**.......................... ThierryThulliez 1 94
(M F De Kock, South Africa) *trckd ldrs: ev ch 1 1/2f out: one pce fnl 110yds* **33/1**

**10** *3/4* **Cat O'Mountain (USA)**[35] 202 4-9-6 **113**.............. MickaelBarzalona 12 107
(Charlie Appleby) *mid-div: rdn 3f out: chsd ldrs 2f out: n.m.r 1 1/2f out: nt rcvr* **11/10**[1]

**11** *2 3/4* **Layali Al Andalus**[7] 593 7-8-6 **98**................................ RichardMullen 4 87
(S Seemar, UAE) *nvr bttr than mid-div* **33/1**

**12** *nk* **Steeler (IRE)**[21] 397 4-9-2 **109**.................................. KierenFallon 9 97
(Charlie Appleby) *trckd ldrs: led briefly 2f out: wknd fnl f* **7/1**[3]

**13** *1 3/4* **Almoonqith (USA)**[19] 440 4-8-5 **95**.............................. PaulHanagan 10 82
(M F De Kock, South Africa) *nvr bttr than mid-div* **16/1**

**14** *3 1/2* **Zain Shamardal (IRE)**[14] 508 6-9-1 **107**...............(t) RoystonFfrench 11 84
(A Al Raihe, UAE) *nvr nr to chal* **25/1**

**15** *1 1/2* **Counterfeiter**[153] 4-8-6 **96** ow1........................................ WilliamBuick 15 73
(Saeed bin Suroor) *settled in rr: nvr nr to chal* **12/1**

**16** *nk* **Samurai Sword**[14] 508 6-8-10 **102**................................(tp) AdriedeVries 5 76
(A bin Harmash, UAE) *sn led: hdd & wknd 2f out* **18/1**

2m 3.07s (-1.63)
**WFA** 4 from 5yo+ 1lb **16** Ran SP% **141.8**
CSF: 330.06; EXACTA: 199.40 TRICAST: 8670.38, TRIFECTA: 5112.10 WIN: 19.90.
**Owner** Damian Lavelle **Bred** P G Lyons **Trained** Bansha, Co Tipperary

**FOCUS**
A terrific handicap.

## 682a BALANCHINE SPONSORED BY DISTRICT ONE (GROUP 2) (F&M) (TURF) 1m 1f

**5:35** (5:35) 3-Y-O+

**£72,289** (£24,096; £12,048; £6,024; £3,614; £2,409)

RPR

**1** **L'Amour De Ma Vie (USA)**[21] 395 5-9-0 109.......................... MaximeGuyon 3 109
(Mme Pia Brandt, France) *trckd ldrs: led 2 1/2f out: r.o wl: comf* **8/1**[3]

**2** *1 3/4* **Flotilla (FR)**[21] 395 4-9-0 116...................... Christophe-PatriceLemaire 4 105+
(M Delzangles, France) *settled in last: nvr nr to chal but r.o fnl 2f: nrst fin* **7/1**[2]

**3** *shd* **Pearl Of Africa (IRE)**[21] 395 4-9-0 105...................... JamieSpencer 1 105
(Edward Lynam, Ire) *s.i.s: rdn 2f out: chsd ldrs 1/2f out: one pce fnl 110yds* **20/1**

**4** *1/2* **Certify (USA)**[21] 395 4-9-3 113............................ MickaelBarzalona 2 107+
(Charlie Appleby) *settled in rr: rdn 2 1/2f out: r.o same pce fnl 1 1/2f but nvr able to chal* **2/5**[1]

**5** *3 3/4* **Moment In Time (IRE)**[116] 7562 5-9-0 108........................ JimCrowley 5 96
(David Simcock) *nvr bttr than mid-div* **12/1**

**6** *2* **Banoffee (IRE)**[28] 307 4-9-0 100.................................. RichardHughes 6 92
(Hughie Morrison) *sn led: rdn 4f out: hdd & wknd 2 1/2f out* **25/1**

1m 50.55s (110.55) **6** Ran SP% **111.3**
CSF: 58.28; EXACTA: 33.10 TRIFECTA: 124.10 WIN: 5.80.
**Owner** Md Bloodstock Limited **Bred** Palides Investments N V Inc **Trained** France

**FOCUS**
There was a turn up here after a modest pace and the form is rated around the winner and third.

## 683a DUBAI MILLENNIUM STKS SPONSORED BY DISTRICT ONE (LISTED RACE) (TURF) 1m 2f

**6:10** (6:10) 3-Y-O+

**£72,289** (£24,096; £12,048; £6,024; £3,614; £2,409)

RPR

**1** **Tasaday (USA)**[21] 397 4-9-0 113.......................... SilvestreDeSousa 5 114
(Saeed bin Suroor) *trckd ldrs: led 2 1/2f out: r.o wl: jst hld on* **7/2**[2]

**2** *nk* **Empoli (GER)**[151] 6678 4-9-0 113.............................. AdriedeVries 7 113
(P Schiergen, Germany) *mid-div: chsd wnr 2f out: r.o fnl 1 1/2f: jst failed* **10/1**

**3** *1 1/4* **Mujaarib (AUS)**[21] 397 6-9-4 115................................ PaulHanagan 2 114+
(M F De Kock, South Africa) *settled in rr: rdn 3f out: r.o wl: nrst fin* **6/4**[1]

**4** *nk* **Jamr**[348] 958 6-9-0 102..........................................(v) MickaelBarzalona 8 109
(A bin Harmash, UAE) *mid-div: chsd wnr 2 1/2f out: nt qckn fnl f* **16/1**

**5** *1 1/4* **Dastarhon (IRE)**[21] 397 4-9-0 113...................................(t) MaximeGuyon 1 108
(Mme Pia Brandt, France) *trckd ldng pair: ev ch 1 1/2f out: one pce fnl f* **8/1**[3]

**6** *1 3/4* **Burano (IRE)**[21] 398 5-9-0 100....................................(b) HarryBentley 13 103
(Brian Meehan) *in rr of mid-div: r.o fnl 1 1/2f but nvr able to chal* **16/1**

**7** *2* **Quick Wit**[148] 6742 7-9-0 107........................................ AhmedAjtebi 11 99
(Saeed bin Suroor) *nvr nr to chal* **10/1**

**8** *hd* **Agent Allison**[21] 394 4-8-9 95..................................... JimCrowley 3 95
(Peter Chapple-Hyam) *settled in rr: nvr nr to chal* **33/1**

**9** *nk* **Rebel Song (IRE)**[21] 394 5-9-0 95...................................(t) WayneSmith 4 98
(A bin Harmash, UAE) *sn led: hdd 7f out: sn btn* **33/1**

**10** *nk* **Without Fear (FR)**[14] 507 6-9-2 106...................... Per-AndersGraberg 9 100
(Niels Petersen, Norway) *nvr able to chal* **25/1**

**11** *1/2* **Mundahesh (IRE)**[19] 442 4-9-0 100............................... DaneO'Neill 10 98
(A Al Raihe, UAE) *nvr bttr than mid-div* **14/1**

**12** *nk* **Robert The Painter (IRE)**[21] 394 6-9-0 95................(v) KierenFallon 12 96
(David O'Meara) *trckd ldrs: led 7f out: hdd & wknd 2 1/2f out* **33/1**

**13** *shd* **Now Spun (USA)**[5] 636 4-9-0 94........................... RoystonFfrench 6 97
(A Al Raihe, UAE) *s.i.s: nvr bttr than mid-div* **25/1**

2m 2.33s (122.33)
**WFA** 4 from 5yo+ 1lb **13** Ran SP% **126.5**
CSF: 48.71; EX: 26.10, TRIFECTA: 83.00 WIN: 4.50; PL: 1.40, 2.10, 1.30 Placepot: £[illegible].70 to a £1 stake.Pool £9010.59 - 1.00 winning unit.Pool of £901.05 carried over to Meydan 27th Feb. Quadpot: £117.60 to a £1 stake.Pool: £635.70 - 4.00 winning units. CSF £27 CT £Owner TOTE £Godolphin: £Bred, £Darley, £Trained, £Newmarket, Suffolk .

**FOCUS**
Not much depth to this Listed contest, but the 'right' three horses contested the finish.

# [662]LINGFIELD (L-H)

Friday, February 21

**OFFICIAL GOING: Standard**
Wind: strong, half behind Weather: dry, breezy

## 684 LADBROKES MOBILE MEDIAN AUCTION MAIDEN STKS 1m 1y(P)

**1:30** (1:31) (Class 6) 3-4-Y-O **£2,726** (£805; £402) **Stalls** High

Form RPR

542 **1** **Zamra (IRE)**[20] 422 3-8-3 67.........................................(p) LukeMorris 9 60+
(James Tate) *in tch in last trio: effrt to chse ldrs on outer bnd 2f out: drvn to ld and edgd lft over 1f out: styd on wl and asserted fnl 100yds: drvn out* **8/11**[1]

35-4 **2** *1 1/4* **Tax Reform (IRE)**[29] 291 4-9-13 67..........................(b[1]) RobertHavlin 3 68
(Mark Hoad) *hld up in tch in midfield: rdn and effrt to press ldr on inner jst over 1f out: nt qckn u.p ins fnl f: outpcd fnl 100yds* **6/1**[2]

0 **3** *1/2* **Jammy Moment**[37] 188 3-8-3 0.......................................... HayleyTurner 8 56
(William Muir) *s.i.s: hld up in rr: hdwy on outer over 1f out: wnt 3rd: edgd lft and flashed tail u.p jst ins fnl f: r.o wl: nt rch ldrs* **14/1**

**4** *1 3/4* **Wings Of Fire (IRE)** 4-9-13 0.............................. StevieDonohoe 5 63?
(Denis Quinn) *s.i.s: hld up in tch in last trio: swtchd rt and hdwy wl over 1f out: styd on fnl f: nvr trbld ldrs* **50/1**

60-4 **5** *4 1/2* **Honiton Lace**[21] 409 3-8-0 65 ow2........................ ShelleyBirkett[(5)] 7 44
(J W Hills) *hld up in tch in midfield on outer: hdwy to join ldrs 3f out: rdn to ld 2f out: hdd over 1f out: outpcd and sltly hmpd ent fnl f: fdd and lost 2 pls ins fnl f* **8/1**

**6** *1* **Moonlit Sky** 3-8-8 0.......................................................... JimmyQuinn 2 44
(James Tate) *in tch in midfield: nt clr run and shuffled bk to rr bnd 2f out: no ch whn swtchd rt and pushed along jst over 1f out: styd on: nvr trbld ldrs* **8/1**

**7** *12* **Brycewise** 3-8-8 0.............................................. RichardKingscote 1 17
(Michael Wigham) *t.k.h: led tl hdd 2f out: sn btn and wknd: bhd fnl f* **7/1**[3]

0 **8** *1/2* **Jazz Bay**[29] 291 3-8-8 0................................................. DavidProbert 6 16
(John Bridger) *chsd ldr: ev ch and rdn over 2f out: btn and wknd over 1f out: bhd fnl f* **100/1**

1m 38.37s (0.17) **Going Correction** +0.05s/f (Slow)
**WFA** 3 from 4yo 19lb **8** Ran SP% **116.5**
Speed ratings (Par 101): **101,99,99,97,93 92,80,79**
CSF £5.83 TOTE £2.00: £1.02, £1.50, £3.30; EX 4.90 Trifecta £37.10.
**Owner** Saif Ali **Bred** T Kimura **Trained** Newmarket, Suffolk

**FOCUS**
A weak maiden and the trio of newcomers failed to make an impact. The winner did not need to match her latest.

## 685 CORAL MOBILE "JUST THREE CLICKS TO BET" (S) STKS 1m 2f (P)

**2:00** (2:00) (Class 6) 4-Y-O+ **£2,385** (£704; £352) **Stalls** Low

Form RPR

305- **1** **Conducting**[65] 8335 6-9-1 65.......................................... DavidProbert 4 71
(Gay Kelleway) *awkward as stalls opened: chsd ldr: rdn and qcknd clr w wnr 2f out: kpt on u.p to ld ins fnl f: rdn out* **4/1**[3]

1-2 **2** *1* **Officer In Command (USA)**[21] 407 8-9-6 75..............(p) LiamKeniry 1 74
(John Butler) *led and set stdy gallop: rdn and qcknd clr w wnr 2f out: kpt on u.p tl hdd and no ex ins fnl f* **9/2**

2161 **3** *2* **Mahadee (IRE)**[7] 601 9-9-1 68..................................(b) LouisSteward[(5)] 7 70+
(Lee Carter) *s.i.s: hld up in rr: 5th and switching rt bnd 2f out: hdwy u.p over 1f out: r.o wl ins fnl f: no ch of rching ldrs* **7/2**[2]

00-0 **4** *3/4* **Lily Edge**[8] 589 5-8-10 62..........................................(p) LukeMorris 3 59?
(John Bridger) *in tch in midfield: rdn 3f out: outpcd and drvn 2f out: chsd clr ldng pair jst over 1f out: kpt on but no threat to ldrs: lost 3rd ins fnl f* **33/1**

-314 **5** *1 1/2* **Matraash (USA)**[21] 407 8-9-6 78...............................(be) ShaneKelly 5 66
(Daniel Mark Loughnane) *hld up in tch in midfield: shuffled bk to last and stuck bhd horses 4f out: swtchd rt bnd 2f out: rdn over 1f out: no ch but kpt on fnl f* **2/1**[1]

-250 **6** *2 3/4* **Copperwood**[22] 379 9-9-6 62.............................................. AmirQuinn 6 60
(Lee Carter) *t.k.h: stdd s: hld up in tch in last pair: hdwy to chse ldrs 4f out: rdn and outpcd 2f out: lost 3rd over 1f out: and wknd fnl f* **16/1**

-660 **7** *2* **Auden (USA)**[18] 458 6-9-6 62................................ FrederikTylicki 2 56
(J R Jenkins) *chsd ldrs: rdn and lost pl over 2f out: bhd 1f out* **10/1**

2m 8.31s (1.71) **Going Correction** +0.05s/f (Slow) **7** Ran SP% **111.7**
Speed ratings (Par 101): **95,94,92,92,90 88,87**
CSF £21.10 TOTE £7.00: £5.90, £2.70; EX 20.90 Trifecta £42.40.There was no bid for the winner. Mahadee was claimed by Mr T. Dascombe for £6,000.
**Owner** John Farley & Ben Parish **Bred** David J Brown **Trained** Exning, Suffolk

**FOCUS**
This seller was run in a crawl. The winner is rated to his latter 2013 form.

## 686 CORAL APP DOWNLOAD FROM THE APP STORE MAIDEN STKS 1m 4f (P)

**2:30** (2:30) (Class 5) 4-Y-O+ **£3,408** (£1,006; £503) **Stalls** Low

Form RPR

2- **1** **Devon Drum**[84] 7158 6-9-5 0.......................... WilliamTwiston-Davies[(3)] 10 67
(Paul Webber) *chsd ldrs: rdn and sltly outpcd jst over 2f out: styd on u.p to ld fnl 100yds: rdn out* **11/4**[2]

**2** *1* **Mister Carrot**[83] 4-9-5 0...............................................(t) RobertHavlin 12 66
(George Baker) *wnt rt s: sn led: rdn and qcknd 3 l clr ent fnl 2f: drvn over 1f out: hdd and no ex fnl 100yds* **33/1**

5 **3** *1/2* **Midnight Chorister**[9] 581 6-9-8 0.................................(t) HayleyTurner 9 65
(Alex Hales) *stdd s: t.k.h: hld up in last trio: sme hdwy over 2f out: 7th and stl plenty to do over 1f out: r.o v strly ins fnl f: wnt 3rd last stride: nt quite rch ldrs* **8/1**

422- **4** *nse* **Song And Dance Man**[145] 6870 4-9-5 73...................(v[1]) GeorgeBaker 8 65
(Gary Moore) *t.k.h: chsd ldr: rdn and sltly outpcd ent fnl 2f: rallied u.p and pressing ldr ins fnl f: no ex and one pce fnl 50yds* **7/4**[1]

**5** *nse* **Ring Eye (IRE)**[147] 6-9-8 0.............................................. LukeMorris 1 65
(John O'Shea) *in tch in midfield: hdwy to chse ldrs 3f out: drvn and slt outpcd 2f out: kpt on again u.p ins fnl f* **33/1**

3 **6** *shd* **Gabrial The Terror (IRE)**[11] 558 4-9-5 0.......................... LiamKeniry 6 65
(David Simcock) *t.k.h: hld up in tch in midfield: rdn and effrt wl over 1f out: swtchd rt 1f out: styd on strly ins fnl f: nt quite rch ldrs* **7/1**[3]

**7** *8* **Cape Breton**[109] 8-9-8 0.................................................. DavidProbert 7 52
(Patrick Chamings) *hld up in last quartet: rdn and sme hdwy into midfield ent fnl 2f: nvr trbld ldrs* **7/1**[3]

8 1 3/4 **Littledean Jimmy (IRE)**[625] 9-9-3 0 DCByrne(5) 5 49
(John O'Shea) *stdd s: hld up in last quartet: rdn and struggling over 3f out: bhd fnl 2f* **50/1**

9 1/2 **Sycophantic (IRE)** 4-9-5 0 TomQueally 2 48
(Jamie Osborne) *s.i.s: rn green and a towards rr: rdn and lost tch 3f out: bhd fnl 2f* **14/1**

10 nk **Hammered Silver (IRE)** 4-9-5 0 ShaneKelly 3 48
(Mike Murphy) *t.k.h: wl in tch in midfield: rdn and outpcd ent fnl 2f: btn over 1f out: wknd fnl f* **25/1**

0/ 11 2 1/4 **Lillioftheballet (IRE)**[49] [4259] 7-9-3 0 GrahamLee 4 39
(Jim Goldie) *in tch in midfield: rdn and outpcd wl over 2f out: wknd 2f out* **33/1**

0 12 72 **Madrinas Prince (IRE)**[27] [341] 5-9-3 0 RyanWhile(5) 11
(Paddy Butler) *t.k.h: chsd ldrs tl lost pl qckly over 3f out: t.o over 1f out* **100/1**

2m 36.05s (3.05) **Going Correction** +0.05s/f (Slow)
**WFA** 4 from 5yo+ 3lb **12 Ran SP% 121.4**
Speed ratings (Par 103): **91,90,90,89,89 89,84,83,83,82 81,33**
CSF £103.67 TOTE £4.70: £1.50, £22.10, £2.60; EX 154.60 Trifecta £1649.80.
**Owner** D G Carrington **Bred** Juddmonte Farms Ltd **Trained** Mollington, Oxon
■ Stewards' Enquiry : Robert Havlin one-day ban: careless riding (Mar 7)

**FOCUS**
They finished in a bunch behind the winner in this ordinary maiden. The form pair were not at their best and the race is rated around the third.

## 687 COMPARE BOOKMAKERS AT BOOKMAKERS.CO.UK H'CAP (DIV I) 6f 1y(P)
**3:00** (3:00) (Class 6) (0-60,61) 4-Y-O+ **£2,726** (£805; £402) **Stalls** Low

Form RPR

6221 1 **Volito**[2] [663] 8-9-8 **61** 6ex GeorgeBaker 7 68
(Anabel K Murphy) *stdd and dropped in bhd after s: hld up in rr: nt clr run 2f out: swtchd rt and clsd over 1f out: gap opened and qcknd 1f out: r.o wl to ld cl home* **9/4**[1]

04-0 2 nk **Hinton Admiral**[19] [449] 10-8-12 **51** JoeFanning 2 57
(Pat Eddery) *chsd ldng trio: rdn and effrt to chal on inner over 1f out: led ins fnl f: kpt on wl but hdd and no ex cl home* **12/1**

4025 3 1/2 **Welsh Inlet (IRE)**[8] [592] 6-9-0 **53** LiamKeniry 4 57
(John Bridger) *dwlt: in tch in last quartet: rdn and effrt 2f out: styd on strly ins fnl f: wnt 3rd towards fin* **7/1**

2-03 4 1/2 **Metropolitan Chief**[21] [402] 10-8-8 **52** (p) DavidKenny(5) 3 55
(Paul Burgoyne) *in tch in midfield: clsd to trck ldrs 2f out: jnd ldrs and stl on bit jst over 1f out: rdn hands and heels and fnd nil ins fnl f: wknd towards fin* **25/1**

61-3 5 1/2 **Assertive Agent**[29] [296] 4-9-4 **57** LukeMorris 1 58
(Tony Carroll) *in tch in midfield: hung rt bnd 2f out: swtchd rt and hdwy to chse ldrs 1f out: styd on same pce u.p ins fnl f* **9/2**[3]

-323 6 3/4 **Hamis Al Bin (IRE)**[19] [448] 5-9-4 **57** (t) RichardKingscote 9 56
(Milton Bradley) *hld up in rr: nt clr run over 1f out: clsng whn nt clr run again jst ins fnl f: pushed along and r.o wl fnl 100yds: nvr able to chal* **3/1**[2]

-464 7 1 **Mossgo (IRE)**[9] [572] 4-9-7 **60** (t) RobertHavlin 8 56
(John Best) *led: rdn and hrd pressed ent fnl f: hdd ins fnl f: wknd fnl 100yds* **8/1**

00-6 8 1/2 **Time For Lambrini (IRE)**[18] [453] 4-9-0 **58** ShirleyTeasdale(5) 10 52
(Lisa Williamson) *chsd ldr tl over 1f out: unable qck and hung rt u.p ent fnl f: wknd ins fnl f* **50/1**

3-40 9 2 1/4 **Microlight**[19] [448] 6-8-7 **46** oh1 (b) JimmyQuinn 11 33
(John E Long) *chsd ldrs: drvn and lost pl whn wd bnd 2f out: wknd over 1f out* **33/1**

000- 10 8 **Waspy**[136] [7092] 5-8-0 **46** oh1 DanielCremin(7) 5 7
(Dr Jeremy Naylor) *in tch in last quartet: rdn and dropped to last wl over 2f out: wknd 2f out* **66/1**

1m 11.4s (-0.50) **Going Correction** +0.05s/f (Slow) **10 Ran SP% 115.5**
Speed ratings (Par 101): **105,104,103,103,102 101,100,99,96,85**
CSF £29.65 CT £165.29 TOTE £2.70: £1.10, £3.00, £2.80; EX 35.00 Trifecta £179.60.
**Owner** Mrs Anabel K Murphy **Bred** A J And Mrs L Brazier **Trained** Wilmcote, Warwicks

**FOCUS**
A run-of-the-mill sprint handicap. The winner rates a bit closer to his old form.

## 688 COMPARE BOOKMAKERS AT BOOKMAKERS.CO.UK H'CAP (DIV II) 6f 1y(P)
**3:30** (3:31) (Class 6) (0-60,58) 4-Y-O+ **£2,726** (£805; £402) **Stalls** Low

Form RPR

-421 1 **Seamster**[21] [402] 7-9-6 **57** (bt) GrahamLee 7 67
(Richard Ford) *mde all: c clr and stl travelling strly over 1f out: pushed along and a doing enough ins fnl f* **2/1**[1]

0-42 2 1/2 **Ghost Train (IRE)**[7] [603] 5-9-6 **57** (p) HayleyTurner 3 65
(Tim McCarthy) *hld up in tch in midfield: rdn and effrt on inner over 1f out: chsd wnr ins fnl f: r.o but comf hld by wnr* **9/4**[2]

355 3 1 1/2 **Avondream**[26] [346] 5-9-4 **55** RichardKingscote 1 59
(Milton Bradley) *chsd ldrs: drvn 2f out: chsd clr wnr over 1f out: no imp and lost 3rd ins fnl f: one pce* **8/1**

0-20 4 1 1/4 **West Leake (IRE)**[9] [576] 8-9-7 **58** (p) TomQueally 2 58
(Paul Burgoyne) *dwlt: hld up inlast pair: hdwy on inner over 1f out: 4th and styd on same pce ins fnl f* **8/1**

50-5 5 2 1/4 **Little Choosey**[14] [510] 4-9-7 **58** GeorgeBaker 6 50
(Anabel K Murphy) *stdd s after s: hld up in rr: sme hdwy over 1f out: swtchd lft 1f out: kpt on same pce after: nvr trbld ldrs* **25/1**

4000 6 shd **Homeboy (IRE)**[10] [563] 6-9-1 **52** (v) StevieDonohoe 9 44
(David Evans) *in tch in midfield: rdn wl over 1f out: edgd lft u.p 1f out: kpt on but no threat to ldrs ins fnl f* **20/1**

-026 7 1 1/4 **Waterloo Dock**[20] [424] 9-9-0 **51** (v) LukeMorris 10 39
(Mick Quinn) *sn bustled along to press wnr: lost 2nd u.p over 1f out: wknd ins fnl f* **25/1**

-413 8 1 **Consistant**[14] [511] 6-9-6 **57** FrederikTylicki 5 42
(Brian Baugh) *hld up in last trio: rdn and no real hdwy over 1f out: n.d* **5/1**[3]

-006 9 1/2 **Chester Deelyte (IRE)**[8] [586] 6-8-3 **45** (v) ShirleyTeasdale(5) 8 28
(Lisa Williamson) *in tch in midfield on outer: rdn and outpcd over 1f out: wknd 1f out* **50/1**

000/ 10 shd **Glenlini**[503] [6887] 8-8-8 **45** JoeFanning 4 28
(Jim Goldie) *chsd ldrs: rdn and struggling wl ovr 1f out: sn btn: wknd fnl f* **33/1**

1m 10.87s (-1.03) **Going Correction** +0.05s/f (Slow) **10 Ran SP% 120.3**
Speed ratings (Par 101): **108,107,105,103,100 100,98,97,96,96**
CSF £6.48 CT £30.25 TOTE £3.20: £2.10, £1.30, £2.80; EX 7.90 Trifecta £51.20.
**Owner** P Bamford **Bred** D G Hardisty Bloodstock **Trained** Garstang, Lancs

**FOCUS**
The second and faster division of the moderate sprint handicap. The winner remains in great form.

## 689 LADBROKES H'CAP 7f 1y(P)
**4:00** (4:03) (Class 4) (0-85,85) 4-Y-O+ **£5,822** (£1,732; £865; £432) **Stalls** Low

Form RPR

6-10 1 **Forceful Appeal (USA)**[28] [314] 6-9-3 **81** GrahamLee 7 91
(Simon Dow) *hld up in midfield: 4th and stl plenty to do whn nt clr run and swtchd rt jst over 1f out: wnt 2nd fnl 100yds: clsd rapidly and led cl home* **3/1**[2]

24-0 2 3/4 **Living The Life (IRE)**[30] [287] 4-8-12 **76** (v[1]) PaddyAspell 3 84
(Phil McEntee) *sn led: wnt clr 4f out: 6 l clr over 2f out: drvn ent fnl f: hdd and no ex cl home* **16/1**

464- 3 2 **Regal Dan (IRE)**[107] [7769] 4-9-7 **85** TomQueally 5 88
(Charles Hills) *racd in midfield: effrt in 3rd 2f out: chsd clr wnr wl over styd on but lost 2nd fnl 100yds: no imp after* **9/4**[1]

5633 4 1 3/4 **Rakaan (IRE)**[7] [602] 7-9-4 **82** (p) GeorgeBaker 4 80
(Jamie Osborne) *stdd s: wl detached in last: niggled along 4f out: rdn and stl plenty to do 2f out: hdwy 1f out: styd on: nvr trbld ldrs* **10/1**

2-52 5 1 1/4 **Pearl Nation (USA)**[17] [479] 5-8-13 **77** FrederikTylicki 9 72
(Brian Baugh) *hld up in rr of main gp: 6th and plenty to do over 1f out: pushed along and kpt on fnl f: nvr trbld ldrs* **4/1**[3]

0-05 6 1 1/4 **Favourite Treat (USA)**[17] [472] 4-9-4 **82** JoeFanning 6 74
(Mark Johnston) *chsd ldr: pushed along as ldr wnt clr over 3f out: hung lft over 2f out: lost 2nd and btn wl over 1f out: wknd fnl f* **6/1**

0206 7 3/4 **Al's Memory (IRE)**[17] [472] 5-9-0 **78** StevieDonohoe 2 68
(David Evans) *restless in stalls: chsd ldrs: outpcd over 3f out: drvn and no hdwy over 2f out: wknd over 1f out* **20/1**

104- 8 7 **Combustible (IRE)**[128] [7297] 4-9-0 **78** StephenCraine 8 50
(Daniel Mark Loughnane) *taken down early: stdd s: plld hrd and hld up in midfield: lost pl and bhd 2f out: lost tch over 1f out* **20/1**

1m 22.5s (-2.30) **Going Correction** +0.05s/f (Slow) **8 Ran SP% 114.6**
Speed ratings (Par 105): **115,114,111,109,108 107,106,98**
CSF £48.65 CT £125.64 TOTE £4.10: £1.40, £4.20, £1.10; EX 55.30 Trifecta £212.20.
**Owner** Simon Caunce **Bred** Juddmonte Farms Inc **Trained** Epsom, Surrey

**FOCUS**
Plenty of pace on in this feature 7f handicap. The form isn't rated too literally, with the winner rated back to his old best.

## 690 DOWNLOAD THE LADBROKES APP H'CAP 1m 1y(P)
**4:30** (4:30) (Class 5) (0-70,70) 4-Y-O+ **£3,408** (£1,006; £503) **Stalls** High

Form RPR

4113 1 **Club House (IRE)**[6] [627] 4-8-10 **66** GeorgeBuckell(7) 5 76
(Robert Mills) *in tch in midfield: clsd to chse ldrs and swtchd rt over 1f out: pushed along to ld ins fnl f: r.o wl: readily* **9/4**[1]

222- 2 2 1/4 **Ifan (IRE)**[195] [5263] 6-9-4 **67** DavidProbert 2 72
(Tim Vaughan) *led: rdn wl over 2f out: battled on wl u.p tl hdd and brushed aside by wnr ins fnl f: hld on for 2nd* **8/1**[3]

0-53 3 1/2 **Cathedral**[9] [583] 5-8-11 **67** AlistairRawlinson(7) 3 71
(Ed de Giles) *dwlt: steadily rcvrd and chsd ldrs 5f out: ev ch and rdn over 2f out: outpcd by wnr and styd on same pce ins fnl f* **8/1**[3]

4226 4 nse **Greensward**[22] [376] 8-9-7 **70** (b) HayleyTurner 11 74
(Conor Dore) *chsd ldr tl over 2f out: rdn and unable qck wl over 1f out: kpt on same pce ins fnl f* **10/1**

4-02 5 1/2 **Swift Cedar (IRE)**[6] [627] 4-9-7 **70** (b) LukeMorris 10 72
(Jeremy Gask) *s.i.s: in tch in rr: effrt on inner ent fnl 2f: hrd drvn and no real imp over tl 1f out tl styd on strly fnl 100yds: nvr trbld ldrs* **11/4**[2]

20-3 6 nse **Lady Sylvia**[19] [451] 5-9-7 **70** GeorgeBaker 6 72
(Joseph Tuite) *hld up wl in tch: rdn over 1f out: unable qck and edgd lft 1f out: styd on same pce fnl f* **8/1**[3]

0-50 7 1 **Gabrial's Wawa**[22] [388] 4-8-13 **62** PaddyAspell 1 62
(Noel Quinlan) *t.k.h: chsd ldrs: rdn and unable qck over 1f out: styd on same pce ins fnl f* **16/1**

-045 8 nk **For Shia And Lula (IRE)**[15] [503] 5-9-1 **64** (be) ShaneKelly 7 63
(Daniel Mark Loughnane) *hld up in tch towards rr: effrt u.p jst over 1f out: edgd lft and sme hdwy ins fnl f: nt clr run and no hdwy towards fin* **20/1**

46-6 9 2 1/2 **South Cape**[35] [211] 11-8-6 **62** HectorCrouch(7) 4 55
(Gary Moore) *hld up in tch in last trio: rdn 3f out: hdwy wl over 1f out: no imp 1f out: wknd ins fnl f* **33/1**

006- 10 1 3/4 **Titan Triumph**[52] [8454] 10-8-11 **60** (t) RobertHavlin 8 49
(Michael Attwater) *hld up in tch towards rr: rdn and no imp over 1f out: n.d* **33/1**

40-0 11 34 **Keene's Pointe**[19] [451] 4-9-4 **67** (b) JoeFanning 9
(J W Hills) *in tch in midfield: lost pl and wd bnd 2f out: bhd and heavily eased ins fnl f: t.o* **16/1**

1m 37.43s (-0.77) **Going Correction** +0.05s/f (Slow) **11 Ran SP% 122.3**
Speed ratings (Par 103): **105,102,102,102,101 101,100,100,97,96 62**
CSF £21.65 CT £126.75 TOTE £2.20: £1.10, £2.90, £3.00; EX 22.00 Trifecta £111.40.
**Owner** Mrs B B Mills A Foreman **Bred** Val & Angela Leeson **Trained** Headley, Surrey
■ Stewards' Enquiry : George Buckell one-day ban each incident: careless riding (Mar 7-8)

**FOCUS**
Modest handicap. The winner was 6lb well in and rates pretty much to form.

## 691 32RED FREE £10 BONUS FILLIES' H'CAP 1m 2f (P)
**5:00** (5:00) (Class 5) (0-70,68) 4-Y-O+ **£3,408** (£1,006; £503) **Stalls** Low

Form RPR

6-21 1 **Waveguide (IRE)**[16] [491] 5-9-0 **68** LewisWalsh(7) 6 74
(David Simcock) *mde all: rdn and qcknd over 1f out: kpt on wl u.p ins fnl f* **7/4**[2]

30-0 2 3/4 **Meddling**[18] [461] 4-8-7 **60** ShelleyBirkett(5) 3 64
(Julia Feilden) *t.k.h: stdd after s: hld up in tch in rr: rdn and effrt on inner over 1f out: chsd wnr fnl 100yds: kpt on but hld towards fin* **10/1**

42-2 3 1 **Candy Kitten**[21] [410] 4-9-5 **67** (p) LukeMorris 4 69
(Alastair Lidderdale) *chsd ldng pair: rdn and effrt wl over 1f out: chsd wnr jst over 1f out tl fnl 100yds: one pce* **6/4**[1]

15-1 4 nse **Litmus (USA)**[17] [469] 5-8-9 **56** (b) HayleyTurner 7 58
(Simon Dow) *chsd wnr: rdn and effrt wl over 1f out: lost 2nd jst over 1f out: styd on same pce ins fnl f* **3/1**[3]

2m 8.41s (1.81) **Going Correction** +0.05s/f (Slow)
**WFA** 4 from 5yo+ 1lb **4 Ran SP% 110.5**
Speed ratings (Par 100): **94,93,92,92**
CSF £15.36 TOTE £2.00; EX 21.30 Trifecta £43.30.
**Owner** Tick Tock Partnership **Bred** T Darcy & Vincent McCarthy **Trained** Newmarket, Suffolk

**FOCUS**
Just four runners went to post for the closing fillies' handicap and they went no pace. Very ordinary form, with doubts.

T/Plt: £34.60 to a £1 stake. Pool: £89198.08 - 1878.49 winning tickets T/Qpdt: £9.20 to a £1 stake. Pool: £6559.29 - 524.02 winning tickets SP

# 670 WOLVERHAMPTON (A.W) (L-H)

Friday, February 21

**OFFICIAL GOING: Standard**

Wind: Fresh behind Weather: Cloudy with sunny spells

## 692 COMPARE BOOKMAKERS AT BOOKMAKERS.CO.UK APPRENTICE H'CAP 5f 216y(P)

5:30 (5:31) (Class 7) (0-50,51) 4-Y-0+ £1,940 (£577; £288; £144) Stalls Low

Form RPR

-555 1 **Lucky Mark (IRE)**[19] [449] 5-9-0 **48**.....(v) BradleyBosley(5) 9 57
(Garry Moss) *trckd ldrs: racd keenly: led over 3f out: pushed clr 2f out: sn rdn: styd on* 11/4[1]

3024 2 1 1/4 **Vale Of Clara (IRE)**[14] [516] 6-9-3 **46**.....(b) JackGarritty 2 51+
(Peter Niven) *s.i.s: hld up: hdwy 2f out: swtchd rt over 1f out: rdn and r.o to go 2nd wl ins fnl f: nt rch wnr* 9/2[2]

01 3 2 1/4 **Lord Buffhead**[11] [556] 5-9-1 **51** 6ex..... MelissaThompson(7) 5 49
(Richard Guest) *chsd ldrs: wnt 2nd over 1f out tl styd on same pce wl ins fnl f* 8/1

240- 4 1 1/4 **Cadmium Loch**[343] [1020] 6-9-1 **49**.....(p) RobHornby(3) 3 43
(Andrew Hollinshead) *a.p: rdn over 1f out: styd on same pce fnl f* 8/1

4-55 5 hd **Methaaly (IRE)**[18] [466] 11-9-0 **50**.....(be) LewisStones(7) 7 43
(Michael Mullineaux) *hld up: rdn and r.o ins fnl f: nvr nrr* 13/2[3]

00-0 6 3/4 **Steel City Boy (IRE)**[8] [586] 11-9-1 **47**..... DavidParkes(3) 6 38
(Ann Stokell) *led: edgd lft and hdd over 3f out: rdn over 1f out: no ex fnl f* 16/1

-605 7 3 **Lexi's Beauty (IRE)**[11] [556] 4-8-13 **45**..... GaryMahon(3) 4 26
(Brian Baugh) *chsd ldrs: hmpd over 3f out: rdn over 1f out: wknd fnl f* 20/1

0600 8 1 **Amis Reunis**[18] [466] 5-9-1 **49**..... JordanHibberd(5) 11 27
(Alan Berry) *mid-div: edgd lft over 3f out: sn pushed along: wknd 2f out* 25/1

0/0- 9 1 **Les Andelys**[54] [8437] 8-8-11 **45**..... JonathanWilletts(5) 8 20
(Michael Murphy) *prom: n.m.r 5f out: hmpd and lost pl over 3f out* 50/1

5400 10 2 3/4 **Upper Lambourn (IRE)**[10] [563] 6-9-3 **46**.....(tp) RobJFitzpatrick 1 12
(Christopher Kellett) *prom tl lost pl over 4f out* 12/1

433/ 11 1/2 **Art Show**[364] [761] 5-9-0 **50**.....(t) KieranShoemark(7) 10 14
(Noel C Kelly, Ire) *plld hrd and prom: rdn and wknd over 1f out* 10/1

1m 16.63s (1.63) **Going Correction** +0.175s/f (Slow) 11 Ran SP% **113.6**

Speed ratings (Par 97): **96,94,91,89,89 88,84,83,81,78 77**

CSF £13.52 CT £87.51 TOTE £3.30: £1.10, £2.50, £2.40; EX 14.60 Trifecta £101.90.

**Owner** Ron Hull **Bred** Mrs Lisa Kelly **Trained** Tickhill, S Yorks

**FOCUS**

A very moderate handicap in which the gallop was ordinary one to the home turn and those held up were at a disadvantage. The winner edged towards the far rail in the closing stages. He's rated to his winter form.

## 693 BEST ODDS AT BOOKMAKERS.CO.UK H'CAP 5f 20y(P)

6:00 (6:00) (Class 7) (0-50,54) 4-Y-0+ £1,940 (£577; £288; £144) Stalls Low

Form RPR

0611 1 **Louis Vee (IRE)**[7] [610] 6-9-11 **54** 6ex.....(t) ChrisCatlin 1 64+
(Roy Brotherton) *mde all: pushed along over 1f out: rdn and edgd lft ins fnl f: styd on* 13/8[1]

/00- 2 1 1/2 **Dear Ben**[371] [670] 5-9-4 **47**..... AndrewMullen 5 52
(Brian Baugh) *chsd wnr over 4f out: rdn over 1f out: styd on* 16/1

-312 3 1 **Ishetoo**[7] [610] 10-9-2 **48**..... SladeO'Hara(3) 4 49
(Peter Grayson) *prom: outpcd over 3f out: hdwy over 1f out: r.o to go 3rd wl ins fnl f* 7/1

200- 4 hd **Exkaliber**[70] [8271] 5-9-5 **48**.....(vt[1]) PaulMulrennan 6 49
(Richard Ford) *hld up: hdwy over 1f out: sn rdn: r.o* 13/2[3]

2043 5 1 1/2 **Flow Chart (IRE)**[7] [610] 7-9-5 **48**..... AdamKirby 8 43
(Peter Grayson) *hld up: hdwy u.p over 1f out: nt trble ldrs* 9/4[2]

4345 6 3/4 **Jiminy**[12] [549] 4-9-6 **49**..... TomEaves 3 42
(Alan Berry) *chsd wnr 1f: rdn 1/2-way: no ex fnl f* 16/1

00-0 7 hd **Athwaab**[19] [449] 7-9-3 **46**.....[1] WilliamCarson 7 38
(Simon Hodgson) *prom: rdn over 1f out: no ex fnl f* 25/1

300- 8 7 **Wicked Wilma (IRE)**[88] [8034] 10-8-9 **45**..... JordanHibberd(7) 2 12
(Alan Berry) *chsd ldrs tl rdn and wknd 1/2-way* 40/1

1m 3.77s (1.47) **Going Correction** +0.175s/f (Slow) 8 Ran SP% **112.7**

Speed ratings (Par 97): **95,92,91,90,88 87,86,75**

CSF £28.82 CT £144.91 TOTE £2.50: £1.10, £7.90, £1.80; EX 34.10 Trifecta £211.60.

**Owner** Mrs P A Wallis & M A Geobey **Bred** Rev James Browne **Trained** Elmley Castle, Worcs

**FOCUS**

A moderate handicap in which the gallop to the home turn was only fair. Very few figured and the progressive winner raced centre-to-far side in the straight. The second is rated to his old form.

## 694 BOOKMAKERS.CO.UK H'CAP 5f 20y(P)

6:30 (6:30) (Class 6) (0-65,65) 4-Y-0+ £2,425 (£721; £360; £180) Stalls Low

Form RPR

-115 1 **Interchoice Star**[14] [511] 9-8-12 **56**.....(p) ChrisCatlin 5 67
(Ray Peacock) *mid-div: hdwy over 1f out: rdn to ld wl ins fnl f: edgd lft: r.o* 12/1

400 2 1 1/4 **Quality Art (USA)**[17] [478] 6-9-1 **62**..... BillyCray(3) 6 68
(Richard Guest) *hld up in tch: rdn over 1f out: edgd rt: r.o* 18/1

55-1 3 1 1/2 **Megaleka**[18] [466] 4-8-13 **62**..... TimClark(5) 3 63+
(Alan Bailey) *mid-div: nt clr run 1/2-way: rdn and hdwy over 1f out: nt clr run and swtchd rt ins fnl f: r.o* 4/1[2]

11-5 4 hd **Give Us A Belle (IRE)**[32] [259] 5-9-7 **65**.....(vt) AdamBeschizza 9 65
(Christine Dunnett) *chsd ldrs: rdn to ld 1f out: hdd and unable qck wl ins fnl f* 6/1[3]

0-65 5 shd **West Coast Dream**[21] [412] 7-9-7 **65**..... TomEaves 4 65
(Roy Brotherton) *trckd ldrs: pushed along 1/2-way: rdn over 1f out: styd on same pce ins fnl f* 13/2

3-30 6 1/2 **Spray Tan**[29] [295] 4-8-13 **62**..... JoeyHaynes(5) 1 60
(Tony Carroll) *hld up: rdn over 1f out: r.o ins fnl f: nvr nrr* 11/1

000- 7 hd **China Excels**[142] [6945] 7-8-5 **54**..... NathanAlison(5) 2 51
(Mandy Rowland) *in rr: rdn and r.o ins fnl f: nrst fin* 16/1

-332 8 nse **Master Of Disguise**[14] [510] 8-9-5 **63**..... GrahamGibbons 11 60
(Brian Baugh) *chsd ldrs: rdn over 1f out: styd on same pce ins fnl f* 7/2[1]

0-60 9 1 **Spic 'n Span**[17] [478] 9-8-8 **52**.....(b) AndreaAtzeni 8 45
(Ronald Harris) *sn pushed along to chse ldr: rdn and ev ch over 1f out: wknd wl ins fnl f* 33/1

-144 10 1 1/4 **I'll Be Good**[21] [412] 5-9-6 **64**..... PaulMulrennan 7 53
(Alan Berry) *led: rdn and hdd 1f out: wknd wl ins fnl f* 15/2

50-0 11 7 **We Have A Dream**[50] [9] 9-8-13 **57**.....(tp) WilliamCarson 10 21
(Ann Stokell) *sn pushed along in rr* 66/1

1m 2.74s (0.44) **Going Correction** +0.175s/f (Slow) 11 Ran SP% **113.2**

Speed ratings (Par 101): **103,101,98,98,98 97,97,96,95,93 82**

CSF £200.89 CT £1015.21 TOTE £16.00: £4.50, £7.00, £1.50; EX 190.00 Trifecta £702.00.

**Owner** John P Evitt **Bred** M Bishop **Trained** Kyre Park, Worcs

**FOCUS**

A modest handicap in which a decent gallop favoured those held up. The winner came down the centre in the straight and is rated only a length off his old best.

## 695 32RED FREE £10 BONUS H'CAP 1m 5f 194y(P)

7:00 (7:00) (Class 6) (0-60,63) 4-Y-0+ £2,425 (£721; £360; £180) Stalls Low

Form RPR

3111 1 **Waving**[7] [606] 5-9-8 **63** 6ex.....(t) JoeyHaynes(5) 9 72
(Tony Carroll) *hld up: hdwy over 3f out: led over 1f out: rdn out* 9/4[1]

/0-2 2 1 3/4 **Pinotage**[14] [513] 6-9-6 **56**.....(p) JamesSullivan 7 63
(Peter Niven) *a.p: chsd ldr 5f out: led over 2f out: rdn and hdd over 1f out: styd on same pce ins fnl f* 4/1[3]

5213 3 2 1/2 **Uncle Bernie (IRE)**[7] [609] 4-9-0 **55**.....(p) JimmyQuinn 2 59
(Andrew Hollinshead) *s.i.s: hld up: hdwy over 2f out: rdn over 1f out: no ex ins fnl f* 7/2[2]

6/2- 4 7 **Street Runner**[112] [7382] 8-9-6 **56**.....(p) LiamKeniry 8 50
(Karl Thornton, Ire) *mid-div: hdwy over 4f out: rdn 3f out: wknd over 1f out* 10/1

5 8 **Celtic Monarch (IRE)**[21] [420] 5-9-3 **53**.....(b[1]) AdamKirby 3 36
(Mark Michael McNiff, Ire) *sn pushed along in rr: hdwy u.p over 2f out: wknd over 1f out* 6/1

4 6 2 3/4 **Alizari (IRE)**[30] [41] 5-9-7 **60**..... RobertTart(3) 5 39
(Barry Brennan) *chsd ldr tl led 6f out: rdn and hdd over 2f out: wknd over 1f out* 33/1

2-23 7 11 **Strandfield Bay (IRE)**[40] [150] 8-9-10 **60**..... PaulMulrennan 6 23
(Sharon Watt) *chsd ldrs: rdn over 3f out: wknd over 2f out* 11/1

000- 8 34 **Top Line Banker**[56] [8418] 4-8-5 **46** oh1..... BenCurtis 4
(Tim Pitt) *led 8f: rdn over 4f out: wknd 3f out* 22/1

34-0 9 29 **Jebulani**[18] [460] 4-8-9 **50**..... BarryMcHugh 10
(Barry Murtagh) *prom: pushed along 7f out: rdn over 4f out: sn wknd* 40/1

3m 7.43s (1.43) **Going Correction** +0.175s/f (Slow)

**WFA** 4 from 5yo+ 5lb 9 Ran SP% **114.4**

Speed ratings (Par 101): **102,101,99,95,91 89,83,63,47**

CSF £10.96 CT £29.74 TOTE £3.60: £1.80, £1.50, £1.40; EX 10.80 Trifecta £26.40.

**Owner** Carl Hodgson **Bred** Theakston Stud **Trained** Cropthorne, Worcs

**FOCUS**

A modest handicap run at an ordinary gallop. The first three pulled clear and the winner came down the centre. He's rated only 5lb off his best.

## 696 32RED MEGA MOOLAH MILLIONAIRES MAIDEN STKS 1m 141y(P)

7:30 (7:31) (Class 5) 3-Y-0 £3,234 (£962; £481; £240) Stalls Low

Form RPR

1 **Lungarno Palace (USA)**[166] [6242] 3-9-5 82..... AdamKirby 8 77
(Marco Botti) *trckd ldr: led 2f out: rdn over 1f out: hung rt ins fnl f: r.o u.p* 5/6[1]

44- 2 hd **Three Cliffs**[113] [7646] 3-9-5 0.....[1] AndreaAtzeni 6 76
(Roger Varian) *hld up: racd keenly: pushed along over 2f out: hdwy over 1f out: rdn: edgd rt and ev ch ins fnl f: r.o* 6/4[2]

3 1 1/2 **Tarrafal (IRE)** 3-9-5 0..... AdrianNicholls 2 72
(Mark Johnston) *set stdy pce tl pushed along and qcknd 3f out: hdd 2f out: rdn and hung rt ins fnl f: no ex towards fin* 10/1[3]

0 4 3 **Sheriff Of Nawton (IRE)**[7] [614] 3-9-5 0..... DavidNolan 4 65
(David O'Meara) *chsd ldrs: rdn over 1f out: nt clr run ins fnl f: styd on same pce* 50/1

1m 56.25s (5.75) **Going Correction** +0.175s/f (Slow) 4 Ran SP% **105.6**

Speed ratings (Par 97): **81,80,79,76**

CSF £2.20 TOTE £1.50; EX 2.30 Trifecta £2.90.

**Owner** Giuliano Manfredini **Bred** Galleria Bloodstock & Samac **Trained** Newmarket, Suffolk

**FOCUS**

A depleted field and just a steady pace but fair form from the principals. The winner came down the centre.

## 697 32RED.COM FREE £10 BONUS FILLIES' H'CAP 1m 141y(P)

8:00 (8:00) (Class 5) (0-70,67) 4-Y-0+ £3,234 (£962; £481; £240) Stalls Low

Form RPR

-003 1 **Queen Aggie (IRE)**[18] [461] 4-9-5 **65**..... AdamKirby 5 74
(David Evans) *trckd ldr tl rdn to ld over 1f out: styd on wl* 7/4[1]

204- 2 2 1/4 **True Pleasure (IRE)**[102] [7836] 7-9-7 **67**..... DaleSwift 1 71
(James Bethell) *a.p: rdn to chse wnr over 1f out: styd on same pce ins fnl f* 11/2[3]

1-40 3 3/4 **Diletta Tommasa (IRE)**[27] [345] 4-9-5 **65**..... AndreaAtzeni 6 67
(John Stimpson) *hld up: pushed along and hdwy over 2f out: rdn over 1f out: styd on same pce ins fnl f* 7/2[2]

04-6 4 3 **Cabal**[44] [88] 7-8-6 **55**.....(b) NeilFarley(3) 4 50
(Andrew Crook) *s.i.s: hld up: rdn over 1f out: nvr trbld ldrs* 7/1

26-5 5 1 1/4 **Awattan**[20] [422] 4-9-3 **63**..... JimmyQuinn 3 55
(Ed Vaughan) *led: pushed along over 2f out: rdn and hdd over 1f out: wknd fnl f* 11/2[3]

-510 6 1 **Dansili Dutch (IRE)**[7] [612] 5-9-0 **63**..... SamJames(3) 2 53
(David O'Meara) *hld up: rdn over 2f out: wknd over 1f out* 10/1

1m 52.05s (1.55) **Going Correction** +0.175s/f (Slow) 6 Ran SP% **110.9**

Speed ratings (Par 100): **100,98,97,94,93 92**

CSF £11.44 TOTE £1.90: £1.10, £2.00; EX 10.20 Trifecta £24.00.

**Owner** Shropshire Wolves 4 **Bred** Mrs Marion Daly **Trained** Pandy, Monmouths

**FOCUS**

A modest fillies handicap in which the pace was on the steady side. The winner raced centre-to-far side in the straight. The form is rated a bit cautiously.

## 698 CORAL APP DOWNLOAD FROM THE APP STORE H'CAP 1m 1f 103y(P)

8:30 (8:31) (Class 4) (0-80,80) 4-Y-0+ £5,175 (£1,540; £769; £384) Stalls Low

Form RPR

-134 1 **Tatting**[32] [256] 5-9-6 **79**..... LiamKeniry 7 88
(Chris Dwyer) *hld up: hdwy over 1f out: shkn up to ld wl ins fnl f: jst hld on* 10/1

0-41 2 nse **Red Shuttle**[15] [498] 7-9-3 **76**..... ChrisCatlin 6 85+
(Andi Brown) *s.i.s: hld up: shkn up over 1f out: r.o wl ins fnl f: jst failed* 10/1

1-16 **3** *nk* **Luv U Whatever**[31] 270 4-9-3 **76** BenCurtis 5 84
(Jo Hughes) *trckd ldr: rdn over 2f out: r.o* **11/2**[3]

2-32 **4** *1* **Excellent Puck (IRE)**[35] 220 4-9-3 **79** WilliamTwiston-Davies(3) 10 85
(Shaun Lycett) *chsd ldrs: led wl over 1f out: sn rdn and hung lft: hdd and unable qck wl ins fnl f* **9/4**[2]

12-3 **5** *2 ¼* **Appease**[11] 560 5-9-4 **77** TomQueally 9 78
(John Butler) *hld up: pushed along and hdwy over 2f out: bmpd sn after: rdn over 1f out: edgd lft and styd on same pce ins fnl f* **7/4**[1]

-034 **6** *1 ¼* **Camachoice (IRE)**[29] 300 4-9-1 **74** (p) AndreaAtzeni 4 73
(Marco Botti) *prom: rdn: nt clr run and swtchd rt over 2f out: styd on same pce fnl f* **12/1**

4-20 **7** *2 ¼* **Pelmanism**[11] 560 7-9-2 **75** DaleSwift 8 69
(Brian Ellison) *hld up: rdn over 1f out: nvr nrr* **33/1**

1 **8** *2* **Hill Fort**[21] 403 4-8-13 **77** DCByrne(5) 1 67
(Ronald Harris) *led: rdn over 2f out: hdd over 1f out: hmpd sn after: wknd ins fnl f* **25/1**

5-06 **9** *4 ½* **Cockney Class (USA)**[21] 408 7-9-7 **80** JamesSullivan 3 60
(Dave Roberts) *hld up: rdn over 2f out: sn wknd* **80/1**

1013 **10** *nk* **Ocean Applause**[5] 623 4-9-3 **76** (t) AdamKirby 2 56
(John Ryan) *chsd ldrs: rdn over 2f out: hmpd over 1f out: sn wknd and eased* **8/1**

2m 1.65s (-0.05) **Going Correction** +0.175s/f (Slow) **10** Ran SP% **127.5**
Speed ratings (Par 105): **107,106,106,105,103 102,100,98,94,94**
CSF £113.14 CT £624.45 TOTE £13.10: £4.40, £5.70, £2.40; EX 124.90 Trifecta £271.50.
**Owner** Mrs K W Sneath **Bred** Darley **Trained** Newmarket, Suffolk
■ Stewards' Enquiry : William Twiston-Davies two-day ban: careless riding (Mar 7-8)

**FOCUS**
A decent race for the grade in which the gallop was reasonable. The winner raced towards the far side in the straight and may do a bit better yet.
T/Plt: £11.60 to a £1 stake. Pool: £108190.96 - 6770.74 winning tickets T/Qpdt: £8.10 to a £1 stake. Pool: £8732.09 - 791.57 winning tickets CR

# 684 LINGFIELD (L-H)

## Saturday, February 22

**OFFICIAL GOING: Standard**
Wind: medium to strong, half behind Weather: dry and breezy

## 713 COMPARE BOOKMAKERS AT BOOKMAKERS.CO.UK CLEVES STKS (FAST TRACK QUALIFIER) (LISTED RACE) 6f 1y(P)

1:45 (1:46) (Class 1) 4-Y-0+

£25,519 (£9,675; £4,842; £2,412; £1,210; £607) Stalls Low

Form RPR

551- **1** **Tarooq (USA)**[66] 8334 8-9-0 104 GrahamGibbons 2 111
(David Barron) *racd off the pce in midfield: rdn and effrt on inner wl over 1f out: strog run to chal ins fnl f: r.o wl u.p to ld cl home* **5/1**[1]

1-21 **2** *hd* **Rivellino**[14] 534 4-9-0 98 DanielTudhope 1 110
(K R Burke) *in tch in midfield: swtchd rt and effrt over 1f out: drvn to ld ins fnl f: kpt on wl u.p tl hdd and no ex cl home* **7/1**[2]

445- **3** *hd* **Hoof It**[66] 8334 7-9-0 105 JamieSpencer 8 109
(Michael Easterby) *bustled along early: off the pce in last trio: hdwy into midfield 2f out: stl plenty to do 1f out: str run ins fnl f: nt quite rch ldrs* **5/1**[1]

42-5 **4** *1 ¼* **Iptisam**[14] 534 5-9-0 91 (p) LukeMorris 4 106
(James Tate) *chsd ldrs: drvn and ev ch over 1f out tl ins fnl f: no ex and outpcd fnl 100yds* **20/1**

2 **5** *¾* **Rummaging (IRE)**[34] 249 6-9-0 99 ShaneFoley 10 103
(M Halford, Ire) *dwlt and short of room sn after s: hdwy u.p on inner ent fnl f: styd on strly: nt rch ldrs* **20/1**

020- **6** *1 ¼* **Ladies Are Forever**[139] 7054 6-9-0 108 (p) RobertTart 11 99+
(Geoffrey Oldroyd) *w ldr: rdn and ev ch 2f out: no ex u.p jst ins fnl f: wknd fnl 100yds* **5/1**[1]

42-4 **7** *1 ¾* **Hawkeyethenoo (IRE)**[29] 314 8-9-0 103 GrahamLee 12 94
(Jim Goldie) *off the pce in last trio: rdn wl over 1f out: hdwy 1f out: styd on ins fnl f: nvr trbld ldrs* **5/1**[1]

01-3 **8** *½* **Ballista (IRE)**[34] 249 6-9-0 104 RichardKingscote 5 92
(Tom Dascombe) *led: drvn over 1f out: hdd and no ex jst ins fnl f: wknd fnl 100yds* **12/1**

00-0 **9** *shd* **Nocturn**[14] 534 5-9-0 98 (p) RyanMoore 6 92
(Jeremy Noseda) *t.k.h: hld up off the pce in midfield: rdn and struggling 2f out: kpt on but no real imp* **10/1**[3]

6-00 **10** *¾* **Hitchens (IRE)**[23] 393 9-9-3 0 PhillipMakin 3 92
(David Barron) *racd off the pce in midfield: rdn and no hdwy wl over 1f out: wknd ins fnl f* **20/1**

4-10 **11** *hd* **Forest Edge (IRE)**[5] 644 5-9-0 104 (b) AdamKirby 7 89
(David Evans) *w ldr: rdn over 2f out: no ex and btn ent fnl f: wknd fnl 150yds* **12/1**

34-0 **12** *1 ¼* **Bravo Echo**[29] 314 8-9-0 91 RobertHavlin 9 85
(Michael Attwater) *in tch in midfield: rdn and lost pl over 1f out: wknd fnl f* **66/1**

1m 8.94s (-2.96) **Going Correction** -0.15s/f (Stan) **12** Ran SP% **119.4**
Speed ratings (Par 111): **113,112,112,110,109 108,105,105,105,104 103,102**
CSF £37.97 TOTE £5.30: £1.80, £2.20, £1.80; EX 39.00 Trifecta £289.90.
**Owner** EPL Investments **Bred** Kirsten Rausing **Trained** Maunby, N Yorks
■ Stewards' Enquiry : Graham Gibbons two-day ban: used whip above permitted level (Mar 8,11)

**FOCUS**
A very competitive sprint, run at a frantic early pace. Solid form.

## 714 BOOKMAKERS.CO.UK SPRINT SERIES FINAL H'CAP 6f 1y(P)

2:15 (2:15) (Class 3) 4-Y-0+ £11,320 (£3,368; £1,683; £841) Stalls Low

Form RPR

-210 **1** **Multitask**[7] 628 4-8-11 **67** LiamKeniry 7 78
(Michael Madgwick) *stdd s: t.k.h: hld up in tch in last pair: stl last over 1f out: sn swtchd rt and effrt: str run on outer ins fnl f to ld cl home* **6/1**[3]

2-11 **2** *¾* **Random Success (IRE)**[28] 340 4-9-0 **70** GeorgeBaker 5 79
(Roger Charlton) *stdd s: t.k.h: hld up in tch in last quartet: hdwy on inner over 1f out: rdn to chal ins fnl f: rdn to ld fnl 50yds: hdd and no ex cl home* **11/4**[1]

0111 **3** *½* **Spellmaker**[7] 628 5-8-5 **66** EoinWalsh(5) 9 73
(Tony Newcombe) *t.k.h: hld up wl in tch in midfield: rdn whn swtchd rt over 1f out: r.o wl u.p ins fnl f: snatched 3rd last stride* **6/1**[3]

-323 **4** *shd* **Pharoh Jake**[21] 424 6-8-2 **63** RyanWhile(5) 6 70
(John Bridger) *led: rdn and qcknd clr over 1f out: drvn and jnd ins fnl f: hdd and lost 3 pls fnl 50yds* **50/1**

2456 **5** *½* **Parisian Pyramid (IRE)**[14] 535 8-8-6 **62** (b[1]) WilliamCarson 3 67
(Lee Carter) *chsd ldrs: rdn and effrt 2f out: drvn and sltly outpcd over 1f out: rallied and styd on again fnl 100yds* **33/1**

-164 **6** *1* **Lujeanie**[14] 535 8-9-2 **72** (p) ShaneKelly 11 74
(Peter Crate) *in tch in midfield on outer: rdn and unable qck over 1f out: styng on same pce and hld whn sltly hmpd ins fnl f* **33/1**

0-11 **7** *nk* **Valmina**[35] 233 7-9-10 **80** (t) JoeFanning 1 81
(Tony Carroll) *stdd s: t.k.h: hld up in tch in last pair: rdn and gd hdwy on inner over 1f out: no imp and styd on same pce fnl 100yds* **10/1**

3-13 **8** *hd* **Chevise (IRE)**[28] 339 6-8-5 **61** (b) LukeMorris 4 62
(Steve Woodman) *chsd ldrs: rdn 1/2-way: drvn and unable qck 2f out: styd on same pce u.p fr over 1f out* **20/1**

1-23 **9** *nk* **Welease Bwian (IRE)**[35] 233 5-9-0 **70** AdamBeschizza 10 70
(Stuart Williams) *in tch in midfield: effrt wl over 1f out: keeping on whn short of room and jostling w rival ins fnl f: no threat to ldrs and one pce after* **8/1**

4320 **10** *1 ¼* **Haadeeth**[7] 628 7-8-2 **65** (t) JoeDoyle(7) 12 61
(David Evans) *hld up in tch in last quartet: rdn and outpcd wl over 1f out: n.d after: plugged on fnl f* **33/1**

-531 **11** *¾* **My Kingdom (IRE)**[14] 535 8-9-3 **73** (v) AndreaAtzeni 8 66
(Stuart Williams) *chsd ldr: rdn and outpcd over 1f out: wkng whn jostling w rival ins fnl f: bhd and eased wl ins fnl f* **7/1**

30-2 **12** *1 ¾* **Glastonberry**[35] 233 6-9-7 **77** JamieSpencer 2 65+
(Geoffrey Deacon) *in tch in midfield: rdn and effrt wl over 1f out: stl nr enough whn nt clr run and snatched up jst over 1f out: nt rcvr and bhd whn eased ins fnl f* **5/1**[2]

1m 10.55s (-1.35) **Going Correction** -0.15s/f (Stan) **12** Ran SP% **120.2**
Speed ratings (Par 107): **103,102,101,101,100 99,98,98,98,96 95,93**
CSF £21.98 CT £106.68 TOTE £7.00: £2.40, £1.10, £2.10; EX 34.20 Trifecta £136.10.
**Owner** Mrs L N Harmes **Bred** Mrs L N Harmes **Trained** Denmead, Hants
■ Stewards' Enquiry : Andrea Atzeni caution: careless riding.

**FOCUS**
A competitive sprint handicap run at a good pace and in a decent time. The winner built on his penultimate C&D win.

## 715 LADBROKES H'CAP 7f 1y(P)

2:50 (2:50) (Class 2) 4-Y-0+ £29,110 (£8,662; £4,329; £2,164) Stalls Low

Form RPR

12-1 **1** **Grey Mirage**[42] 144 5-9-6 **100** (p) RyanMoore 1 110
(Marco Botti) *dwlt and bustled along leaving stalls: sn in tch in midfield: hdwy u.p and edging lft 1f out: led wl ins fnl f: r.o wl: drvn out* **2/1**[1]

-551 **2** *¾* **George Guru**[7] 625 7-9-1 **95** RobertHavlin 5 103
(Michael Attwater) *hld up wl in tch in midfield: travelling wl but nt clr run 2f out: rdn and effrt to chal 1f out: led ins fnl f: hdd and styd on same pce wl ins fnl f* **10/1**

2-30 **3** *½* **Bertiewhittle**[30] 306 6-9-9 **103** (p) GrahamGibbons 3 110
(David Barron) *restless in stalls: in tch in midfield: jostling w rival bnd ent fnl 2f: hdwy u.p to chse ldrs ins fnl f: styd on same pce fnl 100yds* **12/1**

0-12 **4** *hd* **Nassau Storm**[18] 472 5-8-4 **84** AndreaAtzeni 14 90
(William Knight) *stdd and dropped in bhd after s: hld up in tch in rr: rdn and hdwy over 1f out: pressed ldrs ins fnl f: styd on same pce fnl 100yds* **25/1**

1-31 **5** *nk* **Alfred Hutchinson**[29] 314 6-9-3 **100** RobertTart(3) 7 105+
(Geoffrey Oldroyd) *wl in tch in midfield: nt clr run: hmpd and shuffled bk bnd ent fnl 2f: rallied u.p 1f out: styd on* **6/1**[3]

301- **6** *½* **Hasopop (IRE)**[131] 7247 4-9-10 **104** LukeMorris 9 108
(Marco Botti) *hld up in tch in last quartet: rdn and hdwy over 1f out: kpt on u.p ins fnl f: nvr trbld ldrs* **16/1**

1-23 **7** *shd* **Absolutely So (IRE)**[14] 534 4-8-9 **89** DavidProbert 12 93+
(Andrew Balding) *chsd ldrs on outer: rdn and sltly outpcd bnd wl over 1f out: kpt on u.p ins fnl f* **5/1**[2]

005- **8** *nk* **Dr Red Eye**[147] 6826 6-8-8 **88** (p) TomEaves 4 91
(Scott Dixon) *led: rdn and 2 l clr 2f out: drvn and hrd pressed jst ins fnl f: sn hdd & wknd fnl 75yds* **66/1**

0-25 **9** *hd* **Brocklebank (IRE)**[10] 574 5-8-3 **83** NickyMackay 8 85
(Simon Dow) *hld up in tch in rr: stl last 2f out: weaved through and sme hdwy 1f out: styd on ins fnl f: nvr trbld ldrs* **20/1**

300- **10** *1 ¼* **Yeeoow (IRE)**[120] 7495 5-8-11 **91** JimCrowley 10 90
(K R Burke) *in tch in midfield: lost pl bnd 2f out: no threat to ldrs but kpt on u.p ins fnl f* **10/1**

-132 **11** *½* **Apostle (IRE)**[11] 566 5-8-10 **90** JamieSpencer 11 88
(David Simcock) *in tch in midfield but stuck on outer: rdn and outpcd over 1f out: one pce and hld fnl f* **14/1**

-364 **12** *hd* **Verse Of Love**[11] 566 5-7-13 **86** JoeDoyle(7) 13 83
(David Evans) *in tch in last trio: drvn and effrt jst over 1f out: kpt on but nvr trbld ldrs* **66/1**

450- **13** *hd* **Skytrain**[131] 7241 4-8-1 **81** JoeFanning 6 78
(Mark Johnston) *chsd ldr: drvn and outpcd ent fnl 2f: btn ent fnl f: wknd ins fnl f* **33/1**

120- **14** *¾* **Newstead Abbey**[247] 3484 4-9-4 **98** PhillipMakin 2 93
(David Barron) *chsd ldrs: rdn wl over 1f out: no ex u.p 1f out: wknd ins fnl f* **16/1**

1m 21.92s (-2.88) **Going Correction** -0.15s/f (Stan) **14** Ran SP% **123.1**
Speed ratings (Par 109): **110,109,108,108,108 107,107,106,106,105 104,104,104,103**
CSF £22.48 CT £183.03 TOTE £2.80: £1.10, £4.00, £4.10; EX 28.60 Trifecta £181.00.
**Owner** Giuliano Manfredini **Bred** Grundy Bloodstock Srl **Trained** Newmarket, Suffolk

**FOCUS**
A quality handicap. The runner-up set a solid standard and the winner's form could rate a but higher.

## 716 CORAL.CO.UK WINTER DERBY TRIAL STKS (FAST TRACK QUALIFIER) (LISTED RACE) 1m 2f (P)

3:30 (3:33) (Class 1) 4-Y-0+

£25,519 (£9,675; £4,842; £2,412; £1,210; £607) Stalls Low

Form RPR

010- **1** **Grandeur (IRE)**[76] 8211 5-9-3 117 RyanMoore 2 115
(Jeremy Noseda) *chsd ldrs: swtchd out rt and effrt to chse ldr wl over 1f out: led jst over 1f out: r.o wl: drvn out* **4/5**[1]

1-21 **2** *¾* **Modernstone**[36] 212 4-8-8 98 AndreaAtzeni 4 106
(William Knight) *chsd ldrs: effrt u.p wl over 1f out: wnt 3rd 1f out: r.o to chse wnr ins fnl f: kpt on wl towards fin* **12/1**

001- **3** *1 ¼* **Anaconda (FR)**[98] 7926 5-9-0 100 RichardKingscote 1 108
(Tom Dascombe) *led: rdn and hdd jst over 1f out: no ex and lost 2nd ins fnl f: wknd towards fin* **10/1**

6-61 **4** *hd* **Robin Hoods Bay**[28] 344 6-9-0 103 .................................. LukeMorris 9 108
(Ed Vaughan) *in rr: clsd and nt clr run 2f out: effrt and hmpd wl over 1f out: hdwy u.p 1f out: no threat to wnr but stdy on wl ins fnl f* **7/1**[2]

/60- **5** *2 ½* **Hajras (IRE)**[140] 7012 5-9-0 104 .................................. JoeFanning 8 103
(Mark Johnston) *in tch in midfield: rdn and unable qck over 1f out: no threat to wnr and kpt on same pce fnl f* **8/1**[3]

5-23 **6** *1 ½* **Tinshu (IRE)**[28] 344 8-8-9 95 ..................................(p) AndrewMullen 10 95
(Derek Haydn Jones) *hld up in tch in last trio: effrt on outer over 1f out: kpt on but no imp on wnr: n.d* **33/1**

000- **7** *nk* **Sennockian Star**[134] 7174 4-8-13 99 ..................................(v) AdamKirby 7 99
(Mark Johnston) *chsd ldrs: effrt u.p to press ldrs wl over 2f out: outpcd and btn jst over 1f out: wknd ins fnl f* **16/1**

2-21 **8** *1 ¾* **Chookie Royale**[19] 465 6-9-0 107 ..................................(p) TomEaves 5 96
(Keith Dalgleish) *s.i.s: sn rcvrd and in tch in midfield: rdn and unable qck wl over 1f out: wknd fnl f* **8/1**[3]

32-0 **9** *¾* **Uramazin (IRE)**[49] 54 8-9-0 98 .................................. JimCrowley 6 94
(Philip Hide) *hld up in tch in last trio: clsd and nt clr run wl over 1f out: no prog after: n.d* **33/1**

00-4 **10** *7* **Two Days In Paris (FR)**[31] 285 5-8-9 92 .................... JamieSpencer 3 75
(Stuart Williams) *chsd ldr tl over 2f out: losing pl whn hmpd wl over 1f out: sn wknd and bhd fnl f* **33/1**

2m 1.17s (-5.43) **Going Correction** -0.15s/f (Stan)
**WFA** 4 from 5yo+ 1lb **10** Ran SP% **121.8**
Speed ratings (Par 111): **115,114,113,113,111 110,109,108,107,102**
CSF £12.83 TOTE £1.70: £1.10, £2.60, £3.50; EX 13.00 Trifecta £89.40.
**Owner** Miss Yvonne Jacques **Bred** Mrs Cherry Faeste **Trained** Newmarket, Suffolk

**FOCUS**
For the second year running this went to the standout performer on official ratings. The pace was decent and the form makes a fair bit of sense.

## 717 32RED.COM MAIDEN STKS 1m 4f (P)
**4:05** (4:05) (Class 5) 3-Y-O **£4,090** (£1,207; £604) **Stalls** Low

Form RPR

5 **1** **Wildes (IRE)**[40] 167 3-9-5 0 .................................. StevieDonohoe 3 78
(Tim Pitt) *chsd ldr for 2f: wnt 2nd again 6f out: rdn and ev ch 2f out: kpt on to ld fnl 100yds: hld on wl: all out* **8/1**

**2** *nse* **Belfilo (IRE)** 3-9-5 0 .................................. DavidProbert 2 78
(Andrew Balding) *in tch towards rr: rdn and effrt to chse ldng pair jst over 2f out: drvn and ev ch ins fnl f: r.o: jst hld* **6/1**

-222 **3** *½* **Mbhali (IRE)**[14] 536 3-9-5 75 .................................. JoeFanning 4 77
(Mark Johnston) *led: rdn 4f out: drvn wl over 2f out: hdd fnl 100yds: styd on same pce after: n.m.r cl home* **11/10**[1]

5 **4** *3* **New Tarabela**[22] 403 3-9-5 0 .................................. LukeMorris 7 72
(James Tate) *in tch in midfield: rdn and n.m.r over 2f out: chsd ldng trio 2f out: styd on same pce fnl f* **9/2**[3]

**5** *5* **Archiebeau** 3-9-2 0 .................................. MatthewLawson(3) 1 64
(Jonathan Portman) *in tch in rr: rdn along thrght: 6th and drvn over 2f out: no ex and btn over 1f out: wknd fnl f* **50/1**

00- **6** *20* **Storm Of Choice**[213] 4631 3-9-5 0 ..................................(p) RobertHavlin 5 32
(Michael Attwater) *chsd ldrs: rdn and lost pl over 2f out: lost tch wl over 1f out* **66/1**

5 **7** *½* **Patronella (IRE)**[14] 542 3-9-0 0 .................................. JimCrowley 6 26
(David Simcock) *in tch in midfield: rdn and struggling ent fnl 2f: btn wl over 1f out: fdd* **7/2**[2]

0-5 **8** *113* **Lena Player (SWE)**[20] 447 3-9-0 0 ..................................(t[1]) LiamKeniry 8
(Linda Jewell) *chsd ldr 10f out tl 6f out: sn dropped out: t.o fnl 4f* **100/1**

2m 31.35s (-1.65) **Going Correction** -0.15s/f (Stan) **8** Ran SP% **117.9**
Speed ratings (Par 97): **99,98,98,96,93 79,79,**
CSF £55.97 TOTE £11.10: £2.60, £2.20, £1.10; EX 79.90 Trifecta £148.90.
**Owner** Paul Wildes **Bred** Mark & Pippa Hackett **Trained** Market Drayton, Shropshire

**FOCUS**
An ordinary maiden, the standard set by the third, but a slightly positive view has been taken of the third.

## 718 32RED FILLIES' H'CAP 7f 1y(P)
**4:40** (4:40) (Class 5) (0-70,70) 4-Y-O+ **£4,090** (£1,207; £604) **Stalls** Low

Form RPR

0-21 **1** **Fab Lolly (IRE)**[9] 587 4-9-7 **70** ..................................(p) JoeFanning 3 78+
(James Bethell) *in tch in midfield and a gng wl: hdwy to join ldrs on bit over 1f out: rdn hands and heels to ld ins fnl f: r.o wl: comf* **6/4**[1]

3113 **2** *nk* **Medam**[12] 562 5-8-9 **61** .................................. NeilFarley(3) 1 68
(Shaun Harris) *chsd ldr for 2f: chsd ldrs after tl drvn and ev ch jst over 1f out: led ins fnl f: sn hdd: kpt on but a hld* **10/1**

-025 **3** *1 ¾* **Two In The Pink (IRE)**[25] 367 4-8-11 **60** .................... WilliamCarson 10 62
(Ralph J Smith) *t.k.h: hld up in tch in last trio: hdwy on inner wl over 1f out: swtchd rt ent fnl f: r.o wl* **10/1**

60-0 **4** *¾* **Last Minute Lisa (IRE)**[30] 295 4-8-13 **62** .................... LukeMorris 2 62
(Sylvester Kirk) *led: drvn over 1f out: hdd ins fnl f: no ex and wknd towards fin* **20/1**

00-6 **5** *2 ¼* **Angel Cake (IRE)**[9] 589 5-8-10 **59** .................... AndrewMullen 5 53
(Michael Appleby) *chsd ldrs: rdn and unable qck 2f out: outpcd and btn over 1f out: wl hld and one pce fnl f* **9/2**[3]

0-40 **6** *¾* **Bold Ring**[21] 428 8-8-9 **58** .................................. JimmyQuinn 9 50
(Edward Creighton) *in tch in midfield: rdn and unable qck wl over 1f out: wl hld and one pce fnl f* **20/1**

6-44 **7** *3* **Marble Statuette (USA)**[14] 542 4-9-1 **64** ....................(b[1]) RyanMoore 7 48
(Richard Fahey) *chsd ldr after 2f out tl wl over 1f out: sn wknd* **3/1**[2]

/5-0 **8** *½* **Mists Of Time (IRE)**[19] 456 4-8-9 **58** .................... JamesSullivan 6 41
(Pat Eddery) *rrd as stalls opened and s.i.s: a bhd: n.d* **25/1**

40-5 **9** *3 ¼* **Amethyst Dawn (IRE)**[13] 548 8-9-1 **64** ....................(p) TomQueally 4 38
(Alan McCabe) *taken down early: t.k.h: hld up in tch in last trio: rdn and no hdwy over 2f out: wknd over 1f out* **25/1**

1m 23.79s (-1.01) **Going Correction** -0.15s/f (Stan) **9** Ran SP% **118.6**
Speed ratings (Par 100): **99,98,96,95,93 92,88,88,84**
CSF £17.38 CT £113.11 TOTE £2.60: £1.50, £1.80, £3.60; EX 14.90 Trifecta £88.40.
**Owner** James Lambert **Bred** James F Hanly **Trained** Middleham Moor, N Yorks

**FOCUS**
This ordinary fillies' handicap lacked strength in depth but the form makse sense.

## 719 BEST ODDS AT BOOKMAKERS.CO.UK H'CAP 5f 6y(P)
**5:10** (5:10) (Class 4) (0-85,85) 4-Y-O+ **£5,822** (£1,732; £865; £432) **Stalls** High

Form RPR

0-60 **1** **Taajub (IRE)**[14] 534 7-9-7 **85** .................................. ShaneKelly 1 95
(Peter Crate) *broke fast: sn stdd and chsd ldrs: rdn and effrt to chal 1f out: led ins fnl f: r.o wl* **5/2**[1]

30-4 **2** *1* **Royal Bajan (USA)**[52] 4 6-9-4 **82** ..................................(v) JoeFanning 7 88
(James Given) *taken down early: sn led: rdn over 1f out: hdd ins fnl f: styd on same pce fnl 100yds* **25/1**

-430 **3** *1* **Diamond Charlie (IRE)**[14] 534 6-9-7 **85** .................... GrahamLee 5 88+
(Simon Dow) *in tch in midfield: clsd: swtchd lft and nt clr run jst ins fnl f: swtchd bk rt and bmpd rival ins fnl f: wnt 3rd and eased towards fin* **7/2**[2]

2/0- **4** *nk* **We'll Deal Again**[302] 1807 7-9-3 **81** ..................................(b) GrahamGibbons 4 83
(Michael Easterby) *taken down early: sn chsng ldr: rdn and ev ch over 1f out: no ex jst ins fnl f: styng on same pce whn pushed rt ins fnl f: nt given a hrd time after* **25/1**

0-01 **5** *hd* **Sandfrankskipsgo**[10] 572 5-9-4 **82** .................................. GeorgeBaker 6 83
(Peter Crate) *chsd ldrs: rdn and effrt over 1f out: styng on same pce whn pushed rt ins fnl f* **8/1**

24-1 **6** *nk* **Triple Dream**[20] 444 9-9-6 **84** ..................................(tp) RichardKingscote 2 84
(Milton Bradley) *pushed stall open early but stood stl and then moved rt leaving stall: in tch in rr: effrt and hdwy on inner over 1f out: styd on same pce ins fnl f* **12/1**

-060 **7** *¾* **Fratellino**[18] 479 7-9-2 **80** ..................................(tp) TomQueally 8 77
(Alan McCabe) *in tch in midfield: rdn 1/2-way: styd on same pce u.p fnl f* **5/1**

1-61 **8** *nk* **Expose**[22] 412 6-8-8 **79** .................................. AlistairRawlinson(7) 9 75
(Michael Appleby) *hld up in tch in last trio: rdn and effrt on outer over 1f out: kpt on but nvr threatened ldrs* **4/1**[3]

-540 **9** *1 ¼* **Powerful Wind (IRE)**[20] 444 5-9-4 **82** .................................. LukeMorris 3 74
(Ronald Harris) *hmpd s and slowly away: t.k.h: hld up in tch in rr: rdn and no hdwy over 1f out* **20/1**

58.0s (-0.80) **Going Correction** -0.15s/f (Stan) **9** Ran SP% **118.7**
Speed ratings (Par 105): **100,98,96,96,96 95,94,93,91**
CSF £73.77 CT £221.83 TOTE £5.00: £1.30, £4.30, £1.70; EX 66.70 Trifecta £308.30.
**Owner** Peter Crate **Bred** Rabbah Bloodstock Limited **Trained** Newdigate, Surrey

**FOCUS**
A fair sprint handicap. The winner won this off the same mark two years ago and this rates a similar effort.
T/Plt: £11.70 to a £1 stake. Pool: £136325.97 - 8478.85 winning tickets T/Qpdt: £3.60 to a £1 stake. Pool: £5653.69 - 1146.32 winning tickets SP

# 669 CAGNES-SUR-MER
Saturday, February 22

**OFFICIAL GOING: Polytrack: standard; turf: heavy**

## 720a PRIX DES ALPILLES (H'CAP) (3YO) (POLYTRACK) 1m (F)
**12:00** (12:00) 3-Y-O **£9,166** (£3,666; £2,750; £1,833; £916)

RPR

**1** **Visioner (FR)**[42] 3-9-3 **0** .................................. TonyPiccone 12 88
(C Boutin, France) **32/5**[2]

**2** *2* **Manchu (FR)**[57] 3-8-4 **0** ..................................(b) AntoineCoutier 6 71
(F Chappet, France) **12/1**

**3** *snk* **Per (FR)** 3-8-3 **0** .................................. AnthonyCrastus 13 69
(J-P Gauvin, France) **17/1**

**4** *snk* **Denusa (IRE)**[38] 193 3-8-13 **0** .................................. FredericSpanu 4 79
(Laura Grizzetti, Italy) **67/1**

**5** *nk* **Singapore Spur (FR)**[7] 629 3-8-13 **0** ..................................(p) AlexisBadel 10 78
(D De Waele, France) **83/10**

**6** *½* **Sealed (USA)**[10] 585 3-9-5 **0** .................................. MaximeGuyon 3 83
(Gay Kelleway) *slow to stride: sn drvn and rcvrd to r in midfield on inner: short of room and sltly hmpd 2 1/2f out: rdn 2f out: kpt on ins fnl f: nt pce to chal* **9/5**[1]

**7** *2* **Thalie De La Vis (FR)**[49] 3-8-4 **0** .................................. EddyHardouin 11 64
(Mme C Barande-Barbe, France) **31/1**

**8** *½* **Lady Dam's (FR)**[80] 3-8-5 **0** .................... Roberto-CarlosMontenegro 7 63
(C Boutin, France) **31/1**

**9** *¾* **L'Ami Fernand (FR)**[65] 3-8-9 **0** ow1 ....................(p) ThomasMessina 8 66
(D De Waele, France) **41/1**

**10** *shd* **Apsis Dream (FR)**[65] 3-9-0 **0** .................................. RaphaelMarchelli 5 70
(T Castanheira, France) **8/1**[3]

**11** *½* **La Vetus (SPA)**[212] 3-7-12 **0** .................................. ValentinSeguy(2) 14 55
(M Delcher Sanchez, France) **10/1**

**12** *1* **Mitlaa (FR)**[123] 3-8-5 **0** ..................................(b) FabriceVeron 2 58
(P Monfort, France) **10/1**

**13** *1 ½* **Mindsforgemanacles (IRE)**[16] 3-7-11 **0** ..........(p) ValentinGambart(3) 1 50
(C Boutin, France) **36/1**

**14** *1* **Vanvidd (FR)**[55] 3-8-0 **0** ..................................(p) JimmyTastayre 9 47
(C Boutin, France) **70/1**

**15** *1* **Touch Of Honour (FR)**[55] 3-8-13 **0** ..................................(p) SylvainRuis 15 58
(J-M Capitte, France) **25/1**

1m 38.12s (98.12) **15** Ran SP% **120.6**
WIN (incl. 1 euro stake): 6.00 (coupled with Lady Dam's). PLACES: 3.80, 3.70, 4.50. DF: 41.50. SF: 36.20.
**Owner** Stephan Hoffmeister **Bred** P Goral **Trained** France

## 721a PRIX POLICEMAN (LISTED RACE) (3YO) (POLYTRACK) 1m 2f (D)
**12:30** (12:00) 3-Y-O **£25,000** (£10,000; £7,500; £5,000; £2,500)

RPR

**1** **Mr Pommeroy (FR)**[21] 436 3-8-11 0 .................................. FabriceVeron 5 100+
(H-A Pantall, France) **31/10**[2]

**2** *4 ½* **Cockney Bob**[13] 553 3-8-11 0 .................................. FredericSpanu 8 91
(J Parize, France) **10/1**

**3** *½* **God's Speed (IRE)**[15] 515 3-8-11 0 .................................. ChrisCatlin 1 90
(Rae Guest) *scrubbed along leaving stalls to chse ldr on rail: rdn and sltly outpcd 2 1/2f out: styd on to chse ldrs fr 1 1/2f out: one pce ins fnl f* **14/1**

**4** *¾* **Unanimite (FR)**[26] 3-8-11 0 .................................. NicolasPerret 3 89
(K Borgel, France) **26/1**

**5** *shd* **Goldy Espony (FR)**[26] 3-8-8 0 ..................................(p) AnthonyCrastus 12 85
(H-A Pantall, France) **19/1**

**6** *shd* **Dye Fore (USA)**[18] 482 3-8-11 0 ..................................(b) IoritzMendizabal 4 88
(J-C Rouget, France) **2/1**[1]

**7** *2* **Flying Cape (IRE)**[10] 585 3-8-11 0 .................................. EddyHardouin 2 84?
(Andrew Hollinshead) *w.w in midfield on inner: rdn and nt qckn over 2f out: one pce fnl f* **63/10**[3]

**7** *dht* **Royal Sun (FR)** 3-8-11 0 .................................. Francois-XavierBertras 9 84
(F Rohaut, France) **40/1**

9 ½ **Monika Jem (FR)**[21] 436 3-8-8 0................................ FabienLefebvre 13 80
(S Jesus, France) **82/1**
10 shd **Jim (GER)**[55] 3-8-11 0.......................................... AurelienLemaitre 11 83
(Christina Bucher, Switzerland) **43/1**
11 2 ½ **Whitby High Light**[14] 545 3-8-11 0.......................... ThomasMessina 10 78
(Andrew Hollinshead) *hld up towards rr: rdn and short-lived effrt 2 1/2f out: no imp fnl 1 1/2f* **19/1**
12 hd **Stosur (IRE)**[7] 629 3-8-8 0........................................... AlexisBadel 7 75
(Gay Kelleway) *w.w towards rr: nvr in contention* **25/1**
13 1 **Magic Movies (FR)**[55] 3-8-11 0................................(b) MaximeGuyon 6 76
(X Thomas-Demeaulte, France) **9/1**
2m 0.91s (120.91) **13 Ran SP% 120.6**
WIN (incl. 1 euro stake): 4.10. PLACES: 1.60, 2.60, 4.00 DF: 20.70. SF: 35.40.
**Owner** Plersch Breeding Sarl **Bred** Rupert Plersch **Trained** France

## 722a PRIX JACQUES GELIOT (H'CAP) (4YO) (POLYTRACK) 1m (F)
**1:00** (12:00) 4-Y-O **£10,833** (£4,333; £3,250; £2,166; £1,083)

RPR
1 **One And Only (FR)**[55] 8441 4-9-1 0.................. Pierre-CharlesBoudot 9 77
(P Decouz, France) **36/5[3]**
2 1 ½ **Keep The Dream**[42] 4-8-6 0.......................................... EddyHardouin 8 65
(N Caullery, France) **63/10[2]**
3 nk **Asperites (IRE)**[152] 4-8-9 0.......................... MllePaulineDominois(4) 17 71
(D Prod'Homme, France) **15/1**
4 1 ½ **Living Desert**[49] 4-9-6 0............................................... FabriceVeron 12 74
(H-A Pantall, France) **7/2[1]**
5 nse **Tiolache (FR)**[33] 266 4-8-10 0..................................(p) SylvainRuis 10 64
(J-M Capitte, France) **8/1**
6 1 ½ **Diamond Kathi (GER)**[110] 4-8-13 0..........................(b) StefanieHofer 7 64
(Mario Hofer, Germany) **13/1**
7 snk **Knight Charm**[23] 392 4-9-1 0...................................... MaximeGuyon 13 66
(Gay Kelleway) *broke wl: w ldrs: swtchd outside and led over 2f out: sn rdn and hdd bef 1 1/2f out: dropped away ins fnl f* **10/1**
8 ½ **As D'Artois (FR)**[29] 4-8-13 0.................................... JimmyTastayre(3) 18 65
(C Boutin, France) **27/1**
9 ½ **Mon P'Tit Lu (FR)**[327] 4-9-0 0....................... Francois-XavierBertras 11 62
(J-L Foursans-Bourdette, France) **32/1**
10 nk **Style Boreale (FR)**[57] 4-8-9 0...................................... FabienLefebvre 6 57
(M Planard, France) **11/1**
11 ½ **Special Dream (FR)**[33] 266 4-8-6 0............................ AnthonyCrastus 3 52
(H-A Namur, France) **60/1**
12 1 ½ **Pepe Mi Amor (IRE)** 4-8-11 0....................................... TonyPiccone 15 54
(H-A Namur, France) **52/1**
13 nk **Shining Life** 4-8-11 0.................................................... FredericSpanu 1 53
(M Planard, France) **46/1**
14 5 ½ **Zakopane (FR)**[55] 4-9-2 0..................................(b) MickaelForest 4 46
(C Martinon, France) **13/1**
15 1 ½ **Salinas Road (FR)**[23] 392 4-9-5 0............................ IoritzMendizabal 16 45
(M Figge, Germany) **22/1**
16 2 **Proposal (FR)**[57] 4-9-6 0........................(b) Roberto-CarlosMontenegro 14 42
(Mme J Bidgood, France) **21/1**
17 7 **Royale Way (FR)**[42] 4-8-2 0........................................(p) AlexisBadel 5 7
(E Caroux, France) **41/1**
1m 36.21s (96.21) **17 Ran SP% 120.7**
WIN (incl. 1 euro stake): 8.20. PLACES: 2.90, 2.20, 3.80. DF 22.00. SF: 50.70.
**Owner** Julien Phelippon **Bred** Dream With Me Stable Inc, Oceanic Bloodstock & R C **Trained** France

## 723a GRAND PRIX DU CONSEIL GENERAL DES ALPES MARITIMES (LISTED RACE) (4YO+) (TURF) 1m 4f 110y
**1:30** (12:00) 4-Y-O+ **£31,250** (£12,500; £9,375; £6,250; £3,125)

RPR
1 **Narrow Hill (GER)**[18] 6-8-13 0................. Roberto-CarlosMontenegro 2 110+
(P Sogorb, France) **21/10[1]**
2 4 **Salve Hibernia (IRE)** 5-8-9 0.................................. ThomasHenderson 8 99
(D Henderson, France) **47/1**
3 1 **Sant'Alberto (ITY)**[18] 6-8-13 0.............................(p) IoritzMendizabal 7 101
(F Chappet, France) **11/1**
4 1 **Aussi Celebre (IRE)**[33] 5-8-13 0............................(p) AnthonyCrastus 10 100
(E Lellouche, France) **4/1[2]**
5 shd **Griraz (FR)**[99] 7921 9-8-13 0........................ Francois-XavierBertras 6 100
(P Sogorb, France) **5/1[3]**
6 2 ½ **Mister Bawi (FR)**[236] 3912 4-8-9 0.............................. FabriceVeron 9 96
(H-A Pantall, France) **15/1**
7 3 ½ **Zack Hope**[13] 554 6-8-13 0........................................... TonyPiccone 3 91
(N Caullery, France) **12/1**
8 dist **Saint Hilary**[33] 5-8-9 0.............................................. MickaelForest 1
(W Walton, France) **18/1**
9 1 **Swing Alone (IRE)**[21] 427 5-8-13 0.............................. FredericSpanu 5
(Gay Kelleway) *towards rr: short-lived effrt over 3f out: wknd fr over 2f out: sn wl btn* **17/1**
10 8 **Quidamo**[76] 8212 7-8-13 0............................. Pierre-CharlesBoudot 11
(Frau J Mayer, Germany) **9/1**
11 dist **King Of Arnor**[18] 6-8-13 0......................................... MaximeGuyon 4
(S Cerulis, France) **17/1**
2m 51.58s (171.58)
**WFA** 4 from 5yo+ 3lb **11 Ran SP% 120.4**
WIN (incl. 1 euro stake): 3.10. PLACES: 1.80, 8.90, 3.00. DF 92.30. SF: 141.00.
**Owner** Simon Springer **Bred** Gestut Park Wiedingen **Trained** France

726 - 727a (Foreign Racing) - See Raceform Interactive

# 638 ST MORITZ (R-H)
Sunday, February 23

**OFFICIAL GOING: Snow: frozen**

## 728a GRAND PRIX MOYGLARE STUD (CONDITIONS) (4YO+) (SNOW) 6f 110y
**11:40** (12:00) 4-Y-O+
**£8,513** (£4,256; £3,040; £2,027; £1,013; £608)

RPR
1 **Konig Concorde (GER)**[210] 9-9-2 0...............................(p) FilipMinarik 8 90
(Christian Sprengel, Germany) **41/10[3]**
2 2 ½ **Boccalino (GER)**[7] 638 6-9-2 0.................................(b) DanielePorcu 2 83
(P Schaerer, Switzerland) **51/10**
3 1 **Zarras (GER)**[7] 638 5-9-2 0........................................ SilviaCasanova 6 80
(P Schaerer, Switzerland) **9/10[1]**
4 3 ½ **Le Big (GER)**[371] 700 10-9-2 0.................................(p) AndreBest 5 70
(P Schaerer, Switzerland) **74/10**
5 9 **Sheikh The Reins (IRE)**[7] 638 5-8-11 0........................ RobertHavlin 4 39
(John Best) *a towards rr: rdn and no imp ins fnl 3f: wnt 5th post but nvr a factor* **113/10**
6 shd **R Woody**[14] 555 7-8-11 0.................................................... JBojko 3 39
(George Baker) *w ldrs: rdn and lost pl 3f out: dropped to rr and btn in st: lost 5th post* **125/10**
7 dist **The Art Of Racing (IRE)**[14] 555 4-9-2 0................................. APietsch 7
(C Von Der Recke, Germany) **39/10[2]**
F **Ach Was (GER)**[474] 6-8-11 0.................................(p) AlexandraVilmar 1
(W Figge, Germany) **106/10**
1m 20.83s (80.83) **8 Ran SP% 145.1**
PARI-MUTUEL (all including 1 chf stakes): WIN 5.10; PLACE 1.40, 1.30, 1.20; SF 78.60.
**Owner** Wolfgang Frohlich **Bred** Gestut Elsetal **Trained** Germany

## 729a GUBELIN 75. GROSSER PREIS VON ST MORITZ (LOCAL GROUP 2) (4YO+) (SNOW) 1m 2f
**1:10** (12:00) 4-Y-O+
**£42,567** (£21,283; £15,202; £10,135; £5,067; £3,040)

RPR
1 **Future Security (IRE)**[501] 6986 5-8-13 0 ow2.................... APietsch 14 85
(C Von Der Recke, Germany) **181/10**
2 dist **Winterwind (IRE)**[371] 701 9-9-4 0............................(b) FilipMinarik 12
(Carmen Bocskai, Switzerland) **29/10[1]**
3 6 **African Art (USA)**[17] 8-8-11 0...................................(p) DanielePorcu 3
(Mlle B Renk, France) **74/10**
4 3 **Syndic (FR)**[322] 5-9-0 0.............................................. MilanZatloukal 15
(A Schaerer, Switzerland) **106/10**
5 4 **Andreas (GER)**[168] 6248 5-8-11 0...................................... AHelfenbein 10
(Markus Klug, Germany) **7/2[3]**
6 1 ¾ **Fundao (SWI)**[40] 177 5-8-11 0....................................(p) MickaelForest 9
(Carmen Bocskai, Switzerland) **28/1**
7 nk **Ancient Greece**[7] 638 7-8-11 0.................................(p) RobertHavlin 4
(George Baker) *chsd ldr: rdn and lost pl bef st: sn no ex and btn: dropped to last towards fin* **208/10**
U **Cap Sizun (FR)**[147] 5-9-0 0.............................................. SilviaCasanova 11
(P Schaerer, Switzerland) **16/5[2]**
P **Star System (IRE)**[30] 4-9-3 0............................................... JBojko 6
(Frau Agnieszka Klus, Germany) **30/1**
P **Aruaru (GER)**[182] 5-8-11 0........................................ AurelienLemaitre 8
(Christina Bucher, Switzerland) **152/10**
2m 10.97s (130.97)
**WFA** 4 from 5yo+ 1lb **10 Ran SP% 114.9**
PARI-MUTUEL (all including 1 chf stakes): WIN 19.10; PLACE 3.30, 1.60, 1.50; SF 271.50.
**Owner** M-B-A Racing **Bred** Mrs Vanessa Hutch **Trained** Weilerswist, Germany

# 692 WOLVERHAMPTON (A.W) (L-H)
Monday, February 24

**OFFICIAL GOING: Standard**
Wind: Fresh behind Weather: Overcast

## 730 COMPARE BOOKMAKERS AT BOOKMAKERS.CO.UK H'CAP 5f 20y(P)
**3:00** (3:00) (Class 5) (0-75,73) 4-Y-O+ **£3,881** (£1,155; £577; £288) **Stalls** Low

Form RPR
2345 1 **Bapak Bangsawan**[23] 432 4-9-6 72.................................. JamieSpencer 6 77+
(Kevin Ryan) *trckd ldr: shkn up to ld over 1f out: drvn out* **11/10[1]**
5-64 2 ½ **Top Cop**[16] 535 5-9-2 73.........................................(p[1]) DCByrne(5) 1 76
(Ronald Harris) *chsd ldrs: rdn to chse wnr ins fnl f: r.o* **3/1[2]**
3520 3 ½ **Your Gifted (IRE)**[5] 654 7-8-7 59 oh4........................(v) HayleyTurner 4 60
(Lisa Williamson) *dwlt: hdwy 1/2-way: rdn ins fnl f: r.o* **11/2**
-132 4 2 ½ **Shawkantango**[15] 549 7-8-13 72..............................(v) AdamMcLean(7) 2 64
(Derek Shaw) *s.i.s: pushed along in rr early: rdn over 1f out: r.o ins fnl f: nt trble ldrs* **5/1[3]**
-205 5 1 ¾ **Island Legend (IRE)**[12] 572 8-9-5 71...................(p) RichardKingscote 3 57
(Milton Bradley) *led: rdn and hdd over 1f out: wknd ins fnl f* **10/1**
1m 2.93s (0.63) **Going Correction** +0.25s/f (Slow) **5 Ran SP% 113.8**
Speed ratings (Par 103): **104,103,102,98,95**
CSF £4.89 TOTE £1.90: £1.50, £2.30; EX 5.40 Trifecta £22.50.
**Owner** H R H Sultan Ahmad Shah **Bred** Hrh Sultan Ahmad Shah **Trained** Hambleton, N Yorks

**FOCUS**
A small field and this opening handicap didn't take much winning. The third highlights the limitations of the bare form.

## 731 BEST ODDS AT BOOKMAKERS.CO.UK MAIDEN STKS 5f 216y(P)
**3:30** (3:30) (Class 5) 3-Y-O+ **£3,234** (£962; £481; £240) **Stalls** Low

Form RPR
1 **Desert Ranger (IRE)** 3-8-12 0........................................ LukeMorris 10 69+
(James Tate) *hld up: hdwy on outer over 2f out: shkn up to ld ins fnl f: edgd lft: r.o* **5/1[3]**
0- 2 1 ¼ **Crazee Diamond**[150] 6789 3-8-6 0 ow2......... WilliamTwiston-Davies(3) 8 63
(Mick Channon) *trckd ldrs: racd keenly: led over 1f out: rdn and hdd ins fnl f: styd on same pce* **15/2**
3 3 ½ **Sorry Saeed** 3-8-7 0........................................................ JimmyQuinn 5 50+
(James Tate) *s.i.s: hdwy over 2f out: rdn and swtchd rt over 1f out: styd on same pce to go 3rd wl ins fnl f* **6/1**
340- 4 2 **Stoneacre Hull (IRE)**[67] 8338 5-9-5 47............................ SladeO'Hara(3) 4 48
(Peter Grayson) *led: rdn and hdd over 1f out: no ex ins fnl f* **80/1**
55-4 5 2 ½ **Mobley Chaos**[27] 365 4-9-8 40............................................... DCByrne(5) 1 46
(Ronald Harris) *s.i.s: hdwy over 2f out: rdn over 1f out: wknd fnl f* **33/1**
240- 6 ¾ **Travis Bickle (IRE)**[96] 7972 3-8-12 68...................(b[1]) LiamKeniry 3 39
(Sylvester Kirk) *sn drvn along in rr: styd on ins fnl f: nvr nrr* **4/1[2]**
05 7 2 ¾ **Maro**[18] 500 3-8-5 0.......................................(v[1]) AdamMcLean(7) 11 31
(Derek Shaw) *s.i.s: rdn and ev ch over 2f out: wknd over 1f out* **200/1**
0-6 8 shd **Deavin**[9] 622 3-8-5 0.......................................... JordanVaughan(7) 7 31
(Nick Littmoden) *sn pushed along in rr: nvr on terms* **33/1**

 The Form Book, Raceform Ltd, Newbury, RG14 5SJ

5-0 **9** ¾ **High Stand**[24] 416 3-8-12 58..........................(b[1]) ShaneKelly 2 28
(Daniel Mark Loughnane) *chsd ldrs: rdn over 2f out: wknd over 1f out* **14/1**

53-3 **10** 4½ **Brownsville (USA)**[10] 614 3-8-12 69..........................(b[1]) JoeFanning 9 15
(Mark Johnston) *w ldr: rdn and ev ch over 2f out: wkng whn hung lft over 1f out* **7/4**[1]

1m 16.0s (1.00) **Going Correction** +0.25s/f (Slow)
**WFA** 3 from 4yo+ 15lb **10** Ran SP% **113.4**
Speed ratings (Par 103): **103,101,96,94,90 89,86,85,84,78**
CSF £40.06 TOTE £5.00: £2.20, £2.00, £2.60; EX 49.60 Trifecta £459.80.
**Owner** Sheikh Juma Dalmook Al Maktoum **Bred** Tally-Ho Stud **Trained** Newmarket, Suffolk

**FOCUS**
An average maiden for the course and time of year to which a bit of spice was added by a pair of Rabbah Bloodstock newcomers trained by James Tate. The kickback looked atrocious. The bare form is limited by the fourth and fifth but the first three could all rate 7lb+ higher.

## 732 CORAL APP DOWNLOAD FROM THE APP STORE H'CAP 1m 4f 50y(P)
**4:00** (4:00) (Class 5) (0-75,75) 4-Y-O+ **£3,881** (£1,155; £577; £288) **Stalls** Low

Form RPR

00-3 **1** **Lineman**[16] 544 4-8-12 **69**.......................................... ShaneKelly 2 77
(Andrew Hollinshead) *chsd ldr tl led 2f out: sn rdn: styd on wl* **9/2**[3]

-163 **2** 2¼ **Gabrial The Boss (USA)**[12] 582 4-8-11 **68**..................(tp) TomEaves 5 72
(Michael Mullineaux) *a.p: rdn over 2f out: chsd wnr over 1f out: edgd lft and no imp ins fnl f* **10/1**

01/ **3** 2¼ **Fantasy King**[135] 4228 8-9-7 **75**.......................................... TomQueally 6 76
(James Moffatt) *s.i.s: hld up: rdn 3f out: styd on to go 3rd wl ins fnl f: nt trble ldrs* **13/2**

0162 **4** 1¼ **Doldrums (USA)**[7] 641 4-9-4 **75**.......................................... JoeFanning 3 74
(Mark Johnston) *led: rdn and hdd 2f out: no ex fnl f* **11/8**[1]

-302 **5** 4½ **All The Winds (GER)**[16] 544 9-9-1 **72**......(t) WilliamTwiston-Davies(3) 1 64
(Shaun Lycett) *hld up: hdwy 8f out: rdn over 2f out: wknd over 1f out* **3/1**[2]

2m 43.49s (2.39) **Going Correction** +0.25s/f (Slow)
**WFA** 4 from 7yo+ 3lb **5** Ran SP% **107.7**
Speed ratings (Par 103): **102,100,99,98,95**
CSF £39.35 TOTE £5.90: £2.30, £2.10; EX 34.80 Trifecta £165.60.
**Owner** The HRH Trio **Bred** Millsec Limited **Trained** Upper Longdon, Staffs

**FOCUS**
Nothing came into this middle-distance handicap looking to have much in hand on their mark. A minor personal best from the winner.

## 733 CORAL MOBILE "JUST THREE CLICKS TO BET" APPRENTICE H'CAP 1m 1f 103y(P)
**4:30** (4:30) (Class 5) (0-70,69) 4-Y-O+ **£3,557** (£1,058; £529; £264) **Stalls** Low

Form RPR

25-2 **1** **Dubai Celebration**[24] 406 6-9-5 **67**.......................... ConnorBeasley 7 74
(Julie Camacho) *trckd ldrs: rdn over 2f out: edgd lft and styd on u.p to ld wl ins fnl f* **7/2**[2]

4-41 **2** nk **India's Song**[12] 578 4-8-8 **59**..........................(t) GeorgeBuckell(3) 5 65
(David Simcock) *s.i.s: hld up: hdwy over 1f out: n.m.r ins fnl f: styd on* **9/1**

-014 **3** ¾ **Mr Red Clubs (IRE)**[4] 674 5-9-2 **69**..................(p) AlistairRawlinson(5) 4 74
(Michael Appleby) *trckd ldrs: wnt 2nd 6f out: led wl over 1f out: sn rdn: hdd and unable qck wl ins fnl f* **6/5**[1]

-532 **4** ½ **Honey Of A Kitten (USA)**[7] 643 6-8-12 **65**..............(v) HollieDoyle(5) 3 69
(David Evans) *led 1f: led again 7f out: clr 5f out: hdd wl over 1f out: unable qck towards fin* **6/1**[3]

3-20 **5** 4½ **Spanish Plume**[17] 514 6-9-4 **66**..........................(p) LouisSteward 2 61
(Andrew Hollinshead) *hld up: hdwy over 2f out: rdn over 1f out: styd on same pce fnl f* **16/1**

1405 **6** 5 **Outlaw Torn (IRE)**[7] 643 5-9-2 **64**..........................(e) DCByrne 1 50
(Richard Guest) *led after 1f tl 7f out: trckd ldrs: rdn over 2f out: sn wknd* **9/1**

1-00 **7** 16 **Pravda Street**[28] 359 9-9-1 **68**.......................... RobJFitzpatrick(5) 6 23
(Christopher Kellett) *prom: rdn over 3f out: sn wknd* **50/1**

2m 1.99s (0.29) **Going Correction** +0.25s/f (Slow) **7** Ran SP% **109.8**
Speed ratings (Par 103): **108,107,107,106,102 98,83**
CSF £31.12 TOTE £4.00: £2.10, £3.10; EX 22.00 Trifecta £69.80.
**Owner** L Bolingbroke, N Gravett & J Camacho **Bred** Wheelers Land Stud **Trained** Norton, N Yorks

**FOCUS**
A decent handicap for the track and grade in which the best horse finished third. They seemed to go an even pace. Straightforward form.

## 734 32RED FREE £10 BONUS MAIDEN STKS 1m 1f 103y(P)
**5:00** (5:00) (Class 5) 3-Y-O **£3,881** (£1,155; £577; £288) **Stalls** Low

Form RPR

322- **1** **Arantes**[122] 7513 3-9-2 76.......................... WilliamTwiston-Davies(3) 6 72
(Mick Channon) *trckd ldrs: shkn up to ld 1f out: r.o* **4/5**[1]

52 **2** 1¾ **Rose Kazan (IRE)**[16] 542 3-9-0 0.......................... LukeMorris 1 64
(Marco Botti) *trckd ldr: racd keenly: shkn up to ld over 1f out: sn rdn and hdd: hung lft and styd on same pce ins fnl f* **5/2**[2]

5 **3** ¾ **Lockedoutaheaven (IRE)**[38] 218 3-9-5 0.......................... PaoloSirigu 3 67
(Marco Botti) *s.i.s: sn prom: rdn and hung lft over 1f out: styd on same pce ins fnl f* **20/1**

6 **4** 1¼ **Trafalgar Rock**[10] 607 3-9-5 0.......................... JoeFanning 4 65
(Mark Johnston) *led: rdn and hdd over 1f out: no ex ins fnl f* **18/1**

560- **5** ½ **Khee Society**[178] 5951 3-9-5 61.......................... AdamKirby 2 64
(David Evans) *hld up: plld hrd: hdwy over 2f out: shaekn up over 1f out: styd on same pce fnl f* **8/1**[3]

0-0 **6** 24 **Red Wifey (IRE)**[21] 456 3-9-0 0.......................... TomQueally 5 13
(Alan McCabe) *s.i.s: sn pushed along and a in rr: rdn and wknd 3f out* **20/1**

2m 5.7s (4.00) **Going Correction** +0.25s/f (Slow) **6** Ran SP% **110.0**
Speed ratings (Par 97): **92,90,89,88,88 66**
CSF £2.79 TOTE £1.60: £1.10, £1.60; EX 2.90 Trifecta £19.80.
**Owner** M Channon **Bred** Mike Channon Bloodstock Ltd **Trained** West Ilsley, Berks

**FOCUS**
A messy race run at a slow pace, and the bare form is nothing special. The bare form is rated on the negative side.

## 735 LADBROKES MEDIAN AUCTION MAIDEN STKS 1m 141y(P)
**5:30** (5:30) (Class 5) 3-4-Y-O **£3,234** (£962; £481; £240) **Stalls** Low

Form RPR

5 **1** **Fitzgerald (IRE)**[28] 355 3-8-7 0.......................... LukeMorris 4 78+
(Marco Botti) *trckd ldr tl shkn up to ld over 1f out: sn rdn clr: eased ins fnl f* **11/8**[2]

0 **2** 6 **Her Red Devil (IRE)**[19] 486 3-8-2 0.......................... JimmyQuinn 5 56+
(Richard Fahey) *hld up: rdn over 2f out: hdwy over 1f out: wnt 2nd ins fnl f: no ch w wnr* **28/1**

**3** 2 **Stoneham** 3-8-2 0.......................... HayleyTurner 3 52
(Mick Channon) *hld up: rdn over 2f out: wnt 3rd wl ins fnl f: nvr on terms* **11/1**

432 **4** 1¼ **Coillte Cailin (IRE)**[7] 642 4-9-9 67.......................... TomQueally 1 55
(Daniel Mark Loughnane) *trckd ldrs: racd keenly: rdn over 1f out: wknd fnl f* **6/5**[1]

53 **5** 1 **Mount Glenn**[7] 642 3-8-7 0.......................... JoeFanning 2 52
(Mark Johnston) *led: shkn up and hdd over 1f out: wknd fnl f* **9/1**[3]

1m 53.72s (3.22) **Going Correction** +0.25s/f (Slow)
**WFA** 3 from 4yo 21lb **5** Ran SP% **109.3**
Speed ratings (Par 103): **95,89,87,86,85**
CSF £28.46 TOTE £2.70: £1.10, £6.90; EX 48.80 Trifecta £128.60.
**Owner** Al Asayl Bloodstock Ltd **Bred** Sh Sultan Bin Khalifa Al Nahyan **Trained** Newmarket, Suffolk

**FOCUS**
An impressive winner of this auction maiden, who'll go on to better things, but weak form overall.

## 736 LADBROKES H'CAP 1m 141y(P)
**6:00** (6:00) (Class 6) (0-60,60) 4-Y-O+ **£2,587** (£770; £384; £192) **Stalls** Low

Form RPR

0-21 **1** **John Potts**[16] 538 9-9-6 **59**.......................... AdamKirby 1 67
(Brian Baugh) *trckd ldrs: nt clr run and lost pl over 2f out: rallied over 1f out: rdn to ld nr fin* **6/1**[3]

23-1 **2** nk **Reggie Bond**[35] 263 4-9-4 **60**..........................(b) RobertTart(3) 9 67
(Geoffrey Oldroyd) *w ldrs: racd keenly: led over 5f out: rdn over 1f out: hdd nr fin* **1/1**[1]

-450 **3** 1¼ **Delightful Sleep**[20] 467 6-8-11 **57**.......................... HollieDoyle(7) 4 62
(David Evans) *hld up: hdwy over 2f out: rdn over 1f out: unable qck wl ins fnl f* **25/1**

4-63 **4** ½ **Polar Forest**[18] 497 4-8-12 **56**..........................(be[1]) ConnorBeasley(5) 7 60
(Richard Guest) *a.p: chsd ldr over 2f out: rdn and hung lft over 1f out: styd on same pce ins fnl f* **4/1**[2]

653- **5** nk **Dividend Dan (IRE)**[255] 3289 4-9-2 **55**.......................... ShaneKelly 3 58
(Mike Murphy) *s.i.s: hld up: hdwy on outer over 2f out: rdn over 1f out: styd on* **14/1**

6-04 **6** 1¼ **Hot Sugar (USA)**[15] 549 5-8-13 **59**..................(tp) AlistairRawlinson(7) 2 59
(Michael Appleby) *hld up: rdn over 1f out: styd on ins fnl f: nt rch ldrs* **28/1**

-323 **7** ½ **Do More Business (IRE)**[16] 538 7-8-12 **56**..........(vt) PhilipPrince(5) 8 55
(Liam Corcoran) *w ldrs: rdn over 3f out: styd on same pce fr over 2f out* **25/1**

0-65 **8** 5 **Angel Cake (IRE)**[2] 718 5-9-6 **59**.......................... AndrewMullen 5 48
(Michael Appleby) *led 3f: rdn over 3f out: wknd 2f out* **8/1**

1m 51.96s (1.46) **Going Correction** +0.25s/f (Slow) **8** Ran SP% **113.2**
Speed ratings (Par 101): **103,102,101,101,100 99,99,94**
CSF £12.06 CT £138.45 TOTE £6.80: £1.80, £1.10, £6.50; EX 9.50 Trifecta £168.00.
**Owner** Miss S M Potts **Bred** Miss S M Potts **Trained** Audley, Staffs
■ Stewards' Enquiry : Robert Tart two-day ban: used whip above permitted level (Mar 11-12)

**FOCUS**
A few in-form rivals lined up for the closing handicap. The form makes sense.
T/Plt: £319.40 to a £1 stake. Pool: £74367.99 - 169.97 winning tickets T/Qpdt: £42.60 to a £1 stake. Pool: £7662.63 - 132.90 winning tickets CR

# 713 LINGFIELD (L-H)
Tuesday, February 25

**OFFICIAL GOING: Standard**
Wind: medium to strong, half behind Weather: overcast

## 737 CORAL.CO.UK H'CAP 1m 2f (P)
**2:00** (2:00) (Class 6) (0-60,60) 4-Y-O+ **£2,726** (£805; £402) **Stalls** Low

Form RPR

-542 **1** **Standing Strong (IRE)**[20] 490 6-9-2 **55**..........................(p) LiamKeniry 8 63
(Zoe Davison) *hld up in tch in last trio: hdwy on outer wl over 2f out: pushed along to chal ins fnl f: rdn to ld fnl 50yds: r.o* **5/1**[2]

040/ **2** ½ **Orpen'Arry (IRE)**[465] 7767 6-8-11 **55**.......................... DavidKenny(5) 5 62
(Paul Burgoyne) *t.k.h: led: rdn over 1f out: hrd pressed and drvn 1f out: kpt on wl tl hdd and no ex fnl 50yds* **33/1**

00-0 **3** 1 **Scamperdale**[50] 67 12-9-0 **53**..........................(p) AndrewMullen 1 58
(Brian Baugh) *t.k.h: hld up wl in tch in midfield: effrt on inner over 1f out: drvn and ev ch ins fnl f: no ex and one pce wl ins fnl f* **10/1**

3-50 **4** 1½ **Indian Violet (IRE)**[13] 575 8-8-12 **51**..........................(p) JimCrowley 4 53
(Zoe Davison) *bmpd s: t.k.h: hld up wl in tch in midfield: effrt u.p to chse ldr over 1f out: ev ch 1f out: nt qckn ins fnl f: wknd fnl 100yds* **8/1**[3]

11 **5** shd **Stanlow**[24] 435 4-9-2 **56**..........................(v) StephenCraine 2 58+
(Daniel Mark Loughnane) *dwlt: sn in tch in midfield: swtchd rt but hemmed in wl over 2f out: swtchd bk lft and rdn over 2f out: drvn and effrt wl over 1f out: styd on same pce fnl 100yds* **5/4**[1]

0-60 **6** hd **Dreaming Again**[26] 377 4-8-1 **48**.......................... CamHardie(7) 9 50+
(Jimmy Fox) *stdd s: hld up in tch in last pair: rdn and outpcd over 2f out: hdwy and swtchd lft jst ins fnl f: styd on: nvr trbld ldrs* **8/1**[3]

-545 **7** hd **Dazzling Valentine**[11] 612 6-9-2 **60**..........................(v) NatashaEaton(5) 7 61
(Alan Bailey) *dwlt: t.k.h: hld up in tch in last pair: rdn and outpcd over 2f out: hdwy u.p over 1f out: kpt on same pce ins fnl f* **10/1**

0-50 **8** 1½ **Arte Del Calcio**[32] 117 5-8-7 **46** oh1..........................(t) JimmyQuinn 6 44
(Tony Carroll) *in tch in midfield on outer: hdwy to chse ldr over 6f out tl over 1f out: outpcd u.p and btn 1f out: wknd ins fnl f* **33/1**

314- **9** ¾ **Dawn Rock**[178] 5980 4-8-10 **50**.......................... LukeMorris 10 47
(Simon Dow) *chsd ldr tl over 6f out: styd chsng ldrs: drvn and unable qck 2f out: wknd ent fnl f* **12/1**

3-05 **10** 5 **Choral Rhythm (IRE)**[37] 251 4-8-1 **46** oh1.......................... JoeyHaynes(5) 3 33
(Tony Carroll) *wnt rt s: t.k.h: hld up wl in tch in midfield: rdn and losing pl whn short of room 2f out: wknd over 1f out* **25/1**

2m 7.66s (1.06) **Going Correction** +0.05s/f (Slow)
**WFA** 4 from 5yo+ 1lb **10** Ran SP% **118.9**
Speed ratings (Par 101): **97,96,95,94,94 94,94,93,92,88**
CSF £161.16 CT £1585.70 TOTE £6.00: £1.80, £7.30, £3.10; EX 352.70 Trifecta £1454.30.
**Owner** Sussex Racing **Bred** Kilboy Stud **Trained** Hammerwood, E Sussex

**FOCUS**
This was an ordinary race run at a modest tempo, which resulted of many of the runners being too keen. Weak form whioch shouldn't be taken too literally.

## 738 32RED ON THE APP STORE (S) STKS — 1m 2f (P)
**2:30** (2:31) (Class 6) 3-Y-O — **£2,385** (£704; £352) **Stalls** Low

Form — RPR

000- **1** **Lucky Dottie**[147] 6923 3-8-7 39 .................. FrankieMcDonald 4 — 44
(Pat Phelan) *rn green: chsd ldr tl 7f out: styd chsng ldrs tl wnt 2nd again over 3f out: rdn and ev ch 2f out: led over 1f out: pricked ears: hung rt and hdd ins fnl f: kpt on to ld again nr fin* — **20/1**

-546 **2** ½ **Previous Acclaim (IRE)**[7] 653 3-8-2 48 .................. ShelleyBirkett(5) 1 — 43
(Julia Feilden) *led: rdn over 2f out: drvn and hdd over 1f out: kpt on and lft in ld again ins fnl f: hdd and no ex nr fin* — **6/1**[2]

006- **3** ¾ **Polar Express**[69] 8325 3-8-9 50 .................. MatthewLawson(3) 3 — 47
(Jonathan Portman) *stdd s: t.k.h: hld up in last pair: pushed along and clsd over 4f out: wnt 3rd 3f out: rdn and pressed ldrs 2f out: hung lft and nt qckn over 1f out: one pce fnl f* — **7/1**[3]

5-62 **4** 30 **Ultimate Warrior (IRE)**[6] 664 3-8-12 66 ..................(bt) LiamJones 5
(Richard Ford) *s.i.s: rdn along leaving stalls and nvr gng wl: wnt 2nd 7f out: drvn 4f out: dropped to 4th 3f out: sn lost tch* — **1/3**[1]

00 **5** 17 **Jazz Bay**[4] 684 3-8-12 0 .................. LiamKeniry 2
(John Bridger) *stdd s: t.k.h: hld up in tch in rr: rdn over 4f out: sn struggling: t.o over 2f out* — **25/1**

2m 8.77s (2.17) **Going Correction** +0.05s/f (Slow) — **5** Ran SP% **110.4**
Speed ratings (Par 95): **93,92,92,68,54**
CSF £121.10 TOTE £17.30: £8.40, £2.20; EX 79.50 Trifecta £183.60.No claims.
**Owner** Tony Smith **Bred** Tony J Smith **Trained** Epsom, Surrey

**FOCUS**
The first three in this very weak race only contested a close finish because the favourite ran poorly. The winner is rated up a stone.

## 739 32RED THUNDERSTRUCK II SLOT MAIDEN STKS — 6f 1y(P)
**3:00** (3:04) (Class 5) 3-Y-O — **£3,408** (£1,006; £503) **Stalls** Low

Form — RPR

2-2 **1** **Chunghua (USA)**[20] 495 3-9-5 0 .................. GeorgeBaker 2 — 75+
(Ed Walker) *trckd ldng pair: wnt 2nd over 2f out: led over 1f out and sn pushed clr: r.o wl fnl f: easily* — **4/6**[1]

**2** 3 **Advance (FR)** 3-9-5 0 .................. AdamKirby 5 — 64+
(Clive Cox) *dwlt: rdn along and outpcd in 4th: clsd and handy 2f out: drvn and chsd clr wnr ent fnl f: kpt on but no imp* — **6/1**[3]

0 **3** 1¼ **Happydoingnothing**[11] 605 3-9-5 0 .................. AdamBeschizza 1 — 60
(Christine Dunnett) *led tl over 4f out: chsd ldr tl over 2f out: cl 3rd whn swtchd lft and effrt wl over 1f out: styd on same pce fnl f* — **50/1**

-505 **4** 6 **Back On Baileys**[21] 481 3-8-11 46 .................. RyanPowell(3) 4 — 37
(John Ryan) *t.k.h: chsd ldr tl led over 4f out: rdn and hdd over 1f out: 4th and btn 1f out: wknd* — **50/1**

**5** 3¾ **Lindart (ITY)** 3-9-5 0 .................. SeanLevey 3 — 31
(Richard Hannon) *s.i.s: rdn along and sn outpcd in last: reminder after 1f: n.d* — **5/2**[2]

1m 11.23s (-0.67) **Going Correction** +0.05s/f (Slow) — **5** Ran SP% **106.8**
Speed ratings (Par 97): **106,102,100,92,87**
CSF £4.91 TOTE £1.60: £1.10, £2.80; EX 4.70 Trifecta £25.10.
**Owner** Robert Ng **Bred** Lawrence Goichman **Trained** Newmarket, Suffolk

**FOCUS**
This was a reasonable maiden despite the lack of runners. The pace was good and the winner was value for extra. His pre-race form guides the level.

## 740 LADBROKES MOBILE H'CAP — 7f 1y(P)
**3:30** (3:31) (Class 6) (0-60,59) 4-Y-O+ — **£2,726** (£805; £402) **Stalls** Low

Form — RPR

0/16 **1** **Indus Valley (IRE)**[23] 449 7-9-2 54 .................. ShaneKelly 9 — 62
(Des Donovan) *hld up in tch in midfield: hdwy on inner over 1f out: rdn to ld and hung lft u.p ins fnl f: pushed along hands and heels and r.o wl towards fin* — **14/1**

3-03 **2** nk **Warbond**[21] 467 6-9-3 55 ..................(v) LukeMorris 2 — 62
(Michael Madgwick) *chsd ldrs: shkn up to chse ldr 2f out: chal 1f out: ev ch and hrd drvn ins fnl f: nt qckn and hld fnl 100yds* — **8/1**

2111 **3** 1¾ **Bertie Blu Boy**[11] 603 6-9-2 59 ..................(b) EoinWalsh(5) 1 — 61
(Lisa Williamson) *led: rdn 2f out: hrd pressed ent fnl f: hdd and styd on same pce fnl 100yds* — **2/1**[1]

6462 **4** hd **Lutine Charlie (IRE)**[15] 562 7-9-3 55 ..................(p) TomQueally 6 — 57
(Pat Eddery) *t.k.h: wl in tch in midfield: effrt u.p over 1f out: kpt on same pce u.p ins fnl f* — **7/1**[3]

6655 **5** ¾ **Rutterkin (USA)**[14] 563 6-8-7 45 .................. JimmyQuinn 7 — 45
(James Moffatt) *hld up in tch towards rr: hdwy ent fnl f: drvn and kpt on ins fnl f* — **20/1**

-540 **6** 1½ **Annes Rocket (IRE)**[21] 467 9-8-12 57 ..................(p) CamHardie(7) 13 — 53
(Jimmy Fox) *stdd and dropped in bhd after s: hld up in rr: swtchd lft and hdwy ent fnl f: kpt on: nvr trbld ldrs* — **33/1**

-030 **7** ¾ **Sea Soldier (IRE)**[20] 496 6-8-11 56 .................. RobHornby(7) 12 — 50
(Andrew Balding) *in tch in midfield on outer: lost pl and dropped to rr bnd 2f out: rallied u.p 1f out: styd on but no threat to ldrs fnl f* — **16/1**

3-26 **8** shd **Resonare**[24] 425 5-9-6 58 .................. SeanLevey 8 — 52
(Stuart Williams) *chsd ldrs: rdn over 2f out: drvn and outpcd over 1f out: wknd ins fnl f* — **7/1**[3]

0- **9** nse **Until Midnight (IRE)**[137] 6851 4-9-0 55 .................. RobertTart(3) 5 — 48
(Eugene Stanford) *hld up in tch in last quartet: n.m.r on inner and hit rail on bnd 2f out: sme hdwy on inner u.p over 1f out: no imp ins fnl f* — **33/1**

-405 **10** 1¾ **Foie Gras**[13] 576 4-9-7 59 .................. HayleyTurner 11 — 48
(Chris Dwyer) *in tch in midfield: nt clr run and shuffled bk towards rr 2f out: kpt on same pce and no real imp fr over 1f out: nvr trbld ldrs* — **20/1**

65-2 **11** hd **Littlecote Lady**[33] 296 5-8-8 53 .................. CharlotteJenner(7) 10 — 41
(Mark Usher) *hld up in tch in last quartet: nt clr run wl over 1f out: n.d but kpt on fnl f* — **25/1**

0-40 **12** 2 **Vermuyden**[21] 468 5-9-6 58 ..................(t) AdamKirby 3 — 41
(Pam Sly) *chsd ldrs: wnt 2nd over 3f out tl 2f out: drvn and btn over 1f out: wknd fnl f* — **5/1**[2]

60-6 **13** shd **Piccolo Express**[15] 562 8-9-2 54 .................. AndrewMullen 4 — 36
(Brian Baugh) *chsd ldr tl 1/2-way: lost pl u.p over 1f out: wknd fnl f* — **25/1**

1m 23.82s (-0.98) **Going Correction** +0.05s/f (Slow) — **13** Ran SP% **121.8**
Speed ratings (Par 101): **107,106,104,104,103 101,101,100,100,98 98,96,96**
CSF £112.17 CT £335.05 TOTE £17.00: £5.70, £2.90, £1.40; EX 175.00 Trifecta £1051.50.
**Owner** River Racing **Bred** P Morris & B McKenna **Trained** Exning, Suffolk

**FOCUS**
A decent pace set by an in-form front-runner made this a good test for the grade. The second and fourth help set the level.

## 741 LADBROKES MAIDEN STKS — 7f 1y(P)
**4:00** (4:01) (Class 5) 3-Y-O+ — **£3,408** (£1,006; £503) **Stalls** Low

Form — RPR

0- **1** **Chantrea (IRE)**[247] 3605 3-8-5 0 .................. AndreaAtzeni 4 — 65+
(Lady Cecil) *in tch in midfield: nt clr run jst over 2f out: effrt to chse ldrs over 1f out: chalng whn intimidated by rival and faltered ins fnl f: r.o fnl 75yds to ld on post* — **1/1**[1]

2-46 **2** nse **Sebs Sensei (IRE)**[24] 422 3-8-10 70 .................. RobertHavlin 8 — 70
(Mark Hoad) *led: drvn over 1f out: hrd pressed ins fnl f: kpt on and edgd rt ins fnl f: hdd on post* — **8/1**[3]

**3** ¾ **Will** 3-8-10 0 .................. JimmyQuinn 9 — 68
(Gary Harrison) *stdd s: hld up in tch in last trio: hdwy to chse ldrs ent fnl f: str run and pressed ldrs wl ins fnl f: no imp towards fin* — **25/1**

**4** hd **Ermine Ruby** 3-8-5 0 .................. WilliamCarson 5 — 62
(Charles Hills) *hld up in tch in midfield: nt clr run whn swtchd lft and rn green bnd 2f out: hdwy over 1f out: pressed ldrs ins fnl f: styd on same pce towards fin* — **4/1**[2]

5 **5** nse **Spinning Cobblers**[24] 423 3-8-10 0 .................. DavidProbert 1 — 67
(Stuart Williams) *chsd ldrs: rdn to chse ldr 2f out: ev ch over 1f out: unable qck and lost 2nd ins fnl f: one pce and lost 2 pls towards fin* — **33/1**

05-5 **6** 2 **Meridius (IRE)**[10] 628 4-9-13 67 ..................(b) TomQueally 6 — 68
(Gary Harrison) *t.k.h: hld up in tch: rdn and effrt over 1f out: styd on fnl 100yds: nvr gng pce to threaten ldrs* — **4/1**[2]

0-0 **7** 1½ **Madame Mime Artist**[20] 486 3-8-5 0 .................. KieranO'Neill 10 — 53
(Alastair Lidderdale) *chsd ldr tl 2f out: lost pl and btn 1f out: wknd ins fnl f* — **20/1**

05 **8** 6 **Aboody**[11] 614 3-8-10 0 .................. LukeMorris 3 — 42
(Sir Mark Prescott Bt) *dwlt and short of room sn after s: in tch in rr: rdn over 2f out: wknd over 1f out* — **33/1**

05- **9** 1 **K Lightning (IRE)**[235] 4032 4-9-6 0 .................. JackOsborn(7) 7 — 45+
(Gary Harrison) *dwlt: sn rcvrd to chse ldrs after 2f: rdn whn rn wd and lost pl bnd 2f out: sn wknd* — **66/1**

0 **10** 6 **Spin For A Harp (IRE)**[24] 423 3-8-10 0 .................. JimCrowley 2 — 23
(David Dennis) *a towards rr: rdn and btn over 2f out: wknd wl over 1f out* — **50/1**

1m 25.17s (0.37) **Going Correction** +0.05s/f (Slow)
**WFA** 3 from 4yo 17lb — **10** Ran SP% **119.1**
Speed ratings (Par 103): **99,98,98,97,97 95,93,86,85,78**
CSF £9.52 TOTE £1.90: £1.10, £2.10, £7.60; EX 12.10 Trifecta £186.70.
**Owner** Niarchos Family **Bred** Niarchos Family **Trained** Newmarket, Suffolk

**FOCUS**
This was a fair maiden that should yield winners. The pace was average until quickening 3f out. The winner should do a fair bit better.

## 742 32RED FREE £10 BONUS H'CAP — 1m 7f 169y(P)
**4:30** (4:30) (Class 5) (0-70,70) 4-Y-O+ — **£3,234** (£962; £481; £240) **Stalls** Low

Form — RPR

05-1 **1** **King's Request (IRE)**[21] 471 4-9-3 68 .................. LiamJones 5 — 75
(Laura Mongan) *chsd ldng pair for 4f: styd in tch in midfield: hdwy to ld over 2f out: sn rdn: styd on wl u.p ins fnl f* — **5/4**[1]

-101 **2** nk **Keep Kicking (IRE)**[13] 580 7-9-8 67 .................. JimCrowley 7 — 74
(Simon Dow) *stdd s: hld up in last trio: hdwy to chse wnr over 2f out: rdn and ev ch ent fnl f: r.o but hld towards fin* — **9/2**[2]

-342 **3** 5 **Honest Strike (USA)**[28] 361 7-9-4 63 ..................(b) ShaneKelly 2 — 64
(Daniel Mark Loughnane) *stdd s: hld up in rr: clsd 4f out: effrt to chse ldng pair jst over 2f out: no imp fr over 1f out* — **9/2**[2]

-221 **4** 1½ **Cabuchon (GER)**[20] 490 7-9-2 61 .................. SeanLevey 4 — 60
(David Evans) *stdd s: t.k.h: hld up in last trio: clsd over 3f out: effrt in 4th wl over 1f out: no imp over 1f out* — **6/1**[3]

3-60 **5** 6 **Where's Susie**[33] 292 9-9-3 62 .................. LukeMorris 1 — 54
(Michael Madgwick) *chsd ldr tl over 2f out: sn u.p and struggling: wknd wl over 1f out* — **20/1**

54-5 **6** 1¾ **Peachez**[43] 158 6-9-6 65 ..................(b) GeorgeBaker 6 — 55
(Seamus Durack) *stdd s: t.k.h: hld up in midfield: hdwy to chse ldrs 11f out tl nt clr run and shuffled bk towards rr over 2f out: wknd wl over 1f out* — **8/1**

4/0- **7** 10 **Sanctioned**[73] 8298 5-9-11 70 ..................(v[1]) AdamBeschizza 3 — 48
(Robert Stephens) *led tl rdn and hdd over 2f out: sn lost pl and wknd: wl bhd fnl f* — **20/1**

3m 24.14s (-1.56) **Going Correction** +0.05s/f (Slow)
**WFA** 4 from 5yo+ 6lb — **7** Ran SP% **115.7**
Speed ratings (Par 103): **105,104,102,101,98 97,92**
CSF £7.41 TOTE £2.30: £1.20, £2.00; EX 9.70 Trifecta £25.00.
**Owner** Mrs P J Sheen **Bred** Runnymede Farm Inc And Catesby W Clay **Trained** Epsom, Surrey

**FOCUS**
The first two have been in good form, but there was little depth beyond that in a staying race run at a routine early pace for the trip. The third helps set the level.

## 743 32RED CASINO APPRENTICE H'CAP — 1m 2f (P)
**5:00** (5:00) (Class 6) (0-65,58) 3-Y-O — **£2,726** (£805; £402) **Stalls** Low

Form — RPR

5-45 **1** **Duly Acclaimed (IRE)**[6] 665 3-9-2 55 .................. CamHardie(5) 2 — 58
(J S Moore) *chsd ldr: rdn and effrt 2f out: ev ch ins fnl f: r.o to ld wl ins fnl f: hld on cl home* — **11/4**[3]

-061 **2** nse **Shannon Haven (IRE)**[13] 577 3-9-8 56 .................. LouisSteward 5 — 59
(Daniel Mark Loughnane) *t.k.h: hld up in tch: effrt in 3rd wl over 1f out: rdn and ev ch ins fnl f: jst hld cl home* — **5/4**[1]

006 **3** nk **Needs The Run**[39] 218 3-9-2 50 .................. JoeyHaynes 1 — 52
(David Evans) *led and set stdy gallop: qcknd and rdn ent fnl 2f: hrd pressed and kpt on ins fnl f tl hdd and no ex wl ins fnl f* — **8/1**

40-6 **4** 7 **Ventura Reef (IRE)**[21] 477 3-9-10 58 ..................(p) GeorgeChaloner 3 — 47
(Richard Fahey) *chsd ldng pair: dropped to last and rdn wl over 1f out: wknd ins fnl f* — **5/2**[2]

2m 15.91s (9.31) **Going Correction** +0.05s/f (Slow) — **4** Ran SP% **110.8**
Speed ratings (Par 95): **64,63,63,58**
CSF £6.81 TOTE £4.80; EX 6.40 Trifecta £27.20.
**Owner** R Styles, P Grimes & J S Moore **Bred** Rathbarry Stud **Trained** Upper Lambourn, Berks

**FOCUS**
This was weak in quality and quantity, and run at a crawl until the pace suddenly increased 3f out. A personal best from the winner.
T/Plt: £374.20 to a £1 stake. Pool: £61,538.64 - 120.02 winning units. T/Qpdt: £4.00 to a £1 stake. Pool: £8533.78 - 1558.22 winning units. SP

# [654]KEMPTON (A.W) (R-H)

Wednesday, February 26

**OFFICIAL GOING: Standard**

Wind: Virtually nil Weather: dry and mild

## 744 BETDAQ - THE SPORTS BETTING EXCHANGE H'CAP 1m 2f (P)

**5:20** (5:21) (Class 4) (0-85,84) 4-Y-O+ **£4,690** (£1,395; £697; £348) **Stalls** Low

Form RPR

415- **1** **Squire Osbaldeston (IRE)**[117] 7656 4-9-6 **84**................. RyanMoore 6 98+
(Martyn Meade) *hld up in tch: hdwy and wd bnd 2f out: drvn to chal ins fnl f led fnl 25yds: hld on wl* **7/4**[1]

4-60 **2** *nk* **Ishikawa (IRE)**[10] 638 6-8-8 **78**.................. RobJFitzpatrick(7) 8 90+
(K R Burke) *chsd ldrs: led over 1f out: hrd pressed ins fnl f: hdd fnl 25yds: kpt on* **25/1**

-405 **3** *5* **First Post (IRE)**[23] 457 7-9-0 **77**......................... LukeMorris 4 80
(Derek Haydn Jones) *mid-div: hdwy 2f out: styd on to take 3rd fnl 110yds but no ch w ldng duo* **33/1**

1-06 **4** *nk* **Karam Albaari (IRE)**[18] 533 6-9-7 **84**..................... FrederikTylicki 1 86
(J R Jenkins) *in rr: hdwy fr 2f out: styd on fnl f to press for 3rd but no ch w ldng duo* **20/1**

2-06 **5** *nk* **Stevie Thunder**[25] 427 9-9-2 **79**..............................(p) GrahamLee 5 82
(Ian Williams) *chsd ldrs: rdn over 2f out: styd on same pce fnl f* **10/1**

/1-4 **6** *2 ½* **Fujin Dancer (FR)**[49] 85 9-9-2 **79**........................ TomEaves 10 77
(Brian Ellison) *in rr: hdwy over 1f out: sn n.m.r: kpt on cl home* **20/1**

521- **7** *nse* **Busatto (USA)**[151] 6824 4-9-5 **83**.......................... JoeFanning 13 80
(Mark Johnston) *led after 1f: hdd over 1f out: wknd fnl f* **7/1**[3]

126- **8** *nk* **Tight Lipped (IRE)**[236] 4028 5-8-11 **79**.................. RyanTate(5) 11 75
(James Eustace) *chsd ldrs: wknd over 1f out* **25/1**

5 **9** *½* **Ruzeiz (USA)**[36] 270 5-9-0 **80**............................ CharlesBishop(3) 7 75
(Peter Hedger) *s.i.s: in rr: hdwy to cl on ldrs on outside 2f out: outpcd fnl f* **100/1**

0130 **10** *¾* **Ocean Applause**[5] 698 4-8-12 **76**........................(t) JimmyQuinn 14 71
(John Ryan) *s.i.s: in rr: effrt on ins and nt clr run ins fnl 2f: nvr in contention* **25/1**

21-2 **11** *½* **Miguel Grau (USA)**[49] 89 4-9-0 **78**......................(b) AndreaAtzeni 2 75
(Roger Varian) *in rr: hdwy and n.m.r over 1f out: n.d after* **9/4**[2]

655- **12** *6* **Greylami (IRE)**[112] 7765 9-9-6 **83**............................ AdamKirby 9 65
(Clive Cox) *led 1f: chsd ldr to 2f out* **20/1**

452- **13** *4 ½* **Saint Jerome (IRE)**[104] 6379 4-9-2 **80**.................... FergusSweeney 12 53
(Jamie Osborne) *chsd ldrs: wknd appr fnl 2f* **33/1**

2m 4.77s (-3.23) **Going Correction** -0.175s/f (Stan)
**WFA** 4 from 5yo+ 1lb **13** Ran SP% **121.4**
Speed ratings (Par 105): **105,104,100,100,100 98,98,98,97,97 96,91,88**
CSF £56.32 CT £1133.94 TOTE £3.00: £1.20, £11.60, £10.10; EX 85.90 Trifecta £3733.70.
**Owner** P Hickman & G Johns **Bred** Kushnarenkovo Syndicate **Trained** Newmarket, Suffolk
■ Stewards' Enquiry : Frederik Tylicki caution: careless riding.

**FOCUS**
A good, tight-knit handicap with 9lb covering all 13 runners. However, two were clear in the market and the favourite got up late on.

## 745 BOOK NOW FOR SILVER CUPS DAY 15.03.14 H'CAP 6f (P)

**5:50** (5:50) (Class 6) (0-65,64) 3-Y-O **£1,940** (£577; £288; £144) **Stalls** Low

Form RPR

3323 **1** **Global Explorer (USA)**[7] 667 3-9-7 **64**................(t) AdamBeschizza 10 69
(Stuart Williams) *in rr: drvn and hdwy appr fnl 2f: styd on u.p fnl f to ld fnl 110yds: hld on wl* **13/8**[1]

-403 **2** *hd* **Coiste Bodhar (IRE)**[11] 622 3-9-1 **58**..................(p) LukeMorris 5 62
(Joseph Tuite) *chsd ldrs: chal u.p fnl 110yds tl no ex last strides* **8/1**[3]

60-5 **3** *¾* **Wedgewood Estates**[33] 315 3-8-13 **56**..................... DavidProbert 2 58
(Tony Carroll) *towards rr: hdwy whn pushed lft 2f out: styd on ins fnl f: kpt on cl home* **11/4**[2]

4-46 **4** *hd* **Douneedahand**[33] 315 3-9-3 **60**.............................. LiamKeniry 3 61
(Seamus Mullins) *trckd ldrs: chalng whn pushed lft 2f out: sn led and rdn: hdd u.p fnl 110yds: one pce* **11/1**

66-0 **5** *¾* **Crystalized (IRE)**[26] 401 3-8-12 **55**...................... FergusSweeney 6 54
(Dean Ivory) *in rr: drvn and hdwy appr fnl 2f: pressed ldrs 1f out: styd on same pce fnl f* **16/1**

6-60 **6** *4* **Sakhee'Ssquirrel**[12] 608 3-9-0 **57**........................(b[1]) AdamKirby 11 43
(Sean Curran) *in rr: pushed along over 2f out: styd on same pce fnl f* **33/1**

00-0 **7** *1 ½* **Trefnant (IRE)**[22] 477 3-8-2 **50** oh5......................... TimClark(5) 1 31
(Chris Dwyer) *pressed ldr: led over 3f out: rdn and hung lft 2f out: sn hdd and btn appr fnl f* **50/1**

2-33 **8** *¾* **Diamondsinthesky (IRE)**[34] 302 3-9-0 **57**................... DaleSwift 8 36
(Derek Shaw) *chsd ldrs: wknd fr 2f out* **20/1**

305- **9** *¾* **Chanceuse**[68] 8363 3-8-2 **50**.............................. ShelleyBirkett(5) 9 27
(Gay Kelleway) *outpcd most of way* **20/1**

04-6 **10** *1 ¼* **The Boss Of Me**[22] 481 3-8-12 **55**.............................. TomEaves 4 28
(Kevin Ryan) *sn led but hrd pressed: hdd over 3f out: v ch whn pushed lft 2f out: sn wknd* **8/1**[3]

1m 13.32s (0.22) **Going Correction** +0.10s/f (Slow) **10** Ran SP% **115.6**
Speed ratings (Par 95): **102,101,100,100,99 94,92,91,90,88**
CSF £14.53 CT £34.83 TOTE £2.40: £1.10, £2.80, £1.40; EX 14.60 Trifecta £49.50.
**Owner** T W Morley & Mrs J Morley **Bred** James Millar & Janice Millar **Trained** Newmarket, Suffolk
■ Stewards' Enquiry : Tim Clark two-day ban: careless riding (Mar 12-13)

**FOCUS**
Low-grade fare and this is just modest form.

## 746 £500 FREE BETS AT BETDAQ H'CAP 6f (P)

**6:20** (6:20) (Class 5) (0-75,75) 4-Y-O+ **£2,587** (£770; £384; £192) **Stalls** Low

Form RPR

251- **1** **Dutiful Son (IRE)**[84] 8146 4-9-5 **73**............................ RyanMoore 10 87+
(Jeremy Noseda) *trckd ldr: led ins fnl 2f: drvn and styd on wl appr fnl f: readily* **4/5**[1]

120- **2** *1 ½* **Marjong**[146] 6977 4-9-7 **75**..................................... HayleyTurner 9 82+
(Simon Dow) *s.i.s: in rr: drvn and hdwy over 1f out: styd on to take 2nd fnl 110yds but nvr any ch w wnr* **20/1**

-052 **3** *½* **Daring Dragon**[21] 489 4-9-4 **72**........................(b) GeorgeBaker 5 78
(Ed Walker) *in rr: hdwy and swtchd rt over 1f out: kpt on wl fnl 110yds to cl on 2nd but no ch w wnr* **5/1**[2]

5-31 **4** *½* **Rigolleto (IRE)**[38] 248 6-8-10 **71**......................... JackGarritty(7) 7 75
(Anabel K Murphy) *led: rdn and hdd ins fnl 2f: styd chsng wnr tl outpcd fnl 110yds* **8/1**[3]

-600 **5** *nse* **Shaunas Spirit (IRE)**[13] 587 6-9-3 **71**...............(p) RobertWinston 2 75
(Dean Ivory) *chsd ldrs: rdn 2f out: one pce fnl f* **20/1**

0- **6** *¾* **Ceelo**[127] 7444 4-8-13 **67**......................................... LiamKeniry 4 69
(Lydia Pearce) *chsd ldrs: drvn over 2f out: styd on same pce appr fnl f* **14/1**

130- **7** *¾* **Sole Danser (IRE)**[198] 5349 6-9-6 **74**..................(p) RichardKingscote 1 73
(Milton Bradley) *in tch: drvn and hdwy ins fnl 2f: no prog fnl f* **16/1**

-435 **8** *1* **Bajan Bear**[24] 451 6-9-1 **69**.................................. AdamKirby 8 67
(Michael Blanshard) *in rr: hdwy appr fnl f: styng on same pce whn nt clr run fnl 110yds* **8/1**[3]

210- **9** *hd* **Harrogate Fair**[128] 7432 4-8-12 **66**........................... LiamJones 6 62
(Michael Squance) *chsd ldrs: rdn fr 2f out: wknd fnl 110yds* **25/1**

1m 13.35s (0.25) **Going Correction** +0.10s/f (Slow) **9** Ran SP% **120.4**
Speed ratings (Par 103): **102,100,99,98,98 97,96,95,95**
CSF £24.74 CT £61.26 TOTE £1.90: £1.10, £3.80, £1.50; EX 20.00 Trifecta £58.90.
**Owner** Nigel O'Sullivan **Bred** Lodge Park Stud **Trained** Newmarket, Suffolk

**FOCUS**
A fair handicap. The time was nearly identical to the previous race over the same trip.

## 747 MIX BUSINESS WITH PLEASURE AT KEMPTON H'CAP 1m 4f (P)

**6:50** (6:51) (Class 6) (0-65,65) 4-Y-O+ **£1,940** (£577; £288; £144) **Stalls** Centre

Form RPR

440- **1** **Watt Broderick (IRE)**[10] 7169 5-9-5 **63**....................... GrahamLee 6 78+
(Ian Williams) *hld up in rr: stdy hdwy on ins fr 2f out: led appr fnl f: easily* **3/1**[2]

30/3 **2** *4 ½* **Rocky Elsom (USA)**[32] 343 7-9-4 **62**.......................... AdamKirby 3 68
(David Arbuthnot) *led: drvn and hdd appr fnl f: sn outpcd but kpt on wl for 2nd* **10/1**

06-2 **3** *1 ½* **Maison Brillet (IRE)**[12] 606 7-9-2 **60**..................(p) RobertHavlin 5 64
(Clive Drew) *chsd ldrs: rdn 2f out: styd on to take 3rd fnl 110yds: no ch w wnr* **7/1**[3]

20/6 **4** *1 ½* **Grand Gold**[12] 606 5-9-4 **62**..................................(tp) JoeFanning 7 63
(Seamus Durack) *chsd ldr to 2f out: outpcd fr over 1f out* **20/1**

-161 **5** *½* **Fearless Lad (IRE)**[23] 458 4-9-2 **63**......................(t) GeorgeBaker 4 63
(John Best) *chsd ldrs: rdn over 2f out: wknd fnl 110yds* **11/8**[1]

0-25 **6** *1 ½* **Emman Bee (IRE)**[21] 491 5-8-12 **63**................. KieranShoemark(7) 9 61
(Luke Dace) *chsd ldrs: rdn on outside over 2f out: sn btn* **16/1**

36-0 **7** *½* **Vexillum (IRE)**[12] 609 5-8-13 **57**........................(b[1]) LukeMorris 1 54
(Simon Hodgson) *in rr: sme hdwy ins fnl 3f: wknd 2f out* **50/1**

-323 **8** *4 ½* **Lisahane Bog**[18] 530 7-8-7 **54** ow3....................(b) CharlesBishop(3) 10 44
(Peter Hedger) *in rr: sme hdwy 3f out: wknd over 2f out* **14/1**

043- **9** *6* **Silk Route**[135] 7258 4-9-4 **65**................................. WilliamCarson 8 45
(Giles Bravery) *in rr: rdn and sme hdwy over 3f out: sn wknd* **12/1**

2m 35.33s (0.83) **Going Correction** +0.10s/f (Slow)
**WFA** 4 from 5yo+ 3lb **9** Ran SP% **115.7**
Speed ratings (Par 101): **101,98,97,96,95 94,94,91,87**
CSF £33.13 CT £194.46 TOTE £4.10: £1.30, £2.60, £2.20; EX 35.90 Trifecta £149.20.
**Owner** Patrick Kelly **Bred** Joe Fogarty **Trained** Portway, Worcs

**FOCUS**
A distinct lack of pace in this moderate handicap and it turned into a sprint up the straight.

## 748 WINNERS ARE WELCOME AT BETDAQ MAIDEN STKS 1m (P)

**7:20** (7:21) (Class 5) 3-Y-O+ **£2,587** (£770; £384; £192) **Stalls** Low

Form RPR

3 **1** **Born In Bombay**[14] 579 3-8-9 0................................ DavidProbert 8 89+
(Andrew Balding) *t.k.h: trckd ldrs: led over 2f out: c clr appr fnl f: easily* **8/11**[1]

62 **2** *4 ½* **Bobby Benton (IRE)**[22] 468 3-8-9 0........................... LukeMorris 6 78+
(Luke Dace) *chsd ldrs: wnt 2nd ins fnl 2f: sn no ch w wnr but kpt on wl for clr 2nd* **9/2**[2]

0-5 **3** *5* **Hurricane Harry**[22] 468 3-8-9 0............................. AndreaAtzeni 10 64
(William Knight) *sn led: hdd over 2f out: sn no ch w wnr and dropped to wl hld 3rd sn after* **8/1**[3]

62 **4** *hd* **Ambella (IRE)**[7] 660 4-9-4 0............................. GeorgeDowning(5) 7 65
(Ian Williams) *in tch: drvn and styd on fr 2f out: clsd on 4th clsng stages but no ch w ldng duo* **10/1**

**5** *2 ¼* **Mr Soprano** 3-8-9 0............................................ AdamBeschizza 1 59+
(Stuart Williams) *s.i.s: hld up in rr: sme hdwy fr over 1f out* **25/1**

00- **6** *½* **Next Stop**[69] 8340 3-8-4 0...................................... WilliamCarson 2 52
(Lee Carter) *s.i.s: in rr: drvn and mod hdwy fr 2f out* **33/1**

**7** *2 ¼* **Kovolini** 4-9-9 0.................................................. GeorgeBaker 3 55+
(Geoffrey Deacon) *slowly away: in rr: mod prog fr over 1f out* **66/1**

**8** *½* **Al Hanyora** 3-8-4 0............................................. KieranO'Neill 4 46
(Richard Hannon) *slowly away: plld hrd and sn prom: wknd ins fnl 3f* **12/1**

-00 **9** *13* **Literally On Fire (IRE)**[25] 423 3-8-4 0................... RyanTate(5) 9 21
(Brendan Powell) *t.k.h: chsd ldrs to 3f out: sn btn* **66/1**

6 **10** *1 ¾* **Radebe (USA)**[25] 423 3-8-9 0..............................(b[1]) TomEaves 5 17
(Kevin Ryan) *s.i.s: hdwy 1/2-way and sn chsng ldrs: wknd u.p on outside 3f out* **25/1**

1m 40.45s (0.65) **Going Correction** +0.10s/f (Slow)
**WFA** 3 from 4yo 19lb **10** Ran SP% **117.6**
Speed ratings (Par 103): **100,95,90,90,88 87,85,84,71,70**
CSF £3.93 TOTE £1.50: £1.10, £2.00, £2.40; EX 5.20 Trifecta £17.40.
**Owner** George Strawbridge **Bred** George Strawbridge **Trained** Kingsclere, Hants
■ Stewards' Enquiry : Andrea Atzeni ten-day ban (reduced to eight on appeal) : continued on gelding when it appeared to have gone lame (Mar 12-15,17-20)

**FOCUS**
A wide range of abilities on show in this maiden and another favourite winning on the card.

## 749 BETDAQ 1ST UK RACE COMMISSION FREE CONDITIONS STKS 1m (P)

**7:50** (7:51) (Class 2) 4-Y-O+ **£11,827** (£3,541; £1,770; £885; £442) **Stalls** Low

Form RPR

040- **1** **The Rectifier (USA)**[151] 6838 7-9-2 96.....................(t) AdamKirby 1 107
(Seamus Durack) *mde all: drvn and qcknd fr 2f out: styd on strly: unchal* **5/1**

60-4 **2** *2 ¾* **Don't Call Me (IRE)**[23] 465 7-9-2 102...............(t) AdrianNicholls 2 101
(David Nicholls) *racd in 5th: shkn up 3f out: hrd drvn over 1f out: styd on wl fnl 110yds to take 2nd but no ch w wnr* **7/1**

430- **3** *½* **Premio Loco (USA)**[137] 7196 10-9-9 110..................... GeorgeBaker 5 107
(Chris Wall) *trckd wnr: rdn and no imp 2f out: kpt on same pce* **2/1**[2]

6-20 **4** *nk* **Georgian Bay (IRE)**[33] 314 4-9-2 93....................... DanielTudhope 4 99
(K R Burke) *racd in 4th: drvn and hdwy 2f out to chse wnr over 1f out: no imp: outpcd into 4th fnl 50yds* **4/1**[3]

522- **5** *nse* **Emell**242 3839 4-9-2 105 RyanMoore 3 99+
(Richard Hannon) *chsd ldrs: rdn 2f out: effrt over 1f out: nvr nr wnr: outpcd fnl 100yds* **7/4**1
1m 38.75s (-1.05) **Going Correction** +0.10s/f (Slow) **5 Ran SP% 118.9**
Speed ratings (Par 109): **109,106,105,105,105**
CSF £38.08 TOTE £6.30: £2.70, £2.90; EX 36.00 Trifecta £81.60.
**Owner** Mrs Anne Cowley **Bred** Ceka Ireland Ltd **Trained** Baydon, Wilts
**FOCUS**
The highlight race on the card but it disappointed somewhat with tactics playing a big part.

## 750 VISIT AND DINE IN THE PANORAMIC H'CAP 1m (P)
**8:20** (8:20) (Class 6) (0-65,71) 4-Y-0+ **£1,940** (£577; £288; £144) **Stalls** Low

Form RPR
03-5 **1** **Self Employed**8 647 7-9-7 65 GrahamLee 8 77+
(Garry Woodward) *hld up in tch: stdy hdwy 2f out to ld appr fnl f: pushed out in clsng stages* **5/2**1
1-65 **2** *1 ½* **Spirit Of Gondree (IRE)**34 289 6-9-2 60 (b) AdamKirby 3 65+
(Milton Bradley) *in rr: drvn 2f out: hdwy over 1f out: styd on strly fnl f to take 2nd in clsng stages but no ch w wnr* **4/1**2
2021 **3** *nk* **Conry (IRE)**8 647 8-9-8 71 6ex GeorgeDowning(5) 9 76
(Ian Williams) *in tch: drvn 2f out: styd on fr over 1f out: kpt on in clsng stages to press for 2nd: no ch w wnr* **5/1**3
10-2 **4** *½* **Ivor's Princess**49 84 5-9-7 65 (b) SeanLevey 5 68
(Rod Millman) *in rr: drvn over 2f out: styd on fnl f: kpt on in clsng stages* **14/1**
-004 **5** *1* **First Class**13 587 6-9-4 62 (p) DavidProbert 10 63
(Rae Guest) *chsd ldrs: rdn 2f out: pressed ldrs over 1f out: no ex fnl 110yds* **8/1**
31-3 **6** *¾* **Stun Gun**29 367 4-9-1 59 DaleSwift 4 58
(Derek Shaw) *in rr: drvn and hdwy fr 2f out: styd on same pce fnl f* **7/1**
0-04 **7** *hd* **Hill Of Dreams (IRE)**13 589 5-9-6 64 (b) RobertWinston 11 63
(Dean Ivory) *towards rr: rdn over 2f out: sme prog fnl 110yds* **10/1**
6-52 **8** *1 ¼* **Schottische**27 388 4-8-13 57 (v) JoeFanning 7 53
(Derek Haydn Jones) *chsd ldr: rdn over 2f out: wknd appr fnl frlong* **20/1**
-444 **9** *¾* **Safwaan**24 451 7-8-13 57 LiamJones 2 51
(Michael Squance) *led tl hdd & wknd qckly appr fnl f* **10/1**
3-00 **10** *1* **Admirable Art (IRE)**13 589 4-9-0 58 LiamKeniry 6 50
(Tony Carroll) *chsd ldrs: wknd qckly 1f out* **33/1**
1m 40.13s (0.33) **Going Correction** +0.10s/f (Slow) **10 Ran SP% 121.4**
Speed ratings (Par 101): **102,100,100,99,98 97,97,96,95,94**
CSF £12.85 CT £48.91 TOTE £4.10: £1.50, £2.20, £1.50; EX 18.40 Trifecta £67.30.
**Owner** J Pownall **Bred** R G Percival And Mrs A Lockhart **Trained** Bolham, Notts
**FOCUS**
An open handicap and, with some recent winning form on offer from a few of these, it may prove to be slightly better than the grade.
T/Jkpt: £1,457.70 to a £1 stake. Pool of £122140.13 - 59.49 winning tickets. T/Plt: £55.50 to a £1 stake. Pool of £108241.95 - 1422.86 winning tickets. T/Qpdt: £16.80 to a £1 stake. Pool of £11819.82 - 518.09 winning tickets. ST

# LYON-LA SOIE (R-H)
Wednesday, February 26
**OFFICIAL GOING: Viscoride: standard**

## 751a PRIX CARNAVAL (MAIDEN) (3YO COLTS & GELDINGS) (VISCORIDE) 1m 2f 165y(P)
**4:40** (4:40) 3-Y-0 **£6,666** (£2,666; £2,000; £1,333; £666)

RPR
**1** **Souriyan (FR)** 3-9-2 0 IoritzMendizabal 8 74
(J-C Rouget, France) **7/10**1
**2** *¾* **Sindymarch (FR)**117 3-9-2 0 TonyPiccone 10 73
(J Heloury, France) **19/2**3
**3** *½* **Boker Mazal (FR)**59 3-9-2 0 FranckForesi 7 72
(D Chenu, France) **37/1**
**4** *¾* **Flying Cape (IRE)**4 721 3-9-2 0 ThomasMessina 5 70
(Andrew Hollinshead) *broke wl: t.k.h: trckd ldng quartet: sltly outpcd over 2f out: sn rdn: kpt on u.p ins fnl f: nt pce to chal* **3/1**2
**5** *½* **Soulef (FR)**110 3-9-2 0 (b1) AlexisBadel 11 69
(J Heloury, France) **26/1**
**6** *¾* **Zadrak (FR)**4 3-8-10 0 JimmyTastayre(6) 9 68
(C Boutin, France) **39/1**
**7** *6* **A Colorier (FR)** 3-9-2 0 RomainAuray 1 56
(J-P Bourdin, France) **72/1**
**8** *¾* **Hepijeu (FR)**110 3-9-2 0 AntoineHamelin 2 55
(J Heloury, France) **134/10**
**9** *7 ½* **Toxic (SPA)**4 3-9-2 0 (b) AurelienLemaitre 4 40
(C Boutin, France) **18/1**
**10** *dist* **Got Breizh (FR)**234 3-9-2 0 EddyHardouin 3
(J Heloury, France) **28/1**
**0** **Vip (GER)** 3-9-2 0 CyrilleStefan 6
(B Recher, France) **69/1**
2m 14.94s (-3.06) **11 Ran SP% 120.6**
WIN (incl. 1 euro stake): 1.70. PLACES: 1.20, 2.00, 4.30. DF: 6.70. SF: 8.70.
**Owner** H H Aga Khan **Bred** H H The Aga Khan's Studs S C **Trained** Pau, France

## 752a PRIX DE JONAGE (CLAIMER) (4YO+) (VISCORIDE) 1m 1f
**5:40** (5:40) 4-Y-0+ **£5,000** (£2,000; £1,500; £1,000; £500)

RPR
**1** **Tepmokea (IRE)**7 669 8-9-4 0 (p) IoritzMendizabal 6 75
(Andrew Hollinshead) *mde all: pressed thrght: rdn and r.o over 1 1/2f out: drvn clr ins fnl f: wl on top fnl 50yds* **17/5**2
**2** *¾* **Looking**142 5-8-8 0 (p) XavierBergeron(3) 9 66
(P Cottier, France) **99/10**
**3** *hd* **Greatest (FR)**69 5-8-6 0 (p) MickaelForest(5) 4 66
(Mme G Rarick, France) **235/10**
**4** *hd* **Lowengang**65 9-9-2 0 (b) AntoineHamelin 2 70
(Carmen Bocskai, Switzerland) **13/5**1
**5** *1* **Gaelique Show (FR)**314 8-8-11 0 (b) AnthonyCrastus 5 63
(P Khozian, France) **66/10**
**6** *nse* **Happy Monster (FR)**46 6-9-1 0 (b) BriceRaballand 8 67
(M Boutin, France) **96/10**
**7** *1 ½* **Botanique (FR)**163 8-9-5 0 AnthonyTeissieux 3 68
(M Pimbonnet, France) **17/1**
**8** *2 ½* **Prairie City (IRE)** 4-8-11 0 OlivierPlacais 10 55
(G-J Raveneau, Switzerland) **205/10**
**9** *snk* **Nafar (GER)**69 6-9-4 0 (p) TonyPiccone 1 61
(C Boutin, France) **18/5**3
**10** *dist* **Miles Magician (GER)** 5-9-1 0 (p) CyrilleStefan 7
(B Recher, France) **66/1**
1m 51.25s (111.25) **10 Ran SP% 119.8**
WIN (incl. 1 euro stake): 4.40. PLACES: 2.00, 3.10, 5.40. DF: 25.20. SF: 31.90.
**Owner** Hollinshead, Chapman & Evitt **Bred** J H A Baggen **Trained** Upper Longdon, Staffs

# 744 KEMPTON (A.W) (R-H)
Thursday, February 27
**OFFICIAL GOING: Standard**
Wind: light, half behind Weather: showers

## 753 BACK OF THE NET AT BETVICTOR.COM H'CAP 1m (P)
**5:30** (5:31) (Class 6) (0-60,60) 3-Y-0 **£1,940** (£577; £288; £144) **Stalls** Low

Form RPR
00-4 **1** **Kraka Gym (IRE)**16 568 3-9-1 54 GrahamGibbons 4 60+
(Michael Easterby) *hld up in tch in midfield: clsd and nt clr run briefly over 1f out: chsd wnr 1f out: rdn and qcknd to ld wl ins fnl f: r.o wl* **8/1**3
232- **2** *¾* **Byron Gala**121 7604 3-9-5 58 AdamKirby 9 62
(Marco Botti) *led: sn hdd and chsd ldrs after: rdn to ld jst over 1f out: rdn and wandered ins fnl f: hdd and no ex wl ins fnl f* **4/5**1
635- **3** *2* **Baltic Fire (IRE)**170 6275 3-9-0 58 JoeyHaynes(5) 2 57
(K R Burke) *hld up towards rr: n.m.r jst over 2f out: swtchd lft and hdwy over 1f out: wnt 3rd ins fnl f: r.o but no threat to ldrs* **10/1**
006- **4** *1* **Ormer**159 6656 3-8-7 46 oh1 RichardKingscote 13 43
(David Evans) *stdd s: hld up in last: rdn and hdwy over 1f out: r.o wl fnl f: nt rch ldrs* **66/1**
4-42 **5** *nk* **Armelle (FR)**28 378 3-9-1 54 LukeMorris 10 50
(Scott Dixon) *t.k.h: chsd ldr after 2f: ev ch and rdn 2f out: outpcd ent fnl f: wknd fnl 100yds* **11/2**2
-320 **6** *1 ¼* **Bold Max**29 374 3-8-12 51 LiamJones 7 44
(Zoe Davison) *in tch in midfield: rdn and effrt 2f out: no imp and styd on same pce fnl f* **50/1**
3331 **7** *nk* **Day Star Lad**23 480 3-9-5 58 (v) DaleSwift 1 50
(Derek Shaw) *hld up towards rr: rdn and effrt 2f out: swtchd lft 1f out: kpt on u.p ins fnl f* **8/1**3
0-00 **8** *hd* **French Accent**14 588 3-8-8 47 HayleyTurner 6 39
(John Best) *in tch in midfield: rdn and unable qck 2f out: no threat to ldrs and styd on same pce fr over 1f out* **66/1**
55-3 **9** *¾* **Gee Sharp**27 411 3-9-4 57 (p) BarryMcHugh 11 47
(Julie Camacho) *chsd ldrs: rdn and unable qck jst over 2f out: outpcd and btn over 1f out: wknd fnl f* **16/1**
30-6 **10** *1* **La Paiva (FR)**44 174 3-8-5 47 MichaelJMMurphy(3) 12 35
(Scott Dixon) *sn led: rdn and hrd pressed ent fnl f: hdd jst over 1f out: wknd fnl 150yds* **40/1**
000- **11** *9* **Tidal Beauty**232 4164 3-8-7 46 oh1 DavidProbert 8 12
(Tony Carroll) *t.k.h: racd wd: hld up towards rr: hdwy into midfield 1/2-way: wknd 2f out: bhd fnl f* **16/1**
1m 41.59s (1.79) **Going Correction** 0.0s/f (Stan) **11 Ran SP% 121.4**
Speed ratings (Par 95): **91,90,88,87,86 85,85,85,84,83 74**
CSF £15.14 CT £73.48 TOTE £9.70: £1.80, £1.10, £3.70; EX 26.20 Trifecta £208.20.
**Owner** Clark Industrial Service & S Hollings **Bred** E Lonergan **Trained** Sheriff Hutton, N Yorks
**FOCUS**
The market was all over the Marco Botti-trained Byron Gala here, but the odds-on favourite was turned over.

## 754 BETVICTOR NON-RUNNER FREE BET AT CHELTENHAM H'CAP (DIV I) 1m (P)
**6:00** (6:00) (Class 6) (0-55,55) 4-Y-0+ **£1,940** (£577; £288; £144) **Stalls** Low

Form RPR
6631 **1** **Bennelong**8 661 8-8-8 49 (b) PaigeBolton(7) 11 61+
(Lee Carter) *hld up in tch in midfield: hdwy to go 3rd over 2f out: pushed along and steadily clsd on ldr: ev ch ins fnl f: led wl ins fnl f: r.o: pushed out* **15/8**1
2003 **2** *½* **Tijuca (IRE)**15 575 5-9-6 54 FrederikTylicki 1 63
(Ed de Giles) *wl in tch in midfield: hdwy to chse clr ldr jst over 2f out: styd on u.p to ld ins fnl f: hrd drvn and hdd wl ins fnl f: one pce* **7/1**
3222 **3** *2 ¼* **Polydamos**15 570 5-9-4 52 (v) LukeMorris 2 55
(Tony Carroll) *hld up in tch towards rr: hdwy on inner 2f out: swtchd lft over 1f out: styd on u.p ins fnl f: wnt 3rd cl home* **3/1**2
-000 **4** *nk* **Coach Montana (IRE)**7 676 5-8-12 46 oh1 (b) AdamBeschizza 10 49
(Christine Dunnett) *led: wnt clr fr 1/2-way: rdn over 1f out: hdd ins fnl f: wknd fnl 100yds* **40/1**
0-32 **5** *2* **Byrd In Hand (IRE)**25 446 7-8-13 47 (b) LiamKeniry 7 45
(John Bridger) *t.k.h: hld up in tch in midfield: effrt u.p wl over 1f out: edgd rt and no imp fnl f* **7/1**
150- **6** *6* **Wyndham Wave**232 4169 5-9-7 55 (p) AdamKirby 9 38
(Rod Millman) *t.k.h: chsd ldrs: rdn and unable qck ent fnl 2f: wknd over 1f out* **7/2**3
1/0- **7** *1* **Newbury Street**140 7148 7-9-0 55 JackGarritty(7) 8 36
(Patrick Holmes) *t.k.h: hld up in tch in last trio: rdn and no imp 2f out: plugged on fnl f: n.d* **50/1**
00-0 **8** *4* **Beaumont Cooper**15 575 5-9-2 50 GeorgeBaker 5 21
(Anabel K Murphy) *t.k.h: chsd ldrs: wnt 2nd wl over 2f out tl ent fnl 2f: sn btn and wknd over 1f out* **16/1**
050/ **9** *hd* **Curlew (IRE)**329 1310 8-8-7 46 JoeyHaynes(5) 12 17
(Chris Down) *chsd ldr tl wl over 2f out: lost pl and bhd 2f out: sn wknd* **50/1**
500/ **10** *shd* **Kilk**1014 2243 6-9-0 48 GrahamGibbons 4 19
(Stuart Kittow) *hld up in tch towards rr: rdn and no hdwy over 2f out: bhd over 1f out* **66/1**
4-00 **11** *16* **Jackie Love (IRE)**13 602 6-8-5 46 oh1 (v) RhiainIngram(7) 3
(Roger Ingram) *s.i.s: t.k.h: hld up in rr: swtchd lft and hdwy on outer into midfield after 2f: lost pl and bhd over 2f out: lost tch 2f out* **66/1**
1m 39.89s (0.09) **Going Correction** 0.0s/f (Stan) **11 Ran SP% 122.2**
Speed ratings (Par 101): **99,98,96,95,93 87,86,82,82,82 66**
CSF £16.67 CT £40.38 TOTE £3.20: £1.60, £1.90, £1.20; EX 14.20 Trifecta £39.00.
**Owner** Miss Victoria Baalham **Bred** The National Stud **Trained** Epsom, Surrey

**FOCUS**
Very modest form.

## 755 BETVICTOR NON-RUNNER FREE BET AT CHELTENHAM H'CAP (DIV II) 1m (P)
6:30 (6:30) (Class 6) (0-55,55) 4-Y-O+ £1,940 (£577; £288; £144) Stalls Low

Form RPR
0356 1 **Fleetwoodsands (IRE)**[7] 676 7-9-0 48 LiamKeniry 6 58
(David Evans) *t.k.h: hld up bhd: rdn and gd hdwy over 1f out: r.o wl to ld fnl 75yds: rdn out* 14/1
000/ 2 ½ **Minstrels Gallery (IRE)**[442] 8074 5-9-1 52 (p) RobertTart(3) 1 61
(Lucy Wadham) *hld up in last pair: rdn and gd hdwy on inner over 1f out: ev ch wl ins fnl f: kpt on* 3/1[2]
5-02 3 ¾ **Pour La Victoire (IRE)**[15] 575 4-9-3 51 LukeMorris 3 58
(Tony Carroll) *chsd ldrs: jnd ldr on bit ent fnl 2f: rdn to ld overt 1f out: drvn ins fnl f: hdd and no ex fnl 75yds* 5/1[3]
5312 4 2 **Miami Gator (IRE)**[7] 673 7-9-1 54 (v) JoeyHaynes(5) 9 57
(K R Burke) *led for 2f: led again over 3f out: rdn ent fnl 2f: hdd over 1f out: wknd fnl 100yds* 3/1[2]
4165 5 nk **Mr Chocolate Drop (IRE)**[25] 446 10-9-0 48 (t) JimmyQuinn 7 50
(Mandy Rowland) *chsd ldrs: effrt on inner 2f out: no imp 1f out: styd on same pce after* 14/1
306- 6 2¾ **Soubrette**[178] 6038 4-8-12 46 oh1 HayleyTurner 5 42
(Geoffrey Deacon) *t.k.h: hld up wl in tch in midfield: rdn and no imp over 1f out: one pce and wl hld fnl f* 40/1
-005 7 ½ **My Scat Daddy (USA)**[15] 575 5-8-13 47 DavidProbert 2 41
(Zoe Davison) *s.i.s: hld up in tch in last quartet: rdn and effrt 2f out: drvn and sme hdwy over 1f out: no imp fnl f* 14/1
0-05 8 nk **Claude Greenwood**[23] 467 4-9-0 55 NedCurtis(7) 10 49
(Roger Curtis) *hld up in tch in last trio: rdn and no hdwy over 2f out: plugged on ins fnl f: n.d* 20/1
6-0B 9 1½ **Roxy Lane**[16] 563 5-8-12 46 WilliamCarson 4 36
(Peter Hiatt) *chsd ldrs: rdn and unable qck over 2f out: sn lost pl: wknd over 1f out* 66/1
64-6 10 3½ **Abigails Angel**[23] 467 7-9-7 55 (v[1]) AdamKirby 11 37
(Brett Johnson) *s.i.s: rdn and rcvrd to ld after 2f out: hdd over 3f out: wknd 2f out: bhd and eased wl ins fnl f* 11/4[1]

1m 39.39s (-0.41) **Going Correction** 0.0s/f (Stan) 10 Ran SP% **122.0**
Speed ratings (Par 101): **102,101,100,98,98 95,95,94,93,89**
CSF £57.91 CT £255.78 TOTE £14.50: £4.40, £1.70, £2.30; EX 91.20 Trifecta £1198.30.
**Owner** E R Griffiths **Bred** Gary O'Reilly **Trained** Pandy, Monmouths

**FOCUS**
There was a strong gallop on here and it was set up for the closers. The time was 0.5sec quicker than the first division.

## 756 DOWNLOAD THE BETVICTOR APP NOW MAIDEN FILLIES' STKS 6f (P)
7:00 (7:01) (Class 5) 3-Y-O+ £2,911 (£866; £432; £216) Stalls Low

Form RPR
5-4 1 **Walk With An Angel**[15] 579 3-8-13 0 ShaneKelly 6 70+
(Philip McBride) *stdd and dropped in bhd after s: hld up in tch: clsd to press ldrs over 1f out: pushed into ld ins fnl f: r.o wl: comf* 13/8[2]
302- 2 ½ **Mimi Luke (USA)**[160] 6607 3-8-13 69 RobertWinston 1 67
(Alan Bailey) *led for over 1f out: chsd ldrs after: wnt 2nd again 2f out: rdn to ld over 1f out: drvn and hdd ins fnl f: kpt on but a hld* 6/4[1]
00- 3 2¼ **Caminel (IRE)**[148] 6931 3-8-13 0 LiamKeniry 7 60
(Jeremy Gask) *stdd and dropped in bhd after s: hld up in rr: effrt over 2f out: outpcd over 1f out: kpt on ins fnl f* 16/1
0/4 4 2 **Picc Of Burgau**[13] 605 4-10-0 0 GeorgeBaker 5 58
(Geoffrey Deacon) *chsd ldr tl led over 4f out: rdn and hdd over 1f out: wknd ins fnl f* 7/1[3]
0- 5 1 **Perrydot (IRE)**[71] 8326 3-8-13 0 FergusSweeney 4 51
(Jo Crowley) *chsd ldrs: wnt 2nd 4f out tl 2f out: sn hung lft u.p and outpcd: racing against stands' rail and wl hld fnl f* 10/1
6 14 **Virtual Symphony** 3-8-13 0 HayleyTurner 2 9
(John Best) *in tch tl rdn and struggling over 2f out: lost tch over 1f out* 16/1

1m 13.81s (0.71) **Going Correction** 0.0s/f (Stan)
**WFA** 3 from 4yo 15lb 6 Ran SP% **111.5**
Speed ratings (Par 100): **95,94,91,88,87 68**
CSF £4.35 TOTE £2.20: £1.90, £1.10; EX 4.30 Trifecta £28.30.
**Owner** P J McBride **Bred** Michael E Broughton **Trained** Newmarket, Suffolk

**FOCUS**
Just a modest maiden.

## 757 BETVICTOR NON-RUNNER NO BET AT CHELTENHAM 2014 H'CAP 7f (P)
7:30 (7:30) (Class 5) (0-75,75) 4-Y-O+ £2,911 (£866; £432; £216) Stalls Low

Form RPR
-253 1 **Strong Man**[10] 646 6-9-0 68 (b) GrahamGibbons 4 78
(Michael Easterby) *hld up in tch in midfield: rdn and hdwy to ld on inner over 1f out: r.o wl fnl f: rdn out* 9/2[2]
5331 2 1 **Seek The Fair Land**[13] 602 8-9-5 73 (v) AmirQuinn 6 80
(Lee Carter) *in tch in midfield: effrt u.p to chal over 1f out: styd on but outpcd by wnr ins fnl f* 7/1
-010 3 2½ **Kakapuka**[10] 646 7-9-2 70 GeorgeBaker 5 71
(Anabel K Murphy) *led: rdn and hdd over 1f out: no ex and btn jst ins fnl f: plugged on to hold 3rd* 8/1
0-00 4 1¾ **Imperator Augustus (IRE)**[14] 589 6-8-0 61 (p) JackGarritty(7) 8 57
(Patrick Holmes) *hld up in last trio: swtchd lft and hdwy over 1f out: kpt on fnl f: nvr trbld ldrs* 7/1
00/0 5 ¾ **Treadwell (IRE)**[25] 451 7-9-0 68 FergusSweeney 1 62
(Jamie Osborne) *t.k.h: chsd ldrs: rdn and unable qck wl over 1f out: wl hld and plugged on same pce fnl f* 11/2[3]
140- 6 1 **Loud**[114] 7742 4-9-3 71 AdamKirby 11 63
(Mark Johnston) *hld up in tch in midfield: rdn and outpcd 2f out: edging rt and plld out rt over 1f out: n.d but kpt on ins fnl f* 11/4[1]
41-6 7 hd **Illustrious Prince (IRE)**[19] 540 7-9-6 74 BarryMcHugh 9 65
(Julie Camacho) *hld up in tch in last quartet: rdn and no rspnse over 2f out: plugged on fr over 1f out: nvr trbld ldrs* 20/1
0-44 8 2 **Eastern Dragon (IRE)**[19] 540 4-8-13 70 WilliamTwiston-Davies(3) 7 56
(Michael Scudamore) *chsd ldrs: rdn and effrt ent fnl 2f: no ex and btn over 1f out: wknd ins fnl f* 10/1
00-2 9 1½ **Amosite**[30] 362 8-9-5 73 (v) FrederikTylicki 3 55
(J R Jenkins) *chsd ldr tl over 1f out: wknd over 1f out* 20/1
616- 10 ¾ **Spirit Rider (USA)**[206] 5070 4-9-7 75 PatrickDonaghy 2 55
(Giles Bravery) *s.i.s: a bhd* 33/1

1m 25.39s (-0.61) **Going Correction** 0.0s/f (Stan) 10 Ran SP% **117.9**
Speed ratings (Par 103): **103,101,99,97,96 95,94,92,90,89**
CSF £35.40 CT £247.54 TOTE £5.30: £1.80, £1.80, £3.20; EX 33.30 Trifecta £432.40.
**Owner** Mrs Jean Turpin **Bred** Mrs Jean Turpin **Trained** Sheriff Hutton, N Yorks
■ Stewards' Enquiry : Amir Quinn two-day ban: use of whip (13-14 Mar)

**FOCUS**
On paper there appeared the potential for a disputed lead and a good gallop, but it failed to materialise.

## 758 CHELTENHAM 2014 NRFB AT BETVICTOR.COM H'CAP 2m (P)
8:00 (8:01) (Class 4) (0-85,80) 4-Y-O+ £5,175 (£1,540; £769; £384) Stalls Low

Form RPR
-423 1 **Poitin**[29] 369 4-8-11 71 RichardKingscote 4 79
(Harry Dunlop) *hld up in tch in last pair: smooth hdwy 3f out: upsides ldr 2f out: rdn to ld jst ins fnl f: edgd rt u.p: kpt on and a doing enough* 7/1
5-10 2 nk **Java Rose**[25] 450 5-9-7 75 AdamKirby 2 83
(Charlie Longsdon) *chsd ldrs: rdn and effrt over 2f out: styd on u.p to chse wnr ins fnl f: kpt on but a hld* 8/1
22-1 3 1 **Singzak**[20] 513 6-9-8 76 GrahamGibbons 6 82
(Michael Easterby) *led: pressed and rdn ent fnl 2f: hdd jst ins fnl f: styd on same pce after* 3/1[1]
0-23 4 shd **While You Wait (IRE)**[23] 471 5-9-3 71 GeorgeBaker 3 77
(Gary Moore) *stdd s: hld up in tch in rr: swtchd lft and effrt over 2f out: hdwy u.p 1f out: styd on fnl 100yds* 11/2[3]
/1-1 5 hd **Coup De Grace (IRE)**[20] 292 5-9-0 68 ShaneKelly 5 74
(Pat Phelan) *in tch in midfield: rdn 3f out: sltly outpcd u.p over 2f out: rallied 1f out: styd on* 10/3[2]
15-2 6 1¼ **Bramshill Lass**[23] 471 5-9-3 71 HayleyTurner 1 76
(Amanda Perrett) *in tch in midfield: rdn and unable qck over 2f out: styd on same pce and no imp fr over 1f out* 11/2[3]
0-52 7 5 **King Olav (UAE)**[35] 292 9-9-2 70 LukeMorris 7 69
(Tony Carroll) *chsd ldr: rdn over 2f out: sn lost 2nd and unable qck over 1f out: wknd ins fnl f* 12/1
6 8 47 **Vedani (IRE)**[24] 462 5-9-9 80 (t) WilliamTwiston-Davies(3) 8 22
(Tony Carroll) *in tch in last trio: rdn and racd awkwardly bnd over 4f out: lost tch over 1f out: t.o over 1f out* 33/1

3m 29.03s (-1.07) **Going Correction** 0.0s/f (Stan)
**WFA** 4 from 5yo+ 6lb 8 Ran SP% **113.1**
Speed ratings (Par 105): **102,101,101,101,101 100,98,74**
CSF £59.55 CT £202.55 TOTE £7.50: £1.80, £3.10, £1.30; EX 65.00 Trifecta £371.60.
**Owner** David & Paul Hearson **Bred** David & Paul Hearson **Trained** Lambourn, Berks
■ Stewards' Enquiry : Adam Kirby two-day ban: use of whip (13-14 Mar)

**FOCUS**
A competitive staying handicap featuring several in-form horses.

## 759 FAMILY FUN DAY 19.04.14 H'CAP 1m 4f (P)
8:30 (8:32) (Class 7) (0-50,49) 4-Y-O+ £1,617 (£481; £240; £120) Stalls Centre

Form RPR
0/0- 1 **Until The Man (IRE)**[96] 8027 7-9-3 45 (b) StephenCraine 5 50
(Natalie Lloyd-Beavis) *chsd ldrs: rdn to ld ent fnl f: in command and r.o wl fnl 100yds: pushed out* 66/1
0-23 2 1¾ **Dance**[24] 454 5-9-4 46 FrederikTylicki 2 48
(Rod Millman) *led: rdn jst over 2f out: hdd ent fnl f: kpt on same pce fnl 100yds* 11/2[2]
0-35 3 nk **Whiskey N Stout (IRE)**[10] 640 4-9-4 49 (p) AdamKirby 7 51
(Sean Curran) *s.i.s: steadily rcvrd and in tch in midfield 1/2-way: nt clr run 3f out tl hdwy u.p over 1f out: styd on u.p fnl f: no threat to wnr* 10/3[1]
0-64 4 1¼ **Beggers Belief**[39] 247 6-9-6 48 LiamKeniry 11 48
(Zoe Davison) *s.i.s: hld up towards rr: rdn and effrt jst over 2f out: styd on wl u.p ins fnl f: nt rch ldrs* 8/1
-536 5 hd **Ocean Power (IRE)**[8] 656 4-9-2 47 (b[1]) LukeMorris 3 46
(Richard Phillips) *in tch in midfield: effrt u.p to chse ldrs and hit rail over 1f out: hrd drvn and styd on same pce fnl f* 7/1[3]
6234 6 nk **Supa Seeker (USA)**[8] 661 8-9-0 49 (b) MrAidenBlakemore(7) 12 48
(Tony Carroll) *t.k.h: hld up towards rr: effrt and rdn ent fnl 2f: kpt on u.p fnl f: nvr trbld ldrs* 10/1
3-33 7 1½ **Ice Apple**[24] 455 6-9-6 48 JimmyQuinn 14 45
(John E Long) *s.i.s: sn bustled along and nvr gng wl: reminders 1/2-way: swtchd rt and drvn 2f out: kpt on fnl f: nvr trbld ldrs* 8/1
6-54 8 nk **Zelos Diktator**[24] 455 8-9-3 45 GeorgeBaker 6 41
(Sean Curran) *hld up in rr: pushed along and hdwy over 1f out: kpt on ins fnl f: nvr trbld ldrs* 14/1
0-40 9 hd **Illegale (IRE)**[24] 454 8-9-0 45 (bt[1]) MatthewCosham(3) 10 41
(Nikki Evans) *in tch in midfield: effrt and n.m.r ent fnl 2f: kpt on same pce under pressed fr over 1f out* 25/1
0-46 10 ¾ **Beauchamp Sunset**[15] 570 4-9-2 47 RichardKingscote 8 42
(Paul Fitzsimons) *chsd ldrs: rdn wl over 2f out: no ex u.p and btn over 1f out: wknd fnl f* 8/1
0-45 11 1¼ **Kingaroo (IRE)**[9] 648 8-8-13 46 TimClark(5) 4 39
(Garry Woodward) *chsd ldr: rdn over 3f out: pressed ldr over 2f out tl wl over 1f out: sn wknd* 25/1
/00- 12 23 **Golden Groom**[142] 7098 11-8-13 48 JackGarritty(7) 9 6
(Patrick Holmes) *in tch in midfield: hdwy to chse ldrs over 4f out: lost pl qckly u.p over 2f out: t.o* 50/1
00-0 P **Tuxedo**[48] 116 9-9-7 49 (b) WilliamCarson 1
(Peter Hiatt) *a towards rr: eased and p.u 5f out; burst blood vessel* 25/1

2m 34.19s (-0.31) **Going Correction** 0.0s/f (Stan)
**WFA** 4 from 5yo+ 3lb 13 Ran SP% **115.0**
Speed ratings (Par 97): **101,99,99,98,98 98,97,97,97,96 95,80,**
CSF £377.26 CT £1580.00 TOTE £74.50: £13.40, £2.60, £1.60; EX 1227.00 Trifecta £1675.80 Part won..
**Owner** M J Hills **Bred** Tally-Ho Stud **Trained** East Garston, Berks
■ Snowy Valley was withdrawn. Price at time of withdrawal 16-1. Rule 4 does not apply.

**FOCUS**
It's hard to explain this result in this low-grade race.

## 760 GOFFS BREEZE-UP SALE ROYAL ASCOT WEEK H'CAP 6f (P)
9:00 (9:07) (Class 7) (0-50,50) 4-Y-O+ £1,617 (£481; £240; £120) Stalls Low

Form RPR
-303 1 **Bubbly Bailey**[14] 592 4-9-7 50 (v) FrederikTylicki 6 60
(J R Jenkins) *wnt lft s: mde all: clr and rdn over 1f out: drvn 1f out: a holding rivals: rdn out* 7/2[2]

-004 **2** 1 ½ **Christopher Chua (IRE)**[14] 586 5-8-13 **45** WilliamTwiston-Davies(3) 2 51
(Michael Scudamore) *in tch in midfield: effrt to chse clr wnr over 1f out: hung lft 1f out: kpt on fnl f: nvr gng to rch wnr* **12/1**

4323 **3** 2 **Vhujon (IRE)**[14] 586 9-9-0 **46**.......................... SladeO'Hara(3) 1 46
(Peter Grayson) *hld up in rr: hdwy on outer 1f out: r.o wl to snatch 3rd last stride: no threat to wnr* **9/2[3]**

-002 **4** shd **Strategic Action (IRE)**[14] 586 5-9-6 **49**..................(tp) LiamKeniry 12 48
(Linda Jewell) *hld up in last pair: hdwy and swtchd rt wl over 1f out: kpt on fnl f: no ch w wnr* **11/2**

0435 **5** 1 **Flow Chart (IRE)**[6] 693 7-9-5 **48**.......................... StephenCraine 7 44
(Peter Grayson) *restless in stalls: hld up in last trio: hdwy but stl plenty to do over 1f out: kpt on fnl f: nvr trbld ldrs* **14/1**

00-0 **6** 1 **Millies Quest**[14] 592 5-8-12 **48**.......................... GeorgeBuckell(7) 8 41
(Martin Smith) *t.k.h: chsd ldrs: rdn and unable qck jst over 2f out: one pce fr over 1f out* **25/1**

0006 **7** 1 **Homeboy (IRE)**[6] 688 6-9-6 **49**..................(b) AdamKirby 3 39
(David Evans) *t.k.h: chsd ldrs: rdn to chse clr ldr 2f out: no prog and btn over 1f out: wknd fnl f* **5/2[1]**

46-0 **8** ¾ **Fantasy Invader (IRE)**[27] 402 4-9-4 **47**..................(v) GeorgeBaker 5 35
(Gary Moore) *hld up in tch in midfield: rdn and effrt over 1f out: no imp* **8/1**

0066 **9** 1 ¼ **Kaylee**[8] 662 5-8-10 **46**.......................... DanielCremin(7) 4 30
(Kevin Tork) *in tch in midfield: rdn and unable qck 2f out: outpcd and btn over 1f out: wknd fnl f* **33/1**

300- **10** 4 ½ **Mr Man In The Moon (IRE)**[160] 6604 6-9-6 **49**.......... JimmyQuinn 11 20
(Mandy Rowland) *wnt lft s: chsd ldrs: wnt 2nd over 4f out tl jst over 2f out: sn wknd* **16/1**

000/ **11** 5 **Make A Fuss**[769] 228 5-8-10 **46**..................(p) JackGarritty(7) 9 2
(Gerry Enright) *wl in tch in midfield: rdn and lost pl over 2f out: bhd over 1f out* **66/1**

1m 13.0s (-0.10) **Going Correction** 0.0s/f (Stan) **11** Ran SP% **124.0**
Speed ratings (Par 97): **100,98,95,95,93 92,91,90,88,82 75**
CSF £47.31 CT £203.75 TOTE £3.80: £1.50, £3.30, £2.30; EX 57.30 Trifecta £329.50.
**Owner** Mrs S Bowmer **Bred** Bearstone Stud **Trained** Royston, Herts

**FOCUS**
This wasn't going to take much winning.
T/Jkpt: Not won. T/Plt: £50.40 to a £1 stake. Pool: £102,061.34 - 1477.25 winning units. T/Qpdt: £19.20 to a £1 stake. Pool: 10,537.91 - 404.40 winning units. SP

# [647] SOUTHWELL (L-H)
## Thursday, February 27

**OFFICIAL GOING: Standard**
Wind: Strong behind Weather: Cloudy with sunny periods

## 761 32RED TOMB RAIDER SLOT H'CAP 1m (F)
**2:20** (2:20) (Class 5) (0-75,73) 3-Y-O **£3,234** (£962; £481; £240) **Stalls** Low

Form RPR

5151 **1** **Frankthetank (IRE)**[9] 653 3-8-9 **61** 6ex..................(p) TomEaves 3 75
(Keith Dalgleish) *mde most: pushed wl clr over 2f out: rdn over 1f out: styd on strly tl eased fnl 100yds* **2/1[1]**

60-5 **2** 5 **Khee Society**[3] 734 3-8-9 **61**.......................... AndrewMullen 4 63
(David Evans) *chsd ldrs: hdwy on outer over 3f out: rdn wl over 2f out: kpt on to take 2nd appr fnl f: no ch w wnr* **7/1[3]**

45-3 **3** 5 **Turnbury**[13] 607 3-9-2 **68**..................(tp) GrahamLee 5 59
(Robert Mills) *cl up: rdn along wl over 2f out: sn drvn and plugged on one pce* **3/1[2]**

540- **4** 4 ½ **Clever Miss**[127] 7463 3-9-7 **73**.......................... TomQueally 1 53
(Alan McCabe) *sn outpcd and a in rr* **8/1**

025- **5** ½ **Branston De Soto**[84] 8164 3-8-12 **64**.......................... JoeFanning 2 43
(Mark Johnston) *trckd ldng pair: pushed along bef 1/2-way: rdn wl over 3f out: sn lost pl and bhd* **2/1[1]**

1m 44.75s (1.05) **Going Correction** +0.025s/f (Slow) **5** Ran SP% **115.3**
Speed ratings (Par 97): **95,90,85,80,80**
CSF £16.71 TOTE £2.90: £1.70, £3.20; EX 26.10 Trifecta £50.30.
**Owner** Raymond McNeill **Bred** Burgage Stud **Trained** Carluke, S Lanarks

**FOCUS**
In a race run at a fair tempo, a Fibresand specialist easily beat four debutants on the surface. The winner had the run of things here and will receive a hike for this.

## 762 32RED.COM FREE BONUS H'CAP 5f (F)
**2:50** (2:51) (Class 5) (0-75,70) 3-Y-O **£3,234** (£962; £481; £240) **Stalls** High

Form RPR

-221 **1** **Saffire Song**[13] 608 3-9-3 **66**.......................... JoeFanning 3 73
(Alan Bailey) *trckd ldrs: n.m.r: sltly hmpd and lost pl after 1f: hdwy 1/2-way: led wl over 1f out: rdn and kpt on wl fnl f* **5/1[3]**

1222 **2** ¾ **Argent Touch**[9] 650 3-8-4 **60**.......................... AdamMcLean(7) 4 64
(Derek Shaw) *trckd ldrs: effrt 2f out: rdn to chse wnr ent fnl f: sn ev ch tl drvn and no imp towards fin* **7/4[1]**

03-1 **3** 1 ¼ **Monsieur Lavene (IRE)**[12] 622 3-9-7 **70**.......................... TomQueally 6 70
(Robert Mills) *led: rdn along 1/2-way: hdd wl over 1f out: sn drvn: edgd rt and one pce fnl f* **9/4[2]**

2313 **4** 1 ¾ **Ealain Aibrean (IRE)**[9] 650 3-8-13 **67**.......................... EoinWalsh(5) 5 60
(David Evans) *cl up: pushed along and sltly outpcd 1/2-way: swtchd rt to stands' rail and rdn 2f out: keeping on whn n.m.r jst ins fnl f: sn no imp* **10/1**

01-6 **5** shd **Black Geronimo**[16] 568 3-8-11 **65**..................(v) TimClark(5) 2 58
(Roy Bowring) *dwlt: pushed along and outpcd in rr 1/2-way: kpt on u.p fnl f* **5/1[3]**

410- **6** shd **Britain (IRE)**[147] 6967 3-8-9 **58**.......................... AdrianNicholls 1 50
(David C Griffiths) *dwlt: sn prom: rdn along over 2f out: drvn wl over 1f out and sn one pce* **20/1**

1m 0.69s (0.99) **Going Correction** +0.125s/f (Slow) **6** Ran SP% **114.3**
Speed ratings (Par 97): **97,95,93,91,90 90**
CSF £14.63 TOTE £5.50: £2.70, £1.20; EX 13.30 Trifecta £35.60.
**Owner** Mrs A Shone & P Baker **Bred** Mrs A Shone **Trained** Newmarket, Suffolk

**FOCUS**
The first four were in good form beforehand, so this looks solid enough. The winner's best effort yet.

## 763 CORAL APP DOWNLOAD FROM THE APP STORE H'CAP 1m 4f (F)
**3:20** (3:20) (Class 4) (0-85,85) 4-Y-O+ **£5,822** (£1,732; £865; £432) **Stalls** Low

Form RPR

/3-1 **1** **Gogeo (IRE)**[10] 385 7-8-12 **76**.......................... BenCurtis 4 86
(Alan Swinbank) *trckd ldrs: smooth hdwy on outer 4f out: led over 3f out: rdn and edgd lft to inner rail 2f out: sn clr and styd on* **11/8[1]**

12-2 **2** 3 ½ **Honoured (IRE)**[55] 32 7-8-12 **83**..................(t) AlistairRawlinson(7) 1 87
(Michael Appleby) *trckd ldng pair: pushed along over 3f out: rdn to chse wnr 2f out: drvn and edgd lft ent fnl f: sn no imp* **9/2[3]**

-313 **3** 9 **Staff Sergeant**[28] 385 7-9-2 **80**.......................... AndrewMullen 3 70
(Michael Appleby) *hld up in rr: hdwy over 3f out: rdn along to chse ldng pair over 2f out: sn drvn and one pce* **7/2[2]**

6031 **4** 4 ½ **Mica Mika (IRE)**[19] 544 6-8-13 **77**..................(v) TonyHamilton 6 60
(Richard Fahey) *trckd ldr: cl up over 4f out: rdn along over 3f out: wknd over 2f out* **14/1**

0-31 **5** 18 **Blades Lad**[23] 476 5-8-8 **72**.......................... JamesSullivan 2 26
(Peter Niven) *hld up in tch: pushed along 5f out: sn lost pl and bhd* **8/1**

200- **6** 7 **Fort Belvedere**[161] 6551 6-9-7 **85**.......................... TomEaves 5 28
(Keith Dalgleish) *led: rdn along 4f out: hdd over 3f out: sn wknd and bhd* **8/1**

2m 38.36s (-2.64) **Going Correction** +0.025s/f (Slow) **6** Ran SP% **111.4**
Speed ratings (Par 105): **109,106,100,97,85 81**
CSF £7.74 TOTE £3.10: £1.50, £1.60; EX 7.00 Trifecta £15.10.
**Owner** Mrs J Porter **Bred** Peter Nolan **Trained** Melsonby, N Yorks

**FOCUS**
This was an above-average contest for the track, but the pace was modest. The winner is progressive and they finished strung out.

## 764 CORAL.CO.UK BEST ODDS GUARANTEED ON RACING H'CAP 1m 3f (F)
**3:50** (3:50) (Class 2) (0-105,99) 4-Y-O+ **£12,291** (£3,657; £1,827; £913) **Stalls** Low

Form RPR

-224 **1** **The Lock Master (IRE)**[17] 559 7-8-5 **80** oh1.......... AndrewMullen 3 90
(Michael Appleby) *in rr: hdwy over 4f out: rdn to chse ldrs whn swtchd lft 2f out: drvn over 1f out: styd on wl u.p to ld last 110yds: kpt on strly* **12/1**

1661 **2** 2 ¼ **Frontier Fighter**[16] 566 6-9-9 **98**.......................... DanielTudhope 7 104
(David O'Meara) *trckd ldng pair: cl up 1/2-way: led over 2f out: rdn wl over 1f out: drvn ins fnl f: hdd and no ex last 110yds* **4/1**

01-6 **3** nk **Stepping Ahead (FR)**[33] 344 4-9-4 **95**.......................... PhillipMakin 6 101
(K R Burke) *trckd ldrs: hdwy over 3f out: rdn 2f out: drvn and styd on to chal ent fnl f: sn edgd rt and kpt on same pce* **7/2[3]**

0-11 **4** 2 **Masterful Act (USA)**[10] 386 7-9-10 **99**.......................... TomQueally 5 102
(Alan McCabe) *hld up in tch: hdwy on outer over 3f out: rdn over 2f out: drvn to chse ldrs over 1f out: kpt on same pce ins fnl f* **9/4[1]**

-304 **5** 2 **Returntobrecongill**[20] 514 4-8-4 **81**.......................... JamesSullivan 2 81
(James Given) *cl up: led after 3f: rdn along over 3f out: hdd over 2f out: cl up and drvn wl over 1f out: n.m.r and wknd ent fnl f* **3/1[2]**

0-23 **6** 16 **Dewala**[28] 386 5-8-5 **80** oh2.......................... BenCurtis 4 54
(Michael Appleby) *chsd ldrs: rdn along 5f out: sn wknd* **16/1**

-001 **7** 64 **Halfsin (IRE)**[17] 560 6-8-11 **86**..................(t) PaddyAspell 1
(Marco Botti) *slt ld 3f: cl up on inner tl rdn along and lost pl over 4f out: sn bhd* **14/1**

2m 25.62s (-2.38) **Going Correction** +0.025s/f (Slow)
**WFA** 4 from 5yo+ 2lb **7** Ran SP% **118.2**
Speed ratings (Par 109): **109,107,107,105,104 92,46**
CSF £61.78 TOTE £12.40: £4.40, £2.80; EX 49.20 Trifecta £295.00.
**Owner** K G Kitchen **Bred** Patrick F Kelly **Trained** Danethorpe, Notts

**FOCUS**
This was a very good race for the track, contested by some in-form types and run at a solid pace. The winner was entitled to win and the next three showed smart form.

## 765 BOOKMAKERS.CO.UK MEDIAN AUCTION MAIDEN STKS 5f (F)
**4:20** (4:21) (Class 5) 3-4-Y-O **£3,234** (£962; £481; £240) **Stalls** High

Form RPR

2 **1** **Eva Clare (IRE)**[21] 500 3-8-9 0.......................... BenCurtis 2 69
(K R Burke) *prom: cl up 2f out: rdn over 1f out: styd on wl u.p ins fnl f to ld last 50yds* **5/1[3]**

200- **2** nk **Proclamationofwar**[153] 6791 3-9-0 73.......................... TomQueally 3 73
(Kevin Ryan) *led: rdn along wl over 1f out: drvn ins fnl f: hdd and no ex last 50yds* **5/4[1]**

04- **3** 2 ¾ **Camanche Grey (IRE)**[111] 7804 3-9-0 0.......................... JoeFanning 4 63
(Ben Haslam) *chsd ldrs: rdn 2f out: swtchd lft over 1f out: kpt on fnl f: nrst fin* **16/1**

224- **4** 2 ½ **Fredricka**[142] 7095 3-8-6 64.......................... JasonHart(3) 9 49
(Garry Moss) *racd towards stands' rail: prom: rdn along and edgd lft 2f out: sn chsng ldng pair: drvn and edgd lft appr fnl f: sn one pce* **7/2[2]**

0- **5** 5 **Luv U Honey**[325] 1421 3-8-9 0.......................... AndrewMullen 1 31
(Brian Baugh) *dwlt and wnt lft s: in rr tl sme late hdwy* **12/1**

6-05 **6** ½ **Tinchy Ryder**[18] 547 3-9-0 47.......................... PaulMulrennan 6 34
(Bryan Smart) *chsd ldr: rdn along 1/2-way: sn wknd* **12/1**

0 **7** 1 **Incurs Four Faults**[23] 477 3-9-0 0.......................... TomEaves 5 31
(Keith Dalgleish) *s.i.s: a in rr* **14/1**

3330 **8** 3 ½ **Mahon Falls**[13] 608 3-8-4 49.......................... EoinWalsh(5) 8 13
(David Evans) *racd towards stands' rail: prom: rdn along 1/2-way: wkng whn sltly hmpd 2f out* **16/1**

0 **9** 4 ½ **Robbian**[23] 477 3-8-7 0.......................... AdamMcLean(7) 7
(Charles Smith) *a towards rr* **100/1**

59.91s (0.21) **Going Correction** +0.125s/f (Slow) **9** Ran SP% **118.1**
Speed ratings (Par 103): **103,102,98,94,86 85,83,78,70**
CSF £11.90 TOTE £6.80: £2.60, £1.30, £3.10; EX 15.10 Trifecta £97.50.
**Owner** The Mount Racing Club & Mrs E Burke **Bred** Ballyhane Stud **Trained** Middleham Moor, N Yorks

**FOCUS**
This was a routine sprint maiden in which the first four were a cut above the rest. The winner built on her debut effort.

## 766 BEST ODDS AT BOOKMAKERS.CO.UK H'CAP 6f (F)
**4:50** (4:51) (Class 6) (0-65,65) 4-Y-O+ **£2,587** (£770; £384; £192) **Stalls** Low

Form RPR

-510 **1** **Star Up In The Sky (USA)**[25] 448 4-9-4 **62**..................(b) AmyRyan 12 73
(Kevin Ryan) *cl up on outer: led over 2f out: rdn wl over 1f out and sn jnd: drvn ent fnl f: kpt on gamely towards fin* **3/1[1]**

624 **2** ½ **Alpha Tauri (USA)**[9] 651 8-9-2 **65**........................(t) ConnorBeasley(5) 9 75
(Richard Guest) *chsd ldrs: hdwy over 2f out: rdn to chal over 1f out and over ch tl drvn ins fnl f and no ex towards fin* **3/1**[1]
6-65 **3** 3½ **Monnoyer**[35] 297 5-9-2 **60**........................(b) PJMcDonald 6 59
(Scott Dixon) *chsd ldrs: hdwy over 2f out: cl up and rdn wl over 1f out: drvn appr fnl f and kpt on one pce* **10/1**
00-3 **4** 1¼ **Masked Dance (IRE)**[31] 353 7-8-3 **52**........................(b) TimClark(5) 7 47
(Scott Dixon) *in tch: hdwy to chse ldrs 2f out: swtchd lft and rdn over 1f out: drvn and one pce fnl f* **14/1**
2221 **5** 2 **Grace Hull**[20] 511 4-9-5 **63**........................(p) TomQueally 5 52
(Garry Moss) *towards rr: hdwy 2f out: sn rdn and kpt on fnl f: nrst fin* **4/1**[2]
0-40 **6** ¾ **Ferdy (IRE)**[30] 367 5-8-8 **55**........................(v[1]) JasonHart(3) 8 42
(Paul Green) *in rr and reminders early: rdn along and hdwy 2f out: sn swtchd lft and kpt on u.p fnl f: nrst fin* **25/1**
-060 **7** nk **Fathom Five (IRE)**[9] 651 10-8-12 **56**........................ PaddyAspell 11 42
(Shaun Harris) *qckly away and led: rdn along and hdd over 2f out: grad wknd* **33/1**
6033 **8** ½ **Sewn Up**[26] 432 4-9-2 **60**........................(p) TonyHamilton 10 45
(Andrew Hollinshead) *midfield: hdwy wl over 2f out: rdn wl over 1f out and nvr nr ldrs* **7/1**[3]
1240 **9** 7 **Prince Of Passion (CAN)**[9] 651 6-8-12 **63**........... AdamMcLean(7) 4 27
(Derek Shaw) *chsd ldrs on inner: rdn along 1/2-way: sn wknd* **20/1**
-002 **10** ½ **Baltic Prince (IRE)**[21] 503 4-9-0 **58**........................ JoeFanning 13 20
(Paul Green) *racd wd: towards rr: rdn and sme hdwy over 2f out: n.d* **16/1**
603- **11** 1 **Waabel**[369] 775 7-8-13 **62**........................(tp) AnnStokell(5) 2 21
(Ann Stokell) *a in rr* **50/1**
04-6 **12** nse **Tarrsille (IRE)**[35] 297 8-9-2 **65**........................ ShirleyTeasdale(5) 3 24
(Paul Midgley) *a in rr* **50/1**
6-01 **13** 12 **Art Dzeko**[16] 563 5-8-13 **57**........................ TomEaves 1
(Brian Baugh) *in tch on inner: rdn along 1/2-way: sn wknd* **12/1**

1m 16.31s (-0.19) **Going Correction** +0.025s/f (Slow) **13** Ran SP% **127.3**
Speed ratings (Par 101): **102,101,96,95,92 91,90,90,80,80 78,78,62**
CSF £11.77 CT £86.97 TOTE £5.00: £1.40, £1.30, £4.30; EX 19.50 Trifecta £202.70.
**Owner** Matt & Lauren Morgan **Bred** Dixiana Stables Inc **Trained** Hambleton, N Yorks

**FOCUS**
The pace was good around the bend, and only a handful got into it.

## 767 LADBROKES APPRENTICE H'CAP 1m (F)
**5:20** (5:21) (Class 5) (0-75,75) 4-Y-0+ **£3,234** (£962; £481; £240) **Stalls** Low

Form RPR
0-50 **1** **Patriotic (IRE)**[19] 533 6-9-4 **75**........................(p) JoshCrane(3) 4 87
(Chris Dwyer) *hld up in rr: gd hdwy 3f out: led 2f out: rdn over 1f out: edgd lft ins fnl f: hld on wl towards fin* **9/2**[3]
-432 **2** nk **Exclusive Waters (IRE)**[15] 578 4-8-3 **64**........(b) CallumShepherd(7) 3 75
(Charles Hills) *trckd ldrs: gd hdwy on inner and cl up 2f out: rdn and everey ch over 1f out tl no ex towards fin* **10/1**
1216 **3** 8 **Silly Billy (IRE)**[9] 647 6-9-2 **70**........................(p) AdamMcLean 6 63
(John Balding) *cl up: rdn along and ev ch over 2f out: drvn wl over 1f out and kpt on same pce* **8/1**
2122 **4** nk **Queen Of Skies (IRE)**[9] 647 5-8-6 **63**............... AlistairRawlinson(3) 2 55
(Michael Appleby) *cl up: effrt 3f out: sn rdn and ev ch tl drvn 2f out and sn one pce* **7/4**[1]
4132 **5** 4½ **Repetition**[18] 552 4-9-0 **75**........................ GeorginaBaxter(7) 5 57
(Kristin Stubbs) *led: rdn along 3f out: hdd 2f out and sn wknd* **4/1**[2]
5-36 **6** 3 **Alice's Dancer (IRE)**[12] 627 5-9-4 **72**........................ JordanVaughan 7 47
(William Muir) *s.i.s: a in rr* **16/1**
0-11 **7** 3½ **Basingstoke (IRE)**[37] 268 5-9-4 **75**........................ RobJFitzpatrick(3) 1 42
(Simon Hodgson) *cl up: rdn along over 3f out: sn wknd* **5/1**

1m 43.66s (-0.04) **Going Correction** +0.025s/f (Slow) **7** Ran SP% **117.3**
Speed ratings (Par 103): **101,100,92,92,87 84,81**
CSF £48.68 TOTE £4.70: £2.40, £3.60; EX 62.90 Trifecta £588.20.
**Owner** M M Foulger **Bred** Darley **Trained** Newmarket, Suffolk
■ Stewards' Enquiry : Adam McLean four-day ban: use of whip (13-15, 17)

**FOCUS**
Some in-form runners were beaten by a talented rival who had been below his best lately.
T/Plt: £109.50 to a £1 stake. Pool: £69,308.30 - 461.74 winning units. T/Qpdt: £22.10 to a £1 stake. Pool: £5267.19 - 176.20 winning units. JR

# [678] MEYDAN (L-H)
Thursday, February 27
**OFFICIAL GOING: Tapeta: standard; turf: good**

## 768a SMKA TROPHY (H'CAP) (TAPETA) 7f
**2:40** (2:40) (100-110,110) 3-Y-0+
**£43,373** (£14,457; £7,228; £3,614; £2,168; £1,445)

RPR
**1** **Gold City (IRE)**[28] 396 5-8-8 **104**........................(bt) MarcMonaghan(6) 6 112
(S Seemar, UAE) *trckd ldng pair: led 2f out: r.o wl: comf* **6/1**[3]
**2** 2¼ **My Freedom (IRE)**[21] 504 6-9-0 **104**........................ SilvestreDeSousa 3 106+
(Saeed bin Suroor) *mid-div: rdn 3f out: r.o fnl 2f but no ch w wnr* **11/4**[1]
**3** 1¼ **Tamaathul**[14] 597 7-9-6 **110**........................(t) RoystonFfrench 2 109+
(A Al Raihe, UAE) *settled in rr: nvr nr to chal but r.o fnl 2f: nrst fin* **6/1**[3]
**4** 2 **Kanaf (IRE)**[6] 711 7-9-1 **105**........................ PaulHanagan 7 98
(M Al Muhairi, UAE) *settled in rr: rdn 3f out: r.o same pce fnl 2f but nvr able to chal* **5/1**[2]
**5** nk **Barbecue Eddie (USA)**[35] 306 10-8-13 **102**........................(b) DaneO'Neill 8 95
(Doug Watson, UAE) *s.i.s: trckd ldrs tl outpcd 2f out* **20/1**
**6** 1¾ **Modern History (IRE)**[49] 109 6-9-1 **105**........................ MickaelBarzalona 5 93
(Charlie Appleby) *trckd ldrs: led 3f out: hdd & wknd 2f out* **11/4**[1]
**7** 2¼ **Rutland Boy**[385] 557 6-9-5 **109**........................ JamieSpencer 1 91
(Michael Bell) *sn led: hdd & wknd 3f out* **16/1**
**8** 1¼ **Le Drakkar (AUS)**[21] 509 9-9-3 **107**........................(t) TadhgO'Shea 4 85
(A bin Huzaim, UAE) *s.i.s: a in rr* **10/1**

1m 25.53s (0.33) **8** Ran SP% **118.3**
CSF: 23.77; EXACTA: 50.20 TRICAST 105.60; TRIFECTA: 225.80 WIN: 8.40; PL: 2.90, 1.20, 1.40.
**Owner** Sheikh Mansoor bin Mohammed al Maktoum **Bred** Darley **Trained** United Arab Emirates

**FOCUS**
Only eight runners and the clear-cut winner doesn't represent one of powerhouse stables, but the form still looks decent enough. It's rated around the second.

## 769a SWAIDAN TRADING, HEAVY EQUIPMENT DIVISION TROPHY (H'CAP) (TAPETA) 6f
**3:15** (3:15) (95-108,108) 3-Y-0+
**£54,216** (£18,072; £9,036; £4,518; £2,710; £1,807)

RPR
**1** **Medicean Man**[7] 680 8-9-0 **101**........................(tp) MartinLane 3 111+
(Jeremy Gask) *s.i.s: in rr of mid-div: smooth prog 2f out: led over 1f out: comf* **11/4**[1]
**2** 1 **Racy**[7] 680 7-8-11 **99**........................ SilvestreDeSousa 7 105
(Brian Ellison) *in rr of mid-div: r.o fnl 1 1/2f: nrst fin but no ch w wnr* **14/1**
**3** 1½ **Conveyance (USA)**[1069] 997 7-8-7 **100** ow1.......(t) MarcMonaghan(5) 1 100
(S Seemar, UAE) *trckd ldng trio: ev ch 1f out: one pce fnl 110yds* **5/1**[3]
**4** nk **Zee Bros (USA)**[63] 8403 4-9-2 **104**........................(t) ShaneFoley 11 104
(Seth Benzel, U.S.A) *trckd ldng pair: ev ch 1 1/2f out: wknd fnl 110yds* **14/1**
**5** hd **Merhee (AUS)**[28] 393 6-9-5 **107**........................ ChristopheSoumillon 5 106
(M F De Kock, South Africa) *nvr bttr than mid-div but r.o fnl 1 1/2f* **4/1**[2]
**6** nk **Roi De Vitesse (IRE)**[14] 597 7-9-1 **102**........................ WilliamBuick 4 101
(Ali Jan, Qatar) *settled in rr: nvr nr to chal* **14/1**
**7** ¾ **Mujaazef**[20] 526 7-8-11 **99**........................(t) PaulHanagan 2 95
(A Al Raihe, UAE) *trckd ldrs: led 4f: hdd & wknd over 1f out* **14/1**
**8** nk **Abu Sidra (FR)**[103] 7941 5-9-6 **108**........................ JamesDoyle 10 103
(J-F Bernard, France) *nvr bttr than mid-div* **16/1**
**9** 1½ **Masamah (IRE)**[28] 393 8-9-2 **104**........................(p) MartinHarley 9 94
(Marco Botti) *wl away: sn led: hdd 4f out: wknd fnl 2f* **8/1**
**10** 1½ **Lehaaf (ARG)**[12] 636 5-8-9 **97**........................(b) PatCosgrave 6 82
(M F De Kock, South Africa) *nvr bttr than mid-div* **7/1**
**11** 6 **Murbeh (IRE)**[20] 526 6-8-9 **97**........................(t) DaneO'Neill 8 63
(A Al Raihe, UAE) *nvr nr to chal* **25/1**

1m 12.03s (0.43) **11** Ran SP% **123.3**
CSF: 46.69; EXACTA: 101.00 TRICAST 192.90; TRIFECTA: 1,333.20 WIN: 4.30; PL: 1.60, 4.70, 2.60.
**Owner** Stuart Dobb & Miss Kate Dobb **Bred** Barry Taylor **Trained** Sutton Veny, Wilts

**FOCUS**
A decent sprint handicap. The winner was just off his recent turf form.

## 770a MEYDAN CLASSIC SPONSORED BY SWAIDAN TRADING, AUTOMOTIVE DIVISION (LISTED RACE) (TURF) 7f
**3:50** (3:50) 3-Y-0
**£45,180** (£15,060; £7,530; £3,765; £2,259; £1,506)

RPR
**1** **My Catch (IRE)**[14] 594 3-9-0 102........................ PatDobbs 4 102
(Doug Watson, UAE) *trckd ldrs: led 1 1/2f out: r.o wl* **15/2**[2]
**2** 1 **Jallota**[14] 594 3-9-0 102........................ JimCrowley 2 100
(M F De Kock, South Africa) *settled in rr: n.m.r 2f out: r.o wl fnl f: nrst fin* **8/1**[3]
**3** 1¾ **Najm Suhail**[21] 505 3-9-0 95........................ RoystonFfrench 10 95
(A Al Raihe, UAE) *mid-div: chsd ldrs 2 1/2f out: r.o same pce fnl f* **10/1**
**4** nk **Chord Chart (IRE)**[42] 204 3-9-0 89........................ PatCosgrave 3 94
(S Seemar, UAE) *settled in rr: nvr nr to chal but r.o fnl 2f* **50/1**
**5** 2¼ **Dubawi Fun**[21] 505 3-9-0 89........................ WilliamBuick 9 88
(Ismail Mohammed) *trckd ldrs: ev ch 2f out: one pce fnl f* **33/1**
**6** 1¾ **Man Amongst Men (IRE)**[21] 505 3-9-0 85............(bt) JamieSpencer 7 83
(Brian Meehan) *s.i.s: settled in rr: nvr nr to chal but r.o fnl 2f* **8/1**
**7** ¾ **Make It Reel (FR)**[21] 505 3-9-0 95........................ SamHitchcott 6 81
(Doug Watson, UAE) *sn led: hdd & wknd 1 1/2f out* **12/1**
**8** 1¼ **Dolce N Karama (IRE)**[42] 204 3-9-0 105........................ TadhgO'Shea 8 78
(John Patrick Shanahan, Ire) *nvr bttr than mid-div* **10/1**
**9** 2¼ **Eye In The Sky (IRE)**[21] 505 3-9-0 95........................(t) KierenFallon 5 72
(Niels Petersen, Norway) *nvr nr to chal* **8/1**[3]
**10** dist **Wednaan**[14] 594 3-9-0 104........................ ChristopheSoumillon 1
(M F De Kock, South Africa) *mid-div tl virtually p.u 3f out* **8/11**[1]

1m 24.57s (84.57) **10** Ran SP% **125.6**
CSF: 70.31; EXACTA: 39.00; TRIFECTA: 834.30 WIN: 8.60; PL: 2.00, 1.90, 3.70.
**Owner** Valentin Bukhtoyarov & Evgeny Kappushev **Bred** D Noonan & Loughphilip Bloodstock
**Trained** United Arab Emirates

**FOCUS**
The rail was out 15 metres on the turf course. A bang-ordinary Listed contest - the better horses from this age group tend to be aimed at the Tapeta Classics. The gallop was solid early. The winenr and third are rated to their marks.

## 771a UAE OAKS SPONSORED BY SAEED & MOHAMMED AL NABOODAH GROUP (GROUP 3) (FILLIES) (TAPETA) 1m 1f 110y
**4:25** (4:27) 3-Y-0
**£90,361** (£30,120; £15,060; £7,530; £4,518; £3,012)

RPR
**1** **Ihtimal (IRE)**[21] 506 3-8-9 105........................ SilvestreDeSousa 2 113+
(Saeed bin Suroor) *mid-div: smooth prog to ld 1 1/2f out: easily* **4/11**[1]
**2** 10 **Feedyah (USA)**[21] 506 3-8-9 94........................ MickaelBarzalona 5 92
(Charlie Appleby) *settled in rr: chsd wnr 2f out: outpcd 1 1/2f out but r.o same pce* **8/1**[3]
**3** 1½ **Mensoora (SAF)**[21] 506 4-9-5 100........................ ChristopheSoumillon 7 91
(M F De Kock, South Africa) *settled in rr: nvr nr to chal but r.o fnl 1 1/2f* **9/2**[2]
**4** 1½ **Magrooma (AUS)**[21] 506 4-9-5 96........................ RichardHughes 6 88
(M F De Kock, South Africa) *trckd ldrs tl outpcd 2f out: r.o same pce fnl 1 1/2f* **10/1**
**5** shd **More Aspen (USA)**[21] 506 3-8-9 86........................(b) ShaneFoley 3 86
(S Seemar, UAE) *settled in rr: n.m.r 2f out: r.o fnl 1 1/2f: nrst fin* **50/1**
**6** 1¼ **Sign Of Lucky (USA)**[21] 506 3-8-9 85........................ PatDobbs 4 83
(Doug Watson, UAE) *sn led: hdd & wknd 1 1/2f out* **66/1**
**7** 7¾ **Letterfromamerica (USA)**[21] 506 3-8-9 88..............(bt) TadhgO'Shea 1 67
(S Seemar, UAE) *trckd ldrs: rdn 4 1/2f out: wknd fnl 1 1/2f* **33/1**
**8** 8¼ **Illuminating Dream (IRE)**[21] 506 3-8-9 84................ JamieSpencer 9 50
(David Brown) *trckd ldng pair tl outpcd 2f out* **66/1**

1m 58.51s (-0.49)
**WFA** 3 from 4yo 21lb **8** Ran SP% **119.6**
CSF: 4.63; EXACTA: 4.70; TRIFECTA: 13.70 WIN: 1.30; PL: 1.00, 1.90, 1.70.
**Owner** Godolphin **Bred** Darley **Trained** Newmarket, Suffolk
■ Magroora was withdrawn. Price at time of withdrawal 25/1. Rule 4 does not apply.

**FOCUS**
A desperately one-sided running of the UAE Oaks - the winner is genuinely Group class, the others are not.

## 772a ZABEEL MILE SPONSORED BY AL NABOODAH MEP & ENGINEERING GROUP (GROUP 2) (TURF) 1m
**5:00** (5:00) 3-Y-O+

**£90,361** (£30,120; £15,060; £7,530; £4,518; £3,012)

RPR
1 **Mshawish (USA)**[35] 308 4-9-0 113 ............ RichardHughes 6 119+
(M Delzangles, France) *trckd ldrs: led 2 1/2f out: r.o wl: comf* **11/4**[2]
2 2 ½ **Trade Storm**[28] 397 6-9-0 115 ............ JamieSpencer 3 113+
(David Simcock) *s.i.s: settled in rr: r.o wl fnl 1 1/2f but no ch w wnr* **3/1**[3]
3 3 ¼ **Mushreq (AUS)**[28] 397 6-9-0 115 ............ PaulHanagan 5 106
(M F De Kock, South Africa) *trckd ldng pair: rdn 2 1/2f out: outpcd 2f out but r.o same pce fnl f* **15/8**[1]
4 shd **Edu Querido (BRZ)**[21] 509 5-9-0 108 ............(b) MartinHarley 2 106
(Marco Botti) *mid-div: r.o same pce fnl 2f* **14/1**
5 1 **Gabrial (IRE)**[14] 595 5-9-0 109 ............ KierenFallon 4 103
(Richard Fahey) *settled in rr: nvr nr to chal* **9/1**
6 ¾ **Mustaheel (IRE)**[7] 679 5-9-0 104 ............(t) DaneO'Neill 1 102
(A Al Raihe, UAE) *sn led: hdd & wknd 2 1/2f out* **25/1**
7 1 ½ **Gale Force Ten**[14] 595 4-9-0 112 ............(t) PatCosgrave 7 98
(M F De Kock, South Africa) *in rr of mid-div: n.d* **11/1**
1m 37.16s (97.16) **7** Ran SP% **115.3**
CSF: 11.69; EXACTA: 15.30; TRIFECTA: 53.10 WIN: 3.20; PL: 1.00, 1.30, 1.40.
**Owner** Al Shaqab Racing **Bred** OTIF 2007 **Trained** France

**FOCUS**
They went a slow-fast pace. Mshawish rates a personal best.

## 773a AL NABOODAH CARGO CENTRE TROPHY (H'CAP) (TAPETA) 1m 3f
**5:35** (5:35) (100-110,107) 3-Y-O+

**£43,373** (£14,457; £7,228; £3,614; £2,168; £1,445)

RPR
1 **Tha'ir (IRE)**[14] 593 4-9-0 **101** ............ SilvestreDeSousa 2 108
(Saeed bin Suroor) *mid-div: smooth prog 2f out: led 1f out: comf* **7/1**
2 1 **Farrier (USA)**[34] 334 6-8-9 **100** ............ MarcMonaghan(6) 3 105
(S Seemar, UAE) *s.i.s: rdn 3f out: r.o fnl 2f: nrst fin* **14/1**
3 1 **Alexandra Palace (SAF)**[7] 681 5-9-6 **106** ............ ChristopheSoumillon 7 108
(M F De Kock, South Africa) *settled in rr: nvr nr to chal but r.o fnl 2f: nrst fin* **6/1**[3]
4 1 ¼ **Manalapan (IRE)**[21] 507 4-9-5 **107** ............ TedDurcan 9 107
(P J Prendergast, Ire) *trckd ldrs: led briefly 2f out: one pce fnl f* **12/1**
5 ½ **Energia Davos (BRZ)**[14] 593 6-9-3 **102** ............ MartinHarley 5 103+
(Marco Botti) *in rr of mid-div: r.o fnl 2f: nrst fin* **9/2**[2]
6 1 **Starboard**[14] 595 5-9-1 **100** ............ WilliamBuick 4 98
(David Simcock) *trckd ldrs: ev ch 1f out: one pce fnl 110yds* **14/1**
7 1 ½ **Winterlude (IRE)**[14] 593 4-9-0 **101** ............ MickaelBarzalona 1 97
(Charlie Appleby) *mid-div: chsd ldrs 2 1/2f out: wknd fnl f* **6/4**[1]
8 2 **Manchester (FR)**[14] 593 6-9-1 **100** ............(t) KierenFallon 6 92
(Niels Petersen, Norway) *mid-div: chsd ldrs 2f out: wknd fnl f* **33/1**
9 3 **Adroitly (AUS)**[14] 598 7-9-1 **100** ............ AhmedAjtebi 10 87
(Saeed bin Suroor) *a in rr* **33/1**
10 13 ½ **Vasily**[14] 598 6-9-2 **101** ............ RichardHughes 8 63
(M F De Kock, South Africa) *sn led: rdn 3f out: hdd & wknd 2f out* **12/1**
2m 17.63s (-0.77)
**WFA** 4 from 5yo+ 2lb **10** Ran SP% **119.6**
CSF: 102.35; EXACTA: 60.90 TRICAST 625.09; TRIFECTA: 314.40 WIN: 7.10; PL: 1.50, 2.10, 2.40. Placepot: £192.80 to a £1 stake. Pool: £8,465.45 - 32.05 winning units. Quadpot: £22.30 to a £1 stake. Pool: £337.60 - 11.20 winning units..
**Owner** Godolphin **Bred** Lodge Park Stud **Trained** Newmarket, Suffolk

**FOCUS**
A somewhat muddling gallop. The first two were close to their best.

# 737 LINGFIELD (L-H)
## Friday, February 28

**OFFICIAL GOING: Standard**
Wind: virtually nil Weather: showers

## 774 32RED BURNING DESIRE SLOT H'CAP 1m 1y(P)
**1:30** (1:30) (Class 6) (0-65,65) 3-Y-O **£2,726** (£805; £402) **Stalls** High

Form RPR
540- 1 **Tizlove Regardless (USA)**[107] 7855 3-9-0 **58** ............ AdamKirby 8 75+
(Mark Johnston) *chsd ldr tl drvn to ld over 2f out: clr and in command 1f out: edgd rt ins fnl f: comf* **2/1**[2]
06-0 2 2 ½ **Whispering Star (USA)**[45] 174 3-8-7 **51** oh1 ............ DavidProbert 7 61+
(David Simcock) *stdd s: hld up in rr: rdn and stl plenty to do over 2f out: hdwy u.p on outer over 1f out: chsd clr wnr fnl 100yds: r.o but no ch w wnr* **7/4**[1]
40-4 3 3 **Sandy Cove**[9] 665 3-8-13 **57** ............ LukeMorris 6 58
(James Eustace) *hld up in last pair: rdn and effrt to chse ldrs 2f out: drvn and styd on same pce fr over 1f out: wnt 3rd wl ins fnl f* **7/1**
04-1 4 2 ¼ **Barbary (IRE)**[9] 665 3-9-5 **63** 6ex ............ FrederikTylicki 1 59
(Charlie Fellowes) *chsd ldrs: 3rd and unable qck u.p over 1f out: wknd ins fnl f* **7/2**[3]
16-5 5 1 ¼ **Black Vale (IRE)**[20] 541 3-9-0 **65** ............(t) DonnaAspell(7) 2 58
(Phil McEntee) *led: clr 5f out tl hdd over 2f out: outpcd by wnr and btn over 1f out: wknd and lost 3 pls ins fnl f* **66/1**
-215 6 2 **Royal Bushida**[10] 653 3-8-0 **51** oh4 ............ AdamMcLean(7) 4 39
(Derek Shaw) *in tch in midfield: rdn and dropped to rr over 2f out: bhd over 1f out* **25/1**
4-36 7 ½ **Windlass (IRE)**[23] 486 3-9-6 **64** ............ RobertHavlin 5 51
(John Gosden) *in tch in midfield: rdn and dropped to rr 2f out: sn wknd* **8/1**
1m 36.21s (-1.99) **Going Correction** -0.05s/f (Stan) **7** Ran SP% **120.9**
Speed ratings (Par 95): **107,104,101,99,98 96,95**
CSF £6.46 CT £20.24 TOTE £2.70: £2.70, £1.10; EX 11.00 Trifecta £71.40.
**Owner** Crone Stud Farms Ltd **Bred** WinStar Farm LLC **Trained** Middleham Moor, N Yorks

**FOCUS**
A moderate handicap.

## 775 LADBROKES (S) STKS 1m 1y(P)
**2:00** (2:00) (Class 6) 4-Y-O+ **£2,385** (£704; £352) **Stalls** High

Form RPR
0-04 1 **Menelik (IRE)**[32] 359 5-8-12 64 ............(vt) RichardKingscote 1 71
(Tom Dascombe) *mde all: rdn and edgd rt over 1f out: kpt on and holding rivals ins fnl f* **7/2**[3]
0-11 2 1 **Saharia (IRE)**[39] 262 7-9-4 71 ............(v) ShaneKelly 5 75
(Daniel Mark Loughnane) *stdd s: hld up in tch in rr: effrt to chse ldng pair wl over 1f out: drvn and no real imp ins fnl f tl kpt on fnl 100yds to go 2nd towards fin* **6/4**[1]
-22 3 1 ¼ **Officer In Command (USA)**[7] 685 8-9-4 75 ............(p) LiamKeniry 2 73
(John Butler) *in tch: rdn and effrt wl over 1f out: no real imp fr over 1f out: swtchd rt ins fnl f and wnt 3rd towards fin* **3/1**[2]
-012 4 hd **Skidby Mill (IRE)**[24] 467 4-8-13 61 ............ LiamJones 4 66
(Laura Mongan) *t.k.h: chsd ldng pair: effrt to chse ldr over 2f out: swtchd lft and unable qck jst over 1f out: wknd fnl 75yds and lost 2 pls towards fin* **9/2**
2506 5 3 ¼ **Copperwood**[7] 685 9-9-4 62 ............ AmirQuinn 3 63
(Lee Carter) *chsd wnr tl over 2f out: dropped to last and btn over 1f out: wknd fnl f: eased towards fin* **25/1**
1m 36.95s (-1.25) **Going Correction** -0.05s/f (Stan) **5** Ran SP% **109.3**
Speed ratings (Par 101): **104,103,101,101,98**
CSF £9.07 TOTE £5.20: £3.10, £1.10; EX 8.10 Trifecta £32.80.The winner was sold to Lee Carter for 5,000gns.
**Owner** Laurence A Bellman **Bred** Irish National Stud **Trained** Malpas, Cheshire

**FOCUS**
Ordinary form.

## 776 CORAL APP DOWNLOAD FROM THE APP STORE MAIDEN STKS 1m 4f (P)
**2:30** (2:31) (Class 5) 4-Y-O+ **£3,408** (£1,006; £503) **Stalls** Low

Form RPR
1 **Highfields Dancer**[28] 6-9-8 0 ............ GeorgeBaker 3 67+
(Gary Moore) *stdd s: hld up in rr: gd hdwy on inner over 1f out: rdn to ld ins fnl f: styd on wl: rdn out* **16/1**
2 ½ **Neston Grace**[12] 6-9-3 0 ............ RobertWinston 1 60
(Simon Hodgson) *t.k.h early: chsd ldrs: rdn and effrt 2f out: kpt on u.p and pressing ldrs ins fnl f: wnt 2nd towards fin* **7/1**[3]
53 3 hd **Midnight Chorister**[7] 686 6-9-8 0 ............(t) HayleyTurner 6 65
(Alex Hales) *t.k.h: chsd ldrs early: grad stdd bk and in midfield 9f out: swtchd rt over 2f out: styd on u.p to press wnr fnl 100yds: kpt on* **7/2**[2]
-224 4 1 ½ **After The Storm**[16] 581 5-9-8 65 ............(p) LukeMorris 4 63
(John O'Shea) *led: rdn ent fnl 2f: hrd drvn over 1f out: hdd and no ex ins fnl f* **7/2**[2]
3-22 5 1 ½ **Conserve (IRE)**[16] 581 4-9-0 73 ............ RobertHavlin 5 56
(Amy Weaver) *in tch in midfield: drvn and effrt jst over 2f out: swtchd rt and pressed ldrs 1f out: no ex and btn ins fnl f: wknd towards fin* **7/4**[1]
6 1 ¾ **Kilfinichen Bay (IRE)**[51] 6-9-5 0 ............ ThomasBrown(3) 7 57
(Violet M Jordan) *s.i.s: t.k.h in tch in last pair: rdn and effrt over 2f out: outpcd and btn over 1f out: hld but plugged on ins fnl f* **66/1**
20-0 7 1 ½ **Hazzaat (IRE)**[15] 590 4-9-5 58 ............(v[1]) TomQueally 8 55
(Gary Harrison) *dwlt: steadily rcvrd to join ldr after 2f: rdn and ev ch 2f out: btn whn squeezed for room jst ins fnl f: wknd fnl 100yds* **8/1**
6 8 11 **Montjen (IRE)**[20] 542 4-9-0 0 ............ FrederikTylicki 2 32
(Karen Tutty) *chsd ldrs: rdn 3f out: outpcd and struggling over 2f out: wknd over 1f out* **33/1**
2m 32.36s (-0.64) **Going Correction** -0.05s/f (Stan)
**WFA** 4 from 5yo+ 3lb **8** Ran SP% **114.7**
Speed ratings (Par 103): **100,99,99,98,97 96,95,88**
CSF £122.22 TOTE £17.50: £3.60, £2.10, £1.70; EX 48.70 Trifecta £515.00.
**Owner** L Roberts **Bred** L J Roberts **Trained** Lower Beeding, W Sussex

**FOCUS**
This was never going to take much winning.

## 777 COMPARE BOOKMAKERS AT BOOKMAKERS.CO.UK H'CAP 5f 6y(P)
**3:00** (3:01) (Class 5) (0-70,70) 4-Y-O+ **£3,408** (£1,006; £503) **Stalls** High

Form RPR
5-13 1 **Megaleka**[7] 694 4-8-8 **62** ............ TimClark(5) 9 71
(Alan Bailey) *hld up in midfield: rdn and hdwy jst over 1f out: r.o wl to ld towards fin* **8/1**[3]
-506 2 ¾ **Profile Star (IRE)**[26] 444 5-9-7 **70** ............ WilliamCarson 4 76
(Ann Stokell) *led: rdn and wanting to hang lft fr 2f out: kpt on wl tl hdd and no ex towards fin* **20/1**
-230 3 ¾ **Welease Bwian (IRE)**[6] 714 5-9-7 **70** ............ GeorgeBaker 7 74
(Stuart Williams) *hld up in rr: effrt on outer wl over 1f out: kpt on u.p to go 3rd wl ins fnl f* **5/4**[1]
-032 4 1 ¼ **Rise To Glory (IRE)**[9] 663 6-8-11 **60** ............ DuranFentiman 6 59
(Shaun Harris) *chsd ldrs: effrt u.p wl over 1f out: kpt on same pce and n.m.r ins fnl f* **7/1**[2]
4425 5 nk **Desert Strike**[9] 654 8-9-7 **70** ............(p) HayleyTurner 8 72
(Conor Dore) *taken down early: t.k.h: hld up in midfield: effrt over 1f out: keeping on same pce and hld whn swtchd rt and eased towards fin* **7/1**[2]
4640 6 ½ **Mossgo (IRE)**[7] 687 4-8-11 **60** ............(tp) LukeMorris 5 56
(John Best) *chsd ldr: rdn and unable qck over 1f out: lost 2nd and wknd ins fnl f* **14/1**
42-6 7 ¾ **Dawn Catcher**[9] 654 4-8-10 **59** ............ RichardKingscote 3 56
(Geoffrey Deacon) *chsd ldrs: rdn and unable qck over 1f out: keeping on same pce and hld whn squeezed for room and hmpd ins fnl f* **8/1**[3]
166- 8 1 ¼ **Danzoe (IRE)**[59] 8457 7-9-1 **64** ............ TomQueally 2 53
(Christine Dunnett) *sn rdn along in last trio: no imp u.p fr over 1f out* **16/1**
0-04 9 ½ **Bay Knight (IRE)**[19] 552 8-9-7 **70** ............ AdamKirby 1 57
(Ann Stokell) *sn rdn along and a outpcd in rr* **8/1**[3]
58.32s (-0.48) **Going Correction** -0.05s/f (Stan) **9** Ran SP% **120.1**
Speed ratings (Par 103): **101,99,98,96,96 95,94,92,91**
CSF £156.00 CT £336.01 TOTE £8.60: £2.80, £6.20, £1.10; EX 242.30 Trifecta £880.10.
**Owner** North Cheshire Trading & Storage Ltd **Bred** North Cheshire Trading And Storage Ltd **Trained** Newmarket, Suffolk

**FOCUS**
There was a good pace on here.

## 778 32RED FREE £10 BONUS CONDITIONS STKS 6f 1y(P)
3:35 (3:36) (Class 3) 3-Y-O £10,225 (£3,019; £1,510) Stalls Low

| Form | | | | RPR |
|---|---|---|---|---|
| 600- | 1 | | **Ben Hall (IRE)**[146] 7026 3-9-2 97 RobertHavlin 4 | 100 |
| | | | (John Gosden) *sn pushed up to ld and mde rest: rdn over 1f out: drvn and hrd pressed ins fnl f: hld on wl u.p* **5/2**[1] | |
| | 2 | 1/2 | **American Hope (USA)**[84] 8190 3-9-2 0 ShaneKelly 1 | 99 |
| | | | (Mike Murphy) *t.k.h: hld up in tch in last pair: rn green and nt handle bnd 2f out: hdwy on inner over 1f out: str chal and edgd rt ins fnl f: hld towards fin* **10/1** | |
| 40-1 | 3 | 1 | **Major Crispies**[9] 667 3-8-11 79 RyanTate(5) 6 | 96 |
| | | | (James Eustace) *led early: in tch in midfield: effrt to chal 1f out: stl pressing ldrs whn n.m.r ins fnl f: hmpd and btn towards fin* **3/1**[2] | |
| 431- | 4 | 1 1/2 | **Steventon Star**[83] 8203 3-9-2 97 (p) RobertWinston 5 | 91 |
| | | | (Alan Bailey) *in tch in last pair: rdn over 1f out: pushed along and kpt on ins fnl f: nvr gng pce to chal* **5/1** | |
| 43 | 5 | shd | **Golden Amber (IRE)**[13] 624 3-8-11 89 HayleyTurner 2 | 86 |
| | | | (Dean Ivory) *chsd ldrs: rdn to go 2nd over 1f out tl jst ins fnl f: no ex and short of room sn after: wknd wl ins fnl f* **9/2**[3] | |
| 24-1 | 6 | 1 3/4 | **Lady Frances**[22] 501 3-8-8 90 MichaelJMMurphy(3) 7 | 80 |
| | | | (Mark Johnston) *dwlt: rcvrd to chse ldr over 4f out tl over 1f out: sn drvn and lost pl: wknd ins fnl f* **5/1** | |

1m 11.1s (-0.80) **Going Correction** -0.05s/f (Stan) **6 Ran SP% 114.2**
Speed ratings (Par 101): **103,102,101,99,98 96**
CSF £27.49 TOTE £2.70: £1.90, £7.60; EX 32.40 Trifecta £135.00.
**Owner** Saeed Manana **Bred** Ringfort Stud Ltd **Trained** Newmarket, Suffolk
■ Stewards' Enquiry : Shane Kelly one-day ban: careless riding (14 Mar)
**FOCUS**
A competitive conditions event featuring some useful types.

## 779 LADBROKES H'CAP 7f 1y(P)
4:10 (4:10) (Class 4) (0-85,85) 4-Y-O+ £5,822 (£1,732; £865; £432) Stalls Low

| Form | | | | RPR |
|---|---|---|---|---|
| 4-02 | 1 | | **Living The Life (IRE)**[7] 689 4-8-12 76 (v) PaddyAspell 7 | 84 |
| | | | (Phil McEntee) *chsd ldr tl rdn to ld over 1f out: wnt lft u.p ins fnl f: jst hld on* **3/1**[2] | |
| 2-11 | 2 | nse | **Welsh Sunrise**[25] 453 4-8-10 74 RichardKingscote 6 | 82+ |
| | | | (Stuart Williams) *in tch in midfield: swtchd rt and gd hdwy 1f out: rdn to chal ins fnl f: ev ch and rdn hands and heels wl ins fnl f: r.o: jst hld* **7/2**[3] | |
| 000- | 3 | 2 | **Spin Artist (USA)**[140] 7176 4-9-5 83 AdamKirby 4 | 86 |
| | | | (Mark Johnston) *chsd ldrs: rdn ent fnl 2f: drvn and pressed ldrs ent fnl f: no ex and btn whn sltly hmpd ins fnl f: wknd towards fin* **9/4**[1] | |
| 6024 | 4 | 3/4 | **Jay Bee Blue**[9] 658 5-9-2 80 (bt) TomQueally 5 | 80 |
| | | | (Sean Curran) *dwlt: sn rcvrd and in tch in midfield: rdn and effrt 2f out: styd on same pce u.p ins fnl f* **5/1** | |
| 6/0- | 5 | 1 1/4 | **Subtle Knife**[209] 5014 5-9-6 84 LiamJones 3 | 81 |
| | | | (Giles Bravery) *hld up in last pair: rdn and no imp over 1f out: styd on same pce ins fnl f* **16/1** | |
| 022- | 6 | 2 | **Baddilini**[162] 6575 4-9-7 85 RobertWinston 2 | 77 |
| | | | (Alan Bailey) *hld up in last pair: rdn and no hdwy over 1f out: n.d* **7/1** | |
| 6-66 | 7 | nk | **Decent Fella (IRE)**[16] 572 8-8-8 72 (t) WilliamCarson 8 | 63 |
| | | | (Ann Stokell) *led: rdn and hdd over 1f out: wknd ins fnl f* **33/1** | |

1m 23.7s (-1.10) **Going Correction** -0.05s/f (Stan) **7 Ran SP% 116.0**
Speed ratings (Par 105): **104,103,101,100,99 97,96**
CSF £14.38 CT £27.20 TOTE £4.20: £2.20, £2.50; EX 14.20 Trifecta £43.50.
**Owner** Henry R Nothhaft **Bred** Michael Begley **Trained** Newmarket, Suffolk
■ Stewards' Enquiry : Paddy Aspell one-day ban: careless riding (14 Mar)
**FOCUS**
The two in-form fillies in the race had this between them in the closing stages.

## 780 DOWNLOAD THE LADBROKES APP H'CAP 1m 1y(P)
4:45 (4:45) (Class 6) (0-65,65) 4-Y-O+ £2,726 (£805; £402) Stalls High

| Form | | | | RPR |
|---|---|---|---|---|
| -212 | 1 | | **Benandonner (USA)**[8] 672 11-8-10 54 ShaneKelly 8 | 62 |
| | | | (Mike Murphy) *chsd ldrs: wnt 2nd and pressing ldr whn carried wd bnd wl over 1f out: styd on wl u.p ins fnl f: to ld towards fin* **4/1**[3] | |
| 4-55 | 2 | nk | **Hierarch (IRE)**[16] 583 7-9-0 65 (p) GeorgeBuckell(7) 3 | 72 |
| | | | (David Simcock) *chsd ldr tl over 2f out: rdn and ev ch over 1f out: led 1f out: kpt on tl hdd and no ex towards fin* **3/1**[2] | |
| -304 | 3 | 2 3/4 | **Divine Rule (IRE)**[16] 578 6-8-7 58 (v) CharlotteJenner(7) 4 | 59 |
| | | | (Laura Mongan) *hld up in last pair: effrt in 4th and v wd bnd wl over 1f out: styd on to go 3rd wl ins fnl f* **8/1** | |
| 0-62 | 4 | 1/2 | **Midnight Feast**[16] 583 6-9-1 62 (v) ThomasBrown(3) 7 | 61 |
| | | | (Lee Carter) *led: rdn and hung rt bnd wl over 1f out: hdd 1f out: wknd ins fnl f* **7/4**[1] | |
| 56-0 | 5 | 2 | **Not Rigg (USA)**[15] 589 4-9-3 61 (bt) TomQueally 2 | 56 |
| | | | (Gary Harrison) *s.i.s: hld up in rr: rdn and effrt whn carried wd bnd wl over 1f out: swtchd lft and drvn over 1f out: no real imp fnl f* **16/1** | |
| 6-05 | 6 | 1 | **Storm Runner (IRE)**[15] 589 6-9-3 64 RyanPowell(3) 1 | 56 |
| | | | (George Margarson) *in tch in midfield: rdn and lost pl over 2f out: bhd and drvn 2f out: no imp* **5/1** | |

1m 38.33s (0.13) **Going Correction** -0.05s/f (Stan) **6 Ran SP% 115.0**
Speed ratings (Par 101): **97,96,93,93,91 90**
CSF £16.90 CT £90.50 TOTE £4.00: £2.20, £1.90; EX 15.50 Trifecta £42.90.
**Owner** M Murphy **Bred** Gainsborough Farm Llc **Trained** Westoning, Beds
**FOCUS**
The early gallop was steady but it soon picked up.
T/Plt: £235.40 to a £1 stake. Pool: £67258.66 - 208.55 winning tickets T/Qpdt: £61.80 to a £1 stake. Pool: £7377.13 - 88.25 winning tickets SP

# 730 WOLVERHAMPTON (A.W) (L-H)
Friday, February 28

**OFFICIAL GOING: Standard**
Wind: slight half behind Weather: overcast

## 781 CORAL MOBILE "JUST THREE CLICKS TO BET" APPRENTICE H'CAP 1m 4f 50y(P)
5:35 (5:35) (Class 6) (0-55,58) 4-Y-O+ £2,264 (£673; £336; £168) Stalls Low

| Form | | | | RPR |
|---|---|---|---|---|
| 6-46 | 1 | | **Grandiloquent**[14] 609 5-9-1 54 (v) MeganCarberry(5) 7 | 61+ |
| | | | (Brian Ellison) *bustled along leaving stalls to r in midfield: clsd 6f out: rdn 3f out: led appr fnl f: drvn out to hold on* **8/1** | |
| 5-35 | 2 | hd | **Well Owd Mon**[11] 639 4-8-4 46 (p) RobHornby(5) 2 | 53 |
| | | | (Andrew Hollinshead) *in rr: rdn and hdwy on outside over 2f out: chsd wnr ins fnl f: r.o: jst failed* **7/2**[2] | |
| -621 | 3 | 1 3/4 | **Fair Breeze**[11] 639 7-9-6 54 6ex (b) JordanVaughan 6 | 58 |
| | | | (Richard Phillips) *s.s: hld up in rr: hdwy 6f out: rdn over 3f out: styd on ins fnl f* **5/1**[3] | |
| 400- | 4 | 5 | **Rockweiller**[58] 7458 7-8-11 52 (b) AlexHopkinson(7) 1 | 49 |
| | | | (Shaun Harris) *racd keenly: trckd ldrs tl led over 5f out: pushed along over 2f out: hdd appr fnl f: no ex* **20/1** | |
| -323 | 5 | 1 3/4 | **Compton Silver**[9] 661 4-8-8 50 JackGilligan(5) 4 | 44 |
| | | | (Patrick Gilligan) *chsd ldrs: rdn over 2f out: one pce* **6/1** | |
| 2611 | 6 | 10 | **Huzzah (IRE)**[8] 671 9-9-7 58 6ex AlistairRawlinson(3) 9 | 37 |
| | | | (Michael Appleby) *t.k.h: hld up towards rr and racd wd: hdwy over 7f out: rdn 3f out: one pce fnl 2f* **7/4**[1] | |
| 6044 | 7 | 5 | **Mazij**[10] 648 6-9-7 55 DanielCremin 8 | 26 |
| | | | (Peter Hiatt) *led tl over 5f out: rdn 4f out: wknd 2f out* **12/1** | |
| 05/0 | 8 | 10 | **The Right Time**[16] 570 6-8-7 46 oh1 MrAidenBlakemore(5) 3 | 2 |
| | | | (Tony Carroll) *in tch: pushed along 6f out: wknd over 3f out* **50/1** | |
| /000 | 9 | 37 | **Sir Lexington (IRE)**[26] 446 5-8-9 46 oh1 RobJFitzpatrick(3) 5 | |
| | | | (Brian Forsey) *s.i.s: a in rr: niggled along after 6f: lost tch over 4f out: t.o* **100/1** | |

2m 43.85s (2.75) **Going Correction** +0.10s/f (Slow)
**WFA** 4 from 5yo+ 3lb **9 Ran SP% 116.1**
Speed ratings (Par 101): **94,93,92,89,88 81,78,71,46**
CSF £35.94 CT £156.54 TOTE £10.70: £3.00, £1.50, £1.40; EX 50.60 Trifecta £284.10.
**Owner** Mrs June Bownes **Bred** Juddmonte Farms Ltd **Trained** Norton, N Yorks
■ Megan Carberry's first winner in Britain.
**FOCUS**
It paid not to get too overly close to the early pace in this moderate but generously run opener. The winner can probably rate a bit higher.

## 782 CORAL MOBILE "JUST THREE CLICKS TO BET" H'CAP 1m 1f 103y(P)
6:05 (6:05) (Class 5) (0-75,75) 4-Y-O+ £2,911 (£866; £432; £216) Stalls Low

| Form | | | | RPR |
|---|---|---|---|---|
| 01-5 | 1 | | **Spes Nostra**[56] 29 6-9-4 72 (b) GrahamGibbons 8 | 84 |
| | | | (David Barron) *racd keenly: trckd ldr tl led 6f out: kicked over 2f out: drvn out and r.o wl* **11/4**[2] | |
| 5-22 | 2 | 2 1/2 | **Arlecchino (IRE)**[22] 498 4-9-2 70 (b) GrahamLee 3 | 77 |
| | | | (Ed McMahon) *a.p: chsd wnr 5f out: rdn over 2f out: kpt on tl no ex ins fnl f* **5/1** | |
| 14-3 | 3 | hd | **Havelovewilltravel (IRE)**[48] 146 4-9-5 73 JamieSpencer 6 | 80 |
| | | | (Jeremy Noseda) *towards rr: rdn and hdwy 3f out: sn unable qck: styd on ins fnl f* **6/4**[1] | |
| 12-3 | 4 | 1 | **Golden Jubilee (USA)**[11] 641 5-8-13 70(v) WilliamTwiston-Davies(3) 4 | 75 |
| | | | (Nigel Twiston-Davies) *in tch: rdn to chse ldrs 3f out: kpt on one pce fnl 2f* **9/2**[3] | |
| -402 | 5 | 2 | **My Single Malt (IRE)**[20] 539 6-8-12 66 [1] PaulMulrennan 2 | 67 |
| | | | (Julie Camacho) *in tch travelling wl: rdn over 2f out: one pce* **20/1** | |
| 4-33 | 6 | 3/4 | **Lean On Pete (IRE)**[22] 498 5-9-0 73 JacobButterfield(5) 7 | 73 |
| | | | (Ollie Pears) *hld up towards rr: pushed along and outpcd by ldrs over 2f out: modest late hdwy* **8/1** | |
| 1144 | 7 | 7 | **Prime Exhibit**[8] 677 9-9-3 71 (t) StephenCraine 9 | 57 |
| | | | (Daniel Mark Loughnane) *hld up in rr: sme hdwy 4f out: pushed along and outpcd by ldrs over 2f out: no imp* **25/1** | |
| 316- | 8 | 37 | **Great Demeanor (USA)**[12] 2309 4-9-2 75 EmmaSayer(5) 1 | |
| | | | (Dianne Sayer) *led tl 6f out: rdn 4f out: grad wknd: t.o* **50/1** | |

2m 1.49s (-0.21) **Going Correction** +0.10s/f (Slow) **8 Ran SP% 123.2**
Speed ratings (Par 103): **104,101,101,100,98 98,92,59**
CSF £18.10 CT £28.57 TOTE £4.10: £1.50, £1.40, £1.90; EX 21.90 Trifecta £64.10.
**Owner** J Cringan & D Pryde **Bred** James A Cringan **Trained** Maunby, N Yorks
**FOCUS**
This ordinary event was stolen at around halfway by an enterprising move aboard the winner by Graham Gibbons.

## 783 CORAL.CO.UK BEST ODDS GUARANTEED ON RACING H'CAP 1m 1f 103y(P)
6:35 (6:35) (Class 7) (0-50,50) 4-Y-O+ £1,940 (£577; £288; £144) Stalls Low

| Form | | | | RPR |
|---|---|---|---|---|
| 1/05 | 1 | | **Catching Zeds**[8] 671 7-9-4 47 (b) AndreaAtzeni 12 | 54 |
| | | | (Kevin Frost) *s.i.s: sn chsng ldrs: rdn to ld down outside wl over 1f out: r.o* **7/1** | |
| 0-04 | 2 | 1/2 | **Troy Boy**[8] 672 4-8-13 45 NeilFarley(3) 9 | 51 |
| | | | (Robin Bastiman) *chsd ldr: led 2f out: sn hdd: kpt on u.p* **7/2**[2] | |
| 0-00 | 3 | 1/2 | **Edgware Road**[35] 317 6-9-4 50 (b) RossAtkinson(3) 4 | 55+ |
| | | | (Paul Morgan) *s.s and bustled along to r in midfield: dropped towards rr over 4f out: rdn over 3f out: r.o wl u.p ins fnl f* **12/1** | |
| 05-4 | 4 | 1 | **Many Levels**[11] 642 4-9-2 45 TomEaves 2 | 48 |
| | | | (John Quinn) *trckd ldrs: rdn 2f out: kpt on same pce* **9/2**[3] | |
| 5-56 | 5 | 4 | **Silver Fawn (IRE)**[23] 484 4-9-2 45 (be) JimmyQuinn 1 | 41 |
| | | | (John Weymes) *in tch: n.m.r bnd after 2f: rdn over 2f out: one pce* **16/1** | |
| 54-4 | 6 | 1 | **Star Request**[27] 435 4-9-1 49 JacobButterfield(5) 11 | 43 |
| | | | (Ollie Pears) *racd keenly in midfield: lost pl and dropped towards rr 5f out: styd on u.p fnl 2f* **7/1** | |
| 000- | 7 | 4 1/2 | **Call Of Duty (IRE)**[44] 8031 9-9-2 50 (b[1]) EmmaSayer(5) 10 | 35 |
| | | | (Dianne Sayer) *in rr: stdy hdwy 5f out: rdn over 2f out: sn wknd* **16/1** | |
| 42-0 | 8 | shd | **Coastal Passage**[42] 219 6-9-7 50 (t) JamieSpencer 3 | 35 |
| | | | (Gordon Elliott, Ire) *broke wl: sn hld up bhd ldrs: lost pl over 3f out: nt clr run 2f out: unable qck and no imp on ldrs* **3/1**[1] | |
| 00-0 | 9 | 3 | **Gifted Heir (IRE)**[35] 321 10-8-11 45 JoeyHaynes(5) 8 | 24 |
| | | | (Ray Peacock) *a towards rr* **50/1** | |
| 0-00 | 10 | 1 3/4 | **Mistress Shy**[17] 563 7-8-11 45 (t) ShirleyTeasdale(5) 5 | 21 |
| | | | (Peter Hiatt) *in rr: sme hdwy u.p over 3f out: wknd 2f out* **50/1** | |

-000 **11** *11* **Tingle Tangle (USA)**16 575 4-9-5 **48**.............................. LiamKeniry 6 3
(Tony Carroll) *sn led: rdn and hdd 2f out: wknd qckly* **25/1**

2m 3.68s (1.98) **Going Correction** +0.10s/f (Slow) 11 Ran SP% **117.6**
Speed ratings (Par 97): **95,94,94,93,89 88,84,84,82,80 70**
CSF £31.33 CT £291.81 TOTE £8.10: £2.10, £2.50, £3.00; EX 38.60 Trifecta £333.00.
**Owner** The Ferandlin Peaches **Bred** White Horse Bloodstock Ltd **Trained** Stratford-upon-Avon
■ A first training success for Kevin Frost.
■ Stewards' Enquiry : Ross Atkinson four-day ban: use of whip (14, 15, 17, 18 Mar)

**FOCUS**
A basement-grade handicap won with more in hand than the official margin.

## 784 CORAL APP DOWNLOAD FROM APP STORE H'CAP 1m 4f 50y(P)
7:05 (7:05) (Class 2) (0-100,100) 4-Y£01,971 (£3,583; £1,791; £896; £446) Stalls Low

Form RPR
1131 **1** **Blue Wave (IRE)**14 611 4-9-4 **100**.............................. JoeFanning 4 106
(Mark Johnston) *led 1f: styd chsng ldr: rdn to ld over 1f out: r.o wl* **9/2**1
555- **2** *nk* **Nautilus**69 8387 4-8-12 **94** ow2.............................. (p) GrahamLee 10 100
(John Gosden) *led after 1f: rdn and hdd over 1f out: r.o gamely: jst hld* **11/2**3
/-13 **3** *3 ¼* **Bute Hall**21 514 5-8-7 **86** oh8.............................. JimmyQuinn 6 87
(David Thompson) *chsd ldrs: rdn 3f out: kpt on same pce* **25/1**
-514 **4** *¾* **Magika**14 611 4-8-5 **87**.............................. (t) AndreaAtzeni 9 87
(Marco Botti) *chsd ldrs tl lost pl after 4f: hdwy 4f out: rdn over 2f out: styd on one pce* **5/1**2
503- **5** *1 ¼* **Villoresi (IRE)**83 7131 5-8-0 **86** oh1.............................. JoeDoyle(7) 3 84
(John Quinn) *racd keenly: chsd ldrs: rdn over 2f out: kpt on one pce* **10/1**
122 **6** *½* **Echo Brava**23 494 4-7-11 **86** oh6.............................. KieranShoemark(7) 11 83+
(Luke Dace) *towards rr: rdn over 3f out: styd on fnl f: nt rch ldrs* **10/1**
10-2 **7** *2 ½* **Gabrial's Star**13 623 5-8-7 **86** oh2.............................. (b) JamieSpencer 7 80+
(Richard Fahey) *in rr: hdwy 3f out: styd on u.p fnl f: nvr rchd ldrs* **10/1**
0/ **8** *4 ½* **Gretzky**14 621 7-8-6 **88** ow1.............................. (t) WilliamTwiston-Davies(3) 8 75
(Matthew J Smith, Ire) *in tch: effrt over 3f out: no imp on ldrs: wknd fnl f* **10/1**
0222 **9** *hd* **Kashmir Peak (IRE)**14 611 5-8-10 **92**.............................. (v1) OisinMurphy(3) 2 79+
(John Quinn) *racd keenly in midfield: stmbld over 3f out: sn rdn and wknd* **9/2**1
4-24 **10** *8* **Gioia Di Vita**20 544 4-8-1 **86** oh13.............................. NataliaGemelova(3) 5 61+
(David Thompson) *s.s: hld up: sltly hmpd over 3f out: a in rr* **50/1**
134- **11** *18* **Bohemian Rhapsody (IRE)**20 7823 5-8-8 **87**.............................. JohnFahy 1 35
(Seamus Durack) *chsd ldrs: rdn and wkng whn sltly hmpd over 3f out: t.o* **8/1**

2m 38.6s (-2.50) **Going Correction** +0.10s/f (Slow)
**WFA** 4 from 5yo+ 3lb 11 Ran SP% **121.7**
Speed ratings (Par 109): **112,111,109,109,108 107,106,103,103,97 85**
CSF £30.21 CT £571.18 TOTE £7.10: £2.80, £1.70, £5.20; EX 38.30 Trifecta £862.10.
**Owner** Sheikh Hamdan bin Mohammed Al Maktoum **Bred** Tom Darcy And Vincent McCarthy **Trained** Middleham Moor, N Yorks

**FOCUS**
The feature event of the evening by some margin, but very few got meaningfully involved.

## 785 32RED THUNDERSTRUCK II SLOT H'CAP 1m 1f 103y(P)
7:35 (7:35) (Class 4) (0-85,82) 3-Y-O £5,175 (£1,540; £769; £384) Stalls Low

Form RPR
1113 **1** **Swivel**9 659 3-9-7 **82**.............................. JoeFanning 4 91
(Mark Johnston) *chsd ldr tl led over 5f out: hdd over 2f out: rallied to ld ent fnl f: styd on wl* **7/4**1
01-2 **2** *1* **Chinotto (IRE)**9 659 3-9-3 **78**.............................. DavidProbert 2 85
(Andrew Balding) *trckd ldrs: wnt 2nd over 3f out: drvn to ld over 2f out: hdd ent fnl f: kpt on* **2/1**2
-042 **3** *1 ½* **Officer Drivel (IRE)**9 668 3-8-1 **69**.............................. KieranShoemark(7) 5 73
(Luke Dace) *hld up in last: rdn over 2f out: r.o ins fnl f: clsng towards fin* **4/1**3
-154 **4** *9* **Captain Myles (IRE)**14 613 3-9-5 **80**.............................. (vt1) AndreaAtzeni 3 67
(Tim Pitt) *racd in 4th: rdn over 3f out: chsd ldng pair over 2f out: hung rt and wknd fnl f* **8/1**
6-11 **5** *14* **Boogangoo (IRE)**22 499 3-8-9 **73**.............................. OisinMurphy(3) 1 33
(Grace Harris) *led tl over 5f out: rdn 3f out: wknd 2f out: t.o* **10/1**

2m 1.8s (0.10) **Going Correction** +0.10s/f (Slow) 5 Ran SP% **109.9**
Speed ratings (Par 99): **103,102,100,92,80**
CSF £5.54 TOTE £3.60: £1.80, £1.40; EX 5.60 Trifecta £14.40.
**Owner** Sheikh Hamdan bin Mohammed Al Maktoum **Bred** Stratford Place Stud And Watership Down **Trained** Middleham Moor, N Yorks

**FOCUS**
A small-field event won in a time 0.3sec slower than the 72-rated Spes Nostra had recorded in the Class 5 event earlier.

## 786 32RED CASINO H'CAP 5f 216y(P)
8:05 (8:06) (Class 6) (0-55,55) 3-Y-O £2,264 (£673; £336; £168) Stalls Low

Form RPR
00-3 **1** **Emerald Breeze (IRE)**24 480 3-8-12 **46** oh1.............................. (b1) JimmyQuinn 6 65+
(Tim Pitt) *s.s: sn rcvrd to trck ldrs: led wl over 1f out: qckly drvn clr: comf* **14/1**
660- **2** *3* **Hustle Bustle (IRE)**260 3245 3-9-2 **50**.............................. SeanLevey 2 60+
(David Brown) *a.p: rdn to chse wnr over 1f out: kpt on but a being hld* **8/1**
-543 **3** *3 ½* **Biscuiteer**14 608 3-9-7 **55**.............................. (b) LukeMorris 1 56
(Scott Dixon) *led to post: in tch: rdn 3f out: r.o ins fnl f* **5/2**2
00-0 **4** *nk* **Desert Colours**35 311 3-9-3 **51**.............................. JamieSpencer 13 50+
(Kevin Ryan) *towards rr: hung rt early: rdn 2f out: r.o u.p ins fnl f* **9/4**1
6-53 **5** *1 ¼* **River Dreamer (IRE)**22 500 3-8-12 **46** oh1.............................. AndreaAtzeni 10 41
(Robert Stephens) *in tch: rdn 3f out: sn outpcd by ldrs: styd on ins fnl f* **10/1**
05-0 **6** *2 ¼* **Elualla (IRE)**46 165 3-9-3 **51**.............................. AndrewMullen 12 39
(Nigel Tinkler) *in rr: rdn over 1f out: r.o: nvr trbld ldrs* **33/1**
**7** *1 ¼* **Alanna Bheag (IRE)**42 223 3-8-12 **46** oh1.............................. JohnFahy 3 30
(M C Grassick, Ire) *racd keenly: towards rr: rdn over 1f out: modest late hdwy* **20/1**
0-00 **8** *shd* **Limegrove**14 608 3-8-12 **53**.............................. HollieDoyle(7) 7 37
(David Evans) *slowly slowly: towards rr: sme hdwy on outside fnl f* **16/1**
-000 **9** *nk* **Krackerjill (IRE)**9 665 3-8-12 **46** oh1.............................. (p) DavidProbert 11 29
(Mark Usher) *towards rr: rdn 3f out: no imp* **14/1**
0-52 **10** *1* **Streethowlingmama (USA)**10 653 3-8-12 **46** oh1.............................. LiamKeniry 5 26
(Olly Stevens) *led 1f: styd cl up: led 2f out: sn hdd & wknd* **7/1**3
300- **11** *11* **Oakley Dancer**169 6322 3-8-12 **46** oh1.............................. JoeFanning 9
(Tony Carroll) *chsd ldrs: rdn over 2f out: sn wknd* **33/1**

0-60 **12** *9* **Loma Mor**35 315 3-8-11 **48**.............................. NataliaGemelova(3) 8
(Alan McCabe) *racd keenly: led after 1f to 2f out: wknd qckly: t.o* **25/1**

1m 15.77s (0.77) **Going Correction** +0.10s/f (Slow) 12 Ran SP% **125.7**
Speed ratings (Par 95): **98,94,89,88,87 84,82,82,82,80 66,54**
CSF £123.69 CT £381.61 TOTE £15.20: £3.70, £3.50, £1.70; EX 69.10 Trifecta £565.90.
**Owner** Decadent Racing II **Bred** Rathbarry Stud **Trained** Market Drayton, Shropshire

**FOCUS**
An easy success for the winner.

## 787 LADBROKES MEDIAN AUCTION MAIDEN STKS 7f 32y(P)
8:35 (8:35) (Class 5) 3-5-Y-O £2,587 (£770; £384; £192) Stalls High

Form RPR
**1** **Mustajjid** 3-8-11 0.............................. AndreaAtzeni 3 70+
(Roger Varian) *trckd ldr: pushed along over 3f out: relegated to 3rd 2f out: r.o wl u.p fnl f to ld post* **4/5**1
**2** *shd* **Elusive George (IRE)** 3-8-11 0.............................. TomEaves 2 70+
(John Quinn) *racd keenly: trckd ldrs: wnt 2nd 2f out: shkn up to ld narrowly ins fnl f: drvn nr fin: ct post* **10/1**
644 **3** *nk* **Parkhill Star**21 512 3-8-6 63.............................. RichardKingscote 1 64
(Tom Dascombe) *led: narrowly hdd ins fnl f: rdn and r.o* **8/1**3
**4** *8* **Acting Talent (USA)**21 517 4-9-9 69.............................. JamieSpencer 5 50
(M C Grassick, Ire) *hld up: hdwy to chse ldng trio 3f out: sn no imp: wknd fnl f* **3/1**2
0 **5** *½* **Feisty Dragon (IRE)**44 188 3-8-7 0 ow1.............................. FergusSweeney 7 44
(Jamie Osborne) *in tch: rdn over 3f out: sn one pce* **33/1**
4 **6** *nk* **Tashbeeh (IRE)**14 614 3-8-11 0.............................. JamesSullivan 6 47
(Dianne Sayer) *hld up in last: pushed along 3f out: nvr trbld ldrs* **33/1**
4 **7** *8* **Wings Of Fire (IRE)**7 684 4-10-0 0.............................. LiamKeniry 4 34
(Denis Quinn) *hld up: rdn 3f out: wknd 2f out* **14/1**

1m 32.5s (2.90) **Going Correction** +0.10s/f (Slow)
**WFA** 3 from 4yo 17lb 7 Ran SP% **113.3**
Speed ratings (Par 103): **87,86,86,77,76 76,67**
CSF £10.12 TOTE £1.70: £1.40, £3.60; EX 9.10 Trifecta £44.60.
**Owner** Hamdan Al Maktoum **Bred** Rosyground Stud **Trained** Newmarket, Suffolk

**FOCUS**
An exciting finale.
T/Plt: £71.10 to a £1 stake. Pool: £115952.48 - 1189.99 winning tickets T/Qpdt: £19.80 to a £1 stake. Pool: £11386.97 - 423.50 winning tickets RL

# 699 DUNDALK (A.W) (L-H)
Friday, February 28

**OFFICIAL GOING: Standard**

## 788a DUNDALK STADIUM RACECOURSE OF THE YEAR H'CAP 5f (P)
6:15 (6:16) 3-Y-O+ £7,475 (£1,733; £758; £433)

RPR
**1** **Strategic Heights (IRE)**7 699 5-8-3 **72**.............................. RobbieDowney(7) 1 79
(John James Feane, Ire) *chsd ldrs: 4th 1/2-way: hdwy far side to dispute 2f out: rdn to ld over 1f out and kpt on wl towards fin* **9/2**2
**2** *¾* **Queen Grace (IRE)**28 413 7-9-2 **83**.............................. GaryPhillips(5) 2 87
(Michael J Browne, Ire) *disp early tl gained narrow advantage bef 1/2-way: rdn and jnd 2f out: hdd u.p over 1f out: edgd sltly rt u.p and kpt on wl wout matching wnr* **10/1**
**3** *½* **Grey Danube (IRE)**28 413 5-9-7 **83**.............................. (bt) KevinManning 7 85
(D J Bunyan, Ire) *dwlt sltly and racd towards rr: hdwy in 7th over 2f out: tk clsr order in 5th far side 1f out: kpt on u.p into 3rd cl home: nt trble wnr* **9/1**
**4** *hd* **Knock Stars (IRE)**14 618 6-9-5 **81**.............................. (b) ChrisHayes 9 82
(Patrick Martin, Ire) *in tch: hdwy in 8th over 2f out to chse ldrs in 3rd ins fnl f: no ex u.p nr fin and dropped to 4th cl home* **12/1**
**5** *¾* **Ability N Delivery**7 699 9-8-4 **66** oh1.............................. (p) WayneLordan 6 65
(Michael J Browne, Ire) *chsd ldrs: 5th 1/2-way: rdn under 2f out and no ex u.p in 5th ins fnl f: kpt on same pce* **33/1**
**6** *1 ¼* **Caspian Prince (IRE)**11 644 5-10-2 **92**.............................. (t) JosephO'Brien 4 86
(Tony Carroll) *trckd ldrs: cl 3rd 1/2-way: rdn 2f out and sn no imp on ldrs: kpt on one pce in 6th ins fnl f* **11/4**1
**7** *½* **Sylvan Mist (IRE)**28 413 4-9-8 **84**.............................. (tp) PatSmullen 10 76
(Edward Lynam, Ire) *in tch: pushed along in 9th into st: rdn and no imp on ldrs in 7th ins fnl f: kpt on one pce* **6/1**3
**8** *¾* **Harry Trotter (IRE)**14 618 5-9-5 **88**.............................. GaryHalpin(7) 5 78
(David Marnane, Ire) *in rr: pushed along into st and sn swtchd rt: kpt on one pce fnl 2f wout ever threatening* **8/1**
**9** *5 ½* **All Ablaze (IRE)**231 4266 4-9-2 **78**.............................. RoryCleary 8 48
(Damian Joseph English, Ire) *disp early tl settled bhd ldrs: dropped to 6th bef 1/2-way: rdn and wknd 2f out* **25/1**
**10** *4 ¾* **Baytown Kestrel**157 6731 3-8-4 **80**.............................. NGMcCullagh 3 27
(Brian Ellison) *trckd ldrs: cl 2nd 1/2-way: pushed along into st and sn no ex u.p: wknd and eased fr 2f out: stiff post r* **9/2**2

58.73s (58.73)
**WFA** 3 from 4yo+ 14lb 10 Ran SP% **122.0**
CSF £51.45 CT £406.21 TOTE £3.80: £1.30, £3.00, £3.00; DF 36.20 Trifecta £279.70.
**Owner** John James Feane **Bred** Churchtown House Stud **Trained** Kildare, Co Kildare

**FOCUS**
A competitive sprint won in a good time - 58.73 seconds, which was over half a second quicker than the course average.

## 790a CROWNE PLAZA HOTEL RACE & STAY H'CAP 7f (P)
7:15 (7:16) 4-Y-O+ £4,600 (£1,066; £466; £266)

RPR
**1** **Reckless Lad (IRE)**49 132 4-9-1 **65**.............................. (t) AndrewPThornton(3) 1 71
(Patrick Martin, Ire) *in rr of mid-div: 9th 1/2-way: hdwy over 2f out and clsd far side to chal 1 1/2f out: led ent fnl f and styd on wl* **4/1**1
**2** *1 ¼* **Connacht Council (IRE)**233 4187 4-10-0 **75**.............................. (bt) PatSmullen 13 78
(W McCreery, Ire) *chsd ldrs: 4th 1/2-way: rdn in 5th over 1f out and clsd u.p ins fnl f into nvr nrr 2nd fnl stride: nt trble wnr* **15/2**
**3** *shd* **Cheers Buddy (IRE)**21 522 6-9-4 **65**.............................. ChrisHayes 3 68
(Lee Smyth, Ire) *racd in mid-div: 6th 1/2-way: tk clsr order 2f out: sn rdn to chal: wnt 2nd u.p ins fnl f where swtchd rt: no imp on wnr nr fin and denied 2nd fnl stride* **11/2**2
**4** *½* **Badger Daly (IRE)**35 326 8-8-3 **57**.............................. (tp) RossCoakley(7) 10 58
(J R Hagan, Ire) *chsd ldrs tl led after 1f: 3 l clr 1/2-way: reduced advantage 2f out: sn rdn and hdd ent fnl f: no ex u.p and dropped to 4th nr fin* **22/1**

5 1 1/2 **Amazing Star (IRE)**18 562 9-9-2 63......................(t) SeamieHeffernan 2 60
(Denis Gerard Hogan, Ire) *hld up towards rr: prog 2f out into mod 7th 1f: kpt on towards fin: nvr nrr* **10/1**
6 1 1/4 **Ocean Legend (IRE)**25 464 9-9-12 73...................... JosephO'Brien 6 67
(Tony Carroll) *led tl hdd after 1f: 3rd 1/2-way: rdn in 2nd 1 1/2f out and sn no ex u.p: dropped to 6th ins fnl f* **4/1**1
7 2 **Victor's Beach (IRE)**21 520 4-9-10 74.................(bt1) ShaneBKelly(3) 4 63
(M Halford, Ire) *on toes befhand: towards rr: rdn over 2f out and no imp on ldrs in mod 8th ent fnl f: kpt on one pce* **12/1**
8 1 3/4 **Cash Or Casualty (IRE)**21 520 6-9-12 80............(t) LukeDempsey(7) 5 64
(Damian Joseph English, Ire) *hld up: rdn in 11th into st and no imp 2f out: kpt on ins fnl f* **8/1**
9 1/2 **Rigid Rock (IRE)**219 4645 7-8-13 60........................... KevinManning 12 42
(J T Gorman, Ire) *chsd ldrs: 5th 1/2-way: sn pushed along and no ex u.p: wknd fnl 2f* **28/1**
10 hd **Blue Bullet (IRE)**7 701 4-9-11 72........................... MichaelHussey 7 54
(V C Ward, Ire) *chsd ldr in 2nd: rdn and no ex over 2f out: sn wknd* **7/1**3
11 1 3/4 **Pierre D'Or (IRE)**7 701 5-9-3 64.............................. ColmO'Donoghue 8 41
(J T Gorman, Ire) *dwlt and racd towards rr thrght: one pce fnl 2f* **14/1**
12 1 1/2 **Missile Command (IRE)**35 326 6-9-1 62.......(p) EmmetMcNamara 11 35
(Jane M Foley, Ire) *w.w: 8th 1/2-way: rdn and no imp fr 2f out: one pce fnl f* **25/1**
13 3 1/2 **Lightening Stricks (IRE)**119 7672 7-9-5 71..............(t) ConnorKing(5) 9 35
(M J Tynan, Ire) *racd in mid-div: 7th 1/2-way: rdn and wknd fr over 2f out: eased fnl f* **16/1**

1m 24.63s (84.63) **13** Ran SP% **131.7**
CSF £37.18 CT £183.29 TOTE £5.40: £2.10, £2.70, £2.10; DF 29.80 Trifecta £199.50.
**Owner** Derek Molloy **Bred** Ms Patricia Walsh **Trained** Navan, Co Meath

**FOCUS**
Reasonably competitive and the gallop was generous from the outset. Those who were held up benefited.

## 794a JACK'S BIG NIGHT H'CAP 1m 4f (P)
9:15 (9:17) (47-65,69) 4-Y-0+ £4,025 (£933; £408; £233)

RPR
1 **Waving**7 695 5-10-4 69......................................(t) JosephO'Brien 2 73+
(Tony Carroll) *w.w towards rr: 12th 1/2-way: plenty to do appr st: swtchd lft over 2f out and clsd far side to chal ent fnl f: led u.p fnl 100yds and wnt clr nr fin* **6/4**1
2 1 1/4 **Armed Guard (IRE)**28 420 5-9-1 52...............................(t) ChrisHayes 4 54+
(Edward Lynam, Ire) *hld up in rr: plenty to do appr st: sn pushed along and clsd u.p fr 2f out: rdn into 3rd ins fnl f and kpt on wl to go 2nd nr fin: nt trble wnr* **13/2**
3 nk **Only One Galileo (IRE)**138 7231 4-8-0 50..............(t) SeanCorby(10) 12 51+
(J J Lambe, Ire) *hld up in tch: 8th 1/2-way: hdwy between horses over 1f out: r.o wl: nrst fin* **33/1**
4 shd **Boronia (IRE)**28 420 4-8-8 48......................................... NGMcCullagh 8 49
(Charles O'Brien, Ire) *attempted to make all: rdn and stl 2 l clr over 1f out: sn strly pressed and hdd fnl 100yds: sn no ex in 3rd and and dropped to 4th fnl stride* **14/1**
5 3/4 **Akinspirit (IRE)**28 419 10-9-9 60....................................(t) BillyLee 10 60
(Michael Butler, Ire) *chsd ldr: 2nd 1/2-way: rdn fr 2f out and no imp u.p in 4th ins fnl f: dropped to 5th nr fin* **25/1**
6 hd **Juara (IRE)**14 620 4-9-1 62...................................... LukeDempsey(7) 14 61
(Anthony Mulholland, Ire) *hld up in tch: 7th 1/2-way: rdn on outer fr 2f out and no imp on ldrs ins fnl f: kpt on same pce* **6/1**3
7 1/2 **Boxer Beat (IRE)**124 3750 7-8-12 49.............................. FergalLynch 1 48
(Paul W Flynn, Ire) *in rr of mid-div: 9th 1/2-way: rdn far side fr 2f out and wnt 4th briefly u.p over 1f out: sn no ex u.p: wknd* **16/1**
8 nk **General Bunching (USA)**7 704 6-9-3 54.......................(t) RoryCleary 6 52
(Thomas Cleary, Ire) *hld up in tch: 6th 1/2-way: rdn and no ex u.p over 1f out: kpt on one pce* **12/1**
9 nse **Palace Art (IRE)**154 6817 4-8-10 57........................ RobbieDowney(7) 11 55
(Peter Casey, Ire) *towards rr: 12th 1/2-way: hdwy fr 2f out: sn n.m.r bhd horses: swtchd lft ent fnl f and kpt on u.p towards fin* **10/1**
10 1/2 **Horsewithnoname (IRE)**7 705 7-9-5 59..................(p) ColinKeane(3) 5 56
(T G McCourt, Ire) *hld up: 11th 1/2-way: rdn on outer over 2f out and no imp ent fnl f: kpt on one pce* **11/2**2
11 1 3/4 **Charpoy (USA)**7 705 6-8-13 55...............................(tp) GaryPhillips(5) 9 50
(Lee Smyth, Ire) *chsd ldrs: 5th 1/2-way: rdn and wknd 2f out* **33/1**
12 nk **House Limit (IRE)**7 704 5-9-4 55...............................(p) KevinManning 7 49
(J Larkin, Ire) *chsd ldrs: 3rd 1/2-way: rdn and wknd fr 2f out* **14/1**
13 1 1/2 **Danequest (IRE)**13 8010 5-8-10 47............................. WayneLordan 13 39
(Rodger Sweeney, Ire) *chsd ldrs on outer: t.k.h: 4th 1/2-way: pushed along in 3rd 3f out: sn no ex u.p: wknd fr 2f out* **20/1**
14 11 **The Frog Prince (IRE)**35 330 10-8-7 47..................... LeighRoche(3) 3 21
(Sabrina J Harty, Ire) *in rr of mid-div: sme hdwy fr 4f out: rdn into st and no ex: wknd and eased fr 2f out* **40/1**

2m 32.37s (152.37)
**WFA** 4 from 5yo+ 3lb **14** Ran SP% **135.9**
Pick Six: Part won. 17,500.00euro to a 1 euro stake. Tote Aggregate: 2014: 127,393.04euro - 2013: 105,092.39euro. CSF £12.48 CT £273.09 TOTE £3.30: £1.70, £1.90, £16.70; DF 23.40 Trifecta £1055.00.
**Owner** Carl Hodgson **Bred** Theakston Stud **Trained** Cropthorne, Worcs

**FOCUS**
A shrewd move by Tony Carroll to bring across his prolific five-year-old Waving who completed the five-timer.
T/Jkpt: Not won. T/Plt: @46.40. Pool of @34,104.25 - 514.12 winning units. BF

789 - 794a (Foreign Racing) - See Raceform Interactive

# CHANTILLY (R-H)
Friday, February 28
**OFFICIAL GOING: Polytrack: standard**

## 795a PRIX DES TROIS CLAIRIERES (MAIDEN) (3YO) (POLYTRACK) 6f 110y
12:50 (12:00) 3-Y-0 £10,000 (£4,000; £3,000; £2,000; £1,000)

RPR
1 **Ravisseur**216 3-9-2 0................................................... OlivierPeslier 1 101
(F Head, France) **17/5**1
2 6 **Cinquante Nuances (IRE)**22 3-9-2 0.............................. MaximeGuyon 4 83
(Mme Pia Brandt, France) **6/1**3
3 snk **Zantenor (FR)**22 3-9-2 0.............................. Pierre-CharlesBoudot 12 83
(Yves de Nicolay, France) **13/2**
4 1 **Chameur (FR)**94 3-9-2 0.................................................... AlexisBadel 5 80
(Mme M Bollack-Badel, France) **9/2**2
5 nse **Amistades (IRE)** 3-8-13 0................................ StephanePasquier 15 77
(F-X De Chevigny, France) **9/1**
6 1/2 **Square Lamartine (FR)**48 3-9-2 0.....................(p) AurelienLemaitre 6 79
(M Boutin, France) **17/1**
7 1/2 **Such Fun (IRE)** 3-8-13 0..................................................... RonanThomas 11 74
(F-H Graffard, France) **26/1**
8 3/4 **Diamant De Vati (FR)**46 169 3-9-2 0.............................. TheoBachelot 13 75
(S Wattel, France) **20/1**
9 2 **Taleteller (USA)**207 5068 3-8-13 0..............................(p) FabriceVeron 2 66
(H-A Pantall, France) **12/1**
10 3/4 **Linda Garota (FR)**22 3-8-7 0.......................... MllePaulineDominois(6) 8 64
(Mlle V Bougeard, France) **97/1**
11 3 **Haut De L'Affiche (FR)**28 3-8-13 0..................................... FabienLefebvre 9 55
(F Vermeulen, France) **98/1**
12 snk **Rinaldo (FR)**61 3-9-2 0............................................... AnthonyCrastus 10 58
(I Endaltsev, Czech Republic) **54/1**
13 2 **Chesieres (FR)** 3-8-13 0.............................................. ThomasMessina 3 49
(A Le Duff, France) **107/1**
14 shd **Really Wild** 3-8-13 0................................................... IoritzMendizabal 7 49
(X Thomas-Demeaulte, France) **78/10**
15 10 **Soul Of Motion**13 630 3-9-2 0...................................... AntoineHamelin 14 23
(Gay Kelleway) *racd in midfield on outer: c wd and lost pl on bnd: rdn and no imp over 2f out: eased and lost tch ins fnl f* **29/1**

1m 17.0s (77.00) **15** Ran SP% **119.7**
WIN (incl. 1 euro stake): 4.40. PLACES: 2.00, 2.20, 2.30. DF: 15.80. SF: 30.50.
**Owner** Wertheimer & Frere **Bred** Wertheimer Et Frere **Trained** France

## 796a PRIX DE LASSY (H'CAP) (4YO) (POLYTRACK) 7f
2:55 (12:00) 4-Y-0 £8,333 (£3,333; £2,500; £1,666; £833)

RPR
1 **Calamari (FR)**28 4-9-2 0............................................... IoritzMendizabal 6 90
(X Thomas-Demeaulte, France) **3/1**1
2 2 **Contesurmoi (FR)**22 4-8-0 0.............................................. AlexisBadel 3 69
(D De Waele, France) **21/1**
3 2 **Early Run Run (FR)**271 4-8-8 0..................................... FabienLefebvre 8 72
(M Le Forestier, France) **47/1**
4 3/4 **Reine Marie (FR)**35 4-9-2 0......................................(p) AnthonyCrastus 4 78
(F Chappet, France) **8/1**3
5 1 **Barri Gotic (FR)**133 4-8-4 0.................................. ValentinGambart(5) 15 68
(M Boutin, France) **71/1**
6 2 **Keep The Dream**6 722 4-7-13 0...................................... JimmyTastayre(1) 2 53
(N Caullery, France) **17/2**
7 snk **Gaiete (FR)**86 4-9-5 0..................................................... RonanThomas 5 72
(A Bonin, France) **46/1**
8 snk **Cassini (FR)**28 4-9-5 0..............................................(p) MaximeGuyon 16 72
(Mme Pia Brandt, France) **43/10**2
9 3/4 **Fair Moon (FR)**6 4-9-6 0................................................ ThierryThulliez 7 71
(D Smaga, France) **83/10**
10 hd **Whipper Snapper (FR)**22 4-8-13 0.................................... JeromeCabre 1 63
(J-V Toux, France) **20/1**
11 1/2 **Knight Charm**6 722 4-8-7 0............................................... SylvainRuis 12 56
(Gay Kelleway) *midfield: rdn and no imp over 2f out: sme prog ins fnl f: nvr in contention* **46/1**
12 3/4 **Chaudhary (SWI)**22 4-9-1 0........................................ StephanePasquier 11 62
(M Boutin, France) **9/1**
13 nse **Jeremy Road (FR)**28 4-8-9 0........................................... EddyHardouin 14 56
(D Darlix, France) **22/1**
14 1/2 **Lakritze (FR)**149 4-9-5 0.................................................. TheoBachelot 9 64
(E Libaud, France) **25/1**
15 1 **Holy Cesar** 4-8-6 0...................................................... ValentinSeguy(3) 10 52
(C Gourdain, France) **30/1**
16 1 3/4 **Karadargent (FR)**22 4-9-2 0......................................... AntoineHamelin 13 54
(M Boutin, France) **16/1**

1m 25.1s (85.10) **16** Ran SP% **120.6**
WIN (incl. 1 euro stake): 4.00. PLACES: 2.20, 5.40, 11.60. DF: 49.80. SF: 71.20.
**Owner** Roberto Cocheteux Tierno **Bred** Ecurie Serge Bernereau Sarl **Trained** France

# 774 LINGFIELD (L-H)
Saturday, March 1
**OFFICIAL GOING: Standard**
Wind: virtually nil Weather: cloudy, dry

## 797 BEST ODDS AT BOOKMAKERS.CO.UK H'CAP 5f 6y(P)
1:10 (1:11) (Class 6) (0-55,55) 4-Y-0+ £2,726 (£805; £402) Stalls High

Form RPR
-054 1 **Dishy Guru**27 449 5-9-5 53..........................................(b) LiamKeniry 8 63
(Michael Blanshard) *towards rr: jostling match w rivals after 1f: hdwy into midfield and travelling wl 1/2-way: effrt to chal 1f out: rdn to ld wl ins fnl f: comf* **9/4**1
3/45 2 1 **Dissent (IRE)**25 478 5-9-7 55........................................(b1) TomQueally 6 61
(James Given) *dwlt: sn rcvrd and in tch in midfield: hdwy to chse ldrs and drvn wl over 1f out: led fnl 100yds: sn hdd and one pce towards fin* **5/1**3
00-0 3 hd **Sarah Berry**36 313 5-9-4 52.............................................(v) AdamKirby 4 58
(Chris Dwyer) *chsd ldrs: effrt u.p to press ldrs 1f out: kpt on same pce fnl 100yds* **16/1**
5-10 4 3/4 **Volcanic Dust (IRE)**26 466 6-9-6 54....................(t) RichardKingscote 5 57
(Milton Bradley) *pressed ldr: rdn to ld 1f out: hdd fnl 100yds: no ex and wknd towards fin* **12/1**
4-00 4 dht **Outbid**27 448 4-9-3 51....................................................... LukeMorris 10 54
(Tony Carroll) *stuck wd: hld up towards rr: rdn and effrt over 1f out: r.o wl ins fnl f: nt rch ldrs* **25/1**
5203 6 hd **Your Gifted (IRE)**5 730 7-9-7 55...............................(v) HayleyTurner 3 59
(Lisa Williamson) *stdd s: t.k.h: hld up in last trio: jostling match w rivals after 1f: hmpd and swtchd rt wl over 2f out: hdwy 1f out: styd on wl fnl 100yds: nt rch ldrs* **11/4**2
0-60 7 1 **Green Millionaire**27 449 4-9-2 50.................................(t) RobertWinston 2 49
(Jeremy Gask) *in tch in midfield: swtchd lft wl over 2f out: rdn and effrt over 1f out: kpt on same pce and no imp ins fnl f* **10/1**

-600 **8** *hd* **Spic 'n Span**[8] 694 9-9-2 **50**..........(b) LiamJones 9 48
(Ronald Harris) *taken down early: awkward as stalls opened and slowly away: sn rcvrd and in tch in midfield: rdn 2f out: no ex 1f out: wknd ins fnl f* **33/1**

14-4 **9** *½* **College Doll**[50] 114 5-9-5 **53**..........(t) AdamBeschizza 1 49
(Christine Dunnett) *sn bustled up to ld: rdn over 1f out: drvn and hdd 1f out: wknd ins fnl f* **7/1**

3123 **10** *¾* **Ishetoo**[8] 693 10-8-12 **49**.......... SladeO'Hara(3) 7 42
(Peter Grayson) *sn bhd: rdn over 1f out: styd on ins fnl f: n.d* **14/1**

58.87s (0.07) **Going Correction** 0.0s/f (Stan) **10** Ran SP% **122.7**
Speed ratings (Par 101): **99,97,97,95,95 95,93,93,92,91**
CSF £14.81 CT £152.30 TOTE £3.30: £1.10, £1.70, £5.20; EX 19.30 Trifecta £188.90.
**Owner** Clifton Partners **Bred** J W Ford **Trained** Upper Lambourn, Berks

**FOCUS**
A moderate sprint handicap in which several still had a chance entering the last furlong.

## 798 COMPARE BOOKMAKERS AT BOOKMAKERS.CO.UK H'CAP (DIV I) 6f 1y(P)
**1:40** (1:40) (Class 6) (0-55,55) 4-Y-0+ **£2,726** (£805; £402) **Stalls** Low

Form RPR

-550 **1** **Catalinas Diamond (IRE)**[15] 603 6-9-6 **54**..........(t) AdamKirby 5 62
(Pat Murphy) *hld up in last pair: gd hdwy towards inner over 1f out: rdn to ld ins fnl f: r.o strly: drvn out* **11/4**[1]

-062 **2** *½* **Rose Garnet (IRE)**[19] 556 6-9-4 **52**..........(t) LukeMorris 1 58
(Tony Carroll) *rrd as stalls opened and s.i.s: sn in tch in midfield and t.k.h: hdwy and pushed rt jst over 1f out: pressed wnr ins fnl f: kpt on* **9/2**[3]

0253 **3** *nk* **Welsh Inlet (IRE)**[8] 687 6-9-0 **53**.......... RyanWhile(5) 7 58
(John Bridger) *s.i.s: hld up towards rr: hdwy on outer to chse ldrs 2f out: drvn and bmpd jst over 1f out: kpt on ins fnl f* **9/2**[3]

-400 **4** *½* **Microlight**[8] 687 6-8-12 **46** oh1.......... JimmyQuinn 2 50
(John E Long) *chsd ldrs: effrt u.p to chal 1f out: no ex and outpcd but wnr fnl 75yds: wknd towards fin* **16/1**

-030 **5** *1* **Belle Bayardo (IRE)**[22] 511 6-9-7 **55**.......... LiamJones 3 56
(Ronald Harris) *t.k.h: hld up in tch in midfield: shuffled bk towards rr 2f out: kpt on u.p ins fnl f: no threat to ldrs* **4/1**[2]

6-06 **6** *nk* **Renoir's Lady**[27] 448 6-9-4 **52**.......... GeorgeBaker 8 52
(Joseph Tuite) *hld up towards rr: effrt over 1f out: nvr much room ins fnl f: kpt on but nvr able to chal* **6/1**

0540 **7** *nk* **Sherjawy (IRE)**[16] 586 10-8-9 **46** oh1..........(p) RossAtkinson(3) 9 45
(Zoe Davison) *bhd: effrt u.p on inner over 1f out: kpt on but nvr gng pce to rch ldrs* **33/1**

04-5 **8** *½* **Demoiselle Bond**[29] 402 6-9-0 **48**.......... RobertHavlin 4 45
(Lydia Richards) *taken down early: led: rdn over 1f out: hdd ins fnl f: sn wknd* **12/1**

/-50 **9** *¾* **Sweet Piccolo**[17] 575 4-8-7 **46** oh1..........(b) JoeyHaynes(5) 6 41
(Paddy Butler) *chsd ldr: rdn and edgd rt over 1f out: wknd ins fnl f* **100/1**

1m 12.33s (0.43) **Going Correction** 0.0s/f (Stan) **9** Ran SP% **114.8**
Speed ratings (Par 101): **97,96,95,95,93 93,93,92,91**
CSF £15.15 CT £53.36 TOTE £3.60: £1.20, £1.40, £2.00; EX 16.90 Trifecta £49.20.
**Owner** Briton International **Bred** Sean Gorman **Trained** East Garston, Berks

**FOCUS**
Another moderate sprint handicap.

## 799 COMPARE BOOKMAKERS AT BOOKMAKERS.CO.UK H'CAP (DIV II) 6f 1y(P)
**2:15** (2:15) (Class 6) (0-55,55) 4-Y-0+ **£2,726** (£805; £402) **Stalls** Low

Form RPR

-050 **1** **Johnny Splash (IRE)**[35] 340 5-9-4 **52**..........(v) JamieSpencer 8 61
(Roger Teal) *mde all: rdn over 1f out: in command fnl f: r.o wl: rdn out* **7/2**[2]

5-04 **2** *1 ¼* **Diamond Vine (IRE)**[16] 586 6-9-0 **48**..........(p) LukeMorris 1 53
(Ronald Harris) *chsd wnr: rdn and swtchd out rt wl over 1f out: drvn and kpt on same pce ins fnl f* **4/1**[3]

4-02 **3** *1 ¼* **Hinton Admiral**[8] 687 10-9-5 **53**.......... AdamKirby 9 55
(Pat Eddery) *s.i.s: hld up in last trio: hmpd bnd wl over 1f out: hdwy on outer over 1f out: styd on u.p to go 3rd cl home: no ch w wnr* **3/1**[1]

-034 **4** *½* **Metropolitan Chief**[8] 687 10-8-13 **52**..........(p) DavidKenny(5) 3 52
(Paul Burgoyne) *hld up in last trio: hdwy on inner to chse ldng pair 1f out: kpt on but no real imp: lost 3rd cl home* **8/1**

6-65 **5** *¾* **Absolute Bearing (IRE)**[9] 676 5-8-12 **46** oh1.......... JamesSullivan 10 44
(Tim Etherington) *in tch in midfield: rdn and unable qck 2f out: no treat to wnr but kpt on ins fnl f* **16/1**

00-0 **6** *2 ¾* **Senora Lobo (IRE)**[16] 592 4-8-7 **46** oh1.......... ShirleyTeasdale(5) 2 36
(Lisa Williamson) *in tch in midfield: rdn and no hdwy over 1f out: wknd fnl f* **33/1**

6300 **7** *1 ¾* **Ghostwing**[16] 587 7-9-0 **55**..........(t[1]) KieranShoemark(7) 6 39
(Luke Dace) *stdd s: t.k.h: hld up in rr: rdn and no real hdwy 2f out: n.d* **9/2**

0260 **8** *¾* **Waterloo Dock**[8] 688 9-9-2 **50**..........(v) AndreaAtzeni 5 32
(Mick Quinn) *chsd ldrs: rdn and btn over 1f out: lost 3rd 1f out and wknd fnl f* **8/1**

1m 11.66s (-0.24) **Going Correction** 0.0s/f (Stan) **8** Ran SP% **116.4**
Speed ratings (Par 101): **101,99,97,97,96 92,90,89**
CSF £18.33 CT £46.74 TOTE £5.80: £2.00, £2.20, £1.50; EX 19.60 Trifecta £69.20.
**Owner** Barry Kitcherside **Bred** J Connolly **Trained** Ashtead, Surrey

**FOCUS**
Another sprint handicap with the top weight rated 55, in which the winning time was 0.67sec quicker than the first division.

## 800 32RED.COM MAIDEN FILLIES' STKS 1m 1y(P)
**2:50** (2:50) (Class 5) 3-Y-0+ **£3,408** (£1,006; £503) **Stalls** High

Form RPR

0-3 **1** **Trust The Wind**[12] 645 3-8-6 0.......... RobertHavlin 5 73+
(John Gosden) *in tch in midfield: trckd ldng pair 3f out: rdn and swtchd rt over 1f out: styd on u.p fnl f to ld cl home* **7/2**[2]

350- **2** *nk* **Halljoy (IRE)**[161] 6645 3-8-6 93.......... LukeMorris 4 72
(Clive Brittain) *chsd ldrs: wnt 2nd over 5f out: rdn and ev ch 2f out: hrd drvn to ld jst over 1f out: fnd little for press but forged ahd ins fnl f: hdd and no ex cl home* **1/3**[1]

5-0 **3** *1 ½* **Alpine Mist**[26] 456 4-9-10 0.......... FergusSweeney 6 75?
(Pat Murphy) *led: jnd over 2f out: rdn and hdd jst over 1f out: styd on same pce ins fnl f* **25/1**

**4** *8* **Sparkling Ice (IRE)** 3-8-6 0.......... JohnFahy 3 49
(Eve Johnson Houghton) *s.i.s: t.k.h: hld up in last pair: wnt 4th but struggling 3f out: sn outpcd and n.d after* **12/1**[3]

00 **5** *7* **Mrs Burbidge**[10] 660 4-9-10 0.......... LiamKeniry 1 39
(Neil Mulholland) *hld up in rr: 5th and outpcd over 2f out: wl bhd over 1f out* **66/1**

0- **6** *17* **Breezealong Riley**[142] 7154 5-9-7 0.......... RossAtkinson(3) 2
(Zoe Davison) *chsd ldr tl over 5f out: rdn and dropped to last 3f out: sn lost tch: t.o fnl f* **66/1**

1m 37.49s (-0.71) **Going Correction** 0.0s/f (Stan)
**WFA** 3 from 4yo+ 18lb **6** Ran SP% **111.8**
Speed ratings (Par 100): **103,102,101,93,86 69**
CSF £5.04 TOTE £5.60: £1.50, £1.10; EX 5.30 Trifecta £19.70.
**Owner** George Strawbridge **Bred** Highclere Stud & Ms Y Jacques **Trained** Newmarket, Suffolk

**FOCUS**
An uncompetitive maiden and something of a turn-up.

## 801 CORAL.CO.UK H'CAP 1m 4f (P)
**3:25** (3:25) (Class 5) (0-70,70) 4-Y-0+ **£3,408** (£1,006; £503) **Stalls** Low

Form RPR

5/42 **1** **Rowan Ridge**[26] 458 6-9-6 **69**.......... AmirQuinn 5 76
(William Knight) *mde all and dictated stdy gallop: rdn and qcknd 2f out: hld on wl ins fnl f: rdn out* **6/1**[2]

0-16 **2** *½* **My Lord**[30] 379 6-9-3 **66**.......... LukeMorris 11 72
(Luke Dace) *chsd ldr tl 6f out: rdn and effrt 2f out: ev ch ins fnl f: unable qck towards fin* **14/1**

6-00 **3** *hd* **Jewelled**[14] 627 8-9-5 **68**.......... WilliamCarson 1 74
(Ralph J Smith) *hld up in tch in midfield: rdn and effrt over 1f out: styd on wl u.p ins fnl f* **33/1**

5421 **4** *nk* **Standing Strong (IRE)**[4] 737 6-8-12 **61** 6ex..........(p) LiamKeniry 3 67+
(Zoe Davison) *hld up in tch in midfield: switching wd over 2f out: swtchd bk lft and hdwy 1f out: styd on wl ins fnl f* **8/1**

2214 **5** *nk* **Cabuchon (GER)**[4] 742 7-8-5 **61**.......... JoeDoyle(7) 10 66
(David Evans) *hld up in tch in midfield: rdn and effrt over 1f out: styd on u.p ins fnl f* **7/1**[3]

44-6 **6** *¾* **Enriching (USA)**[17] 583 6-9-3 **66**.......... TomQueally 9 70
(Gary Harrison) *chsd ldrs: wnt 2nd 6f out tl over 2f out: styd pressing ldrs tl outpcd fnl 100yds* **8/1**

5-04 **7** *½* **Innoko (FR)**[26] 458 4-9-2 **67**..........(t) DavidProbert 8 70
(Tony Carroll) *t.k.h: hld up wl in tch in midfield: rdn ent fnl 2f: hdwy u.p 1f out: styd on* **8/1**

06-0 **8** *2 ¼* **Thecornishcowboy**[14] 623 5-9-6 **69**..........(t) AdamKirby 2 69
(John Ryan) *chsd ldrs: hdwy and rdn pressed wnr over 2f out tl jst over 1f out: wknd ins fnl f* **11/4**[1]

353- **9** *1 ¾* **Akdam (IRE)**[37] 8184 4-8-11 **67**..........(p) JoeyHaynes(5) 4 64
(Tony Carroll) *hld up in tch in last pair: rdn and outpcd ent fnl 2f: plugged on but n.d after* **16/1**

00/0 **10** *3* **Swampfire (IRE)**[27] 450 6-9-7 **70**..........(v) GeorgeBaker 12 63
(Gary Moore) *hld up in tch in last quartet: switching wd wl over 2f out: lost pl and bhd 2f out: n.d after* **25/1**

-644 **11** *hd* **Zaeem**[17] 582 5-9-3 **66**.......... RobertWinston 7 58
(Dean Ivory) *stdd s: t.k.h: hld up in last trio: swtchd to outer over 3f out: rdn and outpcd wl over 1f out: n.d after* **7/1**[3]

-000 **12** *2* **Planetoid (IRE)**[17] 582 6-9-0 **70**..........[1] AprilKitchener(7) 6 59
(Jim Best) *stdd s: t.k.h: hld up in rr: lost tch whn gallop qcknd 2f out* **33/1**

2m 40.46s (7.46) **Going Correction** 0.0s/f (Stan)
**WFA** 4 from 5yo+ 2lb **12** Ran SP% **121.6**
Speed ratings (Par 103): **75,74,74,74,74 73,73,71,70,68 68,67**
CSF £87.50 CT £2554.15 TOTE £5.00: £1.90, £5.60, £12.90; EX 111.40 Trifecta £2065.30 Part won..
**Owner** Mr & Mrs N Welby **Bred** Rowan Farm Stud **Trained** Patching, W Sussex

**FOCUS**
An ordinary middle-distance handicap and not form to take literally as they dawdled through the early stages and it developed into a 3f sprint.

## 802 BOOKMAKERS.CO.UK H'CAP 5f 6y(P)
**4:00** (4:02) (Class 2) (0-105,102) 4-Y-0+ **£12,938** (£3,850; £1,924; £962) **Stalls** Low

Form RPR

03-5 **1** **Addictive Dream (IRE)**[12] 644 7-9-3 **98**.......... TonyHamilton 1 110
(David Nicholls) *mde all: shkn up and qcknd clr 1f out: in command and r.o wl fnl f: readily* **7/1**[3]

40-4 **2** *2 ¾* **Ubetterbegood (ARG)**[12] 644 6-8-10 **91**..........(p) JimmyQuinn 3 93
(Robert Cowell) *awkward leaving stalls: sn in tch in midfield: rdn and effrt over 1f out: kpt on u.p to go 2nd last stride: no ch w wnr* **16/1**

1-30 **3** *shd* **Ballista (IRE)**[7] 713 6-9-7 **102**.......... RichardKingscote 8 104
(Tom Dascombe) *chsd wnr: rdn over 1f out: drvn and outpcd by wnr 1f out: no ch w wnr but kpt on: lost 2nd last stride* **3/1**[1]

4303 **4** *½* **Diamond Charlie (IRE)**[7] 719 6-8-4 **85**.......... LukeMorris 6 85
(Simon Dow) *hld up in tch in last trio: rdn and effrt over 1f out: styd on wl u.p ins fnl f: no threat to wnr* **8/1**

6-54 **5** *shd* **Picansort**[21] 532 7-8-4 **85**..........(b) AndreaAtzeni 9 84
(Peter Crate) *s.i.s: bhd: rdn over 1f out: styd on wl ins fnl f: nvr trbld ldrs* **8/1**

2132 **6** *hd* **Silken Express (IRE)**[12] 644 5-9-2 **97**.......... AdamKirby 4 96
(Robert Cowell) *chsd ldrs: rdn and effrt 2f out: drvn and outpcd jst over 1f out: no ch w wnr and kpt on same pce fnl f* **9/2**[2]

6-10 **7** *1 ¼* **Swiss Cross**[12] 644 7-9-3 **98**..........(t) PaddyAspell 10 92
(Phil McEntee) *in tch in midfield but stuck wd: rdn and unable qck wl over 1f out: styd on same pce and no ch w wnr fnl f* **25/1**

-601 **8** *shd* **Taajub (IRE)**[7] 719 7-8-9 **90**.......... ShaneKelly 2 84
(Peter Crate) *chsd ldrs: effrt u.p but unable qck on inner over 1f out: wknd ins fnl f* **9/2**[2]

0-30 **9** *½* **Woolfall Sovereign (IRE)**[21] 534 8-8-13 **94**.......... TomQueally 5 86
(George Margarson) *dwlt and bustled along early: in tch in last trio: rdn and no real hdwy over 1f out: n.d* **8/1**

57.15s (-1.65) **Going Correction** 0.0s/f (Stan) **9** Ran SP% **116.9**
Speed ratings (Par 109): **113,108,108,107,107 107,105,105,104**
CSF £111.51 CT £411.25 TOTE £9.90: £2.60, £3.70, £1.30; EX 70.30 Trifecta £712.50.
**Owner** Brian Morton & Pinnacle Dream Partnership **Bred** Eugene Matthews **Trained** Sessay, N Yorks

**FOCUS**
A cracking 85-102 sprint handicap and, not surprisingly, they didn't hang about. Not many got into it.

## 803 32RED CONDITIONS STKS (FAST TRACK QUALIFIER) 1m 7f 169y(P)
**4:35** (4:36) (Class 2) 4-Y-0+ **£16,172** (£4,812; £2,405; £1,202) **Stalls** Low

Form RPR

21- **1** **Litigant**[84] 8202 6-9-2 96.......... GeorgeBaker 2 100+
(Seamus Durack) *hld up wl in tch in midfield: gng wl and nt clr run wl over 1f out: swtchd rt over 1f out: swtchd bk lft ins fnl f: qcknd wl u.p to ld towards fin: r.o wl* **2/1**[1]

360- **2** ½ **Noble Silk**[192] 5655 5-9-2 90....(p) LukeMorris 5 97
(Lucy Wadham) *hld up wl in tch in midfield: rdn and effrt ent fnl 2f: kpt on wl u.p ins fnl f: wnt 2nd on post* **14/1**

312- **3** nse **Duchess Of Gazeley (IRE)**[120] 7659 4-8-6 86.... JimmyQuinn 7 92
(Dean Ivory) *wl in tch in midfield: rdn over 2f out: hdwy u.p to ld jst ins fnl f: hdd and no ex towards fin: lost 2nd on post* **16/1**

5-23 **4** 1¼ **Communicator**[26] 462 6-9-2 90.... DavidProbert 3 96
(Andrew Balding) *hld up in tch in last quartet: rdn and effrt 2f out: hdwy between horses 1f out: chsd ldrs ins fnl f: kpt on same pce fnl 100yds* **5/1**[3]

2-12 **5** ¾ **Castilo Del Diablo (IRE)**[43] 212 5-9-2 98.... JamieSpencer 11 95
(David Simcock) *stdd s: hld up in tch in rr: clsng but forced to switch rt ent fnl f: r.o strly ins fnl f: nt rch ldrs* **3/1**[2]

**6** 1¾ **Ranjaan (FR)**[13] 6-9-2 0....(t) TomQueally 10 94
(Paul Nicholls) *hld up in tch in last trio: hmpd and forced to switch arnd wkng rival 3f out: sn rdn: no imp tl styd on ins fnl f* **8/1**

46/3 **7** hd **Ted Spread**[38] 285 7-9-2 90....(t) AdamKirby 9 93
(Suzy Smith) *chsd ldrs: rdn to press ldr over 3f out: led 2f out and sn drvn: hdd jst ins fnl f: no ex and btn whn hmpd sn after: wknd towards fin* **10/1**

1-10 **8** 2¼ **Mr Burbidge**[38] 285 6-9-2 89....(b) LiamKeniry 6 90
(Neil Mulholland) *stdd s: hld up in rr tl hdwy to ld after 2f: jnd over 3f out: rdn and hdd 2f out: no ex ent fnl f: wknd fnl 150yds* **25/1**

22-1 **9** 5 **Be Perfect (USA)**[26] 462 5-9-2 94.... AdrianNicholls 4 84
(David Nicholls) *led for 2f: chsd ldrs: rdn to join ldr 3f out: ev ch after tl no ex jst ins fnl f: wknd fnl 150yds* **14/1**

500- **10** 2¾ **Tappanappa (IRE)**[248] 3685 7-9-2 90....(t) StephenCraine 1 81
(David Flood) *hld up in tch in rr: struggling over 3f out: bhd fnl 2f* **66/1**

21-6 **11** 39 **Theology**[38] 285 7-9-2 93.... FrederikTylicki 8 34
(Steve Gollings) *chsd ldr tl over 3f out: dropped out rapidly and sn bhd: t.o* **16/1**

3m 21.74s (-3.96) **Going Correction** 0.0s/f (Stan)
**WFA** 4 from 5yo+ 5lb **11** Ran SP% **125.6**
Speed ratings (Par 109): **109,108,108,108,107 106,106,105,103,101 82**
CSF £36.10 TOTE £3.40: £1.40, £4.40, £4.10; EX 55.80 Trifecta £664.50.
**Owner** A A Byrne **Bred** Darley **Trained** Baydon, Wilts

**FOCUS**
A 'Fast Track Qualifier' which guarantees the winner a place in the Marathon Championship Final back here on Good Friday. They went a solid if unspectacular pace and it produced a thrilling finish.

## 804 LADBROKES H'CAP — 1m 1y(P)
**5:10** (5:12) (Class 3) (0-95,95) 4-Y-O+ **£9,703** (£2,887; £1,443; £721) **Stalls High**

Form RPR

-640 **1** **True To Form (IRE)**[28] 426 7-9-1 **89**....(v¹) TomQueally 3 96
(Alan McCabe) *chsd ldrs: chsd clr ldr over 2f out: rdn and clsd over 1f out: led 1f out: hrd pressed wl ins fnl f: jst hld on* **12/1**

00- **2** shd **Atlantis Crossing (IRE)**[100] 7991 5-9-1 **89**.... AdamKirby 5 96
(Jim Boyle) *hld up off the pce in last pair: rdn and gd hdwy on inner over 1f out: str chal wl ins fnl f: r.o: jst hld* **16/1**

33-4 **3** 1 **Veeraya**[35] 342 4-8-5 **84**....(p) ShelleyBirkett(5) 4 88
(Julia Feilden) *racd off the pce in midfield: clsd u.p over 1f out: chsd ldrs and styd on same pce ins fnl f* **10/1**

3640 **4** nse **Verse Of Love**[7] 715 5-8-4 **85**.... JoeDoyle(7) 1 89
(David Evans) *racd off the pce in midfield: rdn and clsd on inner over 1f out: chsd ldrs and styd on same pce ins fnl f* **20/1**

400- **5** ½ **Spiritual Star (IRE)**[154] 6840 5-9-4 **92**.... WilliamCarson 11 97
(Anthony Carson) *stdd s: hld up wl off the pce in rr: clsd over 1f out: swtchd lft 1f out: pushed along and r.o strly ins fnl f: nt rch ldrs* **33/1**

0-41 **6** 1 **Dixie's Dream (IRE)**[26] 457 5-8-12 **91**.... RyanTate(5) 7 93
(William Jarvis) *hld up in midfield: stuck bhd wkng rival and shuffled bk wl over 1f out: swtchd rt over 1f out: r.o wl ins fnl f: unable to rch ldrs* **5/1**[2]

-401 **7** nk **Corporal Maddox**[25] 472 7-8-13 **87**....(p) LukeMorris 8 87
(Ronald Harris) *t.k.h: hld up off the pce in midfield: rdn and effrt over 1f out: no imp ins fnl f* **20/1**

100- **8** nk **Whispering Warrior (IRE)**[182] 6001 5-8-10 **91**.... GeorgeBuckell(7) 9 90+
(David Simcock) *racd in midfield and stuck wd: rdn and effrt wl over 1f out: nt clr run and swtchd rt jst ins fnl f: styd on: unable to rch ldrs* **11/4**[1]

5645 **9** 2¾ **Mia's Boy**[14] 625 10-8-10 **87**.... RobertTart(3) 6 80
(Chris Dwyer) *racd off the pce in midfield: rdn and effrt 2f out: no imp and styd on same pce fr over 1f out* **8/1**

60-0 **10** 1¼ **Burning Blaze**[36] 314 4-8-12 **86**....(b¹) JamieSpencer 12 76
(Olly Stevens) *led and sn clr: rdn over 1f out: hdd 1f out: fdd ins fnl f* **6/1**[3]

/34- **11** 9 **Unsinkable (IRE)**[301] 2023 4-9-7 **95**.... GeorgeBaker 2 63
(Jonjo O'Neill) *restless in stalls: chsd clr ldr tl over 2f out: lost pl qckly wl over 1f out: wl bhd and eased wl ins fnl f* **5/1**[2]

1m 35.98s (-2.22) **Going Correction** 0.0s/f (Stan) **11** Ran SP% **120.5**
Speed ratings (Par 107): **111,110,109,109,109 108,108,107,105,103 94**
CSF £186.70 CT £1999.76 TOTE £13.20: £3.70, £5.80, £2.60; EX 169.60 Trifecta £3521.80 Part won..
**Owner** Craig and Maureen Buckingham **Bred** Sir E J Loder **Trained** Averham Park, Notts

**FOCUS**
A decent handicap run at a strong pace.
T/Plt: £44.20 to a £1 stake. Pool of £95970.22 - 1583.29 winning tickets. T/Qpdt: £12.50 to a £1 stake. Pool of £6621.71 - 391.25 winning tickets. SP

# 169 DEAUVILLE (R-H)
Saturday, March 1

**OFFICIAL GOING: Fibresand: standard**

## 805a PRIX DE LESSARD-LE-CHENE (CLAIMER) (4YO) (FIBRESAND) — 7f 110y
**1:15** (12:00) 4-Y-0 **£7,916** (£3,166; £2,375; £1,583; £791)

RPR

**1** **Jubilee Brig**[15] 602 4-9-2 0....(b) ThierryJarnet 8 79
(Sean Curran) *broke wl but sn restrained and racd in midfield: rdn 2f out: r.o and led ins fnl 100yds: drvn out* **31/10**[1]

**2** nk **Artplace (IRE)**[292] 2334 4-9-1 0....(b) StephanePasquier 6 77
(C Ferland, France) **78/10**

**3** ½ **Windsea (IRE)**[15] 4-9-1 0.... OlivierPeslier 9 76
(Y Barberot, France) **135/10**

**4** ½ **Jolly Old Chap (FR)**[23] 4-9-6 0....(p) MaximeGuyon 11 80
(M Nigge, France) **68/10**

**5** snk **Wight Is Wight (IRE)**[64] 4-9-4 0.... IoritzMendizabal 13 77
(P Nicot, France) **17/5**[2]

**6** 1¾ **Toni Fortebracci (FR)**[15] 4-9-5 0.... SoufyaneMoulin(3) 3 77
(G Botti, France) **31/5**[3]

**7** hd **Ruby Wedding (FR)**[23] 4-8-11 0.... TheoBachelot 5 66
(G Nicot, France) **43/5**

**8** 3½ **Zaadig (FR)**[29] 4-9-1 0.... RonanThomas 10 61
(Y Barberot, France) **51/1**

**9** snk **Bottoms Up (IRE)**[64] 4-8-11 0....(b) SebastienMaillot 7 56
(Robert Collet, France) **158/10**

**10** 1¾ **Perrecalla (FR)**[23] 4-8-8 0.... WilliamsSaraiva 14 49
(D De Waele, France) **40/1**

**11** 1½ **Mlle Agapee (IRE)**[159] 4-8-11 0.... AnthonyCrastus 12 48
(J Rossi, France) **269/10**

**12** 2½ **Al Khisa (IRE)**[15] 4-8-8 0.... SylvainRuis 4 39
(G E Mikhalides, France) **93/1**

**13** 1½ **Valencia (SPA)**[15] 4-8-8 0.... AntonioFresu 1 35
(T Martins, Spain) **120/1**

**14** 2½ **Plovdiv (FR)**[29] 4-8-11 0.... JulienGuillochon(4) 2 36
(E Leenders, France) **72/1**

1m 29.08s (89.08) **14** Ran SP% **119.7**
WIN (incl. 1 euro stake): 4.10. PLACES: 2.00, 2.90, 3.50. DF: 16.20. SF: 28.30.
**Owner** Power Bloodstock Ltd **Bred** Sir Eric Parker **Trained** Hatford, Oxon

## 806a PRIX DE SAINT-JULIEN LE FAUCON (CLAIMER) (5YO+) (AMATEUR RIDERS) (FIBRESAND) — 7f 110y
**2:25** (12:00) 5-Y-0+ **£7,916** (£3,166; £2,375; £1,583; £791)

RPR

**1** **Silverheels (IRE)**[26] 457 5-10-8 0....(b) ClementLefebvre 6 82
(Paul Cole) *trckd ldrs: rdn to chal over 1f out: led ent fnl f and qckned clr: pushed out: readily* **36/5**

**2** 2 **Nova Valorem (IRE)**[23] 6-10-9 0.... MllePaulineBoisgontier 7 78
(Rod Collet, France) **31/10**[1]

**3** hd **Polar Kite (IRE)**[9] 677 6-9-11 0.... MissBHampson(4) 11 70
(Sean Curran) *midfield in tch: smooth hdwy 2f out: rdn over 1f out: wnt 2nd ins fnl f: kpt on and chsd wnr but no imp: dropped to 3rd post* **153/10**

**4** ½ **Mogadishio (FR)**[73] 7-10-6 0.... MrJeanDeMieulle(4) 3 77
(Mlle C Cardenne, France) **54/10**[3]

**5** 1¼ **Mister Segway (IRE)**[68] 6-9-12 0 ow1.... MrAlexisBreton(4) 8 66?
(Robert Collet, France) **63/1**

**6** snk **Handsome Maestro (IRE)**[23] 8-10-4 0.... MrFlorentGuy 1 68
(J Phelippon, France) **51/10**[2]

**7** ½ **Princess Vati (FR)**[20] 5-10-2 0.... MrEdouardMonfort 12 65
(P Monfort, France) **112/10**

**8** snk **Asulaman (GER)**[15] 7-10-6 0....(b) MrPierreJFertillet 4 68
(S Cerulis, France) **87/10**

**9** hd **Kings Canyon (FR)**[23] 7-10-10 0....(b) MrThibaultMarlin 9 72
(S Kobayashi, France) **15/1**

**10** ¾ **Malossol (USA)**[15] 5-10-8 0.... MlleJessicaMarcialis 10 68
(G Botti, France) **146/10**

**11** nk **Carlos Moheba (GER)**[912] 8-10-6 0.... MrTimoDegel 5 65
(R Storp, Germany) **58/1**

**12** 1 **Marangu (IRE)**[73] 8-10-0 0.... MrArthurPean(4) 13 61
(F Pedrono, France) **105/1**

**13** 1¼ **Samyntha (FR)**[36] 5-9-12 0.... MrGuilainBertrand 15 51
(M Maillard, France) **37/1**

**14** ½ **Whip My Heart (IRE)**[73] 5-10-1 0.... MlleDianaLopezLeret 16 53
(M Delcher Sanchez, France) **241/10**

**15** 3½ **Hearts And Minds (IRE)**[72] 5-10-10 0.... MlleBarbaraGuenet 2 53
(Braem Horse Racing Sprl, Belgium) **57/1**

**16** 20 **Mieuquebien (FR)** 6-9-11 0.... MlleMarieRollando(4) 14
(R Limayrac, France) **123/1**

1m 29.79s (89.79) **16** Ran SP% **119.3**
WIN (incl. 1 euro stake): 8.20. PLACES: 2.90, 2.10, 4.40. DF: 13.10. SF: 31.30.
**Owner** P F I Cole Ltd **Bred** Castlemartin Stud And Skymarc Farm **Trained** Whatcombe, Oxon

# 768 MEYDAN (L-H)
Saturday, March 1

**OFFICIAL GOING: Tapeta: standard; turf: good**

## 807a DISTRICT ONE PHASE II (H'CAP) (TAPETA) — 1m 2f
**2:45** (2:45) (100-112,112) 3-Y-0+
**£63,253** (£21,084; £10,542; £5,271; £3,162; £2,108)

RPR

**1** **Samurai Sword**[9] 681 6-8-9 **101**....(tp) MickaelBarzalona 2 106
(A bin Harmash, UAE) *settled in rr: smooth prog 2f out: led 1f out: comf* **9/1**

**2** 2 **Tanfeeth**[16] 598 6-8-8 **100**....(t) PaulHanagan 4 101
(M Al Muhairi, UAE) *sn led: hdd 2f out: r.o gamely: tk 2nd cl home* **16/1**

**3** ¾ **Plantagenet (SPA)**[9] 681 7-8-8 **100**.... Per-AndersGraberg 1 100+
(Niels Petersen, Norway) *trckd ldng pair: ev ch 2 1/2f out: one pce 2f out: r.o fnl 1 1/2f* **7/2**[3]

**4** nse **Ottoman Empire (FR)**[30] 394 8-8-11 **104**.... RichardMullen 6 102
(S Seemar, UAE) *s.i.s: trckd ldrs: led 2f out: hdd 1f out: one pce fnl 110yds* **15/8**[1]

**5** 6 **Busker (USA)**[16] 593 6-8-9 **101**....(t) AdriedeVries 3 88
(A bin Harmash, UAE) *settled in rr: nvr able to chal* **7/1**

**6** 3½ **Mickdaam (IRE)**[16] 595 5-9-6 **112**.... ChristopheSoumillon 5 92
(M F De Kock, South Africa) *mid-div: rdn 4f out: outpcd fnl 2 1/2f* **11/4**[2]

2m 9.2s (4.50) **6** Ran SP% **112.1**
CSF: 120.07; EXACTA: 58.30; TRIFECTA: 374.90; WIN: 10.40;.
**Owner** Sultan Ali **Bred** Darley **Trained** United Arab Emirates

**FOCUS**
Rail out 15m on Turf track. They went slowly early, but the pace picked up prematurely.

## 808a MEYDAN SOBHA (H'CAP) (TAPETA) 7f
**3:20** (3:20) (95-105,105) 3-Y-O+

**£39,759** (£13,253; £6,626; £3,313; £1,987; £1,325)

RPR
1 **Free Wheeling (AUS)**[9] 678 6-9-6 **105**................(t) SilvestreDeSousa 6 109
(Saeed bin Suroor) *trckd ldrs: led 1 1/2f out: r.o wl: comf* **7/1**
2 *1 ½* **Dragon Falls (IRE)**[9] 679 5-9-2 **100**....................... MickaelBarzalona 8 101
(Charlie Appleby) *mid-div: smooth prog 2 1/2f out: r.o fnl 1 1/2f but no ch w wnr* **11/2**[2]
3 *1* **Van Rooney (USA)**[9] 679 5-9-4 **102**............................(t) AdriedeVries 4 100
(Ali Jan, Qatar) *trckd ldng trio: ev ch 1f out: one pce fnl 110yds* **6/1**[3]
4 *nse* **Qatoomah (KSA)**[9] 679 5-9-4 **102**....................... WilliamBuick 9 101+
(N Bachalard, Saudi Arabia) *settled in rr: nvr nr to chal but r.o wl fnl 1 1/2f: nrst fin* **10/1**
5 *½* **Kaiss (USA)**[8] 711 7-9-2 **100**..................................(bt) RichardMullen 11 97
(S Seemar, UAE) *trckd ldng trio: ev ch 1 1/2f out: one pce fnl f* **14/1**
6 *1 ¼* **Ocean Tempest**[9] 679 5-9-4 **102**....................... BrettDoyle 12 95
(John Ryan) *trckd ldrs: t.k.h: ev ch 2 1/2f out: nt qckn fnl f* **10/1**
7 *1 ¼* **Banna Boirche (IRE)**[9] 679 8-9-0 **98**..........................(p) ShaneFoley 2 88
(M Halford, Ire) *a mid-div* **20/1**
8 *hd* **Yaa Wayl (IRE)**[13] 7-9-4 **102**..........................................(t) JamesDoyle 14 91
(D Selvaratnam, UAE) *nvr bttr than mid-div* **14/1**
9 *½* **Derbaas (USA)**[9] 679 8-9-2 **100**..................................(t) RoystonFfrench 5 88
(A Al Raihe, UAE) *nvr bttr than mid-div* **14/1**
10 *shd* **Well Acquainted (IRE)**[162] 6595 4-9-4 **102**....................... MartinLane 13 90
(Charlie Appleby) *sn led: hdd & wknd 1 1/2f out* **16/1**
11 *2 ¼* **Alnashmy (FR)**[23] 504 6-9-2 **100**..................................(tp) PatCosgrave 7 82
(J Peromingo, UAE) *mid-div: chsd ldrs 2 1/2f out: ev ch 1 1/2f out: wknd fnl f* **12/1**
12 *5 ½* **Mister Big Shuffle (GER)**[9] 679 4-9-1 **99**.......... Per-AndersGraberg 3 66
(Niels Petersen, Norway) *nvr bttr than mid-div* **25/1**
13 *35* **Bannock (IRE)**[210] 5013 5-9-2 **100**....................... AhmedAjtebi 10
(Charlie Appleby) *a in rr* **14/1**
U **Tamarkuz (USA)**[30] 396 4-9-6 **105**....................... PaulHanagan 1
(M Al Muhairi, UAE) *uns rdr at s* **9/2**[1]

1m 25.06s (-0.14) **14** Ran SP% **127.4**
CSF: 51.64; EXACTA: 41.00 TRICAST 258.97; TRIFECTA: 457.10; WIN: 6.00; PL: 2.10, 2.60, 2.60.
**Owner** Sheikh Ahmed bin Mohammed Al Maktoum **Bred** Darley **Trained** Newmarket, Suffolk
**FOCUS**
An ordinary handicap. The pace soon steadied, leaving the field well bunched turning into the straight, and it proved hard to make up significant ground. The winner is rated back to his best.

## 809a DISTRICT ONE (H'CAP) (TURF) 6f
**3:55** (3:55) (100-112,112) 3-Y-O+

**£63,253** (£21,084; £10,542; £5,271; £3,162; £2,108)

RPR
1 **Kavanagh (SAF)**[9] 678 7-9-1 **107**..................(tp) ChristopheSoumillon 6 111
(M F De Kock, South Africa) *mid-div: smooth prog 3f out: r.o fnl 1 1/2f: led nr line* **5/1**[2]
2 *nk* **Dux Scholar**[23] 509 6-9-1 **107**..........................................(b) PatDobbs 1 110
(Doug Watson, UAE) *mid-div: smooth prog to ld 2f out: hdd fnl strides* **8/1**
3 *1 ½* **Roicead (USA)**[30] 393 7-9-0 **106**..................................(t) JamesDoyle 7 104
(D Selvaratnam, UAE) *nvr far away: ev ch 1f out: one pce fnl 110yds* **5/1**[2]
4 *5 ¼* **Take Ten**[30] 393 7-8-10 **102**....................... RichardMullen 2 83
(S Seemar, UAE) *led far side: hdd 2f out: r.o same pce fnl 1 1/2f* **6/1**[3]
5 *3* **Nawwaar (USA)**[13] 5-9-6 **112**....................... PaulHanagan 5 84
(A Al Raihe, UAE) *chsd ldrs tl outpcd 1 1/2f out* **3/1**[1]
6 *1 ½* **Glass Office**[211] 4947 4-9-2 **108**....................... JimCrowley 8 75
(David Simcock) *s.i.s: nvr nr to chal* **3/1**[1]
7 *2* **Seachantach (USA)**[30] 393 8-8-7 **104** ow2.......(bt) MarcMonaghan(5) 3 64
(S Seemar, UAE) *s.i.s: trckd ldrs tl outpcd 2f out* **25/1**
8 *4 ½* **Silver Ocean (USA)**[23] 504 6-8-10 **102**....................(tp) WilliamBuick 4 48
(Niels Petersen, Norway) *s.i.s: a in rr* **25/1**

1m 9.74s (69.74) **8** Ran SP% **116.4**
CSF: 44.94; EXACTA: 21.20; TRICAST 207.78; TRIFECTA: 142.70; WIN: 3.30; PL: 1.40, 1.90, 2.60.
**Owner** Wilgerbosdrift Pty Ltd **Bred** Wilgerbosdrift **Trained** South Africa
**FOCUS**
The rail was out 15 metres on the turf course. The main action unfolded stands' side.

## 810a DISTRICT ONE PHASE I (H'CAP) (TAPETA) 1m
**4:30** (4:30) (100-110,110) 3-Y-O+

**£63,253** (£21,084; £10,542; £5,271; £3,162; £2,108)

RPR
1 **Capital Attraction (USA)**[16] 596 7-9-6 **110**....................... TadhgO'Shea 6 114
(Ernst Oertel, UAE) *trckd ldrs: rdn 3 1/2f out: led 1 1/2f out: comf* **7/1**[3]
2 *1 ¾* **Disa Leader (SAF)**[9] 679 9-9-0 **103** ow1.......... ChristopheSoumillon 1 104
(M F De Kock, South Africa) *settled in rr: rdn 3f out: r.o fnl 1 1/2f but no ch w wnr* **7/2**[2]
3 *1 ¼* **Rebel Song (IRE)**[9] 683 5-8-10 **100**..................................(t) AdriedeVries 3 97
(A bin Harmash, UAE) *in rr of mid-div: nvr able to chal but r.o fnl 2f* **14/1**
4 *¾* **Solar Deity (IRE)**[9] 681 5-9-4 **108**....................... MartinHarley 5 103
(Marco Botti) *settled in rr: nvr nr to chal but r.o fnl 2f* **7/2**[2]
5 *½* **Energizer (GER)**[44] 205 5-9-1 **105**....................... MickaelBarzalona 8 99
(Charlie Appleby) *sn led: hdd & wknd 1 1/2f out* **3/1**[1]
6 *nk* **Zain Shamardal (IRE)**[9] 681 6-9-2 **106**..................(t) RoystonFfrench 2 100
(A Al Raihe, UAE) *trckd ldng trio tl outpcd 2f out* **10/1**
7 *2 ¾* **Captain Joy (IRE)**[16] 595 5-9-1 **105**....................... GaryCarroll 7 92
(Tracey Collins, Ire) *trckd ldrs tl wknd 2f out* **7/1**[3]
8 *nk* **Mufarrh (IRE)**[16] 596 7-9-4 **108**....................... PaulHanagan 4 95
(A Al Raihe, UAE) *nvr bttr than mid-div* **9/1**

1m 37.65s (0.15) **8** Ran SP% **120.2**
CSF: 33.46; EXACTA: 39.30; TRICAST 343.61; TRIFECTA: 287.30; WIN: 7.00; PL: 1.70, 1.60, 4.40.
**Owner** H E Sheikh Sultan Bin Khalifa Al Nahyan **Bred** WinStar Farm LLC **Trained** United Arab Emirates

**FOCUS**
The pace slowed significantly rounding the bend into the straight. The winner is rated back to his best.

## 811a NAD AL SHEBA TROPHY SPONSORED BY DISTRICT ONE (GROUP 3) (TURF) 1m 6f 11y
**5:10** (5:10) 3-Y-O+

**£72,289** (£24,096; £12,048; £6,024; £3,614; £2,409)

RPR
1 **Cavalryman**[212] 4919 8-9-2 112....................... SilvestreDeSousa 4 117+
(Saeed bin Suroor) *trckd ldng trio: led 1 1/2f out: comf* **3/1**[1]
2 *5 ½* **Star Empire (SAF)**[23] 507 8-9-2 111.............. ChristopheSoumillon 12 109+
(M F De Kock, South Africa) *s.i.s: settled in rr: swtchd stands' side 2 1/2f out: r.o fnl 1 1/2f but no ch w wnr* **6/1**[2]
3 *1 ½* **Certerach (IRE)**[23] 507 6-9-2 107....................... ShaneFoley 9 107
(M Halford, Ire) *mid-div: r.o fnl 2f but no ch w wnr* **9/1**[3]
4 *1 ¼* **Jutland**[23] 507 7-9-2 104....................... PatDobbs 1 105
(Doug Watson, UAE) *trckd ldng pair: ev ch 1 1/2f out: nt qckn fnl f* **25/1**
5 *¾* **Simenon (IRE)**[83] 8208 7-9-2 113....................... RyanMoore 11 104
(W P Mullins, Ire) *settled in rr: nvr nr to chal but r.o fnl 2f* **3/1**[1]
6 *nk* **Model Pupil**[15] 5-9-2 104....................... LJurado 3 104
(A Mishreff, Saudi Arabia) *s.i.s: settled in rr: nvr nr to chal* **25/1**
7 *shd* **Moment In Time (IRE)**[9] 682 5-8-11 108....................... JimCrowley 8 99
(David Simcock) *nvr bttr than mid-div* **14/1**
8 *hd* **Renew (IRE)**[155] 6800 4-8-11 105....................... MartinHarley 10 103
(Marco Botti) *nvr bttr than mid-div* **9/1**[3]
9 *3* **Buckwheat**[16] 598 4-8-11 110....................... MickaelBarzalona 2 98
(Charlie Appleby) *nvr bttr than mid-div* **14/1**
10 *5 ¼* **Without Fear (FR)**[9] 683 6-9-4 106....................... Per-AndersGraberg 6 94
(Niels Petersen, Norway) *mid-div: chsd ldrs 3f out: wknd fnl 2f* **50/1**
11 *1 ½* **Saddler's Rock (IRE)**[133] 7363 6-9-2 112....................... DeclanMcDonogh 5 90
(John M Oxx, Ire) *sn led: rdn 3f out: hdd & wknd 2 1/2f out* **10/1**
12 *3 ½* **Statutory (IRE)**[23] 507 4-8-11 104....................... WilliamBuick 7 84
(Saeed bin Suroor) *trckd ldrs: led briefly 2 1/2f out: wknd fnl 2f* **18/1**

2m 56.48s (176.48)
**WFA** 4 from 5yo+ 4lb **12** Ran SP% **121.6**
CSF: 20.94; EXACTA: 20.90; TRIFECTA: 130.20; WIN: 4.20; PL: 1.80, 1.60, 2.60.
**Owner** Godolphin **Bred** Darley **Trained** Newmarket, Suffolk
**FOCUS**
A trial for the Dubai Gold Cup - a 2m Group 2 to be run on World Cup day (March 29). The form is sound.

## 812a DISTRICT ONE PHASE III (H'CAP) (TURF) 1m 2f
**5:45** (5:45) (100-110,110) 3-Y-O+

**£63,253** (£21,084; £10,542; £5,271; £2,635; £2,635)

RPR
1 **Sanshaawes (SAF)**[16] 593 5-9-1 **105**.............. ChristopheSoumillon 3 109
(M F De Kock, South Africa) *trckd ldng pair: led 1f out: r.o wl* **5/2**[1]
2 *¾* **Start Right**[9] 681 7-8-11 **101**..................................(p) RichardMullen 11 104
(S Seemar, UAE) *s.i.s: settled in rr: mid-div 4f out: r.o fnl 110yds: nrst fin* **11/1**
3 *½* **Saxo Jack (FR)**[30] 398 4-9-1 **105**..........................(p) SilvestreDeSousa 8 107
(Saeed bin Suroor) *trckd ldrs: led 1 1/2f out: hdd 1f out: r.o same pce* **5/2**[1]
4 *shd* **Regulation (IRE)**[9] 678 5-8-10 **100**....................... ShaneFoley 5 101+
(M Halford, Ire) *settled in rr: nvr able to chal but r.o fnl 2f: nrst fin* **16/1**
5 *nk* **Aussie Reigns (IRE)**[16] 598 4-8-11 **101**....................... RyanMoore 4 102
(William Knight) *mid-div: chsd ldrs 2f out: one pce fnl f* **8/1**[3]
5 *dht* **Al Waab (IRE)**[16] 595 4-9-5 **109**....................... PatDobbs 7 110
(Doug Watson, UAE) *sn led: hdd 1 1/2f out: r.o same pce* **20/1**
7 *1* **Bank Of Burden (USA)**[16] 598 7-8-13 **102**.......(t) Per-AndersGraberg 6 102
(Niels Petersen, Norway) *nvr bttr than mid-div* **33/1**
8 *½* **So Beautiful (FR)**[16] 595 5-8-13 **102**....................... PaulHanagan 12 101
(Doug Watson, UAE) *settled in rr: nvr nr to chal* **25/1**
9 *¾* **Chil The Kite**[23] 509 5-9-3 **107**....................... RichardHughes 2 103
(Hughie Morrison) *in rr of mid-div: nvr nr to chal* **7/1**[2]
10 *½* **Burano (IRE)**[9] 683 5-9-1 **105**....................... HarryBentley 9 100
(Brian Meehan) *trckd ldrs: rdn 3f out: sn btn* **20/1**
11 *1 ¼* **Mutajare (IRE)**[9] 681 6-9-6 **110**..................................(t) RoystonFfrench 10 103
(A Al Raihe, UAE) *nvr bttr than mid-div* **16/1**
12 *6 ¼* **Tarbawi (IRE)**[16] 595 4-8-11 **101**....................... AdriedeVries 1 81
(A bin Harmash, UAE) *settled in rr: a in rr* **10/1**

2CSF.31s2(1;2EXA0CTA: 35.00; TRICAST: 80.47; TRIFECTA: 113.40; WIN2 Ran; PSP% 12633 50, 1.60; TOTE PLACEPOT: £2,247.00 to a £1 stake. Pool of £6310.13 - 2.05 winning units. TOTE QUADPOT: £22.60 to a £1 stake. Pool of £532.10 - 17.40 winning units.27 Owner Trifecta £Sh Ahmed bin Mohd bin Khalifa Al Maktoum Bred Oldlands Stud.
**FOCUS**
Not a strong contest.

# GULFSTREAM PARK (L-H)
Saturday, March 1
**OFFICIAL GOING: Dirt: fast; turf: firm**

## 813a SWALE STKS (GRADE 2) (DIRT) 7f
**10:10** (12:00) 3-Y-O

**£72,289** (£24,096; £12,048; £6,024; £3,614; £2,409)

RPR
1 **Spot (USA)**[28] 3-8-5 0....................... JLezcano 4 108
(Nicholas Zito, U.S.A) **19/2**
2 *2 ½* **No Nay Never (USA)**[195] 5573 3-8-11 0....................... JJCastellano 2 107+
(Wesley A Ward, U.S.A) **2/5**[1]
3 *1 ¼* **Brothersofthetime (USA)** 3-8-9 0....................... JesusMRios 5 102
(Antonio Sano, U.S.A) **29/1**
4 *5* **Prudhoe Bay (USA)** 3-8-9 0....................... PLopez 3 88
(Edward Plesa Jr, U.S.A) **6/1**[3]
5 *13 ¾* **Can't Stop The Kid (USA)**[201] 3-8-5 0..................................(b) LSaez 1 47
(Donna Green, U.S.A) **7/2**[2]
6 *2 ¼* **Breitling Flyer (USA)**[189] 3-8-5 0..................................(b) LContreras 6 41
(Leo Azpurua Jr, U.S.A) **204/10**

1m 22.44s (82.44) **6** Ran SP% **125.5**
PARI-MUTUEL (all including 2 usd stake): WIN 21.00; PLACE (1-2) 4.60, 2.40; SHOW (1-2-3) 3.40, 2.10, 5.20; SF 54.40.

**Owner** Joseph H Moss **Bred** Curtis C Green **Trained** USA

814 - (Foreign Racing) - See Raceform Interactive

# [753]KEMPTON (A.W) (R-H)

Monday, March 3

**OFFICIAL GOING: Standard**

Wind: Almost nil Weather: Mostly fine

## 815 BACK OF THE NET AT BETVICTOR.COM H'CAP 1m (P)

**2:40** (2:41) (Class 6) (0-60,60) 4-Y-O+ **£1,940** (£577; £288; £144) **Stalls** Low

Form RPR

-652 **1** **Spirit Of Gondree (IRE)**[5] [750] 6-9-7 **60**.......................(b) AdamKirby 2 70+
(Milton Bradley) *swtg: slowly away: hld up in last pair: smooth prog jst over 2f out: brought between rivals to ld jst over 1f out: rdn clr* **3/1**[1]

-500 **2** *2 ½* **Gabrial's Wawa**[10] [690] 4-9-7 **60**................................ PaddyAspell 12 64
(Noel Quinlan) *stdd s: hld up in detached last: stdy prog 2f out: pushed along over 1f out: tk 2nd last 100yds: no ch to chal but styd on* **12/1**

3043 **3** *1 ¼* **Divine Rule (IRE)**[3] [780] 6-9-5 **58**..................................(p) LiamJones 3 59
(Laura Mongan) *dwlt: sn chsd ldrs: cajoled along over 2f out: clsd to chal and upsides over 1f out: outpcd after* **8/1**

-032 **4** *½* **Warbond**[6] [740] 6-9-2 **55**.................................................(v) JohnFahy 8 56
(Michael Madgwick) *stdd to rr sn after s: t.k.h: trying to make prog whn nt clr run jst over 2f out and lost pl: rdn and kpt on fr over 1f out* **13/2**

1063 **5** *hd* **Xclusive**[19] [571] 4-9-7 **60**............................................. LukeMorris 5 60
(Ronald Harris) *trckd ldrs: n.m.r briefly on inner over 2f out: drvn and cl up over 1f out: fdd fnl f* **6/1**[3]

-504 **6** *½* **Darnathean**[17] [603] 5-9-5 **58**.......................................(tp) SeanLevey 11 57
(Paul D'Arcy) *dwlt: sn rcvrd to press ldng pair on outer: rdn to ld 2f out: hdd and fdd jst over 1f out* **14/1**

0-00 **7** *3* **Sam Spade (IRE)**[34] [366] 4-8-11 **57**......................... AdamMcLean(7) 4 49
(Derek Shaw) *nvr beyond midfield: urged along and no prog 2f out* **33/1**

520- **8** *hd* **Habeshia**[118] [7740] 4-9-7 **60**........................................(v) HayleyTurner 6 51
(John Best) *t.k.h: pressed ldr: rdn over 3f out: lost 2nd jst over 2f out: wknd over 1f out* **25/1**

/0-5 **9** *nk* **Jambobo**[28] [452] 5-8-4 **46** oh1....................................... RyanPowell(3) 7 37
(Chris Down) *t.k.h: hld up in midfield: rdn and struggling over 2f out: sn btn* **66/1**

6/12 **10** *1 ¾* **Callisto Light**[18] [589] 7-9-6 **59**................................... JimCrowley 10 46
(Michael Squance) *hld up in tch: hmpd and snatched up jst over 2f out: nt rcvr: b.b.v* **9/2**[2]

0-20 **11** *4* **Timothy T**[19] [583] 6-9-7 **60**.......................................(b) LiamKeniry 1 37
(Philip Hide) *led: rdn and hdd 2f out: wknd rapidly jst over 1f out* **9/1**

0-04 **12** *3 ½* **Lily Edge**[10] [685] 5-9-2 **60**........................................ RyanWhile(5) 9 29
(John Bridger) *dwlt: racd wd: towards rr: wd bnd 3f out: sn wknd* **33/1**

1m 38.94s (-0.86) **Going Correction** +0.05s/f (Slow) **12** Ran SP% **117.5**
Speed ratings (Par 101): **106,103,102,101,101 101,98,97,97,95 91,88**
CSF £39.26 CT £269.01 TOTE £4.90: £2.10, £3.00, £3.20; EX 52.30 Trifecta £417.60.
**Owner** Paul & Ann de Weck & Partner **Bred** Windflower Overseas Holdings Inc **Trained** Sedbury, Gloucs

**FOCUS**
A moderate handicap run at a decent pace, suiting those held up. Straightforward enough form.

## 816 BETVICTOR NON-RUNNER FREE BET CHELTENHAM 2014 MAIDEN STKS 1m (P)

**3:10** (3:13) (Class 5) 3-Y-O+ **£2,587** (£770; £384; £192) **Stalls** Low

Form RPR

**1** **Dream Ruler** 3-8-10 **0**...................................................... FergusSweeney 4 71+
(Jo Crowley) *hld up in tch: prog to trck ldng pair 2f out: clsd to ld last 150yds: jst hld on* **10/1**

2 **2** *nk* **Watersmeet**[16] [626] 3-8-7 **0**...................................... MichaelJMMurphy(3) 2 70
(Mark Johnston) *led: hanging and hdd 2f out: continued to hang but led briefly ins fnl f: hung lft and kpt on nr fin* **9/4**[1]

40-3 **3** *1 ¾* **Seven Lucky Seven**[12] [665] 3-8-10 **55**............................ JimmyQuinn 3 66
(Gary Harrison) *t.k.h: trckd ldng pair: prog to ld 2f out: idled in front: hdd and nt qckn jst ins fnl f* **8/1**[3]

U **4** *¾* **Maahir**[17] [614] 3-8-10 **0**.................................................. LukeMorris 8 64+
(Marco Botti) *in tch: sltly impeded jst over 2f out: hrd rdn over 1f out: kpt on same pce* **5/2**[2]

5 **5** *2 ¾* **Khutze (GER)**[16] [626] 3-8-10 **0**........................................... JohnFahy 7 58
(Eve Johnson Houghton) *in tch: rdn over 2f out: sn btn* **16/1**

0 **6** *6* **Jalusive (IRE)**[27] [468] 5-10-0 **0**.............................. AdamBeschizza 5 50
(Christine Dunnett) *t.k.h: pressed ldr: hung lft and wknd jst over 2f out* **66/1**

**7** *3* **Noel's Hope** 4-10-0 **0**........................................................ SebSanders 6 43
(Simon Dow) *s.s and rn green in last: nvr a factor: wknd 2f out* **50/1**

1m 40.37s (0.57) **Going Correction** +0.05s/f (Slow)
**WFA** 3 from 4yo+ 18lb **7** Ran SP% **88.9**
Speed ratings (Par 103): **99,98,96,96,93 87,84**
CSF £19.17 TOTE £7.40: £2.80, £1.50; EX 24.40 Trifecta £101.20.
**Owner** Exors Of The Late Mrs Liz Nelson **Bred** Mrs Liz Nelson **Trained** Whitcombe, Dorset
■ Rule 4 of 25p in the pound applies to all bets; Withdrawn: Mount Shamsan

**FOCUS**
This was run at a fair pace. Mixed messages from the form and the winner can fourth can rate higher.

## 817 DOWNLOAD THE BETVICTOR APP NOW H'CAP 7f (P)

**3:45** (3:45) (Class 5) (0-70,69) 4-Y-O+ **£2,587** (£770; £384; £192) **Stalls** Low

Form RPR

052- **1** **Athletic**[89] [8157] 5-9-2 **64**............................................(v) JimCrowley 6 74
(Andrew Reid) *hld up in rr: stdy prog on inner fr 2f out: cajoled along w hd high but r.o to ld last 120yds: styd on* **8/1**

-643 **2** *1* **Presumido (IRE)**[26] [496] 4-9-1 **63**................................... HayleyTurner 3 70
(Simon Dow) *t.k.h: hld up bhd ldrs: prog to chse ldr over 1f out: clsd to chal ins fnl f: styd on but outpcd by wnr last 100yds* **11/2**

0605 **3** *1 ¼* **Sheikh The Reins (IRE)**[8] [728] 5-9-6 **68**....................(v) RobertHavlin 9 72
(John Best) *led after 1f and set more meaningful pce: sent for home over 2f out: hdd and no ex last 120yds* **16/1**

-001 **4** *1 ½* **Dimitar (USA)**[14] [646] 5-9-7 **69**...................................... LiamKeniry 1 69+
(Johnny Farrelly) *hld up in last pair: pushed along 2f out: prog over 1f out and stl pushed along: tk 4th nr fin and one reminder after: nvr involved* **5/1**[3]

-240 **5** *¾* **Intomist (IRE)**[16] [627] 5-9-7 **69**................................(p) StephenCraine 5 67
(Jim Boyle) *reluctant ldr 1f: trckd ldr after: rdn 2f out: nt qckn over 1f out: steadily fdd* **9/2**[2]

-004 **6** *nk* **Imperator Augustus (IRE)**[4] [757] 6-8-13 **61**...............(p) SeanLevey 11 58
(Patrick Holmes) *hld up in last pair: rdn and nt qckn 2f out: one pce after* **10/1**

30-5 **7** *nk* **Nelson Quay (IRE)**[26] [489] 4-9-6 **68**.................................(p) AdamKirby 2 64
(Jeremy Gask) *t.k.h: trckd ldr after 1f tl wknd 2f out* **5/1**[3]

0-32 **8** *¾* **Russian Ice**[29] [451] 6-9-7 **69**.......................................(b) RobertWinston 7 63
(Dean Ivory) *hld up towards rr: wandered and nt qckn fr 2f out: sn btn* **3/1**[1]

0-54 **9** *½* **Teen Ager (FR)**[12] [663] 10-8-13 **61**............................(p) JimmyQuinn 4 54
(Paul Burgoyne) *t.k.h: hld up in tch: shkn up over 2f out: fdd over 1f out* **20/1**

00-0 **10** *9* **Emperor Julius (IRE)**[18] [587] 4-9-7 **69**...................(p) FergusSweeney 8 38
(Jo Crowley) *t.k.h: in tch on outer tl wknd rapidly over 2f out: t.o* **25/1**

1m 25.6s (-0.40) **Going Correction** +0.05s/f (Slow) **10** Ran SP% **126.6**
Speed ratings (Par 103): **104,102,101,99,98 98,98,97,96,86**
CSF £56.24 CT £730.05 TOTE £7.20: £1.80, £1.60, £6.90; EX 39.50 Trifecta £953.50.
**Owner** A S Reid **Bred** A S Reid **Trained** Mill Hill, London NW7

**FOCUS**
A wide-open looking handicap. It was run at an uneven early pace but the winner came from near last to first. He came here looking pretty exposed.

## 818 CHELTENHAM 2014 NRNB AT BETVICTOR.COM H'CAP 2m (P)

**4:15** (4:16) (Class 5) (0-70,70) 4-Y-O+ **£2,587** (£770; £384; £192) **Stalls** Low

Form RPR

/31- **1** **Ordensritter (GER)**[326] [1502] 6-9-11 **70**................................ JohnFahy 2 79
(Chris Down) *trckd ldr 5f: styd cl up: led over 2f out: rdn clr over 1f out: eased last 50yds* **12/1**

0231 **2** *1 ¾* **Shalambar (IRE)**[12] [656] 8-9-6 **65**..................................(v) JimCrowley 5 71
(Tony Carroll) *trckd ldrs: clsd to chal over 2f out: nt qckn wl over 1f out: kpt on but no real threat to wnr* **2/1**[1]

2/01 **3** *½* **Mighty Mambo**[12] [657] 7-9-2 **61**...............................(tp) WilliamCarson 3 66
(Lawney Hill) *t.k.h: hld up bhd ldrs: prog 2f out: styd on same pce after and unable to throw down a chal* **14/1**

0-13 **4** *shd* **Bert The Alert**[17] [606] 6-8-9 **61**............................ CharlotteJenner(7) 10 66
(Laura Mongan) *t.k.h: hld up in last: prog over 2f out: pushed along and styd on fr over 1f out: no ch to threaten* **4/1**[3]

506- **5** *3 ½* **Guards Chapel**[110] [7863] 6-9-7 **66**...................................(b) SeanLevey 8 67
(Gary Moore) *hld up in last trio: dropped to last and pushed along over 2f out: prog over 1f out but hanging and racd awkwardly: tk 5th ins fnl f: styd on* **3/1**[2]

245 **6** *5* **Teenage Dream (IRE)**[28] [463] 6-8-12 **64**.............(vt) AdamMcLean(7) 7 59
(Derek Shaw) *tk fierce hold: hld up in midfield: rdn over 2f out: steadily wknd* **33/1**

-300 **7** *3 ½* **Wild Desert (FR)**[14] [641] 9-9-10 **69**..................................... AdamKirby 1 60
(Tony Carroll) *led: shkn up 3f out: hdd over 2f out: wknd and eased fnl f* **33/1**

0-35 **8** *8* **Phoenix Flight (IRE)**[39] [292] 9-9-10 **69**................(p) FergusSweeney 6 50
(James Evans) *prog to trck ldr after 5f: rdn and wknd over 2f out* **12/1**

0-50 **9** *6* **Honourable Knight (IRE)**[27] [471] 6-9-9 **68**.................... LiamKeniry 4 42
(Mark Usher) *in tch: rdn 4f out: sn struggling: wl btn fnl 2f* **20/1**

035- **10** *3 ¾* **The Absent Mare**[115] [1502] 6-9-3 **65**.............. WilliamTwiston-Davies(3) 9 34
(Robin Dickin) *hld up in last trio: tried to make prog on wd outside 3f out: sn wknd* **20/1**

3m 29.52s (-0.58) **Going Correction** +0.05s/f (Slow) **10** Ran SP% **115.8**
Speed ratings (Par 103): **103,102,101,101,100 97,95,91,88,86**
CSF £34.57 CT £346.56 TOTE £11.50: £2.90, £1.20, £3.30; EX 41.60 Trifecta £141.40.
**Owner** Red Baron Racing **Bred** Gestut Karlshof **Trained** Mutterton, Devon

**FOCUS**
A moderate staying handicap, run at an ordinary gallop and four in-form horses came clear. The winner could well do better again.

## 819 BACK OF THE NET AT BETVICTOR.COM FILLIES' H'CAP 6f (P)

**4:45** (4:46) (Class 5) (0-70,67) 4-Y-O+ **£2,587** (£770; £384; £192) **Stalls** Low

Form RPR

0-24 **1** **Ray Of Joy**[28] [453] 8-9-7 **67**.....................................(v) FrederikTylicki 1 73
(J R Jenkins) *cl up: led 2f out: shkn up and in command over 1f out: ld dwindled nr fin but nvr in serious danger* **9/2**[3]

-101 **2** *½* **Mill I Am (USA)**[18] [592] 4-8-13 **59**................................ AdamBeschizza 4 64+
(Stuart Williams) *hld up in last pair: rdn and prog over 1f out: wnt 2nd last 100yds: clsd on wnr but a hld* **15/8**[1]

0253 **3** *hd* **Two In The Pink (IRE)**[9] [718] 4-8-13 **59**....................... WilliamCarson 3 63
(Ralph J Smith) *wl in tch: shkn up and nt qckn over 2f out: styd on again fnl f: nrst fin* **10/3**[2]

-623 **4** *1* **Harvest Mist (IRE)**[12] [663] 6-8-10 **59**........... WilliamTwiston-Davies(3) 7 60
(Shaun Lycett) *led to 2f out: nt qckn over 1f out: one pce after* **5/1**

-400 **5** *1 ¼* **Idle Curiosity (IRE)**[17] [603] 4-8-10 **56**......................... HayleyTurner 6 53
(Jim Boyle) *s.s: hld up in last: rdn over 2f out: kpt on u.p fr over 1f out: n.d* **12/1**

0-55 **6** *2 ½* **Little Choosey**[10] [688] 4-8-10 **56**...................................... LiamKeniry 2 46
(Anabel K Murphy) *towards rr: pushed along 2f out: no imp over 1f out: sn rdn and wknd* **16/1**

-306 **7** *¾* **Spray Tan**[10] [694] 4-8-11 **60**................................... CharlesBishop(3) 5 47
(Tony Carroll) *t.k.h: sn chsd ldr on outer: wknd 2f out* **20/1**

1m 12.76s (-0.34) **Going Correction** +0.05s/f (Slow) **7** Ran SP% **111.0**
Speed ratings (Par 100): **104,103,103,101,100 96,95**
CSF £12.58 TOTE £5.50: £2.20, £1.10; EX 14.70 Trifecta £48.60.
**Owner** Robin Stevens **Bred** D R Tucker **Trained** Royston, Herts

**FOCUS**
A modest sprint handicap for fillies, run at a fair pace. The winner is rated to her best efforts of recent years.

## 820 BETVICTOR NONRUNNER NO BET AT CHELTENHAM 2014 H'CAP 6f (P)

**5:15** (5:16) (Class 4) (0-85,85) 4-Y-O+ **£5,175** (£1,540; £769; £384) **Stalls** Low

Form RPR

0-20 **1** **Glastonberry**[9] [714] 6-8-12 **76**........................................ HayleyTurner 2 85
(Geoffrey Deacon) *trckd ldng pair: pushed along to chal wl over 1f out: drvn to ld on inner jst ins fnl f: edgd lft nr fin: hld on wl* **10/1**

0-22 **2** *hd* **Mac's Power (IRE)**[23] [535] 8-8-13 **77**............................ RobertWinston 4 85
(Willie Musson) *trckd ldrs: prog 2f out: rdn to chal jst over 1f out: styd on but jst hld nr fin* **7/2**[2]

344- **3** *½* **Peace Seeker**[73] [8369] 6-9-7 **85**.............................(t) WilliamCarson 3 92
(Anthony Carson) *trckd ldr: rdn to ld wl over 1f out: hdd jst ins fnl f: styd on but hld after* **9/4**[1]

-110 **4** *1 ½* **Valmina**[9] [714] 7-9-1 **79**...................................................(t) JimCrowley 8 81
(Tony Carroll) *stdd s: hld up in last pair: pushed along 2f out: rdn and prog to take 4th fnl f: no imp last 100yds* **12/1**

2624 **5** ½ **Light From Mars**[19] 574 9-9-3 **81**....(p) LiamJones 7 82
(Ronald Harris) *chsd ldrs: rdn over 2f out: nt qckn over 1f out: kpt on same pce fnl f* **10/1**

00-6 **6** nk **Tyfos**[27] 479 9-9-0 **78**.... AndrewMullen 5 78
(Brian Baugh) *led: rdn and hdd wl over 1f out: wknd ins fnl f* **33/1**

0006 **7** ½ **Naabegha**[20] 566 7-9-4 **82**....[1] AdamKirby 11 81
(Alan McCabe) *slowly away then hmpd s: t.k.h in last: shkn up and nt qckn 2f out: kpt on fnl f: n.d* **7/1**[3]

-016 **8** hd **Toymaker**[11] 674 7-8-7 **78**.... DonnaAspell(7) 6 76
(Phil McEntee) *hld up in 8th: rdn and struggling over 2f out: no prog tl styd on last 150yds* **20/1**

63-6 **9** nk **My Son Max**[30] 431 6-9-4 **82**.... DaleSwift 9 79
(Michael Blake) *wnt bdly lft s: chsd ldrs in 7th: rdn over 2f out: no imp over 1f out: fdd last 100yds* **14/1**

0-45 **10** 2½ **Clear Praise (USA)**[12] 658 7-9-3 **81**....[1] SebSanders 1 71
(Simon Dow) *in tch in midfield: rdn and no prog on inner wl over 1f out: wknd fnl f* **9/1**

1m 13.22s (0.12) **Going Correction** +0.05s/f (Slow) **10** Ran SP% **115.7**
Speed ratings (Par 105): **101,100,100,98,97 97,96,96,95,92**
CSF £44.65 CT £108.10 TOTE £10.40: £3.10, £1.50, £1.80; EX 33.80 Trifecta £204.10.
**Owner** Geoffrey Deacon **Bred** Geoffrey Deacon **Trained** Compton, Berks
■ Stewards' Enquiry : Hayley Turner caution: careless riding

**FOCUS**
A modest sprint handicap with a compressed finish. The winner is rated to his best.

## 821 GOFFS BREEZE-UP SALE ROYAL ASCOT WEEK H'CAP 1m 3f (P)
**5:45** (5:45) (Class 6) (0-60,60) 4-Y-O+ **£1,940** (£577; £288; £144) **Stalls** Low

Form RPR

-260 **1** **Thane Of Cawdor (IRE)**[19] 571 5-9-4 **57**.... JimCrowley 6 66
(Joseph Tuite) *w.w in rr: pushed along whn pce lifted 4f out: prog and plld out 2f out: clsd qckly over 1f out to ld last 150yds: r.o wl* **9/2**[1]

-045 **2** 1 **Elegant Ophelia**[26] 490 5-9-5 **58**....(t) AdamKirby 8 65
(Dean Ivory) *trckd ldng pair: prog to ld over 2f out and sharp reminder: styd on but hdd and outpcd last 150yds* **10/1**

-552 **3** 1½ **Petersboden**[19] 571 5-8-13 **52**.... RobertHavlin 4 57
(Michael Blanshard) *trckd ldrs: gng strly over 2f out: prog to chse ldr over 1f out: nt qckn and outpcd fnl f* **6/1**[2]

44/2 **4** 2½ **Ladies Dancing**[18] 590 8-9-1 **54**.... JohnFahy 11 55
(Chris Down) *hld up in midfield: rdn over 2f out: kpt on fr over 1f out: nt pce to threaten* **6/1**[2]

4-03 **5** ½ **Royal Etiquette (IRE)**[28] 459 7-9-2 **55**....(t) WilliamCarson 9 55
(Lawney Hill) *hld up in last pair: tried to make prog fr over 2f out: kpt on fr over 1f out but nvr gng pce to threaten* **7/1**[3]

-550 **6** 1¾ **Time Square (FR)**[19] 571 7-9-1 **57**.... CharlesBishop(3) 10 54
(Tony Carroll) *t.k.h: led at mod pce: racd awkwardly after 4f: tried to kick on 4f out: hdd over 2f out: wknd jst over 1f out* **8/1**

5-14 **7** shd **Litmus (USA)**[10] 691 5-9-2 **55**....(b) HayleyTurner 3 52
(Simon Dow) *trckd ldr to wl over 2f out: steadily wknd* **14/1**

/53- **8** 1½ **Roy Rocket (FR)**[194] 5630 4-8-6 **46**.... JimmyQuinn 5 41
(John Berry) *rring at stalls opened: in tch: prog to chse ldrs 3f out: rdn over 2f out: wknd jst over 1f out* **14/1**

5-20 **9** 1 **Our Golden Girl**[18] 590 4-8-11 **54**....(b) WilliamTwiston-Davies(3) 7 47
(Shaun Lycett) *dwlt: shoved along early and nvr gng wl in last pair: lost tch over 3f out: kpt on fnl f* **20/1**

6600 **10** nk **Auden (USA)**[10] 685 6-9-7 **60**....(p) FrederikTylicki 2 53
(J R Jenkins) *trckd ldng trio: pushed along on inner over 2f out: steadily lost pl fnl 2f* **14/1**

006- **11** 2 **Anjuna Beach (USA)**[72] 8388 4-9-5 **59**.... SeanLevey 1 49
(Gary Moore) *s.s: t.k.h in rr: rdn and no prog over 2f out: wknd* **7/1**[3]

2m 22.33s (0.43) **Going Correction** +0.05s/f (Slow)
**WFA** 4 from 5yo+ 1lb **11** Ran SP% **116.7**
Speed ratings (Par 101): **100,99,98,96,96 94,94,93,92,92 91**
CSF £49.49 CT £273.70 TOTE £4.40: £2.10, £4.00, £1.70; EX 57.80 Trifecta £260.90.
**Owner** Alan & Christine Bright **Bred** Balmerino Bldstock & Newsells Park Stud **Trained** Great Shefford, Berks

**FOCUS**
This was run at an uneven pace. A straightforward level of form.
T/Jkpt: Not won. T/Plt: £58.20 to a £1 stake. Pool: £67549.81 - 845.87 winning tickets T/Qpdt: £17.80 to a £1 stake. Pool: £4923.86 - 204.30 winning tickets JN

# 797 LINGFIELD (L-H)
Monday, March 3

**OFFICIAL GOING: Standard**
Wind: virtually becoming medium behind during showers Weather: heavy showers and brighter spells

## 822 CORAL MOBILE "JUST THREE CLICKS TO BET" H'CAP 1m 2f (P)
**1:45** (1:46) (Class 6) (0-60,60) 4-Y-O+ **£2,726** (£805; £402) **Stalls** Low

Form RPR

00-4 **1** **Cataria Girl (USA)**[54] 92 5-8-8 **54**....(t) JordanVaughan(7) 9 59
(Marcus Tregoning) *hld up in tch in last pair: rdn and gd hdwy on inner over 1f out: ev ch ins fnl f: edgd rt u.p wl ins fnl f: r.o to ld cl home* **7/1**

66-2 **2** hd **Super Duplex**[23] 538 7-9-4 **57**....(t) FrankieMcDonald 4 62
(Roger Teal) *chsd ldng pair: effrt u.p 2f out: drvn and ev ch 1f out: led fnl 100yds: kpt on tl hdd and no ex cl home* **5/1**[3]

3230 **3** 1 **Do More Business (IRE)**[7] 736 7-8-12 **56**....(vt) PhilipPrince(5) 7 59
(Liam Corcoran) *stdd after s: hld up in tch in last trio: hdwy 4f out: drvn and effrt over 1f out: styd on u.p ins fnl f* **16/1**

-412 **4** nk **India's Song**[7] 733 4-8-13 **59**....(t) GeorgeBuckell(7) 1 63
(David Simcock) *chsd ldng pair: nt clr run and hmpd over 1f out: swtchd rt and effrt between horses 1f out: pressing ldrs and keeping on whn pushed rt and bmpd wl ins fnl f* **9/4**[1]

-504 **5** ½ **Indian Violet (IRE)**[6] 737 8-8-12 **51**....(p) DavidProbert 8 52
(Zoe Davison) *in tch in midfield: nt clr run ent fnl 2f: rdn and effrt over 1f out: kpt on ins fnl f* **16/1**

50-4 **6** ½ **Legal Legacy**[27] 469 8-8-10 **52**....(v[1]) ThomasBrown(3) 5 52
(Lee Carter) *sn bustled along to chse ldr: rdn to ld 2f out: hrd pressed and drvn 1f out: hdd fnl 100yds: keeping on same pce whn pushed rt and hmpd wl ins fnl f* **7/1**

5065 **7** ½ **Copperwood**[3] 775 9-9-7 **60**....(v[1]) AmirQuinn 6 61
(Lee Carter) *in tch in midfield: swtchd rt and effrt over 1f out: chsng ldrs and keeping on same pce whn squeezed for room and hmpd wl ins fnl f* **8/1**

05-3 **8** 2¾ **Travel (USA)**[13] 648 4-9-4 **57**.... JoeFanning 2 51
(Mark Johnston) *sn led: hdd 2f out: sn drvn and unable qck: wknd ins fnl f* **9/2**[2]

0 **9** 3¼ **Tide Runner**[14] 639 8-8-9 **48**....(p) JamieSpencer 3 36
(Liam Corcoran) *hld up in tch in rr: drvn and no hdwy wl over 1f out: wknd fnl f* **50/1**

2m 5.38s (-1.22) **Going Correction** -0.05s/f (Stan) **9** Ran SP% **115.5**
Speed ratings (Par 101): **102,101,101,100,100 100,99,97,94**
CSF £41.86 CT £542.64 TOTE £7.50: £2.60, £2.20, £2.90; EX 41.10 Trifecta £294.30.
**Owner** Mr And Mrs A E Pakenham **Bred** Shadwell Farm LLC **Trained** Whitsbury, Hants
■ Stewards' Enquiry : Jordan Vaughan four-day ban: careless riding (17-20 March)

**FOCUS**
A very moderate handicap run at a fair pace. They finished in a bunch. The winner was less exposed than most.

## 823 32RED MEGA MOOLAH MILLIONAIRES CLAIMING STKS 1m 1y(P)
**2:15** (2:16) (Class 6) 3-Y-O **£2,385** (£704; £352) **Stalls** High

Form RPR

6-55 **1** **Black Vale (IRE)**[3] 774 3-8-0 65....(t) DonnaAspell(7) 7 66
(Phil McEntee) *sn led: racd freely and sn wl clr: arnd 12 l clr wl over 1f out: rdn fnl f: a jst hoding on* **6/1**[3]

66 **2** nk **No Refund (IRE)**[27] 468 3-8-6 0.... DavidProbert 8 64+
(David Simcock) *hld up wl off the pce in midfield: rdn and effrt to chse clr ldr wl over 1f out: clsd rapidly fnl f: nt quite rch wnr* **5/4**[1]

0-60 **3** 6 **Prisca**[19] 573 3-8-0 60.... NickyMackay 3 44
(Jamie Osborne) *racd off the pce in midfield: n.m.r and hmpd 2f out: 3rd and kpt on fr over 1f out: nvr trbld wnr* **16/1**

616- **4** 3½ **Autopilot**[146] 7088 3-8-13 72.... JamieSpencer 6 48
(Anabel K Murphy) *stdd s: hld up in rr: swtchd rt and effrt over 1f out: kpt on but n.d* **7/4**[2]

260- **5** 2¼ **Penara**[75] 8332 3-7-7 59.... JackGarritty(7) 5 30
(Philip Hide) *hld up wl off the pce in last trio: rdn ent fnl 2f: no imp: n.d* **14/1**

6 **6** 7 **Diamond Back (IRE)**[16] 626 3-9-5 0.... AndreaAtzeni 4 32
(Denis Quinn) *racd in 3rd but wl off pce: rdn to chse clr wnr briefly 2f out: sn lost pl and wknd* **33/1**

6-00 **7** 1 **Hannah Louise (IRE)**[20] 564 3-8-0 35....(t) KieranO'Neill 1 11
(Roger Ingram) *chsd clr ldr: rdn wl over 2f out: lost pl 2f out: bhd 1f out* **100/1**

1m 37.19s (-1.01) **Going Correction** -0.05s/f (Stan) **7** Ran SP% **111.6**
Speed ratings (Par 96): **103,102,96,93,90 83,82**
CSF £13.27 TOTE £6.00: £4.70, £1.10; EX 15.50 Trifecta £85.50.No Refund was claimed by Mr L. A. Carter for £5,000.
**Owner** Mrs Rebecca McEntee **Bred** Michael Downey & Roalso Ltd **Trained** Newmarket, Suffolk
■ Donna Caldwell's first winner since 2006.

**FOCUS**
They went a sound pace for this uncompetitive claimer. The winner was entitled to run this well.

## 824 BEST ODDS AT BOOKMAKERS.CO.UK MAIDEN STKS 6f 1y(P)
**2:50** (2:52) (Class 5) 3-Y-O+ **£3,408** (£1,006; £503) **Stalls** Low

Form RPR

**1** **Double Up** 3-8-12 0.... AndreaAtzeni 4 71+
(Roger Varian) *in tch in midfield: hdwy to chse ldrs 2f out: rdn hands and heels and chal jst over 1f out: rn green but led fnl 100yds: rdn and r.o wl towards fin* **4/5**[1]

0- **2** 1 **Willy Brennan (IRE)**[129] 7501 3-8-12 0.... DavidProbert 2 68
(Andrew Balding) *chsd ldr: rdn and effrt to press ldr 2f out: sltly outpcd 1f out: kpt on ins fnl f to snatch 2nd last strides* **7/2**[2]

3 **3** hd **Role Reversal**[26] 495 3-8-7 0.... RichardKingscote 6 62
(James Tate) *led: rdn and pressed 2f out: kpt on tl hdd and styd on same pce fnl 100yds: lost 2nd last strides* **5/1**[3]

**4** 2 **Bush Warrior (IRE)** 3-8-12 0.... JamieSpencer 5 61+
(Robert Eddery) *stdd s: t.k.h: hld up in tch in rr: hung lft bnd 2f out: hdwy and edging lft ent fnl f: nudged along and kpt on ins fnl f* **20/1**

5-5 **5** 2¼ **Cocoa's Princess**[48] 174 3-8-7 0.... BarryMcHugh 1 49
(Richard Fahey) *chsd ldrs tl over 2f out: drvn and unable qck ent fnl 2f: styd on same pce fr over 1f out* **50/1**

30 **6** 2½ **Beylerbey (USA)**[12] 660 4-9-7 0.... JoeFanning 7 46
(Mark Johnston) *awkward leaving stalls and s.i.s: in tch in midfield: rdn and struggling ent fnl 2f: wknd over 1f out* **7/1**

60- **7** 13 **O'Raghallaigh (IRE)**[74] 8346 3-8-7 0.... JamesSullivan 3 3
(Richard Fahey) *pushed along and dropped to rr after 1f out: lost tch 2f out* **100/1**

1m 12.07s (0.17) **Going Correction** -0.05s/f (Stan)
**WFA** 3 from 4yo 14lb **7** Ran SP% **114.7**
Speed ratings (Par 103): **96,94,94,91,88 85,68**
CSF £3.91 TOTE £1.70: £1.10, £2.30; EX 4.90 Trifecta £14.70.
**Owner** A D Spence & M B Spence **Bred** Mount Coote New England Barton & Myriad **Trained** Newmarket, Suffolk

**FOCUS**
Some fair stables in opposition for this maiden which was run at a sound pace. The winner is the type to rate plenty higher.

## 825 LADBROKES H'CAP 7f 1y(P)
**3:20** (3:21) (Class 5) (0-75,75) 4-Y-O+ **£3,234** (£962; £481; £240) **Stalls** Low

Form RPR

3-12 **1** **Hillbilly Boy (IRE)**[23] 540 4-9-6 **74**.... AndreaAtzeni 8 81
(Martin Smith) *chsd ldr tl led after 2f: rdn wl over 1f out: hld on gamely u.p ins fnl f* **4/1**[2]

3312 **2** nk **Seek The Fair Land**[4] 757 8-9-5 **73**....(v) AmirQuinn 2 79
(Lee Carter) *wl in tch in midfield: swtchd lft and effrt towards inner over 1f out: str chal ins fnl f: r.o but hld towards fin* **5/1**

6-34 **3** 1 **Gracious George (IRE)**[32] 376 4-9-0 **75**.... CamHardie(7) 4 78
(Jimmy Fox) *chsd ldrs: rdn wl over 1f out: kpt on same pce ins fnl f* **8/1**

1131 **4** nk **Club House (IRE)**[10] 690 4-8-12 **73**.... GeorgeBuckell(7) 1 76
(Robert Mills) *hld up wl in tch in last trio: rdn and effrt on inner over 1f out: kpt on same pce u.p ins fnl f* **9/2**[3]

0-30 **5** nk **Afkar (IRE)**[38] 314 6-9-4 **72**.... TomQueally 3 74
(Clive Brittain) *led for 2f: pressed wnr after: drvn and ev ch over 1f out: no ex ins fnl f: wknd fnl 75yds* **4/1**[2]

0-61 **6** 1 **The Happy Hammer (IRE)**[26] 496 8-8-9 **66** ow1....(b) RobertTart(3) 5 65
(Eugene Stanford) *hld up wl in tch in last trio: rdn and effrt over 1f out: kpt on u.p ins fnl f* **12/1**

21-2 **7** nk **Fanoos**[18] 587 5-9-7 **75**....(p) RichardKingscote 6 73
(Dr Jon Scargill) *led to s: t.k.h: hld up wl in tch in midfield: hdwy to chse ldrs and rdn 2f out: no ex 1f out: wknd ins fnl f* **3/1**[1]

0-00 **8** 2 3/4 **Sulis Minerva (IRE)**[12] 658 7-9-4 72 ....(t) JoeFanning 7 63
(Jeremy Gask) *stdd s: hld up in tch in rr: wdst bnd and rdn wl over 1f out: no real imp: wl hld and eased towards fin* **33/1**
1m 24.16s (-0.64) **Going Correction** -0.05s/f (Stan) 8 Ran SP% **121.6**
Speed ratings (Par 103): **101,100,99,99,98 97,97,94**
CSF £26.05 CT £158.05 TOTE £4.60: £1.40, £1.40, £3.20; EX 26.60 Trifecta £164.10.
**Owner** Macguire's Bloodstock Ltd **Bred** Tipper House Stud **Trained** Newmarket, Suffolk
■ Stewards' Enquiry : Amir Quinn four-day ban: use of whip (17-20 Mar)

**FOCUS**
Not much pace for this competitive handicap. Straightforward, limited form.

## 826 BOOKMAKERS.CO.UK H'CAP 6f 1y(P)
3:55 (3:55) (Class 5) (0-70,69) 4-Y-O+ £3,408 (£1,006; £503) Stalls Low

Form RPR
-033 **1** **Temple Road (IRE)**[16] 628 6-9-7 69 .... RichardKingscote 5 79+
(Milton Bradley) *stdd s: t.k.h: hld up in tch in last trio: shkn up and smooth hdwy ent fnl f: led fnl 100yds: sn clr: readily* **2/1**[1]
4565 **2** 1 1/4 **Parisian Pyramid (IRE)**[9] 714 8-8-10 61 ....(b) ThomasBrown(3) 4 66
(Lee Carter) *chsd ldr: rdn and ev ch wl over 1f out: led ins fnl f: sn hdd and outpcd by wnr fnl f: hld on for 2nd* **6/1**
2211 **3** nk **Volito**[10] 687 8-8-10 65 .... JackGarritty(7) 1 69
(Anabel K Murphy) *stdd s: hld up in rr: hdwy on inner over 1f out: chal and rdn ins fnl f: no ch w wnr and one pce fnl 100yds* **5/1**[3]
0405 **4** shd **The Dancing Lord**[12] 663 5-8-12 60 .... DavidProbert 7 64
(Brett Johnson) *t.k.h: stdd bk to last trio after 1f out: rdn and wdst bnd wl over 1f out: styd on wl ins fnl f: no ch w wnr* **7/1**
6215 **5** 1 1/4 **Where's Reiley (USA)**[12] 662 8-9-2 64 ....(v) JoeFanning 2 64
(Michael Attwater) *led: rdn wl over 1f out: hdd ins fnl f: wknd fnl 100yds* **14/1**
3156 **6** 1/2 **R Woody**[8] 728 7-9-7 69 ....(e) ShaneKelly 3 68
(George Baker) *t.k.h: in tch in midfield: effrt to chse ldrs 2f out: drvn and unable qck over 1f out: hld and styd on same pce fnl f* **9/2**[2]
-060 **7** 4 1/2 **Burnhope**[18] 587 5-9-2 64 ....(b[1]) TomQueally 6 49
(Scott Dixon) *t.k.h: chsd ldng pair tl 2f out: btn over 1f out: wknd fnl f* **6/1**
1m 11.36s (-0.54) **Going Correction** -0.05s/f (Stan) 7 Ran SP% **115.9**
Speed ratings (Par 103): **101,99,98,98,97 96,90**
CSF £14.97 TOTE £3.00: £1.70, £3.00; EX 15.40 Trifecta £86.80.
**Owner** J M Bradley **Bred** Paul Monaghan **Trained** Sedbury, Gloucs

**FOCUS**
The pace was sound for this modest handicap. Straightforward form, with a useful effort for the grade from the winner.

## 827 CORAL.CO.UK MAIDEN STKS 1m 2f (P)
4:25 (4:25) (Class 5) 3-Y-O+ £3,408 (£1,006; £503) Stalls Low

Form RPR
03- **1** **Dance Of Heroes**[123] 7646 3-8-7 0 .... AndreaAtzeni 4 80+
(Jeremy Noseda) *t.k.h early: led briefly: sn settled in 3rd: rdn over 2f out: swtchd rt over 1f out: r.o wl to ld fnl 75yds: gng away at fin* **4/5**[1]
0- **2** 1 1/2 **Moontown**[131] 7460 3-8-8 0 ow1 .... JamieSpencer 2 76
(Charles Hills) *chsd ldr: rdn and ev ch 2f out: led jst ins fnl f: hrd drvn and hdd fnl 75yds: no ex and outpcd by wnr after* **8/1**[3]
023- **3** 1 1/4 **Roskilly (IRE)**[91] 8124 3-8-7 79 .... DavidProbert 5 73
(Andrew Balding) *sn led: rdn 2f out: hrd drvn and hdd jst ins fnl f: wknd fnl 75yds* **9/4**[2]
22-4 **4** 4 1/2 **Song And Dance Man**[10] 686 4-10-0 73 ....(p) TomQueally 6 69
(Gary Moore) *t.k.h: hld up in tch in midfield: rdn 2f out: outpcd by ldng trio over 1f out: wl hld and one pce after* **16/1**
600- **5** hd **Son Of Feyan (IRE)**[160] 6733 3-8-7 68 .... JoeFanning 1 64
(Roger Teal) *t.k.h: hld up in tch in midfield: rdn and unable qck wl over 1f out: no threat to ldrs and one pce after* **16/1**
46 **6** 3/4 **Dark Tsarina (IRE)**[38] 316 3-8-4 0 ow2 .... FrankieMcDonald 7 59
(John Butler) *stdd s: hld up in tch in last: outpcd and rdn over 1f out: no threat to ldrs and one pce fnl f: jockey weighed-in 2lb over* **66/1**
2m 6.39s (-0.21) **Going Correction** -0.05s/f (Stan)
**WFA** 3 from 4yo+ 21lb 6 Ran SP% **110.7**
Speed ratings (Par 103): **98,96,95,92,92 91**
CSF £8.01 TOTE £1.70: £1.10, £3.80; EX 9.30 Trifecta £16.00.
**Owner** Newsells Park Stud **Bred** Newsells Park Stud **Trained** Newmarket, Suffolk
■ Stewards' Enquiry : Frankie McDonald two-day ban: weighed in 2lb heavy (17-18 Mar)

**FOCUS**
Not a strong maiden, run at a steady pace. The front three finished clear. The winner looks better than the bare form.

## 828 32RED.COM H'CAP 1m 2f (P)
4:55 (4:57) (Class 5) (0-75,72) 3-Y-O £3,234 (£962; £481; £240) Stalls Low

Form RPR
40-1 **1** **Tizlove Regardless (USA)**[3] 774 3-8-13 64 6ex .... JoeFanning 4 72+
(Mark Johnston) *awkward leaving stalls: chsd ldr tl rdn to ld 2f out: clr and in command whn rn green: flashed tail and hung lft ins fnl f: pushed out towards fin* **4/7**[1]
5421 **2** 1 1/2 **Zamra (IRE)**[10] 684 3-9-0 65 ....(p) LukeMorris 3 68
(James Tate) *hld up wl in tch: rdn and effrt 2f out: 3rd and drvn over 1f out: chsd wnr and swtchd lft fnl 100yds: kpt on* **6/1**[2]
4-24 **3** 1 3/4 **Samtu (IRE)**[38] 316 3-9-6 71 .... TomQueally 1 71
(Clive Brittain) *wnt rt s: sn led: rdn and hdd 2f out: drvn and outpcd over 1f out: lost 2nd and wknd fnl 100yds* **6/1**[2]
**4** nk **Arianrhod (IRE)**[48] 3-9-7 72 .... AndreaAtzeni 5 71
(Marco Botti) *stdd s: hld up in tch in rr: rdn and effrt in 4th whn swtchd rt over 1f out: kpt on same pce ins fnl f* **20/1**
5-33 **5** 9 **Turnbury**[4] 761 3-8-10 68 ....[1] GeorgeBuckell(7) 6 50
(Robert Mills) *t.k.h: chsd ldrs: rdn and struggling whn edgd lft and bmpd over 1f out: sn wknd* **12/1**[3]
5443 **6** 46 **Izbushka (IRE)**[26] 488 3-8-12 63 .... StevieDonohoe 2
(Ian Williams) *bmpd s: sn rdn along: in tch: rdn 6f out: dropped to last 3f out: lost tch 2f out: t.o and virtually p.u fnl f* **16/1**
2m 5.16s (-1.44) **Going Correction** -0.05s/f (Stan) 6 Ran SP% **110.6**
Speed ratings (Par 98): **103,101,100,100,92 56**
CSF £4.30 TOTE £1.70: £1.10, £2.00; EX 5.10 Trifecta £10.60.
**Owner** Crone Stud Farms Ltd **Bred** WinStar Farm LLC **Trained** Middleham Moor, N Yorks

**FOCUS**
An uncompetitive handicap run at an honest pace. The winner but did this in style of a horse that has the scope to rate considerably higher.
T/Plt: £112.50 to a £1 stake. Pool: £63280.82 - 410.47 winning tickets T/Qpdt: £13.90 to a £1 stake. Pool: £5557.33 - 294.40 winning tickets SP

# [761] SOUTHWELL (L-H)
Tuesday, March 4

**OFFICIAL GOING: Standard**
Wind: Moderate; across Weather: Cloudy with sunny periods

## 829 32RED H'CAP 1m 6f (F)
2:10 (2:10) (Class 5) (0-75,68) 4-Y-O+ £3,234 (£962; £481; £240) Stalls Low

Form RPR
05-1 **1** **Kingscombe (USA)**[14] 648 5-9-3 60 .... SebSanders 4 68
(Linda Jewell) *cl up: led after 2f: pushed along wl over 2f out and sn jnd: rdn wl over 1f out: drvn and hdd ins fnl f: rallied gamely to ld again towards fin* **5/2**[1]
4 **2** nk **Carlanda (FR)**[23] 548 4-9-4 65 ....(p) AndrewMullen 2 73
(Michael Appleby) *trckd ldrs: hdwy 4f out: effrt 2f out: sn cl up: rdn to chal over 1f out: drvn to take slt ld ins fnl f: hdd and no ex towards fin* **6/1**
44-6 **3** 5 **No Such Number**[55] 85 6-9-5 65 ....(p) RossAtkinson(3) 6 66
(Julia Feilden) *trckd ldng pair: hdwy and cl up over 4f out: rdn to chal over 2f out: drvn wl over 1f out and kpt on same pce* **9/2**[3]
2342 **4** 1 1/2 **Yasir (USA)**[16] 567 6-9-11 68 ....(p) HayleyTurner 5 67
(Conor Dore) *racd wd in rr: hdwy 1/2-way: pushed along to chse ldrs 4f out: rdn over 3f out and sn one pce* **3/1**[2]
003- **5** 21 **Star Date (IRE)**[61] 7636 5-8-13 59 .... WilliamTwiston-Davies(3) 3 29
(Oliver Sherwood) *trckd ldrs: pushed along 4f out: rdn over 3f out and sn outpcd* **9/2**[3]
1110 **6** 13 **Fire In Babylon (IRE)**[14] 648 6-9-8 65 ....(b) AdamBeschizza 1 18
(Noel Quinlan) *led 2f: cl up on inner: rdn along 4f out: wknd 3f out* **8/1**
3m 8.12s (-0.18) **Going Correction** 0.0s/f (Stan)
**WFA** 4 from 5yo+ 4lb 6 Ran SP% **115.3**
Speed ratings (Par 103): **100,99,96,96,84 76**
CSF £18.37 TOTE £2.90: £1.30, £6.10; EX 23.50 Trifecta £129.60.
**Owner** Peter Oppenheimer **Bred** Juddmonte Farms Inc **Trained** Sutton Valence, Kent

**FOCUS**
An ordinary staying handicap, but the front pair had a right set-to all the way up the home straight.

## 830 CORAL.CO.UK BEST ODDS GUARANTEED ON RACING (S) STKS 1m 3f (F)
2:40 (2:40) (Class 6) 4-Y-O+ £2,587 (£770; £384; £192) Stalls Low

Form RPR
2112 **1** **Stand Guard**[18] 601 10-9-2 85 .... TomQueally 4 84
(John Butler) *hld up in tch: hdwy on outer 4f out: led wl over 2f out: rdn clr over 1f out: readily* **10/11**[1]
05-1 **2** 8 **Conducting**[11] 685 6-9-2 68 .... DavidProbert 3 71
(Gay Kelleway) *led: pushed along 4f out: rdn over 3f out: hdd wl over 2f out and sn outpcd: kpt on u.p fnl f: tk modest 2nd last 100yds* **10/1**[3]
3133 **3** 3 1/4 **Staff Sergeant**[5] 763 7-9-2 80 .... AndrewMullen 1 66
(Michael Appleby) *trckd ldng pair on inner: effrt and n.m.r over 3f out: rdn along to chse wnr 2f out: sn hung lft to inner rail: drvn and btn over 1f out: lost modest 2nd last 100yds* **5/4**[2]
14/5 **4** 7 **Encore Un Fois**[21] 565 6-8-11 60 .... JamesSullivan 2 50
(Ruth Carr) *trckd ldr: cl up 5f out: rdn along 4f out: wknd 3f out* **50/1**
2m 26.49s (-1.51) **Going Correction** 0.0s/f (Stan) 4 Ran SP% **107.9**
Speed ratings (Par 101): **105,99,96,91**
CSF £9.36 TOTE £1.80; EX 4.80 Trifecta £6.10.There was no bid for the winner. Conducting was claimed by Mr Jim Best for £5,500. Staff Sergeant was subject to a friendly claim by Mr Michael Appleby for £5,500.
**Owner** Maxilead Limited **Bred** Juddmonte Farms Ltd **Trained** Newmarket, Suffolk
■ Stand Guard matched China Castle's record of 25 wins on the AW, set more than 12 years ago.
■ Stewards' Enquiry : Andrew Mullen one-day ban: careless riding (Mar 18)

**FOCUS**
A fascinating clash on paper, which became a one-horse race. The winner was well on top, with the third not hiving his running.

## 831 CORAL MOBILE "JUST THREE CLICKS TO BET" H'CAP 1m 4f (F)
3:10 (3:11) (Class 6) (0-60,60) 4-Y-O+ £2,587 (£770; £384; £192) Stalls Low

Form RPR
2-52 **1** **On The Cusp (IRE)**[23] 546 7-9-6 59 ....(b) WilliamCarson 12 65
(Ann Stokell) *t.k.h: chsd ldr: led 4f out: pushed along over 2f out: rdn wl over 1f out and sn edgd rt: drvn and edgd rt again ins fnl f: kpt on* **7/1**
5-24 **2** 1 **Opus (IRE)**[13] 657 5-9-1 54 .... LukeMorris 2 59
(Lucy Wadham) *trckd ldrs: hdwy 5f out: chsd wnr over 2f out: rdn and ev ch ent fnl f: carried rt and drvn last 100yds: no ex towards fin* **7/2**[1]
4-02 **3** 1 1/2 **Reach The Beach**[28] 475 5-8-8 47 .... StevieDonohoe 9 51
(Brendan Powell) *midfield: pushed along and outpcd over 5f out: hdwy and wd st: sn rdn: chsd ldng pair and styng on wl nr stands' rail whn n.m.r and hmpd ins fnl f: sn swtchd lft: no imp after* **14/1**
6-34 **4** 1 3/4 **Brunello**[25] 513 6-9-4 57 ....(b) RussKennemore 4 57
(Philip Kirby) *chsd ldrs: hdwy over 3f out: rdn over 2f out: sn drvn and kpt on same pce* **7/1**
16-5 **5** 4 1/2 **Bold And Free**[28] 476 4-9-5 60 .... GrahamLee 6 53
(David Thompson) *chsd ldng pair: hdwy 3f out: rdn 2f out: sn drvn and one pce* **8/1**
6546 **6** nse **Monzino (USA)**[14] 652 6-9-0 60 ....(b) PaulBooth(7) 7 53
(Michael Chapman) *s.i.s and bhd: rdn along over 4f out: hdwy 3f out: styd on fnl 2f* **16/1**
0032 **7** 1 3/4 **General Tufto**[15] 640 9-8-13 52 ....(b) TomEaves 10 42
(Charles Smith) *towards rr: hdwy 1/2-way: chsd ldrs 3f out: rdn along over 2f out: sn drvn and no imp* **14/1**
5-30 **8** 4 1/2 **Omega Omega**[40] 303 5-8-7 46 oh1 ....(b) AdamBeschizza 11 29
(Julia Feilden) *midfield: sme hdwy to chse ldrs over 4f out: rdn along over 3f out and sn btn* **16/1**
5500 **9** 1 1/4 **Dontpaytheferryman (USA)**[15] 639 9-8-10 49 ....(b) PaulMulrennan 8 31
(Peter Hiatt) *sn led: rdn along and hdd 4f out: drvn and wknd over 3f out* **25/1**
0132 **10** 9 **Marina Ballerina**[14] 648 6-9-0 58 .... GeorgeDowning(5) 1 26
(Roy Bowring) *midfield: rdn along bef 1/2-way: sn lost pl and bhd* **6/1**[3]
00-4 **11** 15 **Rockweiller**[4] 781 7-8-10 52 ....(b) NeilFarley(3) 3
(Shaun Harris) *prom on inner: rdn along 5f out: sn wknd* **9/2**[2]
56/0 **12** 15 **Cape Safari (IRE)**[56] 73 5-9-2 60 ....(p) HarryPoulton(5) 5
(Tim Vaughan) *sn rdn along in rr: bhd fnl 4f* **20/1**
2m 41.7s (0.70) **Going Correction** 0.0s/f (Stan)
**WFA** 4 from 5yo+ 2lb 12 Ran SP% **124.5**
Speed ratings (Par 101): **97,96,95,94,91 91,89,86,86,80 70,60**
CSF £33.34 CT £349.80 TOTE £7.20: £2.10, £1.40, £4.80; EX 33.10 Trifecta £224.60.
**Owner** Pallet And Recycling Sales Ltd **Bred** J Stan Cosgrove **Trained** Southwell, Notts

**FOCUS**
A low-grade middle-distance handicap, rated around the second.

## 832 LADBROKES H'CAP — 1m (F)
3:40 (3:41) (Class 4) (0-85,85) 4-Y-0+ £5,822 (£1,732; £865; £432) Stalls Low

Form RPR

-1 **1** **Mondlicht (USA)**[21] 564 4-9-2 **80** ........ JoeFanning 2 90+
(Mark Johnston) *prom on inner: green and rdn along over 3f out: sn outpcd: gd hdwy wl over 1f out: styd on strly ent fnl f: led last 75yds* **11/10**[1]

1-33 **2** 1 **Greyfriarschorista**[23] 550 7-9-2 **83** ........ RobertTart(3) 4 90
(Tom Keddy) *prom: cl up 1/2-way: led 3f out: pushed clr 2f out: rdn over 1f out: hung rt ins fnl f: hdd and no ex last 75yds* **5/1**[2]

100- **3** 1½ **Showboating (IRE)**[103] 7992 6-9-7 **85** ........ (tp) TomQueally 6 89
(Alan McCabe) *dwlt: sn trcking ldrs: pushed along and lost pl over 3f out: wd st and hdwy 2f out: sn rdn: styd on to chse ldr ins fnl f: kpt on same pce* **20/1**

000- **4** 2 **Askaud (IRE)**[136] 7368 6-9-2 **80** ........ (p) FrederikTylicki 3 79
(Scott Dixon) *led: rdn along and hdd 3f out: cl up and drvn over 2f out: grad wknd* **16/1**

3216 **5** ¾ **Tartan Trip**[23] 552 7-8-7 **71** ........ (v) AndrewMullen 7 68
(Michael Appleby) *dwlt: sn in tch on outer: hdwy 3f out: rdn 2f out and sn chsng ldr: drvn over 1f out and sn one pce* **20/1**

005- **6** 5 **Karaka Jack**[130] 7499 7-9-1 **79** ........ PaddyAspell 5 65
(David Nicholls) *chsd ldrs: effrt over 2f out and sn swtchd lft: rdn and wknd wl over 1f out* **7/1**

0-45 **7** 2½ **Warfare**[40] 300 5-8-9 **73** ........ (b[1]) TomEaves 9 53
(Kevin Ryan) *dwlt: sn prom on outer: effrt over 2f out: sn rdn and wknd* **12/1**

1341 **8** 6 **Tatting**[11] 698 5-9-5 **83** ........ LiamKeniry 1 49
(Chris Dwyer) *towards rr: rdn along wl over 2f out: n.d* **6/1**[3]

1m 42.09s (-1.61) **Going Correction** 0.0s/f (Stan) **8** Ran SP% **114.2**
Speed ratings (Par 105): **108,107,105,103,102 97,95,89**
CSF £6.76 CT £65.38 TOTE £1.90: £1.10, £2.00, £3.70; EX 7.90 Trifecta £77.80.
**Owner** Sheikh Hamdan bin Mohammed Al Maktoum **Bred** Lazy Lane Farms Llc **Trained** Middleham Moor, N Yorks

**FOCUS**
A decent handicap, run at a solid pace, and won by an unexposed sort, who can do better again from here.

## 833 DOWNLOAD THE LADBROKES APP H'CAP — 7f (F)
4:10 (4:10) (Class 6) (0-52,51) 4-Y-0+ £2,587 (£770; £384; £192) Stalls Low

Form RPR

03-0 **1** **All Right Now**[58] 59 7-9-7 **51** ........ (tp) GrahamLee 5 60
(Tony Newcombe) *mde most: rdn along 2f out: drvn ent fnl f: hld on gamely* **9/2**[3]

5643 **2** nse **Very First Blade**[12] 676 5-9-2 **46** ........ (be) JoeFanning 9 55
(Michael Mullineaux) *prom: cl up 3f out: rdn to chal wl over 1f out: drvn and ev ch ins fnl f: no ex nr line* **6/1**

03-3 **3** 4½ **Shamiana**[12] 671 4-9-7 **51** ........ (b) RichardKingscote 8 50
(Daniel Kubler) *trckd ldrs: hdwy 3f out: rdn over 2f out: drvn over 1f out: kpt on same pce* **6/1**

3203 **4** hd **Mucky Molly**[21] 563 6-9-2 **46** ........ (vt) TomEaves 11 42
(Alison Hutchinson) *prom on outer: effrt to chse ldng pair over 2f out: drvn over 1f out and kpt on same pce* **4/1**[2]

0-14 **5** hd **De Lesseps (USA)**[35] 367 6-9-7 **51** ........ RobertWinston 3 46
(James Moffatt) *chsd ldrs on inner: hdwy 3f out: rdn over 2f out: drvn over 1f out: one pce* **6/4**[1]

/26- **6** 6 **Fast On (IRE)**[11] 8233 5-8-12 **49** ........ (e) DavidParkes(7) 1 28
(Seamus Fahey, Ire) *in rr tl sme late hdwy* **20/1**

-633 **7** shd **Elusive Warrior (USA)**[21] 565 11-9-6 **50** ........ (p) TomQueally 7 29
(Alan McCabe) *dwlt and towards rr: sme hdwy and wd st: sn rdn and n.d* **12/1**

5-40 **8** 8 **Au Renoir**[14] 649 4-9-1 **45** ........ PaulMulrennan 4 2
(Kevin Ryan) *dwlt: in tch: rdn along bef 1/2-way and sn wknd* **33/1**

5-45 **9** 1¾ **Mobley Chaos**[8] 731 4-9-1 **45** ........ LukeMorris 2
(Ronald Harris) *dwlt: a in rr* **33/1**

-0B0 **10** 4 **Roxy Lane**[5] 755 5-9-2 **46** ........ WilliamCarson 6
(Peter Hiatt) *cl up: rdn along over 3f out: sn wknd* **33/1**

1m 30.14s (-0.16) **Going Correction** 0.0s/f (Stan) **10** Ran SP% **128.0**
Speed ratings (Par 101): **100,99,94,94,94 87,87,78,76,71**
CSF £33.71 CT £168.31 TOTE £7.90: £1.90, £1.70, £1.70; EX 41.60 Trifecta £268.40.
**Owner** Justin Hay **Bred** Rolyon Stud **Trained** Yarnscombe, Devon

**FOCUS**
Effectively a 40-51 handicap. The winner is rated back to his better form of recent years.

## 834 COMPARE BOOKMAKERS AT BOOKMAKERS.CO.UK H'CAP — 5f (F)
4:40 (4:40) (Class 5) (0-75,75) 4-Y-0+ £3,234 (£962; £481; £240) Stalls High

Form RPR

0144 **1** **Sir Geoffrey (IRE)**[13] 654 8-8-7 **68** ........ (p) MatthewHopkins(7) 1 78
(Scott Dixon) *trckd ldrs on outer: hdwy 1/2-way and sn cl up: rdn to chal over 1f out: led ent fnl f: kpt on wl* **12/1**

1-65 **2** ½ **Thorpe Bay**[43] 257 5-9-2 **70** ........ AndrewMullen 2 78
(Michael Appleby) *cl up: led 1/2-way: rdn wl over 1f out: drvn and hdd ent fnl f: kpt on* **7/4**[1]

0211 **3** 2½ **Electric Qatar**[23] 549 5-9-1 **72** ........ (p) RossAtkinson(3) 4 71
(Alan McCabe) *qckly away and cl up: rdn along over 2f out: ev ch tl drvn and one pce appr fnl f* **8/1**

-211 **4** 1½ **Iffranesia (FR)**[13] 654 4-9-4 **72** ........ (p) TomQueally 3 66
(Robert Cowell) *dwlt and towards rr: hdwy 2f out: sn rdn and styd on fnl f* **9/2**[3]

5230 **5** 5 **Pull The Pin (IRE)**[13] 654 5-8-13 **67** ........ (bt) WilliamCarson 5 43+
(Ann Stokell) *t.k.h: sn led: hdd 1/2-way: sn rdn and wknd wl over 1f out* **14/1**

3150 **6** nk **Only Ten Per Cent (IRE)**[20] 572 6-9-0 **68** ow1 ........ (v) StephenCraine 8 43+
(J R Jenkins) *cl up: rdn along 2f out: sn wknd* **6/1**

60-2 **7** 2¾ **Rowe Park**[40] 299 11-9-6 **74** ........ (p) LiamKeniry 6 39+
(Linda Jewell) *chsd ldrs: rdn along 1/2-way: sn wknd* **4/1**[2]

000- **8** 2¾ **Lost In Paris (IRE)**[154] 6920 8-9-7 **75** ........ BarryMcHugh 7 30+
(Tony Coyle) *sn outpcd and bhd* **33/1**

59.66s (-0.04) **Going Correction** +0.075s/f (Slow) **8** Ran SP% **117.2**
Speed ratings (Par 103): **103,102,98,95,87 87,82,78**
CSF £34.40 CT £187.56 TOTE £13.80: £3.60, £1.10, £2.20; EX 57.60 Trifecta £479.40.
**Owner** General Sir Geoffrey Howlett **Bred** P Rabbitte **Trained** Babworth, Notts

**FOCUS**
The draw certainly played its part here with those drawn low at a major advantage. The winner is rated back to his best form of recent years.

## 835 BEST ODDS AT BOOKMAKERS.CO.UK H'CAP — 6f (F)
5:10 (5:11) (Class 6) (0-60,60) 4-Y-0+ £2,587 (£770; £384; £192) Stalls Low

Form RPR

-500 **1** **Masai Moon**[19] 589 10-8-13 **59** ........ (b) PatMillman(7) 4 73
(Rod Millman) *towards rr and swtchd rt to outer after 1f: hdwy 1/2-way: rdn to ld over 1f out: clr ins fnl f* **6/1**[3]

0-34 **2** 3 **Masked Dance (IRE)**[5] 766 7-8-13 **52** ........ (b) LukeMorris 7 57
(Scott Dixon) *chsd ldng pair: rdn along to chse ldr over 2f out: drvn wl over 1f out: kpt on same pce fnl f* **6/1**[3]

-045 **3** 2½ **Laughing Rock (IRE)**[14] 651 4-9-1 **54** ........ (p) AndrewMullen 9 52
(Michael Appleby) *chsd ldrs: hdwy wl over 2f out: sn rdn and ev ch wl over 1f out: drvn and one pce appr fnl f* **20/1**

4-52 **4** nse **Solarmaite**[35] 367 5-8-13 **57** ........ (b) GeorgeDowning(5) 5 54
(Roy Bowring) *in tch: rdn along and sltly outpcd wl over 2f out: swtchd lft and styd on u.p appr fnl f: nrst fin* **3/1**[2]

0-53 **5** nse **Caramelita**[35] 362 7-9-7 **60** ........ (v) FrederikTylicki 6 57
(J R Jenkins) *chsd ldr: hdwy to ld wl over 2f out: sn rdn: drvn and hdd over 1f out: grad wknd* **10/1**

13-4 **6** 1½ **Izzy Boy (USA)**[54] 102 4-9-6 **59** ........ LiamJones 3 52
(Mark Johnston) *dwlt and n.m.r shortly after s: sn bhd and rdn along: hdwy 2f out: kpt on fnl f: nrst fin* **11/4**[1]

0330 **7** 1¼ **Sewn Up**[5] 766 4-9-7 **60** ........ (p) TonyHamilton 2 49
(Andrew Hollinshead) *in rr and pushed along whn n.m.r bnd after 2f: sme hdwy wl over 1f out: n.d* **8/1**

63-4 **8** 7 **Dancing Freddy (IRE)**[33] 383 7-9-6 **59** ........ (tp) WilliamCarson 8 27
(Ann Stokell) *qckly away and led: rdn along 1/2-way: sn hdd & wknd* **7/1**

-004 **9** 4 **Avonmore Star**[15] 646 6-9-5 **58** ........ TomQueally 1 14
(Alan McCabe) *a in rr* **25/1**

1m 16.42s (-0.08) **Going Correction** 0.0s/f (Stan) **9** Ran SP% **121.5**
Speed ratings (Par 101): **100,96,92,92,92 90,88,79,74**
CSF £44.14 CT £696.88 TOTE £6.80: £1.70, £1.50, £6.60; EX 47.50 Trifecta £589.20.
**Owner** B R Millman **Bred** Mrs B A Matthews **Trained** Kentisbeare, Devon

**FOCUS**
A moderate sprint handicap, and straightforward form.
T/Jkpt: Not won. T/Plt: £70.80 to a £1 stake. Pool: £104,213.18 - 1,074.07 winning units T/Qpdt: £18.70 to a £1 stake. Pool: £10,144.55 - 400.30 winning units JR

# 795 CHANTILLY (R-H)
Tuesday, March 4

**OFFICIAL GOING: Polytrack: standard**

## 836a PRIX MEYDAN GOLF CLUB (CONDITIONS) (3YO+) (POLYTRACK) — 6f 110y
1:20 (1:20) 3-Y-0+
£20,833 (£8,333; £6,250; £4,166; £1,041; £1,041)

RPR

**1** **Sunny (FR)**[23] 5-9-2 0 ........ ChristopheSoumillon 3 108
(J-C Rouget, France) **23/10**[1]

**2** 1¼ **Complimentor (IRE)**[199] 4-9-2 0 ........ MaximeGuyon 4 104
(X Thomas-Demeaulte, France) **7/1**

**3** ½ **Myasun (FR)**[108] 7941 7-9-6 0 ........ GregoryBenoist 1 107
(C Baillet, France) **27/10**[2]

**4** 2½ **Bravo Echo**[10] 713 8-9-2 0 ........ RobertHavlin 10 95
(Michael Attwater) *broke wl fr wdst draw and led early: trckd ldr on inner after 1f: pushed along 2f out: nt clr run on rail fr over 1f out tl ins fnl f: kpt on wl once clr but ch gone* **199/10**

**5** ½ **Jo De Vati (FR)**[65] 4-9-2 0 ........ TheoBachelot 2 94
(S Wattel, France) **236/10**

**5** dht **Pretty Panther (FR)**[294] 2356 4-8-13 0 ........ Francois-XavierBertras 8 91
(F Rohaut, France) **189/10**

**7** 2½ **Early Ouest (FR)**[18] 4-9-2 0 ........ JeromeCabre 9 87
(P Leray, France) **35/1**

**8** 1½ **Onlyyouknowme (IRE)**[114] 7830 6-9-1 0 ........ FranckBlondel 6 81
(F Rossi, France) **47/10**[3]

**9** ¾ **Aksil (FR)**[103] 7995 4-8-13 0 ........ StephanePasquier 7 77
(M Boutin, France) **15/2**

**10** 1½ **Amberley (FR)**[103] 7995 5-9-2 0 ........ FredericSpanu 5 76
(E Moullec, France) **26/1**

1m 16.73s (76.73) **10** Ran SP% **119.5**
PARI-MUTUEL (all including 1 euro stake): WIN 3.30. PLACE: 1.40, 1.80, 1.50. DF: 13.70. SF: 19.60..
**Owner** Bernard Magrez Horses **Bred** A Bozo, H Bozo, G Bozo & Mme A F Charpy **Trained** Pau, France

# 815 KEMPTON (A.W) (R-H)
Wednesday, March 5

**OFFICIAL GOING: Standard**
Wind: Almost nil Weather: Fine, mild

## 838 SILVER CUPS DAY 15.03.14 H'CAP — 1m 2f (P)
5:30 (5:32) (Class 6) (0-55,55) 4-Y-0+ £1,940 (£577; £288; £144) Stalls Low

Form RPR

53-6 **1** **Sudden Wish (IRE)**[30] 459 5-9-6 **54** ........ RyanMoore 9 61
(Gary Moore) *w ldr in slowly run event: led wl over 1f out: drvn and hld on fnl f* **5/2**[1]

0-61 **2** ½ **My Renaissance**[21] 570 4-9-4 **52** ........ ShaneKelly 3 58
(Ben Case) *trckd ldrs: prog to chal and w wnr over 1f out: nt qckn fnl f: styd on* **13/2**

00-0 **3** nse **Highly Likely (IRE)**[42] 283 5-9-7 **55** ........ JimCrowley 2 61
(Steve Woodman) *t.k.h: hld up in midfield in slowly run r: prog over 1f out: tk 3rd fnl f: r.o and nrly snatched 2nd* **16/1**

3126 **4** 1¼ **Kyle Of Bute**[13] 671 8-9-5 **53** ........ GrahamLee 1 57
(Richard Ford) *trckd ldng pair in slowly run event: rdn over 1f out: kpt on same pce after* **12/1**

2223 **5** ½ **Polydamos**[6] 754 5-9-4 **52**......(v) AdamKirby 10 55
(Tony Carroll) *hld up in last trio in slowly run event: dashed up arnd rivals fr 3f out to chal 2f out: fdd ins fnl f* **11/2**[3]

3324 **6** 1 **Olivers Mount**[31] 446 4-9-7 **55**......(t) JimmyQuinn 7 56
(Ed Vaughan) *racd wd in midfield: dropped to last pair whn pce lifted 2f out and pushed along: rdn and kpt on same pce fnl f* **6/1**

-003 **7** nse **James Pollard (IRE)**[16] 639 9-9-3 **51**......(tp) LiamKeniry 13 52
(Bernard Llewellyn) *t.k.h: hld up in last in slowly run event: rdn over 1f out: kpt on fnl f: no ch* **33/1**

00-1 **8** ¾ **Addikt (IRE)**[28] 484 9-9-4 **52**...... TomEaves 4 51
(John Spearing) *stdd s: plld hrd in midfield: rdn and fnd nil wl over 1f out* **5/1**[2]

5-00 **9** hd **Mists Of Time (IRE)**[11] 718 4-9-6 **54**...... JamesSullivan 8 53
(Pat Eddery) *t.k.h: led at sedate pce: tried to kick on over 2f out: hdd wl over 1f out: wknd* **66/1**

0-54 **10** 1 ¾ **Entrapping**[30] 459 4-9-7 **55**...... LiamJones 11 51
(John E Long) *t.k.h: hld up in last trio in slowly run event: urged along over 1f out: no prog* **16/1**

000- **11** 3 ½ **Three Choirs (IRE)**[172] 6402 4-9-4 **55**......(b¹) RobertTart(3) 5 44
(William Stone) *racd wd: trckd ldrs: lost pl over 2f out: sn btn* **16/1**

2m 12.26s (4.26) **Going Correction** -0.05s/f (Stan) **11** Ran SP% **118.0**
Speed ratings (Par 101): **80,79,79,78,78 77,77,76,76,75 72**
CSF £18.84 CT £217.95 TOTE £3.40: £1.20, £2.20, £4.90; EX 20.90 Trifecta £493.40.
**Owner** M&R Refurbishments Ltd **Bred** Catridge Farm Stud & S Von Schilcher **Trained** Lower Beeding, W Sussex

**FOCUS**
They crawled for most of this race before sprinting up the straight. Moderate form.

## 839 BETDAQ NO LOSE MOBILE BET MEDIAN AUCTION MAIDEN STKS 1m 2f (P)
**6:00** (6:01) (Class 5) 3-Y-O £2,587 (£770; £384; £192) **Stalls** Low

Form RPR

3-2 **1** **Bishop Of Ruscombe**[20] 588 3-9-5 0...... DavidProbert 3 76+
(Andrew Balding) *led 2f: trckd ldr: led on bit over 1f out: pushed clr fnl f* **8/13**[1]

440- **2** 4 ½ **Citizen Kaine (IRE)**[165] 6619 3-8-12 65...... JosephineGordon(7) 2 65
(Jo Hughes) *t.k.h early: trckd ldng pair: pushed along and outpcd 3f out: kpt on fr over 1f out to take 2nd last strides* **10/1**[3]

00-2 **3** hd **Dynamic Ranger (USA)**[40] 316 3-9-5 75...... RyanMoore 4 65
(Gary Moore) *racd freely: led after 2f: rdn and hdd over 1f out: wknd fnl f and lost 2nd last strides* **15/8**[2]

**4** 2 ¾ **Musical Theme** 3-9-0 0...... PaddyAspell 5 55+
(Willie Musson) *difficult to load into stalls: hld up in last pair: outpcd 3f out: shkn up and no prog after* **33/1**

05 **5** ½ **In Seine**[19] 607 3-9-5 0...... FergusSweeney 1 59
(John Best) *hld up in last pair: outpcd 3f out: pushed along and stl looked green after: no prog* **66/1**

2m 8.5s (0.50) **Going Correction** -0.05s/f (Stan) **5** Ran SP% **110.2**
Speed ratings (Par 98): **96,92,92,90,89**
CSF £8.02 TOTE £1.50: £1.10, £3.70; EX 5.80 Trifecta £9.00.
**Owner** David Brownlow **Bred** Whitsbury Manor Stud **Trained** Kingsclere, Hants

**FOCUS**
This was run in quite a slow time and it's likely the winner didn't need to improve. The fifth is perhaps the key.

## 840 BETDAQ - SPORTS BETTING EXCHANGE H'CAP 1m 2f (P)
**6:30** (6:32) (Class 2) (0-100,99) 4-Y-O+
£11,827 (£3,541; £1,770; £885; £442; £222) **Stalls** Low

Form RPR

3114 **1** **Rebellious Guest**[18] 625 5-9-0 **92**...... TomQueally 11 103
(George Margarson) *hld up towards rr: prog over 2f out: clsd qckly to ld jst ins fnl f: shkn up and sn clr* **8/1**

2-00 **2** 2 **Uramazin (IRE)**[11] 716 8-9-3 **95**...... LiamKeniry 12 102
(Philip Hide) *dwlt: hld up in last pair: looking for room on inner over 2f out: prog and eased out over 1f out: r.o to take 2nd last 50yds: no ch to chal* **40/1**

6-23 **3** ¾ **Moonday Sun (USA)**[25] 533 5-9-2 **94**...... RobertHavlin 13 100
(Amanda Perrett) *trckd ldr: led over 5f out: 2 l clr over 1f out: hdd and one pce jst ins fnl f* **12/1**

124- **4** nk **Bancnuanaheireann (IRE)**[91] 8156 7-9-7 **99**...... AndrewMullen 14 104
(Michael Appleby) *hld up in midfield: rdn on outer over 2f out: prog over 1f out: styd on fnl f: nrst fin* **25/1**

-400 **5** 1 ¾ **Emerald Wilderness (IRE)**[32] 426 10-8-9 **87**......(p) WilliamCarson 2 89
(Mark Rimmer) *wl in tch: tried to cl on ldrs on inner over 1f out: outpcd fnl f* **40/1**

0-11 **6** 1 ¾ **Indian Jack (IRE)**[25] 533 6-9-1 **93**...... LukeMorris 7 92
(Ed Walker) *hld up in last trio and racd wd: rdn over 2f out: no prog tl kpt on fnl f* **3/1**[1]

-642 **7** nk **Shavansky**[25] 533 10-8-10 **88**...... AndreaAtzeni 9 86
(Rod Millman) *t.k.h: hld up in rr: pushed along and no ch whn nt clr run briefly wl over 1f out: styd on fnl f: nvr involved* **5/1**[3]

10-3 **8** ½ **Spa's Dancer (IRE)**[18] 625 7-8-12 **90**...... RyanMoore 1 87
(James Eustace) *trckd ldng pair: rdn and steadily wknd fr wl over 1f out* **9/2**[2]

400- **9** ¾ **Born To Surprise**[152] 6989 5-8-10 **88**...... TomEaves 4 84
(Lee Carter) *stdd s: hld up in last pair: stl there 2f out: sme prog and shkn up fnl f: nvr involved* **20/1**

03-0 **10** ½ **Persepolis (IRE)**[60] 54 4-8-8 **86**...... DavidProbert 6 81
(Brett Johnson) *hld up in rr: no ch whn nt clr run briefly wl over 1f out: nvr involved* **12/1**

43-2 **11** 2 **Epic Battle (IRE)**[23] 560 4-8-7 **85** oh1...... LiamJones 3 76
(William Haggas) *trckd ldrs: shoved along fr 4f out: steadily lost pl fr over 2f out* **8/1**

1-03 **12** 1 ¾ **Canadian Run (IRE)**[39] 342 4-8-7 **85** oh2...... HayleyTurner 8 73
(Robert Mills) *led to over 5f out: chsd ldr to over 1f out: wknd qckly* **20/1**

/0-2 **13** 1 **Ansaab**[30] 457 6-8-8 **86**...... JimmyQuinn 10 72
(Alan McCabe) *racd wd: wl in tch: wknd fr 2f out* **12/1**

2m 2.97s (-5.03) **Going Correction** -0.05s/f (Stan) course record **13** Ran SP% **123.4**
Speed ratings (Par 109): **118,116,115,115,114 112,112,112,111,111 109,108,107**
CSF £311.26 CT £3795.13 TOTE £9.70: £3.20, £10.30, £2.90; EX 377.10 Trifecta £2727.30 Part won. Pool of £3636.51 - 0.16 winning units.
**Owner** John Guest Racing **Bred** Equity Bloodstock & Newsells Park Stud **Trained** Newmarket, Suffolk

**FOCUS**
A strong handicap, and a tidy pace, resulting in a course record time, and the race benefited those ridden with a bit of patience. The winner is rated right back to his best.

## 841 BETDAQ IN £500 IN FREE BETS H'CAP 6f (P)
**7:00** (7:01) (Class 6) (0-65,65) 4-Y-O+ £1,940 (£577; £288; £144) **Stalls** Low

Form RPR

-556 **1** **Invigilator**[21] 576 6-9-4 **62**......(t) DaleSwift 10 71
(Derek Shaw) *stdd s: hld up in last and off the pce: prog over 1f out: burst between rivals to chal ins fnl f: sustained effrt to ld last 50yds* **16/1**

-014 **2** nk **Sweet Talking Guy (IRE)**[21] 576 4-9-4 **62**......(t) AdamKirby 12 70
(Lydia Pearce) *hld up in 8th: rdn over 2f out: gd prog over 1f out: led jst ins fnl f: styd on but hdd last 50yds* **11/2**[3]

6236 **3** 2 ¼ **Alnoomaas (IRE)**[20] 587 5-9-7 **65**......(b¹) LukeMorris 8 66
(Luke Dace) *trckd ldrs on outer: rdn over 2f out: hrd drvn to ld jst over 1f out: hdd and outpcd jst ins fnl f* **9/4**[1]

-655 **4** ½ **West Coast Dream**[12] 694 7-9-5 **63**...... TomEaves 5 63
(Roy Brotherton) *pressed ldr: led over 2f out: rdn and hdd jst over 1f out: one pce* **25/1**

1430 **5** ¾ **Insolenceofoffice (IRE)**[21] 576 6-9-2 **60**......(p) GrahamLee 3 58
(Richard Ford) *trckd ldrs: rdn 2f out: chal over 1f out: upsides sn after: fdd fnl f* **12/1**

-253 **6** 1 ½ **Indian Affair**[21] 576 4-9-7 **65**...... DavidProbert 1 58
(Milton Bradley) *led at str pce: hdd over 2f out: stl upsides jst over 1f out: wknd fnl f* **8/1**

-312 **7** shd **Divine Call**[21] 576 7-9-7 **65**...... RichardKingscote 7 58
(Milton Bradley) *stdd s: hld up in last: sme prog on inner 2f out: shkn up over 1f out: kpt on but nvr involved* **9/2**[2]

610- **8** ¾ **Gung Ho Jack**[141] 7263 5-9-7 **65**...... FergusSweeney 4 56
(John Best) *in tch in midfield: shkn up 2f out: no prog over 1f out: wknd fnl f* **16/1**

3200 **9** 1 **Haadeeth**[11] 714 7-9-5 **63**...... JimCrowley 2 51
(David Evans) *pressed ldrs: rdn to chal 2f out: nt qckn over 1f out: wknd fnl f* **8/1**

01-0 **10** hd **Rafaaf (IRE)**[27] 503 6-9-4 **62**...... TomQueally 6 49
(Richard Phillips) *in tch in midfield: lost pl on outer sn after 1/2-way: n.d after* **33/1**

1m 11.53s (-1.57) **Going Correction** -0.05s/f (Stan) **10** Ran SP% **112.8**
Speed ratings (Par 101): **108,107,104,103,102 100,100,99,98,98**
CSF £98.32 CT £256.21 TOTE £22.70: £5.10, £1.80, £1.50; EX 102.30 Trifecta £738.00.
**Owner** The Warren Partnership **Bred** Granham Farm And P Hearson Bloodstock **Trained** Sproxton, Leics

**FOCUS**
Plenty of pace on and the first two came from the rear. Modest form.

## 842 JUMP RACING SILVER CUPS 15.03.14 H'CAP 2m (P)
**7:30** (7:33) (Class 6) (0-60,60) 4-Y-O+ £1,940 (£577; £288; £144) **Stalls** Low

Form RPR

4-10 **1** **Newtown Cross (IRE)**[14] 657 4-8-4 **52**...... CamHardie(7) 3 60
(Jimmy Fox) *reluctant to enter stalls: in tch in midfield: prog over 2f out: rdn to ld over 1f out: jnd fnl f: kpt on gamely* **14/1**

-063 **2** nk **Arashi**[14] 656 8-9-10 **60**......(v) DaleSwift 8 68
(Derek Shaw) *dropped in fr wd draw and hld up in last: prog on outer over 2f out: drvn to join wnr fnl f: outbattled last 100yds* **5/1**[3]

3055 **3** 3 ½ **Willow Island (IRE)**[15] 652 5-8-3 **46** oh1...... HollieDoyle(7) 9 50
(David Evans) *towards rr: rdn over 2f out: prog over 1f out: kpt on to take 3rd ins fnl f: unable to threaten* **66/1**

4-52 **4** 1 **Dr Finley (IRE)**[30] 454 7-9-5 **55**......(v) AdamKirby 5 58
(Lydia Pearce) *led: wound it up fr over 3f out: drvn and hdd over 1f out: fdd fnl f* **3/1**[1]

-313 **5** 1 ¼ **Galiotto (IRE)**[14] 657 8-9-9 **59**......(v) RyanMoore 10 60
(Gary Moore) *trckd ldng pair: wnt 2nd 4f out: rdn to chal and upsides wl over 1f out: wknd fnl f* **7/2**[2]

5365 **6** 5 **Ocean Power (IRE)**[6] 759 4-8-5 **46**...... LukeMorris 6 41
(Richard Phillips) *in tch: rdn and clsd on ldrs jst over 2f out: wknd over 1f out* **8/1**

22-5 **7** ¾ **Rollin 'n Tumblin**[21] 580 10-9-1 **51**...... RobertHavlin 2 45
(Michael Attwater) *hld up in last trio: drvn and prog on inner jst over 2f out: wknd over 1f out* **16/1**

0242 **8** 1 ½ **Ogaritmo**[14] 656 5-9-8 **58**......(t) TomQueally 1 50
(Seamus Durack) *trckd ldrs: rdn to chal 2f out: wknd tamely over 1f out* **3/1**[1]

06-U **9** 2 **Baan (USA)**[33] 405 11-9-4 **57**...... RosieJessop(3) 7 47
(James Eustace) *racd wd: trckd ldrs: dropped to rr and v wd bnd 3f out: no ch after* **25/1**

-660 **10** 26 **Bell'Arte (IRE)**[14] 657 4-8-9 **50**......(p) LiamJones 4 9
(Laura Mongan) *t.k.h: chsd ldr to 4f out: sn lost pl p.u: t.o* **33/1**

3m 30.86s (0.76) **Going Correction** -0.05s/f (Stan)
**WFA** 4 from 5yo+ 5lb **10** Ran SP% **120.8**
Speed ratings (Par 101): **96,95,94,93,92 90,90,89,88,75**
CSF £84.50 CT £4497.84 TOTE £17.60: £4.60, £2.10, £14.90; EX 122.50 Trifecta £2657.60 Part won. Pool of £3543.52 - 0.05 winning units..
**Owner** Mutton & Lamb **Bred** Mrs Anne Coughlan **Trained** Collingbourne Ducis, Wilts
■ Stewards' Enquiry : Dale Swift two-day ban; used whip above permitted level (19th-20th Mar).

**FOCUS**
A very moderate staying contest run at a steady early gallop, but the pace picked up some way out and those held up were advantaged. Weak form.

## 843 BETDAQ NO PREMIUM CHARGE H'CAP (LONDON MILE SERIES QUALIFIER) 1m (P)
**8:00** (8:02) (Class 5) (0-75,74) 4-Y-O+ £2,587 (£770; £384; £192) **Stalls** Low

Form RPR

5-55 **1** **High Time Too (IRE)**[28] 493 4-9-7 **74**...... RyanMoore 1 82
(Hugo Palmer) *trckd ldng trio: prog over 2f out: rdn to ld over 1f out: drvn and styd on* **6/1**

0143 **2** ½ **Mr Red Clubs (IRE)**[9] 733 5-9-2 **69**......[1] AndrewMullen 2 76
(Michael Appleby) *led: kicked on over 2f out: hdd over 1f out: kpt on but readily hld fnl f* **9/2**[2]

0000 **3** ¾ **Ancient Greece**[10] 729 7-9-5 **72**......(tp) LukeMorris 5 77
(George Baker) *in tch in midfield: rdn wl over 2f out: styd on fr over 1f out to take 3rd ins fnl f: nrst fin* **16/1**

0346 **4** ¾ **Camachoice (IRE)**[12] 698 4-9-5 **72**......(p) AndreaAtzeni 7 75
(Marco Botti) *trckd ldr: rdn and nt qckn jst over 2f out: one pce after* **5/1**[3]

53-1 **5** ¾ **Wilfred Pickles (IRE)**[42] 286 8-9-5 **72**......(p) AdamKirby 6 74
(Jo Crowley) *hld up in midfield: rdn and nt qckn jst over 2f out: kpt on one pce after* **8/1**

14-0 **6** ½ **Triple Chocolate**[14] 655 4-9-7 **74** ........ JimmyQuinn 3 75
(Roger Ingram) *t.k.h: trckd ldrs: shkn up and nt qckn 2f out: no imp on ldrs after* **4/1**[1]

-103 **7** 1 **Diplomatic (IRE)**[20] 587 9-9-7 **74** ........ (p) LiamJones 12 72
(Michael Squance) *sn hld up in last: pushed along 1/2-way: no prog whn rdn over 2f out: kpt on fnl f* **8/1**

50-5 **8** *nk* **Al Raqeeb (IRE)**[20] 587 4-9-3 **70** ........ (t) TomQueally 11 68
(Gary Harrison) *s.i.s and hld up in last quartet: rdn over 2f out: no real prog* **33/1**

3-20 **9** *nk* **Flamborough Breeze**[28] 493 5-9-7 **74** ........ (t) LiamKeniry 8 71
(Ed Vaughan) *sn restrained into last quartet: pushed along and sme prog 2f out: no hdwy whn rdn fnl f* **16/1**

4-02 **10** ½ **Bloodsweatandtears**[20] 589 6-8-13 **66** ........ JimCrowley 9 62
(William Knight) *hld up in last quartet: rdn and fnd nil jst over 2f out: no prog* **16/1**

2264 **11** *shd* **Greensward**[12] 690 8-9-2 **69** ........ (b) HayleyTurner 10 64
(Conor Dore) *chsd ldng pair to over 2f out: sn wknd* **25/1**

1m 38.85s (-0.95) **Going Correction** -0.05s/f (Stan) 11 Ran SP% **115.8**
Speed ratings (Par 103): **102,101,100,100,99 98,97,97,97,96 96**
CSF £32.60 CT £330.11 TOTE £7.90: £2.60, £1.40, £5.90; EX 32.50 Trifecta £590.40.
**Owner** Rathordan Partnership **Bred** Christopher Maye **Trained** Newmarket, Suffolk

**FOCUS**
The pace held up pretty well here but they finished compressed. The winner is rated to his mark.

## 844 MIX BUSINESS WITH PLEASURE H'CAP — 1m (P)
**8:30** (8:30) (Class 7) (0-50,54) 4-Y-0+ **£1,617** (£481; £240; £120) **Stalls** Low

Form RPR

60-4 **1** **Fire King**[21] 575 8-9-5 **48** ........ (p) JimmyQuinn 11 55
(Paul Burgoyne) *hld up towards rr: prog jst over 2f out: wnt 2nd over 1f out: rdn to ld last 100yds: edgd rt but fnd jst enough* **9/2**[2]

-325 **2** *nk* **Byrd In Hand (IRE)**[6] 754 7-9-4 **47** ........ (b) WilliamCarson 13 53
(John Bridger) *t.k.h: led after 100yds: rdn 2f out: hdd last 100yds: edgd rt but kpt on: jst hld* **9/2**[2]

550- **3** 3 **Meetha Achar**[73] 8390 4-9-5 **48** ........ (b[1]) StephenCraine 3 47
(Jim Boyle) *hld up in rr: rdn over 2f out: eased to outer sn after: no prog tl styd on fr over 1f out to take 3rd nr fin* **12/1**

040- **4** 1½ **Frosted Off**[81] 8293 4-9-2 **45** ........ TomEaves 9 41
(John Spearing) *led 100yds: chsd ldr: rdn over 2f out: lost 2nd over 1f out: fdd* **25/1**

-030 **5** *nse* **Chandrayaan**[34] 377 7-9-5 **48** ........ (v) RobertHavlin 6 44
(John E Long) *trckd ldrs: drvn over 2f out: kpt on fr over 1f out to chal for 3rd fnl f* **4/1**[1]

0650 **6** 2¾ **The Wonga Coup (IRE)**[14] 661 7-9-2 **45** ........ (p) FergusSweeney 2 34
(Pat Phelan) *hld up in tch: prog 2f out gng bttr than most: rdn and no rspnse over 1f out* **6/1**[3]

-600 **7** *nk* **Fairy Mist (IRE)**[34] 377 7-8-11 **45** ........ RyanWhile(5) 10 34
(John Bridger) *chsd ldng pair: drvn over 2f out: wknd over 1f out* **16/1**

00-0 **8** *shd* **Ficelle (IRE)**[49] 179 5-8-13 **45** ........ (p) MatthewCosham(3) 4 33
(Nikki Evans) *t.k.h: trckd ldrs: rdn over 2f out: wknd over 1f out* **50/1**

0/00 **9** 1½ **Poker Hospital**[13] 676 5-8-11 **45** ........ (p) PhilipPrince(5) 7 30
(John Stimpson) *hld up in last pair: rdn over 2f out: no real prog* **33/1**

-460 **10** *nk* **Ishisoba**[31] 448 4-9-5 **48** ........ LiamJones 5 32
(Ronald Harris) *broke on terms but restrained into last pair: sme prog 2f out: rdn and no hdwy over 1f out: wknd* **20/1**

3-06 **11** 2 **Rigid**[14] 661 7-9-2 **45** ........ (t) JimCrowley 8 25
(Tony Carroll) *t.k.h: hld up in rr: shkn up and no prog over 2f out* **4/1**[1]

1m 39.8s **Going Correction** -0.05s/f (Stan) 11 Ran SP% **117.7**
Speed ratings (Par 97): **98,97,94,93,93 90,90,90,88,88 86**
CSF £24.06 CT £234.16 TOTE £4.80: £1.10, £3.60, £4.00; EX 15.10 Trifecta £284.00.
**Owner** Knowle Rock Racing **Bred** Dr J M Leigh **Trained** Shepton Montague, Somerset
■ Stewards' Enquiry : Tom Eaves one-day ban; weighed in without girth (19th Mar)

**FOCUS**
A weak race but straightforward form.
T/Jkpt: Not won. T/Plt: £455.40 to a £1 stake. Pool of £109312.32 - 175.22 winning tickets.
T/Qpdt: £289.70 to a £1 stake. Pool of £11746.05 - 30.0 winning tickets. JN

# 822 LINGFIELD (L-H)
Wednesday, March 5

**OFFICIAL GOING: Standard**
Wind: medium, across Weather: dry, sunny

## 845 COMPARE BOOKMAKERS AT BOOKMAKERS.CO.UK H'CAP — 5f 6y(P)
**2:00** (2:00) (Class 6) (0-65,64) 4-Y-0+ **£2,726** (£805; £402) **Stalls** High

Form RPR

0520 **1** **Secret Millionaire (IRE)**[21] 576 7-9-6 **63** ........ LukeMorris 5 72
(Tony Carroll) *in tch in midfield: clsd and swtchd lft over 1f out: hrd drvn to ld fnl 100yds: r.o wl: drvn out* **5/2**[1]

3234 **2** 1 **Pharoh Jake**[11] 714 6-9-1 **63** ........ RyanWhile(5) 6 68
(John Bridger) *chsd ldrs: effrt u.p over 1f out: ev ch 1f out: kpt on but nt gng pce of wnr fnl 100yds: wnt 2nd last strides* **3/1**[2]

2-60 **3** *nk* **Dawn Catcher**[5] 777 4-9-1 **58** ........ RichardKingscote 3 62
(Geoffrey Deacon) *led: drvn over 1f out: hdd and one pce fnl 100yds: lost 2nd last strides* **6/1**

-332 **4** 1 **Angelo Poliziano**[29] 478 8-8-13 **63** ........ (bt) JosephineGordon(7) 7 64+
(Jo Hughes) *hood removed late and s.i.s: hld up in last pair: rdn and effrt over 1f out: styd on steadily ins fnl f: nvr trbld ldrs* **7/1**

0324 **5** ¾ **Rise To Glory (IRE)**[5] 777 6-9-4 **61** ........ DuranFentiman 10 59
(Shaun Harris) *chsd ldr: drvn and ev ch over 1f out: no ex and btn ins fnl f: wknd towards fin* **9/2**[3]

1-54 **6** 1¾ **Give Us A Belle (IRE)**[12] 694 5-9-7 **64** ........ (vt) AdamBeschizza 9 56
(Christine Dunnett) *in tch in midfield: rdn 1/2-way: outpcd and struggling 2f out: kpt on same pce and n.d after* **7/1**

64-4 **7** *nk* **Purford Green**[14] 666 5-8-7 **50** oh3 ........ (v) RobertHavlin 1 41
(Michael Attwater) *in tch in midfield: rdn and struggling 2f out: btn over 1f out: wknd fnl f* **66/1**

0-00 **8** 10 **We Have A Dream**[12] 694 9-8-11 **54** ........ (tp) WilliamCarson 8 9
(Ann Stokell) *s.i.s: sn rdn and a outpcd in last* **66/1**

58.1s (-0.70) **Going Correction** -0.05s/f (Stan) 8 Ran SP% **114.0**
Speed ratings (Par 101): **103,101,100,99,98 95,94,78**
CSF £10.12 CT £38.31 TOTE £3.40: £1.10, £1.20, £2.90; EX 9.30 Trifecta £36.00.
**Owner** Robert E Lee Syndicate **Bred** James Delaney **Trained** Cropthorne, Worcs

**FOCUS**
A moderate sprint handicap, and straightforward form.

## 846 DOWNLOAD THE LADBROKES APP H'CAP — 7f 1y(P)
**2:30** (2:31) (Class 6) (0-60,60) 4-Y-0+ **£2,726** (£805; £402) **Stalls** Low

Form RPR

-422 **1** **Ghost Train (IRE)**[12] 688 5-9-6 **59** ........ (p) HayleyTurner 7 66+
(Tim McCarthy) *hmpd s: sn in tch in midfield: hdwy to chse ldrs 5f out: wnt 2nd 2f out: rdn to ld over 1f out: racd awkwardly in front and veered lft ins fnl f: pushed out towards fin* **3/1**[1]

53-6 **2** ½ **Alfresco**[32] 428 10-8-13 **52** ........ (v) RobertHavlin 1 58
(Martin Bosley) *hood removed late and slowly away: sn in tch in midfield: hdwy u.p over 1f out: styd on wl ins fnl f: wnt 2nd towards fin: nvr quite getting to wnr* **33/1**

1113 **3** ¾ **Bertie Blu Boy**[8] 740 6-9-7 **60** ........ (b) RichardKingscote 4 65
(Lisa Williamson) *w ldr tl led after 2f: rdn 2f out: hdd over 1f out: stl pressing wnr but keeping on same pce whn hmpd ins fnl f: no ex* **3/1**[1]

4-40 **4** ¾ **Black Truffle (FR)**[19] 603 4-9-3 **56** ........ (e) LiamKeniry 8 58
(Mark Usher) *hld up towards rr effrt u.p over 1f out: styd on wl ins fnl f: nt rch ldrs* **8/1**[3]

6-30 **5** *nk* **Perfect Pastime**[32] 428 6-9-5 **58** ........ (b) StephenCraine 12 59+
(Jim Boyle) *stdd s: hld up in rr: hdwy into midfield 2f out: styd on u.p fnl f: nt rch ldrs* **33/1**

36-5 **6** *hd* **Gypsy Rider**[32] 428 5-9-0 **53** ........ JimCrowley 6 54
(Roger Curtis) *racd in midfield: effrt whn nt clr run and swtchd rt 1f out: styd on wl ins fnl f: nt rch ldrs* **10/1**

-413 **7** 2 **Starbotton**[26] 516 4-9-0 **53** ........ JoeFanning 5 48
(James Bethell) *chsd ldrs: wnt 2nd 3f out tl 2f out: wknd ins fnl f* **5/1**[2]

060- **8** *nse* **Lewamy (IRE)**[199] 5564 4-9-7 **60** ........ AndreaAtzeni 3 55
(John Best) *racd in midfield: rdn and effrt over 2f out: kpt onins fnl f: nvr trbld ldrs* **33/1**

5-00 **9** ½ **Admirals Walk (IRE)**[19] 603 4-8-13 **52** ........ RenatoSouza 11 46
(Barry Brennan) *hld up in last pair: rdn and effrt over 1f out: kpt on ins fnl f: nvr trbld ldrs* **66/1**

-004 **10** 1½ **Nifty Kier**[20] 592 5-9-1 **54** ow1 ........ AdamKirby 9 44
(Martin Bosley) *midfield: reminders after 1f out and sn dropped to last trio: rdn over 1f out: no imp u.p fr over 1f out* **5/1**[2]

0004 **11** ½ **Coach Montana (IRE)**[6] 754 5-8-7 **46** oh1 ........ (b) AdamBeschizza 2 34
(Christine Dunnett) *taken down early: led for 2f: chsd ldr tl 3f out: wknd u.p over 1f out* **25/1**

0-04 **12** 5 **Last Minute Lisa (IRE)**[11] 718 4-9-7 **60** ........ LukeMorris 10 35
(Sylvester Kirk) *chsd ldrs: rdn along over 4f out: steadily lost pl: bhd fnl f* **14/1**

1m 23.13s (-1.67) **Going Correction** -0.05s/f (Stan) 12 Ran SP% **124.4**
Speed ratings (Par 101): **107,106,105,104,104 104,101,101,101,99 98,93**
CSF £124.57 CT £342.10 TOTE £4.30: £1.40, £14.10, £1.20; EX 117.70 Trifecta £574.60.
**Owner** Surrey Racing Club **Bred** E Puerari, Oceanic B/Stock & Riviera Eq **Trained** Godstone, Surrey
■ Stewards' Enquiry : Richard Kingscote three-day ban; careless riding (19th-21st Mar)

**FOCUS**
Another modest handicap. Ordinary form, but the winner could go in again after a small rise for this.

## 847 32RED CASINO MAIDEN STKS — 7f 1y(P)
**3:00** (3:00) (Class 5) 3-Y-O **£3,408** (£1,006; £503) **Stalls** Low

Form RPR

**1** **Mindurownbusiness (IRE)** 3-9-5 0 ........ JimCrowley 4 75+
(David Simcock) *chsd ldr: rdn to ld jst over 1f out: forged ahd ins fnl f: r.o wl: rdn out* **9/4**[2]

02- **2** 1¼ **Brigliadoro (IRE)**[106] 7960 3-9-5 0 ........ ShaneKelly 1 72
(Philip McBride) *s.i.s: hld up wl in tch in last pair: hdwy and switching rt wl over 1f out: r.o u.p to go 2nd wl ins fnl f: nvr a threat to wnr* **9/2**[3]

330- **3** 1¼ **Sherston**[134] 7451 3-9-5 71 ........ JoeFanning 7 68
(Mark Johnston) *led: hrd pressed and rdn wl over 1f out: hdd jst over 1f out: no ex and outpcd ins fnl f: eased cl home* **1/1**[1]

4- **4** 2 **Woodbridge**[246] 3928 3-9-5 0 ........ TonyHamilton 3 63+
(Richard Fahey) *t.k.h: hld up wl in tch in midfield: swtchd rt ent fnl 2f: rdn and outpcd over 1f out: styd on same pce fnl f* **12/1**

00- **5** 2¾ **Miss Tweedy**[237] 4218 3-9-0 0 ........ AndreaAtzeni 2 50
(Rod Millman) *chsd ldrs: rdn and unable qck ent fnl 2f: wknd over 1f out* **33/1**

**6** 2¼ **Permitted** 3-9-0 0 ........ WilliamCarson 5 44
(Lee Carter) *t.k.h: hld up wl in tch in last trio: rdn and effrt on outer bnd 2f out: sn outpcd and wknd over 1f out* **66/1**

**7** 10 **Roman Riches** 3-9-5 0 ........ AdamKirby 6 22
(Gary Moore) *in tch in last trio: rn green and dropped to last 4f out: sn struggling: bhd over 1f out* **16/1**

1m 25.95s (1.15) **Going Correction** -0.05s/f (Stan) 7 Ran SP% **117.0**
Speed ratings (Par 98): **91,89,88,85,82 80,68**
CSF £13.43 TOTE £3.20: £1.70, £2.60; EX 11.50 Trifecta £21.90.
**Owner** Mrs Julia Annable **Bred** Laundry Cottage Stud Farm **Trained** Newmarket, Suffolk

**FOCUS**
This maiden featured three newcomers against four who were reappearing from lengthy absences, three of whom had been gelded since last seen. They didn't go much of a pace and the time was slow. The winner is the type to rate higher from here.

## 848 32RED IMMORTAL ROMANCE SLOT H'CAP — 1m 5f (P)
**3:30** (3:30) (Class 5) (0-70,69) 4-Y-0+ **£3,408** (£1,006; £503) **Stalls** Low

Form RPR

20-1 **1** **Tokyo Brown (USA)**[19] 609 5-8-11 **59** ........ LukeMorris 1 65
(Heather Main) *t.k.h: hld up in midfield: clsd on ldr over 3f out: swtchd rt and rdn to ld 2f out: styd on wl ins fnl f: drvn out* **12/1**

654- **2** ¾ **Comedy House**[65] 8447 6-9-2 **64** ........ (v) LiamKeniry 7 69
(Michael Madgwick) *hld up in last trio: clsd on ldr over 3f out: drvn chsd wnr fnl 100yds: styd on same pce after* **7/1**[3]

4-22 **3** *shd* **Royal Marskell**[33] 405 5-9-3 **65** ........ TomEaves 8 70
(K F Clutterbuck) *t.k.h: hld up in last trio: clsd on ldr over 3f out: hdwy and swtchd rt jst ins fnl f: styd on wl u.p fnl 100yds* **12/1**

21-3 **4** ½ **Modem**[31] 450 4-9-4 **69** ........ AndreaAtzeni 6 73
(Rod Millman) *t.k.h: led for 1f: chsd clr ldr after: clsd over 3f out: sn rdn: pressed ldrs 2f out: styd on same pce ins fnl f* **11/4**[2]

40-1 **5** *nse* **Watt Broderick (IRE)**[7] 747 5-9-7 **69** 6ex ........ GrahamLee 3 73
(Ian Williams) *hld up in midfield: clsd on ldr over 3f out: rdn and little rspnse over 1f out: styd on ins fnl f: nvr gng pce to chal* **11/10**[1]

50-1 **6** 9 **Gentlemax (FR)**[39] 343 4-9-1 **66**................................ StephenCraine 4 57
(Jim Boyle) *t.k.h: prom in main gp: clsd on ldr over 3f out: lost pl u.p over 2f out: bhd over 1f out* **14/1**

0/06 **7** ½ **Coin Of The Realm (IRE)**[16] 641 9-9-0 **69**.............. DanielCremin(7) 5 60
(Miss Imogen Pickard) *led after 1f: sn wl clr: hdd and rdn 2f out: kpt on: 3rd and styng on same pce whn lost action fnl 100yds: eased and dismntd after fin* **33/1**

4-56 **8** 4½ **Peachez**[8] 742 6-9-3 **65**..............................(b) AdamKirby 2 49
(Seamus Durack) *stdd s: hld up in rr: rdn over 4f out: bhd over 1f out* **20/1**

2m 43.7s (-2.30) **Going Correction** -0.05s/f (Stan)
**WFA** 4 from 5yo+ 3lb **8** Ran SP% **116.5**
Speed ratings (Par 103): **105,104,104,104,104 98,98,95**
CSF £93.87 CT £1039.16 TOTE £12.30: £2.40, £2.20, £2.80; EX 102.50 Trifecta £411.50.

**Owner** Wetumpka Racing **Bred** Monticule **Trained** Kingston Lisle, Oxon

**FOCUS**
An ordinary staying handicap in which the main bunch were inclined to ignore the runaway leader Coin Of The Realm. The runner-up limits the form.

## 849 CORAL.CO.UK BEST ODDS GUARANTEED ON RACING H'CAP 1m 2f (P)
**4:00** (4:02) (Class 5) (0-75,75) 4-Y-O+ **£3,234** (£962; £481; £240) **Stalls** Low

Form RPR

-435 **1** **Munsarim (IRE)**[42] 286 7-9-3 **71**..................................(b) AmirQuinn 11 78
(Lee Carter) *stdd s: t.k.h: hld up in tch towards rr: gd hdwy on inner over 1f out: ev ch ins fnl f: drvn to ld wl ins fnl f: drvn out* **14/1**

265- **2** hd **Manomine**[190] 5855 5-8-13 **67**................................ FrederikTylicki 3 74
(Clive Brittain) *chsd ldrs: rdn and ev ch over 1f out: led 1f out: hdd wl ins fnl f: kpt on wl towards fin* **25/1**

-533 **3** ¾ **Cathedral**[12] 690 5-8-5 **66**.................................. AlistairRawlinson(7) 8 71+
(Ed de Giles) *awkward leaving stalls and v.s.a: rcvrd and in tch in rr after 1f: shkn up and gd hdwy on inner over 1f out: chsd ldrs and reminder fnl 100ys: pushed along and kpt on towards fin* **14/1**

02-6 **4** hd **Perfect Cracker**[56] 79 6-9-4 **72**.............................. AdamKirby 9 79+
(Clive Cox) *stdd after s: t.k.h: hld up in tch towards rr: clsd to chse ldrs but nt clr run over 1f out: swtchd rt ins fnl f: r.o wl fnl 100yds: nt rch ldrs* **3/1**[2]

-554 **5** nk **Arabian Heights**[16] 643 6-8-9 **63**............................. LukeMorris 1 67
(Ian Williams) *t.k.h: hld up wl in tch in midfield: drvn and effrt over 1f out: hrd drvn and kpt on same pce ins fnl f* **14/1**

0522 **6** nk **Lady Lunchalot (USA)**[31] 450 4-9-5 **73**...................(p) LiamJones 10 77
(Laura Mongan) *chsd ldr: rdn wl over 1f out: ev ch and drvn 1f out: unable qck and btn fnl 75yds* **8/1**

0-11 **7** shd **Whitby Jet (IRE)**[21] 582 6-9-5 **73**............................ LiamKeniry 6 76
(Ed Vaughan) *stdd after s: hld up in tch towards rr: rdn and hdwy towards inner 1f out: kpt on wl ins fnl f: nt rch ldrs* **6/1**[3]

0-24 **8** 1 **Apache Glory (USA)**[35] 369 6-9-5 **73**....................(p) AndreaAtzeni 4 75
(John Stimpson) *taken down early: hld up wl in tch in midfield: effrt over 1f out: nt clr run and swtchd rt jst ins fnl f: kpt on: nt trble ldrs* **16/1**

10 **9** 1 **Hill Fort**[12] 698 4-9-2 **75**...................................... DCByrne(5) 2 75
(Ronald Harris) *led and set stdy gallop: rdn and qcknd ent fnl 2f: hdd 1f out: wknd ins fnl f* **25/1**

60-2 **10** 1½ **Steelriver (IRE)**[35] 369 4-9-7 **75**............................ GrahamLee 7 72
(James Bethell) *t.k.h: hld up wl in tch in midfield: effrt and edgd lft wl over 1f out: wknd ins fnl f* **11/4**[1]

50-1 **11** nse **Handsome Stranger (IRE)**[21] 571 4-8-9 **63**...........(p) JoeFanning 12 60
(Alan Bailey) *t.k.h: hld up wl in tch in midfield: rdn and effrt over 1f out: kpt on same pce ins fnl f* **16/1**

2-3 **12** 2¾ **Avidly**[42] 276 4-9-5 **73**........................................ AdamBeschizza 5 65
(Julia Feilden) *t.k.h: chsd ldrs: lost pl and towards rr whn hmpd wl over 1f out: n.d after* **20/1**

2m 6.51s (-0.09) **Going Correction** -0.05s/f (Stan) **12** Ran SP% **121.3**
Speed ratings (Par 103): **98,97,97,97,96 96,96,95,94,93 93,91**
CSF £330.80 CT £4900.53 TOTE £15.40: £4.00, £7.20, £3.50; EX 358.20 Trifecta £5000.90 Part won. Pool of £6667.91- 0.63 winning units..

**Owner** John Joseph Smith **Bred** Shadwell Estate Company Limited **Trained** Epsom, Surrey

**FOCUS**
An ordinary handicap and a messy race, largely due there being no pace on early. The winner is still capable but not reliable.

## 850 32RED H'CAP STKS (BOBIS RACE) 7f 1y(P)
**4:30** (4:32) (Class 3) (0-95,97) 3-Y-O **£9,703** (£2,887; £1,443; £721) **Stalls** Low

Form RPR

2-11 **1** **Pool House**[28] 487 3-8-11 **85**................................ DavidProbert 6 92
(Andrew Balding) *chsd ldr: rdn and ev ch over 1f out: sustained chal to ld wl ins fnl f: r.o wl: rdn out* **11/4**[1]

4-21 **2** hd **Harwoods Volante (IRE)**[18] 624 3-9-1 **89**.................. RobertHavlin 3 95
(Amanda Perrett) *led: hrd pressed and rdn over 1f out: kpt on tl hdd wl ins f: r.o gamely but a jst hld* **3/1**[2]

31-4 **3** 1½ **Steventon Star**[5] 778 3-9-9 **97**............................(v1) RobertWinston 1 99
(Alan Bailey) *hmpd leaving stalls: hld up in tch in last trio: rdn and hdwy over 1f out: chsd clr ldng pair ins fnl f: kpt on* **5/1**

22-1 **4** nk **Outbacker (IRE)**[53] 140 3-8-2 **76**............................. JoeFanning 7 78
(Mark Johnston) *chsd ldrs on outer: rdn and effrt to chse ldng pair and hung lft 1f out: lost 3rd and styd on same pce ins fnl f* **8/1**

-213 **5** hd **Bretherton**[21] 573 3-8-8 **82**.............................(b) BarryMcHugh 5 83
(Richard Fahey) *dwlt: t.k.h: hld up in tch in last pair: rdn and effrt bnd 2f out: kpt on ins fnl f* **16/1**

01-2 **6** ½ **Joohaina (IRE)**[19] 613 3-8-11 **85**............................(b) LukeMorris 2 85
(Marco Botti) *chsd ldrs: rdn and effrt 2f out: hrd drvn and unable qck over 1f out: kpt on same pce ins fnl f* **6/1**

4-15 **7** nk **Can't Change It (IRE)**[33] 404 3-8-4 **78**.................... AndreaAtzeni 4 77
(David Simcock) *wl in tch in midfield: n.m.r ent fnl 2f: rdn and unable qck over 1f out: kpt on same pce ins fnl f* **4/1**[3]

1m 23.08s (-1.72) **Going Correction** -0.05s/f (Stan) **7** Ran SP% **119.6**
Speed ratings (Par 102): **107,106,105,104,104 103,103**
CSF £12.11 TOTE £3.30: £2.30, £1.90; EX 10.70 Trifecta £40.00.

**Owner** David Brownlow **Bred** R, J D & M R Bromley Gardner **Trained** Kingsclere, Hants

**FOCUS**
A decent 3yo handicap in which there was never much separating the front pair and they dominated throughout. Solid form, rated slightly positively.

## 851 LADBROKES ALL-WEATHER "HANDS AND HEELS" APPRENTICE SERIES H'CAP (EXCELLENCE INITIATIVE) 1m 1y(P)
**5:00** (5:00) (Class 6) (0-55,60) 4-Y-O+ **£2,726** (£805; £402) **Stalls** High

Form RPR

0032 **1** **Tijuca (IRE)**[6] 754 5-9-7 **54**..............................(p) AlistairRawlinson 5 61
(Ed de Giles) *hld up in tch in midfield: clsd to chse ldrs 2f out: rdn and qcknd to ld ins fnl f: pricked ears in front and fnd ex whn pressed towards fin* **11/4**[3]

-023 **2** nk **Pour La Victoire (IRE)**[6] 755 4-9-1 **51**.........(p) MrAidenBlakemore(3) 6 57
(Tony Carroll) *t.k.h: hld up in tch in midfield: effrt and nt clr run over 1f out: swtchd rt 1f out: r.o to chal wl ins fnl f: hld towards fin* **5/2**[2]

-012 **3** 1¼ **Zed Candy Girl**[14] 661 4-8-13 **46**..........................(p) RobJFitzpatrick 7 49
(John Stimpson) *chsd ldrs: rdn and hdwy to chal over 2f out: ev ch after tl unable qck and outpcd fnl 100yds* **8/1**

/161 **4** nk **Indus Valley (IRE)**[8] 740 7-9-8 **60** 6ex............. CarolineMurtagh(5) 3 63+
(Des Donovan) *awkward leaving stalls: t.k.h: hld up in tch in rr: rdn and effrt over 1f out: edgd lft ins fnl f: r.o wl fnl 100yds: nvr trbld ldrs* **9/4**[1]

2600 **5** nk **Waterloo Dock**[4] 799 9-9-0 **50**..........................(p) JonathanWilletts(3) 9 52
(Mick Quinn) *led: jnd over 2f out: rdn 2f out: hdd ins fnl f: outpcd fnl 100yds* **25/1**

400- **6** 1¾ **Heart Beat Song**[174] 6339 6-8-12 **45**.......................... GeorgeBuckell 2 43
(James Moffatt) *chsd ldr tl over 2f out: unable qck over 1f out: wknd ins fnl f* **10/1**

0-00 **7** 2 **Cuthbert (IRE)**[42] 288 7-8-9 **45**..........................(b) PaigeBolton(3) 1 38
(Michael Attwater) *stdd after s: t.k.h: hld up in last trio: rdn and effrt over 1f out: no imp* **33/1**

-000 **8** ½ **Jackie Love (IRE)**[6] 754 6-8-7 **45**........................(e1) RhiainIngram(5) 8 37
(Roger Ingram) *s.i.s: bhd: clsd and in tch over 3f out: rdn and no real imp fr over 1f out* **33/1**

1m 39.08s (0.88) **Going Correction** -0.05s/f (Stan) **8** Ran SP% **115.9**
Speed ratings (Par 101): **93,92,91,91,90 89,87,86**
CSF £10.06 CT £46.13 TOTE £2.50: £1.10, £1.60, £2.80; EX 11.20 Trifecta £55.10.
**Owner** E B De Giles **Bred** M Kennelly **Trained** Ledbury, H'fords

**FOCUS**
A very moderate "hands and heels" apprentice handicap. The placed horses highlight the limitations of the bare form.
T/Plt: £1,469.90 to a £1 stake. Pool of £95949.41 - 47.65 winning tickets. T/Qpdt: £294.60 to a £1 stake. Pool of £7486.78 - 18.80 winning tickets. SP

# 838 KEMPTON (A.W) (R-H)
### Thursday, March 6

**OFFICIAL GOING: Standard**
Wind: Almost nil Weather: Cloudy

## 852 MIX BUSINESS WITH PLEASURE AT KEMPTON H'CAP 1m (P)
**5:55** (5:57) (Class 6) (0-65,70) 4-Y-O+ **£1,940** (£577; £288; £144) **Stalls** Low

Form RPR

1430 **1** **Nubar Boy**[23] 565 7-8-11 **60**..............................(p) GeorgeDowning(5) 2 71
(Ian Williams) *mde all: set mod pce: qcknd over 2f out: in control fr over 1f out: rdn out* **12/1**

-552 **2** 1½ **Hierarch (IRE)**[6] 780 7-9-0 **65**.............................(p) GeorgeBuckell(7) 6 72
(David Simcock) *trckd wnr gng wl: chal over 2f out: sn rdn: unable qck* **15/8**[1]

-040 **3** 1¼ **Hill Of Dreams (IRE)**[8] 750 5-9-6 **64**.....................(b) RobertWinston 10 68+
(Dean Ivory) *stdd s: hld up in rr: swtchd lft and hdwy 2f out: styd on u.p: no imp fnl 100yds* **8/1**

0240 **4** 4½ **Dozy Joe**[21] 589 6-9-3 **61**..................................(v) JimCrowley 1 55
(Joseph Tuite) *dwlt: sn chsng ldrs: wknd over 1f out* **9/2**[3]

300- **5** 1¼ **My Guardian Angel**[90] 6721 5-9-7 **65**........................... JoeFanning 9 56
(Mark H Tompkins) *hld up in 5th: rdn and outpcd over 2f out: sn btn* **14/1**

-624 **6** shd **Midnight Feast**[6] 780 6-8-11 **62**...........................(v) PaigeBolton(7) 5 52
(Lee Carter) *s.s: hld up in 6th: hdwy 2f out: wknd over 1f out* **4/1**[2]

00-0 **7** 2 **Pastoral Jet**[57] 88 6-8-10 **57**................................. RyanPowell(3) 7 43
(Richard Rowe) *a towards rr: rdn and n.d fnl 2f* **20/1**

2-25 **8** 1 **Sweet Vintage (IRE)**[24] 562 4-9-0 **58**........................ AdamKirby 3 41
(Mark Brisbourne) *chsd ldrs tl wknd 2f out* **8/1**

1m 41.1s (1.30) **Going Correction** 0.0s/f (Stan) **8** Ran SP% **114.3**
Speed ratings (Par 101): **93,91,90,85,84 84,82,81**
CSF £34.95 CT £199.60 TOTE £8.50: £4.50, £1.30, £2.20; EX 46.60 Trifecta £570.70.
**Owner** Phil Slater **Bred** Low Ground Stud **Trained** Portway, Worcs

**FOCUS**
A steadily run handicap where the order changed little. The winner was left alone in front.

## 853 BETVICTOR NON-RUNNER NO BET CHELTENHAM 2014 FILLIES' H'CAP 1m (P)
**6:25** (6:26) (Class 5) (0-70,69) 4-Y-O+ **£2,587** (£770; £384; £192) **Stalls** Low

Form RPR

15-1 **1** **Compton Bird**[21] 589 5-9-2 **64**................................ JoeFanning 3 76+
(Paul Fitzsimons) *s.s: hld up in rr: smooth hdwy fr 2f out: led jst ins fnl f: rdn clr: comf* **5/1**[2]

04-2 **2** 3 **True Pleasure (IRE)**[13] 697 7-9-5 **67**........................ AdamKirby 1 72
(James Bethell) *chsd ldng pair: rdn and kpt on fnl 2f: jst snatched 2nd* **6/1**[3]

1-23 **3** nse **Pretty Bubbles**[29] 491 5-9-4 **66**............................. FrederikTylicki 6 71
(J R Jenkins) *chsd ldr: led over 2f out tl jst ins fnl f: one pce* **2/1**[1]

1132 **4** 1¾ **Medam**[12] 718 5-8-12 **63**....................................... NeilFarley(3) 9 64
(Shaun Harris) *hld up in rr: rdn over 2f out: hdwy over 1f out: no imp fnl f* **20/1**

0-36 **5** 1¼ **Lady Sylvia**[13] 690 5-9-7 **69**................................... LukeMorris 4 67
(Joseph Tuite) *in tch: hrd rdn 2f out: styd on same pce* **7/1**

/04- **6** nk **Marishi Ten (IRE)**[149] 7108 4-9-3 **65**........................ HayleyTurner 2 62
(Jo Davis) *stdd s: hld up towards rr: hdwy on inner over 2f out: no ex over 1f out* **33/1**

20-0 **7** 4 **Byroness**[57] 84 4-9-3 **65**...................................... AndreaAtzeni 5 52
(Heather Main) *t.k.h: led tl over 2f out: wknd wl over 1f out* **14/1**

20-2 **8** nk **Princess Icicle**[29] 491 6-9-5 **67**............................ FergusSweeney 7 54
(Jo Crowley) *mid-div: rdn and outpcd over 2f out: sn btn* **6/1**[3]

62-6 **9** *8* **Fiducia**[29] 493 4-9-5 **67**........ JimCrowley 8 34
(Simon Dow) *chsd ldrs tl wknd over 2f out* **12/1**

1m 39.01s (-0.79) **Going Correction** 0.0s/f (Stan) **9** Ran SP% **113.1**
Speed ratings (Par 100): **103,100,99,98,96 96,92,92,84**
CSF £34.23 CT £78.66 TOTE £6.30: £1.40, £2.40, £1.20; EX 30.90 Trifecta £85.70.
**Owner** Erik Penser **Bred** Whitsbury Manor Stud **Trained** Upper Lambourn, Berks

**FOCUS**
A competitive race for the level, rated aorund the second and third. The winner looks an improved performer.

## 854 DOWNLOAD THE BETVICTOR APP NOW H'CAP (LONDON MILE SERIES QUALIFIER) (BOBIS RACE) 1m (P)

**6:55** (6:55) (Class 4) (0-85,85) 3-Y-O **£4,851** (£1,443; £721; £360) **Stalls** Low

Form RPR

1 **1** **Passing Star**[22] 579 3-8-11 **75**........ RobertWinston 7 87+
(Charles Hills) *t.k.h in 4th: led 2f out: rdn out: readily* **5/2**[2]

512- **2** *1 1/2* **Never To Be (USA)**[127] 7626 3-9-3 **81**........(t) RobertHavlin 4 87
(John Gosden) *cl up in 3rd: rdn to chse wnr fnl 2f: kpt on: a hld* **11/8**[1]

1221 **3** *1 3/4* **Basil Berry**[15] 659 3-8-12 **76**........ HayleyTurner 3 78
(Chris Dwyer) *t.k.h in rr: rdn and hdwy over 1f out: styd on* **10/1**

061- **4** *1* **Fiftyshadesofgrey (IRE)**[175] 6342 3-9-7 **85**........ AdamKirby 1 84
(George Baker) *hld up in 5th: eased outside and effrt 2f out: edgd rt ins fnl f: styd on same pce* **8/1**[3]

5-21 **5** *2* **Arabian Music (IRE)**[17] 645 3-8-10 **74**........ DavidProbert 5 69
(David Simcock) *chsd ldr tl 2f out: sn outpcd: wknd fnl f* **10/1**

1-23 **6** *3* **Jalingo (IRE)**[36] 375 3-8-13 **77**........ JoeFanning 2 64
(Mark Johnston) *led tl wknd 2f out* **8/1**[3]

1m 40.07s (0.27) **Going Correction** 0.0s/f (Stan) **6** Ran SP% **111.1**
Speed ratings (Par 100): **98,96,94,93,91 88**
CSF £6.19 TOTE £3.10: £2.90, £1.40; EX 7.10 Trifecta £40.60.
**Owner** John C Grant **Bred** Whitsbury Manor Stud & A W M Christie-Miller **Trained** Lambourn, Berks

**FOCUS**
A fair 3-y-o handicap. The winner did this in the style of a horse that will rate higher again.

## 855 BACK OF THE NET AT BETVICTOR.COM MEDIAN AUCTION MAIDEN STKS 6f (P)

**7:25** (7:28) (Class 6) 3-5-Y-O **£1,940** (£577; £288; £144) **Stalls** Low

Form RPR

4-22 **1** **Jolly Red Jeanz (IRE)**[14] 675 3-8-9 65........(b[1]) JoeFanning 5 65
(J W Hills) *prom: led over 2f out: hrd rdn and hld on fnl f* **7/2**[2]

450- **2** *1/2* **Shrewd Bob (IRE)**[184] 6069 3-9-0 55........ AndreaAtzeni 2 69
(Robert Eddery) *towards rr: hdwy fr 2f out: r.o to press wnr ins fnl f: jst hld* **5/1**[3]

44- **3** *1 1/2* **Bereka**[171] 6477 3-8-9 0........ LukeMorris 4 59
(James Tate) *t.k.h: in tch: chsd wnr 2f out tl ins fnl f: one pce* **8/11**[1]

0-00 **4** *7* **Little Red Nell (IRE)**[21] 592 5-9-2 44........(p) AlistairRawlinson(7) 9 42
(Martin Bosley) *hld up in 6th: rdn over 2f out: sn outpcd: wnt mod 4th 1f out* **33/1**

005 **5** *3* **Jazz Bay**[9] 738 3-8-9 0........ RyanWhile(5) 1 34
(John Bridger) *t.k.h: led: rdn and hdd over 2f out: wknd wl over 1f out* **66/1**

4603 **6** *4 1/2* **Countess Lupus (IRE)**[15] 666 3-8-9 47........(b) HayleyTurner 7 16
(Lisa Williamson) *chsd ldr tl over 2f out: sn wknd* **20/1**

-46 **7** *3/4* **Harlequin Jinks**[14] 675 3-8-9 0........ DavidProbert 3 13
(Mark Usher) *sn outpcd and rdn along: a bhd* **40/1**

0 **8** *3 3/4* **Brycewise**[13] 684 3-9-0 0........ JimCrowley 6 7
(Michael Wigham) *stdd in rr s: plld hrd: sn in tch: rdn and wknd over 2f out* **7/1**

1m 12.79s (-0.31) **Going Correction** 0.0s/f (Stan)
**WFA** 3 from 5yo 14lb **8** Ran SP% **120.9**
Speed ratings (Par 101): **102,101,99,90,86 80,79,74**
CSF £21.66 TOTE £4.90: £1.10, £1.60, £1.10; EX 21.70 Trifecta £53.80.
**Owner** MMIMM Racing **Bred** Thomas Creedon **Trained** Upper Lambourn, Berks

**FOCUS**
A weak maiden in which the first three finished clear.

## 856 BETVICTOR NON-RUNNER NO BET CHELTENHAM H'CAP 1m 4f (P)

**7:55** (7:57) (Class 5) (0-75,75) 4-Y-O+ **£2,587** (£770; £384; £192) **Stalls** Centre

Form RPR

01-1 **1** **Swift Blade (IRE)**[34] 405 6-9-5 **73**........ RobertWinston 5 81
(Lady Herries) *hld up in 5th: shkn up and hdwy 2f out: slt ld ins fnl f: hld on narrowly* **9/2**[2]

103- **2** *shd* **Sporting Gold (IRE)**[115] 7840 5-9-7 **75**........(b[1]) AndreaAtzeni 1 83
(Roger Varian) *prom: drvn to ld over 1f out: narrowly hdd ins fnl f: rallied wl* **4/5**[1]

00/4 **3** *1 1/2* **Rasheed**[21] 591 6-9-7 **75**........(v[1]) LukeMorris 4 81
(Lucy Wadham) *chsd ldr: led 6f out tl over 1f out: no ex fnl 75yds* **7/1**[3]

0-55 **4** *1* **Reflect (IRE)**[17] 641 6-9-1 **69**........(vt) JoeFanning 2 73
(Derek Shaw) *dwlt: hld up in rr: effrt in centre 2f out: styd on same pce* **10/1**

5/0 **5** *hd* **Treasure The Ridge (IRE)**[15] 655 5-9-1 **72**(v[1]) WilliamTwiston-Davies(3) 3 76
(Brett Johnson) *led 1f: stdd into 4th: drvn along over 2f out: styd on same pce* **16/1**

005- **6** *12* **Topolski (IRE)**[170] 6173 8-9-2 **70**........ AdamKirby 7 54
(David Arbuthnot) *led after 1f tl 6f out: prom tl wknd 2f out* **14/1**

2m 34.56s (0.06) **Going Correction** 0.0s/f (Stan)
**WFA** 4 from 5yo+ 2lb **6** Ran SP% **107.9**
Speed ratings (Par 103): **99,98,97,97,97 89**
CSF £7.85 TOTE £4.50: £2.10, £1.30; EX 8.50 Trifecta £17.20.
**Owner** Angmering Park **Bred** Messrs Mark Hanly & James Hanly **Trained** Patching, W Sussex

**FOCUS**
Another steadily run handicap. The winner is on a roll and the third fits in.

## 857 DOWNLOAD THE BETVICTOR APP NOW FILLIES' H'CAP 1m 3f (P)

**8:25** (8:28) (Class 5) (0-70,70) 4-Y-O+ **£2,587** (£770; £384; £192) **Stalls** Low

Form RPR

55-3 **1** **Adiynara (IRE)**[20] 612 6-9-8 **68**........(p) LiamKeniry 3 74
(Neil Mulholland) *chsd ldr: led over 2f out: hld on narrowly fnl f* **16/1**

01-0 **2** *nk* **Ssafa**[15] 655 6-9-10 **70**........(p) LukeMorris 4 76
(Alastair Lidderdale) *hld up in 5th: drvn along and no imp over 2f out: styd on fnl f: tk 2nd nr fin* **7/1**

-003 **3** *hd* **Jewelled**[5] 801 8-9-8 **68**........ WilliamCarson 1 73
(Ralph J Smith) *prom: drvn to press wnr over 1f out: str chal fnl f: kpt on* **7/2**[3]

-211 **4** *5* **Waveguide (IRE)**[13] 691 5-9-3 **70**........ GeorgeBuckell(7) 6 67
(David Simcock) *led tl over 2f out: wknd over 1f out* **7/4**[1]

0/50 **5** *6* **Kathleen Frances**[15] 655 7-9-5 **65**........(tp) JimCrowley 2 53
(Ali Stronge) *hld up in rr: rdn and lost tch over 2f out* **33/1**

60-5 **6** *16* **If I Were A Boy (IRE)**[35] 382 7-9-0 **60**........(p) AdamKirby 5 22
(Dominic Ffrench Davis) *in tch tl hrd rdn and wknd over 2f out* **9/4**[2]

2m 20.16s (-1.74) **Going Correction** 0.0s/f (Stan) **6** Ran SP% **110.7**
Speed ratings (Par 100): **106,105,105,102,97 86**
CSF £112.53 TOTE £16.00: £5.20, £5.20; EX 80.80 Trifecta £265.60.
**Owner** J Baigent, D Smith & I Woodward **Bred** His Highness The Aga Khan's Studs S C **Trained** Limpley Stoke, Wilts

**FOCUS**
A moderate mares' handicap lacking depth and run steadily. The winner's best form since December 2012.

## 858 TURFTV H'CAP 7f (P)

**8:55** (8:57) (Class 7) (0-50,50) 4-Y-O+ **£1,617** (£481; £240; £120) **Stalls** Low

Form RPR

4440 **1** **Bladewood Girl**[15] 661 6-9-5 **48**........ FrederikTylicki 2 58
(J R Jenkins) *hld up in midfield: hdwy to ld 1f out: rdn clr* **8/1**

000- **2** *2 1/4* **Vitznau (IRE)**[96] 8118 10-9-7 **50**........ AdamKirby 10 54
(K F Clutterbuck) *s.s: bhd: gd hdwy over 1f out: wnt cl 2nd ent fnl f: unable qck* **5/2**[1]

0050 **3** *1 1/4* **My Scat Daddy (USA)**[7] 755 5-9-4 **47**........(p) DavidProbert 8 48
(Zoe Davison) *led: hrd rdn and hdd 1f out: no ex* **10/1**

0024 **4** *3/4* **Strategic Action (IRE)**[7] 760 5-9-6 **49**........(t) RobertHavlin 4 48
(Linda Jewell) *broke wl: stdd bk into midfield: hdwy over 1f out: styd on same pce* **3/1**[2]

0060 **5** *1/2* **Chester Deelyte (IRE)**[13] 688 6-9-2 **45**........(v) RichardKingscote 6 42
(Lisa Williamson) *chsd ldrs on inner: effrt and clsd 2f out: wknd fnl f* **25/1**

-200 **6** *1 3/4* **Pastoral Dancer**[21] 592 5-9-3 **46**........ RobertWinston 3 38
(Richard Rowe) *towards rr: rdn and sme hdwy over 1f out: nvr able to chal* **12/1**

00-0 **7** *1/2* **Thrasos (IRE)**[46] 244 5-9-6 **49**........ FergusSweeney 1 40
(Jo Crowley) *bhd: rdn 2f out: sme late hdwy* **16/1**

0-30 **8** *1/2* **Buaiteoir (FR)**[42] 290 8-9-3 **49**........ MatthewCosham(3) 14 39
(Nikki Evans) *prom tl wknd over 1f out* **25/1**

0-04 **9** *1/2* **High On The Hog (IRE)**[14] 676 6-9-2 **45**........(p) JimCrowley 5 33
(Mark Brisbourne) *chsd ldrs tl wknd wl over 1f out* **9/2**[3]

60-0 **10** *1 3/4* **Farmers Dream (IRE)**[63] 18 7-9-2 **45**........(p) JohnFahy 7 29
(John Spearing) *a towards rr* **66/1**

-600 **11** *4* **Custom House (IRE)**[42] 290 6-8-13 **45**........ NataliaGemelova(3) 12 18
(John E Long) *dwlt: towards rr: rdn 3f out: sn bhd* **33/1**

0-00 **12** *3/4* **Athwaab**[13] 693 7-9-2 **45**........ WilliamCarson 9 16
(Simon Hodgson) *prom tl wknd qckly over 1f out* **50/1**

0660 **13** *5* **Kaylee**[7] 760 5-8-10 **46**........ NedCurtis(7) 13
(Kevin Tork) *chsd ldrs tl wknd over 2f out* **66/1**

1m 26.2s (0.20) **Going Correction** 0.0s/f (Stan) **13** Ran SP% **121.1**
Speed ratings (Par 97): **98,95,94,93,92 90,90,89,88,86 82,81,75**
CSF £27.34 CT £215.64 TOTE £8.90: £2.60, £1.80, £3.70; EX 37.20 Trifecta £308.40.
**Owner** Byron Boys **Bred** Southill Stud **Trained** Royston, Herts

**FOCUS**
A typical bottom-drawer handicap. Straightforward form behind the winner.
T/Jkpt: Not won. T/Plt: £60.90 to a £1 stake. Pool: £107,340.47 - 1286.22 winning units. T/Qpdt: £28.70 to a £1 stake. Pool: £8,245.06 - 212.40 winning units. LM

# 829 SOUTHWELL (L-H)

Thursday, March 6

**OFFICIAL GOING: Standard**
Wind: Fresh to strong across Weather: Cloudy

## 859 CORAL APP DOWNLOAD FROM THE APP STORE APPRENTICE H'CAP 1m 3f (F)

**2:20** (2:20) (Class 5) (0-75,72) 4-Y-O+ **£3,234** (£962; £481; £240) **Stalls** Low

Form RPR

0-10 **1** **Handsome Stranger (IRE)**[1] 849 4-8-9 **63**........(p) DavidParkes(3) 3 70
(Alan Bailey) *hld up: hdwy 1/2-way: chsd ldng pair over 3f out: pushed along over 2f out: rdn to chal over 1f out: led ent fnl f: kpt on wl towards fin* **8/1**

006- **2** *1 1/4* **Jacobs Son**[191] 5868 6-9-5 **69**........ AlistairRawlinson 4 74
(Michael Appleby) *t.k.h: sn slt ld: hdd narrowly 5f out: rdn along 3f out: n.m.r on inner 2f out and sn swtchd rt out: chal over 1f out: ev ch ent fnl f: kpt on same pce* **1/1**[1]

-603 **3** *2* **Raging Bear (USA)**[16] 647 4-9-4 **69**........(b) CharlotteJenner 5 71
(James Evans) *wnt rt s: sn cl up: slt ld 5f out: rdn along 3f out: edgd lft 2f out: drvn and hdd ent fnl f: one pce* **9/2**[2]

/0-3 **4** *10* **Chain Of Events**[15] 655 7-9-8 **72**........ RobJFitzpatrick 1 58
(Michael Wigham) *cl up on inner: pushed along over 4f out: rdn over 3f out: sn outpcd* **5/1**[3]

234- **5** *3 1/2* **Mixed Message (IRE)**[141] 6297 4-9-0 **70**........ KevinLundie(5) 2 50
(Brian Ellison) *trckd ldrs: pushed along bef 1/2-way: rdn and lost pl 4f out: sn bhd* **7/1**

2m 29.62s (1.62) **Going Correction** +0.175s/f (Slow)
**WFA** 4 from 6yo+ 1lb **5** Ran SP% **108.5**
Speed ratings (Par 103): **101,100,98,91,88**
CSF £16.28 TOTE £12.50: £3.90, £1.30; EX 21.50 Trifecta £88.20.
**Owner** John Stocker **Bred** Gerrardstown House Stud **Trained** Newmarket, Suffolk

**FOCUS**
A modest apprentice handicap lacking depth.

## 860 CORAL MOBILE "JUST THREE CLICKS TO BET" (S) STKS 1m 4f (F)

**2:50** (2:50) (Class 6) 4-Y-O+ **£2,587** (£770) **Stalls** Low

Form RPR

1121 **1** **Stand Guard**[2] 830 10-9-5 85........ TomQueally 1 84
(John Butler) *set stdy pce: qcknd wl over 3f out: rdn clr wl over 1f out: easily* **1/7**[1]

3423 **2** *14* **Honest Strike (USA)**[9] 742 7-8-13 63........(be) ShaneKelly 2 54
(Daniel Mark Loughnane) *trckd wnr: effrt 3f out: rdn 2f out: outpcd and eased over 1f out* **3/1**[2]

2m 51.93s (10.93) **Going Correction** +0.175s/f (Slow)
**WFA** 4 from 6yo+ 2lb **2** Ran SP% **112.5**
Speed ratings (Par 101): **70,60**
TOTE £1.20.There was no bid for the winner.
**Owner** Maxilead Limited **Bred** Juddmonte Farms Ltd **Trained** Newmarket, Suffolk
■ Stand Guard set a new record of 26 wins on the AW.



The Form Book, Raceform Ltd, Newbury, RG14 5SJ

**FOCUS**
This race was reduced to an uncompetitive match after four of the six declared runners were withdrawn.

## 861 LADBROKES MOBILE MEDIAN AUCTION MAIDEN STKS 1m (F)
**3:25** (3:25) (Class 6) 3-5-Y-O **£2,587** (£770; £384; £192) **Stalls** Low

Form RPR
2 **1** **Moonlight Venture**[25] 551 3-8-10 0 TonyHamilton 4 78+
(Kevin Ryan) *t.k.h: cl up: led wl over 2f out: rdn: jnd and rn green over 1f out: kpt on wl towards fin* **11/10**[1]
45- **2** 1 1/4 **Two Moons**[168] 6566 4-10-0 0 BarryMcHugh 3 81
(Tony Coyle) *trckd ldrs: hdwy over 2f out: rdn to chal over 1f out: ev ch tl drvn ins fnl f and kpt on same pce* **8/1**
03-4 **3** 5 **Galaxy (IRE)**[54] 143 3-8-7 72 (v) WilliamTwiston-Davies(3) 2 64
(Alan McCabe) *led: rdn along and hdd wl over 2f out: drvn over 1f out: kpt on one pce fnl f* **5/1**[3]
6- **4** shd **Sea Spear**[78] 8328 3-8-10 0 GrahamGibbons 6 63
(David Barron) *prom on outer: pushed along: rn green: hung rt and outpcd over 3f out: wd st: sn rdn to chse ldrs: kpt on one pce fr over 1f out* **3/1**[2]
3-24 **5** 1/2 **Playtothewhistle**[23] 564 3-8-10 65 PaulMulrennan 5 62
(Bryan Smart) *prom: effrt over 2f out and cl up tl rdn wl over 1f out and sn one pce* **6/1**
6-6 **6** 47 **Cottam Maybel**[17] 642 5-9-2 0 DanielleMooney(7) 1
(Michael Easterby) *a in rr: outpcd wl over 3f out and sn bhd* **100/1**

1m 44.11s (0.41) **Going Correction** +0.175s/f (Slow)
**WFA** 3 from 4yo+ 18lb **6 Ran SP% 115.7**
Speed ratings (Par 101): **104,102,97,97,97 50**
CSF £11.61 TOTE £1.50: £1.10, £4.10; EX 14.60 Trifecta £46.10.
**Owner** Guy Reed Racing **Bred** G Reed **Trained** Hambleton, N Yorks

**FOCUS**
Probably a fair maiden by Fibresand standards. The winner built on a likeable debut.

## 862 LADBROKES H'CAP 7f (F)
**3:55** (3:55) (Class 5) (0-75,75) 4-Y-O+ **£3,234** (£962; £481; £240) **Stalls** Low

Form RPR
1301 **1** **Khajaaly (IRE)**[14] 677 7-9-0 68 (vt) AndrewMullen 2 78
(Michael Appleby) *hld up in rr: hdwy wl over 2f out: swtchd wd and rdn wl over 1f out: styd on strly to chal ent fnl f: sn hung lft: led last 100yds* **6/1**
-454 **2** 2 1/4 **Sofias Number One (USA)**[37] 364 6-8-13 72 (b) PhilipPrince(5) 6 76
(Roy Bowring) *cl up on outer: led after 2f: rdn along over 2f out: hdd wl over 1f out: drvn and rallied to ld again ent fnl f: hdd and no ex last 100yds* **3/1**[2]
5-21 **3** 1/2 **Imaginary World (IRE)**[25] 548 6-8-12 69 (e) BillyCray(3) 5 71
(John Balding) *dwlt: sn in tch: hdwy to chse ldng pair 2f out: sn rdn: drvn and edgd lft ent fnl f: kpt on wl towards fin* **5/1**
6242 **4** 1 1/4 **Alpha Tauri (USA)**[7] 766 8-8-5 64 (t) ConnorBeasley(5) 1 63
(Richard Guest) *slt ld 2f: chsd ldr tl rdn to ld again wl over 1f out: drvn and hdd ent fnl f: sn btn* **5/2**[1]
1325 **5** 4 **Repetition**[7] 767 4-9-7 75 TonyHamilton 3 63
(Kristin Stubbs) *prom: pushed along 1/2-way: rdn 3f out and grad wknd* **7/2**[3]
34-0 **6** 20 **Cape Of Hope (IRE)**[45] 255 4-9-5 73 DanielTudhope 4 7
(David O'Meara) *chsd ldng pair: rdn along 3f out: sn wknd* **12/1**

1m 29.86s (-0.44) **Going Correction** +0.175s/f (Slow) **6 Ran SP% 114.4**
Speed ratings (Par 103): **109,106,105,104,99 77**
CSF £24.83 TOTE £6.70: £3.00, £2.50; EX 26.40 Trifecta £136.50.
**Owner** New Kids On The Trot **Bred** Barry Noonan And Denis Noonan **Trained** Danethorpe, Notts

**FOCUS**
The two leaders took each other on from some way out, setting this up for a closer. Straightforward form.

## 863 COMPARE BOOKMAKERS AT BOOKMAKERS.CO.UK H'CAP 5f (F)
**4:25** (4:26) (Class 4) (0-85,83) 4-Y-O+ **£5,822** (£1,732; £865; £432) **Stalls** High

Form RPR
0-42 **1** **Royal Bajan (USA)**[12] 719 6-9-7 83 (v) TomQueally 8 95
(James Given) *chsd ldr: smooth hdwy 2f out and sn cl up: shkn up to ld appr fnl f: sn clr: readily* **3/1**[1]
0-53 **2** 3 1/4 **Moorhouse Lad**[32] 444 11-9-1 77 GrahamGibbons 1 77
(Garry Moss) *qckly away and sn clr: pushed along wl over 1f out: rdn and hdd appr fnl f: kpt on same pce* **3/1**[1]
03-0 **3** 1 3/4 **O'Gorman**[15] 658 5-9-4 83 WilliamTwiston-Davies(3) 4 77
(Gary Brown) *chsd ldrs: rdn along 2f out: kpt on fnl f* **6/1**[3]
00-1 **4** 1 **Sleepy Blue Ocean**[51] 175 8-9-3 82 (p) JasonHart(3) 10 72
(John Balding) *chsd ldrs: hdwy 2f out: sn rdn and edgd lft appr fnl f: no imp* **7/2**[2]
4520 **5** 3/4 **Pabusar**[15] 658 6-8-10 72 (b) WilliamCarson 3 60
(Ann Stokell) *dwlt and wnt lft s: racd wd and towards rr tl sme late hdwy* **14/1**
530- **6** 4 1/2 **Haajes**[159] 6848 10-8-12 79 ShirleyTeasdale(5) 7 51
(Paul Midgley) *a in rr* **33/1**
012- **7** 1 1/4 **Oldjoesaid**[136] 7420 10-8-12 77 GeorgeChaloner(3) 5 44
(Paul Midgley) *dwlt: a in rr* **14/1**
5400 **8** 1/2 **Powerful Wind (IRE)**[12] 719 5-8-13 80 DCByrne(5) 9 45
(Ronald Harris) *prom: rdn along over 2f out: sn wknd* **8/1**

59.78s (0.08) **Going Correction** +0.15s/f (Slow) **8 Ran SP% 113.9**
Speed ratings (Par 105): **105,99,97,95,94 87,85,84**
CSF £12.01 CT £49.20 TOTE £3.20: £1.60, £1.10, £2.00; EX 14.20 Trifecta £70.60.
**Owner** The Cool Silk Partnership **Bred** West Wind Farm **Trained** Willoughton, Lincs

**FOCUS**
Very few got into this.

## 864 BEST ODDS GUARANTEED AT BOOKMAKERS.CO.UK H'CAP 6f (F)
**4:55** (4:56) (Class 6) (0-52,52) 4-Y-O+ **£2,587** (£770; £384; £192) **Stalls** Low

Form RPR
-362 **1** **Orwellian**[35] 384 5-9-3 48 PaulMulrennan 3 55
(Bryan Smart) *trckd ldrs: hdwy on wd outside over 2f out: rdn to ld wl over 1f out: kpt on* **3/1**[1]
0650 **2** 2 **Novalist**[23] 563 6-8-12 46 oh1 JasonHart(3) 5 47
(Robin Bastiman) *led on inner: hung rt bnd after 2f: hdd 3f out: sn rdn and hung rt: drvn over 1f out: kpt on ins fnl f* **8/1**
-402 **3** 1 **Doctor Hilary**[23] 563 12-8-11 47 (v) PhilipPrince(5) 10 45
(Mark Hoad) *towards rr and sn rdn along: hdwy to chse ldrs 2f out: sn swtchd lft to inner and kpt on fnl f* **4/1**[2]
30-0 **4** hd **Durham Express (IRE)**[23] 563 7-8-10 46 oh1 (v[1]) ConnorBeasley(5) 9 43
(Colin Teague) *cl up on outer: hdwy to ld 3f out: rdn over 2f out: hdd wl over 1f out: sn drvn and one pce* **16/1**
00-0 **5** 1 1/2 **China Excels**[13] 694 7-9-4 52 RossAtkinson(3) 7 45
(Mandy Rowland) *cl up: ev ch 2f out: sn rdn and one pce* **8/1**
0242 **6** 6 **Vale Of Clara (IRE)**[13] 692 6-9-3 48 (be) PJMcDonald 2 23
(Peter Niven) *a towards rr* **8/1**
0-13 **7** nse **Catalyze**[43] 274 6-9-6 51 (t) WilliamCarson 1 26
(Ann Stokell) *s.i.s: a towards rr* **6/1**[3]
4000 **8** 3 1/4 **Upper Lambourn (IRE)**[13] 692 6-9-1 46 oh1 (t) TomQueally 4 11
(Christopher Kellett) *a in rr* **6/1**[3]
0060 **9** 4 1/2 **Homeboy (IRE)**[7] 760 6-8-11 49 (v) HollieDoyle(7) 6
(David Evans) *chsd ldrs on inner: rdn along 1/2-way: sn wknd* **14/1**

1m 17.45s (0.95) **Going Correction** +0.175s/f (Slow) **9 Ran SP% 119.5**
Speed ratings (Par 101): **100,97,96,95,93 85,85,81,75**
CSF £28.79 CT £99.71 TOTE £3.60: £1.60, £5.40, £1.10; EX 38.40 Trifecta £258.10.
**Owner** B Smart **Bred** Mrs Fiona Denniff **Trained** Hambleton, N Yorks

**FOCUS**
A low-grade but competitive 6f handicap, and they raced right across the track in the home straight. Straightforward form.

## 865 32RED MEGA MOOLAH MILLIONAIRES H'CAP 1m (F)
**5:25** (5:25) (Class 6) (0-55,55) 3-Y-O **£2,587** (£770; £384; £192) **Stalls** Low

Form RPR
-523 **1** **Cascadia (IRE)**[16] 653 3-8-11 52 RobJFitzpatrick(7) 8 59
(K R Burke) *cl up: led after 3f: rdn over 2f out: sn jnd: drvn over 1f out: hld on gamely fnl f* **3/1**[1]
0063 **2** nk **Needs The Run**[9] 743 3-9-2 50 AndrewMullen 7 56
(David Evans) *dwlt: sn in tch on outer: hdwy over 3f out: cl up over 2f out: rdn to chal wl over 1f out: ev ch tl drvn ins fnl f and no ex towards fin* **5/1**
400- **3** 4 **Kingsway Lad (IRE)**[148] 7126 3-9-4 52 (t) DaleSwift 6 49
(Derek Shaw) *t.k.h: trckd ldrs: hdwy and cl up 3f out: chal 2f out: sn rdn and ev ch tl drvn and wknd jst ins fnl f* **4/1**[2]
3206 **4** 1 **Bold Max**[7] 753 3-9-3 51 (p) LiamJones 2 46
(Zoe Davison) *towards rr: hdwy wl over 2f out: sn rdn and kpt on fnl f: nrst fin* **16/1**
15-0 **5** 12 **Marlismamma (FR)**[44] 267 3-9-2 50 (v[1]) DanielTudhope 5 17
(David O'Meara) *chsd ldng pair: rdn along over 3f out: wknd wl over 2f out* **20/1**
3-56 **6** 11 **Definite Secret**[25] 547 3-9-7 55 PaulMulrennan 3
(James Tate) *led 3f: cl up tl rdn along over 3f out and sn wknd* **4/1**[2]
050- **7** 11 **Uplifted (IRE)**[122] 7732 3-9-4 52 (b[1]) TomQueally 1
(Kevin Ryan) *chsd ldrs on inner: rdn along 1/2-way: sn outpcd* **8/1**
400- **8** 1 **Redlorryellowlorry (IRE)**[199] 5584 3-9-4 52 (p) ShaneKelly 4
(George Baker) *in rr and sn rdn along: swtchd wd after 2f: sn outpcd and bhd* **9/2**[3]

1m 46.43s (2.73) **Going Correction** +0.175s/f (Slow) **8 Ran SP% 121.6**
Speed ratings (Par 96): **93,92,88,87,75 64,53,52**
CSF £19.76 CT £62.65 TOTE £3.60: £2.10, £2.50, £2.00; EX 17.50 Trifecta £170.10.
**Owner** Mrs Elaine M Burke **Bred** John Wholey **Trained** Middleham Moor, N Yorks

**FOCUS**
A tricky low-grade handicap with three of the eight runners making their handicap and Fibresand debuts on their return to action after being gelded at the end of their mandatory three outings as juveniles. Two of them ran badly, finishing last and second last. Pretty weak form, the first two clear.
T/Plt: £20.00 to 1 £1 stake. Pool: £69,352.71 - 2519.75 winning units. T/Qpdt: £9.10 to a £1 stake. Pool: £6559.21 - 528.19 winning units. JR

# 781 WOLVERHAMPTON (A.W) (L-H)
Friday, March 7

**OFFICIAL GOING: Standard**
Wind: almost nil Weather: fine

## 866 COMPARE BOOKMAKERS AT BOOKMAKERS.CO.UK H'CAP 5f 20y(P)
**5:30** (5:30) (Class 5) (0-70,70) 4-Y-O+ **£2,911** (£866; £432; £216) **Stalls** Low

Form RPR
4255 **1** **Desert Strike**[7] 777 8-9-6 69 (p) HayleyTurner 4 78
(Conor Dore) *mde all: hrd drvn over 1f out: kpt on wl* **7/2**[2]
2036 **2** 1 3/4 **Your Gifted (IRE)**[6] 797 7-8-2 56 oh1 (v) ShirleyTeasdale(5) 2 59
(Lisa Williamson) *dwlt: sn chsng ldrs: styd on down outside appr fnl f: tk 2nd towards fin* **16/1**
-652 **3** 3/4 **Thorpe Bay**[3] 834 5-9-0 70 AlistairRawlinson(7) 1 70
(Michael Appleby) *chsd wnr: chal over 1f out: kpt on same pce last 100yds* **11/8**[1]
-131 **4** nk **Megaleka**[7] 777 4-9-0 68 6ex TimClark(5) 6 67
(Alan Bailey) *in rr: drvn over 3f out: hdwy on ins 2f out: kpt on one pce fnl f* **5/1**[3]
1151 **5** 2 1/2 **Interchoice Star**[14] 694 9-8-12 61 (p) DavidProbert 3 51
(Ray Peacock) *chsd ldrs: hung rt and one pce over 1f out* **5/1**[3]
20-6 **6** 8 **Solemn**[46] 259 9-9-5 68 (v) AdamKirby 5 29
(Milton Bradley) *in rr: sn drvn along: lost pl over 1f out: bhd whn eased clsng stages* **7/1**

1m 1.82s (-0.48) **Going Correction** +0.075s/f (Slow) **6 Ran SP% 116.0**
Speed ratings (Par 103): **106,103,102,101,97 84**
CSF £52.21 TOTE £5.50: £2.20, £4.70; EX 41.10 Trifecta £160.60.
**Owner** Andrew Page **Bred** Mrs Mary Rowlands **Trained** Hubbert's Bridge, Lincs

**FOCUS**
Modest handicap form.

## 867 32RED.COM H'CAP 5f 216y(P)
**6:00** (6:01) (Class 6) (0-65,65) 3-Y-O **£2,264** (£673; £336; £168) **Stalls** Low

Form RPR
0-31 **1** **Emerald Breeze (IRE)**[7] 786 3-8-7 51 6ex (b) StevieDonohoe 3 57
(Tim Pitt) *trckd ldrs: 2nd 2f out: led appr fnl f: pushed out* **11/10**[1]
-431 **2** 1/2 **Rose Buck**[30] 495 3-9-5 63 AdamKirby 5 68+
(Giles Bravery) *chsd ldrs: outpcd over 1f out: styd on strly ins fnl f: tk 2nd nr fin* **9/2**[2]
1-30 **3** 1 1/2 **Under Approval**[17] 650 3-9-4 62 DanielTudhope 4 62
(David O'Meara) *led: hdd appr fnl f: kpt on same pce* **7/1**
2-66 **4** 3/4 **Soul Instinct**[17] 650 3-8-13 62 KevinStott(5) 2 60
(Kevin Ryan) *chsd ldrs: one pce over 1f out* **16/1**
4212 **5** 3/4 **El Duque**[16] 665 3-9-2 65 (v) RyanWhile(5) 1 61
(Bill Turner) *chsd ldrs on inner: outpcd over 2f out: hdwy over 1f out: one pce* **6/1**[3]

4032 6 3 1/4 **Coiste Bodhar (IRE)**[9] 745 3-9-0 58 ..............................(p) GrahamLee 6 44
(Joseph Tuite) *trckd ldrs on outside: drvn over 3f out: sn outpcd: lost pl 2f out* **9/2**[2]

1m 15.08s (0.08) **Going Correction** +0.075s/f (Slow) 6 Ran SP% **116.7**
Speed ratings (Par 96): **102,101,99,98,97 93**
CSF £6.88 TOTE £2.70: £1.60, £1.70; EX 8.70 Trifecta £41.70.
**Owner** Decadent Racing II **Bred** Rathbarry Stud **Trained** Market Drayton, Shropshire

**FOCUS**
An ordinary race lacking depth. The winner was ahead of her mark.

## 868 32RED TOMB RAIDER SLOT H'CAP 2m 119y(P)
**6:30** (6:30) (Class 5) (0-75,74) 4-Y-0+ **£2,911** (£866; £432; £216) **Stalls** Low

Form RPR
0/0- 1 **Bright Abbey**[131] 6585 6-9-6 70 .............................. EmmaSayer(5) 6 75
(Dianne Sayer) *t.k.h: w ldr: led after 4f: qcknd pce over 4f out: edgd rt and styd on gamely ins fnl f* **20/1**
1111 2 1 3/4 **Waving**[7] 794 5-9-10 74 6ex..............................(t) JoeyHaynes(5) 5 77
(Tony Carroll) *hld up in rr: hdwy on outside over 3f out: cl 2nd 2f out: sn upsides and rdn: fdd clsng stages* **7/4**[1]
060- 3 nk **Knightly Escapade**[19] 7342 6-9-12 71 .............................. DaleSwift 7 74
(Brian Ellison) *stdd s: hld up in rr: hdwy on inner over 3f out: chsng ldrs 2f out: kpt on ins fnl f* **3/1**[2]
2-30 4 4 1/2 **Stormy Morning**[28] 513 8-9-2 61..............................(p) RussKennemore 4 59
(Philip Kirby) *chsd ldrs: drvn over 2f out: wknd appr fnl f* **5/1**
661- 5 20 **Estemaala (IRE)**[256] 3627 5-9-12 71..............................(v[1]) DanielTudhope 1 45
(David O'Meara) *led 4f: trckd ldr: drvn over 4f out: lost pl over 2f out: sn bhd and eased* **9/2**[3]
44-6 6 7 **Rapid Heat Lad (IRE)**[64] 16 5-9-9 68..............................(p) GrahamLee 3 33
(Andrew Hollinshead) *trckd ldrs: drvn over 4f out: outpcd over 3f out: lost pl over 2f out: sn bhd* **8/1**

3m 45.77s (3.97) **Going Correction** +0.075s/f (Slow) 6 Ran SP% **112.1**
Speed ratings (Par 103): **93,92,92,89,80 77**
CSF £55.45 TOTE £13.00: £10.00, £1.60; EX 35.20 Trifecta £111.90.
**Owner** Anthony White **Bred** Pendley Farm **Trained** Hackthorpe, Cumbria

**FOCUS**
This track has been a happy hunting ground for front-runners in recent weeks. The winner was entitled to win this on old flat form. Limited form.

## 869 LADBROKES H'CAP 1m 141y(P)
**7:00** (7:01) (Class 7) (0-50,50) 4-Y-0+ **£1,940** (£577; £288; £144) **Stalls** Low

Form RPR
/26- 1 **The Bay Bandit**[149] 3919 7-9-4 47..............................(p) LiamKeniry 1 53+
(Neil Mulholland) *chsd ldrs: n.m.r over 2f out: led over 1f out: hld on towards fin* **12/1**
2346 2 hd **Supa Seeker (USA)**[8] 759 8-9-5 48.............................. GrahamLee 7 54
(Tony Carroll) *mid-div: hdwy over 3f out: chsng ldrs over 1f out: kpt on to take 2nd nr fin* **4/1**[2]
-060 3 nk **Rigid**[2] 844 7-8-11 45..............................(t) JoeyHaynes(5) 11 50
(Tony Carroll) *sn chsng ldrs: upsides over 1f out: kpt on same pce last 50yds* **14/1**
0054 4 3 1/4 **Ellies Image**[15] 673 7-9-2 45.............................. PaulMulrennan 4 43
(Richard Ford) *hld up in rr: hdwy over 2f out: kpt on: nvr a threat* **33/1**
6325 5 1/2 **Amber Moon**[27] 530 9-8-11 45.............................. AnnStokell(5) 9 42
(Ann Stokell) *in rr: outpcd: lost pl and wd over 2f out: hdwy appr fnl f: gng on at fin* **20/1**
06-5 6 1 1/4 **Moves Like Jagger (IRE)**[15] 672 4-9-2 45..............(v) PaddyAspell 3 39
(Phil McEntee) *s.i.s: hdwy on outside over 4f out: 3rd 3f out: wknd appr fnl f* **3/1**[1]
-042 7 1/2 **Troy Boy**[7] 783 4-8-13 45.............................. NeilFarley(3) 5 38
(Robin Bastiman) *in rr: sme hdwy over 2f out: nvr a factor* **3/1**[1]
5-0 8 1 3/4 **Eretara (IRE)**[15] 672 5-9-2 45..............................(b[1]) ShaneKelly 2 35
(S Donohoe, Ire) *mid-div: hdwy over 4f out: 2nd over 3f out: sn led: hdd over 1f out: sn wknd* **8/1**
-003 9 13 **Edgware Road**[7] 783 6-9-4 50..............................(b) RossAtkinson(3) 10 12
(Paul Morgan) *chsd ldr: led after 2f: hdd 3f out: sn lost pl: bhd and eased ins fnl f* **6/1**[3]
060- 10 22 **Benidorm**[19] 7083 6-9-2 45..............................(p) TomEaves 8
(John Wainwright) *led 2f: lost pl 3f out: sn bhd: t.o 2f out* **50/1**

1m 51.89s (1.39) **Going Correction** +0.075s/f (Slow) 10 Ran SP% **119.4**
Speed ratings (Par 97): **96,95,95,92,92 91,90,89,77,58**
CSF £60.10 CT £718.76 TOTE £13.10: £1.90, £1.60, £7.50; EX 67.10 Trifecta £588.00.
**Owner** Neil Mulholland Racing Club **Bred** Darley **Trained** Limpley Stoke, Wilts
■ Stewards' Enquiry : Joey Haynes one-day ban: careless riding (Mar 21)

**FOCUS**
A pretty dire handicap.

## 870 CORAL APP DOWNLOAD FROM THE APP STORE H'CAP 1m 4f 50y(P)
**7:30** (7:30) (Class 4) (0-85,84) 4-Y-0+ **£5,175** (£1,540; £769; £384) **Stalls** Low

Form RPR
034- 1 **Villa Royale**[99] 7596 5-9-0 77..............................[1] AndrewMullen 2 85
(Michael Appleby) *in rr: drvn and hdwy on outer over 4f out: chsng ldrs over 2f out: styd on to ld over 1f out* **12/1**
113- 2 1 3/4 **Aryal**[315] 1803 4-9-2 81..............................(b) JoeFanning 3 88+
(Mark Johnston) *trckd ldrs: nt clr run on inner over 2f out: swtchd rt appr fnl f: styd on wl to take 2nd nr fin* **4/1**[2]
-324 3 hd **Excellent Puck (IRE)**[14] 698 4-9-0 79.............................. AdamKirby 9 84
(Shaun Lycett) *sn trcking ldrs: led over 3f out: hdd over 1f out: no ex* **11/2**
-015 4 4 1/2 **Back Burner (IRE)**[15] 674 6-9-4 81.............................. DanielTudhope 8 79
(David O'Meara) *hld up in mid-div: hdwy 2f out: kpt on ins fnl f* **8/1**
0-63 5 1 1/2 **Flying Power**[21] 611 6-9-7 84.............................. PaddyAspell 6 80
(John Norton) *chsd ldrs: one pce fnl 2f* **9/2**[3]
04/1 6 1 3/4 **Future Security (IRE)**[12] 729 5-8-13 81 6ex.............................. JoeyHaynes(5) 1 74+
(C Von Der Recke, Germany) *hld up in rr: effrt whn hmpd over 2f out: nvr a factor* **7/2**[1]
-430 7 shd **St Ignatius**[20] 623 7-8-8 76..............................(v) NatashaEaton(5) 4 69
(Alan Bailey) *led: hdd over 3f out: lost pl over 2f out* **14/1**
-443 8 nse **Uphold**[23] 584 7-9-0 82..............................(v) JackDuern(5) 5 75
(Gay Kelleway) *s.i.s: sn mid-div: effrt over 4f out: lost pl over 2f out* **8/1**
231- 9 8 **Arizona John (IRE)**[290] 2552 9-9-3 80.............................. StephenCraine 7 61
(John Mackie) *in rr: bhd fnl 2f* **25/1**

2m 39.23s (-1.87) **Going Correction** +0.075s/f (Slow)
**WFA** 4 from 5yo+ 2lb 9 Ran SP% **116.2**
Speed ratings (Par 105): **109,107,107,104,103 102,102,102,97**
CSF £59.96 CT £300.19 TOTE £13.20: £6.30, £1.10, £1.10; EX 62.20 Trifecta £1066.40.
**Owner** David Kuss & Tim Pakyurek **Bred** Lawn Stud **Trained** Danethorpe, Notts

**FOCUS**
A rough race with plenty of hard-luck stories. The first three were clear.

## 871 CORAL.CO.UK BEST ODDS GUARANTEED ON RACING MEDIAN AUCTION MAIDEN STKS 1m 4f 50y(P)
**8:00** (8:01) (Class 5) 3-5-Y-O **£2,587** (£770; £384; £192) **Stalls** Low

Form RPR
22 1 **Puzzle Time**[17] 649 4-9-7 0.............................. WilliamCarson 2 71+
(Giles Bravery) *t.k.h: led 3f: trckd ldrs: led over 2f out: pushed out* **6/5**[1]
64 2 1 1/2 **Trafalgar Rock**[11] 734 3-8-5 0.............................. JoeFanning 7 69+
(Mark Johnston) *in rr: hdwy outer over 5f out: styd on over 1f out: tk 2nd nr fin* **6/1**
6-2 3 2 **Hallouella**[28] 515 3-8-0 0.............................. JimmyQuinn 5 60
(James Tate) *w ldrs: led 7f out: hdd over 2f out: kpt on same pce over 1f out* **11/2**[3]
46 4 1/2 **Tashbeeh (IRE)**[7] 787 3-8-0 0.............................. ShirleyTeasdale(5) 3 65
(Dianne Sayer) *sn chsng ldrs: led after 3f: hdd 7f out: kpt on same pce fnl 2f* **25/1**
36 5 2 1/2 **Gabrial The Terror (IRE)**[14] 686 4-9-12 0.............................. LiamKeniry 4 64
(David Simcock) *trckd ldrs: effrt over 3f out: one pce over 1f out* **9/2**[2]
6 38 **Philosofy**[35] 4-9-7 0.............................. DanielTudhope 6
(David O'Meara) *hld up in mid-div: drvn to chse ldres over 3f out: lost pl over 2f out: bhd and eased over 1f out: virtually p.u* **6/1**
05 7 23 **Mary's Prayer**[18] 642 3-7-10 0 ow1.............................. TimClark(5) 1
(John Holt) *s.i.s: racd in last: reminders 6f out: lost pl over 4f out: sn bhd: t.o and virtually p.u 2f out* **50/1**

2m 41.92s (0.82) **Going Correction** +0.075s/f (Slow)
**WFA** 3 from 4yo 23lb 7 Ran SP% **113.4**
Speed ratings (Par 103): **100,99,97,97,95 70,55**
CSF £8.87 TOTE £2.50: £2.00, £1.70; EX 9.20 Trifecta £33.80.
**Owner** J J May **Bred** Plantation Stud **Trained** Newmarket, Suffolk
■ Stewards' Enquiry : Liam Keniry caution: careless riding.

**FOCUS**
A modest and steadily-run maiden with a compressed finish. The form is rated conservatively.

## 872 CORAL MOBILE "JUST THREE CLICKS TO BET" H'CAP 1m 4f 50y(P)
**8:30** (8:30) (Class 6) (0-65,62) 4-Y-O+ **£2,264** (£673; £336; £168) **Stalls** Low

Form RPR
5-15 1 **Helmsley Flyer (IRE)**[21] 609 4-8-13 56..............................(v) DanielTudhope 3 70+
(David O'Meara) *trckd ldrs: smooth hdwy over 3f out: 2nd 2f out: led over 1f out: pushed along: readily* **4/1**[3]
-241 2 3 1/4 **Sian Gwalia**[21] 612 4-9-5 62.............................. DavidProbert 1 69
(David Simcock) *hld up in rr: hdwy over 2f out: upsides over 1f out: kpt on same pce* **3/1**[2]
0-22 3 3 1/4 **Pinotage**[14] 695 6-9-3 58..............................(p) GrahamLee 5 60
(Peter Niven) *t.k.h: w ldr: led 8f out: drvn over 2f out: hdd over 1f out: kpt on one pce* **7/4**[1]
-461 4 8 **Grandiloquent**[7] 781 5-8-13 54..............................(v) TomEaves 6 44
(Brian Ellison) *trckd ldrs: jnd ldr over 4f out: drvn over 2f out: lost pl over 1f out* **5/1**
-532 5 5 **Rocky Rebel**[16] 657 6-9-7 62.............................. DaleSwift 4 45
(Michael Blake) *led 4f: drvn over 4f out: lost pl over 1f out* **8/1**
/04- 6 18 **No Compromise**[202] 5526 5-9-6 61..............................(b) AdamKirby 2 17
(Richard Phillips) *in rr: drvn over 5f out: lost pl over 3f out: bhd whn eased ins fnl f* **20/1**

2m 42.95s (1.85) **Going Correction** +0.075s/f (Slow)
**WFA** 4 from 5yo+ 2lb 6 Ran SP% **113.9**
Speed ratings (Par 101): **96,93,91,86,83 71**
CSF £16.71 TOTE £3.80: £1.60, £3.30; EX 18.10 Trifecta £51.50.
**Owner** Direct Racing **Bred** Skeaghmore Hill **Trained** Nawton, N Yorks

**FOCUS**
A fair race for the grade, despite the small field. There are more races to be won with the winner.
T/Plt: £284.90 to a £1 stake. Pool: £100217.82 - 256.77 winning tickets T/Qpdt: £27.80 to a £1 stake. Pool: £11260.25 - 299.09 winning tickets WG

873 - 885a (Foreign Racing) - See Raceform Interactive

# [866] WOLVERHAMPTON (A.W) (L-H)
Saturday, March 8

**OFFICIAL GOING: Standard**
Wind: Fresh half-behind Weather: Overcast

## 886 LADBROKES LADY WULFRUNA STKS (FAST TRACK QUALIFIER) (LISTED RACE) 7f 32y(P)
**2:20** (2:21) (Class 1) 4-Y-0+
**£28,355** (£10,750; £5,380; £2,680; £1,345; £675) **Stalls** High

Form RPR
-210 1 **Chookie Royale**[14] 716 6-9-3 107..............................(p) TomEaves 6 113
(Keith Dalgleish) *sn trcking ldrs: wnt 2nd over 5f out: led 3f out: rdn clr fr over 2f out: edgd rt fnl f: styd on* **4/1**[1]
01-6 2 3 1/4 **Hasopop (IRE)**[14] 715 4-9-3 104..............................(p) MartinHarley 10 105+
(Marco Botti) *hld up: t.k.h: hdwy on outer over 2f out: rdn to go 2nd 1f out: no ch w wnr* **9/2**[2]
-303 3 1/2 **Bertiewhittle**[14] 715 6-9-3 103..............................(p) GrahamGibbons 8 104
(David Barron) *a.p: rdn to chse wnr 2f out tl 1f out: styd on same pce* **5/1**[3]
-000 4 1 1/2 **Santefisio**[16] 678 8-9-3 97..............................(p) JoeFanning 4 100
(Keith Dalgleish) *hld up: t.k.h: r.o ins fnl f: nvr nrr* **20/1**
-012 5 1 1/4 **Alben Star (IRE)**[28] 534 6-9-3 100.............................. TonyHamilton 5 97
(Richard Fahey) *hld up: hdwy over 1f out: sn rdn: no imp fnl f* **12/1**
-000 6 nse **Intransigent**[16] 678 5-9-3 100.............................. LiamKeniry 1 100+
(Andrew Balding) *hld up: nt clr run 6f out: hmpd over 2f out: r.o ins fnl f: nvr nrr* **8/1**
205- 7 3/4 **Gabriel's Lad (IRE)**[147] 7190 5-9-3 104.............................. TomQueally 3 95
(Denis Coakley) *mid-div: hdwy over 2f out: rdn over 1f out: no ex fnl f* **5/1**[3]
510- 8 4 1/2 **Highland Knight (IRE)**[112] 7927 7-9-8 108..............................(t) DavidProbert 7 89
(Andrew Balding) *chsd ldr tl over 5f out: remained handy tl rdn and wknd over 1f out* **10/1**
432- 9 1 3/4 **Kenny Powers**[364] 944 5-9-3 0..............................(t) RichardKingscote 2 80
(Tom Dascombe) *prom: plld hrd: nt clr run over 2f out: sn wknd* **6/1**
05-0 10 3 1/2 **Dr Red Eye**[14] 715 6-9-3 87..............................(p) FrederikTylicki 9 71
(Scott Dixon) *led 4f: rdn and wknd over 1f out* **33/1**

1m 27.48s (-2.12) **Going Correction** 0.0s/f (Stan) 10 Ran SP% **121.4**
Speed ratings (Par 111): **112,108,107,106,104 104,103,98,96,92**
CSF £22.98 TOTE £4.70: £1.80, £2.20, £2.50; EX 25.00 Trifecta £71.90.
**Owner** Raeburn Brick Limited **Bred** D And J Raeburn **Trained** Carluke, S Lanarks



The Form Book, Raceform Ltd, Newbury, RG14 5SJ

**FOCUS**
A strong renewal of a Listed race that has been dominated by 4yos in the last two years, in which a guaranteed place in the Mile Final at the All-Weather Championships was an added reward for winning. A personal best from the winner and this could be worth another 4-5lb. Strong form.

## 887 LADBROKES LINCOLN TRIAL H'CAP 1m 141y(P)
2:55 (2:55) (Class 2) (0-105,100) 4-Y-O+
£31,125 (£9,320; £4,660; £2,330; £1,165; £585) Stalls Low

Form RPR
00-0 1 **Whispering Warrior (IRE)**[7] 804 5-9-1 **91** ... JimCrowley 3 99
(David Simcock) *mid-div: hdwy over 2f out: rdn and edgd rt ins fnl f: r.o to ld nr fin* **11/2**[2]
1142 2 ½ **Tellovoi (IRE)**[21] 625 6-9-2 **92** ...(v) WilliamCarson 9 99
(Ann Stokell) *led: rdn and hdd over 1f out: rallied to ld ins fnl f: hdd nr fin* **20/1**
100- 3 ½ **Party Royal**[121] 7793 4-8-9 **85** ... JoeFanning 13 91
(Mark Johnston) *sn chsng ldr: shkn up to ld over 1f out: hdd and unable qck ins fnl f* **33/1**
2-11 4 hd **Fashion Line (IRE)**[16] 674 4-8-7 **88** ... LouisSteward(5) 10 93+
(Michael Bell) *hld up: hdwy 2f out: rdn and edgd rt over 1f out: hung lft wl ins fnl f: r.o: nt rch ldrs* **8/1**
-315 5 ¾ **Alfred Hutchinson**[14] 715 6-9-7 **100** ... RobertTart(3) 7 104
(Geoffrey Oldroyd) *chsd ldrs: rdn and ev ch ins fnl f: styd on same pce* **5/1**[1]
-111 6 hd **Noble Citizen (USA)**[27] 550 9-8-13 **96** ...(b) JoeDoyle(7) 4 100
(David Simcock) *hld up: hdwy over 1f out: nt clr run ins fnl f: styd on* **20/1**
2-41 7 hd **Sky Khan**[16] 674 5-8-6 **87** ...(e) ConnorBeasley(5) 6 90
(Richard Guest) *a.p: t.k.h: rdn over 2f out: styd on same pce ins fnl f* **8/1**
004- 8 2 **Postscript (IRE)**[161] 6834 6-8-13 **89** ... MartinHarley 5 88
(David Simcock) *chsd ldrs: rdn over 1f out: no ex ins fnl f* **20/1**
333- 9 nk **Tres Coronas (IRE)**[161] 6838 7-9-6 **96** ... GrahamGibbons 1 95
(David Barron) *hld up: pushed along over 3f out: nt clr run over 2f out: nt trble ldrs* **6/1**[3]
-121 10 1 **Star Links (USA)**[26] 559 8-9-3 **93** ...(b) ShaneKelly 11 89
(S Donohoe, Ire) *s.i.s: hld up: rdn over 1f out: n.d* **7/1**
006- 11 9 **Global Village (IRE)**[175] 6396 9-9-2 **92** ... DaleSwift 12 69
(Brian Ellison) *hld up: rdn over 2f out: a in rr* **16/1**
-055 12 5 **Strictly Silver (IRE)**[26] 559 5-9-8 **98** ...(v) RobertWinston 2 65
(Alan Bailey) *prom: rdn over 2f out: wknd over 1f out: eased ins fnl f* **7/1**
2-00 13 2¼ **Loyalty**[42] 344 7-8-6 **89** ...(v) AdamMcLean(7) 8 51
(Derek Shaw) *sn pushed along in rr: rdn over 3f out: nt clr run and wknd over 2f out* **20/1**
1m 48.88s (-1.62) **Going Correction** 0.0s/f (Stan) 13 Ran SP% **121.4**
Speed ratings (Par 109): **107,106,106,105,105 105,104,103,102,101 93,89,87**
CSF £117.90 CT £3433.88 TOTE £7.90: £3.10, £8.80, £7.20; EX 139.80 Trifecta £2840.20 Part won..
**Owner** Daniel Pittack **Bred** Epona Bloodstock Ltd **Trained** Newmarket, Suffolk

**FOCUS**
A traditionally competitive renewal of the Lincoln Trial, in which most were in with a chance 1f from home. The pace was surprisingly ordinary. A minor personal best from the winner.

## 888 LADBROKES MAIDEN STKS 1m 141y(P)
3:30 (3:31) (Class 5) 3-Y-O+ £3,881 (£1,155; £577; £288) Stalls Low

Form RPR
324- 1 **Anipa**[166] 6688 3-8-3 74 ...[1] AndreaAtzeni 4 76
(Roger Varian) *a.p: shkn up over 3f out: chsd ldr over 2f out: sn rdn: r.o u.p to ld nr fin* **11/10**[1]
3 2 hd **Tarrafal (IRE)**[15] 696 3-8-8 0 ... JoeFanning 2 81
(Mark Johnston) *led: hdd 6f out: led again 3f out: rdn and edgd rt over 1f out: hdd nr fin* **11/10**[1]
0- 3 9 **Guaracha**[80] 8333 3-8-8 0 ... HayleyTurner 5 61+
(Clive Brittain) *sat last: rdn over 2f out: wknd over 1f out* **7/1**[2]
5 4 4½ **Nellies Quest**[27] 551 5-9-2 0 ... AlistairRawlinson(7) 1 52
(Michael Appleby) *plld hrd: w ldr tl led 6f out: hdd 3f out: rdn and wknd over 1f out* **33/1**[3]
1m 51.01s (0.51) **Going Correction** 0.0s/f (Stan)
**WFA** 3 from 5yo 20lb 4 Ran SP% **110.7**
Speed ratings (Par 103): **97,96,88,84**
CSF £2.63 TOTE £1.90; EX 3.20 Trifecta £5.80.
**Owner** Nurlan Bizakov **Bred** Hesmonds Stud Ltd **Trained** Newmarket, Suffolk

**FOCUS**
Just the four runners went to post in the maiden and they looked a modest bunch. The third and fourth are the key to the level.

## 889 BEST ODDS AT BOOKMAKERS.CO.UK CLASSIFIED CLAIMING STKS 5f 20y(P)
4:05 (4:06) (Class 5) 4-Y-O+ £3,881 (£1,155; £577; £288) Stalls Low

Form RPR
00-2 1 **Come On Dave (IRE)**[17] 662 5-8-8 68 ... AdrianNicholls 2 74
(David Nicholls) *mde all: t.k.h: pushed along 2f out: rdn out* **11/4**[2]
2000 2 ¾ **Haadeeth**[3] 841 7-7-13 63 ...(b) HollieDoyle(7) 4 69
(David Evans) *a.p: chsd wnr 1/2-way: rdn over 1f out: r.o* **9/2**[3]
2155 3 3½ **Where's Reiley (USA)**[5] 826 8-8-10 64 ...(b) GrahamGibbons 3 60
(Michael Attwater) *chsd ldrs: rdn over 1f out: styd on same pce fnl f* **7/1**
3320 4 1¾ **Master Of Disguise**[15] 694 8-8-6 62 ... DuranFentiman 1 50
(Brian Baugh) *chsd wnr to 1/2-way: rdn over 1f out: no ex fnl f* **10/1**
3324 5 3½ **Angelo Poliziano**[3] 845 8-8-0 63 ...(bt) JosephineGordon(7) 6 39
(Jo Hughes) *s.i.s: edgd lft over 1f out: nvr on terms* **6/1**
4002 6 1½ **Quality Art (USA)**[15] 694 6-8-4 63 ow1 ... BillyCray(3) 7 33
(Simon Hodgson) *hld up: hung rt 1/2-way: rdn over 1f out: n.d* **16/1**
1566 7 1¼ **R Woody**[5] 826 7-8-10 69 ...(e) ShaneKelly 5 32
(George Baker) *s.i.s: last and drvn along 3f out: no rspnse* **5/2**[1]
1m 1.43s (-0.87) **Going Correction** 0.0s/f (Stan) 7 Ran SP% **115.2**
Speed ratings (Par 103): **106,104,99,96,90 88,86**
CSF £15.80 TOTE £3.30: £3.30, £1.80; EX 22.10 Trifecta £100.50.
**Owner** Middleham Park Racing XLIV **Bred** Mrs Eithne Hamilton **Trained** Sessay, N Yorks

**FOCUS**
A poor classified claimer, notable for a late gamble on Haadeeth. The winner got closer to last year's turf form.

## 890 COMPARE BOOKMAKERS AT BOOKMAKERS.CO.UK H'CAP 5f 216y(P)
4:40 (4:41) (Class 2) (0-100,102) 4-Y-O+
£15,562 (£4,660; £2,330; £1,165; £582; £292) Stalls Low

Form RPR
22-6 1 **Baddilini**[8] 779 4-8-2 **86** oh4 ...(p) NatashaEaton(5) 5 94
(Alan Bailey) *chsd ldrs: rdn over 1f out: r.o to ld nr fin* **14/1**
4311 2 nk **Trojan Rocket (IRE)**[17] 658 6-8-8 **87** ...(p) RichardKingscote 3 94
(Michael Wigham) *disp ld tl wnt on over 3f out: rdn over 1f out: hdd nr fin* **10/3**[2]
-000 3 nk **Hitchens (IRE)**[14] 713 9-9-2 **102** ... LukeDempsey(7) 7 108
(David Barron) *hld up: rdn and r.o wl ins fnl f: nt rch ldrs* **7/2**[3]
600- 4 1¾ **Pandar**[166] 6699 5-8-10 **89** ... JoeFanning 6 90
(Milton Bradley) *disp ld tl over 3f out: rdn over 1f out: styd on same pce ins fnl f* **16/1**
660- 5 ½ **Regal Parade**[140] 7368 10-8-13 **95** ...(t) RobertTart(3) 8 94
(Milton Bradley) *hld up: r.o ins fnl f: nvr nrr* **4/1**
00-5 6 nk **Joe Eile (IRE)**[25] 566 6-9-0 **93** ...[1] RobertWinston 2 92
(John Quinn) *chsd ldrs: rdn over 2f out: no ex ins fnl f* **3/1**[1]
-500 7 2 **Clockmaker (IRE)**[28] 534 8-8-8 **87** ... HayleyTurner 4 80
(Conor Dore) *hld up: rdn over 2f out: nt trble ldrs* **8/1**
1m 14.43s (-0.57) **Going Correction** 0.0s/f (Stan) 7 Ran SP% **114.0**
Speed ratings (Par 109): **103,102,102,99,99 98,96**
CSF £59.65 CT £203.38 TOTE £10.40: £6.30, £1.10; EX 28.70 Trifecta £147.80.
**Owner** Mrs A Shone **Bred** Mrs A R Ruggles **Trained** Newmarket, Suffolk

**FOCUS**
Not a strong race for the £25,000 pot, with the field made up of mainly out-of-form or veteran performers. The winner is rated back to his best.

## 891 32RED IMMORTAL ROMANCE SLOT H'CAP 1m 5f 194y(P)
5:15 (5:15) (Class 4) (0-85,84) 4-Y-O+ £5,498 (£1,636; £817; £408) Stalls Low

Form RPR
430 1 **Royal Alcor (IRE)**[35] 427 7-9-7 **79** ...(t) DavidProbert 7 87
(Gay Kelleway) *hld up: hdwy over 2f out: rdn to ld wl ins fnl f: styd on* **10/1**
0314 2 ½ **Mica Mika (IRE)**[9] 763 6-9-1 **76** ... GeorgeChaloner(3) 5 83
(Richard Fahey) *a.p: rdn over 2f out: led wl ins fnl f: sn hdd: styd on* **8/1**
-125 3 1 **Sagesse**[21] 623 4-9-2 **78** ... ChrisCatlin 1 84
(Sir Mark Prescott Bt) *led: rdn over 2f out: edgd lft over 1f out: hdd and unable qck wl ins fnl f* **3/1**[2]
1434 4 3 **The Blue Dog (IRE)**[19] 641 7-8-12 **73** ... RobertTart(3) 4 75
(Phil McEntee) *a.p: pushed along 2f out: cl up and n.m.r fr over 1f out tl ins fnl f: no ex* **12/1**
1624 5 3 **Doldrums (USA)**[12] 732 4-8-13 **75** ...(b[1]) JoeFanning 6 73
(Mark Johnston) *chsd ldr: ev ch over 2f out: sn rdn: wknd ins fnl f* **8/1**
-163 6 12 **Luv U Whatever**[15] 698 4-9-3 **79** ... LiamJones 2 60
(Jo Hughes) *chsd ldrs: rdn over 4f out: wknd over 2f out* **4/1**[3]
005- 7 50 **Quixote**[170] 6573 5-9-12 **84** ...(t) FrederikTylicki 3
(Clive Brittain) *hld up: rdn 3f out: sn wknd and eased* **9/4**[1]
3m 3.8s (-2.20) **Going Correction** 0.0s/f (Stan)
**WFA** 4 from 5yo+ 4lb 7 Ran SP% **114.8**
Speed ratings (Par 105): **106,105,105,103,101 94,66**
CSF £84.74 TOTE £15.40: £5.40, £3.70; EX 98.60 Trifecta £612.00.
**Owner** A MacLennan, G Kelleway & P Kerridge **Bred** John Hayes **Trained** Exning, Suffolk

**FOCUS**
Mostly consistent performers lined up for this staying handicap, which was run at just an ordinary gallop. The winner was fully entitled to win on these terms.

## 892 32RED.COM H'CAP (BOBIS RACE) 7f 32y(P)
5:45 (5:48) (Class 4) (0-80,78) 3-Y-O £5,498 (£1,636; £817; £408) Stalls High

Form RPR
1- 1 **Euro Charline**[112] 7934 3-9-7 **78** ... AndreaAtzeni 2 99+
(Marco Botti) *chsd ldrs: led over 1f out: shkn up and sn c clr: easily* **5/4**[1]
45-1 2 9 **Beautiful Stranger (IRE)**[25] 568 3-8-12 **69** ...(p) TomEaves 6 68
(Keith Dalgleish) *disp ld tl wnt on 1/2-way: rdn and hdd over 1f out: sn outpcd* **6/1**[3]
563- 3 nk **Penny's Boy**[113] 7892 3-8-8 **70** ... JoshBaudains(5) 8 68
(Sylvester Kirk) *hld up: hdwy over 2f out: rdn over 1f out: styd on same pce* **6/1**[3]
351- 4 1 **Meaning Of Life (IRE)**[207] 5371 3-9-7 **78** ... MartinHarley 4 75
(Marco Botti) *prom: rdn over 2f out: styd on same pce fr over 1f out* **7/2**[2]
34-0 5 shd **Intermath (IRE)**[21] 624 3-9-6 **77** ... AdamKirby 5 73
(David Evans) *chsd ldr: wnt 2nd over 2f out tl rdn wl over 1f out: no ex* **10/1**
12-4 6 ½ **Poetic Choice**[30] 501 3-8-8 **72** ... JordanVaughan(7) 1 66
(Nick Littmoden) *hld up: rdn over 2f out: n.d* **16/1**
1-50 7 7 **Vodka Time (IRE)**[21] 624 3-9-4 **75** ... ChrisCatlin 7 52
(David Evans) *hld up: rdn and wknd over 2f out* **28/1**
3-1 8 16 **Mon Petit Secret**[16] 675 3-8-4 **66** ... ShaneGray(5) 3 4
(Kevin Ryan) *disputed ld tl pushed along 1/2-way: wknd 2f out* **12/1**
1m 28.62s (-0.98) **Going Correction** 0.0s/f (Stan) 8 Ran SP% **121.4**
Speed ratings (Par 100): **105,94,94,93,93 92,84,66**
CSF £10.24 CT £36.29 TOTE £2.30: £1.10, £2.10, £2.50; EX 12.20 Trifecta £80.10.
**Owner** Scuderia Blueberry **Bred** Brian Liversage **Trained** Newmarket, Suffolk

**FOCUS**
Marco Botti-trained runners dominated the market in this 3yo handicap. The winner destroyed these and showed smart form.
T/Plt: £689.90 to a £1 stake. Pool: £106,003.09 - 112.16 winning units. T/Qpdt: £82.70 to a £1 stake. Pool: £4703.65 - 42.07 winning units. CR

## [807] MEYDAN (L-H)
Saturday, March 8

**OFFICIAL GOING: Tapeta: standard; turf: good**

### 896a AL BASTAKIYA SPONSORED BY EMIRATES SKYWARDS (LISTED RACE) (TAPETA) 1m 1f 110y
**1:10** (1:10) 3-Y-O

**£90,361** (£30,120; £15,060; £7,530; £4,518; £3,012)

RPR
1 **Asmar (IRE)**[23] 594 3-8-8 98 RichardHughes 3 110+
(Fawzi Abdulla Nass, Bahrain) *trckd ldrs: led 6f out: kicked clr 2 1/2f out: comf* **4/1**[3]
2 6 **Emirates Flyer**[23] 594 3-8-8 104 MickaelBarzalona 8 100
(Saeed bin Suroor) *mid-div: chsd ldrs 2 1/2f out: r.o fnl 2f but no ch w wnr* **6/4**[1]
3 3 1/2 **Najm Suhail**[9] 770 3-8-8 95 RoystonFfrench 4 91
(A Al Raihe, UAE) *s.i.s: mid-div: r.o fnl 2f: nrst fin* **12/1**
4 2 **Duke Derby (IRE)**[101] 3-8-8 90 Per-AndersGraberg 10 87
(Niels Petersen, Norway) *settled in rr: nvr nr to chal but r.o fnl 2f* **25/1**
5 1 1/4 **He's No Saint**[30] 505 3-8-8 100 FergalLynch 1 84
(David Marnane, Ire) *mid-div: chsd ldrs 3f out: ev ch 2 1/2f out: wknd fnl f* **3/1**[2]
6 2 **More Aspen (USA)**[9] 771 3-8-5 86 ow1 (b) RichardMullen 6 77
(S Seemar, UAE) *mid-div: chsd ldrs 3f out: outpcd fnl 2f* **33/1**
7 nk **Chord Chart (IRE)**[9] 770 3-8-8 94 MarcMonaghan 2 80
(S Seemar, UAE) *sn led: hdd 6f out: wknd fnl 2f* **20/1**
8 8 1/2 **Full Combat (SAF)**[23] 594 4-9-4 98 PaulHanagan 9 65
(M F De Kock, South Africa) *settled in rr: nvr nr to chal* **7/1**
9 12 1/2 **Letterfromamerica (USA)**[9] 771 3-8-4 88 (t) TadhgO'Shea 7 33
(S Seemar, UAE) *trckd ldrs: rdn 4 1/2f out: wknd fnl 2 1/2f* **50/1**
10 16 1/2 **Eye In The Sky (IRE)**[9] 770 3-8-9 95 ow1 (t) WilliamBuick 5 5
(Niels Petersen, Norway) *a in rr* **16/1**

1m 59.56s (0.56)
**WFA** 3 from 4yo 20lb **10** Ran SP% **124.6**
CSF: 10.81; EXACTA: 18.60; TRIFECTA: 175.70; WIN: 6.40; PL: 2.80, 1.00, 2.60.
**Owner** Fawzi Abdulla Nass **Bred** Eric Puerari And Oceanic Bloodstock **Trained** Bahrain

**FOCUS**
Each split was outside the Trakus par on a day when the Tapeta was riding on the slow side, at least to begin with, as is sometimes the case when racing kicks off in the heat. However, Richard Hughes, who sensibly waited until he'd taken the first bend before sending Asmar to the lead, gradually increased the tempo: 27.99 (400m), 24.79 (800m), 24.35 (1200m), 23.96 (1600m).

### 897a MEYDAN SPRINT SPONSORED BY ARABIAN ADVENTURES (GROUP 3) (TURF) 5f (T)
**1:45** (1:45) 3-Y-0+

**£63,253** (£21,084; £10,542; £5,271; £3,162; £2,108)

RPR
1 **Shea Shea (SAF)**[197] 5726 7-9-4 119 ChristopheSoumillon 6 118
(M F De Kock, South Africa) *mid-div: swtchd stands' side: rdn to ld 1f out: r.o wl* **6/4**[1]
2 hd **Ahtoug**[16] 680 6-9-4 109 MickaelBarzalona 12 117
(Charlie Appleby) *mid-div: smooth prog to ld 1 1/2f out: hdd 1f out: r.o wl* **10/1**
3 1 1/2 **Dux Scholar**[7] 809 6-9-4 111 (b) PatDobbs 5 112
(Doug Watson, UAE) *settled in rr: r.o fnl 2f: nrst fin* **12/1**
4 hd **Sole Power**[90] 8209 7-9-4 115 RyanMoore 13 111+
(Edward Lynam, Ire) *settled in rr: r.o fnl 2f but nvr able to chal* **3/1**[2]
5 1 **Catcall (FR)**[16] 680 5-9-4 113 OlivierPeslier 2 107
(P Sogorb, France) *mid-div: chsd ldrs 2 1/2f: r.o same pce fnl 1 1/2f* **7/1**[3]
6 3/4 **Hototo**[16] 680 4-9-4 105 (v) LukeMorris 7 105
(Fawzi Abdulla Nass, Bahrain) *trckd ldng pair: ev ch 1 1/2f out: one pce fnl f* **16/1**
7 1 1/2 **My Catch (IRE)**[9] 770 3-8-10 102 JamesDoyle 10 98
(Doug Watson, UAE) *nvr bttr than mid-div* **20/1**
8 3/4 **Roi De Vitesse (IRE)**[9] 769 7-9-4 100 (v) AdriedeVries 3 96
(Ali Jan, Qatar) *s.i.s: settled in rr: nvr able to chal* **50/1**
9 nk **Alsaaeqah (KSA)**[37] 393 7-9-0 109 WilliamBuick 11 91
(B Al Shaibani, Saudi Arabia) *nvr bttr than mid-div* **14/1**
10 3/4 **Beat Baby (IRE)**[37] 393 7-9-4 112 (t) Per-AndersGraberg 1 93
(Niels Petersen, Norway) *sn led: hdd 2f out: wknd fnl f* **16/1**
11 nse **Zee Bros (USA)**[9] 769 4-9-4 104 (t) FrankieDettori 4 93
(Seth Benzel, U.S.A) *trckd ldrs tl outpcd 2f* **22/1**
12 hd **Mundahesh (IRE)**[16] 683 4-9-4 98 PaulHanagan 9 92
(A Al Raihe, UAE) *nvr nr to chal* **50/1**
13 5 1/2 **Make It Reel (FR)**[9] 770 3-8-10 95 SamHitchcott 8 71
(Doug Watson, UAE) *nvr nr to chal* **66/1**

57.07s (-1.43)
**WFA** 3 from 4yo+ 13lb **13** Ran SP% **127.2**
CSF: 18.84; EXACTA: 23.90; TRIFECTA: 236.70; WIN: 2.20; PL: 1.40, 3.30, 3.60.
**Owner** Mssrs Brian Joffee & Myron C Berzack **Bred** Klawervlei Stud **Trained** South Africa

**FOCUS**
Another year and another upgrade for this race, which now holds Group 3 status. The key prep for the Al Quoz Sprint. Those who raced middle to far side went off too fast in pursuit of the trailblazing Beat Baby and Zee Bros, while those racing towards the stands' side followed a more even pace set by My Catch and Alsaaeqah. Three of the first four came from the stands' side group while the third came through having been held up in the far-side group. Here are the splits compared to the Trakus pars: 23.95 (24.07), 45.52 (45.87), 57.07 (57.90). The winer is rated in line with last season's British form.

### 898a MAHAB AL SHIMAAL SPONSORED BY EMIRATES SKYWARDS (GROUP 3) (TAPETA) 6f
**2:25** (2:25) 3-Y-0+

**£72,289** (£24,096; £12,048; £6,024; £3,614; £2,409)

RPR
1 **Rich Tapestry (IRE)**[90] 8209 6-9-5 112 (bt) ODoleuze 5 116
(C W Chang, Hong Kong) *wl away: trckd ldng pair: led 1f out: r.o wl* **10/1**
2 1 1/4 **Reynaldothewizard (USA)**[51] 206 8-9-5 118 (bt) RichardMullen 10 112
(S Seemar, UAE) *trckd ldrs: rdn to ld 2 1/2f out: hdd 1f out: r.o wl* **8/1**[3]
3 1 1/4 **Complicate (AUS)**[23] 597 5-9-5 106 KierenFallon 2 108+
(Saeed bin Suroor) *mid-div: r.o fnl 2f: nrst fin* **9/1**
4 1 **Jamesie (IRE)**[23] 597 6-9-5 107 FergalLynch 9 105+
(David Marnane, Ire) *settled in rr: nvr nr to chal but r.o fnl 2f* **9/1**
5 3/4 **Balmont Mast (IRE)**[23] 597 6-9-5 112 RyanMoore 8 102
(Edward Lynam, Ire) *settled in rr: r.o fnl 1 1/2f but nvr able to chal* **10/1**
6 nk **Russian Soul (IRE)**[23] 597 6-9-5 112 (p) ShaneFoley 11 101
(M Halford, Ire) *nvr bttr than mid-div* **6/1**[2]
7 1/2 **Nawwaar (USA)**[7] 809 5-9-5 112 DaneO'Neill 6 100
(A Al Raihe, UAE) *mid-div: r.o same pce fnl 1 1/2f* **50/1**
8 nk **Bello (AUS)**[23] 597 6-9-5 109 (b) MickaelBarzalona 4 99
(Charlie Appleby) *mid-div: r.o same pce fnl 1 1/2f* **16/1**
9 3/4 **Soft Falling Rain (SAF)**[140] 7366 5-9-5 120 PaulHanagan 14 96
(M F De Kock, South Africa) *nvr nr to chal* **3/1**[1]
10 1 3/4 **United Color (USA)**[23] 597 5-9-5 112 (t) JamesDoyle 12 91
(D Selvaratnam, UAE) *nvr nr to chal* **8/1**[3]
11 1/2 **Krypton Factor**[23] 597 6-9-5 111 (b) RichardHughes 7 89
(Fawzi Abdulla Nass, Bahrain) *a in rr* **16/1**
12 3/4 **Gale Force Ten**[9] 772 4-9-5 109 (bt) ChristopheSoumillon 13 87+
(M F De Kock, South Africa) *sn led: hdd 2 1/2f out: wknd fnl 1 1/2f* **25/1**
13 nk **Abu Sidra (FR)**[9] 769 5-9-5 108 FrankieDettori 1 86
(J-F Bernard, France) *s.i.s: n.d* **28/1**
14 1/2 **Tamaathul**[9] 768 7-9-5 108 (t) RoystonFfrench 3 84
(A Al Raihe, UAE) *nvr able to chal* **25/1**

1m 11.7s (0.10)
**WFA** 3 from 4yo+ 14lb **14** Ran SP% **124.6**
CSF: 87.74; EXACTA: 202.10; TRIFECTA: 2285.90; WIN: 15.50; PL: 3.50, 3.40, 2.70.
**Owner** Silas Yang Siu Shun, Wong Tak Wai Et Al **Bred** Moyglare Stud Farm Ltd **Trained** Hong Kong

**FOCUS**
It proved hard to make up significant ground with the pace slowing a touch on the bend, and again each split was above the Trakus par times: 24.69 (400m, from standing start), 23.71 (800m, bend), 23.30 (finish). The last two winners of this race, Krypton Factor and Reynaldothewizard (who were both back for more), followed up in the Golden Shaheen on World Cup day. The winner and third help set the standard.

### 899a BURJ NAHAAR SPONSORED BY EMIRATES HOLIDAYS (GROUP 3) (TAPETA) 1m
**3:00** (3:00) 3-Y-0+

**£72,289** (£24,096; £12,048; £6,024; £3,614; £2,409)

RPR
1 **Shuruq (USA)**[37] 395 4-8-9 109 (p) MickaelBarzalona 12 115+
(Saeed bin Suroor) *mid-div: smooth prog 2 1/2f out: rdn 2f out: led fnl 110yds* **14/1**[3]
2 1 3/4 **Variety Club (SAF)**[23] 596 6-9-0 120 AntonMarcus 11 116
(J Ramsden, South Africa) *trckd ldrs: led 1 1/2f out: hdd fnl 110yds* **4/7**[1]
3 3/4 **Capital Attraction (USA)**[7] 810 7-9-0 113 TadhgO'Shea 5 114
(Ernst Oertel, UAE) *sn led: rdn clr 2 1/2f out: hdd 1 1/2f out: r.o wl* **20/1**
4 2 3/4 **Forjatt (IRE)**[23] 595 6-9-0 112 JamesDoyle 4 108
(D Selvaratnam, UAE) *trckd ldrs: outpcd 2 1/2f out: r.o fnl 2f* **14/1**[3]
5 1 **Gold City (IRE)**[9] 768 5-9-0 109 (bt) RichardMullen 7 105
(S Seemar, UAE) *chsd ldrs: ev ch 2f out: wknd fnl 1 1/2f* **20/1**
6 nse **Avon Pearl**[16] 679 5-9-0 106 (vt) PatDobbs 13 105
(Rune Haugen, Norway) *mid-div: r.o same pce fnl 1 1/2f* **20/1**
7 1 3/4 **Van Rooney (USA)**[7] 808 5-9-0 102 (t) AdriedeVries 3 101
(Ali Jan, Qatar) *nvr bttr than mid-div* **33/1**
8 2 1/2 **Dastarhon (IRE)**[16] 683 4-9-0 109 (t) MaximeGuyon 1 95
(Mme Pia Brandt, France) *trckd ldng pair: ev ch 2 1/2f out: one pce fnl 1 1/2f* **25/1**
9 1 **Gabrial (IRE)**[9] 772 5-9-0 109 JamieSpencer 6 93
(Richard Fahey) *s.i.s: nvr nr to chal* **16/1**
10 nk **Empire Storm (GER)**[23] 596 7-9-0 107 (t) KierenFallon 8 92
(Michael Attwater) *trckd ldng pair: ev ch 3f out: one pce fnl 2f* **25/1**
11 nk **Ocean Tempest**[7] 808 5-9-0 101 BrettDoyle 2 92
(John Ryan) *mid-div: chsd ldrs 3f out: one pce fnl 1 1/2f* **66/1**
12 1 3/4 **Eastern Rules (IRE)**[16] 678 6-9-0 110 ShaneFoley 9 88
(M Halford, Ire) *nvr nr to chal* **16/1**
13 1/2 **Haatheq (USA)**[23] 596 7-9-0 113 PaulHanagan 10 87
(A Al Raihe, UAE) *nvr bttr than mid-div* **12/1**[2]
14 1/2 **Rutland Boy**[9] 768 6-9-0 107 RyanMoore 15 85
(Michael Bell) *settled in rr: nvr able to chal* **66/1**
15 2 **Brendan Brackan (IRE)**[37] 397 5-9-0 115 ColinKeane 16 81
(G M Lyons, Ire) *a in rr* **25/1**
16 4 1/2 **Zahee (NZ)**[16] 678 5-9-0 113 ChristopheSoumillon 14 71
(M F De Kock, South Africa) *a in rr* **16/1**

1m 36.34s (-1.16) **16** Ran SP% **134.1**
CSF: 21.97; EXACTA: 27.10; TRIFECTA: 441.20; WIN: 17.10; PL: 4.50, 1.00, 4.60.
**Owner** Godolphin **Bred** Darley **Trained** Newmarket, Suffolk

**FOCUS**
With the favourite below his best, this is ordinary form. This time each split was well under the Trakus par with the front-running Capital Attraction hassled throughout by Variety Club (25.63, 23.00, 23.49) and, with those two doing too much, the more patiently ridden winner came home in 23.66 compared to 24.32 for the runner-up.

### 900a DUBAI CITY OF GOLD SPONSORED BY EMIRATES SKYCARGO (GROUP 2) (TURF) 1m 4f 11y
**3:35** (3:35) 3-Y-0+

**£90,361** (£30,120; £15,060; £7,530; £4,518; £3,012)

RPR
1 **Excellent Result (IRE)**[30] 507 4-8-11 105 KierenFallon 5 112
(Saeed bin Suroor) *mid-div: rdn 2 1/2f out: r.o fnl 1 1/2f: led fnl 110yds* **9/1**[3]
2 hd **Songcraft (IRE)**[23] 598 6-9-0 109 (p) WilliamBuick 8 113
(Saeed bin Suroor) *trckd ldng pair: led 2 1/2f out: r.o wl hdd cl home* **9/1**[3]
3 nk **Mount Athos (IRE)**[90] 8208 7-9-0 115 JamieSpencer 4 113
(Marco Botti) *in rr of mid-div: smooth prog 2 1/2f out: ev ch 1 1/2f out: nt qckn fnl 110yds* **9/1**[3]
4 1 1/4 **Meandre (FR)**[23] 598 6-9-0 113 PatDobbs 15 110
(Doug Watson, UAE) *trckd ldng pair: ev ch 1f out: nt qckn fnl 110yds* **10/1**
5 1/2 **Dabadiyan (IRE)**[23] 598 4-8-11 105 ShaneFoley 2 108
(M Halford, Ire) *in rr of mid-div: r.o same pce fnl 2f* **20/1**
6 nse **Sheikhzayedroad**[23] 598 5-9-0 110 MartinLane 7 109
(David Simcock) *s.i.s: settled in rr: nvr nr to chal but r.o fnl 2f* **10/1**
7 1 1/2 **Penglai Pavilion (USA)**[153] 7058 4-8-11 118 MickaelBarzalona 10 106
(Charlie Appleby) *trckd ldrs tl wknd qckly 1f out* **7/2**[1]
8 nk **Jamr**[16] 683 6-9-0 110 (v) ChristopheSoumillon 14 106
(A bin Harmash, UAE) *mid-div: chsd ldrs 2 1/2f out: one pce fnl 1 1/2f* **16/1**

9 *shd* **Start Right**[7] 812 7-9-0 102 (p) RichardMullen 12 106
(S Seemar, UAE) *slowly away: settled rr: n.d* **40/1**

10 *½* **Model Pupil**[7] 811 5-9-0 104 RyanMoore 1 105+
(A Mishreff, Saudi Arabia) *settled in rr: nvr able to chal but mod prog last 2f* **33/1**

11 *shd* **Ralston Road (IRE)**[30] 507 4-8-11 102 TadhgO'Shea 11 104
(S Seemar, UAE) *in rr of mid-div: r.o same pce fnl 2 1/2f* **40/1**

12 *1 ½* **Battle Of Marengo (IRE)**[30] 508 4-8-11 117 FrankieDettori 16 102
(David Simcock) *sn led: hdd & wknd 1 1/2f* **16/1**

13 *3 ¾* **Mujaarib (AUS)**[16] 683 6-9-0 115 PaulHanagan 6 97
(M F De Kock, South Africa) *nvr bttr than mid-div* **7/1**[2]

14 *2 ¼* **Heavy Metal (SAF)**[30] 508 6-9-0 118 RichardHughes 9 93
(S G Tarry, South Africa) *nvr bttr than mid-div* **14/1**

15 *36* **Interpret (USA)**[30] 508 6-9-0 110 RoystonFfrench 13 36
(M Al Muhairi, UAE) *s.i.s: a in rr* **40/1**

2m 32.87s (152.87)
**WFA** 4 from 5yo+ 2lb **15** Ran SP% **116.4**
CSF: 72.23; EXACTA: 59.60; TRIFECTA: 481.90; WIN: 11.20; PL: 3.10, 2.90, 3.20..
**Owner** Godolphin **Bred** Tom & Geraldine Molan **Trained** Newmarket, Suffolk
■ Empoli was withdrawn. Price at time of withdrawal 6/1. Rule 4 applies to all bets - deduction 10p in the pound.

**FOCUS**
A prep race for the Sheema Classic for most, but there was no pace on early and it developed into a sprint up the straight. It's questionable how reliable the form is. Here are the splits: 28.90 (400m), 25.86 (800m), 26.29 (1200m), 25.11 (1600m), 23.37 (2000m). The first three all saved ground racing on the rail.

## 901a AL MAKTOUM CHALLENGE R3 SPONSORED BY EMIRATES AIRLINE (GROUP 1) (TAPETA) 1m 2f
**4:10** (4:10) 3-Y-O+

**£144,578** (£48,192; £24,096; £12,048; £7,228; £4,819)

RPR

1 **Prince Bishop (IRE)**[30] 508 7-9-0 117 (v) KierenFallon 1 115+
(Saeed bin Suroor) *mid-div on rail: smooth prog 1 1/2f out: led 1f out: r.o wl* **5/1**[2]

2 *1 ¼* **Sanshaawes (SAF)**[7] 812 5-9-0 109 ChristopheSoumillon 13 113
(M F De Kock, South Africa) *mid-div: r.o wl fnl 2f: nrst fin* **12/1**

3 *¾* **Surfer (USA)**[30] 508 5-9-0 111 (t) RichardMullen 14 111
(S Seemar, UAE) *trckd ldng pair: t.k.h: led 2f out: hdd 21f out: r.o gamely* **25/1**

4 *nk* **Cat O'Mountain (USA)**[16] 681 4-9-0 112 MickaelBarzalona 9 110
(Charlie Appleby) *settled in rr: nvr nr to chal but r.o fnl 2f: nrst fin* **8/1**[3]

5 *nk* **Educate**[37] 397 5-9-0 112 MaximeGuyon 12 110
(Ismail Mohammed) *mid-div: r.o same pce fnl 2f* **16/1**

6 *hd* **Joshua Tree (IRE)**[104] 8033 7-9-0 116 RyanMoore 10 109
(Ed Dunlop) *trckd ldng trio: ev ch 1 1/2f out: one pce fnl f* **16/1**

7 *shd* **Side Glance**[90] 8211 7-9-0 115 JamieSpencer 6 109
(Andrew Balding) *in rr of mid-div: chsd ldrs 2 1/2f out: r.o same pce fnl 1 1/2f* **9/1**

8 *nk* **African Story**[30] 508 7-9-0 119 WilliamBuick 8 109
(Saeed bin Suroor) *in rr of mid-div: rdn 2 1/2f: kpt on fnl 2f but nvr nr to chal* **1/1**[1]

9 *nk* **Limario (GER)**[156] 6987 4-9-0 110 PatDobbs 11 108
(Doug Watson, UAE) *trckd ldrs tl outpcd 42f out* **40/1**

10 *1 ¼* **Zambucca (SAF)**[30] 508 6-9-0 106 RichardHughes 4 106
(S Seemar, UAE) *nvr bttr thsn mid-div* **25/1**

11 *nse* **Ottoman Empire (FR)**[7] 807 8-9-0 104 FrankieDettori 3 105
(S Seemar, UAE) *s.i.s: nvr nr to chal* **50/1**

12 *1 ¼* **Elleval (IRE)**[16] 681 4-9-0 112 FergalLynch 5 103
(David Marnane, Ire) *s.i.s: settled in rr: nvr nr to chal* **12/1**

13 *2 ½* **Alexandra Palace (SAF)**[9] 773 5-9-0 107 PatCosgrave 7 98
(M F De Kock, South Africa) *settled in rr: nvr nr to chal* **40/1**

14 *5 ¼* **Mutajare (IRE)**[7] 812 6-9-0 111 (t) PaulHanagan 2 87
(A Al Raihe, UAE) *sn led: hdd & wknd 2f out* **40/1**

2m 4.23s (-0.47) **14** Ran SP% **131.9**
CSF: 66.21; EXACTA: 28.10; TRIFECTA: 780.30; WIN: 5.10; PL: 2.10, 2.40, 11.20.
**Owner** Sheikh Hamdan bin Mohammed Al Maktoum **Bred** Thurso Ltd **Trained** Newmarket, Suffolk

**FOCUS**
Three horses have won the World Cup following victory in this, Dubai Millennium (2000), Street Cry (2002) and Electrocutionist (2006), while Monterosso (2012) did so after managing only fourth, but it'll be a disappointing running of the world's richest race if we saw the winner this time. The pace was solid through the opening split, but soon slowed and they were quickening in the closing stages: 25.73 (400m), 25.20 (800m), 25.28 (1200m), 24.44 (1600m), 23.58 (finish).

## 902a JEBEL HATTA SPONSORED BY EMIRATES AIRLINE (GROUP 1) (TURF) 1m 1f
**4:45** (4:45) 3-Y-O+

**£108,433** (£36,144; £18,072; £9,036; £5,421; £3,614)

RPR

1 **Vercingetorix (SAF)**[23] 595 5-9-0 113 ChristopheSoumillon 2 115
(M F De Kock, South Africa) *trckd ldrs: led 1 1/2f out: rdn 1f out: r.o wl* **2/1**[1]

2 *1 ¾* **Vancouverite**[174] 6446 4-9-0 116 MickaelBarzalona 3 111
(Charlie Appleby) *mid-div: r.o fnl 2f but no ch w wnr* **7/1**

3 *nk* **Anaerobio (ARG)**[16] 678 7-9-0 112 (t) PatCosgrave 10 110
(M F De Kock, South Africa) *sn led: hdd 1 1/2f out: r.o: lost 2nd cl home* **20/1**

4 *nk* **Trade Storm**[9] 772 6-9-0 115 JamieSpencer 8 110+
(David Simcock) *settled in rr: r.o fnl 2f: nrst fin* **11/4**[2]

5 *nk* **Mushreq (AUS)**[9] 772 6-9-0 113 PaulHanagan 7 109
(M F De Kock, South Africa) *mid-div: r.o same pce fnl 2f* **10/1**

6 *1 ½* **Edu Querido (BRZ)**[9] 772 5-9-0 106 RyanMoore 12 106
(Marco Botti) *settled in rr: r.o fnl 2f but nvr able to chal* **33/1**

7 *¾* **Mars (IRE)**[23] 596 4-9-0 117 (b) RichardHughes 14 104
(M F De Kock, South Africa) *settled in rr: nvr nr to chal* **12/1**

8 *½* **Tanfeeth**[7] 807 6-9-0 101 (t) DaneO'Neill 1 103
(M Al Muhairi, UAE) *slowly away: nvr able to chal* **66/1**

9 *2 ¾* **Quick Wit**[16] 683 7-9-0 107 AhmedAjtebi 9 98
(Saeed bin Suroor) *trckd ldng pair tl outpcd 2f out* **33/1**

10 *shd* **Linton (AUS)**[90] 8210 8-9-0 115 TedDurcan 5 97
(Marco Botti) *nvr bttr than mid-div* **25/1**

11 *5 ½* **L'Amour De Ma Vie (USA)**[16] 682 5-8-9 112 MaximeGuyon 4 81
(Mme Pia Brandt, France) *s.i.s: nvr able to chal* **6/1**[3]

12 *shd* **Al Waab (IRE)**[7] 812 4-9-0 108 (b) PatDobbs 13 86
(Doug Watson, UAE) *nvr bttr than mid-div* **25/1**

13 *16* **Samurai Sword**[7] 807 6-9-0 106 (tp) AdriedeVries 11 52
(A bin Harmash, UAE) *nvr nr to chal* **25/1**

1m 49.26s (109.26) **13** Ran SP% **127.2**
CSF: 16.57; EXACTA: 15.30; TRIFECTA: 259.10; WIN: 1.90; PL: 1.20, 1.80, 7.40. TOTE PLACEPOT: £88.10 to a £1 stake. Pool of £6022.15 - 49.85 winning units. TOTE QUADPOT: £51.00 to a £1 stake. Pool of £448.00 - 6.50 winning units..
**Owner** Sheikh Mohammed Bin Khalifa Al Maktoum **Bred** Klawervlei Stud **Trained** South Africa

**FOCUS**
While a Group 1 in its own right, this is also a key trial for the Dubai Duty Free, run over the same C&D on World Cup night, and only last year the double was completed by Sajjhaa. Few got involved in a race run at a steady early gallop. Here are the splits: 27.31 (400m), 24.27 (800m), 23.66 (1200m), 22.32 (1600m), and the winner came home in 11.70.

903 - 905a (Foreign Racing) - See Raceform Interactive

# 859 SOUTHWELL (L-H)
Tuesday, March 11

**OFFICIAL GOING: Standard**
Wind: Fresh across Weather: Fine and dry

## 906 32RED MAIDEN STKS 6f (F)
**1:55** (1:59) (Class 5) 3-Y-O **£3,234** (£962; £481; £240) **Stalls** Low

Form RPR

2-32 1 **Jaeger Train (IRE)**[35] 477 3-9-5 67 DanielTudhope 6 74
(K R Burke) *trckd ldr: hdwy 1/2-way and sn cl up: led 2f out: sn rdn and green: styd on* **7/4**[2]

033- 2 *2 ¾* **Handwoven (IRE)**[132] 7626 3-9-5 72 JoeFanning 7 67
(Mark Johnston) *led: pushed along 3f out: rdn over 2f out: sn hdd and drvn: one pce* **4/7**[1]

00 3 *12* **Incurs Four Faults**[12] 765 3-9-5 0 TomEaves 3 30
(Keith Dalgleish) *dwlt and in rr: pushed along 1/2-way: rdn over 2f out: styd on to take remote 3rd ins fnl f* **33/1**

0-5 4 *2* **Luv U Honey**[12] 765 3-9-0 0 AndrewMullen 4 19
(Brian Baugh) *trckd ldng pair: rdn along wl over 2f out: sn one pce* **16/1**[3]

-0 5 *2 ¼* **Oriental Maid**[44] 346 3-9-0 0 DaleSwift 1 12
(Brian Ellison) *chsd ldrs: rdn along 1/2-way: sn edgd lft and wknd* **50/1**

00 6 *1* **Brycewise**[5] 855 3-9-5 0 RobertWinston 2 14
(Michael Wigham) *a towards rr* **33/1**

0- 7 *6* **The Brockster**[95] 8188 3-8-12 0 VictorSantos(7) 5
(Richard Ford) *chsd ldrs: rdn along 1/2-way: sn wknd* **100/1**

1m 16.25s (-0.25) **Going Correction** 0.0s/f (Stan) **7** Ran SP% **114.7**
Speed ratings (Par 98): **101,97,81,78,75 74,66**
CSF £3.08 TOTE £3.40: £1.30, £1.10; EX 3.70 Trifecta £18.20.
**Owner** Market Avenue Racing Club & Mrs E Burke **Bred** Ballyhane Stud **Trained** Middleham Moor, N Yorks

**FOCUS**
A moderate and uncompetitive maiden with them betting 16-1 bar two. The two market leaders dominated throughout and pulled a long way clear. The time wasn't bad.

## 907 LADBROKES (S) STKS 7f (F)
**2:30** (2:30) (Class 6) 3-Y-O+ **£2,587** (£770; £384) **Stalls** Low

Form RPR

3-60 1 **My Son Max**[8] 820 6-9-8 82 (v[1]) DaleSwift 2 83
(Michael Blake) *s.i.s and lost 6 l s: hdwy and cl up on outer 1/2-way: rdn to chal over 2f out: sn led and clr over 1f out: styd on* **6/4**[1]

-115 2 *6* **Nick The Odds (IRE)**[28] 568 3-8-12 65 (t) BenCurtis 4 67
(Jo Hughes) *cl up: led 3f out: rdn: hung lft and hdd 2f out: chsd wnr whn drvn and wandered bdly over 1f out: one pce* **5/2**[2]

6211 3 *1 ¾* **Arabian Flight**[28] 565 5-9-9 63 AndrewMullen 1 63
(Michael Appleby) *led: pushed along and hdd 3f out: sn rdn and btn* **6/4**[1]

1m 30.27s (-0.03) **Going Correction** 0.0s/f (Stan)
**WFA** 3 from 5yo+ 16lb **3** Ran SP% **108.6**
Speed ratings (Par 101): **100,93,91**
CSF £5.16 TOTE £2.20; EX 3.90 Trifecta £7.50.The winner was bought in for 8250gns.
**Owner** Kevin Corcoran Aaron Pierce Chris Weare **Bred** Mrs Fiona Denniff **Trained** Trowbridge, Wilts

**FOCUS**
A moderate seller. The winner was different class and the form is rated around the runner-up.

## 908 BEST ODDS AT BOOKMAKERS.CO.UK H'CAP 5f (F)
**3:05** (3:05) (Class 6) (0-60,60) 4-Y-O+ **£2,587** (£770; £384; £192) **Stalls** High

Form RPR

-535 1 **Caramelita**[7] 835 7-9-7 **60** (v) FrederikTylicki 4 69
(J R Jenkins) *chsd ldrs: rdn along wl over 1f out: styd on ins fnl f to ld nr fin* **4/1**[3]

0-23 2 *½* **Heartsong (IRE)**[35] 478 5-9-1 **57** MichaelJMMurphy(3) 1 64
(John Gallagher) *dwlt and in rr: hdwy on outer over 2f out: rdn over 1f out: led ins fnl f: sn drvn: hdd and no ex nr fin* **5/2**[1]

3-40 3 *¾* **Dancing Freddy (IRE)**[7] 835 7-9-6 **59** (tp) BenCurtis 5 63
(Ann Stokell) *cl up: led 2f out: rdn over 1f out: drvn and hdd ins fnl f: one pce towards fin* **9/2**

4-40 4 *1 ¾* **College Doll**[10] 797 5-8-13 **52** (t) AdamBeschizza 3 50
(Christine Dunnett) *slt ld: rdn along 1/2-way: hdd 2f out: cl up and drvn over 1f out: wknd fnl f* **10/1**

6000 5 *1* **Spic 'n Span**[10] 797 9-8-9 **48** (b) LukeMorris 7 42
(Ronald Harris) *racd nr stands' rail: cl up: rdn along 2f out: grad wknd* **16/1**

/452 6 *hd* **Dissent (IRE)**[10] 797 5-9-2 **55** (b) TomEaves 2 49
(James Given) *sn prom: disp ld 1/2-way: rdn along wl over 1f out: wknd ent fnl f* **11/4**[2]

466/ 7 *2 ½* **Incomparable**[799] 13 9-8-12 **58** (p) MatthewHopkins(7) 6 43
(Scott Dixon) *chsd ldrs: rdn along 1/2-way: grad wknd* **16/1**

1m 1.58s (1.88) **Going Correction** +0.425s/f (Slow) **7** Ran SP% **114.3**
Speed ratings (Par 101): **101,100,99,96,94 94,90**
CSF £14.43 TOTE £5.20: £2.10, £2.10; EX 17.40 Trifecta £81.30.
**Owner** La Senoritas **Bred** R B Hill **Trained** Royston, Herts

**FOCUS**
A moderate sprint handicap. The winner is rated basically to her best recent form.

## 909 COMPARE BOOKMAKERS AT BOOKMAKERS.CO.UK H'CAP 6f (F)
**3:45** (3:46) (Class 4) (0-85,83) 4-Y-O+ **£5,822** (£1,732; £865; £432) **Stalls** Low

Form RPR

210- 1 **King Bertie (IRE)**[140] 7452 4-8-11 **80** GeorgeBuckell(7) 13 92
(Michael Wigham) *trckd ldrs: hdwy 1/2-way: led 2f out: rdn over 1f out: drvn and edgd lft ins fnl f: hld on gamely* **7/1**

-314 2 ¾ **Mappin Time (IRE)**[35] [479] 6-9-3 **79**........................(be) RobertWinston 9 89
(Tim Easterby) *in tch: n.m.r 1/2-way: wd st and hdwy over 2f out: rdn to chal over 1f out: drvn and edgd lft ins fnl f: no ex towards fin* **7/2**[1]

22-1 3 shd **Kung Hei Fat Choy (USA)**[63] [75] 5-9-0 **76**...............(b) TomEaves 12 85
(James Given) *midfield: hdwy on outer and wd st: effrt 2f out: sn cl up: rdn over 1f out: kpt on same pce u.p fnl f* **4/1**[2]

5101 4 4 **Star Up In The Sky (USA)**[12] [766] 4-8-2 **69** oh2.......(b) ShaneGray(5) 6 66
(Kevin Ryan) *cl up: led after 2f: rdn along and hdd 2f out: sn drvn and grad wknd appr fnl f* **7/1**

4113 5 3 **Abi Scarlet (IRE)**[30] [552] 5-8-12 **77**............................ RyanPowell(3) 10 65
(Hughie Morrison) *towards rr: hdwy and wd st: sn rdn and styd on fnl 2f: nrst fin* **5/1**[3]

3-03 6 1¾ **O'Gorman**[5] [863] 5-9-2 **83**.............................. ThomasGarner(5) 8 66
(Gary Brown) *dwlt and in rr tl styd on fnl 2f* **10/1**

1015 7 nk **Powerful Pierre**[31] [540] 7-8-13 **80**......................(b) JacobButterfield(5) 2 62
(Ollie Pears) *towards rr tl styd on fnl 2f* **25/1**

010- 8 2¾ **Barkston Ash**[159] [6977] 6-9-2 **81**...............................(p) JasonHart(3) 3 55
(Eric Alston) *sn rdn along and bhd on inner tl sme late hdwy* **25/1**

5062 9 ¾ **Profile Star (IRE)**[11] [777] 5-8-6 **71**............................. OisinMurphy(3) 5 43
(Ann Stokell) *led 2f: cl up: rdn along wl over 2f out: grad wknd* **16/1**

2113 10 3¼ **Electric Qatar**[7] [834] 5-8-8 **70**............................(p) BarryMcHugh 1 32
(Alan McCabe) *chsd ldrs on inner: rdn along wl over 2f out: sn wknd* **12/1**

5-03 11 ½ **Gabrial's Gift (IRE)**[40] [381] 5-8-7 **69**...................(b) LukeMorris 11 30
(Scott Dixon) *chsd ldng pair: rdn along wl over 2f out: grad wknd* **33/1**

101- 12 2¼ **Mysterial**[264] [3507] 4-9-3 **79**........................................ DaleSwift 4 33
(Ruth Carr) *a in rr* **20/1**

0-66 13 2¼ **Tyfos**[8] [820] 9-9-2 **78**........................................... FrederikTylicki 7 25
(Brian Baugh) *chsd ldrs: rdn along wl over 2f out: sn wknd* **33/1**

1m 15.39s (-1.11) **Going Correction** 0.0s/f (Stan) **13 Ran SP% 124.9**
Speed ratings (Par 105): **107,106,105,100,96 94,93,90,89,84 84,81,78**
CSF £31.11 CT £109.66 TOTE £8.00: £1.90, £2.10, £2.60; EX 43.40 Trifecta £223.50.
**Owner** Mrs Jo Brisland **Bred** P J Fahey **Trained** Newmarket, Suffolk

**FOCUS**
A competitive sprint handicap and really solid form for the grade.

## 910 LADBROKES CLASSIFIED CLAIMING STKS 1m (F)
4:25 (4:26) (Class 6) 4-Y-0+ £2,587 (£770; £384; £192) Stalls Low

Form RPR

-304 1 **Dandarrell**[21] [647] 7-8-12 61............................(p) FrederikTylicki 6 69
(Julie Camacho) *trckd ldrs: hdwy 1/2-way: chal on outer over 2f out: sn slt ld: rdn wl over 1f out: drvn ent fnl f: sn edgd lft: styd on towards fin* **5/4**[1]

-502 2 1¼ **Hail Promenader (IRE)**[31] [537] 8-8-7 60..............(tp) PhilipPrince(5) 9 66
(Anthony Carson) *midfield: rdn along: hdwy and wd st: chsd ldrs over 2f out: drvn wl over 1f out: kpt on fnl f: nrst fin* **6/1**[2]

2404 3 nse **Dozy Joe**[5] [852] 6-8-8 61..............................(v) LukeMorris 1 62
(Joseph Tuite) *trckd ldng pair on inner: swtchd rt after 3f and sn cl up: effrt to dispute ld over 2f out and ev ch: drvn over 1f out: one pce ins fnl f* **6/1**[2]

-055 4 2¼ **Ewell Place (IRE)**[46] [320] 5-8-8 63........................(p) PaddyAspell 8 57
(Patrick Morris) *cl up: led after 3f: rdn along 3f out: hdd 2f out: cl up tl drvn and wknd ent fnl f* **8/1**[3]

5106 5 9 **Dansili Dutch (IRE)**[18] [697] 5-8-6 62...................... SamJames(3) 5 37
(David O'Meara) *chsd ldrs: rdn along over 3f out: sn outpcd* **10/1**

0-60 6 7 **Mitchum**[21] [651] 5-7-13 57............................ ShirleyTeasdale(5) 7 16
(Ron Barr) *led 3f: rdn along 1/2-way: wknd 3f out* **16/1**

63-0 7 3¾ **Berkeley Street (USA)**[64] [67] 4-8-7 56.................. DavidKenny(5) 3 15
(Jane Chapple-Hyam) *a towards rr* **6/1**[2]

000- 8 1¼ **Bond Blade**[72] [8438] 6-8-7 40..........................(e[1]) JacobButterfield(5) 4 12
(Suzzanne France) *a towards rr* **100/1**

60-0 9 32 **Shomberg**[31] [538] 5-8-5 45...........................................(p) ChrisCatlin 2
(Dai Burchell) *chsd ldrs to 1/2-way: sn wknd* **25/1**

1m 43.81s (0.11) **Going Correction** 0.0s/f (Stan) **9 Ran SP% 118.2**
Speed ratings (Par 101): **99,97,97,95,86 79,75,74,42**
CSF £9.46 TOTE £1.80: £1.10, £1.60, £2.00; EX 9.10 Trifecta £46.90.
**Owner** Jocelyn Waller **Bred** Peter Onslow **Trained** Norton, N Yorks

**FOCUS**
A moderate claimer. The heavily backed winner is rated to his best.

## 911 CORAL MOBILE H'CAP 1m 4f (F)
5:05 (5:06) (Class 5) (0-75,74) 4-Y-0+ £3,234 (£962; £481; £240) Stalls Low

Form RPR

6101 1 **A Little Bit Dusty**[22] [641] 6-9-7 **74**........................(p) HayleyTurner 6 83
(Conor Dore) *prom: led over 4f out: rdn along 2f out: hdd ent fnl f: rallied to ld again nr line* **4/1**[2]

06-2 2 shd **Jacobs Son**[5] [859] 6-8-9 **69**.............................. AlistairRawlinson(7) 5 78
(Michael Appleby) *trckd ldrs: hdwy over 3f out: cl up on inner over 2f out: sn rdn: drvn to ld ent fnl f: sn edgd rt: hdd and no ex nr line* **8/13**[1]

100- 3 17 **Naburn**[133] [7597] 6-9-1 **68**............................................. BenCurtis 4 50
(Alan Swinbank) *hld up: smooth hdwy on outer over 4f out: chal 3f out: rdn over 2f out: drvn and wknd wl over 1f out* **6/1**[3]

00-5 4 5 **Docofthebay (IRE)**[30] [552] 10-8-8 **68**.................[1] MatthewHopkins(7) 3 42
(Scott Dixon) *t.k.h: trckd ldrs: pushed along 4f out: swtchd wd and rdn over 3f out: sn wknd* **12/1**

322- 5 25 **Flamingo Beat**[147] [7273] 4-9-1 **70**.................................. ChrisCatlin 2 4
(Christine Dunnett) *led: rdn along and hdd over 4f out: wknd over 3f out* **16/1**

2m 40.5s (-0.50) **Going Correction** 0.0s/f (Stan)
**WFA** 4 from 6yo+ 2lb **5 Ran SP% 109.8**
Speed ratings (Par 103): **101,100,89,86,69**
CSF £6.92 TOTE £6.00: £1.60, £1.10; EX 7.60 Trifecta £24.20.
**Owner** David Baldwin & Chris Marsh **Bred** T O C S Limited **Trained** Hubbert's Bridge, Lincs

**FOCUS**
An ordinary middle-distance handicap and a war of attrition between the front pair over the last 2f. They were miles clear and the form is sound.

## 912 CORAL APP DOWNLOAD FROM THE APP STORE APPRENTICE H'CAP 1m 4f (F)
5:35 (5:35) (Class 6) (0-60,65) 4-Y-0+ £2,587 (£770; £384; £192) Stalls Low

Form RPR

6-63 1 **Aureate**[30] [546] 10-8-4 **45**...............................(p) CharlotteJenner(5) 1 50
(Brian Forsey) *trckd ldrs on inner: pushed along 4f out and sn outpcd: swtchd rt and wd st: rdn 2f out: styd on wl fnl f to ld nr fin* **8/1**

60-3 2 shd **Bethan**[69] [1] 5-9-7 57..............................(p) ShelleyBirkett 3 62
(Julia Feilden) *prom: effrt 3f out: chal 2f out: sn rdn: drvn to ld jst ins fnl f: hdd and no ex nr fin* **5/1**

-521 3 ¾ **On The Cusp (IRE)**[7] [831] 7-9-10 **65** 6ex.................(b) DavidParkes(5) 2 69
(Ann Stokell) *t.k.h: cl up: led after 1f: rdn along 2f out: drvn and hdd jst ins fnl f: no ex last 75yds* **3/1**[2]

-023 4 1¼ **Reach The Beach**[7] [831] 5-8-6 **47**..........................(v) JennyPowell(5) 4 49
(Brendan Powell) *trckd ldrs: hdwy 4f out: cl up 3f out: chal 2f out: sn rdn and styd on to ld jst ins fnl f: hdd and no ex nr fin* **2/1**[1]

5000 5 1 **Dontpaytheferryman (USA)**[7] [831] 9-8-10 **49**......(b) DanielCremin(3) 7 49
(Peter Hiatt) *t.k.h: chsd ldrs on outer: cl up 4f out: rdn along 3f out: drvn 2f out and one pce* **16/1**

-426 6 5 **Kyllachykov (IRE)**[36] [460] 6-9-3 **56**............................... KevinStott(3) 8 48
(Robin Bastiman) *hld up: hdwy on inner 5f out: rdn along over 3f out: drvn and outpcd over 2f out* **7/2**[3]

2m 44.49s (3.49) **Going Correction** 0.0s/f (Stan)
**WFA** 4 from 5yo+ 2lb **6 Ran SP% 114.2**
Speed ratings (Par 101): **88,87,87,86,85 82**
CSF £47.22 CT £147.50 TOTE £8.70: £4.00, £3.70; EX 46.20 Trifecta £237.00.
**Owner** B Forsey **Bred** Darley **Trained** Ash Priors, Somerset

**FOCUS**
They went no pace in this messy apprentice handicap and the winning time was almost four seconds slower than the previous contest. A very limited feel to the form.
T/Plt: £19.90 to a £1 stake. Pool: £49,930.60 - 1828.47 winning units. T/Qpdt: £4.00 to a £1 stake. Pool: £3,130.82 - 572.45 winning units. JR

# 886 WOLVERHAMPTON (A.W) (L-H)
Tuesday, March 11

**OFFICIAL GOING: Standard**
Wind: Light against Weather: Fine

## 913 COMPARE BOOKMAKERS AT BOOKMAKERS.CO.UK H'CAP 5f 216y(P)
5:45 (5:45) (Class 5) (0-70,70) 4-Y-0+ £3,234 (£962; £481; £240) Stalls Low

Form RPR

625 1 **Go Far**[34] [496] 4-9-0 **68**....................................(b) TimClark(5) 7 80
(Alan Bailey) *chsd ldrs: rdn to ld 2f out: edgd rt over 1f out: styd on u.p* **5/2**[1]

2215 2 2 **Grace Hull**[12] [766] 4-9-0 **63**.............................(p) TomQueally 3 69
(Garry Moss) *s.i.s: sn pushed along in rr: rdn over 1f out: r.o u.p to go 2nd towards fin: no ch w wnr* **9/2**[3]

-301 3 ½ **Colourbearer (IRE)**[44] [347] 7-9-7 **70**...................(t) RichardKingscote 6 75
(Milton Bradley) *w ldr: rdn and ev ch over 1f out: styd on same pce ins fnl f* **9/2**[3]

15-6 4 ½ **Ad Vitam (IRE)**[64] [65] 6-8-7 **56**................................(bt) DavidProbert 5 59
(David C Griffiths) *prom: pushed along 1/2-way: rdn over 1f out: styd on same pce fnl f* **11/4**[2]

606- 5 1½ **Hazard Warning (IRE)**[302] [2329] 4-9-0 **63**...............(b) DuranFentiman 8 62
(Mandy Rowland) *prom: racd keenly: rdn over 1f out: no ex ins fnl f* **25/1**

456- 6 shd **Red Cape (FR)**[158] [6995] 11-9-2 **65**................................ JamesSullivan 2 63+
(Ruth Carr) *hld up: pushed along over 2f out: styd on fnl f: nvr trbld ldrs* **25/1**

0-00 7 2¾ **Lucky Dan (IRE)**[19] [677] 8-9-6 **69**................................... JoeFanning 4 59
(Paul Green) *prom: shkn up over 1f out: wknd ins fnl f* **12/1**

61-0 8 17 **New Decade**[50] [259] 5-9-4 **67**........................................ AdamKirby 1 6
(Milton Bradley) *sn led: pushed along and hdd 2f out: wknd over 1f out* **8/1**

1m 14.9s (-0.10) **Going Correction** +0.125s/f (Slow) **8 Ran SP% 118.1**
Speed ratings (Par 103): **105,102,101,101,99 98,95,72**
CSF £14.78 CT £47.27 TOTE £2.90: £1.10, £2.10, £1.40; EX 18.20 Trifecta £92.70.
**Owner** R West **Bred** Michael Turner **Trained** Newmarket, Suffolk

**FOCUS**
A modest event. The third is the best guide.

## 914 32REDPOKER.COM FESTIVAL FREEROLL TONIGHT MAIDEN FILLIES' STKS 1m 141y(P)
6:15 (6:16) (Class 5) 3-Y-0+ £2,911 (£866; £432; £216) Stalls Low

Form RPR

62- 1 **Thurayaat**[192] [5983] 3-8-7 0.......................................... AndreaAtzeni 8 74+
(Roger Varian) *mde all: hung rt fr over 1f out: sn rdn: hung rt wl ins fnl f: styd on* **1/2**[1]

00-5 2 1½ **Her Honour (IRE)**[20] [660] 3-8-7 71.................................. WilliamBuick 6 69
(John Gosden) *a.p: chsd wnr 1/2-way: rdn over 1f out: kpt on* **4/1**[2]

20-4 3 ½ **Gratzie**[19] [675] 3-8-7 72 ow3.......................... WilliamTwiston-Davies(3) 1 71
(Mick Channon) *hld up in tch: nt clr run over 2f out: rdn over 1f out: styd on* **10/1**

3-42 4 2¼ **Nixyba**[25] [614] 3-8-7 62................................................. DavidProbert 3 63
(Tim Vaughan) *chsd wnr to 1/2-way: remained handy: rdn over 1f out: styd on same pce ins fnl f* **8/1**[3]

5 9 **Chindeni** 3-8-8 0 ow1.................................................. MartinLane 4 45
(Ed Vaughan) *dwlt: sn pushed along in rr: nvr on terms* **50/1**

6 2¾ **Navajo Dream** 3-8-7 0...................................................... AndrewMullen 7 39
(Michael Appleby) *in tch: rn green and sn pushed along: rdn over 3f out: wknd over 2f out* **20/1**

7 1½ **Puppet Theatre (IRE)** 4-9-13 0.......................................... JoeFanning 5 41
(Mark Johnston) *swvd rt sn after s and wl bhd: shkn up and hdwy over 2f out: hmpd wl over 1f out: no ch after* **12/1**

F **Heavenly River (FR)** 3-8-2 0..................................... JoeyHaynes(5) 2 59
(K R Burke) *hld up: hdwy over 3f out: cl up but pushed along whn clipped heels and fell wl over 1f out* **50/1**

1m 52.79s (2.29) **Going Correction** +0.125s/f (Slow)
**WFA** 3 from 4yo 20lb **8 Ran SP% 123.2**
Speed ratings (Par 100): **94,92,92,90,82 79,78,**
CSF £3.24 TOTE £1.30: £1.02, £1.70, £2.60; EX 4.00 Trifecta £16.50.
**Owner** Hamdan Al Maktoum **Bred** Shadwell Estate Company Limited **Trained** Newmarket, Suffolk

**FOCUS**
A dramatic race but modest form. The winner had the run of things.

## 915 32RED IMMORTAL ROMANCE SLOT H'CAP 2m 119y(P)
6:45 (6:46) (Class 6) (0-60,62) 4-Y-0+ £2,264 (£673; £336; £168) Stalls Low

Form RPR

050/ 1 **Sir Frank Morgan (IRE)**[496] [7492] 4-8-5 **46** oh1.............. JoeFanning 4 59+
(Mark Johnston) *chsd ldr tl led wl over 3f out: sn pushed along and hdd: rallied to ld ins fnl f: styd on strly* **7/2**[2]

3442 2 3¾ **Blazing Desert**[25] [609] 10-9-10 **60**.............................. AdamBeschizza 7 64
(William Kinsey) *trckd ldrs: led over 3f out: rdn and hdd 2f out: ev ch ins fnl f: styd on same pce* **7/2**[2]

-151 **3** *nk* **Helmsley Flyer (IRE)**[4] 872 4-9-7 **62** 6ex..............(v) DanielTudhope 6 66
(David O'Meara) *hld up: hdwy over 4f out: led 2f out: rdn over 1f out: hdd and unable qck ins fnl f* **5/4**[1]
110/ **4** *5* **Fade To Grey (IRE)**[584] 3283 10-9-4 **57**.....(t) WilliamTwiston-Davies(3) 3 55
(Shaun Lycett) *hld up: pushed along over 3f out: rdn over 1f out: nvr nrr* **12/1**
005- **5** *¾* **Amberjam (IRE)**[87] 8298 4-8-5 **46** oh1..........................(tp) AndreaAtzeni 5 43
(Martin Smith) *chsd ldrs: rdn over 3f out: wknd over 2f out* **33/1**
5450 **6** *nk* **Excellent News (IRE)**[25] 609 5-8-3 **46** oh1..............(p) JackGarritty(7) 8 42
(Tony Forbes) *prom: rdn over 3f out: wknd over 2f out* **33/1**
-352 **7** *1 ¼* **Well Owd Mon**[11] 781 4-8-0 **48**..........................(p) RobHornby(7) 2 43
(Andrew Hollinshead) *s.s: hld up: pushed along over 3f out: in rr whn nt clr run over 1f out: no ch whn n.m.r ins fnl f* **6/1**[3]
200- **8** *11* **Dubara Reef (IRE)**[94] 8204 7-8-13 **49**..........................(p) MartinLane 1 31
(Paul Green) *led at stdy pce tl pushed along and qcknd over 4f out: hdd wl over 3f out: wknd over 2f out* **50/1**

3m 48.34s (6.54) **Going Correction** +0.125s/f (Slow)
**WFA** 4 from 5yo+ 5lb **8 Ran SP% 118.7**
Speed ratings (Par 101): **89,87,87,84,84 84,83,78**
CSF £16.70 CT £23.17 TOTE £5.40: £1.30, £1.10, £2.30; EX 20.40 Trifecta £53.10.
**Owner** Mark Johnston Racing Ltd **Bred** Airlie Stud **Trained** Middleham Moor, N Yorks

**FOCUS**
A fair race for the lowly level. There's probably a lot better to come from the winner.

## 916 DOWNLOAD THE LADBROKES APP H'CAP 1m 141y(P)
7:15 (7:16) (Class 6) (0-60,57) 4-Y-O+ **£2,264** (£673; £336; £168) **Stalls** Low

Form RPR
53-5 **1** **Dividend Dan (IRE)**[15] 736 4-9-4 **54**.............................. ShaneKelly 6 60
(Mike Murphy) *mde all: set stdy pce tl qcknd over 3f out: rdn over 1f out: all out* **2/1**[1]
-040 **2** *shd* **Final Delivery**[26] 590 5-9-5 **55**.............................. StephenCraine 1 61
(Jim Boyle) *chsd wnr: shkn up over 2f out: rdn over 1f out: r.o* **7/2**[2]
4624 **3** *1 ¼* **Lutine Charlie (IRE)**[14] 740 7-9-5 **55**..........................(p) TomQueally 2 58
(Pat Eddery) *trckd ldrs: rdn over 1f out: styd on same pce ins fnl f* **9/2**[3]
-565 **4** *6* **Silver Fawn (IRE)**[11] 783 4-8-9 **45**..............................[1] DavidProbert 5 36
(John Weymes) *hld up: pushed along 1/2-way: hdwy u.p over 1f out: n.d* **10/1**
4121 **5** *¾* **Prohibition (IRE)**[19] 673 8-9-7 **57**.............................. AdamKirby 3 46
(Mandy Rowland) *s.i.s: hld up: plld hrd: rdn over 2f out: nvr on terms* **2/1**[1]
-366 **6** *7* **Refuse Colette (IRE)**[19] 672 5-8-9 **45**..........................(v) JoeFanning 4 20
(Paul Green) *hld up: pushed along over 2f out: sn wknd* **25/1**

1m 51.81s (1.31) **Going Correction** +0.125s/f (Slow) **6 Ran SP% 120.0**
Speed ratings (Par 101): **99,98,97,92,91 85**
CSF £10.34 TOTE £3.80: £2.40, £1.70; EX 11.40 Trifecta £29.60.
**Owner** Nick McLeod-Clarke **Bred** Edward Sexton **Trained** Westoning, Beds

**FOCUS**
A moderate contest in which the order barely changed, but it served up a good finish. Not a race to place too much faith in.

## 917 LADBROKES H'CAP 7f 32y(P)
7:45 (7:45) (Class 4) (0-85,85) 4-Y-O+ **£5,175** (£1,540; £769; £384) **Stalls** High

Form RPR
5-23 **1** **Silverware (USA)**[19] 674 6-9-6 **84**.............................. TomEaves 1 93
(Kristin Stubbs) *mde all: pushed along early: rdn over 1f out: styd on gamely* **7/1**
-351 **2** *nk* **Maggie Pink**[36] 461 5-9-0 **78**.............................. AndrewMullen 9 86
(Michael Appleby) *trckd ldrs: rdn and ev ch fr over 1f out: styd on* **8/1**
-525 **3** *1* **Pearl Nation (USA)**[18] 689 5-8-12 **76**.............................. FrederikTylicki 5 82
(Brian Baugh) *a.p: pushed along 1/2-way: rdn over 1f out: styd on* **6/1**[3]
64-3 **4** *½* **Regal Dan (IRE)**[18] 689 4-9-6 **84**.............................. TomQueally 6 89
(Charles Hills) *hld up: hdwy over 1f out: rdn and hung lft ins fnl f: nt rch ldrs* **11/4**[1]
6404 **5** *½* **Verse Of Love**[10] 804 5-9-7 **85**.............................. AdamKirby 8 88
(David Evans) *trckd wnr: rdn over 2f out: ev ch over 1f out: styd on same pce ins fnl f* **3/1**[2]
4-06 **6** *¾* **Cape Of Hope (IRE)**[5] 862 4-8-9 **73**.............................. LukeMorris 3 75
(David O'Meara) *hld up in tch: rdn over 2f out: styd on same pce ins fnl f* **20/1**
204- **7** *1 ½* **Ready (IRE)**[172] 6608 4-9-4 **82**..........................(p) DanielTudhope 7 80
(Garry Moss) *hld up: hdwy over 2f out: rdn over 1f out: no ex ins fnl f* **8/1**
00-3 **8** *1 ½* **Spin Artist (USA)**[11] 779 4-9-4 **82**.............................. JoeFanning 2 76
(Mark Johnston) *hld up: pushed along 1/2-way: nvr on terms* **7/1**
160 **9** *7* **Toymaker**[8] 820 7-8-13 **77**.............................. PaddyAspell 4 54
(Phil McEntee) *hld up: a in rr: wknd over 2f out* **20/1**

1m 28.2s (-1.40) **Going Correction** +0.125s/f (Slow) **9 Ran SP% 122.7**
Speed ratings (Par 105): **113,112,111,110,110 109,107,106,98**
CSF £65.51 CT £361.95 TOTE £10.00: £3.90, £1.90, £2.60; EX 47.20 Trifecta £441.80.
**Owner** Paul & Linda Dixon **Bred** Alliand Equine **Trained** Norton, N Yorks

**FOCUS**
This competitive feature was run at a stern pace throughout. A likeable effort from the winner and the second looks better than ever.

## 918 LADBROKES MOBILE H'CAP 7f 32y(P)
8:15 (8:16) (Class 6) (0-65,64) 4-Y-O+ **£2,264** (£673; £336; £168) **Stalls** High

Form RPR
-021 **1** **Pipers Piping (IRE)**[19] 676 8-8-10 **56**.............................. RossAtkinson(3) 3 66+
(Mandy Rowland) *hld up: hdwy over 1f out: sn rdn: edgd lft and r.o to ld wl ins fnl f* **5/4**[1]
0020 **2** *¾* **Baltic Prince (IRE)**[12] 766 4-9-0 **57**.............................. JoeFanning 4 63
(Paul Green) *sn led: hdd 6f out: chsd ldr tl rdn to ld over 1f out: hdd and unable qck wl ins fnl f* **7/1**
120- **3** *2* **Monte Cassino (IRE)**[91] 8235 9-8-12 **58**..............(e) GeorgeChaloner(3) 9 59
(Bryan Smart) *led 6f out: rdn and hdd over 1f out: styd on same pce ins fnl f* **9/2**[3]
-406 **4** *2 ½* **Ferdy (IRE)**[12] 766 5-8-9 **52**.............................. LukeMorris 8 47
(Paul Green) *hld up: hdwy over 1f out: no ex fnl f* **12/1**
2-00 **5** *¾* **The Mongoose**[39] 399 6-9-7 **64**.............................. AdamKirby 5 57
(David Evans) *trckd ldrs: plld hrd: rdn over 1f out: wknd ins fnl f* **4/1**[2]
-023 **6** *3 ½* **Hinton Admiral**[10] 799 10-8-10 **53**.............................. MartinLane 6 38
(Pat Eddery) *s.i.s: racd keenly and hdwy over 5f out: rdn and wknd over 1f out* **8/1**
00/4 **7** *12* **Spowarticus**[35] 477 5-8-8 **51**.............................. AdamBeschizza 2 6
(Scott Dixon) *chsd ldrs: pushed along 1/2-way: wknd over 2f out* **16/1**

1m 29.34s (-0.26) **Going Correction** +0.125s/f (Slow) **7 Ran SP% 119.8**
Speed ratings (Par 101): **106,105,102,100,99 95,81**
CSF £11.84 CT £32.67 TOTE £2.40: £1.60, £3.10; EX 15.40 Trifecta £47.60.
**Owner** Miss M E Rowland **Bred** Drumhass Stud **Trained** Lower Blidworth, Notts

**FOCUS**
Very few could be fancied for this low-grade handicap and it proved relatively plain sailing for the winner, who can get closer to his old figures.

## 919 32REDBET.COM H'CAP 7f 32y(P)
8:45 (8:45) (Class 6) (0-60,58) 3-Y-O **£2,264** (£673; £336; £168) **Stalls** High

Form RPR
0-04 **1** **Desert Colours**[11] 786 3-8-12 **49**..........................(b) PaulMulrennan 4 61
(Kevin Ryan) *mde virtually all: rdn over 1f out: styd on* **7/2**[3]
54-4 **2** *¾* **Choice Of Destiny**[64] 71 3-9-2 **58**..........................(v[1]) LouisSteward(5) 8 68
(Philip McBride) *hld up: swtchd rt and hdwy over 2f out: rdn and hung rt fr over 1f out: nt run on* **9/4**[1]
0-24 **3** *1 ½* **Romantic Bliss (IRE)**[21] 653 3-8-5 **49**..............(b) RobJFitzpatrick(7) 3 55
(K R Burke) *led early: chsd ldrs: rdn over 1f out: styd on same pce ins fnl f* **7/1**
0-60 **4** *3* **La Paiva (FR)**[12] 753 3-8-8 **45**.............................. AdamBeschizza 9 43
(Scott Dixon) *sn trcking wnr: rdn and ev ch over 1f out: no ex ins fnl f* **12/1**
400- **5** *3 ¾* **Bob Masnicken**[176] 6477 3-9-6 **57**.............................. RichardKingscote 7 46
(Tom Dascombe) *hld up: rdn over 2f out: nt trble ldrs* **5/2**[2]
500- **6** *5* **Brean Splash Susie**[157] 7036 3-8-3 **45**.............................. RyanWhile(5) 10 21
(Bill Turner) *chsd ldrs: rdn and hmpd over 2f out: wknd over 1f out* **33/1**
-000 **7** *6* **Limegrove**[11] 786 3-8-13 **50**.............................. AndrewMullen 6 10
(David Evans) *s.i.s: a in rr: wknd over 2f out* **10/1**

1m 30.78s (1.18) **Going Correction** +0.125s/f (Slow) **7 Ran SP% 113.8**
Speed ratings (Par 96): **98,97,95,92,87 82,75**
CSF £11.70 CT £50.30 TOTE £4.90: £2.20, £1.20; EX 15.10 Trifecta £32.00.
**Owner** Jon Beard **Bred** Rabbah Bloodstock Limited **Trained** Hambleton, N Yorks

**FOCUS**
Very limited but straightforward form.
T/Plt: £48.10 to a £1 stake. Pool: £101,517.64 - 1538.44 winning units. T/Qpdt: £36.10 to a £1 stake. Pool: £7705.95 - 157.91 winning units. CR

# SAINT-CLOUD (L-H)
Tuesday, March 11

**OFFICIAL GOING: Turf: very soft**

## 920a PRIX DE MAGNY EN VEXIN (CLAIMER) (5YO+) (TURF) 1m 4f
2:30 (12:00) 5-Y-O+ **£6,666** (£2,666; £2,000; £1,333; £666)

RPR
**1** **Shining Sun (FR)**[274] 7-9-4 0.............................. ThierryJarnet 10 79
(J Bertran De Balanda, France) **11/2**[2]
**2** *hd* **Speedy Crown (FR)**[39] 8-8-11 0..........................(b) TheoBachelot 3 72
(M Nigge, France) **79/10**
**3** *½* **Windy King**[59] 5-9-5 0.............................. MaximeGuyon 11 79
(J Bertran De Balanda, France) **58/10**[3]
**4** *snk* **Fair Boss (IRE)**[56] 178 6-9-4 0..........................(p) IoritzMendizabal 9 78
(F Chappet, France) **115/10**
**5** *nk* **Incendo**[37] 450 8-9-1 0..........................(b) ChristopheSoumillon 6 74
(Ian Williams) *dwlt: hld up towards rr: prog into midfield sn after 1/2-way: shkn up and styd on fr 1 1/2f out: nvr quite on terms* **12/5**[1]
**6** *3* **Oliandra (FR)** 5-8-13 0.............................. UmbertoRispoli 13 68
(M Figge, Germany) **32/1**
**7** *nk* **Vlatori (FR)**[59] 6-9-4 0.............................. AlexisBadel 2 72
(J Van Handenhove, France) **116/10**
**8** *1* **Matreas (FR)**[39] 7-9-1 0..........................(p) RonanThomas 5 68
(J Phelippon, France) **195/10**
**9** *¾* **Kissavos**[25] 8-8-11 0.............................. LukasDelozier(8) 12 70
(Y Barberot, France) **117/10**
**10** *nk* **Shawnee Saga (FR)**[25] 9-8-11 0.............................. EddyHardouin 8 62
(W Mongil, Germany) **214/10**
**11** *1 ½* **Nijinsky Blood (FR)**[155] 7-8-9 0..........................(p) MlleZoePfeil(6) 7 64
(C Bruno, France) **34/1**
**12** *10* **Touching Kings (FR)**[138] 9-8-11 0.............................. TonyPiccone 4 44
(C Boutin, France) **11/1**
**13** *3 ½* **Dream Youn (FR)**[683] 9-8-6 0.............................. EmmanuelEtienne(5) 1 38
(Mlle C Cardenne, France) **77/1**

2m 40.32s (-0.08) **13 Ran SP% 119.4**
WIN (incl. 1 euro stake): 6.50. PLACES: 2.40, 2.40, 2.10. DF: 40.00. SF: 71.50..
**Owner** David Goncalves **Bred** E A R L Haras Du Camp Benard **Trained** France

# 852 KEMPTON (A.W) (R-H)
Wednesday, March 12

**OFFICIAL GOING: Standard**
Wind: light, half against Weather: dry

## 921 BET LATE AT CHELTENHAM H'CAP 5f (P)
5:45 (5:45) (Class 6) (0-65,65) 4-Y-O+ **£1,940** (£577; £288; £144) **Stalls** Low

Form RPR
35-2 **1** **Novabridge**[21] 654 6-9-7 **65**..........................(b) LiamKeniry 2 73
(Neil Mulholland) *hld up in tch: swtchd lft and effrt ent fnl f: r.o wl to ld wl ins fnl f* **6/4**[1]
0026 **2** *¾* **Quality Art (USA)**[4] 889 6-9-5 **63**.............................. LukeMorris 5 68
(Simon Hodgson) *chsd ldr after 2f: rdn to ld over 1f out: hdd and styd on same pce wl ins fnl f* **5/1**[3]
0501 **3** *1 ½* **Johnny Splash (IRE)**[11] 799 5-8-13 **57**..........................(v) RobertWinston 8 57
(Roger Teal) *led: rdn and hdd over 1f out: no ex and outpcd fnl 100yds* **5/1**[3]
2342 **4** *1* **Pharoh Jake**[7] 845 6-9-0 **63**.............................. RyanWhile(5) 6 59
(John Bridger) *chsd ldrs: rdn and unable qck over 1f out: styd on same pce ins fnl f* **3/1**[2]
02-0 **5** *1* **Max The Machine**[69] 9 4-9-2 **60**.............................. DaleSwift 7 53
(Derek Shaw) *taken down early: dwlt and sn detached in last: clsd and rdn over 1f out: styd on fnl f: nvr trbld ldrs* **12/1**
03-0 **6** *1 ¼* **Waabel**[13] 766 7-9-1 **59**..........................(tp) WilliamCarson 1 47
(Ann Stokell) *chsd ldr for 2f: steadily lost pl: rdn and btn wl over 1f out: sn wknd* **12/1**

59.66s (-0.84) **Going Correction** -0.025s/f (Stan) **6 Ran SP% 113.7**
Speed ratings (Par 101): **105,103,101,99,98 96**
CSF £9.71 CT £29.27 TOTE £2.40: £1.20, £2.20; EX 8.40 Trifecta £36.80.
**Owner** Dajam Ltd **Bred** Bishopswood Bloodstock & Trickledown Stud **Trained** Limpley Stoke, Wilts

**FOCUS**
A modest sprint, and routine form.

## 922 GETTING OUT STKS AT CHELTENHAM H'CAP 1m 2f (P)
6:15 (6:15) (Class 6) (0-65,65) 4-Y-O+ £1,940 (£577; £288; £144) Stalls Low

Form RPR
5545 1 **Arabian Heights**[7] 849 6-9-0 63 ............ GeorgeDowning(5) 3 75+
(Ian Williams) *chsd ldrs tl led over 8f out: mde rest: rdn and qcknd clr over 1f out: r.o wl: comf* 5/2[2]

-101 2 3 ½ **Handsome Stranger (IRE)**[6] 859 4-8-12 63 ......(p) DavidParkes(7) 5 70+
(Alan Bailey) *stdd s: hld up in rr: n.m.r wl over 1f out: rdn and hdwy over 1f out: chsd clr wnr fnl 100yds: r.o wl but no ch w wnr* 9/4[1]

-060 3 2 ¼ **Understory (USA)**[28] 582 7-9-7 65 ............ JoeFanning 2 66
(Tim McCarthy) *chsd wnr: rdn and unable qck over 1f out: 3rd and kpt on same pce ins fnl f* 7/2[3]

366 4 ½ **Mr Lando**[23] 646 5-9-3 61 ............ JimmyQuinn 4 61
(Charles Hills) *taken down early: in tch in midfield: rdn and unable qck over 1f out: styd on same pce ins fnl f* 9/2

65-0 5 nse **Alhaban (IRE)**[38] 445 8-9-4 62 ............(p) LukeMorris 6 62
(Ronald Harris) *in tch in midfield: rdn and no hdwy wl over 1f out: wl hld and one pce fnl f* 20/1

0-02 6 4 ½ **Meddling**[19] 691 4-8-11 60 ............ ShelleyBirkett(5) 7 51
(Julia Feilden) *t.k.h: hld up in tch in last pair: rdn and effrt 2f out: sn btn: wknd over 1f out* 12/1

-000 7 ½ **Sam Spade (IRE)**[9] 815 4-8-13 57 ............ DaleSwift 1 48
(Derek Shaw) *led tl over 8f out: chsd ldrs after: rdn and struggling over 2f out: bhd fnl f* 16/1

2m 5.12s (-2.88) **Going Correction** -0.025s/f (Stan) 7 Ran SP% **118.1**
Speed ratings (Par 101): **110,107,105,105,104 101,100**
CSF £9.06 TOTE £3.80: £2.00, £2.10; EX 12.20 Trifecta £31.80.
**Owner** Macable Partnership **Bred** Biddestone Stud **Trained** Portway, Worcs

**FOCUS**
This didn't look as if it took much winning and the form may not amount to much. Although it was worth noting that the time was okay for the grade. The winner was well in on 2011 form.

## 923 BETBRIGHT.COM MAIDEN STKS 6f (P)
6:45 (6:45) (Class 5) 3-Y-O+ £2,587 (£770; £384; £192) Stalls Low

Form RPR
350- 1 **Almargo (IRE)**[154] 7119 3-9-0 70 ............ AdamKirby 7 80+
(Mark Johnston) *mde all: rdn and qcknd 2f out: r.o wl fnl f: rdn out* 11/10[2]

2 2 ¾ **Elusive George (IRE)**[12] 787 3-9-0 0 ............ RobertWinston 5 77
(John Quinn) *chsd wnr for 2f: wnt 2nd again over 2f out: rdn and qcknd clr w wnr 2f out: r.o but a hld* 10/11[1]

05 3 10 **Feisty Dragon (IRE)**[12] 787 3-8-9 0 ............ FergusSweeney 2 42
(Jamie Osborne) *stdd and wnt lft s: hld up in last pair: rdn jst over 2f out: no ch w ldng pair but styd on to go modest 3rd ins fnl f* 33/1

B0-4 4 1 **Synonym (ITY)**[23] 645 3-8-9 0 ............ JoeFanning 6 39
(J W Hills) *stdd s: t.k.h: hdwy to join ldr after 2f tl jst over 2f out: sn rdn and outpcd: wknd wl over 1f out* 16/1[3]

00- 5 1 **Go Charlie**[252] 3948 3-9-0 0 ............[1] LukeMorris 1 41
(Ronald Harris) *stdd s: t.k.h: chsd ldrs tl outpcd 2f out: sn wl btn and wknd* 25/1

-000 6 1 ¾ **Literally On Fire (IRE)**[14] 748 3-9-0 0 ............ SebSanders 3 36
(Brendan Powell) *stdd s: t.k.h: hld up in last pair: rdn over 2f out: sn outpcd and wknd* 33/1

1m 14.65s (1.55) **Going Correction** -0.025s/f (Stan) 6 Ran SP% **115.6**
Speed ratings (Par 103): **88,87,73,72,71 68**
CSF £2.47 TOTE £3.60: £1.02, £1.80; EX 3.70 Trifecta £42.80.
**Owner** Sheikh Hamdan bin Mohammed Al Maktoum **Bred** Mountarmstrong Stud **Trained** Middleham Moor, N Yorks

**FOCUS**
An uncompetitive weak maiden in which they went no pace at all until they hit the straight. That contributed to a number of horses pulling early and another all-the-way winner on the card. There was little between the first pair on pre-race figures, and they finished well clear.

## 924 BETBRIGHT MONEYBACK OFFERS FILLIES' H'CAP 7f (P)
7:15 (7:15) (Class 5) (0-75,75) 4-Y-O+ £2,587 (£770; £384; £192) Stalls Low

Form RPR
6005 1 **Shaunas Spirit (IRE)**[14] 746 6-9-2 70 ............(p) AdamKirby 1 79
(Dean Ivory) *t.k.h: chsd ldrs: swtchd rt and effrt on inner wl over 1f out: led ins fnl f: hld on wl u.p fnl 100yds* 5/1[3]

-211 2 hd **Fab Lolly (IRE)**[18] 718 4-9-7 75 ............(p) JoeFanning 2 83
(James Bethell) *stdd s: hld up in tch in rr: waiting for gap over 1f out: swtchd lft and rdn ent fnl f: rdn hands and heels and chal ins fnl f: kpt on but a jst hld* 4/5[1]

100- 3 1 ¾ **Broughtons Charm (IRE)**[83] 8345 4-9-5 73 ............ RobertWinston 5 77
(Willie Musson) *wl in tch: rdn and effrt 2f out: styd on u.p ins fnl f: wnt 3rd last stride* 4/1[2]

15-0 4 shd **Sugarformyhoney (IRE)**[67] 57 5-9-6 74 ............(p) LiamKeniry 4 77
(Brendan Powell) *chsd ldr tl rdn to ld jst over 1f out: edgd lft and hdd ins fnl f: no ex and outpcd fnl 100yds* 12/1

-320 5 1 ¼ **Russian Ice**[9] 817 6-9-0 68 ............(b) JimCrowley 3 68
(Dean Ivory) *led: rdn 2f out: hdd jst over 1f out: styng on same pce whn short of room jst ins fnl f: wknd fnl 100yds* 5/1[3]

0-24 6 6 **Ivor's Princess**[14] 750 5-8-11 65 ............(b) LukeMorris 6 49
(Rod Millman) *niggled along leaving stalls: sn wl in tch in midfield: rdn ent fnl 2f: sn outpcd and btn* 8/1

1m 26.66s (0.66) **Going Correction** -0.025s/f (Stan) 6 Ran SP% **127.7**
Speed ratings (Par 100): **95,94,92,92,91 84**
CSF £11.03 TOTE £9.00: £4.60, £1.02; EX 14.20 Trifecta £77.40.
**Owner** Cynthia Smith & Dean Ivory **Bred** Miss Breda Wright **Trained** Radlett, Herts

**FOCUS**
A tight-knit fillies' handicap which could work out well. The winner is rated back to her Doncaster level. Another personal best here.

## 925 BETBRIGHT - LIVE THE MOMENT H'CAP 6f (P)
7:45 (7:47) (Class 5) (0-75,75) 4-Y-O+ £2,587 (£770; £384; £192) Stalls Low

Form RPR
1113 1 **Spellmaker**[18] 714 5-8-7 66 ............ EoinWalsh(5) 4 79+
(Tony Newcombe) *hld up wl in tch in midfield: rdn and qcknd to ld 1f out: clr and r.o wl fnl f: rdn out* 7/4[1]

6251 2 2 **Go Far**[1] 913 4-9-6 74 6ex ............(b) AdamKirby 3 79
(Alan Bailey) *chsd ldrs: swtchd ins and effrt 2f out: chsd wnr ins fnl f: kpt on but no imp* 7/4[1]

003- 3 1 **New Leyf (IRE)**[82] 8365 8-9-5 73 ............(b) MartinHarley 7 75
(Jeremy Gask) *t.k.h: chsd ldr: rdn to ld over 1f out: hdd and no ex 1f out: styd on same pce fnl f* 4/1[2]

140- 4 hd **Gold Beau (FR)**[167] 6774 4-9-0 73 ............(p) JacobButterfield(5) 8 74
(Kristin Stubbs) *chsd ldrs: rdn and pressed ldrs over 1f out: styd on same pce fnl f* 20/1

6053 5 3 ¼ **Sheikh The Reins (IRE)**[9] 817 5-9-0 68 ............(v) RobertHavlin 6 60
(John Best) *led: rdn and hdd over 1f out: wknd ins fnl f* 7/1[3]

-642 6 2 ½ **Top Cop**[16] 730 5-8-13 72 ............(p) DCByrne(5) 2 56
(Ronald Harris) *hld up in last pair: rdn and no hdwy 2f out: wknd ent fnl f* 7/1[3]

601- 7 1 ¼ **Blazing Knight (IRE)**[167] 6777 4-9-7 75 ............ LiamKeniry 5 55
(Chris Gordon) *jostled and short of room sn after s: rdn over 2f out: no prog: bhd fnl f* 33/1

1m 11.87s (-1.23) **Going Correction** -0.025s/f (Stan) 7 Ran SP% **125.4**
Speed ratings (Par 103): **107,104,103,102,98 95,93**
CSF £5.54 CT £11.28 TOTE £2.20: £1.10, £3.80; EX 5.70 Trifecta £28.80.
**Owner** Joli Racing **Bred** Dxb Bloodstock Ltd **Trained** Yarnscombe, Devon

**FOCUS**
A fair race which the market got spot on. The winner was well treated on the balance of his good recent form.

## 926 BETBRIGHT MOBILE H'CAP (BOBIS RACE) 6f (P)
8:15 (8:15) (Class 4) (0-85,81) 3-Y-O £4,690 (£1,395; £697; £348) Stalls Low

Form RPR
5-1 1 **Gone With The Wind (GER)**[49] 284 3-8-10 70 ............ WilliamBuick 1 77+
(Jeremy Noseda) *chsd ldr: rdn and effrt 2f out: clsd and chal 1f out: led ins fnl f: r.o wl and gng away at fin* 8/11[1]

2-21 2 1 ½ **Taquka (IRE)**[32] 531 3-9-0 81 ............ PatrickO'Donnell(7) 6 84
(Ralph Beckett) *led: rdn over 1f out: hdd ins fnl f: styd on same pce after* 7/2[2]

430- 3 ½ **Mick's Yer Man**[179] 6386 3-9-1 80 ............ RyanWhile(5) 2 81
(Bill Turner) *chsd ldng pair: rdn over 2f out: kpt on u.p ins fnl f* 16/1

461- 4 nse **Exceeder**[145] 7349 3-9-6 80 ............ MartinHarley 5 81
(Marco Botti) *hld up in tch in rr: rdn and effrt on inner 2f out: kpt on u.p ins fnl f* 9/2[3]

-134 5 1 ¾ **Artemis (IRE)**[28] 573 3-8-2 62 ............ JoeFanning 4 58
(Conrad Allen) *t.k.h: hld up in tch: rdn and effrt 2f out: no ex ins fnl f: wknd fnl 100yds* 12/1

1m 11.96s (-1.14) **Going Correction** -0.025s/f (Stan) 5 Ran SP% **111.9**
Speed ratings (Par 100): **106,104,103,103,100**
CSF £3.69 TOTE £1.30: £1.10, £2.00; EX 3.40 Trifecta £17.70.
**Owner** Mrs Susan Roy **Bred** Graf And Grafin Von Stauffenberg **Trained** Newmarket, Suffolk

**FOCUS**
Mostly unexposed sorts in this fair handicap. The winner did it quite well and the second more than confirmed his recent winning effort.

## 927 BETBRIGHT H'CAP (LONDON MILE SERIES QUALIFIER) 1m (P)
8:45 (8:45) (Class 5) (0-75,74) 4-Y-O+ £2,587 (£770; £384; £192) Stalls Low

Form RPR
-115 1 **Tee It Up Tommo (IRE)**[25] 627 5-9-5 72 ............ RobertWinston 2 79
(Michael Wigham) *chsd ldng pair: rdn and effrt 2f out: led and edgd lft ins fnl f: r.o* 9/4[2]

-545 2 ¾ **Liberty Jack (IRE)**[21] 655 4-9-3 70 ............ StephenCraine 3 75
(Jim Boyle) *t.k.h: chsd ldr tl led jst over 2f out: drvn and hdd ins fnl f: bmpd and one pce fnl 75yds* 5/4[1]

1030 3 ½ **Diplomatic (IRE)**[7] 843 9-9-7 74 ............(p) AdamKirby 4 80
(Michael Squance) *hld up in tch in rr: rdn and effrt wl over 1f out: kpt on wl ins fnl f* 7/2[3]

5-42 4 4 ½ **Tax Reform (IRE)**[19] 684 4-9-0 67 ............(b) RobertHavlin 5 61
(Mark Hoad) *hld up in last pair: rdn andeffrt 2f out: no hdwy: wknd over 1f out* 10/1

-366 5 3 **Alice's Dancer (IRE)**[13] 767 5-9-2 69 ............(b[1]) LukeMorris 1 56
(William Muir) *t.k.h: sn led: rdn and jst over 2f out: wknd over 1f out* 10/1

1m 40.48s (0.68) **Going Correction** -0.025s/f (Stan) 5 Ran SP% **115.6**
Speed ratings (Par 103): **95,94,93,89,86**
CSF £5.83 TOTE £2.80: £1.30, £1.70; EX 7.80 Trifecta £18.70.
**Owner** Palatinate Thoroughbred Racing Limited **Bred** Oghill House Stud **Trained** Newmarket, Suffolk

**FOCUS**
Predictably tactical and there was little in the way of early pace. The winner only needed to replicate his recent better form.
T/Plt: £4.00 to a £1 stake. Pool: £66749.14 - 12017.49 winning tickets T/Qpdt: £1.80 to a £1 stake. Pool: £5913.25 - 2365.05 winning tickets SP

# [906] SOUTHWELL (L-H)
Wednesday, March 12

**OFFICIAL GOING: Standard**
Wind: Virtually nil Weather: Overcast

## 928 LADBROKES H'CAP 1m (F)
1:55 (1:55) (Class 5) (0-70,70) 4-Y-O+ £3,234 (£962; £481; £240) Stalls Low

Form RPR
4322 1 **Exclusive Waters (IRE)**[13] 767 4-8-12 69 ......(b) CallumShepherd(7) 3 79
(Charles Hills) *dwlt: sn trcking ldrs: swtchd lft to inner and hdwy 2f out: rdn to ld ent fnl f: kpt on* 5/4[1]

2163 2 2 ¾ **Silly Billy (IRE)**[13] 767 6-9-6 70 ............(p) DanielTudhope 5 74
(John Balding) *t.k.h early: cl up on outer: led wl over 2f out: rdn wl over 1f out: hdd ent fnl f: kpt on same pce* 9/2[3]

6033 3 ¾ **Raging Bear (USA)**[6] 859 4-9-0 69 ............(b) RyanTate(5) 4 71
(James Evans) *dwlt: t.k.h: trckd ldrs: hdwy on outer over 2f out: rdn to chse ldng pair over 1f out: drvn and no imp fnl f* 6/4[2]

-000 4 8 **Pravda Street**[16] 733 9-8-9 66 ............ RobJFitzpatrick(7) 2 50
(Christopher Kellett) *cl up: led after 3f: rdn along 3f out: sn hdd: drvn over 2f out and sn wknd* 40/1

100/ 5 ½ **Run Fat Lass Run**[462] 7994 4-8-10 67 ............ EvaMoscrop(7) 1 49
(Philip Kirby) *set stdy pce: hdd after 3f: rdn along over 3f out: sn outpcd and bhd* 25/1

1m 44.41s (0.71) **Going Correction** +0.10s/f (Slow) 5 Ran SP% **108.9**
Speed ratings (Par 103): **100,97,96,88,88**
CSF £7.13 TOTE £1.90: £1.10, £2.00; EX 5.20 Trifecta £6.80.
**Owner** Richard Morecombe&SW Group Logistics Ltd **Bred** M M Sammon **Trained** Lambourn, Berks

■ A first winner on just his second ride for Callum Shepherd, 16.


The Form Book, Raceform Ltd, Newbury, RG14 5SJ

**FOCUS**
A weak handicap, run at a steady pace. The form could be rated a few pounds higher or lower.

## 929 DOWNLOAD THE LADBROKES APP H'CAP 7f (F)
2:30 (2:31) (Class 5) (0-75,74) 4-Y-0+ £3,234 (£962; £481; £240) Stalls Low

Form RPR

40-6 1 **Loud**[13] 757 4-9-2 **69**........ JoeFanning 8 78
(Mark Johnston) *trckd ldng pair: hdwy to ld wl over 2f out: rdn over 1f out: kpt on wl fnl f* **11/4**[2]

4542 2 1 3/4 **Sofias Number One (USA)**[6] 862 6-9-0 **72**........(b) PhilipPrince(5) 3 76
(Roy Bowring) *led: pushed along and hdd wl over 2f out: cl up: drvn over 1f out: styd on same pce fnl f* **2/1**[1]

2165 3 1/2 **Tartan Trip**[8] 832 7-9-4 **71**........(p) AndrewMullen 7 74
(Michael Appleby) *trckd ldrs: hdwy on outer 1/2-way: cl up wl over 2f out: rdn to chal wl over 1f out: drvn and one pce ent fnl f* **7/1**

-213 4 hd **Imaginary World (IRE)**[6] 862 6-8-13 **69**........(e) JasonHart(3) 2 72
(John Balding) *in tch: pushed along 3f out: rdn to chse ldrs and styng on whn n.m.r and hmpd 1 1/2f out: sn swtchd rt: drvn and kpt on fnl f: fin 5th plcd 4th* **5/1**

00-0 5 nk **Blazeofenchantment (USA)**[23] 646 4-8-10 **66**........ BillyCray(3) 1 68
(Richard Guest) *chsd ldr: effrt and cl up on inner 3f out: rdn over 2f out: drvn and edgd rt 1 1/2f out: sn one pce: fin 4th: disqualified and plcd 5th* **33/1**

14-2 6 3 1/2 **Mishrif (USA)**[48] 300 8-9-7 **74**........(v) FrederikTylicki 4 66
(J R Jenkins) *chsd ldrs: rdn along 3f out: sn one pce* **9/2**[3]

1-60 7 2 3/4 **Illustrious Prince (IRE)**[13] 757 7-9-5 **72**........ PaulMulrennan 6 57
(Julie Camacho) *a towards rr* **25/1**

16-0 8 8 **Spirit Rider (USA)**[13] 757 4-9-5 **72**........ PatrickDonaghy 5 35
(Giles Bravery) *sn rdn along and a in rr* **25/1**

1m 29.68s (-0.62) **Going Correction** +0.10s/f (Slow) **8** Ran SP% **118.0**
Speed ratings (Par 103): **107,105,104,103,104 99,96,87**
CSF £8.83 CT £34.41 TOTE £4.20: £2.00, £1.10, £2.30; EX 11.60 Trifecta £50.00.
**Owner** Sheikh Hamdan bin Mohammed Al Maktoum **Bred** P C Hunt **Trained** Middleham Moor, N Yorks

**FOCUS**
A modest handicap. Straightforward form, and the winner may have more to offer on this surface.

## 930 LADBROKES MAIDEN STKS 7f (F)
3:05 (3:07) (Class 5) 3-Y-0+ £3,234 (£962; £481; £240) Stalls Low

Form RPR

45-2 1 **Two Moons**[6] 861 4-10-0 0........ BarryMcHugh 5 81+
(Tony Coyle) *in tch: pushed along 3f out: rdn over 2f out: drvn and styd on wl fnl f to ld nr fin* **7/4**[1]

6-3 2 nk **On Demand**[31] 551 3-8-7 0........ DavidProbert 9 69
(Andrew Balding) *trckd ldrs: hdwy and cl up 3f out: chal over 2f out: rdn to ld over 1f out: drvn and edgd lft ins fnl f: hdd nr fin* **2/1**[2]

2 3 1 1/4 **Streets Of Newyork**[29] 564 7-10-0 0........ TomEaves 7 77+
(Brian Ellison) *s.i.s and bhd: wd st: gd hdwy over 2f out: sn rdn and styd on strly fnl f: nrst fin* **4/1**[3]

4 nse **Pearl Princess (FR)** 3-8-7 0........[1] LiamJones 6 66
(Olly Stevens) *prom: cl up on outer 1/2-way: led wl over 2f out: rdn along and hdd over 1f out: kpt on same pce* **10/1**

2-00 5 nk **Wildcat Lass (USA)**[32] 542 3-8-6 62 ow2........ SamJames(3) 2 67
(David O'Meara) *trckd ldrs: hdwy on inner over 2f out: rdn and ev ch over 1f out: edgd lft and one pce fnl f* **20/1**

6 15 **Ana Ettihady (ITY)** 3-8-12 0........ PaulMulrennan 8 29
(Kevin Ryan) *prom: led 1/2-way: rdn along and hdd over 2f out: wknd wl over 1f out* **8/1**

0 7 3 1/2 **Shades Of Silk**[44] 355 3-8-7 0........ JamesSullivan 4 15
(James Given) *in tch on inner: rdn along 3f out: sn outpcd* **100/1**

04 8 6 **Sheriff Of Nawton (IRE)**[19] 696 3-8-9 0........ JulieBurke(3) 3 9
(David O'Meara) *led: rdn along and hdd 1/2-way: sn wknd* **33/1**

- 9 1/2 **Kate Kelly (IRE)** 3-8-0 0........ JosephineGordon(7) 10
(Jo Hughes) *a in rr* **100/1**

10 21 **Vortex Star**[23] 5-9-7 0........ PaulBooth(7) 1
(Michael Chapman) *sn rdn along in rr: a outpcd and bhd* **100/1**

1m 29.82s (-0.48) **Going Correction** +0.10s/f (Slow)
**WFA** 3 from 4yo+ 16lb **10** Ran SP% **120.6**
Speed ratings (Par 103): **106,105,104,104,103 86,82,75,75,51**
CSF £5.58 TOTE £2.40: £1.20, £1.10, £2.40; EX 7.40 Trifecta £15.20.
**Owner** Tony Coyle **Bred** Mrs M L Parry & P M Steele-Mortimer **Trained** Norton, N Yorks

**FOCUS**
A very ordinary maiden, rated around the second.

## 931 32REDPOKER.COM FESTIVAL FREEROLL TONIGHT (S) STKS 1m (F)
3:45 (3:45) (Class 6) 3-Y-0 £2,587 (£770; £384; £192) Stalls Low

Form RPR

05-0 1 **Chanceuse**[14] 745 3-8-13 48........ DavidProbert 5 56
(Gay Kelleway) *trckd ldrs: hdwy to chse ldr over 3f out: rdn 2f out: drvn ent fnl f: kpt on wl to ld nr fin* **14/1**

5231 2 1/2 **Cascadia (IRE)**[6] 865 3-8-6 52........ RobJFitzpatrick(7) 4 55
(K R Burke) *led: rdn along 2f out: drvn ent fnl f: hdd and no ex nr fin* **7/4**[2]

1-65 3 9 **Black Geronimo**[13] 762 3-8-13 62........ PhilipPrince(5) 3 39
(Roy Bowring) *chsd ldrs: rdn along 3f out: drvn and outpcd fnl 2f* **7/1**[3]

1152 4 18 **Nick The Odds (IRE)**[1] 907 3-9-4 65........(bt) BenCurtis 2
(Jo Hughes) *trckd ldr: pushed along wl over 2f out: sn rdn and btn* **10/11**[1]

1m 45.23s (1.53) **Going Correction** +0.10s/f (Slow) **4** Ran SP% **107.9**
Speed ratings (Par 96): **96,95,86,68**
CSF £37.69 TOTE £10.40; EX 28.70 Trifecta £59.80.There was no bid for the winner. Cascadia was claimed by Miss A. L. Hutchinson for £5,000.
**Owner** Ben Parish **Bred** Gracelands Stud **Trained** Exning, Suffolk

**FOCUS**
A very weak seller run at a steady pace. The two fillies in the field fought out an exciting finish and the form is rated around them.

## 932 32RED IMMORTAL ROMANCE SLOT H'CAP 1m 6f (F)
4:25 (4:25) (Class 5) (0-75,69) 4-Y-0+ £3,234 (£962; £481; £240) Stalls Low

Form RPR

5-11 1 **Kingscombe (USA)**[8] 829 5-9-7 **66** 6ex........ RobertHavlin 3 73
(Linda Jewell) *trckd ldr: cl up 4f out: led over 2f out: jnd and rdn wl over 1f out: drvn ins fnl f: kpt on wl* **6/4**[2]

42 2 1 1/4 **Carlanda (FR)**[8] 829 4-9-2 **65**........(p[1]) AndrewMullen 2 70
(Michael Appleby) *trckd ldrs: hdwy 4f out: effrt to join wnr wl over 1f out: sn rdn: drvn and ev ch ent fnl f: kpt on same pce last 100yds* **10/11**[1]

2456 3 7 **Teenage Dream (IRE)**[9] 818 6-8-12 **64**........(vt) AdamMcLean(7) 4 60
(Derek Shaw) *set stdy pce: pushed along and qcknd over 3f out: rdn and hdd over 2f out: sn drvn and one pce* **20/1**

0/0- 4 5 **Yazdi (IRE)**[24] 3560 5-9-10 **69**........ GrahamLee 1 58
(Henry Oliver) *trckd ldng pair: pushed along over 4f out: rdn over 3f out: sn wknd* **8/1**[3]

3m 15.69s (7.39) **Going Correction** +0.10s/f (Slow)
**WFA** 4 from 5yo+ 4lb **4** Ran SP% **108.3**
Speed ratings (Par 103): **82,81,77,74**
CSF £3.22 TOTE £2.20; EX 3.20 Trifecta £7.90.
**Owner** Peter Oppenheimer **Bred** Juddmonte Farms Inc **Trained** Sutton Valence, Kent

**FOCUS**
This staying handicap looked a match on the book and the market leaders pulled clear up the straight. Very modest form.

## 933 32REDBET.COM H'CAP 5f (F)
5:05 (5:05) (Class 6) (0-60,57) 3-Y-0 £2,587 (£770; £384; £192) Stalls High

Form RPR

606- 1 **Samhain**[148] 7271 3-9-5 **55**........ SeanLevey 2 75+
(David Brown) *mde all: shkn up and clr wl over 1f out: eased ins fnl f: easily* **11/10**[1]

-330 2 4 1/2 **Diamondsinthesky (IRE)**[14] 745 3-9-7 **57**........(v[1]) TomEaves 5 52
(Derek Shaw) *sn chsng wnr: rdn along 2f out: drvn over 1f out: kpt on: no ch w wnr* **6/1**

050 3 3/4 **Maro**[16] 731 3-8-2 **45**........(v) AdamMcLean(7) 3 37
(Derek Shaw) *prom: rdn along: edgd lft and outpcd wl over 1f out: kpt on u.p fnl f* **25/1**

-300 4 1 **Rebel Code (USA)**[36] 481 3-9-3 **53**........(p) GrahamLee 4 42
(James Given) *chsd ldrs: rdn along 1/2-way: sn one pce* **4/1**[2]

10-6 5 5 **Britain (IRE)**[13] 762 3-9-3 **53**........(p) AdrianNicholls 6 24
(David C Griffiths) *dwlt: in tch: sme hdwy 1/2-way: sn rdn and wknd* **9/2**[3]

003- 6 2 1/2 **Who Splashed Me**[75] 8405 3-8-2 **45**........ VictorSantos(7) 1 7
(J R Jenkins) *s.i.s: a bhd* **16/1**

0-00 7 12 **Trefnant (IRE)**[14] 745 3-8-9 **45**........(v[1]) ChrisCatlin 7
(Chris Dwyer) *sn outpcd and a bhd* **20/1**

1m 0.73s (1.03) **Going Correction** +0.125s/f (Slow) **7** Ran SP% **114.6**
Speed ratings (Par 96): **96,88,87,86,78 74,54**
CSF £8.43 TOTE £2.10: £1.40, £2.10; EX 13.40 Trifecta £92.90.
**Owner** J C Fretwell **Bred** Ashburton Property Finance Ltd **Trained** Averham Park, Notts

**FOCUS**
A very weak sprint handicap, run at a fair pace. The impressive winner was value for considerably more than the winning margin.

## 934 COMPARE BOOKMAKERS AT BOOKMAKERS.CO.UK H'CAP 6f (F)
5:35 (5:35) (Class 6) (0-60,65) 4-Y-0+ £2,587 (£770; £384; £192) Stalls Low

Form RPR

5001 1 **Masai Moon**[8] 835 10-9-5 **65** 6ex........(b) PatMillman(7) 10 73
(Rod Millman) *dwlt and in rr: hdwy and wd st: rdn 2f out: styd on strly ent fnl f to ld last 50yds* **7/4**[1]

0453 2 3/4 **Laughing Rock (IRE)**[8] 835 4-9-1 **54**........(v[1]) AndrewMullen 8 60
(Michael Appleby) *chsd ldrs: hdwy wl over 2f out: rdn to chal over 1f out: led jst ins fnl f and sn drvn: hdd and no ex last 50yds* **12/1**

-010 3 1 3/4 **Art Dzeko**[13] 766 5-9-4 **57**........(p) TomEaves 5 58
(Brian Baugh) *prom: cl up 1/2-way: led wl over 2f out: rdn wl over 1f out: hdd jst ins fnl f: kpt on same pce: b.b.v* **10/1**

2-63 4 2 **Pearl Noir**[52] 95 4-8-8 **54**........(b) MatthewHopkins(7) 2 49
(Scott Dixon) *led: rdn along and hdd wl over 2f out: drvn wl over 1f out: sn one pce* **12/1**

0600 5 hd **Fathom Five (IRE)**[13] 766 10-9-0 **53**........ PaddyAspell 7 47
(Shaun Harris) *chsd ldng pair: rdn along over 2f out: drvn wl over 1f out: grad wknd* **50/1**

0-04 6 3/4 **Durham Express (IRE)**[6] 864 7-8-2 **46** oh1........(v) ConnorBeasley(5) 3 38
(Colin Teague) *chsd ldrs: rdn along wl over 2f out: drvn wl over 1f out: grad wknd* **25/1**

000- 7 nk **Hab Reeh**[191] 6053 6-9-0 **60**........ GemmaTutty(7) 6 51
(Ruth Carr) *chsd ldrs: rdn along wl over 2f out: sn no imp* **50/1**

3621 8 nk **Orwellian**[6] 864 5-9-1 **54** 6ex........ PaulMulrennan 4 44
(Bryan Smart) *in rr: rdn along 1/2-way: sme late hdwy* **9/4**[2]

446- 9 1/2 **Camache Queen (IRE)**[120] 7845 6-9-1 **54**........(vt) GrahamLee 9 42
(Joseph Tuite) *midfield: hdwy on outer wl over 2f out: sn rdn and no imp* **25/1**

2-4 10 3 1/4 **Beachwood Bay**[50] 273 6-9-0 **60**........ JosephineGordon(7) 1 39
(Jo Hughes) *chsd ldrs: rdn along wl over 2f out: sn wknd* **6/1**[3]

1m 16.93s (0.43) **Going Correction** +0.10s/f (Slow) **10** Ran SP% **117.5**
Speed ratings (Par 101): **101,100,97,95,94 93,93,92,92,87**
CSF £23.74 CT £169.66 TOTE £2.60: £1.20, £3.40, £3.10; EX 28.30 Trifecta £145.80.
**Owner** B R Millman **Bred** Mrs B A Matthews **Trained** Kentisbeare, Devon
■ Stewards' Enquiry : Andrew Mullen seven-day ban: used whip above permitted level (Mar 26-31,Apr 1)

**FOCUS**
They went a sound gallop in this modest handicap. The winner was well treated under a penalty, and the second is rated to her previous course best.
T/Plt: £275.00 to a £1 stake. Pool of £52026.92 - 138.1 winning tickets T/Qpdt: £137.20 to a £1 stake. Pool of £3505.79 - 18.9 winning tickets JR

# AMIENS (R-H)
Wednesday, March 12

**OFFICIAL GOING: Turf: heavy**

## 935a PRIX DE POULAINVILLE (CONDITIONS) (4YO) (TURF) 1m 3f
6:50 (12:00) 4-Y-0 £6,666 (£2,666; £2,000; £1,333; £666)

RPR

1 **Samuraj (FR)**[98] 4-8-11 0........ FilipMinarik 4 77
(M Munch, Germany) **107/10**

2 3 **Conserve (IRE)**[12] 776 4-8-11 0 ow1........(b) Pierre-CharlesBoudot 12 72
(Amy Weaver) *t.k.h: trckd ldrs: scrubbed along to chse ldr fr 2f out: rdn to chal ins fnl f: edgd lft and getting bttr of battle w long-time ldr whn hdd by str fining wnr 110yds out: no ex* **11/5**[1]

3 nk **Ladalco (FR)**[170] 4-9-0 0........ APietsch 7 74
(Waldemar Hickst, Germany) **41/10**[2]

4 4 **Ana Musica (FR)**[5] 4-8-3 0........ MllePaulineDominois(5) 2 61
(P Demercastel, France) **51/1**

5 2 **Lovely Jee Pee (IRE)**$^{58}$ 4-8-10 0 ThomasMessina 8 60
(Mme Pia Brandt, France) **76/10**
6 3 **Della Star (FR)**$^{176}$ 4-9-0 0 FabienLefebvre 5 58
(A Lyon, France) **31/1**
7 2 **On The Rocks (FR)**$^{34}$ 4-8-8 0 FlavienPrat 6 49
(T Clout, France) **147/10**
8 nk **Yoninaelle (FR)** 4-8-3 0 StephaneLaurent$^{(5)}$ 1 48
(Ecurie Saint Simeon, Belgium) **54/1**
9 6 **Churada (IRE)**$^{12}$ 4-9-4 0 JulienGuillochon$^{(3)}$ 9 50
(J-M Lefebvre, France) **45/1**
10 10 **Topza (FR)**$^{304}$ 4-8-8 0 RonanThomas 3 19
(F-H Graffard, France) **58/10$^{3}$**
11 nk **Zawatar (FR)**$^{47}$ 4-9-2 0 MorganDelalande 10 27
(W Delalande, France) **32/5**
12 2 **Ignis Away (FR)**$^{88}$ 4-8-8 0 SylvainRuis 11 15
(Mme Pia Brandt, France) **178/10**
2m 39.04s (159.04) **12 Ran SP% 120.0**
WIN (incl. 1 euro stake): 11.70. PLACES: 3.00, 1.50, 1.90. DF: 22.60. SF: 45.60.
**Owner** MM Racing **Bred** H Wirth **Trained** Germany

## 913 WOLVERHAMPTON (A.W) (L-H)
Thursday, March 13

**OFFICIAL GOING: Standard**
Wind: Light against Weather: Hazy sunshine

### 936 32RED H'CAP 5f 20y(P)
5:45 (5:45) (Class 5) (0-75,75) 3-Y-O **£3,234** (£962; £481; £240) **Stalls** Low

Form RPR
13 1 **Crisis Averted (IRE)**$^{35}$ 501 3-9-7 **75** TonyHamilton 1 81+
(Richard Fahey) *hld up: hdwy 1/2-way: shkn up and edgd lft over 1f out: rdn and r.o to ld wl ins fnl f* **9/4$^{1}$**
-303 2 hd **Under Approval**$^{6}$ 867 3-8-5 **62** JulieBurke$^{(3)}$ 9 67
(David O'Meara) *sn led: rdn over 1f out: hdd wl ins fnl f* **10/1**
44-0 3 1½ **Lady In Blue (IRE)**$^{29}$ 573 3-8-13 **67** (v$^{1}$) DanielTudhope 10 67
(David O'Meara) *chsd ldr: rdn over 1f out: styd on same pce ins fnl f* **20/1**
2211 4 ½ **Saffire Song**$^{14}$ 762 3-9-5 **73** JoeFanning 6 71
(Alan Bailey) *prom: rdn over 1f out: styd on same pce ins fnl f* **11/2**
255- 5 nse **Inciting Incident (IRE)**$^{243}$ 4289 3-9-2 **70** (b$^{1}$) GrahamGibbons 2 68
(Ed McMahon) *hld up: rdn over 1f out: r.o ins fnl f: nt rch ldrs* **3/1$^{2}$**
63-1 6 2¼ **Castorienta**$^{27}$ 605 3-9-1 **69** HayleyTurner 3 59
(George Baker) *sn pushed along to chse ldrs: rdn over 1f out: no ex ins fnl f* **8/1**
0-55 7 hd **Nova Princesse (GER)**$^{22}$ 667 3-9-5 **73** (bt) MartinHarley 4 62
(Marco Botti) *hld up: hdwy over 1f out: rdn and edgd lft ins fnl f: styd on same pce* **4/1$^{3}$**
3134 8 ¾ **Ealain Aibrean (IRE)**$^{14}$ 762 3-8-4 **65** HollieDoyle$^{(7)}$ 7 51
(David Evans) *mid-div: hung rt 1/2-way: sn lost pl* **16/1**
4-00 9 13 **Song Of Rowland (IRE)**$^{27}$ 608 3-8-3 **57** LukeMorris 5
(Alan Jones) *s.i.s: a in rr: rdn and wknd 1/2-way* **100/1**
1m 1.81s (-0.49) **Going Correction** +0.075s/f (Slow) **9 Ran SP% 123.0**
Speed ratings (Par 98): **106,105,103,102,102 98,98,97,76**
CSF £28.52 CT £381.99 TOTE £3.60: £2.90, £2.70, £6.40; EX 37.00 Trifecta £1140.30.
**Owner** D O'Callaghan **Bred** Sean Gorman **Trained** Musley Bank, N Yorks
■ Stewards' Enquiry : Julie Burke two-day ban: used whip above permitted level (Mar 27-28)
**FOCUS**
Not a bad little handicap.

### 937 BEST ODDS AT BOOKMAKERS.CO.UK H'CAP 5f 20y(P)
6:15 (6:16) (Class 7) (0-50,50) 4-Y-O+ **£1,940** (£577; £288; £144) **Stalls** Low

Form RPR
-004 1 **Outbid**$^{12}$ 797 4-9-7 **50** LukeMorris 2 57
(Tony Carroll) *led 1f: chsd ldrs: wnt 2nd 1/2-way: rdn over 1f out: led ins fnl f: r.o* **5/1$^{2}$**
00-2 2 ½ **Dear Ben**$^{20}$ 693 5-9-5 **48** AndrewMullen 8 53
(Brian Baugh) *led 4f out: rdn over 1f out: hdd ins fnl f: styd on* **8/1**
13 3 ¾ **Lord Buffhead**$^{20}$ 692 5-9-1 **47** (v) BillyCray$^{(3)}$ 1 50
(Richard Guest) *chsd ldr 4f out tl drvn along 1/2-way: styd on* **7/2$^{1}$**
-600 4 1¼ **Green Millionaire**$^{12}$ 797 4-8-12 **48** (t) DavidParkes$^{(7)}$ 7 46
(Jeremy Gask) *chsd ldrs: rdn over 1f out: styd on* **12/1**
-054 5 nse **Speedyfix**$^{48}$ 313 7-9-7 **50** (t) JimmyQuinn 3 48
(Christine Dunnett) *s.i.s: sn pushed along and prom: rdn over 1f out: styd on same pce ins fnl f* **11/2$^{3}$**
00-4 6 ¾ **Exkaliber**$^{20}$ 693 5-9-4 **47** (vt) GrahamLee 4 42
(Richard Ford) *trckd ldrs: rdn over 1f out: no ex ins fnl f: fin 7th: plcd 6th* **7/2$^{1}$**
3233 7 2 **Vhujon (IRE)**$^{14}$ 760 9-9-3 **46** StephenCraine 6 34
(Peter Grayson) *s.i.s: hld up: nvr on terms: fin 8th: plcd 7th* **10/1**
00-5 8 shd **Jemimaville (IRE)**$^{36}$ 483 7-8-13 **45** (v) RyanPowell$^{(3)}$ 12 32
(Giles Bravery) *s.i.s: sn pushed along in rr: rdn over 1f out: n.d: fin 9th: plcd 8th* **50/1**
1230 9 1½ **Ishetoo**$^{12}$ 797 10-9-2 **48** SladeO'Hara$^{(3)}$ 11 30
(Peter Grayson) *sn pushed along in rr: nvr on terms: fin 10th: plcd 9th* **25/1**
0-06 10 1 **Steel City Boy (IRE)**$^{20}$ 692 11-8-11 **45** AnnStokell$^{(5)}$ 5 23
(Ann Stokell) *mid-div: sn pushed along: n.m.r and lost pl over 3f out: bhd fr 1/2-way: fin 11th: plcd 10th* **25/1**
-555 D shd **Methaaly (IRE)**$^{20}$ 692 11-9-0 **50** (be) LewisStones$^{(7)}$ 10 45
(Michael Mullineaux) *s.i.s: r.o ins fnl f: nrst fin: fin 6th: disqualified and plcd last: rdr failed to weigh in* **16/1**
1m 2.66s (0.36) **Going Correction** +0.075s/f (Slow) **11 Ran SP% 119.9**
Speed ratings (Par 97): **100,99,98,96,95 94,91,91,88,87 95**
CSF £44.84 CT £162.95 TOTE £4.80: £2.00, £2.00, £1.40; EX 68.60 Trifecta £472.80.
**Owner** Richard Ward **Bred** Llety Stud **Trained** Cropthorne, Worcs
■ Stewards' Enquiry : Lewis Stones two-day ban: failed to weigh-in (Mar 27-28)
**FOCUS**
A weak handicap and very few got involved.

### 938 COMPARE BOOKMAKERS AT BOOKMAKERS.CO.UK H'CAP 5f 216y(P)
6:45 (6:45) (Class 5) (0-70,70) 4-Y-O+ **£2,911** (£866; £432; £216) **Stalls** Low

Form RPR
5430 1 **Greenhead High**$^{22}$ 663 6-8-13 **62** (v) AdrianNicholls 7 69
(David Nicholls) *mde virtually all: rdn over 1f out: all out* **11/2$^{2}$**
2536 2 shd **Indian Affair**$^{8}$ 841 4-8-9 **65** LeroyLynch$^{(7)}$ 5 72
(Milton Bradley) *chsd ldrs: pushed along over 1f out: hung lft ins fnl f: r.o* **6/1$^{3}$**
3300 3 2¼ **Sewn Up**$^{9}$ 835 4-8-8 **57** (p) ShaneKelly 1 57
(Andrew Hollinshead) *prom: rdn over 1f out: styd on same pce ins fnl f* **6/1$^{3}$**
3013 4 shd **Colourbearer (IRE)**$^{2}$ 913 7-9-7 **70** (t) RichardKingscote 4 70
(Milton Bradley) *chsd ldrs: swtchd lft over 1f out: sn rdn: no ex ins fnl f* **5/4$^{1}$**
456 5 4½ **Dark Lane**$^{47}$ 339 8-8-10 **62** DeclanBates$^{(3)}$ 8 48
(David Evans) *trckd ldrs: racd keenly: rdn over 2f out: wknd ins fnl f* **7/1**
-000 6 1 **Lucky Dan (IRE)**$^{2}$ 913 8-9-6 **69** JoeFanning 3 52
(Paul Green) *broke wl: sn lost pl: rdn over 2f out: wknd over 1f out* **10/1**
220- 7 34 **Saga Lout**$^{134}$ 7633 4-9-6 **69** ChrisCatlin 6
(Ray Peacock) *sn pushed along in rr: wknd over 2f out* **25/1**
1m 14.83s (-0.17) **Going Correction** +0.075s/f (Slow) **7 Ran SP% 113.8**
Speed ratings (Par 103): **104,103,100,100,94 93,48**
CSF £37.36 CT £203.52 TOTE £9.10: £7.00, £3.50; EX 45.00 Trifecta £244.10.
**Owner** David Nicholls Racing Club **Bred** Wyck Hall Stud Ltd **Trained** Sessay, N Yorks
**FOCUS**
Again it was an advantage to race handily out of the kickback.

### 939 DOWNLOAD THE LADBROKES APP (S) H'CAP 1m 141y(P)
7:15 (7:15) (Class 6) (0-60,60) 4-Y-O+ **£2,264** (£673; £336; £168) **Stalls** Low

Form RPR
3462 1 **Supa Seeker (USA)**$^{6}$ 869 8-8-9 **48** LukeMorris 6 55
(Tony Carroll) *hld up: drvn along over 2f out: hdwy over 1f out: edgd lft and styd on to ld wl ins fnl f* **9/4$^{1}$**
6116 2 ¾ **Huzzah (IRE)**$^{13}$ 781 9-9-0 **60** AlistairRawlinson$^{(7)}$ 1 65
(Michael Appleby) *plld hrd: sn trcking ldr: led 2f out: rdn over 1f out: hdd wl ins fnl f* **5/2$^{2}$**
6543 3 1 **One Way Or Another (AUS)**$^{27}$ 603 11-9-6 **59** (t) MartinHarley 3 62
(David Evans) *chsd ldrs: rdn over 1f out: nt clr run ins fnl f: styd on* **3/1$^{3}$**
0603 4 nk **Rigid**$^{6}$ 869 7-8-2 **46** oh1 (t) JoeyHaynes$^{(5)}$ 4 50
(Tony Carroll) *trckd ldrs: pushed along over 3f out: nt clr run over 1f out: sn rdn and edgd lft: styd on* **8/1**
1420 5 4 **Greek Islands (IRE)**$^{37}$ 467 6-9-3 **56** ChrisCatlin 5 50
(Edward Creighton) *hld up: pushed along over 2f out: nvr trbld ldrs* **11/2**
0/4- 6 6 **Unbreak My Heart (IRE)**$^{276}$ 3152 9-8-7 **46** (tp) WilliamCarson 2 28
(Ann Stokell) *led: plld hrd: hdd 2f out: wknd fnl f* **33/1**
1m 52.18s (1.68) **Going Correction** +0.075s/f (Slow) **6 Ran SP% 113.8**
Speed ratings (Par 101): **95,94,93,93,89 84**
CSF £8.41 TOTE £2.00: £1.20, £1.20; EX 6.90 Trifecta £19.00.There was no bid for the winner.
**Owner** A W Carroll **Bred** Arbib Bloodstock Partnership **Trained** Cropthorne, Worcs
**FOCUS**
The pace picked up some way out here with Unbreak My Heart being given a forceful ride, and that suited the winner.

### 940 LADBROKES H'CAP 1m 141y(P)
7:45 (7:46) (Class 5) (0-70,70) 4-Y-O+ **£2,911** (£866; £432; £216) **Stalls** Low

Form RPR
1432 1 **Mr Red Clubs (IRE)**$^{8}$ 843 5-9-6 **69** AndrewMullen 5 77
(Michael Appleby) *chsd ldrs: rdn to ld ins fnl f: edgd lft: styd on* **7/4$^{1}$**
0202 2 nk **Baltic Prince (IRE)**$^{2}$ 918 4-8-8 **57** JoeFanning 6 64
(Paul Green) *led: hdd 7f out: chsd ldr tl led again 2f out: hdd ins fnl f: styd on* **11/2$^{3}$**
3344 3 2½ **Run It Twice (IRE)**$^{26}$ 627 4-9-6 **69** (b) MartinHarley 8 71+
(David Evans) *hld up: hdwy over 1f out: sn rdn: styd on same pce ins fnl f* **9/4$^{2}$**
1440 4 ½ **Prime Exhibit**$^{13}$ 782 9-9-7 **70** (t) ShaneKelly 1 71
(Daniel Mark Loughnane) *prom: rdn over 1f out: styd on same pce ins fnl f* **25/1**
52-5 5 1½ **Special Mix**$^{62}$ 120 6-9-4 **67** MartinLane 3 65
(Martin Smith) *s.i.s: sn prom: led 7f out: rdn and hdd 2f out: no ex fnl f* **10/1**
550- 6 nk **Egotist (IRE)**$^{83}$ 8360 6-8-11 **63** ow1 (t) RobertTart$^{(3)}$ 2 60
(Milton Bradley) *s.s: styd on ins fnl f: nvr nrr* **12/1**
3-60 7 1½ **Kelpie Blitz (IRE)**$^{22}$ 655 5-9-3 **69** (t) RossAtkinson$^{(3)}$ 7 63
(Paul Morgan) *hld up: pushed along over 2f out: hmpd wl over 1f out: nvr trbld ldrs* **7/1**
1m 51.19s (0.69) **Going Correction** +0.075s/f (Slow) **7 Ran SP% 115.6**
Speed ratings (Par 103): **99,98,96,96,94 94,93**
CSF £12.32 CT £22.00 TOTE £3.60: £1.60, £2.50; EX 11.50 Trifecta £25.40.
**Owner** Ferrybank Properties Limited **Bred** Tally-Ho Stud **Trained** Danethorpe, Notts
**FOCUS**
Very few got into this.

### 941 CORAL MOBILE "JUST THREE CLICKS TO BET" MAIDEN STKS 1m 1f 103y(P)
8:15 (8:16) (Class 5) 3-Y-O+ **£2,587** (£770; £384; £192) **Stalls** Low

Form RPR
1 **Genius Boy** 4-9-13 0 LukeMorris 7 76+
(James Tate) *a.p: trckd ldr over 6f out tl led over 2f out: hdd over 1f out: rallied u.p to ld nr fin* **8/13$^{1}$**
53 2 shd **Lockedoutaheaven (IRE)**$^{17}$ 734 3-8-7 0 PaoloSirigu 5 70
(Marco Botti) *hld up: hdwy over 5f out: shkn up to ld over 1f out: hdd nr fin* **5/1$^{2}$**
02 3 6 **Her Red Devil (IRE)**$^{17}$ 735 3-8-2 0 JimmyQuinn 1 54+
(Richard Fahey) *hld up: pushed along and hdwy over 1f out: styd on u.p to go 3rd nr fin: nt trble ldrs* **16/1**
4 nse **All Reddy** 3-8-7 0 RichardKingscote 10 59
(Tom Dascombe) *plld hrd: trckd ldr tl over 6f out: remained handy: rdn over 2f out: styd on same pce fr over 1f out* **5/1$^{2}$**
3 5 3½ **Stoneham**$^{17}$ 735 3-8-2 0 HayleyTurner 6 47
(Mick Channon) *chsd ldrs: pushed along over 2f out: wknd over 1f out* **12/1$^{3}$**
54 6 ½ **Nellies Quest**$^{5}$ 888 5-9-1 0 AlistairRawlinson$^{(7)}$ 4 52
(Michael Appleby) *prom: plld hrd: rdn over 2f out: wknd over 1f out* **20/1**
3-5 7 1 **Acton Gold**$^{70}$ 13 5-9-8 0 AndrewMullen 9 50?
(Brian Baugh) *plld hrd: led at stdy pce tl pushed along and hdd over 2f out: wknd fnl f* **33/1**
0 8 2 **Sycophantic (IRE)**$^{20}$ 686 4-9-13 0 FergusSweeney 8 51
(Jamie Osborne) *hld up: pushed along over 2f out: sn wknd* **25/1**
00 9 2¾ **Premier Jack's**$^{21}$ 675 3-8-4 0 MatthewCosham$^{(3)}$ 3 40
(Nikki Evans) *hld up: hdwy over 2f out: hung rt and wknd over 1f out* **66/1**

0 **10** *13* **Flamenco Flyer**[31] 558 5-9-8 0 EoinWalsh(5) 2 21
(Edward Bevan) *hld up: rdn over 3f out: sn wknd* **100/1**
2m 4.04s (2.34) **Going Correction** +0.075s/f (Slow)
**WFA** 3 from 4yo+ 20lb **10** Ran SP% **122.9**
Speed ratings (Par 103): **92,91,86,86,83 82,82,80,77,66**
CSF £4.19 TOTE £1.80: £1.10, £1.90, £4.10; EX 5.80 Trifecta £26.60.
**Owner** Sheikh Juma Dalmook Al Maktoum **Bred** Meon Valley Stud **Trained** Newmarket, Suffolk
**FOCUS**
Two came clear in this maiden, which was run at a steady early pace. The market only wanted to know about one horse.

## 942 CORAL APP DOWNLOAD FROM THE APP STORE H'CAP 1m 1f 103y(P)
**8:45** (8:45) (Class 4) (0-85,82) 4-Y-O+ **£5,175** (£1,540; £769; £384) **Stalls** Low

Form RPR
1-51 **1** **Spes Nostra**[13] 782 6-9-2 **78** (b) GrahamGibbons 5 88
(David Barron) *hmpd s: mde all: rdn over 1f out: styd on* **2/1**[1]
141- **2** *1 1/4* **Mubtadi**[267] 3468 6-9-5 **81** MartinHarley 1 89+
(Ismail Mohammed) *hld up: hdwy over 1f out: rdn to chse wnr ins fnl f: styd on* **8/1**
-602 **3** *3 1/4* **Ishikawa (IRE)**[15] 744 6-8-13 **82** RobJFitzpatrick(7) 2 83
(K R Burke) *trckd ldrs: racd keenly: rdn to chse wnr over 1f out tl styd on same pce ins fnl f* **7/2**[3]
23-1 **4** *3* **Secular Society**[52] 265 4-9-4 **80** FergusSweeney 3 76
(George Baker) *prom: rdn over 2f out: styd on same pce fr over 1f out* **5/1**
21-0 **5** *1 3/4* **Busatto (USA)**[15] 744 4-9-6 **82** JoeFanning 4 74
(Mark Johnston) *edgd rt s: sn trcking wnr: rdn over 2f out: wknd fnl f* **5/2**[2]
1m 59.98s (-1.72) **Going Correction** +0.075s/f (Slow) **5** Ran SP% **111.9**
Speed ratings (Par 105): **110,108,106,103,101**
CSF £17.61 TOTE £2.70: £2.70, £1.50; EX 14.00 Trifecta £29.80.
**Owner** J Cringan & D Pryde **Bred** James A Cringan **Trained** Maunby, N Yorks
**FOCUS**
An interesting little handicap.
T/Plt: £37.00 to a £1 stake. Pool of £117310.92 - 2309.54 winning tickets. T/Qpdt: £10.80 to a £1 stake. Pool of £9458.53 - 643.49 winning tickets. CR

943 - 950a (Foreign Racing) - See Raceform Interactive

845
# LINGFIELD (L-H)
Friday, March 14

**OFFICIAL GOING: Standard**
Wind: very light, across Weather: bright and sunny

## 951 32REDBET.COM MAIDEN STKS 1m 4f (P)
**1:55** (1:58) (Class 5) 3-Y-O **£3,408** (£1,006; £503) **Stalls** Low

Form RPR
2 **1** **Belfilo (IRE)**[20] 717 3-9-5 0 JimCrowley 8 81+
(Andrew Balding) *hld up in midfield: hdwy to chse ldrs 7f out: rdn and ev ch 2f out: edgd lft and led over 1f out: fnd ex whn pressed wl ins fnl f: r.o* **8/11**[1]
54 **2** *3/4* **New Tarabela**[20] 717 3-9-5 0 LukeMorris 5 80
(James Tate) *wl in tch in midfield: rdn 5f out: swtchd rt and clr in ldng quintet 3f out: hdwy u.p 1f out: pressed wnr wl ins fnl f: styd on same pce fnl 50yds* **14/1**
**3** *3 1/4* **Lake Alfred (USA)** 3-9-5 0 JamesDoyle 1 75
(Lady Cecil) *chsd ldrs: rdn and clr in ldng quintet 3f out: chsd ldng pair and swtchd rt 1f out: styd on same pce ins fnl f* **8/1**
0-2 **4** *nk* **Moontown**[11] 827 3-9-5 0 WilliamBuick 2 74
(Charles Hills) *led: rdn and hrd pressed 2f out: hdd over 1f out: wknd ins fnl f* **5/1**[3]
022- **5** *8* **Ujagar (IRE)**[130] 7732 3-9-5 72 KierenFallon 9 61
(Tom Dascombe) *t.k.h: chsd ldr after 2f out tl over 2f out: btn over 1f out: fdd ins fnl f* **9/2**[2]
45- **6** *6* **Softly She Treads (IRE)**[148] 7327 3-8-11 0 JemmaMarshall(3) 10 47
(Pat Phelan) *hld up in tch in midfield: 6th and wl outpcd by ldng quintet 3f out: n.d after: plugged on* **50/1**
**7** *1 3/4* **Moriond (USA)** 3-9-5 0 MartinLane 3 49+
(David Simcock) *s.i.s: in tch in last pair: outpcd by ldng quintet 3f out: n.d after* **25/1**
00-0 **8** *5* **Foxie Girl**[55] 230 3-9-0 41 FergusSweeney 4 36
(John Best) *in tch in last trio: rdn 5f out: outpcd over 3f out: bhd fnl 3f* **150/1**
00-6 **9** *1 3/4* **Storm Of Choice**[20] 717 3-9-5 28 (p) RobertHavlin 6 38
(Michael Attwater) *t.k.h: chsd ldr for 2f: lost pl and rdn 4f out: bhd fnl 2f* **150/1**
5 **10** *2 1/4* **Archiebeau**[20] 717 3-9-2 0 MatthewLawson(3) 7 35
(Jonathan Portman) *s.i.s: in tch in rr: rdn 5f out: bhd over 2f out* **66/1**
2m 30.93s (-2.07) **Going Correction** -0.075s/f (Stan) **10** Ran SP% **119.2**
Speed ratings (Par 98): **103,102,100,100,94 90,89,86,85,83**
CSF £13.92 TOTE £2.10: £1.10, £4.10, £2.70; EX 12.10 Trifecta £76.70.
**Owner** Mrs Fitri Hay **Bred** E O'Leary **Trained** Kingsclere, Hants
**FOCUS**
A fair maiden run at an honest pace.

## 952 32RED FILLIES' H'CAP 1m 1y(P)
**2:30** (2:30) (Class 5) (0-75,72) 4-Y-O+ **£3,408** (£1,006; £503) **Stalls** High

Form RPR
6-45 **1** **Serenity Spa**[44] 369 4-9-7 **72** JamesDoyle 2 78
(Tony Carroll) *chsd ldr tl over 2f out: wnt 2nd again and travelling wl 2f: rdn and ev ch 1f out: led ins fnl f: r.o wl: drvn out* **9/2**[3]
0124 **2** *1/2* **Skidby Mill (IRE)**[14] 775 4-8-10 **61** LiamJones 1 66
(Laura Mongan) *stdd s: hld up in tch in rr: gd hdwy on inner to chal over 1f out: ev ch fnl f: kpt on but unable qck cl home* **8/1**
0031 **3** *nse* **Queen Aggie (IRE)**[21] 697 4-9-6 **71** AdamKirby 3 76
(David Evans) *sn led: hrd pressed and drvn jst over 1f out: hdd ins fnl f: kpt on but unable qck cl home* **7/2**[2]
2533 **4** *2 1/4* **Two In The Pink (IRE)**[11] 819 4-8-8 **59** WilliamCarson 5 59
(Ralph J Smith) *stdd s: hld up in tch: rdn and effrt but wd bnd wl over 1f out: styd on same pce and no imp ins fnl f* **8/1**
-233 **5** *hd* **Pretty Bubbles**[8] 853 5-9-1 **66** FrederikTylicki 6 65
(J R Jenkins) *stdd after s: chsd ldrs tl rdn to chse ldr over 2f out tl 2f out: outpcd and btn 1f out: wknd ins fnl f* **5/4**[1]
1324 **6** *1 1/2* **Medam**[8] 853 5-8-9 **63** NeilFarley(3) 7 59
(Shaun Harris) *stdd after s: hld up in tch: rdn and effrt on outer bnd wl over 1f out: no imp: wknd ins fnl f* **12/1**
1m 38.03s (-0.17) **Going Correction** -0.075s/f (Stan) **6** Ran SP% **114.8**
Speed ratings (Par 100): **97,96,96,94,94 92**
CSF £38.93 TOTE £8.50: £2.30, £3.10; EX 46.80 Trifecta £175.50.
**Owner** Seasons Holidays **Bred** Barry Hurley **Trained** Cropthorne, Worcs
**FOCUS**
A fair fillies' handicap run at a steady pace.

## 953 CORAL.CO.UK CLASSIFIED CLAIMING STKS 1m 2f (P)
**3:05** (3:08) (Class 5) 4-Y-O+ **£3,408** (£1,006; £503) **Stalls** Low

Form RPR
4351 **1** **Munsarim (IRE)**[9] 849 7-9-6 71 (b) AmirQuinn 5 80
(Lee Carter) *stdd s: hld up in midfield: effrt on inner over 1f out: chal and edgd rt ins fnl f: led wl ins fnl f: r.o wl* **3/1**[3]
40-1 **2** *3/4* **Gaelic Silver (FR)**[41] 421 8-9-2 71 GeorgeBaker 1 75
(Gary Moore) *chsd ldr tl rdn to ld over 1f out: hrd pressed and carried rt ins fnl f: hdd and no ex wl ins fnl f* **5/4**[1]
1613 **3** *1 1/2* **Mahadee (IRE)**[21] 685 9-8-9 71 (b) JennyPowell(7) 2 72
(Tom Dascombe) *stdd s: hld up in tch: hdwy to go 3rd 6f out: rdn wl over 1f out: struggling to qckn whn edgd lft and bmpd rival 1f out: outpcd ins fnl f* **11/4**[2]
223 **4** *3 1/4* **Officer In Command (USA)**[14] 775 8-9-6 71 (p) LiamKeniry 3 70
(John Butler) *stdd s: hld up in tch in rr: rdn and effrt wl over 1f out: kpt on but no real imp* **8/1**
0650 **5** *3/4* **Copperwood**[11] 822 9-8-5 60 (v) WilliamCarson 4 53
(Lee Carter) *led: rdn and hdd over 1f out: struggling whn bmpd 1f out: sn wknd* **20/1**
2m 6.8s (0.20) **Going Correction** -0.075s/f (Stan) **5** Ran SP% **112.0**
Speed ratings (Par 103): **96,95,94,91,91**
CSF £7.36 TOTE £3.90: £2.40, £1.50; EX 5.30 Trifecta £21.10.
**Owner** John Joseph Smith **Bred** Shadwell Estate Company Limited **Trained** Epsom, Surrey
**FOCUS**
They went a steady gallop for this tight claimer.

## 954 32RED ON THE APP STORE MAIDEN STKS 1m 1y(P)
**3:45** (3:53) (Class 5) 3-Y-O **£3,408** (£1,006; £503) **Stalls** High

Form RPR
**1** **Equitable** 3-9-5 0 JamesDoyle 7 77+
(Lady Cecil) *in tch in midfield: clsd to trck ldrs 3f out: rdn over 1f out: reminder and chal 1f out: r.o wl under hands and heels to ld wl ins fnl f: gng away at fin* **1/1**[1]
622 **2** *nk* **Bobby Benton (IRE)**[16] 748 3-9-5 72 LukeMorris 4 76
(Luke Dace) *chsd ldr: rdn and ev ch 2f out: led 1f out: r.o wl tl hdd and no ex wl ins fnl f* **6/1**[3]
44-2 **3** *2 1/2* **Three Cliffs**[21] 696 3-9-5 77 WilliamBuick 1 70
(Roger Varian) *led: rdn wl over 1f out: hdd 1f out: outpcd ins fnl f: kpt on* **5/2**[2]
**4** *2 1/4* **Obstinate (IRE)** 3-9-5 0 JimCrowley 2 65+
(Andrew Balding) *chsd ldng pair tl 4th and rdn over 2f out: outpcd and btn over 1f out: plugged on same pce fnl f* **8/1**
55- **5** *1 1/4* **Cotton Club (IRE)**[257] 3853 3-9-5 0 DavidProbert 5 64+
(Rod Millman) *stdd after s: hld up in tch in last pair: 5th and outpcd over 2f out: n.d and kpt on same pce fnl 2f* **20/1**
0- **6** *8* **Graphene**[290] 2741 3-9-5 0 FrederikTylicki 6 44
(Rod Millman) *dropped to rr sn after s and rn green: rdn and outpcd over 2f out: bhd fnl 2f* **33/1**
0 **7** *3 1/4* **Roman Riches**[9] 847 3-8-12 0 HectorCrouch(7) 3 36
(Gary Moore) *in tch in midfield: rdn over 4f out: dropped to rr 3f out: lost tch over 2f out* **100/1**
1m 37.01s (-1.19) **Going Correction** -0.075s/f (Stan) **7** Ran SP% **112.7**
Speed ratings (Par 98): **102,101,99,96,95 87,84**
CSF £7.43 TOTE £2.10: £1.50, £1.70; EX 7.00 Trifecta £17.10.
**Owner** K Abdullah **Bred** Juddmonte Farms Ltd **Trained** Newmarket, Suffolk
**FOCUS**
They went a fair gallop for this maiden.

## 955 32RED IMMORTAL ROMANCE SLOT H'CAP 1m 1y(P)
**4:25** (4:28) (Class 5) (0-75,73) 3-Y-O **£3,408** (£1,006; £503) **Stalls** High

Form RPR
6-21 **1** **Crowdmania**[56] 217 3-9-6 **72** JoeFanning 1 82+
(Mark Johnston) *mde all: rdn and qcknd clr over 1f out: in command and flashed tail ins fnl f: readily* **2/1**[2]
435- **2** *3 1/2* **Ifrika**[86] 8332 3-9-4 **70** KierenFallon 4 71
(Clive Brittain) *in tch in midfield: rdn and lost pl bnd wl over 1f out: no ch w wnr but styd on u.p fnl 100yds: snatched 2nd on post* **8/1**
-115 **3** *shd* **Boogangoo (IRE)**[14] 785 3-9-7 **73** DavidProbert 3 74
(Grace Harris) *hld up in tch in last pair: rdn and hdwy on inner over 1f out: no ch w wnr but wnt 2nd jst ins fnl f: kpt on: lost 2nd on post* **33/1**
1 **4** *1* **Mustajjid**[14] 787 3-9-4 **70** WilliamBuick 2 68
(Roger Varian) *chsd ldrs: rdn over 2f out: outpcd by wnr and btn over 1f out: wnt 2nd briefly 1f out: one pce after* **6/4**[1]
615- **5** *nk* **Relation Alexander (IRE)**[179] 6474 3-9-2 **68** SeanLevey 5 66
(Paul D'Arcy) *hld up in tch in last pair: effrt and n.m.r ent fnl f: no ch w wnr and styd on same pce fnl f* **8/1**
51- **6** *5* **Poker Gold (FR)**[95] 8213 3-9-6 **72** LiamKeniry 6 58
(Heather Main) *t.k.h: chsd wnr tl outpcd u.p over 1f out: lost 2nd 1f out and sn wknd* **6/1**[3]
1m 36.15s (-2.05) **Going Correction** -0.075s/f (Stan) **6** Ran SP% **112.8**
Speed ratings (Par 98): **107,103,103,102,102 97**
CSF £17.99 TOTE £2.50: £1.40, £4.70; EX 15.20 Trifecta £91.20.
**Owner** Sheikh Hamdan bin Mohammed Al Maktoum **Bred** Car Colston Hall Stud **Trained** Middleham Moor, N Yorks
**FOCUS**
A number of unexposed types lined up for this handicap, which was run at a steady pace.

## 956 CORAL MOBILE "JUST THREE CLICKS TO BET" H'CAP 1m 4f (P)
**5:05** (5:05) (Class 2) (0-105,102) 4-Y-O+ **£12,938** (£3,850; £1,924; £962) **Stalls** Low

Form RPR
6420 **1** **Shavansky**[9] 840 10-8-5 **88** ShelleyBirkett(5) 1 96
(Rod Millman) *in tch in midfield: smooth hdwy to join ldrs travelling wl over 1f out: rdn to ld jst ins fnl f: edgd rt but qcknd again whn pressed ins fnl f: comf* **16/1**
-451 **2** *3/4* **Grendisar (IRE)**[41] 427 4-9-1 **95** (p) MartinHarley 4 102
(Marco Botti) *hld up in tch in last pair: rdn and gd hdwy over 1f out: drvn and pressed wnr fnl 100yds: no ex and one pce fnl 75yds* **7/4**[1]
12-3 **3** *3/4* **Duchess Of Gazeley (IRE)**[13] 803 4-8-6 **86** JimmyQuinn 8 92
(Dean Ivory) *chsd ldrs: drvn and sltly outpcd over 1f out: rallied and kpt on again ins fnl f* **5/1**

006- **4** ½ **Angel Gabriel (IRE)**[244] 4310 5-8-11 **89**.......................... KierenFallon 3 94
(Richard Fahey) *in tch in midfield: effrt and n.m.r over 1f out: kpt on u.p ins fnl f* **14/1**

1311 **5** *nse* **Blue Wave (IRE)**[14] 784 4-9-8 **102**.......................... JoeFanning 9 107
(Mark Johnston) *chsd ldr tl rdn to ld 2f out: drvn and hdd jst ins fnl f: no ex and btn whn n.m.r wl ins fnl f* **3/1**[2]

-540 **6** *shd* **Presburg (IRE)**[27] 623 5-8-7 **85**.......................... LukeMorris 2 90
(Joseph Tuite) *wl in tch in midfield: rdn and effrt on outer wl over 1f out: swtchd rt over 1f out: kpt on same pce u.p ins fnl f* **14/1**

24-0 **7** 4½ **Knockgraffon Lad (USA)**[27] 623 7-8-5 **83** oh4..............(t) ChrisCatlin 5 81
(Brendan Powell) *stdd s: t.k.h: hld up in rr: hdwy on outer to press ldrs over 2f out: no ex u.p jst over 1f out: wknd ins fnl f* **50/1**

1-63 **8** 3¼ **Stepping Ahead (FR)**[15] 764 4-9-0 **94**.......................... DanielTudhope 6 86
(K R Burke) *led: rdn and hdd 2f out: lost pl and rdr looking down ent fnl f: sn bhd and eased ins fnl f* **9/2**[3]

2m 28.58s (-4.42) **Going Correction** -0.075s/f (Stan)
**WFA** 4 from 5yo+ 2lb **8** Ran SP% **117.4**
Speed ratings (Par 109): **111,110,110,109,109 109,106,104**
CSF £45.77 CT £170.47 TOTE £17.90: £3.40, £1.20, £2.10; EX 76.30 Trifecta £777.40.
**Owner** The Links Partnership **Bred** George Strawbridge **Trained** Kentisbeare, Devon

**FOCUS**
This decent handicap was run at a solid pace. It suited those coming from the rear.

## 957 32REDPOKER.COM FESTIVAL FREEROLL TONIGHT H'CAP 7f 1y(P)
**5:40** (5:40) (Class 5) (0-70,70) 3-Y-O **£3,408** (£1,006; £503) **Stalls** Low

Form RPR

4-13 **1** **First Experience**[37] 487 3-9-5 **70**.......................... ChrisCatlin 2 74
(Rae Guest) *stdd s: hld up in tch in rr: rdn and hdwy on inner over 1f out: ev ch ins fnl f: r.o wl to ld nr fin* **10/1**

0-1 **2** *hd* **Chantrea (IRE)**[17] 741 3-9-2 **67**.......................... JamesDoyle 4 70
(Lady Cecil) *chsd ldr: upsides over 2f out: rdn and led 1f out: edgd lft ins fnl f: hdd and no ex nr fin* **1/1**[1]

444- **3** ½ **Iseemist (IRE)**[123] 7837 3-9-0 **68**.......................... MichaelJMMurphy(3) 3 70
(John Gallagher) *t.k.h: chsd ldrs: hdwy u.p on inner over 1f out: ev ch ins fnl f: no ex cl home* **16/1**

3231 **4** ½ **Global Explorer (USA)**[16] 745 3-9-2 **67**..........................(t) SeanLevey 5 68
(Stuart Williams) *t.k.h: led: rdn wl over 1f out: hdd 1f out: ev ch after: no ex towards fin* **4/1**[3]

5-41 **5** *shd* **Walk With An Angel**[15] 756 3-9-5 **70**.......................... ShaneKelly 1 70
(Philip McBride) *in tch: hdwy on outer to press ldrs over 2f out: kpt on same pce u.p fnl f: sddle slipped* **3/1**[2]

1m 28.6s (3.80) **Going Correction** -0.075s/f (Stan) **5** Ran SP% **110.0**
Speed ratings (Par 98): **75,74,74,73,73**
CSF £20.85 TOTE £9.70: £2.90, £1.30; EX 20.80 Trifecta £110.00.
**Owner** Fitorfat Racing & Guy Carstairs **Bred** Northmore Stud **Trained** Newmarket, Suffolk

**FOCUS**
Only 3lb covered the field for this handicap which was run at a steady pace.
T/Plt: £80.10 to a £1 stake. Pool: £64623.92 - 588.69 winning tickets T/Qpdt: £14.30 to a £1 stake. Pool: £3262.22 - 167.75 winning tickets SP

# [936] WOLVERHAMPTON (A.W) (L-H)
Friday, March 14

**OFFICIAL GOING: Standard**
Wind: Fresh behind Weather: Overcast

## 958 CORAL APP DOWNLOAD FROM THE APP STORE APPRENTICE H'CAP 1m 1f 103y(P)
**5:55** (5:55) (Class 5) (0-70,69) 4-Y-O+ **£2,911** (£866; £432; £216) **Stalls** Low

Form RPR

2511 **1** **Kindlelight Storm (USA)**[25] 643 4-9-2 **68**.........(b) JordanVaughan(5) 1 73+
(Nick Littmoden) *hld up: hdwy over 1f out: sn hung rt: r.o to ld nr fin* **1/1**[1]

4010 **2** 1 **Attain**[25] 643 5-8-12 **62**.......................... LouisSteward(3) 7 65
(Julia Feilden) *set stdy pce over 5f: pushed along over 2f out: led again over 1f out: hdd nr fin* **6/1**[3]

2533 **3** 1¾ **Yourinthewill (USA)**[25] 643 6-8-13 **63**.......................... PhilipPrince(3) 3 63
(Daniel Mark Loughnane) *trckd ldrs: racd keenly: led 4f out: rdn and hdd over 1f out: no ex towards fin* **7/1**

-040 **4** 1¼ **Innoko (FR)**[13] 801 4-9-2 **66**..........................(t) JoeyHaynes(3) 2 63
(Tony Carroll) *trckd ldr 5f: remained handy: rdn over 2f out: styd on same pce fnl f* **7/1**

/145 **5** 8 **Blackthorn Stick (IRE)**[49] 319 5-8-12 **62**.......................... TimClark(3) 4 44
(John Butler) *s.s: hld up: plld hrd: hdwy 5f out: rdn and wknd over 1f out* **7/2**[2]

2m 8.93s (7.23) **Going Correction** +0.125s/f (Slow) **5** Ran SP% **111.5**
Speed ratings (Par 103): **72,71,69,68,61**
CSF £7.63 TOTE £1.50: £1.10, £4.90; EX 7.70 Trifecta £20.40.
**Owner** Kindlelight Ltd, N Shields & N Littmoden **Bred** Kirsten Rausing **Trained** Newmarket, Suffolk

**FOCUS**
They went no gallop at all early on causing most of the field to race freely and this turned into a bit of a sprint. So although the in-form horse won, the form probably isn't very reliable.

## 959 CORAL MOBILE "JUST THREE CLICKS TO BET" H'CAP 1m 4f 50y(P)
**6:30** (6:30) (Class 7) (0-50,50) 4-Y-O+ **£1,940** (£577; £288; £144) **Stalls** Low

Form RPR

-531 **1** **Goldmadchen (GER)**[25] 640 6-9-7 **50**.......................... GrahamLee 4 60
(James Given) *trckd ldrs: lost pl over 5f out: pushed along and hdwy over 2f out: chsd ldr over 1f out: styd on to ld wl ins fnl f* **9/4**[1]

-200 **2** 1¼ **Ice Tres**[28] 609 5-9-7 **50**.......................... MartinLane 5 58
(Rod Millman) *chsd ldrs: wnt 2nd over 3f out: led wl over 1f out: sn rdn: hdd and unable qck wl ins fnl f* **7/1**[3]

6654 **3** 3¼ **Poste Restante**[30] 580 4-8-9 **47**..........................(p) GeorgeBuckell(7) 12 50
(David Simcock) *hld up: rdn and hdwy over 1f out: styd on: nt rch ldrs* **7/1**[3]

0/0- **4** 1½ **Oliver's Gold**[202] 3727 6-8-13 **45**..........................(p) JasonHart(3) 10 45
(Mark Walford) *hld up: hdwy 1/2-way: rdn over 2f out: styd on same pce fr over 1f out* **4/1**[2]

3-00 **5** 7 **Layla's Boy**[33] 546 7-9-4 **50**..........................(b) RobertTart(3) 1 39
(Simon West) *prom: rdn over 2f out: wknd over 1f out* **20/1**

-500 **6** 2½ **Arte Del Calcio**[17] 737 5-8-11 **45**.......................... JoeyHaynes(5) 3 30
(Tony Carroll) *s.i.s: hld up: pushed along and racd wd fr over 3f out: nvr on terms* **16/1**

0005 **7** 3½ **Dontpaytheferryman (USA)**[3] 912 9-8-13 **49**......(b) DanielCremin(7) 2 29
(Peter Hiatt) *led: plld hrd: clr 8f out tl rdn over 2f out: hdd & wknd wl over 1f out* **14/1**

000- **8** 1¼ **Jewelled Dagger (IRE)**[165] 6895 10-9-2 **45**..................(t) PaddyAspell 6 23
(Sharon Watt) *chsd ldr tl drvn along over 3f out: wknd over 2f out* **16/1**

-644 **9** ½ **Beggers Belief**[15] 759 6-9-5 **48**.......................... LiamJones 11 25
(Zoe Davison) *sn pushed along and a in rr* **7/1**[3]

3656 **10** 1½ **Ocean Power (IRE)**[9] 842 4-8-8 **46**.......................... JordanVaughan(7) 7 20
(Richard Phillips) *mid-div: rdn over 3f out: wknd over 2f out* **14/1**

2m 40.72s (-0.38) **Going Correction** +0.125s/f (Slow)
**WFA** 4 from 5yo+ 2lb **10** Ran SP% **118.1**
Speed ratings (Par 97): **106,105,103,102,97 95,93,92,92,91**
CSF £18.68 CT £97.45 TOTE £2.00: £1.02, £1.80, £3.20; EX 14.30 Trifecta £58.00.
**Owner** Andy Clarke **Bred** Gestut Gorlsdorf **Trained** Willoughton, Lincs

**FOCUS**
A weak handicap and no surprise the only in-form runner in the line-up prevailed.

## 960 32RED CASINO H'CAP 1m 1f 103y(P)
**7:00** (7:00) (Class 6) (0-60,59) 3-Y-O **£2,264** (£673; £336; £168) **Stalls** Low

Form RPR

060- **1** **Enquiring**[152] 7219 3-8-12 **50**.......................... SilvestreDeSousa 1 60+
(Mark Johnston) *sn pushed along to chse ldrs: wnt 2nd over 2f out: styd on u.p to ld wl ins fnl f* **6/4**[1]

-323 **2** 1 **Frederic Chopin**[30] 577 3-9-6 **58**.......................... GrahamLee 5 66
(Stuart Williams) *hld up: hdwy over 5f out: nt clr run 3f out: rdn and hung lft fr over 1f out: styd on to go 2nd nr fin* **3/1**[3]

50-0 **3** ¾ **Uplifted (IRE)**[8] 865 3-9-0 **52**..........................(b) AmyRyan 9 58
(Kevin Ryan) *chsd ldr tl led over 2f out: sn clr: rdn over 1f out: hdd wl ins fnl f* **33/1**

200- **4** 2½ **Suni Dancer**[116] 7944 3-8-7 **45**.......................... MartinLane 4 46
(Paul Green) *trckd ldrs: rdn over 1f out: styd on* **50/1**

0-41 **5** *nk* **Kraka Gym (IRE)**[15] 753 3-9-7 **59**.......................... GrahamGibbons 7 59
(Michael Easterby) *hld up in tch: rdn over 2f out: styd on: nt rch ldrs* **9/4**[2]

435 **6** 3½ **Trinity Lorraine (IRE)**[42] 411 3-8-7 **50**..................(v) NatashaEaton(5) 6 43
(Alan Bailey) *hld up: rdn over 1f out: nvr trbld ldrs* **14/1**

5462 **7** 11 **Previous Acclaim (IRE)**[17] 738 3-8-8 **46**.......................... AdamBeschizza 2 16
(Julia Feilden) *sn led: rdn and hdd over 2f out: wknd over 1f out* **33/1**

06-4 **8** 7 **Ormer**[15] 753 3-8-7 **45**.......................... AndrewMullen 8
(David Evans) *hld up: drvn along over 3f out: sn wknd* **14/1**

2m 1.71s (0.01) **Going Correction** +0.125s/f (Slow) **8** Ran SP% **116.9**
Speed ratings (Par 96): **104,103,102,100,99 96,87,80**
CSF £6.44 CT £99.34 TOTE £3.10: £1.20, £1.90, £5.60; EX 8.00 Trifecta £73.90.
**Owner** Sheikh Hamdan bin Mohammed Al Maktoum **Bred** D J Bloodstock, G Roddick & Wrottesley Ltd **Trained** Middleham Moor, N Yorks

**FOCUS**
A moderate handicap.

## 961 32REDPOKER.COM FESTIVAL FREEROLL TONIGHT H'CAP 2m 119y(P)
**7:30** (7:30) (Class 4) (0-85,83) 4-Y-O+ **£5,175** (£1,540; £769; £384) **Stalls** Low

Form RPR

34-1 **1** **Villa Royale**[7] 870 5-9-11 **83** 6ex.......................... AndrewMullen 3 94+
(Michael Appleby) *a.p: pushed along to ld and edgd lft over 2f out: rdn clr fr over 1f out: eased nr fin* **6/1**

13-2 **2** 4½ **Aryal**[7] 870 4-9-4 **81**..........................(b) SilvestreDeSousa 2 86
(Mark Johnston) *led 1f: trckd ldr: racd keenly: led over 3f out: pushed along whn hdd and hmpd over 2f out: styd on same pce* **5/4**[1]

0-51 **3** 3 **Arr' Kid (USA)**[31] 567 4-9-2 **79**..........................(b) TomEaves 4 79
(Keith Dalgleish) *led after 1f: rdn and hdd over 3f out: outpcd fr over 2f out* **7/2**[3]

416- **4** 18 **Capellanus (IRE)**[26] 3726 8-9-4 **76**.......................... DaleSwift 1 54
(Brian Ellison) *s.s: hld up: rdn and wknd over 3f out* **11/4**[2]

3m 42.48s (0.68) **Going Correction** +0.125s/f (Slow)
**WFA** 4 from 5yo+ 5lb **4** Ran SP% **107.6**
Speed ratings (Par 105): **103,100,99,91**
CSF £13.93 TOTE £7.10; EX 13.10 Trifecta £20.80.
**Owner** David Kuss & Tim Pakyurek **Bred** Lawn Stud **Trained** Danethorpe, Notts

**FOCUS**
A fair little staying handicap.

## 962 32REDBET.COM MAIDEN FILLIES' STKS 7f 32y(P)
**8:00** (8:00) (Class 5) 3-Y-O+ **£2,587** (£770; £384; £192) **Stalls** High

Form RPR

2 **1** **Joie De Reve (IRE)**[37] 486 3-8-10 0.......................... FergusSweeney 1 78+
(David Simcock) *a.p: chsd ldr 1/2-way: shkn up to ld over 1f out: pushed clr fnl f: eased nr fin* **2/5**[1]

306 **2** 7 **Beylerbey (USA)**[11] 824 4-9-12 0.......................... SilvestreDeSousa 3 63
(Mark Johnston) *led: plld hrd: rdn over 2f out: hdd over 1f out: no ex fnl f* **3/1**[2]

03- **3** ½ **Speedbird One**[200] 5819 3-8-10 0.......................... TomEaves 2 56
(James Given) *chsd ldr to 1/2-way: sn rdn: styd on same pce fnl 2f* **8/1**[3]

**4** 25 **Dutch Lady Roseane** 3-8-10 0.......................... AdamBeschizza 5
(James Unett) *s.s: sn pushed along in rr: lost tch fr 1/2-way* **33/1**

1m 31.09s (1.49) **Going Correction** +0.125s/f (Slow)
**WFA** 3 from 4yo 16lb **4** Ran SP% **110.5**
Speed ratings (Par 100): **96,88,87,58**
CSF £1.99 TOTE £1.20; EX 2.10 Trifecta £2.80.
**Owner** Al Asayl Bloodstock Ltd **Bred** Maurice Craig **Trained** Newmarket, Suffolk

**FOCUS**
Probably fairly weak maiden form overall.

## 963 DOWNLOAD THE LADBROKES APP H'CAP 7f 32y(P)
**8:30** (8:31) (Class 6) (0-55,55) 4-Y-O+ **£2,264** (£673; £336; £168) **Stalls** High

Form RPR

-505 **1** **Exceedexpectations (IRE)**[36] 497 5-9-6 **54**..........(vt[1]) GeorgeBaker 6 62+
(John Butler) *mde all: shkn up over 1f out: styd on u.p* **7/4**[1]

6243 **2** 1½ **Lutine Charlie (IRE)**[3] 916 7-9-7 **55**..........................(p) TomQueally 4 59
(Pat Eddery) *hld up: nt clr run over 2f out: hdwy over 1f out: rdn and r.o to go 2nd nr fin: nt rch wnr* **2/1**[2]

55-0 **3** ½ **Triple Aitch (USA)**[43] 384 4-9-0 **55**.......................... JordanVaughan(7) 10 58
(Conrad Allen) *hld up: hdwy over 2f out: rdn to chse wnr over 1f out: edgd lft and styd on same pce ins fnl f* **16/1**

/20- **4** ½ **Red Invader (IRE)**[151] 7253 4-8-13 **54**.......................... JackBudge(7) 1 58+
(Charles Hills) *n.m.r after s: in rr whn stmbld wl over 5f out: nt clr run over 2f out: swtchd rt and hdwy over 1f out: shkn up and r.o ins fnl f: nt rch ldrs* **11/4**[3]

0-60 **5** 4½ **Piccolo Express**[17] 740 8-9-4 **52**..........................(p) AndrewMullen 8 43
(Brian Baugh) *prom: racd keenly: rdn to chse wnr 2f out tl over 1f out: wknd fnl f* **16/1**



The Form Book, Raceform Ltd, Newbury, RG14 5SJ

0503 **6** 3 ¾ **My Scat Daddy (USA)**[8] 858 5-8-12 **46** oh1..................(p) LiamJones 5 28
(Zoe Davison) *dwlt: sn pushed along in rr: nvr nrr* **14/1**

0-06 **7** 3 ¼ **Senora Lobo (IRE)**[13] 799 4-8-7 **46** oh1..................... ShirleyTeasdale(5) 7 20
(Lisa Williamson) *chsd wnr tl rdn 2f out: wknd over 1f out* **50/1**

-040 **8** 1 ¾ **High On The Hog (IRE)**[8] 858 6-8-12 **46** oh1......(p) GrahamGibbons 2 15
(Mark Brisbourne) *prom: pushed along 1/2-way: wknd over 2f out* **16/1**

000- **9** 4 **Basle**[74] 8446 7-9-4 **52**..........................................(t) TomEaves 3 12
(Roy Brotherton) *awkward leaving stalls: sn chsng ldrs: rdn over 2f out: wknd over 1f out* **33/1**

1m 30.01s (0.41) **Going Correction** +0.125s/f (Slow) **9** Ran SP% **125.6**
Speed ratings (Par 101): **102,100,99,99,94 89,86,84,79**
CSF £6.13 CT £44.76 TOTE £3.70: £1.20, £1.90, £3.30; EX 7.10 Trifecta £31.60.
**Owner** Wildcard Racing Syndicate **Bred** R S Cockerill (farms) Ltd & Peter Dodd **Trained** Newmarket, Suffolk

**FOCUS**
Most of these were out of form and the market proved spot-on.

## 964 LADBROKES H'CAP — 1m 141y(P)
**9:00** (9:00) (Class 6) (0-55,55) 4-Y-O+ **£2,264** (£673; £336; £168) **Stalls** Low

Form RPR

000- **1** **Overrider**[74] 8443 4-9-7 **55**..........................................(t) GeorgeBaker 7 62
(Alastair Lidderdale) *mde all: shkn up over 1f out: rdn ins fnl f: jst hld on* **11/4**[2]

42-1 **2** *nk* **Bond Artist (IRE)**[22] 672 5-9-3 **54**................................ RobertTart(3) 9 60
(Geoffrey Oldroyd) *hld up: hdwy over 2f out: rdn over 1f out: r.o wl* **6/4**[1]

1020 **3** *nk* **Katmai River (IRE)**[22] 671 7-8-10 **51**...................... CharlotteJenner(7) 5 56
(Mark Usher) *chsd wnr tl over 6f out: remained handy: rdn over 1f out: r.o* **6/1**

-634 **4** ¾ **Polar Forest**[18] 736 4-9-2 **55**...................................(e) ConnorBeasley(5) 4 59
(Richard Guest) *hld up: nt clr run fr over 2f out tl swtchd lft over 1f out: rdn and r.o: nt rch ldrs* **7/2**[3]

2303 **5** 1 ½ **Do More Business (IRE)**[11] 822 7-9-2 **55**..............(vt) PhilipPrince(5) 1 56
(Liam Corcoran) *hld up: pushed along over 3f out: rdn and r.o ins fnl f: nvr nrr* **8/1**

000- **6** 1 ¾ **Odd Ball (IRE)**[207] 5596 7-8-7 **46** oh1....................... ShirleyTeasdale(5) 8 43
(Lisa Williamson) *prom: chsd wnr over 6f out: rdn and ev ch 2f out: no ex ins fnl f* **50/1**

3255 **7** 1 **Amber Moon**[7] 869 9-8-7 **46** oh1.................................... AnnStokell(5) 3 41
(Ann Stokell) *prom: pushed along over 3f out: no ex fnl f* **33/1**

04-6 **8** 1 ¼ **Limon Squeezy**[66] 76 5-8-12 **46** oh1............................ MartinLane 6 38
(Mike Murphy) *chsd ldrs: rdn over 1f out: styd on same pce* **16/1**

1m 51.6s (1.10) **Going Correction** +0.125s/f (Slow) **8** Ran SP% **125.1**
Speed ratings (Par 101): **100,99,99,98,97 95,95,93**
CSF £8.12 CT £24.23 TOTE £4.90: £1.80, £1.10, £1.50; EX 13.20 Trifecta £54.50.
**Owner** Jersey Royals **Bred** P M Cunningham **Trained** Lambourn, Berks

**FOCUS**
A moderate handicap.
T/Plt: £33.40 to a £1 stake. Pool: £84066.43 - 1833.63 winning tickets T/Qpdt: £16.70 to a £1 stake. Pool: £6308.72 - 277.90 winning tickets CR

965 - 971a (Foreign Racing) - See Raceform Interactive

# [958]WOLVERHAMPTON (A.W) (L-H)
Saturday, March 15

**OFFICIAL GOING: Standard**
Wind: Light against, changing to fresh across after race 4 Weather: Fine

## 972 COMPARE BOOKMAKERS AT BOOKMAKERS.CO.UK H'CAP (DIV I) — 5f 216y(P)
**5:40** (5:40) (Class 6) (0-52,56) 4-Y-O+ **£1,940** (£577; £288; £144) **Stalls** Low

Form RPR

-130 **1** **Catalyze**[9] 864 6-9-6 **51**..........................................(t) MartinHarley 6 57
(Ann Stokell) *mde all: set stdy pce: edgd lft over 3f out: qcknd over 2f out: rdn and edgd rt over 1f out: jst hld on* **5/4**[1]

042 **2** *shd* **Diamond Vine (IRE)**[14] 799 6-9-4 **49**..........................(p) LukeMorris 4 55
(Ronald Harris) *chsd ldrs: wnt 2nd over 3f out: rdn and ev ch fnl f: r.o* **9/4**[2]

0041 **3** 2 ½ **Outbid**[2] 937 4-9-6 **56** 6ex......................................... JoeyHaynes(5) 2 54
(Tony Carroll) *trckd wnr tl hmpd over 3f out: remained handy: rdn and edgd rt fnl f: styd on same pce* **11/4**[3]

-000 **4** 2 **Athwaab**[9] 858 7-9-1 **46** oh1....................................... WilliamCarson 7 38
(Simon Hodgson) *hld up: hdwy u.p over 2f out: styd on same pce fr over 1f out* **33/1**

2300 **5** 1 ¼ **Ishetoo**[2] 937 10-9-0 **48**............................................ SladeO'Hara(3) 5 36
(Peter Grayson) *s.i.s: sn prom: lost pl over 2f out: n.d after* **14/1**

1m 15.72s (0.72) **Going Correction** +0.075s/f (Slow) **5** Ran SP% **111.5**
Speed ratings (Par 101): **98,97,94,91,90**
CSF £4.44 TOTE £2.90: £1.60, £1.70; EX 4.80 Trifecta £9.90.
**Owner** Stephen Arnold **Bred** The Hon Robert Hanson **Trained** Southwell, Notts

**FOCUS**
Not much depth to this.

## 973 COMPARE BOOKMAKERS AT BOOKMAKERS.CO.UK H'CAP (DIV II) — 5f 216y(P)
**6:10** (6:10) (Class 6) (0-52,52) 4-Y-O+ **£1,940** (£577; £288; £144) **Stalls** Low

Form RPR

40-4 **1** **Cadmium Loch**[22] 692 6-8-12 **48**................................(p) JackDuern(5) 9 61
(Andrew Hollinshead) *broke wl: sn stdd and lost pl: hdwy on outer over 2f out: led over 1f out: shkn up and r.o wl* **14/1**

4355 **2** 2 ¾ **Flow Chart (IRE)**[16] 760 7-8-13 **47**.............................. SladeO'Hara(3) 1 52
(Peter Grayson) *sn pushed along to ld: rdn and hdd over 1f out: styd on same pce ins fnl f* **16/1**

6432 **3** *hd* **Very First Blade**[11] 833 5-9-4 **49**................................(be) JoeFanning 7 53
(Michael Mullineaux) *hld up: pushed along 1/2-way: rdn over 1f out: r.o wl ins fnl f* **9/2**[2]

0622 **4** 1 ¾ **Rose Garnet (IRE)**[14] 798 6-9-7 **52**................................(t) LukeMorris 4 51
(Tony Carroll) *chsd ldrs: rdn over 1f out: styd on same pce fnl f* **9/2**[2]

-060 **5** ½ **Steel City Boy (IRE)**[2] 937 11-8-10 **46** oh1................... AnnStokell(5) 6 43
(Ann Stokell) *led early: chsd ldrs: pushed along over 3f out: rdn and lost pl over 2f out: n.d after* **33/1**

-342 **6** *nse* **Masked Dance (IRE)**[11] 835 7-9-6 **51**...................(b) SilvestreDeSousa 2 48
(Scott Dixon) *prom: racd keenly: n.m.r and swtchd lft over 5f out: wnt 2nd over 4f out: rdn and ev ch over 2f out: no ex ins fnl f* **7/4**[1]

1-23 **7** ½ **Daneglow (IRE)**[40] 466 4-9-4 **49**................................(e) TomQueally 3 45
(Mike Murphy) *plld hrd and prom: rdn over 2f out: no ex fnl f* **5/1**[3]

-066 **8** 3 **Renoir's Lady**[14] 798 6-9-5 **50**.................................... GeorgeBaker 8 37
(Joseph Tuite) *hld up: nt clr run over 2f out: n.d* **8/1**

2300 **9** 12 **Red Star Lady (IRE)**[37] 502 4-8-12 **46** oh1..................... NeilFarley(3) 5
(Shaun Harris) *broke wl: sn lost pl: pushed along to go prom again over 4f out: rdn over 2f out: wknd over 1f out* **33/1**

1m 15.49s (0.49) **Going Correction** +0.075s/f (Slow) **9** Ran SP% **118.9**
Speed ratings (Par 101): **99,95,95,92,92 92,91,87,71**
CSF £218.13 CT £1176.98 TOTE £22.40: £4.00, £5.40, £3.40; EX 237.70 Trifecta £1481.70.
**Owner** M Johnson **Bred** R Hollinshead And M Johnson **Trained** Upper Longdon, Staffs

**FOCUS**
They looked to go a solid gallop and no reason why this form shouldn't stand up at this level.

## 974 32RED THUNDERSTRUCK II SLOT H'CAP — 1m 5f 194y(P)
**6:40** (6:43) (Class 6) (0-60,62) 4-Y-O+ **£2,264** (£673; £336; £168) **Stalls** Low

Form RPR

003- **1** **Divea**[180] 6479 5-9-10 **60**............................................. WilliamCarson 6 68+
(Anthony Carson) *hld up: hdwy over 3f out: nt clr run and swtchd rt over 1f out: shkn up to ld wl ins fnl f: readily* **5/4**[2]

4-53 **2** 1 **Celebrian**[26] 640 7-8-10 **46** oh1....................................(t) ChrisCatlin 5 51
(Alex Hales) *chsd ldr after 2f: rdn to ld over 1f out: hdd wl ins fnl f* **14/1**

0-11 **3** 2 ½ **Tokyo Brown (USA)**[10] 848 5-9-12 **62**............................ LukeMorris 2 63
(Heather Main) *trckd ldrs: pushed along over 3f out: rdn and ev ch over 1f out: styd on same pce ins fnl f* **11/10**[1]

611- **4** 2 **Vertueux (FR)**[100] 6099 9-9-8 **58**................................(p) LiamKeniry 7 56
(Tony Carroll) *led: rdn and hdd over 1f out: no ex ins fnl f* **12/1**[3]

6/00 **5** 7 **Cape Safari (IRE)**[11] 831 5-9-5 **55**...................................[1] DavidProbert 4 44
(Tim Vaughan) *hld up: rdn over 2f out: n.d* **25/1**

66-0 **6** 10 **Somerton Star**[38] 484 4-8-6 **46** oh1.............................(v[1]) JoeFanning 1 21
(Pat Eddery) *hld up: rdn over 3f out: wknd over 2f out* **25/1**

00/0 **7** 76 **Muzey's Princess**[31] 580 8-8-10 **46** oh1................. SilvestreDeSousa 3
(Michael Mullineaux) *chsd ldr 2f: remained handy: rdn over 5f out: wknd 4f out: eased* **100/1**

3m 7.46s (1.46) **Going Correction** +0.075s/f (Slow)
**WFA** 4 from 5yo+ 4lb **7** Ran SP% **115.1**
Speed ratings (Par 101): **98,97,96,94,90 85,41**
CSF £18.49 TOTE £2.50: £1.20, £4.30; EX 20.70 Trifecta £39.20.
**Owner** W H Carson **Bred** Lady Bamford **Trained** Newmarket, Suffolk

**FOCUS**
A modest staying handicap.

## 975 32RED H'CAP (BOBIS RACE) — 1m 141y(P)
**7:10** (7:10) (Class 3) (0-95,87) 3-Y-O **£7,246** (£2,168; £1,084; £542; £270) **Stalls** Low

Form RPR

51 **1** **Fitzgerald (IRE)**[19] 735 3-9-0 **80**.................................... MartinHarley 4 87+
(Marco Botti) *trckd ldr: shkn up to ld over 1f out: rdn: edgd lft and hdd ins fnl f: rallied to ld post* **11/10**[1]

331 **2** *hd* **Jaahiez (USA)**[28] 626 3-8-6 **72**...................................... ChrisCatlin 2 79+
(Roger Varian) *hld up: hdwy over 2f out: rdn to ld ins fnl f: hdd post* **5/2**[2]

-321 **3** 2 ¼ **Upholland**[23] 670 3-8-11 **77**........................................(p) TonyHamilton 5 77
(Richard Fahey) *s.s: hdwy over 7f out: rdn over 2f out: styd on* **5/2**[2]

1511 **4** 3 ½ **Frankthetank (IRE)**[16] 761 3-8-7 **73**...............................(p) TomEaves 3 66
(Keith Dalgleish) *led: rdn and hdd over 1f out: no ex ins fnl f* **12/1**[3]

35-0 **5** 14 **Lone Warrior (IRE)**[28] 624 3-9-4 **87**.............................. DeclanBates(3) 1 51
(David Evans) *chsd ldrs: rdn over 3f out: wknd over 2f out* **16/1**

1m 49.7s (-0.80) **Going Correction** +0.075s/f (Slow) **5** Ran SP% **118.3**
Speed ratings (Par 102): **106,105,103,100,88**
CSF £4.66 TOTE £2.00: £1.10, £1.80; EX 4.20 Trifecta £9.90.
**Owner** Al Asayl Bloodstock Ltd **Bred** Sh Sultan Bin Khalifa Al Nahyan **Trained** Newmarket, Suffolk

**FOCUS**
A cracking little contest with four of the five runners winning last time out and all bar the top horse had a progressive profile. The pace was solid and the form looks useful.

## 976 32RED.COM MEDIAN AUCTION MAIDEN STKS — 1m 141y(P)
**7:40** (7:41) (Class 5) 3-Y-O **£2,911** (£866; £432; £216) **Stalls** Low

Form RPR

330- **1** **Arrowzone**[140] 7529 3-9-5 71........................................... AdamKirby 2 74
(Garry Moss) *trckd ldr tl qcknd to ld over 2f out: rdn over 1f out: r.o wl: comf* **10/11**[1]

**2** 5 **Drifter (IRE)** 3-9-5 0............................................... StephenCraine 3 63+
(Tom Dascombe) *trckd ldrs: plld hrd: rdn over 1f out: styd on same pce fnl f* **9/4**[2]

033- **3** *shd* **Solo Hunter**[152] 7243 3-9-2 69...................................... DeclanBates(3) 1 62
(David Evans) *sn pushed along to ld: rdn and hdd over 2f out: styd on same pce fnl f* **9/2**[3]

0-45 **4** 3 ½ **Honiton Lace**[22] 684 3-9-0 62.......................................... JoeFanning 5 50
(J W Hills) *hld up: rdn over 1f out: sn outpcd: eased whn hld ins fnl f* **8/1**

1m 51.47s (0.97) **Going Correction** +0.075s/f (Slow) **4** Ran SP% **112.4**
Speed ratings (Par 98): **98,93,93,90**
CSF £3.42 TOTE £1.60; EX 3.60 Trifecta £6.70.
**Owner** Ron Hull **Bred** J K Beckitt And Son **Trained** Tickhill, S Yorks

**FOCUS**
A modest maiden.

## 977 CORAL MOBILE "JUST THREE CLICKS TO BET" H'CAP — 1m 1f 103y(P)
**8:10** (8:10) (Class 3) (0-95,93) 4-Y-O+ **£7,439** (£2,213; £1,106; £553) **Stalls** Low

Form RPR

0-15 **1** **Thatchmaster (USA)**[34] 550 4-8-7 **79**............................... JoeFanning 6 90
(Mark Johnston) *trckd ldr after 1f: racd keenly: shkn up to ld over 1f out: edgd lft ins fnl f: rdn out* **10/1**

0001 **2** 1 **Tepmokea (IRE)**[17] 752 8-9-4 **90**...............................(p) ShaneKelly 2 99
(Andrew Hollinshead) *led: shkn up over 2f out: rdn and hdd over 1f out: styd on* **16/1**

353- **3** 1 **Centurius**[154] 7205 4-9-7 **93**...................................... MartinHarley 1 100
(Marco Botti) *trckd ldrs: rdn over 2f out: styd on same pce ins fnl f* **5/4**[1]

5-12 **4** 1 ¼ **Commissar**[24] 655 5-8-8 **80**...............................(t) SilvestreDeSousa 7 85
(Ian Williams) *hld up: hdwy over 2f out: rdn over 1f out: hung lft and styd on same pce ins fnl f* **7/2**[3]

1210 **5** *hd* **Star Links (USA)**[7] 887 8-9-6 **92**.................................(b) LukeMorris 4 96
(S Donohoe, Ire) *chsd ldr 1f: remained handy: rdn over 3f out: styd on same pce fnl f* **3/1**[2]

3410 **6** 6 **Tatting**[11] 832 5-8-10 **82**............................................ LiamKeniry 8 75
(Chris Dwyer) *hld up: rdn over 2f out: nt trble ldrs* **16/1**

300- **7** 22 **Lord Of The Dance (IRE)**[148] 7337 8-9-0 **86**.................... TomEaves 3 37
(Michael Mullineaux) *s.i.s: hld up: rdn and wknd over 2f out* **50/1**

1m 59.13s (-2.57) **Going Correction** +0.075s/f (Slow) **7** Ran SP% **114.5**
Speed ratings (Par 107): **114,113,112,111,110 105,86**
CSF £144.00 CT £336.37 TOTE £6.50: £6.00, £3.40; EX 128.40 Trifecta £358.90.
**Owner** Sheikh Hamdan bin Mohammed Al Maktoum **Bred** Darley **Trained** Middleham Moor, N Yorks

**FOCUS**
This decent contest looked to be run at a fairly sound gallop and, given the quality and age of animal involved, it was no surprise it produced the best time performance (per furlong) of the evening. However, nothing got into it from off the pace and the front two filled those positions throughout.

**978 CORAL APP DOWNLOAD FROM THE APP STORE H'CAP** 1m 4f 50y(P)
**8:40** (8:40) (Class 5) (0-70,66) 4-Y-0+ **£2,911** (£866; £432) **Stalls** Low

Form RPR
2412 1 **Sian Gwalia**[8] 872 4-9-2 **63** MartinLane 4 72+
(David Simcock) *trckd ldrs: a gng wl: hmpd wl over 1f out: led on bit 1f out: easily* **8/15**[1]
-035 2 2 ¼ **Star Of Namibia (IRE)**[32] 567 4-9-0 **61** (v[1]) SilvestreDeSousa 1 64
(Michael Mullineaux) *led: rdn over 3f out: hdd 1f out: styd on same pce* **4/1**[3]
300- 3 2 ¼ **Nadema Rose (IRE)**[316] 1993 5-9-3 **62** TomEaves 3 61
(Keith Dalgleish) *chsd ldr: rdn over 2f out: no ex ins fnl f* **7/2**[2]
2m 41.23s (0.13) **Going Correction** +0.075s/f (Slow)
**WFA** 4 from 5yo+ 2lb 3 Ran SP% **107.5**
Speed ratings (Par 103): **102,100,99**
CSF £2.90 TOTE £1.80; EX 2.40 Trifecta £2.10.
**Owner** Mrs Ann Simcock **Bred** Mrs A E Simcock **Trained** Newmarket, Suffolk
**FOCUS**
A weak race.

**979 LADBROKES H'CAP** 7f 32y(P)
**9:10** (9:10) (Class 5) (0-70,74) 4-Y-0+ **£2,911** (£866; £432) **Stalls** High

Form RPR
5522 1 **Hierarch (IRE)**[9] 852 7-8-11 **67** (p) GeorgeBuckell(7) 3 72
(David Simcock) *trckd ldr tl led over 1f out: rdn and edgd lft ins fnl f: r.o* **5/2**[2]
3011 2 *hd* **Khajaaly (IRE)**[9] 862 7-9-11 **74** (vt) AndrewMullen 1 79
(Michael Appleby) *trckd ldrs: racd keenly: rdn over 1f out: chsd wnr ins fnl f: r.o* **8/11**[1]
3300 3 3 ¼ **Kyllachy Star**[26] 646 8-9-5 **68** (v) TomEaves 4 65
(Richard Fahey) *led: rdn and hdd over 1f out: no ex ins fnl f* **4/1**[3]
1m 30.78s (1.18) **Going Correction** +0.075s/f (Slow) 3 Ran SP% **106.5**
Speed ratings (Par 103): **96,95,92**
CSF £4.75 TOTE £2.90; EX 4.70 Trifecta £5.20.
**Owner** Tick Tock Partnership **Bred** Castlemartin Stud And Skymarc Farm **Trained** Newmarket, Suffolk
**FOCUS**
The finish was fought out by the two in-form runners.
T/Plt: £599.50 to a £1 stake. Pool: £69,814.92 - 85.0 winning tickets. T/Qpdt: £109.50 to a £1 stake. Pool: £7,488.72 - 50.60 winning tickets. CR

980 - 983a (Foreign Racing) - See Raceform Interactive

## 920 SAINT-CLOUD (L-H)
Saturday, March 15

**OFFICIAL GOING: Turf: soft**

**984a PRIX EXBURY (GROUP 3) (4YO+) (TURF)** 1m 2f
**1:30** (12:00) 4-Y-0+ **£33,333** (£13,333; £10,000; £6,666; £3,333)

RPR
1 **Norse King (FR)**[146] 7410 5-9-2 0 AlexisBadel 7 116+
(Mme M Bollack-Badel, France) *midfield in tch: rdn and swtchd rt over 1f out: drifted lft u.p but styd on strly and led ent fnl 100yds: pushed out and drew clr: readily* **9/5**[1]
2 1 ¾ **Singing (FR)**[143] 7572 4-8-9 0 OlivierPeslier 8 106
(C Laffon-Parias, France) *led: pushed along over 2f out: rdn over 1f out: styd on but hdd ent fnl 100yds and readily outpcd by wnr: no ex* **107/10**
3 *snk* **Rose Vista (FR)**[138] 5-8-6 0 Christophe-PatriceLemaire 3 102+
(J-L Guillochon, France) *hld up towards rr on inner: last 2f out: swtchd rt and rdn over 1f out: styd on strly towards fin and wnt 3rd fnl strides: nvr nrr* **31/1**
4 *hd* **Au Revoir (IRE)**[188] 6250 4-8-9 0 MaximeGuyon 6 105
(A Fabre, France) *trckd ldr on outer: rdn over 2f out: styd on wl u.p but nt quite pce to chal and dropped to 4th fnl strides* **6/1**[3]
5 ¾ **Vanishing Cupid (SWI)**[133] 7705 4-8-11 0 (p) FabriceVeron 1 105
(H-A Pantall, France) *trckd ldr on inner: rdn 2f out: styd on wl against rail but nt quite pce to chal: no ex and dropped to 5th cl home* **31/5**
6 1 ¼ **Zagros (FR)**[24] 669 5-8-9 0 CristianDemuro 4 101
(J Heloury, France) *hld up and sn towards rr: rdn over 2f out: styd on same pce u.p and nvr able to chal* **18/1**
7 ¾ **Vally Jem (FR)**[137] 7613 5-8-8 0 (p) AntoineHamelin 10 98
(D Sepulchre, France) *dropped in fr wdst draw and hld up towards rr early: midfield on outer 1/2-way: rdn over 2f out: outpcd ins fnl f: n.d* **83/10**
8 *nk* **Spirit's Revench (FR)**[97] 8212 4-8-9 0 ThierryJarnet 9 99
(P Demercastel, France) *dwlt sltly but qckly rcvrd: midfield in tch on outer: prom 1/2-way: rdn and effrt to chal 2f out: no ex and wknd ins fnl f* **201/10**
9 *shd* **Aussi Celebre (IRE)**[21] 723 5-8-9 0 (b) GregoryBenoist 5 99
(E Lellouche, France) *midfield on inner: rdn 2f out: sn outpcd and btn: n.d* **9/2**[2]
10 *hd* **Superplex (FR)**[161] 7049 4-9-0 0 UmbertoRispoli 2 103
(M Figge, Germany) *hld up and a in rr: rdn over 2f out: sn outpcd: nvr a factor* **187/10**
2m 10.19s (-5.81) 10 Ran SP% **119.6**
WIN (incl. 1 euro stake): 2.80. PLACES: 1.50, 3.20, 5.40. DF: 16.00. SF: 23.40.
**Owner** J C Smith **Bred** Littleton Stud **Trained** Lamorlaye, France

985 - 986a (Foreign Racing) - See Raceform Interactive

## 921 KEMPTON (A.W) (R-H)
Monday, March 17

**OFFICIAL GOING: Standard**
Wind: Light; across Weather: Dry and bright

**987 TURFTV H'CAP** 5f (P)
**2:20** (2:20) (Class 5) (0-70,69) 4-Y-0+ **£2,587** (£770; £384; £192) **Stalls** Low

Form RPR
5201 1 **Secret Millionaire (IRE)**[12] 845 7-9-4 **66** RichardHughes 3 73
(Tony Carroll) *chsd ldrs tl wnt 2nd after 1f out: rdn to chal over 1f out: led wl ins fnl f: r.o wl* **4/1**[2]
2055 2 ¾ **Island Legend (IRE)**[21] 730 8-9-6 **68** (b) RichardKingscote 6 72
(Milton Bradley) *led: rdn and hrd pressed over 1f out: hdd and styd on same pce wl ins fnl f* **12/1**[3]
211 3 *hd* **Seamster**[24] 688 7-9-0 **62** (bt) GrahamLee 1 67
(Richard Ford) *chsd ldr tl hmpd and dropped to 3rd after 1f: waiting for gap on inner over 1f out: gap opened and effrt 1f out: ev ch ins fnl f: styd on same pce fnl 75yds* **15/8**[1]
0541 4 1 ¾ **Dishy Guru**[16] 797 5-8-9 **57** (b) LiamKeniry 4 54
(Michael Blanshard) *hld up in tch: rdn and effrt to chse ldng trio over 1f out: styd on same pce and no imp* **4/1**[2]
2303 5 ¾ **Welease Bwian (IRE)**[17] 777 5-9-7 **69** AdamBeschizza 7 64
(Stuart Williams) *v.s.a: detached in last: rdn and hdwy on inner over 1f out: kpt on but n.d* **4/1**[2]
452- 6 ¾ **Ladweb**[151] 7324 4-9-1 **66** MichaelJMMurphy(3) 2 58
(John Gallagher) *t.k.h: hld up in tch in midfield: rdn and no hdwy over 1f out: 6th and wl hld fnl f* **14/1**
2533 7 1 ½ **Welsh Inlet (IRE)**[16] 798 6-8-2 **55** oh2 RyanWhile(5) 5 41
(John Bridger) *in tch in midfield: rdn and dropped to rr over 1f out: wl hld after* **25/1**
59.54s (-0.96) **Going Correction** 0.0s/f (Stan) 7 Ran SP% **113.0**
Speed ratings (Par 103): **107,105,105,102,101 100,97**
CSF £47.30 TOTE £3.80: £2.50, £4.40; EX 21.10 Trifecta £52.60.
**Owner** Robert E Lee Syndicate **Bred** James Delaney **Trained** Cropthorne, Worcs
**FOCUS**
Fair form for the level and the pace held up well. The winner is clearly in good form.

**988 KEMPTON FREE ENTRY WITH BETVICTOR APP MEDIAN AUCTION MAIDEN STKS** 1m 2f (P)
**2:50** (2:50) (Class 5) 3-5-Y-0 **£2,587** (£770; £384; £192) **Stalls** Low

Form RPR
1 **Wonder Weapon (GER)** 3-8-8 0 DavidProbert 1 73+
(Andrew Balding) *led for over 1f: stdd and in tch in midfield after: rdn and effrt to chse clr ldr over 1f out: 3 l down jst ins fnl f: styd on wl to ld nr fin* **1/1**[1]
2 *nk* **Russian Remarque** 3-8-8 0 ShaneKelly 8 72+
(Jonathan Portman) *s.i.s: sn rcvrd and pressed ldr over 8f out: led 2f out: rdn: rn green but qcknd clr over 1f out: 3 l clr jst ins fnl f: tired fnl 100yds and hdd nr fin* **20/1**
3 ½ **Dream Big (IRE)** 3-8-5 0 ow2 ChrisCatlin 7 68+
(Jo Crowley) *s.i.s: hld up in tch in last pair: effrt in 5th over 1f out: styd on to go 3rd wl ins fnl f: rn green and hung lft towards fin* **14/1**
4 4 1 ½ **Arianrhod (IRE)**[14] 828 3-8-3 72 (b[1]) PaoloSirigu 5 63
(Marco Botti) *t.k.h: hld up wl in tch in midfield: rdn and effrt to chse ldrs over 1f out: kpt on ins fnl f* **3/1**[2]
056- 5 3 **Buy Out Boy**[176] 6666 3-8-8 63 BenCurtis 6 62
(Jo Hughes) *t.k.h: chsd ldr tl led over 8f out: set stdy gallop tl hdd and rdn 2f out: outpcd over 1f out: wknd ins fnl f* **25/1**
6 5 **Sea Tiger**[29] 4-10-0 0 FergusSweeney 4 57
(Alan King) *hld up wl in tch in midfield: rdn and outpcd wl over 1f out: sn wknd* **6/1**[3]
66 7 8 **Diamond Back (IRE)**[14] 823 3-8-3 0 TimClark(5) 3 37
(Denis Quinn) *chsd ldrs: rdn and lost pl jst over 2f out: wknd and bhd over 1f out* **50/1**
40 8 14 **Wings Of Fire (IRE)**[17] 787 4-10-0 0 AdamKirby 2
(Denis Quinn) *t.k.h: chsd ldrs tl stdd in to last pair after 2f: rdn and lost tch over 2f out* **16/1**
2m 9.06s (1.06) **Going Correction** 0.0s/f (Stan)
**WFA** 3 from 4yo 20lb 8 Ran SP% **112.4**
Speed ratings (Par 103): **95,94,94,93,90 86,80,69**
CSF £26.38 TOTE £1.90: £1.02, £4.50, £3.10; EX 19.90 Trifecta £157.30.
**Owner** N Botica, Rex & Mrs Wendy Gorell **Bred** Stiftung Gestut Fahrhof **Trained** Kingsclere, Hants
**FOCUS**
A moderate maiden dominated by newcomers. The form could easily be worth another 5lb or so.

**989 GEORGE BATTLE CELEBRATORY H'CAP** 1m 4f (P)
**3:20** (3:20) (Class 6) (0-60,60) 4-Y-0+ **£1,940** (£577; £288; £144) **Stalls** Centre

Form RPR
2601 1 **Thane Of Cawdor (IRE)**[14] 821 5-9-7 **60** (p) JimCrowley 4 67
(Joseph Tuite) *hld up in tch: swtchd lft and effrt over 2f out: ev ch over 1f out: led jst ins fnl f: kpt on wl u.p* **3/1**[2]
0452 2 ½ **Elegant Ophelia**[14] 821 5-9-6 **59** (t) AdamKirby 5 65
(Dean Ivory) *chsd ldrs: rdn and effrt jst over 2f out: ev ch over 1f out: styd on same pce wl ins fnl f* **7/1**[3]
40/2 3 ½ **Orpen'Arry (IRE)**[20] 737 6-8-13 **57** DavidKenny(5) 6 62
(Paul Burgoyne) *led and set stdy gallop tl hdd 5f out: rdn over 2f out: ev ch over 1f out: styd on same pce fnl 100yds* **16/1**
40-6 4 *nk* **Booktheband (IRE)**[56] 252 4-8-9 **50** HayleyTurner 10 55
(Clive Brittain) *chsd ldrs tl wnt 2nd over 4f out: rdn jst over 2f out: drvn and ev ch over 1f out: styd on same pce fnl 100yds* **8/1**
-232 5 1 ½ **Dance**[18] 759 5-8-9 **48** FrederikTylicki 8 51
(Rod Millman) *chsd ldr tl led 5f out: hrd pressed and rdn ent fnl 2f: hdd jst ins fnl f: outpcd fnl 100yds* **7/1**[3]
6-23 6 ½ **Maison Brillet (IRE)**[19] 747 7-9-7 **60** (p) RobertHavlin 1 62
(Clive Drew) *hld up in tch in midfield: rdn and effrt on inner 2f out: hdwy and pressed ldrs ent fnl f: outpcd fnl 100yds* **7/1**[3]
0030 7 1 **James Pollard (IRE)**[12] 838 9-8-12 **51** (t) MartinLane 3 51
(Bernard Llewellyn) *stdd s: hld up in last pair: rdn and effrt over 2f out: no imp tl styd on steadily ins fnl f: nvr gng pce to trble ldrs* **25/1**
6-22 8 1 **Super Duplex**[14] 822 7-9-6 **59** (t) RichardHughes 2 58
(Roger Teal) *in tch in midfield: rdn and unable qck over 1f out: one pce and no imp fnl f* **11/4**[1]

-040 **9** *1 ½* **Lily Edge**[14] 815 5-9-3 **56**.................. GrahamLee 9 52
(John Bridger) *in tch in last trio: rdn and no imp over 2f out: n.d after* **25/1**
2m 34.97s (0.47) **Going Correction** 0.0s/f (Stan)
**WFA** 4 from 5yo+ 2lb **9** Ran SP% **113.9**
Speed ratings (Par 101): **98,97,97,97,96 95,95,94,93**
CSF £24.00 CT £280.81 TOTE £5.10: £2.20, £2.00, £2.90; EX 21.10 Trifecta £179.90.
**Owner** Alan & Christine Bright **Bred** Balmerino Bldstock & Newsells Park Stud **Trained** Great Shefford, Berks

**FOCUS**
A weak handicap run at a stop-star gallop. Straightforward form.

## 990 BETVICTOR.COM H'CAP 1m 3f (P)
3:50 (3:50) (Class 5) (0-75,72) 4-Y-0+ £2,587 (£770; £384; £192) Stalls Low

Form RPR
0/32 **1** **Rocky Elsom (USA)**[19] 747 7-8-11 **62**.................. JimCrowley 3 71
(David Arbuthnot) *led tl 8f out: rdn and effrt ent fnl 2f: led jst over 1f out: clr ins fnl f: r.o wl* **13/2**[3]
-554 **2** *2 ¾* **Reflect (IRE)**[11] 856 6-9-2 **67**..................(vt) DaleSwift 6 72
(Derek Shaw) *stdd s: t.k.h: hld up in last pair: rdn and effrt on inner 2f out: styd on to go 2nd fnl 75yds: no threat to wnr* **4/1**[2]
6-42 **3** *½* **Aldeburgh**[33] 582 5-9-2 **67**.................. GeorgeBaker 7 71
(Jim Old) *stdd s: hld up in midfield tl hdwy to ld 8f out: rdn and hdd jst over 1f out: no ex and one pce fnl f* **2/1**[1]
65-2 **4** *nk* **Manomine**[12] 849 5-9-4 **69**.................. FrederikTylicki 5 73
(Clive Brittain) *chsd ldrs tl rdn and outpcd over 2f out: rallied and kpt on again ins fnl f: no threat to wnr* **4/1**[2]
6-00 **5** *2* **Thecornishcowboy**[16] 801 5-9-3 **68**..................(t) AdamKirby 4 69
(John Ryan) *chsd ldr tl 8f out: rdn and outpcd over 2f out: plugged on same pce fr over 1f out: eased cl home* **4/1**[2]
0000 **6** *2 ½* **Planetoid (IRE)**[16] 801 6-8-10 **68**.................. AprilKitchener(7) 1 65
(Jim Best) *stdd s: hld up in last: rdn and outpcd over 2f out: n.d after* **25/1**
2m 21.77s (-0.13) **Going Correction** 0.0s/f (Stan) **6** Ran SP% **110.5**
Speed ratings (Par 103): **100,98,97,97,95 94**
CSF £31.03 TOTE £7.40: £5.30, £2.70; EX 36.10 Trifecta £54.90.
**Owner** A T A Wates & J G M Wates **Bred** Michael Ryan **Trained** Beare Green, Surrey

**FOCUS**
The pace was steady for this modest handicap. Straightforward form.

## 991 £25 FREE BET AT BETVICTOR.COM H'CAP 6f (P)
4:20 (4:20) (Class 3) (0-95,94) 4-Y-0+
£7,158 (£2,143; £1,071; £535; £267; £134) Stalls Low

Form RPR
16-0 **1** **Upavon**[58] 235 4-8-13 **86**.................. LiamKeniry 1 94
(David Elsworth) *chsd ldng trio: rdn and effrt to chal between horses ent fnl f: hld on gamely ins fnl f: all out* **9/1**
2-61 **2** *nk* **Baddilini**[9] 890 4-9-1 **88**..................(p) RichardHughes 9 95
(Alan Bailey) *hld up in tch in midfield: swtchd lft and effrt 2f out: drvn and styd on wl ins fnl f: wnt 2nd cl home: nt quite rch wnr* **7/1**[3]
4010 **3** *¾* **Corporal Maddox**[16] 804 7-9-0 **87**..................(p) AdamKirby 4 92
(Ronald Harris) *hld up in tch in midfield: rdn and effrt wl over 1f out: styd on wl ins fnl f: wnt 3rd last strides* **12/1**
3112 **4** *hd* **Trojan Rocket (IRE)**[9] 890 6-9-1 **88**..................(p) RichardKingscote 10 92
(Michael Wigham) *chsd ldr: rdn and ev ch over 1f out: styd on same pce ins fnl f* **7/1**[3]
000- **5** *nk* **Another Wise Kid (IRE)**[175] 6699 6-8-13 **86**.................. GrahamLee 5 89
(Paul Midgley) *hld up in tch towards rr: hdwy on inner over 1f out: chsng ldrs whn swtchd lft and nt clr run ins fnl f: nvr much room but kpt on towards fin* **33/1**
-450 **6** *½* **Clear Praise (USA)**[14] 820 7-8-7 **80**.................. HayleyTurner 2 82
(Simon Dow) *taken down early: led: rdn over 1f out: hdd ins fnl f: no ex and wknd towards fin* **25/1**
00-0 **7** *nk* **Piscean (USA)**[37] 534 9-9-6 **93**.................. GeorgeBaker 6 95
(Tom Keddy) *stdd after s: hld up in tch in rr: hdwy jst over 1f out: swtchd lft 1f out: kpt on: nt rch ldrs* **7/1**[3]
00-0 **8** *3* **Yeeoow (IRE)**[23] 715 5-9-3 **90**.................. MartinHarley 8 82
(K R Burke) *chsd ldng trio: rdn and effrt over 2f out: unable qck over 1f out: wknd ins fnl f* **7/4**[1]
505- **9** *nk* **Barnet Fair**[170] 6830 6-9-4 **94**.................. OisinMurphy(3) 7 85
(Lee Carter) *taken down early: hld up in tch towards rr: rdn and effrt over 2f out: no imp: nvr trbld ldrs* **13/2**[2]
1-56 **10** *2 ½* **Novellen Lad (IRE)**[26] 658 9-8-9 **82**.................. ChrisCatlin 3 66
(Willie Musson) *hld up in tch towards rr: rdn and no hdwy over 2f out: nvr trbld ldrs* **16/1**
1m 11.39s (-1.71) **Going Correction** 0.0s/f (Stan) **10** Ran SP% **117.6**
Speed ratings (Par 107): **111,110,109,109,108 108,107,103,103,100**
CSF £71.17 CT £782.32 TOTE £10.10: £3.20, £2.90, £3.90; EX 87.40 Trifecta £2009.50 Part won..
**Owner** McPabb Racing **Bred** Major-Gen Guy Watkins **Trained** Newmarket, Suffolk

**FOCUS**
A competitive sprint handicap run at a good gallop with a compressed finish. Straightforward form at the level.

## 992 DOWNLOAD THE BETVICTOR APP NOW H'CAP 2m (P)
4:50 (4:50) (Class 5) (0-70,70) 4-Y-0+ £2,587 (£770; £384; £192) Stalls Low

Form RPR
02-3 **1** **Arty Campbell (IRE)**[53] 292 4-9-7 **70**.................. MartinLane 2 79+
(Bernard Llewellyn) *hld up in tch in last quartet: gd hdwy on outer and edging rt ent fnl 2f: led wl over 1f out: clr and in command 1f out: r.o wl* **7/2**[1]
24-5 **2** *2 ½* **Montjess (IRE)**[56] 260 4-9-7 **70**..................(p) LiamJones 5 76
(Laura Mongan) *chsd ldrs: rdn and unable qck whn sltly hmpd 2f out: rallied u.p ins fnl f: wnt 2nd wl ins fnl f: no threat to wnr* **12/1**
0632 **3** *¾* **Arashi**[12] 842 8-9-5 **63**..................(v) DaleSwift 4 68
(Derek Shaw) *hld up in last pair: rdn and hdwy towards inner ent fnl 2f: battling for 2nd but no threat to wnr* **7/1**
-215 **4** *nk* **Graylyn Ruby (FR)**[32] 590 9-8-9 **53**.................. FrederikTylicki 10 58
(Robert Eddery) *in tch in midfield: hdwy over 3f out: rdn to ld over 2f out: hdd and outpcd by wnr wl over 1f out: battled on tl lost 2 pls wl ins fnl f* **9/1**
/013 **5** *3 ¼* **Mighty Mambo**[14] 818 7-9-3 **61**..................(tp) GeorgeBaker 1 62
(Lawney Hill) *hld up in tch in midfield: nt clr run and shuffled bk 4f out: swtchd lft and hdwy over 2f out: battling for 2nd but no ch w wnr over 1f out: hmpd and wknd ins fnl f* **6/1**
35-0 **6** *5* **The Absent Mare**[14] 818 6-9-3 **61**.................. AdamKirby 9 56
(Robin Dickin) *stdd s: hld up in last quartet: rdn and sme hdwy jst over 2f out: plugged on but n.d* **25/1**
5-26 **7** *2 ½* **Bramshill Lass**[18] 758 5-9-12 **70**.................. JimCrowley 6 62
(Amanda Perrett) *hld up in last quartet: rdn and no real imp jst over 2f out: plugged on but n.d* **4/1**[2]
2312 **8** *7* **Shalambar (IRE)**[14] 818 8-9-8 **66**..................(v) JamesDoyle 11 49
(Tony Carroll) *chsd ldrs: wnt 2nd over 4f out tl over 2f out: wknd u.p wl over 1f out: wl btn and eased fnl f* **5/1**[3]
3000 **9** *1 ¾* **Wild Desert (FR)**[14] 818 9-9-8 **66**.................. SteveDrowne 7 48
(Tony Carroll) *led tl rdn and hdd over 2f out: wknd u.p over 1f out: bhd and eased ins fnl f* **33/1**
05-6 **10** *¾* **Topolski (IRE)**[11] 856 8-9-8 **66**.................. GrahamLee 3 48
(David Arbuthnot) *chsd ldrs: rdn and unable qck over 2f out: wknd over 1f out: bhd and eased ins fnl f* **16/1**
060/ **11** *17* **Young Lou**[24] 7132 5-8-13 **57**.................. LiamKeniry 8 18
(Robin Dickin) *chsd ldr: rdn 6f out: lost 2nd 4f out and sn struggling: t.o over 1f out* **66/1**
3m 28.52s (-1.58) **Going Correction** 0.0s/f (Stan)
**WFA** 4 from 5yo+ 5lb **11** Ran SP% **117.5**
Speed ratings (Par 103): **103,101,101,101,99 97,95,92,91,91 83**
CSF £45.85 CT £282.61 TOTE £4.80: £2.00, £5.20, £2.70; EX 50.60 Trifecta £243.40.
**Owner** Alex James **Bred** Airlie Stud **Trained** Fochriw, Caerphilly

**FOCUS**
An ordinary staying handicap. The form fits in behind the impressive winner.

## 993 FOLLOW @BETVICTORRACING ON TWITTER H'CAP 6f (P)
5:20 (5:22) (Class 6) (0-65,65) 4-Y-0+ £1,940 (£577; £288; £144) Stalls Low

Form RPR
4050 **1** **Foie Gras**[20] 740 4-8-9 **58**.................. ConnorBeasley(5) 7 68
(Chris Dwyer) *in tch in midfield: effrt u.p over 1f out: styd on u.p to ld fnl 75yds: gng away at fin* **8/1**
-540 **2** *2* **Teen Ager (FR)**[14] 817 10-9-1 **59**..................(p) JimmyQuinn 9 63
(Paul Burgoyne) *hld up in tch in midfield: rdn and effrt 2f out: styd on to press ldrs ins fnl f: wnt 2nd but outpcd by wnr fnl 50yds* **20/1**
-410 **3** *½* **Compton Prince**[30] 628 5-9-4 **65**..................(b) RobertTart(3) 6 68
(Milton Bradley) *chsd ldr tl rdn to ld over 1f out: hdd and no ex fnl 75yds* **12/1**
025- **4** *½* **Sakhee's Rose**[165] 6982 4-9-6 **64**..................(b) GeorgeBaker 5 65
(Ed McMahon) *hld up towards rr: swtchd lft and hdwy 2f out: kpt on wl ins fnl f* **7/1**
-531 **5** *nk* **New Rich**[33] 576 4-9-5 **63**..................(p) JohnFahy 1 63
(Eve Johnson Houghton) *chsd ldrs: rdn and effrt 2f out: styd on same pce ins fnl f* **7/2**[1]
2400 **6** *¾* **Prince Of Passion (CAN)**[18] 766 6-9-3 **61**..................(v) MartinLane 2 59
(Derek Shaw) *led: rdn and hdd over 1f out: wknd ins fnl f* **33/1**
0-6 **7** *1 ¾* **Ceelo**[19] 746 4-9-7 **65**.................. LiamKeniry 4 58
(Lydia Pearce) *in tch in midfield: rdn and no hdwy on inner over 1f out: plugged on same pce fnl f* **5/1**[2]
10-0 **8** *½* **Harrogate Fair**[19] 746 4-9-7 **65**.................. LiamJones 10 56
(Michael Squance) *hld up towards rr: swtchd to outer and effrt over 2f out: kpt on but nvr a threat to ldrs* **12/1**
-040 **9** *nk* **Last Minute Lisa (IRE)**[12] 846 4-9-0 **58**.................. RichardHughes 8 48
(Sylvester Kirk) *stdd s: hld up off the pce in last pair: rdn and effrt 2f out: kpt on but nvr a threat to ldrs* **20/1**
4020 **10** *1 ¼* **Climaxfortackle (IRE)**[33] 576 6-9-3 **61**.................. DaleSwift 12 47+
(Derek Shaw) *stdd and dropped in bhd after s: hld up wl off the pce in rr: rdn and effrt over 1f out: nvr trbld ldrs* **12/1**
10-0 **11** *1* **Gung Ho Jack**[12] 841 5-9-6 **64**.................. SteveDrowne 11 47
(John Best) *hld up in tch in midfield: rdn and no hdwy over 2f out: wknd over 1f out* **16/1**
-000 **12** *1 ¾* **El Mirage (IRE)**[30] 628 4-9-6 **64**.................. JimCrowley 3 42
(Dean Ivory) *chsd ldrs: rdn over 2f out: wknd over 1f out: fdd ins fnl f* **13/2**[3]
1m 12.58s (-0.52) **Going Correction** 0.0s/f (Stan) **12** Ran SP% **117.3**
Speed ratings (Par 101): **103,100,99,99,98 97,95,94,94,92 91,88**
CSF £158.70 CT £1905.92 TOTE £8.00: £2.50, £4.60, £4.40; EX 196.70 Trifecta £2404.40 Part won..
**Owner** Mrs Shelley Dwyer **Bred** Sir Eric Parker **Trained** Newmarket, Suffolk

**FOCUS**
A moderate sprint handicap run at an even pace. The winner has a pretty good record here.
T/Jkpt: Not won. T/Plt: £361.20 to a £1 stake. Pool: £92829.50 - 187.59 winning tickets T/Qpdt: £72.60 to a £1 stake. Pool: £5633.24 - 57.35 winning tickets SP

# 972 WOLVERHAMPTON (A.W) (L-H)
Monday, March 17

**OFFICIAL GOING: Standard**
Wind: Light behind Weather: Cloudy with sunny spells

## 994 COMPARE BOOKMAKERS AT BOOKMAKERS.CO.UK MAIDEN STKS 5f 216y(P)
3:00 (3:00) (Class 5) 3-Y-O+ £2,911 (£866; £432; £216) Stalls Low

Form RPR
0-2 **1** **Crazee Diamond**[21] 731 3-8-7 0 ow2.................. WilliamTwiston-Davies(3) 2 70+
(Mick Channon) *hld up in tch: led over 1f out: shkn up and r.o wl: comf* **9/4**[2]
**2** *3 ¼* **Jan Van Hoof (IRE)** 3-8-13 0.................. TonyHamilton 4 62+
(Richard Fahey) *s.i.s and green early on: hdwy over 2f out: rdn to chse wnr ins fnl f: no imp* **5/4**[1]
33 **3** *2 ¾* **Role Reversal**[14] 824 3-8-8 0.................. LukeMorris 1 48+
(James Tate) *trckd ldr tl led over 2f out: rdn and hdd over 1f out: wknd ins fnl f* **7/2**[3]
40-4 **4** *1 ½* **Stoneacre Hull (IRE)**[21] 731 5-9-4 47.................. SladeO'Hara(3) 5 48
(Peter Grayson) *chsd ldrs: rdn over 1f out: hung lft and wknd fnl f* **50/1**
**5** *6* **Torridon** 3-8-13 0.................. JoeFanning 6 31
(Mark Johnston) *prom: n.m.r and lost pl 4f out: wknd 2f out* **7/1**
6036 **6** *nk* **Countess Lupus (IRE)**[17] 855 3-8-3 47..................(b) ShirleyTeasdale(5) 3 25
(Lisa Williamson) *sn led: rdn and hdd over 2f out: wknd over 1f out* **66/1**
0000 **7** *11* **Mrs Medley**[28] 645 8-9-2 20..................(v) AnnStokell(5) 7
(Ann Stokell) *prom tl rdn and wknd over 2f out* **100/1**
1m 15.24s (0.24) **Going Correction** +0.10s/f (Slow)
**WFA** 3 from 5yo+ 13lb **7** Ran SP% **114.4**
Speed ratings (Par 103): **102,97,94,92,84 83,68**
CSF £5.46 TOTE £3.20: £1.80, £1.20; EX 8.80 Trifecta £18.50.
**Owner** Nick & Olga Dhandsa & John & Zoe Webster **Bred** Mrs G S Rees **Trained** West Ilsley, Berks

**FOCUS**
A weak and slowly run maiden with Stoneacre Hull, officially rated just 47, not beaten all that far in fourth. The winner won with something in hand.

## 995 LADBROKES H'CAP 1m 141y(P)
**3:30** (3:30) (Class 5) (0-75,78) 4-Y-0+ **£2,911** (£866; £432) **Stalls** Low

Form RPR
1151 **1** **Tee It Up Tommo (IRE)**[5] 927 5-9-10 **78** 6ex............ RobertWinston 5 85+
(Michael Wigham) *trckd ldr: wnt upsides on bit over 2f out: shkn up to ld over 1f out: sn hung lft: c clr ins fnl f* **8/11**[1]
316- **2** *5* **Who's Shirl**[179] 6567 8-9-7 **75**.......................... PaulMulrennan 3 70
(Chris Fairhurst) *prom: pushed along over 3f out: rdn to go 2nd ins fnl f: no ch w wnr* **14/1**[3]
3-23 **3** *3 ¼* **Canon Law (IRE)**[37] 539 4-9-6 **74**...................... DanielTudhope 2 63
(David O'Meara) *led: rdn over 2f out: hdd over 1f out: hung lft and nt clr run sn after: wknd wl ins fnl f* **6/4**[2]
1m 51.9s (1.40) **Going Correction** +0.10s/f (Slow) **3** Ran SP% **104.6**
Speed ratings (Par 103): **97,92,89**
CSF £6.99 TOTE £1.50; EX 7.50 Trifecta £5.90.
**Owner** Palatinate Thoroughbred Racing Limited **Bred** Oghill House Stud **Trained** Newmarket, Suffolk
**FOCUS**
With his main market rival looking one to avoid, Tee It Up Tommo had little to beat and did the job with considerable ease. It's not hard to have reservations about the form.

## 996 DOWNLOAD THE LADBROKES APP H'CAP 7f 32y(P)
**4:00** (4:00) (Class 6) (0-60,59) 4-Y-0+ **£2,264** (£673; £336; £168) **Stalls** High

Form RPR
5046 **1** **Darnathean**[14] 815 5-9-5 **57**..............................(p) SeanLevey 4 65
(Paul D'Arcy) *hld up: hdwy 1/2-way: rdn to chse ldr ins fnl f: edgd lft and r.o to ld post* **9/2**[3]
0040 **2** *shd* **Coach Montana (IRE)**[12] 846 5-8-7 **45**..............(b) LukeMorris 9 53
(Christine Dunnett) *mde all: qcknd clr over 2f out: rdn over 1f out: hdd post* **25/1**
1-13 **3** *hd* **Kasbhom**[44] 425 4-9-7 **59**...............................(t) WilliamCarson 5 67
(Anthony Carson) *hld up: hdwy over 2f out: nt clr run and swtchd lft over 1f out: rdn and r.o wl* **2/1**[1]
-065 **4** *3 ¼* **Hold The Star**[49] 358 8-8-2 **45**.................. ShirleyTeasdale(5) 6 44
(Ann Stokell) *chsd wnr: rdn over 2f out: no ex and lost 2nd ins fnl f* **50/1**
300- **5** *nk* **Prigsnov Dancer (IRE)**[80] 8411 9-8-11 **56**...........(p) DavidParkes(7) 3 55
(Deborah Sanderson) *chsd ldrs: rdn over 2f out: styd on same pce fnl f* **25/1**
3-46 **6** *1* **Izzy Boy (USA)**[13] 835 4-9-6 **58**........................... JoeFanning 2 54
(Mark Johnston) *prom: rdn over 2f out: no ex ins fnl f* **5/2**[2]
20-3 **7** *3 ¼* **Monte Cassino (IRE)**[6] 918 9-9-3 **58**.........(e) GeorgeChaloner(3) 7 46
(Bryan Smart) *hld up: rdn over 2f out: nvr trbld ldrs* **9/2**[3]
6005 **8** *12* **Waterloo Dock**[12] 851 9-8-9 **47**.......................(p) PaddyAspell 8 6
(Mick Quinn) *chsd ldrs: rdn 1/2-way: wknd over 2f out* **33/1**
05-0 **9** *26* **Glenridding**[35] 562 10-9-6 **58**.........................(p) TomQueally 1
(James Given) *s.i.s: sn pushed along in rr: bhd fnl 4f* **16/1**
1m 30.04s (0.44) **Going Correction** +0.10s/f (Slow) **9** Ran SP% **116.7**
Speed ratings (Par 101): **101,100,100,96,96 95,91,78,48**
CSF £109.05 CT £295.84 TOTE £6.10: £1.60, £4.60, £1.90; EX 74.80 Trifecta £375.40.
**Owner** K Snell **Bred** K Snell **Trained** Newmarket, Suffolk
**FOCUS**
A tight finish and moderate form, rated around the second.

## 997 32RED H'CAP 2m 119y(P)
**4:30** (4:30) (Class 6) (0-55,54) 4-Y-0+ **£2,264** (£673; £336; £168) **Stalls** Low

Form RPR
50/1 **1** **Sir Frank Morgan (IRE)**[6] 915 4-8-13 **51** 6ex.............. JoeFanning 3 61+
(Mark Johnston) *trckd ldr tl led over 6f out: rdn over 1f out: styd on wl: eased nr fin* **1/4**[1]
0/0- **2** *2 ½* **Tallulah Mai**[20] 4605 7-9-2 **49**........................... LukeMorris 5 56
(Alastair Lidderdale) *hld up: hdwy 12f out: rdn to chse wnr over 2f out: ev ch over 1f out: no ex ins fnl f* **20/1**
6543 **3** *4* **Poste Restante**[3] 959 4-8-2 **47**.....................(p) GeorgeBuckell(7) 6 49
(David Simcock) *hld up: hdwy on outer over 2f out: rdn over 1f out: styd on same pce* **6/1**[2]
4506 **4** *15* **Excellent News (IRE)**[6] 915 5-8-5 **45**..............(b[1]) JackGarritty(7) 4 29
(Tony Forbes) *chsd ldrs: wnt 2nd over 5f out tl rdn over 2f out: sn wknd* **33/1**
6213 **5** *½* **Fair Breeze**[17] 781 7-9-0 **54**.....................(b) KieranShoemark(7) 2 37
(Richard Phillips) *s.i.s: sn prom: rdn and wknd over 3f out* **10/1**[3]
06/- **6** *11* **Maid Of Silk (IRE)**[151] 6769 8-9-4 **51**..................(t) PaddyAspell 1 21
(Neil Mulholland) *led 10f: rdn and wknd over 3f out* **25/1**
3m 41.17s (-0.63) **Going Correction** +0.10s/f (Slow)
**WFA** 4 from 5yo+ 5lb **6** Ran SP% **114.9**
Speed ratings (Par 101): **105,103,101,94,94 89**
CSF £9.62 TOTE £1.20: £1.10, £6.40; EX 8.40 Trifecta £25.80.
**Owner** Paul Dean **Bred** Airlie Stud **Trained** Middleham Moor, N Yorks
**FOCUS**
Uncompetitive stuff. The winner has the scope to do better.

## 998 CORAL.CO.UK BEST ODDS GUARANTEED ON RACING H'CAP 1m 1f 103y(P)
**5:00** (5:01) (Class 6) (0-60,60) 4-Y-0+ **£2,264** (£673; £336; £168) **Stalls** Low

Form RPR
5-54 **1** **Teide Peak (IRE)**[37] 538 5-9-5 **58**.......................... SeanLevey 7 66
(Paul D'Arcy) *hld up: pushed along over 2f out: hdwy over 1f out: r.o to ld wl ins fnl f* **6/4**[1]
4124 **2** *1* **India's Song**[14] 822 4-9-0 **60**.....................(t) GeorgeBuckell(7) 5 66
(David Simcock) *hld up: hdwy on outer over 2f out: led over 1f out: rdn and hdd wl ins fnl f* **2/1**[2]
0320 **3** *1 ¼* **General Tufto**[13] 831 9-8-12 **51**.....................(b) TomQueally 6 55
(Charles Smith) *pushed along in rr early: shkn up 1/2-way: rdn over 1f out: r.o ins fnl f: nt rch ldrs* **16/1**
-230 **4** *4 ½* **Strandfield Bay (IRE)**[24] 695 8-9-4 **57**..................(p) JoeFanning 1 52
(Sharon Watt) *chsd ldr tl led 2f out: rdn and hdd over 1f out: wknd ins fnl f* **10/1**
3035 **5** *1 ¾* **Do More Business (IRE)**[3] 964 7-8-12 **56**...........(vt) PhilipPrince(5) 3 48
(Liam Corcoran) *prom: rdn over 2f out: wknd over 1f out* **10/1**
000 **6** *1 ¾* **Kristal Hart**[26] 660 5-9-5 **58**.......................... PaddyAspell 2 47
(Neil Mulholland) *led: rdn and hdd 2f out: wknd fnl f* **20/1**
4503 **7** *1 ¼* **Delightful Sleep**[21] 736 6-8-13 **57**........................ EoinWalsh(5) 4 43
(David Evans) *trckd ldrs: ev ch over 1f out: wknd ins fnl f* **6/1**[3]
2m 2.26s (0.56) **Going Correction** +0.10s/f (Slow) **7** Ran SP% **116.4**
Speed ratings (Par 101): **101,100,99,95,93 91,90**
CSF £4.88 CT £30.99 TOTE £2.50: £1.10, £1.70; EX 7.30 Trifecta £48.00.
**Owner** C M Wilson **Bred** Blue Bloodstock Ltd **Trained** Newmarket, Suffolk
**FOCUS**
A moderate handicap in which the first three came from the rear. The winner took advantage of a good mark.

## 999 CORAL APP DOWNLOAD FROM THE APP STORE H'CAP 1m 4f 50y(P)
**5:30** (5:30) (Class 4) (0-85,83) 4-Y-0+ **£5,175** (£1,540; £769; £384) **Stalls** Low

Form RPR
2241 **1** **The Lock Master (IRE)**[18] 764 7-9-7 **83**.................. AndrewMullen 5 92
(Michael Appleby) *trckd ldr tl led wl over 3f out: rdn over 2f out: edgd rt fnl f: styd on* **7/2**[3]
3142 **2** *2* **Mica Mika (IRE)**[9] 891 6-9-1 **77**......................... TonyHamilton 4 83
(Richard Fahey) *led tl wl over 3f out: sn rdn: styd on same pce ins fnl f: wnt 2nd post* **9/2**
0-31 **3** *shd* **Lineman**[21] 732 4-8-9 **73**................................ ShaneKelly 3 79
(Andrew Hollinshead) *trckd ldrs: rdn to go 2nd over 3f out: styd on same pce ins fnl f: lost 2nd post* **5/2**[2]
301 **4** *½* **Royal Alcor (IRE)**[9] 891 7-9-5 **81**........................(t) TomQueally 1 86
(Gay Kelleway) *hld up: pushed along over 3f out: hdwy over 1f out: sn rdn: styd on same pce ins fnl f* **2/1**[1]
3025 **5** *1* **All The Winds (GER)**[21] 732 9-8-7 **72** ow1(t) WilliamTwiston-Davies(3) 2 75
(Shaun Lycett) *hld up: hdwy over 4f out: rdn over 1f out: no ex ins fnl f* **10/1**
2m 41.94s (0.84) **Going Correction** +0.10s/f (Slow)
**WFA** 4 from 6yo+ 2lb **5** Ran SP% **111.4**
Speed ratings (Par 105): **101,99,99,99,98**
CSF £18.91 TOTE £3.50: £3.10, £1.80; EX 15.00 Trifecta £53.30.
**Owner** K G Kitchen **Bred** Patrick F Kelly **Trained** Danethorpe, Notts
**FOCUS**
A fair handicap, but all bar the favourite bunched up leaving the back straight and the time was more than a second slower than the following Class 6. A minor career best from the winner.

## 1000 CORAL MOBILE "JUST THREE CLICKS TO BET" H'CAP 1m 4f 50y(P)
**6:00** (6:00) (Class 6) (0-65,68) 4-Y-0+ **£2,264** (£673; £336; £168) **Stalls** Low

Form RPR
-205 **1** **Spanish Plume**[21] 733 6-9-2 **65**.......................(p) JackDuern(5) 5 70
(Andrew Hollinshead) *hld up: hdwy over 2f out: led on bit 1f out: sn shkn up: styd on* **7/1**[3]
0440 **2** *½* **Mazij**[17] 781 6-8-7 **51**.................................... LukeMorris 1 55
(Peter Hiatt) *trckd ldrs: nt clr run over 2f out: rdn over 1f out: r.o to go 2nd post* **12/1**
0352 **3** *hd* **Star Of Namibia (IRE)**[2] 978 4-9-1 **61**................(v) JoeFanning 4 65
(Michael Mullineaux) *pushed along in rr early: hdwy to chse ldr over 9f out: led 2f out: rdn and hdd 1f out: kpt on* **7/1**[3]
5451 **4** *1 ¼* **Arabian Heights**[5] 922 6-9-5 **68** 6ex.................... GeorgeDowning(5) 3 70
(Ian Williams) *hld up: rdn over 2f out: hdwy over 1f out: styd on same pce ins fnl f* **5/6**[1]
23-4 **5** *shd* **Alborz (IRE)**[71] 64 5-9-7 **65**.............................. LeeTopliss 6 67
(Tim Vaughan) *trckd ldrs: rdn over 2f out: hmpd and lost pl wl over 1f out: styd on ins fnl f* **9/2**[2]
43-0 **6** *½* **Silk Route**[19] 747 4-9-4 **64**.............................. WilliamCarson 2 65
(Giles Bravery) *led: rdn and hdd 2f out: no ex ins fnl f* **20/1**
2m 40.74s (-0.36) **Going Correction** +0.10s/f (Slow)
**WFA** 4 from 5yo+ 2lb **6** Ran SP% **110.2**
Speed ratings (Par 101): **105,104,104,103,103 103**
CSF £74.97 TOTE £8.10: £3.00, £6.70; EX 55.00 Trifecta £179.10.
**Owner** The Three R'S **Bred** Mrs J A Prescott **Trained** Upper Longdon, Staffs
■ Stewards' Enquiry : Lee Topliss two-day ban: careless riding
**FOCUS**
A moderate contest. The winner can rate a bit higher.
T/Plt: £11.50 to a £1 stake. Pool: £53472.51 - 3366.84 winning tickets T/Qpdt: £5.50 to a £1 stake. Pool: £5179.76 - 688.00 winning tickets CR

# 928 SOUTHWELL (L-H)
Tuesday, March 18

**OFFICIAL GOING: Standard**
Wind: Fresh; half behind Weather: Cloudy with showers

## 1001 BOOKMAKERS.CO.UK H'CAP 5f (F)
**2:20** (2:20) (Class 6) (0-58,64) 4-Y-0+ **£2,587** (£770; £384; £192) **Stalls** High

Form RPR
5351 **1** **Caramelita**[7] 908 7-9-13 **64** 6ex.....................(v) FrederikTylicki 6 72
(J R Jenkins) *trckd ldrs: hdwy over 2f out: chal over 1f out: rdn to take slt ld ins fnl f: kpt on wl* **6/1**
-403 **2** *hd* **Dancing Freddy (IRE)**[7] 908 7-9-6 **57**...............(tp) WilliamCarson 7 64
(Ann Stokell) *prom: cl up 1/2-way: led wl over 1f out: sn jnd and rdn: hdd and drvn ins fnl f: kpt on* **5/1**[3]
-232 **3** *1* **Heartsong (IRE)**[7] 908 5-9-6 **57**.......................... TomQueally 1 61
(John Gallagher) *dwlt and in rr: pushed along on wd outside 1/2-way: hdwy wl over 1f out: sn rdn and styd on fnl f: nrst fin* **7/2**[2]
0-05 **4** *hd* **China Excels**[12] 864 7-8-8 **50**........................ NathanAlison(5) 3 53
(Mandy Rowland) *dwlt and in rr: hdwy over 2f out: sn rdn and styd on wl appr fnl f: nrst fin* **8/1**
5551 **5** *¾* **Lucky Mark (IRE)**[25] 692 5-9-2 **53**....................(v) AdamKirby 8 53
(Garry Moss) *racd towards stands' rail: prom: rdn along 2f out: drvn appr fnl f and sn one pce* **3/1**[1]
6005 **6** *2* **Fathom Five (IRE)**[6] 934 10-9-2 **53**....................... PaddyAspell 5 46
(Shaun Harris) *sn led: rdn along 2f out: sn hdd and grad wknd appr fnl f* **14/1**
0000 **7** *1* **Upper Lambourn (IRE)**[12] 864 6-8-9 **46** oh1...............(t) JoeFanning 4 35
(Christopher Kellett) *in tch: rdn along over 2f out: sn wknd* **14/1**
6-00 **8** *½* **Two Turtle Doves (IRE)**[43] 466 8-9-3 **54**.............. SilvestreDeSousa 2 42
(Michael Mullineaux) *dwlt: a towards rr* **20/1**
-634 **9** *1 ¾* **Pearl Noir**[6] 934 4-9-3 **54**................................(b) LukeMorris 9 35
(Scott Dixon) *racd towards stands' rail: prom: rdn along 1/2-way: sn wknd* **11/2**
59.59s (-0.11) **Going Correction** -0.025s/f (Stan) **9** Ran SP% **122.8**
Speed ratings (Par 101): **99,98,97,96,95 92,90,89,87**
CSF £38.51 CT £125.27 TOTE £7.50: £2.10, £2.60, £1.20; EX 26.90 Trifecta £69.00.


The Form Book, Raceform Ltd, Newbury, RG14 5SJ

**Owner** La Senoritas **Bred** R B Hill **Trained** Royston, Herts
■ Stewards' Enquiry : William Carson two-day ban: used whip above permitted level (Apr 1-2)
Frederik Tylicki two-day ban: used whip above permitted level (Apr 1-2)

**FOCUS**
A competitive race given the lowly grade and it served up an exciting finish. The winner could do a bit better than this.

## 1002 LADBROKES MOBILE MEDIAN AUCTION MAIDEN STKS 1m (F)
**2:50** (2:50) (Class 6) 3-5-Y-O **£2,587** (£770; £384; £192) **Stalls** Low

Form RPR
0-30 **1** **Soul Of Motion**[18] 795 3-8-11 68 ...[1] DavidProbert 3 70
(Gay Kelleway) *trckd ldrs: hdwy on outer 3f out: chal over 2f out: rdn to ld wl over 1f out: styd on wl fnl f* **9/2**[3]
6 **2** *1* **Moonlit Sky**[25] 684 3-8-11 0 ... LukeMorris 5 68
(James Tate) *trckd ldng pair on outer: hdwy over 3f out: led wl over 2f out: sn jnd and rdn: hdd wl over 1f out: sn drvn and kpt on same pce fnl f* **5/4**[1]
4-64 **3** *12* **Flying Author (IRE)**[34] 577 3-8-11 45 ... PaddyAspell 4 40
(Phil McEntee) *sn slt ld: rdn along and hdd wl over 2f out: drvn wl over 1f out and one pce* **12/1**
**4** *6* **Lince Suertudo (FR)** 3-8-11 0 ... DaleSwift 1 26
(Michael Blake) *cl up: rdn along 3f out: sn rn green and outpcd fnl 2f* **10/1**
0- **5** *18* **Born To Reign**[137] 7654 3-8-11 0 ... TomQueally 2
(Michael Bell) *in rr and pushed along after 2f: rdn 1/2-way: sn outpcd and bhd* **9/4**[2]
1m 45.76s (2.06) **Going Correction** +0.10s/f (Slow) 5 Ran SP% **110.2**
Speed ratings (Par 101): **93,92,80,74,56**
CSF £10.68 TOTE £4.00: £2.00, £1.10; EX 10.00 Trifecta £22.10.
**Owner** Matt Bartram, Gay Kelleway & Adrian Parr **Bred** A Christou **Trained** Exning, Suffolk

**FOCUS**
A weak race that took little winning. The first two were clear.

## 1003 CORAL APP DOWNLOAD FROM THE APP STORE H'CAP 1m 3f (F)
**3:25** (3:26) (Class 5) (0-75,80) 4-Y-O+ **£3,234** (£962; £481; £240) **Stalls** Low

Form RPR
-336 **1** **Lean On Pete (IRE)**[18] 782 5-9-0 72 ... JacobButterfield(5) 6 81
(Ollie Pears) *hld up in rr: hdwy 4f out: rdn to chse ldr over 1f out: styd on wl fnl f to ld last 50yds* **8/1**[3]
6245 **2** *1¼* **Doldrums (USA)**[10] 891 4-9-6 74 ... JoeFanning 5 81
(Mark Johnston) *trckd ldrs: cl up 4f out: led wl over 2f out: rdn clr wl over 1f out: drvn ins fnl f: hdd and no ex last 50yds* **3/1**[1]
1011 **3** *7* **A Little Bit Dusty**[7] 911 6-9-13 80 6ex ... (p) HayleyTurner 7 76
(Conor Dore) *trckd ldr: hdwy to ld 3f out: sn rdn and hdd: drvn and one pce fr wl over 1f out* **7/2**[2]
100- **4** *11* **He's A Striker (IRE)**[174] 6743 4-9-3 71 ... DaleSwift 2 49
(Michael Blake) *dwlt and hld up in rr: hdwy on outer over 4f out: chsd ldng pair over 2f out: sn rdn and btn* **3/1**[1]
026- **5** *11* **Brockfield**[94] 8299 8-8-13 66 ... SilvestreDeSousa 4 27
(Mel Brittain) *led: pushed along 4f out: rdn and hdd 3f out: sn wknd: eased over 1f out* **7/2**[2]
500- **6** *6* **Al Enbess (IRE)**[261] 3861 4-8-9 63 ... JamesSullivan 8 14
(Ruth Carr) *trckd ldrs on outer: rdn along wl over 3f out: sn wknd* **33/1**
244 **7** *7* **After The Storm**[18] 776 5-8-12 65 ... (p) LukeMorris 3 5
(John O'Shea) *hld up towards rr: sme hdwy over 4f out: sn rdn along and wknd over 3f out* **10/1**
**8** *13* **Longshadow**[253] 4133 4-9-2 70 ... PJMcDonald 1
(Jason Ward) *chsd ldrs on inner: rdn along over 5f out: sn lost pl and bhd* **25/1**
2m 26.91s (-1.09) **Going Correction** +0.10s/f (Slow)
**WFA** 4 from 5yo+ 1lb 8 Ran SP% **121.4**
Speed ratings (Par 103): **107,106,101,93,85 80,75,66**
CSF £34.40 CT £103.38 TOTE £8.50: £2.50, £1.90, £1.30; EX 52.50 Trifecta £105.70.
**Owner** K C West **Bred** Mrs T Mahon **Trained** Norton, N Yorks

**FOCUS**
They went off plenty hard enough in this handicap and there's a suspicion the race fell apart. The first two took well to the surface.

## 1004 CORAL MOBILE "JUST THREE CLICKS TO BET" (S) STKS 1m 4f (F)
**4:00** (4:03) (Class 6) 4-Y-O+ **£2,587** (£770; £384; £192) **Stalls** Low

Form RPR
-100 **1** **Mr Burbidge**[17] 803 6-9-5 88 ... (b) LiamKeniry 6 90
(Neil Mulholland) *trckd ldr: smooth hdwy to ld over 4f out: pushed clr 3f out: easily* **1/10**[1]
**2** *9* **Teajaybe (USA)**[74] 46 6-8-13 63 ... BenCurtis 4 65
(Chris Dwyer) *trckd ldng pair: hdwy to chse wnr 4f out: rdn 3f out: drvn 2f out and sn no imp* **8/1**[2]
00/ **3** *18* **Freedom Flying**[91] 1231 11-8-8 0 ... (t) JamesSullivan 5 31
(Lee James) *bhd: pushed along after 4f: rdn 1/2-way: styd on fnl 3f to take remote 3rd ins fnl f* **80/1**
0050 **4** *4½* **Dontpaytheferryman (USA)**[4] 959 9-8-13 45 ... (b) WilliamCarson 1 29
(Peter Hiatt) *led: rdn along and hdd over 4f out: sn wknd: lost remote 3rd ins fnl f* **20/1**[3]
0 **5** *74* **Vortex Star**[6] 930 5-8-13 0 ... RussKennemore 2
(Michael Chapman) *a in rr: outpcd and bhd after 4f: t.o fnl 5f* **80/1**
2m 40.17s (-0.83) **Going Correction** +0.10s/f (Slow) 5 Ran SP% **109.3**
Speed ratings (Par 101): **106,100,88,85,35**
CSF £1.39 TOTE £1.10: £1.10, £1.40; EX 1.50 Trifecta £13.50.The winner was bought in for 20,500gns
**Owner** Dajam Ltd **Bred** M Burbidge **Trained** Limpley Stoke, Wilts

**FOCUS**
Stand Guard's controversial absence provided a mere penalty kick for the winner, who is too good for this level.

## 1005 32RED.COM H'CAP (BOBIS RACE) 5f (F)
**4:30** (4:30) (Class 4) (0-85,72) 3-Y-O **£5,822** (£1,732; £865; £432) **Stalls** High

Form RPR
13-1 **1** **Razin' Hell**[54] 302 3-8-12 63 ... (v) SilvestreDeSousa 1 69
(Alan McCabe) *mde most: rdn and edgd rt jst over 1f out: drvn ins fnl f: jst hld on* **4/1**[2]
0-31 **2** *nse* **Fuel Injection**[28] 650 3-9-0 65 ... (p) JamesSullivan 5 71
(Paul Midgley) *chsd wnr: cl up 1/2-way: rdn and edging lft whn sltly hmpd and swtchd lft jst over 1f out: drvn and hung lft ins fnl f: styd on wl towards fin: jst failed* **10/1**
21 **3** *1¾* **Eva Clare (IRE)**[19] 765 3-9-4 69 ... BenCurtis 3 69
(K R Burke) *chsd ldng pair: swtchd lft and rdn wl over 1f out: hld whn sltly hmpd and swtchd rt ins fnl f: kpt on same pce* **4/1**[2]
2222 **4** *4* **Argent Touch**[19] 762 3-9-0 65 ... DaleSwift 2 50
(Derek Shaw) *chsd ldrs: rdn along 2f out: sn one pce* **7/1**[3]
1-24 **5** *12* **National Service (USA)**[31] 624 3-9-7 72 ... SeanLevey 4 14
(Stuart Williams) *dwlt and sn rdn along: a bhd* **10/11**[1]
59.33s (-0.37) **Going Correction** -0.025s/f (Stan) 5 Ran SP% **114.0**
Speed ratings (Par 100): **101,100,98,91,72**
CSF £37.94 TOTE £5.90: £2.80, £6.40; EX 32.80 Trifecta £96.80.
**Owner** Timms, Timms, McCabe & Warke **Bred** Alan J McCabe **Trained** Averham Park, Notts

**FOCUS**
Some progressive sprinters locked horns in this feature handicap. The winner's task was eased by the favourite's no-show.

## 1006 32RED IMMORTAL ROMANCE SLOT H'CAP 6f (F)
**5:05** (5:05) (Class 5) (0-75,72) 3-Y-O **£3,234** (£962; £481; £240) **Stalls** Low

Form RPR
3111 **1** **Alumina (IRE)**[32] 613 3-9-7 72 ... DavidProbert 2 83
(Andrew Balding) *mde most: qcknd clr over 2f out: rdn wl over 1f out: drvn ins fnl f: kpt on wl towards fin* **4/6**[1]
3-30 **2** *¾* **Brownsville (USA)**[22] 731 3-9-0 65 ... JoeFanning 5 74
(Mark Johnston) *trckd ldng pair: hdwy on outer to chse wnr over 2f out: rdn wl over 1f out: styd on fnl f: no imp towards fin* **5/1**[3]
4312 **3** *6* **Rose Buck**[11] 867 3-9-1 66 ... AdamKirby 1 57
(Giles Bravery) *cl up on inner: rdn along 3f out: kpt on one pce fnl 2f* **4/1**[2]
360- **4** *3* **Rostrum Farewell**[123] 7901 3-9-0 65 ... SeanLevey 4 47
(David Brown) *trckd ldrs: effrt 3f out: rdn over 2f out: sn btn* **6/1**
16- **5** *½* **Value (IRE)**[201] 5927 3-9-5 70 ... TomQueally 3 50
(Gay Kelleway) *trckd ldrs on inner: effrt 3f out: sn rdn along and wknd fnl 2f* **16/1**
1m 17.01s (0.51) **Going Correction** +0.10s/f (Slow) 5 Ran SP% **116.8**
Speed ratings (Par 98): **100,99,91,87,86**
CSF £5.04 TOTE £1.40: £1.10, £2.10; EX 4.50 Trifecta £10.20.
**Owner** Shapoor Mistry **Bred** Eimear Mulhern & Abbeville Stud **Trained** Kingsclere, Hants

**FOCUS**
The market had spoken heavily in the favour of the progressive winner. The form is rated a shade positively.

## 1007 32RED MEGA MOOLAH MILLIONAIRES APPRENTICE H'CAP 1m (F)
**5:35** (5:36) (Class 6) (0-60,60) 3-Y-O **£2,587** (£770; £384; £192) **Stalls** Low

Form RPR
3310 **1** **Day Star Lad**[19] 753 3-9-5 58 ... (v) JacobButterfield 5 70+
(Derek Shaw) *hld up: smooth hdwy 1/2-way and sn trcking ldrs: cl up over 2f out: shkn up ent fnl f: sn led and rdn clr: readily* **3/1**[2]
33-0 **2** *7* **Sky Ranger (IRE)**[35] 568 3-9-4 60 ... GeorgeBuckell(3) 4 55
(James Tate) *chsd ldrs: pushed along after 2f: lost pl and in rr after 3f: swtchd wd st and hdwy over 2f out: kpt on u.p fnl f: no ch w wnr* **16/1**
-503 **3** *½* **Evacusafe Lady**[35] 568 3-9-7 60 ... (tp) NathanAlison 7 54
(John Ryan) *cl up on outer: led 3f out: rdn along 2f out: drvn ent fnl f: sn hdd and one pce* **9/4**[1]
4336 **4** *1¼* **Indira**[27] 665 3-9-7 60 ... JoeyHaynes 1 51
(John Berry) *trckd ldrs: effrt whn n.m.r and swtchd rt 3f out: sn rdn and one pce* **5/1**[3]
00-5 **5** *¾* **Miss Tweedy**[13] 847 3-9-2 58 ... PatMillman(3) 2 47
(Rod Millman) *trckd ldrs: rdn along 3f out: sn one pce* **14/1**
2064 **6** *17* **Bold Max**[12] 865 3-8-9 48 ... (b[1]) TimClark 6
(Zoe Davison) *cl up: rdn along 3f out: sn wknd* **8/1**
-520 **7** *4½* **Streethowlingmama (USA)**[18] 786 3-8-0 46 ... KieranShoemark(7) 3
(Olly Stevens) *slt ld: rdn along and hdd 3f out: sn wknd* **5/1**[3]
1m 46.75s (3.05) **Going Correction** +0.10s/f (Slow) 7 Ran SP% **112.8**
Speed ratings (Par 96): **88,81,80,79,78 61,57**
CSF £45.41 TOTE £4.90: £1.90, £4.50; EX 42.80 Trifecta £167.90.
**Owner** Brian Johnson (Northamptonshire) **Bred** Mrs S J Somner **Trained** Sproxton, Leics

**FOCUS**
A desperately weak finale and one-way traffic. It's doubtful the winner was flattered.
T/Plt: £19.20 to a £1 stake. Pool: £72,030.48 - 2,738.23 winning units T/Qpdt: £9.80 to a £1 stake. Pool: £5,689.26 - 429.37 winning units JR

# 987 KEMPTON (A.W) (R-H)
## Wednesday, March 19

**OFFICIAL GOING: Standard**
Wind: Moderate, across Weather: Fine, warm

## 1008 BETBRIGHT.COM MEDIAN AUCTION MAIDEN STKS 7f (P)
**5:40** (5:45) (Class 5) 3-5-Y-O **£2,587** (£770; £384; £192) **Stalls** Low

Form RPR
554- **1** **Jeremos (IRE)**[124] 7892 3-8-13 68 ... RichardHughes 5 71
(Richard Hannon) *mde most and set stdy pce: kicked on over 2f out: rdn and hanging rt over 1f out: narrowly hdd ins fnl f: kpt on to ld again nr fin* **11/4**[1]
- **2** *nse* **Zain Dream (IRE)** 3-8-13 0 ... SteveDrowne 2 71+
(Robert Cowell) *sn trckd ldrs: wnt 2nd jst over 2f out: shkn up to take narrow ld ins fnl f: hdd nr fin: jst pipped* **9/2**[3]
25 **3** *1¼* **Sleipnir**[35] 579 3-8-13 0 ... TomEaves 1 67
(Philip Hide) *trckd ldrs: wnt 3rd 2f out but rdn and nt qckn: cl up bhd ldng pair after but nvr able to throw down a chal* **3/1**[2]
**4** *4½* **Gaelic O'Reagan** 3-8-13 0 ... JimmyQuinn 8 55+
(Robert Eddery) *hld up in last: pushed along over 2f out: kpt on fr over 1f out to take 4th nr fin: n.d* **50/1**
0 **5** *nk* **Pouncing Tiger**[46] 422 3-8-8 0 ... AdamBeschizza 10 50
(Stuart Williams) *slowly away: hld up in rr: pushed along and outpcd over 2f out: hdwy to take modest 4th over 1f out tl nr fin* **33/1**
-462 **6** *3¼* **Sebs Sensei (IRE)**[22] 741 3-8-13 71 ... FergusSweeney 9 46
(Mark Hoad) *chsd ldrs: fnd nil whn rdn over 2f out and sn bdly outpcd: tried to keep on over 1f out: wknd fnl f* **5/1**
60- **7** *1¾* **Eugenic**[167] 6975 3-8-13 0 ... FrederikTylicki 4 41
(Rod Millman) *a in rr: rdn and struggling over 2f out: sn wknd* **10/1**
**8** *3¼* **Adam Forever** 3-8-13 0 ... RichardKingscote 6 32
(Michael Wigham) *plld hrd: chsd wnr 4f out to jst over 2f out: wknd qckly* **11/1**
0U- **9** *½* **Pendo**[162] 7111 3-8-13 0 ... LukeMorris 7 31
(Alastair Lidderdale) *restless in stalls: plld hrd: chsd wnr to 4f out: wknd qckly over 2f out* **6/1**
1m 27.01s (1.01) **Going Correction** -0.05s/f (Stan) 9 Ran SP% **123.1**
Speed ratings (Par 103): **92,91,90,85,85 81,79,75,75**
CSF £16.80 TOTE £4.50: £1.70, £1.20, £1.90; EX 25.10 Trifecta £79.00.
**Owner** Gerald Moss **Bred** R Hannon & J Cullinan **Trained** East Everleigh, Wilts

■ Nouvelle Ere (20-1) was withdrawn. Rule 4 does not apply.

**FOCUS**
A modest maiden run at a steady early pace. The winner had a good trip up front.

## 1009 GOFFS LONDON SALE - KEMPTON-BREEZE/KENSINGTON-SALE H'CAP (DIV I) 6f (P)
**6:10** (6:11) (Class 6) (0-55,57) 4-Y-0+ **£1,940** (£577; £288; £144) **Stalls** Low

Form RPR
1 **Mr Bounty**[33] 617 4-8-11 **52**........(p) DavidParkes(7) 7 63+
(M D O'Callaghan, Ire) *trckd ldr in slowly run racwe: led 2f out and kicked on: decisive move and wl in command fnl f* **7/2**[1]

5-20 2 2 **Littlecote Lady**[22] 740 5-8-12 **53**........ CharlotteJenner(7) 10 58
(Mark Usher) *chsd ldng pair in slowly run event: rdn over 2f out: kpt on to win battle for 2nd nr fin* **20/1**

1301 3 hd **Catalyze**[4] 972 6-9-9 **57** 6ex........(t) TomEaves 2 61+
(Ann Stokell) *hld up towards rr in slowly run r: prog on inner 2f out: drvn to dispute 2nd fnl f: kpt on* **5/1**[2]

5-01 4 ½ **Torres Del Paine**[34] 586 7-9-6 **54**........ TomQueally 3 57+
(Brett Johnson) *hld up in rr in slowly run r: rdn 2f out: kpt on fr over 1f out: n.d but nrst fin* **7/2**[1]

00-2 5 1 **Vitznau (IRE)**[13] 858 10-9-2 **50**........ RichardHughes 1 50
(K F Clutterbuck) *hld up in midfield: rdn and tried to make prog wl over 1f out: one pce after* **6/1**[3]

-556 6 nse **Little Choosey**[16] 819 4-9-6 **54**........ GeorgeBaker 9 54
(Anabel K Murphy) *led at mod pce: hdd and nt qckn 2f out: wknd fnl f* **20/1**

-040 7 ¾ **Captain Scooby**[58] 258 8-9-0 **53**........(e) ConnorBeasley(5) 8 51
(Richard Guest) *chsd ldrs: urged along and nt qckn 2f out: one pce and n.d after* **8/1**

0660 8 1¼ **Renoir's Lady**[4] 973 6-8-11 **50**........ JoeyHaynes(5) 4 44
(Joseph Tuite) *nvr bttr than midfield: shkn up and no prog 2f out: fdd* **25/1**

2-06 9 nk **Celestial Dawn**[59] 244 5-8-13 **55**........(bt) CamHardie(7) 5 47
(John Weymes) *dwlt: t.k.h in rr: tried to make prog on wd outside over 3f out: wknd 2f out* **16/1**

0-00 10 2 **Mambo Spirit (IRE)**[59] 248 10-9-2 **55**........ EoinWalsh(5) 6 42
(Tony Newcombe) *dwlt and rrd s: t.k.h: hld up in last: c wd bnd 3f out: sn btn* **5/1**[2]

1m 14.15s (1.05) **Going Correction** -0.05s/f (Stan) **10** Ran SP% **122.4**
Speed ratings (Par 101): **91,88,88,87,86 86,85,83,82,80**
CSF £82.83 CT £368.61 TOTE £5.30: £2.50, £5.70, £1.20; EX 67.10 Trifecta £773.40.
**Owner** Michael O'Callaghan **Bred** Alvediston Stud **Trained** The Curragh, Co. Kildare

**FOCUS**
There was very little pace on early and it paid to race handily. The winner was well treated on the pick of his Irish form.

## 1010 GOFFS LONDON SALE - KEMPTON-BREEZE/KENSINGTON-SALE H'CAP (DIV II) 6f (P)
**6:40** (6:40) (Class 6) (0-55,55) 4-Y-0+ **£1,940** (£577; £288; £144) **Stalls** Low

Form RPR
20-0 1 **Time Medicean**[28] 663 8-9-4 **52**........ RobertWinston 3 63
(Tony Carroll) *hld up in rr: prog over 2f out: clsd qckly over 1f out to ld 150yds out: styd on wl* **9/4**[1]

3031 2 2 **Bubbly Bailey**[20] 760 4-9-7 **55**........(v) FrederikTylicki 8 60
(J R Jenkins) *led at str pce: kpt on whn rdn 2f out: hdd and outpcd 150yds out: hld on for 2nd* **7/2**[2]

0305 3 hd **Belle Bayardo (IRE)**[18] 798 6-9-6 **54**........ LukeMorris 12 58
(Ronald Harris) *restrained fr wdst draw s but racd awkwardly early: hld up in last: prog wl over 1f out: drvn and r.o fnl f: nrly snatched 2nd* **10/1**

-504 4 ½ **Ivestar (IRE)**[40] 511 9-9-5 **53**........(v) GrahamGibbons 6 56
(Michael Easterby) *prom: rdn to chse ldr 2f out to 1f out: one pce* **7/2**[2]

0-03 5 ¾ **Sarah Berry**[18] 797 5-8-13 **52**........(v) ConnorBeasley(5) 5 54
(Chris Dwyer) *chsd ldrs: rdn and nt qckn jst over 2f out: kpt on fr over 1f out: nt pce to threaten* **14/1**

46-0 6 2 **Camache Queen (IRE)**[7] 934 6-8-13 **54**........(bt) DanielCremin(7) 9 49
(Joseph Tuite) *racd wd: prog fr midfield to chse ldrs 1/2-way: rdn to dispute 2nd 2f out: hanging and nt qckn sn after: one pce* **33/1**

/0-0 7 3¾ **Newbury Street**[20] 754 7-8-11 **52**........(p) JackGarritty(7) 7 35
(Patrick Holmes) *hld up in midfield: brief prog on inner wl over 1f out: wknd fnl f* **33/1**

4005 8 3½ **Idle Curiosity (IRE)**[16] 819 4-9-7 **55**........(p[1]) StephenCraine 1 28
(Jim Boyle) *hld up in rr: nt clr run briefly over 2f out: no real prog whn swtchd lft over 1f out: wknd* **12/1**

-000 9 5 **We Have A Dream**[14] 845 9-9-2 **50**........(p) TomEaves 2 8
(Ann Stokell) *t.k.h: chsd ldr to 2f out: wknd rapidly: eased* **8/1**[3]

0-06 10 ½ **Millies Quest**[20] 760 5-8-7 **46**........ NathanAlison(5) 10 2
(Martin Smith) *a in rr: struggling over 2f out: sn btn* **50/1**

6004 11 5 **Green Millionaire**[6] 937 4-9-0 **48**........(t) SteveDrowne 11
(Jeremy Gask) *chsd ldrs: rdn bef 1/2-way: wknd wl over 2f out: t.o* **25/1**

1m 12.22s (-0.88) **Going Correction** -0.05s/f (Stan) **11** Ran SP% **121.5**
Speed ratings (Par 101): **103,100,100,99,98 95,90,86,79,78 72**
CSF £10.04 CT £69.05 TOTE £3.40: £1.30, £1.30, £4.40; EX 17.70 Trifecta £183.50.
**Owner** A W Carroll **Bred** C A Cyzer **Trained** Cropthorne, Worcs

**FOCUS**
With the leader going off at a scorching pace (roughly 3.7sec quicker to the 3f pole than in the first division), this was set up for a closer. The final time was 1.93sec quicker than the first division. Straightforward form, the third helping pin the standard.

## 1011 GOFFS LONDON SALE - KEMPTON-BREEZE/KENSINGTON-SALE MEDIAN AUCTION MAIDEN STKS 1m 4f (P)
**7:10** (7:11) (Class 6) 3-5-Y-0 **£1,940** (£577; £288; £144) **Stalls** Centre

Form RPR
0423 1 **Officer Drivel (IRE)**[19] 785 3-8-6 70........[1] LukeMorris 2 70
(Luke Dace) *t.k.h: mde all: rdn 2f out: edgd lft but styd on fnl f: unchal* **3/1**[3]

2 2¼ **Amourita (IRE)** 3-8-1 0........ NickyMackay 1 61
(Jonathan Portman) *chsd wnr 2f: rdn 3f out: wnt 2nd again 2f out: kpt on but no imp* **25/1**

642 3 1½ **Trafalgar Rock**[12] 871 3-8-6 70........ SilvestreDeSousa 5 64
(Mark Johnston) *chsd wnr after 2f but nvr gng sweetly: rdn over 3f out: lost 2nd and one pce 2f out* **11/8**[1]

4 1¼ **Bergan (GER)** 3-8-6 0 ow3........ WilliamTwiston-Davies(3) 6 65
(Mick Channon) *hld up in last pair: rdn over 2f out: plugged on but nvr able to threaten* **8/1**

5 6 **Sawwala** 4-9-7 0........ FrederikTylicki 4 49
(J R Jenkins) *hld up in last pair: shkn up 4f out: rdn and no imp over 2f out: wknd over 1f out* **40/1**

6 60 **Dubai Kiss**[172] 5-10-0 0........ GeorgeBaker 3
(Harry Whittington) *trckd ldng trio: rdn and wknd rapidly 3f out: sn t.o and eased* **11/4**[2]

2m 34.44s (-0.06) **Going Correction** -0.05s/f (Stan)
**WFA** 3 from 4yo 22lb 4 from 5yo 2lb **6** Ran SP% **111.2**
Speed ratings (Par 101): **98,96,95,94,90 50**
CSF £58.75 TOTE £4.70: £2.40, £7.10; EX 40.90 Trifecta £187.80.
**Owner** Mark Benton **Bred** Patrick Keane **Trained** Five Oaks, W Sussex

**FOCUS**
With one of the two with previous form running disappointingly this maiden didn't take much winning. The winner was allowed to dictate a steady tempo.

## 1012 BETBRIGHT MONEYBACK OFFERS H'CAP 1m 3f (P)
**7:40** (7:41) (Class 6) (0-55,55) 4-Y-0+ **£1,940** (£577; £288; £144) **Stalls** Low

Form RPR
361- 1 **I'm Harry**[147] 7458 5-9-6 **54**........(vt) RichardHughes 3 66+
(George Baker) *trckd ldrs: rdn to go 2nd on inner 2f out: clsd fr over 1f out: styd on to ld nr fin* **2/1**[1]

5506 2 hd **Time Square (FR)**[16] 821 7-9-2 **55**........ JoeyHaynes(5) 14 67
(Tony Carroll) *sn trckd ldr fr wdst draw: led 6f out: skipped clr fr 3f out: 4 l up 2f out: styd on but collared nr fin* **7/1**[3]

6344 3 4½ **Polar Forest**[5] 964 4-9-1 **55**........(e) ConnorBeasley(5) 1 61+
(Richard Guest) *hld up in midfield: nt clr run fr over 2f out to over 1f out w ldng pair already clr: r.o wl fnl f to take 3rd last 100yds: no ch* **7/2**[2]

-540 4 2 **Entrapping**[14] 838 4-9-6 **55**........ JimmyQuinn 7 56
(John E Long) *t.k.h: trckd ldrs on outer: rdn to dispute 2nd over 2f out but w hd high: chsd clr ldng pair over 1f out to last 100yds: nt qckn* **12/1**

060 5 1½ **Pembroke Pride**[28] 660 4-9-1 **50**........ TomEaves 10 51
(Philip Hide) *hld up in last quartet: pushed along in last pair and no ch whn hmpd wl over 1f out: drvn and styd on wl fnl f* **50/1**

050- 6 1 **Voice From Above (IRE)**[91] 8329 5-9-0 **55**........ JackGarritty(7) 2 52
(Patrick Holmes) *hld up in last quartet: shkn up on inner over 2f out: kpt on one pce and no threat* **33/1**

3230 7 hd **Lisahane Bog**[21] 747 7-9-3 **51**........(v) AdamKirby 11 50
(Peter Hedger) *squeezed out s: hld up in last pair: urged along 4f out: no prog whn hmpd wl over 1f out: styd on fnl f* **7/1**[3]

/0-0 8 1½ **Hardy Plume**[35] 570 5-8-12 **46** oh1........ RobertWinston 5 42
(Denis Coakley) *awkward s then squeezed out: hld up in last pair: pushed along over 2f out: nt clr run over 1f out: stl pushed along and kpt on steadily fnl f* **25/1**

36-0 9 nk **She's A Honey**[35] 581 4-8-11 **46** oh1........ LukeMorris 6 40
(Kevin Morgan) *nvr bttr than midfield: rdn and no prog over 2f out* **33/1**

/0-1 10 2¾ **Until The Man (IRE)**[20] 759 7-9-2 **50**........(b) StephenCraine 8 40
(Natalie Lloyd-Beavis) *trckd ldrs: rdn over 3f out and dropped to midfield: swtchd lft 2f out: wknd* **12/1**

00-0 11 1¼ **Gung Ho (FR)**[45] 446 5-9-3 **51**........(p) ChrisCatlin 13 39
(Tony Newcombe) *t.k.h: trckd ldng pair after 3f: disp 2nd over 2f out: sn wknd rapidly* **16/1**

14-0 12 10 **Dawn Rock**[22] 737 4-8-13 **48**........ SilvestreDeSousa 4 20
(Simon Dow) *led to 6f out: chsd ldr to over 2f out: wknd rapidly* **12/1**

2m 21.12s (-0.78) **Going Correction** -0.05s/f (Stan)
**WFA** 4 from 5yo+ 1lb **12** Ran SP% **121.2**
Speed ratings (Par 101): **100,99,96,95,94 93,93,92,91,89 88,81**
CSF £16.29 CT £48.68 TOTE £2.80: £2.00, £1.40, £1.40; EX 17.50 Trifecta £52.90.
**Owner** Wickfield Stud And Hartshill Stud **Bred** Wickfield Stud And Hartshill Stud **Trained** Manton, Wilts

**FOCUS**
Very few got into this. A fair effort for the grade from the winner.

## 1013 BETBRIGHT - LIVE THE MOMENT H'CAP (BOBIS RACE) 7f (P)
**8:10** (8:10) (Class 4) (0-85,81) 3-Y-0 **£4,690** (£1,395; £697; £348) **Stalls** Low

Form RPR
-211 1 **Crowdmania**[5] 955 3-9-4 **78** 6ex........ SilvestreDeSousa 4 87+
(Mark Johnston) *mde all: kicked more than 2 l clr over 2f out: wandered u.p fr over 1f out: styd on and nvr in serious danger* **11/10**[1]

1 2 1½ **Khatiba (IRE)**[42] 486 3-9-1 **75**........ WilliamBuick 3 80
(Roger Varian) *trckd ldng pair: rdn to chse wnr jst over 2f out: kpt on but nvr able to chal* **11/4**[2]

2213 3 ½ **Basil Berry**[13] 854 3-9-2 **76**........[1] LukeMorris 1 80
(Chris Dwyer) *hld up in 4th: waiting for room on inner over 2f out: drvn to dispute 2nd over 1f out: kpt on but nvr able to chal* **10/1**

-322 4 nse **Drive On (IRE)**[28] 667 3-9-6 **80**........(p) JohnFahy 2 83
(Eve Johnson Houghton) *hld up in 5th: rdn over 2f out: disp 2nd over 1f out: kpt on but nvr able to chal* **7/1**[3]

1- 5 1¾ **Announcement**[268] 3624 3-9-2 **76**........ StevieDonohoe 6 75
(Ian Williams) *wnt lft s: hld up in last and detached 1/2-way: sme prog over 1f out: no imp fnl f* **16/1**

2135 6 3 **Bretherton**[14] 850 3-9-7 **81**........(b) AdamKirby 5 72
(Richard Fahey) *t.k.h: chsd wnr to jst over 2f out: wknd over 1f out* **9/1**

1m 25.13s (-0.87) **Going Correction** -0.05s/f (Stan) **6** Ran SP% **111.8**
Speed ratings (Par 100): **102,100,99,99,97 94**
CSF £4.22 TOTE £1.90: £1.10, £1.70; EX 5.40 Trifecta £36.70.
**Owner** Sheikh Hamdan bin Mohammed Al Maktoum **Bred** Car Colston Hall Stud **Trained** Middleham Moor, N Yorks

**FOCUS**
Fairly useful form. The winner did this well and can keep improving.

## 1014 BETBRIGHT MOBILE H'CAP (LONDON MILE SERIES QUALIFIER) 1m (P)
**8:40** (8:41) (Class 4) (0-85,85) 4-Y-0+ **£4,690** (£1,395; £697; £348) **Stalls** Low

Form RPR
-641 1 **Silverheels (IRE)**[18] 806 5-9-1 **79**........(b) JimCrowley 9 90
(Paul Cole) *trckd ldng trio: gng strly whn clsd 2f out: rdn to ld 1f out: styd on wl: readily* **11/4**[1]

2-35 2 2¼ **Appease**[26] 698 5-8-12 **76**........(p) TomQueally 11 82
(John Butler) *chsd ldr: rdn over 2f out: clsd to chal jst over 1f out: wnr sn wnt by: kpt on* **6/1**[3]

0-42 3 ¾ **Sound Advice**[38] 550 5-9-1 **79**........ TomEaves 2 83
(Keith Dalgleish) *led at str pce: drvn 2f out: hdd 1f out: outpcd but kpt on* **4/1**[2]

0-03 4 ½ **Toga Tiger (IRE)**[35] 574 7-9-0 **78**........ RobertWinston 6 81
(Jeremy Gask) *hld up towards rr on outer: rdn 2f out: styd on fr over 1f out: nrst fin* **7/1**

/0-5 5 nse **Subtle Knife**[19] 779 5-9-3 **81**........ WilliamCarson 4 84
(Giles Bravery) *hld up in midfield: prog to chse ldrs 2f out: styd on same pce fr over 1f out* **25/1**



The Form Book, Raceform Ltd, Newbury, RG14 5SJ

6450 **6** ¾ **Mia's Boy**[18] 804 10-9-7 **85**.............................. LukeMorris 7 86
(Chris Dwyer) *a in midfield: rdn 2f out: no real prog but styd on fnl f: nrst fin* **8/1**

50 **7** 1½ **Ruzeiz (USA)**[21] 744 5-8-10 **77**.............................. CharlesBishop(3) 8 75
(Peter Hedger) *s.s: hld up in last and wl off the pce early: pushed along and sme prog on inner over 1f out: reminder and kpt on fnl f: nvr involved* **14/1**

0244 **8** nk **Jay Bee Blue**[19] 779 5-9-1 **79**..............................(bt) AdamKirby 5 76
(Sean Curran) *dwlt: hld up in midfield: sme prog on inner 2f out: reminders and no hdwy fnl f* **12/1**

206- **9** nk **Myboyalfie (USA)**[130] 7820 7-9-6 **84**.............................. FrederikTylicki 10 80
(J R Jenkins) *hld up in last trio and wl off the pce early: last and pushed along 2f out: nvr involved but styd on quite takingly fnl f* **20/1**

461- **10** 2¼ **Coincidently**[171] 6875 4-8-7 **76**.............................. TimClark(5) 3 67
(Alan Bailey) *chsd ldng pair: lost pl and rdn over 2f out: sn wknd* **10/1**

250- **11** 2¾ **Idol Deputy (FR)**[194] 6167 8-9-2 **80**.............................. GeorgeBaker 1 65
(James Bennett) *hld up in last trio and wl off the pce early: shkn up over 2f out: no prog over 1f out: wknd* **33/1**

1m 36.9s (-2.90) **Going Correction** -0.05s/f (Stan) **11** Ran SP% **119.6**
Speed ratings (Par 105): **112,109,109,108,108 107,106,105,105,103 100**
CSF £19.14 CT £68.15 TOTE £3.30: £1.80, £1.30, £1.70; EX 19.50 Trifecta £114.00.
**Owner** P F I Cole Ltd **Bred** Castlemartin Stud And Skymarc Farm **Trained** Whatcombe, Oxon

**FOCUS**
The pace held up pretty well here. Straightforward form rated around the placed horses.

## 1015 BETBRIGHT.COM H'CAP 1m (P)
9:10 (9:10) (Class 7) (0-50,50) 4-Y-O+ £1,617 (£481; £240; £120) Stalls Low

Form RPR

04 **1** **Appyjack**[42] 484 6-8-13 **45**.............................. RobertTart(3) 9 59
(Tony Carroll) *hld up in last pair and wl off the pce: pushed along and prog over 2f out: styd on past toiling rivals to ld jst ins fnl f: sn clr* **3/1**[1]

050- **2** 3½ **Just Five (IRE)**[120] 7963 8-9-2 **45**..............................(v) DavidProbert 5 51
(John Weymes) *wl in tch: clsd over 2f out: rdn to ld over 1f out: hdd and outpcd jst ins fnl f* **12/1**

-220 **3** 1¾ **Chez Vrony**[56] 281 8-9-6 **49**.............................. TomQueally 10 51
(Dave Morris) *wl in rr: rdn 1/2-way: prog on inner over 2f out: drvn to chal over 1f out: wnr sn swept past* **14/1**

5036 **4** 2¼ **My Scat Daddy (USA)**[5] 963 5-9-2 **45**..............................(p) LiamKeniry 8 42
(Zoe Davison) *towards rr: rdn 1/2-way: nvr a threat but plugged on fr over 1f out* **16/1**

-035 **5** 1¼ **Claude Monet (BRZ)**[28] 661 5-9-6 **49**.............................. JimCrowley 4 43
(Simon Dow) *trckd ldr 2f: styd prom: clsd to dispute ld over 2f out: sn nt qckn: fdd fnl f* **3/1**[1]

0123 **6** ¾ **Zed Candy Girl**[14] 851 4-9-3 **46**..............................(p) LukeMorris 3 38
(John Stimpson) *nvr bttr than midfield: rdn and no imp on ldrs fr 2f out* **6/1**[2]

3252 **7** 2 **Byrd In Hand (IRE)**[14] 844 7-9-7 **50**..............................(b) WilliamCarson 11 38
(John Bridger) *t.k.h: trckd ldrs: clsd to ld over 2f out: idled in front and hdd over 1f out: wknd* **8/1**[3]

152/ **8** 2 **Palladius**[103] 8192 4-8-11 **47**..............................(p) DavidParkes(7) 13 30
(M D O'Callaghan, Ire) *restrained into last after s: urged along sn after 1/2-way: no real prog* **25/1**

-000 **9** ¾ **Admirals Walk (IRE)**[14] 846 4-9-7 **50**..............................(p) GeorgeBaker 12 31
(Barry Brennan) *hld up in rr: tried to make prog over 2f out: rdn and fnd nil over 1f out* **20/1**

3235 **10** 1½ **Compton Silver**[19] 781 4-8-13 **49**..............................(b) JackGilligan(7) 6 27
(Patrick Gilligan) *led at str pce: hdd over 2f out: wknd over 1f out* **8/1**[3]

/00- **11** 57 **Royal Intruder**[155] 7265 9-9-5 **48**..............................(bt) BenCurtis 7
(Ann Stokell) *plld hrd: pressed ldr after 2f to over 3f out: wknd rapidly and sn t.o* **33/1**

00R- **R** **Sakhee's Alround**[119] 7980 4-9-5 **48**.............................. AdamKirby 2
(K F Clutterbuck) *ref to r: tk no part* **16/1**

1m 38.64s (-1.16) **Going Correction** -0.05s/f (Stan) **12** Ran SP% **124.2**
Speed ratings (Par 97): **103,99,97,95,94 93,91,89,88,87 30,**
CSF £43.82 CT £464.28 TOTE £4.50: £1.90, £8.00, £3.50; EX 71.20 Trifecta £1036.20.
**Owner** Mayden Stud **Bred** Mayden Stud, J A And D S Dewhurst **Trained** Cropthorne, Worcs

**FOCUS**
With Royal Intruder hassling Compton Silver up front, the pace built up a fair way out and that set things up for those ridden with more restraint. The winner bounced back to some of his better form.
T/Plt: £33.80 to a £1 stake. Pool: £79,239.83 - 1,711.25 winning tickets. T/Qpdt: £12.80 to a £1 stake. Pool: £9,104.21 - 551.54 winning tickets. JN

951 **LINGFIELD** (L-H)
Wednesday, March 19

**OFFICIAL GOING: Standard**
Wind: light to medium, half behind Weather: dry, overcast

## 1016 CORAL MOBILE "JUST THREE CLICKS TO BET" H'CAP 1m 2f (P)
2:00 (2:00) (Class 6) (0-55,55) 4-Y-O+ £2,045 (£603; £302) Stalls Low

Form RPR

00/2 **1** **Minstrels Gallery (IRE)**[20] 755 5-9-4 **55**..............................(p) RobertTart(3) 8 66+
(Lucy Wadham) *t.k.h: chsd ldrs: rdn to chse ldr 2f out: led ent fnl f: r.o wl: readily* **9/4**[2]

-140 **2** 3 **Litmus (USA)**[16] 821 5-9-6 **54**..............................(b) LukeMorris 10 59
(Simon Dow) *chsd ldr tl rdn to ld over 2f out: hdd ent fnl f: outpcd by wnr but kpt on for clr 2nd fnl f* **14/1**

4-60 **3** 1¾ **Abigails Angel**[20] 755 7-8-11 **52**.............................. DavidParkes(7) 9 54
(Brett Johnson) *hld up in tch towards rr: hdwy on outer 3f out: styd on u.p to go 3rd ins fnl f: no threat to wnr* **14/1**

5523 **4** hd **Petersboden**[16] 821 5-9-4 **52**.............................. RobertHavlin 5 53
(Michael Blanshard) *chsd ldng pair: rdn and effrt ent fnl 2f: outpcd and btn 1f out: lost 3rd and one pce ins fnl f* **5/1**[3]

-606 **5** ¾ **Dreaming Again**[22] 737 4-8-6 **47**.............................. CamHardie(7) 7 47
(Jimmy Fox) *hld up in tch in midfield: rdn and unable qck wl over 1f out: no threat to wnr and kpt on same pce fnl f* **10/1**

5045 **6** ½ **Indian Violet (IRE)**[16] 822 8-9-2 **50**..............................(p) JimCrowley 11 49
(Zoe Davison) *hld up in tch towards rr: nt clr run 2f out: swtchd rt and hdwy u.p over 1f out: styd on fnl f: nvr trbld ldrs* **20/1**

05-0 **7** 1 **Querido (GER)**[48] 377 10-8-7 **46** oh1..............................(tp) JoeyHaynes(5) 1 43
(Paddy Butler) *s.i.s: t.k.h: hld up in tch in last pair: effrt u.p on outer over 1f out: kpt on but nvr trbld ldrs* **100/1**

1503 **8** nk **Daniel Thomas (IRE)**[46] 435 12-9-3 **51**..............................(tp) MartinHarley 6 49
(Ann Stokell) *s.i.s: in tch in last pair: stuck bhd wall of horses and rdn jst over 2f out: sme hdwy fnl f: n.d* **2/1**[1]

0-03 **9** ¾ **Scamperdale**[22] 737 12-9-5 **53**..............................(p) AndrewMullen 2 48
(Brian Baugh) *stdd after s: t.k.h: hld up in midfield: effrt u.p in 6th over 1f out: no hdwy: wknd ins fnl f* **10/1**

-050 **10** 3¼ **Claude Greenwood**[20] 755 4-8-12 **53**.............................. NedCurtis(7) 4 44
(Roger Curtis) *in tch in midfield: rdn 4f out: struggling whn hmpd and dropped to rr 2f out: n.d after* **66/1**

/4-6 **11** 23 **Unbreak My Heart (IRE)**[6] 939 9-8-12 **46**..........(b[1]) WilliamCarson 12
(Ann Stokell) *t.k.h: led tl hdd jst over 2f out: sn dropped out: wl bhd and eased ins fnl f* **33/1**

2m 8.02s (1.42) **Going Correction** +0.125s/f (Slow) **11** Ran SP% **122.5**
Speed ratings (Par 101): **99,96,95,95,94 94,93,93,92,89 71**
CSF £34.67 CT £379.60 TOTE £2.50: £1.20, £3.90, £2.90; EX 35.40 Trifecta £286.80.
**Owner** G Pascoe & S Brewer **Bred** Morecool Stud **Trained** Newmarket, Suffolk

**FOCUS**
A modest handicap run at a steady pace, and the first three raced prominently. The bare level of the form makes sense.

## 1017 LADBROKES MOBILE H'CAP 7f 1y(P)
2:30 (2:30) (Class 6) (0-65,65) 4-Y-O+ £2,045 (£603; £302) Stalls Low

Form RPR

6432 **1** **Presumido (IRE)**[16] 817 4-9-2 **65**.............................. JackDuern(5) 6 74
(Simon Dow) *stdd s: hld up in rr: swtchd rt and hdwy on outer over 1f out: racd awkwardly but str run ins fnl f to ld fnl 75yds: rdn out* **5/1**[3]

2363 **2** ½ **Alnoomaas (IRE)**[14] 841 5-9-7 **65**.............................. RichardHughes 10 73
(Luke Dace) *hld up in tch in midfield: effrt u.p to chal 1f out: led fnl 100yds: sn hdd and styd on same pce* **4/1**[2]

-204 **3** 1 **West Leake (IRE)**[26] 688 8-8-13 **57**.............................. LiamKeniry 8 62
(Paul Burgoyne) *in tch in midfield: rdn and effrt to chse ldrs 2f out: ev ch ins fnl f: styd on same pce fnl 100yds* **16/1**

1133 **4** ½ **Bertie Blu Boy**[14] 846 6-9-2 **60**..............................(b) RichardKingscote 12 64
(Lisa Williamson) *broke fast fr outside draw: led and grad crossed to inner: rdn ent fnl 2f: hrd pressed 1f out: hdd and no ex fnl 100yds* **4/1**[2]

0024 **5** 2 **Shifting Star (IRE)**[32] 628 9-9-4 **62**..............................(b) WilliamCarson 7 61
(John Bridger) *hld up in tch in midfield: hdwy u.p on inner to press ldrs 1f out: no ex and outpcd fnl 100yds* **10/1**

1553 **6** 5 **Where's Reiley (USA)**[11] 889 8-9-4 **62**..............................(v) AdamKirby 5 47
(Michael Attwater) *chsd ldrs: rdn to chse ldr over 2f out tl over 1f out: wknd fnl f* **25/1**

600/ **7** 1¾ **The Cash Generator (IRE)**[533] 6770 6-8-9 **60**.............................. DanielCremin(7) 2 40
(Ralph J Smith) *towards rr: rdn and struggling over 2f out: modest hdwy ins fnl f: nvr trbld ldrs* **66/1**

3-01 **8** 1¾ **All Right Now**[15] 833 7-8-6 **55**..............................(tp) EoinWalsh(5) 3 31
(Tony Newcombe) *bustled along early: chsd ldr tl over 2f out: sn lost pl and wl btn over 1f out* **20/1**

-130 **9** 1 **Chevise (IRE)**[25] 714 6-9-2 **60**..............................(b) LukeMorris 11 33
(Steve Woodman) *in tch towards rr: rdn and struggling over 2f out: n.d fnl 2f* **25/1**

5-00 **10** 1¾ **Amenable (IRE)**[58] 258 7-9-0 **58**..............................(p) BenCurtis 1 26
(Ann Stokell) *bustled along early: chsd ldrs tl lost pl over 2f out: bhd over 1f out* **50/1**

5-60 **F** **Red Art (IRE)**[59] 245 5-9-5 **63**.............................. MartinHarley 4 71
(Tony Newcombe) *in tch in midfield: rdn and effrt over 1f out: swtchd rt 1f out: styd on u.p and pressing ldrs whn short of room: clipped heels and fell heavily fnl 50yds: fatally injured* **7/4**[1]

1m 24.63s (-0.17) **Going Correction** +0.125s/f (Slow) **11** Ran SP% **123.9**
Speed ratings (Par 101): **105,104,103,102,100 94,92,90,89,87**
CSF £25.45 CT £310.39 TOTE £5.20: £2.10, £2.00, £4.70; EX 31.50 Trifecta £245.50.
**Owner** R Moss & J Page **Bred** Lynn Lodge Stud **Trained** Epsom, Surrey

**FOCUS**
The gallop was solid for this open handicap with the race marred by a terrible fall for Red Art and Martin Harley inside the final furlong. The winner looks the type that needs things to fall right.

## 1018 BOOKMAKERS.CO.UK MAIDEN STKS 5f 6y(P)
3:00 (4:25) (Class 5) 3-Y-O+ £2,726 (£805; £402) Stalls High

Form RPR

333- **1** **Rock N Rouge (IRE)**[162] 7095 3-8-9 72..............................[1] JimCrowley 6 61
(Olly Stevens) *mde all: rdn and clr whn racd awkwardly and edgd rt jst ins fnl f: drvn and kpt on fnl 100yds* **5/4**[1]

4 **2** 1 **Bush Warrior (IRE)**[16] 824 3-9-0 0.............................. FrederikTylicki 2 63+
(Robert Eddery) *t.k.h to post: v.s.a: wnt bdly lft leaving stalls and lost many l: rn green but grad rcvrd: rdn and hdwy ent fnl f: r.o wl to snatch 2nd last strides* **9/4**[2]

02-2 **3** nk **Narborough**[28] 666 3-8-11 60.............................. WilliamTwiston-Davies(3) 3 61
(Mick Channon) *chsd ldrs: rdn and effrt over 1f out: chsd clr wnr 1f out: kpt on same pce fnl 100yds: lost 2nd last strides* **8/1**

4-40 **4** 1 **Purford Green**[14] 845 5-9-7 45..............................(v) RobertHavlin 4 58?
(Michael Attwater) *chsd wnr: rdn and unable qck 2f out: lost 2nd 1f out and styd on same pce fnl f* **100/1**

55 **5** 1½ **Spinning Cobblers**[22] 741 3-9-0 0.............................. AdamBeschizza 1 52
(Stuart Williams) *in tch in midfield: rdn and unable qck wl over 1f out: styd on same pce and no imp after* **3/1**[3]

6 **6** 24 **Virtual Symphony**[20] 756 3-8-9 0.............................. FergusSweeney 5
(John Best) *v keen to post: outpcd in last pair after 1f: dropped to last 1/2-way: sn lost tch* **66/1**

59.87s (1.07) **Going Correction** +0.125s/f (Slow)
**WFA** 3 from 5yo 12lb **6** Ran SP% **113.8**
Speed ratings (Par 103): **96,94,93,92,89 51**
CSF £4.47 TOTE £2.40: £1.90, £1.90; EX 5.10 Trifecta £12.60.
**Owner** Qatar Racing Limited **Bred** Michael D Ryan **Trained** Chiddingfold, Surrey

**FOCUS**
Racing was delayed by 85 minutes, awaiting the return of the course ambulance. The pace looked fair for this weak maiden but the time was slow and the fourth finished close enough.

## 1019 COMPARE BOOKMAKERS AT BOOKMAKERS.CO.UK H'CAP 5f 6y(P)
3:30 (4:49) (Class 5) (0-75,75) 4-Y-O+ £2,726 (£805; £402) Stalls High

Form RPR

0620 **1** **Profile Star (IRE)**[8] 909 5-9-3 **71**.............................. WilliamCarson 4 79+
(Ann Stokell) *stdd after s: hld up in last pair: swtchd ins and effrt wl over 1f out: led and edgd rt ins fnl f: drvn and qcknd clr fnl 75yds: r.o wl* **3/1**[2]

322- **2** 1¼ **Shirley's Pride**[225] 5094 4-9-1 **69**..............................(t) AndrewMullen 6 73
(Michael Appleby) *taken down early: dwlt: niggled along in rr: hdwy u.p on inner over 1f out: styd on to go 2nd wl ins fnl f: no threat to wnr* **6/1**

4-42 **3** 1/2 **Ask The Guru**[39] 532 4-9-4 **72**..........................................(v) KierenFox 5 74
(Michael Attwater) *hld up in tch in midfield: rdn and effrt to press ldrs 1f out: styd on same pce fnl 100yds* **7/2**[3]

2551 **4** *nse* **Desert Strike**[12] 866 8-9-6 **74**..........................................(p) LiamKeniry 1 76
(Conor Dore) *taken down early: dwlt: sn rcvrd to r in midfield: rdn and effrt to chal 1f out: outpcd by wnr fnl 100yds: lost 2 pls towards fin* **8/1**

350- **5** 2 **Silvanus (IRE)**[154] 7314 9-9-7 **75**.......................... PaulMulrennan 8 69
(Paul Midgley) *taken down early: hld up in tch in midfield: rdn and effrt 2f out: n.m.r 1f out: styd on same pce after* **25/1**

1123 **6** *nk* **Roy's Legacy**[28] 654 5-9-0 **71**.......................... MichaelJMMurphy(3) 3 64
(Shaun Harris) *w ldr: carried rt bnd wl over 1f out: sn rdn to ld: hdd ins fnl f: no ex: wknd towards fin* **5/2**[1]

150- **7** 2 1/2 **Alpha Delta Whisky**[140] 7634 6-9-4 **72**..........................(v) TomQueally 9 56
(John Gallagher) *pressed ldrs on outer: rdn and wd bnd 2f out: lost pl and drvn over 1f out: no prog fnl f* **10/1**

2305 **8** *hd* **Pull The Pin (IRE)**[15] 834 5-8-11 **65**..........................(bt) BenCurtis 2 49
(Ann Stokell) *wnt rt s: led: shifted rt bnd wl over 1f out: sn hdd: wknd fnl f* **16/1**

58.49s (-0.31) **Going Correction** +0.125s/f (Slow) **8** Ran SP% **120.0**
Speed ratings (Par 103): **107,105,104,104,100 100,96,96**
CSF £22.65 CT £67.08 TOTE £4.10: £1.40, £2.50, £1.90; EX 46.00 Trifecta £194.80.
**Owner** J Robinson (Leicester) **Bred** Knocklong House Stud **Trained** Southwell, Notts

**FOCUS**
This was run at a fierce pace with plenty of prominent runners in the field. The winner has obvious scope to win another couple.

## 1020 DOWNLOAD THE LADBROKES APP H'CAP 7f 1y(P)
**4:05** (5:15) (Class 4) (0-85,85) 4-Y-0+ **£5,175** (£1,540; £769; £384) **Stalls** Low

Form RPR

1-22 **1** **Firmdecisions (IRE)**[28] 658 4-9-6 **84**.......................... AdamKirby 8 96
(Brett Johnson) *in tch in midfield: rdn to chse clr ldr over 1f out: drvn and clsd to ld fnl 100yds: idled in front: rdn out* **7/1**[3]

-250 **2** 1/2 **Brocklebank (IRE)**[25] 715 5-8-13 **82**.......................... JackDuern(5) 3 93
(Simon Dow) *wl off the pce in rr: wd and effrt bnd 2f out: hdwy over 1f out: styd on strly to go 2nd wl ins fnl f: nvr quite getting to wnr* **3/1**[2]

-021 **3** 1 3/4 **Living The Life (IRE)**[19] 779 4-9-0 **78**..........................(v) PaddyAspell 6 84
(Phil McEntee) *chsd ldrs: wnt 2nd wl over 2f out: led 2f out and sn rdn clr: drvn and hdd fnl 100yds: wknd towards fin* **8/1**

-124 **4** 1 **Nassau Storm**[25] 715 5-9-6 **84**.......................... RyanMoore 11 89
(William Knight) *hld up off the pce towards rr: clsd whn nt clr run and swtchd rt over 1f out: kpt on u.p ins fnl f: no threat to wnr* **7/4**[1]

404- **5** 1 1/4 **Saucy Minx (IRE)**[182] 6524 4-9-2 **80**.......................... JimCrowley 1 80
(Amanda Perrett) *racd in midfield: effrt in 5th bnd 2f out: chsd clr ldng pair 1f out: no imp on ldrs and lost 2 pls ins fnl f* **10/1**

10-5 **6** 1 **Yojojo (IRE)**[65] 163 5-9-7 **85**.......................... DavidProbert 9 82
(Gay Kelleway) *racd in midfield: rdn and effrt 2f out: kpt on same pce and no imp after* **12/1**

60-6 **7** 3/4 **Al Khan (IRE)**[38] 549 5-9-2 **80**..........................(p) BenCurtis 7 75
(Ann Stokell) *racd off the pce in last pair: rdn and effrt wl over 1f out: styd on fnl f: nvr trbld ldrs* **20/1**

2060 **8** 3 3/4 **Al's Memory (IRE)**[26] 689 5-8-9 **76**.......................... DeclanBates(3) 2 61
(David Evans) *chsd ldrs early: dropped to midfield after 2f: rdn and no hdwy ent fnl 2f: wknd over 1f out* **33/1**

3016 **9** 1 **Bowstar**[35] 574 5-8-13 **77**..........................(b) RobertHavlin 5 59
(Michael Attwater) *chsd ldrs: rdn and no hdwy over 1f out: wknd fnl f* **20/1**

5205 **10** 6 **Pabusar**[13] 863 6-8-7 **71** oh1..........................(b) WilliamCarson 4 37
(Ann Stokell) *sn rdn along to ld: hdd and rdn 2f out: sn btn: fdd fnl f* **12/1**

000- **11** 2 1/2 **Snow Bay**[159] 7176 8-8-13 **82**.......................... ShirleyTeasdale(5) 10 41
(Paul Midgley) *chsd ldr tl wl over 2f out: sn rdn and lost pl: bhd 1f out* **66/1**

1m 24.16s (-0.64) **Going Correction** +0.125s/f (Slow) **11** Ran SP% **123.4**
Speed ratings (Par 105): **108,107,105,104,102 101,100,96,95,88 85**
CSF £28.67 CT £182.45 TOTE £5.70: £2.50, £1.60, £1.70; EX 33.70 Trifecta £116.40.
**Owner** White Bear Racing **Bred** Thomas O'Meara **Trained** Epsom, Surrey
■ Stewards' Enquiry : William Carson Fine: £140, failed to declare gelding did not wear declared tongue-tie.

**FOCUS**
A competitive handicap run at a strong pace. The form makes sense.

## 1021 LADBROKES H'CAP 1m 1y(P)
**4:40** (5:38) (Class 5) (0-70,76) 4-Y-0+ **£2,726** (£805; £402) **Stalls** High

Form RPR

5452 **1** **Liberty Jack (IRE)**[7] 927 4-9-7 **70**.......................... WilliamCarson 5 80
(Jim Boyle) *s.i.s: t.k.h: hld up in rr: clsd and travelling strly whn nt clr run 2f out: swtchd rt and effrt over 1f out: hung lft but qcknd to ld ins fnl f: r.o wl: readily* **11/4**[1]

4321 **2** 2 **Mr Red Clubs (IRE)**[6] 940 5-9-13 **76** 6ex.......................... AndrewMullen 4 81
(Michael Appleby) *hld up in midfield: rdn and qcknd to ld 1f out: hdd and outpcd by wnr fnl 100yds: r.o for clr 2nd* **3/1**[2]

3113 **3** 2 1/4 **Wishformore (IRE)**[27] 672 7-8-11 **60**..........................(v[1]) StevieDonohoe 10 60
(Ian Williams) *chsd ldng pair: clsd and rdn ent fnl 2f: pressed ldrs 1f out: 3rd and outpcd ins fnl f* **12/1**

3443 **4** 2 1/2 **Run It Twice (IRE)**[6] 940 4-9-3 **69**..........................(b) DeclanBates(3) 1 63
(David Evans) *dwlt and rdn along leaving stalls: racd in last trio: hdwy on inner over 2f out: drvn and chsd ldrs over 1f out: outpcd fnl f* **5/1**[3]

2640 **5** 1 **Greensward**[14] 843 8-9-5 **68**..........................(b) LiamKeniry 11 60
(Conor Dore) *hld up in midfield on outer: clsd 3f out: rdn and unable qck over 1f out: wknd fnl f* **12/1**

3-16 **6** 1/2 **Ostralegus**[58] 255 4-9-3 **69**.......................... MichaelJMMurphy(3) 6 60
(John Gallagher) *chsd clr ldr: clsd 3f out: rdn to ld ent fnl 2f: hdd 1f out: wknd ins fnl f* **16/1**

000- **7** 1 1/2 **Choral Festival**[126] 7865 8-8-12 **66**.......................... RyanWhile(5) 9 54
(John Bridger) *midfield tl dropped to rr 5f out: rdn and sme hdwy over 1f out: styd on but no threat to ldrs* **40/1**

-660 **8** 2 1/2 **Decent Fella (IRE)**[19] 779 8-9-5 **68**..........................(t) AdamKirby 3 50
(Ann Stokell) *hld up in last trio: clsd 3f out: rdn and no imp over 1f out: nvr trbld ldrs* **3/1**[2]

0-00 **9** 13 **Fairy Wing (IRE)**[48] 383 7-8-8 **57**..........................(b) BenCurtis 2 9
(Ann Stokell) *led and sn clr: rdn and hdd ent fnl 2f: wknd over 1f out: fdd fnl f* **50/1**

00-0 **10** 2 1/2 **Rezwaan**[53] 345 7-9-3 **66**..........................(b) ShaneKelly 7 12
(Murty McGrath) *racd in midfield: rdn and lost pl 3f out: bhd 2f out: sn lost tch* **33/1**

1m 38.09s (-0.11) **Going Correction** +0.125s/f (Slow) **10** Ran SP% **121.9**
Speed ratings (Par 103): **105,103,100,98,97 96,95,92,79,77**
CSF £11.72 CT £89.94 TOTE £3.70: £1.50, £1.50, £3.10; EX 13.10 Trifecta £100.60.
**Owner** M Fitzgerald **Bred** D J And Mrs Deer **Trained** Epsom, Surrey

**FOCUS**
Another strongly run affair that suited the closers. The form is rated around the second.

## 1022 CORAL.CO.UK H'CAP 1m 2f (P)
**5:10** (6:01) (Class 5) (0-75,75) 4-Y-0+ **£2,726** (£805; £402) **Stalls** Low

Form RPR

4-33 **1** **Havelovewilltravel (IRE)**[19] 782 4-9-5 **73**.......................... RyanMoore 7 80
(Jeremy Noseda) *chsd ldr: drvn to ld jst over 1f out: hrd pressed fnl 100yds: hld on gamely: all out* **2/1**[1]

2-64 **2** *nse* **Perfect Cracker**[14] 849 6-9-4 **72**.......................... AdamKirby 6 79
(Clive Cox) *hld up in tch in midfield: swtchd out rt and effrt over 1f out: str chal ins fnl f: r.o u.p: jst hld* **9/4**[2]

13-0 **3** *hd* **Syncopate**[70] 89 5-9-5 **73**.......................... LiamKeniry 4 80
(Pam Sly) *chsd ldrs: rdn and effrt on inner over 1f out: ev ch fnl 100yds: r.o but no ex cl home* **20/1**

5333 **4** 1 3/4 **Cathedral**[14] 849 5-8-5 **66**.......................... AlistairRawlinson(7) 2 69
(Ed de Giles) *dwlt: hld up in tch towards rr: swtchd lft ent fnl f: styd on same pce fnl 100yds* **9/2**[3]

5226 **5** 1/2 **Lady Lunchalot (USA)**[14] 849 4-9-5 **73**..........................(p) LiamJones 8 75
(Laura Mongan) *in tch in midfield: effrt u.p 2f out: styd on same pce ins fnl f* **14/1**

525- **6** 1 3/4 **Strong Conviction**[19] 6867 4-9-4 **72**.......................... JimCrowley 9 71
(Simon Hodgson) *led: rdn ent fnl 2f: hdd over 1f out: wknd ins fnl f* **33/1**

-240 **7** 1/2 **Apache Glory (USA)**[14] 849 6-9-5 **73**..........................(p) ShaneKelly 1 71
(John Stimpson) *hld up in tch: rdn and effrt 2f out: styd on same pce and no imp fr over 1f out* **20/1**

2-00 **8** 2 1/2 **Palus San Marco (IRE)**[45] 450 5-9-1 **72**.......................... RobertTart(3) 5 65
(Tony Carroll) *stdd s: hld up in rr: rdn over 2f out: kpt on but no imp fnl 2f* **33/1**

-523 **9** 2 3/4 **Smokethatthunders (IRE)**[49] 372 4-9-7 **75**.......................... StevieDonohoe 3 63
(Tim Pitt) *stdd s: t.k.h: hld up in last trio: hdwy into midfield 1/2-way: chsd ldrs and rdn 2f out: wknd over 1f out* **10/1**

2m 8.87s (2.27) **Going Correction** +0.125s/f (Slow) **9** Ran SP% **113.4**
Speed ratings (Par 103): **95,94,94,93,93 91,91,89,87**
CSF £6.13 CT £61.49 TOTE £2.50: £1.10, £1.10, £6.50; EX 7.60 Trifecta £96.00.
**Owner** Joseph Barton **Bred** Lynch Bages Ltd **Trained** Newmarket, Suffolk

**FOCUS**
A fair handicap for the grade run at a steady pace. The front three fought out a thrilling finish. The third helps anchor the level.
T/Plt: £37.60 to a £1 stake. Pool: £76,781.06 - 1,488.02 winning tickets. T/Qpdt: £6.20 to a £1 stake. Pool: £8,176.82 - 967.45 winning tickets. SP

# 1008 KEMPTON (A.W) (R-H)
### Thursday, March 20

**OFFICIAL GOING: Standard**
Wind: Strong across (away from stands) Weather: Overcast, raining after race 2

## 1023 GOFFS LONDON SALE - KEMPTON-BREEZE/KENSINGTON-SALE H'CAP 1m (P)
**5:55** (5:55) (Class 6) (0-60,60) 4-Y-0+ **£1,940** (£577; £288; £144) **Stalls** Low

Form RPR

06-0 **1** **Anjuna Beach (USA)**[17] 821 4-9-3 **56**.......................... GeorgeBaker 5 65+
(Gary Moore) *slowly away: hld up in last: rdn and gd prog on inner over 2f out: styd on wl fnl f to ld last 75yds: won gng away* **9/1**

6311 **2** 1 1/4 **Bennelong**[21] 754 8-8-11 **57**..........................(b) PaigeBolton(7) 3 63
(Lee Carter) *prom: chsd ldr 1/2-way: pushed along and clsd fr 2f out: led jst ins fnl f: hdd and nt qckn last 75yds* **9/2**[2]

0433 **3** 1 1/4 **Divine Rule (IRE)**[17] 815 6-9-5 **58**..........................(p) LiamJones 8 61
(Laura Mongan) *hld up towards rr: urged along over 2f out: kpt on fr over 1f out to take 3rd nr fin* **10/1**

4-31 **4** 3/4 **Pearl Ransom (IRE)**[44] 467 4-9-0 **60**..........................(v) AlistairRawlinson(7) 1 61
(Ed de Giles) *sn pushed up to ld: 5 l clr over 3f out: rdn and hung lft 2f out: hdd & wknd jst ins fnl f* **7/2**[1]

561 **5** *nk* **Fleetwoodsands (IRE)**[21] 755 7-8-10 **52**.......................... DeclanBates(3) 13 53
(David Evans) *racd wd in rr: urged along over 2f out: styd on wl fnl f: nrst fin* **16/1**

22-4 **6** *shd* **Up Tipp**[71] 90 4-9-4 **57**.......................... RichardHughes 9 57
(Mike Murphy) *chsd ldrs: pushed along over 2f out: kpt on same pce fr over 1f out: no real danger* **7/2**[1]

50-6 **7** 1 1/4 **Wyndham Wave**[21] 754 5-9-0 **53**..........................(p) FrederikTylicki 10 51
(Rod Millman) *chsd ldr to 1/2-way: sn pushed along: wknd over 1f out* **10/1**

20-0 **8** 3 1/2 **Habeshia**[17] 815 4-9-4 **57**..........................(v) RobertHavlin 11 47
(John Best) *chsd ldrs: u.p and no prog over 2f out: sn wknd* **25/1**

0-41 **9** 3 1/4 **Fire King**[15] 844 8-8-13 **52**..........................(p) JimmyQuinn 4 34
(Paul Burgoyne) *chsd ldrs: rdn and no prog over 2f out: wknd over 1f out: eased* **12/1**

-406 **10** 1 3/4 **Bold Ring**[26] 718 8-9-3 **56**.......................... TomQueally 6 34
(Edward Creighton) *hld up in rr: brief effrt over 2f out: no hdwy over 1f out: wknd* **25/1**

660- **11** 19 **Uncle Fred**[120] 7981 9-9-0 **53**.......................... JimCrowley 14
(Patrick Chamings) *hung lft and ended on outer rail after 3f: sn t.o* **8/1**[3]

1m 40.76s (0.96) **Going Correction** +0.10s/f (Slow) **11** Ran SP% **123.2**
Speed ratings (Par 101): **99,97,96,95,95 95,94,90,87,85 66**
CSF £51.71 CT £422.67 TOTE £12.30: £3.80, £1.30, £3.60; EX 70.30 Trifecta £617.20.
**Owner** C E Stedman **Bred** Daniel J Yates **Trained** Lower Beeding, W Sussex

**FOCUS**
A modest handicap, but it was competitive and the pace was strong. It produced a slow-motion finish but the form makes sense.

## 1024 BETVICTOR 6 PLACES GRAND NATIONAL MEDIAN AUCTION MAIDEN FILLIES' STKS 1m (P)
**6:25** (6:29) (Class 5) 3-5-Y-0 **£2,587** (£770; £384; £192) **Stalls** Low

Form RPR

6- **1** **Emaratiya Ana (IRE)**[183] 6523 3-8-11 0.......................... WilliamBuick 6 71+
(Roger Varian) *reluctant to enter stalls: led 1f: trckd ldrs: shkn up 2f out: clsd to ld jst over 1f out: pushed along and styd on wl* **5/4**[1]

4 **2** 2 **Sparkling Ice (IRE)**[19] 800 3-8-11 0.......................... JohnFahy 3 64
(Eve Johnson Houghton) *hld up in 6th: clsd on ldrs over 2f out: prog over 1f out to chse wnr ins fnl f: styd on but no imp* **10/1**

0- **3** 2 **Rio Yuma (ITY)**[156] 7260 3-8-6 0.......................... JacobButterfield(5) 2 60
(Kristin Stubbs) *trckd ldng pair after 1f: effrt on inner 2f out: outpcd fr jst over 1f out* **66/1**

23 **4** 1 ¼ **Blacke Forest**[41] 512 3-8-11 0 ...................... RichardHughes 5 57
(William Muir) *led after 1f: shkn up over 2f out: hdd jst over 1f out: pushed along and fdd* **7/2**[2]

0-44 **5** 1 **Joyful Risk (IRE)**[29] 660 4-10-0 69 ...................... GeorgeBaker 7 60
(Martin Bosley) *trckd ldr after 1f: shkn up 2f out: nt qckn over 1f out: fdd* **7/1**[3]

0 **6** ¾ **Purana**[29] 660 3-8-11 0 ...................... DavidProbert 9 53
(Tony Carroll) *t.k.h: hld up in 5th: shkn up 2f out: no imp on ldrs over 1f out* **10/1**

0 **7** nk **Kovolini**[22] 748 4-10-0 0 ...................... SteveDrowne 10 57
(Geoffrey Deacon) *settled in 7th and off the pce: pushed along over 2f out: threatened to cl over 1f out: one pce after* **66/1**

**8** 4 ½ **Cypress Point (FR)** 3-8-11 0 ...................... JimmyQuinn 4 42
(Ed Vaughan) *awkward s: a in last trio: nvr really figured* **8/1**

**9** 7 **Flying By** 3-8-11 0 ...................... ChrisCatlin 8 26
(Rae Guest) *dwlt: rn green and a wl in rr* **16/1**

0 **10** 50 **Amelia George**[47] 422 4-10-0 0 ...................... AdamBeschizza 1
(Julia Feilden) *sn bhd: wl t.o* **33/1**

1m 42.02s (2.22) **Going Correction** +0.10s/f (Slow)
**WFA** 3 from 4yo 17lb **10** Ran SP% **120.3**
Speed ratings (Par 100): **92,90,88,86,85 85,84,80,73,23**
CSF £16.21 TOTE £2.20: £1.10, £2.80, £13.20; EX 21.00 Trifecta £1587.00.
**Owner** Ahmad Abdulla Al Shaikh **Bred** Lynch Bages Ltd **Trained** Newmarket, Suffolk

**FOCUS**
Just an ordinary fillies' maiden. The principals were unexposed and the winner could well rate a good deal higher.

## 1025 GOFFS LONDON SALE IN JUNE CLAIMING STKS 7f (P)
6:55 (6:56) (Class 6) 4-Y-0+ £1,940 (£577; £288; £144) Stalls Low

Form RPR

3122 **1** **Seek The Fair Land**[17] 825 8-8-11 75 ...................... (b) LouisSteward(5) 3 70+
(Lee Carter) *trckd ldng pair: led on inner wl over 1f out and sent for home: hrd rdn fnl f: jst hld on* **5/4**[2]

-523 **2** hd **Polar Kite (IRE)**[19] 806 6-9-5 75 ...................... AdamKirby 4 73+
(Sean Curran) *dwlt: hld up in last pair: sltly outpcd wl over 1f out: hrd rdn and styd on to take 2nd 150yds out: grad clsd on wnr: jst failed* **1/1**[1]

-200 **3** nk **Timothy T**[17] 815 6-8-9 58 ...................... (b) LiamKeniry 5 62
(Philip Hide) *t.k.h: trckd ldr: led jst over 2f out to wl over 1f out: sn hrd rdn: lost 2nd 150yds out but kpt on wl nr fin* **10/1**[3]

0/6- **4** 6 **Viva Vettori**[325] 1890 10-8-10 87 ...................... CharlesBishop(3) 1 50
(Brian Forsey) *hld up in last pair: outpcd 2f out: drvn and no imp on ldrs over 1f out: fdd* **10/1**[3]

0-50 **5** 1 ½ **Jambobo**[17] 815 5-8-10 37 ...................... (b) JohnFahy 2 43
(Chris Down) *pushed up to ld: stdd pce after 2f: rdn and hdd jst over 2f out: wknd* **66/1**

0 **6** 7 **Park Dancer**[29] 660 7-8-3 0 ...................... JackGarritty(7) 6 24
(Martin Bosley) *trckd ldrs tl wknd over 2f out: t.o* **66/1**

1m 26.35s (0.35) **Going Correction** +0.10s/f (Slow) **6** Ran SP% **115.6**
Speed ratings (Par 101): **102,101,101,94,92 84**
.Polar Kite was claimed for £12,000 by Mr Christian Main\n\x\x Timothy T was claimed for £2000 by Mr William Muir
**Owner** John Joseph Smith **Bred** Raimon Bloodstock **Trained** Epsom, Surrey

**FOCUS**
An uncompetitive claimer run in a poor time. The fifth suggests the bare form is no better than rated.

## 1026 GRAND NATIONAL 6 PLACES AT BETVICTOR.COM H'CAP 7f (P)
7:25 (7:25) (Class 5) (0-75,75) 4-Y-0+ £2,587 (£770; £384; £192) Stalls Low

Form RPR

1-20 **1** **Fanoos**[17] 825 5-9-6 74 ...................... (p) RichardKingscote 3 86
(Dr Jon Scargill) *hld up in 6th: prog on inner over 2f out: rdn to ld jst over 1f out: styd on wl* **5/1**[3]

2531 **2** 1 ½ **Strong Man**[21] 757 6-9-5 73 ...................... (b) GrahamGibbons 6 81
(Michael Easterby) *led: rdn and pressed 2f out: hdd jst over 1f out: dropped to 3rd ins fnl f: kpt on to take 2nd last strides* **2/1**[1]

3226 **3** hd **Ocean Legend (IRE)**[20] 790 9-9-4 72 ...................... TomQueally 4 79
(Tony Carroll) *trckd ldrs: clsd 2f out: rdn to chal and upsides jst over 1f out: nt qckn and lost 2nd nr fin* **4/1**[2]

235- **4** 3 ½ **Light Rose (IRE)**[149] 7438 4-9-4 72 ...................... AdamKirby 2 70
(Jeremy Gask) *cl up: wnt 2nd over 2f out and sn chalng: shkn up and nt qckn over 1f out: fdd fnl f* **6/1**

340- **5** 5 **George Baker (IRE)**[148] 7462 7-9-2 70 ...................... WilliamBuick 1 54
(George Baker) *hld up in last pair: lost tch 3f out: shkn up 2f out: no prog* **8/1**

410- **6** 3 **Bountybeamadam**[131] 7824 4-9-4 72 ...................... (p) RichardHughes 7 48
(George Baker) *racd v wd early: chsd ldr to over 2f out: sn wknd* **16/1**

0535 **7** ½ **Sheikh The Reins (IRE)**[8] 925 5-9-0 68 ...................... (v) RobertHavlin 8 43
(John Best) *restless in stalls: dwlt: prog fr rr on outer to press ldng pair after 3f: wknd over 2f out* **16/1**

-110 **8** 6 **Basingstoke (IRE)**[21] 767 5-9-7 75 ...................... SteveDrowne 5 34
(Simon Hodgson) *a in last pair: bhd fr 3f out: t.o* **10/1**

1m 25.36s (-0.64) **Going Correction** +0.10s/f (Slow) **8** Ran SP% **116.3**
Speed ratings (Par 103): **107,105,105,101,95 91,91,84**
CSF £15.73 CT £43.93 TOTE £5.60: £2.50, £1.10, £2.00; EX 19.60 Trifecta £49.60.
**Owner** Theme Tune Partnership **Bred** Miss Otis Partnership **Trained** Newmarket, Suffolk

**FOCUS**
A fair handicap. The form fits.

## 1027 6 PLACES AT AINTREE AT BETVICTOR.COM H'CAP 1m 4f (P)
7:55 (7:56) (Class 5) (0-70,68) 4-Y-0+ £2,587 (£770; £384; £192) Stalls Centre

Form RPR

302- **1** **Grey Blue (IRE)**[32] 7091 4-9-0 63 ...................... TomQueally 5 75+
(Nicky Henderson) *led after nthing else wanted to: mde all at stdy pce: skipped away wl over 2f out: wandered briefly u.p over 1f out: styd on: unchal* **2/1**[2]

-162 **2** 2 ¾ **My Lord**[19] 801 6-9-6 67 ...................... LukeMorris 6 73
(Luke Dace) *hld up in 4th: prog to chse wnr over 2f out: tried to cl over 1f out: styd on but no imp fnl f* **11/2**

-041 **3** 2 **Menelik (IRE)**[20] 775 5-9-5 66 ...................... (v) AdamKirby 8 68
(Lee Carter) *stdd s: hld up in last pair in slowly run event: prog over 2f out but ldng pair already gone: drvn to go 3rd jst over 1f out: kpt on* **9/2**[3]

012 **4** 1 ¼ **Handsome Stranger (IRE)**[8] 922 4-8-9 65 ...................... (p) DavidParkes(7) 3 65
(Alan Bailey) *trckd wnr 2f: rdn and nt qckn wl over 2f out: sn outpcd: kpt on fnl f* **7/4**[1]

43-0 **5** 2 ½ **See And Be Seen**[35] 590 4-8-9 58 ...................... (p) RenatoSouza 9 54
(Sylvester Kirk) *hld up in last pair: struggling 3f out: sn outpcd: no ch after* **14/1**

0/00 **6** nk **Swampfire (IRE)**[19] 801 6-9-6 67 ...................... GeorgeBaker 2 63
(Gary Moore) *prog to trck wnr after 2f: shkn up and nt qckn wl over 2f out: sn lost 2nd and btn* **25/1**

560- **7** 1 **Marcus Antonius**[66] 4679 7-9-1 62 ...................... StephenCraine 4 56
(Jim Boyle) *stdd s: hld up in 5th: rdn and nt qckn wl over 2f out: outpcd and no ch after* **20/1**

2m 36.52s (2.02) **Going Correction** +0.10s/f (Slow)
**WFA** 4 from 5yo+ 2lb **7** Ran SP% **118.5**
Speed ratings (Par 103): **97,95,93,93,91 91,90**
CSF £14.36 CT £45.40 TOTE £3.10: £1.70, £3.60; EX 13.50 Trifecta £63.70.
**Owner** A D Spence **Bred** Twelve Oaks Stud **Trained** Upper Lambourn, Berks

**FOCUS**
A modest handicap, but it was a tactical affair and the pace was steady. The winner had the run of the race but can rate higher still.

## 1028 FOLLOW @BETVICTORRACING ON TWITTER H'CAP (LONDON MIDDLE DISTANCE QUALIFIER) (BOBIS RACE) 1m 3f (P)
8:25 (8:25) (Class 4) (0-85,82) 3-Y-O £4,690 (£1,395; £697) Stalls Low

Form RPR

0-11 **1** **Tizlove Regardless (USA)**[17] 828 3-8-10 71 ...................... SilvestreDeSousa 3 83+
(Mark Johnston) *mde all: stretched on over 3f out: rdn 2f out: styd on after and drew away nr fin* **4/9**[1]

053- **2** 2 ¾ **Libeccio (FR)**[171] 6896 3-8-10 71 ...................... DavidProbert 4 74+
(Andrew Balding) *trckd wnr: shkn up 3f out: hanging whn asked to cl 2f out: in tch 1f out: one pce after* **11/4**[2]

001- **3** 4 ½ **Rite To Reign**[117] 8026 3-9-2 77 ...................... RichardHughes 2 74
(Philip McBride) *cl up in 3rd: rdn over 3f out: no imp 2f out: eased whn btn fnl f* **7/1**[3]

2m 19.35s (-2.55) **Going Correction** +0.10s/f (Slow) **3** Ran SP% **108.4**
Speed ratings (Par 100): **113,111,107**
CSF £2.00 TOTE £1.90; EX 1.60 Trifecta £1.60.
**Owner** Crone Stud Farms Ltd **Bred** WinStar Farm LLC **Trained** Middleham Moor, N Yorks

**FOCUS**
Only three runners and an uncompetitive race for the grade, but the winner is progressive. Not the easiest form to contemplate.

## 1029 VISIT VICTOR'S LIVE CASINO AT BETVICTOR.COM H'CAP 1m 3f (P)
8:55 (8:56) (Class 6) (0-60,59) 3-Y-O £1,940 (£577; £288; £144) Stalls Low

Form RPR

033- **1** **Jarlath**[127] 7855 3-9-3 55 ...................... SteveDrowne 7 60
(Seamus Mullins) *trckd ldr: rdn over 2f out: chal over 2f out: chsd new ldr ins fnl f: styd on to ld last strides* **4/1**[3]

0612 **2** hd **Shannon Haven (IRE)**[23] 743 3-9-4 56 ...................... ShaneKelly 2 61
(Daniel Mark Loughnane) *hld up in 6th: clsd on ldrs fr 2f out: gap appeared and rdn to ld last 150yds: edgd lft and hdd fnl strides* **5/2**[2]

0632 **3** 1 ½ **Needs The Run**[14] 865 3-9-1 53 ...................... AdamKirby 5 55
(David Evans) *led: rdn over 2f out: kpt on same pce fr over 1f out: hdd and no ex last 150yds* **7/1**

00-1 **4** ½ **Lucky Dottie**[23] 738 3-8-9 47 ...................... FrankieMcDonald 4 48
(Pat Phelan) *t.k.h: trckd ldng pair: rdn over 2f out: tried to chal over 1f out: nt qckn* **33/1**

0-62 **5** 4 ½ **Beastfromtheeast**[44] 480 3-8-11 49 ...................... LukeMorris 3 43
(Ed Walker) *chsd ldrs: pushed along 4f out: no imp fr over 2f out* **2/1**[1]

605- **6** 8 **Vera Lou (IRE)**[90] 8362 3-9-1 53 ......................[1] TomQueally 1 34
(Pat Eddery) *mostly in last and nt gng wl after 3f: wknd over 2f out* **16/1**

6-46 **7** 17 **Amontillado (IRE)**[61] 236 3-9-7 59 ...................... (b) RichardHughes 6 13
(Richard Hannon) *trckd ldng trio: urged along 3f out: hung lft sn after and btn: eased over 1f out: t.o: lame* **10/1**

2m 24.11s (2.21) **Going Correction** +0.10s/f (Slow) **7** Ran SP% **112.3**
Speed ratings (Par 96): **95,94,93,93,90 84,71**
CSF £13.90 TOTE £4.40: £2.30, £2.20; EX 18.10 Trifecta £59.40.
**Owner** Phoenix Bloodstock **Bred** D & C Bloodstock **Trained** Wilsford-Cum-Lake, Wilts

**FOCUS**
A moderate handicap, but fair form for the lowly grade.
T/Plt: £17.70 to a £1 stake. Pool: £96,030.79 - 3942.82 winning units. T/Qpdt: £3.00 to a £1 stake. Pool: £8785.16 - 2140.22 winning units. JN

# 994 WOLVERHAMPTON (A.W) (L-H)
Thursday, March 20

**OFFICIAL GOING: Standard**
Wind: Fresh behind Weather: Overcast turning showery after race 4

## 1030 BOOKMAKERS.CO.UK H'CAP 5f 20y(P)
2:10 (2:10) (Class 6) (0-65,65) 4-Y-0+ £2,587 (£770; £384; £192) Stalls Low

Form RPR

6554 **1** **West Coast Dream**[15] 841 7-9-4 62 ...................... TomEaves 4 72
(Roy Brotherton) *mde virtually all: rdn and edgd lft fr over 1f out: styd on* **2/1**[1]

6224 **2** 2 ¼ **Rose Garnet (IRE)**[5] 973 6-8-8 52 ...................... LukeMorris 2 56
(Tony Carroll) *sn w wnr: pushed along 1/2-way: rdn over 1f out: styng on same pce whn hmpd wl ins fnl f* **5/1**[2]

0002 **3** 1 ¾ **Haadeeth**[12] 889 7-9-7 65 ...................... (vt) AdamKirby 3 61
(David Evans) *chsd ldrs: pushed along 1/2-way: rdn over 1f out: styd on same pce* **2/1**[1]

06-5 **4** 1 ¾ **Hazard Warning (IRE)**[9] 913 4-9-5 63 ...................... (b) DuranFentiman 1 52
(Mandy Rowland) *hld up: rdn over 1f out: nvr on terms* **14/1**

0362 **5** 3 **Your Gifted (IRE)**[13] 866 7-8-7 56 ...................... (v) ShirleyTeasdale(5) 6 35
(Lisa Williamson) *prom: rdn over 1f out: wknd fnl f* **6/1**[3]

0-60 **6** 3 **Time For Lambrini (IRE)**[27] 687 4-8-11 55 ...................... JoeFanning 5 23
(Lisa Williamson) *sn pushed along in rr: wknd 1/2-way* **10/1**

1m 3.01s (0.71) **Going Correction** +0.15s/f (Slow) **6** Ran SP% **113.4**
Speed ratings (Par 101): **100,96,93,90,86 81**
CSF £12.81 TOTE £3.50: £2.00, £1.70; EX 15.00 Trifecta £43.40.
**Owner** Miss Emma Byrd **Bred** Eurostrait Ltd **Trained** Elmley Castle, Worcs

**FOCUS**
Moderate form. The winner has dropped a long way in the past year.

## 1031 COMPARE BOOKMAKERS AT BOOKMAKERS.CO.UK H'CAP 5f 216y(P)
2:40 (2:40) (Class 5) (0-75,75) 4-Y-0+ £3,881 (£1,155; £577; £288) Stalls Low

Form RPR
2512 1 **Go Far**[8] 925 4-9-6 74 6ex....(b) RobertWinston 5 87
(Alan Bailey) *chsd ldr: shkn up to ld over 1f out: rdn ins fnl f: r.o: eased nr fin* 3/1[3]
0-62 2 3 1/4 **Point North (IRE)**[47] 432 7-9-2 70.... DanielTudhope 2 73
(John Balding) *trckd ldrs: rdn and edgd lft over 1f out: chsd wnr ins fnl f: styd on same pce* 11/4[2]
05-3 3 1 1/2 **Bogsnog (IRE)**[77] 20 4-9-6 74.... TomEaves 3 73
(Kristin Stubbs) *led: rdn and hdd over 1f out: no ex ins fnl f* 7/1
6426 4 1 1/2 **Top Cop**[8] 925 5-9-4 72....(p) LukeMorris 1 66
(Ronald Harris) *prom: pushed along over 2f out: rdn over 1f out: wknd ins fnl f* 14/1
5561 5 1 **Invigilator**[15] 841 6-8-12 66....(t) StephenCraine 7 57
(Derek Shaw) *s.i.s: hld up: rdn over 1f out: nvr trbld ldrs* 8/1
0-61 6 1/2 **Loud**[8] 929 4-9-7 75 6ex.... JoeFanning 8 65
(Mark Johnston) *chsd ldrs: pushed along 4f out: wknd over 1f out* 5/2[1]
1m 15.39s (0.39) **Going Correction** +0.15s/f (Slow) 6 Ran SP% **110.5**
Speed ratings (Par 103): **103,98,96,94,93 92**
CSF £11.27 CT £47.50 TOTE £3.90: £2.20, £1.30; EX 14.30 Trifecta £54.80.
**Owner** R West **Bred** Michael Turner **Trained** Newmarket, Suffolk

**FOCUS**
Once again it paid to race with wind in the hair rather than with kickback in the face. A step up from the winner.

## 1032 32RED IMMORTAL ROMANCE SLOT H'CAP 1m 4f 50y(P)
3:15 (3:15) (Class 6) (0-65,62) 3-Y-O £2,587 (£770; £384; £192) Stalls Low

Form RPR
505- 1 **Piton**[124] 7936 3-9-5 60.... JoeFanning 3 76+
(Mark Johnston) *hld up in tch: led on bit over 3f out: clr fnl 2f: eased ins fnl f* 8/11[1]
6-23 2 12 **Hallouella**[13] 871 3-9-7 62....(p) LukeMorris 5 59
(James Tate) *chsd ldr: rdn and ev ch over 3f out: sn outpcd: eased ins fnl f* 9/2[3]
0-52 3 7 **Khee Society**[21] 761 3-9-6 61.... AdamKirby 4 43
(David Evans) *led: racd keenly: rdn and hdd over 3f out: wknd over 2f out* 7/2[2]
-600 4 3 **Deano's Devil (IRE)**[44] 480 3-8-5 46.... BarryMcHugh 2 23
(Richard Fahey) *hld up: a in rr: rdn and wknd wl over 2f out* 25/1
000- 5 59 **Bed Bed**[92] 8332 3-8-12 53.... StevieDonohoe 1
(Michael Bell) *chsd ldrs: rdn over 4f out: wknd 3f out: eased fnl 2f* 14/1
2m 42.5s (1.40) **Going Correction** +0.15s/f (Slow) 5 Ran SP% **108.8**
Speed ratings (Par 96): **101,93,88,86,47**
CSF £4.26 TOTE £1.60: £1.10, £2.70; EX 4.90 Trifecta £9.90.
**Owner** T T Bloodstocks **Bred** Miss K Rausing **Trained** Middleham Moor, N Yorks

**FOCUS**
This proved a simple task for handicap debutant Piton, who looked miles ahead of his mark on this evidence.

## 1033 32RED.COM H'CAP 1m 1f 103y(P)
3:50 (3:50) (Class 5) (0-75,68) 3-Y-O £3,881 (£1,155; £577; £288) Stalls Low

Form RPR
P5-4 1 **Maxie T**[29] 668 3-9-5 66.... JoeFanning 1 71
(Mark Johnston) *mde all: rdn over 1f out: styd on* 5/1[3]
4212 2 1/2 **Zamra (IRE)**[17] 828 3-9-7 68....(p) LukeMorris 3 72
(James Tate) *a.p: chsd wnr over 2f out: rdn over 1f out: styd on u.p* 3/1[2]
32-2 3 1 1/2 **Byron Gala**[21] 753 3-9-0 61....(b[1]) AdamKirby 2 62
(Marco Botti) *trckd wnr tl over 2f out: rdn over 1f out: styd on same pce ins fnl f* 2/1[1]
1113 4 1 **Masterpaver**[29] 668 3-9-7 68....(v) RobertWinston 4 67
(Alan Bailey) *hld up: rdn over 2f out: hung lft fr over 1f out: nt trble ldrs* 2/1[1]
2m 5.44s (3.74) **Going Correction** +0.15s/f (Slow) 4 Ran SP% **108.3**
Speed ratings (Par 98): **89,88,87,86**
CSF £18.82 TOTE £8.30; EX 16.10 Trifecta £44.60.
**Owner** Christopher W T Johnston **Bred** Meon Valley Stud **Trained** Middleham Moor, N Yorks

**FOCUS**
Mark Johnston enhanced his record in 3yo handicaps at this venue this season to a staggering 9-11 with the success of Maxie T in this four-runner affair. The winner was entitled to win on his peak 2yo form.

## 1034 CORAL MOBILE "JUST THREE CLICKS TO BET" (S) STKS 1m 1f 103y(P)
4:25 (4:25) (Class 6) 4-Y-O+ £2,587 (£770; £384; £192) Stalls Low

Form RPR
4043 1 **Dozy Joe**[9] 910 6-8-12 59....(b) LukeMorris 4 71
(Joseph Tuite) *chsd clr ldr: tk clsr order 1/2-way: shkn up to ld over 1f out: drvn out* 7/1
5333 2 3 3/4 **Yourinthewill (USA)**[6] 958 6-8-12 63.... StephenCraine 3 64
(Daniel Mark Loughnane) *sn led and clr to 1/2-way: rdn and hdd over 1f out: styd on same pce ins fnl f* 3/1[3]
3145 3 6 **Matraash (USA)**[27] 685 8-9-4 75....(be) ShaneKelly 1 58
(Daniel Mark Loughnane) *hld up: nt clr run over 3f out: hdwy over 2f out: rdn and wknd over 1f out* 2/1[1]
4 2 1/4 **Daily Advertiser (USA)** 6-8-12 0.... GrahamLee 5 48
(Tony Carroll) *s.s: hld up: rdn and wknd over 2f out* 10/1
2051 5 1 1/4 **Spanish Plume**[3] 1000 6-8-13 65....(p) JackDuern[(5)] 2 52
(Andrew Hollinshead) *hld up: hdwy over 3f out: rdn and wknd 2f out* 9/4[2]
2m 2.36s (0.66) **Going Correction** +0.15s/f (Slow) 5 Ran SP% **110.7**
Speed ratings (Par 101): **103,99,94,92,91**
CSF £27.70 TOTE £6.50: £3.50, £2.00; EX 14.40 Trifecta £26.60.There was no bid for the winner.
**Owner** Paddy Barrett **Bred** John Morton **Trained** Great Shefford, Berks

**FOCUS**
A moderate seller run at a fair pace. The form is rated a little cautiously.

## 1035 LADBROKES MAIDEN STKS 1m 141y(P)
5:00 (5:00) (Class 5) 3-Y-O+ £3,234 (£962; £481; £240) Stalls Low

Form RPR
U4 1 **Maahir**[17] 816 3-8-9 0.... LukeMorris 5 76
(Marco Botti) *broke wl and led early: sn lost pl: pushed along and hdwy over 3f out: rdn to ld ins fnl f: r.o* 11/4[2]
22 2 1 3/4 **Watersmeet**[17] 816 3-8-9 0.... JoeFanning 1 72
(Mark Johnston) *sn trcking ldrs: led over 3f out: shkn up over 1f out: hdd ins fnl f: styd on same pce: hung rt towards fin* 2/5[1]
3 6 **Arcamante (ITY)** 3-8-9 0....(b[1]) AntonioFresu 2 60
(Marco Botti) *prom: rdn over 2f out: hung lft and wknd over 1f out* 14/1[3]
00 4 10 **Sycophantic (IRE)**[7] 941 4-10-0 0.... FergusSweeney 6 44
(Jamie Osborne) *hld up: a in rr: wknd over 2f out* 33/1
4 5 nk **Crooked Arrow (IRE)**[30] 649 6-9-9 0.... ShirleyTeasdale[(5)] 3 43
(Marjorie Fife) *sn led: hdd 6f out: chsd ldr tl 4f out: wknd over 2f out* 25/1
2043 6 15 **Island Express (IRE)**[40] 531 7-9-9 45....(t) AnnStokell[(5)] 4 12
(Ann Stokell) *plld hrd: sn trcking ldr: led 6f out: hdd over 3f out: wknd over 2f out* 100/1
1m 52.44s (1.94) **Going Correction** +0.15s/f (Slow)
**WFA** 3 from 4yo+ 19lb 6 Ran SP% **112.5**
Speed ratings (Par 103): **97,95,90,81,80 67**
CSF £4.22 TOTE £3.30: £1.30, £1.10; EX 6.40 Trifecta £23.20.
**Owner** Sheikh Mohammed Bin Khalifa Al Maktoum **Bred** Peter Onslow **Trained** Newmarket, Suffolk

**FOCUS**
A modest maiden. The winner reversed Kempton form with the runner-up, who was a little below his best.

## 1036 LADBROKES H'CAP 1m 141y(P)
5:30 (5:30) (Class 6) (0-65,65) 4-Y-O+ £2,587 (£770; £384; £192) Stalls Low

Form RPR
4025 1 **My Single Malt (IRE)**[20] 782 6-9-7 65....(p[1]) PaulMulrennan 5 75
(Julie Camacho) *sn trcking ldr: led over 2f out: rdn clr fr over 1f out* 5/2[1]
2121 2 2 1/4 **Benandonner (USA)**[20] 780 11-8-13 57.... ShaneKelly 6 62
(Mike Murphy) *hld up: hdwy over 1f out: sn rdn: wnt 2nd ins fnl f: nt trble wnr* 3/1[2]
4-26 3 3 1/4 **Colour My World**[31] 643 4-9-4 62.... GrahamLee 2 60
(Ed McMahon) *led: rdn and hdd over 2f out: no ex fnl f* 7/2[3]
-206 4 nk **Ellaal**[58] 269 5-8-13 57.... JamesSullivan 1 55
(Ruth Carr) *prom: rdn over 2f out: styd on same pce fr over 1f out* 10/1
2550 5 2 1/2 **Amber Moon**[6] 964 9-8-2 51 oh6.... ShirleyTeasdale[(5)] 4 43
(Ann Stokell) *plld hrd and prom: rdn over 2f out: wknd over 1f out* 50/1
0211 6 16 **Pipers Piping (IRE)**[9] 918 8-9-1 62 6ex.... RossAtkinson[(3)] 3 21
(Mandy Rowland) *hld up: plld hrd: rdn over 3f out: sn wknd* 5/2[1]
1m 51.34s (0.84) **Going Correction** +0.15s/f (Slow) 6 Ran SP% **115.4**
Speed ratings (Par 101): **102,100,97,96,94 80**
CSF £10.79 TOTE £3.10: £1.60, £2.40; EX 10.60 Trifecta £42.70.
**Owner** Nigel Gravett **Bred** Ballylinch Stud **Trained** Norton, N Yorks

**FOCUS**
Once again it paid to race out of the kickback. Ordinary form.
T/Plt: £102.10 to a £1 stake. Pool: £58,088.50 - 415.28 winning units. T/Qpdt: £22.00 to a £1 stake. Pool: £3884.95 - 130.60 winning units. CR

1037 - (Foreign Racing) - See Raceform Interactive

# 1016 LINGFIELD (L-H)
Friday, March 21

**OFFICIAL GOING: Standard**
Wind: Fresh, half behind Weather: Fine

## 1038 BEST ODDS AT BOOKMAKERS.CO.UK CLAIMING STKS 6f 1y(P)
2:00 (2:00) (Class 6) 4-Y-O+ £2,385 (£704; £352) Stalls Low

Form RPR
2121 1 **Jubilee Brig**[20] 805 4-9-5 76....(v) AdamKirby 4 83
(Sean Curran) *trckd ldr: shkn up over 2f out: drvn and styd on to ld last 150yds: sn clr* 4/7[1]
0651 2 2 3/4 **Kuanyao (IRE)**[30] 662 8-9-2 78....(b) LouisSteward[(5)] 1 77
(Lee Carter) *led: shkn up 2f out: hdd last 150yds: wknd nr fin* 2/1[2]
2-16 3 1 1/4 **Song Of Parkes**[41] 532 7-8-9 73.... SladeO'Hara[(3)] 3 64
(Peter Grayson) *hld up in last: pushed along and outpcd over 2f out: rdn and one pce over 1f out* 10/1[3]
1m 11.05s (-0.85) **Going Correction** +0.025s/f (Slow) 3 Ran SP% **106.1**
Speed ratings (Par 101): **106,102,100**
CSF £1.94 TOTE £1.60; EX 1.70 Trifecta £2.00.
**Owner** Power Bloodstock Ltd **Bred** Sir Eric Parker **Trained** Hatford, Oxon

**FOCUS**
With all three runners officially rated in the 70s, this was a decent claimer in quality if not quantity, and there was nothing between the first two based on their current handicap marks. Despite the lack of competition, the pace was good. The winner is rated to his recent standard.

## 1039 32RED THUNDERSTRUCK II SLOT CASINO H'CAP 5f 6y(P)
2:30 (2:32) (Class 6) (0-65,62) 3-Y-O £2,726 (£805; £402) Stalls High

Form RPR
5433 1 **Biscuiteer**[21] 786 3-8-12 53....(b) FrederikTylicki 5 58
(Scott Dixon) *led to post: mde all: hung rt bnd wl over 1f out: drvn and styd on fnl f* 6/1[3]
0-42 2 3/4 **Katja**[34] 622 3-9-4 59.... JoeFanning 7 61
(J W Hills) *chsd wnr: carried rt and sltly impeded wl over 1f out: nt qckn fnl f: styd on nr fin* 2/1[1]
3302 3 3/4 **Diamondsinthesky (IRE)**[9] 933 3-9-2 57....(v) DaleSwift 1 57
(Derek Shaw) *chsd ldng pair: styd on inner in st: nt qckn fnl f: kpt on* 25/1
00-3 4 nk **Caminel (IRE)**[22] 756 3-9-7 62.... LiamKeniry 8 61
(Jeremy Gask) *hld up in 6th: rdn wl over 1f out: styd on fnl f: nrly snatched 3rd* 14/1
1345 5 1/2 **Artemis (IRE)**[9] 926 3-9-7 62.... AndreaAtzeni 10 59
(Conrad Allen) *s.i.s: hld up in 8th: rdn wl over 1f out: styd on fnl f: nrst fin but no ch* 6/1[3]
0-36 6 nk **Jalebi**[71] 94 3-9-1 56.... JimCrowley 3 52
(Jim Boyle) *chsd ldng trio: rdn and nt qckn over 1f out: one pce fnl f* 16/1
000- 7 1 1/2 **Sutton Sioux**[157] 7261 3-8-6 47.... LiamJones 2 37
(Jeremy Gask) *awkward s: chsd ldng trio: rdn wl over 1f out: wknd fnl f* 33/1
604- 8 1 1/4 **Dancing Juice**[156] 7293 3-9-2 57.... GrahamLee 9 43
(Alan Jarvis) *s.i.s: hld up in last: nvr a factor* 12/1
0-22 9 7 **Precariously Good**[57] 298 3-9-2 57.... RichardHughes 4 18+
(Paul Cole) *hld up in 7th: shkn up and no prog 2f out: eased whn no ch fnl f* 11/4[2]
59.03s (0.23) **Going Correction** +0.025s/f (Slow) 9 Ran SP% **115.6**
Speed ratings (Par 96): **99,97,96,96,95 94,92,90,79**
CSF £18.41 CT £284.15 TOTE £7.90: £2.00, £1.10, £3.90; EX 20.80 Trifecta £168.30.
**Owner** P J Dixon & Partners **Bred** Mrs Fiona Denniff **Trained** Babworth, Notts


The Form Book, Raceform Ltd, Newbury, RG14 5SJ

**FOCUS**
Many of these were in decent form and it wasn't a bad race of its type, though with one exception all the runners were fillies. The winner made all at a good pace, so it looked a solid performance. She was entitled to win off one standout run.

## 1040 LADBROKES H'CAP — 1m 1y(P)
3:00 (3:01) (Class 6) (0-65,65) 4-Y-0+ £2,726 (£805; £402) Stalls High

Form RPR
53-0 **1** **Cravat**30 [655] 5-9-7 **65**.................................................. AndreaAtzeni 3 73
(Ed de Giles) *chsd ldr after 3f: rdn over 2f out: led over 1f out: drvn and asserted fnl f* **2/1**1
-020 **2** 1 **Bloodsweatandtears**16 [843] 6-9-7 **65**.................................... GeorgeBaker 6 71
(William Knight) *led: rdn 2f out: hdd and nt qckn over 1f out: kpt on same pce* **9/4**2
1242 **3** 1 ¼ **Skidby Mill (IRE)**7 [952] 4-9-3 **61**........................................ LiamJones 4 64
(Laura Mongan) *dwlt: hld up in last trio: prog on inner wl over 1f out: drvn to try to chal fnl f: nt qckn* **9/2**3
- **4** ½ **The Firm (IRE)**35 [616] 5-9-7 **65**........................................ StephenCraine 2 67
(Daniel Mark Loughnane) *t.k.h: hld up in 4th: moved clsr 2f out: sn rdn and nt qckn: one pce fnl f* **6/1**
06-0 **5** nk **Titan Triumph**28 [690] 10-9-0 **58**........................................(t) RobertHavlin 7 59
(Michael Attwater) *hld up in last: stl there 2f out but gng bttr than many: rdn over 1f out: kpt on but no ch* **25/1**
5-05 **6** ½ **Alhaban (IRE)**9 [922] 8-9-4 **62**........................................(p) AdamKirby 1 63
(Ronald Harris) *chsd ldr 3f: rdn 3f out: no imp over 1f out: fdd* **16/1**
60-0 **7** 1 ¼ **Lewamy (IRE)**16 [846] 4-9-0 **58**........................................ FergusSweeney 5 55
(John Best) *mostly in last trio on outer: rdn over 2f out: no prog over 1f out: wl btn after* **20/1**
1m 39.54s (1.34) **Going Correction** +0.025s/f (Slow) **7** Ran SP% **111.1**
Speed ratings (Par 101): **94,93,91,91,90 90,89**
CSF £6.32 TOTE £2.90: £1.20, £4.20; EX 7.50 Trifecta £28.30.
**Owner** T Gould **Bred** Darley **Trained** Ledbury, H'fords

**FOCUS**
Only two of these ran well on their previous outings, and the pace was ordinary, so this isn't a race to get excited about. The second helps with the level.

## 1041 COMPARE BOOKMAKERS AT BOOKMAKERS.CO.UK H'CAP — 6f 1y(P)
3:35 (3:35) (Class 4) (0-85,85) 4-Y-0+ £5,822 (£1,732; £865; £432) Stalls Low

Form RPR
144- **1** **Breccbennach**143 [7603] 4-8-13 **77**........................................(tp) RichardHughes 8 85
(Seamus Durack) *gd spd fr wd draw: mde all: hrd pressed and drvn fnl f: hld on wl* **4/1**2
2-33 **2** shd **Palace Moon**30 [658] 9-9-4 **82**........................................(t) JimCrowley 1 90
(William Knight) *chsd ldng pair to over 2f out: shkn up on inner sn after: clsd over 1f out: tried to chal ins fnl f: kpt on to take 2nd last strides* **11/4**1
-545 **3** hd **Picansort**20 [802] 7-9-6 **84**........................................(v) ShaneKelly 2 91
(Peter Crate) *in tch: prog on outer fr 1/2-way: chsd wnr 2f out: str chal fnl f: nt qckn last 75yds: lost 2nd fnl strides* **6/1**
5000 **4** 1 ¼ **Clockmaker (IRE)**13 [890] 8-9-7 **85**........................................ TomQueally 4 89
(Conor Dore) *dwlt: t.k.h: hld up in rr: shkn up over 2f out: prog to go 4th ins fnl f: styd on but unable to chal* **14/1**
000- **5** 1 ¾ **Vincentti (IRE)**135 [7777] 4-9-2 **80**........................................ AdamKirby 5 78
(Ronald Harris) *chsd ldng trio: lost pl over 2f out: sn shkn up: no prog and btn over 1f out* **5/1**3
1104 **6** 1 **Valmina**18 [820] 7-9-1 **79**........................................(t) SteveDrowne 6 74
(Tony Carroll) *hld up in last pair: stl there 2f out: rdn over 1f out: one pce and no ch* **14/1**
3034 **7** 1 ¼ **Diamond Charlie (IRE)**20 [802] 6-9-6 **84**........................................ GrahamLee 9 76
(Simon Dow) *chsd wnr: lost pl sltly then bdly hmpd over 2f out: in rr whn nt clr run over 1f out: no ch after* **7/1**
0 **8** ½ **Bainne (IRE)**57 [294] 4-9-2 **80**........................................ AndreaAtzeni 3 70
(Jeremy Gask) *n.m.r s: hld up: prog on wd outside 3f out: chsd wnr briefly jst over 2f out: wknd over 1f out* **25/1**
0331 **9** ¾ **Temple Road (IRE)**18 [826] 6-8-10 **74**........................................ JoeFanning 7 62
(Milton Bradley) *hld up in last pair: tried to make prog on outer 2f out: no hdwy over 1f out: fdd* **8/1**
1m 11.41s (-0.49) **Going Correction** +0.025s/f (Slow) **9** Ran SP% **118.4**
Speed ratings (Par 105): **104,103,103,101,99 98,96,95,94**
CSF £15.88 CT £66.36 TOTE £4.60: £1.40, £1.60, £2.30; EX 23.70 Trifecta £156.10.
**Owner** Mrs Anne Cowley **Bred** Bloomsbury Stud **Trained** Baydon, Wilts

**FOCUS**
A mixed bunch, but the overall standard was above average for Polytrack and the winner is the one going in the right direction. The gallop wasn't bad considering lack of front-runners, with the winner taking up the role and Richard Hughes judging it well. Improved form from the winner.

## 1042 LADBROKES MOBILE H'CAP — 7f 1y(P)
4:10 (4:10) (Class 3) (0-95,92) 4-Y-0+ £9,703 (£2,887; £1,443; £721) Stalls Low

Form RPR
134- **1** **Purcell (IRE)**168 [6993] 4-9-0 **88**........................................ OisinMurphy(3) 4 96
(Andrew Balding) *trckd ldng trio: clsd 2f out: rdn to ld jst over 1f out: hrd pressed fnl f: edgd lft nr fin* **3/1**1
150- **2** hd **Brownsea Brink**120 [7991] 4-9-6 **91**........................................ RichardHughes 6 98
(Richard Hannon) *trckd ldr: rdn over 2f out: led briefly over 1f out: kpt on wl to press wnr fnl f: nudged nr fin: jst hld* **6/1**3
0-0 **3** ¾ **Chilworth Icon**64 [207] 4-9-4 **92**.................. WilliamTwiston-Davies(3) 3 98
(Mick Channon) *hld up in last quartet: shkn up over 2f out: tried to cl on ldrs over 1f out: styd on to take 3rd nr fin* **20/1**
0103 **4** shd **Corporal Maddox**4 [991] 7-9-2 **87**........................................(p) AdamKirby 8 92
(Ronald Harris) *trckd ldng quartet: shkn up over 2f out: nt qckn over 1f out: kpt on fnl f: nt pce to chal* **8/1**
-004 **5** ½ **Bravo Echo**17 [836] 8-9-6 **91**........................................ RobertHavlin 1 95
(Michael Attwater) *trckd ldng pair: rdn on inner 2f out: nt qckn over 1f out: one pce after* **25/1**
-101 **6** hd **Forceful Appeal (USA)**28 [689] 6-9-2 **87**........................................ GrahamLee 9 90
(Simon Dow) *off the pce in last quartet: rdn over 2f out: no prog tl styd on ins fnl f: nrst fin* **9/2**2
600- **7** 1 ¾ **Jack Of Diamonds (IRE)**181 [6647] 5-9-2 **87**.............. RobertWinston 2 88
(Roger Teal) *dwlt: mostly in last: pushed along fr 1/2-way: nvr involved but kpt on steadily on inner fr over 1f out* **6/1**3
560- **8** 1 **Heavy Metal**181 [6650] 4-8-13 **84**........................................ JoeFanning 5 80
(Mark Johnston) *restless stalls: a in last quartet: pushed along 1/2-way: no prog and wl btn over 1f out* **9/2**2
5-00 **9** nk **Dr Red Eye**13 [886] 6-9-2 **87**........................................(p) FrederikTylicki 7 83
(Scott Dixon) *led at fast pce to over 1f out: wknd qckly* **10/1**
1m 23.07s (-1.73) **Going Correction** +0.025s/f (Slow) **9** Ran SP% **118.7**
Speed ratings (Par 107): **110,109,108,108,108 108,106,104,104**
CSF £22.02 CT £310.27 TOTE £5.20: £1.70, £2.30, £9.60; EX 22.60 Trifecta £361.00.
**Owner** Highclere Thoroughbred Racing-JohnPorter **Bred** Rathbarry Stud **Trained** Kingsclere, Hants
■ Stewards' Enquiry : Oisin Murphy one-day ban: careless riding (Apr 4)

**FOCUS**
Run at a decent pace, this was a competitive race, with the first two setting themselves up for a good year on their seasonal debuts. The winner edged into the runner-up near the finish but it came too late to affect the result. The form could be rated a little higher.

## 1043 32RED MERMAIDS MILLIONS SLOT H'CAP — 1m 7f 169y(P)
4:45 (4:47) (Class 5) (0-75,74) 4-Y-0+ £3,408 (£1,006; £503) Stalls Low

Form RPR
5-11 **1** **King's Request (IRE)**24 [742] 4-9-6 **73**........................................ LiamJones 3 80
(Laura Mongan) *trckd ldng trio: rdn whn pce lifted over 3f out: responded to go 2nd over 2f out: drvn to ld 1f out: grad asserted* **6/4**1
31-1 **2** ¾ **Ordensritter (GER)**18 [818] 6-9-12 **74**........................................ JohnFahy 1 80
(Chris Down) *trckd ldr: led 3f out gng strly: rdn 2f out: hdd 1f out: kpt on but hld after* **9/2**3
1012 **3** 1 ½ **Keep Kicking (IRE)**24 [742] 7-9-8 **70**........................................ JimCrowley 6 74
(Simon Dow) *hld up in last pair: tried to make prog fr 3f out: drvn and kpt on to take 3rd fnl f: nvr able to chal* **4/1**2
6323 **4** ½ **Arashi**4 [992] 8-9-1 **63**........................................(v) DaleSwift 2 67
(Derek Shaw) *hld up in last pair: outpcd and pushed along 3f out: sme prog and shkn up over 1f out: kpt on but nvr threatened* **14/1**
1-3 **5** 4 **Outrageous Request**38 [567] 8-9-6 **73**........................................ LouisSteward(5) 4 72
(William Stone) *chsd ldng pair: rdn whn pce lifted over 3f out: wknd fr 2f out* **10/1**
404- **6** 7 **Miss Tiger Lily**152 [7395] 4-9-5 **72**........................................ RichardHughes 5 62
(Harry Dunlop) *led: tried to kick on over 3f out: sn hdd: wknd and eased over 1f out* **9/2**3
3m 27.2s (1.50) **Going Correction** +0.025s/f (Slow)
**WFA** 4 from 6yo+ 5lb **6** Ran SP% **112.1**
Speed ratings (Par 103): **97,96,95,95,93 90**
CSF £8.55 TOTE £2.60: £1.30, £2.20; EX 10.70 Trifecta £22.20.
**Owner** Mrs P J Sheen **Bred** Runnymede Farm Inc And Catesby W Clay **Trained** Epsom, Surrey

**FOCUS**
This was tactical, with a weak pace until 3f out. Though this could have led to a false result, it probably didn't suit any of the runners, with the short-priced favourite still winning and the placed horses also making sense. The winner continues to progress.

## 1044 32RED.COM MAIDEN STKS — 1m 2f (P)
5:15 (5:16) (Class 5) 3-Y-0 £3,408 (£1,006; £503) Stalls Low

Form RPR
**1** **Moonrise Landing (IRE)** 3-9-0 0........................................ JimCrowley 3 73+
(Ralph Beckett) *hld up in tch: prog on outer to go 3rd over 2f out: shkn up and clsd to ld 1f out: styd on wl: readily* **16/1**
32- **2** 1 ¼ **El Najmm (IRE)**174 [6829] 3-9-5 0........................................1 AndreaAtzeni 1 74
(Roger Varian) *trckd ldng pair to over 2f out: shkn up and nt qckn wl over 1f out: kpt on to take 2nd ins fnl f: no match for wnr* **4/11**1
23-3 **3** ½ **Roskilly (IRE)**18 [827] 3-9-5 78........................................ DavidProbert 5 73
(Andrew Balding) *led: jnd 4f out: rdn 2f out: hdd and one pce 1f out* **6/1**3
0-3 **4** 1 ¼ **Guaracha**13 [888] 3-9-5 0........................................ FrederikTylicki 6 71
(Clive Brittain) *hld up in tch: pushed along over 2f out: kpt on steadily fnl f: nt disgracd* **50/1**
0- **5** nk **Rookery (IRE)**164 [7089] 3-9-5 0........................................ JoeFanning 7 70
(Mark Johnston) *trckd ldr: upsides fr 4f out to wl over 1f out: fdd fnl f* **5/1**2
0 **6** 1 ½ **Bongo Beat**62 [231] 3-9-5 0........................................ RobertHavlin 4 67?
(Michael Attwater) *hld up in tch: pushed along on inner over 2f out: one pce and nvr able to threaten* **66/1**
**7** 45 **Carnt Cash Sorry** 3-9-5 0........................................ TomQueally 2
(Ed Vaughan) *greento post: v.s.a: rn green and a last: wknd 3f out: t.o* **33/1**
2m 7.82s (1.22) **Going Correction** +0.025s/f (Slow) **7** Ran SP% **116.5**
Speed ratings (Par 98): **96,95,94,93,93 92,56**
CSF £23.55 TOTE £11.90: £8.50, £1.10; EX 26.50 Trifecta £161.30.
**Owner** P D Savill **Bred** Oak Hill Stud **Trained** Kimpton, Hants

**FOCUS**
The runners were typical Polytrack maiden quality and the pace was ordinary, but the big finish of the winner makes her one to look out for next time. She's capable of much better than this bare form.
T/Plt: £35.90 to a £1 stake. Pool: £64138.88 - 1301.25 winning tickets T/Qpdt: £14.40 to a £1 stake. Pool: £5085.51 - 259.88 winning tickets JN

# 1030 WOLVERHAMPTON (A.W) (L-H)
Friday, March 21

**OFFICIAL GOING: Standard**
Wind: Fresh behind Weather: Cloudy with sunny spells

## 1045 32RED CASINO MAIDEN FILLIES' STKS — 5f 216y(P)
5:35 (5:35) (Class 5) 3-Y-0+ £2,911 (£866; £432; £216) Stalls Low

Form RPR
626- **1** **Moonspring (IRE)**155 [7327] 3-8-12 60........................................(e1) SeanLevey 1 64
(Robert Cowell) *led 1f: chsd ldr tl led again over 2f out: rdn and hung rt fnl f: jst hld on* **4/1**3
44-3 **2** shd **Bereka**15 [855] 3-8-12 65........................................ LukeMorris 5 64
(James Tate) *chsd ldrs: nt clr run 2f out: wnt 2nd over 1f out: rdn and carried rt ins fnl f: r.o* **1/1**1
5- **3** 8 **Sitting Pretty (IRE)**196 [6160] 3-8-12 0..................(v1) RichardKingscote 2 40
(Tom Dascombe) *led 5f out: hdd over 2f out: rdn and wknd over 1f out* **6/4**2
-0 **4** 8 **Kate Kelly (IRE)**9 [930] 3-8-12 0........................................ BenCurtis 4 16
(Jo Hughes) *outpcd: drvn along 1/2-way: sn lost tch* **50/1**
1m 16.52s (1.52) **Going Correction** +0.225s/f (Slow) **4** Ran SP% **112.0**
Speed ratings (Par 100): **98,97,87,76**
CSF £8.86 TOTE £1.90; EX 10.10 Trifecta £14.30.
**Owner** P Foster & Friends **Bred** R N Auld **Trained** Six Mile Bottom, Cambs

**FOCUS**
A weak fillies' maiden. The first two are rated to their respective marks.

## 1046 32RED THUNDERSTRUCK II SLOT H'CAP — 1m 5f 194y(P)
6:05 (6:06) (Class 5) (0-75,72) 4-Y-0+ £2,911 (£866; £432; £216) Stalls Low

Form RPR
5-30 **1** **Travel (USA)**18 [822] 4-8-4 **57**........................................ MichaelJMMurphy(3) 5 64+
(Mark Johnston) *led: hdd over 8f out: remained handy: rdn to ld ins fnl f: r.o wl* **9/2**3

03-1 **2** 2 1/4 **Divea**6 974 5-9-6 **66** 6ex........ WilliamCarson 2 70
(Anthony Carson) *trckd ldrs: plld hrd: wnt 2nd over 7f out tl led over 2f out: sn rdn: hdd and unable qck ins fnl f* **11/10**1
4344 **3** 2 3/4 **The Blue Dog (IRE)**13 891 7-9-9 **72**........ RobertTart(3) 1 72
(Phil McEntee) *a.p: pushed along and ev ch fr over 2f out tl rdn and no ex wl ins fnl f* **6/1**
3424 **4** *nk* **Yasir (USA)**17 829 6-9-7 **67**........(p) LiamKeniry 3 67
(Conor Dore) *s.i.s: hdwy to chse wnr after 1f tl led over 8f out: rdn and hdd over 2f out: swtchd rt and styd on same pce ins fnl f* **8/1**
10-3 **5** *2* **Lacey**42 513 5-8-12 **63**........ JackDuern(5) 4 60
(Andrew Hollinshead) *hld up: pushed along over 2f out: sn outpcd* **3/1**2
3m 10.52s (4.52) **Going Correction** +0.225s/f (Slow)
**WFA** 4 from 5yo+ 4lb **5** Ran SP% **116.2**
Speed ratings (Par 103): **96,94,93,92,91**
CSF £10.63 TOTE £4.70: £5.10, £1.10; EX 12.90 Trifecta £58.10.
**Owner** Sheikh Hamdan bin Mohammed Al Maktoum **Bred** Darley **Trained** Middleham Moor, N Yorks

**FOCUS**
An ordinary handicap run at a stop-start gallop. The winner might have more to offer.

## 1047 32RED BURNING DESIRE SLOT H'CAP 5f 216y(P)
**6:35** (6:35) (Class 6) (0-60,60) 3-Y-O **£1,940** (£577; £288; £144) **Stalls** Low

Form RPR
-311 **1** **Emerald Breeze (IRE)**14 867 3-9-5 **58**........(b) StevieDonohoe 6 74+
(Tim Pitt) *trckd ldr tl led over 1f out: shkn up and c clr fnl f: easily* **10/11**1
-464 **2** *5* **Douneedahand**23 745 3-9-2 **60**........ JoeyHaynes(5) 9 61
(Seamus Mullins) *trckd ldrs: racd keenly: rdn over 1f out: styd on same pce: wnt 2nd wl ins fnl f* **4/1**3
-664 **3** *1/2* **Soul Instinct**14 867 3-9-2 **60**........(b1) KevinStott(5) 2 60
(Kevin Ryan) *led: rdn and hdd over 1f out: no ex fnl f* **9/4**2
00-0 **4** *1 3/4* **Tidal Beauty**22 753 3-8-7 **46** oh1........1 LukeMorris 1 40
(Tony Carroll) *sn pushed along in rr: outpcd 4f out: styd on ins fnl f* **25/1**
0366 **5** *11* **Countess Lupus (IRE)**4 994 3-8-3 **47**........(b) ShirleyTeasdale(5) 7 8
(Lisa Williamson) *s.i.s: hdwy over 4f out: rdn and wknd over 2f out* **25/1**
1m 16.15s (1.15) **Going Correction** +0.225s/f (Slow) **5** Ran SP% **110.8**
Speed ratings (Par 96): **101,94,93,91,76**
CSF £5.07 TOTE £1.60: £1.10, £3.50; EX 5.40 Trifecta £6.20.
**Owner** Decadent Racing II **Bred** Rathbarry Stud **Trained** Market Drayton, Shropshire

**FOCUS**
A winner to follow in this 3yo handicap. The second and third are rated near their recent marks.

## 1048 32RED ON THE APP STORE H'CAP 7f 32y(P)
**7:05** (7:05) (Class 6) (0-60,57) 3-Y-O **£1,940** (£577; £288; £144) **Stalls** High

Form RPR
-041 **1** **Desert Colours**10 919 3-9-5 **55** 6ex........(b) PaulMulrennan 4 66
(Kevin Ryan) *mde all: rdn over 1f out: styd on u.p* **11/4**2
60-2 **2** *1 3/4* **Hustle Bustle (IRE)**21 786 3-9-2 **52**........ SeanLevey 5 58
(David Brown) *plld hrd: trckd wnr tl over 5f out: wnt 2nd again over 3f out: rdn over 1f out: styd on same pce ins fnl f* **10/11**1
-034 **3** *7* **Clapperboard**41 541 3-9-6 **56**........(b) RichardKingscote 3 44
(Paul Fitzsimons) *prom: rdn 1/2-way: styd on same pce fr over 1f out* **16/1**
000- **4** *1/2* **Caledonia Laird**150 7451 3-9-7 **57**........ BenCurtis 1 44
(Jo Hughes) *hld up: nt clr run over 2f out: hdwy over 1f out: no ex fnl f* **14/1**
-425 **5** *nse* **Armelle (FR)**22 753 3-9-4 **54**........(p) LukeMorris 6 41
(Scott Dixon) *hld up: rdn 1/2-way: hdwy over 2f out: styd on same pce fr over 1f out* **5/1**3
0000 **6** *11* **Krackerjill (IRE)**21 786 3-8-2 **45**........(e1) CharlotteJenner(7) 7
(Mark Usher) *prom: chsd wnr over 5f out tl over 3f out: wknd over 2f out* **33/1**
1m 30.89s (1.29) **Going Correction** +0.225s/f (Slow) **6** Ran SP% **111.2**
Speed ratings (Par 96): **101,99,91,90,90 77**
CSF £5.51 TOTE £5.10: £3.20, £1.02; EX 5.60 Trifecta £23.00.
**Owner** Jon Beard **Bred** Rabbah Bloodstock Limited **Trained** Hambleton, N Yorks

**FOCUS**
A 3yo handicap with little depth that turned into a two-horse battle as the market suggested. Improvement from the winner.

## 1049 COMPARE BOOKMAKERS AT BOOKMAKERS.CO.UK H'CAP 5f 20y(P)
**7:35** (7:35) (Class 4) (0-85,82) 4-Y-O+ **£5,175** (£1,540; £769; £384) **Stalls** Low

Form RPR
426 **1** **Muhdiq (USA)**32 644 5-9-5 **80**........ ShaneKelly 4 87
(Mike Murphy) *trckd ldr: racd keenly: led 1/2-way: rdn over 1f out: r.o: eased nr fin* **7/2**2
1-23 **2** *1 1/4* **Dangerous Age**32 644 4-9-7 **82**........ GeorgeBaker 5 85
(J W Hills) *trckd ldrs: plld hrd: rdn to chse wnr over 1f out: hung lft ins fnl f: styd on same pce* **5/6**1
000- **3** *1 3/4* **Top Boy**151 7420 4-8-13 **74**........(v) TomEaves 3 70
(Derek Shaw) *hld up: hdwy over 1f out: sn rdn: styd on* **10/1**
/0-4 **4** *shd* **We'll Deal Again**27 719 7-9-5 **80**........(b) GrahamGibbons 2 76
(Michael Easterby) *stmbld s: sn trcking ldrs: nt clr run 1/2-way: rdn over 1f out: styd on* **8/1**
000- **5** *3/4* **Bapak Chinta (USA)**161 7171 5-9-7 **82**........ AmyRyan 7 75
(Kevin Ryan) *hld up: r.o ins fnl f: nvr nrr* **6/1**3
1441 **6** *1* **Sir Geoffrey (IRE)**17 834 8-8-5 **73**........(p) MatthewHopkins(7) 1 63
(Scott Dixon) *led to 1/2-way: rdn over 1f out: no ex fnl f* **16/1**
6/0- **7** *6* **Almanack**128 7869 4-8-13 **79**........ GeorgeDowning(5) 6 47
(Ian Williams) *prom: rdn 1/2-way: wknd over 1f out* **14/1**
1m 2.05s (-0.25) **Going Correction** +0.225s/f (Slow) **7** Ran SP% **123.8**
Speed ratings (Par 105): **111,109,106,106,104 103,93**
CSF £7.56 TOTE £6.20: £2.60, £1.10; EX 9.00 Trifecta £59.40.
**Owner** Ms Denise Tibbett **Bred** Shadwell Farm LLC **Trained** Westoning, Beds

**FOCUS**
The feature on the card and the scene of the ride of the evening from Shane Kelly. The winner is rated back to his best in an ordinary race for the grade.

## 1050 CORAL MOBILE "JUST THREE CLICKS TO BET" H'CAP 1m 1f 103y(P)
**8:05** (8:05) (Class 7) (0-50,56) 4-Y-O+ **£1,940** (£577; £288; £144) **Stalls** Low

Form RPR
/051 **1** **Catching Zeds**21 783 7-9-7 **50**........(b) StevieDonohoe 1 55
(Kevin Frost) *pushed along in rr early: hdwy out wd over 1f out: r.o to ld wl ins fnl f* **6/1**3
26-1 **2** *1 1/4* **The Bay Bandit**14 869 7-9-7 **50**........(p) LiamKeniry 7 53
(Neil Mulholland) *a.p: chsd ldr 4f out: rdn over 1f out: styd on: wnt 2nd nr fin* **5/2**1
0-40 **3** *nk* **Rockweiller**17 831 7-8-12 **48**........(b) AlexHopkinson(7) 2 50
(Shaun Harris) *led over 8f out: pushed along over 1f out: hdd wl ins fnl f* **11/4**2
/000 **4** *4* **Devote Myself (IRE)**48 435 5-9-7 **50**........ LukeMorris 3 44
(Tony Carroll) *hld up: hdwy 2f out: rdn over 1f out: no ex fnl f* **11/4**2
0420 **5** *12* **Troy Boy**14 869 4-9-0 **46**........ NeilFarley(3) 4 18
(Robin Bastiman) *racd keenly: led 1f: trckd ldr tl 4f out: rdn over 2f out: wknd over 1f out* **7/1**
2m 4.04s (2.34) **Going Correction** +0.225s/f (Slow) **5** Ran SP% **108.7**
Speed ratings (Par 97): **98,96,96,93,82**
CSF £20.55 TOTE £5.30: £1.90, £1.30; EX 11.70 Trifecta £50.30.
**Owner** The Ferandlin Peaches **Bred** White Horse Bloodstock Ltd **Trained** Stratford-upon-Avon

**FOCUS**
A lot of non-runners weakened this handicap.

## 1051 CORAL APP DOWNLOAD FROM THE APP STORE H'CAP 1m 1f 103y(P)
**8:35** (8:35) (Class 5) (0-70,70) 4-Y-O+ **£2,911** (£866; £432; £216) **Stalls** Low

Form RPR
5111 **1** **Kindlelight Storm (USA)**7 958 4-9-5 **68**........(b) GeorgeBaker 3 75
(Nick Littmoden) *trckd ldrs: wnt 2nd 7f out: led 1f out: rdn ins fnl f: jhust hld on* **11/10**1
3332 **2** *nk* **Yourinthewill (USA)**1 1034 6-9-0 **63**........ ShaneKelly 2 68
(Daniel Mark Loughnane) *hld up: ehadway over 1f out: r.o: wnt 2nd post: nt quite rch wnr* **14/1**
-222 **3** *1/2* **Arlecchino (IRE)**21 782 4-9-7 **70**........(b) AdamKirby 4 74
(Ed McMahon) *set stdy pce tl qcknd 3f out: rdn and hdd 1f out: kpt on* **7/4**2
1242 **4** *8* **India's Song**4 998 4-8-4 **60**........(t) GeorgeBuckell(7) 1 49
(David Simcock) *trckd ldr over 2f: remained handy: rdn and hung lft over 1f out: wkng whn rdr dropped whip ins fnl f* **9/2**3
2m 5.22s (3.52) **Going Correction** +0.225s/f (Slow) **4** Ran SP% **108.8**
Speed ratings (Par 103): **93,92,92,85**
CSF £13.58 TOTE £1.20; EX 9.20 Trifecta £19.40.
**Owner** Kindlelight Ltd, N Shields & N Littmoden **Bred** Kirsten Rausing **Trained** Newmarket, Suffolk

**FOCUS**
Just the four runners but still a strong handicap for the grade. However it was run at a very steady pace. Another personal best from the winner.
T/Plt: £25.50 to a £1 stake. Pool: £63760.09 - 1824.82 winning tickets T/Qpdt: £2.00 to a £1 stake. Pool: £8345.12 - 3046.47 winning tickets CR

# 1038 LINGFIELD (L-H)
Saturday, March 22

**OFFICIAL GOING: Standard**
Wind: medium, half behind Weather: overcast

## 1065 32RED.COM ALL WEATHER "HANDS AND HEELS" APPRENTICE SERIES FINAL H'CAP (RACING EXCELLENCE) 1m 5f (P)
**2:10** (2:10) (Class 5) (0-75,74) 4-Y-O+ **£4,090** (£1,207; £604) **Stalls** Low

Form RPR
6133 **1** **Mahadee (IRE)**8 953 9-9-0 **69**........(b) JennyPowell(3) 6 78
(Tom Dascombe) *stdd s: t.k.h: hld up in midfield: hdwy to chse ldr over 6f out: upsides ldr 5f out tl led 2f out: rdn and qcknd clr over 1f out: r.o wl* **7/1**
-005 **2** *2 3/4* **Thecornishcowboy**5 990 5-8-13 **68**........(t) JordonMcMurray(3) 5 73
(John Ryan) *stdd s: chsd ldng pair: nt clr run 2f out: swtchd rt and effrt over 1f out: chsd clr wnr fnl 150yds: styd on but no ch w wnr* **8/1**
-134 **3** *3/4* **Bert The Alert**19 818 6-8-9 **61**........ CharlotteJenner 2 65
(Laura Mongan) *stdd s: t.k.h: hld up in last pair: rdn and effrt over 2f out: styd on to go 3rd fnl 100yds: no ch w wnr* **7/2**2
3511 **4** *1/2* **Munsarim (IRE)**8 953 7-9-8 **74**........(b) LouisSteward 4 77
(Lee Carter) *stdd s: hld up in rr: rdn and effrt wl over 1f out: hung rt and kpt on same pce ins fnl f: no ch w wnr* **7/2**2
4121 **5** *1/2* **Sian Gwalia**7 978 4-9-0 **69**........ GeorgeBuckell 1 71
(David Simcock) *chsd ldr tl over 6f out: styd wl in tch in midfield: rdn and effrt over 1f out: outpcd by wnr but wnt 2nd over 1f out tl fnl 150yds: one pce* **3/1**1
/421 **6** *3/4* **Rowan Ridge**21 801 6-9-0 **71**........ MrJamieCoates(5) 3 72
(William Knight) *led and set stdy gallop: hdd 2f out: rdn and unable qck and lost 2nd over 1f out: wknd ins fnl f* **9/2**3
2m 50.88s (4.88) **Going Correction** -0.10s/f (Stan)
**WFA** 4 from 5yo+ 3lb **6** Ran SP% **111.2**
Speed ratings (Par 103): **80,78,77,77,77 76**
CSF £56.54 TOTE £6.40: £4.30, £6.20; EX 55.80 Trifecta £971.70.
**Owner** T Dascombe **Bred** Darley **Trained** Malpas, Cheshire

**FOCUS**
The final of this series turned out to be a messy affair with the six runners going no pace for much of the journey (it took them over 56sec to cover the first half-mile) and it developed into a sprint. The winner will be of interest if running without a penalty.

## 1066 BOOKMAKERS.CO.UK HEVER SPRINT STKS (FAST TRACK QUALIFIER) (LISTED RACE) 5f 6y(P)
**2:40** (2:40) (Class 1) 4-Y-O+
**£25,519** (£9,675; £4,842; £2,412; £1,210; £607) **Stalls** High

Form RPR
140- **1** **Stepper Point**167 7054 5-9-3 108........(p) MartinDwyer 6 116
(William Muir) *pressed ldrs: rdn to chal over 1f out: led 1f out: clr fnl 100yds: r.o wl: readily* **16/1**
2-54 **2** *2* **Iptisam**28 713 5-9-0 100........(p) LukeMorris 10 106
(James Tate) *hld up in tch in midfield: n.m.r over 2f out: swtchd out rt and effrt bnd 2f out: switching bk lft and hdwy 1f out: r.o wl u.p to snatch 2nd last strides* **8/1**
1421 **3** *nk* **Even Stevens**33 644 6-9-0 102........(v) FrederikTylicki 1 105
(Scott Dixon) *led: rdn and hrd pressed wl over 1f out: hdd 1f out: kpt on same pce after: lost 2nd last strides* **16/1**
3-51 **4** *nk* **Addictive Dream (IRE)**21 802 7-9-0 105........ TonyHamilton 3 104
(David Nicholls) *restless in stalls and nt best away: sn reovered to press ldr: rdn and ev ch wl over 1f out: outpcd by wnr and one pce u.p ins fnl f* **5/1**2
20-6 **5** *hd* **Ladies Are Forever**28 713 6-9-0 108........(p) RobertTart 4 105+
(Geoffrey Oldroyd) *wl in tch in midfield: hmpd bnd ent fnl 2f: pushed rt and lost further grnd bnd wl over 1f out: 6th and looked wl hld 1f out: r.o strly u.p fnl 100yds: no threat to wnr* **3/1**1


The Form Book, Raceform Ltd, Newbury, RG14 5SJ

440- **6** *1 ¾* **Kingsgate Choice (IRE)**[167] 7054 7-9-0 107 JimCrowley 8 97
(Ed de Giles) *dwlt: sn niggled along and racd off the pce in last trio: styd on ins fnl f: nvr trbld ldrs* **3/1**[1]

1326 **7** *½* **Silken Express (IRE)**[21] 802 5-8-9 97 RichardHughes 2 90
(Robert Cowell) *chsd ldng trio: rdn and edgd out rt bnd 2f out: unable qck over 1f out: wknd ins fnl f* **12/1**

-100 **8** *1* **Swiss Cross**[21] 802 7-9-0 97 (t) PaddyAspell 5 91
(Phil McEntee) *in tch in midfield: rdn and unable qck ent fnl 2f: outpcd and btn over 1f out: wl hld fnl f* **33/1**

-606 **9** *¾* **Monsieur Joe (IRE)**[30] 680 7-9-0 101 (v) WilliamBuick 9 89
(Paul Midgley) *stdd after s: hld up off the pce in last pair: rdn and no imp wl over 1f out* **20/1**

-100 **10** *nk* **Forest Edge (IRE)**[28] 713 5-9-0 102 (b) AdamKirby 7 88
(David Evans) *restless in stalls: s.i.s: a bhd* **7/1**[3]

57.12s (-1.68) **Going Correction** -0.10s/f (Stan) **10** Ran SP% **117.4**
Speed ratings (Par 111): **109,105,105,104,104 101,100,99,98,97**
CSF £138.85 TOTE £15.40: £4.80, £3.00, £3.70; EX 169.40 Trifecta £2250.40 Part won..
**Owner** C L A Edginton **Bred** Whitsbury Manor Stud **Trained** Lambourn, Berks

**FOCUS**
The last of the three 'Fast Track Qualifiers' for the Sprint Championship Final over 6f back here on Good Friday and a decent Listed race in its own right. Not surprisingly there was no hanging about, with a three-way battle for the lead for most of the way, and it proved hard to make up ground from off the pace. They dipped inside standard time. Another personal best from the winner.

## 1067 32RED SPRING CUP (FAST TRACK QUALIFIER) (LISTED RACE) 7f 1y(P)
**3:15** (3:16) (Class 1) 3-Y-O

**£25,519** (£9,675; £4,842; £2,412; £1,210; £607) **Stalls** Low

Form RPR

21- **1** **Ertijaal (IRE)**[268] 3737 3-9-1 98 PaulHanagan 13 101
(William Haggas) *chsd ldr tl led ent fnl 2f: rdn and qcknd over 1f out: r.o wl but flashed tail ins fnl f: a holding on* **5/4**[1]

2 **2** *hd* **American Hope (USA)**[22] 778 3-9-1 95 ShaneKelly 1 100
(Mike Murphy) *stdd after s: t.k.h: hld up in tch in last pair: hdwy and switching rt ent fnl 2f: str run u.p ins fnl f: wnt 2nd wl ins fnl f: clsng but nvr quite getting to wnr* **16/1**

0-13 **3** *1 ¼* **Major Crispies**[22] 778 3-9-1 94 RyanTate 11 97
(James Eustace) *chsd ldrs: rdn and effrt to press wnr 2f out: nt quite gng pce of wnr over 1f out: r.o same pce fnl f: lost 2nd wl ins fnl f* **50/1**

312- **4** *¾* **Sir Robert Cheval**[119] 8018 3-9-1 90 AdamKirby 7 95
(Marco Botti) *hld up in tch towards rr: rdn and hdwy over 1f out: styd on wl u.p ins fnl f* **12/1**

351- **5** *nk* **Expert (IRE)**[141] 7658 3-9-1 99 RichardHughes 2 94
(Richard Hannon) *wl in tch in midfield: nt clr run on inner ent fnl 2f: swtchd rt and effrt u.p over 1f out: kpt on same pce ins fnl f* **10/1**[3]

-111 **6** *¾* **Pool House**[17] 850 3-9-1 89 DavidProbert 3 92
(Andrew Balding) *chsd ldrs: rdn and effrt wl over 1f out: 3rd and no ex u.p 1f out: wknd fnl 75yds* **14/1**

40-1 **7** *nk* **Alutiq (IRE)**[66] 183 3-8-10 95 JamieSpencer 4 86
(Eve Johnson Houghton) *hld up in last trio: rdn and swtchd rt ent fnl f: styd on wl u.p: nvr trbld ldrs* **8/1**[2]

544- **8** *1 ¾* **Brazos (IRE)**[177] 6765 3-9-1 95 RyanMoore 5 87
(Clive Brittain) *in tch in midfield: n.m.r and shuffled bk towards rr ent fnl 2f: hdwy under presssure 1f out: styd on but no threat to ldrs* **8/1**[2]

014- **9** *nk* **Bow Creek (IRE)**[152] 7421 3-9-1 98 SilvestreDeSousa 10 86
(Mark Johnston) *towards rr: hdwy on outer fr 5f out: chsd ldrs and rdn jst over 2f out: outpcd and btn over 1f out: wknd ins fnl f* **8/1**[2]

543- **10** *3 ¼* **Wee Jean**[84] 8426 3-8-10 91 WilliamTwiston-Davies 12 72
(Mick Channon) *stdd after s: hld up in tch in rr: rdn and effrt wl over 1f out: kpt on but n.d* **33/1**

1-21 **11** *1 ¼* **Oriental Relation (IRE)**[59] 279 3-9-1 93 (b) GrahamLee 8 74
(James Given) *t.k.h: in tch in midfield: rdn and unable qck ent fnl 2f: outpcd and btn over 1f out: wknd fnl f* **33/1**

1-43 **12** *hd* **Steventon Star**[17] 850 3-9-1 97 (v) RobertWinston 6 73
(Alan Bailey) *in tch in midfield: rdn and struggling over 2f out: wknd over 1f out* **25/1**

326- **13** *6* **Lilbourne Lass**[198] 6142 3-8-10 93 JimCrowley 9 52
(K R Burke) *led tl ent fnl 2f: sn lost pl u.p: bhd fnl f* **50/1**

1m 22.72s (-2.08) **Going Correction** -0.10s/f (Stan) **13** Ran SP% **120.8**
Speed ratings (Par 106): **107,106,105,104,104 103,102,100,100,96 95,95,88**
CSF £23.55 TOTE £2.30: £1.10, £5.00, £14.60; EX 24.20 Trifecta £1341.00.
**Owner** Hamdan Al Maktoum **Bred** Shadwell Estate Company Limited **Trained** Newmarket, Suffolk

**FOCUS**
A fascinating Listed race and the last of the three 'Fast Track Qualifiers' for the Three-Year-Old Championship Final over C&D next month. They appeared to go a good pace. The winner built on his Yarmouth form and can rate higher again.

## 1068 CORAL.CO.UK WINTER DERBY (FAST TRACK QUALIFIER) (GROUP 3) 1m 2f (P)
**3:50** (3:51) (Class 1) 4-Y-O+

**£56,710** (£21,500; £10,760; £5,360; £2,690; £1,350) **Stalls** Low

Form RPR

-614 **1** **Robin Hoods Bay**[28] 716 6-9-0 103 LukeMorris 8 112
(Ed Vaughan) *dwlt and rdn along leaving stalls: in tch in last quartet: rdn and hdwy 2f out: str run u.p to chal whn bmpd and pushed rt ins fnl f: sn led and r.o wl* **10/1**

22-1 **2** *¾* **Windhoek**[58] 307 4-9-0 105 SilvestreDeSousa 7 111
(Saeed bin Suroor) *hld up in tch towards rr: gd hdwy on outer 3f out: rdn to ld over 1f out: hung rt and bmpd chalr ins fnl f: sn hdd and one pce* **11/4**[2]

2505 **3** *1* **Aussie Reigns (IRE)**[21] 812 4-9-0 102 AdamKirby 4 109
(William Knight) *hld up in tch in midfield: hdwy u.p over 1f out: chsd ldrs and nt clr run wl ins fnl f: kpt on towards fin* **33/1**

521- **4** *1* **Dick Doughtywylie**[91] 8386 6-9-0 102 (t) WilliamBuick 12 107
(John Gosden) *chsd ldr: rdn and ev ch over 1f out: no ex u.p whn hung rt ins fnl f: sn lost 3rd and one pce* **25/1**

/15- **5** *1* **Farraaj (IRE)**[208] 5849 5-9-0 105 AndreaAtzeni 9 105
(Roger Varian) *t.k.h: chsd ldrs: rdn and effrt wl over 1f out: stl chsng ldrs but styng on same pce whn nt clr run ins fnl f: no hdwy fnl 75yds* **5/1**[3]

666- **6** *½* **Circumvent**[183] 6596 7-9-0 95 JimCrowley 5 104
(Paul Cole) *hld up in tch in last pair: rdn and hdwy over 1f out: styd on wl u.p ins fnl f: nt rch ldrs* **66/1**

1141 **7** *nk* **Rebellious Guest**[17] 840 5-9-0 92 TomQueally 3 103
(George Margarson) *hld up in tch in midfield: nt clr run wl over 1f out: swtchd lft and hdwy jst over 1f out: kpt on u.p: nt trble ldrs* **16/1**

10-1 **8** *1* **Grandeur (IRE)**[28] 716 5-9-0 117 (p) RyanMoore 14 101
(Jeremy Noseda) *wl in tch in midfield: drvn and unable qck wl over 1f out: outpcd whn sltly hmpd 1f out: no prog fnl f* **7/4**[1]

-000 **9** *1 ¾* **Chil The Kite**[21] 812 5-9-0 105 RichardHughes 13 98
(Hughie Morrison) *stdd s: hld up in tch towards rr: effrt towards outer bnd wl over 1f out: styd on same pce and no imp ins fnl f* **20/1**

01-3 **10** *hd* **Anaconda (FR)**[28] 716 5-9-0 102 RichardKingscote 11 98
(Tom Dascombe) *led: rdn wl over 1f out: hdd over 1f out: wknd ins fnl f* **25/1**

5/ **11** *1 ½* **Vodkato (FR)**[18] 837 6-9-0 100 (p) TheoBachelot 6 95
(S Wattel, France) *wnt rt s: hld up towards rr and stuck on outer: rdn and effrt bnd 2f out: no real prog: nvr trbld ldrs* **14/1**

30-3 **12** *1 ¼* **Premio Loco (USA)**[24] 749 10-9-0 110 GeorgeBaker 1 93
(Chris Wall) *hld up in tch in midfield: nt clr run and shuffled bk on inner 2f out: rdn and effrt over 1f out: no real prog and wl hld whn swtchd rt ins fnl f* **20/1**

-236 **13** *5* **Tinshu (IRE)**[28] 716 8-8-11 95 (p) JamieSpencer 2 80
(Derek Haydn Jones) *chsd ldrs: rdn and struggling ent fnl 2f: wknd and bhd ins fnl f* **66/1**

100- **14** *1 ½* **Mirsaale**[260] 4027 4-9-0 105 JoeFanning 10 80
(James Tate) *in tch in midfield: rdn and struggling to qckn whn nt clr run and dropped to rr bnd 2f: n.d after* **50/1**

2m 1.41s (-5.19) **Going Correction** -0.10s/f (Stan) **14** Ran SP% **126.4**
Speed ratings (Par 113): **116,115,114,113,113 112,112,111,110,110 108,107,103,102**
CSF £36.54 TOTE £11.30: £3.20, £1.80, £9.80; EX 59.00 Trifecta £1291.70.
**Owner** A M Pickering **Bred** Palm Tree Thoroughbreds **Trained** Newmarket, Suffolk
■ Stewards' Enquiry : Andrea Atzeni three-day ban: careless riding (Apr 5,7,8)

**FOCUS**
The 17th running of the Winter Derby and the ninth as a Group 3. This year's renewal looked well up to scratch too, with the last two winners back again plus a challenger from France and a Godolphin representative alongside a strong domestic field. The race took on an extra significance this year as it was the last of the three 'Fast Track Qualifiers' for the Middle Distance Championship Final over C&D in four weeks' time. The pace set by the leader Anaconda was a good one and again they dipped inside standard time. The form makes sense.

## 1069 DOWNLOAD THE LADBROKES APP MAIDEN STKS 1m 1y(P)
**4:25** (4:28) (Class 5) 3-Y-O+ **£4,090** (£1,207; £604) **Stalls** High

Form RPR

25- **1** **Shafrah (IRE)**[205] 5924 3-8-10 0 PaulHanagan 8 85+
(Richard Hannon) *mde all: wnt clr and rdn over 1f out: in n.d and r.o wl fnl f: comf* **9/4**[1]

6- **2** *4* **L'Importante**[287] 3112 3-8-10 0 LukeMorris 5 75+
(Marco Botti) *restless in stalls: in tch towards rr of main gp: rdn and rn green bnd 2f out: hdwy jst over 1f out: styd on to go 2nd wl ins fnl f: no ch w wnr* **11/4**[2]

66- **3** *½* **Sea Here**[115] 8067 3-8-10 0 JimCrowley 7 74
(Ralph Beckett) *chsd wnr: rdn wl over 1f out: sn outpcd and btn: plugged on same pce and lost 2nd wl ins fnl f* **8/1**

**4** *nk* **Court Room (IRE)** 3-8-10 0 WilliamBuick 3 73
(John Gosden) *hld up in tch towards rr of main gp: rdn and rn green bnd 2f out: swtchd lft and sme hdwy ent fnl f: battling for 2nd and kpt on ins fnl f* **6/1**

**5** *1 ½* **Mount Shamsan** 4-9-13 0 RyanMoore 2 75
(William Haggas) *chsd ldrs: rn green and outpcd bnd ent fnl 2f: no ch w wnr and styd on same pce fr over 1f out* **3/1**[3]

00- **6** *1 ¾* **Dylan's Centenary**[282] 3245 3-8-10 0 FrederikTylicki 1 65
(Rod Millman) *chsd ldrs: 3rd and effrt u.p 2f out: sn outpcd and btn over 1f out: wknd fnl f* **66/1**

50 **7** *11* **Patronella (IRE)**[28] 717 3-8-5 0 ChrisCatlin 9 35
(David Simcock) *hld up in tch in rr of main gp: rdn and no hdwy ent fnl 2f: sn wknd: bhd fnl f* **50/1**

0 **8** *22* **Puppet Theatre (IRE)**[11] 914 4-9-8 0 (b[1]) JoeFanning 6 +
(Mark Johnston) *veered bdly rt leaving stalls and virtually ref to r: continued t.o thrght* **16/1**

00 **9** *19* **Madrinas Prince (IRE)**[29] 686 5-9-8 0 RyanWhile(5) 4
(Paddy Butler) *in tch in midfield: rdn over 4f out: lost tch qckly 3f out: t.o over 1f out* **100/1**

1m 37.44s (-0.76) **Going Correction** -0.10s/f (Stan)
**WFA** 3 from 4yo+ 17lb **9** Ran SP% **118.2**
Speed ratings (Par 103): **99,95,94,94,92 90,79,57,38**
CSF £8.90 TOTE £3.00: £1.10, £2.20, £2.10; EX 8.90 Trifecta £40.10.
**Owner** Hamdan Al Maktoum **Bred** Mrs Eleanor Kent **Trained** East Everleigh, Wilts

**FOCUS**
An ordinary maiden which became a one-horse race. The winner is clearly useful but there's nothing much to anchor the form on.

## 1070 LADBROKES H'CAP 1m 1y(P)
**5:00** (5:01) (Class 2) (0-100,108) 4-Y-O+ **£16,172** (£4,812; £2,405; £1,202) **Stalls** High

Form RPR

5512 **1** **George Guru**[28] 715 7-9-3 **96** RobertHavlin 9 104
(Michael Attwater) *wl in tch in midfield: hdwy to press ldrs over 2f out: led wl over 1f out: sn rdn: rdr dropped whip and edgd lft: clr 1f out: r.o and a jst lasting home* **4/1**[1]

2502 **2** *shd* **Brocklebank (IRE)**[3] 1020 5-8-3 **87** oh4 ow1 JackDuern(5) 5 95
(Simon Dow) *hld up in last trio: clsd and nt clr run over 1f out: sn swtchd rt and gd hdwy ent fnl f: chsd clr wnr ins fnl f: clsd rapidly towards fin: nvr quite getting to wnr* **10/1**

00-5 **3** *2 ¾* **Spiritual Star (IRE)**[21] 804 5-8-13 **92** WilliamCarson 8 93
(Anthony Carson) *stdd s: hld up in last pair: rdn and hdwy on outer over 1f out: kpt on wl ins fnl f: snatched 3rd last stride* **8/1**[3]

00-2 **4** *shd* **Atlantis Crossing (IRE)**[21] 804 5-8-12 **91** AdamKirby 3 92
(Jim Boyle) *hld up in tch in midfield: rdn and effrt whn edgd lft over 1f out: hdwy to go 3rd ins fnl f: no imp and lost 3rd last stride* **10/1**

0-32 **5** *3 ¾* **Stasio (USA)**[40] 559 4-8-9 **88** LiamKeniry 6 81
(David Simcock) *stdd s: hld up in tch towards rr: rdn and hdwy into midfield 2f out: no prog over 1f out: wknd ins fnl f* **9/2**[2]

10-0 **6** *1 ¼* **Highland Knight (IRE)**[14] 886 7-9-12 **108** (t) OisinMurphy(3) 1 98
(Andrew Balding) *chsd ldr tl led 2f out: sn rdn and hdd: wknd fnl f* **12/1**

00-3 **7** *2* **Party Royal**[14] 887 4-8-7 **86** oh1 SilvestreDeSousa 7 71
(Mark Johnston) *wl in tch in midfield: rdn and unable qck 2f out: wknd ent fnl f* **10/1**

-230 **8** *1* **Luhaif**[35] 625 4-8-11 **95** (p) ShelleyBirkett(5) 11 78
(Julia Feilden) *rdn along early: hdwy to chse ldrs after 1f: rdn and outpcd wl over 1f out: wknd fnl f* **20/1**

160- **9** *1 ¾* **Azrur (IRE)**[184] 6571 4-8-8 **87** SeanLevey 4 66
(David Brown) *led tl 2f out: sn lost pl: wknd 1f out* **33/1**

6401 **P** **True To Form (IRE)**$^{21}$ 804 7-8-13 **92**..........................(v) TomQueally 10
(Alan McCabe) *chsd ldrs tl lost action and dropped out rapidly 4f out: p.u over 3f out: fatally injured* **20/1**

1m 35.49s (-2.71) **Going Correction** -0.10s/f (Stan) **10 Ran SP% 96.7**
Speed ratings (Par 109): **109,108,106,106,102 101,99,98,96,**
CSF £28.23 CT £156.44 TOTE £3.80: £1.40, £3.50, £3.00; EX 32.50 Trifecta £181.90.
**Owner** T M Jones **Bred** T M Jones **Trained** Epsom, Surrey
■ Mondlicht was withdrawn. Price at time of withdrawal 4/1J. Rule 4 applies to all bets - deduct 20p in the pound.

**FOCUS**
A decent handicap, but weakened by the withdrawal of Mondlicht at the start and marred by the awful injury suffered by True To Form at around halfway. The front pair are in the form of their lives.

## 1071 CORAL MOBILE "JUST THREE CLICKS TO BET" H'CAP — 1m 4f (P)
**5:35** (5:35) (Class 3) (0-95,95) 4-Y-0+ **£9,703** (£2,887; £1,443; £721) **Stalls** Low

Form RPR

355- **1** **Lord Van Percy**$^{147}$ 7526 4-8-8 **87**.................................. OisinMurphy(3) 6 95
(Andrew Balding) *stdd s: hld up in last pair: rdn and stl plenty to do jst over 2f out: hdwy 1f out and str run ins fnl f: led on post* **5/4**$^{1}$

-311 **2** *nse* **Scottish Star**$^{35}$ 623 6-8-2 **81**.................................. RyanTate(5) 7 89
(James Eustace) *in tch in midfield: rdn and effrt to chal over 1f out: led ins fnl f: r.o wl: hdd on post* **10/1**

3120 **3** *1/2* **Swing Alone (IRE)**$^{28}$ 723 5-9-7 **95**.................................. LukeMorris 2 102
(Gay Kelleway) *hld up in tch in last trio: hdwy u.p over 1f out: r.o wl u.p to press ldng pair wl ins fnl f: no ex cl home* **9/2**$^{3}$

4-11 **4** *3/4* **Villa Royale**$^{8}$ 961 5-9-0 **88**.................................. AndrewMullen 9 94
(Michael Appleby) *chsd ldng trio: rdn along over 4f out: hdwy to chse ldr and edgd lft ent fnl 2f: rdn to ld over 1f out: hdd ins fnl f: outpcd towards fin* **14/1**

400- **5** *1 1/2* **Viewpoint (IRE)**$^{100}$ 8263 5-9-1 **89**.................................. RichardHughes 5 95
(Richard Hannon) *hld in tch in midfield: rdn whn squeezed for room: hmpd and dropped to rr 2f out: rallied and styd on wl ins fnl f: no threat to ldrs* **12/1**

4430 **6** *1* **Uphold**$^{15}$ 870 7-8-7 **81** oh1.................................(v) DavidProbert 8 83
(Gay Kelleway) *led: drvn and hdd over 1f out: no ex and btn 1f out: wknd ins fnl f* **25/1**

55-2 **7** *2* **Nautilus**$^{22}$ 784 4-9-5 **95**..................................(p) WilliamBuick 4 94
(John Gosden) *chsd ldrs: wnt 2nd 10f out tl rdn: hmpd and lost pl ent fnl 2f: sn rdn and hung rt: plugged on but n.d after* **4/1**$^{2}$

-000 **8** *3/4* **Loyalty**$^{14}$ 887 7-8-13 **87**..................................(v) DaleSwift 1 85
(Derek Shaw) *stdd s: hld up in last pair: rdn over 3f out: sme hdwy on inner over 1f out: no imp ins fnl f: nvr trbld ldrs* **25/1**

05-0 **9** *3 3/4* **Quixote**$^{14}$ 891 5-8-8 **82**.................................. SilvestreDeSousa 3 74
(Clive Brittain) *chsd ldr for 2f: styd chsng ldrs: short of room and hmpd 2f out: rdn and no hdwy over 1f out: wknd ins fnl f* **25/1**

2m 29.2s (-3.80) **Going Correction** -0.10s/f (Stan)
**WFA** 4 from 5yo+ 2lb **9 Ran SP% 117.6**
Speed ratings (Par 107): **108,107,107,107,106 105,104,103,101**
CSF £15.33 CT £42.86 TOTE £2.30: £1.10, £2.20, £2.30; EX 15.30 Trifecta £84.30.
**Owner** Mrs L E Ramsden & Richard Morecombe **Bred** Mr & Mrs A E Pakenham **Trained** Kingsclere, Hants
■ Stewards' Enquiry : Oisin Murphy two-day ban: used whip above permitted level (Apr 5,7)

**FOCUS**
They went a solid pace in this decent middle-distance handicap and it was a case of gamble landed, if only just. Sound form.
T/Plt: £2,320.10 to a £1 stake. Pool of £133868.77 - 42.12 winning tickets. T/Qpdt: £20.20 to a £1 stake. Pool of £10807.60 - 394.80 winning tickets. SP

1072 - 1075a (Foreign Racing) - See Raceform Interactive

# CURRAGH (R-H)
Sunday, March 23

**OFFICIAL GOING: Soft to heavy**

## 1076a LODGE PARK STUD EUROPEAN BREEDERS FUND PARK EXPRESS STKS (FILLIES) (GROUP 3) — 1m
**3:40** (3:41) 3-Y-0+ **£41,979** (£12,270; £5,812; £1,937)

RPR

**1** **Vote Often**$^{154}$ 7402 3-8-9 94.................................. PatSmullen 2 102
(D K Weld, Ire) *prom early: settled bhd ldrs: 4th 1/2-way: rdn into 2nd 1 1/2f out and sn disp: led narrowly u.p ins fnl 50yds: all out* **10/1**

**2** *hd* **Odeliz (IRE)**$^{132}$ 7843 4-9-11 101.................................. DanielTudhope 6 106
(K R Burke) *chsd ldrs: clsr in 3rd fr 1/2-way: travelling wl 2f out and led narrowly 1 1/2f out: sn jnd and rdn: hdd u.p ins fnl 50yds: jst denied* **4/1**$^{2}$

**3** *3 3/4* **Achnaha (IRE)**$^{140}$ 7720 3-8-9 93..................................(p) JamieSpencer 12 93?
(P D Deegan, Ire) *wnt sltly lft s and racd towards rr: pushed along in 7th over 3f out and clsd u.p to chal in 3rd over 1f out: sn no imp on principals: kpt on same pce* **8/1**

**4** *nk* **Pop Art (IRE)**$^{140}$ 7719 4-9-11 97.................................. FMBerry 5 97
(Charles O'Brien, Ire) *w.w towards rr: hdwy fr 3f out to chse ldrs over 1f out: rdn in 4th ins fnl f and no imp on principals: kpt on same pce* **16/1**

**5** *1 3/4* **Morga (IRE)**$^{140}$ 7721 4-9-11 93.................................. KevinManning 10 93
(J S Bolger, Ire) *towards rr: tk clsr order in 8th over 3f out: clsd u.p nr side fr 2f out: n.m.r on inner over 1f out and swtchd rt: kpt on towards fin* **16/1**

**6** *2 1/2* **Wannabe Better (IRE)**$^{154}$ 7404 4-9-11 109.................................. WayneLordan 3 87
(T Stack, Ire) *in rr of mid-div: pushed along in 8th fr 3f out to chse ldrs on outer over 1f out: no ex u.p in 5th ins fnl f: kpt on one pce* **9/4**$^{1}$

**7** *5* **Asgardella (IRE)**$^{153}$ 7424 4-9-11 82.................................. BillyLee 4 75
(W McCreery, Ire) *hld up towards rr: tk clsr order 2f out: rdn in 8th ent fnl f and sn no imp on ldrs: kpt on one pce* **33/1**

**8** *3/4* **Euphrasia (IRE)**$^{148}$ 7550 5-10-0 107.................................. GaryCarroll 9 77
(Joseph G Murphy, Ire) *sn trckd ldrs tl got on terms bef 1/2-way: sn led narrowly: rdn over 2f out and sn hdd: wknd over 1f out* **10/1**

**9** *7* **Akira (IRE)**$^{168}$ 7051 4-9-11 94.................................. NGMcCullagh 1 58
(J R Barry, Ire) *racd in mid-div: tk clsr order bhd ldrs 1/2-way: rdn 2f out and sn no ex u.p: wknd* **40/1**

**10** *nse* **Dance With Another (IRE)**$^{159}$ 7284 3-8-9 89....... ColmO'Donoghue 11 53
(A P O'Brien, Ire) *chsd ldrs: pushed along in 5th after 1/2-way and sn no ex: wknd fnl 2f* **10/1**

**11** *4 1/2* **Indigo Lady**$^{172}$ 6962 4-9-11 90.................................. JosephO'Brien 8 47
(W McCreery, Ire) *sn led tl jnd bef 1/2-way: sn hdd narrowly: rdn and wknd over 2f out: eased over 1f out* **25/1**

**12** *3* **Majenta (IRE)**$^{140}$ 7723 4-9-11 98.................................. ChrisHayes 7 40
(Kevin Prendergast, Ire) *in rr of mid-div: rdn 3f out and sn no imp: wknd* **7/1**$^{3}$

1m 49.47s (3.47) **Going Correction** +0.70s/f (Yiel)
**WFA** 3 from 4yo+ 17lb **12 Ran SP% 122.6**
Speed ratings: **110,109,106,105,104 101,96,95,88,88 84,81**
CSF £50.78 TOTE £9.80: £2.40, £1.70, £2.80; DF 64.70 Trifecta £369.80.
**Owner** K Abdullah **Bred** Juddmonte Farms Ltd **Trained** The Curragh, Co Kildare
■ Stewards' Enquiry : Jamie Spencer caution: use of whip

**FOCUS**
A smart contest.

## 1078a WWW.THETOTE.COM IRISH LINCOLNSHIRE (PREMIER H'CAP) — 1m
**4:40** (4:40) 4-Y-0+
**£50,000** (£15,833; £7,500; £2,500; £1,666; £833)

RPR

**1** **Stuccodor (IRE)**$^{56}$ 7550 5-9-9 **102**..................................(v) PatSmullen 18 111+
(D K Weld, Ire) *hld up in tch: tk clsr order 2f out: hdwy into 2nd ent fnl f: rdn to ld ins fnl 100yds and kpt on wl* **11/2**$^{1}$

**2** *3/4* **That's Plenty (IRE)**$^{93}$ 8378 5-8-7 **86**.................................. WayneLordan 5 93
(John Patrick Shanahan, Ire) *a.p: narrow advantage 1/2-way: strly pressed ent fnl f and hdd u.p ins fnl 100yds: kpt on wl wout matching wnr* **12/1**

**3** *1 1/4* **Canary Row (IRE)**$^{168}$ 7052 4-8-6 **85**.................................. BenDawson(10) 7 99
(P J Prendergast, Ire) *chsd ldrs: effrt over 1f out: rdn in cl 3rd ins fnl f and sn no ex u.p: kpt on same pce* **10/1**

**4** *2 1/2* **Bold Thady Quill (IRE)**$^{140}$ 7719 7-9-4 **100**............(p) ConorHoban(3) 17 98+
(K J Condon, Ire) *in rr of mid-div: rdn and clsd u.p fr 2f out to chse ldrs in 7th ent fnl f: kpt on wl into mod 4th nr fin: nvr nrr* **25/1**

**5** *3/4* **Lord Aeryn (IRE)**$^{163}$ 7172 7-8-4 **83**.................................. BarryMcHugh 13 80
(Richard Fahey) *on toes befhand: chsd ldrs: niggled along in 6th over 3f out: clsd u.p into 4th over 1f out: sn no imp on principals and dropped to 5th nr fin* **10/1**

**6** *3/4* **Defining Year (IRE)**$^{37}$ 621 6-9-0 **96**.................................. LeighRoche(3) 11 91
(D K Weld, Ire) *chsd ldrs: tk clsr order 1 1/2f out: rdn in 5th ent fnl f and sn no imp on ldrs: dropped to 6th nr fin* **14/1**

**7** *2* **Chapter Seven**$^{38}$ 593 5-9-9 **102**..................................(b[1]) JamieSpencer 12 92
(G M Lyons, Ire) *hld up towards rr: prog fr 2f out where nt clr run: styd on wl ins fnl f into nvr nrr 7th* **15/2**$^{2}$

**8** *1 1/2* **Smoker**$^{297}$ 2820 4-8-4 **83** oh1.................................. RoryCleary 2 70
(P J Prendergast, Ire) *chsd ldrs: tk clsr order fr 2f out: sn rdn and no ex in 6th ent fnl f: one pce towards fin* **33/1**

**9** *2 3/4* **Captain Cullen (IRE)**$^{16}$ 877 5-8-2 **86**.................................. ConnorKing(5) 6 66
(Gerard Keane, Ire) *hld up in tch: pushed along fr 3f out and sn no imp on ldrs u.p: kpt on one pce ins fnl f* **25/1**

**10** *2* **Cheval Rouge (IRE)**$^{184}$ 6617 7-8-6 **85**..................................(tp) DannyGrant 1 61
(H Rogers, Ire) *in rr of mid-div: sme hdwy on outer over 2f out: no ex ent fnl f: kpt on one pce* **20/1**

**11** *1/2* **Saratoga Baby (IRE)**$^{190}$ 6419 6-7-9 **84** oh3 ow1......(t) SeanCorby(10) 3 58
(Peter Fahey, Ire) *racd in mid-div: hdwy over 2f out to chse ldrs far side: no ex u.p ent fnl f: one pce towards fin* **33/1**

**12** *nk* **Regulation (IRE)**$^{22}$ 812 5-9-7 **100**.................................. ShaneFoley 15 74
(M Halford, Ire) *in rr of mid-div: sme hdwy fr 2f out: n.m.r over 1f out: kpt on one pce* **10/1**

**13** *1 1/2* **We'll Go Walking (IRE)**$^{195}$ 6266 4-9-9 **102**.................. NGMcCullagh 9 73
(J P Murtagh, Ire) *in rr of mid-div: rdn over 2f out and no imp: one pce fnl f* **14/1**

**14** *4 1/2* **Trail Blaze (IRE)**$^{155}$ 7368 5-8-8 **92**.................................. ShaneGray(5) 4 52
(Kevin Ryan) *sn led narrowly: cl 2nd 1/2-way: sn rdn and wknd fr 2f out* **9/1**

**15** *nse* **Einsteins Folly (IRE)**$^{140}$ 7719 4-8-11 **90**.................. KevinManning 20 50
(J S Bolger, Ire) *chsd ldrs: cl 5th 3f out: rdn over 2f out and sn no ex u.p: wknd and eased ins fnl f* **16/1**

**16** *nk* **Strandfield Lady (IRE)**$^{9}$ 970 9-8-4 **83** oh2..................(p) BenCurtis 8 42
(H Rogers, Ire) *a towards rr: rdn and no imp fr 3f out* **50/1**

**17** *5 1/2* **Man Of Erin (IRE)**$^{28}$ 5775 6-7-8 **83** oh7..........................[1] IanQueally(10) 21 30
(J F Levins, Ire) *sn chsd ldrs: racd keenly: rdn and wknd 3f out* **33/1**

**18** *2 1/2* **Shipyard (USA)**$^{148}$ 7552 5-8-4 **83**.................................. ChrisHayes 19 24
(A Oliver, Ire) *in rr of mid-div: pushed along over 3f out and sn no imp u.p: wknd and eased ins fnl f* **8/1**$^{3}$

**19** *6 1/2* **Afonso De Sousa (USA)**$^{156}$ 7361 4-10-0 **107**.......... JosephO'Brien 10 33
(A P O'Brien, Ire) *hld up: rdn towards rr fr after 1/2-way and no ex: wknd and eased fnl 2f* **12/1**

**20** *1* **Beacon Lodge (IRE)**$^{140}$ 7719 9-9-2 **102**.................. TomMadden(7) 16 26
(T Stack, Ire) *wnt bdly rt s and bmpd rival: racd in rr tl tk clsr order 1/2-way: rdn and wknd 3f out* **16/1**

**U** **Diesel Ten (IRE)**$^{43}$ 7477 4-8-6 **85** ow1..................(b) MichaelHussey 14
(Patrick O Brady, Ire) *bdly hmpd s and uns rdr* **40/1**

1m 49.3s (3.30) **Going Correction** +0.70s/f (Yiel) **21 Ran SP% 141.7**
Speed ratings: **111,110,109,106,105 105,103,101,98,96 96,95,94,89,89 89,84,81,75,74**
CSF £73.51 CT £701.99 TOTE £8.20: £1.50, £3.70, £4.10, £5.70; DF 134.00 Trifecta £2678.90.
**Owner** Dominick Glennane **Bred** Castleton Lyons & Kilboy Estat **Trained** The Curragh, Co Kildare
■ Stewards' Enquiry : Ben Dawson one race day: weighed in heavy

**FOCUS**
The first two ran to personal bests, while the third and fourth ran to what they did at the back-end of 2013.

1077 - 1079a (Foreign Racing) - See Raceform Interactive

# 1045 WOLVERHAMPTON (A.W) (L-H)
Monday, March 24

**OFFICIAL GOING: Standard**
Wind: Fresh behind Weather: Cloudy with sunny spells

## 1080 32RED MERMAIDS MILLIONS SLOT FILLIES' H'CAP — 5f 216y(P)
**2:40** (2:40) (Class 5) (0-75,72) 4-Y-0+ **£3,881** (£1,155; £577; £288) **Stalls** Low

Form RPR

1014 **1** **Star Up In The Sky (USA)**$^{13}$ 909 4-8-11 **67**............(b) KevinStott(5) 4 77
(Kevin Ryan) *a.p: led over 1f out: rdn out* **3/1**$^{1}$

220- **2** *2 3/4* **Oasis Spirit**$^{121}$ 8020 4-9-0 **72**.................................. KieranShoemark(7) 7 74
(Andrew Balding) *hld up: hdwy over 2f out: nt clr run wl over 1f out: sn rdn and edgd lft: styd on same pce ins fnl f* **7/2**$^{2}$

4532 **3** *nk* **Laughing Rock (IRE)**$^{12}$ 934 4-8-7 **58** oh2..............(v) AndrewMullen 5 59
(Michael Appleby) *chsd ldrs: wnt 2nd 1/2-way: tl rdn 2f out: styd on same pce ins fnl f* **10/1**

1314 **4** *8* **Megaleka**$^{17}$ 866 4-8-10 **66**.................................. TimClark(5) 1 43
(Alan Bailey) *s.i.s: pushed along 1/2-way: effrt over 1f out: wknd fnl f* **8/1**

0-20 **5** *hd* **Amosite**[25] [757] 8-9-2 **72**..........(v) ShelleyBirkett(5) 6 48
(J R Jenkins) *led: rdn and hdd over 1f out: wknd ins fnl f* **7/1**
0200 **6** *2 ½* **Climaxfortackle (IRE)**[7] [993] 6-8-10 **61**..........(v) DaleSwift 3 30
(Derek Shaw) *s.s: outpcd* **9/2**[3]
3062 **7** *3 ½* **Beylerbey (USA)**[10] [962] 4-9-0 **65**.......... JoeFanning 2 23
(Mark Johnston) *chsd ldr to 1/2-way: rdn and wknd wl over 1f out* **5/1**
1m 15.43s (0.43) **Going Correction** +0.225s/f (Slow) **7** Ran SP% **114.8**
Speed ratings (Par 100): **106,102,101,91,91 87,83**
CSF £13.81 TOTE £4.20: £2.60, £2.60; EX 16.60 Trifecta £96.10.
**Owner** Matt & Lauren Morgan **Bred** Dixiana Stables Inc **Trained** Hambleton, N Yorks

**FOCUS**
An open-looking fillies' handicap run at a decent pace. The winner confirmed she's back to her best.

## 1081 DOWNLOAD THE LADBROKES APP H'CAP 7f 32y(P)
**3:10** (3:10) (Class 6) (0-52,52) 4-Y-0+ **£2,587** (£770; £384; £192) **Stalls** High

Form RPR
050/ **1** **Mont Signal**[461] [8155] 4-9-7 **52**..........(t) RichardKingscote 8 63+
(Daniel Kubler) *a.p: nt clr run over 1f out: shkn up to ld wl ins fnl f: r.o* **5/1**[2]
3005 **2** *1 ¼* **Ishetoo**[9] [972] 10-9-1 **46**.......... AdamKirby 11 52
(Peter Grayson) *hld up: hdwy over 2f out: rdn over 1f out: r.o* **25/1**
-605 **3** *nse* **Piccolo Express**[10] [963] 8-9-5 **50**.......... AndrewMullen 9 56
(Brian Baugh) *hld up: hdwy over 1f out: sn rdn: r.o* **8/1**
4323 **4** *nse* **Very First Blade**[9] [973] 5-9-4 **49**..........(be) JoeFanning 7 55
(Michael Mullineaux) *trckd ldr tl led 2f out: rdn over 1f out: hdd and unable qck wl ins fnl f* **5/2**[1]
0000 **5** *1 ½* **Sam Spade (IRE)**[12] [922] 4-9-7 **52**..........(v[1]) DaleSwift 10 54
(Derek Shaw) *chsd ldrs: rdn over 2f out: styd on same pce ins fnl f* **7/1**[3]
2330 **6** *3* **Vhujon (IRE)**[11] [937] 9-8-12 **46** oh1.......... SladeO'Hara(3) 4 41
(Peter Grayson) *s.i.s: hld up: r.o ins fnl f: nvr nrr* **16/1**
0056 **7** *1 ¾* **Fathom Five (IRE)**[6] [1001] 10-9-6 **51**.......... PaddyAspell 2 41
(Shaun Harris) *led: pushed along and hdd 2f out: wknd ins fnl f* **16/1**
0336 **8** *7* **Partner's Gold (IRE)**[55] [367] 4-9-1 **46** oh1..........(b) LukeMorris 5 19
(Alan Berry) *chsd ldrs: rdn over 2f out: wknd over 1f out* **5/1**[2]
-606 **9** *12* **David's Secret**[45] [516] 4-9-1 **46**.......... ChrisCatlin 3
(Roy Brotherton) *sn outpcd* **12/1**
-450 **10** *10* **Mobley Chaos**[20] [833] 4-9-1 **46** oh1..........(b[1]) DavidProbert 1
(Ronald Harris) *s.i.s: a in rr: drvn along 1/2-way: sn wknd* **10/1**
2034 **P** **Mucky Molly**[20] [833] 6-9-1 **46**..........(vt) TomEaves 6
(Alison Hutchinson) *mid-div: hdwy u.p over 2f out: ev ch whn wnt wrong over 1f out: sn p.u and dismntd: fatally injured* **8/1**
1m 31.29s (1.69) **Going Correction** +0.225s/f (Slow) **11** Ran SP% **129.0**
Speed ratings (Par 101): **99,97,97,97,95 92,90,82,68,57**
CSF £133.23 CT £756.03 TOTE £6.70: £2.00, £7.20, £1.80; EX 312.60 Trifecta £2653.30 Part won..
**Owner** Mr & Mrs G Middlebrook **Bred** Mr & Mrs G Middlebrook & Cheveley Park **Trained** Lambourn, Berks

**FOCUS**
A fair race for the lowly grade and the winner might go on from here.

## 1082 LADBROKES H'CAP 7f 32y(P)
**3:40** (3:40) (Class 5) (0-70,70) 4-Y-0+ **£3,881** (£1,155; £577; £288) **Stalls** High

Form RPR
2152 **1** **Grace Hull**[13] [913] 4-9-0 **63**..........(p) AdamKirby 6 71
(Garry Moss) *hld up: rdn over 1f out: edgd lft and r.o u.p to ld nr fin* **6/1**
5221 **2** *½* **Hierarch (IRE)**[9] [979] 7-8-12 **68**..........(p) LewisWalsh(7) 7 74
(David Simcock) *a.p: rdn to ld ins fnl f: edgd lft and hdd nr fin* **5/1**[3]
21-0 **3** *½* **Sakash**[64] [245] 4-9-4 **67**.......... FrederikTylicki 2 72
(J R Jenkins) *chsd ldrs: rdn and ev ch ins fnl f: styd on same pce* **2/1**[1]
2100 **4** *1 ¾* **Hellbender (IRE)**[37] [627] 8-9-6 **69**.......... DavidProbert 5 69
(Shaun Harris) *led: rdn over 1f out: hdd and unable qck ins fnl f* **7/1**
-600 **5** *shd* **Illustrious Prince (IRE)**[12] [929] 7-9-7 **70**..........(p) PaulMulrennan 8 70
(Julie Camacho) *trckd ldr: plld hrd: rdn and ev ch over 1f out: styd on same pce ins fnl f* **16/1**
0-04 **6** *½* **Blazeofenchantment (USA)**[12] [929] 4-9-0 **66**.......... BillyCray(3) 1 65
(Richard Guest) *hld up: drvn along 1/2-way: kpt on ins fnl f: nt trble ldrs* **3/1**[2]
3204 **7** *1 ¼* **Master Of Disguise**[16] [889] 8-8-11 **60**.......... DuranFentiman 3 56+
(Brian Baugh) *hld up: rdn over 1f out: n.d* **25/1**
0-05 **8** *¾* **See The Storm**[32] [677] 6-9-3 **69**.......... JasonHart(3) 4 63
(Eric Alston) *plld hrd and prom: rdn over 1f out: no ex fnl f* **16/1**
1m 30.75s (1.15) **Going Correction** +0.225s/f (Slow) **8** Ran SP% **117.4**
Speed ratings (Par 103): **102,101,100,98,98 98,96,95**
CSF £36.95 CT £81.88 TOTE £5.60: £1.50, £1.70, £1.40; EX 16.00 Trifecta £30.70.
**Owner** Ron Hull **Bred** Whitsbury Manor Stud & Pigeon House Stud **Trained** Tickhill, S Yorks

**FOCUS**
A modest handicap. The winning time was just over half a second quicker than the Class 6 event over the same C&D earlier in the card. The winner is starting to assemble good record here.

## 1083 LADBROKES (S) STKS 1m 141y(P)
**4:10** (4:10) (Class 6) 3-Y-0+ **£2,556** (£754; £377) **Stalls** Low

Form RPR
3464 **1** **Camachoice (IRE)**[19] [843] 4-9-10 **71**..........(p) AdamKirby 4 71
(Marco Botti) *chsd ldr: rdn to ld over 1f out: hdd ins fnl f: rallied to ld nr fin: all out* **1/2**[1]
0-06 **2** *hd* **Red Wifey (IRE)**[28] [734] 3-8-0 **56**..........(b[1]) LukeMorris 5 61
(Alan McCabe) *chsd ldrs: hung rt 7f out: drvn along over 3f out: sn lost pl: rallied 2f out: styd on u.p to ld ins fnl f: hdd nr fin* **20/1**
2234 **3** *1 ¼* **Officer In Command (USA)**[10] [953] 8-10-2 **69**..........(p) LiamKeniry 1 74
(John Butler) *hld up: hdwy 3f out: outpcd 2f out: sn swtchd rt: hung lft and styd on ins fnl f* **11/2**[2]
450 **4** *2 ¼* **For Shia And Lula (IRE)**[31] [690] 5-9-5 **63**..........(p) PhilipPrince(5) 3 63
(Daniel Mark Loughnane) *led: clr 6f out: c bk to the field over 2f out: rdn and hdd over 1f out: no ex ins fnl f* **8/1**
4404 **5** *nse* **Prime Exhibit**[11] [940] 9-10-2 **69**..........(t) ShaneKelly 2 69
(Daniel Mark Loughnane) *hld up: hdwy 3f out: rdn over 1f out: styd on same pce fnl f* **6/1**[3]
500/ **6** *41* **Drummers Drumming (USA)**[547] [33] 8-9-7 **45**.......... SladeO'Hara(3) 7
(Alan Berry) *sn outpcd* **66/1**
1m 52.71s (2.21) **Going Correction** +0.225s/f (Slow)
**WFA** 3 from 4yo+ 19lb **6** Ran SP% **113.7**
Speed ratings (Par 101): **99,98,97,95,95 59**
CSF £13.67 TOTE £1.70: £1.10, £6.90; EX 10.90 Trifecta £43.00.Th winner was sold to Jamie Snowden for 6,750gns. Red Wifey was subject to a friendly claim.
**Owner** Jonny Allison **Bred** Doc Bloodstock **Trained** Newmarket, Suffolk

**FOCUS**
An uncompetitive seller, but the odds-on favourite had to work hard to get the win. Straightforward form.

## 1084 LADBROKES MEDIAN AUCTION MAIDEN STKS 1m 141y(P)
**4:40** (4:41) (Class 5) 3-5-Y-0 **£3,234** (£962; £481; £240) **Stalls** Low

Form RPR
2- **1** **Indian Trifone (IRE)**[308] [2507] 4-10-0 **0**.......... LukeMorris 6 71+
(Ed Walker) *trckd ldr: rdn over 1f out: styd on to ld nr fin* **1/2**[1]
35 **2** *½* **Stoneham**[11] [941] 3-8-4 **0**.......... HayleyTurner 5 60
(Mick Channon) *led: rdn over 1f out: edgd rt ins fnl f: hdd nr fin* **11/2**[3]
**3** *1 ¾* **Nothing Special** 3-8-4 **0**.......... KieranO'Neill 2 56+
(Tom Dascombe) *s.i.s: sn prom: rdn over 1f out: styd on same pce ins fnl f* **10/1**
60-0 **4** *14* **O'Raghallaigh (IRE)**[21] [824] 3-8-4 **0**.......... JoeFanning 4 27
(Richard Fahey) *s.i.s: hdwy 1/2-way: rdn and wknd over 2f out* **33/1**
0-60 **5** *2 ½* **Deavin**[28] [731] 3-8-2 **37**.......... JordanVaughan(7) 3 27
(Nick Littmoden) *chsd ldrs tl rdn and wknd over 3f out* **33/1**
**6** *11* **Mink Coat** 3-8-4 **0**.......... ChrisCatlin 1
(Rae Guest) *rn green and sn pushed along in rr: bhd fnl 6f* **4/1**[2]
1m 53.93s (3.43) **Going Correction** +0.225s/f (Slow)
**WFA** 3 from 4yo 19lb **6** Ran SP% **117.0**
Speed ratings (Par 103): **93,92,91,78,76 66**
CSF £4.27 TOTE £1.70: £1.10, £2.20; EX 3.90 Trifecta £10.90.
**Owner** Forza Azzurri **Bred** P J Gleeson **Trained** Newmarket, Suffolk

**FOCUS**
A very modest maiden and the bare form is little better. The first three finished well clear.

## 1085 LADBROKES MOBILE H'CAP 1m 141y(P)
**5:10** (5:10) (Class 5) (0-70,72) 4-Y-0+ **£3,557** (£1,058; £529; £264) **Stalls** Low

Form RPR
400- **1** **Life And Times (USA)**[154] [7424] 6-9-7 **70**.......... JoeFanning 4 81+
(Mark Johnston) *s.i.s: hld up: nt clr run over 2f out: hdwy over 1f out: shkn up and r.o to ld towards fin: readily* **2/1**[1]
0251 **2** *1* **My Single Malt (IRE)**[4] [1036] 6-9-9 **72** 7ex..........(p) PaulMulrennan 3 79
(Julie Camacho) *trckd ldr tl led over 3f out: clr over 1f out: rdn and hdd towards fin* **2/1**[1]
-520 **3** *1 ½* **Schottische**[26] [750] 4-8-0 **56**..........(v) JoeDoyle(7) 5 60
(Derek Haydn Jones) *a.p: nt clr run and swtchd rt wl over 1f out: sn rdn: styd on* **12/1**
4-45 **4** *2 ¾* **One Scoop Or Two**[35] [646] 8-9-5 **68**..........(v) GrahamGibbons 6 66
(Andrew Hollinshead) *hld up: pushed along and hmpd wl over 1f out: sn rdn and hung lft: nt trble ldrs* **4/1**[2]
4056 **5** *3 ¼* **Outlaw Torn (IRE)**[28] [733] 5-8-10 **62**..........(e) BillyCray(3) 2 53
(Richard Guest) *led 5f: sn rdn: wknd over 1f out* **14/1**
0004 **6** *½* **Pravda Street**[12] [928] 9-8-8 **62**..........(b) JackDuern(5) 7 52
(Christopher Kellett) *chsd ldrs: rdn over 2f out: wknd fnl f* **33/1**
440 **7** *3 ½* **Safwaan**[26] [750] 7-8-7 **56**.......... LukeMorris 1 39
(Michael Squance) *chsd ldrs: rdn over 1f out: wknd fnl f* **10/1**[3]
1m 51.19s (0.69) **Going Correction** +0.225s/f (Slow) **7** Ran SP% **113.1**
Speed ratings (Par 103): **105,104,102,100,97 97,93**
CSF £5.80 TOTE £2.90: £1.90, £1.70; EX 6.90 Trifecta £50.40.
**Owner** Sheikh Hamdan bin Mohammed Al Maktoum **Bred** Vision Bloodstock Et Al **Trained** Middleham Moor, N Yorks

**FOCUS**
A modest handicap run at an ordinary pace, but the form looks straightforward rated around the second.

## 1086 CORAL APP DOWNLOAD FROM THE APP STORE H'CAP 1m 1f 103y(P)
**5:40** (5:40) (Class 6) (0-60,63) 4-Y-0+ **£2,587** (£770; £384; £192) **Stalls** Low

Form RPR
0431 **1** **Dozy Joe**[4] [1034] 6-9-11 **63** 6ex..........(b) LukeMorris 1 71
(Joseph Tuite) *chsd ldrs: pushed along over 2f out: hmpd over 1f out: led 1f out: rdn out* **10/11**[1]
3203 **2** *1 ¼* **General Tufto**[7] [998] 9-8-8 **51**..........(b) JoeyHaynes(5) 3 57
(Charles Smith) *hld up: hdwy over 2f out: rdn over 1f out: styd on to go 2nd post: nt rch wnr* **4/1**[3]
546 **3** *nse* **Nellies Quest**[11] [941] 5-8-8 **46**.......... AndrewMullen 2 52
(Michael Appleby) *trckd ldrs: plld hrd: wnt 2nd over 3f out: rdn to ld and hung lft fr over 1f out: hdd 1f out: styd on same pce: lost 2nd post* **10/1**
3666 **4** *3 ½* **Refuse Colette (IRE)**[13] [916] 5-8-7 **45**.......... JoeFanning 4 44
(Paul Green) *trckd ldr after 1f tl led over 3f out: rdn: hdd and hmpd over 1f out: no ex ins fnl f* **25/1**
**5** *7* **Ferryview Place**[88] [8399] 5-8-12 **50**..........(tp) StevieDonohoe 7 36
(Ian Williams) *hld up: rdn over 2f out: nvr on terms* **9/4**[2]
00-0 **6** *14* **Moissanite**[46] [497] 5-8-0 **45**.......... JordanVaughan(7) 6 4
(Sean Regan) *led: racd keenly: rdn and hdd over 3f out: wknd over 2f out* **50/1**
2m 3.37s (1.67) **Going Correction** +0.225s/f (Slow) **6** Ran SP% **118.1**
Speed ratings (Par 101): **101,99,99,96,90 78**
CSF £5.57 TOTE £1.70: £1.10, £2.60; EX 4.80 Trifecta £13.10.
**Owner** Paddy Barrett **Bred** John Morton **Trained** Great Shefford, Berks

**FOCUS**
A weak handicap lacking much depth. Straightforward form.
T/Plt: £41.90 to a £1 stake. Pool: £69468.90 - 1207.48 winning tickets T/Qpdt: £2.30 to a £1 stake. Pool: £5611.69 - 1759.30 winning tickets CR

# 1001 SOUTHWELL (L-H)
Tuesday, March 25

**OFFICIAL GOING: Standard**
Wind: Virtually nil Weather: Heavy cloud

## 1087 LADBROKES H'CAP 1m (F)
**2:20** (2:21) (Class 6) (0-60,60) 4-Y-0+ **£2,587** (£770; £384; £192) **Stalls** Low

Form RPR
5022 **1** **Hail Promenader (IRE)**[14] [910] 8-9-7 **60**..........(tp) WilliamCarson 2 70
(Anthony Carson) *trckd ldrs: swtchd rt to outer after 2f: gd hdwy over 3f out: chal over 2f out: rdn over 1f out: led ent fnl f: sn edgd lft and kpt on* **3/1**[3]
6000 **2** *2* **Auden (USA)**[22] [821] 6-9-4 **57**..........(v) JoeFanning 5 62
(J R Jenkins) *trckd ldrs: hdwy 3f out: effrt to chse ldng pair wl over 1f out: sn rdn: kpt on u.p fnl f* **5/2**[1]

6210 **3** ½ **Bapak Pesta (IRE)**[40] 590 4-9-2 **55**..............................(p) GrahamLee 6 59
(Kevin Ryan) *cl up: led 3f out: jnd and rdn 2f out: drvn and hdd ent fnl f: kpt on same pce* **6/1**

-524 **4** 7 **Solarmaite**[21] 835 5-8-12 **56**..............................(b) PhilipPrince(5) 3 44
(Roy Bowring) *led: rdn along and hdd 3f out: drvn over 2f out and sn wknd* **8/1**

0635 **5** 9 **Xclusive**[22] 815 4-9-6 **59**..............................(p) LukeMorris 1 26
(Ronald Harris) *chsd ldrs on inner: rdn along over 3f out: drvn and wknd wl over 2f out* **11/4**[2]

6330 **6** 5 **Elusive Warrior (USA)**[21] 833 11-8-10 **49**....................(p) BenCurtis 4 5
(Alan McCabe) *n.m.r shortly after s and sn rdn along: a in rr* **25/1**

5654 **7** 2 **Silver Fawn (IRE)**[14] 916 4-8-7 **46** oh1....................(be) JimmyQuinn 8
(John Weymes) *t.k.h: in tch on wd outside: rdn along wl over 3f out and sn wknd* **16/1**

-000 **8** 12 **Mists Of Time (IRE)**[20] 838 4-9-1 **54**.......................... JamesSullivan 7
(Pat Eddery) *dwlt and a in rr: outpcd and bhd fr wl over 3f out* **20/1**

1m 42.88s (-0.82) **Going Correction** +0.05s/f (Slow) **8 Ran SP% 120.1**
Speed ratings (Par 101): **106,104,103,96,87 82,80,68**
CSF £11.64 CT £43.32 TOTE £3.70: £1.10, £1.10, £4.30; EX 13.80 Trifecta £80.60.
**Owner** Richard Prince **Bred** Rathbarry Stud **Trained** Newmarket, Suffolk

**FOCUS**
A moderate handicap in which the principals pulled clear. The third is the best guide.

## 1088 CORAL.CO.UK BEST ODDS GUARANTEED ON RACING MEDIAN AUCTION MAIDEN STKS — 1m 4f (F)
**2:50** (2:50) (Class 5) 3-5-Y-O **£3,234** (£962; £481; £240) **Stalls Low**

Form RPR

**1** **From Frost** 3-8-5 0..............................(t) DavidProbert 4 81+
(Andrew Balding) *trckd ldrs: green and pushed along briefly over 5f out: cl up over 3f out: hdwy on outer to ld wl over 2f out: sn rdn clr: edgd lft over 1f out: styd on strly: readily* **11/4**[2]

4- **2** 6 **Ridgeway Storm (IRE)**[227] 5286 4-9-11 0.......................... TomQueally 3 70+
(Alan King) *trckd ldr: cl up 1/2-way: effrt to chal 3f out and sn ev ch: rdn and edgd lft wl over 1f out: kpt on: no ch w wnr* **8/13**[1]

6-2 **3** 12 **Sheila's Heart**[75] 97 4-9-6 0.......................... ShelleyBirkett(5) 1 51
(Julia Feilden) *trckd ldng pair on inner: effrt over 3f out: sn rdn along and outpcd over 2f out: kpt on u.p fnl f to take modest 3rd nr fin* **7/1**[3]

-643 **4** ¾ **Flying Author (IRE)**[7] 1002 3-8-5 45..............................(t) LukeMorris 2 48
(Phil McEntee) *led: pushed along 4f out: rdn 3f out: sn hdd and gradually wknd: lost modest 3rd towards fin* **25/1**

6 **5** 30 **Philosofy**[18] 871 4-9-6 0.......................... DanielTudhope 6
(David O'Meara) *trckd ldrs: pushed along over 4f out: sn rdn and wknd* **25/1**

6-06 **6** 99 **Somerton Star**[10] 974 4-9-11 39..............................(b[1]) JoeFanning 5
(Pat Eddery) *dwlt: in tch: rdn along 1/2-way: sn outpcd and wl bhd* **50/1**

2m 39.82s (-1.18) **Going Correction** +0.05s/f (Slow)
**WFA** 3 from 4yo 22lb **6 Ran SP% 110.7**
Speed ratings (Par 103): **105,101,93,92,72 6**
CSF £4.68 TOTE £5.90: £2.00, £1.40; EX 7.00 Trifecta £13.00.
**Owner** George Strawbridge **Bred** George Strawbridge **Trained** Kingsclere, Hants

**FOCUS**
Fibresand maidens for older horses at this time of year can be modest affairs, but this one may be above average with an impressive debut winner. The fourth and the time offer perspective to the worth of the bare form.

## 1089 COMPARE BOOKMAKERS AT BOOKMAKERS.CO.UK H'CAP — 5f (F)
**3:25** (3:25) (Class 6) (0-60,59) 4-Y-0+ **£2,587** (£770; £384; £192) **Stalls High**

Form RPR

0005 **1** **Spic 'n Span**[14] 908 9-8-8 **46**..............................(v) LukeMorris 8 58
(Ronald Harris) *sn led: rdn over 1f out: edgd rt ins fnl f: kpt on strly* **16/1**

4032 **2** 2 **Dancing Freddy (IRE)**[7] 1001 7-9-6 **58**....................(tp) AdamKirby 9 63
(Ann Stokell) *trckd wnr: effrt 1/2-way: rdn along wl over 1f out: swtchd lft and drvn appr fnl f: no imp* **5/4**[1]

-263 **3** 3 **Imaginary Diva**[34] 662 8-9-7 **59**.......................... TomQueally 5 53
(George Margarson) *chsd ldrs: swtchd rt 2f out: sn rdn along and kpt on same pce fnl f* **7/1**

0400 **4** ¾ **Captain Scooby**[6] 1009 8-8-12 **53**..............................(e) BillyCray(3) 1 45
(Richard Guest) *chsd ldrs: rdn along wl over 1f out: drvn and one pce appr fnl f* **6/1**[3]

-054 **5** 2 ¼ **China Excels**[7] 1001 7-8-9 **50**.......................... RossAtkinson(3) 7 33
(Mandy Rowland) *racd nr stands' rail: in tch: rdn along bef 1/2-way: sn outpcd* **7/2**[2]

0-50 **6** 2 ½ **Jemimaville (IRE)**[12] 937 7-8-4 **45**..............................(v) RyanPowell(3) 2 19+
(Giles Bravery) *blind removed late and dwlt: s.i.s: rdn along and hdwy on outer after 2f: in tch over 2f out: sn wknd* **50/1**

-046 **7** 1 ¼ **Durham Express (IRE)**[13] 934 7-8-2 **45**.............(b) ConnorBeasley(5) 4 15
(Colin Teague) *sn rdn along and outpcd in rr* **6/1**[3]

100- **8** 2 **Sophie's Beau (USA)**[102] 8272 7-8-0 **45**....................(b) PaulBooth(7) 3 8
(Michael Chapman) *chsd ldrs: rdn along bef 1/2-way: sn wknd* **33/1**

59.67s (-0.03) **Going Correction** +0.025s/f (Slow) **8 Ran SP% 118.5**
Speed ratings (Par 101): **101,97,93,91,88 84,82,79**
CSF £38.06 CT £167.25 TOTE £11.30: £3.40, £1.30, £1.90; EX 41.30 Trifecta £105.80.
**Owner** P Nurcombe **Bred** C A Cyzer **Trained** Earlswood, Monmouths

**FOCUS**
A moderate sprint handicap. A high draw is often a disadvantage over the straight 5f here, but the two berthed closest to the stands' rail dominated the finish thanks to being manoeuvred towards the centre of the track in the early stages. The winner improved 10lb on recent peak efforts.

## 1090 32RED BURNING DESIRE SLOT MAIDEN STKS — 1m (F)
**4:00** (4:00) (Class 5) 3-Y-0 **£3,234** (£962; £481; £240) **Stalls Low**

Form RPR

6222 **1** **Bobby Benton (IRE)**[11] 954 3-9-5 75.......................... LukeMorris 3 70
(Luke Dace) *cl up: led after 2f: rdn over 2f out: styd on strly fnl f* **6/4**[2]

63-0 **2** 1 ½ **Outback Warrior (IRE)**[60] 316 3-9-5 68.......................... PaulMulrennan 4 65
(Kevin Ryan) *dwlt and sn pushed along: cl up on outer after 2f: rdn along and sltly outpcd over 2f out: kpt on u.p fnl f* **8/1**[3]

66- **3** hd **Zephyr**[181] 6740 3-9-5 0.......................... DanielTudhope 2 64
(K R Burke) *trckd ldrs: effrt whn n.m.r and swtchd lft to inner rail wl over 2f out: sn rdn along and sltly kpt on fnl f* **16/1**

32 **4** 1 ½ **Tarrafal (IRE)**[17] 888 3-9-5 0.......................... JoeFanning 1 62
(Mark Johnston) *led 2f: trckd ldng pair: swtchd rt and rdn to chal wl over 2f out: drvn over 1f out: sn btn and eased towards fin* **10/11**[1]

1m 45.4s (1.70) **Going Correction** +0.05s/f (Slow) **4 Ran SP% 109.4**
Speed ratings (Par 98): **93,91,91,89**
CSF £11.75 TOTE £3.20; EX 7.40 Trifecta £24.00.
**Owner** Mark Benton **Bred** Old Carhue & Graeng Bloodstock **Trained** Five Oaks, W Sussex

**FOCUS**
A modest maiden and there wasn't that much covering the four runners at the line. The winner was value for a little extra.

## 1091 32RED THUNDERSTRUCK II SLOT H'CAP — 1m 6f (F)
**4:35** (4:35) (Class 4) (0-85,83) 4-Y-0+ **£5,822** (£1,732; £865; £432) **Stalls Low**

Form RPR

-513 **1** **Arr' Kid (USA)**[11] 961 4-9-3 **78**..............................(b) TomEaves 7 91+
(Keith Dalgleish) *mde all: pushed clr over 3f out: styd on strly: unchal* **6/4**[1]

0-61 **2** 12 **Noguchi (IRE)**[35] 652 9-9-5 **76**..............................(b) TomQueally 2 68
(George Margarson) *trckd ldrs: hdwy 5f out: rdn along and outpcd 3f out: styd on u.p fnl 2f: tk modest 2nd towards fin* **8/1**

014 **3** ½ **Royal Alcor (IRE)**[8] 999 7-9-10 **81**..............................(t) DavidProbert 6 73
(Gay Kelleway) *hld up: hdwy 1/2-way: chsd wnr 4f out: drvn and hung lft to inner rail wl over 2f out: sn no imp: lost 2nd towards fin* **5/1**[3]

/00- **4** 2 ½ **Recession Proof (FR)**[26] 7193 8-9-6 **77**....................(b) RobertWinston 3 66
(John Quinn) *sn rdn along in rr: drvn and bhd 1/2-way: styd on u.p fr over 3f out* **16/1**

436- **5** 7 **Lyric Street (IRE)**[31] 7115 6-9-12 **83**.......................... PhillipMakin 4 62
(Donald McCain) *in tch: rdn along 1/2-way: wknd 5f out* **20/1**

3045 **6** 14 **Returntobrecongill**[26] 764 4-9-6 **81**.......................... GrahamLee 1 42
(James Given) *prom: pushed along 1/2-way: rdn and lost pl 5f out: sn bhd* **3/1**[2]

422 **7** 4 ½ **Carlanda (FR)**[13] 932 4-8-6 **67**..............................(p) AndrewMullen 5 22
(Michael Appleby) *prom: pushed along over 5f out: rdn along over 4f out: sn wknd* **7/1**

000/ **8** 27 **Storm Hawk (IRE)**[688] 1890 7-9-6 **77**..............................(b) JoeFanning 8
(Pat Eddery) *in tch: pushed along 1/2-way: sn rdn and wknd: wl bhd fnl 3f* **25/1**

3m 9.92s (1.62) **Going Correction** +0.05s/f (Slow)
**WFA** 4 from 6yo+ 4lb **8 Ran SP% 119.8**
Speed ratings (Par 105): **97,90,89,88,84 76,73,58**
CSF £15.69 CT £51.54 TOTE £2.40: £1.10, £2.00, £1.50; EX 17.00 Trifecta £54.40.
**Owner** Weldspec Glasgow Limited **Bred** Chestnut Farm **Trained** Carluke, S Lanarks
■ Stewards' Enquiry : Andrew Mullen one-day ban: careless riding (Apr 8)

**FOCUS**
The favourite made this a proper test from the start and it proved too severe a test for many. The winner demolished them and this effort could be worth more.

## 1092 32RED ON THE APP STORE H'CAP — 2m (F)
**5:05** (5:05) (Class 6) (0-65,63) 4-Y-0+ **£2,587** (£770; £384; £192) **Stalls Low**

Form RPR

2 **1** **Teajaybe (USA)**[7] 1004 6-9-12 **63**.......................... BenCurtis 5 78+
(Chris Dwyer) *trckd ldrs: hdwy over 4f out: led 3f out: wd st: sn clr: pushed out* **7/2**[2]

5-54 **2** 8 **Adili (IRE)**[42] 567 5-9-1 **52**.......................... AndrewMullen 2 56
(Michael Appleby) *trckd ldr: cl up 7f out: led over 4f out: sn rdn along and hdd 3f out:: drvn and kpt on fnl 2f: no ch w wnr* **9/2**[3]

040- **3** 4 **Joyful Motive**[147] 7597 5-8-3 **47**.......................... PaulBooth(7) 3 47
(Michael Chapman) *in tch on inner: pushed along over 5f out: rdn along and outpcd over 4f out: swtchd rt and drvn wl over 1f out: styd on fnl f to take modest 3rd nr fin* **50/1**

00-3 **4** nk **Nadema Rose (IRE)**[10] 978 5-9-8 **59**.......................... TomEaves 4 58
(Keith Dalgleish) *hld up in tch: hdwy 5f out: rdn along over 3f out: drvn 3f out: sn btn* **7/1**

0/11 **5** ¾ **Sir Frank Morgan (IRE)**[8] 997 4-9-2 **58** 6ex.................... JoeFanning 1 56
(Mark Johnston) *led: pushed along and hdd over 4f out: rdn along over 3f out: sn drvn and wknd* **8/11**[1]

3m 47.49s (1.99) **Going Correction** +0.05s/f (Slow)
**WFA** 4 from 5yo+ 5lb **5 Ran SP% 112.8**
Speed ratings (Par 101): **97,93,91,90,90**
CSF £19.16 TOTE £4.60: £2.10, £2.70; EX 17.50 Trifecta £135.40.
**Owner** Mrs C Sandall **Bred** J S Bolger **Trained** Newmarket, Suffolk

**FOCUS**
Another severe test of stamina and another easy winner. It was a weak race with the favourite disappointing.

## 1093 32RED IMMORTAL ROMANCE SLOT H'CAP — 7f (F)
**5:35** (5:36) (Class 5) (0-75,78) 3-Y-0 **£3,234** (£962; £481; £240) **Stalls Low**

Form RPR

1111 **1** **Alumina (IRE)**[7] 1006 3-9-6 **78** 6ex.......................... JackGarritty(7) 4 88+
(Andrew Balding) *trckd ldng pair: smooth hdwy 3f out: cl up over 2f out: led over 1f out: sn pushed clr: readily* **8/13**[1]

-551 **2** 7 **Black Vale (IRE)**[22] 823 3-8-9 **67**..............................(t) DonnaAspell(7) 3 58
(Phil McEntee) *led and sn rdn: jnd over 2f out and sn rdn along: hdd and drvn over 1f out: kpt on: no ch w wnr* **7/2**[2]

14 **3** 7 **Glace (IRE)**[39] 604 3-9-1 **66**.......................... JoeFanning 2 38
(Mark Johnston) *chsd ldr on inner: rdn along 3f out: sn outpcd* **5/1**[3]

5033 **4** 2 ½ **Evacusafe Lady**[7] 1007 3-8-6 **60**..............................(t) RyanPowell(3) 1 25
(John Ryan) *in tch: rdn along after 3f: outpcd fr over 3f out* **14/1**

1m 30.2s (-0.10) **Going Correction** +0.05s/f (Slow) **4 Ran SP% 107.5**
Speed ratings (Par 98): **102,94,86,83**
CSF £3.01 TOTE £1.40; EX 3.20 Trifecta £5.00.
**Owner** Shapoor Mistry **Bred** Eimear Mulhern & Abbeville Stud **Trained** Kingsclere, Hants

**FOCUS**
A one-sided contest. The winner outclassed her rivals and this could underrate her a fair bit.
T/Plt: £52.10 to a £1 stake. Pool: £71,689.94 - 1004.11 winning units. T/Qpdt: £22.00 to a £1 stake. Pool: 4446.56 - 149.50 winning units. JR

# 1037 SAINT-CLOUD (L-H)
Tuesday, March 25

**OFFICIAL GOING: Turf: good**

## 1094a PRIX DU DEBUT (MAIDEN) (UNRACED 2YO) (TURF) — 4f 110y
**11:45** (12:00) 2-Y-0 **£10,416** (£4,166; £3,125; £2,083; £1,041)

RPR

**1** **Hesat (FR)** 2-8-13 0.......................... Christophe-PatriceLemaire 3 83
(M Boutin, France) **104/10**

**2** 1 ½ **Goken (FR)** 2-9-2 0.......................... FabriceVeron 6 80
(H-A Pantall, France) **23/5**[2]

**3** 3 **Acantos (FR)** 2-8-13 0.......................... CristianDemuro 9 65
(J Heloury, France) **233/10**



The Form Book, Raceform Ltd, Newbury, RG14 5SJ

4 1 ½ **Mylenachope (FR)** 2-8-13 0 ........ JulienGrosjean 4 59
(A De Watrigant, France) **28/1**

5 shd **Showmethemoney (FR)** 2-8-13 0 ........ Roberto-CarlosMontenegro 5 59
(P Sogorb, France) **107/10**

6 ¾ **Ma Ptite Sarah (FR)** 2-8-13 0 ........ SebastienMaillot 12 56
(E Caroux, France) **39/1**

7 nk **Royal Dolois (FR)** 2-9-2 0 ........ RonanThomas 8 57
(A Bonin, France) **161/10**

8 nk **Nomos (FR)** 2-9-2 0 ........ FilipMinarik 1 56
(N Sauer, Germany) **5/2**[1]

9 1 ½ **Liberte Mon Amour (FR)** 2-8-13 0 ........ IoritzMendizabal 10 47
(J Heloury, France) **144/10**

10 shd **Voila Baileys (FR)** 2-8-13 0 ........ MickaelForest 15 47
(W Walton, France) **183/10**

11 2 ½ **Elizabeth March (IRE)** 2-8-13 0 ........ GregoryBenoist 11 37
(E J O'Neill, France) **152/10**

12 shd **Caritas (GER)** 2-8-13 0 ........(p) MorganDelalande 13 36
(M Nigge, France) **40/1**

13 nk **Clever Love (FR)** 2-9-2 0 ........ ThomasHenderson 14 38
(Jo Hughes) *in tch: rdn and outpcd fr 2f out: sn btn: dropped to rr ins fnl f* **164/10**

14 nk **Michachope (FR)** 2-8-13 0 ........ JulienAuge 7 34
(A De Watrigant, France) **57/10**[3]

54.21s (54.21) **14** Ran SP% **120.6**
WIN (incl. 1 euro stake): 11.40. PLACES: 3.20, 2.40, 5.60. DF: 26.00. SF: 79.40.
**Owner** M Boutin **Bred** M Boutin, H Boutin & M Boutin **Trained** France

## 1096a PRIX LA CAMARGO (LISTED RACE) (3YO FILLIES) (TURF) 1m
**1:20** (12:00) 3-Y-O **£22,916** (£9,166; £6,875; £4,583; £2,291)

RPR

1 **Stormyra (FR)**[153] 7571 3-9-0 0 ........ UmbertoRispoli 3 108+
(J-P Gallorini, France) **13/2**

2 nk **Stellar Path (FR)**[153] 7571 3-9-0 0 ........ MaximeGuyon 2 107+
(X Thomas-Demeaulte, France) **7/5**[1]

3 ¾ **Victoria Regina (IRE)**[9] 3-9-0 0 ........ EddyHardouin 6 105
(J Heloury, France) **114/10**

4 ½ **Kenzadargent (FR)**[153] 7571 3-9-0 0 ........ ChristopheSoumillon 1 104+
(J-C Rouget, France) **14/5**[2]

5 3 **Vallicola (IRE)**[18] 3-9-0 0 ........ AntoineHamelin 4 97
(F Vermeulen, France) **113/10**

6 6 **Laurelita (IRE)**[194] 6318 3-9-0 0 ........ IoritzMendizabal 5 83
(George Baker) *led: rdn and hdd 2f out: sn no ex and btn: wknd and dropped to last: eased* **18/5**[3]

1m 43.51s (-3.99) **6** Ran SP% **119.2**
WIN (incl. 1 euro stake): 7.50. PLACES: 2.40, 1.50. SF: 28.70.
**Owner** Guy Pariente **Bred** G Pariente & G Pariente **Trained** France

1095 - 1096a (Foreign Racing) - See Raceform Interactive

# 1023 KEMPTON (A.W) (R-H)
## Wednesday, March 26

**OFFICIAL GOING: Standard**
Wind: Moderate, behind Weather: Rain before racing, then mainly clear

## 1097 FAMILY FUN AT KEMPTON 19.04.13 APPRENTICE H'CAP 1m 2f (P)
**5:30** (5:30) (Class 6) (0-65,65) 4-Y-O+ **£1,940** (£577; £288; £144) **Stalls** Low

Form RPR

0-41 1 **Cataria Girl (USA)**[23] 822 5-8-8 **57** ........(t) PatrickO'Donnell(5) 6 64
(Marcus Tregoning) *prom: rdn 2f out: edgd lft 1f out: styd on to ld nr fin* **10/3**[2]

6-60 2 ½ **South Cape**[33] 690 11-8-9 **60** ........ HectorCrouch(7) 1 66
(Gary Moore) *hld up in 5th: effrt and hrd rdn over 1f out: styd on to take 2nd nr fin: jst hld* **8/1**

3112 3 ½ **Bennelong**[6] 1023 8-8-8 **57** ........(b) PaigeBolton(5) 4 62
(Lee Carter) *plld hrd in 4th: hdwy to ld 3f out: shkn up over 1f out: ct nr fin* **6/4**[1]

6-00 4 1 ¼ **Raamz (IRE)**[42] 571 7-8-8 **55** ........[1] CamHardie(3) 2 58
(Kevin Morgan) *chsd ldrs: wnt 2nd over 2f out tl 1f out: one pce* **12/1**

-403 5 2 **Diletta Tommasa (IRE)**[33] 697 4-9-6 **64** ........(p) JackGarritty 7 63
(John Stimpson) *hld up towards rr: pushed along and no hdwy fnl 2f* **10/1**

0404 6 7 **Innoko (FR)**[12] 958 4-9-2 **65** ........(t) MrAidenBlakemore(5) 3 51
(Tony Carroll) *led tl 3f out: wknd over 2f out* **6/1**[3]

600- 7 4 ½ **Back On The Trail**[180] 6810 4-9-4 **65** ........ JennyPowell(3) 5 42
(Michael Blake) *s.s: wd on bnd 4f out: a bhd* **20/1**

2m 8.53s (0.53) **Going Correction** 0.0s/f (Stan) **7** Ran SP% **110.0**
Speed ratings (Par 101): **97,96,96,95,93 88,84**
CSF £27.11 TOTE £5.30: £1.80, £4.50; EX 27.30 Trifecta £60.80.
**Owner** Mr And Mrs A E Pakenham **Bred** Shadwell Farm LLC **Trained** Whitsbury, Hants
■ Patrick O'Donnell's first winner in Britain, to go with one in Ireland.
■ Stewards' Enquiry : Mr Aiden Blakemore four-day ban: careless riding (9-12 Apr)

**FOCUS**
A moderate handicap, confined to apprentice jockeys. It was run at a modest pace and saw changing fortunes up the home straight. The winner should be competitive again next time.

## 1098 HAPPY 80TH BIRTHDAY RAY HALL H'CAP 1m 2f (P)
**6:00** (6:01) (Class 6) (0-60,60) 3-Y-O **£1,940** (£577; £288; £144) **Stalls** Low

Form RPR

60-1 1 **Enquiring**[12] 960 3-9-3 **56** ........ AdamKirby 4 64+
(Mark Johnston) *led at modest pce: qcknd over 2f out: narrowly hdd over 1f out: regained ld ins fnl f: gamely* **2/1**[2]

6-02 2 nk **Whispering Star (USA)**[26] 774 3-9-1 **54** ........ AndreaAtzeni 3 62+
(David Simcock) *trckd ldrs: effrt and swtchd rt over 1f out: r.o to take 2nd fnl strides* **11/10**[1]

3364 3 hd **Indira**[8] 1007 3-9-7 **60** ........ JimCrowley 6 67+
(John Berry) *trckd ldr: slt ld over 1f out tl ins fnl f: kpt on* **20/1**

6122 4 3 **Shannon Haven (IRE)**[6] 1029 3-9-3 **56** ........(p) ShaneKelly 1 57
(Daniel Mark Loughnane) *hld up: effrt on inner 2f out: no ex fnl f* **9/2**[3]

020- 5 4 ½ **Assoluta (IRE)**[166] 7168 3-8-13 **57** ........ JoshBaudains(5) 2 49
(Sylvester Kirk) *stdd s: hld up in rr: hdwy 5f out: wknd over 1f out* **25/1**

6-40 6 7 **Ormer**[12] 960 3-8-7 **46** oh1 ........ ChrisCatlin 5 25
(David Evans) *sn rdn along: in tch tl outpcd and btn over 2f out* **66/1**

2m 10.54s (2.54) **Going Correction** 0.0s/f (Stan) **6** Ran SP% **109.2**
Speed ratings (Par 96): **89,88,88,86,82 77**
CSF £4.27 TOTE £2.70: £1.40, £1.20; EX 5.30 Trifecta £32.10.
**Owner** Sheikh Hamdan bin Mohammed Al Maktoum **Bred** D J Bloodstock, G Roddick & Wrottesley Ltd **Trained** Middleham Moor, N Yorks

**FOCUS**
Not a bad handicap for the class. It was run at a fair early pace, but slowed up markedly on the far side and most were off the bridle turning for home as it increased seriously. The form makes sense at face value.

## 1099 BETDAQ FREE £25 NO LOSE BET FILLIES' H'CAP 1m 2f (P)
**6:30** (6:33) (Class 5) (0-75,74) 4-Y-O+ **£2,587** (£770; £384; £192) **Stalls** Low

Form RPR

221 1 **Puzzle Time**[19] 871 4-9-6 **73** ........ WilliamCarson 2 80+
(Giles Bravery) *trckd ldrs: hmpd and swtchd rt wl over 1f out: led ins fnl f: rdn out* **6/4**[1]

-246 2 1 ½ **Ivor's Princess**[14] 924 5-8-10 **63** ........(b) SeanLevey 4 67
(Rod Millman) *hld up in 6th: shkn up and hdwy over 1f out: styd on fnl f: jst snatched 2nd* **12/1**

1-44 3 nse **Wakeup Little Suzy (IRE)**[51] 461 4-9-3 **70** ........(t) AndreaAtzeni 6 74
(Marco Botti) *hld up in 4th: hdwy on outer to ld wl over 1f out: hdd ins fnl f: one pce: lost 2nd on line* **7/2**[2]

1-02 4 5 **Ssafa**[20] 857 6-9-4 **71** ........(p) LukeMorris 1 66
(Alastair Lidderdale) *led: rdn over 2f out: hdd wl over 1f out: sn wknd* **9/2**[3]

060- 5 ½ **Movementneverlies**[123] 8020 4-9-0 **67** ........ JimCrowley 3 61
(Richard Phillips) *plld hrd in rr: rdn over 2f out: n.d* **16/1**

6-36 6 shd **Remix (IRE)**[40] 612 5-8-5 **58** ........(v) ChrisCatlin 7 51
(Ian Williams) *in tch: rdn 3f out: sn outpcd in rr* **14/1**

116- 7 1 ½ **Sureness (IRE)**[16] 6832 4-9-7 **74** ........(t) AdamKirby 5 65
(Charlie Mann) *dwlt: sn trcking ldr: rdn and wknd 2f out* **7/1**

2m 6.91s (-1.09) **Going Correction** 0.0s/f (Stan) **7** Ran SP% **113.1**
Speed ratings (Par 100): **104,102,102,98,98 98,97**
CSF £20.81 TOTE £2.10: £1.20, £5.70; EX 25.10 Trifecta £100.00.
**Owner** J J May **Bred** Plantation Stud **Trained** Newmarket, Suffolk

**FOCUS**
A modest fillies' handicap. It was another race run at an uneven pace but the form looks fair with the principals coming clear. The winner can do better still.

## 1100 BETDAQ £500 IN FREE BETS H'CAP 1m 4f (P)
**7:00** (7:00) (Class 6) (0-65,64) 4-Y-O+ **£1,940** (£577; £288; £144) **Stalls** Centre

Form RPR

50-1 1 **Able Dash**[41] 590 4-9-5 **64** ........ RichardKingscote 1 75+
(Michael Blake) *prom: rdn 3f out: led jst over 1f out: drvn out* **8/11**[1]

54-2 2 2 ¼ **Comedy House**[21] 848 6-9-7 **64** ........(v) GeorgeBaker 4 69
(Michael Madgwick) *in tch: rdn and styd on fr over 1f out: tk 2nd nr fin* **4/1**[2]

4214 3 ½ **Standing Strong (IRE)**[25] 801 6-9-4 **61** ........(p) LiamKeniry 5 66
(Zoe Davison) *stdd s: t.k.h in rr: hdwy to press ldng pair over 1f out: one pce* **8/1**[3]

66-6 4 ¾ **Gravitate**[35] 655 5-9-7 **64** ........(t) RobertHavlin 7 67
(Paul Webber) *sn led: set modest pce: qcknd 3f out: hdd jst over 1f out: no ex* **9/1**

106- 5 4 **Chella Thriller (SPA)**[317] 2311 5-9-7 **64** ........(b) AdamKirby 6 61
(Alastair Lidderdale) *pressed ldr tl outpcd 2f out: sn btn* **20/1**

2235 6 7 **Polydamos**[21] 838 5-8-8 **51** ........(v) LukeMorris 2 37
(Tony Carroll) *in tch: effrt 2f out: sn wknd* **14/1**

50/0 7 6 **Curlew (IRE)**[27] 754 8-8-2 **50** oh5 ........ JoeyHaynes(5) 3 26
(Chris Down) *hld up in 6th: rdn 3f out: sn bhd* **66/1**

2m 35.36s (0.86) **Going Correction** 0.0s/f (Stan)
**WFA** 4 from 5yo+ 2lb **7** Ran SP% **111.9**
Speed ratings (Par 101): **97,95,95,94,92 87,83**
CSF £3.66 TOTE £1.60: £1.20, £1.50; EX 4.20 Trifecta £15.00.
**Owner** West Wilts Hockey Lads **Bred** Cheveley Park Stud Ltd **Trained** Trowbridge, Wilts

**FOCUS**
This modest handicap was run at no more than an average pace and the tempo only got really serious going into the home bend. The placed horses set a very straightforward level.

## 1101 NEW JUMP FIXTURE ON 05.05.14 H'CAP 7f (P)
**7:30** (7:32) (Class 6) (0-65,65) 3-Y-O **£1,940** (£577; £288; £144) **Stalls** Low

Form RPR

0411 1 **Desert Colours**[5] 1048 3-8-10 **59** 6ex ........(b) KevinStott(5) 8 69
(Kevin Ryan) *chsd ldr: pushed lft 2f out: led wl over 1f out: rdn and r.o wl* **2/1**[1]

-243 2 1 ¼ **Romantic Bliss (IRE)**[15] 919 3-8-0 **51** oh3 ........(b) RobJFitzpatrick(7) 7 58
(K R Burke) *chsd ldrs: carried lft 2f out: styd on to chse wnr fnl f: a hld* **25/1**

334- 3 1 ¼ **The Dukkerer (IRE)**[165] 7198 3-9-4 **62** ........ JimCrowley 3 65
(Garry Moss) *off the pce in 5th: rdn 3f out: styd on fnl f* **14/1**

-220 4 ¾ **Witchy Woman**[35] 665 3-9-4 **62** ........(t) GeorgeBaker 10 63
(Geoffrey Deacon) *outpcd towards rr: sme hdwy 2f out: styd on fnl f* **16/1**

4-42 5 ½ **Choice Of Destiny**[15] 919 3-8-11 **60** ........ LouisSteward(5) 6 60
(Philip McBride) *chsd ldng pair: wnt 2nd over 1f out: one pce* **13/2**

006- 6 nk **Prim And Proper**[133] 7855 3-8-10 **54** ........ RobertWinston 4 53
(Brendan Powell) *outpcd and bhd: sme hdwy 2f out: no imp over 1f out* **33/1**

-302 7 2 ½ **Brownsville (USA)**[8] 1006 3-9-7 **65** ........ AdamKirby 1 57+
(Mark Johnston) *outpcd towards rr: sme hdwy 2f out: wknd over 1f out* **3/1**[2]

536- 8 ½ **Baker Man (IRE)**[163] 7243 3-9-0 **63** ........(t) JoshBaudains(5) 2 54
(Sylvester Kirk) *led at gd pce: edgd lft 2f out: hdd wl over 1f out: sn wknd* **7/2**[3]

-466 9 8 **Howz The Family (IRE)**[34] 670 3-9-5 **63** ........ JohnFahy 9 32
(John Spearing) *outpcd: a wl bhd* **33/1**

1m 25.27s (-0.73) **Going Correction** 0.0s/f (Stan) **9** Ran SP% **116.2**
Speed ratings (Par 96): **104,102,101,100,99 99,96,95,86**
CSF £58.94 CT £555.20 TOTE £3.30: £1.10, £5.10, £2.60; EX 50.80 Trifecta £729.30.
**Owner** Jon Beard **Bred** Rabbah Bloodstock Limited **Trained** Hambleton, N Yorks

**FOCUS**
There was a brisk pace on in this ordinary handicap. The winner continues on the upgrade.

## 1102 BETDAQ NO PREMIUM CHARGE H'CAP 7f (P)
**8:00** (8:01) (Class 4) (0-80,80) 4-Y-O+ **£4,690** (£1,395; £697; £348) **Stalls** Low

Form RPR

6245 1 **Light From Mars**[23] 820 9-9-7 **80** ........(p) LiamJones 8 90
(Ronald Harris) *chsd ldr: led 4f out: rdn and in control fnl 2f: r.o wl* **20/1**

0160 2 2 **Bowstar**[7] 1020 5-9-4 **77** ........(b) RobertHavlin 1 82
(Michael Attwater) *cl up: rdn over 2f out: styd on to chse wnr fnl f: a hld* **7/1**[3]

52-1 **3** 1/2 **Athletic**[23] 817 5-8-9 **68**..........(v) JimCrowley 2 71
(Andrew Reid) *hld up in tch: effrt and rdn over 1f out: styd on same pce* **3/1**[2]
2112 **4** *nk* **Fab Lolly (IRE)**[14] 924 4-9-6 **79**..........(p[1]) TedDurcan 5 81
(James Bethell) *dwlt: hld up in rr: hdwy 2f out: one pce fnl f* **3/1**[2]
06-6 **5** 1/2 **Lionheart**[60] 342 4-9-6 **79**.......... ShaneKelly 4 80
(Peter Crate) *chsd ldrs: one pce fnl 2f* **14/1**
3-36 **6** 2 **Malaysian Boleh**[34] 677 4-9-0 **73**.......... LukeMorris 7 69
(Simon Dow) *dwlt: hld up towards rr: rdn over 2f out: nvr able to chal* **8/1**
0-30 **7** 2 3/4 **Spin Artist (USA)**[15] 917 4-9-7 **80**.......... AdamKirby 6 68
(Mark Johnston) *led 3f: chsd wnr after tl wknd over 1f out* **11/4**[1]
1m 24.64s (-1.36) **Going Correction** 0.0s/f (Stan) **7** Ran SP% **118.1**
Speed ratings (Par 105): **107,104,104,103,103 100,97**
CSF £63.88 CT £208.56 TOTE £12.30: £4.60, £3.50; EX 53.10 Trifecta £210.70.
**Owner** Mrs N Macauley **Bred** Harts Farm And Stud **Trained** Earlswood, Monmouths
**FOCUS**
A modest handicap, run at a sound pace. Straightforward form.

## 1103 BETDAQ - THE SPORTS BETTING EXCHANGE H'CAP (LONDON MILE SERIES QUALIFIER) 1m (P)
**8:30** (8:30) (Class 4) (0-85,85) 4-Y-O+ **£4,690** (£1,395; £697; £348) **Stalls** Low

Form RPR
300- **1** **Tigers Tale (IRE)**[130] 7926 5-9-7 **85**..........(v) GeorgeBaker 2 92
(Roger Teal) *led: rdn and hdd over 1f out: rallied gamely to ld again nr fin* **11/4**[1]
4521 **2** *nk* **Liberty Jack (IRE)**[7] 1021 4-8-12 **76** 6ex.......... WilliamCarson 3 82
(Jim Boyle) *dwlt: hld up in 5th: hdwy 2f out: led over 1f out: hrd rdn fnl f: ct nr fin* **7/2**[3]
0-20 **3** 1 1/2 **Steelriver (IRE)**[21] 849 4-8-11 **75**..........[1] TedDurcan 7 78
(James Bethell) *chsd ldrs: rdn over 2f out: styd on fnl f* **7/1**
04-0 **4** *shd* **Ready (IRE)**[15] 917 4-9-2 **80**..........(p) JimCrowley 5 83
(Garry Moss) *t.k.h towards rr: rdn over 2f out: styd on wl fnl f* **12/1**
144- **5** 1/2 **Bold Prediction (IRE)**[170] 7063 4-8-11 **80**..........[1] JoeyHaynes(5) 4 81
(K R Burke) *chsd ldr: hrd rdn 2f out: kpt on same pce* **9/2**
-401 **6** *nk* **The Great Gabrial**[45] 552 5-9-4 **82**..........(p) AdamKirby 6 83
(Alan McCabe) *hld up in rr: hdwy 2f out: one pce fnl f* **10/1**
1511 **7** 1 **Tee It Up Tommo (IRE)**[9] 995 5-9-2 **80** 6ex.......... RobertWinston 1 78
(Michael Wigham) *prom: 5th and btn whn n.m.r ins fnl f* **3/1**[2]
1m 37.9s (-1.90) **Going Correction** 0.0s/f (Stan) **7** Ran SP% **121.4**
Speed ratings (Par 105): **109,108,107,107,106 106,105**
CSF £13.87 TOTE £5.90: £2.50, £2.10; EX 15.30 Trifecta £109.40.
**Owner** B Kitcherside & Big Cat Partnership **Bred** Butlersgrove Stud **Trained** Ashtead, Surrey
**FOCUS**
An open-looking handicap, run at a stop-start pace. The form has a pretty straightforward feel.
T/Plt: £340.80 to a £1 stake. Pool of £68039.85 - 145.70 winning tickets. T/Qpdt: £36.40 to a £1 stake. Pool of £8426.72 - 171.30 winning tickets. LM

# 1065 LINGFIELD (L-H)
Wednesday, March 26
**OFFICIAL GOING: Standard**
Wind: light, half against Weather: dry, rain for races 6 and 7

## 1104 BOOKMAKERS.CO.UK (S) STKS 6f 1y(P)
**2:00** (2:00) (Class 6) 3-Y-O+ **£2,385** (£704; £352) **Stalls** Low

Form RPR
-204 **1** **Drawnfromthepast (IRE)**[35] 662 9-9-9 67..........(p) FergusSweeney 3 63
(Luke Dace) *chsd ldng trio: clsd over 2f out: drvn and chsd ldr ins fnl f: styd on u.p to ld cl home* **9/2**[2]
1-40 **2** *hd* **Hamoody (USA)**[68] 208 10-10-0 77.......... TonyHamilton 2 67
(David Nicholls) *taken down early: chsd ldr: pushed along and hdwy to ld over 1f out: clr ins fnl f: pressed and drvn fnl 50yds: hdd cl home* **10/11**[1]
3053 **3** 3/4 **Belle Bayardo (IRE)**[7] 1010 6-9-9 54.......... LukeMorris 7 60+
(Ronald Harris) *stdd after s: hld up off the pce in last trio: rdn over 3f out: clsd and swtchd lft over 1f out: styd on u.p and pressed ldr wl ins fnl f: kpt on* **9/2**[2]
0050 **4** 3 1/2 **Waterloo Dock**[9] 996 9-9-9 47..........(v) MartinDwyer 6 50
(Mick Quinn) *sn rdn along: chsd ldrs and reminders after 1f: styd on same pce fr over 1f out* **33/1**
505- **5** 2 1/4 **Alhaarth Beauty (IRE)**[134] 7845 4-9-4 64..........(be[1]) PaddyAspell 1 38
(Phil McEntee) *sn led: hdd and racd awkwardly u.p over 1f out: nt run on and lost 2nd ins fnl f: wknd* **8/1**[3]
00-6 **6** 1 3/4 **Brean Splash Susie**[15] 919 3-8-2 42 ow2.......... RyanWhile(5) 5 31
(Bill Turner) *sn outpcd in rr: rdn and no hdwy 3f out: n.d* **100/1**
04-5 **7** 1/2 **Charleys Angel**[56] 374 3-8-2 43.......... JemmaMarshall(3) 4 27
(Pat Phelan) *sn outpcd in last pair: n.d* **16/1**
1m 11.96s (0.06) **Going Correction** +0.075s/f (Slow)
**WFA** 3 from 4yo+ 13lb **7** Ran SP% **109.7**
Speed ratings (Par 101): **102,101,100,96,93 90,90**
CSF £8.22 TOTE £4.90: £1.90, £1.20; EX 10.10 Trifecta £21.40.The winner was bought in for 5,200gns. Belle Bayardo was claimed by A. W. Carroll for £6000. Hamoody was claimed by J Tuite for £6000.
**Owner** Mark Benton **Bred** D And Mrs D Veitch **Trained** Five Oaks, W Sussex
**FOCUS**
A weak seller in which they went a true pace. The winner is rated below his best.

## 1105 DOWNLOAD THE LADBROKES APP H'CAP 1m 1y(P)
**2:30** (2:32) (Class 6) (0-55,55) 4-Y-O+ **£2,726** (£805; £402) **Stalls** High

Form RPR
0-0 **1** **Until Midnight (IRE)**[29] 740 4-9-4 **52**.......... MartinDwyer 9 58
(Eugene Stanford) *chsd ldrs: rdn to chal over 1f out: drvn to ld ins fnl f: hld on wl towards fin* **25/1**
0456 **2** *shd* **Indian Violet (IRE)**[7] 1016 8-9-2 **50**..........(p) JimCrowley 8 56
(Zoe Davison) *hld up in tch in midfield: rdn and hdwy over 1f out: drvn and str chal fnl 100yds: kpt on but hld towards fin* **16/1**
0232 **3** 1 1/2 **Pour La Victoire (IRE)**[21] 851 4-9-5 **53**..........(p) LukeMorris 2 55
(Tony Carroll) *wl in tch in midfield: rdn and effrt over 2f out: pressed ldrs ins fnl f: kpt on same pce fnl 100yds: wnt 3rd towards fin* **7/2**[2]
000- **4** *nk* **Bajan Story**[168] 7124 5-9-2 **50**.......... LiamKeniry 6 52
(Michael Blanshard) *w ldr tl led wl over 1f out: sn drvn: hdd ins fnl f: no ex fnl 100yds* **12/1**
0040 **5** *hd* **Nifty Kier**[21] 846 5-9-5 **53**.......... GeorgeBaker 10 54
(Martin Bosley) *stdd s: hld up in tch towards rr: rdn and hdwy ent fnl f: kpt on wl: nt rch ldrs* **8/1**
4205 **6** *nk* **Greek Islands (IRE)**[13] 939 6-9-7 **55**.......... ChrisCatlin 4 55
(Edward Creighton) *hld up in tch in midfield: shuffled bk towards rr jst over 2f out: rdn and effrt over 1f out: styd on wl u.p ins fnl f: nvr trbld ldrs* **14/1**
20-4 **7** 1 **Red Invader (IRE)**[12] 963 4-8-13 **54**.......... JackBudge(7) 7 52+
(Charles Hills) *dwlt: hld up in tch in last quartet: hdwy on outer into midfield 1/2-way: wd bnd 2f out: kpt on fnl f: no threat to ldrs* **11/4**[1]
5-64 **8** 3/4 **Ad Vitam (IRE)**[15] 913 6-9-0 **55**..........(tp) DavidParkes(7) 1 51
(David C Griffiths) *led and set stdy gallop tl hdd wl over 1f out: sn rdn and unable qck: wknd ins fnl f* **20/1**
0-46 **9** 1/2 **Legal Legacy**[23] 822 8-9-3 **51**..........(v) AdamKirby 3 46
(Lee Carter) *hld up in tch in midfield: rdn and unable qck over 1f out: kpt on but n.d fnl f* **5/1**[3]
3-62 **10** 1 1/4 **Alfresco**[21] 846 10-9-6 **54**..........(v) RobertHavlin 5 46
(Martin Bosley) *plld hrd: chsd ldrs: drvn and btn ent fnl f: wknd fnl 150yds* **8/1**
63-0 **11** 1/2 **Holli Deya**[83] 17 4-8-12 **46**.......... AdamBeschizza 11 37
(Andi Brown) *in tch in last quartet: rdn and no hdwy 2f out: nvr trbld ldrs* **33/1**
006- **12** 44 **Mastered (IRE)**[229] 5217 4-8-12 **46** oh1.......... FergusSweeney 12
(John Best) *v.s.a: in tch in rr tl lost tch jst over 2f out: t.o fnl f* **100/1**
1m 39.22s (1.02) **Going Correction** +0.075s/f (Slow) **12** Ran SP% **120.6**
Speed ratings (Par 101): **97,96,95,95,94 94,93,92,92,91 90,46**
CSF £372.17 CT £1783.16 TOTE £26.90: £7.20, £3.20, £2.10; EX 297.20 Trifecta £897.90.
**Owner** newmarketracingclub.co.uk **Bred** Rathbarry Stud **Trained** Newmarket, Suffolk
**FOCUS**
A modest sort of race, there was little in the way of pace and this looks to be unreliable form. The winner is rated back to his Irish figures.

## 1106 32RED.COM MEDIAN AUCTION MAIDEN STKS 5f 6y(P)
**3:00** (3:01) (Class 6) 3-Y-O **£2,726** (£805; £402) **Stalls** High

Form RPR
**1** **Jaywalker (IRE)** 3-9-2 0.......... WilliamTwiston-Davies(3) 4 79+
(Mick Channon) *in tch: hdwy to trck ldr after 1f: rdn to ld over 1f out: qcknd wl clr fnl f: readily* **Evs**[1]
02-2 **2** 4 1/2 **Mimi Luke (USA)**[27] 756 3-9-0 68.......... RobertWinston 5 55
(Alan Bailey) *led: rdn ent fnl 2f: drvn to and hdd over 1f out: wl btn ins fnl f but kpt on for clr 2nd* **Evs**[1]
-435 **3** 3 3/4 **Rosie Prospects**[39] 622 3-8-7 56..........(p) RhiainIngram(7) 3 42
(Roger Ingram) *hld up in tch in 4th: rdn and effrt over 1f out: outpcd and btn 1f out: no ch but plugged on to snatch 3rd last strides* **16/1**[2]
0055 **4** *hd* **Jazz Bay**[20] 855 3-9-0 36.......... RyanWhile(5) 2 46
(John Bridger) *t.k.h: chsd ldr for 1f: chsd ldng pair after: rdn and btn over 1f out: wknd fnl f: lost 3rd last strides* **66/1**[3]
66 **5** 7 **Virtual Symphony**[7] 1018 3-9-0 0.......... FergusSweeney 1 16
(John Best) *stdd s: t.k.h: hld up in tch in rr: rdn wl over 1f out: sn wknd* **66/1**[3]
59.53s (0.73) **Going Correction** +0.075s/f (Slow) **5** Ran SP% **108.9**
Speed ratings (Par 96): **97,89,83,83,72**
CSF £2.12 TOTE £2.70: £1.30, £1.10; EX 2.30 Trifecta £4.40.
**Owner** Insignia Racing (Crest) **Bred** Kilfrush Stud **Trained** West Ilsley, Berks
**FOCUS**
An uncompetitive modest maiden, which was effectively a match. It will take a while until the true worth of this form becomes clear.

## 1107 32RED MAIDEN STKS 7f 1y(P)
**3:30** (3:30) (Class 5) 3-Y-O **£3,234** (£962; £481; £240) **Stalls** Low

Form RPR
33- **1** **Passing By**[98] 8332 3-9-0 0.......... SeanLevey 6 75
(Richard Hannon) *mde all: rdn over 1f out: pressed ins fnl f: kpt on and a holding runner-up: pushed out* **11/4**[2]
324- **2** 3/4 **Munfallet (IRE)**[239] 4858 3-9-5 83.......... AdamKirby 8 78
(David Brown) *t.k.h: hld up in tch in midfield: rdn and effrt to chse wnr wl over 1f out: chal but edging lft ins fnl f: fnd little and a hld* **4/6**[1]
4 **3** 3 1/2 **Pearl Princess (FR)**[14] 930 3-9-0 0.......... JimCrowley 7 64
(Olly Stevens) *t.k.h: chsd ldrs: hdwy to go 2nd 4f out: rdn and outpcd in 3rd over 1f out: wl btn but plugged on for clr 3rd ins fnl f* **5/1**[3]
00 **4** 5 **Spin For A Harp (IRE)**[29] 741 3-9-5 0.......... FergusSweeney 2 55
(David Dennis) *chsd ldrs: outpcd ent fnl 2f: modest 4th and plugged on same pce fnl f* **100/1**
0- **5** *nk* **Percys Princess**[250] 4491 3-9-0 0.......... SteveDrowne 4 49
(Pat Murphy) *hld up off the pce in last trio: rdn over 1f out: no ch but plugged on ins fnl f* **50/1**
00 **6** *nse* **Roman Riches**[12] 954 3-9-5 0.......... GeorgeBaker 5 54+
(Gary Moore) *hld up off the pce in last trio: pushed along over 1f out: plugged on but nvr trbld ldrs* **33/1**
-606 **7** 3 1/4 **Sakhee'Ssquirrel**[28] 745 3-9-0 55..........(b) JohnFahy 1 40
(Sean Curran) *t.k.h: chsd ldr tl 4f out: rdn and struggling 2f out: 4th and btn over 1f out: fdd ins fnl f* **33/1**
0 **8** 1 **Adam Forever**[7] 1008 3-9-5 0.......... RichardKingscote 9 43+
(Michael Wigham) *stdd and dropped in bhd after s: t.k.h: hld up off the pce in last trio: rdn over 1f out: no hdwy n.d* **33/1**
1m 25.43s (0.63) **Going Correction** +0.075s/f (Slow) **8** Ran SP% **115.1**
Speed ratings (Par 98): **99,98,94,88,88 88,84,83**
CSF £4.90 TOTE £3.20: £1.30, £1.10, £1.10; EX 6.10 Trifecta £13.10.
**Owner** Saeed Manana **Bred** C J Mills **Trained** East Everleigh, Wilts
■ Tashtu was withdrawn. Price at time of withdrawal 100/1. Rule 4 does not apply.
**FOCUS**
Three horses dominated both the market and the race itself in this fair maiden. Improved form from the winner.

## 1108 CORAL APP DOWNLOAD FROM THE APP STORE H'CAP 1m 4f (P)
**4:00** (4:00) (Class 5) (0-75,75) 4-Y-O+ **£3,234** (£962; £481; £240) **Stalls** Low

Form RPR
2265 **1** **Lady Lunchalot (USA)**[7] 1022 4-9-3 **73**.......... LiamJones 3 80
(Laura Mongan) *hld up in tch: swtchd rt and hdwy on outer over 2f out: led and edgd lft ent fnl f: r.o wl: rdn out* **7/1**[3]
0413 **2** 2 **Menelik (IRE)**[6] 1027 5-8-12 **66**..........(b[1]) WilliamCarson 1 71
(Lee Carter) *hld up in tch in midfield: nt clr run and shuffled bk over 2f out: rdn and hdwy to chse wnr 1f out: keeping on same pce and hld whn swtchd rt wl ins fnl f* **12/1**
5114 **3** 3/4 **Munsarim (IRE)**[4] 1065 7-9-6 **74**..........(v[1]) AmirQuinn 5 77
(Lee Carter) *stdd and dropped in bhd after s: swtchd rt and effrt ent fnl f: r.o wl u.p fnl 150yds: nt rch ldrs* **8/1**

46-6 **4** 1 3/4 **The Holyman (IRE)**72 158 6-9-3 **71**.......................... FergusSweeney 8 71
(Jo Crowley) *t.k.h: chsd ldng pair tl 5f out: styd wl in tch: effrt and pressing ldrs whn nt clr run and hmpd over 1f out: one pce fnl f* **10/1**

454- **5** 2 1/4 **Angus Glens**163 7257 4-9-5 **75**.......................... JimCrowley 4 71
(David Dennis) *led: drvn wl over 1f out: hdd ent fnl f: sn btn and wknd ins fnl f* **7/4**1

1622 **6** nk **My Lord**6 1027 6-8-13 **67**.......................... SteveDrowne 6 63
(Luke Dace) *dwlt: hdwy to join ldr after 1f: rdn and ev ch 2f out tl no ex 1f out: sn wknd* **8/1**

2452 **7** 5 **Doldrums (USA)**8 1003 4-9-4 **74**.......................... AdamKirby 2 62
(Mark Johnston) *in tch: chsd ldng pair 5f out tl lost pl u.p over 2f out: bhd 1f out: wknd* **3/1**2

2m 36.35s (3.35) **Going Correction** +0.075s/f (Slow)
**WFA** 4 from 5yo+ 2lb **7** Ran SP% **112.9**
Speed ratings (Par 103): **91,89,89,88,86 86,82**
CSF £80.14 CT £681.53 TOTE £8.70: £4.60, £6.30; EX 78.50 Trifecta £885.30.
**Owner** Charlie's Starrs **Bred** Fred W Hertrich III **Trained** Epsom, Surrey

**FOCUS**
A fair race, but there seemed to be a distinct lack of pace and it turned into a bit of a sprint up the home straight. The winner is rated to her mark.

## 1109 COMPARE BOOKMAKERS AT BOOKMAKERS.CO.UK H'CAP 5f 6y(P)
**4:30** (4:30) (Class 5) (0-75,74) 4-Y-0+ **£3,234** (£962; £481; £240) **Stalls** High

Form RPR

1236 **1** **Roy's Legacy**7 1019 5-9-1 **71**.......................... MichaelJMurphy(3) 3 78
(Shaun Harris) *mde all: rdn and fnd ex over 1f out: pressed fnl 100yds: a jst lasting home: drvn out* **2/1**1

5514 **2** hd **Desert Strike**7 1019 8-9-7 **74**..........................(p) HayleyTurner 2 80
(Conor Dore) *taken down early: t.k.h: hld up in tch in last pair: rdn and effrt on inner to chse wnr 1f out: kpt on fnl 100yds and grad clsd on wnr: nvr quite getting up* **7/2**2

-423 **3** 2 3/4 **Ask The Guru**7 1019 4-9-5 **72**..........................(v) KierenFox 5 68
(Michael Attwater) *chsd ldrs on outer: rdn and unable qck over 1f out: drvn and styd on same pce ins fnl f* **2/1**1

3424 **4** 3/4 **Pharoh Jake**14 921 6-8-5 **63**.......................... RyanWhile(5) 4 57
(John Bridger) *pressed wnr tl drvn and unable qck over 1f out: wknd ins fnl f* **7/1**3

-050 **5** 3 **Billy Red**50 470 10-9-1 **68**..........................(b) FergusSweeney 1 51
(J R Jenkins) *dwlt: in tch in rr: rdn and no hdwy over 1f out: wknd ins fnl f* **12/1**

58.86s (0.06) **Going Correction** +0.075s/f (Slow) **5** Ran SP% **109.1**
Speed ratings (Par 103): **102,101,97,96,91**
CSF £9.08 TOTE £2.10: £1.10, £3.10; EX 9.20 Trifecta £14.20.
**Owner** P Birley,S Mohammed,S Rowley,K Blackwell **Bred** A Christou **Trained** Carburton, Notts

**FOCUS**
A small field, but most of these had shown form this winter and the pace was sound. The runner-up is the best guide.

## 1110 LADBROKES H'CAP 7f 1y(P)
**5:00** (5:01) (Class 6) (0-60,60) 4-Y-0+ **£2,726** (£805; £402) **Stalls** Low

Form RPR

4060 **1** **Bold Ring**6 1023 8-8-10 **56**.......................... JenniferFerguson(7) 4 63
(Edward Creighton) *in tch in midfield: rdn and hdwy over 1f out: led fnl 100yds: r.o wl: rdn out* **20/1**

5402 **2** nk **Teen Ager (FR)**9 993 10-9-6 **59**..........................(p) LukeMorris 1 65
(Paul Burgoyne) *chsd ldrs: effrt u.p over 1f out: ev ch ins fnl f: r.o but hld towards fin* **9/2**3

2043 **3** 1/2 **West Leake (IRE)**7 1017 8-9-4 **57**.......................... LiamKeniry 2 62
(Paul Burgoyne) *t.k.h: chsd ldrs: wnt 2nd over 2f out: drvn and ev ch fnl f: styd on same pce cl home* **16/1**

5501 **4** 3/4 **Catalinas Diamond (IRE)**25 798 6-9-3 **56**..........................(t) SteveDrowne 10 59+
(Pat Murphy) *stdd s: hld up in tch towards rr: rdn and gd hdwy towards inner 1f out: chsd ldrs and no imp wl ins fnl f* **10/1**

1300 **5** hd **Chevise (IRE)**7 1017 6-9-2 **60**..........................(b) RyanTate(5) 7 62
(Steve Woodman) *broke fast: led and crossed to rail: rdn over 1f out: drvn and hdd fnl 100yds: outpcd towards fin* **12/1**

-305 **6** hd **Perfect Pastime**21 846 6-9-4 **57**..........................(b) StephenCraine 9 60+
(Jim Boyle) *t.k.h: hld up in tch towards rr: nt clr run ent fnl 2f: rdn and hdwy 1f out: kpt on fnl f: nt rch ldrs* **5/1**

5330 **7** 1/2 **Welsh Inlet (IRE)**9 987 6-9-0 **53**.......................... WilliamCarson 8 53
(John Bridger) *in tch in midfiel: rdn and effrt over 1f out: keeping on whn nt clr run towards fin* **16/1**

-004 **8** nk **Little Red Nell (IRE)**20 855 5-8-4 **46** oh1......(p) MichaelJMurphy(3) 3 46
(Martin Bosley) *in tch in midfield: rdn and effrt on inner over 1f out: no imp ins fnl f* **66/1**

-404 **9** 1 1/4 **Black Truffle (FR)**21 846 4-8-9 **55**..........................(e) CharlotteJenner(7) 6 51
(Mark Usher) *t.k.h: hld up in tch towards rr: rdn and effrt over 1f out: keeping on whn nt clr run and hmpd ins fnl f: nvr trbld ldrs* **4/1**2

0236 **10** hd **Hinton Admiral**15 918 10-8-13 **52**..........................1 RobertWinston 12 48
(Pat Eddery) *stdd s: hld up in tch in rr: hdwy and wd whn hmpd bnd wl over 1f out: kpt on but no threat to ldrs after* **12/1**

000- **11** 3/4 **Baytown Bertie**169 7093 5-8-7 **46** oh1.......................... RobertHavlin 14 40
(Lydia Richards) *stdd and dropped in bhd after s: rdn and effrt ent fnl f: styd on same pce ins fnl f* **100/1**

606- **12** 3 1/4 **Zammy**308 2578 5-8-7 **46** oh1.......................... RichardKingscote 11 31
(Michael Wigham) *t.k.h: hld up in tch in midfield: shuffled bk and towards rr whn n.m.r over 1f out: no hdwy* **14/1**

000- **13** 1 1/4 **Fishlake Rebel**264 4008 4-8-7 **46** oh1..........................(p) HayleyTurner 5 27
(David C Griffiths) *t.k.h: chsd ldr tl over 2f out: shifted rt and lost pl bnd 2f out: bhd fnl f* **25/1**

1m 25.26s (0.46) **Going Correction** +0.075s/f (Slow) **13** Ran SP% **125.2**
Speed ratings (Par 101): **100,99,99,98,98 97,97,96,95,95 94,90,89**
CSF £110.74 CT £349.62 TOTE £23.70: £6.00, £1.30, £1.70; EX 107.40 Trifecta £586.40.
**Owner** Miss Charlotte Harper **Bred** J A Pickering & T Pears **Trained** Wormshill, Kent

■ Stewards' Enquiry : William Carson one-day ban: careless riding (9 Apr)
Stephen Craine one-day ban: careless riding (9 Apr)

**FOCUS**
No more than a modest handicap, but most of these held a chance coming into the race and it was still wide open at the top of the straight. Not form to dwell on.
T/Plt: £51.20 to a £1 stake. Pool of £57783.47 - 822.30 winning tickets. T/Qpdt: £15.80 to a £1 stake. Pool of £4110.48 - 191.90 winning tickets. SP

# 1087 SOUTHWELL (L-H)
## Wednesday, March 26

**OFFICIAL GOING: Standard**
Wind: Moderate across Weather: Cloudy

## 1111 CORAL.CO.UK BEST ODDS GUARANTEED CLAIMING STKS 1m 4f (F)
**2:20** (2:20) (Class 6) 4-Y-0+ **£2,716** (£808; £404; £202) **Stalls** Low

Form RPR

2-22 **1** **Honoured (IRE)**27 763 7-9-7 84..........................(t) TomQueally 4 84+
(Michael Appleby) *cl up: led over 8f out: pushed clr wl over 2f out: unchal* **1/12**1

360/ **2** 11 **Bivouac (UAE)**24 285 10-8-13 70.......................... BenCurtis 3 56
(Alan Swinbank) *trckd ldrs: hdwy on outer over 4f out: sn chsng wnr: rdn along wl over 2f out and sn no imp* **8/1**2

6/-6 **3** 1 3/4 **Maid Of Silk (IRE)**9 997 8-8-3 51..........................(bt1) JoeDoyle(7) 1 50
(Neil Mulholland) *trckd ldrs on inner: effrt over 4f out: rdn along over 3f out: drvn along on inner rail over 2f out: sn one pce* **33/1**3

00 **4** 17 **Flamenco Flyer**13 941 5-8-13 0.......................... DavidProbert 2 26
(Edward Bevan) *slt ld tl hdd over 8f out: cl up tl rdn along over 4f out: sn wknd* **100/1**

2m 44.19s (3.19) **Going Correction** -0.025s/f (Stan) **4** Ran SP% **107.4**
Speed ratings (Par 101): **88,80,79,68**
CSF £1.29 TOTE £1.10; EX 1.40 Trifecta £2.10.
**Owner** Dallas Racing **Bred** Kilfrush Stud **Trained** Danethorpe, Notts

**FOCUS**
This was little more than an exercise canter for long odds-on favourite.

## 1112 DOWNLOAD THE LADBROKES APP MAIDEN STKS 7f (F)
**2:50** (2:50) (Class 5) 3-Y-0+ **£3,363** (£1,001; £500; £250) **Stalls** Low

Form RPR

**1** **Cloverdale** 4-9-9 0.......................... JoeFanning 2 86+
(Mark Johnston) *cl up: led 3f out: rdn clr wl over 1f out: styd on* **3/1**2

0- **2** 5 **Molly Ahoy**166 7162 3-8-8 0.......................... BenCurtis 4 64
(Alan McCabe) *dwlt and towards rr: hdwy on outer over 3f out: rdn to chse wnr 2f out: drvn and edgd lft over 1f out: no imp fnl f* **50/1**

6-32 **3** 3 1/2 **On Demand**14 930 3-8-8 71.......................... DavidProbert 1 55
(Andrew Balding) *led: pushed along and hdd 3f out: sn rdn and btn over 2f out* **1/2**1

00- **4** 8 **Soul Artist (IRE)**207 5983 3-8-8 0.......................... DuranFentiman 6 33
(Tim Easterby) *trckd ldrs: hdwy 1/2-way: rdn along wl over 2f out: sn wknd* **14/1**

0- **5** 10 **Cards**376 1019 4-9-9 0.......................... PaulMulrennan 5 11
(Kevin Ryan) *dwlt and swtchd lft s: trckd ldrs on inner: rdn along 1/2-way: sn wknd* **7/1**3

000- **6** 8 **Samoan (IRE)**159 7346 5-9-11 52..........................(b) SladeO'Hara(3) 3
(Alan Berry) *awkward s: sn outpcd and a bhd* **80/1**

1m 29.81s (-0.49) **Going Correction** -0.025s/f (Stan)
**WFA** 3 from 4yo+ 15lb **6** Ran SP% **114.0**
Speed ratings (Par 103): **101,95,91,82,70 61**
CSF £92.40 TOTE £3.30: £1.70, £18.60; EX 59.90 Trifecta £117.00.
**Owner** Sheikh Hamdan bin Mohammed Al Maktoum **Bred** Darley **Trained** Middleham Moor, N Yorks

**FOCUS**
A fair maiden for the track but the favourite disappointed. Hard form to pin down.

## 1113 DOWNLOAD THE LADBROKES APP H'CAP 1m (F)
**3:20** (3:21) (Class 4) (0-80,80) 4-Y-0+ **£5,822** (£1,732; £865; £432) **Stalls** Low

Form RPR

-423 **1** **Sound Advice**7 1014 5-9-6 **79**.......................... TomEaves 4 94+
(Keith Dalgleish) *mde most: rdn clr over 2f out: readily* **6/4**1

-601 **2** 6 **My Son Max**15 907 6-9-7 **80**..........................(v) DaleSwift 5 80
(Michael Blake) *dwlt: sn in tch on outer: hdwy 3f out: rdn 2f out: styd on to chse wnr appr fnl f: sn no imp* **12/1**

50-0 **3** 2 1/4 **Skytrain**32 715 4-9-7 **80**.......................... JoeFanning 7 75
(Mark Johnston) *prom: cl up 1/2-way: rdn along over 2f out: drvn wl over 1f out and sn one pce* **9/2**2

1632 **4** nk **Silly Billy (IRE)**14 928 6-8-5 **69**..........................(p) JacobButterfield(5) 6 63
(John Balding) *trckd ldrs: hdwy 3f out: rdn over 2f out: drvn wl over 1f out: sn one pce* **8/1**3

330- **5** shd **Caledonia Prince**308 2580 6-9-2 **75**..........................(tp) BenCurtis 8 69
(Jo Hughes) *in tch on outer: hdwy over 3f out: rdn along over 2f out: sn one pce* **12/1**

02-0 **6** 13 **Hydrant**44 560 8-8-12 **76**.......................... ConnorBeasley(5) 3 40
(Richard Guest) *cl up: rdn along 1/2-way: sn wknd* **33/1**

0-20 **7** 2 1/4 **Piceno (IRE)**78 75 6-8-9 **75**..........................(p) MatthewHopkins(7) 1 34
(Scott Dixon) *s.i.s: hdwy on inner to chse ldrs after 3f: rdn along over 3f out and sn wknd* **25/1**

1m 41.25s (-2.45) **Going Correction** -0.025s/f (Stan) **7** Ran SP% **91.5**
Speed ratings (Par 105): **111,105,102,102,102 89,87**
CSF £12.12 CT £27.38 TOTE £1.60: £1.40, £3.90; EX 11.80 Trifecta £29.60.
**Owner** G L S Partnership **Bred** G L S Partnership **Trained** Carluke, S Lanarks

■ Exclusive Waters was withdrawn. Price at time of withdrawal 7/2. Rule 4 applies to all bets - deduct 20p in the pound.

**FOCUS**
The enforced withdrawal of Exclusive Waters meant this wasn't as strong as previously advertised. However, it has to rate a personal best from the winner.

## 1114 LADBROKES H'CAP 7f (F)
**3:50** (3:50) (Class 2) (0-105,99) 4-Y-0+ **£13,584** (£4,042; £2,020; £1,010) **Stalls** Low

Form RPR

6612 **1** **Frontier Fighter**27 764 6-9-6 **98**.......................... DanielTudhope 5 108
(David O'Meara) *trckd ldr: smooth hdwy 1/2-way: led over 2f out: rdn over 1f out: kpt on wl ins fnl f* **7/4**1

1116 **2** 1 1/2 **Noble Citizen (USA)**18 887 9-8-11 **96**..........................(be) GeorgeBuckell(7) 3 102
(David Simcock) *dwlt and in rr: hdwy 1/2-way: rdn over 2f out: drvn to chse wnr over 1f out: kpt on fnl f* **3/1**3

-332 **3** 1/2 **Greyfriarschorista**22 832 7-8-7 **85**.......................... JimmyQuinn 6 90
(Tom Keddy) *trckd ldrs: hdwy on outer 3f out: rdn over 2f out: drvn and kpt on same pce appr fnl f* **10/1**

013- **4** 12 **Dubai Hills**88 8428 8-9-7 **99**.......................... TomEaves 4 71
(David O'Meara) *trckd ldrs: effrt 3f out: sn rdn and wknd 2f out* **9/4**2

-000 **5** *7* **Dr Red Eye**[5] 1042 6-8-2 **87**................................(v[1]) MatthewHopkins(7) 2 40
(Scott Dixon) *led and clr: rdn along 3f out: hdd over 2f out and sn wknd* **14/1**

60-5 **6** *1 1/4* **Regal Parade**[18] 890 10-8-13 **94**..................................(t) RobertTart(3) 1 44
(Milton Bradley) *chsd ldrs: rdn along over 3f out: sn wknd* **16/1**

1m 27.59s (-2.71) **Going Correction** -0.025s/f (Stan) **6** Ran SP% **113.8**
Speed ratings (Par 109): **114,112,111,98,90 88**
CSF £7.55 TOTE £2.10: £2.20, £2.00; EX 8.10 Trifecta £22.70.

**Owner** Walker Nicholson **Bred** Darley **Trained** Nawton, N Yorks

**FOCUS**
A hotly contested feature, despite the small field, run at a good pace. The winner has a finr profile here.

## 1115 COMPARE BOOKMAKERS AT BOOKMAKERS.CO.UK H'CAP 6f (F)
**4:20** (4:20) (Class 5) (0-70,69) 4-Y-0+ **£3,363** (£1,001; £500; £250) **Stalls** Low

Form RPR

1506 **1** **Only Ten Per Cent (IRE)**[22] 834 6-9-3 **65**..............(v) FrederikTylicki 6 82
(J R Jenkins) *trckd ldrs: smooth hdwy 1/2-way: led over 2f out: clr appr fnl f: readily* **9/4**[1]

5362 **2** *6* **Indian Affair**[13] 938 4-8-10 **65**.............................. LeroyLynch(7) 2 64
(Milton Bradley) *chsd ldrs: hdwy 2f out: styd on to chse wnr over 1f out: sn edgd lft: kpt on: no ch w wnr* **8/1**

0011 **3** *1* **Masai Moon**[14] 934 10-9-0 **69**..............................(b) PatMillman(7) 5 65
(Rod Millman) *dwlt and sn outpcd in rr: rdn and hdwy 2f out: styd on fnl f: nrst fin* **4/1**[3]

00-0 **4** *1/2* **Hab Reeh**[14] 934 6-8-3 **58**.............................. GemmaTutty(7) 7 53
(Ruth Carr) *towards rr: rdn and hdwy over 2f out: edgd lft and no imp appr fnl f* **50/1**

01-1 **5** *2* **Pick A Little**[82] 34 6-9-2 **67**.............................. RobertTart(3) 3 56
(Michael Blake) *towards rr: rdn along 1/2-way: n.d* **3/1**[2]

-653 **6** *3/4* **Monnoyer**[27] 766 5-8-4 **59**..............................(b) MatthewHopkins(7) 1 45
(Scott Dixon) *cl up on inner: led after 2f: rdn 3f out: hdd and drvn over 2f out: sn wknd* **12/1**

4301 **7** *1/2* **Greenhead High**[13] 938 6-9-1 **63**..............................(v) AdrianNicholls 4 48
(David Nicholls) *led 2f: cl up: rdn wl over 2f out: drvn and wknd wl over 1f out* **9/2**

1m 15.47s (-1.03) **Going Correction** -0.025s/f (Stan) **7** Ran SP% **114.7**
Speed ratings (Par 103): **105,97,95,95,92 91,90**
CSF £21.17 TOTE £3.60: £1.40, £3.00; EX 25.90 Trifecta £117.70.

**Owner** B Silkman **Bred** Sandro Garavelli **Trained** Royston, Herts

**FOCUS**
This has looked a competitive sprint handicap on paper, but it was turned into a procession. The winner governs the standard.

## 1116 32RED IMMORTAL ROMANCE SLOT H'CAP 1m (F)
**4:50** (4:50) (Class 5) (0-75,75) 3-Y-0 **£3,363** (£1,001; £500; £250) **Stalls** Low

Form RPR

551- **1** **Framed Masterpiece**[127] 7955 3-9-7 **75**..................(p) DanielTudhope 4 80+
(Paul Fitzsimons) *cl up on outer: effrt 3f out: chal over 2f out: rdn to ld wl over 1f out: edgd lft ins fnl f: kpt on* **9/2**[3]

5114 **2** *2 1/2* **Frankthetank (IRE)**[11] 975 3-9-5 **73**..............................(p) TomEaves 3 71
(Keith Dalgleish) *led: jnd and rdn along over 2f out: hdd wl over 1f out and sn drvn: swtchd rt ins fnl f: no imp* **7/4**[2]

3101 **3** *12* **Day Star Lad**[8] 1007 3-8-4 **58**..............................(v) DuranFentiman 5 32
(Derek Shaw) *s.i.s and sn pushed along: t.k.h and in tch after 2f: hung rt and wd st: sn rdn and n.d* **11/10**[1]

1 **4** *10* **Nellie The Elegant**[46] 542 3-8-13 **67**.............................. DavidProbert 2 12
(Tim Vaughan) *cl up on inner: rdn along wl over 3f out: sn wknd* **14/1**

1m 43.36s (-0.34) **Going Correction** -0.025s/f (Stan) **4** Ran SP% **108.8**
Speed ratings (Par 98): **100,97,85,75**
CSF £12.65 TOTE £7.40; EX 14.10 Trifecta £21.90.

**Owner** Saxon Gate Bloodstock (Helene Moller) **Bred** Mrs Hugh Maitland-Jones **Trained** Upper Lambourn, Berks

**FOCUS**
A fair contest. The winner did this quite well from a fair yardstick.

## 1117 32RED THUNDERSTRUCK II SLOT AMATEUR RIDERS' H'CAP 1m 6f (F)
**5:20** (5:20) (Class 6) (0-65,65) 4-Y-0+ **£2,620** (£812; £406; £203) **Stalls** Low

Form RPR

40-3 **1** **Joyful Motive**[1] 1092 5-9-5 **47**.............................. MissLWilson(5) 8 55
(Michael Chapman) *prom on outer: cl up 4f out: led 3f out: sn rdn clr and edgd lft to inner rail: kpt on wl ins fnl f* **10/1**

/3-4 **2** *4* **Ballyheigue (IRE)**[68] 209 5-10-0 **58**..............................(p) MissHHeal(7) 4 61
(Liam Corcoran) *cl up: rdn along over 3f out: kpt on same pce fnl 2f* **33/1**

4232 **3** *2 1/4* **Honest Strike (USA)**[20] 860 7-10-11 **62**..............................(b) FreddieMitchell 6 62
(Daniel Mark Loughnane) *hld up in tch: hdwy over 4f out: chsd ldrs 3f out: swtchd rt to wd outside and rdn 2f out: kpt on one pce* **5/1**[3]

51-6 **4** *8* **Goodlukin Lucy**[71] 176 7-10-2 **53**.............................. MrSWalker 7 42
(Keith Dalgleish) *led: pushed along over 4f out: rdn and hdd 3f out: sn drvn and wknd* **11/4**[2]

0-32 **5** *1 1/2* **Bethan**[15] 912 5-10-7 **58**..............................(p) MrRBirkett 2 46
(Julia Feilden) *trckd ldrs on inner: pushed along over 4f out: rdn wl over 3f out: wknd over 2f out* **8/1**

5466 **6** *3* **Monzino (USA)**[22] 831 6-10-3 **57**..............................(b) MrChrisMartin(3) 3 41
(Michael Chapman) *in rr: rdn along 5f out: nvr a factor* **10/1**

-242 **7** *31* **Opus (IRE)**[22] 831 5-9-11 **55**.............................. MrSamDavis(7) 5
(Lucy Wadham) *trckd ldrs: effrt over 5f out: rdn along over 4f out and sn wknd* **6/4**[1]

3m 11.43s (3.13) **Going Correction** -0.025s/f (Stan) **7** Ran SP% **115.6**
Speed ratings (Par 101): **90,87,86,81,81 79,61**
CSF £243.00 CT £1837.45 TOTE £19.80: £7.50, £9.40; EX 589.60 Trifecta £768.10.

**Owner** Mrs M Chapman **Bred** Hesmonds Stud Ltd **Trained** Market Rasen, Lincs

**FOCUS**
A desperately weak finale with a number of the market principals failing to perform. The winner is rated back to his pre-race best.

T/Plt: £240.00 to a £1 stake. Pool of £58064.57 - 176.60 winning tickets. T/Qpdt: £39.80 to a £1 stake. Pool of £5277.21 - 98.10 winning tickets JR

# 1097 KEMPTON (A.W) (R-H)
Thursday, March 27

**OFFICIAL GOING: Standard**
Wind: Light, across Weather: Grey

## 1118 DINE IN THE PANORAMIC RESTAURANT MEDIAN AUCTION MAIDEN STKS 1m 3f (P)
**5:35** (5:35) (Class 6) 3-5-Y-0 **£1,940** (£577; £288; £144) **Stalls** Low

Form RPR

**1** **Votary (IRE)** 3-8-7 0.............................. RobertHavlin 2 77+
(John Gosden) *dwlt: trckd ldrs: gng wl 3f out: led over 2f out: hung bdly lft fr wl over 1f out and ended against nr side rail: kpt on* **5/1**[3]

00- **2** *1/2* **Norse Star (IRE)**[165] 7219 3-8-7 0.............................. LiamKeniry 6 76
(Sylvester Kirk) *trckd ldr to over 5f out: pushed along over 3f out: rallied 2f out: chsd wnr over 1f out: kpt on fnl f* **10/1**

**3** *1 1/4* **Full Moon Fever (IRE)** 3-8-2 0.............................. NickyMackay 4 69
(Ed Walker) *hld up: pushed along 4f out and rn green: rallied on outer over 2f out: hmpd by wnr over 1f out: keeping on but hld whn tightened up again ins fnl f* **8/1**

03- **4** *1* **Wannabe Your Man**[157] 7422 4-9-13 0.............................. ChrisCatlin 1 75
(Roger Varian) *led: shkn up over 2f out: sn hdd and nt qckn w hd high: kpt on same pce after* **7/4**[1]

**5** *hd* **Gallic Destiny (IRE)** 3-8-7 0.............................. HayleyTurner 3 72
(Andrew Balding) *dwlt: rn green in last pair: pushed along over 2f out: tried to cl on ldrs over 1f out: one pce* **3/1**[2]

064- **6** *24* **Martinas Delight (USA)**[98] 8343 4-9-8 67.............................. RobertWinston 7 26
(Alan Jarvis) *hld up: t.k.h and prog to press ldr over 5f out: lost pl over 2f out: hld whn short of room over 1f out: wknd rapidly: t.o* **15/2**

2m 22.45s (0.55) **Going Correction** -0.025s/f (Stan)
**WFA** 3 from 4yo 21lb **6** Ran SP% **110.0**
Speed ratings (Par 101): **97,96,95,95,94 77**
CSF £47.49 TOTE £5.20: £1.80, £4.90; EX 48.30 Trifecta £205.80.

**Owner** HRH Princess Haya Of Jordan **Bred** J Dorrian **Trained** Newmarket, Suffolk
■ Stewards' Enquiry : Robert Havlin three-day ban: careless riding (10-12 Apr)

**FOCUS**
An ordinary maiden in which a slow gallop to the home turn means the form isn't reliable. The winner ended up against the stands' rail in the straight.

## 1119 BETDAQ - THE SPORTS BETTING EXCHANGE MAIDEN STKS 1m 3f (P)
**6:05** (6:05) (Class 5) 3-Y-0+ **£2,587** (£770; £384; £192) **Stalls** Low

Form RPR

422- **1** **Liberty Red (GER)**[171] 7061 3-8-7 76.............................. ShaneKelly 2 70+
(Ed Dunlop) *trckd ldng pair: led wl over 2f out: sn clr: easily* **2/11**[1]

0/ **2** *3 1/4* **Pentameter**[876] 7233 5-10-0 0.............................. LiamKeniry 3 68
(John Butler) *hld up in 5th: prog to chse wnr over 2f out: shkn up and drew clr of rest but no imp* **8/1**[3]

0 **3** *5* **Moriond (USA)**[13] 951 3-8-7 0.............................. ChrisCatlin 5 57
(David Simcock) *hld up in last: outpcd whn prog over 2f out: pushed along and tk 3rd wl over 1f out: no imp after* **7/1**[2]

**4** *3 1/4* **Medburn Cutler**[26] 4-9-13 0.............................. FergusSweeney 1 55
(George Baker) *led: v wd bnd 3f out: sn hdd: steadily wknd over 1f out and ended against nr side rail* **16/1**

50 **5** *6* **Fleetwood Nix**[55] 403 4-9-1 0.............................. SophieRalston(7) 4 40
(Pat Phelan) *chsd ldr: pushed along 4f out: wd bnd 3f out: sn lost pl: wknd 2f out* **50/1**

00 **6** *17* **Laguna Belle**[50] 486 4-9-5 0.............................. JemmaMarshall(3) 6 13
(Pat Phelan) *in tch tl wknd over 2f out: t.o* **50/1**

2m 22.65s (0.75) **Going Correction** -0.025s/f (Stan)
**WFA** 3 from 4yo 21lb 4 from 5yo 1lb **6** Ran SP% **118.0**
Speed ratings (Par 103): **96,93,90,87,83 70**
CSF £3.04 TOTE £1.10: £1.02, £3.80; EX 5.30 Trifecta £6.00.

**Owner** The Hon R J Arculli **Bred** Gestut Hof Ittlingen **Trained** Newmarket, Suffolk

**FOCUS**
A most uncompetitive maiden in which the market leader won with plenty in hand. The gallop was an ordinary one and the winner raced towards the far rail in the straight.

## 1120 BETDAQ FREE BET £25 NO LOSE H'CAP 1m 3f (P)
**6:35** (6:36) (Class 5) (0-70,70) 4-Y-0+ **£2,587** (£770; £384; £192) **Stalls** Low

Form RPR

-520 **1** **King Olav (UAE)**[28] 758 9-9-6 **69**.............................. LiamKeniry 5 76
(Tony Carroll) *hld up in 4th: rdn 3f out and looked in trble: rallied to chse ldr over 1f out: edgd rt but drvn and styd on to ld last 100yds* **11/4**[3]

0-34 **2** *nk* **Chain Of Events**[21] 859 7-9-7 **70**.............................. GeorgeBaker 3 77
(Michael Wigham) *led: rdn over 2f out: kpt on u.p but hdd fnl 100yds: jst outpcd* **2/1**[1]

0400 **3** *2 1/2* **Lily Edge**[10] 989 5-8-7 **56**..............................(v[1]) KieranO'Neill 2 59
(John Bridger) *t.k.h: cl up: urged along 4f out: responded to chse ldr over 2f out to over 1f out: one pce fnl f* **33/1**

533 **4** *1 3/4* **Midnight Chorister**[27] 776 6-9-5 **68**..............................(t) HayleyTurner 6 68
(Alex Hales) *awkward s: hld up in last: prog jst over 2f out: sn rdn: carried rt and nt clr run jst over 1f out: nt qckn after* **9/4**[2]

1615 **5** *9* **Fearless Lad (IRE)**[29] 747 4-8-13 **63**..............................(t) SteveDrowne 4 48
(John Best) *chsd ldr to over 2f out: sn rdn and wknd* **4/1**

2m 20.23s (-1.67) **Going Correction** -0.025s/f (Stan)
**WFA** 4 from 5yo+ 1lb **5** Ran SP% **113.7**
Speed ratings (Par 103): **105,104,102,101,95**
CSF £9.01 TOTE £3.30: £2.10, £1.10; EX 10.80 Trifecta £89.60.

**Owner** Cover Point Racing **Bred** Darley **Trained** Cropthorne, Worcs

**FOCUS**
A modest handicap in which the gallop was on the steady side to the intersection. The winner came down the centre in the straight.

## 1121 FAMILY FUN AT KEMPTON ON 19.04.14 H'CAP 1m (P)
**7:05** (7:06) (Class 6) (0-65,71) 4-Y-0+ **£1,940** (£577; £288; £144) **Stalls** Low

Form RPR

0403 **1** **Hill Of Dreams (IRE)**[21] 852 5-9-5 **63**..............................(b) RobertWinston 4 73
(Dean Ivory) *trckd ldng pair: dashed into ld over 2f out and sent for home: wl in command after: rdn out* **11/4**[2]

4301 **2** *3* **Nubar Boy**[21] 852 7-9-2 **65**..............................(p) GeorgeDowning(5) 1 68
(Ian Williams) *fast away: led 1f: chsd ldr to 3f out: rdn to go 2nd again 2f out: no imp on wnr* **7/1**

1455 **3** *nk* **Blackthorn Stick (IRE)**13 958 5-9-3 **61** ........................ LiamKeniry 3 63
(John Butler) *hld up in 5th: smooth prog to dispute 2nd 2f out: shuffled along after and no imp: one reminder fnl f: nvr chal* **8/1**

0-00 **4** *2 3/4* **Byroness**21 853 4-8-13 **62** ........................1 RyanTate(5) 6 58
(Heather Main) *hld up in last and sn wl detached: latched on to field 3f out: sn outpcd and drvn: kpt on ins fnl f* **12/1**

3-01 **5** *nk* **Cravat**6 1040 5-9-8 **71** 6ex ........................ EoinWalsh(5) 5 66
(Ed de Giles) *hld up in 4th: impeded after 2f: rdn over 2f out: no prog and wl btn over 1f out* **15/8**1

3-51 **6** *4* **Dividend Dan (IRE)**16 916 4-8-12 **56** ........................ ShaneKelly 2 42
(Mike Murphy) *pushed up to ld after 1f: hdd over 2f out: sn btn* **9/2**3

1m 38.26s (-1.54) **Going Correction** -0.025s/f (Stan) 6 Ran SP% **110.9**
Speed ratings (Par 101): **106,103,102,99,99 95**
CSF £20.96 TOTE £3.70: £2.00, £1.90; EX 12.50 Trifecta £72.60.
**Owner** I Gethin & R Gethin **Bred** Miss Breda Wright **Trained** Radlett, Herts

**FOCUS**
A modest handicap in which an ordinary gallop increased passing the intersection. The winner raced centre-to-far side in the straight.

## 1122 BETDAQ £500 IN FREE BETS H'CAP (LONDON MILE SERIES QUALIFIER) (BOBIS RACE) 1m (P)
**7:35** (7:35) (Class 4) (0-85,85) 3-Y-O **£4,690** (£1,395; £697; £348) **Stalls** Low

Form RPR
11 **1** **Passing Star**21 854 3-9-5 **83** ........................ RobertWinston 1 90
(Charles Hills) *tk fierce hold: hld up bhd ldrs: prog to go 2nd 2f out: cajoled along to chal over 1f out: led 150yds: wanted to hang rt but a fnd enough* **11/10**1

536- **2** *nk* **Zampa Manos (USA)**176 6935 3-9-4 **85** ........................ OisinMurphy(3) 6 91
(Andrew Balding) *led after 100yds and set mod pce: kicked on over 2f out: drvn and hdd 150yds out: styd on wl but a jst hld* **16/1**

1- **3** *2 1/2* **Tree Of Grace (FR)**162 7302 3-9-5 **83** ........................ FrankieDettori 4 83
(Richard Hannon) *t.k.h: trckd ldr after 2f: nt qckn and lost pl 2f out: kpt on same pce after* **6/4**2

166- **4** *1/2* **Dovil's Duel (IRE)**165 7221 3-8-8 **72** ........................ HayleyTurner 2 71
(Rod Millman) *led 100yds: t.k.h after and cl up: effrt on inner 2f out: outpcd over 1f out* **66/1**

63-3 **5** *1* **Penny's Boy**19 892 3-8-7 **71** oh1 ........................(t) LukeMorris 5 67
(Sylvester Kirk) *hld up in last in modly run event: rdn and nt qckn whn pce lifted over 2f out: no imp after* **33/1**

1 **6** *2 3/4* **Tigers In Red (USA)**46 551 3-9-7 **85** ........................ AdamKirby 3 75
(David Simcock) *hld up in tch: quite wd bnd 4f out: rdn and wl outpcd fr 2f out* **11/2**3

30-3 **7** *1/2* **Mick's Yer Man**15 926 3-8-11 **80** ........................ RyanWhile(5) 7 69
(Bill Turner) *awkward after s: hld up: wd bnd 4f out to 3f out: sn outpcd: no ch after* **40/1**

1m 39.92s (0.12) **Going Correction** -0.025s/f (Stan) 7 Ran SP% **115.8**
Speed ratings (Par 100): **98,97,95,94,93 90,90**
CSF £20.28 TOTE £2.20: £1.30, £5.80; EX 20.50 Trifecta £54.60.
**Owner** John C Grant **Bred** Whitsbury Manor Stud & A W M Christie-Miller **Trained** Lambourn, Berks

**FOCUS**
A useful and interesting handicap in which three of the runners boasted unbeaten records. Howver a steady gallop saw several fail to settle was and this bare form may not be entirely reliable. The winner came down the in the straight.

## 1123 BETDAQ NO PREMIUM CHARGE FILLIES' H'CAP 7f (P)
**8:05** (8:05) (Class 5) (0-70,66) 4-Y-O+ **£2,587** (£770; £288; £288) **Stalls** Low

Form RPR
343 **1** **Ishiamber**42 588 4-9-7 **66** ........................ LukeMorris 2 76
(George Baker) *trckd ldng pair: wnt 2nd jst over 2f out: rdn to ld jst over 1f out: edgd lft fnl f: drvn out* **11/4**2

5334 **2** *1 1/4* **Two In The Pink (IRE)**13 952 4-9-2 **61** ow2 ........................ AdamKirby 6 68
(Ralph J Smith) *t.k.h early: trckd ldr: nt qckn and lost pl jst over 2f out: rdn and kpt on again fr over 1f out to take 2nd nr fin* **7/2**3

3246 **3** *3/4* **Medam**13 952 5-9-0 **62** ........................ NeilFarley(3) 3 67
(Shaun Harris) *led: kicked on over 2f out: hdd jst over 1f out: one pce and lost 2nd nr fin* **9/1**

0321 **3** *dht* **Tijuca (IRE)**22 851 5-8-12 **57** ........................(p) ChrisCatlin 7 62
(Ed de Giles) *s.i.s: t.k.h hld up in last: pushed along and stl there 2f out: grad clsd and shkn up fnl f: nrst fin* **11/1**

1012 **5** *3/4* **Mill I Am (USA)**24 819 4-9-1 **60** ........................ AdamBeschizza 4 63
(Stuart Williams) *hld up in 4th: pushed along and no prog over 2f out: reminders after: kpt on fnl f: nvr really threatened* **13/8**1

0050 **6** *1/2* **Idle Curiosity (IRE)**8 1010 4-8-10 **55** ........................(b1) HayleyTurner 5 56
(Jim Boyle) *dwlt: t.k.h: hld up in last pair: rdn over 2f out: one pce and no imp on ldrs after* **16/1**

1m 25.89s (-0.11) **Going Correction** -0.025s/f (Stan) 6 Ran SP% **111.2**
Speed ratings (Par 100): **99,97,96,96,95 95**
CSF £12.47 TOTE £2.80: £2.60, £2.30; EX 13.60 TRIFECTA I/TITP/M £51.90, I/TITP/T £40.30.
**Owner** Mrs P Scott-Dunn **Bred** Patricia Ann Scott-Dunn **Trained** Manton, Wilts

**FOCUS**
A modest fillies' handicap which, in keeping with several races earlier on the card, was run at just a steady gallop to the intersection. The winner raced towards the inside rail throughout.

## 1124 NEW JUMP FIXTURE ON 05.05.14 H'CAP 1m 3f (P)
**8:35** (8:35) (Class 6) (0-65,66) 3-Y-O **£1,940** (£577; £288; £144) **Stalls** Low

Form RPR
05-1 **1** **Piton**7 1032 3-9-8 **66** 6ex ........................ AdamKirby 3 74+
(Mark Johnston) *trckd ldr: pushed into ld jst over 2f out: styd on wl and in n.d over 1f out* **30/100**1

6013 **2** *3 1/2* **Blue Oyster**45 561 3-9-7 **65** ........................ ShaneKelly 8 67
(Philip McBride) *led: rdn and hdd jst over 2f out: wl clr of rest but no ch w wnr* **10/1**3

400- **3** *8* **Kaizen Factor**178 6897 3-9-2 **60** ........................ SeanLevey 6 48
(Rod Millman) *chsd ldng pair to 5f out: sn urged along: wl outpcd over 2f out: kpt on to take modest 3rd again 1f out* **33/1**

4-56 **4** *1 3/4* **Marphilly (IRE)**42 588 3-8-12 **56** ........................ SteveDrowne 2 41
(John Best) *hld up: outpcd whn pushed along and prog to chse clr ldng pair 2f out: shkn up and lost 3rd 1f out* **33/1**

-631 **5** *1 3/4* **Plough Boy (IRE)**43 577 3-9-3 **61** ........................ ChrisCatlin 4 44
(Willie Musson) *hld up in last: pushed along over 3f out: sn lft bhd and no ch* **6/1**2

466 **6** *5* **Dark Tsarina (IRE)**24 827 3-9-6 **64** ........................ LiamKeniry 1 38
(John Butler) *in tch: chsd ldng pair 5f out: lost 3rd and shkn up briefly 2f out: wknd and eased* **20/1**

56-5 **7** *8* **Buy Out Boy**10 988 3-9-5 **63** ........................ BenCurtis 7 23
(Jo Hughes) *racd wd: in tch: shkn up wl over 3f out: wknd over 2f out: sn bhd* **33/1**

2m 20.69s (-1.21) **Going Correction** -0.025s/f (Stan) 7 Ran SP% **113.9**
Speed ratings (Par 96): **103,100,94,93,92 88,82**
CSF £3.87 CT £35.33 TOTE £1.40: £1.10, £3.60; EX 3.60 Trifecta £45.50.
**Owner** T T Bloodstocks **Bred** Miss K Rausing **Trained** Middleham Moor, N Yorks
■ Stewards' Enquiry : Sean Levey five-day ban: improper riding (May 21-24,26)

**FOCUS**
An uncompetitive handicap run at a reasonable gallop and one in which the first two, who raced in the centre, pulled clear in the home straight.
T/Plt: £125.50 to a £1 stake. Pool: £65,914.88 - 383.34 winning units. T/Qpdt: £10.80 to a £1 stake. Pool: £10,746.85 - 730.20 winning units. JN

# 1111 SOUTHWELL (L-H)
Thursday, March 27

**OFFICIAL GOING: Standard**
Wind: Moderate to fresh across Weather: Cloudy with showers

## 1125 LADBROKES H'CAP 7f (F)
**2:00** (2:00) (Class 5) (0-65,65) 4-Y-O+ **£2,587** (£770; £384; £192) **Stalls** Low

Form RPR
00-0 **1** **Welliesinthewater (IRE)**50 489 4-9-1 **59** ........................(v1) DaleSwift 8 64
(Derek Shaw) *chsd ldrs: rdn along 3f out: styd on to chal over 1f out: drvn ent fnl f: kpt on wl to ld last 50yds* **6/1**

520- **2** *nk* **Rio Cobolo (IRE)**192 6464 8-8-13 **64** ........................(e1) EvaMoscrop(7) 3 68
(Philip Kirby) *hld up towards rr: gd hdwy over 2f out and sn swtchd to outer: led over 1f out: sn rdn: hdd and no ex last 50yds* **4/1**2

000- **3** *4 1/2* **Thrust Control (IRE)**198 6276 7-8-7 **51** oh4 ........................(p) BarryMcHugh 7 43
(Tracy Waggott) *cl up: led 3f out: sn rdn: hdd and drvn 2f out: one pce appr fnl f* **12/1**

6234 **4** *3 1/4* **Harvest Mist (IRE)**24 819 6-8-9 **58** ........................ LouisSteward(5) 5 41
(Shaun Lycett) *trckd ldrs: hdwy 3f out: rdn to ld 2f out: sn hdd & wknd appr fnl f* **9/2**3

1-00 **5** *1/2* **Rafaaf (IRE)**22 841 6-9-2 **60** ........................ StevieDonohoe 6 42
(Richard Phillips) *towards rr: hdwy on outer and wd st: rdn to chse ldrs 2f out: sn drvn and no imp* **10/1**

2113 **6** *2 1/4* **Arabian Flight**16 907 5-9-5 **63** ........................ TomQueally 4 39
(Michael Appleby) *slt ld: rdn along 1/2-way: sn hdd: drvn over 2f out and sn wknd* **9/4**1

130- **7** *18* **Marcus Caesar (IRE)**209 5975 4-9-7 **65** ........................ JamesSullivan 9
(Ruth Carr) *cl up on outer: ev ch wl over 2f out: sn rdn and wknd* **6/1**

400/ **8** *24* **Belle Intrigue**555 6332 4-8-12 **61** ........................ ShirleyTeasdale(5) 2
(Marjorie Fife) *a in rr: bhd fr 1/2-way* **33/1**

1m 30.68s (0.38) **Going Correction** +0.05s/f (Slow) 8 Ran SP% **117.2**
Speed ratings (Par 103): **99,98,93,89,89 86,66,38**
CSF £31.03 CT £284.24 TOTE £8.00: £3.50, £1.40, £6.50; EX 41.30 Trifecta £507.80.
**Owner** The Whiteman Partnership **Bred** Brendan Ryan **Trained** Sproxton, Leics

**FOCUS**
A very modest event in which they went an even gallop. Straightforward form.

## 1126 BOOKMAKERS.CO.UK MAIDEN STKS 6f (F)
**2:30** (2:31) (Class 5) 3-Y-O+ **£2,781** (£827; £413; £206) **Stalls** Low

Form RPR
0-2 **1** **Willy Brennan (IRE)**24 824 3-8-13 0 ........................ DavidProbert 6 89+
(Andrew Balding) *trckd ldrs: gd hdwy on outer 1/2-way: led 2f out: sn pushed clr: readily* **10/11**1

-005 **2** *7* **Wildcat Lass (USA)**15 930 3-8-6 67 ow1 ........................ SamJames(3) 3 64
(David O'Meara) *cl up: pushed along and sltly outpcd wl over 2f out: styd on fr over 1f out: tk 2nd ins fnl f: no ch w wnr* **9/2**3

33-2 **3** *2 3/4* **Handwoven (IRE)**16 906 3-8-10 70 ........................ MichaelJMMurphy(3) 1 60
(Mark Johnston) *led: rdn along 1/2-way: hdd 2f out: sn drvn and wknd over 1f out* **3/1**2

6- **4** *8* **Best Tamayuz**110 8201 3-8-13 0 ........................(p) FrederikTylicki 5 36
(Scott Dixon) *cl up: rdn along 1/2-way: drvn over 2f out and sn wknd* **20/1**

6 **5** *4 1/2* **Ana Ettihady (ITY)**15 930 3-8-13 0 ........................ PaulMulrennan 4 23
(Kevin Ryan) *cl up: rdn along 1/2-way: sn wknd* **8/1**

1m 15.9s (-0.60) **Going Correction** +0.05s/f (Slow) 5 Ran SP% **111.4**
Speed ratings (Par 103): **106,96,93,82,76**
CSF £5.54 TOTE £1.70: £1.10, £3.30; EX 4.70 Trifecta £12.40.
**Owner** Dr Philip Brown **Bred** J Costello **Trained** Kingsclere, Hants

**FOCUS**
A fair small-field maiden in which they went a proper gallop. The winner routed them.

## 1127 BEST ODDS AT BOOKMAKERS.CO.UK H'CAP 5f (F)
**3:05** (3:05) (Class 5) (0-70,70) 4-Y-O+ **£2,587** (£770; £384; £192) **Stalls** High

Form RPR
2424 **1** **Alpha Tauri (USA)**21 862 8-8-12 **68** ........................(t) AlistairRawlinson(7) 2 77
(Richard Guest) *cl up: led after 2f: rdn over 1f out: sn edgd lft: kpt on wl towards fin* **7/2**2

213- **2** *1* **Keep It Dark**148 7634 5-9-6 **69** ........................ BarryMcHugh 1 74
(Tony Coyle) *trckd ldrs on outer: hdwy 2f out: swtchd rt and rdn to chse wnr over 1f out: drvn and carried hd high ins fnl f: no imp* **5/2**1

1-03 **3** *1/2* **Beacon Tarn**63 299 4-9-4 **70** ........................ JasonHart(3) 7 74
(Eric Alston) *prom: pushed along and sltly outpcd over 2f out: sn rdn: styd on fnl f* **7/2**2

4006 **4** *hd* **Prince Of Passion (CAN)**10 993 6-8-12 **61** ........................ DaleSwift 5 64
(Derek Shaw) *sn rdn along and outpcd in rr: hdwy wl over 1f out: kpt on fnl f: nrst fin* **14/1**

3-06 **5** *1/2* **Waabel**15 921 7-8-4 **56** ........................(t) MichaelJMMurphy(3) 3 57
(Ann Stokell) *sn rdn along and outpcd in rr: swtchd lft to outer over 3f out: styd on appr fnl f: nrst fin* **33/1**

3050 **6** *nk* **Pull The Pin (IRE)**8 1019 5-9-2 **65** ........................(bt) PaulMulrennan 4 65
(Ann Stokell) *led 2f: cl up: rdn along 2f out: sn drvn and wknd ent fnl f* **6/1**3

0-40 **7** *1/2* **Flash City (ITY)**60 347 6-9-4 **67** ........................ JamesSullivan 6 65
(Ruth Carr) *prom: rdn along over 2f out: drvn over 1f out: wknd ent fnl f* **20/1**

1324 **8** *3/4* **Shawkantango**31 730 7-9-0 **70** ........................(p) AdamMcLean(7) 8 66
(Derek Shaw) *racd nr stands' rail: in tch: rdn along after 2f: drvn wl over 1f out: no hdwy* **6/1**3

1m 1.02s (1.32) **Going Correction** +0.35s/f (Slow) 8 Ran SP% **116.0**
Speed ratings (Par 103): **103,101,100,100,99 99,98,97**
CSF £12.91 CT £32.37 TOTE £4.00: £1.50, £1.10, £2.40; EX 17.00 Trifecta £83.00.
**Owner** John Wilkinson **Bred** Flaxman Holdings Ltd **Trained** Wetherby, W Yorks

■ Stewards' Enquiry : Adam McLean two-day ban: use of whip (10-11 Apr)
**FOCUS**
A fair sprint handicap for older horses. Straightforward form.

## 1128 CORAL APP DOWNLOAD FROM THE APP STORE H'CAP 1m 3f (F)
**3:40** (3:40) (Class 4) (0-85,89) 4-Y-O+ **£5,175** (£1,540; £769; £384) **Stalls** Low

Form RPR
2411 1 **The Lock Master (IRE)**[10] 999 7-9-13 **89** 6ex.................. TomQueally 2 97
(Michael Appleby) *hld up: stdy hdwy on outer over 4f out: led over 2f out: sn rdn and styd on strly* **4/1**[3]
21-4 2 3 **First Warning**[71] 182 4-9-0 **77**..............................(b[1]) StevieDonohoe 4 80
(Tim Pitt) *trckd ldrs on inner: hdwy over 2f out: rdn wl over 1f out: kpt on to chse wnr fnl f: no imp* **10/1**
-151 3 3 **Thatchmaster (USA)**[12] 977 4-9-2 **82**.............. MichaelJMMurphy(3) 1 80
(Mark Johnston) *slt ld at str pce: rdn along over 4f out: hdd over 2f out and sn drvn: one pce and hld whn hung rt ent fnl f* **7/4**[1]
0456 4 ½ **Returntobrecongill**[2] 1091 4-9-4 **81**.............................. JamesSullivan 5 78
(James Given) *disp ld at str pce for 2f: t.k.h and cl up: rdn along over 3f out and ev ch: drvn wl over 1f out: sn one pce and hld whn swtchd lft ent fnl f* **2/1**[2]
554- 5 99 **Anton Chigurh**[21] 7536 5-9-0 **83**............................ CamHardie(7) 3
(Brendan Powell) *in rr: rdn along 5f out: sn outpcd and bhd whn virtually p.u 2f out* **7/1**

2m 27.21s (-0.79) **Going Correction** +0.05s/f (Slow)
**WFA** 4 from 5yo+ 1lb 5 Ran SP% **111.3**
Speed ratings (Par 105): **104,101,99,99,27**
CSF £37.15 TOTE £4.40: £2.50, £1.70; EX 24.30 Trifecta £26.50.
**Owner** K G Kitchen **Bred** Patrick F Kelly **Trained** Danethorpe, Notts
**FOCUS**
A decent middle-distance handicap, in which they went a contested gallop. The winner is in fine form.

## 1129 CORAL MOBILE JUST THREE CLICKS TO BET H'CAP 1m 3f (F)
**4:10** (4:10) (Class 6) (0-60,58) 4-Y-O+ **£1,940** (£577; £288; £144) **Stalls** Low

Form RPR
1320 1 **Marina Ballerina**[23] 831 6-9-1 **57**..............................(p) PhilipPrince(5) 3 68
(Roy Bowring) *trckd ldr: cl up after 2f: led 7f out: rdn over 2f out: clr over 1f out: styd on strly* **12/1**
0002 2 6 **Auden (USA)**[2] 1087 6-9-6 **57**..............................(v) FrederikTylicki 5 58
(J R Jenkins) *t.k.h: chsd ldrs: hdwy over 3f out: effrt over 2f out: sn rdn and chsd wnr fr wl over 1f out: drvn and no imp ent fnl f* **10/11**[1]
2-20 3 6 **Amtired**[58] 366 8-9-7 **58**..............................(p) DanielTudhope 6 50
(Marjorie Fife) *hld up in rr: hdwy on outer over 2f out and sn rdn: chsd ldng pair: drvn and btn whn hung lft over 1f out* **2/1**[2]
-022 4 5 **Gabrial's Hope (FR)**[56] 379 5-9-7 **58**............................ DaleSwift 7 42
(Tracy Waggott) *t.k.h: chsd ldrs: hdwy 4f out: chsd wnr 3f out: sn rdn and wknd 2f out* **8/1**[3]
0234 5 4½ **Reach The Beach**[16] 912 5-8-9 **46**..............................(b[1]) StevieDonohoe 2 23
(Brendan Powell) *led: jnd after 2f: hdd over 7f out: rdn along 4f out: drvn wl over 2f out and sn wknd* **14/1**

2m 27.89s (-0.11) **Going Correction** +0.05s/f (Slow) 5 Ran SP% **111.2**
Speed ratings (Par 101): **102,97,93,89,86**
CSF £24.21 TOTE £9.70: £4.10, £1.40; EX 27.50 Trifecta £53.50.
**Owner** S R Bowring **Bred** S R Bowring **Trained** Edwinstowe, Notts
**FOCUS**
A moderate middle-distance handicap in which they went an even gallop. Improvement from the winner, but hard form to quantify.

## 1130 32RED IMMORTAL ROMANCE SLOT H'CAP 6f (F)
**4:45** (4:45) (Class 6) (0-65,69) 3-Y-O **£2,045** (£603; £302) **Stalls** Low

Form RPR
415- 1 **Scarborough (IRE)**[175] 6967 3-8-4 **53**.............. AlistairRawlinson(7) 1 70
(Michael Appleby) *t.k.h early: trckd ldng pair: swtchd lft and hdwy 2f out: rdn to ld over 1f out: clr ent fnl f* **8/1**
12-0 2 6 **Mornin Mr Norris**[44] 568 3-8-1 **50**.............................. JoeDoyle(7) 3 49
(John Quinn) *towards rr: rdn along: outpcd and bhd over 3f out: hdwy wl over 1f out: styd on wl u.p fnl f to take 2nd towards fin* **8/1**
3-11 3 1 **Razin' Hell**[9] 1005 3-9-13 **69** 6ex..............................(v) TomQueally 5 65
(Alan McCabe) *qckly away and set str pce: wd st and sn rdn: drvn and hdd over 1f out: sn hung lft and wknd* **5/4**[1]
-653 4 nk **Black Geronimo**[15] 931 3-8-13 **60**..............................(v) PhilipPrince(5) 6 55
(Roy Bowring) *dwlt and in rr: hdwy over 3f out: rdn and edgd lft to inner rail over 2f out: sn drvn and n.d* **5/1**[3]
3111 5 5 **Emerald Breeze (IRE)**[6] 1047 3-9-8 **64** 6ex..............(b) StevieDonohoe 2 44
(Tim Pitt) *t.k.h: trckd ldr: cl up 1/2-way: wd st: chal over 2f out: sn rdn and ev ch: drvn and edgd rt to stands' rail wl over 1f out: wknd* **5/2**[2]

1m 16.53s (0.03) **Going Correction** +0.05s/f (Slow) 5 Ran SP% **111.9**
Speed ratings (Par 96): **101,93,91,91,84**
CSF £61.47 TOTE £13.70: £6.90, £7.60; EX 60.30 Trifecta £250.40.
**Owner** M Wainman **Bred** Tom Foley **Trained** Danethorpe, Notts
**FOCUS**
A modest 6f handicap in which they went a decent gallop. The winner did it well.

## 1131 32RED THUNDERSTRUCK II SLOT FILLIES' H'CAP 1m (F)
**5:15** (5:15) (Class 5) (0-70,66) 4-Y-O+ **£2,726** (£805; £402) **Stalls** Low

Form RPR
0-12 1 **Hot Right Now**[46] 548 4-9-0 **66**.............................. RobJFitzpatrick(7) 2 72
(K R Burke) *slt ld: rdn along 2f out: drvn over 1f out: hld on gamely towards fin* **2/5**[1]
4401 2 ½ **Bladewood Girl**[21] 858 6-8-1 **53**.............................. JoeDoyle(7) 1 58
(J R Jenkins) *trckd wnr on inner: effrt over 2f out: sn ev ch: rdn wl over 1f out: drvn ins fnl f: no ex towards fin* **9/2**[2]
-026 3 1½ **Meddling**[15] 922 4-8-11 **59**..............................[1] RossAtkinson(3) 3 61
(Julia Feilden) *trckd wnr on outer: cl up 3f out: rdn over 2f out and ev ch: drvn and edgd lft jst over 1f out: sn swtchd lft and one pce* **7/1**[3]
00/5 4 ¾ **Run Fat Lass Run**[15] 928 4-8-13 **65**..............................(e[1]) EvaMoscrop(7) 4 65+
(Philip Kirby) *stdd s: hld up and 12 l bhd over 3f out: wd st: pushed along over 2f out: rdn and styd on strly fnl f: nrst fin* **16/1**

1m 46.26s (2.56) **Going Correction** +0.05s/f (Slow) 4 Ran SP% **108.0**
Speed ratings (Par 100): **89,88,87,86**
CSF £2.54 TOTE £1.30; EX 1.80 Trifecta £4.00.
**Owner** Mrs Elaine M Burke **Bred** Hillwood Bloodstock **Trained** Middleham Moor, N Yorks
■ Stewards' Enquiry : Joe Doyle two-day ban: use of whip (10-11 Apr)
**FOCUS**
A modest fillies' handicap lacking depth. The winner's recent course form was enough.
T/Plt: £674.30 to a £1 stake. Pool: £62,635.10 - 67.80 winning units. T/Qpdt: £238.20 to a £1 stake. Pool: £5,293.95 - 16.44 winning units. JR

# 1080 WOLVERHAMPTON (A.W) (L-H)
Thursday, March 27

**OFFICIAL GOING: Standard**
Wind: Fresh against Weather: Overcast

## 1132 CORAL MOBILE "JUST THREE CLICKS TO BET" H'CAP 1m 4f 50y(P)
**2:10** (2:10) (Class 6) (0-60,60) 4-Y-O+ **£2,264** (£673; £336; £168) **Stalls** Low

Form RPR
664- 1 **Precision Strike**[118] 7881 4-9-0 **60**..............................(v) ConnorBeasley(5) 6 67
(Richard Guest) *hld up: hdwy to ld over 2f out: rdn over 1f out: jst hld on* **8/1**
5311 2 nse **Goldmadchen (GER)**[13] 959 6-9-2 **55**.............................. GrahamLee 5 61
(James Given) *hld up: pushed along 6f out: hdwy over 2f out: rdn over 1f out: r.o* **2/1**[1]
3520 3 nk **Well Owd Mon**[16] 915 4-8-6 **47**..............................(p) LiamJones 4 53
(Andrew Hollinshead) *s.i.s: hld up: hdwy on outer to chse wnr over 2f out: rdn and ev ch ins fnl f: styd on* **11/2**[3]
2-22 4 3¼ **Shirazz**[63] 303 5-9-7 **60**..............................(t) GeorgeBaker 1 61
(Seamus Durack) *prom: lost pl over 3f out: nt clr run over 2f out: hdwy over 1f out: sn rdn and hung lft: styd on* **7/2**[2]
02-0 5 1 **Impeccability**[80] 68 4-8-5 **46**.............................. LukeMorris 7 45
(John Mackie) *chsd ldrs: rdn over 3f out: no ex ins fnl f* **20/1**
445- 6 4 **Qibtee (FR)**[179] 6870 4-9-5 **60**.............................. DavidAllan 3 53
(Les Eyre) *plld hrd: led after 1f tl 10f out: trckd ldr tl led again over 3f out: rdn and hdd over 2f out: wknd fnl f* **7/1**
4402 7 ¾ **Mazij**[10] 1000 6-8-12 **51**.............................. WilliamCarson 8 43
(Peter Hiatt) *led 1f: chsd ldrs tl wknd 2f out* **6/1**
00-4 8 14 **Felice (IRE)**[84] 13 4-8-5 **46** oh1..............................(p) NickyMackay 2 15
(Scott Dixon) *chsd ldrs: led 10f out tl over 3f out: wknd over 2f out* **50/1**

2m 43.24s (2.14) **Going Correction** +0.15s/f (Slow)
**WFA** 4 from 5yo+ 2lb 8 Ran SP% **115.6**
Speed ratings (Par 101): **98,97,97,95,94 92,91,82**
CSF £24.73 CT £97.59 TOTE £8.20: £1.60, £1.10, £2.90; EX 36.90 Trifecta £203.40.
**Owner** Resdev **Bred** Mickley Stud **Trained** Wetherby, W Yorks
■ Stewards' Enquiry : Connor Beasley four-day ban: use of whip (10-14 Apr)
**FOCUS**
The principals came from behind here.

## 1133 CORAL APP DOWNLOAD FROM THE APP STORE H'CAP 1m 4f 50y(P)
**2:40** (2:40) (Class 4) (0-85,83) 4-Y-O+ **£5,175** (£1,540; £769; £384) **Stalls** Low

Form RPR
-511 1 **Spes Nostra**[14] 942 6-9-7 **83**..............................(b) GrahamGibbons 4 94+
(David Barron) *mde all: racd keenly: clr 8f out tl stdd 6f out: qcknd over 2f out: clr over 1f out: comf* **1/1**[1]
-635 2 5 **Flying Power**[20] 870 6-9-7 **83**.............................. PaddyAspell 3 86
(John Norton) *chsd wnr: rdn over 2f out: styd on same pce fr over 1f out* **11/4**[2]
-313 3 ¾ **Lineman**[10] 999 4-8-9 **73**.............................. ShaneKelly 1 75
(Andrew Hollinshead) *chsd ldrs: rdn over 3f out: styd on same pce fnl 2f* **7/2**[3]
31-0 4 17 **Arizona John (IRE)**[20] 870 9-9-1 **77**.............................. StephenCraine 5 52
(John Mackie) *hld up: rdn and wknd over 2f out* **16/1**
0-45 5 49 **Wildomar**[55] 407 5-8-11 **73**.............................. WilliamCarson 2
(Peter Hiatt) *hld up: hdwy over 5f out: rdn over 3f out: sn wknd* **25/1**

2m 41.29s (0.19) **Going Correction** +0.15s/f (Slow)
**WFA** 4 from 5yo+ 2lb 5 Ran SP% **108.6**
Speed ratings (Par 105): **105,101,101,89,57**
CSF £3.87 TOTE £1.70: £1.10, £2.00; EX 4.60 Trifecta £7.90.
**Owner** J Cringan & D Pryde **Bred** James A Cringan **Trained** Maunby, N Yorks
**FOCUS**
A useful effort from the winner.

## 1134 CORAL.CO.UK BEST ODDS GUARANTEED ON RACING H'CAP 1m 1f 103y(P)
**3:15** (3:15) (Class 5) (0-75,73) 4-Y-O+ **£2,911** (£866; £432) **Stalls** Low

Form RPR
5-21 1 **Dubai Celebration**[31] 733 6-8-12 **69**.............................. ConnorBeasley(5) 3 75
(Julie Camacho) *mde all: set stdy pce tl qcknd over 2f out: rdn out* **5/6**[1]
035- 2 2½ **Silver Alliance**[149] 7608 6-9-2 **73**..............................(p) ShelleyBirkett(5) 4 74
(Julia Feilden) *hld up: hdwy to chse wnr 2f out: rdn over 1f out: styd on same pce fnl f* **6/4**[2]
/36- 3 ¾ **Keep Calm**[309] 2564 4-9-1 **67**.............................. GrahamLee 1 67
(John Mackie) *trckd wnr tl rdn 2f out: styd on same pce fnl f* **6/1**[3]

2m 5.93s (4.23) **Going Correction** +0.15s/f (Slow) 3 Ran SP% **108.8**
Speed ratings (Par 103): **87,84,84**
CSF £2.43 TOTE £1.60; EX 2.20 Trifecta £2.00.
**Owner** L Bolingbroke, N Gravett & J Camacho **Bred** Wheelers Land Stud **Trained** Norton, N Yorks
**FOCUS**
A straightforward success for the favourite.

## 1135 32RED IMMORTAL ROMANCE SLOT H'CAP 1m 1f 103y(P)
**3:50** (3:50) (Class 5) (0-75,74) 3-Y-O **£3,234** (£962; £481; £240) **Stalls** Low

Form RPR
001- 1 **Collaboration**[161] 7320 3-9-7 **74**..............................(t) JimCrowley 3 84+
(Andrew Balding) *hld up: hdwy over 1f out: shkn up to ld wl ins fnl f: r.o wl* **5/4**[1]
431- 2 2 **Shimba Hills**[141] 7774 3-9-2 **72**.............. WilliamTwiston-Davies(3) 7 76
(Mick Channon) *trckd ldrs: wnt 2nd over 6f out: led over 1f out: rdn and hdd wl ins fnl f: styd on same pce* **7/1**
1-33 3 nk **Power Up**[50] 492 3-9-0 **67**.............................. JoeFanning 2 71
(Mark Johnston) *chsd ldr tl over 6f out: remained handy: rdn over 1f out: styd on* **10/1**
2122 4 shd **Zamra (IRE)**[7] 1033 3-9-1 **68**..............................(p) GrahamLee 6 71
(James Tate) *hld up: hdwy over 5f out: rdn over 1f out: styd on* **7/2**[2]
1-25 5 1¾ **Aramadyh**[51] 473 3-9-5 **72**..............................(p) LukeMorris 4 72
(James Tate) *led: rdn over 2f out: hdd over 1f out: no ex ins fnl f* **9/2**[3]
1153 6 4½ **Boogangoo (IRE)**[13] 955 3-9-6 **73**.............................. PaddyAspell 1 65
(Grace Harris) *prom: rdn over 2f out: wknd ins fnl f* **33/1**

2m 2.99s (1.29) **Going Correction** +0.15s/f (Slow) 6 Ran SP% **109.4**
Speed ratings (Par 98): **100,98,97,97,96 92**
CSF £10.09 TOTE £2.00: £1.60, £5.10; EX 12.30 Trifecta £54.20.
**Owner** Another Bottle Racing 2 **Bred** Shareef Racing & Redmyre Bloodstock **Trained** Kingsclere, Hants

**FOCUS**
Fair form.

## 1136 32RED H'CAP (BOBIS RACE) 5f 216y(P)
4:20 (4:20) (Class 3) (0-95,93) 3-Y-O £7,439 (£2,213; £1,106; £553) Stalls Low

Form RPR

21-1 1 **Captain Secret**[81] [62] 3-9-6 **92** .......... AdamKirby 7 97
(Marco Botti) *mde all: qcknd 2f out: hrd rdn ins fnl f: all out* **3/1**[3]

2-14 2 *hd* **Outbacker (IRE)**[22] [850] 3-8-4 **76** .......... JoeFanning 2 80
(Mark Johnston) *a.p: chsd wnr 4f out: rdn and hung lft over 1f out: r.o* **8/1**

210- 3 *nk* **Lincoln (IRE)**[173] [7026] 3-8-6 **81** ow1 .......... WilliamTwiston-Davies(3) 1 84
(Mick Channon) *racd keenly: trckd wnr 2f: remained handy: rdn over 1f out: r.o* **11/4**[2]

130- 4 *2 1/4* **Muir Lodge**[173] [7017] 3-9-7 **93** .......... (t) JimCrowley 4 89
(Andrew Balding) *s.i.s: hdwy over 2f out: outpcd wl over 1f out: r.o ins fnl f* **7/4**[1]

525- 5 *3/4* **Captain Midnight (IRE)**[131] [7933] 3-8-13 **85** .......... GrahamLee 5 79
(David Brown) *a.p: rdn over 2f out: styd on same pce fnl f* **25/1**

331- 6 *8* **Ribbleton**[157] [7419] 3-8-5 **77** .......... BenCurtis 3 45
(David Barron) *s.i.s: sn outpcd: bhd fr 1/2-way* **12/1**

1m 14.55s (-0.45) **Going Correction** +0.15s/f (Slow) **6** Ran SP% **110.7**
Speed ratings (Par 102): **109,108,108,105,104 93**
CSF £25.09 TOTE £4.10: £2.30, £3.50; EX 13.20 Trifecta £58.90.
**Owner** Scuderia Blueberry **Bred** R G Percival **Trained** Newmarket, Suffolk

**FOCUS**
A decent handicap. The early pace wasn't hectic and it paid to race handily.

## 1137 COMPARE BOOKMAKERS AT BOOKMAKERS.CO.UK MAIDEN STKS 5f 20y(P)
4:55 (4:55) (Class 5) 3-Y-O+ £2,587 (£770; £384; £192) Stalls Low

Form RPR

00-2 1 **Proclamationofwar**[28] [765] 3-8-10 **73** .......... ShaneGray(5) 2 71
(Kevin Ryan) *mde virtually all: shkn up and clr fr over 1f out* **4/11**[1]

2 *3 1/4* **Dreams Of Reality** 3-8-10 0 .......... RichardKingscote 7 54+
(Tom Dascombe) *s.i.s: hdwy over 1f out: edgd lft and r.o to go 2nd wl ins fnl f: no ch w wnr* **5/1**[2]

5 3 *1 1/2* **Torridon**[10] [994] 3-9-1 0 .......... JoeFanning 6 54
(Mark Johnston) *sn pushed along in rr: hdwy 1/2-way: rdn to chse wnr over 1f out tl no ex wl ins fnl f* **8/1**[3]

0-44 4 *1* **Stoneacre Hull (IRE)**[10] [994] 5-9-5 **47** .......... SladeO'Hara(3) 1 50
(Peter Grayson) *prom: pushed along 1/2-way: styd on same pce fnl f* **25/1**

3004 5 *7* **Rebel Code (USA)**[15] [933] 3-8-10 **51** .......... (p) ConnorBeasley(5) 3 25
(James Given) *chsd wnr: rdn 1/2-way: lost 2nd over 1f out: wknd fnl f* **14/1**

/65- 6 *3 1/4* **Stoneacre Thirsk (IRE)**[154] [7484] 5-9-8 **38** .......... StephenCraine 4 13
(Peter Grayson) *chsd ldrs: pushed along over 3f out: wknd over 1f out* **66/1**

1m 2.89s (0.59) **Going Correction** +0.15s/f (Slow)
**WFA** 3 from 5yo 12lb **6** Ran SP% **113.1**
Speed ratings (Par 103): **101,95,93,91,80 75**
CSF £2.73 TOTE £1.50: £1.10, £2.10; EX 2.80 Trifecta £7.10.
**Owner** Michael Beaumont **Bred** Abingdon & Witney College **Trained** Hambleton, N Yorks

**FOCUS**
Weak maiden form.

## 1138 LADBROKES H'CAP 1m 141y(P)
5:25 (5:27) (Class 6) (0-52,52) 4-Y-O+ £2,264 (£673; £336; £168) Stalls Low

Form RPR

50-2 1 **Just Five (IRE)**[8] [1015] 8-8-10 **46** oh1 .......... (v) ConnorBeasley(5) 9 53
(John Weymes) *hld up: pushed along over 2f out: hdwy over 1f out: r.o to ld post* **7/2**[1]

0203 2 *hd* **Katmai River (IRE)**[13] [964] 7-8-13 **51** .......... CharlotteJenner(7) 12 58
(Mark Usher) *a.p: shkn up to ld wl ins fnl f: hdd post* **7/2**[1]

3-33 3 *1* **Shamiana**[23] [833] 4-9-6 **51** .......... (b) RichardKingscote 11 55
(Daniel Kubler) *a.p: rdn and ev ch ins fnl f: styd on same pce towards fin* **6/1**[3]

4064 4 *1/2* **Ferdy (IRE)**[16] [918] 5-9-5 **50** .......... JoeFanning 10 53
(Paul Green) *s.i.s: hld up: hdwy over 2f out: rdn and ev ch ins fnl f: styd on same pce* **10/1**

0004 5 *1/2* **Devote Myself (IRE)**[6] [1050] 5-9-5 **50** .......... (t) KierenFox 5 52
(Tony Carroll) *led after 1f: rdn over 1f out: hdd and no ex wl ins fnl f* **12/1**

002- 6 *3 1/4* **Thewestwalian (USA)**[154] [7485] 6-9-2 **47** .......... WilliamCarson 4 43
(Peter Hiatt) *led 1f: chsd ldrs: wnt 2nd over 2f out: sn rdn: no ex ins fnl f* **16/1**

5030 7 *1 1/2* **Daniel Thomas (IRE)**[8] [1016] 12-9-6 **51** .......... (tp) GrahamGibbons 2 43
(Ann Stokell) *hld up: rdn over 2f out: nvr on terms* **5/1**[2]

0544 8 *nk* **Ellies Image**[20] [869] 7-9-1 **46** oh1 .......... GrahamLee 3 38
(Richard Ford) *hld up: pushed along over 3f out: n.d* **25/1**

3-50 9 *1 3/4* **Acton Gold**[14] [941] 5-9-1 **46** oh1 .......... TomEaves 8 34
(Brian Baugh) *trckd ldr: plld hrd: pushed along and lost 2nd over 2f out: rdn whn hung lft and rt ins fnl f: sn wknd* **10/1**

00-6 10 *4 1/2* **Odd Ball (IRE)**[13] [964] 7-8-10 **46** oh1 .......... ShirleyTeasdale(5) 6 25
(Lisa Williamson) *chsd ldrs tl rdn and wknd over 2f out* **25/1**

0-10 11 *3/4* **Addikt (IRE)**[22] [838] 9-9-7 **52** .......... JohnFahy 7 29
(John Spearing) *s.i.s: hld up and a in rr: rdn and wknd over 3f out* **14/1**

0/0- 12 *2 1/2* **The Kernigal (IRE)**[416] [517] 5-9-1 **46** .......... (vt[1]) DavidProbert 1 18
(Bernard Llewellyn) *hld up: pushed along and hdwy 3f out: wknd wl over 1f out* **33/1**

1m 51.47s (0.97) **Going Correction** +0.15s/f (Slow) **12** Ran SP% **124.5**
Speed ratings (Par 101): **101,100,99,99,99 96,94,94,93,89 88,86**
CSF £15.43 CT £73.95 TOTE £4.50: £1.30, £1.60, £2.00; EX 20.40 Trifecta £103.50.
**Owner** Hoofbeats Racing Club 4 **Bred** Rathbarry Stud **Trained** Middleham Moor, N Yorks

**FOCUS**
A fairly open handicap.

T/Plt: £13.50 to a £1 stake. Pool: £58,115.66 - 3121.36 winning units. T/Qpdt: £8.60 to a £1 stake. Pool: £4140.04 - 352.45 winning units. CR

# COMPIEGNE (L-H)
Thursday, March 27

**OFFICIAL GOING: Turf: very soft**

## 1139a PRIX ATALANTE (MAIDEN) (3YO FILLIES) (TURF) 1m 4f
1:20 (12:00) 3-Y-O £10,416 (£4,166; £3,125; £2,083; £1,041)

RPR

1 **Akalmia (FR)**[82] 3-9-0 0 .......... FlavienPrat 12 77
(J-M Lefebvre, France) **198/10**

2 *1/2* **Donavista (FR)** 3-8-10 0 .......... RonanThomas 1 72
(F-H Graffard, France) **10/1**

3 *3/4* **Isabella Liberty (FR)**[42] [599] 3-9-0 0 .......... JimmyQuinn 6 75
(Robert Eddery) *sn prom on outer: led 1/2-way: rdn and strly pressed over 2f out: sn jst hdd: styd on gamely u.p and battled bk to hold ev ch tl hld and dropped to 3rd cl home* **48/10**[2]

4 *1 1/4* **Laderia (FR)**[181] 3-9-0 0 .......... MlleTatianaPuitg 11 73
(Mlle T Puitg, France) **46/1**

5 *snk* **Mauny (FR)** 3-8-10 0 .......... FabienLefebvre 4 69
(Mlle A Voraz, France) **47/1**

6 *hd* **Ganny (FR)**[138] 3-9-0 0 .......... AnthonyCrastus 3 72
(E Lellouche, France) **48/10**[2]

7 *1* **Peace Mine (CAN)** 3-9-0 0 .......... FranckBlondel 9 71
(M Mace, France) **9/1**[3]

8 *1 1/2* **Heartily (IRE)**[198] [6281] 3-9-0 0 .......... FabriceVeron 2 68
(H-A Pantall, France) **9/1**[3]

9 *5* **Anymore (FR)** 3-8-10 0 .......... EddyHardouin 10 56
(J-Y Artu, France) **64/1**

10 *3* **Heights Of Glory (FR)** 3-8-10 0 .......... MarcLerner 7 52
(C Lerner, France) **14/1**

11 *4* **Olymnia**[152] [7533] 3-9-0 0 .......... IoritzMendizabal 8 49
(Robert Eddery) *hld up and a towards rr: rdn 3f out: no imp and btn over 1f out: eased ins fnl f: nvr a factor* **26/1**

12 *6* **Mediteranea (FR)**[9] 3-9-0 0 .......... AurelienLemaitre 5 40
(F-M Cottin, France) **31/1**

13 *nk* **Larabesque (IRE)** 3-8-10 0 .......... MaximeGuyon 13 35
(A Fabre, France) **2/1**[1]

2m 46.74s (166.74) **13** Ran SP% **121.0**
WIN (incl. 1 euro stake): 20.80. PLACES: 5.10, 3.70, 2.50. DF: 113.80. SF: 344.90.
**Owner** Athanase Poulopoulos **Bred** A Poulopoulos **Trained** France

# 1104 LINGFIELD (L-H)
Friday, March 28

**OFFICIAL GOING: Standard**
Wind: Fresh, across (away from stands) Weather: Cloudy

## 1140 32RED CASINO CLAIMING STKS 1m 5f (P)
2:00 (2:00) (Class 6) 4-Y-O+ £2,045 (£603; £302) Stalls Low

Form RPR

-265 1 **Incendo**[17] [920] 8-9-2 **74** .......... (p) StevieDonohoe 4 73
(Ian Williams) *hld up in last: gng easily and cl up 2f out: smooth prog on inner to ld 1f out: sn clr* **5/2**[1]

5-43 2 *3 1/4* **Daring Indian**[55] [430] 6-9-6 **68** .......... (p) RichardKingscote 3 73
(Tom Dascombe) *hld up in tch: gng strly alongside wnr and cl up 2f out: stuck bhd rivals tl swtchd rt 130yds out: r.o to take 2nd post: no ch* **4/1**[2]

506- 3 *nse* **Ampleforth**[27] [7947] 6-8-6 **67** .......... (v) GeorgeDowning(5) 5 65
(Ian Williams) *pressed ldr: shkn up to take narrow ld over 3f out to 1f out: easily outpcd* **12/1**

1343 4 *hd* **Bert The Alert**[6] [1065] 6-9-1 **61** .......... LiamJones 6 67
(Laura Mongan) *hld up in tch: pushed up on wd outside to chal 3f out: nt qckn over 1f out: sn outpcd* **5/1**

0113 5 *1 1/4* **A Little Bit Dusty**[10] [1003] 6-9-8 **76** .......... (p) HayleyTurner 1 72
(Conor Dore) *mde most: narrowly hdd over 3f out: shkn up and stl upsides jst over 1f out: sn outpcd: fdd nr fin* **5/2**[1]

00-0 6 *8* **Tappanappa (IRE)**[27] [803] 7-9-8 **85** .......... (bt) StephenCraine 2 60
(David Flood) *trckd ldng pair: pushed up to chal 4f out: drvn over 2f out: sn wknd* **9/2**[3]

2m 45.11s (-0.89) **Going Correction** +0.05s/f (Slow) **6** Ran SP% **119.7**
Speed ratings (Par 101): **104,102,101,101,101 96**
CSF £13.97 TOTE £2.90: £1.10, £4.90; EX 16.20 Trifecta £135.20.
**Owner** Ian Williams **Bred** London Thoroughbred Services Ltd **Trained** Portway, Worcs

**FOCUS**
An ordinary claimer.

## 1141 DOWNLOAD THE LADBROKES APP H'CAP 1m 1y(P)
2:30 (2:31) (Class 6) (0-60,60) 4-Y-O+ £2,045 (£603; £302) Stalls High

Form RPR

4333 1 **Divine Rule (IRE)**[8] [1023] 6-9-5 **58** .......... (p) LiamJones 7 64
(Laura Mongan) *hld up in last: brought wdst of all bnd 2f out: drvn and r.o fnl f to ld last 50yds* **4/1**[3]

04-0 2 *nk* **Fair Comment**[68] [246] 4-9-0 **53** .......... LiamKeniry 4 58
(Michael Blanshard) *hld up in last trio: brought wd bnd 2f out: prog over 1f out: drvn to ld 100yds out: hdd and outpcd last 50yds* **8/1**

6065 3 *1/2* **Dreaming Again**[9] [1016] 4-8-8 **47** .......... DavidProbert 6 51
(Jimmy Fox) *racd on outer: led 1f: chsd ldr to 1/2-way: pushed along 3f out: kpt on u.p to ld 1f out: hdd and outpcd last 100yds* **5/1**

0324 4 *1 1/2* **Warbond**[25] [815] 6-9-5 **58** .......... (v) AdamKirby 1 59
(Michael Madgwick) *hld up in last trio: cl up over 1f out: nt qckn jst ins fnl f: sn outpcd* **11/4**[1]

1133 5 *1/2* **Wishformore (IRE)**[9] [1021] 7-9-7 **60** .......... (b[1]) StevieDonohoe 2 60
(Ian Williams) *trckd ldng trio: drvn and tried to chal 1f out: outpcd last 150yds* **3/1**[2]

6000 6 *1/2* **Fairy Mist (IRE)**[23] [844] 7-8-2 **46** oh1 .......... RyanWhile(5) 5 44
(John Bridger) *cl up: trckd ldr 1/2-way: drvn to ld briefly jst over 1f out: outpcd fnl f* **33/1**

/06- 7 *9* **Addictive Nature (IRE)**[284] [3401] 4-9-5 **58** .......... MartinDwyer 3 36
(John Gallagher) *nt that wl away but pushed up to ld after 1f: styd on inner and hdd jst over 1f out: wknd rapidly* **8/1**

1m 38.1s (-0.10) **Going Correction** +0.05s/f (Slow) **7** Ran SP% **113.5**
Speed ratings (Par 101): **102,101,101,99,99 98,89**
CSF £34.44 TOTE £4.80: £2.90, £5.40; EX 42.60 Trifecta £264.70.

**Owner** Mrs L J Mongan **Bred** Car Colston Hall Stud **Trained** Epsom, Surrey
**FOCUS**
A moderate handicap, but something of a messy race and the pace was steady.

## 1142 LADBROKES H'CAP — 1m 1y(P)
**3:00** (3:00) (Class 5) (0-75,75) 4-Y-O+ **£2,726** (£805; £402) **Stalls** High

Form / RPR
135- **1** **Tenor (IRE)**[198] 6313 4-9-3 **71**.....(t) DavidProbert 3 81
(John Ryan) *mde all: kicked on over 2f out: drew away over 1f out: styd on wl* **20/1**
604- **2** 1 1/4 **The Best Doctor (IRE)**[165] 7253 4-9-4 **72**..... SebSanders 5 80
(Jeremy Noseda) *trckd wnr 2f: styd cl up: rdn over 2f out: wnt 2nd again jst over 1f out: hrd rdn and styd on but unable to chal* **11/10**[1]
0-12 **3** 2 **Gaelic Silver (FR)**[14] 953 8-9-2 **70**..... GeorgeBaker 4 73
(Gary Moore) *hld up in last pair: wd bnd 2f out: tried to make prog over 1f out but ldrs nt stopping: kpt on to take 3rd last stride* **6/1**[3]
1314 **4** nse **Club House (IRE)**[25] 825 4-8-12 **73**..... GeorgeBuckell(7) 7 76
(Robert Mills) *t.k.h: hld up in last: tried to make prog wl over 1f out but ldrs nt stopping: kpt on same pce* **7/2**[2]
-343 **5** nse **Gracious George (IRE)**[25] 825 4-9-7 **75**..... LiamKeniry 6 78
(Jimmy Fox) *trckd wnr after 2f: upsides sn after: rdn over 2f out: outpcd and lost 2nd jst over 1f out: fdd* **6/1**[3]
3-15 **6** 4 1/2 **Wilfred Pickles (IRE)**[23] 843 8-9-4 **72**.....(p) AdamKirby 2 64
(Jo Crowley) *cl up: rdn over 2f out: nt qckn and btn over 1f out: wknd and eased fnl f* **10/1**

1m 37.61s (-0.59) **Going Correction** +0.05s/f (Slow) **6** Ran SP% **112.3**
Speed ratings (Par 103): **104,102,100,100,100 96**
CSF £43.17 TOTE £18.70: £7.00, £1.20; EX 62.80 Trifecta £462.20.
**Owner** Kilco (International) Ltd **Bred** Epona Bloodstock Ltd And P A Byrne **Trained** Newmarket, Suffolk
**FOCUS**
A fair handicap.

## 1143 32RED MAIDEN FILLIES' STKS — 1m 2f (P)
**3:30** (3:30) (Class 5) 3-Y-O+ **£2,726** (£805; £402) **Stalls** Low

Form / RPR
50- **1** **Zanouska (USA)**[157] 7435 3-8-6 0..... AdrianNicholls 1 66+
(Mark Johnston) *led at v slow pce 2f: styd cl up: rdn to go 2nd over 2f out and veered rt: drvn to ld 1f out: veered rt and lft: styd on* **5/2**[2]
**2** 1 **Elpida (USA)** 3-8-6 0..... HayleyTurner 3 64+
(David Simcock) *hld up in last trio: pushed along and prog on inner fr 3f out: clsd to chal 1f out: styd on same pce* **4/1**[3]
**3** nk **Martinette (USA)** 3-8-6 0..... MartinDwyer 7 63+
(Charles Hills) *hld up and sn t.k.h: last whn dash for home sed 3f out: swtchd wd and prog 2f out: rn green but clsd on ldrs fnl f: nvr able to chal and hmpd cl home* **6/4**[1]
**4** 4 **Labyrinthine (IRE)**[256] 4-9-12 0..... DavidProbert 4 59
(James Unett) *prog to ld after 2f but set mod pce: dashed for home 3f out: hdd & wknd 1f out* **10/1**
**5** 3 1/4 **Double Dealites**[30] 4-9-12 0..... RobertHavlin 2 53
(Jamie Poulton) *hld up: prog to chse ldr over 3f out to over 2f out: sn wknd* **14/1**
2-30 **6** 1 3/4 **Avidly**[23] 849 4-9-12 71.....[1] AdamBeschizza 5 49
(Julia Feilden) *s.i.s: hld up in last pair: prog on outer 4f out: rdn whn hmpd over 2f out: sn wknd* **12/1**
00- **7** 1/2 **Petale Noir**[163] 7310 3-8-6 0..... NickyMackay 6 44
(Jonathan Portman) *cl up: chsd ldr 6f out to over 3f out: sn wknd* **66/1**

2m 11.37s (4.77) **Going Correction** +0.05s/f (Slow)
**WFA** 3 from 4yo 20lb **7** Ran SP% **113.5**
Speed ratings (Par 100): **82,81,80,77,75 73,73**
CSF £12.76 TOTE £2.70: £2.20, £2.60; EX 19.00 Trifecta £37.20.
**Owner** Nabil Mourad **Bred** Rabbah Bloodstock Llc **Trained** Middleham Moor, N Yorks
**FOCUS**
An interesting maiden that should produce winners.

## 1144 BEST ODDS AT BOOKMAKERS.CO.UK H'CAP — 6f 1y(P)
**4:05** (4:05) (Class 5) (0-75,75) 4-Y-O+ **£2,726** (£805; £402) **Stalls** Low

Form / RPR
2101 **1** **Multitask**[34] 714 4-9-4 **72**..... LiamKeniry 3 81+
(Michael Madgwick) *hld up in 5th: prog over 1f out: rdn and r.o fnl f to ld last 50yds* **11/10**[1]
-314 **2** 3/4 **Rigolleto (IRE)**[30] 746 6-9-2 **70**..... GeorgeBaker 5 76
(Anabel K Murphy) *led: sent for home 2f out: rdn fnl f: hdd and outpcd last 50yds* **6/1**[3]
00-0 **3** nk **Langley Vale**[37] 658 5-9-6 **74**..... SebSanders 6 79
(Roger Teal) *trckd ldr: shkn up 2f out: rdn to chal fnl f: styd on same pce last 100yds* **8/1**
3310 **4** hd **Temple Road (IRE)**[7] 1041 6-9-6 **74**..... RichardKingscote 1 78
(Milton Bradley) *hld up disputing 6th: prog over 1f out: reminder and styd on ins fnl f: nvr quite rchd ldrs* **5/1**[2]
02- **5** hd **Diamondhead (IRE)**[215] 5798 5-9-4 **72**..... FrederikTylicki 2 75
(Ed de Giles) *trckd ldng pair: rdn 2f out: tried to chal on inner 1f out: one pce after* **7/1**
2113 **6** 3 **Volito**[25] 826 8-8-4 **65**..... JackGarritty(7) 8 59
(Anabel K Murphy) *t.k.h: hld up in last pair: pushed along 2f out: kpt on fnl f: nvr involved* **20/1**
30/6 **7** 3 **Tarara**[42] 605 4-9-0 **68**..... FergusSweeney 9 52
(Michael Blanshard) *chsd ldng trio: rdn over 2f out: wknd over 1f out* **66/1**
010- **8** hd **Pettochside**[164] 7264 5-9-7 **75**..... AdamKirby 4 59
(Chris Gordon) *hld up disputing 6th: rdn jst over 2f out: wknd over 1f out* **14/1**
01-0 **9** nk **Blazing Knight (IRE)**[16] 925 4-9-6 **74**..... HayleyTurner 7 57
(Chris Gordon) *hld up in last pair: pushed along and struggling over 2f out: nvr on terms* **33/1**

1m 12.27s (0.37) **Going Correction** +0.05s/f (Slow) **9** Ran SP% **118.0**
Speed ratings (Par 103): **99,98,97,97,97 93,89,88,88**
CSF £8.24 CT £37.53 TOTE £2.60: £1.40, £1.60, £2.50; EX 11.00 Trifecta £61.10.
**Owner** Mrs L N Harmes **Bred** Mrs L N Harmes **Trained** Denmead, Hants
**FOCUS**
A tight sprint and a progressive winner.

## 1145 COMPARE BOOKMAKERS AT BOOKMAKERS.CO.UK H'CAP — 5f 6y(P)
**4:40** (4:40) (Class 4) (0-85,84) 4-Y-O+ **£4,690** (£1,395; £697; £348) **Stalls** High

Form / RPR
5453 **1** **Picansort**[7] 1041 7-9-6 **84**.....(v) ShaneKelly 5 93
(Peter Crate) *trckd ldrs: cl up fr 2f out: rdn to ld 1f out: styd on wl* **3/1**[1]
510- **2** 1 **Go Nani Go**[246] 4675 8-9-3 **81**..... FrederikTylicki 2 86
(Ed de Giles) *slowly away: wl in rr: prog on inner over 1f out: styd on wl to take 2nd nr fin* **14/1**
40-3 **3** 1/2 **Fair Value (IRE)**[48] 532 6-9-6 **84**..... GeorgeBaker 8 88
(Simon Dow) *fast away: led: rdn and hdd 1f out: kpt on same pce* **9/2**[3]
-036 **4** 3/4 **O'Gorman**[17] 909 5-9-3 **81**..... LiamKeniry 4 82
(Gary Brown) *n.m.r sn after s and snatched up: mostly in last tl prog over 1f out: styd on strly towards fin* **10/1**
4-16 **5** hd **Triple Dream**[34] 719 9-9-5 **83**.....(tp) RichardKingscote 1 83
(Milton Bradley) *trckd ldrs: cl up on inner over 1f out: nt qckn sn after: one pce* **16/1**
005- **6** hd **Lady Ibrox**[235] 5057 4-9-4 **82**..... RobertHavlin 9 81
(Alan Brown) *chsd ldr on outer after 1f to over 1f out: edgd lft and one pce* **8/1**
310- **7** nk **Monumental Man**[202] 6189 5-9-3 **81**.....(p) DavidProbert 6 79
(James Unett) *racd wd: in tch: drvn 2f out: kpt on but nvr able to threaten ldrs* **5/1**
32-6 **8** 1 3/4 **Nafa (IRE)**[75] 148 6-9-5 **83**..... AdamKirby 3 75
(Daniel Mark Loughnane) *w.w towards rr: pushed along and limited prog over 1f out: reminders and no hdwy ins fnl f: eased last 75yds* **16/1**
-232 **9** hd **Dangerous Age**[7] 1049 4-9-4 **82**..... HayleyTurner 7 76
(J W Hills) *chsd ldr 1f: lost pl and in midfield by 1/2-way: pushed along and no prog over 1f out: eased ins fnl f* **4/1**[2]
00 **10** 3 **Bainne (IRE)**[7] 1041 4-9-2 **80**..... SteveDrowne 10 61
(Jeremy Gask) *wl in rr fr wd draw: no prog 2f out: wknd over 1f out* **33/1**

58.5s (-0.30) **Going Correction** +0.05s/f (Slow) **10** Ran SP% **121.4**
Speed ratings (Par 105): **104,102,101,100,100 99,99,96,96,91**
CSF £49.78 CT £198.82 TOTE £4.20: £1.60, £5.50, £2.80; EX 53.30 Trifecta £615.90.
**Owner** Peter Crate **Bred** Miss Brooke Sanders **Trained** Newdigate, Surrey
**FOCUS**
A very tight sprint handicap.

## 1146 32RED.COM H'CAP — 6f 1y(P)
**5:15** (5:15) (Class 5) (0-75,73) 3-Y-O **£2,726** (£805; £402) **Stalls** Low

Form / RPR
50-1 **1** **Almargo (IRE)**[16] 923 3-9-6 **72**..... AdamKirby 3 77+
(Mark Johnston) *led to over 4f out: cl up: rdn to ld over 1f out whn veered lft and bmpd rival: hung lft ins fnl f: styd on wl nr fin* **1/1**[1]
60-6 **2** 1 **Minley**[37] 667 3-9-7 **73**..... FrederikTylicki 1 75
(Charlie Fellowes) *in tch: prog to chse ldng pair over 2f out: chal on inner whn bmpd over 1f out: pressed wnr tl no ex last 100yds* **10/1**
55-5 **3** 2 **Inciting Incident (IRE)**[15] 936 3-9-4 **70**.....(b) GeorgeBaker 6 66
(Ed McMahon) *t.k.h: prog to ld over 4f out: hdd and bmpd over 1f out: nt rcvr* **6/1**[3]
0-1 **4** 1 1/4 **Monashka Bay (IRE)**[37] 666 3-8-10 **62**..... DavidProbert 2 54
(Michael Blanshard) *t.k.h: bmpd after 1f and dropped to last pair: effrt on inner over 1f out: no prog fnl f* **16/1**
621- **5** 1/2 **Flashy Queen (IRE)**[125] 8017 3-9-1 **67**..... SteveDrowne 5 57
(Joseph Tuite) *pressed ldr to over 4f out: steadily lost pl fr over 2f out: reminder over 1f out: fdd* **20/1**
-245 **6** 3/4 **National Service (USA)**[10] 1005 3-9-6 **72**..... SeanLevey 4 60
(Stuart Williams) *dwlt: plld v hrd and bmpd rival after 1f: in tch: rdn 2f out: fdd over 1f out* **5/2**[2]
65- **7** 1 1/2 **Robynelle**[206] 6082 3-8-12 **67**..... RobertTart(3) 7 50
(Alan Jarvis) *a in last pair: struggling over 2f out: no prog* **33/1**

1m 11.71s (-0.19) **Going Correction** +0.05s/f (Slow) **7** Ran SP% **115.5**
Speed ratings (Par 98): **103,101,99,97,96 95,93**
CSF £13.02 TOTE £1.70: £1.10, £3.50; EX 14.70 Trifecta £64.40.
**Owner** Sheikh Hamdan bin Mohammed Al Maktoum **Bred** Mountarmstrong Stud **Trained** Middleham Moor, N Yorks
**FOCUS**
A modest sprint handicap for 3-y-os.
T/Plt: £74.10 to a £1 stake. Pool: £69216.13 - 681.32 winning tickets T/Qpdt: £12.10 to a £1 stake. Pool: £5635.61 - 343.73 winning tickets JN

# 1132 WOLVERHAMPTON (A.W) (L-H)
Friday, March 28

**OFFICIAL GOING: Standard**
Wind: Light against Weather: Showers

## 1147 BEST ODDS AT BOOKMAKERS.CO.UK MEDIAN AUCTION MAIDEN STKS — 5f 216y(P)
**5:55** (5:56) (Class 6) 3-5-Y-O **£1,940** (£577; £288; £144) **Stalls** Low

Form / RPR
3- **1** **Dreese (IRE)**[136] 7844 3-9-0 0..... GrahamLee 3 67+
(James Tate) *s.i.s: rn green in rr: hdwy and nt clr run wl over 1f out: shkn up to ld 1f out: r.o: comf* **1/4**[1]
500- **2** 3 3/4 **Baltic Gin (IRE)**[179] 6902 4-9-8 49..... DuranFentiman 7 54
(Malcolm Saunders) *sn chsng ldr: led over 2f out: rdn and hdd 1f out: styd on same pce ins fnl f* **33/1**
6443 **3** 1 1/2 **Parkhill Star**[28] 787 3-8-9 63.....(p) KieranO'Neill 2 45
(Tom Dascombe) *chsd ldrs: rdn over 2f out: styd on same pce fnl f* **4/1**[2]
-4 **4** 4 **Captain T**[50] 500 3-9-0 0..... PaulMulrennan 6 37
(Richard Ford) *sn led: rdn and hdd over 2f out: wknd fnl f* **33/1**
5604 **5** 2 3/4 **Busy Bimbo (IRE)**[42] 610 5-9-5 43.....[1] SladeO'Hara(3) 1 28
(Alan Berry) *chsd ldrs: pushed along over 2f out: wknd over 1f out* **50/1**
**6** 8 **Lucky Clover** 3-8-4 0..... PhilipPrince(5) 4
(Malcolm Saunders) *s.s: outpcd* **16/1**[3]

1m 16.44s (1.44) **Going Correction** +0.125s/f (Slow)
**WFA** 3 from 4yo+ 13lb **6** Ran SP% **113.7**
Speed ratings (Par 101): **95,90,88,82,79 68**
CSF £15.99 TOTE £1.20: £1.10, £9.00; EX 10.40 Trifecta £28.50.
**Owner** Saeed Manana **Bred** W Shaughnessy **Trained** Newmarket, Suffolk
**FOCUS**
A very weak maiden run at a steady pace.

## 1148 COMPARE BOOKMAKERS AT BOOKMAKERS.CO.UK H'CAP — 5f 216y(P)
**6:30** (6:30) (Class 6) (0-60,60) 4-Y-O+ **£2,264** (£673; £336; £168) **Stalls** Low

Form / RPR
0-41 **1** **Cadmium Loch**[13] 973 6-8-11 **55**.....(p) JackDuern(5) 8 63
(Andrew Hollinshead) *hld up: hdwy over 2f out: shkn up to ld ins fnl f: r.o* **7/1**[3]
023- **2** nk **Whipphound**[167] 7197 6-9-7 **60**..... PaulMulrennan 12 67
(Mark Brisbourne) *a.p: shkn up to ld 1f out: sn rdn and hdd: r.o* **8/1**

565 **3** ¾ **Dark Lane**[15] 938 8-9-2 **60** EoinWalsh(5) 11 65
(David Evans) *hld up: hdwy over 1f out: sn rdn: r.o* **7/1**[3]

3003 **4** *nk* **Sewn Up**[15] 938 4-9-2 **55** (p[1]) DanielTudhope 10 59
(Andrew Hollinshead) *hld up: hdwy and hung lft fr over 1f out: nt clr run wl ins fnl f: styd on* **3/1**[1]

4130 **5** ¾ **Consistant**[35] 688 6-9-4 **57** TomEaves 9 61+
(Brian Baugh) *chsd ldrs: pushed along whn hmpd over 1f out: sn lost pl: styd on towards fin* **6/1**[2]

00-5 **6** *nk* **Prigsnov Dancer (IRE)**[11] 996 9-8-10 **56** (p) DavidParkes(7) 6 56
(Deborah Sanderson) *led 1f: w ldr tl led again 1/2-way: rdn and edgd lft over 1f out: sn hdd: styd on same pce* **33/1**

422 **7** *nse* **Diamond Vine (IRE)**[13] 972 6-8-11 **50** (p) GrahamLee 1 50
(Ronald Harris) *prom: pushed along and lost pl after 1f: hdwy over 1f out: r.o* **10/1**

6502 **8** 4 ½ **Novalist**[22] 864 6-8-4 **46** NeilFarley(3) 3 32
(Robin Bastiman) *sn pushed along and prom: lost pl 4f out: n.d after* **16/1**

3245 **9** *23* **Rise To Glory (IRE)**[23] 845 6-9-6 **59** DuranFentiman 4
(Shaun Harris) *s.i.s: rcvrd to ld 5f out: hdd 1/2-way: sn rdn: wknd wl over 1f out* **6/1**[2]

1m 16.46s (1.46) **Going Correction** +0.125s/f (Slow) **9** Ran SP% **107.6**
Speed ratings (Par 101): **95,94,93,93,92 91,91,85,55**
CSF £51.90 CT £302.16 TOTE £5.60: £2.30, £1.90, £2.40; EX 34.60 Trifecta £351.30.
**Owner** M Johnson **Bred** R Hollinshead And M Johnson **Trained** Upper Longdon, Staffs
■ Rule 4 of 10p in the pound applies to all bets; Withdrawn: Louis Vee
■ Stewards' Enquiry : David Parkes two-day ban; careless riding (11th-12th Apr)

**FOCUS**
A competitive if moderate handicap run in a heavy shower. The gallop was sound.

## 1149 32RED THUNDERSTRUCK II SLOT CLASSIFIED STKS 5f 216y(P)
**7:00** (7:00) (Class 5) 3-Y-O **£2,587** (£770; £384; £192) **Stalls** Low

Form RPR

1 **1** **Desert Ranger (IRE)**[32] 731 3-9-0 70 GrahamLee 3 78+
(James Tate) *trckd ldrs: wnt 2nd over 3f out: rdn over 1f out: hung lft and led ins fnl f: r.o* **8/15**[1]

01-0 **2** 1 ½ **Chookie's Lass**[44] 573 3-8-11 66 JasonHart(3) 5 72
(Keith Dalgleish) *led: pushed along over 2f out: sn clr: rdn and hung lft over 1f out: hdd and hmpd ins fnl f: styd on same pce* **25/1**

5-12 **3** *6* **Beautiful Stranger (IRE)**[20] 892 3-9-0 70 (v[1]) TomEaves 2 53
(Keith Dalgleish) *chsd ldrs: rdn over 2f out: wknd over 1f out* **7/1**[3]

30-3 **4** *12* **Sherston**[23] 847 3-9-0 70 JoeFanning 4 23
(Mark Johnston) *sn chsng ldr: pushed along and lost 2nd over 3f out: rdn and wknd 2f out* **11/4**[2]

1m 15.7s (0.70) **Going Correction** +0.125s/f (Slow) **4** Ran SP% **108.2**
Speed ratings (Par 98): **100,98,90,74**
CSF £12.63 TOTE £1.30; EX 7.90 Trifecta £19.50.
**Owner** Sheikh Juma Dalmook Al Maktoum **Bred** Tally-Ho Stud **Trained** Newmarket, Suffolk

**FOCUS**
A decent pace for the paucity of runners. Fair form.

## 1150 32RED IMMORTAL ROMANCE SLOT H'CAP 1m 5f 194y(P)
**7:30** (7:30) (Class 6) (0-60,63) 4-Y-O+ **£2,264** (£673; £336; £168) **Stalls** Low

Form RPR

45-0 **1** **Royal Defence (IRE)**[70] 214 8-8-2 **46** oh1 (t) ConnorBeasley(5) 1 60
(Richard Ford) *chsd ldr tl over 11f out: remained handy: drvn along over 2f out: led wl over 1f out: sn hung lft: styd on wl* **14/1**

-301 **2** 4 ½ **Travel (USA)**[7] 1046 4-9-3 **63** 6ex MichaelJMMurphy(3) 2 71
(Mark Johnston) *sn led: rdn and hdd wl over 1f out: styd on same pce fnl f* **8/13**[1]

11-4 **3** 3 ¾ **Vertueux (FR)**[13] 974 9-9-4 **57** (p) JoeFanning 5 59
(Tony Carroll) *prom: chsd ldr over 11f out: wnt upsides over 8f out tl rdn over 2f out: wknd ins fnl f* **11/4**[2]

/50- **4** *99* **Brabazon (IRE)**[135] 7863 11-9-7 **60** (bt) GrahamGibbons 4
(Emmet Michael Butterly, Ire) *s.s: tk clsr order over 10f out: rdn over 6f out: wknd over 4f out* **5/1**[3]

3m 3.75s (-2.25) **Going Correction** +0.125s/f (Slow)
**WFA** 4 from 7yo+ 4lb **4** Ran SP% **111.9**
Speed ratings (Par 101): **111,108,106,49**
CSF £24.86 TOTE £6.40; EX 37.70 Trifecta £54.00.
**Owner** Winks Racing **Bred** Joseph Rogers **Trained** Garstang, Lancs

**FOCUS**
They came off the final turn three in a line and this modest staying handicap produced a surprise winner.

## 1151 32RED MERMAIDS MILLIONS SLOT H'CAP 2m 119y(P)
**8:00** (8:00) (Class 4) (0-85,76) 4-Y-O+ **£4,851** (£1,443; £721) **Stalls** Low

Form RPR

1331 **1** **Mahadee (IRE)**[6] 1065 9-8-12 **69** JennyPowell(7) 3 78
(Tom Dascombe) *hld up: hdwy to chse ldr 5f out: rdn over 2f out: led over 1f out: edgd lft ins fnl f: styd on wl* **9/4**[2]

2-13 **2** 2 ¼ **Singzak**[29] 758 6-9-12 **76** GrahamGibbons 2 82
(Michael Easterby) *led: rdn and hdd over 1f out: nt clr run ins fnl f: styd on same pce* **1/2**[1]

10/4 **3** *30* **Fade To Grey (IRE)**[17] 915 10-8-7 **57** oh2 (t) ChrisCatlin 1 27
(Shaun Lycett) *chsd ldr: pushed along over 6f out: lost 2nd 5f out: rdn and wknd 3f out* **8/1**[3]

3m 43.11s (1.31) **Going Correction** +0.125s/f (Slow) **3** Ran SP% **108.5**
Speed ratings (Par 105): **101,99,85**
CSF £3.95 TOTE £3.00; EX 3.90 Trifecta £3.10.
**Owner** T Dascombe **Bred** Darley **Trained** Malpas, Cheshire

**FOCUS**
They went a reasonable clip despite the small field. Useful form.

## 1152 LADBROKES H'CAP 7f 32y(P)
**8:30** (8:30) (Class 5) (0-75,75) 4-Y-O+ **£3,234** (£962; £481; £240) **Stalls** High

Form RPR

5-33 **1** **Bogsnog (IRE)**[8] 1031 4-9-6 **74** TomEaves 4 81
(Kristin Stubbs) *mde all: rdn over 1f out: styd on gamely* **7/1**

-066 **2** *nk* **Cape Of Hope (IRE)**[17] 917 4-9-3 **71** DanielTudhope 1 77
(David O'Meara) *a.p: chsd wnr over 2f out: rdn and ev ch ins fnl f: styd on* **5/2**[2]

-111 **3** ½ **Caramack**[48] 540 4-9-2 **75** EoinWalsh(5) 2 80
(Richard Lee) *a.p: rdn over 1f out: styd on* **5/4**[1]

0014 **4** *5* **Dimitar (USA)**[25] 817 5-9-1 **69** StevieDonohoe 5 60
(Johnny Farrelly) *stdd s: in rr: shkn up over 1f out: nvr on terms* **5/1**[3]

600 **5** ½ **Toymaker**[17] 917 7-9-7 **75** PaddyAspell 3 65
(Phil McEntee) *s.i.s: hdwy to chse wnr 6f out tl rdn over 2f out: wknd ins fnl f* **12/1**

1m 28.96s (-0.64) **Going Correction** +0.125s/f (Slow) **5** Ran SP% **109.9**
Speed ratings (Par 103): **108,107,107,101,100**
CSF £24.40 TOTE £10.70: £2.70, £1.80; EX 22.80 Trifecta £55.60.
**Owner** Facts & Figures **Bred** J R Weston **Trained** Norton, N Yorks

**FOCUS**
On the front was the place to be, although and the pace was reasonable enough for this fair handicap.

## 1153 CORAL MOBILE "JUST THREE CLICKS TO BET" MAIDEN STKS 1m 1f 103y(P)
**9:00** (9:01) (Class 5) 3-Y-O+ **£2,911** (£866; £432; £216) **Stalls** Low

Form RPR

2-2 **1** **L'Avenue (IRE)**[74] 167 3-8-4 0 JimmyQuinn 3 70
(James Tate) *s.i.s: sn rcvrd to chse ldr: shkn up over 2f out: rdn to ld and hung lft ins fnl f: r.o* **11/10**[1]

2- **2** 1 ¼ **Passionate Affair (IRE)**[171] 7111 3-8-9 0 (tp) RichardKingscote 5 72
(Tom Dascombe) *sn led: rdn over 1f out: hung lft and hdd ins fnl f: styd on same pce* **3/1**[2]

0-5 **3** *5* **Rookery (IRE)**[7] 1044 3-8-9 0 JoeFanning 4 62
(Mark Johnston) *prom: rdn over 2f out: styd on same pce fr over 1f out* **6/1**

62 **4** *nk* **Moonlit Sky**[10] 1002 3-8-9 0 PaulMulrennan 2 61
(James Tate) *prom: lost pl after 1f: hdwy over 3f out: rdn over 1f out: no ex fnl f* **5/1**[3]

0- **5** *35* **Omotesando**[403] 708 4-10-0 0 GrahamGibbons 1
(Mark Brisbourne) *chsd ldrs: rdn 1/2-way: wknd 3f out* **16/1**

2m 1.55s (-0.15) **Going Correction** +0.125s/f (Slow)
**WFA** 3 from 4yo 19lb **5** Ran SP% **109.5**
Speed ratings (Par 103): **105,103,99,99,68**
CSF £4.55 TOTE £1.70: £1.10, £1.80; EX 4.00 Trifecta £17.60.
**Owner** Saeed Manana **Bred** Carrigdownane Stud **Trained** Newmarket, Suffolk

**FOCUS**
The pace was solid for this ordinary maiden.
T/Plt: £510.00 to a £1 stake. Pool: £78827.03 - 112.82 winning tickets T/Qpdt: £85.20 to a £1 stake. Pool: £6612.29 - 57.40 winning tickets CR

# DONCASTER (L-H)
Saturday, March 29

**OFFICIAL GOING: Soft (6.0)**
Wind: Light half behind Weather: Fine & dry

## 1161 WILLIAM HILL DOWNLOAD THE APP BROCKLESBY CONDITIONS STKS (BOBIS RACE) 5f
**1:30** (1:33) (Class 4) 2-Y-O **£6,469** (£1,925; £962; £481) **Stalls** High

Form RPR

**1** **Cock Of The North** 2-8-10 0 MatthewHopkins(7) 2 87
(Scott Dixon) *towards rr: hdwy on outer and in tch 1/2-way: effrt to chse ldrs 2f out: chal over 1f out: rdn to ld jst ins fnl f: kpt on strly* **14/1**

**2** *3* **Paddy Again (IRE)** 2-8-7 0 RyanWhile(5) 6 71
(Bill Turner) *led: rdn along: edgd rt and hdd over 1f out: rallied u.p ins fnl f: kpt on* **9/1**

**3** 2 ¼ **Flyball** 2-9-3 0 JimmyFortune 8 68
(Richard Hannon) *trckd ldng pair: effrt 2f out: sn rdn and edgd rt over 1f out: kpt on same pce* **6/1**[2]

**4** 1 ½ **Magic Florence (IRE)** 2-8-12 0 GrahamLee 1 58+
(James Given) *cl up: effrt 2f out: rdn to ld briefly over 1f out: hdd jst ins fnl f: sn wknd* **14/1**

**5** 2 ½ **Horsforth** 2-8-12 0 BarryMcHugh 11 49
(Tony Coyle) *chsd ldrs: hdwy 2f out: rdn: green and edgd lft 1 1/2f out: kpt on same pce after* **8/1**[3]

**6** *hd* **Red Connect** 2-9-3 0 WilliamCarson 4 53
(Alan McCabe) *dwlt and in rr: hdwy 1/2-way: rdn wl over 1f out: kpt on appr fnl f: nrst fin* **50/1**

**7** 1 ½ **Escalating** 2-9-3 0 TomQueally 3 47
(Pat Eddery) *in tch: hdwy to trck ldrs 1/2-way: effrt over 2f out: sn rdn and wknd wl over 1f out* **9/2**[1]

**8** *1* **Well Fleeced** 2-9-3 0 DavidProbert 13 44+
(J S Moore) *towards rr: sme hdwy whn sltly hmpd and swtchd lft wl over 1f out: kpt on: n.d* **20/1**

**9** *shd* **Penalty Scorer** 2-8-9 0 BillyCray(3) 14 39
(Richard Guest) *in tch: pushed along 1/2-way: sn rdn and no imp* **66/1**

**10** *hd* **Mountain Man** 2-9-3 0 GrahamGibbons 17 43+
(Michael Easterby) *in tch: rdn along 1/2-way: n.d* **12/1**

**11** ¾ **Cornwallville (IRE)** 2-9-3 0 JohnFahy 15 40
(J S Moore) *a towards rr* **25/1**

**12** *7* **Toytown (IRE)** 2-9-3 0 DaleSwift 5 17
(Derek Shaw) *in tch: pushed along 1/2-way: rdn: green and sltly hmpd whn hung lft 1 1/2f out: sn wknd* **40/1**

**13** ½ **Hoofithully** 2-9-3 0 PaulMulrennan 12 13
(Michael Easterby) *midfield: rdn along and no hdwy whn rn green and hung lft wl over 1f out* **20/1**

**14** *5* **Endislie (IRE)** 2-9-3 0 LiamJones 9
(J S Moore) *dwlt: sn rdn along: a towards rr* **66/1**

**15** 4 ½ **Duquesa Penguin** 2-9-3 0 JoeFanning 19
(Jo Hughes) *s.i.s: a bhd* **8/1**[3]

**16** 2 ½ **Monsieur Jimmy** 2-9-0 0 NeilFarley(3) 10
(Declan Carroll) *a towards rr* **11/1**

**17** 1 ½ **Johnny Sorrento** 2-9-3 0 StevieDonohoe 18
(Tim Pitt) *s.i.s: a bhd* **16/1**

1m 1.84s (1.34) **Going Correction** +0.325s/f (Good) **17** Ran SP% **120.7**
Speed ratings (Par 94): **102,97,93,91,87 86,84,82,82,82 81,70,69,61,54 50,47**
CSF £124.03 TOTE £17.00: £4.90, £2.40, £2.20; EX 126.90 Trifecta £663.90.
**Owner** Amey Cope Dixon Kennerly **Bred** G E Amey **Trained** Babworth, Notts
■ Stewards' Enquiry : Ryan While two-day ban; used whip above permitted level (12th & 14th April)

**FOCUS**
This was the first 2yo race in Great Britain of the year and it paid to race handy. Most jockeys said afterwards that the ground was riding dead. Joe Fanning said it was "terrible ground, really tacky."

## 1162 WILLIAM HILL IN THE APP STORE DONCASTER MILE STKS (LISTED RACE) 1m (S)
**2:05** (2:09) (Class 1) 4-Y-0+ **£21,904** (£8,284; £4,140; £2,068) **Stalls** Low

Form RPR
115- **1** **Graphic (IRE)**[129] 7974 5-9-0 110 ..............................(p) SebSanders 8 113
(William Haggas) *led 2f: led over 3f out: hrd drvn 2f out: hld on towards fin* **7/2**[2]
166- **2** *nk* **Fencing (USA)**[242] 4856 5-9-0 112 ........................ RobertHavlin 6 112
(John Gosden) *t.k.h towards rr: hdwy and 3rd 2f out: edgd lft and styd on to take 2nd towards fin* **11/4**[1]
640- **3** *3/4* **Custom Cut (IRE)**[216] 5794 5-9-0 108 ........................ DanielTudhope 4 111
(David O'Meara) *trckd ldrs: 2nd over 2f out: kpt on same pce fnl 100yds* **9/1**
300- **4** *4* **Guest Of Honour (IRE)**[183] 6797 5-9-0 110 ..................(p) AdamKirby 9 101
(Marco Botti) *hld up in last: effrt over 2f out: kpt on fnl f: nvr a threat* **11/4**[1]
-400 **5** *3 1/2* **Tales Of Grimm (USA)**[37] 679 5-9-0 102 ........................ TonyHamilton 5 93
(Richard Fahey) *hld up in rr: hdwy 3f out: rdn and fdd over 1f out* **12/1**
22-5 **6** *9* **Emell**[31] 749 4-9-0 105 ........................ JimmyFortune 3 73
(Richard Hannon) *trckd ldrs: effrt over 2f out: wknd 2f out* **20/1**
520- **7** *12* **Butterfly McQueen (USA)**[168] 7205 4-8-9 97 ........................ DavidProbert 1 40
(Andrew Balding) *drvn to sn join ldr: led after 2f: hdd over 3f out: edgd rt and lost pl over 2f out: sn bhd* **11/2**[3]

1m 40.12s (0.82) **Going Correction** +0.325s/f (Good) **7 Ran SP% 113.4**
Speed ratings (Par 111): **108,107,106,102,99 90,78**
CSF £13.33 TOTE £3.90: £2.00, £1.90; EX 10.60 Trifecta £69.00.
**Owner** The Royal Ascot Racing Club **Bred** Kevin & Meta Cullen **Trained** Newmarket, Suffolk

**FOCUS**
This Listed event was a fairly tight affair on paper and they went a solid early gallop. The principals dominated from 2f out.

## 1163 WILLIAM HILL - BET ON THE MOVE CAMMIDGE TROPHY (LISTED RACE) 6f
**2:40** (2:40) (Class 1) 3-Y-0+ **£20,982** (£7,955; £3,981; £1,983; £995; £499) **Stalls** High

Form RPR
056- **1** **Dinkum Diamond (IRE)**[140] 7821 6-9-5 100 ........................ OisinMurphy 3 110
(Henry Candy) *prom: cl up over 2f out: rdn and slt ld jst over 1f out: drvn ins fnl f: kpt on wl towards fin* **12/1**
260- **2** *1* **Captain Ramius (IRE)**[224] 5545 8-9-5 105 ........................ PhillipMakin 9 107
(Kevin Ryan) *slt ld: rdn 2f out: hdd jst over 1f out: sn drvn and ev ch tl no ex last 75yds* **12/1**
321- **3** *2 1/4* **Jack Dexter**[140] 7821 5-9-10 114 ........................ GrahamLee 5 105
(Jim Goldie) *trckd ldrs: effrt 2f out: sn rdn and kpt on same pce fnl f* **13/8**[1]
004- **4** *shd* **Jimmy Styles**[168] 7208 10-9-5 103 ..............................(p) AdamKirby 6 99
(Clive Cox) *trckd ldrs: hdwy 2f out: rdn over 1f out and ev ch tl drvn and wknd ins fnl f* **20/1**
054- **5** *1 1/2* **Maureen (IRE)**[183] 6796 4-9-0 107 ........................ KieranO'Neill 10 89
(Richard Hannon) *towards rr: hdwy over 2f out: rdn along wl over 1f out: kpt on fnl f: nrst fin* **9/2**[3]
410- **6** *shd* **Heaven's Guest (IRE)**[161] 7364 4-9-5 104 ........................ TonyHamilton 8 94
(Richard Fahey) *trckd ldrs on outer: effrt over 2f out: sn rdn and edgd lft wl over 1f out: sn btn* **7/1**
101- **7** *7* **Tropics (USA)**[175] 7013 6-9-10 116 ........................ RobertWinston 2 77
(Dean Ivory) *stdd s: t.k.h and hld up towards rr: hdwy and in tch over 2f out: shkn up wl over 1f out: sn btn* **4/1**[2]
020- **8** *4 1/2* **Inxile (IRE)**[210] 5984 9-9-5 100 ..............................(p) AdrianNicholls 1 57
(David Nicholls) *cl up: disp ld 1/2-way: sn rdn and wknd over 2f out* **50/1**
160- **9** *2* **Mass Rally (IRE)**[140] 7821 7-9-5 107 ..............................(b) PaulMulrennan 7 51
(Michael Dods) *dwlt: hld up: a in rr* **20/1**

1m 13.48s (-0.12) **Going Correction** +0.325s/f (Good) **9 Ran SP% 115.6**
Speed ratings (Par 111): **113,111,108,108,106 106,97,91,88**
CSF £139.68 TOTE £13.70: £3.10, £3.50, £1.10; EX 171.90 Trifecta £465.90.
**Owner** Eight Star Syndicate **Bred** Ms H W Topping **Trained** Kingston Warren, Oxon

**FOCUS**
This looked a decent field for a Listed event, but plenty of the fancied horses couldn't get to the leaders. The early gallop appeared strong.

## 1164 WILLIAM HILL SPRING MILE (H'CAP) 1m (S)
**3:15** (3:16) (Class 2) 4-Y-0+ **£28,012** (£8,388; £4,194; £2,097; £1,048; £526) **Stalls** High

Form RPR
200- **1** **Brae Hill (IRE)**[169] 7172 8-9-9 **91** ........................ DavidNolan 15 104
(Richard Fahey) *trckd ldr towards stands' side: led over 2f out: hld on gamely clsng stages* **10/1**
034- **2** *1/2* **Stand My Ground (IRE)**[143] 7775 7-9-8 **90** ........................ DanielTudhope 16 102
(David O'Meara) *hld up towards rr: hdwy and edgd lft over 2f out: chsd wnr over 1f out: no ex clsng stages* **18/1**
400- **3** *2 1/4* **Yourartisonfire**[176] 6988 4-9-1 **83** ........................ PhillipMakin 18 90
(K R Burke) *hld up towards rr: hdwy towards stands' side over 3f out: sn chsng ldrs: 3rd over 1f out: kpt on same pce* **28/1**
025- **4** *3/4* **Farlow (IRE)**[190] 6586 6-9-4 **86** ........................ TonyHamilton 14 91
(Richard Fahey) *hld up towards rr: hdwy towards stands' side over 2f out: styd on fnl f: tk 4th last 75yds* **12/1**
00-3 **5** *2 1/4* **Showboating (IRE)**[25] 832 6-9-6 **88** ..............................(tp) TomQueally 19 88
(Alan McCabe) *prom: drvn over 2f out: one pce* **25/1**
0-20 **6** *2 3/4* **Ansaab**[24] 840 6-9-1 **86** ..............................(t) WilliamTwiston-Davies(3) 4 79
(Alan McCabe) *chsd ldrs towards far side: drvn over 2f out: fdd fnl f* **20/1**
210- **7** *1 3/4* **Silvery Moon (IRE)**[238] 4979 7-9-7 **89** ........................ RobertWinston 22 78
(Tim Easterby) *hld up in rr: hdwy stands' side over 2f out: kpt on same pce appr fnl f* **14/1**
1422 **8** *hd* **Tellovoi (IRE)**[21] 887 6-9-7 **92** ..............................(v) GeorgeChaloner(3) 20 81
(Ann Stokell) *led towards stands' side: hdd over 2f out: fdd appr fnl f* **16/1**
06-0 **9** *shd* **Global Village (IRE)**[21] 887 9-9-10 **92** ..............................(p) DaleSwift 13 81
(Brian Ellison) *mid-div: hdwy over 2f out: kpt on same pce* **14/1**
06-3 **10** *1 3/4* **Dance And Dance (IRE)**[70] 235 8-9-5 **90** ........................ OisinMurphy(3) 9 75
(Ed Vaughan) *mid-div: swtchd rt 5f out: sme hdwy over 2f out: nvr a factor* **6/1**[1]
0060 **11** *3/4* **Naabegha**[26] 820 7-9-2 **84** ........................ WilliamCarson 21 67
(Alan McCabe) *s.i.s: hdwy stands' side over 2f out: nvr nr ldrs* **66/1**
410- **12** *1 1/2* **Dream Walker (FR)**[183] 6801 5-8-9 **84** ........................ MeganCarberry(7) 11 64
(Brian Ellison) *in tch: drvn over 3f out: wknd fnl 2f* **9/1**[3]
00-0 **13** *2* **Born To Surprise**[24] 840 5-9-6 **88** ........................ AmirQuinn 1 63
(Lee Carter) *s.i.s: in rr: hdwy towards far side over 2f out: nvr a factor* **25/1**
-416 **14** *2* **Dixie's Dream (IRE)**[28] 804 5-9-9 **91** ........................ JoeFanning 10 61
(William Jarvis) *in rr: sme hdwy over 2f out: sn wknd* **20/1**
50- **15** *7* **Freewheel (IRE)**[98] 8385 4-9-3 **85** ........................ JimmyFortune 2 39
(David Nicholls) *mid-div: drvn and hdwy towards far side over 3f out: wknd over 1f out* **33/1**
356- **16** *hd* **Boots And Spurs**[161] 7368 5-9-9 **91** ........................ AdamBeschizza 17 45
(Stuart Williams) *chsd ldrs: drvn 3f out: sn lost pl* **11/1**
231- **17** *nk* **Gworn**[162] 7337 4-9-8 **90** ........................ GrahamLee 6 43
(Ed Dunlop) *hld up in mid-div: effrt over 2f out: sn wknd* **8/1**[2]
010- **18** *nk* **Weapon Of Choice (IRE)**[164] 7312 6-9-5 **87** ........................ AdamKirby 7 39
(Stuart Kittow) *chsd ldrs: drvn 3f out: sn wknd* **25/1**
000- **19** *5* **Nameitwhatyoulike**[169] 7172 5-9-5 **87** ........................ PaulMulrennan 12 28
(Michael Easterby) *t.k.h towards rr: bhd fnl 2f* **20/1**
025- **20** *1 1/4* **Amaze**[164] 7312 6-9-2 **84** ........................ BarryMcHugh 8 22
(Brian Ellison) *mid-div: drvn over 4f out: sn wknd* **20/1**
00-4 **21** *4* **Askaud (IRE)**[25] 832 6-9-8 **90** ..............................(p) TomEaves 3 19
(Scott Dixon) *chsd ldrs towards far side: lost pl over 2f out* **50/1**
04-0 **22** *11* **Postscript (IRE)**[21] 887 6-9-7 **89** ........................ FergusSweeney 5
(David Simcock) *chsd ldrs: drvn over 3f out: wknd 2f out: sn eased* **25/1**

1m 40.15s (0.85) **Going Correction** +0.325s/f (Good) **22 Ran SP% 129.3**
Speed ratings (Par 109): **108,107,105,104,102 99,97,97,97,95 94,93,91,89,82 82,81,81,76,75 71,60**
CSF £149.92 CT £4873.02 TOTE £11.10: £2.90, £6.40, £10.40, £2.20; EX 242.30 TRIFECTA Not won..
**Owner** Dr Marwan Koukash **Bred** James Doyle **Trained** Musley Bank, N Yorks

**FOCUS**
A consolation handicap for those not getting a run in the Lincoln, but a valuable race in its own right and it looked most competitive. Predictably they ignored either rail and the main action was more towards the stands' side, with few landing a blow in the final furlong.

## 1165 WILLIAM HILL LINCOLN (HERITAGE H'CAP) 1m (S)
**3:50** (3:51) (Class 2) 4-Y-0+ **£62,250** (£18,640; £9,320; £4,660; £2,330; £1,170) **Stalls** High

Form RPR
0360 **1** **Ocean Tempest**[21] 899 5-9-3 **102** ........................ AdamKirby 3 114
(John Ryan) *in tch on wd outside: hdwy 1/2-way: cl up 3f out: led 2f out: rdn wl over 1f out: edgd rt ent fnl f: sn drvn and kpt on wl towards fin* **20/1**
030- **2** *1 3/4* **Tullius (IRE)**[129] 7974 6-9-7 **109** ........................ OisinMurphy(3) 22 117
(Andrew Balding) *hld up in tch on outer: smooth hdwy over 2f out: ev ch over 1f out: sn rdn: drvn ent fnl f: no ex last 100yds* **7/1**[1]
-000 **3** *1/2* **Robert The Painter (IRE)**[37] 683 6-8-7 **95** ..................[1] JulieBurke(3) 20 102
(David O'Meara) *chsd ldrs: hdwy and cl up over 2f out: rdn along and sltly outpcd 1 1/2f out: n.m.r and swtchd lft ent fnl f: kpt on* **25/1**
-000 **4** *nse* **Sweet Lightning**[37] 681 9-8-13 **98** ..............................(t) DanielTudhope 18 105
(David O'Meara) *hld up towards rr gng wl: hdwy wl over 2f out: rdn wl over 1f out: n.m.r and swtchd lft ent fnl f: sn drvn and one pce* **11/1**
111- **5** *1/2* **Off Art**[280] 3563 4-8-8 **93** ........................ DavidAllan 14 99
(Tim Easterby) *trckd ldrs: hdwy over 2f out: rdn along wl over 1f out: kpt on same pce fnl f* **7/1**[1]
252- **6** *2 1/4* **Gabrial's Kaka (IRE)**[168] 7205 4-8-10 **95** ........................ TonyHamilton 16 95
(Richard Fahey) *prom: cl up 1/2-way: led 3f out: sn rdn and hdd 2f out: drvn and wknd appr fnl f* **8/1**[2]
020- **7** *hd* **Jack's Revenge (IRE)**[161] 7368 6-8-10 **95** ..........(bt) FergusSweeney 11 95
(George Baker) *hld up towards rr: hdwy wl over 2f out: rdn wl over 1f out: styd on fnl f: nrst fin* **16/1**
33-0 **8** *nk* **Tres Coronas (IRE)**[21] 887 7-8-11 **96** ........................ GrahamGibbons 7 95
(David Barron) *hld up in midfield: pushed along over 3f out: rdn wl over 2f out: swtchd lft over 1f out: styd on strly fnl f: nrst fin* **16/1**
0-30 **9** *3/4* **Spa's Dancer (IRE)**[24] 840 7-8-7 **97** ........................ RyanTate(5) 2 95
(James Eustace) *hld up towards rr: hdwy over 2f out: sn rdn: styd on fnl f: nrst fin* **25/1**
110- **10** *1* **Hi There (IRE)**[140] 7823 5-8-10 **98** ........................ GeorgeChaloner(3) 4 93
(Richard Fahey) *towards rr: hdwy wl over 2f out: rdn wl over 1f out: kpt on fnl f: nrst fin* **16/1**
0-01 **11** *5* **Whispering Warrior (IRE)**[21] 887 5-8-11 **96** 6ex ....... RobertWinston 6 80
(David Simcock) *a towards rr* **11/1**
220- **12** *2 1/4* **Balty Boys (IRE)**[161] 7368 5-8-10 **95** ..............................(b) DaleSwift 9 74
(Brian Ellison) *prom: rdn along over 3f out: sn wknd* **25/1**
10-6 **13** *2 1/2* **Consign**[42] 625 4-8-10 **95** ..............................(v) GrahamLee 13 68
(Jeremy Noseda) *s.i.s: a bhd* **10/1**
34-0 **14** *1 3/4* **Unsinkable (IRE)**[28] 804 4-8-7 **95** ..................[1] JasonHart(3) 19 64
(Jonjo O'Neill) *led: rdn along and hdd 3f out: sn wknd* **25/1**
141- **15** *1 1/4* **Levitate**[140] 7820 6-9-0 **106** ..............................(v) JoeDoyle(7) 8 72
(John Quinn) *trckd ldrs: rdn along 3f out: sn wknd* **9/1**[3]
012- **16** *8* **Mezzotint (IRE)**[182] 6840 5-9-0 **99** ........................ PaulMulrennan 1 46
(Stuart Williams) *chsd ldrs: rdn along 3f out: sn wknd* **33/1**
2101 **17** *19* **Chookie Royale**[21] 886 6-9-13 **112** 5ex ..............................(p) TomEaves 12 16
(Keith Dalgleish) *t.k.h: chsd ldrs: rdn along over 3f out: sn wknd* **22/1**

1m 40.17s (0.87) **Going Correction** +0.325s/f (Good) **17 Ran SP% 117.0**
Speed ratings (Par 109): **108,106,105,105,105 102,102,102,101,100 95,93,90,89,87 79,60**
CSF £129.68 CT £3146.82 TOTE £24.10: £5.50, £2.00, £4.90, £3.50; EX 261.60 Trifecta £4953.10 Part won..
**Owner** W McLuskey & C Little **Bred** Old Mill Stud Ltd And Oomswell Ltd **Trained** Newmarket, Suffolk

■ One Word More was withdrawn. Price at time of withdrawal 10/1. Rule 4 applies to all bets - deduct 5p in the pound.

**FOCUS**
The first major turf handicap of the season was predictably a strong-looking field, even following four horses (one of them the ante-post favourite Captain Cat) coming out after being declared due to the ground easing and One Word More being withdrawn to the start for being unruly in the stalls. The field were bunched towards the stands' side early, ignoring the far rail.

## 1166 PARK HILL HOSPITAL MAIDEN STKS 1m 2f 60y
**4:25** (4:26) (Class 5) 3-Y-O **£3,234** (£962; £481; £240) **Stalls** Low

Form RPR
23- **1** **Hymenaios (IRE)**[218] 5698 3-9-5 0 ........................ JimmyFortune 8 89
(Richard Hannon) *s.i.s: sn mid-div: hdwy over 4f out: 2nd over 2f out: led over 1f out: edgd lft: drvn out* **2/1**[1]
3- **2** *1 1/4* **Cape Caster (IRE)**[186] 6733 3-9-2 0 ........................ OisinMurphy(3) 11 86
(Ralph Beckett) *s.i.s: t.k.h in rr: hdwy over 3f out: 3rd 2f out: styd on to take 2nd last 75yds* **3/1**[2]
**3** *1 1/4* **Romsdal** 3-9-5 0 ........................ RobertHavlin 9 83
(John Gosden) *dwlt: sn trcking ldrs: led over 2f out: hdd over 1f out: kpt on same pce* **7/2**[3]

5- **4** *11* **Kisanji**[178] 6953 3-9-2 0 WilliamTwiston-Davies(3) 6 62
(Mick Channon) *chsd ldr: drvn 3f out: wknd over 1f out* **8/1**

54- **5** *3 1/4* **The Kid**[267] 4021 3-9-5 0 StephenCraine 13 56
(Tom Dascombe) *hld up in rr: effrt over 2f out: wknd over 1f out* **14/1**

3-43 **6** *8* **Galaxy (IRE)**[23] 861 3-9-5 70 (b[1]) WilliamCarson 4 41
(Alan McCabe) *t.k.h: led: hdd over 2f out: lost pl over 1f out* **25/1**

00- **7** *4* **Tawan**[162] 7339 3-9-5 0 BarryMcHugh 5 33
(Brian Rothwell) *in rr: nvr on terms* **150/1**

- **8** *2* **Nagambie (IRE)** 3-9-0 0 JoeFanning 1 25
(Mark Johnston) *dwlt: sn chsng ldrs: drvn over 3f out: lost pl over 2f out* **14/1**

**9** *3 1/2* **Inca Drum (USA)** 3-9-5 0 TomQueally 7 23
(Pat Eddery) *s.i.s: in rr: pushed along over 8f out: sme hdwy over 3f out: sn wknd* **20/1**

**10** *16* **Enniscorthy Myles (USA)** 3-9-5 0 StevieDonohoe 3
(Tim Pitt) *chsd ldrs: drvn over 4f out: sn lost pl and bhd* **40/1**

2m 14.49s (5.09) **Going Correction** +0.75s/f (Yiel) **10** Ran SP% **116.7**
Speed ratings (Par 98): **109,108,107,98,95 89,86,84,81,68**
CSF £7.71 TOTE £2.80: £1.30, £2.00, £1.20; EX 9.10 Trifecta £19.30.
**Owner** H H Sheikh Mohammed Bin Khalifa Al Thani **Bred** Michael Lowry **Trained** East Everleigh, Wilts

**FOCUS**
They appeared to go a sound pace in this 3yo maiden and the market leaders fought it out from the two-furlong marker.

## 1167 HARRIET DE-VERE POWELL APPRENTICE H'CAP (DIV I) (ROUND 1 GO RACING IN YORKSHIRE FUTURE STARS SERIES) 1m 2f 60y
**5:00** (5:00) (Class 5) (0-70,70) 4-Y-O+ **£3,234** (£962; £481; £240) **Stalls Low**

Form RPR

5-00 **1** **Magnolia Ridge (IRE)**[45] 582 4-9-4 **67** (p) JacobButterfield 11 75
(Kristin Stubbs) *chsd ldrs: led wl over 1f out: drvn out* **12/1**

0565 **2** *1* **Outlaw Torn (IRE)**[5] 1085 5-8-9 **58** (e) ConnorBeasley 2 64
(Richard Guest) *chsd ldrs on inner: outpcd over 2f out: hdwy over 1f out: styd on to take 2nd ins fnl f* **10/1**

034- **3** *1* **Hector's Chance**[138] 7840 5-9-4 **67** RyanTate 5 71
(Heather Main) *led: hdd over 4f out: kpt on fnl f: tk 3rd nr fin* **9/2[1]**

050- **4** *nk* **King Of The Celts (IRE)**[148] 7656 6-9-2 **70** RachelRichardson(5) 6 74
(Tim Easterby) *chsd ldrs: styd on same pce fnl f* **16/1**

0333 **5** *1* **Raging Bear (USA)**[17] 928 4-9-5 **68** (v) DavidKenny 3 70
(James Evans) *s.v.s: in tch7f out: hdwy over 3f out: styd on same pce fnl f* **10/1**

510/ **6** *2 1/4* **Frontline Phantom (IRE)**[882] 7178 7-8-8 **60** RobJFitzpatrick(3) 8 57
(K R Burke) *chsd ldrs: drvn over 2f out: wknd fnl 75yds* **6/1[2]**

633- **7** *2 3/4* **Henpecked**[187] 6686 4-8-6 **58** KevinStott(3) 7 51
(Alistair Whillans) *hld up in rr: hdwy 3f out: one pce over 1f out* **6/1[2]**

053- **8** *1/2* **Triple Eight (IRE)**[14] 8400 6-9-2 **70** (b) EvaMoscrop(5) 10 62
(Philip Kirby) *s.i.s: gd hdwy on outside over 7f out: led over 4f out: hdd wl over 1f out: wknd and eased ins fnl f* **9/1[3]**

5- **9** *nse* **Cropley (IRE)**[16] 5542 5-9-5 **68** GeorgeDowning 9 60
(Ian Williams) *mid-div: pushed along over 5f out: lost pl over 3f out: styd on ins fnl f* **10/1**

-200 **10** *3* **Pelmanism**[36] 698 7-8-12 **66** (p) MeganCarberry(5) 1 52
(Brian Ellison) *hld up in rr: hdwy over 3f out: sn drvn: wknd over 1f out* **9/1[3]**

0-54 **11** *5* **Docofthebay (IRE)**[18] 911 10-8-13 **65** (b) MatthewHopkins(3) 4 42
(Scott Dixon) *t.k.h towards rr: hdwy on outer over 3f out: chsng ldrs over 2f out: sn wknd* **16/1**

333- **12** *2 3/4* **My Destination (IRE)**[64] 7881 5-8-8 **62** LukeLeadbitter(5) 12 34
(Declan Carroll) *mid-div: drvn over 3f out: sn lost pl and bhd* **14/1**

2m 16.07s (6.67) **Going Correction** +0.75s/f (Yiel) **12** Ran SP% **120.1**
Speed ratings (Par 103): **103,102,101,101,100 98,96,96,96,93 89,87**
CSF £128.38 CT £631.61 TOTE £16.20: £4.10, £3.10, £2.40; EX 165.70 Trifecta £1209.60 Part won..
**Owner** David Grieve **Bred** S Coughlan **Trained** Norton, N Yorks

**FOCUS**
The first division of a mainly modest handicap for apprentice riders, in which the early fractions didn't appear particularly strong.

## 1168 HARRIET DE-VERE POWELL APPRENTICE H'CAP (DIV II)(ROUND 1 GO RACING IN YORKSHIRE FUTURE STARS SERIES) 1m 2f 60y
**5:35** (5:36) (Class 5) (0-70,70) 4-Y-O+ **£3,234** (£962; £481; £240) **Stalls Low**

Form RPR

500- **1** **Memory Cloth**[77] 7131 7-9-2 **70** MeganCarberry(5) 6 82
(Brian Ellison) *trckd ldrs: hdwy and cl up 4f out: chal over 2f out: rdn to ld ent fnl f: kpt on wl towards fin* **3/1[1]**

500- **2** *1 1/4* **Zafranagar (IRE)**[42] 1836 9-9-2 **65** GeorgeDowning 10 75
(Ian Williams) *trckd ldrs: hdwy over 4f out: cl up 3f out: sn led and rdn 2f out: hdd and drvn ent fnl f: sn edgd lft and no ex last 100yds* **3/1[1]**

5062 **3** *4 1/2* **Time Square (FR)**[10] 1012 7-8-4 **58** JackGarritty(5) 2 59
(Tony Carroll) *led: rdn along wl over 3f out: hdd wl over 2f out: drvn and wknd over 1f out* **10/1**

00-5 **4** *1 1/2* **Seaside Rock (IRE)**[45] 582 4-9-3 **66** (b) ConnorBeasley 11 65
(Keith Dalgleish) *in tch: hdwy to track ldrs over 5f out: rdn along 3f out: drvn and no imp fnl 2f* **10/1**

2064 **5** *nse* **Ellaal**[9] 1036 5-8-4 **56** oh1 GemmaTutty(3) 7 55
(Ruth Carr) *trckd ldrs on outer: hdwy 1/2-way: rdn to chse ldrs 3f out: one pce fnl 2f* **28/1**

0052 **6** *3/4* **Thecornishcowboy**[7] 1065 5-9-0 **68** (t) JordonMcMurray(5) 8 65
(John Ryan) *t.k.h: hld up towards rr: hdwy over 3f out: rdn along over 2f out: no imp and eased ins fnl f* **7/1[3]**

100- **7** *3 1/4* **He's No Angel (IRE)**[263] 4150 5-9-5 **68** RyanTate 3 59
(Clive Cox) *prom: cl up 5f out: rdn along over 3f out: drvn and plugged on one pce fr over 2f out* **5/1[2]**

1-36 **8** *1 1/4* **Stun Gun**[31] 750 4-8-6 **58** AdamMcLean(3) 12 47
(Derek Shaw) *a towards rr* **12/1**

030- **9** *12* **City Ground (USA)**[155] 7498 7-8-10 **64** DanielleMooney(5) 4 30
(Michael Easterby) *t.k.h early: a towards rr* **25/1**

4-10 **10** *4 1/2* **Roger Thorpe**[58] 388 5-8-13 **62** JackDuern 9 19
(Deborah Sanderson) *t.k.h in rr whn stmbld after 1f: sme hdwy 1/2-way: sn rdn and nvr a factor* **33/1**

13-5 **11** *8* **Elspeth's Boy (USA)**[51] 498 7-8-13 **67** EvaMoscrop(5) 1 9
(Philip Kirby) *cl up: rdn along over 4f out: wknd over 3f out* **16/1**

50- **12** *19* **Lateral Thinking (IRE)**[107] 8260 4-9-5 **68** DavidKenny 5
(James Evans) *chsd ldrs: rdn along over 4f out: wknd qckly* **33/1**

2m 16.3s (6.90) **Going Correction** +0.75s/f (Yiel) **12** Ran SP% **124.1**
Speed ratings (Par 103): **102,101,97,96,96 95,92,91,82,78 72,57**
CSF £11.33 CT £82.02 TOTE £4.40: £1.60, £1.80, £2.70; EX 14.00 Trifecta £184.30.
**Owner** Racing Management & Training Ltd **Bred** Darley **Trained** Norton, N Yorks
■ Stewards' Enquiry : Megan Carberry four-day ban; used whip above permitted level and in the incorrect place (12th,14th-16th Apr)
Jordon McMurray four-day ban; failed to ride out (12th,14th-16th Apr)

**FOCUS**
The second division of the modest apprentice riders' handicap. They went a fair pace and two pulled clear nearing the final furlong.
T/Jkpt: Not won. T/Plt: £71.00 to a £1 stake. Pool: £236904.15 - 2433.90 winning tickets T/Qpdt: £19.30 to a £1 stake. Pool: £16921.80 - 648.62 winning tickets JR

# 1118 KEMPTON (A.W) (R-H)
Saturday, March 29

**OFFICIAL GOING: Standard**
Wind: Strong, behind, becoming moderate last 2 races Weather: Sunny, warm

## 1169 SARA'S SUPER SMASHING GREAT 40TH BIRTHDAY MAIDEN FILLIES' STKS (BOBIS RACE) 5f (P)
**1:50** (1:50) (Class 4) 2-Y-O **£3,881** (£1,155; £577; £288) **Stalls Low**

Form RPR

**1** **Tiggy Wiggy (IRE)** 2-9-0 0 SeanLevey 4 90+
(Richard Hannon) *mde all: easily drew rt away fr 1/2-way: eased last 150yds* **8/13[1]**

**2** *7* **Charlie's Star** 2-9-0 0 ChrisCatlin 5 62
(David Evans) *chsd wnr: easily lft bhd fr 1/2-way: kpt on wl enough* **10/1**

**3** *1/2* **Just Marion (IRE)** 2-8-11 0 DeclanBates(3) 2 60+
(David Evans) *chsd ldng pair: easily lft bhd by wnr fr 1/2-way: kpt on fnl f* **16/1**

**4** *2 3/4* **Low Cut Affair (IRE)** 2-9-0 0 LiamKeniry 6 49
(David Evans) *rn green but chsd ldrs in 5th: wnt 4th jst over 2f out: no hdwy after* **50/1**

**5** *3 1/4* **Beautifull Mind (IRE)** 2-8-9 0 NatashaEaton(5) 8 36
(Alan Bailey) *outpcd in 6th: sme prog on inner 2f out: no hdwy over 1f out: wknd* **8/1[3]**

**6** *2* **Keep 'r Lit** 2-8-9 0 EoinWalsh(5) 3 28
(David Evans) *slowly away: a wl in rr* **25/1**

**7** *1 1/4* **Baileys Pursuit** 2-9-0 0 MartinDwyer 1 23
(Chris Dwyer) *slowly away: outpcd and a wl off the pce* **6/1[2]**

**8** *9* **Ciaras Cookie (IRE)** 2-8-11 0 RossAtkinson(3) 10
(David Evans) *wnt lft s: a wl bhd: rn v wd bnd 2f out: t.o* **25/1**

**9** *1/2* **Powerfulstorm** 2-9-0 0 FrederikTylicki 7
(Ronald Harris) *chsd ldng trio but rn green: wnt wd bnd 2f out and wknd rapidly: t.o* **9/1**

1m 0.22s (-0.28) **Going Correction** -0.125s/f (Stan) **9** Ran SP% **121.9**
Speed ratings (Par 91): **97,85,85,80,75 72,70,55,55**
CSF £8.68 TOTE £1.80: £1.10, £2.70, £2.00; EX 11.40 Trifecta £81.70.
**Owner** Potensis Ltd & Ms Elaine Chivers **Bred** Cbs Bloodstock **Trained** East Everleigh, Wilts

**FOCUS**
The second 2-y-o race of the campaign, for fillies, and it saw an impressive winner.

## 1170 6 PLACES AT AINTREE AT BETVICTOR MAGNOLIA STKS (LISTED RACE) 1m 2f (P)
**2:20** (2:20) (Class 1) 4-Y-O+
**£20,982** (£7,955; £3,981; £1,983; £995; £499) **Stalls Low**

Form RPR

224- **1** **Contributer (IRE)**[281] 3523 4-9-0 101 GeorgeBaker 1 108+
(Ed Dunlop) *trckd ldr: clsd to ld wl over 1f out: rdn and wl in command fnl f* **2/1[1]**

-212 **2** *2* **Modernstone**[35] 716 4-8-9 99 ShaneKelly 6 99
(William Knight) *led at v mod pce: hung lft bnd 6f out: kicked on over 3f out: hdd wl over 1f out and sn dropped to 3rd: kpt on to take 2nd last strides* **7/2[3]**

15-1 **3** *hd* **Squire Osbaldeston (IRE)**[31] 744 4-9-0 90 JamesDoyle 4 104
(Martyn Meade) *hld up in 5th: prog to go 3rd over 2f out: chsd wnr over 1f out: no imp fnl f: lost 2nd last strides* **7/1**

2360 **4** *3 3/4* **Tinshu (IRE)**[7] 1068 8-8-9 94 (p) FrederikTylicki 5 91
(Derek Haydn Jones) *hld up in last: rdn and outpcd over 3f out: no ch after: tk 4th fnl f* **33/1**

066- **5** *1/2* **Trumpet Major (IRE)**[168] 7190 5-9-0 110 SeanLevey 2 95
(Richard Hannon) *trckd ldrs in 4th: rdn and fnd nil 3f out: hung lft bnd 2f out: wl btn after* **9/4[2]**

-335 **6** *3/4* **Energia Davos (BRZ)**[30] 773 6-9-0 102 PaddyAspell 3 94
(Marco Botti) *trckd ldng pair: rdn whn pce lifted over 3f out: sn outpcd and btn* **12/1**

2m 6.89s (-1.11) **Going Correction** -0.125s/f (Stan) **6** Ran SP% **109.5**
Speed ratings (Par 111): **99,97,97,94,93 93**
CSF £8.85 TOTE £3.40: £1.10, £2.30; EX 8.70 Trifecta £25.00.
**Owner** George Bolton **Bred** Petra Bloodstock Agency Ltd **Trained** Newmarket, Suffolk

**FOCUS**
Not the most competitive Listed event.

## 1171 BETVICTOR 6 PLACES GRAND NATIONAL ROSEBERY H'CAP (LONDON MIDDLE DISTANCE SERIES QUALIFIER) 1m 3f (P)
**2:55** (2:55) (Class 2) (0-10£26,012 (£8,388; £4,194; £2,097; £1,048; £526) **Stalls Low**

060- **1** **Salutation (IRE)**[154] 7536 4-8-7 87 MichaelJMMurphy(3) 8 102
(Mark Johnston) *mde all: shkn up and in command 2f out: drew rt away w str wind bhd him fnl f* **15/2**

4512 **2** *6* **Grendisar (IRE)**[15] 956 4-9-5 96 (p) AntonioFresu 3 100
(Marco Botti) *hld up towards rr: rdn and prog over 2f out: styd on u.p to take 2nd last 150yds: no ch w wnr* **8/1**

1410 **3** *nk* **Rebellious Guest**[7] 1068 5-9-10 100 GeorgeBaker 2 104
(George Margarson) *hld up in tch: prog over 2f out gng wl: rdn to chse wnr over 1f out: no imp: lost 2nd last 150yds: kpt on* **7/2[1]**

4201 **4** *1 3/4* **Shavansky**[15] 956 10-8-10 91 ShelleyBirkett(5) 7 92
(Rod Millman) *trckd ldrs in 5th: nvr clrest of runs fr over 2f out: pushed along and kpt on same pce* **16/1**

541- **5** *1/2* **Vital Evidence (USA)**[159] 7431 4-8-13 90 (p) JamesDoyle 4 90
(Sir Michael Stoute) *trckd ldng trio: rdn 3f out: outpcd fr 2f out: kpt on* **5/1[2]**

3-22 **6** *1 1/4* **Aryal**[15] 961 4-8-5 82 (b) MartinDwyer 13 79
(Mark Johnston) *prom: chsd wnr 5f out: drvn wl over 2f out: wknd over 1f out* **14/1**

5406 **7** *nk* **Presburg (IRE)**[15] 956 5-8-3 84 JoeyHaynes(5) 11 81
(Joseph Tuite) *rel to r and lft at least 10 l: ct up in last pair after 3f: rdn over 2f out: kpt on fr over 1f out: no ch* **20/1**

23 **8** *1 ½* **Streets Of Newyork**[17] 930 7-8-1 77 NickyMackay 6 71
(Brian Ellison) *hld up in last pair: rdn and struggling over 3f out: modest late prog* **16/1**

-002 **9** *½* **Uramazin (IRE)**[24] 840 8-9-7 97 LiamKeniry 1 90
(Philip Hide) *hld up towards rr: shkn up on inner over 2f out: no prog and sn btn* **11/1**

123- **10** *¾* **Bishop's Castle (USA)**[202] 6236 5-8-2 78 JimmyQuinn 10 70
(Brian Ellison) *dwlt: hld up in rr: sme prog on outer 4f out: no hdwy over 2f out: fdd* **7/1**[3]

/0-0 **11** *8* **Media Hype**[84] 54 7-9-10 100 BenCurtis 9 77
(K R Burke) *chsd ldrs tl wknd wl over 3f out: t.o* **25/1**

630- **12** *1 ½* **Awake My Soul (IRE)**[140] 7823 5-9-0 93 SamJames(3) 5 68
(David O'Meara) *chsd wnr to 5f out: wknd wl over 2f out: t.o* **14/1**

2m 16.09s (-5.81) **Going Correction** -0.125s/f (Stan) course record
**WFA** 4 from 5yo+ 1lb **12** Ran SP% **116.3**
Speed ratings (Par 109): **116,111,111,110,109 108,108,107,107,106 100,99**
CSF £65.04 CT £248.35 TOTE £8.50: £2.10, £2.30, £1.40; EX 83.40 Trifecta £524.30.
**Owner** Sheikh Hamdan bin Mohammed Al Maktoum **Bred** Foursome Thoroughbreds, Muir & Waldron **Trained** Middleham Moor, N Yorks

■ Stewards' Enquiry : Antonio Fresu three-day ban; used whip without giving horse time to respond (12th, 14th-15th Apr)

**FOCUS**
A competitive running of this well-established handicap.

## 1172 GRAND NATIONAL 6 PLACES AT BETVICTOR.COM H'CAP 6f (P)
**3:30** (3:30) (Class 2) (0-105,105) 4-Y-0+
**£11,827** (£3,541; £1,770; £885; £442; £222) **Stalls** Low

Form RPR
-212 **1** **Trinityelitedotcom (IRE)**[62] 348 4-8-11 95 RichardKingscote 6 106
(Tom Dascombe) *mde all: drew 3 l clr over 1f out w str wind bhd: drvn fnl f: hld on wl* **9/2**[3]

-230 **2** *¾* **Absolutely So (IRE)**[35] 715 4-8-5 **89** MartinDwyer 4 98+
(Andrew Balding) *chsd ldrs: rdn over 2f out: prog to go 2nd 1f out: clsd on wnr but a hld* **4/1**[2]

45-3 **3** *1 ¾* **Hoof It**[35] 713 7-9-7 **105** FrederikTylicki 1 108
(Michael Easterby) *prom: rdn to chse wnr 2f out: no imp and lost 2nd 1f out: kpt on* **7/2**[1]

414- **4** *½* **Annunciation**[215] 5844 4-9-1 **99** SeanLevey 2 100
(Richard Hannon) *in tch: drvn and nt qckn jst over 2f out: kpt on fr over 1f out to take 4th nr fin* **16/1**

313- **5** *hd* **Lancelot Du Lac (ITY)**[101] 8334 4-9-5 **103** GeorgeBaker 5 104+
(Dean Ivory) *stdd s: hld up in midfield: prog 2f out: drvn to dispute 4th 1f out: no ex and pushed along fnl f* **7/2**[1]

000- **6** *3 ¾* **Pearl Ice**[155] 7495 6-8-9 **93** ShaneKelly 3 82
(Charlie Fellowes) *chsd wnr: hrd rdn over 2f out: sn lost 2nd: wknd and hanging fnl f* **16/1**

-612 **7** *2 ¾* **Baddilini**[12] 991 4-8-1 **90** (p) NatashaEaton(5) 12 70
(Alan Bailey) *chsd ldrs: shkn up and easily outpcd fr 2f out: modest 7th over 1f out* **16/1**

1000 **8** *3* **Forest Edge (IRE)**[7] 1066 5-8-13 **100** (b) DeclanBates(3) 7 70
(David Evans) *s.i.s: sn rousted along: nvr on terms* **16/1**

-000 **9** *1 ¼* **Tennessee Wildcat (IRE)**[58] 396 4-9-0 **98** JamesDoyle 10 64
(Robert Cowell) *a wl in rr: no ch fnl 2f* **33/1**

000- **10** *2* **Polski Max**[169] 7171 4-8-8 **92** TedDurcan 8 52
(Richard Fahey) *a wl in rr: no ch fnl 2f* **16/1**

0-00 **11** *3 ¾* **Piscean (USA)**[12] 991 9-8-8 **92** JimmyQuinn 9 40
(Tom Keddy) *hld up in last trio: nvr any prog* **14/1**

-421 **12** *4* **Royal Bajan (USA)**[23] 863 6-8-6 **90** JamesSullivan 11 25
(James Given) *spd fr wd draw on outer: wknd sn after 1/2-way* **33/1**

1m 9.79s (-3.31) **Going Correction** -0.125s/f (Stan) course record **12** Ran SP% **124.6**
Speed ratings (Par 109): **117,116,113,113,112 107,104,100,98,95 90,85**
CSF £24.16 CT £73.26 TOTE £5.20: £1.20, £2.10, £1.60; EX 24.00 Trifecta £137.90.
**Owner** Manor House Racing Club **Bred** Natasha Newsome **Trained** Malpas, Cheshire

**FOCUS**
A decent sprint handicap that broke the previous course record time.

## 1173 BETVICTOR.COM MAIDEN STKS 7f (P)
**4:05** (4:05) (Class 4) 3-Y-0+ **£5,175** (£1,540; £769; £384) **Stalls** Low

Form RPR
62- **1** **Crystal Lake (IRE)**[151] 7602 3-8-13 0 RichardKingscote 4 79
(Ralph Beckett) *trckd ldng pair: shkn up 2f out: clsd to ld 1f out: rdn out and styd on wl* **11/2**

6- **2** *1 ¼* **Zerfaal**[225] 5473 3-8-13 0 NickyMackay 2 76+
(John Gosden) *hld up in last trio: shkn up wl over 2f out: prog wl over 1f out: styd on to take 2nd ins fnl f: unable to chal* **6/5**[1]

6- **3** *1* **Knockroon**[244] 4795 3-8-13 0 LiamKeniry 7 73
(Andrew Balding) *plld hrd early: led 1f: led again over 2f out to 1f out: no ex* **9/2**[3]

05- **4** *1 ¾* **War Spirit**[217] 5744 3-8-13 0 SeanLevey 6 68
(Richard Hannon) *trckd ldng pair: rdn on outer 2f out: nt qckn over 1f out: fdd* **3/1**[2]

0/4- **5** *2 ¼* **Lawmans Thunder**[236] 5069 4-9-9 0 TimClark(5) 5 67
(Ismail Mohammed) *trckd ldrs: cl enough 2f out: shkn up and nt qckn over 1f out: fdd* **33/1**

**6** *2* **More Beau (USA)** 3-8-13 0 PaddyAspell 1 57
(Ed Dunlop) *t.k.h: hld up in last pair: brief effrt on inner 2f out: sn no prog* **25/1**

00- **7** *½* **Company Secretary (USA)**[192] 6513 3-8-13 0 BenCurtis 8 55
(Jo Hughes) *led after 1f to over 2f out: sn wknd* **66/1**

05- **8** *8* **Sweet Cherry (IRE)**[115] 8145 3-8-8 0 JimmyQuinn 3 29
(Jo Hughes) *t.k.h early: hld up in last pair: wknd over 2f out: t.o* **33/1**

1m 24.73s (-1.27) **Going Correction** -0.125s/f (Stan)
**WFA** 3 from 4yo 15lb **8** Ran SP% **115.2**
Speed ratings (Par 105): **102,100,99,97,94 92,92,82**
CSF £12.44 TOTE £4.60: £1.50, £1.10, £1.10; EX 14.40 Trifecta £57.50.
**Owner** The Pickford Hill Partnership **Bred** B Holland, S Hillen & J Cullinan **Trained** Kimpton, Hants

**FOCUS**
A modest maiden.

## 1174 DOWNLOAD THE BETVICTOR APP NOW CONDITIONS STKS 7f (P)
**4:40** (4:42) (Class 4) 4-Y-0+ **£5,175** (£1,540; £769; £384) **Stalls** Low

Form RPR
0045 **1** **Bravo Echo**[8] 1042 8-8-13 90 MichaelJMMurphy(3) 3 98
(Michael Attwater) *mde all: shkn up 2f out: fnd plenty fr over 1f out: edgd rt and hld on wl* **10/1**

1-62 **2** *1 ½* **Hasopop (IRE)**[21] 886 4-9-2 104 (p) JamesDoyle 4 96
(Marco Botti) *trckd wnr: shkn up over 1f out: tried to chal on inner fnl f: wl hld whn short of room nr fin* **10/11**[1]

0006 **3** *1* **Intransigent**[21] 886 5-9-2 100 LiamKeniry 5 91
(Andrew Balding) *stdd s: hld up in 3rd: shkn up and nt qckn over 1f out: kpt on same pce after* **2/1**[2]

461- **4** *2 ¾* **Set The Trend**[196] 6411 8-9-2 101 GeorgeBaker 1 84
(David Dennis) *stdd s: hld up in last: pushed along over 1f out: no prog and wl btn fnl f* **6/1**[3]

1m 24.08s (-1.92) **Going Correction** -0.125s/f (Stan) **4** Ran SP% **109.1**
Speed ratings (Par 105): **105,103,102,99**
CSF £20.17 TOTE £8.90; EX 20.60 Trifecta £54.70.
**Owner** Canisbay Bloodstock **Bred** Juddmonte Farms Ltd **Trained** Epsom, Surrey
■ Stewards' Enquiry : Michael J M Murphy two-day ban; careless riding (12th, 14th Apr)

**FOCUS**
This unsurprisingly proved tactical.

## 1175 BRIAN MATTHEWS 50TH BIRTHDAY H'CAP (QUALIFIER FOR LONDON MIDDLE DISTANCE SERIES FINAL) 1m 3f (P)
**5:15** (5:15) (Class 4) (0-85,83) 4-Y-0+ **£5,175** (£1,540; £769; £384) **Stalls** Low

Form RPR
-124 **1** **Commissar**[14] 977 5-9-4 **80** (t) JamesDoyle 1 87
(Ian Williams) *trckd ldrs: clsd over 2f out towards inner: rdn to ld over 1f out: hld on wl* **7/2**[1]

321- **2** *nk* **Certavi (IRE)**[138] 7840 5-9-4 **80** LiamKeniry 4 86
(Brendan Powell) *t.k.h: hld up in 5th tl prog to trck ldr 7f out: led over 2f out: rdn and hdd over 1f out: kpt on wl but jst hld* **5/1**[3]

0-35 **3** *¾* **Chapter And Verse (IRE)**[49] 533 8-9-7 **83** ShaneKelly 2 88
(Mike Murphy) *dwlt and stdd s: hld up in last: prog wl over 1f out: threaded through to chse ldng pair ins fnl f: effrt flattened out last 100yds* **8/1**

1300 **4** *½* **Ocean Applause**[31] 744 4-8-12 **75** (t) JimmyQuinn 5 79
(John Ryan) *trckd ldrs: rt there 2f out: drvn and nt qckn over 1f out: styd on ins fnl f* **16/1**

162- **5** *nse* **Noble Protector**[150] 7627 4-9-3 **80** MartinDwyer 3 84
(Stuart Kittow) *hld up in 6th: pushed along over 4f out: no prog u.p 2f out: styd on fnl f* **4/1**[2]

4053 **6** *2 ¾* **First Post (IRE)**[31] 744 7-9-0 **76** RichardKingscote 7 75
(Derek Haydn Jones) *fast away: trckd ldr 4f: cl up whn shkn up over 2f out: nt qckn over 1f out: wknd fnl f* **12/1**

-064 **7** *1 ½* **Karam Albaari (IRE)**[31] 744 6-9-7 **83** FrederikTylicki 8 79
(J R Jenkins) *t.k.h: hld up in 7th: sme prog on inner 2f out: shkn up over 1f out: wknd fnl f* **11/2**

200- **8** *4 ½* **Flashman**[168] 7193 5-9-4 **80** GeorgeBaker 6 68
(Gary Moore) *led: rdn and hdd over 2f out: sn wknd* **11/2**

2m 21.05s (-0.85) **Going Correction** -0.125s/f (Stan)
**WFA** 4 from 5yo+ 1lb **8** Ran SP% **114.3**
Speed ratings (Par 105): **98,97,97,96,96 94,93,90**
CSF £21.17 CT £129.14 TOTE £3.30: £1.20, £2.40, £2.50; EX 20.00 Trifecta £146.00.
**Owner** S Hassiakos **Bred** R A Instone **Trained** Portway, Worcs

**FOCUS**
A decent handicap.
T/Plt: £145.10 to a £1 stake. Pool: £82482.36 - 414.91 winning tickets T/Qpdt: £64.00 to a £1 stake. Pool: £5797.74 - 67.00 winning tickets JN

# 945 MEYDAN (L-H)
Saturday, March 29

**OFFICIAL GOING: Turf: good; tapeta: standard**

## 1176a GODOLPHIN MILE SPONSORED BY MEYDAN SOBHA (GROUP 2) (TAPETA) 1m
**1:10** (1:10) 3-Y-0+
**£361,445** (£120,481; £60,240; £30,120; £18,072; £12,048)

RPR
**1** **Variety Club (SAF)**[21] 899 6-9-0 120 AntonMarcus 15 117
(J Ramsden, South Africa) *sn led: mde rest: rdn 3f out: r.o wl: comf* **11/2**[3]

**2** *1* **Soft Falling Rain (SAF)**[21] 898 5-9-0 120 PaulHanagan 5 115
(M F De Kock, South Africa) *trckd ldrs: ev ch 1 1/2f out: nt qckn fnl f* **11/4**[1]

**3** *nse* **Flotilla (FR)**[37] 682 4-8-9 111 Christophe-PatriceLemaire 9 110+
(M Delzangles, France) *in rr of mid-div: r.o fnl 2f: nrst fin* **9/1**

**4** *1 ¼* **Gold City (IRE)**[21] 899 5-9-0 109 (bt) RichardMullen 8 112
(S Seemar, UAE) *chsd ldrs: ev ch 2f out: nt qckn fnl f* **33/1**

**5** *shd* **Brightline (JPN)**[34] 5-9-0 110 YuichiFukunaga 14 112
(Ippo Sameshima, Japan) *mid-div: chsd ldrs 2 1/2f out: kpt on same pce fnl 1 1/2f* **16/1**

**6** *nk* **Limario (GER)**[21] 901 4-9-0 110 PatDobbs 16 111
(Doug Watson, UAE) *mid-div: wd: r.o fnl 2f: nrst fin* **40/1**

**7** *¾* **Elleval (IRE)**[21] 901 4-9-0 112 FergalLynch 6 109
(David Marnane, Ire) *nvr bttr than mid-div* **16/1**

**8** *nk* **Shuruq (USA)**[21] 899 4-8-9 115 (p) SilvestreDeSousa 10 104
(Saeed bin Suroor) *in rr of mid-div: nvr able to chal* **3/1**[2]

**9** *nk* **Eastern Rules (IRE)**[21] 899 6-9-0 110 ShaneFoley 4 108
(M Halford, Ire) *nvr bttr than mid-div* **33/1**

**10** *nk* **Haatheq (USA)**[21] 899 7-9-0 113 DaneO'Neill 13 107
(A Al Raihe, UAE) *nvr bttr than mid-div* **20/1**

**11** *1 ½* **Gabrial (IRE)**[21] 899 5-9-0 106 RichardHughes 2 104
(Richard Fahey) *settled in rr: nvr nr to chal* **33/1**

**12** *shd* **Mull Of Killough (IRE)**[140] 7826 8-9-0 115 RyanMoore 11 104
(Jane Chapple-Hyam) *nvr bttr than mid-div* **11/1**

**13** *1* **Glory Awaits (IRE)**[183] 6797 4-9-0 112 (b) JamieSpencer 3 101
(Kevin Ryan) *trckd ldrs tl outpcd 2 1/2f out: wknd fnl f* **25/1**

**14** *2 ½* **Penitent**[147] 7698 8-9-0 113 JosephO'Brien 1 96
(David O'Meara) *nvr bttr than mid-div* **16/1**



The Form Book, Raceform Ltd, Newbury, RG14 5SJ

15 6 1/4 **Capital Attraction (USA)**21 899 7-9-0 113 ............ TadhgO'Shea 12 81
(Ernst Oertel, UAE) *s.i.s: a in rr* **20/1**
1m 37.28s (-0.22) **15** Ran SP% **127.7**
CSF: 20.28; EXACTA: 19.40; TRICAST: 143.68; TRIFECTA: 156.80; WIN: 3.80; PL: 1.80, 1.50, 2.60..
**Owner** Mrs Ingrid Jooste & Markus Jooste **Bred** Beaumont Stud **Trained** South Africa

**FOCUS**
Times showed the Tapeta was riding much faster than at last year's meeting - this was 2.69 seconds quicker than the 2013 running - with heavy rain earlier in the week seemingly having tightened up the surface. Something of a bunch finish.

## 1177a DUBAI GOLD CUP SPONSORED BY AL TAYER MOTORS (GROUP 2) (TURF) 2m
**1:45** (1:45) 3-Y-0+
**£361,445** (£120,481; £60,240; £30,120; £18,072; £12,048)

RPR
1 **Certerach (IRE)**28 811 6-9-0 107 ............ JamieSpencer 14 113
(M Halford, Ire) *settled in rr: smooth prog 3f out: led 1 1/2f out: jst hld on* **33/1**
2 nk **Cavalryman**28 811 8-9-0 115 ............ SilvestreDeSousa 7 114+
(Saeed bin Suroor) *trckd ldrs: n.m.r 2f out: r.o fnl f: jst failed* **7/4**1
3 2 1/4 **Star Empire (SAF)**28 811 8-9-0 111 ............ ChristopheSoumillon 2 111
(M F De Kock, South Africa) *mid-div: r.o fnl 2f: nrst fin* **14/1**
4 1/2 **Moment In Time (IRE)**28 811 5-8-9 108 ............ JimCrowley 4 105
(David Simcock) *in rr of mid-div: smooth prog 3f out: ev ch 2f out: one pce fnl f* **20/1**
5 3/4 **Ralston Road (IRE)**21 900 4-8-8 104 ............ TadhgO'Shea 5 108?
(S Seemar, UAE) *trckd ldrs: led 8f out: rdn 5f out: hdd 1 1/2f out: r.o gamely* **40/1**
6 nk **Dabadiyan (IRE)**21 900 4-8-8 110 ............ ShaneFoley 1 108
(M Halford, Ire) *mid-div: kpt on fnl 2f: nrst fin* **12/1**
7 nk **Songcraft (IRE)**21 900 6-9-0 113 ............(p) MickaelBarzalona 6 108
(Saeed bin Suroor) *trckd ldrs: ev ch 2f out: outpcd fnl f* **12/1**
8 nse **Ernest Hemingway (IRE)**195 6441 5-9-0 116 ............ JosephO'Brien 3 108
(A P O'Brien, Ire) *nvr bttr than mid-div* **7/1**2
9 1/2 **Sheikhzayedroad**21 900 5-9-0 110 ............ MartinLane 13 108
(David Simcock) *settled in rr: nvr nr to chal* **16/1**
10 nk **Seismos (IRE)**34 6-9-0 115 ............ AndreaAtzeni 9 108
(A Wohler, Germany) *settled in rr: nr to chal* **25/1**
11 hd **Joshua Tree (IRE)**21 901 7-9-0 116 ............ RyanMoore 8 107
(Ed Dunlop) *sn led: hdd 9f out: wknd fnl 4f* **9/1**
12 1 **Now We Can**25 837 5-9-0 112 ............ ThierryThulliez 12 106
(N Clement, France) *trckd ldrs: led 9f out: hdd 8f out: wknd fnl 3f* **12/1**
13 1/2 **Saddler's Rock (IRE)**28 811 6-9-0 112 ............ DeclanMcDonogh 11 106
(John M Oxx, Ire) *settled in rr: nvr nr to chal* **25/1**
14 hd **Jamr**13 986 6-9-0 108 ............ AdriedeVries 10 105
(A bin Harmash, UAE) *s.i.s: settled in rr: n.d* **40/1**
15 1/2 **Simenon (IRE)**28 811 7-9-0 113 ............ PatSmullen 15 105
(W P Mullins, Ire) *trckd ldrs tl wknd 2f out* **15/2**3
3m 23.14s (203.14)
**WFA** 4 from 5yo+ 5lb **15** Ran SP% **126.5**
CSF: 89.55; EXACTA: 73.50; TRICAST: 932.14; TRIFECTA: 358.90; WIN: 31.10; PL: 5.90, 1.40, 2.20..
**Owner** Paul Rooney **Bred** Newberry Stud Company **Trained** Doneany, Co Kildare

**FOCUS**
There was no Trakus information, but this was clearly a messy race. Nothing wanted to go on and the early pace was sedate, but things picked up as the lead changed hands down the back. The winner improved for the rise in trip and the second ran to last year's figure in this race.

## 1178a UAE DERBY SPONSORED BY THE SAEED & MOHAMMED AL NABOODAH GROUP (GROUP 2) (TAPETA) 1m 1f 110y
**2:25** (2:25) 3-Y-0
**£722,891** (£240,963; £120,481; £60,240; £36,144; £24,096)

RPR
1 **Toast Of New York (USA)**148 7662 3-8-9 102 ............ JamieSpencer 8 115
(Jamie Osborne) *trckd ldrs: led 2f out: r.o wl: comf* **11/1**3
2 2 1/2 **Asmar (IRE)**21 896 3-8-9 113 ............ RichardHughes 9 110
(Fawzi Abdulla Nass, Bahrain) *s.i.s: chsd ldrs 3f out: r.o fnl 1 1/2f but no ch w wnr* **6/1**2
3 1 1/4 **Emirates Flyer**21 896 3-8-9 104 ............ KierenFallon 6 107
(Saeed bin Suroor) *mid-div: r.o fnl 2f but no ch w first two* **20/1**
4 nse **Giovanni Boldini (USA)**148 7688 3-8-9 115 ............ RyanMoore 5 107
(A P O'Brien, Ire) *settled in rr: nvr nr to chal but r.o fnl 2f: nrst fin* **2/1**1
5 6 1/4 **Cooptado (ARG)**105 4-9-5 113 ............ PatDobbs 3 97
(Doug Watson, UAE) *settled in rr: nvr nr to chal but r.o fnl 2f* **20/1**
6 shd **Long John (AUS)**44 594 4-9-5 115 ............(b) MickaelBarzalona 4 96
(Charlie Appleby) *in rr of mid-div: rdn 3f out: n.d* **2/1**1
7 3/4 **Paximadia (AUS)**44 594 4-9-5 108 ............(tp) SilvestreDeSousa 2 95
(Saeed bin Suroor) *trckd ldrs tl outpcd 2 1/2f out* **16/1**
8 1 **Sir Jack Layden**182 6835 3-8-9 106 ............ FrankieDettori 7 91
(David Brown) *nvr bttr than mid-div* **20/1**
9 3 3/4 **King Rubi**15 3-8-9 100 ............ AntoineHamelin 12 83
(Matthieu Palussiere, France) *trckd ldng pair tl outpcd 2 1/2f out* **40/1**
10 1 1/4 **Safety Check (IRE)**44 594 3-8-9 101 ............ WilliamBuick 1 80+
(Charlie Appleby) *wl away: sn led: kicked clr 4f out: hdd 2f out: sn wknd* **50/1**
11 2 1/4 **Jallota**30 770 3-8-9 100 ............ JimCrowley 11 76
(M F De Kock, South Africa) *s.i.s: nvr nr to chal* **50/1**
12 31 **Sir John Hawkins (USA)**247 4694 3-8-9 104 ............ ColmO'Donoghue 10 12
(A P O'Brien, Ire) *trckd ldrs tl outpcd 2 1/2f out* **14/1**
1m 57.92s (-1.08)
**WFA** 3 from 4yo 19lb **12** Ran SP% **122.5**
CSF: 71.84; EXACTA: 125.80; TRICAST: 1325.62; TRIFECTA: 1232.70; WIN: 12.60; PL: 3.40, 2.30, 4.10..
**Owner** Michael Buckley **Bred** Ashleigh Stud, Frank Ramos & Jackie Ramos **Trained** Upper Lambourn, Berks

**FOCUS**
On a track that was riding much faster than 12 months ago, they went just an ordinary, even pace and it proved hard to make up ground: 26.17 (400m), 24.13 (800m), 24.58 (1200m), 24.66 (1600m). The form fits the race averages.

## 1179a AL QUOZ SPRINT EMPOWERED BY IPIC (GROUP 1) (TURF) 5f
**3:03** (3:03) 3-Y-0+
**£361,445** (£120,481; £60,240; £30,120; £18,072; £12,048)

RPR
1 **Amber Sky (AUS)**62 5-9-0 115 ............(t) JoaoMoreira 8 119
(P F Yiu, Hong Kong) *wl away: sn led: clr 3f out: r.o wl* **5/2**2
2 nk **Ahtoug**21 897 6-9-0 115 ............ MickaelBarzalona 11 118
(Charlie Appleby) *chsd ldrs: ev ch 1 1/2f out: nt qckn ins fnl f* **12/1**
3 hd **Shea Shea (SAF)**21 897 7-9-0 119 ............ ChristopheSoumillon 12 117+
(M F De Kock, South Africa) *settled in rr: smooth prog 2 1/2f out: r.o fnl 2f: nrst fin* **11/10**1
4 1 1/4 **Medicean Man**30 769 8-9-0 112 ............(tp) HarryBentley 4 113
(Jeremy Gask) *broke awkwardly: settled in rr: r.o fnl 2f but nvr able to chal* **16/1**
5 shd **Catcall (FR)**21 897 5-9-0 113 ............ OlivierPeslier 10 112
(P Sogorb, France) *mid-div: r.o same pce fnl 1 1/2f* **14/1**
6 1/2 **Hamza (IRE)**174 7054 5-9-0 108 ............(b) NeilCallan 6 111
(Kevin Ryan) *trckd ldrs tl outpcd 2f out: kpt on same pce fnl 1 1/2f* **28/1**
7 shd **Sole Power**21 897 7-9-0 115 ............ RyanMoore 2 110
(Edward Lynam, Ire) *nvr bttr than mid-div* **7/1**3
8 3/4 **Dux Scholar**21 897 6-9-0 111 ............(b) PatDobbs 9 107
(Doug Watson, UAE) *nvr bttr than mid-div* **25/1**
9 hd **Joy And Fun (NZ)**111 8209 11-9-0 117 ............(p) BrettDoyle 1 107
(D Cruz, Hong Kong) *nvr bttr than mid-div* **33/1**
10 shd **Sholaan (IRE)**22 882 5-9-0 108 ............(b) WilliamBuick 3 106
(D Selvaratnam, UAE) *broke awkwardly: nvr nr to chal* **50/1**
11 nk **Berlino Di Tiger (BRZ)**56 6-9-0 111 ............ LRGoncalves 7 105
(Eduardo Caramori, U.S.A) *trckd ldrs tl outpcd 1 1/2f out* **33/1**
12 2 1/2 **Beat Baby (IRE)**21 897 7-9-0 111 ............(t) Per-AndersGraberg 5 96
(Niels Petersen, Norway) *nvr nr to chal* **66/1**
56.21s (56.21) **12** Ran SP% **125.6**
CSF: 32.43; EXACTA: 45.30; TRICAST: 52.49; TRIFECTA: 133.50; WIN: 3.90; PL: 1.60, 2.90, 1.00..
**Owner** Hung Kam Po **Bred** D E & D R Pope Pty Ltd **Trained** Hong Kong

**FOCUS**
The stalls were positioned on the far side, but the field gradually edged over to the stands' rail. The winning time of 56.21 was a new track record, 0.2sec quicker than that recorded by Shea Shea in this race last year. The fourth is a good guide to the form.

## 1180a DUBAI GOLDEN SHAHEEN SPONSORED BY GULF NEWS (GROUP 1) (TAPETA) 6f
**3:41** (3:41) 3-Y-0+
**£722,891** (£240,963; £120,481; £60,240; £36,144; £24,096)

RPR
1 **Sterling City (AUS)**41 6-9-6 116 ............ JoaoMoreira 4 121+
(J Moore, Hong Kong) *trckd ldrs: n.m.r 2 1/2f out: r.o wl fnl f: led 110yds out* **9/4**1
2 3/4 **Rich Tapestry (IRE)**21 898 6-9-6 117 ............(bt) ODoleuze 12 119
(C W Chang, Hong Kong) *trckd ldrs: smooth prog 2 1/2f out: led 1 1/2f out: hdd 110yds out* **7/2**2
3 2 1/4 **United Color (USA)**21 898 5-9-6 110 ............(t) WilliamBuick 7 112
(D Selvaratnam, UAE) *nvr able to chal but r.o fnl 2f* **16/1**
4 1 **Reynaldothewizard (USA)**21 898 8-9-6 116 .........(bt) RichardMullen 5 109
(S Seemar, UAE) *racd in rr: nvr able to chal but r.o fnl 2f: nrst fin* **5/1**3
5 1 1/4 **Nawwaar (USA)**21 898 5-9-6 109 ............ PaulHanagan 3 105
(A Al Raihe, UAE) *nvr able to chal but r.o fnl 2f* **50/1**
6 hd **Zee Bros (USA)**21 897 4-9-6 104 ............(t) FrankieDettori 6 104
(Seth Benzel, U.S.A) *sn led: hdd & wknd 1 1/2f out* **28/1**
7 shd **Russian Soul (IRE)**21 898 6-9-6 112 ............(b) ShaneFoley 9 104
(M Halford, Ire) *s.i.s: n.d* **11/1**
8 3/4 **Balmont Mast (IRE)**21 898 6-9-6 109 ............(p) RyanMoore 2 101
(Edward Lynam, Ire) *nvr bttr than mid-div* **10/1**
9 hd **Complicate (AUS)**21 898 5-9-6 111 ............ SilvestreDeSousa 8 101
(Saeed bin Suroor) *trckd ldrs tl wknd fnl f* **8/1**
10 1/2 **Krypton Factor**21 898 6-9-6 107 ............(v) LukeMorris 1 99
(Fawzi Abdulla Nass, Bahrain) *s.i.s: nvr able to chal* **25/1**
11 3 **Jamesie (IRE)**21 898 6-9-6 109 ............ FergalLynch 10 89
(David Marnane, Ire) *nvr bttr than mid-div* **14/1**
12 3 1/2 **My Catch (IRE)**21 897 3-8-11 102 ............ PatDobbs 11 78
(Doug Watson, UAE) *nvr nr to chal* **40/1**
13 shd **Bello (AUS)**21 898 6-9-6 107 ............(b) MickaelBarzalona 13 78
(Charlie Appleby) *trckd ldrs tl outpcd 2f out* **33/1**
1m 10.88s (-0.72)
**WFA** 3 from 4yo+ 13lb **13** Ran SP% **125.4**
CSF: 9.74; EXACTA: 16.60; TRICAST: 108.28; TRIFECTA: 314.40; WIN: 3.70; PL: 1.50, 2.00, 7.80..
**Owner** Ling Chiu Shing & Gary Ling Kay Wai **Bred** Mr Dpr Esplin **Trained** Hong Kong

**FOCUS**
Each split was inside the Trakus par - 24.42 (24.48), 47.13 (47.44), 1:10.88 (1:11.57) - and again the time was much faster than 12 months ago. A one-two for Hong Kong, but not form to go overboard on as the locals aren't a great bunch. The third and sixth hekp with the standard.

## 1181a DUBAI DUTY FREE SPONSORED BY DUBAI DUTY FREE (GROUP 1) (TURF) 1m 1f
**4:39** (4:39) 3-Y-0+
**£1,807,228** (£602,409; £301,204; £150,602; £90,361; £60,240)

RPR
1 **Just A Way (JPN)**27 5-9-0 123 ............(t) YuichiFukunaga 2 130+
(Naosuke Sugai, Japan) *settled in rr: smooth prog 2 1/2f out: led 1 1/2f out: comf* **3/1**1
2 6 1/4 **Vercingetorix (SAF)**21 902 5-9-0 117 ............ ChristopheSoumillon 11 117+
(M F De Kock, South Africa) *in rr of mid-div: smooth prog 3f out: led 2f out: hdd 1 1/2f out but no ch w wnr* **5/1**3
3 1 3/4 **Dank**147 7708 5-8-9 117 ............ RyanMoore 10 110+
(Sir Michael Stoute) *settled in rr: nvr nr to chal but r.o fnl 2f: nrst fin* **6/1**
4 1 1/4 **Mshawish (USA)**30 772 4-9-0 116 ............ FrankieDettori 1 113+
(M Delzangles, France) *mid-div: kpt on same pce fnl 2f but nvr able to chal* **8/1**

5 *1* **Anaerobio (ARG)**[21] 902 7-9-0 112..............................(t) AntonMarcus 3 110
(M F De Kock, South Africa) *mid-div: kpt on same pce fnl 2f but n.d* **50/1**
6 *4* **Logotype (JPN)**[27] 4-9-0 117.............................. CristianDemuro 12 100
(Tsuyoshi Tanaka, Japan) *mid-div: chsd ldrs 2 1/2f out: one pce fnl f* **16/1**
7 *1* **Tokei Halo (JPN)**[27] 5-9-0 117.............................. YutakaTake 6 98
(Hisashi Shimizu, Japan) *sn led: hdd & wknd 2f out* **16/1**
8 *nk* **Hunter's Light (IRE)**[51] 508 6-9-0 113..............................(v) KierenFallon 13 97
(Saeed bin Suroor) *mid-div: smooth prog 3f out: ev ch 1 1/2f out: wknd fnl f* **33/1**
9 *6 3/4* **Tasaday (USA)**[37] 683 4-8-9 113.............................. SilvestreDeSousa 8 78
(Saeed bin Suroor) *trckd ldrs tl wknd 2f out* **16/1**
10 *3 1/4* **Blazing Speed**[34] 727 5-9-0 118..............................(t) JoaoMoreira 9 76
(A S Cruz, Hong Kong) *trckd ldrs tl outpcd 2f out* **25/1**
11 *3/4* **The Fugue**[111] 8208 5-8-9 123.............................. WilliamBuick 4 70
(John Gosden) *trckd ldrs tl outpcd and wknd 2f out* **7/2[2]**
12 *3/4* **Trade Storm**[21] 902 6-9-0 115.............................. JamieSpencer 7 73
(David Simcock) *s.i.s: settled in rr: nvr nr to chal* **16/1**
13 *1 1/2* **Educate**[21] 901 5-9-0 113.............................. MaximeGuyon 5 70
(Ismail Mohammed) *trckd ldrs tl outpcd and wknd 3f out* **40/1**

1m 45.52s (105.52) **13** Ran SP% **124.0**
CSF: 18.20; EXACTA: 23.10; TRICAST: 89.03; TRIFECTA: 114.80; WIN: 4.30; PL: 1.60, 1.90, 2.10..
**Owner** Akatsuki Yamatoya **Bred** Shadai Corporation Inc **Trained** Japan

**FOCUS**
An incredible performance from a Japanese runner, who lowered the course record. The fifth helps the standard and the winner improved.

## 1182a DUBAI SHEEMA CLASSIC PRESENTED BY LONGINES (GROUP 1) (TURF) 1m 4f 11y

**5:17** (5:17) 3-Y-O+

**£1,807,228** (£602,409; £301,204; £150,602; £90,361; £60,240)

RPR

1 **Gentildonna (JPN)**[41] 5-8-9 117.............................. RyanMoore 12 116+
(Sei Ishizaka, Japan) *in rr of mid-div: smooth prog 3f out: n.m.r 2f out: led ent fnl f: comf* **4/1[2]**
2 *1 1/2* **Cirrus Des Aigles (FR)**[25] 837 8-9-0 123........ ChristopheSoumillon 15 117
(Mme C Barande-Barbe, France) *in rr of mid-div: smooth prog 2 1/2f out: led 1 1/2f out: hdd ent fnl f: no ch w wnr* **9/1**
3 *1/2* **My Ambivalent (IRE)**[202] 6253 5-8-9 108.............................. AndreaAtzeni 7 111
(Roger Varian) *s.i.s: chsd ldrs: led 2f out: hdd 1 1/2f out: kpt on same pce ins fnl f* **50/1**
4 *1/2* **Empoli (GER)**[37] 683 4-8-13 113.............................. AdriedeVries 13 116
(P Schiergen, Germany) *settled in rr: nvr nr to chal but r.o fnl 2f* **25/1**
5 *shd* **Dominant (IRE)**[34] 727 6-9-0 119.............................. JoaoMoreira 14 115
(J Moore, Hong Kong) *settled in rr: last of main gp 3f out: r.o fnl 2f: nrst fin* **12/1**
6 *nk* **Magician (IRE)**[147] 7712 4-8-13 123.............................. JosephO'Brien 4 116
(A P O'Brien, Ire) *settled in rr: nvr nr to chal but r.o fnl 2f* **5/2[1]**
7 *shd* **Meandre (FR)**[21] 900 6-9-0 113.............................. PatDobbs 8 115
(Doug Watson, UAE) *in rr of mid-div: nvr able to chal* **33/1**
8 *shd* **Mount Athos (IRE)**[21] 900 7-9-0 115.............................. KierenFallon 5 114
(Marco Botti) *settled in rr: nvr nr to chal* **16/1**
9 *2 1/4* **Dunaden (FR)**[51] 508 8-9-0 117.............................. JamieSpencer 6 111
(M Delzangles, France) *nvr bttr than mid-div* **16/1**
10 *4* **Denim And Ruby (JPN)**[125] 8033 4-8-8 116.......... SuguruHamanaka 3 100
(Katsuhiko Sumii, Japan) *sn led: hdd & wknd 2f out* **13/2[3]**
11 *3/4* **Excellent Result (IRE)**[21] 900 4-8-13 115............ SilvestreDeSousa 1 104
(Saeed bin Suroor) *trckd ldng trio tl outpcd 2 1/2f out* **12/1**
12 *2* **Twilight Eclipse (USA)**[42] 5-9-0 117..............................(t) JLezcano 11 100
(Thomas Albertrani, U.S.A) *trckd ldrs tl one pce fnl 2 1/2f* **33/1**
13 *dist* **Festive Cheer (FR)**[273] 3849 4-8-13 113.............................. SeamieHeffernan 9
(A P O'Brien, Ire) *trckd ldrs tl outpcd 2 1/2f out* **20/1**
14 *dist* **Dubday**[30] 4-8-13 115.............................. FrankieDettori 10
(Jassim Al Ghazali, Qatar) *settled in rr: virtually p.u 3f out* **25/1**
P **Mars (IRE)**[21] 902 4-8-13 113.............................. RichardHughes 2
(M F De Kock, South Africa) *p.u after 2f: collapsed fatally* **25/1**

2m 27.25s (147.25)
**WFA** 4 from 5yo+ 2lb **15** Ran SP% **123.2**
CSF: 37.11; EXACTA: 38.20; TRICAST: 1604.06; TRIFECTA: 1965.30; WIN: 4.30; PL: 1.80, 3.50, 17.30..
**Owner** Sunday Racing Co Ltd **Bred** Northern Racing **Trained** Japan

**FOCUS**
The splits were as follows: 27.30 (400m), 50.87 (800m), 1:14.74 (1200m), 1:39.04 (1600m), 2:03.32 (2000m) and the winner came home in 23.72. This was a rough race with a bunched finish. Gentildonna is rated to her bset bar one standout run.

## 1183a DUBAI WORLD CUP SPONSORED BY EMIRATES AIRLINE (GROUP 1) (TAPETA) 1m 2f

**6:05** (6:05) 3-Y-O+

**£3,614,457** (£1,204,819; £602,409; £301,204; £180,722; £120,481)

RPR

1 **African Story**[21] 901 7-9-0 119.............................. SilvestreDeSousa 6 124
(Saeed bin Suroor) *trckd ldrs: led 1f out: comf* **12/1**
2 *2 3/4* **Mukhadram**[161] 7367 5-9-0 122.............................. PaulHanagan 13 119+
(William Haggas) *sn led: t.k.h: kicked clr 3 1/2f out: hdd 1f out: r.o but no ch w wnr* **14/1**
3 *4 1/4* **Cat O'Mountain (USA)**[21] 901 4-9-0 113.............. MickaelBarzalona 15 111
(Charlie Appleby) *settled in rr: nvr nr to chal but r.o fnl 2f: nrst fin* **25/1**
4 *3/4* **Side Glance**[21] 901 7-9-0 115.............................. JamieSpencer 9 110
(Andrew Balding) *in rr of mid-div: r.o fnl 2f* **33/1**
5 *shd* **Akeed Mofeed**[34] 727 5-9-0 123.............................. DouglasWhyte 4 109+
(R Gibson, Hong Kong) *mid-div: chsd ldrs 3f out: nt qckn fnl 2f* **8/1[3]**
6 *nse* **Red Cadeaux**[111] 8208 8-9-0 120.............................. GeraldMosse 14 109
(Ed Dunlop) *s.i.s: settled in rr: nvr able to chal but r.o fnl 2f* **16/1**
7 *1 1/4* **Sanshaawes (SAF)**[21] 901 5-9-0 115.............. ChristopheSoumillon 5 107
(M F De Kock, South Africa) *nvr bttr than mid-div* **12/1**
8 *2 1/4* **Vancouverite**[21] 902 4-9-0 116.............................. WilliamBuick 3 102+
(Charlie Appleby) *in rr of mid-div: nvr able to chal* **16/1**
9 *nk* **Prince Bishop (IRE)**[21] 901 7-9-0 117..............................(v) KierenFallon 1 102
(Saeed bin Suroor) *s.i.s: nvr nr to chal* **8/1[3]**
10 *1 1/4* **Military Attack (IRE)**[34] 727 6-9-0 123.............................. JoaoMoreira 8 99+
(J Moore, Hong Kong) *nvr bttr than mid-div* **3/1[1]**
11 *2* **Belshazzar (JPN)**[34] 6-9-0 116................(t) Christophe-PatriceLemaire 2 95+
(Kunihide Matsuda, Japan) *in rr of mid-div: nvr able to chal* **16/1**
12 *1 1/2* **Ron The Greek (USA)**[42] 7-9-0 122..............................(t) JLezcano 16 92+
(N Bachalard, Saudi Arabia) *trckd ldrs tl outpcd 3f out* **25/1**
13 *hd* **Ruler Of The World (IRE)**[161] 7367 4-9-0 122........(p) JosephO'Brien 12 92+
(A P O'Brien, Ire) *trckd ldrs tl wknd 3 1/2f out* **6/1[2]**
14 *1/2* **Hillstar**[161] 7367 4-9-0 118.............................. RyanMoore 7 91+
(Sir Michael Stoute) *a in rr* **14/1**
15 *1 1/2* **Surfer (USA)**[21] 901 5-9-0 113..............................(t) RichardMullen 10 88
(S Seemar, UAE) *mid-div: r.o same pce fnl 2f* **40/1**
16 *2 1/2* **Hokko Tarumae (JPN)**[34] 5-9-0 117.............................. HideakiMiyuki 11 83+
(Katsuichi Nishiura, Japan) *chsd ldrs: rdn 4f out: sn btn* **16/1**

2m 1.61s (121.61) CSF: 179.73; EXACTA: 754.80; TRICAST: 4128.61; TRIFECTA: 12847.60; **16** Ran SP% **126.8** WIN: 13.40; PL: 6.30, 8.30, 11.30. Placepot: £1,053.70 to a £1 stake. Pool: £14,925.53 - 10.34 winning units. Quadpot: £142.00 to a £1 stake. Pool: £1,228.40 - 6.40 winning units. 27 Trifecta £Owner Godolphin Bred.

**FOCUS**
If the rumours are to be believed then this may have been the last Dubai World Cup before they rip up the Tapeta and start again, and it went to a synthetic-track specialist. Typically a few found trouble and several of the beaten runners failed to produce their best. African Story is rated to the best view of his previous form.

# 1072 ROSEHILL
Saturday, March 29

**OFFICIAL GOING: Turf: heavy changing to soft**

## 1186a GEORGE RYDER STKS (GROUP 1) (3YO+) (TURF) 7f 110y

**5:00** (12:00) 3-Y-O+

**£325,268** (£107,526; £53,763; £26,881; £10,752; £5,376)

RPR

1 **Gordon Lord Byron (IRE)**[111] 8210 6-9-4 0.............. CraigAWilliams 5 118
(T Hogan, Ire) *settled in midfield: rdn 2f out: r.o strly ins fnl f and led cl home* **18/1**
2 *hd* **Speediness (AUS)**[14] 981 7-9-4 0..............................(bt) DamienOliver 6 118
(Colin Scott, Australia) *midfield on inner: rdn 2f out: hdwy to chal ent fnl f and sn led: r.o but hdd cl home* **25/1**
3 *3/4* **El Roca (AUS)**[14] 980 4-8-11 0..............................(bt) HughBowman 11 113
(Trent Busuttin & Natalie Young, New Zealand) *led: rdn 2f out: strly pressed ent fnl f and sn hdd: kpt on wl but dropped to 3rd ins fnl 100yds and hld* **6/1[2]**
4 *1/2* **Sacred Falls (NZ)**[14] 981 5-9-4 0..............................(b) ZacPurton 2 114
(Chris Waller, Australia) *midfield in tch on inner: rdn 2f out: kpt on same pce and nvr quite able to chal* **6/1[2]**
5 *1* **Toydini (AUS)**[14] 981 5-9-4 0.............................. BlakeShinn 4 112
(Guy Walter, Australia) *hld up in rr on inner: rdn 2f out: kpt on and tk n.d 5th fnl strides* **20/1**
6 *shd* **Streama (AUS)**[14] 981 6-9-0 0.............................. KerrinMcEvoy 3 108
(Guy Walter, Australia) *prom early: sn midfield in tch: rdn over 2f out: kpt on but nt pce to chal: dropped to 6th fnl strides* **10/1**
7 *1 3/4* **Boban (AUS)**[21] 903 5-9-4 0..............................(t) GlynSchofield 9 107
(Chris Waller, Australia) *t.k.h: hld up in rr: fanned wd into st: rdn over 1f out: r.o ins fnl f and wnt 7th cl home: nvr nrr* **7/1[3]**
8 *1/2* **Ninth Legion (AUS)**[21] 5-9-4 0..............................(bt) JamesMcDonald 7 106
(Michael, Wayne & John Hawkes, Australia) *trckd ldr on outer: rdn to chal 2f out: cl up and ev ch ent fnl f: sn no ex: steadily fdd and dropped to 8th cl home* **40/1**
9 *1/2* **Lidari (FR)**[21] 5-9-4 0.............................. ChadSchofield 10 105
(Peter G Moody, Australia) *restrained and hld up towards rr: rdn over 2f out: kpt on same pce in st and nvr threatened* **50/1**
10 *3/4* **Red Tracer (AUS)**[14] 981 7-9-0 0..............................(b) MichaelRodd 13 99
(Chris Waller, Australia) *midfield in tch on outer: shkn up 2f out: nt qckn and rdn over 1f out: no ex and btn ins fnl f* **27/10[1]**
11 *nk* **Terravista (AUS)**[21] 5-9-4 0.............................. JasonCollett 12 102
(Joseph Pride, Australia) *prom on outer: rdn 2f out: kpt on tl no ex and fdd ins fnl f* **12/1**
12 *2 1/2* **Fat Al (AUS)**[14] 6-9-4 0..............................(b) CraigNewitt 15 96
(Peter G Moody, Australia) *sn midfield on outer: rdn over 2f out: no imp and btn over 1f out* **70/1**
13 *1* **Tres Blue (IRE)**[144] 7761 4-9-3 0.............................. TommyBerry 8 92
(Gai Waterhouse, Australia) *hld up and a in rr: rdn 3f out: no imp and sn btn: nvr a factor* **30/1**
14 *3/4* **My Kingdom Of Fife**[14] 981 9-9-4 0.............................. NashRawiller 14 92
(Chris Waller, Australia) *stdd fr wd draw and hld up towards rr: fanned wd and rdn on turn into st: sn no imp and btn: nvr a factor* **30/1**
15 *2* **Eurozone (AUS)**[14] 980 4-8-11 0..............................(b[1]) JimCassidy 1 84
(Bart & James Cummings, Australia) *prom on inner: rdn over 2f out: no ex and btn over 1f out: wknd: eased and dropped to last towards fin* **11/1**

1m 30.95s (90.95) **15** Ran SP% **119.3**
PARI-MUTUEL (NSW TAB - all including 1 aud stake): WIN 20.40; PLACE 5.00, 6.70, 2.70; DF 286.50; SF 534.70.
**Owner** Morgan J Cahalan **Bred** Roland H Alder **Trained** Nenagh, Co Tipperary

# 1161 DONCASTER (L-H)
Sunday, March 30

**OFFICIAL GOING: Soft (6.4)**
Wind: light 1/2 behind Weather: fine

## 1190 WILLIAM HILL DOWNLOAD THE APP H'CAP (DIV I) 7f

**1:40** (1:44) (Class 4) (0-85,86) 4-Y-O+ **£5,175** (£1,540; £769; £384) **Stalls** High

Form RPR

124- 1 **Manchester**[178] 6976 4-8-9 **72**..............................[1] TonyHamilton 21 90
(Richard Fahey) *hld up stands' side: pushed along over 3f out: hdwy 2f out: swtchd lft and rdn over 1f out: led ins fnl f: kpt on* **7/1[3]**
400- 2 *1 3/4* **Johnny Cavagin**[101] 8350 5-8-10 **73**..............................(t) BarryMcHugh 2 86
(Richard Guest) *t.k.h early: prom far side: hdwy to ld that gp over 2f out: rdn to take overall ld over 1f out: sn edgd rt: hdd ins fnl f: kpt on same pce 1st of 12 in gp* **16/1**
005- 3 *3 1/2* **Trade Secret**[185] 6774 7-8-7 **70**.............................. DuranFentiman 15 74
(Mel Brittain) *prom stands' side: effrt over 2f out: sn rdn and ev ch tl drvn and one pce ent fnl f: 2nd of 7 in gp* **25/1**

341/ **4** 1 1/4 **Compton Park**[119] 7-9-5 **82**..............................(t) DavidAllan 4 83
(Les Eyre) *dwlt and towards rr on far side: hdwy wl over 2f out: sn rdn: styd on fnl f: nrst fin: 2nd of 12 in gp* **25/1**

200- **5** *shd* **Pashan Garh**[131] 7964 5-8-7 **70**..............................[1] JoeFanning 8 71
(Pat Eddery) *cl up far side: led that gp after 2f: hdd over 2f out and sn rdn along: drvn and one pce fr over 1f out: 3rd of 12 in gp* **16/1**

006- **6** 3 1/2 **King Of Eden (IRE)**[170] 7176 8-9-2 **82**.............. JasonHart(3) 18 74
(Eric Alston) *prom stands' side: hdwy to ld that gp and overall ldr over 2f out: sn rdn: hdd over 1f out and sn wknd: 3rd of 7 in gp* **25/1**

05-6 **7** 1/2 **Karaka Jack**[26] 832 7-9-1 **78**.............................. PaddyAspell 9 68
(David Nicholls) *in tch far side: hdwy over 2f out: sn rdn along and no imp: 4th of 12 in gp* **12/1**

126- **8** 1 1/4 **Teetotal (IRE)**[155] 7531 4-8-4 **74**.............................. JoeDoyle(7) 5 61
(Nigel Tinkler) *chsd ldrs far side: rdn along over 2f out: grad wknd: 5th of 12 in gp* **33/1**

040- **9** 2 **Commanche**[89] 8455 5-8-9 **77**.............. ConnorBeasley(5) 16 59
(Chris Dwyer) *in rr stands' side: rdn along over 2f out: sme late hdwy: 4th of 7 in gp* **16/1**

01-0 **10** 1/2 **Mysterial**[19] 909 4-9-0 **77**.............................. DaleSwift 17 58
(Ruth Carr) *chsd ldrs stands' side: rdn along and outpcd over 3f out: kpt on u.p fnl 2f: n.d: 5th of 7 in gp* **20/1**

000- **11** 6 **Mon Brav**[144] 7777 7-8-13 **76**.............................. PaulPickard 12 41
(Brian Ellison) *in rr far side tl sme late hdwy: 6th of 12 in gp* **33/1**

020- **12** 1 1/4 **Act Your Shoe Size**[182] 6875 5-8-13 **76**.............. TomEaves 3 38
(Keith Dalgleish) *a towards rr far side: 7th of 12 in gp* **20/1**

005- **13** 3/4 **Banovallum**[166] 7264 4-8-9 **72**.............................. JamesSullivan 14 32
(Michael Easterby) *a in rr stands' side: 6th of 7 in gp* **20/1**

2451 **14** *nse* **Light From Mars**[4] 1102 9-9-9 **86** 6ex..............(p) LiamJones 20 46
(Ronald Harris) *led stands' side gp and overall ldr: rdn along and hdd over 2f out: wknd wl over 1f out: 7th of 7 in gp* **16/1**

065- **15** *nk* **Fieldgunner Kirkup (GER)**[124] 8053 6-9-3 **80**........ GrahamGibbons 10 39
(David Barron) *chsd ldrs far side: rdn along 3f out: sn wknd: 8th of 12 in gp* **12/1**

000- **16** 3 1/2 **Rocket Ronnie (IRE)**[169] 7211 4-9-4 **81**.............. AdrianNicholls 6 31
(David Nicholls) *a in rr far side: 9th of 12 in gp* **25/1**

0-00 **17** 3/4 **Burning Blaze**[29] 804 4-9-4 **84**.............. OisinMurphy(3) 11 32
(Olly Stevens) *racd towards far side: chsd ldrs: rdn along 1/2-way: sn wknd: 10th of 12 in gp* **5/1[2]**

4016 **18** 5 **The Great Gabrial**[4] 1103 5-8-12 **82**.........(p) NatalieHambling-Yates(7) 1 17
(Alan McCabe) *led far side 2f: prom tl rdn along 3f out and sn wknd: 11th of 12 in gp* **16/1**

0-13 **19** 19 **Compton**[67] 287 5-9-6 **83**..............................(t) GeorgeBaker 13
(Stuart Williams) *a in rr far side: 12th of 12 in gp* **4/1[1]**

1m 28.94s (2.64) **Going Correction** +0.375s/f (Good) **19** Ran SP% **127.7**
Speed ratings (Par 105): **99,97,93,91,91 87,86,85,83,82 75,74,73,73,73 69,68,62,40**
CSF £100.89 CT £2724.46 TOTE £7.10: £1.90, £4.90, £8.50, £6.10; EX 145.70 TRIFECTA Not won..
**Owner** Mr & Mrs G Calder **Bred** Mr & Mrs G Calder **Trained** Musley Bank, N Yorks
■ Stewards' Enquiry : Graham Gibbons caution; failed to obtain best possible placing

**FOCUS**
Although there was no overnight rain there was a heavy due and the going was left as soft all over. This was a wide-open handicap. The field spread across the track, although the far rail was shunned, and the first pair were clear at the finish down the centre.

## 1191 WILLIAM HILL DOWNLOAD THE APP H'CAP (DIV II) 7f
**2:15** (2:17) (Class 4) (0-85,84) 4-Y-0+ **£5,175** (£1,540; £769; £384) **Stalls** High

Form RPR

-121 **1** **Hillbilly Boy (IRE)**[27] 825 4-9-5 **82**.............................. AndreaAtzeni 16 94
(Martin Smith) *mde all: edgd rt fnl f: hld on towards fin* **11/1**

206- **2** 1/2 **Khelman (IRE)**[141] 7824 4-8-6 **72** ow2.............. GeorgeChaloner(3) 11 83
(Richard Fahey) *trckd ldrs: 2nd over 2f out: no ex clsng stages* **8/1**

-244 **3** 1 1/4 **Capaill Liath (IRE)**[44] 602 6-8-10 **78**..............(p) ShaneGray(5) 7 86
(Kevin Ryan) *trckd ldrs: effrt over 2f out: 3rd 1f out: kpt on same pce* **14/1**

4-24 **4** 1/2 **Royal Holiday (IRE)**[58] 408 7-8-8 **71**..............(p) BarryMcHugh 19 77
(Marjorie Fife) *w ldrs stands' side: styd on same pce fnl f* **20/1**

**5** 3/4 **Baraweez (IRE)**[190] 4-9-0 **77**.............................. DaleSwift 20 82
(Brian Ellison) *chsd ldrs stands' side: kpt on same pce over 1f out* **15/2[3]**

330- **6** 1 1/4 **Dubai Dynamo**[163] 7337 9-9-5 **82**.............................. PJMcDonald 3 83+
(Ruth Carr) *mid-div: hdwy 2f out: n.m.r and kpt on ins fnl f* **25/1**

000- **7** *hd* **Victoire De Lyphar (IRE)**[162] 7374 7-8-13 **76**........(e) JamesSullivan 17 77
(Ruth Carr) *mid-div: drvn 3f out: hdwy over 1f out: kpt on ins fnl f* **25/1**

332- **8** 1 3/4 **Millkwood**[145] 7759 4-8-12 **75**..............................(p) GrahamLee 18 71
(John Davies) *in rr stands' side: hdwy over 2f out: nvr nr ldrs* **25/1**

4-34 **9** 3/4 **Regal Dan (IRE)**[19] 917 4-9-7 **84**.............................. TomQueally 2 78
(Charles Hills) *mid-div towards far side: effrt over 2f out: edgd lft over 1f out: edgd rt and wknd fnl 150yds* **5/1[1]**

000- **10** 2 1/2 **Justonefortheroad**[136] 7885 8-9-3 **80**.............. TonyHamilton 14 68
(Richard Fahey) *in rr-div stands' side: effrt over 2f out: nvr a factor* **13/2[2]**

110- **11** 4 1/2 **Baron Run**[178] 6977 4-8-5 **73**.............................. JoeyHaynes(5) 15 49
(K R Burke) *w ldrs: drvn over 3f out: lost pl over 1f out* **20/1**

420- **12** 1 **Shesastar**[170] 7176 6-8-12 **82**.............................. LukeDempsey(7) 6 55
(David Barron) *in rr stands' side: nvr on terms* **20/1**

001- **13** *nse* **Johnno**[165] 7307 5-9-0 **77**.............................. AdrianNicholls 4 50
(David Nicholls) *in rr on outside: nvr a factor* **16/1**

210- **14** 2 1/2 **Just Paul (IRE)**[162] 7374 4-9-0 **77**.............................. RussKennemore 9 44
(Philip Kirby) *in tch: drvn over 3f out: wknd over 2f out* **25/1**

110- **15** 1 1/4 **Evanescent (IRE)**[170] 7176 5-9-3 **83**.............. IanBrennan(3) 5 47
(John Quinn) *mid-div on outer: wknd over 2f out* **14/1**

041- **16** 1 1/4 **Invincible Hero (IRE)**[117] 7632 7-9-1 **81**.............. JasonHart(3) 13 41
(Declan Carroll) *w ldrs: drvn over 3f out: hung rt and wknd 2f out: sn heavily eased* **14/1**

0523 **17** 3/4 **Daring Dragon**[32] 746 4-8-9 **72**..............................(b) LukeMorris 12 30
(Ed Walker) *s.i.s: a in rr* **14/1**

R3R- **R** **Defence Council (IRE)**[181] 6908 6-8-11 **74**.............. DuranFentiman 8
(Mel Brittain) *ref to r: lft at s* **33/1**

1m 28.06s (1.76) **Going Correction** +0.375s/f (Good) **18** Ran SP% **126.4**
Speed ratings (Par 105): **104,103,102,101,100 99,98,96,96,93 88,86,86,84,82 81,80,**
CSF £86.07 CT £1306.81 TOTE £11.40: £2.60, £3.40, £4.20, £5.60; EX 111.70 Trifecta £1537.30.
**Owner** Macguire's Bloodstock Ltd **Bred** Tipper House Stud **Trained** Newmarket, Suffolk

**FOCUS**
This second division of the 7f handicap saw the field race middle-to-stands' side and they went a sound pace, but it favoured those racing handy.

## 1192 JOHN SMITH'S EXTRA SMOOTH MAIDEN STKS 7f
**2:45** (2:49) (Class 5) 3-Y-O **£3,234** (£962; £481; £240) **Stalls** High

Form RPR

**1** **That Is The Spirit** 3-9-5 0.............................. DanielTudhope 13 96+
(David O'Meara) *mde all: shkn up and qcknd clr wl over 1f out: readily* **6/1[3]**

- **2** 1 1/2 **Provident Spirit** 3-9-5 0.............................. WilliamBuick 9 91
(John Gosden) *dwlt sltly s: sn trcking ldrs: hdwy over 2f out: chsd wnr wl over 1f out: sn rdn and no imp fnl f* **4/1[2]**

4- **3** 3 1/2 **Marmoom**[226] 5473 3-9-5 0.............................. DaneO'Neill 1 82+
(Charles Hills) *n.m.r shortly after s and hld up in rr: hdwy on wd outside 2f out: rdn to chse ldng pair over 1f out: sn no imp* **6/5[1]**

0- **4** 5 **Sighora (IRE)**[239] 5003 3-9-0 0.............................. TomQueally 6 64
(Ismail Mohammed) *towards rr: hdwy after 2f and sn in tch: rdn to chse ldrs 2f out: sn one pce* **25/1**

003- **5** 1 **Ravenous**[156] 7500 3-9-5 77.............................. JimCrowley 4 66
(Ralph Beckett) *in tch: gd hdwy on outer over 2f out: sn chsng ldng pair: rdn wl over 1f out and sn one pce* **8/1**

**6** 1 1/4 **Hesketh Bank** 3-9-5 0.............................. LeeTopliss 10 63
(Richard Fahey) *cl up: rdn along wl over 2f out: grad wknd* **50/1**

653- **7** 2 1/2 **Full Day**[165] 7310 3-9-0 72.............................. DaleSwift 2 52
(Brian Ellison) *in rr tl sme late hdwy* **14/1**

40- **8** 2 **Aran Sky (IRE)**[141] 7817 3-9-5 0.............................. PhillipMakin 5 51
(K R Burke) *dwlt and in rr: effrt over 2f out: n.m.r and swtchd lft wl over 1f out: nvr a factor* **33/1**

60- **9** 1 **Orient Sky**[320] 2337 3-9-5 0.............................. GrahamLee 7 49
(Paul Midgley) *chsd ldrs: rdn along wl over 2f out: sn wknd* **100/1**

**10** *nk* **Election Night** 3-9-0 0.............................. DuranFentiman 8 43
(Tim Easterby) *t.k.h: in tch: hdwy 4f out: rdn 3f out and sn wknd* **66/1**

4-4 **11** 4 **Woodbridge**[25] 847 3-9-5 0.............................. TonyHamilton 3 38
(Richard Fahey) *a towards rr* **33/1**

**12** *shd* **To Begin** 3-9-5 0.............................. GrahamGibbons 12 37
(Tim Easterby) *in tch: pushed along over 3f out: sn wknd* **66/1**

420- **13** 16 **Supersta**[159] 7451 3-9-5 74.............................. LukeMorris 11
(Ronald Harris) *uns rdr and loose bef s: t.k.h: cl up: rdn along over 3f out and sn wknd* **16/1**

1m 29.12s (2.82) **Going Correction** +0.375s/f (Good) **13** Ran SP% **119.1**
Speed ratings (Par 98): **98,96,92,86,85 84,81,78,77,77 72,72,54**
CSF £28.95 TOTE £8.80: £2.50, £1.80, £1.10; EX 33.70 Trifecta £108.60.
**Owner** F Gillespie **Bred** Cliveden Stud Ltd **Trained** Nawton, N Yorks

**FOCUS**
The runners favoured the stands' side early on in this 3yo maiden. There was a fair pace on and they got sorted out from the two-furlong pole.

## 1193 WILLIAM HILL BET ON THE MOVE H'CAP 6f
**3:20** (3:23) (Class 3) (0-95,95) 4-Y-O+ **£7,762** (£2,310; £1,154; £577) **Stalls** High

Form RPR

303- **1** **Flyman**[156] 7495 4-9-2 **90**..............................(b) TonyHamilton 1 104
(Richard Fahey) *chsd ldrs far side: led 1f out: drvn out* **7/1[2]**

113- **2** 3/4 **Joey's Destiny (IRE)**[167] 7255 4-8-7 **81** oh1.............. MartinDwyer 7 93+
(George Baker) *mid-div: drvn over 3f out: hdwy over 2f out: edgd rt and n.m.r 1f out: styd on to take 2nd last 50yds* **8/1[3]**

10-0 **3** 2 **Barkston Ash**[19] 909 6-8-4 **81**..............................(p) JasonHart(3) 2 87
(Eric Alston) *led tl over 2f out: led over 1f out: sn hdd: kpt on same pce* **33/1**

06-3 **4** *shd* **Sir Reginald**[86] 38 6-9-4 **92**.............................. BarryMcHugh 16 97+
(Richard Fahey) *s.i.s: hld up in rr towards stands' side: hdwy 2f out: styd on wl ins fnl f* **11/2[1]**

100- **5** 1 1/4 **Hadaj**[178] 6977 5-8-11 **85**.............................. JamesSullivan 17 87
(Ruth Carr) *in tch: hdwy over 2f out: kpt on same pce fnl f* **33/1**

365- **6** *hd* **Baby Strange**[183] 6831 10-8-5 **86**.............. AdamMcLean(7) 5 87
(Derek Shaw) *hld up in mid-div: hdwy and swtchd lft over 1f out: kpt on ins fnl f* **16/1**

00-5 **7** 3/4 **Another Wise Kid (IRE)**[13] 991 6-8-12 **86**.............. GrahamLee 8 85+
(Paul Midgley) *in tch: effrt over 2f out: n.m.r jst ins fnl f: styd on* **14/1**

000- **8** 3/4 **Secret Witness**[155] 7527 8-9-7 **95**..............................(b) LiamJones 10 92
(Ronald Harris) *s.i.s: in rr: sme hdwy over 1f out: nvr a factor* **25/1**

020- **9** 1 1/4 **Kimberella**[191] 6586 4-8-9 **83**.............................. AdrianNicholls 9 76
(David Nicholls) *chsd ldrs: led over 2f out: hdd over 1f out: edgd rt and sn wknd* **11/1**

-050 **10** 2 **Doctor Parkes**[41] 644 8-8-9 **83**.............................. AndreaAtzeni 19 70
(Stuart Williams) *in rr towards stands' side: hdwy over 2f out: kpt on fnl f* **25/1**

021- **11** *hd* **Can You Conga**[225] 5538 4-8-7 **88**.............. DanielleMooney(7) 13 74
(Michael Easterby) *s.i.s: in rr: sme hdwy over 2f out: kpt on steadily fnl f* **16/1**

1-4 **12** 1 1/2 **Bedloe's Island (IRE)**[68] 271 9-8-13 **87**..............(p) TomQueally 18 69
(Alan McCabe) *hld up towards rr towards stands' side: effrt 2f out: nvr a factor* **20/1**

1034 **13** 1/2 **Corporal Maddox**[9] 1042 7-8-13 **87**..............(p) LukeMorris 6 67
(Ronald Harris) *sn chsng ldrs towards far side: rdn and outpcd over 2f out* **16/1**

4213 **14** 2 **Even Stevens**[8] 1066 6-9-3 **91**..............(v) FrederikTylicki 15 65
(Scott Dixon) *chsd ldrs: upsides over 2f out: wknd appr fnl f* **8/1[3]**

001- **15** 1 1/2 **Chooseday (IRE)**[159] 7452 5-8-13 **87**.............. PaulMulrennan 4 57
(Kevin Ryan) *chsd ldrs far side: wknd 2f out* **9/1**

030- **16** 1 1/4 **Chosen Character (IRE)**[141] 7820 6-8-12 **93**........(tp) JennyPowell(7) 20 59
(Tom Dascombe) *racd alone stands' side: mid-div: edgd lft and wknd 2f out* **16/1**

600- **17** *nse* **Lastchancelucas**[160] 7420 4-8-4 **81** oh1.............. NeilFarley(3) 11 47
(Declan Carroll) *mid-div: lost pl over 2f out* **33/1**

0-56 **18** 3/4 **Joe Eile (IRE)**[22] 890 6-9-3 **91**.............................. RobertWinston 14 55
(John Quinn) *mid-div: towards stands' side: sn drvn along: lost pl over 2f out* **9/1**

1m 14.46s (0.86) **Going Correction** +0.375s/f (Good) **18** Ran SP% **129.9**
Speed ratings (Par 107): **109,108,105,105,103 103,102,101,99,96 96,94,94,91,89 87,87,86**
CSF £59.98 CT £1140.45 TOTE £8.40: £2.30, £2.60, £8.60, £1.90; EX 60.10 Trifecta £3200.40 Part won..
**Owner** George Murray **Bred** Coln Valley Stud **Trained** Musley Bank, N Yorks

**FOCUS**
A competitive sprint handicap in which it paid to be handy and was a race where finally those drawn low on the straight track came out on top.

## 1194 WILLIAM HILL NO 1 DOWNLOADED BETTING APP DONCASTER SHIELD (CONDITIONS STKS) 1m 4f
3:55 (3:55) (Class 2) 4-Y-0+ £12,938 (£3,850; £1,924; £962) Stalls Low

Form RPR
502- **1** **Area Fifty One**65 7206 6-9-0 103 JamieSpencer 1 108
(Nicky Henderson) *chsd ldng pair: pushed along 5f out: hdwy 3f out: rdn to chal 2f out: slt ld over 1f out: sn drvn and edgd lft: styd on wl towards fin* **11/4**2
322- **2** 1 3/4 **Gatewood**99 8386 6-9-0 106 WilliamBuick 2 106
(John Gosden) *trckd ldr: led over 7f out: pushed clr wl over 2f out: jnd and rdn 2f out: drvn and hdd over 1f out: n.m.r ent fnl f: sn one pce* **5/6**1
140- **3** 8 **Chancery (USA)**170 7174 6-9-0 98 DanielTudhope 4 93
(David O'Meara) *hld up in rr: rdn along 4f out: nvr a factor* **11/2**3
345- **4** 18 **Romantic Settings**141 7822 4-8-7 92 BarryMcHugh 5 61
(Richard Fahey) *led: hdd over 7f out: rdn along over 3f out: sn one pce* **17/2**

2m 39.22s (4.32) **Going Correction** +0.475s/f (Yiel)
**WFA** 4 from 6yo+ 2lb 4 Ran SP% **107.1**
Speed ratings (Par 109): **104,102,97,85**
CSF £5.45 TOTE £3.80; EX 6.60 Trifecta £11.20.
**Owner** Middleham Park Racing Iii **Bred** Carmel Stud **Trained** Upper Lambourn, Berks
■ Stewards' Enquiry : William Buick caution; careless riding

**FOCUS**
It's a shame that Conduct defected, but this was still a good-quality conditions event. The first pair locked horns from 2f out as they went clear.

## 1195 WEARAHATDAY - BRAIN TUMOUR RESEARCH H'CAP (BOBIS RACE) 1m 2f 60y
4:30 (4:30) (Class 3) (0-95,87) 3-Y-0 £7,762 (£2,310; £1,154; £577) Stalls Low

Form RPR
52-1 **1** **Rudi Five One (FR)**45 600 3-8-12 78 AndreaAtzeni 1 86
(Robert Eddery) *dwlt: hld up in rr: hdwy over 2f out: swtchd ins over 1f out: squeezed through to ld last 150yds: styd on wl* **12/1**
413- **2** 1 **Mr Gallivanter (IRE)**156 7492 3-9-0 80 RobertWinston 2 86
(John Quinn) *chsd ldr: upsides over 7f out: drvn over 3f out: led over 1f out: hdd and no ex ins fnl f* **3/1**2
611- **3** 3/4 **Latenightrequest**163 7336 3-8-12 78 TonyHamilton 6 83
(Richard Fahey) *trckd ldrs: drvn over 3f out: kpt on to take 3rd clsng stages* **6/1**
013- **4** 1 1/4 **Notarised**158 7471 3-8-10 76 JoeFanning 7 78
(Mark Johnston) *led: increased pce over 3f out: hdd over 1f out: kpt on same pce* **9/4**1
211- **5** 1 3/4 **Killing Time (IRE)**150 7640 3-8-13 79 JimCrowley 4 78
(Ralph Beckett) *hld up in rr: hdwy on outside over 3f out: 4th and chsng ldrs over 1f out: fdd jst ins fnl f* **7/2**3
250- **6** 9 **Rising Breeze (FR)**161 7409 3-9-7 87 DanielTudhope 3 69
(K R Burke) *trckd ldrs: effrt 3f out: wknd 2f out* **8/1**

2m 14.55s (5.15) **Going Correction** +0.475s/f (Yiel) 6 Ran SP% **111.1**
Speed ratings (Par 102): **98,97,96,95,94 87**
CSF £46.56 TOTE £6.40: £3.70, £2.10; EX 56.40 Trifecta £246.30.
**Owner** Anderson, Mathews & Kerve **Bred** Mme Catherine Niederhauser **Trained** Newmarket, Suffolk

**FOCUS**
This fair 3yo handicap was another race weakened by a non-runner. It was run at an average pace and saw something of a bunched finish.

## 1196 UNIVERSAL RECYCLING H'CAP 1m 2f 60y
5:00 (5:02) (Class 4) (0-85,85) 4-Y-0+ £5,175 (£1,540; £769; £384) Stalls Low

Form RPR
310- **1** **Dark Ruler (IRE)**138 7849 5-8-12 76 BenCurtis 3 87
(Alan Swinbank) *trckd ldrs on inner: hdwy over 3f out: chal over 2f out: rdn to ld over 1f out: drvn and edgd rt ins fnl f: kpt on wl towards fin* **9/2**2
040- **2** 1 **High Office**142 7805 8-8-8 72 BarryMcHugh 6 81
(Richard Fahey) *hld up towards rr: stdy hdwy on inner over 3f out: chsd ldng pair over 1f out: swtchd rt to outer and chal ent fnl f: sn drvn and ev ch tl no ex last 75yds* **8/1**
012- **3** 1 **Handheld**149 7661 7-8-7 76 (p) ShelleyBirkett(5) 17 83
(Julia Feilden) *sn led: pushed along 4f out: rdn 3f out: drvn and hdd over 1f out: kpt on same pce fnl f* **8/1**
1422 **4** 5 **Mica Mika (IRE)**13 999 6-8-13 77 TonyHamilton 14 75
(Richard Fahey) *trckd ldrs: hdwy 4f out: rdn along wl over 2f out: drvn wl over 1f out and sn one pce* **7/1**3
040- **5** 1 3/4 **Ardmay (IRE)**135 7906 5-9-4 82 GrahamLee 16 76
(Kevin Ryan) *hld up towards rr: hdwy over 3f out: rdn over 2f out: kpt on one pce* **16/1**
160- **6** 2 **Maven**163 7337 6-9-7 85 DuranFentiman 7 76
(Tim Easterby) *hld up in rr: hdwy on inner over 3f out: swtchd rt and rdn 2f out and kpt on: nrst fin* **20/1**
4005 **7** 4 1/2 **Emerald Wilderness (IRE)**25 840 10-8-13 77 (p) FrederikTylicki 4 59
(Mark Rimmer) *trckd ldrs: hdwy 4f out: rdn along 3f out: wknd fnl 2f* **18/1**
100- **8** 1 3/4 **San Cassiano (IRE)**160 7424 7-9-1 79 JamesSullivan 2 58
(Ruth Carr) *trckd ldrs: pushed along on inner over 3f out: sn rdn and grad wknd* **50/1**
26-0 **9** 1/2 **Tight Lipped (IRE)**32 744 5-8-8 77 RyanTate(5) 10 55
(James Eustace) *trckd ldrs: hdwy on outer and cl up 4f out: rdn along 3f out and grad wknd* **10/1**
2-55 **10** 5 **Special Mix**17 940 6-8-7 71 oh5 AndreaAtzeni 12 39
(Martin Smith) *hld up towards rr: sme hdwy on wd outside over 4f out: rdn along over 3f out and sn wknd* **33/1**
100 **11** 1 1/4 **Hill Fort**25 849 4-8-10 74 LukeMorris 9 40
(Ronald Harris) *midfield: rdn along 4f out: sn wknd* **25/1**
330- **12** 3 **War Poet**156 7499 7-8-11 82 MeganCarberry(7) 1 42
(Brian Ellison) *hld up towards rr: pushed along on inner 4f out: rdn over 3f out and sn btn: lame* **7/2**1
536- **13** 2 **Zeus Magic**284 3470 4-8-12 76 PaulPickard 18 32
(Brian Ellison) *rrd s and s.i.s: a bhd* **12/1**
000- **14** 1/2 **Ex Oriente (IRE)**141 7823 5-9-1 79 AdamBeschizza 5 34
(Stuart Williams) *v.s.i.s and a bhd* **33/1**
450- **15** shd **Le Deluge (FR)**170 7188 4-9-1 79 GrahamGibbons 13 34
(Michael Easterby) *trckd ldr: rdn along 4f out: sn wknd* **20/1**
026- **16** 1 1/2 **Hard Core Debt**247 4729 4-8-12 76 TomEaves 11 28
(Brian Ellison) *in tch: hdwy on outer 5f out: rdn along wl over 3f out: sn wknd* **33/1**

2m 12.81s (3.41) **Going Correction** +0.475s/f (Yiel) 16 Ran SP% **127.2**
Speed ratings (Par 105): **105,104,103,99,98 96,92,91,91,87 86,83,82,81,81 80**
CSF £38.83 CT £293.53 TOTE £7.20: £1.70, £2.00, £2.20, £1.90; EX 47.70 Trifecta £436.60.
**Owner** Kenneth Walters **Bred** John Thompson **Trained** Melsonby, N Yorks
■ Stewards' Enquiry : Barry McHugh four-day ban; used whip above permitted level (14th-17th Apr)

**FOCUS**
The principals dominated the latter stages of this modest handicap.

## 1197 CROWNHOTEL-BAWTRY.COM GENTLEMAN AMATEUR RIDERS' H'CAP 1m 4f
5:30 (5:31) (Class 5) (0-70,70) 4-Y-0+ £2,495 (£774; £386; £193) Stalls Low

Form RPR
000- **1** **Arthurs Secret**283 3502 4-11-3 68 MrSWalker 2 78+
(John Quinn) *mid-div: hdwy to trck ldrs over 3f out: 2nd over 1f out: styd on to ld last 100yds: drvn out* **7/4**1
102- **2** 2 **Aficionado**116 3535 4-11-5 70 (p) MrDHDunsdon 9 75
(Keith Dalgleish) *hld up in rr: hdwy over 3f out: 3rd over 1f out: styd on to chse wnr last 75yds* **4/1**2
-403 **3** 2 1/4 **Rockweiller**9 1050 7-10-2 56 oh8 (b) MrGrahamCarson(5) 8 58
(Shaun Harris) *mid-div: hmpd and rdr briefly lost iron after 1f: hdwy 7f out: led over 2f out: sn drvn 3 l clr: hdd and fdd last 100yds* **25/1**
042- **4** 1 3/4 **Choisan (IRE)**14 7778 5-11-2 70 (tp) MrWEasterby(5) 7 69
(Tim Easterby) *towards rr: sn pushed along: swtchd ins and hdwy over 2f out: kpt on one pce* **7/1**3
36-6 **5** 1 1/4 **Father Shine (IRE)**13 14 11-10-2 56 oh7 MrJohnWilley(5) 4 54
(Shaun Harris) *in tch: sn pushed along: chsng ldrs over 4f out: led over 3f out: hdd over 2f out: one pce* **40/1**
-223 **6** hd **Royal Marskell**25 848 5-11-2 65 MrPCollington 12 62
(Alison Hutchinson) *in rr: hdwy over 3f out: sn chsng ldrs: one pce fnl 2f* **15/2**
404- **7** 5 **Cavalieri (IRE)**299 2957 4-10-13 69 PhillipDennis(5) 6 59
(Philip Kirby) *in tch: hdwy to chse ldrs 7f out: wknd over 1f out* **17/2**
6-U0 **8** 5 **Baan (USA)**25 842 11-10-0 56 oh1 MrDeanSmith(7) 11 38
(James Eustace) *in rr: sme hdwy over 3f out: wknd over 2f out* **40/1**
614- **9** 5 **Dynastic**106 8299 5-10-9 65 MrKWood(7) 17 40
(Tony Coyle) *swtchd lft after s: hld up in rr: hdwy on outside over 4f out: wknd over 1f out* **14/1**
102- **10** 3 1/2 **Tinseltown**149 6631 8-10-13 67 MrDLevey(5) 3 36
(Brian Rothwell) *led: hdd over 3f out: lost pl over 2f out* **16/1**
43 **11** 9 **Candesta (USA)**46 581 4-11-0 65 MrRBirkett 5 21
(Julia Feilden) *in rr: sn drvn along: bhd fnl 3f* **20/1**
0 **12** 2 **Longshadow**12 1003 4-10-10 64 MrMichaelJMurphy(3) 13 17
(Jason Ward) *sn chsng ldr: sn drvn along: wknd over 4f out: sn bhd* **33/1**
202/ **13** 2 1/4 **Spruzzo**512 6407 8-10-13 62 MrWHogg 16 12
(Chris Fairhurst) *chsd ldrs: drvn 7f out: outpcd 5f out: lost pl over 3f out: sn bhd* **50/1**

2m 41.2s (6.30) **Going Correction** +0.475s/f (Yiel)
**WFA** 4 from 5yo+ 2lb 13 Ran SP% **122.1**
Speed ratings (Par 103): **98,96,95,94,93 93,89,86,83,80 74,73,71**
CSF £7.71 CT £135.08 TOTE £3.50: £1.80, £2.10, £3.50; EX 13.00 Trifecta £288.70.
**Owner** David Scott and Co (Pattern Makers) Ltd **Bred** Howard Barton Stud **Trained** Settrington, N Yorks
■ Stewards' Enquiry : Mr S Walker two-day ban; used whip above permitted level (18th Apr - 12th May)
Mr P Collington caution; failed to obtain best possible placing

**FOCUS**
A moderate handicap, confined to gentleman amatuer riders, that was run at a solid pace.
T/Plt: £2002.40 to a £1 stake. Pool: £110,795.73 - 40.39 winning units. T/Qpdt: £108.90 to a £1 stake. Pool: 9641.62 - 65.50 winning units. WG

1198 - 1199a (Foreign Racing) - See Raceform Interactive

# LEOPARDSTOWN (L-H)
Sunday, March 30
**OFFICIAL GOING: Soft to heavy**

## 1200a LEOPARDSTOWN 2,000 GUINEAS TRIAL STKS (LISTED RACE) 1m
3:10 (3:11) 3-Y-0 £21,666 (£6,333; £3,000; £1,000)

RPR
**1** **Go For Goal (IRE)**7 1077 3-9-3 94 (b) PatSmullen 9 109
(D K Weld, Ire) *led tl jnd 1/2-way: narrow advantage into st and wnt 1 l clr 1 1/2f out: kpt on wl u.p ins fnl f* **7/1**3
**2** 3/4 **Shining Emerald**155 7548 3-9-3 110 ChrisHayes 5 107
(P D Deegan, Ire) *chsd ldrs: 3rd 1/2-way: rdn 2f out and wnt 2nd u.p 1 1/2f out: pressed wnr ins fnl f: a hld* **5/2**2
**3** 2 1/2 **Ebanoran (IRE)**166 7287 3-9-3 DeclanMcDonogh 10 102+
(John M Oxx, Ire) *w.w in rr: plenty to do 3f out: hdwy into mod 5th over 1f out and clsd u.p into nvr nrr 3rd cl home: nt trble principals* **7/1**3
**4** hd **Davids Park**155 7548 3-9-3 90 FMBerry 1 101
(John Joseph Murphy, Ire) *chsd ldrs: 4th 1/2-way: rdn 2f out and wnt 3rd u.p ins fnl f: no imp on ldrs and denied 3rd cl home* **33/1**
**5** 2 3/4 **Buonarroti (IRE)**155 7528 3-9-3 105 SeamieHeffernan 7 96+
(A P O'Brien, Ire) *chsd ldrs tl pushed along into cl 2nd after 2f: disp 1/2-way: rdn in cl 2nd into st and sn no ex u.p in 3rd: wknd ins fnl f* **9/1**
**6** nk **All Set To Go (IRE)**155 7548 3-9-3 98 GaryCarroll 3 94
(A Oliver, Ire) *hld up towards rr: 8th 1/2-way: rdn into mod 7th ins fnl f and kpt on u.p: nrst fin* **50/1**
**7** 3/4 **Highly Toxic (IRE)**175 7050 3-9-3 DannyGrant 2 92
(Patrick J Flynn, Ire) *on toes befhand: hld up in tch: 6th 1/2-way: pushed along over 3f out and sn no ex u.p: kpt on one pce fnl 2f* **100/1**
**8** 3 1/4 **Indian Maharaja (IRE)**233 5251 3-9-3 99 JosephO'Brien 6 85
(A P O'Brien, Ire) *hld up in tch: 7th 1/2-way: pushed along into st and no imp on ldrs 2f out: kpt on one pce: stiff bhd post r* **11/8**1
**9** 1/2 **Quadrivium (USA)**109 8253 3-9-3 WayneLordan 4 84
(David Wachman, Ire) *chsd ldrs: 5th 1/2-way: pushed along 3f out and no ex into st: dropped towards rr over 1f out and kpt on one pce* **16/1**
**10** 14 **Stirabout (USA)**255 4460 3-9-3 88 KevinManning 8 52
(J S Bolger, Ire) *hld up: racd keenly early: 9th 1/2-way: rdn and no imp fr 3f out: sn dropped to rr: eased fnl f* **25/1**

1m 44.88s (3.68) **Going Correction** +0.625s/f (Yiel) 10 Ran SP% **121.3**
Speed ratings: **106,105,102,102,99 99,98,95,95,81**
CSF £25.51 TOTE £7.90: £2.30, £1.20, £2.10; DF 32.20 Trifecta £176.90.

**Owner** Glen Devlin **Bred** Moyglare Stud Farm Ltd **Trained** The Curragh, Co Kildare
**FOCUS**
This was up to the standard of the habitual trial, even if it were surprising that a horse coming in off a defeat in a handicap off a mark of 90 could score.

## 1201a LEOPARDSTOWN 1,000 GUINEAS TRIAL STKS (GROUP 3) 7f
3:45 (3:46) 3-Y-O £32,500 (£9,500; £4,500; £1,500)

RPR
1 **Bracelet (IRE)**290 3260 3-9-0 97 JosephO'Brien 2 105+
(A P O'Brien, Ire) *hld up in tch: cl 8th 1/2-way: hdwy over 2f out to chal in 2nd 1f out: clsd u.p to ld ins fnl 100yds: kpt on wl* 7/1³
2 1 **Balansiya (IRE)**147 7716 3-9-0 PatSmullen 7 102
(D K Weld, Ire) *chsd ldrs: 4th 1/2-way: tk clsr order gng wl in 3rd into st: led fr under 2f out: rdn ins fnl f and hdd u.p ins fnl 100yds: no ex* 9/10¹
3 ½ **Avenue Gabriel**184 6798 3-9-0 103 ChrisHayes 5 101
(P D Deegan, Ire) *led: narrow advantage 1/2-way: brought wd into st and sn jnd: hdd fr under 2f out: no imp on ldrs u.p in 3rd ins fnl f: kpt on same pce* 5/1²
4 1 **Harry's Princess (IRE)**137 7867 3-9-0 DeclanMcDonogh 1 98
(John M Oxx, Ire) *chsd ldrs: cl 2nd bef 1/2-way: on terms far side into st: sn rdn and no ex u.p in 4th ins fnl f: kpt on same pce* 12/1
5 hd **Queen Of Power (IRE)**298 2999 3-9-0 FergalLynch 4 98
(M D O'Callaghan, Ire) *chsd ldrs: 5th 1/2-way: rdn 2f out and sn swtchd rt: no imp on ldrs u.p ins fnl f: kpt on same pce* 20/1
6 1¼ **Marvellous (IRE)**172 7136 3-9-0 SeamieHeffernan 8 94
(A P O'Brien, Ire) *hld up in tch: 6th 1/2-way: pushed along fr 3f out: no imp and dropped to 8th 2f out: kpt on again ins fnl f* 8/1
7 2 **Remember You (IRE)**190 6622 3-9-0 97 WayneLordan 9 89
(David Wachman, Ire) *chsd ldrs: cl 3rd bef 1/2-way: rdn into st and wknd fr 2f out* 12/1
8 nk **Sparrow (IRE)**166 7285 3-9-0 96 ColmO'Donoghue 6 88
(A P O'Brien, Ire) *w.w: 7th 1/2-way: rdn into st and no imp u.p in 6th ent fnl f: one pce towards fin* 16/1
9 2¼ **Tirghra (IRE)**155 7547 3-9-0 79 KevinManning 3 82
(J S Bolger, Ire) *hld up towards rr: pushed along in rr 1/2-way: no imp into st: kpt on one pce fnl 2f* 50/1

1m 33.7s (5.00) **Going Correction** +0.70s/f (Yiel) 9 Ran SP% 120.9
Speed ratings: **99,97,97,96,95 94,92,91,89**
CSF £14.35 TOTE £6.00: £1.50, £1.02, £1.70; DF 12.40 Trifecta £24.50.
**Owner** Michael Tabor & Derrick Smith & Mrs John Magnier **Bred** Roncon & Chelston **Trained** Ballydoyle, Co Tipperary
**FOCUS**
Probably a decent race.

1202 - 1206a (Foreign Racing) - See Raceform Interactive

# FONTAINEBLEAU
Friday, March 28
**OFFICIAL GOING: Turf: very soft**

## 1207a PRIX COR DE CHASSE (LISTED RACE) (3YO+) (TURF) 5f 110y
2:20 (12:00) 3-Y-O+ £21,666 (£8,666; £6,500; £4,333; £2,166)

RPR
1 **Eton Rifles (IRE)**127 7995 9-9-10 0 IoritzMendizabal 6 112
(Stuart Williams) *pressed ldr on outer: shkn up to ld appr fnl f: drvn out: won a shade cosily* 9/5¹
2 1¼ **Myasun (FR)**24 836 7-9-13 0 GregoryBenoist 1 111
(C Baillet, France) 12/5²
3 snk **Another Party (FR)**15 943 3-8-8 0 UmbertoRispoli 5 100
(Matthieu Palussiere, France) 13/5³
4 3 **Sorry Woman (FR)**132 7941 4-9-3 0 AntoineWerle 2 90
(H-A Pantall, France) 174/10
5 hd **Paiza (IRE)**345 1633 4-9-6 0 FabriceVeron 3 93
(H-A Pantall, France) 93/10
6 5 **Aksil (FR)**24 836 4-9-3 0 StephanePasquier 4 73
(M Boutin, France) 71/10

1m 4.2s (64.20)
**WFA** 3 from 4yo+ 12lb 6 Ran SP% 120.4
WIN (incl. 1 euro stake): 2.80. PLACES: 1.60, 1.80. SF: 7.80.
**Owner** The Eton Riflemen **Bred** Grangecon Stud **Trained** Newmarket, Suffolk

# 1169 KEMPTON (A.W) (R-H)
Monday, March 31
**OFFICIAL GOING: Standard**
Wind: Light, half behind Weather: Cloudy, warm

## 1208 DOWNLOAD THE BETVICTOR APP NOW MAIDEN STKS 1m 2f (P)
2:30 (2:31) (Class 5) 3-Y-O+ £2,587 (£770; £384; £192) Stalls Low

Form RPR
2- 1 **Arab Spring (IRE)**319 2384 4-10-0 0 RyanMoore 3 83+
(Sir Michael Stoute) *trckd ldr: pushed along whn pce qcknd over 2f out: clsd to ld 150yds out: shkn up and sn asserted* 4/6¹
00- 2 1½ **Arable**186 6762 3-8-8 0 JamesDoyle 2 76
(Charles Hills) *led at v mod pce: kicked on over 2f out: styd on but hdd and outpcd last 150yds* 7/1³
02- 3 1¾ **Mr Greenspan (USA)**131 7972 3-8-8 0 SeanLevey 9 73+
(Richard Hannon) *racd on outer: t.k.h: trckd ldng trio: rdn over 2f out: kpt on same pce to take 3rd ins fnl f* 5/2²
4 nk **Miyachiku** 3-8-8 0 JamieSpencer 1 72
(Ed Dunlop) *t.k.h: trckd ldng pair: gng wl enough whn pce qcknd over 2f out: waiting for room sn after: rn green over 1f out: pushed along and jst lost out in r for 3rd* 14/1
00- 5 2¾ **Pershing**184 6829 3-8-8 0 ¹ AndreaAtzeni 6 66
(Marco Botti) *t.k.h: hld up in 5th: pushed along over 2f out: wl outpcd over 1f out: one pce after* 14/1
6 5 **Suerte Al Salto (IRE)**113 7-10-0 0 AdamKirby 4 60
(Chris Gordon) *dwlt: hld up in last pair: outpcd and pushed along over 2f out: nvr on terms* 25/1
7 nk **Flight Fight** 3-8-8 0 TedDurcan 8 56
(Chris Wall) *dwlt: hld up in 7th in slowly run event: pushed along and outpcd over 2f out: hanging and green over 1f out: wknd* 25/1
0-6 8 1½ **Graphene**17 954 3-8-8 0 DavidProbert 5 53
(Rod Millman) *in tch in 6th: pushed along and outpcd over 2f out: wknd over 1f out* 50/1
04 9 7 **Abdication**40 664 3-8-8 0 ChrisCatlin 7 39
(Gary Moore) *tk fierce hold early: hld up in last pair: pushed along and outpcd over 2f out: wknd* 50/1

2m 10.94s (2.94) **Going Correction** -0.10s/f (Stan)
**WFA** 3 from 4yo+ 20lb 9 Ran SP% 126.0
Speed ratings (Par 103): **84,82,81,81,78 74,74,73,67**
CSF £7.21 TOTE £1.60: £1.10, £2.10, £1.10; EX 7.80 Trifecta £18.00.
**Owner** Ballymacoll Stud **Bred** Ballymacoll Stud Farm Ltd **Trained** Newmarket, Suffolk
**FOCUS**
The hot favourite showed a good attitude to score with something in hand in this steadily-run maiden. The form of the principals is sound enough.

## 1209 BETVICTOR 6 PLACE GRAND NATIONAL H'CAP 1m 2f (P)
3:00 (3:04) (Class 5) (0-70,70) 4-Y-O+ £2,587 (£770; £384; £192) Stalls Low

Form RPR
3334 1 **Cathedral**12 1022 5-9-0 66 OisinMurphy(3) 7 79
(Ed de Giles) *slowly away and sltly awkward: rcvrd to ld after 1f: mde rest: wound it up fr 3f out: clr 2f out: drvn out* 7/2³
0/21 2 6 **Minstrels Gallery (IRE)**12 1016 5-8-9 61 (p) RobertTart(3) 1 63+
(Lucy Wadham) *dwlt: hld up in last trio: gng wl enough on inner whn nowhere to go as wnr was striking for home: kpt on to take 2nd jst over 1f out: no ch* 15/8¹
001- 3 2½ **Posh Boy (IRE)**160 7434 4-9-5 68 GeorgeBaker 4 65+
(Chris Wall) *hld up in last trio: brought wd into st 2f out and already outpcd: kpt on to take 3rd fnl f* 9/4²
035- 4 ½ **Balmoral Castle**161 7430 5-8-9 65 NedCurtis(7) 6 61
(Jonathan Portman) *hld up in last trio: brought v wd bnd 2f out whn already outpcd: kpt on same pce after* 14/1
2-23 5 2½ **Candy Kitten**38 691 4-8-13 67 (p) ShelleyBirkett(5) 5 58
(Alastair Lidderdale) *chsd ldrs: rdn 3f out: sn outpcd: fdd fnl f* 12/1
25-6 6 1½ **Strong Conviction**12 1022 4-9-7 70 JimCrowley 3 58
(Simon Hodgson) *led 1f: chsd wnr: rdn 3f out: lost 2nd and btn 2f out: steadily wknd* 14/1
306- 7 3½ **Sabre Rock**222 5632 4-9-6 69 SteveDrowne 2 51
(John Best) *fractious preliminaries: chsd ldng pair: rdn 3f out: wnt 2nd 2f out to jst over 1f out: wknd* 33/1

2m 4.33s (-3.67) **Going Correction** -0.10s/f (Stan) 7 Ran SP% 111.7
Speed ratings (Par 103): **110,105,103,102,100 99,96**
CSF £9.99 TOTE £3.40: £1.50, £1.90; EX 12.30 Trifecta £25.00.
**Owner** T & Z Racing Club **Bred** Kincorth Investments Inc **Trained** Ledbury, H'fords
**FOCUS**
There was an emphatic front-running winner in this handicap and the favourite didn't get the breaks when he needed them. Hard form to pin downm the winner rated close to his early level.

## 1210 GRAND NATIONAL 6 PLACES AT BETVICTOR.COM FILLIES' H'CAP 1m 4f (P)
3:30 (3:33) (Class 5) (0-70,70) 4-Y-O+ £2,587 (£770; £384; £192) Stalls Centre

Form RPR
5450 1 **Dazzling Valentine**34 737 6-8-4 58 (v) NatashaEaton(5) 1 66
(Alan Bailey) *trckd ldrs: allowed others to fight it out fr 4f out: pld out jst ins fnl 2f: rdn to ld 1f out: sn clr* 11/2³
030- 2 3¾ **Kenny's Girl (IRE)**185 6809 4-8-12 63 MartinDwyer 7 65
(William Muir) *trckd ldr: quick move to go upsides 1/2-way: disp tl def advantage 3f out: hdd 2f out: upsides 1f out: sn btn* 5/2²
4003 3 nk **Lily Edge**4 1120 5-8-0 56 oh4 (v) CamHardie(7) 5 58
(John Bridger) *trckd ldrs: rdn wl over 3f out: clsd to ld 2f out: hdd 1f out: sn btn* 10/1
0605 4 4 **Pembroke Pride**12 1012 4-7-12 56 oh6 JackGarritty(7) 4 51
(Philip Hide) *mostly in last: nvr gng that wl: struggling fr 4f out: no imp on ldrs fnl 2f* 10/1
5-31 5 7 **Adiynara (IRE)**25 857 6-9-7 70 (p) LiamKeniry 6 54
(Neil Mulholland) *led: jnd and rousted along 1/2-way: duelled for ld tl btn u.p over 2f out: wknd* 11/10¹

2m 32.44s (-2.06) **Going Correction** -0.10s/f (Stan)
**WFA** 4 from 5yo+ 2lb 5 Ran SP% 109.8
Speed ratings (Par 100): **102,99,99,96,91**
CSF £19.27 TOTE £7.40: £3.10, £2.10; EX 24.20 Trifecta £133.20.
**Owner** The Glenbuccaneers **Bred** Chippenham Lodge Stud Ltd **Trained** Newmarket, Suffolk
**FOCUS**
The two market leaders got involved in a battle up front and the winner surged to victory from off the pace in this middle-distance handicap. Weak fillies' form.

## 1211 FAMILY FUN AT KEMPTON ON 19.04.14 H'CAP 6f (P)
4:00 (4:01) (Class 6) (0-55,55) 3-Y-O £1,940 (£577; £288; £144) Stalls Low

Form RPR
400- 1 **Biotic**192 6589 3-9-7 55 AndreaAtzeni 2 64
(Rod Millman) *mde all: gng strly whn pressed over 2f out: shkn up and asserted over 1f out: rdn out* 5/4¹
-366 2 2 **Jalebi**10 1039 3-9-6 54 HayleyTurner 10 56
(Jim Boyle) *chsd wnr: chal over 2f out: kpt on whn drvn over 1f out but readily hld after* 14/1
006- 3 1 **Febrayer Star (IRE)**108 8273 3-9-1 49 (p) AdamKirby 3 48
(Robert Cowell) *trckd ldrs: cl 3rd jst over 2f out: drvn and outpcd over 1f out: kpt on: bttr for r* 14/1
6-05 4 2¾ **Crystalized (IRE)**33 745 3-9-5 53 (p) RobertWinston 9 43
(Dean Ivory) *trckd ldrs: cl up and t.k.h 1/2-way: rdn over 2f out: nt qckn and sn outpcd* 7/2²
-553 5 1½ **This Charming Man (IRE)**49 557 3-9-7 55 (b) TomEaves 5 40
(Keith Dalgleish) *rrd s: bhd: lft in 7th pl 4f out: nvr on terms but plugged on fnl 2f* 12/1
4-50 6 2¾ **Charleys Angel**5 1104 3-8-9 46 oh1 JemmaMarshall(3) 6 22+
(Pat Phelan) *towards rr: hmpd over 4f out: bhd after: kpt on fnl 2f: no ch* 25/1
040- 7 ¾ **Morgans Bluff**215 5891 3-9-0 48 FergusSweeney 7 22+
(Pat Phelan) *hld up: hmpd over 4f out: detached after and no ch: modest late hdwy* 33/1
5054 8 2½ **Back On Baileys**34 739 3-8-7 48 ow2 ¹ JordonMcMurray(7) 8 14+
(John Ryan) *dwlt: bhd whn hmpd over 4f out: no ch after* 20/1
0-44 9 4½ **Synonym (ITY)**19 923 3-9-6 54 JoeFanning 11 6
(J W Hills) *prom: rdn 1/2-way: wknd rapidly over 2f out* 16/1
630- P **Idamante**206 6175 3-9-7 55 SeanLevey 4
(Kristin Stubbs) *prom tl lost action bdly and p.u over 4f out* 7/1³

556 **P** **Jenny Sparks**[51] [541] 3-9-0 **51**.................... WilliamTwiston-Davies(3) 1
(Mick Channon) *a in midfield: wl hld in 5th whn lost action over 1f out: p.u* **16/1**

1m 12.85s (-0.25) **Going Correction** -0.10s/f (Stan) **11 Ran SP% 123.5**
Speed ratings (Par 96): **97,94,93,89,87 83,82,79,73,**
CSF £22.96 CT £192.18 TOTE £2.50: £1.10, £3.00, £4.20; EX 21.70 Trifecta £264.10.
**Owner** Mrs Mette Campbell-Andenaes **Bred** Mette Campbell-Andenaes **Trained** Kentisbeare, Devon

**FOCUS**
A big gamble was landed by an unexposed type in this low-grade handicap. A clear personal best from the winner.

## 1212 6 PLACES AT AINTREE AT BETVICTOR.COM H'CAP 6f (P)
**4:30** (4:33) (Class 4) (0-85,86) 4-Y-0+ **£4,690** (£1,395; £697; £348) **Stalls** Low

Form RPR
51-1 **1** **Dutiful Son (IRE)**[33] [746] 4-9-3 **81**.................... RyanMoore 6 92+
(Jeremy Noseda) *sltly awkward s: trckd ldrs: pushed along over 2f out: clsd to ld jst over 1f out: rdn clr: readily* **1/2**[1]

00-5 **2** 1 3/4 **Vincentti (IRE)**[10] [1041] 4-9-0 **78**.................... AdamKirby 3 83
(Ronald Harris) *led 1f: rdn to ld again 2f out: hdd jst over 1f out: one pce after* **20/1**

150- **3** *shd* **Nenge Mboko**[191] [6647] 4-9-7 **85**....................(v) JimCrowley 10 90
(George Baker) *chsd ldrs: rdn over 2f out: kpt on u.p fr over 1f out: pressed runner-up nr fin* **25/1**

03-3 **4** 1/2 **New Leyf (IRE)**[19] [925] 8-8-8 **72**....................(b) SeanLevey 5 75+
(Jeremy Gask) *towards rr: dropped to last and rdn over 2f out: styd on fr over 1f out: gaining on plcd horses at fin* **20/1**

5121 **5** 1 1/4 **Go Far**[11] [1031] 4-8-12 **81**....................(b) TimClark(5) 2 80
(Alan Bailey) *chsd ldrs: rdn over 2f out: trying to cl whn hung rt 1f out: btn after* **10/1**

20-2 **6** 1/2 **Marjong**[33] [746] 4-8-13 **77**.................... HayleyTurner 7 75
(Simon Dow) *c slowly out of stalls: t.k.h and hld up in last pair: taken wd and no real hdwy over 2f out: kpt on fr over 1f out: nrst fin* **10/1**

-222 **7** 2 1/4 **Mac's Power (IRE)**[28] [820] 8-9-0 **78**.................... RobertWinston 1 69
(Willie Musson) *hld up in last pair: sme prog on inner wl over 1f out: no hdwy and btn whn hmpd jst ins fnl f: eased* **9/1**[3]

0550 **8** 1 **Tax Free (IRE)**[40] [658] 12-9-6 **84**.................... AdrianNicholls 8 71
(David Nicholls) *led after 1f to 2f out: wknd qckly* **50/1**

000- **9** 1 3/4 **Line Of Reason (IRE)**[184] [6831] 4-9-6 **84**....................(p) FrederikTylicki 4 66
(Paul Midgley) *in tch: pushed along and no prog over 2f out: wknd over 1f out* **4/1**[2]

1m 12.21s (-0.89) **Going Correction** -0.10s/f (Stan) 9 Ran SP% **130.2**
Speed ratings (Par 105): **101,98,98,97,96 95,92,91,88**
CSF £21.32 CT £182.23 TOTE £1.80: £1.10, £7.40, £4.40; EX 25.40 Trifecta £246.10.
**Owner** Nigel O'Sullivan **Bred** Lodge Park Stud **Trained** Newmarket, Suffolk
■ Stewards' Enquiry : Tim Clark two-day ban: careless riding (Apr 14-15)

**FOCUS**
The pace was not very strong in this fair handicap but the progressive favourite delivered in good style under a waiting ride. There's more to come from him but the placed horses are not entirely solid.

## 1213 BETVICTOR.COM CONDITIONS STKS (FAST TRACK QUALIFIER) 2m (P)
**5:00** (5:02) (Class 2) 4-Y-0+
**£11,827** (£3,541; £1,770; £885; £442; £222) **Stalls** Low

Form RPR
-125 **1** **Castilo Del Diablo (IRE)**[30] [803] 5-9-2 **98**....................(p) JamieSpencer 1 97
(David Simcock) *trckd ldrs in 5th: prog on inner 2f out: drvn over 1f out: edgd ahd last 100yds: hld on* **6/1**

60-2 **2** *hd* **Noble Silk**[30] [803] 5-9-2 **91**....................(p) DavidProbert 2 97
(Lucy Wadham) *hld up in 7th: prog wl over 1f out: drvn and styd on fnl f: tk 2nd last stride: jst hld* **14/1**

320- **3** *nse* **Clowance Estate (IRE)**[170] [7193] 5-9-2 **95**.................... JamesDoyle 4 97
(Roger Charlton) *led: jnd after shying 6f out: drvn over 2f out: hrd pressed after: hdd last 100yds: kpt on wl but lost 2nd fnl stride* **11/4**[1]

6 **4** 1 **Ranjaan (FR)**[30] [803] 6-9-2 **89**....................(t) GeorgeBaker 6 96
(Paul Nicholls) *trckd ldng trio: wnt 2nd wl over 1f out and sn chalng: nt qckn jst ins fnl f: one pce after* **16/1**

000- **5** 3/4 **Sir Graham Wade (IRE)**[244] [4857] 5-9-2 **99**.................... JoeFanning 3 95
(Mark Johnston) *trckd ldng pair: nt clr run briefly 2f out whn cl up: drvn and one pce over 1f out: kpt on* **7/2**[3]

146- **6** *shd* **Glenard**[185] [6793] 4-8-11 **93**.................... RyanMoore 7 94+
(Charles Hills) *hld up in 9th: rdn over 2f out: kpt on fr over 1f out: nvr able to chal* **3/1**[2]

1-12 **7** 1 1/4 **Ordensritter (GER)**[10] [1043] 6-9-2 **75**.................... JohnFahy 10 93?
(Chris Down) *hld up in 6th: rdn 2f out: one pce and no imp* **50/1**

0/ **8** 1/2 **Tzora**[17] [1851] 9-9-2 **0**.................... JimCrowley 5 92?
(Martin Hill) *hld up in 8th: rdn over 2f out: one pce and no imp on ldrs* **66/1**

2-33 **9** 5 **Duchess Of Gazeley (IRE)**[17] [956] 4-8-6 **86**.................... JimmyQuinn 9 81
(Dean Ivory) *trckd ldr: chal and upsides fr 6f out to 2f out: wknd qckly* **16/1**

1-00 **P** **Thecornishcockney**[53] [507] 5-9-2 **100**....................(p) AdamKirby 11
(John Ryan) *t.k.h: hld up in last: appeared to pull himself up 1/2-way* **6/1**

3m 27.64s (-2.46) **Going Correction** -0.10s/f (Stan)
**WFA** 4 from 5yo+ 5lb **10 Ran SP% 124.3**
Speed ratings (Par 109): **102,101,101,101,101 100,100,100,97,**
CSF £92.06 TOTE £7.40: £1.90, £3.10, £1.70; EX 47.70 Trifecta £282.10.
**Owner** The Khat Partnership **Bred** Ennistown Stud **Trained** Newmarket, Suffolk

**FOCUS**
There was an exciting finish in this interesting conditions event for stayers. The second and fourth limit the form among the principals.

## 1214 TURFTV H'CAP 1m (P)
**5:30** (5:32) (Class 6) (0-65,65) 3-Y-0 **£1,940** (£577; £288; £144) **Stalls** Low

Form RPR
054- **1** **Si Senor (IRE)**[151] [7647] 3-9-7 **65**.................... FrederikTylicki 1 73+
(Ed Vaughan) *trckd ldrs: gng much bttr than rest 2f out: nudged along to ld 1f out: rdn whn pressed and fnd enough last 100yds* **2/1**[1]

35-3 **2** *nk* **Baltic Fire (IRE)**[32] [753] 3-8-8 **57**.................... JoeyHaynes(5) 6 64
(K R Burke) *led 1f: styd prom: rdn over 2f out: led over 1f out: hdd 1f out: fought on wl but jst hld* **10/1**

3-24 **3** 1 3/4 **Needless Shouting (IRE)**[39] [670] 3-9-4 **65** WilliamTwiston-Davies(3) 7 68
(Mick Channon) *led after 1f: drvn and pressed over 2f out: hdd and one pce over 1f out* **5/1**[3]

55-5 **4** *nk* **Cotton Club (IRE)**[17] [954] 3-9-7 **65**.................... DavidProbert 3 67
(Rod Millman) *t.k.h: hld up in rr: pushed along over 3f out: prog u.p 2f out: clsd on ldrs jst ins fnl f: one pce after* **9/2**[2]

2-23 **5** 3 1/4 **Byron Gala**[11] [1033] 3-9-3 **61**....................(b) AdamKirby 8 56
(Marco Botti) *prog and prom after 2f: drvn to chal and w ldr 2f out: nt qckn over 1f out: wknd fnl f* **6/1**

03-5 **6** 3 1/4 **Confiture**[56] [456] 3-9-2 **60**.................... LiamKeniry 2 47
(Michael Blanshard) *t.k.h: hld up in rr: rdn and no prog over 2f out* **20/1**

004- **7** 5 **Manor Way (IRE)**[152] [7623] 3-9-4 **62**.................... RyanMoore 4 38
(Richard Hannon) *chsd ldrs: u.p sn after 1/2-way: wl btn in rr over 2f out* **6/1**

660- **8** 3 **Hostile Fire (IRE)**[173] [7119] 3-9-5 **63**.................... ChrisCatlin 5 32
(Ed de Giles) *a last: lost tch by 1/2-way: bhd after* **20/1**

1m 38.2s (-1.60) **Going Correction** -0.10s/f (Stan) **8 Ran SP% 115.4**
Speed ratings (Par 96): **104,103,101,101,98 95,90,87**
CSF £23.94 CT £86.81 TOTE £3.50: £1.70, £3.50, £1.50; EX 35.70 Trifecta £184.10.
**Owner** A E Oppenheimer **Bred** Hascombe And Valiant Studs **Trained** Newmarket, Suffolk

**FOCUS**
The favourite was probably value for a bit more than the winning margin in this sound run handicap. The winner is probably a bit better than the bare form.
T/Plt: £43.60 to a £1 stake. Pool: £69,197.60 - 1158.01 winning units. T/Qpdt: £33.30 to a £1 stake. Pool: 4540.27 - 100.60 winning units. JN

# 1208 KEMPTON (A.W) (R-H)
Tuesday, April 1

**OFFICIAL GOING: Standard**
Wind: Almost Nil Weather: Sunny, warm

## 1215 FAMILY FUN AT KEMPTON 19.04.14 H'CAP 1m (P)
**2:20** (2:22) (Class 6) (0-65,69) 4-Y-0+ **£1,940** (£577; £288; £144) **Stalls** Low

Form RPR
/30- **1** **Burnt Fingers (IRE)**[347] [1660] 4-9-2 **60**.................... AndreaAtzeni 5 70
(Rod Millman) *sn chsd ldrs: shkn up over 2f out: prog to ld over 1f out: edgd rt but styd on wl* **33/1**

0300 **2** 2 1/4 **Sea Soldier (IRE)**[35] [740] 6-8-3 **54**.................... RobHornby(7) 2 59
(Andrew Balding) *lw: t.k.h: trckd ldr after 3f: chal 2f out: nt qckn over 1f out: styd on but no imp on wnr* **10/1**

615 **3** 1 3/4 **Fleetwoodsands (IRE)**[12] [1023] 7-8-8 **52**.................... LiamKeniry 3 53
(David Evans) *t.k.h: hld up in last trio: pushed along and outpcd over 2f out: rdn over 1f out: kpt on to take 3rd last strides* **16/1**

6-01 **4** *nk* **Anjuna Beach (USA)**[12] [1023] 4-9-2 **60**.................... RyanMoore 8 60
(Gary Moore) *lw: s.s and lost abt 8 l: ct up in rr of field after 3f: shkn up and outpcd over 2f out: styd on fr over 1f out: nrly tk 3rd* **9/2**[3]

4031 **5** *shd* **Hill Of Dreams (IRE)**[5] [1121] 5-9-11 **69** 6ex..............(b) RobertWinston 1 69
(Dean Ivory) *lw: trckd ldr 3f: styd cl up: led over 2f out: hanging and hdd over 1f out: fdd and lost pls nr fin* **3/1**[2]

5002 **6** 1 **Gabrial's Wawa**[29] [815] 4-9-2 **60**.................... AdamKirby 7 58
(Noel Quinlan) *broke on terms but stdd into 7th: shkn up and outpcd over 2f out: rdn and one pce fr over 1f out: n.d* **6/4**[1]

0202 **7** *shd* **Bloodsweatandtears**[11] [1040] 6-9-7 **65**.................... GeorgeBaker 6 63
(William Knight) *led: rdn and hdd over 2f out: wl hld whn squeezed out jst over 1f out: no ch after* **8/1**

-410 **8** 1 1/2 **Fire King**[12] [1023] 8-8-7 **51**....................(p) JimmyQuinn 4 45
(Paul Burgoyne) *wl in tch: rdn and nt qckn on inner wl over 1f out: wknd fnl f* **20/1**

1m 38.94s (-0.86) **Going Correction** -0.05s/f (Stan) **8 Ran SP% 117.0**
Speed ratings (Par 101): **102,99,98,97,97 96,96,95**
CSF £328.53 CT £5411.52 TOTE £35.30: £6.30, £3.40, £3.20; EX 417.10 Trifecta £2453.00.
**Owner** Miss Gloria Abbey **Bred** Miss G Abbey **Trained** Kentisbeare, Devon
■ Stewards' Enquiry : Andrea Atzeni two-day ban: careless riding (Apr 15-16)

**FOCUS**
A modest 1m handicap for older horses in which they went an even gallop. The form is rated around the runner-up.

## 1216 BETDAQ £25 NO LOSE MOBILE BETS MAIDEN STKS 1m (P)
**2:50** (2:51) (Class 5) 3-Y-0+ **£2,587** (£770; £384; £192) **Stalls** Low

Form RPR
2- **1** **Bustopher (USA)**[59] [438] 4-10-0 **0**.................... MickaelBarzalona 8 93
(Charlie Appleby) *mde all: pushed along over 2f out: sn pressed: rdn and styd on fr over 1f out* **6/5**[1]

**2** 2 1/2 **Heisman (IRE)** 3-8-13 **0**.................... JamieSpencer 5 83
(Olly Stevens) *tall: lengthy: coltish preliminaries: sn prom: trckd wnr 1/2-way: pushed along to chal 2f out: rdn and nt qckn over 1f out: no imp fnl f* **7/2**[2]

**3** 1 1/4 **Abseil (USA)** 4-10-0 **0**.................... JamesDoyle 11 84+
(Sir Michael Stoute) *str: lengthy: bit bkwd: hld up in last trio: pushed along and prog over 2f out: shkn up to take 3rd jst over 1f out: styd on quite encouragingly* **14/1**

06- **4** 1 3/4 **Tall Ship (IRE)**[165] [7335] 3-8-13 **0**.................... RyanMoore 7 76
(Sir Michael Stoute) *trckd ldng trio: pushed along and outpcd over 2f out: kpt on fr over 1f out: nt disgracd* **11/2**

6- **5** 2 1/2 **Aldborough (IRE)**[346] [1678] 4-10-0 **0**.................... JimCrowley 1 75
(Ralph Beckett) *str: b.bkwd: trckd ldng trio: shkn up over 2f out: chsd clr ldng pair briefly over 1f out: one pce after* **4/1**[3]

**6** 1 3/4 **Thanks Harry** 3-8-13 **0**.................... JimmyFortune 6 67
(Gary Moore) *s.i.s: hld up in midfield: outpcd and pushed along over 2f out: n.d after but kpt on fr over 1f out* **66/1**

0- **7** 3/4 **Lord Brantwood**[170] [7219] 3-8-10 **0**.............. WilliamTwiston-Davies(3) 65
(Mick Channon) *chsd wnr to 1/2-way: lost 3rd pl and wknd over 1f out* **66/1**

620- **8** 3 **Bison Grass**[159] [7490] 4-10-0 **65**.................... PatrickDonaghy 2 62
(Giles Bravery) *s.i.s: t.k.h early: hld up in last pair: wl outpcd over 2f out: shkn up and no ch after: plugged on* **33/1**

00- **9** 9 **Updated (FR)**[190] [6691] 3-8-8 **0**.................... DavidProbert 12 32
(Ismail Mohammed) *chsd ldrs: wknd 3f out: t.o* **100/1**

06- **10** 3/4 **Zambeasy**[238] [5101] 3-8-13 **0**.................... LiamKeniry 4 36
(Philip Hide) *plld hrd in midfield early: wknd 3f out: t.o* **100/1**

0 **11** 3 3/4 **Noel's Hope**[29] [816] 4-10-0 **0**.................... SebSanders 9 31
(Simon Dow) *t.k.h early: a in last pair: wknd over 2f out: t.o* **100/1**

1m 39.22s (-0.58) **Going Correction** -0.05s/f (Stan)
**WFA** 3 from 4yo 15lb **11 Ran SP% 118.6**
Speed ratings (Par 103): **100,97,96,94,92 90,89,86,77,76 73**
CSF £5.56 TOTE £2.70: £1.50, £1.40, £4.40; EX 7.10 Trifecta £46.20.
**Owner** Godolphin **Bred** Darley **Trained** Newmarket, Suffolk

**FOCUS**
A decent maiden in which the winner made all at an even tempo. The winner stood out on his debut effort last year.

## 1217 BETDAQ £500 IN FREE BETS H'CAP 7f (P)
**3:20** (3:20) (Class 5) (0-75,75) 4-Y-0+ **£2,587** (£770; £384; £192) **Stalls** Low

Form RPR
3120 **1** **Shaolin (IRE)**[47] 587 4-9-7 **75**..........................(t) GeorgeBaker 7 82
(Seamus Durack) *sltly impeded s: hld up in rr: prog on inner 2f out: clsd on ldrs over 1f out: rdn to ld last 100yds: kpt on* **11/4**[2]
40-4 **2** *nk* **Gold Beau (FR)**[20] 925 4-9-4 **72**..............................(p) HayleyTurner 3 78
(Kristin Stubbs) *wnt lft s: led at decent pce: hrd pressed and urged along jst over 2f out: kpt on but hdd and hld last 100yds* **10/1**
0045 **3** *nk* **First Class**[34] 750 6-8-7 **61**.........................................(p) DavidProbert 4 66
(Rae Guest) *sltly impeded s: hld up in tch: prog wl over 1f out: rdn to chal jst ins fnl f: nt qckn* **5/1**[3]
0245 **4** *1* **Shifting Star (IRE)**[13] 1017 9-8-4 **61**...............(vt) MichaelJMMurphy(3) 8 63
(John Bridger) *trckd ldr: rdn and upsides 2f out: nt qckn over 1f out: lost 2nd and one pce fnl f* **14/1**
5232 **5** *½* **Polar Kite (IRE)**[12] 1025 6-9-7 **75**.............................. RobertWinston 10 76
(Roger Ingram) *s.s: hld up in last: making sme prog whn stuck bhd rivals 2f out to 1f out: urged along and styd on: shade unlucky* **10/1**
-112 **6** *¾* **Welsh Sunrise**[32] 779 4-9-7 **75**...................................... RyanMoore 1 74
(Stuart Williams) *trckd ldng pair: tried to chal 2f out: nt qckn over 1f out: wl hld fnl f* **6/4**[1]
0051 **7** *4½* **Shaunas Spirit (IRE)**[20] 924 6-9-7 **75**.......................(p) AdamKirby 9 62
(Dean Ivory) *t.k.h: hld up in rr: effrt on outer over 2f out: nt qckn over 1f out: wknd* **14/1**
1100 **8** *6* **Basingstoke (IRE)**[12] 1026 5-9-4 **72**........................... SteveDrowne 6 43
(Simon Hodgson) *in tch tl wknd wl over 2f out: sn bhd* **33/1**

1m 25.34s (-0.66) **Going Correction** -0.05s/f (Stan) **8** Ran SP% **117.8**
Speed ratings (Par 103): **101,100,100,99,98 97,92,85**
CSF £31.21 CT £133.29 TOTE £3.00: £1.80, £4.30, £1.20; EX 27.50 Trifecta £152.40.
**Owner** P A Deal **Bred** Joe Fogarty **Trained** Baydon, Wilts

**FOCUS**
A fair 7f handicap for older horses in which they went an honest gallop. The winner resumed his progress, with the second to form.

## 1218 BETDAQ NO PREMIUM CHARGE MAIDEN STKS 1m 4f (P)
**3:50** (3:50) (Class 5) 3-Y-0+ **£2,587** (£770; £384; £192) **Stalls** Centre

Form RPR
2- **1** **Economy**[251] 4632 4-9-13 0........................................ JamesDoyle 6 77+
(Sir Michael Stoute) *athletic: racd wd: trckd ldng pair: shkn up 3f out: led 2f out: idled and jnd ins fnl f: jst hld on* **1/4**[1]
**2** *3¾* **Earls Quarter (IRE)**[34] 4666 8-10-0 0.......................(t) RyanMoore 4 70
(Ian Williams) *trckd ldr: led over 3f out: drvn and hdd 2f out: lost 2nd and fdd over 1f out: fin 3rd: plcd 2nd* **8/1**[2]
0- **3** *1* **Alzammaar (USA)**[160] 7469 3-8-7 0................................ PaulHanagan 2 67
(Charles Hills) *led to over 3f out: shkn up and one pce after: steadily lost grnd on ldrs over 1f out: fin 4th: plcd 3rd* **8/1**[2]
00-5 **4** *nk* **Son Of Feyan (IRE)**[29] 827 3-8-7 68................................ MartinLane 1 66
(Roger Teal) *trckd ldng pair: shkn up over 3f out: steadily lost grnd fnl 2f: fin 5th: plcd 4th* **33/1**
00/ **5** *78* **Morgana**[916] 6459 6-9-9 0........................................ SteveDrowne 3
(Simon Hodgson) *a in last: wknd 4f out: t.o: fin 6th: plcd 5th* **100/1**
2 **D** *shd* **Neston Grace**[32] 776 6-9-2 0.................................... RobertWinston 5 64
(Simon Hodgson) *hld up in tch: shkn up over 3f out: prog to take 2nd over 1f out: str chal fnl f and upsides last 100yds: edgd lft nr fin: jst hld: fin 2nd, shd: disq: jockey weighed in 7lb light (carried 9st 2lb nt 9st 9lb)* **14/1**[3]

2m 34.85s (0.35) **Going Correction** -0.05s/f (Stan)
**WFA** 3 from 4yo 21lb 4 from 6yo+ 1lb **6** Ran SP% **112.8**
Speed ratings (Par 103): **96,93,92,92,40 95**
CSF £3.15 TOTE £1.10: £1.10, £3.00; EX 3.80 Trifecta £8.80.
**Owner** K Abdullah **Bred** Juddmonte Farms Ltd **Trained** Newmarket, Suffolk

**FOCUS**
A fair small-field middle-distance maiden in which they went a modest gallop. Muddling form, rated around the fifth.

## 1219 BETDAQ - THE SPORTS BETTING EXCHANGE H'CAP 1m 4f (P)
**4:20** (4:20) (Class 4) (0-80,80) 4-Y-0+ **£5,175** (£1,540; £769; £384) **Stalls** Centre

Form RPR
/10- **1** **Jakey (IRE)**[169] 7257 4-9-2 **76**........................................ RyanMoore 5 85
(Pat Phelan) *t.k.h: sn trckd ldr: led 2f out: rdn and edgd lft fnl f: styd on* **11/4**[2]
221- **2** *1¼* **Flemish School**[134] 7947 4-9-5 **79**................................ LiamKeniry 6 86
(David Elsworth) *trckd ldrs: rdn over 2f out: chsd wnr over 1f out: styd on but no imp last 150yds* **8/1**
2-1 **3** *2* **Devon Drum**[17] 686 6-9-1 **77**........................ WilliamTwiston-Davies(3) 2 81+
(Paul Webber) *hld up in 5th: rdn and nt qckn over 2f out: hanging over 1f out but kpt on to take 3rd fnl f* **10/1**
03-2 **4** *2* **Sporting Gold (IRE)**[26] 856 5-9-4 **77**.......................(b) AndreaAtzeni 7 78
(Roger Varian) *hld up in last: rdn and fnd nil over 2f out: wl btn after: plugged on into 4th fnl f* **11/10**[1]
4300 **5** *1¼* **St Ignatius**[18] 870 7-8-11 **75**.................................(v) TimClark(5) 3 74
(Alan Bailey) *led: rdn and hdd 2f out: steadily wknd* **25/1**
1-11 **6** *3½* **Swift Blade (IRE)**[26] 856 6-9-4 **77**.............................. RobertWinston 1 70
(Lady Herries) *plld hrd: sn in 3rd: shuffled along and nt qckn over 2f out: wknd over 1f out: eased* **5/1**[3]

2m 33.95s (-0.55) **Going Correction** -0.05s/f (Stan)
**WFA** 4 from 5yo+ 1lb **6** Ran SP% **115.0**
Speed ratings (Par 105): **99,98,96,95,94 92**
CSF £24.68 CT £191.36 TOTE £3.50: £1.50, £5.10; EX 18.30 Trifecta £94.80.
**Owner** Allen B Pope **Bred** Cliveden Stud Ltd **Trained** Epsom, Surrey

**FOCUS**
A fair middle-distance handicap for older horses in which they went an, at best, even gallop. The form is taken at face value.

## 1220 KEMPTON.CO.UK H'CAP (LONDON MIDDLE DISTANCE SERIES QUALIFIER) 1m 3f (P)
**4:50** (4:50) (Class 5) (0-75,75) 3-Y-0 **£2,587** (£770; £384; £192) **Stalls** Low

Form RPR
335- **1** **Storm Force Ten**[162] 7428 3-9-5 **73**............................ DavidProbert 7 81
(Andrew Balding) *lengthy: lw: mde all and enjoyed untrbld ld: stretched on over 3f out: hung lft fr 2f out: rdn out: unchal* **9/4**[1]
314- **2** *1¾* **Castle Combe (IRE)**[118] 8147 3-9-7 **75**...................... MartinDwyer 2 79
(Marcus Tregoning) *str: lw: hld up: mostly in 5th fr 1/2-way and off the pce: prog and hung lft 2f out: chsd wnr over 1f out: styd on but nvr cl enough to chal* **5/1**[2]
1134 **3** *½* **Masterpaver**[12] 1033 3-9-0 **68**...........................(v) RobertWinston 8 71
(Alan Bailey) *awkward s: hld up in last: prog on outer jst over 3f out: rdn and hdwy to take 3rd jst over 1f out: styd on but nvr cl enough to chal* **8/1**
-425 **4** *6* **Mary Le Bow**[41] 668 3-8-12 **66**................................(p) RyanMoore 6 58
(Lucy Wadham) *hld up: chsd clr ldng trio fr 1/2-way: pushed along and no hdwy over 2f out: nt on over 1f out: rdn into modest 4th nr fin* **11/2**[3]
40-2 **5** *nk* **Citizen Kaine (IRE)**[27] 839 3-8-8 **69**........................ JosephineGordon(7) 1 61
(Jo Hughes) *w'like: chsd wnr: shkn up and no imp over 2f out: lost 2nd and wknd over 1f out* **25/1**
-031 **6** *1* **Captain Mo**[41] 668 3-8-11 **65**........................................ AndreaAtzeni 3 55
(Marco Botti) *hld up in last trio: shkn up and dropped to last 3f out: no ch after* **5/1**[2]
0-46 **7** *2* **Last Echo (IRE)**[41] 660 3-8-11 **65**................................ JimCrowley 4 51
(Ralph Beckett) *hld up in last trio: rdn and no prog wl over 2f out: no ch after* **13/2**
401- **8** *1* **Encore Encore (FR)**[148] 7732 3-9-0 **68**........................ JamesDoyle 5 53
(Harry Dunlop) *trckd ldng pair: nudged along over 2f out: steadily wknd: eased ins fnl f* **25/1**

2m 19.78s (-2.12) **Going Correction** -0.05s/f (Stan) **8** Ran SP% **111.6**
Speed ratings (Par 98): **105,103,103,99,98 98,96,95**
CSF £12.82 CT £72.35 TOTE £2.60: £1.50, £1.10, £2.60; EX 13.30 Trifecta £115.20.
**Owner** Robert Waley-Cohen **Bred** Upton Viva Stud **Trained** Kingsclere, Hants
■ Stewards' Enquiry : Ryan Moore one-day ban: careless riding (Apr 15)

**FOCUS**
A fair middle-distance 3yo handicap in which they went an honest gallop. The winner made all to step up on his 2yo form.

## 1221 NEW JUMP FIXTURE ON 05.05.14 H'CAP 6f (P)
**5:20** (5:20) (Class 6) (0-65,65) 4-Y-0+ **£1,940** (£577; £288; £144) **Stalls** Low

Form RPR
0142 **1** **Sweet Talking Guy (IRE)**[27] 841 4-9-4 **65**.............(t) SimonPearce(3) 1 74
(Lydia Pearce) *trckd ldrs: prog to ld over 1f out: rdn and hrd pressed fnl f: hld on wl* **3/1**[2]
4221 **2** *½* **Ghost Train (IRE)**[27] 846 5-9-4 **62**..............................(p) HayleyTurner 7 69
(Tim McCarthy) *trckd ldrs: prog 2f out: wnt 2nd jst over 1f out: drvn to chal fnl f: nt qckn nr fin* **6/1**[3]
0023 **3** *1¾* **Haadeeth**[12] 1030 7-9-5 **63**............................................ AdamKirby 6 65
(David Evans) *led 100yds: trckd ldr: rdn to ld briefly wl over 1f out: outpcd by ldng pair fnl f* **20/1**
0501 **4** *hd* **Foie Gras**[15] 993 4-9-1 **64**.................................... ConnorBeasley(5) 2 67+
(Chris Dwyer) *hld up in rr: prog 2f out: nt clr run and swtchd lft over 1f out: drvn and styd on: unable to threaten* **12/1**
0-01 **5** *1* **Time Medicean**[13] 1010 8-9-0 **58**................................ RobertWinston 5 56
(Tony Carroll) *hld up in rr: effrt over 2f out: drvn and sme prog fr over 1f out: nvr a threat* **7/4**[1]
1136 **6** *1¾* **Volito**[4] 1144 8-9-7 **65**................................................ GeorgeBaker 4 57
(Anabel K Murphy) *slowly out of stalls: hld up in last pair: prog on inner 2f out: jst pushed along and no hdwy fnl f: nvr involved* **12/1**
645- **7** *shd* **Encapsulated**[258] 4410 4-8-12 **56**................................ MartinLane 3 48
(Roger Ingram) *a in midfield: cl enough bhd ldrs 2f out: rdn and steadily outpcd over 1f out* **25/1**
660- **8** *nk* **Commandingpresence (USA)**[162] 7432 8-8-10 **57** MichaelJMMurphy(3) 8 48
(John Bridger) *sweating: led after 100yds: hdd wl over 1f out: wknd fnl f* **33/1**
000- **9** *nk* **Fortrose Academy (IRE)**[104] 8330 5-9-1 **59**.................. DavidProbert 9 49
(Andrew Balding) *nvr beyond midfield: shkn up and no prog jst over 2f out: wl hld over 1f out* **10/1**
000- **10** *2* **Taurus Twins**[147] 7743 8-9-6 **64**..........................(v) JamesDoyle 11 48
(Richard Price) *spd fr wd draw to dispute 2nd: lost pl fr 2f out* **50/1**
5315 **11** *1* **New Rich**[15] 993 4-9-0 **63**................................(p) GeorgeDowning(5) 12 44
(Eve Johnson Houghton) *v awkward s: hld up in last pair: rdn and no prog over 2f out* **14/1**
0-00 **12** *6* **Gung Ho Jack**[15] 993 5-9-4 **62**.................................... SteveDrowne 10 23
(John Best) *racd on outer: nvr beyond midfield: struggling fr 1/2-way: wl bhd fnl 2f* **33/1**

1m 11.62s (-1.48) **Going Correction** -0.05s/f (Stan) **12** Ran SP% **123.2**
Speed ratings (Par 101): **107,106,104,103,102 100,99,99,99,96 95,87**
CSF £21.10 CT £324.00 TOTE £5.90: £2.20, £2.40, £4.40; EX 21.60 Trifecta £151.80.
**Owner** Killarney Glen **Bred** Churchtown House Stud **Trained** Newmarket, Suffolk

**FOCUS**
The concluding contest was a modest 6f handicap for older horses in which they went a strong pace. The winner posted a length personal best.
T/Jkpt: £19,908.90 to a £1 stake. Pool of £70101.76 - 2.50 winning tickets. T/Plt: £827.00 to a £1 stake. Pool of £78964.67 - 69.70 winning tickets. T/Qpdt: £23.50 to a £1 stake. Pool of £7409.41 - 232.98 winning tickets. JN

# 1125 SOUTHWELL (L-H)
### Tuesday, April 1

**OFFICIAL GOING: Standard**
Wind: Virtually nil Weather: Hazy sunshine

## 1222 CORAL APP DOWNLOAD FROM THE APP STORE H'CAP 1m 3f (F)
**2:00** (2:00) (Class 5) (0-75,75) 4-Y-0+ **£2,587** (£770; £384; £192) **Stalls** Low

Form RPR
6-22 **1** **Jacobs Son**[21] 911 6-9-2 **70**........................................ TomQueally 2 78
(Michael Appleby) *hld up: hdwy over 4f out: led 3f out: rdn wl over 1f out: edgd lft ins fnl f: kpt on wl u.p towards fin* **11/10**[1]
3361 **2** *½* **Lean On Pete (IRE)**[14] 1003 5-9-2 **75**...................... JacobButterfield(5) 4 82
(Ollie Pears) *hld up in rr: hdwy over 3f out: chsd wnr over 2f out: rdn over 1f out: styd on fnl f* **5/4**[2]
4-26 **3** *8* **Mishrif (USA)**[20] 929 8-9-6 **74**................................(v) JoeFanning 1 68
(J R Jenkins) *trckd ldrs: effrt 4f out: pushed along and hdwy 3f out: rdn and one pce fnl 2f* **10/1**[3]
22-5 **4** *27* **Flamingo Beat**[21] 911 4-8-11 **68**................................ OisinMurphy(3) 3 16
(Christine Dunnett) *led 3f: cl up: pushed along over 4f out: rdn wl over 3f out and sn wknd* **14/1**

00-6 **5** *8* **Al Enbess (IRE)**[14] 1003 4-8-7 **61** oh1 JamesSullivan 5
(Ruth Carr) *cl up: led after 3f: rdn along 4f out: hdd 3f out and sn wknd* **50/1**

2m 26.14s (-1.86) **Going Correction** -0.05s/f (Stan) **5** Ran SP% **109.8**
Speed ratings (Par 103): **104,103,97,78,72**
CSF £2.72 TOTE £2.30: £1.10, £1.10; EX 2.90 Trifecta £5.60.
**Owner** The Rain Dancers **Bred** Stowell Park Stud **Trained** Danethorpe, Notts

**FOCUS**
An uncompetitive handicap dominated by the two market leaders. The first two ran basically to form.

## 1223 BEST ODDS AT BOOKMAKERS.CO.UK MEDIAN AUCTION MAIDEN STKS 6f (F)
**2:30** (2:30) (Class 6) 3-5-Y-O **£1,940** (£577; £288; £144) **Stalls** Low

Form RPR
**1** **Red Primo (IRE)** 3-9-0 0 TomQueally 6 71+
(Alan McCabe) *in tch: gd hdwy on outer over 3f out: led over 2f out: rdn and green over 1f out: kpt on* **1/1**[1]

003 **2** *1 1/4* **Incurs Four Faults**[21] 906 3-9-0 39 TomEaves 7 65
(Keith Dalgleish) *towards rr and pushed along early: hdwy to ld after 2f: rdn along and hdd over 2f out: drvn over 1f out: kpt on u.p fnl f* **16/1**

552- **3** *4 1/2* **Lendal Bridge**[164] 7371 3-9-0 62 BarryMcHugh 5 52
(Tony Coyle) *prom: rdn along and outpcd over 2f out: drvn and plugged on fr over 1f out: edgd lft fnl f* **9/2**[3]

422 **4** *3* **Meebo (IRE)**[42] 651 3-8-4 60 ShelleyBirkett(5) 4 38+
(J R Jenkins) *prom on inner: rdn along wl over 2f out: sn one pce* **3/1**[2]

00-0 **5** *2 1/4* **Fishlake Rebel**[6] 1110 4-9-9 42 (v[1]) OisinMurphy(3) 9 39
(David C Griffiths) *towards rr: hdwy on outer to chse ldrs after 2f: rdn along 3f out: sn drvn and wknd* **33/1**

**6** *1 1/2* **Fizzolo** 3-8-9 0 AdamBeschizza 3 26
(Noel Quinlan) *in tch: rdn along and sme hdwy 3f out: sn btn* **20/1**

4600 **7** *2* **Ishisoba**[27] 844 4-9-7 46 LiamJones 8 23
(Ronald Harris) *sn led: hdd 4f out: cl up: rdn along wl over 2f out: sn wknd* **25/1**

00-4 **8** *9* **Caledonia Laird**[11] 1048 3-9-0 55 (p) BenCurtis 1
(Jo Hughes) *a towards rr* **14/1**

1m 15.66s (-0.84) **Going Correction** -0.05s/f (Stan)
**WFA** 3 from 4yo+ 12lb **8** Ran SP% **117.3**
Speed ratings (Par 101): **103,101,95,91,88 86,83,71**
CSF £20.43 TOTE £1.80: £1.10, £3.60, £1.80; EX 27.80 Trifecta £106.10.
**Owner** Craig and Maureen Buckingham **Bred** E O'Gorman **Trained** Averham Park, Notts

**FOCUS**
A moderate maiden in which those to have run before didn't set a very high standard and a newcomer took advantage. The runner-up is probably the key to the form.

## 1224 COMPARE BOOKMAKERS AT BOOKMAKERS.CO.UK H'CAP 6f (F)
**3:00** (3:01) (Class 5) (0-75,75) 4-Y-O+ **£2,587** (£770; £384; £192) **Stalls** Low

Form RPR
000- **1** **Klynch**[183] 6908 8-9-7 **75** (b) JamesSullivan 4 85
(Ruth Carr) *in tch: hdwy over 3f out: chsd ldng pair over 2f out: sn swtchd lft and rdn wl over 1f out: styd on strly to ld ins fnl f: r.o* **3/1**[2]

0506 **2** *2 1/4* **Pull The Pin (IRE)**[5] 1127 5-8-10 **64** (bt) PaulMulrennan 1 67
(Ann Stokell) *slt ld: wd st: rdn over 2f out: sltly hmpd over 1f out: drvn ent fnl f: sn edgd rt and hdd: kpt on same pce* **5/1**[3]

-205 **3** *hd* **Amosite**[8] 1080 8-9-4 **72** (v) JoeFanning 7 75
(J R Jenkins) *sn cl up: wd st and chal wl over 2f out: sn rdn and disp ld whn edgd lft over 1f out: drvn and ev ch whn sltly hmpd ins fnl f sn one pce* **5/1**[3]

00-0 **4** *6* **Lost In Paris (IRE)**[28] 834 8-8-11 **72** LauraBarry(7) 2 57
(Tony Coyle) *in tch: rdn along and outpcd wl over 2f out: styd on appr fnl f: n.d* **33/1**

6600 **5** *1 1/2* **Decent Fella (IRE)**[13] 1021 8-8-10 **67** (t) OisinMurphy(3) 6 47
(Ann Stokell) *dwlt and in rr: wd st: sn rdn and sme late hdwy* **6/1**

510- **6** *5* **Beau Mistral (IRE)**[153] 7634 5-9-5 **73** LukeMorris 5 38
(Paul Green) *chsd ldng pair: rdn along 1/2-way: drvn over 2f out and sn wknd* **14/1**

313 **7** *7* **Layla's Hero (IRE)**[61] 384 7-8-9 **63** (v) AdrianNicholls 3 7
(David Nicholls) *dwlt: sn rdn along: a in rr* **2/1**[1]

1m 15.31s (-1.19) **Going Correction** -0.05s/f (Stan) **7** Ran SP% **115.6**
Speed ratings (Par 103): **105,102,101,93,91 85,75**
CSF £18.75 TOTE £3.40: £2.50, £2.40; EX 22.80 Trifecta £113.40.
**Owner** Douglas Renton **Bred** J C S Wilson Bloodstock **Trained** Huby, N Yorks

**FOCUS**
An ordinary sprint handicap, but they didn't hang about with the second and third horses going hard at it from the start. The winner is rated to last year's C&D reappearance figure.

## 1225 32RED THUNDERSTRUCK II SLOT H'CAP (BOBIS RACE) 7f (F)
**3:30** (3:30) (Class 4) (0-80,84) 3-Y-O **£4,690** (£1,395; £697; £348) **Stalls** Low

Form RPR
1111 **1** **Alumina (IRE)**[7] 1093 3-9-6 **84** 6ex JackGarritty(7) 5 88
(Andrew Balding) *hld up: hdwy on outer 3f out: wd st: effrt to chal wl over 1f out: rdn to ld ent fnl f: edgd lft and kpt on wl towards fin* **11/10**[1]

10-2 **2** *hd* **Aspirant**[73] 232 3-9-4 **75** (t) DaleSwift 6 78
(Brian Ellison) *trckd ldrs: hdwy 3f out: cl up over 2f out: rdn to ld 1 1/2f out: sn jnd and drvn hdd ent fnl f: kpt on u.p tl no ex nr fin* **9/2**[3]

-142 **3** *2 3/4* **Outbacker (IRE)**[5] 1136 3-9-5 **76** JoeFanning 1 72
(Mark Johnston) *slt ld on inner: rdn along 3f out: sn hdd and hung lft to inner rail: cl up and drvn 2f out: rdr dropped whip over 1f out and kpt on same pce* **5/2**[2]

1- **4** *4 1/2* **Royal Warrior**[363] 1328 3-9-7 **78** BenCurtis 3 63
(Alan McCabe) *cl up: led wl over 2f out: sn rdn: hdd and drvn 1 1/2f out: sn wknd* **14/1**

5512 **5** *2 1/2* **Black Vale (IRE)**[7] 1093 3-8-3 **67** (t) DonnaAspell(7) 2 45
(Phil McEntee) *dwlt: t.k.h and chsd ldrs: rdn along 3f out: sn wknd* **20/1**

110- **6** *9* **Hala Hala (IRE)**[185] 6839 3-9-7 **78** TomQueally 4 33
(Michael Bell) *hld up in rr: effrt over 3f out: sn rdn and wknd over 2f out* **16/1**

1m 29.8s (-0.50) **Going Correction** -0.05s/f (Stan) **6** Ran SP% **111.7**
Speed ratings (Par 100): **100,99,96,91,88 78**
CSF £6.45 TOTE £2.30: £1.30, £3.10; EX 7.80 Trifecta £17.20.
**Owner** Shapoor Mistry **Bred** Eimear Mulhern & Abbeville Stud **Trained** Kingsclere, Hants

**FOCUS**
A decent 3yo handicap. The winner was 6lb well in and did not look to have that amount in hand.

## 1226 32RED FREE £10 BONUS H'CAP 1m 6f (F)
**4:00** (4:00) (Class 5) (0-75,72) 4-Y-O+ **£2,587** (£770; £384; £192) **Stalls** Low

Form RPR
-111 **1** **Kingscombe (USA)**[20] 932 5-9-8 **70** RobertHavlin 3 80
(Linda Jewell) *dwlt: t.k.h and trckd ldrs: hdwy 4f out: chsd ldr 3f out: rdn to chal 2f out: drvn to ld ent fnl f: kpt on strly* **11/10**[1]

4-63 **2** *3 1/4* **No Such Number**[17] 829 6-8-10 **63** (p) ShelleyBirkett(5) 5 68
(Julia Feilden) *trckd ldng pair: hdwy on outer and cl up over 5f out: led over 4f out: pushed along over 2f out: sn jnd and rdn: hdd ent fnl f: sn one pce* **9/4**[2]

210- **3** *20* **Coconell**[103] 8343 4-9-7 **72** GrahamLee 4 49
(Peter Hiatt) *slt ld: hdd over 4f out and sn pushed along: rdn over 3f out: sn drvn and wknd* **25/1**

2420 **4** *4 1/2* **Opus (IRE)**[6] 1117 5-8-7 **55** LukeMorris 2 26
(Lucy Wadham) *cl up on inner: pushed along 1/2-way: rdn along over 4f out: sn wknd* **7/2**[3]

60/2 **5** *22* **Bivouac (UAE)**[6] 1111 10-9-8 **70** BenCurtis 1 10
(Alan Swinbank) *hld up in rr: pushed along on inner 1/2-way: swtchd rt to outer 6f out: sn rdn along: outpcd and bhd* **14/1**

3m 7.66s (-0.64) **Going Correction** -0.05s/f (Stan)
**WFA** 4 from 5yo+ 3lb **5** Ran SP% **111.1**
Speed ratings (Par 103): **99,97,85,83,70**
CSF £3.89 TOTE £1.90: £1.10, £1.60; EX 5.00 Trifecta £27.30.
**Owner** Peter Oppenheimer **Bred** Juddmonte Farms Inc **Trained** Sutton Valence, Kent

**FOCUS**
A modest staying handicap and another race won by a course specialist on a roll. They finished very well spread out and the form is rated around the second.

## 1227 LADBROKES MOBILE H'CAP 7f (F)
**4:30** (4:30) (Class 6) (0-60,60) 4-Y-O+ **£1,940** (£577; £288; £144) **Stalls** Low

Form RPR
-133 **1** **Kasbhom**[15] 996 4-9-7 **60** (t) LukeMorris 4 69
(Anthony Carson) *trckd ldrs: hdwy on inner 3f out: rdn to chse ldr over 2f out: drvn over 1f out: styd on to ld jst ins fnl f: sn edgd rt: drvn out* **2/1**[1]

/-2 **2** *1* **Chapellerie (IRE)**[60] 402 5-8-11 **53** (b) OisinMurphy(3) 5 59
(Tony Newcombe) *cl up: led 3f out: rdn over 2f out: drvn over 1f out: hdd jst ins fnl f: kpt on towards fin* **7/2**[3]

62-3 **3** *1 1/4* **Bitaphon (IRE)**[88] 30 5-8-11 **57** (t) AlistairRawlinson(7) 2 60
(Michael Appleby) *chsd ldrs: hdwy 3f out: rdn over 2f out: drvn to chse ldng pair over 1f out: edgd lft and one pce fnl f* **5/2**[2]

2022 **4** *3 1/4* **Baltic Prince (IRE)**[19] 940 4-9-7 **60** TomQueally 6 55
(Paul Green) *cl up: rdn along 1/2-way: drvn wl over 2f out: sn wknd* **5/1**

000- **5** *1 3/4* **Master Of Song**[102] 8360 7-9-1 **59** (p) PhilipPrince(5) 1 49
(Roy Bowring) *s.i.s and bhd: rdn along 1/2-way: kpt on fnl 2f* **10/1**

150- **6** *3* **Look On By**[210] 6083 4-9-4 **57** JamesSullivan 3 39
(Ruth Carr) *led: rdn along and hdd 3f out: wknd over 2f out* **16/1**

1m 30.43s (0.13) **Going Correction** -0.05s/f (Stan) **6** Ran SP% **115.8**
Speed ratings (Par 101): **97,95,94,90,88 85**
CSF £9.82 TOTE £2.70: £1.40, £2.50; EX 10.60 Trifecta £25.20.
**Owner** Macattack, William Lea Screed & Form IT **Bred** Darley **Trained** Newmarket, Suffolk

**FOCUS**
A moderate handicap. The winner is rated to his best.

## 1228 LADBROKES H'CAP 1m (F)
**5:00** (5:02) (Class 6) (0-55,58) 4-Y-O+ **£1,940** (£577; £288; £144) **Stalls** Low

Form RPR
0005 **1** **Sam Spade (IRE)**[8] 1081 4-9-7 **52** (v) DaleSwift 4 70
(Derek Shaw) *led 2f: cl up: led again wl over 2f out: rdn wl over 1f out: drvn ins fnl f and kpt on strly* **12/1**

2032 **2** *3* **General Tufto**[8] 1086 9-9-6 **51** (b) TomQueally 8 62
(Charles Smith) *sn outpcd and rdn along in rr: gd hdwy on outer over 3f out: wd st and chal over 2f out: sn rdn and ev ch tl drvn ent fnl f and one pce* **6/1**

6555 **3** *4 1/2* **Rutterkin (USA)**[35] 740 6-9-0 **45** GrahamLee 2 46
(James Moffatt) *chsd ldrs: rdn along and outpcd 1/2-way: hdwy 2f out: swtchd rt and rdn over 1f out: styd on to take 3rd ins fnl f: rn wout declared tongue strap* **8/1**

5463 **4** *3/4* **Nellies Quest**[8] 1086 5-8-8 **46** AlistairRawlinson(7) 5 45
(Michael Appleby) *chsd ldrs: rdn along and outpcd 1/2-way: hdwy 3f out: rdn to chse ldng pair wl over 1f out: sn drvn: edgd lft and wknd* **7/2**[2]

50/1 **5** *2 1/4* **Mont Signal**[8] 1081 4-9-13 **58** 6ex (t) RichardKingscote 7 52
(Daniel Kubler) *blind removed late and awkward s: sn trcking ldrs: hdwy and cl up after 3f: rdn along 3f out: drvn 2f out and grad wknd* **7/4**[1]

0000 **6** *3* **Upper Lambourn (IRE)**[14] 1001 6-9-0 **45** (t) JoeFanning 3 32
(Christopher Kellett) *sn rdn along and a in rr* **33/1**

6540 **7** *6* **Silver Fawn (IRE)**[7] 1087 4-9-0 **45** (be) LukeMorris 6 18
(John Weymes) *cl up: led after 2f: rdn along 3f out: sn hdd & wknd* **25/1**

0-21 **8** *33* **Just Five (IRE)**[5] 1138 8-9-3 **51** 6ex (v) OisinMurphy(3) 1
(John Weymes) *pushed along to chse ldrs on inner: rdn along bef 1/2-way: sn wknd and bhd whn eased over 1f out* **5/1**[3]

1m 43.37s (-0.33) **Going Correction** -0.05s/f (Stan) **8** Ran SP% **115.1**
Speed ratings (Par 101): **99,96,91,90,88 85,79,46**
CSF £82.04 CT £621.43 TOTE £23.60: £3.10, £2.00, £2.50; EX 93.20 Trifecta £547.80.
**Owner** The Warren Partnership **Bred** Newhall Ltd **Trained** Sproxton, Leics

**FOCUS**
A moderate handicap in which they finished well spread out. The winner's best form for his current yard.
T/Plt: £13.60 to a £1 stake. Pool of £54944.16 - 2928.02 winning tickets. T/Qpdt: £8.60 to a £1 stake. Pool of £4126.48 - 351.38 winning tickets. JR

# 1215 KEMPTON (A.W) (R-H)
Wednesday, April 2

**OFFICIAL GOING: Standard**
Wind: Light, half behind Weather: Muggy

## 1229 BETBRIGHT.COM MAIDEN STKS 6f (P)
**5:55** (5:56) (Class 5) 3-Y-O+ **£2,587** (£770) **Stalls** Low

Form RPR
224- **1** **Speedfiend**[172] 7191 3-9-2 105 AdamKirby 1 95+
(Noel Quinlan) *mde all: shkn up and qcknd wl clr over 1f out: unchal* **1/33**[1]

03 2 11 **Happydoingnothing**[36] 739 3-9-2 0 .......................... AdamBeschizza 2 60
(Christine Dunnett) *a 2nd: rdn over 2f out: sn outpcd* **16/1**[2]

1m 12.39s (-0.71) **Going Correction** 0.0s/f (Stan) **2** Ran SP% **103.0**
Speed ratings (Par 103): **104,89**
TOTE £1.02.
**Owner** Newtown Anner Stud Farm Ltd **Bred** Glebe Stud, J F Dean & Lady Trenchard **Trained** Newmarket, Suffolk

**FOCUS**
Little more than an exercise gallop for the winner, who unsurprisingly outclassed his sole rival. The runner-up is rated to his latest effort.

## 1230 BETBRIGHT.COM FILLIES' H'CAP 7f (P)
**6:25** (6:25) (Class 5) (0-70,72) 4-Y-0+ **£2,587** (£770; £384; £192) **Stalls** Low

Form RPR
3431 1 **Ishiamber**[6] 1123 4-9-11 **72** 6ex .......................... LukeMorris 3 83
(George Baker) *t.k.h: in tch: effrt 2f out: led over 1f out: drvn out* **13/8**[1]
065- 2 ½ **Meet Me Halfway**[180] 6998 4-9-3 **67** .......................... AshleyMorgan(3) 5 76
(Chris Wall) *rrd s: hld up in rr: rdn 2f out: clsd on wnr fnl f: jst hld* **14/1**
123- 3 1 **Princess Spirit**[119] 8151 5-8-5 **59** .......................... (p) JenniferFerguson(7) 4 65
(Edward Creighton) *plld hrd: pressed ldr: slt ld 3f out tl over 1f out: unable qck* **4/1**[3]
0125 4 ¾ **Mill I Am (USA)**[6] 1123 4-8-8 **60** .......................... RyanTate(5) 1 64
(Stuart Williams) *cl up: rdn over 2f out: one pce fnl f* **9/2**
-365 5 1 ¼ **Lady Sylvia**[27] 853 5-9-7 **68** .......................... AdamKirby 2 69
(Joseph Tuite) *led and set modest pce: hdd 3f out: no ex fnl f: eased whn btn* **11/4**[2]

1m 28.08s (2.08) **Going Correction** 0.0s/f (Stan) **5** Ran SP% **109.6**
Speed ratings (Par 100): **88,87,86,85,84**
CSF £22.17 TOTE £1.90: £1.70, £6.00; EX 24.80 Trifecta £46.00.
**Owner** Mrs P Scott-Dunn **Bred** Patricia Ann Scott-Dunn **Trained** Manton, Wilts

**FOCUS**
A fair fillies' handicap run at a steady pace. Muddling form.

## 1231 BETBRIGHT - LIVE THE MOMENT H'CAP 1m 4f (P)
**6:55** (6:55) (Class 5) (0-70,70) 4-Y-0+ **£2,587** (£770; £384; £192) **Stalls** Centre

Form RPR
200- 1 **Emulating (IRE)**[133] 7970 4-9-6 **70** .......................... ShaneKelly 1 77+
(James Fanshawe) *hld up in 4th: qcknd to ld over 1f out: pushed out: comf* **11/8**[1]
-500 2 1 ¼ **Honourable Knight (IRE)**[30] 818 6-9-2 **65** .......................... DavidProbert 3 70
(Mark Usher) *trckd ldr: led briefly wl over 1f out: unable qck fnl f* **12/1**
5542 3 shd **Reflect (IRE)**[16] 990 6-9-4 **67** .......................... (vt) DaleSwift 6 72
(Derek Shaw) *stdd s: t.k.h in rr: rdn and hdwy over 1f out: r.o fnl f* **11/2**[3]
0000 4 2 ¾ **Wild Desert (FR)**[16] 992 9-9-0 **63** .......................... LukeMorris 2 63
(Tony Carroll) *led tl wl over 1f out: no ex fnl f* **20/1**
5-00 5 hd **Shirataki (IRE)**[69] 293 6-8-13 **62** .......................... ChrisCatlin 7 62
(Peter Hiatt) *t.k.h: chsd ldrs: chal wl over 1f out: no ex fnl f* **10/1**
1 P **Highfields Dancer**[33] 776 6-9-6 **69** .......................... RyanMoore 5
(Gary Moore) *in tch: 5th whn p.u lame over 2f out: fatally injured* **9/4**[2]

2m 39.15s (4.65) **Going Correction** 0.0s/f (Stan)
**WFA** 4 from 6yo+ 1lb **6** Ran SP% **109.8**
Speed ratings (Par 103): **84,83,83,81,81**
CSF £17.71 TOTE £2.60: £2.20, £3.10; EX 20.00 Trifecta £71.30.
**Owner** Ben CM Wong **Bred** Mrs E J O'Grady **Trained** Newmarket, Suffolk

**FOCUS**
A fair handicap run at a steady pace. It is rated around the fourth.

## 1232 FAMILY FUN ON 19.04.14 H'CAP 1m 3f (P)
**7:25** (7:25) (Class 6) (0-60,60) 4-Y-0+ **£1,940** (£577; £288; £144) **Stalls** Low

Form RPR
-236 1 **Maison Brillet (IRE)**[16] 989 7-9-6 **59** .......................... (p) RobertHavlin 4 67
(Clive Drew) *in tch: effrt 2f out: chal fnl f: led fnl strides* **10/1**
0/23 2 shd **Orpen'Arry (IRE)**[16] 989 6-8-13 **57** .......................... (p) DavidKenny(5) 12 65
(Paul Burgoyne) *led: kpt on wl u.p fnl f: hdd fnl strides* **16/1**
1123 3 nk **Bennelong**[7] 1097 8-9-2 **58** .......................... (v) OisinMurphy(3) 8 65
(Lee Carter) *hld up towards rr: hdwy 2f out: chal fnl f: r.o* **7/2**[1]
0-60 4 ½ **Wyndham Wave**[13] 1023 5-8-12 **51** .......................... (b[1]) DavidProbert 9 57
(Rod Millman) *stdd s: hld up towards rr: hdwy 2f out: pressed ldrs fnl f: r.o* **6/1**[2]
4522 5 2 ½ **Elegant Ophelia**[16] 989 5-9-7 **60** .......................... (t) AdamKirby 5 63+
(Dean Ivory) *in tch: lost pl and n.m.r over 2f out: r.o again fr over 1f out* **7/1**[3]
0-56 6 hd **If I Were A Boy (IRE)**[27] 857 7-9-6 **59** .......................... (be) JamesDoyle 11 61
(Dominic Ffrench Davis) *hld up in rr: promising hdwy 2f out: no imp fnl f* **16/1**
5404 7 ¾ **Entrapping**[14] 1012 4-9-1 **54** .......................... JimmyQuinn 2 54
(John E Long) *t.k.h: prom on rail tl no ex jst over 1f out* **16/1**
455- 8 1 **Greyemkay**[119] 8148 6-8-7 **49** .......................... ThomasBrown(3) 3 47
(Richard Price) *prom tl outpcd over 2f out* **20/1**
050- 9 1 ½ **Capetown Kid**[130] 8031 4-8-8 **52** .......................... JoshBaudains(5) 7 48
(Sylvester Kirk) *chsd ldr tl wknd 2f out* **25/1**
526- 10 4 ½ **Party Palace**[174] 3953 10-8-6 **50** .......................... NatashaEaton(5) 6 38
(Stuart Howe) *mid-div: wd st: n.d after* **33/1**
-411 11 2 ¼ **Cataria Girl (USA)**[7] 1097 5-8-11 **57** .......................... (t) JordanVaughan(7) 10 41
(Marcus Tregoning) *s.s: towards rr: wd st: n.d* **7/2**[1]
-612 12 15 **My Renaissance**[28] 838 4-9-1 **54** .......................... ShaneKelly 13 11
(Ben Case) *in tch tl wknd over 2f out* **15/2**
00/0 13 1 ¼ **Make A Fuss**[34] 760 5-8-7 **46** oh1 ..........................[1] ChrisCatlin 1
(Gerry Enright) *s.i.s: a wl bhd* **100/1**

2m 20.12s (-1.78) **Going Correction** 0.0s/f (Stan) **13** Ran SP% **122.3**
Speed ratings (Par 101): **106,105,105,105,103 103,102,102,101,97 96,85,84**
CSF £157.15 CT £681.57 TOTE £10.00: £3.00, £1.70, £2.30; EX 284.20 Trifecta £1118.70.
**Owner** C Drew **Bred** Liam Webb **Trained** Rampton, Cambs

**FOCUS**
They went a steady pace for this moderate contest which saw a thrilling finish. Sound, regulation form.

## 1233 BETBRIGHT MOBILE MAIDEN FILLIES' STKS 1m (P)
**7:55** (7:56) (Class 5) 3-Y-0+ **£2,587** (£770; £384; £192) **Stalls** Low

Form RPR
30- 1 **Cameo Tiara (IRE)**[158] 7532 3-8-13 0 .......................... RyanMoore 3 80
(Richard Hannon) *settled in 4th: rdn to chse clr ldr 2f out: styd on to ld ins fnl f* **9/2**[3]
0- 2 2 ½ **Arctic Moon (USA)**[210] 6112 3-8-13 0 .......................... MickaelBarzalona 7 74
(Charlie Appleby) *led and racd freely: sn 4 l clr: rdn 2f out: hdd and no ex ins fnl f* **7/1**
3 3 ¾ **Labise (IRE)**[56] 486 3-8-13 0 .......................... (t) JimCrowley 11 72
(Ralph Beckett) *chsd ldng pair: rdn over 3f out: kpt on fnl 2f* **15/8**[1]
4 hd **Reesha** 3-8-13 0 .......................... PaulHanagan 8 72+
(Roger Varian) *chsd ldrs: rdn over 2f out: kpt on fr over 1f out* **12/1**
5 1 ¼ **Betty Bere (FR)** 3-8-13 0 .......................... DanielTudhope 4 69+
(K R Burke) *towards rr: rdn and hdwy over 1f out: styd on: nvr rchd ldrs* **11/4**[2]
42 6 nk **Sparkling Ice (IRE)**[13] 1024 3-8-13 0 .......................... JohnFahy 5 68
(Eve Johnson Houghton) *chsd clr ldr tl 2f out: sn wknd* **16/1**
7 3 **Mountain Dew** 3-8-13 0 .......................... RichardKingscote 10 61
(Ralph Beckett) *towards rr: sme hdwy 2f out: nvr nr to chal* **20/1**
00 8 4 ½ **Kovolini**[13] 1024 4-10-0 0 .......................... GeorgeBaker 1 54
(Geoffrey Deacon) *mid-div tl wknd 2f out* **66/1**
9 ¾ **Semaral (IRE)** 3-8-13 0 .......................... TedDurcan 9 48
(Chris Wall) *mid-div tl wknd over 2f out* **50/1**
6 10 4 ½ **Permitted**[28] 847 3-8-13 0 .......................... WilliamCarson 6 37
(Lee Carter) *s.i.s: a bhd* **100/1**
0- 11 9 **Summerling (IRE)**[193] 6641 3-8-10 0 .......................... MatthewLawson(3) 12 16
(Jonathan Portman) *towards rr: rdn over 3f out: sn bhd* **100/1**

1m 38.66s (-1.14) **Going Correction** 0.0s/f (Stan)
**WFA** 3 from 4yo 15lb **11** Ran SP% **115.9**
Speed ratings (Par 100): **105,102,101,101,100 100,97,92,91,87 78**
CSF £34.33 TOTE £5.30: £1.20, £2.20, £1.50; EX 40.60 Trifecta £112.40.
**Owner** Mrs J Wood **Bred** Robert Norton **Trained** East Everleigh, Wilts
■ Stewards' Enquiry : Daniel Tudhope one-day ban: careless riding (Apr 16)

**FOCUS**
Plenty of pace on for this interesting fillies' maiden, but the time was modest. The winner improved a bit on her debut effort.

## 1234 BETBRIGHT MONEYBACK OFFERS H'CAP (LONDON MILE SERIES QUALIFIER) 1m (P)
**8:25** (8:25) (Class 4) (0-80,85) 4-Y-0+ **£4,690** (£1,395; £697; £348) **Stalls** Low

Form RPR
-551 1 **High Time Too (IRE)**[28] 843 4-9-4 **77** .......................... RyanMoore 2 88
(Hugo Palmer) *chsd ldng pair: wnt 4 l 2nd wl over 1f out: r.o to ld ins fnl f: rdn out* **10/1**
4231 2 1 **Sound Advice**[7] 1113 5-9-9 **85** 6ex .......................... JasonHart(3) 7 94
(Keith Dalgleish) *broke wl: led and sn 4 l clr: hdd and no ex ins fnl f* **3/1**[2]
5212 3 4 **Liberty Jack (IRE)**[7] 1103 4-9-4 **77** .......................... WilliamCarson 1 77
(Jim Boyle) *dwlt: hld up towards rr: shkn up and hdwy over 1f out: r.o* **6/1**[3]
51- 4 1 ¼ **Love Excel**[109] 8303 4-9-4 **77** .......................... JamieSpencer 6 74
(Charles Hills) *chsd clr ldr tl wl over 1f out: one pce* **11/8**[1]
2440 5 3 ½ **Jay Bee Blue**[14] 1014 5-9-5 **78** .......................... (t) JamesDoyle 9 67
(Sean Curran) *mid-div: rdn and no hdwy fnl 2f* **33/1**
3144 6 1 **Club House (IRE)**[5] 1142 4-8-11 **73** .......................... WilliamTwiston-Davies(3) 4 60
(Robert Mills) *bhd: rdn over 2f out: nvr nr ldrs* **25/1**
-025 7 3 ¼ **Swift Cedar (IRE)**[40] 690 4-8-12 **71** .......................... (b) LukeMorris 3 50
(Jeremy Gask) *chsd clr ldrs tl wknd 2f out* **20/1**
0-55 8 2 ¼ **Subtle Knife**[14] 1014 5-9-7 **80** .......................... AdamKirby 8 54
(Giles Bravery) *sn bhd: mod effrt over 2f out: n.d* **7/1**
6-00 9 10 **Spirit Rider (USA)**[21] 929 4-8-10 **69** .......................... LiamKeniry 5 20
(Giles Bravery) *a bhd* **100/1**

1m 37.78s (-2.02) **Going Correction** 0.0s/f (Stan) **9** Ran SP% **115.5**
Speed ratings (Par 105): **110,109,105,103,100 99,96,93,83**
CSF £38.91 CT £201.28 TOTE £11.00: £2.50, £1.40, £2.60; EX 39.30 Trifecta £129.60.
**Owner** Rathordan Partnership **Bred** Christopher Maye **Trained** Newmarket, Suffolk

**FOCUS**
The pace was strong for this fair handicap. A clear personal best from the winner.

## 1235 VISIT AND DINE IN THE PANORAMIC H'CAP 1m (P)
**8:55** (8:56) (Class 6) (0-60,60) 3-Y-0 **£1,940** (£577; £288; £144) **Stalls** Low

Form RPR
00-6 1 **Next Stop**[35] 748 3-9-4 **57** .......................... AmirQuinn 6 67
(Lee Carter) *in tch: effrt over 2f out: wnt 4 l 2nd wl over 1f out: r.o to ld wl ins fnl f* **8/1**
2432 2 2 ¼ **Romantic Bliss (IRE)**[7] 1101 3-8-2 **48** .......................... (b) RobJFitzpatrick(7) 11 52
(K R Burke) *broke wl: led: 4 l clr 2f out: hrd rdn over 1f out: hdd and no ex wl ins fnl f* **9/2**[3]
0-43 3 hd **Sandy Cove**[33] 774 3-9-2 **55** .......................... LukeMorris 3 59
(James Eustace) *t.k.h: in tch: effrt over 2f out: styd on fnl f* **2/1**[1]
2156 4 2 **Royal Bushida**[33] 774 3-8-9 **48** ow1 .......................... (v[1]) DaleSwift 1 47
(Derek Shaw) *towards rr: rdn and hdwy 2f out: styd on same pce fnl f* **20/1**
0-55 5 4 ½ **Miss Tweedy**[15] 1007 3-9-2 **55** .......................... DavidProbert 9 44
(Rod Millman) *prom tl wknd over 1f out* **16/1**
1-55 6 nk **Jazri**[41] 670 3-9-7 **60** .......................... DanielTudhope 7 48
(Milton Bradley) *mid-div on outer: outpcd fnl 2f* **20/1**
0-14 7 2 ¼ **Lucky Dottie**[13] 1029 3-8-8 **47** .......................... FrankieMcDonald 4 30
(Pat Phelan) *prom tl wknd 2f out* **25/1**
6323 8 1 ¼ **Needs The Run**[13] 1029 3-9-1 **54** .......................... AdamKirby 5 34
(David Evans) *bhd: rdn over 2f out: nvr nr ldrs* **7/1**
0-00 9 1 ½ **Madame Mime Artist**[36] 741 3-9-6 **59** .......................... (t) GeorgeBaker 10 36
(Alastair Lidderdale) *sn bhd* **4/1**[2]
-535 10 10 **River Dreamer (IRE)**[33] 786 3-8-7 **46** oh1 .......................... AdamBeschizza 2
(Robert Stephens) *mid-div on rail: wknd 3f out* **12/1**
00-0 11 8 **Redlorryellowlorry (IRE)**[27] 865 3-8-13 **52** .......................... FergusSweeney 8
(George Baker) *chsd ldrs: wknd qckly 3f out: sn bhd* **25/1**

1m 38.82s (-0.98) **Going Correction** 0.0s/f (Stan) **11** Ran SP% **125.9**
Speed ratings (Par 96): **104,101,101,99,95 94,92,91,89,79 71**
CSF £44.77 CT £104.05 TOTE £9.60: £3.40, £1.80, £1.10; EX 95.20 Trifecta £205.40.
**Owner** S Hussey **Bred** Millsec Limited **Trained** Epsom, Surrey
■ Stewards' Enquiry : Amir Quinn four-day ban: used whip above permitted level (Apr 16-19)

**FOCUS**
A moderate handicap run at a messy pace until the runner-up went on. The winner improved on her maiden form.

T/Plt: £67.90 to a £1 stake. Pool: £60,372.95 - 648.29 winning units. T/Qpdt: £16.90 to a £1 stake. Pool: £8668.15 - 378.80 winning units. LM

# [1140] LINGFIELD (L-H)

Wednesday, April 2

**OFFICIAL GOING: Standard**

Wind: light, across Weather: overcast

## 1236 LADBROKES CLAIMING STKS — 1m 1y(P)

2:25 (2:25) (Class 6) 3-Y-O+ — £2,045 (£603; £302) Stalls High

Form — RPR

-123 **1** **Gaelic Silver (FR)**[5] [1142] 8-9-11 70 ..... RyanMoore 3 — 72
(Gary Moore) *in tch in midfield: hdwy to ld wl over 1f out: sn rdn and qcknd clr: r.o wl: rdn out* **1/2**[1]

2343 **2** *5* **Officer In Command (USA)**[9] [1083] 8-9-13 69 ..... (p) LiamKeniry 7 — 63
(John Butler) *s.i.s: niggled along in last pair: rdn and hdwy on outer ent fnl 2f: wnt 2nd fnl 100yds: no ch w wnr: eased towards fin* **9/2**[2]

-603 **3** *1 1/2* **Abigails Angel**[14] [1016] 7-8-10 51 ..... DavidParkes(7) 2 — 49
(Brett Johnson) *dwlt: sn rcvrd and racd in midfield: rdn and hdwy wl over 1f out: wnt 3rd fnl 100yds: kpt on but no ch w wnr* **14/1**

0355 **4** *1* **Claude Monet (BRZ)**[14] [1015] 5-9-4 48 ..... JackDuern(5) 1 — 53
(Simon Dow) *led tl hdd and unable qck u.p wl over 1f out: no ch w wnr and plugged on same pce after* **25/1**

-005 **5** *1 3/4* **The Mongoose**[22] [918] 6-9-7 62 ..... (t) AdamKirby 4 — 47
(David Evans) *chsd ldrs: rdn and chsd clr wnr over 1f out: no imp: lost 2nd and wknd fnl 100yds* **8/1**[3]

5-00 **6** *3/4* **Querido (GER)**[14] [1016] 10-9-1 41 ..... (tp) ShelleyBirkett(5) 5 — 44
(Paddy Butler) *in tch in last pair: nt clr run ent fnl 2f: rdn and effrt on inner over 1f out: no hdwy: wknd ins fnl f* **100/1**

0504 **7** *12* **Waterloo Dock**[7] [1104] 9-9-6 45 ..... (v) MartinDwyer 6 — 16
(Mick Quinn) *t.k.h: chsd ldr tl 2f out: wkng whn n.m.r over 1f out: bhd and eased wl ins fnl f* **50/1**

1m 37.47s (-0.73) **Going Correction** 0.0s/f (Stan) — 7 Ran SP% **109.4**
Speed ratings (Par 101): **103,98,96,95,93 93,81**
CSF £2.66 TOTE £1.60: £1.50, £1.20; EX 3.30 Trifecta £9.20.

**Owner** The Winning Hand **Bred** Earl Haras Du Camp Bernard Et Al **Trained** Lower Beeding, W Sussex

**FOCUS**
The well-backed favourite, who was best in at the weights, won easily. The poor and sixth limit the form.

## 1237 LADBROKES MOBILE MEDIAN AUCTION MAIDEN STKS — 7f 1y(P)

2:55 (2:56) (Class 6) 3-5-Y-O — £2,249 (£664; £332) Stalls Low

Form — RPR

254- **1** **Sacha Park (IRE)**[206] [6234] 3-8-12 92 ..... RyanMoore 2 — 81
(Richard Hannon) *mde all: rdn wl over 1f out: forged ahd fnl 75yds: r.o: rdn out* **2/5**[1]

53- **2** *3/4* **Three Peaks**[166] [7335] 3-8-12 0 ..... JamesDoyle 5 — 79
(Charles Hills) *chsd ldng pair: swtchd to inner over 4f out: rdn and effrt to chse wnr wl over 1f out: ev ch whn edgd lft and flashed tail u.p ins fnl f: no ex and btn fnl 75yds* **11/4**[2]

33/ **3** *4 1/2* **Rome**[474] [8102] 4-9-12 0 ..... GeorgeBaker 4 — 72
(Gary Moore) *stdd after s: hld up in tch in rr: effrt wl over 1f out: chsd ldng pair jst over 1f out: wknd ins fnl f* **12/1**[3]

554- **4** *hd* **Serena Grae**[105] [8332] 3-8-7 70 ..... MartinDwyer 3 — 61
(Marcus Tregoning) *taken down early: chsd wnr tl wl over 1f out: sn outpcd and btn 1f out: plugged on* **14/1**

1m 25.11s (0.31) **Going Correction** 0.0s/f (Stan)
**WFA** 3 from 4yo 14lb — 4 Ran SP% **112.5**
Speed ratings (Par 101): **98,97,92,91**
CSF £1.95 TOTE £1.40; EX 1.80 Trifecta £4.40.

**Owner** Middleham Park Racing XLI **Bred** Kildaragh Stud **Trained** East Everleigh, Wilts

**FOCUS**
The winner did not need to match his best to make all.

## 1238 COMPARE BOOKMAKERS AT BOOKMAKERS.CO.UK H'CAP — 5f 6y(P)

3:25 (3:25) (Class 6) (0-65,65) 4-Y-O+ — £2,726 (£805; £402) Stalls High

Form — RPR

5414 **1** **Dishy Guru**[16] [987] 5-8-13 57 ..... (b) LiamKeniry 4 — 71
(Michael Blanshard) *a travelling strly: hld up in tch in midfield: cruised upsides ldrs ent fnl f: rdn and readily qcknd clr ins fnl f: easily* **5/2**[1]

5013 **2** *2* **Johnny Splash (IRE)**[21] [921] 5-8-13 57 ..... (v) RyanMoore 5 — 64
(Roger Teal) *led: drvn wl over 1f out: hdd and brushed aside by wnr ins fnl f: kpt on for clr 2nd* **3/1**[2]

66-0 **3** *1 3/4* **Danzoe (IRE)**[33] [777] 7-8-13 62 ..... EoinWalsh(5) 1 — 63
(Christine Dunnett) *chsd ldrs: effrt u.p over 1f out: kpt on same pce ins fnl f* **14/1**

0262 **4** *1/2* **Quality Art (USA)**[21] [921] 6-9-6 64 ..... SteveDrowne 9 — 63
(Simon Hodgson) *hld up in tch in midfield: effrt u.p over 1f out: kpt on ins fnl f: no threat to wnr* **16/1**

0-60 **5** *1* **Ceelo**[16] [993] 4-9-3 64 ..... [1] SimonPearce(3) 6 — 59
(Lydia Pearce) *hld up in tch in rr of main gp: rdn and effrt over 1f out: no imp: nvr trbld ldrs* **6/1**[3]

-404 **6** *1 1/4* **Purford Green**[14] [1018] 5-8-8 52 oh4 ow1 ..... (v) RobertHavlin 2 — 43
(Michael Attwater) *pressed ldrs on inner: rdn and unable qck over 1f out: wknd ins fnl f* **66/1**

300 **7** *3/4* **Dorback**[56] [489] 7-9-7 65 ..... (t) DaneO'Neill 8 — 53
(Tony Newcombe) *pressed ldrs on outer: drvn and outpcd over 1f out: wknd ins fnl f* **3/1**[2]

236- **8** *2 1/2* **Trending (IRE)**[114] [8216] 5-9-0 65 ..... (bt) DavidParkes(7) 3 — 44+
(Jeremy Gask) *awkward leaving stalls and v.s.a: wl bhd: clsd 1/2-way: rdn and wknd over 1f out* **14/1**

05-5 **9** *hd* **Alhaarth Beauty (IRE)**[7] [1104] 4-8-13 64 ..... DonnaAspell(7) 7 — 42+
(Phil McEntee) *stdd after s and v.s.i.s: wl bhd in last pair: clsd 1/2-way: rdn and wknd over 1f out* **20/1**

59.41s (0.61) **Going Correction** 0.0s/f (Stan) — 9 Ran SP% **118.3**
Speed ratings (Par 101): **95,91,89,88,86 84,83,79,79**
CSF £10.45 CT £87.97 TOTE £2.80: £1.50, £1.50, £4.30; EX 12.30 Trifecta £85.50.

**Owner** Clifton Partners **Bred** J W Ford **Trained** Upper Lambourn, Berks

**FOCUS**
The form makes enough sense around the first and second.

## 1239 32RED H'CAP — 1m 4f (P)

3:55 (3:55) (Class 6) (0-65,65) 3-Y-O — £2,726 (£805; £402) Stalls Low

Form — RPR

606- **1** **Late Shipment**[137] [7936] 3-9-7 65 ..... JoeFanning 1 — 79
(Mark Johnston) *t.k.h: led for 1f: chsd ldrs after tl effrt to ld 2f out: rdn and drew clr over 1f out: r.o strly: easily* **6/4**[2]

6434 **2** *10* **Flying Author (IRE)**[8] [1088] 3-8-0 51 oh6 ..... (tp) DonnaAspell(7) 4 — 49
(Phil McEntee) *wnt rt s: hdwy to ld after 1f: rdn and hdd 2f out: outpcd and no ch w wnr 1f out: kpt on for clr 2nd* **33/1**

0132 **3** *3 1/2* **Blue Oyster**[6] [1124] 3-9-7 65 ..... ShaneKelly 5 — 57
(Philip McBride) *pushed rt s: sn rcvrd: chsd ldr 9f out: rdn and ev ch over 2f out: 3rd and outpcd 2f out: wl btn over 1f out* **5/4**[1]

-451 **4** *2 3/4* **Duly Acclaimed (IRE)**[36] [743] 3-8-4 55 ..... CamHardie(7) 3 — 43
(J S Moore) *hld up in rr: rdn 4f out: outpcd and btn over 2f out: no ch over 1f out* **7/1**[3]

-625 **5** *1/2* **Beastfromtheeast**[13] [1029] 3-8-7 51 oh2 ..... (b) HayleyTurner 2 — 38
(Ed Walker) *rdn along early: chsd ldr after 1f tl 9f out: rdn over 3f out: 4th and btn 2f out: sn wknd* **8/1**

2m 31.09s (-1.91) **Going Correction** 0.0s/f (Stan) — 5 Ran SP% **111.0**
Speed ratings (Par 96): **106,99,97,95,94**
CSF £34.06 TOTE £2.40: £1.80, £4.00; EX 35.60 Trifecta £86.90.

**Owner** R Barnett **Bred** W And R Barnett Ltd **Trained** Middleham Moor, N Yorks

**FOCUS**
Not a competitive race, but the pace was alright. The third and fourth disappointed.

## 1240 32RED.COM FILLIES' H'CAP (BOBIS RACE) — 1m 2f (P)

4:25 (4:25) (Class 4) (0-80,80) 3-Y-O — £5,175 (£1,540; £769; £384) Stalls Low

Form — RPR

31- **1** **Sequined (USA)**[169] [7260] 3-9-5 78 ..... MickaelBarzalona 2 — 84+
(Charlie Appleby) *t.k.h: trckd ldrs: nt clr run ent fnl 2f: rdn and qcknd to ld on inner ent fnl f: hrd drvn fnl 100yds: hld on cl home* **7/4**[1]

11-1 **2** *hd* **Groovejet**[83] [99] 3-9-7 80 ..... JamesDoyle 3 — 84
(Peter Chapple-Hyam) *led: rdn ent fnl 2f: hdd ent fnl f: edgd rt u.p ins fnl f: rallied gamely towards fin* **5/1**

000- **3** *1 3/4* **Mollasses**[193] [6643] 3-8-11 70 ..... TomQueally 8 — 71+
(Jonathan Portman) *rn green: s.i.s: hld up in tch in rr: rn green and racd awkwardly bnd 2f: nt clr run jst over 1f out: hdwy 1f out: wnt rt but styd on ins fnl f: wnt 3rd nr fin* **25/1**

62-1 **4** *nk* **Thurayaat**[22] [914] 3-9-1 74 ..... PaulHanagan 4 — 74
(Roger Varian) *stdd s: t.k.h: hld up in tch: nt clr run jst over 2f out: rdn and hdwy over 1f out: chsd ldng pair 1f out: no imp: lost 3rd nr fin* **9/2**[3]

101- **5** *3/4* **Hedge End (IRE)**[119] [8147] 3-9-7 80 ..... RyanMoore 5 — 78
(Richard Hannon) *wl in tch in midfield: rdn and unable qck 2f out: trying to rally wwhn hmpd jst ins fnl f: kpt on same pce after* **10/1**

35-2 **6** *1/2* **Ifrika**[19] [955] 3-8-11 70 ..... KierenFallon 7 — 67
(Clive Brittain) *stdd bk after s: hld up in tch towards rr: rdn and hdwy to chse ldrs 3f out: outpcd bnd 2f out: keeping on same pce whn hmpd jst ins fnl f* **7/1**

636- **7** *1 1/4* **Layla's Red Devil (IRE)**[159] [7493] 3-8-9 68 ..... JamieSpencer 6 — 65
(Richard Fahey) *w ldr tl edgd rt bnd 2f out: drvn and unable qck over 1f out: btn whn hmpd jst ins fnl f: n.d after* **4/1**[2]

2m 8.58s (1.98) **Going Correction** 0.0s/f (Stan) — 7 Ran SP% **116.6**
Speed ratings (Par 97): **92,91,90,90,89 89,88**
CSF £11.37 CT £160.96 TOTE £2.60: £1.20, £3.00; EX 12.70 Trifecta £164.40.

**Owner** Godolphin **Bred** Darley **Trained** Newmarket, Suffolk

**FOCUS**
Half of these had won last time out and this looked an interesting handicap, but the early pace was fairly steady. It's hard to be too positive about the form.

## 1241 CORAL.CO.UK H'CAP — 1m 2f (P)

4:55 (4:55) (Class 4) (0-85,84) 4-Y-O+ — £5,175 (£1,540; £769; £384) Stalls Low

Form — RPR

650- **1** **Red Runaway**[175] [7121] 4-8-13 76 ..... RyanMoore 6 — 86
(Ed Dunlop) *w ldr: rdn and ev ch ent fnl 2f: forged ahd 1f out: styd on wl: rdn out* **6/4**[1]

-352 **2** *2 1/2* **Appease**[14] [1014] 5-9-0 77 ..... (p) TomQueally 5 — 82
(John Butler) *sn led: rdn ent fnl 2f: no ex u.p 1f out: kpt on same pce and hung rt ins fnl f: hld on for 2nd cl home* **7/2**[2]

3-03 **3** *hd* **Syncopate**[14] [1022] 5-8-11 74 ..... LiamKeniry 3 — 79
(Pam Sly) *wl in tch in midfield: rdn and effrt over 1f out: keeping on same pce whn carried rt ins fnl f* **8/1**

645- **4** *1/2* **Ree's Rascal (IRE)**[132] [7989] 6-9-6 83 ..... StephenCraine 7 — 87
(Jim Boyle) *wl in tch in midfield: rdn and effrt jst over 2f out: sltly outpcd over 1f out: kpt on and pressing for placings towards fin* **14/1**

4506 **5** *3 1/4* **Mia's Boy**[14] [1014] 10-9-6 83 ..... GeorgeBaker 1 — 80
(Chris Dwyer) *stdd after s: hld up in tch in rr: rdn and effrt over 1f out: wknd ins fnl f* **8/1**

3-43 **6** *8* **Veeraya**[32] [804] 4-9-2 84 ..... (p) ShelleyBirkett(5) 2 — 65
(Julia Feilden) *chsd ldrs: rdn and struggling over 2f out: wknd u.p over 1f out* **4/1**[3]

235- **7** *nk* **Fairyinthewind (IRE)**[125] [7651] 5-8-10 73 ..... KierenFallon 4 — 54
(Brendan Powell) *in tch in last pair: rdn wl over 3f out: wd and btn bnd 2f out: sn wknd* **20/1**

2m 3.4s (-3.20) **Going Correction** 0.0s/f (Stan) — 7 Ran SP% **115.9**
Speed ratings (Par 105): **112,110,109,109,106 100,100**
CSF £7.13 CT £30.69 TOTE £2.70: £1.60, £2.10; EX 10.90 Trifecta £45.80.

**Owner** The Hon R J Arculli **Bred** Lofts Hall, M Philipson & Cheveley Park **Trained** Newmarket, Suffolk

■ Stewards' Enquiry : Tom Queally one-day ban: careless riding (Apr 16)

**FOCUS**
It paid to race handily in a race lacking early pace. The winner is rated back to his early 3yo form.

## 1242 32RED TOMB RAIDER SLOT H'CAP — 1m 7f 169y(P)

5:25 (5:25) (Class 6) (0-60,60) 4-Y-O+ — £2,726 (£805; £402) Stalls Low

Form — RPR

-524 **1** **Dr Finley (IRE)**[28] [842] 7-9-1 54 ..... (v) SimonPearce(3) 6 — 61
(Lydia Pearce) *chsd ldr: rdn and ev ch 3f out: squeezed ent fnl 2f: led over 1f out: styd on u.p and forged ahd fnl 50yds* **9/2**[3]

41-0 **2** *1/2* **Annaluna (IRE)**[31] [349] 5-9-1 54 ..... (v) DeclanBates(3) 2 — 60
(David Evans) *led: rdn and jnd 3f out: squeezed ent fnl 2f: hdd over 1f out: kpt on tl no ex and btn fnl 50yds* **14/1**

3434 **3** *1 ¼* **Bert The Alert**[5] 1140 6-9-10 **60**........ LiamJones 4 65
(Laura Mongan) *hld up in last pair: hdwy to chse ldrs 5f out: rdn and ev ch whn carried lft and sltly hmpd ent fnl 2f: no ex and btn ins fnl f* **7/4**[1]

50-4 **4** *31* **Brabazon (IRE)**[5] 1150 11-9-10 **60**........ JamieSpencer 3 28
(Emmet Michael Butterly, Ire) *hld up in last pair: 4th and drvn wl over 3f out: no hdwy and wknd 2f out: eased ent fnl f: t.o* **10/1**

466 **5** *21* **Ceevee**[49] 581 4-9-2 **56**........ (t) DavidProbert 5
(Tim Vaughan) *chsd ldrs tl dropped to rr and drvn over 4f out: lost tch 3f out: t.o* **8/1**

2154 **U** **Graylyn Ruby (FR)**[16] 992 9-9-2 **52**........ AndreaAtzeni 1
(Robert Eddery) *stmbld and uns rdr after s* **5/2**[2]

3m 25.63s (-0.07) **Going Correction** 0.0s/f (Stan)
**WFA** 4 from 5yo+ 4lb **6** Ran SP% **110.0**
Speed ratings (Par 101): **100,99,99,83,73**
CSF £55.22 TOTE £5.10: £1.70, £5.20; EX 56.70 Trifecta £108.10.
**Owner** Killarney Glen **Bred** Darley **Trained** Newmarket, Suffolk

**FOCUS**
Drama at the start here as Graylyn Ruby stumbled and ditched his rider after the stalls opened. The loose horse also had a part to play later on in the race when cutting across the three principals as they headed for the turn in. Very modest form.
T/Plt: £14.30 to a £1 stake. Pool: £60,867.80 - 3104.57 winning units. T/Qpdt: £9.40 to a £1 stake. Pool: 3708.06 - 291.28 winning units. SP

# 1222 SOUTHWELL (L-H)
## Wednesday, April 2

**OFFICIAL GOING: Standard**
Wind: Moderate across Weather: Cloudy

## 1243 BOOKMAKERS.CO.UK MAIDEN STKS 5f (F)
**2:35** (2:36) (Class 5) 3-Y-O+ **£2,587** (£770; £384; £192) **Stalls** High

Form RPR

04- **1** **Walta (IRE)**[236] 5215 3-8-11 0........ (b[1]) PhilipPrince(5) 5 65
(Roy Bowring) *dwlt and swtchd lft s to r centre: gd hdwy on outer to ld after 2f: rdn over 1f out: kpt on strly* **25/1**

0- **2** *2 ½* **Roomie**[144] 7818 3-8-11 0........ DuranFentiman 1 51
(Tim Easterby) *dwlt: sn trcking ldrs on outer: hdwy 1/2-way: rdn to chse wnr and ev ch wl over 1f out: drvn and kpt on same pce fnl f* **8/1**[2]

433- **3** *1* **Steele Ranger**[243] 4963 3-9-2 74........ LukeMorris 3 52
(Peter Chapple-Hyam) *trckd ldrs: pushed along wl over 3f out: rdn 2f out: sn drvn and one pce* **2/9**[1]

5- **4** *5* **Pusey Street Vale**[289] 3408 3-8-8 0........ MichaelJMMurphy(3) 4 29
(John Gallagher) *racd nr stands' rail: led 2f: cl up: rdn along wl over 2f out: sn btn* **8/1**[2]

3456 **5** *6* **Jiminy**[40] 693 4-9-13 47........ (b) RobertWinston 2 18
(Alan Berry) *prom: rdn along 1/2-way: sn wknd* **14/1**[3]

655- **6** *5* **Elusive**[407] 712 8-9-3 29........ AnnStokell(5) 6
(Ann Stokell) *sn in rr: outpcd and bhd fr 1/2-way* **100/1**

1m 1.17s (1.47) **Going Correction** +0.075s/f (Slow)
**WFA** 3 from 4yo+ 11lb **6** Ran SP% **115.6**
Speed ratings (Par 103): **91,87,85,77,67 59**
CSF £201.31 TOTE £25.10: £10.40, £3.10; EX 248.70 Trifecta £836.70.
**Owner** S R Bowring **Bred** John Webb **Trained** Edwinstowe, Notts

**FOCUS**
Maidens don't come much weaker than this and short-priced favourite backers got their fingers well and truly burned. Little form to go on, and it's hard to know what the winner achieved.

## 1244 BOOKMAKERS.CO.UK H'CAP 5f (F)
**3:05** (3:05) (Class 5) (0-75,74) 4-Y-O+ **£2,587** (£770; £384; £192) **Stalls** High

Form RPR

641- **1** **Foxy Music**[154] 7634 10-9-4 **74**........ JasonHart(3) 3 89
(Eric Alston) *cl up centre: led after 1 1/2f: rdn clr over 1f out: kpt on strly* **8/1**

24-1 **2** *3 ¼* **Rambo Will**[69] 299 6-9-3 **73**........ NataliaGemelova(3) 2 76
(J R Jenkins) *racd centre: trckd ldrs: hdwy 1/2-way: rdn to chse wnr wl over 1f out: drvn: edgd rt and no imp fnl f* **11/4**[2]

5062 **3** *2* **Pull The Pin (IRE)**[1] 1224 5-8-11 **64**........ (bt) PaulMulrennan 10 60
(Ann Stokell) *racd towards stands' rail: qckly away and led 1 1/2f: cl up: rdn along and edgd lft 2f out: drvn and kpt on one pce fnl f* **12/1**

4416 **4** *½* **Sir Geoffrey (IRE)**[12] 1049 8-8-12 **72**........ (p) MatthewHopkins(7) 9 66+
(Scott Dixon) *racd towards stands' rail: in tch: rdn along and sltly outpcd 1/2-way: kpt on u.p fnl f: nrst fin* **10/1**

2050 **5** *nk* **Pabusar**[14] 1020 6-9-0 **70**........ (bt) OisinMurphy(3) 1 63
(Ann Stokell) *dwlt: hdwy on outer over 2f out: sn rdn: styd on fnl f: nrst fin* **5/1**[3]

52-6 **6** *½* **Ladweb**[16] 987 4-8-8 **64**........ MichaelJMMurphy(3) 6 55
(John Gallagher) *racd centre: chsd ldrs: rdn along over 2f out: drvn wl over 1f out and sn one pce* **14/1**

0-04 **7** *shd* **Lost In Paris (IRE)**[1] 1224 8-8-12 **72**........ LauraBarry(7) 8 63
(Tony Coyle) *outpcd in rr tl sme late hdwy* **33/1**

000- **8** *2 ¼* **Exotic Guest**[162] 7445 4-9-2 **69**........ JamesSullivan 4 52
(Ruth Carr) *racd centre: chsd ldrs: rdn along over 2f out: sn wknd* **33/1**

13-2 **9** *¾* **Keep It Dark**[6] 1127 5-9-2 **69**........ BarryMcHugh 7 49
(Tony Coyle) *hld up in tch: effrt over 2f out: sn rdn along: carried hd high and sn btn* **5/2**[1]

0F0- **10** *1 ¾* **Boxing Shadows**[155] 7601 4-9-3 **70**........ DavidAllan 5 44
(Les Eyre) *racd centre: chsd ldrs: rdn along over 2f out: sn wknd* **16/1**

59.7s **Going Correction** +0.075s/f (Slow) **10** Ran SP% **118.2**
Speed ratings (Par 103): **103,97,94,93,93 92,92,88,87,84**
CSF £30.72 CT £271.19 TOTE £11.20: £2.80, £1.30, £5.10; EX 35.60 Trifecta £503.50.
**Owner** G M & Mrs C Baillie **Bred** G M & C Baillie & Springs Equestrian **Trained** Longton, Lancs
■ Stewards' Enquiry : Natalia Gemelova four-day ban: used whip above permitted level (Apr 16-19)

**FOCUS**
An ordinary sprint handicap and again the centre of the track was the place to be. This rates the winner's best form since 2012.

## 1245 LADBROKES H'CAP 1m (F)
**3:35** (3:35) (Class 5) (0-70,70) 4-Y-O+ **£2,587** (£770; £384; £192) **Stalls** Low

Form RPR

2335 **1** **Pretty Bubbles**[19] 952 5-9-2 **65**........ FrederikTylicki 5 73
(J R Jenkins) *trckd ldrs: smooth hdwy 3f out: chal 2f out: rdn to ld appr fnl f: sn edgd rt and drvn out* **7/2**[2]

550- **2** *½* **Midaz**[231] 5392 4-9-2 **65**........ GrahamLee 8 72
(Hughie Morrison) *hld up towards rr: hdwy 3f out: chsd ldrs over 2f out: rdn wl over 1f out: styd on wl fnl f* **7/4**[1]

450- **3** *½* **I'm Super Too (IRE)**[182] 6943 7-9-2 **65**........ BenCurtis 6 71
(Alan Swinbank) *trckd ldrs: hdwy on outer over 3f out: chal over 2f out and sn rdn: edgd lft and swtchd lft to inner over 1f out: drvn and kpt on same pce fnl f* **5/1**[3]

**4** *4 ½* **Real Tigress (IRE)**[299] 5-8-9 **58**........ DavidAllan 2 53
(Les Eyre) *prom: cl up 1/2-way: led 3f out: jnd and rdn 2f out: drvn and hdd appr fnl f: sn wknd* **6/1**

050- **5** *6* **Wyldfire (IRE)**[189] 6758 4-9-2 **65**........ JamesSullivan 3 47
(Ruth Carr) *cl up: effrt 3f out: sn rdn and wknd 2f out* **8/1**

02-4 **6** *2* **Tight Knit (USA)**[47] 601 4-8-10 **64**........ (b) JoeyHaynes(5) 4 41
(John Weymes) *in rr: sme hdwy 3f out: rdn along over 2f out: nvr a factor* **8/1**

16-0 **7** *15* **Great Demeanor (USA)**[33] 782 4-9-2 **70**........ EmmaSayer(5) 7 12
(Dianne Sayer) *chsd ldrs on outer: rdn along 1/2-way: sn wknd* **16/1**

-000 **8** *13* **Fairy Wing (IRE)**[14] 1021 7-8-5 **57**........ (b) OisinMurphy(3) 1
(Ann Stokell) *slt ld on inner: rdn along and hdd 3f out: wknd qckly and sn bhd: eased* **50/1**

1m 42.84s (-0.86) **Going Correction** +0.05s/f (Slow) **8** Ran SP% **119.6**
Speed ratings (Par 103): **106,105,105,100,94 92,77,64**
CSF £10.59 CT £30.84 TOTE £3.40: £1.20, £1.30, £1.60; EX 11.80 Trifecta £31.00.
**Owner** Mark Goldstein **Bred** Southill Stud **Trained** Royston, Herts

**FOCUS**
A modest handicap in which those held up were favoured. The winner is rated back to her best.

## 1246 32RED THUNDERSTRUCK II SLOT H'CAP 5f (F)
**4:05** (4:05) (Class 5) (0-70,69) 3-Y-O **£2,587** (£770; £384; £192) **Stalls** High

Form RPR

15-1 **1** **Scarborough (IRE)**[6] 1130 3-8-4 **59** 6ex........ AlistairRawlinson(7) 4 83
(Michael Appleby) *mde all: shkn up 2f out: rdn clr and hung bdly lft to far rail 1f out: easily* **1/2**[1]

3032 **2** *10* **Under Approval**[20] 936 3-9-0 **65**........ SamJames(3) 5 53
(David O'Meara) *cl up: rdn 2f out: kpt on: no ch w wnr* **7/2**[2]

065- **3** *¾* **Miss Acclaimed (IRE)**[175] 7125 3-8-13 **68**........ MeganCarberry(7) 6 53
(Brian Ellison) *chsd ldrs: rdn along 2f out: sn one pce* **16/1**

04-0 **4** *1* **Dancing Juice**[12] 1039 3-8-0 **55**........ MatthewHopkins(7) 1 37
(Alan Jarvis) *dwlt: sn cl up on outer: rdn along 1/2-way: sn drvn and one pce* **8/1**[3]

0503 **5** *6* **Maro**[21] 933 3-8-0 **55** oh10........ (v) AdamMcLean(7) 3 15
(Derek Shaw) *chsd ldrs: rdn along bef 1/2-way: sn outpcd and bhd* **25/1**

59.91s (0.21) **Going Correction** +0.075s/f (Slow) **5** Ran SP% **109.7**
Speed ratings (Par 98): **101,85,83,82,72**
CSF £2.51 TOTE £1.40: £1.10, £1.10; EX 2.40 Trifecta £9.40.
**Owner** M Wainman **Bred** Tom Foley **Trained** Danethorpe, Notts
■ Stewards' Enquiry : Alistair Rawlinson two-day ban: used whip when clearly winning (Apr 16-17)

**FOCUS**
A one-sided handicap and not many 5f races are won by such a margin. The time was good and the winner more than confirmed last week's win here.

## 1247 32RED FILLIES' H'CAP 7f (F)
**4:35** (4:36) (Class 4) (0-85,84) 4-Y-O+ **£5,175** (£1,540; £769; £384) **Stalls** Low

Form RPR

00-3 **1** **Broughtons Charm (IRE)**[21] 924 4-8-10 **73**........ RobertWinston 3 81
(Willie Musson) *cl up on outer: led over 2f out: jnd and rdn over 1f out: sn hdd: drvn ent fnl f: styd on wl to ld last 100yds* **5/2**[2]

1233 **2** *1 ¼* **Hannahs Turn**[50] 566 4-9-2 **84**........ ConnorBeasley(5) 2 89
(Chris Dwyer) *t.k.h: trckd ldrs: hdwy over 2f out: rdn to ld over 1f out: drvn ent fnl f: hdd and no ex last 100yds* **11/10**[1]

1136 **3** *3 ½* **Arabian Flight**[6] 1125 5-8-7 **70** oh7........ AndrewMullen 4 66
(Michael Appleby) *led: rdn along and hdd over 2f out: sn drvn and kpt on same pce* **6/1**[3]

451- **4** *11* **Gold Chain (IRE)**[28] 6407 4-8-9 **72**........ JamesSullivan 5 39
(Dianne Sayer) *dwlt: sn rdn along and outpcd in rr tl styd on fnl 2f* **14/1**

540- **5** *nk* **Penny Garcia**[195] 6564 4-9-0 **77**........ DuranFentiman 1 43
(Tim Easterby) *trckd ldrs on inner: effrt 3f out: rdn along over 2f out: sn wknd* **7/1**

1m 28.49s (-1.81) **Going Correction** +0.05s/f (Slow) **5** Ran SP% **109.6**
Speed ratings (Par 102): **112,110,106,94,93**
CSF £5.62 TOTE £5.00: £1.90, £1.10; EX 5.70 Trifecta £16.90.
**Owner** Broughton Thermal Insulation **Bred** West Dereham Abbey Stud **Trained** Newmarket, Suffolk

**FOCUS**
A fair little fillies' handicap in which stamina proved key. A small personal best from the winner.

## 1248 32RED TOMB RAIDER SLOT H'CAP 1m 6f (F)
**5:05** (5:05) (Class 6) (0-55,53) 4-Y-O+ **£1,940** (£577; £288; £144) **Stalls** Low

Form RPR

-542 **1** **Adili (IRE)**[8] 1092 5-9-7 **52**........ AndrewMullen 5 62
(Michael Appleby) *trckd ldng pair: hdwy and cl up over 3f out: rdn to chal and swtchd lft 2f out: drvn over 1f out: styd on to ld appr fnl f: drvn out* **5/4**[1]

-631 **2** *¾* **Aureate**[22] 912 10-8-9 **47**........ (p) CharlotteJenner(7) 6 56
(Brian Forsey) *trckd ldrs: hdwy 5f out: smooth prog on inner to ld 3f out: swung wd st: jnd and rdn 2f out: hdd appr fnl f: kpt on same pce* **3/1**[2]

0-31 **3** *7* **Joyful Motive**[7] 1117 5-9-1 **53** 6ex........ PaulBooth(7) 2 52
(Michael Chapman) *trckd ldrs: pushed along after 4f: sn lost pl and in rr: rdn along 5f out: styd on fnl 3f: tk 3rd ins fnl f* **3/1**[2]

/005 **4** *4 ½* **Cape Safari (IRE)**[18] 974 5-9-7 **52**........ (b[1]) GrahamLee 4 45
(Tim Vaughan) *cl up: led 5f out: rdn along and hdd 3f out: sn drvn and wknd fnl 2f* **8/1**[3]

0/0- **5** *22* **Solis (GER)**[20] 4614 11-8-9 **45**........ EmmaSayer(5) 7 7
(Dianne Sayer) *a in rr: rdn along 1/2-way: sn outpcd and bhd* **16/1**

040- **6** *69* **Overrule (USA)**[134] 7951 10-9-4 **49**........ (p) FrederikTylicki 1
(Chris Bealby) *slt ld: pushed along 1/2-way: hdd 5f out: sn rdn and wknd qckly 4f out* **16/1**

3m 9.62s (1.32) **Going Correction** +0.05s/f (Slow) **6** Ran SP% **117.3**
Speed ratings (Par 101): **98,97,93,91,78 39**
CSF £5.67 TOTE £2.80: £1.40, £1.80; EX 5.80 Trifecta £10.60.
**Owner** Dallas Racing **Bred** His Highness The Aga Khan's Studs S C **Trained** Danethorpe, Notts

**FOCUS**
A moderate handicap and a dour test of stamina. The winner got closer to his old figures and the runner-up stepped up on his latest form.

## 1249 CORAL APP DOWNLOAD FROM THE APP STORE H'CAP — 1m 3f (F)
5:35 (5:35) (Class 6) (0-55,55) 4-Y-0+ — £1,940 (£577; £288; £144) Stalls Low

Form — RPR

-230 **1** **Geeaitch**[48] [590] 5-9-7 55 ........ RobertWinston 5 63+
(Peter Hiatt) *trckd ldrs: smooth hdwy over 4f out: effrt on outer 3f out: slt ld wl over 1f out and sn rdn: drvn and wandered ins jst ins fnl f: kpt on u.p towards fin* **7/4**[1]

4/54 **2** *1 1/4* **Encore Un Fois**[29] [830] 6-9-6 54 ........ JamesSullivan 7 60
(Ruth Carr) *hld up towards rr: tk clsr order over 4f out: stdy hdwy 3f out: rdn over 1f out: styd on fnl f: nrst fin* **16/1**

3112 **3** *nk* **Goldmadchen (GER)**[6] [1132] 6-9-7 55 ........ GrahamLee 1 60
(James Given) *led: jnd 5f out and sn pushed along: rdn 3f out and sn jnd: hdd and drvn wl over 1f out: ev ch tl no ex ins fnl f* **9/4**[2]

4266 **4** *2 1/4* **Kyllachykov (IRE)**[22] [912] 6-9-3 54 ........ NeilFarley(3) 9 55
(Robin Bastiman) *chsd ldrs: rdn along and outpcd over 5f out: hdwy wl over 2f out: kpt on u.p fnl f* **8/1**

-030 **5** *2 1/4* **Scamperdale**[14] [1016] 12-9-5 53 ........(p) AndrewMullen 6 50
(Brian Baugh) *awkward s: chsd ldrs on outer after 1f: cl up 1/2-way: rdn along 3f out: drvn and hld whn n.m.r and swtchd lft 1 1/2f out: sn one pce* **20/1**

2304 **6** *5* **Strandfield Bay (IRE)**[16] [998] 8-9-7 55 ........(p) PaddyAspell 4 44
(Sharon Watt) *towards rr: sme hdwy 5f out: rdn along over 3f out: n.d* **12/1**

000- **7** *3/4* **Bitusa (USA)**[179] [7027] 4-8-12 53 ........ GemmaTutty(7) 2 41
(Karen Tutty) *chsd ldr: pushed along 5f out: rdn along wl over 3f out and sn wknd* **20/1**

2002 **8** *8* **Ice Tres**[19] [959] 5-9-4 52 ........ MartinLane 3 26
(Rod Millman) *in tch on inner: pushed along 5f out: rdn 4f out and sn wknd* **7/1**[3]

00-0 **9** *6* **Call Of Duty (IRE)**[33] [783] 9-8-8 47 ........ EmmaSayer(5) 8 11
(Dianne Sayer) *a in rr: outpcd fr 1/2-way: bhd fnl 4f* **33/1**

2m 29.76s (1.76) **Going Correction** +0.05s/f (Slow) **9** Ran SP% **116.8**
Speed ratings (Par 101): **95,94,93,92,90 86,86,80,76**
CSF £31.08 CT £66.77 TOTE £2.40: £1.10, £4.90, £1.40; EX 44.90 Trifecta £180.00.
**Owner** P J R Gardner **Bred** G Houghton **Trained** Hook Norton, Oxon

**FOCUS**
Another moderate handicap. The winner looks capable of a bit better around here.
T/Plt: £216.60 to a £1 stake. Pool: £51,978.71 - 175.13 winning units. T/Qpdt: £2.20 to a £1 stake. Pool: £5877.59 - 1915.91 winning units. JR

# 1198 LEOPARDSTOWN (L-H)
Wednesday, April 2

**OFFICIAL GOING: Heavy**

## 1252a HERITAGE STKS (LISTED RACE) — 1m
4:40 (4:40) 4-Y-0+ — £21,666 (£6,333; £3,000; £1,000)

RPR

**1** **Qewy (IRE)**[234] [5317] 4-9-5 98 ........ DeclanMcDonogh 3 104
(John M Oxx, Ire) *sn led: 1 l clr 1/2-way: rdn 2f out and kpt on wl u.p ins fnl f* **11/1**

**2** *3/4* **Pop Art (IRE)**[10] [1076] 4-9-0 97 ........ FMBerry 4 97+
(Charles O'Brien, Ire) *w.w in rr: hdwy 2f out to chse ldrs gng wl in 3rd 1 1/2f out: sn rdn and kpt on wl u.p ins fnl f into 2nd cl home wout really troubling wnr* **4/1**[2]

**3** *1/2* **Kingsbarns (IRE)**[165] [7366] 4-9-5 117 ........ JosephO'Brien 5 101+
(A P O'Brien, Ire) *prom: sn settled bhd ldr: gng wl in 2nd 2f out: sn pushed along and no imp on wnr wl ins fnl f: dropped to 3rd cl home* **4/6**[1]

**4** *3 3/4* **Light Heavy (IRE)**[405] [741] 5-9-5 104 ........(p) KevinManning 1 92
(J S Bolger, Ire) *chsd ldrs: 3rd 1/2-way: pushed along 3f out and no ex u.p in 4th fr 2f out: kpt on one pce* **7/1**

**5** *2 3/4* **Bold Thady Quill (IRE)**[10] [1078] 7-9-5 100 ........(p) ShaneFoley 6 86
(K J Condon, Ire) *chsd ldrs: 4th 1/2-way: pushed along 3f out and sn no ex u.p: dropped to rr fr 2f out: kpt on one pce* **6/1**[3]

1m 49.46s (8.26) **Going Correction** +1.00s/f (Soft) **5** Ran SP% **115.1**
Speed ratings: **98,97,96,93,90**
CSF £53.81 TOTE £9.30: £2.90, £2.00; DF 36.60 Trifecta £50.20.
**Owner** Sheikh Mohammed Obaid Al Maktoum **Bred** Darley **Trained** Currabeg, Co Kildare

**FOCUS**
All eyes were on the favourite, but a good positive ride from Declan McDonogh on Qewy paid dividends and he found plenty on a surface he acted very well on. The runner-up helps with the standard.

# 1236 LINGFIELD (L-H)
Thursday, April 3

**OFFICIAL GOING: Standard**
Wind: light, half behind Weather: dry, bright spells

## 1257 32RED ON THE APP STORE (S) STKS — 1m 2f (P)
1:50 (1:50) (Class 6) 3-Y-0 — £2,079 (£613; £307) Stalls Low

Form — RPR

3361 **1** **Big Kenny**[43] [664] 3-9-3 66 ........(b[1]) AdamKirby 3 61
(David Evans) *pushed along leaving stalls: chsd ldrs: rdn and effrt to ld over 2f out: asserted ent fnl f: styd on: eased towards fin* **4/6**[1]

5-01 **2** *1 3/4* **Chanceuse**[22] [931] 3-8-12 57 ........ DavidProbert 6 53
(Gay Kelleway) *in tch in rr: rdn and effrt to chse ldng pair 2f out: kpt on u.p fnl f to go 2nd towards fin: no threat to wnr* **9/2**[2]

0343 **3** *hd* **Clapperboard**[13] [1048] 3-8-7 54 ........ RichardKingscote 4 47
(Paul Fitzsimons) *chsd ldrs: rdn to chse wnr over 2f out: drvn and styd on same pce fr over 1f out: lost 2nd towards fin* **6/1**[3]

4620 **4** *21* **Previous Acclaim (IRE)**[20] [960] 3-8-2 45 ........ ShelleyBirkett(5) 1 5
(Julia Feilden) *led tl rdn and hdd over 2f out: sn btn: wl bhd 1f out* **16/1**

06-3 **5** *33* **Polar Express**[37] [738] 3-8-9 50 ........(p) MatthewLawson(3) 5
(Jonathan Portman) *chsd ldr tl rdn and qckly dropped to last over 4f out: sn lost tch: t.o over 1f out* **8/1**

2m 5.8s (-0.80) **Going Correction** -0.05s/f (Stan) **5** Ran SP% **109.4**
Speed ratings (Par 96): **101,99,99,82,56**
CSF £3.95 TOTE £1.50: £1.10, £2.20; EX 1.90 Trifecta £5.90.The winner was bought by N King for 6,600gns.
**Owner** P D Evans **Bred** O J Williams **Trained** Pandy, Monmouths

**FOCUS**
A low-key opener and it went the way of the form book. The winner did not need to match his best and the form is rated on the cautious side.

## 1258 32RED.COM MAIDEN STKS — 1m 2f (P)
2:20 (2:21) (Class 5) 3-Y-0 — £2,726 (£805; £402) Stalls Low

Form — RPR

3- **1** **Shama (IRE)**[140] [7875] 3-9-0 0 ........ RyanMoore 5 83
(Sir Michael Stoute) *mde all: rdn and wnt clr 2f out: in command and styd on wl fnl f: rdn out* **6/4**[1]

4 **2** *4 1/2* **Court Room (IRE)**[12] [1069] 3-9-5 0 ........ WilliamBuick 8 79
(John Gosden) *dwlt: t.k.h: hdwy into midfield after 2f: rdn and outpcd 2f out: 4th and wl hld over 1f out: styd on ins fnl f to go 2nd towards fin: no threat to wnr* **2/1**[2]

0- **3** *1* **Classic Devotion (USA)**[143] [7834] 3-9-5 0 ........ MickaelBarzalona 2 77
(Charlie Appleby) *chsd ldrs: rdn and effrt 2f out: chsd clr wnr over 1f out: plugged on same pce fnl f: lost 2nd towards fin* **3/1**[3]

03- **4** *3* **Magnus Romeo**[202] [6365] 3-9-5 0 ........ AdamKirby 6 71
(Marco Botti) *taken down early: chsd ldrs: rdn and unable qck 2f out: 3rd and btn over 1f out: wknd ins fnl f* **10/1**

5-5 **5** *3* **Ganymede**[83] [119] 3-9-5 0 ........ JimCrowley 7 65
(Eve Johnson Houghton) *wl in tch in midfield: rdn and outpcd over 2f out: 5th and n.d fnl 2f: wknd over 1f out* **25/1**

06 **6** *1/2* **Bongo Beat**[13] [1044] 3-9-5 0 ........ RobertHavlin 4 64
(Michael Attwater) *stdd s: hld up in tch in rr: outpcd over 2f out: n.d fnl 2f: plugged on* **66/1**

**7** *12* **Effect (IRE)** 3-9-5 0 ........ BenCurtis 3 40
(Jo Hughes) *hld up in tch in last pair: rdn and struggling over 3f out: lost tch over 2f out* **33/1**

2m 4.46s (-2.14) **Going Correction** -0.05s/f (Stan) **7** Ran SP% **115.7**
Speed ratings (Par 98): **106,102,101,99,96 96,86**
CSF £4.85 TOTE £2.00: £1.20, £2.70; EX 5.30 Trifecta £8.00.
**Owner** The Queen **Bred** His Highness The Aga Khan's Studs S C **Trained** Newmarket, Suffolk

**FOCUS**
Probably an above-average maiden for the track with some big yards on show. The fifth and sixth help with the level.

## 1259 BOOKMAKERS.CO.UK MEDIAN AUCTION MAIDEN STKS — 5f 6y(P)
2:55 (2:57) (Class 5) 2-Y-0 — £2,726 (£805; £402) Stalls High

Form — RPR

**1** **Cheerio Sweetie (IRE)** 2-9-0 0 ........ AdamKirby 7 84+
(David Evans) *mde all: pushed clr ent fnl 2f: wl clr over 1f out: r.o strly: impressive* **3/1**[1]

0 **2** *9* **Johnny Sorrento**[5] [1161] 2-9-5 0 ........ StevieDonohoe 8 53
(Tim Pitt) *chsd ldr tl outpcd ent fnl 2f: no ch w wnr after but kpt on u.p for clr 2nd* **10/1**

**3** *1 1/2* **Designate (IRE)** 2-9-5 0 ........ JimCrowley 9 47+
(Ralph Beckett) *restless in stalls: rn green and hung rt thrght: chsd ldng pair: struggling and hung rt bnd 2f out: n.d after: plugged on* **7/1**[3]

**4** *2 1/4* **Hell Of A Lord** 2-9-0 0 ........ RyanWhile(5) 1 38
(Bill Turner) *chsd ldr but sn bustled along and outpcd after 1f out: nvr on terms after: plugged on to go 4th ins fnl f* **9/2**[2]

**5** *2* **Don Sigfredo (IRE)** 2-9-5 0 ........ RichardKingscote 10 30+
(Tom Dascombe) *s.i.s: rn green and wl off the pce in rr: no ch but hdwy 1f out: rdn and swtchd rt ins fnl f: n.d* **3/1**[1]

**6** *1 1/2* **Mount Isa (IRE)** 2-9-5 0 ........ LiamJones 5 24
(J S Moore) *sn pushed along and outpcd in midfield: n.d* **20/1**

**7** *shd* **Rose Of Kiev (IRE)** 2-9-0 0 ........ JoeFanning 4 19
(Mark Johnston) *dwlt: sn rcvrd and racd in 4th: nvr on terms w ldrs: no ch fnl 2f: wknd and lost 2 pls ins fnl f* **12/1**

**8** *1* **Jet Mate (IRE)** 2-9-5 0 ........ MartinDwyer 6 20
(William Muir) *s.i.s: a wl off the pce in rr* **7/1**[3]

**9** *5* **Pickle Lilly Pearl** 2-9-0 0 ........ AdrianNicholls 3
(David C Griffiths) *s.i.s: rcvrd into midfield after 1f but nvr on terms w ldrs: hung rt and lost pl bnd 2f out: bhd after* **16/1**

59.34s (0.54) **Going Correction** -0.05s/f (Stan) **9** Ran SP% **120.6**
Speed ratings (Par 92): **93,78,76,72,69 67,66,65,57**
CSF £36.42 TOTE £3.80: £1.90, £3.70, £2.20; EX 43.80 Trifecta £407.20.
**Owner** Walters Plant Hire Ltd **Bred** Knocktoran Stud & Maura Purcell **Trained** Pandy, Monmouths

**FOCUS**
All bar one of these were newcomers and most didn't seem to know their job first time. They were strung out like three-mile chasers by halfway, but one filly certainly did know her job. A guessy level of the form but the winner is clearly pretty good.

## 1260 32RED IMMORTAL ROMANCE SLOT H'CAP — 6f 1y(P)
3:30 (3:30) (Class 5) (0-75,74) 3-Y-0 — £3,234 (£962; £481; £240) Stalls Low

Form — RPR

-550 **1** **Nova Princesse (GER)**[21] [936] 3-9-5 72 ........(t) AdamKirby 4 77
(Marco Botti) *chsd ldng pair: swtchd ins and rdn to chal over 1f out: led jst ins fnl f: kpt on wl fnl 100yds: drvn out* **16/1**

202- **2** *nk* **Nakuti (IRE)**[172] [7218] 3-9-7 74 ........ RyanMoore 5 78
(Sylvester Kirk) *in tch in rr but niggled along early: rdn and hdwy to press ldng pair 1f out: n.m.r briefly jst ins fnl f: drvn and strly chal fnl 100yds: r.o wl* **11/4**[2]

-011 **3** *1 3/4* **Dont Have It Then**[50] [573] 3-9-1 68 ........ RobertWinston 1 67
(Willie Musson) *stdd after s: t.k.h: hld up in tch in last pair: rdn and effrt over 1f out: switchd rt but nt clrest of runs ins fnl f: kpt on* **6/1**

006- **4** *3/4* **Sir Guy Porteous (IRE)**[170] [7270] 3-9-2 69 ........ JoeFanning 2 66
(Mark Johnston) *led: rdn and edgd out rt wl over 1f out: hdd jst ins fnl f: edgd rt and wknd fnl 75yds* **5/4**[1]

453- **5** *1 3/4* **Quantum Dot (IRE)**[183] [6931] 3-9-4 71 ........ RichardKingscote 3 62
(Tom Dascombe) *chsd ldr tl wl over 1f out: drvn and outpcd ent fnl f* **7/2**[3]

1m 11.7s (-0.20) **Going Correction** -0.05s/f (Stan) **5** Ran SP% **113.5**
Speed ratings (Par 98): **99,98,96,95,92**
CSF £60.02 TOTE £12.90: £4.40, £2.20; EX 53.70 Trifecta £86.70.
**Owner** Scuderia Blueberry **Bred** Gestut Isarland **Trained** Newmarket, Suffolk

**FOCUS**
Just ordinary handicap form, with the favourite disappointing. The winner is rated back to her best.

## 1261 COMPARE BOOKMAKERS AT BOOKMAKERS.CO.UK H'CAP 6f 1y(P)
4:05 (4:05) (Class 4) (0-80,80) 4-Y-0+ £5,175 (£1,540; £769; £384) Stalls Low

Form RPR
4-31 1 **Gregori (IRE)**[54] 532 4-9-4 77 (tp) JimmyFortune 1 87
(Brian Meehan) *mde all: wnt clr w runner-up ent fnl 2f: rdn and fnd ex over 1f out: styd on wl fnl f: rdn out* 9/2[2]
1211 2 1 1/4 **Jubilee Brig**[13] 1038 4-9-5 78 (v) AdamKirby 6 84
(Sean Curran) *hld up in tch in midfield: rdn gd hdwy to join wnr and wnt clr ent fnl 2f: edgd lft and unable qck ent fnl f: hld and styd on same pce fnl f* 2/1[1]
010- 3 3/4 **Secret Missile**[177] 7112 4-9-6 79 MartinDwyer 4 83
(William Muir) *hld up in tch in midfield: rdn and effrt wl over 1f out: chsd ldng pair fnl 100yds: kpt on* 7/1
4506 4 shd **Clear Praise (USA)**[17] 991 7-9-6 79 HayleyTurner 2 82
(Simon Dow) *taken down early: t.k.h: chsd ldrs: effrt to chse clr ldng pair and edgd rt wl over 1f out: styd on same pce and lost 3rd fnl 100yds* 8/1
135- 5 shd **Jungle Bay**[96] 8431 7-8-13 77 (p) DavidKenny(5) 11 80
(Jane Chapple-Hyam) *hld up in tch in midfield: rdn and effrt whn carried rt wl over 1f out: no imp tl kpt on u.p fnl 100yds* 16/1
1046 6 1 1/2 **Valmina**[13] 1041 7-9-5 78 (t) JoeFanning 12 76
(Tony Carroll) *stdd after s: hld up in rr: plenty to do but hdwy 1f out: kpt on but nvr a threat to ldrs: eased cl home* 12/1
1221 7 1 **Seek The Fair Land**[14] 1025 8-9-2 75 (v) WilliamCarson 9 70
(Lee Carter) *stdd and dropped in bhd after s: rdn and effrt but stl plenty to do wl over 1f out: kpt on ins fnl f: nvr trbld ldrs* 10/1
6512 8 3/4 **Kuanyao (IRE)**[13] 1038 8-9-4 77 (b) AmirQuinn 8 70
(Lee Carter) *chsd ldrs: rdn and outpcd whn carried rt wl over 1f out: btn and swtchd lft jst ins fnl f: wknd ins fnl f* 20/1
00-5 9 1/2 **Bapak Chinta (USA)**[13] 1049 5-9-7 80 AmyRyan 7 71
(Kevin Ryan) *chsd ldr tl over 2f out: short of room and lost pl ent fnl 2f: wknd 1f out* 6/1[3]
006- 10 2 1/4 **Lady Phill**[260] 4413 4-9-6 79 KierenFox 5 63
(Michael Attwater) *stdd s: hld up in rr: rdn and no hdwy over 1f out: n.d* 50/1

1m 12.41s (0.51) **Going Correction** -0.05s/f (Stan) 10 Ran SP% 118.8
Speed ratings (Par 105): **94,92,91,91,91 89,87,86,86,83**
CSF £14.16 CT £63.31 TOTE £4.20: £1.80, £1.10, £2.70; EX 11.00 Trifecta £137.50.
**Owner** Stephen Tucker **Bred** Mrs James Wigan **Trained** Manton, Wilts

**FOCUS**
A competitive sprint handicap featuring several in-form contenders, but nothing could get into it from off the pace. The winner is probably worth a personal best.

## 1262 32RED THUNDERSTRUCK II SLOT H'CAP 1m 7f 169y(P)
4:40 (4:40) (Class 5) (0-70,67) 4-Y-0+ £3,234 (£962; £481; £240) Stalls Low

Form RPR
-101 1 **Newtown Cross (IRE)**[29] 842 4-8-4 56 CamHardie(7) 4 62
(Jimmy Fox) *chsd ldr after 2f tl led over 2f out: rdn and readily wnt clr over 1f out: in command and r.o wl fnl f: comf* 3/1[3]
2323 2 3 1/4 **Honest Strike (USA)**[8] 1117 7-9-7 62 (b) AdamKirby 2 64
(Daniel Mark Loughnane) *stdd s: hld up in tch in last: swtchd rt and effrt to chal wl over 2f out: unable qck over 1f out: no ch w wnr but hld on for 2nd ins fnl f* 5/4[1]
3120 3 3/4 **Shalambar (IRE)**[17] 992 8-9-10 65 (v) JimCrowley 3 66
(Tony Carroll) *led tl hdd and rdn over 2f out: 3rd and outpcd 2f out: no ch w wnr but kpt on and pressing for 2nd towards fin* 5/2[2]
456- 4 1 **Freddy Q (IRE)**[38] 7217 5-9-12 67 GeorgeBaker 1 67?
(Roger Teal) *chsd ldr for 2f: 3rd and wl in tch after: dropped to last and outpcd over 2f out: kpt on same pce u.p fnl f* 5/1

3m 26.92s (1.22) **Going Correction** -0.05s/f (Stan)
**WFA** 4 from 5yo+ 4lb 4 Ran SP% 114.7
Speed ratings (Par 103): **94,92,92,91**
CSF £7.68 TOTE £5.10; EX 11.00 Trifecta £13.70.
**Owner** Mutton & Lamb **Bred** Mrs Anne Coughlan **Trained** Collingbourne Ducis, Wilts

**FOCUS**
They looked to go fairly steady here and the form is weak and muddling.

## 1263 CORAL.CO.UK APPRENTICE H'CAP 1m 4f (P)
5:15 (5:15) (Class 6) (0-60,57) 4-Y-0+ £2,726 (£805; £402) Stalls Low

Form RPR
-040 1 **Novel Dancer**[43] 656 6-8-7 45 JennyPowell(3) 6 54
(Lydia Richards) *chsd ldr for 2f: wl in tch in midfield after: rdn and effrt to chal ent fnl 2f: led over 1f out: edgd lft jst ins fnl f: hld on towards fin* 12/1
-425 2 hd **Magicalmysterytour (IRE)**[43] 656 11-8-12 52 PatrickO'Donnell(5) 1 60
(Willie Musson) *hld up in midfield: rdn and hdwy to chse ldng pair wl over 1f out: chsd wnr fnl 100yds: kpt on wl: jst hld* 9/2[2]
-004 3 3 1/2 **Salient**[57] 490 10-8-6 48 RhiainIngram(7) 10 51
(Michael Attwater) *midfield tl hdwy to chse ldrs after 2f: led over 2f out: rdn and hdd over 1f out: keeping on same pce whn nt clr run and hmpd ins fnl f: wknd fnl 100yds* 8/1
500- 4 6 **Dorry K (IRE)**[36] 1789 5-8-13 55 AprilKitchener(7) 8 48
(Jim Best) *stdd s: hld up in rr: hdwy 4f out: outpcd over 2f out and wd bnd 2f out: pushed along and styd on fnl f: wnt 4th nr fin: nvr trbld ldrs* 7/2[1]
3-05 5 nk **See And Be Seen**[14] 1027 4-9-4 57 (p) GaryMahon(3) 2 49
(Sylvester Kirk) *wl in tch in midfield: rdn and effrt wl over 1f out: wnt modest 4th 1f out: no prog: lost 4th nr fin* 5/1[3]
53-0 6 3/4 **Roy Rocket (FR)**[31] 821 4-8-6 45 CamHardie(3) 3 36
(John Berry) *chsd ldrs: nt clr run and shuffled bk ent fnl 2f: drvn and no hdwy over 1f out: no ch but plugged on fnl f* 9/2[2]
440- 7 5 **Snowy Valley**[379] 1090 5-8-8 48 JoshQuinn(5) 7 31
(Paul Burgoyne) *t.k.h: led tl hdd and rdn over 2f out: 4th and btn over 1f out: fdd* 16/1
6-00 8 2 1/2 **Mayan Flight (IRE)**[59] 459 6-8-10 45 JackGarritty 9 24
(Tony Carroll) *hld up towards rr: rdn and struggling over 2f out: wknd 2f out* 16/1
-460 9 5 **Legal Legacy**[8] 1105 8-8-11 51[1] PaigeBolton(5) 5 22
(Lee Carter) *s.i.s: hld up in rr: rdn and no hdwy over 2f out: wknd 2f out* 9/2[2]
0-0 10 8 **Big City Boy (IRE)**[45] 639 6-8-6 46 ow1 (t) JordonMcMurray(5) 4 4
(Phil McEntee) *stdd s: t.k.h: hdwy to chse ldr after 2f: rdn and lost pl ent fnl 2f: sn wknd: wl bhd fnl f* 66/1

2m 31.3s (-1.70) **Going Correction** -0.05s/f (Stan)
**WFA** 4 from 5yo+ 1lb 10 Ran SP% 125.5
Speed ratings (Par 101): **103,102,100,96,96 95,92,90,87,82**
CSF £70.41 CT £478.50 TOTE £14.10: £3.80, £1.30, £3.20; EX 90.80 Trifecta £864.00.
**Owner** Mrs Lydia Richards **Bred** The Queen **Trained** Funtington, W Sussex
■ Stewards' Enquiry : Jenny Powell two-day ban: careless riding (Apr 17-18)
April Kitchener 16-day ban: failed to take all reasonable and permissable measures to obtain best possible placing (Apr 17-May 2)

**FOCUS**
The form seems sound enough, if very limited. The 1-2 are rated close to their bests for the past couple of years.
T/Plt: £83.60 to a £1 stake. Pool of £44597.50 - 389.02 winning tickets. T/Qpdt: £75.90 to a £1 stake. Pool of £2679.28 - 26.10 winning tickets. SP

# 1147 WOLVERHAMPTON (A.W) (L-H)
Thursday, April 3

**OFFICIAL GOING: Standard**
Wind: Fresh against Weather: Misty

## 1264 32RED.COM H'CAP 5f 216y(P)
5:45 (5:45) (Class 6) (0-60,60) 3-Y-O £2,264 (£673; £336; £168) Stalls Low

Form RPR
0-22 1 **Hustle Bustle (IRE)**[13] 1048 3-9-2 55 SeanLevey 5 66
(David Brown) *mde all: pushed clr 2f out: eased nr fin* 4/7[1]
-153 2 6 **Dandys Perier (IRE)**[53] 547 3-9-7 60 LukeMorris 6 52
(Ronald Harris) *sn pushed along and prom: drvn along 1/2-way: chsd wnr over 1f out* 5/2[2]
3455 3 3/4 **Artemis (IRE)**[13] 1039 3-9-2 60 ShelleyBirkett(5) 3 49
(Conrad Allen) *s.i.s: hld up: hdwy over 1f out: shkn up ins fnl f: nvr nr to chal* 8/1[3]
00-4 4 2 3/4 **Notnow Penny**[48] 608 3-8-2 48 JordanVaughan(7) 4 29
(Milton Bradley) *chsd ldrs: wnt 2nd 4f out tl rdn and wknd over 1f out* 25/1
0-54 5 nk **Luv U Honey**[23] 906 3-8-7 46 oh1 AndrewMullen 1 26
(Brian Baugh) *plld hrd: trckd wnr 2f: pushed along over 2f out: rdn and wknd over 1f out* 25/1
00-0 6 2 1/2 **Oakley Dancer**[34] 786 3-8-8 47 oh1 ow1 (v1) LiamKeniry 2 19
(Tony Carroll) *hld up: rdn and wknd over 1f out* 100/1

1m 15.28s (0.28) **Going Correction** +0.025s/f (Slow) 6 Ran SP% 112.0
Speed ratings (Par 96): **99,91,90,86,85 82**
CSF £2.19 TOTE £1.60: £1.10, £1.60; EX 2.70 Trifecta £4.80.
**Owner** J C Fretwell **Bred** Graeng & Old Carhue Stud **Trained** Averham Park, Notts

**FOCUS**
A moderate and uncompetitive handicap in which the pace was steady for a sprint. The winner came down the centre in the straight. This rating could underestimate her.

## 1265 32RED THUNDERSTRUCK II SLOT H'CAP 1m 5f 194y(P)
6:15 (6:15) (Class 6) (0-65,61) 4-Y-0+ £2,264 (£673; £336; £168) Stalls Low

Form RPR
3012 1 **Travel (USA)**[6] 1150 4-9-4 61 MichaelJMMurphy(3) 1 69
(Mark Johnston) *mde all: rdn and hung rt fnl f: jst hld on* 5/4[1]
212- 2 hd **Tracks Of My Tears**[115] 8225 4-9-6 60 PatrickDonaghy 2 67
(Giles Bravery) *chsd wnr over 5f: remained handy: rdn to go 2nd again over 1f out: r.o* 2/1[2]
0-35 3 4 1/2 **Lacey**[13] 1046 5-9-5 61 JackDuern(5) 3 61
(Andrew Hollinshead) *hld up: hdwy to chse wnr over 8f out: rdn over 2f out: lost 2nd over 1f out: styd on same pce* 4/1[3]
005- 4 1 1/4 **Mr Vendman (IRE)**[26] 7770 4-8-5 45 (p) LukeMorris 5 44
(Ian Williams) *prom: drvn along over 5f out: styd on same pce fr over 1f out* 8/1

3m 11.0s (5.00) **Going Correction** +0.025s/f (Slow)
**WFA** 4 from 5yo+ 3lb 4 Ran SP% 108.9
Speed ratings (Par 101): **86,85,83,82**
CSF £4.05 TOTE £1.80; EX 3.30 Trifecta £4.20.
**Owner** Sheikh Hamdan bin Mohammed Al Maktoum **Bred** Darley **Trained** Middleham Moor, N Yorks

**FOCUS**
A modest handicap in which the pace was on the steady side to the home turn. The winner came down the centre and is rated to form.

## 1266 32RED FILLIES' H'CAP 5f 216y(P)
6:45 (6:45) (Class 5) (0-75,75) 4-Y-0+ £2,911 (£866; £432; £216) Stalls Low

Form RPR
0141 1 **Star Up In The Sky (USA)**[10] 1080 4-9-0 73 6ex (b) KevinStott(5) 1 81
(Kevin Ryan) *mde all: clr over 2f out: shkn up and edgd rt fr over 1f out: styd on* 4/11[1]
10-6 2 1 1/4 **Beau Mistral (IRE)**[2] 1224 5-9-5 73 LukeMorris 4 76
(Paul Green) *trckd ldrs: plld hrd: pushed along to go 2nd over 2f out: rdn over 1f out: styd on* 8/1[3]
-241 3 8 **Ray Of Joy**[31] 819 8-9-2 70 (v) FrederikTylicki 5 47
(J R Jenkins) *sn pushed along in rr: outpcd fnl 2f* 4/1[2]
1/0- 4 11 **Pira Palace (IRE)**[302] 2983 4-9-7 75 StephenCraine 3 17
(Jim Boyle) *chsd wnr tl rdn over 2f out: sn wknd* 20/1

1m 15.01s (0.01) **Going Correction** +0.025s/f (Slow) 4 Ran SP% 109.2
Speed ratings (Par 100): **100,98,87,73**
CSF £3.99 TOTE £1.10; EX 4.20 Trifecta £6.60.
**Owner** Matt & Lauren Morgan **Bred** Dixiana Stables Inc **Trained** Hambleton, N Yorks

**FOCUS**
Another uncompetitive handicap and one in which the gallop was reasonable. The winner edged towards the stands' side in the closing stages and the first two pulled clear. The winner confirmed her latest C&D win.

## 1267 LADBROKES H'CAP 1m 141y(P)
7:15 (7:15) (Class 4) (0-80,80) 4-Y-0+ £5,175 (£1,540; £769; £384) Stalls Low

Form RPR
240- 1 **Angelic Upstart (IRE)**[176] 7131 6-9-0 76 OisinMurphy(3) 6 85
(Andrew Balding) *chsd ldrs: pushed along over 3f out: rdn to ld 1f out: edgd lft: styd on* 11/10[1]
0-03 2 1 **Skytrain**[8] 1113 4-9-7 80 SilvestreDeSousa 2 87
(Mark Johnston) *prom: sn pushed along: lost pl over 7f out: hdwy u.p over 1f out: r.o to go 2nd nr fin: nt rch wnr* 4/1[2]

2512 **3** ½ **My Single Malt (IRE)**[10] 1085 6-8-11 **70**..................(p) PaulMulrennan 5 76
(Julie Camacho) *led 1f: trckd ldr tl led again over 2f out: rdn and hdd 1f out: unable qck towards fin* **6/1**

0213 **4** ½ **Conry (IRE)**[36] 750 8-8-12 **71**........................................ StevieDonohoe 3 75
(Ian Williams) *hmpd s: hld up: hdwy over 1f out: sn rdn: r.o* **16/1**

5253 **5** 1 ½ **Pearl Nation (USA)**[23] 917 5-9-3 **76**............................ FrederikTylicki 1 77
(Brian Baugh) *trckd ldrs: racd keenly: rdn over 1f out: no ex ins fnl f* **5/1**[3]

50-0 **6** 3 ½ **Idol Deputy (FR)**[15] 1014 8-8-12 **78**...................(e[1]) CharlotteJenner(7) 7 71
(James Bennett) *hld up and bhd: nvr nrr* **20/1**

-233 **7** 14 **Canon Law (IRE)**[17] 995 4-9-0 **73**..........................(v[1]) DanielTudhope 4 34
(David O'Meara) *s.i.s: hdwy to ld over 7f out: rdn and hdd over 2f out: wknd over 1f out* **20/1**

1m 49.12s (-1.38) **Going Correction** +0.025s/f (Slow) 7 Ran SP% **114.0**
Speed ratings (Par 105): **107,106,105,105,103 100,88**
CSF £5.69 TOTE £2.30: £1.20, £3.20; EX 6.80 Trifecta £29.50.
**Owner** Barry Burdett **Bred** Swordlestown Stud **Trained** Kingsclere, Hants

**FOCUS**
A fair handicap in which the gallop was soon reasonable. The winner came down the centre in the straight and ran pretty much to form.

## 1268 CORAL APP DOWNLOAD FROM THE APP STORE CLAIMING STKS 1f 103y(P)
**7:45** (7:45) (Class 5) 4-Y-O+ **£3,234** (£962; £481; £240) **Stalls** Low

Form RPR

/35- **1** **Cai Shen (IRE)**[369] 1241 6-9-6 **99**........................................ JamieSpencer 2 100
(Jamie Osborne) *trckd ldrs: racd keenly: wnt 2nd wl over 1f out: rdn to ld ins fnl f: pushed out* **6/5**[2]

0012 **2** nk **Tepmokea (IRE)**[19] 977 8-9-6 **91**..............................(p) ShaneKelly 4 99
(Andrew Hollinshead) *sn led: rdn over 2f out: hung rt over 1f out: hdd ins fnl f: styd on u.p* **1/1**[1]

0154 **3** 7 **Back Burner (IRE)**[27] 870 6-9-1 **80**.................................. AdrianNicholls 8 79
(David Nicholls) *trckd ldrs: wnt 2nd over 5f out tl rdn wl over 1f out: no ex fnl f* **7/1**[3]

0-5 **4** 9 **Kay Gee Be (IRE)**[54] 539 10-8-9 **67** ow1...................... SladeO'Hara(3) 6 57
(Alan Berry) *chsd ldr tl over 5f out: pushed along and wknd over 2f out* **50/1**

030- **5** 5 **Lambert Pen (USA)**[121] 8142 4-8-6 **52**........................ ShelleyBirkett(5) 5 46
(Peter Hiatt) *hld up: pushed along and wknd over 3f out* **100/1**

4 **6** 15 **Daily Advertiser (USA)**[14] 1034 6-8-10 **0**............................ SeanLevey 7 13
(Tony Carroll) *s.i.s: hld up: rdn and wknd over 2f out* **100/1**

1m 59.51s (-2.19) **Going Correction** +0.025s/f (Slow) 6 Ran SP% **111.9**
Speed ratings (Par 103): **110,109,103,95,91 77**
CSF £2.70 TOTE £2.40: £1.10, £1.10; EX 3.00 Trifecta £4.50.Cai Shen was claimed by A. G. Newcombe for £16000.Tepmokea was claimed by C Dore for £16000.
**Owner** J A Osborne **Bred** Wardstown Stud Ltd **Trained** Upper Lambourn, Berks

**FOCUS**
A couple of very useful sorts came to the fore in an uncompetitive claimer. The gallop was ordinary and the first two came down the centre. The form is rated around the runner-up.

## 1269 CORAL MOBILE "JUST THREE CLICKS TO BET" MAIDEN STKS 1m 4f 50y(P)
**8:15** (8:17) (Class 5) 3-5-Y-O **£2,911** (£866; £432; £216) **Stalls** Low

Form RPR

6- **1** **Galizzi (USA)**[183] 6953 3-8-7 **0**........................................ JamieSpencer 7 83+
(Michael Bell) *hld up: hdwy over 3f out: chsd ldr over 2f out: shkn up to ld over 1f out: hrd rdn ins fnl f: styd on* **11/10**[1]

542 **2** ¾ **New Tarabela**[20] 951 3-8-7 **75**........................................ LukeMorris 1 80
(James Tate) *chsd ldrs: lost pl over 9f out: hdwy over 5f out: led over 2f out: rdn and hdd over 1f out: styd on* **15/8**[2]

00- **3** 29 **Nam Ma Prow**[216] 5968 3-8-7 **0**........................................ AndrewElliott 2 34
(Simon West) *led 2f: chsd ldr tl over 6f out: nt clr run and lost pl over 4f out: rdn and wknd over 2f out* **100/1**

00- **4** ½ **Crafty Spell**[178] 7061 3-8-2 **0**........................................ SilvestreDeSousa 3 28
(Mark Johnston) *chsd ldr 2f: wnt 2nd again over 6f out tl led 5f out: rdn and hdd over 2f out: wknd wl over 1f out* **6/1**[3]

06-0 **5** 8 **Chief Executive (IRE)**[79] 171 4-9-6 **53**.................. AlistairRawlinson(7) 6 22
(Mandy Rowland) *hld up: hdwy over 8f out: chsd ldr over 4f out tl rdn 3f out: wknd over 2f out* **66/1**

**6** 34 **Sturmwind (GER)** 3-8-2 **0**........................................ PhilipPrince(5) 4
(J S Moore) *hld up: a in rr: pushed along over 6f out: wknd 5f out* **50/1**

2 **7** 45 **Drifter (IRE)**[19] 976 3-8-7 **0**........................................ RichardKingscote 5
(Tom Dascombe) *bolted to post: s.s: hld up: plld hrd: hdwy to ld 10f out: sn clr: c bk to field over 6f out: hdd & wknd 5f out* **8/1**

2m 40.8s (-0.30) **Going Correction** +0.025s/f (Slow)
**WFA** 3 from 4yo 21lb 7 Ran SP% **112.2**
Speed ratings (Par 103): **102,101,82,81,76 53,23**
CSF £3.22 TOTE £2.10: £1.30, £1.30; EX 5.00 Trifecta £389.80.
**Owner** Sheikh Marwan Al Maktoum **Bred** Darley **Trained** Newmarket, Suffolk

**FOCUS**
An uncompetitive maiden that concerned only the two market leaders in the last quarter mile. The gallop was fair and the first two, who pulled well clear, came down the centre. The form is rated around the runner-up.

## 1270 BEST ODDS AT BOOKMAKERS.CO.UK H'CAP 5f 20y(P)
**8:45** (8:46) (Class 6) (0-55,55) 4-Y-O+ **£2,264** (£673; £336; £168) **Stalls** Low

Form RPR

4526 **1** **Dissent (IRE)**[23] 908 5-9-2 **55**..............................(b) ConnorBeasley(5) 1 63
(James Given) *mde virtually all: clr 2f out: sn rdn: jst hld on* **5/4**[1]

-404 **2** ½ **College Doll**[23] 908 5-8-12 **51**..............................(t) EoinWalsh(5) 9 57
(Christine Dunnett) *hld up: hdwy over 1f out: sn rdn: r.o* **16/1**

5044 **3** hd **Ivestar (IRE)**[15] 1010 9-9-4 **52**..............................(v) GrahamGibbons 4 57
(Michael Easterby) *sn pushed along and prom: rdn over 1f out: r.o* **11/4**[2]

-104 **4** shd **Volcanic Dust (IRE)**[33] 797 6-9-6 **54**......................(t) RichardKingscote 2 59
(Milton Bradley) *chsd wnr 2f: remained handy: rdn over 1f out: r.o* **25/1**

133 **5** nk **Lord Buffhead**[21] 937 5-8-10 **47**..............................(v) BillyCray(3) 12 51
(Richard Guest) *s.i.s: sn pushed along in rr: rdn over 1f out: r.o ins fnl f: nrst fin* **10/1**

000- **6** 2 ¼ **Evens And Odds (IRE)**[129] 8035 10-9-3 **54**.................. SladeO'Hara(3) 3 50
(Peter Grayson) *sn pushed along in rr: r.o ins fnl f: nt rch ldrs* **33/1**

6000 **7** ½ **Amis Reunis**[41] 692 5-8-13 **47**..............................(p) PaulMulrennan 11 41
(Alan Berry) *sn pushed along in rr: r.o towards fin: nvr nrr* **50/1**

0051 **8** ½ **Spic 'n Span**[9] 1089 9-9-4 **52** 6ex..............................(v) LukeMorris 7 44
(Ronald Harris) *prom: chsd wnr 3f out: rdn 2f out: no ex ins fnl f* **10/1**

0413 **9** nk **Outbid**[19] 972 4-9-6 **54**........................................ SilvestreDeSousa 8 45
(Tony Carroll) *mid-div: rdn over 1f out: hung lft ins fnl f: nt trble ldrs* **7/1**[3]

056- **10** 2 ¾ **Harpers Ruby**[127] 8070 4-8-9 **46** oh1...................... MichaelJMMurphy(3) 5 27
(Neville Bycroft) *chsd ldrs: rdn 1/2-way: wknd over 1f out* **25/1**

0-22 **11** 3 ½ **Dear Ben**[21] 937 5-9-2 **50**........................................ AndrewMullen 6 19
(Brian Baugh) *chsd ldrs 3f* **14/1**

1m 2.43s (0.13) **Going Correction** +0.025s/f (Slow) 11 Ran SP% **126.9**
Speed ratings (Par 101): **99,98,97,97,97 93,92,92,91,87 81**
CSF £27.20 CT £57.06 TOTE £2.80: £2.20, £4.60, £1.10; EX 34.30 Trifecta £192.30.
**Owner** The Cool Silk Partnership **Bred** Corduff Stud Ltd & J Corcoran **Trained** Willoughton, Lincs
■ Stewards' Enquiry : Luke Morris two-day ban: careless riding (Apr 17-18)

**FOCUS**
A moderate handicap but, although the gallop was sound, very few figured. The winner raced centre-to-far side in the straight. Ordinary if sound form.
T/Plt: £5.70 to a £1 stake. Pool of £56348.62 -7117.20 winning tickets. T/Qpdt: £3.00 to a £1 stake. Pool of £5677.50 - 1397.93 winning tickets. CR

# MAISONS-LAFFITTE (R-H)
Thursday, April 3

**OFFICIAL GOING: Turf: good**

## 1271a PRIX D'ORGEVAL (CLAIMER) (2YO) (TURF) 5f
**11:45** (12:00) 2-Y-O **£9,583** (£3,833; £2,875; £1,916; £958)

RPR

**1** **Belle Du Jour (FR)** 2-9-1 **0**........................................ AntoineHamelin 10 64
(Matthieu Palussiere, France) **23/5**[3]

**2** nk **Little Mask (FR)**[19] 2-8-8 **0**........................................ ThierryJarnet 1 56
(J Heloury, France) **79/10**

**3** nk **Duquesa Penguin**[5] 1161 2-9-4 **0**........................ ThomasHenderson 2 65
(Jo Hughes) *dwlt sltly and pushed along early: towards rr whn rdn 2f out: r.o strly against rail ins fnl 150yds and wnt 3rd cl home: nrst fin* **32/1**

**4** 1 **Rivolochop (FR)** 2-9-4 **0**..............................(p) TonyPiccone 7 61
(C Boutin, France) **5/2**[1]

**5** hd **Mocky Glaz (FR)**[19] 2-9-4 **0**........................................ FlavienPrat 12 60
(D Windrif, France) **167/10**

**6** nk **Zebedeedoodah (IRE)**[19] 2-8-11 **0**................................ MickaelForest 11 52
(Matthieu Palussiere, France) **30/1**

**7** snk **Candy Kendall (FR)** 2-8-6 **0**........................ MatthiasLauron(5) 9 52
(T Lemer, France) **129/10**

**8** 2 **Princesse Rebelle (FR)** 2-8-11 **0**................................ AlexisBadel 8 44
(F-X De Chevigny, France) **52/1**

**9** shd **Lorenza Chope (FR)**[19] 2-9-1 **0**..............................(p) MaximeGuyon 3 48
(C Boutin, France) **31/10**[2]

**10** nk **Twin Mix (FR)**[19] 2-8-6 **0**..............................(b) JimmyTastayre(5) 5 43
(Y Gourraud, France) **51/1**

**11** 6 **Miss Doina (FR)** 2-8-8 **0**........................................ FabriceVeron 4 18
(E Nicoleau, France) **49/1**

**12** 6 **Iambertie** 2-8-11 **0**........................................ IoritzMendizabal 6
(J S Moore) *nvr travelling and sn in rr: lost tch and btn over 1f out: eased ins fnl f* **7/1**

1m 1.2s (61.20) 12 Ran SP% **119.5**
WIN (incl. 1 euro stake): 4.70 (Belle Du Jour coupled with Zebedeedoodah). PLACES: 2.20, 2.60, 9.30. DF: 26.80. SF: 60.50.
**Owner** Mrs Theresa Marnane **Bred** S.L. Muvisolar Ecologic **Trained** France

## 1272a PRIX DJEBEL (GROUP 3) (3YO COLTS & GELDINGS) (STRAIGHT) (TURF) 7f (S)
**1:20** (12:00) 3-Y-O **£33,333** (£13,333; £10,000; £6,666; £3,333)

RPR

**1** **Charm Spirit (IRE)**[179] 7056 3-9-2 **0**................................ OlivierPeslier 4 112+
(F Head, France) *midfield in tch: rdn and hdwy to chal over 1f out: r.o and led narrowly towards fin: jst hld on all out* **7/2**[3]

**2** shd **Kiram (FR)**[138] 7939 3-9-2 **0**........................ ChristopheSoumillon 1 112+
(J-C Rouget, France) *midfield in tch: rdn over 1f out: r.o strly against rail towards fin and wnt 2nd post: jst failed* **6/4**[1]

**3** shd **Imperiator**[21] 943 3-9-2 **0**........................................ FranckBlondel 6 112?
(P Decouz, France) *crossed to rail and led: rdn and strly pressed fr 2f out: hung rt u.p but r.o: hdd narrowly ins fnl f: jst hld and dropped to 3rd post* **108/10**

**4** shd **Bookrunner (USA)**[128] 3-9-2 **0**.................. Christophe-PatriceLemaire 3 112
(M Delzangles, France) *sn prom on outer: rdn to chal 2f out: r.o and ev ch tl jst hld and dropped to 4th post* **68/10**

**5** 3 ½ **Earnshaw (USA)**[153] 7686 3-9-2 **0**................................ MaximeGuyon 2 102
(A Fabre, France) *dwlt sltly and hld up towards rr: swtchd to outer and rdn 2f out: outpcd and btn ins fnl f* **14/5**[2]

**6** snk **See You Soon (FR)**[21] 3-9-2 **0**........................................ FabriceVeron 5 102
(H-A Pantall, France) *t.k.h: trckd ldr: rdn to chal 2f out: sltly short of room whn no ex ins fnl f: fdd* **123/10**

**7** 2 ½ **Zygmunt (FR)**[133] 7994 3-9-2 **0**........................................ AlexisBadel 7 95
(Mme M Bollack-Badel, France) *hld up and last thrght: rdn 2f out: outpcd and btn ins fnl f: nvr a factor* **27/1**

1m 24.3s (-3.70) **Going Correction** -0.325s/f (Firm) 7 Ran SP% **120.9**
Speed ratings: **108,107,107,107,103 103,100**
WIN (incl. 1 euro stake): 4.50. PLACES: 2.00, 1.80. SF: 12.20.
**Owner** H H Sheikh Abdulla Bin Khalifa Al Thani **Bred** Ecurie Des Monceaux **Trained** France

**FOCUS**
A race that has twice had a big impact on the English 2,000 Guineas in recent years, with Makfi following up his win here in 2010 and French Fifteen (winner of this in 2012) going on to finish second at Newmarket. A blanket finish but the form fits the averages for the race.

## 1273a PRIX IMPRUDENCE (GROUP 3) (3YO FILLIES) (STRAIGHT) (TURF) 7f (S)
**1:50** (12:00) 3-Y-O **£33,333** (£13,333; £10,000; £6,666; £3,333)

RPR

**1** **Xcellence (FR)**[138] 7940 3-9-0 **0**................................ CristianDemuro 5 114+
(F Doumen, France) *midfield in tch on inner: rdn and swtchd rt for clr run over 1f out: r.o and chal ins fnl f: wore down eventual runner-up and led cl home* **229/10**

**2** snk **Vorda (FR)**[153] 7690 3-9-0 **0**........................ Christophe-PatriceLemaire 1 113
(P Sogorb, France) *sn trcking ldr: shkn up to ld over 1f out: rdn and strly pressed ins fnl f: r.o but worn down and hdd cl home* **19/10**[2]

**3** 2 ½ **Dancing Sands (IRE)**[21] 944 3-9-0 **0**................................ OlivierPeslier 3 106+
(H-A Pantall, France) *t.k.h: sn midfield in tch: rdn over 1f out: r.o and wnt 3rd cl home: nt pce of front pair* **141/10**

4 1/2 **This Time (FR)**[138] [7939] 3-9-0 0 ........ FabriceVeron 7 105
(H-A Pantall, France) *hld up in rr: rdn and hdwy on outer 1f out: r.o ins fnl f but nt pce of front pair: jst hld on for 4th* **69/10**[3]

5 nse **Marbre Rose (IRE)**[175] [7160] 3-9-0 0 ........ ThierryJarnet 6 105
(F Head, France) *plld hrd early: sn prom: rdn over 1f out: outpcd by front pair ins fnl f: kpt on: jst denied 4th* **15/1**

6 1/2 **Miss France (IRE)**[188] [6795] 3-9-0 0 ........ MaximeGuyon 4 104
(A Fabre, France) *t.k.h: midfield in tch: pushed along and sltly outpcd whn nt clrest of runs over 1f out: kpt on under hands and heels ins fnl f but nvr threatened* **8/5**[1]

7 1 1/4 **Ice Love (FR)**[21] [944] 3-9-0 0 ........ RaphaelMarchelli 10 100
(T Castanheira, France) *wnt rt s: hld up in rr: hdwy 2f out: ev ch whn rdn over 1f out: no ex and fdd ins fnl f* **128/10**

8 1 1/4 **Early Prime (FR)**[27] 3-9-0 0 ........ UmbertoRispoli 8 97
(H-A Pantall, France) *t.k.h: midfield in tch on outer: prom and ev ch whn rdn over 1f out: no ex and fdd ins fnl f* **39/1**

9 1 **Fresles (IRE)**[256] 3-9-0 0 ........ GregoryBenoist 9 94
(Mme Pia Brandt, France) *restless stalls and dwlt sltly: hld up and a in rr: rdn over 1f out: sn on imp and btn: nvr a factor* **214/10**

10 2 **Fetan Joa (FR)**[174] [7184] 3-9-0 0 ........ IoritzMendizabal 2 89
(J Heloury, France) *sn led: rdn and hdd over 1f out: wknd: eased and dropped to last ins fnl f* **43/1**

1m 27.4s (-0.60) **Going Correction** -0.325s/f (Firm) **10** Ran SP% **119.1**
Speed ratings: **90,89,86,86,86 85,84,82,81,79**
WIN (incl. 1 euro stake): 23.90. PLACES: 4.50, 1.60, 3.50. DF: 37.70. SF: 107.40.
**Owner** Henri De Pracomtal **Bred** Haras D'Ecouves & Henri De Pracomtal **Trained** Bouce, France

**FOCUS**
A race that often produces high-class fillies, as well as the occasional top-notch one, but there was a bit up a turn up this time. The form was 5lb slower than the bunch finish of the Djebel.

1274 - (Foreign Racing) - See Raceform Interactive

# LEICESTER (R-H)
Friday, April 4

**OFFICIAL GOING: Good to soft (6.4)**
Wind: Light across Weather: Overcast

## 1275 YOUR EXPERT GUIDE TO LEICESTER LEICESTERRACECOURSETIPS.CO.UK H'CAP 7f 9y
**1:50** (1:50) (Class 4) (0-85,84) 4-Y-0+ **£4,690** (£1,395; £697; £348) **Stalls** High

Form RPR

5310 1 **My Kingdom (IRE)**[41] [714] 8-8-10 **73** ........(t) HarryBentley 1 83
(Stuart Williams) *hld up: hdwy 2f out: shkn up to ld 1f out: r.o wl* **16/1**

211- 2 3 **Bousatet (FR)**[196] [6602] 4-8-6 **74** ........ KevinStott(5) 2 76
(Kevin Ryan) *a.p: led over 1f out: sn rdn and hdd: styd on same pce ins fnl f* **9/2**

530- 3 1 1/2 **Red Refraction (IRE)**[208] [6238] 4-9-5 **82** ........ RyanMoore 7 80
(Richard Hannon) *plld hrd: trckd ldr tl over 5f out: remained handy: pushed along over 2f out: nt clr run over 1f out: swtchd rt and styd on same pce fnl f* **4/1**[3]

535- 4 1/2 **Accession (IRE)**[184] [6959] 5-9-2 **79** ........ MartinLane 8 76
(Charlie Fellowes) *hld up: pushed along over 1f out: nt clr run and swtchd rt ins fnl f: r.o: nt rch ldrs* **7/2**[2]

023- 5 nse **Al Mukhdam**[184] [6951] 4-9-7 **84** ........ DaneO'Neill 3 81
(Ed de Giles) *led to 1/2-way: chsd ldr: rdn and ev ch over 1f out: no ex ins fnl f* **10/3**[1]

20-4 6 shd **Great Expectations**[64] [389] 6-8-12 **75** ........ FrederikTylicki 4 72
(J R Jenkins) *trckd ldrs: racd keenly: rdn over 1f out: styd on same pce fnl f* **12/1**

0-60 7 6 **Al Khan (IRE)**[16] [1020] 5-8-12 **78** ........ OisinMurphy(3) 6 59
(Ann Stokell) *prom: chsd ldr 5f out tl led 1/2-way: rdn over 2f out: hdd over 1f out: wknd fnl f* **11/1**

300- 8 17 **Front Page News**[153] [7699] 4-8-9 **72** ........ AndreaAtzeni 5 9
(Robert Eddery) *hld up: rdn over 2f out: wknd over 1f out* **18/1**

1m 27.25s (1.05) **Going Correction** 0.0s/f (Good) **8** Ran SP% **110.7**
Speed ratings (Par 105): **94,90,88,88,88 88,81,61**
CSF £80.77 CT £335.25 TOTE £14.60: £4.00, £1.30, £2.20; EX 81.10 Trifecta £212.10.
**Owner** My Kingdom For A Horse **Bred** Irish National Stud **Trained** Newmarket, Suffolk

**FOCUS**
There was a false rail from the top of the hill on the back straight all the way to the winning line, increasing distances on the round course by 17 yards. They raced stands' side in this fair handicap, but the winner was positioned away from the rail for the most part. The pace looked solid. The winner is the best guide to the form.

## 1276 KNIGHTON MAIDEN STKS 5f 2y
**2:20** (2:23) (Class 5) 2-Y-0 **£2,587** (£770; £384; £192) **Stalls** High

Form RPR

3 1 **Flyball**[6] [1161] 2-9-5 0 ........ SeanLevey 1 77
(Richard Hannon) *led: rdn and hdd over 1f out: rallied to ld post* **2/1**[1]

2 nse **Burtonwood** 2-9-5 0 ........ RyanMoore 3 77+
(Richard Fahey) *chsd wnr tl led over 1f out: rdn and edgd lft ins fnl f: hdd post* **2/1**[1]

3 nk **Harry Hurricane** 2-9-5 0 ........ FergusSweeney 6 76
(George Baker) *pushed along in rr early: hdwy over 3f out: rdn and ev ch over 1f out: styd on* **14/1**[3]

4 1 **Come Uppence** 2-9-2 0 ........ DeclanBates(3) 4 72
(David Evans) *chsd ldrs: pushed along over 3f out: styd on* **50/1**

5 1 1/2 **Fast Act (IRE)** 2-9-5 0 ........ JamieSpencer 7 67
(Kevin Ryan) *chsd ldrs: pushed along 3f out: styd on same pce ins fnl f* **7/2**[2]

6 1/2 **Brazen Spirit** 2-9-5 0 ........ AdamKirby 13 67+
(Clive Cox) *prom: pushed along and outpcd 1/2-way: styd on ins fnl f* **20/1**

7 2 1/4 **London Life (IRE)** 2-9-0 0 ........ RichardKingscote 9 52
(Tom Dascombe) *chsd ldrs: outpcd 1/2-way: n.d after* **20/1**

8 1 1/2 **Chester Deal** 2-9-5 0 ........ BenCurtis 8 51
(Jo Hughes) *sn outpcd: r.o ins fnl f: nvr nrr* **100/1**

9 nk **Josie Joe** 2-9-0 0 ........ LiamKeniry 10 45
(David Evans) *sn outpcd* **50/1**

10 1 1/2 **Lady Bling** 2-8-9 0 ........ RyanWhile(5) 12 40
(Bill Turner) *s.i.s: outpcd* **33/1**

11 1 **Verchild Lad (IRE)** 2-9-2 0 ........ OisinMurphy(3) 5 41
(David Evans) *s.i.s: outpcd* **50/1**

12 6 **Hard To Find (IRE)** 2-9-5 0 ........ ChrisCatlin 2 20
(David Evans) *s.i.s: outpcd* **66/1**

1m 2.9s (2.90) **Going Correction** 0.0s/f (Good) **12** Ran SP% **116.4**
Speed ratings (Par 92): **76,75,75,73,71 70,67,64,64,61 60,50**
CSF £5.27 TOTE £3.00: £1.80, £1.20, £7.10; EX 7.20 Trifecta £51.70.
**Owner** Middleham Park Racing LXXIX **Bred** Gracelands Stud **Trained** East Everleigh, Wilts

**FOCUS**
They raced middle-to-stands' side. There were a few fancied in this and it's a maiden that ought to produce plenty of winners. It went to the only one with experience.

## 1277 BURTON OVERY (S) STKS 5f 218y
**2:55** (2:55) (Class 6) 3-Y-O **£1,940** (£577; £288; £144) **Stalls** High

Form RPR

0326 1 **Coiste Bodhar (IRE)**[28] [867] 3-9-0 60 ........(p) LukeMorris 11 65
(Joseph Tuite) *chsd ldr tl rdn to ld over 1f out: styd on wl* **17/2**

-420 2 2 **Intense Feeling (IRE)**[52] [568] 3-8-11 70 ........ DeclanBates(3) 3 59
(David Evans) *sn pushed along in rr: hdwy 2f out: rdn to chse wnr and edgd rt ins fnl f: r.o* **7/2**[2]

033- 3 2 1/4 **Hipz (IRE)**[104] [8383] 3-8-9 71 ........ DavidKenny(5) 4 51
(George Baker) *trckd ldrs: rdn and ev ch over 1f out: no ex ins fnl f* **13/8**[1]

0-66 4 2 **Brean Splash Susie**[9] [1104] 3-8-4 40 ........(v[1]) RyanWhile(5) 1 40
(Bill Turner) *led: rdn and hdd over 1f out: wknd ins fnl f* **66/1**

-000 5 5 **Trefnant (IRE)**[23] [933] 3-8-4 33 ........ ConnorBeasley(5) 2 24
(Chris Dwyer) *sn pushed along in rr: sme hdwy u.p over 1f out: wknd fnl f* **100/1**

00 6 2 **Robbian**[36] [765] 3-9-0 0 ........ MartinLane 6 23
(Charles Smith) *prom: rdn over 2f out: wknd over 1f out* **150/1**

65-0 7 2 3/4 **Robynelle**[7] [1146] 3-8-7 67 ........(v[1]) MatthewHopkins(7) 5 14
(Alan Jarvis) *plld hrd and prom: rdn over 2f out: sn wknd* **10/1**

2-23 8 hd **Narborough**[16] [1018] 3-8-11 60 ........ WilliamTwiston-Davies(3) 9 13
(Mick Channon) *hld up: rdn and hung lft over 1f out: sn wknd* **6/1**[3]

-5U6 9 2 1/2 **Sand Stormer (IRE)**[49] [614] 3-9-0 62 ........ MartinDwyer 7 5
(William Muir) *rdr removed hood late: dwlt: a in rr: rdn and wknd over 2f out* **12/1**

5-06 10 6 **Elualla (IRE)**[35] [786] 3-8-9 49 ........ SilvestreDeSousa 10
(Nigel Tinkler) *chsd ldrs: rdn 1/2-way: wknd over 2f out* **12/1**

1m 13.68s (0.68) **Going Correction** 0.0s/f (Good) **10** Ran SP% **112.7**
Speed ratings (Par 96): **95,92,89,86,80 77,73,73,70,62**
CSF £37.15 TOTE £10.20: £3.40, £1.40, £1.10; EX 40.70 Trifecta £80.10.No bid for the winner.
**Owner** Shefford Valley Racing **Bred** C Amerian **Trained** Great Shefford, Berks

**FOCUS**
Again, the action unfolded middle-to-stands' side. Just a moderate seller, in which the winner probably didn't improve.

## 1278 LODDINGTON CONDITIONS STKS (BOBIS RACE) 5f 218y
**3:30** (3:32) (Class 3) 3-Y-O **£7,561** (£2,263; £1,131; £566; £282) **Stalls** High

Form RPR

0-30 1 **Mick's Yer Man**[8] [1122] 3-9-4 80 ........ RyanWhile(5) 1 102
(Bill Turner) *a.p: chsd ldr 4f out: led over 1f out: edgd rt: rdn out* **16/1**

43-0 2 3 **Wee Jean**[13] [1067] 3-8-10 90 ........ WilliamTwiston-Davies(3) 2 82
(Mick Channon) *chsd ldrs: rdn and swtchd rt over 1f out: styd on same pce ins fnl f* **4/1**[3]

323- 3 nse **Beau Nash (IRE)**[177] [7122] 3-9-4 86 ........ RyanMoore 4 87
(Richard Hannon) *s.i.s: pushed along and hdwy over 3f out: rdn over 1f out: styd on same pce ins fnl f* **11/4**[2]

10- 4 nk **Canyari (IRE)**[267] [4212] 3-9-4 0 ........ PaulHanagan 3 86+
(Richard Fahey) *led: rdn and hdd over 1f out: styd on same pce ins fnl f* **5/4**[1]

4-23 5 9 **Bonjour Steve**[79] [187] 3-9-2 65 ........ JamesDoyle 5 55
(Richard Price) *hld up: rdn over 1f out: sn wknd* **80/1**

-346 6 29 **Scruffy Tramp (IRE)**[48] [624] 3-9-2 88 ........[1] AdamKirby 6
(Alan Bailey) *trckd ldr 2f: rdn and hung rt over 2f out: wknd and eased over 1f out* **7/1**

1m 12.7s (-0.30) **Going Correction** 0.0s/f (Good) **6** Ran SP% **110.7**
Speed ratings (Par 102): **102,98,97,97,85 46**
CSF £75.03 TOTE £18.60: £8.80, £4.20; EX 76.30 Trifecta £235.80.
**Owner** Mrs Tracy Turner & E A Brook **Bred** Heather Raw **Trained** Sigwells, Somerset

**FOCUS**
They raced middle-to-far side. This was a very useful performance from the winner, who'd been a smart early 2yo. Most of his rivals here were a bit disappointing.

## 1279 SIMON DE MONTFORT H'CAP (BOBIS RACE) 1m 1f 218y
**4:05** (4:05) (Class 4) (0-85,85) 3-Y-O **£4,690** (£1,395; £697; £348) **Stalls** Low

Form RPR

512- 1 **Montaly**[153] [7694] 3-9-1 **79** ........ DavidProbert 4 88+
(Andrew Balding) *hld up: hdwy over 2f out: rdn to ld wl ins fnl f: r.o* **6/1**[3]

22-1 2 1/2 **Arantes**[39] [734] 3-8-9 **76** ........ WilliamTwiston-Davies(3) 7 83
(Mick Channon) *s.i.s: hld up: hdwy over 1f out: sn rdn: r.o* **16/1**

021- 3 hd **Dragoon Guard (IRE)**[116] [8221] 3-8-13 **77** ........ AdamKirby 2 84
(Marco Botti) *hld up: nt clr run over 1f out: rdn and r.o wl ins fnl f: nt quite rch ldrs* **16/1**

31- 4 1 **Alex Vino (IRE)**[192] [6733] 3-9-2 **80** ........ RyanMoore 9 85
(Sir Michael Stoute) *trckd ldr after 1f: shkn up to ld over 2f out: rdn over 1f out: hdd and unable qck wl ins fnl f* **3/1**[2]

41- 5 1 1/4 **Idder (IRE)**[154] [7655] 3-9-2 **80** ........ AndreaAtzeni 6 82
(Roger Varian) *hld up: racd keenly: hdwy on outer over 6f out: rdn and ev ch ins fnl f: styd on same pce* **5/4**[1]

2404 6 11 **Flying Cape (IRE)**[37] [751] 3-9-4 **82** ........ WilliamBuick 3 63
(Andrew Hollinshead) *trckd ldrs: rdn over 2f out: wknd over 1f out* **50/1**

31 7 3/4 **Dubawi Light**[59] [468] 3-8-11 **75** ........ LukeMorris 5 55
(James Tate) *chsd ldrs: shkn up 1/2-way: rdn: hung lft and wknd over 1f out* **10/1**

534- 8 3/4 **Malachim Mist (IRE)**[160] [7529] 3-9-7 **85** ........ SeanLevey 1 64
(Richard Hannon) *led: rdn and hdd over 2f out: wknd over 1f out* **20/1**

2m 12.0s (4.10) **Going Correction** +0.425s/f (Yiel) **8** Ran SP% **111.3**
Speed ratings (Par 100): **100,99,99,98,97 88,88,87**
CSF £88.05 CT £1408.71 TOTE £6.40: £1.80, £3.30, £3.80; EX 75.80 Trifecta £565.10.
**Owner** The Farleigh Court Racing Partnership **Bred** Farleigh Court Racing Partnership **Trained** Kingsclere, Hants

**FOCUS**
An interesting 3yo handicap, but it rather fell apart late on with the front two in the market failing to see it out and the first three home coming from the last three places. A slightly positive view has been taken of the form.

## 1280 BARKBY MAIDEN FILLIES' STKS (BOBIS RACE) 7f 9y
4:40 (4:41) (Class 5) 3-Y-O £3,234 (£962; £481; £240) Stalls High

Form RPR
0- **1** **Nirva (IRE)**[193] 6689 3-9-0 0 ... JimCrowley 3 80
(Ralph Beckett) *a.p: trckd ldr 1/2-way: rdn to ld over 1f out: r.o* **14/1**
0- **2** 2 1/2 **Polar Eyes**[259] 4484 3-9-0 0 ... JamieSpencer 7 74
(Peter Chapple-Hyam) *s.i.s and wnt rt s: hld up: swtchd rt and hdwy over 1f out: r.o to go 2nd wl ins fnl f: no ch w wnr* **12/1**
02- **3** 2 **Stereo Love (FR)**[170] 7310 3-9-0 0 ... AdamKirby 10 68
(Clive Cox) *trckd ldrs: shkn up over 1f out: styd on same pce fnl f: wnt 3rd post* **7/1**[3]
**4** shd **Royal Seal** 3-9-0 0 ... RyanMoore 5 68
(Sir Michael Stoute) *trckd ldr tl led over 4f out: shkn up and hdd over 1f out: no ex ins fnl f: lost 3rd post* **11/4**[2]
**5** 3/4 **Cape Karli (IRE)** 3-9-0 0 ... RobertWinston 2 66
(Charles Hills) *hld up: hdwy over 4f out: shkn up over 1f out: styd on same pce fnl f* **25/1**
33- **6** 1 1/2 **Rocksee (IRE)**[196] 6607 3-9-0 0 ... RichardKingscote 4 62
(Tom Dascombe) *prom: rdn over 2f out: wknd ins fnl f* **22/1**
0- **7** 2 3/4 **Insight (IRE)**[223] 5773 3-9-0 0 ... JohnFahy 1 55
(John Spearing) *s.i.s: in rr: rdn over 2f out: wknd over 1f out* **100/1**
60 **8** 2 1/2 **Bikini Club**[44] 660 3-9-0 0 ... SeanLevey 6 49
(Paul D'Arcy) *chsd ldrs: lost pl over 4f out: wknd wl over 1f out* **150/1**
**9** 1/2 **Lisanor** 3-9-0 0 ... WilliamBuick 9 47
(John Gosden) *in rr: pushed along over 4f out: wknd over 2f out* **10/1**
3- **10** 6 **Shasta Daisy**[155] 7645 3-9-0 0 ... JamesDoyle 8 32
(Lady Cecil) *led: hdd over 4f out: pushed along over 2f out: wknd and eased fnl f* **11/8**[1]

1m 28.29s (2.09) **Going Correction** 0.0s/f (Good) **10** Ran SP% **114.6**
Speed ratings (Par 95): **88,85,82,82,81 80,77,74,73,66**
CSF £159.52 TOTE £19.10: £5.00, £5.00, £2.20; EX 266.00 Trifecta £1761.00 Part won. Pool: £2,348.05 - 0.50 winning tickets..
**Owner** Gillian, Lady Howard De Walden **Bred** Avington Manor Stud **Trained** Kimpton, Hants

**FOCUS**
They raced stands' side in this fillies' maiden and although the favourite blew out, a slightly positive view has been taken of the form.

## 1281 GRANBY H'CAP 1m 60y
5:15 (5:15) (Class 5) (0-75,74) 4-Y-0+ £3,234 (£962; £481; £240) Stalls Low

Form RPR
00-1 **1** **Memory Cloth**[6] 1168 7-8-10 **70** ... MeganCarberry(7) 10 84
(Brian Ellison) *mid-div: hdwy 1/2-way: rdn over 2f out: led ins fnl f: styd on wl* **3/1**[2]
511- **2** 1 1/4 **Sword Of The Lord**[169] 7322 4-9-4 **74** ... WilliamTwiston-Davies(3) 7 85
(Michael Bell) *hld up: hdwy over 2f out: rdn: edgd lft and ev ch ins fnl f: styd on same pce* **10/1**
210- **3** 1 1/2 **Uncle Dermot (IRE)**[105] 8360 6-9-0 **67** ... KierenFallon 4 75
(Brendan Powell) *led over 2f: led again 5f out: rdn over 1f out: hdd and unable qck ins fnl f* **11/1**
613- **4** 1 **Jaladee**[116] 8227 4-9-6 **73** ... AndreaAtzeni 5 78
(Roger Varian) *hld up in tch: rdn over 2f out: styd on* **9/2**[3]
-423 **5** 1/2 **Aldeburgh**[18] 990 5-9-0 **67** ... AdamKirby 2 71
(Jim Old) *hld up: hdwy u.p over 1f out: styd on same pce ins fnl f* **22/1**
131- **6** 3 1/4 **Bling King**[181] 7027 5-9-5 **72** ... SilvestreDeSousa 8 69
(Geoffrey Harker) *chsd ldrs: rdn over 2f out: wknd ins fnl f* **16/1**
515- **7** 1 **Imperial Glance**[283] 3665 4-8-12 **68** ... OisinMurphy(3) 1 62
(Andrew Balding) *plld hrd and prom: led 6f out tl 5f out: rdn over 2f out: wknd fnl f* **5/2**[1]
0003 **8** 13 **Ancient Greece**[30] 843 7-9-5 **72** ... (tp) JimCrowley 6 37
(George Baker) *hld up: a in rr: rdn over 2f out: sn wknd* **12/1**
542- **9** 1 3/4 **Aomen Rock**[109] 8313 4-9-1 **68** ... HayleyTurner 3 29
(James Fanshawe) *trckd ldrs: plld hrd: rdn over 3f out: wknd over 2f out* **9/1**

1m 47.54s (2.44) **Going Correction** +0.425s/f (Yiel) **9** Ran SP% **117.1**
Speed ratings (Par 103): **104,102,101,100,99 96,95,82,80**
CSF £33.62 CT £295.53 TOTE £4.00: £1.20, £2.10, £4.30; EX 16.70 Trifecta £225.00.
**Owner** Racing Management & Training Ltd **Bred** Darley **Trained** Norton, N Yorks

**FOCUS**
They raced up the middle in the straight. This is probably fair enough form for the level, a horse ahead of the handicapper defeating a progressive hat-trick seeker. The third is the key.
T/Plt: £306.10 to a £1 stake. Pool: £62,239.31 - 148.43 winning tickets. T/Qpdt: £93.20 to a £1 stake. Pool: £4,182.25 - 33.20 winning tickets. CR

# 1264 WOLVERHAMPTON (A.W) (L-H)
Friday, April 4

**OFFICIAL GOING: Standard**
Wind: light, behind Weather: overcast, dry

## 1282 BEST ODDS AT BOOKMAKERS.CO.UK H'CAP 5f 216y(P)
5:50 (5:53) (Class 6) (0-55,55) 4-Y-0+ £2,264 (£673; £336; £168) Stalls Low

Form RPR
0034 **1** **Sewn Up**[7] 1148 4-9-7 **55** ... (p) ShaneKelly 6 62
(Andrew Hollinshead) *taken down early: in tch towards rr: rdn along over 2f out: swtchd rt and hdwy over 1f out: racd awkwardly but r.o to chal and hld hd high towards fin: pushed ahd last stride* **3/1**[1]
5515 **2** shd **Lucky Mark (IRE)**[17] 1001 5-8-12 **53** ... (v) BradleyBosley(7) 10 60
(Garry Moss) *hdwy to ld and crossed to inner rail after 1f: rdn over 1f out: drvn ins fnl f: hrd pressed towards fin: hdd last stride* **9/1**
5-03 **3** hd **Triple Aitch (USA)**[21] 963 4-9-0 **55** ... JordanVaughan(7) 4 61
(Conrad Allen) *in tch in midfield: swtchd rt and effrt to chse ldr over 1f out: flashed tail u.p but r.o and ev ch wl ins fnl f: kpt on* **8/1**
0-56 **4** shd **Prigsnov Dancer (IRE)**[7] 1148 9-9-0 **55** ... DavidParkes(7) 3 61
(Deborah Sanderson) *in tch in midfield: effrt to chse ldrs and n.m.r over 1f out: hdwy u.p and ev ch wl ins fnl f: kpt on* **33/1**
4004 **5** 1 3/4 **Captain Scooby**[10] 1089 8-8-12 **51** ... (e) ConnorBeasley(5) 1 51
(Richard Guest) *in tch in midfield: effrt u.p wl over 1f out: styd on same pce ins fnl f* **20/1**
3234 **6** 3/4 **Very First Blade**[11] 1081 5-9-1 **49** ... (be) JoeFanning 12 47
(Michael Mullineaux) *in tch in midfield: effrt and rdn 2f out: styd on same pce fnl f* **12/1**
-230 **7** 1 1/2 **Daneglow (IRE)**[20] 973 4-9-0 **48** ... (e) LukeMorris 9 41
(Mike Murphy) *stdd after s: hld up in tch in last quartet: rdn and hdwy over 1f out: styd on but nvr trbld ldrs* **25/1**
0443 **8** 2 1/4 **Ivestar (IRE)**[1] 1270 9-9-4 **52** ... (v) JamesSullivan 11 38
(Michael Easterby) *chsd ldr tl no ex u.p and lost pl over 1f out: wknd ins fnl f* **5/1**[3]
3552 **9** shd **Flow Chart (IRE)**[20] 973 7-8-10 **47** ... SladeO'Hara(3) 7 32
(Peter Grayson) *in tch in last quartet but stuck wd: v wd and rdn bnd 2f out: kpt on fnl f: n.d* **25/1**
22-4 **10** 1 1/2 **Errigal Lad**[89] 58 9-8-10 **51** ... JackGarritty(7) 5 32
(Garry Woodward) *stdd s: effrt but forced to switch a long way rt over 1f out: no imp: n.d* **25/1**
00-2 **11** 3/4 **Baltic Gin (IRE)**[7] 1147 4-9-1 **49** ... DuranFentiman 2 27
(Malcolm Saunders) *chsd ldrs tl no ex u.p over 1f out: wknd ins fnl f* **20/1**
3553 **12** 1 1/4 **Avondream**[42] 688 5-9-4 **55** ... RobertTart(3) 8 29
(Milton Bradley) *in tch in midfield: rdn 4f out: lost pl and bhd wl over 1f out: wknd fnl f* **4/1**[2]

1m 15.22s (0.22) **Going Correction** +0.025s/f (Slow) **12** Ran SP% **114.5**
Speed ratings (Par 101): **99,98,98,98,96 95,93,90,90,88 87,85**
CSF £24.63 CT £174.72 TOTE £5.10: £2.30, £4.10, £2.10; EX 36.00 Trifecta £426.60.
**Owner** John L Marriott **Bred** M E Broughton **Trained** Upper Longdon, Staffs
■ Lord Buffhead (10-1) was withdrawn. Rule 4 applies to all bets. Deduction - 5p in the pound.

**FOCUS**
They went a decent pace in this handicap and there was a tight four-way finish. Standard form.

## 1283 COMPARE BOOKMAKERS AT BOOKMAKERS.CO.UK H'CAP 5f 20y(P)
6:25 (6:26) (Class 4) (0-80,80) 4-Y-0+ £5,175 (£1,540; £769; £384) Stalls Low

Form RPR
00-3 **1** **Top Boy**[14] 1049 4-9-0 **73** ... (v) DaleSwift 5 86
(Derek Shaw) *t.k.h: chsd ldrs: rdn and effrt 2f out: chal and edgd lft 1f out: led ins fnl f: stl edging lft but sn clr: r.o* **3/1**[1]
3451 **2** 2 1/4 **Bapak Bangsawan**[39] 730 4-9-0 **73** ... AmyRyan 7 78
(Kevin Ryan) *chsd ldr tl led over 2f out: rdn over 1f out: carried lft and hdd ins fnl f: sn outpcd by wnr but hld on for 2nd* **5/1**[3]
5142 **3** hd **Desert Strike**[9] 1109 8-9-1 **74** ... (p) LiamKeniry 4 78
(Conor Dore) *taken down early: led tl hdd over 2f out: drvn and stl ev ch over 1f out: carried lft and no ex ins fnl f* **16/1**
350- **4** 3/4 **Intrepid (IRE)**[199] 6488 4-9-2 **75** ... StevieDonohoe 9 77
(Tim Pitt) *stdd after s: hld up in rr: hdwy and swtchd rt over 1f out: styd on wl ins fnl f: nvr trbld ldrs* **7/1**
100- **5** 3/4 **Red Baron (IRE)**[196] 6583 5-9-4 **80** ... NeilFarley(3) 1 79
(Eric Alston) *t.k.h: chsd ldrs: rdn and unable qck over 1f out: outpcd and btn ins fnl f* **14/1**
0-00 **6** 3/4 **Harrogate Fair**[18] 993 4-8-7 **66** oh2 ... JoeFanning 3 62
(Michael Squance) *in tch in midfield: effrt u.p 2f out: keeping on same pce whn nt clr run and hmpd ins fnl f: one pce after* **33/1**
0-44 **7** 1 3/4 **We'll Deal Again**[14] 1049 7-9-5 **78** ... (b) GrahamGibbons 6 68
(Michael Easterby) *t.k.h: stdd after s: hld up in midfield: rdn and no hdwy 2f out: wl btn fnl f* **7/2**[2]
6201 **8** 1 3/4 **Profile Star (IRE)**[16] 1019 5-9-4 **77** ... LukeMorris 8 61
(Ann Stokell) *in tch in midfield on outer: rdn over 3f out: no rspnse: outpcd and dropped to last pair ent fnl 2f: n.d after* **6/1**
035- **9** 2 **Rylee Mooch**[165] 7420 6-8-13 **77** ... (e) ConnorBeasley(5) 2 53
(Richard Guest) *taken down early: short of room sn after s: a in rr: rdn and struggling over 2f out: no ch over 1f out* **17/2**

1m 2.02s (-0.28) **Going Correction** +0.025s/f (Slow) **9** Ran SP% **116.7**
Speed ratings (Par 105): **103,99,99,97,96 95,92,89,86**
CSF £18.47 CT £205.97 TOTE £3.50: £1.50, £2.20, £2.90; EX 21.20 Trifecta £193.80.
**Owner** Brian Johnson (Northamptonshire) **Bred** Mrs C R Philipson & Mrs H G Lascelles **Trained** Sproxton, Leics

**FOCUS**
The pace was not very strong in this sprint handicap but the well-handicapped favourite scored in good style and the form looks solid enough. The winner was close to his 3yo best.

## 1284 32RED BURNING DESIRE SLOT H'CAP 2m 119y(P)
7:00 (7:00) (Class 6) (0-60,60) 4-Y-0+ £2,264 (£673; £336; £168) Stalls Low

Form RPR
/115 **1** **Sir Frank Morgan (IRE)**[10] 1092 4-9-6 **60** ... JoeFanning 2 73+
(Mark Johnston) *chsd ldr tl led and grg best over 2f out: in command and edging rt fr over 1f out: styd on: comf* **8/13**[1]
5-01 **2** 3 1/4 **Royal Defence (IRE)**[7] 1150 8-8-10 **51** 6ex ... (t) ConnorBeasley(5) 7 60
(Richard Ford) *chsd ldrs: rdn and effrt to chse ldr wl over 1f out: edgd lft and no imp 1f out: plugged on* **5/2**[2]
066- **3** 5 **William Hogarth**[254] 3271 9-8-5 **46** ... DanielMuscutt(5) 4 49
(Keith Goldsworthy) *sn led and set stdy gallop: rdn and hdd over 2f out: 3rd and outpcd over 1f out: wknd ins fnl f* **15/2**[3]
4-06 **4** 5 **Go Amwell**[16] 657 11-8-3 **46** oh1 ... (v) VictorSantos(7) 1 43
(J R Jenkins) *v.s.a: sn rcvrd and in tch in last pair: t.k.h after 4f: rdn and outpcd over 2f out: 4th and wl hld fnl 2f* **66/1**
00-4 **5** 2 **Inside Knowledge (USA)**[40] 2 8-8-11 **47** ... (p) LukeMorris 6 42
(Garry Woodward) *t.k.h: chsd ldrs: rdn over 3f out: outpcd and btn over 2f out: wknd over 1f out* **33/1**
500 **6** 3/4 **Hejaz (IRE)**[46] 646 4-9-5 **59** ... (t[1]) StevieDonohoe 5 53
(Tim Pitt) *stdd s: t.k.h: hld up in last pair: rdn over 2f out: sn outpcd and btn: wknd over 1f out* **20/1**

3m 45.52s (3.72) **Going Correction** +0.025s/f (Slow)
**WFA** 4 from 8yo+ 4lb **6** Ran SP% **111.5**
Speed ratings (Par 101): **92,90,88,85,84 84**
CSF £2.30 TOTE £1.20: £1.10, £1.90; EX 2.10 Trifecta £5.00.
**Owner** Paul Dean **Bred** Airlie Stud **Trained** Middleham Moor, N Yorks

**FOCUS**
The hot favourite beat his main market rival with something in hand in this staying handicap. Weak, muddling form.

## 1285 32RED.COM H'CAP 7f 32y(P)
7:30 (7:31) (Class 6) (0-60,60) 3-Y-0 £2,264 (£673; £336; £168) Stalls High

Form RPR
656- **1** **Speed Society**[205] 6311 3-9-1 **54** ... AdamKirby 4 63
(Jim Boyle) *racd in midfield: 4th and effrt over 2f out: chsd ldr and clsng 2f out: led and edgd rt over 1f out: edgd bk lft and kpt on wl fnl f: rdn out* **15/8**[1]

5-14 **2** *1 ½* **It's All A Game**[73] 267 3-8-8 **50**....................(e) BillyCray(3) 3 54
(Richard Guest) *taken down early: chsd clr ldr: rdn and clsd over 2f out: chsd wnr and swtchd lft 1f out: keeping on same pce whn swtchd rt towards fin* **9/2**[3]

2-02 **3** *3 ¾* **Mornin Mr Norris**[8] 1130 3-8-4 **50**.................... JoeDoyle(7) 9 44
(John Quinn) *racd off the pce in midfield: rdn and no hdwy 3f out: modest 5th over 1f out: styd on fnl f to go 3rd nr fin: no threat to ldrs* **5/2**[2]

056- **4** *½* **Tamayuz Magic (IRE)**[199] 6487 3-9-7 **60**.................... GrahamGibbons 5 53
(Michael Easterby) *chsd ldng pair: rdn and effrt over 2f out: no hdwy and btn ent fnl f: wnt 3rd fnl 150yds: no imp and lost 3rd nr fin* **12/1**

0-04 **5** *2 ½* **Tidal Beauty**[14] 1047 3-8-7 **46** oh1.................... LukeMorris 2 32
(Tony Carroll) *fly-jmpd as stalls opened and s.i.s: t.k.h and hld up off the pce in last trio: r.o to heels and hmpd over 4f out: effrt u.p over 2f out: no hdwy over 1f out* **8/1**

0006 **6** *8* **Literally On Fire (IRE)**[23] 923 3-8-0 **46** oh1.................... JennyPowell(7) 1 12
(Brendan Powell) *led: wnt wl clr after 1f: 6 l clr 4f out: rdn and hdd over 1f out: sn btn and fdd fnl f* **25/1**

000- **7** *5* **Poco Piccolo**[178] 7096 3-8-7 **46** oh1....................(t) JoeFanning 7
(Deborah Sanderson) *stdd after s: t.k.h: hld up off the pce in last trio: swtchd to outer over 5f out: rdn and no hdwy 3f out: bhd over 1f out* **40/1**

5-00 **8** *5* **High Stand**[39] 731 3-9-2 **55**....................(b) ShaneKelly 6
(Daniel Mark Loughnane) *stdd s: t.k.h: hld up off the pce in rr: rdn over 3f out no hdwy: lost tch wl over 1f out* **10/1**

1m 30.37s (0.77) **Going Correction** +0.025s/f (Slow) 8 Ran SP% **115.7**
Speed ratings (Par 96): **96,94,90,89,86 77,71,66**
CSF £10.92 CT £21.20 TOTE £2.80: £1.10, £1.70, £1.60; EX 10.60 Trifecta £21.70.
**Owner** The 'In Recovery' Partnership **Bred** J B J Richards **Trained** Epsom, Surrey

**FOCUS**
They went a strong pace in this minor handicap and a big gamble was landed by an unexposed type. He's rated up a length on his 2yo form.

## 1286 DOWNLOAD THE LADBROKES APP H'CAP 7f 32y(P)
**8:00** (8:01) (Class 5) (0-75,75) 4-Y-0+ **£2,911** (£866; £432; £216) **Stalls High**

Form RPR

1-03 **1** **Sakash**[11] 1082 4-8-13 **67**.................... FrederikTylicki 5 77
(J R Jenkins) *wl in tch in midfield: effrt and qcknd to ld ent fnl f: in command fnl 150yds: comf* **2/1**[2]

5230 **2** *2* **Smokethatthunders (IRE)**[16] 1022 4-9-6 **74**....................[1] StevieDonohoe 6 79
(Tim Pitt) *hld up in tch in rr: rdn and swtchd rt 2f out: hdwy u.p over 1f out: kpt on wl fnl f to go 2nd towards fin: no threat to wnr* **11/4**[3]

5312 **3** *½* **Strong Man**[15] 1026 6-9-5 **73**....................(b) GrahamGibbons 4 77
(Michael Easterby) *pressed ldr tl rdn to ld wl over 1f out: hdd ent fnl f: outpcd by wnr jst ins fnl f: styd on same pce and lost 2nd towards fin* **15/8**[1]

354- **4** *4 ½* **Ginzan**[202] 6381 6-9-7 **75**.................... DaneO'Neill 1 67
(Malcolm Saunders) *t.k.h: chsd ldng pair: rdn and unable qck over 1f out: wknd ins fnl f* **33/1**

620- **5** *1* **Ted's Brother (IRE)**[146] 7824 6-8-12 **69**....................(e) BillyCray(3) 3 58
(Richard Guest) *stdd s: plld hrd: hld up in tch in last pair: rdn and no hdwy 2f out: wl hld and edgd lft ins fnl f* **16/1**

-616 **6** *1 ¾* **Loud**[15] 1031 4-9-7 **75**.................... JoeFanning 2 60
(Mark Johnston) *led tl hdd and rdn wl over 1f out: 3rd and btn 1f out: fdd ins fnl f* **7/1**

1m 28.99s (-0.61) **Going Correction** +0.025s/f (Slow) 6 Ran SP% **116.1**
Speed ratings (Par 103): **104,101,101,96,94 92**
CSF £8.37 TOTE £2.30: £3.00, £1.60; EX 9.40 Trifecta £22.30.
**Owner** Mr & Mrs C Schwick **Bred** Mr & Mrs C Schwick **Trained** Royston, Herts

**FOCUS**
The pace was decent in this handicap and the well-backed winner scored in good style. Straightforward form.

## 1287 LADBROKES MAIDEN STKS 7f 32y(P)
**8:30** (8:30) (Class 5) 3-Y-0+ **£2,911** (£866; £432; £216) **Stalls High**

Form RPR

2- **1** **Hagree (IRE)**[189] 6807 3-8-12 0.................... AntonioFresu 1 88
(Marco Botti) *sn led and mde rest: readily wnt clr ent fnl 2f: in command over 1f out: pushed out: easily* **4/7**[1]

4 **2** *7* **All Reddy**[22] 941 3-8-12 0.................... RichardKingscote 4 70
(Tom Dascombe) *led: sn hdd and chsd wnr after: rdn over 2f out: outpcd and no ch w wnr over 1f out: kpt on for 2nd fnl f* **8/1**[3]

-2 **3** *2* **Zain Dream (IRE)**[16] 1008 3-8-12 0.................... TomQueally 3 65
(Robert Cowell) *in tch in 4th: wnt 3rd and rdn over 2f out: 3rd and no imp fr over 1f out* **3/1**[2]

**4** *7* **Regal Selection** 3-8-7 0.................... LukeMorris 2 41
(James Tate) *chsd ldrs: rdn over 3f out: 4th and btn 2f out: sn wknd* **14/1**

00- **5** *9* **Permsiri (IRE)**[210] 6152 3-8-7 0.................... DuranFentiman 5 18
(Malcolm Saunders) *dropped to last and rdn after 1f: sn struggling: lost tch 1/2-way* **150/1**

1m 28.4s (-1.20) **Going Correction** +0.025s/f (Slow) 5 Ran SP% **107.1**
Speed ratings (Par 103): **107,99,96,88,78**
CSF £5.51 TOTE £1.30: £1.10, £6.80; EX 5.80 Trifecta £14.10.
**Owner** Manfredini & Mohamed Albousi Alghufli **Bred** J F Tuthill **Trained** Newmarket, Suffolk

**FOCUS**
The was an emphatic odds-on winner in this maiden who made all in a relatively good time. There was no depth to the race.

## 1288 LADBROKES H'CAP 1m 141y(P)
**9:00** (9:00) (Class 6) (0-60,60) 4-Y-0+ **£2,264** (£673; £336; £168) **Stalls Low**

Form RPR

0645 **1** **Ellaal**[6] 1168 5-9-2 **55**.................... DaleSwift 8 65
(Ruth Carr) *hld up in tch in midfield: rdn and effrt ent fnl 2f: led ins fnl f: kpt on wl: rdn out* **9/2**[2]

-263 **2** *1 ½* **Colour My World**[15] 1036 4-9-7 **60**....................(b[1]) GrahamLee 2 67
(Ed McMahon) *led: 3 l clr 3f out: rdn wl over 1f out: hdd ins fnl f: styd on same pce after* **9/2**[2]

0224 **3** *2* **Baltic Prince (IRE)**[3] 1227 4-9-7 **60**.................... TomQueally 6 62
(Paul Green) *chsd ldng pair: wnt 2nd and effrt ent fnl 2f: 3rd and no ex ent fnl f: wknd fnl 75yds* **11/4**[1]

0-6 **4** *1 ¼* **Brown Pete (IRE)**[82] 152 6-8-8 **50**.................... OisinMurphy(3) 7 49
(Ann Stokell) *in tch in midfield: effrt u.p but no imp over 2f out: styd on ins fnl f: nvr trbld ldrs* **11/4**[1]

000- **5** *5* **Daisie Cutter**[123] 8122 4-8-7 **46** oh1.................... JoeFanning 9 34
(Graeme McPherson) *hld up in last trio: rdn over 3f out: no real imp: wl hld whn swtchd lft jst ins fnl f* **100/1**

0045 **6** *2 ¼* **Devote Myself (IRE)**[8] 1138 5-8-7 **46**....................(t[1]) KierenFox 3 28
(Tony Carroll) *chsd ldr tl jst over 2f out: 4th and btn over 1f out: wknd fnl f* **9/1**[3]

5 **7** *¾* **Ferryview Place**[11] 1086 5-8-11 **50**....................(v) StevieDonohoe 4 31
(Ian Williams) *led to post: stdd s: t.k.h: hld up in last pair: rdn and no hdwy 3f out: bhd fnl f* **20/1**

1215 **8** *1 ½* **Prohibition (IRE)**[24] 916 8-9-4 **57**....................(t) AdamKirby 1 34
(Mandy Rowland) *dwlt and rdn along leaving stalls: hld up in last pair: rdn and no hdwy 3f out: n.d* **11/1**

400 **P** **Safwaan**[11] 1085 7-9-3 **56**.................... LukeMorris 5
(Michael Squance) *hld up in tch in midfield tl lost action and p.u 6f out* **11/1**

1m 49.96s (-0.54) **Going Correction** +0.025s/f (Slow) 9 Ran SP% **122.1**
Speed ratings (Par 101): **103,101,99,98,94 92,91,90,**
CSF £26.73 CT £68.13 TOTE £6.70: £2.10, £1.40, £1.50; EX 29.30 Trifecta £115.60.
**Owner** The Bottom Liners & Paul Saxton **Bred** W And R Barnett Ltd **Trained** Huby, N Yorks

**FOCUS**
They went a fair pace in this handicap but not many got involved and they finished quite well strung out.The winner is rated back to his January C&D run.
T/Plt: £13.70 to a £1 stake. Pool: £77,799.35 - 4,135.01 winning tickets. T/Qpdt: £2.70 to a £1 stake. Pool: £7,916.09 - 2,159.90 winning tickets. SP

# 1257 LINGFIELD (L-H)
Saturday, April 5

**OFFICIAL GOING: Standard**
Wind: Moderate, behind Weather: Overcast

## 1296 32RED TOMB RAIDER SLOT MAIDEN STKS 7f 1y(P)
**1:15** (1:15) (Class 5) 3-Y-0 **£3,340** (£986; £493) **Stalls Low**

Form RPR

422- **1** **Exchequer (IRE)**[173] 7251 3-9-5 76.................... FrankieDettori 4 89
(Richard Hannon) *mde all: rdn clr wl over 1f out: readily* **11/10**[1]

34- **2** *3 ¾* **Twin Point**[124] 8123 3-9-5 0....................[1] WilliamBuick 2 79
(John Gosden) *t.k.h in 3rd: rdn over 2f out: kpt on to take 2nd ins fnl f: nt trble wnr* **6/1**[3]

632- **3** *¾* **Intermedium**[145] 7835 3-9-5 83.................... MickaelBarzalona 5 77
(Charlie Appleby) *t.k.h: chsd wnr: rdn 2f out: one pce: lost 2nd ins fnl f* **5/4**[2]

5- **4** *4 ½* **Foxford**[149] 7780 3-9-0 0.................... DavidProbert 1 60
(Patrick Chamings) *chsd ldrs: rdn over 2f out: sn outpcd* **33/1**

00 **5** *16* **Adam Forever**[10] 1107 3-9-5 0.................... RichardKingscote 7 24
(Michael Wigham) *stdd s: hld up in rr: sme hdwy and pushed along 3f out: sn wknd* **100/1**

**6** *13* **Fleetwood Bella** 3-9-0 0.................... KierenFox 6
(Michael Attwater) *dwlt: outpcd and rdn along in rr: bhd fnl 4f* **66/1**

0- **7** *27* **Little Herbert**[133] 8017 3-9-0 0.................... RyanWhile(5) 3
(John Bridger) *in tch: rdn 4f out: sn bhd* **200/1**

1m 23.33s (-1.47) **Going Correction** -0.10s/f (Stan) 7 Ran SP% **112.3**
Speed ratings (Par 98): **104,99,98,93,75 60,29**
CSF £7.91 TOTE £1.80: £1.10, £2.60; EX 8.20 Trifecta £9.80.
**Owner** HighclereThoroughbredRacing-LakeConiston **Bred** B Holland, S Hillen & J Cullinan **Trained** East Everleigh, Wilts

**FOCUS**
Ignore the official ratings in this one, Exchequer is a pretty useful sort and the second and third are not straightforward. A clear personal best from the winner.

## 1297 DOWNLOAD THE LADBROKES APP H'CAP 7f 1y(P)
**1:50** (1:50) (Class 5) (0-70,68) 4-Y-0+ **£3,408** (£1,006; £503) **Stalls Low**

Form RPR

4321 **1** **Presumido (IRE)**[17] 1017 4-9-2 **68**.................... JackDuern(5) 10 77
(Simon Dow) *dwlt: bhd: pushed along 3f out: swtchd wd and gd hdwy over 1f out: r.o to ld fnl 75yds* **3/1**[1]

2-13 **2** *½* **Athletic**[10] 1102 5-9-7 **68**....................(v) JimCrowley 1 76
(Andrew Reid) *dwlt: patiently rdn towards rr: hdwy on bit over 1f out: led ins fnl f: hung lft and hdd fnl 75yds* **3/1**[1]

504 **3** *2 ½* **For Shia And Lula (IRE)**[12] 1083 5-9-1 **62**....................(p) ShaneKelly 5 63
(Daniel Mark Loughnane) *t.k.h: in tch: rdn to chse ldrs over 1f out: one pce fnl f* **12/1**

1334 **4** *½* **Bertie Blu Boy**[17] 1017 6-8-13 **60**....................(b) RichardKingscote 2 60+
(Lisa Williamson) *led: rdn over 2f out: hdd and no ex ins fnl f* **7/2**[2]

-166 **5** *3 ½* **Ostralegus**[17] 1021 4-9-6 **67**.................... JamesDoyle 9 57
(John Gallagher) *prom: chsd ldr 3f out tl over 1f out: sn wknd* **14/1**

0400 **6** *1* **Last Minute Lisa (IRE)**[19] 993 4-8-9 **56**.................... LukeMorris 8 44
(Sylvester Kirk) *sn bhd: rdn over 2f out: nvr nr to chal* **33/1**

330/ **7** *hd* **La Danza**[484] 8018 4-8-13 **65**.................... TimClark(5) 4 52
(Lisa Williamson) *chsd ldrs on inner tl wknd over 1f out* **66/1**

506- **8** *¾* **Eager To Bow (IRE)**[122] 8158 8-9-3 **67**.................... OisinMurphy(3) 7 52
(Patrick Chamings) *in tch tl wknd 2f out* **6/1**[3]

0103 **9** *1 ¼* **Kakapuka**[37] 757 7-9-7 **68**.................... GeorgeBaker 6 50
(Anabel K Murphy) *chsd ldr 4f: wknd over 1f out* **8/1**

1m 23.74s (-1.06) **Going Correction** -0.10s/f (Stan) 9 Ran SP% **116.4**
Speed ratings (Par 103): **102,101,98,98,94 92,92,91,90**
CSF £12.18 CT £93.62 TOTE £4.50: £1.50, £1.10, £5.00; EX 15.20 Trifecta £190.10.
**Owner** R Moss & J Page **Bred** Lynn Lodge Stud **Trained** Epsom, Surrey

**FOCUS**
As usual, Bertie Blu Boy blasted off in front but he did too much, TurfTrax showing he was quite bit quicker to the half-mile point than the leaders in the other two races at this trip, and the winner and second filled the last two places early on. The form is taken at something like face value.

## 1298 32RED FREE £10 BONUS MAIDEN STKS 6f 1y(P)
**2:25** (2:28) (Class 5) 3-Y-0 **£3,340** (£986; £493) **Stalls Low**

Form RPR

64- **1** **Mutawathea**[185] 6931 3-9-5 .................... PaulHanagan 3 85+
(Richard Hannon) *t.k.h in 4th: effrt and nt handle bnd into st: rallied and led 1f out: rdn clr* **11/10**[1]

23- **2** *2* **Dark Leopard**[162] 7501 3-9-5 .................... JamesDoyle 2 77
(Roger Charlton) *cl up: led briefly jst over 1f out: unable qck fnl f* **9/4**[2]

24-2 **3** *1* **Munfallet (IRE)**[10] 1107 3-9-5 83....................(b[1]) SeanLevey 1 74
(David Brown) *led tl jst over 1f out: one pce* **5/2**[3]

0-5 **4** *9* **Perrydot (IRE)**[37] 756 3-9-0 .................... FergusSweeney 5 40
(Jo Crowley) *trckd ldr tl 2f out: wknd over 1f out* **66/1**

5 6 **Dorset Gift** 3-9-0 ........ HayleyTurner 4 21
(Michael Bell) *s.i.s: a in last: rdn and lost tch 3f out* 25/1

1m 11.23s (-0.67) **Going Correction** -0.10s/f (Stan) 5 Ran SP% **112.3**
Speed ratings (Par 98): **100,97,96,84,76**
CSF £4.02 TOTE £2.00: £1.10, £1.50; EX 5.30 Trifecta £5.80.
**Owner** Hamdan Al Maktoum **Bred** Genesis Green Stud & P Scott **Trained** East Everleigh, Wilts

**FOCUS**
The third didn't run to his mark, but still not a terrible maiden and Mutawathea is potentially quite a nice horse. He showed considerable improvement.

## 1299 CORAL.CO.UK H'CAP 1m 4f (P)
**3:00** (3:01) (Class 2) (0-105,97) 4-Y-O+ **£12,938** (£3,850; £1,924; £962) **Stalls** Low

Form RPR
511- 1 **Brass Ring**[322] 2457 4-9-2 **90** ........ JamesDoyle 1 102+
(John Gosden) *hld up in 4th: effrt 2f out: rdn to ld nr fin* 5/6[1]
00-5 2 nk **Viewpoint (IRE)**[14] 1071 5-9-2 **89** ........ RyanMoore 3 100
(Richard Hannon) *sn chsng ldr: led 1f out: kpt on u.p fnl f: hdd nr fin* 8/1[3]
322- 3 ½ **Glorious Protector (IRE)**[174] 7223 4-8-12 **86** ........ WilliamBuick 7 96+
(Ed Walker) *t.k.h in 5th: rdn 2f out: r.o wl fnl f: clsng at fin* 4/1[2]
0-12 4 2½ **Hunting Ground (USA)**[65] 386 4-9-9 **97** ........ JoeFanning 2 103
(Mark Johnston) *led: rdn and hdd 1f out: no ex* 8/1[3]
1203 5 ½ **Swing Alone (IRE)**[14] 1071 5-9-9 **96** ........ LukeMorris 4 101
(Gay Kelleway) *hld up in 6th: rdn 2f out: styd on same pce* 8/1[3]
1241 6 ½ **Commissar**[7] 1175 5-8-9 **82** ........ (t) PaulHanagan 6 87
(Ian Williams) *hld up in rr: rdn 2f out: nvr able to chal* 14/1
104- 7 1¾ **Opera Box**[150] 7768 6-8-12 **88** ........ OisinMurphy(3) 5 90
(Marcus Tregoning) *prom on outer: rdn over 2f out: wknd wl over 1f out* 20/1

2m 31.45s (-1.55) **Going Correction** -0.10s/f (Stan)
**WFA** 4 from 5yo+ 1lb 7 Ran SP% **119.3**
Speed ratings (Par 109): **101,100,100,98,98 98,96**
CSF £9.32 TOTE £1.70: £1.20, £4.00; EX 10.10 Trifecta £51.20.
**Owner** K Abdullah **Bred** Millsec Limited **Trained** Newmarket, Suffolk

**FOCUS**
Quite strong-looking form, with the form rated slightly positively.

## 1300 32RED INTERNATIONAL TRIAL STKS (LISTED RACE) 1m 1y(P)
**3:40** (3:42) (Class 1) 3-Y-O **£20,982** (£7,955; £3,981) **Stalls** High

Form RPR
14-0 1 **Bow Creek (IRE)**[14] 1067 3-9-0 97 ........ JoeFanning 5 108
(Mark Johnston) *mde all: rdn and qcknd 2f out: hld on wl u.p fnl f* 10/1[3]
125- 2 ½ **Barley Mow (IRE)**[181] 7056 3-9-0 110 ........ RyanMoore 1 107
(Richard Hannon) *trckd wnr: drvn to chal fnl f: r.o: jst hld* 8/13[1]
22 3 1¾ **American Hope (USA)**[14] 1067 3-9-0 99 ........ ShaneKelly 2 103
(Mike Murphy) *t.k.h in 3rd: effrt on inner ent st: one pce fnl f* 6/1[2]

1m 35.71s (-2.49) **Going Correction** -0.10s/f (Stan) 3 Ran SP% **85.3**
Speed ratings (Par 106): **108,107,105**
CSF £10.47 TOTE £8.90; EX 8.50 Trifecta £7.30.
**Owner** Sheikh Hamdan bin Mohammed Al Maktoum **Bred** Roundhill Stud **Trained** Middleham Moor, N Yorks
■ Rule 4 of 25p in the pound applies to all bets; Withdrawn: Sloane Avenue

**FOCUS**
A far from ideal situation with the interesting Sloane Avenue and outsider Zampa Manos both having to be withdrawn after bursting through the stalls, despite the pair of them travelling no more than a few yards. The winner reversed reapparance form with the third, and the second was 8lb off last season's French form.

## 1301 LADBROKES H'CAP 7f 1y(P)
**4:45** (4:46) (Class 3) (0-95,91) 4-Y-O+ **£7,439** (£2,213; £1,106; £553) **Stalls** Low

Form RPR
34-1 1 **Purcell (IRE)**[15] 1042 4-9-4 **91** ........ OisinMurphy(3) 4 104
(Andrew Balding) *led after 1f: qcknd clr ent st: easily* 9/4[1]
1244 2 3 **Nassau Storm**[17] 1020 5-9-0 **84** ........ RyanMoore 7 89
(William Knight) *hld up towards rr: rdn 2f out: r.o wl to snatch 2nd on line* 7/2[2]
136- 3 shd **Big Whiskey (IRE)**[136] 7974 4-8-12 **82** ........ KierenFallon 3 87
(Edward Creighton) *in tch: rdn 2f out: wnt 6 l 2nd 1f out: r.o: no ch w wnr: lost 2nd on line* 6/1[3]
0-00 4 nk **Born To Surprise**[7] 1164 5-9-1 **85** ........ AmirQuinn 9 89
(Lee Carter) *s.i.s: hld up in rr: rdn 2f out: fin strly* 6/1[3]
-000 5 ½ **Piscean (USA)**[7] 1172 9-9-6 **90** ........ GeorgeBaker 2 93
(Tom Keddy) *hld up in rr: shkn up over 1f out: nrest at fin* 25/1
-441 6 ½ **Stonefield Flyer**[52] 574 5-9-5 **89** ........ WilliamBuick 5 90
(Keith Dalgleish) *prom tl fdd over 1f out* 10/1
24-0 7 nse **Talented Kid**[49] 625 5-9-6 **90** ........ JoeFanning 6 92
(Mark Johnston) *t.k.h: chsd ldrs tl no ex over 1f out* 12/1
1016 8 nk **Forceful Appeal (USA)**[15] 1042 6-9-3 **87** ........ HayleyTurner 1 87
(Simon Dow) *led 1f: chsd wnr after tl wknd 1f out* 10/1
000- 9 ¾ **Zacynthus (IRE)**[173] 7241 6-8-9 **84** ........ LouisSteward(5) 8 83
(Michael Bell) *chsd ldrs on outer: outpcd fnl 2f* 16/1

1m 23.62s (-1.18) **Going Correction** -0.10s/f (Stan) 9 Ran SP% **117.2**
Speed ratings (Par 107): **102,98,98,98,97 96,96,96,95**
CSF £10.16 CT £41.63 TOTE £2.80: £1.40, £1.20, £2.10; EX 10.70 Trifecta £45.50.
**Owner** Highclere Thoroughbred Racing-JohnPorter **Bred** Rathbarry Stud **Trained** Kingsclere, Hants

**FOCUS**
Form to be wary of as Purcell was allowed a totally uncontested lead and, sensibly ridden, TurfTrax sectional times showed he was much slower to the half-mile point than the leaders in the two previous races at this distance (50.33 compared to 49.56 for Exchequer in race one and 48.52 for Bertie Blu Boy in race two). He is progressive on Polytrack.

## 1302 CORAL.CO.UK BEST ODDS GUARANTEED ON RACING H'CAP 1m 2f (P)
**5:20** (5:21) (Class 6) (0-65,65) 4-Y-O+ **£2,726** (£805; £402) **Stalls** Low

Form RPR
0-50 1 **Nelson Quay (IRE)**[33] 817 4-9-7 **65** ........ SteveDrowne 8 72
(Jeremy Gask) *t.k.h: prom: rdn 2f out: r.o to ld nr fin* 16/1
-436 2 hd **Minstrel Lad**[52] 571 6-8-10 **57** ........ SimonPearce(3) 1 64
(Lydia Pearce) *in tch: effrt 2f out: led ins fnl f: kpt on u.p: hdd nr fin* 8/1
2143 3 nk **Standing Strong (IRE)**[10] 1100 6-9-3 **61** ........ (p) LiamKeniry 7 67+
(Zoe Davison) *hld up towards rr: n.m.r over 2f out: gd hdwy fr over 1f out: fin wl* 7/1[3]
-4 4 shd **The Firm (IRE)**[15] 1040 5-9-7 **65** ........ ShaneKelly 3 71
(Daniel Mark Loughnane) *hld up towards rr: hdwy 2f out: r.o wl fnl f* 12/1
-220 5 ¾ **Super Duplex**[19] 989 7-9-0 **58** ........ (t) FrankieMcDonald 5 62
(Roger Teal) *chsd ldrs: rdn over 2f out: kpt on fnl f* 16/1
0603 6 1 **Understory (USA)**[24] 922 7-9-6 **64** ........ (b) HayleyTurner 4 67
(Tim McCarthy) *led: hrd rdn and hdd ins fnl f: one pce* 5/1[2]

6505 7 3¾ **Copperwood**[22] 953 9-8-13 **57** ........ WilliamCarson 6 52
(Lee Carter) *mid-div: rdn over 2f out: no imp* 20/1
316- 8 shd **Buster Brown (IRE)**[140] 7922 5-9-7 **65** ........ RyanMoore 2 60
(Gary Moore) *prom: sltly outpcd over 1f out: rallied and nt clr run on rail jst ins fnl f: nt rcvr* 6/4[1]
000- 9 2 **L'Hirondelle (IRE)**[402] 813 10-9-4 **62** ........ JoeFanning 9 53
(Michael Attwater) *a towards rr* 50/1
6-05 10 ½ **Titan Triumph**[15] 1040 10-8-12 **56** ........ (t) RobertHavlin 10 46
(Michael Attwater) *a towards rr* 25/1
1402 11 1¼ **Litmus (USA)**[17] 1016 5-8-6 **55** ........ (b) LouisSteward(5) 11 43
(Simon Dow) *t.k.h: sn prom: wknd 2f out* 20/1
366- 12 3 **Loucal**[227] 5650 4-8-12 **59** ........ (p) RossAtkinson(3) 13 41
(Noel Quinlan) *stdd and swtchd lft s: a bhd* 33/1
400 13 18 **Wings Of Fire (IRE)**[19] 988 4-8-11 **60** ........ (v[1]) TimClark(5) 12 8
(Denis Quinn) *s.s: prom on outer after 2f: hrd rdn 3f out: sn wknd* 66/1

2m 5.71s (-0.89) **Going Correction** -0.10s/f (Stan) 13 Ran SP% **119.5**
Speed ratings (Par 101): **99,98,98,98,97 97,94,94,92,92 91,88,74**
CSF £127.90 CT £993.79 TOTE £24.80: £3.50, £3.00, £2.50; EX 218.00 Trifecta £1061.00.
**Owner** S T Brankin **Bred** Albert Conneally **Trained** Sutton Veny, Wilts

**FOCUS**
There was a bunch finish to this moderate handicap off an ordinary pace.
T/Plt: £322.30 to a £1 stake. Pool: £50262.95 - 113.83 winning tickets T/Qpdt: £223.50 to a £1 stake. Pool: £3051.22 - 10.10 winning tickets LM

# NEWCASTLE (L-H)
Saturday, April 5

**OFFICIAL GOING: Soft changing to soft (heavy in places) after race 1 (1:40)**
Wind: Breezy, half against Weather: Overcast, showers

## 1303 VERTEM ASSET MANAGEMENT MAIDEN FILLIES' STKS 1m 3y(S)
**1:40** (1:41) (Class 5) 3-4-Y-O **£3,234** (£962; £481; £240) **Stalls** Centre

Form RPR
1 **Barleycorn Lady (IRE)** 3-8-9 0 ........ JasonHart(3) 9 59
(Mark Walford) *dwlt: sn in tch: hdwy to ld wl over 1f out: pushed along and styd on wl fnl f* 25/1
4- 2 ½ **Missy Wells**[107] 8348 4-9-13 0 ........ DuranFentiman 4 62
(Mark Walford) *chsd ldrs: rdn and outpcd wl over 1f out: rallied to chse wnr ins fnl f: kpt on: hld nr fin* 66/1
3 1½ **Conveyor Belt (IRE)** 3-8-9 0 ........ SamJames(3) 10 55
(David O'Meara) *dwlt: sn midfield: outpcd over 2f out: shkn up and rallied over 1f out on steadily fnl f: no ex towards fin* 4/1[2]
0-60 4 2 **Sicilian Bay (IRE)**[46] 651 3-8-7 29 ........ ShirleyTeasdale(5) 6 50
(Paul Midgley) *hld up in tch: pushed along over 2f out: styd on fnl f: nrst fin* 100/1
5 2 **Queens Park (FR)** 3-8-12 0 ........ PJMcDonald 5 45
(John Davies) *dwlt: hld up in midfield: hdwy and ev ch over 1f out to ins fnl f: wknd last 50yds* 40/1
F 6 hd **Heavenly River (FR)**[25] 914 3-8-12 0 ........ BenCurtis 3 45
(K R Burke) *t.k.h: cl up: led 3f out to wl over 1f out: sn rdn: no ex ins fnl f* 12/1
362- 7 2½ **Vivere (IRE)**[195] 6666 3-8-12 76 ........ DanielTudhope 12 39
(David O'Meara) *t.k.h: led to 3f out: rdn and wknd wl over 1f out* 4/5[1]
0-3 8 ¾ **Rio Yuma (ITY)**[16] 1024 3-8-7 0 ........ JacobButterfield(5) 11 37
(Kristin Stubbs) *midfield: outpcd after 3f: styd on fr over 1f out: nvr able to chal* 11/1[3]
9 4½ **Come On Lulu** 3-8-9 0 ........ MichaelJMMurphy(3) 7 27
(Shaun Harris) *hld up: rdn over 3f out: no imp fr 2f out* 50/1
50- 10 2½ **Moon Over Rio (IRE)**[197] 6597 3-8-12 0 ........ AndrewElliott 1 21
(Ben Haslam) *dwlt: sn prom on outside: struggling 3f out: sn btn* 33/1
11 ½ **Belle Caroline (USA)** 3-8-12 0 ........ StevieDonohoe 13 20
(Tim Pitt) *bhd: struggling over 3f out: nvr on terms* 11/1[3]
00- 12 31 **Magical Mischief**[171] 7311 4-9-13 0 ........ PaulMulrennan 2
(Chris Fairhurst) *prom on outside: struggling 3f out: sn btn: t.o* 100/1
13 47 **Siouxsie Gee** 4-9-13 0 ........ GrahamLee 8
(Jim Goldie) *bhd and sn pushed along: lost tch over 4f out: t.o* 25/1
00- 14 ½ **How Rude**[253] 4731 3-8-12 0 ........ DavidAllan 14
(Mel Brittain) *racd towards stands' rail: in tch 3f: sn struggling: t.o* 66/1

1m 51.93s (8.53) **Going Correction** +0.65s/f (Yiel)
**WFA** 3 from 4yo 15lb 14 Ran SP% **119.9**
Speed ratings (Par 100): **83,82,81,79,77 76,74,73,69,66 66,35,,**
CSF £1078.80 TOTE £26.40: £5.70, £10.40, £1.60; EX 576.90 Trifecta £1224.00 Part won..
**Owner** G Mett Racing **Bred** G Strawbridge & London Thoroughbred Services Ltd **Trained** Sherriff Hutton, N Yorks
■ A first winner for trainer Mark Walford, who also had the runner-up. He took over the licence from his father Tim.

**FOCUS**
The ground was described as 'verging on heavy' and 'bottomless' by the first two riders and the official going was changed to soft, heavy in places from soft after this race. This may prove to be no more than an ordinary contest, highlighted by the fact that the fourth home, Sicilian Bay came into the race with a mark of just 29.

## 1304 R F HENDERSON LTD MAIDEN STKS 6f
**2:15** (2:16) (Class 5) 3-Y-O+ **£3,234** (£962; £481; £240) **Stalls** Centre

Form RPR
52- 1 **Shared Equity**[198] 6561 3-9-0 0 ........ GrahamLee 3 81
(Jedd O'Keeffe) *t.k.h: chsd ldrs: hdwy to ld over 1f out: rdn and r.o strly fnl f* 7/2[3]
0- 2 1¼ **Soul Brother (IRE)**[295] 3295 3-9-0 0 ........ DuranFentiman 4 77
(Tim Easterby) *t.k.h early: chsd ldr: smooth hdwy to chal over 1f out: sn rdn: kpt on same pce ins fnl f* 13/8[2]
56- 3 5 **Jimmy Crackle (IRE)**[318] 2577 3-9-0 ........ PaulPickard 5 62+
(Brian Ellison) *in tch: rdn and outpcd 1/2-way: styd on fnl f: nt rch first two* 50/1
-05 4 2¼ **Oriental Maid**[25] 906 3-8-9 0 ........ DaleSwift 2 50
(Brian Ellison) *hld up: rdn wl over 2f out: sn outpcd: n.d after* 66/1
553- 5 ½ **Highland Acclaim (IRE)**[178] 7125 3-9-0 84 ........ DanielTudhope 6 54
(David O'Meara) *plld hrd: led to over 1f out: wkng whn drifted markedly lft ins fnl f* 11/8[1]
03- 6 11 **Sleeper Class**[169] 7341 3-8-6 0 ........ IanBrennan(3) 1 16
(Jim Goldie) *in tch: struggling wl over 2f out: sn btn* 20/1

1m 19.55s (4.95) **Going Correction** +0.65s/f (Yiel) 6 Ran SP% **110.6**
Speed ratings (Par 103): **93,91,84,81,81 66**
CSF £9.34 TOTE £5.30: £2.40, £1.90; EX 13.20 Trifecta £75.30.
**Owner** Paul & Dale Chapman Racing **Bred** Trickledown Stud Limited **Trained** Middleham Moor, N Yorks


The Form Book, Raceform Ltd, Newbury, RG14 5SJ

**FOCUS**
This looked a fair maiden but the early pace was slow. The winner was a bigger improver than the runner-up.

## 1305 VERTEM ASSET MANAGEMENT H'CAP 5f
**2:45** (2:46) (Class 3) (0-95,95) 4-Y-O+ **£9,056** (£2,695; £1,346; £673) **Stalls** Centre

Form RPR
233- **1** **Aetna**[168] [7373] 4-8-12 **86**.................. GrahamGibbons 2 97+
(Michael Easterby) *in tch: smooth hdwy 2f out: shkn up to ld ins fnl f: rdn out towards fin* **3/1**[2]
01-0 **2** *1 ¾* **Rusty Rocket (IRE)**[94] [4] 5-8-11 **85**.................. PJMcDonald 4 90
(Paul Green) *led: rdn 2f out: hdd ins fnl f: kpt on same pce* **22/1**
306- **3** *1 ½* **Jamaican Bolt (IRE)**[161] [7527] 6-9-2 **93**.................. RobertTart(3) 8 92
(Geoffrey Oldroyd) *hld up bhd ldng gp: stdy hdwy over 1f out: sn rdn: kpt on fnl f to take 3rd cl home* **11/4**[1]
00-0 **4** *nk* **Lastchancelucas**[6] [1193] 4-8-5 **82** oh1 ow1..................(b[1]) JasonHart(3) 9 80
(Declan Carroll) *in tch: effrt and rdn 2f out: kpt on same pce ins fnl f* **25/1**
211- **5** *shd* **Da'Quonde (IRE)**[171] [7313] 6-8-13 **87**.................. PaulMulrennan 5 85
(Bryan Smart) *fly-jmpd s: trckd ldrs: chal gng wl over 1f out: rdn and kpt on same pce ins fnl f* **8/1**
010/ **6** *¾* **Bond Fastrac**[518] [7559] 7-8-2 **81**.................. NatashaEaton(5) 7 76
(Geoffrey Oldroyd) *hld up: shkn up and hdwy over 1f out: styd on steadily fnl f: nrst fin* **66/1**
0-50 **7** *1* **Another Wise Kid (IRE)**[6] [1193] 6-8-12 **86**.................. GrahamLee 6 78
(Paul Midgley) *in tch: rdn and effrt over 2f out: no imp fr over 1f out* **11/2**[3]
004- **8** *1* **Singeur (IRE)**[168] [7373] 7-8-11 **88**.................. NeilFarley(3) 11 76
(Robin Bastiman) *bhd and sn outpcd: hdwy over 1f out: nvr on terms* **20/1**
206- **9** *1* **Fast Shot**[162] [7495] 6-9-1 **89**.................. DavidAllan 1 73
(Tim Easterby) *hld up bhd ldng gp: pushed along over 2f out: sn outpcd: n.d after* **8/1**
106- **10** *3 ¼* **Angus Og**[168] [7373] 4-8-5 **84**.................. JoeyHaynes(5) 10 57+
(K R Burke) *missed break: bhd and outpcd: no ch fr 1/2-way* **16/1**
030- **11** *½* **Bear Behind (IRE)**[189] [6830] 5-9-7 **95**..................(e[1]) StephenCraine 3 66
(Tom Dascombe) *taken early to post: cl up tl rdn and wknd fr 2f out* **20/1**

1m 3.25s (2.15) **Going Correction** +0.65s/f (Yiel) **11 Ran SP% 114.4**
Speed ratings (Par 107): **108,105,102,102,102 100,99,97,96,90 90**
CSF £72.51 CT £203.71 TOTE £4.00: £1.60, £4.30, £1.10; EX 57.60 Trifecta £408.30.
**Owner** B Padgett **Bred** Bearstone Stud **Trained** Sheriff Hutton, N Yorks

**FOCUS**
A competitive sprint handicap. The winner is the type to rate higher this year.

## 1306 VERTEMASSETMANAGEMENT.COM H'CAP 1m 2f 32y
**3:15** (3:15) (Class 4) (0-85,85) 4-Y-O+ **£5,822** (£1,732; £865; £432) **Stalls** Centre

Form RPR
421- **1** **Esteaming**[229] [5582] 4-9-7 **85**.................. GrahamGibbons 5 98+
(David Barron) *cl up in chsng gp: smooth hdwy 3f out: led gng wl over 1f out: sn pushed clr: eased last 100yds: readily* **11/4**[2]
111- **2** *2* **Ebony Express**[150] [7778] 5-9-6 **84**.................. BenCurtis 4 89
(Alan Swinbank) *cl up chsng gp: effrt wl over 2f out: wnt 2nd appr fnl f: kpt on: flattered by proximity to eased-down wnr* **5/2**[1]
231- **3** *6* **King Of Paradise (IRE)**[195] [6668] 5-8-12 **79**.................. JasonHart(3) 2 73
(Eric Alston) *led and sn clr: rdn 3f out: hdd over 1f out: lost 2nd appr fnl f: sn btn* **11/2**
25-0 **4** *4 ½* **Amaze**[7] [1164] 6-9-4 **82**.................. BarryMcHugh 1 67
(Brian Ellison) *hld up in tch: rdn over 3f out: no imp fr 2f out* **7/2**[3]
111- **5** *1 ½* **Mr Snoozy**[281] [3765] 5-9-3 **81**..................(p) DuranFentiman 6 63
(Mark Walford) *hld up in tch: rdn and edgd lft wl over 2f out: sn outpcd* **7/1**
106- **6** *31* **Shamaheart (IRE)**[179] [7105] 4-8-13 **77**.................. GrahamLee 3
(Geoffrey Harker) *t.k.h: hld up: shkn up over 2f out: sn wknd: t.o* **20/1**

2m 23.12s (11.22) **Going Correction** +1.125s/f (Soft) **6 Ran SP% 110.1**
Speed ratings (Par 105): **100,98,93,90,88 64**
CSF £9.63 TOTE £3.30: £1.40, £1.70; EX 9.10 Trifecta £39.50.
**Owner** D E Cook **Bred** Mr & Mrs A E Pakenham & Daniel James **Trained** Maunby, N Yorks

**FOCUS**
This looked a competitive little handicap and it was run at a good gallop. This rating could underestimate the winner.

## 1307 VERTEM MANAGEMENT H'CAP 1m 4f 93y
**3:55** (3:55) (Class 5) (0-75,75) 4-Y-O+ **£3,234** (£962; £481; £240) **Stalls** Centre

Form RPR
516- **1** **Forced Family Fun**[26] [7338] 4-9-0 **72**.................. IanBrennan(3) 9 83
(John Quinn) *t.k.h: hld up in midfield on outside: hdwy over 2f out: led 1f out: kpt on strly: eased nr fin* **3/1**[1]
230- **2** *3 ½* **Rosie Rebel**[162] [7504] 4-9-4 **73**.................. ChrisCatlin 6 79
(Rae Guest) *t.k.h: hld up in tch: stdy hdwy to chse ldr over 2f out: effrt and led briefly appr fnl f: kpt on same pce last 150yds* **13/2**[3]
050- **3** *3* **Entihaa**[158] [7596] 6-9-7 **75**.................. BenCurtis 3 77
(Alan Swinbank) *hld up: pushed along 3f out: swtchd rt and hdwy over 1f out: styd on fnl f: nt rch first two* **11/1**
-240 **4** *½* **Gioia Di Vita**[36] [784] 4-9-4 **73**..................(p) GrahamLee 5 74
(David Thompson) *t.k.h: led: rdn and qcknd over 3f out: hdd appr fnl f: sn outpcd* **18/1**
02-2 **5** *6* **Aficionado**[6] [1197] 4-9-1 **70**..................(p) TomEaves 7 62
(Keith Dalgleish) *hld up: pushed along and hdwy over 2f out: drvn and outpcd over 1f out* **7/2**[2]
010- **6** *5* **El Massivo (IRE)**[86] [7066] 4-8-9 **64**.................. DaleSwift 10 48
(Brian Ellison) *hld up: rdn and outpcd over 3f out: n.d after* **7/1**
433- **7** *1* **Uncle Brit**[112] [8295] 8-8-7 **61**.................. PJMcDonald 1 44
(Malcolm Jefferson) *in tch on ins: struggling over 2f out: sn btn* **20/1**
10- **8** *4 ½* **Medieval Bishop (IRE)**[209] [6237] 5-8-9 **66**..................(p) JasonHart(3) 4 42
(Mark Walford) *chsd ldrs: rdn and edgd lft over 2f out: sn wknd* **16/1**
103- **9** *¾* **Danehill Flyer (IRE)**[223] [5786] 4-9-2 **71**.................. PhillipMakin 8 46
(Philip Kirby) *hld up: pushed along and hdwy over 2f out: rdn and wknd wl over 1f out* **16/1**
-001 **10** *3 ½* **Magnolia Ridge (IRE)**[7] [1167] 4-8-11 **71**..................(p) JacobButterfield(5) 2 41
(Kristin Stubbs) *chsd ldr: rdn over 2f out: sn btn* **7/1**

2m 57.68s (12.08) **Going Correction** +1.125s/f (Soft)
**WFA** 4 from 5yo+ 1lb **10 Ran SP% 115.7**
Speed ratings (Par 103): **104,101,99,99,95 92,91,88,87,85**
CSF £22.58 CT £188.56 TOTE £4.70: £1.70, £2.60, £2.90; EX 31.10 Trifecta £291.50.
**Owner** The Top Silk Syndicate **Bred** M B Hawtin **Trained** Settrington, N Yorks

**FOCUS**
A dawdling gallop to this handicap but the form makes sense.

## 1308 VERTEM H'CAP 1m 3y(S)
**5:00** (5:01) (Class 6) (0-65,64) 3-Y-O **£2,264** (£673; £336; £168) **Stalls** Centre

Form RPR
0-03 **1** **Uplifted (IRE)**[22] [960] 3-8-10 **53**..................(b) PaulMulrennan 5 63
(Kevin Ryan) *mde all: pushed along and qcknd wl over 2f out: kpt on wl fnl f: unchal* **9/2**[3]
00-4 **2** *6* **Suni Dancer**[22] [960] 3-8-7 **50** oh1.................. DuranFentiman 4 46
(Paul Green) *hld up on outside: smooth hdwy over 3f out: chsd (clr) wnr over 1f out: no imp* **25/1**
000- **3** *1* **Where's Tiger**[185] [6939] 3-9-0 **57**.................. PhillipMakin 10 51
(Jedd O'Keeffe) *dwlt: hld up: shkn up and stdy hdwy fr over 2f out: kpt on fnl f: nvr nr to chal* **11/1**
-415 **4** *3 ¼* **Kraka Gym (IRE)**[22] [960] 3-9-2 **59**.................. GrahamGibbons 7 45
(Michael Easterby) *t.k.h: prom: chsd wnr over 3f out to over 1f out: sn outpcd* **11/2**
023 **5** *6* **Her Red Devil (IRE)**[23] [941] 3-9-1 **58**.................. DavidNolan 3 31
(Richard Fahey) *in tch: drvn and outpcd over 3f out: edgd lft: no imp fr over 1f out* **6/1**
03-3 **6** *1 ¾* **Lynngale**[53] [564] 3-8-13 **61**.................. JacobButterfield(5) 1 30
(Kristin Stubbs) *t.k.h: cl up tl rdn and wknd over 1f out* **4/1**[2]
356- **7** *8* **Wilberfoss (IRE)**[131] [8040] 3-9-3 **60**.................. DavidAllan 11 10
(Mel Brittain) *hld up: rdn along and outpcd over 3f out: n.d after* **40/1**
040- **8** *14* **Miguela McGuire**[169] [7352] 3-8-5 **51**.................. NeilFarley(3) 9
(Eric Alston) *t.k.h: cl up: struggling over 3f out: sn btn* **16/1**
000- **9** *3 ½* **Mariners Moon (IRE)**[173] [7237] 3-9-7 **64**.................. DanielTudhope 6
(David O'Meara) *t.k.h: hld up: stdy hdwy over 3f out: rdn and edgd lft over 2f out: sn btn* **11/4**[1]
064- **10** *shd* **Greenbury (IRE)**[169] [7340] 3-8-12 **55**..................(p) PJMcDonald 8
(Ann Duffield) *t.k.h: prom tl rdn and wknd over 2f out* **50/1**

1m 50.39s (6.99) **Going Correction** +0.975s/f (Soft) **10 Ran SP% 117.0**
Speed ratings (Par 96): **104,98,97,93,87 86,78,64,60,60**
CSF £110.60 CT £1204.02 TOTE £4.70: £1.50, £4.50, £3.90; EX 81.30 Trifecta £1001.30.
**Owner** Slaters Arms Racing Club **Bred** Michael McGlynn **Trained** Hambleton, N Yorks

**FOCUS**
Probably no more than an ordinary handicap and it was run at a sedate pace, but there were several unexposed sorts in the line-up and it could throw up a winner or two. The first, second and fourth all ran in the same race at Wolverhampton last month, and they finished in the same order. The winner stepped up again.

## 1309 VERTEM ASSET MANAGEMENT APPRENTICE H'CAP (DIV I) 7f
**5:35** (5:36) (Class 6) (0-65,65) 4-Y-O+ **£2,264** (£673; £336; £168) **Stalls** Centre

Form RPR
300- **1** **Graceful Act**[169] [7345] 6-8-5 **52**.................. ShirleyTeasdale(3) 1 62
(Ron Barr) *hld up: hdwy and swtchd lft 2f out: edgd rt and led over 1f out: rdn out fnl f* **14/1**
003- **2** *2 ¼* **Mitchell**[106] [8360] 4-8-9 **56**.................. ConnorBeasley(3) 2 60
(David Thompson) *prom: hdwy and ev ch over 2f out to over 1f out: kpt on same pce ins fnl f* **7/1**[2]
000- **3** *¾* **Secret City (IRE)**[169] [7343] 8-9-0 **63**.................. LukeLeadbitter(5) 4 65
(Robin Bastiman) *prom: hdwy to ld over 2f out: hdd over 1f out: kpt on same pce ins fnl f* **25/1**
600- **4** *9* **Hayek**[197] [6600] 7-8-1 **52**..................(b) RachelRichardson(7) 6 31
(Tim Easterby) *in tch: effrt over 2f out: outpcd wl over 1f out* **8/1**[3]
640 **5** *1* **Ad Vitam (IRE)**[10] [1105] 6-8-5 **54**..................(bt) DavidParkes(5) 8 30
(David C Griffiths) *dwlt: bhd: hdwy and prom over 3f out: rdn and wknd over 1f out* **20/1**
055- **6** *1 ¾* **Alluring Star**[155] [7663] 6-8-7 **58**.................. DanielleMooney(7) 9 30
(Michael Easterby) *t.k.h: cl up tl rdn and wknd 2f out* **12/1**
/44- **7** *2 ½* **Grand Jipeck (IRE)**[383] [1066] 4-8-6 **55**.................. MeganCarberry(5) 7 20
(Brian Ellison) *t.k.h: cl up: led after 2f: hdd over 2f out: wknd over 1f out* **6/5**[1]
0-00 **8** *14* **Newbury Street**[17] [1010] 7-8-2 **51** oh2..................(p) JackGarritty(5) 3
(Patrick Holmes) *bhd: drvn over 3f out: btn fnl 2f* **66/1**
3426 **9** *9* **Masked Dance (IRE)**[21] [973] 7-8-12 **61**..................(b) MatthewHopkins(5) 10
(Scott Dixon) *t.k.h: led 2f: cl up tl wknd over 2f out* **7/1**[2]
005- **10** *24* **Mick Slates (IRE)**[309] [2836] 5-9-7 **65**.................. JasonHart 5
(Declan Carroll) *in tch tl wknd qckly 1/2-way: sn struggling: t.o* **11/1**

1m 34.49s (6.69) **Going Correction** +0.975s/f (Soft) **10 Ran SP% 114.4**
Speed ratings (Par 101): **100,97,96,86,85 83,80,64,54,26**
CSF £104.10 CT £1613.53 TOTE £17.30: £2.60, £2.10, £7.10; EX 103.40 Trifecta £932.40.
**Owner** D Thomson **Bred** Mayden Stud, J A And D S Dewhurst **Trained** Seamer, N Yorks
■ Stewards' Enquiry : Shirley Teasdale two-day ban: use of whip (19-20 Apr)

**FOCUS**
This looks ordinary form, with little depth to the race.

## 1310 VERTEM ASSET MANAGEMENT APPRENTICE H'CAP (DIV II) 7f
**6:05** (6:05) (Class 6) (0-65,64) 4-Y-O+ **£2,264** (£673; £336; £168) **Stalls** Centre

Form RPR
212- **1** **Trixie Malone**[172] [7283] 4-9-4 **64**.................. JoeyHaynes(5) 10 81
(K R Burke) *cl up: effrt and led over 1f out: rdn and hld on wl ins fnl f* **5/4**[1]
000- **2** *½* **Echo Of Lightning**[197] [6587] 4-8-0 **50**..................[1] KevinLundie(7) 1 65
(Brian Ellison) *t.k.h: led: rdn over 2f out: hdd over 1f out: rallied: kpt on: hld towards fin* **9/2**[2]
025- **3** *4* **Clumber Place**[148] [7808] 8-8-12 **55**.................. MichaelJMMurphy 7 60
(Shaun Harris) *chsd ldrs: drvn over 2f out: outpcd by first two fr over 1f out* **7/1**[3]
04-4 **4** *3* **Violent Velocity (IRE)**[83] [152] 11-9-0 **62**.................. JoeDoyle(5) 4 59
(John Quinn) *hld up: pushed along over 2f out: styd on fnl f: nvr on terms* **11/1**
630- **5** *hd* **Monel**[177] [7148] 6-8-9 **52**.................. IanBrennan 9 48
(Jim Goldie) *plld hrd: hld up: stdy hdwy 2f out: sn rdn and no imp* **11/1**
0644 **6** *1 ½* **Ferdy (IRE)**[9] [1138] 5-9-3 **60**.................. JasonHart 5 52
(Paul Green) *hld up: rdn along wl over 2f out: no imp* **10/1**
000- **7** *½* **Liliargh (IRE)**[169] [7344] 5-8-9 **52**.................. GeorgeChaloner 6 43
(Ben Haslam) *in tch: drvn over 3f out: wknd 2f out* **16/1**
/60- **8** *11* **Grey Destiny**[329] [2274] 4-8-6 **56**.................. RobertDodsworth(7) 2 18
(Mel Brittain) *dwlt: t.k.h and sn prom: struggling wl over 2f out: sn btn* **22/1**
2/0- **9** *3 ¼* **Cheeky Wee Red**[186] [6919] 6-8-9 **57**.................. LauraBarry(5) 8 11
(Alistair Whillans) *hld up on outside: struggling over 2f out: sn btn* **25/1**

1m 34.33s (6.53) **Going Correction** +0.975s/f (Soft) **9 Ran SP% 115.0**
Speed ratings (Par 101): **101,100,95,92,92 90,89,77,73**
CSF £6.73 CT £27.76 TOTE £2.20: £1.10, £2.10, £2.20; EX 9.30 Trifecta £37.40.
**Owner** Mrs Elaine M Burke **Bred** Llety Farms **Trained** Middleham Moor, N Yorks

■ Stewards' Enquiry : Kevin Lundie seven-day ban: use of whip (19-25 Apr) three-day ban: weighed in 2lb heavy (26-28 Apr)

**FOCUS**

This looked the better of the two divisions of the apprentice handicap, though the time was only marginally faster. The form is rated slightly positively.

T/Plt: £354.90 to a £1 stake. Pool: £50076.66 - 103.00 winning tickets T/Qpdt: £11.10 to a £1 stake. Pool: £4784.59 - 318.46 winning tickets RY

# [1282]WOLVERHAMPTON (A.W) (L-H)

Saturday, April 5

**OFFICIAL GOING: Standard**

Wind: Light behind Weather: Overcast

## 1311 BEST ODDS AT BOOKMAKERS.CO.UK H'CAP 5f 216y(P)

5:50 (5:50) (Class 5) (0-70,73) 4-Y-O+ £2,911 (£866; £432; £216) Stalls Low

Form RPR

4264 1 **Top Cop**[16] 1031 5-9-2 **70**....................(be) DCByrne(5) 8 77
(Ronald Harris) *w ldr tl led over 4f out: rdn over 1f out: jst hld on* **8/1**

56-6 2 shd **Red Cape (FR)**[25] 913 11-9-0 **63**....................(b) JamesSullivan 10 70
(Ruth Carr) *a.p: rdn over 2f out: r.o* **14/1**

0233 3 nk **Haadeeth**[4] 1221 7-8-7 **63**....................(t) HollieDoyle(7) 4 69
(David Evans) *chsd ldrs: rdn and edgd lft ins fnl f: r.o* **4/1**[2]

0134 4 nk **Colourbearer (IRE)**[23] 938 7-9-6 **69**....................(t) DavidProbert 1 74
(Milton Bradley) *sn led: hdd over 4f out: chsd wnr: rdn over 1f out: r.o* **4/1**[2]

0-04 5 3 1/2 **Hab Reeh**[10] 1115 6-8-0 **56**.................... GemmaTutty(7) 7 50
(Ruth Carr) *s.i.s: hld up: r.o ins fnl f: nvr nrr* **12/1**

2361 6 1 1/2 **Roy's Legacy**[10] 1109 5-9-10 **73**.................... AdamKirby 9 62
(Shaun Harris) *chsd ldrs: rdn over 1f out: no ex fnl f* **3/1**[1]

-411 7 hd **Cadmium Loch**[8] 1148 6-8-4 **58**....................(p) JackDuern(5) 3 46
(Andrew Hollinshead) *hld up: rdn over 2f out: nvr on terms* **6/1**[3]

5433 8 6 **One Way Or Another (AUS)**[23] 939 11-8-4 **58**..........(t) EoinWalsh(5) 6 27
(David Evans) *s.i.s: pushed along 1/2-way: a in rr* **9/1**

1m 14.97s (-0.03) **Going Correction** 0.0s/f (Stan) 8 Ran SP% **114.8**

Speed ratings (Par 103): **100,99,99,99,94 92,92,84**

CSF £109.85 CT £516.71 TOTE £12.20: £4.60, £5.20, £1.90; EX 114.10 Trifecta £219.90.

**Owner** Ridge House Stables Ltd **Bred** Littleton Stud **Trained** Earlswood, Monmouths

**FOCUS**

A strongly run, if only modest opener. The first four were close to their marks.

## 1312 BOOKMAKERS.CO.UK (S) H'CAP 5f 216y(P)

6:20 (6:20) (Class 6) (0-60,61) 3-Y-O+ £2,264 (£673; £336; £168) Stalls Low

Form RPR

5051 1 **Exceedexpectations (IRE)**[22] 963 5-9-11 **58**.........(vt) JamieSpencer 1 65
(John Butler) *pushed along early: led 5f out: rdn and hung rt over 1f out: edgd lft ins fnl f: styd on u.p* **11/10**[1]

5536 2 3/4 **Where's Reiley (USA)**[17] 1017 8-9-13 **60**....................(v) SebSanders 10 65
(Michael Attwater) *a.p: pushed along 1/2-way: rdn to chse wnr over 1f out: r.o* **12/1**

3013 3 nk **Catalyze**[17] 1009 6-9-10 **57**....................(t) AdamKirby 6 61
(Ann Stokell) *trckd ldrs: racd keenly: rdn over 1f out: r.o* **9/2**[3]

0341 4 hd **Sewn Up**[1] 1282 4-9-9 **61** 6ex....................(p) JackDuern(5) 8 64
(Andrew Hollinshead) *hld up: hdwy over 2f out: rdn and edgd lft ins fnl f: styd on* **5/2**[2]

2360 5 2 1/4 **Hinton Admiral**[10] 1110 10-9-4 **51**.................... JamesSullivan 3 47
(Pat Eddery) *s.i.s: sn pushed along in rr: r.o ins fnl f: nvr nrr* **20/1**

4220 6 1 **Diamond Vine (IRE)**[8] 1148 6-9-2 **49**....................(v) LukeMorris 2 42
(Ronald Harris) *chsd ldrs: pushed along thrght: rdn over 2f out: styd on same pce fr over 1f out* **14/1**

454- 7 4 **Dancing Welcome**[192] 6752 8-9-4 **58**....................(b) LeroyLynch(7) 4 38
(Milton Bradley) *hmpd sn after s: a in rr* **33/1**

2450 8 14 **Rise To Glory (IRE)**[8] 1148 6-9-10 **57**.................... RobertWinston 7
(Shaun Harris) *led 1f: chsd wnr: rdn over 2f out: wknd over 1f out* **16/1**

1m 15.77s (0.77) **Going Correction** 0.0s/f (Stan) 8 Ran SP% **122.3**

Speed ratings (Par 101): **94,93,92,92,89 88,82,64**

CSF £18.54 CT £50.43 TOTE £3.00: £1.10, £2.40, £1.60; EX 14.20 Trifecta £101.90.

**Owner** Wildcard Racing Syndicate **Bred** R S Cockerill (farms) Ltd & Peter Dodd **Trained** Newmarket, Suffolk

**FOCUS**

The market can often prove the best guide in races at this basement level and that certainly proved the case. The placed form is ordinary.

## 1313 BOOKMAKERS.CO.UK H'CAP 5f 216y(P)

6:50 (6:51) (Class 3) (0-95,93) 4-Y-O-£7,246 (£2,168; £1,084; £542; £270) Stalls Low

Form RPR

320- 1 **Barracuda Boy (IRE)**[189] 6830 4-9-7 **93**.................... RichardKingscote 6 106
(Tom Dascombe) *chsd ldr tl shkn up to ld over 1f out: rdn and edgd rt ins fnl f: r.o* **5/4**[1]

3142 2 3/4 **Mappin Time (IRE)**[25] 909 6-8-9 **81**....................(be) RobertWinston 4 92
(Tim Easterby) *chsd ldrs: shkn up and edgd lft over 1f out: rdn and ev ch ins fnl f: unable qck nr fin* **9/4**[2]

1-40 3 6 **Bedloe's Island (IRE)**[6] 1193 9-9-1 **87**.................... AdamKirby 5 79
(Alan McCabe) *s.i.s: pushed along over 2f out: styd on u.p to go 3rd wl ins fnl f: nt trble ldrs* **10/1**

106 4 2 1/4 **Caspian Prince (IRE)**[36] 788 5-9-5 **91**....................(t) DavidProbert 2 76
(Tony Carroll) *led: rdn and hdd over 1f out: wknd ins fnl f* **7/2**[3]

00-4 5 11 **Pandar**[28] 890 5-9-2 **88**.................... JamieSpencer 1 37
(Milton Bradley) *chsd ldrs: rdn over 2f out: wknd and eased over 1f out* **10/1**

1m 14.16s (-0.84) **Going Correction** 0.0s/f (Stan) 5 Ran SP% **115.6**

Speed ratings (Par 107): **105,104,96,93,78**

CSF £4.66 TOTE £2.00: £1.10, £1.30; EX 4.00 Trifecta £22.00.

**Owner** Laurence A Bellman **Bred** Mount Coote Partnership **Trained** Malpas, Cheshire

■ Stewards' Enquiry : Richard Kingscote caution: careless riding

**FOCUS**

A briskly run feature and much to like about the winner. The second is rated in line with his winter best.

## 1314 32RED EBF STALLIONS MAIDEN FILLIES' STKS (BOBIS RACE) 5f 20y(P)

7:20 (7:22) (Class 5) 2-Y-O £3,234 (£962; £481; £240) Stalls Low

Form RPR

1 **Patience Alexander (IRE)** 2-9-0 0.................... AdamKirby 8 87+
(David Evans) *trckd ldrs: carried rt over 2f out: pushed along to ld over 1f out: sn clr: easily* **10/11**[1]

2 9 **Zermintrudee (IRE)** 2-8-11 0.................... DeclanBates(3) 7 55+
(David Evans) *sn outpcd: r.o to go 2nd wl ins fnl f: no ch w wnr* **33/1**

3 3/4 **Sparbrook (IRE)** 2-9-0 0.................... MartinDwyer 12 52
(George Baker) *mid-div: pushed along 1/2-way: styd on to go 3rd ins fnl f: n.d* **12/1**

4 3/4 **Macarthurs Park (IRE)** 2-9-0 0.................... RichardKingscote 13 49
(Tom Dascombe) *s.s: outpcd and flashed tail at times: styd on fnl f: nvr nrr* **4/1**[2]

5 1 **Mark's Whisper (IRE)** 2-8-9 0.................... RyanWhile(5) 6 46
(Bill Turner) *chsd ldr: pushed along and hmpd over 2f out: rdn and wkng whn hung lft ins fnl f* **6/1**[3]

6 1 1/4 **Multi Quest** 2-9-0 0.................... JohnFahy 1 41
(Jo Hughes) *sn outpcd: kpt on ins fnl f: nvr nrr* **33/1**

7 1/2 **Shamrock Sheila (IRE)** 2-8-9 0.................... PhilipPrince(5) 3 39
(J S Moore) *chsd ldrs: swtchd rt over 2f out: chsd wnr over 1f out: sn hung lft: wknd ins fnl f* **16/1**

8 1/2 **Seamoor Secret** 2-9-0 0.................... StephenCraine 10 39
(Alex Hales) *mid-div: pushed along 1/2-way: sme hdwy sn after: btn whn hmpd ins fnl f* **25/1**

9 8 **Wiggle** 2-9-0 0.................... StevieDonohoe 5 9
(Tim Pitt) *led: rdn and hdd over 1f out: wkng whn hmpd ins fnl f* **8/1**

10 1 **Lady Armada** 2-9-0 0.................... LukeMorris 9 5
(Jo Hughes) *s.s: outpcd* **33/1**

1m 3.07s (0.77) **Going Correction** 0.0s/f (Stan) 10 Ran SP% **124.0**

Speed ratings (Par 89): **93,78,77,76,74 72,71,71,58,56**

CSF £51.49 TOTE £1.80: £1.10, £10.90, £2.70; EX 46.20 Trifecta £673.50.

**Owner** Noel O'Callaghan **Bred** Mountarmstrong Stud **Trained** Pandy, Monmouths

■ Stewards' Enquiry : Philip Prince one-day ban: careless riding (19 Apr)

**FOCUS**

A hugely impressive debut for the heavily supported winner.

## 1315 32RED.COM H'CAP 7f 32y(P)

7:50 (7:51) (Class 5) (0-75,78) 3-Y-O £2,911 (£866; £432; £216) Stalls High

Form RPR

0-11 1 **Almargo (IRE)**[8] 1146 3-9-10 **78**.................... SilvestreDeSousa 5 88
(Mark Johnston) *trckd ldr tl led 2f out: rdn over 1f out: wandered arnd ins fnl f: r.o wl: comf* **4/7**[1]

0-14 2 4 **Secret Suspect**[54] 561 3-9-5 **73**.................... LukeMorris 3 73
(James Tate) *a.p: rdn over 2f out: chsd wnr over 1f out: styd on same pce ins fnl f* **8/1**

032- 3 2 **Quincel**[243] 5068 3-9-0 **68**.................... RichardKingscote 4 63
(Tom Dascombe) *led: plld hrd: rdn and hdd 2f out: no ex ins fnl f* **5/1**[3]

010- 4 1 **Picks Pinta**[196] 6628 3-8-11 **65**.................... DaneO'Neill 1 57
(Jo Hughes) *chsd ldrs: rdn over 2f out: no ex fnl f* **16/1**

60-4 5 3 1/4 **Rostrum Farewell**[18] 1006 3-8-8 **62**.................... AndrewElliott 2 46
(David Brown) *hld up: pushed along 1/2-way: n.d* **50/1**

530- 6 2 3/4 **Big Boned (USA)**[165] 7435 3-9-0 **68**.................... JamieSpencer 6 45
(Ed Dunlop) *hld up: hdwy on outer over 2f out: shkn up and wknd over 1f out* **4/1**[2]

1m 29.89s (0.29) **Going Correction** 0.0s/f (Stan) 6 Ran SP% **119.3**

Speed ratings (Par 98): **98,93,91,90,86 83**

CSF £7.06 TOTE £1.40: £1.10, £3.10; EX 5.60 Trifecta £14.80.

**Owner** Sheikh Hamdan bin Mohammed Al Maktoum **Bred** Mountarmstrong Stud **Trained** Middleham Moor, N Yorks

**FOCUS**

Fitness doubts surrounded many of these. Another step up from the winner.

## 1316 LADBROKES H'CAP 1m 141y(P)

8:20 (8:20) (Class 3) (0-95,93) 4-Y-O-£7,246 (£2,168; £1,084; £542; £270) Stalls Low

Form RPR

561- 1 **Capo Rosso (IRE)**[130] 8053 4-9-2 **88**.................... RichardKingscote 3 102
(Tom Dascombe) *disp ld at str pce tl wnt on over 3f out: clr over 1f out: styd on wl* **6/1**[3]

31-0 2 5 **Gworn**[7] 1164 4-9-4 **90**.................... JamieSpencer 4 93
(Ed Dunlop) *sn outpcd: hdwy over 2f out: rdn to chse wnr over 1f out: no imp fnl f* **11/8**[1]

2134 3 2 1/2 **Conry (IRE)**[2] 1267 8-8-2 **79** oh8.................... SammyJoBell(5) 2 76
(Ian Williams) *s.i.s: hld up: hdwy over 2f out: rdn over 1f out: no ex fnl f* **16/1**

-231 4 12 **Silverware (USA)**[25] 917 6-9-1 **87**.................... TonyHamilton 5 56
(Kristin Stubbs) *disp ld at str pce tl rdn over 3f out: wknd over 1f out* **6/1**[3]

0-30 5 14 **Party Royal**[14] 1070 4-8-13 **85**.................... SilvestreDeSousa 1 22
(Mark Johnston) *pushed along in 4th and off the pce: rdn and wknd 3f out* **8/1**

4220 6 12 **Tellovoi (IRE)**[7] 1164 6-9-4 **93**....................(v) OisinMurphy(3) 6
(Ann Stokell) *disp ld at str pce tl rdn wl over 3f out: wknd over 2f out* **10/3**[2]

1m 48.24s (-2.26) **Going Correction** 0.0s/f (Stan) 6 Ran SP% **110.7**

Speed ratings (Par 107): **110,105,103,92,80 69**

CSF £14.38 TOTE £7.30: £2.20, £2.40; EX 15.20 Trifecta £99.10.

**Owner** Deva Racing Red Clubs Partnership **Bred** Michael Wiley **Trained** Malpas, Cheshire

**FOCUS**

This was run at a scorching early pace and it required a strong, tough staying effort from the winner, who posted a personal best.

## 1317 CORAL APP DOWNLOAD FROM THE APP STORE H'CAP 1m 1f 103y(P)

8:50 (8:50) (Class 5) (0-75,76) 4-Y-O+ £2,911 (£866; £432; £216) Stalls Low

Form RPR

00-1 1 **Life And Times (USA)**[12] 1085 6-9-7 **75**.................... SilvestreDeSousa 1 93+
(Mark Johnston) *s.i.s: racd keenly and rcvrd to trck ldr after 1f: shkn up to ld over 1f out: r.o wl to come clr ins fnl f: easily* **4/11**[1]

-134 2 10 **Tiger Reigns**[58] 498 8-9-5 **73**....................(tp) JamieSpencer 2 77
(John Butler) *led: pushed along and hdd over 1f out: eased whn btn ins fnl f* **8/1**[3]

-455 3 10 **Wildomar**[9] 1133 5-9-0 **68**.................... StephenCraine 5 51
(Peter Hiatt) *s.i.s: hld up: rdn and wknd over 2f out* **50/1**

35-1 4 6 **Tenor (IRE)**[8] 1142 4-9-8 **76**....................(t) AdamKirby 3 46
(John Ryan) *chsd ldrs: rdn over 3f out: wknd over 2f out* **5/2**[2]

140- 5 5 **Tevez**[211] 6167 9-9-4 **75**.................... OisinMurphy(3) 4 35
(Des Donovan) *wnt rt s: hld up: rdn and wknd over 3f out* **14/1**

1m 59.5s (-2.20) **Going Correction** 0.0s/f (Stan) 5 Ran SP% **121.6**

Speed ratings (Par 103): **109,100,91,85,81**

CSF £5.47 TOTE £1.60: £1.10, £3.10; EX 6.20 Trifecta £76.90.

**Owner** Sheikh Hamdan bin Mohammed Al Maktoum **Bred** Vision Bloodstock Et Al **Trained** Middleham Moor, N Yorks

**FOCUS**
An intriguing finale was turned into a procession by the winner. He's rated as scoring by 6l, as the runner-up was eased.
T/Plt: £57.10 to a £1 stake. Pool: £57656.74 - 736.26 winning tickets T/Qpdt: £3.60 to a £1 stake. Pool: £8759.85 - 1800.45 winning tickets CR

1318 - 1332a (Foreign Racing) - See Raceform Interactive

## CORK (R-H)
Sunday, April 6

**OFFICIAL GOING: Heavy**

### 1333a CORK STKS (LISTED RACE) 6f
2:55 (2:56) 3-Y-O+ **£21,666** (£6,333; £3,000; £1,000)

RPR
1 **An Saighdiur (IRE)**[30] 873 7-9-7 99 BillyLee 10 111
(Andrew Slattery, Ire) *broke wl and sn led: rdn clr ent fnl f: styd on strly to extend advantage ins fnl 100yds: comf* **12/1**
2 5 **Scream Blue Murder (IRE)**[175] 7227 4-9-5 104 WayneLordan 9 93
(T Stack, Ire) *trckd ldrs in 3rd: rdn along appr fnl f: sn chsd wnr in 2nd: no imp ins fnl f: kpt on same pce* **5/1**[2]
3 1 **Remember You (IRE)**[7] 1201 3-8-4 96 ConnorKing 6 84
(David Wachman, Ire) *trckd ldr in 2nd tl rdn along and dropped to 3rd 1f out: kpt on same pce* **14/1**
4 3 **Bold Thady Quill (IRE)**[4] 1252 7-9-7 99 (p) JosephO'Brien 4 82
(K J Condon, Ire) *hld up in rr: niggled along 1/2-way: prog into 7th 1f out: styd on wl into 4th clsng stages: nvr nrr* **11/1**
5 3/4 **Arctic (IRE)**[154] 7719 7-9-7 97 (t) PatSmullen 7 80
(Tracey Collins, Ire) *chsd ldrs: rdn along under 2f out in 5th: no imp ent fnl f* **14/1**
6 1/2 **Bubbly Bellini (IRE)**[14] 1075 7-9-7 98 (p) FergalLynch 2 78
(Adrian McGuinness, Ire) *chsd ldrs in 4th: rdn along over 2f out: no ex ins fnl f and dropped to 6th clsng stages* **25/1**
7 3 1/2 **Maarek**[169] 7364 7-10-0 114 DeclanMcDonogh 3 74
(Miss Evanna McCutcheon, Ire) *w.w: sme prog towards outer 2f out: wnt 6th 1f out: sn no imp* **11/8**[1]
8 12 **Smoothtalkinrascal (IRE)**[210] 6235 4-9-7 105 DanielTudhope 8 29
(David O'Meara) *chsd ldrs tl rdn along 2f out: nt qckn appr fnl f: sn no ex* **11/2**[3]
9 22 **Sendmylovetorose**[238] 5320 4-9-2 97 ShaneFoley 1
(M Halford, Ire) *w.w towards outer: pushed along 1/2-way: dropped towards rr under 2f out: sn no ex* **20/1**
10 31 **Morning Frost (IRE)**[113] 8307 4-9-2 104 ConorHoban 5
(M Halford, Ire) *slowly away and a in rr: adrift under 2f out* **16/1**

1m 22.69s (10.09)
**WFA** 3 from 4yo+ 12lb **10** Ran SP% **118.0**
CSF £71.90 TOTE £9.40: £3.20, £4.10, £2.00; DF 92.70 Trifecta £803.80.
**Owner** Men Of Forty Eight Syndicate **Bred** S Ross **Trained** Thurles, Co Tipperary

**FOCUS**
A horse who made his name as a tough sprint handicapper at a high level, An Saigdiur took a convincing step up to Listed level.

1334 - 1339a (Foreign Racing) - See Raceform Interactive

## LONGCHAMP (R-H)
Sunday, April 6

**OFFICIAL GOING: Turf: good**

### 1340a PRIX LA FORCE (GROUP 3) (3YO) (TURF) 1m 2f
1:30 (12:00) 3-Y-O **£33,333** (£13,333; £10,000; £6,666; £3,333)

RPR
1 **Gailo Chop (FR)**[22] 982 3-9-2 0 JulienAuge 3 110+
(A De Watrigant, France) *t.k.h: trckd ldr: pushed along and short of room fr 2f out: swtchd outside and nudged Elliptique whn chalng between horses over 1f out: r.o to ld fnl 120yds: readily* **15/2**
2 3/4 **Free Port Lux**[20] 3-9-2 0 ThierryJarnet 2 109+
(F Head, France) *t.k.h: hld up in midfield: rdn and hdwy on outer over 1 1/2f out: styd on u.p appr fnl f: tk 2nd fnl strides: nvr quite on terms w wnr* **13/2**
3 hd **Mr Pommeroy (FR)**[43] 721 3-9-2 0 FabriceVeron 4 108
(H-A Pantall, France) *led: rousted along fr 2f out: rallied gamely: hdd 120yds out: no ex: lost 2nd fnl strides* **13/2**
4 1 3/4 **Diaghan (FR)**[168] 7409 3-9-2 0 ChristopheSoumillon 5 105
(M Delzangles, France) *s.s: w.w towards rr: pushed along and sme prog fr 2f out: styd on ins fnl f: nvr on terms* **4/1**[2]
5 nk **Elliptique (IRE)**[168] 7409 3-9-2 0 MaximeGuyon 8 104
(A Fabre, France) *hld up towards rr: sn plld himself onto quarters of ldr: rdn 1 1/2f out: ev ch whn nudged by eventual wnr over 1f out: one pce u.p fnl f* **15/8**[1]
6 shd **Nabbaash**[36] 3-9-2 0 IoritzMendizabal 1 104
(J-C Rouget, France) *t.k.h: hld up in tch bef dropping to midfield after 3f: rdn 2f out and nt qckn: kpt on at one pce fnl f* **5/1**[3]
7 1 3/4 **Double Look (IRE)**[22] 982 3-9-2 0 Christophe-PatriceLemaire 6 100
(D Guillemin, France) *racd in tch on outer: pushed along fr 2f out: wknd u.p appr fnl f* **20/1**
8 9 **Cockney Bob**[23] 3-9-2 0 (p) ThomasMessina 7 82
(J Parize, France) *hld up in rr: swtchd outside and shortlived effrt 3f out: hld in last whn eased ins fnl f* **40/1**

2m 2.96s (-1.04) **8** Ran SP% **117.1**
WIN (incl. 1 euro stake): 8.40. PLACES: 2.60, 2.40, 2.40. DF: 22.80. SF: 46.20.
**Owner** Alain Chopard **Bred** A Chopard **Trained** France

### 1341a PRIX D'HARCOURT (GROUP 2) (4YO+) (TURF) 1m 2f
2:40 (12:00) 4-Y-O+ **£61,750** (£23,833; £11,375; £7,583; £3,791)

RPR
1 **Smoking Sun (USA)**[124] 8144 5-8-11 0 (b1) StephanePasquier 4 115+
(P Bary, France) *settled in 5th: swtchd outside and gd hdwy 1 1/2f out: rdn to ld fnl 150yds: drvn out: readily* **7/1**
2 1 1/2 **Norse King (FR)**[22] 984 5-9-1 0 AlexisBadel 7 116
(Mme M Bollack-Badel, France) *trckd ldng pair on outer: pushed along to chal ldrs fr 1 1/2f out: r.o fnl f: nt pce of wnr* **6/5**[1]
3 1/2 **Triple Threat (FR)**[169] 7367 4-9-1 0 MaximeGuyon 5 115
(A Fabre, France) *w.w towards rr: last and rdn 1 1/2f out: styd on ins fnl f: nvr on terms* **10/3**[2]
4 1/2 **Baltic Baroness (GER)**[183] 7048 4-8-9 0 ow1 Pierre-CharlesBoudot 6 108
(A Fabre, France) *t.k.h: hld up in rr: hdwy on inner over 2f out: 4th and styng on 1 1/2f out: kpt on ins fnl f: nt pce to chal* **10/1**
5 hd **Singing (FR)**[22] 984 4-8-11 0 OlivierPeslier 1 110
(C Laffon-Parias, France) *led on inner: rdn and increased tempo fr 2f out: hrd rdn and hdd fnl 150yds: no ex* **6/1**[3]
6 6 **Superplex (FR)**[22] 984 4-8-11 0 UmbertoRispoli 2 98
(M Figge, Germany) *trckd ldng pair on inner: rdn 2 1/2f out and nt qckn: wknd appr fnl f* **25/1**
7 2 1/2 **Royal Prize**[50] 625 4-8-11 0 GregoryBenoist 3 93
(Mme M Bollack-Badel, France) *dwlt: sn rcvrd to press ldr on outer after 1f: rdn 2 1/2f out: chsd ldrs tl grad dropped away fnl 1 1/2f* **40/1**

2m 1.96s (-2.04) **7** Ran SP% **110.7**
WIN (incl. 1 euro stake): 6.20. PLACES: 2.10, 1.30. SF: 17.90.
**Owner** Niarchos Family **Bred** Flaxman Holdings Limited **Trained** Chantilly, France

## REDCAR (L-H)
Monday, April 7

**OFFICIAL GOING: Good to soft (6.6)**
Wind: Light half behind Weather: Cloudy with sunny periods

### 1342 REDCAR RACECOURSE CHEAPEST ADMISSION IN GREAT BRITIAN MAIDEN AUCTION STKS 5f
2:20 (2:22) (Class 5) 2-Y-O **£2,587** (£770; £384; £192) **Stalls** Centre

Form RPR
2 1 **Paddy Again (IRE)**[9] 1161 2-8-1 0 RyanWhile(5) 5 74
(Bill Turner) *qckly away: mde all: rdn fnl f and kpt on wl* **10/11**[1]
2 1 1/4 **Sarista (IRE)** 2-8-9 0 RobertWinston 3 73+
(David Barron) *chsd wnr: green and pushed along bef 1/2-way: rdn and hung lft fr wl over 1f out: kpt on u.p fnl f* **5/2**[2]
0 3 6 **Penalty Scorer**[9] 1161 2-8-3 0 BillyCray(3) 4 48
(Richard Guest) *t.k.h early: chsd ldng pair: rdn along wl over 1f out: kpt on same pce* **9/1**[3]
4 nk **Binky Blue (IRE)** 2-8-9 0 BarryMcHugh 11 50+
(Tony Coyle) *towards rr: green and pushed along bef 1/2-way: hdwy 2f out: styd on appr fnl f: nrst fin* **50/1**
5 1 **Reet Petite (IRE)** 2-8-4 0 ConnorBeasley(5) 2 46+
(Michael Dods) *in tch: green: pushed along and outpcd towards rr after 1 1/2f: hdwy 2f out: swtchd lft ent fnl f: kpt on nrst fin* **16/1**
6 1/2 **Compton River** 2-9-0 0 PaulMulrennan 8 49
(Bryan Smart) *chsd ldrs: rdn along over 2f out: grad wknd* **25/1**
7 2 1/4 **Dragline** 2-9-4 0 DavidAllan 10 45
(Tim Easterby) *s.i.s: a towards rr* **40/1**
8 2 1/2 **Lazy Days In Loule (IRE)** 2-8-6 0 DuranFentiman 7 24
(Noel Wilson) *dwlt: sn in tch: rdn along wl over 2f out: sn wknd* **50/1**
9 1 1/4 **Esk Valley Lady** 2-8-6 0 PJMcDonald 12 20+
(Philip Kirby) *sn outpcd and a bhd* **50/1**
10 1/2 **Diatomic (IRE)** 2-9-0 0 StephenCraine 9 26
(Tom Dascombe) *sn in tch: rdn along 1/2-way: sn wknd* **20/1**
11 4 1/2 **Tagtale (IRE)** 2-8-6 0 PatrickMathers 1 2
(Richard Fahey) *wnt lft s: a in rr* **16/1**

58.67s (0.07) **Going Correction** +0.075s/f (Good) **11** Ran SP% **119.6**
Speed ratings (Par 92): **102,100,90,89,88 87,83,79,77,77 69**
CSF £2.95 TOTE £1.70: £1.10, £1.10, £2.20; EX 4.90 Trifecta £18.10.
**Owner** Mrs Sheila Clarke **Bred** Ballybrennan Stud **Trained** Sigwells, Somerset

**FOCUS**
A moderate 2yo maiden dominated by the first pair. The form rates a bit better than the race average.

### 1343 DOWNLOAD THE NEW RACING UK IPAD APP (S) STKS 5f
2:50 (2:57) (Class 6) 3-Y-O+ **£2,045** (£603; £302) **Stalls** Centre

Form RPR
0-34 1 **Dodina (IRE)**[81] 196 4-9-4 68 (p) TomEaves 2 69
(Brian Ellison) *qckly away: mde all: rdn clr wl over 1f out: readily* **11/8**[1]
0-65 2 3 1/2 **Britain (IRE)**[26] 933 3-8-7 50 (v1) LukeMorris 1 51
(David C Griffiths) *chsd wnr: rdn along over 2f out: drvn over 1f out: kpt on one pce* **10/1**[3]
6643 3 hd **Soul Instinct**[17] 1047 3-8-7 59 (p) ShaneGray(5) 4 56
(Kevin Ryan) *sn chsng wnr: rdn along over 2f out: drvn over 1f out: one pce* **3/1**[2]
00-5 4 1/2 **Bond Club**[63] 464 4-9-6 62 (b) RobertTart(3) 3 59
(Geoffrey Oldroyd) *chsd ldrs: rdn along 2f out: drvn and kpt on fnl f: nrst fin* **3/1**[2]
4565 5 6 **Jiminy**[5] 1243 4-9-6 47 (b) SladeO'Hara(3) 9 37
(Alan Berry) *in tch: rdn along over 2f out: sn outpcd* **50/1**
-44 6 1 **Captain T**[10] 1147 3-8-12 0 PaulMulrennan 6 29
(Richard Ford) *in rr: rdn along and outpcd fr 1/2-way* **33/1**
360- 7 shd **Balinka**[152] 7772 4-8-11 56 (p1) RobertDodsworth(7) 7 28
(Mel Brittain) *blind removed late: s.i.s: a in rr* **12/1**

58.51s (-0.09) **Going Correction** +0.075s/f (Good)
**WFA** 3 from 4yo 11lb **7** Ran SP% **113.8**
Speed ratings (Par 101): **103,97,97,96,86 85,84**
CSF £16.74 TOTE £1.70: £1.20, £4.40; EX 11.60 Trifecta £54.10.There was no bid for the winner.
**Owner** Ontoawinner 9 & Brian Ellison **Bred** Rathbarry Stud **Trained** Norton, N Yorks

**FOCUS**
A weak seller in which the winner did not need to match her best.

### 1344 BECOME AN ANNUAL BADGE HOLDER TODAY MEDIAN AUCTION MAIDEN STKS 7f
3:20 (3:24) (Class 5) 3-Y-O **£2,587** (£770; £384; £192) **Stalls** Centre

Form RPR
1 **Cornborough** 3-9-2 0 JasonHart(3) 7 74
(Mark Walford) *hld up: swtchd rt to outer and trckd ldrs after 3f: hdwy wl over 2f out: led wl over 1f out and sn rdn: drvn and edgd lft ins fnl f: kpt on wl towards fin* **10/1**
420- 2 1 **Rough Courte (IRE)**[178] 7175 3-8-11 73 CharlesBishop(3) 5 66
(Mick Channon) *hld up towards rr: swtchd lft to wd outside and tk clsr order 3f out: effrt over 2f out: rdn to chal over 1f out: drvn and edgd rt ins fnl f: ev ch tl no ex towards fin* **5/2**[2]

6- **3** *1 ½* **White Rose Runner**[149] 7818 3-9-0 0 DavidAllan 2 62
(Mel Brittain) *slt ld: pushed along 3f out: rdn over 2f out: hdd wl over 1f out: drvn and kpt on same pce fnl f* **3/1**[3]

63- **4** *2* **Stanarley Pic**[174] 7276 3-9-5 0 BenCurtis 9 62
(Alan Swinbank) *trckd ldrs: cl up 1/2-way: chal over 2f out: sn rdn and hung lft over 1f out: sn one pce* **9/4**[1]

00- **5** *4 ½* **Highway Pursuit**[174] 7276 3-8-12 0 KieranSchofield(7) 4 50
(George Moore) *chsd ldrs: rdn along 3f out: grad wknd* **100/1**

406- **6** *shd* **Lady Liz**[181] 7097 3-9-0 58 PJMcDonald 1 45
(George Moore) *prom: rdn along wl over 2f out: grad wknd* **28/1**

030- **7** *15* **Too Elusive**[174] 7261 3-9-5 69 (p) TomEaves 6 11
(Kristin Stubbs) *t.k.h early: chsd ldrs: rdn along 3f out: sn wknd* **8/1**

**8** *12* **Notaprayer** 3-9-5 0 DuranFentiman 3
(Tim Easterby) *sn outpcd in rr: bhd fr 1/2-way* **18/1**

1m 27.14s (2.64) **Going Correction** +0.575s/f (Yiel) **8** Ran SP% **114.2**
Speed ratings (Par 98): **107,105,104,101,96 96,79,65**
CSF £35.27 TOTE £13.20: £2.60, £1.40, £1.40; EX 39.70 Trifecta £206.90.
**Owner** Cornborough Racing Club **Bred** Mr & Mrs A E Pakenham **Trained** Sherriff Hutton, N Yorks

**FOCUS**
The forecast rain arrived just before this modest maiden. The form is rated around the runner-up towards the lower end of her 2yo figures.

## 1345 BOOK TICKETS ONLINE @ REDCARRACING.CO.UK H'CAP 1m
**3:50** (3:51) (Class 4) (0-85,85) 4-Y-0+ **£5,983** (£1,780; £889; £444) **Stalls** Centre

Form RPR

005- **1** **Kiwi Bay**[149] 7824 9-8-3 **72** ConnorBeasley(5) 7 83
(Michael Dods) *t.k.h: trckd ldrs: hdwy 3f out: led over 2f out: rdn over 1f out: kpt on strly fnl f* **12/1**

420- **2** *1 ½* **Lazarus Bell**[146] 7849 4-8-12 **81** JacobButterfield(5) 5 89
(Alan Brown) *midfield: hdwy 3f out: trckd ldrs wl over 1f out: rdn to chal over 1f out: drvn ins fnl f: kpt on same pce* **14/1**

311- **3** *4* **Knight Owl**[196] 6701 4-9-1 **79** ShaneKelly 11 77
(James Fanshawe) *hld up: hdwy 3f out: chsd ldrs 2f out: sn swtchd rt and rdn to chal over 1f out: drvn ent fnl f: sn edgd lft and one pce* **7/2**[1]

166- **4** *nk* **Fazza**[164] 7499 7-8-8 **77** KevinStott(5) 4 75
(Edwin Tuer) *hld up in rr: hdwy wl over 2f out: rdn wl over 1f out: styd on fnl f: nrst fin* **33/1**

2443 **5** *1 ½* **Capaill Liath (IRE)**[8] 1191 6-9-0 **78** (p) AmyRyan 14 72
(Kevin Ryan) *trckd ldrs: hdwy to chse ldr 3f out: rdn along over 2f out: grad wknd* **7/2**[1]

420- **6** *hd* **Spavento (IRE)**[247] 4994 8-8-5 **72** NeilFarley(3) 16 66
(Eric Alston) *chsd ldrs: rdn along wl over 2f out: sn no imp* **33/1**

020- **7** *1 ½* **No Poppy (IRE)**[178] 7172 6-9-0 **83** AdamCarter(5) 8 73
(Tim Easterby) *hld up towards rr: hdwy 3f out: rdn 2f out: no imp appr fnl f* **16/1**

00-0 **8** *shd* **Snow Bay**[19] 1020 8-8-10 **79** ShirleyTeasdale(5) 9 69
(Paul Midgley) *led: rdn along and hdd over 2f out: sn drvn and grad wknd* **66/1**

300- **9** *nk* **Destiny Blue (IRE)**[129] 7849 7-8-10 **74** DaleSwift 15 63
(Brian Ellison) *in rr tl sme late hdwy* **28/1**

245- **10** *2 ¼* **Al Muheer (IRE)**[184] 7031 9-9-2 **80** JamesSullivan 1 64
(Ruth Carr) *hld up: effrt and sme hdwy 2f out: sn rdn and n.d* **25/1**

530- **11** *hd* **Nurpur (IRE)**[192] 6796 4-9-7 **85** DanielTudhope 2 69
(David O'Meara) *hld up: a towards rr* **11/1**[3]

146- **12** *1* **Save The Bees**[73] 7425 6-8-11 **78** JasonHart(3) 12 59
(Declan Carroll) *a towards rr* **20/1**

234- **13** *1 ½* **Staffhoss**[416] 674 4-8-7 **78** PaulaMuir(7) 10 56
(Mark Johnston) *plld hrd: in tch: pushed along wl over 2f out: sn btn* **33/1**

00-6 **14** *3* **Fort Belvedere**[39] 763 6-9-4 **82** [1] TomEaves 6 53
(Keith Dalgleish) *prom: rdn along 3f out: sn edgd lft and wknd* **12/1**

00-0 **15** *nk* **Justonefortheroad**[8] 1191 8-9-2 **80** TonyHamilton 3 50
(Richard Fahey) *prom: rdn along 3f out: sn wknd* **12/1**

1 **16** *17* **Cloverdale**[12] 1112 4-9-6 **84** JoeFanning 13 15
(Mark Johnston) *cl up: rdn along over 3f out: sn wknd* **8/1**[2]

1m 39.97s (3.37) **Going Correction** +0.575s/f (Yiel) **16** Ran SP% **121.9**
Speed ratings (Par 105): **106,104,100,100,98 98,97,96,96,94 94,93,91,88,88 71**
CSF £157.47 CT £723.03 TOTE £17.10: £4.30, £3.90, £1.30, £6.70; EX 259.70 Trifecta £930.40.

**Owner** Kiwi Racing **Bred** Templeton Stud **Trained** Denton, Co Durham

**FOCUS**
A competitive big-field handicap, run at a solid pace, and most of the action developed towards the stands' side. The winner is rated around last year's best.

## 1346 RACINGUK.COM/ANYWHERE: 3DEVICES, 1PRICE H'CAP (STRAIGHT-MILE CHAMPIONSHIP QUALIFIER) 1m
**4:20** (4:20) (Class 5) (0-75,75) 3-Y-0 **£2,587** (£770; £384; £192) **Stalls** Centre

Form RPR

30-1 **1** **Arrowzone**[23] 976 3-9-0 **71** BillyCray(3) 9 81
(Garry Moss) *led 1f: trckd ldrs tl effrt to chse ldr wl over 1f out and sn rdn: drvn to chal ent fnl f: styd on to ld last 100yds* **7/1**[2]

1-43 **2** *¾* **Lesha (IRE)**[70] 357 3-9-2 **70** TomEaves 15 78
(Kevin Ryan) *awkward s: sn rcvrd and hdwy to ld after 1f: pushed clr wl over 1f out: sn rdn and jnd ent fnl f: drvn: hdd and no ex last 100yds* **9/1**

652- **3** *1* **Alquimia (IRE)**[226] 5740 3-8-12 **66** TonyHamilton 4 72
(Richard Fahey) *hld up in tch: hdwy wl over 2f out: rdn to chse ldng pair over 1f out: ev ch ent fnl f: sn drvn and kpt on same pce* **9/1**

0-43 **4** *4* **Gratzie**[27] 914 3-9-1 **72** CharlesBishop(3) 11 69
(Mick Channon) *hld up in midfield: smooth hdwy wl over 2f out and sn chsng ldrs: rdn over 1f out: edgd lft and one pce fnl f* **14/1**

000- **5** *4 ½* **Petergate**[164] 7494 3-8-8 **62** JamesSullivan 1 48
(Brian Rothwell) *hld up in rr: swtchd rt to r nr stands' rail and hdwy wl over 2f out: rdn wl over 1f out: kpt on fnl f: nrst fin* **66/1**

536- **6** *1 ¼* **Sketch Map (IRE)**[198] 6627 3-8-11 **65** RussKennemore 5 49
(Jedd O'Keeffe) *chsd ldrs: rdn along wl over 2f out: drvn wl over 1f out and grad wknd* **9/1**

360- **7** *shd* **Ralphy Lad (IRE)**[208] 6299 3-9-4 **72** BenCurtis 6 55
(Alan Swinbank) *hld up in rr: hdwy over 2f out: sn rdn and no imp fnl f* **14/1**

-455 **8** *1 ¼* **Eddiemaurice (IRE)**[56] 561 3-9-0 **68** RobbieFitzpatrick 14 48
(Richard Guest) *in rr tl sme late hdwy* **33/1**

334- **9** *½* **Caridadi (IRE)**[171] 7335 3-9-7 **75** MartinLane 12 54
(Charlie Appleby) *trckd ldrs: effrt wl over 2f out: sn rdn and btn* **6/1**[1]

021- **10** *hd* **Toboggan Star**[242] 5193 3-8-13 **67** PJMcDonald 17 46
(Ann Duffield) *prom: trckd ldr after 1f: rdn along wl over 2f out: sn drvn and wknd* **10/1**

013- **11** *3* **Shirocco Passion**[193] 6770 3-8-11 **72** LauraBarry(7) 3 44
(Tony Coyle) *hld up: a towards rr* **8/1**

052- **12** *1 ¼* **Tancred (IRE)**[163] 7529 3-9-4 **72** BarryMcHugh 7 41
(Tony Coyle) *dwlt: a towards rr* **15/2**[3]

**13** *2 ½* **Taanif**[232] 5566 3-8-9 **63** GrahamGibbons 10 26
(Michael Easterby) *a towards rr* **33/1**

050- **14** *2 ¼* **Green Zone (IRE)**[164] 7494 3-9-0 **68** AndrewMullen 2 26
(Nigel Tinkler) *a in rr* **20/1**

1m 42.18s (5.58) **Going Correction** +0.575s/f (Yiel) **14** Ran SP% **114.2**
Speed ratings (Par 98): **95,94,93,89,84 83,83,82,81,81 78,77,74,72**
CSF £62.56 TOTE £10.30: £4.50, £3.90, £2.80; EX 62.20 Trifecta £585.99.

**Owner** Ron Hull **Bred** J K Beckitt And Son **Trained** Tickhill, S Yorks

**FOCUS**
A modest 3yo handicap in which the first three were always prominent and were among the more feasible improvers.

## 1347 FOLLOW REDCARRACING ON FACEBOOK & TWITTER APPRENTICE MEDIAN AUCTION MAIDEN STKS 6f
**4:50** (4:52) (Class 6) 3-4-Y-0 **£2,045** (£603; £302) **Stalls** Centre

Form RPR

22 **1** **Elusive George (IRE)**[26] 923 3-9-2 0 IanBrennan 9 68+
(John Quinn) *trckd ldrs: cl up on outer 1/2-way: rdn to ld over 1f out: edgd lft ins fnl f: kpt on* **12/5**[2]

550- **2** *¾* **False Witness (IRE)**[179] 7147 3-8-12 68 AnnaHesketh(4) 3 66
(David Nicholls) *sn led: rdn along 2f out: hdd over 1f out: rallied ins fnl f: one pce last 100yds* **20/1**

24- **3** *1* **Yagheer (IRE)**[135] 8018 3-9-2 0 RossAtkinson 8 63
(Roger Varian) *t.k.h early: trckd ldrs: hdwy 1/2-way: cl up over 2f out: rdn to chal over 1f out and ev ch tl drvn and one pce ins fnl f* **1/1**[1]

30- **4** *6* **Tears And Rain (IRE)**[184] 7023 3-8-7 0 RachelRichardson(4) 4 39
(Tim Easterby) *trckd ldrs: rdn along and outpcd 1/2-way: kpt on u.p appr fnl f* **22/1**

00- **5** *4 ½* **Unfinishedbusiness**[184] 7023 3-8-12 0 SammyJoBell(4) 6 29
(Richard Fahey) *awkward s: sn rcvrd to trck ldrs: rdn along wl over 2f out and sn wknd* **11/2**[3]

65- **6** *½* **Spring Willow (IRE)**[279] 3928 3-9-2 0 NeilFarley 5 28
(Eric Alston) *prom: trckd ldr after 2f: rdn along wl over 2f out: sn wandered and wknd: lame* **50/1**

600- **7** *2 ¼* **Emily Davison (IRE)**[177] 7199 3-8-7 55 GemmaTutty(4) 7 15
(Karen Tutty) *prom 2f: rdn along 1/2-way: sn wknd* **20/1**

-40 **8** *28* **Daring Pursuit**[83] 174 4-9-5 0 BTTreanor(4) 2
(K R Burke) *sn outpcd and bhd* **50/1**

0- **U** **Naggers (IRE)**[193] 6769 3-9-0 0 JacobButterfield(2) 1
(Paul Midgley) *in tch whn clipped heels, stmbld and uns rdr 1/2-way* **33/1**

1m 14.9s (3.10) **Going Correction** +0.575s/f (Yiel)
**WFA** 3 from 4yo 12lb **9** Ran SP% **115.5**
Speed ratings (Par 101): **102,101,99,91,85 85,82,44,**
CSF £49.04 TOTE £3.20: £1.10, £5.20, £1.10; EX 32.50 Trifecta £110.20.

**Owner** S A T Quinn **Bred** H Etreham,Vision Bloods,Pontchartrain S **Trained** Settrington, N Yorks

**FOCUS**
A modest maiden lacking depth and dominated by the principals. The winner didn't need to match his latest form.

## 1348 RACING AGAIN ON EASTER MONDAY FILLIES' H'CAP 1m 2f
**5:20** (5:22) (Class 5) (0-70,69) 3-Y-0+ **£2,587** (£770; £384; £192) **Stalls** Low

Form RPR

354- **1** **Lady Yeats**[174] 7277 3-8-8 **68** PJMcDonald 1 75+
(George Moore) *dwlt and in rr: stdy hdwy 4f out: swtchd rt to outer and effrt to ld over 2f out: rdn clr over 1f out: drvn out* **9/2**[2]

522 **2** *2* **Rose Kazan (IRE)**[42] 734 3-8-7 **67** LukeMorris 2 70+
(Marco Botti) *trckd ldrs: nt clr run on inner over 2f out and sn swtchd rt: rdn to chse ldrs whn n.m.r and swtchd lft ent fnl f: sn drvn and kpt on: nt rch wnr* **7/2**[1]

410- **3** *½* **Ana Shababiya (IRE)**[139] 7961 4-9-8 **68** TimClark(5) 3 73
(Ismail Mohammed) *t.k.h: trckd ldrs: hdwy over 3f out: rdn 2f out: sn ev ch tl drvn appr fnl f and kpt on same pce* **14/1**

**4** *4* **Patty Fingers (IRE)**[81] 8197 4-8-11 **55** oh10 NeilFarley(3) 10 52
(Declan Carroll) *trckd ldrs: effrt and cl up 4f out: rdn along 3f out: ev ch 2f out: drvn wl over 1f out and sn one pce* **66/1**

346- **5** *5* **Magic Skyline (IRE)**[42] 6601 4-9-8 **63** (tp) DaleSwift 5 51
(Brian Ellison) *slt ld on inner: rdn along over 3f out: hdd over 2f out: sn drvn and grad wknd* **6/1**

446- **6** *hd* **Irondale Express**[224] 5829 3-8-9 **69** BarryMcHugh 4 53
(Tony Coyle) *dwlt and towards rr whn nt much on inner bnd after 4f: hdwy over 3f out: in tch whn n.m.r and swtchd rt 2f out: sn rdn along and no imp* **8/1**

50-6 **7** *1* **Voice From Above (IRE)**[19] 1012 5-8-7 **55** oh2 JackGarritty(7) 6 41
(Patrick Holmes) *in tch: hdwy on outer to chse ldrs whn n.m.r over 3f out: sn rdn and wknd 2f out* **25/1**

350- **8** *¾* **Newgate Queen**[207] 6330 3-7-7 **60** oh3 JoeDoyle(7) 8 40
(Tony Coyle) *chsd ldrs: rdn along over 3f out: wknd wl over 2f out* **5/1**[3]

50-1 **9** *1 ¾* **Zanouska (USA)**[10] 1143 3-8-5 **65** JoeFanning 11 42
(Mark Johnston) *cl up: rdn along 3f out: drvn over 2f out: wknd wl over 1f out* **8/1**

343- **10** *2 ¾* **Lady Artiste (IRE)**[299] 3202 4-10-0 **69** BenCurtis 9 45
(Alan Swinbank) *chsd ldrs on outer: rdn along over 3f out: wknd over 2f out* **8/1**

2m 13.1s (6.00) **Going Correction** +0.575s/f (Yiel)
**WFA** 3 from 4yo+ 19lb **10** Ran SP% **116.7**
Speed ratings (Par 100): **99,97,97,93,89 89,88,88,86,84**
CSF £20.66 CT £204.75 TOTE £5.30: £1.90, £1.50, £2.80; EX 30.30 Trifecta £279.90.

**Owner** A Crute & Partners **Bred** Biddestone Stud **Trained** Middleham Moor, N Yorks

**FOCUS**
A weak fillies' handicap.

T/Plt: £15.70 to a £1 stake. Pool: £64195.02 - 2975.63 winning tickets T/Qpdt: £11.00 to a £1 stake. Pool: £4436.18 - 295.86 winning tickets JR

# WINDSOR (R-H)

Monday, April 7

**OFFICIAL GOING: Good to soft (good in places) changing to soft after race 1 (2:10)**

Wind: Almost Nil Weather: Overcast, drizzly

## 1349 BRITISH STALLION STUDS EBF MAIDEN STKS 5f 10y

2:10 (2:11) (Class 5) 2-Y-O £2,911 (£866; £432; £216) Stalls Low

Form RPR

1 **Magical Roundabout (IRE)** 2-9-5 0 RyanMoore 13 77+
(Richard Hannon) *sn pressed ldrs: shkn up 2f out: led over 1f out: jnd fnl f: drvn and styd on wl* **4/6[1]**

2 ½ **Fine Prince (IRE)** 2-9-5 0 JimmyFortune 12 74+
(Robert Mills) *jinked lft s: rcvrd to chse ldng quartet after 2f: prog 2f out: jnd wnr fnl f: styd on but jst hld nr fin* **20/1**

3 2½ **Sportlobster (IRE)** 2-9-5 0 RichardKingscote 5 65
(Tom Dascombe) *w ldrs: rdn and rt on terms over 1f out: one pce after* **20/1**

4 ¾ **As A Dream (IRE)** 2-8-9 0 EoinWalsh(5) 9 58+
(David Evans) *rn green in rr: reminder after 1f: prog on outer fr 1/2-way: chsd clr ldng quartet over 1f out: pushed along and styd on: shaped w promise* **33/1**

5 hd **Jersey Bull (IRE)** 2-9-2 0 WilliamTwiston-Davies(3) 6 62
(Mick Channon) *fractious preliminaries and taken down early: gd spd and w ldrs: pushed along over 1f out: one pce fnl f* **14/1[3]**

6 7 **Tommys Geal** 2-9-0 0 LiamKeniry 11 32
(Michael Madgwick) *nt that wl away: pushed along in rr: nvr on terms but kpt on fnl f* **80/1**

6 7 1 **Keep 'r Lit**[9] 1169 2-9-0 0 AdamKirby 3 28
(David Evans) *led to over 1f out: wknd and eased fnl f* **16/1**

8 1 **Air Of York (IRE)** 2-9-5 0 DavidProbert 2 29
(Ronald Harris) *rn green and sn pushed along in rr: nt on terms fr 1/2-way: no ch after* **40/1**

9 1¾ **Go Gently (IRE)** 2-9-5 0 FergusSweeney 8 23
(George Baker) *a towards rr: pushed along and nt on terms fr 1/2-way: nt totally disgracd* **16/1**

10 1 **Zebs Lad (IRE)** 2-9-5 0 SteveDrowne 1 19
(Ronald Harris) *awkwardly away: bdly outpcd and t.o after 2f: kpt on fr over 1f out* **20/1**

11 ½ **Nimble (IRE)** 2-9-0 0 LiamJones 7 13
(J S Moore) *sn pushed along in rr: nvr on terms* **100/1**

12 3½ **Habibah (IRE)** 2-9-0 0 MartinDwyer 10
(Hugo Palmer) *moved poorly to post: sn pushed along to stay in tch: wknd 2f out* **9/2[2]**

1m 3.31s (3.01) **Going Correction** +0.30s/f (Good) **12 Ran SP% 118.5**
Speed ratings (Par 92): **87,86,82,81,80 69,67,66,63,61 61,55**
CSF £21.87 TOTE £1.80: £1.10, £7.10, £4.40; EX 23.20 Trifecta £266.20.
**Owner** Mrs J Wood **Bred** Oliver Donlon **Trained** East Everleigh, Wilts

**FOCUS**
The top bend had been dolled out 3yds from the normal inner configuration, adding 10yds to race distances of 1m and over. Despite the softening ground (officially changed to soft following this contest), the runners stayed stands' side for what looked quite an ordinary juvenile maiden. The winner is the type to do better.

## 1350 DOWNLOAD THE UNIBET PRO APP H'CAP (BOBIS RACE) 6f

2:40 (2:41) (Class 4) (0-85,85) 3-Y-O £4,851 (£1,443; £721; £360) Stalls Low

Form RPR

363- 1 **Stomp**[144] 7879 3-8-9 73 JamesDoyle 10 81
(Roger Charlton) *s.i.s: hld up in last pair: prog on outer over 2f out: hanging lft but sustained effrt to ld last 100yds: r.o wl* **5/1[3]**

452- 2 2 **Montaigne**[152] 7771 3-9-5 83 JimCrowley 7 85
(Ralph Beckett) *pressed ldng pair: chsd ldr 1/2-way tl jst ins fnl f: kpt on to take 2nd again post* **8/1**

130- 3 hd **Desert Ace (IRE)**[171] 7333 3-9-7 85 AdamKirby 6 86
(Clive Cox) *led: gng strly 2f out: shkn up over 1f out: hdd and fdd last 100yds: lost 2nd post* **16/1**

61-4 4 ½ **Fiftyshadesofgrey (IRE)**[32] 854 3-9-4 82 (t) FergusSweeney 9 82
(George Baker) *hld up in rr: sme prog 2f out: shkn up over 1f out: styd on fnl f: nrst fin* **14/1**

201- 5 shd **Honey Meadow**[123] 8166 3-8-7 71 oh1 JimmyQuinn 11 71
(Robert Eddery) *chsd ldrs: rdn 2f out: kpt on fnl f: nvr able to chal* **50/1**

314- 6 1 **Star Code (IRE)**[158] 7640 3-9-0 78 RyanMoore 5 75+
(Richard Hannon) *dwlt: hld up in last pair: stl last wl over 1f out: shkn up and styd on fnl f: nvr involved* **6/1**

5-11 7 3¾ **Gone With The Wind (GER)**[26] 926 3-8-12 76 (p) FrankieDettori 2 61
(Jeremy Noseda) *pushed along early in rr: effrt over 2f out: no prog over 1f out: wknd* **3/1[2]**

550- 8 nse **Tableforten**[149] 7819 3-8-7 71 (b) LiamJones 4 56
(J S Moore) *in tch: rdn over 2f out: no prog over 1f out: wknd fnl f* **33/1**

215- 9 5 **Classic Pursuit**[237] 5371 3-8-11 75 SteveDrowne 1 45
(Ronald Harris) *t.k.h: trckd ldrs tl wknd qckly 2f out* **25/1**

123- 10 6 **King Of Macedon (IRE)**[166] 7463 3-9-5 83 SilvestreDeSousa 3 35
(Mark Johnston) *chsd ldr to 1/2-way: wknd rapidly 2f out: eased: t.o* **11/4[1]**

1m 14.56s (1.56) **Going Correction** +0.30s/f (Good) **10 Ran SP% 115.0**
Speed ratings (Par 100): **101,98,98,97,97 95,90,90,84,76**
CSF £43.13 CT £593.98 TOTE £6.10: £1.90, £3.50, £4.60; EX 56.20 Trifecta £396.10.
**Owner** Lady Rothschild **Bred** The Rt Hon Lord Rothschild **Trained** Beckhampton, Wilts

**FOCUS**
Not a particularly strong race for the level, especially with a couple of the key contenders disappointing. The form is best rated around the fifth.

## 1351 FEDERATION OF BLOODSTOCK AGENTS H'CAP 1m 67y

3:10 (3:11) (Class 4) (0-85,85) 4-Y-O+ £4,851 (£1,443; £721; £360) Stalls Low

Form RPR

140- 1 **Tobacco Road (IRE)**[176] 7224 4-9-6 84 RyanMoore 5 96
(Richard Hannon) *mde all: rdn 2f out: styd on wl fnl f* **5/1[3]**

114- 2 1¼ **Saigon City**[160] 7611 4-9-0 78 (b) AdamKirby 2 87+
(Luca Cumani) *wl in tch: awkward bnd over 5f out: rdn 2f out: prog over 1f out: styd on to take 2nd ins fnl f: unable to chal* **4/1[1]**

000- 3 1¼ **Starwatch**[168] 7431 7-8-9 73 (v) WilliamCarson 1 79
(John Bridger) *prom: rdn 2f out: styd on same pce fr over 1f out: nvr able to chal* **25/1**

06-0 4 1½ **Myboyalfie (USA)**[19] 1014 7-9-6 84 FrederikTylicki 10 87
(J R Jenkins) *hld up in rr: prog over 2f out towards outer: shkn up over 1f out: styd on fnl f: nvr really threatened* **8/1**

11-5 5 ¾ **Fleckerl (IRE)**[56] 560 4-8-12 76 MartinDwyer 11 77
(William Muir) *sn trckd ldng pair: rdn to chse wnr jst over 2f out: hanging lft and nt qckn over 1f out: wknd ins fnl f* **8/1**

462- 6 1¼ **Aint Got A Scooby (IRE)**[195] 6734 4-8-5 74 RyanTate(5) 9 72
(Clive Cox) *in tch in midfield: rdn over 2f out: no imp over 1f out: steadily wknd* **12/1**

6012 7 ¾ **My Son Max**[12] 1113 6-8-10 74 SilvestreDeSousa 3 70
(Michael Blake) *s.i.s: hld up in last trio: rdn and sme prog on outer over 2f out: no hdwy fnl f* **15/2**

240- 8 nk **Lunar Deity**[166] 7464 5-9-4 82 JamesDoyle 4 78
(Stuart Williams) *hld up towards rr: lost pl and last over 2f out: reminder and styd on again fnl f* **12/1**

3-00 9 4 **Persepolis (IRE)**[33] 840 4-9-7 85 JimmyFortune 6 71
(Brett Johnson) *chsd wnr: drvn and lost 2nd jst over 2f out: wknd* **14/1**

530- 10 ¾ **Ogbourne Downs**[156] 7696 4-9-2 80 SteveDrowne 7 65
(Charles Hills) *hld up towards rr: brief prog jst over 2f out: shkn up over 1f out: sn lost pl and eased* **9/2[2]**

21- 11 7 **Eurato (FR)**[169] 7412 4-9-7 85 PaddyAspell 12 54
(Alan Jones) *s.i.s: hld up in last trio: prog into midfield 3f out: lost pl and wknd over 2f out: t.o* **50/1**

2300 12 ¾ **Luhaif**[16] 1070 4-9-7 85 (p) JimCrowley 8 52
(Julia Feilden) *chsd ldrs tl wknd rapidly over 2f out: t.o* **20/1**

1m 45.1s (0.40) **Going Correction** +0.20s/f (Good) **12 Ran SP% 121.5**
Speed ratings (Par 105): **106,104,103,102,101 100,99,98,94,94 87,86**
CSF £25.44 CT £468.91 TOTE £5.10: £1.80, £1.20, £12.30; EX 25.70 Trifecta £831.10.
**Owner** Noodles Racing **Bred** Minch Bloodstock **Trained** East Everleigh, Wilts

**FOCUS**
Little got into this. The winner posted a 4lb personal best with the second to form.

## 1352 NEW HORSERACING ODDS AT UNIBET.CO.UK H'CAP (BOBIS RACE) 1m 67y

3:40 (3:42) (Class 4) (0-85,85) 3-Y-O £4,851 (£1,443; £721; £360) Stalls Low

Form RPR

610- 1 **Grevillea (IRE)**[233] 5530 3-8-10 77 WilliamTwiston-Davies(3) 3 86
(Mick Channon) *free to post: trckd ldrs: led jst over 2f out: edgd lft but drew clr fr over 1f out* **33/1**

4-05 2 5 **Intermath (IRE)**[30] 892 3-9-2 80 AdamKirby 11 77
(David Evans) *prom whn hanging lft on bnd over 5f out: chsd ldrs after: prog on outer over 2f out: wnt 2nd jst over 1f out: no imp on wnr* **33/1**

3312 3 1¾ **Jaahiez (USA)**[23] 975 3-8-12 76 TomQueally 9 69
(Roger Varian) *hld up towards rr: prog 3f out: rdn to chse wnr 2f out to jst over 1f out: one pce* **8/1**

215- 4 ¾ **Black Schnapps (IRE)**[157] 7662 3-9-1 79 MartinDwyer 2 70+
(William Muir) *led briefly after 2f: chsd ldr: led over 3f out to jst over 2f out: nt qckn and sn btn* **11/2**

3213 5 1½ **Upholland**[23] 975 3-8-13 77 (v[1]) RyanMoore 8 65
(Richard Fahey) *t.k.h: hld up in midfield: sme prog 2f out: drvn and nt qckn over 1f out: hanging and fdd fnl f* **3/1[1]**

365- 6 1½ **Mendacious Harpy (IRE)**[157] 7657 3-8-11 75 JimCrowley 10 59
(George Baker) *hld up in last: sme prog on outer 3f out: reminder and flashed tail over 2f out: no hdwy after* **33/1**

1-3 7 nk **Tree Of Grace (FR)**[11] 1122 3-9-5 83 FrankieDettori 7 67+
(Richard Hannon) *t.k.h in midfield: hanging lft bnd over 5f out: racd awkwardly fr 1/2-way: wl btn over 2f out* **7/2[2]**

013- 8 ½ **Peacemaker (IRE)**[201] 6529 3-8-7 71 oh1 JohnFahy 12 54
(Eve Johnson Houghton) *hld up in rr: rdn over 2f out: no prog over 1f out* **33/1**

324 9 8 **Tarrafal (IRE)**[13] 1090 3-8-12 76 SilvestreDeSousa 1 40
(Mark Johnston) *nipped through on inner to ld over 5f out: hdd over 3f out: upsides over 2f out: sn wknd qckly and eased* **14/1**

061- 10 24 **Westminster (IRE)**[115] 8266 3-9-7 85 WilliamBuick 5
(John Gosden) *led 2f: hanging lft bnd after and lost pl: shkn up and wknd 3f out: eased and t.o* **5/1[3]**

1m 45.65s (0.95) **Going Correction** +0.20s/f (Good) **10 Ran SP% 108.8**
Speed ratings (Par 100): **103,98,96,95,94 92,92,91,83,59**
CSF £761.40 CT £8712.04 TOTE £37.40: £10.60, £7.00, £1.90; EX 606.90 Trifecta £3067.70.
**Owner** N J Hitchins **Bred** Mr & Mrs Nick Hitchins **Trained** West Ilsley, Berks

**FOCUS**
What had looked quite a competitive handicap was won readily by one of the outsiders. A clear personal best from the winner in something of a messy race.

## 1353 WINDSOR VEHICLE LEASING WVL.CO.UK MAIDEN STKS 1m 2f 7y

4:10 (4:15) (Class 5) 3-Y-O £2,587 (£770; £384; £192) Stalls Centre

Form RPR

2- 1 **Cannock Chase (USA)**[180] 7119 3-9-5 0 RyanMoore 4 89+
(Sir Michael Stoute) *trckd ldrs: bustled along and quick move on inner to ld over 2f out: drew away over 1f out: comf* **5/4[1]**

52 2 4 **Late Night Mark (IRE)**[52] 607 3-9-5 0 GeorgeBaker 5 78+
(Charles Hills) *wl in tch: pushed along over 2f out: kpt on wl fnl 2f to take 2nd nr fin* **20/1**

3- 3 nk **Loving Home**[157] 7654 3-9-5 0 WilliamBuick 9 78
(John Gosden) *pressed ldr: led 4f out: shkn up and hdd over 2f out: no ch w wnr after: lost 2nd nr fin* **7/2[2]**

6- 4 1 **Rydan (IRE)**[147] 7834 3-9-5 0 JimmyFortune 7 76
(Robert Mills) *hld up towards rr: pushed along and stdy prog fr wl over 2f out: kpt on wl fnl f: should improve* **20/1**

5 nk **Fastnet Red** 3-9-5 0 RobertHavlin 1 75+
(John Gosden) *s.i.s: sn in midfield: pushed along fr 3f out: kpt on steadily fnl 2f: shaped w sme promise* **50/1**

42- 6 nk **Damascene**[109] 8340 3-9-5 0 AdamKirby 6 75
(Marco Botti) *t.k.h in midfield: prog to press ldrs 3f out: drvn and outpcd fnl 2f* **10/1**

05- 7 5 **Good Value**[220] 5968 3-9-5 0 JamesDoyle 3 65+
(Sir Michael Stoute) *s.i.s: hld up in last: nvr in it: light reminder over 1f out and passed several stragglers* **16/1**

33-3 8 nk **Solo Hunter**[23] 976 3-9-2 68 DeclanBates(3) 2 65
(David Evans) *led to 4f out: shkn up and steadily wknd fr 3f out* **40/1**

9 1½ **Nam Hai (IRE)** 3-9-5 0 JimCrowley 8 62
(Michael Bell) *dwlt: a in rr: pushed along and lost tch fr 3f out* **66/1**

10 nse **Princess Ombu (IRE)** 3-9-0 0 SteveDrowne 10 57
(Charles Hills) *hld up: a in rr: lost tch 3f out* **50/1**

00- **11** *1 ½* **Oracle Boy**[151] 7780 3-9-5 0 ............................ MartinDwyer 12 59
(William Muir) *t.k.h early: prom: urged along fr 4f out: wknd over 2f out* **100/1**

4- **12** *3* **Elusive Guest (FR)**[182] 7070 3-9-5 0 ............................ TomQueally 11 53
(George Margarson) *t.k.h early: hld up in rr: prog on wd outside to chse ldrs 4f out: wknd 3f out* **9/2**[3]

2m 11.04s (2.34) **Going Correction** +0.20s/f (Good) **12 Ran SP% 118.2**
Speed ratings (Par 98): **98,94,94,93,93 93,89,89,87,87 86,84**
CSF £34.86 TOTE £2.20: £1.10, £3.70, £1.50; EX 23.00.
**Owner** Saeed Suhail **Bred** Hascombe Stud **Trained** Newmarket, Suffolk

**FOCUS**
Just a fair maiden, but it should produce winners. Cannock Chase impressed.

## 1354 UNIBET - BY PLAYERS FOR PLAYERS H'CAP — 1m 2f 7y
**4:40** (4:44) (Class 5) (0-75,74) 4-Y-O+ **£2,911** (£866; £432; £216) **Stalls** Centre

Form RPR

010- **1** **Heezararity**[112] 8314 6-9-0 **67** ............................ JimmyFortune 5 75
(Jonathan Geake) *trckd ldr to 1/2-way: rdn to go 2nd again over 2f out: led 1f out: drvn rt out* **16/1**

-000 **2** *½* **Palus San Marco (IRE)**[19] 1022 5-8-12 **70** ............ RyanTate(5) 10 77
(Tony Carroll) *hld up in last pair: rdn and prog on wd outside fr 3f out: tk 2nd ins fnl f and pressed wnr: jst hld nr fin* **20/1**

00-4 **3** *2* **He's A Striker (IRE)**[20] 1003 4-9-3 **70** ............ RichardKingscote 15 73
(Michael Blake) *led: rdn wl over 2f out: hdd and one pce 1f out* **5/1**[2]

00-0 **4** *½* **Choral Festival**[19] 1021 8-8-11 **64** ............................ WilliamCarson 13 66
(John Bridger) *hld up wl in rr: stdy prog over 2f out: rdn to chse ldrs over 1f out: one pce after* **16/1**

340- **5** *hd* **Barwick**[160] 7608 6-9-7 **74** ............................ SebSanders 1 76
(Lady Herries) *dwlt: pushed up to go prom and then t.k.h: rdn to press ldrs 2f out: nt qckn on inner over 1f out* **5/1**[2]

54-5 **6** *1* **Angus Glens**[12] 1108 4-9-7 **74** ............................ JimCrowley 2 74
(David Dennis) *nvr beyond midfield: rdn 3f out: kpt on fnl f: nrst fin* **7/1**[3]

0124 **7** *½* **Handsome Stranger (IRE)**[18] 1027 4-8-5 **65** ..........(p) DavidParkes(7) 3 64
(Alan Bailey) *trckd ldrs: rdn 3f out: nt qckn over 2f out: wl hld whn nt clr run over 1f out: kpt on* **16/1**

-110 **8** *shd* **Whitby Jet (IRE)**[33] 849 6-9-6 **73** ............................ LiamKeniry 8 72
(Ed Vaughan) *hld up in rr: rdn 3f out: sme prog on inner 2f out: no hdwy over 1f out* **14/1**

400- **9** *hd* **Significant Move**[207] 6336 7-9-4 **71** ............................ TomQueally 4 70
(Stuart Kittow) *trapped out wd in midfield on bnd over 5f out: rdn over 3f out: no prog over 2f out: sn btn* **11/4**[1]

233- **10** *2 ½* **Dark Amber**[159] 7625 4-9-1 **68** ............................ SilvestreDeSousa 11 62
(Brendan Powell) *prom: chsd ldr 1/2-way to over 2f out: steadily wknd* **16/1**

3004 **11** *3 ¾* **Ocean Applause**[9] 1175 4-9-7 **74** ............................(tp) DavidProbert 7 61
(John Ryan) *a towards rr: shkn up and no prog 3f out: wl btn fnl 2f* **14/1**

6405 **12** *2 ½* **Greensward**[19] 1021 8-8-13 **66** ............................(b) HayleyTurner 14 48
(Conor Dore) *hld up in last: shkn up and lost tch over 3f out: bhd after* **33/1**

06-5 **13** *7* **Chella Thriller (SPA)**[12] 1100 5-8-2 **60** oh3.........(b) DanielMuscutt(5) 12 29
(Alastair Lidderdale) *slowly away: quick rcvry and sn prom: wknd 3f out: t.o* **50/1**

2m 10.75s (2.05) **Going Correction** +0.20s/f (Good) **13 Ran SP% 119.0**
Speed ratings (Par 103): **99,98,97,96,96 95,95,95,95,93 90,88,82**
CSF £303.24 CT £1838.42 TOTE £17.80: £4.80, £7.90, £2.10; EX 443.10 Trifecta £2667.70.
**Owner** Miss E J Tanner **Bred** D J Weston **Trained** Marlborough, Wilts

**FOCUS**
Modest handicap form, rated around the third..

## 1355 UNIBET OFFER DAILY JOCKEY & TRAINER SPECIALS H'CAP — 1m 3f 135y
**5:10** (5:12) (Class 5) (0-75,75) 4-Y-O+ **£2,911** (£866; £432; £216) **Stalls** Centre

Form RPR

**1** **Civil War (IRE)**[42] 7289 5-8-12 **66** ............................ RyanMoore 2 78
(Gary Moore) *hld up and last tl over 4f out: stl plenty to do and shoved along over 3f out: relentless prog over 2f out: clsd to ld last 150yds: drvn out* **13/8**[1]

260- **2** *1 ¾* **Yul Finegold (IRE)**[140] 7950 4-9-1 **70** ............................ FergusSweeney 3 79
(George Baker) *led at gd pce: rdn and fended off nrest chalrs fr over 2f out: hdd last 150yds: styd on* **8/1**[2]

0526 **3** *4 ½* **Thecornishcowboy**[9] 1168 5-9-0 **68** ............................(tp) AdamKirby 1 69
(John Ryan) *hld up in midfield: rdn over 3f out: prog over 2f out: disp 2nd wl over 1f out: sn no imp* **20/1**

1-34 **4** *nk* **Modem**[33] 848 4-8-13 **68** ............................(b) SeanLevey 9 69
(Rod Millman) *hld up in tch: chsd ldng pair over 3f out: drvn to dispute 2nd 2f out: one pce after* **8/1**[2]

140- **5** *½* **Guilded Spirit**[174] 7275 4-9-1 **70** ............................ TomQueally 8 70
(Stuart Kittow) *hld up in rr: nt clr run over 3f out: rdn and struggling after: sme prog over 1f out: n.d* **10/1**[3]

2-34 **6** *6* **Golden Jubilee (USA)**[38] 782 5-8-12 **69**(v) WilliamTwiston-Davies(3) 11 59
(Nigel Twiston-Davies) *mostly chsd ldr: rdn wl over 2f out: wl hld and lost 2nd wl over 1f out: wknd qckly* **8/1**[2]

3-12 **7** *1* **Afro**[77] 253 4-8-7 **65** ............................(p[1]) MichaelJMMurphy(3) 7 53
(Peter Hedger) *hld up in rr: rdn 5f out: sn struggling: bhd over 3f out: no ch after* **8/1**[2]

5/05 **8** *hd* **Treasure The Ridge (IRE)**[32] 856 5-9-2 **70** .............(v) JimmyFortune 5 58
(Brett Johnson) *hld up in midfield: prog over 3f out: drvn to dispute 2nd 2f out: nt qckn after: wl hld whn n.m.r on inner jst ins fnl f* **12/1**

000- **9** *11* **Bondi Mist (IRE)**[173] 7305 5-8-2 **61** oh4............................ RyanTate(5) 6 30
(Jonathan Geake) *trckd ldng pair to over 3f out: wknd qckly over 2f out: t.o* **66/1**

/60- **10** *6* **Shades Of Silver**[298] 3250 4-8-8 **68** ............................ DavidKenny(5) 4 27
(Michael Scudamore) *hld up in rr: prog after 4f: wknd 4f out: t.o* **33/1**

4520 **11** *99* **Doldrums (USA)**[12] 1108 4-9-6 **75** ............................ SilvestreDeSousa 10
(Mark Johnston) *chsd ldrs: rdn 1/2-way: wknd 4f out: wl t.o* **16/1**

2m 31.24s (1.74) **Going Correction** +0.20s/f (Good)
**WFA** 4 from 5yo 1lb **11 Ran SP% 114.4**
Speed ratings (Par 103): **102,100,97,97,97 93,92,92,85,81 15**
CSF £13.95 CT £188.47 TOTE £1.90: £1.10, £3.80, £4.10; EX 18.50 Trifecta £159.30.
**Owner** Ashley Head **Bred** Grangemore Stud **Trained** Lower Beeding, W Sussex

**FOCUS**
Run at a decent gallop, Ryan Moore judged it perfectly aboard the favourite. He's rated back to his early level.
T/Jkpt: Not won. T/Plt: £1,222.00 to a £1 stake. Pool: £90533.07 - 54.08 winning tickets T/Qpdt: £248.90 to a £1 stake. Pool: £7536.06 - 22.40 winning tickets JN

# PONTEFRACT (L-H)
Tuesday, April 8

**OFFICIAL GOING: Good to soft (soft in places) changing to soft after race 1 (2.10)**
Wind: strong 1/2 behind Weather: fine and sunny but very windy

## 1356 PONTEFRACT LOYALTY CARD H'CAP — 1m 4y
**2:10** (2:11) (Class 5) (0-75,81) 4-Y-O+ **£3,234** (£962; £481; £240) **Stalls** Low

Form RPR

425- **1** **Dark Ocean (IRE)**[183] 7065 4-8-12 **66** ............................ GrahamLee 2 77
(Jedd O'Keeffe) *trckd ldrs: hung lft and led over 1f out: drvn out* **11/1**

3003 **2** *2 ½* **Kyllachy Star**[24] 979 8-8-13 **67** ............................(v) PaulHanagan 4 72
(Richard Fahey) *mid-div: hdwy and swtchd outside 2f out: chsd wnr 1f out: styd on same pce* **7/1**[3]

45-6 **3** *3* **Qibtee (FR)**[12] 1132 4-8-7 **61** oh3............................ JimmyQuinn 5 59+
(Les Eyre) *chsd ldrs: kpt on ins fnl f: tk 3rd post* **33/1**

322- **4** *hd* **Lord Franklin**[198] 6667 5-8-12 **69** ............................ JasonHart(3) 7 67
(Eric Alston) *led: hdd over 1f out: kpt on same pce* **5/1**[2]

020- **5** *nk* **Surround Sound**[185] 7024 4-9-0 **68** ............................ DavidAllan 6 65+
(Tim Easterby) *hld up in rr: effrt 2f out: styd on fnl f* **25/1**

000- **6** *¾* **Merchant Of Medici**[242] 5245 7-8-7 **61** oh4............................ PJMcDonald 3 56
(Micky Hammond) *in rr: hdwy over 2f out: one pce fnl f* **25/1**

230- **7** *3 ½* **Blue Maisey**[172] 7344 6-8-6 **65** ow1............................ KevinStott(5) 8 52
(Edwin Tuer) *mid-div: hdwy over 2f out: wknd over 1f out* **16/1**

530- **8** *1 ½* **Barren Brook**[178] 7211 7-9-7 **75** ............................ GrahamGibbons 13 59
(Michael Easterby) *mid-div: effrt 2f out: nvr a threat* **20/1**

-450 **9** *3 ¼* **Warfare**[35] 832 5-9-2 **70** ............................ PaulMulrennan 14 47
(Kevin Ryan) *swtchd lft sfter s: hld up in rr: hdwy over 2f out: wknd over 1f out* **20/1**

000- **10** *1 ¾* **Cono Zur (FR)**[180] 7152 7-8-12 **66** ............................ JamesSullivan 10 38
(Ruth Carr) *chsd ldrs: lost pl over 1f out* **50/1**

053- **11** *¾* **Hakuna Matata**[185] 7024 7-9-2 **75** ............................(b) ConnorBeasley(5) 9 46
(Michael Dods) *in rr-div: hdwy over 2f out: lost pl over 1f out* **9/1**

34-5 **12** *7* **Mixed Message (IRE)**[33] 859 4-8-8 **69** ow1.......(p) MeganCarberry(7) 1 24
(Brian Ellison) *s.i.s: drvn to sn chse ldrs: lost pl 2f out* **11/1**

0-11 **13** *11* **Life And Times (USA)**[3] 1317 6-9-13 **81** 6ex............................ JoeFanning 12 10
(Mark Johnston) *dwlt: hdwy on outside to chse ldrs over 5f out: lost pl over 2f out: bhd over 1f out: eased* **15/8**[1]

1m 50.45s (4.55) **Going Correction** +0.70s/f (Yiel) **13 Ran SP% 118.6**
Speed ratings (Par 103): **105,102,99,99,99 98,94,93,90,88 87,80,69**
CSF £77.44 CT £1612.56 TOTE £14.60: £4.50, £2.40, £7.90; EX 98.60 Trifecta £2301.70 Part won. Pool of £3069.06 - 0.71 winning units..
**Owner** The Fatalists **Bred** Mrs T Mahon **Trained** Middleham Moor, N Yorks

**FOCUS**
There was 16mm of rain over the previous week, 3mm of rain the previous day and a further 0.5mm overnight, and the going was given as good to soft, soft in places (GoingStick 5.7). Paul Mulrennan said 'it's testing', while Jimmy Quinn said it was 'tacky and hard work'. A modest handicap, with a small personal best from the winner.

## 1357 HIGH-RISE MAIDEN STKS (BOBIS RACE) — 1m 2f 6y
**2:40** (2:41) (Class 4) 3-Y-O **£5,175** (£1,540; £769; £384) **Stalls** Low

Form RPR

4- **1** **Champagne Rules**[290] 3588 3-9-5 0 ............................ PaddyAspell 3 78
(Sharon Watt) *t.k.h in mid-div: hdwy over 3f out: 3rd over 2f out: led over 1f out: hung bdly rt: styd on towards fin* **100/1**

6- **2** *nk* **Galuppi**[110] 8340 3-9-5 0 ............................ AdamKirby 4 77
(Luca Cumani) *in rr: effrt and nt clr run over 2f out: swtchd ins: styd on and upsides last 100yds: r.o* **20/1**

- **3** *2* **Munatas** 3-9-5 0 ............................ JackMitchell 9 74+
(Roger Varian) *in rr-div: gd hdwy on ins to chse ldrs 2f out: upsides ins fnl f: kpt on same pce* **28/1**

2- **4** *5* **Sufranel (IRE)**[127] 8123 3-9-5 0 ............................ LukeMorris 10 64
(Marco Botti) *led: hdd over 1f out: wknd fnl 75yds* **8/1**[3]

3- **5** *4* **Munaaser**[202] 6534 3-9-5 0 ............................ PaulHanagan 8 57+
(Sir Michael Stoute) *t.k.h: sn trcking ldr hanging rt: led over 2f out: hdd over 1f out: sn wknd* **4/6**[1]

52- **6** *1 ½* **Zee Zeely**[158] 7655 3-9-5 0 ............................ RyanMoore 7 54
(William Haggas) *s.i.s: hdwy 5f out: chsng ldrs on outer over 1f out: fdd fnl 200yds* **5/2**[2]

03- **7** *1 ¾* **Arbaab**[172] 7339 3-9-5 0 ............................ DaneO'Neill 11 50
(Sir Michael Stoute) *chsd ldrs: drvn 3f out: wknd over 1f out* **16/1**

34- **8** *1* **In Vino Veritas (IRE)**[209] 6299 3-9-5 0 ............................ PJMcDonald 5 48
(Ann Duffield) *in rr: sme hdwy over 2f out: wknd over 1f out* **66/1**

0- **9** *4* **Burmese Breeze**[177] 7219 3-9-5 0 ............................ TedDurcan 1 41
(Chris Wall) *chsd ldrs: lost pl over 1f out* **100/1**

3 **10** *¾* **Nothing Special**[15] 1084 3-9-0 0 ............................ StephenCraine 2 34
(Tom Dascombe) *chsd ldrs: drvn 3f out: lost pl over 1f out* **50/1**

**11** *8* **High Love (IRE)** 3-9-0 0 ............................[1] JimCrowley 6 19
(Tom Dascombe) *s.i.s: in rr: reminders over 5f out: bhd fnl 3f* **33/1**

2m 25.52s (11.82) **Going Correction** +0.80s/f (Soft) **11 Ran SP% 122.1**
Speed ratings (Par 100): **84,83,82,78,74 73,72,71,68,67 61**
CSF £1388.11 TOTE £67.80: £14.80, £3.20, £7.80; EX 1344.70 Trifecta £4518.90 Part won. Pool of £6025.22 - 0.08 winning units..
**Owner** Rosey Hill Partnership **Bred** Heather Raw **Trained** Brompton-on-Swale, N Yorks

**FOCUS**
A steadily run maiden and right turn-up. The time was slow and the worth of the form is hard to gauge.

## 1358 NEW RACING UK ANYWHERE AVAILABLE NOW H'CAP (BOBIS RACE) — 6f
**3:10** (3:10) (Class 3) (0-95,87) 3-Y-O **£7,762** (£2,310; £1,154; £577) **Stalls** Low

Form RPR

300- **1** **New Bidder**[183] 7062 3-8-13 **79** ............................ RussKennemore 3 87
(Jedd O'Keeffe) *chsd ldrs: drvn over 2f out: 2nd jst ins fnl f: styd on to ld nr fin* **10/1**

102- **2** *hd* **See The Sun**[172] 7334 3-9-7 **87** ............................ DavidAllan 4 94
(Tim Easterby) *led: edgd lft ins fnl f: hdd and no ex nr fin* **12/1**

5U0- **3** *1 ¼* **Mr Matthews (IRE)**[179] 7170 3-9-1 **81** ............................ DanielTudhope 1 84
(K R Burke) *s.i.s: hld up: hdwy over 2f out: kpt on to take 3rd last 75yds* **16/1**

013- **4** *2 ½* **Quickaswecan**[143] 7933 3-9-2 **82** ............................ JoeFanning 2 77
(Mark Johnston) *sn chsng ldrs: upsides over 2f out: wkng whn sltly hmpd 100yds out* **9/2**[2]

233- **5** 1 1/4 **Instant Attraction (IRE)**[150] 7819 3-8-11 **77**............. PaulMulrennan 10 68+
(Jedd O'Keeffe) *chsd ldrs: outpcd over 2f out: kpt on fnl f* **25/1**

300- **6** *nk* **Kickboxer (IRE)**[164] 7534 3-9-2 **85**............. WilliamTwiston-Davies(3) 13 75+
(Mick Channon) *s.s: hdwy over 2f out: edgd rt over 1f out: styd on fnl f* **9/1**

331- **7** *6* **Jazz (IRE)**[150] 7817 3-9-6 **86**............................................ JimCrowley 6 57
(Charles Hills) *sn trcking ldrs: drvn over 2f out: wknd over 1f out* **11/4**[1]

411- **8** 3 1/2 **Kenny The Captain (IRE)**[150] 7819 3-9-6 **86**............. DuranFentiman 5 46
(Tim Easterby) *mid-div: effrt over 2f out: wkng whn n.m.r 1f out* **15/2**[3]

201- **9** 3 1/4 **Milly's Secret (IRE)**[190] 6904 3-8-11 **77**......................... PJMcDonald 12 26
(Ann Duffield) *in rr on outer: sme hdwy over 2f out: sn lost pl* **33/1**

110- **10** *16* **Khalice**[208] 6328 3-9-2 **82**........................................ TonyHamilton 7
(Richard Fahey) *chsd ldrs: lost pl over 2f out: sn bhd and eased: t.o* **16/1**

060- **11** *13* **Foxy Clarets (IRE)**[185] 7026 3-8-11 **77**........................... PaulHanagan 9
(Richard Fahey) *w ldrs on outer: lost pl over 2f out: sn bhd and eased: t.o: struck into* **10/1**

0-22 **12** *4* **Aspirant**[7] 1225 3-8-9 **75**..................................................(tp) SeanLevey 11
(Brian Ellison) *chsd ldrs on outer: lost pl over 2f out: sn bhd and eased: t.o* **9/1**

1m 20.91s (4.01) **Going Correction** +0.80s/f (Soft) **12** Ran SP% **121.0**
Speed ratings (Par 102): **105,104,103,99,98 97,89,85,80,59 42,36**
CSF £126.93 CT £1245.14 TOTE £8.00: £2.50, £3.80, £7.20; EX 148.90 Trifecta £1199.80.
**Owner** Highbeck Racing **Bred** West Is Best Syndicate **Trained** Middleham Moor, N Yorks

**FOCUS**
A 0-95, but the top-weight was rated 8lb below the ceiling for the race. They seemed to go a decent pace but the first two were never far away. The first four were the four best drawn, who all raced on the inside rail.

## 1359 JAMAICAN FLIGHT H'CAP 2m 1f 216y
3:40 (3:40) (Class 5) (0-75,72) 4-Y-0+ £3,234 (£962; £481; £240) Stalls Low

Form RPR

/00- **1** **Suprise Vendor (IRE)**[38] 3709 8-8-6 **55** oh7 ow2........... JasonHart(3) 4 66
(Stuart Coltherd) *mde all: drvn over 3f out: styd on: hld on towards fin* **20/1**

231- **2** 3/4 **Fitzwilly**[17] 7395 4-8-10 **64**........................... WilliamTwiston-Davies(3) 10 74
(Mick Channon) *trckd ldr after 3f: chal over 4f out: drvn over 2f out: kpt on same pce last 50yds* **2/1**[2]

616- **3** 1/2 **Calculated Risk**[27] 7239 5-9-12 **72**.................................. RyanMoore 3 81+
(John Quinn) *mid-div: drvn over 4f out: n.m.r over 2f out: styd on and 3rd last 150yds: fin strly* **15/8**[1]

/14- **4** *3* **Iron Butterfly**[20] 7597 5-8-12 **58**............................. GrahamGibbons 8 64
(James Eustace) *t.k.h in mid-div: hdwy over 3f out: modest 3rd over 1f out: one pce* **9/1**[3]

-313 **5** *8* **Joyful Motive**[6] 1248 5-8-0 **53** oh2................................ JoeDoyle(7) 2 50
(Michael Chapman) *chsd wnr 3f: wknd over 1f out* **16/1**

/11- **6** *3* **Madam Lilibet (IRE)**[37] 7423 5-9-3 **63**.............................. PaulQuinn 6 57
(Sharon Watt) *in rr: drvn 5f out: sme hdwy over 1f out: nvr on terms* **10/1**

30-6 **7** *2* **Iktiview**[16] 260 6-8-5 **58**.................................................(p) EvaMoscrop(7) 9 50
(Philip Kirby) *hld up in rr: drvn and sme hdwy 3f out: nvr on terms* **9/1**

5/0- **8** *10* **All That Remains (IRE)**[51] 1445 9-8-9 **55**........................ JimmyQuinn 5 36
(Brian Ellison) *mid-div: sme hdwy 4f out: wknd over 2f out* **25/1**

162- **9** 3 1/2 **Cowslip**[169] 7423 5-8-10 **56**.......................................... PJMcDonald 11 33
(George Moore) *in rr: sme hdwy over 5f out: lost pl 3f out* **20/1**

326- **10** *3* **Stickleback**[26] 7597 5-8-10 **56**.......................................(v) GrahamLee 7 30
(Micky Hammond) *mid-div: hdwy 8f out: drvn over 5f out: lost pl 3f out: sn bhd* **20/1**

-432 **11** *17* **Daring Indian**[11] 1140 6-9-2 **69**......................................(p) JennyPowell(7) 1 24
(Tom Dascombe) *s.s: in rr: hdwy over 5f out: lost pl 3f out: sn bhd: t.o* **22/1**

4m 20.61s (24.41) **Going Correction** +0.80s/f (Soft)
**WFA** 4 from 5yo+ 5lb **11** Ran SP% **118.0**
Speed ratings (Par 103): **77,76,76,75,71 70,69,64,63,62 54**
CSF £56.03 CT £117.67 TOTE £24.30: £4.80, £1.40, £1.60; EX 93.40 Trifecta £515.90.
**Owner** Aidan Gunning **Bred** P Travers **Trained** Selkirk, Borders

**FOCUS**
The first two formed a breakaway from the main bunch here and, while they both tired in the closing stages, they had just enough in hand to hold off the best of those coming from out of the pack. Both were on fair marks on their jumps form.

## 1360 NEW BETTING HALL H'CAP 1m 2f 6y
4:15 (4:15) (Class 2) (0-105,97) 4-Y-0+
£12,450 (£3,728; £1,864; £932; £466; £234) Stalls Low

Form RPR

134- **1** **Clayton**[201] 6551 5-9-6 **96**........................................... PaulMulrennan 4 107
(Kevin Ryan) *trckd ldrs: challenged over 2f out: led over 1f out: edgd lft: hrd drvn: all out* **9/2**[2]

-630 **2** 3/4 **Stepping Ahead (FR)**[25] 956 4-9-4 **94**........................ DanielTudhope 3 103
(K R Burke) *led: hdd over 1f out: n.m.r and swtchd rt jst ins fnl f: styd on in clsng stages: jst hld* **5/1**[3]

00-0 **3** 4 1/2 **Sennockian Star**[45] 716 4-9-7 **97**....................................(v) JoeFanning 5 97
(Mark Johnston) *chsd ldrs: drvn over 3f out: one pce fnl 2f* **9/1**

**4** 1 3/4 **Safe Home (IRE)**[26] 7405 4-8-10 **89**............................... IanBrennan(3) 1 86
(John Quinn) *sn chsng ldrs: one pce whn edgd rt 1f out* **20/1**

/0-0 **5** *2* **Gunner Lindley (IRE)**[24] 559 7-8-8 **87**............................ JasonHart(3) 2 80+
(Stuart Coltherd) *mid-div: drvn 3f out: kpt on fnl 2f: tk 5th last 50yds* **33/1**

45-4 **6** *2* **Romantic Settings**[9] 1194 4-9-2 **92**................................... RyanMoore 6 81
(Richard Fahey) *chsd ldrs: drvn and outpcd 4f out: kpt on fnl f* **5/1**[3]

53-3 **7** *11* **Centurius**[24] 977 4-9-3 **93**..............................................(p) LukeMorris 7 61
(Marco Botti) *hld up towards rr: effrt 3f out: rdn and hung lft: wknd over 1f out* **7/2**[1]

420- **8** 2 1/2 **Las Verglas Star (IRE)**[158] 7656 6-8-8 **84**........................ PaulHanagan 10 47
(Richard Fahey) *s.i.s: in rr: bhd fnl 2f* **8/1**

004- **9** *2* **Easy Terms**[196] 6729 7-8-13 **89**...................................... PhillipMakin 11 49
(Edwin Tuer) *s.i.s: brief effrt 3f out: bhd fnl 2f* **11/1**

**10** *44* **Zip Wire (IRE)**[51] 7479 5-8-3 **79**................................... DuranFentiman 12
(Donald McCain) *chsd ldrs: lost pl after 2f: reminders over 3f out: sn bhd: t.o over 1f out: virtually p.u* **16/1**

2m 19.33s (5.63) **Going Correction** +0.80s/f (Soft) **10** Ran SP% **116.8**
Speed ratings (Par 109): **109,108,104,103,101 100,91,89,87,52**
CSF £27.37 CT £195.33 TOTE £5.50: £1.70, £2.50, £3.50; EX 28.50 Trifecta £214.10.
**Owner** Guy Reed Racing **Bred** G Reed **Trained** Hambleton, N Yorks

**FOCUS**
Very few got involved and the pace held up. The winner is rated in line with the better view of his form.

## 1361 RACING UK ON SKY CHANNEL 432 MAIDEN FILLIES' STKS (BOBIS RACE) 6f
4:45 (4:45) (Class 5) 3-Y-O £3,234 (£962; £481; £240) Stalls Low

Form RPR

**1** **Danehill Revival** 3-9-0 0............................................... RyanMoore 4 92+
(William Haggas) *mde all: pushed along over 2f out: drvn clr fnl f: v readily* **8/11**[1]

600- **2** *6* **Two Smart (IRE)**[185] 7016 3-9-0 79.................................. PhillipMakin 7 76
(K R Burke) *w wnr: rdn over 1f out: eased whn no match last 50yds* **7/4**[2]

052- **3** *9* **Princess Rose**[181] 7117 3-9-0 69....................................... LukeMorris 5 49
(John Weymes) *half rrd s: sn chsng ldrs: effrt over 2f out: one pce* **12/1**[3]

**4** 3 1/2 **My Escapade (IRE)** 3-8-9 0................................ GarryWhillans(5) 6 39
(Simon Waugh) *s.i.s: in last: drvn over 3f out: outpcd over 2f out* **50/1**

6- **5** 3 1/4 **Spinner Lane**[196] 6718 3-9-0 0......................................... PaulQuinn 1 42
(Richard Whitaker) *chsd ldrs: drvn over 2f out: wknd fnl f* **33/1**

1m 21.98s (5.08) **Going Correction** +0.80s/f (Soft) **5** Ran SP% **106.9**
Speed ratings (Par 95): **98,90,78,73,69**
CSF £2.03 TOTE £2.00: £1.10, £1.10; EX 2.20 Trifecta £4.10.
**Owner** Cheveley Park Stud **Bred** Cheveley Park Stud Ltd **Trained** Newmarket, Suffolk

**FOCUS**
The runner-up set a fair standard but the winner, who was value for 5l, proved much too good.

## 1362 RACING ON MONDAY 14TH APRIL H'CAP 1m 2f 6y
5:15 (5:15) (Class 5) (0-75,72) 4-Y-0+ £3,234 (£962; £481; £240) Stalls Low

Form RPR

024- **1** **Pertuis (IRE)**[87] 7346 8-8-13 **64**................................... GrahamLee 2 74
(Micky Hammond) *in rr: hdwy 5f out: effrt and nt clr run over 2f out: 2nd over 1f out: led jst ins fnl f: drvn out* **8/1**

3341 **2** 1 1/2 **Cathedral**[8] 1209 5-9-7 **72** 6ex......................................... RyanMoore 5 79
(Ed de Giles) *led: increased pce over 2f out: led jst ins fnl f: kpt on wl* **3/1**[2]

063- **3** 1 3/4 **Gold Show**[39] 7346 5-8-9 **65**....................................... KevinStott(5) 1 69
(Edwin Tuer) *chsd ldrs: drvn over 2f out: 3rd and kpt on same pce over 1f out* **5/1**[3]

40-2 **4** 3/4 **High Office**[9] 1196 8-9-0 **72**.......................................... JoshQuinn(7) 6 74
(Richard Fahey) *s.i.s: in rr: hdwy 5f out: styd on fnl f: tk 4th towards fin* **7/1**

123- **5** 1 1/4 **Mash Potato (IRE)**[175] 7275 4-9-1 **71**........................ ConnorBeasley(5) 4 71
(Michael Dods) *chsd ldrs effrt over 2f out: one pce over 1f out* **2/1**[1]

015/ **6** *1* **Switched Off**[14] 6802 9-9-5 **70**...................................(bt) StevieDonohoe 9 68
(Kevin Frost) *s.i.s: hdwy and swtchd wd over 2f out: chsng ldrs over 1f out: one pce* **50/1**

046- **7** *6* **Eutropius (IRE)**[187] 6970 5-9-7 **72**................................... BenCurtis 13 59
(Alan Swinbank) *in rr: hdwy 4f out: lost pl over 2f out* **25/1**

/26- **8** *7* **Ze King**[253] 4831 5-9-1 **66**............................................. TedDurcan 11 39
(Chris Wall) *in rr: effrt over 2f out: sn wknd: bhd whn eased ins fnl f* **25/1**

000- **9** *54* **Carragold**[254] 4810 8-9-3 **68**........................................... DavidAllan 14
(Mel Brittain) *racd wd: drvn to sn chse ldrs: lost pl over 2f out: eased whn bhd over 1f out: virtually p.u: hopelessly t.o* **33/1**

02-6 **10** 4 1/2 **Bavarian Nordic (USA)**[75] 303 9-8-0 **58** oh2.........(b) GemmaTutty(7) 8
(Richard Whitaker) *chsd ldrs: lost pl over 2f out: bhd and eased over 1f out: virtually p.u: hopelessly t.o* **33/1**

240- **P** **Pivotman**[153] 7778 6-9-6 **71**..........................................(t) GrahamGibbons 7
(Michael Easterby) *w ldr: drvn over 2f out: hung lft and lost pl over 1f out: eased and sn bhd: p.u ins fnl f* **20/1**

2m 21.83s (8.13) **Going Correction** +0.80s/f (Soft) **11** Ran SP% **118.9**
Speed ratings (Par 103): **99,97,96,95,94 94,89,83,40,36**
CSF £30.18 CT £136.29 TOTE £9.80: £2.90, £1.20, £2.30; EX 38.60 Trifecta £167.20.
**Owner** M H O G **Bred** Killeen Castle Stud **Trained** Middleham Moor, N Yorks

**FOCUS**
The first three saved ground on the rail into the straight. The winner is rated up a length on last year's best.
T/Jkpt: Not won. T/Plt: £26,272.90 to a £1 stake. Pool of £93574.82 - 2.60 winning tickets.
T/Qpdt: £45.90 to a £1 stake. Pool of £9721.11 - 156.50 winning tickets. WG

# 1243 SOUTHWELL (L-H)
Tuesday, April 8

**OFFICIAL GOING: Standard**
Wind: Strong behind Weather: Cloudy with sunny periods

## 1363 BRITISH STALLION STUDS EBF BOOKMAKERS.CO.UK MAIDEN STKS 5f (F)
2:00 (2:01) (Class 5) 2-Y-O £2,911 (£866; £432; £216) Stalls High

Form RPR

**1** **Absent Friends** 2-9-0 0.............................................. RyanWhile(5) 6 71
(Bill Turner) *mde virtually all: shkn up over 1f out: kpt on strly* **4/1**[2]

**2** 1 1/2 **Spindle (IRE)** 2-9-0 0.................................................... LiamKeniry 4 60
(Mark Usher) *racd towards centre: in tch: hdwy 2f out: sn rdn: chsd ldrs over 1f out: kpt on wl fnl f* **25/1**

**3** 2 1/4 **Basil The Great** 2-9-5 0......................................... RichardKingscote 7 56
(Tom Dascombe) *in tch: sn rn green and pushed along: hdwy 2f out: styd on fnl f: nrst fin* **10/1**

0 **4** 3/4 **Toytown (IRE)**[10] 1161 2-9-5 0....................................... DaleSwift 2 53
(Derek Shaw) *cl up: rdn along wl over 1f out: grad wknd* **8/1**

0 **5** *hd* **Josie Joe**[4] 1276 2-8-11 0.......................................... DeclanBates(3) 5 47+
(David Evans) *sn rdn along and outpcd in rr: green and bhd 1/2-way: hdwy wl over 1f out: sn edgd lft: kpt on fnl f: nrst fin* **12/1**

**6** 1/2 **Ko Cache (IRE)** 2-9-0 0.................................................. TomEaves 8 45
(Keith Dalgleish) *racd nr stands' rail: cl up: effrt 2f out and ev ch tl rdn wl over 1f out and grad wknd* **11/4**[1]

**7** *1* **Smugglers Lane (IRE)** 2-9-5 0...................................... ChrisCatlin 1 46+
(David Evans) *s.i.s and in rr: pushed along: green and edgd lft 1/2-way: rdn wl over 1f out: n.d* **9/2**[3]

**8** *hd* **Lunar Knot** 2-9-0 0.......................................................... TomQueally 3 40+
(Alan McCabe) *s.i.s and racd centre: sn in tch: pushed along over 2f out: rdn green and edgd lft over 1f out: sn wknd* **5/1**

1m 0.48s (0.78) **Going Correction** -0.025s/f (Stan) **8** Ran SP% **113.3**
Speed ratings (Par 92): **92,89,86,84,84 83,82,81**
CSF £89.47 TOTE £4.50: £1.50, £6.70, £1.40; EX 99.20 Trifecta £600.40.
**Owner** Mrs Tracy Turner **Bred** Miss Jackie Penny **Trained** Sigwells, Somerset

**FOCUS**
A moderate 2yo maiden with a pretty compressed finish and the bare form can't rate much better.

## 1364 LADBROKES MEDIAN AUCTION MAIDEN STKS — 7f (F)
2:30 (2:30) (Class 6) 3-4-Y-O — £2,045 (£603; £302) Stalls Low

Form — RPR

0- **1** **Deep Resolve (IRE)**[194] 6773 3-8-13 0 ............ BenCurtis 5 — 67+
(Alan Swinbank) *trckd ldng pair on outer: led over 4f out: rdn clr over 2f out: styd on wl ins fnl f* — **11/4**[3]

**2** *2 ½* **Va Benny** 3-8-13 0 ............ FrederikTylicki 4 — 61+
(J R Jenkins) *dwlt: green and sn outpcd in rr: bhd and rdn along 1/2-way: hdwy over 2f out: drvn and styd on to chse ldng pair whn edgd lft over 1f out: kpt on: nt rch wnr* — **5/2**[2]

0 **3** *1 ½* **Flying By**[19] 1024 3-8-8 0 ............ ChrisCatlin 3 — 52
(Rae Guest) *trckd ldrs: hdwy to chse wnr 3f out: rdn over 2f out: drvn wl over 1f out: sn no imp* — **16/1**

0-2 **4** *24* **Molly Ahoy**[13] 1112 3-8-8 0 ............ WilliamCarson 2
(Alan McCabe) *led: hdd over 4f out and sn pushed along: rdn 1/2-way: drvn 3f out and sn wknd* — **5/4**[1]

6 **5** *23* **Fizzolo**[7] 1223 3-8-6 0 ow1 ............ OisinMurphy(3) 1
(Noel Quinlan) *cl up on inner: rdn along 1/2-way: sn wknd and bhd whn eased wl over 1f out* — **12/1**

1m 30.33s (0.03) **Going Correction** -0.05s/f (Stan) — 5 Ran SP% 113.3
Speed ratings (Par 101): **97,94,92,65,38**
CSF £10.32 TOTE £3.90: £1.20, £2.10; EX 10.70 Trifecta £77.70.
**Owner** Panther Racing Ltd **Bred** Dermot & Catherine Dwan **Trained** Melsonby, N Yorks

**FOCUS**
A moderate 3yo maiden run in a modest time. Guessy form.

## 1365 LADBROKES H'CAP — 7f (F)
3:00 (3:01) (Class 6) (0-55,56) 4-Y-O+ — £1,940 (£577; £288; £144) Stalls Low

Form — RPR

0-40 **1** **Red Invader (IRE)**[13] 1105 4-9-5 53 ............ RobertWinston 8 — 67
(Charles Hills) *trckd ldng pair: hdwy 1/2-way: led wl over 2f out: rdn wl over 1f out: drvn and edgd lft ent fnl f: styd on* — **11/8**[1]

2346 **2** *2* **Very First Blade**[4] 1282 5-9-1 49 ............(be) SilvestreDeSousa 9 — 57
(Michael Mullineaux) *trckd ldr: hdwy 3f out: rdn to chse wnr over 2f out: drvn over 1f out: kpt on same pce fnl f* — **6/1**[3]

0051 **3** *3 ½* **Sam Spade (IRE)**[7] 1228 4-9-8 56 6ex ............(v) DaleSwift 10 — 55
(Derek Shaw) *in tch on wd outside: rdn along 1/2-way: hdwy to chse ldrs wl over 2f out: drvn over 1f out: no imp* — **7/2**[2]

4012 **4** *3 ¾* **Bladewood Girl**[12] 1131 6-9-5 53 ............ FrederikTylicki 4 — 42
(J R Jenkins) *towards rr: hdwy and wd st: rdn to chse ldrs over 2f out: no imp appr fnl f* — **12/1**

02-6 **5** *6* **Thewestwalian (USA)**[12] 1138 6-8-12 46 oh1 ............ WilliamCarson 11 — 20
(Peter Hiatt) *chsd ldrs: rdn along wl over 2f out: sn btn* — **12/1**

0560 **6** *3 ½* **Fathom Five (IRE)**[15] 1081 10-9-1 49 ............ DavidProbert 3 — 13
(Shaun Harris) *led: rdn along 1/2-way: hdd wl over 2f out: grad wknd* — **33/1**

-010 **7** *1 ¼* **All Right Now**[20] 1017 7-9-7 55 ............(tp) HarryBentley 7 — 16
(Tony Newcombe) *chsd ldrs: rdn along 1/2-way: sn wknd* — **8/1**

402- **8** *1 ½* **Kalithea**[129] 8119 4-9-7 55 ............(e[1]) BarryMcHugh 5 — 12
(Julie Camacho) *dwlt: a in rr* — **12/1**

/0-0 **9** *1* **Les Andelys**[46] 692 8-8-9 46 oh1 ............(p) MichaelJMMurphy(3) 6
(Michael Murphy) *a towards rr* — **50/1**

0460 **10** *4* **Durham Express (IRE)**[14] 1089 7-8-12 46 oh1 ............(b) ChrisCatlin 2
(Colin Teague) *towards rr: sme hdwy and in tch 1/2-way: rdn along wl over 2f out and sn wknd* — **50/1**

040- **11** *36* **Sairaam (IRE)**[258] 4623 8-8-12 46 oh1 ............ MartinLane 1
(Charles Smith) *cl up on inner: rdn along bef 1/2-way: sn wknd and bhd* — **50/1**

1m 29.35s (-0.95) **Going Correction** -0.05s/f (Stan) — 11 Ran SP% 121.6
Speed ratings (Par 101): **103,100,96,92,85 81,80,78,77,72 31**
CSF £10.32 CT £25.03 TOTE £2.70: £1.10, £2.80, £1.10; EX 12.70 Trifecta £43.00.
**Owner** The Hon R J Arculli **Bred** Tally-Ho Stud **Trained** Lambourn, Berks

**FOCUS**
A weak handicap in which the winner ran pretty much to his best.

## 1366 32RED FREE £10 BONUS H'CAP — 2m (F)
3:30 (3:30) (Class 4) (0-85,84) 4-Y-O+ — £4,690 (£1,395; £697; £348) Stalls Low

Form — RPR

000- **1** **Tartan Jura**[188] 6942 6-8-12 70 ............(p) SilvestreDeSousa 6 — 80+
(Mark Johnston) *slt ld: pushed along after 5f: hdd after 7f and cl up tl led again 5f out: jnd and rdn over 2f out: drvn over 1f out: kpt on wl fnl f* — **7/4**[1]

21 **2** *½* **Teajaybe (USA)**[14] 1092 6-8-13 71 ............ BenCurtis 2 — 80
(Chris Dwyer) *trckd ldrs: smooth hdwy 4f out: effrt on outer to chal over 2f out: rdn over 1f out and ev ch: drvn and edgd lft ins fnl f: no extyra last 75yds* — **5/2**[2]

00-4 **3** *8* **Recession Proof (FR)**[14] 1091 8-9-2 74 ............ RobertWinston 3 — 73
(John Quinn) *trckd ldrs: effrt 4f out: rdn 3f out: drvn 2f out and sn one pce* — **7/1**

-221 **4** *9* **Honoured (IRE)**[13] 1111 7-9-12 84 ............(t) AndrewMullen 5 — 72
(Michael Appleby) *hld up in tch: hdwy to chse ldrs over 4f out: rdn along over 3f out: drvn wl over 2f out and sn outpcd* — **3/1**[3]

0/0- **5** *34* **Lady Amakhala**[338] 2040 6-9-0 72 ............ TomEaves 4 — 19
(George Moore) *stdd and swtchd rt to outer s: hld up in rr: pushed along and outpcd over 6f out: hdwy and in tch over 4f out: sn rdn and wknd* — **50/1**

-612 **6** *21* **Noguchi (IRE)**[14] 1091 9-9-4 76 ............(b) TomQueally 1
(George Margarson) *cl up on inner: slt ld after 7f: pushed along and hdd 5f out: rdn 4f out and sn wknd* — **8/1**

3m 41.36s (-4.14) **Going Correction** -0.05s/f (Stan) — 6 Ran SP% 115.5
Speed ratings (Par 105): **108,107,103,99,82 71**
CSF £6.71 TOTE £3.50: £2.30, £1.40; EX 8.80 Trifecta £34.20.
**Owner** Frank Bird **Bred** Newsells Park Stud **Trained** Middleham Moor, N Yorks

**FOCUS**
A modest staying handicap. The winner is rated to his latter 2013 form.

## 1367 32RED CASINO H'CAP — 1m 4f (F)
4:05 (4:05) (Class 5) (0-75,73) 3-Y-O — £2,587 (£770; £384) Stalls Low

Form — RPR

22-5 **1** **Ujagar (IRE)**[25] 951 3-9-6 72 ............(b[1]) RichardKingscote 5 — 79
(Tom Dascombe) *cl up: led wl over 2f out: rdn clr over 1f out: edgd lft ent fnl f: styd on strly* — **8/1**[3]

53-2 **2** *2 ¼* **Libeccio (FR)**[19] 1028 3-9-5 71 ............ DavidProbert 3 — 74
(Andrew Balding) *trckd ldng pair: hdwy on outer over 3f out: rdn to chse wnr 2f out: drvn over 1f out: kpt on u.p fnl f* — **1/1**[1]

00-1 **3** *15* **Right Of Appeal**[82] 198 3-9-1 67 ............ SilvestreDeSousa 1 — 57
(Mark Johnston) *slt ld on inner: pushed along 5f out: rdn 4f out: drvn and hdd wl over 2f out: sn wknd and eased over 1f out* — **11/10**[2]

2m 41.46s (0.46) **Going Correction** -0.05s/f (Stan) — 3 Ran SP% 108.7
Speed ratings (Par 98): **96,94,84**
CSF £16.01 TOTE £5.30; EX 8.70 Trifecta £6.50.
**Owner** Denarius Consulting Ltd **Bred** Mogeely Stud **Trained** Malpas, Cheshire

**FOCUS**
Just a trio of runners but still an interesting 3yo handicap. A bit of a turn-up but the form is taken at face value.

## 1368 BEST ODDS AT BOOKMAKERS.CO.UK CLAIMING STKS — 6f (F)
4:35 (4:35) (Class 6) 3-Y-O+ — £1,940 (£577; £288; £144) Stalls Low

Form — RPR

-402 **1** **Hamoody (USA)**[13] 1104 10-9-3 72 ............ OisinMurphy(3) 5 — 82
(Joseph Tuite) *mde all: rdn clr wl over 1f out: readily* — **5/4**[1]

150 **2** *1 ¾* **Powerful Pierre**[28] 909 7-9-4 79 ............(b) JacobButterfield(5) 2 — 78
(Ollie Pears) *sltly hmpd at s and sn in rr: pushed along and outpcd after 2f: wd st and hdwy over 2f out: sn rdn and styd on wl fnl f: nt rch wnr* — **6/1**

2-32 **3** *6* **Spitfire**[68] 387 9-9-5 68 ............(t) FrederikTylicki 4 — 55
(J R Jenkins) *dwlt: wnt lft s: trckd wnr for 2f: pushed along 1/2-way: rdn wl over 2f out: sn one pce* — **7/2**[3]

1-4 **4** *nk* **Royal Warrior**[7] 1225 3-8-11 78 ............(p) TomQueally 3 — 55
(Alan McCabe) *dwlt sltly and swtchd rt to outer after s: hdwy to chse wnr after 2f: rdn along 1/2-way: drvn wl over 1f out: sn wknd* — **5/2**[2]

1m 16.05s (-0.45) **Going Correction** -0.05s/f (Stan)
**WFA** 3 from 7yo+ 12lb — 4 Ran SP% 109.5
Speed ratings (Par 101): **101,98,90,90**
CSF £8.67 TOTE £2.30; EX 9.60 Trifecta £12.60.
**Owner** Andrew Liddiard **Bred** Ragged Mountain Farm **Trained** Great Shefford, Berks

**FOCUS**
A fair claimer. Not easy form to assess, with the third and fourth no guides.

## 1369 COMPARE BOOKMAKERS AT BOOKMAKERS.CO.UK H'CAP — 6f (F)
5:05 (5:06) (Class 6) (0-60,60) 4-Y-O+ — £1,940 (£577; £288; £144) Stalls Low

Form — RPR

4023 **1** **Doctor Hilary**[33] 864 12-8-8 47 ............(v) RobertHavlin 7 — 55
(Mark Hoad) *in tch: wd st: hdwy to chse ldrs over 2f out: rdn to chal over 1f out: drvn to ld ent fnl f: sn edgd lft: styd on wl towards fin* — **10/1**

645- **2** *1 ½* **Meshardal (GER)**[189] 6916 4-9-1 54 ............ JamesSullivan 3 — 57
(Ruth Carr) *trckd ldrs: hdwy and cl up over 3f out: led wl over 2f out: rdn wl over 1f out: drvn and hdd ent fnl f: kpt on* — **7/2**[2]

0064 **3** *¾* **Prince Of Passion (CAN)**[12] 1127 6-9-7 60 ............(v) DaleSwift 10 — 61
(Derek Shaw) *prom: hdwy 1/2-way: rdn to chse ldng pair over 2f out: drvn over 1f out: kpt on same pce fnl f* — **5/1**[3]

-065 **4** *4* **Waabel**[12] 1127 7-8-9 55 ............(t) NatalieHambling-Yates(7) 5 — 43
(Ann Stokell) *dwlt and in rr: hdwy wl over 2f out: styd on appr fnl f: nrst fin* — **25/1**

-060 **5** *2 ¼* **Celestial Dawn**[20] 1009 5-8-13 52 ............(b) DavidProbert 8 — 33
(John Weymes) *in tch: wd st: rdn to chse ldrs 2f out: sn drvn and no imp* — **14/1**

0312 **6** *½* **Bubbly Bailey**[20] 1010 4-9-2 55 ............(v) FrederikTylicki 2 — 34
(J R Jenkins) *chsd ldr on inner: rdn along 1/2-way: sn wknd* — **3/1**[1]

0322 **7** *1 ½* **Dancing Freddy (IRE)**[14] 1089 7-9-3 59 ............(tp) MichaelJMMurphy(3) 4 — 33
(Ann Stokell) *led: rdn along 3f out: sn hdd & wknd fnl 2f* — **8/1**

-22 **8** *hd* **Chapellerie (IRE)**[7] 1227 5-8-11 53 ............(b) OisinMurphy(3) 1 — 27
(Tony Newcombe) *a in rr* — **7/2**[2]

-506 **9** *10* **Jemimaville (IRE)**[14] 1089 7-8-4 46 oh1 ............(v) RyanPowell(3) 6
(Giles Bravery) *a towards rr* — **50/1**

1m 16.35s (-0.15) **Going Correction** -0.05s/f (Stan) — 9 Ran SP% 118.8
Speed ratings (Par 101): **99,97,96,90,87 87,85,84,71**
CSF £46.35 CT £202.58 TOTE £11.70: £2.80, £1.40, £1.80; EX 56.30 Trifecta £415.60.
**Owner** J Baden White **Bred** The Lavington Stud **Trained** Lewes, E Sussex

**FOCUS**
A competitive low-grade handicap to close the card. The winner's best form since November 2012.
T/Plt: £626.90 to a £1 stake. Pool of £59504.10 - 69.28 winning tickets. T/Qpdt: £65.90 to a £1 stake. Pool of £6331.94 - 71.0 winning tickets. JR

1370 - (Foreign Racing) - See Raceform Interactive

# 1205 SAINT-CLOUD (L-H)
Tuesday, April 8

**OFFICIAL GOING: Turf: good**

## 1371a PRIX EDMOND BLANC (GROUP 3) (4YO+) (TURF) — 1m
1:50 (1:50) 4-Y-O+ — £33,333 (£13,333; £10,000; £6,666; £3,333)

RPR

**1** **Sommerabend**[47] 678 7-8-11 0 ............ GeraldMosse 7 — 113
(M Rulec, Germany) *broke wl and trckd ldr on outer: led 2f out: rdn over 1f out: r.o: rapidly diminishing advantage cl home but a jst doing enough* — **63/10**[3]

**2** *hd* **Kokaltash (FR)**[19] 1037 4-8-11 0 ............ UmbertoRispoli 9 — 113
(M Delzangles, France) *dwlt sltly and hld up in last pair: rdn and hdwy on outer fr over 1f out: hung lft u.p but r.o strly and wnt 2nd towards fin: clsd rapidly on wnr: jst failed* — **43/5**

**3** *1 ¼* **Silas Marner (FR)**[35] 7-9-0 0 ............ Jean-BernardEyquem 1 — 113
(J-C Rouget, France) *prom on inner: rdn to chal and ev ch over 1f out: outpcd by wnr ins fnl f: kpt on but dropped to 3rd towards fin* — **18/5**[2]

**4** *½* **Esoterique (IRE)**[19] 1037 4-8-10 0 ............ MaximeGuyon 10 — 108
(A Fabre, France) *sn prom on outer: rdn to chal over 1f out: outpcd by wnr and dropped to 4th ins fnl f: kpt on but hld* — **14/5**[1]

**5** *1 ¼* **Pilote (IRE)**[200] 6618 4-8-11 0 ............ OlivierPeslier 3 — 106
(A Fabre, France) *midfield on outer: rdn over 1f out: keeping on same pce whn short of room briefly ins fnl f: hld after* — **63/10**[3]

**6** *nk* **Peace At Last (IRE)**[35] 4-9-2 0 ............ FabriceVeron 6 — 110
(H-A Pantall, France) *dwlt sltly and hld up in last: rdn 2f out: stl last ent fnl f: kpt on and wnt 6th towards fin: nvr nrr* — **33/1**

**7** *1 ¼* **Coup De Theatre (FR)**[35] 5-8-11 0 ............ JeromeCabre 2 — 103
(P Van De Poele, France) *midfield in tch: rdn over 2f out: outpcd and fdd ins fnl f* — **196/10**

8 ½ **Kenhope (FR)**[213] 6224 4-8-10 0................ Christophe-PatriceLemaire 8 100
(H-A Pantall, France) *hld up towards rr: rdn 2f out: sn outpcd and btn: nvr a factor* **103/10**

9 ½ **Don Bosco (FR)**[185] 7047 7-9-2 0................................ GregoryBenoist 4 105
(D Smaga, France) *broke wl and led: rdn whn hdd 2f out: sn no ex and btn: wknd* **161/10**

10 4 **King Air (FR)**[12] 7-8-11 0................................ RonanThomas 5 91
(Rod Collet, France) *sn midfield on inner: rdn 2f out: outpcd and btn ent fnl f: wknd and dropped to last: eased* **83/10**

1m 42.51s (-4.99) **10** Ran SP% **119.1**
WIN (incl. 1 euro stake): 7.30. PLACES: 2.20, 2.40, 1.70. DF: 29.30. SF: 63.40.
**Owner** Stall Am Alten Flies **Bred** Gestut Schlenderhan **Trained** Germany

# CATTERICK (L-H)

## Wednesday, April 9

**OFFICIAL GOING: Soft (good to soft in places; 6.3)**
Wind: light across Weather: overcast

## 1372 WELCOME TO CATTERICK'S FLAT SEASON 2014 H'CAP 1m 3f 214y

**2:20** (2:22) (Class 5) (0-70,71) 3-Y-O **£2,911** (£866; £432; £216) **Stalls** Low

Form RPR

5-41 **1** **Maxie T**[20] 1033 3-9-7 68................................ GrahamLee 3 79
(Mark Johnston) *mde all: drvn over 2f out: styd on strly to forge clr fnl f* **3/1**[2]

06-1 **2** 2½ **Late Shipment**[7] 1239 3-9-10 71 6ex................................ JoeFanning 2 78
(Mark Johnston) *chsd wnr: drvn over 4f out: styd on same pce appr fnl f* **11/8**[1]

000- **3** 3¾ **Bentons Lad**[170] 7418 3-8-5 52................................ JamesSullivan 5 53
(George Moore) *chsd ldrs: drvn 4f out: one pce fnl 2f* **20/1**

650- **4** 6 **Mister Uno (IRE)**[186] 7032 3-8-3 50................................ PJMcDonald 6 41
(Ann Duffield) *in rr: reminders over 4f out: hdwy over 2f out: sn chsng ldrs: wknd fnl 150yds* **16/1**

053- **5** 11 **Blue Talisman (IRE)**[189] 6946 3-8-9 56................................ DuranFentiman 1 30
(Tim Easterby) *chsd ldrs: drvn over 3f out: wknd 2f out* **12/1**

0-04 **6** 39 **O'Raghallaigh (IRE)**[16] 1084 3-8-2 49 oh4................................ PatrickMathers 4
(Richard Fahey) *sn drvn along in last: bhd fnl 6f: t.o 3f out: eased over 1f out* **14/1**

650- **P** **Sirpertan**[211] 6275 3-7-10 50................................[1] JoeDoyle(7) 7
(Mark Walford) *swtchd lft s: t.k.h: sn trcking ldrs: hood c loose: eased and p.u after 3f* **4/1**[3]

2m 47.06s (8.16) **Going Correction** +0.675s/f (Yiel) **7** Ran SP% **112.1**
Speed ratings (Par 98): **99,97,94,90,83 57,**
CSF £7.20 TOTE £5.20: £2.50, £1.10; EX 7.90 Trifecta £119.20.
**Owner** Christopher W T Johnston **Bred** Meon Valley Stud **Trained** Middleham Moor, N Yorks

**FOCUS**
A moderate 3yo handicap with a 1-2 for Mark Johnston. Little depth but the winner is entitled to be at least this good.

## 1373 YORKSHIRE-OUTDOORS.CO.UK ADVENTURE ACTIVITIES H'CAP 5f

**2:50** (2:51) (Class 6) (0-60,59) 3-Y-O **£2,385** (£704; £352) **Stalls** Low

Form RPR

506- **1** **Orient Class**[183] 7095 3-9-3 55................................(v[1]) GrahamLee 8 65
(Paul Midgley) *chsd ldrs: led over 2f out: drvn out* **6/1**[2]

660- **2** 1¼ **Straight Gin**[192] 6872 3-8-7 45................................(t) BarryMcHugh 7 50
(Alan Berry) *chsd ldrs: 2nd 1f out: styd on same pce* **12/1**

550- **3** ¾ **Lady Mai (IRE)**[286] 3724 3-8-13 56................................ SammyJoBell(5) 1 58
(Richard Fahey) *chsd ldrs: 3rd 1f out: kpt on same pce* **9/4**[1]

360- **4** 3¾ **Lady Montenegro**[153] 7788 3-8-13 51................................ PJMcDonald 3 40
(Ann Duffield) *rr-div: hdwy 2f out: kpt on fnl f* **6/1**[2]

004- **5** 4½ **Lady Dancer (IRE)**[172] 7370 3-8-0 45................................ KieranSchofield(7) 2 18
(George Moore) *in rr-div: sme hdwy over 1f out: nvr a factor* **66/1**

000- **6** 1½ **Dream Sika (IRE)**[182] 7127 3-9-1 53................................ JamesSullivan 6 20
(Ruth Carr) *led tl over 2f out: wknd fnl f* **15/2**[3]

61-0 **7** nk **Kinkohyo**[64] 481 3-9-3 55................................ PaulMulrennan 4 21
(Bryan Smart) *in rr-div: drvn over 2f out: nvr on terms* **10/1**

300- **8** 1¼ **Classical Diva**[154] 7771 3-9-4 59................................ NeilFarley(3) 9 21
(Declan Carroll) *half-rrd s: sn chsng ldrs towards centre: edgd rt and lost pl 2f out* **15/2**[3]

5535 **9** 12 **This Charming Man (IRE)**[9] 1211 3-9-3 55................................(b) TomEaves 10
(Keith Dalgleish) *mid-div: hung rt and lost pl after 2f: racd stands' side and sn bhd* **8/1**

5035 **10** 8 **Maro**[7] 1246 3-8-0 45................................(v) AdamMcLean(7) 5
(Derek Shaw) *sn drvn along: lost pl over 3f out: sn wl bhd* **25/1**

1m 3.7s (3.90) **Going Correction** +0.675s/f (Yiel) **10** Ran SP% **116.1**
Speed ratings (Par 96): **95,93,91,85,78 76,75,73,54,41**
CSF £75.06 CT £214.34 TOTE £7.20: £2.90, £4.80, £1.10; EX 46.70 Trifecta £444.30.
**Owner** Frank & Annette Brady **Bred** Frank Brady **Trained** Westow, N Yorks

**FOCUS**
A moderate sprint handicap, with not much winning form on show, but the form has been given a bit of a chance.

## 1374 RACINGUK.COM/ANYWHERE 3 DEVICES 1 PRICE H'CAP 1m 5f 175y

**3:20** (3:24) (Class 5) (0-75,75) 4-Y-O+ **£2,911** (£866; £432; £216) **Stalls** Low

Form RPR

00-3 **1** **Naburn**[29] 911 6-9-4 67................................ BenCurtis 6 75
(Alan Swinbank) *trckd ldrs: drvn over 3f out: led 2f out: hld on towards fin* **4/1**[2]

650- **2** nk **Waltz Darling (IRE)**[23] 7342 6-8-8 57................................ TomEaves 2 65
(Keith Reveley) *reminders after s: sn chsng ldrs: swtchd lft and 2nd over 1f out: no ex in clsng stages* **5/2**[1]

33-0 **3** 1¼ **My Destination (IRE)**[11] 1167 5-8-6 62................................ LukeLeadbitter(7) 10 68
(Declan Carroll) *bhd: hdwy over 3f out: edgd lft and chsng ldng pair over 1f out: kpt on same pce last 100yds* **16/1**

000- **4** 6 **Patavium (IRE)**[19] 4969 11-8-7 56 oh1................................ JamesSullivan 9 53
(Edwin Tuer) *mid-div: drvn 7f out: outpcd over 4f out: kpt on fnl f* **12/1**

600- **5** nk **Anne's Valentino**[120] 8229 4-7-11 56 oh11................................ JoeDoyle(7) 5 53
(Malcolm Jefferson) *chsd ldrs: outpcd over 4f out: one pce fnl 3f* **28/1**

020- **6** 1¼ **Rosairlie (IRE)**[162] 7596 6-9-12 75................................ PJMcDonald 4 70
(Micky Hammond) *in rr: hdwy over 6f out: nvr nr ldrs* **8/1**

225- **7** 2 **Jan Smuts (IRE)**[118] 6466 6-9-2 65................................(tp) GrahamLee 11 57
(Wilf Storey) *rrd s: mid-div: lost pl and drvn 6f out: kpt on fnl 2f* **9/1**

035- **8** nk **Kathlatino**[36] 7372 7-8-7 56 oh1................................ DuranFentiman 1 48
(Micky Hammond) *mid-div: hdwy over 4f out: hung rt and lost pl 3f out* **28/1**

3234 **9** 1¾ **Arashi**[19] 1043 8-8-13 62................................(v) DaleSwift 7 52
(Derek Shaw) *hld up in rr: effrt 4f out: lost pl over 2f out* **7/1**[3]

2-54 **10** 9 **Flamingo Beat**[8] 1222 4-9-2 68................................ AdamBeschizza 3 45
(Christine Dunnett) *led: hdd 2f out: sn lost pl and bhd* **12/1**

000- **11** 46 **Moheebb (IRE)**[25] 6598 10-8-4 56 oh3................................[1] IanBrennan(3) 8
(Robert Johnson) *sn chsng ldrs: reminders and lost pl over 7f out: sn wl bhd: t.o 5f out: virtually p.u over 1f out: eventually completed* **16/1**

3m 14.57s (10.97) **Going Correction** +0.675s/f (Yiel)
**WFA** 4 from 5yo+ 3lb **11** Ran SP% **116.2**
Speed ratings (Par 103): **95,94,94,90,90 89,88,88,87,82 56**
CSF £14.17 CT £139.28 TOTE £4.30: £2.20, £1.20, £4.20; EX 16.90 Trifecta £320.20.
**Owner** Elsa Crankshaw & G Allan **Bred** Old Mill Stud **Trained** Melsonby, N Yorks

**FOCUS**
An average staying handicap, and although the first and second were towards the head of affairs throughout, this was run at a slick pace. The winner is rated to last year's C&D win.

## 1375 DOWNLOAD NEW RACING UK IPAD APP CLAIMING STKS 7f

**3:50** (3:52) (Class 6) 3-Y-O+ **£2,385** (£704; £352) **Stalls** Low

Form RPR

335- **1** **Llewellyn**[146] 7885 6-9-8 75................................ JoeFanning 7 77
(David Nicholls) *sn led: hdd after 2f: upsides whn jinked rt wl over 1f out: sn led: fnd ex in clsng stages* **2/1**[1]

000- **2** nk **Solar Spirit (IRE)**[195] 6774 9-9-8 77................................ IanBrennan(3) 3 79
(Tracy Waggott) *t.k.h in mid-div: hdwy over 2f out: chal over 1f out: no ex in clsng stages* **8/1**

3665 **3** ½ **Alice's Dancer (IRE)**[28] 927 5-9-7 76................................ PhillipMakin 4 74
(William Muir) *dwlt: in rr: drvn over 3f out: hdwy over 2f out: kpt on and 3rd ins fnl f* **8/1**

500- **4** 1¼ **Sunraider (IRE)**[191] 6908 7-9-12 76................................ GrahamLee 2 76
(Paul Midgley) *mid-div: effrt over 2f out: kpt on one pce* **9/2**[3]

000- **5** 1¼ **Elle West**[166] 7494 3-8-2 37................................ JamesSullivan 5 57
(Michael Easterby) *dwlt: in rr: drvn and hdwy over 3f out: n.m.r over 1f out: swtchd lft ins fnl f: one pce* **100/1**

010- **6** 3½ **Tajneed (IRE)**[162] 7594 11-9-7 77................................ PaulQuinn 8 58
(David Nicholls) *led early: chsd ldrs: wknd over 1f out* **6/1**

0662 **7** ¾ **Cape Of Hope (IRE)**[12] 1152 4-9-11 72................................(v[1]) SamJames(3) 1 63
(David O'Meara) *chsd ldrs: led after 2f: hdd over 1f out: sn wknd* **7/2**[2]

0-05 **8** 1½ **Viking Warrior (IRE)**[92] 77 7-9-0 52................................ AlexHopkinson(7) 9 52
(Shaun Harris) *chsd ldrs 2f: sn mid-div: lost pl over 2f out* **66/1**

1m 31.28s (4.28) **Going Correction** +0.675s/f (Yiel)
**WFA** 3 from 4yo+ 14lb **8** Ran SP% **112.7**
Speed ratings (Par 101): **102,101,101,99,98 94,93,91**
CSF £18.56 TOTE £3.30: £1.30, £4.10, £3.10; EX 20.90 Trifecta £120.80.Llewellyn was claimed by Mr D Carroll for £6000.
**Owner** David Nicholls Racing Club **Bred** Elite Racing Club **Trained** Sessay, N Yorks

**FOCUS**
A moderate claimer that became an open affair due to the absence of likely short-priced favourite Joe Eile.

## 1376 CATTERICKBRIDGE.CO.UK H'CAP 7f

**4:20** (4:23) (Class 5) (0-75,75) 4-Y-O+ **£2,911** (£866; £432; £216) **Stalls** Low

Form RPR

-200 **1** **Piceno (IRE)**[14] 1113 6-8-12 73................................(p) MatthewHopkins(7) 7 83
(Scott Dixon) *mde all: drvn clr over 2f out: styd on* **10/1**

32-0 **2** 2¾ **Millkwood**[10] 1191 4-9-7 75................................(p) PJMcDonald 8 78
(John Davies) *chsd ldrs: drvn over 2f out: styd on to take 2nd ins fnl f* **7/1**[1]

206- **3** nk **Mystical Moment**[166] 7505 4-8-11 70................................ KevinStott(5) 6 72
(Edwin Tuer) *mid-div: hdwy over 2f out: 2nd over 1f out: kpt on same pce* **11/1**

140- **4** 2½ **Beckermet (IRE)**[151] 7824 12-9-4 72................................ JamesSullivan 14 68
(Ruth Carr) *chsd ldrs on outer: kpt onone pce fnl 2f* **16/1**

055- **5** ½ **Running Reef (IRE)**[197] 6720 5-8-9 66................................ IanBrennan(3) 5 60
(Tracy Waggott) *mid-div: hdwy 4f out: effrt over 2f out: kpt on one pce* **8/1**[2]

430- **6** ½ **Perfect Words (IRE)**[173] 7343 4-8-2 61 oh1................................ ShirleyTeasdale(5) 11 54
(Marjorie Fife) *mid-div: hdwy to chse ldrs over 2f out: one pce* **25/1**

666- **7** 1 **Old Man Clegg**[201] 6588 4-8-8 62................................(t) TomEaves 10 52
(Michael Easterby) *chsd ldrs: one pce over 1f out* **14/1**

040- **8** shd **Desert Creek (IRE)**[197] 6720 8-9-6 74................................ PaulQuinn 1 64
(David Nicholls) *s.s: in rr: hdwy over 2f out: kpt on: nvr nr ldrs* **17/2**[3]

000- **9** ¾ **West Leake Hare (IRE)**[162] 7595 5-8-13 74................................ AnnaHesketh(7) 9 62
(David Nicholls) *mid-div: effrt over 2f out: kpt on: nvr a threat* **8/1**[2]

05-0 **10** 1½ **Banovallum**[10] 1190 4-8-11 72................................ DanielleMooney(7) 2 56
(Michael Easterby) *in rr: kpt on fnl 2f: nvr a factor* **25/1**

0/0- **11** 6 **Charles De Mille**[201] 6600 6-8-7 61 oh1................................ AndrewElliott 15 30
(George Moore) *chsd ldrs on outer: edgd lft and lost pl 2f out* **33/1**

511- **12** hd **Fleurtille**[162] 7598 5-8-9 63................................ AndrewMullen 4 31
(Robert Johnson) *s.i.s: a in rr* **14/1**

060- **13** 4 **Thistleandtworoses (USA)**[139] 7989 4-9-1 72................................ SamJames(3) 13 30
(David O'Meara) *mid-div: sme hdwy over 2f out: sn wknd* **16/1**

014- **14** 2 **Alexandrakollontai (IRE)**[173] 7344 4-8-11 68................................ JulieBurke(3) 12 21
(Alistair Whillans) *a in rr* **14/1**

253- **15** 6 **Delores Rocket**[128] 8134 4-8-12 66................................(b) PaulMulrennan 3 3
(Kevin Ryan) *s.i.s: in rr: bhd fnl 2f* **7/1**[1]

1m 30.95s (3.95) **Going Correction** +0.675s/f (Yiel) **15** Ran SP% **117.6**
Speed ratings (Par 103): **104,100,100,97,97 96,95,95,94,92 85,85,81,78,71**
CSF £74.25 CT £792.65 TOTE £11.10: £2.80, £2.00, £3.40; EX 79.90 Trifecta £1088.50.
**Owner** Ontoawinner 4 **Bred** Miss Wendy Fox **Trained** Babworth, Notts

**FOCUS**
A wide-open 7f handicap in which few got involved. The winner is rated to his best.

## 1377 2014 CATTERICK TWELVE FURLONG SERIES H'CAP (QUALIFIER) 1m 3f 214y

**4:50** (4:51) (Class 4) (0-85,83) 4-Y-O+ **£6,469** (£1,925; £962; £481) **Stalls** Low

Form RPR

2-00 **1** **Brigadoon**[61] 514 7-9-5 81................................ AndrewMullen 8 89
(Michael Appleby) *hld up in mid-div: smooth hdwy over 3f out: led over 2f out: hld on towards fin* **10/1**

0-25 **2** ½ **Fly Solo**[61] 514 5-8-7 69................................ BenCurtis 3 76
(Alan Swinbank) *chsd ldrs: lost pl bnd after 3f: hdwy over 3f out: chsng wnr over 1f out: no ex towards fin* **11/4**[1]

102- **3** 1¾ **Pixie Cut (IRE)**[27] 8184 4-8-7 70................................ BarryMcHugh 9 74
(Alistair Whillans) *hld up in rr: drvn over 3f out: styd on fnl 2f: tk 3rd nr fin* **14/1**

0-20 4 nk **Gabrial's Star**[40] 784 5-9-7 83..............................(b) DavidNolan 7 87
(Richard Fahey) *mid-div: hdwy over 3f out: kpt on same pce over 1f out* 15/2

230 5 6 **Streets Of Newyork**[11] 1171 7-9-0 76.............................. TomEaves 10 70
(Brian Ellison) *in rr: hdwy over 5f out: drvn over 3f out: chsng ldrs over 1f out: fdd last 100yds* 9/2[3]

541- 6 1 1/4 **Satanic Beat (IRE)**[25] 6567 5-9-5 81.............................. PhillipMakin 5 73
(Jedd O'Keeffe) *sn chsng ldrs: drvn 4f out: fdd fnl f* 3/1[2]

344- 7 hd **Gran Maestro (USA)**[183] 7100 5-8-10 72..............................(b) PJMcDonald 4 64
(Ruth Carr) *chsd ldrs: rdn over 2f out: fdd fnl f* 10/1

8 44 **Baccalaureate (FR)**[234] 8-9-4 80.............................. RussKennemore 1
(Sue Smith) *sn drvn along: chsd ldrs: lost pl over 5f out: sn bhd: t.o whn eased 3f out: virtually p.u: eventually completed* 40/1

25-0 9 2 **Sherman McCoy**[97] 16 8-9-0 76.............................. RobertWinston 2
(Marjorie Fife) *led: drvn over 4f out: hdd over 2f out: sn lost pl and bhd: heavily eased ins fnl f: t.o* 14/1

2m 46.21s (7.31) **Going Correction** +0.675s/f (Yiel)
**WFA** 4 from 5yo+ 1lb 9 Ran SP% **115.6**
Speed ratings (Par 105): **102,101,100,100,96 95,95,66,64**
CSF £37.77 CT £393.12 TOTE £5.20: £3.20, £1.10, £3.60; EX 36.90 Trifecta £604.70.
**Owner** Robin Oliver **Bred** Biddestone Stud **Trained** Danethorpe, Notts

**FOCUS**
This was a decent 1m4f handicap in which the front four opened up a gap between themselves and the remainder of the field. The winner was better than ever on this first start for a new yard.

## 1378 RACING AGAIN 23RD APRIL APPRENTICE H'CAP 5f
**5:20** (5:22) (Class 6) (0-65,65) 4-Y-0+ **£2,385** (£704; £352) **Stalls** Low

Form RPR

3144 1 **Megaleka**[16] 1080 4-9-4 65.............................. TimClark(3) 13 78
(Alan Bailey) *hmpd s: hdwy and swtchd lft 3f out: led over 1f out: kpt on wl* 9/1

3010 2 1 1/2 **Greenhead High**[14] 1115 6-8-2 53..............................(v) AnnaHesketh(7) 7 61
(David Nicholls) *chsd ldrs: led wl over 1f out: sn hdd: no ex* 10/3[1]

-546 3 1/2 **Give Us A Belle (IRE)**[35] 845 5-8-10 57..............................(vt) JacobButterfield(3) 11 63
(Christine Dunnett) *chsd ldrs on outer: outpcd over 2f out: hdwy out wd over 1f out: kpt on same pce ins fnl f* 12/1

-000 4 2 **Two Turtle Doves (IRE)**[22] 1001 8-8-10 57.............. ShirleyTeasdale(3) 1 56
(Michael Mullineaux) *chsd ldrs: kpt on same pce over 1f out* 28/1

046- 5 nk **Spring Bird**[189] 6940 5-8-0 51 oh3.............................. GaryMahon(7) 10 49
(David Nicholls) *chsd ldrs: one pce over 1f out* 50/1

335 6 1 1/4 **Lord Buffhead**[6] 1270 5-8-8 52..............................(v) BillyCray 15 45
(Richard Guest) *in rr: hdwy whn nt clr run over 1f out: nvr a factor* 12/1

330- 7 1/2 **Here Now And Why (IRE)**[156] 7728 7-8-8 57..............................(p) EvaMoscrop(5) 2 48
(Philip Kirby) *outpcd and lost pl over 3f out: kpt on fnl f* 8/1[3]

240- 8 2 3/4 **Tuibama (IRE)**[175] 7315 5-9-3 61..............................(p) GeorgeChaloner 3 42
(Tracy Waggott) *led: edgd rt and hdd wl over 1f out: sn wknd* 14/1

-560 9 1/2 **Cadeaux Pearl**[69] 383 6-8-8 57..............................(v) MatthewHopkins(5) 14 37
(Scott Dixon) *wnt lft s: in rr: nvr on terms* 11/2[2]

000- 10 nk **Chosen One (IRE)**[186] 7029 9-9-1 64.............................. GemmaTutty(5) 8 42
(Ruth Carr) *chsd ldrs: wknd over 1f out* 22/1

1440 11 3 1/2 **I'll Be Good**[47] 694 5-8-13 62.............................. JoeDoyle(5) 5 28
(Alan Berry) *w ldr: lost pl over 1f out* 8/1[3]

1m 4.23s (4.43) **Going Correction** +0.675s/f (Yiel) 11 Ran SP% **102.5**
Speed ratings (Par 101): **91,88,87,84,84 82,81,76,76,75 70**
CSF £30.32 CT £263.06 TOTE £7.70: £2.30, £1.10, £3.60; EX 50.60 Trifecta £298.80.
**Owner** North Cheshire Trading & Storage Ltd **Bred** North Cheshire Trading And Storage Ltd **Trained** Newmarket, Suffolk
■ Rule 4 of 10p in the pound applies to all bets; Withdrawn: Flash City
■ Stewards' Enquiry : Gary Mahon caution: careless riding.

**FOCUS**
A moderate sprint handicap. Flash City was withdrawn at the start after breaking through the stalls. The winner is rated in line with a better view of his AW form.
T/Jkpt: £100,957.60 to a £1 stake. Pool of £853163.0 - 6.0 winning tickets. T/Plt: £28.50 to a £1 stake. Pool of £81895.88 - 2092.04 winning tickets. T/Qpdt: £14.30 to a £1 stake. Pool of £5288.82 - 273.05 winning tickets. WG

# 1229 KEMPTON (A.W) (R-H)
## Wednesday, April 9

**OFFICIAL GOING: Standard**
Wind: Moderate, across Weather: Fine, warm

## 1379 BETDAQ £500 IN FREE BETS H'CAP 6f (P)
**5:30** (5:30) (Class 5) (0-70,69) 3-Y-0 **£2,587** (£770; £384; £192) **Stalls** Low

Form RPR

5-23 1 **Android (IRE)**[54] 605 3-9-7 69.............................. AdamKirby 8 78
(Clive Cox) *pushed up to go prom: chsd ldr after 2f: rdn to ld 2f out: styd on wl after* 9/2[3]

00-1 2 2 1/2 **Biotic**[9] 1211 3-8-13 61 6ex.............................. SeanLevey 5 62
(Rod Millman) *led: rdn and hdd 2f out: wandered sltly but chsd wnr after: n.d fnl f* 5/1

50-2 3 1 **Shrewd Bob (IRE)**[34] 855 3-9-6 68.............................. JimCrowley 6 66
(Robert Eddery) *chsd ldrs: pushed along 1/2-way: rdn and hung fr 2f out tl styd on fnl f to take 3rd nr fin* 10/1

005- 4 1/2 **Syrian Pearl**[162] 7609 3-8-9 60.............................. AshleyMorgan(3) 3 56
(Chris Wall) *hld up in last: prog on inner fr 2f out: shkn up and styd on fnl f: nrly snatched 3rd* 25/1

023- 5 nk **Smidgen (IRE)**[177] 7251 3-9-5 67.............................. FrederikTylicki 2 62
(Ed de Giles) *t.k.h: hld up: prog on outer over 3f out: cl enough 2f out: nt qckn and sn hld: one pce* 9/4[1]

0-14 6 hd **Monashka Bay (IRE)**[12] 1146 3-9-0 62.............................. DavidProbert 4 57
(Michael Blanshard) *chsd ldr 2f: styd prom: rdn 2f out: fdd fnl f* 25/1

0-21 7 hd **Crazee Diamond**[23] 994 3-9-4 69.............. WilliamTwiston-Davies(3) 1 63
(Mick Channon) *t.k.h: hld up in tch: gng bttr than many 2f out: shkn up over 1f out: nt qckn and lost pls nr fin* 5/2[2]

0-34 8 1 1/2 **Caminel (IRE)**[19] 1039 3-9-0 62.............................. SteveDrowne 7 51
(Jeremy Gask) *sn in rr: last and struggling over 2f out* 20/1

1m 12.76s (-0.34) **Going Correction** -0.075s/f (Stan) 8 Ran SP% **115.7**
Speed ratings (Par 98): **99,95,94,93,93 93,92,90**
CSF £26.64 CT £209.31 TOTE £5.20: £1.60, £1.10, £3.40; EX 14.10 Trifecta £98.10.
**Owner** Al Asayl Bloodstock Ltd **Bred** Ballyhane Stud **Trained** Lambourn, Berks

**FOCUS**
Potentially a fair 3yo sprint handicap for the class, and the form makes plenty of sense.

## 1380 KEMPTON FOR SUMMER WEDDINGS MEDIAN AUCTION MAIDEN STKS 1m 3f (P)
**6:00** (6:02) (Class 6) 3-5-Y-0 **£1,940** (£577; £288; £144) **Stalls** Low

Form RPR

3 1 **Romsdal**[11] 1166 3-8-8 0.............................. RobertHavlin 4 96+
(John Gosden) *trckd ldr: led wl over 2f out: sn pushed wl clr: eased fnl 75yds* 1/3[1]

46- 2 5 **Big Orange**[168] 7469 3-8-8 0.............................. SeanLevey 1 82
(Michael Bell) *t.k.h: trckd ldrs: outpcd over 2f out: pushed into 2nd wl over 1f out: no ch w wnr but styd on* 10/1

2- 3 6 **Invasor Luck (USA)**[169] 7442 3-8-8 0.............................. FrederikTylicki 2 71+
(James Fanshawe) *hld up in last pair: lft bhd fr wl over 2f out: pushed along and styd on to take modest 3rd jst ins fnl f: do bttr* 11/2[2]

264- 4 5 **Chattanooga Line**[181] 7158 4-9-9 66..............................(t) FergusSweeney 6 60
(George Baker) *led to wl over 2f out: sn btn: wknd over 1f out* 25/1

3 5 7 **Dream Big (IRE)**[23] 988 3-8-3 0.............................. DavidProbert 5 45
(Jo Crowley) *stdd s: t.k.h: hld up in last pair: easily lft bhd fr over 2f out* 8/1[3]

2 6 10 **Amourita (IRE)**[21] 1011 3-8-3 0.............................. NickyMackay 3 27
(Jonathan Portman) *chsd ldng pair on outer after 3f: rdn over 3f out: sn wknd: t.o* 50/1

00- 7 3 1/4 **Macnamara**[190] 6922 3-8-3 0.............................. WilliamCarson 7 21
(Harry Dunlop) *t.k.h: trckd ldrs: rdn over 3f out: sn wknd: t.o* 66/1

2m 20.05s (-1.85) **Going Correction** -0.075s/f (Stan)
**WFA** 3 from 4yo 20lb 7 Ran SP% **117.9**
Speed ratings (Par 101): **103,99,95,91,86 79,76**
CSF £5.31 TOTE £1.10: £1.02, £4.80; EX 5.30 Trifecta £16.10.
**Owner** HRH Princess Haya Of Jordan **Bred** W And R Barnett Ltd **Trained** Newmarket, Suffolk
■ Stewards' Enquiry : Frederik Tylicki two-day ban: careless riding (Apr 23-24)

**FOCUS**
A modest maiden with little depth. The winner is afforded nominal improvement on his debut run.

## 1381 BETDAQ £25 NO LOSE BET CLASSIFIED STKS 7f (P)
**6:30** (6:31) (Class 5) 3-Y-0 **£2,587** (£770; £384; £192) **Stalls** Low

Form RPR

41- 1 **Brown Eyed Honey**[260] 4610 3-9-0 75.............................. AdamKirby 2 78+
(William Haggas) *mde all: kicked on over 2f out: drvn and pressed over 1f out: styd on wl* 7/2[2]

05-6 2 1 **Seaham**[57] 564 3-9-0 73.............................. PaulHanagan 1 75
(Rod Millman) *t.k.h: hld up towards rr: pushed along and prog 2f out: rdn and styd on fnl f to take 2nd last 50yds* 33/1

251- 3 3/4 **Got To Dance**[198] 6695 3-9-0 72.............................. JimCrowley 3 73
(Ralph Beckett) *trckd ldng pair: chsd wnr 2f out: drvn to chal jst over 1f out: hld ins fnl f: lost 2nd last 50yds* 4/1[3]

001- 4 1 **Royal Preserve**[147] 7859 3-9-0 75.............................. DavidProbert 7 70
(Andrew Balding) *hld up in last pair: outpcd over 2f out: pushed along and prog over 1f out: rdn and styd on fnl f to take 4th nr fin* 9/2

0-1 5 1/2 **Platinum Pearl**[77] 275 3-9-0 74.............................. RobertHavlin 4 69
(Peter Chapple-Hyam) *t.k.h early: trckd ldrs: shkn up and nt qckn 2f out: kpt on same pce after* 16/1

620- 6 2 1/4 **Jive**[170] 7418 3-9-0 69.............................. SeanLevey 5 63
(Richard Hannon) *t.k.h: chsd wnr to 2f out: steadily wknd over 1f out* 25/1

1- 7 6 **Don't**[175] 7296 3-9-0 75.............................. AndreaAtzeni 6 48+
(Luca Cumani) *dwlt: t.k.h: hld up towards rr: rdn and no rspnse wl over 2f out: sn bhd* 9/4[1]

361- 8 4 1/2 **Zugzwang (IRE)**[153] 7782 3-9-0 74.............................. FrederikTylicki 8 36
(Ed de Giles) *a in last pair: struggling 3f out: sn bhd* 10/1

1m 26.33s (0.33) **Going Correction** -0.075s/f (Stan) 8 Ran SP% **112.9**
Speed ratings (Par 98): **95,93,93,91,91 88,81,76**
CSF £97.97 TOTE £3.10: £1.50, £5.70, £2.70; EX 82.00 Trifecta £502.20.
**Owner** M S Bloodstock Ltd **Bred** Mike Smith **Trained** Newmarket, Suffolk

**FOCUS**
Classified races are always tight affairs and this 3yo edition featured six last-time-out winners. Muddling form, but the winner is the type to do better.

## 1382 BOOK FOR 05.05.14 ON 0844 579 3008 H'CAP 1m 4f (P)
**7:00** (7:00) (Class 6) (0-60,58) 3-Y-0 **£1,940** (£577; £288; £144) **Stalls** Centre

Form RPR

33-1 1 **Jarlath**[20] 1029 3-9-7 58.............................. SteveDrowne 2 64+
(Seamus Mullins) *trckd ldrs: moved up to ld jst over 2f out: rdn and edgd lft over 1f out: kpt on wl* 4/1[2]

000- 2 3/4 **Bold Runner**[166] 7502 3-9-6 57.............................. FrankieMcDonald 6 61
(Sean Curran) *dwlt and pushed along early: rapid prog fr last trio to press ldr 7f out: drvn to ld briefly over 2f out: chsd wnr after: kpt on wl* 25/1

0-11 3 nse **Enquiring**[14] 1098 3-9-7 58.............................. AdamKirby 7 62
(Mark Johnston) *trckd ldr 5f: styd cl up: rdn and nt qckn over 2f out: kpt on u.p fnl f: nrly tk 2nd* 1/1[1]

060- 4 1 1/2 **Musalaha (IRE)**[237] 5435 3-9-6 57.............................. PaulHanagan 4 59
(Ed Dunlop) *w.w and dropped to last trio by 1/2-way: prog over 2f out: chsd ldrs over 1f out: one pce fnl f* 10/1

000- 5 1 **Coastal Storm**[154] 7764 3-9-7 58.............................. GeorgeBaker 3 58+
(Hughie Morrison) *hld up in last trio: smooth prog to trck ldrs 2f out: shkn up and nt qckn over 1f out: fdd fnl f* 14/1

0-54 6 12 **Witch From Rome**[60] 536 3-9-7 58.............................. JimCrowley 8 39
(Ralph Beckett) *trckd ldrs on outer: rdn over 3f out: wknd over 2f out: t.o* 9/2[3]

0-60 7 1 **Storm Of Choice**[26] 951 3-8-8 45..............................(p) RobertHavlin 5 24
(Michael Attwater) *a in last trio: rdn and lost tch by 3f out: t.o* 50/1

000- 8 hd **Satin Waters**[211] 6281 3-8-10 47.............................. JohnFahy 1 26
(Eve Johnson Houghton) *led to over 2f out: sn wknd: t.o* 25/1

2m 34.69s (0.19) **Going Correction** -0.075s/f (Stan) 8 Ran SP% **113.6**
Speed ratings (Par 96): **96,95,95,94,93 85,85,85**
CSF £91.91 CT £169.19 TOTE £3.30: £1.10, £4.10, £1.10; EX 92.00 Trifecta £313.10.
**Owner** Phoenix Bloodstock **Bred** D & C Bloodstock **Trained** Wilsford-Cum-Lake, Wilts

**FOCUS**
An interesting 3yo handicap for the class. There was a relatively compressed finish, but the pace was true and the form seems sound.

## 1383 BETDAQ 3% COMMISSION H'CAP 2m (P)
7:30 (7:30) (Class 3) (0-95,91) 4-Y-O+
£7,158 (£2,143; £1,071; £535; £267; £134) Stalls Low

Form RPR
441- 1 **White Nile (IRE)**[166] 7496 5-9-6 **85** AdamKirby 5 98+
(Ed Dunlop) *hld up in 4th: clsd on ldrs over 3f out: quick move to ld over 2f out: rdn and r.o wl fnl 2f: readily* **6/4**[1]
303- 2 3 ¼ **Masquerading (IRE)**[81] 6751 4-9-4 **87** GeorgeBaker 6 95
(Jonjo O'Neill) *hld up in 5th: clsd on ldrs over 3f out: prog to chse wnr wl over 1f out: r.o and clr of rest but no imp* **11/2**[3]
1001 3 6 **Mr Burbidge**[22] 1004 6-9-9 **88** (b) LiamKeniry 4 89
(Neil Mulholland) *led and sn 10 l clr: c bk to field fr 1/2-way: urged along over 3f out: hdd over 2f out: readily outpcd* **7/1**
503- 4 ¾ **Spice Fair**[178] 7217 7-8-13 **78** SeanLevey 7 78
(Mark Usher) *dwlt: hld up in last: pushed along and outpcd over 2f out: no ch after: rdn and styd on fr over 1f out: pressed for 3rd nr fin* **16/1**
4231 5 1 ½ **Poitin**[41] 758 4-8-5 **74** DavidProbert 2 72
(Harry Dunlop) *trckd ldr: poised to chal gng strly over 2f out whn wnr shot past: sn rdn and fnd nil* **4/1**[2]
103- 6 1 ¾ **Argent Knight**[187] 6992 4-9-7 **90** (v) SteveDrowne 1 86
(William Jarvis) *disp 2nd pl to over 4f out: rdn and stl in tch over 2f out: sn lft bhd* **11/2**[3]
410- 7 12 **Ascendant**[339] 2052 8-9-3 **82** JimCrowley 8 64
(Andrew Reid) *a in last pair: wknd wl over 2f out: t.o* **33/1**
3m 26.59s (-3.51) **Going Correction** -0.075s/f (Stan)
**WFA** 4 from 5yo+ 4lb 7 Ran SP% **112.1**
Speed ratings (Par 107): **105,103,100,100,99 98,92**
CSF £9.74 CT £42.29 TOTE £2.50: £2.00, £2.20; EX 9.70 Trifecta £36.00.
**Owner** Sir Robert Ogden **Bred** Super Gift Syndicate **Trained** Newmarket, Suffolk
**FOCUS**
Not a bad staying handicap. The winner stepped up on his progressive 4yo form.

## 1384 BETDAQ - THE SPORTS BETTING EXCHANGE H'CAP 1m (P)
8:00 (8:00) (Class 6) (0-60,60) 3-Y-O £1,940 (£577; £288; £144) Stalls Low

Form RPR
06-6 1 **Prim And Proper**[14] 1101 3-8-13 **52** RichardKingscote 5 56
(Brendan Powell) *hld up in midfield: prog jst over 2f out: drvn to ld jst over 1f out: kpt on wl* **9/2**[3]
202- 2 1 **Choral Clan (IRE)**[147] 7855 3-9-6 **59** JackMitchell 7 61
(Philip Mitchell) *hld up in last trio: hanging whn asked for effrt over 2f out: prog wl over 1f out: chsd wnr last 150yds: styd on but no imp* **3/1**[1]
0334 3 hd **Evacusafe Lady**[15] 1093 3-9-5 **58** (tp) AdamKirby 9 60
(John Ryan) *hld up in last pair: rdn and prog wl over 1f out: wnt 3rd and clsd ins fnl f: styd on but nvr quite able to chal* **4/1**[2]
006- 4 3 **Picanight**[171] 7393 3-8-2 **46** oh1 JoeyHaynes(5) 2 41
(Eve Johnson Houghton) *sn led: rdn over 2f out: hdd jst over 1f out: wknd ins fnl f* **25/1**
556P 5 3 ¾ **Jenny Sparks**[9] 1211 3-8-9 **51** WilliamTwiston-Davies(3) 8 37
(Mick Channon) *hld up in last pair: sme prog on inner jst over 2f out: wknd over 1f out* **33/1**
000- 6 1 ½ **Spring Lady**[183] 7102 3-8-12 **51** JimCrowley 1 34
(Alan Jarvis) *prom: rdn to chse ldr 2f out to over 1f out: wknd quite qckly* **10/1**
60-0 7 1 **Eugenic**[21] 1008 3-9-4 **57** FrederikTylicki 3 37
(Rod Millman) *chsd ldr to 2f out: sn wknd* **4/1**[2]
224 8 hd **Meebo (IRE)**[8] 1223 3-9-2 **60** ShelleyBirkett(5) 6 40
(J R Jenkins) *racd wd: chsd ldng pair: rdn and wknd over 2f out* **8/1**
004 9 15 **Spin For A Harp (IRE)**[14] 1107 3-9-6 **59** FergusSweeney 4 4
(David Dennis) *chsd ldrs: pushed along 1/2-way: wknd qckly over 2f out: t.o* **14/1**
1m 40.19s (0.39) **Going Correction** -0.075s/f (Stan) 9 Ran SP% **116.8**
Speed ratings (Par 96): **95,94,93,90,87 85,84,84,69**
CSF £18.66 CT £58.86 TOTE £5.30: £1.70, £1.60, £1.20; EX 23.80 Trifecta £81.00.
**Owner** Mr & Mrs A J Mutch **Bred** Mrs J L Egan **Trained** Upper Lambourn, Berks
**FOCUS**
A weak 3yo handicap, run at a routine pace. The winner reversed November's C&D form with the runner-up.

## 1385 NEW JUMP FIXTURE 05.05.14 H'CAP 1m (P)
8:30 (8:30) (Class 6) (0-65,63) 4-Y-O+ £1,940 (£577; £288; £144) Stalls Low

Form RPR
310- 1 **Secret Success**[183] 7092 4-9-6 **62** AdamKirby 6 71+
(Paul Cole) *trckd ldng trio: clsd to ld wl over 1f out: sn rdn: pressed after but a holding on* **13/8**[1]
3213 2 ½ **Tijuca (IRE)**[13] 1123 5-8-12 **57** OisinMurphy(3) 2 64
(Ed de Giles) *trckd ldrs in 5th: rdn and prog to chse wnr over 1f out: tried to chal but a hld* **11/2**[2]
2454 3 ½ **Shifting Star (IRE)**[8] 1217 9-9-5 **61** (bt) WilliamCarson 1 67
(John Bridger) *t.k.h: trckd ldng pair: shkn up and nt qckn over 1f out: kpt on fnl f: a hld* **16/1**
050- 4 hd **Keep The Secret**[197] 6734 4-9-7 **63** AndreaAtzeni 11 68+
(William Knight) *s.s: hld up in last: stl there 2f out: prog and shkn up over 1f out: styd on fnl f: nrst fin* **12/1**
130- 5 ¾ **Automotive**[194] 6794 6-9-1 **62** ShelleyBirkett(5) 9 66
(Julia Feilden) *hld up disputing 6th: gng wl enough on inner over 2f out: prog to press for a pl 1f out: nt qckn* **8/1**[3]
3331 6 2 ½ **Divine Rule (IRE)**[12] 1141 6-9-5 **61** (p) LiamJones 4 59
(Laura Mongan) *hld up in last pair: rdn and no prog over 2f out: styd on fr jst over 1f out* **12/1**
-211 7 ¾ **John Potts**[44] 736 9-9-7 **63** JimCrowley 10 59
(Brian Baugh) *hld up in last quartet: pushed along 2f out: shkn up and mod prog over 1f out: nvr on terms* **10/1**
3-30 8 nk **Little Indian**[56] 583 4-9-5 **61** FrederikTylicki 8 57
(J R Jenkins) *chsd ldrs disputing 6th: rdn over 3f out: lost pl and struggling 2f out: nvr on terms after* **12/1**
00-0 9 1 ¼ **Back On The Trail**[14] 1097 4-9-6 **62** (p[1]) RichardKingscote 7 55
(Michael Blake) *chsd ldr: lost pl u.p over 2f out: sn btn* **20/1**
2032 10 nk **Katmai River (IRE)**[13] 1138 7-8-4 **53** CharlotteJenner(7) 5 45
(Mark Usher) *hld up in last quartet: pushed along over 2f out: no prog and btn over 1f out* **10/1**
240- 11 ½ **Shahrazad (IRE)**[169] 7439 5-8-13 **62** (t) JackGilligan(7) 3 53
(Patrick Gilligan) *sn led at fair pce: hdd & wknd wl over 1f out* **14/1**
1m 38.71s (-1.09) **Going Correction** -0.075s/f (Stan) 11 Ran SP% **123.2**
Speed ratings (Par 101): **102,101,101,100,100 97,96,96,95,94 94**
CSF £10.81 CT £115.64 TOTE £2.50: £1.10, £2.70, £4.60; EX 13.10 Trifecta £174.60.
**Owner** P F I Cole Ltd **Bred** Ray Bailey **Trained** Whatcombe, Oxon
**FOCUS**
A moderate handicap, but not bad form for the grade. The winner built on a decent Polytrack profile.
T/Plt: £20.80 to a £1 stake. Pool of £70334.49 - 2463.21 winning tickets. T/Qpdt: £5.50 to a £1 stake. Pool of £8504.17 - 1143.49 winning tickets. JN

# 1296 LINGFIELD (L-H)
Wednesday, April 9

**OFFICIAL GOING: Standard**
Wind: light, across Weather: dry, bright spells

## 1386 LADBROKES H'CAP (DIV I) 1m 1y(P)
2:00 (2:01) (Class 6) (0-55,55) 4-Y-O+ £2,726 (£805; £402) Stalls High

Form RPR
4562 1 **Indian Violet (IRE)**[14] 1105 8-9-5 **53** (p) JimCrowley 10 61
(Zoe Davison) *stdd s: t.k.h: hld up in tch in midfield: rdn and hdwy ent fnl f: chal fnl 100yds: led fnl 50yds: r.o: rdn out* **8/1**
2056 2 nk **Greek Islands (IRE)**[14] 1105 6-9-0 **55** JenniferFerguson(7) 6 62
(Edward Creighton) *in tch in midfield: effrt on inner to chse ldr over 1f out: drvn and ev ch ins fnl f: led wl ins fnl f: hdd and no ex fnl 50yds* **4/1**[2]
3554 3 nk **Claude Monet (BRZ)**[7] 1236 5-8-9 **48** JackDuern(5) 1 55
(Simon Dow) *led: rdn ent fnl 2f: drvn 1f out: kpt on tl hdd and one pce wl ins fnl f* **5/1**[3]
4040 4 2 ¼ **Black Truffle (FR)**[14] 1110 4-8-13 **54** (e) CharlotteJenner(7) 8 55
(Mark Usher) *hld up in tch in last trio: swtchd lft and effrt over 1f out: hdwy to chse ldrs ins fnl f: styd on same pce fnl 100yds* **7/2**[1]
0405 5 ½ **Nifty Kier**[14] 1105 5-9-4 **52** GeorgeBaker 4 52
(Martin Bosley) *broke wl: stdd and chsd ldng pair: wnt 2nd over 2f out tl drvn and unable qck over 1f out: styd on same pce ins fnl f* **7/2**[1]
0406 6 1 ½ **Glennten**[70] 370 5-9-0 **48** RenatoSouza 9 45
(Sean Curran) *chsd ldrs: rdn and unable qck over 1f out: wknd ins fnl f* **20/1**
0000 7 ¾ **Admirals Walk (IRE)**[21] 1015 4-8-10 **47** OisinMurphy(3) 12 42
(Barry Brennan) *hld up in tch in last quartet: swtchd rt and effrt bnd wl over 1f out: styd on: nvr trbld ldrs* **16/1**
-006 8 hd **Querido (GER)**[7] 1236 10-8-7 **46** oh1 (vt) JoeyHaynes(5) 11 41
(Paddy Butler) *s.i.s: hld up in tch in rr: rdn and effrt over 1f out: kpt on ins fnl f: nvr trbld ldrs* **50/1**
5505 9 2 ¼ **Amber Moon**[20] 1036 9-8-7 **46** oh1 AnnStokell(5) 5 35
(Ann Stokell) *chsd ldr tl over 2f out: sn lost pl u.p: wknd over 1f out* **66/1**
0506 10 shd **Idle Curiosity (IRE)**[13] 1123 4-9-4 **52** (b) StephenCraine 7 41
(Jim Boyle) *in tch in midfield: nt clr run over 2f out: rdn and no rspnse ent fnl 2f: dropped to rr and btn over 1f out* **20/1**
-000 11 8 **Cuthbert (IRE)**[35] 851 7-8-12 **46** oh1 (b) RobertHavlin 3 17
(Michael Attwater) *dwlt: a in rr: rdn over 1f out: sn btn and bhd fnl f* **25/1**
1m 37.85s (-0.35) **Going Correction** -0.10s/f (Stan) 11 Ran SP% **114.9**
Speed ratings (Par 101): **97,96,96,94,93 92,91,91,88,88 80**
CSF £36.71 CT £181.56 TOTE £5.40: £2.20, £1.40, £1.80; EX 20.10 Trifecta £99.80.
**Owner** Macable Partnership **Bred** James F Hanly **Trained** Hammerwood, E Sussex
**FOCUS**
A weak handicap but straightforward form.

## 1387 LADBROKES H'CAP (DIV II) 1m 1y(P)
2:30 (2:31) (Class 6) (0-55,55) 4-Y-O+ £2,726 (£805; £402) Stalls High

Form RPR
3246 1 **Olivers Mount**[35] 838 4-9-3 **54** OisinMurphy(3) 2 62
(Ed Vaughan) *sn pushed up to ld: rdn and qcknd ent fnl 2f: forged jst over 1 l clr over 1f out: edgd rt ins fnl f: hld on cl home* **6/4**[1]
06-0 2 nk **Zammy**[14] 1110 5-8-12 **46** oh1 [1] JimCrowley 6 53
(Michael Wigham) *sn pushed up to chse wnr after 1f: rdn and ev ch 2f out: sltly outpcd over 1f out: rallied and carried sltly rt ins fnl f: r.o wl: jst hld* **10/1**
0-25 3 1 ¼ **Vitznau (IRE)**[21] 1009 10-9-2 **50** PatDobbs 3 54
(K F Clutterbuck) *chsd ldrs: effrt u.p over 1f out: chsd ldng pair jst ins fnl f: r.o same pce fnl 100yds* **20/1**
4-02 4 shd **Fair Comment**[12] 1141 4-9-7 **55** LiamKeniry 4 59
(Michael Blanshard) *wl in tch in midfield: rdn to chse ldrs 1f out: styd on same pce wl ins fnl f* **8/1**[3]
05-0 5 1 ½ **K Lightning (IRE)**[43] 741 4-8-9 **50** ow2 GeorgeBuckell(7) 12 50
(Denis Quinn) *stdd and dropped in bhd after s: swtchd rt and hdwy on outer over 1f out: running on whn swtchd lft ins fnl f: gng on wl at fin: nvr trbld ldrs* **33/1**
0244 6 ½ **Strategic Action (IRE)**[34] 858 5-9-0 **48** (t) RobertHavlin 1 47
(Linda Jewell) *led briefly: stdd and chsd ldrs after 1f: rdn and effrt over 1f out: no ex and wknd fnl 100yds* **10/1**
0305 7 ¾ **Chandrayaan**[35] 844 7-8-10 **47** (v) SimonPearce(3) 10 44
(John E Long) *chsd ldrs: rdn and unable qck over 1f out: wknd ins fnl f* **20/1**
41 8 ¾ **Appyjack**[21] 1015 6-9-0 **51** RobertTart(3) 8 47
(Tony Carroll) *hld up in tch in last quartet: edging out rt and effrt bnd wl over 1f out: kpt on ins fnl f: nvr trbld ldrs* **7/2**[2]
6153 9 nk **Fleetwoodsands (IRE)**[8] 1215 7-9-1 **52** DeclanBates(3) 11 47
(David Evans) *taken down early: hld up in tch in midfield: rdn and no hdwy over 1f out: kpt on same pce fnl f* **12/1**
0-00 10 ½ **Pastoral Jet**[34] 852 6-9-5 **53** JamesDoyle 7 47
(Richard Rowe) *in tch towards rr: rdn and no imp over 1f out: styd on same pce fnl f* **16/1**
00-0 11 7 **Baytown Bertie**[14] 1110 5-8-12 **46** oh1 SteveDrowne 5 24
(Lydia Richards) *restless in stalls: in tch towards rr: rdn over 1f out: sn wknd* **66/1**
0000 12 shd **Jackie Love (IRE)**[35] 851 6-8-5 **46** oh1 (b) RhiainIngram(7) 9 24
(Roger Ingram) *stdd and v.s.a: t.k.h: hdwy on outer 5f out: rdn over 3f out: wknd wl over 1f out* **66/1**
1m 38.72s (0.52) **Going Correction** -0.10s/f (Stan) 12 Ran SP% **120.5**
Speed ratings (Par 101): **93,92,91,91,89 89,88,87,87,87 80,79**
CSF £17.27 CT £225.17 TOTE £2.80: £1.20, £4.40, £8.60; EX 17.70 Trifecta £383.00.
**Owner** A M Pickering **Bred** Mrs A D Bourne **Trained** Newmarket, Suffolk
■ Stewards' Enquiry : George Buckell one-day ban: careless riding (Apr 23)
Oisin Murphy three-day ban: careless riding (Apr 23-25)

**FOCUS**
The second division of a weak 1m handicap. Muddling form.

## 1388 COMPARE BOOKMAKERS AT BOOKMAKERS.CO.UK CLASSIFIED CLAIMING STKS 6f 1y(P)
3:00 (3:00) (Class 6) 3-Y-0+ £2,079 (£613; £307) Stalls Low

Form RPR
2041 1 **Drawnfromthepast (IRE)**[14] 1104 9-9-2 67..........(p) FergusSweeney 6 62
(Luke Dace) *chsd ldr tl rdn to ld wl over 1f out: hld on wl u.p fnl 75yds: rdn out* **14/1**
3632 2 ½ **Alnoomaas (IRE)**[21] 1017 5-9-5 67.......................... OisinMurphy(3) 2 66
(Luke Dace) *hld up in tch towards rr: hdwy over 1f out: drvn and pressed wnr fnl 100yds: no ex and hld towards fin* **5/4**[1]
4434 3 ½ **Run It Twice (IRE)**[21] 1021 4-9-4 68..........................(b) LiamKeniry 1 61
(David Evans) *s.i.s: detached in last: rdn over 4f out: hdwy u.p 1f out: r.o wl to go 3rd towards fin: nt rch ldrs* **6/1**
1646 4 ½ **Lujeanie**[46] 714 8-9-3 70..........................................(p) ShaneKelly 4 58
(Peter Crate) *in tch in midfield: edgd out rt and effrt wl over 1f out: drvn 1f out: kpt on same pce ins fnl f* **3/1**[2]
3605 5 *nk* **Hinton Admiral**[4] 1312 10-8-10 51.............................. JoeyHaynes(5) 7 55
(Pat Eddery) *in tch in midfield: rdn and swtchd lft over 1f out: kpt on u.p ins fnl f: nvr gng pce to threaten ldrs* **50/1**
2333 6 ¾ **Haadeeth**[4] 1311 7-8-12 63..........................................(t) DeclanBates(3) 3 53
(David Evans) *chsd ldrs: rdn and effrt on inner over 1f out: no ex jst ins fnl f: wknd towards fin* **9/2**[3]
5-50 7 2 ¼ **Alhaarth Beauty (IRE)**[7] 1238 4-8-10 60..................(be) RyanTate(5) 5 45
(Phil McEntee) *t.k.h: led and crossed to inner: led tl hdd and rdn wl over 1f out: wknd ins fnl f* **66/1**

1m 11.64s (-0.26) **Going Correction** -0.10s/f (Stan) 7 Ran SP% **112.0**
Speed ratings (Par 101): **97,96,95,95,94 93,90**
CSF £30.90 TOTE £9.20: £3.10, £1.80; EX 22.00 Trifecta £138.00.Drawnfromthepast was claimed by E for Walker £6000.
**Owner** Mark Benton **Bred** D And Mrs D Veitch **Trained** Five Oaks, W Sussex

**FOCUS**
A modest claimer and a bunched finish. The fifth finished close enough and the form horses were 10lb+ off.

## 1389 32RED FREE £10 BONUS H'CAP 7f 1y(P)
3:30 (3:30) (Class 5) (0-70,70) 3-Y-0 £3,234 (£962; £481; £240) Stalls Low

Form RPR
220- 1 **Nimble Kimble**[198] 6695 3-9-0 68.............................. RyanTate(5) 6 76
(James Eustace) *chsd ldrs: outpcd whn ldng trio qcknd 3f out: rdn and clsd over 1f out: str chal ins fnl f: led wl ins fnl f: r.o wl: rdn out* **16/1**
0-12 2 ½ **Chantrea (IRE)**[26] 957 3-9-5 68.......................................... JamesDoyle 2 74
(Lady Cecil) *chsd ldrs: ev ch and qcknd clr in ldng trio 3f out: rdn to ld wl over 1f out: hdd and styd on same pce wl ins fnl f* **4/1**[2]
621- 3 1 ¾ **Sahra Al Khadra**[188] 6972 3-9-7 70.................................... PaulHanagan 7 71+
(Charles Hills) *in tch in midfield on outer: outpcd whn ldrs qcknd and pushed along 3f out: widish bnd and plenty to do in 5th wl over 1f out: rallied and styd on wl ins fnl f: no threat to ldng pair* **5/4**[1]
44-3 4 1 ¼ **Iseemist (IRE)**[26] 957 3-9-2 68.................... MichaelJMMurphy(3) 11 66
(John Gallagher) *chsd ldr and sn crossed to inner: wnt clr in ldng trio and ev ch u.p 2f out: no ex and wknd ins fnl f* **20/1**
3-35 5 2 ¼ **Penny's Boy**[13] 1122 3-9-2 70..............................(t) JoshBaudains(5) 5 62
(Sylvester Kirk) *in tch in midfield: outpcd whn ldrs qcknd 3f out: 6th and plenty to do 2f out: kpt on but no threat to ldrs fnl f* **8/1**
0-34 6 ½ **Sherston**[12] 1149 3-9-5 68.............................................. AdrianNicholls 9 59
(Mark Johnston) *led and crossed to inner: wnt clr w 2 rivals 3f out: drvn and hdd wl over 1f out: fdd ins fnl f* **16/1**
16-4 7 3 **Autopilot**[37] 823 3-9-5 68................................................ GeorgeBaker 3 51
(Anabel K Murphy) *hld up in rr: outpcd 3f out: wl bhd and effrt 2f out: sme hdwy over 1f out: nvr trbld ldrs* **14/1**
404- 8 1 ¼ **Double Czech (IRE)**[209] 6322 3-9-2 68.................. OisinMurphy(3) 1 47
(Patrick Chamings) *in tch in midfield: outpcd 3f out: 7th and wl hld u.p 2f out: wknd fnl f* **5/1**[3]
300- 9 4 **Kinloss**[149] 7837 3-8-11 67.......................................... CamHardie(7) 10 35
(Richard Hannon) *in tch in last: struggling whn pce qcknd and rdn 3f out: bhd fnl 2f* **33/1**
00-6 10 ½ **Dylan's Centenary**[18] 1069 3-9-4 67.............................. FrederikTylicki 4 34
(Rod Millman) *in tch in midfield: outpcd 3f out and sn nudged along: bhd fnl 2f* **20/1**
4353 11 *nk* **Rosie Prospects**[14] 1106 3-8-0 56 oh1...................... RhiainIngram(7) 8 22
(Roger Ingram) *wd: hld up in last quartet: rdn and outpcd 3f out: n.d after* **66/1**

1m 24.51s (-0.29) **Going Correction** -0.10s/f (Stan) 11 Ran SP% **124.6**
Speed ratings (Par 98): **97,96,94,93,90 89,86,85,80,79 79**
CSF £80.94 CT £147.56 TOTE £17.40: £4.90, £1.80, £1.10; EX 135.10 Trifecta £430.00.
**Owner** Ian Rushby **Bred** Stowell Hill Ltd **Trained** Newmarket, Suffolk

**FOCUS**
A modest 3yo handicap but the first three hadn't had many chances. The winner is rated up a length or so.

## 1390 32RED TOMB RAIDER SLOT H'CAP (BOBIS RACE) 7f 1y(P)
4:00 (4:02) (Class 4) (0-85,82) 3-Y-0 £5,175 (£1,540; £769; £384) Stalls Low

Form RPR
1- 1 **Glorious Empire (IRE)**[133] 8061 3-9-2 77......................... GeorgeBaker 5 89
(Ed Walker) *t.k.h: chsd ldr: rdn and ev ch wl over 1f out: led ent fnl f: styd on wl and asserted fnl 100yds* **5/4**[1]
411- 2 1 ¾ **Outback Traveller (IRE)**[175] 7300 3-9-5 80..................... JamesDoyle 2 87
(Jeremy Noseda) *in tch in midfield: chsd ldrs 3f out: rdn and ev ch wl over 1f out: no ex and outpcd fnl 100yds* **9/2**[3]
134- 3 2 **Black Caesar (IRE)**[151] 7819 3-9-5 80.............................. PatDobbs 7 82
(Richard Hannon) *led: drvn and hrd pressed wl over 1f out: hdd ent fnl f: 3rd and outpcd fnl 150yds* **16/1**
2133 4 3 ¼ **Basil Berry**[21] 1013 3-8-12 76.................................... RobertTart(3) 3 69
(Chris Dwyer) *hld up in tch in last pair: rdn and effrt towards inner over 1f out: 4th and no imp 1f out: wknd ins fnl f* **12/1**
232- 5 1 ½ **Ice Slice (IRE)**[197] 6731 3-8-9 75.............................. RyanTate(5) 1 64
(James Eustace) *in tch in midfield: rdn and effrt on inner wl over 1f out: 5th and btn ent fnl f: sn wknd* **25/1**
51- 6 1 ¼ **Grandest**[111] 8346 3-9-7 82........................................(p) RobertHavlin 4 68
(John Gosden) *hld up in tch in midfield: rdn and outpcd ent fnl f: drvn and wl btn 6th over 1f out: wknd* **7/2**[2]
66-4 7 ¾ **Dovil's Duel (IRE)**[13] 1122 3-8-11 72.............................. DavidProbert 8 56
(Rod Millman) *stdd and dropped in bhd after s: hld up in rr: rdn 4f out: hung rt and struggling bnd 2f out: sn wknd* **25/1**
140- P **Rizal Park (IRE)**[249] 4988 3-8-13 77........................... OisinMurphy(3) 6
(Andrew Balding) *chsd ldrs tl rdn and dropped out rapidly over 3f out: t.o whn eased and p.u 2f out: burst blood vessel* **6/1**

1m 23.21s (-1.59) **Going Correction** -0.10s/f (Stan) 8 Ran SP% **120.4**
Speed ratings (Par 100): **105,103,100,97,95 93,93,**
CSF £7.76 CT £61.07 TOTE £2.40: £1.10, £1.10, £6.00; EX 10.50 Trifecta £114.00.
**Owner** Ms Judy Yap & Ms Salina Yang **Bred** Patrick Grogan **Trained** Newmarket, Suffolk

**FOCUS**
An interesting 3yo handicap run in a relatively good time. The first two were unexposed and improved again.

## 1391 32RED ON THE APP STORE MAIDEN STKS 1m 4f (P)
4:30 (4:30) (Class 5) 3-Y-0 £2,726 (£805; £402) Stalls Low

Form RPR
3- 1 **Morning Watch (IRE)**[147] 7854 3-9-5 0.............................. JamesDoyle 4 81+
(Lady Cecil) *in tch in midfield: trcking ldrs and n.m.r over 2f out: rdn and effrt to chse ldr over 1f out: qcknd u.p to ld ins fnl f: pushed out towards fin* **6/1**[3]
44- 2 1 ¼ **Belrog**[149] 7834 3-9-5 0................................................ HarryBentley 2 79
(Ralph Beckett) *chsd ldrs tl lft in ld 9f out: hdd 8f out: chsd ldr tl swtchd rt and led again wl over 2f out: rdn over 1f out: hdd and one pce ins fnl f* **6/4**[1]
3 ½ **Saarrem (USA)** 3-9-5 0................................................ PaulHanagan 7 78+
(John Gosden) *rn green: wnt rt s and slowly: steadily rcvrd: clsd and wl in tch 1/2-way: rdn and effrt wl over 1f out: wnt 3rd 1f out: kpt on wl* **11/4**[2]
0- 4 8 **Tactical Strike**[162] 7607 3-9-5 0...................................(t) SebSanders 6 65
(Hugo Palmer) *awkward leaving stalls and slowly away: sn rcvrd and in tch in midfield: rdn and effrt to chal wl over 2f out: btn over 1f out: wknd fnl f* **8/1**
525- 5 1 **Mambo Rhythm**[154] 7774 3-9-0 69.................................... LiamJones 5 59
(Mark Johnston) *led tl hung bdly rt at paddock bnd 9f out and hdd: rcvrd to chse ldrs but stuck wd 8f out: drvn and ev ch wl over 2f out tl 2f out: wknd over 1f out* **8/1**
6423 6 *nse* **Trafalgar Rock**[21] 1011 3-9-2 70...................... MichaelJMMurphy(3) 3 64
(Mark Johnston) *chsd ldr tl carried rt and lost pl 9f out: in tch in midfield after: rdn 4f out: wknd wl over 1f out* **20/1**
2-2 7 8 **Passionate Affair (IRE)**[12] 1153 3-9-5 0.................(tp) StephenCraine 8 51
(Tom Dascombe) *in tch in midfield: swtchd lft and lft chsng ldr 9f out: led 8f out tl wl over 2f out: wknd 2f out* **14/1**
8 36 **Oakbank (USA)** 3-8-12 0.............................................. DavidParkes(7) 1
(Brett Johnson) *s.i.s: a bhd: lost tch 1/2-way: sn t.o* **66/1**

2m 31.09s (-1.91) **Going Correction** -0.10s/f (Stan) 8 Ran SP% **116.1**
Speed ratings (Par 98): **102,101,100,95,94 94,89,65**
CSF £15.70 TOTE £7.30: £2.10, £1.40, £1.10; EX 15.70 Trifecta £55.60.
**Owner** De La Warr Racing **Bred** Mrs J Norris **Trained** Newmarket, Suffolk

**FOCUS**
The principals dominated this fair 3yo maiden. Improvement from the winner.

## 1392 32RED IMMORTAL ROMANCE SLOT FILLIES' H'CAP 1m 1y(P)
5:00 (5:00) (Class 5) (0-75,75) 4-Y-0+ £3,234 (£962; £481; £240) Stalls High

Form RPR
1- 1 **Grasped**[126] 8154 4-9-4 72.............................................. JamesDoyle 5 79+
(Lady Cecil) *chsd ldng pair tl wnt 2nd wl over 1f out: pressing ldr but no immediate rspnse whn rdn 2f out: drvn 1f out: styd on fnl f 100yds to ld cl home* **1/3**[1]
-451 2 *nk* **Serenity Spa**[26] 952 4-9-2 73.................................. OisinMurphy(3) 1 79
(Tony Carroll) *t.k.h: led: rdn over 1f out: hrd pressed and edgd lft u.p fnl 100yds: hdd and no ex cl home* **5/1**[2]
205- 3 *hd* **Starlight Symphony (IRE)**[184] 7075 4-9-7 75...............(b) JohnFahy 4 81+
(Eve Johnson Houghton) *hld up in tch in last pair: rdn and effrt u.p on inner ent fnl f: ev ch wl ins fnl f: kpt on* **12/1**[3]
2423 4 1 ¼ **Skidby Mill (IRE)**[19] 1040 4-8-7 61.................................. LiamJones 2 66+
(Laura Mongan) *stdd s: t.k.h: hld up in tch in last pair: clsd to trck ldrs and nt clr run over 1f out: swtchd lft 1f out: pressing ldrs and keeping on whn short of room and hmpd wl ins fnl f: no hdwy after* **12/1**[3]
23-3 5 1 ½ **Princess Spirit**[7] 1230 5-8-7 61 oh2..........................(p) SamHitchcott 3 62+
(Edward Creighton) *chsd ldr tl wl over 2f out: 3rd and rdn ent fnl 2f: keeping on same pce whn short of room and hmpd wl ins fnl f* **20/1**

1m 37.37s (-0.83) **Going Correction** -0.10s/f (Stan) 5 Ran SP% **111.8**
Speed ratings (Par 100): **100,99,99,98,96**
CSF £2.53 TOTE £1.30: £1.10, £2.10; EX 2.40 Trifecta £9.30.
**Owner** K Abdullah **Bred** Juddmonte Farms Ltd **Trained** Newmarket, Suffolk
■ Stewards' Enquiry : Oisin Murphy one-day ban: careless riding (Apr 26)

**FOCUS**
A steadily run, muddling fillies' handicap. The winner again looked better than the bare form.

## 1393 32RED.COM FILLIES' H'CAP 1m 2f (P)
5:35 (5:35) (Class 5) (0-75,75) 4-Y-0+ £3,408 (£1,006; £503) Stalls Low

Form RPR
300- 1 **Tilstarr (IRE)**[166] 7505 4-8-13 70.............................. OisinMurphy(3) 1 79
(Roger Teal) *hld up in tch in rr: nt clr run ent fnl 2f: gap opened and hdwy over 1f out: str chal fnl 100yds: r.o wl to ld nr fin* **4/1**[2]
-331 2 *nk* **Havelovewilltravel (IRE)**[21] 1022 4-9-7 75...............(p) JamesDoyle 4 83
(Jeremy Noseda) *chsd ldr tl led over 2f out: rdn and edgd lft u.p fr over 1f out: hrd pressed fnl 100yds: kpt on tl hdd and no ex nr fin* **4/7**[1]
530- 3 2 ¾ **Happy Families**[132] 8089 4-8-4 63.................................. RyanTate(5) 3 66
(Heather Main) *chsd ldrs: rdn over 2f out: chsd wnr over 1f out tl 1f out: 3rd and outpcd ins fnl f* **10/1**
332- 4 4 ½ **Kingston Eucalypt**[118] 8260 4-9-5 73.............................. LiamKeniry 2 67
(David Elsworth) *in tch in last pair: rdn over 3f out: drvn and no hdwy over 1f out: wknd fnl f* **8/1**[3]
0313 5 5 **Queen Aggie (IRE)**[26] 952 4-9-0 71.......................... DeclanBates(3) 5 55
(David Evans) *sn pushed up to ld: hdd and rdn over 2f out: btn over 1f out: fdd fnl f* **10/1**

2m 4.03s (-2.57) **Going Correction** -0.10s/f (Stan) 5 Ran SP% **112.9**
Speed ratings (Par 100): **106,105,103,99,95**
CSF £6.99 TOTE £10.70: £2.60, £1.10; EX 10.60 Trifecta £37.80.
**Owner** Homecroft Wealth Racing **Bred** Ronnie Boland **Trained** Ashtead, Surrey

**FOCUS**
A modest fillies' handicap, rated around the runner-up.
T/Plt: £17.10 to a £1 stake. Pool of £66966.26 - 2847.44 winning tickets. T/Qpdt: £3.30 to a £1 stake. Pool of £5276.27 - 1155.40 winning tickets. SP



The Form Book, Raceform Ltd, Newbury, RG14 5SJ

# NOTTINGHAM (L-H)

Wednesday, April 9

**OFFICIAL GOING: Soft (good to soft in places; 6.6)**

Wind: Light half against Weather: Cloudy with sunny periods

## 1394 TOTEJACKPOT GO FOR THE BIG ONE MAIDEN STKS (DIV I) 1m 75y

2:10 (2:12) (Class 5) 3-Y-O £3,881 (£1,155; £577; £288) Stalls Centre

Form RPR

1 **Sacred Act** 3-9-5 0 WilliamBuick 9 96+
(John Gosden) *hld up in rr: tk clsr order 3f out: swtchd rt and green 2f out: sn chsng ldrs: shkn up over 1f out: str run ent fnl f to ld last 50yds* **10/1[2]**

4- 2 1 3/4 **Fast Delivery**[209] 6330 3-9-5 0 SilvestreDeSousa 1 90
(Saeed bin Suroor) *dwlt sltly: t.k.h and sn cl up: led over 2f out: rdn clr over 1f out: hdd and no ex last 50yds* **13/8[1]**

2- 3 3/4 **Art Of War (IRE)**[214] 6184 3-9-5 0 RichardKingscote 2 88
(Tom Dascombe) *dwlt sltly: sn trcking ldrs: hdwy over 3f out: rdn 2f out and sn one pce* **13/8[1]**

4 1 1/2 **Slemy (IRE)** 3-9-5 0 FrankieDettori 10 85
(Richard Hannon) *sn led: pushed along over 3f out: hdd over 2f out: sn rdn and kpt on same pce* **14/1**

54- 5 4 **Courageous Rock (USA)**[169] 7442 3-9-5 0 JimmyFortune 8 75
(Ed Vaughan) *trckd ldrs: effrt over 3f out: rdn along wl over 2f out: sn one pce* **12/1[3]**

0- 6 2 **Light Of Asia (IRE)**[133] 8066 3-9-5 0 PaddyAspell 4 71
(Ed Dunlop) *a towards rr* **25/1**

3- 7 1 1/4 **She's Gorgeous (IRE)**[169] 7450 3-9-0 0 HayleyTurner 6 63
(James Fanshawe) *trckd ldrs: effrt on inner over 3f out: pushed along wl over 2f out: grad wknd* **10/1[2]**

8 3 3/4 **Tzharr (IRE)** 3-9-5 0 AntonioFresu 5 59
(Marco Botti) *dwlt: a towards rr* **50/1**

00- 9 9 **Bourbon Prince**[154] 7774 3-9-5 0 JamieSpencer 3 39
(Michael Bell) *chsd ldrs: rdn along wl over 3f out: wknd over 2f out* **50/1**

1m 50.09s (1.09) **Going Correction** -0.025s/f (Good) 9 Ran SP% **116.5**

Speed ratings (Par 98): **93,91,90,89,85 83,81,78,69**

CSF £26.71 TOTE £15.20: £2.80, £1.10, £1.50; EX 39.00 Trifecta £105.80.

**Owner** Lady Bamford **Bred** Lady Bamford **Trained** Newmarket, Suffolk

**FOCUS**

Inner track used. It was dry overnight and the going was soft, good to soft in places (GoignStick 6.6). Frankie Dettori and Silvestre de Sousa described it as sticky and holding. This had the look of a pretty good maiden, and while there wasn't much pace on early, it picked up in the straight and the final time was much quicker than the second division. The winner looks sure to improve.

## 1395 TOTEJACKPOT GO FOR THE BIG ONE MAIDEN STKS (DIV II) 1m 75y

2:40 (2:41) (Class 5) 3-Y-O £3,881 (£1,155; £577; £288) Stalls Centre

Form RPR

40- 1 **Gm Hopkins**[305] 3112 3-9-5 0 WilliamBuick 2 77+
(John Gosden) *t.k.h early: trckd ldng pair on inner: smooth hdwy 3f out: cl up wl over 1f out: rdn to ld ent fnl f: kpt on strly* **11/4[2]**

- 2 2 **Lacan (IRE)** 3-9-5 0 FrankieDettori 8 72
(Clive Cox) *set stdy pce: qcknd 3f out: jnd and rdn over 1f out: hdd ent fnl f: kpt on same pce* **10/1**

02- 3 nk **Roseburg (IRE)**[249] 4977 3-9-5 0 AndreaAtzeni 4 71+
(Luca Cumani) *t.k.h early: trckd ldng pair: effrt over 2f out: rdn and ev ch over 1f out: one pce fnl f* **6/4[1]**

32- 4 1 1/4 **Spirit Or Soul (FR)**[112] 8328 3-9-5 0 LukeMorris 3 68
(Marco Botti) *in tch: hdwy over 2f out: sn rdn and edgd lft over 1f out: kpt on one pce fnl f* **10/1**

60- 5 2 **Kashmiri Sunset**[154] 7773 3-9-5 0 DaneO'Neill 6 64
(Ed de Giles) *dwlt and in rr: hdwy on outer wl over 2f out: sn rdn and styd on wl fnl f: nrst fin* **50/1**

0- 6 hd **Stampede (IRE)**[222] 5957 3-9-5 0 RyanMoore 10 63
(Sir Michael Stoute) *hld up: hdwy over 3f out: chsd ldrs over 2f out: rdn wl over 1f out: sn no imp* **7/2[3]**

0- 7 nk **Buckland Beau**[301] 3211 3-9-5 0 HayleyTurner 9 62
(Charlie Fellowes) *cl up: rdn along wl over 2f out: wknd wl over 1f out* **40/1**

00- 8 6 **Rock Of Leon**[154] 7773 3-9-5 0 MartinLane 1 49
(Michael Bell) *in tch: rdn along 3f out: sn wknd* **50/1**

9 1 3/4 **Distant Shadow** 3-9-0 0 TedDurcan 5 40
(Chris Wall) *midfield: pushed along bef 1/2-way: sn towards rr* **50/1**

0 10 shd **Sound Of Life (IRE)**[49] 660 3-9-0 0 ChrisCatlin 7 39
(Rae Guest) *dwlt: a in rr* **80/1**

1m 53.27s (4.27) **Going Correction** -0.025s/f (Good) 10 Ran SP% **116.6**

Speed ratings (Par 98): **77,75,74,73,71 71,70,64,63,63**

CSF £28.99 TOTE £4.10: £1.40, £3.70, £1.10; EX 24.20 Trifecta £63.60.

**Owner** R J H Geffen **Bred** Cadran-Earl Blot-Scea Des Bissons **Trained** Newmarket, Suffolk

**FOCUS**

The pace held up here and it was the slower of the two divisions by 3.18sec. More doubts over the form than the first division, but the winner and third have been rated close to their 2yo levels.

## 1396 TOTEPLACEPOT RACING'S FAVOURITE BET H'CAP (BOBIS RACE) 5f 13y

3:10 (3:10) (Class 4) (0-80,80) 3-Y-O £5,175 (£1,540; £769; £384) Stalls High

Form RPR

031- 1 **Signore Piccolo**[183] 7094 3-8-7 69 JasonHart(3) 9 87+
(Eric Alston) *racd towards stands' rail: sn led: rdn clr over 1f out: hung lft ins fnl f: kpt on: readily* **6/1[2]**

012- 2 2 1/4 **Piazon**[299] 3267 3-9-2 75 WilliamBuick 6 83
(Michael Bell) *s.i.s and awkward s: in rr tl hdwy wl over 1f out: rdn and styd on wl fnl f* **8/1[3]**

150- 3 nse **One Boy (IRE)**[186] 7026 3-8-10 74 ConnorBeasley(5) 7 82
(Michael Dods) *in rr: effrt 2f out: sn rdn and styd on fnl f* **8/1[3]**

160- 4 3/4 **Skye's The Limit**[173] 7333 3-8-13 72 TonyHamilton 13 77
(Richard Fahey) *dwlt: sn trcking ldrs nr stands' rail: hdwy 2f out: rdn to chse wnr over 1f out: drvn and one pce fnl f* **16/1**

5-11 5 3 1/4 **Scarborough (IRE)**[7] 1246 3-8-3 69 6ex AlistairRawlinson(7) 3 62
(Michael Appleby) *prom centre: effrt and cl up 2f out: sn rdn and hung lft over 1f out: wknd ent fnl f* **5/1[1]**

0-21 6 hd **Proclamationofwar**[13] 1137 3-8-9 73 ShaneGray(5) 12 66
(Kevin Ryan) *racd towards stands' rail: trckd wnr: rdn along wl over 1f out: drvn and wknd appr fnl f* **10/1**

101- 7 1/2 **Flying Bear (IRE)**[214] 6187 3-9-5 78 RyanMoore 4 69
(Jeremy Gask) *wnt lft s: towards rr: rdn along 2f out: swtchd towards stands' rail wl over 1f out: sme late hdwy* **6/1[2]**

411- 8 1 1/4 **Touch The Clouds**[103] 8405 3-9-2 80 LouisSteward(5) 2 66
(William Stone) *midfield: rdn along 1/2-way: n.d* **25/1**

154- 9 nk **Tinsill**[182] 7127 3-8-4 68 (v) ShelleyBirkett(5) 11 53
(Nigel Tinkler) *racd towards stands' rail: prom: rdn along over 2f out: sn wknd* **33/1**

021- 10 4 1/2 **Nova Champ (IRE)**[125] 8165 3-8-13 72 JamieSpencer 8 41
(Stuart Williams) *racd centre: prom: rdn along over 2f out: sn wknd* **5/1[1]**

100- 11 3/4 **De Repente (IRE)**[182] 7127 3-8-12 71 SilvestreDeSousa 1 37
(Paul Green) *racd centre: cl up on wd outside: rdn along 1/2-way: sn wknd* **8/1[3]**

1m 1.88s (0.38) **Going Correction** +0.10s/f (Good) 11 Ran SP% **117.0**

Speed ratings (Par 100): **100,96,96,95,89 89,88,86,86,79 77**

CSF £53.13 CT £389.11 TOTE £6.80: £2.00, £2.70, £4.30; EX 74.10 Trifecta £621.60.

**Owner** Lancashire Lads Partnership **Bred** Capt J H Wilson **Trained** Longton, Lancs

**FOCUS**

This is a quick 5f and it often pays to be up there. The winner impressed and could improve again, and the form is rated around the placed horses.

## 1397 TOTEPOOL LOLA FAULKNER CONDITIONS STKS 5f 13y

3:40 (3:41) (Class 3) 3-Y-O+ £7,470 (£2,236; £1,118; £559; £279) Stalls High

Form RPR

0/3- 1 **Pearl Secret**[295] 3420 5-9-1 110 JamieSpencer 3 112
(David Barron) *stdd s: t.k.h and hld up in rr: hdwy 1/2-way: trckd ldrs and nt clr run 2f out: sn swtchd lft to outer: shkn up and qcknd to ld jst ins fnl f: edgd rt: readily* **30/100[1]**

350- 2 2 3/4 **Graphic Guest**[313] 2843 4-8-10 92 SilvestreDeSousa 4 97
(Robert Cowell) *trckd ldng pair: hdwy 2f out: rdn to ld wl over 1f out: drvn and hdd jst ins fnl f: kpt on same pce* **8/1[2]**

600- 3 2 **Doc Hay (USA)**[165] 7527 7-9-1 102 DanielTudhope 5 95
(David O'Meara) *trckd ldrs: hdwy over 2f out: rdn over 1f out: kpt on same pce* **14/1**

20-0 4 3 3/4 **Inxile (IRE)**[11] 1163 9-9-1 99 (p) KierenFallon 6 81
(David Nicholls) *chsd ldr: cl up 1/2-way: rdn along 2f out: sn edgd lft and wknd over 1f out* **20/1**

215- 5 9 **Fine 'n Dandy (IRE)**[278] 4025 3-8-7 96 RichardKingscote 2 47
(Tom Dascombe) *led: jnd 1/2-way and sn rdn along: hdd wl over 1f out: sn wknd* **10/1[3]**

1m 1.48s (-0.02) **Going Correction** +0.10s/f (Good)

**WFA** 3 from 4yo+ 11lb 5 Ran SP% **108.6**

Speed ratings (Par 107): **104,99,96,90,76**

CSF £3.17 TOTE £1.20: £1.10, £2.30; EX 3.70 Trifecta £13.80.

**Owner** Qatar Racing Limited **Bred** Whitsbury Manor Stud & Pigeon House Stud **Trained** Maunby, N Yorks

**FOCUS**

Pearl Secret looked as good as ever and there's every chance of more to come.

## 1398 TOTEPOOL EBF STALLIONS BARRY HILLS FURTHER FLIGHT STKS (LISTED RACE) 1m 6f 15y

4:10 (4:10) (Class 1) 4-Y-O+

£22,684 (£8,600; £4,304; £2,144; £1,076; £540) Stalls Low

Form RPR

0/1- 1 **Flying Officer (USA)**[283] 3862 4-8-12 100 WilliamBuick 7 105+
(John Gosden) *trckd ldrs: hdwy 4f out: cl up 3f out: rdn to chal wl over 1f out: drvn and styd on to ld ins fnl f: kpt on gamely* **11/4[1]**

200- 2 1/2 **Earth Amber**[76] 7193 5-8-10 92 KierenFallon 10 99
(Nicky Henderson) *prom: trckd ldr fr 1/2-way: cl up over 4f out: led over 3f out: rdn over 2f out: jnd and drvn over 1f out: hdd ins fnl f: no ex towards fin* **14/1**

250- 3 3 3/4 **High Jinx (IRE)**[172] 7363 6-9-1 110 RyanMoore 5 99
(James Fanshawe) *led: rdn along and hdd over 3f out: sn outpcd: rallied u.p over 1f out: styng on whn hmpd on inner ent fnl f: kpt on same pce after* **11/4[1]**

266- 4 1 1/2 **Continuum**[180] 7174 5-9-1 94 DaneO'Neill 4 98
(Peter Hedger) *hld up in rr: hdwy 4f out: rdn to chse ldrs over 2f out: drvn and no imp appr fnl f* **25/1**

364- 5 shd **Repeater**[186] 7012 5-9-1 107 DanielTudhope 2 97
(David O'Meara) *hld up towards rr: smooth hdwy 5f out: trckd ldrs on bit 4f out: effrt and cl up 3f out: sn shkn up and btn 2f out* **10/1**

23-6 6 2 3/4 **Gabrial's King (IRE)**[89] 125 5-9-1 87 SilvestreDeSousa 1 94
(David Simcock) *chsd ldrs: effrt over 3f out: rdn along over 2f out: drvn and wkng whn hung lft ent fnl f* **66/1**

1/1- 7 1 1/2 **Mighty Yar (IRE)**[266] 4416 4-8-12 88 JamieSpencer 9 92
(Lady Cecil) *hld up towards rr: pushed along over 6f out: hdwy on outer over 4f out: chsd ldrs on outer over 3f out: rdn wl over 2f out: sn drvn and outpcd* **9/2[3]**

046- 8 14 **Biographer**[172] 7363 5-9-1 110 (p) TedDurcan 3 82
(David Lanigan) *prom: trckd ldr after 2f: effrt over 3f out: rdn over 2f out: sn drvn and wknd: bhd and eased over 1f out* **7/2[2]**

3m 9.0s (2.00) **Going Correction** -0.025s/f (Good)

**WFA** 4 from 5yo+ 3lb 8 Ran SP% **114.8**

Speed ratings (Par 111): **93,92,90,89,89 88,87,79**

CSF £42.87 TOTE £3.60: £1.10, £5.30, £1.60; EX 50.10 Trifecta £200.00.

**Owner** George Strawbridge **Bred** George Strawbridge Jr **Trained** Newmarket, Suffolk

## 1399 TOTETRIFECTA AVAILABLE ON ALL RACES H'CAP 1m 75y

4:40 (4:41) (Class 3) (0-95,95) 4-Y-O+ £7,762 (£2,310; £1,154; £577) Stalls Centre

Form RPR

0003 1 **Robert The Painter (IRE)**[11] 1165 6-9-7 95 DanielTudhope 1 104
(David O'Meara) *trckd ldng pair: hdwy to ld over 3f out: rdn along 2f out: drvn over 1f out: styd on gamely towards fin* **11/4[1]**

505- 2 1/2 **Roserrow**[118] 8263 5-9-2 90 JimmyFortune 7 98
(Andrew Balding) *hld up in tch: hdwy on outer over 3f out: cl up over 2f out: rdn to chal wl over 1f out: drvn and ev ch ins fnl f: edgd lft and no ex towards fin* **3/1[2]**

00-5 3 1 1/2 **Lord Aeryn (IRE)**[17] 1078 7-8-9 83 TonyHamilton 4 87
(Richard Fahey) *hld up towards rr: hdwy 4f out: cl up over 2f out: rdn wl over 1f out and ev ch tl drvn: edgd lft and one pce ins fnl f* **9/2[3]**

633- 4 2 **Woody Bay**[138] 8007 4-8-2 76 LukeMorris 5 76
(James Given) *hld up in rr: pushed along over 3f out: rdn wl over 2f out: styd on fnl f: nrst fin* **14/1**

351- **5** *nk* **Multi Bene**[216] 6126 5-9-2 **90** ........ GrahamGibbons 2 89
(Ed McMahon) *hld up in tch: hdwy over 4f out: chal over 2f out: sn rdn and ev ch: drvn and hld whn n.m.r and hmpd ins fnl f* **5/1**

112- **6** *16* **Croquembouche (IRE)**[195] 6772 5-9-0 **88** ........ ChrisCatlin 8 50
(Ed de Giles) *sn led: hdd after 2f and cl up tl rdn along over 3f out and sn wknd* **8/1**

**7** *nk* **Malicho**[214] 5-8-10 **84** ........ JamieSpencer 6 46
(Dean Ivory) *cl up: slt ld after 2f: rdn along and hdd over 3f out: sn wknd* **18/1**

1m 47.02s (-1.98) **Going Correction** -0.025s/f (Good) **7 Ran SP% 109.6**
Speed ratings (Par 107): **108,107,106,104,103 87,87**
CSF £10.23 CT £30.87 TOTE £2.90: £1.60, £2.20; EX 12.50 Trifecta £32.70.
**Owner** Stephen Humphreys **Bred** Ballylinch Stud **Trained** Nawton, N Yorks

**FOCUS**
They went a contested pace in this decent handicap, in which the winner is the best guide to the form.

## 1400 BEST ODDS GUARANTEED AT TOTEPOOL.COM H'CAP 1m 75y
**5:10** (5:14) (Class 5) (0-75,75) 3-Y-O **£2,726** (£805; £402) **Stalls** Centre

Form RPR

0-21 **1** **Secret Pursuit (IRE)**[74] 341 3-9-0 **68** ........ HayleyTurner 7 84+
(Marcus Tregoning) *in tch: smooth hdwy over 4f out: chsd clr ldr over 2f out: led wl over 1f out: sn clr: readily* **5/1**[3]

1536 **2** *5* **Boogangoo (IRE)**[13] 1135 3-9-5 **73** ........ StevieDonohoe 8 76
(Grace Harris) *dwlt and bhd: hdwy over 3f out: swtchd rt and rdn over 2f out: str run on outer fr over 1f out: tk 2nd nr fin: no ch w wnr* **25/1**

31-2 **3** *nk* **Shimba Hills**[13] 1135 3-9-2 **73** ........ CharlesBishop(3) 2 75+
(Mick Channon) *cl up: led after 2f: pushed clr 4f out: rdn over 2f out: hdd wl over 1f out: wknd fnl f: lost 2nd nr fin* **3/1**[1]

512- **4** *2¼* **Tyrsal (IRE)**[128] 8133 3-8-11 **65** ........ JimmyQuinn 6 62
(Robert Eddery) *chsd ldrs: rdn along 3f out: drvn 2f out: sn one pce* **25/1**

024- **5** *4½* **Alexanor (IRE)**[137] 8026 3-9-0 **73** ........(b[1]) DanielMuscutt(5) 10 60
(Marco Botti) *in tch: hdwy to chse ldrs over 3f out: rdn along 2f out: sn one pce* **8/1**

410- **6** *3¾* **Golden Spear**[184] 7062 3-9-7 **75** ........(p) PaddyAspell 9 53
(Noel Quinlan) *hld up towards rr: sme hdwy on inner 3f out: rdn wl over 1f out: n.d* **20/1**

605- **7** *1¼* **Gannicus**[168] 7467 3-9-1 **69** ........(t) KierenFallon 5 44
(Brendan Powell) *nvr bttr than midfield* **16/1**

0-03 **8** *1* **Sweet Alibi (IRE)**[84] 190 3-8-10 **64** ........ LukeMorris 3 37
(J S Moore) *chsd ldrs: rdn along 3f out: sn wknd* **33/1**

062- **9** *2¼* **Master Dan**[116] 8297 3-8-7 **66** ........ ConnorBeasley(5) 12 34
(James Given) *a towards rr* **10/1**

232- **10** *5* **Miss Brazil (IRE)**[155] 7737 3-9-3 **71** ........ RyanMoore 13 27
(Richard Hannon) *dwlt: a in rr* **9/2**[2]

003- **11** *10* **Miss Sophisticated**[211] 6271 3-8-12 **66** ........ GrahamGibbons 4
(David Barron) *prom: chsd ldng pair after 2f: rdn along over 3f out: sn wknd* **10/1**

330- **12** *2¾* **Miaplacidus (IRE)**[221] 6002 3-9-0 **68** ........ TonyHamilton 11
(Richard Fahey) *a in rr* **16/1**

231- **13** *¾* **Hickster (IRE)**[188] 6983 3-8-11 **70** ........ PhilipPrince(5) 1
(Roy Bowring) *led 2f: cl up: rdn along over 3f out: sn wknd* **20/1**

1m 47.37s (-1.63) **Going Correction** -0.025s/f (Good) **13 Ran SP% 121.1**
Speed ratings (Par 98): **107,102,101,99,94 91,89,88,86,81 71,68,68**
CSF £133.31 CT £459.71 TOTE £6.70: £2.70, £7.10, £1.30; EX 113.20 Trifecta £355.70.
**Owner** Guy Brook **Bred** Petra Bloodstock Agency Ltd **Trained** Whitsbury, Hants

**FOCUS**
There was a good gallop on here and the race was taken apart by the winner in the best relative time of the four C&D races. A step up from the impressive winner.

## 1401 TEN TO FOLLOW OPENS APRIL 19TH H'CAP 1m 2f 50y
**5:40** (5:44) (Class 5) (0-70,70) 3-Y-O **£2,587** (£770; £384; £192) **Stalls** Low

Form RPR

4-24 **1** **Old Town Boy**[54] 607 3-9-7 **70** ........ SilvestreDeSousa 12 81
(Philip McBride) *prom: cl up 1/2-way: led wl over 2f out: sn rdn clr: kpt on fnl f* **16/1**

326- **2** *2¾* **Ultimate Act**[173] 7332 3-9-6 **69** ........ JamieSpencer 7 78+
(Seamus Mullins) *dwlt and in rr: hdwy 3f out: n.m.r wl over 2f out: sn swtchd rt and rdn wl over 1f out: styd on strly fr over 1f out: nt rch wnr* **4/1**[3]

011- **3** *1½* **Emerahldz (IRE)**[186] 7032 3-9-2 **65** ........ TonyHamilton 8 68
(Richard Fahey) *trckd ldrs: hdwy 3f out: rdn 2f out: drvn over 1f out: kpt on same pce* **16/1**

305- **4** *3¼* **Lightning Shower (USA)**[198] 6688 3-9-1 **69** ........ DanielMuscutt(5) 11 66
(Marco Botti) *towards rr: hdwy 4f out: rdn to chse ldrs: whn n.m.r 2f out: sn swtchd rt and kpt on fnl f: nrst fin* **33/1**

060- **5** *hd* **Mustadrik (USA)**[145] 7902 3-9-2 **65** ........ DaneO'Neill 1 61
(J W Hills) *in tch: hdwy over 4f out: chsd ldrs over 3f out: rdn to chse wnr 2f out: sn rdn and one pce appr fnl f* **25/1**

000- **6** *1½* **Dalarosso**[140] 7972 3-9-7 **70** ........ KierenFallon 2 64
(Ed Dunlop) *dwlt: sn in midfield: hdwy 1/2-way: chsd ldrs over 2f out: sn rdn and one pce* **20/1**

605- **7** *1¾* **Sahara Desert (IRE)**[154] 7773 3-9-2 **65** ........ RyanMoore 6 55
(Sir Michael Stoute) *hld up: hdwy over 4f out: effrt to chse ldrs over 2f out: rdn and n.m.r over 1f out: sn drvn and btn* **13/8**[1]

003- **8** *10* **Supachap**[154] 7773 3-9-3 **66** ........ JimmyFortune 4 37
(Hughie Morrison) *in tch: effrt on outer to chse ldrs over 3f out: sn rdn and wknd* **7/2**[2]

401- **9** *2½* **New Colours**[112] 8328 3-9-5 **68** ........ MartinDwyer 3 35
(Marcus Tregoning) *prom: effrt over 3f out: sn rdn along and wknd over 2f out* **20/1**

050- **10** *2* **Lucky Jim**[128] 8123 3-9-7 **70** ........ TedDurcan 5 33
(Chris Wall) *a in rr* **16/1**

6315 **11** *2¾* **Plough Boy (IRE)**[13] 1124 3-8-12 **61** ........ ChrisCatlin 9 18
(Willie Musson) *led: rdn along over 3f out: hdd wl over 2f out and sn wknd* **50/1**

2m 14.72s (0.42) **Going Correction** -0.025s/f (Good) **11 Ran SP% 116.2**
Speed ratings (Par 98): **97,94,93,91,90 89,88,80,78,76 74**
CSF £73.25 CT £1061.62 TOTE £12.50: £4.10, £2.30, £3.80; EX 88.80 Trifecta £1320.40.
**Owner** Richard Wilson (Hertfordshire) **Bred** Wood Farm Stud (Waresley) **Trained** Newmarket, Suffolk

**FOCUS**
A modest handicap, in which the market leaders both disappointed. Improvement from the winner, but maybe there wasn't much depth to the race.
T/Plt: £18.20 to a £1 stake. Pool of £65414.73 - 2611.45 winning tickets. T/Qpdt: £15.80 to a £1 stake. Pool of £3230.71 - 150.60 winning tickets. JR

# 943 CHANTILLY (R-H)
Wednesday, April 9

**OFFICIAL GOING: Turf: good; polytrack: standard**

## 1402a PRIX DU PREMIER PAS (MAIDEN) (UNRACED 2YO) (TURF) 5f
**3:20** (12:00) 2-Y-O **£10,416** (£4,166; £3,125; £2,083; £1,041)

RPR

**1** **El Suizo (FR)** 2-9-2 0 ........ FabriceVeron 8 87
(H-A Pantall, France) **14/5**[1]

**2** *3½* **Super Eria (FR)** 2-8-13 0 ........ AlexandreGavilan 9 71
(D Guillemin, France) **28/1**

**3** *nk* **Dame Des Lys (FR)** 2-8-13 0 ........ ThierryJarnet 4 70
(J Heloury, France) **192/10**

**4** *¾* **Pomone (IRE)** 2-8-13 0 ........ MaximeGuyon 2 68
(D De Watrigant, France) **51/10**[2]

**5** *½* **Queen Bee (FR)** 2-8-13 0 ........ AntoineHamelin 5 66
(Matthieu Palussiere, France) **11/2**[3]

**6** *snk* **Seradora (FR)** 2-8-13 0 ........ CristianDemuro 3 65
(E J O'Neill, France) **158/10**

**7** *3* **Grise De Gris (FR)** 2-8-13 0 ........ UmbertoRispoli 1 54
(J-L Pelletan, France) **227/10**

**8** *shd* **Benouville (FR)** 2-8-13 0 ........ GregoryBenoist 11 54
(C Baillet, France) **56/10**

**9** *2½* **Hyakuman (FR)** 2-9-2 0 ........ Christophe-PatriceLemaire 6 48
(M Boutin, France) **114/10**

**10** *2* **Frostman (FR)** 2-9-2 0 ........ IoritzMendizabal 7 41
(Jo Hughes) *bmpd s: led early: remained prom once hdd tl rdn and wknd ins fnl 2f* **94/10**

**11** *2* **Intuitif (FR)** 2-9-2 0 ........ Pierre-CharlesBoudot 10 34
(H-F Devin, France) **19/2**

59.16s (0.86) **11 Ran SP% 119.0**
WIN (incl. 1 euro stake): 3.80. Places: 1.90, 5.70, 4.40. DF: 54.00. SF: 61.60..
**Owner** Peter Rechsteiner **Bred** P Rechsteiner **Trained** France

# 1379 KEMPTON (A.W) (R-H)
Thursday, April 10

**OFFICIAL GOING: Standard**
Wind: Virtually nil Weather: Fine

## 1403 DOWNLOAD THE BETVICTOR APP NOW H'CAP 1m (P)
**5:40** (5:41) (Class 6) (0-65,65) 3-Y-O **£1,940** (£577; £288; £144) **Stalls** Low

Form RPR

4111 **1** **Desert Colours**[15] 1101 3-9-1 **64** ........(b) KevinStott(5) 10 68
(Kevin Ryan) *mde all: rdn over 2f out: kpt on: edgd rt ins fnl f* **3/1**[1]

-235 **2** *1¼* **Byron Gala**[10] 1214 3-8-12 **61** ........ DanielMuscutt(5) 5 62
(Marco Botti) *midfield: pushed along and hdwy over 1f out: sn chsd ldrs: rdn and hung rt ins fnl f: wnt 2nd 110yds out: kpt on* **8/1**[3]

-243 **3** *½* **Needless Shouting (IRE)**[10] 1214 3-9-4 **65** WilliamTwiston-Davies(3) 4 65
(Mick Channon) *trckd ldrs: rdn over 2f out: kpt on* **9/2**[2]

004- **4** *shd* **Starlit Cantata**[170] 7435 3-9-7 **65** ........ JohnFahy 6 68+
(Eve Johnson Houghton) *in tch on inner: rdn and hdwy to chse wnr over 1f out: ¾ l down and keeping on whn short of room on rail 110yds out: no ch after* **16/1**

000- **5** *¾* **Mister Mayday (IRE)**[233] 5610 3-9-3 **61** ........ MartinDwyer 8 59
(George Baker) *midfield: rdn over 2f out: kpt on fnl f: nvr threatened ldrs* **20/1**

06-6 **6** *shd* **Harry's Summer (USA)**[85] 188 3-9-3 **61** ........(b[1]) GeorgeBaker 2 59+
(Nick Littmoden) *dwlt: hld up: rdn over 2f out: kpt on fnl f: nvr threatened ldrs* **9/2**[2]

4-14 **7** *nk* **Barbary (IRE)**[41] 774 3-9-3 **61** ........ FrederikTylicki 12 58
(Charlie Fellowes) *in tch on outer: rdn 3f out: one pce and no imp on ldrs* **8/1**[3]

34-3 **8** *¾* **The Dukkerer (IRE)**[15] 1101 3-9-4 **62** ........ JimCrowley 11 57
(Garry Moss) *trckd ldrs: rdn over 2f out: wknd ins fnl f* **14/1**

004- **9** *1¾* **Majestic Sun (IRE)**[177] 7271 3-9-6 **64** ........ ShaneKelly 1 55
(Peter Chapple-Hyam) *stdd s: hld up: racd keenly: rdn over 2f out: nvr threatened* **8/1**[3]

3-56 **10** *½* **Confiture**[10] 1214 3-9-2 **60** ........ LiamKeniry 7 50
(Michael Blanshard) *hld up: nvr threatened* **50/1**

000- **11** *1¼* **Dover The Moon (IRE)**[183] 7119 3-8-13 **62** ........ JoshBaudains(5) 3 49
(Sylvester Kirk) *midfield on inner: rdn over 2f out: sn btn* **50/1**

4-42 **12** *2¾* **River Goddess (IRE)**[52] 645 3-9-7 **65** ........ WilliamBuick 13 46
(Charles Hills) *in tch on outer: wnt prom 1/2-way: rdn over 2f out: wknd appr fnl f* **20/1**

400- **13** *10* **Plucky Dip**[169] 7471 3-8-13 **57** ........ KierenFallon 9 15
(John Ryan) *chsd ldrs: rdn over 3f out: wknd over 1f out: eased* **25/1**

054- **14** *9* **Cameley Dawn**[210] 6334 3-9-5 **63** ........ DaneO'Neill 14
(Malcolm Saunders) *hld up in rr: a bhd* **40/1**

1m 39.43s (-0.37) **Going Correction** -0.025s/f (Stan) **14 Ran SP% 127.0**
Speed ratings (Par 96): **100,98,98,98,97 97,97,96,94,94 92,90,80,71**
CSF £27.07 CT £114.85 TOTE £6.10: £2.40, £2.30, £2.00; EX 48.20 Trifecta £107.00.
**Owner** Jon Beard **Bred** Rabbah Bloodstock Limited **Trained** Hambleton, N Yorks
■ Stewards' Enquiry : Kevin Stott four-day ban: careless riding (Apr 24-27)

**FOCUS**
Bright, mild, dry conditions for this seven-race card. The field were fairly well bunched up to halfway in this opener, but the winner came well away.

## 1404 BETVICTOR.COM MAIDEN AUCTION STKS 6f (P)
**6:10** (6:11) (Class 5) 3-Y-O **£2,587** (£770; £384; £192) **Stalls** Low

Form RPR

00- **1** **Strategic Force (IRE)**[182] 7155 3-9-4 0 ........ AdamKirby 3 79+
(Clive Cox) *mde all: hld narrow ld tl over 2f out: pushed along and edgd lft 2f out: in command over 1f out: kpt on: comf* **5/1**[3]

2- **2** *2¾* **Misstemper (IRE)**[156] 7756 3-8-7 0 ow1 ........ JohnFahy 7 60
(Sean Curran) *racd keenly: hld up in tch: rdn over 2f out: wnt 2nd appr fnl f: one pce and no ch w wnr* **8/1**

34- **3** *½* **Space Walker (IRE)**[181] 7162 3-8-13 0 ........ TomQueally 2 64
(Harry Dunlop) *dwlt: hld up: rdn over 2f out: wnt 3rd appr fnl f: one pce* **9/4**[1]

0U-0 **4** ½ **Pendo**[22] [1008] 3-8-11 0.....1 SteveDrowne 5 60+
(Alastair Lidderdale) *dwlt: hld up: pushed along 1/2-way: sme hdwy to go 4th ins fnl f: nvr threatened* **20/1**

002- **5** 2¼ **Pastoral Witness**[259] [4686] 3-8-8 69..... FrederikTylicki 1 50
(Clive Brittain) *trckd ldng pair: rdn over 2f out: wknd fnl f* **5/1**[3]

024- **6** hd **Baars Causeway (IRE)**[170] [7441] 3-8-1 72..... JoeyHaynes(5) 4 48
(Alan Jarvis) *w ldr: rdn over 2f out: wknd fnl f* **4/1**[2]

2-22 **7** 3½ **Mimi Luke (USA)**[15] [1106] 3-8-13 67..... KierenFallon 6 43
(Alan Bailey) *racd keenly: trckd ldng pair: rdn 1/2-way: wknd over 1f out* **4/1**[2]

1m 13.49s (0.39) **Going Correction** -0.025s/f (Stan) **7** Ran SP% **120.0**
Speed ratings (Par 98): **96,92,91,91,88 87,83**
CSF £46.07 TOTE £7.60: £3.60, £6.60; EX 67.30 Trifecta £305.80.
**Owner** Peter Ridgers **Bred** D J Sweeney **Trained** Lambourn, Berks

**FOCUS**
A moderate maiden.

## 1405 £25 FREE BET AT BETVICTOR.COM FILLIES' H'CAP 6f (P)

**6:40** (6:41) (Class 5) (0-70,70) 4-Y-O+ **£2,587** (£770; £384; £192) **Stalls** Low

Form RPR

56-6 **1** **Aeolian Blue**[78] [275] 4-8-9 **58**..... ShaneKelly 1 69+
(William Knight) *hld up in tch: smooth hdwy over 2f out: rdn to ld appr fnl f: kpt on wl* **11/4**[1]

2413 **2** 1 **Ray Of Joy**[7] [1266] 8-9-7 **70**.....(v) FrederikTylicki 4 76
(J R Jenkins) *chsd ldng pair: rdn over 2f out: kpt on: wnt 2nd 50yds out* **3/1**[2]

3005 **3** 1½ **Chevise (IRE)**[15] [1110] 6-8-10 **59**.....(b) HarryBentley 6 60
(Steve Woodman) *led narrowly: hdd 4f out: rdn to ld again over 2f out: hdd appr fnl f: no ex: lost 2nd 50yds out* **6/1**

5014 **4** 2¼ **Catalinas Diamond (IRE)**[15] [1110] 6-8-7 **56**.....(t) JohnFahy 3 50
(Pat Murphy) *rrd s and slowly away: pushed along 1/2-way: sme hdwy over 1f out: nvr threatened* **8/1**

2323 **5** ¾ **Heartsong (IRE)**[23] [1001] 5-8-6 **58**..... MichaelJMMurphy(3) 5 50
(John Gallagher) *hld up: rdn 1/2-way: nvr threatened* **11/2**[3]

0/60 **6** nk **Tarara**[13] [1144] 4-9-2 **65**..... FergusSweeney 2 56
(Michael Blanshard) *hld up: rdn over 2f out: nvr threatened* **25/1**

60-0 **7** 1½ **Commandingpresence (USA)**[9] [1221] 8-8-8 **57**..... WilliamCarson 8 43
(John Bridger) *trckd ldng pair: rdn over 2f out: sn wknd* **25/1**

325- **8** 16 **Maltease Ah**[242] [5305] 5-8-10 **59**..... JimCrowley 7
(Andrew Reid) *w ldr: led 4f out: hdd over 2f out: wknd qckly and eased* **8/1**

1m 12.77s (-0.33) **Going Correction** -0.025s/f (Stan) **8** Ran SP% **111.3**
Speed ratings (Par 100): **101,99,97,94,93 93,91,69**
CSF £10.52 CT £42.34 TOTE £3.80: £1.30, £1.20, £2.30; EX 12.40 Trifecta £142.60.
**Owner** Mrs Sheila Mitchell **Bred** Mrs S M Mitchell **Trained** Patching, W Sussex

**FOCUS**
Just a modest 0-70 fillies' handicap, but it did go to the least exposed in the field in a winning time nearly 0.8 seconds faster than that of the preceding maiden.

## 1406 DOWNLOAD THE BETVICTOR INSTABET APP H'CAP 1m 3f (P)

**7:10** (7:10) (Class 6) (0-65,65) 4-Y-O+ **£1,940** (£577; £288; £144) **Stalls** Far side

Form RPR

0623 **1** **Time Square (FR)**[12] [1168] 7-8-12 **58**..... JoeyHaynes(5) 3 67
(Tony Carroll) *chsd clr ldr: rdn over 2f out: led over 1f out: kpt on wl* **8/1**

6011 **2** 1½ **Thane Of Cawdor (IRE)**[24] [989] 5-9-7 **62**.....(p) JimCrowley 8 68
(Joseph Tuite) *hld up: rdn over 5f out: fnlly responded to press to cl over 1f out: wnt 2nd 75yds out* **4/1**[2]

0033 **3** ¾ **Lily Edge**[10] [1210] 5-8-5 **53**.....(v) CamHardie(7) 4 58
(John Bridger) *midfield: rdn over 2f out: hdwy to chse ldr appr fnl f: one pce: lost 2nd 75yds out* **25/1**

-604 **4** hd **Wyndham Wave**[8] [1232] 5-8-10 **51**.....(b) DavidProbert 6 56
(Rod Millman) *midfield: hdwy to chse ldrs 3f out: rdn over 2f out: carried hd bit awkwardly and one pce* **11/2**[3]

0-03 **5** 1 **Highly Likely (IRE)**[36] [838] 5-9-2 **57**..... AdamKirby 1 60
(Steve Woodman) *hld up in midfield: rdn over 2f out: one pce and nvr threatened* **16/1**

-541 **6** 1 **Teide Peak (IRE)**[24] [998] 5-9-7 **62**..... SeanLevey 7 63
(Paul D'Arcy) *hld up: rdn over 2f out: nvr threatened* **6/4**[1]

1233 **7** 10 **Bennelong**[8] [1232] 8-9-0 **58**.....(b) OisinMurphy(3) 2 41
(Lee Carter) *led: racd keenly and sn clr: rdn whn hdd over 1f out: wknd* **4/1**[2]

40-0 **8** 2½ **Snowy Valley**[7] [1263] 5-8-7 **48**..... JimmyQuinn 5 26
(Paul Burgoyne) *in tch: rdn over 3f out: wknd over 2f out* **50/1**

2m 20.71s (-1.19) **Going Correction** -0.025s/f (Stan) **8** Ran SP% **118.2**
Speed ratings (Par 101): **103,101,101,101,100 99,92,90**
CSF £41.38 CT £778.44 TOTE £9.00: £1.90, £1.50, £5.30; EX 34.90 Trifecta £241.60.
**Owner** M S Cooke **Bred** Mme Therese Bouche & Isabelle Roussel **Trained** Cropthorne, Worcs

**FOCUS**
No surprise to see the complexion of this contest change completely from the 2f pole, as the overly generous pace set by Bennelong, ignored by his rivals, finally collapsed.

## 1407 FOLLOW @BETVICTORRACING ON TWITTER H'CAP (BOBIS RACE) 1m 4f (P)

**7:40** (7:40) (Class 3) (0-90,85) 3-Y-O **£7,158** (£2,143; £1,071; £535) **Stalls** Centre

Form RPR

3-21 **1** **Anglo Irish**[76] [316] 3-8-13 **77**..... WilliamBuick 1 81+
(John Gosden) *chsd ldr: rdn to ld appr fnl f: edgd rt ins fnl f: a holding on* **10/11**[1]

1 **2** ½ **Wonder Weapon (GER)**[24] [988] 3-8-13 **77**..... DavidProbert 4 80+
(Andrew Balding) *hld up in tch in 3rd: rdn 2f out: wnt 2nd 110yds out: kpt on but a hld* **8/1**[3]

231 **3** 2 **Officer Drivel (IRE)**[22] [1011] 3-8-9 **73**..... FergusSweeney 3 73
(Luke Dace) *rrd s: sn led: rdn over 2f out: hdd appr fnl f: no ex: lost 2nd 110yds out* **16/1**

41- **4** 3½ **Festival Theatre (IRE)**[247] [5101] 3-9-7 **85**..... RyanMoore 2 81
(Sir Michael Stoute) *hld up in 4th: rdn over 2f out: sme hdwy over 1f out: wknd ins fnl f* **7/4**[2]

2m 33.07s (-1.43) **Going Correction** -0.025s/f (Stan) **4** Ran SP% **105.7**
Speed ratings (Par 102): **103,102,101,99**
CSF £7.73 TOTE £1.70; EX 8.00 Trifecta £30.00.
**Owner** George Strawbridge **Bred** George Strawbridge **Trained** Newmarket, Suffolk

**FOCUS**
The evening's highlight and not the falsely run affair that such small-field races can often degenerate into, as the outsider of the party quickly imbued the race with a fair degree of pace.

## 1408 BOOK KEMPTON TICKETS ON 0844 579 3008 H'CAP 7f (P)

**8:10** (8:10) (Class 6) (0-60,60) 4-Y-O+ **£1,940** (£577; £288; £144) **Stalls** Low

Form RPR

0-01 **1** **Until Midnight (IRE)**[15] [1105] 4-9-3 **56**..... MartinDwyer 7 67
(Eugene Stanford) *trckd ldrs: rdn to chal over 1f out: edgd in front 110yds out: kpt on wl* **7/2**[1]

50P- **2** nk **Substantivo (IRE)**[112] [8341] 4-9-2 **55**..... KierenFallon 5 65
(Alan Jarvis) *prom: led over 2f out: rdn and strly pressed fr over 1f out: hdd 110yds out: kpt on wl: jst failed* **10/1**

4022 **3** 3¾ **Teen Ager (FR)**[15] [1110] 10-9-7 **60**.....(p) JimmyQuinn 6 60
(Paul Burgoyne) *hld up in tch: rdn and hdwy over 1f out: wnt 3rd jst ins fnl f: one pce and no threat to ldng pair* **5/1**[3]

0433 **4** hd **West Leake (IRE)**[15] [1110] 8-9-4 **57**..... LiamKeniry 3 57
(Paul Burgoyne) *trckd ldrs: rdn and outpcd over 1f out: plugged on ins fnl f* **7/2**[1]

3056 **5** ½ **Perfect Pastime**[15] [1110] 6-9-4 **57**.....(b) StephenCraine 4 55
(Jim Boyle) *hld up: rdn and hdwy 2f out: briefly chsd ldng pair appr fnl f: wknd ins fnl f* **15/2**

3300 **6** 1¼ **Welsh Inlet (IRE)**[15] [1110] 6-8-13 **52**..... WilliamCarson 8 47
(John Bridger) *dwlt: hld up in tch: pushed along whn short of room over 1f out and swtchd: no ch after* **12/1**

40- **7** 7 **With Hindsight (IRE)**[175] [1716] 6-9-2 **55**..... JohnFahy 12 32
(John Spearing) *racd keenly: chsd ldrs on outside: rdn over 2f out: sn wknd* **10/1**

3000 **8** 3¾ **Knight Charm**[24] 4-9-1 **59**..... DanielMuscutt(5) 2 26
(Gay Kelleway) *racd keenly: led: rdn whn hdd over 2f out: wknd* **4/1**[2]

1m 25.58s (-0.42) **Going Correction** -0.025s/f (Stan) **8** Ran SP% **118.7**
Speed ratings (Par 101): **101,100,96,96,95 94,86,81**
CSF £40.47 CT £177.65 TOTE £5.50: £1.70, £3.50, £1.60; EX 52.70 Trifecta £729.30 Part won..
**Owner** newmarketracingclub.co.uk **Bred** Rathbarry Stud **Trained** Newmarket, Suffolk
■ Darnathean was withdrawn. Price at time of withdrawal 100/30. Rule 4 applies to bets struck prior to withdrawal but not to SP bets. Deduct 20p in the pound. New market formed.
■ Stewards' Enquiry : Jimmy Quinn one-day ban: careless riding (Apr 24)

**FOCUS**
A contest already thinned out by five absentees lost a sixth participant in the shape of the late withdrawal Darnathean.

## 1409 INTERACTIVE FILLIES' H'CAP 6f (P)

**8:40** (8:40) (Class 4) (0-80,77) 3-Y-O **£4,690** (£1,395; £697; £348) **Stalls** Low

Form RPR

321- **1** **Perfect Alchemy (IRE)**[218] [6107] 3-9-4 **75**..... JimCrowley 1 81+
(Ralph Beckett) *in tch in 3rd: pushed along to ld appr fnl f: kpt on: cosily* **15/8**[2]

1-23 **2** 1 **Queenie's Home**[83] [217] 3-9-2 **73**..... MartinDwyer 4 74
(James Given) *trckd ldr: rdn to chal 2f out: kpt on: wnt 2nd 50yds out: a hld by wnr* **8/1**[3]

21- **3** ½ **Invoke (IRE)**[184] [7095] 3-9-3 **74**..... TomQueally 3 73
(Michael Bell) *led: rdn over 2f out: hdd appr fnl f: lost 2nd 50yds out: no ex* **10/1**

061- **4** ¾ **Terhaab (USA)**[161] [7638] 3-9-6 **77**..... PaulHanagan 5 74
(John Gosden) *racd keenly: hld up in tch in 4th: rdn 2f out: sn one pce* **5/6**[1]

1m 13.64s (0.54) **Going Correction** -0.025s/f (Stan) **4** Ran SP% **109.5**
Speed ratings (Par 97): **95,93,93,92**
CSF £14.14 TOTE £2.90; EX 16.00 Trifecta £25.30.
**Owner** The Perfect Partnership & D H Caslon **Bred** W Maxwell Ervine **Trained** Kimpton, Hants

**FOCUS**
A tight contest on paper with just 3lb separating the quarter on RPRs and the pace was pretty fair.
T/Plt: £711.40 to a £1 stake. Pool of £76709.07 - 78.71 winning tickets. T/Qpdt: £37.50 to a £1 stake. Pool of £8992.11 - 177.22 winning tickets. AS

# NEWBURY (L-H)

Friday, April 11

**OFFICIAL GOING: Good to soft (good in places; 6.1)**
Wind: virtuall nil Weather: sunny periods

## 1417 AL BASTI EQUIWORLD EBF STALLIONS MAIDEN STKS (BOBIS RACE) 5f 34y

**2:00** (2:02) (Class 4) 2-Y-O **£6,469** (£1,925; £962; £481) **Stalls** Centre

Form RPR

**1** **Kasb (IRE)** 2-9-5 0..... DaneO'Neill 10 88+
(John Gosden) *lengthy: tall: s.i.s: running green and bhd: gd hdwy fr 2f out: r.o strly to ld fnl 120yds: readily* **10/1**

2 **2** 1 **Charlie's Star**[13] [1169] 2-8-11 0..... DeclanBates(3) 4 77
(David Evans) *leggy: prom: rdn over 2f out: led v briefly ins fnl f: kpt on but nt pce of wnr clsng stages* **25/1**

**3** nk **Ballymore Castle (IRE)** 2-9-5 0..... TonyHamilton 8 81
(Richard Fahey) *cmpt: prom: rdn to ld over 1f out: hdd fnl 120yds: kpt on* **12/1**

**4** 2½ **The Paco Kid** 2-9-5 0..... MickaelBarzalona 9 72
(Olly Stevens) *w'like: chsd ldrs: rdn over 2f out: ch ent fnl f: no ex fnl 120yds* **8/1**[3]

**5** 2½ **Be Bold** 2-9-5 0..... SeanLevey 14 64
(Richard Hannon) *lengthy: tall: bit bkwd: mid-div: hdwy 3f out: sn rdn: sltly hmpd ent fnl f: kpt on same pce* **16/1**

**6** hd **Justice Good (IRE)** 2-9-5 0..... LiamKeniry 3 63
(David Elsworth) *w'like: chsd ldrs: rdn 2f out: fdd ins fnl f* **9/4**[2]

**7** ½ **Magical Memory (IRE)** 2-9-5 0..... GeorgeBaker 12 62
(Charles Hills) *str: prom: rdn w ev ch over 1f out: hld whn sltly hmpd ent fnl f: fdd* **85/40**[1]

**8** shd **Kibaar** 2-9-5 0..... PaulHanagan 7 60
(J W Hills) *str: tall: sltly awkward leaving stalls: sn led: rdn and hdd over 1f out: wknd fnl f* **9/1**

**9** 6 **Now Say Boooom** 2-9-0 0..... FergusSweeney 11 34
(Luke Dace) *leggy: wnt rt and slowly away: a outpcd in rr* **100/1**

**10** hd **Arlecchino's Leap** 2-9-5 0..... DavidProbert 6 38
(Mark Usher) *leggy: scope: tall: chsd ldrs: rdn 2f out: wknd over 1f out* **50/1**

11 2 1/4 **Diamond Sam** 2-9-5 0........................................ PatDobbs 5 30
(Sylvester Kirk) *w'like: mid-div: rdn 3f out: hung lft and wknd over 1f out*
**66/1**

12 16 **King Crimson** 2-9-2 0.................................. WilliamTwiston-Davies(3) 1
(Mick Channon) *leggy: wnt rt s: in tch tl wknd wl over 2f out* **14/1**

13 7 **Royal Street** 2-9-5 0........................................ JamesDoyle 13
(Seamus Durack) *w'like: bit bkwd: sn hung lft and a outpcd towards rr*
**20/1**

1m 4.52s (3.12) **Going Correction** +0.35s/f (Good) **13** Ran SP% **126.3**
Speed ratings (Par 94): **89,87,86,82,78 78,77,77,68,67 64,38,27**
CSF £250.05 TOTE £9.30: £3.90, £3.80, £3.50; EX 111.90 Trifecta £1877.40.
**Owner** Hamdan Al Maktoum **Bred** J O'Connor **Trained** Newmarket, Suffolk

**FOCUS**

Rails on round course moved out between 8f and 5f adding 26m to races on Round course. The ground had dried out slightly and was given as Good to soft, good in places. Jockeys in the opener described conditions as "on the easy side of good" and "dead". This maiden has been won by some nice sorts in recent years (the form of last year's race worked out amazingly well) and this year's renewal should produce its fair share of winners too. Kasb did it nicely but the bare form can't be rated much higher than this.

## 1418 BATHWICK TYRES H'CAP 2m

**2:30** (2:30) (Class 4) (0-80,80) 4-Y-O+ **£4,690** (£1,395; £697; £348) **Stalls** High

Form RPR

560/ 1 **Bob's World**[14] 5373 5-9-1 **69**........................(tp) PaulHanagan 3 81
(Jennie Candlish) *mid-div: hdwy 3f out: sn rdn: swtchd rt 2f out: str run to ld over 1f out: edgd lft but styd on wl to draw clr fnl f* **20/1**

454- 2 4 **Our Folly**[161] 7660 6-9-4 **72**..............................(t) TomQueally 4 79
(Stuart Kittow) *lw: mid-div: hdwy over 3f out: led 2f out: rdn: hdd and sn hld by wnr over 1f out: kpt on same pce* **13/2[2]**

2-31 3 3/4 **Arty Campbell (IRE)**[25] 992 4-9-3 **75**.................. MartinLane 1 81
(Bernard Llewellyn) *trckd ldrs: rdn 3f out: chal for 2nd ent fnl f: styd on but no ex fnl 120yds* **11/1**

1-15 4 1/2 **Coup De Grace (IRE)**[27] 758 5-9-0 **68**................... ShaneKelly 9 74
(Pat Phelan) *in tch: trckd ldrs over 3f out: rdn over 2f out: styd on same pce fnl f* **8/1**

221- 5 1/2 **Story Writer**[225] 5933 5-9-2 **70**........................ JimCrowley 12 75
(William Knight) *lw: hld up towards rr of mid-div: hdwy 3f out: sn rdn to chse ldrs: styd on same pce fnl f* **7/1[3]**

003- 6 4 1/2 **Desert Recluse (IRE)**[163] 7635 7-9-9 **77**.............. KierenFallon 8 77
(Brendan Powell) *racd keenly in mid-div: hdwy to join ldr after 6f: led over 5f out: kicked clr and racd alone on farside rails: rdn: edging lft and hdd 2f out: kpt on tl no ex fnl f* **10/1**

020- 7 1 1/4 **Jezza**[149] 7863 8-8-13 **67**...............................(bt) JamieSpencer 5 65
(Karen George) *v.s.a: bhd: hdwy into midfield on outer over 3f out: sn rdn: nvr threatened: styd on same pce fnl 2f* **33/1**

1-35 8 1/2 **Outrageous Request**[21] 1043 8-8-13 **72**.............. LouisSteward(5) 13 70
(William Stone) *hld up towards rr: hdwy over 3f out: sn rdn: nvr threatened ldrs: wknd ent fnl f* **50/1**

-102 9 13 **Java Rose**[23] 758 5-9-8 **76**..................................(p) AdamKirby 7 58
(Charlie Longsdon) *lw: trckd ldrs: clsd on ldng pair over 3f out: rdn over 2f out: wknd over 1f out* **9/1**

6/0- 10 2 **Leo Luna**[28] 6926 5-9-8 **76**.................................. RyanMoore 2 56
(Gary Moore) *swtg: trckd ldrs: rdn 4f out: sn btn: wknd 2f out* **11/4[1]**

660- 11 1 1/2 **Mombasa**[178] 7275 4-8-10 **68**................................. JamesDoyle 10 46
(Harry Dunlop) *hld up towards rr of mid-div: rdn over 3f out: wknd wl over 1f out* **25/1**

450- 12 6 **Kashgar**[173] 7396 5-8-13 **74**............................ DavidParkes(7) 14 45
(Bernard Llewellyn) *a towards rr* **33/1**

105- 13 1 3/4 **Albonny (IRE)**[246] 5185 5-9-4 **72**......................... DaneO'Neill 6 41
(Alan Jarvis) *hld up towards rr of mid-div tl wknd over 2f out* **16/1**

100/ 14 2 1/2 **Moon Trip**[169] 6031 5-9-12 **80**............................ GeorgeBaker 11 46
(Geoffrey Deacon) *led tl over 5f out: wknd 3f out* **28/1**

3m 43.09s (11.09) **Going Correction** +0.475s/f (Yiel)
**WFA** 4 from 5yo+ 4lb **14** Ran SP% **116.8**
Speed ratings (Par 105): **91,89,88,88,88 85,85,85,78,77 76,73,72,71**
CSF £133.22 CT £1521.59 TOTE £23.40: £5.60, £2.00, £3.40; EX 183.80 Trifecta £2067.60 Part won..
**Owner** Bob Cant **Bred** Robert J Cant **Trained** Basford Green, Staffs

**FOCUS**

A fair staying handicap, though the pace didn't look strong until things quickened up turning for home. The bulk of the field came up the centre in the straight. The form is rated around the runner-up.

## 1419 DUBAI DUTY FREE GOLF WORLD CUP EBF STALLIONS CONDITIONS STKS (BOBIS RACE) 1m 2f 6y

**3:05** (3:05) (Class 3) 3-Y-O

**£9,337** (£2,796; £1,398; £699; £349; £175) **Stalls** Centre

Form RPR

1- 1 **Western Hymn**[130] 8124 3-8-13 92........................ WilliamBuick 4 107+
(John Gosden) *athletic: hld up in last pair: swtchd lft over 2f out: sn nudged along and prog: pushed into ld ent fnl f: qcknd clr: impressive* **11/8[1]**

410- 2 2 1/4 **Snow Sky**[167] 7528 3-8-13 95.................................. JamesDoyle 1 101
(Sir Michael Stoute) *trckd ldrs: rdn over 2f out: styd on ins fnl f: snatched 2nd fnl stride: no ch w wnr* **7/1[3]**

216- 3 shd **Double Bluff (IRE)**[173] 7409 3-8-13 94.............. SilvestreDeSousa 7 101
(Mark Johnston) *led for 1f: trckd ldr: rdn to ld 2f out: drifted lft and hdd ent fnl f: nt pce of wnr: lost 2nd fnl stride* **9/1**

31- 4 4 **Scotland (GER)**[194] 6866 3-9-1 96.......................... JimCrowley 5 95
(Andrew Balding) *hld up in last trio: hdwy fr 3f out: rdn 2f out: nt pce to chal: no ex fnl f* **11/4[2]**

-213 5 7 **God's Speed (IRE)**[48] 721 3-8-13 0........................ ChrisCatlin 3 80
(Rae Guest) *trckd ldrs: rdn over 2f out: nt pce to chal: wknd jst over 1f out* **25/1**

21 6 1 3/4 **Belfilo (IRE)**[28] 951 3-8-10 78........................ OisinMurphy(3) 6 77
(Andrew Balding) *str: pushed along leaving stalss: led after 1f: clr 5f out: rdn 3f out: hdd 2f out: wknd over 1f out* **14/1**

10- 7 8 **Shankly**[153] 7828 3-8-13 81................................... JamieSpencer 2 61
(Clive Cox) *swtg: stdd s: nvr settled in last: wknd 2f out* **10/1**

2m 12.56s (3.76) **Going Correction** +0.475s/f (Yiel) **7** Ran SP% **110.9**
Speed ratings (Par 102): **103,101,101,97,92 90,84**
CSF £10.95 TOTE £1.90: £1.50, £2.90; EX 11.80 Trifecta £88.40.
**Owner** RJH Geffen and Rachel Hood **Bred** Newsells Park Stud **Trained** Newmarket, Suffolk

**FOCUS**

This race has gone to some nice sorts in recent years, including the Oaks winner Light Shift in 2007, and this year's winner looks a bit special too. He can better this already smart form. They went a good gallop thanks to the pacemaker but the time was ordinary.

## 1420 DUBAI DUTY FREE FULL OF SURPRISES H'CAP (BOBIS RACE) 7f (S)

**3:40** (3:40) (Class 2) (0-100,95) 3-Y-O

**£11,827** (£3,541; £1,770; £885; £442; £222) **Stalls** Centre

Form RPR

1- 1 **Muwaary**[266] 4483 3-8-8 **82**................................. PaulHanagan 8 98+
(John Gosden) *str: racd stands' side: trckd ldr: led 2f out: qcknd up wl to draw clr fnl f: readily* **2/1[1]**

41- 2 2 3/4 **Zarwaan**[266] 4477 3-9-4 **92**................................. DaneO'Neill 7 100
(Ed Dunlop) *lw: racd stands' side: hld up: pushed along and hdwy 2f out: sn rdn: r.o to chse wnr ins fnl f but a being readily hld* **12/1**

44-0 3 1 1/4 **Brazos (IRE)**[20] 1067 3-9-7 **95**........................... JamesDoyle 6 100
(Clive Brittain) *swtg: racd in centre: trckd ldr: rdn and ev ch 2f out: nt pce of wnr ent fnl f: no ex fnl 75yds* **20/1**

015- 4 3/4 **Showpiece**[209] 6395 3-8-10 **84**........................... RyanMoore 9 87
(Richard Hannon) *racd stands' side: hld up: pushed along over 3f out: steadily swtchd rt fr over 2f out: r.o ent fnl f: fin in centre but snatched 4th fnl stride* **20/1**

12- 5 nse **Hors De Combat**[216] 6197 3-9-3 **91**................. FrederikTylicki 5 94+
(James Fanshawe) *racd centre: trckd ldrs: rdn 3f out: ev ch 2f out: kpt on same pce fnl f* **12/1**

10-3 6 2 1/4 **Lincoln (IRE)**[15] 1136 3-8-6 **83** ow1............. WilliamTwiston-Davies(3) 4 80
(Mick Channon) *wnt to s early: hld up in centre: swtchd rt 2f out: sn rdn to chse ldrs: one pce fnl f* **16/1**

610- 7 3 **Extremity (IRE)**[188] 7017 3-8-4 **78**.................... MartinDwyer 10 67
(Hugo Palmer) *lw: racd stands' side: overall ldr tl rdn 2f out: wknd fnl f* **3/1[2]**

162- 8 1 1/4 **Torchlighter (IRE)**[153] 7819 3-8-13 **87**........ SilvestreDeSousa 1 73
(Mark Johnston) *disp ld in centre tl rdn over 2f out: wknd fnl f* **16/1**

103- 9 3/4 **Baby Bush (IRE)**[191] 6955 3-7-13 **80**.................. CamHardie(7) 2 64
(Richard Hannon) *racd centre: trckd ldrs: rdn and ev ch 2f out: wknd ent fnl f* **33/1**

22-1 10 3 1/4 **Exchequer (IRE)**[6] 1296 3-8-8 **82** 6ex.................. SeanLevey 3 57
(Richard Hannon) *lw: led centre gp tl rdn 2f out: sn hung lft: wknd fnl f* **9/2[3]**

1m 26.48s (0.78) **Going Correction** +0.35s/f (Good) **10** Ran SP% **116.1**
Speed ratings (Par 104): **109,105,104,103,103 100,97,96,95,91**
CSF £26.94 CT £377.13 TOTE £3.40: £1.40, £3.60, £5.10; EX 25.40 Trifecta £476.90.
**Owner** Hamdan Al Maktoum **Bred** Shadwell Estate Company Limited **Trained** Newmarket, Suffolk

**FOCUS**

This looked a decent 3yo handicap, won by a nice prospect. The field split into two early with the main bunch coming up the centre, but four were taken to race against the nearside rail and they included the winner, second and fourth. The form is rated on the positive side.

## 1421 DUBAI DUTY FREE H'CAP 5f 34y

**4:15** (4:15) (Class 2) (0-110,110) 4-Y-O+

**£11,827** (£3,541; £1,770; £885; £442; £222) **Stalls** Centre

Form RPR

150- 1 **Lucky Beggar (IRE)**[189] 6990 4-8-13 **102**............ WilliamBuick 2 110
(Charles Hills) *racd centre: overall ldr thrght: r.o strly fnl f: rdn out* **5/1[3]**

04-4 2 1 1/4 **Jimmy Styles**[13] 1163 10-9-0 **103**........................(p) AdamKirby 4 107
(Clive Cox) *lw: trckd wnr in centre: rdn 2f out: kpt on but a being hld fnl f* **6/1**

010- 3 nk **Steps (IRE)**[167] 7527 6-8-13 **105**...................... OisinMurphy(3) 3 107
(Roger Varian) *racd centre: trckd ldrs: rdn 2f out: kpt on but nt gng pce to chal* **7/2[2]**

060- 4 1 1/4 **El Viento (FR)**[174] 7373 6-8-2 **96**...................... SammyJoBell(5) 1 94
(Richard Fahey) *racd centre: trckd ldrs: rdn 2f out: kpt on same pce fnl f* **8/1**

000- 5 nse **Ballesteros**[153] 7821 5-8-13 **102**.......................... JimmyFortune 8 100+
(Richard Fahey) *racd stands' side: chsd ldrs: pushed along over 2f out: kpt on fnl f wout ever threatening to get involved* **10/1**

220- 6 3/4 **Kyleakin Lass**[167] 7527 5-8-7 **96** oh3.................... DavidProbert 6 91
(Jonathan Portman) *lw: disp ld on stands' side: rdn over 1f out: fdd fnl 120yds* **10/1**

0000 7 3 3/4 **Tennessee Wildcat (IRE)**[13] 1172 4-8-7 **96** oh1........(p) AndreaAtzeni 5 78
(Robert Cowell) *racd stands' side: trckd ldrs: rdn 2f out: wknd fnl f* **25/1**

10- 8 2 1/2 **Dutch Masterpiece**[187] 7054 4-9-7 **110**................ RyanMoore 7 83
(Gary Moore) *lw: disp ld on stands' side tl rdn 2f out: sn hung rt and btn* **11/4[1]**

1m 2.35s (0.95) **Going Correction** +0.35s/f (Good) **8** Ran SP% **113.0**
Speed ratings (Par 109): **106,104,103,101,101 100,94,90**
CSF £33.96 CT £116.94 TOTE £6.50: £2.10, £2.40, £1.50; EX 43.10 Trifecta £119.80.
**Owner** Hon Mrs Corbett, C Wright, Mrs B W Hills **Bred** Mrs Cherry Faeste **Trained** Lambourn, Berks

**FOCUS**

A decent sprint handicap with the field soon splitting into two groups of four. The roles were reversed in comparison to the previous race, with the four who raced up to centre beating the quartet who raced closer to the nearside rail. The winner seemed better than ever.

## 1422 COLN VALLEY STUD BRIDGET MAIDEN FILLIES' STKS (BOBIS RACE) 7f (S)

**4:45** (4:49) (Class 4) 3-Y-O **£4,851** (£1,443; £721; £360) **Stalls** Centre

Form RPR

1 **Evita Peron** 3-9-0 ............................................. JimCrowley 12 78
(Ralph Beckett) *str: lw: trckd ldrs: pushed along 2f out: r.o wl to ld fnl 40yds: pushed out: readily* **4/1[1]**

2 1 1/4 **Childesplay** 3-8-9 ........................................... RyanTate(5) 14 75
(Heather Main) *w'like: sn led: rdn ent fnl f: kpt on gamely: hdd fnl 40yds* **100/1**

3 1 3/4 **Perfect Blessings (IRE)** 3-9-0 .......................... AdamKirby 19 70
(Clive Cox) *w'like: lengthy: trckd ldrs: pushed along 2f out: kpt on fnl f but nvr threatening to rch ldrs* **20/1**

- 4 2 1/4 **Ski Lift** 3-9-0 ............................................... JamesDoyle 16 65+
(John Gosden) *w'like: s.i.s: bhd: rdn over 2f out: hdwy over 1f out: fin wl to go 4th on stands' side rail but nvr rching ldrs* **9/2[2]**

5 hd **Wojha (IRE)** 3-9-0 ........................................... PaulHanagan 13 64
(William Haggas) *unf: lw: s.i.s: sn mid-div: stdy prog fr over 2f out: r.o fnl f: nvr trbld ldrs* **4/1[1]**

6 ¾ **Zaawia (IRE)** 3-9-0 DaneO'Neill 10 62+
(Ed Dunlop) *w'like: str: mid-div: stdy hdwy over 1f out: r.o fnl f: nvr trbld ldrs* **33/1**
7 1 **Enliven** 3-9-0 DavidProbert 18 60
(Andrew Balding) *leggy: prom: rdn 2f out: hld 4th ent fnl f: no ex and lost three pls fnl 70yds* **8/1**[3]
8 ½ **Palerma** 3-8-11 WilliamTwiston-Davies(3) 6 58
(Mick Channon) *unf: prom: rdn 2f out: fdd fnl f* **40/1**
9 ¾ **Native Heart** 3-8-11 CharlesBishop(3) 17 56
(Mick Channon) *leggy: hmpd s: sn mid-div: effrt 2f out: kpt on same pce fnl f* **100/1**
10 1 ¼ **Scillonian Sunset (IRE)** 3-9-0 FrankieDettori 15 53
(Charles Hills) *unf: lengthy: rdn 2f out: a mid-div* **12/1**
11 ¾ **Temptress (IRE)** 3-8-9 [1] JoeyHaynes(5) 1 51
(Roger Charlton) *str: lw: a in mid-div* **20/1**
12 1 ¾ **Scarlet Plum** 3-9-0 SteveDrowne 8 47+
(Roger Charlton) *str: tall: slowly away: bhd: sme late prog: nvr any danger* **16/1**
13 3 **Southern Cross** 3-9-0 JimmyFortune 4 39
(Hughie Morrison) *athletic: mid-div tl wknd 2f out* **40/1**
14 ½ **Scariff Hornet (IRE)** 3-9-0 PatDobbs 11 37
(Sylvester Kirk) *unf: trckd ldrs: rdn 2f out: sn wknd* **50/1**
15 4 ½ **Swiss Lait** 3-9-0 LiamKeniry 5 26
(David Elsworth) *leggy: unf: s.i.s: a towards rr* **66/1**
16 5 **Sand Dancer (IRE)** 3-9-0 SeanLevey 20 13
(Richard Hannon) *lengthy: bit bkwd: mid-div tl wknd 2f out* **25/1**
17 1 ½ **Nutbush** 3-9-0 SamHitchcott 7 9
(Mick Channon) *leggy: trckd ldrs tl rdn 2f out: sn wknd* **100/1**
18 1 ¼ **Zman Awal (IRE)** 3-9-0 HayleyTurner 3 6
(James Fanshawe) *w'like: mid-div tl wknd wl over 1f out* **20/1**
19 8 **Brown Glaze (USA)** 3-9-0 JamieSpencer 9
(Richard Hannon) *w'like: scope: mid-div tl wknd over 2f out* **8/1**[3]

1m 28.3s (2.60) **Going Correction** +0.35s/f (Good) 19 Ran SP% **126.4**
Speed ratings (Par 97): **99,97,95,93,92 91,90,90,89,87 87,85,81,81,75 70,68,67,57**
CSF £443.31 TOTE £5.90: £2.10, £18.30, £5.50; EX 276.50 Trifecta £2650.50 Part won..
**Owner** Newsells Park Stud **Bred** Newsells Park Stud **Trained** Kimpton, Hants

**FOCUS**
A complete head-scratcher for punters with 19 fillies, all newcomers, going to post. The winning time was 1.82sec slower than the earlier 3yo handicap, but the winner did it nicely and a few caught the eye. A slightly cautious view has been taken of the form.

## 1423 WHITLEY STUD MAIDEN FILLIES' STKS (BOBIS RACE) (DIV II) 1m 2f 6y
5:15 (5:18) (Class 4) 3-Y-O £4,851 (£1,443; £721; £360) Stalls Centre

Form RPR
1 **Bright Approach (IRE)** 3-9-0 0 WilliamBuick 7 90+
(John Gosden) *str: lw: hld up bhd: hdwy over 3f out: nt clrest of runs tl 2f out: swtchd lft: qcknd up wl whn asked ent fnl f: led fnl 140yds: readily* **11/4**[2]
2- 2 1 ½ **Be My Gal**[130] 8124 3-9-0 0 SilvestreDeSousa 9 87+
(Roger Charlton) *unf: lw: mid-div: hdwy 3f out: rdn to dispute 2f out: narrow advantage ent fnl f: hdd and outpcd by wnr fnl 140yds* **13/8**[1]
0- 3 ½ **Talmada (USA)**[156] 7763 3-9-0 0 AndreaAtzeni 12 86
(Roger Varian) *lengthy: tall: trckd ldr: disp ld 2f out: sn rdn narrowly hdd ent fnl f: kpt on but no ex* **12/1**
4 2 ¼ **Marsh Daisy** 3-9-0 0 JimmyFortune 8 82+
(Hughie Morrison) *w'like: hld up towards rr: hdwy over 3f out: nt clr run fr over 2f out tl swtchd rt wl over 1f out: sn rdn: r.o wl fnl f: clsng on ldrs at fin* **33/1**
5 4 ½ **Fiery Sunset** 3-9-0 0 [1] TomQueally 11 73
(Michael Bell) *athletic: mid-div: hdwy 3f out: sn rdn to chse ldrs: fdd ins fnl f* **28/1**
352- 6 7 **Makruma**[160] 7692 3-9-0 80 PaulHanagan 1 60
(J W Hills) *lw: led: rdn and hdd 2f out: wknd over 1f out* **11/2**[3]
4- 7 nk **Intense Tango**[178] 7274 3-9-0 0 KierenFallon 2 60
(Alan Jarvis) *w'like: mid-div: hdwy 3f out: sn rdn: wknd over 1f out* **40/1**
0- 8 1 ½ **Interject (USA)**[156] 7764 3-9-0 0 JamesDoyle 4 57
(Charles Hills) *lengthy: mid-div: hdwy 3f out: sn rdn: wknd over 1f out* **20/1**
4- 9 1 **Pink And Black (IRE)**[156] 7763 3-9-0 0 MartinDwyer 10 55
(William Muir) *athletic: trckd ldrs: rdn over 2f out: sn wknd* **25/1**
10 ¾ **En Reve** 3-9-0 0 DaneO'Neill 6 53
(Seamus Durack) *w'like: leggy: a towards rr* **66/1**
43- 11 nk **Charmy Dukesse (IRE)**[105] 8415 3-9-0 0 AdamKirby 5 53
(Marco Botti) *w'like: trckd ldrs: rdn over 2f out: sn wknd* **20/1**
06- 12 nse **Cradle Of Life (IRE)**[167] 7532 3-9-0 0 FrankieDettori 3 53
(Ed Dunlop) *lw: hld up towards rr: hdwy 3f out: sn rdn: edgd lft and wknd 2f out* **20/1**

2m 11.2s (2.40) **Going Correction** +0.475s/f (Yiel) 12 Ran SP% **116.3**
Speed ratings (Par 97): **109,107,107,105,102 96,96,94,94,93 93,93**
CSF £6.43 TOTE £3.70: £2.10, £1.10, £2.90; EX 10.60 Trifecta £72.30.
**Owner** Saeed Manana **Bred** Rabbah Bloodstock Limited **Trained** Newmarket, Suffolk

**FOCUS**
The second division of this maiden was run before the first in order to fit in with the visit of The Queen, who had a runner in this leg following Enliven in the previous race. The Oaks winner Dancing Rain took a division of this race in 2011 and this year it went to another nice prospect. As in the earlier races on the round course, they spurned the inside rail in the straight. It was the fastest of the four C&D races, the first four finished clear, and the form is rated on the positive side.

## 1424 WHITLEY STUD MAIDEN FILLIES' STKS (BOBIS RACE) (DIV I) 1m 2f 6y
5:45 (5:48) (Class 4) 3-Y-O £4,851 (£1,443; £721; £360) Stalls Centre

Form RPR
23- 1 **Inchila**[238] 5488 3-9-0 0 JamieSpencer 4 84+
(Peter Chapple-Hyam) *lw: t.k.h early: hld up: gng best w nt clr run fr over 2f out: swtchd rt jst over 1f out: quicked up wl ent fnl f: sn led: r.o: comf* **9/2**[2]
43- 2 1 ¼ **Cascading**[167] 7532 3-9-0 0 JimmyFortune 1 79
(Hughie Morrison) *led: rdn over 1f out: hdd jst ins fnl f: kpt on gamely but sn hld by wnr* **12/1**
45- 3 ¾ **Criteria (IRE)**[202] 6643 3-9-0 0 WilliamBuick 9 78
(John Gosden) *bit bkwd: restrained bk into mid-div after 3f: hdwy 3f out: chsd ldr 2f out: sn rdn: kpt on same pce ins fnl f* **9/2**[2]
4 1 **Nancy From Nairobi** 3-8-11 0 WilliamTwiston-Davies(3) 8 76
(Mick Channon) *str: lw: hld up towards rr: hdwy over 3f out: rdn to chse ldrs over 2f out: kpt on same pce fnl f* **40/1**
52- 5 1 ¼ **Dorset Cream**[171] 7449 3-9-0 0 JamesDoyle 12 74
(Lady Cecil) *str: in tch: chsd ldr 2f out: sn rdn: one pce fnl f* **8/1**

5- 6 ¾ **Almashooqa (USA)**[156] 7764 3-9-0 0 PaulHanagan 13 72
(Roger Varian) *w'like: scope: bit bkwd: hld up towards rr: pushed along and hdwy over 3f out: rdn over 2f out: kpt on but nvr finding pce to get involved* **8/1**
7 1 ¼ **Approaching Star (FR)** 3-9-0 0 RyanMoore 2 70
(William Haggas) *athletic: str: mid-div: hdwy over 3f out: sn chsng ldrs: rdn over 2f out: wknd ins fnl f* **7/2**[1]
253- 8 8 **Tinga (IRE)**[220] 6063 3-9-0 0 [1] JimCrowley 6 55
(Ralph Beckett) *trckd ldrs: rdn wl over 2f out: wknd over 1f out* **5/1**[3]
0- 9 14 **Magic Shoes (IRE)**[162] 7645 3-9-0 0 SilvestreDeSousa 3 28
(Roger Charlton) *w'like: trckd ldrs: effrt over 3f out: wknd 2f out* **28/1**
10 17 **Lady Day** 3-9-0 0 SeanLevey 10
(Richard Hannon) *angular: tall: s.i.s: a towards rr: t.o* **40/1**
3 11 ½ **Martinette (USA)**[14] 1143 3-9-0 0 FrankieDettori 5
(Charles Hills) *tall: trckd ldr: rdn over 3f out: wknd 2f out: t.o* **16/1**

2m 12.69s (3.89) **Going Correction** +0.475s/f (Yiel) 11 Ran SP% **119.4**
Speed ratings (Par 97): **103,102,101,100,99 99,98,91,80,66 66**
CSF £57.41 TOTE £5.60: £2.20, £3.20, £1.70; EX 56.90 Trifecta £308.20.
**Owner** Woodcote Stud Ltd **Bred** Woodcote Stud Ltd **Trained** Newmarket, Suffolk

**FOCUS**
The winning time was 1.49sec slower than the other division and again they came up the centre.
T/Jkpt: Not won. T/Plt: £670.00 to a £1 stake. Pool: £88935.70 - 96.90 winning tickets T/Qpdt: £27.10 to a £1 stake. Pool: £6766.57 - 184.25 winning tickets TM

# 1311 WOLVERHAMPTON (A.W) (L-H)
Friday, April 11

**OFFICIAL GOING: Standard**
Wind: Fresh against Weather: Fine

## 1425 32RED FREE £10 BONUS H'CAP 5f 20y(P)
5:35 (5:36) (Class 5) (20-50,66) 3-Y-O £2,911 (£866; £432; £216) Stalls Low

Form RPR
614- 1 **Dynamo Walt (IRE)**[147] 7900 3-9-3 62 (v) DaleSwift 1 70+
(Derek Shaw) *plld hrd and prom: rdn over 1f out: led ins fnl f: r.o* **9/2**[2]
4642 2 1 ¾ **Douneedahand**[21] 1047 3-8-8 60 GaryMahon(7) 5 62
(Seamus Mullins) *a.p: chsd ldr over 3f out: led over 2f out: rdn over 1f out: edgd lft and hdd ins fnl f: styd on same pce* **8/1**
36-0 3 nk **Baker Man (IRE)**[16] 1101 3-8-12 62 JoshBaudains(5) 2 63
(Sylvester Kirk) *sn led: pushed along and hdd over 2f out: n.m.r and styd on same pce ins fnl f* **9/4**[1]
24-4 4 ½ **Fredricka**[43] 765 3-9-1 63 BillyCray(3) 4 62
(Garry Moss) *hld up: rdn over 1f out: sn hung lft: hung rt ins fnl f: r.o: nt rch ldrs* **14/1**
3123 5 2 ¼ **Rose Buck**[24] 1006 3-9-7 66 WilliamCarson 6 57
(Giles Bravery) *sn pushed along in rr: styd on ins fnl f: nvr trbld ldrs* **13/2**[3]
4331 6 2 **Biscuiteer**[21] 1039 3-8-12 57 (b) LukeMorris 3 41
(Scott Dixon) *chsd ldr tl over 3f out: sn rdn: wknd over 1f out* **9/4**[1]

1m 2.57s (0.27) **Going Correction** +0.075s/f (Slow) 6 Ran SP% **110.8**
Speed ratings (Par 98): **100,97,96,95,92 89**
CSF £36.85 TOTE £7.30: £3.10, £3.80; EX 29.00 Trifecta £132.60.
**Owner** Brian Johnson (Northamptonshire) **Bred** Dan Major **Trained** Sproxton, Leics

**FOCUS**
The opening sprint handicap for 3yos was notable for a gamble going astray. The form is rated around the runner-up.

## 1426 32RED.COM H'CAP 1m 5f 194y(P)
6:05 (6:06) (Class 6) (0-60,66) 4-Y-O+ £2,264 (£673; £336; £168) Stalls Low

Form RPR
-223 1 **Pinotage**[35] 872 6-9-5 58 (p) JamesSullivan 4 66
(Peter Niven) *trckd ldrs: pushed along over 2f out: r.o to ld nr fin* **6/1**[3]
0-00 2 nk **Hazzaat (IRE)**[42] 776 4-9-2 58 JimmyQuinn 2 65
(Nick Littmoden) *s.i.s: hld up: hdwy over 4f out: rdn to ld ins fnl f: edgd rt: hdd nr fin* **20/1**
1151 3 ¾ **Sir Frank Morgan (IRE)**[7] 1284 4-9-10 66 6ex JoeFanning 1 72
(Mark Johnston) *led at stdy pce tl qcknd over 3f out: rdn over 1f out: hdd ins fnl f: unable qck towards fin* **8/13**[1]
12-2 4 ¾ **Tracks Of My Tears**[8] 1265 4-9-4 60 PatrickDonaghy 3 64
(Giles Bravery) *trckd ldr: rdn and ev ch over 2f out: no ex wl ins fnl f* **5/2**[2]

3m 8.63s (2.63) **Going Correction** +0.075s/f (Slow)
**WFA** 4 from 5yo+ 3lb 4 Ran SP% **109.5**
Speed ratings (Par 101): **95,94,94,93**
CSF £59.21 TOTE £10.50; EX 16.90 Trifecta £63.50.
**Owner** S Bowett **Bred** Hellwood Stud Farm **Trained** Barton-le-Street, N Yorks
■ Stewards' Enquiry : Jimmy Quinn four-day ban: used whip above permitted level down shoulder in the forehand (Apr 25-28)

**FOCUS**
A good staying handicap for the grade with a couple of the runners due to race off higher marks in future. The leader set a slow gallop that played into the winner's hands, and this is muddling form, with the market leaders disappointing.

## 1427 32RED CASINO MAIDEN FILLIES' STKS 1m 141y(P)
6:35 (6:36) (Class 5) 3-Y-O+ £2,587 (£770; £384; £192) Stalls Low

Form RPR
0- 1 **Saltwater Creek (IRE)**[170] 7466 3-8-10 0 JoeFanning 6 75
(Michael Bell) *hld up: hdwy over 1f out: shkn up to ld wl ins fnl f: r.o: readily* **25/1**
00- 2 1 ¼ **Dalmarella Dancer (IRE)**[195] 6828 3-8-10 0 BenCurtis 3 72
(K R Burke) *dwlt: hld up: hdwy over 3f out: rdn over 2f out: hung lft fr over 1f out: led ins fnl f: sn hdd and unable qck* **20/1**
64- 3 1 **Gold Approach**[171] 7449 3-8-10 0 [1] LiamJones 5 70
(William Haggas) *chsd ldrs: sn pushed along: outpcd over 2f out: r.o ins fnl f* **10/11**[1]
35- 4 ½ **Weekend Getaway (IRE)**[185] 7102 3-8-10 0 WilliamCarson 2 69
(Clive Brittain) *led 1f: trckd ldr: rdn over 2f out: styd on same pce ins fnl f* **8/1**[3]
6- 5 nk **Alphabetique**[126] 8175 3-8-10 0 ShaneKelly 4 68
(Peter Chapple-Hyam) *chsd ldrs: rdn over 1f out: no ex ins fnl f* **20/1**
42- 6 2 ¼ **Alpine Storm (IRE)**[146] 7934 3-8-10 0 MartinLane 1 63
(Charlie Appleby) *plld hrd: led over 7f out: rdn over 1f out: hdd & wknd ins fnl f* **7/4**[2]

1m 50.63s (0.13) **Going Correction** +0.075s/f (Slow) 6 Ran SP% **113.2**
Speed ratings (Par 100): **102,100,100,99,99 97**
CSF £355.28 TOTE £21.50: £15.30, £16.80; EX 153.90 Trifecta £508.70.
**Owner** Dr Ali Ridha **Bred** Keelogue Stables **Trained** Newmarket, Suffolk

**FOCUS**
With the two market leaders bombing out this was a weak fillies' maiden and they finished in a bit of a heap. The form is rated cautiously.

## 1428 CORAL APP DOWNLOAD FROM THE APP STORE H'CAP 1m 1f 103y(P)
**7:05** (7:05) (Class 6) (0-60,57) 4-Y-0+ **£2,264** (£673; £336; £168) **Stalls** Low

Form RPR
3443 **1** **Polar Forest**[23] 1012 4-9-5 55 (e) RobertWinston 9 62
(Richard Guest) *a.p: shkn up over 1f out: r.o u.p to ld towards fin* **4/1**[2]
0322 **2** *nse* **General Tufto**[10] 1228 9-9-1 51 (b) MartinLane 3 58
(Charles Smith) *hld up: hdwy over 2f out: rdn over 1f out: r.o wl* **10/1**
02 **3** *nk* **Final Delivery**[31] 916 5-9-6 56 WilliamCarson 6 62
(Jim Boyle) *trckd ldrs: wnt 2nd over 1f out: rdn to ld ins fnl f: edgd rt: hdd towards fin* **6/4**[1]
4033 **4** *1 1/4* **Rockweiller**[12] 1197 7-8-9 48 (b) MichaelJMMurphy(3) 4 52
(Shaun Harris) *led: rdn over 1f out: hdd and unable qck ins fnl f* **9/2**[3]
30-5 **5** *1 1/2* **Lambert Pen (USA)**[8] 1268 4-8-11 52 ShelleyBirkett(5) 7 52
(Peter Hiatt) *chsd ldr tl rdn over 1f out: styd on same pce ins fnl f* **25/1**
0511 **6** *8* **Catching Zeds**[21] 1050 7-9-3 53 (b) StevieDonohoe 2 37
(Kevin Frost) *s.i.s: hld up: rdn over 2f out: n.d* **8/1**
-450 **7** *1 1/4* **Cantor**[58] 571 6-9-4 57 (tp) RossAtkinson(3) 1 38
(Paul Morgan) *mid-div: rdn over 3f out: wknd over 1f out* **20/1**
040- **8** *2 3/4* **Barton Bounty**[182] 7169 7-9-5 55 TomEaves 5 30
(Peter Niven) *hld up: pushed along over 3f out: hdwy u.p over 2f out: wknd fnl f* **8/1**
6-66 **9** *8* **Cottam Maybel**[36] 861 5-8-11 47 GrahamGibbons 8 5
(Michael Easterby) *s.i.s: hdwy over 7f out: rdn over 2f out: wknd over 1f out* **33/1**

2m 3.3s (1.60) **Going Correction** +0.075s/f (Slow) 9 Ran SP% **121.0**
Speed ratings (Par 101): **95,94,94,93,92 85,84,81,74**
CSF £44.13 CT £87.18 TOTE £3.80: £1.20, £3.70, £1.10; EX 42.40 Trifecta £253.60.
**Owner** Maze Rattan Limited **Bred** Worksop Manor Stud **Trained** Wetherby, W Yorks

**FOCUS**
A low-grade handicap with a surprisingly short-priced favourite. Straightforward form.

## 1429 COMPARE BOOKMAKERS AT BOOKMAKERS.CO.UK H'CAP 5f 216y(P)
**7:35** (7:35) (Class 4) (0-85,81) 4-Y-0+ **£5,175** (£1,540; £769; £384) **Stalls** Low

Form RPR
2112 **1** **Jubilee Brig**[8] 1261 4-9-1 78 (v) RossAtkinson(3) 2 88
(Sean Curran) *chsd ldrs: rdn over 1f out: r.o to ld nr fin* **5/1**[2]
1422 **2** *shd* **Mappin Time (IRE)**[6] 1313 6-9-7 81 (be) RobertWinston 3 91+
(Tim Easterby) *broke wl: sn stdd and lost pl: hdwy over 2f out: shkn up to ld over 1f out: rdn ins fnl f: hdd nr fin* **10/11**[1]
0-52 **3** *3* **Vincentti (IRE)**[11] 1212 4-9-4 78 LukeMorris 5 78
(Ronald Harris) *sn pushed along in rr: styd on u.p fnl f: nt trble ldrs* **7/1**[3]
0-50 **4** *3/4* **Bapak Chinta (USA)**[8] 1261 5-9-6 80 (b[1]) AmyRyan 6 78
(Kevin Ryan) *trckd ldr tl rdn to ld over 1f out: sn hdd: styd on same pce ins fnl f* **10/1**
50-4 **5** *2 3/4* **Intrepid (IRE)**[7] 1283 4-9-1 75 StevieDonohoe 1 64
(Tim Pitt) *chsd ldrs: rdn over 1f out: wknd fnl f* **8/1**
-331 **6** *1/2* **Bogsnog (IRE)**[14] 1152 4-9-2 76 TomEaves 4 63
(Kristin Stubbs) *sn led: rdn and hdd over 1f out: wknd ins fnl f* **8/1**

1m 14.46s (-0.54) **Going Correction** +0.075s/f (Slow) 6 Ran SP% **112.9**
Speed ratings (Par 105): **106,105,101,100,97 96**
CSF £10.16 TOTE £4.10: £1.80, £1.30; EX 8.10 Trifecta £33.10.
**Owner** Power Bloodstock Ltd **Bred** Sir Eric Parker **Trained** Hatford, Oxon

**FOCUS**
A personal best from the winner in this fair handicap.

## 1430 BOOKMAKERS.CO.UK MAIDEN STKS 5f 20y(P)
**8:05** (8:05) (Class 5) 3-Y-0+ **£2,587** (£770; £384; £192) **Stalls** Low

Form RPR
2 **1** **Dreams Of Reality**[15] 1137 3-8-10 0 (e[1]) RichardKingscote 5 74
(Tom Dascombe) *trckd ldr: shkn up to ld ins fnl f: r.o wl* **7/1**
-422 **2** *2 3/4* **Katja**[21] 1039 3-8-7 60 OisinMurphy(3) 3 64
(J W Hills) *led: rdn over 1f out: hdd and unable qck ins fnl f* **10/11**[1]
5-56 **3** *2 1/4* **Meridius (IRE)**[45] 741 4-9-5 65 (b) JordanVaughan(7) 4 66
(Nick Littmoden) *mid-div: hdwy over 1f out: styd on: nt trble ldrs* **7/2**[2]
333 **4** *2 3/4* **Role Reversal**[25] 994 3-8-10 62 (p) LukeMorris 6 46
(James Tate) *sn drvn along in rr: styd on ins fnl f: nvr nrr* **5/1**[3]
53 **5** *1* **Torridon**[15] 1137 3-9-1 0 JoeFanning 2 47
(Mark Johnston) *chsd ldrs: rdn 1/2-way: wknd fnl f* **14/1**
-444 **6** *1 3/4* **Stoneacre Hull (IRE)**[15] 1137 5-9-7 47 StephenCraine 1 41
(Peter Grayson) *hld up: sme hdwy over 1f out: sn wknd* **50/1**
00-0 **7** *2* **Sutton Sioux**[21] 1039 3-8-10 45 SteveDrowne 8 29
(Jeremy Gask) *s.i.s: nvr on terms* **50/1**
23-0 **8** *3/4* **Mid Yorkshire Golf**[91] 121 5-9-4 47 SladeO'Hara(3) 9 31
(Peter Grayson) *hld up: rdn over 1f out: n.d* **33/1**
55-6 **9** *4* **Elusive**[9] 1243 8-9-2 29 AnnStokell(5) 7 17
(Ann Stokell) *sn pushed along and prom: wknd 2f out* **100/1**

1m 2.04s (-0.26) **Going Correction** +0.075s/f (Slow)
**WFA** 3 from 4yo+ 11lb 9 Ran SP% **118.3**
Speed ratings (Par 103): **105,100,97,92,91 88,85,83,77**
CSF £14.11 TOTE £8.40: £2.40, £1.10, £2.10; EX 16.80 Trifecta £85.50.
**Owner** John A Duffy **Bred** J A And Mrs Duffy **Trained** Malpas, Cheshire

**FOCUS**
With a 60-rated filly sent off odds-on favourite, this was a weak maiden, but the time wasn't bad. The form is rated around the runner-up.

## 1431 BEST ODDS AT BOOKMAKERS.CO.UK H'CAP 5f 20y(P)
**8:35** (8:36) (Class 5) (0-75,78) 4-Y-0+ **£3,072** (£914; £456; £228) **Stalls** Low

Form RPR
6-62 **1** **Red Cape (FR)**[6] 1311 11-8-9 63 (b) JamesSullivan 8 71
(Ruth Carr) *outpcd: rdn and r.o ins fnl f: led nr fin* **6/1**
-660 **2** *3/4* **Tyfos**[31] 909 9-9-7 75 AndrewMullen 1 80
(Brian Baugh) *chsd ldrs: pushed along 3f out: rdn to ld wl ins fnl f: hdd nr fin* **8/1**
400- **3** *shd* **Storm Lightning**[163] 7634 5-9-5 73 (b) GrahamGibbons 5 78
(Mark Brisbourne) *chsd ldrs: rdn 1/2-way: led 1f out: hdd wl ins fnl f: kpt on* **8/1**
5541 **4** *1 1/2* **West Coast Dream**[22] 1030 7-8-13 67 TomEaves 7 67
(Roy Brotherton) *jnd ldr 4f out tl led 2f out: rdn and hdd 1f out: styd on same pce* **5/1**[3]
4021 **5** *nk* **Hamoody (USA)**[3] 1368 10-9-7 78 6ex OisinMurphy(3) 4 76
(Joseph Tuite) *s.i.s: sn pushed along in rr: hdwy over 1f out: nt trble ldrs* **7/4**[1]
2011 **6** *2* **Secret Millionaire (IRE)**[25] 987 7-9-2 70 LukeMorris 6 61
(Tony Carroll) *prom: pushed along 1/2-way: nt clr run over 1f out: styd on same pce fnl f* **3/1**[2]
140- **7** *3 1/2* **Royal Acquisition**[232] 5673 4-9-6 74 SteveDrowne 3 53
(Robert Cowell) *led 3f: sn rdn: wknd ins fnl f* **20/1**

1m 2.18s (-0.12) **Going Correction** +0.075s/f (Slow) 7 Ran SP% **119.3**
Speed ratings (Par 103): **103,101,101,99,98 95,89**
CSF £54.45 CT £392.22 TOTE £7.60: £3.20, £4.00; EX 44.40 Trifecta £407.70.
**Owner** Middleham Park Racing LVI **Bred** Gilles And Mrs Forien **Trained** Huby, N Yorks

**FOCUS**
The pace was furious in this handicap over the minimum trip. The third looks the best guide.
T/Plt: £5,122.30 to a £1 stake. Pool: £71923.87 - 10.25 winning tickets T/Qpdt: £172.00 to a £1 stake. Pool: £11137.73 - 47.90 winning tickets CR

1432 - (Foreign Racing) - See Raceform Interactive

# 1417 NEWBURY (L-H)
Saturday, April 12

**OFFICIAL GOING: Good (good to soft in places; 6.4)**
Wind: mild breeze half across Weather: cloudy

## 1433 DUBAI DUTY FREE TENNIS CHAMPIONSHIPS MAIDEN STKS (BOBIS RACE) 1m (S)
**1:20** (1:23) (Class 4) 3-Y-0 **£5,175** (£1,540; £769; £384) **Stalls** Centre

Form RPR
**1** **Matalleb (USA)** 3-9-5 0 DaneO'Neill 4 87+
(John Gosden) *w'like: scope: str: mid-div: hdwy over 2f out: pushed into ld over 1f out: qcknd ahed ent fnl f: kpt up to work: hld on w a little in hand* **7/1**[3]
2- **2** *hd* **Mutakayyef**[171] 7467 3-9-5 0 PaulHanagan 11 84
(William Haggas) *lw: sn prom: rdn to chal 2f out: briefly outpcd by wnr ent fnl f: kpt on towards fin: nvr quite getting there* **1/1**[1]
4- **3** *1 1/4* **Brown Diamond (IRE)**[203] 6643 3-9-0 0 JamieSpencer 1 76
(Charles Hills) *leggy: hld up bhd: hdwy 2f out: sn rdn: fin wl to go 3rd up stands' side rail fnl f* **8/1**
03- **4** *1 3/4* **Hanno (USA)**[143] 7971 3-9-5 0 AdamKirby 3 77
(Ed Dunlop) *tall: mid-div: hdwy over 2f out to chse ldrs: sn rdn: kpt on fnl f* **25/1**
**5** *1 1/4* **Hoy Hoy (IRE)** 3-9-5 0 SilvestreDeSousa 9 74+
(Mick Channon) *w'like: led for 1f: led over 3f out: rdn 2f out: hdd over 1f out: no ex fnl 100yds* **20/1**
**6** *1* **Elite Force (IRE)** 3-9-5 0 GeorgeBaker 13 72+
(Roger Charlton) *w'like: scope: lw: hld up towards rr: hdwy 2f out: sn rdn: kpt on but nt pce to get involved* **33/1**
**7** *shd* **Silver Duke (IRE)** 3-9-5 0 KierenFallon 10 72
(Alan Jarvis) *str: mid-div: pushed along over 2f out: hdwy whn swtchd rt over 1f out: kpt on same pce fnl f* **66/1**
45- **8** *3/4* **Isabella Bird**[184] 7155 3-9-0 0 JamesDoyle 14 65
(Mick Channon) *mid-div: hdwy 2f out: effrt over 1f out: fdd fnl f* **16/1**
**9** *2 1/2* **Inspector Norse** 3-9-5 0 LiamKeniry 6 64
(Sylvester Kirk) *unf: trckd ldrs: rdn over 2f out: wknd jst over 1f out* **66/1**
**10** *3/4* **I Am Not Here (IRE)** 3-9-5 0 LukeMorris 2 62
(Alan Jarvis) *w'like: hld up towards rr: rdn and sme prog over 2f out: no further imp fnl f* **100/1**
**11** *5* **Sleeper** 3-9-0 0 JimCrowley 5 46
(Ralph Beckett) *unf: trckd ldrs: rdn over 2f out: wknd over 1f out* **33/1**
**11** *dht* **Villainous (IRE)** 3-9-5 0 WilliamBuick 12 51
(John Gosden) *w'like: mid-div tl wknd 2f out* **11/1**
**13** *4* **Triple Chief (IRE)** 3-9-5 0 FrederikTylicki 8 42
(Rod Millman) *w'like: tall: trckd ldrs tl wknd over 2f out* **100/1**
2- **14** *16* **Dursey Island (USA)**[200] 6733 3-9-5 0 RyanMoore 15 5
(Richard Hannon) *athletic: prom: led after 1f tl over 3f out: wknd tamely over 2f out: eased fnl f* **6/1**[2]
**15** *23* **Leftrightleftright (IRE)** 3-9-5 0 MarcHalford 7
(Luke Dace) *leggy: s.i.s: sn struggling in rr: a bhd* **125/1**

1m 44.01s (4.31) **Going Correction** +0.525s/f (Yiel) 15 Ran SP% **122.4**
Speed ratings (Par 100): **99,98,97,95,94 93,93,92,90,89 84,84,80,64,41**
CSF £13.65 TOTE £8.90: £2.30, £1.10, £2.40; EX 22.10 Trifecta £212.60.
**Owner** Hamdan Al Maktoum **Bred** Kilroy Thoroughbred Partnership **Trained** Newmarket, Suffolk

**FOCUS**
Rails on round course moved out overnight between 8f and 5f adding 30 metres to races on Round course. The ground had dried out further since the previous day's meeting and was now Good, good to soft in places. They raced centre-to-stands' side in this interesting maiden which should produce its share of winners. However the form is rated below the race average. The winner was value for extra on the day. As in the opening 2yo maiden here the previous day, Paul Hanagan's loss was Dane O'Neill's gain.

## 1434 DUBAI DUTY FREE FINEST SURPRISE STKS (REGISTERED AS THE JOHN PORTER STAKES) (GROUP 3) 1m 4f 5y
**1:50** (1:51) (Class 1) 4-Y-0+
**£34,026** (£12,900; £6,456; £3,216; £1,614; £810) **Stalls** Centre

Form RPR
321- **1** **Cubanita**[168] 7535 5-9-0 107 JimCrowley 2 111
(Ralph Beckett) *trckd ldrs: chal gng wl over 2f out: led wl over 1f out: sn rdn and hrd pressed: hld on gamely fnl f: drvn out* **7/1**
434- **2** *nk* **Noble Mission**[189] 7049 5-9-0 111 JamesDoyle 3 110
(Lady Cecil) *little slowly away: in last pair: hdwy over 2f out: edgd rt whn rdn to press wnr wl over 1f out: str chal thrght fnl f: hld nring fin* **11/4**[1]
350- **3** *1 1/4* **Rawaki (IRE)**[174] 7407 6-9-0 99 LiamKeniry 6 108
(Andrew Balding) *trckd ldrs: rdn 2f out: kpt on ins fnl f but nt pce to chal* **33/1**
221- **4** *1 1/2* **Astonishing (IRE)**[198] 6764 4-8-10 109 RyanMoore 9 102+
(Sir Michael Stoute) *lw: hld up: pushed along and hdwy 3f out: nt clrest of runs whn rdn wl over 1f out: styd on same pce fnl f* **9/2**[3]
4/1- **5** *3/4* **Khione**[343] 2012 5-8-11 105 AndreaAtzeni 5 101+
(Luca Cumani) *mid-div: rdn to cl 2f out: sn short of room and lost pl: swtchd rt: styd on ins fnl f* **9/1**
032- **6** *2* **Cocktail Queen (IRE)**[154] 7822 4-8-10 97 DaneO'Neill 10 98
(David Elsworth) *trckd ldr: rdn and ev ch briefly 2f out: sn one pce* **16/1**
014- **7** *1 1/2* **Quiz Mistress**[168] 7535 6-8-11 105 TomQueally 4 95
(Hughie Morrison) *hld up: rdn 2f out: nvr finding pce to get involved* **16/1**
/13- **8** *3 3/4* **Mutashaded (USA)**[295] 3523 4-8-13 104 PaulHanagan 1 92
(Roger Varian) *lw: mid-div: hdwy 3f out: rdn to chse ldrs 2f out: wknd ins fnl f* **3/1**[2]


The Form Book, Raceform Ltd, Newbury, RG14 5SJ

160- **9** 2 ½ **Nearly Caught (IRE)**[154] 7823 4-8-13 99.................. SilvestreDeSousa 8 88
(Hughie Morrison) *led: rdn over 2f out: hdd wl over 1f out: wknd ent fnl f*
**16/1**

2m 37.98s (2.48) **Going Correction** +0.525s/f (Yiel)
**WFA** 4 from 5yo+ 1lb **9** Ran SP% **112.9**
Speed ratings (Par 113): **112,111,110,109,109 108,107,104,102**
CSF £25.94 TOTE £8.00: £2.30, £1.50, £6.60; EX 30.90 Trifecta £503.80.
**Owner** Miss K Rausing **Bred** Miss K Rausing **Trained** Kimpton, Hants

**FOCUS**
The form is ordinary for the grade but some of these are still improving, notably the winner. They raced up the middle in the straight.

## 1435 DUBAI DUTY FREE STKS (REGISTERED AS THE FRED DARLING STAKES) (GROUP 3) (FILLIES) 7f (S)
**2:20** (2:21) (Class 1) 3-Y-O
**£34,026** (£12,900; £6,456; £3,216; £1,614; £810) **Stalls** Centre

Form RPR
110- **1** **J Wonder (USA)**[233] 5680 3-9-0 94.................. JimmyFortune 4 106+
(Brian Meehan) *mid-div: nt clr run fr over 2f out tl swtchd lft jst over 1f out: qcknd up wl to ld jst ins fnl f: r.o*
**4/1**[2]

110- **2** *hd* **Al Thakhira**[162] 7690 3-9-0 107.................. FrankieDettori 12 105
(Marco Botti) *lw: mid-div: swtchd lft 2f out: hdwy sn after: rdn for str chal jst ins fnl f: drifted rt fnl 70yds: kpt on: jst hld*
**11/4**[1]

316- **3** 1 ¼ **Joyeuse**[196] 6836 3-9-0 104.................. JamesDoyle 1 101
(Lady Cecil) *hld up last: swtchd lft 2f out: sn rdn and hdwy: r.o fnl f but nvr rching ldng pair*
**4/1**[2]

431- **4** ½ **Lady Lara (IRE)**[204] 6594 3-9-0 95.................. KierenFallon 11 100
(Alan Jarvis) *trckd ldrs: chal 2f out: sn rdn: led jst over 1f out: hdd ins fnl f: kpt on*
**20/1**

302- **5** 1 **Manderley (IRE)**[189] 7016 3-9-0 91.................. SeanLevey 13 97
(Richard Hannon) *trckd ldr: rdn to chal 2f out tl no ex ins fnl f*
**33/1**

211- **6** 2 ¼ **Dutch Courage**[273] 4300 3-9-0 93.................. RyanMoore 7 91
(Richard Fahey) *racd keenly: trckd ldrs: effrt to chal 2f out: one pce fnl f*
**8/1**[3]

311- **7** ½ **Coral Mist**[203] 6622 3-9-0 99.................. TomQueally 9 90+
(Charles Hills) *hld up: nt clr run and swtchd lft whn hmpd 2f out: no imp after*
**10/1**

143- **8** ¾ **Valonia**[182] 7194 3-9-0 98.................. JamieSpencer 5 88
(Henry Candy) *lw: led: rdn 2f out: hdd jst over 1f out: wknd*
**8/1**[3]

422- **9** ½ **Alys Love**[191] 6973 3-9-0 79.................. MartinDwyer 8 87?
(William Muir) *in tch: rdn 2f out: nt pce to get on terms w ldrs*
**66/1**

413- **10** 1 ½ **Dutch Romance**[168] 7537 3-9-0 93.................. WilliamBuick 3 82
(Charles Hills) *hld up: rdn 2f out: nvr threatened: wknd fnl f*
**16/1**

110- **11** *hd* **Beldale Memory (IRE)**[297] 3459 3-9-0 91.................. HarryBentley 2 82
(Clive Cox) *in tch: hung lft whn rdn 2f out: wknd fnl f*
**16/1**

1m 28.83s (3.13) **Going Correction** +0.525s/f (Yiel) **11** Ran SP% **118.9**
Speed ratings (Par 105): **103,102,101,100,99 97,96,95,95,93 93**
CSF £15.32 TOTE £5.60: £2.20, £1.30, £2.40; EX 19.40 Trifecta £79.10.
**Owner** Andrew Rosen **Bred** Canterbury Lace Syndicate **Trained** Manton, Wilts
■ Stewards' Enquiry : James Doyle one-day ban: careless riding (Apr 26)

**FOCUS**
No winner of the Fred Darling has followed up in the 1,000 Guineas since Wince in 1999. This didn't look a particularly strong race but some of the likelier types came to the fore and the front two were well on top at the line off what appeared just an ordinary gallop. They raced stands' side throughout and the time was almost two seconds slower than Kingman managed in the Greenham, in which the action initially unfolded up the middle of the track. Just an ordinary renewal, and the winner needs to find 10lb or so in the Guineas.

## 1436 AON GREENHAM STKS (GROUP 3) (C&G) 7f (S)
**2:55** (2:55) (Class 1) 3-Y-O
**£34,026** (£12,900; £6,456; £3,216; £1,614; £810) **Stalls** Centre

Form RPR
11- **1** **Kingman**[224] 5999 3-9-0 111.................. JamesDoyle 8 123+
(John Gosden) *str: travelled wl: hld up in tch: smooth prog to ld jst ins fnl f: qcknd clr: impressive*
**15/8**[1]

11- **2** 4 ½ **Night Of Thunder (IRE)**[168] 7525 3-9-0 109.................. RyanMoore 7 111
(Richard Hannon) *lw: trckd ldr: rdn wl over 1f out: wnt clr 2nd ins fnl f but nt pce of impressive wnr*
**11/4**[2]

023- **3** 2 ¾ **Master Carpenter (IRE)**[203] 6640 3-9-0 91.................. AndreaAtzeni 9 103
(Rod Millman) *hld up: rdn over 1f out: r.o wl ins fnl f: snatched 3rd fnl strides*
**80/1**

1- **4** ½ **Lat Hawill (IRE)**[192] 6939 3-9-0 0.................. JamieSpencer 6 102+
(Marco Botti) *w'like: scope: hld up: hdwy 2f out: sn rdn: kpt on fnl f but nt pce to threaten: lost 3rd fnl strides*
**8/1**

111- **5** *hd* **Astaire (IRE)**[182] 7191 3-9-0 114.................. KierenFallon 2 101
(Kevin Ryan) *led: rdn wl over 1f out: sn edgd rt: hdd jst ins fnl f: sn no ex*
**11/2**[3]

41- **6** ¾ **Golden Town (IRE)**[232] 5727 3-9-0 93.................. (t) SilvestreDeSousa 1 99+
(Saeed bin Suroor) *plld hrd: in tch: swtchd lft 2f out: sn rdn: chsng ldrs whn veered lft jst over 1f out: one pce fnl f*
**14/1**

21- **7** 2 **Windfast (IRE)**[326] 2543 3-9-0 97.................. JimmyFortune 5 94
(Brian Meehan) *in tch: rdn 2f out: nvr gng pce to chal: fdd ins fnl f*
**33/1**

320- **8** 6 **No Leaf Clover (IRE)**[147] 7939 3-9-0 99.................. RobertWinston 10 78
(Ollie Pears) *v awkward leaving stalls: towards rr: sme hdwy whn swtchd lft 2f out: nvr threatened: wknd fnl f*
**66/1**

311- **9** 2 ½ **Berkshire (IRE)**[196] 6835 3-9-0 113.................. JimCrowley 4 71
(Paul Cole) *racd keenly: trckd ldr: rdn over 1f out: sn wknd*
**9/1**

116- **10** 1 ¾ **Supplicant**[182] 7191 3-9-0 110.................. PaulHanagan 3 66
(Richard Fahey) *racd keenly: trckd ldrs: pushed along 3f out: wknd over 1f out*
**25/1**

1m 26.95s (1.25) **Going Correction** +0.525s/f (Yiel) **10** Ran SP% **114.1**
Speed ratings (Par 108): **113,107,104,104,103 103,100,93,91,89**
CSF £6.61 TOTE £2.70: £1.10, £1.50, £11.20; EX 6.80 Trifecta £349.20.
**Owner** K Abdullah **Bred** Juddmonte Farms Ltd **Trained** Newmarket, Suffolk

**FOCUS**
The way Kingman won this so impressively brought back memories of the 2011 winner Frankel. Kingman's form verges on Guineas standard, with Night Of Thunder improving a little.

## 1437 BERRY BROS & RUDD MAGNUM SPRING CUP (H'CAP) 1m (S)
**3:30** (3:31) (Class 2) 4-Y-O+
**£31,125** (£9,320; £4,660; £2,330; £1,165; £585) **Stalls** Centre

Form RPR
52-6 **1** **Gabrial's Kaka (IRE)**[14] 1165 4-8-12 95.................. JamieSpencer 11 108
(Richard Fahey) *racd centre: hld up bhd: travelling wl but nt clr run tl over 1f out: swtchd lft and r.o strly to ld jst ins fnl f: drifted rt: readily*
**8/1**[1]

-300 **2** 1 ½ **Spa's Dancer (IRE)**[14] 1165 7-8-13 96.................. JimCrowley 25 106
(James Eustace) *racd stands' side: hld up: travelling strly but nowhere to go fr 2f out tl gap appeared jst ins fnl f: fin v strly to go 2nd but nvr rching wnr in time*
**25/1**

50-2 **3** ¾ **Brownsea Brink**[22] 1042 4-8-10 93.................. RyanMoore 3 101
(Richard Hannon) *lw: racd centre: mid-div: hdwy fr 2f out: chal over 1f out: sn shkn up: shied away fr wnr whn w ev ch jst ins fnl f: kpt on same pce*
**8/1**[1]

3601 **4** *nk* **Ocean Tempest**[14] 1165 5-9-10 107.................. AdamKirby 6 114
(John Ryan) *racd centre: trckd ldr: rdn to ld and hung rt over 1f out: hdd jst ins fnl f: kpt on same pce*
**16/1**

0004 **5** *nse* **Sweet Lightning**[14] 1165 9-9-1 98.................. (t) DanielTudhope 21 105
(David O'Meara) *racd stands' side: hld up: rdn and hdwy 2f out: chsd ldrs ent fnl f: kpt on same pce*
**14/1**[3]

660- **6** 1 ¾ **Charles Camoin (IRE)**[147] 7927 6-8-7 90.................. LiamKeniry 24 93
(Sylvester Kirk) *racd stands' side: trckd ldr: nt clr run briefly 2f out: sn rdn: kpt on ins fnl f*
**16/1**

000- **7** *hd* **Bronze Angel (IRE)**[147] 7926 5-8-13 96.................. (b[1]) HayleyTurner 20 99
(Marcus Tregoning) *racd stands' side tl swtchd to centre 3f out: hld up: hdwy over 3f out: rdn to chse ldrs 2f out: styd on same pce fnl f*
**14/1**[3]

360 **8** *nk* **Burano (IRE)**[42] 812 5-9-5 102.................. JimmyFortune 12 104
(Brian Meehan) *racd centre: hld up towards rr: hdwy over 2f out: nt clr run over 1f out: rdn to kpt on same pce fnl f*
**33/1**

531- **9** 1 ¼ **Highland Duke (IRE)**[254] 4923 5-8-0 88 ow1.................. RyanTate[(5)] 23 87
(Clive Cox) *racd stands' side: mid-div: rdn over 2f out: kpt on ins fnl f but n.d*
**16/1**

/00- **10** ½ **Foxtrot Romeo (IRE)**[307] 3142 5-8-11 94.................. (t) FrankieDettori 16 92+
(Marco Botti) *racd stands' side: prom: rdn over 2f out: wknd ent fnl f*
**14/1**[3]

146- **11** ½ **Amulet**[154] 7822 4-8-3 86.................. SilvestreDeSousa 18 83
(Eve Johnson Houghton) *led stands' side gp: rdn over 2f out: wknd fnl f*
**20/1**

020- **12** 1 ¼ **One Word More (IRE)**[175] 7368 4-9-0 97.................. WilliamBuick 8 91
(Charles Hills) *racd centre: trckd ldrs: rdn over 2f out: wknd ent fnl f* **12/1**[2]

000- **13** ½ **Dubawi Sound**[175] 7368 6-8-11 94.................. (t[1]) MartinDwyer 9 87
(Hugo Palmer) *wnt to s early: racd centre: mid-div: hld whn sltly hmpd ins fnl f*
**16/1**

002- **14** ½ **Magic City (IRE)**[150] 7856 5-9-2 99.................. SeanLevey 10 90
(Richard Hannon) *racd centre: s.i.s: towards rr: sme hdwy into midfield over 2f out: no further imp fr over 1f out*
**33/1**

4160 **15** *shd* **Dixie's Dream (IRE)**[14] 1164 5-8-4 90.................. (v[1]) MichaelJMMurphy[(3)] 2 81
(William Jarvis) *racd centre: towards rr: hdwy over 2f out: chsd ldrs over 1f out: wknd ins fnl f*
**66/1**

150- **16** *hd* **Enobled**[225] 5958 4-8-3 86.................. DavidProbert 7 77
(Sir Michael Stoute) *racd centre: overall ldr: rdn and hdd over 1f out: wknd fnl f*
**16/1**

340- **17** ¾ **Secret Art (IRE)**[213] 6308 4-8-3 86.................. AndreaAtzeni 5 75
(William Knight) *racd centre: mid-div: rdn over 2f out: wknd over 1f out*
**12/1**[2]

-233 **18** *nk* **Moonday Sun (USA)**[38] 840 5-8-12 95.................. PatDobbs 4 83
(Amanda Perrett) *racd centre: mid-div: hdwy over 2f out: sn rdn: ch over 1f out: wknd fnl f*
**25/1**

000- **19** ¾ **Jacob Cats**[227] 5894 5-8-4 87.................. PaulHanagan 22 74
(William Knight) *racd stands' side: mid-div: sltly hmpd whn u.p 2f out: sn wknd*
**33/1**

516- **20** 10 **Tinghir (IRE)**[161] 7696 4-8-11 94.................. TedDurcan 17 58
(David Lanigan) *racd stands' side: mid-div: rdn over 2f out: wknd over 1f out*
**14/1**[3]

5022 **21** 3 ½ **Brocklebank (IRE)**[21] 1070 5-8-4 92.................. JackDuern[(5)] 1 48
(Simon Dow) *racd centre: stdd s: a bhd*
**33/1**

313- **22** 2 ¾ **Bluegrass Blues (IRE)**[210] 6403 4-8-5 88.................. LukeMorris 13 37
(Paul Cole) *racd stands' side: trckd ldrs tl wknd over 2f out*
**33/1**

103- **23** 21 **So Beloved**[255] 4897 4-8-4 90.................. OisinMurphy[(3)] 15
(Roger Charlton) *lw: racd stands' side: mid-div: rdn wl over 2f out: wknd over 1f out*
**8/1**[1]

1m 42.17s (2.47) **Going Correction** +0.525s/f (Yiel) **23** Ran SP% **133.4**
Speed ratings (Par 109): **108,106,105,105,105 103,103,103,101,101 100,99,99,98,98 98,97,97,96,86 83,80,59**
CSF £216.18 CT £1719.71 TOTE £8.90: £2.40, £5.50, £2.00, £5.20; EX 378.80 Trifecta £2801.70 Part won..
**Owner** Dr Marwan Koukash **Bred** Dave Orme **Trained** Musley Bank, N Yorks

**FOCUS**
Four of the first five contested the previous month's Lincoln, but they came home in a different order this time in what was another really competitive handicap. There were two groups early, a bunch near side and the others up the middle, but they merged soon enough and there was no noticeable bias. The winner continued his 3yo progress and the second ran as well as ever on the face of things.

## 1438 AL BASTI EQUIWORLD MAIDEN STKS (BOBIS RACE) 1m 3f 5y
**4:05** (4:09) (Class 4) 3-Y-O **£6,469** (£1,925; £962; £481) **Stalls** Centre

Form RPR
**1** **Eagle Top** 3-9-5 0.................. WilliamBuick 10 92+
(John Gosden) *cmpt: hld up towards rr: pushed along but no imp fr 3f out: swtchd lft and stdy prog fr over 1f out: r.o wl ins fnl f: led fnl 40yds: comf*
**4/6**[1]

63- **2** ½ **Automated**[161] 7694 3-9-5 0.................. FrederikTylicki 2 91
(Clive Brittain) *led: rdn clr 2f out: kpt on but no ex whn hdd fnl 40yds* **40/1**

**3** 3 **Le Maitre Chat (USA)** 3-9-5 0.................. SteveDrowne 13 86
(Clive Cox) *str: mid-div: hdwy 2f out but hanging lft: wnt 3rd ins fnl f: styd on*
**50/1**

4- **4** 3 ¼ **Sayed Youmzain**[157] 7774 3-9-5 0.................. RyanMoore 12 80
(Marco Botti) *unf: scope: trckd ldrs: rdn over 1f out: hung lft: styd on same pce*
**8/1**[2]

4- **5** 1 ½ **Norab (GER)**[157] 7773 3-9-5 0.................. AdamKirby 5 77
(Marco Botti) *str: mid-div: pushed along over 2f out: no imp tl styd on fnl f*
**12/1**[3]

4- **6** 1 ¼ **Sternrubin (GER)**[165] 7607 3-9-5 0.................. JamieSpencer 8 75+
(Peter Chapple-Hyam) *racd keenly: hld up: swtchd rt 2f out: kpt on but little imp on ldrs*
**8/1**[2]

**7** ½ **Limousine** 3-9-0 0.................. JamesDoyle 9 69+
(Charles Hills) *w'like: bit bkwd: rdn 3f out: nvr bttr than mid-div* **12/1**[3]

0- **8** 1 ¼ **Cinnilla**[168] 7532 3-9-0 0.................. JimCrowley 4 67
(Ralph Beckett) *leggy: trckd ldrs: rdn 2f out: wknd ent fnl f* **12/1**[3]

**9** 1 ¾ **Catadupa** 3-9-0 0..................[1] LukeMorris 11 64
(Roger Charlton) *unf: a towards rr*
**33/1**

5-4 **10** 2 3/4 **Kisanji**[14] 1166 3-9-5 0 GeorgeBaker 6 65
(Mick Channon) *trckd ldr: rdn wl over 2f out: wknd over 1f out* **25/1**

**11** 2 **Dark Days** 3-9-5 0 DavidProbert 7 61
(Paul Cole) *a towards rr* **20/1**

**12** 6 **Fort Berkeley (IRE)** 3-9-5 0 TomQueally 3 51
(Paul Cole) *w'like: s.i.s: sn mid-div: rdn 3f out: wknd 2f out* **50/1**

4 **13** 9 **Bergan (GER)**[24] 1011 3-9-5 0 SilvestreDeSousa 1 47
(Mick Channon) *w'like: mid-div: rdn over 2f out: wknd over 1f out* **40/1**

2m 27.68s (6.48) **Going Correction** +0.525s/f (Yiel) 13 Ran SP% **125.6**
Speed ratings (Par 100): **97,96,94,92,91 90,89,88,87,85 84,79,73**
CSF £53.00 TOTE £1.90: £1.30, £7.90, £9.00; EX 56.40 Trifecta £1043.20.
**Owner** Lady Bamford **Bred** Lady Bamford **Trained** Newmarket, Suffolk

**FOCUS**
They raced up the middle in the straight. Sectional times would be handy given the winner stayed on from miles back, whereas the runner-up led for most of the way. Visually, though, this was a taking performance from the winner, who can rate a lot better than the bare form.

## 1439 DUBAI DUTY FREE MILLENNIUM MILLIONAIRE H'CAP 1m 2f 6y
**4:40** (4:40) (Class 4) (0-85,85) 4-Y-0+ **£5,175** (£1,540; £769; £384) **Stalls** Centre

Form RPR

-011 **1** **Top Diktat**[52] 655 6-9-0 78 RyanMoore 11 88
(Gary Moore) *lw: mid-div: hdwy over 2f out: rdn over 1f out: chal between horses jst ins fnl f: led fnl 70yds: r.o* **7/1**[3]

011- **2** 3/4 **Gone Dutch**[177] 7330 4-9-3 81 FrederikTylicki 4 90
(James Fanshawe) *mid-div: hdwy 3f out: rdn for str chal fr 2f out: upsides ent fnl f: kpt on* **8/1**

0536 **3** 1/2 **First Post (IRE)**[14] 1175 7-8-10 74 DaneO'Neill 2 82
(Derek Haydn Jones) *in tch: hdwy 3f out: tk narrow advantage 2f out: sn rdn: kpt on tl no ex and hdd fnl 70yds* **16/1**

000- **4** 1 3/4 **Oetzi**[204] 6596 6-8-7 71 LukeMorris 9 75
(Alan Jarvis) *hld up towards rr: pushed along and hdwy 2f out: sn rdn: styd on ins fnl f: wnt 4th towards fin* **50/1**

320- **5** nk **Sheila's Buddy**[182] 7211 5-8-13 77 LiamKeniry 13 81
(J S Moore) *hld up towards rr: hdwy 2f out: sn rdn: edgd lft ins fnl f: kpt on same pce* **8/1**

66-6 **6** 2 3/4 **Circumvent**[21] 1068 7-9-7 85 TomQueally 8 84
(Paul Cole) *lw: trckd ldrs: led briefly over 2f out: sn rdn: styd pressing ldrs tl fdd ent fnl f* **9/2**[2]

-034 **7** 5 **Toga Tiger (IRE)**[24] 1014 7-8-12 76 SeanLevey 5 65
(Jeremy Gask) *in tch: hdwy 3f out: sn rdn: wknd jst over 1f out* **20/1**

363- **8** 2 1/4 **Noble Gift**[192] 6957 4-9-6 84 JimCrowley 3 69
(William Knight) *hld up towards rr: hdwy 2f out: sn rdn: nvr threatened: wknd fnl f* **4/1**[1]

-340 **9** 3 1/2 **Red Dragon (IRE)**[69] 450 4-8-8 72 DavidProbert 7 50
(Michael Blanshard) *mid-div: pushed along over 3f out: hung lft and wknd over 1f out* **25/1**

54-5 **10** 10 **Anton Chigurh**[16] 1128 5-8-11 82 CamHardie(7) 12 41
(Brendan Powell) *trckd ldr: rdn over 2f out: wknd over 1f out* **14/1**

551- **11** 1 1/4 **Rossetti**[212] 6336 6-8-6 77 (p) HectorCrouch(7) 6 34
(Gary Moore) *wnt lft s: trckd ldrs: rdn and hung lft over 2f out: sn wknd* **20/1**

014- **12** 12 **Northern Star (IRE)**[259] 4777 4-9-5 83 PaulHanagan 1 17
(John Mackie) *led: rdn and hdd over 2f out: sn wknd* **12/1**

**13** 3/4 **Minister Of Mayhem**[149] 4740 4-8-10 74 SteveDrowne 14 6
(Nick Mitchell) *a towards rr* **25/1**

41-2 **14** 1 1/2 **Mubtadi**[30] 942 6-9-6 84 WilliamBuick 10 14
(Ismail Mohammed) *a towards rr* **8/1**

2m 11.83s (3.03) **Going Correction** +0.525s/f (Yiel) 14 Ran SP% **123.4**
Speed ratings (Par 105): **108,107,107,105,105 103,99,97,94,86 85,75,75,74**
CSF £59.17 CT £885.92 TOTE £4.40: £2.20, £2.40, £5.30; EX 23.20 Trifecta £489.50.
**Owner** Miss T R Hale **Bred** Wretham Stud **Trained** Lower Beeding, W Sussex

**FOCUS**
A competitive handicap and the field came centre-to-far side up the straight. The winner rates better than ever.
T/Plt: £19.00 to a £1 stake. Pool: £128306.97 - 4922.10 winning tickets T/Qpdt: £4.60 to a £1 stake. Pool: £8361.01 - 1324.36 winning tickets TM

# THIRSK (L-H)
Saturday, April 12
**OFFICIAL GOING: Good to soft (good in places; 7.2)**
Wind: Virtually nil Weather: Heavy cloud

## 1440 JACK BERRY HOUSE H'CAP (DIV I) 6f
**2:15** (2:15) (Class 5) (0-75,80) 4-Y-0+ **£2,587** (£770; £384; £192) **Stalls** High

Form RPR

456- **1** **My Name Is Rio (IRE)**[271] 4354 4-8-13 67 PaulMulrennan 3 84
(Michael Dods) *trckd ldrs: smooth hdwy over 2f out: swtchd rt wl over 1f out and sn cl up: rdn to ld jst ins fnl f: kpt on strly* **12/1**

6060 **2** 2 1/4 **Clubland (IRE)**[62] 552 5-8-9 68 PhilipPrince(5) 6 78
(Roy Bowring) *slt ld: pushed along 2f out: rdn over 1f out: hdd and drvn jst ins fnl f: kpt on same pce* **13/2**[2]

26-0 **3** 1 1/2 **Teetotal (IRE)**[13] 1190 4-8-12 73 JoeDoyle(7) 4 78
(Nigel Tinkler) *in rr: hdwy to trck ldrs 1/2-way: effrt to chse ldng pair over 1f out: sn rdn and kpt on same pce* **12/1**

320- **4** 1 3/4 **Lucky Lodge**[138] 8037 4-8-11 65 (b) DavidAllan 9 64
(Mel Brittain) *prom: rdn along over 2f out: drvn over 1f out: one pce fnl f* **28/1**

411- **5** 1 3/4 **Thatcherite (IRE)**[189] 7030 6-9-3 71 (t) StephenCraine 2 65
(Tony Coyle) *in rr: hdwy on outer wl over 2f out: rdn to chse ldrs over 1f out: sn one pce* **14/1**

253- **6** shd **Go Go Green (IRE)**[157] 7777 8-9-5 73 GaryBartley 8 66
(Jim Goldie) *dwlt and in rr: hdwy over 2f out: rdn and kpt on fnl f: nrst fin* **16/1**

2-30 **7** 1/2 **Severiano (USA)**[58] 589 4-8-7 64 (b[1]) WilliamTwiston-Davies(3) 13 56
(Roger Varian) *midfield: swtchd lft to outer and hdwy over 2f out: rdn wl over 1f out and sn no imp* **8/1**[3]

135- **8** 1/2 **Dream Ally (IRE)**[190] 6995 4-8-13 67 PJMcDonald 1 57
(Micky Hammond) *chsd ldrs: rdn alongt and sltly outpcd wl over 2f out: kpt on fnl f* **40/1**

00-1 **9** hd **Klynch**[11] 1224 8-9-12 80 (b) JamesSullivan 12 70+
(Ruth Carr) *towards rr: hdwy over 2f out: n.m.r and rdn wl over 1f out: no imp* **10/3**[1]

316- **10** hd **Kylladdie**[164] 7634 7-9-6 74 (b) MickaelBarzalona 15 63
(Steve Gollings) *chsd ldrs: rdn along wl over 2f out: sn wknd* **10/1**

53-0 **11** 3 1/2 **Delores Rocket**[3] 1376 4-8-12 66 (p) AmyRyan 11 44
(Kevin Ryan) *a towards rr* **14/1**

032- **12** 1 1/2 **Sunny Side Up (IRE)**[165] 7593 5-8-11 72 GemmaTutty(7) 10 45
(Karen Tutty) *cl up: disp ld 1/2-way: sn rdn along and wknd fnl 2f* **14/1**

143- **13** 3 3/4 **Holy Angel (IRE)**[165] 7594 5-9-7 75 (e) DuranFentiman 5 36
(Tim Easterby) *rrd and dwlt s: a in rr* **33/1**

322- **14** 8 **Dartrix**[232] 5714 5-9-2 70 TomEaves 7
(Michael Dods) *t.k.h: hld up towards rr and plld hrd after 2f: nvr a factor* **14/1**

600- **15** nk **Sunrise Dance**[165] 7594 5-9-5 73 AndrewMullen 14
(Robert Johnson) *a towards rr: bhd fnl 2f* **22/1**

1m 14.47s (1.77) **Going Correction** +0.425s/f (Yiel) 15 Ran SP% **117.7**
Speed ratings (Par 103): **105,102,100,97,95 95,94,93,93,93 88,86,81,71,70**
CSF £82.16 CT £968.89 TOTE £19.10: £5.40, £2.30, £3.50; EX 134.80 Trifecta £1197.00 Part won..
**Owner** K Kirkup & Mrs T Galletley **Bred** Anthony J Keane **Trained** Denton, Co Durham

**FOCUS**
The ground was just on the easy side of good. A high draw is often an advantage over the straight course here as they come up the stands rail but the first three home in the opener were drawn 3, 6 and 4. It paid to be prominent with nothing making any kind of impact from off the pace. The winner is rated back to his early level.

## 1441 NEW PREMIER "SHRIMP & STIRRUP BAR" MEDIAN AUCTION MAIDEN STKS 6f
**2:50** (2:52) (Class 5) 3-4-Y-0 **£2,587** (£770; £384; £192) **Stalls** High

Form RPR

620- **1** **Red Pike (IRE)**[189] 7026 3-9-0 77 PaulMulrennan 4 80
(Bryan Smart) *trckd ldrs: effrt 2f out: upsides jst ins fnl f: led last 50yds: all out* **11/8**[1]

025- **2** hd **Royal Connoisseur (IRE)**[183] 7173 3-9-0 75 TonyHamilton 6 79
(Richard Fahey) *trckd ldr: led over 1f out: edgd lft ins fnl f: sn hdd: rallied and jst hld nr fin* **10/3**[2]

0- **3** 7 **Storyline (IRE)**[192] 6947 3-8-9 0 DavidAllan 8 52
(Tim Easterby) *led: hdd over 1f out: hung lft and wknd fnl 150yds* **11/1**

50- **4** 1/2 **Traditionelle**[206] 6517 3-8-9 0 TomEaves 1 50+
(Tim Easterby) *swtchd rt after s: sn trcking ldrs: outpcd 2f out: kpt on ins fnl f* **80/1**

6-3 **5** 1/2 **White Rose Runner**[5] 1344 3-8-9 0 PJMcDonald 3 49
(Mel Brittain) *chsd ldrs: rdn over 3f out: lost pl over 2f out* **13/2**[3]

56- **6** 2 3/4 **Singing Star (IRE)**[141] 8005 3-8-9 0 AndrewElliott 2 40
(Mel Brittain) *racd wd: prom: rdn over 2f out: wknd over 1f out* **20/1**

04- **7** 3 **Edward Elgar**[196] 6842 3-8-11 0 GeorgeChaloner(3) 9 35
(Richard Whitaker) *s.i.s: sn outpcd and drvn along in rr: nvr on terms* **25/1**

0-2 **8** 10 **Roomie**[10] 1243 3-8-9 0 DuranFentiman 7
(Tim Easterby) *chsd ldrs: lost pl over 2f out: sn bhd* **16/1**

**9** nk **Cavallo Bella** 3-8-9 0 GrahamGibbons 5
(David Barron) *resteless in stalls: s.i.s: in rr: bhd fnl 2f* **15/2**

1m 15.06s (2.36) **Going Correction** +0.425s/f (Yiel) 9 Ran SP% **114.3**
Speed ratings (Par 103): **101,100,91,90,90 86,82,69,68**
CSF £5.62 TOTE £2.60: £1.10, £1.30, £3.90; EX 7.30 Trifecta £64.30.
**Owner** Sir A Ferguson, P Deal & G Lowe **Bred** Mrs M Marnane **Trained** Hambleton, N Yorks

**FOCUS**
This thinned right out in the closing stages and the two that dominated the market did so in the race itself by drawing 7l clear in the closing stages. Both improved a little on their 2yo form.

## 1442 INJURED JOCKEYS' FUND 50TH ANNIVERSARY YEAR H'CAP 7f
**3:25** (3:25) (Class 3) (0-95,95) 4-Y-0+ **£7,439** (£2,213; £1,106; £553) **Stalls** Low

Form RPR

25-4 **1** **Farlow (IRE)**[14] 1164 6-8-12 86 TonyHamilton 9 95
(Richard Fahey) *pushed along into midfield sn after s: hdwy on outer 3f out: chsd ldrs 2f out: rdn to ld ent fnl f: sn edgd lft and drvn: jst hld on* **11/4**[1]

0-40 **2** shd **Askaud (IRE)**[14] 1164 6-8-7 88 (p) MatthewHopkins(7) 6 97
(Scott Dixon) *trckd ldr: effrt 2f out: rdn along and sltly outpcd over 1f out: swtchd rt and drvn ins fnl f: styd on strly: jst failed* **16/1**

0-35 **3** nk **Showboating (IRE)**[14] 1164 6-9-0 88 (tp) MickaelBarzalona 16 96
(Alan McCabe) *stdd and swtchd lft s: hld up and bhd: hdwy on outer over 2f out: rdn wl over 1f out: styd on wl fnl f* **9/1**

3/0- **4** 2 **Grissom (IRE)**[273] 4285 8-8-13 87 DavidAllan 7 90
(Tim Easterby) *led: pushed along over 2f out: rdn wl over 1f out: hdd and drvn ent fnl f: kpt on same pce* **40/1**

154- **5** 1/2 **Dusky Queen (IRE)**[154] 7820 4-8-7 86 SammyJoBell(5) 2 87
(Richard Fahey) *hld up towards rr: hdwy on inner whn n.m.r and hmpd 2f out: styd on fnl f: nrst fin* **10/1**

000- **6** shd **Fort Bastion (IRE)**[182] 7206 5-9-6 94 JamesSullivan 5 95+
(Ruth Carr) *hld up towards rr: effrt on inner and nt clr run wl over 2f out: swtchd rt to outer wl over 1f out: sn rdn and styd on fnl f: nrst fin* **22/1**

03 **7** nk **Chilworth Icon**[22] 1042 4-9-1 92 WilliamTwiston-Davies(3) 4 92
(Mick Channon) *in tch: hdwy to chse ldrs 3f out: effrt and swtchd lft towards inner 2f out: sn n.m.r and swtchd rt over 1f out: rdn and styd on one pce fnl f* **10/1**

000- **8** 1 **Norse Blues**[203] 6624 6-9-7 95 GrahamGibbons 11 93+
(David Barron) *hld up: hdwy whn nt clr run over 2f out: chsd ldrs whn hmpd over 1f out: one pce after* **16/1**

410- **9** 4 **Lilac Lace (IRE)**[154] 7820 4-8-12 86 DuranFentiman 8 73
(Tim Easterby) *t.k.h early: prom: cl up 1/2-way: rdn along over 2f out: drvn and hld whn n.m.r ent fnl f: wknd* **16/1**

4-00 **10** 1/2 **Talented Kid**[7] 1301 5-9-2 90 JoeFanning 3 76
(Mark Johnston) *chsd ldrs: rdn along over 2f out: hld whn bmpd over 1f out: sn wknd* **15/2**[3]

30-0 **11** 1 3/4 **Bear Behind (IRE)**[7] 1305 5-9-5 93 RichardKingscote 13 75
(Tom Dascombe) *swtchd lft s: hld up: a towards rr* **28/1**

10/ **12** 3 1/2 **Englishman**[662] 3240 4-9-2 90 GrahamLee 10 62
(Charles Hills) *cl up: pushed along 3f out: rdn along over 2f out and sn wknd* **5/1**[2]

040- **13** 1/2 **Shahdaroba (IRE)**[175] 7368 4-8-13 87 PJMcDonald 12 58
(Micky Hammond) *nvr bttr than midfield* **22/1**

30-0 **14** nk **Chosen Character (IRE)**[13] 1193 6-8-11 92 (vt) JennyPowell(7) 14 62
(Tom Dascombe) *in tch on outer: sme hdwy wl over 2f out: sn rdn and wknd* **33/1**

000- **15** 4 1/2 **Osteopathic Remedy (IRE)**[176] 7337 10-9-6 94 TomEaves 15 53
(Michael Dods) *a towards rr* **25/1**

1m 29.16s (1.96) **Going Correction** +0.50s/f (Yiel) 15 Ran SP% **122.3**
Speed ratings (Par 107): **108,107,107,105,104 104,104,103,98,97 95,91,91,91,85**
CSF £46.08 CT £373.88 TOTE £3.20: £1.70, £5.30, £2.20; EX 56.20 Trifecta £575.10.
**Owner** Red Sky Partnership 1 **Bred** Patrick J Monahan **Trained** Musley Bank, N Yorks
■ Stewards' Enquiry : William Twiston-Davies three-day ban: careless riding (Apr 26-28)

**FOCUS**
A competitive handicap run at an even enough pace and form that should stand up. The winner is rated basically back to his best.

## 1443 EBFSTALLIONS.COM MICHAEL FOSTER EBF CONDITIONS STKS 7f
4:00 (4:03) (Class 3) 4-Y-O+

£9,337 (£2,796; £1,398; £699; £349; £175) Stalls Low

Form RPR
312- **1** **Breton Rock (IRE)**[157] 7775 4-9-0 103 MartinLane 5 110
(David Simcock) *trckd ldrs: hdwy on outer wl over 2f out: led over 1f out: rdn out* 5/2[2]
150- **2** 1 1/4 **Baccarat (IRE)**[182] 7208 5-9-0 101 TonyHamilton 4 107
(Richard Fahey) *t.k.h early: trckd ldng pair: hdwy 3f out: chal over 2f out: sn rdn and ev ch tl drvn: edgd lft and one pce ins fnl f* 15/8[1]
120- **3** nk **Tariq Too**[142] 7995 7-9-0 104 JoeFanning 2 106
(Amy Weaver) *dwlt: hdwy and in tch 1/2-way: effrt on inner over 2f out: rdn to chal over 1f out: ev ch tl drvn and one pce ins fnl f* 6/1
60-2 **4** 6 **Captain Ramius (IRE)**[14] 1163 8-9-0 105 PhillipMakin 6 90
(Kevin Ryan) *chsd ldr: hdwy to ld wl over 2f out: rdn along and hdd wl over 1f out: grad wknd* 4/1[3]
060- **5** 6 **Pintura**[168] 7540 7-9-5 101 AmyRyan 1 80
(Kevin Ryan) *hld up: effrt over 3f out: rdn along wl over 2f out and sn btn* 25/1
32-0 **6** 8 **Kenny Powers**[35] 886 5-9-0 102 (tp) RichardKingscote 7 54
(Tom Dascombe) *led: rdn along and hdd wl over 2f out: sn wknd* 11/1
1m 28.65s (1.45) **Going Correction** +0.50s/f (Yiel) 6 Ran SP% 109.8
Speed ratings (Par 107): **111,109,109,102,95 86**
CSF £7.24 TOTE £2.40: £1.10, £1.60; EX 8.00 Trifecta £16.70.
**Owner** John Cook **Bred** George Kent **Trained** Newmarket, Suffolk

**FOCUS**
A tight but warm conditions race with only 4lb separating the six runners on official ratings. The pace looked fairly steady but it was the fastest of the three C&D races. The form looks sound.

## 1444 NEW "THOMAS LORD DINE & VIEW RESTAURANT" H'CAP 1m 4f
4:35 (4:35) (Class 2) (0-100,100) 4-Y-O+ £12,938 (£3,850; £1,924; £962) Stalls High

Form RPR
003- **1** **Elidor**[197] 6793 4-8-12 92 WilliamTwiston-Davies(3) 15 103
(Mick Channon) *trckd ldrs: smooth hdwy over 3f out: led wl over 2f out: rdn clr over 1f out: readily* 11/1
10-1 **2** 2 3/4 **Dark Ruler (IRE)**[13] 1196 5-8-5 81 BenCurtis 3 88+
(Alan Swinbank) *midfield: hdwy and in tch 1/2-way: effrt wl over 2f out: swtchd lft and rdn to chse ldrs over 1f out: drvn ins fnl f: styd on wl: nrst fin* 13/2[3]
-133 **3** 3/4 **Bute Hall**[43] 784 5-8-7 83 JimmyQuinn 1 87
(David Thompson) *in tch: hdwy over 4f out: rdn to chse ldrs over 2f out: drvn over 1f out and kpt on same pce* 33/1
511- **4** 1/2 **Stomachion (IRE)**[172] 7453 4-8-7 84 ow1 ShaneKelly 11 88
(Sir Michael Stoute) *hld up in rr: hdwy on wd outside 3f out: chsd ldrs 2f out: sn rdn and edgd lft: drvn ins fnl f: sn edgd lft and one pce* 7/2[2]
100- **5** 1 1/2 **Sirvino**[169] 7496 9-8-7 90 PaulMcGiff(7) 7 91
(David Barron) *hld up in rr: hdwy on inner over 2f out: rdn to chse ldrs over 1f out: n.m.r ins fnl f: kpt on same pce* 40/1
50-0 **6** 1/2 **Freewheel (IRE)**[14] 1164 4-8-5 82 AndrewMullen 13 82
(David Nicholls) *prom: rdn along and sltly outpcd over 4f out: cl up over 3f out: drvn wl over 1f out: wknd and hmpd ins fnl f* 66/1
600- **7** 2 1/4 **O Ma Lad (IRE)**[168] 7526 6-8-7 86 IanBrennan(3) 16 83
(John Quinn) *hld up towards rr: hdwy and swtchd lft 2f out: n.m.r and swtchd rt over 1f out: rdn whn n.m.r ins fnl f: kpt on* 18/1
100- **8** 2 **Herostatus**[136] 4873 7-8-6 87 JoeyHaynes(5) 10 81
(Jason Ward) *dwlt and bhd tl sme late hdwy* 66/1
011- **9** 8 **Retirement Plan**[253] 4950 4-9-9 100 GrahamLee 4 81
(Lady Cecil) *midfield: in tch whn pushed along briefly 7f out: effrt to chse ldrs over 4f out: rdn along 3f out: drvn 2f out and sn btn* 15/8[1]
601- **10** 5 **A Star In My Eye (IRE)**[206] 6514 4-8-7 84 BarryMcHugh 8 57
(Kevin Ryan) *t.k.h: led over 3f: cl up tl led again over 3f out: rdn along and hdd wl over 2f out: sn drvn and wknd wl over 1f out* 14/1
052/ **11** 2 3/4 **Aviator (GER)**[177] 6-9-2 92 [1] GrahamGibbons 14 60
(James Eustace) *hld up: a towards rr* 20/1
105- **12** hd **Linguine (FR)**[169] 7496 4-8-12 89 PaulMulrennan 2 57
(Paul Midgley) *cl up: led after 3f: rdn along over 3f out: hdd wl over 2f out and sn wknd* 33/1
0122 **13** 1 3/4 **Tepmokea (IRE)**[9] 1268 8-8-12 88 (p) PhillipMakin 5 53
(Conor Dore) *chsd ldrs: rdn along on inner 5f out: wknd over 3f out* 25/1
011- **14** 8 **Bayan Kasirga (IRE)**[180] 7239 4-8-3 85 SammyJoBell(5) 6 37
(Richard Fahey) *dwlt: a in rr* 14/1
2m 40.11s (3.91) **Going Correction** +0.50s/f (Yiel)
**WFA** 4 from 5yo+ 1lb 14 Ran SP% 117.2
Speed ratings (Par 109): **106,104,103,103,102 102,100,99,93,90 88,88,87,82**
CSF £73.85 CT £2283.78 TOTE £11.90: £4.80, £2.50, £5.00; EX 94.40 Trifecta £1068.90 Part won..
**Owner** Jon and Julia Aisbitt **Bred** Ashley House Stud **Trained** West Ilsley, Berks

**FOCUS**
This looked a very warm handicap on paper with a whole host of potential winners. The pace held up and the third and sixth limit the form.

## 1445 DONATE £5 - TEXT IJF TO 70800 H'CAP (BOBIS RACE) 5f
5:10 (5:10) (Class 3) (0-95,95) 3-Y-O £7,439 (£2,213; £1,106; £553) Stalls High

Form RPR
224- **1** **Mecca's Angel (IRE)**[189] 7026 3-9-7 95 PaulMulrennan 3 104
(Michael Dods) *trckd ldrs: cl up 1/2-way: led wl over 1f out: pushed clr ins fnl f: readily* 9/2[2]
161- **2** 4 1/2 **Blithe Spirit**[196] 6825 3-8-12 89 JasonHart(3) 7 82
(Eric Alston) *slt ld: rdn along and jnd over 2f out: hdd wl over 1f out: drvn and kpt on same pce fnl f* 6/1[3]
110- **3** shd **Deeds Not Words (IRE)**[189] 7026 3-9-1 92 WilliamTwiston-Davies(3) 4 84
(Mick Channon) *chsd ldng pair: hdwy 1/2-way: rdn wl over 1f out: drvn and kpt on same pce fnl f* 9/2[2]
501- **4** 1 3/4 **The Hooded Claw (IRE)**[165] 7592 3-8-8 82 DuranFentiman 1 68
(Tim Easterby) *in tch on outer: rdn along and outpcd 1/2-way: swtchd rt and rdn wl over 1f out: kpt on ins fnl f: nrst fin* 9/1
10- **5** 2 **Distant Past**[126] 8203 3-8-2 76 oh1 JimmyQuinn 2 55
(Kevin Ryan) *chsd ldrs on outer: rdn along wl over 2f out: wknd wl over 1f out* 7/1
13- **6** 1 1/4 **Eastern Impact (IRE)**[317] 2809 3-9-5 93 TonyHamilton 8 67
(Richard Fahey) *chsd ldr on inner: rdn along over 2f out: sn wknd* 7/2[1]
614- **7** 2 1/2 **Meadway**[176] 7333 3-8-11 85 RoystonFfrench 5 50
(Bryan Smart) *a towards rr* 7/1
01-0 **8** 2 **Baytown Kestrel**[43] 788 3-8-6 80 PaulPickard 6 38
(Brian Ellison) *a towards rr* 25/1
59.95s (0.35) **Going Correction** +0.425s/f (Yiel) 8 Ran SP% 111.7
Speed ratings (Par 102): **114,106,106,103,100 98,94,91**
CSF £29.95 CT £125.81 TOTE £3.60: £1.40, £2.50, £1.10; EX 29.80 Trifecta £93.20.
**Owner** David T J Metcalfe **Bred** Yeomanstown Stud & Doc Bloodstock **Trained** Denton, Co Durham

**FOCUS**
A warmish sprint featuring a few horses with potential this season, but they were all blown away by the winner. The form has a fluid look to it.

## 1446 THIRSKRACECOURSE.NET FOR DISCOUNTED TICKETS ONLINE H'CAP 7f
5:45 (5:48) (Class 5) (0-70,69) 4-Y-O+ £2,726 (£805; £402) Stalls Low

Form RPR
403- **1** **Flexible Flyer**[259] 4772 5-9-4 69 (t) JasonHart(3) 11 82
(Mark Walford) *hld up in rr: hdwy on outer over 2f out: led over 1f out: styd on wl* 6/1[1]
02-1 **2** 2 1/2 **Icy Blue**[79] 289 6-8-11 62 (p) GeorgeChaloner(3) 3 69
(Richard Whitaker) *s.i.s: hdwy over 3f out: chsng ldrs 2f out: styd on same pce fnl f* 8/1
000- **3** 3/4 **Steel Stockholder**[144] 7965 8-9-5 67 DavidAllan 6 72
(Mel Brittain) *chsd ldrs: styd on same pce fnl f* 16/1
20-5 **4** nse **Ted's Brother (IRE)**[8] 1286 6-8-13 68 (e) AlistairRawlinson(7) 4 72
(Richard Guest) *mid-div: hdwy over 3f out: narrow ld over 2f out: hdd over 1f out: kpt on same pce* 7/1[3]
4 **5** 1 1/2 **Real Tigress (IRE)**[10] 1245 5-8-10 58 TonyHamilton 1 59
(Les Eyre) *mid-div: hdwy on outside over 2f out: kpt on same pce fnl f* 13/2[2]
404- **6** 3 3/4 **Space War**[176] 7343 7-9-4 66 GrahamGibbons 5 57
(Michael Easterby) *s.i.s: hld up in rr: hdwy over 2f out: nvr trbld ldrs* 14/1
423- **7** 3 1/2 **Duke Of Grazeon (IRE)**[102] 8454 4-9-7 69 RoystonFfrench 15 51
(Mrs Ilka Gansera-Leveque) *sn chsng ldrs on outer: hung lft and wknd over 1f out* 9/1
000- **8** 1 3/4 **Day Of The Eagle (IRE)**[154] 7824 8-9-7 69 DuranFentiman 13 46
(Michael Easterby) *in rr: kpt on fnl 2f: nvr a factor* 33/1
330- **9** hd **Lothair (IRE)**[189] 7030 5-9-7 69 BenCurtis 9 46
(Alan Swinbank) *chsd ldrs: wknd over 1f out: eased whn n.m.r ins fnl f* 12/1
0/54 **10** 1 **Run Fat Lass Run**[16] 1131 4-9-3 65 PhillipMakin 7 42
(Philip Kirby) *chsd ldrs: wknd fnl 2f* 11/1
/0-0 **11** 2 1/2 **Almanack**[22] 1049 4-9-2 69 (tp) GeorgeDowning(5) 12 37
(Ian Williams) *chsd ldrs on outer: lost pl over 2f out* 20/1
350- **12** 1/2 **Mowhoob**[204] 6588 4-8-12 60 GrahamLee 16 26
(Jim Goldie) *a towards rr* 33/1
3-10 **13** 1/2 **Ace Master**[62] 552 6-9-1 68 (b) PhilipPrince(5) 14 36
(Roy Bowring) *t.k.h: led: hdd over 2f out: lost pl and eased over 1f out* 14/1
434- **14** hd **Loyal N Trusted**[155] 7808 6-8-3 58 (p) GemmaTutty(7) 10 22
(Karen Tutty) *a in rr* 25/1
30-0 **15** 11 **Marcus Caesar (IRE)**[16] 1125 4-9-3 65 JamesSullivan 8
(Ruth Carr) *chsd ldrs: drvn over 3f out: sn wknd: bhd whn eased ins fnl f* 16/1
040- **16** 5 **Meandmyshadow**[165] 7593 6-9-6 68 PaulMulrennan 2
(Alan Brown) *chsd ldrs: wknd qckly 3f out: bhd whn eased ins fnl f* 8/1
1m 30.67s (3.47) **Going Correction** +0.50s/f (Yiel) 16 Ran SP% 128.0
Speed ratings (Par 103): **100,97,96,96,94 90,86,84,84,82 80,79,78,78,66 60**
CSF £53.05 CT £780.38 TOTE £7.60: £2.20, £2.30, £4.00, £2.00; EX 59.00 Trifecta £1274.00.
**Owner** A Quirke & T Heseltine **Bred** Glebe Stud **Trained** Sherriff Hutton, N Yorks

**FOCUS**
A sound gallop to this handicap and the action unfolded towards the centre of the track in the straight. The runner-up gives the form substance.

## 1447 JACK BERRY HOUSE H'CAP (DIV II) 6f
6:15 (6:16) (Class 5) (0-75,75) 4-Y-O+ £2,587 (£770; £384; £192) Stalls High

Form RPR
05-3 **1** **Trade Secret**[13] 1190 7-9-2 70 DavidAllan 13 86
(Mel Brittain) *in tch: pushed along and hdwy to chse ldrs 1/2-way: rdn to ld over 1f out: clr ins fnl f and kpt on strly* 7/2[1]
100- **2** 4 **Pastureyes**[178] 7315 4-8-2 63 MatthewHopkins(7) 9 66
(Scott Dixon) *racd towards centre: led to 1/2-way: cl up: rdn and ev ch over 1f out: drvn and kpt on same pce fnl f* 50/1
40- **3** nk **Orbit The Moon (IRE)**[154] 7824 6-9-3 71 (tp) PaulMulrennan 1 73
(Michael Dods) *chsd ldrs on wd outside: cl up 1/2-way: rdn and ev ch over 1f out: drvn and one pce ins fnl f* 14/1
0-00 **4** 2 1/4 **Bapak Muda (USA)**[75] 359 4-8-8 67 ShaneGray(5) 15 62
(Kevin Ryan) *racd nr stands' rail: cl up: rdn wl over 1f out: drvn over 1f out and one pce fnl f* 14/1
006- **5** nk **Adam's Ale**[198] 6771 5-9-0 73 ShirleyTeasdale(5) 14 67
(Paul Midgley) *t.k.h early: cl up: led 1/2-way: rdn and hdd over 1f out: wknd ins fnl f* 8/1[3]
010- **6** hd **Mercers Row**[176] 7344 7-8-6 67 GemmaTutty(7) 8 60
(Karen Tutty) *chsd ldrs: rdn along wl over 1f out: grad wknd* 33/1
3-20 **7** 1 1/4 **Keep It Dark**[10] 1244 5-9-2 70 BarryMcHugh 2 59
(Tony Coyle) *dwlt and towards rr: hdwy 2f out: sn rdn and kpt on fnl f: n.d* 11/1
660- **8** shd **Diamond Blue**[155] 7801 6-8-12 66 TonyHamilton 11 55
(Richard Fahey) *towards rr: hdwy wl over 1f out: kpt on fnl f: n.d* 14/1
122- **9** 3 3/4 **Mishaal (IRE)**[195] 6874 4-9-5 73 PhillipMakin 3 50
(Michael Herrington) *dwlt and swtchd rt s: in rr tl sme late hdwy* 8/1[3]
10-0 **10** 1 1/2 **Baron Run**[13] 1191 4-8-13 72 JoeyHaynes(5) 6 44
(K R Burke) *chsd ldrs: rdn along 2f out: grad wknd over 1f out* 9/1
425- **11** 1 1/2 **Verus Delicia (IRE)**[159] 7728 5-8-6 65 PhilipPrince(5) 5 33
(Daniel Mark Loughnane) *a towards rr* 22/1
2-5 **12** 2 3/4 **Diamondhead (IRE)**[15] 1144 5-9-4 75 RobertTart(3) 10 34
(Ed de Giles) *a in rr* 11/2[2]
-040 **13** 2 **Lost In Paris (IRE)**[10] 1244 8-8-13 74 LauraBarry(7) 12 26
(Tony Coyle) *chsd ldrs: rdn along over 2f out: sn wknd* 40/1
606- **14** 1 1/4 **Funding Deficit (IRE)**[140] 8029 4-8-11 65 GrahamLee 4 13
(Jim Goldie) *a towards rr* 20/1
150- **15** 3 3/4 **The Strig**[172] 7452 7-9-7 75 (v) AndrewMullen 7 11
(Nigel Tinkler) *wnt rt s: a in rr* 33/1
1m 14.78s (2.08) **Going Correction** +0.425s/f (Yiel) 15 Ran SP% 117.6
Speed ratings (Par 103): **103,97,97,94,93 93,91,91,86,84 82,79,76,74,69**
CSF £218.30 CT £2240.50 TOTE £4.70: £1.10, £12.60, £6.30; EX 277.10 Trifecta £1714.10.

**Owner** Mel Brittain **Bred** Whitsbury Manor Stud **Trained** Warthill, N Yorks

**FOCUS**

Just a modest handicap to finish, run 0.31sec slower than the first division. The winner's best effort since his summer 2012 peak.

T/Plt: £787.90 to a £1 stake. Pool: £59,854.89 - 55.45 winning tickets. T/Qpdt: £41.20 to a £1 stake. Pool: £4,378.92 - 78.50 winning tickets. JR

# [1425]WOLVERHAMPTON (A.W) (L-H)

Saturday, April 12

**OFFICIAL GOING: Standard**

Wind: Fresh behind Weather: Cloudy with sunny spells

## 1448 COMPARE BOOKMAKERS AT BOOKMAKERS.CO.UK AMATEUR RIDERS' H'CAP 5f 216y(P)

**5:50** (5:50) (Class 5) (0-70,70) 4-Y-0+ **£2,807** (£870; £435; £217) **Stalls** Low

Form RPR

6464 **1** **Lujeanie**[3] 1388 8-10-9 **70** MrGeorgeCrate(5) 7 79
(Peter Crate) *s.i.s: hld up: hdwy over 1f out: r.o to ld nr fin* **10/1**

6340 **2** *nk* **Pearl Noir**[25] 1001 4-9-9 **56** oh4 (b) MrKLocking(5) 4 64
(Scott Dixon) *led and sn clr: rdn over 1f out: hdd nr fin* **22/1**

006- **3** *¾* **Iggy**[239] 5471 4-10-12 **68** (bt) MissSBrotherton 6 74
(Michael Easterby) *chsd clr ldr: rdn over 1f out: hung lft ins fnl f: styd on* **2/1[1]**

1305 **4** *1 ½* **Consistant**[15] 1148 6-9-10 **57** MrGrahamCarson(5) 10 58
(Brian Baugh) *a.p: rdn over 1f out: styd on* **6/1[2]**

3414 **5** *½* **Sewn Up**[7] 1312 4-10-4 **60** (p) FreddieMitchell 2 59
(Andrew Hollinshead) *chsd ldrs: pushed along over 2f out: kpt on* **6/1[2]**

00-0 **6** *1 ½* **Fortrose Academy (IRE)**[11] 1221 5-9-8 **57** MrHHunt(7) 5 51
(Andrew Balding) *mid-div: sn pushed along: rdn over 1f out: nt trble ldrs* **8/1[3]**

23-2 **7** *½* **Whipphound**[15] 1148 6-10-3 **62** BeckyBrisbourne(3) 11 55
(Mark Brisbourne) *mid-div: rdn over 1f out: nvr trbld ldrs* **9/1**

3245 **8** *1 ¼* **Angelo Poliziano**[35] 889 8-10-3 **62** (b) MrChrisMartin(3) 9 51
(Jo Hughes) *s.i.s: hld up: rdn over 1f out: nvr on terms* **33/1**

0623 **9** *4 ½* **Pull The Pin (IRE)**[10] 1244 5-10-1 **64** (bt) MissEllaSmith(7) 1 38
(Ann Stokell) *s.i.s: hld up: n.d* **16/1**

40 **10** *1 ¼* **Beachwood Bay**[31] 934 6-9-11 **58** (p) MrJamesHughes(5) 13 28
(Jo Hughes) *rdr lost iron leaving stalls: a towards rr* **22/1**

1-00 **11** *1 ¼* **New Decade**[32] 913 5-10-10 **66** (t) MissADeniel 3 32
(Milton Bradley) *hld up: a in rr* **33/1**

1m 15.65s (0.65) **Going Correction** 0.0s/f (Stan) 11 Ran SP% **112.6**

Speed ratings (Par 103): **95,94,93,91,90 88,88,86,80,78 77**

CSF £207.23 CT £612.49 TOTE £13.10: £3.10, £4.00, £2.00; EX 230.90 Trifecta £626.50 Part won..

**Owner** Peter Crate & Gallagher Equine Ltd **Bred** K T Ivory **Trained** Newdigate, Surrey

**FOCUS**

A moderate sprint handicap, confined to amateur riders and run at a good pace. The winner ran to his best form for the yard.

## 1449 32RED H'CAP 5f 216y(P)

**6:20** (6:22) (Class 6) (0-60,65) 3-Y-O **£2,264** (£673; £336; £168) **Stalls** Low

Form RPR

6422 **1** **Douneedahand**[1] 1425 3-9-0 **60** GaryMahon(7) 3 61
(Seamus Mullins) *s.i.s: hld up: hdwy 2f out: rdn to ld and hung lft fr over 1f out: styd on* **13/2[3]**

-221 **2** *nk* **Hustle Bustle (IRE)**[9] 1264 3-9-7 **65** KevinStott(5) 7 65
(David Brown) *w ldrs: led over 3f out: rdn and hdd over 1f out: edgd lft ins fnl f: styd on* **4/5[1]**

0-04 **3** *nk* **Aussie Sky (IRE)**[71] 411 3-8-7 **46** oh1 LiamJones 8 45
(Daniel Mark Loughnane) *chsd ldrs: rdn over 2f out: sn outpcd: r.o wl towards fin* **33/1**

0066 **4** *½* **Literally On Fire (IRE)**[8] 1285 3-8-2 **46** oh1 (p) RyanTate(5) 1 43
(Brendan Powell) *trckd ldrs: hmpd 4f out: rdn over 1f out: r.o* **40/1**

3662 **5** *nse* **Jalebi**[12] 1211 3-9-1 **54** HayleyTurner 2 51
(Jim Boyle) *w ldrs: drifted rt over 1f out: rdn and carried lft ins fnl f: unable qck towards fin* **9/1**

024- **6** *10* **Goadby**[156] 7788 3-9-6 **59** StevieDonohoe 5 24
(John Holt) *prom: lost pl 4f out: rdn and wknd over 2f out* **20/1**

06-3 **7** *3 ¾* **Febrayer Star (IRE)**[12] 1211 3-8-9 **48** (p) PaddyAspell 4 1
(Robert Cowell) *sn pushed along in rr: rdn and wknd over 2f out* **20/1**

-425 **8** *2 ¾* **Choice Of Destiny**[17] 1101 3-9-2 **60** (v) LouisSteward(5) 6 5
(Philip McBride) *sn led: rdn and hdd over 3f out: wknd wl over 1f out* **7/2[2]**

1m 16.03s (1.03) **Going Correction** 0.0s/f (Stan) 8 Ran SP% **116.0**

Speed ratings (Par 96): **93,92,92,91,91 78,73,69**

CSF £11.95 CT £166.17 TOTE £8.20: £1.60, £1.10, £6.40; EX 18.20 Trifecta £310.40.

**Owner** Caloona Racing **Bred** New England, Myriad B/S And Barton Stud **Trained** Wilsford-Cum-Lake, Wilts

**FOCUS**

A weak sprint handicap run at an uneven pace, and doubts over the form.

## 1450 LADBROKES CLASSIFIED (S) STKS 1m 141y(P)

**6:50** (6:50) (Class 6) 3-Y-O+ **£2,264** (£673; £336; £168) **Stalls** Low

Form RPR

00-0 **1** **Poor Duke (IRE)**[98] 49 4-9-8 65 (p) JoeFanning 7 69
(Jamie Osborne) *chsd ldr over 7f out tl led over 2f out: shkn up and clr fr over 1f out: comf* **9/1**

-454 **2** *3* **One Scoop Or Two**[19] 1085 8-9-3 65 (p) JackDuern(5) 4 62
(Andrew Hollinshead) *a.p: shkn up to chse wnr over 1f out: edgd lft fnl f: no imp* **6/4[1]**

30-0 **3** *½* **City Ground (USA)**[14] 1168 7-9-1 64 DanielleMooney(7) 6 61
(Michael Easterby) *trckd ldr 1f: remained handy: rdn over 1f out: styd on same pce fnl f* **12/1**

2424 **4** *2 ¼* **India's Song**[22] 1051 4-9-6 61 (t) GeorgeBuckell(7) 3 61
(David Simcock) *hld up: r.o ins fnl f: nvr nrr* **9/1**

0102 **5** *2 ¼* **Attain**[29] 958 5-9-8 62 ShelleyBirkett(5) 5 56
(Julia Feilden) *hld up: rdn over 1f out: n.d* **9/2[2]**

1363 **6** *2 ¼* **Arabian Flight**[10] 1247 5-9-13 62 RobbieFitzpatrick 9 50
(Michael Appleby) *led: racd keenly: rdn and hdd over 2f out: wknd fnl f* **5/1[3]**

0046 **7** *¾* **Pravda Street**[19] 1085 9-9-13 60 (b) HayleyTurner 8 49
(Christopher Kellett) *hld up: a in rr* **22/1**

-516 **8** *1* **Dividend Dan (IRE)**[16] 1121 4-9-13 56 PaddyAspell 2 46
(Mike Murphy) *s.i.s: hmpd after 1f: hld up and racd keenly: rdn over 2f out: wknd wl over 1f out* **20/1**

1m 50.66s (0.16) **Going Correction** 0.0s/f (Stan) 8 Ran SP% **111.7**

Speed ratings (Par 101): **99,96,95,93,91 89,89,88**

CSF £21.88 TOTE £11.10: £2.50, £1.20, £3.70; EX 19.10 Trifecta £288.60.Winner bought by Crewe & Nantwich Racing Club for 6000gns.

**Owner** The Duke's Partnership **Bred** Corrin Stud **Trained** Upper Lambourn, Berks

■ Stewards' Enquiry : Danielle Mooney one-day ban: careless riding (Apr 26)

**FOCUS**

A typically moderate race of its type. The winner is rated close to his 3yo turf form.

## 1451 LADBROKES H'CAP 1m 141y(P)

**7:20** (7:20) (Class 4) (0-85,82) 4-Y-0+ **£5,175** (£1,540; £769; £384) **Stalls** Low

Form RPR

-032 **1** **Skytrain**[9] 1267 4-9-7 **82** JoeFanning 1 92
(Mark Johnston) *mde all: rdn over 1f out: r.o* **2/1[1]**

6023 **2** *1* **Ishikawa (IRE)**[30] 942 6-9-0 **82** RobJFitzpatrick(7) 2 90
(K R Burke) *chsd ldrs: hmpd over 3f out: rdn to chse wnr fnl f: r.o* **11/4[2]**

202- **3** *4 ½* **Moccasin (FR)**[173] 7425 5-9-4 **79** TomEaves 3 76
(Geoffrey Harker) *trckd wnr: rdn over 2f out: lost 2nd 1f out: sn hung lft and no ex* **10/1**

30-6 **4** *nk* **Dubai Dynamo**[13] 1191 9-9-6 **81** PJMcDonald 5 78
(Ruth Carr) *prom: lost pl whn hmpd over 3f out: n.d after* **11/2[3]**

2302 **5** *hd* **Smokethatthunders (IRE)**[8] 1286 4-8-13 **74** StevieDonohoe 4 70
(Tim Pitt) *s.i.s: hdwy over 6f out: rdn over 2f out: no ex fnl f* **7/1**

210- **6** *7* **Our Boy Jack (IRE)**[183] 7176 5-9-5 **80** LeeTopliss 6 60
(Richard Fahey) *hld up: rdn over 3f out: wknd 2f out* **15/2**

1m 49.05s (-1.45) **Going Correction** 0.0s/f (Stan) 6 Ran SP% **108.7**

Speed ratings (Par 105): **106,105,101,100,100 94**

CSF £7.13 TOTE £3.60: £2.50, £1.50; EX 9.60 Trifecta £56.00.

**Owner** Ready To Run Partnership **Bred** Brook Stud Bloodstock Ltd **Trained** Middleham Moor, N Yorks

**FOCUS**

A modest handicap dominated by the winner, who posted a personal best.

## 1452 CORAL MOBILE "JUST THREE CLICKS TO BET" MAIDEN STKS 1m 4f 50y(P)

**7:50** (7:50) (Class 5) 3-Y-O+ **£2,911** (£866; £432; £216) **Stalls** Low

Form RPR

3 **1** **Full Moon Fever (IRE)**[16] 1118 3-8-2 0 NickyMackay 2 71+
(Ed Walker) *sn pushed along in rr: hdwy over 8f out: chsd ldr 4f out: led 2f out: sn pushed clr: comf* **5/2[2]**

5 **2** *1 ¾* **Gallic Destiny (IRE)**[16] 1118 3-8-7 0 HayleyTurner 1 73+
(Andrew Balding) *chsd ldrs: rdn to chse wnr over 1f out: styd on* **3/1[3]**

530- **3** *15* **Testing (FR)**[179] 7260 3-8-2 70 JoeFanning 4 44
(Mark Johnston) *led: racd keenly: rdn and hdd 2f out: sn wknd* **2/1[1]**

0-5 **4** *shd* **Omotesando**[15] 1153 4-9-13 0 ShaneKelly 3 51
(Mark Brisbourne) *hld up: hdwy over 3f out: rdn over 2f out: wknd wl over 1f out* **33/1**

03 **5** *13* **Moriond (USA)**[16] 1119 3-8-7 0 (b[1]) MartinLane 5 28
(David Simcock) *hld up: hdwy over 4f out: rdn over 2f out: sn wknd* **5/1**

6-46 **6** *32* **Rocky Hill Ridge**[53] 649 3-8-7 32 LukeMorris 7
(Alan McCabe) *racd keenly: trckd ldr tl over 8f out: pushed along over 5f out: wknd 4f out* **66/1**

7 *1 ¾* **Lower Lake (FR)**[333] 4-9-13 0 WilliamCarson 6
(Mark Brisbourne) *prom: chsd ldr over 8f out: pushed along 4f out: sn wknd* **40/1**

2m 40.24s (-0.86) **Going Correction** 0.0s/f (Stan)

**WFA** 3 from 4yo 21lb 7 Ran SP% **110.4**

Speed ratings (Par 103): **102,100,90,90,82 60,59**

CSF £9.62 TOTE £4.40: £2.60, £1.90; EX 11.90 Trifecta £19.30.

**Owner** Bellman, Donald, Walker & Walker **Bred** T Boylan **Trained** Newmarket, Suffolk

**FOCUS**

An ordinary maiden. The first ran similar to their Kempton meeting last month.

## 1453 CORAL.CO.UK BEST ODDS GUARANTEED ON RACING H'CAP 1m 4f 50y(P)

**8:20** (8:20) (Class 6) (0-60,57) 4-Y-O+ **£2,264** (£673; £336; £168) **Stalls** Low

Form RPR

5203 **1** **Well Owd Mon**[16] 1132 4-8-7 **49** JackDuern(5) 1 61
(Andrew Hollinshead) *hld up: hdwy on outer to ld 2f out: rdn clr fnl f* **4/1[3]**

-035 **2** *8* **Herbalist**[59] 571 4-9-6 **57** (p) AdamKirby 7 56
(Sean Curran) *led: rdn and hdd 2f out: no ex fnl f* **5/2[2]**

1123 **3** *2 ¼* **Goldmadchen (GER)**[10] 1249 6-9-7 **57** JoeFanning 5 53
(James Given) *prom: rdn over 2f out: wknd ins fnl f* **9/4[1]**

5064 **4** *1 ¾* **Excellent News (IRE)**[26] 997 5-8-2 **45** (p) JackGarritty(7) 6 38
(Tony Forbes) *hld up: hdwy on outer 3f out: rdn and wknd over 1f out* **25/1**

2-05 **5** *1 ¾* **Impeccability**[16] 1132 4-8-8 **45** JimmyQuinn 3 35
(John Mackie) *hld up: rdn over 2f out: wknd over 1f out* **25/1**

030- **6** *2 ¾* **Camelopardalis**[205] 6558 5-9-5 **55** ShaneKelly 2 41
(Philip McBride) *hld up: hdwy to chse ldr over 8f out tl rdn over 2f out: wknd over 1f out* **13/2**

55-0 **7** *11* **Greyemkay**[10] 1232 6-8-7 **48** (p) DanielMuscutt(5) 9 16
(Richard Price) *chsd ldr tl over 8f out: rdn over 3f out: wknd over 2f out* **16/1**

4020 **8** *3 ¾* **Mazij**[16] 1132 6-9-1 **51** WilliamCarson 8 13
(Peter Hiatt) *chsd ldrs: rdn over 2f out: wknd over 1f out* **12/1**

566- **9** *26* **Ella Motiva (IRE)**[189] 7034 4-8-8 **45** LukeMorris 4
(Mark Brisbourne) *mid-div: pushed along over 5f out: wknd 3f out* **22/1**

2m 40.46s (-0.64) **Going Correction** 0.0s/f (Stan)

**WFA** 4 from 5yo+ 1lb 9 Ran SP% **118.3**

Speed ratings (Par 101): **102,96,95,94,92 91,83,81,63**

CSF £14.46 CT £27.01 TOTE £4.60: £1.20, £2.50, £1.30; EX 15.90 Trifecta £49.50.

**Owner** The Giddy Gang **Bred** Mr & Mrs W Hodge **Trained** Upper Longdon, Staffs

**FOCUS**

A weak handicap and one-way traffic for the winner, who's rated back to early form.

## 1454 CORAL APP DOWNLOAD FROM THE APP STORE H'CAP 1m 1f 103y(P)

**8:50** (8:50) (Class 5) (0-70,70) 4-Y-O+ **£2,911** (£866; £432; £216) **Stalls** Low

Form RPR

22-2 **1** **Ifan (IRE)**[50] 690 6-8-13 **67** DanielMuscutt(5) 7 77
(Tim Vaughan) *trckd ldrs: racd keenly: wnt 2nd over 3f out: led 2f out: and edgd lft ins fnl f: jst hld on* **6/1[3]**

6451 **2** *nk* **Ellaal**[8] 1288 5-8-11 **60** DaleSwift 9 69
(Ruth Carr) *mid-div: hdwy 1/2-way: rdn to chse wnr fnl f: r.o* **14/1**

2223 **3** 2 3/4 **Arlecchino (IRE)**[22] 1051 4-9-7 **70**....................(b) JoeFanning 3 74
(Ed McMahon) *hld up in tch: rdn over 1f out: styd on to go 3rd ins fnl f* **9/2**[2]

522- **4** 2 3/4 **Taro Tywod (IRE)**[214] 6283 5-8-11 **65**.................... JackDuern(5) 8 62
(Mark Brisbourne) *chsd ldr tl led over 4f out: rdn and hdd 2f out: no ex fnl f* **16/1**

3322 **5** 3/4 **Yourinthewill (USA)**[22] 1051 6-8-13 **62**.................... ShaneKelly 10 58
(Daniel Mark Loughnane) *hld up: hdwy over 2f out: sn rdn: styd on same pce fr over 1f out* **7/1**

4311 **6** 3 **Dozy Joe**[19] 1086 6-9-3 **66**....................(b) LukeMorris 2 56
(Joseph Tuite) *chsd ldrs: rdn over 2f out: wknd fnl f* **4/1**[1]

5-66 **7** 4 1/2 **Strong Conviction**[12] 1209 4-9-3 **69**.................... CharlesBishop(3) 1 49
(Simon Hodgson) *led 5f: rdn and wkng whn n.m.r over 2f out* **28/1**

-134 **8** 2 3/4 **Sutton Sid**[72] 379 4-8-13 **65**....................(bt) BillyCray(3) 11 39
(John Balding) *s.i.s: a in rr* **17/2**

-004 **9** 4 **Byroness**[16] 1121 4-8-8 **62**.................... RyanTate(5) 6 28
(Heather Main) *hld up: a in rr* **16/1**

6521 **10** 8 **Spirit Of Gondree (IRE)**[40] 815 6-9-3 **66**....................(b) AdamKirby 5 15
(Milton Bradley) *s.i.s: hld up: rdn over 3f out: sn wknd* **9/2**[2]

510- **11** 3/4 **First Sargeant**[252] 4995 4-9-1 **64**.................... TomEaves 4 12
(Geoffrey Harker) *hld up: a in rr: wkng whn hmpd wl over 2f out* **33/1**

2m 0.33s (-1.37) **Going Correction** 0.0s/f (Stan) **11** Ran SP% **118.5**
Speed ratings (Par 103): **106,105,103,100,100 97,93,91,87,80 79**
CSF £87.46 CT £417.38 TOTE £6.60: £2.50, £4.00, £1.30; EX 84.50 Trifecta £502.20.
**Owner** WRB Racing 61 and Derek & Jean Clee **Bred** Dr John Waldron **Trained** Aberthin, Vale of Glamorgan

**FOCUS**
A moderate handicap but the form looks sound.
T/Plt: £24.90 to a £1 stake. Pool: £91,616.67 - 2,680.08 winning tickets. T/Qpdt: £5.10 to a £1 stake. Pool: £8,477.50 - 1,212.10 winning tickets. CR

## NAVAN (L-H)
Saturday, April 12

**OFFICIAL GOING: Yielding to soft**

### 1458a P.W. MCGRATH MEMORIAL BALLYSAX STKS (GROUP 3) 1m 2f
3:35 (3:35) 3-Y-O **£32,500** (£9,500; £4,500; £1,500)

RPR

**1** **Fascinating Rock (IRE)**[13] 1199 3-9-3 .................... PatSmullen 4 110+
(D K Weld, Ire) *hld up in tch: 6th 1/2-way: hdwy fr 4f out to chse ldrs: gng best in 3rd on outer 1 1/2f out: led ent fnl f and sn rdn clr: kpt on wl* **5/2**[2]

**2** 2 1/2 **Answered**[20] 1079 3-9-3 .................... KevinManning 2 105
(J S Bolger, Ire) *chsd ldrs: 5th 1/2-way: outpcd over 2f out: sn rdn in 6th and wnt 4th over 1f out: kpt on wl towards fin into nvr nrr 2nd fnl stride: nt trble wnr* **7/4**[1]

**3** shd **All Set To Go (IRE)**[13] 1200 3-9-3 97.................... GaryCarroll 3 105
(A Oliver, Ire) *chsd ldr tl clsd to ld fr under 3f out: sn rdn and strly pressed: hdd ent fnl f and sn no imp on wnr in 2nd: denied 2nd fnl stride* **25/1**

**4** 1 **Carlo Bugatti (IRE)**[215] 6262 3-9-3 .................... JosephO'Brien 7 103
(A P O'Brien, Ire) *chsd ldrs: 4th 1/2-way: rdn into 3rd 3f out and clsd between horses to chal over 1f out: sn no imp on wnr and dropped to 4th nr fin* **4/1**[3]

**5** 4 3/4 **Kingfisher (IRE)**[196] 6835 3-9-3 99.................... SeamieHeffernan 5 96
(A P O'Brien, Ire) *w.w towards rr: checked sltly after 2f: 7th 1/2-way: rdn 1 1/2f out and no imp on ldrs: wnt mod 5th ins fnl f: kpt on* **14/1**

**6** 3 **Ebasani (IRE)**[185] 7137 3-9-3 .................... DeclanMcDonogh 1 88
(John M Oxx, Ire) *chsd ldrs tl 3rd 1/2-way: 3rd tl lost pl fr 3f out: sn rdn and no ex u.p in mod 6th ent fnl f: kpt on one pce* **13/2**

**7** 4 1/2 **Davids Park**[13] 1200 3-9-3 97.................... FMBerry 6 79
(John Joseph Murphy, Ire) *hld up in rr: last 1/2-way: rdn and no imp 3f out: kpt on one pce fnl 2f* **25/1**

**8** 3/4 **Stirabout (USA)**[13] 1200 3-9-3 87.................... RonanWhelan 8 77
(J S Bolger, Ire) *led: pushed along into st and hdd fr under 3f out: wknd and eased fr 2f out* **66/1**

2m 16.89s (1.09) **8** Ran SP% **114.1**
CSF £7.13 TOTE £3.40: £1.30, £1.80, £4.30; DF 8.10 Trifecta £140.10.
**Owner** Newtown Anner Stud Farm Ltd **Bred** Newtown Anner Stud **Trained** The Curragh, Co Kildare

**FOCUS**
Run at Leopardstown since 1993, the Ballysax Stakes was switched for this year to Navan for 'calendar' reasons as the Leopardstown fixture came too early in the season for the race to be an effective Classic trial. This became a bit of a sprint up the straight and the principals improved in line with the race averages.

1459 - 1467a (Foreign Racing) - See Raceform Interactive

## 980 RANDWICK (L-H)
Saturday, April 12

**OFFICIAL GOING: Turf: heavy**

### 1468a DARLEY T J SMITH STKS (GROUP 1) (2YO+) (TURF) 6f
6:50 (12:00) 2-Y-O+
**£843,951** (£268,817; £134,408; £67,204; £26,881; £13,440)

RPR

**1** **Lankan Rupee (AUS)**[35] 894 5-9-3 0.................... CraigNewitt 1 121+
(Mick Price, Australia) *broke wl and mde all: rdn 2f out: r.o strly and asserted: in control whn drifted rt ins fnl f: v readily* **14/5**[1]

**2** 2 **Rebel Dane (AUS)**[154] 7825 5-9-3 0.................... GlenBoss 5 114
(Gary Portelli, Australia) *midfield: rdn over 2f out: r.o and wnt 2nd cl home: no ch w wnr* **8/1**

**3** shd **Buffering (AUS)**[28] 7-9-3 0....................(b) DamianBrowne 2 114
(Robert Heathcote, Australia) *trckd ldr: rdn to try and chal 2f out: sn outpcd by wnr: kpt on but dropped to 3rd cl home* **9/1**

**4** 1 1/2 **Tiger Tees (NZ)**[14] 1185 7-9-3 0.................... NashRawiller 3 109
(Joseph Pride, Australia) *in tch on inner: rdn 2f out: kpt on same pce and no threat to wnr* **18/1**

**5** shd **See The World (AUS)**[14] 1185 8-9-3 0....................(b) ChristianReith 12 109
(Joseph Pride, Australia) *dwlt sltly and racd in rr: rdn over 2f out: str late run and wnt 5th fnl strides: nvr nrr* **60/1**

**6** shd **Gordon Lord Byron (IRE)**[14] 1186 6-9-3 0.................... CraigAWilliams 8 108
(T Hogan, Ire) *midfield: rdn over 2f out: kpt on u.p in st but n.d* **9/2**[2]

**7** 1 **Shamexpress (NZ)**[22] 5-9-3 0....................(t) DamienOliver 11 105
(Danny O'Brien, Australia) *dwlt sltly and racd in rr: rdn 2f out: kpt on but n.d* **25/1**

**8** 1 **Villa Verde (AUS)**[14] 1185 4-8-8 0.................... JamesMcDonald 9 93
(Anthony Cummings, Australia) *midfield: rdn over 2f out: kpt on same pce and n.d* **9/1**

**9** 1/2 **Sweet Idea (AUS)**[21] 4-8-8 0....................(b) TommyBerry 13 91
(Gai Waterhouse, Australia) *midfield: rdn over 2f out: kpt on same pce u.p and n.d* **15/2**[3]

**10** 1 **Sessions (AUS)**[14] 1185 5-9-3 0....................(t) KerrinMcEvoy 14 97
(Peter Snowden, Australia) *a towards rr: rdn over 1f out: no imp and btn: nvr a factor* **25/1**

**11** 3/4 **Famous Seamus (NZ)**[14] 1185 6-9-3 0.................... TimothyClark 6 95
(Noel Mayfield-Smith, Australia) *stdd and hld up in last: fanned wd and rdn into st: no imp and sn btn: nvr a factor* **40/1**

**12** 1 **Snitzerland (AUS)**[28] 5-8-13 0....................(b) BrentonAvdulla 15 87
(Gerald Ryan, Australia) *prom on outer: rdn over 2f out: no ex and btn ent fnl f: wknd and eased* **15/1**

**13** 3/4 **Steps In Time (AUS)**[21] 7-8-13 0.................... BlakeShinn 10 85
(Joseph Pride, Australia) *in tch on outer: rdn 2f out: no ex and btn ent fnl f: wknd* **20/1**

**14** 1 **Bel Sprinter (AUS)**[14] 1185 7-9-3 0....................(tp) ChadSchofield 7 86
(Jason Warren, Australia) *dwlt and a towards rr: rdn over 2f out: no imp and btn in st: nvr a factor* **50/1**

**15** 1 1/2 **Aeronautical (AUS)**[56] 631 6-9-3 0.................... JohnKissick 4 81
(Lionel Cohen, Australia) *a towards rr: rdn over 2f out: last and btn ent fnl f: nvr a factor* **100/1**

1m 12.14s (72.14) **15** Ran SP% **118.4**
PARI-MUTUEL (NSW TAB - all including 1 aud stake): WIN 3.70; PLACE 1.90, 2.70, 3.10; DF 15.30; SF 24.80.
**Owner** Teeley Assets Ltd Syndicate **Bred** Teeley Assets Ltd **Trained** Australia

1469 - 1472a (Foreign Racing) - See Raceform Interactive

## 1073 CURRAGH (R-H)
Sunday, April 13

**OFFICIAL GOING: Round course - yielding; straight course - yielding to soft**

### 1473a BIG BAD BOB GLADNESS STKS (GROUP 3) 7f
3:55 (3:57) 3-Y-O+ **£33,854** (£9,895; £4,687; £1,562)

RPR

**1** **Sruthan (IRE)**[189] 7051 4-9-10 111....................[1] ChrisHayes 6 114
(P D Deegan, Ire) *chsd ldrs: cl 3rd 1/2-way: hdwy nr side gng wl to chal ent fnl f: rdn to ld ins fnl 150yds and kpt on wl towards fin* **9/4**[1]

**2** 1 1/2 **Custom Cut (IRE)**[15] 1162 5-9-10 .................... DanielTudhope 4 110
(David O'Meara) *led: narrow advantage 1/2-way: rdn 1 1/2f out and sn strly pressed: hdd ins fnl 150yds and kpt on wl towards fin wout matching wnr: jst hld 2nd* **4/1**[2]

**3** nse **Wannabe Better (IRE)**[21] 1076 4-9-4 108.................... WayneLordan 7 104
(T Stack, Ire) *chsd ldrs: 6th 1/2-way: rdn 2f out and clsd u.p nr side into 3rd ins fnl 150yds: kpt on wl towards fin and jst failed for 2nd: nt trble wnr* **4/1**[2]

**4** 2 **Cristoforo Colombo (USA)**[162] 7714 4-9-7 108......(p) JosephO'Brien 1 101
(A P O'Brien, Ire) *trckd ldr in cl 2nd: rdn fr 2f out and no ex ent fnl f: sn dropped to 4th: kpt on same pce* **4/1**[2]

**5** hd **Pop Art (IRE)**[11] 1252 4-9-4 100.................... FMBerry 5 98
(Charles O'Brien, Ire) *chsd ldrs: 4th 1/2-way: clsd bhd ldrs over 1f out where nt clr run: sn rdn in 5th and no imp on ldrs: kpt on same pce* **13/2**[3]

**6** 1/2 **Bubbly Bellini (IRE)**[7] 1333 7-9-7 96....................(p) FergalLynch 8 100
(Adrian McGuinness, Ire) *w.w towards rr: 7th 1/2-way: tk clsr order bhd ldrs 2f out: sn rdn and no imp over 1f out: kpt on towards fin* **33/1**

**7** 1 1/4 **Tobann (IRE)**[163] 7673 4-9-4 101....................(t) RoryCleary 3 93
(J S Bolger, Ire) *chsd ldrs: t.k.h: 5th 1/2-way: rdn over 1f out and sn no ex u.p: kpt on one pce* **16/1**

**8** nk **Bold Thady Quill (IRE)**[7] 1333 7-9-7 98....................(v) ShaneFoley 2 95
(K J Condon, Ire) *s.i.s and racd in rr: last 1/2-way: tk clsr order far side over 2f out: sn rdn and no imp over 1f out: kpt on one pce* **25/1**

1m 28.4s (-2.40) **Going Correction** 0.0s/f (Good) **8** Ran SP% **116.8**
Speed ratings: **113,111,111,108,108 108,106,106**
CSF £11.73 TOTE £3.40: £1.40, £1.70, £1.60; DF 11.90 Trifecta £59.10.
**Owner** Robert Ng **Bred** Messrs J , R & J Hyland **Trained** The Curragh, Co Kildare

**FOCUS**
Apart from 2012 when Excelebration made a winning Irish debut for Aidan O'Brien, this rarely attracts a genuine Group 1 performer and this year's renewal was in keeping with most recent runnings. The runner-up, as expected, dictated the fractions from the front but couldn't retain his crown. The standard is set around the winner, fifth and sixth.

1474 - 1476a (Foreign Racing) - See Raceform Interactive

## CAPANNELLE (R-H)
Sunday, April 13

**OFFICIAL GOING: Turf: good to soft**

### 1477a PREMIO CARLO CHIESA (GROUP 3) (3YO+ FILLIES & MARES) (TURF) 6f
3:55 (12:00) 3-Y-O+ **£29,166** (£12,833; £7,000; £3,500)

RPR

**1** **Clorofilla (IRE)**[175] 7416 4-9-5 0.................... LManiezzi 1 105
(Marco Gasparini, Italy) *mde all: rdn appr fnl f: drvn out ins fnl f: hld on wl* **87/20**[2]

**2** hd **Universo Star (IRE)** 4-9-3 0.................... MEsposito 6 102
(A Marcialis, Italy) *towards rr: swtchd outside and hdwy 2f out: rdn to chse ldrs over 1f out: r.o u.p fnl f: hld cl home* **118/10**

**3** 2 1/4 **Chiara Wells (IRE)**[154] 7830 5-9-3 0.................... SBasile 10 95
(A Floris, Italy) *a.p wd of other runners: sltly outpcd and scrubbed along over 2f out: rallied to chse ldrs over 1f out: kpt on at same pce fnl f* **42/1**

**4** snk **Bettolle (ITY)**[154] 7830 5-9-3 0.................... StefanoLandi 9 95
(Jessica Lari, Italy) *midfield: tk clsr order bef 1/2-way: rdn to chse ldr 2f out: sn no further imp and outpcd appr 1f out: one pce fnl f* **58/10**

**5** 1 1/2 **Alfkona (GER)**[518] 7697 6-9-3 0.................... TBitala 11 90
(Jozef Roszival, Hungary) *trckd Chiara Wells on wd outside: rdn and nt qckn 2f out: kpt on u.p fnl f: nt pce to trble ldrs* **234/10**

6 *6* **Jadel**[23] 3-8-5 0 GBietolini 5 68
(D Camuffo, Italy) *in rr: rdn and shortlived effrt over 2f out: no further imp fr 1 1/2f out: eased ins fnl f* **113/10**
7 *1/2* **Grain De Beaute (IRE)** 3-8-5 0 GianlucaSanna 2 66
(Marco Gasparini, Italy) *midfield on inner: rdn and no imp over 2f out: one pce ent fnl f: sn eased* **81/10**
8 *6* **Sgomma (IRE)** 4-9-3 0 (b) PBorrelli 8 50
(Pamela Demuro, Italy) *midfield: rdn and no imp over 2f out: sn wknd: eased ins fnl f* **68/1**
9 *shd* **Naxos Beach (IRE)**[204] 5-9-3 0 (b) GMarcelli 3 49
(A Di Dio, Italy) *a towards rr: rdn and no imp fr 2 1/2f out: eased over 1 1/2f out* **37/1**
10 *4* **Girl Of The Rain (IRE)**[532] 7428 4-9-3 0 FabioBranca 7 37
(Stefano Botti, Italy) *chsd ldrs: rdn and lost pl 2 1/2f out: sn wl btn* **48/10**[3]
11 *5* **Omaticaya (IRE)**[23] 3-8-5 0 DarioVargiu 4 18
(Manila Illuminati, Italy) *rrd as stalls opened and missed break: wl adrift but rushed up to chse ldng pair after 2f: rdn and no imp sn after 1/2-way: wknd over 2f out: heavily eased fnl 1 1/2f* **7/10**[1]

1m 10.01s (-0.29)
**WFA** 3 from 4yo+ 12lb **11** Ran SP% **146.9**
WIN (incl. 1 euro stake): 5.34. PLACES: 2.21, 3.91, 7.34. DF: 112.75.
**Owner** Vincenzo Caldarola **Bred** Francesca Turri **Trained** Italy

# DUSSELDORF (R-H)

Sunday, April 13

**OFFICIAL GOING: Turf: good to soft**

## 1478a WETTENLEIP FRUHJAHRSMEILE (GROUP 3) (4YO+) (TURF) 1m

4:25 (12:00) 4-Y-0+

**£26,666** (£9,166; £4,583; £2,500; £1,666; £1,250)

RPR

1 **Amaron**[163] 7685 5-9-2 0 FabienLefebvre 3 117
(Andreas Lowe, Germany) *led early: hdd bef end of 1f: settled in 2nd: clsd on clr ldr fr 2f out: hrd rdn to ld ent fnl f: r.o u.p and a holding runner-up* **12/5**[2]
2 *1 1/4* **Chopin (GER)**[297] 3485 4-9-2 0 JamieSpencer 2 114
(A Wohler, Germany) *trckd ldng pair on inner: sn settled in 4th: rdn and nt qckn immediately 2f out: chsd eventual wnr fr over 1f out: r.o u.p fnl f but a hld by wnr* **19/10**[1]
3 *1 3/4* **Combat Zone (IRE)**[24] 1037 8-9-0 0 (p) NRichter 4 108
(Mario Hofer, Germany) *led bef end of 1f: 4 l clr 1/2-way: grad reeled in by wnr fr 2f out: hdd ent fnl f: kpt on at same pce* **148/10**
4 *nk* **Neatico (GER)**[126] 8211 7-9-6 0 DanielePorcu 5 113
(P Schiergen, Germany) *midfield in tch: rdn and effrt on outer over 2f out: kpt on fnl f: nt pce to chal* **14/5**[3]
5 *1/2* **Zazou (GER)**[40] 837 7-9-2 0 FilipMinarik 6 108
(Waldemar Hickst, Germany) *w.w in rr: rdn to chse ldng gp fr over 1 1/2f out: one pce fnl f* **18/5**
6 *1 1/2* **Global Thrill**[120] 8307 5-9-2 0 AndreaAtzeni 7 105
(J Hirschberger, Germany) *racd in 3rd: rdn and nt qckn over 1 1/2f out: fdd ins fnl f* **133/10**
7 *15* **Daring Storm (GER)**[145] 7968 4-9-0 0 SHellyn 1 68
(J Hirschberger, Germany) *towards rr: rdn and shortlived effrt on ins over 2f out: sn wknd* **129/10**

1m 37.58s (-3.58) **7** Ran SP% **132.5**
WIN (incl. 10 euro stake): 34. PLACES: 13, 10. SF: 112.
**Owner** Gestut Winterhauch **Bred** Genesis Green Stud Ltd **Trained** Germany

1479 - (Foreign Racing) - See Raceform Interactive

# 1339 LONGCHAMP (R-H)

Sunday, April 13

**OFFICIAL GOING: Turf: good**

## 1480a PRIX DE LA GROTTE (GROUP 3) (3YO FILLIES) (TURF) 1m

1:30 (12:00) 3-Y-0 **£33,333** (£13,333; £10,000; £6,666; £3,333)

RPR

1 **Lesstalk In Paris (IRE)**[189] 7055 3-9-0 0 ChristopheSoumillon 4 107
(J-C Rouget, France) *mde all: set slow pce: shkn up and qcknd whn pressed 2f out: rdn ent fnl f: r.o strly and a in control: pushed out towards fin* **6/4**[2]
2 *3/4* **Straight Thinking (USA)**[215] 6292 3-9-0 0 MaximeGuyon 5 105
(A Fabre, France) *trckd ldr on outer: pushed along to chal 2f out: rdn over 1f out: r.o wl but a being hld by wnr* **9/2**[3]
3 *1/2* **Indonesienne (IRE)**[189] 7055 3-9-0 0 OlivierPeslier 2 104+
(C Ferland, France) *dwlt sltly but qckly rcvrd: midfield in tch: pushed along 2f out: rdn and wnt 3rd ins fnl f: r.o but nvr able to chal* **5/4**[1]
4 *3/4* **Bocaiuva (IRE)**[27] 3-9-0 0 CristianDemuro 3 102
(F Chappet, France) *restrained and hld up in tch in last: rdn and sltly outpcd as tempo lifted 2f out: kpt on ins fnl f and wnt 4th fnl strides: nvr able to chal* **12/1**
5 *snk* **Ultradargent (FR)**[31] 944 3-9-0 0 UmbertoRispoli 1 102?
(Yannick Fouin, France) *t.k.h: trckd ldr on inner: rdn 2f out: kpt on same pce and sn hld: dropped to last fnl strides* **25/1**

1m 50.64s (12.24) **5** Ran SP% **114.2**
WIN (incl. 1 euro stake): 2.80. PLACES: 1.50, 1.60. SF: 6.10.
**Owner** Sarl Ecurie J L Tepper **Bred** Skymarc Farm Inc **Trained** Pau, France

**FOCUS**
They went a very steady pace and it became a sprint with the positions hardly changing. The time was extremely slow.

## 1481a PRIX DE FONTAINEBLEAU (GROUP 3) (3YO COLTS) (TURF) 1m

2:40 (12:00) 3-Y-0 **£33,333** (£13,333; £10,000; £6,666; £3,333)

RPR

1 **Ectot**[163] 7686 3-9-2 0 GregoryBenoist 7 118+
(E Lellouche, France) *sn trcking ldr in 2nd: chal gng strly 2f out and sn led: pushed along over 1f out: r.o strly under firm hands and heels ins fnl f and a doing enough to repel runner-up: front two clr* **2/1**[2]
2 *nk* **Karakontie (JPN)**[189] 7056 3-9-2 0 StephanePasquier 3 117+
(J E Pease, France) *in tch on inner early: clr 3rd after 2f: pushed along 2f out: wnt 2nd over 1f out: rdn to chal and pressed wnr ins fnl f: r.o wl and drew clr of remainder but a being hld* **6/4**[1]
3 *3 1/2* **Galiway**[169] 7534 3-9-2 0 OlivierPeslier 4 109
(A Fabre, France) *hld up in midfield on outer: pushed along over 2f out: r.o under hands and heels and wnt 3rd towards fin: nt pce of front pair: do bttr* **8/1**
4 *snk* **Prestige Vendome (FR)**[163] 7686 3-9-2 0 (p) ThierryThulliez 6 109
(N Clement, France) *t.k.h early: midfield in tch: pushed along 2f out: rdn and wnt 3rd ent fnl f: kpt on but nt pce of front pair and dropped to 4th towards fin* **10/1**
5 *1* **Daraybi (FR)**[14] 3-9-2 0 ChristopheSoumillon 2 107
(A De Royer-Dupre, France) *dwlt sltly and hld up in last pair: pushed along and hdwy on outer 1f out: rdn ins fnl f: kpt on same pce and n.d* **6/1**[3]
6 *1 1/4* **Kenbest (FR)**[20] 3-9-2 0 ThierryJarnet 1 104
(H-A Pantall, France) *hld up in midfield on inner: rdn over 2f out: kpt on same pce and nvr threatened* **20/1**
7 *3* **Serans (FR)**[46] 3-9-2 0 (b[1]) CyrilleStefan 5 99
(E Lellouche, France) *dwlt sltly: pushed along to rcvr and sn led: rdn and strly pressed 2f out: sn hdd & wknd on rail* **66/1**
8 *hd* **Apache Spirit**[27] 3-9-2 0 MaximeGuyon 8 96
(A Fabre, France) *dwlt sltly: hld up and a in rr: rdn whn nt clr run on rail ent fnl f: nt rcvr and eased* **14/1**

1m 39.13s (0.73) **8** Ran SP% **120.7**
WIN (incl. 1 euro stake): 2.70 (Ectot coupled with Serans). PLACES: 1.20, 1.20, 1.60. DF: 2.80. SF: 4.90.
**Owner** G Augustin-Normand & Mme E Vidal **Bred** Skymarc Farm Inc And Ecurie Des Monceaux **Trained** Lamorlaye, France

**FOCUS**
This was run in a much quicker time than the fillies' trial.

# 1356 PONTEFRACT (L-H)

Monday, April 14

**OFFICIAL GOING: Final mile - good; remainder - good (good to soft in places; 7.1)**
Wind: fresh 1/2 behind Weather: fine and sunny

## 1482 RACING UK EASTER HOLIDAY MAIDEN FILLIES' STKS (BOBIS RACE) 5f

2:10 (2:11) (Class 5) 2-Y-O **£3,234** (£962; £481; £240) **Stalls** Low

Form RPR

1 **Don't Tell Annie** 2-9-0 0 DavidAllan 2 72+
(Tim Easterby) *trckd ldrs: led 1f out: pushed out* **4/1**[3]
5 2 *2* **Horsforth**[16] 1161 2-9-0 0 StephenCraine 6 65
(Tony Coyle) *led: hdd 1f out: kpt on same pce* **15/8**[1]
3 *1/2* **War Paint (IRE)** 2-9-0 0 RichardKingscote 8 63
(Tom Dascombe) *sn chsng ldrs on outer: drvn over 2f out: swtchd lft over 1f out: styd on towards fin* **7/2**[2]
4 *1* **Ar Colleen Aine** 2-9-0 0 SamHitchcott 7 59
(Mick Channon) *w ldr: effrt over 2f out: kpt on same pce appr fnl f* **16/1**
5 *2 3/4* **Lotara** 2-9-0 0 RobbieFitzpatrick 5 50
(Michael Appleby) *rera-div: hdwy over 2f out: chsng ldrs over 1f out: fdd towards fin* **14/1**
6 *1 3/4* **Appleberry (IRE)** 2-9-0 0 AndrewMullen 9 43
(Michael Appleby) *sn chsng ldrs on outside: drvn over 2f out: wknd fnl f* **33/1**
7 *8* **Is She Any Good (IRE)** 2-8-11 0 DeclanBates[(3)] 1 14
(David Evans) *s.i.s: in rr: bhd fnl 2f* **12/1**
8 *8* **Freida** 2-8-11 0 IanBrennan[(3)] 3
(Karen Tutty) *s.s: outpcd in rr: bhd fnl 2f* **80/1**
9 *14* **Little Sista** 2-9-0 0 PaulMulrennan 4
(Bryan Smart) *w ldrs: drvn and lost pl over 2f out: sn bhd: eased ins fnl f: t.o* **9/1**

1m 4.92s (1.62) **Going Correction** +0.025s/f (Good) **9** Ran SP% **111.4**
Speed ratings (Par 89): **88,84,84,82,78 75,62,49,27**
CSF £11.23 TOTE £4.60: £1.50, £1.10, £1.50; EX 13.50 Trifecta £50.90.
**Owner** Dale & Ann Wilsdon & Partner **Bred** Wilsdon & Habton **Trained** Great Habton, N Yorks

**FOCUS**
Probably not a maiden with a great deal of depth to it, but a taking performance from the winner. The form has been rated in line with the averages for this race.

## 1483 THE FULL PONTE PACKAGE - NEW FOR 2014 H'CAP 1m 4y

2:40 (2:40) (Class 4) (0-85,85) 4-Y-O+ **£6,469** (£1,925; £962; £481) **Stalls** Low

Form RPR

-206 1 **Ansaab**[16] 1164 6-9-7 **85** (t) SilvestreDeSousa 5 93
(Alan McCabe) *trckd ldrs: led over 1f out: jst hld on* **5/2**[1]
550- 2 *nse* **Stellar Express (IRE)**[165] 7651 5-9-5 **83** AndrewMullen 2 91
(Michael Appleby) *chsd ldrs: 2nd jst ins fnl f: styd on clsng stages: jst denied* **9/2**[2]
326- 3 *3/4* **Kalk Bay (IRE)**[164] 7661 7-9-4 **82** (t) JamesSullivan 7 89+
(Michael Easterby) *in rr: hdwy over 2f out: bdly hmpd 1f out: styd on strly: tk 3rd clsng stages* **18/1**
125- 4 *1* **Zeyran (IRE)**[273] 4348 5-9-1 **82** [1] RobertTart[(3)] 6 87+
(Hugo Palmer) *hld up in mid-div: hdwy 2f out: chsng ldrs whn hmpd 1f out: kpt on to take 3rd last 50yds* **8/1**[3]
432- 5 *3* **Talent Scout (IRE)**[202] 6727 8-9-0 **85** (p) GemmaTutty[(7)] 9 82
(Karen Tutty) *led: hdd over 1f out: sn swtchd rt: wknd last 100yds* **25/1**
26-0 6 *1 3/4* **Hard Core Debt**[15] 1196 4-8-11 **75** TomEaves 3 68
(Brian Ellison) *s.i.s: hdwy on inner 3f out: nt clr run over 2f out: kpt on same pce over 1f out* **16/1**
5-21 7 *hd* **Two Moons**[33] 930 4-8-12 **76** StephenCraine 4 69
(Tony Coyle) *chsd ldrs: one pce over 1f out* **12/1**
01-0 8 *2 1/4* **Johnno**[15] 1191 5-8-6 **77** AnnaHesketh[(7)] 12 64
(David Nicholls) *mid-div: effrt over 2f out: kpt on: nvr a threat* **33/1**
00-0 9 *nk* **Rocket Ronnie (IRE)**[15] 1190 4-9-2 **80** AdrianNicholls 1 67
(David Nicholls) *in rr: sme hdwy over 1f out: edgd lft: nvr a factor* **20/1**
220- 10 *1/2* **Topamichi**[166] 7632 4-9-1 **79** BenCurtis 16 65
(Mark H Tompkins) *s.s: swtchd lft s: bhd: hdwy whn hmpd 1f out: styng on at fin* **50/1**
620- 11 *5* **Prophesy (IRE)**[184] 7211 5-8-11 **78** NeilFarley[(3)] 8 52
(Tim Easterby) *in rr: sn drvn along: sme hdwy over 2f out: lost pl over 1f out* **14/1**

265- **12** 1 1/4 **The Osteopath (IRE)**[216] 6288 11-8-11 **75**.................. PJMcDonald 17 46
(John Davies) *rr-div: sme hdwy on outer over 2f out: nvr a factor* **33/1**

240- **13** 4 **Kingscroft (IRE)**[220] 6161 6-9-0 **83**.................. JacobButterfield(5) 15 45
(Michael Herrington) *in rr: bhd fnl 2f* **50/1**

163- **14** hd **Bartack (IRE)**[195] 6925 4-9-4 **82**.................. DanielTudhope 14 44
(David O'Meara) *chsd ldrs on outer: drvn 3f out: lost pl over 2f out* **20/1**

500- **15** nk **Dolphin Rock**[166] 7632 7-8-12 **76**.................. DaleSwift 11 37
(Brian Ellison) *chsd ldrs: drvn 4f out: lost pl 2f out* **10/1**

**16** 8 **Bob**[183] 4-9-2 **80**.................. DavidAllan 10 22
(Les Eyre) *chsd ldrs: lost pl over 2f out: sn bhd* **14/1**

1513 **17** 76 **Thatchmaster (USA)**[18] 1128 4-8-13 **77**.................. JoeFanning 13
(Mark Johnston) *mid-div on outer: reminders 3f out: sn lost pl and bhd: t.o over 1f out: virtually p.u* **12/1**

1m 44.6s (-1.30) **Going Correction** +0.025s/f (Good) **17** Ran SP% **130.0**
Speed ratings (Par 105): **107,106,106,105,102 100,100,98,97,97 92,90,86,86,86 78,2**
CSF £12.16 CT £180.25 TOTE £4.00: £1.20, £1.60, £4.70, £2.70; EX 19.90 Trifecta £293.20.
**Owner** Craig and Maureen Buckingham **Bred** Castlemartin Stud And Skymarc Farm **Trained** Averham Park, Notts

■ Stewards' Enquiry : Gemma Tutty three-day ban: careless riding (Apr 28-30)

**FOCUS**
A fairly useful handicap which was soundly run. The runner-up has been rated to his best.

## 1484 RIU PALACE MELONERAS H'CAP 6f
**3:10** (3:10) (Class 2) (0-100,100) 4-Y-0+
**£12,450** (£3,728; £1,864; £932; £466; £234) **Stalls** Low

Form RPR

06-0 **1** **Fast Shot**[9] 1305 6-8-2 **88**.................. RachelRichardson(7) 3 98
(Tim Easterby) *trckd ldrs: styd on to ld jst ins fnl f: pushed out* **7/1**[3]

14-4 **2** 1/2 **Annunciation**[16] 1172 4-9-6 **99**.................. PatDobbs 7 107
(Richard Hannon) *chsd ldrs: edgd rt 1f out: styd on to take 2nd last 100yds: no ex nr fin* **8/1**

0-00 **3** 3/4 **Yeeoow (IRE)**[28] 991 5-8-4 **88**.................. JoeyHaynes(5) 8 94
(K R Burke) *mid-div: hdwy over 2f out: swtchd outside over 1f out: kpt on wl: tk 3rd last 40yds: gng on at fin* **9/2**[1]

600- **4** 1 1/2 **Majestic Myles (IRE)**[205] 6623 6-9-1 **94**.................. TonyHamilton 11 95
(Richard Fahey) *w ldr: led briefly 1f out: styd on same pce* **12/1**

20-0 **5** 3/4 **Newstead Abbey**[51] 715 4-9-4 **97**.................. PhillipMakin 9 95
(David Barron) *mid-div: effrt over 2f out: kpt on same pce fnl f* **11/1**

/00- **6** nk **Royal Rascal**[191] 7025 4-9-4 **97**.................. DavidAllan 12 94
(Tim Easterby) *in rr on outer: hdwy over 1f out: styd on ins fnl f* **33/1**

200- **7** 3/4 **Louis The Pious**[171] 7495 6-9-5 **98**.................. DanielTudhope 10 93
(David O'Meara) *mid-div: drvn and outpcd over 2f out: hdwy over 1f out: kpt on* **6/1**[2]

65-6 **8** shd **Baby Strange**[15] 1193 10-8-0 **86** oh1.................. AdamMcLean(7) 5 81
(Derek Shaw) *in rr: hdwy over 1f out: keeping on at fin* **12/1**

0000 **9** 2 **Forest Edge (IRE)**[16] 1172 5-8-12 **94**.................. DeclanBates(3) 1 82
(David Evans) *chsd ldrs: sn drvn along: wknd fnl f* **15/2**

21-0 **10** 1 1/2 **Can You Conga**[15] 1193 4-8-2 **88**.................. DanielleMooney(7) 4 72
(Michael Easterby) *mid-div: sme hdwy over 1f out: wknd last 150yds* **16/1**

203- **11** nk **Colonel Mak**[203] 6685 7-9-2 **95**.................. AndrewMullen 2 78
(David Barron) *led: hdd 1f out: sn wknd* **15/2**

100- **12** 4 **Ancient Cross**[171] 7495 10-9-7 **100**..................(t) JamesSullivan 6 70
(Michael Easterby) *s.i.s: swtchd lft sn after s: in rr: sme hdwy over 1f out: sn wknd* **33/1**

1m 15.67s (-1.23) **Going Correction** +0.025s/f (Good) **12** Ran SP% **115.1**
Speed ratings (Par 109): **109,108,107,105,104 103,102,102,100,98 97,92**
CSF £60.14 CT £281.46 TOTE £8.70: £3.60, £2.40, £2.10; EX 79.30 Trifecta £306.00.
**Owner** Ontoawinner & Partners **Bred** Whitsbury Manor Stud & Pigeon House Stud **Trained** Great Habton, N Yorks

**FOCUS**
A useful sprint, albeit one which not many ever threatened to get into, three of the first four home all handy throughout. The winner has been rated as running a small personal best, with the runner-up pretty much to form.

## 1485 PETER REEK 70TH BIRTHDAY PONTEFRACT MARATHON H'CAP 2m 5f 122y
**3:40** (3:41) (Class 5) (0-75,76) 4-Y-0+ **£3,881** (£1,155; £577; £288) **Stalls** Low

Form RPR

000- **1** **New Youmzain (FR)**[178] 7338 5-9-12 **74**.................. AndrewMullen 2 86
(Michael Appleby) *t.k.h: w ldr: led after 2f: styd on u.p over 1f out: fnd ex nr fin* **1/1**[1]

00 **2** nk **Longshadow**[15] 1197 4-8-0 **59**..................(p) JoeyHaynes(5) 1 70
(Jason Ward) *trckd ldrs: 2nd 12f out: chal 3f out: edgd rt over 1f out: no ex clsng stages* **33/1**

1-23 **3** 12 **Jawaab (IRE)**[22] 73 10-8-7 **55**..................(v) PJMcDonald 3 54
(Philip Kirby) *trckd ldrs: drvn 6f out: modest 3rd over 4f out: one pce* **12/1**

/10- **4** 22 **Rock Relief (IRE)**[17] 3726 8-9-6 **68**.................. PaulMulrennan 10 45
(Chris Grant) *chsd ldrs: drvn 10f out: lost pl over 3f out: sn bhd* **9/1**

0/43 **5** 4 1/2 **Fade To Grey (IRE)**[17] 1151 10-8-7 **55** oh2..........(t) SilvestreDeSousa 5 28
(Shaun Lycett) *in rr: hdwy 9f out: poor 4th over 3f out: wknd fnl 3f* **7/1**[2]

3/6- **6** 13 **Rockawango (FR)**[7] 7423 8-9-3 **65**..................(t) GrahamLee 4 25
(James Ewart) *in rr: drvn 9f out: sme hdwy 5f out: lost pl over 3f out* **16/1**

02/0 **7** 6 **Spruzzo**[15] 1197 8-8-11 **59**.................. DuranFentiman 9 13
(Chris Fairhurst) *led 2f: chsd ldrs: drvn 11f out: lost pl over 8f out: bhd fnl 6f* **14/1**

3135 **8** 58 **Joyful Motive**[6] 1359 5-8-0 **55** oh4.................. PaulBooth(7) 6
(Michael Chapman) *sn pushed along in rr: sme hdwy13f out: lost pl over 3f out: t.o and eased 2f out: virtually p.u* **20/1**

-225 **9** 25 **Scribe (IRE)**[27] 513 6-8-13 **64**..................(vt) DeclanBates(3) 7
(David Evans) *wnt rt s: in rr: sn pushed along: sme hdwy 7f out: lost pl over 4f out: sn bhd: t.o over 2f out: virtually p.u* **16/1**

00-1 **10** 11 **Tartan Jura**[6] 1366 6-10-0 **76** 6ex..................(p) JoeFanning 8
(Mark Johnston) *n.m.r s: sn mid-div: modest 3rd and drvn 9f out: lost pl over 3f out: sn bhd: t.o whn eased ins fnl f: virtually p.u* **8/1**[3]

4m 56.67s (5.67) **Going Correction** +0.025s/f (Good)
**WFA** 4 from 5yo+ 6lb **10** Ran SP% **117.4**
Speed ratings (Par 103): **90,89,85,77,75 71,68,47,38,34**
CSF £44.05 CT £278.57 TOTE £2.00: £1.02, £11.60, £3.20; EX 49.30 Trifecta £543.40.
**Owner** C L Bacon **Bred** Sarl Haras De Saint-Faust **Trained** Danethorpe, Notts

■ Stewards' Enquiry : Andrew Mullen nine-day ban: used whip above permitted level (Apr 28-May 6)

**FOCUS**
Hardly a contest that will provide many pointers to future races but the front two clearly deserve some credit for having the rest well strung out. The winner has been rated close to his 3yo form, with the runner-up to last year's Irish 3yo figure.

## 1486 SUBSCRIBE ONLINE @ RACINGUK.COM MAIDEN STKS 6f
**4:10** (4:11) (Class 5) 3-Y-0+ **£3,881** (£1,155; £577; £288) **Stalls** Low

Form RPR

**1** **Active Spirit (IRE)** 3-9-0 0.................. SilvestreDeSousa 11 87+
(Saeed bin Suroor) *in rr on outer: edgd lft over 2f out: swtchd to outside 2f out: gd hdwy over 1f: hung lft and sn led: drew clr* **5/1**[2]

0-U **2** 5 **Naggers (IRE)**[7] 1347 3-9-0 0.................. GrahamLee 6 71
(Paul Midgley) *mid-div: hdwy over 2f out: w ldrs 1f out: styd on same pce* **33/1**

3- **3** 5 **Al Senad**[207] 6569 3-9-0 0.................. RobertHavlin 9 55
(Peter Chapple-Hyam) *trckd ldrs: rdn and led briefly over 1f out: kpt on same pce* **6/5**[1]

6 **4** 3 **More Beau (USA)**[16] 1173 3-9-0 0.................. PaddyAspell 3 45+
(Ed Dunlop) *dwlt: hdwy on ins and nt clr run 2f out: hung rt and kpt on one pce fnl f* **10/1**

**5** 1/2 **Sleeping Apache (IRE)** 4-9-12 0.................. PhillipMakin 8 47+
(Philip Kirby) *in rr: carried wd over 2f out: hdwy over 1f out: edgd lft ins fnl f: nvr a factor* **33/1**

500- **6** 2 1/4 **Bahamian C**[185] 7170 3-9-0 68.................. TonyHamilton 10 37
(Richard Fahey) *mid-div: outpcd and lost pl over 3f out: sme hdwy over 1f out: no imp whn hmpd wl ins fnl f* **17/2**

00- **7** 1 **Locky Taylor (IRE)**[145] 7978 3-9-0 0..................(b[1]) TomEaves 1 33
(Kevin Ryan) *led: hung rt and hdd over 1f out: sn wknd* **7/1**[3]

**8** 1 **Little Shambles** 3-8-9 0.................. JoeFanning 7 25
(Mark Johnston) *chsd ldrs: drvn over 2f out: lost pl over 1f out* **9/1**

0436 **9** 3/4 **Island Express (IRE)**[25] 1035 7-9-7 45..................(tp) AnnStokell(5) 5 31
(Ann Stokell) *chsd ldrs: rdn over 2f out: hung rt and wknd over 1f out* **100/1**

000- **10** 2 **Jack Barker**[174] 7455 5-9-9 44.................. NeilFarley(3) 2 24
(Robin Bastiman) *drvn to chse ldrs: wknd appr fnl f* **66/1**

0- **11** 34 **Kalani's Diamond**[216] 6289 4-9-7 0.................. PaulMulrennan 4
(Bryan Smart) *mid-div: lost pl over 1f out: heavily eased ins fnl f: virtually p.u: t.o* **33/1**

1m 17.07s (0.17) **Going Correction** +0.025s/f (Good)
**WFA** 3 from 4yo+ 12lb **11** Ran SP% **115.5**
Speed ratings (Par 103): **99,92,85,81,81 78,76,75,74,71 26**
CSF £160.68 TOTE £4.70: £2.00, £10.10, £1.10; EX 168.90 Trifecta £669.30.
**Owner** Godolphin **Bred** Darley **Trained** Newmarket, Suffolk

**FOCUS**
An ordinary sprint maiden overall, but a promising effort from the winner, who overcame clear inexperience to score easily. The runner-up surprised and is the key to the form - he's clearly improved but it's hard to gauge by how much.

## 1487 80'S NIGHT ON FRIDAY EVENING 23RD MAY H'CAP 5f
**4:40** (4:40) (Class 5) (0-70,69) 4-Y-0+ **£3,881** (£1,155; £577; £288) **Stalls** Low

Form RPR

200- **1** **Shillito**[178] 7345 4-8-9 **57**.................. PJMcDonald 2 67
(Tony Coyle) *chsd ldrs: n.m.r over 3f out: str run fnl 100yds: led nr fin* **8/1**[3]

3220 **2** nk **Dancing Freddy (IRE)**[6] 1369 7-9-7 **69**..................(tp) PaulMulrennan 8 78
(Ann Stokell) *swtchd lft after s: led over 3f out: drvn fnl f: hdd nr fin* **12/1**

6523 **3** 3 **Thorpe Bay**[38] 866 5-9-4 **66**.................. AndrewMullen 3 64
(Michael Appleby) *led: hmpd and hdd over 3f out: chsd ldr 2f out: styd on same pce last 150yds* **3/1**[1]

-050 **4** 1/2 **See The Storm**[21] 1082 6-9-2 **67**.................. JasonHart(3) 6 63+
(Eric Alston) *mid-div: hdwy and n.m.r over 1f out: kpt on fnl f* **9/1**

F0-0 **5** 1 1/2 **Boxing Shadows**[12] 1244 4-8-12 **60**.................. DavidAllan 7 51
(Les Eyre) *chsd ldrs: edgd lft and one pce over 1f out* **16/1**

060- **6** 1 1/2 **See Clearly**[159] 7772 5-8-9 **57**..................(p) DuranFentiman 1 43
(Tim Easterby) *rr-div: hdwy on ins 2f out: sn chsng ldrs: one pce over 1f out* **8/1**[3]

00-0 **7** 2 **Exotic Guest**[12] 1244 4-9-5 **67**.................. JamesSullivan 4 45
(Ruth Carr) *chsd ldrs: nt clr run over 1f out: one pce* **20/1**

513- **8** 1/2 **Manatee Bay**[196] 6903 4-8-9 **57**.................. AdrianNicholls 14 34
(David Nicholls) *s.i.s: swtchd lft after s: sme hdwy over 1f out: nvr a factor* **12/1**

0-06 **9** 2 3/4 **Mey Blossom**[81] 296 9-8-9 **57**..................(p) PaulQuinn 5 24
(Richard Whitaker) *dwlt: in rr: nvr on terms* **22/1**

53 **10** nse **Dark Lane**[17] 1148 8-8-12 **60**..................(v) GrahamLee 9 26
(David Evans) *mid-div: hdwy over 2f out: wknd over 1f out* **15/2**[2]

1130 **11** 1 **Electric Qatar**[34] 909 5-9-4 **66**..................(p) SilvestreDeSousa 13 29
(Alan McCabe) *swtchd lft after s: drvn to chse ldrs: wkng whn n.m.r over 1f out* **10/1**

0643 **12** 3 **Prince Of Passion (CAN)**[6] 1369 6-8-8 **56**..................(v) DaleSwift 11 8
(Derek Shaw) *swtchd lft s: in rr: rdn over 2f out: nvr on terms* **12/1**

311- **13** 2 3/4 **Windforpower (IRE)**[194] 6944 4-8-12 **60**..................(p) JoeFanning 12 2
(Tracy Waggott) *swtchd lft after s: chsd ldrs: lost pl over 1f out* **14/1**

1m 3.92s (0.62) **Going Correction** +0.025s/f (Good) **13** Ran SP% **122.8**
Speed ratings (Par 103): **96,95,90,89,87 85,81,81,76,76 75,70,65**
CSF £103.41 CT £370.64 TOTE £12.30: £3.70, £4.10, £1.70; EX 163.70 Trifecta £706.40.
**Owner** Tony Coyle **Bred** L M Cumani **Trained** Norton, N Yorks

■ Stewards' Enquiry : Paul Mulrennan two-day ban: careless riding (Apr 28-29)

**FOCUS**
A run-of-the-mill sprint. It was run at a good pace courtesy of the second but not many got into it. The winner has been rated to last year's reappearance run and the third as running his best turf race.

T/Plt: £15.70 to a £1 stake. Pool: £74225.67 - 3446.49 winning tickets T/Qpdt: £9.80 to a £1 stake. Pool: £4446.55 - 333.96 winning tickets WG

# [1349]WINDSOR (R-H)

Monday, April 14

**OFFICIAL GOING: Good (good to firm in places; 8.5)**

Wind: Light, behind Weather: Fine

## 1488 GRANT THORNTON MAIDEN AUCTION FILLIES' STKS (BOBIS RACE) 5f 10y

**2:20** (2:21) (Class 5) 2-Y-O **£2,587** (£770; £384; £192) **Stalls** Low

Form RPR

4 **1** **Low Cut Affair (IRE)**[16] 1169 2-8-6 0 MartinLane 1 74+
(David Evans) *fast away: mde all and racd against nr side rail: shkn up and drew clr jst over 1f out* **8/1**[3]

**2** 3 1/4 **Polar Vortex (IRE)** 2-9-1 0 AdamKirby 10 71+
(Clive Cox) *prom: pushed along 1/2-way: rdn to chse wnr 1f out: kpt on but no imp* **9/2**[1]

**3** 1 **No One Knows** 2-8-13 0 ow1 SebSanders 11 66+
(J W Hills) *s.i.s: racd wdst of all: prog fr rr 1/2-way: shkn up over 1f out: kpt on to take 3rd ins fnl f* **20/1**

2 **4** 3/4 **Zermintrudee (IRE)**[9] 1314 2-8-6 0 ChrisCatlin 3 56
(David Evans) *prom: drvn 2f out: chsd wnr briefly jst over 1f out: one pce fnl f* **13/2**[2]

**5** 1 3/4 **June's Moon** 2-8-10 0 ShaneKelly 5 54
(Jonathan Portman) *chsd ldrs: rdn 2f out: tried to cl over 1f out: no prog fnl f* **20/1**

**6** hd **Itsindebag** 2-8-6 0 LiamJones 12 49
(J S Moore) *dwlt: swtchd to r against nr side rail: rdn and wl in rr: swtchd lft fnl f and kpt on* **66/1**

**7** 1/2 **Mylaporyours (IRE)** 2-8-6 0 AndreaAtzeni 2 54+
(Rod Millman) *trckd ldrs: shkn up and wl in tch whn hmpd more than once fr over 1f out: no ch after: r.o nr fin* **9/2**[1]

**8** hd **Frozen Princess** 2-8-8 0 FergusSweeney 13 48
(Jamie Osborne) *dwlt: hld up in last pair: sme prog over 1f out: pushed along and no hdwy fnl f* **16/1**

**9** nk **Karluk (IRE)** 2-8-9 0 ow1 JohnFahy 7 48
(Eve Johnson Houghton) *nvr beyond midfield: pushed along over 1f out: no real prog* **16/1**

3 **10** nk **Sparbrook (IRE)**[9] 1314 2-8-8 0 MartinDwyer 6 46
(George Baker) *chsd wnr: drvn 2f out: hung rt over 1f out: sn lost 2nd and wknd* **9/2**[1]

**11** 4 **Arousal** 2-8-3 0 LouisSteward(5) 8 32
(Michael Bell) *sn pushed along in last and rn green: nvr a factor* **8/1**[3]

**12** 1/2 **Kidmeforever** 2-8-6 0 DavidProbert 9 28
(J S Moore) *a towards rr: wknd over 1f out* **33/1**

1m 0.84s (0.54) **Going Correction** -0.175s/f (Firm) **12 Ran SP% 115.8**
Speed ratings (Par 89): **88,82,81,80,77 76,76,75,75,74 68,67**
CSF £40.99 TOTE £10.60: £3.10, £1.80, £5.70; EX 57.90 Trifecta £933.90.
**Owner** Mrs T Burns **Bred** D Donegan **Trained** Pandy, Monmouths

**FOCUS**
Top bend dolled out 3yds from normal inner configuration adding 10yds to race distances of 1m or more. The ground was soft at the previous meeting, but following a dry week the going had changed to good, good to firm in places. Not a strong-looking maiden, but good to see a 5f sprint at this track won in old-school fashion, with early speed from stall one and grabbing the stands' rail proving decisive.

## 1489 DOWNLOAD THE UNIBET PRO APP H'CAP (DIV I) 5f 10y

**2:50** (2:51) (Class 4) (0-85,85) 4-Y-O+ **£4,851** (£1,443; £721; £360) **Stalls** Low

Form RPR

351- **1** **Pal Of The Cat**[254] 4989 4-8-10 77 (tp) OisinMurphy(3) 6 86
(Brian Gubby) *pressed ldr: led after 2f: racd against nr side rail after: drvn and hld on wl fnl f: jinked and uns rdr after* **5/1**[2]

0F0- **2** 3/4 **Arctic Lynx (IRE)**[189] 7080 7-9-2 80 AndreaAtzeni 11 86
(Robert Cowell) *prom on outer: prog to chse wnr fnl f: styd on but a hld* **10/1**

5120 **3** 1 **Kuanyao (IRE)**[11] 1261 8-8-6 75 (b) LouisSteward(5) 3 77
(Lee Carter) *trckd ldrs: rdn over 1f out: kpt on fnl f to take 3rd last strides* **10/1**

261 **4** nk **Muhdiq (USA)**[24] 1049 5-8-13 77 ShaneKelly 9 78
(Mike Murphy) *led 2f: chsd wnr: one pce fnl f* **7/2**[1]

614- **5** shd **Waseem Faris (IRE)**[175] 7420 5-8-11 78 WilliamTwiston-Davies(3) 2 79
(Mick Channon) *s.i.s: hld up in last: stl there 2f out: prog over 1f out: shkn up and r.o fnl f: nrst fin but nvr involved* **8/1**[3]

466 **6** 2 **Valmina**[11] 1261 7-8-10 74 (t) LukeMorris 7 68
(Tony Carroll) *sn pushed along in rr: drvn and one pce fr 2f out: no threat* **10/1**

206- **7** 1 1/4 **Rebecca Romero**[203] 6699 7-9-3 81 RobertWinston 4 70
(Denis Coakley) *w.w towards rr: pushed along and no imp on ldrs fr over 1f out: nvr involved* **8/1**[3]

4233 **8** nk **Ask The Guru**[19] 1109 4-8-8 72 (v) KierenFox 8 60
(Michael Attwater) *chsd ldrs: pushed along 1/2-way: rdn and nt qckn over 1f out: wknd fnl f* **20/1**

0-45 **9** 1/2 **Pandar**[9] 1313 5-9-7 85 AdamKirby 10 71
(Milton Bradley) *racd wd towards rr: shkn up and no prog over 1f out: nvr involved* **25/1**

000 **10** 2 1/2 **Bainne (IRE)**[17] 1145 4-9-4 82 (t) SeanLevey 1 59
(Jeremy Gask) *hld up in rr: nudged along and no prog fr 2f out* **25/1**

0-42 **11** 1 **Ubetterbegood (ARG)**[44] 802 6-9-6 84 (p) JimmyQuinn 5 58
(Robert Cowell) *s.i.s: towards rr: hanging whn pushed along 1/2-way: sn lost pl and struggling* **5/1**[2]

58.69s (-1.61) **Going Correction** -0.175s/f (Firm) **11 Ran SP% 117.5**
Speed ratings (Par 105): **105,103,102,101,101 98,96,95,95,91 89**
CSF £52.56 CT £487.66 TOTE £4.80: £2.00, £5.90, £5.10; EX 66.40 Trifecta £723.70.
**Owner** Brian Gubby **Bred** B Gubby **Trained** Bagshot, Surrey

**FOCUS**
The pick of the C&D times. Just like in the opening maiden, early speed and grabbing the stands' rail proved key. The winner backed up a clear personal best on his final 2yo start.

## 1490 DOWNLOAD THE UNIBET PRO APP H'CAP (DIV II) 5f 10y

**3:20** (3:21) (Class 4) (0-85,85) 4-Y-O+ **£4,851** (£1,443; £721; £360) **Stalls** Low

Form RPR

44-1 **1** **Breccbennach**[24] 1041 4-8-11 75 (tp) DaneO'Neill 3 87
(Seamus Durack) *w ldr: led 1/2-way: racd against nr side rail after: shkn up and in command fnl f* **5/2**[1]

44-3 **2** 1 3/4 **Peace Seeker**[42] 820 6-9-7 85 (t) WilliamCarson 10 92
(Anthony Carson) *chsd ldng pair: wnt 2nd over 1f out: rdn and kpt on fnl f: unable to chal* **5/1**[2]

111- **3** hd **Marmalady (IRE)**[196] 6900 4-9-2 80 RyanMoore 9 86+
(Gary Moore) *hld up in midfield: prog 2f out: shkn up over 1f out: tk 3rd fnl f: kpt on and pressed runner-up nr fin* **5/1**[2]

0364 **4** 2 1/4 **O'Gorman**[17] 1145 5-9-3 81 LiamKeniry 2 83+
(Gary Brown) *hld up towards rr: stl there and no ch whn hmpd 1f out: r.o fnl f to take 4th last stride* **10/1**

006- **5** 1/2 **Lupo D'Oro (IRE)**[180] 7313 5-9-4 82 SteveDrowne 7 79
(John Best) *pushed along in last trio: kpt on fr over 1f out: n.d* **25/1**

4405 **6** shd **Jay Bee Blue**[12] 1234 5-8-13 77 (bt) JamesDoyle 8 74
(Sean Curran) *dwlt: hld up in last trio: pushed along over 1f out: kpt on but nvr involved* **14/1**

4-12 **7** nk **Rambo Will**[12] 1244 6-8-6 73 NataliaGemelova(3) 1 69
(J R Jenkins) *chsd ldng pair: pushed along 1/2-way: rdn and wknd jst over 1f out* **12/1**

-165 **8** nse **Triple Dream**[17] 1145 9-8-12 76 (tp) HayleyTurner 4 72
(Milton Bradley) *fastest away but hld up in 5th: pushed along 2f out: no ch whn hmpd 1f out* **20/1**

10-3 **9** 1 3/4 **Secret Missile**[11] 1261 4-9-1 79 MartinDwyer 6 69
(William Muir) *dwlt: hld up in last: stl there whn nt clr run 1f out: no real prog* **8/1**[3]

36-5 **10** 3 3/4 **Sir Pedro**[65] 532 5-9-0 78 LiamJones 5 56
(Robert Cowell) *fractious in stalls: narrow ldr to 1/2-way: lost 2nd and wknd rapidly over 1f out* **10/1**

59.08s (-1.22) **Going Correction** -0.175s/f (Firm) **10 Ran SP% 114.2**
Speed ratings (Par 105): **102,99,98,95,94 94,93,93,90,84**
CSF £14.11 CT £58.30 TOTE £2.80: £1.10, £2.50, £1.50; EX 16.00 Trifecta £63.10.
**Owner** Mrs Anne Cowley **Bred** Bloomsbury Stud **Trained** Baydon, Wilts

**FOCUS**
The slower of the two divisions by 0.39sec, but the more interesting form. The winner is progressing.

## 1491 INJURED JOCKEYS FUND MAIDEN STKS 1m 2f 7y

**3:50** (3:52) (Class 5) 3-Y-O+ **£2,587** (£770; £384; £192) **Stalls** Centre

Form RPR

3- **1** **Arod (IRE)**[154] 7835 3-8-8 0 JamieSpencer 10 88+
(Peter Chapple-Hyam) *racd freely: led after 2f: mde rest: drew clr fr over 2f out: easily* **4/5**[1]

4- **2** 5 **Sea The Bloom**[163] 7692 3-8-3 0 AndreaAtzeni 7 68+
(Sir Michael Stoute) *t.k.h: trckd ldng pair: shkn up over 2f out: wnt 2nd over 1f out: one pce and no ch w wnr* **3/1**[2]

4-2 **3** 3/4 **Ridgeway Storm (IRE)**[20] 1088 4-9-13 0 TomQueally 11 76+
(Alan King) *stdd s: t.k.h: hld up disputing 5th: pushed along 3f out: clsd on those chsng wnr fr 2f out: reminders and styd on to take 3rd nr fin* **16/1**

**4** nse **Kinshasa** 3-8-8 0 LemosdeSouza 2 72+
(Luca Cumani) *slowly away: hld up wl in rr: prog and pushed along over 2f out: light reminder over 1f out: styd on and nrly snatched 3rd* **20/1**

00- **5** nse **Filosofo (IRE)**[254] 4987 3-8-1 0 CamHardie(7) 6 72
(Richard Hannon) *t.k.h early: chsd ldng pair: shkn up over 2f out: no imp on wnr but kpt on* **66/1**

**6** 1 3/4 **Holberg Suite** 3-8-3 0 NickyMackay 5 63+
(John Gosden) *slowly away: hld up in rr: prog on outer over 2f out: encouraged along and one pce fr over 1f out* **10/1**[3]

22 **7** hd **Neston Grace**[13] 1218 6-9-8 0 RobertWinston 8 67
(Simon Hodgson) *led 2f: chsd wnr to over 1f out: fdd fnl f* **33/1**

0- **8** 7 **Malory Towers**[205] 6643 3-8-3 0 HayleyTurner 12 50
(James Fanshawe) *hld up disputing 5th: lost pl and pushed along over 3f out: steadily fdd* **33/1**

0-0 **9** nk **Lord Brantwood**[13] 1216 3-8-6 0 ow1 WilliamTwiston-Davies(3) 13 55
(Mick Channon) *hld up wl in rr: no real prog fr 3f out* **66/1**

0/2 **10** 1 1/4 **Pentameter**[18] 1119 5-9-13 0 LiamKeniry 4 56
(John Butler) *hld up wl in rr: pushed along and no prog 3f out* **66/1**

0 **11** 23 **Flight Fight**[14] 1208 3-8-8 0 TedDurcan 3 8
(Chris Wall) *hld up in rr: wknd 3f out: t.o* **66/1**

000- **12** 23 **Echoes Of War**[107] 8427 5-9-13 45 DavidProbert 9
(John Bridger) *nvr beyond midfield: wknd over 3f out: wl t.o* **100/1**

2m 5.87s (-2.83) **Going Correction** -0.275s/f (Firm)
**WFA** 3 from 4yo+ 19lb **12 Ran SP% 113.1**
Speed ratings (Par 103): **100,96,95,95,95 93,93,88,87,86 68,50**
CSF £2.57 TOTE £1.50: £1.10, £1.10, £3.10; EX 3.80 Trifecta £18.50.
**Owner** Qatar Racing Limited **Bred** Kabansk Ltd & Rathbarry Stud **Trained** Newmarket, Suffolk
■ Rule 4 of 5p in the pound applies to all bets; Withdrawn: Mr Greenspan

**FOCUS**
There was no depth to this but the winner impressed. There are some doubts over the bare form.

## 1492 UNIBET - BY PLAYERS FOR PLAYERS H'CAP 6f

**4:20** (4:22) (Class 3) (0-90,90) 4-Y-O+ **£8,086** (£2,406; £1,202; £601) **Stalls** Low

Form RPR

030- **1** **Huntsmans Close**[170] 7531 4-9-0 83 [1] JamesDoyle 5 93
(Roger Charlton) *slowest away: wl in rr: prog nr side fr 1/2-way: gap appeared fnl f: str run to ld last stride* **20/1**

13-2 **2** hd **Joey's Destiny (IRE)**[15] 1193 4-9-2 85 MartinDwyer 8 95
(George Baker) *in tch in midfield: rdn and prog fr over 2f out: chsd ldng pair over 1f out: clsd to ld ins fnl f: hdd last stride* **7/1**[3]

11-1 **3** 3/4 **Discussiontofollow (IRE)**[81] 294 4-9-3 86 ShaneKelly 15 93+
(Mike Murphy) *hld up in midfield: prog on outer 2f out: drvn and tried to chal fnl f: styd on but jst outpcd* **9/2**[1]

006- **4** 3/4 **Robot Boy (IRE)**[192] 6990 4-9-4 87 GrahamGibbons 1 92
(David Barron) *racd against nr side rail: led and clr w one rival: edgd lft jst over 1f out: hdd and no ex ins fnl f* **5/1**[2]

43-3 **5** 3/4 **Blessington (IRE)**[96] 80 4-9-4 87 (t) WilliamBuick 12 90
(John Gosden) *w.w in midfield: prog 2f out: rdn over 1f out: styd on same pce fnl f: nrst fin* **9/2**[1]

000- **6** 1/2 **Good Authority (IRE)**[133] 8127 7-9-1 87 ThomasBrown(3) 3 88
(Karen George) *chsd ldrs: rdn bef 1/2-way against nr side rail: wnt 3rd 2f out: tried to cl and swtchd lft ins fnl f: kpt on* **33/1**

600- **7** 1/2 **Monsieur Chevalier (IRE)**[156] 7820 7-9-7 90 JamieSpencer 9 89
(P J O'Gorman) *hld up in last quartet and sn wl off the pce: nudged along and styd on steadily fnl 2f: nrst fin* **14/1**

430- **8** 1/2 **Slip Sliding Away (IRE)**[123] 8264 7-8-12 81 LiamKeniry 6 79
(Peter Hedger) *chsd ldrs: pushed along over 2f out: lost pl over 1f out: shkn up and one pce fnl f* **33/1**

600- **9** 1 1/4 **Dominate**[218] 6238 4-9-3 **86** SeanLevey 2 80
(Richard Hannon) *pressed ldr and clr of rest: rdn over 2f out: lost 2nd and wknd fnl f* **16/1**

0340 **10** hd **Corporal Maddox**[15] 1193 7-9-2 **85** (p) LukeMorris 14 78
(Ronald Harris) *stdd s: off the pce in last quartet: rdn over 2f out: no prog tl styd on ins fnl f: gng on at fin* **33/1**

-560 **11** 1 1/4 **Novellen Lad (IRE)**[28] 991 9-8-12 **81** ChrisCatlin 7 70
(Willie Musson) *nvr beyond midfield: pushed along and no prog fr 2f out* **66/1**

-332 **12** 3 3/4 **Palace Moon**[24] 1041 9-9-0 **83** (t) JimCrowley 4 60
(William Knight) *chsd ldng pair to 2f out: wknd* **8/1**

360- **13** 3 **Midnight Rider (IRE)**[173] 7464 6-9-1 **84** TedDurcan 13 52
(Chris Wall) *stdd s: hld up in last: no real prog and nvr a factor* **33/1**

000- **14** 3 3/4 **Freddy With A Y (IRE)**[171] 7507 4-8-13 **82** RyanMoore 10 38
(Gary Moore) *spd on outer to 1/2-way: sn lost pl: eased over 1f out* **16/1**

000- **15** nk **Links Drive Lady**[183] 7222 6-9-3 **86** RobertWinston 11 41
(Dean Ivory) *settled in rr: shkn up and no prog over 1f out: sn eased* **33/1**

110- **16** hd **Trucanini**[192] 6993 4-9-4 **87** GeorgeBaker 16 41
(Chris Wall) *in tch on wd outside to 1/2-way: wknd qckly 2f out: eased* **12/1**

1m 10.83s (-2.17) **Going Correction** -0.175s/f (Firm) **16** Ran SP% **123.7**
Speed ratings (Par 107): **107,106,105,104,103 103,102,101,100,99 98,93,89,84,83 83**
CSF £149.27 CT £790.37 TOTE £37.30: £4.30, £1.90, £1.20, £1.40; EX 142.90 Trifecta £1458.30.
**Owner** Brook House **Bred** Darley **Trained** Beckhampton, Wilts

**FOCUS**
Given the evidence of the earlier races it was understandable there was a mad dash to claim the lead on the rail, but Robot Boy and Dominate, from the two lowest stalls, rather took each other on and the result was that the race was set up for a closer. Intreseting form that reads sound enough.

## 1493 NEW HORSERACING ODDS AT UNIBET.CO.UK H'CAP 1m 3f 135y
**4:50** (4:52) (Class 4) (0-85,85) 4-Y-0+ **£4,851** (£1,443; £721; £360) **Stalls** Centre

Form RPR

3/0- **1** **Christopher Wren (USA)**[32] 6596 7-9-7 **85** GeorgeBaker 7 95
(Nick Gifford) *hld up in last pair and wl off the pce: prog on outer over 2f out: clsd to ld jst ins fnl f as all rivals bmpd into each other: edgd lft and r.o* **25/1**

544- **2** 1 3/4 **Burnham**[145] 7976 5-9-0 **78** (p) JimmyFortune 1 85
(Hughie Morrison) *hld up off the pce in midfield: prog to go 3rd 3f out: drvn 2f out: clsd to chal whn bmpd 1f out: chsd wnr ins fnl f: styd on* **11/2**[3]

133- **3** 2 3/4 **Quest For More (IRE)**[166] 7627 4-9-1 **80** JamesDoyle 9 88+
(Roger Charlton) *dwlt: hld up in last pair and wl off the pce: prog over 3f out: trckd ldrs 2f out and waiting for room: chal on inner 1f out but gap clsd and bdly hmpd: styd on to take 3rd last stride* **5/2**[2]

2651 **4** 1/2 **Lady Lunchalot (USA)**[19] 1108 4-8-11 **76** LiamJones 4 78
(Laura Mongan) *hld up off the pce towards rr: prog to chse ldr 3f out: rdn to ld over 2f out: fnd little in front: edgd lft then bmpd 1f out: sn hdd and nt rcvr* **25/1**

0/5- **5** 1 3/4 **Kleitomachos (IRE)**[360] 1670 6-9-1 **79** TomQueally 10 78
(Stuart Kittow) *hld up off the pce in midfield: rdn to cl on ldrs whn bmpd over 3f out: nt qckn 2f out: lost pl and btn over 1f out* **16/1**

060- **6** 5 **Jupiter Storm**[189] 7072 5-8-13 **77** RyanMoore 6 77+
(Gary Moore) *led at gd pce: hdd after 2f: led again after 4f and clr w one rival: rdn and hdd 2f out: stl upsides whn bdly bmpd 1f out: nt rcvr and eased* **6/4**[1]

1636 **7** 1 1/2 **Luv U Whatever**[37] 891 4-8-4 **72** OisinMurphy[(3)] 2 59
(Jo Hughes) *t.k.h: chsd clr ldng pair: pushed along whn bdly bmpd over 3f out: lost pl and btn after* **25/1**

253- **8** 1/2 **Obstacle**[181] 7279 4-8-11 **76** DaneO'Neill 3 63
(Paul Webber) *trckd clr ldng pair: trying to cl whn bmpd over 3f out: lost pl and btn after* **14/1**

354- **9** 3/4 **Australia Day (IRE)**[157] 6252 11-9-6 **84** MartinDwyer 5 69
(Paul Webber) *pushed up to ld after 2f but unable to dominate: hdd after 4f: chsd ldr and clr of rest tl lost pl and fdd 3f out* **16/1**

2m 24.35s (-5.15) **Going Correction** -0.275s/f (Firm)
**WFA** 4 from 5yo+ 1lb **9** Ran SP% **113.9**
Speed ratings (Par 105): **106,104,103,102,101 98,97,96,96**
CSF £151.62 CT £472.40 TOTE £27.50: £8.60, £1.80, £1.10; EX 165.60 Trifecta £756.80.
**Owner** John P McManus **Bred** Rod D'Elia **Trained** Findon, W Sussex

**FOCUS**
A messy finish to a race run at a strong pace. The winner is rated close to his 3yo mark.

## 1494 WINDSOR VEHICLE LEASING WVL.CO.UK H'CAP 1m 3f 135y
**5:20** (5:21) (Class 5) (0-75,75) 3-Y-O **£2,911** (£866; £432; £216) **Stalls** Centre

Form RPR

24-1 **1** **Anipa**[37] 888 3-9-6 **74** AndreaAtzeni 7 82
(Roger Varian) *sn trckd ldr: rdn to ld over 2f out: steadily asserted fnl 2f: drvn out* **6/1**[3]

00-2 **2** 1 1/2 **Norse Star (IRE)**[18] 1118 3-9-3 **71** LiamKeniry 1 76
(Sylvester Kirk) *sn chsd ldng pair: drvn over 2f out: kpt on fr over 1f out to take 2nd nr fin: no threat to wnr* **8/1**

01- **3** 3/4 **Love Tangle (IRE)**[159] 7773 3-9-3 **71** JimmyFortune 8 75
(Brian Meehan) *racd freely: led: drvn and hdd over 2f out: hld over 1f out: pushed along and lost 2nd nr fin* **5/2**[2]

1- **4** 1 **Wylye**[170] 7532 3-9-7 **75** DavidProbert 3 77
(Andrew Balding) *wl in tch: rdn over 2f out: unable to cl on ldrs u.p: kpt on* **6/4**[1]

51-6 **5** 2 1/2 **Poker Gold (FR)**[31] 955 3-9-4 **72** (t) LiamJones 9 70
(Heather Main) *hld up in 6th: rdn and struggling 3f out: nvr on terms after: plugged on* **20/1**

352 **6** shd **Stoneham**[21] 1084 3-8-8 **65** WilliamTwiston-Davies[(3)] 6 63
(Mick Channon) *hld up in 7th: pushed along and sme prog 3f out: no imp after: shkn up fnl f* **16/1**

0-55 **7** 6 **Son Of Feyan (IRE)**[13] 1218 3-9-0 **68** RobertWinston 2 56
(Roger Teal) *mostly chsd ldng trio: rdn 3f out: lost pl and btn wl over 1f out: wknd* **33/1**

14- **8** 4 1/2 **Improvized**[188] 7110 3-8-10 **64** MartinDwyer 10 44
(William Muir) *slowly away: a in last: bustled along fr 4f out: no prog* **16/1**

2m 28.71s (-0.79) **Going Correction** -0.275s/f (Firm) **8** Ran SP% **113.4**
Speed ratings (Par 98): **91,90,89,88,87 87,83,80**
CSF £51.64 CT £149.51 TOTE £5.60: £1.80, £3.20, £1.10; EX 44.80 Trifecta £148.10.
**Owner** Nurlan Bizakov **Bred** Hesmonds Stud Ltd **Trained** Newmarket, Suffolk

**FOCUS**
The early pace wasn't strong and it paid to race handily. The time was 4.36sec slower than the previous race on the card, a 0-85 handicap. The form makes a fair bit of sense.

T/Jkpt: Not won. T/Plt: £50.70 to a £1 stake. Pool: £93,937.75 - 1,300.44 winning tickets T/Qpdt: £2.90 to a £1 stake. Pool: £8,916.07 - 2,213.78 winning tickets JN

# 1363 SOUTHWELL (L-H)
Tuesday, April 15

**OFFICIAL GOING: Standard**
Wind: Light, slightly against Weather: Fine and dry

## 1495 CORAL APP DOWNLOAD FROM THE APP STORE CLAIMING STKS 1m 3f (F)
**2:20** (2:20) (Class 6) 4-Y-0+ **£1,940** (£577; £288; £144) **Stalls** Low

Form RPR

1543 **1** **Back Burner (IRE)**[12] 1268 6-9-2 79 AdrianNicholls 5 86
(David Nicholls) *trckd ldr: smooth hdwy over 3f out: led wl over 2f out: rdn wl over 1f out: kpt on strly fnl f* **14/1**[3]

1211 **2** 4 **Stand Guard**[40] 860 10-9-7 85 TomQueally 4 84
(John Butler) *hld up in tch: hdwy on outer to trck ldrs 1/2-way: effrt over 3f out: chsd wnr over 2f out: rdn wl over 1f out: no imp fnl f* **7/4**[1]

3612 **3** 4 **Lean On Pete (IRE)**[14] 1222 5-9-0 77 JacobButterfield[(5)] 1 75
(Ollie Pears) *hld up in tch: hdwy 3f out: chsd ldng pair 2f out: sn rdn along and kpt on same pce* **9/4**[2]

/50- **4** 6 **Licence To Till (USA)**[346] 2018 7-9-1 84 JoeFanning 3 61
(Mark Johnston) *led: rdn along over 3f out: hdd wl over 2f out and sn wknd* **7/4**[1]

45 **5** 42 **Crooked Arrow (IRE)**[26] 1035 6-9-1 0 (p) RussKennemore 2
(Marjorie Fife) *trckd ldr on inner: rdn along 5f out: sn outpcd and bhd fnl 3f* **100/1**

2m 26.59s (-1.41) **Going Correction** 0.0s/f (Stan) **5** Ran SP% **111.2**
Speed ratings (Par 101): **105,102,99,94,64**
CSF £39.31 TOTE £9.10: £3.40, £1.30; EX 27.20 Trifecta £56.30.
**Owner** Middleham Park Racing LXXV **Bred** Anamoine Ltd **Trained** Sessay, N Yorks

**FOCUS**
A dry, bright and sunny afternoon with a light wind across the track. A fair claimer, run at modest early pace. This rating could underestimate the winner.

## 1496 CORAL JUST THREE CLICKS TO BET H'CAP 1m 3f (F)
**2:50** (2:50) (Class 6) (0-65,65) 4-Y-0+ **£1,940** (£577; £288; £144) **Stalls** Low

Form RPR

2301 **1** **Geeaitch**[13] 1249 5-9-2 **60** RobertWinston 5 73+
(Peter Hiatt) *in tch: hdwy on wd outside over 4f out: cl up over 3f out: led on bit jst over 2f out: shkn up over 1f out: carried hd high and kpt on fnl f* **6/4**[1]

-120 **2** 2 1/4 **Afro**[8] 1355 4-9-7 **65** (p) LukeMorris 4 72
(Peter Hedger) *pushed along s: sn trcking ldrs: cl up 4f out: slt ld 3f out: sn rdn: hdd over 2f out: cl up and sn drvn: kpt on same pce fnl f* **4/1**[3]

5244 **3** 2 1/2 **Solarmaite**[21] 1087 5-8-6 **55** (b) PhilipPrince[(5)] 2 58
(Roy Bowring) *led 2f: cl up on inner: pushed along 4f out: rdn and outpcd over 3f out: swtchd rt to outer over 2f out: sn drvn and kpt on appr fnl f* **20/1**

/542 **4** 1/2 **Encore Un Fois**[13] 1249 6-8-12 **56** JamesSullivan 6 58
(Ruth Carr) *hld up in rr: sme hdwy wl over 3f out: sn rdn along and outpcd wl over 2f out: kpt on u.p appr fnl f: nrst fin* **10/1**

30-2 **5** 2 **Kenny's Girl (IRE)**[15] 1210 4-9-5 **63** MartinDwyer 3 62
(William Muir) *prom: effrt and cl up 3f out: sn rdn and wknd over 1f out* **16/1**

5213 **6** 11 **On The Cusp (IRE)**[35] 912 7-9-4 **65** (b) OisinMurphy[(3)] 7 45
(Ann Stokell) *plld hrd: cl up: led after 2f: rdn along wl over 3f out: hdd wl over 2f out and sn wknd* **7/2**[2]

0-16 **7** 28 **Samoset**[56] 648 4-8-13 **57** TomQueally 1
(Alan Swinbank) *in rr: pushed along 1/2-way: rdn 4f out and sn outpcd* **8/1**

2m 29.01s (1.01) **Going Correction** 0.0s/f (Stan) **7** Ran SP% **113.1**
Speed ratings (Par 101): **96,94,92,92,90 82,62**
CSF £7.51 TOTE £2.20: £1.30, £3.10; EX 7.30 Trifecta £49.80.
**Owner** P J R Gardner **Bred** G Houghton **Trained** Hook Norton, Oxon

**FOCUS**
A modest handicap. The winner is rated back to his early best.

## 1497 BOOKMAKERS.CO.UK (S) STKS 6f (F)
**3:25** (3:25) (Class 6) 4-Y-0+ **£2,045** (£603; £302) **Stalls** Low

Form RPR

-323 **1** **Spitfire**[7] 1368 9-8-11 68 (t) VictorSantos[(7)] 2 75
(J R Jenkins) *dwlt and in rr: hdwy on outer wl over 2f out: rdn to chse ldr over 1f out: drvn fnl f: kpt on to ld nr line* **16/1**

1135 **2** hd **Abi Scarlet (IRE)**[35] 909 5-8-6 76 CharlieBennett[(7)] 5 69
(Hughie Morrison) *cl up on outer: led wl over 2f out: rdn wl over 1f out: edgd lft ins fnl f: hdd and no ex nr line* **8/11**[1]

-600 **3** 4 1/2 **Al Khan (IRE)**[11] 1275 5-8-9 76 (p) OisinMurphy[(3)] 4 54
(Ann Stokell) *cl up: effrt wl over 2f out: rdn wl over 1f out and ev ch: drvn and one pce ins fnl f* **2/1**[2]

2643 **4** 5 **George Fenton**[75] 389 5-9-4 72 (p) HayleyTurner 3 44
(Conor Dore) *led: rdn along 1/2-way: sn hdd: drvn wl over 1f out and sn one pce* **7/1**[3]

0000 **5** 4 1/2 **Amis Reunis**[12] 1270 5-8-2 45 (p) ConnorBeasley[(5)] 1 19
(Alan Berry) *chsd ldrs on inner: rdn along 1/2-way: sn outpcd* **100/1**

1m 16.33s (-0.17) **Going Correction** 0.0s/f (Stan) **5** Ran SP% **110.6**
Speed ratings (Par 101): **101,100,94,88,82**
CSF £29.16 TOTE £7.50: £3.50, £1.10; EX 14.30 Trifecta £53.80.There was no bid for winner. Al Khan was claimed by O Pears for £6,000.
**Owner** Mrs Wendy Jenkins **Bred** R B Hill **Trained** Royston, Herts

**FOCUS**
A fair seller in which two inexperienced riders fought out the finish. There are doubts over the form.

## 1498 LADBROKES MEDIAN AUCTION MAIDEN STKS 1m (F)
**4:00** (4:02) (Class 6) 3-5-Y-0 **£1,940** (£577; £288; £144) **Stalls** Low

Form RPR

6 **1** **Thanks Harry**[14] 1216 3-8-12 0 JimmyFortune 2 76
(Gary Moore) *hld up in tch: hdwy on outer over 3f out: wd st: chal 2f out: rdn and slt ld jst ins fnl f: drvn and hld on wl towards fin* **8/1**[3]

43 **2** nse **Pearl Princess (FR)**[20] 1107 3-8-7 0 HarryBentley 5 71
(Olly Stevens) *cl up: wd st: effrt over 2f out: led wl over 1f out and sn rdn: hdd jst ins fnl f: drvn and rallied wl towards fin: jst failed* **11/4**[2]

**3** 3 **Glorious Star (IRE)** 4-9-13 0 GeorgeBaker 4 73
(Ed Walker) *cl up: led wl over 2f out: rdn and hdd wl over 1f out: one pce fnl f* **9/4**[1]

063- **4** *6* **Bajan Beauty (IRE)**[227] 5983 3-8-7 70 WilliamCarson 3 50
(Charles Hills) *trckd ldrs: effrt 3f out: rdn over 2f out: drvn wl over 1f out and sn wknd* **9/4**[1]

30- **5** *5* **Smart Alec (IRE)**[192] 7023 3-8-12 0 BenCurtis 1 44
(Alan Swinbank) *slt ld: rdn along over 3f out: hdd wl over 2f out: sn wknd* **8/1**[3]

1m 42.81s (-0.89) **Going Correction** 0.0s/f (Stan)
**WFA** 3 from 4yo 15lb 5 Ran SP% **110.4**
Speed ratings (Par 101): **104,103,100,94,89**
CSF £29.74 TOTE £9.00: £3.90, £1.90; EX 25.10 Trifecta £87.30.
**Owner** Ms Trish Hall **Bred** J A Knox **Trained** Lower Beeding, W Sussex

**FOCUS**
A true pace for this modest maiden and a tight finish with the front pair coming widest of the quintet. The fourth sets the standard.

## 1499 LADBROKES H'CAP — 7f (F)
**4:30** (4:31) (Class 4) (0-80,78) 4-Y-0+ **£4,690** (£1,395; £697; £348) **Stalls** Low

Form RPR

133- **1** **Realize**[256] 4962 4-9-4 75 JimmyFortune 5 85
(Hughie Morrison) *hld up: gd hdwy on outer 1/2-way: wd st: chal 2f out: rdn to ld jst over 1f out: sn edgd lft: drvn and hung lft ins fnl f: kpt on wl towards fin* **6/1**

-244 **2** *1* **Royal Holiday (IRE)**[16] 1191 7-8-13 70 (p) DanielTudhope 4 77
(Marjorie Fife) *cl up: led after 2f: rdn along 2f out: hdd over 1f out: drvn and n.m.r ins fnl f: kpt on same pce towards fin* **3/1**[3]

1004 **3** *1 3/4* **Hellbender (IRE)**[22] 1082 8-8-11 68 DavidProbert 1 70
(Shaun Harris) *led 2f: cl up: rdn along 2f out: drvn and one pce fnl f* **14/1**

6166 **4** *shd* **Loud**[11] 1286 4-9-3 74 JoeFanning 8 76
(Mark Johnston) *trckd ldng pair: wd st: rdn along wl over 2f out: drvn and hld whn n.m.r over 1f out: one pce* **8/1**

2-13 **5** *3/4* **Kung Hei Fat Choy (USA)**[35] 909 5-9-7 78 (b) GrahamLee 3 78
(James Given) *trckd ldrs on inner: effrt wl over 2f out: sn rdn: swtchd rt and drvn over 1f out: one pce* **9/4**[1]

00-0 **6** *3 3/4* **Cash Or Casualty (IRE)**[9] 1334 6-8-12 72 (t) OisinMurphy(3) 7 62
(Damian Joseph English, Ire) *chsd ldrs: rdn along over 3f out: sn drvn and wknd: in rr whn hung rt over 1f out* **5/2**[2]

1m 29.23s (-1.07) **Going Correction** 0.0s/f (Stan) 6 Ran SP% **116.4**
Speed ratings (Par 105): **106,104,102,102,101 97**
CSF £25.27 CT £243.89 TOTE £6.60: £3.30, £1.60; EX 21.30 Trifecta £118.60.
**Owner** Deborah Collett & M J Watson **Bred** M J Watson **Trained** East Ilsley, Berks
■ Pearl Nation was withdrawn. Price at time of withdrawal 4/1. Rule 4 applies to bets struck prior to withdrawal but not to SP bets. Deduct 20p in the pound. New market formed.
■ Stewards' Enquiry : Jimmy Fortune one-day ban: careless riding (Apr 29)

**FOCUS**
A fair and tight-knit handicap, despite two late withdrawals. The pace was true. The winner was the least exposed runner.

## 1500 32RED FILLIES' H'CAP — 5f (F)
**5:00** (5:00) (Class 5) (0-70,70) 4-Y-0+ **£2,587** (£770; £384; £192) **Stalls** High

Form RPR

4042 **1** **College Doll**[12] 1270 5-8-7 56 oh4 (t) JimmyQuinn 5 61
(Christine Dunnett) *qckly away: mde all: rdn ent fnl f: kpt on* **8/1**

4132 **2** *3/4* **Ray Of Joy**[5] 1405 8-9-7 70 (v) FrederikTylicki 2 72
(J R Jenkins) *dwlt: towards rr whn n.m.r and swtchd lft after 1f: rdn along 1/2-way: hdwy and edgd lft 2f out: drvn and hung lft towards stands' over 1f out: styd on fnl f: nrst fin* **6/4**[1]

306- **3** *3/4* **Foreign Rhythm (IRE)**[168] 7599 9-8-6 60 ShirleyTeasdale(5) 3 60
(Ron Barr) *towards rr: rdn along 1/2-way: hdwy wl over 1f out: chsd wnr ins fnl f: kpt on same pce* **8/1**

600- **4** *2* **Mandy Layla (IRE)**[202] 6757 4-8-11 60 RoystonFfrench 4 52
(Bryan Smart) *prom: cl up 1/2-way: rdn along 2f out: drvn over 1f out: one pce ent fnl f* **11/4**[2]

300- **5** *1 3/4* **Perfect Blossom**[147] 7959 7-9-7 70 GrahamLee 1 56
(Alan Berry) *racd centre: chsd ldrs: rdn along over 2f out: grad wknd* **8/1**

5100 **6** *3 1/4* **Take The Lead**[56] 651 4-9-2 65 AdrianNicholls 6 39
(David Nicholls) *racd nr stands' rail: chsd wnr: rdn along 2f out: sn wknd* **7/1**[3]

1m 0.78s (1.08) **Going Correction** +0.30s/f (Slow) 6 Ran SP% **112.5**
Speed ratings (Par 100): **103,101,100,97,94 89**
CSF £20.69 TOTE £6.20: £3.70, £2.00; EX 11.20 Trifecta £46.90.
**Owner** P D West, A S Machin & C A Dunnett **Bred** Christine Dunnett & Brian Green **Trained** Hingham, Norfolk

**FOCUS**
The track was riding fairly deep and stamina came into play in this weak fillies' sprint handicap. The form is rated cautiously.

## 1501 32RED.COM APPRENTICE H'CAP — 1m 6f (F)
**5:35** (5:35) (Class 5) (0-70,67) 4-Y-0+ **£2,587** (£770; £384; £192) **Stalls** Low

Form RPR

0121 **1** **Travel (USA)**[12] 1265 4-9-10 66 JackGarritty 5 83
(Mark Johnston) *trckd ldr: cl up 4f out: led wl over 2f out: sn rdn clr: easily* **3/1**[2]

3201 **2** *11* **Marina Ballerina**[19] 1129 6-9-8 65 (p) JonathanWilletts(4) 4 67
(Roy Bowring) *led: pushed along over 3f out: hdd wl over 2f out: sn rdn and kpt on same pce: no ch w wnr* **8/1**

14-0 **3** *1 1/4* **Dynastic**[16] 1197 5-9-7 64 JoshQuinn(4) 1 64
(Tony Coyle) *hld up in rr: hdwy over 3f out: swtchd rt and rdn 2f out: kpt on fnl f* **8/1**

212- **4** *1 3/4* **Aiyana**[148] 7947 4-9-7 67 CharlieBennett(4) 6 65
(Hughie Morrison) *trckd ldrs on outer: effrt 4f out: rdn along 3f out: sn one pce* **5/4**[1]

6312 **5** *9* **Aureate**[13] 1248 10-8-12 51 (p) CharlotteJenner 3 36
(Brian Forsey) *hld up in rr: effrt over 4f out: sn pushed along and bhd whn wd st: nvr a factor* **8/1**

-632 **6** *5* **No Such Number**[14] 1226 6-9-11 64 (p) DavidParkes 2 42
(Julia Feilden) *trckd ldrs on inner: effrt 4f out: rdn along over 3f out: sn wknd* **5/1**[3]

3m 8.54s (0.24) **Going Correction** 0.0s/f (Stan)
**WFA** 4 from 5yo+ 3lb 6 Ran SP% **119.4**
Speed ratings (Par 103): **99,92,92,91,85 83**
CSF £27.86 TOTE £5.00: £1.70, £2.40; EX 23.20 Trifecta £133.90.
**Owner** Sheikh Hamdan bin Mohammed Al Maktoum **Bred** Darley **Trained** Middleham Moor, N Yorks
■ Stewards' Enquiry : Jack Garritty two-day ban: used whip when clearly winning (Apr 29-30)

**FOCUS**
A sensible pace for this ordinary apprentices' handicap. The favourite disappointed and there was little depth, but the winner impressed.

T/Plt: £77.30 to a £1 stake. Pool of £61522.33 - 580.86 winning tickets. T/Qpdt: £13.50 to a £1 stake. Pool of £5024.39 - 275.40 winning tickets. JR

# 1370 SAINT-CLOUD (L-H)
### Tuesday, April 15
**OFFICIAL GOING: Turf: good**

## 1502a PRIX PENELOPE (GROUP 3) (3YO FILLIES) (TURF) — 1m 2f 110y
**1:20** (12:00) 3-Y-O **£33,333** (£13,333; £10,000; £6,666; £3,333)

RPR

**1** **Goldy Espony (FR)**[31] 983 3-9-0 0 FabriceVeron 2 108
(H-A Pantall, France) *trckd ldr on outer: shkn up to chal 2 1/2f out: led 2f out: reminders 1 1/2f out: rn an on under hands and heels ins fnl f: a holding runner-up: won a shade cosily* **17/2**

**2** *1/2* **Hug And A Kiss (USA)**[26] 3-9-0 0 Pierre-CharlesBoudot 7 107+
(A Fabre, France) *t.k.h: hld up in midfield: rdn to chse ldr over 1 1/2f out: kpt on u.p fnl f: a hld by wnr* **8/5**[1]

**3** *1 1/4* **Stormyra (FR)**[21] 1096 3-9-0 0 UmbertoRispoli 8 105+
(J-P Gallorini, France) *t.k.h: hld up in rr: rdn and hdwy over 1f out: styd on ins fnl f: nt pce to chal* **13/2**

**4** *1* **Green Speed (FR)**[31] 983 3-9-0 0 AlexisBadel 6 103
(Mme M Bollack-Badel, France) *hld up towards rr: effrt on outside 1 1/2f out: kpt on u.p fnl f: nvr on terms* **192/10**

**5** *2 1/2* **Bereni Ka (FR)**[31] 983 3-9-0 0 TonyPiccone 4 98
(Y Gourraud, France) *t.k.h: hld up in midfield: 5th and rdn 2 1/2f out: kpt on fr over 1f out: nvr trbld ldrs* **47/10**[3]

**6** *3/4* **Whim**[204] 3-9-0 0 ThierryJarnet 3 97
(F Head, France) *w.w towards rr: short of room fr over 2f out: swtchd outside and styd on past btn horses fnl f: nvr in contention* **89/10**

**7** *3 1/2* **My Jolie (IRE)**[31] 983 3-9-0 0 MaximeGuyon 1 90
(A Fabre, France) *trckd ldr on inner: 3rd and rdn 2f out: wknd fnl 1 1/2f* **18/5**[2]

**8** *10* **Bondi (GER)**[177] 7409 3-9-0 0 StephanePasquier 5 71
(Frau J Mayer, Germany) *reluctant to enter stalls: sn led: rousted along 2 1/2f out: hdd 2f out: sn wknd* **25/1**

2m 17.16s (-2.44) 8 Ran SP% **120.5**
WIN (incl. 1 euro stake): 9.50. PLACES: 2.00, 1.40, 1.90. DF: 10.90. SF: 33.90.
**Owner** Henri-Alex Pantall **Bred** Henri Alex Pantall & Mme Yvette Chabot **Trained** France

# BEVERLEY (R-H)
### Wednesday, April 16
**OFFICIAL GOING: Good (good to firm in places; 8.1)**
Wind: Moderate slightly against Weather: Fine and dry

## 1503 PROMOTE YOUR HORSE PRE-AUCTION AT RACEHORSETRADER.COM (S) STKS — 1m 100y
**1:25** (1:25) (Class 6) 3-Y-0+ **£2,264** (£673; £336; £168) **Stalls** Low

Form RPR

0-00 **1** **Justonefortheroad**[9] 1345 8-9-6 78 (p) TonyHamilton 4 68
(Richard Fahey) *hld up in tch: smooth hdwy on outer 2f out: chal over 1f out: rdn to ld ent fnl f: drvn and kpt on towards fin* **6/4**[1]

3012 **2** *nk* **Nubar Boy**[20] 1121 7-9-7 66 (p) GeorgeDowning(5) 5 73
(Ian Williams) *trckd ldrs: hdwy wl over 1f out: rdn to ld briefly jst over 1f out: hdd narrowly ent fnl f: sn drvn and ev ch tl no ex nr fin* **9/2**[3]

004- **3** *8* **Hello Sweetness**[148] 7954 3-8-3 45 ow2 JamesSullivan 1 42
(Jason Ward) *hld up towards rr: swtchd lft to outer and hdwy wl over 2f out: rdn over 1f out: styd on fnl f: nrst fin* **50/1**

00-3 **4** *3/4* **Thrust Control (IRE)**[20] 1125 7-9-1 47 (p) ConnorBeasley(5) 12 47
(Tracy Waggott) *sn led: rdn along over 2f out: drvn and hdd jst over 1f out: wknd fnl f* **7/1**

006- **5** *1 3/4* **Betty Boo (IRE)**[169] 7610 4-8-10 39 ShirleyTeasdale(5) 9 38
(Shaun Harris) *trckd ldng pair: hdwy to chse ldr over 2f out: rdn wl over 1f out: grad wknd* **100/1**

/60- **6** *2* **Spithead**[132] 2957 4-9-6 60 PJMcDonald 10 38
(Mike Sowersby) *chsd ldr: rdn along wl over 2f out: wknd wl over 1f out* **20/1**

5050 **7** *1 1/4* **Amber Moon**[7] 1386 9-8-10 41 AnnStokell(5) 2 30
(Ann Stokell) *nvr bttr than midfield* **66/1**

230- **8** *3 1/4* **Juvenal (IRE)**[182] 7306 5-9-6 70 (p) TomEaves 3 28
(Geoffrey Harker) *midfield: effrt wl over 2f out: sn rdn and n.d* **7/2**[2]

4-46 **9** *1* **Star Request**[47] 783 4-8-10 47 JacobButterfield(5) 11 21
(Ollie Pears) *swtchd rt s: hld up: a towards rr* **25/1**

0-6P **10** *11* **Volodina (IRE)**[67] 543 3-8-2 57 ow1 (v) PatrickMathers 7
(Alan McCabe) *dwlt and sn rdn along into midfield: in tch 1/2-way: rdn along wl over 2f out: sn wknd* **16/1**

2-46 **11** *1* **Tight Knit (USA)**[14] 1245 4-9-1 57 (b) JoeyHaynes(5) 6
(John Weymes) *t.k.h in midfield: pushed along over 3f out: sn rdn and wknd* **16/1**

1m 45.05s (-2.55) **Going Correction** -0.275s/f (Firm)
**WFA** 3 from 4yo+ 14lb 11 Ran SP% **117.7**
Speed ratings (Par 101): **101,100,92,91,90 88,86,83,82,71 70**
CSF £7.95 TOTE £2.40: £1.10, £1.80, £6.20; EX 10.40 Trifecta £306.60.There was no bid for the winner.
**Owner** Middleham Park Racing LXV **Bred** Wellsummers Farm & Hammarsfield B'Stock **Trained** Musley Bank, N Yorks

**FOCUS**
Track at widest configuration all around. Drying ground, with the official description amended before the opener. They went a fair gallop in this ordinary seller, in which the first two pulled clear. The winner was best in and this level was below even his latter 2013 form.

## 1504 NEW CLEVERLY'S BAR AND BISTRO MAIDEN AUCTION STKS (DIV I) — 5f
**1:55** (1:57) (Class 5) 2-Y-O **£3,234** (£962; £481; £240) **Stalls** Low

Form RPR

**1** **Buccaneers Vault (IRE)** 2-9-1 0 PaulMulrennan 1 78+
(Michael Dods) *trckd ldrs on inner: hdwy over 1f out: effrt whn n.m.r ent fnl f: sn rdn to chal: styd on wl to ld nr fin* **12/1**

**2** *hd* **Realtra (IRE)** 2-8-8 0 TonyHamilton 4 71+
(Richard Fahey) *trckd ldrs: hdwy wl over 1f out: chal ent fnl f: sn rdn to take slt ld tl hdd and no ex nr fin* **6/1**[2]

6 **3** *3 1/2* **Red Connect**[18] 1161 2-8-13 0 GrahamGibbons 8 63
(Alan McCabe) *in tch: hdwy 2f out: chsd ldrs over 1f out: styng on whn nt clr run and swtchd lft ins fnl f: kpt on wl towards fin* **8/1**[3]

03 **4** *1 1/2* **Penalty Scorer**[9] 1342 2-8-1 0 ConnorBeasley(3) 3 51
(Richard Guest) *chsd ldr: rdn along to chal over 1f out: ev ch tl drvn and wknd ins fnl f* **18/1**

**5** *3/4* **Bahamian Art** 2-8-8 0 FrannyNorton 2 50
(Mark Johnston) *qckly away and set str pce: rdn over 1f out: hdd ins fnl f: sn wknd* **11/10**[1]

**6** *3/4* **Upward Trend (IRE)** 2-8-13 0 DavidAllan 12 52+
(Tim Easterby) *in rr: pushed along 1/2-way: hdwy wl over 1f out: styd on fnl f: nrst fin* **33/1**

0 **7** *1/2* **Well Fleeced**[18] 1161 2-8-11 0 JohnFahy 9 48
(J S Moore) *in rr: hdwy 2f out: styd on fnl f: nrst fin* **16/1**

3 **8** *5* **Sportlobster (IRE)**[9] 1349 2-9-4 0 RichardKingscote 11 37
(Tom Dascombe) *in tch on wd outside: rdn along over 2f out: sn no imp* **6/1**[2]

**9** *1/2* **Bahango (IRE)** 2-9-1 0 KierenFallon 5 33
(Kristin Stubbs) *in tch: rdn along over 2f out: sn hung bdly lft and wknd* **9/1**

**10** *2 1/2* **Royal Roman** 2-8-6 0 PJMcDonald 10 15
(Mel Brittain) *dwlt and wnt lft s: a towards rr* **66/1**

**11** *1* **On Appro** 2-8-6 0 JamesSullivan 7
(Tim Easterby) *in tch: pushed along 1/2-way: hmpd over 2f out: sn edgd rt and wknd* **50/1**

0 **12** *9* **Esk Valley Lady**[9] 1342 2-8-1 0 JoeyHaynes(5) 6
(Philip Kirby) *a in rr* **66/1**

1m 3.2s (-0.30) **Going Correction** -0.125s/f (Firm) **12** Ran SP% **124.0**
Speed ratings (Par 92): **97,96,91,88,87 86,85,77,76,72 71,56**
CSF £85.23 TOTE £14.70: £4.20, £2.00, £2.40; EX 84.10 Trifecta £1161.10.
**Owner** D Neale **Bred** Kilfrush Stud **Trained** Denton, Co Durham

**FOCUS**
The first, and quicker, division of this modest median auction was dominated by those drawn low.

## 1505 NEW CLEVERLY'S BAR AND BISTRO MAIDEN AUCTION STKS (DIV II) 5f
**2:30** (2:31) (Class 5) 2-Y-O **£3,234** (£962; £481; £240) **Stalls** Low

Form RPR

0 **1** **Lazy Days In Loule (IRE)**[9] 1342 2-8-1 0 JoeyHaynes(5) 5 62+
(Noel Wilson) *qckly away: mde all: rdn clr ent fnl f: kpt on wl* **33/1**

**2** *2 1/4* **Kylach Me If U Can** 2-9-1 0 TomEaves 2 63
(Kevin Ryan) *chsd wnr: rdn to chal over 1f out: edgd lft and kpt on same pce ins fnl f* **11/2**[3]

**3** *1 1/4* **Multiplier** 2-8-11 0 JamesSullivan 1 54
(Kristin Stubbs) *towards rr: pushed along 1/2-way: hdwy wl over 1f out: rdn and styd on fnl f: nrst fin* **16/1**

**4** *nk* **Pomme De Terre (IRE)** 2-9-4 0 PaulMulrennan 3 60
(Michael Dods) *trckd ldrs: hdwy 2f out: rdn over 1f out: kpt on fnl f* **9/2**[2]

**5** *1/2* **Ythan Waters** 2-9-4 0 RoystonFfrench 7 59
(Bryan Smart) *dwlt and in rr: rdn along 1/2-way: hdwy whn hmpd 1 1/2f out: styd on fnl f: nrst fin* **7/1**

3 **6** *3/4* **Basil The Great**[8] 1363 2-8-11 0 RichardKingscote 11 49+
(Tom Dascombe) *cl up: pushed along over 2f out: rdn 1 1/2f out and sn wknd* **7/1**

**7** *2 1/4* **Johnny B Goode (IRE)** 2-8-12 0 GeorgeChaloner(3) 4 45
(Richard Fahey) *t.k.h: trckd ldrs: effrt 2f out: rdn whn hit in face by opponents whip and edgd lft 1 1/2f out: sn btn* **5/2**[1]

**8** *1 1/4* **Mister York** 2-8-11 0 DavidAllan 8 36
(Mel Brittain) *wnt lft s and towards rr: sme hdwy on wd outside over 1f out: sn rdn and n.d* **25/1**

4 **9** *nk* **Binky Blue (IRE)**[9] 1342 2-8-8 0 PJMcDonald 6 32
(Tony Coyle) *prom: effrt and cl up 2f out: sn rdn and wknd over 1f out* **17/2**

**10** *6* **Sparkle Girl** 2-8-6 0 PaulQuinn 10 9
(Tim Easterby) *dwlt and a in rr* **12/1**

0 **11** *3 3/4* **Iambertie**[13] 1271 2-8-8 0 (b[1]) PhilipPrince(5) 9 2
(J S Moore) *wnt lft s: sn outpcd and bhd* **50/1**

1m 4.4s (0.90) **Going Correction** -0.125s/f (Firm) **11** Ran SP% **120.0**
Speed ratings (Par 92): **87,83,81,80,80 78,75,73,72,63 57**
CSF £207.95 TOTE £37.60: £8.20, £2.90, £5.90; EX 442.80 Trifecta £2629.50 Part won..
**Owner** Pow Partnership **Bred** Lazy Lady Partnership **Trained** Middleham, N Yorks

**FOCUS**
The slower division by 1.2sec.

## 1506 WORLD'S FIRST EASTER EGG TREE H'CAP 5f
**3:05** (3:09) (Class 3) (0-95,95) 4-Y-O+ **£7,439** (£2,213; £1,106; £553) **Stalls** Low

Form RPR

152- **1** **Bondesire**[179] 7373 4-8-9 **86** SamJames(3) 2 97
(David O'Meara) *slt ld to 1/2-way: cl up: rdn over 1f out: swtchd lft ins fnl f and styd on strly to ld nr fin* **14/1**

01-0 **2** *1/2* **Chooseday (IRE)**[17] 1193 5-8-13 **87** (p) PaulMulrennan 3 96
(Kevin Ryan) *cl up: led 1/2-way: rdn over 1f out: drvn and edgd rt ins fnl f: hdd and no ex towards fin* **9/1**

0-31 **3** *3/4* **Top Boy**[12] 1283 4-8-8 **82** oh1 ow1 (v) DaleSwift 4 88
(Derek Shaw) *dwlt: swtchd rt s and sn trcking ldrs: effrt over 1f out: rdn ent fnl f: kpt on wl towards fin* **10/1**

04-0 **4** *hd* **Singeur (IRE)**[11] 1305 7-8-10 **87** JasonHart(3) 1 93
(Robin Bastiman) *hld up towards rr: hdwy on inner wl over 1f out: rdn to chse ldrs ent fnl f: sn drvn and kpt on* **9/2**[2]

000- **5** *hd* **Blaine**[242] 5545 4-9-7 **95** AmyRyan 10 100+
(Kevin Ryan) *in tch on wd outside: hdwy 2f out: sn rdn and styd on fnl f: nrst fin* **8/1**[3]

00-5 **6** *1/2* **Hadaj**[17] 1193 5-8-10 **84** JamesSullivan 5 87
(Ruth Carr) *in tch: hdwy 1/2-way: rdn to chse ldrs over 1f out: swtchd rt jst ins fnl f and kpt on same pce* **8/1**[3]

566- **7** *1 3/4* **Arctic Feeling (IRE)**[117] 8369 6-8-3 **82** SammyJoBell(5) 6 79
(Richard Fahey) *hld up towards rr: hdwy over 2f out: sn nt clr run and swtchd rt to inner: sn rdn and no imp fnl f* **22/1**

632- **8** *4 1/2* **Tumblewind**[200] 6848 4-8-8 **85** GeorgeChaloner(3) 11 66
(Richard Whitaker) *in tch: rdn along over 2f out: sn no hdwy* **25/1**

0-04 **9** *2 3/4* **Lastchancelucas**[11] 1305 4-8-4 **81** oh1 (b) NeilFarley(3) 9 52
(Declan Carroll) *chsd ldrs: rdn along 2f out: sn wknd* **25/1**

33-1 **10** *shd* **Aetna**[11] 1305 4-9-4 **92** GrahamGibbons 8 62
(Michael Easterby) *trckd ldng pair: pushed along over 2f out: rdn and n.m.r wl over 1f out: sn btn* **9/4**[1]

540- **11** *5* **Normal Equilibrium**[185] 7222 4-8-13 **87** (p) ShaneKelly 7 39
(Robert Cowell) *chsd ldrs: rdn along over 2f out: sn wknd* **12/1**

403 **12** *10* **Bedloe's Island (IRE)**[11] 1313 9-8-11 **85** (p) KierenFallon 12
(Alan McCabe) *dwlt: a outpcd and bhd fr 1/2-way* **33/1**

1m 1.85s (-1.65) **Going Correction** -0.125s/f (Firm) **12** Ran SP% **119.6**
Speed ratings (Par 107): **108,107,106,105,105 104,101,94,90,90 82,66**
CSF £129.22 CT £903.62 TOTE £13.60: £4.10, £3.30, £3.20; EX 77.10 Trifecta £554.90.
**Owner** Geoff & Sandra Turnbull **Bred** A C M Spalding **Trained** Nawton, N Yorks

**FOCUS**
A fair handicap in which the first two were always to the fore and those drawn low dominated. The form is rated around the third and fourth.

## 1507 RANDALL'S FOLLY STKS (H'CAP) 7f 100y
**3:40** (3:40) (Class 5) (0-75,75) 3-Y-O **£3,234** (£962; £481; £240) **Stalls** Low

Form RPR

020- **1** **Flycatcher (IRE)**[195] 6972 3-9-1 **69** TonyHamilton 5 77
(Richard Fahey) *hld up in tch on inner: effrt 2f out: swtchd lft and hdwy over 1f out: swtchd rt and rdn ent fnl f: styd on strly to ld nr fin* **3/1**[2]

656- **2** *nk* **Mfiftythreedotcom (IRE)**[228] 5995 3-8-8 **65** GeorgeChaloner(3) 8 72
(Richard Fahey) *hld up in rr: stdy hdwy 2f out: chsd ldrs over 1f out: sn rdn and ev ch ins fnl f: kpt on* **12/1**

3-23 **3** *1 1/4* **Handwoven (IRE)**[20] 1126 3-9-0 **68** FrannyNorton 6 72
(Mark Johnston) *trckd ldrs: hdwy over 2f out: rdn to ld 1 1/2f out: drvn and hung lft ins fnl f: hdd & wknd towards fin* **11/2**[3]

031- **4** *3* **Rock Of Dreams (IRE)**[183] 7270 3-9-7 **75** GeorgeBaker 2 72
(Charles Hills) *prom: effrt on inner over 2f out: rdn wl over 1f out: one pce fnl f* **15/8**[1]

-142 **5** *1/2* **Secret Suspect**[11] 1315 3-9-6 **74** PaulMulrennan 7 69
(James Tate) *trckd ldrs: hdwy over 2f out: rdn to chse ldr over 1f out: drvn and wknd fnl f* **10/1**

222- **6** *nk* **Madame Mirasol (IRE)**[124] 8267 3-9-0 **73** KevinStott(5) 10 68
(Kevin Ryan) *dwlt and bhd: hdwy on outer over 2f out: rdn to chse ldrs over 1f out: drvn ent fnl f: sn wknd* **11/1**

40-4 **7** *2 1/4* **Clever Miss**[48] 761 3-9-3 **71** KierenFallon 9 60
(Alan McCabe) *hld up towards rr: hdwy on wd outside 2f out: rdn to chse ldrs over 1f out: sn wknd* **18/1**

020- **8** *2 1/4* **Palace Princess (FR)**[169] 7609 3-8-10 **64** ShaneKelly 3 47
(Ed Dunlop) *t.k.h early: trckd ldrs: hdwy 3f out: rdn over 2f out: sn drvn and wknd* **9/1**

0 **9** *10* **Taanif**[9] 1346 3-8-9 **63** GrahamGibbons 4 21
(Michael Easterby) *led 2f: cl up: rdn along 3f out: sn wknd* **50/1**

3-10 **10** *3 3/4* **Mon Petit Secret**[39] 892 3-8-7 **66** ShaneGray(5) 1 15
(Kevin Ryan) *cl up on inner: led after 2f: rdn along over 2f out: drvn and hdd 1 1/2f out: sn wknd* **25/1**

1m 32.41s (-1.39) **Going Correction** -0.275s/f (Firm) **10** Ran SP% **121.4**
Speed ratings (Par 98): **96,95,94,90,90 89,87,84,73,69**
CSF £40.95 CT £195.93 TOTE £5.00: £1.80, £4.50, £3.40; EX 49.60 Trifecta £772.50.
**Owner** Mrs P B E P Farr **Bred** Worksop Manor Stud **Trained** Musley Bank, N Yorks
■ Stewards' Enquiry : Franny Norton caution: careless riding.

**FOCUS**
A muddling handicap in which the first two, both from the Richard Fahey yard, came from the rear. The form is rated around the runner-up.

## 1508 MANOR FARM FEEDS FED WOODHOUSE PIGS H'CAP 1m 4f 16y
**4:15** (4:15) (Class 5) (0-75,76) 3-Y-O **£2,098** (£2,098; £481; £240) **Stalls** Low

Form RPR

233- **1** **Blue Atlantic (USA)**[218] 6275 3-9-7 **72** FrannyNorton 2 78
(Mark Johnston) *mde most: hung lft bnd after 1 1/2f: rdn along 2f out: drvn and edgd lft ins fnl f: hdd last 30yds: rallied u.p nr line* **10/3**[2]

1224 **1** *dht* **Zamra (IRE)**[20] 1135 3-9-4 **69** (p) PaulMulrennan 3 75
(James Tate) *dwlt: hld up in rr: hdwy 2f out: swtchd ins and effrt over 1f out: rdn to chal ins fnl f: led last 30yds: ct on line* **13/2**

2-51 **3** *2 1/2* **Ujagar (IRE)**[8] 1367 3-9-11 **76** 6ex (b) RichardKingscote 7 78
(Tom Dascombe) *trckd ldr: effrt over 2f out: rdn wl over 1f out: drvn and edgd rt appr fnl f: sn one pce* **6/1**[3]

36-0 **4** *1/2* **Layla's Red Devil (IRE)**[14] 1240 3-9-1 **66** DavidNolan 6 67
(Richard Fahey) *hld up towards rr: hdwy on outer 2f out: rdn to chse ldrs and edgd lft ent fnl f: kpt on wl towards fin* **9/1**

010- **5** *2 1/4* **Running Wolf (IRE)**[177] 7418 3-9-1 **71** ConnorBeasley(5) 1 69
(Michael Dods) *trckd ldrs on inner: effrt 2f out: rdn along over 1f out: sn drvn grad wknd* **8/1**

534- **6** *1/2* **Loch Ma Naire (IRE)**[151] 7936 3-9-5 **70** ShaneKelly 5 67
(Ed Dunlop) *trckd ldrs: hdwy wl over 2f out: rdn wl over 1f out: one pce* **3/1**[1]

50-P **7** *3 1/4* **Sirpertan**[7] 1372 3-8-4 **58** oh8 NeilFarley(3) 8 50
(Mark Walford) *cl up on outer: edgd lft bnd after 1 1/2f: effrt 3f out: rdn along over 2f out: wknd over 1f out* **14/1**

004- **8** *10* **Come On Sunshine**[180] 7332 3-9-2 **67** TomEaves 4 43
(Brian Ellison) *hld up towards rr: rdn along over 2f out: sn outpcd* **8/1**

2m 40.25s (0.45) **Going Correction** -0.275s/f (Firm) **8** Ran SP% **114.6**
Speed ratings (Par 98): **87,87,85,85,83 83,81,74**
WIN: 2.50 Blue Atlantic, 3.50 Zamra; PL: 1.70 Ujagar, 2.50 Blue Atlantic, 1.90 Zamra; EX: 9.90, 11.00; CSF: 12.64, 14.26; TC: 61.95, 68.54; TF: 26.70, 26.10;.
**Owner** R S Brookhouse **Bred** Skymarc Farm Inc **Trained** Middleham Moor, N Yorks
**Owner** Saif Ali **Bred** T Kimura **Trained** Newmarket, Suffolk

**FOCUS**
A fine finish to this fair handicap. Blue Atlantic is the type to progress and Zamra improved again on her AW form.

## 1509 SELL RACEHORSES ONLINE @RACEHORSETRADER H'CAP (BOBIS RACE) 1m 1f 207y
**4:50** (4:51) (Class 4) (0-80,79) 3-Y-O **£4,851** (£1,443; £721; £360) **Stalls** Low

Form RPR

334- **1** **Al Busayyir (IRE)**[118] 8340 3-9-0 **72** PaddyAspell 5 86
(Marco Botti) *trckd ldng pair: cl up 1/2-way: chal over 2f out: rdn to ld over 1f out: clr ins fnl f: kpt on strly* **14/1**

132- **2** *2 1/2* **Solidarity**[177] 7418 3-9-4 **76** MartinLane 1 85
(Charlie Appleby) *trckd ldrs on inner: effrt 2f out: swtchd rt and rdn over 1f out: chsd wnr ins fnl f: sn drvn and no imp* **7/2**[1]

22-1 **3** *nse* **Liberty Red (GER)**[20] 1119 3-9-7 **79** ShaneKelly 4 88
(Ed Dunlop) *hld up towards rr: hdwy over 2f out: rdn to chse ldrs over 1f out: drvn ins fnl f: kpt on* **6/1**[3]

445- **4** *2 1/4* **Innocent Touch (IRE)**[217] 6299 3-8-9 **67** TonyHamilton 2 72
(Richard Fahey) *prom: effrt over 2f out: rdn along wl over 1f out: kpt on same pce fnl f* **8/1**

414- **5** *nk* **Adventure Seeker (IRE)**[196] 6935 3-9-6 **78** KierenFallon 3 82
(Ed Vaughan) *in tch: hdwy on inner over 2f out: rdn to chse ldrs over 1f out: drvn ent fnl f and sn one pce* **13/2**

645- **6** *½* **Lovelocks (IRE)**[183] 7277 3-9-1 **73** GeorgeBaker 9 76
(Charles Hills) *dwlt and bhd: hdwy over 2f out: n.m.r over 1f out: swtchd rt and rdn ent fnl f: kpt on: nrst fin* **10/1**

400- **7** *¾* **Emaad (USA)**[182] 7309 3-8-10 **68** FrannyNorton 7 70
(Mark Johnston) *t.k.h: led: pushed along over 2f out: rdn wl over 1f out: sn hdd & wknd* **4/1**[2]

53-0 **8** *hd* **Full Day**[17] 1192 3-8-13 **71** DaleSwift 8 72
(Brian Ellison) *hld up towards rr: hdwy over 2f out: rdn wl over 1f out: sn one pce* **25/1**

650- **9** *½* **Penhill**[187] 7175 3-8-9 **67** PJMcDonald 6 67
(James Bethell) *in tch: effrt over 2f out: rdn along whn n.m.r over 1f out: sn no imp* **20/1**

441- **10** *2 ½* **Sbraase**[173] 7513 3-9-6 **78** PaulMulrennan 11 74
(James Tate) *trckd ldrs: cl up 3f out: rdn along over 2f out: drvn and wknd over 1f out* **10/1**

2-21 **11** *1 ½* **L'Avenue (IRE)**[19] 1153 3-8-13 **71** JimmyQuinn 10 64
(James Tate) *hld up towards rr: hdwy on wd outside over 2f out: rdn along wl over 1f out: sn wknd* **11/1**

2m 3.31s (-3.69) **Going Correction** -0.275s/f (Firm) **11** Ran SP% **122.7**
Speed ratings (Par 100): **103,101,100,99,98 98,97,97,97,95 94**
CSF £65.39 CT £341.20 TOTE £21.50: £5.40, £1.70, £1.10; EX 86.00 Trifecta £375.40.
**Owner** Mubarak Al Naemi **Bred** Jim Halligan **Trained** Newmarket, Suffolk

**FOCUS**
A decent 3yo handicap run in the best time on the card. A clear personal best from the winner.

## 1510 SYNDICATE YOUR HORSE AT RACEHORSETRADER.COM FILLIES' STKS (H'CAP) 1m 100y

**5:25** (5:25) (Class 5) (0-70,70) 4-Y-O+ **£3,234** (£962; £481; £240) **Stalls** Low

Form RPR

45 **1** **Real Tigress (IRE)**[4] 1446 5-8-9 **58** DavidAllan 9 69
(Les Eyre) *trckd ldrs: hdwy on outer 3f out: cl up over 2f out: led 1 1/2f out and sn rdn: drvn ins fnl f: kpt on wl towards fin* **9/4**[1]

056- **2** *½* **Simply Shining (IRE)**[160] 7785 4-9-2 **70** SammyJoBell(5) 3 80
(Richard Fahey) *t.k.h: trckd ldng pair: effrt on inner 2f out: swtchd lft and rdn to chse wnr jst over 1f out: kpt on* **5/2**[2]

2135 **3** *6* **Imaginary World (IRE)**[35] 929 6-9-3 **69** (p) JasonHart(3) 1 65
(John Balding) *trckd ldrs: hdwy over 2f out: rdn wl over 1f out: one pce fnl f* **3/1**[3]

065 **4** *1 ¼* **Dansili Dutch (IRE)**[36] 910 5-8-9 **61** JulieBurke(3) 8 54
(David O'Meara) *prom: rdn along over 2f out: drvn 1 1/2f out: sn one pce* **16/1**

624 **5** *7* **Ambella (IRE)**[49] 748 4-9-2 **70** GeorgeDowning(5) 6 47
(Ian Williams) *dwlt: a in rr* **8/1**

0620 **6** *1 ¾* **Beylerbey (USA)**[23] 1080 4-8-13 **62** FrannyNorton 5 35
(Mark Johnston) *led: rdn along over 2f out: hdd 1 1/2f out and sn wknd* **10/1**

51-4 **7** *3 ¾* **Gold Chain (IRE)**[14] 1247 4-9-2 **70** EmmaSayer(5) 4 35
(Dianne Sayer) *dwlt: a bhd* **20/1**

1m 44.73s (-2.87) **Going Correction** -0.275s/f (Firm) **7** Ran SP% **115.2**
Speed ratings (Par 100): **103,102,96,95,88 86,82**
CSF £8.31 CT £16.17 TOTE £3.00: £1.80, £2.40; EX 10.30 Trifecta £25.70.
**Owner** GIB Bloodstock Limited **Bred** Atacama Bloodstock Ltd **Trained** Catton, North Yorkshire
■ Les Eyre's first winner since returning to this country.
■ Stewards' Enquiry : David Allan four-day ban: used whip above permitted level (Apr 30,May1-2,5)

**FOCUS**
A very modest fillies' handicap, run at a solid gallop. The first two were clear but there was little depth.
T/Plt: £1,034.90 to a £1 stake. Pool of £53733.20 - 37.90 winning tickets. T/Qpdt: £86.80 to a £1 stake. Pool of £4764.28 - 40.60 winning tickets. JR

# NEWMARKET (R-H)

Wednesday, April 16

**OFFICIAL GOING: Good (good to firm in places; 7.5)**
Wind: medium half against Weather: bright and sunn

## 1511 ALEX SCOTT MAIDEN STKS (BOBIS RACE) (C&G) 7f

**1:45** (1:47) (Class 4) 3-Y-O **£5,175** (£1,540; £769; £384) **Stalls** High

Form RPR

-2 **1** **Provident Spirit**[17] 1192 3-9-0 0 WilliamBuick 8 88+
(John Gosden) *t.k.h: chsd ldrs tl led 2f out: rdn over 1f out: styd on strly fnl f* **4/5**[1]

**2** *2 ¼* **Between Wickets** 3-9-0 0 HayleyTurner 5 82+
(Marcus Tregoning) *bhd: effrt and swtchd lft over 1f out: styd on wl to go 2nd nr fin: no ch w wnr* **25/1**

6- **3** *¾* **Zilber (GER)**[173] 7494 3-9-0 0 AdamKirby 9 80
(Ed Dunlop) *in tch in last trio: hdwy 2f out: chsd wnr and rdn ent fnl f: styd on same pce* **3/1**[2]

34- **4** *½* **Master Of Suspense**[173] 7501 3-9-0 0 JimCrowley 4 79
(Peter Chapple-Hyam) *stdd s and t.k.h: in tch in last trio: effrt in centre to chse ldrs over 1f out: one pce* **10/1**[3]

55- **5** *1* **Ganges (IRE)**[167] 7647 3-8-11 0 RobertTart(3) 7 76+
(James Toller) *pressed ldr: ev ch 3f out: outpcd u.p wl over 1f out: rallied and kpt on again fnl f* **33/1**

**6** *½* **Emirati Spirit** 3-9-0 0 AndreaAtzeni 3 75+
(Roger Varian) *wl in tch in midfield: n.m.r wl over 1f out: rdn and unable qck over 1f out: plugged on same pce fnl f* **11/1**

05- **7** *½* **Speculative Bid (IRE)**[312] 3112 3-9-0 0 LiamKeniry 1 74
(David Elsworth) *wl in tch in midfield: n.m.r wl over 1f out: drvn and unable qck ent fnl f* **12/1**

6-3 **8** *2 ½* **Knockroon**[18] 1173 3-9-0 0 DavidProbert 2 67
(Andrew Balding) *t.k.h: hld up wl in tch in midfield: hdwy to ld 3f out: hdd 2f out: unable qck over 1f out: wknd fnl f* **14/1**

**9** *1 ½* **Dynamic Vision (IRE)** 3-9-0 0 JackMitchell 6 63
(Roger Varian) *led tl 3f out: sn lost pl and in rr 2f out* **66/1**

1m 28.26s (2.86) **Going Correction** +0.35s/f (Good) **9** Ran SP% **120.6**
Speed ratings (Par 100): **97,94,93,93,91 91,90,87,86**
CSF £31.32 TOTE £1.70: £1.10, £4.90, £1.70; EX 24.20 Trifecta £120.00.
**Owner** George Strawbridge **Bred** David & Paul Hearson **Trained** Newmarket, Suffolk

**FOCUS**
Far Side track used and stalls on stands' side. The going was on the firm side of good despite having been watered earlier in the week. The jockeys exercising before racing described it as "beautiful ground". This maiden has been mainly a source of handicappers, although Virtual went on to score at Grade 1 level. The winner didn't have to improve to win and has been rated as a standard winner of this race.

## 1512 HORSESOURCE SEABUCKTHORN CONDITIONS STKS (BOBIS RACE) 5f

**2:20** (2:20) (Class 3) 2-Y-O **£7,762** (£2,310; £1,154; £577) **Stalls** High

Form RPR

**1** **Mind Of Madness (IRE)** 2-8-9 0 JamieSpencer 7 97+
(David Brown) *chsd clr ldng trio: clsd smoothly to trck ldrs over 1f out: swtchd lft and qcknd to ld fnl 100yds: sn clr: impressive* **13/2**[3]

1 **2** *4 ½* **Abscent Friends**[8] 1363 2-8-10 0 RyanWhile(5) 4 85
(Bill Turner) *chsd ldr and clr in ldng trio: led u.p 2f out: hdd fnl 100yds: no ch w wnr but battled on wl to hold 2nd* **8/1**

3 **3** *½* **Harry Hurricane**[12] 1276 2-8-12 0 FergusSweeney 2 80
(George Baker) *chsd ldrs and clr in ldng trio: ev ch u.p over 1f out: outpcd by wnr ins fnl f* **5/2**[1]

31 **4** *1 ¾* **Flyball**[12] 1276 2-9-1 0 RyanMoore 1 77
(Richard Hannon) *led: drvn over 1f out: hdd 1f out: wknd ins fnl f* **5/2**[1]

**5** *3 ¾* **Portamento (IRE)** 2-8-9 0 MickaelBarzalona 6 57+
(Charlie Appleby) *outpcd in midfield: styd on steadily fnl f: nvr trbld ldrs* **9/2**[2]

**6** *7* **Big McIntosh (IRE)** 2-8-9 0 (t) DavidProbert 3 32
(John Ryan) *outpcd in midfield: n.d* **11/1**

**7** *11* **Framley Garth (IRE)** 2-8-9 0 LiamKeniry 5
(David Elsworth) *rn green: sn outpcd: n.d* **40/1**

**8** *21* **Ralph McTell** 2-8-4 0 LouisSteward(5) 8
(Alan Coogan) *v.s.a: outpcd: a wl bhd* **100/1**

1m 1.03s (1.93) **Going Correction** +0.35s/f (Good) **8** Ran SP% **111.5**
Speed ratings (Par 96): **98,90,90,87,81 70,52,18**
CSF £53.89 TOTE £6.00: £1.90, £1.80, £1.50; EX 43.80 Trifecta £207.20.
**Owner** Qatar Racing Limited **Bred** Mrs Jacqueline Norris **Trained** Averham Park, Notts

**FOCUS**
Eight of the previous ten winners benefited from having previous experience, and the market once again gravitated towards those contenders, but they rather took each other on in front, and the race set up nicely for the winner, who sat in behind and pounced late. Nevertheless, the suspicion is that the winner will rate higher next time and looks up to contesting Listed races at least.

## 1513 £100,000 TATTERSALLS MILLIONS 3-Y-O SPRINT (BOBIS RACE) 6f

**2:55** (2:55) (Class 2) 3-Y-O
**£54,100** (£24,590; £9,840; £4,910; £2,960; £1,970) **Stalls** High

Form RPR

301- **1** **Magnus Maximus**[188] 7155 3-9-5 85 PatDobbs 4 104
(Richard Hannon) *mde virtually all: rdn over 1f out: edgd lft ins fnl f: readily holding runner-up fnl 100yds* **25/1**

216- **2** *¾* **Toofi (FR)**[193] 7017 3-9-5 98 AndreaAtzeni 7 101
(Roger Varian) *hld up in midfield: hdwy 2f out: swtchd rt and chsd wnr ins fnl f: r.o: jst hld* **9/4**[1]

01- **3** *2 ¼* **Naadirr (IRE)**[147] 7972 3-9-5 82 LukeMorris 1 94
(Marco Botti) *hld up in tch: rdn to chse wnr 2f out: lost 2nd ins fnl f: one pce* **8/1**

53-5 **4** *2 ¾* **Highland Acclaim (IRE)**[11] 1304 3-9-5 80 DanielTudhope 8 85
(David O'Meara) *mid-div: rdn over 2f out: styd on fnl f: no imp* **100/1**

130- **5** *¾* **One Chance (IRE)**[278] 4253 3-9-0 97 WilliamBuick 3 78
(John Butler) *prom tl wknd over 1f out* **20/1**

1-14 **6** *2 ¼* **Wedding Ring (IRE)**[69] 506 3-9-0 97 MickaelBarzalona 13 70
(Charlie Appleby) *mid-div: rdn and styd on same pce fnl 2f: nvr able to chal* **11/4**[2]

434- **7** *1 ¾* **Bon Voyage**[173] 7494 3-9-5 95 RyanMoore 5 70
(Richard Hannon) *mid-div: rdn and outpcd 2f out: n.d after* **6/1**[3]

13-4 **8** *½* **Quickaswecan**[8] 1358 3-9-5 82 JoeFanning 6 68
(Mark Johnston) *prom tl wknd wl over 1f out* **20/1**

30-4 **9** *hd* **Muir Lodge**[20] 1136 3-9-5 92 (t) JimCrowley 10 68
(Andrew Balding) *bmpd s: towards rr: rdn over 2f out: n.d* **14/1**

2111 **10** *hd* **Crowdmania**[28] 1013 3-9-5 84 AdamKirby 2 67
(Mark Johnston) *sn prom: wknd 2f out* **25/1**

33-3 **11** *2* **Steele Ranger**[14] 1243 3-9-5 70 JamieSpencer 12 61
(Peter Chapple-Hyam) *bhd: rdn and n.d fnl 2f* **100/1**

152- **12** *2 ½* **Hatha Hooh**[244] 5438 3-9-5 85 TomQueally 9 53
(Ismail Mohammed) *wnt lft s: sn w wnr on stands' rail tl wknd 2f out* **66/1**

01- **13** *5* **Scrutiny**[173] 7501 3-9-5 SilvestreDeSousa 11 37
(William Haggas) *bhd: rdn over 2f out: no ch after* **16/1**

1m 13.23s (1.03) **Going Correction** +0.35s/f (Good) **13** Ran SP% **116.1**
Speed ratings (Par 104): **107,106,103,99,98 95,93,92,92,91 89,85,79**
CSF £75.55 TOTE £28.20: £8.60, £1.20, £2.60; EX 163.50 Trifecta £2531.10 Part won. Pool of £3374.90 - 0.67 winning units..
**Owner** Carmichael Humber **Bred** St Albans Bloodstock Llp **Trained** East Everleigh, Wilts

**FOCUS**
A valuable sales race but not that strong a contest on paper, with more than half the field rated below 90, and a surprise winner. The time was good and the level looks pretty solid.

## 1514 CSP EUROPEAN FREE H'CAP (LISTED RACE) 7f

**3:30** (3:30) (Class 1) 3-Y-O
**£20,982** (£7,955; £3,981; £1,983; £995; £499) **Stalls** High

Form RPR

11- **1** **Shifting Power**[257] 4959 3-9-1 **105** RyanMoore 3 107
(Richard Hannon) *chsd ldrs: rdn and unable qck ent fnl 2f: rallied u.p to chal over 1f out: styd on wl u.p to ld nr fin* **13/8**[1]

11- **2** *hd* **Mushir**[186] 7207 3-8-10 **100** PaulHanagan 2 102
(Roger Varian) *in tch: effrt towards centre ent fnl 2f: drvn to ld over 1f out: kpt on wl u.p tl hdd and no ex nr fin* **3/1**[2]

112- **3** *nk* **Aeolus**[172] 7525 3-8-11 **101** GrahamLee 4 103+
(Ed McMahon) *chsd ldrs: nt clr run over 1f out: effrt and stl nt enough room ins fnl f tl r.o wl towards fin: nt quite rch ldrs* **8/1**

016- **4** *¾* **Saayerr**[235] 5765 3-9-4 **108** [1] JamieSpencer 6 107
(William Haggas) *stdd and shifted rt leaving stalls: hld up in rr: swtchd rt and effrt over 1f out: hdwy to chse ldrs jst ins fnl f: styd on same pce fnl 100yds* **10/1**

233- **5** *hd* **Parbold (IRE)**[235] 5765 3-9-7 **111** JimmyFortune 5 109
(Richard Fahey) *led: pressed fr 1/2-way: rdn over 2f out: hdd and drvn over 1f out: styd on same pce ins fnl f* **4/1**[3]

001- 6 6 **Miracle Of Medinah**[202] 6765 3-9-0 **104**............................ LiamKeniry 1 86
(Mark Usher) *chsd ldrs tl pressed ldr 1/2-way: rdn and ev ch over 1f out tl 1f out: wknd ins fnl f* **12/1**

1m 26.72s (1.32) **Going Correction** +0.35s/f (Good) 6 Ran SP% **111.0**
Speed ratings (Par 106): **106,105,105,104,104 97**
CSF £6.50 TOTE £2.10: £1.20, £2.00; EX 6.50 Trifecta £32.60.
**Owner** Ms Elaine Chivers & Potensis Ltd **Bred** John And Susan Davis **Trained** East Everleigh, Wilts

**FOCUS**
A bunched finish and it's unlikely the race will have much of an impact on the 2,000 Guineas. The winner, second, fourth and fifth have been rated pretty much to their marks.

## 1515 LANWADES STUD NELL GWYN STKS (GROUP 3) (FILLIES) 7f
**4:05** (4:06) (Class 1) 3-Y-O
**£36,861** (£13,975; £6,994; £3,484; £1,748; £877) **Stalls** High

Form RPR

210- 1 **Sandiva (IRE)**[192] 7055 3-9-0 109.............................. FrankieDettori 4 106
(Richard Fahey) *hld up tch: hdwy wl over 2f out: rdn and chal over 1f out: led ins fnl f: styd on wl u.p* **7/2**[1]

1-1 2 1/2 **Euro Charline**[39] 892 3-9-0 98.............................. AndreaAtzeni 14 104
(Marco Botti) *t.k.h: chsd ldrs: short of room over 1f out: swtchd rt ins fnl f: styd on wl to snatch 2nd last stride* **5/1**[2]

201- 3 shd **Majeyda (USA)**[165] 7695 3-9-0 99.............................. SilvestreDeSousa 12 103
(Charlie Appleby) *chsd ldrs: effrt u.p to ld over 1f out: hdd ins fnl f: kpt on but unable qck: lost 2nd last stride* **6/1**[3]

365- 4 2 1/4 **Lamar (IRE)**[223] 6142 3-9-0 92.............................. LukeMorris 1 98
(James Tate) *in tch towards rr: hdwy and n.m.r over 1f out: drvn and styd on wl ins fnl f: nvr trbld ldrs* **66/1**

223- 5 nse **Queen Catrine (IRE)**[192] 7055 3-9-0 106.............................. JamieSpencer 13 97
(Charles Hills) *led: rdn and hdd over 1f out: no ex u.p jst ins fnl f: outpcd fnl 100yds* **8/1**

123- 6 nk **Lily Rules (IRE)**[221] 6195 3-9-0 94.............................. StephenCraine 10 97
(Tony Coyle) *in tch towards rr: nt clr run over 2f out: hdwy ent fnl f: styd on wl ins fnl f: nvr trbld ldrs* **50/1**

132- 7 1/2 **Wind Fire (USA)**[215] 6347 3-9-0 100.............................. HarryBentley 8 95
(David Brown) *in tch towards rr: rdn and hdwy over 1f out: kpt on ins fnl f but nvr a threat to ldrs* **16/1**

1- 8 1 **Folk Melody (IRE)**[271] 4491 3-9-0 95.............................. MickaelBarzalona 6 93
(Charlie Appleby) *s.i.s: in tch towards rr: hdwy u.p over 1f out: styd on ins fnl f but no threat to ldrs* **8/1**

060- 9 4 **Azagal (IRE)**[172] 7537 3-9-0 89.............................. DuranFentiman 9 82
(Tim Easterby) *in tch in midfield: rdn over 2f out: no imp and struggling wl over 1f out: wknd fnl f* **100/1**

201- 10 1/2 **Miss Lillie**[165] 7693 3-9-0 79.............................. OisinMurphy 15 81
(Roger Teal) *s.i.s: sn rcvrd and in tch: rdn and effrt over 2f out: no imp and wknd over 1f out* **66/1**

1- 11 2 3/4 **Pelerin (IRE)**[182] 7295 3-9-0 81.............................. AdamKirby 2 74
(Marco Botti) *in tch towards rr: effrt towards centre over 2f out: no prog and btn over 1f out: wknd fnl f* **10/1**

102- 12 1 1/2 **Blockade (IRE)**[186] 7194 3-9-0 100.............................. GrahamLee 7 70
(James Tate) *chsd ldrs: u.p over 2f out: struggling and wknd over 1f out* **33/1**

125- 13 1 **Dorothy B (IRE)**[200] 6836 3-9-0 107.............................. WilliamBuick 11 67
(John Gosden) *in tch: effrt whn short of room and bdly hmpd over 1f out: sn btn and eased fnl f* **6/1**[3]

231- 14 4 **Artistic Charm**[195] 6974 3-9-0 85.............................. JimCrowley 3 57
(David Simcock) *in tch towards rr: rdn and no hdwy over 2f out: wknd over 1f out* **40/1**

213- 15 3/4 **Along Again (IRE)**[263] 4742 3-9-0 99.............................. RyanMoore 5 52
(Sir Michael Stoute) *restless in stalls: in tch in midfield: hdwy to join ldrs over 2f out: rdn whn short of room and btn over 1f out: eased fnl f* **20/1**

1m 26.93s (1.53) **Going Correction** +0.35s/f (Good) 15 Ran SP% **120.7**
Speed ratings (Par 105): **105,104,104,101,101 101,100,99,95,94 91,89,88,83,83**
CSF £19.18 TOTE £3.70: £1.40, £2.20, £2.10; EX 27.00 Trifecta £177.70.
**Owner** Al Shaqab Racing **Bred** Denis McDonnell **Trained** Musley Bank, N Yorks

**FOCUS**
Arguably the premier British 1,000 Guineas trial, although Speciosa was the last filly to win this and then take the first fillies' classic. That said, Sky Lantern finished runner-up here before taking the 1,000 Guineas last year. There were runners representing the best of last season's juvenile fillies' form and two of those filled the first three places. The time was slightly slower than the preceding Free Handicap, they raced towards the stands' rail, and there were a few hard-luck stories as Blockade and Along Again dropped back and caused traffic problems in behind.

## 1516 EBM-PAPST FEILDEN STKS (LISTED RACE) 1m 1f
**4:40** (4:44) (Class 1) 3-Y-O
**£20,982** (£7,955; £3,981; £1,983; £995; £499) **Stalls** High

Form RPR

21- 1 **True Story**[278] 4256 3-9-0 100.............................. SilvestreDeSousa 8 114
(Saeed bin Suroor) *s.i.s: t.k.h: hld up towards rr: hdwy 6f out: chsd ldrs 3f out: rdn and ev ch over 1f out: led ins fnl f: styd on strly and sn clr: impressive* **5/2**[2]

2 7 **Obliterator (IRE)**[214] 6413 3-9-0 0.............................. JamieSpencer 5 106
(G M Lyons, Ire) *hld up in rr: pushed along 4f out: hdwy over 3f out: drvn to ld over 1f out: hdd ins fnl f: sn btn but stl clr 2nd: eased cl home* **15/8**[1]

113- 3 6 **Truth Or Dare**[186] 7195 3-9-0 107.............................. MartinDwyer 7 87
(Richard Hannon) *in tch in midfield: rdn over 2f out: styd on over 1f out: wnt 3rd ins fnl f: kpt on but no ch w ldng pair* **16/1**

25-2 4 nk **Barley Mow (IRE)**[11] 1300 3-9-0 110.............................. RyanMoore 2 86
(Richard Hannon) *chsd ldrs: outpcd u.p and btn over 1f out: rallied and plugged on ins fnl f: no ch w ldrs* **13/2**[3]

120- 5 3/4 **Somewhat (USA)**[172] 7528 3-9-3 112.............................. JoeFanning 1 87
(Mark Johnston) *chsd ldrs: rdn over 2f out: outpcd and btn over 1f out: wl btn and plugged on same pce fnl f* **15/2**

21- 6 3 1/2 **Madeed**[236] 5698 3-9-0 89.............................. PaulHanagan 4 77
(Brian Meehan) *t.k.h: chsd ldr tl rdn to ld over 2f out: hdd and btn over 1f out: fdd fnl f* **14/1**

214- 7 2 3/4 **Cordite (IRE)**[172] 7534 3-9-0 94.............................. AndrewMullen 9 71
(Michael Appleby) *t.k.h: hld up in rr: rdn and effrt 3f out: no prog: n.d* **20/1**

36-1 8 6 **Rock 'N' Roll Star**[75] 409 3-9-0 80.............................. LukeMorris 10 59
(Peter Chapple-Hyam) *s.i.s: hld up in rr: rdn and no hdwy 3f out: wl btn over 1f out* **66/1**

251- 9 3 1/4 **Master The World (IRE)**[202] 6762 3-9-0 92.............................. LiamKeniry 3 52
(David Elsworth) *led: rdn and hdd over 2f out: sn btn and wknd* **20/1**

135- 10 37 **Stormardal (IRE)**[186] 7192 3-9-0 93.............................. WilliamBuick 6
(Ismail Mohammed) *chsd ldr: rdn and pressed ldr briefly 3f out: sn btn: t.o fnl f* **40/1**

1m 51.6s (-0.10) **Going Correction** +0.35s/f (Good) 10 Ran SP% **114.5**
Speed ratings (Par 106): **114,107,102,102,101 98,95,90,87,54**
CSF £7.04 TOTE £3.40: £1.40, £1.30, £3.30; EX 8.00 Trifecta £130.20.
**Owner** Godolphin **Bred** Darley **Trained** Newmarket, Suffolk

**FOCUS**
Intello won this easily last year on his way to taking the French Derby, and it's entirely possible that True Story could emulate him in winning a Classic. A strong renewal and the winner has been rated up with the better winners of this race.

## 1517 NGK SPARK PLUGS EBF STALLIONS MAIDEN STKS (BOBIS RACE) 1m 2f
**5:10** (5:16) (Class 4) 3-Y-O
**£5,498** (£1,636; £817; £408) **Stalls** High

Form RPR

32- 1 **Munjaz**[175] 7469 3-9-5 0.............................. PaulHanagan 2 92
(John Gosden) *racd in centre tl gps merged 3f out: in tch in midfield: hdwy to join ldr 3f out: rdn to ld over 1f out: hung lft but kpt on wl fnl f* **11/8**[1]

43- 2 1/2 **Venezia (IRE)**[193] 7019 3-9-5 0.............................. RyanMoore 5 91
(Martyn Meade) *racd in centre tl gps merged 3f out: chsd ldrs: effrt u.p and ev ch over 1f out: kpt on wl but no ex and hld towards fin* **6/1**[3]

3 3 **Connecticut** 3-9-5 0.............................. AndreaAtzeni 16 85+
(Luca Cumani) *racd stands' side tl gps merged 3f out: hld up towards rr: stdy hdwy 3f out: kpt on wl ins fnl f* **20/1**

5- 4 3/4 **Mustadaam (IRE)**[202] 6762 3-9-5 0.............................. DaneO'Neill 8 84
(Brian Meehan) *racd in centre tl gps merged 3f out: overall ldr tl rdn and hdd over 1f out: outpcd and btn ins fnl f* **8/1**

5 1/2 **Ayrad (IRE)** 3-9-5 0.............................. WilliamBuick 17 83
(Roger Varian) *racd stands' side tl gps merged 3f out: chsd ldrs: hdwy to press ldrs 3f out: outpcd and btn ins fnl f* **9/1**

6 1 1/4 **Min Alemarat (IRE)** 3-9-5 0.............................. AdamKirby 9 81
(Marco Botti) *racd in centre tl gps merged 3f out: towards rr: pushed along over 2f out: kpt on ins fnl f: nvr trbld ldrs* **33/1**

7 nk **Every Time** 3-9-0 0.............................. DavidProbert 6 75
(Andrew Balding) *racd in centre tl gps merged 3f out: in tch in midfield: effrt and no imp over 1f out: styd on same pce after* **40/1**

3- 8 4 1/2 **Wrangler**[169] 7607 3-9-5 0.............................. JamieSpencer 14 71
(William Haggas) *racd stands' side tl gps merged 3f out: led gp and prom overall: chsd ldr 3f out tl wknd u.p over 1f out* **4/1**[2]

24- 9 2 1/2 **Mustamir (IRE)**[210] 6528 3-9-5 0.............................. LukeMorris 4 67
(James Tate) *racd in centre tl gps merged 3f out: chsd ldrs: rdn and unable qck over 2f out: sn struggling: wknd wl over 1f out* **33/1**

0- 10 nk **Telegraphy (USA)**[173] 7493 3-9-0 0..............................[1] GrahamLee 10 61
(Ed Dunlop) *racd in centre tl gps merged 3f out: hld up towards rr: n.d* **66/1**

11 14 **Austerian** 3-9-5 0.............................. JoeFanning 11 40
(Gay Kelleway) *racd in centre tl gps merged 3f out: hld up towards rr: rdn and effrt 3f out: edgd lft and btn 2f out: sn wknd* **66/1**

0- 12 7 **Eye Contact**[243] 5472 3-9-5 0.............................. JamesDoyle 1 26
(Sir Michael Stoute) *racd in centre tl gps merged 3f out: sn rdn and wknd wl over 1f out: t.o* **25/1**

6- 13 39 **Lara Lipton (IRE)**[131] 8176 3-8-9 0.............................. DavidKenny(5) 15
(Jane Chapple-Hyam) *racd stands' side tl gps merged 3f out: bhd 7f out: t.o* **100/1**

2m 9.23s (3.43) **Going Correction** +0.35s/f (Good) 13 Ran SP% **118.4**
Speed ratings (Par 100): **100,99,97,96,96 95,94,91,89,89 77,72,41**
CSF £8.86 TOTE £2.30: £1.10, £2.20, £5.10; EX 10.20 Trifecta £98.60.
**Owner** Hamdan Al Maktoum **Bred** Shadwell Estate Company Limited **Trained** Newmarket, Suffolk

**FOCUS**
A maiden that usually throws up some useful types. They were quite bunched at the finish, though, so the bare form can't be rated quite up to standard.

## 1518 BLUE FROG SUPPLIED BY NP NUNN H'CAP (BOBIS RACE) 6f
**5:40** (5:46) (Class 2) (0-100,99) 3-Y-O **£12,938** (£3,850; £1,924; £962) **Stalls** High

Form RPR

01- 1 **Danzeno**[180] 7341 3-8-12 **90**.............................. AndrewMullen 6 105
(Michael Appleby) *t.k.h: chsd ldr: rdn to ld but wnt rt over 1f out: sn clr w runner-up: r.o strly and drew clr ins fnl f* **6/1**[2]

51-5 2 3 **Expert (IRE)**[25] 1067 3-9-7 **99**.............................. RyanMoore 4 104
(Richard Hannon) *chsd ldr: rdn and ev ch over 1f out: sn wnt clr wnr: no ex and btn ins fnl f: wknd towards fin but stl clr 2nd* **7/1**[3]

41- 3 2 1/2 **Greeb**[238] 5646 3-8-5 **83**.............................. JoeFanning 5 80
(Charles Hills) *stdd s: t.k.h: hld up in tch towards rr: hdwy ent fnl 2f: hdwy to chse clr ldng pair over 1f out: kpt on* **7/1**[3]

-301 4 hd **Mick's Yer Man**[12] 1278 3-8-12 **95**.............................. RyanWhile(5) 9 91+
(Bill Turner) *stdd and bdly hmpd s: steadily rcvrd and hdwy into midfield 1/2-way: rdn and effrt 2f out: battling for 3rd over 1f out: kpt on but no threat to ldrs* **14/1**

001- 5 4 1/2 **Meritocracy (IRE)**[181] 7329 3-8-12 **90**.............................. JamieSpencer 1 72
(Paul Cole) *stdd s: hld up in last trio: n.m.r and swtchd rt over 1f out: sn drvn: no ch w ldrs but kpt on* **25/1**

21- 6 1/2 **Quiet Warrior (IRE)**[119] 8326 3-8-5 **83**.............................. AndreaAtzeni 11 63+
(Marco Botti) *hmpd s: in tch in tch: rdn and effrt ent fnl 2f: sn outpcd and no ch w ldrs 1f out: plugged on* **11/2**[1]

120- 7 nk **Outer Space**[186] 7207 3-9-2 **94**.............................. JamesDoyle 12 73+
(Jamie Osborne) *hmpd s: sn reovered to chse ldrs: rdn ent fnl 2f: outpcd and btn over 1f out: wl hld fnl f* **6/1**[2]

031- 8 1 **Sleepy Sioux**[180] 7333 3-8-4 **82**.............................. SilvestreDeSousa 2 58
(David Elsworth) *led: rdn and hdd whn squeezed for room over 1f out: sn outpcd by ldng pair: wknd fnl f* **14/1**

310- 9 1 1/4 **Ventura Mist**[186] 7194 3-9-5 **97**..............................(p) DuranFentiman 8 69+
(Tim Easterby) *stdd and veered bdly lft leaving stalls: hld up in tch in midfield: rdn and btn ent fnl 2f: wknd over 1f out* **16/1**

11 10 nk **Desert Ranger (IRE)**[19] 1149 3-8-2 **80** oh4.............................. LukeMorris 10 51+
(James Tate) *bdly hmpd s: nvr rcvrd and a bhd* **11/1**

612- 11 4 1/2 **Claim The Roses (USA)**[189] 7122 3-8-8 **89**.............................. OisinMurphy(3) 7 46
(Ed Vaughan) *t.k.h: chsd ldrs: rdn and no ex ent fnl 2f: sn wknd: bhd fnl f* **14/1**

01- 12 1 3/4 **Kaab (IRE)**[176] 7448 3-8-7 **85**.............................. PaulHanagan 3 36
(Ed Dunlop) *hld up in tch towards rr: rdn over 2f out: sn btn: bhd fnl f* **8/1**

1m 13.2s (1.00) **Going Correction** +0.35s/f (Good) 12 Ran SP% **118.1**
Speed ratings (Par 104): **107,103,99,99,93 92,92,91,89,88 82,80**
CSF £47.53 CT £304.16 TOTE £8.80: £3.20, £2.00, £3.00; EX 56.70 Trifecta £695.20.
**Owner** A M Wragg **Bred** A M Wragg **Trained** Danethorpe, Notts

**FOCUS**
A smart sprint handicap that has thrown up the Group level sprinters Sakhee's Secret and Prohibit in the last ten years. Several runners were badly hampered when Ventura Mist went sharply left coming out of the stalls, but the time was better than the earlier sales race. The form makes sense, with the winner improving again, the second pretty exposed and the third, whose maiden has worked out well, giving it substance.
T/Plt: £25.30 to a £1 stake. Pool of £98033.14 - 2827.89 winning tickets. T/Qpdt: £8.70 to a £1 stake. Pool of £5359.30 - 454.90 winning tickets. SP

1511 **NEWMARKET** (R-H)
Thursday, April 17
**OFFICIAL GOING: Good (good to firm in places; 7.5)**
Wind: medium, behind Weather: dry, bright spells

## 1528 MONTAZ RESTAURANT EBF STALLIONS MAIDEN FILLIES' STKS (BOBIS RACE) 5f
1:45 (1:48) (Class 4) 2-Y-O **£5,175** (£1,540; £769; £384) **Stalls** Low

Form RPR
1 **Spirit Of Xian (IRE)** 2-9-0 0 PatDobbs 15 78+
(Richard Hannon) *wnt lft s: in tch in midfield: rdn and effrt over 1f out: pressing ldrs whn carried lftins fnl f: r.o wl to ld last stride* **8/1**
2 *shd* **Al Ghuwariyah (IRE)** 2-9-0 0 JamesDoyle 12 78+
(Kevin Ryan) *chsd ldr tl led wl over 1f out: hrd pressed after but battled on wl u.p: edgd lft ins fnl f: hdd last stride* **25/1**
3 *hd* **El Che** 2-8-11 0 CharlesBishop(3) 4 77
(Mick Channon) *chsd ldrs: rdn and hdwy over 1f out: ev ch ins fnl f: no ex nr fin* **40/1**
0 4 *hd* **London Life (IRE)**[13] 1276 2-9-0 0 KierenFallon 8 76
(Tom Dascombe) *chsd ldrs: rdn and ev ch over 1f out: no ex towards fin* **18/1**
5 *3/4* **Belle Fille** 2-9-0 0 SilvestreDeSousa 5 74
(David Brown) *in tch in midfield: rdn over 2f out: hdwy to chse ldrs over 1f out: pressing ldrs ins fnl f: one pce and hld whn short of room and eased cl home* **11/1**
6 *1/2* **Rise Up Lotus (IRE)** 2-9-0 0 PaulHanagan 1 72
(Charles Hills) *dwlt sn rcvrd to chse ldrs: rdn and ev ch wl over 1f out: no ex fnl 100yds: hld whn short of room and eased towards fin* **20/1**
7 *1/2* **Granny Alice** 2-9-0 0 AndreaAtzeni 7 70
(Noel Quinlan) *chsd ldrs: rdn and ev ch wl over 1f out: no ex ins fnl f: wknd fnl 100yds* **50/1**
8 *1 1/4* **Lacing** 2-9-0 0 RyanMoore 14 65+
(Richard Fahey) *rn green in midfield: lost pl 1/2-way: stl plenty to do but hdwy jst over 1f out: styd on wl ins fnl f: nvr trbld ldrs* **9/4**[1]
9 *1* **Tarando** 2-9-0 0 TomQueally 2 62
(Michael Bell) *led tl hdd wl over 1f out: sn rdn: wknd ins fnl f* **20/1**
10 *2* **Mary McPhee** 2-9-0 0 JamieSpencer 16 55+
(Charles Hills) *pushed lft s: bhd: styd on to pass btn rivals ins fnl f: nvr trbld ldrs* **10/1**
11 *1 1/4* **Gold Waltz** 2-9-0 0[1] JimCrowley 10 50
(Ralph Beckett) *in toouch in midfield: rdn 1/2-way: sn struggling: wknd wl over 1f out* **7/1**[3]
12 *1 3/4* **Artfilly (IRE)** 2-9-0 0 WilliamBuick 6 44
(Ed Walker) *chsd ldrs tl 1/2-way: sn struggling: wknd wl over 1f out* **14/1**
13 *2 1/2* **Kodestiny (IRE)** 2-9-0 0 LiamJones 11 35
(Ismail Mohammed) *in tch in midfield: rdn ent fnl 2f: green: racd awkwardly on downhill run and lost pl wl over 1f out: sn wknd* **66/1**
14 *2 1/4* **No Delusion (USA)** 2-9-0 0 MickaelBarzalona 3 27
(Charlie Appleby) *s.i.s: a bhd* **11/2**[2]
0 15 *1* **Baileys Pursuit**[19] 1169 2-9-0 0 MartinDwyer 13 23
(Chris Dwyer) *restless in stalls: bhd: struggling 1/2-way: no ch fnl 2f* **66/1**
16 *15* **Julia Stardust** 2-8-9 0 LouisSteward(5) 9
(Alan Coogan) *wnt rt s and s.i.s: a bhd: lost tch 1/2-way: t.o* **150/1**

1m 0.6s (1.50) **Going Correction** -0.05s/f (Good) 16 Ran **SP% 119.8**
Speed ratings (Par 91): **86,85,85,85,84 83,82,80,78,75 73,70,66,63,61 37**
CSF £200.60 TOTE £9.50: £3.30, £7.40, £7.80; EX 253.10 Trifecta £2791.80 Part won..
**Owner** Rockcliffe Stud **Bred** B Kennedy **Trained** East Everleigh, Wilts
■ Stewards' Enquiry : Charles Bishop three-day ban: careless riding (May 1,2,5)

**FOCUS**
Far Side track used and stalls on far side. A total of 3mm of water had been applied after racing the previous day and the ground remained Good, good to firm in places. There was a tailwind in the straight. They raced centre-field in a race that's thrown up some useful types in recent years, although the main action unfolded nearer the stands' side late on.

## 1529 SWAN AT LAVENHAM WOOD DITTON STKS (BOBIS RACE) 1m
2:20 (2:23) (Class 4) 3-Y-O **£6,469** (£1,925; £962; £481) **Stalls** Low

Form RPR
1 **Basem** 3-9-5 0 SilvestreDeSousa 11 89+
(Saeed bin Suroor) *wl in tch in midfield: rdn wl over 2f out: 5th and outpcd wl over 1f out: rallied and swtchd lft jst ins fnl f: str run fnl 100yds to ld cl home* **5/2**[1]
2 *1/2* **Made With Love** 3-9-5 0 AndreaAtzeni 3 88
(Roger Varian) *led and set stdy gallop: rdn and qcknd wl over 1f out: battled on wl u.p ins fnl f: hdd and no ex cl home* **16/1**
3 *3/4* **Moonvoy** 3-9-0 0 SebSanders 8 81
(Jeremy Noseda) *wl in tch midfield: rdn and chsd ldng trio wl over 1f out: swtchd rt and chal ent fnl f: no ex and one pce fnl 100yds* **20/1**
4 *2 1/2* **Famous Kid (USA)** 3-9-5 0 KierenFallon 10 81
(Saeed bin Suroor) *pressed ldr: rdn wl over 1f out: no ex 1f out: wknd fnl 100yds* **12/1**
5 *1/2* **Prince Of Stars** 3-9-5 0 GrahamLee 4 79+
(John Gosden) *chsd ldrs: lost pl over 2f out: 8th and looked wl hld over 1f out: rallied and styd on wl ifnl 150yds: no threat to ldrs* **13/2**[3]
6 *1/2* **Tabreek (USA)** 3-9-5 0 PaulHanagan 15 78+
(Richard Hannon) *in tch in midfield: pushed along 3f out: rdn and outpcd 2f out: rallied and styd on wl ins fnl f: no threat to ldrs* **9/1**
7 *1/2* **Computer (USA)** 3-9-5 0 JamesDoyle 18 77
(Charles Hills) *chsd ldrs: rdn to press ldrs wl over 1f out: no ex jst ins fnl f: wknd fnl 100yds* **20/1**
8 *1 3/4* **Randwick (IRE)** 3-9-5 0 RobertWinston 1 73
(Charles Hills) *chsd ldrs: 6th and outpcd wl over 1f out: styd on same pce after* **50/1**
9 *3/4* **Tercel (IRE)** 3-9-5 0 RyanMoore 5 71
(Sir Michael Stoute) *t.k.h: hld up in tch in rr: pushed along and outpcd ent fnl 2f: hdwy over 1f out: styd on steadily ins fnl f: nvr trbld ldrs* **11/1**
10 *1/2* **Mawaseel** 3-9-5 0 DaneO'Neill 7 70
(J W Hills) *wl in tch in midfield: pushed along and outpcd ent fnl 2f: plugged on same pce and no imp after* **14/1**
11 *3 3/4* **Censorius** 3-9-5 0 GeorgeBaker 12 62
(Ed Walker) *hld up in tch in rr: rdn and outpcd over 2f out: n.d after* **66/1**
12 *2* **Fine Tune (IRE)** 3-9-5 0 RobertHavlin 14 57
(John Gosden) *wnt lft s: sn swtchd rt and hdwy into midfield: rdn and struggling over 2f out: wkng and hung lft wl over 1f out* **25/1**
13 *1/2* **Injun Sands** 3-9-0 0 DavidKenny(5) 9 56
(Jane Chapple-Hyam) *in tch in rr: rdn 3f out: sn struggling: n.d fnl 2f* **100/1**
14 *4* **Fallen In Line (IRE)** 3-9-5 0 WilliamBuick 6 47
(John Gosden) *in tch towards rr: struggling over 2f out: no prog whn hmpd wl over 1f out: bhd after* **9/2**[2]
15 *6* **Wild Affaire (IRE)** 3-9-0 0 (b[1]) JimCrowley 16 28
(Charles Hills) *in tch in midfield: pushed along 1/2-way: rdn and lost pl ent fnl 2f: lost tch over 1f out* **66/1**

1m 40.8s (2.20) **Going Correction** -0.05s/f (Good) 15 Ran **SP% 118.0**
Speed ratings (Par 100): **87,86,85,83,82 82,81,80,79,78 75,73,72,68,62**
CSF £41.88 TOTE £3.80: £2.00, £3.70, £6.10; EX 45.90 Trifecta £1530.90.
**Owner** Godolphin **Bred** Darley **Trained** Newmarket, Suffolk

**FOCUS**
A big field for this long-established newcomers' race, but they went very steadily early and the time was modest, despite a tailwind. It's been rated around the averages for the race.

## 1530 £200,000 TATTERSALLS MILLIONS 3-Y-O TROPHY (BOBIS RACE) 1m 2f
2:55 (3:05) (Class 2) 3-Y-O
**£108,220** (£44,280; £19,700; £9,820; £4,920; £1,960) **Stalls** Low

Form RPR
421- 1 **Sudden Wonder (IRE)**[176] 7468 3-9-5 96 MickaelBarzalona 2 104
(Charlie Appleby) *in tch in midfield: effrt on far side to chal over 1f out: drew clr w ldr fnl f: sustained effrt u.p to ld wl ins fnl f: styd on* **7/1**
2- 2 *hd* **Observational**[174] 7502 3-9-5 0 JamesDoyle 13 103
(Roger Charlton) *hld up in tch in last quartet: pushed along and hdwy to press ldrs 3f out: led over 1f out: hung rt but drew clr w wnr fnl f: hdd wl ins fnl f: kpt on* **9/1**
1- 3 *3 1/2* **Seagull Star**[194] 7019 3-9-5 81 GrahamLee 8 96
(William Haggas) *in tch in midfield: hdwy to press ldrs over 2f out: rdn and ev ch over 1f out: 3rd and outpcd fnl f* **10/3**[2]
6-1 4 *1 1/2* **Emaratiya Ana (IRE)**[28] 1024 3-9-0 75 AndreaAtzeni 15 88
(Roger Varian) *in tch in midfield: hdwy to press ldrs u.p 2f out: no ex and btn 1f out: wknd ins fnl f* **66/1**
100- 5 *1 1/4* **Lyn Valley**[173] 7534 3-9-5 94 JoeFanning 10 91
(Mark Johnston) *in tch in midfield: rdn and effrt 2f out: shifting lft over 1f out: styd on same pce u.p ins fnl f* **25/1**
42- 6 *1* **Johann Strauss**[15] 1251 3-9-5 108 JosephO'Brien 7 89
(A P O'Brien, Ire) *restless in stalls: stdd s: hld up in last pair: clsd 3f out: rdn and unable qck on downhill run wl over 1f out: sn swtchd lft and no imp after* **13/8**[1]
144- 7 *2* **Hunters Creek (IRE)**[194] 7017 3-9-5 94 WilliamBuick 12 85
(John Gosden) *in tch in midfield: rdn and unable qck whn short of room wl over 1f out: no imp after* **11/2**[3]
5- 8 *1 1/4* **Cadeaux Power**[166] 7692 3-9-0 0 RyanMoore 5 78
(Clive Brittain) *chsd ldr tl led ent fnl 3f: drvn and hdd over 1f out: fdd ins fnl f* **66/1**
4-23 9 *3 3/4* **Munfallet (IRE)**[12] 1298 3-9-5 80 JamieSpencer 16 76
(David Brown) *stdd s: hld up in last pair: sme hdwy 2f out: sn rdn and no imp nvr trbld ldrs* **100/1**
-411 10 *4* **Maxie T**[8] 1372 3-9-5 68 SilvestreDeSousa 11 68
(Mark Johnston) *chsd ldrs: rdn to chse ldr over 3f out tl over 2f out: struggling whn sltly hmpd wl over 1f out: sn wknd* **66/1**
3-33 11 *1 1/4* **Roskilly (IRE)**[27] 1044 3-9-5 77 DavidProbert 3 66
(Andrew Balding) *hld up in tch in last quartet: rdn over 2f out: no hdwy and sn btn: wknd wl over 1f out* **66/1**
600- 12 *3/4* **Lanark (IRE)**[194] 7017 3-9-5 90 AdamKirby 1 64
(Mark Johnston) *racd solo on far side tl jnd rivals 7f out: chsd ldrs: struggling u.p wl over 2f out: bhd over 1f out* **33/1**
5-55 13 *11* **Ganymede**[14] 1258 3-9-5 68 JimCrowley 9 44
(Eve Johnson Houghton) *led tl ent fnl 3f: sn lost pl: towards rr whn n.m.r 2f out: sn bhd: t.o* **100/1**
135- 14 *15* **Dancealot**[212] 6501 3-9-0 82 FrederikTylicki 14 10
(Clive Brittain) *in tch in last quartet: struggling 3f out: sn lost tch: t.o* **66/1**

2m 4.0s (-1.80) **Going Correction** -0.05s/f (Good) 14 Ran **SP% 115.3**
Speed ratings (Par 104): **105,104,102,100,99 99,97,96,93,90 89,88,79,67**
CSF £62.08 TOTE £7.50: £2.10, £2.90, £1.80; EX 76.10 Trifecta £288.70.
**Owner** Godolphin **Bred** Rabbah Bloodstock Limited **Trained** Newmarket, Suffolk

**FOCUS**
This wasn't as competitive as the field size suggested, with only a handful being seriously considered, and although the front pair drew clear it isn't form to be putting much stock into going forward. They raced centre-field and the pace was an even one. The runner-up, third and fourth have all been rated as improving, with the fifth close to his 2yo form.

## 1531 CONNAUGHT ACCESS FLOORING ABERNANT STKS (GROUP 3) 6f
3:30 (3:34) (Class 1) 3-Y-O+
**£36,861** (£13,975; £6,994; £3,484; £1,748; £877) **Stalls** Low

Form RPR
03-6 1 **Hamza (IRE)**[19] 1179 5-9-6 110 (b) JamieSpencer 6 114
(Kevin Ryan) *mde all: rdn over 2f out: drvn wl over 1f out: hdd ins fnl f: sn led again: styd on wl and outbattled runner-up towards fin* **11/4**[2]
230- 2 *1/2* **Es Que Love (IRE)**[194] 7014 5-9-6 103 AdamKirby 3 112
(Clive Cox) *travelled wl: trckd ldrs: chsd wnr over 1f out: rdn to chal 1f out: led ins fnl f: sn hdd: drvn and nt qckn: jst hld 2nd* **9/1**[3]
210- 3 *shd* **Aljamaaheer (IRE)**[249] 5314 5-9-6 116 PaulHanagan 5 112+
(Roger Varian) *dwlt: in tch in last pair: plenty to do wl over 1f out: swtchd rt and hdwy between horses ent fnl f: chsd clr ldng pair and swtchd lft ins fnl f: r.o strly: nt quite rch ldrs* **5/4**[1]
56-1 4 *3* **Dinkum Diamond (IRE)**[19] 1163 6-9-6 108 OisinMurphy 4 102
(Henry Candy) *chsd ldr tl over 1f out: outpcd u.p ent fnl f: one pce and no imp after* **10/1**
01-0 5 *1/2* **Tropics (USA)**[19] 1163 6-9-10 116 RobertWinston 2 105
(Dean Ivory) *stdd s: hld up in tch: rdn and effrt wl over 1f out: styd on same pce and no imp fnl f* **9/1**[3]

10-6 **6** 3/4 **Heaven's Guest (IRE)**[19] 1163 4-9-6 104 RyanMoore 8 98
(Richard Fahey) *chsd ldrs: rdn and outpcd over 1f out: styng on at same pce and wl hld whn sltly impeded ins fnl f* **12/1**

0003 **7** 1 **Hitchens (IRE)**[40] 890 9-9-6 102 SilvestreDeSousa 1 95
(David Barron) *in tch in midfield: rdn ent fnl 2f: outpcd and btn over 1f out: plugged on same pce after* **33/1**

6502 **8** nk **Racy**[49] 769 7-9-6 94 GeorgeBaker 7 94
(Brian Ellison) *taken down early: hld up in rr: rdn and effrt wl over 1f out: kpt on but no imp* **33/1**

1m 9.88s (-2.32) **Going Correction** -0.05s/f (Good) **8** Ran SP% **113.8**
Speed ratings (Par 113): **113,112,112,108,107 106,105,104**
CSF £27.25 TOTE £3.70: £1.40, £2.60, £1.10; EX 21.50 Trifecta £48.00.
**Owner** Mubarak Al Naemi **Bred** Castlemartin Stud And Skymarc Farm **Trained** Hambleton, N Yorks

**FOCUS**
Often the starting point for the season for some of the top sprinters, Equiano and Mayson won this before going on to take the Group 1 King's Stand and July Cup respectively. The winner has been rated to form on a track that suits.

## 1532 NOVAE BLOODSTOCK INSURANCE CRAVEN STKS (C&G) (GROUP 3) 1m

4:05 (4:05) (Class 1) 3-Y-O

**£36,861** (£13,975; £6,994; £3,484; £1,748; £877) **Stalls** Low

Form RPR

111- **1** **Toormore (IRE)**[214] 6442 3-9-3 122 RyanMoore 1 117
(Richard Hannon) *t.k.h: chsd ldr tl led over 6f out: jnd 3f out: bmpd and hdd wl over 1f out: led again over 1f out: doing little in front but in command ins fnl f: drvn out fnl 100yds* **1/1**[1]

220- **2** 2 **The Grey Gatsby (IRE)**[173] 7528 3-9-0 110 JamieSpencer 4 109
(Kevin Ryan) *led tl over 6f out: jnd ldr again 3f out: rdn and edgd rt wl over 1f out: sn led again: wandered lft u.p and hdd over 1f out: shifting rt and styd on same pce ins fnl f* **16/1**

512- **3** 1 3/4 **Postponed (IRE)**[194] 7017 3-9-0 96 AndreaAtzeni 3 105
(Luca Cumani) *stdd s: hld up in tch: hdwy 3f out: rdn and effrt over 2f out: outpcd over 1f out: kpt on but no threat to ldrs ins fnl f* **8/1**[3]

1- **4** 2 1/4 **Patentar (FR)**[187] 7209 3-9-0 87 WilliamBuick 2 100
(Marco Botti) *chsd ldrs: rdn and unable qck over 2f out: no imp u.p fr over 1f out* **40/1**

114- **5** 7 **Anjaal**[187] 7192 3-9-3 111 PaulHanagan 5 87
(Richard Hannon) *t.k.h: hld up wl in tch: rdn and unable qck wl over 2f out: wknd over 1f out* **16/1**

21- **6** 28 **Be Ready (IRE)**[216] 6351 3-9-0 111 SilvestreDeSousa 6 19
(Saeed bin Suroor) *plld hrd: hld up in tch in rr: rdn 3f out: sn btn and rdr looking down: eased fnl f: t.o* **7/4**[2]

1m 35.42s (-3.18) **Going Correction** -0.05s/f (Good) **6** Ran SP% **111.7**
Speed ratings (Par 108): **113,111,109,107,100 72**
CSF £18.25 TOTE £1.80: £1.10, £3.30; EX 17.90 Trifecta £33.10.
**Owner** Middleham Park Racing IX & James Pak **Bred** BEC Bloodstock **Trained** East Everleigh, Wilts

**FOCUS**
The leading 2,000 Guineas trial, which was run at an ordinary gallop. The winner didn't have to improve to win under his penalty. The third and fourth have been rated as improving in line with the place averages for the race.

## 1533 WEATHERBYS HAMILTON INSURANCE EARL OF SEFTON STKS (GROUP 3) 1m 1f

4:40 (4:42) (Class 1) 4-Y-O+

**£36,861** (£13,975; £6,994; £3,484; £1,748; £877) **Stalls** Low

Form RPR

34-0 **1** **Mull Of Killough (IRE)**[19] 1176 8-8-13 114 AdamKirby 8 117
(Jane Chapple-Hyam) *chsd ldr: jnd ldr 6f out tl led 3f out: drvn and forged clr over 1f out: tiring fnl 100yds but a holding on: drvn out* **4/1**[2]

242- **2** 1 **French Navy**[166] 7698 6-8-13 112 MickaelBarzalona 9 115
(Charlie Appleby) *awkward leaving stalls: hld up in last pair: rdn and hdwy in centre wl over 1f out: chsd clr wnr ins fnl f: r.o but nvr gng to rch wnr* **11/2**[3]

66-2 **3** 1 1/4 **Fencing (USA)**[19] 1162 5-8-13 110 WilliamBuick 7 112
(John Gosden) *t.k.h: hld up in tch in midfield: hdwy to press wnr 3f out: racd awkwardly u.p and nt qckn wl over 1f out: drifted lft and outpcd over 1f out: one pce and lost 2nd ins fnl f* **7/2**[1]

015- **4** shd **Gospel Choir**[194] 7012 5-8-13 104 RyanMoore 2 112
(Sir Michael Stoute) *hld up in tch in rr: rdn and sme hdwy over 1f out: r.o strly ins fnl f: nt rch ldrs* **11/1**

306- **5** 1 3/4 **Just The Judge (IRE)**[201] 6837 4-8-10 110 JamieSpencer 3 105
(Charles Hills) *hld up in tch in last trio: rdn and hdwy over 2f out: chsd ldrs but unable qck over 1f out: styd on same pce after* **6/1**

621- **6** 3 **Danadana (IRE)**[222] 6232 6-9-4 114 AndreaAtzeni 1 106
(Luca Cumani) *in tch in midfield: rdn and effrt over 2f out: no imp and drifted rt over 1f out: wknd ins fnl f* **8/1**

055- **7** 1/2 **First Mohican**[33] 7206 6-8-13 106 TomQueally 4 100
(Alan King) *in tch in midfield: rdn and outpcd over 2f out: n.d and one pce fnl 2f* **16/1**

156- **8** 11 **Elkaayed (USA)**[260] 4874 4-8-13 106 PaulHanagan 6 76
(Roger Varian) *t.k.h: in tch in midfield: rdn and struggling 3f: bhd over 1f out* **7/1**

225- **9** 1/2 **Boom And Bust (IRE)**[202] 6797 7-8-13 108 HayleyTurner 5 75
(Marcus Tregoning) *t.k.h: led tl over 3f out: sn rdn and dropped out: bhd over 1f out* **25/1**

1m 48.44s (-3.26) **Going Correction** -0.05s/f (Good) **9** Ran SP% **113.6**
Speed ratings (Par 113): **112,111,110,109,108 105,105,95,95**
CSF £25.81 TOTE £4.70: £1.70, £2.00, £1.50; EX 28.70 Trifecta £116.40.
**Owner** Invictus **Bred** Owenstown Stud **Trained** Dalham, Suffolk
■ Stewards' Enquiry : Adam Kirby four-day ban: used whip above permitted level (May 1-2,5-6)

**FOCUS**
Usually a strong Group 3, despite the relatively unusual intermediate distance, that has thrown up a number of smart performers in recent years, notably subsequent multiple Group 1 winners Notnowcato and Manduro. This year's line-up looked up to par and it fell to the horse with the highest adjusted official rating. He has been given the same rating as when winning it last year.

## 1534 ROSSDALES MAIDEN FILLIES' STKS (BOBIS RACE) 7f

5:10 (5:15) (Class 4) 3-Y-O **£5,175** (£1,540; £769; £384) **Stalls** Low

Form RPR

**1** **Hadaatha (IRE)** 3-9-0 0 PaulHanagan 7 84+
(Roger Varian) *racd stands' side: in tch in midfield: rdn and effrt 2f out: ev ch over 1f out: led ins fnl f: styd on wl: rdn out* **7/2**[2]

32- **2** 1 1/4 **Eastern Belle**[166] 7693 3-9-0 0 WilliamBuick 3 81
(John Gosden) *racd far side: led gp and chsd ldrs overall: rdn wl over 1f out: ev ch ins fnl f: no ex and one pce fnl 75yds* **10/3**[1]

0-4 **3** shd **Sighora (IRE)**[18] 1192 3-9-0 0 LiamJones 12 81
(Ismail Mohammed) *racd stands' side: chsd ldrs: rdn to ld over 1f out: hdd ins fnl f: styd on same pce fnl 75yds* **66/1**

**4** shd **Solar Magic** 3-9-0 0 RobertHavlin 1 81+
(John Gosden) *racd far side: hld up towards rr: pushed along and hdwy over 1f out: r.o wl ins fnl f* **16/1**

**5** 1 1/4 **Ramshackle** 3-9-0 0 JamesDoyle 5 77
(Sir Michael Stoute) *racd far side: midfield overall: rdn and hdwy 2f out: chsd ldrs and styd on same pce ins fnl f* **33/1**

**6** shd **Etaab (USA)** 3-9-0 0 DaneO'Neill 19 77+
(William Haggas) *racd stands' side: in tch in midfield: rdn and effrt 2f out: swtchd lft over 1f out: kpt on ins fnl f* **25/1**

**7** 1 1/2 **Red Velour** 3-9-0 0 SebSanders 9 73+
(Jeremy Noseda) *racd stands' side: in tch in midfield: rdn and hdwy to chse ldrs 2f out: styd on same pce ins fnl f* **25/1**

33- **8** 1 1/4 **Lady Horatia**[164] 7732 3-9-0 0 MartinDwyer 10 70
(William Muir) *chsd ldrs: rdn ent fnl 2f: unable qck over 1f out: wknd ins fnl f* **100/1**

**9** 1 3/4 **Margaret's Mission (IRE)** 3-9-0 0 ShaneKelly 4 65
(Jeremy Noseda) *racd far side: in tch overall: swtchd to join stands' side gp and midfield 4f out: rdn and outpcd 2f out: rn green and styd on same pce fr over 1f out* **33/1**

42- **10** 1/2 **Venus Grace**[140] 8084 3-9-0 0 JimCrowley 20 64
(Ralph Beckett) *racd stands' side: chsd ldr tl led ent fnl 2f: rdn and hdd over 1f out: wknd ins fnl f* **12/1**

6- **11** 3/4 **Spring Fling**[141] 8061 3-9-0 0 FergusSweeney 15 62
(Henry Candy) *racd stands' side: t.k.h: hld up in tch in midfield: rdn and no hdwy ent fnl 2f: wknd over 1f out* **10/1**

**12** 7 **Solar Moon** 3-9-0 0 MickaelBarzalona 16 44
(Charlie Appleby) *v free to post: racd stands' side: overall ldr tl ent fnl 2f: wknd over 1f out* **8/1**

**13** 3/4 **Dorraar (IRE)** 3-9-0 0 AndreaAtzeni 6 42
(Roger Varian) *racd stands' side: in tch towards rr: struggling 3f out: wl btn over 1f out* **25/1**

**14** 1/2 **Executrix** 3-9-0 0 RyanMoore 18 41
(Sir Michael Stoute) *racd stands' side: s.i.s: bhd: rdn over 2f out: sn btn* **16/1**

4 **15** nse **Ermine Ruby**[51] 741 3-9-0 0 JamieSpencer 2 41
(Charles Hills) *racd far side: in tch in midfield: rdn and effrt 2f out: no ex and btn over 1f out: wknd fnl f* **25/1**

54- **16** 1 1/2 **Sotise (IRE)**[132] 8175 3-8-9 0 DanielMuscutt(5) 14 37
(Marco Botti) *racd stands' side: in tch in midfield: rdn and struggling over 2f out: bhd over 1f out* **50/1**

0- **17** 7 **Popping Candy**[168] 7645 3-9-0 0 JackMitchell 11 19
(Roger Varian) *racd stands' side: t.k.h: hld up in rr: lost tch over 2f out* **66/1**

0- **18** nk **Emporium**[235] 5797 3-9-0 0 JFEgan 17 18
(Nick Littmoden) *racd stands' side: t.k.h: chsd ldrs early: steadily lost pl: rdn 3f out: sn wl btn: bhd over 1f out* **100/1**

045- **19** 1 1/2 **Wedding Wish (IRE)**[194] 7016 3-9-0 86 TomQueally 8 14
(Michael Bell) *racd stands' side: chsd ldrs: rdn and lost pl over 2f out: wl bhd and eased ins fnl f* **15/2**[3]

1m 24.8s (-0.60) **Going Correction** -0.05s/f (Good) **19** Ran SP% **124.9**
Speed ratings (Par 97): **101,99,99,99,97 97,96,94,92,92 91,83,82,81,81 80,72,71,69**
CSF £13.94 TOTE £4.80: £2.30, £1.90, £15.80; EX 15.40 Trifecta £1267.90.
**Owner** Hamdan Al Maktoum **Bred** Shadwell Estate Company Limited **Trained** Newmarket, Suffolk

**FOCUS**
No end of well bred, unexposed and unraced fillies, yet the two at the head of the market came to the fore late. There were many promising performances in behind and it's a race that should produce more than its share of winners. They split into two groups, with the much smaller bunch being on the far side, but looking at how they finished there was no advantage. The field was quiet compressed at the finish and, while the runner-up gives a bit of a guide to the level, the form is a little questionable.

## 1535 NEWMARKETRACECOURSES.CO.UK H'CAP (BOBIS RACE) 1m 2f

5:40 (5:44) (Class 3) (0-95,90) 3-Y-O **£9,703** (£2,887; £1,443; £721) **Stalls** Low

Form RPR

1- **1** **Cloudscape (IRE)**[136] 8123 3-9-2 85 WilliamBuick 3 103
(John Gosden) *trckd ldrs: rdn and effrt to chal 2f out: led over 1f out: styd on strly and asserted ins fnl f: rdn out* **7/4**[1]

1- **2** 3/4 **Windshear**[216] 6355 3-8-11 80 PatDobbs 5 96
(Richard Hannon) *led: jnd 3f out: rdn and hrd pressed 2f out: hdd over 1f out: stl ev ch tl no ex and btn fnl 75yds* **4/1**[2]

311- **3** 2 1/4 **Volume**[190] 7129 3-9-3 86 AndreaAtzeni 2 98
(Luca Cumani) *t.k.h: chsd ldrs: rdn and ev ch wl over 1f out: no ex 1f out: 3rd and outpcd fnl f* **13/2**

31- **4** 5 **Raven Ridge (IRE)**[197] 6938 3-9-2 85 TomQueally 9 88
(Michael Bell) *t.k.h: hld up in tch in midfield: rdn and unable qck whn edgd rt wl over 1f out: no threat to ldrs after: kpt on* **10/1**

2-11 **5** nse **Rudi Five One (FR)**[18] 1195 3-8-13 82 JimmyQuinn 6 84
(Robert Eddery) *hld up in last pair: rdn and effrt wl over 1f out: battling for 4th but no ch w ldrs over 1f out: kpt on* **12/1**

312- **6** 2 3/4 **Top Tug (IRE)**[197] 6935 3-9-2 85 RyanMoore 1 82
(Sir Michael Stoute) *in tch in midfield: rdn 3f out: sn struggling and outpcd over 2f out: 6th and wl hld over 1f out* **5/1**[3]

124- **7** nk **Rosehill Artist (IRE)**[166] 7695 3-9-2 85 JamieSpencer 8 82
(Charles Hills) *hld up in last pair: rdn and short-lived effrt over 2f out: wknd wl over 1f out* **40/1**

216- **8** 22 **Laugharne**[159] 7828 3-9-7 90 JamesDoyle 7 45
(Roger Charlton) *chsd ldr: clsd to join ldr 3f out tl rdn and lost pl qckly ent fnl 2f: t.o and eased ins fnl f* **12/1**

2m 3.87s (-1.93) **Going Correction** -0.05s/f (Good) **8** Ran SP% **113.3**
Speed ratings (Par 102): **105,104,102,98,98 96,96,78**
CSF £8.52 CT £35.18 TOTE £2.70: £1.20, £1.60, £1.80; EX 8.30 Trifecta £54.60.
**Owner** Lady Rothschild **Bred** Carwell Equities Ltd **Trained** Newmarket, Suffolk

**FOCUS**
A strong 3yo handicap that has thrown up a number of high-class performers, including Group 1 winner Wigmore Hall, Group 2 winners Papal Bull and Bronze Cannon, plus Derby runner-up Main Sequence. This year's contest looked a typical renewal, featuring a number of unexposed and promising performers, and the finish was fought out between two previously unbeaten runners. This again looks form to follow. The time was good versus the earlier sales race and the form has been rated positively, with the first two unexposed and the third progressive at two.
T/Plt: £165.00 to a £1 stake. Pool: £98,148.02 - 434.10 winning tickets. T/Qpdt: £7.50 to a £1 stake. Pool: £10,057.06 - 991.40 winning units. SP

# RIPON (R-H)

Thursday, April 17

**OFFICIAL GOING: Good (8.2)**

Wind: moderate 1/2 behind Weather: overcast, very cool, breezy, becoming fine

## 1536 EBF EAT SLEEP & DRINK AT NAGS HEAD PICKHILL MAIDEN STKS 5f

1:55 (1:57) (Class 5) 2-Y-O **£3,881** (£1,155; £577; £288) **Stalls** High

Form RPR

1 **Roudee** 2-9-5 0 ........ RichardKingscote 6 81+
(Tom Dascombe) *w ldr: led 2f out: kpt on wl towards fin* **4/1**[2]

2 *1* **Midterm Break (IRE)** 2-9-5 0 ........ GrahamGibbons 3 77
(David Barron) *chsd ldrs: styd on ins fnl f: tk 2nd nr fin* **11/2**[3]

3 *hd* **Collosium (IRE)** 2-9-0 0 ........ ConnorBeasley(5) 4 77
(Michael Dods) *mid-div: hdwy over 2f out: chsng ldrs over 1f out: kpt on same pce last 50yds* **16/1**

4 *5* **Elizabeth Flynn (IRE)** 2-9-0 0 ........ DanielTudhope 5 54
(K R Burke) *uns rdr and rn loose gng to s: chsd ldrs: swtchd rt over 1f out: wknd fnl 150yds* **20/1**

5 *1 3/4* **Reassert** 2-9-5 0 ........ DavidAllan 8 52+
(Tim Easterby) *chsd ldrs: wknd last 150yds* **11/2**[3]

6 *2* **Spirit Of Zeb (IRE)** 2-9-5 0 ........ TonyHamilton 2 45
(Richard Fahey) *dwlt: swtchd lft after s: in rr: sme hdwy over 1f out: nvr on terms* **15/2**

7 *3 1/2* **Sudest (IRE)** 2-9-5 0 ........ PaulMulrennan 1 33
(Kevin Ryan) *swvd bdly rt s: swtchd lft after s: in rr: sme hdwy over 1f out: sn wknd* **20/1**

8 *5* **Mistress Makfi (IRE)** 2-9-0 0 ........ FrannyNorton 7 10
(Mark Johnston) *dwlt: sn drvn along: outpcd after 1f: sn in rr* **25/1**

9 *2 1/2* **Mandarin Girl** 2-9-0 0 ........ SeanLevey 10
(Richard Hannon) *led: hdd 2f out: sn lost pl* **2/1**[1]

10 *7* **Magh Meall** 2-9-0 0 ........ AdrianNicholls 9
(David Nicholls) *uns rdr and rn loose gng to s: dwlt: v green and sn bhd* **33/1**

1m 0.57s (0.57) **Going Correction** -0.125s/f (Firm) **10** Ran SP% **118.1**
Speed ratings (Par 92): **90,88,88,80,77 74,68,60,56,45**
CSF £25.12 TOTE £3.60: £1.20, £2.10, £6.00; EX 27.80 Trifecta £245.90.
**Owner** Edwards Hughes Jenkins Roberts & Partner **Bred** Miss D Fleming **Trained** Malpas, Cheshire

**FOCUS**
Rail on bend from back to home straight moved out six metres, increasing distances on Round course by about 12yds. A couple of the more likely types on paper proved a little disappointing, but it's probably still best to view the first three, who came nicely clear, in a positive light.

## 1537 PPR FOUNDATION H'CAP (DIV I) 6f

2:30 (2:30) (Class 4) (0-85,83) 4-Y-O+ **£4,851** (£1,443; £721; £360) **Stalls** High

Form RPR

0-03 1 **Barkston Ash**[18] 1193 6-9-2 **81** ........(p) JasonHart(3) 5 96
(Eric Alston) *w ldr: led over 4f out: drvn over 2f out: hung rt over 1f out: styd on towards fin* **4/1**[3]

130- 2 *1 1/4* **Right Touch**[209] 6586 4-9-4 **83** ........ GeorgeChaloner(3) 6 94
(Richard Fahey) *chsd ldrs: 2nd over 3f out: upsides over 1f out: kpt on same pce last 75yds* **10/3**[1]

600- 3 *2 3/4* **Powerful Presence (IRE)**[188] 7176 8-9-6 **82** ........ DanielTudhope 9 84
(David O'Meara) *led over 1f: chsd ldrs: kpt on same pce over 1f out* **25/1**

065- 4 *2* **Duke Cosimo**[190] 7123 4-9-3 **79** ........ GrahamGibbons 8 75
(David Barron) *chsd ldrs: drvn over 2f out: kpt on one pce over 1f out* **4/1**[3]

255- 5 *3/4* **Lulu The Zulu (IRE)**[177] 7452 6-8-13 **75** ........ AndrewMullen 2 68
(Michael Appleby) *chsd ldrs: one pce fnl 2f* **7/2**[2]

10-6 6 *4 1/2* **Tajneed (IRE)**[8] 1375 11-8-8 **77** ........ AnnaHesketh(7) 7 56
(David Nicholls) *half-rrd s: sn chsng ldrs: outpcd over 2f out: grad wknd* **16/1**

0600 7 *5* **Naabegha**[19] 1164 7-9-4 **80** ........ WilliamCarson 4 43
(Alan McCabe) *s.s: nvr on terms* **9/1**

1-00 8 *6* **Mysterial**[18] 1190 4-8-13 **75** ........ DaleSwift 3 19
(Ruth Carr) *chsd ldrs: lost pl 2f out* **28/1**

300- 9 *1 1/4* **Dark Castle**[188] 7176 5-9-7 **83** ........ PJMcDonald 1 23
(Micky Hammond) *swvd lft s: hdwy to chse ldrs over 4f out: lost pl over 2f out* **11/1**

1m 11.33s (-1.67) **Going Correction** -0.125s/f (Firm) **9** Ran SP% **116.8**
Speed ratings (Par 105): **106,104,100,98,97 91,84,76,74**
CSF £18.00 CT £296.64 TOTE £5.80: £2.10, £1.30, £4.90; EX 19.70 Trifecta £240.10.
**Owner** The Selebians **Bred** Jonathan Shack **Trained** Longton, Lancs

**FOCUS**
The first division of a fairly useful sprint. As is often the case over this C&D a prominent position proved vital, the winner bagging the rail to make all. The winner has returned better than ever and the runner-up has been rated in line with his 3yo form.

## 1538 PPR FOUNDATION H'CAP (DIV II) 6f

3:05 (3:08) (Class 4) (0-85,83) 4-Y-O+ **£4,851** (£1,443; £721; £360) **Stalls** High

Form RPR

20-0 1 **Kimberella**[18] 1193 4-9-6 **82** ........ AdrianNicholls 3 96
(David Nicholls) *swtchd lft after s: mde all: t.k.h: drvn clr appr fnl f* **9/2**[2]

30-3 2 *4* **Red Refraction (IRE)**[13] 1275 4-9-6 **82** ........ SeanLevey 1 83
(Richard Hannon) *trckd ldrs: effrt over 1f out: styd on to take 2nd last 50yds* **10/1**

06-5 3 *3/4* **Adam's Ale**[5] 1447 5-8-11 **73** ........ PaulMulrennan 5 72
(Paul Midgley) *chsd wnr: kpt on same pce over 1f out* **5/1**[3]

240- 4 *1 1/2* **Green Howard**[177] 7452 6-9-4 **83** ........ JasonHart(3) 8 77
(Robin Bastiman) *strated slowly: sn drvn along: hdwy over 2f out: 4th appr fnl f: kpt on same pce* **7/1**

322- 5 *1 3/4* **Vallarta (IRE)**[199] 6900 4-8-11 **76** ........ WilliamTwiston-Davies(3) 9 64
(Mick Channon) *in rr: sme hdwy over 2f out: nvr a factor* **5/1**[3]

350- 6 *2* **Bonnie Charlie**[199] 6908 8-8-13 **75** ........ PaulQuinn 4 57
(David Nicholls) *mid-div: drvn over 2f out: wknd over 1f out* **28/1**

0-10 7 *3/4* **Klynch**[5] 1440 8-9-4 **80** ........(b) JamesSullivan 6 59
(Ruth Carr) *n.m.r sn after s: hdwy on wd outside over 2f out: wknd over 1f out* **11/2**

41/4 8 *4 1/2* **Compton Park**[18] 1190 7-9-5 **81** ........(t) DavidAllan 2 46
(Les Eyre) *dwlt: hld up in mid-div: drvn over 2f out: wknd over 1f out; b.b.v* **7/2**[1]

020- 9 *3 1/4* **Towbee**[183] 7314 5-8-10 **79** ........ DanielleMooney(7) 7 34
(Michael Easterby) *wnt rt s: sn trcking ldrs: n.m.r on inner over 2f out: hung rt and sn wknd* **33/1**

1m 11.66s (-1.34) **Going Correction** -0.125s/f (Firm) **9** Ran SP% **117.1**
Speed ratings (Par 105): **103,97,96,94,92 89,88,82,78**
CSF £49.31 CT £236.24 TOTE £4.60: £1.40, £2.20, £2.40; EX 46.80 Trifecta £349.90.
**Owner** C Titcomb **Bred** P And Mrs A G Venner **Trained** Sessay, N Yorks

**FOCUS**
A similar story to the first division, with a prominent position vital. The winner has been rated as running a personal best, with the runner-up a length off his 3yo form.

## 1539 RIPONBET SILVER BOWL H'CAP 1m 1f 170y

3:40 (3:40) (Class 3) (0-95,95) 4-Y-O+ **£7,762** (£2,310; £1,154; £577) **Stalls** Low

Form RPR

201- 1 **Wall Of Sound**[201] 6832 4-9-2 **90** ........ RichardKingscote 2 99+
(Tom Dascombe) *trckd ldrs: drvn 4f out: styd on to ld jst ins fnl f: styd on wl* **9/4**[1]

60-6 2 *1 1/4* **Maven**[18] 1196 6-8-9 **83** ........ GrahamGibbons 7 89
(Tim Easterby) *sn trcking ldr: led over 2f out: hdd jst ins fnl f: no ex* **9/2**[3]

046- 3 *nk* **Marcret (ITY)**[139] 8094 7-9-7 **95** ........ DanielTudhope 3 100+
(David O'Meara) *hld up in mid-div: hdwy on ins 4f out: nt clr run and hung rt over 2f out: swtchd lft over 1f out: kpt on to take 3rd nr line* **9/1**

00-0 4 *nk* **San Cassiano (IRE)**[18] 1196 7-8-3 **77** ........ JamesSullivan 4 82
(Ruth Carr) *led: hdd over 2f out: kpt on same pce over 1f out* **16/1**

36-0 5 *1 1/2* **Zeus Magic**[18] 1196 4-8-2 **76** oh2 ........[1] AndrewMullen 6 78
(Brian Ellison) *s.i.s: detached in last: hdwy over 3f out: one pce over 1f out* **14/1**

40-5 6 *1 3/4* **Ardmay (IRE)**[18] 1196 5-8-3 **82** ........(p) ShaneGray(5) 5 80
(Kevin Ryan) *t.k.h: trckd ldrs: stdd after 2f: effrt over 3f out: one pce fnl 2f* **10/1**

140- 7 *7* **King Of The Danes**[187] 7205 4-8-13 **87** ........ FrannyNorton 8 71
(Mark Johnston) *trckd ldrs after 3f: drvn over 3f out: lost pl over 1f out: eased clsng stages* **5/2**[2]

210- 8 *17* **Dance King**[194] 7028 4-8-4 **78** ........ DuranFentiman 1 27
(Tim Easterby) *in rr: pushed along over 5f out: bhd fnl 3f: eased ins fnl f* **16/1**

2m 4.45s (-0.95) **Going Correction** +0.125s/f (Good) **8** Ran SP% **115.0**
Speed ratings (Par 107): **108,107,106,106,105 103,98,84**
CSF £12.90 CT £75.21 TOTE £2.50: £1.10, £2.30, £2.60; EX 9.80 Trifecta £73.80.
**Owner** Chasemore Farm **Bred** A Black **Trained** Malpas, Cheshire

**FOCUS**
A fairly useful contest which appeared to be soundly run. The runner-up and fourth have been rated close to their best.

## 1540 RIPON "COCK O' THE NORTH" H'CAP (BOBIS RACE) 1m

4:15 (4:16) (Class 3) (0-90,86) 3-Y-O **£7,561** (£2,263; £1,131; £566; £282) **Stalls** Low

Form RPR

62-1 1 **Crystal Lake (IRE)**[19] 1173 3-8-10 **75** ........ RichardKingscote 5 89+
(Ralph Beckett) *trckd ldrs: drvn 3f out: led wl over 1f out: kpt on wl* **5/2**[1]

262- 2 *1* **Shot In The Sun (IRE)**[222] 6207 3-8-11 **76** ........ TonyHamilton 3 87
(Richard Fahey) *trckd ldrs: nt clr run over 2f out: swtchd lft: chsd wnr over 1f out: styd on towards fin* **10/1**

10-1 3 *4 1/2* **Grevillea (IRE)**[10] 1352 3-9-1 **83** 6ex ........ WilliamTwiston-Davies(3) 1 84
(Mick Channon) *dwlt: hld up: hdwy to chse ldrs over 2f out: 3rd over 1f out: kpt on one pce* **5/1**[2]

100- 4 *2 1/4* **Comino (IRE)**[173] 7529 3-9-3 **82** ........ PaulMulrennan 2 78
(Kevin Ryan) *led tl 3f out: led briefly 2f out: fdd over 1f out* **5/1**[2]

1- 5 *1/2* **Champagne Sydney (IRE)**[198] 6922 3-9-7 **86** ........ SeanLevey 6 81
(Richard Hannon) *hld up in rr: hdwy u.p 3f out: one pce over 1f out* **8/1**

233- 6 *6* **Snow Squall**[210] 6572 3-9-4 **83** ........ AndrewMullen 9 64
(Charlie Appleby) *dwlt: hld up in rr: hdwy 4f out: sn chsng ldrs: wknd over 2f out: hung rt over 1f out* **6/1**[3]

230- 7 *4 1/2* **Xanthos**[182] 7326 3-9-3 **82** ........ DanielTudhope 4 53
(Ed Walker) *w ldr: led narrowly 3f out: hdd 2f out: sn lost pl: bhd whn eased towards fin* **6/1**[3]

010- 8 *2 3/4* **Maid In Rio (IRE)**[186] 7221 3-8-6 **71** ........ FrannyNorton 7 35
(Mark Johnston) *chsd ldrs: drvn over 4f out: lost pl over 3f out: bhd whn eased ins fnl f* **33/1**

1m 41.75s (0.35) **Going Correction** +0.125s/f (Good) **8** Ran SP% **113.6**
Speed ratings (Par 102): **103,102,97,95,94 88,84,81**
CSF £28.59 CT £116.78 TOTE £3.40: £1.40, £2.50, £2.00; EX 24.60 Trifecta £77.70.
**Owner** The Pickford Hill Partnership **Bred** B Holland, S Hillen & J Cullinan **Trained** Kimpton, Hants

**FOCUS**
Form to view fairly positively, the leading pair drawing clear off a sound pace. There's scope for this to be rated a bit better.

## 1541 MALOSA MEDICAL APPRENTICE H'CAP (PART OF THE GO RACING IN YORKSHIRE FUTURE STARS SERIES) 5f

4:50 (4:50) (Class 4) (0-80,79) 4-Y-O+ **£4,851** (£1,443; £721; £360) **Stalls** High

Form RPR

000- 1 **Ruby's Day**[154] 7887 5-8-13 **76** ........ ClaireMurray(8) 8 83
(David Brown) *dwlt: sn drvn along: hdwy over 2f out: swtchd lft jst ins fnl f: styd on to ld post* **20/1**

026- 2 *shd* **Willbeme**[194] 7029 6-8-13 **71** ........ MeganCarberry(3) 9 78
(Neville Bycroft) *chsd ldrs: chal over 1f out: led jst ins fnl f: hdd post* **9/2**[3]

-610 3 *nk* **Expose**[54] 719 6-9-4 **78** ........ PaulMcGiff(5) 10 84
(Michael Appleby) *chsd ldrs: upsides ins fnl f: no ex nr fin* **3/1**[1]

14-5 4 *hd* **Waseem Faris (IRE)**[3] 1489 5-9-6 **78** ........ DanielCremin(3) 11 83
(Mick Channon) *uns rdr and rn loose gng to s: hld up in rr: hdwy over 2f out: chsng ldrs ins fnl f: no ex clsng stages* **4/1**[2]

00-0 5 *3/4* **Mon Brav**[18] 1190 7-8-12 **75** ........ KevinLundie(8) 5 77+
(Brian Ellison) *in rr on outer: sn drvn along: hdwy over 2f out: kpt on same pce ins fnl f* **11/1**

6-66 6 *2 1/4* **Majestic Manannan (IRE)**[76] 412 5-9-1 **70** ........(p) KevinStott 7 64
(David Nicholls) *led: hdd jst ins fnl f: sn wknd* **9/1**

4164 7 *1 3/4* **Sir Geoffrey (IRE)**[15] 1244 8-8-10 **68** ........(p) MatthewHopkins(3) 2 56
(Scott Dixon) *chsd ldr: one pce appr fnl f* **12/1**

000- 8 *2 3/4* **Medici Time**[197] 6948 9-8-6 **69** ........ RachelRichardson(8) 1 47
(Tim Easterby) *sn bhd: kpt on appr fnl f: nvr on terms* **12/1**

0-00 9 *2 1/4* **Mister Manannan (IRE)**[84] 299 7-9-1 **78** ........(v[1]) AnnaHesketh(8) 4 48
(David Nicholls) *s.s: swtchd lft after s: hdwy over 3f out: lost pl over 1f out* **9/1**

000- **10** 3 1/4 **First In Command (IRE)**162 7777 9-9-0 79..............(t) LouiseDay(10) 3 37
(Daniel Mark Loughnane) *mid-div: hdwy on outer over 2f out: hung lft and lost pl over 1f out* **33/1**

59.49s (-0.51) **Going Correction** -0.125s/f (Firm) **10** Ran SP% **114.6**
Speed ratings (Par 105): **99,98,98,98,96 93,90,86,82,77**
CSF £106.11 CT £315.35 TOTE £22.90: £4.90, £1.60, £1.40; EX 154.10 Trifecta £536.50.
**Owner** Mrs Rachael Archer **Bred** A Archer Electrical Ltd **Trained** Averham Park, Notts

**FOCUS**
A run-of-the-mill apprentice event. The leaders went off hard and there was a blanket finish. The form looks ordinary, with the first three close to last year's form.

## 1542 SIS LIVE MAIDEN STKS 1m
5:25 (5:27) (Class 5) 3-Y-O £3,234 (£962; £481; £240) Stalls Low

Form RPR
4- **1** **Yenhaab (IRE)**230 5941 3-9-5 0.............................. HarryBentley 12 85+
(William Haggas) *swtchd rt after s: sn chsng ldr: effrt 3f out: chal over 1f out: styd on to ld last 150yds* **5/6**1

**2** 1 3/4 **Lord Of The Nile (IRE)**202 6813 3-9-5 0.................. DanielTudhope 3 81
(David O'Meara) *set str pce: drvn over 2f out: hdd and no ex ins fnl f* **5/2**2

0- **3** 5 **Master Clockmaker (IRE)**204 6754 3-9-5 0.................. PJMcDonald 8 70
(Ann Duffield) *chsd ldrs: 3rd after 1f: kpt on same pce fnl 3f* **50/1**

30 **4** 1 1/2 **Nothing Special**9 1357 3-9-0 0.............................. RichardKingscote 7 61
(Tom Dascombe) *mid-div: hdwy and 4th 3f out: one pce* **22/1**

44- **5** 7 **Twin Appeal (IRE)**167 7664 3-9-5 0.......................... GrahamGibbons 13 50
(David Barron) *swtchd rt after s: hld up in rr: hdwy over 2f out: nvr a factor* **8/1**

4 **6** 2 3/4 **My Escapade (IRE)**9 1361 3-8-9 0.......................... GarryWhillans(5) 4 39
(Simon Waugh) *in tch: drvn over 4f out: nvr a factor* **66/1**

0- **7** 1/2 **Minionette (IRE)**174 7493 3-9-0 0.............................. BenCurtis 5 37
(Alan Swinbank) *mid-div: kpt on fnl 2f: nvr nr ldrs* **66/1**

0 **8** 1/2 **To Begin**18 1192 3-9-0 0.............................. AdamCarter(5) 10 41
(Tim Easterby) *s.i.s: sme hdwy over 2f out: nvr on terms* **66/1**

**9** 2 1/4 **Mendelita** 3-9-0 0.............................. DavidNolan 11 31
(Richard Fahey) *s.s: detached in rr: sme hdwy over 2f out: nvr on terms* **16/1**

0- **10** 3 1/2 **Solid Justice (IRE)**192 7069 3-9-0 0.......................... JoeyHaynes(5) 9 28
(Jason Ward) *hld up in rr: sme hdwy over 2f out: nvr on terms* **40/1**

20- **11** 2 **Craggaknock**259 4925 3-9-2 0.............................. JasonHart(3) 1 24
(Mark Walford) *chsd ldrs: 4th after 1f: drvn over 4f out: hung rt and lost pl over 2f out* **15/2**3

56- **12** 4 1/2 **Sleet (IRE)**109 8435 3-9-5 0.............................. AndrewMullen 6 13
(Michael Appleby) *in tch: hung rt and lost pl 3f out* **66/1**

**13** 2 **Im Dapper Too** 3-9-5 0.............................. TomEaves 2 9
(John Davies) *hld up in rr: bhd fnl 4f* **66/1**

1m 41.89s (0.49) **Going Correction** +0.125s/f (Good) **13** Ran SP% **128.1**
Speed ratings (Par 98): **102,100,95,93,86 84,83,83,80,77 75,70,68**
CSF £3.09 TOTE £1.80: £1.10, £1.10, £10.10; EX 4.70 Trifecta £108.30.
**Owner** Essafinaat & Qatar Racing **Bred** Albert Conneally **Trained** Newmarket, Suffolk

**FOCUS**
They went a good pace for a maiden, the field being well strung out from an early stage and the leading pair dominated throughout. The raced lacked depth. The first two have been rated as improving a stone on their 2yo runs.

## 1543 RIPONBET PLACE 6 H'CAP 6f
5:55 (5:55) (Class 5) (0-75,74) 3-Y-O £3,234 (£962; £481; £240) Stalls High

Form RPR
453- **1** **Two Shades Of Grey (IRE)**198 6914 3-8-8 61............ TonyHamilton 8 70
(Richard Fahey) *chsd ldrs on inner: chal over 1f out: led jst ins fnl f: drvn and styd on strly* **9/2**1

1- **2** 2 1/2 **Tea Leaf (IRE)**239 5635 3-9-0 74.............................. JaneElliott(7) 9 75
(Ralph Beckett) *in rr: hdwy 2f out: styd on to take 2nd nr line* **7/1**3

050- **3** hd **Lorimer's Lot (IRE)**244 5468 3-9-1 71.......................... JasonHart(3) 5 71
(Mark Walford) *swtchd lft after s: led: hdd jst ins fnl f: kpt on same pce* **11/2**2

564- **4** 2 **Injaz**161 7789 3-8-12 65.............................. PaulMulrennan 6 59
(Kevin Ryan) *s.i.s: sn chsng ldrs: rdn and wnt rt over 1f out: kpt on same pce* **10/1**

-131 **5** 2 3/4 **First Experience**34 957 3-9-5 72.............................. ChrisCatlin 3 57
(Rae Guest) *hmpd s: sn mid-div: one pce fnl 2f* **12/1**

366- **6** 3 1/2 **Margrets Gift**190 7126 3-9-0 67.............................. DavidAllan 7 41
(Tim Easterby) *chsd ldrs: drvn over 2f out: wknd appr fnl f* **8/1**

202- **7** 3/4 **Sartori**191 7096 3-8-13 66.............................. RussKennemore 10 38
(Marjorie Fife) *stdd s: hld up in rr: hdwy over 1f out: nvr a factor* **8/1**

440- **8** 3/4 **Native Falls (IRE)**178 7418 3-8-12 65.......................... BenCurtis 2 34
(Alan Swinbank) *t.k.h: sn trcking ldrs: wkng whn hmpd over 1f out* **20/1**

200- **9** 2 **Secret Kode (IRE)**184 7261 3-8-9 62.......................... WilliamCarson 11 25
(Simon Waugh) *in rr: sn pushed along: hdwy over 2f out: wknd over 1f out* **16/1**

4-03 **10** 1/2 **Lady In Blue (IRE)**35 936 3-8-11 67..........................(v) SamJames(3) 1 28
(David O'Meara) *chsd ldrs: weakwning whn hmpd over 1f out* **11/1**

50-2 **11** 19 **False Witness (IRE)**10 1347 3-9-1 68.......................... AdrianNicholls 4
(David Nicholls) *wnt rt s: chsd ldrs: drvn over 2f out: sn lost pl: bhd whn hung rt ins fnl f: heavily eased* **15/2**

1m 13.54s (0.54) **Going Correction** -0.125s/f (Firm) **11** Ran SP% **115.8**
Speed ratings (Par 98): **91,87,87,84,81 76,75,74,71,71 45**
CSF £34.92 CT £177.12 TOTE £6.50: £1.80, £1.90, £2.70; EX 50.80 Trifecta £380.80.
**Owner** McCreary, Harrison, Astrop & Partner **Bred** Martin Donovan **Trained** Musley Bank, N Yorks

**FOCUS**
Another race over this C&D which was dominated by those who raced prominently towards the rail. The runner-up has been rated as matching her debut effort.
T/Plt: £81.80 to a £1 stake. Pool: £68,937.39 - 614.92 winning units. T/Qpdt: £13.10 to a £1 stake. Pool: £7,723.26 - 433.222 winning units. WG

1544 - 1550a (Foreign Racing) - See Raceform Interactive

# 1480 LONGCHAMP (R-H)
Thursday, April 17

**OFFICIAL GOING: Turf: good**

## 1551a PRIX DU MUSEE CARNAVALET (MAIDEN) (3YO COLTS & GELDINGS) (TURF) 7f
1:20 (12:00) 3-Y-O £10,416 (£4,166; £3,125; £2,083; £1,041)

RPR
**1** **Helwan (FR)**191 3-9-2 0.............................. FrankieDettori 4 89
(J-F Bernard, France) **21/10**1

**2** 1 1/2 **Sailing Club (USA)**218 3-9-2 0.............................. GregoryBenoist 2 85
(D Smaga, France) **4/1**3

**3** nse **Silver Treasure (FR)**147 7994 3-9-2 0.......................... IoritzMendizabal 8 85
(Amy Weaver) *hld up in midfield: pushed along and hdwy on outer fr 2f out: rdn and wnt 3rd ins fnl f: r.o wl but nt pce of wnr: almost snatched 2nd post* **16/5**2

**4** 1 1/4 **Itoobeboss (IRE)**149 7967 3-9-2 0.......................... StephanePasquier 3 82
(Rod Collet, France) **23/5**

**5** 1 1/4 **Diamant De Vati (FR)**48 795 3-9-2 0.......................... TheoBachelot 7 78
(S Wattel, France) **146/10**

**6** 3/4 **Levoila (FR)** 3-9-2 0..............................(b) JulienAuge 5 76
(L Larrigade, France) **166/10**

**7** 1 1/2 **Mr Hawk (FR)** 3-8-13 0.............................. UmbertoRispoli 9 69
(Yannick Fouin, France) **31/1**

**8** 1 3/4 **Little Rainbow (FR)**47 3-9-2 0.............................. GeraldMosse 1 67
(V Luka Jr, Czech Republic) **30/1**

**9** 1 1/2 **Split Step** 3-8-13 0..............................(p) FabriceVeron 6 60
(H-A Pantall, France) **131/10**

1m 22.92s (2.22) **9** Ran SP% **119.5**
WIN (incl. 1 euro stake): 3.10. PLACES: 1.30, 1.40, 1.40. DF: 7.20. SF: 11.80.
**Owner** Al Shaqab Racing **Bred** Mme G Forien & G Forien **Trained** France

1552 - (Foreign Racing) - See Raceform Interactive

# 1386 LINGFIELD (L-H)
Friday, April 18

**OFFICIAL GOING: Standard**
Wind: light, half against Weather: dry, bright spells

## 1553 CORAL.CO.UK ALL-WEATHER CHAMPIONSHIPS APPRENTICE H'CAP 1m 4f (P)
1:45 (1:48) (Class 2) (0-105,97) 4-Y-O+
£31,125 (£9,320; £4,660; £2,330; £1,165; £585) Stalls Low

Form RPR
0-52 **1** **Viewpoint (IRE)**13 1299 5-9-3 92.............................. CamHardie(3) 2 103
(Richard Hannon) *chsd ldrs: effrt to chse ldng pair 2f out: rdn to ld ent fnl f: kpt on and a jst holding on towards fin: rdn out* **5/1**3

5122 **2** nk **Grendisar (IRE)**20 1171 4-9-10 97..........................(p) DanielMuscutt 4 107
(Marco Botti) *hld up in midfield: effrt to chse ldrs wl over 1f out: chsd wnr ins fnl f: kpt on wl towards fin but nvr quite getting to wnr* **7/2**1

4224 **3** 3 **Mica Mika (IRE)**19 1196 6-8-2 77..........................(p) SammyJoBell(3) 8 82
(Richard Fahey) *chsd ldr: rdn and effrt to press ldr on inner wl over 1f out: no ex u.p 1f out: outpcd fnl 100yds* **20/1**

-226 **4** 3/4 **Aryal**20 1171 4-8-8 81..............................(b) MichaelJMMurphy 1 85
(Mark Johnston) *led: stl travelling wl ent fnl 2f: rdn over 1f out: hdd ent fnl f: sn no ex and outpcd fnl 100yds* **15/2**

6514 **5** 2 1/2 **Lady Lunchalot (USA)**4 1493 4-8-0 76.................. CharlotteJenner(3) 7 76
(Laura Mongan) *hld up in rr of main gp: effrt on outer over 2f out: lost pl bnd 2f out: wnt 5th 1f out: styd on but no threat to ldrs* **20/1**

11-1 **6** 1/2 **Asia Minor (IRE)**75 450 5-8-1 76..........................(t) JackGarritty(3) 3 75
(Dr Jon Scargill) *hld up in rr of main gp: clsd and wl in tch but stuck bhd horses over 2f out: effrt u.p wl over 1f out: no imp* **10/1**

2416 **7** 1 **Commissar**13 1299 5-8-10 82..........................(t) GeorgeDowning 6 79
(Ian Williams) *in tch in midfield: hdwy to chse ldrs 4f out: rdn: edgd lft and unable qck ent fnl 2f: sn outpcd and no threat to ldrs over 1f out* **16/1**

2214 **8** 2 1/4 **Honoured (IRE)**10 1366 7-8-12 84..........................(t) OisinMurphy 10 78
(Michael Appleby) *chsd ldrs: rdn and outpcd ent fnl 2f: wknd u.p over 1f out* **20/1**

3112 **9** 1/2 **Scottish Star**27 1071 6-8-11 83.............................. RyanTate 9 76
(James Eustace) *in tch in midfield: short of room and lost pl jst over 2f out: sn rdn and struggling: wknd over 1f out* **9/2**2

4111 **10** 6 **The Lock Master (IRE)**22 1128 7-9-4 93............ AlistairRawlinson(3) 5 76
(Michael Appleby) *t.k.h: hld up in tch in midfield: dropped to rr and u.p 4f out: lost tch 2f out* **14/1**

5-25 **11** 11 **Icebuster**78 386 6-8-12 84.............................. ShelleyBirkett 11 50
(Rod Millman) *v.s.a and lost many l: steadily rcvrd and in tch in rr 8f out: rdn and struggling over 3f out: wl bhd fnl 2f* **7/1**

2m 28.38s (-4.62) **Going Correction** -0.15s/f (Stan)
**WFA** 4 from 5yo+ 1lb **11** Ran SP% **117.3**
Speed ratings (Par 109): **109,108,106,106,104 104,103,102,101,97 90**
CSF £21.98 CT £314.71 TOTE £6.00: £2.70, £1.40, £5.20; EX 18.60 Trifecta £586.30.
**Owner** The Heffer Syndicate **Bred** F Dunne **Trained** East Everleigh, Wilts

**FOCUS**
£1 million in prize-money up for grabs for the inaugural running of All-Weather Finals day, and on the first day that racing took place in Britain on Good Friday. The only handicap on the card and one confined to apprentices, but a very useful event and, although improving types were thin on the ground, the gallop was an even one and the first two deserve credit for pulling clear late on. The winner came down the centre in the straight. The sectional times were: first 2f (25.70), 4f (50.33s), 6f (1m14.88), 1m (1m40.00), 1m2f (2m04.31) with a finishing time of 2m28.29. The winner did well to split unexposed rivals last time out and this performance confirmed the merit of that run.

## 1554 32RED.COM ALL-WEATHER FILLIES' AND MARES' CHAMPIONSHIPS CONDITIONS STKS 7f 1y(P)
2:20 (2:22) (Class 2) 4-Y-O+
£93,375 (£27,960; £13,980; £6,990; £3,495; £1,755) Stalls Low

Form RPR
0213 **1** **Living The Life (IRE)**30 1020 4-9-0 78..........................(v) AdamKirby 8 90
(Phil McEntee) *mde all: rdn and kicked 3 l clr ent fnl 2f: in command after: rdn out* **8/1**3

5511 **2** 3 1/2 **High Time Too (IRE)**16 1234 4-9-0 77.......................... RyanMoore 6 81
(Hugo Palmer) *chsd wnr thrght: rdn and outpcd whn wnr qcknd ent fnl 2f: kpt on but no imp after* **3/1**1

3512 **3** nk **Maggie Pink**38 917 5-9-0 80.............................. AndrewMullen 3 80
(Michael Appleby) *taken down early: chsd ldng pair: rdn and outpcd whn wnr qcknd 2f out: no ch w wnr after: styd on fnl 100yds and pressing for 2nd cl home* **7/1**2

-114 **4** 1 **Fashion Line (IRE)**41 887 4-9-0 88.......................... JamieSpencer 11 77+
(Michael Bell) *hld up in midfield: n.m.r and shuffled bk jst over 2f out: hdwy u.p over 1f out: wnt 4th ins fnl f: styd on but no ch w wnr* **3/1**1

111- **5** 1/2 **Interception (IRE)**141 8088 4-9-0 84.......................... TedDurcan 14 76+
(David Lanigan) *mounted on crse: dropped in bhd after s: hld up in last pair: stl last 2f out: hdwy ent fnl f: impossible task but r.o strly fnl100yds: nvr trbld ldrs* **7/1**2

-201 **6** *nk* **Fanoos**[29] 1026 5-9-0 78....(p) RichardKingscote 10 75+
(Dr Jon Scargill) *taken down early: s.i.s and bustled along early: hld up in last pair: nt clr run ent fnl 2f: hdwy wl over 1f out: r.o wl ins fnl f: nvr trbld ldrs* **10/1**

1124 **7** *1 ½* **Fab Lolly (IRE)**[23] 1102 4-9-0 79....(p) JoeFanning 1 71
(James Bethell) *hld up in tch in midfield: effrt on inner but immediately outpcd 2f out: wnt 4th over 1f out but no prog after: wknd ins fnl f* **20/1**

3-35 **8** *shd* **Princess Spirit**[9] 1392 5-9-0 59....(p) JenniferFerguson 4 71?
(Edward Creighton) *in tch in midfield: rdn and outpcd 2f out: trying to rally and swtchd lft 1f out: kpt on same pce after* **100/1**

1126 **9** *1* **Welsh Sunrise**[17] 1217 4-9-0 75.... JamesDoyle 9 68
(Stuart Williams) *hld up in tch towards rr: sme hdwy jst over 2f out: drvn and no hdwy over 1f out: wl hld whn n.m.r ins fnl f* **25/1**

-201 **10** *nk* **Glastonberry**[46] 820 6-9-0 78.... GrahamLee 2 68+
(Geoffrey Deacon) *hld up in tch towards rr: sme hdwy on inner over 1f out: no threat to wnr whn hmpd jst ins fnl f: nvr trbld ldrs* **20/1**

20-2 **11** *½* **Oasis Spirit**[25] 1080 4-9-0 72....(v) OisinMurphy 5 66
(Andrew Balding) *t.k.h: chsd ldrs: 4th and outpcd wl over 1f out: racd awkwardly u.p and btn 1f out: fdd fnl 150yds* **20/1**

2332 **12** *5* **Hannahs Turn**[16] 1247 4-9-0 84.... LukeMorris 12 53+
(Chris Dwyer) *taken down early: hld up in tch towards rr but stuck wd: rdn ent fnl 2f: wknd over 1f out* **16/1**

0601 **13** *3 ¾* **Bold Ring**[23] 1110 8-9-0 58.... KierenFallon 7 44
(Edward Creighton) *chsd ldrs: rdn and lost pl ent fnl 2f: wknd over 1f out* **66/1**

2-15 **14** *2 ¾* **Burren View Lady (IRE)**[82] 348 4-9-0 82....(e) GrahamGibbons 13 36
(Tim Easterby) *wl in tch in midfield: hdwy to chse ldrs on outer 4f out: rdn 2f out: sn btn and bhd over 1f out* **14/1**

1m 22.84s (-1.96) **Going Correction** -0.15s/f (Stan) **14 Ran SP% 128.4**
Speed ratings (Par 96): **105,101,100,99,98 98,96,96,95,95 94,89,84,81**
CSF £31.91 CT £188.92 TOTE £11.70: £3.50, £1.20, £3.00; EX 45.30 Trifecta £392.50.
**Owner** Henry R Nothhaft **Bred** Michael Begley **Trained** Newmarket, Suffolk

**FOCUS**
A clutch of progressive sorts in a useful event for fillies. The gallop was just an ordinary one though (sectional times: first 2f (24.47s), 4f (48.71s), 6f (1m10.71) and a finishing time of 1m22.69s) and those held up were at a big disadvantage. The enterprisingly ridden winner raced against the far rail in the straight. He has been rated as running a personal best, but perhaps it shouldn't be taken too literally.

## 1555 32RED ALL-WEATHER 3 YEAR OLD CHAMPIONSHIPS CONDITIONS STKS (BOBIS RACE) 7f 1y(P)
**2:55** (2:58) (Class 2) 3-Y-O

**£93,375** (£27,960; £13,980; £6,990; £3,495; £1,755) **Stalls** Low

Form RPR

21-1 **1** **Ertijaal (IRE)**[27] 1067 3-9-5 100.... PaulHanagan 4 105+
(William Haggas) *bmpd s: sn bustled along and rcvrd to chse ldrs: nt clr run ent fnl 2f: rdn and qcknd smartly to ld 1f out: flashed tail but r.o wl fnl f: a holding runner-up* **4/5**[1]

111 **2** *¾* **Passing Star**[22] 1122 3-9-5 89.... RobertWinston 2 103
(Charles Hills) *hld up in tch in midfield: hdwy on inner to chal ent fnl f: ev ch fnl thrght fnl f: r.o but a hld by wnr* **7/1**[2]

1116 **3** *2* **Pool House**[27] 1067 3-9-5 93.... DavidProbert 10 98
(Andrew Balding) *in tch in midfield: effrt u.p wl over 1f out: styd on u.p to snatch 3rd on post* **25/1**

223 **4** *nse* **American Hope (USA)**[13] 1300 3-9-5 99.... ShaneKelly 3 98
(Mike Murphy) *broke wl: stdd bk to chse ldrs and t.k.h: wnt 2nd and shifted rt 2f out: drvn and ev ch over 1f out: outpcd and btn fnl 100yds: lost 2nd on post* **10/1**[3]

12-4 **5** *3 ¼* **Sir Robert Cheval**[27] 1067 3-9-5 95.... RyanMoore 5 90
(Marco Botti) *wnt lft s: wl in tch in midfield: rdn and outpcd over 1f out: no threat to ldrs but kpt on again u.p fnl 100yds* **7/1**[2]

0-10 **6** *nk* **Alutiq (IRE)**[27] 1067 3-9-0 95.... JamieSpencer 14 84+
(Eve Johnson Houghton) *pushed rt s: in tch towards rr: sme hdwy ent fnl 2f: drvn wl over 1f out: styd on u.p fnl f: nvr trbld ldrs* **16/1**

4-16 **7** *1 ¼* **Lady Frances**[49] 778 3-9-0 90.... JoeFanning 11 81
(Mark Johnston) *chsd ldr tl 2f out: sn carried rt and unable qck: outpcd and btn over 1f out: wknd ins fnl f* **50/1**

1-11 **8** *¾* **Captain Secret**[22] 1136 3-9-0 95.... AdamKirby 7 79
(Marco Botti) *led: drvn and hrd pressed wl over 1f out: hdd and hmpd 1f out: sn btn and wknd ins fnl f* **20/1**

-212 **9** *½* **Harwoods Volante (IRE)**[44] 850 3-9-5 92.... RobertHavlin 15 82
(Amanda Perrett) *s.i.s: in tch towards rr: rdn and sme hdwy over 1f out: no imp fnl f* **50/1**

-133 **10** *nk* **Major Crispies**[27] 1067 3-9-5 97.... RyanTate 12 81
(James Eustace) *stdd and shifted rt s: hld up in rr: stl plenty to do whn effrt wl over 1f out: sn intimidated by rivals whip and clipped heels: styd on fnl f: nvr trbld ldrs* **33/1**

211- **11** *½* **Complicit (IRE)**[136] 8143 3-9-5 95.... GrahamLee 6 80
(Paul Cole) *in tch in midfield but stuck wd: lost pl and dropped towards rr 2f out: plugged on but n.d after* **14/1**

435 **12** *6* **Golden Amber (IRE)**[49] 778 3-9-0 89....[1] JimCrowley 9 60
(Dean Ivory) *in tch towards rr: effrt on inner wl over 1f out: no real imp and wl hld 1f out: wknd* **66/1**

-210 **13** *2* **Oriental Relation (IRE)**[27] 1067 3-9-5 92....(b) TomQueally 8 59
(James Given) *t.k.h: hdwy to press ldrs on outer after 2f: struggling and rdn ent fnl 2f: wknd over 1f out* **100/1**

-430 **14** *1 ¼* **Steventon Star**[27] 1067 3-9-5 97....(p) KierenFallon 16 56
(Alan Bailey) *sltly hmpd s and s.i.s: nvr travelling in rr: n.d* **50/1**

1m 23.19s (-1.61) **Going Correction** -0.15s/f (Stan) **14 Ran SP% 122.1**
Speed ratings (Par 104): **103,102,99,99,96 95,94,93,92,92 91,85,82,81**
CSF £6.11 CT £92.42 TOTE £1.90: £1.10, £1.90, £5.30; EX 8.30 Trifecta £91.90.
**Owner** Hamdan Al Maktoum **Bred** Shadwell Estate Company Limited **Trained** Newmarket, Suffolk

**FOCUS**
Several very useful sorts on show but, although the betting suggested this was a one-sided event, the smart winner had to work hard to maintain his unbeaten record on Polytrack. The gallop was a reasonable one (sectional times: first 2f (23.91s), 4f (47.43s), 6f (1m10.79) and finishing time of 1m23.12) and the leaders didn't get home. The winner raced centre to far side in the straight. This was basically a reworking of a C&D Listed event held here last month, with the winner, third, fourth and fifth all from that race.

## 1556 32RED CASINO ALL-WEATHER MARATHON CHAMPIONSHIPS CONDITIONS STKS 1m 7f 169y(P)
**3:30** (3:32) (Class 2) 4-Y-O+

**£93,375** (£27,960; £13,980; £6,990; £3,495; £1,755) **Stalls** Low

Form RPR

21-1 **1** **Litigant**[48] 803 6-9-5 96.... GeorgeBaker 8 104
(Seamus Durack) *chsd ldrs: wnt 2nd and kicked clr of field 2f out: drvn and chal ins fnl f: r.o to ld towards fin* **2/1**[1]

14-1 **2** *½* **Arch Villain (IRE)**[86] 285 5-9-5 94....(b) JimCrowley 12 103
(Amanda Perrett) *dwlt and rdn along leaving stalls: sn rcvrd to chse ldr: led over 2f out: rdn and kicked on w wnr 2f out: drvn over 1f out: hdd and no ex towards fin* **8/1**

-234 **3** *4* **Communicator**[48] 803 6-9-5 90.... OisinMurphy 6 98
(Andrew Balding) *hld up in last trio: switching out rt over 2f out: rdn and effrt over 1f out: styd on wl ins fnl f to go 3rd fnl 75yds: no threat to ldng pair* **8/1**

1251 **4** *¾* **Castilo Del Diablo (IRE)**[18] 1213 5-9-5 98....(p) JamieSpencer 14 97
(David Simcock) *stdd and dropped in bhd after s: in tch in rr: hdwy on outer ent fnl 2f: edgd lft but styd on wl u.p fnl f: wnt 4th fnl 75yds: no threat to ldng pair* **11/2**[3]

-114 **5** *¾* **Villa Royale**[27] 1071 5-9-0 88.... AndrewMullen 11 91
(Michael Appleby) *in tch in midfield: rdn along over 4f out: hdwy to chse ldrs over 2f out: outpcd and drvn 2f out: wnt 3rd 1f out: no imp and lost 2 pls fnl 75yds* **25/1**

2035 **6** *3 ¼* **Swing Alone (IRE)**[13] 1299 5-9-5 96.... LukeMorris 1 93
(Gay Kelleway) *hld up towards rr: sme hdwy over 2f out: drvn and no imp over 1f out: plugged on same pce after* **20/1**

-330 **7** *½* **Duchess Of Gazeley (IRE)**[18] 1213 4-8-10 86.... JimmyQuinn 10 87
(Dean Ivory) *in tch in midfield: stuck bhd rivals over 2f out: rdn and effrt over 1f out: no imp fnl f* **33/1**

3115 **8** *¾* **Blue Wave (IRE)**[35] 956 4-9-1 102.... AdamKirby 13 91
(Mark Johnston) *chsd ldr: wnt 3rd 2f out: sn drvn and outpcd by ldng pair: wknd ins fnl f* **13/2**

4060 **9** *2 ¼* **Presburg (IRE)**[20] 1171 5-9-5 83.... JamesDoyle 2 88
(Joseph Tuite) *in tch in midfield: swtchd lft and effrt towards inner over 1f out: no imp: wknd ins fnl f* **40/1**

0013 **10** *3* **Mr Burbidge**[9] 1383 6-9-5 88....(b) LiamKeniry 3 85
(Neil Mulholland) *chsd ldrs tl drvn and outpcd 2f out: btn over 1f out: fdd ins fnl f* **66/1**

-111 **11** *4* **King's Request (IRE)**[28] 1043 4-9-1 76.... LiamJones 9 80
(Laura Mongan) *in tch in midfield: rdn and struggling over 2f out: bhd fnl f* **50/1**

-124 **12** *5* **Hunting Ground (USA)**[13] 1299 4-9-1 96.... JoeFanning 5 74
(Mark Johnston) *led tl hdd and drvn over 2f out: wknd ent fnl 2f: bhd fnl f* **5/1**[2]

5131 **13** *17* **Arr' Kid (USA)**[24] 1091 4-9-1 90....(b) TomEaves 4 54
(Keith Dalgleish) *dwlt and rdn along early: in tch towards rr: rdn 4f out: sn struggling: lost tch 2f out: t.o fnl f* **33/1**

-114 **14** *10* **Masterful Act (USA)**[50] 764 7-9-5 98.... TomQueally 7 42
(Alan McCabe) *in tch in midfield: rdn 5f out: bhd over 2f out: t.o fnl f* **33/1**

3m 17.3s (-8.40) **Going Correction** -0.15s/f (Stan)
**WFA** 4 from 5yo+ 4lb **14 Ran SP% 124.3**
Speed ratings (Par 109): **115,114,112,112,112 110,110,109,108,107 105,102,94,89**
CSF £17.88 CT £114.17 TOTE £2.80: £1.20, £3.00, £3.10; EX 22.20 Trifecta £125.40.
**Owner** A A Byrne **Bred** Darley **Trained** Baydon, Wilts

**FOCUS**
Several last-time out winners in a very useful conditions event. The gallop was an ordinary one (sectionals: first 2f (22.93), 4f (48.41), 6f (1m13.88), 1m (1m39.89), 1m2f (2m04.95), 1m4f (2m29.50), 1m6f (2m53.12) and finishing time of 3m17.16) and this suited the prominent-racers. The first two pulled clear turning for home and the winner came down the centre in the straight. The form makes a fair bit of sense among the front four.

## 1557 BOOKMAKERS.CO.UK ALL-WEATHER SPRINT CHAMPIONSHIPS CONDITIONS STKS 6f 1y(P)
**4:05** (4:08) (Class 2) 4-Y-O+

**£93,375** (£27,960; £13,980; £6,990; £3,495; £1,755) **Stalls** Low

Form RPR

0125 **1** **Alben Star (IRE)**[41] 886 6-9-5 100.... PaulHanagan 7 110
(Richard Fahey) *hld up in midfield: clsd on ldrs and gng wl whn nt clr run 2f out: hdwy u.p 1f out: chsd clr ldr fnl 100yds: r.o strly to ld last strides* **25/1**

2121 **2** *hd* **Trinityelitedotcom (IRE)**[20] 1172 4-9-5 101.... RichardKingscote 5 109
(Tom Dascombe) *led: rdn and qcknd clr over 1f out: 3 l clr ins fnl f: kpt on but hdd and no ex last strides* **5/1**[2]

-212 **3** *½* **Rivellino**[55] 713 4-9-5 104.... DanielTudhope 13 108
(K R Burke) *hld up off the pce in midfield: clsd ent fnl 2f: swtchd rt wl over 1f out: swtchd lft and hdwy ent fnl f: wnt 3rd wl ins fnl f: r.o strly and pressing ldrs cl home* **10/1**

2-40 **4** *3* **Hawkeyethenoo (IRE)**[55] 713 8-9-5 103.... GrahamLee 4 98
(Jim Goldie) *wl off pce in last trio: pushed along over 4f out: clsd on inner over 2f out: hmpd and swtchd rt over 1f out: r.o wl u.p fnl f to go 4th towards fin: nvr trbld ldrs* **8/1**

40-1 **5** *1* **Stepper Point**[27] 1066 5-9-5 112....(p) MartinDwyer 8 95
(William Muir) *chsd ldrs and clr in ldng quartet: wnt 2nd over 2f out: ev ch 2f out: sn rdn and outpcd by wnr: btn 1f out: wknd and lost 3 pls fnl 100yds* **7/1**[3]

-303 **6** *½* **Ballista (IRE)**[48] 802 6-9-5 102.... StephenCraine 3 93
(Tom Dascombe) *chsd clr ldng quartet: clsd and n.m.r ent fnl 2f: 3rd and edgd lft u.p 1f out: wknd and lost 3 pls fnl 100yds* **33/1**

-622 **7** *hd* **Hasopop (IRE)**[20] 1174 4-9-5 104....(p) LukeMorris 12 93
(Marco Botti) *racd off the pce in rr: clsd jst over 2f out: hrd drvn over 1f out: plugged on but no threat to ldrs* **16/1**

13-5 **8** *½* **Lancelot Du Lac (ITY)**[20] 1172 4-9-5 103.... JimCrowley 2 103+
(Dean Ivory) *hld up in midfield: clsd on inner and nt clr run 2f out: edgd lft and effrt u.p over 1f out: keeping on but looked hld whn hmpd ins fnl f: n.d after* **5/1**[2]

51-1 **9** *nk* **Tarooq (USA)**[55] 713 8-9-5 105........................ GrahamGibbons 11 90
(David Barron) *dropped in bhd after s: hld up off the pce in rr: stl last 2f out: edging lft and hdwy u.p ent fnl f: styd on but nvr trbld ldrs* **5/1**[2]

601- **10** *4 ½* **Valbchek (IRE)**[153] 7928 5-9-5 104...............................(b) RyanMoore 6 76
(Jeremy Noseda) *dwlt: nvr travelling wl and off the pce in rr: clsd jst over 1f out: rdn and no hdwy wl over 1f out: wknd fnl f* **3/1**[1]

2130 **11** *4 ½* **Even Stevens**[19] 1193 6-9-5 102...................................(v) TomEaves 1 61
(Scott Dixon) *chsd ldrs and clr in ldng quartet tl lost pl 2f out: wknd over 1f out: fdd fnl f* **50/1**

-514 **12** *6* **Addictive Dream (IRE)**[27] 1066 7-9-5 105.................. AndrewMullen 14 42
(David Nicholls) *chsd ldr and clr in ldng quartet: lost 2nd over 2f out and lost pl qckly 2f out: bhd 1f out* **33/1**

1m 9.73s (-2.17) **Going Correction** -0.15s/f (Stan) **12** Ran SP% **125.3**
Speed ratings (Par 109): **108,107,107,103,101 101,100,100,99,93 87,79**
CSF £150.59 CT £1403.27 TOTE £25.10: £6.30, £2.30, £4.10; EX 213.80 Trifecta £3482.50.
**Owner** J K Shannon & M A Scaife **Bred** Rathasker Stud **Trained** Musley Bank, N Yorks
■ Stewards' Enquiry : Stephen Craine two-day ban: careless riding (2, 5 May)

**FOCUS**
A smart and competitive sprint on paper and this form should prove reliable, despite a couple of the market leaders underperforming. The gallop was sound (sectionals: first 2f (24.15s), 4f (46.20s) and finishing time of 1m09.60) but not too many figured. The winner came down the centre and the first three pulled clear. The third has been rated a shade off his best.

## 1558 LADBROKES ALL-WEATHER MILE CHAMPIONSHIPS CONDITIONS STKS 1m 1y(P)

**4:40** (4:40) (Class 2) 4-Y-O+
**£93,375** (£27,960; £13,980; £6,990; £3,495; £1,755) **Stalls** High

Form RPR

12-2 **1** **Captain Cat (IRE)**[83] 344 5-9-5 99............................ JamesDoyle 8 111
(Roger Charlton) *hld up in last pair: swtchd to outer and hdwy over 1f out: str run fnl f to ld fnl 75yds: sn in command and r.o wl* **4/1**[2]

0-06 **2** *1 ¼* **Highland Knight (IRE)**[27] 1070 7-9-5 105.................(t) DavidProbert 11 108
(Andrew Balding) *wl in tch in midfield: rdn over 2f out: rallied u.p ent fnl f: led ins fnl f: sn hdd and outpcd by wnr: kpt on* **25/1**

3155 **3** *1 ¼* **Alfred Hutchinson**[41] 887 6-9-5 100.......................... RobertTart 4 105
(Geoffrey Oldroyd) *in tch in midfield: hdwy u.p on inner over 1f out: ev ch ins fnl f: no ex and outpcd fnl 75yds* **12/1**

2-11 **4** *¾* **Grey Mirage**[55] 715 5-9-5 103...................................(p) RyanMoore 12 104
(Marco Botti) *hld up in tch towards rr: prog over 3f out: hdwy u.p to chse ldrs whn short of room and hmpd jst ins fnl f: kpt on again fnl 100yds* **5/2**[1]

5121 **5** *¾* **George Guru**[27] 1070 7-9-5 102................................ RobertHavlin 10 102
(Michael Attwater) *chsd ldrs: rdn and effrt 2f out: chsng ldrs and keeping on whn short of room and hmpd ins fnl f: styd on same pce fnl 100yds* **14/1**

1162 **6** *nse* **Noble Citizen (USA)**[23] 1114 9-9-5 97....................(be) JamieSpencer 6 102
(David Simcock) *dwlt: bhd: rdn over 1f out: no prog tl r.o strly ins fnl f: nvr trbld ldrs* **25/1**

051- **7** *nse* **Sirius Prospect (USA)**[149] 7974 6-9-5 106.............. RobertWinston 14 102
(Dean Ivory) *hld up in tch in midfield: rdn and effrt wl over 1f out: sltly hmpd jst ins fnl f: styd on but no threat to ldrs fnl 100yds* **9/1**

1010 **8** *1 ¼* **Chookie Royale**[20] 1165 6-9-5 111..............................(p) TomEaves 9 99
(Keith Dalgleish) *taken down early: chsd ldrs: rdn and ev ch over 1f out tl ins fnl f: wknd fnl 75yds* **6/1**

1-30 **9** *hd* **Anaconda (FR)**[27] 1068 5-9-5 102.......................... RichardKingscote 2 98
(Tom Dascombe) *led: rdn 2f out: hrd drvn and hdd ins fnl f: sn wknd* **5/1**[3]

6121 **10** *1 ½* **Frontier Fighter**[23] 1114 6-9-5 103........................ DanielTudhope 13 95
(David O'Meara) *chsd ldr tl over 1f out: sn drvn and no ex: btn whn n.m.r ins fnl f: sn wknd* **20/1**

2330 **11** *nk* **Moonday Sun (USA)**[6] 1437 5-9-5 95.............................. PatDobbs 1 94
(Amanda Perrett) *in tch towards rr: no hdwy u.p over 1f out: nvr trbld ldrs* **33/1**

6411 **12** *11* **Silverheels (IRE)**[30] 1014 5-9-5 85.........................(b) JimCrowley 3 69
(Paul Cole) *chsd ldrs: lost pl u.p over 2f out: bhd 1f out: fdd fnl f* **33/1**

1m 34.51s (-3.69) **Going Correction** -0.15s/f (Stan) **12** Ran SP% **122.2**
Speed ratings (Par 109): **112,110,109,108,108 107,107,106,106,104 104,93**
CSF £109.85 CT £1135.41 TOTE £5.60: £2.10, £9.20, £3.10; EX 84.20 Trifecta £789.50.
**Owner** Seasons Holidays **Bred** Azienda Agricola Mediterranea **Trained** Beckhampton, Wilts

**FOCUS**
Several in-form sorts in a good-quality event. The gallop was a solid one (sectionals: first 2f (23.66), 4f (46.78), 6f (1m10.31) and a course-record finishing time of 1m34.36) and those up with the pace not surprisingly failed to last home. The winner came down the centre in the straight. The winner has been rated as running a 6lb personal best, with the third and fifth close to form.

## 1559 CORAL EASTER CLASSIC ALL-WEATHER MIDDLE DISTANCE CHAMPIONSHIPS CONDITIONS STKS 1m 2f (P)

**5:20** (5:21) (Class 2) 4-Y-O+
**£124,500** (£37,280; £18,640; £9,320; £4,660; £2,340) **Stalls** Low

Form RPR

0-10 **1** **Grandeur (IRE)**[27] 1068 5-9-5 115.............................. RyanMoore 2 108
(Jeremy Noseda) *chsd ldrs: wnt 2nd and shifting rt 2f out: chal over 1f out: sustained duel w runner-up after: drvn ins fnl f: r.o to ld towards fin* **6/4**[1]

21-4 **2** *hd* **Dick Doughtywylie**[27] 1068 6-9-5 102....................(t) WilliamBuick 6 107
(John Gosden) *chsd ldr tl rdn to ld and qcknd ent fnl 2f: hrd pressed and sustained duel w wnr fr over 1f out: r.o wl tl hdd and no ex towards fin* **7/1**

6141 **3** *1* **Robin Hoods Bay**[27] 1068 6-9-5 107............................. LukeMorris 7 105+
(Ed Vaughan) *hld up in tch towards rr: n.m.r ent fnl 2f tl rdn and hdwy ent fnl f: edging lft u.p but r.o wl fnl 150yds: nvr gng to rch ldng pair* **7/2**[2]

-564 **4** *1* **Solar Deity (IRE)**[48] 810 5-9-5 107............................. AdamKirby 3 103
(Marco Botti) *in tch in midfield: n.m.r jst over 2f out: hdwy u.p over 1f out: kpt on same pce ins fnl f* **6/1**[3]

24-4 **5** *1* **Bancnuanaheireann (IRE)**[44] 840 7-9-5 99.............. AndrewMullen 12 101
(Michael Appleby) *chsd ldrs: 3rd and unable qck u.p over 1f out: styd on same pce fnl f* **25/1**

5053 **6** *¾* **Aussie Reigns (IRE)**[27] 1068 4-9-5 104..................... GeorgeBaker 11 100+
(William Knight) *stdd after s: hld up in rr: clsd and wl in tch but stuck bhd rivals 2f out: gap opened and hdwy 1f out: r.o u.p: nvr trbld ldrs* **14/1**

4103 **7** *¾* **Rebellious Guest**[20] 1171 5-9-5 100........................... TomQueally 10 98
(George Margarson) *hld up towards rr: clsd and in tch 4f out: swtchd rt and effrt wl over 1f out: no imp tl kpt on wl u.p ins fnl f: nvr trbld ldrs* **16/1**

-436 **8** *¾* **Veeraya**[16] 1241 4-9-5 84...............................(b[1]) AdamBeschizza 13 97?
(Julia Feilden) *hld up in midfield: clsd and in tch 4f out: rdn over 2f out: outpcd wl over 1f out: no threat to ldrs but rallied and styd on u.p fnl f* **100/1**

3604 **9** *1 ½* **Tinshu (IRE)**[20] 1170 8-9-0 93..................................(p) PaulHanagan 4 89
(Derek Haydn Jones) *stdd after s: hld up in midfield: clsd and in tch 4f out: effrt on inner over 1f out: no prog 1f out: wknd ins fnl f* **50/1**

311- **10** *½* **Marshgate Lane (USA)**[125] 8301 5-9-5 104................... JoeFanning 9 93
(Mark Johnston) *stdd s: hld up in last trio: clsd and in tch 4f out: hdwy on outer over 2f out: styd on same pce ins fnl f* **14/1**

-305 **11** *2* **Party Royal**[13] 1316 4-9-5 83...................................... GrahamLee 8 89
(Mark Johnston) *led: clr tl 4f out: rdn and hdd ent fnl 2f: wknd fnl f* **100/1**

0020 **12** *2 ¾* **Uramazin (IRE)**[20] 1171 8-9-5 97.................................. LiamKeniry 1 84
(Philip Hide) *stdd s: hld up in rr: clsd 4f out: effrt on inner and forced to switch rt over 1f out: wknd fnl f* **66/1**

2m 5.59s (-1.01) **Going Correction** -0.15s/f (Stan) **12** Ran SP% **117.5**
Speed ratings (Par 109): **98,97,97,96,95 94,94,93,92,92 90,88**
CSF £12.24 CT £32.47 TOTE £1.90: £1.10, £3.00, £1.60; EX 13.00 Trifecta £36.40.
**Owner** Miss Yvonne Jacques **Bred** Mrs Cherry Faeste **Trained** Newmarket, Suffolk
■ Stewards' Enquiry : Luke Morris two-day ban: careless riding (2, 5 May)

**FOCUS**
The most valuable race ever staged on the AW in Britain but a muddling gallop (sectionals: first 2f (27.56s), 4f (53.06), 6f (1m19.24), 1m (1m43.11) and finishing time of 2m05.40s) favoured those up with the pace and this bare form doesn't look entirely reliable. The winner came down the centre in the straight. The winner didn't have to run to his best to win, while the well-placed runner-up has been rated to form.
T/Jkpt: Not won. T/Plt: £169.70 to a £1 stake. Pool: £210547.52 - 905.23 winning tickets T/Qpdt: £30.90 to a £1 stake. Pool: £14760.14 - 352.40 winning tickets SP

# MUSSELBURGH (R-H)

Friday, April 18

**OFFICIAL GOING: Good to firm (good in places on 5f course; 8.7)**
Wind: Light across Weather: Bright and sunny

## 1560 BET TOTEPLACEPOT SCOTTISH BROCKLESBY CONDITIONS STKS (BOBIS RACE) 5f

**2:10** (2:11) (Class 2) 2-Y-O **£9,703** (£2,887; £1,443; £721) **Stalls** High

Form RPR

**1** **Mukhmal (IRE)** 2-9-3 0.............................................. DaneO'Neill 1 87
(Mark Johnston) *w ldr: rdn to ld over 1f out: kpt on wl* **11/2**[3]

1 **2** *1 ½* **Cheerio Sweetie (IRE)**[15] 1259 2-8-12 0.................... DeclanBates 5 77
(David Evans) *trckd ldr on inner: angled rt ent fnl f: kpt on but no ch w wnr* **5/4**[1]

4 **3** *2 ½* **Magic Florence (IRE)**[20] 1161 2-8-12 0.................. JamesSullivan 3 68
(James Given) *led narrowly: rdn whn hdd over 1f out: sn no ex* **15/8**[2]

**4** *1 ¾* **Bowson Fred** 2-9-3 0............................................ PaulMulrennan 6 66
(Michael Easterby) *dwlt: hld up in tch: rdn to chse ldrs over 1f out: wknd ins fnl f* **33/1**

**5** *3 ½* **Casterbridge** 2-9-3 0.................................................... JasonHart 4 54
(Eric Alston) *hld up in tch on outer: rdn and briefly chsd ldrs 2f out: wknd fnl f* **8/1**

**6** *31* **Kepple's Best (IRE)** 2-9-3 0........................................ SladeO'Hara 2
(Alan Berry) *slowly away: a wl bhd* **100/1**

58.84s (-1.56) **Going Correction** -0.325s/f (Firm) **6** Ran SP% **109.7**
Speed ratings (Par 98): **99,96,92,89,84 34**
CSF £12.28 TOTE £6.20: £3.00, £1.10; EX 13.70 Trifecta £31.00.
**Owner** Hamdan Al Maktoum **Bred** Pier House Stud & Martinstown **Trained** Middleham Moor, N Yorks

**FOCUS**
The first ever turf meeting on Good Friday, with the eight races carrying total prize money of £158,000. The ground continued to dry out, and after the opener the riders reckoned it was quick ground. A Class 2 2yo conditions race and an impressive winner. The winner was quite professional, while the second had been a wide-margin AW winner on debut and the fourth and fith are well enough bred to think the form is sound.

## 1561 TOTEPOOL.COM BORDERLESCOTT SPRINT TROPHY (A CONDITIONS RACE) 5f

**2:40** (2:41) (Class 2) 3-Y-O+ **£16,172** (£4,812; £2,405; £1,202) **Stalls** High

Form RPR

06-0 **1** **Smoothtalkinrascal (IRE)**[12] 1333 4-9-7 105.......... SilvestreDeSousa 5 106
(David O'Meara) *sn outpcd in rr: stl in last over 1f out: swtchd rt ins fnl f: r.o to ld post* **7/1**

540- **2** *nse* **Borderlescott**[188] 7208 12-9-2 100............................... NeilFarley 7 101
(Robin Bastiman) *in tch: outpcd 1/2-way: hdwy to chse ldrs over 1f out: led 75yds out: kpt on: hdd post* **33/1**

0-04 **3** *1 ½* **Inxile (IRE)**[9] 1397 9-9-2 99.................................(p) AdrianNicholls 8 96
(David Nicholls) *hld up in tch: rdn over 1f out: kpt on: wnt 3rd nr fin* **66/1**

503- **4** *shd* **Tangerine Trees**[135] 8155 9-9-2 99............................(v) PaulMulrennan 1 95
(Bryan Smart) *led narrowly on outer: rdn over 1f out: hdd 75yds out: no ex and lost 2 more pls* **6/1**[3]

104- **5** *1* **Heeraat (IRE)**[195] 7013 5-9-9 110.................................. DaneO'Neill 6 99
(William Haggas) *w ldr: rdn over 1f out: wknd fnl 100yds* **6/4**[1]

0/0- **6** *2* **Fire Eyes**[349] 2019 4-9-2 99....................................... HarryBentley 2 84
(David Brown) *pressed ldr: rdn over 1f out: wknd ins fnl f* **9/1**

613- **7** *9* **Morawij**[293] 3848 4-9-9 106........................................ AndreaAtzeni 4 59
(Roger Varian) *awkward s: hld up: rdn over 1f out: wknd and eased* **9/4**[2]

57.71s (-2.69) **Going Correction** -0.325s/f (Firm) **7** Ran SP% **112.0**
Speed ratings (Par 109): **108,107,105,105,103 100,86**
CSF £166.64 TOTE £5.90: £2.70, £6.30; EX 73.90 Trifecta £659.20.
**Owner** Cheveley Park Stud **Bred** Tony Kilduff **Trained** Nawton, N Yorks

**FOCUS**
The second running of this Class 2 conditions sprint named in honour of dual Nunthorpe winner Borderlescott. Three took each other on up front and the first three home came from off the pace. A length or so best from the winner. The runner-up has been rated to last year's best.

## 1562 DOWNLOAD THE TOTEPOOL LIVE INFO APP H'CAP 1m 6f

**3:15** (3:15) (Class 2) (0-105,95) 4-Y-O+ **£19,407** (£5,775; £2,886; £1,443) **Stalls** Low

Form RPR

300- **1** **Jonny Delta**[175] 7496 7-8-5 79................................ IanBrennan(3) 4 87
(Jim Goldie) *hld up: pushed along and stdy hdwy fr over 2f out: rdn to ld 110yds out: styd on* **12/1**

00-5 **2** *nk* **Sirvino**[6] 1444 9-9-5 90....................................... PaulMulrennan 2 98
(David Barron) *hld up in midfield on inner: hdwy over 4f out: angled lft to outer wl over 1f out: kpt on wl: jst failed* **8/1**

163- **3** *½* **Special Meaning**[204] 6764 4-9-5 92............................. FrannyNorton 7 99
(Mark Johnston) *trckd ldr: rdn to ld over 2f out: hdd over 1f out: kpt on* **11/2**[2]

06-4 **4** ¾ **Angel Gabriel (IRE)**[35] 956 5-9-3 **88** .............................. DavidNolan 8 94
(Richard Fahey) *trckd ldrs: rdn to ld narrowly over 1f out: hdd 110yds out: no ex* **5/1**[1]

050- **5** 1¼ **Love Marmalade (IRE)**[42] 7028 4-8-3 **76** ........................ PJMcDonald 1 80
(Alistair Whillans) *midfield: hdwy and in tch over 3f out: rdn 2f out: one pce* **25/1**

000- **6** ½ **Itlaaq**[160] 7823 8-8-11 **82** .............................(t) JamesSullivan 9 85
(Michael Easterby) *midfield: pushed along whn carried sltly lft wl over 1f out: rdn and kpt on fnl f: nvr threatened ldrs* **10/1**

500- **7** nk **Chicago (IRE)**[62] 3073 5-9-10 **95** ..................................... TadhgO'Shea 3 98
(John Patrick Shanahan, Ire) *dwlt: hld up: rdn over 2f out: kpt on: nvr threatened ldrs* **20/1**

206- **8** 2 **Lady Kashaan (IRE)**[307] 3333 5-9-6 **91** ............................ BenCurtis 13 91
(Alan Swinbank) *in tch on outer: rdn and hdwy to chal over 2f out: stl ev ch over 1f out: wknd ins fnl f* **12/1**

100- **9** 10 **Eagle Rock (IRE)**[188] 7193 6-8-11 **82** ..................(p) SilvestreDeSousa 12 68
(Tom Tate) *prom: rdn over 3f out: wknd over 1f out* **7/1**[3]

31-3 **10** 13 **King Of Paradise (IRE)**[13] 1306 5-8-5 **79** ..................... JasonHart(3) 11 47
(Eric Alston) *sn led: rdn whn hdd over 2f out: wknd* **12/1**

2-10 **11** ¾ **Be Perfect (USA)**[48] 803 5-9-9 **94** ............................ AdrianNicholls 10 61
(David Nicholls) *hld up: rdn over 3f out: sn btn* **22/1**

240- **12** 2¼ **Moidore**[188] 7193 5-9-4 **89** ........................................... BarryMcHugh 5 53
(John Quinn) *chsd ldrs: rdn over 4f out: sn wknd* **11/2**[2]

2m 57.98s (-7.32) **Going Correction** -0.325s/f (Firm)
**WFA** 4 from 5yo+ 2lb 12 Ran SP% **116.2**
Speed ratings (Par 109): **107,106,106,106,105 105,104,103,98,90 90,88**
CSF £99.71 CT £593.75 TOTE £13.90: £6.70, £2.60, £1.90; EX 157.30 Trifecta £1016.70.
**Owner** Johnnie Delta Racing **Bred** Miss Gill Quincey **Trained** Uplawmoor, E Renfrews

**FOCUS**
A highly competitive stayers' handicap run at a strong pace on fast ground with the winner lowering the track record by over a second. The first two came from off the pace and wide. The runner-up helps set the standard, with the winner recording a small personal best.

## 1563 TOTEPOOL ROYAL MILE H'CAP (BOBIS RACE) 1m
3:50 (3:51) (Class 2) 3-Y-O £32,345 (£9,625; £4,810; £2,405) Stalls Low

Form RPR

041- **1** **Bilimbi (IRE)**[171] 7606 3-8-0 **83** oh1 ............................ JamesSullivan 6 95
(William Haggas) *trckd ldrs: pushed along over 2f out: rdn to ld over 1f out: kpt on wl* **7/1**[3]

216- **2** 2¼ **Extra Noble**[174] 7534 3-8-7 **90** ........................................ AndreaAtzeni 3 96
(Ralph Beckett) *in tch: pushed along and hdwy over 2f out: rdn and ev ch over 1f out: kpt on but hld in 2nd ins fnl f* **13/8**[1]

521- **3** 1½ **Finn Class (IRE)**[191] 7122 3-8-0 **83** oh1 ....................... NickyMackay 10 86
(Michael Bell) *hld up: rdn and hdwy on outside over 1f out: wnt 3rd ins fnl f: kpt on: edgd rt* **25/1**

-111 **4** 2 **Almargo (IRE)**[13] 1315 3-8-5 **88** ............................ SilvestreDeSousa 12 86
(Mark Johnston) *w ldr on outer: led over 2f out: sn rdn: hdd over 1f out: wknd ins fnl f* **10/1**

4-01 **5** nk **Bow Creek (IRE)**[13] 1300 3-9-7 **104** ................................ FrannyNorton 4 102
(Mark Johnston) *led narrowly: hdd over 2f out: remained w ev ch tl wknd fnl f* **10/1**

101- **6** ½ **Ventura Quest (USA)**[192] 7097 3-8-2 **85** ..................... PatrickMathers 7 82
(Richard Fahey) *midfield: rdn over 2f out: one pce and nvr threatened ldrs* **14/1**

131- **7** 1 **Roachdale House (IRE)**[174] 7529 3-8-8 **91** .................. TonyHamilton 5 85
(Richard Fahey) *midfield: rdn over 2f out: no imp* **7/2**[2]

23-6 **8** ½ **Ticking Katie (IRE)**[93] 183 3-8-1 **89** ........................... JoeyHaynes(5) 1 82
(K R Burke) *trckd ldrs: rdn over 2f out: wknd over 1f out* **20/1**

325- **9** 1¼ **Cool Bahamian (IRE)**[217] 6351 3-8-7 **90** ........................... JohnFahy 8 80
(Eve Johnson Houghton) *half-rrd s and s.i.s: hld up: rdn over 2f out: nvr threatened* **25/1**

414- **10** ¾ **Miss Buckshot (IRE)**[170] 7626 3-7-9 **83** oh3 ................ NoelGarbutt(5) 2 72
(Rae Guest) *in tch on inner: rdn over 2f out: wknd over 1f out* **40/1**

12-3 **11** 9 **Resolute**[85] 301 3-7-12 **86** oh2 ow3 ............................... TimClark(5) 9 54
(Ed de Giles) *hld up: a bhd* **33/1**

1131 **12** 9 **Swivel**[49] 785 3-8-4 **87** ................................................ AdrianNicholls 11 34
(Mark Johnston) *dwlt: sn pushed along in rr: a bhd* **20/1**

1m 37.27s (-3.93) **Going Correction** -0.325s/f (Firm) 12 Ran SP% **120.3**
Speed ratings (Par 104): **106,103,102,100,99 99,98,97,96,95 86,77**
CSF £17.32 CT £287.19 TOTE £10.30: £2.30, £1.10, £10.70; EX 29.40 Trifecta £739.10.
**Owner** The Starship Partnership **Bred** T Hirschfeld **Trained** Newmarket, Suffolk

**FOCUS**
A strongly contested 3yo handicap carrying £50,000 guarenteed prize money. Again the pace was unrelenting, though it largely held up. Good form.

## 1564 TOTEEXACTA PICK THE 1ST AND 2ND H'CAP 7f 30y
4:25 (4:25) (Class 3) (0-95,90) 4-Y-O+ £10,997 (£3,272; £1,635; £817) Stalls Low

Form RPR

14-2 **1** **That's Plenty (IRE)**[26] 1078 5-9-7 **90** .............................. TadhgO'Shea 5 99
(John Patrick Shanahan, Ire) *chsd ldrs: rdn to ld 2f out: kpt on wl* **11/2**[3]

60-0 **2** 2 **Azrur (IRE)**[27] 1070 4-9-2 **85** ........................................ AndrewElliott 4 89
(David Brown) *midfield: rdn and hdwy on outer over 2f out: kpt on to go 2nd 110yds out: no ch w wnr* **25/1**

000- **3** ¾ **Toto Skyllachy**[179] 7424 9-8-11 **85** ........................ JacobButterfield(5) 2 87
(David O'Meara) *midfield: rdn and hdwy over 2f out: kpt on to go 3rd 110yds out* **33/1**

4045 **4** 1 **Verse Of Love**[38] 917 5-8-10 **82** ................................. DeclanBates(3) 11 81
(David Evans) *chsd ldrs: rdn over 2f out: kpt on* **25/1**

20-2 **5** 1¼ **Lazarus Bell**[11] 1345 4-8-12 **81** ............................ SilvestreDeSousa 6 77
(Alan Brown) *hld up: rdn over 2f out: kpt on fnl f: nrst fin* **9/2**[2]

26-3 **6** ½ **Kalk Bay (IRE)**[4] 1483 7-8-13 **82** ...............................(t) JamesSullivan 10 86+
(Michael Easterby) *hld up: nudged along and hdwy on inner whn short of room wl over 1f out tl ent fnl f: swtchd lft: kpt on but no ch after* **9/2**[2]

4416 **7** ¾ **Stonefield Flyer**[13] 1301 5-9-2 **88** ................................ JasonHart(3) 12 81
(Keith Dalgleish) *trckd ldrs on outer: rdn over 2f out: chsd wnr over 1f out: wknd fnl f* **12/1**

102- **8** 2 **Silver Rime (FR)**[186] 7241 9-9-4 **87** ................................ PhillipMakin 8 75
(Linda Perratt) *hld up: nvr threatened* **33/1**

640- **9** 1¾ **Majestic Moon (IRE)**[181] 7368 4-9-7 **90** ....................(b) TonyHamilton 7 73
(Richard Fahey) *w ldr: rdn over 2f out: wknd over 1f out* **3/1**[1]

65-0 **10** nk **Fieldgunner Kirkup (GER)**[19] 1190 6-8-9 **78** ............ PaulMulrennan 9 60
(David Barron) *hld up: a towards rr* **40/1**

23-5 **11** 1½ **Al Mukhdam**[14] 1275 4-9-1 **84** ........................................ FrederikTylicki 3 62
(Ed de Giles) *led narrowly: rdn whn hdd 2f out: sn wknd* **17/2**

10 **12** 3½ **Cloverdale**[11] 1345 4-9-1 **84** ........................................ FrannyNorton 1 53
(Mark Johnston) *hld up: a towards rr* **28/1**

1m 26.66s (-2.34) **Going Correction** -0.325s/f (Firm) 12 Ran SP% **114.4**
Speed ratings (Par 107): **100,97,96,95,94 93,92,90,88,88 86,82**
CSF £139.62 CT £4060.14 TOTE £5.40: £2.50, £6.10, £9.70; EX 133.10 Trifecta £2024.10.
**Owner** Thistle Bloodstock Limited **Bred** Denis Brosnan **Trained** Viper Kells, Co Kilkenny

**FOCUS**
In another strongly run race five horses turned for home clear of the remainder. The winner has posted a personal best and the third rated as being close to matching his best reappearance figure.

## 1565 TOTETRIFECTA AVAILABLE ON ALL RACES H'CAP (DIV I) 5f
4:55 (4:56) (Class 4) (0-85,83) 4-Y-O+ £5,175 (£1,540; £769; £384) Stalls High

Form RPR

50-5 **1** **Silvanus (IRE)**[30] 1019 9-8-12 **74** ................................ PaulMulrennan 7 88
(Paul Midgley) *chsd ldr: rdn to chal appr fnl f: kpt on to ld towards fin* **9/1**

00-5 **2** nk **Red Baron (IRE)**[14] 1283 5-9-0 **79** ................................ NeilFarley(3) 5 92
(Eric Alston) *led: rdn over 1f out: carried hd bit awkwardly whn pressed by wnr ins fnl f: hdd towards fin* **3/1**[1]

050- **3** 3½ **Jinky**[186] 7240 6-8-5 **72** ............................................ ConnorBeasley(5) 6 72
(Linda Perratt) *hld up: rdn 1/2-way: kpt on into 3rd ins fnl f: no threat to ldng pair* **9/1**

5500 **4** ½ **Tax Free (IRE)**[18] 1212 12-9-6 **82** ................................ AdrianNicholls 9 81
(David Nicholls) *midfield: rdn 1/2-way: kpt on: nvr threatened* **16/1**

-532 **5** 3 **Moorhouse Lad**[43] 863 11-8-8 **77** ................................ BradleyBosley(7) 1 65
(Garry Moss) *in tch: rdn 2f out: grad wknd* **5/1**[2]

040- **6** ¾ **Economic Crisis (IRE)**[143] 8052 5-8-2 **64** oh1 ............ JamesSullivan 3 49
(Alan Berry) *hld up: rdn and hung rt over 1f out: nvr threatened* **33/1**

154- **7** hd **Opt Out**[186] 7240 4-8-4 **66** ........................................... PJMcDonald 8 50
(Alistair Whillans) *hld up: rdn 1/2-way: nvr threatened* **8/1**[3]

05-6 **8** 2½ **Lady Ibrox**[21] 1145 4-9-5 **81** ................................ SilvestreDeSousa 10 56
(Alan Brown) *chsd ldrs: wknd 2f out* **5/1**[2]

544- **9** 5 **L'Ami Louis (IRE)**[230] 5991 6-9-2 **83** ......................... GarryWhillans(5) 2 40
(Ian Semple) *dwlt: midfield on outer: rdn 1/2-way: wknd over 1f out* **5/1**[2]

57.67s (-2.73) **Going Correction** -0.325s/f (Firm) 9 Ran SP% **114.9**
Speed ratings (Par 105): **108,107,101,101,96 95,94,90,82**
CSF £36.04 CT £253.76 TOTE £10.80: £2.90, £1.10, £3.60; EX 39.20 Trifecta £311.90.
**Owner** Colin Alton **Bred** Barronstown Stud And Mrs T Stack **Trained** Westow, N Yorks

**FOCUS**
Just two seriously involved soon after halfway in part one of this sprint handicap. The winner was running off his lowest mark for nearly two years and was still 10lb off his best in winning.

## 1566 TOTETRIFECTA AVAILABLE ON ALL RACES H'CAP (DIV II) 5f
5:30 (5:32) (Class 4) (0-85,83) 4-Y-O+ £5,175 (£1,540; £769; £384) Stalls High

Form RPR

10-2 **1** **Go Nani Go**[21] 1145 8-9-6 **82** ........................................ FrederikTylicki 3 91
(Ed de Giles) *trckd ldrs: gng wl but n.m.r over 1f out: angled lft into clr jst ins fnl f: kpt on wl: led 50yds out* **5/2**[1]

000- **2** 1¼ **Bronze Beau**[165] 7731 7-8-10 **77** ..........................(t) JacobButterfield(5) 7 82
(Kristin Stubbs) *led narrowly: rdn 2f out: kpt on: hdd 50yds out* **12/1**

-440 **3** 1¼ **We'll Deal Again**[14] 1283 7-9-0 **76** ow2 .......................(b) PhillipMakin 6 74
(Michael Easterby) *hld up: rdn 2f out: kpt on to go 3rd towards fin* **9/1**

06-0 **4** hd **Angus Og**[13] 1305 4-9-2 **83** ........................................ JoeyHaynes(5) 5 82
(K R Burke) *chsd ldrs: rdn 1/2-way: kpt on* **6/1**

143- **5** ½ **Space Artist (IRE)**[165] 7731 4-9-4 **80** .......................... PaulMulrennan 2 77
(Bryan Smart) *chsd ldrs on outer: rdn 2f out: no ex fnl 110yds* **4/1**[2]

000- **6** 1 **Findog**[214] 6471 4-8-0 **67** ow2 .................................... ConnorBeasley(5) 8 61
(Linda Perratt) *hld up: rdn 2f out: nvr threatened* **5/1**[3]

14-0 **7** 1¾ **Alexandrakollontai (IRE)**[9] 1376 4-8-3 **68** .................... JulieBurke(3) 9 56
(Alistair Whillans) *dwlt: sn pushed along in rr: nvr threatened* **20/1**

4210 **8** hd **Royal Bajan (USA)**[20] 1172 6-9-2 **78** ......................(b) JamesSullivan 4 65
(James Given) *w ldr: rdn 2f out: wknd ins fnl f* **4/1**[2]

58.11s (-2.29) **Going Correction** -0.325s/f (Firm) 8 Ran SP% **122.0**
Speed ratings (Par 105): **105,103,101,100,99 98,95,95**
CSF £37.14 CT £246.24 TOTE £3.50: £1.20, £5.80, £3.40; EX 46.30 Trifecta £310.80.
**Owner** T Gould **Bred** D J And Mrs Deer **Trained** Ledbury, H'fords
■ Stewards' Enquiry : Phillip Makin 10-day ban: weighed in 2lb heavy (3rd breach of rule in 12-month period) (May 23-Jun 2)

**FOCUS**
Part two and a more competitive affair. It's been rated as ordinary form, with the winner at least as good as ever as an 8yo.

## 1567 FLAT TEN TO FOLLOW OPENS TOMORROW AMATEUR RIDERS' H'CAP 1m 6f
6:00 (6:01) (Class 5) (0-70,73) 4-Y-O+ £3,119 (£967; £483; £242) Stalls Low

Form RPR

3-42 **1** **Ballyheigue (IRE)**[23] 1117 5-9-4 **53** ................................(p) MissHHeal(7) 6 61
(Liam Corcoran) *led: hdd 7f out: trckd ldr: rdn to ld again over 2f out: kpt on: strly pressed towards fin: jst hld on* **8/1**

/00- **2** shd **Categorical**[21] 7342 11-11-0 **70** ................................ MissSBrotherton 8 78
(Keith Reveley) *hld up: pushed along and hdwy on inner over 2f out: sn chsd wnr: kpt on: chal strly towards fin: jst hld* **11/2**

0-31 **3** 8 **Naburn**[9] 1374 6-10-12 **73** 6ex ................................ MrORJSangster(5) 5 70
(Alan Swinbank) *hld up: rdn and hdwy over 2f out: wnt 3rd over 1f out: edgd rt and wknd ins fnl f* **5/2**[1]

0/6- **4** 4½ **Leroy Parker (IRE)**[104] 2706 6-10-13 **69** ........................ MrJHamilton 2 59
(Barry Murtagh) *midfield: rdn over 3f out: sn one pce: wknd ins fnl f* **25/1**

-304 **5** 9 **Stormy Morning**[42] 868 8-9-13 **60** ..........................(p) PhillipDennis(5) 7 38
(Philip Kirby) *midfield: rdn 3f out: sn no imp: wknd fnl f* **4/1**[3]

1-64 **6** 14 **Goodlukin Lucy**[5] 1117 7-9-10 **52** ................................ MrsCBartley 3 10
(Keith Dalgleish) *sn prom: led 7f out: hdd over 2f out: wknd* **3/1**[2]

004- **7** 8 **Silver Tigress**[181] 7372 6-9-2 **51** ................................ MissKMabon(7) 4
(Iain Jardine) *racd keenly: trckd ldrs: wknd 3f out* **11/1**

3m 3.4s (-1.90) **Going Correction** -0.325s/f (Firm)
**WFA** 4 from 5yo+ 2lb 7 Ran SP% **112.2**
Speed ratings (Par 103): **92,91,87,84,79 71,67**
Anne's Valentino was withdrawn. Price at time of withdrawal 8/1. Rule 4 applies to bets placed prior to withdrawal but not to SP bets - deduction 10p in the pound. New market formed. CSF £48.75 CT £140.88 TOTE £13.60: £5.60, £3.40; EX 51.90 Trifecta £209.80.
**Owner** Mrs Elizabeth Heal **Bred** Gerry Flannery Developments **Trained** Lovington, Somerset

**FOCUS**
They went very steady early on in this modest amateur riders' handicap. The winner has been rated as matching his latest AW mark.
T/Plt: £923.80 to £1 stake. Pool: £111,300.84 - 87.95 winning tickets T/Qpdt: £83.70 to a £1 stake. Pool: £9253.07 - 81.76 winning tickets AS

# BATH (L-H)

Saturday, April 19

**OFFICIAL GOING: Firm (good to firm in places)**

Wind: Light behind Weather: Cloudy with sunny spells

## 1568 32RED THUNDERSTRUCK II SLOT FILLIES' H'CAP 1m 2f 46y

4:55 (4:55) (Class 4) (0-80,79) 4-Y-O+ £4,690 (£1,395; £697; £348) Stalls Low

Form RPR

62-5 1 **Noble Protector**[21] 1175 4-9-2 **79** ShelleyBirkett(5) 6 91
(Stuart Kittow) *trckd ldrs: wnt 2nd 7f out: rdn to ld over 1f out: r.o* 6/4[1]

044- 2 2 1/2 **Sinaadi (IRE)**[192] 7121 4-9-4 **76** JimmyFortune 2 83
(Brian Meehan) *led: rdn and hdd over 1f out: styd on same pce ins fnl f* 3/1[2]

124- 3 4 1/2 **Play Street**[216] 6433 5-9-1 **76** MatthewLawson(3) 1 75
(Jonathan Portman) *trckd ldr over 3f: remained handy: rdn over 2f out: no ex fnl f* 6/1

61-0 4 2 1/4 **Coincidently**[31] 1014 4-8-13 **76** TimClark(5) 3 70
(Alan Bailey) *hld up: rdn over 2f out: nvr trbld ldrs* 9/2[3]

1335 5 4 1/2 **Wishformore (IRE)**[22] 1141 7-8-0 **65** oh6 JennyPowell(7) 4 51
(Ian Williams) *prom: rdn over 2f out: wknd fnl f* 8/1

-306 6 7 **Avidly**[22] 1143 4-8-6 **67** RossAtkinson(3) 5 40
(Julia Feilden) *hld up: hung rt 1/2-way: rdn over 2f out: wknd over 1f out* 20/1

2m 9.67s (-1.33) **Going Correction** -0.15s/f (Firm) **6** Ran SP% **113.3**
Speed ratings (Par 102): **99,97,93,91,88 82**
CSF £6.33 TOTE £2.20: £1.40, £1.40; EX 5.10 Trifecta £22.20.
**Owner** The Black Type Partnership III **Bred** D R Tucker **Trained** Blackborough, Devon

**FOCUS**
All races incorporating bottom bend increased by 10yds. The opening contest of an interesting seven-race card was a fair handicap for older fillies in which they went an even gallop on drying ground officially described as firm, good to firm in places. The runner-up has been rated close to the balance of her form.

## 1569 32RED FREE £10 BONUS MAIDEN STKS 5f 161y

5:25 (5:26) (Class 5) 3-Y-O+ £2,587 (£770; £384; £192) Stalls Centre

Form RPR

5- 1 **Ashkari (IRE)**[186] 7270 3-9-1 0 SteveDrowne 2 82+
(Clive Cox) *sn trcking ldrs: edgd lft over 1f out: rdn to ld ins fnl f: r.o wl* 5/4[1]

334- 2 3 1/2 **Kuala Queen (IRE)**[208] 6697 3-8-10 73 JohnFahy 6 65
(Denis Coakley) *trckd ldrs: racd keenly: shkn up to ld over 2f out: hdd and unable qck ins fnl f* 5/1[3]

034- 3 1 **Broadway Ranger (IRE)**[114] 8396 3-9-1 72 WilliamCarson 3 67
(Charles Hills) *w ldr: rdn and ev ch over 1f out: no ex ins fnl f* 7/1

453- 4 1 1/4 **Groundworker (IRE)**[162] 7804 3-9-1 68 JimmyFortune 1 63
(Sylvester Kirk) *led 3f: hmpd wl over 1f out: no ex fnl f* 12/1

5 nk **Dubawi Coast** 3-8-10 0 LukeMorris 5 57+
(James Tate) *dwlt: hdwy over 3f out: swtchd rt wl over 2f out: sn rdn: styd on same pce fr over 1f out* 3/1[2]

050- 6 7 **Zafraaj**[149] 7986 3-9-1 62 DavidProbert 9 38
(Ronald Harris) *prom tl rdn and wknd over 2f out* 20/1

6 7 nk **Lucky Clover**[22] 1147 3-8-5 0 RyanWhile(5) 10 32
(Malcolm Saunders) *prom: hung rt and lost pl over 3f out: n.d after* 33/1

00-5 8 3/4 **Go Charlie**[38] 923 3-8-10 44 DCByrne(5) 8 35
(Ronald Harris) *hld up: plld hrd: hdwy 3f out: sn rdn: wknd over 1f out* 66/1

9 8 **Border Guard** 3-9-1 0 SebSanders 7 9
(Milton Bradley) *s.i.s: sn pushed along and a in rr* 50/1

1m 10.17s (-1.03) **Going Correction** -0.175s/f (Firm) **9** Ran SP% **117.5**
Speed ratings (Par 103): **99,94,93,91,90 81,81,80,69**
CSF £7.88 TOTE £1.90: £1.02, £1.60, £2.60; EX 8.80 Trifecta £49.60.
**Owner** Al Asayl Bloodstock Ltd **Bred** Sheikh Sultan Bin Khalifa Al Nahyan **Trained** Lambourn, Berks

**FOCUS**
A fair sprint maiden. The second, third and fourth set only a modest standard.

## 1570 32RED.COM H'CAP (BOBIS RACE) 5f 161y

6:00 (6:00) (Class 4) (0-80,78) 3-Y-O £4,690 (£1,395; £697; £348) Stalls Centre

Form RPR

012- 1 **Fear Or Favour (IRE)**[217] 6376 3-9-2 **78** RyanTate(5) 9 88
(Clive Cox) *trckd ldrs: rdn to ld over 1f out: r.o* 6/4[1]

1-25 2 1 **Amahoro**[64] 613 3-9-3 **77** WilliamTwiston-Davies(3) 1 84
(Mick Channon) *a.p: nt clr run over 1f out: rdn to chse wnr ins fnl f: r.o* 8/1[3]

20-6 3 1 3/4 **Jive**[10] 1381 3-8-12 **69** SeanLevey 2 70
(Richard Hannon) *s.i.s: hld up: no0t clr run fr over 2f out tl r.o ins fnl f: nvr able to chal* 16/1

056- 4 nk **Concrete Mac**[147] 8024 3-8-9 **73** CharlieBennett(7) 4 73
(Hughie Morrison) *chsd ldr: shkn up to ld 2f out: sn hdd: edgd rt and styd on same pce ins fnl f* 20/1

423- 5 1/2 **Telegraph (IRE)**[203] 6825 3-8-11 **68** DavidProbert 3 67
(Andrew Balding) *led: rdn and hdd 2f out: no ex ins fnl f* 7/4[2]

4202 6 1/2 **Intense Feeling (IRE)**[15] 1277 3-8-1 **65** (v) HollieDoyle(7) 10 62
(David Evans) *chsd ldrs: rdn over 1f out: no ex ins fnl f* 14/1

15-0 7 5 **Classic Pursuit**[12] 1350 3-9-2 **73** TomQueally 8 53
(Ronald Harris) *s.i.s: hdwy over 3f out: rdn over 2f out: wknd fnl f* 16/1

23-5 8 2 3/4 **Kodafine (IRE)**[100] 103 3-8-5 **67** EoinWalsh(5) 6 38
(David Evans) *hld up: hmpd 4f out: hdwy over 2f out: wknd and eased fnl f* 25/1

-220 9 3/4 **Mimi Luke (USA)**[9] 1404 3-8-3 **65** (v1) TimClark(5) 7 34
(Alan Bailey) *prom: pushed along and lost pl 4f out: sn bhd* 25/1

50-0 10 3/4 **Tableforten**[12] 1350 3-8-12 **69** (b) LiamJones 5 35
(J S Moore) *s.i.s: outpcd* 25/1

1m 10.15s (-1.05) **Going Correction** -0.175s/f (Firm) **10** Ran SP% **122.2**
Speed ratings (Par 100): **100,98,96,95,95 94,87,84,83,82**
CSF £14.55 CT £139.86 TOTE £2.70: £1.40, £2.40, £3.30; EX 19.80 Trifecta £110.20.
**Owner** Alan G Craddock **Bred** Shadwell Estate Company Limited **Trained** Lambourn, Berks
■ Stewards' Enquiry : Hollie Doyle three-day ban: careless riding (May 5-7)

**FOCUS**
A fair 3yo sprint handicap. The third has been rated close to her 2yo form and the fourth to form.

## 1571 32RED TOMB RAIDER SLOT EBF MEDIAN AUCTION MAIDEN STKS 5f 11y

6:30 (6:36) (Class 5) 2-Y-O £3,067 (£905; £453) Stalls Centre

Form RPR

1 **Ahlan Emarati (IRE)** 2-9-5 0 JimmyFortune 11 82+
(Peter Chapple-Hyam) *a.p: shkn up to ld over 1f out: rdn out* 13/2

2 1 1/2 **Stinky Socks (IRE)** 2-9-0 0 TomQueally 2 72
(Charles Hills) *s.i.s: hdwy over 2f out: ev ch fr over 1f out tl unable qck wl ins fnl f* 5/1[2]

5 3 2 **Jersey Bull (IRE)**[12] 1349 2-9-2 0 WilliamTwiston-Davies(3) 1 69
(Mick Channon) *trckd ldrs: rdn and ev ch over 1f out: styd on same pce ins fnl f* 7/2[1]

4 2 1/2 **Simply Magic (IRE)** 2-9-0 0 SeanLevey 7 55+
(Richard Hannon) *chsd ldrs: led 1/2-way: rdn and hdd over 1f out: no ex ins fnl f* 6/1[3]

0 5 1 3/4 **Chester Deal**[15] 1276 2-9-5 0 LiamJones 15 54
(Jo Hughes) *sn pushed along in rr: r.o ins fnl f: nvr nrr* 25/1

0 6 1 1/4 **Clever Love (FR)**[25] 1094 2-9-5 0 MartinDwyer 9 50
(Jo Hughes) *sn pushed along in rr: nvr on terms* 33/1

6 7 1 1/4 **Multi Quest**[14] 1314 2-9-0 0 JohnFahy 13 40
(Jo Hughes) *chsd ldrs: rdn over 1f out: wknd fnl f* 50/1

8 1/2 **Union Rose** 2-9-5 0 DavidProbert 17 43
(Ronald Harris) *hmpd and swvd rt sn after s: outpcd: nvr nrr* 33/1

0 9 2 **Seamoor Secret**[14] 1314 2-9-0 0 ChrisCatlin 4 31
(Alex Hales) *sn led: hdd 1/2-way: wknd over 1f out* 66/1

10 3/4 **May One** 2-9-0 0 SamHitchcott 10 28
(Mick Channon) *sn outpcd* 25/1

11 3 1/4 **Majenski (IRE)** 2-9-5 0 FergusSweeney 6 22
(Jamie Osborne) *s.i.s: outpcd* 8/1

12 1 1/2 **Sarah Catherine** 2-9-0 0 MartinLane 14 11
(Mark Usher) *sn pushed along in mid-div: bhd fr 1/2-way* 66/1

4 13 3/4 **As A Dream (IRE)**[12] 1349 2-8-9 0 EoinWalsh(5) 12 39+
(David Evans) *prom: pushed along and lost pl over 3f out: sn bhd* 8/1

0 14 1 1/4 **Lady Bling**[15] 1276 2-8-9 0 RyanWhile(5) 5 4
(Bill Turner) *prom: pushed along and lost pl over 3f out: bhd fr 1/2-way* 33/1

1m 2.3s (-0.20) **Going Correction** -0.175s/f (Firm) **14** Ran SP% **110.2**
Speed ratings (Par 92): **94,91,88,84,81 79,77,76,73,72 67,64,63,61**
CSF £26.87 TOTE £6.10: £2.30, £2.90, £1.60; EX 45.30 Trifecta £252.90.
**Owner** Ahmad Abdulla Al Shaikh **Bred** Patrick F Kelly **Trained** Newmarket, Suffolk
■ Come Uppence was withdrawn. Price at time of withdrawal 4/1. Rule 4 applies to all bets - deduction 20p in the pound.

**FOCUS**
A fair juvenile maiden. The third and fifth offer the form some substance.

## 1572 WHITSBURY MANOR STUD & EBF STALLIONS LANSDOWN FILLIES' STKS (LISTED RACE) 5f 11y

7:00 (7:03) (Class 1) 3-Y-O+

£22,684 (£8,600; £4,304; £2,144; £1,076; £540) Stalls Centre

Form RPR

0-65 1 **Ladies Are Forever**[28] 1066 6-9-0 108 (b) RobertTart 6 107
(Geoffrey Oldroyd) *trckd ldrs: nt clr run over 1f out: rdn to ld ins fnl f: r.o wl* 7/4[1]

60- 2 1 1/4 **Reroute (IRE)**[240] 5680 3-8-4 90 HayleyTurner 9 98
(Ed Walker) *hld up: swtchd rt and hdwy over 1f out: rdn ins fnl f: r.o* 10/1

005- 3 hd **Caledonia Lady**[161] 7821 5-9-0 98 LiamJones 4 101
(Jo Hughes) *hmpd sn after s: sn pushed along in rr: hdwy over 1f out: r.o wl towards fin: nvr nrr* 20/1

310- 4 1 1/4 **Swan Song**[220] 6305 5-9-0 93 JimmyFortune 14 97
(Andrew Balding) *chsd ldrs: nt clr run over 1f out: sn rdn: styd on* 10/1

101/ 5 1 1/2 **Kune Kune**[238] 5-9-0 98 MartinDwyer 1 91
(Rae Guest) *sn led: hdd 1/2-way: rdn and ev ch ins fnl f: no ex* 50/1

230- 6 nk **March**[244] 5561 4-9-0 100 SteveDrowne 11 90
(Robert Cowell) *hld up: hmpd over 1f out: r.o ins fnl f: nvr nrr* 8/1[3]

260- 7 nk **Jillnextdoor (IRE)**[224] 6189 4-9-0 90 WilliamTwiston-Davies 3 89
(Mick Channon) *s.i.s: in rr: r.o ins fnl f: nvr nrr* 33/1

444- 8 1/2 **Exceptionelle**[170] 7642 4-9-0 87 AndreaAtzeni 8 87
(Roger Varian) *prom: rdn over 1f out: bmpd and no ex ins fnl f* 10/1

114- 9 1/2 **Riskit Fora Biskit (IRE)**[216] 6445 4-9-0 100 TomQueally 5 86
(Michael Bell) *prom: n.m.r over 3f out: rdn over 1f out: no ex ins fnl f* 7/1[2]

245- 10 1 **Excel's Beauty**[196] 7011 3-8-4 95 (b) LukeMorris 7 78
(James Tate) *chsd ldr tl led 1/2-way: rdn over 1f out: hdd and no ex ins fnl f* 16/1

110- 11 2 **Cincinnati Kit**[258] 5027 5-9-0 80 (t) DavidProbert 12 75
(Stuart Williams) *prom: nt clr run over 1f out: wknd ins fnl f* 33/1

21- 12 2 **Hurryupharriet (IRE)**[211] 6584 3-8-8 97 SeanLevey 10 68
(W McCreery, Ire) *prom: drvn along 1/2-way: wknd fnl f* 10/1

400- 13 2 3/4 **Gladiatrix**[224] 6189 5-9-0 87 MichaelJMMurphy 15 71
(Rod Millman) *sn pushed along in rr: sme hdwy whn hmpd ins fnl f: eased* 33/1

26-0 14 6 **Lilbourne Lass**[28] 1067 3-8-4 90 MartinLane 2 32
(K R Burke) *sn pushed along to chse ldrs: rdn and wkng whn hmpd over 1f out* 25/1

2215 15 8 **Three D Alexander (IRE)**[63] 624 3-8-4 85 ChrisCatlin 13
(David Evans) *sn pushed along in rr: bhd fr 1/2-way* 66/1

59.88s (-2.62) **Going Correction** -0.175s/f (Firm)
**WFA** 3 from 4yo+ 10lb **15** Ran SP% **123.1**
Speed ratings (Par 108): **113,111,110,108,106 105,105,104,103,102 98,95,91,81,68**
CSF £18.59 TOTE £3.00: £1.50, £3.20, £4.20; EX 23.60 Trifecta £658.40.
**Owner** R C Bond **Bred** Bond Thoroughbred Corporation **Trained** Brawby, N Yorks
■ Stewards' Enquiry : Robert Tart two-day ban: careless riding (May 5-6)
Hayley Turner three-day ban: careless riding (May 5-7)

**FOCUS**
The feature race was a decent Listed sprint for fillies and mares. The runner-up has been rated back to her early 2yo form, and the level looks pretty sound.

## 1573 32RED ON THE APP STORE H'CAP 5f 161y

7:30 (7:34) (Class 6) (0-60,60) 4-Y-O+ £1,940 (£433; £433; £144) Stalls Centre

Form RPR

45-0 1 **Encapsulated**[18] 1221 4-9-1 **54** (p) MartinLane 12 62
(Roger Ingram) *mid-div: rdn 1/2-way: hdwy sn after: led 1f out: r.o* 16/1

0133 2 1 **Catalyze**14 1312 6-9-1 **57**....(t) OisinMurphy(3) 7 62
(Ann Stokell) *chsd ldrs: led 2f out: rdn and hdd 1f out: styd on same pce* **8/1**
3236 2 dht **Hamis Al Bin (IRE)**57 687 5-9-4 **57**....(t) LukeMorris 6 62
(Milton Bradley) *mid-div: hdwy 1/2-way: rdn and ev ch 1f out: styd on same pce ins fnl f* **7/1**3
0/44 4 1 1/4 **Picc Of Burgau**51 756 4-9-5 **58**.... FergusSweeney 15 59
(Geoffrey Deacon) *hld up: swtchd rt and hdwy over 1f out: r.o: nt rch ldrs* **25/1**
-000 5 1/2 **Mambo Spirit (IRE)**31 1009 10-9-5 **58**.... ChrisCatlin 3 57+
(Tony Newcombe) *hld up in tch: plld hrd: hmpd 1/2-way: nt clr run over 1f out: shkn up ins fnl f: styd on same pce* **16/1**
0144 6 1 3/4 **Catalinas Diamond (IRE)**9 1405 6-9-2 **55**....(t) SteveDrowne 10 48
(Pat Murphy) *mid-div: rdn and hdwy 2f out: styd on: nt trble ldrs* **10/1**
5362 7 2 3/4 **Where's Reiley (USA)**14 1312 8-9-2 **55**....(v) SebSanders 4 39
(Michael Attwater) *chsd ldrs: rdn over 1f out: wknd ins fnl f* **4/1**2
5566 8 hd **Little Choosey**31 1009 4-8-13 **52**.... SamHitchcott 17 36
(Anabel K Murphy) *hld up: r.o ins fnl f: nvr trbld ldrs* **25/1**
103 9 1 1/4 **Art Dzeko**38 934 5-9-4 **57**....(p) LiamJones 2 37
(Brian Baugh) *s.s: hdwy 1/2-way: wknd fnl f* **8/1**
530 10 1 **Dark Lane**5 1487 8-9-2 **60**.... EoinWalsh(5) 1 36
(David Evans) *chsd ldr: led over 3f out: rdn and hdd 2f out: edgd rt and wknd ins fnl f* **7/2**1
314- 11 2 **Chester'slittlegem (IRE)**209 6669 5-8-6 **52**.... JosephineGordon(7) 14 22
(Jo Hughes) *mid-div: pushed along 1/2-way: wknd over 1f out* **16/1**
4110 12 1 **Cadmium Loch**14 1311 6-9-0 **58**....(p) JackDuern(5) 13 24
(Andrew Hollinshead) *hld up: pushed along 1/2-way: n.d* **10/1**
345/ 13 1 1/2 **Stand Beside Me (IRE)**1146 709 7-8-13 **55**.... RossAtkinson(3) 11 16
(Tony Newcombe) *s.s: hld up: plld hrd: nvr on terms* **33/1**
5530 14 1 1/4 **Avondream**15 1282 5-9-1 **54**.... DavidProbert 8 11
(Milton Bradley) *prom: rdn 1/2-way: wknd fnl f* **20/1**
0-20 15 7 **Baltic Gin (IRE)**15 1282 4-8-10 **49**....(b1) MartinDwyer 5
(Malcolm Saunders) *led 2f: rdn and wknd over 1f out* **25/1**

1m 10.95s (-0.25) **Going Correction** -0.175s/f (Firm) **15** Ran SP% **132.0**
Speed ratings (Par 101): **94,92,92,91,90 88,84,84,82,81 78,77,75,73,64**
WIN: 22.60 Encapsulated; PL: 5.50, Hamis Al Bin 2.50, Catalyze 3.10; EX: E&HAB 88.60, E&C 129.50; CSF: E&HAB 63.43, E&C 70.90; TC: E&HAB&C 500.73, E&C&HAB 506.81; TF: 702.10 TRIFECTA Part won..
**Owner** Mrs E N Nield **Bred** Juddmonte Farms Ltd **Trained** Epsom, Surrey

**FOCUS**
A moderate sprint handicap. Straightforward form, with the runner-up rated in line with his recent AW form.

## 1574 32RED CASINO H'CAP 2m 1f 34y
**8:00** (8:00) (Class 6) (0-65,68) 4-Y-0+ **£1,940** (£577; £288; £144) **Stalls** Centre

Form RPR
-055 1 **See And Be Seen**16 1263 4-8-13 **56**....(p) RenatoSouza 14 63
(Sylvester Kirk) *a.p: chsd ldr 6f out: rdn over 2f out: led ins fnl f: styd on* **25/1**
31-2 2 1 1/4 **Fitzwilly**11 1359 4-9-8 **68**.... WilliamTwiston-Davies(3) 9 74
(Mick Channon) *led: clr 3f out: rdn over 1f out: hdd ins fnl f: styd on same pce* **5/6**1
1-02 3 1 3/4 **Annaluna (IRE)**17 1242 5-9-2 **58**....(v) DeclanBates(3) 5 62
(David Evans) *a.p: rdn over 2f out: styd on* **8/1**3
0/0- 4 7 **Eastern Magic**322 2860 7-8-11 **55**.... JackDuern(5) 3 51
(Andrew Hollinshead) *hld up: hdwy over 7f out: rdn over 3f out: sn outpcd* **10/1**
2420 5 3/4 **Ogaritmo**45 842 5-9-2 **55**....(t) SeanLevey 10 51
(Seamus Durack) *hld up: rdn over 4f out: n.d* **14/1**
05-5 6 20 **Amberjam (IRE)**39 915 4-8-6 **49** oh1 ow3....(tp) KierenFox 6 23
(Martin Smith) *hld up: rdn over 4f out: sn wknd* **33/1**
505- 7 nse **On Stage**180 7433 5-9-4 **57**.... TomQueally 12 30
(Stuart Kittow) *s.i.s: hld up: rdn over 4f out: wknd 3f out* **11/2**2
0-60 8 45 **Be A Rebel**59 657 4-8-3 **46** oh1....(p) FrankieMcDonald 2
(John E Long) *hld up: wknd over 4f out* **66/1**
-113 9 nk **Tokyo Brown (USA)**35 974 5-9-9 **62**.... LukeMorris 8
(Heather Main) *hld up: hdwy over 6f out: rdn and wknd over 2f out: eased* **8/1**3
2145 10 73 **Cabuchon (GER)**49 801 7-9-3 **61**.... EoinWalsh(5) 4
(David Evans) *chsd ldr 11f: wknd 5f out: eased* **14/1**

3m 47.31s (-4.59) **Going Correction** -0.15s/f (Firm)
**WFA** 4 from 5yo+ 4lb **10** Ran SP% **122.9**
Speed ratings (Par 101): **104,103,102,99,98 89,89,68,68,33**
CSF £48.53 CT £217.93 TOTE £21.80: £2.80, £1.30, £2.40; EX 68.50 Trifecta £252.40.
**Owner** Timothy Pearson **Bred** Exors Of The Late T E Pocock **Trained** Upper Lambourn, Berks

**FOCUS**
A modest staying handicap in which they went, at best, an even gallop. It's been rated around the first three.
T/Plt: £20.40 to a £1 stake. Pool: £59522.25 - 2122.27 winning tickets T/Qpdt: £16.20 to a £1 stake. Pool: £5981.26 - 271.98 winning tickets CR

# 1403 KEMPTON (A.W) (R-H)
Saturday, April 19

**OFFICIAL GOING: Standard**
Wind: medium, half behind Weather: dry, bright spells

## 1575 BETFRED TV/BRITISH STALLION STUDS EBF MAIDEN STKS (BOBIS RACE) 5f (P)
**1:45** (1:46) (Class 4) 2-Y-0 **£4,075** (£1,212; £606; £303) **Stalls** Low

Form RPR
0 1 **Escalating**21 1161 2-9-5 0.... JamesDoyle 6 88+
(Pat Eddery) *mde all: rdn and qcknd clr over 1f out: in command and r.o wl fnl f: comf* **9/2**3
5 2 2 3/4 **Be Bold**8 1417 2-9-5 0.... RyanMoore 4 77
(Richard Hannon) *chsd wnr: rdn and unable qck w wnr over 1f out: no imp but kpt on for clr 2nd* **7/4**1
3 1 1/2 **Colour Catcher** 2-9-5 0.... MickaelBarzalona 1 72+
(Charlie Appleby) *s.i.s: racd in last pair and niggled along: hdwy wl over 1f out: kpt on fnl f to snatch 3rd cl home* **5/2**2
0 4 hd **King Crimson**8 1417 2-9-2 0.... WilliamTwiston-Davies(3) 7 71+
(Mick Channon) *wnt lft s: rn green and t.k.h in midfield: effrt in 3rd 2f out: styd on same pce fr over 1f out: lost 3rd cl home* **11/1**
3 5 2 1/4 **Designate (IRE)**16 1259 2-9-5 0.... JimCrowley 2 63
(Ralph Beckett) *in tch in midfield: rn green on bnd 4f out: nt clr run 3f out: effrt on inner wl over 1f out: no imp* **6/1**
6 1 **Ivors Rebel** 2-9-5 0.... LiamKeniry 8 59
(David Elsworth) *bmpd s and s.i.s: rn green: sn rdn along and outpcd in rr: kpt on ins fnl f: n.d* **50/1**
5 7 8 **Mark's Whisper (IRE)**14 1314 2-8-9 0.... RyanWhile(5) 5 25
(Bill Turner) *chsd ldrs tl 2f out: sn struggling: bhd 1f out* **25/1**

1m 0.41s (-0.09) **Going Correction** +0.025s/f (Slow) **7** Ran SP% **111.5**
Speed ratings (Par 94): **101,96,94,93,90 88,75**
CSF £12.16 TOTE £7.30: £2.40, £1.10; EX 13.20 Trifecta £38.60.
**Owner** K Abdullah **Bred** Juddmonte Farms Ltd **Trained** Nether Winchendon, Bucks

**FOCUS**
An ordinary-looking juvenile maiden. It's been rated towards the upper end of the averages for the race, though.

## 1576 BETFRED "GOALS GALORE EXTRA" H'CAP 7f (P)
**2:20** (2:20) (Class 2) (0-105,97) 4-Y-0+
**£12,450** (£3,728; £1,864; £699; £699; £234) **Stalls** Low

Form RPR
-204 1 **Georgian Bay (IRE)**52 749 4-9-3 **93**....(v1) DanielTudhope 4 105
(K R Burke) *a travelling strly: chsd ldr: upsides and gng best 2f out: led over 1f out: sn pushed along and qcknd clr ent fnl f: r.o wl: readily* **11/2**3
000- 2 2 **Glen Moss (IRE)**196 7014 5-9-6 **96**.... SeanLevey 5 103
(David Brown) *in tch in midfield: rdn and effrt wl over 1f out: chsd clr wnr ins fnl f: r.o but nvr a threat* **11/4**1
001- 3 1 1/2 **Ayaar (IRE)**203 6840 4-9-7 **97**.... FrankieDettori 8 100+
(Luca Cumani) *t.k.h: hld up in tch towards rr: swtchd lft and effrt over 2f out: kpt on wl u.p ins fnl f: no threat to wnr* **7/2**2
0451 4 3/4 **Bravo Echo**21 1174 8-9-5 **95**.... RobertHavlin 3 96
(Michael Attwater) *led: rdn and hdd over 1f out: outpcd by wnr 1f out: plugged on same pce and lost 2 pls ins fnl f* **9/1**
13-0 4 dht **Bluegrass Blues (IRE)**7 1437 4-8-12 **88**.... LukeMorris 7 89
(Paul Cole) *chsd ldng trio: effrt u.p ent fnl 2f: no imp and styd on same pce fnl f* **9/1**
30 6 1 1/2 **Chilworth Icon**7 1442 4-8-13 **92**.... WilliamTwiston-Davies(3) 1 89
(Mick Channon) *in tch in midfield: effrt on inner over 2f out: no imp fr over 1f out* **8/1**
0005 7 2 1/2 **Piscean (USA)**14 1301 9-8-9 **88**.... OisinMurphy(3) 6 79
(Tom Keddy) *stdd and dropped in after s: hld up in last pair: rdn and effrt wl over 1f out: no imp: n.d* **11/1**
6-01 8 7 **Upavon**33 991 4-8-13 **89**.... LiamKeniry 9 61
(David Elsworth) *t.k.h: hld up in last pair: rdn over 2f out: no hdwy and wknd over 1f out* **12/1**
411- 9 6 **Rocksilla**212 6575 4-8-11 **87**.... TedDurcan 2 44
(Chris Wall) *dwlt: sn rcvrd and in tch in midfield: rdn and struggling ent fnl 2f: wknd over 1f out* **20/1**

1m 23.98s (-2.02) **Going Correction** +0.025s/f (Slow) **9** Ran SP% **116.2**
Speed ratings (Par 109): **112,109,108,107,107 105,102,94,87**
CSF £21.15 CT £61.15 TOTE £8.00: £2.00, £1.50, £1.50; EX 24.80 Trifecta £131.70.
**Owner** Market Avenue Racing Club & Mrs E Burke **Bred** Old Carhue & Graeng Bloodstock **Trained** Middleham Moor, N Yorks

**FOCUS**
The runner-up has been rated close to his best.

## 1577 BETFRED MOBILE LOTTO SNOWDROP FILLIES' STKS (LISTED RACE) 1m (P)
**2:55** (2:55) (Class 1) 4-Y-0+
**£20,982** (£7,955; £3,981; £1,983; £995; £499) **Stalls** Low

Form RPR
113- 1 1 1/4 **Ribbons**213 6536 4-9-0 95.... HayleyTurner 2 98+
(James Fanshawe) *broke wl: stdd bk into last pair after 1f: rdn and effrt but stl plenty to do wl over 1f out: r.o u.p to go 2nd ins fnl f: no threat to wnr* **7/2**2
120- 2 3/4 **Magic Of Reality (FR)**204 6792 4-9-0 90....1 AndreaAtzeni 3 96
(Lady Cecil) *in tch in midfield: effrt and sltly hmpd wl over 1f out: rallied and hdwy ent fnl f: r.o wl to snatch 3rd last stride: no threat to wnr* **15/2**
302- 3 shd **Broadway Duchess (IRE)**211 6596 4-9-0 83.... SeanLevey 1 96
(Richard Hannon) *in tch in midfield: effrt u.p ent fnl 2f: chsd ldng pair over 1f out: styd on same pce ins fnl f* **16/1**
300- 4 3/4 **Senafe**296 3734 4-9-0 95.... LukeMorris 9 94
(Marco Botti) *led: rdn ent fnl 2f: drvn over 1f out: hdd 1f out: outpcd and lost 3 pls ins fnl f* **33/1**
5-11 5 4 **Compton Bird**44 853 5-9-0 72.... FrankieDettori 6 85
(Paul Fitzsimons) *stdd s: hld up in rr: effrt u.p on inner ent fnl 2f: no hdwy: n.d* **25/1**
240- 6 1 1/2 **Auction (IRE)**267 4705 4-9-0 99.... JamieSpencer 8 81
(Ed Dunlop) *chsd ldrs tl wnt 2nd over 6f out: rdn and bmpd wl over 1f out: fnd nil and sn lost pl and racing awkwardly: bhd ins fnl f* **7/1**3
061- D **Zurigha (IRE)**204 6796 4-9-3 109.... RyanMoore 7 104
(Richard Hannon) *t.k.h: chsd ldder tl over 6f out: trckd ldng pair after: swtchd lft and effrt wl over 1f out: drvn to ld 1f out: r.o wl: rdn out* **10/11**1

1m 38.54s (-1.26) **Going Correction** +0.025s/f (Slow) **7** Ran SP% **111.5**
Speed ratings (Par 108): **105,105,104,104,100 98,107**
CSF £3.98 TOTE £1.60: £1.30, £1.90; EX 4.50 Trifecta £13.00.
**Owner** Elite Racing Club **Bred** Elite Racing Club **Trained** Newmarket, Suffolk
■ Stewards' Enquiry : Ryan Moore caution: careless riding.

**FOCUS**
The form isn't entirely solid, but the third has been rated close to her form and the fourth as running a personal best.

## 1578 BETFRED MOBILE SPORTS H'CAP (LONDON MILE QUALIFIER) 1m (P)
**3:30** (3:30) (Class 2) (0-105,100) 4-Y-0+
**£12,450** (£3,728; £1,864; £932; £466; £234) **Stalls** Low

Form RPR
244- 1 **Sea Shanty (USA)**170 7641 4-8-12 **91**.... RyanMoore 7 98
(Richard Hannon) *t.k.h: w ldr: rdn 2f out: drvn over 1f out: led ins fnl f: styd on wl: drvn out* **5/1**2
00-1 2 3/4 **Tigers Tale (IRE)**24 1103 5-8-6 **88**....(v) OisinMurphy(3) 4 93
(Roger Teal) *led and set stdy gallop: rdn 2f out: hdd 1f out: styd pressing ldrs: kpt on* **10/1**
0004 3 shd **Santefisio**42 886 8-9-7 **100**....(p) TomEaves 3 105
(Keith Dalgleish) *dwlt: sn pushed along and hdwy into midfield: rdn and effrt 2f out: drvn to ld 1f out: hdd ins fnl f: kpt on same pce after* **20/1**



The Form Book, Raceform Ltd, Newbury, RG14 5SJ

6-66 **4** *shd* **Circumvent**[7] 1439 7-9-6 **99**..............................(b) TomQueally 5 104
(Paul Cole) *chsd ldrs: rdn and effrt ent fnl 2f: kpt on wl u.p ins fnl f* **12/1**

033- **5** *¾* **Loving Spirit**[196] 7014 6-9-4 **100**.............................. RobertTart(3) 6 103
(James Toller) *stdd s: hld up in last pair: rdn and effrt jst over 2f out: hdwy u.p ent fnl f: kpt on but nvr quite gng pce to chal* **3/1**[1]

400- **6** *¾* **George Cinq**[183] 7337 4-8-8 **87** ow1.............................. JamieSpencer 9 88+
(Michael Bell) *stdd s: hld up in last pair: effrt whn nt clr run and swtchd rt over 1f out: pushed along and hdwy 1f out: kpt on wl: nvr trbld ldrs* **8/1**

36-3 **7** *1 ¾* **Big Whiskey (IRE)**[14] 1301 4-8-3 **82**.............................. JimmyQuinn 2 79
(Edward Creighton) *chsd ldrs: effrt u.p on inner to press ldrs wl over 1f out: no ex jst ins fnl f: wknd fnl 100yds* **14/1**

/26- **8** *2* **Frasers Hill**[349] 2041 5-8-6 **85**.............................. AndreaAtzeni 11 78
(Roger Varian) *in tch in midfield: effrt but wd wl over 2f out: no imp over 1f out: plugged on same pce fnl f* **7/1**[3]

-110 **9** *¾* **Life And Times (USA)**[11] 1356 6-8-8 **87**.............................. FrannyNorton 1 78
(Mark Johnston) *t.k.h: in tch in midfield: rdn and no hdwy 2f out: sn outpcd and btn over 1f out* **5/1**[2]

0000 **10** *2* **Loyalty**[28] 1071 7-8-8 **87** ow1..............................(v) DaleSwift 10 73
(Derek Shaw) *hld up in tch in last trio: rdn and effrt wl over 1f out: no hdwy: n.d* **25/1**

400- **11** *1 ¾* **Cavaleiro (IRE)**[175] 7542 5-8-11 **90**.............................. HayleyTurner 8 72
(Marcus Tregoning) *chsd ldrs: rdn 3f out: lost pl over 2f out: bhd fnl f* **33/1**

1m 38.31s (-1.49) **Going Correction** +0.025s/f (Slow) **11** Ran SP% **116.9**
Speed ratings (Par 109): **108,107,107,107,106 105,103,101,101,99 97**
CSF £52.43 CT £923.00 TOTE £5.00: £1.60, £4.40, £5.70; EX 49.60 Trifecta £602.50.
**Owner** The Queen **Bred** Her Majesty The Queen **Trained** East Everleigh, Wilts

**FOCUS**
A competitive contest, although it paid to be handy. Ordinary pace and time, coupled with a bunched finish mean the form cannot be rated highly.

## 1579 BETFRED SUPPORTS JACK BERRY HOUSE FILLIES' CONDITIONS STKS (BOBIS RACE) 1m (P)

**4:00** (4:02) (Class 2) 3-Y-O **£12,450** (£3,728; £1,864; £932) **Stalls** Low

Form RPR

1- **1** **Queen Of Ice**[168] 7692 3-9-0 82.............................. RyanMoore 2 92+
(William Haggas) *mde all: rdn and qcknd clr ent fnl 2f: a doing enough after: rdn out* **11/10**[1]

246- **2** *1 ¾* **Midnite Angel (IRE)**[204] 6795 3-9-0 95.............................. FrankieDettori 3 89+
(Richard Hannon) *in tch in rr: rdn and effrt over 2f out: hdwy to chse clr wnr and edgd rt over 1f out: kpt on u.p but nvr gng to rch wnr: eased cl home* **13/8**[2]

253- **3** *5* **Acclio (IRE)**[175] 7533 3-9-0 71.............................. FrederikTylicki 1 77
(Clive Brittain) *chsd ldng trio: rdn and outpcd 2f out: wl hld 3rd and one pce fr over 1f out* **25/1**

21 **4** *1 ¾* **Joie De Reve (IRE)**[36] 962 3-9-0 76.............................. JamieSpencer 4 72
(David Simcock) *chsd wnr: rdn and outpcd 2f out: 4th and wl hld over 1f out* **9/2**[3]

1m 37.87s (-1.93) **Going Correction** +0.025s/f (Slow) **4** Ran SP% **107.7**
Speed ratings (Par 101): **110,108,103,101**
CSF £3.15 TOTE £2.60; EX 3.00 Trifecta £17.90.
**Owner** Cheveley Park Stud **Bred** Cheveley Park Stud Ltd **Trained** Newmarket, Suffolk

**FOCUS**
The winner had the run of the race. The runner-up has been rated a bit off her 2yo form but could rate higher.

## 1580 BETFRED "RACING'S BIGGEST SUPPORTER" CONDITIONS STKS (BOBIS RACE) 1m (P)

**4:35** (4:36) (Class 2) 3-Y-O
**£12,450** (£3,728; £1,864; £932; £466; £234) **Stalls** Low

Form RPR

36-2 **1** **Zampa Manos (USA)**[23] 1122 3-9-0 90.............................. OisinMurphy 5 91
(Andrew Balding) *mde all: jnd 2f out: sn drvn: sustained duel w runner-up after: r.o gamely and maintained narrow ld* **22/1**

31- **2** *shd* **Snow Trouble (USA)**[259] 4987 3-9-0 84.............................. HayleyTurner 2 91
(Marcus Tregoning) *chsd wnr: rdn to chal 2f out: sustained duel w wnr after: r.o gamely but jst hld* **7/1**

2-1 **3** *1 ¾* **Hagree (IRE)**[15] 1287 3-9-0 0.............................. AntonioFresu 4 87
(Marco Botti) *chsd ldrs: rdn and effrt 2f out: styd on same pce ins fnl f* **11/4**[2]

154- **4** *nk* **God Willing**[189] 7195 3-9-0 105.............................. JamieSpencer 3 86
(Ed Dunlop) *t.k.h: hld up in tch: hdwy to chse ldrs 4f out: effrt u.p on inner over 1f out: styd on same pce fnl f* **5/4**[1]

1 **5** *¾* **Mindurownbusiness (IRE)**[45] 847 3-9-0 76.............................. JimCrowley 6 84
(David Simcock) *stdd after s: hld up in rr: rdn and effrt ent fnl 2f: kpt on ins fnl f: nvr trbld ldrs* **25/1**

106- **6** *26* **Championship (IRE)**[205] 6765 3-9-0 89.............................. RyanMoore 1 25
(Richard Hannon) *stdd s: hld up in last pair: rdn and effrt 2f out: rdr sn looking down and eased over 1f out: t.o* **4/1**[3]

1m 40.19s (0.39) **Going Correction** +0.025s/f (Slow) **6** Ran SP% **111.8**
Speed ratings (Par 104): **99,98,97,96,96 70**
CSF £155.87 TOTE £13.70: £8.30, £6.70; EX 50.30 Trifecta £217.60.
**Owner** N M Watts **Bred** Hunter Valley Farm Et Al **Trained** Kingsclere, Hants

**FOCUS**
A fine advert of Oisin Murphy's talents in the saddle. The winner had an easy lead, it was the slowest time of the four C&D races on the card and the form is rated around the winner.

## 1581 BETFRED "STILL TREBLE ODDS ON LUCKY 15'S" QUEEN'S PRIZE (H'CAP) 2m (P)

**5:05** (5:05) (Class 2) (0-105,97) 4-Y-O+
**£12,450** (£3,728; £1,864; £932; £466; £234) **Stalls** Low

Form RPR

330- **1** **Seaside Sizzler**[189] 7193 7-9-1 **86**..............................(vt) JimCrowley 5 94
(Ralph Beckett) *in tch in midfield: rdn over 3f out: styd on to chal 1f out: led ins fnl f: r.o wl* **11/2**

20-3 **2** *nk* **Clowance Estate (IRE)**[19] 1213 5-9-10 **95**..............................(b[1]) JamieSpencer 6 103
(Roger Charlton) *hld up in tch in last pair: swtchd lft and racd wd of rivals 7f out tl chsd ldr 4f out: rdn to ld 2f out: hdd ins fnl f: kpt on wl* **9/2**[3]

125- **3** *2* **Shwaiman (IRE)**[197] 6991 4-9-8 **97**.............................. FrederikTylicki 7 102
(James Fanshawe) *v.s.a: rcvrd and in tch in rr: rdn and effrt on outer wl over 3f out: styd on fnl f: wnt 3rd fnl 100yds* **7/2**[2]

0-22 **4** *nk* **Noble Silk**[19] 1213 5-9-3 **91**..............................(p) OisinMurphy(3) 3 96
(Lucy Wadham) *in tch in midfield: rdn to chse ldrs and n.m.r ent fnl f: styd on same pce fnl 100yds* **7/1**

00-0 **5** *½* **Flashman**[21] 1175 5-8-8 **79**.............................. TedDurcan 2 83
(Gary Moore) *chsd ldrs: rdn and ev ch wl over 1f out tl ins fnl f: wknd fnl 100yds* **33/1**

41-1 **6** *2 ¾* **White Nile (IRE)**[10] 1383 5-9-7 **92**.............................. RyanMoore 4 93
(Ed Dunlop) *chsd ldrs: rdn and effrt ent fnl 2f: pressed ldr over 1f out tl jst ins fnl f: wknd fnl 100yds* **5/2**[1]

00-5 **7** *3 ¾* **Sir Graham Wade (IRE)**[19] 1213 5-9-12 **97**.............................. FrannyNorton 1 93
(Mark Johnston) *led tl hdd and rdn 2f out: no ex u.p over 1f out: wknd fnl f* **8/1**

3m 28.7s (-1.40) **Going Correction** +0.025s/f (Slow)
**WFA** 4 from 5yo+ 4lb **7** Ran SP% **110.9**
Speed ratings (Par 109): **104,103,102,102,102 101,99**
CSF £28.31 TOTE £7.30: £3.60, £4.70; EX 34.40 Trifecta £130.50.
**Owner** I J Heseltine **Bred** Redmyre Bloodstock And S Hillen **Trained** Kimpton, Hants

**FOCUS**
An interesting running of the Queen's Prize, but the disappointing Sir Graham Wade cut out just a steady pace and only around 3l covered the first five at the line. The fourth and fifth have been rated close to their marks.
T/Plt: £141.30 to a £1 stake. Pool: £89383.44 - 461.59 winning tickets T/Qpdt: £31.90 to a £1 stake. Pool: £4500.54 - 104.30 winning tickets SP

# 1394 NOTTINGHAM (L-H)

Saturday, April 19

**OFFICIAL GOING: Good to firm (good in places; 8.5)**
Wind: Moderate half behind Weather: Sunny periods

## 1582 NOTTINGHAM RACECOURSE LADIES DAY 10TH MAY MAIDEN STKS 1m 75y

**4:45** (4:47) (Class 5) 3-Y-O **£3,234** (£962; £481; £240) **Stalls** Centre

Form RPR

6-2 **1** **Zerfaal**[21] 1173 3-9-5 0.............................. PaulHanagan 11 82+
(John Gosden) *trckd ldrs: hdwy over 3f out: cl up 2f out: rdn to chal over 1f out: drvn and edgd rt ent fnl f: led last 110yds: kpt on* **10/11**[1]

56- **2** *½* **Maracuja**[178] 7466 3-9-0 0.............................. JoeFanning 4 75
(Mark Johnston) *sn led: pushed along wl over 2f out: jnd and rdn over 1f out: drvn ent fnl f: hdd and no ex last 110yds* **100/1**

**3** *1 ½* **Karraar** 3-9-5 0.............................. PatDobbs 6 77
(Richard Hannon) *chsd ldrs: effrt 3f out: rdn along 2f out: kpt on same pce fnl f* **25/1**

02- **4** *hd* **Rapid Advance**[159] 7834 3-9-5 0.............................. WilliamBuick 13 77+
(Roger Varian) *in tch on outer: hdwy 3f out: rdn to chse ldng pair wl over 1f out: drvn ent fnl f: kpt on same pce* **3/1**[2]

0- **5** *2 ¼* **Heho**[208] 6690 3-9-0 0.............................. ShaneKelly 1 66
(Sir Michael Stoute) *in tch: hdwy 3f out: rdn to chse ldrs 2f out: kpt on one pce appr fnl f* **20/1**

053- **6** *1 ¾* **Glasgow Central**[194] 7070 3-9-5 73.............................. RobertWinston 5 67
(Charles Hills) *cl up: rdn along 3f out: drvn 2f out: grad wknd* **20/1**

**7** *¾* **High Church (IRE)** 3-9-5 0.............................. GeorgeBaker 7 68+
(Roger Charlton) *dwlt and bhd: stdy hdwy on inner over 3f out: effrt and green 2f out: sn rdn and kpt on fnl f: nrst fin* **33/1**

05- **8** *2 ½* **Kinema (IRE)**[269] 4640 3-9-5 0.............................. GrahamLee 3 60
(Ed Walker) *towards rr: hdwy on outer over 3f out: in tch over 2f out: sn rdn and no imp* **33/1**

0- **9** *¾* **Mantonize (USA)**[281] 4256 3-9-5 0.............................. SilvestreDeSousa 10 58+
(Brian Meehan) *a in midfield* **33/1**

0- **10** *1* **Saxon Princess (IRE)**[274] 4484 3-9-0 0.............................. JamesDoyle 2 51
(Roger Charlton) *in tch: rdn along over 3f out: sn wknd* **20/1**

**11** *hd* **Gang Warfare** 3-9-5 0.............................. HarryBentley 12 55
(Olly Stevens) *dwlt: a in rr* **50/1**

0 **12** *2* **Mountain Dew**[17] 1233 3-9-0 0.............................. RichardKingscote 8 46+
(Ralph Beckett) *a towards rr* **25/1**

**13** *15* **Saalib (USA)** 3-9-5 0..............................(t) DaneO'Neill 9 16
(Brian Meehan) *dwlt: a in rr* **12/1**[3]

1m 44.66s (-4.34) **Going Correction** -0.525s/f (Hard) **13** Ran SP% **118.8**
Speed ratings (Par 98): **100,99,98,97,95 93,93,90,89,88 88,86,71**
CSF £179.92 TOTE £1.60: £1.10, £6.90, £4.40; EX 66.40 Trifecta £1074.00.
**Owner** Hamdan Al Maktoum **Bred** Shadwell Estate Company Limited **Trained** Newmarket, Suffolk

**FOCUS**
All races on Inner track. Rail in back straight and home bend moved out two metres onto fresh ground, increasing distances on Round course by 10yds. It was dry overnight but the ground had been watered. A fair maiden, won a shade cosily by the favourite. The initial level is set around the fourth and sixth.

## 1583 IJF 50TH ANNIVERSARY MAIDEN STKS 5f 13y

**5:15** (5:15) (Class 5) 2-Y-O **£3,234** (£962; £481; £240) **Stalls** High

Form RPR

2 **1** **Burtonwood**[15] 1276 2-9-5 0.............................. AdamKirby 3 79
(Richard Fahey) *cl up: effrt 2f out: rdn over 1f out: led jst ins fnl f: kpt on wl towards fin* **1/1**[1]

**2** *¾* **Clouds Rest** 2-9-0 0.............................. TonyHamilton 5 71
(Richard Fahey) *slt ld: pushed along 2f out: rdn and edgd lft ent fnl f: sn hdd and no ex last 75yds* **25/1**

**3** *1 ¾* **Celestial Vision (USA)** 2-9-5 0.............................. RichardKingscote 6 70+
(Tom Dascombe) *green and sn outpcd in rr: pushed along 1/2-way: gd hdwy over 1f out: rn in strly ins fnl f: nrst fin* **8/1**[3]

0 **4** *shd* **Rose Of Kiev (IRE)**[16] 1259 2-9-0 0.............................. JoeFanning 1 65
(Mark Johnston) *wnt lft s: sn rcvrd to chse ldng pair: effrt and cl up wl over 1f out: sn rdn: wknd ins fnl f* **50/1**

**5** *hd* **Dr No** 2-9-5 0.............................. PatDobbs 7 69+
(Richard Hannon) *trckd ldrs on inner: effrt 2f out: rdn over 1f out: one pce ins fnl f* **13/8**[2]

**6** *2 ¼* **Makin A Statement (IRE)** 2-9-5 0.............................. RobertWinston 4 62+
(John Quinn) *trckd ldrs: effrt over 2f out: sn rdn and wknd ent fnl f: hld whn sltly hmpd last 100yds and eased towards fin* **25/1**

**7** *3 ¾* **Muzarkash** 2-9-5 0.............................. PaulHanagan 8 47
(J W Hills) *s.i.s and wnt lft s: green and a bhd* **16/1**

59.43s (-2.07) **Going Correction** -0.525s/f (Hard) 2y crse rec **7** Ran SP% **114.7**
Speed ratings (Par 92): **95,93,91,90,90 86,80**
CSF £30.90 TOTE £1.50: £1.10, £9.60; EX 18.30 Trifecta £159.50.
**Owner** D W Armstrong & Cheveley Park Stud **Bred** Brightwalton Stud **Trained** Musley Bank, N Yorks

**FOCUS**
A one-two for Richard Fahey. The level is a bit guessy but the winner looks the type to do better, as well as the third.

## 1584 HAPPY EASTER FROM NOTTINGHAM RACECOURSE H'CAP 5f 13y
5:45 (5:46) (Class 6) (0-65,65) 4-Y-O+ £1,940 (£577; £288; £144) Stalls High

Form RPR
-603 1 **Dawn Catcher**45 845 4-9-4 62 GeorgeBaker 1 73
(Geoffrey Deacon) *mde all far side: rdn clr wl over 1f out: readily* 7/1[2]
0-00 2 1 1/4 **Dancing Maite**88 273 9-8-4 53 (b) PhilipPrince(5) 9 60
(Roy Bowring) *racd towards centre: prom: rdn along 2f out: chsd wnr over 1f out: kpt on: 1st of 7 in gp* 25/1
0006 3 2 **Lucky Dan (IRE)**37 938 8-9-7 65 RaulDaSilva 4 64
(Paul Green) *trckd ldng pair far side: hdwy to chse wnr over 1f out: sn rdn and no imp fnl f: 2nd of 4 in gp* 12/1
6-03 4 hd **Danzoe (IRE)**17 1238 7-9-3 61 AdamKirby 14 60
(Christine Dunnett) *cl up stands' rail: rdn along 2f out: drvn over 1f out: kpt on same pce: 2nd of 7 in gp* 8/1[3]
0040 5 3/4 **Avonmore Star**46 835 6-8-12 56 BenCurtis 10 52
(Alan McCabe) *rrd s and s.i.s: in rr: hdwy 2f out: swtchd rt to stands' rail and rdn wl over 1f out: styd on fnl f: nrst fin: 3rd of 7 in gp* 16/1
0545 6 hd **China Excels**25 1089 7-8-2 51 oh2 NoelGarbutt(5) 15 46
(Mandy Rowland) *racd nr stands' rail: led stands' side gp: rdn along 2f out: sn hdd and grad wknd: 4th of 7 in gp* 8/1[3]
5463 7 1 **Give Us A Belle (IRE)**10 1378 5-8-13 57 (vt) AdamBeschizza 8 49
(Christine Dunnett) *hmpd s: chsd ldrs stands' side: rdn along 2f out: keeping on whn n.m.r ent fnl f: no imp: 5th of 7 in gp* 7/1[2]
0600 8 1/2 **Fratellino**56 719 7-9-2 60 (vt) SilvestreDeSousa 13 50
(Alan McCabe) *chsd ldrs stands' side: rdn along 1/2-way: sn no imp: 6th of 7 in gp* 6/4[1]
2-40 9 1 1/4 **Errigal Lad**15 1282 9-8-0 51 oh1 JackGarritty(7) 7 36
(Garry Woodward) *wnt rt s: a in rr towards stands' side: 7th of 7 in gp* 18/1
00-0 10 4 1/2 **Sophie's Beau (USA)**25 1089 7-8-9 53 (bt) RussKennemore 5 22
(Michael Chapman) *chsd wnr far side: rdn along 2f out: sn wknd: 3rd of 4 in gp* 50/1
41-0 11 2 1/4 **My Time**97 147 5-8-10 54 GrahamLee 6 15
(Michael Mullineaux) *racd far side: a in rr: 4th of 4 in gp* 25/1
58.81s (-2.69) **Going Correction** -0.525s/f (Hard) 11 Ran SP% 115.7
Speed ratings (Par 101): **100,98,94,94,93 92,91,90,88,81 77**
CSF £168.00 CT £2083.41 TOTE £6.20: £2.30, £13.20, £8.50; EX 198.90 Trifecta £786.90.
**Owner** Mayden Stud & Associates **Bred** Mayden Stud, J A And D S Dewhurst **Trained** Compton, Berks

**FOCUS**
They raced all over the track in this sprint. The winner made all on the far side, the runner-up came up the centre and the first home on the stands' side was only narrowly beaten for third, so it's hard to know if the draw had an impact. The winner has been rated as running a length personal best.

## 1585 NEW RACING UK ANYWHERE AVAILABLE NOW H'CAP 5f 13y
6:15 (6:15) (Class 5) (0-75,75) 3-Y-O £2,587 (£770; £384; £192) Stalls High

Form RPR
60-4 1 **Skye's The Limit**10 1396 3-9-4 72 PaulHanagan 11 79
(Richard Fahey) *towards rr: hdwy on stands' rail over 2f out: effrt on inner to join ldr over 1f out: sn rdn and qcknd to ld last 100yds: kpt on* 5/2[1]
144- 2 1/2 **Captain Whoosh (IRE)**236 5842 3-9-2 70 RichardKingscote 3 75
(Tom Dascombe) *wnt rt s: trckd ldrs: hdwy 2f out: rdn over 1f out: ev ch ins fnl f: drvn and kpt on towards fin* 7/1[3]
210- 3 1/2 **Shilla (IRE)**208 6695 3-9-2 70 DaneO'Neill 2 73
(Henry Candy) *in tch on wd outside: hdwy 2f out: rdn over 1f out: ev ch ins fnl f: kpt on* 7/2[2]
2-31 4 1/2 **Searchlight**92 213 3-9-7 75 JamesDoyle 10 77
(Kevin Ryan) *racd towards stands' rail: trckd ldrs: smooth hdwy to ld 1 1/2f out: rdn and jnd ent fnl f: drvn and hdd last 100yds: one pce* 7/2[2]
3023 5 3 **Diamondsinthesky (IRE)**29 1039 3-7-11 58 ow2 (v) AdamMcLean(7) 6 49
(Derek Shaw) *prom: rdn along 2f out: grad wknd* 25/1
113 6 nk **Razin' Hell**23 1130 3-8-13 67 (v) SilvestreDeSousa 1 57
(Alan McCabe) *sn led: rdn along 2f out: hdd 1 1/2f out and sn drvn: wknd ent fnl f* 10/1
65-4 7 6 **Danfazi (IRE)**82 354 3-8-13 72 JacobButterfield(5) 5 40
(Kristin Stubbs) *wnt lft s: a towards rr* 25/1
04-1 8 2 3/4 **Walta (IRE)**17 1243 3-8-8 67 PhilipPrince(5) 4 25
(Roy Bowring) *sltly hmpd s and sn swtchd lft to far rail: sn outpcd and wl bhd tl kpt on fr over 1f out: nvr a factor* 25/1
035- 9 2 **Lexington Rose**175 7545 3-9-5 73 RoystonFfrench 7 24
(Bryan Smart) *chsd ldrs: rdn along 1/2-way: wknd fnl 2f* 14/1
58.6s (-2.90) **Going Correction** -0.525s/f (Hard) 9 Ran SP% 112.8
Speed ratings (Par 98): **102,101,100,99,94 94,84,80,77**
CSF £19.49 CT £59.58 TOTE £2.50: £1.10, £4.40, £1.20; EX 31.40 Trifecta £133.10.
**Owner** The Fairweather Foursome **Bred** Whatton Manor Stud **Trained** Musley Bank, N Yorks

**FOCUS**
The leaders set a good gallop. The runner-up and third have had a few chances but have been rated as improving a length or so.

## 1586 IJF 50TH ANNIVERSARY H'CAP (BOBIS RACE) 1m 75y
6:45 (6:46) (Class 4) (0-80,80) 3-Y-O £5,175 (£1,540; £769; £384) Stalls Centre

Form RPR
340- 1 **Donny Rover (IRE)**161 7819 3-9-6 79 AndrewMullen 1 84
(Michael Appleby) *hld up in rr: pushed along and hdwy on inner 3f out: sn chsng ldrs: rdn to squeeze through 2f out: drvn to chal ent fnl f: styd on to ld last 100yds* 16/1
01- 2 1/2 **Secret Archive (USA)**150 7971 3-9-5 78 RichardKingscote 9 82
(Ralph Beckett) *a.p: cl up wl over 2f out: led wl over 1f out: jnd and rdn ent fnl f: sn drvn: hdd and no ex last 100yds* 8/1
312- 3 1/2 **Emef Diamond**183 7336 3-9-6 79 SilvestreDeSousa 8 82
(Mick Channon) *sn chsng ldr: hdwy and cl up 3f out: rdn along wl over 1f out: drvn and ev ch ent fnl f: kpt on same pce last 100yds* 14/1
301- 4 1/2 **Gilbey's Mate**182 7371 3-9-6 79 WilliamBuick 6 81
(John Gosden) *hld up in rr: hdwy on wd outside over 2f out: rdn along wl over 1f out: styd on strly fnl f: nrst fin* 5/1[2]
412- 5 1/2 **Meteoroid (USA)**210 6640 3-9-7 80 JamesDoyle 2 80
(Lady Cecil) *t.k.h: trckd ldrs: hdwy 3f out: rdn along to chse ldrs 2f out: kpt on same pce fnl f* 2/1[1]
420- 6 1/2 **Raise Your Gaze**221 6277 3-9-4 77 AdamKirby 10 76+
(Clive Cox) *hld up towards rr: hdwy 3f out: rdn wl over 1f out: styd on fnl f: nrst fin* 20/1
536- 7 3/4 **Cornish Path**203 6839 3-9-2 75 DaneO'Neill 5 75+
(Henry Candy) *hld up towards rr: hdwy over 3f out: effrt over 2f out: chsng ldrs whn bdly hmpd towards inner 2f out: sn swtchd rt and rdn to chse ldrs over 1f out: kpt on same pce fnl f* 16/1
-052 8 3 1/4 **Intermath (IRE)**12 1352 3-9-4 80 JasonHart(3) 11 70
(David Evans) *set gd pce: rdn along over 2f out: drvn and hdd wl over 1f out: sn wknd* 16/1
022- 9 3/4 **Maraayill (IRE)**170 7647 3-9-3 76 PaddyAspell 3 64
(Marco Botti) *dwlt: t.k.h and sn chsng ldrs on inner: hdwy 3f out: effrt 2f out: rdn to chal over 1f out: ev ch tl drvn and wknd ent fnl f* 7/1[3]
435- 10 1 1/2 **Canova (IRE)**143 8067 3-9-2 75 GeorgeBaker 4 60
(Roger Charlton) *dwlt: a towards rr* 10/1
5-21 11 28 **Excellent Royale (IRE)**94 188 3-9-4 77 RobertWinston 7
(Charles Hills) *chsd ldrs: rdn along 3f out: wknd 2f out* 50/1
1m 44.02s (-4.98) **Going Correction** -0.525s/f (Hard) 11 Ran SP% 113.7
Speed ratings (Par 100): **103,102,102,101,101 100,99,96,95,94 66**
CSF £133.90 CT £1865.98 TOTE £23.10: £4.60, £3.60, £3.50; EX 272.00 Trifecta £1047.10.
**Owner** C L Bacon **Bred** Lynn Lodge Stud **Trained** Danethorpe, Notts

**FOCUS**
A few interesting, lightly raced sorts lined up in this handicap, but it went the way of the most experienced horse in the race. The level is a bit fluid with the second-sixth all unexposed.

## 1587 JOIN US FOR LADIES DAY MAIDEN STKS 1m 2f 50y
7:15 (7:19) (Class 5) 3-Y-O £3,234 (£962; £481; £240) Stalls Low

Form RPR
1 **Zaeemah (IRE)** 3-9-0 0 SilvestreDeSousa 2 83+
(Saeed bin Suroor) *chsd ldrs: hdwy 1/2-way and sn cl up: effrt 3f out: slt ld 2f out and sn rdn: drvn ins fnl f and kpt on wl towards fin* 11/8[1]
2- 2 3/4 **Saab Almanal**192 7128 3-9-5 0 ShaneKelly 3 86+
(James Fanshawe) *led 2f: prom: effrt 2f out: sn rdn and ev ch tl drvn ins fnl f and no ex last 75yds* 6/1[3]
3 1 **Moohaarib (IRE)** 3-9-5 0 PaddyAspell 1 84+
(Marco Botti) *in tch: hdwy 3f out: chsd ldrs 2f out: rdn over 1f out: ev ch ins fnl f: n.m.r on inner and no ex last 100yds* 33/1
53-2 4 2 3/4 **Three Peaks**17 1237 3-9-5 80 JamesDoyle 10 79
(Charles Hills) *prom: hdwy 3f out: chal 2f out: sn rdn and ev ch tl drvn and one pce ent fnl f* 8/1
03- 5 1 **Battersea**183 7332 3-9-5 0 DaneO'Neill 5 77
(Roger Varian) *t.k.h early: trckd ldrs: hdwy 3f out: rdn along 2f out: kpt on same pce fnl f* 8/1
6 1 1/4 **Prairie Rose (GER)** 3-9-0 0 HarryBentley 9 70
(Olly Stevens) *dwlt and towards rr: hdwy 3f out: rdn to chse ldrs 2f out: no imp fr over 1f out* 100/1
3 7 1 1/4 **Arcamante (ITY)**30 1035 3-9-0 0 (b) DanielMuscutt(5) 8 72?
(Marco Botti) *chsd ldrs: led after 2f: rdn along 3f out: hdd 2f out: grad wknd* 100/1
8 3/4 **Altaayil (IRE)** 3-9-5 0 PaulHanagan 12 71
(Sir Michael Stoute) *dwlt: a towards rr* 4/1[2]
9 3/4 **Do Wah Diddy Diddy** 3-9-5 0 AdamKirby 4 70
(Clive Cox) *a towards rr* 20/1
10 2 1/4 **Seagull (IRE)** 3-9-0 0 WilliamBuick 11 60
(John Gosden) *dwlt: a towards rr* 10/1
5- 11 14 **Sweet Summer**126 8297 3-9-0 0 StevieDonohoe 7 34
(John Holt) *midfield: rdn along 4f out: sn wknd* 100/1
2m 16.29s (1.99) **Going Correction** -0.525s/f (Hard) 11 Ran SP% 118.4
Speed ratings (Par 98): **71,70,69,67,66 65,64,64,63,61 50**
CSF £9.83 TOTE £2.20: £1.30, £1.80, £8.60; EX 14.80 Trifecta £159.60.
**Owner** Godolphin **Bred** Darley **Trained** Newmarket, Suffolk

**FOCUS**
An interesting maiden, but they went no pace early and it was an advantage to race handily. It's been rated around the third, fourth and averages for the race.

## 1588 DOWNLOAD NEW RACING UK IPAD APP H'CAP 1m 2f 50y
7:45 (7:46) (Class 6) (0-65,65) 3-Y-O £1,940 (£577; £288; £144) Stalls Low

Form RPR
5-54 1 **Cotton Club (IRE)**19 1214 3-8-13 64 PatMillman(7) 8 72
(Rod Millman) *hld up towards rr: swtchd to wd outside and gd hdwy over 2f out: rdn and str run to ld ent fnl f: styd on strly* 12/1
-523 2 2 **Khee Society**30 1032 3-9-3 61 GeorgeBaker 4 65
(David Evans) *bhd: hdwy over 3f out: effrt whn nt clr run 2f out: sn swtchd rt to outer and rdn: styd on to chse wnr ins fnl f: kpt on* 16/1
000- 3 1 **Winter Spice (IRE)**199 6953 3-9-6 64 AdamKirby 16 66+
(Clive Cox) *hld up towards rr: hdwy over 3f out: rdn to chse ldrs wl over 1f out: drvn and ev ch appr fnl f: sn edgd lft and kpt on same pce* 11/2[3]
4-06 4 1 **Ronya (IRE)**79 378 3-8-11 60 JoeyHaynes(5) 5 60
(K R Burke) *trckd ldrs on inner: hdwy 3f out: effrt 2f out: sn rdn and ev ch tl drvn and one pce fnl f* 50/1
530- 5 3/4 **Sellingallthetime (IRE)**161 7819 3-9-7 65 AndrewMullen 13 64
(Michael Appleby) *in rr: hdwy on outer over 3f out: chsd ldrs 2f out: sn rdn and edgd lft: drvn and one pce appr fnl f* 7/4[1]
036- 6 1/2 **Bognor (USA)**150 7979 3-9-7 65 BenCurtis 10 63
(Jo Hughes) *prom: hdwy over 3f out: chsd ldr over 2f out: sn rdn and ev ch tl drvn and one pce appr fnl f* 33/1
54-5 7 3/4 **The Kid**21 1166 3-9-7 65 RichardKingscote 12 63+
(Tom Dascombe) *hld up: hdwy 3f out: chsd ldrs 2f out: sn rdn and no imp fnl f* 9/2[2]
0235 8 1 **Her Red Devil (IRE)**14 1308 3-8-12 56 PaulHanagan 2 51
(Richard Fahey) *led: pushed along over 3f out: rdn over 2f out: drvn over 1f out: hdd & wknd ent fnl f* 20/1
0-42 9 7 **Suni Dancer**14 1308 3-8-7 51 oh2 DuranFentiman 3 32
(Paul Green) *a towards rr* 33/1
-113 10 1 1/2 **Enquiring**10 1382 3-9-2 60 JoeFanning 14 39
(Mark Johnston) *prom: trckd ldr 1/2-way: cl up 4f out: rdn along 3f out: sn wknd* 7/1
4666 11 6 **Dark Tsarina (IRE)**23 1124 3-9-4 62 LiamKeniry 6 29
(John Butler) *a towards rr* 100/1
004- 12 hd **Kashstaree**180 7418 3-8-7 51 oh2 RoystonFfrench 11 18
(David Barron) *a bhd* 33/1
50-3 13 1 1/4 **Goleador (USA)**58 670 3-9-6 64 (b) JamesDoyle 9 28
(Marco Botti) *hld up: hdwy and in tch over 3f out: rdn along whn n.m.r wl over 2f out: sn wknd* 16/1
000- 14 1 1/4 **Moxey**178 7467 3-8-12 56 PJMcDonald 7 18
(John Davies) *chsd ldrs: effrt 3f out: rdn 2f out: sn drvn and wknd* 66/1

-062 **15** *16* **Red Wifey (IRE)**[26] 1083 3-9-2 **60**.........................(b) SilvestreDeSousa 1
(Alan McCabe) *dwlt: rapid hdwy on inner and sn chsng ldrs: effrt over 3f out: rdn along over 2f out: sn wknd and bhd* **25/1**

2m 12.34s (-1.96) **Going Correction** -0.525s/f (Hard) **15** Ran SP% **123.8**
Speed ratings (Par 96): **86,84,83,82,82 81,81,80,74,73 68,68,67,66,53**
CSF £179.09 CT £1192.67 TOTE £18.30: £3.90, £4.10, £1.80; EX 114.80 Trifecta £1012.00.
**Owner** The Links Partnership **Bred** Patrick Gleeson **Trained** Kentisbeare, Devon

**FOCUS**
There was competition for the lead here, resulting in a good pace, and the race was set up for the closers. The third-seventh have all been rated within a length or so of their marks.
T/Plt: £294.40 to a £1 stake. Pool: £50515.32 - 125.23 winning tickets T/Qpdt: £107.20 to a £1 stake. Pool: £4261.89 - 29.40 winning tickets JR

# 1560 MUSSELBURGH (R-H)

Sunday, April 20

**OFFICIAL GOING: Good to firm (8.7)**
Wind: Breezy, half behind Weather: Cloudy, bright

## 1596 2,000 GUINEAS ANTE POST AT TOTEPOOL.COM H'CAP — 1m
**2:05** (2:08) (Class 6) (0-60,60) 4-Y-O+ **£3,234** (£962; £481; £240) **Stalls Low**

Form RPR

00-2 **1** **Echo Of Lightning**[15] 1310 4-9-1 **54**.......................... PaulPickard 9 65
(Brian Ellison) *taken early to post: mde al: pushed along 2f out: styd on strly fnl f* **2/1**[1]

50-0 **2** *2 1/4* **Mowhoob**[8] 1446 4-9-4 **57**.......................... GrahamLee 2 63
(Jim Goldie) *trckd ldrs: effrt and wnt 2nd over 1f out: kpt on fnl f: nt rch wnr* **12/1**

0-00 **3** *nk* **Call Of Duty (IRE)**[18] 1249 9-8-5 **49** oh1 ow3............(b) EmmaSayer(5) 5 54
(Dianne Sayer) *bhd and sn pushed along: gd hdwy wl over 1f out: kpt on strly fnl f: nrst fin* **40/1**

4-00 **4** *2 3/4* **Taxiformissbyron**[29] 289 4-9-0 **53**..........................(p) TomEaves 7 52
(Iain Jardine) *in tch: drvn and outpcd over 2f out: kpt on ins fnl f: nvr able to chal* **22/1**

4540 **5** *nk* **Cyflymder (IRE)**[59] 671 8-9-0 **53**..........................(b) LukeMorris 4 51
(David C Griffiths) *chsd wnr: rdn over 2f out: hung rt and lost 2nd over 1f out: kpt on same pce* **20/1**

663- **6** *3/4* **Midnight Warrior**[214] 6518 4-8-11 **50**.......................... DaleSwift 8 46
(Ron Barr) *plld hrd in midfield: rdn and outpcd over 2f out: kpt on fnl f: no imp* **7/1**[3]

063- **7** *1 3/4* **Joshua The First**[149] 8006 5-9-1 **59**.......................... GarryWhillans(5) 3 51
(Ian Semple) *hld up on ins: rdn over 3f out: no imp fr 2f out* **16/1**

1655 **8** *1 1/4* **Mr Chocolate Drop (IRE)**[52] 755 10-8-8 **47**.............(t) AndrewMullen 1 36
(Mandy Rowland) *hld up on ins: drvn over 3f out: nvr able to chal* **20/1**

0-00 **9** *2 3/4* **Buzz Law (IRE)**[59] 677 6-9-7 **60**.......................... PhillipMakin 6 43
(K R Burke) *bhd and sn pushed along: drvn 3f out: no imp whn nt clr run wl over 1f out* **9/2**[2]

2103 **10** *2 1/2* **Bapak Pesta (IRE)**[26] 1087 4-9-2 **55**..........................(p) PaulMulrennan 12 32
(Kevin Ryan) *t.k.h: prom on outside: drvn over 2f out: btn over 1f out* **9/1**

-040 **11** *shd* **My Manekineko**[67] 571 5-9-5 **58**.......................... StephenCraine 10 35
(J R Jenkins) *s.i.s: sn midfield on outside: struggling over 2f out: sn btn* **14/1**

30-6 **12** *3* **Perfect Words (IRE)**[11] 1376 4-9-2 **60**.................. ShirleyTeasdale(5) 11 30
(Marjorie Fife) *hld up on outside: drvn wl over 2f out: sn btn* **14/1**

1m 39.99s (-1.21) **Going Correction** -0.075s/f (Good) **12** Ran SP% **117.2**
Speed ratings (Par 101): **103,100,100,97,97 96,94,93,90,88 88,85**
CSF £25.74 CT £751.85 TOTE £2.90: £1.10, £3.70, £11.80; EX 30.80 Trifecta £939.10.
**Owner** VictoriaGreetham,EmilyBeasley,NickSmith **Bred** Gracelands Stud **Trained** Norton, N Yorks

**FOCUS**
The GoingStick reading for the watered ground was 8.7. Very few got involved here.

## 1597 BEST ODDS AT TOTEPOOL.COM MAIDEN STKS — 7f 30y
**2:35** (2:35) (Class 5) 3-Y-O+ **£3,234** (£962; £481; £240) **Stalls Low**

Form RPR

**1** **Libran (IRE)** 3-9-0 0.......................... BenCurtis 1 74
(Alan Swinbank) *trckd ldrs: effrt and rdn over 2f out: hdwy to ld ins fnl f: kpt on strly* **4/1**[3]

05- **2** *1 1/4* **Insaany**[188] 7237 3-9-0 0.......................... JoeFanning 5 71
(Mark Johnston) *led at ordinary gallop: rdn 2f out: edgd lft and hdd ins fnl f: kpt on same pce* **8/13**[1]

**3** *1 1/4* **Maid Of The Glens (IRE)** 3-8-9 0.......................... TadhgO'Shea 3 63
(John Patrick Shanahan, Ire) *pressed ldr: drvn and ev ch over 1f out: nt qckn ins fnl f* **10/3**[2]

0 **4** *24* **Come On Lulu**[15] 1303 3-8-9 0.......................... DuranFentiman 4
(Shaun Harris) *rn green in tch: struggling over 2f out: sn btn: t.o* **25/1**

1m 29.1s (0.10) **Going Correction** -0.075s/f (Good) **4** Ran SP% **108.8**
Speed ratings (Par 103): **96,94,93,65**
CSF £7.11 TOTE £6.70; EX 5.50 Trifecta £11.50.
**Owner** Mrs J Porter **Bred** Roundhill Stud **Trained** Melsonby, N Yorks

**FOCUS**
This didn't look a strong maiden.

## 1598 WIN BIG WITH TOTEJACKPOT H'CAP — 1m 1f
**3:05** (3:05) (Class 4) (0-80,79) 4-Y-O+ **£6,469** (£1,925; £962; £481) **Stalls Low**

Form RPR

46-0 **1** **Eutropius (IRE)**[12] 1362 5-8-12 **70**.......................... BenCurtis 11 79
(Alan Swinbank) *prom: effrt and rdn over 2f out: led over 1f out: drvn out fnl f* **8/1**

511- **2** *1 1/4* **Dancing Cosmos (IRE)**[23] 1157 4-9-7 **79**.......................... TadhgO'Shea 4 87
(John Patrick Shanahan, Ire) *hld up in midfield: hdwy whn n.m.r over 2f out to over 1f out: wnt 2nd last 100yds: kpt on: nt rch wnr* **8/1**

5-60 **3** *nk* **Karaka Jack**[21] 1190 7-9-4 **76**.......................... AdrianNicholls 6 82
(David Nicholls) *bhd: pushed along over 3f out: gd hdwy and edgd rt wl over 1f out: plld out and styd on wl fnl f: nrst fin* **5/1**[3]

105- **4** *1/2* **Red Charmer (IRE)**[204] 6846 4-9-2 **74**.......................... PJMcDonald 3 79
(Ann Duffield) *in tch: effrt and rdn 2f out: kpt on same pce ins fnl f* **9/1**

30-0 **5** *3 1/2* **Zaitsev (IRE)**[107] 29 4-9-0 **72**.......................... RobertWinston 5 70
(Ollie Pears) *led: rdn over 2f out: hdd over 1f out: outpcd ins fnl f* **16/1**

22-4 **6** *1 3/4* **Lord Franklin**[12] 1356 5-8-8 **69**.......................... JasonHart(3) 12 63
(Eric Alston) *t.k.h early: pressed ldr: ev ch over 2f out tl n.m.r and fdd over 1f out* **7/2**[1]

50-0 **7** *2 3/4* **Le Deluge (FR)**[21] 1196 4-9-5 **77**.......................... GrahamGibbons 8 66
(Michael Easterby) *taken early to post: hld up: pushed along 3f out: no imp fr 2f out* **25/1**

-300 **8** *3* **Spin Artist (USA)**[25] 1102 4-9-6 **78**.......................... JoeFanning 7 61
(Mark Johnston) *midfield: drvn and outpcd 3f out: n.d after* **12/1**

400- **9** *1 3/4* **Another For Joe**[177] 7498 6-8-5 **66**.......................... IanBrennan(3) 9 45
(Jim Goldie) *s.i.s: bhd on ins: rdn over 3f out: nvr able to chal* **16/1**

20-0 **10** *2 1/2* **Act Your Shoe Size**[21] 1190 5-9-3 **75**.......................... TomEaves 1 49
(Keith Dalgleish) *hld up towards rr: struggling over 2f out: sn btn* **22/1**

15-1 **11** *22* **Swehan (IRE)**[102] 79 4-9-6 **78**.......................... PaulMulrennan 2 8
(Kevin Ryan) *trckd ldrs: effrt on ins 3f out: wknd qckly over 1f out: t.o* **9/2**[2]

1m 52.02s (-1.88) **Going Correction** -0.075s/f (Good) **11** Ran SP% **116.9**
Speed ratings (Par 105): **105,103,103,103,100 98,96,93,91,89 70**
CSF £70.17 CT £361.80 TOTE £9.30: £2.90, £2.90, £2.00; EX 105.60 Trifecta £405.60.
**Owner** Andrew Sparks **Bred** Grangemore Stud **Trained** Melsonby, N Yorks

**FOCUS**
Modest form.

## 1599 TOTEPOOL MUSSELBURGH GOLD CUP (H'CAP) — 2m
**3:35** (3:35) (Class 4) (0-85,83) 4-Y-O+ **£12,938** (£3,850; £1,924; £962) **Stalls High**

Form RPR

342/ **1** **Pass Muster**[37] 8148 7-9-1 **74**.......................... PhillipMakin 3 83
(Philip Kirby) *t.k.h: hld up in tch: stdy hdwy whn n.m.r briefly over 1f out: rdn to ld ins fnl f: edgd rt: hld on wl* **17/2**

/0-1 **2** *shd* **Bright Abbey**[44] 868 6-9-0 **73**.......................... GrahamLee 8 82
(Dianne Sayer) *led: rdn over 2f out: hdd ins fnl f: rallied u.p: jst hld* **20/1**

0-24 **3** *3 1/4* **High Office**[12] 1362 8-8-12 **74**.......................... GeorgeChaloner(3) 10 79
(Richard Fahey) *hld up in midfield: drvn along over 3f out: hdwy 2f out: styd on fnl f: nt rch first two* **5/1**[2]

1513 **4** *1/2* **Sir Frank Morgan (IRE)**[9] 1426 4-8-7 **70**.......................... JoeFanning 5 74
(Mark Johnston) *cl up: effrt and ev ch over 2f out: kpt on same pce ins fnl f* **14/1**

**5** *3 1/2* **King Of The Picts (IRE)**[16] 7280 5-9-5 **78**.......................... TadhgO'Shea 6 78
(John Patrick Shanahan, Ire) *pressed ldr: drvn over 3f out: rallied: wknd wl over 1f out* **5/4**[1]

130- **6** *3/4* **Dr Irv**[190] 7210 5-9-5 **78**.......................... RussKennemore 4 77
(Philip Kirby) *t.k.h: hld up: smooth hdwy and cl up over 2f out: rdn and wknd over 1f out* **9/1**

343- **7** *5* **Corton Lad**[164] 7794 4-8-12 **75**..........................(tp) TomEaves 2 68
(Keith Dalgleish) *hld up bhd ldng gp: drvn along 3f out: no imp fr 2f out* **16/1**

354- **8** *1/2* **Caledonia**[64] 7210 7-8-5 **67**.......................... IanBrennan(3) 9 60
(Jim Goldie) *prom on outside: drvn and outpcd wl over 2f out: sn btn* **11/1**

010- **9** *1* **Twelve Strings (IRE)**[162] 7823 5-9-10 **83**.......................... HayleyTurner 7 74
(Brian Ellison) *hld up: drvn along wl over 2f out: nvr on terms* **8/1**[3]

3m 29.95s (-3.55) **Going Correction** -0.075s/f (Good)
**WFA** 4 from 5yo+ 4lb **9** Ran SP% **118.4**
Speed ratings (Par 105): **105,104,103,103,101 100,98,98,97**
CSF £162.93 CT £945.86 TOTE £8.60: £2.40, £4.30, £1.90; EX 187.70 Trifecta £573.00.
**Owner** C B Construction (Cleveland) Limited **Bred** Darley **Trained** Middleham, N Yorks

**FOCUS**
The front pair pulled clear in this modest staying handicap.

## 1600 TOTE TENTOFOLLOW.COM ENTER NOW EBF STALLIONS MAIDEN STKS — 1m 4f 100y
**4:05** (4:05) (Class 4) 3-Y-O+ **£5,175** (£1,540; £769; £384) **Stalls Low**

Form RPR

2- **1** **Alex My Boy (IRE)**[187] 7274 3-8-8 0.......................... JoeFanning 6 84
(Mark Johnston) *t.k.h: in tch: stdy hdwy 1/2-way: led over 3f out: rdn over 2f out: styd on wl fnl f* **1/1**[1]

5422 **2** *3* **New Tarabela**[17] 1269 3-8-8 77.......................... LukeMorris 5 79
(James Tate) *in tch: pushed along almost thrght: drvn and outpcd over 4f out: rallied to chse wnr and effrt over 2f out: sn ev ch: kpt on same pce fnl f* **7/4**[2]

**3** *9* **Molly Cat**[16] 4-9-8 0.......................... BenCurtis 1 62
(Alan Swinbank) *t.k.h: trckd ldrs: effrt and rdn over 2f out: sn outpcd by first two* **11/2**[3]

0- **4** *3 1/4* **Petite Madame (IRE)**[195] 7061 3-8-3 0.......................... PJMcDonald 4 55
(Ann Duffield) *pressed ldr: rdn over 3f out: edgd rt and wknd 2f out* **40/1**

**5** *11* **Haames (IRE)** 7-10-0 0.......................... GrahamLee 3 45
(Kevin Morgan) *hld up in tch: stdy hdwy over 3f out: rdn and wknd 2f out* **25/1**

**6** *19* **Classic Orange**[196] 4-9-3 0.......................... GarryWhillans(5) 2 11
(Simon Waugh) *led at stdy pce: rdn and hdd over 3f out: sn wknd: t.o* **100/1**

2m 44.78s (2.78) **Going Correction** -0.075s/f (Good)
**WFA** 3 from 4yo 20lb 4 from 7yo 1lb **6** Ran SP% **109.0**
Speed ratings (Par 105): **87,85,79,76,69 56**
CSF £2.75 TOTE £1.70: £1.10, £1.20; EX 3.10 Trifecta £6.70.
**Owner** Jaber Abdullah **Bred** Orpendale, Chelston & Wynatt **Trained** Middleham Moor, N Yorks

**FOCUS**
They went no pace early.

## 1601 DOWNLOAD THE TOTEPOOL LIVE INFO APP H'CAP — 7f 30y
**4:35** (4:35) (Class 5) (0-75,75) 3-Y-O **£4,528** (£1,347; £673; £336) **Stalls Low**

Form RPR

1111 **1** **Desert Colours**[10] 1403 3-8-10 **69**..........................(b) KevinStott(5) 6 76
(Kevin Ryan) *mde all: rdn over 2f out: sn hrd pressed: kpt on gamely fnl f* **6/1**

06-4 **2** *1/2* **Sir Guy Porteous (IRE)**[17] 1260 3-9-0 **68**.......................... JoeFanning 5 74
(Mark Johnston) *t.k.h: cl up: effrt and chal over 1f out: edgd rt ins fnl f: kpt on: hld nr fin* **7/2**[2]

000- **3** *3/4* **Regiment**[176] 7529 3-9-4 **72**.......................... TonyHamilton 8 76
(Richard Fahey) *t.k.h: prom on outside: effrt over 2f out: sn rdn: kpt on ins fnl f* **3/1**[1]

4- **4** *2 1/4* **Tiffany Bay (IRE)**[121] 8376 3-9-7 **75**.......................... TadhgO'Shea 2 73
(John Patrick Shanahan, Ire) *trckd ldrs: effrt and rdn over 2f out: edgd rt and outpcd over 1f out* **7/2**[2]

513- **5** *2 1/2* **Imshivalla (IRE)**[224] 6233 3-9-0 **73**.......................... SammyJoBell(5) 7 64
(Richard Fahey) *plld hrd: hld up in tch: pushed along over 2f out: edgd rt and no imp fr over 1f out* **5/1**[3]

020- **6** *2 1/4* **Bajan Rebel**[158] 7855 3-8-2 **56** oh1.......................... JamesSullivan 4 41
(Michael Easterby) *hld up: rdn over 2f out: nvr able to chal* **18/1**

631- **7** *5* **Dark Crystal**[184] 7340 3-8-8 **62**.......................... PJMcDonald 1 34
(Linda Perratt) *t.k.h: hld up in tch on ins: struggling over 2f out: sn btn* **14/1**

1m 28.42s (-0.58) **Going Correction** -0.075s/f (Good) **7** Ran SP% **112.3**
Speed ratings (Par 98): **100,99,98,96,93 90,84**
CSF £26.19 CT £74.22 TOTE £4.60: £2.40, £2.90; EX 17.70 Trifecta £95.20.
**Owner** Jon Beard **Bred** Rabbah Bloodstock Limited **Trained** Hambleton, N Yorks

**FOCUS**
The first two held their positions throughout in a race in which the pace held up.

## 1602 1,000 GUINEAS ANTE POST AT TOTEPOOL.COM APPRENTICE H'CAP 5f
5:05 (5:06) (Class 6) (0-60,59) 4-Y-0+ £3,234 (£962; £481; £240) Stalls High

Form RPR
102- 1 **Little Eli**220 6345 4-9-7 59 JasonHart 9 69
(Eric Alston) mde all: rdn over 1f out: edgd lft ins fnl f: hld on wl towards fin 6/1²
3616 2 nk **Roy's Legacy**15 1311 5-9-2 54 MichaelJMMurphy 14 63
(Shaun Harris) w wnr: rdn over 1f out: swtchd rt ins fnl f: kpt on wl: hld nr fin 5/1¹
0102 3 nk **Greenhead High**11 1378 6-8-9 54 (v) AnnaHesketh(7) 1 62
(David Nicholls) cl up: effrt and pushed along over 1f out: edgd lft ins fnl f: kpt on: hld towards fin 5/1¹
06-3 4 1 1/4 **Iggy**8 1448 4-9-0 59 (tp) DanielleMooney(7) 10 62
(Michael Easterby) hld up: rdn and hdwy over 1f out: swtchd rt and styd on wl fnl f: nrst fin 6/1²
46-5 5 nse **Spring Bird**11 1378 5-8-5 48 AlistairRawlinson(5) 12 51
(David Nicholls) prom: rdn along 2f out: kpt on same pce ins fnl f 12/1
2-52 6 1/2 **Commandable (AUS)**90 258 10-9-3 55 SamJames 11 56
(Ian Semple) prom: rdn 2f out: nt qckn ins fnl f 8/1
4-40 7 1 1/4 **Confidential Creek**90 258 4-9-1 56 (p) JacobButterfield(3) 7 53
(Ollie Pears) in tch: effrt and pushed along 2f out: one pce appr fnl f 16/1
606- 8 nse **Lizzy's Dream**188 7236 6-9-5 57 NeilFarley 4 54
(Robin Bastiman) bhd and outpcd: hdwy on outside over 1f out: kpt on: nvr able to chal 14/1
30-0 9 hd **Here Now And Why (IRE)**11 1378 7-9-0 57 (p) EvaMoscrop(5) 6 53
(Philip Kirby) towards rr: hdwy on outside 2f out: kpt on fnl f: no imp 13/2³
401- 10 1 1/2 **Tadalavil**188 7236 9-8-13 56 SammyJoBell(5) 8 47
(Linda Perratt) midfield: pushed along over 2f out: nvr able to chal 18/1
366- 11 2 1/2 **Saxonette**192 7149 6-8-11 52 ConnorBeasley(3) 2 34
(Linda Perratt) bhd and outpcd: hdwy on outside 1/2-way: wknd over 1f out 28/1
600- 12 11 **Pavers Star**146 8035 5-8-12 53 (p) JoeyHaynes(3) 5
(Noel Wilson) s.i.s: bhd and outpcd: nvr on terms 20/1

58.74s (-1.66) **Going Correction** -0.30s/f (Firm) 12 Ran SP% 120.1
Speed ratings (Par 101): **101,100,100,98,97 97,95,95,94,92 88,70**
CSF £36.57 CT £166.86 TOTE £8.60: £2.20, £2.10, £2.00; EX 50.50 Trifecta £188.70.
**Owner** Whittle Racing Partnership **Bred** J E Jackson **Trained** Longton, Lancs

**FOCUS**
Early speed won the day here, the first two being up there throughout.
T/Jkpt: £34,256.40 to a £1 stake. Pool: £217118.19 - 4.50 winning tickets T/Plt: £278.80 to a £1 stake. Pool: £75300.19 - 197.10 winning tickets T/Qpdt: £28.60 to a £1 stake. Pool: £4067.62 - 105.10 winning tickets RY

# SAN SIRO (R-H)
Sunday, April 20

**OFFICIAL GOING: Turf: soft**

## 1603a PREMIO AMBROSIANO (GROUP 3) (4YO+) (TURF) 1m 2f
4:00 (12:00) 4-Y-0+ £23,333 (£10,266; £5,600; £2,800)

RPR
1 **Orpello (IRE)**294 3881 5-9-0 0 (b) FabioBranca 1 107
(Stefano Botti, Italy) led: hdd after 2f and trckd ldr: rdn to ld over 2f out: hrd pressed fr 1 1/2f out: dug in gamely u.p fnl f: all out 79/50¹
2 hd **Occhio Della Mente (IRE)**28 7-8-11 0 (p) MickaelBarzalona 7 104
(E Botti, Italy) trckd ldng pair: 8 l 3rd 1/2-way: tk clsr over 2 1/2f out: trckd wnr fr 2f out: rdn to press eventual wnr 1 1/2f out: virtually jnd wnr 100yds out: no ex cl home 48/10
3 1 1/4 **Targaryen (IRE)**14 4-8-11 0 (p) FBossa 3 101
(Sebastiano Latina, Italy) towards rr: outpcd in last 4f out: hrd rdn and hdwy 2f out: wnt 3rd ins fnl f: styd on u.p: nvr on terms w first two 231/10
4 3 **Storming Loose**182 7413 7-8-11 0 DarioVargiu 2 95
(B Grizzetti, Italy) settled towards rr: rdn and no imp fr over 2 1/2f out: styd on ins fnl 1 1/2f: nvr in contention 41/10³
5 1 1/2 **Nabucco (GER)**168 7725 4-9-0 0 GeraldMosse 6 95
(R Rohne, Germany) t.k.h: hld up in rr: prog 3 1/2f out: cl 3rd and ev ch 2f out: sn rdn and nt qckn: wknd ins fnl f 17/10²
6 1/2 **Prato Mariante (ITY)** 5-8-11 0 AntonioFresu 4 91
(M Corradini, Italy) midfield: rdn and short of room 3f out: effrt u.p 1 1/2f out: plugged on at one pce fnl f 18/1
7 4 **Duca Di Mantova**28 5-8-11 0 (b) MircoDemuro 5 83
(R Biondi, Italy) tk v t.k.h: led after 2f and sn 3 l clr: hdd over 2f out: sn wknd and eased fnl f 114/10

2m 3.7s (-3.00) 7 Ran SP% 130.1
WIN (incl. 1 euro stake): 2.58. PLACES: 1.69, 2.36. DF: 8.30.
**Owner** Scuderia Effevi SRL **Bred** Deni Srl & Effevi Snc **Trained** Italy

# 1342 REDCAR (L-H)
Monday, April 21

**OFFICIAL GOING: Good to firm (good in places; 8.3)**

## 1604 MARKET CROSS JEWELLERS FILLIES' H'CAP 5f
2:10 (2:10) (Class 5) (0-75,73) 4-Y-0+ £2,587 (£770; £384; £192) Stalls Centre

Form RPR
06-3 1 **Foreign Rhythm (IRE)**6 1500 9-8-8 60 DaleSwift 6 68
(Ron Barr) trckd ldrs: effrt and hdwy whn n.m.r and swtchd rt over 1f out: rdn to take slt ld appr fnl f: sn drvn: edgd lft towards fin: jst hld on 8/1
321- 2 nse **Be Lucky**233 5989 4-9-6 72 GrahamGibbons 1 80
(Michael Easterby) towards rr: pushed along 1/2-way: hdwy 2f out: swtchd lft and rdn whn edgd lft ent fnl f: sn drvn and styd on strly: edgd rt nr line: jst failed 9/4¹
5-50 3 1 1/4 **Lady Poppy**91 259 4-8-6 58 PJMcDonald 2 61
(George Moore) cl up on wd outside: effrt 2f out and sn ev ch: drvn ent fnl f: hld whn n.m.r nr line 14/1
0-62 4 shd **Beau Mistral (IRE)**18 1266 5-9-7 73 RaulDaSilva 8 76
(Paul Green) trckd ldrs: hdwy 2f out: sn rdn and carried sltly rt appr fnl f: sn ev ch tl drvn and kpt on same pce fnl f 6/1³
-060 5 1 1/4 **Mey Blossom**7 1487 9-8-0 57 (v) ConnorBeasley(5) 5 55
(Richard Whitaker) hld up: hdwy 2f out: sn rdn: drvn and kpt on fnl f: nrst fin 22/1
256- 6 3 **Ballarina**253 5305 8-8-6 61 JasonHart(3) 9 48
(Eric Alston) sn led: rdn and hung bdly lft over 1f out: sn edgd rt: drvn and hdd appr fnl f: sn edgd rt and wknd 11/1
22-2 7 1 **Shirley's Pride**33 1019 4-9-4 70 (t) AndrewMullen 4 54
(Michael Appleby) trckd ldrs: hdwy over 2f out: rdn whn n.m.r over 1f out: sn ev ch tl drvn and wknd ins fnl f 3/1²
410- 8 3 3/4 **Irish Girls Spirit (IRE)**195 7101 5-8-1 58 (p) ShirleyTeasdale(5) 10 28
(Paul Midgley) prom: rdn along 2f out: sn wknd 16/1
00-0 9 13 **Sunrise Dance**9 1440 5-9-5 71 RobertWinston 3
(Robert Johnson) a towards rr: outpcd and bhd fnl 2f 12/1

1m 1.48s (2.88) **Going Correction** +0.575s/f (Yiel) 9 Ran SP% 114.1
Speed ratings (Par 100): **99,98,96,96,94 89,88,82,61**
CSF £26.02 CT £252.01 TOTE £8.10: £1.70, £1.60, £2.50; EX 37.10 Trifecta £641.40.
**Owner** R E Barr **Bred** Yeomanstown Stud **Trained** Seamer, N Yorks
■ Stewards' Enquiry : Dale Swift one-day ban: careless riding (May 5)

**FOCUS**
A fair sprint to kick things off. They went a good pace. The winner produced a similar effort as when winning this last year.

## 1605 JAMES CROWTHER DESIGNED TODAY'S RACECARD COVER H'CAP 2m 4y
2:45 (2:45) (Class 6) (0-65,63) 4-Y-0+ £1,940 (£577; £288; £144) Stalls Low

Form RPR
00-0 1 **Dubara Reef (IRE)**41 915 7-8-9 46 RaulDaSilva 1 56
(Paul Green) mde all at gd pce: pushed along 3f out: jnd 2f out: sn rdn: drvn ent fnl f and sn edgd rt: kpt on wl towards fin 22/1
25-0 2 1 **Jan Smuts (IRE)**12 1374 6-9-12 63 (tp) GrahamLee 3 72
(Wilf Storey) trckd ldrs: hdwy 4f out: chsd ldng pair over 2f out: sn rdn: styd on wl fnl f: tk 2nd nr line 14/1
002 3 nk **Longshadow**7 1485 4-8-13 59 (p) JoeyHaynes(5) 7 67
(Jason Ward) a chsng wnr: hdwy over 3f out: cl up wl over 2f out: rdn to chal wl over 1f out and ev ch tl no ex ins fnl f: lost 2nd nr fin 5/2¹
450- 4 11 **Miss Macnamara (IRE)**238 5831 5-9-10 61 PhillipMakin 12 56
(Martin Todhunter) hld up in rr: hdwy on outer over 3f out: swtchd lft to inner wl over 1f out: sn pushed along: styd on appr fnl f: nrst fin 12/1
62-0 5 hd **Cowslip**13 1359 5-9-4 55 PJMcDonald 9 50
(George Moore) in tch: hdwy on inner to chse ldrs over 4f out: rdn along over 3f out: drvn and no imp fnl 2f 9/1³
06-0 6 6 **Summerlea (IRE)**34 639 8-8-11 48 TomEaves 15 36
(Micky Hammond) chsd ldrs: rdn along over 4f out: drvn over 3f out: grad wknd 11/1
11-6 7 6 **Madam Lilibet (IRE)**13 1359 5-9-11 62 PaulQuinn 6 43
(Sharon Watt) a towards rr 12/1
3-03 8 nk **My Destination (IRE)**12 1374 5-9-9 63 JasonHart(3) 2 43
(Declan Carroll) dwlt: a towards rr 17/2²
5421 9 27 **Adili (IRE)**19 1248 5-9-5 56 AndrewMullen 14 4
(Michael Appleby) in tch: pushed along over 7f out: lost pl over 5f out: sn bhd 12/1
045- 10 1 1/2 **Authentication**133 8223 5-9-2 53 DavidAllan 5
(Mel Brittain) chsd ldrs: rdn along over 4f out: sn wknd 16/1
200- 11 1 **Petella**201 6942 8-9-0 58 KieranSchofield(7) 4 3
(George Moore) in tch: pushed along 1/2-way: lost pl over 6f out and sn bhd 28/1
050- 12 3/4 **Transfer**139 6283 9-8-7 49 JacobButterfield(5) 11
(Richard Price) a in rr: bhd fnl 4f 33/1
210- 13 15 **Golden Future**143 5786 11-9-5 59 GeorgeChaloner(3) 10
(Peter Niven) chsd ldrs: rdn along over 4f out: wknd over 3f over 3f out 16/1
3232 14 12 **Honest Strike (USA)**18 1262 7-9-7 58 (b) ShaneKelly 8
(Daniel Mark Loughnane) midfield: sme hdwy 6f out: rdn along over 4f out: sn wknd and bhd 11/1
4563 15 8 **Teenage Dream (IRE)**34 932 6-9-4 62 (vt) AdamMcLean(7) 13
(Derek Shaw) v s.i.s: a bhd 33/1

3m 31.3s (-0.10) **Going Correction** +0.05s/f (Good)
**WFA** 4 from 5yo+ 4lb 15 Ran SP% 121.0
Speed ratings (Par 101): **102,101,101,95,95 92,89,89,76,75 74,74,66,60,56**
CSF £293.57 CT £1050.12 TOTE £32.20: £7.50, £4.00, £1.80; EX 199.60 Trifecta £495.30.
**Owner** Oaklea Aces **Bred** M Duffy **Trained** Lydiate, Merseyside
■ Stewards' Enquiry : Raul Da Silva seven-day ban: used whip above permitted level (May 5-10,12)

**FOCUS**
A run-of-the-mill staying event, though it was at least soundly run, the field well strung out a long way from home. The winner was close to his best form from last year.

## 1606 NEW RACING UK ANYWHERE AVAILABLE NOW CLASSIFIED (S) STKS 7f
3:20 (3:22) (Class 6) 3-Y-0+ £1,940 (£577; £288; £144) Stalls Centre

Form RPR
405 1 **Ad Vitam (IRE)**16 1309 6-9-4 53 (vt) MartinDwyer 7 61
(David C Griffiths) hld up in rr: pushed along over 3f out: rdn 2f out: drvn ent fnl f: styd on to ld last 50yds 16/1
-606 2 hd **Mitchum**41 910 5-9-4 55 DaleSwift 4 60
(Ron Barr) chsd ldrs: hdwy over 2f out: rdn over 1f out: drvn and ev ch ins fnl f: no ex towards fin 25/1
360- 3 3/4 **Whispered Times (USA)**201 6943 7-9-4 60 (p) PaulPickard 5 59
(Tracy Waggott) led: rdn along 2f out: drvn ent fnl f: hdd and no ex last 50yds 7/1³
200- 4 1/2 **Dialogue**203 6907 8-9-4 64 PJMcDonald 3 57
(Geoffrey Harker) hld up towards rr: pushed along over 3f out: hdwy over 2f out: rdn to chse ldrs over 1f out: drvn and ev ch ins fnl f: one pce last 75yds 9/1
350- 5 nse **Kirkstall Abbey (IRE)**258 5083 3-8-5 60 BarryMcHugh 6 52
(Tony Coyle) towards rr: pushed along over 2f out: rdn and hdwy whn nt much room jst over 1f out: swtchd lft and drvn: styd on: nrst fin 14/1
200- 6 2 1/2 **No Quarter (IRE)**212 6633 7-9-4 63 FrannyNorton 8 51
(Tracy Waggott) chsd ldrs: hdwy over 2f out: rdn and ch over 1f out: sn drvn and wknd fnl f 7/1³
043 7 1 3/4 **For Shia And Lula (IRE)**16 1297 5-9-4 61 (p) ShaneKelly 2 46
(Daniel Mark Loughnane) hld up in tch: hdwy over 2f out: sn rdn: drvn and no imp fnl f 7/2¹



The Form Book, Raceform Ltd, Newbury, RG14 5SJ

2-33 **8** ½ **Bitaphon (IRE)**[20] 1227 5-9-4 57 (t) AndrewMullen 1 45
(Michael Appleby) *racd wd: in tch: rdn along over 2f out: sn no imp* **13/2**[2]

660- **9** *nk* **Bunce (IRE)**[132] 8230 6-8-11 61 GemmaTutty(7) 12 44
(Karen Tutty) *dwlt and in rr: stdy hdwy towards stands' rail over 2f out: chsd ldrs over 1f out: sn rdn and wknd* **14/1**

2125 **10** *5* **El Duque**[45] 867 3-8-6 65 (v) RyanWhile(5) 10 32
(Bill Turner) *chsd ldr: rdn along wl over 2f out: drvn wl over 1f out: sn wknd* **8/1**

-000 **11** 2½ **Newbury Street**[16] 1309 7-8-11 45 JackGarritty(7) 9 24
(Patrick Holmes) *a towards rr* **66/1**

0-00 **12** *shd* **Marcus Caesar (IRE)**[9] 1446 4-9-4 63 JamesSullivan 11 24
(Ruth Carr) *prom: rdn along over 2f out: grad wknd* **12/1**

1m 29.77s (5.27) **Going Correction** +0.575s/f (Yiel)
**WFA** 3 from 4yo+ 13lb **12 Ran SP% 113.9**
Speed ratings (Par 101): **92,91,90,90,90 87,85,84,84,78 75,75**
CSF £348.58 TOTE £15.60: £5.30, £8.10, £2.10; EX 335.20 Trifecta £499.20.There was no bid for the winner. Kirkstall Abbey was claimed by S P Hodgson for £6000.
**Owner** Eros Bloodstock **Bred** Michelle Morgan **Trained** Bawtry, S Yorks
■ Stewards' Enquiry : Paul Pickard four-day ban: used whip above permitted level (May 5-8)

**FOCUS**
Distinctly modest fare in this classified seller. The third home went off pretty hard in front, the other principals all coming from off the pace. Not form to be too literal about.

## 1607 DOWNLOAD THE NEW RACING UK IPAD APP H'CAP (STRAIGHT-MILE CHAMPIONSHIP QUALIFIER) 1m
**3:55** (3:55) (Class 4) (0-80,80) 4-Y-0+ **£6,469** (£1,925; £962; £481) **Stalls** Centre

Form RPR

24-1 **1** **Manchester**[22] 1190 4-9-5 78 TonyHamilton 10 87+
(Richard Fahey) *mde virtually all: rdn wl over 1f out: drvn and hung lft ins fnl f: hld on wl towards fin* **4/1**[1]

31-6 **2** *nk* **Bling King**[17] 1281 5-8-13 72 PJMcDonald 9 80
(Geoffrey Harker) *prom: effrt over 2f out and sn cl up: rdn over 1f out and ev ch tl drvn ins fnl f and no ex last 50yds* **16/1**

10-0 **3** *nk* **Just Paul (IRE)**[22] 1191 4-9-3 76 RussKennemore 7 83
(Philip Kirby) *midfield: hdwy 3f out: swtchd rt and chsd ldrs 2f out: rdn to chal over 1f out: ev ch tl drvn ins fnl f and no ex last 50yds* **20/1**

601- **4** 1¼ **No Dominion (IRE)**[150] 8008 5-9-6 79 GrahamLee 15 83
(James Given) *hld up in rr: hdwy over 2f out: rdn over 1f out: styd on strly fnl f: nrst fin* **14/1**

023- **5** ½ **King Pin**[213] 6600 9-8-8 67 BarryMcHugh 6 70
(Tracy Waggott) *hld up in rr: hdwy 3f out: chsd ldrs wl over 1f out: sn rdn and kpt on same pce fnl f* **20/1**

23-0 **6** ½ **Bishop's Castle (USA)**[23] 1171 5-9-4 77 (t) PaulPickard 5 79
(Brian Ellison) *hld up towards rr: stdy hdwy over 3f out: chsd ldrs 2f out: sn rdn: drvn and ch ent fnl f: kpt on same pce* **7/1**[3]

20-5 **7** ¾ **Surround Sound**[13] 1356 4-8-9 68 DavidAllan 8 68+
(Tim Easterby) *midfield: hdwy 3f out: swtchd rt over 2f out and sn rdn to chse ldrs: drvn and kpt on same pce ins fnl f* **12/1**

313- **8** ¾ **Eurystheus (IRE)**[115] 8416 5-9-6 79 AndrewMullen 4 78
(Michael Appleby) *chsd ldrs on outer: rdn along 2f out: drvn over 1f out: sn one pce* **13/2**[2]

05-1 **9** *shd* **Kiwi Bay**[14] 1345 9-9-0 78 ConnorBeasley(5) 1 76
(Michael Dods) *cl up: pushed along 3f out: rdn over 2f out: drvn wl over 1f out and grad wknd* **8/1**

11-2 **10** *4* **Bousatet (FR)**[17] 1275 4-8-10 74 KevinStott(5) 13 63
(Kevin Ryan) *trckd ldrs: hdwy and cl up 1/2-way: chal over 2f out: sn rdn and wknd appr fnl f* **17/2**

20-6 **11** 2¼ **Spavento (IRE)**[14] 1345 8-8-10 72 JasonHart(3) 2 56
(Eric Alston) *in tch: hdwy to chse ldrs whn n.m.r 2f out: sn btn* **20/1**

34-0 **12** 2¼ **Staffhoss**[14] 1345 4-8-9 75 PaulaMuir(7) 12 54
(Mark Johnston) *in tch on wd outside: rdn along 1/2-way: sn wknd* **50/1**

00-0 **13** *nk* **Destiny Blue (IRE)**[14] 1345 7-8-13 72 (t) TomEaves 17 50
(Brian Ellison) *dwlt: a towards rr* **33/1**

-203 **14** 4½ **Steelriver (IRE)**[26] 1103 4-9-2 75 (p[1]) JoeFanning 18 43
(James Bethell) *chsd ldrs: rdn along over 3f out: sn wknd* **20/1**

160- **15** *nk* **Artful Prince**[182] 7424 4-9-5 78 DaleSwift 11 45
(James Given) *midfield: rdn along 1/2-way: sn lost pl and bhd* **20/1**

0160 **16** *3* **The Great Gabrial**[22] 1190 5-9-6 79 (p) ShaneKelly 16 39
(Alan McCabe) *a towards rr* **33/1**

06-3 **17** ¾ **Mystical Moment**[12] 1376 4-8-11 70 PaulMulrennan 3 29
(Edwin Tuer) *prom: rdn along wl over 2f out: sn wknd* **20/1**

321/ **18** *12* **Engrossing**[593] 5942 5-9-7 80 JamesSullivan 14 11
(Ruth Carr) *chsd ldrs to 1/2-way: sn wknd* **33/1**

1m 41.75s (5.15) **Going Correction** +0.575s/f (Yiel) **18 Ran SP% 127.1**
Speed ratings (Par 105): **97,96,96,95,94 94,93,92,92,88 86,84,83,79,78 75,75,63**
CSF £61.52 CT £1190.81 TOTE £5.40: £1.60, £4.90, £4.80, £3.90; EX 100.90 Trifecta £598.70.
**Owner** Mr & Mrs G Calder **Bred** Mr & Mrs G Calder **Trained** Musley Bank, N Yorks

**FOCUS**
A fairly useful and competitive handicap. The gallop wasn't as strong as might have been expected given the size of the field, the pace taking around 2f or so to pick up. The winner built on his Doncaster run and should rate higher.

## 1608 WIN A VIP DAY OUT @ REDCARRACING.CO.UK MAIDEN STKS 1m 1f
**4:30** (4:33) (Class 5) 3-Y-0+ **£2,587** (£770; £384; £192) **Stalls** Low

Form RPR

5- **1** **Odeon**[185] 7339 3-8-13 0 GrahamLee 1 99
(James Given) *trckd ldr on inner: led 6f out: pushed along 3f out: rdn clr wl over 1f out: styd on strly* **6/1**[3]

**2** *9* **Easter Sky (IRE)**[201] 4-10-0 84 DanielTudhope 12 90
(David O'Meara) *trckd ldng pair: hdwy to chse wnr 4f out: rdn to chal wl over 2f out: sn drvn and plugged on same pce fr wl over 1f out* **11/4**[2]

000- **3** *10* **Frosty The Snowman (IRE)**[201] 6954 3-8-13 0 JamesSullivan 2 59
(Ruth Carr) *trckd ldrs: hdwy over 3f out: sn rdn along: kpt on to take mod 3rd ins fnl 2f: n.d* **40/1**

**4** 1¼ **Silver Craftsman (IRE)** 3-8-13 0 MartinDwyer 3 56
(Alan Swinbank) *towards rr: stdy hdwy 4f out: rdn wl over 2f out: styd on to take modest 4th over 1f out: nvr a factor* **11/1**

332- **5** *8* **Legal Waves (IRE)**[196] 7075 4-10-0 79 BenCurtis 11 43
(Alan Swinbank) *trckd ldrs: hdwy to chse ldng pair 4f out: rdn along over 3f out: sn drvn and btn* **1/1**[1]

60 **6** 1¼ **Radebe (USA)**[54] 748 3-8-13 0 (p) PaulMulrennan 6 37
(Kevin Ryan) *chsd ldrs: rdn along 1/2-way: outpcd 4f out* **33/1**

**7** 2¼ **Two B'S** 3-8-13 0 DavidAllan 9 32
(Tim Easterby) *s.i.s: a bhd* **20/1**

00-0 **8** *2* **Bitusa (USA)**[19] 1249 4-9-7 50 (b) GemmaTutty(7) 4 31
(Karen Tutty) *led 3f: cl up: rdn along 4f out: sn wknd* **66/1**

00 **9** 4½ **Miss Bella Rose**[62] 649 7-9-6 0 BillyCray(3) 8 17
(Richard Guest) *s.i.s: a bhd* **80/1**

**10** 2¼ **Yorkshire Monarch (IRE)** 3-8-13 0 DuranFentiman 10 14
(Tim Easterby) *s.i.s: a towards rr* **25/1**

**11** *4* **Shadow Of The Day**[179] 7-10-0 0 RussKennemore 14
(Lee James) *s.i.s: a bhd* **100/1**

000- **12** 1½ **Oriental Dream (IRE)**[198] 7023 3-8-13 0 AndrewMullen 13
(Nigel Tinkler) *a in rr* **80/1**

00-0 **13** *32* **How Rude**[16] 1303 3-8-8 22 PJMcDonald 7
(Mel Brittain) *a towards rr* **100/1**

1m 53.97s (0.97) **Going Correction** +0.05s/f (Good)
**WFA** 3 from 4yo+ 15lb **13 Ran SP% 119.2**
Speed ratings (Par 103): **97,89,80,79,71 70,68,67,63,61 57,56,27**
CSF £21.60 TOTE £8.30: £2.00, £1.60, £11.00; EX 21.20 Trifecta £611.20.
**Owner** Alex Owen **Bred** Northmore Stud **Trained** Willoughton, Lincs

**FOCUS**
No depth to this maiden but it was still hard not to be taken with the performance of the winner, who can rate higher. The runner-up was eased when held.

## 1609 FOLLOW REDCARRACING ON FACEBOOK AND TWITTER H'CAP (DIV I) 7f
**5:05** (5:06) (Class 5) (0-75,75) 4-Y-0+ **£2,587** (£770; £384; £192) **Stalls** Centre

Form RPR

00-0 **1** **Victoire De Lyphar (IRE)**[22] 1191 7-9-7 75 (e) JamesSullivan 6 89
(Ruth Carr) *trckd ldrs on outer: hdwy 3f out: led wl over 1f out: sn rdn and edgd rt: rdr dropped whip 1f out: clr ins fnl f: kpt on strly* **9/2**[1]

16-2 **2** *5* **Who's Shirl**[35] 995 8-9-6 74 PaulMulrennan 10 75
(Chris Fairhurst) *in rr: pushed along wl over 2f out: swtchd rt and hdwy wl over 1f out: rdn to chse ldrs over 1f out: drvn and kpt on same pce ins fnl f* **12/1**

00-3 **3** 1¼ **Steel Stockholder**[9] 1446 8-8-13 67 DavidAllan 7 65
(Mel Brittain) *in tch: hdwy to chse ldrs over 2f out: n.m.r and swtchd lft over 1f out: drvn and kpt on same pce fnl f* **11/2**[3]

15-0 **4** 1¾ **Camerooney**[80] 406 11-8-11 65 RussKennemore 8 58
(Marjorie Fife) *led: rdn along over 2f out: drvn and hdd wl over 1f out: grad wknd appr fnl f* **16/1**

055- **5** 1¼ **Broctune Papa Gio**[48] 7344 7-9-0 68 TomEaves 5 58
(Keith Reveley) *hld up in rr: hdwy wl over 2f out: swtchd rt and rdn to chse ldrs wl over 1f out: drvn appr fnl f and sn wknd* **8/1**

6620 **6** *2* **Cape Of Hope (IRE)**[12] 1375 4-9-4 72 DanielTudhope 11 57
(David O'Meara) *trckd ldrs: hdwy 3f out sn cl up: rdn along wl over 1f out: sn wknd* **5/1**[2]

1653 **7** 2½ **Tartan Trip**[40] 929 7-9-3 71 (v) AndrewMullen 4 49
(Michael Appleby) *towards rr: effrt and sme hdwy over 3f out: rdn along wl over 2f out: sn btn* **8/1**

020- **8** ½ **Relight My Fire**[153] 7965 4-9-0 75 RachelRichardson(7) 3 52
(Tim Easterby) *hld up: a towards rr* **16/1**

6-00 **9** *hd* **Great Demeanor (USA)**[19] 1245 4-8-6 65 ow3 (b[1]) EmmaSayer(5) 1 41
(Dianne Sayer) *cl up: rdn along over 3f out: wknd over 2f out* **33/1**

55-5 **10** *hd* **Running Reef (IRE)**[12] 1376 5-8-8 65 IanBrennan(3) 9 41
(Tracy Waggott) *trckd ldrs: hdwy to chse ldr 3f out: rdn along over 2f out: sn swtchd lft and wknd over 1f out* **8/1**

520- **11** *10* **Ypres**[158] 7887 5-9-2 75 JoeyHaynes(5) 2 25
(Jason Ward) *t.k.h: prom: pushed along 3f out: wknd over 2f out* **12/1**

1m 28.05s (3.55) **Going Correction** +0.575s/f (Yiel) **11 Ran SP% 113.7**
Speed ratings (Par 103): **102,96,94,92,91 89,86,85,85,85 73**
CSF £56.56 CT £301.20 TOTE £5.20: £2.00, £3.80, £2.20; EX 53.60 Trifecta £426.70.
**Owner** The Beer Stalkers & Ruth Carr **Bred** Mrs Monica Hackett **Trained** Huby, N Yorks

**FOCUS**
This looked quite a tight affair beforehand. The slightly slower division. The winner is rated around his better 2013 form.

## 1610 FOLLOW REDCARRACING ON FACEBOOK AND TWITTER H'CAP (DIV II) 7f
**5:40** (5:42) (Class 5) (0-75,75) 4-Y-0+ **£2,587** (£770; £384; £192) **Stalls** Centre

Form RPR

330- **1** **Escape To Glory (USA)**[129] 8269 6-9-7 75 PaulMulrennan 6 88
(Michael Dods) *hld up in tch: rdn along over 2f out: drvn and hdwy over 1f out: drifted lft and led ins fnl f: kpt on strly* **11/2**[2]

35-1 **2** *3* **Llewellyn**[12] 1375 6-9-4 75 NeilFarley(3) 1 80
(Declan Carroll) *t.k.h: cl up: rdn to ld over 1f out: hdd ins fnl f: kpt on same pce* **15/2**

20-4 **3** 2¾ **Lucky Lodge**[9] 1440 4-8-10 64 (b) DavidAllan 3 62
(Mel Brittain) *hld up: rdn along over 2f out: hdwy u.p over 1f out: kpt on fnl f: nvr able to chal* **12/1**

40-4 **4** *nk* **Beckermet (IRE)**[12] 1376 12-9-3 71 JamesSullivan 5 68
(Ruth Carr) *led: rdn over 2f out: hdd over 1f out: kpt on same pce fnl f* **14/1**

2-02 **5** *nse* **Millkwood**[12] 1376 4-9-7 75 (p) PJMcDonald 11 72
(John Davies) *hld up: pushed along and outpcd 1/2-way: hdwy and hung lft over 1f out: kpt on fnl f: nvr able to chal* **15/2**

636- **6** 3½ **Shearian**[249] 5425 4-8-7 61 BarryMcHugh 7 49
(Tracy Waggott) *cl up: effrt and rdn over 2f out: wknd ent fnl f* **20/1**

0-54 **7** 4½ **Ted's Brother (IRE)**[9] 1446 6-8-7 68 (e) AlistairRawlinson(7) 2 44
(Richard Guest) *prom tl rdn and wknd wl over 1f out* **6/1**[3]

230- **8** 3½ **Ralphy Boy (IRE)**[193] 7152 5-8-9 68 KevinStott(5) 4 35
(Alistair Whillans) *in tch: effrt and rdn over 2f out: wknd over 1f out* **5/1**[1]

0-42 **9** 2½ **Gold Beau (FR)**[20] 1217 4-9-1 74 (p) JacobButterfield(5) 9 35
(Kristin Stubbs) *bhd and sn pushed along: drvn 1/2-way: nvr on terms* **7/1**

2243 **10** *13* **Baltic Prince (IRE)**[17] 1288 4-8-11 65 RaulDaSilva 10
(Paul Green) *hld up in tch: rdn and struggling over 3f out: sn btn: eased whn no ch over 1f out* **12/1**

200- **11** *39* **Majestic Dream (IRE)**[163] 7824 6-9-3 71 (v) GrahamGibbons 8
(Michael Easterby) *prom 3f: sn drvn and struggling: no ch and eased fr 2f out* **20/1**

1m 27.82s (3.32) **Going Correction** +0.575s/f (Yiel) **11 Ran SP% 113.9**
Speed ratings (Par 103): **104,100,97,97,97 93,87,83,81,66 21**
CSF £44.90 CT £476.47 TOTE £5.60: £3.00, £2.30, £4.40; EX 44.70 Trifecta £775.90.
**Owner** Pearson, Lamb, Wynn Williams **Bred** Castleton Lyons **Trained** Denton, Co Durham

**FOCUS**
A fair handicap which was soundly run, in a slightly quicker time than the first division. The form is rated around the runner-up.

## 1611 RACINGUK.COM/ANYWHERE: 3 DEVICES, 1 PRICE H'CAP 6f
**6:10** (6:10) (Class 6) (0-65,65) 3-Y-O **£1,940** (£577; £288; £144) **Stalls** Centre

Form RPR
633- **1** **Le Laitier (FR)**[130] 8261 3-9-5 **63**........................ GrahamLee 1 71
(Scott Dixon) *prom on far side of gp: hdwy to ld 2f out: rdn out fnl f* **8/1**
400- **2** *1 1/4* **Tell Me When**[195] 7094 3-8-9 **53**........................ BarryMcHugh 2 57
(Brian Rothwell) *dwlt: hld up on far side of gp: hdwy to chse wnr over 1f out: kpt on fnl f: nt pce to chal* **50/1**
333- **3** *2* **Another Royal**[195] 7096 3-9-0 **58**........................(p) DuranFentiman 16 56+
(Tim Easterby) *hld up in tch in centre of gp: hdwy and ev ch whn carried rt 2f out: rdn and edgd lft ins fnl f: r.o* **14/1**
3261 **4** *1/2* **Coiste Bodhar (IRE)**[17] 1277 3-9-3 **61**........................(p) JoeFanning 6 57
(Joseph Tuite) *in tch centre of gp: pushed along over 2f out: hdwy over 1f out: kpt on fnl f* **11/2**[2]
045- **5** *2* **Bearskin (IRE)**[182] 7419 3-9-2 **60**........................(p) PJMcDonald 14 50
(Ann Duffield) *bhd and outpcd in centre of gp: hdwy over 1f out: styd on fnl f: nrst fin* **12/1**
1-00 **6** *1 1/4* **Kinkohyo**[12] 1373 3-8-9 **53**........................ PaulMulrennan 10 39
(Bryan Smart) *bhd and rdn towards far side of gp: edgd lft over 2f out: styd on fnl f: nvr rchd ldrs* **33/1**
-604 **7** *1 1/4* **La Paiva (FR)**[41] 919 3-8-0 **51** oh6........................(p) MatthewHopkins(7) 12 33
(Scott Dixon) *led in centre of gp: hung rt: rdn and hdd 2f out: btn fnl f* **33/1**
50-3 **8** *1* **Lady Mai (IRE)**[12] 1373 3-8-7 **56**........................ SammyJoBell(5) 8 34
(Richard Fahey) *cl up in centre of gp: drvn over 2f out: wknd over 1f out* **9/2**[1]
006- **9** *1* **Bashiba (IRE)**[193] 7147 3-8-7 **51** oh6........................(v) AndrewMullen 5 26
(Nigel Tinkler) *plld hrd: hld up in centre of gp: effrt over 2f out: wknd over 1f out* **50/1**
366- **10** *nse* **China In My Hands**[191] 7202 3-9-1 **62**........................ JasonHart(3) 4 37
(James Bethell) *prom towards far side of gp: drvn and lost pl over 2f out: n.d after* **12/1**
4433 **11** *nk* **Parkhill Star**[24] 1147 3-8-12 **63**........................(p) JennyPowell(7) 18 37
(Tom Dascombe) *bhd and outpcd towards nr side of gp: sme hdwy fnl f: nvr on terms* **33/1**
550- **12** *nse* **Nelson's Pride**[230] 6085 3-9-1 **64**........................ ShaneGray(5) 17 38
(Kevin Ryan) *in tch nr side of gp: struggling over 2f out: btn over 1f out* **20/1**
060- **13** *2 3/4* **Snugfit Sam**[243] 5646 3-8-11 **55**........................ GrahamGibbons 19 20
(John Quinn) *hld up in tch on nr side of gp: effrt over 2f out: sn wknd* **7/1**[3]
-232 **14** *1/2* **Queenie's Home**[11] 1409 3-9-7 **65**........................ MartinDwyer 3 29
(James Given) *cl up in far side of gp tl rdn and wknd wl over 1f out* **9/2**[1]
020- **15** *1* **Secret Applause**[195] 7096 3-9-0 **63**........................ ConnorBeasley(5) 9 23
(Michael Dods) *hld up in centre of gp: hdwy 1/2-way: rdn and wknd 2f out* **14/1**
000- **16** *9* **San Remo Rose (IRE)**[163] 7818 3-8-8 **52** oh6 ow1........ TomEaves 15
(Nigel Tinkler) *prom in nr side of gp tl rdn and wknd over 2f out* **50/1**

1m 15.98s (4.18) **Going Correction** +0.575s/f (Yiel) **16** Ran SP% **123.5**
Speed ratings (Par 96): **95,93,90,90,87 85,84,82,81,81 80,80,77,76,75 63**
CSF £378.27 CT £5620.99 TOTE £10.40: £2.20, £6.10, £3.80, £1.30; EX 455.60 Trifecta £911.20.
**Owner** Paul J Dixon **Bred** J Vittori & Mme Y Dixon **Trained** Babworth, Notts

**FOCUS**
A modest sprint, full of largely exposed types. Those racing on the far side of the group fared best with the winner rated around his better 2yo efforts.
T/Jkpt: Not won. T/Plt: £508.50 to a £1 stake. Pool of £71970.35 - 103.32 winning tickets.
T/Qpdt: £239.60 to a £1 stake. Pool of £4112.30 - 12.70 winning tickets JR

# YARMOUTH (L-H)
Monday, April 21

**OFFICIAL GOING: Good (good to firm in places; 7.5)**
Wind: medium, half behind Weather: overcast, light rain at times

## 1612 WIN BIG WITH THE TOTEJACKPOT MAIDEN STKS 1m 3y
**1:50** (1:55) (Class 5) 3-Y-O+ **£3,493** (£1,039; £519; £259) **Stalls** Centre

Form RPR
3 **1** **Abseil (USA)**[20] 1216 4-9-13 0........................ JamesDoyle 13 99+
(Sir Michael Stoute) *hld up wl in tch and a travelling wl: jnd ldrs 2f out: pushed into ld 1f out: r.o strly and drew clr fnl f: easily* **5/4**[1]
40- **2** *4 1/2* **Joys Of Spring (IRE)**[178] 7493 3-8-8 0........................ AndreaAtzeni 10 79
(Luca Cumani) *t.k.h: hld up in tch in midfield: hdwy to press ldr 2f out: ev ch u.p over 1f out: outpcd by wnr and one pce fnl f* **10/1**
05/ **3** *1* **Putra Eton (IRE)**[535] 7517 4-9-13 0........................ JackMitchell 12 86+
(Roger Varian) *stdd s: hld up in tch in last pair: hdwy ent fnl 2f: modest 5th over 1f out: styd on wl to go 3rd towards fin: no ch w wnr* **33/1**
34-2 **4** *1 1/4* **Twin Point**[16] 1296 3-8-13 76........................ WilliamBuick 7 79
(John Gosden) *led: rdn over 2f out: drvn and hdd 1f out: outpcd by wnr and plugged on same pce fnl f: lost 3rd towards fin* **3/1**[2]
**5** *1 3/4* **Halation (IRE)** 3-9-0 ow1........................ AdamKirby 1 76
(Marco Botti) *hld up in tch in last quartet: hdwy over 3f out: pressed ldrs and rdn 2f out: 4th and btn over 1f out: wknd fnl f* **16/1**
5- **6** *6* **Surety (IRE)**[328] 2758 3-8-13 0........................ FrederikTylicki 3 61
(Clive Brittain) *hld up in midfield: hdwy to chse ldrs 3f out: rdn and no ex ent fnl f: wknd over 1f out* **16/1**
0- **7** *shd* **Windy Citi**[180] 7466 3-8-8 0........................ LukeMorris 11 56
(Chris Wall) *t.k.h: hld up in tch in midield: rdn and effrt 3f out: sn struggling: wknd 2f out* **50/1**
0 **8** *1/2* **Semaral (IRE)**[19] 1233 3-8-8 0........................ TedDurcan 2 55
(Chris Wall) *stdd s: t.k.h: rn green and hld up in rr: effrt over 2f out: sn btn and wknd 2f out* **100/1**
**9** *3/4* **Fresh Kingdom (IRE)** 3-8-13 0........................ HayleyTurner 8 58
(James Fanshawe) *sn pushed along in midfield: struggling 3f out: wl btn fnl 2f* **33/1**
0- **10** *hd* **Daydreamer**[180] 7467 3-8-13 0........................ SebSanders 6 58
(William Haggas) *wl in tch in midfield: rdn and struggling 3 out: wknd ent fnl 2f* **11/2**[3]
06 **11** *13* **Jalusive (IRE)**[49] 816 5-9-13 0........................ AdamBeschizza 4 32
(Christine Dunnett) *chsd ldr tl 3f out: sn dropped out: bhd over 1f out* **100/1**
12 *12* **Jay Gee Speedfit (IRE)** 3-8-13 0........................ TomQueally 9
(George Margarson) *chsd ldrs tl 1/2-way: sn bhd: t.o over 1f out* **66/1**
13 *23* **Tellatail** 4-9-6 0........................ ThomasHemsley(7) 5
(Chris Dwyer) *in tch in midfield: struggling 1/2-way: t.o fnl 2f* **100/1**

1m 36.26s (-4.34) **Going Correction** -0.425s/f (Firm)
**WFA** 3 from 4yo+ 14lb **13** Ran SP% **118.0**
Speed ratings (Par 103): **104,99,98,97,95 89,89,88,88,87 74,62,39**
CSF £15.10 TOTE £2.70: £1.10, £2.40, £8.90; EX 16.70 Trifecta £263.50.
**Owner** K Abdullah **Bred** Juddmonte Farms Inc **Trained** Newmarket, Suffolk

**FOCUS**
Both Luke Morris and Hayley Turner felt the ground was good. An ordinary maiden, but a ready winner who should do better from here.

## 1613 TOTEEXACTA PICK THE 1ST AND 2ND H'CAP 7f 3y
**2:25** (2:26) (Class 6) (0-65,65) 4-Y-O+ **£2,587** (£770; £384; £192) **Stalls** Centre

Form RPR
1331 **1** **Kasbhom**[20] 1227 4-9-6 **64**........................(t) WilliamCarson 3 74
(Anthony Carson) *racd towards far side tl 1/2-way: chsd ldrs tl led 1/2-way: mde rest but edging rt after: stl gng rt u.p 1f out: racing nr stands' rail and styd on fnl 150yds: drvn out* **11/2**[2]
/00- **2** *3/4* **Specialty (IRE)**[138] 8157 4-9-2 **60**........................ AdamKirby 4 68
(Pam Sly) *led tl 1/2-way: rdn and lost pl ent fnl 2f: looked wl hld over 1f out: rallied u.p fnl f: styd on wl to go 2nd cl home* **22/1**
5350 **3** *nk* **Sheikh The Reins (IRE)**[32] 1026 5-9-7 **65**........................(v) RobertHavlin 1 72
(John Best) *hld up in tch in midfield: rdn and effrt ent fnl 2f: chsd wnr over 1f out: carried rt 1f out: swtchd lft and styd on same pce fnl 100yds: lost 2nd cl home* **16/1**
1614 **4** *1 1/4* **Indus Valley (IRE)**[47] 851 7-9-1 **59**........................ AndreaAtzeni 8 63
(Des Donovan) *hld up in tch towards rr: rdn and effrt to chse ldr wl over 1f out tl over 1f out: styd on same pce fnl f* **9/2**[1]
-300 **5** *nk* **Little Indian**[12] 1385 4-9-2 **60**........................ FrederikTylicki 13 65+
(J R Jenkins) *hld up in tch in rr: hdwy towards stands' side over 1f out: forced to swtchd lft ins fnl f: styng on whn squeezed for room and hmpd wl ins fnl f: one pce after* **7/1**
0461 **6** *2 1/4* **Darnathean**[35] 996 5-9-1 **59**........................(p) SeanLevey 7 56
(Paul D'Arcy) *taken down early: hld up in tch in midfield: rdn and unable qck over 2f out: hld and one pce fr over 1f out* **13/2**
0453 **7** *shd* **First Class**[20] 1217 6-9-5 **63**........................(p) DavidProbert 12 60
(Rae Guest) *in tch in midfield: rdn and effrt to chse ldrs ent fnl 2f: no ex ent fnl f: plugged on same pce after* **15/2**
-605 **8** *1* **Ceelo**[19] 1238 4-9-1 **62**........................ SimonPearce(3) 9 57
(Lydia Pearce) *taken down early: chsd ldrs: rdn and ev ch over 2f out tl wl over 1f out: wknd jst over 1f out* **6/1**[3]
10-0 **9** *8* **First Sargeant**[9] 1454 4-9-3 **61**........................ SilvestreDeSousa 2 35
(Geoffrey Harker) *urged along in tch in rr early: rdn and hdwy over 2f out: btn jst over 1f out: eased ins fnl f* **16/1**
4/2- **10** *15* **Kashmiri Star**[440] 523 5-8-11 **58**........................(v) WilliamTwiston-Davies(3) 6
(Mick Quinn) *chsd ldrs tl 1/2-way: lost pl u.p over 2f out: wl bhd fnl f* **16/1**
046- **11** *94* **Fever Few**[158] 7880 5-8-13 **64**........................ SamuelClarke(7) 10
(Chris Wall) *throwing hd arnd and v awkward leaving stalls: immediately wl t.o* **14/1**

1m 24.54s (-2.06) **Going Correction** -0.425s/f (Firm) **11** Ran SP% **114.1**
Speed ratings (Par 101): **94,93,92,91,91 88,88,87,78,60**
CSF £114.89 CT £1233.39 TOTE £5.40: £2.00, £5.40, £6.90; EX 144.20 Trifecta £660.70.
**Owner** Macattack, William Lea Screed & Form IT **Bred** Darley **Trained** Newmarket, Suffolk
■ Stewards' Enquiry : William Carson two-day ban: careless riding (May 5-6)

**FOCUS**
They raced centre-field, with the exception of the winner, who continued his progress from the AW.

## 1614 TRY A TOTETRIFECTA H'CAP (BOBIS RACE) 7f 3y
**3:00** (3:02) (Class 3) (0-90,90) 3-Y-O **£8,191** (£2,451; £1,225; £613; £305) **Stalls** Centre

Form RPR
134- **1** **Shyron**[174] 7609 3-8-0 **76** oh3........................ JordanVaughan(7) 9 84+
(George Margarson) *wl in tch in midfield: effrt to chal and wnt lft u.p 1f out: rdr dropped rein and wnt further lft: regained reins and kpt on under hands and heels fnl 100yds* **25/1**
1356 **2** *nk* **Bretherton**[33] 1013 3-8-11 **80**........................(b) PaulHanagan 4 85
(Richard Fahey) *racd keenly: led: rdn and hdd over 1f out: lft w ev ch ins fnl f: kpt on but hld fnl 75yds* **10/1**
3-02 **3** *2* **Wee Jean**[17] 1278 3-8-13 **85**........................ WilliamTwiston-Davies(3) 7 89+
(Mick Channon) *chsd ldr: drvn to ld over 1f out: hdd and carried lft ins fnl f: hmpd and dropped to 3rd ins fnl f: one pce after* **8/1**[3]
011- **4** *1* **Lawyer (IRE)**[191] 7202 3-8-12 **81**........................ AndreaAtzeni 6 78
(Luca Cumani) *chsd ldrs: rdn and effrt ent fnl 2f: 4th and styd on same pce fnl f* **7/4**[1]
035- **5** *hd* **Legend Rising (IRE)**[238] 5837 3-9-4 **87**........................ NickyMackay 2 84
(Martyn Meade) *in tch in midfield: effrt u.p ent fnl 2f: styd on same pce fnl f* **25/1**
165- **6** *2 1/4* **Free Code (IRE)**[222] 6304 3-9-7 **90**........................ LukeMorris 8 81
(James Tate) *s.i.s: nvr really travelling wl in rr: struggling u.p 1/2-way: styd on past btn horses fnl f: n.d* **16/1**
164- **7** *1 3/4* **Valen (IRE)**[171] 7657 3-9-3 **86**........................ TomQueally 11 73
(Michael Bell) *in tch in midfield: effrt u.p over 2f out: no prog over 1f out: wknd fnl f* **12/1**
24-3 **8** *1/2* **Yagheer (IRE)**[14] 1347 3-8-7 **76**........................ FrederikTylicki 10 61
(Roger Varian) *t.k.h: hld up in tch in midfield: rdn and effrt over 2f out: no imp and wl hld over 1f out* **11/2**[2]
61-0 **9** *2 1/4* **Westminster (IRE)**[14] 1352 3-9-2 **85**........................ WilliamBuick 3 64
(John Gosden) *chsd ldrs: rdn and unable qck ent fnl 2f: wknd over 1f out* **9/1**
400- **10** *1 1/2* **Diamond Lady**[178] 7503 3-9-0 **83**........................ JamieSpencer 5 58
(William Stone) *stdd s: hld up in tch in rr: rdn and no imp ent fnl 2f: wknd over 1f out* **25/1**
1423 **11** *3/4* **Outbacker (IRE)**[20] 1225 3-8-9 **78**........................ SilvestreDeSousa 1 52
(Mark Johnston) *s.i.s: in tch in last trio: rdn and hdwy 3f out: wknd u.p over 1f out* **8/1**[3]

1m 23.27s (-3.33) **Going Correction** -0.425s/f (Firm) **11** Ran SP% **118.2**
Speed ratings (Par 102): **102,101,99,98,98 95,93,92,90,88 87**
CSF £252.26 CT £2224.49 TOTE £29.30: £6.30, £1.70, £3.60; EX 423.80 Trifecta £1786.30.
**Owner** F Butler **Bred** F Butler **Trained** Newmarket, Suffolk

**FOCUS**
Bit of a messy finish to what was a decent handicap The winner resumed his progress from the AW last year.

## 1615 YOUR FAVOURITE POOL BETS AT TOTEPOOL.COM H'CAP (BOBIS RACE) 5f 43y
**3:35** (3:37) (Class 4) (0-80,78) 3-Y-O **£5,433** (£1,617; £808; £404) **Stalls** Centre

Form RPR
12-2 **1** **Piazon**[12] 1396 3-9-0 **76** ........ LouisSteward(5) 4 91+
(Michael Bell) *taken down early: t.k.h early: clsd to ld 2f out: rdn to go clr but hung lft fr over 1f out: r.o: comf* **8/11**[1]
21-0 **2** *2 1/4* **Nova Champ (IRE)**[12] 1396 3-9-1 **72** ........ JamieSpencer 1 76
(Stuart Williams) *led for 1f: chsd ldr tl outpcd u.p ent fnl 2f: plugged on to chse clr wnr 1f out: no ch but kpt on u.p* **11/2**[3]
213 **3** *5* **Eva Clare (IRE)**[34] 1005 3-8-12 **69** ........ SeanLevey 5 56
(K R Burke) *chsd ldr tl led after 1f: rdn and hdd 2f out: 3rd and btn over 1f out* **10/1**
140- **4** *nk* **Kalon Brama (IRE)**[166] 7771 3-8-0 **64** oh1 ........ BradleyBosley(7) 3 49
(Peter Charalambous) *in tch in rr: rdn and struggling 1/2-way: plugged on fnl f and pressing for 3rd towards fin: no ch w wnr* **50/1**
035- **5** *1* **Finflash (IRE)**[178] 7503 3-9-4 **78** ........ WilliamTwiston-Davies(3) 6 60
(Mick Channon) *chsd ldrs: effrt u.p to press ldrs 2f out: sn outpcd and btn: wknd 1f out* **3/1**[2]
1m 1.19s (-1.51) **Going Correction** -0.425s/f (Firm) **5** Ran SP% **109.3**
Speed ratings (Par 100): **95,91,83,82,81**
CSF £5.19 TOTE £1.80: £1.10, £2.50; EX 5.70 Trifecta £18.00.
**Owner** R P B Michaelson **Bred** Peter Baldwin **Trained** Newmarket, Suffolk

**FOCUS**
No depth and a good opportunity for the winner, who did it well and produced a step up.

## 1616 BEST ODDS GUARANTEED AT TOTEPOOL.COM MAIDEN AUCTION STKS 1m 2f 21y
**4:10** (4:12) (Class 5) 3-Y-O **£3,493** (£1,039; £519; £259) **Stalls** Low

Form RPR
**1** **Der Meister (IRE)** 3-8-12 0 ........ OisinMurphy(3) 4 72+
(Andrew Balding) *in tch in midfield: rdn and effrt over 3f out: hdwy to chal over 1f out: kpt on u.p to ld wl ins fnl f: rdn out* **9/2**[2]
20-2 **2** *nk* **Rough Courte (IRE)**[14] 1344 3-8-10 69 ........ SamHitchcott 8 66
(Mick Channon) *taken down early: led: rdn 3f out: changing legs and wandering u.p after: kpt on tl hdd and no ex wl ins fnl f* **10/1**
2433 **3** *hd* **Needless Shouting (IRE)**[11] 1403 3-8-8 65(v[1]) WilliamTwiston-Davies(3) 7 67
(Mick Channon) *t.k.h: hld up in midfield: clsd to join ldr wl over 3f out: rdn over 1f out: ev ch after but nt finding as much as looked likely u.p: hld cl home* **9/2**[2]
**4** *1 1/4* **Affaire De Coeur** 3-8-13 0 ........ JamieSpencer 6 67+
(David Simcock) *t.k.h: hld up in last pair: hld up in tch in last pair: hdwy to chse ldrs 2f out: rdn over 1f out: styd on same pce ins fnl f* **9/4**[1]
645- **5** *1/2* **L Ge R**[130] 8259 3-8-2 60 ow1 ........ ShelleyBirkett(5) 2 60+
(Peter Charalambous) *chsd ldrs: travelling wl enough but trapped on inner 4f out: swtchd rt ins fnl f: stl nt enough room and no imp fnl 100yds* **25/1**
4- **6** *5* **Lifejacket (IRE)**[187] 7301 3-8-13 0 ........ AdamKirby 1 56
(Ed Dunlop) *t.k.h: hld up in tch in midfield: rdn over 2f out: no ex jst over 1f out: wknd fnl f* **9/2**[2]
4 **7** *2* **Musical Theme**[47] 839 3-8-6 0 ........ ChrisCatlin 5 45
(Willie Musson) *s.i.s: a in rr: struggling 3f out: no ch but kpt on ins fnl f* **25/1**
5- **8** *11* **Ice Falcon (IRE)**[220] 6365 3-8-13 0 ........ LukeMorris 3 31
(James Tate) *chsd ldr tl wl over 3f out: lost pl u.p over 2f out: bhd fnl f* **8/1**[3]
2m 8.81s (-1.69) **Going Correction** -0.20s/f (Firm) **8** Ran SP% **113.2**
Speed ratings (Par 98): **98,97,97,96,96 92,90,81**
CSF £46.94 TOTE £5.20: £2.40, £2.70, £1.90; EX 18.90 Trifecta £100.80.
**Owner** James/Michaelson/Greenwood 1 **Bred** Mrs C L Weld **Trained** Kingsclere, Hants

**FOCUS**
Quite a modest maiden, with 69 and 65-rated runners filling the places. The form is set around the third.

## 1617 DOWNLOAD THE TOTEPOOL LIVE INFO APP H'CAP 1m 2f 21y
**4:45** (4:47) (Class 5) (0-70,69) 4-Y-O+ **£3,493** (£1,039; £519; £259) **Stalls** Low

Form RPR
320- **1** **Ela Goog La Mou**[174] 7608 5-8-4 **55** oh2 ........ RosieJessop(3) 7 63
(Peter Charalambous) *t.k.h: hld up in midfield: swtchd rt and hdwy to ld 7f out: sn clr: rdn 2f out: stl 4 l clr 1f out: nvr gng to be ct: rdn out* **20/1**
46-0 **2** *1 1/4* **Mcbirney (USA)**[61] 655 7-9-3 **65** ........ SeanLevey 4 71
(Paul D'Arcy) *t.k.h: hld up in midfield: effrt to go prom in main gp 3f out: chsd clr wnr 1f out: styd on but nvr gng to rch wnr* **16/1**
-004 **3** *1 1/4* **Sixties Queen**[60] 671 4-8-2 **55** oh3 ........ NatashaEaton(5) 3 58
(Alan Bailey) *t.k.h: chsd ldr tl 7f out: styd prom in main gp: rdn and chsd clr wnr 2f out tl 1f out: kpt on same pce* **11/1**
133- **4** *shd* **The Ducking Stool**[174] 7611 7-9-2 **69** ........ ShelleyBirkett(5) 2 72
(Julia Feilden) *hld up in midfield: rdn and effrt over 2f out: swtchd rt 1f out: styd on fnl f: no threat to wnr* **11/2**[2]
/212 **5** *1/2* **Minstrels Gallery (IRE)**[21] 1209 5-8-10 **61** ........(p) RobertTart(3) 5 63
(Lucy Wadham) *stdd s: t.k.h: hld up in last trio: rdn and effrt 3f out: hdwy in centre over 1f out: styd on fnl f: no threat to winner* **7/4**[1]
365 **6** *1 1/4* **Gabrial The Terror (IRE)**[45] 871 4-9-6 **68** ........ JamieSpencer 1 68
(David Simcock) *stdd s: t.k.h: hld up in rr: rdn and hdwy over 1f out: kpt on but no ch w wnr* **9/1**
10/6 **7** *2 1/4* **Frontline Phantom (IRE)**[23] 1167 7-8-3 **58** ........ RobJFitzpatrick(7) 9 53
(K R Burke) *t.k.h: chsd ldr tl 7f out: styd handy in main gp: rdn over 2f out: no imp and btn 1f out* **15/2**
006- **8** *3 1/2* **Super Cookie**[42] 7437 4-9-2 **64** ........ WilliamCarson 6 53
(Noel Quinlan) *led and set stdy gallop tl hdd 7f out: chsd clr ldr after: rdn and no imp over 2f out: lost 2nd 2f out and sn wknd* **28/1**
4362 **9** *5* **Minstrel Lad**[16] 1302 6-8-8 **59** ........ SimonPearce(3) 8 38
(Lydia Pearce) *t.k.h: hld up in midfield: dropped in bhd over 7f out: n.d after: bhd fnl 2f* **16/1**
10-3 **10** *5* **Ana Shababiya (IRE)**[14] 1348 4-9-6 **68** ........ WilliamBuick 10 38
(Ismail Mohammed) *t.k.h: chsd ldrs tl 7f out: styd handy in main gp tl rdn 4f out: bhd fnl 2f* **7/1**[3]
2m 9.87s (-0.63) **Going Correction** -0.20s/f (Firm) **10** Ran SP% **114.3**
Speed ratings (Par 103): **94,93,92,91,91 90,88,85,81,77**
CSF £296.58 CT £3658.36 TOTE £21.00: £8.00, £4.30, £5.00; EX 283.40 Trifecta £2568.10.
**Owner** pcracing.co.uk **Bred** Peter Charles **Trained** Newmarket, Suffolk

**FOCUS**
A moderate handicap that was run at just a steady gallop. The form is rated at face value.

## 1618 FOLLOW @TOTEPOOL ON TWITTER H'CAP 5f 43y
**5:20** (5:21) (Class 5) (0-75,75) 4-Y-O+ **£3,493** (£1,039; £519; £259) **Stalls** Centre

Form RPR
1441 **1** **Megaleka**[12] 1378 4-8-12 **71** ........ TimClark(5) 1 79+
(Alan Bailey) *travelled wl: pressed ldr tl lft in ld 1/2-way: rdn over 1f out: edgd lft but kpt on wl fnl 100yds* **5/1**
40-0 **2** *nk* **Commanche**[22] 1190 5-9-7 **75** ........ LukeMorris 2 82
(Chris Dwyer) *chsd ldrs: lft pressing wnr 1/2-way: ev ch and drvn over 1f out: kpt on wl ins fnl f* **9/2**[3]
220- **3** *3/4* **Indian Tinker**[173] 7634 5-8-13 **67** ........ AndreaAtzeni 6 71
(Robert Cowell) *chsd ldrs: lft cl 3rd 1/2-way: ev ch u.p over 1f out: styd on same pce ins fnl f* **9/2**[3]
-006 **4** *3 1/2* **Harrogate Fair**[17] 1283 4-8-7 **61** oh3 ........ LiamJones 4 52
(Michael Squance) *in tch in last pair: effrt 2f out: stl cl 4th whn hung lft jst ins fnl f: sn btn and wknd fnl 100yds* **12/1**
5-03 **5** *42* **Monsieur Jamie**[71] 549 6-9-7 **75** ........(v) FrederikTylicki 3
(J R Jenkins) *dwlt: hld up in tch in rr: rdn 1/2-way: sn btn: t.o fnl f* **4/1**[2]
2202 **P** **Dancing Freddy (IRE)**[7] 1487 7-8-12 **69** ........(tp) OisinMurphy(3) 5
(Ann Stokell) *taken down early: led tl lost action and hdd 1/2-way: p.u and dismntd* **5/2**[1]
1m 1.05s (-1.65) **Going Correction** -0.425s/f (Firm) **6** Ran SP% **109.3**
Speed ratings (Par 103): **96,95,94,88,21**
CSF £25.65 TOTE £5.10: £2.40, £2.70; EX 26.80 Trifecta £190.50.
**Owner** North Cheshire Trading & Storage Ltd **Bred** North Cheshire Trading And Storage Ltd **Trained** Newmarket, Suffolk

**FOCUS**
Modest sprinting form, with the favourite. The winner's Catterick run had been franked.
T/Plt: £2,868.90 to a £1 stake. Pool of £54352.29- 13.83 winning tickets. T/Qpdt: £129.60 to a £1 stake. Pool of £3697.43- 21.10 winning tickets. SP

# COLOGNE (R-H)
Monday, April 21

**OFFICIAL GOING: Turf: good**

## 1619a KARIN BARONIN VON ULLMANN - SCHWARZGOLD-RENNEN (GROUP 3) (3YO FILLIES) (TURF) 1m
**4:20** (12:00) 3-Y-O
**£26,666** (£9,166; £4,583; £2,500; £1,666; £1,250)

RPR
**1** **Meerjungfrau (GER)**[176] 7559 3-9-2 0 ........ HarryBentley 3 102
(A Wohler, Germany) *stdd and hld up in rr: last 3f out: rdn and hdwy on wd outside fr 2f out: hung rt u.p but r.o strly and chal ent fnl f: sn led and qcknd clr: readily* **2/1**[1]
**2** *1 3/4* **Ajaxana (GER)**[172] 3-9-2 0 ........ AndreBest 7 98
(Waldemar Hickst, Germany) *t.k.h: trckd ldr on outer: rdn over 2f out: r.o and wnt 2nd ins fnl f: nt pce of wnr* **16/5**[2]
**3** *1 1/2* **Emerald Star**[22] 3-9-2 0 ........ DanielePorcu 1 95
(P Schiergen, Germany) *led: rdn and qcknd over 2f out: reeled in ent fnl f and sn hdd: no ex and dropped to 2nd* **54/10**[3]
**4** *1 1/2* **Turfmaid (GER)**[183] 7406 3-9-2 0 ........ SHellyn 5 91
(J Hirschberger, Germany) *reluctant to load: hld up in midfield on inner: rdn over 2f out: kpt on and wnt 4th ins fnl f: nt pce to chal* **132/10**
**5** *1* **Papagena Star (IRE)**[176] 7559 3-9-2 0 ........ MartinSeidl 9 89
(Markus Klug, Germany) *hld up in midfield on outer: rdn over 2f out: kpt on and wnt 5th post: nt pce to chal* **61/10**
**6** *hd* **Wild Step (GER)**[183] 7406 3-9-2 0 ........ MichaelCadeddu 2 88
(Markus Klug, Germany) *prom on inner: rdn over 2f out: kpt on same pce u.p and sn hld: dropped to 6th post* **171/10**
**7** *1/2* **Goiania**[176] 7559 3-9-2 0 ........ FMBerry 4 87
(P Schiergen, Germany) *dwlt and hld up in rr on inner: rdn and swtchd lft over 2f out: nt clr run and squeezed for room over 1f out: kpt on ins fnl f but nvr able to chal* **7/1**
**8** *2* **Mariele (IRE)**[175] 3-9-2 0 ........ J-PLopez 8 83
(W Hefter, Germany) *t.k.h: hld up in midfield: rdn over 2f out: outpcd whn bmpd over 1f out: sn no ex and btn* **207/10**
**9** *2 1/2* **Elora Princess (GER)**[211] 3-9-2 0 ........ BGanbat 6 77
(Markus Klug, Germany) *midfield in tch: rdn 3f out: outpcd and btn over 1f out: wknd* **41/1**
**10** *3* **She Bang (FR)**[22] 3-9-2 0 ........ AdriedeVries 10 70
(Jean-Pierre Carvalho, Germany) *midfield in tch on outer: rdn 3f out: shifted lft and bmpd rival over 1f out: sn no ex and wknd: dropped to last and eased* **78/10**
1m 34.91s (-3.48) **10** Ran SP% **130.3**
WIN (incl. 10 euro stake): 30, PLACES: 14, 17, 16. SF: 76,.
**Owner** Rennstall Wohler **Bred** Gestut Gorlsdorf **Trained** Germany

# LE LION-D'ANGERS (R-H)
Monday, April 21

**OFFICIAL GOING: Turf: good to soft**

## 1620a PRIX OLIVIER BOURGEAIS (MAIDEN) (3YO COLTS & GELDINGS) (TURF) 7f
**5:20** (12:00) 3-Y-O **£6,666** (£2,666; £2,000; £1,333; £666)

RPR
**1** **Steel Train (FR)**[44] 3-8-10 0 ........ SebastienMartino(6) 78
(H-A Pantall, France) **16/5**[2]
**2** *2 1/2* **Poudlard Express (FR)**[81] 390 3-9-2 0 ........ ThomasHenderson 71
(D De Watrigant, France) **6/4**[1]
**3** *5* **Wefeen (FR)**[128] 3-9-2 0 ........ AntoineCoutier 58
(F Chappet, France) **44/1**
**4** *1* **In For Dinner (FR)**[11] 3-9-2 0 ........ MathieuAndrouin 55
(P Monfort, France) **149/10**
**5** *2 1/2* **Adventurer (FR)**[12] 3-9-2 0 ........ RonanThomas 48
(F-H Graffard, France) **51/10**[3]

6 5 **Parfum De Roi (FR)** 3-9-2 0 StevanBourgois 35
(Y-M Porzier, France) 11/2
7 10 **Craftsmanship (FR)**[181] 7451 3-9-2 0 TheoBachelot 8
(Robert Eddery) *hld up towards rr on outer: rdn over 2f out: outpcd and btn ent fnl f: eased* 83/10
8 8 **Bill Jem (FR)**[124] 3-9-2 0 ArnaudBourgeais
(D Sepulchre, France) 204/10
1m 26.98s (86.98) 8 Ran SP% 119.5
WIN (incl. 1 euro stake): 4.20. PLACES: 1.60, 1.30, 4.50. DF: 4.70. SF: 11.50.
**Owner** Erich Schmid **Bred** E Schmid **Trained** France

# 1551 LONGCHAMP (R-H)
Monday, April 21

**OFFICIAL GOING: Turf: good**

## 1621a PRIX NOAILLES (GROUP 3) (3YO) (TURF) 1m 2f 110y
1:50 (12:00) 3-Y-0 £33,333 (£13,333; £10,000; £6,666; £3,333)

RPR
1 **Gailo Chop (FR)**[15] 1340 3-9-2 0 JulienAuge 4 112+
(A De Watrigant, France) *mde all: pushed along and qcknd ent fnl f: kpt on strly: comf* 7/10[1]
2 1 1/4 **Aventador (FR)**[22] 3-9-2 0 RaphaelMarchelli 1 108
(T Castanheira, France) *trckd ldr on inner: pushed along and nt clr run 2f out: swtchd lft and bmpd rival over 1f out: rdn in 2nd ent fnl f: styd on wl but a comf hld by wnr* 129/10
3 2 1/2 **Gallante (IRE)**[222] 3-9-2 0 Pierre-CharlesBoudot 5 103
(A Fabre, France) *t.k.h early: in tch in 4th: pushed along 3f out: wnt 3rd ent fnl f: styd on u.p but nt pce to chal* 7/2[3]
4 1 **A Soldier's Life (IRE)**[19] 3-9-2 0 MaximeGuyon 3 101
(A Fabre, France) *t.k.h early: trckd ldr on outer: pushed along and effrt to chal 2f out: rdn and outpcd by wnr whn bmpd by rival over 1f out: plugged on but wl hld after* 27/10[2]
5 12 **Bal De France (FR)**[16] 3-9-2 0 Christophe-PatriceLemaire 2 78
(S Kobayashi, France) *hld up and last thrght: bhd 1/2-way: no imp u.p in st and eased whn btn: nvr a factor* 168/10
2m 9.33s (-0.87) 5 Ran SP% 120.9
WIN (incl. 1 euro stake): 1.70.PLACES: 1.40, 2.70. SF: 6.10.
**Owner** Oti Management Pty Ltd & A Chopard **Bred** A Chopard **Trained** France

# LES LANDES
Monday, April 21

**OFFICIAL GOING: Good (good to soft in places)**

## 1622a LIBERATION BREWERY H'CAP 1m 4f
3:05 (3:05) (0-65,) 3-Y-0+ £1,460 (£525; £315)

RPR
1 **I'm Harry**[33] 1012 5-10-10 (vt1) MattieBatchelor 2 70
(George Baker) 5/4[1]
2 3 **Midnight Sequel**[52] 459 5-10-3 (tp) HarryPoulton 8 58
(Neil Mulholland) 7/2[3]
3 6 **Reach The Beach**[25] 1129 5-9-8 (v) MatthewLawson 9 40
(Brendan Powell) 5/1
4 6 **River Du Nord (FR)**[135] 8204 7-9-4 JemmaMarshall 5 26
(Sue Gardner) 5/1
5 2 **Mr Opulence**[238] 7145 5-9-8 (b) MrRHodson 1 27
(T Le Brocq, Jersey) 8/1
6 3 1/2 **Neuilly**[238] 7144 7-10-11 MrPCollington 6 38
(Mrs A Malzard, Jersey) 3/1[2]
7 5 **Bollin Fergus**[238] 7144 10-8-6 ow1 JenniferFerguson 7
(Mrs A Corson, Jersey) 10/1
8 6 **Lady Petrus**[238] 7145 9-8-8 ow3 MichaelStainton 4
(K Kukk, Jersey) 16/1
9 7 **Major Maximus**[238] 7144 7-10-12 DavidCuthbert 3 10
(Mrs C Gilbert, Jersey) 3/1[2]
2m 48.0s (-2.00) 9 Ran SP% 176.1
**Owner** Wickfield Stud And Hartshill Stud **Bred** Wickfield Stud And Hartshill Stud **Trained** Manton, Wilts

## 1623a JERSEY BOOKMAKERS H'CAP 7f
3:40 (3:40) 3-Y-0+ £1,900 (£685; £415)

RPR
1 **Copper Falls**[329] 1738 5-8-11 MatthewLawson 3 50
(Brendan Powell) 5/1
2 1 **George Baker (IRE)**[32] 1026 7-10-12 MattieBatchelor 2 76
(Mrs A Malzard, Jersey) 1/1[1]
3 4 **First Cat**[238] 7143 7-9-6 MichaelStainton 1 45
(K Kukk, Jersey) 5/1
4 3 1/2 **Pas D'Action**[238] 7145 6-9-0 JemmaMarshall 9 30
(Mrs A Malzard, Jersey) 7/4[2]
5 7 **Fast Freddie**[238] 7143 10-9-2 ow1 (p) MrPCollington 8 13
(Mrs A Corson, Jersey) 6/1
6 1/2 **Spanish Bounty**[238] 7143 9-10-6 MrRHodson 6 29
(Mrs A Malzard, Jersey) 4/1[3]
7 1 **Lively Little Lady**[253] 5327 4-8-6 ow1 JenniferFerguson 4
(Mrs A Corson, Jersey) 16/1
8 6 **Country Blue (FR)**[238] 7143 5-9-3 HarryPoulton 5
(Mrs A Malzard, Jersey) 8/1
9 dist **Esprit De Midas**[210] 6702 8-10-7 ow2 MrHJFCruickshank 7
(K Kukk, Jersey) 11/2
1m 32.0s (2.00) 9 Ran SP% 186.4
**Owner** P Banfield & J Hackett **Bred** P Banfield **Trained** Upper Lambourn, Berks

## 1624a LA VERTE RUE H'CAP 1m 2f
4:15 (4:15) 3-Y-0+ £1,460 (£525; £315)

RPR
1 **Ancient Greece**[17] 1281 7-10-12 (t) MattieBatchelor 2
(George Baker) 4/5[1]
2 10 **King Kenny**[238] 7144 9-8-6 JenniferFerguson 6
(Mrs A Corson, Jersey) 4/1
3 5 **Steely**[209] 6736 6-10-0 MichaelStainton 5
(K Kukk, Jersey) 2/1[2]
4 6 **Beck's Bolero (IRE)**[238] 7145 8-9-3 (p) MrPCollington 3
(Mrs A Corson, Jersey) 3/1[3]
5 10 **Constanzina (FR)**[152] 5-10-0 JemmaMarshall 1
(Mrs A Malzard, Jersey) 11/2
2m 18.0s (5.00) 5 Ran SP% 149.3
**Owner** Inkin, Inkin, Byng, Baker & Partners **Bred** Darley **Trained** Manton, Wilts

## 1625a HENRY THE VII H'CAP 1m 100y
4:50 (4:50) (0-50,) 3-Y-0+ £950 (£345; £205)

RPR
1 **Jackpot**[238] 7145 4-10-3 MatthewLawson 4 34
(Brendan Powell) 5/4[1]
2 7 **Grey Panel (FR)**[281] 6-10-12 MrRHodson 2 28
(T Le Brocq, Jersey) 5/2[3]
3 6 **Rebel Woman**[238] 7145 8-10-5 JenniferFerguson 6 7
(Mrs A Corson, Jersey) 6/1
4 5 **Rocquaine (IRE)**[238] 5-9-9 MichaelStainton 5
(Mrs A Malzard, Jersey) 10/1
5 2 **Athania (IRE)**[238] 7145 8-10-6 MrPCollington 1
(Mrs A Corson, Jersey) 6/1
6 1 1/2 **Lucifers Shadow (IRE)**[238] 7145 5-10-12 MattieBatchelor 3
(Mrs C Gilbert, Jersey) 2/1[2]
1m 56.0s (116.00) 6 Ran SP% 144.0
**Owner** P Banfield & J Hackett **Bred** P Banfield **Trained** Upper Lambourn, Berks

# 1448 WOLVERHAMPTON (A.W) (L-H)
Tuesday, April 22

**OFFICIAL GOING: Standard**
Wind: Light behind Weather: Overcast

## 1626 QUICKSILVERSLOTS PLAY £500 JACKPOT RAINBOW RICHES H'CAP 5f 20y(P)
5:45 (5:45) (Class 6) (0-60,58) 3-Y-0 £2,264 (£673; £336; £168) Stalls Low

Form RPR
3316 1 **Biscuiteer**[11] 1425 3-9-6 57 (b) LukeMorris 7 59
(Scott Dixon) *mde all: rdn over 1f out: styd on* 15/8[1]
046- 2 3/4 **Clear Focus (IRE)**[154] 7956 3-8-1 45 JennyPowell(7) 8 44
(Brendan Powell) *a.p: rdn to chse wnr over 1f out: styd on* 10/1[3]
0554 3 hd **Jazz Bay**[27] 1106 3-8-8 45 WilliamCarson 4 44
(John Bridger) *chsd ldr tl rdn over 1f out: styd on* 20/1
-664 4 3/4 **Brean Splash Susie**[18] 1277 3-8-4 46 ow1 (b1) RyanWhile(5) 3 42
(Bill Turner) *sn outpcd: hdwy over 1f out: hung lft and r.o ins fnl f: nt rch ldrs* 14/1
0005 5 1/2 **Trefnant (IRE)**[18] 1277 3-8-3 45 ConnorBeasley(5) 1 39
(Chris Dwyer) *prom: pushed along and nt clr run over 2f out: styd on same pce ins fnl f* 20/1
0664 6 7 **Literally On Fire (IRE)**[10] 1449 3-8-9 46 (p) RobertWinston 5 15
(Brendan Powell) *trckd ldrs: rdn over 1f out: wknd ins fnl f* 11/4[2]
0350 7 6 **Maro**[13] 1373 3-8-8 45 (t) DaleSwift 6
(Derek Shaw) *sn drvn along in rr: bhd fnl 3f* 16/1
1m 3.3s (1.00) **Going Correction** +0.075s/f (Slow) 7 Ran SP% 92.6
Speed ratings (Par 96): **95,93,93,92,91 80,70**
CSF £13.00 CT £121.28 TOTE £1.70: £1.10, £4.00; EX 9.00 Trifecta £71.70.
**Owner** P J Dixon & Partners **Bred** Mrs Fiona Denniff **Trained** Babworth, Notts
■ Rule 4 of 20p in the pound applies to all bets; Withdrawn: Bountiful Forest

**FOCUS**
They favourite made all in this modest handicap, and didn't need to improve. Bountiful Forest reared and unseated her rider at the start before being withdrawn.

## 1627 QUICKSILVERSLOTS PLAY FROM 10P TO £2 MAIDEN STKS 1m 4f 50y(P)
6:15 (6:15) (Class 5) 3-Y-0+ £2,911 (£866; £432; £216) Stalls Low

Form RPR
0 1 **Nam Hai (IRE)**[15] 1353 3-8-7 0 LukeMorris 1 73
(Michael Bell) *a.p: shkn up to ld and hung lft ins fnl f: r.o: readily* 2/1[2]
0-4 2 1 1/4 **Alzammaar (USA)**[21] 1218 3-8-7 0 DaneO'Neill 4 71
(Charles Hills) *trckd ldr: rdn to ld over 2f out: hdd and unable qck wl ins fnl f* 15/8[1]
3 shd **First Move** 4-9-12 0 JoeFanning 2 73
(Mark Johnston) *hld up: hdwy on outer over 2f out: rdn and ev ch fr over 1f out tl styd on same pce wl ins fnl f* 2/1[2]
0 4 21 **Hammered Silver (IRE)**[60] 686 4-9-12 0 ShaneKelly 3 53
(Mike Murphy) *led: rdn and hdd over 2f out: wknd over 1f out* 16/1[3]
2m 42.26s (1.16) **Going Correction** +0.075s/f (Slow)
**WFA** 3 from 4yo 20lb 4 Ran SP% 107.3
Speed ratings (Par 103): **99,98,98,84**
CSF £6.01 TOTE £2.40; EX 4.40 Trifecta £11.80.
**Owner** J Barnett & L Caine **Bred** Michael D Ryan **Trained** Newmarket, Suffolk

**FOCUS**
There was an open market for this small-field maiden. They went a fair pace and there was not much separating the three market leaders at the finish. Modest form, rated around the runner-up.

## 1628 QUICKSILVERSLOTS OPEN AFTER 10PM H'CAP 1m 4f 50y(P)
6:45 (6:45) (Class 5) (0-75,75) 4-Y-0+ £2,911 (£866; £432; £216) Stalls Low

Form RPR
0255 1 **All The Winds (GER)**[20] 999 9-9-2 70 (t) LukeMorris 2 78
(Shaun Lycett) *hld up: hdwy 2f out: rdn to ld ins fnl f: styd on* 10/1
1215 2 3/4 **Sian Gwalia**[31] 1065 4-9-0 69 MartinLane 4 76
(David Simcock) *hld up: hdwy on outer over 2f out: rdn and ev ch fr over 1f out: styd on* 5/1

/321 **3** 1 1/4 **Rocky Elsom (USA)**36 990 7-8-13 **67** JimCrowley 7 72
(David Arbuthnot) *trckd ldr tl over 8f out: remained handy: ev ch fr over 2f out tl rdn and styd on same pce ins fnl f* **11/4**1

126- **4** *hd* **Gabrial The Duke (IRE)**263 4961 4-9-2 **71** RobertWinston 5 75
(David Simcock) *a.p: hung lft almost thrght: chsd ldr over 8f out tl rdn over 2f out: led over 1f out: hdd and unable qck ins fnl f* **3/1**2

0515 **5** 3 **Spanish Plume**33 1034 6-8-7 **66** (p) JackDuern(5) 3 66
(Andrew Hollinshead) *hld up: rdn over 2f out: nt trble ldrs* **17/2**

1135 **6** 9 **A Little Bit Dusty**25 1140 6-9-7 **75** (p) HayleyTurner 1 60
(Conor Dore) *chsd ldrs: pushed along whn hmpd over 2f out: wknd over 1f out* **9/1**

1342 **7** 1/2 **Tiger Reigns**17 1317 8-9-2 **73** (t) OisinMurphy(3) 6 57
(John Butler) *led: rdn and hdd over 1f out: wknd fnl f* **4/1**3

2m 40.93s (-0.17) **Going Correction** +0.075s/f (Slow)
**WFA** 4 from 6yo+ 1lb **7 Ran SP% 118.0**
Speed ratings (Par 103): **103,102,101,101,99 93,93**
CSF £61.03 TOTE £16.10: £7.70, £4.00; EX 56.30 Trifecta £172.80.
**Owner** Nicholls Family **Bred** Stall Tralopp **Trained** Clapton-on-the-Hill, Gloucs

**FOCUS**
They went a decent gallop in this handicap and first two came from off the pace. The winner was a little below his winter best.

## 1629 QUICKSILVERSLOTS £1 TO WIN £500 H'CAP 2m 119y(P)
**7:15** (7:15) (Class 5) (0-75,71) 4-Y-O+ **£2,911** (£866; £432) **Stalls** Low

Form RPR
1211 **1** **Travel (USA)**7 1501 4-9-2 **66** JoeFanning 2 79+
(Mark Johnston) *trckd ldr tl led on bit 3f out: clr 2f out: easily* **1/3**1

4244 **2** 3 3/4 **Yasir (USA)**11 1046 6-9-6 **66** (p) HayleyTurner 1 72
(Conor Dore) *s.i.s: hld up: pushed along and hdwy to chse wnr over 2f out: rdn over 1f out: styd on same pce* **17/2**3

04-6 **3** 22 **Miss Tiger Lily**32 1043 4-9-7 **71** LukeMorris 3 68
(Harry Dunlop) *led: rdn and hdd 3f out: wknd and eased fnl f* **9/2**2

3m 43.42s (1.62) **Going Correction** +0.075s/f (Slow)
**WFA** 4 from 6yo 4lb **3 Ran SP% 103.7**
Speed ratings (Par 103): **99,97,86**
CSF £3.15 TOTE £1.70; EX 1.50 Trifecta £2.70.
**Owner** Sheikh Hamdan bin Mohammed Al Maktoum **Bred** Darley **Trained** Middleham Moor, N Yorks

**FOCUS**
The hot favourite scored with plenty in hand in this small-field event. The winner did not need to match her Southwell romp.

## 1630 QUICKSILVERSLOTS PLAY YOUR FAVOURITE £500 JACKPOT H'CAP 7f 32y(P)
**7:45** (7:46) (Class 4) (0-80,78) 4-Y-O+ **£5,175** (£1,540; £769; £384) **Stalls** High

Form RPR
-135 **1** **Kung Hei Fat Choy (USA)**7 1499 5-9-2 **78** (b) ConnorBeasley(5) 4 89
(James Given) *hld up: drvn along 1/2-way: hdwy on outer over 2f out: led over 1f out: styd on u.p* **7/1**

-031 **2** 1 1/2 **Sakash**18 1286 4-9-1 **72** FrederikTylicki 9 79
(J R Jenkins) *hld up: hdwy over 1f out: rdn to chse wnr fnl f: styd on* **6/1**3

51-4 **3** *nk* **Love Excel**20 1234 4-9-6 **77** GeorgeBaker 5 83
(Charles Hills) *hld up in tch: rdn over 1f out: styd on* **6/5**1

1113 **4** 1/2 **Caramack**25 1152 4-8-13 **75** EoinWalsh(5) 1 80
(Richard Lee) *s.i.s: outpcd: hdwy over 1f out: styd on* **10/1**

2535 **5** 2 1/4 **Pearl Nation (USA)**19 1267 5-9-5 **76**1 RobertWinston 3 75
(Brian Baugh) *led early: trckd ldrs: nt clr run and swtchd rt over 1f out: kpt on* **11/2**2

0505 **6** 8 **Pabusar**20 1244 6-8-8 **68** OisinMurphy(3) 2 46
(Ann Stokell) *trckd ldrs: rdn to ld over 2f out: hdd over 1f out: wknd and eased ins fnl f* **50/1**

2001 **7** 1/2 **Piceno (IRE)**13 1376 6-8-11 **75** (p) MatthewHopkins(7) 8 52
(Scott Dixon) *trckd ldr: plld hrd: rdn over 2f out: wknd wl over 1f out* **28/1**

3316 **8** 4 **Bogsnog (IRE)**11 1429 4-9-5 **76** TomEaves 6 43
(Kristin Stubbs) *sn led: rdn and hdd over 2f out: wknd wl over 1f out* **28/1**

0600 **9** 3/4 **Al's Memory (IRE)**34 1020 5-9-0 **74** DeclanBates(3) 7 39
(David Evans) *prom: drvn along 1/2-way: wknd over 2f out* **16/1**

1m 28.45s (-1.15) **Going Correction** +0.075s/f (Slow) **9 Ran SP% 111.5**
Speed ratings (Par 105): **109,107,106,106,103 94,94,89,88**
CSF £45.68 CT £82.65 TOTE £6.80: £2.10, £1.20, £1.10; EX 49.80 Trifecta £155.80.
**Owner** The Cool Silk Partnership **Bred** Gilgai Farm **Trained** Willoughton, Lincs
■ Stewards' Enquiry : Frederik Tylicki two-day ban: used whip down shoulder in the forehand (May 6-7)

**FOCUS**
They went a good pace in this handicap and the winner came from some way back. The winner is rated close to his best.

## 1631 QUICKSILVERSLOTS MORE JACKPOTS MORE MACHINES H'CAP 7f 32y(P)
**8:15** (8:15) (Class 6) (0-55,54) 4-Y-O+ **£2,264** (£673; £336; £168) **Stalls** High

Form RPR
55-6 **1** **Global Leader (IRE)**109 40 4-9-2 **49** PatrickDonaghy 6 71
(Paul D'Arcy) *mde all: clr 1/2-way: easily* **7/4**1

3006 **2** 8 **Welsh Inlet (IRE)**12 1408 6-9-3 **50** WilliamCarson 8 51
(John Bridger) *chsd ldrs: wnt 2nd 1/2-way: sn rdn: outpcd fnl 2f* **11/1**

004- **3** 3 **Lucilla**220 6406 4-9-4 **51** LukeMorris 4 44
(Michael Squance) *chsd wnr tl rdn 1/2-way: outpcd fr over 2f out* **16/1**

404- **4** 3 **Clary (IRE)**152 7987 4-9-7 **54** DavidProbert 7 40
(James Unett) *mid-div: drvn along 1/2-way: n.d* **11/2**3

3462 **5** *hd* **Very First Blade**14 1365 5-9-2 **49** (be) TomEaves 5 34
(Michael Mullineaux) *trckd ldrs: rdn and outpcd fr over 2f out* **4/1**2

6055 **6** 1 3/4 **Hinton Admiral**13 1388 10-9-5 **52** JoeFanning 1 33
(Pat Eddery) *s.i.s: pushed along over 2f out: nvr nrr* **14/1**

203 **7** *nk* **Chez Vrony**34 1015 8-9-1 **48** BenCurtis 11 28
(Dave Morris) *mid-div: drvn along 3f out: n.d after* **6/1**

0654 **8** 1 1/2 **Hold The Star**36 996 8-8-8 **46** ow1 AnnStokell(5) 3 22
(Ann Stokell) *hld up: a in rr* **40/1**

0-60 **9** 2 1/4 **Odd Ball (IRE)**26 1138 7-8-7 **45** ShirleyTeasdale(5) 12 15
(Lisa Williamson) *s.i.s: a in rr* **66/1**

1m 29.61s (0.01) **Going Correction** +0.075s/f (Slow) **9 Ran SP% 110.8**
Speed ratings (Par 101): **102,92,89,86,85 83,83,81,79**
CSF £21.41 CT £220.33 TOTE £2.60: £1.10, £3.60, £3.90; EX 20.80 Trifecta £235.10.
**Owner** Dr J S Kinnear **Bred** Thomas J Murphy **Trained** Newmarket, Suffolk

**FOCUS**
The favourite hammered his rivals in this low-grade handicap. The second and third are a bit below their recent figures.

## 1632 QUICKSILVERSLOTS FUN ON HIGH STREET H'CAP 1m 1f 103y(P)
**8:45** (8:46) (Class 6) (0-60,60) 3-Y-O **£2,264** (£673; £336; £168) **Stalls** Low

Form RPR
605- **1** **Vosne Romanee**168 7755 3-8-8 **47** (p) TomEaves 3 54
(Keith Dalgleish) *trckd ldrs: plld hrd: lost pl 7f out: nt clr run over 2f out: hdwy over 1f out: rdn to ld ins fnl f: r.o wl* **9/1**

-022 **2** 1 1/4 **Whispering Star (USA)**27 1098 3-9-2 **55** MartinLane 5 59
(David Simcock) *plld hrd: led 2f: trckd ldrs: rdn to ld over 1f out: hdd ins fnl f: styd on same pce* **4/6**1

00-0 **3** *hd* **Company Secretary (USA)**24 1173 3-9-2 **55** (b1) BenCurtis 2 59
(Jo Hughes) *hld up: hdwy over 1f out: sn rdn: r.o* **5/1**3

000- **4** 2 1/2 **Aldreth**193 7175 3-9-4 **57** GrahamGibbons 6 56
(Michael Easterby) *hdwy over 7f out: chsd ldr over 6f out: led over 2f out: rdn and hdd over 1f out: styd on same pce ins fnl f* **4/1**2

000- **5** 1 3/4 **Halloween Moon**227 6206 3-8-2 **46** oh1 1 ShirleyTeasdale(5) 9 41
(James Bethell) *wnt rt s: hdwy over 7f out: ev ch over 1f out: no ex ins fnl f* **50/1**

3230 **6** 3/4 **Needs The Run**20 1235 3-8-11 **53** DeclanBates(3) 4 47
(David Evans) *sn pushed along in rr: hdwy u.p over 2f out: styd on same pce fr over 1f out* **25/1**

00-0 **7** 2 3/4 **Dover The Moon (IRE)**12 1403 3-9-2 **60** JoshBaudains(5) 7 48
(Sylvester Kirk) *plld hrd: w ldr tl over 6f out: remained handy: rdn over 2f out: wknd over 1f out* **40/1**

3-02 **8** 2 1/4 **Sky Ranger (IRE)**35 1007 3-9-7 **60** LukeMorris 8 43
(James Tate) *w ldr tl led over 7f out: rdn and hdd over 2f out: wknd fnl f* **12/1**

600 **9** 18 **Bikini Club**18 1280 3-9-4 **57** SeanLevey 1
(Paul D'Arcy) *prom: n.m.r and lost pl over 7f out: hdwy over 2f out: sn rdn and wknd* **50/1**

2m 2.99s (1.29) **Going Correction** +0.075s/f (Slow) **9 Ran SP% 124.6**
Speed ratings (Par 96): **97,95,95,93,91 91,88,86,70**
CSF £16.58 CT £39.40 TOTE £10.50: £2.40, £1.02, £4.20; EX 34.00 Trifecta £70.40.
**Owner** Straightline Construction Ltd **Bred** Mrs L M G Walsh **Trained** Carluke, S Lanarks

**FOCUS**
They went a steady pace in this handicap and the odds-on favourite was held. A clear best from the winner.
T/Plt: £63.50 to a £1 stake. Pool: £60,373.53 - 693.72 winning units. T/Qpdt: £15.40 to a £1 stake. Pool: £5353.91 - 255.90 winning units. CR

# 1612 YARMOUTH (L-H)
Tuesday, April 22

**OFFICIAL GOING: Good (good to firm in places; 7.3)**
Wind: medium, half against Weather: overcast and brightening up

## 1633 GROSVENOR CASINO AT GREAT YARMOUTH MAIDEN AUCTION STKS 5f 43y
**4:20** (4:22) (Class 6) 2-Y-O **£2,264** (£673; £336; £168) **Stalls** Centre

Form RPR
22 **1** **Charlie's Star**11 1417 2-8-6 0 ChrisCatlin 2 72
(David Evans) *mde all: pushed along and wnt 2 l clr over 1f out: in command fnl f: pushed out: comf* **4/11**1

**2** 2 1/4 **Brown Velvet** 2-8-10 0 (v1) AndreaAtzeni 7 67
(Hugo Palmer) *dwlt: in tch in last pair: rdn and effrt 1/2-way: chsd wnr 2f out: hung lft and no imp on wnr ins fnl f: kpt on for clr 2nd* **12/1**

0 **3** 2 3/4 **Lunar Knot**14 1363 2-8-7 0 SilvestreDeSousa 4 54
(Alan McCabe) *chsd ldr tl 2f out: outpcd u.p over 1f out: 3rd and wl hld whn edgd lft ins fnl f* **15/2**2

**4** 1 3/4 **Madamoiselle Bond** 2-8-1 0 NoelGarbutt(5) 8 47
(William Jarvis) *in tch in last pair: rdn and effrt jst over 2f out: hdwy u.p wl over 1f out: btn 1f out: wknd ins fnl f* **14/1**

0 **5** 1 **Arousal**8 1488 2-8-4 0 ow1 LouisSteward(5) 1 46
(Michael Bell) *chsd ldrs: rdn and effrt over 2f out: no ex and btn over 1f out: wknd fnl f* **10/1**3

1m 3.98s (1.28) **Going Correction** -0.10s/f (Good) **5 Ran SP% 108.5**
Speed ratings (Par 90): **85,81,77,74,72**
CSF £5.48 TOTE £1.20: £1.10, £2.70; EX 4.90 Trifecta £10.20.
**Owner** J A Wilcox **Bred** David Allan And Bucklands Farm And Stud **Trained** Pandy, Monmouths

**FOCUS**
Quite a lowly juvenile maiden and hard to gauge the form. The race average is not exactly encouraging.

## 1634 BOOK A PARTY GREAT YARMOUTH RACECOURSE MEDIAN AUCTION MAIDEN STKS 6f 3y
**4:55** (4:55) (Class 5) 3-4-Y-O **£2,975** (£885; £442; £221) **Stalls** Centre

Form RPR
2- **1** **Golden Steps (FR)**138 8165 3-9-1 0 FrankieDettori 9 83+
(Marco Botti) *taken down early: sltly hmpd leaving stalls: travelled strly: hld up in tch in rr: stdy hdwy to ld wl over 1f out: edgd lft but readily wnt clr over 1f out: r.o wl: easily* **5/6**1

000- **2** 7 **Yankee Red**244 5635 3-9-1 0 SteveDrowne 10 61
(John Best) *in tch in midfield: rdn and effrt over 2f out: chsd wnr wl over 1f out: sn outpcd and brushed aside: kpt on for clr 2nd* **66/1**

**3** 1 3/4 **Eleusis** 3-8-10 0 TedDurcan 3 50
(Chris Wall) *stdd and short of room leaving stalls: hld up in tch in rr: hdwy 3f out: rdn to go 3rd over 1f out: no ch w wnr and kpt on same pce fnl f: eased cl home* **9/1**3

0- **4** 2 **Starlite Jewel**208 6769 3-8-7 0 RyanPowell(3) 4 44
(George Margarson) *in tch towards rr: rdn and effrt over 2f out: wnt 4th ent fnl f: kpt on but no ch w wnr* **10/1**

032 **5** 1/2 **Happydoingnothing**20 1229 3-9-1 **64** AdamBeschizza 2 47
(Christine Dunnett) *sn niggled along in midfield: u.p 1/2-way: swtchd rt and styd on u.p fnl f: no ch w wnr* **12/1**

-500 **6** 2 1/4 **Appellez Baileys (FR)**77 473 3-9-1 **50**1 LiamKeniry 6 40
(Chris Dwyer) *chsd ldr tl 1/2-way: styd chsng ldrs tl no ex u.p wl over 1f out: wknd fnl f* **25/1**

**7** 3 **Goldfellow** 3-9-1 0 WilliamBuick 1 30+
(Peter Chapple-Hyam) *s.i.s: rn green and detached in last: reminders over 4f out: rdn 1/2-way: no ch but past btn horses fnl f: n.d* **5/1**2

8 ¾ **Happy Jack (IRE)** 3-9-1 0 AndreaAtzeni 7 28
(Michael Wigham) *in tch in midfield: rdn and effrt over 2f out: sn struggling: wknd over 1f out* **25/1**

65 9 2¼ **Fizzolo**[14] 1364 3-8-10 0 MickaelBarzalona 5 16
(Noel Quinlan) *led tl rdn and hdd wl over 1f out: sn btn and fdd over 1f out* **25/1**

00- 10 2½ **Triple O Seven (IRE)**[306] 3493 3-9-1 0 PaulHanagan 8 13
(John Best) *chsd ldrs: wnt 2nd 1/2-way tl wl over 1f out: sn wknd* **28/1**

1m 13.79s (-0.61) **Going Correction** -0.10s/f (Good) **10** Ran SP% **114.5**
Speed ratings (Par 103): **100,90,88,85,85 82,78,77,74,70**
CSF £99.60 TOTE £1.50: £1.10, £10.40, £2.30; EX 56.80 Trifecta £798.00.
**Owner** M A A Al-Mannai **Bred** T Jeffroy, B Jeffroy Et Al **Trained** Newmarket, Suffolk

**FOCUS**
A weak sprint maiden with no depth. The winner built on debut promise but the form isn't solid.

## 1635 BURLINGTON PALM HOTEL H'CAP 1m 2f 21y
**5:25** (5:26) (Class 5) (0-75,75) 3-Y-O **£2,846** (£847; £423; £211) **Stalls** Low

Form RPR

2-14 1 **Thurayaat**[20] 1240 3-9-6 74 [1] PaulHanagan 4 79
(Roger Varian) *mde all: rdn over 2f out: kpt on u.p and a holding rivals ins fnl f: rdn out* **13/2**[3]

00-5 2 ¾ **Pershing**[22] 1208 3-9-4 72 AndreaAtzeni 6 75
(Marco Botti) *chsd wnr: rdn and pressing over 2f out: styd on same pce ins fnl f* **16/1**

1-23 3 hd **Shimba Hills**[13] 1400 3-9-2 73 WilliamTwiston-Davies(3) 2 76+
(Mick Channon) *in tch in midfield: chsd ldrs but nvr much room on inner fnl 2f: swtchd lft and styd on fnl 75yds* **10/3**[2]

056- 4 hd **Mairise**[134] 8214 3-9-2 70 RyanMoore 3 73+
(Sir Michael Stoute) *hld up wl in tch in midfield: rdn and sltly outpcd 2f out: 6th and swtchd rt over 1f out: styd on steadily u.p ins fnl f* **5/2**[1]

420- 5 1¼ **Lucky Visione**[190] 7252 3-9-1 74 DanielMuscutt(5) 1 74
(Gay Kelleway) *in tch in midfield: chsng ldrs but nvr enough room on inner fr 3f out: stl nt enough room and one pce fnl f* **16/1**

00-6 6 1¼ **Dalarosso**[13] 1401 3-8-13 67 KierenFallon 8 65
(Ed Dunlop) *in tch in midfield: rdn and effrt over 2f out: styd on same pce u.p fr over 1f out* **8/1**

01- 7 ¾ **Crystal Pearl**[159] 7874 3-9-7 75 LiamJones 10 73+
(Mark H Tompkins) *dwlt: rcvrd and chsd ldrs on outer after 2f: outpcd and losing pl whn hmpd over 2f out: no threat to wnr but styd on again fnl f* **25/1**

1343 8 ½ **Masterpaver**[21] 1220 3-8-10 69 (v) TimClark(5) 5 64
(Alan Bailey) *in tch in last quartet: rdn over 3f out: styd on same pce and no imp fr over 1f out* **16/1**

-436 9 ½ **Galaxy (IRE)**[24] 1166 3-9-0 68 (p) TomQueally 7 63
(Alan McCabe) *in tch in last trio: rdn and effrt over 3f out: no imp tl kpt on ins fnl f: nvr trbld ldrs* **33/1**

0-53 10 19 **Rookery (IRE)**[25] 1153 3-9-3 71 SilvestreDeSousa 9 29
(Mark Johnston) *a towards rr: rdn 4f out: no hdwy and lost tch over 1f out* **20/1**

66-3 11 17 **Zephyr**[28] 1090 3-8-13 67 DanielTudhope 11
(K R Burke) *dropped in bhd after s: rdn and no hdwy 4f out: bhd and rdr looking down over 2f out: t.o fnl f* **10/1**

2m 8.26s (-2.24) **Going Correction** -0.15s/f (Firm) **11** Ran SP% **114.4**
Speed ratings (Par 98): **102,101,101,101,100 99,98,98,97,82 68**
CSF £98.87 CT £405.50 TOTE £4.90: £2.00, £5.00, £1.70; EX 100.10 Trifecta £325.60.
**Owner** Hamdan Al Maktoum **Bred** Shadwell Estate Company Limited **Trained** Newmarket, Suffolk
■ Stewards' Enquiry : Andrea Atzeni two-day ban: used whip above permitted level (May 6-7)

**FOCUS**
A fair handicap, run at just an ordinary gallop, and Paul Hanagan judged it perfectly from the front. Not entirely convincing form.

## 1636 1954-2014 MICHAEL FOULGER BIRTHDAY H'CAP 1m 2f 21y
**5:55** (5:56) (Class 4) (0-80,80) 4-Y-O+ **£4,690** (£1,046; £1,046; £348) **Stalls** Low

Form RPR

023- 1 **Red Warrior (IRE)**[160] 7864 4-9-4 77 TomQueally 6 85
(Ismail Mohammed) *in tch in midfield: chsng ldrs 3f out: effrt to chal over 1f out: led 1f out: drvn to assert ins fnl f: r.o wl: drvn out* **25/1**

4306 2 1¾ **Uphold**[31] 1071 7-9-6 79 (v) RyanMoore 2 84
(Gay Kelleway) *led: rdn over 2f out: drvn and hdd 1f out: styd on same pce fnl 100yds* **9/1**

521- 2 dht **Freedom's Light**[158] 7894 4-9-7 80 WilliamBuick 3 85+
(John Gosden) *t.k.h: chsd ldr tl over 4f out: styd chsng ldrs: nt clr run on inner ent fnl 2f: swtchd rt ins fnl f and fnlly in the clr 100yds out: r.o towards fin* **6/4**[1]

232- 4 1 **Raskova (USA)**[172] 7656 4-9-3 76 FrankieDettori 12 79
(William Jarvis) *dropped in bhd after s: rdn and effrt 2f out: drvn and styd on wl ins fnl f* **6/1**[2]

40-5 5 ½ **Barwick**[15] 1354 6-9-0 73 SebSanders 4 75
(Lady Herries) *chsd ldrs: rdn and effrt ent fnl 2f: styd on same pce fnl f* **8/1**[3]

5263 6 nk **Thecornishcowboy**[15] 1355 5-8-8 67 (tp) SilvestreDeSousa 10 69
(John Ryan) *hld up in tch: rdn and clsd on inner whn nt clr run over 1f out: swtchd rt arnd many horses 1f out: kpt on u.p ins fnl f* **20/1**

-342 7 ¾ **Chain Of Events**[26] 1120 7-8-12 71 AndreaAtzeni 8 71
(Michael Wigham) *chsd ldrs: wnt 2nd over 4f out tl over 1f out: wknd ins fnl f* **25/1**

35-2 8 3¾ **Silver Alliance**[26] 1134 6-8-9 73 (p) ShelleyBirkett(5) 9 66
(Julia Feilden) *in tch in midfield: rdn and effrt ent fnl 2f: wknd fnl f* **20/1**

166- 9 2¾ **Qanan**[195] 7121 5-9-1 74 TedDurcan 7 62
(Chris Wall) *in tch in midfield: rdn and effrt over 2f out: no imp and btn over 1f out* **16/1**

000- 10 2¼ **Laughing Jack**[205] 6869 6-8-10 74 GeorgeDowning(5) 5 58
(George Baker) *stdd s: t.k.h: hld up in rr tl gd hdwy on outer 5f out: pressed ldrs and rdn 4f out: wknd wl over 1f out* **10/1**

-412 11 4 **Red Shuttle**[60] 698 7-9-5 78 ChrisCatlin 1 54
(Andi Brown) *stdd s: t.k.h: hld up in tch in rr: rdn and effrt 2f out: no real imp: wl btn 1f out: eased towards fin* **14/1**

2m 7.56s (-2.94) **Going Correction** -0.15s/f (Firm) **11** Ran SP% **114.3**
Speed ratings (Par 105): **105,103,103,102,102 102,101,98,96,94 91**
WIN: 47.90 Red Warrior; PL: 9.60 Red Warrior, 1.10 Freedom's Light, 2.70 Uphold; EX: 46.60, 91.60; CSF: 109.00, 29.27; TC: 190.76, 274.60; TF: 338.20, 348.70;.
**Owner** Ismail Mohammed **Bred** Pat Roach **Trained** Newmarket, Suffolk

**FOCUS**
A race that revolved around the red-hot favourite, but it all got rather congested down on the inside. Freedom's Light is the key to the form.

## 1637 SEADELL SHOPS AND CHALETS AT HEMSBY H'CAP 1m 3y
**6:25** (6:26) (Class 4) (0-85,84) 4-Y-O+ **£4,690** (£1,395; £697; £348) **Stalls** Centre

Form RPR

543- 1 **Sir Mike**[181] 7464 5-9-7 84 FrankieDettori 3 95+
(Luca Cumani) *stdd after s: t.k.h: hld up in tch in midfield: swtchd lft and hdwy 2f out: jnd ldrs over 1f out: rdn to ld ins fnl f: qcknd u.p and r.o wl* **3/1**[2]

10-0 2 ¾ **Dream Walker (FR)**[24] 1164 5-9-7 84 RyanMoore 5 93+
(Brian Ellison) *hld up in tch in rr: effrt 2f out: swtchd lft and chsd ldng trio over 1f out: chsd wnr ins fnl f: r.o but a hld* **5/2**[1]

44-5 3 2½ **Bold Prediction (IRE)**[27] 1103 4-9-3 80 DanielTudhope 2 84
(K R Burke) *chsd ldr tl rdn to ld over 2f out: drvn and hrd pressed over 1f out: hdd ins fnl f: outpcd fnl 100yds* **13/2**

00-0 4 ½ **Zacynthus (IRE)**[17] 1301 6-9-1 83 LouisSteward(5) 1 85
(Michael Bell) *dwlt: sn rcvrd to chse ldrs: rdn and effrt to press ldr 2f out: ev ch over 1f out tl outpcd ins fnl f* **10/1**

3212 5 6 **Mr Red Clubs (IRE)**[34] 1021 5-9-1 78 AndrewMullen 7 67
(Michael Appleby) *wl in tch in midfield: lost pl u.p over 2f out: wknd over 1f out* **4/1**[3]

000- 6 1¾ **Jonnie Skull (IRE)**[171] 7699 8-8-11 74 (vt) JimmyQuinn 6 59
(Lydia Pearce) *led tl hdd and rdn over 2f out: sn struggling u.p: wknd over 1f out* **20/1**

0040 7 2¼ **Ocean Applause**[15] 1354 4-8-11 74 (bt) KierenFallon 4 53
(John Ryan) *in tch in last pair: rdn over 3f out: drvn and struggling ent fnl 2f: wknd over 1f out: eased towards fin* **10/1**

1m 38.56s (-2.04) **Going Correction** -0.10s/f (Good) **7** Ran SP% **109.8**
Speed ratings (Par 105): **106,105,102,102,96 94,92**
CSF £10.02 TOTE £4.10: £2.30, £1.90; EX 10.80 Trifecta £40.20.
**Owner** Al Shaqab Racing **Bred** M H And Mrs G Tourle **Trained** Newmarket, Suffolk

**FOCUS**
They raced stands' side in what was quite an ordinary 0-85, but the right two came to the fore. A length step up from the winner.

## 1638 INJURED JOCKEYS FUND H'CAP 1m 3y
**6:55** (6:55) (Class 6) (0-65,65) 4-Y-O+ **£1,940** (£577; £288; £144) **Stalls** Centre

Form RPR

0400 1 **My Manekineko**[2] 1596 5-9-0 58 KierenFallon 5 68
(J R Jenkins) *t.k.h: hld up wl in tch in midfield: hdwy and pushed into ld over 1f out: reminder ins fnl f: r.o wl: comf* **12/1**

40-4 2 ¾ **Push Me (IRE)**[111] 1 7-9-4 65 JasonHart(3) 6 73
(Iain Jardine) *hld up in tch in last pair: clsd and nt clr run over 1f out: swtchd lft and hdwy to chse wnr ins fnl f: r.o but a hld* **6/1**[3]

0043 3 4½ **Sixties Queen**[1] 1617 4-8-3 52 NatashaEaton(5) 3 50
(Alan Bailey) *led: rdn ent fnl 2f: edgd lft and unable qck over 1f out: outpcd by ldng pair ins fnl f: plugged on to hold 3rd* **10/3**[2]

3355 4 shd **Wishformore (IRE)**[3] 1568 7-9-1 59 (p) SilvestreDeSousa 7 57
(Ian Williams) *t.k.h: chsd ldr: rdn and ev ch 2f out tl outpcd and btn ins fnl f: plugged on* **3/1**[1]

300- 5 nk **Hot Mustard**[139] 8151 4-9-2 60 TomQueally 10 57
(Michael Bell) *wl in tch in midfield: rdn and effrt to press ldrs wl over 1f out: outpcd and btn ins fnl f: plugged on* **15/2**

1240 6 1 **Handsome Stranger (IRE)**[15] 1354 4-8-13 64 (p) DavidParkes(7) 2 59
(Alan Bailey) *dwlt: sn rcvrd and chsd ldrs: rdn ent fnl 2f: outpcd and btn 1f out: plugged on same pce after* **3/1**[1]

-000 7 6 **Spirit Rider (USA)**[20] 1234 4-9-4 62 LiamKeniry 8 43
(Giles Bravery) *hld up in tch in rr: rdn over 2f out: sn struggling and wknd over 1f out* **14/1**

1m 40.49s (-0.11) **Going Correction** -0.10s/f (Good) **7** Ran SP% **113.5**
Speed ratings (Par 101): **96,95,90,90,90 89,83**
CSF £79.05 CT £296.11 TOTE £13.60: £5.20, £2.80; EX 94.10 Trifecta £455.30.
**Owner** Bond Street General Services Ltd **Bred** Cannon Bloodstock And Newsells Park Stud **Trained** Royston, Herts

**FOCUS**
Run at a steady gallop, they reverted to racing centre-field. Weak handicap form, the runner-up the initial guide.

## 1639 ANNUAL BADGES ON SALE AT YARMOUTH RACECOURSE APPRENTICE H'CAP 6f 3y
**7:25** (7:25) (Class 6) (0-60,60) 4-Y-O+ **£1,940** (£577; £288; £144) **Stalls** Centre

Form RPR

5606 1 **Fathom Five (IRE)**[14] 1365 10-8-7 46 oh1 JoshQuinn 7 57
(Shaun Harris) *mde all: rdn over 1f out: edgd rt but styd on wl ins fnl f: rdn out* **20/1**

5300 2 1¼ **Dark Lane**[3] 1573 8-9-4 60 HollieDoyle(3) 4 67
(David Evans) *chsd ldrs: wnt 2nd ent fnl 2f: kpt on u.p ins fnl f: a hld by wnr* **4/1**[2]

0533 3 ¾ **Belle Bayardo (IRE)**[27] 1104 6-8-12 54 MrAidenBlakemore(3) 3 59
(Tony Carroll) *stmbld s: sn rcvrd and in tch in midfield: rdn and effrt 2f out: chsd ldng pair over 1f out: kpt on* **6/1**

5-01 4 4½ **Encapsulated**[3] 1573 4-8-13 60 6ex (p) RhiainIngram(8) 6 50
(Roger Ingram) *in tch in midfield: rdn and effrt 2f out: 4th and no imp 1f out: one pce and wl hld after* **15/8**[1]

40-0 5 3½ **Sairaam (IRE)**[14] 1365 8-8-7 46 oh1 AaronJones 8 25
(Charles Smith) *in tch in midfield: rdn and effrt ent fnl 2f: outpcd and btn over 1f out: wknd fnl f* **66/1**

500- 6 2¾ **Misty Pearl**[336] 2547 4-8-7 46 oh1 GaryMahon 5 16
(Michael Appleby) *in tch in last pair: rdn over 3f out: outpcd and struggling u.p 2f out: wl btn after* **8/1**

2633 7 2½ **Imaginary Diva**[28] 1089 8-9-2 58 AlfieWarwick(3) 2 20
(George Margarson) *chsd ldr tl ent fnl 2f: sn rdn and struggling: bhd 1f out* **12/1**

4055 8 2½ **Nifty Kier**[13] 1386 5-8-12 51 (vt[1]) JordonMcMurray 9 5
(Phil McEntee) *s.i.s: a in rr: rdn over 2f out: sn bhd* **9/2**[3]

1m 13.88s (-0.52) **Going Correction** -0.10s/f (Good) **8** Ran SP% **112.3**
Speed ratings (Par 101): **99,97,96,90,85 82,78,75**
CSF £94.71 CT £553.86 TOTE £7.20: £4.20, £1.20, £1.10; EX 124.50 Trifecta £346.40.
**Owner** Nottinghamshire Racing **Bred** Eamonn Connolly **Trained** Carburton, Notts

**FOCUS**
They raced stands' side in this lowly sprint. The first three were down to career-low marks.
T/Plt: £28.70 to a £1 stake. Pool: £47,188.78 - 1197.35 winning units. T/Qpdt: £26.90 to a £1 stake. Pool: £5457.05 - 150.10 winning units. SP

1640 - 1641a (Foreign Racing) - See Raceform Interactive

# 1372 CATTERICK (L-H)

Wednesday, April 23

**OFFICIAL GOING: Good (good to firm in places; 8.3)**

Wind: Moderate behind Weather: Fine and dry

## 1642 ST GEORGE'S DAY H'CAP 5f

**1:30** (1:32) (Class 6) (0-65,65) 3-Y-O £2,385 (£704; £352) Stalls Low

Form RPR

616- **1** **Gulland Rock**175 7623 3-9-3 **61** MartinDwyer 7 66
(William Muir) *in tch: pushed along 1/2-way: hdwy on outer wl over 1f out: rdn to chal ent fnl f: led last 100yds: kpt on* **9/2**1

4-44 **2** 1 1/4 **Fredricka**12 1425 3-9-4 **62** GrahamGibbons 10 63
(Garry Moss) *trckd ldrs: hdwy 2f out: rdn to ld 1 1/2f out: edgd lft and drvn ent fnl f: hdd and no ex last 100yds* **7/1**

-230 **3** nk **Narborough**19 1277 3-9-1 **59** SamHitchcott 1 58+
(Mick Channon) *towards rr: gd hdwy on inner 1/2-way: trckd ldrs and nt clr run 2f out and over 1f out: swtchd rt and rdn ent fnl f: kpt on* **12/1**

402- **4** 1/2 **Baltic Spirit (IRE)**206 6872 3-9-7 **65** TomEaves 6 63+
(Keith Dalgleish) *sn rdn along and outpcd in rr: bhd 1/2-way: hdwy wl over 1f out: sn swtchd rt to outer and rdn 1f out: styd on fnl f: nrst fin* **8/1**

444- **5** nk **Princess Myla (IRE)**206 6872 3-8-13 **57** (p) PaulMulrennan 4 54
(Paul Midgley) *chsd ldrs: rdn along 2f out: drvn appr fnl f: sn one pce* **8/1**

1340 **6** nse **Ealain Aibrean (IRE)**41 936 3-8-12 **63** HollieDoyle(7) 5 59+
(David Evans) *in tch: effrt and nt clr run 2f out and over 1f out: swtchd rt and rdn appr fnl f: kpt on: nrst fin* **12/1**

-652 **7** 1 **Britain (IRE)**16 1343 3-8-9 **53** (v) FrannyNorton 2 46
(David C Griffiths) *slt ld on inner: rdn along 2f out: drvn and hdd 1 1/2f out: wknd ent fnl f* **11/2**2

00-6 **8** 1 3/4 **Dream Sika (IRE)**14 1373 3-8-7 **51** JamesSullivan 9 37
(Ruth Carr) *cl up: rdn along wl over 1f out: sn edgd lft and hld whn n.m.r ent fnl f* **16/1**

0322 **9** 4 **Under Approval**21 1246 3-9-7 **65** DanielTudhope 11 37
(David O'Meara) *in tch on wd outside: rdn along 1/2-way: sn wknd* **6/1**3

-600 **10** 1 3/4 **Loma Mor**54 786 3-8-11 **55** 1 AndrewMullen 3 21
(Alan McCabe) *cl up: ev ch 2f out: sn rdn and wknd over 1f out* **33/1**

59.96s (0.16) **Going Correction** -0.125s/f (Firm) **10** Ran SP% **106.8**

Speed ratings (Par 96): **93,91,90,89,89 89,87,84,78,75**

CSF £30.93 CT £300.08 TOTE £3.60: £1.10, £2.20, £4.50; EX 33.00 Trifecta £347.40.

**Owner** C L A Edginton & K Mercer **Bred** Whitsbury Manor Stud **Trained** Lambourn, Berks

■ Rule 4 of 5p in the pound applies to all bets; Withdrawn: Dancing Juice

**FOCUS**

The ground had eased slightly from that forecast following 2mm of overnight rain and was now good, good to firm in places. A moderate 3yo sprint handicap run in a slow time after an overstrong pace. The winner confirmed Musselburgh form with the fourth and fifth.

## 1643 CATTERICKBRIDGE.CO.UK H'CAP 5f

**2:00** (2:01) (Class 5) (0-70,70) 4-Y-O+ £3,067 (£905; £453) Stalls Low

Form RPR

0-05 **1** **Boxing Shadows**9 1487 4-8-11 **60** DavidAllan 6 71
(Les Eyre) *prom: cl up over 2f out: rdn to ld jst over 1f out: drvn ins fnl f: jst hld on* **11/2**2

11-0 **2** nse **Windforpower (IRE)**9 1487 4-8-11 **60** (p) JoeFanning 2 70
(Tracy Waggott) *trckd ldrs: hdwy wl over 1f out: chal ent fnl f: sn rdn: styd on wl towards fin: jst failed* **16/1**

6602 **3** 2 1/4 **Tyfos**12 1431 9-9-7 **70** AndrewMullen 3 72
(Brian Baugh) *led: rdn along 2f out: hdd ent fnl f: kpt on same pce* **8/1**

11-0 **4** 1 1/2 **Fleurtille**14 1376 5-8-8 **62** ConnorBeasley(5) 5 59
(Robert Johnson) *towards rr: hdwy and in tch over 2f out: swtchd lft and rdn over 1f out: kpt on fnl f* **17/2**

00-0 **5** 2 3/4 **Chosen One (IRE)**14 1378 9-8-13 **62** JamesSullivan 1 49
(Ruth Carr) *trckd ldrs on inner: rdn along wl over 1f out: wknd fnl f* **15/2**

11-5 **6** 1 **Thatcherite (IRE)**11 1440 6-9-7 **70** (t) StephenCraine 9 53+
(Tony Coyle) *dwlt and in rr: rdn along 1/2-way: hdwy over 1f out: styd on wl fnl f: nrst fin* **5/1**1

10-6 **7** nk **Mercers Row**11 1447 7-8-10 **66** GemmaTutty(7) 7 48
(Karen Tutty) *prom: rdn along wl over 1f out: grad wknd* **12/1**

35-0 **8** 1 3/4 **Dream Ally (IRE)**11 1440 4-9-3 **66** PJMcDonald 10 42
(Micky Hammond) *in tch: rdn along and outpcd after 2f: in rr tl sme late hdwy* **11/1**

200- **9** nse **Choc'A'Moca (IRE)**210 6757 7-8-11 **60** (v) GrahamLee 11 35
(Paul Midgley) *blind removed late and wnt rt s: chsd ldrs on outer: rdn along 2f out: sn wknd* **12/1**

-503 **10** 1 **Lady Poppy**2 1604 4-8-2 **58** KieranSchofield(7) 8 30
(George Moore) *prom: rdn along 2f out: sn drvn and wknd* **13/2**3

40-0 **11** 2 1/2 **Tuibama (IRE)**14 1378 5-8-10 **59** (p) DaleSwift 12 22
(Tracy Waggott) *sltly hmpd s: chsd ldrs on outer to 1/2-way: sn wknd* **20/1**

240- **12** hd **One Kool Dude**187 7347 5-8-8 **57** oh1 ow1 TomEaves 4 19
(Micky Hammond) *sn outpcd and a in rr* **25/1**

58.69s (-1.11) **Going Correction** -0.125s/f (Firm) **12** Ran SP% **117.0**

Speed ratings (Par 103): **103,102,99,96,92 90,90,87,87,85 81,81**

CSF £89.00 CT £704.61 TOTE £5.00: £2.20, £5.00, £2.90; EX 105.70 Trifecta £1589.70.

**Owner** Billy Parker **Bred** Catridge Farm Stud Ltd **Trained** Catton, North Yorkshire

**FOCUS**

An ordinary sprint handicap for older horses and not many got into it. The time was good. The first two were both on good marks based on early 3yo form.

## 1644 2014 CATTERICK TWELVE FURLONG SERIES H'CAP (QUALIFIER) 1m 3f 214y

**2:30** (2:31) (Class 5) (0-70,70) 4-Y-O+ £3,881 (£1,155; £577; £288) Stalls Low

Form RPR

04-0 **1** **Cavalieri (IRE)**24 1197 4-8-10 **67** EvaMoscrop(7) 1 75
(Philip Kirby) *in tch on inner: hdwy over 2f out: rdn to clr over 1f out: clr ins fnl f: kpt on* **6/1**3

200- **2** 1 3/4 **Al Furat (USA)**214 6632 6-8-9 **58** ow2 DavidAllan 12 61
(Ron Barr) *hld up towards rr: hdwy 4f out: chsd ldrs 3f out: swtchd rt to outer and rdn 2f out: disp ld and ev ch over 1f out: sn drvn and kpt on same pce* **6/1**3

02-0 **3** hd **Tinseltown**24 1197 8-8-12 **66** ShirleyTeasdale(5) 4 71
(Brian Rothwell) *trckd ldr: cl up 5f out: rdn over 2f out: drvn to dispute ld and ev ch over 1f out: kpt on same pce* **8/1**

600- **4** 1/2 **Hot Spice**175 7635 6-8-13 **62** GrahamGibbons 5 66
(Michael Easterby) *trckd ldrs: hdwy 3f out: cl up on outer whn bmpd 2f out: sn rdn and kpt on same pce fnl f* **8/1**

212- **5** 1 **Grayswood**183 7439 4-9-1 **65** MartinDwyer 7 68
(William Muir) *in rr: hdwy over 3f out: rdn along 2f out: kpt on fnl f: nrst fin* **9/2**1

44-0 **6** 1/2 **Gran Maestro (USA)**14 1377 5-9-7 **70** (b) PJMcDonald 9 72
(Ruth Carr) *trckd ldrs: hdwy over 4f out: led wl over 2f out and sn rdn: drvn and hdd over 1f out: grad wknd* **11/2**2

356- **7** 6 **Madrasa (IRE)**240 5831 6-9-6 **69** TomEaves 8 61
(Keith Reveley) *in rr tl sme late hdwy* **20/1**

0334 **8** 7 **Rockweiller**12 1428 7-8-1 **57** oh6 ow1 (b) GaryMahon(7) 11 38
(Shaun Harris) *sn led: rdn along over 3f out: hdd wl over 2f out and sn wknd* **16/1**

03-0 **9** 9 **Danehill Flyer (IRE)**18 1307 4-9-5 **69** PhillipMakin 2 36
(Philip Kirby) *in tch: effrt over 4f out: rdn along over 3f out: sn btn* **6/1**3

002- **10** 20 **Khelac**36 7322 4-9-0 **64** (b) GrahamLee 10
(Micky Hammond) *midfield: rdn along over 4f out: sn wknd* **22/1**

2m 36.97s (-1.93) **Going Correction** +0.075s/f (Good)

**WFA** 4 from 5yo+ 1lb **10** Ran SP% **113.6**

Speed ratings (Par 103): **109,107,107,107,106 106,102,97,91,78**

CSF £40.73 CT £288.31 TOTE £9.00: £3.10, £3.00, £2.70; EX 64.50 Trifecta £876.00.

**Owner** The Cavalieri Partnership **Bred** Grange & Manister House Studs **Trained** Middleham, N Yorks

**FOCUS**

A modest handicap, but run at a decent pace with four soon skipping clear of the others. The winner was the least exposed runner and the form seems sound.

## 1645 BREEDERS BACKING RACING EBF MAIDEN FILLIES' STKS (BOBIS RACE) 7f

**3:05** (3:06) (Class 5) 3-Y-O £3,881 (£1,155; £577; £288) Stalls Low

Form RPR

0 **1** **Little Shambles**9 1486 3-9-0 0 JoeFanning 5 74
(Mark Johnston) *mde all: rdn 2f out: styd on wl fnl f* **12/1**

0-2 **2** 1 1/2 **Polar Eyes**19 1280 3-9-0 0 PaulMulrennan 4 71
(Peter Chapple-Hyam) *t.k.h: trckd ldrs: hdwy and cl up 4f out: effrt 2f out: sn rdn and edgd lft over 1f out: drvn and edgd lft ins fnl f: sn one pce* **4/9**1

54- **3** 2 1/2 **Shushu Sugartown (IRE)**140 8145 3-9-0 0 RobertWinston 2 64
(Ian Williams) *t.k.h: trckd ldrs: pushed along over 2f out: rdn over 1f out: styng on whn n.m.r and sltly hmpd ins fnl f: one pce after* **10/1**3

0 **4** 5 **Nutbush**12 1422 3-9-0 0 SamHitchcott 1 51
(Mick Channon) *in rr: effrt and sme hdwy 3f out: sn rdn along and n.d* **66/1**

00- **5** 3 3/4 **Danzig In The Dark (IRE)**299 3760 3-9-0 0 PhillipMakin 6 41
(Tim Easterby) *t.k.h: chsd ldrs: pushed along over 4f out: sn outpcd* **33/1**

3 **6** 7 **Conveyor Belt (IRE)**18 1303 3-9-0 0 DanielTudhope 3 23
(David O'Meara) *chsd ldrs: pushed along and lost pl over 4f out: sn outpcd and in rr: lame* **7/2**2

1m 27.24s (0.24) **Going Correction** +0.075s/f (Good) **6** Ran SP% **112.7**

Speed ratings (Par 95): **101,99,96,90,86 78**

CSF £18.30 TOTE £10.20: £4.00, £1.10; EX 18.30 Trifecta £97.30.

**Owner** Sheikh Hamdan bin Mohammed Al Maktoum **Bred** Darley **Trained** Middleham Moor, N Yorks

**FOCUS**

A moderate fillies' maiden, but the time wasn't bad and backs the winner's effort to some extent.

## 1646 PIN POINT RECRUITMENT H'CAP 7f

**3:40** (3:40) (Class 3) (0-90,90) 4-Y-O+ £7,762 (£2,310; £1,154; £577) Stalls Low

Form RPR

536- **1** **Music In The Rain (IRE)**301 3684 6-9-2 **85** DanielTudhope 6 97
(David O'Meara) *trckd ldng pair: effrt whn nt clr run 2f out: sn swtchd lft to inner: squeezed through to ld ent fnl f: sn rdn and styd on wl* **7/2**1

10-6 **2** 2 3/4 **Our Boy Jack (IRE)**11 1451 5-8-8 **80** GeorgeChaloner(3) 9 85
(Richard Fahey) *in tch: pushed along on outer 3f out: rdn to chse ldrs wl over 1f out: drvn ins fnl f: styd on* **9/1**

030- **3** nse **Wannabe King**172 7696 8-9-5 **88** (p) PJMcDonald 12 93
(Geoffrey Harker) *trckd ldrs: hdwy 3f out: rdn and ev ch wl over 1f out: drvn and kpt on same pce fnl f* **25/1**

0454 **4** hd **Verse Of Love**5 1564 5-8-13 **82** GrahamGibbons 8 86
(David Evans) *trckd ldrs on inner: hdwy over 2f out: rdn over 1f out: drvn and one pce ins fnl f* **5/1**3

-353 **5** nk **Showboating (IRE)**11 1442 6-9-7 **90** (tp) TomQueally 1 93+
(Alan McCabe) *s.i.s and bhd: hdwy over 2f out: swtchd rt to wd outside over 1f out: styd on strly fnl f: nrst fin* **4/1**2

-560 **6** nk **Joe Eile (IRE)**24 1193 6-9-5 **88** RobertWinston 10 91
(John Quinn) *dwlt: hld up towards rr: hdwy wl over 2f out: swtchd rt and rdn over 1f out: ev ch tl drvn and one pce ins fnl f* **16/1**

0321 **7** nk **Skytrain**11 1451 4-9-4 **87** JoeFanning 5 89
(Mark Johnston) *cl up: chal 2f out: sn rdn: drvn to ld briefly jst over 1f out: hdd ent fnl f and sn wknd* **6/1**

00-2 **8** 3 **Solar Spirit (IRE)**14 1375 9-8-5 **77** IanBrennan(3) 11 71
(Tracy Waggott) *in tch: hdwy on outer to trck ldrs 1/2-way: effrt 2f out: sn rdn and ev ch tl drvn and wknd ent fnl f* **16/1**

45-0 **9** 3 **Al Muheer (IRE)**16 1345 9-8-11 **80** JamesSullivan 7 66
(Ruth Carr) *t.k.h: trckd ldrs: lost pl 1/2-way: sn in rr* **33/1**

10-0 **10** 2 **Evanescent (IRE)**24 1191 5-8-13 **82** RaulDaSilva 4 63
(John Quinn) *slt ld: rdn along over 2f out: drvn and edgd rt over 1f out: hdd & wknd appr fnl f* **8/1**

000- **11** 1 3/4 **Xilerator (IRE)**194 7176 7-8-8 **77** AdrianNicholls 2 54
(David Nicholls) *s.i.s: a in rr* **20/1**

1m 26.16s (-0.84) **Going Correction** +0.075s/f (Good) **11** Ran SP% **117.6**

Speed ratings (Par 107): **107,103,103,103,103 102,102,99,95,93 91**

CSF £34.63 CT £700.40 TOTE £7.10: £1.60, £3.40, £4.70; EX 49.40 Trifecta £509.20.

**Owner** Colne Valley Racing **Bred** Maddenstown Equine Enterprise Ltd **Trained** Nawton, N Yorks

**FOCUS**

A decent handicap run at a good pace with a bunch finish for the places, but the winner was impressive. The form makes sense.

## 1647 RACINGUK.COM/ANYWHERE 3 DEVICES 1 PRICE H'CAP (DIV I) 7f

**4:15** (4:16) (Class 6) (0-60,60) 3-Y-O £2,385 (£704; £352) Stalls Low

Form RPR

040 **1** **Sheriff Of Nawton (IRE)**42 930 3-9-4 **57** DanielTudhope 7 69
(David O'Meara) *hld up: hdwy over 3f out: chsd ldrs wl over 1f out: sn rdn: styd on wl fnl f to ld last 50yds* **7/2**2

4322 **2** 1 1/4 **Romantic Bliss (IRE)**21 1235 3-8-5 **51** (b) RobJFitzpatrick(7) 8 60
(K R Burke) *trckd ldrs: wd and hdwy wl over 2f out: led 1 1/2f out: rdn clr whn wandered ins fnl f: hdd and no ex last 50yds* **5/2**1

64-0 **3** *4* **Greenbury (IRE)**18 [1308] 3-9-0 **53**..............................(p) PJMcDonald 11 51
(Ann Duffield) *led: rdn along over 2f out: hdd 1 1/2f out and sn drvn: kpt on one pce* **33/1**

466- **4** *1 1/4* **Maysville (IRE)**205 [6897] 3-9-1 **54**.............................. BarryMcHugh 3 49
(Tony Coyle) *dwlt and towards rr: hdwy on inner over 2f out: swtchd rt and rdn over 1f out: styd on fnl f: nrst fin* **13/2**[3]

000- **5** *shd* **Dutch Lady**167 [7789] 3-9-1 **54**.............................. StevieDonohoe 1 49
(John Holt) *prom on inner: effrt 2f out: sn rdn and grad wknd* **66/1**

023 **6** *hd* **Mornin Mr Norris**19 [1285] 3-8-7 **49**.............................. IanBrennan(3) 6 43
(John Quinn) *trckd ldrs: effrt and hdwy over 2f out: rdn wl over 1f out: edgd lft ent fnl f: sn wknd* **7/1**

00-0 **7** *1 3/4* **Emily Davison (IRE)**16 [1347] 3-8-7 **53**.............................. GemmaTutty(7) 2 43
(Karen Tutty) *chsd ldrs: n.m.r and swtchd lft to inner wl over 1f out: sn rdn and wknd appr fnl f* **22/1**

-054 **8** *7* **Oriental Maid**18 [1304] 3-8-11 **50**.............................. DaleSwift 9 22
(Brian Ellison) *hld up: a towards rr* **16/1**

00-5 **9** *2 1/4* **Elle West**14 [1375] 3-9-7 **60**.............................. JamesSullivan 13 26
(Michael Easterby) *t.k.h: in rr tl sme late hdwy* **20/1**

00-6 **10** *1* **Spring Lady**14 [1384] 3-8-9 **48**.............................. JoeFanning 10 11
(Alan Jarvis) *a towards rr* **8/1**

-545 **11** *3/4* **Luv U Honey**20 [1264] 3-8-7 **46** oh1.............................. AndrewMullen 12 7
(Brian Baugh) *cl up: rdn along over 2f out: sn wknd* **33/1**

30-4 **12** *1* **Tears And Rain (IRE)**16 [1347] 3-9-5 **58**.............................. DuranFentiman 4 17
(Tim Easterby) *hld up: a towards rr* **20/1**

04-5 **13** *1 1/4* **Lady Dancer (IRE)**14 [1373] 3-8-0 **46** oh1.............................. KieranSchofield(7) 5
(George Moore) *a towards rr* **66/1**

1m 28.01s (1.01) **Going Correction** +0.075s/f (Good) **13** Ran SP% **116.4**
Speed ratings (Par 96): **97,95,88,87,87 84,82,74,72,70 70,68,67**
CSF £11.15 CT £240.74 TOTE £8.30: £2.00, £1.20, £8.80; EX 14.30 Trifecta £455.80.
**Owner** Direct Racing **Bred** Lawman Syndicate & Pipe View Stud **Trained** Nawton, N Yorks

**FOCUS**
A moderate 3yo handicap in which only one of these had been successful before. The winner backed up his shaky AW figure and the first two were clear.

## 1648 RACINGUK.COM/ANYWHERE 3 DEVICES 1 PRICE H'CAP (DIV II) 7f
**4:50** (4:53) (Class 6) (0-60,59) 3-Y-O £2,385 (£704; £352) **Stalls** Low

Form RPR

004- **1** **Cahal (IRE)**176 [7592] 3-9-1 **53**.............................. AdrianNicholls 6 60
(David Nicholls) *mde all: rdn 2f out: drvn ent fnl f: kpt on strly towards fin* **12/1**

56-4 **2** *1 1/2* **Tamayuz Magic (IRE)**19 [1285] 3-9-6 **58**..............................(b[1]) GrahamGibbons 7 61
(Michael Easterby) *trckd ldrs: hdwy over 2f out: sn chsng ldr: cl up over 1f out: drvn and ev ch ent fnl f tl no ex last 75yds* **20/1**

5-05 **3** *2 1/4* **Marlismamma (FR)**48 [865] 3-9-2 **54**.............................. DanielTudhope 9 51
(David O'Meara) *hld up towards rr: hdwy 3f out: swtchd rt 2f out and sn rdn: styd on appr fnl f: nrst fin* **11/1**

00-4 **4** *shd* **Soul Artist (IRE)**28 [1112] 3-9-1 **53**.............................. DavidAllan 2 50
(Tim Easterby) *chsd ldrs: rdn along on inner wl over 2f out: drvn over 1f out: one pce* **14/1**

005- **5** *shd* **Trinity Star (IRE)**229 [6175] 3-9-2 **59**.............................. ConnorBeasley(5) 10 56+
(Michael Dods) *s.i.s and bhd: hdwy on outer wl over 1f out: sn rdn and kpt on fnl f: nrst fin* **15/8**[1]

-142 **6** *1/2* **It's All A Game**19 [1285] 3-8-11 **52**..............................(v) BillyCray(3) 1 47
(Richard Guest) *cl up: rdn along over 2f out and sltly outpcd: n.m.r and swtchd rt over 1f out: kpt on u.p fnl f* **7/2**[2]

60-4 **7** *1 1/2* **Lady Montenegro**14 [1373] 3-8-12 **50**.............................. PJMcDonald 12 41
(Ann Duffield) *in tch: hdwy to chse ldrs wl over 2f out: drvn along wl over 1f out and sn no imp* **10/1**

-043 **8** *2 3/4* **Aussie Sky (IRE)**11 [1449] 3-8-4 **47**.............................. PhilipPrince(5) 11 31
(Daniel Mark Loughnane) *in tch: rdn along bef 1/2-way: sn towards rr* **20/1**

600- **9** *nk* **Nu Form Fire (IRE)**193 [7209] 3-8-12 **50**.............................. AndrewMullen 8 34
(Nigel Tinkler) *a towards rr* **33/1**

000- **10** *3/4* **Skinny Latte**125 [8346] 3-8-7 **45**.............................. DuranFentiman 5 27
(Micky Hammond) *a towards rr* **100/1**

535 **11** *17* **Torridon**12 [1430] 3-9-3 **55**.............................. JoeFanning 3
(Mark Johnston) *chsd ldrs: rdn along 1/2-way: sn wknd* **17/2**[3]

56P5 **12** *3/4* **Jenny Sparks**14 [1384] 3-8-10 **48**.............................. SamHitchcott 4
(Mick Channon) *in tch: rdn along bef 1/2-way: sn wknd* **25/1**

1m 27.77s (0.77) **Going Correction** +0.075s/f (Good) **12** Ran SP% **116.6**
Speed ratings (Par 96): **98,96,93,93,93 92,91,88,87,86 67,66**
CSF £231.71 CT £2697.79 TOTE £15.80: £4.20, £5.10, £3.10; EX 243.10 Trifecta £1548.50.
**Owner** J Law **Bred** Tally-Ho Stud **Trained** Sessay, N Yorks

**FOCUS**
At least there were three previous winners in this division and the winning time was 0.24sec quicker than the first leg. Not many figured, though. The winner built on his modest 2yo progress.

## 1649 WE RACE AGAIN 6TH MAY APPRENTICE H'CAP 7f
**5:20** (5:24) (Class 6) (0-65,65) 4-Y-O+ £2,385 (£704; £352) **Stalls** Low

Form RPR

55-6 **1** **Alluring Star**18 [1309] 6-8-8 **57**.............................. DanielleMooney(5) 3 66+
(Michael Easterby) *trckd ldrs: hdwy over 2f out: chal over 1f out: rdn to ld ent fnl f: styd on* **8/1**

2426 **2** *1* **Vale Of Clara (IRE)**48 [864] 6-8-7 **51** oh3..............................(p) LauraBarry 9 57
(Peter Niven) *hld up towards rr: hdwy over 2f out: rdn to chse ldrs over 1f out: kpt on to chse wnr ins fnl f: no imp towards fin* **12/1**

045- **3** *1/2* **Mysterious Wonder**124 [8361] 4-8-11 **55**.............................. RobJFitzpatrick 11 60
(Philip Kirby) *hld up towards rr: swtchd rt and hdwy on wd outside 2f out: sn rdn and styd on fnl f: nrst fin* **10/1**

-050 **4** *3 1/4* **Viking Warrior (IRE)**14 [1375] 7-8-3 **52**.............................. GaryMahon(5) 12 49
(Shaun Harris) *in tch: hdwy 3f out: rdn to chse ldrs wl over 1f out: drvn and edgd lft ent fnl f: kpt on same pce* **16/1**

0055 **5** *1 3/4* **The Mongoose**21 [1236] 6-8-11 **60**..............................(t) HollieDoyle(5) 4 52
(David Evans) *slt ld: rdn along 2f out: hdd ent fnl f: sn wknd* **11/2**[3]

0-34 **6** *nk* **Thrust Control (IRE)**7 [1503] 7-8-7 **51** oh4..............................(p) KevinStott 8 42
(Tracy Waggott) *cl up: rdn along over 2f out: drvn and wknd over 1f out* **4/1**[1]

20-2 **7** *2 1/2* **Rio Cobolo (IRE)**27 [1125] 8-9-4 **65**..............................(be) EvaMoscrop(3) 1 50
(Philip Kirby) *in rr: hdwy on inner 2f out: rdn wl over 1f out: sn no imp* **9/2**[2]

00-3 **8** *1* **Secret City (IRE)**18 [1309] 8-9-2 **63**.............................. LukeLeadbitter(3) 7 45
(Robin Bastiman) *midfield: effrt 3f out: sn rdn along and n.d* **9/2**[2]

00-0 **9** *1 1/4* **Jack Barker**9 [1486] 5-8-4 **51** oh6.............................. JackGarritty(3) 10 30
(Robin Bastiman) *prom: rdn along 3f out: wknd 2f out* **50/1**

000/ **10** *3* **Morna's Glory**480 [8291] 5-8-6 **55**.............................. AnnaHesketh(5) 2 26
(Michael Herrington) *midfield: rdn along 1/2-way: sn wknd* **66/1**

-000 **11** *1 3/4* **Marcus Caesar (IRE)**2 [1606] 4-9-5 **63**.............................. GemmaTutty 5 30
(Ruth Carr) *chsd ldrs: rdn along over 2f out: sn wknd* **16/1**

000- **12** *5* **Red Joker (IRE)**10 [8294] 4-9-1 **62**..............................(p) MeganCarberry(3) 6 16
(Andrew Crook) *a in rr* **28/1**

1m 26.48s (-0.52) **Going Correction** +0.075s/f (Good) **12** Ran SP% **118.3**
Speed ratings (Par 101): **105,103,103,99,97 97,94,93,91,88 86,80**
CSF £98.81 CT £991.08 TOTE £10.70: £3.00, £5.30, £3.70; EX 67.20 Trifecta £620.00.
**Owner** Jeff Hamer & Bernard Bargh **Bred** B Bargh **Trained** Sheriff Hutton, N Yorks

**FOCUS**
A moderate apprentice handicap in which they didn't hang about. Relatively the best time of the five C&D races. The winner was back to his form of this time last year.
T/Plt: £364.30 to a £1 stake. Pool: £53164.24 - 106.52 winning tickets T/Qpdt: £37.80 to a £1 stake. Pool: £3892.85 - 76.10 winning tickets JR

# EPSOM (L-H)
## Wednesday, April 23

**OFFICIAL GOING: Good to soft (soft in places; overall 6.5, home straight: stands' side 5.9, far side 6.3)**
Railed out up to 10yds from 1m to Winning Post adding 31yds to all distances except 5f.
Wind: Fresh, across (towards stands) Weather: Fine but cloudy

## 1650 INVESTEC WEALTH & INVESTMENT H'CAP 5f
**1:45** (1:47) (Class 3) (0-95,93) 4-Y-O+
£12,450 (£3,728; £1,864; £932; £466; £234) **Stalls** High

Form RPR

064 **1** **Caspian Prince (IRE)**18 [1313] 5-9-4 **90**..............................(t) AdamKirby 15 103
(Tony Carroll) *awkward s but mde all and racd against nr side rail: rdn clr fnl f: readily* **13/2**[3]

0-03 **2** *2 1/4* **Elusivity (IRE)**87 [348] 6-9-2 **88**.............................. JamieSpencer 7 93
(Peter Crate) *lw: hld up: sn outpcd in last trio: gd prog over 1f out: r.o to take 2nd last 75yds: no ch to threaten wnr* **5/1**[2]

0-33 **3** *3/4* **Fair Value (IRE)**26 [1145] 6-8-12 **84**.............................. HayleyTurner 5 86
(Simon Dow) *chsd wnr: clr of rest but rdn and no imp over 1f out: fdd and lost 2nd last 75yds* **7/1**

434- **4** *nk* **Pearl Blue (IRE)**179 [7527] 6-9-6 **92**.............................. GeorgeBaker 6 93+
(Chris Wall) *lw: hld up and sn bdly outpcd in last: stl last 1f out: gd prog fnl f: nrly snatched 3rd: no ch* **7/1**

0340 **5** *1 1/4* **Diamond Charlie (IRE)**33 [1041] 6-8-7 **79**.............................. MickaelBarzalona 13 76
(Simon Dow) *a abt same pl: nt qckn over 1f out: no imp after* **8/1**

260- **6** *1* **Imperial Legend (IRE)**186 [7373] 5-9-1 **87**..............................(p) PaulHanagan 12 80
(David Nicholls) *chsd ldng pair against nr side rail: no imp over 1f out: fdd fnl f* **10/1**

4-32 **7** *nk* **Peace Seeker**9 [1490] 6-8-13 **85**..............................(t) WilliamCarson 10 77
(Anthony Carson) *lw: a towards rr: effrt on outer over 1f out: no hdwy fnl f* **7/2**[1]

0000 **8** *3/4* **Tennessee Wildcat (IRE)**12 [1421] 4-9-6 **92**..............................(p) AndreaAtzeni 4 81
(Robert Cowell) *outpcd in last trio: no prog whn nt clr run jst over 1f out* **25/1**

6010 **9** *1/2* **Taajub (IRE)**53 [802] 7-9-4 **90**.............................. ShaneKelly 3 83
(Peter Crate) *racd on outer in midfield: tried to cl over 1f out: wknd qckly last 50yds: dismntd: b.b.v* **8/1**

200- **10** *4 1/2* **Fitz Flyer (IRE)**161 [7851] 8-9-2 **88**..............................(v) KierenFallon 8 65
(David Nicholls) *prom: rdn 2f out: wknd over 1f out: short of room fnl f and eased* **18/1**

55.8s (0.10) **Going Correction** +0.20s/f (Good) **10** Ran SP% **117.6**
Speed ratings (Par 107): **107,103,102,101,99 98,97,96,95,88**
CSF £39.40 CT £242.74 TOTE £7.70: £2.70, £2.10, £1.90; EX 41.90 Trifecta £421.10.
**Owner** Stephen Louch **Bred** Ballygallon Stud Limited **Trained** Cropthorne, Worcs
■ Stewards' Enquiry : Jamie Spencer one-day ban: careless riding (May 7)

**FOCUS**
A total of 25mm of rain fell on Monday night but it had been dry since and the going had dried up a little to good to soft, soft in places (GoingStick 6.7; stands' side home straight 6.1; far side 6.5). The rail was out up to 10 yards from the mile point to the winning post, adding 31 yards to all races except the 5f. Despite the GoingStick suggesting the ground was quicker away from the rail, they stayed together stands' side in this sprint handicap. A personal best from the winner, worth a bit more at face value.

## 1651 INVESTEC GREAT METROPOLITAN H'CAP 1m 4f 10y
**2:20** (2:22) (Class 3) (0-95,91) 4-Y-O+
£14,006 (£4,194; £2,097; £1,048; £524; £263) **Stalls** Centre

Form RPR

400- **1** **Beacon Lady**191 [7250] 5-8-9 **84**.............................. JackDuern(5) 5 99
(William Knight) *stdd s: hld up in last: stl there st: rapid prog on outer 3f out to ld over 1f out: sn rdn clr: eased last 150yds* **14/1**

210- **2** *7* **Da Do Run Run**306 [3526] 4-8-9 **80**.............................. MartinLane 6 84
(Brian Meehan) *lw: led: rdn wl over 2f out: hdd and outpcd wl over 1f out: kpt on* **20/1**

0-12 **3** *3/4* **Dark Ruler (IRE)**11 [1444] 5-8-13 **83**.............................. BenCurtis 11 86
(Alan Swinbank) *prom: stdd bk into midfield after 3f: 6th st: rdn and prog 3f out: clsd on ldr 2f out but wnr shot past: one pce after* **3/1**[1]

50-1 **4** *1* **Red Runaway**21 [1241] 4-8-10 **81**.............................. RyanMoore 3 84
(Ed Dunlop) *lw: trckd ldrs: 5th st: effrt on inner whn hmpd wl over 2f out: no ch after: kpt on fr over 1f out* **4/1**[2]

10-1 **5** *1* **Jakey (IRE)**22 [1219] 4-8-10 **81**.............................. LiamJones 7 80
(Pat Phelan) *trckd ldrs: prog and 3rd st: chsd ldr 3f out to 2f out: sn outpcd* **8/1**[3]

550- **6** *nk* **Another Cocktail**228 [6186] 4-9-6 **91**.............................. JimmyFortune 2 90
(Hughie Morrison) *in tch: 7th and rdn st: prog to chse ldrs 2f out: sn outpcd: plugged on* **8/1**[3]

51-0 **7** *2 1/4* **Rossetti**11 [1439] 6-8-7 **77** oh1..............................(p) MickaelBarzalona 8 72
(Gary Moore) *hld up: 8th st: hanging bdly lft whn asked for effrt 3f out: sme prog 2f out: hung lft to far rail over 1f out: nvr a factor* **14/1**

11-0 **8** *10* **Bayan Kasirga (IRE)**11 [1444] 4-8-9 **85**.............................. SammyJoBell(5) 1 64
(Richard Fahey) *stdd s: hld up in last pair: 9th st: sn shkn up and no prog* **25/1**

41-5 **9** *18* **Vital Evidence (USA)**25 [1171] 4-9-5 **90**..............................(v) JamesDoyle 10 41
(Sir Michael Stoute) *lw: awkward s: trckd ldng pair: chal on outer over 4f out: dropped to 4th and rdn st: sn btn: eased over 1f out: t.o* **4/1**[2]

2264 **10** 7 **Aryal**[5] 1553 4-8-10 **81**..........(b) SilvestreDeSousa 13 20
(Mark Johnston) *pressed ldr tl wknd rapidly 3f out: t.o and eased* **8/1**[3]

2m 40.65s (1.75) **Going Correction** +0.20s/f (Good)
**WFA** 4 from 5yo+ 1lb **10** Ran SP% **120.3**
Speed ratings (Par 107): **102,97,96,96,95 95,93,87,75,70**
CSF £266.73 CT £1072.23 TOTE £15.70: £3.40, £5.10, £1.50; EX 350.00 Trifecta £2251.80 Part won..
**Owner** The Pro-Claimers **Bred** Ashley House Stud **Trained** Patching, W Sussex
■ Stewards' Enquiry : Liam Jones three-day ban: careless riding (May 7-9)

**FOCUS**
This looked competitive beforehand but the winner scored with ease.

## 1652 INVESTEC DERBY TRIAL (CONDITIONS RACE) (BOBIS RACE) 1m 2f 18y
2:50 (2:55) (Class 2) 3-Y-O
£31,125 (£9,320; £4,660; £2,330; £1,165; £585) Stalls Low

Form RPR
321- **1** **Our Channel (USA)**[211] 6716 3-8-13 85..........RyanMoore 6 99
(William Haggas) *neat: mde all: styd against far rail in st: rdn over 2f out: hung rt fnl f: jst hld on* **14/1**

1- **2** *hd* **Marzocco (USA)**[182] 7460 3-8-13 83..........WilliamBuick 4 99+
(John Gosden) *str: tall: lw: settled in 6th: pushed along 4f out: rdn and limited prog over 2f out: r.o fnl f: tk 2nd and cl on wnr: jst failed* **7/2**[2]

115- **3** ¾ **Stars Over The Sea (USA)**[228] 6195 3-8-13 91..........KierenFallon 8 97
(Mark Johnston) *t.k.h: trckd wnr: brought wd in st: rdn over 2f out: stl disputing 2nd fr over 1f out: kpt on but a hld* **14/1**

110- **4** *hd* **Signposted (IRE)**[200] 7017 3-8-13 90..........DavidProbert 5 97
(Andrew Balding) *bit bkwd: trckd ldng trio: brought wd in st: rdn over 2f out: tried to chal over 1f out: kpt on but a hld* **8/1**[3]

113- **5** *1* **Hartnell**[165] 7828 3-9-1 103..........SilvestreDeSousa 1 97
(Mark Johnston) *lw: t.k.h: trckd ldng pair: brought wd in st: rdn over 2f out: chal but nt qckn over 1f out: lost 2nd and sltly impeded ins fnl f* **6/4**[1]

2-12 **6** *5* **Arantes**[19] 1279 3-8-13 79..........WilliamTwiston-Davies 9 85
(Mick Channon) *restrained into last: jst pushed along and no prog fr 3f out: rdn and no imp fnl f* **25/1**

012- **7** *hd* **Trip To Paris (IRE)**[243] 5717 3-8-13 88..........(b) AdamKirby 3 85
(Ed Dunlop) *bit bkwd: settled in 7th: shkn up and no prog 3f out: wl btn 2f out* **14/1**

1- **8** *nk* **Moontime**[182] 7469 3-8-13 0..........MickaelBarzalona 2 84
(Charlie Appleby) *w'like: trckd ldrs in 5th: pushed along 4f out: no prog 3f out: sn btn* **8/1**[3]

**9** 1½ **Nonno Giulio (IRE)**[232] 3-8-13 0..........RobertHavlin 7 82
(John Gosden) *leggy: lengthy: dwlt: hld up in 8th: shkn up 3f out: no prog and wl btn 2f out* **16/1**

2m 10.57s (0.87) **Going Correction** +0.20s/f (Good) **9** Ran SP% **114.2**
Speed ratings (Par 104): **104,103,103,103,102 98,98,97,96**
CSF £61.95 TOTE £14.70: £3.60, £1.30, £3.70; EX 79.30 Trifecta £833.70.
**Owner** Abdulla Al Mansoori **Bred** Bluegrass Hall Llc **Trained** Newmarket, Suffolk

**FOCUS**
Despite its title this is not a race that has had much of an impact on the Derby itself. The favourite disappointed and Our Channel made all. The form rates a bit below the race standard.

## 1653 INVESTEC PROPERTY INVESTMENTS CITY AND SUBURBAN STKS (H'CAP) 1m 2f 18y
3:25 (3:28) (Class 2) (0-105,102) 4-Y-O+
£31,125 (£9,320; £4,660; £2,330; £1,165; £585) Stalls Low

Form RPR
0-03 **1** **Sennockian Star**[15] 1360 4-9-1 **96**..........(v) SilvestreDeSousa 3 106
(Mark Johnston) *prom: 3rd st: rdn to go 2nd 3f out: led wl over 1f out and sn chal: drvn and styd on wl* **12/1**

34-1 **2** 1¼ **Clayton**[15] 1360 5-9-7 **102**..........JamieSpencer 10 110
(Kevin Ryan) *hld up in tch: 6th st: prog 3f out: wnt 2nd over 1f out and chal: drvn and nt qckn fnl f* **8/1**

005- **3** 1¼ **Soviet Rock (IRE)**[179] 7536 4-8-11 **92**..........DavidProbert 5 97
(Andrew Balding) *lw: led: gng strly over 2f out: rdn and hdd wl over 1f out: one pce* **9/2**[1]

10-0 **4** *nk* **Hi There (IRE)**[25] 1165 5-8-12 **98**..........SammyJoBell(5) 7 103
(Richard Fahey) *lw: dwlt: hld up in midfield and off the pce: 8th st: prog whn nt clr run over 2f out: rdn to go 4th over 1f out: kpt on but nt gng pce to threaten* **12/1**

3-00 **5** 2¼ **Tres Coronas (IRE)**[25] 1165 7-9-0 **95**..........MickaelBarzalona 12 95+
(David Barron) *hld up in rr and wl off the pce: 10th st: drvn on outer wl over 2f out: styd on fr over 1f out: nrst fin* **6/1**[2]

0R6- **6** *nk* **King's Warrior (FR)**[30] 7536 7-8-9 **95**..........ShelleyBirkett(5) 4 95
(Tom George) *s.s: hld up in last trio: 13th st: pushed along and stdy prog fr 3f out: nrst fin* **33/1**

60-6 **7** *1* **Charles Camoin (IRE)**[11] 1437 6-8-9 **90**..........LiamKeniry 17 88
(Sylvester Kirk) *hld up in tch: 7th st: tried to cl on ldrs over 2f out: fdd over 1f out* **10/1**

401- **8** 2½ **Pasaka Boy**[215] 6596 4-8-5 **86**..........PaulHanagan 16 79
(Jonathan Portman) *off the pce in midfield: 9th and rdn st: plugged on u.p fnl 2f* **14/1**

441- **9** 2¼ **Cactus Valley (IRE)**[317] 3157 5-8-9 **90**..........JamesDoyle 15 79
(Roger Charlton) *hld up wl in rr and wl off the pce: 12th st: rdn and no hdwy 3f out* **12/1**

060- **10** ½ **Resurge (IRE)**[179] 7536 9-8-11 **92**..........(t) JimCrowley 6 80
(Stuart Kittow) *dwlt: hld up in last and wl off the pce: shkn up on outer 3f out: nvr involved* **7/1**[3]

11-2 **11** 3¼ **Ebony Express**[18] 1306 5-8-3 **84**..........BenCurtis 8 66
(Alan Swinbank) *pressed ldr to 3f out: wknd* **12/1**

250- **12** ¾ **Red Avenger (USA)**[207] 6838 4-9-4 **99**..........WilliamBuick 2 79
(Ed Dunlop) *a in rr and off the pce: 11th st: drvn and no prog 3f out: wl btn 2f out* **20/1**

10-0 **13** 2¼ **Weapon Of Choice (IRE)**[25] 1164 6-8-6 **87**..........MartinLane 9 63
(Stuart Kittow) *prom: 4th st: rdn 3f out: wknd rapidly 2f out* **25/1**

60-1 **14** 1¾ **Salutation (IRE)**[25] 1171 4-8-13 **97**..........MichaelJMMurphy(3) 11 70
(Mark Johnston) *pressed ldng trio tl 5th and wkng st: sn bhd* **20/1**

2m 8.96s (-0.74) **Going Correction** +0.20s/f (Good) **14** Ran SP% **118.9**
Speed ratings (Par 109): **110,109,108,107,105 105,104,102,101,100 98,97,95,94**
CSF £98.26 CT £505.65 TOTE £14.50: £3.70, £2.50, £2.40; EX 81.80 Trifecta £354.00.
**Owner** The Vine Accord **Bred** Cheveley Park Stud Ltd **Trained** Middleham Moor, N Yorks

**FOCUS**
The time was 1.61sec quicker than the Derby Trial, but it was another race where it paid to race handily. The winner, who reversed Pontefract form with the second, is rated back to his best.

## 1654 INVESTEC SPECIALIST CASH PRODUCTS MAIDEN STKS 1m 114y
4:00 (4:02) (Class 4) 3-4-Y-O £4,851 (£1,443; £721; £360) Stalls Low

Form RPR
03-5 **1** **Ravenous**[24] 1192 3-8-11 75..........JimCrowley 3 79
(Ralph Beckett) *trckd ldr: led gng wl 2f out: rdn to assert over 1f out: styd on* **5/2**[2]

6- **2** 1½ **Moshe (IRE)**[180] 7502 3-8-11 0..........JimmyFortune 2 76
(Hughie Morrison) *bit bkwd: trckd ldng pair: pushed along 3f out and no imp: pushed along firmly and tk 2nd last 150yds: steadily clsd on wnr tl veered rt nr fin* **6/1**

050- **3** 4½ **After The Goldrush**[197] 7088 3-8-11 71..........RyanMoore 1 65
(Richard Hannon) *lw: led: shkn up and hdd 2f out: steadily outpcd and lost 2nd fnl 150yds* **9/2**[3]

53- **4** 4½ **D'Avignon (USA)**[154] 7971 3-8-11 0..........WilliamBuick 5 55
(John Gosden) *w'like: restless in stalls: a in 4th and nvr gng wl: urged along bef 1/2-way: wl btn fnl 2f* **1/1**[1]

60 **5** 3¾ **Permitted**[21] 1233 3-8-6 0..........WilliamCarson 4 41
(Lee Carter) *w'like: a in last: swtchd fr far rail to wd outside 2f out: pushed along after: nvr involved* **66/1**

1m 49.06s (2.96) **Going Correction** +0.20s/f (Good) **5** Ran SP% **112.5**
Speed ratings (Par 105): **94,92,88,84,81**
CSF £17.16 TOTE £3.80: £2.00, £3.10; EX 13.50 Trifecta £46.00.
**Owner** Prince Of Wales And Duchess Of Cornwall **Bred** Prince Of Wales And Duchess Of Cornwall **Trained** Kimpton, Hants

**FOCUS**
An ordinary maiden rated around the winner with the favourite disappointing.

## 1655 INVESTEC SPECIALIST BANK H'CAP (BOBIS RACE) 1m 114y
4:35 (4:35) (Class 4) (0-80,80) 3-Y-O £6,469 (£1,925; £962; £481) Stalls Low

Form RPR
331- **1** **Chatez (IRE)**[180] 7502 3-9-5 **78**..........FergusSweeney 10 91+
(Alan King) *lw: hld up in tch: 7th st: gd prog to ld 2f out: drvn and styd on wl fr over 1f out* **7/2**[1]

051- **2** *2* **Beach Bar (IRE)**[167] 7779 3-9-7 **80**..........AndreaAtzeni 3 88
(William Knight) *taken down early and steadily to post: hld up in tch: 6th st: prog over 2f out: drvn to chse wnr over 1f out: styd on but no real imp fnl f* **8/1**

-434 **3** *4* **Gratzie**[16] 1346 3-8-10 **72**..........WilliamTwiston-Davies(3) 5 71
(Mick Channon) *hld up: 8th st: shkn up over 2f out: no prog tl jst over 1f out: r.o to take 3rd last stride* **25/1**

-432 **4** *nk* **Lesha (IRE)**[16] 1346 3-9-0 **73**..........JamieSpencer 13 71
(Kevin Ryan) *pushed up fr wdst draw to ld after 1f: rdn and hdd 2f out: outpcd after: fdd and lost 3rd last stride* **7/1**

100- **5** 1¾ **Bureau (IRE)**[196] 7129 3-9-3 **76**..........SilvestreDeSousa 1 70
(Mark Johnston) *led 1f: cl up: 3rd st: sn rdn: outpcd 2f out: no imp after* **14/1**

124- **6** *hd* **Mime Dance**[196] 7122 3-9-4 **77**..........DavidProbert 2 71
(Andrew Balding) *trckd ldr 7f out: chal but nt qckn 2f out: steadily wknd over 1f out* **5/1**[3]

11-5 **7** 2½ **Killing Time (IRE)**[24] 1195 3-9-6 **79**..........(b) JimCrowley 12 67
(Ralph Beckett) *hld up in last pair: 9th st: prog and reminder 2f out: 6th over 1f out: pushed along and no hdwy after* **4/1**[2]

21- **8** *6* **Isabella Beeton**[132] 8259 3-8-8 **70**..........JemmaMarshall(3) 11 44
(Pat Phelan) *leggy: swtg: t.k.h: trckd ldrs: 4th st: wknd over 2f out* **25/1**

006- **9** *1* **Golden Journey (IRE)**[198] 7070 3-8-13 **72**..........AdamKirby 8 44
(Clive Cox) *lw: sn restrained into last pair: last st: reminders and no prog 2f out* **7/1**

130- **10** *12* **Dance Bid**[207] 6839 3-9-4 **77**..........MickaelBarzalona 4 21
(Clive Brittain) *chsd ldrs: 5th st: wknd wl over 2f out: eased and t.o fnl f* **16/1**

1m 46.93s (0.83) **Going Correction** +0.20s/f (Good) **10** Ran SP% **115.2**
Speed ratings (Par 100): **104,102,98,98,96 96,94,89,88,77**
CSF £31.50 CT £591.55 TOTE £5.70: £1.60, £3.30, £3.50; EX 34.50 Trifecta £689.50.
**Owner** Mrs Peter Andrews **Bred** Colin Kennedy **Trained** Barbury Castle, Wilts

**FOCUS**
There was a bit of competition for the early lead, and those that got involved in that eventually paid the price. The time was 2.13sec quicker than the earlier maiden contested by 3yos. A slightly positive view has been taken of the form.
T/Jkpt: Not won. T/Plt: £386.00 to a £1 stake. Pool: £99143.78 - 187.47 winning tickets T/Qpdt: £49.90 to a £1 stake. Pool: £6971.86 - 103.30 winning tickets JN

# 1503 BEVERLEY (R-H)
## Thursday, April 24

**OFFICIAL GOING: Good to firm (good in places; 8.4)**
Wind: Virtually nil Weather: Sunny periods

## 1656 BEVERLEY MINSTER MAIDEN AUCTION FILLIES' STKS 5f
1:55 (1:56) (Class 6) 2-Y-O £2,264 (£673; £336; £168) Stalls Low

Form RPR
**1** **Bond's Girl** 2-8-6 0..........PaulHanagan 2 73
(Richard Fahey) *trckd ldrs: hdwy 2f out: chal over 1f out: sn rdn: styd on to ld ins fnl f: r.o* **4/1**[2]

**2** 1½ **Mecca's Mirage (IRE)** 2-8-1 0..........ConnorBeasley(5) 8 68
(Michael Dods) *midfield: hdwy 2f out: rdn over 1f out: styd on wl to take 2nd towards fin* **7/1**

**3** ½ **Magic Time (IRE)** 2-8-12 0..........PJMcDonald 5 72
(Ann Duffield) *qckly away and led: jnd and rdn jst over 1f out: hdd ins fnl f: kpt on same pce* **7/1**

**4** 2½ **Make On Madam (IRE)** 2-8-6 0..........PaulPickard 1 57+
(Brian Ellison) *s.i.s and bhd: swtchd lft to outer and rdn 2f out: gd hdwy wl over 1f out: swtchd rt appr fnl f: kpt on wl: nrst fin* **6/1**

**5** *2* **Millar Rose (IRE)** 2-8-6 0..........LukeMorris 7 50
(K R Burke) *prom: rdn along wl over 1f out: grad wknd appr fnl f* **5/1**[3]

**6** 2¼ **Astrea** 2-8-6 0..........AndrewMullen 9 42
(Nigel Tinkler) *chsd ldrs: rdn along 2f out: grad wknd appr fnl f* **50/1**

**7** *1* **Debt Free Dame** 2-8-6 0..........JamesSullivan 6 38
(Michael Easterby) *a towards rr* **33/1**

034 **8** *2* **Penalty Scorer**[8] 1504 2-8-3 0..........BillyCray(3) 10 31
(Richard Guest) *chsd ldrs on outer: rdn along over 1f out: drvn wl over 1f out: sn wknd* **12/1**

5 **9** 2½ **Reet Petite (IRE)**$^{17}$ 1342 2-8-9 0 ........ PaulMulrennan 4 25
(Michael Dods) *in tch: rdn along 1/2-way: sn wknd* **7/2**$^{1}$

00 **10** 7 **Esk Valley Lady**$^{8}$ 1504 2-8-1 0 ........ JoeyHaynes(5) 11
(Philip Kirby) *a in rr* **100/1**

**11** 10 **Mini Minstrel** 2-8-9 0 ........ BenCurtis 3
(Alan McCabe) *a in rr: bhd fr 1/2-way* **10/1**

1m 3.01s (-0.49) **Going Correction** -0.325s/f (Firm) **11** Ran SP% **120.8**
Speed ratings (Par 87): **90,87,86,82,79 76,74,71,67,56 40**
CSF £33.03 TOTE £4.80: £2.20, £2.60, £3.50; EX 38.30 Trifecta £224.60.
**Owner** Crown Select **Bred** David Holgate **Trained** Musley Bank, N Yorks

**FOCUS**
A modest fillies' maiden auction event in which three had previous experience, but none of them figured. The form matches the race standard.

## 1657 MAYDAY RACEDAY HERE MONDAY 5TH MAY H'CAP 7f 100y
**2:30** (2:30) (Class 5) (0-70,68) 3-Y-O **£3,234** (£962; £481; £240) **Stalls** Low

Form RPR

205- **1** **Dalaki (IRE)**$^{181}$ 7492 3-9-5 **66** ........ KierenFallon 3 73
(Clive Brittain) *dwlt and sn pushed along into midfield: in tch 1/2-way: rdn along to chse ldrs 2f out: styd on ent fnl f: led nr fin* **7/1**

00-0 **2** nk **Mariners Moon (IRE)**$^{19}$ 1308 3-9-1 **62** ........ DanielTudhope 5 68+
(David O'Meara) *trckd ldrs: hdwy over 2f out: rdn to ld jst over 1f out: edgd lft ins fnl f: sn drvn: hdd and no ex towards fin* **7/1**

4154 **3** ¾ **Kraka Gym (IRE)**$^{19}$ 1308 3-8-11 **58** ........ (b$^{1}$) BarryMcHugh 12 62
(Michael Easterby) *towards rr: pushed along 3f out: rdn and hdwy 2f out: swtchd rt to inner and styd on ent fnl f: nrst fin* **16/1**

065- **4** 2 **Kalahari Kingdom (IRE)**$^{187}$ 7371 3-9-0 **61** ........ PaulHanagan 7 60
(Richard Fahey) *trckd ldrs: hdwy 2f out: sn rdn: kpt on same pce u.p fnl f* **9/2**$^{1}$

-233 **5** 2½ **Handwoven (IRE)**$^{8}$ 1507 3-9-7 **68** ........ JoeFanning 13 61
(Mark Johnston) *prom: effrt to chse ldr over 2f out: sn rdn and one pce* **6/1**$^{3}$

5-32 **6** 2½ **Baltic Fire (IRE)**$^{24}$ 1214 3-8-8 **60** ........ (b) JoeyHaynes(5) 4 47
(K R Burke) *chsd ldr: hdwy to ld 3f out: rdn along 2f out: hdd jst over 1f out: sn drvn and wknd* **11/2**$^{2}$

5350 **7** 3 **This Charming Man (IRE)**$^{15}$ 1373 3-8-7 **54** oh2 ........ (p) PJMcDonald 9 33
(Keith Dalgleish) *t.k.h early: hld up: a towards rr* **33/1**

055- **8** ¾ **Street Boss (IRE)**$^{240}$ 5858 3-8-6 **60** ........ RachelRichardson(7) 2 37
(Tim Easterby) *dwlt: a towards rr* **12/1**

50-0 **9** ¾ **Green Zone (IRE)**$^{17}$ 1346 3-9-4 **65** ........ AndrewMullen 1 40
(Nigel Tinkler) *dwlt and in rr: effrt and sme hdwy whn hmpd 2f out: nt rcvr* **25/1**

03-0 **10** 2¾ **Miss Sophisticated**$^{15}$ 1400 3-9-4 **65** ........ (b$^{1}$) PhillipMakin 11 33
(David Barron) *hld up in midfield: effrt 3f out: rdn along and edgd lft 2f out: sn wknd* **20/1**

546- **11** 7 **Henke (IRE)**$^{206}$ 6904 3-8-6 **60** ........ JoeDoyle(7) 14 11
(Nigel Tinkler) *chsd ldrs on outer: rdn along wl over 2f out: sn wknd* **16/1**

-031 **12** 7 **Uplifted (IRE)**$^{19}$ 1308 3-9-1 **62** ........ (b) PaulMulrennan 8
(Kevin Ryan) *sn led: rdn along and hdd 3f out: wknd qckly 2f out* **9/2**$^{1}$

1m 31.87s (-1.93) **Going Correction** -0.325s/f (Firm) **12** Ran SP% **122.0**
Speed ratings (Par 98): **98,97,96,94,91 88,85,84,83,80 72,64**
CSF £55.79 CT £785.43 TOTE £8.70: £3.10, £2.70, £5.40; EX 96.00 Trifecta £1414.00 Part won..
**Owner** Saeed Manana **Bred** Rabbah Bloodstock Limited **Trained** Newmarket, Suffolk

**FOCUS**
A modest handicap, but they went a strong pace which eventually took its toll on a few. The winner is rated in line with a best view of his 2yo form.

## 1658 HAPPY BIRTHDAY DADIE OUGHTRED STKS (H'CAP) (BOBIS RACE) 7f 100y
**3:00** (3:02) (Class 3) (0-95,92) 3-Y-O **£7,439** (£2,213; £1,106; £553) **Stalls** Low

Form RPR

1- **1** **Muteela**$^{175}$ 7645 3-8-7 **78** ........ PaulHanagan 1 92
(Mark Johnston) *set stdy pce: qcknd wl over 2f out: shkn up appr fnl f: styd on strly* **2/1**$^{1}$

0-36 **2** 4 **Lincoln (IRE)**$^{13}$ 1420 3-8-8 **82** ........ WilliamTwiston-Davies(3) 5 86
(Mick Channon) *trckd ldrs on outer: edgd lft 1/2-way: hdwy to join wnr 3f out: rdn wl over 1f out: drvn and kpt on same pce ent fnl f* **11/4**$^{2}$

2135 **3** 3½ **Upholland**$^{17}$ 1352 3-8-4 **75** ........ (p) LukeMorris 6 70
(Richard Fahey) *t.k.h: trckd ldrs: hdwy 3f out: rdn along to chse ldng pair wl over 1f out: sn one pce* **9/2**$^{3}$

13- **4** ½ **Red Stargazer (IRE)**$^{188}$ 7334 3-9-7 **92** ........ PhillipMakin 3 86
(David Barron) *unruly in stalls: in rr: pushed along over 2f out: sn rdn: styd on fnl f: nrst fin* **10/1**

2-00 **5** hd **Illuminating Dream (IRE)**$^{56}$ 771 3-8-13 **84** ........ HarryBentley 4 78
(David Brown) *cl up: rdn along wl over 2f out: wknd wl over 1f out* **7/1**

030- **6** 7 **Belayer (IRE)**$^{181}$ 7492 3-8-8 **79** ........ PaulMulrennan 2 55
(Kevin Ryan) *trckd ldng pair: rdn along wl over 2f out: wknd wl over 1f out* **13/2**

1m 31.0s (-2.80) **Going Correction** -0.325s/f (Firm) **6** Ran SP% **113.1**
Speed ratings (Par 102): **103,98,94,93,93 85**
CSF £7.85 TOTE £2.70: £1.40, £1.70; EX 7.90 Trifecta £16.00.
**Owner** Hamdan Al Maktoum **Bred** Shadwell Estate Company Limited **Trained** Middleham Moor, N Yorks

**FOCUS**
A decent 3yo handicap, but ultimately a one-horse race. Despite the early pace not looking that strong, the winning time was still 0.87sec quicker than the previous contest. The winner should do better still.

## 1659 IN MEMORY OF BARRY LINLEY H'CAP 1m 4f 16y
**3:30** (3:30) (Class 4) (0-85,84) 4-Y-O+ **£4,690** (£1,395; £697; £348) **Stalls** Low

Form RPR

1-04 **1** **Arizona John (IRE)**$^{28}$ 1133 9-8-13 **76** ........ JoeFanning 7 84
(John Mackie) *trckd ldr: cl up 1/2-way: slt ld 2f out: rdn over 1f out: kpt on fnl f: hld on gamely towards fin* **12/1**

3-24 **2** hd **Sporting Gold (IRE)**$^{23}$ 1219 5-8-13 **76** ........ (b) TomQueally 3 84
(Roger Varian) *trckd ldrs: hdwy wl over 2f out: rdn to chal over 1f out: ev ch tl drvn ins fnl f and no ex nr fin* **7/2**$^{3}$

-001 **3** 2¾ **Brigadoon**$^{15}$ 1377 7-9-7 **84** ........ AndrewMullen 2 87
(Michael Appleby) *trckd ldrs: hdwy to chse ldng pair wl over 1f out: sn rdn and no imp fnl f* **11/8**$^{1}$

1-46 **4** ¾ **Fujin Dancer (FR)**$^{14}$ 744 9-9-0 **77** ........ PaulPickard 1 79
(Brian Ellison) *hld up in rr: hdwy 2f out: sn rdn: drvn and kpt on same pce fnl f* **8/1**

213- **5** 1½ **Omnipresent**$^{218}$ 6514 4-8-13 **80** ........ SamJames(3) 4 80
(David O'Meara) *led: pushed along and jnd 3f out: rdn and hdd 2f out: grad wknd* **3/1**$^{2}$

122- **6** 2¾ **Aneedh**$^{11}$ 6601 4-8-13 **77** ........ RussKennemore 6 72
(Jedd O'Keeffe) *trckd ldng pair on inner: effrt over 3f out: rdn along over 2f out: sn drvn and wknd* **12/1**

2m 37.09s (-2.71) **Going Correction** -0.325s/f (Firm)
**WFA** 4 from 5yo+ 1lb **6** Ran SP% **115.8**
Speed ratings (Par 105): **96,95,94,93,92 90**
CSF £54.91 TOTE £14.30: £4.40, £1.90; EX 51.00 Trifecta £218.90.
**Owner** Derbyshire Racing **Bred** Abergwaun Farms **Trained** Church Broughton , Derbys

**FOCUS**
They didn't go much of a gallop in this fair middle-distance handicap and all six horses were still within a couple of lengths of each other coming to the last furlong. The steady pace counted against a few. Ordinary form, with the winner setting the standard.

## 1660 RAPID LAD H'CAP 1m 1f 207y
**4:00** (4:00) (Class 5) (0-75,74) 4-Y-O+ **£3,234** (£962; £481; £240) **Stalls** Low

Form RPR

435- **1** **Hit The Jackpot (IRE)**$^{194}$ 7210 5-9-4 **74** ........ JulieBurke(3) 8 96
(David O'Meara) *cl up: led over 6f out: pushed clr 2f out: styd on strly: unchal* **14/1**

1 **2** 9 **Genius Boy**$^{42}$ 941 4-9-4 **71** ........ LukeMorris 3 76
(James Tate) *trckd ldrs: pushed along wl over 3f out: rdn over 2f out: sn chsng wnr: drvn over 1f out and no imp* **5/4**$^{1}$

0010 **3** 3¾ **Magnolia Ridge (IRE)**$^{19}$ 1307 4-8-13 **71** ........ (p) JacobButterfield(5) 11 69
(Kristin Stubbs) *hld up towards rr: hdwy 3f out: swtchd to outer and rdn along 2f out: kpt on to take mod 3rd ins fnl f* **20/1**

50-4 **4** 2½ **King Of The Celts (IRE)**$^{26}$ 1167 6-9-3 **70** ........ PhillipMakin 12 63
(Tim Easterby) *hld up and bhd: hdwy over 2f out: sn rdn and plugged on same pce fr over 1f out: n.d* **12/1**

000- **5** 1 **Maybeme**$^{231}$ 6130 8-8-6 **66** ow1 ........ (p) MeganCarberry(7) 10 57
(Neville Bycroft) *sn outpcd in rr: pushed along 5f out: rdn and sme hdwy over 2f out: plugged on one pce: n.d* **33/1**

150- **6** 1¼ **Judicious**$^{187}$ 7369 7-9-0 **67** ........ AndrewMullen 7 56
(Geoffrey Harker) *hld up in tch: hdwy to chse ldrs 3f out: rdn along over 2f out: sn drvn and wknd* **40/1**

/30- **7** 2 **Hurry Home Poppa (IRE)**$^{199}$ 7066 4-9-1 **68** ........ TomQueally 1 53
(John Mackie) *hld up: a towards rr* **33/1**

1-62 **8** nk **Bling King**$^{3}$ 1607 5-9-5 **72** ........ (p) PJMcDonald 9 56
(Geoffrey Harker) *chsd ldrs: effrt 3f out: rdn along over 2f out: drvn wl over 1f out and sn wknd* **5/1**$^{2}$

244- **9** 1 **Saint Thomas (IRE)**$^{167}$ 5382 7-9-3 **70** ........ LiamJones 6 52
(John Mackie) *trckd ldrs: pushed along 4f out: rdn 3f out: sn wknd* **9/1**

5-63 **10** 3¾ **Qibtee (FR)**$^{16}$ 1356 4-8-7 **60** oh2 ........ JoeFanning 2 35
(Les Eyre) *led: hdd over 6f out: rdn along over 3f out: wknd over 2f out* **7/1**$^{3}$

50-5 **11** 44 **Wyldfire (IRE)**$^{22}$ 1245 4-8-10 **63** ........ BenCurtis 5
(Ruth Carr) *rrd s and s.i.s: t.k.h and sddle sn slipped: hdwy on outer to chse ldrs 1/2-way: wd st: sn bhd and eased fnl 2f* **33/1**

2m 1.79s (-5.21) **Going Correction** -0.325s/f (Firm) **11** Ran SP% **114.0**
Speed ratings (Par 103): **107,99,96,94,94 93,91,91,90,87 52**
CSF £28.34 CT £326.64 TOTE £18.40: £5.30, £1.10, £3.80; EX 45.00 Trifecta £827.80.
**Owner** Hambleton Racing Ltd XXX **Bred** Moyglare Stud Farm Ltd **Trained** Nawton, N Yorks
■ Rule 4 of 5p in the pound applies to all bets; Withdrawn: Apache Glory

**FOCUS**
The market only wanted to know one horse in this ordinary handicap and although the race was won by a wide margin, it wasn't by the short-priced favourite. They went a strong gallop and recorded a decent time. Tricky form to pin down, the winner recording his best effort since his early 3yo days.

## 1661 FOLLOW US ON TWITTER @BEVERLEY_RACES H'CAP 1m 1f 207y
**4:30** (4:31) (Class 5) (0-70,75) 3-Y-O **£3,234** (£962; £481; £240) **Stalls** Low

Form RPR

244- **1** **Opera Fan (FR)**$^{216}$ 6605 3-9-0 **62** ........ JoeFanning 6 68
(Mark Johnston) *trckd ldr: hdwy over 2f out: rdn to ld over 1f out: drvn and kpt on wl fnl f* **5/2**$^{2}$

053- **2** 1 **Lunar Spirit**$^{191}$ 7260 3-9-4 **66** ........ PaulHanagan 2 70
(Ralph Beckett) *trckd ldng pair: pushed along wl over 2f out: rdn wl over 1f out: styd on to chse wnr ent fnl f: drvn whn sltly hmpd last 100yds: one pce towards fin* **5/2**$^{2}$

30-5 **3** 1 **Sellingallthetime (IRE)**$^{5}$ 1588 3-9-3 **65** ........$^{1}$ AndrewMullen 1 69+
(Michael Appleby) *carried hd high and t.k.h: hld up in rr: hdwy to chse ldrs wl over 1f out: effrt on inner ent fnl f: sn rdn: n.m.r: tried to swtchd lft and hmpd last 100yds: one pce after* **2/1**$^{1}$

34-0 **4** 1¼ **In Vino Veritas (IRE)**$^{16}$ 1357 3-9-5 **67** ........ PJMcDonald 5 67
(Ann Duffield) *trckd ldng pair: rdn along wl over 2f out: drvn and sltly outpcd wl over 1f out: kpt on u.p fnl f* **12/1**

2241 **5** ¾ **Zamra (IRE)**$^{8}$ 1508 3-9-13 **75** 6ex ........ (p) LukeMorris 3 73
(James Tate) *hld up in rr: hdwy on outer over 3f out: chsd ldng pair over 2f out and sn rdn: drvn over 1f out and sn one pce* **6/1**$^{3}$

5-03 **6** 10 **Casper Lee (IRE)**$^{64}$ 664 3-8-10 **58** ........ PaulPickard 7 37
(Michael Herrington) *led: rdn along 2f out: hdd over 1f out: sn wknd* **33/1**

2m 5.47s (-1.53) **Going Correction** -0.325s/f (Firm) **6** Ran SP% **115.4**
Speed ratings (Par 98): **93,92,91,90,89 81**
CSF £9.58 TOTE £4.20: £2.40, £1.30; EX 14.50 Trifecta £34.00.
**Owner** Sheikh Majid bin Mohammed Al Maktoum **Bred** T , D & A De La Heronniere **Trained** Middleham Moor, N Yorks

**FOCUS**
A modest 3yo handicap and the winning time was 3.68sec slower than the preceding race. The form looks sound.

## 1662 BEVERLEY FOLK FESTIVAL HERE IN JUNE MAIDEN STKS 1m 100y
**5:00** (5:04) (Class 5) 3-Y-O+ **£3,234** (£962; £481; £240) **Stalls** Low

Form RPR

24- **1** **Night Party (IRE)**$^{244}$ 5716 3-8-8 0 ow1 ........ KierenFallon 2 76+
(Saeed bin Suroor) *trckd ldng pair: sltly hmpd 5f out: pushed along over 3f out: hdwy to chal over 2f out: led wl over 1f out: rdn clr ent fnl f: kpt on* **1/4**$^{1}$

00-3 **2** 2 **Notebook**$^{101}$ 167 3-8-12 72 ........ (p) LiamJones 3 74
(William Haggas) *led: pushed along 3f out: rdn over 2f out: hdd wl over 1f out: kpt on same pce* **5/1**$^{2}$

3240 **3** 5 **Tarrafal (IRE)**$^{17}$ 1352 3-8-12 74 ........ AdrianNicholls 4 63
(Mark Johnston) *trckd ldr: effrt 3f out: rdn along and ch over 2f out: drvn wl over 1f out: sn one pce* **16/1**

4 30 **Cayjo** 3-8-12 0 ........ JoeFanning 1 35
(Mark Johnston) *hld up in rr: effrt and sme hdwy on outer over 3f out: rdn along wl over 2f out: wknd and eased wl over 1f out* **8/1[3]**

1m 47.77s (0.17) **Going Correction** -0.325s/f (Firm) **4** Ran SP% **113.7**
Speed ratings (Par 103): **86,84,79,49**
CSF £2.26 TOTE £1.20; EX 2.50 Trifecta £5.90.
**Owner** Godolphin **Bred** Stiftung Gestut Fahrhof **Trained** Newmarket, Suffolk

**FOCUS**
An uncompetitive maiden run at a modest pace and in a slow time. The winner's pre-race form was already good enough to take this.
T/Jkpt: Not won. T/Plt: £228.80 to a £1 stake. Pool: £57,402.02 - 182.10 winning units. T/Qpdt: £14.80 to a £1 stake. Pool: £3923.18 - 195.82 winning units. JR

# BRIGHTON (L-H)
Thursday, April 24

**OFFICIAL GOING: Good to soft (good in places; 6.3)**
Wind: Moderate, half against Weather: Fine

## 1663 STEPHANIE LEIGHTON 50TH BIRTHDAY MAIDEN STKS 5f 59y
4:50 (4:52) (Class 5) 2-Y-O £2,587 (£770; £384; £192) Stalls Low

Form RPR

1 **Bronze Maquette (IRE)** 2-9-0 0 ........ WilliamBuick 4 72+
(Gary Moore) *dwlt: green and pushed along in rr: hdwy 2f out: hung lft over 1f out: led ins fnl f: sn clr* **2/1[1]**

4 2 5 **Macarthurs Park (IRE)**[19] 1314 2-9-0 0 ........ RichardKingscote 7 54
(Tom Dascombe) *led tl ins fnl f: flashed tail and qckly outpcd by wnr* **2/1[1]**

0 3 2 ¾ **Mandarin Girl**[17] 1536 2-9-0 0 ........ SeanLevey 5 44
(Richard Hannon) *in tch: rdn to chse ldrs whn n.m.r wl over 1f out: sn outpcd* **5/2[2]**

6 4 2 **Tommys Geal**[17] 1349 2-9-0 0 ........ LiamKeniry 3 37
(Michael Madgwick) *s.s: towards rr: rdn and nt trble ldrs fnl 2f* **16/1[3]**

5 3 ½ **Please Don't Tease (IRE)** 2-9-0 0 ........ RyanWhile(5) 1 29
(Bill Turner) *chsd ldrs tl wknd 2f out* **16/1[3]**

60 6 3 ¾ **Keep 'r Lit**[17] 1349 2-9-0 0 ........ SteveDrowne 6 11
(David Evans) *chsd ldr tl wknd wl over 1f out* **33/1**

1m 3.55s (1.25) **Going Correction** +0.125s/f (Good) **6** Ran SP% **109.9**
Speed ratings (Par 92): **95,87,82,79,73 67**
CSF £5.98 TOTE £2.50: £1.10, £1.40; EX 7.10 Trifecta £12.20.
**Owner** R A Green **Bred** Rosetown Bloodstock Ltd **Trained** Lower Beeding, W Sussex

**FOCUS**
They went hard early on in this modest 2yo maiden. The winner did it well and is clearly capable of better than the bare form.

## 1664 HARRINGTONSLETTINGS.CO.UK H'CAP 1m 1f 209y
5:25 (5:26) (Class 6) (0-60,59) 4-Y-O+ £1,940 (£577; £288; £144) Stalls High

Form RPR

040- 1 **Megalala (IRE)**[189] 7321 13-8-11 **49** ........ WilliamCarson 3 67
(John Bridger) *mde all: wnt clr 5f out: kpt on gamely fnl 3f: unchal* **10/1**

-501 2 9 **Nelson Quay (IRE)**[19] 1302 4-9-7 **59** ........ SteveDrowne 9 60
(Jeremy Gask) *prom in chsng gp: rdn and lost pl over 2f out: styd on to take 2nd nr fin* **7/2[1]**

0-00 3 nk **Rezwaan**[36] 1021 7-9-2 **54** ........(b) ShaneKelly 13 54
(Murty McGrath) *hld up in midfield: hdwy 3f out: wnt 7 l 2nd over 2f out: one pce and nvr trbld wnr: lost 2nd nr fin* **7/2[1]**

3664 4 1 **Mr Lando**[43] 922 5-9-2 **59** ........ RyanTate(5) 1 57
(Tony Carroll) *mid-div: hdwy on inner 5f out: styd on same pce fnl 3f* **4/1[2]**

404- 5 shd **Lindsay's Dream**[24] 3655 8-8-4 **45** ........(p) SimonPearce(3) 4 43
(Zoe Davison) *bhd: rdn and hdwy 2f out: nvr nr to chal* **33/1**

102- 6 nk **Who's That Chick (IRE)**[192] 7246 5-8-12 **57** ........ DanielCremin(7) 6 55
(Ralph J Smith) *t.k.h towards rr: hdwy and prom in chsng gp 3f out: rdn over 2f out: one pce* **5/1[3]**

4020 7 1 ¾ **Litmus (USA)**[19] 1302 5-8-7 **50** ........(b) JackDuern(5) 11 44
(Simon Dow) *towards rr: rdn over 3f out: nvr nrr* **14/1**

34- 8 4 ½ **Hypnotism**[139] 8186 4-8-7 **45** ........[1] RobertHavlin 2 31
(Ronald Harris) *chsd ldrs tl wknd wl over 1f out* **14/1**

/25- 9 1 **Hail To Princess**[296] 3918 4-8-7 **45** ........ DavidProbert 8 29
(Patrick Chamings) *towards rr: rdn and struggling fnl 3f* **20/1**

450- 10 ½ **Hawk Moth (IRE)**[189] 7321 6-9-6 **58** ........(b) SamHitchcott 12 41
(John Spearing) *stdd s: plld hrd in rr: rdn and modest hdwy 2f out: n.d* **20/1**

0000 11 5 **Mists Of Time (IRE)**[30] 1087 4-8-7 **50** ........ TimClark(5) 10 23
(Pat Eddery) *mid-div tl lost pl and btn over 2f out* **33/1**

000- 12 18 **Anginola (IRE)**[212] 6737 5-9-5 **57** ........ LiamKeniry 14
(Laura Mongan) *chsd ldrs tl wknd 3f out* **25/1**

0-00 13 2 ¼ **Back On The Trail**[15] 1385 4-9-5 **57** ........(p) RichardKingscote 5
(Michael Blake) *chsd wnr tl wknd qckly over 2f out* **16/1**

2m 3.95s (0.35) **Going Correction** +0.125s/f (Good) **13** Ran SP% **128.7**
Speed ratings (Par 101): **103,95,95,94,94 94,93,89,88,88 84,69,68**
CSF £45.50 CT £155.09 TOTE £9.30: £2.80, £1.90, £1.90; EX 63.50 Trifecta £673.00.
**Owner** Trevor Wallace **Bred** Joseph Gallagher **Trained** Liphook, Hants

**FOCUS**
This was taken apart by 13yo course specialist Megalala, who is rated to last year's best.

## 1665 BRIGHTON & HOVE STREAMLINE TAXIS H'CAP 7f 214y
5:55 (5:59) (Class 5) (0-75,74) 4-Y-O+ £2,587 (£770; £384; £192) Stalls Low

Form RPR

10-3 1 **Uncle Dermot (IRE)**[20] 1281 6-9-0 **67** ........ RichardKingscote 1 76
(Brendan Powell) *mde all: clr over 1f out: comf* **6/4[1]**

1231 2 2 ¾ **Gaelic Silver (FR)**[22] 1236 8-8-12 **72** ........ HectorCrouch(7) 8 75
(Gary Moore) *in tch: effrt over 2f out: styd on to chse wnr over 1f out: no imp* **7/1**

1100 3 1 ¼ **Whitby Jet (IRE)**[17] 1354 6-9-6 **73** ........ LiamKeniry 2 73
(Ed Vaughan) *chsd ldr: rdn over 2f out: kpt on fnl f* **6/1[3]**

500- 4 2 ½ **Siouxperhero (IRE)**[190] 7306 5-9-1 **68** ........(p) MartinDwyer 3 62
(William Muir) *dwlt: towards rr: rdn 3f out: nvr able to chal* **14/1**

0-00 5 1 ¾ **Keene's Pointe**[62] 690 4-9-0 **67** ........ SebSanders 4 57
(J W Hills) *chsd wnr tl wknd over 1f out* **8/1**

3135 6 ½ **Queen Aggie (IRE)**[15] 1393 4-9-4 **71** ........ SteveDrowne 9 60
(David Evans) *towards rr: rdn and nt trble ldrs fnl 2f* **10/1**

2020 7 ½ **Bloodsweatandtears**[23] 1215 6-8-9 **65** ........ MichaelJMMurphy(3) 5 53
(William Knight) *sn bhd: rdn and carried hd high fnl 2f: nvr nr ldrs* **5/1[2]**

005 8 4 **Toymaker**[27] 1152 7-9-2 **74** ........(v[1]) RyanTate(5) 10 53
(Phil McEntee) *chsd ldrs tl wknd 2f out* **16/1**

1m 36.61s (0.61) **Going Correction** +0.125s/f (Good) **8** Ran SP% **116.2**
Speed ratings (Par 103): **101,98,97,94,92 92,91,87**
CSF £12.89 CT £50.68 TOTE £2.20: £1.10, £2.20, £2.10; EX 12.10 Trifecta £43.60.
**Owner** K Rhatigan **Bred** Ballyhane Stud **Trained** Upper Lambourn, Berks

**FOCUS**
A modest handicap and another winner from the front. The form is rated around the second and third.

## 1666 STREAMLINETAXIS.ORG CLASSIFIED STKS 7f 214y
6:25 (6:26) (Class 6) 3-Y-O+ £1,940 (£577; £288; £144) Stalls Low

Form RPR

2323 1 **Pour La Victoire (IRE)**[29] 1105 4-9-3 53 ........ RobertTart(3) 7 65+
(Tony Carroll) *in tch: chsd ldr 5f out: led over 1f out: drvn clr: coasted in nr fin* **11/10[1]**

3433 2 1 ¾ **Clapperboard**[21] 1257 3-8-6 52 ........(b) WilliamCarson 1 53
(Paul Fitzsimons) *led at gd pce: 3 l clr 5f out: hdd over 1f out: one pce: clsd on easing wnr nr fin* **8/1**

0000 3 3 **Knight Charm**[14] 1408 4-9-6 55 ........ DavidProbert 5 50
(Gay Kelleway) *in tch: effrt and hung bdly lft fr over 2f out: hrd rdn: one pce* **7/1[3]**

0000 4 6 **Admirals Walk (IRE)**[15] 1386 4-9-6 44 ........ LiamKeniry 2 36
(Barry Brennan) *prom: hrd rdn over 2f out: sn wknd* **16/1**

6060 5 3 ¼ **Sakhee'Ssquirrel**[29] 1107 3-8-6 50 ........ FrankieMcDonald 4 25
(Sean Curran) *outpcd in rr: drvn along 4f out: n.d* **8/1**

0550 6 11 **Nifty Kier**[2] 1639 5-9-1 51 ........(vt) RyanTate(5) 6
(Phil McEntee) *towards rr: rdn 3f out: n.d after* **4/1[2]**

06-6 7 8 **Soubrette**[56] 755 4-9-6 40 ........(p[1]) SteveDrowne 3
(Geoffrey Deacon) *chsd wnr 3f: wknd 3f out* **33/1**

1m 37.5s (1.50) **Going Correction** +0.125s/f (Good)
**WFA** 3 from 4yo+ 14lb **7** Ran SP% **111.2**
Speed ratings (Par 101): **97,95,92,86,83 72,64**
CSF £10.10 TOTE £1.90: £1.20, £2.60; EX 5.20 Trifecta £14.90.
**Owner** Curry House Corner **Bred** L Fox **Trained** Cropthorne, Worcs

**FOCUS**
A weak classified event, run at a sound pace. The form is rated around the winner.

## 1667 PAPA JOHN'S PIZZA IN BRIGHTON H'CAP 6f 209y
6:55 (6:57) (Class 4) (0-85,85) 4-Y-O+ £4,690 (£1,395; £697; £348) Stalls Low

Form RPR

3400 1 **Corporal Maddox**[10] 1492 7-9-7 **85** ........(p) SteveDrowne 5 93
(Ronald Harris) *hld up in rr: hdwy and swtchd rt over 1f out: str run u.p to ld fnl 100yds* **8/1**

2-23 2 ¾ **Aqua Ardens (GER)**[91] 300 6-8-12 **76** ........(t) SeanLevey 7 82
(George Baker) *chsd ldr: hrd rdn over 1f out: r.o* **11/4[2]**

1/0- 3 nse **Kosika (USA)**[462] 243 4-8-9 **73** ........ WilliamBuick 1 79
(Mark Johnston) *led: hrd rdn and kpt on fnl f: hdd fnl 100yds* **5/2[1]**

0-46 4 3 **Great Expectations**[20] 1275 6-8-10 **74** ........ DavidProbert 4 72
(J R Jenkins) *in tch: effrt over 2f out: one pce* **4/1**

1-00 5 5 **Blazing Knight (IRE)**[27] 1144 4-8-8 **72** ........(p) RichardKingscote 6 57
(Chris Gordon) *in tch tl wknd 2f out* **33/1**

6-65 6 2 ½ **Lionheart**[29] 1102 4-8-13 **77** ........ ShaneKelly 3 56
(Peter Crate) *chsd ldrs tl wknd 2f out* **3/1[3]**

1m 22.76s (-0.34) **Going Correction** +0.125s/f (Good) **6** Ran SP% **114.3**
Speed ratings (Par 105): **106,105,105,101,95 93**
CSF £30.89 TOTE £8.10: £3.20, £1.30; EX 25.20 Trifecta £83.10.
**Owner** Robert & Nina Bailey **Bred** Theobalds Stud **Trained** Earlswood, Monmouths
■ Stewards' Enquiry : Steve Drowne one-day ban: careless riding (May 8)

**FOCUS**
There was a fair pace on in this modest handicap. The winner is rated in line with his winter AW form.

## 1668 FROSTS4CARS.CO.UK H'CAP 6f 209y
7:25 (7:26) (Class 6) (0-60,60) 4-Y-O+ £1,940 (£577; £288; £144) Stalls Low

Form RPR

-132 1 **Athletic**[19] 1297 5-9-7 **60** ........(v) JimCrowley 1 69
(Andrew Reid) *dwlt: t.k.h in rr: hdwy and nt clr run over 1f out: fnd room: str run to ld fnl stride* **4/1[2]**

50-0 2 shd **Mrs Warren**[104] 114 4-9-5 **58** ........ MartinDwyer 6 67
(George Baker) *mid-div: hdwy 2f out: led ins fnl f: kpt on u.p: hdd fnl stride* **20/1**

4006 3 2 **Last Minute Lisa (IRE)**[19] 1297 4-8-10 **49** ........ SeanLevey 12 53
(Sylvester Kirk) *hld up towards rr: nt clr run 2f out: shkn up and hdwy over 1f out: gng on at fin* **16/1**

40-4 4 hd **Frosted Off**[50] 844 4-8-7 **46** oh1 ........ SamHitchcott 10 49
(John Spearing) *sn chsng ldr: led over 2f out tl ins fnl f: one pce* **50/1**

0565 5 1 ¾ **Perfect Pastime**[14] 1408 6-8-10 **56** ........(b) DanielCremin(7) 3 55
(Jim Boyle) *plld hrd towards rr: rdn and hdwy 2f out: n.m.r wl over 1f out: styd on* **12/1**

2-65 6 2 ¼ **Thewestwalian (USA)**[16] 1365 6-8-7 **46** oh1 ........[1] WilliamCarson 2 39
(Peter Hiatt) *led 1f: prom tl no ex over 1f out* **25/1**

0006 7 ½ **Fairy Mist (IRE)**[27] 1141 7-8-2 **46** oh1 ........(v) RyanWhile(5) 8 38
(John Bridger) *prom: led after 1f tl over 2f out: wknd 1f out* **20/1**

2432 8 1 ¼ **Lutine Charlie (IRE)**[41] 963 7-9-2 **55** ........(p) LiamKeniry 5 43
(Pat Eddery) *in tch on rail: rdn and no hdwy fnl 2f* **8/1[3]**

5650 9 nk **Minimee**[82] 424 4-9-2 **55** ........(v) DavidProbert 13 43
(Phil McEntee) *in tch tl outpcd fnl 2f* **16/1**

-401 10 nk **Red Invader (IRE)**[16] 1365 4-9-6 **59** ........ WilliamBuick 4 46
(Charles Hills) *chsd ldrs tl wknd fnl f* **6/4[1]**

1332 11 6 **Catalyze**[5] 1573 6-9-4 **57** ........(t) SteveDrowne 11 28
(Ann Stokell) *dwlt: drvn along over 2f out: a towards rr* **10/1**

0000 12 6 **Cuthbert (IRE)**[15] 1386 7-8-4 **46** oh1 ........ JemmaMarshall(3) 9 2
(Michael Attwater) *a bhd* **66/1**

5060 13 ½ **Idle Curiosity (IRE)**[15] 1386 4-8-11 **50** ........ ShaneKelly 7 4
(Jim Boyle) *chsd ldrs tl rdn and wknd wl over 1f out: eased whn btn* **20/1**

1m 23.33s (0.23) **Going Correction** +0.125s/f (Good) **13** Ran SP% **121.2**
Speed ratings (Par 101): **103,102,100,100,98 95,95,93,93,93 86,79,78**
CSF £89.89 CT £1213.36 TOTE £3.80: £1.30, £6.90, £5.60; EX 81.70 Trifecta £858.00.
**Owner** A S Reid **Bred** A S Reid **Trained** Mill Hill, London NW7

**FOCUS**
An ordinary sprint handicap, run at a sound pace in the best relative time on the card. A stone turf best from the winner.

## 1669 STREAMLINE TAXIS H'CAP — 5f 213y
7:55 (7:55) (Class 5) (0-70,70) 3-Y-O — £2,587 (£770; £384; £192) Stalls Low

Form — RPR
4-34 1 **Iseemist (IRE)**[15] 1389 3-9-2 68 MichaelJMMurphy(3) 6 77
(John Gallagher) *chsd ldr: led over 2f out: drvn out* 5/1[3]
32-0 2 3/4 **Miss Brazil (IRE)**[15] 1400 3-9-7 70 SeanLevey 4 76
(Richard Hannon) *cl up in 4th: drvn to chse wnr over 1f out: r.o* 6/1
21-5 3 3/4 **Flashy Queen (IRE)**[27] 1146 3-9-7 70 SteveDrowne 7 74
(Joseph Tuite) *chsd ldrs: hrd rdn and sltly outpcd 2f out: styd on fnl f* 7/1
443- 4 1 1/4 **Baltic Brave (IRE)**[168] 7790 3-9-6 69 (t) WilliamBuick 2 69
(Hughie Morrison) *off the pce in 5th: effrt 2f out: styd on fnl f* 5/2[1]
300- 5 2 1/4 **Bowsers Bold**[226] 6285 3-9-1 64 HayleyTurner 3 57
(Marcus Tregoning) *dwlt: bhd: rdn over 2f out: styd on fnl f* 9/2[2]
0-33 6 4 **Seven Lucky Seven**[52] 816 3-9-1 64 SebSanders 1 44
(Nick Littmoden) *off the pce in 6th: effrt 2f out: wknd fnl f* 9/2[2]
25 7 6 **Black Vale (IRE)**[23] 1225 3-9-3 66 (t) DavidProbert 5 27
(Phil McEntee) *led at gd pce tl over 2f out: wknd over 1f out* 20/1

1m 11.21s (1.01) **Going Correction** +0.125s/f (Good) 7 Ran SP% 113.1
Speed ratings (Par 98): **98,97,96,94,91 86,78**
CSF £33.67 TOTE £9.70: £4.80, £3.30; EX 28.90 Trifecta £144.50.
**Owner** K Marsden **Bred** J P Lim,K Marsden & South Hatch Racing **Trained** Chastleton, Oxon

**FOCUS**
There was no hanging about in this modest 3yo sprint handicap. The form is rated around the better 2yo efforts of the first three.
T/Plt: £24.60 to a £1 stake. Pool: £52,181.47 - 1547.61 winning units. T/Qpdt: £12.10 to a £1 stake. Pool: £5,581.80 - 338.60 winning units. LM

# 1303 NEWCASTLE (L-H)
Thursday, April 24

**OFFICIAL GOING: Good (good to firm in places; 7.5)**
Wind: light half behind Weather: Fine

## 1670 EBF/H MALONE & SONS NOVICE STKS (BOBIS RACE) — 5f
5:05 (5:07) (Class 4) 2-Y-O — £6,469 (£1,925; £962; £481) Stalls High

Form — RPR
6 1 **Ko Cache (IRE)**[16] 1363 2-8-9 0 TomEaves 4 75
(Keith Dalgleish) *mde all: pressed thrght: rdn 2f out: kpt on: jst hld on* 16/1
2 nse **Littlemissblakeney** 2-8-4 0 NoelGarbutt(5) 6 75
(Hugo Palmer) *trckd ldng pair: rdn 2f out: chal strly ins fnl f: kpt on: jst hld* 16/1
6 3 3/4 **Makin A Statement (IRE)**[5] 1583 2-8-11 0 IanBrennan(3) 8 77
(John Quinn) *trckd ldng pair: gng wl whn n.m.r over 1f out: swtchd lft appr fnl f: kpt on* 11/4[2]
3 4 1/2 **No One Knows**[10] 1488 2-8-9 0 GrahamLee 3 70
(J W Hills) *trckd ldng pair towards outer: rdn and hung lft over 1f out: kpt on fnl f* 9/2
5 1 1/4 **Mignolino (IRE)** 2-9-0 0 GrahamGibbons 1 71+
(David Barron) *dwlt: hld up: pushed along 1/2-way: kpt on fnl f* 10/3[3]
41 6 1 **Low Cut Affair (IRE)**[10] 1488 2-8-11 0 MartinLane 7 64
(David Evans) *racd keenly: pressed ldr: rdn 2f out: wknd ins fnl f* 5/2[1]
0 7 1 1/4 **Bahango (IRE)**[8] 1504 2-9-0 0 JamesSullivan 2 62
(Kristin Stubbs) *hld up in tch: pushed along 1/2-way: nvr threatened* 28/1
8 1 3/4 **The Card Players (IRE)** 2-9-0 0 DaleSwift 5 56
(Brian Ellison) *hld up: nvr threatened* 50/1

1m 0.89s (-0.21) **Going Correction** -0.675s/f (Hard) 8 Ran SP% 113.7
Speed ratings (Par 94): **74,73,72,71,69 68,66,63**
CSF £231.97 TOTE £15.20: £3.90, £4.50, £2.50; EX 78.80 Trifecta £1346.90 Part won..
**Owner** Straightline Construction Ltd **Bred** Tally-Ho Stud **Trained** Carluke, S Lanarks

**FOCUS**
After 8mm overnight rain the ground had eased slightly but was still on the fast side. A 2yo novice event with one previous winner in the line-up. The time and compressed finish don't help the form, which could be rated higher.

## 1671 CRABBIE'S SCOTTISH RASPBERRY MAIDEN STKS — 5f
5:40 (5:40) (Class 5) 3-Y-O+ — £2,587 (£770; £384; £192) Stalls High

Form — RPR
2- 1 **G Force (IRE)**[181] 7501 3-9-3 0 DanielTudhope 4 91+
(David O'Meara) *dwlt: midfield: pushed along and hdwy 2f out: rdn to ld jst ins fnl f: kpt on* 1/2[1]
0-2 2 1/2 **Soul Brother (IRE)**[19] 1304 3-9-3 0 DuranFentiman 8 89
(Tim Easterby) *trckd ldrs: rdn to ld appr fnl f: sn hdd: kpt on but a hld* 9/2[2]
3 4 **Saakhen (IRE)**[344] 2373 3-9-3 0 TonyHamilton 1 75
(Richard Fahey) *chsd ldrs: rdn 2f out: one pce and no ch w ldng pair fnl f* 7/1[3]
0-3 4 5 **Storyline (IRE)**[12] 1441 3-8-12 0 DavidAllan 5 52
(Tim Easterby) *prom: rdn 2f out: wknd fnl f* 20/1
350- 5 1/2 **Reet Thicknstrong**[295] 3942 3-8-12 0 RoystonFfrench 7 50
(Bryan Smart) *led: racd keenly: rdn whn hd appr fnl f: wknd* 66/1
6 3/4 **Carnamoney** 3-9-3 0 GrahamGibbons 3 52
(David Barron) *dwlt: hld up: rdn and outpcd 1/2-way: minor late hdwy* 50/1
323- 7 1/2 **Lord Clyde**[320] 3077 3-9-3 76 PatrickMathers 10 51
(Richard Fahey) *dwlt: midfield: rdn 2f out: wknd fnl f* 8/1
8 6 **Mossy Marie (IRE)** 3-8-9 0 JasonHart(3) 2 24
(Eric Alston) *hld up: nvr threatened* 50/1
6-5 9 3/4 **Spinner Lane**[16] 1361 3-8-12 0 PaulQuinn 6 21
(Richard Whitaker) *midfield: rdn 1/2-way: sn wknd* 66/1
10 1/2 **Fujin** 3-9-3 0 GrahamLee 9 24
(Noel Wilson) *slowly away: hld up: a towards rr* 33/1

57.81s (-3.29) **Going Correction** -0.675s/f (Hard) course record 10 Ran SP% 123.1
Speed ratings (Par 103): **99,98,91,83,83 81,81,71,70,69**
CSF £3.22 TOTE £1.50: £1.10, £1.80, £1.60; EX 4.60 Trifecta £13.60.
**Owner** Middleham Park Racing XVIII & Partner **Bred** Kildaragh Stud & Twelve Oaks Stud Est **Trained** Nawton, N Yorks

**FOCUS**
The first two pulled clear in this and look above average. The form is rated on the positive side.

## 1672 LORDS TAVERNERS H'CAP — 6f
6:15 (6:15) (Class 4) (0-85,85) 4-Y-O+ — £4,690 (£1,395; £697; £348) Stalls High

Form — RPR
56-1 1 **My Name Is Rio (IRE)**[12] 1440 4-8-10 74 PaulMulrennan 9 87
(Michael Dods) *trckd ldr: rdn to chal over 1f out: kpt on: led 50yds out* 11/4[1]
0-3 2 nk **Orbit The Moon (IRE)**[12] 1447 6-8-2 71 (tp) ConnorBeasley(5) 5 83
(Michael Dods) *trckd ldr: rdn to ld 2f out: sn pressed: kpt on: hdd 50yds out* 13/2
06-6 3 7 **King Of Eden (IRE)**[25] 1190 8-9-0 81 (p) JasonHart(3) 7 71+
(Eric Alston) *hld up: rdn over 3f out: hdwy over 2f out: one pce: wnt 3rd 110yds out* 4/1[2]
5-31 4 1/2 **Trade Secret**[12] 1447 7-9-1 79 DavidAllan 11 67
(Mel Brittain) *in tch: rdn 3f out: one pce and nvr threatened* 11/2[3]
00-0 5 nse **Line Of Reason (IRE)**[24] 1212 4-9-4 82 GrahamLee 1 70
(Paul Midgley) *midfield: rdn over 2f out: one pce and nvr threatened* 16/1
1411 6 1 **Star Up In The Sky (USA)**[21] 1266 4-8-8 77 (b) ShaneGray(5) 6 62
(Kevin Ryan) *led: rdn whn hdd 2f out: wknd fnl f* 20/1
024- 7 1 **Time And Place**[272] 4734 4-9-1 79 DavidNolan 3 60
(Richard Fahey) *sltly hmpd s: hld up in midfield: pushed along over 2f out: keeping on one pce whn n.m.r 50yds out* 17/2
360- 8 1 3/4 **Head Space (IRE)**[208] 6831 6-9-7 85 (p) JamesSullivan 10 61
(Ruth Carr) *hld up: n.m.r on rail 3f out tl over 1f out: no ch after* 14/1
010- 9 4 **Just The Tonic**[156] 7964 7-8-13 77 DanielTudhope 8 40
(Marjorie Fife) *hld up: nvr threatened* 40/1
00-5 10 2 **Trader Jack**[106] 80 5-9-5 83 StephenCraine 2 40
(David Flood) *in tch: rdn 3f out: wknd over 1f out* 12/1
056- 11 3 **Enderby Spirit (GR)**[117] 8431 8-8-13 77 (t) RoystonFfrench 4 24
(Bryan Smart) *rrd s: hld up: nvr threatened* 25/1

1m 11.44s (-3.16) **Going Correction** -0.375s/f (Firm) 11 Ran SP% 117.2
Speed ratings (Par 105): **106,105,96,95,95 94,92,90,85,82 78**
CSF £20.15 CT £71.54 TOTE £3.80: £2.00, £1.90, £1.70; EX 28.00 Trifecta £160.70.
**Owner** K Kirkup & Mrs T Galletley **Bred** Anthony J Keane **Trained** Denton, Co Durham
■ Stewards' Enquiry : Stephen Craine four-day ban: careless riding (May 8-10,12)

**FOCUS**
An unsatisfactory sprint handicap with plenty of trouble leaving the stalls. A 1-2 for Michael Dods with the winner progressing from Thirsk.

## 1673 RUTHERFORD & CO H'CAP — 1m (R)
6:45 (6:45) (Class 6) (0-65,65) 4-Y-O+ — £1,940 (£577; £288; £144) Stalls Centre

Form — RPR
/0-0 1 **Charles De Mille**[15] 1376 6-9-0 58 AndrewElliott 3 68
(George Moore) *hld up in rr: stl plenty to do over 2f out: angled rt to outside over 1f out: r.o strly: led towards fin* 25/1
5652 2 3/4 **Outlaw Torn (IRE)**[26] 1167 5-9-2 60 (e) RobbieFitzpatrick 2 68
(Richard Guest) *miefield: rdn and hdwy over 2f out: led 1f out: kpt on: hdd towards fin* 9/2[1]
4-44 3 2 **Violent Velocity (IRE)**[19] 1310 11-9-1 62 IanBrennan(3) 14 65
(John Quinn) *hld up: hdwy over 2f out: rdn 2f out: kpt on* 9/1
000- 4 1 **Nelson's Bay**[156] 7952 5-9-4 62 GrahamLee 7 63
(Wilf Storey) *trckd ldrs: rdn and ev ch over 1f out: one pce fnl f* 16/1
00-1 5 1/2 **Graceful Act**[19] 1309 6-8-8 57 ShirleyTeasdale(5) 8 57
(Ron Barr) *midfield: rdn and hdwy 2f out: one pce fnl f* 5/1[2]
405- 6 1 **Tanawar (IRE)**[199] 7067 4-9-4 62 JamesSullivan 16 60
(Ruth Carr) *t.k.h in midfield: hdwy over 2f out: rdn to ld over 1f out: hdd 1f out: no ex* 7/1[3]
0-65 7 1 **Al Enbess (IRE)**[23] 1222 4-8-8 55 JasonHart(3) 1 50
(Ruth Carr) *midfield: briefly n.m.r over 2f out: rdn and hdwy over 1f out: no further imp fnl f* 20/1
35- 8 3 1/2 **Seldom (IRE)**[319] 3138 8-8-13 57 DavidAllan 11 44
(Mel Brittain) *midfield: n.m.r over 2f out: nvr threatened* 10/1
210/ 9 1 3/4 **Aseela (IRE)**[565] 6873 4-8-13 64 KieranSchofield(7) 6 47
(George Moore) *hld up: nvr threatened* 22/1
060- 10 nk **Eastlands Lad (IRE)**[188] 7343 5-8-9 53 TomEaves 10 36
(Micky Hammond) *in tch: rdn over 3f out: wknd over 1f out* 33/1
60-0 11 2 3/4 **Mcmonagle (USA)**[11] 96 6-9-4 62 (tp) GrahamGibbons 9 38
(Alan Brown) *prom: rdn to ld 3f out: hdd over 1f out: wknd* 16/1
50-6 12 5 **Look On By**[23] 1227 4-8-13 57 RaulDaSilva 5 22
(Ruth Carr) *led: hdd 3f out: sn wknd* 9/1
566- 13 1 1/2 **Eastward Ho**[289] 4135 6-9-5 63 TonyHamilton 4 24
(Michael Herrington) *in tch on inner: rdn over 2f out: wknd over 1f out* 7/1[3]
/0-0 14 9 **Cheeky Wee Red**[19] 1310 6-8-10 54 PaulMulrennan 15
(Alistair Whillans) *trckd ldrs: rdn over 3f out: sn wknd* 33/1

1m 44.13s (-1.17) **Going Correction** -0.075s/f (Good) 14 Ran SP% 119.5
Speed ratings (Par 101): **102,101,99,98,97 96,95,92,90,90 87,82,80,71**
CSF £126.81 CT £1144.45 TOTE £43.20: £15.20, £2.20, £3.90; EX 284.70 Trifecta £600.40.
**Owner** Mrs Liz Ingham **Bred** St Clare Hall Stud **Trained** Middleham Moor, N Yorks

**FOCUS**
The first three came from the rear in this modest handicap. The winner rates back to his best.

## 1674 DSE NORTHERN LTD H'CAP — 1m 4f 93y
7:15 (7:15) (Class 6) (0-60,60) 4-Y-O+ — £1,940 (£577; £288; £144) Stalls Centre

Form — RPR
203- 1 **Frosty Berry**[193] 7220 5-9-7 60 GrahamLee 2 70+
(Paul Midgley) *hld up in midfield: pushed along and hdwy over 2f out: led ins fnl f: pushed out: idled nr fin but a holding on* 7/2[1]
35-0 2 hd **Kathlatino**[15] 1374 7-8-13 52 (v[1]) DuranFentiman 6 59+
(Micky Hammond) *hld up: n.m.r over 2f out: rdn and stl plenty to do over 1f out: r.o wl* 25/1
-005 3 2 1/4 **Stamp Duty (IRE)**[75] 538 6-8-0 46 oh1 JordanVaughan(7) 12 49
(Suzzanne France) *hld up: smooth hdwy 3f out: rdn to ld over 1f out: hdd ins fnl f: no ex* 40/1
045- 4 hd **Rocky Two (IRE)**[174] 7667 4-8-10 50 TomEaves 9 53
(Philip Kirby) *midfield: trckd ldrs gng wl over 2f out: rdn and ev ch over 1f out: no ex fnl f* 8/1
422- 5 1 3/4 **Tobrata**[126] 8349 8-9-4 57 DavidAllan 4 57
(Mel Brittain) *trckd ldr: led 3f out: sn rdn: hdd over 1f out: no ex* 5/1[3]
0-60 6 2 1/2 **Voice From Above (IRE)**[17] 1348 5-8-13 52 PaulMulrennan 8 48
(Patrick Holmes) *hld up: pushed along over 4f out: sme hdwy over 2f out: plugged on* 14/1
430- 7 4 1/2 **Operateur (IRE)**[124] 7375 6-9-2 55 AndrewElliott 11 44
(Ben Haslam) *prom: rdn 3f out: wknd over 1f out* 12/1

246- 8 nk **Noosa Sound**[176] 7636 4-8-9 **49**...(t) RoystonFfrench 10 38
(John Davies) *midfield: rdn to chse ldrs over 2f out: wknd over 1f out* **14/1**
-203 9 1 1/4 **Amtired**[28] 1129 8-9-0 **53**...(p) DanielTudhope 3 40
(Marjorie Fife) *miefield: rdn 2f out: sn wknd* **9/2**[2]
134- 10 16 **Valantino Oyster (IRE)**[220] 6470 7-9-6 **59**...(p) DaleSwift 1 20
(Tracy Waggott) *trckd ldrs: rdn 3f out: wknd over 1f out* **7/1**
00-0 11 2 3/4 **Jewelled Dagger (IRE)**[41] 959 10-8-10 **49**...(tp) PaulQuinn 5 6
(Sharon Watt) *sn led: hdd 3f out: sn wknd* **20/1**
2-60 12 75 **Bavarian Nordic (USA)**[16] 1362 9-8-13 **55**...(b) GeorgeChaloner(3) 7
(Richard Whitaker) *hld up in midfield: rdn over 5f out: sn struggling: eased and t.o* **14/1**

2m 45.31s (-0.29) **Going Correction** -0.075s/f (Good)
**WFA** 4 from 5yo+ 1lb **12 Ran SP% 119.4**
Speed ratings (Par 101): **97,96,95,95,94 92,89,89,88,77 75,25**
CSF £100.46 CT £3010.32 TOTE £4.00: £1.40, £8.50, £14.10; EX 92.20 Trifecta £931.30 Part won..
**Owner** Ms Julie French **Bred** J H Widdows **Trained** Westow, N Yorks

**FOCUS**
Good recent form was thin on the ground and the gallop was just modest until the home turn. The first three all came from the rear and the winner looks back to something like her best.

## 1675 SIS H'CAP 1m 2f 32y
**7:45** (7:45) (Class 6) (0-65,65) 4-Y-O+ **£1,940** (£577; £288; £144) **Stalls** Centre

Form RPR
010- 1 **Hussar Ballad (USA)**[135] 8233 5-9-0 **58**... DavidAllan 1 66
(Mel Brittain) *hld up: pushed along and hdwy over 2f out: drvn to ld over 1f out: kpt on* **16/1**
4431 2 3/4 **Polar Forest**[13] 1428 4-8-13 **57**...(e) GrahamLee 14 64
(Richard Guest) *trckd ldrs: rdn over 2f out: kpt on* **9/1**
00-6 3 1/2 **Merchant Of Medici**[16] 1356 7-8-13 **57**... PJMcDonald 7 63
(Micky Hammond) *midfield: rdn over 3f out: stl only 8th over 1f out: kpt on wl* **7/1**[3]
064- 4 hd **Kolonel Kirkup**[34] 6587 4-8-9 **58**... ConnorBeasley(5) 5 64
(Michael Dods) *midfield: hdwy over 2f out: rdn to chse ldrs over 1f out: kpt on* **4/1**[1]
0224 5 3/4 **Gabrial's Hope (FR)**[28] 1129 5-8-9 **53**... BarryMcHugh 13 57
(Tracy Waggott) *dwlt: hld up: rdn hdwy over 1f out: kpt on fnl f* **16/1**
4512 6 1 1/4 **Ellaal**[12] 1454 5-9-5 **63**... DaleSwift 8 65
(Ruth Carr) *led for 1f: trckd ldr: rdn to ld again over 2f out: hdd over 1f out: wknd fnl 110yds* **11/2**[2]
50-3 7 3 1/2 **I'm Super Too (IRE)**[22] 1245 7-9-7 **65**... BenCurtis 9 60
(Alan Swinbank) *in tch: rdn over 3f out: wknd fnl f* **15/2**
/00- 8 1 1/2 **Comical**[316] 3199 5-8-8 **52**... PaulMulrennan 2 44
(George Moore) *hld up: rdn over 2f out: nvr threatened* **20/1**
1340 9 1/2 **Sutton Sid**[12] 1454 4-9-7 **65**...(v) GrahamGibbons 6 56
(John Balding) *miefield: rdn over 3f out: nvr threatened* **14/1**
000- 10 1/2 **Euston Square**[169] 7778 8-8-12 **61**... GarryWhillans(5) 11 51
(Alistair Whillans) *v.s.a: hld up in rr: nvr threatened* **25/1**
0-54 11 4 1/2 **Seaside Rock (IRE)**[26] 1168 4-9-5 **63**...(b) TomEaves 4 45
(Keith Dalgleish) *miefield on inner: rdn 3f out: wknd over 1f out* **8/1**
000- 12 2 1/4 **Amazing Blue Sky**[216] 6598 8-8-10 **54**... JamesSullivan 16 32
(Ruth Carr) *led after 1f: rdn whn hdd over 2f out: wknd* **25/1**
6-05 13 4 1/2 **Chief Executive (IRE)**[21] 1269 4-8-7 **51** oh3... AndrewMullen 12 20
(Mandy Rowland) *prom: rdn over 3f out: sn wknd* **25/1**
050- 14 1 **Monthly Medal**[92] 7498 11-8-6 **53** oh3 ow2...(t) GeorgeChaloner(3) 10 20
(Wilf Storey) *prom: rdn over 3f out: wknd 2f out* **50/1**

2m 13.61s (1.71) **Going Correction** -0.075s/f (Good) **14 Ran SP% 117.5**
Speed ratings (Par 101): **90,89,89,88,88 87,84,83,82,82 78,77,73,72**
CSF £139.67 CT £1111.66 TOTE £18.80: £6.50, £2.10, £1.90; EX 163.50 Trifecta £1541.00 Part won..
**Owner** Mel Brittain **Bred** Darley **Trained** Warthill, N Yorks

**FOCUS**
Mist and fog descended on Gosforth Park ahead of this wide-open 1m2f handicap. The runner-up sets the standard.

## 1676 SIS LIVE H'CAP 5f
**8:15** (8:15) (Class 5) (0-75,75) 3-Y-O **£2,587** (£770; £384; £192) **Stalls** High

Form RPR
50-3 1 **One Boy (IRE)**[15] 1396 3-9-2 **75**... ConnorBeasley(5) 8 86+
(Michael Dods) *trckd ldrs: rdn to ld over 1f out: kpt on: edgd rt towards fin: comf* **4/5**[1]
06-1 2 2 1/4 **Orient Class**[15] 1373 3-8-8 **62**...(v) PaulMulrennan 5 65
(Paul Midgley) *w ldr: rdn to ld 2f out: sn hdd: kpt on but no ch w wnr* **4/1**[2]
265- 3 1 1/4 **Noble Asset**[220] 6467 3-9-0 **68**... RaulDaSilva 2 66
(John Quinn) *trckd ldrs: rdn and outpcd 1/2-way: kpt on to go modest 3rd ins fnl f* **5/1**[3]
54-0 4 1/2 **Tinsill**[15] 1396 3-8-11 **65**...(v) AndrewMullen 1 62
(Nigel Tinkler) *slowly away: hld up: rdn 1/2-way: nvr threatened* **14/1**
5-40 5 shd **Danfazi (IRE)**[5] 1585 3-9-1 **72**... NataliaGemelova(3) 7 68
(Kristin Stubbs) *led narrowly: rdn whn hdd 2f out: wknd* **14/1**
04-3 6 3 **Camanche Grey (IRE)**[56] 765 3-8-11 **65**... AndrewElliott 6 50
(Ben Haslam) *hld up: rdn 1/2-way: nvr threatened* **25/1**

59.84s (-1.26) **Going Correction** -0.375s/f (Firm) **6 Ran SP% 109.4**
Speed ratings (Par 98): **95,91,89,88,88 83**
CSF £3.98 CT £7.66 TOTE £1.50: £1.10, £2.20; EX 4.40 Trifecta £8.40.
**Owner** Sekura Group **Bred** Tom Radley **Trained** Denton, Co Durham

**FOCUS**
A modest race. The winner is rated in line with his Nottingham form, which is working out well.
T/Plt: £140.20 to a £1 stake. Pool: £63,341.22 - 329.80 winning units. T/Qpdt: £28.80 to a £1 stake. Pool: £8093.68 - 207.66 winning units. AS

# WARWICK (L-H)
### Thursday, April 24

**OFFICIAL GOING: Good (6.5)**
Wind: Light across Weather: Sunny spells

## 1677 BREEDERS BACKING RACING EBF MAIDEN STKS 6f
**2:10** (2:10) (Class 5) 3-Y-O+ **£3,881** (£1,155; £577; £288) **Stalls** Low

Form RPR
1 **Dinneratmidnight** 3-9-0 0... JimCrowley 7 81+
(Ralph Beckett) *sn pushed along in rr: hdwy over 1f out: shkn up to ld ins fnl f: edgd rt: r.o* **9/2**[3]
44- 2 1 **Byron's Gold**[170] 7737 3-8-9 0... MickaelBarzalona 10 73
(Ben De Haan) *w ldr tl led over 3f out: rdn and hdd over 1f out: ev ch ins fnl f: edgd rt: styd on same pce* **33/1**
34-4 3 3/4 **Master Of Suspense**[8] 1511 3-9-0 0... AdamKirby 8 76
(Peter Chapple-Hyam) *trckd ldrs: rdn to ld over 1f out: edgd rt and hdd ins fnl f: styd on same pce* **6/5**[1]
4 2 **Backstage Gossip** 3-8-9 0... RobertHavlin 5 64
(Hughie Morrison) *a.p: racd keenly: rdn over 1f out: no ex ins fnl f* **50/1**
2- 5 3/4 **Garraun (IRE)**[141] 8145 3-8-9 0...[1] AndreaAtzeni 4 62
(Jeremy Noseda) *mid-div: sn pushed along: outpcd over 2f out: styd on ins fnl f* **8/1**
5-2 6 3/4 **Touzr**[69] 605 3-9-0 0... FrankieDettori 1 64
(Richard Hannon) *s.i.s: sn chsng ldrs: rdn over 2f out: styd on same pce appr fnl f* **11/4**[2]
44- 7 2 1/4 **Stroll On (IRE)**[218] 6517 3-8-9 0... ChrisCatlin 2 52
(Rae Guest) *stdd s: hld up: shkn up over 2f out: nvr on terms* **11/1**
4360 8 22 **Island Express (IRE)**[10] 1486 7-9-6 45...(tp[1]) AnnStokell(5) 3
(Ann Stokell) *sn led: hdd over 3f out: wknd wl over 1f out* **200/1**

1m 12.78s (0.98) **Going Correction** +0.15s/f (Good)
**WFA** 3 from 7yo 11lb **8 Ran SP% 115.1**
Speed ratings (Par 103): **99,97,96,94,93 92,89,59**
CSF £117.70 TOTE £5.40: £2.30, £4.30, £1.10; EX 105.60 Trifecta £355.40.
**Owner** The Rat Pack Partnership **Bred** Bumble Bloodstock Ltd **Trained** Kimpton, Hants

**FOCUS**
A newcomer scored in decent style in this maiden, and should improve. The favourite disappointed but the form makes sense.

## 1678 TURFTV H'CAP 6f
**2:40** (2:40) (Class 5) (0-75,75) 4-Y-O+ **£2,587** (£770; £384; £192) **Stalls** Low

Form RPR
515- 1 **Apricot Sky**[211] 6744 4-9-6 **74**... DaneO'Neill 1 89+
(Henry Candy) *trckd ldrs: led over 1f out: rdn clr ins fnl f: eased towards fin* **9/4**[1]
0602 2 3 1/4 **Clubland (IRE)**[12] 1440 5-8-10 **69**... PhilipPrince(5) 5 74
(Roy Bowring) *mid-div: pushed along over 2f out: hdwy over 1f out: r.o: no ch w wnr* **5/1**[2]
205- 3 1 **Dream Catcher (FR)**[170] 7743 6-9-0 **68**... FergusSweeney 11 69
(Henry Candy) *hld up: rdn over 1f out: r.o ins fnl f: nt rch ldrs* **20/1**
00-0 4 1/2 **Panther Patrol (IRE)**[106] 91 4-9-0 **68**...(v[1]) JohnFahy 2 68
(Eve Johnson Houghton) *trckd ldrs: rdn over 1f out: styd on same pce ins fnl f* **8/1**[3]
1203 5 nse **Kuanyao (IRE)**[10] 1489 8-9-7 **75**...(b) AmirQuinn 6 75
(Lee Carter) *sn pushed along to ld: rdn: edgd lft and hdd wl over 1f out: no ex ins fnl f* **16/1**
0-02 6 hd **Commanche**[3] 1618 5-9-0 **75**... ThomasHemsley(7) 4 74
(Chris Dwyer) *mid-div: hmpd over 4f out: rdn over 1f out: styd on ins fnl f: nt trble ldrs* **5/1**[2]
3142 7 1 **Rigolleto (IRE)**[27] 1144 6-9-3 **71**... GeorgeBaker 10 67+
(Anabel K Murphy) *s.s: bhd tl r.o ins fnl f* **10/1**
310- 8 8 **Fossa**[202] 6998 4-9-5 **73**... RobertWinston 8 43
(Dean Ivory) *trckd ldrs: plld hrd: rdn over 1f out: wknd fnl f* **16/1**
-015 9 1 1/4 **Time Medicean**[23] 1221 8-9-4 **72**... FrannyNorton 7 38
(Tony Carroll) *hld up: bhd fr 1/2-way* **20/1**
26-4 10 16 **Foxtrot Jubilee (IRE)**[84] 381 4-9-6 **74**... JimCrowley 9
(Ralph Beckett) *hld up: pushed along 1/2-way: a in rr* **9/1**
3104 11 2 **Temple Road (IRE)**[27] 1144 6-9-6 **74**... AdamKirby 3
(Milton Bradley) *hld up in tch: plld hrd: rdn over 1f out: sn wknd and eased* **16/1**

1m 12.53s (0.73) **Going Correction** +0.15s/f (Good) **11 Ran SP% 121.5**
Speed ratings (Par 103): **101,96,95,94,94 94,93,82,80,59 56**
CSF £13.43 CT £181.62 TOTE £3.10: £1.30, £2.80, £7.20; EX 18.20 Trifecta £461.80.
**Owner** Simon Broke & Partners III **Bred** Mrs James Bethell **Trained** Kingston Warren, Oxon
■ Stewards' Enquiry : Amir Quinn two-day ban: used whip above permitted level (May 8-9)

**FOCUS**
A big gamble was landed in emphatic style in this sprint handicap. A clear personal best from the winner with the second close to his latest.

## 1679 FOLLOW US ON TWITTER @WARWICKRACES CONDITIONS STKS 6f
**3:10** (3:10) (Class 3) 4-Y-O+ **£7,762** (£2,310; £1,154; £577) **Stalls** Low

Form RPR
202- 1 **Music Master**[201] 7013 4-8-12 108... DaneO'Neill 3 113+
(Henry Candy) *trckd ldr tl led 4f out: shkn up over 1f out: clr fnl f: easily* **8/13**[1]
422- 2 2 1/4 **Mar Mar (IRE)**[174] 7658 4-8-3 96...(p) SilvestreDeSousa 4 96
(Saeed bin Suroor) *trckd ldrs: wnt 2nd over 3f out: rdn and edgd lft over 1f out: styd on same pce* **11/2**[3]
100- 3 4 1/2 **Royal Rock**[181] 7495 10-9-4 102... GeorgeBaker 5 96
(Chris Wall) *hld up: rdn to go 3rd 1f out: no ex ins fnl f* **20/1**
015- 4 6 **Redvers (IRE)**[201] 7014 6-8-8 98... FrederikTylicki 1 75
(Ed Vaughan) *trckd ldrs: shkn up over 1f out: wknd and eased fnl f* **3/1**[2]
0605 5 10 **Steel City Boy (IRE)**[40] 973 11-8-3 37... PhilipPrince(5) 6 35
(Ann Stokell) *led 2f: rdn and wknd over 2f out* **200/1**

1m 10.95s (-0.85) **Going Correction** +0.15s/f (Good) **5 Ran SP% 107.6**
Speed ratings (Par 107): **111,108,102,94,80**
CSF £4.29 TOTE £2.00: £1.10, £2.70; EX 4.70 Trifecta £11.50.
**Owner** Godfrey Wilson **Bred** Mrs C R D Wilson **Trained** Kingston Warren, Oxon

**FOCUS**
The hot favourite was an easy winner of this steadily-run conditions event. Music Master is rated in line with a better virew of his 3yo form.

## 1680 REWARDS4RACING.COM MAIDEN STKS (DIV I) 7f 26y
**3:40** (3:40) (Class 5) 3-Y-O **£2,587** (£770; £384; £192) **Stalls** Low

Form RPR
0- 1 **Battle Command (USA)**[183] 7467 3-9-5 0... FrankieDettori 7 80
(Peter Chapple-Hyam) *mde all: set stdy pce tl qcknd over 2f out: rdn ins fnl f: r.o* **4/1**[3]
42 2 1 1/2 **Voyageofdiscovery (USA)**[82] 423 3-9-5 0... AdamKirby 1 76
(Clive Cox) *trckd ldrs: rdn to chse wnr over 1f out: edgd rt ins fnl f: styd on same pce towards fin* **1/1**[1]
3 2 **Old Guard** 3-9-5 0... JamesDoyle 3 71
(Roger Charlton) *prom: plld hrd: shkn up over 1f out: styd on* **10/1**
40- 4 1 3/4 **Pipe Dream**[191] 7270 3-9-5 0... JimmyFortune 8 66
(Brian Meehan) *chsd wnr tl rdn over 1f out: no ex ins fnl f* **16/1**
0- 5 3/4 **Crafty Exit**[244] 5718 3-9-5 0... JimCrowley 9 64+
(William Knight) *s.i.s: pushed along in rr early: r.o ins fnl f: nvr nrr* **7/2**[2]

0-0 **6** *2 ½* **Buckland Beau**[15] 1395 3-9-5 0 FrederikTylicki 5 58
(Charlie Fellowes) *prom: rdn over 1f out: wknd ins fnl f* **25/1**
06 **7** *3* **Purana**[35] 1024 3-9-0 0 RobertWinston 2 45+
(Tony Carroll) *s.s: hld up: nvr on terms* **50/1**
05 **8** *nk* **Pouncing Tiger**[36] 1008 3-9-0 0 AdamBeschizza 6 44
(Stuart Williams) *hld up: rdn over 1f out: n.d* **50/1**
**9** *11* **Crucible** 3-9-5 0 MickaelBarzalona 4 20
(Daniel Kubler) *s.s: a in rr* **20/1**
1m 28.56s (5.36) **Going Correction** +0.525s/f (Yiel) **9** Ran SP% **119.7**
Speed ratings (Par 98): **90,88,86,84,83 80,76,76,63**
CSF £8.46 TOTE £6.70: £1.60, £1.10, £2.60; EX 13.60 Trifecta £60.50.
**Owner** Clipper Logistics **Bred** Marc Keller **Trained** Newmarket, Suffolk
**FOCUS**
They went a steady pace in the maiden and the winner made all under a good ride. The form does make a bit of sense.

## 1681 REWARDS4RACING.COM MAIDEN STKS (DIV II) 7f 26y
**4:10** (4:12) (Class 5) 3-Y-O **£2,587** (£770; £384; £192) **Stalls** Low

Form RPR
220- **1** **Captain Bob (IRE)**[224] 6328 3-9-5 75 FrankieDettori 5 82
(Charles Hills) *mde all: set stdy pce tl qckng over 2f out: shkn up over 1f out: r.o: eased nr fin* **15/8**[2]
0 **2** *1* **Triple Chief (IRE)**[12] 1433 3-9-5 0 AndreaAtzeni 7 79
(Rod Millman) *mid-div: rdn over 2f out: r.o to go 2nd wl ins fnl f: no ch w wnr* **25/1**
22- **3** *1 ¼* **Potentate (IRE)**[189] 7328 3-9-5 0 PatDobbs 3 76
(Richard Hannon) *trckd wnr tl wnt upsides 1/2-way: rdn over 2f out: styd on same pce ins fnl f* **5/6**[1]
34- **4** *5* **Marmarus**[192] 7243 3-9-5 0 AdamKirby 9 63
(Clive Cox) *chsd ldrs: rdn and hung lft over 2f out: wknd ins fnl f* **8/1**[3]
66- **5** *3 ½* **Strike A Light**[184] 7448 3-9-0 0 ChrisCatlin 2 49
(Rae Guest) *chsd ldrs: rdn over 2f out: wknd over 1f out* **25/1**
**6** *hd* **Nouvelle Ere** 3-9-5 0 RobertWinston 6 54
(Tony Carroll) *s.s: in rr whn hung rt 1/2-way: styd on ins fnl f: nvr on terms* **33/1**
0-0 **7** *shd* **Insight (IRE)**[20] 1280 3-9-0 0 JohnFahy 8 48
(John Spearing) *sn bhd: rdn over 1f out: n.d* **50/1**
**7** *dht* **Captain George (IRE)** 3-9-5 0 HayleyTurner 4 53
(James Fanshawe) *chsd ldrs: rdn over 2f out: wknd over 1f out* **14/1**
**9** *24* **Ballyfarsoon (IRE)** 3-9-5 0 StevieDonohoe 1
(Ian Williams) *s.s: outpcd* **50/1**
1m 26.91s (3.71) **Going Correction** +0.525s/f (Yiel) **9** Ran SP% **121.7**
Speed ratings (Par 98): **99,97,96,90,86 86,86,86,58**
CSF £53.30 TOTE £3.10: £1.10, £6.00, £1.10; EX 61.30 Trifecta £148.00.
**Owner** A L R Morton **Bred** Martyn J McEnery **Trained** Lambourn, Berks
**FOCUS**
One of the main form contenders scored with authority under a positive ride in this maiden. The winner is rated close to his best.

## 1682 RACING UK H'CAP 1m 22y
**4:40** (4:42) (Class 4) (0-85,83) 4-Y-O+ **£6,469** (£1,925; £962; £481) **Stalls** Low

Form RPR
6-04 **1** **Myboyalfie (USA)**[17] 1351 7-9-7 83 FrederikTylicki 2 91
(J R Jenkins) *a.p: chsd ldr over 5f out: rdn to ld 1f out: edgd rt: r.o* **9/4**[1]
5-14 **2** *nk* **Tenor (IRE)**[19] 1317 4-9-0 76 (t) AdamKirby 6 83
(John Ryan) *led: rdn and hdd 1f out: r.o* **5/1**[3]
3435 **3** *4 ½* **Gracious George (IRE)**[27] 1142 4-8-6 75 CamHardie(7) 5 72
(Jimmy Fox) *hld up: hdwy u.p 2f out: styd on same pce fnl f* **7/1**
3221 **4** *1* **Exclusive Waters (IRE)**[43] 928 4-8-4 73 (b) CallumShepherd(7) 3 68
(Charles Hills) *hld up: rdn over 1f out: nvr trbld ldrs* **11/4**[2]
60-0 **5** *½* **Heavy Metal**[34] 1042 4-9-6 82 FrannyNorton 4 76
(Mark Johnston) *chsd ldr tl over 5f out: remained handy: pushed along 1/2-way: wknd ins fnl f* **6/1**
**6** *2 ¼* **Rayak (IRE)**[27] 4-9-4 80 GeorgeBaker 1 68
(Jonjo O'Neill) *hld up: rdn over 2f out: wknd fnl f* **8/1**
1m 40.79s (-0.21) **Going Correction** +0.125s/f (Good) **6** Ran SP% **112.0**
Speed ratings (Par 105): **106,105,101,100,99 97**
CSF £13.71 TOTE £2.80: £1.60, £2.80; EX 14.40 Trifecta £112.90.
**Owner** Sweet Sugar Racing Club **Bred** Robert Pierz & Robert Brooks **Trained** Royston, Herts
**FOCUS**
The pacesetters had a good battle in this handicap and pulled clear. The winner is rated to last year's form.

## 1683 GEORGE AND IRENE RUBY ANNIVERSARY H'CAP (DIV I) 1m 22y
**5:15** (5:18) (Class 6) (0-60,60) 3-Y-O **£1,940** (£577; £288; £144) **Stalls** Low

Form RPR
60-0 **1** **Hostile Fire (IRE)**[24] 1214 3-9-5 58 ChrisCatlin 9 65
(Ed de Giles) *hld up: hdwy over 1f out: r.o u.p to ld wl ins fnl f* **10/1**
00-0 **2** *¾* **Bourbon Prince**[15] 1394 3-8-5 49 LouisSteward(5) 4 54+
(Michael Bell) *hld up: hdwy over 2f out: led over 1f out: rdn: edgd lft and hdd wl ins fnl f* **8/1**[3]
-556 **3** *2 ½* **Jazri**[22] 1235 3-9-4 57 FrederikTylicki 10 57
(Milton Bradley) *hld up: hdwy over 1f out: styd on same pce and wnt 3rd ins fnl f* **8/1**[3]
56-1 **4** *2* **Speed Society**[20] 1285 3-9-7 60 AdamKirby 2 55
(Jim Boyle) *chsd ldrs: rdn and ev ch over 1f out: no ex ins fnl f* **2/1**[1]
6-61 **5** *2 ¼* **Prim And Proper**[15] 1384 3-9-2 55 RobertWinston 5 45
(Brendan Powell) *chsd ldrs: rdn and hung lft over 1f out: no ex fnl f* **5/1**[2]
-454 **6** *¾* **Honiton Lace**[40] 976 3-9-5 58 GeorgeBaker 1 46
(J W Hills) *disp ld tl wnt on over 2f out: rdn and hdd over 1f out: wknd ins fnl f* **25/1**
06-4 **7** *10* **Picanight**[15] 1384 3-8-7 46 oh1 AndreaAtzeni 6 11
(Eve Johnson Houghton) *plld hrd: disp ld tl rdn over 2f out: wknd over 1f out* **20/1**
00-0 **8** *6* **Plucky Dip**[14] 1403 3-8-13 52 DaneO'Neill 8 3
(John Ryan) *chsd ldrs: rdn over 2f out: sn wknd* **10/1**
030- **9** *3 ¼* **Gold Class**[190] 7309 3-9-6 59 FrannyNorton 3 3
(Ed McMahon) *s.i.s: sn pushed along in rr: wknd over 3f out* **5/1**[2]
050- **10** *18* **Reflection**[171] 7732 3-8-11 50 AdamBeschizza 7
(Brian Baugh) *trckd ldrs: racd keenly: rdn over 3f out: sn wknd* **50/1**
1m 41.93s (0.93) **Going Correction** +0.125s/f (Good) **10** Ran SP% **117.6**
Speed ratings (Par 96): **100,99,96,94,92 91,81,75,72,54**
CSF £86.04 CT £693.67 TOTE £10.60: £3.10, £3.00, £2.80; EX 126.70 Trifecta £603.40.
**Owner** Ali Mortazavi **Bred** Thomas Hassett **Trained** Ledbury, H'fords
■ Stewards' Enquiry : Chris Catlin two-day ban: used whip above permitted level (May 8-9)

**FOCUS**
The winner swooped late from a long way back in this minor handicap. It was the faster division by 1.52sec and the winner is rated to his standout 2yo run.

## 1684 GEORGE AND IRENE RUBY ANNIVERSARY H'CAP (DIV II) 1m 22y
**5:45** (5:48) (Class 6) (0-60,59) 3-Y-O **£1,940** (£577; £288; £144) **Stalls** Low

Form RPR
030- **1** **Aurelia Cotta (IRE)**[169] 7763 3-9-7 59 RobertWinston 5 63
(Charles Hills) *a.p: shkn up over 2f out: r.o u.p to ld nr fin* **7/1**
320- **2** *hd* **Tunnel Tiger (IRE)**[188] 7352 3-9-5 57 AndreaAtzeni 7 61
(William Knight) *a.p: chsd ldr 1/2-way: led 2f out: sn rdn: hdd nr fin* **5/1**[3]
340- **3** *1 ½* **Nissaki Kasta**[142] 8138 3-9-7 59 JimmyFortune 8 60
(Hughie Morrison) *hld up in tch: rdn over 1f out: styd on* **9/2**[2]
0032 **4** *hd* **Incurs Four Faults**[23] 1223 3-9-5 57 SilvestreDeSousa 3 57+
(Keith Dalgleish) *s.i.s: hld up: pushed along over 3f out: hdwy u.p over 1f out: nt rch ldrs* **7/4**[1]
0-46 **5** *2* **Water For Life**[98] 198 3-8-10 48 JackMitchell 9 43
(Dave Morris) *trckd ldr tl nt clr run 1/2-way: rdn over 1f out: no ex ins fnl f* **16/1**
053 **6** *1 ¼* **Feisty Dragon (IRE)**[43] 923 3-8-7 45 FergusSweeney 4 38
(Jamie Osborne) *hld up: swtchd rt over 1f out: sn rdn: nvr trbld ldrs* **14/1**
5006 **7** *2* **Appellez Baileys (FR)**[2] 1634 3-8-12 50 (b) FrannyNorton 2 38
(Chris Dwyer) *sn pushed along and prom: hmpd 1/2-way: wknd fnl f* **10/1**
600- **8** *1 ¼* **D'Arcy Indiana**[147] 8085 3-8-8 51 DavidKenny(5) 6 36
(Amy Weaver) *s.i.s: hld up: rdn over 2f out: wknd fnl f* **33/1**
0-43 **9** *3* **Jessy Mae**[94] 254 3-9-1 53 DaneO'Neill 10 31
(Derek Haydn Jones) *led: rdn and hdd 2f out: wknd fnl f* **12/1**
1m 43.45s (2.45) **Going Correction** +0.125s/f (Good) **9** Ran SP% **116.0**
Speed ratings (Par 96): **92,91,90,90,88 86,84,83,80**
CSF £42.06 CT £176.21 TOTE £8.90: £2.50, £1.50, £2.00; EX 49.20 Trifecta £203.60.
**Owner** Decadent Racing II **Bred** W J Kennedy **Trained** Lambourn, Berks
■ Stewards' Enquiry : Robert Winston two-day ban: used whip above permitted level (May 8-9)
**FOCUS**
They went a stop-start gallop in this second division of an ordinary handicap and there was a tight finish. The slower leg, with the winner rated to a better view of his 2yo form.
T/Plt: £8.90 to a £1 stake. Pool: £47,624.71 - 3898.71 winning units. T/Qpdt: £3.00 to a £1 stake. Pool: £2824.34 - 686.44 winning units. CR

1685 - 1688a (Foreign Racing) - See Raceform Interactive

# [1190]DONCASTER (L-H)
Friday, April 25

**OFFICIAL GOING: Good to soft (good in places) changing to soft after race 1 (1:20)**
Course railed out from 10f start to where Round joins straight, increasing distances on Round course by about 18yds.
Wind: Moderate half behind Weather: Heavy cloud and rain

## 1689 MOBILE BETTING @ FREEBETS.CO.UK H'CAP 7f
**1:20** (1:21) (Class 5) (0-70,69) 4-Y-O+ **£2,587** (£770; £384; £192) **Stalls** High

Form RPR
3255 **1** **Repetition**[50] 862 4-9-5 67 TomEaves 10 77
(Kristin Stubbs) *racd nr stands' rail: cl up: slt ld wl over 1f out: sn rdn and edgd lft ent fnl f: kpt on wl* **9/1**
1665 **2** *2* **Ostralegus**[20] 1297 4-8-12 63 MichaelJMMurphy(3) 5 68
(John Gallagher) *slt ld: pushed along over 2f out: rdn and hdd wl over 1f out: drvn and kpt on same pce fnl f* **20/1**
-000 **3** *hd* **Amenable (IRE)**[37] 1017 7-9-6 68 (p) PaulMulrennan 1 72
(Ann Stokell) *in tch: hdwy on outer to chse ldrs wl over 2f out: rdn to chse ldng pair wl over 1f out: sn rdn: kpt on same pce fnl f* **25/1**
135- **4** *1 ½* **Red Paladin (IRE)**[214] 6702 4-9-7 69 (p) GrahamLee 4 70
(Kevin Ryan) *dwlt and hld up in rr: hdwy over 2f out: rdn over 1f out: styd on fnl f: nrst fin* **11/4**[1]
1-15 **5** *nk* **Pick A Little**[30] 1115 6-9-5 67 LukeMorris 3 67
(Michael Blake) *in tch: chsd ldrs 1/2-way: rdn along over 2f out: drvn and one pce fr over 1f out* **25/1**
6324 **6** *½* **Silly Billy (IRE)**[30] 1113 6-8-10 61 (p) JasonHart(3) 6 60
(John Balding) *trckd ldrs: pushed along 2 1/2f out: rdn wl over 1f out: grad wknd* **5/1**[2]
000- **7** *5* **Frognal (IRE)**[168] 7801 8-8-11 59 (bt) SeanLevey 2 45
(Ann Stokell) *in rr: sme hdwy 3f out: sn rdn along and n.d* **25/1**
020/ **8** *nk* **Audacious**[143] 6250 6-9-1 63 AdamBeschizza 14 48
(Charles Pogson) *in tch on inner: rdn along 1/2-way: sn wknd* **80/1**
/20- **9** *1 ½* **Byron's Dream**[199] 7109 4-8-11 59 RussKennemore 11 40
(Jedd O'Keeffe) *chsd ldrs: rdn along 3f out: wknd 2f out* **9/1**
0113 **10** *hd* **Masai Moon**[30] 1115 10-9-0 69 (b) PatMillman(7) 13 49
(Rod Millman) *hld up in rr: swtchd lft to wd outside and sme hdwy over 2f out: sn rdn along and n.d* **10/1**
/40- **11** *3 ¼* **Dazeen**[250] 5564 7-9-0 67 JacobButterfield(5) 8 39
(Michael Herrington) *a towards rr: pushed along 1/2-way: rdn wl over 2f out: sn outpcd* **7/1**
0P-2 **12** *24* **Substantivo (IRE)**[15] 1408 4-8-12 60 KierenFallon 9
(Alan Jarvis) *chsd ldrs: rdn along 3f out: sn wknd: bhd and eased fnl f* **6/1**[3]
1m 27.9s (1.60) **Going Correction** +0.175s/f (Good) **12** Ran SP% **116.7**
Speed ratings (Par 103): **97,94,94,92,92 91,86,85,84,83 80,52**
CSF £178.65 CT £4335.25 TOTE £8.40: £3.40, £5.70, £6.40; EX 208.10 Trifecta £1286.60 Part won..
**Owner** The B P J Partnership **Bred** G Reed **Trained** Norton, N Yorks
**FOCUS**
The course was railed out from the 1m2f start to where the round course joins the straight, adding approximately 18 yards to races of 1m2f-plus. The ground was eased to an official description of soft following this opening contest. They raced stands' side and it proved hard to make up significant ground. The form is rated around the second.

## 1690 VIRGIN MEDIA FIELD SALES TALENT CHASER H'CAP (BOBIS RACE) 1m 2f 60y
**1:50** (1:50) (Class 4) (0-80,80) 3-Y-O **£5,175** (£1,540; £769; £384) **Stalls** Low

Form RPR
15-4 **1** **Black Schnapps (IRE)**[18] 1352 3-9-5 78 MartinDwyer 5 88
(William Muir) *prom: cl up over 4f out: led 2f out: rdn clr over 1f out: styd on wl* **12/1**
31- **2** *2 ¾* **Latin Charm (IRE)**[189] 7339 3-9-1 74 LukeMorris 9 79+
(Marco Botti) *s.i.s and reminders in rr: pushed along 6f out: hdwy on outer wl over 2f out: sn rdn and styd on strly fnl f: tk 2nd towards fin* **3/1**[1]

 The Form Book, Raceform Ltd, Newbury, RG14 5SJ

623- **3** *1* **Carthage (IRE)**[182] 7502 3-9-5 **78** SeanLevey 10 81
(Richard Hannon) *trckd ldrs: cl up over 4f out: rdn along over 2f out: drvn and kpt on same pce fnl f* **5/1**[2]

125- **4** *hd* **Mutatis Mutandis (IRE)**[174] 7695 3-9-6 **79** GrahamLee 1 82
(Ed Walker) *led 2f: prom: effrt over 2f out: rdn and n.m.r over 1f out: chsd wnr ins fnl f: kpt on same pce* **10/1**

1- **5** *½* **Billingsgate (IRE)**[184] 7461 3-9-7 **80** MickaelBarzalona 8 82
(Charlie Appleby) *hld up in tch: hdwy on inner 4f out: effrt over 2f out: rdn to chse ldrs on inner wl over 1f out: one pce appr fnl f* **8/1**

1-12 **6** *6* **Kantara Castle (IRE)**[88] 356 3-9-1 **74** (t) PaulMulrennan 3 64
(John Mackie) *hld up in rr: hdwy on inner and in tch over 3f out: rdn along over 2f out: sn no imp* **66/1**

41- **7** *hd* **Natural Choice**[170] 7764 3-9-7 **80** [1] KierenFallon 11 70
(Saeed bin Suroor) *towards rr: rapid hdwy on outer to ld after 2f: pushed along over 3f out: rdn and hdd 2f out: wknd over 1f out* **6/1**[3]

1 **8** *1¼* **Votary (IRE)**[29] 1118 3-9-7 **80** RobertHavlin 7 68
(John Gosden) *hld up in midfield: hdwy on outer 3f out: rdn to chse ldrs 2f out: sn wknd* **5/1**[2]

0-1 **9** *2½* **The Silver Kebaya (FR)**[65] 660 3-9-4 **77** ShaneKelly 4 67
(Jeremy Noseda) *hld up towards rr: effrt and sme hdwy on outer over 3f out: sn rdn and n.d* **10/1**

416- **10** *1½* **Top Of The Glas (IRE)**[198] 7129 3-9-6 **79** AndrewMullen 2 59
(Alan Jarvis) *t.k.h: chsd ldrs: rdn along over 3f out: sn wknd* **16/1**

2m 16.18s (6.78) **Going Correction** +0.30s/f (Good) **10** Ran SP% **117.0**
Speed ratings (Par 100): **84,81,81,80,80 75,75,74,72,71**
CSF £48.20 CT £209.87 TOTE £7.20: £2.60, £1.70, £2.00; EX 73.90 Trifecta £318.50.
**Owner** O'Mulloy, Collenette, Quaintance, Clark **Bred** J & J Waldron **Trained** Lambourn, Berks

**FOCUS**
An interesting 3yo handicap, but the ground wouldn't have suited all and a few can rate higher in due course. It's a race that sometimes throws up a useful performer.

## 1691 ONLINE CASINOS @ BONUS.CO.UK MAIDEN STKS 1m 4f
**2:20** (2:24) (Class 5) 3-Y-O+ **£2,587** (£770; £384; £192) **Stalls** Low

Form RPR

**1** **Clever Cookie**[13] 6-9-13 0 GrahamLee 5 93+
(Peter Niven) *hld up towards rr: stdy hdwy 1/2-way: trckd ldrs over 3f out: effrt to chse ldng pair 2f out: swtchd rt and rdn jst over 1f out: styd on to ld ins fnl f: kpt on strly* **9/2**[3]

**2** *1¾* **Air Pilot**[675] 5-9-6 0 PatrickO'Donnell(7) 9 90
(Ralph Beckett) *trckd ldng pair: hdwy over 3f out: chal over 2f out: led wl over 1f out and sn rdn: drvn and hdd ins fnl f: kpt on same pce* **13/2**

-3 **3** *7* **Munatas**[17] 1357 3-8-7 0 AndreaAtzeni 1 77
(Roger Varian) *slt ld: rdn along wl over 2f out: hdd wl over 1f out: sn drvn and wknd aqpproaching fnl f* **3/1**[2]

00-0 **4** *6* **Olymnia**[29] 1139 3-8-2 0 NickyMackay 2 62
(Robert Eddery) *trckd ldrs on inner: pushed along 4f out: rdn 3f out: drvn and plugged on one pce fnl 2f* **100/1**

**5** *5* **Ronald Gee (IRE)**[201] 7-9-10 0 IanBrennan(3) 10 61
(Jim Goldie) *hld up and bhd: hdwy 4f out: rdn along wl over 2f out: nvr nr ldrs* **100/1**

42- **6** *26* **Shanti**[211] 6781 4-9-12 0 TomQueally 7 20
(Michael Bell) *plld hrd: cl up: rdn along over 3f out: wknd qckly wl over 2f out* **14/1**

**7** *19* **Hazel Brook**[196] 5-9-8 0 HayleyTurner 8
(Mary Hambro) *trckd ldrs: rdn along on outer over 4f out: sn lost pl and bhd* **50/1**

3 **8** *14* **Saarrem (USA)**[16] 1391 3-8-7 0 PaulHanagan 6
(John Gosden) *hld up in tch: effrt over 4f out: rdn along 3f out: sn wknd* **5/4**[1]

0-4 **9** *nk* **Tactical Strike**[16] 1391 3-8-7 0 (t) MickaelBarzalona 4
(Hugo Palmer) *towards rr: rdn along 4f out: sn outpcd and bhd* **20/1**

60- **10** *93* **Foiled**[249] 5588 4-9-9 0 MatthewCosham(3) 3
(Nikki Evans) *in tch on inner: pushed along 1/2-way: rdn over 4f out and sn wknd: bhd and heavily eased fnl 2f* **100/1**

2m 39.4s (4.50) **Going Correction** +0.30s/f (Good)
**WFA** 3 from 4yo 20lb 4 from 5yo+ 1lb **10** Ran SP% **117.3**
Speed ratings (Par 103): **97,95,91,87,83 66,53,44,44,**
CSF £32.87 TOTE £5.60: £1.60, £2.10, £1.40; EX 42.40 Trifecta £224.30.
**Owner** Francis Green Racing Ltd **Bred** Mrs J A Niven **Trained** Barton-le-Street, N Yorks

**FOCUS**
The testing ground wasn't for everyone, but the front two relished the conditions and probably ran to a fair enough level. The winenr is a potential mid-90s horse on his jumps form.

## 1692 TRENT REFRACTORIES LTD 25TH ANNIVERSARY H'CAP 2m 110y
**2:55** (2:57) (Class 4) (0-85,85) 4-Y-O+ **£5,175** (£1,540; £769; £384) **Stalls** Low

Form RPR

261- **1** **Perfect Heart**[189] 7338 5-9-12 **85** AndreaAtzeni 4 100+
(Roger Varian) *trckd ldrs: hdwy 5f out: chsd clr ldr over 3f out: effrt over 2f out: rdn to ld 1 1/2f out: sn clr and styd on wl* **11/8**[1]

60/1 **2** *3¾* **Bob's World**[14] 1418 5-9-2 **75** (tp) PaulHanagan 2 84
(Jennie Candlish) *hld up and bhd: hdwy on outer 4f out: chsd ldng pair wl over 2f out: sn rdn and styd on to chse wnr appr fnl f: sn drvn and no imp* **5/1**[2]

11-5 **3** *3¼* **Mr Snoozy**[20] 1306 5-9-5 **81** (p) JasonHart(3) 5 86
(Mark Walford) *prom: hdwy to ld over 4f out: rdn clr over 3f out: drvn and hdd 1 1/2f out: sn one pce* **13/2**[3]

240- **4** *9* **Teak (IRE)**[188] 6646 7-8-11 **75** GeorgeDowning(5) 1 69
(Ian Williams) *midfield: effrt and sme hdwy over 4f out: rdn along to chse ldrs over 3f out: sn one pce* **20/1**

05-0 **5** *9* **Albonny (IRE)**[14] 1418 5-8-12 **71** KierenFallon 6 55
(Alan Jarvis) *hld up: a in rr* **25/1**

-132 **6** *10* **Singzak**[28] 1151 6-9-3 **76** GrahamGibbons 7 48
(Michael Easterby) *hld up towards rr: sme hdwy over 4f out: rdn along wl over 3f out and n.d* **25/1**

60-3 **7** *nk* **Knightly Escapade**[35] 868 6-8-12 **71** BenCurtis 3 42
(Brian Ellison) *hld up towards rr: effrt and sme hdwy 5f out: rdn along over 4f out: sn outpcd and bhd* **14/1**

00-1 **8** *6* **New Youmzain (FR)**[11] 1485 5-9-7 **80** 6ex AndrewMullen 10 44
(Michael Appleby) *led: rdn along 5f out: sn hdd & wknd* **8/1**

2111 **9** *dist* **Travel (USA)**[3] 1629 4-8-6 **72** 6ex MichaelJMMurphy(3) 8
(Mark Johnston) *prom: rdn along 1/2-way: drvn along over 5f out and wknd qckly: sn bhd and eased* **9/1**

3m 42.72s (2.32) **Going Correction** +0.30s/f (Good)
**WFA** 4 from 5yo+ 4lb **9** Ran SP% **112.3**
Speed ratings (Par 105): **106,104,102,98,94 89,89,86,**
CSF £7.56 CT £31.70 TOTE £2.50: £1.40, £1.70, £1.90; EX 8.80 Trifecta £28.80.
**Owner** Normandie Stud Ltd **Bred** Normandie Stud Ltd **Trained** Newmarket, Suffolk

**FOCUS**
They finished strung out behind the smart-looking winner off what seemed a quick pace in the conditions.

## 1693 GET FREE BETS @ FREEBETS.CO.UK H'CAP (BOBIS RACE) 6f
**3:25** (3:25) (Class 3) (0-90,89) 3-Y-O **£7,762** (£2,310; £1,154; £577) **Stalls** High

Form RPR

00-1 **1** **New Bidder**[17] 1358 3-9-1 **83** RussKennemore 7 88
(Jedd O'Keeffe) *prom: effrt 2f out: sn rdn: drvn to chse ldr ent fnl f: led last 75yds: hld on gamely towards fin* **5/1**[3]

4350 **2** *hd* **Golden Amber (IRE)**[7] 1555 3-9-7 **89** RobertWinston 4 93
(Dean Ivory) *trckd ldrs: hdwy 2f out: rdn over 1f out: drvn and kpt on wl fnl f: jst hld* **10/1**

01- **3** *1½* **You're Fired (IRE)**[192] 7261 3-8-10 **78** PaulHanagan 9 78
(Alan Jarvis) *chsd ldrs: rdn along and sltly outpcd over 1f out: drvn and kpt on wl fnl f: nrst fin* **10/1**

451- **4** *hd* **Lexington Abbey**[198] 7125 3-9-3 **85** PaulMulrennan 6 84
(Kevin Ryan) *slt ld: hdd 1/2-way: cl up and ev ch wl over 1f out: drvn ent fnl f: one pce last 100yds* **10/1**

31-0 **5** *hd* **Jazz (IRE)**[17] 1358 3-9-4 **86** TomQueally 1 84
(Charles Hills) *cl up: led 1/2-way: rdn over 1f out: drvn ins fnl f: hdd & wknd last 75yds* **3/1**[1]

01-4 **6** *nk* **The Hooded Claw (IRE)**[13] 1445 3-8-12 **80** DuranFentiman 11 77
(Tim Easterby) *hld up in rr: hdwy 2f out: rdn over 1f out: kpt on ins fnl f: nrst fin* **4/1**[2]

U0-3 **7** *2¼* **Mr Matthews (IRE)**[17] 1358 3-8-8 **81** JoeyHaynes(5) 3 72
(K R Burke) *in tch: hdwy on outer over 2f out: rdn wl over 1f out: grad wknd* **6/1**

513- **8** *nk* **Centre Haafhd**[294] 4019 3-8-9 **77** GrahamGibbons 5 67
(David Barron) *towards rr and pushed along 1/2-way: rdn and sme hdwy over 2f out: wknd over 1f out* **12/1**

10-0 **9** *6* **Khalice**[17] 1358 3-8-12 **80** TonyHamilton 10 52
(Richard Fahey) *racd cl to stands' rail: prom: rdn along over 2f out: wknd wl over 1f out* **20/1**

1m 14.31s (0.71) **Going Correction** +0.175s/f (Good) **9** Ran SP% **115.7**
Speed ratings (Par 102): **102,101,99,99,99 98,95,95,87**
CSF £53.80 CT £484.56 TOTE £5.20: £2.40, £3.20, £3.80; EX 64.40 Trifecta £1294.80.
**Owner** Highbeck Racing **Bred** West Is Best Syndicate **Trained** Middleham Moor, N Yorks
■ Stewards' Enquiry : Russ Kennemore seven-day ban: used whip above permitted level (May 9-10,12-16)

**FOCUS**
The action unfolded stands' side. This briefly looked between Lexington Abbey and Jazz entering the final furlong, but they ran out of steam and there was little more than two lengths covering the first six at the line, so probably form to treat with a bit of caution.

## 1694 PEGLER YORKSHIRE FILLIES' H'CAP 6f
**4:00** (4:00) (Class 5) (0-70,70) 4-Y-O+ **£2,587** (£770; £384; £192) **Stalls** High

Form RPR

3235 **1** **Heartsong (IRE)**[15] 1405 5-8-10 **62** MichaelJMMurphy(3) 5 72+
(John Gallagher) *trckd ldrs: hdwy 2f out: effrt whn n.m.r jst over 1f out: rdn and hmpd ins fnl f: swtchd lft last 100yds and kpt on wl to ld nr fin* **5/1**[3]

60-6 **2** *½* **See Clearly**[11] 1487 5-8-8 **57** (p) DuranFentiman 3 63
(Tim Easterby) *hld up: gd hdwy on outer over 2f out: rdn to chal over 1f out: drvn to ld and edgd rt ins fnl f: hdd and no ex nr fin* **5/1**[3]

40-0 **3** *2¼* **Meandmyshadow**[13] 1446 6-9-4 **67** RobertWinston 8 66
(Alan Brown) *cl up: rdn to ld 2f out: drvn ent fnl f and sn hdd: wknd last 100yds* **13/2**

401- **4** *2¾* **Next Door (IRE)**[291] 4114 4-9-7 **70** GrahamGibbons 9 61
(David Barron) *dwlt: sn trcking ldrs: effrt 2f out: rdn and n.m.r over 1f out: sn drvn and btn* **2/1**[1]

-033 **5** *1* **Beacon Tarn**[29] 1127 4-9-4 **70** JasonHart(3) 10 58
(Eric Alston) *slt ld: rdn and hdd 2f out: wknd over 1f out* **4/1**[2]

60-0 **6** *4* **Balinka**[18] 1343 4-8-7 **56** DavidAllan 4 32
(Mel Brittain) *cl up: rdn and ev ch 2f out: sn drvn and wknd over 1f out* **8/1**

1m 15.13s (1.53) **Going Correction** +0.175s/f (Good) **6** Ran SP% **111.1**
Speed ratings (Par 100): **96,95,92,88,87 82**
CSF £28.70 CT £156.78 TOTE £6.70: £3.30, £3.20; EX 28.30 Trifecta £154.20.
**Owner** Colin Rashbrook **Bred** Gerry And John Rowley **Trained** Chastleton, Oxon
■ Stewards' Enquiry : Michael J M Murphy one-day ban: careless riding (May 9)

**FOCUS**
Again, they raced stands' side in this modest fillies' handicap. The winner rates better than the bare form.

## 1695 RHINORECRUITMENT.COM CONSTRUCTION SPECIALISTS H'CAP 5f
**4:35** (4:37) (Class 4) (0-85,85) 4-Y-O+ **£5,175** (£1,540; £769; £384) **Stalls** High

Form RPR

0-52 **1** **Red Baron (IRE)**[7] 1565 5-8-12 **79** NeilFarley(3) 7 92
(Eric Alston) *prom: cl up 1/2-way: led 1 1/2f out: rdn clr ent fnl f: kpt on* **5/1**[2]

5004 **2** *1¾* **Tax Free (IRE)**[7] 1565 12-9-4 **82** AdrianNicholls 3 89
(David Nicholls) *sn in tch: chsd ldrs over 2f out: rdn wl over 1f out: kpt on wl fnl f* **16/1**

-500 **3** *nk* **Another Wise Kid (IRE)**[20] 1305 6-9-7 **85** GrahamLee 13 90+
(Paul Midgley) *towards rr: hdwy wl over 1f out: sn rdn and styd on strly fnl f: nrst fin* **4/1**[1]

0-14 **4** *¾* **Sleepy Blue Ocean**[50] 863 8-9-1 **79** (p) RobertWinston 4 82
(John Balding) *prom: cl up 2f out: sn rdn: drvn and n.m.r ent fnl f: kpt on one pce* **10/1**

-200 **5** *hd* **Keep It Dark**[13] 1447 5-8-7 **71** oh2 BarryMcHugh 2 73
(Tony Coyle) *sn in tch on wd outside: hdwy 2f out: rdn to chse ldrs over 1f out: carried hd high and edgd lft ent fnl f: no imp* **9/1**

524- **6** *shd* **Six Wives**[245] 5701 7-8-1 **72** (p) MatthewHopkins(7) 1 74
(Scott Dixon) *led: rdn along 2f out: hdd 1 1/2f out: sn drvn and edgd rt: wknd fnl f* **20/1**

53-6 **7** *½* **Go Go Green (IRE)**[13] 1440 8-8-4 **71** IanBrennan(3) 8 71
(Jim Goldie) *towards rr: hdwy 2f out: rdn wl over 1f out: kpt on fnl f: nrst fin* **11/1**

10-0 **8** *3¼* **Monumental Man**[28] 1145 5-9-2 **80** (p) HayleyTurner 11 68
(James Unett) *chsd ldrs: rdn 2f out: drvn over 1f out: grad wknd* **14/1**

000- **9** *1½* **Bosun Breese**[288] 4217 9-9-3 **81** PaulMulrennan 5 64
(Paul Midgley) *dwlt: hdwy and in tch after 1f: rdn along 2f out: sn wknd* **25/1**

5325 **10** *½* **Moorhouse Lad**[7] 1565 11-8-13 **77** AndrewMullen 15 58
(Garry Moss) *qckly away and prom: pushed along and lost pl after 1 1/2f: rdn 1/2-way and n.d* **16/1**

313/ **11** *nk* **Just Charlie**[564] 6929 4-9-7 **85** DaneO'Neill 9 65
(Henry Candy) *chsd ldrs: rdn along 2f out: sn wknd* **6/1**[3]
060- **12** *½* **Captain Dunne (IRE)**[209] 6848 9-9-0 **78** DavidAllan 14 56
(Tim Easterby) *in tch: rdn along 1/2-way: sn wknd* **17/2**
50-0 **13** *hd* **The Strig**[13] 1447 7-8-3 **74** (v) JoeDoyle(7) 6 51
(Nigel Tinkler) *a towards rr* **50/1**
050- **14** *4½* **Noodles Blue Boy**[178] 7593 8-8-7 **76** JacobButterfield(5) 12 37
(Ollie Pears) *dwlt: a in rr* **25/1**

1m 0.59s (0.09) **Going Correction** +0.175s/f (Good) **14** Ran SP% **121.7**
Speed ratings (Par 105): **106,103,102,101,101 101,100,95,92,91 91,90,90,83**
CSF £79.72 CT £367.68 TOTE £4.80: £1.30, £6.90, £1.70; EX 111.40 Trifecta £542.50.
**Owner** J Stephenson **Bred** Mrs C A Moore **Trained** Longton, Lancs

**FOCUS**
They raced middle-to-far side in this fair handicap. The winner was well in after his reappearance.
T/Plt: £3,701.90 to a £1 stake. Pool: £73277.65 - 14.45 winning tickets T/Qpdt: £66.20 to a £1 stake. Pool: £8552.36 - 95.60 winning tickets JR

# SANDOWN (R-H)

Friday, April 25

**OFFICIAL GOING: Soft (sprint 5.5, round 6.0)**
Round course at outermost configuration down back straight and around bend, increasing distances on Round course by about 10yds.
Wind: Moderate, half against Weather: Very overcast, drizzly

## 1696 BET365 ESHER CUP (H'CAP) (BOBIS RACE) 1m 14y
**1:40** (1:45) (Class 2) (0-100,90) 3-Y-O
**£15,562** (£4,660; £2,330; £1,165; £582; £292) **Stalls** Low

Form RPR
314- **1** **What About Carlo (FR)**[217] 6593 3-9-2 **85** JimmyFortune 5 99
(Eve Johnson Houghton) *trckd ldr: led over 2f out: pushed clr over 1f out: rdn out* **12/1**
1- **2** *4* **End Of Line**[182] 7494 3-9-6 **89** JamieSpencer 3 97+
(Andrew Balding) *dwlt: hld up in last: reminder over 3f out: shkn up and prog whn nt clr run over 1f out: r.o fnl f to take 2nd last 50yds* **5/2**[2]
16- **3** *¾* **First Flight (IRE)**[247] 5652 3-9-7 **90** SilvestreDeSousa 1 93+
(Saeed bin Suroor) *dwlt: hld up in last: gd prog fr 3f out to chse wnr 2f out: rdn and no imp over 1f out: lost 2nd last 50yds* **8/1**
11- **4** *3¾* **Cricklewood Green (USA)**[264] 5034 3-9-0 **83** RyanMoore 7 77
(Richard Hannon) *chsd ldr: rdn over 3f out: outpcd fr 2f out: plugged on* **7/1**[3]
1 **5** *1¼* **Sacred Act**[16] 1394 3-9-7 **90** WilliamBuick 6 82
(John Gosden) *dwlt: hld up in last trio: shkn up over 2f out: no prog and wl btn over 1f out* **6/4**[1]
104- **6** *6* **Art Official (IRE)**[189] 7336 3-9-5 **88** RichardHughes 4 66
(Richard Hannon) *led: pushed along and hdd over 2f out: wknd over 1f out: eased nr fin* **14/1**
1114 **7** *16* **Almargo (IRE)**[7] 1563 3-9-5 **88** JoeFanning 2 29
(Mark Johnston) *trckd ldrs: cl enough and shkn up over 2f out: wknd rapidly wl over 1f out: t.o* **20/1**
605- **8** *18* **Street Force (USA)**[208] 6865 3-8-13 **82** JamesDoyle 8
(Clive Brittain) *in tch: rdn wl over 2f out: sn wknd rapidly: wl t.o* **40/1**

1m 48.42s (5.12) **Going Correction** +0.70s/f (Yiel) **8** Ran SP% **113.7**
Speed ratings (Par 104): **102,98,97,93,92 86,70,52**
CSF £41.84 CT £261.00 TOTE £14.10: £2.70, £1.70, £1.50; EX 49.50 Trifecta £499.20.
**Owner** Anthony Pye-Jeary **Bred** Earl Haras Du Logis & J Ince **Trained** Blewbury, Oxon
■ The Gordon Richards Stakes and Classic Trial were previously held on a mixed Saturday card.

**FOCUS**
A decent 3yo handicap. It proved hard to get involved from off the pace. The winner stepped up on his 2yo form and is possibly worth more at face value.

## 1697 BET365 GORDON RICHARDS STKS (GROUP 3) 1m 2f 7y
**2:10** (2:14) (Class 1) 4-Y-O+ **£35,443** (£13,437; £6,725; £3,350; £1,681) **Stalls** Low

Form RPR
34-2 **1** **Noble Mission**[13] 1434 5-9-0 **111** JamesDoyle 5 123
(Lady Cecil) *sn led: mde rest: shkn up over 2f out: rdn clr over 1f out: styd on wl* **4/1**[3]
121- **2** *9* **Telescope (IRE)**[247] 5653 4-9-0 **115** RyanMoore 1 107
(Sir Michael Stoute) *hld up in tch: chsd wnr 4f out: rdn and no imp over 1f out: one pce after* **5/2**[2]
24-1 **3** *9* **Contributer (IRE)**[27] 1170 4-9-0 **106** GeorgeBaker 2 91
(Ed Dunlop) *hld up in last: prog to dispute 2nd 3f out: rdn over 1f out: wknd qckly: fin tired* **9/1**
13- **4** *nk* **Sky Hunter**[284] 4362 4-9-0 **115** SilvestreDeSousa 3 90
(Saeed bin Suroor) *broke wl but restrained: effrt 3f out: sn rdn: floundering wl over 1f out: wl btn after* **6/5**[1]
2030 **5** *34* **Empire Storm (GER)**[48] 899 7-9-0 **107** (t[1]) JoeFanning 4 29
(Michael Attwater) *led briefly early: trckd wnr to 4f out: sn wknd: wl t.o* **33/1**

2m 15.89s (5.39) **Going Correction** +0.80s/f (Soft) **5** Ran SP% **107.0**
Speed ratings (Par 113): **110,102,95,95,68**
CSF £13.43 TOTE £6.20: £2.20, £1.30; EX 14.20 Trifecta £51.50.
**Owner** K Abdullah **Bred** Juddmonte Farms Ltd **Trained** Newmarket, Suffolk

**FOCUS**
This Group 3, boosted by Al Kazeem's success last year, was always likely to prove tactical and the winner dictated. He was the only one to show his form.

## 1698 BET365 MILE (GROUP 2) 1m 14y
**2:45** (2:46) (Class 1) 4-Y-O+
**£53,874** (£20,425; £10,222; £5,092; £2,555; £1,282) **Stalls** Low

Form RPR
30-2 **1** **Tullius (IRE)**[27] 1165 6-9-1 **110** JimmyFortune 4 119
(Andrew Balding) *hld up disputing 4th: smooth prog 2f out: led jst over 1f out and dashed for home: sn clr and styd on wl* **9/2**[3]
152- **2** *3¾* **Montiridge (IRE)**[210] 6797 4-9-1 **115** RichardHughes 2 110+
(Richard Hannon) *hld up disputing 4th: prog 2f out to look a threat jst over 1f out: no answer to wnr's thrust but sn in 2nd and styd on* **3/1**[2]
01-0 **3** *2¾* **Penitent**[27] 1176 8-9-1 **113** DanielTudhope 5 104
(David O'Meara) *led: shkn up 2f out: hdd and outpcd jst over 1f out* **5/1**
112- **4** *½* **Top Notch Tonto (IRE)**[188] 7366 4-9-1 **118** DaleSwift 1 103
(Brian Ellison) *t.k.h early: trckd ldr 3f: shkn up and outpcd fr 2f out: kpt on* **9/2**[3]

163- **5** *2¼* **Garswood**[201] 7059 4-9-1 **117** RyanMoore 7 98
(Richard Fahey) *hld up in detached last: shkn up 2f out: no real prog and no ch* **5/2**[1]
510- **6** *1¾* **Fire Ship**[202] 7047 5-9-1 **107** JimCrowley 3 94
(William Knight) *trckd ldr after 3f tl drvn and wknd over 1f out* **14/1**

1m 48.1s (4.80) **Going Correction** +0.90s/f (Soft) **6** Ran SP% **113.3**
Speed ratings (Par 115): **112,108,105,105,102 101**
CSF £18.60 TOTE £5.90: £3.00, £1.80; EX 23.30 Trifecta £97.30.
**Owner** Kennet Valley Thoroughbreds VI **Bred** Sc Archi Romani **Trained** Kingsclere, Hants

**FOCUS**
A tight Group 2 but not many showed their form on the ground. The time was relatively slow and the winner is rated to his old best.

## 1699 BET365 CLASSIC TRIAL (GROUP 3) 1m 2f 7y
**3:15** (3:16) (Class 1) 3-Y-O
**£35,443** (£13,437; £6,725; £3,350; £1,681; £843) **Stalls** Low

Form RPR
1-1 **1** **Western Hymn**[14] 1419 3-9-1 **104** WilliamBuick 3 109+
(John Gosden) *dwlt: hld up in 5th: pushed along and prog on outer over 2f out: led over 1f out: carried hd high: reminder and hung lft ins fnl f: styd on* **1/2**[1]
51- **2** *1¾* **Impulsive Moment (IRE)**[125] 8382 3-9-1 **80** DavidProbert 5 105
(Andrew Balding) *trckd ldrs: pushed along over 2f out: clsd to chal and upsides wl over 1f out: chsd wnr after: kpt on but a hld* **25/1**
23-3 **3** *2* **Master Carpenter (IRE)**[13] 1436 3-9-1 **103** RyanMoore 8 101
(Rod Millman) *hld up in last: pushed along over 2f out: prog wl over 1f out: rdn and styd on to take 3rd last 100yds* **8/1**[3]
221- **4** *1¼* **Red Galileo**[205] 6934 3-9-1 **90** GeorgeBaker 7 99
(Ed Dunlop) *t.k.h: led over 7f out: shkn up and hdd over 1f out: steadily fdd* **7/1**[2]
63-2 **5** *2½* **Automated**[13] 1438 3-9-1 **88** JamesDoyle 6 94
(Clive Brittain) *led to over 7f out: trckd ldr: tried to chal over 2f out: sn lost 2nd and steadily fdd* **14/1**
13-3 **6** *26* **Truth Or Dare**[9] 1516 3-9-1 **107** RichardHughes 2 44
(Richard Hannon) *chsd ldng pair: rdn over 3f out: wknd rapidly over 2f out: t.o* **10/1**

2m 19.53s (9.03) **Going Correction** +1.00s/f (Soft) **6** Ran SP% **109.9**
Speed ratings (Par 108): **103,101,100,99,97 76**
CSF £14.88 TOTE £1.60: £1.30, £3.60; EX 13.90 Trifecta £59.90.
**Owner** RJH Geffen and Rachel Hood **Bred** Newsells Park Stud **Trained** Newmarket, Suffolk

**FOCUS**
Often just a Classic trial in name only and there was no Ballydoyle representative. The third filled the same place behind Kingman in the Greenham, however, and this year's race may work out to be a decent affair. The form makes some sense and the winner is still improving.

## 1700 BET365.COM H'CAP (BOBIS RACE) 5f 6y
**3:50** (3:51) (Class 2) (0-100,92) 3-Y-O
**£12,450** (£3,728; £1,864; £932; £466; £234) **Stalls** Low

Form RPR
106- **1** **Eccleston**[279] 4528 3-9-3 **88** DanielTudhope 3 99
(David O'Meara) *hld up in midfield and racd against far rail: nt clr run and swtchd lft wl over 1f out: prog to ld last 150yds: rdn out: decisively* **7/2**[1]
110- **2** *1¼* **Hay Chewed (IRE)**[202] 7011 3-9-7 **92** FrankieDettori 1 98
(Conrad Allen) *led and racd against far rail: edgd lft whn rdn over 1f out: hdd and outpcd last 150yds* **14/1**
52-2 **3** *1¼* **Montaigne**[18] 1350 3-8-12 **83** JimCrowley 5 85
(Ralph Beckett) *trckd ldrs towards far rail: angled out over 1f out: rdn and kpt on to take 3rd last 100yds: nt pce to chal* **7/1**
213- **4** *¾* **Charles Molson**[175] 7658 3-9-6 **91** FergusSweeney 2 90
(Henry Candy) *trckd ldrs and racd against far rail: shkn up and kpt on same pce fnl f: nvr able to chal* **13/2**
00-6 **5** *1½* **Kickboxer (IRE)**[17] 1358 3-8-9 **83** WilliamTwiston-Davies(3) 4 76
(Mick Channon) *dwlt: rcvrd and sn prom but racd three off far rail: rdn to chse ldr wl over 1f out to 1f out: wknd* **5/1**[2]
01-0 **6** *2½* **Flying Bear (IRE)**[16] 1396 3-8-6 **77** HarryBentley 10 61
(Jeremy Gask) *dwlt: racd wd: nvr on terms: plugged on fr over 1f out* **20/1**
3466 **7** *7* **Scruffy Tramp (IRE)**[21] 1278 3-8-9 **85** (b[1]) NatashaEaton(5) 12 44
(Alan Bailey) *racd wdst of all: struggling bef 1/2-way: sn bhd* **66/1**
30-3 **8** *½* **Desert Ace (IRE)**[18] 1350 3-9-0 **85** AdamKirby 9 42
(Clive Cox) *spd fr wd draw to press ldr: drvn 2f out: wknd over 1f out* **11/2**[3]
54-1 **9** *2¾* **Sacha Park (IRE)**[23] 1237 3-8-12 **90** CamHardie(7) 7 38
(Richard Hannon) *a towards rr: struggling sn after 1/2-way: bhd over 1f out* **16/1**
112- **10** *3¾* **Pushkin Museum (IRE)**[119] 8404 3-8-11 **82** RyanMoore 8 16
(Richard Fahey) *racd wd: nvr on terms w ldrs: struggling fr 1/2-way: bhd over 1f out* **8/1**
1224 **11** *3½* **Spreadable (IRE)**[65] 667 3-8-4 **75** (b) SilvestreDeSousa 6
(Nick Littmoden) *racd wd: chsd ldrs 2f: sn lost pl and struggling: bhd over 1f out* **25/1**

1m 6.73s (5.13) **Going Correction** +1.125s/f (Soft) **11** Ran SP% **113.9**
Speed ratings (Par 104): **103,101,99,97,95 91,80,79,75,69 63**
CSF £51.77 CT £323.97 TOTE £4.90: £1.40, £3.60, £2.40; EX 49.10 Trifecta £412.70.
**Owner** David W Armstrong **Bred** Highfield Farm Llp **Trained** Nawton, N Yorks

**FOCUS**
A decent 3yo sprint handicap. Once again at this venue, especially on demanding ground, a low draw proved a massive advantage. A positive view has still been taken of the form.

## 1701 NORDOFF ROBBINS WILLIE ROBERTSON MEMORIAL MAIDEN FILLIES' STKS (BOBIS RACE) 1m 2f 7y
**4:25** (4:28) (Class 4) 3-Y-O **£6,469** (£1,925; £962; £481) **Stalls** Low

Form RPR
**1** **Kallisha** 3-9-0 0 JimCrowley 1 83+
(Ralph Beckett) *dwlt but rcvrd to trck ldr: led jst over 2f out gng wl: rdn over 1f out: 2 l clr fnl f: pressed last 100yds but hld on wl* **5/1**[2]
4 **2** *½* **Nancy From Nairobi**[14] 1424 3-8-11 0 WilliamTwiston-Davies(3) 17 79
(Mick Channon) *trckd ldng trio: rdn over 2f out: wnt 2nd jst over 1f out: drvn to chal 100yds out: kpt on but hld nr fin* **8/1**
0- **3** *3¼* **What A Scorcher**[181] 7533 3-9-0 0 AdamKirby 7 73
(Clive Cox) *chsd ldng trio: rdn over 2f out: kpt on fr over 1f out to take 3rd nr fin* **20/1**
**4** *1* **Grace And Favour** 3-9-0 0 DavidProbert 8 71
(Andrew Balding) *led: shkn up and hdd jst over 2f out: lost 2nd jst over 1f out: steadily fdd* **6/1**

- 5 3/4 **Allegria (IRE)** 3-9-0 0 FrankieDettori 11 70+
(John Gosden) *hld up wl in rr and wl off the pce: prog on outer fr 3f out: disp 4th over 1f out: one pce after: only one to make real hdwy fr the rr* **17/2**

6 4 **Perfect Light (IRE)** 3-9-0 0 RyanMoore 14 62
(William Haggas) *hld up off the pce disputing 6th: clsd on inner over 2f out: no hdwy over 1f out: fdd* **7/2[1]**

7 1 3/4 **Time Signal** 3-9-0 0 JamesDoyle 15 59
(Sir Michael Stoute) *hld up in midfield disputing 6th: shkn up and no prog over 2f out: n.d after* **12/1**

0-0 8 1 1/2 **Telegraphy (USA)**[9] 1517 3-9-0 0 PaddyAspell 12 56
(Ed Dunlop) *wl in rr and wl off the pce: shkn up and sme prog over 2f out: no hdwy over 1f out: fdd* **66/1**

9 3 1/2 **Millionaires Row (USA)** 3-9-0 0 WilliamBuick 6 49
(John Gosden) *uns rdr on way to post: slowly away: nvr really gng and a wl in rr: modest late prog* **11/2[3]**

10 2 1/2 **Strawberry Martini** 3-9-0 0 FergusSweeney 10 44
(William Muir) *slowly away: mostly in last and wl off the pce: no ch fnl 3f: modest late hdwy* **66/1**

11 3/4 **Fire Spinner (IRE)** 3-9-0 0 RichardHughes 5 43
(Ed Dunlop) *slowly away: hld up wl in rr and wl off the pce: pushed along and no prog over 2f out* **20/1**

12 1 1/4 **Dino Mite** 3-9-0 0 JamieSpencer 9 41
(Peter Chapple-Hyam) *a wl in rr and wl off the pce: shkn up and no prog over 2f out* **12/1**

13 3/4 **Petticoat Lane** 3-9-0 0 LemosdeSouza 16 39
(Luca Cumani) *trckd ldng quartet and clr of rest: pushed along over 2f out: sn wknd* **33/1**

2m 24.47s (13.97) **Going Correction** +1.10s/f (Soft) 13 Ran SP% **121.0**
Speed ratings (Par 97): **88,87,85,84,83 80,79,77,75,73 72,71,70**
CSF £42.91 TOTE £5.40: £2.00, £2.80, £7.80; EX 59.10 Trifecta £1091.20.
**Owner** D & J Newell **Bred** Derek & Judith Newell **Trained** Kimpton, Hants

**FOCUS**
Often a good-quality fillies' maiden and it was won by top-class Dar Re Me in 2008. It was run at a routine pace, favouring again those racing handily, and the form is rated around the runner-up.

## 1702 BET365 H'CAP (BOBIS RACE) 1m 2f 7y
4:55 (4:58) (Class 3) (0-95,89) 3-Y-O
£9,337 (£2,796; £1,398; £699; £349; £175) Stalls Low

Form RPR

1-2 1 **Windshear**[8] 1535 3-8-12 **80** RichardHughes 9 94+
(Richard Hannon) *led: racd wd in bk st: hdd 1/2-way: led again jst over 2f out: rdn clr over 1f out: styd on wl* **13/8[1]**

01-1 2 4 1/2 **Collaboration**[29] 1135 3-8-13 **81** (t) JimmyFortune 10 86
(Andrew Balding) *trckd ldrs: racd wd in bk st: chsd ldng pair over 2f out: rdn and outpcd wl over 1f out: styd on wl to take 2nd last 75yds* **10/1**

1- 3 1 3/4 **Elite Army**[165] 7835 3-9-4 **86** SilvestreDeSousa 11 88+
(Saeed bin Suroor) *t.k.h: trckd ldr: led 1/2-way: rdn and hdd jst over 2f out: btn over 1f out: lost 2nd last 75yds* **5/2[2]**

61- 4 13 **Gothic**[192] 7274 3-9-3 **85** RyanMoore 7 62
(Sir Michael Stoute) *trckd ldng pair: stl cl enough over 2f out: wknd wl over 1f out* **9/1**

23-1 5 1 1/4 **Hymenaios (IRE)**[27] 1166 3-9-4 **86** PatDobbs 4 61
(Richard Hannon) *dwlt: hld up in tch: racd wd in bk st: brief effrt wl over 2f out: sn rdn and wknd* **6/1[3]**

41- 6 5 **Oasis Fantasy (IRE)**[200] 7070 3-8-9 **77** ow1 JamieSpencer 5 43
(Ed Dunlop) *hld up in tch: rdn jst over 3f out: sn struggling and btn* **22/1**

10- 7 11 **Farquhar (IRE)**[157] 7967 3-9-3 **85** WilliamBuick 6 30
(Peter Chapple-Hyam) *awkward s: t.k.h: hld up in tch: rdn and wknd wl over 2f out: t.o* **25/1**

1- 8 24 **Mannaro (IRE)**[178] 7607 3-9-3 **85** AdamKirby 1
(Marco Botti) *a last: struggling fr 1/2-way: wl t.o* **20/1**

2m 21.16s (10.66) **Going Correction** +1.20s/f (Soft) 8 Ran SP% **113.0**
Speed ratings (Par 102): **105,101,100,89,88 84,75,56**
CSF £18.05 CT £39.01 TOTE £2.50: £1.10, £3.40, £1.10; EX 17.40 Trifecta £64.90.
**Owner** Michael Daniels **Bred** Cheveley Park Stud Ltd **Trained** East Everleigh, Wilts

**FOCUS**
A good 3yo handicap. It was run at a fair pace with two of the trio that elected to race wide for better ground on the far side filling the first two places. The winner is rated to his Newmarket form.
T/Jkpt: Not won. T/Plt: £379.40 to a £1 stake. Pool: £116502.62 - 224.15 winning tickets T/Qpdt: £50.00 to a £1 stake. Pool: £9029.86 - 133.49 winning tickets JN

1703 - 1709a (Foreign Racing) - See Raceform Interactive

# 1689 DONCASTER (L-H)
Saturday, April 26

**OFFICIAL GOING: Soft (7.4)**
Course railed out from 10f start to where Round joins straight, increasing distances on Round course by about 18yds
Wind: Moderate; across Weather: Sunny periods

## 1710 BOOKMAKER OFFERS AT FREEBETS.CO.UK AJA LADY RIDERS' H'CAP (LADY AMATEUR RIDERS) 7f
4:55 (4:56) (Class 4) (0-80,79) 4-Y-O+ £4,991 (£1,548; £773; £387) Stalls High

Form RPR

3101 1 **My Kingdom (IRE)**[22] 1275 8-10-1 **78** (t) MissKMargarson(5) 11 87
(Stuart Williams) *swtchd lft s: midfield: hdwy on outer 2f out: chsd ldrs over 1f out: rdn to challanmge ent fnl f: kpt on to ld last 75yds* **9/1**

06-2 2 1/2 **Khelman (IRE)**[27] 1191 4-10-3 **75** MissADeniel 9 83
(Richard Fahey) *cl up: led after 3f: rdn over 1f out: hdd and no ex last 75yds* **2/1[1]**

6005 3 1 **Illustrious Prince (IRE)**[33] 1082 7-9-11 **74** (p) MissLWilson(5) 6 79
(Julie Camacho) *trckd ldrs: hdwy 2f out: n.m.r and swtchd lft jst over 1f out: rdn and kpt on fnl f* **16/1**

40-0 4 nk **Desert Creek (IRE)**[17] 1376 8-10-1 **73** MrsCBartley 1 79
(David Nicholls) *trckd ldrs: hdwy 3f out: cl up 2f out: rdn to chal over 1f out and ev ch tl one pce ins fnl f: eased and lost 3rd nr line* **10/1**

0120 5 2 **My Son Max**[19] 1351 6-10-1 **73** MissSBrotherton 13 72
(Michael Blake) *towards rr: hdwy into midfield 1/2-way: rdn along 2f out: styd on appr fnl f: nrst fin* **5/1[2]**

30-0 6 1/2 **Lothair (IRE)**[14] 1446 5-9-6 **69** MissHHeal(5) 8 67
(Alan Swinbank) *led 3f: cl up: rdn along 2f out: wknd ent fnl f* **16/1**

210- 7 1 **Checkpoint**[189] 7369 5-9-4 **67** MissHDukes(5) 4 63
(Tony Coyle) *hld up in rr: sme hdwy 2f out: rdn and kpt on fnl f: nrst fin* **20/1**

006- 8 1 **Tapis Libre**[182] 7539 6-9-12 **73** MissJoannaMason(3) 5 66
(Michael Easterby) *nvr bttr than midfield* **20/1**

1343 9 hd **Conry (IRE)**[21] 1316 8-10-7 **79** MissCWalton 15 71
(Ian Williams) *n.m.r after s: a towards rr* **8/1[3]**

000- 10 2 1/4 **Jontleman (IRE)**[205] 6977 4-10-4 **76** MissEJJones 10 63
(Mick Channon) *n.m.r jst after s: in tch: effrt and hdwy to chse ldrs 3f out: sn rdn and no imp* **28/1**

2000 11 3 **Pelmanism**[28] 1167 7-9-0 **65** (p) MissAnne-SophieCrombez(7) 14 44
(Gay Kelleway) *a in rr* **20/1**

6-06 12 19 **Hard Core Debt**[12] 1483 4-10-1 **73** MissHBethell 16
(Brian Ellison) *a in rr* **12/1**

1m 30.04s (3.74) **Going Correction** +0.25s/f (Good) 12 Ran SP% **117.4**
Speed ratings (Par 105): **88,87,86,85,83 83,81,80,80,78 74,52**
CSF £25.40 CT £294.04 TOTE £7.10: £3.00, £1.10, £5.50; EX 21.60 Trifecta £196.20.
**Owner** My Kingdom For A Horse **Bred** Irish National Stud **Trained** Newmarket, Suffolk
■ Stewards' Enquiry : Mrs C Bartley seven-day ban: failed to take all reasonable and permissable measures to obtain best possible placing (May 12,19,23,27,29,31,Jun 6)
Miss A Deniel one-day ban: failed to ride to draw (May 12); three-day ban: careless riding (May 19,23,27)

**FOCUS**
Course railed out from 10f start to where Round joins straight increasing distances on Round course by about 18yds. This looked to be run at a sound enough pace. The winner's best run for two years.

## 1711 FREE BETS AT FREEBETS.CO.UK FILLIES' H'CAP 7f
5:25 (5:25) (Class 4) (0-80,79) 3-Y-O £4,690 (£1,395; £697; £348) Stalls High

Form RPR

330- 1 **Cay Dancer**[182] 7533 3-9-2 74 PatDobbs 1 84
(Richard Hannon) *trckd ldrs on outer: hdwy over 2f out: sn cl up: rdn to ld over 1f out: clr whn edgd rt ins fnl f: kpt on* **13/2**

20-1 2 2 1/4 **Nimble Kimble**[17] 1389 3-8-10 73 RyanTate(5) 2 77
(James Eustace) *cl up: rdn along 2f out: ev ch tl drvn and one pce ent fnl f* **9/2[3]**

1 3 3/4 **Divine (IRE)**[83] 447 3-9-6 78 MickaelBarzalona 5 80+
(Mick Channon) *trckd ldrs: smooth hdwy to ld wl over 2f out: rdn wl over 1f out: sn drvn and hdd over 1f out: kpt on one pce* **4/1[2]**

214- 4 nk **Starlight Serenade**[222] 6474 3-8-0 65 JaneElliott(7) 3 66+
(Ralph Beckett) *rrd s and bhd: hdwy over 2f out: sn rdn and kpt on appr fnl f: nrst fin* **6/1**

13-5 5 1 1/2 **Imshivalla (IRE)**[6] 1601 3-9-1 73 TonyHamilton 8 70
(Richard Fahey) *sn led: pushed along 1/2-way: rdn and hdd wl over 2f out: sn wknd* **8/1**

331- 6 7 **Rayoumti (IRE)**[190] 7352 3-8-13 71 AdamKirby 7 50
(Marco Botti) *trckd ldrs: pushed along over 3f out: rdn wl over 2f out and sn btn* **10/3[1]**

002- 7 22 **Thatchereen (IRE)**[226] 6334 3-8-10 68 DavidProbert 6
(Michael Bell) *dwlt: a in rr: rdn along wl over 2f out: sn outpcd and bhd* **8/1**

1m 28.71s (2.41) **Going Correction** +0.25s/f (Good) 7 Ran SP% **111.1**
Speed ratings (Par 97): **96,93,92,92,90 82,57**
CSF £33.42 CT £126.86 TOTE £7.30: £3.20, £2.40; EX 43.60 Trifecta £209.10.
**Owner** R Barnett **Bred** W And R Barnett Ltd **Trained** East Everleigh, Wilts

**FOCUS**
An interesting fillies' handicap featuring a handful of horses with potential. The winner stepped up on her 2yo form.

## 1712 POLYPIPE MAIDEN STKS 5f
6:00 (6:05) (Class 5) 2-Y-O £3,234 (£962; £481; £240) Stalls High

Form RPR

1 **Sea Wolf (IRE)** 2-9-5 0 PaulMulrennan 2 76
(Michael Dods) *prom: cl up 1/2-way: led wl over 1f out: jnd and rdn ent fnl f: kpt on wl towards fin* **7/2[3]**

2 hd **Mattmu** 2-9-5 0 RobertWinston 4 75
(Tim Easterby) *trckd ldrs: hdwy wl over 1f out: rdn to chal ent fnl f: ev ch tl no ex nr fin* **20/1**

3 2 1/2 **Agadoo** 2-8-11 0 MichaelJMMurphy(3) 8 61
(Shaun Harris) *green and towards rr: pushed along over 2f out: hdwy over 1f out: styd on strly fnl f: nrst fin* **50/1**

4 nk **Beacon** 2-9-5 0 RichardHughes 5 65+
(Richard Hannon) *cl up: led 1/2-way: rdn and hdd wl over 1f out: wknd fnl f* **1/1[1]**

0 5 hd **Mountain Man**[28] 1161 2-8-12 0 DanielleMooney(7) 1 64
(Michael Easterby) *led to 1/2-way: rdn along on outer 2f out: grad wknd* **20/1**

6 nk **Roossey (IRE)** 2-9-5 0 RyanMoore 6 63
(William Haggas) *prom: cl up 1/2-way: pushed along 2f out: sn rdn and wknd over 1f out* **11/4[2]**

7 16 **Phoenix Phil** 2-9-5 0 PaddyAspell 7 6
(Shaun Harris) *dwlt: green and a in rr: outpcd and bhd fnl 2f* **50/1**

1m 4.12s (3.62) **Going Correction** +0.25s/f (Good) 7 Ran SP% **112.3**
Speed ratings (Par 92): **81,80,76,76,75 75,49**
CSF £54.82 TOTE £4.70: £3.40, £4.90; EX 50.50 Trifecta £340.10.
**Owner** Mr & Mrs Paul Gaffney **Bred** Irish National Stud **Trained** Denton, Co Durham
■ Grand Beauty was withdrawn. Price at time of withdrawal 10-1. Rule 4 applies to all bets - deduction 5p in the pound.

**FOCUS**
Some nicely bred sorts on show. The winner is from a yard that has its 2yos well forward and looks a fair recruit.

## 1713 DOWNLOAD THE FREEBETS.CO.UK APP MAIDEN FILLIES' STKS 6f
6:30 (6:31) (Class 5) 3-Y-O+ £3,234 (£962; £481; £240) Stalls High

Form RPR

3 1 **Perfect Blessings (IRE)**[15] 1422 3-8-13 0 AdamKirby 3 92
(Clive Cox) *mde all: rdn clr appr fnl f: kpt on strly* **11/4[2]**

322- 2 3 3/4 **Penny Drops**[168] 7818 3-8-13 88 RyanMoore 1 81
(William Haggas) *t.k.h early and prom: sn trcking wnr: effrt 2f out and sn rdn: drvn ent fnl f and kpt on one pce* **2/5[1]**

0-5 3 10 **Cards**[31] 1112 4-9-10 0 (p) PaulMulrennan 12 54
(Kevin Ryan) *prom: rdn along over 2f out: sn outpcd: plugged on one pce to take modest 3rd ins fnl f* **25/1**

23- 4 2 **Alpine Flower (IRE)**[316] 3280 3-8-13 0 RobertWinston 5 45
(Tim Easterby) *hld up towards rr: hdwy 3f out: rdn to chse ldng pair wl over 1f out: wknd fnl f* **8/1[3]**

5 nk **Champagne Charley** 3-8-13 0 AdamBeschizza 2 44
(Des Donovan) *trckd ldrs: pushed along and green 1/2-way: rdn wl over 2f out: sn one pce* **20/1**

0-0 **6** ½ **Minionette (IRE)**[9] 1542 3-8-13 0 BenCurtis 10 43
(Alan Swinbank) *towards rr tl sme late hdwy* **50/1**
400- **7** 4 **Lazy Sioux**[212] 6778 3-8-6 55 EvaMoscrop(7) 9 31
(Philip Kirby) *in tch: rdn and sme hdwy over 2f out: sn edgd lft and wknd* **20/1**
5 **8** 2¾ **Dorset Gift**[21] 1298 3-8-13 0 DavidProbert 4 22
(Michael Bell) *prom: rdn along 1/2-way: sn wknd* **25/1**
**9** 24 **Sirnita**[40] 5-9-7 0 BillyCray(3) 8
(Richard Guest) *s.i.s: green and a in rr: outpcd and bhd fnl 3f* **66/1**
1m 13.58s (-0.02) **Going Correction** +0.25s/f (Good)
**WFA** 3 from 4yo+ 11lb **9** Ran SP% **129.9**
Speed ratings (Par 100): **110,105,91,89,88 87,82,78,46**
CSF £4.54 TOTE £4.20: £1.20, £1.02, £5.60; EX 5.70 Trifecta £55.10.
**Owner** John Drew & Ian M Brown **Bred** Diomed Bloodstock Ltd **Trained** Lambourn, Berks
**FOCUS**
Not much depth to this maiden and it only ever concerned the top two in the market who drew a mile clear. A fair time from the winner, who was worth more at face value.

## 1714 GET FREEBETS.CO.UK ON YOUR MOBILE H'CAP (BOBIS RACE) 1m (S)
**7:05** (7:05) (Class 3) (0-90,87) 3-Y-O **£8,409** (£2,502; £1,250; £625) **Stalls** High

Form RPR
1334 **1** **Basil Berry**[17] 1390 3-8-5 71 BenCurtis 3 83
(Chris Dwyer) *racd centre and set stdy pce: shkn up and qcknd wl clr 2f out: kpt on strly fnl f* **14/1**
15-4 **2** 4½ **Showpiece**[15] 1420 3-9-3 83 RichardHughes 7 86
(Richard Hannon) *racd towards stands' rail: hld up: effrt and hdwy to chse clr ldr wl over 1f out: sn rdn and no imp fnl f* **6/4**[1]
21 **3** 2¼ **Moonlight Venture**[51] 861 3-8-12 78 PaulMulrennan 6 74
(Kevin Ryan) *t.k.h early: racd towards stands' rail: prom: effrt wl over 2f out: sn rdn and one pce* **8/1**
1 **4** nse **Cornborough**[19] 1344 3-8-6 75 JasonHart(3) 2 71
(Mark Walford) *trckd wnr in centre: shkn up wl over 2f out: sn rdn and one pce* **4/1**[3]
16- **5** 29 **Almuheet**[215] 6697 3-9-5 85 PaulHanagan 4 15
(Sir Michael Stoute) *t.k.h early: hld up: rdn along wl over 2f out: sn btn and eased* **9/4**[2]
1m 41.2s (1.90) **Going Correction** +0.25s/f (Good) **5** Ran SP% **108.5**
Speed ratings (Par 102): **100,95,93,93,64**
CSF £34.76 TOTE £9.50: £4.10, £1.10; EX 50.90 Trifecta £74.70.
**Owner** Strawberry Fields Stud **Bred** Strawberry Fields Stud **Trained** Newmarket, Suffolk
**FOCUS**
Some unexposed horses from powerful stables dominated the betting for this handicap, but it was won by the most exposed runner, who was tackling turf for the first time. He's rated in line with his AW form.

## 1715 CASINO SIGN UP BONUSES AT BONUS.CO.UK H'CAP 1m 2f 60y
**7:35** (7:35) (Class 3) (0-95,95) 4-Y-0+ **£8,409** (£2,502; £1,250; £625) **Stalls** Low

Form RPR
2-1 **1** **Arab Spring (IRE)**[26] 1208 4-8-11 85 RyanMoore 12 100+
(Sir Michael Stoute) *trckd ldrs: smooth hdwy over 2f out: swtchd lft and effrt to chal wl over 1f out: sn led: rdn clr ent fnl f: readily* **1/1**[1]
016- **2** 2½ **Jazz Master**[129] 8327 4-8-11 85 AndreaAtzeni 6 92
(Luca Cumani) *trckd ldng pair: pushed along over 3f out: rdn and sltly outpcd wl over 1f out: kpt on u.p fnl f* **6/1**[2]
500- **3** nk **Storm King**[217] 6650 5-9-4 92 DavidProbert 14 98
(David C Griffiths) *led: rdn and qcknd 3f out: drvn and hdd over 1f out: kpt on same pce fnl f* **20/1**
6-00 **4** hd **Global Village (IRE)**[28] 1164 9-9-1 89 SteveDrowne 2 95
(Brian Ellison) *hld up: hdwy and in tch 1/2-way: rdn to chse ldrs over 2f out: drvn and kpt on same pce fnl f* **20/1**
/32- **5** 1¼ **Magic Hurricane (IRE)**[233] 6133 4-8-10 84 FrederikTylicki 16 88
(James Fanshawe) *in tch: hdwy on outer over 3f out: rdn to chse ldng pair 2f out: drvn and one pce appr fnl f* **8/1**
20-0 **6** 1¼ **Las Verglas Star (IRE)**[18] 1360 6-8-4 83 SammyJoBell(5) 3 84
(Richard Fahey) *hld up towards rr: hdwy over 2f out: sn rdn and kpt on fnl f: nrst fin* **14/1**
310- **7** 1 **Spirit Of The Law (IRE)**[133] 8301 5-8-7 88 JoshQuinn(7) 7 87
(Richard Fahey) *chsd ldr: rdn along 3f out: wknd 2f out* **22/1**
2061 **8** 1¼ **Ansaab**[12] 1483 6-8-13 87 (t) TomQueally 5 84
(Alan McCabe) *hld up in rr: effrt and sme hdwy 3f out: rdn along 2f out: n.d* **7/1**[3]
4 **9** hd **Safe Home (IRE)**[18] 1360 4-8-6 87 JoeDoyle(7) 4 84
(John Quinn) *hld up in rr: effrt and sme hdwy on inner 3f out: sn rdn and btn* **14/1**
21-0 **10** 7 **Eurato (FR)**[19] 1351 4-8-8 82 PaddyAspell 13 65
(Alan Jones) *hld up: a towards rr* **50/1**
2m 16.0s (6.60) **Going Correction** +0.875s/f (Soft) **10** Ran SP% **117.1**
Speed ratings (Par 107): **108,106,105,105,104 103,102,101,101,96**
CSF £6.66 CT £75.92 TOTE £1.70: £1.10, £2.00, £5.70; EX 8.70 Trifecta £123.90.
**Owner** Ballymacoll Stud **Bred** Ballymacoll Stud Farm Ltd **Trained** Newmarket, Suffolk
**FOCUS**
This was entitled to be a competitive event, but it was turned into a procession by the completely unexposed and clearly very well handicapped winner. The placed form is only ordinary.

## 1716 ONLINE CASINOS AT BONUS.CO.UK FILLIES' H'CAP 1m (S)
**8:05** (8:05) (Class 4) (0-80,80) 4-Y-0+ **£5,175** (£1,540; £769; £384) **Stalls** High

Form RPR
12-1 **1** **Trixie Malone**[21] 1310 4-8-5 69 JoeyHaynes(5) 2 81
(K R Burke) *mde all: rdn along wl over 1f out: sn jnd and drvn ent fnl f: hld on gamely towards fin* **5/2**[2]
124- **2** nk **Cosseted**[185] 7470 4-9-2 75 RyanMoore 1 86
(James Fanshawe) *hld up: hdwy to trck ldrs over 3f out: rdn to chse ldng pair 2f out: drvn to chal ent fnl f: ev ch tl no ex nr fin* **6/4**[1]
30-1 **3** 1½ **Burnt Fingers (IRE)**[25] 1215 4-8-7 66 AndreaAtzeni 6 74
(Rod Millman) *t.k.h early: trckd wnr: hdwy over 2f out: rdn to chal over 1f out: drvn and ev ch ins fnl f tl wknd towards fin* **9/1**
320- **4** 7 **Al Manaal**[262] 5125 4-9-4 80 CharlesBishop(3) 7 72
(Mick Channon) *trckd ldrs: rdn along 3f out: wknd 2f out* **20/1**
100- **5** ½ **Cosmic Halo**[171] 7765 5-9-0 78 SammyJoBell(5) 3 69
(Richard Fahey) *hld up: hdwy to trck ldng pair 1/2-way: effrt wl over 2f out: sn rdn and one pce* **7/1**[3]
43-0 **6** 2½ **Lady Artiste (IRE)**[19] 1348 4-8-7 66 oh1 BenCurtis 8 51
(Alan Swinbank) *towards rr: rdn along over 3f out: outpcd and bhd fnl 2f* **20/1**

600- **7** 5 **Rosaceous**[163] 7891 4-9-7 80 (b) SteveDrowne 9 54
(Daniel Kubler) *dwlt: sn prom: rdn along 3f out: sn wknd* **8/1**
1m 40.76s (1.46) **Going Correction** +0.25s/f (Good) **7** Ran SP% **111.7**
Speed ratings (Par 102): **102,101,100,93,92 90,85**
CSF £6.30 CT £24.95 TOTE £3.00: £1.10, £2.00; EX 6.30 Trifecta £32.60.
**Owner** Mrs Elaine M Burke **Bred** Llety Farms **Trained** Middleham Moor, N Yorks
**FOCUS**
A few of these look open to improvement this season. The winner is progressive.
T/Plt: £186.20 to a £1 stake. Pool: £52,591.39 - 206.11 winning units T/Qpdt: £20.20 to a £1 stake. Pool: £6,934.50 - 252.83 winning units JR

# HAYDOCK (L-H)
### Saturday, April 26

**OFFICIAL GOING: Good (good to firm in places; watered; 7.9)**
All races on Stands' side home straight. Rail realignment around bends increased distances of all races by 37yds.
Wind: fresh 1/2 behind Weather: changeable, becoming fine and sunny, breezy

## 1717 PAUL MERSON SPORTMAN'S DINNER 27TH MAY H'CAP (DIV I) 1m
**1:20** (1:21) (Class 5) (0-70,70) 4-Y-0+ **£4,851** (£1,443; £721; £360) **Stalls** Low

Form RPR
-015 **1** **Cravat**[30] 1121 5-9-2 68 OisinMurphy(3) 7 78
(Ed de Giles) *mid-div: pushed along 6f out: hdwy on outer over 2f out: led jst ins fnl f: styd on* **6/1**
-540 **2** 1¼ **Docofthebay (IRE)**[28] 1167 10-9-0 63 LukeMorris 1 70
(Scott Dixon) *dwlt: sn mid-div: effrt over 3f out: sn chsng ldrs: kpt on to take 2nd last 100yds* **9/1**
0554 **3** 3½ **Ewell Place (IRE)**[46] 910 5-9-2 65 RyanMoore 2 64
(Patrick Morris) *trckd ldrs: effrt over 3f out: kpt on one pce fnl 150yds* **9/2**[1]
2632 **4** 2 **Colour My World**[22] 1288 4-8-13 62 (b) SteveDrowne 6 56
(Ed McMahon) *t.k.h: led: hdd jst ins fnl f: wknd towards fin* **5/1**[2]
6-30 **5** 6 **McCool Bannanas**[92] 319 6-8-9 58 HayleyTurner 5 39
(James Unett) *s.s: drvn and hdwy on ins over 3f out: wknd over 1f out* **8/1**
0122 **6** ½ **Nubar Boy**[10] 1503 7-9-1 69 (p) GeorgeDowning(5) 4 49
(Ian Williams) *hld up in rr: effrt 3f out: wknd over 1f out* **9/2**[1]
60-0 **7** 1¼ **Thistleandtworoses (USA)**[17] 1376 4-9-7 70 DanielTudhope 9 47
(David O'Meara) *hld up in rr: effrt over 3f out: rdn and wnt lft over 2f out: nvr a factor* **11/1**
-660 **8** 1¾ **Strong Conviction**[14] 1454 4-9-2 68 CharlesBishop(3) 8 41
(Simon Hodgson) *sn chsng ldr: wknd 2f out* **25/1**
-004 **9** 24 **Bapak Muda (USA)**[14] 1447 4-9-3 66 JamieSpencer 3
(Kevin Ryan) *chsd ldrs: lost pl over 2f out: bhd whn eased 1f out: t.o* **11/2**[3]
1m 43.85s (0.15) **Going Correction** -0.10s/f (Good) **9** Ran SP% **116.0**
Speed ratings (Par 103): **95,93,90,88,82 81,80,78,54**
CSF £58.79 CT £268.44 TOTE £7.50: £2.60, £2.30, £1.90; EX 70.00 Trifecta £352.30.
**Owner** T Gould **Bred** Darley **Trained** Ledbury, H'fords
**FOCUS**
There was 10mm of overnight rain in the 24 hours prior to racing, but course officials were pleased with the state of the ground, which had not been used since last October. The jockeys were also complimentary about it after the first. A moderate handicap that looked wide open. They went an average gallop early on and began to wind up nearing 3f out. A similar time to division II, and ordinary form.

## 1718 80'S MUSIC NIGHT HERE 21ST JUNE H'CAP (DIV II OF 1:20) 1m
**1:50** (1:50) (Class 5) (0-70,70) 4-Y-0+ **£4,851** (£1,443; £721; £360) **Stalls** Low

Form RPR
3-12 **1** **Reggie Bond**[61] 736 4-8-10 62 (b) RobertTart(3) 6 72
(Geoffrey Oldroyd) *mid-div: hdwy over 3f out: sn chsng ldrs: led over 1f out: styd on ins fnl f* **9/4**[1]
-355 **2** 2 **Prince Of Burma (IRE)**[85] 399 6-9-0 66 (v) DeclanBates(3) 3 71
(David Evans) *s.s: hdwy on ins over 2f out: swtchd rt ins fnl f: kpt on* **16/1**
0032 **3** ½ **Kyllachy Star**[18] 1356 8-9-5 68 (v) RyanMoore 4 72
(Richard Fahey) *dwlt: hld up in rr: drvn over 3f out: styd on appr fnl f* **5/2**[2]
4542 **4** 1 **One Scoop Or Two**[14] 1450 8-9-0 68 (p) JackDuern(5) 2 70
(Andrew Hollinshead) *trckd ldrs on inner: upsides over 1f out: kpt on same pce* **6/1**[3]
30/0 **5** ½ **La Danza**[21] 1297 4-8-8 62 ShirleyTeasdale(5) 1 62
(Lisa Williamson) *dwlt: sn chsng ldrs: drvn over 3f out: one pce over 1f out* **66/1**
3-42 **6** 1¼ **Tukitinyasok (IRE)**[65] 671 7-8-7 56 oh2 RoystonFfrench 5 54
(Clive Mulhall) *chsd ldrs: drvn over 3f out: one pce fnl 2f* **11/1**
4- **7** ½ **Janaab (IRE)**[107] 4-9-4 67 (t) TomEaves 8 63
(Tim Easterby) *swtchd lft after s: hld up in rr: effrt 3f out: nvr a factor* **20/1**
00-0 **8** ¾ **Cono Zur (FR)**[18] 1356 7-9-2 65 JamesSullivan 9 60
(Ruth Carr) *led: hdd over 1f out: wknd jst ins fnl f* **12/1**
200- **9** 11 **Kuwait Star**[250] 5580 5-9-7 70 PaulHanagan 7 39
(Michael Herrington) *sn trcking ldrs on outside: drvn over 3f out: lost pl 2f out: sn bhd* **8/1**
1m 43.81s (0.11) **Going Correction** -0.10s/f (Good) **9** Ran SP% **112.9**
Speed ratings (Par 103): **95,93,92,91,91 89,89,88,77**
CSF £38.41 CT £94.98 TOTE £2.70: £1.20, £5.20, £1.50; EX 49.70 Trifecta £191.00.
**Owner** R C Bond **Bred** R C Bond **Trained** Brawby, N Yorks
**FOCUS**
The second division of the moderate 1m handicap. It was run at a fair enough pace and most of the field held a chance nearing 2f out. The winner progressed again from the AW.

## 1719 £25 FREE BET AT CORBETTSPORTS.COM H'CAP 7f
**2:20** (2:20) (Class 2) (0-105,103) 4-Y-0+ **£32,345** (£9,625; £4,810; £2,405) **Stalls** Low

Form RPR
00-2 **1** **Glen Moss (IRE)**[7] 1576 5-9-0 96 SeanLevey 5 106
(David Brown) *trckd ldrs: led over 2f out: kpt on wl ins fnl f* **13/2**[3]
00-0 **2** ¾ **Louis The Pious**[12] 1484 6-9-0 96 [1] DanielTudhope 8 104
(David O'Meara) *rr-div: effrt over 3f out: edgd rt 1f out: styd on to take 2nd clsng stages* **8/1**
0-05 **3** 1 **Newstead Abbey**[12] 1484 4-9-0 96 TomEaves 12 101
(David Barron) *chsd ldrs: nt clr run over 2f out: kpt on fnl f* **11/1**
050- **4** ¾ **Dont Bother Me (IRE)**[202] 7051 4-9-3 99 FrankieDettori 3 103
(Marco Botti) *chsd ldrs: upsides over 2f out: kpt on same pce fnl f* **7/1**
20-0 **5** nk **Balty Boys (IRE)**[28] 1165 5-8-13 95 DaleSwift 10 98
(Brian Ellison) *mid-div: sn drvn along: hdwy on outer over 2f out: kpt on fnl f* **16/1**



The Form Book, Raceform Ltd, Newbury, RG14 5SJ

3033 **6** *nk* **Bertiewhittle**[49] [886] 6-9-0 **103**........................ JackGarritty(7) 13 105
(David Barron) *dwlt: in rr: hdwy on outer over 2f out: kpt on fnl f* **11/1**

00-6 **7** *3/4* **Fort Bastion (IRE)**[14] [1442] 5-8-10 **92**........................ JamesSullivan 11 92
(Ruth Carr) *swtchd lft s: in rr: hdwy on outside over 2f out: kpt on fnl f* **16/1**

6-34 **8** *3* **Sir Reginald**[27] [1193] 6-8-11 **93**........................ RyanMoore 9 85+
(Richard Fahey) *swtchd lft s: in rr: sme hdwy over 2f out: nvr a factor* **6/1**[2]

2-06 **9** *hd* **Kenny Powers**[14] [1443] 5-9-4 **100**........................(t) StephenCraine 6 92
(Tom Dascombe) *trckd ldrs: t.k.h: effrt over 2f out: wknd fnl f* **50/1**

0-60 **10** *3 3/4* **Consign**[28] [1165] 4-8-12 **94**........................(v) SebSanders 4 76
(Jeremy Noseda) *mid-div: drvn over 3f out: wknd over 1f out* **8/1**

0-56 **11** *1/2* **Regal Parade**[31] [1114] 10-8-12 **94**........................(t) LukeMorris 7 75
(Milton Bradley) *in tch: effrt over 2f out: wknd over 1f out* **33/1**

030- **12** *5* **Gramercy (IRE)**[183] [7495] 7-8-12 **94**........................ JamieSpencer 14 62
(David Simcock) *swtchd lft s: a in rr* **20/1**

110- **13** *9* **Big Johnny D (IRE)**[203] [7014] 5-9-1 **97**........................ PaulHanagan 2 41
(David Barron) *stmbld s: led: hdd over 2f out: lost pl and eased over 1f out* **11/2**[1]

61-4 **14** *66* **Set The Trend**[28] [1174] 8-9-1 **100**........................ OisinMurphy(3) 1
(David Dennis) *chsd ldrs: lost pl over 3f out: sn wl bhd: virtually p.u: hopelessly t.o* **20/1**

1m 28.18s (-2.52) **Going Correction** -0.10s/f (Good) **14** Ran SP% **120.6**
Speed ratings (Par 109): **110,109,108,107,106 106,105,102,101,97 97,91,81,5**
CSF £55.28 CT £586.95 TOTE £6.60: £2.20, £2.60, £4.00; EX 45.40 Trifecta £868.50.
**Owner** J C Fretwell **Bred** Rathbarry Stud **Trained** Averham Park, Notts

**FOCUS**
A highly competitive handicap run at a sound pace and it produced a tight finish. Those racing handily seemed at an advantage. The winner rates back to his best.

## 1720 WATCH RACING UK ON SKY CHANNEL 432 MAIDEN STKS 1m 3f 200y
**2:55** (2:56) (Class 5) 3-Y-O+ **£3,881** (£1,155; £577; £288) **Stalls** High

Form RPR

0-3 **1** **Talmada (USA)**[15] [1423] 3-8-3 0........................ PaulHanagan 4 91+
(Roger Varian) *led 1f: trckd ldng pair: shkn up to ld over 2f out: drvn clr 1f out: eased towards fin* **10/11**[1]

6-2 **2** *7* **Galuppi**[18] [1357] 3-8-9 0 ow1........................ RyanMoore 3 83
(Luca Cumani) *dwlt: hld up in last: effrt 4f out: 2nd over 1f out: no ch w wnr* **13/8**[2]

4-5 **3** *3* **Norab (GER)**[14] [1438] 3-8-8 0........................ LukeMorris 1 78
(Marco Botti) *chsd ldr after 1f: led over 3f out: sn rdn: hdd over 2f out: one pce* **6/1**[3]

624- **4** *57* **Market Storm (FR)**[120] [8415] 3-8-8 72........................(v[1]) TomEaves 5
(Michael Mullineaux) *t.k.h: led after 1f: drvn over 4f out: hdd over 3f out: wknd qckly: t.o 2f out: eventually completed* **28/1**

2m 33.72s (-0.08) **Going Correction** -0.10s/f (Good) **4** Ran SP% **108.2**
Speed ratings (Par 103): **96,91,89,51**
CSF £2.65 TOTE £2.10; EX 3.30 Trifecta £4.30.
**Owner** Sheikh Ahmed Al Maktoum **Bred** Darley **Trained** Newmarket, Suffolk

**FOCUS**
A small field but the form makes sense. The winner has the potential to rate a fair bit higher.

## 1721 BEST ODDS GUARANTEED AT CORBETTSPORTS.COM H'CAP 1m
**3:25** (3:28) (Class 2) (0-105,101) 4-Y-O+**£29,110** (£8,662; £4,329; £2,164) **Stalls** Low

Form RPR

00-3 **1** **Yourartisonfire**[28] [1164] 4-7-12 **83**........................(v) JoeyHaynes(5) 10 92
(K R Burke) *trckd ldrs on outer: t.k.h: effrt over 2f out: r.o to ld last 100yds* **7/1**[3]

2-61 **2** *3/4* **Gabrial's Kaka (IRE)**[14] [1437] 4-9-7 **101**........................ JamieSpencer 6 109+
(Richard Fahey) *hld up in rr: drvn on outer over 3f out: gd hdwy over 1f out: fin wl to take 2nd nr fin* **11/4**[1]

40-1 **3** *3/4* **The Rectifier (USA)**[59] [749] 7-9-6 **100**........................(t) GeorgeBaker 9 106
(Seamus Durack) *trckd ldrs: led 3f out: hdd and no ex ins fnl f* **16/1**

2206 **4** *1 1/4* **Tellovoi (IRE)**[21] [1316] 6-8-9 **92**........................(v) OisinMurphy(3) 11 95
(Ann Stokell) *t.k.h: sn trckd ldrs: upsides over 2f out: kpt on same pce fnl f* **50/1**

110- **5** *3/4* **Ingleby Angel (IRE)**[198] [7152] 5-9-2 **96**........................ RyanMoore 12 97+
(David O'Meara) *s.i.s: t.k.h in rr: hdwy on outer over 2f out: styd on fnl f: tk 5th nr fin* **14/1**

00-0 **6** *1* **Foxtrot Romeo (IRE)**[14] [1437] 5-8-12 **92**........................(t) FrankieDettori 5 91
(Marco Botti) *mid-div: hdwy over 3f out: one pce over 1f out* **13/2**[2]

2312 **7** *2* **Sound Advice**[24] [1234] 5-8-10 **90**........................ TomEaves 16 85
(Keith Dalgleish) *hld up in rr on outer: hdwy over 2f out: kpt on fnl f* **20/1**

0031 **8** *nse* **Robert The Painter (IRE)**[17] [1399] 6-9-1 **98**........................ JulieBurke(3) 8 92
(David O'Meara) *chsd ldrs: one pce fnl 2f* **16/1**

-000 **9** *1 1/4* **Talented Kid**[14] [1442] 5-8-5 **88**........................ MichaelJMMurphy(3) 2 80
(Mark Johnston) *in rr: hdwy on inner over 3f out: one pce fnl 2f* **20/1**

0-00 **10** *nk* **Chosen Character (IRE)**[14] [1442] 6-8-3 **90**........................(vt) JennyPowell(7) 4 81
(Tom Dascombe) *s.s: chsd ldrs after 2f: fdd fnl 100yds* **33/1**

124- **11** *1 3/4* **Frog Hollow**[247] [5681] 5-8-11 **91**........................ SeanLevey 15 78
(David O'Meara) *mid-div: sme hdwy 3f out: fdd over 1f out* **14/1**

00-1 **12** *3 1/2* **Brae Hill (IRE)**[28] [1164] 8-9-3 **97**........................ PaulHanagan 1 76
(Richard Fahey) *chsd ldrs: lost pl over 1f out: eased clsng stages* **9/1**

4-00 **13** *1 3/4* **Postscript (IRE)**[28] [1164] 6-8-9 **89**........................ LukeMorris 14 64
(David Simcock) *mid-div: effrt 3f out: wknd 2f out* **33/1**

0045 **14** *1* **Sweet Lightning**[14] [1437] 9-9-4 **98**........................(t) DanielTudhope 13 70
(David O'Meara) *in rr: bhd fnl 2f* **9/1**

0-42 **15** *8* **Don't Call Me (IRE)**[59] [749] 7-9-5 **99**........................(t) AdrianNicholls 3 53
(David Nicholls) *mid-div: hdwy on inner over 3f out: sn drvn: wknd 2f out: sn eased* **12/1**

3210 **16** *8* **Skytrain**[3] [1646] 4-8-7 **87**........................ JoeFanning 7 23
(Mark Johnston) *led: hdd 3f out: sn lost pl: eased over 1f out* **25/1**

1m 41.92s (-1.78) **Going Correction** -0.10s/f (Good) **16** Ran SP% **126.5**
Speed ratings (Par 109): **104,103,102,101,100 99,97,97,96,95 94,90,88,87,79 71**
CSF £25.13 CT £316.90 TOTE £8.70: £2.20, £1.60, £2.70, £8.10; EX 32.30 Trifecta £829.40.
**Owner** J O'Shea, W Rooney & Ontoawinner **Bred** J A And Mrs M A Knox **Trained** Middleham Moor, N Yorks

**FOCUS**
A decent and competitive handicap. It was run at a solid pace, but, yet again, those placed handily 2f out had an advantage over the hold-up horses. It was the fastest of the five C&D races and the winner posted a small personal best.

## 1722 BET AT CORBETTSPORTS.COM MAIDEN FILLIES' STKS 1m
**4:00** (4:03) (Class 5) 3-Y-O+ **£4,204** (£1,251; £625; £312) **Stalls** Low

Form RPR

**1** **Belle De Lawers** 3-9-0 0........................ JoeFanning 10 85+
(James Bethell) *in rr: hdwy into mid-div 6f out: hdwy on outer over 3f out: led over 1f out: drvn clr* **50/1**

45-0 **2** *4* **Isabella Bird**[14] [1433] 3-8-11 72........................ CharlesBishop(3) 14 76
(Mick Channon) *swtchd lft after s: led: hdd over 1f out: kpt on same pce* **8/1**

22- **3** *2 1/4* **Song Of Norway**[177] [7645] 3-9-0 0........................ SteveDrowne 8 71
(Peter Makin) *trckd ldrs: t.k.h: drvn over 2f out: kpt on wl fnl f to take 3rd nr fin* **13/2**

0- **4** *3/4* **Spirit Raiser (IRE)**[192] [7296] 3-9-0 0........................ HayleyTurner 7 69+
(James Fanshawe) *s.i.s: hdwy over 4f out: sn drvn: kpt on wl fnl f: tk 4th nr fin: will improve* **16/1**

**5** *3/4* **Elshaadin** 3-9-0 0........................ PaulHanagan 5 67
(Roger Varian) *trckd ldrs: t.k.h: effrt over 3f out: kpt on ins fnl f* **6/1**[3]

30- **6** *nse* **Seek A Star (USA)**[171] [7764] 3-9-0 0........................ LukeMorris 2 67
(Luca Cumani) *t.k.h: trckd ldrs: 2nd and drvn over 3f out: one pce over 1f out* **10/1**

4 **7** *3/4* **Royal Seal**[22] [1280] 3-9-0 0........................ RyanMoore 1 65
(Sir Michael Stoute) *chsd ldrs: 2nd 2f out: wknd last 100yds* **5/1**[2]

-4 **8** *3 1/2* **Ski Lift**[15] [1422] 3-9-0 0........................ RobertHavlin 9 57
(John Gosden) *mid-div: drvn over 4f out: sme hdwy over 2f out: nvr a factor* **6/4**[1]

**9** *3 1/4* **Adaptability** 3-9-0 0........................ JamieSpencer 6 50
(Brian Meehan) *sn in tch: drvn 4f out: wknd over 1f out* **20/1**

00- **10** *12* **Mystical Maze**[211] [6789] 3-9-0 0........................ ShaneKelly 12 22
(Mark Brisbourne) *in rr: bhd fnl 2f* **100/1**

04- **11** *32* **Princess Kheleyf**[437] [641] 5-9-11 0........................ RobertTart(3) 4
(Geoffrey Oldroyd) *s.i.s: in rr: bhd fnl 3f: t.o* **200/1**

0/6- **12** *dist* **Smirfys Blackcat (IRE)**[308] [3572] 5-10-0 0........................ TomEaves 13
(Michael Mullineaux) *in rr: lost tch 5f out: sn t.o: virtually p.u over 1f out* **200/1**

1m 43.95s (0.25) **Going Correction** -0.10s/f (Good)
**WFA** 3 from 5yo 14lb **12** Ran SP% **119.1**
Speed ratings (Par 100): **94,90,87,87,86 86,85,81,78,66 34,**
CSF £411.54 TOTE £36.30: £8.10, £2.40, £2.10; EX 558.40 Trifecta £2022.30 Part won..
**Owner** J A Tabet **Bred** Robert Gibbons **Trained** Middleham Moor, N Yorks

**FOCUS**
An ordinary fillies' maiden run at a fair pace. Sound form, the winner doing it well.

## 1723 FOLLOW @HAYDOCKRACES ON TWITTER H'CAP 1m
**4:35** (4:35) (Class 5) (0-75,74) 3-Y-O **£4,851** (£1,443; £721; £360) **Stalls** Low

Form RPR

52-3 **1** **Alquimia (IRE)**[19] [1346] 3-9-0 **67**........................ PaulHanagan 1 77+
(Richard Fahey) *trckd ldr: drvn over 3f out: led over 1f out: styd on* **11/4**[1]

035- **2** *2 3/4* **Ghinia (IRE)**[210] [6828] 3-8-13 **69**........................ RossAtkinson(3) 10 72
(Pam Sly) *in rr: drvn over 3f out: hdwy on outside 2f out: edgd lft ins fnl f: kpt on to take 2nd nr fin* **10/1**

1 **3** *nk* **Bridie ffrench**[82] [456] 3-9-7 **74**........................ FrankieDettori 2 77
(Mick Channon) *trckd ldrs: effrt over 2f out: nt clr run and swtchd lft over 2f out: chsd wnr over 1f out: kpt on same pce* **8/1**

16-6 **4** *2* **Know Your Name**[71] [613] 3-9-4 **74**........................(v) DeclanBates(3) 6 72
(David Evans) *in rr: drvn and hdwy 3f out: kpt on same pce appr fnl f* **22/1**

61-0 **5** *nk* **Zugzwang (IRE)**[17] [1381] 3-9-2 **74**........................ TimClark(5) 7 71
(Ed de Giles) *hld up in mid-div: hdwy over 2f out: one pce over 1f out* **8/1**

100- **6** *3 1/2* **We'll Shake Hands (FR)**[228] [6285] 3-8-13 **73**.......... RobJFitzpatrick(7) 5 62
(K R Burke) *mid-div: effrt over 3f out: sn chsng ldrs: fdd fnl f* **11/1**

41- **7** *5* **Approach The West (IRE)**[213] [6754] 3-9-7 **74**........................ LukeMorris 4 52
(James Tate) *chsd ldrs: drvn 4f out: wknd over 1f out* **3/1**[2]

1142 **8** *1 3/4* **Frankthetank (IRE)**[31] [1116] 3-9-6 **73**........................(p) TomEaves 3 47
(Keith Dalgleish) *t.k.h: led: clr over 4f out: wknd and hdd over 1f out* **6/1**[3]

32-3 **9** *18* **Quincel**[21] [1315] 3-9-1 **68**........................ StephenCraine 8
(Tom Dascombe) *stdd and swtchd lft s: hld up in rr: drvn over 3f out: wl bhd fnl 2f* **22/1**

1m 43.91s (0.21) **Going Correction** -0.10s/f (Good) **9** Ran SP% **114.3**
Speed ratings (Par 98): **94,91,90,88,88 85,80,78,60**
CSF £30.55 CT £193.56 TOTE £3.80: £1.10, £4.00, £2.60; EX 37.90 Trifecta £322.70.
**Owner** Sir Robert Ogden **Bred** Sir Robert Ogden **Trained** Musley Bank, N Yorks

**FOCUS**
An ordinary handicap run at a solid pace. The form is rated around the fourth.

## 1724 BET ON YOUR MOBILE AT CORBETTSPORTS.COM H'CAP 1m 2f 95y
**5:10** (5:10) (Class 4) (0-80,80) 4-Y-O+ **£8,086** (£2,406; £1,202; £601) **Stalls** Centre

Form RPR

0-11 **1** **Memory Cloth**[22] [1281] 7-8-11 **77**........................ MeganCarberry(7) 16 85+
(Brian Ellison) *in tch: drvn and chsd ldrs over 3f out: edgd rt over 1f out: styd on to ld last 50yds* **9/1**

-033 **2** *nk* **Syncopate**[24] [1241] 5-8-13 **75**........................ RossAtkinson(3) 8 82
(Pam Sly) *t.k.h: trckd ldrs: led narrowly jst ins fnl f: hdd and no ex clsng stages* **16/1**

-603 **3** *1* **Karaka Jack**[6] [1598] 7-9-3 **76**........................ AdrianNicholls 7 81+
(David Nicholls) *s.i.s: hdwy on outer over 2f out: styd on fnl f* **7/1**[3]

2233 **4** *nk* **Arlecchino (IRE)**[14] [1454] 4-8-10 **71** oh2........................(b) SeanLevey 14 74
(Ed McMahon) *chsd ldrs: led 2f out: hdd jst ins fnl f: no ex* **16/1**

00-1 **5** *3 1/4* **Emulating (IRE)**[24] [1231] 4-9-2 **75**........................ ShaneKelly 17 73
(James Fanshawe) *trckd ldrs: dropped mid-div over 6f out: drvn to chse ldrs 3f out: sn outpcd: kpt on ins fnl f* **14/1**

024- **6** *3/4* **Aldwick Bay (IRE)**[131] [8308] 6-8-3 **71** oh2........................ JennyPowell(7) 10 66
(Tom Dascombe) *in rr: hdwy to chse ldrs 5f out: wknd appr fnl f* **20/1**

000- **7** *5* **St Moritz (IRE)**[196] [7211] 8-9-5 **78**........................ DanielTudhope 13 65
(David O'Meara) *w ldrs: led briefly over 2f out: wknd fnl f* **4/1**[2]

0-04 **8** *1 3/4* **San Cassiano (IRE)**[9] [1539] 7-9-3 **76**........................ JamesSullivan 15 60
(Ruth Carr) *led 2f: chsd ldr: led over 3f out: hdd over 2f out: wknd over 1f out* **16/1**

144- **9** *nk* **Soul Intent (IRE)**[138] [8218] 4-9-4 **77**........................ JamieSpencer 2 61
(J W Hills) *in rr: reminders and sme hdwy over 3f out: sn lost pl* **16/1**

/21- **10** *1* **Llanarmon Lad (IRE)**[232] [6178] 5-9-4 **80**........................ GeorgeChaloner(3) 1 62
(Brian Ellison) *s.i.s: in rr: nvr on terms* **12/1**

602/ **11** *2 ¾* **Deepsand (IRE)**[63] 7032 5-9-6 **79**.......................... LucyAlexander 3 55
(Tim Easterby) *in rr: drvn over 5f out: nvr a factor* **33/1**

2404 **12** *10* **Gioia Di Vita**[21] 1307 4-8-12 **71**..........................(b[1]) BarryMcHugh 9 28
(David Thompson) *w ldrs: led after 2f: hdd over 3f out: wknd 2f out* **16/1**

5200 **13** *1 ¼* **Doldrums (USA)**[19] 1355 4-8-13 **72**.......................... JoeFanning 6 27
(Mark Johnston) *in rr: sme hdwy on outer 3f out: sn lost pl* **33/1**

0- **14** *1 ½* **Cloud Monkey (IRE)**[196] 7211 4-9-6 **79**..........................(p) RoystonFfrench 4 31
(Martin Todhunter) *prom: drvn over 3f out: sn lost pl* **33/1**

140- **15** *15* **Argaki (IRE)**[219] 6551 4-9-7 **80**.......................... TomEaves 5 4
(Keith Dalgleish) *chsd ldrs: lost pl over 3f out: sn bhd: t.o* **28/1**

434- **16** *2 ¾* **Pleasure Bent**[186] 7438 4-9-7 **80**.......................... FrankieDettori 12
(Luca Cumani) *t.k.h: trckd ldrs: dropped bk over 7f out: in rr and drvn over 5f out: bhd whn eased over 1f out: t.o* **3/1**[1]

2m 14.38s (-1.12) **Going Correction** -0.10s/f (Good) **16** Ran SP% **128.3**
Speed ratings (Par 105): **100,99,98,98,96 95,91,90,89,89 86,78,77,76,64 62**
CSF £144.06 CT £1081.36 TOTE £9.10: £1.90, £4.60, £1.50, £4.50; EX 223.60 Trifecta £2390.80 Part won..
**Owner** Racing Management & Training Ltd **Bred** Darley **Trained** Norton, N Yorks
■ Stewards' Enquiry : Adrian Nicholls two-day ban: used whip above permitted level (May 10,12)
Ross Atkinson two-day ban: used whip above permitted level (May 10,12)

**FOCUS**
This looked wide-open. There was a sound pace and the first four were a little way clear at the finish. The overall form makes sense.
T/Plt: £398.00 to a £1 stake. Pool: £86002.21 - 157.71 winning tickets T/Qpdt: £56.90 to a £1 stake. Pool: £5795.02 - 75.30 winning tickets WG

# [1275] LEICESTER (R-H)

Saturday, April 26

**OFFICIAL GOING: Good (7.3)**
False rail from top of hill in back straight to Winning Post, increasing distances on Round course by about 17yds.
Wind: Light behind Weather: Overcast

## 1725 £4 MILLION TOTESCOOP6 TODAY H'CAP — 7f 9y
**2:00** (2:00) (Class 5) (0-75,75) 3-Y-O **£3,234** (£962; £481; £240) **Stalls** High

Form RPR

02-2 **1** **Nakuti (IRE)**[23] 1260 3-9-7 **75**.......................... JamesDoyle 9 84
(Sylvester Kirk) *hld up: hdwy 1/2-way: rdn to ld over 1f out: styd on* **13/2**

33-5 **2** *nk* **Instant Attraction (IRE)**[18] 1358 3-9-7 **75**.......................... RussKennemore 12 83
(Jedd O'Keeffe) *trckd ldrs: rdn and ev ch fr over 1f out: styd on* **5/1**[3]

1- **3** *4* **Argot**[199] 7126 3-9-5 **73**.......................... WilliamCarson 5 71+
(Anthony Carson) *hld up: hdwy and hung lft over 1f out: sn rdn: styd on same pce wl ins fnl f* **8/1**

160- **4** *1 ½* **Ninety Minutes (IRE)**[170] 7782 3-9-3 **71**.......................... MartinDwyer 8 65
(John Best) *trckd ldrs: racd keenly: rdn and hung lft over 1f out: styd on same pce* **33/1**

345- **5** *nk* **Tubeanie (IRE)**[223] 6426 3-8-9 **63**.......................... JohnFahy 6 56
(Clive Cox) *hld up: hdwy and hung lft over 1f out: nt trble ldrs* **50/1**

65-6 **6** *3 ¾* **Mendacious Harpy (IRE)**[19] 1352 3-9-5 **73**.......................... MartinLane 7 56
(George Baker) *mid-div: rdn over 2f out: styd on same pce fr over 1f out* **25/1**

10-6 **7** *¾* **Golden Spear**[17] 1400 3-9-5 **73**..........................(p) AdamBeschizza 10 54
(Noel Quinlan) *sn pushed along in rr: styd on fr over 1f out: nvr nrr* **25/1**

31-0 **8** *½* **Hickster (IRE)**[17] 1400 3-8-6 **65**..........................(v) PhilipPrince[(5)] 2 45
(Roy Bowring) *trckd ldr tl led over 4f out: hdd 3f out: wknd fnl f* **66/1**

620- **9** *hd* **Llyrical**[199] 7125 3-8-11 **65**.......................... LiamKeniry 1 45
(Derek Haydn Jones) *s.i.s: sn prom: rdn over 2f out: wknd over 1f out* **100/1**

042- **10** *1 ¼* **Red Cossack (CAN)**[191] 7327 3-9-5 **73**.......................... JimmyFortune 11 49
(Paul Webber) *plld hrd: led: hdd over 4f out: led again 3f out: rdn and hdd over 1f out: wknd ins fnl f* **25/1**

23-2 **11** *8* **Dark Leopard**[21] 1298 3-9-6 **74**.......................... RichardHughes 4 38
(Roger Charlton) *hld up: hung rt 4f out: sme hdwy wl over 1f out: sn wknd and eased* **7/2**[2]

526- **12** *4 ½* **Sakhalin Star (IRE)**[197] 7168 3-8-8 **65**.......................... BillyCray[(3)] 14 9
(Richard Guest) *hld up: rdn 1/2-way: wknd 2f out* **66/1**

064- **13** *8* **Faure Island**[194] 7251 3-9-1 **69**.......................... FergusSweeney 13
(Henry Candy) *hld up: rdn over 2f out: sn wknd* **11/4**[1]

14 **14** *11* **Mustajjid**[43] 955 3-9-2 **70**..........................(b[1]) DaneO'Neill 15
(Roger Varian) *hld up: rdn 1/2-way: wknd over 2f out* **11/1**

265- **15** *3 ¾* **Calrissian (IRE)**[186] 7442 3-9-3 **71**.......................... KierenFallon 3
(Alan Jarvis) *prom: rdn over 2f out: wknd over 1f out* **33/1**

1m 26.2s **Going Correction** -0.05s/f (Good) **15** Ran SP% **121.7**
Speed ratings (Par 98): **98,97,93,91,91 86,85,85,85,83 74,69,60,47,43**
CSF £36.03 CT £276.34 TOTE £8.60: £3.00, £2.20, £2.30; EX 50.60 Trifecta £482.30.
**Owner** Nelius Hayes **Bred** Eamonn McEvoy **Trained** Upper Lambourn, Berks

**FOCUS**
There was a false rail from the top of the hill on the back straight all the way to the winning line, increasing race distances on the round course by approximately 17yards. After riding in the opener the general opinion was that it rode like good ground, although Richard Hughes described it as "just on the easy side". A competitive handicap for 3yos, but not the strongest. The 1-2 deserve some credit for pulling clear.

## 1726 TOTESCOOP6 THE MILLIONAIRE MAKER MEDIAN AUCTION MAIDEN STKS — 5f 2y
**2:30** (2:34) (Class 5) 2-Y-O **£3,234** (£962; £481; £240) **Stalls** High

Form RPR

**1** **Kool Kompany (IRE)** 2-9-5 **0**.......................... RichardHughes 12 86+
(Richard Hannon) *a.p: rdn to ld wl ins fnl f: r.o: hung rt towards fin* **6/4**[1]

**2** *1* **Haxby (IRE)** 2-9-5 **0**.......................... AndreaAtzeni 4 80+
(Roger Varian) *trckd ldr: led over 1f out: rdn and hdd wl ins fnl f* **7/1**[3]

4 **3** *½* **Hell Of A Lord**[23] 1259 2-9-0 **0**.......................... RyanWhile[(5)] 9 78
(Bill Turner) *led: rdn and hdd over 1f out: styd on same pce wl ins fnl f* **20/1**

**4** *5* **Majestic Hero (IRE)** 2-9-5 **0**.......................... DavidProbert 10 60
(Ronald Harris) *chsd ldrs: rdn over 1f out: wknd ins fnl f* **20/1**

**5** *1 ¼* **Vimy Ridge** 2-9-5 **0**.......................... LeeTopliss 2 56
(Richard Fahey) *prom: rdn over 1f out: wknd ins fnl f* **9/1**

**6** *½* **Alpha Spirit** 2-9-0 **0**.......................... SamHitchcott 7 49
(Mick Channon) *prom: rdn 1/2-way: wknd fnl f* **12/1**

**7** *¾* **Grazed Knees (IRE)** 2-9-5 **0**.......................... AndrewElliott 5 51
(David Brown) *prom: pushed along whn nt clr run and lost pl 1/2-way: n.d after* **7/1**[3]

0 **8** *1 ¼* **Lyfka** 2-9-0 **0**.......................... DaneO'Neill 6 42
(J W Hills) *s.i.s: sn pushed along towards rr: n.d* **66/1**

0 **9** *2 ¼* **Johnny B Goode (IRE)**[10] 1505 2-9-2 **0**.......................... GeorgeChaloner[(3)] 1 39
(Richard Fahey) *chsd ldrs: rdn 1/2-way: wknd over 1f out* **5/1**[2]

**10** *3 ¾* **Tobougg an Run** 2-9-5 **0**.......................... AndrewMullen 8 25
(Michael Appleby) *s.i.s: outpcd* **50/1**

**11** *2 ¼* **Whoopie Do** 2-9-0 **0**.......................... FergusSweeney 11
(John Gallagher) *s.s: outpcd* **16/1**

**12** *17* **Striking Stone** 2-9-5 **0**.......................... JohnFahy 3
(Jo Hughes) *s.i.s: outpcd* **66/1**

1m 0.86s (0.86) **Going Correction** -0.05s/f (Good) **12** Ran SP% **119.7**
Speed ratings (Par 92): **91,89,88,80,78 77,76,74,71,65 61,34**
CSF £11.71 TOTE £2.10: £1.10, £2.70, £4.70; EX 12.10 Trifecta £83.70.
**Owner** Middleham Park Racing LXXXVI **Bred** Miss Imelda O'Shaughnessy **Trained** East Everleigh, Wilts

**FOCUS**
An ordinary looking maiden, won with a bit in hand by the well-backed favourite. The first three were clear and the third will be key.

## 1727 TOTEPOOL.COM H'CAP (BOBIS RACE) — 1m 3f 183y
**3:05** (3:05) (Class 3) (0-95,92) 3-Y-O **£7,561** (£2,263; £1,131; £566; £282) **Stalls** Low

Form RPR

631- **1** **Fun Mac (GER)**[190] 7332 3-8-8 **79**.......................... MickaelBarzalona 6 86+
(Hughie Morrison) *a.p: rdn to ld 1f out: sn hung rt: styd on* **7/2**[2]

12-1 **2** *nk* **Montaly**[22] 1279 3-8-13 **84**.......................... DavidProbert 4 90+
(Andrew Balding) *hld up: hdwy over 3f out: led over 2f out: sn rdn: hdd 1f out: sn hung rt: styd on u.p* **4/1**[3]

01-3 **3** *1 ¼* **Rite To Reign**[37] 1028 3-8-0 **76**.......................... DannyBrock[(5)] 2 80
(Philip McBride) *a.p: led 3f out: hdd over 2f out: sn rdn: styd on* **50/1**

1 **4** *nk* **Eagle Top**[14] 1438 3-9-7 **92**.......................... WilliamBuick 1 95+
(John Gosden) *hld up: hdwy over 3f out: jnd ldrs over 2f out: rdn and edgd rt ins fnl f: styd on same pce* **11/8**[1]

14-2 **5** *11* **Castle Combe (IRE)**[25] 1220 3-8-6 **77**.......................... MartinDwyer 3 63
(Marcus Tregoning) *trckd ldrs: plld hrd: rdn over 2f out: wknd over 1f out* **25/1**

32-2 **6** *9* **El Najmm (IRE)**[36] 1044 3-8-8 **79**.......................... AndreaAtzeni 7 51
(Roger Varian) *sn led: hdd 3f out: wknd 2f out* **8/1**

-111 **7** *26* **Tizlove Regardless (USA)**[37] 1028 3-8-6 **77**.......................... SilvestreDeSousa 5
(Mark Johnston) *chsd ldr tl pushed along over 3f out: sn wknd* **7/1**

2m 34.93s (1.03) **Going Correction** +0.175s/f (Good) **7** Ran SP% **113.7**
Speed ratings (Par 102): **103,102,101,101,94 88,71**
CSF £17.66 TOTE £5.40: £2.60, £2.50; EX 14.90 Trifecta £329.20.
**Owner** Mrs Angela McAlpine & Partners **Bred** Gestut Gorlsdorf **Trained** East Ilsley, Berks

**FOCUS**
Not the strongest handicap for the grade and they went a steady pace, with the tempo only increasing in the home straight. The third is the key to the form.

## 1728 TOTEPOOL EBF STALLIONS KING RICHARD III STKS (FORMERLY THE LEICESTERSHIRE STAKES) (LISTED RACE) — 7f 9y
**3:40** (3:40) (Class 1) 4-Y-O+
**£25,519** (£9,675; £4,842; £2,412; £1,210; £607) **Stalls** High

Form RPR

/15- **1** **Eton Forever (IRE)**[322] 3101 7-9-3 **112**.......................... AndreaAtzeni 2 112
(Roger Varian) *a.p: chsd ldr over 2f out: shkn up to ld over 1f out: r.o wl* **7/2**[3]

-402 **2** *3* **Askaud (IRE)**[14] 1442 6-8-12 **91**..........................(p) FrederikTylicki 5 99
(Scott Dixon) *trckd ldr tl rdn over 2f out: styd on same pce fnl f* **25/1**

12-1 **3** *nse* **Breton Rock (IRE)**[14] 1443 4-9-3 **107**.......................... MartinLane 7 104
(David Simcock) *hld up: hdwy over 2f out: rdn over 1f out: styd on* **11/4**[1]

033- **4** *hd* **Professor**[244] 5794 4-9-3 **109**.......................... RichardHughes 9 104
(Richard Hannon) *a.p: shkn up over 1f out: styd on same pce ins fnl f* **3/1**[2]

05-0 **5** *2 ½* **Gabriel's Lad (IRE)**[49] 886 5-9-3 **104**.......................... JimmyFortune 6 97
(Denis Coakley) *s.s: hld up: hdwy over 1f out: no ex ins fnl f* **7/1**

00-0 **6** *½* **Dubawi Sound**[14] 1437 6-9-3 **92**..........................(bt[1]) MartinDwyer 1 96
(Hugo Palmer) *led: clr 5f out: rdn and hdd over 1f out: wknd ins fnl f* **33/1**

6220 **7** *2 ¾* **Hasopop (IRE)**[8] 1557 4-9-3 **104**..........................(p) AntonioFresu 3 89
(Marco Botti) *hld up: rdn over 2f out: wknd over 1f out* **10/1**

540- **8** *4* **Pavlosk (USA)**[196] 7196 4-8-12 **101**.......................... JamesDoyle 4 73
(Sir Michael Stoute) *hld up: rdn over 2f out: wknd over 1f out: eased* **9/1**

1m 23.96s (-2.24) **Going Correction** -0.05s/f (Good) **8** Ran SP% **112.3**
Speed ratings (Par 111): **110,106,106,106,103 102,99,95**
CSF £77.76 TOTE £4.30: £1.60, £4.00, £1.10; EX 73.10 Trifecta £181.10.
**Owner** H R H Sultan Ahmad Shah **Bred** Mrs Brid Cosgrove **Trained** Newmarket, Suffolk

**FOCUS**
An interesting Listed event in which the pace was strong throughout. The winner is rated to something like his best and the second outran her odds.

## 1729 BET TOTEEXACTA H'CAP — 1m 1f 218y
**4:15** (4:15) (Class 5) (0-70,70) 4-Y-O+ **£3,234** (£962; £481; £240) **Stalls** Low

Form RPR

06- **1** **Stockhill Diva**[221] 6491 4-8-11 **60**.......................... LiamKeniry 10 71
(Brendan Powell) *chsd ldrs: rdn to ld ins fnl f: r.o* **25/1**

322- **2** *nk* **Kastini**[186] 7447 4-9-5 **68**.......................... JimmyFortune 13 79+
(Denis Coakley) *hld up: hdwy over 2f out: hung rt and ev ch fr over 1f out: sn rdn: nt run on* **5/2**[1]

-44 **3** *2* **The Firm (IRE)**[21] 1302 5-9-3 **66**.......................... JamesDoyle 11 73
(Daniel Mark Loughnane) *chsd ldrs: led over 6f out: hdd over 5f out: led again 3f out: rdn over 1f out: hdd ins fnl f: styng on same pce whn hmpd towards fin* **9/1**[3]

0/3- **4** *4* **Favorite Girl (GER)**[13] 1076 6-8-7 **63**.......................... AlistairRawlinson[(7)] 3 62
(Michael Appleby) *hld up: nt clr run over 2f out: rdn over 1f out: styd on ins fnl f: nvr nrr* **12/1**

4035 **5** *hd* **Diletta Tommasa (IRE)**[31] 1097 4-9-0 **63**..........................(p) AndreaAtzeni 9 62
(John Stimpson) *chsd ldrs: rdn and ev ch 2f out: wknd ins fnl f* **28/1**

-221 **6** *½* **Jacobs Son**[25] 1222 6-9-7 **70**.......................... AndrewMullen 7 68
(Michael Appleby) *led: hdd over 6f out: led again over 5f out tl hdd 3f out: rdn over 1f out: wknd fnl f* **10/1**

64-6 **7** *3* **Martinas Delight (USA)**[30] 1118 4-9-4 **67**.......................... KierenFallon 2 59
(Alan Jarvis) *trckd ldrs: rdn over 1f out: wknd ins fnl f* **33/1**

5423 **8** *7* **Reflect (IRE)**[24] 1231 6-9-4 **67**..........................(vt) DaneO'Neill 12 46
(Derek Shaw) *hld up: rdn and hung rt over 1f out: n.d* **14/1**

36-3 **9** *½* **Keep Calm**[30] 1134 4-9-3 **66**.......................... SilvestreDeSousa 8 44
(John Mackie) *prom: rdn over 2f out: wknd over 1f out* **12/1**

15/6 **10** *1 ½* **Switched Off**[18] 1362 9-9-5 **68**..........................(t[1]) StevieDonohoe 14 43
(Kevin Frost) *s.i.s: hld up: rdn over 2f out: a in rr* **20/1**

4501 **11** 2 1/4 **Dazzling Valentine**[26] 1210 6-8-7 61........................(v) NatashaEaton(5) 6 32
(Alan Bailey) *s.i.s: hld up: nvr on terms* **20/1**

604- **12** 11 **Woolston Ferry (IRE)**[150] 8059 8-9-5 68................... FergusSweeney 4 18
(Henry Candy) *hld up: effrt over 2f out: sn wknd* **18/1**

00-2 **13** 14 **Zafranagar (IRE)**[16] 1168 9-9-1 69.................. GeorgeDowning(5) 1 +
(Ian Williams) *hld up: sddle slipped 1/2-way: wknd and eased over 2f out* **10/3**[2]

5225 **14** 2 3/4 **Elegant Ophelia**[24] 1232 5-8-11 60.............................(t) JimCrowley 5
(Dean Ivory) *prom: rdn over 2f out: sn hung rt and wknd* **25/1**

2m 9.87s (1.97) **Going Correction** +0.175s/f (Good) **14** Ran SP% **121.7**
Speed ratings (Par 103): **99,98,97,93,93 93,91,85,85,83 82,73,62,59**
CSF £81.80 CT £644.77 TOTE £37.00: £10.60, £1.40, £3.70; EX 160.00 Trifecta £699.50 Part won..

**Owner** Mrs M Fairbairn & E Gadsden **Bred** Mrs M Fairbairn And E Gadsden **Trained** Upper Lambourn, Berks

**FOCUS**
A modest handicap that suited those who raced prominently. A step up from the winner.

## 1730 BET TOTETRIFECTA MAIDEN STKS 1m 1f 218y
**4:50** (4:50) (Class 5) 3-Y-O+ **£2,911** (£866; £432; £216) **Stalls** Low

Form RPR

4 **1** **Reesha**[24] 1233 3-8-5 0.............................................[1] MartinDwyer 8 77+
(Roger Varian) *hld up: racd keenly: hdwy over 2f out: rdn over 1f out: r.o to ld wl ins fnl f* **11/1**

3-2 **2** 1 **Cape Caster (IRE)**[28] 1166 3-8-10 0.............................. JimCrowley 3 80
(Ralph Beckett) *trckd ldr tl led 3f out: rdn over 1f out: hdd and unable qck wl ins fnl f* **10/11**[1]

3-3 **3** nk **Loving Home**[19] 1353 3-8-10 0................................. WilliamBuick 9 80
(John Gosden) *hld up: pushed along and hdwy over 2f out: rdn over 1f out: edgd rt ins fnl f: styd on* **7/2**[2]

523- **4** 2 **Early Morning (IRE)**[220] 6528 3-8-10 77.................. JimmyFortune 6 76
(Harry Dunlop) *chsd ldrs: rdn and ev ch over 1f out: edgd lft and styd on same pce ins fnl f* **12/1**

0- **5** 1 1/4 **Hallbeck**[243] 5812 3-8-5 0........................... SilvestreDeSousa 10 69
(Henry Candy) *chsd ldrs: pushed along 3f out: styng on same pce whn nt clr run ins fnl f* **25/1**

**6** 5 **Race To Glory (FR)** 3-8-10 0.................................. JamesDoyle 4 64+
(Roger Charlton) *s.s: rn green in rr: swtchd lft over 2f out: sme hdwy and hung rt over 1f out: nvr trbld ldrs* **25/1**

**7** 8 **Comedy King (IRE)** 3-8-10 0................................. AndreaAtzeni 7 49
(Luca Cumani) *dwlt: in rr: pushed along and sme hdwy over 2f out: wknd over 1f out* **8/1**[3]

2- **8** 4 1/2 **Gambol (FR)**[119] 8427 4-9-13 0............................ DaneO'Neill 2 43
(J W Hills) *led 7f: wknd 2f out* **20/1**

4 **9** 44 **Gaelic O'Reagan**[38] 1008 3-8-10 0.......................... FrederikTylicki 1
(Robert Eddery) *mid-div: wknd 3f out* **80/1**

2m 9.5s (1.60) **Going Correction** +0.175s/f (Good)
**WFA** 3 from 4yo 17lb **9** Ran SP% **115.4**
Speed ratings (Par 103): **100,99,98,97,96 92,85,82,47**
CSF £20.87 TOTE £14.70: £3.90, £1.02, £1.50; EX 30.30 Trifecta £105.20.

**Owner** Hamdan Al Maktoum **Bred** Shadwell Estate Company Limited **Trained** Newmarket, Suffolk

**FOCUS**
Not a bad maiden and it should produce winners. The form makes sense around the second and fourth.

## 1731 TOTETENTOFOLLOW.COM ENTER NOW H'CAP 5f 218y
**5:20** (5:21) (Class 4) (0-85,85) 4-Y-O+ **£4,690** (£1,395; £697; £348) **Stalls** High

Form RPR

410- **1** **Mutafaakir (IRE)**[218] 6586 5-8-11 75....................... SilvestreDeSousa 4 87
(Ruth Carr) *mde all: rdn over 1f out: r.o* **4/1**[1]

140- **2** nk **Tight Fit**[206] 6959 4-9-5 83............................................ DaneO'Neill 12 94
(Henry Candy) *a.p: rdn to chse wnr fnl f: sn ev ch: r.o* **5/1**[2]

151- **3** 3 1/4 **Prince Regal**[194] 7254 4-9-0 78................................ KierenFallon 2 79
(Alan Jarvis) *racd keenly: trckd ldr: rdn over 1f out: no ex ins fnl f* **9/1**

6000 **4** 1 1/4 **Naabegha**[9] 1537 7-9-1 79...................................... JimmyFortune 3 76
(Alan McCabe) *hld up: hdwy over 1f out: sn rdn: styd on same pce ins fnl f* **16/1**

35-5 **5** 4 1/2 **Jungle Bay**[23] 1261 7-8-8 77.................................(p) DavidKenny(5) 13 59
(Jane Chapple-Hyam) *mid-div: hdwy over 2f out: sn rdn: wknd fnl f* **20/1**

335- **6** 1 1/2 **Extrasolar**[224] 6403 4-9-7 85..........................................(t) JamesDoyle 1 62
(Amanda Perrett) *prom: rdn o0ver 1f out: hung lft and wknd fnl f* **15/2**[3]

22-5 **7** 3/4 **Vallarta (IRE)**[9] 1538 4-8-12 76..................................(v[1]) SamHitchcott 14 51
(Mick Channon) *mid-div: rdn over 2f out: n.d* **9/1**

510 **8** 1/2 **Light From Mars**[27] 1190 9-9-3 81.................................(p) LiamJones 7 56
(Ronald Harris) *chsd ldrs: rdn over 2f out: wkng whn hmpd ins fnl f* **25/1**

660- **9** 2 **Dominium (USA)**[141] 8181 7-8-5 76............................ DavidParkes(7) 9 43
(Jeremy Gask) *s.s: n.d* **33/1**

616- **10** 3/4 **Gravitational (IRE)**[194] 7255 4-9-1 79............................ SebSanders 10 44
(Chris Wall) *mid-div: rdn over 2f out: wknd over 1f out* **5/1**[2]

35-4 **11** 5 **Light Rose (IRE)**[37] 1026 4-8-8 72................................ AndrewMullen 5 21
(Jeremy Gask) *chsd ldrs: rdn over 2f out: wknd over 1f out* **20/1**

020- **12** 19 **Springinmystep (IRE)**[301] 3846 5-9-6 84......................... FrederikTylicki 6
(Ed de Giles) *sn pushed along in rr: bhd fr 1/2-way* **16/1**

3-34 **13** 15 **New Leyf (IRE)**[26] 1212 8-8-7 71 oh2...........................(b) ChrisCatlin 8
(Jeremy Gask) *bhd fnl 4f* **16/1**

1m 11.72s (-1.28) **Going Correction** -0.05s/f (Good) **13** Ran SP% **119.1**
Speed ratings (Par 105): **106,105,101,99,93 91,90,89,87,86 79,54,34**
CSF £21.72 CT £177.52 TOTE £4.70: £1.60, £3.40, £2.40; EX 38.40 Trifecta £463.00.

**Owner** Michael Hill **Bred** Shadwell Estate Company Limited **Trained** Huby, N Yorks

**FOCUS**
A competitive handicap in which the first two pulled nicely clear. The winner rates better than ever.

T/Plt: £122.20 to a £1 stake. Pool: £60354.91 - 360.31 winning tickets T/Qpdt: £18.10 to a £1 stake. Pool: £4434.92 - 181.00 winning tickets CR

# 1536 RIPON (R-H)
## Saturday, April 26

**OFFICIAL GOING: Good changing to good to soft after race 1 (1:40)**
Rail on bend from back st to home st moved out 6m, increasing distances on Round course by about 12yds.
Wind: Fresh, across Weather: Cloudy

## 1732 RIPONBET YANKEE MAIDEN AUCTION STKS (BOBIS RACE) 5f
**1:40** (1:43) (Class 4) 2-Y-O **£5,175** (£1,540; £769; £384) **Stalls** High

Form RPR

2 **1** **Sarista (IRE)**[19] 1342 2-8-10 0..................................... RobertWinston 5 85+
(David Barron) *mde all: sn crossed to stands' rail: rdn and clr over 1f out: kpt on fnl f: jst hld on* **11/10**[1]

2 **2** nse **Realtra (IRE)**[10] 1504 2-8-8 0.................................. TonyHamilton 6 83+
(Richard Fahey) *in tch: pushed along and hdwy to chse wnr over 1f out: kpt on wl fnl f: jst hld* **5/2**[2]

2 **3** 7 **Kylach Me If U Can**[10] 1505 2-9-1 0.......................... PaulMulrennan 7 65
(Kevin Ryan) *in tch: effrt and shkn up 2f out: kpt on fnl f: no ch w first two* **7/1**[3]

**4** 2 **Alaskan Wing (IRE)** 2-9-1 0....................................... BarryMcHugh 3 57+
(Tony Coyle) *pressed wnr: rdn over 2f out: wknd appr fnl f* **40/1**

**5** 1 3/4 **Gamesters Lad** 2-8-11 0.................................... RichardKingscote 1 47
(Tom Dascombe) *dwlt: sn in tch on outside: rdn over 2f out: wknd wl over 1f out* **20/1**

5 **6** 4 1/2 **Reassert**[9] 1536 2-9-1 0............................................ DavidAllan 9 35
(Tim Easterby) *dwlt: bhd and sn pushed along: rdn over 2f out: nvr able to chal* **9/1**

**7** 3 1/2 **Bahamian Sunrise** 2-8-11 0................................... PatrickMathers 4 18
(Richard Fahey) *dwlt: bhd and outpcd: nvr on terms* **25/1**

**8** 6 **Overstone Lass (IRE)** 2-8-3 0.................................. IanBrennan(3) 8
(John Spearing) *s.i.s: sn wl bhd: nvr on terms* **66/1**

**9** 1 1/4 **Arcossi** 2-8-10 0................................................... PJMcDonald 2
(Ann Duffield) *bhd and sn outpcd: no ch fr 1/2-way* **50/1**

1m 0.57s (0.57) **Going Correction** +0.125s/f (Good) **9** Ran SP% **113.2**
Speed ratings (Par 94): **100,99,88,85,82 75,69,60,58**
CSF £3.53 TOTE £2.00: £1.30, £1.10, £1.50; EX 4.30 Trifecta £8.30.

**Owner** S Rudolf **Bred** Tally-Ho Stud **Trained** Maunby, N Yorks

**FOCUS**
After 4mm of rain overnight, the going remained officially good. The rail on the bend into the home straight had been moved out six metres, adding about 12 yards to race distances on the round course. An interesting maiden auction to start with, in which the first three home had all finished runner-up on their respective debuts, and it produced a thrilling finish. The winner improved from her Redcar run.

## 1733 RIPONBET OUR PROFITS STAY IN RACING H'CAP 1m
**2:15** (2:16) (Class 3) (0-90,90) 4-Y-O+
**£10,582** (£3,168; £1,584; £792; £396; £198) **Stalls** Low

Form RPR

40-0 **1** **Trail Blaze (IRE)**[34] 1078 5-9-2 90.........................(p) ShaneGray(5) 11 96
(Kevin Ryan) *mde all and sn crossed to ins rail: rdn over 2f out: edgd lft over 1f out: hld on gamely fnl f* **15/2**

000- **2** nk **Ginger Jack**[197] 7172 7-9-3 86..................................... PJMcDonald 6 91
(Geoffrey Harker) *hld up: rdn and gd hdwy over 1f out: chal ins fnl f: kpt on: hld nr fin* **9/1**

0-53 **3** 3/4 **Lord Aeryn (IRE)**[17] 1399 7-9-0 83............................ TonyHamilton 1 87
(Richard Fahey) *trckd ldrs on ins: effrt and rdn over 2f out: ev ch ins fnl f: kpt on: hld towards fin* **11/4**[1]

640- **4** 1 1/4 **Swiftly Done (IRE)**[120] 7820 7-9-3 89............................ JasonHart(3) 2 90
(Declan Carroll) *in tch on ins: nt clr run over 3f out to over 2f out: rallied over 1f out: kpt on: nvr able to chal* **20/1**

0-25 **5** 1/2 **Lazarus Bell**[8] 1564 4-8-10 84.......................... JacobButterfield(5) 7 84
(Alan Brown) *hld up in midfield: hdwy to chse ldrs over 2f out: rdn over 1f out: kpt on same pce* **9/1**

000- **6** 3/4 **Anderiego (IRE)**[197] 7172 6-9-0 86.............................. SamJames(3) 3 84
(David O'Meara) *prom: rdn and outpcd over 2f out: no imp fr over 1f out* **6/1**[3]

402- **7** 1 **Head Of Steam (USA)**[185] 7464 7-9-4 87.......................[1] PaulMulrennan 8 83
(Micky Hammond) *hld up: smooth hdwy and prom over 2f out: rdn and outpcd over 1f out* **14/1**

66-4 **8** 3/4 **Fazza**[19] 1345 7-8-3 77........................................... ConnorBeasley(5) 10 71
(Edwin Tuer) *s.i.s: hld up: hdwy on outside 3f out: rdn and no ex wl over 1f out* **16/1**

1-02 **9** 1 1/4 **Gworn**[21] 1316 4-9-7 90.................................................... GrahamLee 9 81
(Ed Dunlop) *hld up: angled to outside wl over 2f out: sn rdn and no imp* **9/2**[2]

10-0 **10** 1 1/2 **Lilac Lace (IRE)**[14] 1442 4-9-2 85............................. DuranFentiman 5 72
(Tim Easterby) *plld hrd towards rr: effrt and rdn on outside over 2f out: sn btn* **14/1**

100 **11** 23 **Cloverdale**[8] 1564 4-8-11 80....................................... FrannyNorton 12 15
(Mark Johnston) *chsd wnr: rdn over 3f out: wknd 2f out: t.o* **40/1**

1m 43.46s (2.06) **Going Correction** +0.225s/f (Good) **11** Ran SP% **117.3**
Speed ratings (Par 107): **98,97,96,95,95 94,93,92,91,89 66**
CSF £73.12 CT £237.15 TOTE £13.00: £3.20, £3.30, £1.20; EX 151.90 Trifecta £617.40.

**Owner** Mr & Mrs Julian And Rosie Richer **Bred** Edmond Kent **Trained** Hambleton, N Yorks

**FOCUS**
The ground was changed to good to soft before this race. They didn't go a great pace early in his decent handicap and, as is often the case at Ripon, it proved hard to come from behind. The winner was on a good mark based on last year's best.

## 1734 VISIT ATTHERACES.COM/PUNCHESTOWN H'CAP 6f
**2:50** (2:51) (Class 2) (0-105,105) 4-Y-O+
**£15,562** (£4,660; £2,330; £1,165; £582; £292) **Stalls** High

Form RPR

6-01 **1** **Fast Shot**[12] 1484 6-8-2 93.............................. RachelRichardson(7) 1 103
(Tim Easterby) *prom far side: effrt and hdwy over 1f out: styd on wl fnl f to ld nr fin: 1st of 7 in gp* **10/1**

-031 **2** nk **Barkston Ash**[9] 1537 6-8-2 86.................................(p) FrannyNorton 4 95
(Eric Alston) *cl up far side: led and edgd rt over 1f out: drifted lft u.p and kpt on ins fnl f: 2nd of 7 in gp* **6/1**[1]

1211 **3** 3/4 **Hillbilly Boy (IRE)**[27] 1191 4-8-2 86............................. NickyMackay 10 93
(Martin Smith) *cl up on outside of stands' side gp: led that bunch 2f out: kpt on wl fnl f: nt rch far side: 1st of 9 in gp* **7/1**[3]

200- **4** *hd* **Clear Spring (IRE)**[183] 7495 6-8-8 **92**........................ PaulMulrennan 14 98
(John Spearing) *cl up stands' side: effrt and wnt 2nd in that gp over 1f out: kpt on fnl f: hld nr fin: 2nd of 9 in gp* **11/1**

0-24 **5** *1* **Captain Ramius (IRE)**[14] 1443 8-9-7 **105**........................ PhillipMakin 5 108
(Kevin Ryan) *in tch far side: effrt and rdn over 1f out: kpt on same pce ins fnl f: 3rd of 7 in gp* **14/1**

451- **6** *nse* **Best Trip (IRE)**[171] 7776 7-8-3 **87** ow1.............................. PaulPickard 3 90
(Brian Ellison) *in tch far side: rdn over 2f out: edgd rt over 1f out: kpt on same pce ins fnl f: 4th of 7 in gp* **22/1**

340- **7** *¾* **Cosmic Chatter**[245] 5769 4-8-13 **97**........................ GrahamGibbons 2 97
(David Barron) *led far side to over 1f out: sn one pce: 5th of 7 in gp* **20/1**

03-0 **8** *2¼* **Colonel Mak**[12] 1484 7-8-6 **93**........................................ JasonHart(3) 15 86
(David Barron) *midfield stands' side: drvn along 1/2-way: plugged on fnl f: no imp: 3rd of 9 in gp* **20/1**

516- **9** *2½* **Body And Soul (IRE)**[288] 4260 4-9-3 **101**.................. DuranFentiman 12 86+
(Tim Easterby) *hld up in tch on outside of stands' side gp: effrt over 2f out: outpcd over 1f out: 4th of 9 in gp* **13/2**[2]

110- **10** *½* **Hopes N Dreams (IRE)**[203] 7021 6-9-1 **99**.................... GrahamLee 17 82
(Kevin Ryan) *led stands' side to 2f out: sn outpcd: 5th of 9 in gp* **14/1**

60-4 **11** *hd* **El Viento (FR)**[15] 1421 6-8-11 **95**.................................(v) TonyHamilton 6 78
(Richard Fahey) *hld up in tch far side: drvn along over 2f out: no imp over 1f out: 6th of 7 in gp* **10/1**

025- **12** *1½* **Love Island**[150] 8064 5-8-8 **92**........................................ PaulQuinn 16 70
(Richard Whitaker) *hld up bhd ldng gp stands' side: pushed along over 2f out: no imp over 1f out: 6th of 9 in gp* **22/1**

00-3 **13** *¾* **Doc Hay (USA)**[17] 1397 7-9-3 **101**.............................. DavidNolan 7 77
(David O'Meara) *dwlt: hld up far side: struggling over 2f out: n.d after: last of 7 in gp* **10/1**

030- **14** *¾* **Misplaced Fortune**[168] 7820 9-7-11 **88**........................ JoeDoyle(7) 11 61
(Nigel Tinkler) *dwlt: hld up stands' side: rdn over 2f out: sn btn: 7th of 9 in gp* **25/1**

00-6 **15** *3¾* **Pearl Ice**[28] 1172 6-8-8 **92**..........................................(v[1]) TedDurcan 13 53
(Charlie Fellowes) *in tch stands' side: drvn along 1/2-way: wknd 2f out: 8th of 9 in gp* **9/1**

00-0 **16** *1½* **Ancient Cross**[12] 1484 10-8-7 **98**..........................(t) DanielleMooney(7) 8 54
(Michael Easterby) *bhd stands' side: pushed along over 2f out: sn btn: last of 9 in gp* **40/1**

1m 12.14s (-0.86) **Going Correction** +0.125s/f (Good) **16** Ran SP% **123.6**
Speed ratings (Par 109): **110,109,108,108,107 106,105,102,99,98 98,96,95,94,89 87**
CSF £62.60 CT £479.21 TOTE £11.70: £3.20, £1.60, £1.50, £2.90; EX 78.30 Trifecta £576.50.

**Owner** Ontoawinner & Partners **Bred** Whitsbury Manor Stud & Pigeon House Stud **Trained** Great Habton, N Yorks

**FOCUS**
A hot sprint handicap, in which the field soon split into two. Although the front pair raced far side, the third and fourth horses finished close enough, having raced stands' side, to suggest there was no great bias. The form makes enough sense overall.

## 1735 AT THE RACES SKY 415 H'CAP 2m
**3:30** (3:31) (Class 2) (0-105,96) 4-Y-0+
**£24,900** (£7,456; £3,728; £1,864; £932; £468) **Stalls** Low

Form RPR

6-44 **1** **Angel Gabrial (IRE)**[8] 1562 5-9-3 **88**.............................. DavidNolan 14 101
(Richard Fahey) *hld up: smooth hdwy and weaved through fr over 3f out: effrt and rdn over 1f out: styd on to ld wl towards fin: sn edgd rt and bmpd rival* **14/1**

343- **2** *nk* **Mubaraza (IRE)**[301] 3824 5-9-9 **94**........................ PaulMulrennan 11 106
(Ed Dunlop) *hld up: smooth hdwy and weaved through over 3f out: led and rdn over 1f out: hdd and bmpd towards fin* **17/2**

312- **3** *7* **Chocala (IRE)**[76] 7250 4-8-11 **86**............................ HarryBentley 7 90
(Alan King) *prom: smooth hdwy over 3f out: rdn and ev ch wl over 1f out: sn outpcd by first two* **7/1**[3]

411- **4** *1¾* **Sizzler**[194] 7250 4-9-7 **96**........................................ RichardKingscote 2 98
(Ralph Beckett) *cl up: led over 3f out: rdn and hdd over 1f out: sn outpcd* **9/2**[2]

21-1 **5** *1¼* **Esteaming**[21] 1306 4-9-5 **94**................................... GrahamGibbons 10 95
(David Barron) *hld up towards rr: pushed along 6f out: hdwy whn nt clr run over 3f out to over 2f out: rdn and no imp over 1f out* **17/2**

044- **6** *3* **Saptapadi (IRE)**[174] 7723 8-9-5 **90**..............................(t) PaulPickard 6 86
(Brian Ellison) *hld up: stdy hdwy whn nt clr run over 3f out to over 2f out: effrt and hung rt wl over 1f out: nvr rchd ldrs* **25/1**

411/ **7** *8* **Huff And Puff**[35] 6776 7-9-1 **86**................................ GrahamLee 4 73
(Venetia Williams) *hld up in midfield on ins: n.m.r 3f out: sn rdn and outpcd: btn fnl 2f* **10/1**

/63- **8** *4½* **Bayan (IRE)**[45] 7723 5-8-10 **81**..............................(tp) RobertWinston 12 62
(Gordon Elliott, Ire) *hld up towards rr: effrt and pushed along over 3f out: wknd fr 2f out* **11/4**[1]

100- **9** *4½* **Ardlui (IRE)**[175] 4857 6-9-10 **95**............................. DavidAllan 3 71
(Tim Easterby) *hld up in tch: pushed along 1/2-way: rallied: n.m.r briefly and wknd wl over 2f out* **20/1**

40-0 **10** *nk* **Moidore**[8] 1562 5-8-13 **87**........................................ IanBrennan(3) 9 63
(John Quinn) *in tch on outside: stdy hdwy over 4f out: rdn and wknd over 3f out* **22/1**

1240 **11** *5* **Hunting Ground (USA)**[8] 1556 4-8-7 **82**.................. FrannyNorton 1 52
(Mark Johnston) *prom: drvn over 4f out: wknd wl over 2f out* **12/1**

-100 **12** *36* **Be Perfect (USA)**[8] 1562 5-9-4 **89**......................... TonyHamilton 5 15
(David Nicholls) *led tl hdd over 3f out: sn wknd: t.o* **40/1**

00-0 **13** *5* **Herostatus**[14] 1444 7-9-1 **86**.................................... PJMcDonald 13 6
(Jason Ward) *midfield on outside: struggling 6f out: sn lost tch: t.o* **50/1**

3m 31.15s (-0.65) **Going Correction** +0.225s/f (Good)
**WFA** 4 from 5yo+ 4lb **13** Ran SP% **119.2**
Speed ratings (Par 109): **110,109,106,105,104 103,99,97,94,94 92,74,71**
CSF £119.94 CT £917.24 TOTE £16.20: £5.40, £2.00, £2.10; EX 130.40 Trifecta £660.10 Not won..

**Owner** Dr Marwan Koukash **Bred** K And Mrs Cullen **Trained** Musley Bank, N Yorks

■ Stewards' Enquiry : Paul Mulrennan two-day ban: used whip in incorrect place (May 15-16)

**FOCUS**
A competitive and valuable staying handicap, although the topweight was 10lb below the race ceiling. They went a decent pace and the first two, who eventually pulled clear, were towards the back of the field early. The first five are progressive.

## 1736 RIPONBET PATENT H'CAP 1m 4f 10y
**4:05** (4:07) (Class 2) (0-112,108) 4-Y-0+
**£15,562** (£4,660; £2,330; £1,165; £582; £292) **Stalls** Low

Form RPR

113- **1** **Battalion (IRE)**[175] 7705 4-9-0 **102**.......................... GrahamGibbons 8 112+
(William Haggas) *cl up: led after 2f and maintained ordinary gallop: qcknd 4f out: clr 2f out: kpt on strly: unchal* **7/4**[1]

40-3 **2** *2½* **Chancery (USA)**[27] 1194 6-8-7 **97**............................ SamJames(3) 4 103
(David O'Meara) *hld up: hdwy to chse (clr) wnr 2f out: kpt on fnl f: no imp* **8/1**

252- **3** *3¾* **Suegioo (FR)**[210] 6833 5-8-7 **94** oh1..............................(p) PaoloSirigu 6 94
(Marco Botti) *hld up: hdwy on outside over 3f out: edgd rt and kpt on fr over 1f out: no imp* **9/1**

30-0 **4** *6* **Awake My Soul (IRE)**[28] 1171 5-8-4 **94** oh2................ JasonHart(3) 3 84
(David O'Meara) *plld hrd: led 2f: cl up: drvn over 2f out: hung rt and wknd over 1f out* **10/1**

50-3 **5** *2* **Rawaki (IRE)**[14] 1434 6-9-4 **108**............................ ThomasBrown(3) 5 95
(Andrew Balding) *hld up towards rr: smooth hdwy 3f out: rdn and outpcd whn n.m.r briefly wl over 1f out: hung rt and sn btn* **6/1**[3]

0-00 **6** *1* **Media Hype**[28] 1171 7-8-8 **95**..........................................(v[1]) BenCurtis 9 81
(K R Burke) *t.k.h: prom: rdn 3f out: hung rt and wknd 2f out* **40/1**

605- **7** *2¾* **Golden Bowl (FR)**[219] 6580 4-8-11 **99**........................ GrahamLee 1 80
(Ian Williams) *in tch: drvn and outpcd 3f out: sn btn* **11/1**

1150 **8** *2¼* **Blue Wave (IRE)**[8] 1556 4-8-13 **101**........................ FrannyNorton 2 79
(Mark Johnston) *cl up tl rdn and wknd over 2f out* **14/1**

221- **9** *16* **De Rigueur**[322] 3099 6-8-8 **95**.........................................(tp) PaddyAspell 7 47
(Marco Botti) *hld up in tch: rdn on outside over 3f out: wknd over 2f out: t.o* **5/1**[2]

2m 37.74s (1.04) **Going Correction** +0.225s/f (Good)
**WFA** 4 from 5yo+ 1lb **9** Ran SP% **115.0**
Speed ratings (Par 109): **105,103,100,96,95 94,93,91,80**
CSF £16.39 CT £99.30 TOTE £2.90: £1.10, £2.10, £3.90; EX 20.60 Trifecta £90.00.

**Owner** Sheikh Juma Dalmook Al Maktoum **Bred** Kildaragh Stud **Trained** Newmarket, Suffolk

**FOCUS**
Another decent handicap, albeit run at an ordinary pace, but an impressive winner. Sound form.

## 1737 RIPONBET PLACE6 H'CAP (BOBIS RACE) 5f
**4:40** (4:40) (Class 4) (0-85,84) 3-Y-O **£7,561** (£2,263; £1,131; £566; £282) **Stalls** High

Form RPR

50-3 **1** **Lorimer's Lot (IRE)**[9] 1543 3-8-8 **71**........................ DuranFentiman 6 74
(Mark Walford) *hld up bhd ldng gp: pushed along 1/2-way: effrt on outside over 1f out: led ins fnl f: drvn out* **12/1**

-212 **2** *¾* **Taquka (IRE)**[45] 926 3-9-5 **82**.............................. RichardKingscote 2 82
(Ralph Beckett) *cl up: led over 1f out to ins fnl f: kpt on: hld nr fin* **5/2**[2]

14-0 **3** *½* **Meadway**[14] 1445 3-9-7 **84**........................................ GrahamLee 5 85+
(Bryan Smart) *in tch: effrt and pushed along whn nt clr run over 1f out: swtchd rt and styd on fnl f: tk 3rd cl home* **8/1**[3]

31-1 **4** *hd* **Signore Piccolo**[17] 1396 3-9-0 **80**.......................... JasonHart(3) 4 78
(Eric Alston) *prom: stdy hdwy and ev ch over 1f out: sn rdn: no ex ins fnl f* **1/1**[1]

00-0 **5** *4* **De Repente (IRE)**[17] 1396 3-8-7 **70**........................ RaulDaSilva 3 53
(Paul Green) *bhd on outside: drvn and shortlived effrt 1/2-way: sn btn* **25/1**

-312 **6** *¾* **Fuel Injection**[39] 1005 3-8-7 **70** oh2..............................(b[1]) PJMcDonald 1 51
(Paul Midgley) *led at decent gallop: rdn and hdd over 1f out: sn btn* **9/1**

1m 0.66s (0.66) **Going Correction** +0.125s/f (Good) **6** Ran SP% **111.2**
Speed ratings (Par 100): **99,97,97,96,90 89**
CSF £41.28 TOTE £12.80: £6.30, £1.40; EX 56.70 Trifecta £664.90.

**Owner** Lorimer Walford **Bred** Roundhill Stud & Gleadhill House Stud Ltd **Trained** Sherriff Hutton, N Yorks

**FOCUS**
Punters only wanted to know about two horses in this good 3yo sprint handicap, but it didn't work out that way. The time was ordinary and form is rated around the runner-up.

## 1738 RIPONBET FORECAST MAIDEN STKS 1m 1f 170y
**5:15** (5:15) (Class 5) 3-Y-O **£5,175** (£1,540; £769; £384) **Stalls** Low

Form RPR

**1** **Satellite (IRE)** 3-9-5 0........................................ GrahamGibbons 3 91+
(William Haggas) *s.i.s: t.k.h in tch: smooth hdwy over 3f out: led gng wl over 1f out: pushed clr fnl f: readily* **6/5**[1]

56-2 **2** *5* **Maracuja**[7] 1582 3-9-0 74........................................ FrannyNorton 5 72
(Mark Johnston) *led at ordinary gallop: rdn and hdd over 1f out: kpt on fnl f: no ch w wnr* **10/3**[2]

6 **3** *1¾* **Hesketh Bank**[27] 1192 3-9-5 0.................................... DavidNolan 2 73
(Richard Fahey) *hld up in tch: pushed along over 4f out: hdwy 2f out: chsd clr ldng pair ins fnl f: kpt on: no imp* **11/1**

42 **4** *1* **All Reddy**[22] 1287 3-9-5 0...................................... RichardKingscote 4 71
(Tom Dascombe) *trckd ldrs: drvn over 2f out: edgd rt and outpcd wl over 1f out* **8/1**

5 **5** *1¾* **Fiery Sunset**[15] 1423 3-9-0 0.................................... TomQueally 1 63
(Michael Bell) *t.k.h: pressed ldr: drvn over 2f out: hung rt and wknd over 1f out* **4/1**[3]

00- **6** *18* **Kirkman (IRE)**[128] 8340 3-9-5 0.................................... TedDurcan 6 31
(James Bethell) *bhd: struggling over 3f out: sn btn: t.o* **40/1**

2m 7.71s (2.31) **Going Correction** +0.225s/f (Good) **6** Ran SP% **110.4**
Speed ratings (Par 98): **99,95,93,92,91 77**
CSF £5.19 TOTE £2.20: £1.50, £1.90; EX 5.80 Trifecta £32.80.

**Owner** Highclere Thoroughbred Racing - Distinction **Bred** Whisperview Trading Ltd **Trained** Newmarket, Suffolk

**FOCUS**
Not a particularly competitive maiden, but an imposing winner who looks sure do better.

T/Plt: £53.90 to a £1 stake. Pool: £72261.94 - 978.45 winning tickets T/Qpdt: £24.40 to a £1 stake. Pool: £4210.57 - 127.45 winning tickets RY

1626 **WOLVERHAMPTON (A.W)** (L-H)
Saturday, April 26

**OFFICIAL GOING: Standard**
Wind: Strong across Weather: Sunny; with the odd shower

## 1739 QUICKSILVERSLOTS PLAY £500 JACKPOT RAINBOW RICHES APPRENTICE H'CAP — 5f 216y(P)
**5:45** (5:45) (Class 5) (0-75,75) 4-Y-O+ **£2,911** (£866; £432; £216) **Stalls** Low

Form RPR
1423 **1** **Desert Strike**[22] 1283 8-9-7 **75**.......................(p) LouisSteward 8 82
(Conor Dore) *chsd ldrs towards outer: rdn 2f out: kpt on: led post* **14/1**
2641 **2** *hd* **Top Cop**[21] 1311 5-9-4 **72**.......................(p) DCByrne 1 78
(Ronald Harris) *trckd ldr: stl gng wl over 1f out: pushed along to ld ins fnl f: rdn and one pce fnl 110yds: hdd post* **6/1**
2053 **3** *1/2* **Amosite**[25] 1224 8-9-3 **71**.......................(v) ConnorBeasley 2 76
(J R Jenkins) *prom: rdn over 2f out: kpt on* **11/1**
6230 **4** *1/2* **Pull The Pin (IRE)**[14] 1448 5-8-8 **62**.......................(bt) ShirleyTeasdale 3 65
(Ann Stokell) *led: rdn whn hdd ins fnl f: no ex* **28/1**
5615 **5** *1 3/4* **Invigilator**[37] 1031 6-8-9 **66**.......................(t) AdamMcLean(3) 4 64
(Derek Shaw) *hld up: rdn over 2f out: kpt on fnl f: nvr threatened* **9/1**
5230 **6** *1 1/4* **Daring Dragon**[27] 1191 4-8-13 **72**.......................(b) BradleyBosley(5) 7 66
(Ed Walker) *s.i.s: hld up in tch: rdn 2f out: sn no imp* **2/1**[1]
321- **7** *hd* **Kimbali (IRE)**[152] 8037 5-9-2 **70**....................... EoinWalsh 6 63
(David Evans) *v.s.a: sn pushed along in rr: bhd tl minor late hdwy* **11/2**[3]
0-45 **8** *3 1/4* **Intrepid (IRE)**[15] 1429 4-9-2 **73**.......................(b[1]) GeorgeBuckell(3) 5 56
(Tim Pitt) *hld up: pushed along 1/2-way: nvr threatened* **4/1**[2]

1m 14.61s (-0.39) **Going Correction** +0.075s/f (Slow) 8 Ran SP% **111.5**
Speed ratings (Par 103): **105,104,104,103,101 99,99,94**
CSF £89.98 CT £952.00 TOTE £10.80: £3.30, £1.70, £3.20; EX 37.80 Trifecta £223.20.
**Owner** Andrew Page **Bred** Mrs Mary Rowlands **Trained** Hubbert's Bridge, Lincs

**FOCUS**
All but one wore some form of headgear in what was a modest sprint. Straightforward form.

## 1740 QUICKSILVERSLOTS £1 TO WIN £500 H'CAP — 1m 5f 194y(P)
**6:15** (6:16) (Class 6) (0-65,64) 4-Y-O+ **£2,264** (£673; £336; £168) **Stalls** Low

Form RPR
64-1 **1** **Precision Strike**[30] 1132 4-9-2 **63**.......................(v) ConnorBeasley(5) 7 71
(Richard Guest) *prom: rdn to ld over 2f out: drvn and kpt on fnl f* **3/1**[1]
-002 **2** *1 1/2* **Hazzaat (IRE)**[15] 1426 4-9-2 **58**....................... LukeMorris 6 65
(Nick Littmoden) *hld up in tch: rdn and hdwy over 2f out: drvn to chse wnr appr fnl f: l down whn edgd lft and attempted to bite winning rdr's whip 50yds out: nt run on* **9/2**
1233 **3** *4* **Goldmadchen (GER)**[14] 1453 6-9-3 **57**....................... DaleSwift 2 57
(James Given) *t.k.h early: trckd ldrs: rdn 3f out: one pce* **8/1**
235- **4** *1* **Nolecce**[183] 7510 7-9-2 **61**....................... JackDuern(5) 3 60
(Tony Forbes) *led: rdn whn hdd over 2f out: grad wknd* **8/1**
-224 **5** *4* **Shirazz**[30] 1132 5-8-13 **60**.......................(t) CamHardie(7) 4 53
(Seamus Durack) *trckd ldrs: rdn over 2f out: wknd over 1f out* **4/1**[3]
2133 **6** *2 1/4* **Uncle Bernie (IRE)**[64] 695 4-9-0 **56**.......................(p) JohnFahy 5 46
(Andrew Hollinshead) *s.i.s: hld up: rdn over 2f out: sn btn* **7/2**[2]
000/ **7** *23* **Scotsbrook Cloud**[598] 5124 9-9-1 **60**....................... EoinWalsh(5) 8 18
(David Evans) *hld up: rdn over 4f out: sn struggling* **40/1**

3m 9.27s (3.27) **Going Correction** +0.075s/f (Slow)
**WFA** 4 from 5yo+ 2lb 7 Ran SP% **110.1**
Speed ratings (Par 101): **93,92,89,89,87 85,72**
CSF £15.42 CT £88.23 TOTE £3.10: £2.70, £2.00; EX 14.70 Trifecta £124.80.
**Owner** Resdev **Bred** Mickley Stud **Trained** Wetherby, W Yorks

**FOCUS**
A weak and muddling handicap. The winner rates a small personal best.

## 1741 QUICKSILVERSLOTS OPEN AFTER 10PM EBF STALLIONS MAIDEN STKS — 5f 20y(P)
**6:45** (6:45) (Class 5) 2-Y-O **£3,234** (£962; £481; £240) **Stalls** Low

Form RPR
4 **1** **Elizabeth Flynn (IRE)**[9] 1536 2-9-0 **0**....................... MartinLane 6 70
(K R Burke) *pressed ldr: led gng wl 2f out: rdn clr over 1f out: wandered ins fnl f: comf* **3/1**[2]
5 **2** *2* **Don Sigfredo (IRE)**[23] 1259 2-9-5 **0**....................... StephenCraine 4 70+
(Tom Dascombe) *s.i.s: hld up: rdn 2f out: r.o wl fnl f: wnt 2nd towards fin* **6/4**[1]
**3** *1/2* **Perardua** 2-9-0 **0**....................... LeeTopliss 7 61+
(Richard Fahey) *chsd ldng pair: rdn 1/2-way: wnt 2nd appr fnl f: one pce: lost 2nd towards fin* **9/2**[3]
**4** *2* **Arizona Snow** 2-9-5 **0**....................... LukeMorris 2 59
(Ronald Harris) *s.i.s: hld up: sn pushed along: kpt on fr over 1f out* **16/1**
02 **5** *1 1/4* **Johnny Sorrento**[23] 1259 2-9-5 **0**....................... StevieDonohoe 3 54
(Tim Pitt) *led narrowly: rdn whn hdd 2f out: wknd fnl f* **3/1**[2]
0 **6** *1 3/4* **Is She Any Good (IRE)**[12] 1482 2-9-0 **0**....................... AndrewMullen 5 43
(David Evans) *sn pushed along in rr: nvr threatened* **25/1**
0 **7** *shd* **Ciaras Cookie (IRE)**[28] 1169 2-9-0 **0**....................... LiamKeniry 9 43
(David Evans) *racd keenly in tch: pushed along 1/2-way: wknd over 1f out* **50/1**
0 **8** *6* **Lady Armada**[21] 1314 2-9-0 **0**....................... JohnFahy 1 21
(Jo Hughes) *in tch: rdn 1/2-way: wknd over 1f out* **33/1**

1m 3.94s (1.64) **Going Correction** +0.075s/f (Slow) 8 Ran SP% **122.8**
Speed ratings (Par 92): **89,85,85,81,79 77,76,67**
CSF £8.51 TOTE £4.60: £1.40, £1.10, £1.80; EX 10.40 Trifecta £44.00.
**Owner** Norton Common Farm Racing **Bred** Philip Hore Jnr **Trained** Middleham Moor, N Yorks

**FOCUS**
The favourite fluffed his line again in this weak 2yo maiden. Improvement from the winner.

## 1742 QUICKSILVERSLOTS MORE JACKPOTS MORE MACHINES H'CAP — 5f 20y(P)
**7:20** (7:21) (Class 2) (0-100,96) 4-Y-O+
**£11,827** (£3,541; £1,770; £885; £442; £222) **Stalls** Low

Form RPR
4222 **1** **Mappin Time (IRE)**[15] 1429 6-9-1 **85**.......................(be) KierenFallon 10 95
(Tim Easterby) *dwlt: hld up: sn pushed along: hdwy on outside 1/2-way: drvn to ld ins fnl f: sn jnd: edgd lft: jst hld on* **9/2**[2]
-313 **2** *shd* **Top Boy**[10] 1506 4-8-12 **82**.......................(v) DaleSwift 8 92
(Derek Shaw) *dwlt: hld up: rdn and gd hdwy on ins over 1f out: upsides 110yds out: kpt on: jst failed* **11/2**[3]
0641 **3** *1 1/2* **Caspian Prince (IRE)**[3] 1650 5-9-12 **96** 6ex.......................(t) LiamKeniry 3 100
(Tony Carroll) *sn led: rdn 2f out: hdd ins fnl f: no ex* **2/1**[1]
1-02 **4** *1 1/4* **Rusty Rocket (IRE)**[21] 1305 5-8-13 **83**....................... LukeMorris 1 83
(Paul Green) *trckd ldr: rdn 1/2-way: one pce* **20/1**
2614 **5** *shd* **Muhdiq (USA)**[12] 1489 5-9-0 **84**....................... ShaneKelly 7 83
(Mike Murphy) *chsd ldr: rdn 2f out: one pce: sltly hmpd ins fnl f* **7/1**
2100 **6** *3/4* **Royal Bajan (USA)**[8] 1566 6-9-1 **90**.......................(v) ConnorBeasley(5) 9 87
(James Given) *chsd ldr: rdn 1/2-way: no ex ins fnl f* **22/1**
1215 **7** *1/2* **Go Far**[26] 1212 4-8-6 **81**.......................(b) TimClark(5) 4 76
(Alan Bailey) *s.i.s: sn outpcd in rr: minor late hdwy: nvr threatened* **14/1**
2320 **8** *1/2* **Dangerous Age**[29] 1145 4-8-12 **82**....................... JoeFanning 2 75
(J W Hills) *in tch on inner: rdn 2f out: wknd ins fnl f* **11/1**
-420 **9** *1 1/4* **Ubetterbegood (ARG)**[12] 1489 6-9-7 **91**.......................(p) MartinLane 5 80
(Robert Cowell) *midfield: rdn 1/2-way: wknd over 1f out* **16/1**
000- **10** *5* **Sacrosanctus**[266] 4983 6-8-10 **87**.......................(p) MatthewHopkins(7) 6 58
(Scott Dixon) *sn outpcd in rr: hung rt on bnd 2f out: a bhd* **50/1**

1m 1.1s (-1.20) **Going Correction** +0.075s/f (Slow) **10** Ran SP% **111.4**
Speed ratings (Par 109): **112,111,109,107,107 106,105,104,102,94**
CSF £27.25 CT £62.77 TOTE £6.00: £2.00, £2.50, £1.20; EX 25.00 Trifecta £110.40.
**Owner** P Baillie **Bred** J Jamgotchian **Trained** Great Habton, N Yorks

**FOCUS**
An ultra-competitive sprint handicap run at a furious gallop. The winner was marginally better than ever.

## 1743 QUICKSILVERSLOTS PLAY YOUR FAVOURITE £500 JACKPOT CLAIMING STKS — 1m 4f 50y(P)
**7:50** (7:50) (Class 6) 4-Y-O+ **£2,264** (£673; £336; £168) **Stalls** Low

Form RPR
23-1 **1** **Reve De Nuit (USA)**[115] 2 8-9-6 **94**....................... DanielTudhope 3 82+
(K R Burke) *trckd ldr: led over 4f out: pushed clr over 1f out: easily* **1/3**[1]
4320 **2** *2 3/4* **Daring Indian**[18] 1359 6-8-8 **66**.......................(p) JennyPowell(7) 4 73
(Tom Dascombe) *hld up in tch: rdn over 2f out: hdwy into 2nd wl over 1f out: no ch w easy wnr* **11/1**[3]
4334 **3** *7* **Layline (IRE)**[80] 494 7-9-6 **76**....................... LukeMorris 5 71
(Gay Kelleway) *in tch: drvn to chse wnr 3f out: btn in 3rd fr over 1f out* **8/1**[2]
6-24 **4** *11* **Easydoesit (IRE)**[16] 168 6-8-10 **62**....................... LiamKeniry 2 39
(Tony Carroll) *in tch: rdn and outpcd over 3f out: sn btn* **25/1**
0/0- **5** *11* **Stormy Weather (FR)**[14] 5147 8-9-1 **84**.......................(t) DaleSwift 1 27
(Brian Ellison) *led: hdd over 4f out: sn rdn and wknd* **11/1**[3]

2m 38.42s (-2.68) **Going Correction** +0.075s/f (Slow) 5 Ran SP% **106.6**
Speed ratings (Par 101): **111,109,104,97,89**
CSF £4.34 TOTE £1.10: £1.10, £3.80; EX 4.90 Trifecta £18.00.
**Owner** Mrs Z Wentworth **Bred** Ecurie Du Haras De Meautry **Trained** Middleham Moor, N Yorks

**FOCUS**
A claimer that featured a long odds-on favourite bidding to prove his effectiveness on this surface. He didn't need to approach his best.

## 1744 QUICKSILVERSLOTS PLAY FROM 10P TO £2 H'CAP — 1m 141y(P)
**8:20** (8:20) (Class 4) (0-85,89) 4-Y-O+ **£5,175** (£1,540; £769; £384) **Stalls** Low

Form RPR
4-53 **1** **Bold Prediction (IRE)**[4] 1637 4-9-4 **80**....................... DanielTudhope 2 89
(K R Burke) *trckd ldr: rdn to chal strly fr over 2f out: led ins fnl f: kpt on* **11/10**[1]
5123 **2** *1 3/4* **My Single Malt (IRE)**[23] 1267 6-8-7 **74**.......................(p) ConnorBeasley(5) 1 79
(Julie Camacho) *led at stdy pce: rdn and strly pressed fr over 2f out: hdd ins fnl f: no ex* **5/2**[2]
-060 **3** *1* **Cockney Class (USA)**[64] 698 7-8-8 **75**....................... GeorgeDowning(5) 6 78
(Dave Roberts) *trckd ldng pair towards outer: rdn over 2f out: sn one pce in 3rd* **16/1**
014- **4** *5* **Goldstorm**[249] 5613 6-9-6 **82**.......................(p) AndrewMullen 4 73
(Brian Baugh) *slowly away and bit rel to r early: sn bk in tch w pce stdy: rdn 3f out: sn no imp: wknd ins fnl f* **9/2**[3]
1664 **5** *8* **Loud**[11] 1499 4-8-10 **72**....................... JoeFanning 3 52
(Mark Johnston) *hld up: rdn and outpcd 3f out: sn btn: eased over 1f out* **7/1**

1m 50.33s (-0.17) **Going Correction** +0.075s/f (Slow) 5 Ran SP% **112.8**
Speed ratings (Par 105): **103,101,100,96,89**
CSF £4.25 TOTE £2.00: £1.20, £1.50; EX 6.00 Trifecta £39.60.
**Owner** Mrs Elaine M Burke **Bred** Mountarmstrong Stud **Trained** Middleham Moor, N Yorks

**FOCUS**
A weak race, and muddling form.

## 1745 QUICKSILVERSLOTS FUN ON THE HIGH STREET H'CAP — 1m 141y(P)
**8:50** (8:50) (Class 6) (0-60,59) 4-Y-O+ **£2,264** (£673; £336; £168) **Stalls** Low

Form RPR
0433 **1** **Sixties Queen**[4] 1638 4-9-0 **52**....................... KierenFallon 6 60
(Alan Bailey) *prom: led over 2f out: rdn over 1f out: kpt on* **6/4**[1]
40-0 **2** *1* **Jumbo Prado (USA)**[85] 406 5-9-7 **59**.......................(p) ShaneKelly 3 65
(John Stimpson) *hld up: pushed along and hdwy over 1f out: rdn to chse wnr ins fnl f: kpt on but a hld* **7/1**
-210 **3** *3/4* **Just Five (IRE)**[25] 1228 8-8-5 **48**.......................(v) ConnorBeasley(5) 5 52
(John Weymes) *trckd ldng pair: rdn over 2f out: one pce* **9/4**[2]
0355 **4** *1/2* **Do More Business (IRE)**[40] 998 7-8-11 **54**.......................(vt) PhilipPrince(5) 2 57
(Liam Corcoran) *trckd ldng pair: rdn over 2f out: one pce* **11/2**[3]
-500 **5** *1 1/4* **Acton Gold**[30] 1138 5-8-7 **45**.......................(p) AndrewMullen 1 45
(Brian Baugh) *stdd sed: hld up in tch: racd keenly: rdn over 2f out: no imp* **20/1**
650- **6** *3/4* **Glan Lady (IRE)**[220] 6518 8-8-7 **45**....................... StevieDonohoe 4 43
(Ian Williams) *led: rdn whn hdd over 2f out: sn wknd* **12/1**

1m 51.76s (1.26) **Going Correction** +0.075s/f (Slow) 6 Ran SP% **111.1**
Speed ratings (Par 101): **97,96,95,95,93 93**
CSF £12.33 TOTE £3.00: £1.50, £3.90; EX 10.60 Trifecta £40.10.
**Owner** Tregarth Racing & Partner **Bred** R L Williams **Trained** Newmarket, Suffolk

**FOCUS**
A straightforward success for the favourite in this weak handicap, backing up her recent efforts.
T/Plt: £11.60 to a £1 stake. Pool: £57,402.8 - 3,585.31 winning units T/Qpdt: £2.50 to a £1 stake. Pool: £7,167.40 - 2,080.68 winning units AS

1740 - 1749a (Foreign Racing) - See Raceform Interactive

1410 **LIMERICK** (R-H)

Saturday, April 26

**OFFICIAL GOING: Yielding to soft**

**1750a** **MARTIN MOLONY STKS (LISTED RACE)** **1m 4f 110y**
**4:45** (4:46) 4-Y-O+ **£21,666** (£6,333; £3,000; £1,000)

RPR

1 **Tarana (IRE)**[13] 1474 4-9-0 98 .................................... DeclanMcDonogh 3 104+
(John M Oxx, Ire) *trckd ldr in 2nd: clsd to press ldr 3f out: styd on wl to ld ins fnl 100yds: jst hld on* **10/3**[3]

2 *nse* **El Salvador (IRE)**[16] 1416 5-9-6 106 ............................ JosephO'Brien 1 109+
(A P O'Brien, Ire) *chsd ldrs in 3rd: rdn along to press ldrs appr fnl f: styd on wl into 2nd ins fnl 100yds: jst hld* **5/2**[2]

3 *1 ¼* **Inis Meain (USA)**[13] 1474 7-9-9 110 ............................ DannyMullins 2 110
(Denis Gerard Hogan, Ire) *led: clly pressed fr 3f out: kpt on wl fr 2f out tl hdd ins fnl 100yds and dropped to 3rd: no ex* **7/4**[1]

4 *3* **Sir Ector (USA)**[41] 7723 7-9-6 104 ............................ ChrisHayes 9 103
(J J Lambe, Ire) *w.w: pushed along in 6th 2f out: kpt on wl into 4th appr fnl f: nt rch principals* **12/1**

5 *1* **Ebazziyr (IRE)**[120] 6-9-6 ........................................(t) FMBerry 5 101
(James Leavy, Ire) *slowly away and racd in rr tl kpt on wl towards outer ins fnl 2f: nvr nrr* **50/1**

6 *3 ¼* **Parish Hall (IRE)**[13] 1474 5-9-11 112 ............................ KevinManning 8 101
(J S Bolger, Ire) *chsd ldrs in 4th towards outer tl rdn along over 2f out: sn no imp and wknd* **13/2**

7 *9* **Storm Away (IRE)**[199] 7135 5-9-1 76 ............................ DannyGrant 6 78
(Patrick J Flynn, Ire) *hld up: sme prog under 4f out on inner: wnt 4th 2f out: sn no ex and wknd* **66/1**

8 *1 ¾* **Valbucca (IRE)**[7] 1592 7-9-1 92 ............................(b) WayneLordan 4 75
(W McCreery, Ire) *w.w in 5th: rdn along over 2f out: sn no ex* **33/1**

2m 52.47s (172.47)
**WFA** 4 from 5yo+ 1lb **8** Ran SP% **115.4**
CSF £12.17 TOTE £4.40: £2.40, £1.02, £1.02; DF 14.50 Trifecta £41.90.
**Owner** H H Aga Khan **Bred** His Highness The Aga Khan's Studs S C **Trained** Currabeg, Co Kildare

**FOCUS**
A filly only having her fourth career start, perhaps Tarana can now make up for lost time. The way she battled her way to victory here certainly augurs well.

1751 - 1756a (Foreign Racing) - See Raceform Interactive

**AYR** (L-H)

Sunday, April 27

**OFFICIAL GOING: Good (good to firm in places; 9.0) changing to good to firm (good in places) after race 2 (2.30)**
Track on innermost line, Stands' side rail in 10m and distances as advertised.
Wind: Breezy; half behind Weather: Overcast

**1757** **DOWNLOAD THE FREE FREEBETS.CO.UK APP MAIDEN STKS** **6f**
**2:00** (2:01) (Class 5) 3-Y-O+ **£2,911** (£866; £432; £216) **Stalls** High

Form RPR

3- 1 **Watchable**[191] 7345 4-10-0 0 ............................ DanielTudhope 2 96
(David O'Meara) *pressed ldr: shkn up to ld over 1f out: pushed out fnl f: readily* **9/4**[2]

023- 2 *3 ½* **Galvanize**[198] 7173 3-9-3 86 ............................ PaulMulrennan 1 82
(Kevin Ryan) *led: rdn: edgd lft and hdd over 1f out: kpt on same pce fnl f* **2/5**[1]

3 *6* **Poetree In Motion** 3-8-12 0 ............................ TomEaves 6 58
(Keith Dalgleish) *trckd ldrs: shkn up wl over 1f out: sn outpcd by first two* **33/1**[3]

- 4 *4 ½* **Haidees Reflection** 4-9-9 0 ............................ PJMcDonald 4 46
(Lucy Normile) *dwlt: rn green in rr: rdn and wknd fr 2f out* **150/1**

1m 12.26s (-0.14) **Going Correction** -0.275s/f (Firm)
**WFA** 3 from 4yo 11lb **4** Ran SP% **105.8**
Speed ratings (Par 103): **89,84,76,70**
CSF £3.41 TOTE £3.10; EX 3.80 Trifecta £4.50.
**Owner** P Bamford **Bred** Cheveley Park Stud Ltd **Trained** Nawton, N Yorks

**FOCUS**
There had been 9.5mm of rain over the previous five days, the majority of it falling on Wednesday and Friday, but it had been dry for 24 hours and the ground had dried out to good, good to firm in places (GoingStick 9.0). The track was on its innermost line and the stands' rail was in by 10m with all distances as advertised. This looked pretty uncompetitive, but there was a minor turn-up. It's hard to gauge what the winner achieved.

**1758** **EXCLUSIVE FREE BETS AT FREEBETS.CO.UK H'CAP** **6f**
**2:30** (2:32) (Class 6) (0-65,65) 3-Y-O+ **£1,940** (£577; £288; £144) **Stalls** High

Form RPR

166- 1 **Dashwood**[10] 1546 7-9-10 61 ............................(t) DavidNolan 12 82
(J F Levins, Ire) *trckd ldrs gng wl stands' side: smooth hdwy to ld over 1f out: pushed clr fnl f: readily: 1st of 9 in gp* **3/1**[1]

60-0 2 *8* **Diamond Blue**[15] 1447 6-9-13 64 ............................(p) TonyHamilton 3 61
(Richard Fahey) *prom centre: effrt and rdn 2f out: led that gp ins fnl f: no ch w ready stands' side wnr: 1st of 6 in gp* **9/1**

606/ 3 *nk* **New Lease Of Life**[658] 3892 5-9-5 56 ............................ DanielTudhope 5 52
(Jim Goldie) *prom centre: effrt and drvn along 2f out: kpt on ins fnl f: nrst fin: 2nd of 6 in gp* **50/1**

06-0 4 *nse* **Funding Deficit (IRE)**[15] 1447 4-9-8 62 ............................ IanBrennan(3) 9 58
(Jim Goldie) *w stands' side ldr: drvn over 2f out: kpt on same pce fnl f: 2nd of 9 in gp* **22/1**

006- 5 *¾* **Goninodaethat**[199] 7153 6-9-0 54 ............................ JasonHart(3) 10 48
(Jim Goldie) *led stands' side to over 1f out: drvn and kpt on same pce fnl f: 3rd of 9 in gp* **12/1**

40-6 6 *hd* **Economic Crisis (IRE)**[9] 1565 5-9-11 62 ............................ JamesSullivan 13 55
(Alan Berry) *taken early and unruly to post: trckd stands' side ldrs: rdn and edgd lft wl over 1f out: kpt on same pce: 4th of 9 in gp* **14/1**

02-4 7 *1 ½* **Baltic Spirit (IRE)**[4] 1642 3-9-3 65 ............................ TomEaves 15 51
(Keith Dalgleish) *hld up bhd ldng gp stands' side: rdn 2f out: no imp over 1f out: 5th of 9 in gp* **9/2**[2]

30-5 8 *hd* **Monel**[22] 1310 6-9-1 52 ............................ GrahamLee 8 40
(Jim Goldie) *blindfold slow to remove and s.i.s: hld up on outside of stands' side gp: effrt and hdwy over 2f out: wknd ins fnl f: 6th of 9 in gp* **7/1**[3]

-526 9 *¾* **Commandable (AUS)**[7] 1602 10-8-13 55 ............................ GarryWhillans(5) 4 41
(Ian Semple) *led centre: rdn over 2f out: hung lft and hdd ins fnl f: sn btn: 3rd of 6 in gp* **10/1**

66-0 10 *¾* **Saxonette**[7] 1602 6-9-1 52 ............................ PJMcDonald 6 36
(Linda Perratt) *pressed centre ldr: rdn and ev ch over 1f out to ins fnl f: nt qckn: 4th of 6 in gp* **33/1**

25-0 11 *hd* **Verus Delicia (IRE)**[15] 1447 5-9-13 64 ............................ StephenCraine 2 47
(Daniel Mark Loughnane) *bhd centre: rdn along 1/2-way: sme late hdwy: nvr on terms: 5th of 6 in gp* **28/1**

006- 12 *½* **Fife Jo**[199] 7150 4-9-0 51 oh6 ............................(v) PaulMulrennan 16 32
(Jim Goldie) *hld up stands' side: effrt and swtchd lft over 2f out: sn no imp: 7th of 9 in gp* **33/1**

004- 13 *hd* **Classy Anne**[199] 7150 4-9-0 51 oh6 ............................ RussKennemore 11 32
(Jim Goldie) *in tch on outside of stands' side gp: rdn over 2f out: wknd over 1f out: 8th of 9 in gp* **50/1**

060/ 14 *4 ½* **Karens Legacy (IRE)**[858] 7845 6-9-0 51 oh6 ............................ GaryBartley 7 18
(Jim Goldie) *hld up centre: struggling over 2f out: sn btn: last of 6 in gp* **22/1**

005- 15 *1* **Spirit Of Alsace (IRE)**[214] 6746 3-9-1 63 ............................ PhillipMakin 14 24
(Jim Goldie) *t.k.h: hld up bhd ldng gp stands' side: rdn over 2f out: sn wknd: last of 9 in gp* **25/1**

1m 10.51s (-1.89) **Going Correction** -0.275s/f (Firm)
**WFA** 3 from 4yo+ 11lb **15** Ran SP% **114.9**
Speed ratings (Par 101): **101,90,89,89,88 88,86,86,85,84 84,83,83,77,75**
CSF £24.91 CT £1113.82 TOTE £3.80: £1.50, £4.20, £6.70; EX 29.90 Trifecta £1550.90.
**Owner** Seamus Mannion **Bred** Darley **Trained** The Curragh, Co Kildare
■ Jim Goldie sent out no fewer than eight runners.

**FOCUS**
They split into two groups here but there looked to be no bias. The well backed winner is rated to last year's best.

**1759** **BEST ONLINE CASINOS AT BONUS.CO.UK H'CAP** **5f**
**3:00** (3:02) (Class 5) (0-75,77) 4-Y-O+ **£2,781** (£827; £413; £206) **Stalls** High

Form RPR

4411 1 **Megaleka**[6] 1618 4-9-6 77 6ex ............................ TimClark(5) 2 88
(Alan Bailey) *prom on outside: hdwy to ld over 1f out: drvn: edgd lft and drew clr ins fnl f* **10/3**[1]

320- 2 *3* **Rothesay Chancer**[157] 7985 6-9-7 73 ............................ GrahamLee 7 73
(Jim Goldie) *hld up: rdn and hdwy over 1f out: chsd (clr) wnr ins fnl f: kpt on: no imp* **10/1**

204- 3 *¾* **Salvatore Fury (IRE)**[215] 6728 4-9-2 68 ............................(p) TomEaves 3 66
(Keith Dalgleish) *t.k.h: cl up: led over 2f out to over 1f out: kpt on same pce ins fnl f* **7/2**[2]

50-3 4 *¾* **Jinky**[9] 1565 6-9-5 71 ............................ DaleSwift 1 66
(Linda Perratt) *bhd and sn pushed along: hdwy on outside over 2f out: rdn and no imp fnl f* **7/2**[2]

00-5 5 *1 ½* **Perfect Blossom**[12] 1500 7-9-7 73 ............................ PaulMulrennan 6 62
(Alan Berry) *cl up: rdn and ev ch over 2f out to over 1f out: sn outpcd* **12/1**

54-0 6 *½* **Opt Out**[9] 1565 4-9-0 66 ............................ PJMcDonald 5 54
(Alistair Whillans) *hld up bhd ldng gp: rdn over 2f out: no imp fr over 1f out* **8/1**

610- 7 *3 ¼* **Chloe's Dream (IRE)**[217] 6669 4-8-9 64 ............................ JasonHart(3) 4 40
(Ian Semple) *led to over 2f out: rdn and wknd over 1f out* **6/1**[3]

58.59s (-0.81) **Going Correction** -0.275s/f (Firm) **7** Ran SP% **109.7**
Speed ratings (Par 103): **95,90,89,87,85 84,79**
CSF £32.80 CT £112.45 TOTE £4.00: £2.50, £5.70; EX 27.60 Trifecta £82.40.
**Owner** North Cheshire Trading & Storage Ltd **Bred** North Cheshire Trading And Storage Ltd **Trained** Newmarket, Suffolk

**FOCUS**
The going was changed to good to firm, good in places before this race. A modest sprint, and unclear what winning this took with doubts over the field.

**1760** **CASINO BONUSES AT BONUS.CO.UK H'CAP** **7f 50y**
**3:30** (3:30) (Class 5) (0-75,74) 4-Y-O+ **£2,716** (£808; £404; £202) **Stalls** High

Form RPR

306- 1 **Patrona Ciana (FR)**[180] 7603 4-9-6 73 ............................ DanielTudhope 2 82
(David O'Meara) *in tch: hdwy and angled to outside over 2f out: led 1f out: rdn out* **15/8**[1]

520- 2 *1 ¼* **Thorntoun Lady (USA)**[242] 5878 4-8-13 66 ............................ GrahamLee 1 71
(Jim Goldie) *hld up: rdn and hdwy 2f out: chsd wnr wl ins fnl f: r.o* **4/1**[3]

0- 3 *1 ½* **Jumbo Steps (IRE)**[186] 7474 7-8-13 71 ............................ GarryWhillans(5) 5 72
(Jim Goldie) *chsd clr ldr: effrt and rdn 2f out: kpt on same pce ins fnl f* **9/4**[2]

-000 4 *1 ¼* **Great Demeanor (USA)**[6] 1609 4-8-4 62 ............................(b) EmmaSayer(5) 4 60?
(Dianne Sayer) *led: clr after 2f: rdn and hdd 1f out: sn outpcd* **16/1**

5 *1 ¼* **Alanos (IRE)**[270] 5-9-7 74 ............................ PaulMulrennan 3 69
(James Ewart) *prom: effrt and rdn 2f out: outpcd fnl f* **12/1**

006- 6 *5* **Good Boy Jackson**[171] 6906 6-8-12 70 ............................ NoelGarbutt(5) 6 52
(R Mike Smith) *stdd s: hld up: rdn along 3f out: wknd fr 2f out* **8/1**

1m 31.1s (-2.30) **Going Correction** -0.275s/f (Firm) **6** Ran SP% **110.2**
Speed ratings (Par 103): **102,100,98,97,96 90**
CSF £9.36 TOTE £3.00: £1.60, £2.20; EX 7.20 Trifecta £19.50.
**Owner** Middleham Park Racing LII & Partner **Bred** Mlle Francoise Perree **Trained** Nawton, N Yorks

**FOCUS**
This was run at a good gallop thanks to Great Demeanor, who went off fast in front. Limited form.

**1761** **BETTING ODDS AT COMPAREBETTING.COM H'CAP** **1m 2f**
**4:00** (4:00) (Class 6) (0-60,60) 4-Y-O+ **£1,940** (£577; £288; £144) **Stalls** Low

Form RPR

-003 1 **Call Of Duty (IRE)**[7] 1596 9-8-4 48 oh1 ow2 ............................(b) EmmaSayer(5) 2 57
(Dianne Sayer) *hld up: hdwy and angled to outside 2f out: kpt on to ld wl ins fnl f: r.o* **11/2**[3]

040- 2 *½* **Eilean Mor**[199] 7153 6-8-2 46 oh1 ............................ NoelGarbutt(5) 6 54
(R Mike Smith) *chsd ldrs: n.m.r and lost pl over 2f out: kpt on u.p fnl f: tk 2nd cl home* **10/1**

5-05 3 *nk* **K Lightning (IRE)**[18] 1387 4-8-3 49 ow1 ............................ GeorgeBuckell(7) 8 56
(Denis Quinn) *hld up: rdn and hdwy on outside to ld over 1f out: hdd wl ins fnl f: no ex nr fin* **3/1**[1]

605- 4 *1 ½* **Elizabeth Coffee (IRE)**[142] 8183 6-8-3 47 ............................ JoeyHaynes(5) 4 52
(John Weymes) *hld up: rdn over 2f out: hdwy on outside over 1f out: kpt on fnl f: nrst fin* **12/1**

434/ 5 *1 ¼* **Snooker (GER)**[530] 4958 8-9-2 55 ............................ JamesSullivan 5 57
(Rose Dobbin) *hld up in tch: hdwy and ev ch over 1f out: sn rdn: outpcd ins fnl f* **16/1**

523- **6** *1 ½* **Latin Rebel (IRE)**[199] 7151 7-9-5 **58**.................................. GrahamLee 3 57
(Jim Goldie) *hld up: pushed along whn n.m.r over 2f out: hdwy over 1f out: kpt on: nvr able to chal* **4/1**[2]

4-64 **7** *1* **Cabal**[65] 697 7-8-10 **52**.................................................(b) NeilFarley(3) 7 50
(Andrew Crook) *s.i.s: hld up: rdn over 2f out: sme late hdwy: nvr on terms* **14/1**

3225 **8** *2 ¾* **Yourinthewill (USA)**[15] 1454 6-9-7 **60**........................ StephenCraine 11 52
(Daniel Mark Loughnane) *hld up on outside: hdwy and prom 3f out: rdn 2f out: wknd fnl f* **9/1**

046 **9** *1* **Strandfield Bay (IRE)**[25] 1249 8-8-13 **52**.......................(p) PaulQuinn 12 42
(Sharon Watt) *chsd ldrs tl rdn and lost pl over 2f out: n.d after* **25/1**

500- **10** *3 ¾* **Gadobout Dancer**[173] 7752 7-8-7 **46** oh1.................. TomEaves 9 29
(Keith Dalgleish) *prom: hdwy to ld 3f out: rdn and hdd over 1f out: sn btn* **10/1**

4/5- **11** *57* **She's Some Girl (IRE)**[448] 507 4-8-4 **46** oh1............... IanBrennan(3) 1
(Ian Semple) *led: rdn and hdd 3f out: wknd 2f out: eased and sn lost tch* **28/1**

2m 11.27s (-0.73) **Going Correction** -0.275s/f (Firm) **11 Ran SP% 116.1**
Speed ratings (Par 101): **91,90,90,89,88 86,86,83,83,80 34**
CSF £58.71 CT £195.67 TOTE £8.30: £2.70, £4.80, £1.80; EX 79.30 Trifecta £805.50.
**Owner** T W Rebanks **Bred** Gainsborough Stud Management Ltd **Trained** Hackthorpe, Cumbria

**FOCUS**
The early pace wasn't strong but three of the first four came from the rear. The second was possibly unlucky.

## 1762 FREE BETS AT FREEBETS.CO.UK H'CAP — 1m
**4:30** (4:30) (Class 4) (0-85,85) 4-Y-0+ **£5,175** (£1,540; £769; £384) **Stalls Low**

Form / RPR

5 **1** **Baraweez (IRE)**[28] 1191 4-8-12 **76**.................................... DaleSwift 5 85
(Brian Ellison) *prom: hdwy to ld over 1f out: sn rdn: edgd rt: hld on wl fnl f* **7/4**[1]

610- **2** *¾* **Ingleby Symphony (IRE)**[184] 7499 4-8-7 **71**.............. PatrickMathers 4 78
(Richard Fahey) *hld up: effrt and hdwy on outside over 1f out: chal ins fnl f: kpt on: hld nr fin* **12/1**

30-0 **3** *2 ¼* **Nurpur (IRE)**[20] 1345 4-9-7 **85**.................................... DanielTudhope 1 88
(David O'Meara) *hld up: shkn up and hdwy wl over 1f out: edgd lft: cl 3rd and keeping on whn n.m.r ins fnl f: one pce last 75yds* **8/1**

1-04 **4** *nk* **Coincidently**[8] 1568 4-8-6 **75**.................................... TimClark(5) 7 76
(Alan Bailey) *cl up: ev ch over 1f out: sn rdn: kpt on same pce ins fnl f* **16/1**

0-64 **5** *nk* **Dubai Dynamo**[15] 1451 9-9-2 **80**................................ PJMcDonald 2 80+
(Ruth Carr) *hld up in tch on ins: pushed along and edgd lft over 2f out: rallying whn n.m.r and swtchd rt appr fnl f: kpt on: no imp* **7/2**[2]

400- **6** *2 ½* **Order Of Service**[202] 7075 4-8-10 **74**.......................... GrahamLee 3 69
(Jim Goldie) *chsd ldrs: rdn over 2f out: wknd over 1f out* **14/1**

150- **7** *¾* **Blighty (IRE)**[195] 7257 4-9-0 **81**................................ SamJames(3) 6 74
(David O'Meara) *t.k.h: led tl rdn and hdd over 1f out: sn btn* **4/1**[3]

1m 40.3s (-3.50) **Going Correction** -0.275s/f (Firm) **7 Ran SP% 109.9**
Speed ratings (Par 105): **106,105,103,102,102 99,99**
CSF £22.19 TOTE £2.60: £1.30, £4.60; EX 16.50 Trifecta £62.60.
**Owner** A Barnes **Bred** Sunderland Holdings Inc **Trained** Norton, N Yorks

**FOCUS**
Whether the best horse won this race is open to debate. The winner's Doncaster race is working out.

## 1763 BETTING OFFERS AT ONLINEBETTINGOFFERS.CO.UK H'CAP — 1m 5f 13y
**5:00** (5:00) (Class 6) (0-65,64) 4-Y-0+ **£1,940** (£577; £288; £144) **Stalls Low**

Form / RPR

230- **1** **A Southside Boy (GER)**[220] 6552 6-9-9 **64**...................... GrahamLee 3 69
(Jim Goldie) *t.k.h: in tch on ins: effrt whn nt clr run over 2f out: swtchd rt and effrt wl over 1f out: carried hd high: styd on wl to ld cl home* **11/8**[1]

350- **2** *hd* **Vicky Valentine**[158] 7757 4-9-4 **63**................................ JulieBurke(3) 7 67
(Alistair Whillans) *in tch: hdwy on outside to ld 2f out: sn pushed along: edgd lft ins fnl f: hdd cl home* **5/1**[2]

556- **3** *1* **Geanie Mac (IRE)**[149] 7668 5-9-3 **58**...........................(p) PJMcDonald 6 60
(Linda Perratt) *cl up: effrt and ev ch 2f out: sn rdn: kpt on ins fnl f* **12/1**

62-0 **4** *½* **Sergeant Pink (IRE)**[19] 609 8-8-8 **54**...........................(p) EmmaSayer(5) 2 55
(Dianne Sayer) *cl up: effrt and ev ch 2f out: sn rdn: kpt on same pce ins fnl f* **7/1**[3]

300- **5** *¾* **Forrest Flyer (IRE)**[177] 7668 10-9-3 **58**........................ PhillipMakin 5 58
(Jim Goldie) *led at modest gallop: rdn and hdd 2f out: kpt on same pce* **5/1**[2]

610- **6** *5* **Grand Diamond (IRE)**[195] 7239 10-9-6 **61**...................... GaryBartley 1 54
(Jim Goldie) *hld up in tch: rdn and outpcd over 2f out: n.d after* **9/1**

50-6 **7** *1 ¼* **Sohcahtoa (IRE)**[77] 546 8-8-13 **57**...........................(p) NeilFarley(3) 4 48
(Andrew Crook) *hld up in tch: drvn and outpcd wl over 2f out: n.d after* **25/1**

2m 59.31s (5.31) **Going Correction** -0.275s/f (Firm)
**WFA** 4 from 5yo+ 1lb **7 Ran SP% 109.5**
Speed ratings (Par 101): **72,71,71,70,70 67,66**
CSF £7.62 TOTE £2.10: £1.60, £3.10; EX 7.80 Trifecta £40.60.
**Owner** Connor & Dunne **Bred** Gestut Karlshof **Trained** Uplawmoor, E Renfrews
■ Stewards' Enquiry : Julie Burke two-day ban: used whip above permitted level (May 12-13)

**FOCUS**
A race of changing fortunes with a bunch finish. It's hard to have too much confidence in this.
T/Jkpt: £946.60 to a £1 stake. Pool: £10,000.00 - 7.50 winning units T/Plt: £96.10 to a £1 stake. Pool: £79,865.63 - 606.44 winning units T/Qpdt: £11.50 to a £1 stake. Pool: £5,997.19 - 382.74 winning units RY

# 1575 KEMPTON (A.W) (R-H)
Sunday, April 27

**OFFICIAL GOING: Standard**
Wind: Light; behind Weather: Cloudy

## 1764 BETBRIGHT.COM MAIDEN FILLIES' STKS (BOBIS RACE) — 5f (P)
**2:15** (2:16) (Class 5) 2-Y-0 **£2,587** (£770; £384; £192) **Stalls Low**

Form / RPR

**1** **Dittander** 2-9-0 .................................................. RichardHughes 6 74+
(Richard Hannon) *w'like: chsd ldrs: sltly wd on bnd over 3f out: swtchd to ins rail ent st: led 1f out: rdn out* **11/8**[1]

4 **2** *1 ¼* **Ar Colleen Aine**[13] 1482 2-9-0 .................................. RyanMoore 4 67
(Mick Channon) *leggy: lw: chsd ldr: led briefly over 1f out: kpt on same pce fnl f* **7/4**[2]

**3** *1 ¾* **Howlin'For You** 2-9-0 .................................................. SeanLevey 3 60
(David Brown) *athletic: led: edgd lft and hdd over 1f out: one pce* **11/2**[3]

**4** *3 ¼* **Jersey Belle** 2-9-0 .................................................. SamHitchcott 7 49
(Mick Channon) *w'like: bit bkwd: sn rdn along and bhd: styd on u.p fnl f* **33/1**

0 **5** *nk* **Kodestiny (IRE)**[10] 1528 2-9-0 .................................... LiamJones 5 47
(Ismail Mohammed) *cl up in 3rd: pressing ldrs whn squeezed out over 1f out: nt rcvr* **12/1**

**6** *3* **Amber Crystal** 2-9-0 .................................................. TomQueally 1 37
(John Gallagher) *tall: str: s.i.s: rn green and wl bhd: styng on at fin* **33/1**

0 **7** *21* **Julia Stardust**[10] 1528 2-9-0 ........................................ LiamKeniry 2
(Alan Coogan) *bit bkwd: outpcd and struggling after 2f: no ch fnl 2f* **100/1**

1m 0.57s (0.07) **Going Correction** -0.125s/f (Stan) **7 Ran SP% 108.4**
Speed ratings (Par 89): **94,92,89,84,83 78,45**
CSF £3.50 TOTE £2.30: £1.30, £1.10; EX 4.40 Trifecta £10.10.
**Owner** Rockcliffe Stud **Bred** Rockcliffe Stud **Trained** East Everleigh, Wilts

**FOCUS**
A two-horse market, and that played out in the race. The well-bred winner made a pleasing start.

## 1765 BETBRIGHT MOBILE CLASSIFIED STKS — 1m 2f (P)
**2:45** (2:45) (Class 5) 3-Y-0 **£2,587** (£770; £384; £192) **Stalls Low**

Form / RPR

05-0 **1** **Good Value**[20] 1353 3-9-0 67 ........................................ JamesDoyle 7 84+
(Sir Michael Stoute) *lw: hld up in 5th: hdwy on outer ent st: led over 1f out: pushed clr: easily* **2/1**[2]

655- **2** *3 ¼* **High Master (IRE)**[178] 7646 3-9-0 70 ...................... RichardHughes 4 77
(Richard Hannon) *lw: chsd ldrs: chal 2f out: hrd rdn over 1f out: one pce* **6/4**[1]

5222 **3** *nse* **Rose Kazan (IRE)**[20] 1348 3-8-9 68 ...................... DanielMuscutt(5) 5 77
(Marco Botti) *athletic: cl up: rdn to press ldrs 2f out: one pce appr fnl f* **12/1**

402- **4** *3 ¼* **Merry Me (IRE)**[142] 8175 3-9-0 70 .................................... JimCrowley 6 71
(Andrew Balding) *t.k.h: sn pressing ldr: led 2f out tl over 1f out: sn wknd* **8/1**

00-5 **5** *5* **Mister Mayday (IRE)**[17] 1403 3-9-0 61 ...................... MartinDwyer 2 61
(George Baker) *towards rr: rdn over 3f out: sn struggling* **28/1**

646- **6** *3 ¼* **Charlie Wells (IRE)**[218] 6640 3-9-0 67 ...................... TomQueally 1 54
(Eve Johnson Houghton) *str: lengthy: put hd over side of stall and and lost 12 l s: bhd: pushed along 4f out: no ch fnl 2f* **6/1**[3]

624- **7** *22* **Sydney James (IRE)**[132] 8311 3-9-0 68 ...................... DavidProbert 3
(Dai Burchell) *led tl wknd qckly 2f out* **100/1**

2m 6.62s (-1.38) **Going Correction** -0.125s/f (Stan) **7 Ran SP% 110.9**
Speed ratings (Par 98): **100,97,97,94,90 88,70**
CSF £5.00 TOTE £3.50: £1.50, £1.50; EX 6.60 Trifecta £34.20.
**Owner** K Abdullah **Bred** Millsec Limited **Trained** Newmarket, Suffolk

**FOCUS**
They didn't go a great pace in this ordinary classified event, but the winner was impressive. The third and fourth help with the standard.

## 1766 MIX BUSINESS WITH PLEASURE AT KEMPTON H'CAP — 6f (P)
**3:15** (3:16) (Class 6) (0-65,65) 4-Y-0+ **£1,940** (£577; £288; £144) **Stalls Low**

Form / RPR

0404 **1** **Black Truffle (FR)**[18] 1386 4-8-2 **53**.....................(v) CharlotteJenner(7) 3 62
(Mark Usher) *disp 2nd tl led 1f out: rdn out and hld on narrowly* **8/1**[3]

0-00 **2** *shd* **Commandingpresence (USA)**[17] 1405 8-8-10 **54**...... WilliamCarson 4 63
(John Bridger) *led: rdn and edgd lft 2f out: hdd 1f out: w wnr fnl f: hrd rdn: kpt on wl* **50/1**

4334 **3** *1 ¾* **West Leake (IRE)**[17] 1408 8-8-13 **57**..........................(p) LiamKeniry 5 60
(Paul Burgoyne) *t.k.h in midfield: effrt 2f out: styd on fnl f* **8/1**[3]

0000 **4** *½* **El Mirage (IRE)**[41] 993 4-8-11 **62**.................................... PaulBooth(7) 1 64
(Dean Ivory) *in tch on rail: rdn to press ldrs 2f out: one pce fnl f* **33/1**

-000 **5** *nk* **Valdaw**[79] 511 6-9-0 **58**.................................................. ShaneKelly 6 59
(Mike Murphy) *chsd ldrs: rdn 2f out: one pce fnl f* **9/1**

-563 **6** *1 ¼* **Meridius (IRE)**[16] 1430 4-9-7 **65**.................................... GeorgeBaker 2 62
(Nick Littmoden) *mid-div: rdn over 2f out: styd on same pce* **7/2**[1]

3622 **7** *2* **Indian Affair**[32] 1115 4-9-4 **65**.................................... OisinMurphy(3) 8 55
(Milton Bradley) *disp 2nd tl lost pl over 2f out: hung rt: n.d after* **7/2**[1]

3120 **8** *nse* **Divine Call**[53] 841 7-9-7 **65**.......................................... LiamJones 9 55
(Milton Bradley) *hmpd s: t.k.h in rr: rdn 2f out: nvr able to chal* **12/1**

-033 **9** *¾* **Triple Aitch (USA)**[23] 1282 4-8-5 **56**.......................... JordanVaughan(7) 11 44
(Conrad Allen) *in tch tl outpcd fnl 2f* **10/1**

5014 **10** *shd* **Foie Gras**[26] 1221 4-9-1 **64**.................................... ConnorBeasley(5) 12 52
(Chris Dwyer) *dwlt: towards rr on outer: rdn over 2f out: sn struggling* **7/1**[2]

364- **11** *8* **Mack's Sister**[405] 1063 7-8-11 **55**...........................(p) JimCrowley 7 17
(Dean Ivory) *dwlt: t.k.h in rr: rdn and struggling over 2f out* **20/1**

1m 12.51s (-0.59) **Going Correction** -0.125s/f (Stan) **11 Ran SP% 115.6**
Speed ratings (Par 101): **98,97,95,94,94 92,90,90,89,88 78**
CSF £353.75 CT £3262.41 TOTE £10.40: £3.00, £9.00, £2.40; EX 370.20 Trifecta £2937.00.
**Owner** Ushers Court **Bred** Peter Harris **Trained** Upper Lambourn, Berks
■ Stewards' Enquiry : Jordan Vaughan two-day ban: careless riding (May 12-13)

**FOCUS**
A moderate sprint handicap in which the first two were always up there. Straightforward form.

## 1767 BETBRIGHT - LIVE THE MOMENT MAIDEN FILLIES' STKS (DIV I) — 7f (P)
**3:45** (3:45) (Class 5) 3-Y-0+ **£2,587** (£770; £384; £192) **Stalls Low**

Form / RPR

3- **1** **Angelic Air**[176] 7692 3-9-0 ..................................................1 JamesDoyle 4 85+
(John Gosden) *lw: hld up in 5th: hdwy over 2f out: chsd clr ldr wl over 1f out: styd on to ld fnl 75yds* **5/4**[1]

0-2 **2** *1 ½* **Arctic Moon (USA)**[25] 1233 3-9-0 .......................... SilvestreDeSousa 9 81
(Charlie Appleby) *w'like: str: led and sn 5 l clr: hrd rdn over 1f out: no ex and hdd fnl 75yds* **7/2**[3]

0 **3** *9* **Southern Cross**[16] 1422 3-9-0 .......................................... JimmyFortune 1 58
(Hughie Morrison) *chsd clr ldr after 2f tl wl over 1f out: one pce* **33/1**

03- **4** *shd* **Gracie Hart**[187] 7449 3-8-7 ...................................... JosephineGordon(7) 3 57
(Jo Hughes) *w'like: tall: dwlt: sn in midfield: pushed along over 3f out: styd on same pce: unable to chal* **16/1**

6- **5** *hd* **Inheritance**[176] 7693 3-9-0 .............................................. RyanMoore 10 57
(Sir Michael Stoute) *chsd ldr 2f: prom in chsng gp after: one pce fnl 2f: lost 3rd fnl strides* **5/2**[2]

**6** *¾* **Byrae** 4-9-13 .................................................................. SamHitchcott 2 60
(Polly Gundry) *w'like: chsd ldrs tl rdn and btn 2f out* **50/1**

0 **7** *2* **Swiss Lait**[16] 1422 3-9-0 .............................................. LiamKeniry 5 50
(David Elsworth) *dwlt: bhd and rdn along: styng on at fin* **50/1**

00- **8** 1 1/4 **Borough Belle**[130] 8332 3-8-9 ... AmyScott(5) 8 47
(Henry Candy) *mid-div: outpcd 3f out: n.d after* **33/1**
0-0 **9** nse **Popping Candy**[10] 1534 3-9-0 ... JackMitchell 6 46
(Roger Varian) *a bhd* **25/1**
0-6 **10** 19 **Breezealong Riley**[57] 800 5-9-10 ... SimonPearce(3) 7
(Zoe Davison) *outpcd towards rr: drvn along 3f out: sn no ch* **100/1**
1m 24.62s (-1.38) **Going Correction** -0.125s/f (Stan)
**WFA** 3 from 4yo+ 13lb 10 Ran SP% **115.8**
Speed ratings (Par 100): **102,100,90,89,89 88,86,85,85,63**
CSF £5.54 TOTE £1.70: £1.10, £1.10, £7.40; EX 6.30 Trifecta £95.30.
**Owner** K Abdullah **Bred** Juddmonte Farms Ltd **Trained** Newmarket, Suffolk
**FOCUS**
An interesting fillies' maiden in which the first two were a long way clear of the rest. The time was quick.

## 1768 BETBRIGHT - LIVE THE MOMENT MAIDEN FILLIES' STKS (DIV II) 7f (P)
**4:15** (4:16) (Class 5) 3-Y-0+ **£2,587** (£770; £384; £192) **Stalls** Low

Form RPR
**1** **Rekdhat (IRE)** 3-9-0 ... JackMitchell 5 73+
(Roger Varian) *w'like: str: disp 2nd: led jst over 1f out: rdn out* **1/1**[1]
3-0 **2** 1 1/4 **Shasta Daisy**[23] 1280 3-9-0 ... JamesDoyle 6 69
(Lady Cecil) *w'like: leggy: hld up in tch: eased outside and effrt 2f out: r.o wl to take 2nd nr fin* **5/1**[3]
5/ **3** 3/4 **Sandaura (IRE)**[526] 7778 4-9-13 ... AdamKirby 8 72
(Clive Cox) *lengthy: led at modest pce: rdn and qcknd over 2f out: hdd jst over 1f out: kpt on same pce* **25/1**
6- **4** 1/2 **Darting**[195] 7244 3-9-0 ... DavidProbert 3 66
(Andrew Balding) *w'like: lengthy: bit bkwd: disp 2nd tl over 1f out: kpt on same pce* **16/1**
**5** 3/4 **Miss Moppet** 3-9-0 ... JimmyFortune 7 64+
(Hughie Morrison) *hld up in midfield: shkn up and hdwy fnl 2f: gng on at fin: should improve* **33/1**
4 **6** 1 **Marweena (IRE)**[111] 70 3-9-0 ... TomQueally 4 61
(Michael Bell) *athletic: hld up towards rr: pushed along and sme hdwy over 1f out: no imp fnl f* **20/1**
**7** 1 1/4 **Zynah (IRE)** 3-9-0 ...[1] SilvestreDeSousa 2 58
(Saeed bin Suroor) *leggy: chsd ldrs tl outpcd fnl 2f* **11/4**[2]
0 **8** 1/2 **Scariff Hornet (IRE)**[16] 1422 3-9-0 ... LiamKeniry 9 57
(Sylvester Kirk) *hld up in rr: pushed along 2f out: n.d* **66/1**
**9** 11 **Ascending Angel (IRE)** 3-9-0 ... SeanLevey 1 28
(Richard Hannon) *w'like: lengthy: bit bkwd: s.s: rdn along: a bhd* **14/1**
1m 27.75s (1.75) **Going Correction** -0.125s/f (Stan)
**WFA** 3 from 4yo 13lb 9 Ran SP% **118.9**
Speed ratings (Par 100): **85,83,82,82,81 80,78,78,65**
CSF £6.48 TOTE £2.60: £1.70, £1.10, £4.50; EX 7.00 Trifecta £79.80.
**Owner** Sheikh Ahmed Al Maktoum **Bred** Darley **Trained** Newmarket, Suffolk
**FOCUS**
They went no pace early in this division and it developed into a 2f sprint. Not surprisingly, the winning time was 3.13sec slower than the first leg. Inconclusive form.

## 1769 BETBRIGHT MONEYBACK OFFERS H'CAP 7f (P)
**4:45** (4:47) (Class 5) (0-70,70) 3-Y-0 **£2,587** (£770; £384; £192) **Stalls** Low

Form RPR
043- **1** **Despot (IRE)**[194] 7271 3-9-4 **67** ... RyanMoore 2 89
(Charles Hills) *mde all: rdn clr wl over 1f out: r.o strly* **2/1**[1]
15-5 **2** 6 **Relation Alexander (IRE)**[44] 955 3-9-4 **67** ... SeanLevey 5 73
(Paul D'Arcy) *hld up in rr: rdn and hdwy over 1f out: r.o to take 2nd ins fnl f: nt trble wnr* **8/1**
564- **3** 2 1/2 **Glebe Spirit (IRE)**[222] 6487 3-9-4 **67** ... RichardHughes 6 67
(Richard Hannon) *hld up towards rr: rdn over 2f out: hdwy over 1f out: no imp fnl f* **4/1**[3]
2-46 **4** 1 3/4 **Poetic Choice**[50] 892 3-9-7 **70** ... GeorgeBaker 8 65
(Nick Littmoden) *chsd wnr: outpcd wl over 1f out: lost 2nd and wknd 1f out* **12/1**
000- **5** 1 1/4 **Movie Magic**[265] 5061 3-8-7 **56** oh11 ... WilliamCarson 4 48?
(John Bridger) *t.k.h in rr gp: rdn over 2f out: nvr trbld ldrs* **100/1**
U-04 **6** 1/2 **Pendo**[17] 1404 3-9-7 **70** ... SilvestreDeSousa 7 60
(Alastair Lidderdale) *chsd ldrs on outer: hrd rdn 2f out: sn wknd* **25/1**
23-5 **7** nk **Telegraph (IRE)**[8] 1570 3-9-2 **68** ... OisinMurphy(3) 3 58
(Andrew Balding) *hld up in 5th: rdn over 2f out: wknd over 1f out* **11/4**[2]
40-3 **8** 4 **Why Not Now**[88] 371 3-8-13 **62** ... JamesDoyle 1 41
(Roger Charlton) *dwlt: t.k.h: sn chsng ldrs: wknd over 1f out* **8/1**
1m 25.28s (-0.72) **Going Correction** -0.125s/f (Stan) 8 Ran SP% **114.8**
Speed ratings (Par 98): **99,92,89,87,85 85,84,80**
CSF £19.15 CT £59.04 TOTE £3.20: £1.70, £2.50, £1.70; EX 20.80 Trifecta £91.30.
**Owner** Hon Mrs Corbett, C Wright, Mrs B W Hills **Bred** Michael G Daly **Trained** Lambourn, Berks
**FOCUS**
This handicap proved extremely one-sided, but the form has something of a sound feel.

## 1770 BETBRIGHT.COM H'CAP 2m (P)
**5:15** (5:16) (Class 3) (0-95,94) 4-Y-0+
**£7,158** (£2,143; £1,071; £535; £267; £134) **Stalls** Low

Form RPR
306- **1** **Presto Volante (IRE)**[177] 7660 6-8-11 **79** ...(p) JamesDoyle 6 93
(Amanda Perrett) *chsd ldrs: led jst ins fnl 2f: rdn clr: comf* **9/2**[3]
021- **2** 7 **Dark Ranger**[298] 3959 8-9-0 **82** ... StevieDonohoe 4 88
(Tim Pitt) *hld up in midfield: effrt 2f out: wnt 5 l 2nd over 1f out: no ch w wnr* **12/1**
00/0 **3** 3 1/4 **Storm Hawk (IRE)**[33] 1091 7-8-4 **75** oh2 ...(v) OisinMurphy(3) 1 77
(Pat Eddery) *s.s: bhd: rdn 3f out: styd on fr over 1f out* **33/1**
21-2 **4** nk **Flemish School**[26] 1219 4-8-9 **81** ... LiamKeniry 8 83
(David Elsworth) *mid-div early: chsd ldrs after 4f: one pce fnl 2f* **5/1**
64 **5** nse **Ranjaan (FR)**[27] 1213 6-9-8 **90** ...(t) RyanMoore 7 92
(Paul Nicholls) *chsd clr ldr: led 3f out tl jst ins fnl 2f: wknd over 1f out* **11/8**[1]
40-5 **6** 1/2 **First Avenue**[12] 591 9-8-5 **80** ...(p) CharlotteJenner(7) 9 81
(Laura Mongan) *mid-div: effrt 3f out: btn 2f out* **25/1**
S/5- **7** 7 **Romeo Montague**[333] 2775 6-9-10 **92** ... PaddyAspell 2 85
(Ed Dunlop) *dwlt: hld up towards rr: hdwy on inner 2f out: wknd over 1f out* **16/1**
030- **8** 47 **Highland Castle**[169] 7823 6-9-12 **94** ... JimmyFortune 5 30
(Brian Meehan) *lw: led at gd pce: sn 4 l clr: hdd 3f out: wknd rapidly over 2f out: sn bhd and eased* **4/1**[2]
3m 26.14s (-3.96) **Going Correction** -0.125s/f (Stan)
**WFA** 4 from 6yo+ 4lb 8 Ran SP% **117.3**
Speed ratings (Par 107): **104,100,98,98,98 98,94,71**
CSF £57.36 CT £1589.91 TOTE £6.80: £2.30, £2.10, £6.90; EX 62.80 Trifecta £1004.30.
**Owner** Mrs S Conway Mr & Mrs M Swayne Mr A Brooke Mrs R D **Bred** R A Major **Trained** Pulborough, W Sussex
**FOCUS**
This decent staying handicap was run at a better pace than many contests over this trip, so the form looks solid. The winner is progressive.

## 1771 MASCOT GRAND NATIONAL TRANSFERRED TO EPSOM H'CAP 1m (P)
**5:45** (5:47) (Class 6) (0-65,65) 4-Y-0+ **£1,940** (£577; £288; £144) **Stalls** Low

Form RPR
/4-5 **1** **Lawmans Thunder**[29] 1173 4-9-7 **65** ... TomQueally 1 79
(Ismail Mohammed) *w'like: str: lw: hld up towards rr: hdwy over 2f out: led over 1f out: rdn clr* **13/2**[3]
2330 **2** 2 3/4 **Bennelong**[17] 1406 8-9-1 **59** ...(b) AmirQuinn 7 66
(Lee Carter) *hld up in midfield: stdy hdwy over 2f out: rdn to chal over 1f out: unable qck* **14/1**
10-1 **3** 1 3/4 **Secret Success**[18] 1385 4-9-7 **65** ... AdamKirby 4 68+
(Paul Cole) *hld up in midfield: rdn and styd on fnl 2f: wnt 3rd ins fnl f* **5/4**[1]
4543 **4** 1/2 **Shifting Star (IRE)**[18] 1385 9-9-3 **61** ...(bt) WilliamCarson 9 63
(John Bridger) *chsd ldr: led over 2f out tl over 1f out: no ex fnl f* **25/1**
50-4 **5** 2 3/4 **Keep The Secret**[18] 1385 4-9-5 **63** ... JimCrowley 13 58
(William Knight) *lw: stdd wl in rr s: t.k.h: rdn and hdwy over 1f out: no further prog* **5/1**[2]
3316 **6** 3 1/2 **Divine Rule (IRE)**[18] 1385 6-9-3 **61** ...(p) LiamJones 10 48
(Laura Mongan) *lw: in tch: effrt over 2f out: wknd over 1f out* **33/1**
4320 **7** 1 **Lutine Charlie (IRE)**[3] 1668 7-8-8 **55** ...(p) OisinMurphy(3) 8 39
(Pat Eddery) *led 2f: prom tl wknd over 1f out* **10/1**
00-4 **8** 3 3/4 **Bajan Story**[32] 1105 5-8-7 **51** oh2 ... DavidProbert 12 26
(Michael Blanshard) *chsd ldrs tl hrd rdn and wknd wl over 1f out* **25/1**
525/ **9** 1 1/4 **Royal Mizar (SPA)**[639] 4540 4-9-2 **65** ... DanielMuscutt(5) 3 37
(Alastair Lidderdale) *towards rr: rdn 3f out: nvr trbld ldrs* **66/1**
045- **10** 3/4 **Port Lairge**[171] 7787 4-9-2 **60** ... JimmyFortune 2 30
(Jonjo O'Neill) *bhd: rdn over 2f out: n.d* **25/1**
2-46 **11** 7 **Up Tipp**[38] 1023 4-8-12 **56** ...(b[1]) ShaneKelly 6 10
(Mike Murphy) *led after 2f tl wknd over 2f out* **8/1**
/232 **12** 13 **Orpen'Arry (IRE)**[25] 1232 6-8-9 **58** ...(p) DavidKenny(5) 5
(Paul Burgoyne) *prom tl wknd qckly over 2f out: sn bhd* **16/1**
1m 38.57s (-1.23) **Going Correction** -0.125s/f (Stan) 12 Ran SP% **123.2**
Speed ratings (Par 101): **101,98,96,96,93 89,88,85,83,83 76,63**
CSF £90.77 CT £191.19 TOTE £9.00: £2.60, £3.70, £1.30; EX 147.10 Trifecta £537.70.
**Owner** Sheikh Juma Dalmook Al Maktoum **Bred** Foursome Thoroughbreds **Trained** Newmarket, Suffolk
■ Stewards' Enquiry : Adam Kirby one-day ban: careless riding (May 12)
**FOCUS**
A moderate handicap with little depth, but the winner is unexposed. The form is rated around the second.
T/Plt: £31.20 to a £1 stake. Pool: £83,036.63 - 1,939.68 winning units T/Qpdt: £24.40 to a £1 stake. Pool: £5,289.85 - 160.08 winning units LM

1772 - 1778a (Foreign Racing) - See Raceform Interactive

# [1477] CAPANNELLE (R-H)
Sunday, April 27

**OFFICIAL GOING: Turf: heavy**

## 1779a PREMIO PARIOLI SISAL MATCHPOINT (GROUP 3) (3YO) (TURF) 1m
**2:35** (12:00) 3-Y-0 **£50,000** (£22,000; £12,000; £6,000)

RPR
**1** **Salford Secret (IRE)**[35] 3-9-2 ... DPerovic 5 105
(Riccardo Santini, Italy) *w.w in midfield: hdwy over 2 1/2f out: led appr 1 1/2f out: drvn out fnl f: a holding runner-up* **19/5**[2]
**2** 1/2 **Priore Philip (ITY)**[196] 7235 3-9-2 ... CristianDemuro 4 104
(Stefano Botti, Italy) *tk a t.k.h in 5th: prog 2 1/2f out: chsd eventual wnr appr 1 1/2f out: u.p fnl f: nvr quite on terms w wnr* **152/100**[1]
**3** 2 1/2 **Hoovergetthekeys (USA)**[140] 3-9-2 ... SSulas 6 98
(M Narduzzi, Italy) *among bkmarkers: hdwy on outside 2 1/2f out: rdn to chse ldng pair over 1f out: kpt on u.p ent fnl f: run flattened out fnl 100yds* **17/2**
**4** 2 **Dress Drive (IRE)**[21] 3-9-2 ... MircoDemuro 1 94
(M Arienti, Italy) *disp 3rd on inner: rdn to press ldrs over 2f out: nt qckn w front two fr 1 1/2f out: one pce u.p fnl f* **27/1**
**5** 2 1/2 **Mujas**[35] 3-9-2 ... CColombi 3 88
(F Turner, Italy) *among bkmarkers: rdn and hdwy on inner 3f out: kpt on u.p ins fnl f: nt pce to trble ldrs* **30/1**
**6** 8 **Collateral Risk (IRE)**[21] 3-9-2 ... FabioBranca 11 69
(Stefano Botti, Italy) *disp 3rd on outer: rdn and nt qckn appr 2f out: sn wknd: eased ins fnl f* **19/5**[2]
**7** 1 1/2 **Il Pittore (FR)**[37] 3-9-2 ... MickaelBarzalona 12 66
(G Botti, France) *settled in midfield: rdn and no imp fnl 2f* **41/10**[3]
**8** 3/4 **Grey Greezly (FR)**[42] 3-9-2 ... DarioVargiu 10 64
(B Grizzetti, Italy) *hld up in fnl 3rd: rdn and shortlived effrt over 2f out: sn btn* **705/100**
**9** 4 **Gulfstream Kitten (USA)** 3-9-2 ... GBietolini 8 55
(Gianluca Bietolini, Italy) *hld up towards rr: rdn an no imp fr over 2 1/2f out: nvr in contention* **50/1**
**10** 1/2 **Big Bradon (IRE)** 3-9-2 ... MEsposito 9 54
(Agostino Affe', Italy) *a towards rr: rdn and no imp over 2f out: sn btn* **195/10**
**11** 3 1/2 **Laguna Drive (IRE)**[35] 3-9-2 ... NicolaPinna 2 46
(Stefano Botti, Italy) *dwlt: led after 1 1/2f: hdd over 1 1/2f out: sn wknd* **19/5**[2]
**12** 5 **Guizzo Vincente**[140] 3-9-2 ... CFiocchi 7 34
(F Saggiomo, Italy) *led: hdd after 1 1/2f: chsd clr ldr: rdn and wknd over 2f out: eased ins fnl f* **30/1**
1m 39.63s (-0.17) 12 Ran SP% **161.6**
WIN (incl. 1 euro stake): 4.80. PLACES: 1.71, 1.32, 2.07. DF: 11.42.
**Owner** Carlo Lanfranchi **Bred** Hyphen Bloodstock **Trained** Italy

## 1780a PREMIO REGINA ELENA (GROUP 3) (3YO FILLIES) (TURF) 1m
**4:25** (12:00) 3-Y-0 **£50,000** (£22,000; £12,000; £6,000)

RPR
**1** **Vague Nouvelle (IRE)**[21] 3-8-11 ... MircoDemuro 5 99
(R Biondi, Italy) *trckd ldrs: scrubbed along to ld 2f out: rdn 1 1/2f out: r.o u.p fnl f: hld on wl cl home* **67/20**[1]

2 *nk* **Lady Dutch**[21] 3-8-11 0........................................ AndreaAtzeni 17 98
(B Grizzetti, Italy) *t.k.h: hld up towards rr: hdwy on inner over 2 1/2f out: chsd ldrs appr fnl f: r.o u.p: nvr quite gng to get up* **112/10**

3 *2* **Felcine (IRE)**[37] 3-8-11 0........................................ MickaelBarzalona 13 94
(G Botti, France) *midfield: shkn up and prog 2 1/2f out: 6th and hrd rdn 2f out: styd on u.p fnl f: nvr on terms w front two* **48/10**[3]

4 *3/4* **Nearly Not Mine**[35] 3-8-11 0........................................ SSulas 1 92
(Giada Ligas, Italy) *midfield on inner: 8th and rdn 2 1/2f out: styd on u.p fnl f: nt pce to chal* **35/4**

5 *nk* **Finidaprest (IRE)**[189] 7415 3-8-11 0........................................ IRossi 7 91
(B Grizzetti, Italy) *trckd ldr: cl 3rd and ev ch 2f out: one pce u.p fr over 1f out* **87/20**[2]

6 *2* **Fair Dubawi (IRE)**[21] 3-8-11 0........................................ DarioVargiu 8 87
(B Grizzetti, Italy) *a trcking ldng gp: rdn and nt qckn over 2f out: one pce fnl f* **87/20**[2]

7 *2 1/2* **Noblesse Anime (IRE)**[224] 3-8-11 0........................................ FrancescoDettori 9 81
(L Riccardi, Italy) *midfield: rdn and lost pl 1/2-way: styd on u.p fr over 2f out: no further imp ins fnl f* **57/1**

8 *1 3/4* **Grey Bet (IRE)**[175] 3-8-11 0........................................ SGuerrieri 6 77
(S Lanteri, Italy) *towards rr: hdwy over 2f out: hrd rdn and one pce appr fnl f: nvr in contention* **65/1**

9 *1/2* **Konkan (IRE)**[140] 3-8-11 0........................................ DPerovic 16 76
(L Riccardi, Italy) *chsd ldrs on outer: 4th and styng on 2 1/2f out: hrd rdn and no further imp 1 1/2f out: grad fdd fnl f* **98/10**

10 *3* **Kitten's Lady (USA)**[147] 3-8-11 0........................................ GBietolini 15 69
(Gianluca Bietolini, Italy) *towards rr: sme hdwy over 1 1/2f out: nvr a factor* **44/5**

11 *6* **Donna Prassede (ITY)**[189] 7415 3-8-11 0........................................ CristianDemuro 12 55
(Stefano Botti, Italy) *midfield: rdn and no imp over 2f out: eased whn wl hld over 1f out* **5/1**

12 *3* **Jadel**[14] 1477 3-8-11 0........................................ MEsposito 3 48
(D Camuffo, Italy) *towards rr: rdn and sme hdwy 3f out: sn no further imp: wl btn whn eased over 1f out* **33/1**

13 *3* **Tucci (ITY)**[175] 3-8-11 0........................................ NicolaPinna 2 41
(M Guarnieri, Italy) *towards rr: rdn and no imp fr 2 1/2f out: sn wknd* **79/1**

14 *2* **Passionateshepherd (ITY)**[147] 3-8-11 0........................................ PBorrelli 10 37
(C Impelluso, Italy) *awkward leaving stalls: a among bkmarkers* **177/1**

15 *1* **Sweet Fede** 3-8-11 0........................................ FabioBranca 4 34
(Stefano Botti, Italy) *led: rdn 2 1/2f out: hdd appr 2f out: sn wknd: eased over 1f out* **105/10**

16 *hd* **Hurrimera (ITY)** 3-8-11 0........................................ GMarcelli 14 34
(R Menichetti, Italy) *chsd ldng gp: wknd u.p fr 3f out* **192/10**

17 *15* **Francine (IRE)** 3-8-11 0........................................ CFiocchi 11
(Stefano Botti, Italy) *midfield: bhd fnl 2 1/2f* **158/10**

1m 42.52s (2.72) **17** Ran SP% **159.8**
WIN (incl. 1 euro stake): 4.37. PLACES: 1.98, 4.06, 2.38. DF: 42.68.
**Owner** Incolinx **Bred** Scuderia Incolinx **Trained** Italy

# KREFELD (R-H)
## Sunday, April 27
**OFFICIAL GOING: Turf: good to soft**

## 1781a GROSSER PREIS DES KREFELDER RENNCLUB 1997 - DR. BUSCH-MEMORIAL (GROUP 3) (3YO) (TURF) 1m 110y
**3:40** (12:00) 3-Y-O
**£26,666** (£9,166; £4,583; £2,500; £1,666; £1,250)

RPR

1 **Lucky Lion**[35] 3-9-2 0........................................ AlexanderWeis 5 105
(Andreas Lowe, Germany) *hld up towards rr: hdwy on outside 2f out: rdn 1 1/2f out to chse ldr appr fnl f: r.o to ld 75yds out: won a shade cosily* **19/5**[1]

2 *1 3/4* **Nordico (GER)**[175] 7726 3-9-2 0........................................(p) FrederikTylicki 1 101
(Mario Hofer, Germany) *led: pushed along and qcknd 3 l clr 2f out: edgd lft and hdd 75yds out: no ex* **68/10**

3 *nk* **Andoyas (GER)**[169] 3-9-2 0........................................ SHellyn 8 100
(J Hirschberger, Germany) *towards rr: last rdn over 2f out: hdwy on ins over 1 1/2f out: styng on whn edgd lft appr fnl f: kpt on u.p whn stened out: nt pce to chal* **66/10**

4 *1 3/4* **Kerosin (GER)**[242] 5911 3-9-2 0........................................ AdriedeVries 10 96
(Jean-Pierre Carvalho, Germany) *in rr: hdwy 2 1/2f out: 3rd and hrd rdn 1 1/2f out: one pce u.p fnl f* **57/10**

5 *2* **Nadelwald**[35] 3-9-2 0........................................ DanielePorcu 7 92
(P Schiergen, Germany) *midfield on outer: rdn to chse ldrs over 2f out: 4th and hrd rdn appr fnl f: no further imp: one pce fr 1f out* **5/1**[3]

6 *3 1/2* **Stillman (FR)**[177] 7686 3-9-2 0........................................ EddyHardouin 3 84
(Mario Hofer, Germany) *midfield on inner: pushed along 3f out: plugged on at one pce fnl 1 1/2f: nvr in contention* **39/10**[2]

7 *1 1/4* **Eric (GER)**[14] 3-9-2 0........................................ FilipMinarik 2 82
(C Von Der Recke, Germany) *trckd ldr on inner: rdn and wknd fr over 2f out* **7/1**

8 *10* **Speedy Approach**[21] 3-9-2 0........................................ JBojko 4 60
(A Wohler, Germany) *trckd ldr on outer: rdn and wknd over 2f out: sn wl bhd* **11/2**

9 *6* **Rock Of Cashel (GER)**[196] 7232 3-9-2 0........................................ AHelfenbein 9 46
(Waldemar Hickst, Germany) *towards rr on outer: lost tch fr over 2f out* **212/10**

1m 48.21s (1.61) **9** Ran SP% **131.2**
WIN (incl. 10 euro stake): 48. PLACES: 21,35,30. SF: 426.
**Owner** Gestut Winterhauch **Bred** Stall Parthenaue **Trained** Germany

# 1621 LONGCHAMP (R-H)
## Sunday, April 27
**OFFICIAL GOING: Turf: very soft**

## 1782a PRIX VANTEAUX (GROUP 3) (3YO FILLIES) (TURF) 1m 1f 55y
**1:30** (12:00) 3-Y-O **£33,333** (£13,333; £10,000; £6,666; £3,333)

RPR

1 **Vazira (FR)**[27] 3-9-0 0........................................ ChristopheSoumillon 5 108+
(A De Royer-Dupre, France) *midfield in tch on outer: pushed along over 2f out: rdn to chal over 1f out: led jst ins fnl f and edgd rt to rail: strly pressed all the way to fin but styd on wl and a jst doing enough* **8/11**[1]

2 *snk* **Kenzadargent (FR)**[33] 1096 3-9-0 0........................................ IoritzMendizabal 4 107
(J-C Rouget, France) *t.k.h: hld up in tch: rdn 2f out: hdwy to chal ent fnl f and sn wnt 2nd: styd on wl and pressed wnr all the way to fin but a jst being hld* **9/1**

3 *3* **Crisolles (FR)**[37] 3-9-0 0........................................ GregoryBenoist 6 101
(J-C Rouget, France) *stdd and hld up in last: rdn 2f out: styd on and wnt 3rd towards fin: nt pce of front pair* **4/1**[2]

4 *1/2* **Chocolatier (FR)**[21] 1339 3-9-0 0........................................ UmbertoRispoli 1 100
(M Delzangles, France) *led: pushed along 2f out: rdn and hdd jst ins fnl f: sn no ex: fdd and dropped to 4th towards fin* **8/1**

5 *2* **Momo No Sekku (FR)**[28] 3-9-0 0........................................ OlivierPeslier 3 95
(S Kobayashi, France) *trckd ldr on outer: rdn and effrt to chal 2f out: ev ch tl no ex and fdd ins fnl f* **20/1**

6 *5* **Privet Hedge (USA)**[24] 3-9-0 0........................................ Christophe-PatriceLemaire 2 85
(D Smaga, France) *prom on inner: rdn 2f out: no ex over 1f out: fdd and dropped to last ent fnl f: sn eased* **7/1**[3]

1m 58.91s (3.61) **Going Correction** +0.80s/f (Soft) **6** Ran SP% **116.3**
Speed ratings: **115,114,112,111,109 105**
WIN (incl. 1 euro stake): 2.00. PLACES: 1.50, 2.40. SF: 6.60.
**Owner** H H Aga Khan **Bred** Haras De Son Altesse L'Aga Khan Scea **Trained** Chantilly, France

## 1783a PRIX GANAY (GROUP 1) (4YO+) (TURF) 1m 2f 110y
**2:40** (12:00) 4-Y-0+ **£142,850** (£57,150; £28,575; £14,275; £7,150)

RPR

1 **Cirrus Des Aigles (FR)**[29] 1182 8-9-2 0........................................ ChristopheSoumillon 4 126
(Mme C Barande-Barbe, France) *prom in main body of field: clsd to chal 3f out and sn led gng strly: rdn and jnd by eventual runner-up 2f out: styd on strly and sustained battled w rival: edgd ahd cl home: jst prevailed* **7/2**[2]

2 *snk* **Treve (FR)**[203] 7058 4-8-13 0........................................ FrankieDettori 2 123
(Mme C Head-Maarek, France) *restrained and hld up in last: hdwy into midfield on outer 1/2-way: pushed along and clsd into st: rdn to chal and jnd eventual wnr 2f out: styd on strly and sustained battle w rival: hdd cl home: jst hld* **30/100**[1]

3 *4 1/2* **Norse King (FR)**[21] 1341 5-9-2 0........................................ AlexisBadel 8 117
(Mme M Bollack-Badel, France) *hld up towards rr: last 1/2-way: rdn over 2f out: styd on steadily u.p and wnt 3rd ins fnl f: no match for front pair* **20/1**[3]

4 *1 1/4* **Smoking Sun (USA)**[21] 1341 5-9-2 0........................................(b) StephanePasquier 1 115
(P Bary, France) *stdd and hld up towards rr on inner: rdn over 2f out: styd on same pce fr over 1f out and no match for front pair* **20/1**[3]

5 *1 1/4* **Joshua Tree (IRE)**[29] 1177 7-9-2 0........................................ ThierryThulliez 6 112
(Ed Dunlop) *chsd clr ldr: clsd to chal 3f out and sn rdn: outpcd by front pair fr 2f out and dropped to 5th ent fnl f: plugged on* **50/1**

6 *5* **Baltic Baroness (GER)**[21] 1341 4-8-13 0........................................ Pierre-CharlesBoudot 3 99
(A Fabre, France) *midfield on inner: pushed along into st: outpcd and btn over 1f out: fdd* **66/1**

7 *20* **Triple Threat (FR)**[21] 1341 4-9-2 0........................................ MaximeGuyon 7 63
(A Fabre, France) *restrained and hld up: a towards rr: pushed along 3f out: rdn and outpcd 2f out: sn btn and eased: t.o* **20/1**[3]

8 *1 1/2* **Belle De Crecy (IRE)**[190] 7365 5-8-13 0........................................ ThierryJarnet 5 57
(Mme C Head-Maarek, France) *led and sn clr: reeled in 3f out and sn hdd: wknd qckly and dropped to last: eased and t.o* **66/1**

2m 14.13s (3.93) **Going Correction** +0.80s/f (Soft) **8** Ran SP% **118.4**
Speed ratings: **117,116,113,112,111 108,93,92**
WIN (incl. 1 euro stake): 4.30. PLACES: 1.10, 1.10, 1.10. DF: 2.00. SF: 8.00.
**Owner** Jean-Claude-Alain Dupouy **Bred** M Yvon Lelimouzin & M Benoit Deschamps **Trained** France

**FOCUS**
A race that saw the eagerly anticipated reappearance of last season's brilliant Arc winner Treve. Cirrus Des Aigles is rated in line with last year's best, with Treve 8lb off her Arc figure.

## 1784a PRIX DE BARBEVILLE (GROUP 3) (4YO+) (TURF) 1m 7f 110y
**3:15** (12:00) 4-Y-0+ **£33,333** (£13,333; £10,000; £6,666; £3,333)

RPR

1 **Montclair (IRE)**[19] 1370 4-8-13 0........................................ Pierre-CharlesBoudot 6 110
(A Fabre, France) *midfield in tch: pushed along to chal over 2f out: rdn and w ldrs over 1f out: styd on and led narrowly 100yds out: drvn as runner-up rallied and jst prevailed on hd bob post: all out* **6/1**[3]

2 *nse* **Terrubi (IRE)**[28] 1206 4-8-13 0........................................ ThierryJarnet 4 110
(P Bary, France) *hld up in midfield: clsd into st and rdn to chal 2f out: w ldrs over 1f out: styd on but narrowly hdd 100yds out: battled bk gamely u.p and jst lost out on hd bob post* **6/1**[3]

3 *1 1/4* **Fly With Me (FR)**[41] 4-8-9 0........................................(p) FabriceVeron 2 105
(E Libaud, France) *led early stages: sn restrained in midfield: rdn over 2f out: styd on and wnt 3rd cl home: nt pce of front pair* **7/1**

4 *nk* **Goldtara (FR)**[19] 1370 6-8-11 0........................................ Christophe-PatriceLemaire 7 102
(A Lyon, France) *sn trcking ldr: rdn 2f out: swtchd lft off rail ins fnl f and styd on wl for 4th: nt pce of front pair* **25/1**

5 *hd* **Narrow Hill (GER)**[64] 723 6-9-1 0........................................ Roberto-CarlosMontenegro 8 106
(P Sogorb, France) *t.k.h: hld up in rr: last 2f out: swtchd lft to outer and rdn over 1f out: styd on strly ins fnl f and wnt 5th post: nrst fin* **4/1**[2]

6 *snk* **Green Byron (FR)**[28] 1206 4-8-13 0........................................ IoritzMendizabal 10 108
(Mme Pia Brandt, France) *sn led: rdn over 2f out: jnd over 1f out and hdd jst ins fnl f: styd on but sn hld by front pair and lost three pls cl home* **33/1**

7 *1 3/4* **Ebiyza (IRE)**[140] 8208 4-9-0 0........................................ ChristopheSoumillon 9 107
(A De Royer-Dupre, France) *hld up in rr: last 1/2-way: rdn over 2f out: styd on same pce and nvr on terms w ldrs: nt given hrd time once hld ins fnl 150yds* **13/2**

8 *nse* **Les Beaufs (FR)**[19] 1370 5-9-1 0.................................. JulienGuillochon 1 104
(Mme V Seignoux, France) *midfield: rdn whn nt clr run on rail 2f out: swtchd lft and shuffled bk over 1f out: styd on ins fnl f but nvr able to chal: nt rcvr* **10/1**

9 *2* **Aussi Celebre (IRE)**[19] 1370 5-9-1 0.................(p) GregoryBenoist 3 101
(E Lellouche, France) *t.k.h: hld up towards rr: rdn over 2f out: sn outpcd: plugged on but nvr a factor* **7/1**

10 *1 ¼* **Going Somewhere (BRZ)**[19] 1370 5-9-1 0.................... OlivierPeslier 5 100
(D Smaga, France) *trckd ldr: rdn and effrt to chal over 2f out: lost pl over 1f out: sn no ex and btn: fdd and dropped to last* **3/1**[1]

3m 37.44s (15.94) **Going Correction** +0.80s/f (Soft)
**WFA** 4 from 5yo+ 3lb **10 Ran SP% 127.8**
Speed ratings: **92,91,91,91,91 91,90,90,89,88**
WIN (incl. 1 euro stake): 7.20. PLACES: 2.10, 2.10, 2.60. DF: 24.90. SF: 51.70.
**Owner** Oti Management Pty Ltd & M Watt **Bred** Elisabeth Fabre **Trained** Chantilly, France

1785 - (Foreign Racing) - See Raceform Interactive

## 1568 BATH (L-H)

### Monday, April 28

**OFFICIAL GOING: Soft (5.8)**
Races incorporating bottom bend increased in distance by about 10yds.
Wind: mild breeze behind Weather: overcast with showers

## 1786 32RED THUNDERSTRUCK II SLOT H'CAP — 1m 5y

**1:30** (1:33) (Class 5) (0-70,68) 3-Y-O **£2,587** (£770; £384; £192) **Stalls Low**

Form — RPR

3-30 1 **Solo Hunter**[21] 1353 3-9-6 67...................................(v[1]) AdamKirby 8 71
(David Evans) *s.i.s: sn pushed along: led after 1f: rdn, sltly hmpd and hdd over 1f out: sn looked hld: rallied ins fnl f: led fnl stride* **5/1**[3]

04-0 2 *nse* **Double Czech (IRE)**[19] 1389 3-9-5 66............................ DavidProbert 5 70
(Patrick Chamings) *led for over 1f: trckd wnr: rdn over 2f out: sn hanging lft: led and drifted lft to far rails over 1f out: kpt on: hdd fnl stride* **20/1**

465- 3 *1 ½* **Spectator**[140] 8214 3-8-12 66.......................... KieranShoemark[(7)] 4 67
(Andrew Balding) *racd keenly: trckd ldrs: rdn over 2f out: chalng whn hanging rt over 1f out: kpt on same pce* **6/4**[1]

01-0 4 *2 ¼* **Encore Encore (FR)**[27] 1220 3-9-2 66.................... ThomasBrown[(3)] 9 61
(Harry Dunlop) *trckd ldrs: rdn over 2f out: chalng whn squeezed up over 1f out: no ex fnl f* **14/1**

-355 5 *1* **Penny's Boy**[19] 1389 3-9-7 68................................ LiamKeniry 1 61
(Sylvester Kirk) *in tch: rdn over 2f out: ev ch over 1f out tl ent fnl f: no ex* **3/1**[2]

6-40 6 *3 ½* **Autopilot**[19] 1389 3-8-11 65................................ JackGarritty[(7)] 6 50
(Anabel K Murphy) *hld up: rdn over 3f out: nvr threatened* **16/1**

055- 7 *1 ¼* **Classic Mission**[215] 6739 3-9-7 68........................ RichardKingscote 3 50
(Jonathan Portman) *hld up: pushed along over 4f out: nvr threatened* **8/1**

020- 8 *25* **Stan Nineteen (IRE)**[121] 8426 3-8-13 67.......................... RobHornby[(7)] 7
(Simon Hodgson) *trckd ldrs: rdn 3f out: wknd 2f out* **25/1**

4-55 9 *69* **Lady Kathian (IRE)**[74] 588 3-9-2 63.............................. SteveDrowne 2
(Joseph Tuite) *chsd ldrs tl pushed along over 4f out: sn in rr: t.o* **40/1**

1m 45.22s (4.42) **Going Correction** +0.475s/f (Yiel) **9 Ran SP% 116.4**
Speed ratings (Par 98): **96,95,94,92,91 87,86,61,**
CSF £98.34 CT £221.67 TOTE £4.70: £1.20, £4.00, £1.20; EX 75.60 Trifecta £284.70.
**Owner** Wayne Clifford **Bred** Willie Musson Racing Ltd **Trained** Pandy, Monmouths

**FOCUS**
Races incorporating bottom bend increased in distance by about 10yds. There was 21mm of rain in the 24 hours prior to racing and a total of 55mm since the last meeting just over a week earlier, leading to an official description of soft ground. Moderate stuff, with the first two 1-2 throughout. The winner is rated to his 2yo mark.

## 1787 32RED FREE £10 BONUS SLOT H'CAP — 5f 11y

**2:00** (2:02) (Class 6) (0-65,65) 4-Y-O+ **£1,940** (£577; £288; £144) **Stalls Centre**

Form — RPR

3-20 1 **Whipphound**[16] 1448 6-9-3 61.................................... JamesDoyle 9 75
(Mark Brisbourne) *hld up bhd: pushed along and hdwy fr 2f out: str run ins fnl f: led fnl 70yds: r.o wl* **8/1**

522- 2 *2* **Perfect Muse**[180] 7634 4-9-3 61................................ AdamKirby 5 68
(Clive Cox) *chsd ldrs: rdn to ld over 1f out: sn drifted lft: no ex whn hdd fnl 70yds* **6/4**[1]

0020 3 *2 ¼* **One Last Dream**[73] 603 5-8-13 57............................ DavidProbert 13 56
(Ron Hodges) *chsd ldrs: rdn over 2f out: styd on but nvr gng pce to chal: wnt 3rd fnl strides* **4/1**[2]

0-66 4 *hd* **Solemn**[52] 866 9-9-7 65............................(v) RichardKingscote 10 63
(Milton Bradley) *trckd ldr: rdn 2f out: sn ev ch: no ex ent fnl f: lost 3rd fnl strides* **10/1**

4141 5 *2* **Dishy Guru**[26] 1238 5-9-7 65.............................(b) LiamKeniry 8 56
(Michael Blanshard) *sn mid-div: rdn and stdy prog fr over 2f out: styd on but nvr rchd ldrs* **5/1**[3]

0-00 6 *nk* **Ficelle (IRE)**[54] 844 5-8-5 52 oh2 ow1.............(p) MatthewCosham[(3)] 14 42
(Nikki Evans) *mid-div: rdn over 3f out: styd on same pce* **33/1**

2624 7 *1 ¼* **Quality Art (USA)**[26] 1238 6-9-5 63............................ SteveDrowne 1 49
(Simon Hodgson) *trckd ldrs: rdn over 2f out: led briefly over 1f out: fdd fnl f* **25/1**

320- 8 *1 ¼* **First Rebellion**[348] 2364 5-8-10 57.................... MichaelJMMurphy[(3)] 11 39
(Tony Carroll) *trckd ldrs: rdn over 2f out: wknd ent fnl f* **33/1**

36-0 9 *2* **Trending (IRE)**[26] 1238 5-9-0 65...................(bt) DavidParkes[(7)] 6 40
(Jeremy Gask) *slowly away and hmpd s: a towards rr* **28/1**

14-0 10 *nk* **Chester'slittlegem (IRE)**[9] 1573 5-8-1 52........... JosephineGordon[(7)] 4 26
(Jo Hughes) *mid-div: rdn 3f out: wknd over 1f out* **16/1**

0552 11 *6* **Island Legend (IRE)**[42] 987 8-8-8 52 oh2 ow1......(b) FergusSweeney 3
(Milton Bradley) *led: rdn and hdd over 1f out: sn wknd* **12/1**

1m 3.11s (0.61) **Going Correction** +0.25s/f (Good) **11 Ran SP% 123.6**
Speed ratings (Par 101): **105,101,98,97,94 94,92,90,87,86 76**
CSF £20.78 CT £59.80 TOTE £8.30: £2.50, £1.10, £1.40; EX 27.90 Trifecta £148.10.
**Owner** W M Clare **Bred** Mrs B Skinner **Trained** Great Ness, Shropshire
■ Stewards' Enquiry : Adam Kirby one-day ban: careless riding (13 May)

**FOCUS**
They went fast and that played into the hands of the patiently ridden winner. Modest form, the winner back to his best at face value.

## 1788 CB SECURITY FILLIES' MAIDEN AUCTION STKS (BOBIS RACE) — 5f 11y

**2:30** (2:33) (Class 5) 2-Y-O **£2,587** (£770; £384; £192) **Stalls Centre**

Form — RPR

0 1 **Mylaporyours (IRE)**[14] 1488 2-8-6 0.............................. DavidProbert 7 71
(Rod Millman) *trckd ldr: led over 1f out: kpt on wl: rdn out* **5/4**[1]

2 *2 ¼* **Doomah (IRE)** 2-8-9 0................................................ SeanLevey 1 66
(Richard Hannon) *led: rdn and hdd over 1f out: kpt on same pce fnl f* **5/1**[3]

0 3 *2* **Kidmeforever**[14] 1488 2-8-1 0.................................. PhilipPrince[(5)] 8 56
(J S Moore) *mid-div: rdn over 2f out: chsd ldrs over 1f out: styd on same pce fnl f* **40/1**

4 *shd* **Fujiano** 2-8-9 0 ow1............................................... FergusSweeney 10 58+
(Derek Haydn Jones) *unshipped jockey in paddock: rn green: wnt rt s and sn 20 l adrift: hdwy fr 2f out: kpt on wl fnl f: wnt 4th towards fin* **33/1**

5 *nk* **Red Perdita (IRE)** 2-8-9 0......................................... MartinDwyer 9 57
(George Baker) *s.i.s: rn green: sn pushed along towards rr: stdy prog fr 2f out: styd on same pce fnl f* **10/3**[2]

6 *1 ½* **River Spirit** 2-8-6 0............................................ SamHitchcott 4 49
(Mick Channon) *mid-div: pushed along 3f out: nvr any imp* **10/1**

0 7 *2 ½* **Sarah Catherine**[9] 1571 2-8-7 0 ow1........................... RenatoSouza 3 41
(Mark Usher) *rn green: sn pushed along in rr: nvr any danger* **66/1**

8 *3 ¼* **Featsdontfailmenow** 2-8-1 0.............................. ShirleyTeasdale[(5)] 6 28
(Lisa Williamson) *prom: rdn 2f out: wknd over 1f out* **80/1**

9 *hd* **Cajoling (IRE)** 2-8-8 0 ow1................................ RichardKingscote 2 29
(Jonathan Portman) *prom: rdn over 1f out: sn wknd* **10/1**

10 *1 ½* **Areion (IRE)** 2-8-6 0................................................ LiamJones 5 22
(J S Moore) *sn pushed along towards rr: sme prog 2f out: wknd over 1f out* **25/1**

1m 5.31s (2.81) **Going Correction** +0.25s/f (Good) **10 Ran SP% 114.3**
Speed ratings (Par 89): **87,83,80,80,79 77,73,67,67,65**
CSF £7.26 TOTE £1.90: £1.10, £2.20, £11.40; EX 8.00 Trifecta £106.40.
**Owner** Mrs Nerys Dutfield **Bred** Michael J Ryan & Red Hill Partners **Trained** Kentisbeare, Devon

**FOCUS**
All bar three of these fillies were making their racecourse debuts and Fujiano played up in the paddock, running loose and setting off several of her rivals.

## 1789 32RED.COM H'CAP — 5f 161y

**3:00** (3:00) (Class 4) (0-80,80) 4-Y-O+ **£5,175** (£1,540; £769; £384) **Stalls Centre**

Form — RPR

322- 1 **Desert Command**[188] 7445 4-9-7 80.............................. LiamKeniry 3 88+
(Andrew Balding) *taken to s early: a.p: led over 1f out: sn rdn and hrd pressed: kpt on wl to assert cl home* **2/1**[1]

-523 2 *½* **Vincentti (IRE)**[17] 1429 4-9-5 78................................ AdamKirby 7 84
(Ronald Harris) *in tch: hdwy over 2f out: rdn for str chal ent fnl f: kpt on tl no ex towards fin* **9/2**[2]

10-0 3 *¾* **Pettochside**[31] 1144 5-8-7 66.................................. SamHitchcott 1 70
(Chris Gordon) *trckd ldrs: nt clr run over 1f out tl squeezed through ent fnl f: kpt on* **25/1**

00-0 4 *3 ¼* **First In Command (IRE)**[11] 1541 9-9-5 78...............(t) StephenCraine 4 71
(Daniel Mark Loughnane) *mid-div: hdwy to chse ldrs over 1f out: sn rdn: kpt on but nt gng pce to get involved* **40/1**

243- 5 *1 ¼* **Edged Out**[210] 6900 4-9-0 73................................... DavidProbert 2 62
(Christopher Mason) *led: rdn and hdd over 1f out: fdd ins fnl f* **8/1**[3]

465- 6 *hd* **Alcando (IRE)**[254] 5541 4-8-11 70............................. JamesDoyle 11 58+
(Denis Coakley) *trckd ldrs: rdn over 2f out: one pce fnl f* **9/2**[2]

54-4 7 *½* **Ginzan**[24] 1286 6-9-2 75.......................................... SteveDrowne 8 61
(Malcolm Saunders) *mid-div: rdn over 2f out: nvr threatened* **8/1**[3]

000 8 *1* **Bainne (IRE)**[14] 1489 4-9-6 79.................................... SeanLevey 6 62
(Jeremy Gask) *towards rr: hdwy over 2f out: sn rdn: wknd fnl f* **20/1**

06-0 9 *4* **Lady Phill**[25] 1261 4-9-2 75.......................................... KierenFox 10 45
(Michael Attwater) *mid-div: rdn over 2f out: wknd jst over 1f out* **33/1**

500- 10 *16* **Federal Blue (USA)**[224] 6466 4-9-0 73..................... RichardKingscote 9
(Milton Bradley) *trckd ldrs: rdn over 2f out: sn wknd: eased fnl f* **16/1**

10-0 11 *8* **Steel Rain**[108] 122 6-9-0 76.............................. MatthewCosham[(3)] 5
(Nikki Evans) *v awkward away: bhd: hdwy on outer over 2f out: sn rdn: wknd fnl f: eased* **20/1**

1m 13.05s (1.85) **Going Correction** +0.25s/f (Good) **11 Ran SP% 116.6**
Speed ratings (Par 105): **97,96,95,91,89 89,88,87,81,60 49**
CSF £9.65 CT £173.65 TOTE £2.60: £1.40, £2.20, £7.30; EX 12.30 Trifecta £190.70.
**Owner** J C Smith **Bred** Littleton Stud **Trained** Kingsclere, Hants

**FOCUS**
A fair sprint handicap. the winner is rated to his final AW mark.

## 1790 32RED TOMB RAIDER SLOT MAIDEN STKS — 5f 161y

**3:30** (3:31) (Class 5) 3-Y-O+ **£2,587** (£770; £384; £192) **Stalls Centre**

Form — RPR

1 **Sleep Walk** 3-8-10 0................................................. JamesDoyle 2 66+
(Roger Charlton) *hld up bhd ldng trio: smooth prog 2f out: led over 1f out: nudged clr: easily* **1/9**[1]

06-0 2 *4* **Addictive Nature (IRE)**[31] 1141 4-9-9 54.......... MichaelJMMurphy[(3)] 4 54
(John Gallagher) *broke wl: led: rdn and hdd over 1f out: kpt on but sn hld by easy wnr* **7/1**[2]

0 3 *16* **Border Guard**[9] 1569 3-9-1 0................................. RichardKingscote 3
(Milton Bradley) *chsd ldrs: rdn over 2f out: wknd over 1f out* **33/1**[3]

4 *4 ½* **La Brava** 4-9-2 0................................................ ShirleyTeasdale[(5)] 1
(Lisa Williamson) *racd keenly: trckd ldr: rdn over 2f out: wknd over 1f out* **33/1**[3]

1m 14.38s (3.18) **Going Correction** +0.25s/f (Good)
**WFA** 3 from 4yo 11lb **4 Ran SP% 108.4**
Speed ratings (Par 103): **88,82,61,55**
CSF £1.44 TOTE £1.10; EX 1.40 Trifecta £3.60.
**Owner** K Abdullah **Bred** Juddmonte Farms Ltd **Trained** Beckhampton, Wilts

**FOCUS**
An uncompetitive maiden. The time was 1.33secs slower than the preceding Class 4 handicap. The winner is bred to be smart and likely leave this bare form well behind.

## 1791 32RED ON THE APP STORE H'CAP — 1m 2f 46y

**4:00** (4:00) (Class 5) (0-75,75) 4-Y-O+ **£2,587** (£770; £384; £96; £96) **Stalls Low**

Form — RPR

-013 1 **Eco Warrior**[88] 382 4-8-13 67.................................(b) JamesDoyle 8 78
(J W Hills) *trckd ldr: chal over 2f out: rdn to ld over 1f out: styd on: rdn out* **12/1**

005- 2 *nk* **The Quarterjack**[197] 7220 5-8-9 63........................ RichardKingscote 7 73
(Ron Hodges) *trckd ldrs: rdn over 2f out: chsd wnr over 1f out: styd on and clsng on wnr fnl 75yds: a being hld* **7/2**[2]

2462 3 *3 ¼* **Ivor's Princess**[33] 1099 5-8-10 64................................(b) SeanLevey 4 68
(Rod Millman) *s.i.s: in last pair: rdn 4f out: hld 5th ent fnl f: styd on to go 3rd cl home* **12/1**

60-2 4 *½* **Yul Finegold (IRE)**[21] 1355 4-9-4 72.............................[1] FergusSweeney 6 75
(George Baker) *led: rdn wl over 2f out: sn jnd: hdd over 1f out: styd on same pce: lost 3rd nring fin* **5/4**[1]

4-56 **4** *dht* **Angus Glens**[21] 1354 4-9-4 **72** ........ SteveDrowne 5 75
(David Dennis) *trckd ldrs: rdn over 2f out: styd on same pce fr over 1f out* **5/1**[3]

3400 **6** *22* **Red Dragon (IRE)**[16] 1439 4-9-2 **70** ........ AdamKirby 3
(Michael Blanshard) *in last pair: rdn wl over 3f out: wknd 2f out: t.o* **11/2**

2m 14.65s (3.65) **Going Correction** +0.475s/f (Yiel) **6** Ran SP% **114.1**
Speed ratings (Par 103): **104,103,101,100,100 83**
CSF £54.12 CT £522.24 TOTE £6.70: £4.90, £5.60; EX 60.50 Trifecta £158.90.
**Owner** D J Deer **Bred** D J And Mrs Deer **Trained** Upper Lambourn, Berks

**FOCUS**
A modest handicap. The form makes sense around the front three.

## 1792 32RED CASINO H'CAP 1m 3f 144y
**4:30** (4:30) (Class 6) (0-60,60) 3-Y-O **£1,940** (£577; £288; £144) **Stalls** Low

Form RPR

000- **1** **Gimme Five**[194] 7308 3-9-1 **54** ........ FergusSweeney 9 63+
(Alan King) *hld up: rdn and hdwy fr 3f out: wnt 4th over 2f out: styd on strly ent fnl f: led nring fin* **7/2**[2]

00-2 **2** *½* **Bold Runner**[19] 1382 3-9-6 **59** ........ FrankieMcDonald 6 67
(Sean Curran) *pushed along briefly to sit prom: disp over 6f out: clr ldr 4f out: rdn over 2f out: hdd over 1f out: rallied fnl 120yds: regained 2nd fnl stride* **7/1**

530- **3** *hd* **Cape Arrow**[179] 7640 3-9-7 **60** ........ AdamKirby 2 68+
(Paul Cole) *trckd ldrs: rdn over 2f out: led over 1f out: no ex whn hdd and lost 2 pls nring fin* **5/2**[1]

000- **4** *5* **Norse Legend**[173] 7774 3-8-9 **48** ........ RichardKingscote 7 47
(Daniel Kubler) *trckd ldrs: rdn over 2f out: nt quite able to mount chal: styd on same pce tl no ex fnl 120yds* **33/1**

1130 **5** *8* **Enquiring**[9] 1588 3-9-2 **58** ........ MichaelJMMurphy(3) 8 44
(Mark Johnston) *chsd ldrs briefly: sn last: rdn over 5f out: hdwy on outer 4f out but nvr bk on terms w ldrs* **4/1**[3]

000- **6** *2* **Kelamita (IRE)**[185] 7501 3-8-12 **51** ........ LiamJones 4 33
(Hughie Morrison) *hld up: rdn 3f out: wknd 2f out* **8/1**

54-0 **7** *12* **Cameley Dawn**[18] 1403 3-9-5 **58** ........ (p) SteveDrowne 3 20
(Malcolm Saunders) *led tl over 6f out: chsd ldrs: rdn over 4f out: wknd 2f out* **33/1**

000- **8** *4* **Squaw King**[188] 7442 3-8-11 **55** ........ GeorgeDowning(5) 1 10
(Eve Johnson Houghton) *hld up: rdn over 4f out: nvr any imp: wknd 2f out* **12/1**

00-3 **9** *7* **Kaizen Factor**[32] 1124 3-9-4 **57** ........ (b[1]) SeanLevey 5
(Rod Millman) *rousted along to sit promly: disp over 6f out tl drvn over 4f out: sn hld: wknd 2f out* **10/1**

2m 37.69s (7.09) **Going Correction** +0.475s/f (Yiel) **9** Ran SP% **117.1**
Speed ratings (Par 96): **95,94,94,91,85 84,76,73,69**
CSF £28.72 CT £70.58 TOTE £7.10: £2.20, £1.70, £1.10; EX 44.50 Trifecta £270.40.
**Owner** McNeill Family **Bred** Granham Farm Partnership **Trained** Barbury Castle, Wilts

■ Stewards' Enquiry : Frankie McDonald two-day ban: use of whip (12-13 May)

Fergus Sweeney trainer said, regarding the apparent improvment of form, that his charge had been gelded and had strengthened up over the winter

**FOCUS**
A low-grade handicap, but it featured some potential improvers. The form is rated around the second.
T/Plt: £26.70 to a £1 stake. Pool of £48776.29 - 1329.21 winning tickets. T/Qpdt: £9.60 to a £1 stake. Pool of £3423.47 - 262.96 winning tickets. TM

# 1764 KEMPTON (A.W) (R-H)
Monday, April 28

**OFFICIAL GOING: Standard**
Wind: medium, half behind Weather: dry, light cloud

## 1793 KEMPTON FOR SUMMER WEDDINGS H'CAP 1m 3f (P)
**1:40** (1:44) (Class 6) (0-60,59) 3-Y-O **£1,940** (£577; £288; £144) **Stalls** Low

Form RPR

005- **1** **Nyanza (GER)**[194] 7309 3-9-6 **58** ........ RichardHughes 2 65+
(Alan King) *prom in main gp: rdn and effrt over 2f out: chsd clr ldr over 1f out: clsd qckly 1f out and led fnl 150yds: in command after: r.o* **11/4**[1]

000- **2** *1½* **Snow Conditions**[203] 7070 3-9-5 **57** ........ RobertWinston 6 62
(Philip Hide) *hld up in rr: swtchd lft and effrt over 2f out: gd hdwy over 1f out: r.o wl to go 2nd wl ins fnl f: nvr trbld ldrs* **20/1**

006 **3** *¾* **Roman Riches**[33] 1107 3-9-6 **58** ........ GeorgeBaker 11 61
(Gary Moore) *stdd s: hld up wl in rr: stl poor 11th 3f out: hdwy on outer over 1f out: r.o strly fnl f to go 3rd towards fin: nvr trbld ldrs* **12/1**

000- **4** *½* **Sweetheart Abbey**[173] 7764 3-9-7 **59** ........ TedDurcan 8 62
(William Knight) *awkward leaving stalls and s.i.s: sn rcvrd and racd in midfield: plenty to do whn swtchd ins fnl effrt 2f out: r.o strly fnl f: nvr trbld ldrs* **20/1**

00-0 **5** *½* **Satin Waters**[19] 1382 3-8-7 **45** ........ (b[1]) JohnFahy 9 47
(Eve Johnson Houghton) *led: grad drew clr fr 8f out: rdn: reminders and wnt wl clr 5f out: rdn over 2f out: stl 10 l clr 2f out: hdd fnl 150yds: no ex and wknd towards fin* **66/1**

00-0 **6** *2* **Astrovirtue**[114] 50 3-9-3 **55** ........ MickaelBarzalona 1 53
(Mark H Tompkins) *chsd ldr: rdn and effrt over 2f out: 3rd over 1f out: plugged on but lost 3 pls ins fnl f* **33/1**

20-5 **7** *2¼* **Assoluta (IRE)**[33] 1098 3-8-13 **56** ........ JoshBaudains(5) 7 50
(Sylvester Kirk) *s.i.s: steadily rcvrd: prom in main gp over 4f out: rdn and effrt over 2f out: plugged on but no real imp fnl f* **25/1**

-012 **8** *½* **Chanceuse**[25] 1257 3-9-2 **57** ........ OisinMurphy(3) 3 50
(Gay Kelleway) *racd in midfield: rdn and effrt ent fnl 2f: hdwy whn hmpd and swtchd rt 1f out: kpt on: nvr trbld ldrs* **9/1**

60-4 **9** *½* **Musalaha (IRE)**[19] 1382 3-9-5 **57** ........ PaulHanagan 10 49
(Ed Dunlop) *racd in midfield: rdn and effrt over 2f out: no real rspnse: plugged on same pce and n.d fnl f* **4/1**[2]

0-60 **10** *¾* **Graphene**[28] 1208 3-9-5 **57** ........ AndreaAtzeni 4 48
(Rod Millman) *racd in midfield: rdn over 3f out: plugged on but n.d fnl 2f* **8/1**

00-0 **11** *13* **Oracle Boy**[21] 1353 3-9-4 **56** ........ TomQueally 12 23
(William Muir) *dwlt and bustled along early: in rr: rdn over 4f out: sme hdwy over 2f out: wknd over 1f out* **9/2**[3]

00-0 **12** *18* **Updated (FR)**[27] 1216 3-8-11 **49** ........ JamieSpencer 5
(Ismail Mohammed) *prom in main gp: rdn over 2f out: wknd wl over 1f out: eased ins fnl f: t.o* **11/1**

2m 21.88s (-0.02) **Going Correction** +0.075s/f (Slow) **12** Ran SP% **119.8**
Speed ratings (Par 96): **103,101,101,101,100 99,97,97,96,96 86,73**
CSF £66.85 CT £585.66 TOTE £3.70: £1.40, £9.40, £4.10; EX 73.40 Trifecta £1140.60.
**Owner** Hunscote Stud **Bred** Gestut Ebbesloh **Trained** Barbury Castle, Wilts

**FOCUS**
Plenty of unexposed types lined up for this modest handicap, which was run at a fierce pace. The winner is in good hands to expect progress.

## 1794 DOWNLOAD THE BETVICTOR APP NOW H'CAP 1m (P)
**2:10** (2:13) (Class 6) (0-65,65) 3-Y-O **£1,940** (£577; £288; £144) **Stalls** Low

Form RPR

06-0 **1** **Zambeasy**[27] 1216 3-9-4 **62** ........ GeorgeBaker 13 72
(Philip Hide) *mde all: styd wd early: rdn and 4 l clr wl over 1f out: in command and styd on wl: rdn out* **20/1**

12-4 **2** *3¼* **Tyrsal (IRE)**[19] 1400 3-9-6 **64** ........ AndreaAtzeni 6 67
(Robert Eddery) *in tch in midfield: rdn and effrt to chse clr wnr wl over 1f out: kpt on but no real imp ins fnl f* **5/1**[2]

04-4 **3** *1* **Starlit Cantata**[18] 1403 3-9-7 **65** ........ JohnFahy 3 66
(Eve Johnson Houghton) *in tch in midfield: swtchd rt and effrt on inner ent fnl 2f: wnt 3rd 1f out: kpt on but no threat to wnr* **7/2**[1]

006- **4** *1¾* **Allergic Reaction (IRE)**[209] 6924 3-8-13 **57** ........ ShaneKelly 1 54
(William Knight) *chsd ldrs: rdn and effrt ent fnl 2f: 4th and no imp whn edgd lft 1f out: styd on same pce fnl f* **13/2**

055- **5** *3¼* **Pink Mirage (IRE)**[266] 5061 3-9-4 **65** ........ MatthewLawson(3) 2 54
(Jonathan Portman) *hld up in rr: effrt on inner 2f out: sme hdwy over 1f out: no threat to ldrs but styd on steadily fnl f* **25/1**

662 **6** *shd* **No Refund (IRE)**[56] 823 3-9-7 **65** ........ AmirQuinn 8 57
(Lee Carter) *dwlt: hld up in tch in last quartet: hmpd over 3f out: rdn and hdwy 2f out: no imp fnl f: eased towards fin* **6/1**[3]

3343 **7** *1¾* **Evacusafe Lady**[19] 1384 3-8-12 **59** ........ (p) OisinMurphy(3) 5 44
(John Ryan) *in tch midfield: effrt ent fnl 2f: keeping on same pce whn short of room and hmpd 1f out: no imp after* **10/1**

0-30 **8** *1* **Rio Yuma (ITY)**[23] 1303 3-9-1 **64** ........ JacobButterfield(5) 11 47
(Kristin Stubbs) *chsd ldng trio: rdn and effrt to chse clr wnr jst over 2f out tl wl over 1f out: wknd fnl f* **33/1**

006- **9** *1* **Rehanaat (USA)**[194] 7295 3-9-1 **59** ........ PaulHanagan 4 39
(Ed Dunlop) *in tch in midfield: rdn and no real imp ent fnl 2f: n.d fr over 1f out* **11/1**

6-66 **10** *5* **Harry's Summer (USA)**[18] 1403 3-9-0 **61** ........ (b) RobertTart(3) 9 30
(Nick Littmoden) *s.i.s: hld in tch in last quartet: effrt wd wl over no real imp: wknd over 1f out* **5/1**[2]

-564 **11** *1* **Marphilly (IRE)**[32] 1124 3-8-9 **53** ........ MickaelBarzalona 10 20
(John Best) *in tch in midfield: rdn and no hdwy over 2f out: wknd over 1f out* **20/1**

00-0 **12** *3¾* **Charlies Mate**[94] 311 3-8-11 **55** ........ HayleyTurner 7 13
(John Best) *chsd wnr tl over 2f out: wknd over 1f out: bhd fnl f* **50/1**

006- **13** *16* **Rosina Jay (IRE)**[237] 6069 3-9-4 **62** ........ RichardHughes 12
(Simon Dow) *stdd to rr after 1f: rdn and no hdwy over 2f out: wl bhd and eased ins fnl f: t.o* **25/1**

1m 39.62s (-0.18) **Going Correction** +0.075s/f (Slow) **13** Ran SP% **122.7**
Speed ratings (Par 96): **103,99,98,97,93 93,91,90,89,84 83,80,64**
CSF £112.61 CT £463.57 TOTE £50.00: £9.00, £1.90, £1.50; EX 184.70 Trifecta £2491.60.
**Owner** Heart Of The South Racing **Bred** Frank Brady **Trained** Findon, W Sussex

■ Stewards' Enquiry : Shane Kelly two-day ban: careless riding (12-13 May)

**FOCUS**
An open contest with a number of the field making their handicap debuts. The winner made all in a good time. The form is rated around the runner-up.

## 1795 BRITISH STALLION STUDS EBF MAIDEN STKS 1m (P)
**2:40** (2:42) (Class 5) 3-Y-O **£3,881** (£1,155; £577; £288) **Stalls** Low

Form RPR

2 **1** **Heisman (IRE)**[27] 1216 3-9-5 0 ........ JamieSpencer 11 82+
(Olly Stevens) *chsd ldr tl led after 1f: mde rest: rdn ent fnl 2f: r.o wl u.p fnl f: drvn out* **6/4**[1]

05-0 **2** *¾* **Speculative Bid (IRE)**[12] 1511 3-9-5 77 ........ DaneO'Neill 3 80
(David Elsworth) *in tch in midfield: effrt and rdn wl over 1f out: hdwy to press wnr 1f out: r.o wl but a hld* **20/1**

02- **3** *1¼* **Lisamour (IRE)**[165] 7874 3-9-0 0 ........ RaulDaSilva 10 72
(Paul Cole) *t.k.h: led for 1f: chsd wnr tl 5f out: styd chsng ldrs: rdn wl over 1f out: kpt on same pce fnl f* **33/1**

0-6 **4** *1¼* **Stampede (IRE)**[19] 1395 3-9-5 0 ........ RyanMoore 8 74+
(Sir Michael Stoute) *stdd s: hld up in tch in last trio: swtchd lft and effrt wl over 1f out: r.o strly fnl f: nt rch ldrs* **14/1**

4- **5** *nk* **Nigel's Destiny (USA)**[194] 7302 3-9-5 0 ........ ShaneKelly 6 73
(Jeremy Noseda) *s.i.s: rcvrd and wl in tch in midfield after 2f: rdn and effrt wl over 1f out: 4th and n.m.r whn edgd lft 1f out: one pce fnl f* **11/2**[3]

346- **6** *½* **Munjally**[268] 4988 3-9-5 78 ........ PaulHanagan 12 72
(Richard Hannon) *chsd ldr tl chsd wnr 5f out: rdn and effrt to chal 2f out: unable qck and lost 2nd ent fnl f: sn carried lft and outpcd fnl 150yds* **12/1**

0- **7** *1¼* **Orion's Bow**[208] 6953 3-9-5 0 ........ (t) WilliamBuick 5 69+
(John Gosden) *in tch in rr: rdn and struggling whn gallop qcknd over 2f out: swtchd rt to inner rail 2f out: styd on past btn horses fnl f: nvr trbld ldrs* **8/1**

44- **8** *¾* **Ian's Memory (USA)**[187] 7461 3-9-5 0 ........ SebSanders 2 68
(Jeremy Noseda) *t.k.h: in tch in midfield: rdn and effrt over 2f out: no prog over 1f out: one pce and wl hld fnl f* **10/1**

**9** *1* **Incredible Fresh (IRE)** 3-9-5 0 ........ HayleyTurner 1 65
(James Fanshawe) *in tch in midfield: rdn and effrt ent fnl 2f: outpcd and btn over 1f out: plugged on same pce after* **50/1**

6 **10** *nk* **Elite Force (IRE)**[16] 1433 3-9-5 0 ........ GeorgeBaker 4 65
(Roger Charlton) *wl in tch in midfield: effrt ent fnl 2f: outpacd and btn over 1f out: wknd ins fnl f* **9/2**[2]

00-5 **11** *nk* **Filosofo (IRE)**[14] 1491 3-9-5 79 ........ RichardHughes 9 64
(Richard Hannon) *chsd ldrs: effrt and rdn to press ldrs ent fnl 2f: outpcd and btn 1f out: wknd fnl f* **20/1**

02- **12** *3* **Classical Art (IRE)**[193] 7320 3-9-5 0 ........ AndreaAtzeni 7 57
(Roger Varian) *in tch in midfield: rdn 1/2-way: lost pl ent fnl 2f: bhd ins fnl f* **10/1**

1m 39.68s (-0.12) **Going Correction** +0.075s/f (Slow) **12** Ran SP% **131.6**
Speed ratings (Par 98): **103,102,101,99,99 98,97,96,95,95 95,92**
CSF £45.46 TOTE £2.80: £1.10, £9.50, £8.40; EX 52.70 Trifecta £740.10.
**Owner** Qatar Racing Limited **Bred** Keatly Overseas Ltd **Trained** Chiddingfold, Surrey

**FOCUS**
A decent maiden for the track, but run at a steady pace and muddling. The winner didn't need to improve on his debut form.

## 1796 BETVICTOR.COM H'CAP 1m (P)
3:10 (3:11) (Class 4) (0-80,80) 4-Y-0+ £4,690 (£1,395; £697; £348) Stalls Low

Form RPR
165- **1** **Whipper Snapper (IRE)**[185] 7507 4-9-6 79 AndreaAtzeni 2 88+
(William Knight) *chsd ldrs: effrt wl over 1f out: n.m.r ent fnl f: hdwy to chse ldr wl ins fnl f: str run u.p to ld last stride* 3/1[1]

33/3 **2** shd **Rome**[26] 1237 4-9-1 74 RyanMoore 7 82
(Gary Moore) *chsd ldr tl rdn to ld 2f out: drvn and forged ahd ins fnl f: r.o wl but hdd last stride* 8/1[3]

1201 **3** 1 1/2 **Shaolin (IRE)**[27] 1217 4-9-5 78 (t) GeorgeBaker 1 82
(Seamus Durack) *in tch in midfield: effrt on inner and chsd ldrs u.p over 1f out: wnt 2nd briefly ins fnl f: r.o same pce fnl 75yds* 3/1[1]

35-4 **4** shd **Accession (IRE)**[24] 1275 5-9-6 79 [1] RichardHughes 6 83
(Charlie Fellowes) *in tch in midfield: effrt u.p wl over 1f out: styd on wl fnl 100yds but nvr getting to ldrs* 5/1[2]

05-3 **5** nk **Starlight Symphony (IRE)**[19] 1392 4-9-2 75 (b) JohnFahy 5 78
(Eve Johnson Houghton) *dwlt: in tch in rr: effrt on inner 2f out: chsd ldrs 1f out: kpt on u.p but nvr gng pce to chal* 10/1

2210 **6** shd **Seek The Fair Land**[25] 1261 8-9-1 74 (b) AmirQuinn 8 77
(Lee Carter) *t.k.h: chsd ldrs: upsides wnr 2f out: rdn and effrt over 1f out: no ex and btn ins fnl f: wknd towards fin* 16/1

3211 **7** 3/4 **Presumido (IRE)**[23] 1297 4-8-9 73 JackDuern(5) 9 74+
(Simon Dow) *stdd s: hld up in tch in rr: rdn and effrt ent fnl 2f: wd and kpt on fnl f: nvr trbld ldrs* 5/1[2]

003- **8** 3/4 **Breakheart (IRE)**[213] 6802 7-8-9 75 JonathanWilletts(7) 4 75
(Andrew Balding) *in tch in last trio: swtchd lft and effrt wd over 2f out: kpt on but nvr gng pce to chal* 14/1

0 **9** 6 **Malicho**[19] 1399 5-9-7 80 RobertWinston 3 66
(Dean Ivory) *led tl 2f out: sn rdn and unable qck: lost pl ent fnl f: wknd fnl 150yds* 33/1

1m 40.45s (0.65) **Going Correction** +0.075s/f (Slow) 9 Ran SP% **119.0**
Speed ratings (Par 105): **99,98,97,97,97 96,96,95,89**
CSF £29.20 CT £79.58 TOTE £4.10: £1.20, £2.50, £1.90; EX 39.50 Trifecta £205.30.
**Owner** The Oil Merchants **Bred** Michael Mullins **Trained** Patching, W Sussex
■ Stewards' Enquiry : John Fahy £80 fine: entered the wrong stallsx

**FOCUS**
A tight handicap run at a steady pace, with a bunch finish. The form is rated around the third and fourth.

## 1797 £25 FREE BET AT BETVICTOR.COM MAIDEN STKS 1m 4f (P)
3:40 (3:43) (Class 5) 3-4-Y-0 £2,587 (£770; £384; £192) Stalls Centre

Form RPR
45-3 **1** **Criteria (IRE)**[17] 1424 3-8-3 77 NickyMackay 6 76
(John Gosden) *mde all: rdn and qcknd 2f out: clr w runner-up over 1f out: r.o wl: rdn out* 11/8[1]

0-3 **2** 1 **Classic Devotion (USA)**[25] 1258 3-8-8 0 MickaelBarzalona 4 79
(Charlie Appleby) *chsd wnr for 2f: styd chsng ldrs tl wnt 2nd again over 2f out: rdn and chal 2f out: clr w wnr over 1f out: kpt on but nt gng pce of wnr ins fnl f* 3/1[2]

**3** 2 **Smiling Stranger (IRE)** 3-8-5 0 OisinMurphy(3) 10 76+
(Andrew Balding) *s.i.s: in tch in rr: hdwy on inner ent fnl 2f: wnt 3rd 1f out: kpt on* 5/1

**4** 3 1/4 **Nusantara** 3-8-3 0 AndreaAtzeni 1 66
(Paul Cole) *in tch in midfield: effrt and rdn to press ldrs ent fnl 2f: 3rd and outpcd over 1f out: wknd ins fnl f* 12/1

53- **5** 3 1/4 **Vent De Force**[197] 7219 3-8-8 0 PaulHanagan 8 66+
(Hughie Morrison) *dropped to last and pushed along after 2f out: rdn over 2f out: hdwy past btn horses over 1f out: kpt on: nvr trbld ldrs* 7/2[3]

0-0 **6** 1 3/4 **Malory Towers**[14] 1491 3-8-3 0 HayleyTurner 7 58+
(James Fanshawe) *in tch in midfield: rdn ent fnl 2f: sn outpcd and no threat to ldrs fr over 1f out* 25/1

5 **7** 3/4 **Sawwala**[40] 1011 4-9-9 0 FrederikTylicki 2 60
(J R Jenkins) *in tch in midfield: effrt u.p ent fnl 2f: no prog and outpcd wl over 1f out: n.d after* 50/1

0 **8** shd **Abyaat (IRE)**[70] 642 3-8-1 0 CamHardie(7) 9 62
(Richard Hannon) *chsd ldrs: wnt 2nd 10f out tl 9f out: steadily dropped towards rr: rdn and effrt over 2f out: no prog: wl btn over 1f out* 25/1

0 **9** 3/4 **Inca Drum (USA)**[30] 1166 3-8-8 0 (b[1]) TedDurcan 5 60
(Pat Eddery) *awkward and wnt lft leaving stalls: early reminders: hdwy into midfield 1/2-way: no hdwy under pressure over 2f out: bhd fnl f* 33/1

0 **10** 14 **Oakbank (USA)**[19] 1391 3-8-3 0 DanielMuscutt(5) 3 38
(Brett Johnson) *chsd ldrs tl wnt 2nd 9f out tl over 2f out: sn dropped out: bhd fnl f* 66/1

2m 35.51s (1.01) **Going Correction** +0.075s/f (Slow)
**WFA** 3 from 4yo 20lb 10 Ran SP% **127.8**
Speed ratings (Par 103): **99,98,97,94,92 91,91,90,90,81**
CSF £6.16 TOTE £2.50: £1.10, £1.90, £2.60; EX 10.40 Trifecta £30.60.
**Owner** Cheveley Park Stud **Bred** Lynch - Bages & Longfield Stud **Trained** Newmarket, Suffolk

**FOCUS**
The pace was steady for this uncompetitive maiden, which had a compressed finish. The first two were always 1-2.

## 1798 DOWNLOAD THE BETVICTOR INSTABET APP H'CAP 1m 3f (P)
4:10 (4:12) (Class 5) (0-70,70) 4-Y-0+ £2,587 (£770; £384; £192) Stalls Low

Form RPR
300- **1** **Conquestadim**[233] 6202 4-9-4 67 JimmyFortune 9 76
(Hughie Morrison) *mde all and dictated stdy gallop: rdn and qcknd over 2f out: in command and r.o wl ins fnl f* 4/1[1]

160- **2** 1 1/4 **Warrigal (IRE)**[201] 7121 4-9-7 70 RyanMoore 1 76+
(Jeremy Noseda) *wl in tch in midfield: rdn and effrt ent fnl 2f: hdwy to chse clr wnr jst ins fnl f: r.o but nvr getting to wnr* 7/1

500- **3** 2 **Tingo In The Tale (IRE)**[208] 6960 5-9-3 66 WilliamBuick 7 69
(David Arbuthnot) *chsd wnr: rdn ent fnl 2f: outpcd by wnr over 1f out: 3rd and kpt on same pce fnl f* 10/1

0112 **4** 1 **Thane Of Cawdor (IRE)**[18] 1406 5-8-10 62 OisinMurphy(3) 5 63
(Joseph Tuite) *hld up in tch in midfield: rdn and sltly outpcd ent fnl 2f: rallied and styd on u.p ins fnl f: no threat to ldrs* 10/1

6155 **5** nk **Fearless Lad (IRE)**[32] 1120 4-8-13 62 (t) TedDurcan 6 62
(John Best) *chsd ldrs: rdn over 1f out: styd on same pce ins fnl f* 33/1

2636 **6** shd **Thecornishcowboy**[6] 1636 5-9-4 67 (t) RichardHughes 8 67
(John Ryan) *in tch in midfield: effrt u.p over 2f out: no threat to wnr and styd on same pce fnl f* 11/1

02-1 **7** hd **Grey Blue (IRE)**[22] 1027 4-9-5 68 TomQueally 10 68
(Nicky Henderson) *chsd ldrs: rdn: edgd rt and slty outpcd ent fnl 2f: no threat to wnr and styd on same pce fnl f* 7/1

01-3 **8** 1/2 **Posh Boy (IRE)**[28] 1209 4-9-5 68 GeorgeBaker 11 67+
(Chris Wall) *hld up in tch in last quartet: rdn and effrt on inner 2f out: kpt on same pce fnl f: nvr trbld ldrs* 9/2[2]

5334 **9** 2 3/4 **Midnight Chorister**[32] 1120 6-9-4 67 (t) HayleyTurner 12 62
(Alex Hales) *t.k.h: hld up in tch in last pair: rdn over 2f out: plugged on fnl f: nvr trbld ldrs* 20/1

431- **10** 2 3/4 **Wall Street Boss (USA)**[168] 7839 4-9-5 68 FrederikTylicki 14 58+
(James Fanshawe) *hld up in tch in last quartet: effrt and rdn wl over 2f out: no prog: nvr trbld ldrs* 5/1[3]

035- **11** 4 **Spring Tonic**[131] 8323 5-9-0 68 JackDuern(5) 3 51
(Simon Dow) *s.i.s: hld up in rr: n.d* 14/1

-005 **12** 3 1/4 **Shirataki (IRE)**[26] 1231 6-8-11 60 [1] ChrisCatlin 4 37
(Peter Hiatt) *t.k.h: chsd ldrs: rdn and effrt over 2f out: lost pl wl over 1f out: wknd fnl f* 25/1

2m 22.68s (0.78) **Going Correction** +0.075s/f (Slow) 12 Ran SP% **124.6**
Speed ratings (Par 103): **100,99,97,96,96 96,96,96,94,92 89,87**
CSF £33.10 CT £272.70 TOTE £7.20: £3.20, £3.20, £5.00; EX 59.80 Trifecta £873.90.
**Owner** The Fairy Story Partnership **Bred** Deepwood Farm Stud **Trained** East Ilsley, Berks

**FOCUS**
They went a steady pace for this open handicap, the winner having an easy lead. The form is taken at something like face value.

## 1799 FOLLOW @BETVICTORRACING ON TWITTER H'CAP 7f (P)
4:40 (4:40) (Class 5) (0-70,70) 4-Y-0+ £2,587 (£770; £384; £192) Stalls Low

Form RPR
-011 **1** **Until Midnight (IRE)**[18] 1408 4-8-10 62 RobertTart(3) 3 70+
(Eugene Stanford) *mde all: rdn and qcknd 2f out: drvn and hld on wl fnl f* 1/1[1]

000- **2** shd **Bayleyf (IRE)**[187] 7462 5-9-7 70 AmirQuinn 2 78
(Lee Carter) *dwlt: sn rcvrd and chsd ldrs: upsides wnr 2f out: rdn and effrt ent fnl f: kpt on but a jst hld fnl 100yds* 9/1

000- **3** 3/4 **Orders From Rome (IRE)**[194] 7303 5-8-11 60 [1] MickaelBarzalona 1 66
(Charlie Fellowes) *wl in tch in midfield: rdn and effrt 2f out: kpt on but no imp on ldng pair fnl 100yds* 8/1[3]

42-0 **4** 3/4 **Aomen Rock**[24] 1281 4-9-5 68 HayleyTurner 5 72
(James Fanshawe) *chsd wnr: rdn ent fnl 2f: 3rd and sltly outpcd jst over 1f out: kpt on same pce fnl f* 11/4[2]

0223 **5** 1 **Teen Ager (FR)**[18] 1408 10-8-6 60 (p) DavidKenny(5) 4 61
(Paul Burgoyne) *t.k.h: hld up wl in tch in midfield: effrt on inner over 1f out: styd on same pce ins fnl f* 16/1

010- **6** 3/4 **Barnmore**[257] 5387 6-9-2 68 CharlesBishop(3) 8 67
(Peter Hedger) *taken down early: hld up in last pair: rdn and effrt 2f out: no imp tl kpt on ins fnl f: nvr trbld ldrs* 33/1

3205 **7** 1/2 **Russian Ice**[47] 924 6-9-3 66 (p) RobertWinston 6 64
(Dean Ivory) *wl in tch in midfield: rdn and effrt 2f out: outpcd jst over 1f out: wknd ins fnl f* 10/1

0144 **8** 3 1/2 **Dimitar (USA)**[31] 1152 5-9-3 69 DeclanBates(3) 7 58
(Johnny Farrelly) *s.i.s: hld up in tch in last pair: effrt u.p ent fnl 2f: no imp and btn 1f out: wknd ins fnl f* 14/1

55-0 **9** 11 **Captain Kendall (IRE)**[95] 294 5-9-7 70 ChrisCatlin 9 30
(Harry Chisman) *in tch towards rr: rdn over 2f out: no hdwy and sn struggling: bhd fnl f* 20/1

1m 26.8s (0.80) **Going Correction** +0.075s/f (Slow) 9 Ran SP% **127.1**
Speed ratings (Par 103): **98,97,96,95 94,93,89,77**
CSF £13.45 CT £57.65 TOTE £2.70: £1.02, £5.20, £4.20; EX 18.40 Trifecta £169.50.
**Owner** newmarketracingclub.co.uk **Bred** Rathbarry Stud **Trained** Newmarket, Suffolk
■ Stewards' Enquiry : Amir Quinn seven-day ban: use of whip (12-18 May)
Robert Tart four-day ban: use of whip (12-15 May)

**FOCUS**
A steadily run handicap, with the winner again making all. There's every chance the winner will do better.
T/Jkpt: Not won. T/Plt: £17.30 to a £1 stake. Pool of £49028.27 - 2066.87 winning tickets.
T/Qpdt: £9.30 to a £1 stake. Pool of £4484.46 - 356.30 winning tickets. SP

# 1495 SOUTHWELL (L-H)
Monday, April 28

**OFFICIAL GOING: Standard**
Wind: Light half against Weather: Cloudy but warm

## 1800 WIN BIG WITH THE TOTEJACKPOT H'CAP 1m (F)
5:15 (5:17) (Class 6) (0-60,60) 4-Y-0+ £2,264 (£673; £336; £168) Stalls Low

Form RPR
0513 **1** **Sam Spade (IRE)**[20] 1365 4-9-6 59 (v) DaleSwift 5 71
(Derek Shaw) *led 1f: cl up: led again wl over 2f out: rdn wl over 1f out and sn jnd: drvn ent fnl f: styd on wl towards fin* 3/1[2]

3222 **2** 1 **General Tufto**[17] 1428 9-8-8 52 (b) JoeyHaynes(5) 6 62
(Charles Smith) *broke wl: sn pushed along: rdn along: lost pl and outpcd after 2f: hdwy on outer 3f out: chal 2f out: rdn and ev ch appr fnl f tl one pce last 100yds* 5/1

-100 **3** 7 **Roger Thorpe**[30] 1168 5-9-4 60 NeilFarley(3) 7 54
(Deborah Sanderson) *s.i.s and reminders s: hdwy to chse ldrs after 1f: rdn along wl over 2f out: sn one pce* 5/1

0-5P **4** 1 1/4 **Botanist**[92] 352 7-8-7 46 oh1 DuranFentiman 1 37
(Shaun Harris) *chsd ldrs on inner: rdn along 3f out: drvn wl over 1f out: sn outpcd* 50/1

014- **5** 1 **Barista (IRE)**[137] 7430 6-8-11 57 DanielCremin(7) 3 46
(Brian Forsey) *chsd ldrs: rdn along 1/2-way: drvn 3f out and sn wknd* 20/1

34-0 **6** 1 1/4 **Loyal N Trusted**[16] 1446 6-8-13 57 ConnorBeasley(5) 4 43
(Karen Tutty) *chsd ldrs: rdn along over 3f out: sn btn* 9/2[3]

-330 **7** 2 1/2 **Bitaphon (IRE)**[7] 1606 5-8-11 57 (vt[1]) AlistairRawlinson(7) 2 37
(Michael Appleby) *cl up on inner: led after 1f: rdn along 3f out: sn hdd and drvn: wknd fnl 2f* 7/4[1]

1m 45.6s (1.90) **Going Correction** +0.275s/f (Slow) 7 Ran SP% **119.6**
Speed ratings (Par 101): **101,100,93,91,90 89,87**
CSF £19.58 TOTE £2.70: £1.40, £5.50; EX 13.60 Trifecta £66.70.
**Owner** The Warren Partnership **Bred** Newhall Ltd **Trained** Sproxton, Leics

**FOCUS**
A modest handicap in which the winner backed up his earlier C&D win.

## 1801 TOTEEXACTA ON ALL RACES CLASSIFIED STKS 6f (F)
5:45 (5:45) (Class 6) 3-Y-O £2,264 (£673; £336; £168) Stalls Low

Form RPR
1 1 **Red Primo (IRE)**27 1223 3-9-0 64 BenCurtis 1 78+
(Alan McCabe) *trckd ldr: cl up 1/2-way: led wl over 1f out: pushed clr appr fnl f: easily* 1/3[1]
3220 2 8 **Under Approval**5 1642 3-9-0 65 DanielTudhope 5 52
(David O'Meara) *led: rdn along and jnd wl over 2f out: hdd wl over 1f out: drvn and one pce fnl f: wl hld whn eased towards fin* 5/2[2]
060- 3 1 **Booloo (IRE)**154 8039 3-8-11 47 (v[1]) BillyCray(3) 4 49
(Garry Moss) *chsd ldrs: pushed along and outpcd after 2f: hdwy wl over 2f out: sn rdn along and one pce* 25/1[3]
000- 4 5 **Notts So Blue**222 6513 3-9-0 47 DuranFentiman 3 33
(Shaun Harris) *chsd ldng pair: rdn along 1/2-way: sn outpcd* 50/1
00-0 5 9 **Poco Piccolo**24 1285 3-8-11 40 (tp) NeilFarley(3) 2 4
(Deborah Sanderson) *in rr: rdn along bef 1/2-way: sn outpcd* 33/1
1m 18.1s (1.60) **Going Correction** +0.275s/f (Slow) 5 Ran SP% **112.3**
Speed ratings (Par 96): **100,89,88,81,69**
CSF £1.47 TOTE £1.50: £1.10, £1.30; EX 1.50 Trifecta £3.80.
**Owner** Craig and Maureen Buckingham **Bred** E O'Gorman **Trained** Averham Park, Notts
**FOCUS**
Any price bar two in this 0-65 3yo classified race. Weak form, the winner building on his debut win.

## 1802 BEST ODDS GUARANTEED AT TOTEPOOL.COM MAIDEN STKS 6f (F)
6:15 (6:15) (Class 5) 3-Y-O £2,587 (£770; £384; £192) Stalls Low

Form RPR
0052 1 **Wildcat Lass (USA)**32 1126 3-9-0 67 DanielTudhope 3 70
(David O'Meara) *slt ld: jnd over 2f out and sn rdn: styd on wl and clr whn edgd lft ins fnl f* 5/2[2]
25-2 2 5 **Royal Connoisseur (IRE)**16 1441 3-9-5 76 TonyHamilton 4 59
(Richard Fahey) *cl up: effrt wl over 2f out: sn rdn and ev ch tl drvn: edgd rt and lft and one pce appr fnl f* 1/3[1]
0646 3 8 **Bold Max**41 1007 3-9-2 46 (p) RossAtkinson(3) 1 33
(Zoe Davison) *chsd ldng pair on inner: rdn along 1/2-way: sn drvn and outpcd* 33/1[3]
03-6 4 nk **Who Splashed Me**47 933 3-8-7 40 VictorSantos(7) 2 27
(J R Jenkins) *awkward s: chsd ldrs on outer: hung rt bnd at 1/2-way: sn rdn and outpcd fnl 2f* 33/1[3]
1m 18.52s (2.02) **Going Correction** +0.275s/f (Slow) 4 Ran SP% **109.5**
Speed ratings (Par 98): **97,90,79,79**
CSF £3.82 TOTE £3.00; EX 6.20 Trifecta £8.80.
**Owner** R G Fell **Bred** Mount Brilliant Farm & Ranch, Llc **Trained** Nawton, N Yorks
**FOCUS**
What turned out to be another two-horse race but not the result the betting indicated. Weak form.

## 1803 EXCLUSIVE TICKET GIVEAWAYS @TOTEPOOL H'CAP 7f (F)
6:45 (6:45) (Class 4) (0-85,85) 4-Y-O+ £5,175 (£1,540; £769; £384) Stalls Low

Form RPR
0-00 1 **Tasrih (USA)**78 550 5-9-3 81 BenCurtis 3 91+
(Alan McCabe) *cl up: led after 2f: rdn clr wl over 1f out: drvn fnl f: kpt on wl* 14/1
1351 2 3/4 **Kung Hei Fat Choy (USA)**6 1630 5-9-1 84 6ex..(b) ConnorBeasley(5) 4 92
(James Given) *trckd ldrs: pushed along and lost pl after 2f: in rr and rdn along 1/2-way: hdwy and wd st: drvn to chse wnr appr fnl f: kpt on* 3/1[2]
-100 3 6 **Ace Master**16 1446 6-8-10 79 (b) PhilipPrince(5) 5 71
(Roy Bowring) *prom: rdn along over 2f out: n.m.r and swtchd rt over 1f out: kpt on same pce fnl f* 12/1[3]
3323 4 3 1/4 **Greyfriarschorista**33 1114 7-9-7 85 PaddyAspell 6 69
(Tom Keddy) *trckd ldrs: hdwy 3f out: rdn to chse wnr over 2f out: drvn and edgd lft over 1f out: sn wknd* 2/1[1]
33-1 5 6 **Realize**13 1499 4-9-0 78 RobertHavlin 1 46
(Hughie Morrison) *trckd ldrs: effrt wl over 2f out: sn rdn along and wknd wl over 1f out* 2/1[1]
0215 6 4 **Hamoody (USA)**17 1431 10-8-9 76 JasonHart(3) 2 34
(Joseph Tuite) *slt ld: hdd after 2f: cl up: rdn along 3f out: wknd 2f out* 14/1
1m 30.43s (0.13) **Going Correction** +0.275s/f (Slow) 6 Ran SP% **112.7**
Speed ratings (Par 105): **110,109,102,98,91 87**
CSF £55.72 TOTE £8.70: £4.30, £1.80; EX 28.40 Trifecta £149.20.
**Owner** Craig and Maureen Buckingham **Bred** G Bolton, D Dipietro & R W Honour **Trained** Averham Park, Notts
**FOCUS**
The winner is rated up a length on his Kempton December win. The first two showed very useful form to pull clear.

## 1804 2,000 GUINEAS ANTE POST AT TOTEPOOL.COM H'CAP 6f (F)
7:15 (7:16) (Class 6) (0-55,55) 4-Y-O+ £2,264 (£673; £336; £168) Stalls Low

Form RPR
45-2 1 **Meshardal (GER)**20 1369 4-9-7 55 JamesSullivan 2 73+
(Ruth Carr) *trckd ldr: smooth hdwy to ld wl over 2f out: rdn clr over 1f out: readily* 6/4[1]
0231 2 4 1/2 **Doctor Hilary**20 1369 12-9-4 52 (v) RobertHavlin 7 56
(Mark Hoad) *dwlt and in rr: pushed along after 3f: wd st: rdn and hdwy 2f out: styd on to take 2nd ins fnl f: no ch w wnr* 11/4[2]
5520 3 1 **Flow Chart (IRE)**24 1282 7-8-10 47 SladeO'Hara(3) 8 47
(Peter Grayson) *towards rr: hdwy over 2f out: sn rdn and styd on appr fnl f: nrst fin* 7/1[3]
356 4 1 3/4 **Lord Buffhead**19 1378 5-8-13 47 (v) RobbieFitzpatrick 4 42
(Richard Guest) *dwlt and towards rr: hdwy over 2f out: sn rdn: styd on fnl f: nrst fin* 10/1
0000 5 hd **Fairy Wing (IRE)**26 1245 7-9-6 54 (b) LukeMorris 3 48
(Ann Stokell) *led: rdn along over 3f out: hdd wl over 2f out and sn drvn: wknd ent fnl f* 12/1
4430 6 5 **Ivestar (IRE)**24 1282 9-9-4 52 (v) GrahamGibbons 1 30
(Michael Easterby) *dwlt: hdwy and in tch on inner 1/2-way: rdn along wl over 2f out: sn wknd* 10/1
6-06 7 1 **Camache Queen (IRE)**40 1010 6-8-13 52 (bt) JoeyHaynes(5) 5 27
(Joseph Tuite) *chsd ldrs: rdn along wl over 2f out: wknd over 1f out* 12/1
-220 8 2 3/4 **Dear Ben**25 1270 5-9-2 50 TomEaves 6 16
(Brian Baugh) *prom: wd st: rdn along wl over 2f out: sn wknd* 16/1
1m 18.28s (1.78) **Going Correction** +0.275s/f (Slow) 8 Ran SP% **118.6**
Speed ratings (Par 101): **99,93,91,89,89 82,81,77**
CSF £5.93 CT £21.85 TOTE £2.60: £1.10, £1.40, £2.10; EX 6.80 Trifecta £27.20.
**Owner** The Hollinbridge Partnership & Ruth Carr **Bred** Gestut Hofgut Heymann **Trained** Huby, N Yorks
**FOCUS**
A moderate handicap, but a good chance the winner can do better.

## 1805 COLLECT TOTEPOOL WINNINGS AT BETFRED SHOPS MAIDEN STKS 1m (F)
7:45 (7:46) (Class 5) 3-Y-O+ £2,587 (£770; £384; £192) Stalls Low

Form RPR
432 1 **Pearl Princess (FR)**13 1498 3-8-7 68 HarryBentley 2 69
(Olly Stevens) *cl up: swtchd wd over 2f out and sn rdn: led wl over 1f out: clr ent fnl f* 4/6[1]
4-2 2 11 **Missy Wells**23 1303 4-9-4 0 JasonHart(3) 4 48
(Mark Walford) *chsd ldng pair on outer: green and pushed along over 4f out: rdn along and outpcd wl over 2f out: styd on u.p fnl f to take modest 2nd nr line* 7/2[3]
60- 3 1/2 **Crafted (IRE)**173 7766 3-8-12 0 JoeFanning 1 54
(Mark Johnston) *led: rdn along towards inner whn green and jinked lft 2f out: sn hdd: drvn and wkng whn swvd bdly rt jst ins fnl f: lost modest 2nd nr line* 9/4[2]
00-5 4 20 **Lenderking (IRE)**97 268 6-9-12 26 StevieDonohoe 3 6
(Michael Chapman) *chsd ldng pair: rdn along after 3f: outpcd and bhd fnl 3f* 100/1
1m 45.91s (2.21) **Going Correction** +0.275s/f (Slow)
**WFA** 3 from 4yo+ 14lb 4 Ran SP% **114.0**
Speed ratings (Par 103): **99,88,87,67**
CSF £3.77 TOTE £1.20; EX 2.50 Trifecta £3.00.
**Owner** Pearl Bloodstock Ltd **Bred** Aliette Forien & Gilles Forien **Trained** Chiddingfold, Surrey
**FOCUS**
What turned out to be a very weak maiden. The winner is rated to form.

## 1806 PUNCHESTOWN FESTIVAL POOLS FROM TOMORROW H'CAP 2m (F)
8:15 (8:15) (Class 6) (0-65,65) 4-Y-O+ £2,264 (£673; £336; £168) Stalls Low

Form RPR
4-03 1 **Dynastic**13 1501 5-9-3 63 LauraBarry(7) 5 73
(Tony Coyle) *t.k.h: trckd ldrs: effrt and slipped through on inner to ld 3f out: rdn clr 2f out: styd on wl* 3/1[3]
4210 2 2 1/2 **Adili (IRE)**7 1605 5-9-3 56 LukeMorris 6 63
(Michael Appleby) *trckd ldng pair: effrt and hdwy 3f out: rdn to chse wnr over 2f out: drvn over 1f out and sn no imp* 2/1[1]
2236 3 6 **Royal Marskell**29 1197 5-9-11 64 TomEaves 3 64
(Alison Hutchinson) *swtchd rt s: hld up in rr: smooth hdwy on outer over 3f out: wd st: rdn to chse ldng pair 2f out: drvn over 1f out: sn edgd lft and no imp* 11/4[2]
2012 4 3 1/4 **Marina Ballerina**13 1501 6-9-7 65 (p) PhilipPrince(5) 4 61
(Roy Bowring) *t.k.h: cl up: led after 4f: pushed along 4f out: rdn and hdd 3f out: sn wknd* 6/1
2320 5 6 **Honest Strike (USA)**7 1605 7-9-9 62 (be) StephenCraine 2 51
(Daniel Mark Loughnane) *trckd ldrs: hdwy over 4f out: rdn along 3f out: sn wknd* 12/1
1350 6 8 **Joyful Motive**14 1485 5-8-11 50 StevieDonohoe 1 29
(Michael Chapman) *led 4f: cl up on inner: pushed along and lost pl over 5f out: sn rdn and outpcd fnl 4f* 14/1
3m 51.66s (6.16) **Going Correction** +0.275s/f (Slow) 6 Ran SP% **113.6**
Speed ratings (Par 101): **95,93,90,89,86 82**
CSF £9.65 TOTE £8.00: £3.40, £1.60; EX 14.60 Trifecta £58.90.
**Owner** Michael Anthony O'Donnell **Bred** Castleton Lyons & Kilboy Estate **Trained** Norton, N Yorks
**FOCUS**
A very modest stayers' handicap run at a very steady pace until the final three-quarters of a mile. The winner is rated to the best of last season's form.
T/Plt: £46.10 to a £1 stake. Pool of £45334.92 - 716.95 winning tickets. T/Qpdt: £44.50 to a £1 stake. Pool of £3774.70 - 62.70 winning tickets. JR

# 1488 WINDSOR (R-H)
### Monday, April 28

**OFFICIAL GOING: Soft (heavy in places) (final 3f soft) changing to soft after race 2 (6.05)**
Top bend dolled out 3yds, adding 10yds to races of one mile and beyond
Wind: Light, against Weather: Cloudy

## 1807 UNIBET - BY PLAYERS FOR PLAYERS EBF MAIDEN STKS 5f 10y
5:35 (5:35) (Class 5) 2-Y-O £2,911 (£866; £432; £216) Stalls Low

Form RPR
6 1 **Justice Good (IRE)**17 1417 2-9-5 0 LiamKeniry 5 87
(David Elsworth) *led after 150yds and racd against nr side rail: shkn up ins fnl f: nvr seriously threatened* 1/1[1]
2 1 **Dougal (IRE)** 2-9-5 0 RichardHughes 2 84
(Richard Hannon) *broke wl: led 150yds: sn in 3rd: trckd wnr 2f out: plld out ins fnl f: shkn up and no imp nr fin* 5/4[2]
0 3 6 1/4 **Arlecchino's Leap**17 1417 2-9-5 0 DavidProbert 3 61
(Mark Usher) *trckd wnr over 3f out to 2f out: hung lft over 1f out: wknd* 16/1[3]
4 8 **Storming Harry** 2-9-5 0 WilliamCarson 4 32
(Robin Dickin) *s.s: in tch: hung lft fr 2f out: wknd* 66/1
5 6 **Edmund Halley (FR)** 2-9-5 0 DaneO'Neill 1 11
(Harry Dunlop) *s.i.s: sn in last: hanging bdly lft fr 2f out: sn wl bhd* 20/1
1m 4.57s (4.27) **Going Correction** +0.725s/f (Yiel) 5 Ran SP% **106.6**
Speed ratings (Par 92): **94,92,82,69,60**
CSF £2.29 TOTE £2.40: £1.10, £1.10; EX 2.30 Trifecta £6.10.
**Owner** Robert Ng **Bred** Mrs C Regalado-Gonzalez **Trained** Newmarket, Suffolk
**FOCUS**
Top bend dolled out 3yds, adding 10yds to races of 1m and beyond. The betting suggested this concerned only two horses, and that's how it turned out, but they both look useful types.

## 1808 NEW HORSE RACING ODDS AT UNIBET.CO.UK MAIDEN STKS 1m 67y
6:05 (6:06) (Class 5) 3-Y-O £2,587 (£770; £384; £192) Stalls Low

Form RPR
2- 1 **Man Of Harlech**214 6773 3-9-5 0 DavidProbert 3 89
(Andrew Balding) *trckd ldrs in 5th: prog over 2f out: wnt 2nd wl over 1f out and sn chalng: rdn to ld ins fnl f: styd on wl* 5/4[1]
2 3/4 **Principle Equation (IRE)** 3-9-0 0 JimCrowley 2 82
(Ralph Beckett) *trckd ldng trio: smooth prog to ld jst over 2f out: sent for home but sn hrd pressed: hdd ins fnl f: styd on but hld after* 4/1[2]

05- **3** *8* **Curbyourenthusiasm (IRE)**[147] 8123 3-9-5 0 MartinDwyer 4 69
(David Simcock) *hld up in midfield: shkn up over 3f out: outpcd over 2f out: kpt on fnl 2f to take 3rd last strides* **6/1**[3]

2 **4** *½* **Russian Remarque**[42] 988 3-9-5 0 ShaneKelly 1 67
(Jonathan Portman) *prom: gng wl 3f out: outpcd whn pushed along to chse clr ldng pair over 1f out: no imp: lost 3rd last strides* **16/1**

0- **5** *7* **Storm Rider (IRE)**[219] 6635 3-9-5 0 RichardHughes 11 51
(Richard Hannon) *nvr bttr than midfield: shkn up and no prog wl over 2f out: n.d after* **10/1**

5- **6** *1 ½* **Rapunzal**[196] 7243 3-9-0 0 DaneO'Neill 8 43
(Henry Candy) *trckd ldr: led over 3f out to jst over 2f out: wknd* **25/1**

**7** *1* **Mad Endeavour** 3-9-5 0 TomQueally 12 46
(Stuart Kittow) *nvr beyond midfield: pushed along 3f out: sn outpcd and btn* **33/1**

**8** *2* **Deadline Day (IRE)** 3-9-5 0 JackMitchell 5 41
(Roger Varian) *s.s: rn green and mostly in last: nvr a factor but modest late prog* **20/1**

0 **9** *7* **Villainous (IRE)**[16] 1433 3-9-5 0 WilliamBuick 10 25
(John Gosden) *v awkward s: mostly in last pair: shkn up and struggling over 3f out* **8/1**

**10** *4* **Beauchamp Melba** 3-9-0 0 LiamKeniry 9 11
(Paul Fitzsimons) *a in rr: struggling fr 1/2-way* **100/1**

040 **11** *3 ¾* **Abdication**[28] 1208 3-9-5 0 GeorgeBaker 6 7
(Gary Moore) *led to over 3f out: wknd qckly* **100/1**

1m 47.26s (2.56) **Going Correction** +0.425s/f (Yiel) 11 Ran SP% **118.3**
Speed ratings (Par 98): **104,103,95,94,87 86,85,83,76,72 68**
CSF £5.82 TOTE £2.10: £1.10, £2.20, £2.90; EX 8.50 Trifecta £37.50.
**Owner** Elite Racing Club **Bred** Elite Racing Club **Trained** Kingsclere, Hants

**FOCUS**
Once again the first two in the market came clear, and both look promising types. The form makes sense around the winner.

## 1809 FIRST £10 MOBILE BET RISK-FREE AT UNIBET.CO.UK MAIDEN STKS 1m 2f 7y
**6:35** (6:36) (Class 5) 3-Y-O+ £2,587 (£770; £384; £192) **Stalls** Centre

Form RPR

03- **1** **Honor Bound**[203] 7069 3-8-6 0 AndreaAtzeni 4 80+
(Ralph Beckett) *dwlt: hld up in last trio: prog 3f out: chsd clr ldr wl over 1f out: clsd to ld last 100yds: rdn out* **14/1**

6- **2** *1* **Black Shadow**[194] 7302 3-8-11 0 TomQueally 7 84
(Amanda Perrett) *t.k.h early: hld up in midfield: rdn and prog on outer fr 3f out: clsd and upsides ins fnl f: jst outpcd* **7/2**[2]

552- **3** *nk* **Tioga Pass**[184] 7533 3-8-6 73 RaulDaSilva 11 78
(Paul Cole) *t.k.h: trckd ldrs: rdn and outpcd 3f out: clsd on wd outside fr 2f out: upsides ins fnl f: jst outpcd* **20/1**

6-4 **4** *½* **Rydan (IRE)**[21] 1353 3-8-11 0 JimmyFortune 6 82
(Robert Mills) *mde most: kicked for home over 3f out: clr against nr side rail over 2f out: wilted and hdd last 100yds* **9/4**[1]

5- **5** *7* **Micras**[185] 7493 3-8-6 0 DavidProbert 8 64+
(Andrew Balding) *hld up in last trio: outpcd and rn green 3f out: urged along and modest prog fr over 1f out* **6/1**[3]

6-5 **6** *nk* **Aldborough (IRE)**[27] 1216 4-10-0 0 JimCrowley 9 71
(Ralph Beckett) *chsd ldr: rdn over 3f out: sn outpcd: lost 2nd and wknd wl over 1f out* **6/1**[3]

**7** *shd* **Rocket Ship** 3-8-11 0 JamesDoyle 5 68+
(Sir Michael Stoute) *t.k.h: hld up in midfield: outpcd and shkn up 3f out: n.d after* **8/1**

**8** *2 ¼* **Ophir** 3-8-11 0 MartinDwyer 3 64
(William Muir) *wl in tch: shkn up over 3f out: sn outpcd: n.d over 2f out* **50/1**

02- **9** *1* **White Russian**[196] 7244 3-8-6 0 HayleyTurner 1 57
(Henry Candy) *trckd ldng pair to 3f out: pushed along and steadily wknd* **10/1**

**10** *3* **Nelson Of The Nile** 3-8-11 0 ShaneKelly 2 56
(Jonathan Portman) *dwlt: a in last trio: shkn up and no prog 3f out: n.d after* **100/1**

2m 13.16s (4.46) **Going Correction** +0.425s/f (Yiel)
**WFA** 3 from 4yo 17lb 10 Ran SP% **116.1**
Speed ratings (Par 103): **99,98,97,97,91 91,91,89,89,86**
CSF £61.80 TOTE £14.10: £2.90, £1.60, £3.80; EX 96.50 Trifecta £1395.00.
**Owner** Ashley House Stud **Bred** Ashley House Stud **Trained** Kimpton, Hants
■ Stewards' Enquiry : Raul Da Silva one-day ban: careless riding (13 May)

**FOCUS**
They went steady early but the pace picked up in the mid-section of the race and those that kicked on at the top of the straight were eventually run down by the winner. The form is rated around the fourth.

## 1810 DOWNLOAD THE UNIBET PRO APP H'CAP 1m 2f 7y
**7:05** (7:05) (Class 4) (0-85,84) 4-Y-O+ £5,175 (£1,540; £769; £384) **Stalls** Centre

Form RPR

0111 **1** **Top Diktat**[16] 1439 6-9-7 84 RyanMoore 4 94
(Gary Moore) *hld up in last trio: pushed along and prog wl over 2f out: clsd to ld 1f out: drvn out* **9/4**[1]

00-3 **2** *1 ¼* **Starwatch**[21] 1351 7-8-10 73 WilliamCarson 8 80
(John Bridger) *trckd ldr: rdn 3f out: hrd drvn to cl and upsides whn wnr wnt past 1f out: kpt on* **20/1**

604- **3** *hd* **Number One London (IRE)**[166] 7864 4-9-0 77 MartinDwyer 1 83
(Brian Meehan) *trckd ldng pair: cl enough 2f out: drvn and nt qckn over 1f out: styd on again ins fnl f* **5/1**[3]

12-3 **4** *1 ¼* **Handheld**[29] 1196 7-8-8 76 (p) ShelleyBirkett(5) 3 80
(Julia Feilden) *led at decent pce: rdn over 2f out: hdd and fdd 1f out* **3/1**[2]

044- **5** *5* **Top Set (IRE)**[293] 4151 4-8-11 74 AndreaAtzeni 2 68
(Marco Botti) *wl in tch: shkn up over 3f out: no imp on ldrs 2f out: fdd* **9/1**

6-00 **6** *3* **Tight Lipped (IRE)**[29] 1196 5-8-7 75 RyanTate(5) 7 63
(James Eustace) *trckd ldng trio: urged along 3f out: steadily wknd over 2f out* **8/1**

632- **7** *nk* **Red Pilgrim (IRE)**[188] 7453 4-8-8 74 [1] RobertTart(3) 6 62
(James Toller) *a in last trio: pushed along 4f out: taken wd but no prog 3f out* **8/1**

**8** *21* **Santo Thomas (FR)**[32] 8-9-5 82 RichardHughes 5 30
(Venetia Williams) *hld up in last trio: shkn up and no prog over 3f out: wl btn after: heavily eased fnl f* **20/1**

2m 11.39s (2.69) **Going Correction** +0.425s/f (Yiel) 8 Ran SP% **114.2**
Speed ratings (Par 105): **106,105,104,103,99 97,97,80**
CSF £48.42 CT £202.66 TOTE £2.80: £1.10, £4.30, £2.40; EX 36.70 Trifecta £352.30.
**Owner** Miss T R Hale **Bred** Wretham Stud **Trained** Lower Beeding, W Sussex

**FOCUS**
An ordinary race for the grade. The winner is rated better than ever.

## 1811 DAILY UNIBET EARLY PRICES FROM 9AM H'CAP 1m 3f 135y
**7:35** (7:36) (Class 4) (0-80,80) 4-Y-O+ £5,175 (£1,540; £769; £384) **Stalls** Centre

Form RPR

414- **1** **Running Deer (IRE)**[185] 7504 5-9-1 79 LouisSteward(5) 5 88+
(Eve Johnson Houghton) *hld up bhd ldrs: gng best whn clsd 3f out: shkn up to ld over 1f out: idled sltly but rdn to assert fnl f: eased last strides* **5/1**[3]

-212 **2** *¾* **Wilhana (IRE)**[73] 612 4-9-3 77 AdamKirby 3 83
(Pam Sly) *trckd ldrs: urged along and nt qckn wl over 2f out: drvn wl over 1f out: styd on to take 2nd nr fin* **9/2**[2]

126- **3** *nk* **Opera Buff**[180] 7635 5-9-7 80 (p) JamesDoyle 2 85
(Sean Curran) *trckd ldr to 7f out: styd cl up: drvn and prog to ld over 2f out: hdd over 1f out: one pce and lost 2nd nr fin* **3/1**[1]

0002 **4** *6* **Palus San Marco (IRE)**[21] 1354 5-8-8 72 RyanTate(5) 4 70
(Tony Carroll) *prom: trckd ldr 7f out: led 4f out: rdn and hdd over 2f out: wknd over 1f out* **9/2**[2]

4-50 **5** *1 ¾* **Anton Chigurh**[16] 1439 5-9-0 80 (p) CamHardie(7) 7 72
(Brendan Powell) *dwlt: t.k.h: hld up in last: shkn up over 3f out: no prog over 2f out: wl btn after* **12/1**

1-05 **6** *1 ¾* **Busatto (USA)**[46] 942 4-9-6 80 FrannyNorton 1 69
(Mark Johnston) *sn led: hdd 4f out: stl nrly upsides over 2f out: wknd* **7/1**

00-0 **7** *10* **Significant Move**[21] 1354 7-8-12 71 TomQueally 6 48
(Stuart Kittow) *hld up in tch: shkn up and no prog over 3f out: wl btn 2f out: eased* **11/2**

2m 34.08s (4.58) **Going Correction** +0.425s/f (Yiel)
**WFA** 4 from 5yo+ 1lb 7 Ran SP% **113.6**
Speed ratings (Par 105): **101,100,100,96,95 93,87**
CSF £27.14 TOTE £6.10: £2.90, £2.80; EX 23.30 Trifecta £86.40.
**Owner** W H Ponsonby **Bred** Mrs E Henry **Trained** Blewbury, Oxon

**FOCUS**
Just a fair handicap, but an interesting betting heat and sound form.

## 1812 UNIBET OFFER DAILY JOCKEY & TRAINERS SPECIALS H'CAP 1m 3f 135y
**8:05** (8:05) (Class 5) (0-70,68) 3-Y-O £2,587 (£770; £384; £192) **Stalls** Centre

Form RPR

044- **1** **Cosette (IRE)**[208] 6954 3-9-4 65 DaneO'Neill 7 77+
(Henry Candy) *trckd ldrs: chal over 3f out: rdn to ld over 1f out: drew clr fnl f* **9/4**[1]

-233 **2** *4* **Yeah Baby (IRE)**[69] 649 3-9-7 68 RichardHughes 6 72
(Charles Hills) *hld up in last pair: quick move on inner to ld over 2f out: hdd over 1f out: no ch w wnr fnl f* **7/2**[3]

3-11 **3** *3* **Jarlath**[19] 1382 3-9-1 62 SteveDrowne 1 61
(Seamus Mullins) *trckd ldrs: stuck bhd rivals over 2f out as r was unfolding: shkn up and kpt on to take 3rd fnl f: nvr nr to chal* **5/1**

05-4 **4** *¾* **Lightning Shower (USA)**[19] 1401 3-9-2 68 DanielMuscutt(5) 5 66
(Marco Botti) *hld up in last pair: shkn up over 3f out: tried to cl on ldrs over 2f out: one pce after* **3/1**[2]

45-6 **5** *7* **Softly She Treads (IRE)**[45] 951 3-9-0 64 JemmaMarshall(3) 2 50
(Pat Phelan) *led to 8f out: led again over 3f out to over 2f out: steadily wknd* **14/1**

-546 **6** *9* **Witch From Rome**[19] 1382 3-8-3 57 (v[1]) PatrickO'Donnell(7) 3 27
(Ralph Beckett) *in tch: shkn up over 3f out: no prog over 2f out: eased whn btn over 1f out* **8/1**

5-65 **7** *21* **Confucius Legend (IRE)**[82] 488 3-8-11 58 (p) WilliamCarson 4
(Jim Boyle) *pressed ldr: led 8f out: reminder over 4f out: hdd over 3f out: wknd qckly over 2f out: t.o* **25/1**

2m 38.08s (8.58) **Going Correction** +0.425s/f (Yiel) 7 Ran SP% **116.3**
Speed ratings (Par 98): **88,85,83,82,78 72,58**
CSF £10.80 TOTE £2.30: £1.10, £3.40; EX 14.50 Trifecta £37.70.
**Owner** P A Deal/H Candy **Bred** R N Auld **Trained** Kingston Warren, Oxon

**FOCUS**
The early pace was much slower in this race than the preceding 0-80 handicap, resulting in a time 4.00sec slower. The form is rated around the runner-up.
T/Plt: £63.40 to a £1 stake. Pool of £89,592.06 - 1031.12 winning units. T/Qpdt: £30.50 to a £1 stake. Pool of £5,792.90 - 140.50 winning units. JN

# 1739 WOLVERHAMPTON (A.W) (L-H)
Monday, April 28

**OFFICIAL GOING: Standard**
Wind: Almost nil Weather: Overcast

## 1813 QUICKSILVERSLOTS MORE JACKPOTS MORE MACHINES H'CAP 7f 32y(P)
**1:50** (1:51) (Class 6) (0-60,59) 4-Y-O+ £2,264 (£673; £336; £168) **Stalls** High

Form RPR

5-61 **1** **Global Leader (IRE)**[6] 1631 4-9-3 55 6ex PatrickDonaghy 4 68+
(Paul D'Arcy) *hld up: hdwy on outer over 2f out: led wl over 1f out: pushed out* **4/11**[1]

5203 **2** *2 ½* **Schottische**[35] 1085 4-9-4 56 (v) JoeFanning 5 62
(Derek Haydn Jones) *trckd ldrs: rdn and ev ch wl over 1f out: styd on same pce fnl f* **10/1**[3]

4145 **3** *5* **Sewn Up**[16] 1448 4-9-7 59 (p) DanielTudhope 1 52
(Andrew Hollinshead) *hld up: hdwy over 1f out: no ex fnl f* **10/1**[3]

5160 **4** *nk* **Dividend Dan (IRE)**[16] 1450 4-9-4 56 PaddyAspell 6 48
(Mike Murphy) *dwlt: hdwy to chse ldr over 5f out: led 2f out: sn rdn and hdd: no ex fnl f* **25/1**

0/15 **5** *1 ¾* **Mont Signal**[27] 1228 4-9-4 56 (t) LukeMorris 3 44
(Daniel Kubler) *chsd ldrs: rdn over 2f out: edgd lft and wknd fnl f* **6/1**[2]

00-6 **6** *9* **Heart Beat Song**[54] 851 6-8-7 45 JamesSullivan 7 9
(James Moffatt) *sn led: rdn and hdd 2f out: wknd over 1f out* **33/1**

260- **7** *½* **Gladsome**[299] 3946 6-9-7 59 TomEaves 2 22
(Michael Herrington) *hld up: bhd fnl 3f* **40/1**

1m 29.04s (-0.56) **Going Correction** -0.025s/f (Stan) 7 Ran SP% **115.0**
Speed ratings (Par 101): **102,99,93,93,91 80,80**
CSF £5.11 TOTE £1.30: £1.10, £3.10; EX 4.20 Trifecta £15.70.
**Owner** Dr J S Kinnear **Bred** Thomas J Murphy **Trained** Newmarket, Suffolk

**FOCUS**
This race revolved around the favourite, who looked well treated under a penalty and recorded a similar figure.

## 1814 QUICKSILVERSLOTS PLAY FROM 10P TO £2 CLASSIFIED CLAIMING STKS 5f 20y(P)
**2:20** (2:20) (Class 6) 3-Y-O+ **£2,264** (£673; £336; £168) **Stalls** Low

Form RPR
0-21 **1** **Come On Dave (IRE)**[51] 889 5-9-5 70........................ AdrianNicholls 4 72
(David Nicholls) *mde all and sn clr: shkn up 2f out: drvn out* **8/11**[1]
040- **2** *1 3/4* **Speightowns Kid (USA)**[140] 8224 6-9-9 63........................ TomEaves 5 70
(Michael Herrington) *trckd wnr tl over 3f out: rdn to go 2nd again ins fnl f: r.o* **25/1**
-621 **3** *3/4* **Red Cape (FR)**[17] 1431 11-9-1 66........................(b) JamesSullivan 3 59
(Ruth Carr) *hld up: rdn over 1f out: r.o ins fnl f: nvr nrr* **5/1**[3]
045- **4** *1 3/4* **Avonvalley**[273] 4837 7-8-10 63........................ SladeO'Hara[(3)] 2 51
(Peter Grayson) *sn pushed along and prom: chsd wnr who was clr over 3f out: rdn and lost 2nd ins fnl f: no ex* **12/1**
-030 **5** *2 1/4* **Lady In Blue (IRE)**[11] 1543 3-8-13 65........................(v) DanielTudhope 1 49
(David O'Meara) *s.i.s: hld up: rdn 1/2-way: n.d* **3/1**[2]
1m 1.84s (-0.46) **Going Correction** -0.025s/f (Stan)
**WFA** 3 from 5yo+ 10lb 5 Ran SP% 111.1
Speed ratings (Par 101): **102,99,98,95,91**
CSF £19.57 TOTE £1.40: £1.10, £6.40; EX 11.80 Trifecta £43.30.
**Owner** Middleham Park Racing XLIV **Bred** Mrs Eithne Hamilton **Trained** Sessay, N Yorks

**FOCUS**
This was a weak 5f claimer and the favourite was a clear-cut winner. He's rated close to form.

## 1815 QUICKSILVERSLOTS PLAY £500 JACKPOT RAINBOW RICHES H'CAP 1m 4f 50y(P)
**2:50** (2:50) (Class 5) (0-70,69) 4-Y-O+ **£2,587** (£770; £384; £192) **Stalls** Low

Form RPR
5155 **1** **Spanish Plume**[6] 1628 6-9-4 66........................(p) DanielTudhope 4 75
(Andrew Hollinshead) *mde all: clr 5f out: rdn out* **11/2**
2152 **2** *3* **Sian Gwalia**[6] 1628 4-9-6 69........................ MartinLane 6 73
(David Simcock) *racd keenly: hdwy to go 3rd 10f out: chsd wnr over 2f out: rdn over 1f out: styd on same pce ins fnl f* **2/1**[1]
6-02 **3** *hd* **Mcbirney (USA)**[7] 1617 7-9-3 65........................ PatrickDonaghy 2 69
(Paul D'Arcy) *hld up: hdwy over 4f out: rdn over 1f out: styd on* **9/4**[2]
604- **4** *6* **Petrify**[191] 7383 4-8-8 57........................ StevieDonohoe 5 51
(Bernard Llewellyn) *trckd wnr: plld hrd: rdn 3f out: sn lost 2nd: wknd fnl f* **10/1**
2031 **5** *6* **Well Owd Mon**[16] 1453 4-8-11 60........................ JamesSullivan 3 45
(Andrew Hollinshead) *prom: plld hrd: rdn over 4f out: wknd 3f out* **7/2**[3]
2m 43.2s (2.10) **Going Correction** -0.025s/f (Stan)
**WFA** 4 from 6yo+ 1lb 5 Ran SP% 110.8
Speed ratings (Par 103): **92,90,89,85,81**
CSF £17.00 TOTE £10.10: £4.20, £1.30; EX 20.90 Trifecta £45.60.
**Owner** The Three R'S **Bred** Mrs J A Prescott **Trained** Upper Longdon, Staffs

**FOCUS**
The winner got an easy lead and this isn't form to take too literally.

## 1816 QUICKSILVERSLOTS OPEN AFTER 10PM CLAIMING STKS 1m 1f 103y(P)
**3:20** (3:22) (Class 6) 4-Y-O+ **£2,264** (£673; £336; £168) **Stalls** Low

Form RPR
50-4 **1** **Licence To Till (USA)**[13] 1495 7-9-3 78........................ JoeFanning 4 87
(Mark Johnston) *mde all: shkn up over 1f out: styd on wl* **5/1**[3]
30-0 **2** *3/4* **War Poet**[29] 1196 7-9-3 80........................ SilvestreDeSousa 6 86
(Brian Ellison) *a.p: rdn over 2f out: chsd wnr ins fnl f: styd on* **6/5**[1]
5431 **3** *3/4* **Back Burner (IRE)**[13] 1495 6-9-4 79........................ AdrianNicholls 2 85
(David Nicholls) *plld hrd: trckd wnr: rdn and ev ch over 2f out: styd on u.p* **7/4**[2]
5010 **4** *14* **Dazzling Valentine**[2] 1729 6-7-13 61........................(v) NatashaEaton[(5)] 3 42
(Alan Bailey) *sn pushed along to chse ldrs: rdn over 2f out: wknd over 1f out* **12/1**
0 **5** *9* **Lower Lake (FR)**[16] 1452 4-9-9 0........................ LukeMorris 5 42
(Mark Brisbourne) *hld up: rdn over 3f out: sn wknd* **100/1**
2m 0.58s (-1.12) **Going Correction** -0.025s/f (Stan) 5 Ran SP% 107.2
Speed ratings (Par 101): **103,102,101,89,81**
CSF £10.81 TOTE £7.00: £2.60, £1.10; EX 12.30 Trifecta £22.00.Back Burner was claimed by D Burchell for £10500. Licence To Till was claimed by T Dascombe for £10000.
**Owner** The Vine Accord **Bred** John Hettinger **Trained** Middleham Moor, N Yorks
■ Exemplary was withdrawn. Price at time of withdrawal 14/1. Rule 4 applies to all bets - deduct 5p in the pound.

**FOCUS**
This was a good claimer on paper and, after Exemplary was withdrawn at the start, the three highest-rated horses in the field finished clear. There are doubts over the form, however.

## 1817 QUICKSILVERSLOTS £1 TO WIN £500 MEDIAN AUCTION MAIDEN STKS 1m 141y(P)
**3:50** (3:52) (Class 5) 3-5-Y-O **£2,587** (£770; £384; £192) **Stalls** Low

Form RPR
**1** **Luck Of The Game (USA)** 3-8-12 0........................ MartinLane 7 76+
(David Simcock) *sn pushed along and rn green in rr: rdn over 2f out: hdwy to ld and hung rt over 1f out: r.o* **13/8**[1]
3020 **2** *1/2* **Brownsville (USA)**[33] 1101 3-8-12 69........................ JoeFanning 3 72+
(Mark Johnston) *led: rdn and hung rt wl over 1f out: sn hdd: r.o* **6/1**[3]
5- **3** *6* **Interconnection**[255] 5488 3-8-12 0........................ LukeMorris 4 65+
(Ed Vaughan) *chsd ldrs: rdn over 2f out: ev ch whn hmpd ins fnl f: nt rcvr* **7/4**[2]
0-6 **4** *3/4* **Light Of Asia (IRE)**[19] 1394 3-8-12 0........................ PaddyAspell 5 56
(Ed Dunlop) *s.i.s: sn prom: rdn over 2f out: styd on same pce fr over 1f out* **10/1**
44 **5** *4 1/2* **Arianrhod (IRE)**[42] 988 3-8-8 71 ow1........................(p) AntonioFresu 1 42
(Marco Botti) *trckd ldr: rdn over 2f out: sn edgd rt: wknd fnl f* **7/1**
0 **6** *16* **Enniscorthy Myles (USA)**[30] 1166 3-8-12 0........................ StevieDonohoe 6 9
(Tim Pitt) *hld up: racd keenly: rdn over 3f out: sn wknd* **33/1**
1m 50.07s (-0.43) **Going Correction** -0.025s/f (Stan) 6 Ran SP% 113.3
Speed ratings (Par 103): **100,99,94,93,89 75**
CSF £12.09 TOTE £3.20: £2.00, £3.10; EX 7.90 Trifecta £21.80.
**Owner** Michael Tabor **Bred** Chelston **Trained** Newmarket, Suffolk

**FOCUS**
This maiden was a race full of incident that eventually saw the well-backed favourite get up to win. He was very green and looks sure to improve.

## 1818 QUICKSILVERSLOTS PLAY YOUR FAVOURITE £500 JACKPOT H'CAP (BOBIS RACE) 5f 216y(P)
**4:20** (4:21) (Class 4) (0-80,80) 3-Y-O **£5,175** (£1,540; £769; £384) **Stalls** Low

Form RPR
3-1 **1** **Dreese (IRE)**[31] 1147 3-9-4 77........................ LukeMorris 2 86+
(James Tate) *s.i.s: sn pushed along in rr: hdwy over 2f out: led over 1f out: drvn out* **7/4**[1]
213- **2** *3/4* **Miss Atomic Bomb**[178] 7662 3-9-0 78........................ MarcMonaghan[(5)] 5 84
(Marco Botti) *hld up in tch: rdn and ev ch over 1f out: hung lft and flashed tail ins fnl f: styd on* **8/1**
2240 **3** *2 1/4* **Spreadable (IRE)**[3] 1700 3-8-9 75........................(b) JordanVaughan[(7)] 8 74
(Nick Littmoden) *stdd s: hld up: r.o ins fnl f: wnt 3rd nr fin: nt trble ldrs* **3/1**[2]
21-3 **4** *1/2* **Invoke (IRE)**[18] 1409 3-9-0 73........................ StevieDonohoe 3 70
(Michael Bell) *w ldr tl led over 3f out: rdn and hdd over 1f out: no ex ins fnl f* **16/1**
0-62 **5** *1/2* **Minley**[31] 1146 3-8-11 75........................ LouisSteward[(5)] 1 71
(Charlie Fellowes) *trckd ldrs: rdn and ev ch over 1f out: no ex ins fnl f* **7/1**
303- **6** *3 1/2* **Straits Of Malacca**[200] 7147 3-8-5 69........................ KevinStott[(5)] 6 53
(Kevin Ryan) *s.i.s: sn rcvrd to ld: hdd over 3f out: rdn and ev ch over 1f out: wknd ins fnl f* **8/1**
-220 **7** *7* **Aspirant**[20] 1358 3-9-7 80........................(tp) SilvestreDeSousa 4 42
(Brian Ellison) *plld hrd and prom: rdn and wknd over 1f out* **6/1**[3]
1m 14.37s (-0.63) **Going Correction** -0.025s/f (Stan) 7 Ran SP% 116.3
Speed ratings (Par 100): **103,102,99,98,97 93,83**
CSF £17.27 CT £40.25 TOTE £2.80: £1.90, £2.30; EX 9.30 Trifecta £43.30.
**Owner** Saeed Manana **Bred** W Shaughnessy **Trained** Newmarket, Suffolk

**FOCUS**
This was a competitive 3yo handicap with plenty of previous winners and there were five in with a chance in the straight. The winner was well on top at the line despite doing plenty wrong.

## 1819 QUICKSILVERSLOTS FUN ON THE HIGH STREET APPRENTICE H'CAP 1m 141y(P)
**4:50** (4:51) (Class 6) (0-55,54) 4-Y-O+ **£2,264** (£673; £336; £168) **Stalls** Low

Form RPR
0320 **1** **Katmai River (IRE)**[19] 1385 7-9-5 52........................ CharlotteJenner 6 58
(Mark Usher) *hld up: hdwy over 3f out: chsd ldr 2f out: sn rdn: r.o to ld wl ins fnl f* **5/2**[1]
0300 **2** *nk* **Daniel Thomas (IRE)**[32] 1138 12-8-10 50(tp) NatalieHambling-Yates[(7)] 7 55
(Ann Stokell) *s.i.s: hld up: hdwy 2f out: r.o* **14/1**
0456 **3** *3/4* **Devote Myself (IRE)**[24] 1288 5-9-1 48........................(bt[1]) JackGarritty 5 51
(John Flint) *trckd ldr tl led over 3f out: rdn over 1f out: hdd and unable qck wl ins fnl f* **9/1**
4621 **4** *2* **Supa Seeker (USA)**[46] 939 8-8-13 51........................ MrAidenBlakemore[(5)] 3 50
(Tony Carroll) *hld up: hdwy over 1f out: rdn and hung lft ins fnl f: nt trble ldrs* **7/1**[3]
-145 **5** *3 3/4* **De Lesseps (USA)**[55] 833 6-8-12 50........................ JoshQuinn[(5)] 8 40
(James Moffatt) *chsd ldrs: lost pl over 3f out: hmpd over 2f out: n.d after* **5/2**[1]
000- **6** *1* **Alberto**[141] 7266 4-8-11 47........................ PaulBooth[(3)] 1 35
(Alastair Lidderdale) *hld up: hdwy 1/2-way: chsd ldr over 3f out tl rdn 2f out: wknd fnl f* **25/1**
6-20 **7** *2 3/4* **Flying Giant (IRE)**[97] 269 4-9-0 54........................ KieranShoemark[(7)] 4 35
(Jo Hughes) *chsd ldrs: rdn over 2f out: wknd wl over 1f out* **7/2**[2]
5006 **8** *11* **Hejaz (IRE)**[24] 1284 4-9-6 53........................(tp) JennyPowell 2 9
(Tim Pitt) *led 5f: wknd over 2f out* **20/1**
1m 50.96s (0.46) **Going Correction** -0.025s/f (Stan) 8 Ran SP% 117.1
Speed ratings (Par 101): **96,95,95,93,89 89,86,76**
CSF £40.56 CT £277.26 TOTE £3.00: £1.10, £4.40, £3.00; EX 37.50 Trifecta £284.40.
**Owner** M D I Usher **Bred** Mrs S M Roy **Trained** Upper Lambourn, Berks
■ Stewards' Enquiry : Josh Quinn one-day ban: careless riding (12 May)

**FOCUS**
A weak apprentice handicap. The 1-2-3 are rated pretty much to recent marks.
T/Plt: £16.60 to a £1 stake. Pool: £40849.4, 1791.04 winning tickets T/Qpdt: £9.50 to a £1 stake. Pool of £2560.65 - 199.30 winning tickets. CR

# NAAS (L-H)
Monday, April 28
**OFFICIAL GOING: Round course - good to yielding; straight course - good**

## 1824a WOODLANDS STKS (LISTED RACE) 5f
**6:55** (6:57) 3-Y-O+ **£21,666** (£6,333; £3,000; £1,000)

RPR
**1** **Guerre (USA)**[211] 6882 3-9-0 103 ow1........................ JosephO'Brien 4 108
(A P O'Brien, Ire) *chsd ldrs: tk clsr order in 2nd bef 1/2-way: led 2f out and rdn clr ent fnl f: styd on wl towards fin: readily* **11/4**[1]
**2** *1 1/2* **Maarek**[22] 1333 7-10-0 113........................ DeclanMcDonogh 1 111
(Miss Evanna McCutcheon, Ire) *dwlt sltly and racd towards rr: tk clsr order fr 1/2-way: rdn in 4th under 2f out and clsd u.p between horses into 2nd fnl 100yds: kpt on wl wout troubling wnr* **7/2**[2]
**3** *hd* **Nocturnal Affair (SAF)**[185] 7521 8-9-9 103........................ FergalLynch 3 105
(David Marnane, Ire) *chsd ldrs: swtchd in 4th 1 1/2f out and clsd u.p to dispute 2nd ins fnl f: no imp on wnr in 3rd ins fnl 100yds: kpt on wl* **20/1**
**4** *2 1/4* **Timeless Call (IRE)**[185] 7521 6-9-7 101........................ PatSmullen 8 95+
(Reginald Roberts, Ire) *prom on nr side: rdn in 2nd ent fnl f and sn no imp on wnr in 4th: kpt on one pce* **14/1**
**5** *nk* **Scream Blue Murder (IRE)**[22] 1333 4-9-7 104........................ WayneLordan 9 94+
(T Stack, Ire) *in tch: rdn in 6th 1 1/2f out and no imp on ldrs u.p in 5th ins fnl f: kpt on one pce* **7/2**[2]
**6** *3/4* **Leitir Mor (IRE)**[191] 7366 4-9-12 109........................(p) KevinManning 10 96
(J S Bolger, Ire) *dwlt and racd towards rr: rdn in 9th fr 2f out and wnt mod 6th ins fnl f: kpt on towards fin wout ever troubling principals* **16/1**
**7** *1 1/4* **Srucahan (IRE)**[15] 1475 5-9-9 94........................(v) ChrisHayes 5 89
(P D Deegan, Ire) *dwlt sltly and racd towards rr: rdn in 7th under 2f out and no imp on ldrs: kpt on one pce* **14/1**
**8** *1* **An Saighdiur (IRE)**[22] 1333 7-9-12 107........................ BillyLee 6 88
(Andrew Slattery, Ire) *chsd ldrs on nr side: rdn and no ex fr after 1/2-way: one pce fnl 2f* **9/2**[3]

9 2 **Lottie Dod (IRE)**45 965 4-9-4 93 FMBerry 7 73
(Charles O'Brien, Ire) *chsd ldrs early tl dropped towards rr at 1/2-way: no imp after: one pce fnl 2f* **25/1**

10 shd **Allegra Tak (ITY)**15 1475 8-9-4 82 (tp) DannyGrant 2 72
(H Rogers, Ire) *prom on far side: pushed along w narrow advantage 1/2-way: hdd u.p 2f out: sn wknd* **100/1**

57.84s (-4.16)
**WFA** 3 from 4yo+ 10lb **10** Ran SP% **118.1**
CSF £12.35 TOTE £3.10: £1.02, £2.20, £4.30; DF 11.60 Trifecta £174.60.
**Owner** Derrick Smith & Mrs John Magnier & Michael Tabor **Bred** Ponder Hill Inc **Trained** Cashel, Co Tipperary
**FOCUS**
It's premature to say Guerre is a candidate for top sprinting honours this year but it was hard not to be impressed with this performance.

1825 - 1826a (Foreign Racing) - See Raceform Interactive

## 1527 CHANTILLY (R-H)
Monday, April 28
**OFFICIAL GOING: Turf: very soft; polytrack: standard**

### 1827a PRIX ALLEZ FRANCE (GROUP 3) (4YO+ FILLIES & MARES) (TURF) 1m 2f
**2:55** (12:00) 4-Y-O+ **£33,333** (£13,333; £10,000; £6,666; £3,333)

RPR

1 **Daksha (FR)**22 4-8-7 0 ThierryThulliez 5 106
(Waldemar Hickst, Germany) *in midfield: 8th and short of room 2 1/2f out: rdn to qckn through gap under 2f out: r.o wl under hands and heels fnl f: led cl home* **27/1**

2 snk **Entree**25 1274 4-8-7 0 StephanePasquier 10 106
(P Bary, France) *t.k.h: trckd ldr: shkn up to chal 1 1/2f out: rdn to ld over 1f out: r.o u.p fnl f: hdd cl home* **5/1**2

3 1 1/2 **Siljan's Saga (FR)**29 4-8-8 0 ow1 Pierre-CharlesBoudot 9 104
(J-P Gauvin, France) *w.w towards rr on outer: pushed along over 2f out and sed to pick up 1 1/2f out: styd on wl fnl f to take 3rd fnl strides* **113/10**

4 snk **Ipswich (IRE)**25 1274 4-8-7 0 GeraldMosse 13 102
(A De Royer-Dupre, France) *prom on outer: led appr 2f out: rdn 1 1/2f out: hdd appr fnl f: one pce u.p fnl f: lost 3rd fnl strides* **67/10**

5 nk **Gaga A (URU)**29 5-8-9 0 GregoryBenoist 3 104
(D Smaga, France) *hld up bhd ldng gp: rdn and briefly short of room 1 1/2f out: kpt on fnl f: nt gng pce to threaten ldrs* **141/10**

6 snk **Sparkling Beam (IRE)**251 5629 4-9-0 0 ThierryJarnet 8 109
(J E Pease, France) *dwlt: settled towards rr: hdwy into midfield 1/2-way: 6th whn forced to switch to outside over 2f out: bmpd 1 1/2f out: kpt on under driving fnl f: nt pce to trble ldrs* **58/10**3

7 1 1/4 **Venturous Spirit (FR)**22 4-8-7 0 (b) Christophe-PatriceLemaire 2 99
(M Delzangles, France) *prom on ins: rdn and nt qckn 1 1/2f out: one pce fnl f* **31/1**

8 1/2 **No News (FR)**29 4-8-7 0 ThomasMessina 1 98
(X Nakkachdji, France) *wnt rt leaving stalls: w.w towards rr: effrt on ins over 1 1/2f out: one pce fnl f* **59/10**

9 1/2 **Vally Jem (FR)**44 984 5-8-9 0 AntoineHamelin 11 99
(D Sepulchre, France) *in rr: last and rdn 1 1/2f out: nt clr run over 1f out: styd on fnl 150yds: nvr in contention* **27/1**

10 nk **Alumna (USA)**29 4-8-9 0 MaximeGuyon 4 98
(A Fabre, France) *w.w towards rr: pushed along over 3f out: n.m.r and hmpd 2f out: kpt on fnl f but nt persevered w fnl 50yds* **23/5**1

11 nk **Intimhir (IRE)**29 4-8-7 0 FlavienPrat 6 96
(F Head, France) *t.k.h: hld up towards rr: rdn and no imp fr 2f out* **142/10**

12 2 1/2 **Nausica Time (GER)**22 4-8-7 0 BGanbat 12 91
(S Smrczek, Germany) *rousted along to ld: hdd appr 2f out: sn wknd* **133/10**

13 7 **Adriana (GER)**169 7831 6-9-0 0 AHelfenbein 7 84
(Markus Klug, Germany) *tk v t.k.h in midfield: trckd ldrs fr 1/2-way: 4th and rdn over 2f out: reminder and wnt lft and bmpd rival 1 1/2f out: sn wknd* **247/10**

2m 3.9s (-0.90) **13** Ran SP% **119.2**
WIN (incl. 1 euro stake): 28.30. PLACES: 8.20, 2.40, 3.60. DF: 107.10. SF: 225.30.
**Owner** Gestut Ittlingen **Bred** Gestut Hof Ittlingen **Trained** Germany

## 1271 MAISONS-LAFFITTE (R-H)
Tuesday, April 22
**OFFICIAL GOING: Turf: good to soft**

### 1828a PRIX DE TRIE-CHATEAU (CLAIMER) (5YO+) (TURF) 1m 4f 110y
**2:20** (12:00) 5-Y-O+ **£7,916** (£3,166; £2,375; £1,583; £791)

RPR

1 **Le Roumois (FR)**40 8-8-11 0 (b) MaximeGuyon 4 81
(E Libaud, France) **5/2**1

2 1 1/4 **Val De Majorque (FR)**194 6-8-11 0 (b) TheoBachelot 5 79
(D Sepulchre, France) **205/10**

3 nk **Le Reverend (FR)**7 5-9-1 0 (p) FlavienPrat 7 83
(D Windrif, France) **10/1**

4 1 1/4 **Cabaretune (FR)**23 9-9-1 0 CristianDemuro 3 81
(F Doumen, France) **31/5**

5 hd **Roxy De Vindecy (FR)**23 9-9-2 0 RonanThomas 10 82
(J Phelippon, France) **57/10**3

6 snk **Incendo**25 1140 8-9-2 0 (p) StevieDonohoe 8 81
(Ian Williams) *dwlt sltly and hld up in rr on inner: rdn and looking for room over 2f out: swtchd lft over 1f out: styd on ins fnl f but nt pce to chal* **11/1**

7 nk **Ranyan (SPA)**370 5-9-2 0 BFayosMartin 11 81
(E Buzon Bobillo, Spain) **26/1**

8 nk **Lord Emery (GER)**23 6-8-11 0 UmbertoRispoli 1 75
(M Figge, Germany) **163/10**

9 9 **Barongo (IRE)**33 9-9-1 0 GeraldMosse 2 66
(Mme B Suter, France) **47/10**2

10 7 **Monsynn (FR)**22 5-8-11 0 (b) MarcLerner 6 51
(C Lerner, France) **132/10**

11 2 1/2 **Aristote**116 8-9-4 0 JeromeCabre 9 55
(P Van De Poele, France) **161/10**

2m 43.22s (163.22) **11** Ran SP% **119.4**
WIN (incl. 1 euro stake): 3.50. PLACES: 1.90, 5.10, 2.70. DF: 33.70. SF: 60.10.
**Owner** Mme Olivier Lecerf **Bred** Olivier & Jean Lecerf **Trained** France

## 1553 LINGFIELD (L-H)
Tuesday, April 29
**OFFICIAL GOING: Standard**
Wind: Light; half against Weather: Cloudy becoming fine

### 1829 BREATHE SPA AT LINGFIELD PARK RESORT CLAIMING STKS 7f 1y(P)
**1:25** (1:25) (Class 6) 3-Y-O **£2,045** (£603; £302) **Stalls** Low

Form RPR

2615 1 **Little Big Man**76 573 3-9-1 67 (b) RichardHughes 4 69
(Sylvester Kirk) *t.k.h: chsd ldr: clr of rest 1/2-way: 3 l down 2f out: rdn and clsd over 1f out: led ins fnl f: styd on* **1/1**1

250 2 1 1/4 **Black Vale (IRE)**5 1669 3-8-13 66 (t) DavidProbert 1 64
(Phil McEntee) *racd freely: led: 3 l clr 2f out: sn rdn: hdd and no ex ins fnl f* **5/4**2

-440 3 9 **Synonym (ITY)**29 1211 3-8-4 50 HarryBentley 2 31
(J W Hills) *outpcd in last and pushed along after 3f: no ch: kpt on to take remote 3rd nr fin* **16/1**

5U60 4 3/4 **Sand Stormer (IRE)**25 1277 3-9-1 60 MartinDwyer 5 40
(William Muir) *racd in 4th: rdn to chse ldng pair 1/2-way but outpcd: no imp: lost 3rd nr fin* **12/1**3

060- 5 1 **Fenella Foghorn**197 7243 3-8-13 50 MatthewLawson(3) 3 39
(Jonathan Portman) *chsd ldng pair: outpcd and dropped to 4th 1/2-way: no ch after* **50/1**

1m 24.24s (-0.56) **Going Correction** -0.075s/f (Stan) **5** Ran SP% **110.0**
Speed ratings (Par 96): **100,98,88,87,86**
CSF £2.50 TOTE £1.30: £1.10, £1.40; EX 2.50 Trifecta £8.20.
**Owner** N Simpson & S Kirk **Bred** Paul Merritt **Trained** Upper Lambourn, Berks
**FOCUS**
Essentially a match and so it played out. The winner is rated to his Polytrack best.

### 1830 FELCOURT MEDIAN AUCTION MAIDEN STKS 1m 2f (P)
**1:55** (1:56) (Class 6) 3-4-Y-O **£2,420** (£714; £357) **Stalls** Low

Form RPR

46-2 1 **Big Orange**20 1380 3-8-11 83 TomQueally 7 80
(Michael Bell) *mde all: gng best fr 3f out: rdn fnl f: edgd rt but styd on* **8/11**1

3- 2 1 1/2 **Royal Warranty**141 8213 3-8-6 0 DavidProbert 6 73
(Andrew Balding) *mostly chsd wnr: shkn up 3f out: kpt on but nvr able to chal* **5/1**3

2-3 3 nk **Invasor Luck (USA)**20 1380 3-8-11 0 FrederikTylicki 5 77
(James Fanshawe) *trckd ldng pair: cl enough over 2f out: rdn to dispute 2nd over 1f out: one pce* **7/2**2

4 4 1/2 **Sixties Love** 3-8-6 0 MickaelBarzalona 3 63
(Simon Dow) *a in 4th: shoved along and outpcd 3f out: no imp after* **50/1**

5 4 **Monsieur Chabal** 3-8-11 0 FergusSweeney 8 61?
(Jamie Osborne) *dwlt: hld up in 6th: outpcd and pushed along 3f out: reminder fnl f: no threat* **100/1**

20 6 1/2 **Drifter (IRE)**26 1269 3-8-11 0 1 StephenCraine 2 60
(Tom Dascombe) *s.s: t.k.h early: hld up in last: outpcd and pushed along 3f out: reminder fnl f: nvr in it* **16/1**

00- 7 2 **Lochalsh (IRE)**204 7069 3-8-11 0 JimCrowley 1 56
(William Knight) *s.i.s: hld up in 5th: shkn up and outpcd 3f out: wknd over 1f out* **25/1**

2m 6.81s (0.21) **Going Correction** -0.075s/f (Stan) **7** Ran SP% **109.5**
Speed ratings (Par 101): **96,94,94,90,87 87,85**
CSF £4.27 TOTE £1.80: £1.02, £4.80; EX 5.10 Trifecta £7.80.
**Owner** W J Gredley **Bred** Stetchworth & Middle Park Studs **Trained** Newmarket, Suffolk
**FOCUS**
An ordinary maiden but the winner and third set a fair standard. The time was slow.

### 1831 DOWNLOAD THE 888SPORT.COM MOBILE APP MAIDEN STKS 7f 1y(P)
**2:25** (2:26) (Class 5) 3-Y-O **£2,726** (£805; £402) **Stalls** Low

Form RPR

4 1 **Slemy (IRE)**20 1394 3-9-5 0 FrankieDettori 1 83
(Richard Hannon) *mde all: kicked clr wl over 1f out: wl in command after: rdn out* **11/10**2

0 2 1 3/4 **Red Velour**12 1534 3-9-0 0 SebSanders 3 73
(Jeremy Noseda) *a in 2nd: nt qckn whn wnr kicked on wl over 1f out: kpt on but nvr able to threaten* **10/11**1

0 3 3 **Dynamic Vision (IRE)**13 1511 3-9-5 0 JackMitchell 4 71
(Roger Varian) *in tch in last: rdn 3f out: sn outpcd: kpt on u.p to take 3rd ins fnl f* **25/1**

0 4 2 1/4 **Native Heart**18 1422 3-9-0 0 LiamKeniry 2 60
(Mick Channon) *chsd ldng pair: rdn and outpcd fr 2f out: lost 3rd and fdd ins fnl f* **20/1**3

5 5 **Crafty Business (IRE)** 3-9-5 0 RobertHavlin 5 52?
(Mark Hoad) *s.i.s: in tch in 4th: rdn over 2f out: sn outpcd: wknd fnl f* **100/1**

1m 24.51s (-0.29) **Going Correction** -0.075s/f (Stan) **5** Ran SP% **109.6**
Speed ratings (Par 98): **98,96,92,90,84**
CSF £2.35 TOTE £1.90: £1.10, £1.10; EX 2.60 Trifecta £7.50.
**Owner** Al Shaqab Racing **Bred** Derek Veitch **Trained** East Everleigh, Wilts
**FOCUS**
A modest maiden. The form is rated around the winner to his debut.

### 1832 "CASH IN EARLY" AT 888SPORT.COM FILLIES' H'CAP 7f 1y(P)
**2:55** (2:55) (Class 5) (0-70,69) 3-Y-O **£3,234** (£962; £481; £240) **Stalls** Low

Form RPR

05-4 1 **Syrian Pearl**20 1379 3-8-8 59 AshleyMorgan(3) 6 64
(Chris Wall) *chsd ldr: rdn over 1f out: clsd to ld ins fnl f: drvn and styd on* **20/1**

-420 2 nk **River Goddess (IRE)**19 1403 3-9-2 64 (b1) SebSanders 3 68
(Charles Hills) *led: rdn 2f out: hdd ins fnl f: kpt on wl but a jst hld* **14/1**

33-6 3 1 3/4 **Rocksee (IRE)**25 1280 3-9-6 68 StephenCraine 2 67
(Tom Dascombe) *chsd ldng pair: rdn over 2f out: tried to chal on inner but nt qckn over 1f out: styd on same pce* **14/1**

055- **4** 1 3/4 **Cueca (FR)**[190] 7426 3-8-8 **56** MickaelBarzalona 9 51
(Jonathan Portman) *mostly in midfield: reminder over 3f out: rdn and kpt on fr over 1f out to take 4th nr fin* **25/1**

063- **5** 1/2 **Goodwood Storm**[195] 7294 3-9-7 **69** JimCrowley 11 63+
(William Knight) *stdd fr wd draw and hld up in last pair: prog 2f out: nt clr run 1f out and swtchd rt: styd on but no ch* **9/2**[2]

26-1 **6** 1/2 **Moonspring (IRE)**[39] 1045 3-9-0 **62** (e) SeanLevey 12 54+
(Robert Cowell) *dropped in fr wd draw and hld up in rr: wd and drvn bnd 2f out: styd on fnl f: no ch* **8/1**

055- **7** hd **Cadmium**[210] 6923 3-9-2 **64** DavidProbert 1 56
(Harry Dunlop) *chsd ldrs: rdn and no imp on ldng trio fr 2f out: fdd ins fnl f* **25/1**

0-63 **8** 1 3/4 **Jive**[10] 1570 3-9-7 **69** RichardHughes 10 56
(Richard Hannon) *dropped in fr wd draw and hld up in rr: prog over 2f out: pushed along and no imp on ldrs over 1f out: fdd last 100yds* **5/2**[1]

0-40 **9** 2 1/2 **Clever Miss**[13] 1507 3-9-7 **69** (p) MartinDwyer 4 50
(Alan McCabe) *pushed along early to chse ldrs: rdn over 2f out: nt qckn and no prog: wknd fnl f* **8/1**

54-0 **10** 4 1/2 **Sotise (IRE)**[12] 1534 3-9-2 **69** DanielMuscutt(5) 7 38
(Marco Botti) *hmpd over 5f out and dropped to rr: nvr on terms after: no prog over 1f out* **14/1**

642- **11** 32 **Castagna Girl**[237] 6095 3-9-2 **64** JamesDoyle 5
(Denis Coakley) *hmpd over 5f out and dropped to rr: nvr on terms after: wknd and virtually p.u over 1f out* **7/1**[3]

050- **12** 12 **Setai**[195] 7294 3-9-6 **68** FrankieDettori 8
(Brian Meehan) *pressed ldrs on outer: wknd and v wd bnd 2f out: virtually p.u* **10/1**

1m 24.61s (-0.19) **Going Correction** -0.075s/f (Stan) 12 Ran SP% **123.0**
Speed ratings (Par 95): **98,97,95,93,93 92,92,90,87,82 45,32**
CSF £278.57 CT £4017.91 TOTE £26.20: £7.40, £7.00, £5.70; EX 427.60 Trifecta £1732.50 Part won..
**Owner** The Clodhoppers **Bred** Jeremy Green And Sons **Trained** Newmarket, Suffolk

**FOCUS**
A moderate fillies' handicap in which few became involved. The bare form looks ordinary.

## 1833 £88 IN FREE BETS AT 888SPORT.COM H'CAP 6f 1y(P)
**3:25** (3:26) (Class 6) (0-60,60) 3-Y-O **£2,726** (£805; £402) **Stalls** Low

Form RPR

540- **1** **Frangipanni (IRE)**[153] 8061 3-9-7 **60** JamesDoyle 5 69+
(Roger Charlton) *dwlt: w.w in last pair: plenty to do over 2f out: gap opened and prog on inner to go 2nd wl over 1f out: angled out and hrd rdn to cl on clr ldr: styd on to ld last strides* **4/5**[1]

6-30 **2** nk **Febrayer Star (IRE)**[17] 1449 3-8-8 **47** (v) LiamKeniry 2 51
(Robert Cowell) *led and racd keenly: 4 l clr over 2f out: drvn over 1f out: collared last strides* **14/1**

-054 **3** 2 1/4 **Crystalized (IRE)**[29] 1211 3-8-13 **52** JimCrowley 6 49
(Dean Ivory) *hld up in last pair: plenty to do over 2f out: nt clr run briefly wl over 1f out: shkn up to take 3rd fnl f: nvr able to chal* **5/2**[2]

600- **4** 2 **Golly Miss Molly**[195] 7293 3-8-9 **51** RobertTart(3) 1 41
(Jeremy Gask) *chsd ldng pair on inner: eased off rail 2f out: nt qckn over 1f out: one pce* **8/1**[3]

0-00 **5** 1 3/4 **Sutton Sioux**[18] 1430 3-8-7 **46** oh1 HarryBentley 3 31
(Jeremy Gask) *chsd ldng pair on outer: rdn 2f out: steadily fdd* **25/1**

000- **6** 6 **Khloe**[198] 7218 3-8-7 **46** oh1 DavidProbert 4 12
(Michael Blanshard) *chsd ldr and sn pushed along: lost 2nd and wknd qckly wl over 1f out* **25/1**

1m 12.59s (0.69) **Going Correction** -0.075s/f (Stan) 6 Ran SP% **109.6**
Speed ratings (Par 96): **92,91,88,85,83 75**
CSF £13.10 TOTE £1.50: £1.10, £4.90; EX 12.00 Trifecta £15.90.
**Owner** Lady Rothschild **Bred** Kincorth Investments Inc **Trained** Beckhampton, Wilts

**FOCUS**
A weak 3yo sprint handicap. The winner is a bit better than the bare form.

## 1834 "BET AND WATCH" AT 888SPORT.COM H'CAP 1m 1y(P)
**3:55** (3:56) (Class 3) (0-95,94) 4-Y-O+ **£8,409** (£2,502; £1,250; £625) **Stalls** High

Form RPR

03-0 **1** **So Beloved**[17] 1437 4-9-3 **90** JamesDoyle 6 98
(Roger Charlton) *racd wd early: led after 2f: mde rest: 2 l clr and hld together wl over 1f out: hanging and looked awkward whn rdn fnl f: kpt on wl enough* **7/1**

100- **2** 3/4 **Yeager (USA)**[220] 6650 4-9-7 **94** FrankieDettori 1 100+
(Jeremy Noseda) *hld up in last pair: prog on inner wl over 1f out: rdn and r.o to take 2nd last 50yds: nt rch wnr* **5/1**[2]

2-1 **3** 1/2 **Bustopher (USA)**[28] 1216 4-9-1 **88** MickaelBarzalona 3 93
(Charlie Appleby) *led 2f: chsd wnr: rdn and nt qckn over 1f out: hld whn impeded and lost 2nd last 50yds* **5/4**[1]

00-0 **4** 1 1/4 **Jack Of Diamonds (IRE)**[39] 1042 5-8-12 **85** RichardHughes 7 87
(Roger Teal) *chsd ldrs: rdn on outer 2f out: clsd over 1f out: no imp and pushed along last 100yds* **6/1**[3]

00-0 **5** 1 1/2 **Jacob Cats**[17] 1437 5-8-11 **84** JimCrowley 2 83
(William Knight) *chsd ldrs: rdn over 2f out: tried to cl over 1f out: fdd ins fnl f* **16/1**

0-24 **6** 3/4 **Atlantis Crossing (IRE)**[38] 1070 5-9-4 **91** StephenCraine 4 88
(Jim Boyle) *chsd ldrs: rdn over 2f out: no imp on ldrs jst over 1f out: wknd* **16/1**

5065 **7** hd **Mia's Boy**[27] 1241 10-8-9 **82** LiamKeniry 8 78
(Chris Dwyer) *hld up in 6th: shkn up and no prog over 1f out* **20/1**

0220 **8** 2 **Brocklebank (IRE)**[17] 1437 5-9-0 **92** JackDuern(5) 5 84
(Simon Dow) *stdd s: hld up in last: lost tch over 3f out: wl bhd over 2f out: drvn and plugged on fnl f* **8/1**

1m 35.93s (-2.27) **Going Correction** -0.075s/f (Stan) 8 Ran SP% **115.5**
Speed ratings (Par 107): **108,107,106,105,104 103,103,101**
CSF £42.18 CT £71.99 TOTE £9.70: £2.60, £1.60, £1.10; EX 51.30 Trifecta £246.60.
**Owner** K Abdullah **Bred** Juddmonte Farms Ltd **Trained** Beckhampton, Wilts

**FOCUS**
A fair handicap, run at a sound pace. The form is rated on the positive side.

## 1835 LINGFIELD PARK OWNERS GROUP H'CAP (DIV I) 1m 2f (P)
**4:30** (4:30) (Class 6) (0-55,55) 4-Y-O+ **£2,726** (£805; £402) **Stalls** Low

Form RPR

600/ **1** **Black Minstrel (IRE)**[573] 6792 5-9-7 **55** JimCrowley 9 69+
(Amanda Perrett) *hld up in last pair: trapped bhd rivals over 3f out tl prog on inner 2f out: chsd clr ldr over 1f out: no imp tl eased off rail fnl f: clsd qckly u.str.p to ld last strides* **4/5**[1]

0043 **2** 1/2 **Salient**[26] 1263 10-8-13 **47** KierenFox 7 55
(Michael Attwater) *prog and prom after 4f: led over 3f out and sent for home: 4 l clr and drvn over 1f out: kpt on wl but hdd last strides* **8/1**

0333 **3** 4 **Lily Edge**[19] 1406 5-8-12 **53** (v) CamHardie(7) 1 53
(John Bridger) *hld up in tch: rdn and prog on outer over 2f out: tk 3rd fnl f but nvr on terms* **16/1**

0030 **4** 1 3/4 **Edgware Road**[53] 869 6-9-2 **50** (b) JamesDoyle 3 47
(Sean Curran) *trckd ldrs: shkn up 2f out: nt qckn and no imp over 1f out: pushed along and one pce fnl f* **6/1**[2]

-024 **5** 1 1/4 **Fair Comment**[20] 1387 4-9-7 **55** LiamKeniry 8 50
(Michael Blanshard) *hld up in tch: outpcd fr 3f out: no prog fr over 1f out* **10/1**

50-0 **6** 3 3/4 **Capetown Kid**[27] 1232 4-9-2 **50** RichardHughes 6 38
(Sylvester Kirk) *pressed ldr after 3f: upsides fr 1/2-way to over 3f out: chsd new ldr after: no imp: lost 2nd and fdd over 1f out* **7/1**[3]

4-00 **7** 5 **Dawn Rock**[41] 1012 4-8-7 **46** JackDuern(5) 5 24
(Simon Dow) *pressed ldr 3f: lost pl over 3f out: wknd over 2f out* **16/1**

0-00 **8** 9 **Hardy Plume**[41] 1012 5-8-12 **46** oh1 JohnFahy 2
(Denis Coakley) *mde most to over 3f out: wknd rapidly over 2f out* **50/1**

0006 **9** 99 **Kristal Hart**[43] 998 5-9-1 **54** RyanWhile(5) 4
(Neil Mulholland) *in tch tl dropped away rapidly 1/2-way: sn t.o: virtually p.u: dismntd after fin* **33/1**

2m 5.1s (-1.50) **Going Correction** -0.075s/f (Stan) 9 Ran SP% **119.2**
Speed ratings (Par 101): **103,102,99,98,97 94,90,82,3**
CSF £8.51 CT £64.81 TOTE £2.70: £1.20, £1.50, £2.70; EX 11.40 Trifecta £63.30.
**Owner** M B Spence & Partners **Bred** Corduff Stud Ltd **Trained** Pulborough, W Sussex

**FOCUS**
A weak handicap, with the runner-up the best guide.

## 1836 LINGFIELD PARK OWNERS GROUP H'CAP (DIV II) 1m 2f (P)
**5:00** (5:02) (Class 6) (0-55,55) 4-Y-O+ **£2,726** (£805; £402) **Stalls** Low

Form RPR

4066 **1** **Glennten**[20] 1386 5-8-12 **46** JamesDoyle 1 56+
(Sean Curran) *fast away: led 100yds: chsd ldr: led 3f out and gng best: drvn and steadily drew clr fr 2f out* **12/1**

6033 **2** 3 1/4 **Abigails Angel**[27] 1236 7-8-9 **50** DavidParkes(7) 7 54
(Brett Johnson) *hld up: prog 1/2-way: pressed ldr 3f out: sn rdn: nt qckn 2f out: kpt on* **10/1**

0562 **3** 1/2 **Greek Islands (IRE)**[20] 1386 6-9-0 **55** JenniferFerguson(7) 5 58
(Edward Creighton) *hld up towards rr: chsd ldng quartet 3f out but nt on terms: pushed along and no imp over 2f out: shkn up over 1f out: r.o to press for 2nd nr fin* **9/2**[2]

5543 **4** nk **Claude Monet (BRZ)**[20] 1386 5-8-9 **48** JackDuern(5) 4 50
(Simon Dow) *led after 100yds: set str pce and sn clr: hdd 3f out: steadily lft bhd fr 2f out* **5/1**[3]

3-00 **5** 7 **Berkeley Street (USA)**[49] 910 4-9-7 **55** MartinDwyer 6 44
(Jane Chapple-Hyam) *in tch: outpcd and shkn up over 3f out: nvr on terms after* **9/2**[2]

0305 **6** 1 1/2 **Scamperdale**[27] 1249 12-9-3 **51** (p) KierenFox 3 45
(Brian Baugh) *prom in chsng gp: rdn 3f out: btn over 1f out: heavily eased last 100yds* **16/1**

-400 **7** 1/2 **Illegale (IRE)**[61] 759 8-8-9 **46** oh1 (p) MatthewCosham(3) 2 31
(Nikki Evans) *in tch tl rdn and struggling sn after 1/2-way: bhd over 3f out* **33/1**

3050 **8** 2 1/4 **Chandrayaan**[20] 1387 7-8-9 **46** oh1 (v) SimonPearce(3) 9 27
(John E Long) *detached in last and nt gng wl after 3f: a bhd* **25/1**

6120 **9** 13 **My Renaissance**[27] 1232 4-9-6 **54** RichardHughes 8 10
(Ben Case) *hld up off fast pce: tried to make prog 5f out but sn urged along w no rspnse: no hdwy in 8th 2f out: heavily eased over 1f out* **2/1**[1]

2m 5.28s (-1.32) **Going Correction** -0.075s/f (Stan) 9 Ran SP% **115.8**
Speed ratings (Par 101): **102,99,99,98,93 91,91,89,79**
CSF £124.99 CT £626.27 TOTE £7.00: £1.10, £3.30, £1.20; EX 73.30 Trifecta £300.40.
**Owner** Bob Cooper & Val Dean **Bred** The Hon Mrs R Pease **Trained** Hatford, Oxon

**FOCUS**
The second division of the weak 1m2f handicap, and a length slower than the first. The winner's best form since early last year.
T/Plt: £22.60 to a £1 stake. Pool: £43,728.59 - 1,406.86 winning units T/Qpdt: £19.20 to a £1 stake. Pool: £2,756.48 - 105.72 winning units JN

# 1670 NEWCASTLE (L-H)
Tuesday, April 29

**OFFICIAL GOING: Soft (5.8)**
Wind: Light; half behind Weather: Sunny

## 1837 EBF STALLIONS ESH GROUP FILLIES' MAIDEN STKS (BOBIS RACE) 5f
**5:20** (5:20) (Class 5) 2-Y-O **£2,911** (£866; £432; £216) **Stalls** Centre

Form RPR

**1** **Moving Melody** 2-9-0 0 PaulHanagan 2 71+
(Richard Fahey) *t.k.h: trckd ldrs: effrt and rdn over 1f out: led ins fnl f: kpt on wl* **4/1**[3]

**2** 3/4 **Cabbies Lou** 2-9-0 0 DuranFentiman 1 68
(Noel Wilson) *sn prom on outside: rdn 1/2-way: hdwy to chse wnr wl ins fnl f: r.o* **50/1**

3 **3** 1/2 **El Che**[12] 1528 2-8-11 0 CharlesBishop(3) 7 66
(Mick Channon) *t.k.h: trckd ldr: led and rdn over 1f out: hdd ins fnl f: kpt on same pce* **7/4**[2]

**4** 2 1/2 **Indian Keys** 2-9-0 0 TomEaves 5 57
(Kevin Ryan) *dwlt: sn prom: effrt and ch 2f out: sn rdn: outpcd ins fnl f* **12/1**

5 **5** 1 1/4 **Bahamian Art**[13] 1504 2-9-0 0 JoeFanning 3 53
(Mark Johnston) *t.k.h: led tl rdn and hdd over 1f out: wknd ins fnl f* **6/5**[1]

**6** 4 **Celestial Dancer (FR)** 2-8-11 0 MichaelJMMurphy(3) 6 38
(Michael Appleby) *s.i.s: bhd and outpcd: nvr on terms* **33/1**

1m 4.59s (3.49) **Going Correction** +0.325s/f (Good) 6 Ran SP% **114.4**
Speed ratings (Par 89): **85,83,83,79,77 70**
CSF £117.48 TOTE £11.30: £7.30, £19.90; EX 79.30 Trifecta £187.10.
**Owner** Mrs H Steel **Bred** Sean Gorman **Trained** Musley Bank, N Yorks

**FOCUS**
Only the six runners but an interesting fillies' maiden.

## 1838 COREPEOPLE RECRUITMENT H'CAP — 6f
5:50 (5:51) (Class 6) (0-60,60) 4-Y-O+ — £1,940 (£577; £288; £144) Stalls Centre

Form — RPR

-045 **1** **Hab Reeh**[24] [1311] 6-8-11 **50**........ JamesSullivan 5 — 64
(Ruth Carr) *t.k.h: chsd ldr in main centre gp: led over 1f out: sn clr: edgd lft ins fnl f: kpt on wl* **25/1**

03- **2** 2 ¼ **Niceonemyson**[216] [6761] 5-9-1 **59**........ KevinStott(5) 12 — 66
(Christopher Wilson) *prom in main centre gp: hdwy to chse wnr over 1f out: kpt on fnl f: nt pce to chal* **20/1**

03-2 **3** 1 ¼ **Mitchell**[24] [1309] 4-8-12 **56**........ ConnorBeasley(5) 15 — 59+
(David Thompson) *led stands' side quartet: rdn clr of that gp wl over 1f out: edgd lft: kpt on fnl f: nt rch first two* **7/2**[2]

0-50 **4** nk **Monel**[2] [1758] 6-8-10 **52**........ IanBrennan(3) 11 — 54
(Jim Goldie) *dwlt: sn midfield centre gp: smooth hdwy over 2f out: rdn over 1f out: edgd rt: kpt on same pce ins fnl f* **10/1**

4262 **5** ½ **Vale Of Clara (IRE)**[6] [1649] 6-8-9 **48**........(p) PaulHanagan 6 — 48
(Peter Niven) *towards rr main centre gp: drvn and outpcd over 2f out: n.d* **3/1**[1]

1023 **6** 2 ¼ **Greenhead High**[9] [1602] 6-9-1 **54**........(v) AdrianNicholls 7 — 47
(David Nicholls) *led main centre gp: rdn and hdd over 1f out: wknd ins fnl f* **8/1**

035- **7** 1 ¾ **Mission Impossible**[182] [7599] 9-9-6 **59**........(p) DougieCostello 2 — 46
(Tracy Waggott) *dwlt: hld up main centre gp: drvn and effrt over 2f out: no imp over 1f out* **14/1**

4306 **8** ½ **Ivestar (IRE)**[1] [1804] 9-8-2 **48**........(v) DanielleMooney(7) 10 — 34
(Michael Easterby) *hld up main centre gp: shkn up 2f out: nvr able to chal* **25/1**

040- **9** ½ **Lees Anthem**[154] [8049] 7-9-2 **55**........ PJMcDonald 3 — 39
(Mel Brittain) *in tch main centre gp: rdn over 2f out: wknd over 1f out* **33/1**

4-60 **10** 2 ¾ **Tarrsille (IRE)**[61] [766] 8-9-2 **60**........ ShirleyTeasdale(5) 4 — 35
(Paul Midgley) *prom on far side of main centre gp: rdn and hung lft over 2f out: wknd over 1f out* **20/1**

0605 **11** 1 **Celestial Dawn**[21] [1369] 5-8-11 **50**........(b) JimmyQuinn 9 — 22
(John Weymes) *missed break: bhd main centre gp: drvn along 1/2-way: nvr rchd ldrs* **25/1**

666- **12** hd **Pivotal Prospect**[182] [7598] 6-8-13 **52**........ RoystonFfrench 1 — 24
(Tracy Waggott) *hld up in tch on outside of main centre gp: struggling over 2f out: sn btn* **20/1**

0654 **13** 7 **Waabel**[21] [1369] 7-8-12 **54**........(tp) DeclanBates(3) 14
(Ann Stokell) *chsd stands' side ldr: drvn and outpcd over 2f out: btn over 1f out* **33/1**

020- **14** 2 ½ **Black Douglas**[201] [7149] 5-9-5 **58**........ TomEaves 13
(Jim Goldie) *dwlt: in tch stands' side: rdn along over 2f out: no imp* **20/1**

44-0 **15** 14 **Grand Jipeck (IRE)**[24] [1309] 4-9-2 **55**........[1] PaulPickard 16
(Brian Ellison) *chsd stands' side ldrs: rdn over 2f out: wknd over 1f out: eased whn no ch fnl f* **6/1**[3]

1m 16.24s (1.64) **Going Correction** +0.325s/f (Good) — **15** Ran SP% **124.8**
Speed ratings (Par 101): **102,99,97,96,96 93,90,90,89,85 84,84,75,71,53**
CSF £433.15 CT £2238.17 TOTE £30.00: £5.80, £4.10, £3.00; EX 472.00 Trifecta £1295.30 Part won..
**Owner** Grange Park Racing & Mrs B Taylor **Bred** The Anglo Irish Choral Society **Trained** Huby, N Yorks

**FOCUS**
A competitive low-grade sprint handicap, where the field split into two groups. The majority opted to race up the centre but only a handful managed to get involved. The winner is rated close to last year's turf best.

## 1839 JEWSONS H'CAP — 7f
6:20 (6:21) (Class 5) (0-75,81) 4-Y-O+ — £2,587 (£770; £384; £192) Stalls Centre

Form — RPR

0-01 **1** **Victoire De Lyphar (IRE)**[8] [1609] 7-9-13 **81** 6ex......(e) JamesSullivan 10 — 96
(Ruth Carr) *hld up in tch: stdy hdwy and edgd lft over 2f out: rdn over 1f out: led wl ins fnl f: r.o* **4/1**[3]

0-32 **2** 1 **Orbit The Moon (IRE)**[5] [1672] 6-8-12 **71**........(tp) ConnorBeasley(5) 1 — 83
(Michael Dods) *pressed ldr: led over 2f out: rdn and edgd rt fr over 1f out: hdd and no ex wl ins fnl f* **10/11**[1]

2442 **3** 5 **Royal Holiday (IRE)**[14] [1499] 7-9-3 **71**........(p) RussKennemore 7 — 70
(Marjorie Fife) *led: rdn and hdd over 2f out: rallied: outpcd fnl f* **7/2**[2]

6005 **4** 17 **Decent Fella (IRE)**[28] [1224] 8-8-13 **70**........(t) DeclanBates(3) 3 — 25
(Ann Stokell) *fly-jmpd s: hld up: rdn along and effrt over 2f out: sn no imp* **28/1**

-000 **5** 5 **Mysterial**[12] [1537] 4-9-1 **72**........(b) JasonHart(3) 6 — 14
(Ruth Carr) *chsd ldrs: drvn over 3f out: wknd over 2f out* **16/1**

66-0 **6** ½ **Old Man Clegg**[20] [1376] 4-8-0 **61**........(t) DanielleMooney(7) 4
(Michael Easterby) *fly-jmpd s: hld up: drvn and edgd lft over 2f out: sn btn* **10/1**

0-00 **7** ¾ **Sunrise Dance**[8] [1604] 5-9-0 **71**........ IanBrennan(3) 2
(Robert Johnson) *t.k.h: cl up tl wknd fr 3f out* **50/1**

1m 29.04s (1.24) **Going Correction** +0.325s/f (Good) — **7** Ran SP% **115.0**
Speed ratings (Par 103): **105,103,98,78,73 72,71**
CSF £8.12 CT £13.15 TOTE £5.80: £3.40, £1.10; EX 9.70 Trifecta £15.70.
**Owner** The Beer Stalkers & Ruth Carr **Bred** Mrs Monica Hackett **Trained** Huby, N Yorks

**FOCUS**
An ordinary handicap where the complexion of the race was changed when the pace was noticeably upped with over 3f to go and effectively knocking all but the three principals out of the race. The winner's best form since he was a 3yo.

## 1840 ULTIMATE CONTRACTORS H'CAP — 1m 4f 93y
6:50 (6:51) (Class 6) (0-60,55) 3-Y-O — £1,940 (£577; £288; £144) Stalls Centre

Form — RPR

0-P0 **1** **Sirpertan**[13] [1508] 3-8-13 **50**........ JasonHart(3) 2 — 57
(Mark Walford) *t.k.h: hld up: swtchd rt and hdwy over 2f out: led last 100yds: hld on wl* **7/4**[1]

05-1 **2** hd **Vosne Romanee**[7] [1632] 3-9-5 **53** 6ex........(p) TomEaves 8 — 59
(Keith Dalgleish) *t.k.h: hld up in tch: hdwy to ld over 1f out: sn rdn: hdd last 100yds: rallied: jst hld* **4/1**[2]

50-0 **3** 2 ¼ **Newgate Queen**[22] [1348] 3-9-7 **55**........ PJMcDonald 3 — 57
(Tony Coyle) *chsd ldr: effrt and rdn over 2f out: ch on ins over 1f out to ins fnl f: outpcd last 100yds* **10/1**

000- **4** 1 ¼ **Barbara Elizabeth**[216] [6755] 3-8-11 **45**........ BarryMcHugh 7 — 45
(Tony Coyle) *chsd ldrs: hdwy to ld over 2f out: rdn and hdd over 1f out: outpcd ins fnl f* **9/2**[3]

00-3 **5** 3 ½ **Bentons Lad**[20] [1372] 3-9-4 **52**........ DougieCostello 6 — 46
(George Moore) *led: rdn and hdd over 2f out: wknd appr fnl f* **5/1**

00-3 **6** 11 **Nam Ma Prow**[26] [1269] 3-9-7 **55**........ AndrewElliott 4 — 32
(Simon West) *dwlt: sn prom: rdn over 3f out: edgd lft and wknd 2f out* **25/1**

00-0 **7** nk **Tawan**[31] [1166] 3-8-11 **45**........ JamesSullivan 5 — 21
(Brian Rothwell) *hld up: drvn and outpcd over 3f out: hung lft and wknd over 2f out* **50/1**

00-4 **8** 10 **Crafty Spell**[26] [1269] 3-9-1 **49**........ JoeFanning 1 — 9
(Mark Johnston) *hld up: rdn 3f out: sn wknd* **14/1**

2m 56.58s (10.98) **Going Correction** +0.80s/f (Soft) — **8** Ran SP% **112.8**
Speed ratings (Par 96): **95,94,93,92,90 82,82,76**
CSF £8.52 CT £51.26 TOTE £6.50: £3.60, £1.10, £2.30; EX 10.10 Trifecta £73.40.
**Owner** D & S Woodall **Bred** John James **Trained** Sherriff Hutton, N Yorks

**FOCUS**
A low-grade handicap run at just an ordinary pace but a good battle to the line. A step up from the winner.

## 1841 SWINBURNE MADDISON MAIDEN STKS — 1m 2f 32y
7:20 (7:21) (Class 5) 3-Y-O+ — £2,587 (£770; £384; £192) Stalls Centre

Form — RPR

4-4 **1** **Sayed Youmzain**[17] [1438] 3-8-10 0........ PaddyAspell 4 — 83
(Marco Botti) *mde all at stdy gallop: shkn up and qcknd clr over 2f out: drvn out fnl f* **1/1**[1]

6- **2** 2 **Shama's Song (IRE)**[180] [7645] 3-8-5 0........ JimmyQuinn 3 — 74
(Sir Michael Stoute) *trckd ldrs: effrt and wnt 2nd over 3f out: drvn and clsd on wnr over 1f out: no further imp last 100yds* **11/4**[2]

**3** nk **Miss Tree** 3-8-2 0........ IanBrennan(3) 2 — 73
(John Quinn) *hld up last but in tch: stdy hdwy over 2f out: rdn over 1f out: kpt on same pce ins fnl f* **33/1**

**4** 7 **Taqneen (IRE)** 3-8-10 0........ PaulHanagan 1 — 65
(Ed Dunlop) *in tch: rdn and outpcd wl over 2f out: sn n.d* **4/1**[3]

**5** 31 **Ballyhurst (IRE)** 3-8-10 0........ TonyHamilton 7
(Richard Fahey) *chsd wnr to over 3f out: sn rdn: hung lft and lost pl: t.o* **9/1**

2m 22.98s (11.08) **Going Correction** +0.80s/f (Soft)
**WFA** 3 from 5yo 17lb — **5** Ran SP% **109.6**
Speed ratings (Par 103): **87,85,85,79,54**
CSF £3.95 TOTE £1.30: £1.10, £2.30; EX 4.40 Trifecta £35.20.
**Owner** Jaber Abdullah **Bred** Rabbah Bloodstock Limited **Trained** Newmarket, Suffolk

**FOCUS**
An ordinary gallop for a fair-looking maiden. The form is rated around the winner.

## 1842 SOLUTION GROUP H'CAP — 1m 3y(S)
7:50 (7:50) (Class 4) (0-80,80) 4-Y-O+ — £4,851 (£1,443; £721; £360) Stalls Centre

Form — RPR

53-0 **1** **Hakuna Matata**[21] [1356] 7-8-11 **75**........(b) ConnorBeasley(5) 2 — 85
(Michael Dods) *trckd ldrs: shkn up to ld over 1f out: sn clr: rdn out fnl f* **11/4**[2]

30-0 **2** 2 **Barren Brook**[21] [1356] 7-9-1 **74**........ JamesSullivan 8 — 79
(Michael Easterby) *t.k.h: chsd ldr: rdn 2f out: styd on fnl f to take 2nd nr fin: nt rch wnr* **7/1**

56-2 **3** nk **Simply Shining (IRE)**[13] [1510] 4-9-1 **74**........ PaulHanagan 6 — 79
(Richard Fahey) *t.k.h: led at stdy gallop: rdn over 2f out: hdd over 1f out: kpt on same pce ins fnl f* **7/4**[1]

65-0 **4** 1 ½ **The Osteopath (IRE)**[15] [1483] 11-9-1 **74**........ PJMcDonald 9 — 75
(John Davies) *t.k.h: hld up in tch: rdn 2f out: no imp fnl f* **15/2**

4500 **5** 8 **Warfare**[21] [1356] 5-8-3 **67**........ ShaneGray(5) 3 — 50
(Kevin Ryan) *hld up in tch: stdy hdwy over 2f out: rdn and wknd over 1f out* **7/2**[3]

1m 45.58s (2.18) **Going Correction** +0.325s/f (Good) — **5** Ran SP% **109.5**
Speed ratings (Par 105): **102,100,99,98,90**
CSF £20.17 TOTE £3.60: £1.80, £5.20; EX 19.90 Trifecta £49.10.
**Owner** Sekura Group **Bred** Mrs J A Chapman **Trained** Denton, Co Durham

**FOCUS**
Only a reasonable pace for this fairly uncompetitive handicap. The winner is rated back to form.

## 1843 JAMES BURRELL H'CAP — 5f
8:20 (8:21) (Class 5) (0-70,70) 4-Y-O+ — £2,587 (£770; £384; £192) Stalls Centre

Form — RPR

1-04 **1** **Fleurtille**[6] [1643] 5-8-8 **62**........ ConnorBeasley(5) 3 — 76
(Robert Johnson) *taken early to post: midfield: hdwy 2f out: led last 50yds: kpt on wl* **5/1**[2]

2005 **2** nk **Keep It Dark**[4] [1695] 5-9-6 **69**........ BarryMcHugh 9 — 82
(Tony Coyle) *led: shkn up: drifted lft and hdd last 50yds: no ex* **7/2**[1]

0064 **3** 2 **Harrogate Fair**[8] [1618] 4-8-9 **58**........ JoeFanning 8 — 64
(Michael Squance) *prom: effrt and ev ch over 1f out to ins fnl f: one pce last 100yds* **10/1**

0-00 **4** 2 **Exotic Guest**[15] [1487] 4-9-2 **65**........ JamesSullivan 6 — 64+
(Ruth Carr) *dwlt: bhd: hdwy over 2f out: rdn over 1f out: kpt on fnl f: nvr able to chal* **20/1**

301- **5** 1 ¾ **Dark Opal (IRE)**[201] [7150] 4-9-7 **70**........ DanielTudhope 2 — 62
(John Weymes) *in tch: rdn and hdwy over 2f out: one pce appr fnl f* **11/1**

535- **6** 1 **Ingenti**[206] [7029] 6-9-0 **68**........ KevinStott(5) 10 — 57
(Christopher Wilson) *prom: effrt and rdn over 2f out: outpcd appr fnl f* **20/1**

642- **7** ½ **Captain Royale (IRE)**[182] [7594] 9-9-5 **68**........(p) DougieCostello 5 — 55
(Tracy Waggott) *hld up bhd ldng gp: drvn over 2f out: sn no imp* **16/1**

5233 **8** hd **Thorpe Bay**[15] [1487] 5-9-0 **66**........ MichaelJMMurphy(3) 4 — 52
(Michael Appleby) *chsd ldrs tl rdn and wknd appr fnl f* **13/2**

450- **9** 2 ½ **Arch Walker (IRE)**[211] [6901] 7-8-7 **56**........ JimmyQuinn 7 — 33
(John Weymes) *bhd: drvn along over 2f out: nvr able to chal* **40/1**

2010 **10** 2 ¼ **Profile Star (IRE)**[25] [1283] 5-9-2 **68**........ DeclanBates(3) 13 — 37
(Ann Stokell) *midfield: drvn and outpcd 1/2-way: n.d after* **14/1**

0-06 **11** 1 **Balinka**[4] [1694] 4-8-7 **56**........(b[1]) PJMcDonald 12 — 21
(Mel Brittain) *t.k.h: prom tl rdn and wknd 2f out* **20/1**

-341 **12** 2 ¾ **Dodina (IRE)**[22] [1343] 4-9-5 **68**........(p) TomEaves 1 — 24
(Brian Ellison) *cl up on far side of gp tl rdn and wknd 2f out* **11/2**[3]

300- **13** 1 ¾ **Marabout (IRE)**[165] [7904] 4-8-7 **56** oh3........(b[1]) DuranFentiman 11 — 5
(Mel Brittain) *towards rr: struggling over 2f out: sn btn* **25/1**

1m 2.26s (1.16) **Going Correction** +0.325s/f (Good) — **13** Ran SP% **118.2**
Speed ratings (Par 103): **103,102,99,96,93 91,90,90,86,83 81,77,74**
CSF £20.57 CT £175.97 TOTE £4.70: £1.60, £1.40, £3.00; EX 28.60 Trifecta £638.30.
**Owner** Ray Craggs **Bred** Ray Craggs **Trained** Newburn, Tyne & Wear

**FOCUS**
A competitive sprint handicap with a fierce gallop, run in a good time. Another step forward from the winner.

T/Plt: £271.00 to a £1 stake. Pool: £48,013.29 - 129.31 winning units T/Qpdt: £5.70 to a £1 stake. Pool: £6,071.40 - 779.92 winning units RY

# 1582 NOTTINGHAM (L-H)

Tuesday, April 29

**OFFICIAL GOING: Good (8.2)**

All races on Inner track. Rail out 2m on Home bend increasing distances on Round course by 10yds.

Wind: Very light breeze; across Weather: Warm sunshine

## 1844 WATCH RACING UK ON SKY CHANNEL 432 MEDIAN AUCTION MAIDEN STKS 1m 75y

1:45 (1:46) (Class 5) 3-Y-O £2,726 (£805; £402) Stalls Centre

Form RPR

1 **Cape Icon** 3-9-5 0 AdamKirby 4 82+
(Clive Cox) *trckd ldrs: hdwy 3f out: effrt 2f out: rdn to ld appr fnl f: kpt on strly* **10/1**

434- 2 2 ¾ **Sebastian Beach (IRE)**[216] 6740 3-9-5 75 PatDobbs 2 74
(Richard Hannon) *trckd ldrs: hdwy over 3f out: rdn wl over 1f out: kpt on fnl f* **9/2**[3]

0-22 3 nk **Rough Courte (IRE)**[8] 1616 3-9-0 69 SamHitchcott 3 68
(Mick Channon) *led: rdn along 2f out: drvn and hdd appr fnl f: kpt on same pce: lost 2nd nr line* **13/2**

4 nk **Discreetly** 3-9-0 0 AndreaAtzeni 8 68+
(Hughie Morrison) *towards rr: hdwy 3f out: pushed along and green 2f out: styd on appr fnl f: nrst fin* **12/1**

34- 5 1 **Majorities**[171] 7818 3-9-5 0 JimmyFortune 10 70+
(Brian Meehan) *dwlt and hld up in rr: hdwy 4f out: swtchd rt wl over 2f out: rdn to chse ldrs over 1f out: styd on same pce fnl f* **4/1**[2]

0 6 4 **Censorius**[12] 1529 3-9-5 0 GrahamLee 1 61
(Ed Walker) *midfield: sme hdwy to chse ldrs 3f out: sn rdn along and wknd fnl 2f* **33/1**

0 7 ½ **Silver Duke (IRE)**[17] 1433 3-9-5 0 KierenFallon 7 60
(Alan Jarvis) *trckd ldr: effrt over 2f out: rdn wl over 1f out: grad wknd* **7/2**[1]

8 5 **Slunovrat (FR)** 3-9-5 0 TedDurcan 6 48
(David Menuisier) *dwlt: a towards rr* **50/1**

4-6 9 1 ½ **Lifejacket (IRE)**[8] 1616 3-9-5 0 PaulMulrennan 11 45
(Ed Dunlop) *trckd ldrs: pushed along wl over 2f out: rdn wl over 1f out and sn wknd* **25/1**

0- 10 7 **Venus Marina**[178] 7693 3-9-0 0 LukeMorris 12 24
(Chris Wall) *dwlt: sme hdwy into midfield after 3f: rdn along 3f out: sn wknd* **100/1**

3 11 1 ¼ **Silent Pursuit**[104] 188 3-9-0 0 RobertWinston 5 21
(Philip Hide) *trckd ldng pair: pushed along 3f out: rdn over 2f out: sn wknd* **8/1**

03 12 25 **Flying By**[21] 1364 3-9-0 0 ChrisCatlin 9
(Rae Guest) *a in rr: outpcd and bhd fnl 3f* **50/1**

1m 45.59s (-3.41) **Going Correction** -0.475s/f (Firm) 12 Ran SP% 113.3
Speed ratings (Par 98): **98,95,94,94,93 89,89,84,82,75 74,49**
CSF £50.49 TOTE £12.70: £2.90, £2.00, £2.00; EX 81.10 Trifecta £233.60.
**Owner** R Haim **Bred** J Bernstein & R Haim **Trained** Lambourn, Berks

**FOCUS**

The rail was moved out two metres on the home bend, increasing round course distances by ten yards. After a dry morning the going was changed to good. The pace was honest for this open maiden. Ordinary form but a nice start from the winner.

## 1845 ROA OWNERS JACKPOT H'CAP 1m 75y

2:15 (2:46) (Class 5) (0-75,73) 4-Y-O+ £2,726 (£805; £402) Stalls Centre

Form RPR

405- 1 **Celtic Sixpence (IRE)**[161] 7964 6-9-7 73 MichaelStainton 4 82
(Nick Kent) *mde all: rdn along over 2f out: drvn ins fnl f: hld on gamely* **20/1**

640- 2 nk **Mister Marcasite**[141] 8227 4-8-10 62 DavidAllan 9 70
(Mel Brittain) *trckd ldr: cl up over 3f out: chal over 2f out: rdn over 1f out: drvn and ev ch ins fnl f: kpt on* **10/1**

0-31 3 1 ½ **Uncle Dermot (IRE)**[5] 1665 6-9-7 73 6ex KierenFallon 2 78
(Brendan Powell) *trckd ldng pair: swtchd rt and effrt 3f out: rdn wl over 1f out: no imp fnl f* **2/1**[1]

3335 4 5 **Raging Bear (USA)**[31] 1167 4-8-11 68 (p) DavidKenny(5) 1 61
(James Evans) *hld up in rr: hdwy over 2f out: sn rdn and styd on fnl f: nvr nr ldrs* **8/1**

/6-4 5 shd **Viva Vettori**[40] 1025 10-8-8 67 DanielCremin(7) 3 60
(Brian Forsey) *dwlt: t.k.h and hld up in rr: hdwy 1/2-way: chsd ldrs 3f out: sn rdn and one pce* **50/1**

2214 6 ¾ **Exclusive Waters (IRE)**[5] 1682 4-9-0 73 (b) CallumShepherd(7) 5 64
(Charles Hills) *dwlt: sn in tch and t.k.h: hdwy to chse ldrs 4f out: rdn along wl over 2f out: drvn wl over 1f out: sn wknd* **8/1**

006- 7 2 ½ **Granell (IRE)**[174] 7765 4-9-7 73 JimmyFortune 8 58
(Brian Meehan) *trckd ldrs on outer: pushed along over 3f out: rdn wl over 2f out and sn btn* **9/2**[2]

246- 8 4 ½ **Duke Of Destiny (IRE)**[144] 8178 5-9-0 73 (p) CliffordLee(7) 6 48
(Ed Walker) *t.k.h early: chsd ldrs: rdn along wl 3f out: sn wknd* **10/1**

2-1 9 4 ½ **Indian Trifone (IRE)**[36] 1084 4-9-6 72 LukeMorris 10 37
(Ed Walker) *in rr and rdn along bef 1/2-way: sn bhd* **6/1**[3]

1m 44.36s (-4.64) **Going Correction** -0.475s/f (Firm) 9 Ran SP% 112.9
Speed ratings (Par 103): **104,103,102,97,97 96,93,89,84**
CSF £199.33 CT £583.76 TOTE £25.80: £5.80, £2.10, £1.90; EX 210.00 Trifecta £794.90.
**Owner** Cynthia Commons, Nick Kent **Bred** Burns Farm Stud **Trained** Brigg, Lincs

**FOCUS**

The rail turning into the home straight was realigned after the first race, as the bend was deemed too sharp. Not a strong contest for the grade, run at a fair pace. It paid to race handy. The winner seems back to her old best.

## 1846 WATCH ON 3 DEVICES RACINGUK.COM/ANYWHERE FILLIES' H'CAP 1m 75y

2:45 (3:16) (Class 5) (0-70,70) 3-Y-O+ £2,587 (£770; £384; £192) Stalls Centre

Form RPR

356- 1 **Lady Tiana**[238] 6070 3-8-11 67 LukeMorris 12 75
(Lucy Wadham) *trckd ldrs: hdwy on outer and cl up over 3f out: led over 2f out: rdn over 1f out: drvn and kpt on wl fnl f* **12/1**

323- 2 1 ¼ **Lady Guinevere**[146] 8154 4-9-8 64 GrahamGibbons 1 73
(Stuart Williams) *trckd ldrs: hdwy wl over 2f out: chsd wnr wl over 1f out: sn rdn to chal: drvn and ev ch ins fnl f: kpt on same pce towards fin* **9/2**[1]

044- 3 nk **Crystal Nymph (IRE)**[185] 7532 3-9-0 70 PatDobbs 6 74
(Richard Hannon) *trckd ldr: cl up 3f out: rdn along over 2f out: drvn and ch over 1f out: kpt on same pce* **5/1**[2]

-362 4 3 **Fruit Pastille**[77] 568 3-8-12 68 JimmyFortune 3 66
(Hughie Morrison) *trckd ldng pair on inner: pushed along wl over 2f out: rdn wl over 1f out: sn drvn and kpt on same pce* **5/1**[2]

360- 5 1 **Sweet Martoni**[189] 7439 4-9-9 65 AndreaAtzeni 7 64
(William Knight) *towards rr: hdwy over 3f out: rdn to chse ldrs 2f out: drvn and no imp appr fnl f* **9/2**[1]

264- 6 1 ¼ **Lady Red Oak**[246] 5812 3-8-12 68 RichardKingscote 2 60
(Tom Dascombe) *n.m.r s and towards rr: hdwy 4f out: chsd ldrs over 2f out: sn rdn and no imp* **6/1**[3]

600- 7 5 **Tenbridge**[161] 7952 5-9-6 62 (v) AdamKirby 4 47
(Derek Haydn Jones) *led: rdn along 3f out: hdd over 2f out: sn wknd* **25/1**

6245 8 2 **Ambella (IRE)**[13] 1510 4-9-6 67 GeorgeDowning(5) 11 47
(Ian Williams) *dwlt and sn pushed along into midfield: hdwy on outer over 3f out: rdn wl over 2f out and sn wknd* **33/1**

41- 9 1 ½ **Reimpose (USA)**[131] 8342 3-8-10 66 DaneO'Neill 8 39
(Pat Eddery) *dwlt: a towards rr* **12/1**

3-00 10 ½ **Delores Rocket**[17] 1440 4-9-7 63 (p) PaulMulrennan 10 39
(Kevin Ryan) *a in rr* **25/1**

43-0 11 ¾ **Charmy Dukesse (IRE)**[18] 1423 3-9-0 70 (b[1]) AntonioFresu 9 40
(Marco Botti) *in tch: hdwy on outer over 3f out: rdn along wl over 2f out: sn wknd* **20/1**

1m 45.32s (-3.68) **Going Correction** -0.475s/f (Firm)
**WFA** 3 from 4yo+ 14lb 11 Ran SP% 114.8
Speed ratings (Par 100): **99,97,97,94,93 92,87,85,83,83 82**
CSF £60.70 CT £315.96 TOTE £9.70: £2.50, £1.40, £2.20; EX 98.30 Trifecta £570.10.
**Owner** The FOPS **Bred** Mr & Mrs A E Pakenham **Trained** Newmarket, Suffolk

**FOCUS**

They went a steady pace for this open fillies' handicap. Again it paid to race handy. The winner stepped up a bit.

## 1847 FOLLOW US ON FACEBOOK AND TWITTER H'CAP 1m 2f 50y

3:15 (3:50) (Class 5) (0-65,65) 3-Y-O £2,726 (£805; £402) Stalls Low

Form RPR

50-0 1 **Penhill**[13] 1509 3-9-7 65 TedDurcan 14 79
(James Bethell) *trckd ldr: cl up 1/2-way: led 3f out: rdn wl over 1f out: drvn fnl f: hld on gamely towards fin* **7/1**

660- 2 nk **Gavlar**[204] 7070 3-9-2 60[1] AndreaAtzeni 15 73
(William Knight) *trckd ldrs: hdwy to chse wnr over 2f out: rdn to chal over 1f out: drvn and ev ch ins fnl f: no ex towards fin* **11/2**[2]

60-5 3 5 **Kashmiri Sunset**[20] 1395 3-9-5 63 ChrisCatlin 4 67+
(Ed de Giles) *hld up in rr: hdwy on outer 3f out: effrt over 2f out: sn rdn and styd on to chse ldng pair ent fnl f: sn drvn: edgd lft and no imp* **6/1**[3]

04-0 4 3 ¾ **Majestic Sun (IRE)**[19] 1403 3-9-4 62 JimmyFortune 11 59
(Peter Chapple-Hyam) *in tch: hdwy to trck ldrs over 4f out: effrt over 2f out: rdn whn n.m.r and swtchd lft over 1f out: sn drvn and one pce* **7/1**

5232 5 ½ **Khee Society**[10] 1588 3-9-5 63 AdamKirby 12 59
(David Evans) *hld up towards rr: hdwy on outer 3f out: rdn to chse ldrs 2f out: sn drvn and one pce* **7/2**[1]

00 6 3 **Taanif**[13] 1507 3-9-1 59 GrahamGibbons 2 49
(Michael Easterby) *nvr bttr than midfield* **80/1**

064- 7 ½ **Twenty Roses (IRE)**[148] 8133 3-9-2 60 GrahamLee 13 49
(Ed Walker) *led: rdn along and hdd 3f out: drvn 2f out: grad wknd* **14/1**

4550 8 2 ¾ **Eddiemaurice (IRE)**[22] 1346 3-9-7 65 RobbieFitzpatrick 6 49
(Richard Guest) *s.i.s: a towards rr* **16/1**

400- 9 1 ¾ **Weisse Girl**[195] 7293 3-8-1 52 AdamMcLean(7) 5 33
(Nick Kent) *rrd and dwlt s: a towards rr* **50/1**

3526 10 5 **Stoneham**[15] 1494 3-9-6 64 SamHitchcott 9 35
(Mick Channon) *trckd ldng pair on inner: effrt over 3f out: rdn along over 2f out: sn drvn and wknd* **25/1**

62-0 11 1 ¼ **Master Dan**[20] 1400 3-9-7 65 DaleSwift 7 34
(James Given) *chsd ldrs on outer: rdn along 3f out: sn wknd* **25/1**

000- 12 10 **Always Resolute**[220] 6635 3-9-7 65 KierenFallon 1 15
(Alan Jarvis) *chsd ldrs: rdn along 3f out: sn wknd* **12/1**

2-46 13 6 **Lady Knight (IRE)**[104] 190 3-9-7 65 LukeMorris 10 3
(J S Moore) *a towards rr* **40/1**

20-0 14 14 **Palace Princess (FR)**[13] 1507 3-9-4 62 PaulMulrennan 8
(Ed Dunlop) *t.k.h: hld up: a towards rr* **25/1**

2m 12.56s (-1.74) **Going Correction** -0.475s/f (Firm) 14 Ran SP% 114.3
Speed ratings (Par 98): **87,86,82,79,79 76,76,74,72,68 67,59,55,43**
CSF £39.93 CT £244.89 TOTE £11.10: £4.10, £3.70, £1.70; EX 71.80 Trifecta £568.50.
**Owner** Clarendon Thoroughbred Racing **Bred** Newsells Park Stud & Equity Bloodstock **Trained** Middleham Moor, N Yorks

**FOCUS**

Plenty of unexposed types in this handicap which was run at a fair pace. The front two were always handy and a positive view has been taken of them.

## 1848 LADS NIGHT OUT ON 9TH MAY H'CAP (DIV I) 1m 6f 15y

3:45 (4:16) (Class 4) (0-80,80) 4-Y-O+ £4,690 (£1,395; £697; £348) Stalls Low

Form RPR

213- 1 **Hassle (IRE)**[204] 7072 5-9-10 80 (p) AdamKirby 10 91+
(Clive Cox) *hld up in tch: gd hdwy on outer over 3f out: led wl over 2f out: rdn over 1f out: drvn ins fnl f: hld on wl towards fin* **5/4**[1]

50-3 2 ½ **Entihaa**[24] 1307 6-9-5 75 BenCurtis 1 83
(Alan Swinbank) *hld up in tch: hdwy over 3f out: cl up 2f out: sn rdn: drvn and ev ch ins fnl f tl no ex towards fin* **5/1**[2]

/5-5 3 3 ½ **Kleitomachos (IRE)**[15] 1493 6-9-7 77 KierenFallon 6 80
(Stuart Kittow) *led: rdn along over 3f out: hdd wl over 2f out: drvn along wl over 1f out: kpt on same pce* **8/1**[3]

0-25 4 1 ¼ **Kenny's Girl (IRE)**[14] 1496 4-8-3 61 AndreaAtzeni 7 62
(William Muir) *trckd ldrs: effrt and hdwy over 3f out: rdn along over 2f out: sn drvn and kpt on one pce* **18/1**

00-4 5 ¾ **Oetzi**[17] 1439 6-9-1 71 DaneO'Neill 4 71
(Alan Jarvis) *dwlt and hld up in rr: hdwy wl over 2f out: sn rdn and styd on appr fnl f: nrst fin* **12/1**

6/0- 6 ½ **Kayaan**[41] 2435 7-8-4 63 RossAtkinson(3) 5 63
(Pam Sly) *s.i.s and hld up in rr: hdwy wl over 2f out: rdn wl over 1f out: styd on fnl f: nrst fin* **20/1**

1111 7 4 ½ **Kingscombe (USA)**[28] 1226 5-8-6 62 HayleyTurner 2 55
(Linda Jewell) *trckd ldng pair on inner: pushed along over 4f out: rdn over 3f out and sn wknd* **10/1**

652- 8 1 ¼ **Musikhani**[235] 6158 4-8-12 70 PhillipMakin 3 61
(Philip Kirby) *t.k.h early: in tch: pushed along and lost pl bef 1/2-way: sn towards rr* **8/1**[3]

2-56 **9** *nk* **Eshtyaaq**[84] 471 7-9-2 **72**........ JimmyFortune 9 63
(David Evans) *trckd ldr: rdn along over 3f out: wknd over 2f out* **14/1**

3m 6.45s (-0.55) **Going Correction** -0.475s/f (Firm)
**WFA** 4 from 5yo+ 2lb 9 Ran SP% **116.8**
Speed ratings (Par 105): **82,81,79,79,78 78,75,75,74**
CSF £7.61 CT £35.89 TOTE £2.80: £1.10, £1.20, £2.70; EX 10.20 Trifecta £51.00.
**Owner** A D Spence **Bred** Cheval Court Stud **Trained** Lambourn, Berks

**FOCUS**
A fair pace for division one of this staying handicap. The winner stepped up on last year's form.

## 1849 LADS NIGHT OUT ON 9TH MAY H'CAP (DIV II) 1m 6f 15y
**4:15** (4:45) (Class 4) (0-80,77) 4-Y-O+ **£4,690** (£1,395; £697; £348) **Stalls** Low

Form RPR
03-4 **1** **Wannabe Your Man**[33] 1118 4-9-0 **70**........ AndreaAtzeni 8 79+
(Roger Varian) *hld up towards rr: smooth hdwy over 3f out: chal 2f out: led and sn rdn whn edgd lft wl over 1f out: drvn: carried hd high and edgd lft ins fnl f: kpt on wl towards fin* **11/4**[2]

132- **2** *1 1/4* **Ashdown Lad**[19] 3765 5-9-9 **77**........ GrahamLee 5 83
(Tom Symonds) *prom: cl up 1/2-way: effrt to chal 3f out: rdn along over 2f out: n.m.r and sltly outpcd wl over 1f out: styd on fnl f: tk 2nd nr fin* **8/1**

3133 **3** *hd* **Lineman**[33] 1133 4-8-12 **68**........ RobertWinston 2 73
(Andrew Hollinshead) *hld up: hdwy 3f out: effrt to chal whn carried lft wl over 1f out: sn rdn: drvn and ev ch whn n.m.r on inner wl ins fnl f: no ex last 50yds* **10/1**

-350 **4** *1* **Outrageous Request**[18] 1418 8-9-3 **71**........ DaneO'Neill 1 74
(William Stone) *hld up in rr: hdwy wl over 2f out: rdn to chse ldrs over 1f out: sn drvn and no imp ins fnl f* **16/1**

03-6 **5** *3 1/4* **Desert Recluse (IRE)**[18] 1418 7-9-8 **76**........ KierenFallon 4 75
(Brendan Powell) *led: rdn along over 3f out: hdd and drvn wl over 1f out: grad wknd* **5/2**[1]

404- **6** *hd* **Pearl Spice (IRE)**[223] 6540 4-9-7 **77**........(p) StevieDonohoe 6 75
(Tim Pitt) *towards rr: hdwy to trck ldrs after 3f: effrt on outer over 3f out: rdn along wl over 2f out and sn one pce* **10/1**

544- **7** *1* **Mount Macedon**[165] 7894 4-9-1 **71**........ PatDobbs 9 68
(Luca Cumani) *trckd ldrs: effrt over 3f out: rdn along wl over 2f out: sn btn* **9/2**[3]

002 **8** *1/2* **Honourable Knight (IRE)**[27] 1231 6-8-8 **62**........ HayleyTurner 7 58
(Mark Usher) *trckd ldrs: effrt over 3f out: rdn along wl over 2f out: sn drvn and wknd* **20/1**

3m 4.23s (-2.77) **Going Correction** -0.475s/f (Firm)
**WFA** 4 from 5yo+ 2lb 8 Ran SP% **113.4**
Speed ratings (Par 105): **88,87,87,86,84 84,84,83**
CSF £24.48 CT £189.18 TOTE £3.50: £1.70, £2.20, £1.90; EX 20.40 Trifecta £231.10.
**Owner** Normandie Stud Ltd **Bred** Normandie Stud Ltd **Trained** Newmarket, Suffolk

**FOCUS**
Division two of this handicap was run at a steady pace, in a slightly faster time than division I. The form is rated around the second.

## 1850 NEW RACING UK ANYWHERE AVAILABLE NOW FILLIES' H'CAP 5f 13y
**4:50** (5:15) (Class 4) (0-85,81) 4-Y-O+ **£4,690** (£1,395; £697; £348) **Stalls** High

Form RPR
2114 **1** **Iffranesia (FR)**[56] 834 4-8-12 **72**........(p) GrahamLee 4 81
(Robert Cowell) *chsd ldrs: rdn along and outpcd 1/2-way: hdwy over 1f out: styd on to ld last 100yds* **12/1**

500- **2** *3/4* **Mayfield Girl (IRE)**[234] 6212 4-9-1 **75**........ DavidAllan 3 82
(Mel Brittain) *chsd ldrs: rdn along and outpcd 1/2-way: hdwy over 1f out: styd on u.p and ev ch ins fnl f: nt qckn towards fin* **6/1**

24-6 **3** *1 1/4* **Six Wives**[4] 1695 7-8-5 **72**........(p) MatthewHopkins(7) 7 74
(Scott Dixon) *led and set str pce: clr 1/2-way: rdn over 1f out: wknd qckly ent fnl f: hdd last 100yds* **9/2**[3]

655- **4** *nk* **Whitecrest**[194] 7324 6-8-12 **72**........ SamHitchcott 5 73
(John Spearing) *sn outpcd in rr: rdn along 1/2-way: hdwy over 1f out: styd on fnl f: nrst fin* **16/1**

326- **5** *1 3/4* **Jofranka**[234] 6212 4-9-3 **77**........ GrahamGibbons 1 72
(David Barron) *chsd ldrs on outer: hdwy 2f out: sn rdn and wknd ent fnl f* **9/2**[3]

305- **6** *1/2* **Cheworee**[136] 8305 5-9-7 **81**........ RichardKingscote 6 74
(Tom Dascombe) *chsd ldr: rdn along 2f out: drvn and wknd appr fnl f* **4/1**[2]

544- **D** *3 3/4* **Gowanharry (IRE)**[195] 7314 5-9-2 **76**........ PaulMulrennan 2 55
(Michael Dods) *chsd ldng pair: hdwy to chse ldr 1/2-way: rdn wl over 1f out: edgd lft and enterting fnl f and sn wknd* **11/4**[1]

59.46s (-2.04) **Going Correction** -0.475s/f (Firm) 7 Ran SP% **110.9**
Speed ratings (Par 102): **97,95,93,93,90 89,83**
CSF £75.55 TOTE £6.30: £3.20, £9.10; EX 78.90 Trifecta £270.60.
**Owner** Cyril Humphris **Bred** Cyril Humphris **Trained** Six Mile Bottom, Cambs
■ Stewards' Enquiry : Matthew Hopkins two-day ban: use of whip (13-14 May)

**FOCUS**
A fair fillies' sprint handicap run at a decent pace. The winner carried over her AW progress.

## 1851 BDN CONSTRUCTION H'CAP 5f 13y
**5:25** (5:46) (Class 5) (0-70,70) 3-Y-O **£2,587** (£770; £384; £192) **Stalls** High

Form RPR
-115 **1** **Scarborough (IRE)**[20] 1396 3-9-0 **70**........ AlistairRawlinson(7) 6 83
(Michael Appleby) *trckd ldng pair: hdwy 2f out: led over 1f out: rdn and styd on wl fnl f* **9/2**[3]

10- **2** *1 1/4* **Rozene (IRE)**[200] 7170 3-9-3 **66**........ GrahamGibbons 1 74
(David Barron) *cl up: led over 3f out: rdn and hdd over 1f out: drvn ins fnl f: kpt on same pce* **4/1**[2]

14-1 **3** *2 1/4* **Dynamo Walt (IRE)**[18] 1425 3-9-5 **68**........(v) DaleSwift 9 68
(Derek Shaw) *towards rr: hdwy 2f out: rdn over 1f out: kpt on fnl f* **9/2**[3]

5-53 **4** *nk* **Inciting Incident (IRE)**[32] 1146 3-9-7 **70**........(b) GrahamLee 7 69
(Ed McMahon) *chsd ldrs: effrt wl over 1f out: sn rdn and kpt on same pce fnl f* **7/2**[1]

415- **5** *1/2* **Kiss From A Rose**[169] 7837 3-8-12 **61**........ ChrisCatlin 2 58
(Rae Guest) *dwlt and towards rr: hdwy on wd outside wl over 1f out: sn rdn and no imp fnl f* **7/1**

3406 **6** *2 1/4* **Ealain Aibrean (IRE)**[6] 1642 3-9-0 **63**........ JimmyFortune 10 52
(David Evans) *chsd ldrs: rdn along over 2f out: sn drvn and wknd over 1f out* **12/1**

-235 **7** *1 3/4* **Bonjour Steve**[25] 1278 3-9-2 **65**........ StevieDonohoe 3 48
(Richard Price) *dwlt: a in rr* **16/1**

-221 **8** *3/4* **Jolly Red Jeanz (IRE)**[54] 855 3-9-2 **65**........(b) DaneO'Neill 4 45
(J W Hills) *in tch: rdn along 1/2-way: sn wknd* **12/1**

053- **9** *11* **Little Briar Rose**[190] 7426 3-8-10 **59**........ SamHitchcott 5
(John Spearing) *led: hdd over 3f out and sn pushed along: rdn wl over 2f out and sn wknd* **50/1**

59.12s (-2.38) **Going Correction** -0.475s/f (Firm) 9 Ran SP% **114.3**
Speed ratings (Par 98): **100,98,94,93,93 89,86,85,67**
CSF £22.61 CT £85.07 TOTE £4.80: £1.70, £1.90, £1.90; EX 27.10 Trifecta £133.60.
**Owner** M Wainman **Bred** Tom Foley **Trained** Danethorpe, Notts

**FOCUS**
An open sprint handicap run at a sound pace. The front two were always handy and the form looks solid.
T/Jkpt: Not won. T/Plt: £73.70 to a £1 stake. Pool: £61,858.06 - 612.05 winning units T/Qpdt: £17.60 to a £1 stake. Pool: £4,237.74 - 177.86 winning units JR

# 1813 WOLVERHAMPTON (A.W) (L-H)
### Tuesday, April 29

**OFFICIAL GOING: Standard**
The final meeting at Wolverhampton until August. The degraded Polytrack surface is to be replaced by Tapeta.
Wind: Light across Weather: Fine

## 1852 QUICKSILVERSLOTS MORE JACKPOTS MORE MACHINES H'CAP 1m 141y(P)
**6:00** (6:01) (Class 6) (0-60,60) 3-Y-O **£2,264** (£673; £336; £168) **Stalls** Low

Form RPR
00-0 **1** **Oly'Roccs (IRE)**[92] 355 3-8-0 **46** oh1........ EvaMoscrop(7) 5 52
(Philip Kirby) *chsd ldr tl led over 6f out: hdd over 3f out: led again over 1f out: shkn up and hung rt ins fnl f: styd on* **14/1**[3]

0-03 **2** *3/4* **Company Secretary (USA)**[7] 1632 3-9-2 **55**........(b) FrannyNorton 2 59
(Jo Hughes) *a.p: chsd wnr over 1f out: rdn and ev ch ins fnl f: edgd lft: kpt on* **6/4**[2]

0-02 **3** *1* **Bourbon Prince**[5] 1683 3-8-5 **49**........ LouisSteward(5) 6 51
(Michael Bell) *hld up: hdwy over 1f out: styd on: nt trble ldrs* **10/11**[1]

04-3 **4** *5* **Hello Sweetness**[13] 1503 3-8-2 **46**........ JoeyHaynes(5) 4 36
(Jason Ward) *hld up in tch: rdn over 2f out: wknd fnl f* **25/1**

050- **5** *1 3/4* **Motamayezah**[130] 8368 3-8-7 **46** oh1........(p) LukeMorris 3 32
(Alan McCabe) *sn led: hdd over 6f out: led again over 3f out: rdn and hdd over 1f out: wknd fnl f* **40/1**

0620 **6** *7* **Red Wifey (IRE)**[10] 1588 3-9-7 **60**........(v[1]) SilvestreDeSousa 1 30
(Alan McCabe) *hld up: hdwy over 3f out: sn rdn: wknd over 1f out* **16/1**

1m 52.39s (1.89) **Going Correction** +0.075s/f (Slow) 6 Ran SP% **111.2**
Speed ratings (Par 96): **94,93,92,88,86 80**
CSF £35.09 TOTE £22.50: £13.30, £1.10; EX 45.30 Trifecta £88.10.
**Owner** Claudio Michael Grech **Bred** Elton Lodge Stud **Trained** Middleham, N Yorks

**FOCUS**
This weak handicap was the scene of an upset, the winner showing his first real form. The time was slow.

## 1853 QUICKSILVERSLOTS OPEN AFTER 10PM MEDIAN AUCTION MAIDEN STKS 7f 32y(P)
**6:30** (6:30) (Class 5) 3-4-Y-O **£2,911** (£866; £432; £216) **Stalls** High

Form RPR
4-2 **1** **Fast Delivery**[20] 1394 3-8-13 0........ SilvestreDeSousa 3 81+
(Saeed bin Suroor) *mde all: racd keenly and set stdy pce tl qcknd over 2f out: shkn up over 1f out: r.o* **1/8**[1]

4- **2** *2 3/4* **Serata Di Gala (FR)**[272] 4880 3-8-8 0........ LukeMorris 5 68
(Marco Botti) *trckd wnr: plld hrd: rdn over 2f out: hung lft ins fnl f: styd on same pce* **8/1**[2]

**3** *5* **Highland Rebel (IRE)** 3-8-13 0........ LeeTopliss 1 60
(Richard Fahey) *trckd ldrs: plld hrd: rdn 2f out: styd on same pce fr over 1f out* **20/1**[3]

**4** *3* **Notgordonitsrodger (IRE)** 4-9-5 0........ BradleyBosley(7) 2 57?
(Phil McEntee) *s.i.s: hld up: plld hrd: effrt over 2f out: sn outpcd* **50/1**

1m 30.29s (0.69) **Going Correction** +0.075s/f (Slow)
**WFA** 3 from 4yo 13lb 4 Ran SP% **106.7**
Speed ratings (Par 103): **99,95,90,86**
CSF £1.58 TOTE £1.10; EX 1.80 Trifecta £2.40.
**Owner** Godolphin **Bred** Gestut Wittekindshof **Trained** Newmarket, Suffolk

**FOCUS**
An uncompetitive maiden in which the winner made all in a slow time. Rather shaky form.

## 1854 QUICKSILVERSLOTS FUN ON THE HIGH STREET CLASSIFIED STKS 7f 32y(P)
**7:00** (7:00) (Class 6) 3-Y-O+ **£2,264** (£673; £336; £168) **Stalls** High

Form RPR
3222 **1** **Romantic Bliss (IRE)**[6] 1647 3-8-0 **51**........(b) RobJFitzpatrick(7) 1 58
(K R Burke) *led to 1/2-way: led again over 2f out: rdn over 1f out: r.o* **4/7**[1]

-650 **2** *2 1/4* **Al Enbess (IRE)**[5] 1673 4-9-6 **55**........ SilvestreDeSousa 3 57
(Ruth Carr) *a.p: rdn to chse wnr over 1f out: edgd rt: styd on same pce ins fnl f* **4/1**[2]

05-0 **3** *4 1/2* **Sweet Cherry (IRE)**[31] 1173 3-8-7 **55**........ FrannyNorton 4 40
(Peter Makin) *prom: rdn 1/2-way: styd on same pce fr over 1f out* **16/1**

0003 **4** *2 3/4* **Knight Charm**[5] 1666 4-9-6 **55**........ DavidProbert 2 38
(Gay Kelleway) *chsd wnr tl led 1/2-way: hdd over 2f out: wknd fnl f* **9/2**[3]

1m 29.49s (-0.11) **Going Correction** +0.075s/f (Slow)
**WFA** 3 from 4yo 13lb 4 Ran SP% **107.7**
Speed ratings (Par 101): **103,100,95,92**
CSF £3.14 TOTE £1.10; EX 2.30 Trifecta £17.70.
**Owner** Mrs Elaine M Burke **Bred** A Hanahoe **Trained** Middleham Moor, N Yorks

**FOCUS**
A weak, uncompetitive low-grade classified contest. The form is rated around the winner.

## 1855 QUICKSILVERSLOTS PLAY FROM 10P TO £2 (S) H'CAP 5f 216y(P)
**7:35** (7:36) (Class 6) (0-60,59) 3-Y-O **£1,940** (£577; £288; £144) **Stalls** Low

Form RPR
5350 **1** **River Dreamer (IRE)**[27] 1235 3-8-7 **45**........(t) AdamBeschizza 1 47
(Robert Stephens) *led: hdd briefly wl over 1f out: sn rdn: r.o* **16/1**

0055 **2** *hd* **Trefnant (IRE)**[7] 1626 3-8-7 **45**........ BenCurtis 7 46
(Chris Dwyer) *a.p: chsd wnr over 2f out: led briefly wl over 1f out: sn rdn: r.o* **22/1**

342- **3** *2 1/2* **Sexy Secret**[131] 8347 3-9-7 **59**........ RobertHavlin 3 52
(Lydia Pearce) *hld up in tch: rdn over 1f out: styd on* **4/1**[3]

62- **4** *1/2* **Jaeger Connoisseur (IRE)**[147] 8137 3-8-9 **52**........ JoeyHaynes(5) 2 43
(K R Burke) *sn chsng ldrs: rdn over 1f out: styd on same pce ins fnl f* **3/1**[2]

0-40 **5** *nk* **Lady Montenegro**[6] 1648 3-8-5 **50** RowanScott(7) 5 40
(Ann Duffield) *prom: lost pl 4f out: styd on fr over 1f out: nt trble ldrs* **9/1**
0430 **6** *2* **Aussie Sky (IRE)**[6] 1648 3-8-9 **47** LukeMorris 6 31
(Daniel Mark Loughnane) *w wnr over 3f: sn rdn: wknd fnl f* **5/1**
003- **7** *8* **Gauchita**[151] 8090 3-8-11 **54** LouisSteward(5) 4 12
(Michael Bell) *hld up: effrt over 2f out: wknd over 1f out* **9/4**[1]
1m 15.92s (0.92) **Going Correction** +0.075s/f (Slow) **7** Ran SP% **112.7**
Speed ratings (Par 96): **96,95,92,91,91 88,78**
CSF £273.19 TOTE £22.00: £10.50, £15.00; EX 194.70 Trifecta £560.90.There was no bid for the winner.
**Owner** R Stephens **Bred** Round Hill Stud **Trained** Penhow, Newport
**FOCUS**
A poor 3yo selling handicap marred by the atrocious kickback. The winner and the runner-up were both rated 42 coming into this which illustrates the strength of the contest, and the form is shaky. It paid to be on the pace.

## 1856 QUICKSILVERSLOTS PLAY £500 JACKPOT RAINBOW RICHES H'CAP (BOBIS RACE) 1m 4f 50y(P)
**8:05** (8:05) (Class 4) (0-80,80) 3-Y-O **£5,175** (£1,540; £769; £384) **Stalls** Low

Form RPR
521- **1** **Personal Opinion**[164] 7936 3-9-4 **77** MickaelBarzalona 1 89
(Charlie Appleby) *chsd clr ldr: shkn up to take clsr order over 2f out: led over 1f out: sn rdn: styd on* **4/6**[1]
6-1 **2** *3/4* **Galizzi (USA)**[26] 1269 3-9-6 **79** TomQueally 5 89
(Michael Bell) *s.i.s: hld up: hdwy over 2f out: chsd wnr over 1f out: hrd rdn ins fnl f: styd on* **7/4**[2]
4046 **3** *10* **Flying Cape (IRE)**[25] 1279 3-9-6 **79** TedDurcan 2 73
(Andrew Hollinshead) *hld up: effrt over 2f out: wknd over 1f out* **40/1**
2313 **4** *3/4* **Officer Drivel (IRE)**[19] 1407 3-8-13 **72** LukeMorris 4 65
(Luke Dace) *led: clr 10f out tl rdn over 2f out: wknd fnl f* **10/1**[3]
2m 38.58s (-2.52) **Going Correction** +0.075s/f (Slow) **4** Ran SP% **107.9**
Speed ratings (Par 100): **111,110,103,103**
CSF £2.06 TOTE £1.60; EX 1.80 Trifecta £12.50.
**Owner** Godolphin **Bred** Whitley Stud **Trained** Newmarket, Suffolk
**FOCUS**
Two well-bred, unexposed colts fought out a tight finish, clear of the other pair. Both have the potential to be better than their marks.

## 1857 QUICKSILVERSLOTS £1 TO WIN £500 FILLIES' H'CAP 1m 141y(P)
**8:35** (8:35) (Class 5) (0-70,69) 4-Y-O+ **£2,911** (£866; £432; £216) **Stalls** Low

Form RPR
40-0 **1** **Shahrazad (IRE)**[20] 1385 5-8-5 **60** (t) JackGilligan(7) 5 68
(Patrick Gilligan) *led over 7f out: shkn up over 1f out: r.o* **15/2**
1353 **2** *1* **Imaginary World (IRE)**[13] 1510 6-9-7 **69** (p) SilvestreDeSousa 2 75
(John Balding) *a.p: chsd wnr over 5f out: rdn over 1f out: ev ch ins fnl f: styd on* **11/4**[3]
3351 **3** *1 1/4* **Pretty Bubbles**[27] 1245 5-9-6 **68** FrederikTylicki 4 71
(J R Jenkins) *a.p: rdn and nt clr run over 1f out: swtchd lft ins fnl f: styd on* **13/8**[1]
/540 **4** *3 1/4* **Run Fat Lass Run**[17] 1446 4-8-7 **62** (e) EvaMoscrop(7) 3 57
(Philip Kirby) *hld up: rdn over 1f out: n.d* **25/1**
441- **5** *nse* **Thankyou Very Much**[153] 8060 4-9-2 **64** TedDurcan 1 59
(James Bethell) *led 1f: chsd ldrs: rdn over 2f out: no ex fnl f* **5/2**[2]
1m 51.47s (0.97) **Going Correction** +0.075s/f (Slow) **5** Ran SP% **108.9**
Speed ratings (Par 100): **98,97,96,93,93**
CSF £27.27 TOTE £13.60: £5.30, £2.40; EX 31.00 Trifecta £95.10.
**Owner** Linton Doolan **Bred** Shadwell Estate Company Limited **Trained** Newmarket, Suffolk
**FOCUS**
The penultimate contest gathered just a small field of fillies and mares together. However, it was competitive. The winner did not need to match her best.

## 1858 QUICKSILVERSLOTS PLAY YOUR FAVOURITE £500 JACKPOT H'CAP 1m 1f 103y(P)
**9:05** (9:05) (Class 5) (0-70,68) 3-Y-O **£2,911** (£866; £432; £216) **Stalls** Low

Form RPR
550- **1** **Arabian Comet (IRE)**[221] 6597 3-9-7 **68** SilvestreDeSousa 4 78
(William Haggas) *chsd ldr tl shkn up to ld over 1f out: r.o wl* **1/1**[1]
0-30 **2** *4 1/2* **Goleador (USA)**[10] 1588 3-9-1 **62** (p) LukeMorris 3 63
(Marco Botti) *led: rdn and hdd over 1f out: styd on same pce fnl f* **11/4**[2]
40-0 **3** *3* **Aran Sky (IRE)**[30] 1192 3-9-7 **68** PhillipMakin 1 63
(K R Burke) *trckd ldrs: pushed along over 3f out: no ex fnl f* **4/1**[3]
020- **4** *4 1/2* **Gift Of Rain (IRE)**[166] 7874 3-9-7 **68** TomQueally 2 53
(Ed Dunlop) *hld up: hdwy over 2f out: sn rdn: wknd over 1f out* **7/1**
2m 2.13s (0.43) **Going Correction** +0.075s/f (Slow) **4** Ran SP% **109.2**
Speed ratings (Par 98): **101,97,94,90**
CSF £4.04 TOTE £1.70; EX 3.80 Trifecta £10.60.
**Owner** Abdulla Al Mansoori **Bred** Darley **Trained** Newmarket, Suffolk
**FOCUS**
Some of the lesser lights from top yards fought out this closing 3yo handicap. Not form to be too confident about.
T/Plt: £738.50 to a £1 stake. Pool: £40,743.04 - 40.27 winning units T/Qpdt: £299.60 to a £1 stake. Pool: £3,279.73 - 8.10 winning units CR

# 1633 YARMOUTH (L-H)
Tuesday, April 29
**OFFICIAL GOING: Good to firm (good in places; watered; 7.6)**
Wind: Light to medium; half behind Weather: Overcast; dry

## 1859 TRAFALGAR RESTAURANT AT YARMOUTH RACECOURSE MAIDEN STKS 5f 43y
**2:05** (2:05) (Class 5) 2-Y-O **£2,911** (£866; £432; £216) **Stalls** Centre

Form RPR
**1** **Zuhoor Baynoona (IRE)** 2-9-0 0 RyanMoore 7 80+
(Richard Fahey) *dwlt: sn rcvrd and pressed ldr after 1f: led 1/2-way: pushed along and asserted 1f out: r.o wl: pushed out: comf* **8/11**[1]
04 **2** *2 3/4* **King Crimson**[10] 1575 2-9-2 0 WilliamTwiston-Davies(3) 1 72
(Mick Channon) *t.k.h early: in tch in midfield: clsd to trck ldng pair ent fnl 2f: effrt to chse wnr jst ins fnl f: no imp but kpt on for clr 2nd* **11/4**[2]
**3** *6* **Wolfofwallstreet (IRE)** 2-9-5 0 WilliamBuick 3 50
(Ed Walker) *led for 1f: chsd ldrs after: chsd wnr ent fnl 2f: rdn and btn jst over 1f out: wknd ins fnl f* **6/1**[3]
00 **4** *2* **Baileys Pursuit**[12] 1528 2-9-0 0 (p[1]) NickyMackay 5 38
(Chris Dwyer) *chsd ldrs: rdn and struggling 2f out: sn btn: no ch fnl f* **66/1**
**5** *1/2* **Mr Shekells** 2-9-0 0 DannyBrock(5) 4 41
(Philip McBride) *s.i.s: rn green and outpcd in rr: modest hdwy over 1f out: n.d* **22/1**
**6** *9* **Mary Ann Bugg (IRE)** 2-8-11 0 RyanPowell(3) 6
(Phil McEntee) *chsd ldr tl led after 1f: hdd 1/2-way and sn struggling u.p: wl bhd fnl f* **25/1**
0 **7** *1* **Ralph McTell**[13] 1512 2-9-5 0 LiamJones 2
(Alan Coogan) *s.i.s: a outpcd and wl bhd* **100/1**
1m 1.7s (-1.00) **Going Correction** -0.40s/f (Firm) **7** Ran SP% **109.5**
Speed ratings (Par 92): **92,87,78,74,74 59,58**
CSF £2.54 TOTE £1.50: £1.02, £3.80; EX 2.90 Trifecta £5.70.
**Owner** Jaber Abdullah **Bred** Rabbah Bloodstock Limited **Trained** Musley Bank, N Yorks
**FOCUS**
The front pair drew clear in a maiden lacking depth.

## 1860 CAN'T BELIEVE GARY HOLMES IS 50 MEDIAN AUCTION MAIDEN STKS 5f 43y
**2:35** (2:36) (Class 6) 3-4-Y-O **£2,264** (£673; £336; £168) **Stalls** Centre

Form RPR
**1** **Boy Wonder** 3-9-0 0 WilliamTwiston-Davies(3) 6 68+
(Mick Channon) *in tch in midfield: effrt to chal over 1f out: rdn to ld ins fnl f: r.o: pushed out towards fin* **4/7**[1]
45-6 **2** *hd* **Vodka Chaser (IRE)**[111] 86 3-8-7 60 PhilipPrince(5) 8 62
(Alison Hutchinson) *chsd ldrs: rdn and ev ch over 1f out: hung lft and hdd ins fnl f: kpt on but hld fnl 75yds* **16/1**
00- **3** *3 3/4* **Tete Orange**[178] 7692 3-8-12 0 AdamBeschizza 9 49
(Stuart Williams) *s.i.s: in tch in rr but sn niggled along: edging lft and hdwy jst over 1f out: styd on to go 3rd wl ins fnl f: no threat to ldng pair* **16/1**
240 **4** *1* **Meebo (IRE)**[20] 1384 3-8-12 58 (v) ShaneKelly 7 45
(J R Jenkins) *towards rr: hdwy over 1f out: styd on steadily ins fnl f: nvr trbld ldrs* **8/1**[3]
650 **5** *1/2* **Fizzolo**[7] 1634 3-8-9 0 OisinMurphy(3) 4 43
(Noel Quinlan) *chsd ldr tl led 3f out: rdn and hrd pressed over 1f out: hdd 1f out: wknd ins fnl f* **50/1**
-564 **6** *1 1/2* **Anfield**[84] 481 3-8-12 50 JamieSpencer 2 38
(Mick Quinn) *dwlt: sn rcvrd and chsd ldrs: rdn and ev ch over 1f out tl no ex 1f out: racd awkwardly and wknd ins fnl f: eased cl home* **14/1**
**7** *1 1/4* **Khelfan** 3-8-12 0 NickyMackay 1 33
(Martin Smith) *s.i.s: bhd: rdn and hdwy on far side over 2f out: no ex over 1f out: wknd ins fnl f* **7/1**[2]
0-4 **8** *3* **Starlite Jewel**[7] 1634 3-8-9 0 RyanPowell(3) 3 22
(George Margarson) *dwlt: in tch in midfield: struggling and losing pl 1/2-way: bhd over 1f out* **16/1**
04-0 **9** *3 1/2* **Princess Bounty**[102] 215 4-9-3 44 RachealKneller(5) 5 14
(Phil McEntee) *led for 2f: sn rdn and lost pl: bhd 1f out* **100/1**
1m 1.96s (-0.74) **Going Correction** -0.40s/f (Firm)
**WFA** 3 from 4yo 10lb **9** Ran SP% **114.5**
Speed ratings (Par 101): **89,88,82,81,80 77,75,71,65**
CSF £12.01 TOTE £1.40: £1.10, £2.40, £3.30; EX 12.60 Trifecta £130.30.
**Owner** Dark Horse Racing Partnership 7 **Bred** F D Harvey **Trained** West Ilsley, Berks
**FOCUS**
A very weak maiden run in a slow time. It doesn't look a race to be giving chances to.

## 1861 FOLLOW US ON TWITTER AT YARMOUTH H'CAP (BOBIS RACE) 1m 3y
**3:05** (3:06) (Class 4) (0-85,84) 3-Y-O **£4,690** (£1,395; £697; £348) **Stalls** Centre

Form RPR
15 **1** **Mindurownbusiness (IRE)**[10] 1580 3-9-0 **80** OisinMurphy(3) 4 89+
(David Simcock) *t.k.h: chsd ldrs tl wnt 2nd after 2f: rdn 3f out: ev ch wl over 1f out: led ins fnl f: styd on wl and forged ahd fnl 100yds* **7/1**[3]
1110 **2** *1 1/2* **Crowdmania**[13] 1513 3-9-7 **84** LiamJones 6 90
(Mark Johnston) *led: rdn ent fnl 2f: drvn and hdd ins fnl f: no ex and btn fnl 100yds: kpt on same pce after* **12/1**
02-2 **3** *3/4* **Brigliadoro (IRE)**[55] 847 3-8-9 **72** ShaneKelly 5 76
(Philip McBride) *stdd s: hld up in tch in last pair: hdwy 3f out: chsd ldng pair over 1f out: kpt on same pce ins fnl f* **11/1**
42-6 **4** *1 1/4* **Damascene**[22] 1353 3-8-6 **74** MarcMonaghan(5) 9 75
(Marco Botti) *chsd ldr for 2f: styd chsng ldrs: rdn ent fnl 2f: kpt on same pce u.p fnl f* **12/1**
214- **5** *hd* **New Street (IRE)**[246] 5829 3-8-11 **74** RyanMoore 8 75
(Richard Fahey) *t.k.h: wl in tch in midfield tl lost pl 1/2-way: bhd and struggling u.p over 2f out: rallied and styd on ins fnl f: no threat to wnr* **8/1**
34-1 **6** *4* **Shyron**[8] 1614 3-8-9 **79** 6ex JordanVaughan(7) 3 70
(George Margarson) *chsd ldrs: rdn 2f out: sn struggling and outpcd: wknd ent fnl f* **6/1**[2]
51-6 **7** *nk* **Grandest**[20] 1390 3-9-5 **82** WilliamBuick 7 73
(John Gosden) *hld up in tch in last pair: rdn and effrt ent fnl 2f: no real prog: wl hld fnl f* **6/1**[2]
1 **8** *1 3/4* **Equitable**[46] 954 3-9-0 **77** MartinLane 1 64
(Lady Cecil) *in tch in midfield: rdn 3f out: no hdwy and struggling 2f out: wl btn 1f out: bhd and eased cl home* **7/4**[1]
1m 35.99s (-4.61) **Going Correction** -0.40s/f (Firm) **8** Ran SP% **112.3**
Speed ratings (Par 100): **107,105,104,103,103 99,99,97**
CSF £81.91 CT £906.11 TOTE £9.10: £2.90, £3.90, £2.20; EX 62.00 Trifecta £994.50.
**Owner** Mrs Julia Annable **Bred** Laundry Cottage Stud Farm **Trained** Newmarket, Suffolk
**FOCUS**
A fair handicap, although it was run at a steady early pace and little got involved. The winner is progressing.

## 1862 RIVERSIDE RENTALS AT HORNING H'CAP 7f 3y
**3:35** (3:35) (Class 3) (0-95,95) 4-Y-O **£7,246** (£2,168; £1,084; £542; £270) **Stalls** Centre

Form RPR
113- **1** **Horsted Keynes (FR)**[174] 7769 4-9-1 **89** JamieSpencer 4 104+
(Roger Varian) *trckd ldng pair and a gng wl: led on bit ent fnl f: nudged along and in command ins fnl f: comf* **6/4**[1]
2064 **2** *1* **Tellovoi (IRE)**[3] 1721 6-9-1 **92** (v) OisinMurphy(3) 3 97
(Ann Stokell) *led: rdn wl over 1f out: hdd ent fnl f: kpt on u.p but no threat to wnr* **5/2**[2]
052- **3** *1 1/4* **Kakatosi**[119] 8455 7-8-9 **83** ShaneKelly 6 85
(Mike Murphy) *stdd s: t.k.h: hld up in last pair: rdn and effrt ent fnl 2f: hdwy u.p over 1f out: kpt on ins fnl f: no threat to wnr* **10/1**
411- **4** *1 1/4* **Mabait**[206] 7018 8-9-0 **95** GeorgeBuckell(7) 5 93
(David Simcock) *racd in midfield: rdn over 2f out: kpt on same pce u.p ins fnl f: no threat to wnr* **8/1**[3]

1000 5 6 **Swiss Cross**[38] 1066 7-9-0 **88**..............................(t) WilliamBuick 2 70
(Phil McEntee) *chsd ldr: rdn over 2f out: 3rd and btn over 1f out: fdd ins fnl f* **12/1**

510- 6 ½ **Vainglory (USA)**[318] 3339 10-8-9 **90**.................. LewisWalsh(7) 7 71
(David Simcock) *a towards rr: rdn 3f out: sn struggling and outpcd ent fnl 2f: n.d after* **25/1**

306 7 nk **Chilworth Icon**[10] 1576 4-9-0 **91**.................. WilliamTwiston-Davies(3) 1 71
(Mick Channon) *stdd s: hld up in midfield: effrt 2f out: sn btn: wknd ent fnl f* **8/1**[3]

1m 23.44s (-3.16) **Going Correction** -0.40s/f (Firm) **7** Ran SP% **111.4**
Speed ratings (Par 107): **102,100,99,98,91 90,90**
CSF £5.02 TOTE £1.60: £1.10, £2.60; EX 6.10 Trifecta £34.50.
**Owner** Mrs Fitri Hay **Bred** Oceanic Bloodstock & Mme A Gravereaux **Trained** Newmarket, Suffolk
**FOCUS**
A decent handicap. The winner impressed and the form is rated around the runner-up.

## 1863 CONFERENCES AT GREAT YARMOUTH RACECOURSE FILLIES' H'CAP 7f 3y
**4:05** (4:07) (Class 5) (0-70,68) 4-Y-0+ **£2,587** (£770; £384; £192) **Stalls** Centre

Form RPR

65-2 1 **Meet Me Halfway**[27] 1230 4-9-7 **68**.................. GeorgeBaker 5 79+
(Chris Wall) *hld up in tch: effrt to chal over 1f out: rn green and wandering arnd whn led jst ins fnl f: kpt on* **9/4**[1]

0124 2 1½ **Bladewood Girl**[21] 1365 6-8-4 **54** oh1.................. OisinMurphy(3) 4 61
(J R Jenkins) *chsd ldr: rdn and effrt to chal over 1f out: led jst over 1f out tl hdd jst ins fnl f: styd on same pce after* **11/4**[2]

150- 3 2½ **Gift Of Silence**[209] 6941 5-9-6 **67**.................. JamieSpencer 3 68
(John Berry) *stdd s: hld up in tch in rr: rdn and effrt over 1f out: wnt 3rd but styd on same pce ins fnl f* **9/4**[1]

126- 4 3¼ **Tiger's Home**[154] 8052 4-8-5 **57**.................. ShelleyBirkett(5) 2 49
(Julia Feilden) *mounted on crse: broke wl: led for 1f: chsd ldr after tl led again over 2f out: rdn and hdd jst over 1f out: fdd ins fnl f* **8/1**[3]

6206 5 11 **Beylerbey (USA)**[13] 1510 4-8-12 **59**.................. LiamJones 1 22
(Mark Johnston) *pushed along early: hdwy to ld after 1f: rdn and hdd over 2f out: sn struggling and btn wl over 1f out: bhd fnl f* **10/1**

1m 23.63s (-2.97) **Going Correction** -0.40s/f (Firm) **5** Ran SP% **108.4**
Speed ratings (Par 100): **100,98,95,91,79**
CSF £8.41 TOTE £3.30: £1.60, £3.40; EX 7.10 Trifecta £14.20.
**Owner** Des Thurlby **Bred** Stratford Place Stud And Watership Down **Trained** Newmarket, Suffolk
**FOCUS**
A modest fillies' race, but Beylerbey took them along at a good gallop and the time was only 0.19sec slower than the preceding 0-95 handicap. The winner progressed from her reappearance.

## 1864 HAVEN SEASHORE AT CAISTER H'CAP 1m 1f
**4:40** (4:41) (Class 5) (0-70,69) 4-Y-0+ **£2,587** (£770; £384; £192) **Stalls** Low

Form RPR

22-4 1 **Taro Tywod (IRE)**[17] 1454 5-9-3 **65**.................. ShaneKelly 1 74
(Mark Brisbourne) *chsd ldr: upside ldr and travelling strly 4f out: led over 2f out: rdn clr wl over 1f out: clr but doing little in front whn rdn 1f out: drvn ins fnl f: a doing enough* **5/1**[3]

20-1 2 nk **Ela Goog La Mou**[8] 1617 5-8-8 **59** 6ex.................. RosieJessop(3) 4 67
(Peter Charalambous) *stdd s: hld up off the pce in last pair: hdwy to chse ldng trio 6f out: clsd and wl in tch over 4f out: rdn and effrt over 2f out: chsd clr wnr 1f out: kpt on ins fnl f: nvr quite getting to wnr* **4/1**[2]

30-5 3 1¾ **Automotive**[20] 1385 6-8-9 **62**.................. ShelleyBirkett(5) 6 66
(Julia Feilden) *hld up off the pce in rr: clsd and in tch 4f out: rdn and effrt on inner ent fnl 2f: kpt on ins fnl f* **4/1**[2]

040- 4 ¾ **Gabrial The Thug (FR)**[141] 8223 4-8-9 **57**.................. JamieSpencer 5 60
(Richard Fahey) *hld up off the pce in last quartet: clsd and in tch 4f out: rdn over 2f out: no imp tl swtchd rt and plugged on ins fnl f* **5/2**[1]

06-0 5 shd **Super Cookie**[8] 1617 4-8-13 **64**.................. OisinMurphy(3) 7 67
(Noel Quinlan) *led for 1f: chsd ldng pair and clr of rivals tl 4f out: rdn and effrt over 2f out: plugged on same pce fnl f* **14/1**

14-0 6 1¾ **Two No Bids (IRE)**[117] 11 4-9-3 **65**.................. GeorgeBaker 3 64
(Phil McEntee) *led after 1f: jnd 4f out: rdn and hdd over 2f out: edgd rt and outpcd over 1f out: wknd ins fnl f* **11/2**

-426 7 4½ **Funky Cold Medina**[85] 461 4-9-7 **69**.................. WilliamCarson 2 58
(Tom Keddy) *hld up off the pce in last quartet: clsd and in tch 4f out: rdn and btn over 2f out: bhd over 1f out* **16/1**

1m 54.54s (-1.26) **Going Correction** -0.05s/f (Good) **7** Ran SP% **113.2**
Speed ratings (Par 103): **103,102,101,100,100 98,94**
CSF £24.62 TOTE £5.20: £2.60, £1.30; EX 21.90 Trifecta £44.70.
**Owner** Rasio Cymru Racing 1 **Bred** Pat Fullam **Trained** Great Ness, Shropshire
**FOCUS**
The pace was sound throughout for this low-grade handicap and they finished in a heap. The winner is rated better than ever.

## 1865 ANNUAL BADGES AT GREAT YARMOUTH RACECOURSE H'CAP 1m 3f 101y
**5:10** (5:10) (Class 6) (0-55,53) 4-Y-0+ **£1,940** (£577; £288; £144) **Stalls** Low

Form RPR

30-6 1 **Camelopardalis**[17] 1453 5-9-1 **52**.................. DannyBrock(5) 9 63
(Philip McBride) *chsd ldrs tl hdwy to ld 9f out: mde rest: wnt clr 4f out: in n.d after: rdn 2f out: eased towards fin* **4/1**[2]

0-64 2 3½ **Brown Pete (IRE)**[25] 1288 6-8-13 **48**.................. OisinMurphy(3) 8 52
(Ann Stokell) *hld up off the pce in last trio: rdn and effrt but plenty to do over 2f out: wnt 3rd over 1f out: chsd wnr ins fnl f: kpt on but nvr a threat to wnr* **5/2**[1]

222- 3 1½ **Zinnobar**[181] 7636 4-9-4 **50**.................. MartinLane 10 52
(Jonathan Portman) *racd in midfield: rdn and effrt in modest 3rd over 3f out: chsd wnr over 2f out: plugged on but nvr a threat to wnr: lost 2nd ins fnl f* **8/1**[3]

/33- 4 5 **Wasabi (IRE)**[36] 2642 5-9-5 **51**.................. JamieSpencer 2 45
(John Berry) *jostled leaving stalls: hld up off the pce in rr: rdn and effrt over 2f out: plugged on to go 4th 1f out: nvr trbld ldrs* **8/1**[3]

0-54 5 6 **Omotesando**[17] 1452 4-9-6 **52**.................. ShaneKelly 7 36
(Mark Brisbourne) *hld up off the pce in midfield: rdn and effrt 3f out: no imp: nvr trbld ldrs* **14/1**

-333 6 3¼ **Shamiana**[33] 1138 4-9-5 **51**..............................(b) GeorgeBaker 4 30
(Daniel Kubler) *jostled leaving stalls: hld up off the pce in last trio: hdwy 4f out: modest 3rd and rdn over 2f out: no prog: wknd over 1f out* **4/1**[2]

00-5 7 7 **Daisie Cutter**[25] 1288 4-8-10 **45**.................. WilliamTwiston-Davies(3) 5 13
(Graeme McPherson) *short of room leaving stalls: hdwy to ld 10f out tl 9f out: chsd ldrs after: rdn and struggling 4f out: bhd fnl 2f* **33/1**

5-00 8 16 **Greyemkay**[17] 1453 6-8-13 **45**.................. WilliamCarson 6 10
(Richard Price) *led tl 10f out: chsd ldr: rdn 4f out: lost 2nd and 2f out and wll btn: t.o and eased ins fnl f* **10/1**

000- 9 10 **Market Puzzle (IRE)**[214] 6794 7-8-7 **46**..............(p) GaryMahon(7) 1
(Mark Brisbourne) *racd in midfield: rdn and lost pl over 3f out: sn bhd: t.o and eased ins fnl f* **20/1**

2m 27.78s (-0.92) **Going Correction** -0.05s/f (Good) **9** Ran SP% **114.3**
Speed ratings (Par 101): **101,98,97,93,89 87,81,70,63**
CSF £14.24 CT £74.68 TOTE £2.80: £1.10, £2.80, £2.10; EX 16.90 Trifecta £209.90.
**Owner** Budgett, Fleming, Hamilton **Bred** Miss Harriet Budgett **Trained** Newmarket, Suffolk
■ Stewards' Enquiry : Danny Brock three-day ban: used whip without giving mare time to respond (13-15 May)
**FOCUS**
A weak handicap in which the winner was given an enterprising ride from the front. The form is rated around the third.
T/Plt: £61.30 to a £1 stake. Pool: £47,002.14 - 559.60 winning units T/Qpdt: £34.90 to a £1 stake. Pool: £2,899.58 - 61.35 winning units SP

# ASCOT (R-H)
Wednesday, April 30

**OFFICIAL GOING: Soft (str 6.2, rnd 5.8)**
Rail on Round course moved in 3yds from 12f to Home straight adding 3yd to Old Mile and 16yds to 2m race.
Wind: light, half against Weather: dry, mainly sunny

## 1866 INJURED JOCKEYS FUND 50TH ANNIVERSARY CELEBRATION CONDITIONS STKS (BOBIS RACE) 5f
**2:00** (2:02) (Class 2) 2-Y-O **£8,715** (£2,609; £1,304; £652) **Stalls** Centre

Form RPR

01 1 **Escalating**[11] 1575 2-9-1 0.................. JamesDoyle 3 89
(Pat Eddery) *rn green: mde virtually all: rdn over 1f out: swvd lft and bmpd runner-up jst over 1f out: kpt on wl ins fnl f* **13/8**[1]

0 2 ½ **Kibaar**[19] 1417 2-8-11 0.................. PaulHanagan 4 85
(J W Hills) *rn green: in tch in rr: clsd and trckd ldrs 2f out: swtchd lft and effrt whn bmpd and pushed lft jst over 1f out: rallied to chse wnr fnl 75yds: styd on but nvr quite getting to wnr* **3/1**[3]

12 3 ¾ **Abscent Friends**[14] 1512 2-9-1 0.................. RyanWhile 2 85
(Bill Turner) *w ldr: rdn and ev ch over 1f out tl lost 2nd and one pce fnl 75yds* **8/1**

1 4 2 **Magical Roundabout (IRE)**[23] 1349 2-9-1 0.................. RichardHughes 1 77
(Richard Hannon) *chsd ldrs: rdn and effrt whn hung bdly rt over 1f out: styd pressing ldrs tl no ex and btn fnl 100yds* **15/8**[2]

1m 4.24s (3.74) **Going Correction** +0.55s/f (Yiel) **4** Ran SP% **109.0**
Speed ratings (Par 98): **92,91,90,86**
CSF £6.72 TOTE £2.80; EX 6.70 Trifecta £50.10.
**Owner** K Abdullah **Bred** Juddmonte Farms Ltd **Trained** Nether Winchendon, Bucks
**FOCUS**
Rail on Round course moved in 3yds from 1m4f to Home straight adding 3yd to Old Mile and 16yds to 2m race. The GoingStick suggested the ground was slower on the Round course (5.8) compared to the straight (6.2). Those who rode in the opener agreed with the official description of 'soft'. They raced centre-field in a conditions race that has fallen to some smart juveniles in recent years, and three of the four runners this time around were previous winners, but it was the one who hadn't scored previously, Kibaar, who almost certainly would have won had Escalating not swerved in front of him. The result stood after an enquiry. The form is rated at the lower end of the race averages.

## 1867 RACING POST MOBILE APP PAVILION STKS (LISTED RACE) 6f
**2:35** (2:36) (Class 1) 3-Y-O
**£20,982** (£7,955; £3,981; £1,983; £995; £499) **Stalls** Centre

Form RPR

3014 1 **Mick's Yer Man**[14] 1518 3-9-0 **95**.................. RyanWhile 5 106
(Bill Turner) *wl in tch in midfield: effrt to chse ldr whn carried rt and n.m.r ent fnl 2f: rdn and chal over 1f out: sustained effrt u.p to ld fnl 50yds: rdn out* **16/1**

211- 2 nk **Musical Comedy**[187] 7503 3-9-0 **106**.................. RyanMoore 3 105
(Richard Hannon) *chsd ldr tl led over 2f out: a edging rt after: rdn 2f out: drvn ins fnl f: hdd and no ex fnl 50yds* **2/1**[1]

254- 3 2 **Rufford (IRE)**[186] 7525 3-9-0 **105**.................. JimmyFortune 4 99
(Richard Fahey) *led tl over 2f out: sn drvn: outpcd over 1f out: rallied and styd on again ins fnl f: wnt 3rd towards fin* **5/1**[3]

1 4 hd **Danehill Revival**[22] 1361 3-8-9 0.................. PaulHanagan 2 93
(William Haggas) *racd apart fr rivals for 3f: chsd ldrs: rdn and pressing ldrs ent fnl 2f: no ex and outpcd ins fnl f: lost 3rd towards fin* **5/1**[3]

1-52 5 2¼ **Expert (IRE)**[14] 1518 3-9-0 **101**.................. RichardHughes 6 92
(Richard Hannon) *stdd s: hld up in tch in last pair: rdn and effrt to chse ldrs wl over 1f out: no imp: wknd ins fnl f* **11/4**[2]

30-5 6 ½ **One Chance (IRE)**[14] 1513 3-8-9 **94**.................. TomQueally 1 85
(John Butler) *swtchd lft sn after s: hld up in tch in last pair: clsd to trck ldrs whn n.m.r ent fnl 2f: rdn and chsd ldrs wl over 1f out tl ent fnl f: wknd fnl f* **25/1**

24-1 7 14 **Speedfiend**[28] 1229 3-9-0 **105**.................. AdamKirby 7 48
(Noel Quinlan) *t.k.h: hld up wl in tch in midfield: dropped to last pair 1/2-way: rdn and btn 2f out: bhd and eased ins fnl f* **6/1**

1m 16.81s (2.31) **Going Correction** +0.55s/f (Yiel) **7** Ran SP% **117.3**
Speed ratings (Par 106): **106,105,102,102,99 99,80**
CSF £50.36 TOTE £17.70: £4.80, £1.50; EX 31.30 Trifecta £470.90.
**Owner** Mrs Tracy Turner & E A Brook **Bred** Heather Raw **Trained** Sigwells, Somerset
**FOCUS**
This didn't appeal as a particularly strong Listed event and there was a bit of a turn up. They ended up nearer the far side, having started off more down the middle. The form is rated a bit cautiously.

## 1868 SPINAL INJURIES ASSOCIATION EBF STALLIONS STKS (CONDITIONS RACE) (BOBIS RACE) (FILLIES) 1m (R)
**3:10** (3:12) (Class 3) 3-Y-O
**£9,337** (£2,796; £1,398; £699; £349; £175) **Stalls** Low

Form RPR

422- 1 **Adhwaa**[179] 7695 3-8-12 92.................. PaulHanagan 9 94
(J W Hills) *hld up wl in tch in midfield: rdn and effrt to chal 2f out: drvn to ld over 1f out: hdd ins fnl f: rallied gamely u.p to ld again towards fin* **4/1**[3]

1 2 nk **Evita Peron**[19] 1422 3-8-12 0.................. JimCrowley 7 93
(Ralph Beckett) *rrd as stalls opened: hld up in tch in last pair: hdwy on outer jst over 2f out: rdn and chal over 1f out: drvn to ld ins fnl f: hdd and no ex towards fin* **2/1**[1]

4 **3** *shd* **Solar Magic**[13] 1534 3-8-12 0 WilliamBuick 8 93
(John Gosden) *chsd ldrs tl wnt 2nd 1/2-way: rdn to ld 2f out: edgd rt u.p and hdd over 1f out: ev ch after: no ex cl home* **5/2**[2]

052- **4** *2 1/4* **Rasheeda**[250] 5699 3-8-12 86 LukeMorris 4 88
(Marco Botti) *wnt rt s: hld up wl in tch in midfield: effrt and n.m.r ent fnl 2f: hdwy u.p to chse ldng trio 1f out: kpt on but no real imp* **16/1**

140- **5** *2 1/4* **Lustrous**[200] 7194 3-8-12 93 RichardHughes 2 83+
(Richard Hannon) *hld up in tch in midfield: hmpd and hit rail 4f out: travelling wl but nt clr run on 2f out: swtchd lft and stl nt clr run 1f out: swtchd further lft sn after: 7th and no ch fnl 150yds: nudged along and kpt on after* **14/1**

-130 **6** *1* **Stosur (IRE)**[67] 721 3-9-1 82 DavidProbert 6 83
(Gay Kelleway) *chsd ldr tl 1/2-way: rdn jst over 2f out: 4th and outpcd u.p over 1f out: wknd fnl f* **50/1**

01- **7** *2 3/4* **Bright Cecily (IRE)**[258] 5443 3-8-12 80 SteveDrowne 3 74+
(Clive Cox) *stdd s: hld up in last pair: switching out lft and effrt ent fnl 2f: no progrss wknd jst over 1f out* **16/1**

1- **8** *4* **Kind Invitation**[167] 7875 3-8-12 81 MickaelBarzalona 5 65
(Charlie Appleby) *led: rdn and hdd 2f out: drvn and btn over 1f out: wknd fnl f* **8/1**

1m 45.64s (4.94) **Going Correction** +0.65s/f (Yiel) **8** Ran SP% **113.4**
Speed ratings (Par 99): **101,100,100,98,96 95,92,88**
CSF £12.20 TOTE £4.80: £1.30, £1.10, £1.50; EX 12.00 Trifecta £27.40.
**Owner** Hamdan Al Maktoum **Bred** Shadwell Estate Company Limited **Trained** Upper Lambourn, Berks

**FOCUS**
An interesting fillies' conditions event, run at a fair pace. The winner set the standard on her 2yo form and is rated around that.

## 1869 LONGINES SAGARO STKS (GROUP 3) 2m
3:45 (3:46) (Class 1) 4-Y-O+
**£34,026** (£12,900; £6,456; £3,216; £1,614; £810) **Stalls** Low

Form RPR

121- **1** **Tac De Boistron (FR)**[185] 7566 7-9-9 117 FrankieDettori 3 119
(Marco Botti) *hld up in tch in last trio: clsd to trck ldrs over 2f out: rdn and qcknd to ld over 1f out: r.o strly and drew clr fnl f: impressive* **7/2**[2]

00-2 **2** *5* **Earth Amber**[21] 1398 5-8-13 95 KierenFallon 6 103
(Nicky Henderson) *chsd ldr tl rdn to ld wl over 2f out: drvn and hdd 2f out: outpcd by wnr over 1f out: 2nd and kpt on same pce fnl f* **16/1**

016- **3** *1* **Oriental Fox (GER)**[200] 7193 6-9-2 106 JoeFanning 4 105
(Mark Johnston) *in tch in midfield: effrt u.p to chal over 2f out: led 2f out tl hdd and over 1f out: sn outpcd by wnr: 3rd and one pce fnl f* **14/1**

23- **4** *4* **Missunited (IRE)**[20] 1416 7-8-13 107 RichardHughes 5 97
(Michael Winters, Ire) *stdd s: hdwy to chse ldrs after 1f: n.m.r over 2f out: sn rdn: 4th and no imp over 1f out* **9/2**[3]

32-6 **5** *3 1/4* **Cocktail Queen (IRE)**[18] 1434 4-8-9 97 DaneO'Neill 1 93
(David Elsworth) *hld up in tch in last trio: switching out lft and effrt over 2f out: sn drvn and outpcd 2f out: sn wknd* **22/1**

5-50 **6** *9* **Simenon (IRE)**[32] 1177 7-9-2 111 RyanMoore 2 85
(W P Mullins, Ire) *hld up in rr: short-lived effrt and no hdwy over 2f out: n.d: bhd fnl f* **5/1**

112- **7** *32* **Harris Tweed**[193] 7363 7-9-2 112 (p) GeorgeBaker 7 75
(William Haggas) *led tl hdd and rdn wl over 2f out: dropped out and btn 2f: wl bhd and heavily eased fnl f: t.o* **15/8**[1]

3m 34.07s (5.07) **Going Correction** +0.65s/f (Yiel)
**WFA** 4 from 5yo+ 4lb **7** Ran SP% **108.8**
Speed ratings (Par 113): **113,110,110,108,106 101,85**
CSF £48.60 TOTE £3.70: £2.30, £4.10; EX 45.90 Trifecta £354.10.
**Owner** Australian Thoroughbred Bloodstock **Bred** Mme Isabelle Reverseau **Trained** Newmarket, Suffolk

**FOCUS**
This is often a good staying event, indeed the last two Gold Cup winners have taken it en route to the royal meeting, and although a couple of the key contenders failed to give their running this time around, it was hard not to be impressed with the performance of Tac De Boistron. He produced another career bset, with the runner-up the key.

## 1870 BET365 PARADISE STKS (LISTED RACE) 1m (S)
4:15 (4:18) (Class 1) 4-Y-O+
**£20,982** (£7,955; £3,981; £1,983; £995; £499) **Stalls** Centre

Form RPR

6014 **1** **Ocean Tempest**[18] 1437 5-9-0 107 AdamKirby 10 116
(John Ryan) *chsd ldrs: rdn to ld over 1f out: edging rt after: forged ahd ins fnl f: styd on wl and asserted fnl 100yds* **5/1**[3]

15-1 **2** *2* **Graphic (IRE)**[32] 1162 5-9-3 110 (p) SebSanders 3 114
(William Haggas) *mostly chsd ldr: rdn and ev ch 2f out: stl ev ch and carried rt over 1f out: no ex and btn fnl 100yds* **3/1**[1]

42-2 **3** *3/4* **French Navy**[13] 1533 6-9-0 112 MickaelBarzalona 8 110
(Charlie Appleby) *wl in tch in midfield: clsd to press ldrs 3f out: outpcd u.p over 1f out: rallied and kpt on again ins fnl f* **7/2**[2]

6-23 **4** *1/2* **Fencing (USA)**[13] 1533 5-9-0 110 WilliamBuick 1 109
(John Gosden) *racd along on far rail: w ldrs: overall ldr over 4f: rdn over 2f out: hdd over 1f out: no ex and styd on same pce ins fnl f* **5/1**[3]

042- **5** *3 1/4* **Boomshackerlacker (IRE)**[162] 7968 4-9-0 105 (p) JamesDoyle 7 101
(George Baker) *hld up in tch in midfield: effrt u.p over 2f out: 5th and btn over 1f out: wknd ins fnl f* **25/1**

51-0 **6** *2 1/2* **Sirius Prospect (USA)**[12] 1558 6-9-3 106 RobertWinston 9 98
(Dean Ivory) *hld up in tch in last pair: rdn and effrt over 2f out: no prog and btn 2f out: 6th and wl hld over 1f out* **20/1**

41-0 **7** *3 1/4* **Levitate**[32] 1165 6-9-0 106 (v) RyanMoore 5 88
(John Quinn) *chsd ldrs: rdn and unable qck over 2f out: sn struggling: wknd wl over 1f out* **10/1**

030- **8** *hd* **Mister Music**[186] 7536 5-9-0 100 (b) JimmyFortune 4 87
(Brian Meehan) *hld up in tch in midfield: rdn and no hdwy over 2f out: sn btn: wknd wl over 1f out* **40/1**

210- **9** *5* **Baltic Knight (IRE)**[271] 4945 4-9-0 111 RichardHughes 6 76
(Richard Hannon) *led tl over 4f out: lost pl and bhd over 2f out: sn wknd* **11/1**

3/6- **10** *2 1/4* **Race And Status (IRE)**[378] 1623 4-9-0 102 DavidProbert 2 71
(Andrew Balding) *t.k.h: hld up in tch in last pair: rdn over 2f out: no hdwy and sn btn: wknd wl over 1f out* **12/1**

1m 44.9s (4.10) **Going Correction** +0.80s/f (Soft) **10** Ran SP% **116.7**
Speed ratings (Par 111): **111,109,108,107,104 102,98,98,93,91**
CSF £19.94 TOTE £6.70: £2.00, £1.40, £1.70; EX 20.70 Trifecta £98.70.
**Owner** W McLuskey & C Little **Bred** Old Mill Stud Ltd And Oomswell Ltd **Trained** Newmarket, Suffolk
■ Stewards' Enquiry : Adam Kirby caution: careless riding

**FOCUS**
A competitive Listed event, the form of which looks solid. Ocean Tempest found a bit on his handicap form. They raced centre-field, with the exception of Fencing, who raced on his own far side.

## 1871 REDCENTRIC H'CAP 1m (S)
4:45 (4:48) (Class 4) (0-85,89) 4-Y-O+ **£6,469** (£1,925; £962; £481) **Stalls** Centre

Form RPR

0232 **1** **Ishikawa (IRE)**[18] 1451 6-8-4 75 RobJFitzpatrick(7) 9 86
(K R Burke) *mde all: racd keenly and set stdy gallop tl wnt clr 1/2-way: rdn and edging rt fr wl over 1f out: a holding on: rdn out* **15/2**[3]

312- **2** *1 1/2* **Russian Realm**[229] 6356 4-9-7 85 RyanMoore 3 93+
(Sir Michael Stoute) *t.k.h: hld up wl in tch in midfield: rdn and effrt to chse clr ldr over 2f out: stl 4 l down over 1f out: steadily clsd u.p but nvr getting to wnr* **7/4**[1]

63-0 **3** *2* **Noble Gift**[18] 1439 4-9-5 83 JimCrowley 13 86
(William Knight) *hld up in tch in rr: rdn and effrt ent fnl 2f: styd on over 1f out: wnt 3rd ins fnl f: kpt on but nvr gng to rch wnr* **8/1**

4106 **4** *1 1/4* **Tatting**[46] 977 5-9-3 81 AdamKirby 5 84+
(Chris Dwyer) *hld up in tch towards rr: stl travelling wl and nt clr run over 2f out: plenty to do whn hdwy u.p over 1f out: kpt on: no threat to wnr* **40/1**

61-0 **5** *3/4* **The Tichborne (IRE)**[95] 342 6-8-11 75 (v) RobertWinston 1 73
(Roger Teal) *hld up in tch: chsd ldrs and drvn ent fnl 2f: no imp and btn over 1f out: plugged on same pce and lost 2 pls fnl f* **50/1**

220- **6** *1 1/4* **Good Luck Charm**[249] 5759 5-9-4 82 GeorgeBaker 4 78
(Gary Moore) *stdd after s: t.k.h: hld up in tch: clsd and squeezed between horses over 2f out: no prog over 1f out* **33/1**

-041 **7** *nk* **Myboyalfie (USA)**[6] 1682 7-9-11 89 6ex FrederikTylicki 2 84
(J R Jenkins) *in tch in midfield: rdn over 2f out: n.m.r jst over 2f out: no threat to wnr and kpt on same pce after* **11/1**

5363 **8** *3 3/4* **First Post (IRE)**[18] 1439 7-8-13 77 DaneO'Neill 12 63
(Derek Haydn Jones) *wl in tch in midfield: effrt u.p over 2f out: no prog 2f out: wknd over 1f out* **8/1**

11-2 **9** *3/4* **Sword Of The Lord**[26] 1281 4-8-13 77 TomQueally 11 61
(Michael Bell) *hld up wl in tch in midfield: rdn and no rspnse wl over 2f out lost pl and hrd drvn 2f out: no prog* **5/1**[2]

20-5 **10** *7* **Sheila's Buddy**[18] 1439 5-8-13 77 LiamKeniry 8 45
(J S Moore) *wl in tch in midfield: rdn over 2f out: drvn and btn ent fnl 2f: sn wknd* **16/1**

3-14 **11** *34* **Secular Society**[48] 942 4-9-2 80 FrankieDettori 7
(George Baker) *chsd ldrs: chsd wnr 1/2-way tl over 2f out: sn btn and dropped out: virtually p.u fnl f: t.o* **16/1**

6-30 **12** *6* **Big Whiskey (IRE)**[11] 1578 4-9-4 82 KierenFallon 10
(Edward Creighton) *chsd wnr tl 1/2-way: lost pl u.p 3f out: sn bhd: virtually p.u fnl f: t.o* **16/1**

1m 47.44s (6.64) **Going Correction** +0.80s/f (Soft) **12** Ran SP% **120.3**
Speed ratings (Par 105): **98,96,94,93,92 91,90,87,86,79 45,39**
CSF £21.00 CT £115.11 TOTE £9.40: £3.20, £1.10, £2.80; EX 28.20 Trifecta £204.30.
**Owner** Tim Dykes **Bred** Ken Carroll **Trained** Middleham Moor, N Yorks

**FOCUS**
Little got into this decent handicap, which was run at a steady pace. A clear turf best from the all-the-way winner.
T/Plt: £68.90 to a £1 stake. Pool of £96965.86 - 1026.90 winning tickets. T/Qpdt: £9.80 to a £1 stake. Pool of £8484.46 - 638.20 winning tickets. SP

# 1663 BRIGHTON (L-H)
Wednesday, April 30

**OFFICIAL GOING: Good (good to soft in places; 6.1)**
All races on inner line and distances as advertised.
Wind: Almost nil Weather: Fine

## 1872 BRITISH STALLION STUDS EBF MEDIAN AUCTION MAIDEN STKS 5f 59y
4:50 (4:50) (Class 5) 2-Y-O **£2,911** (£866; £432; £216) **Stalls** Low

Form RPR

**1** **Loretta Martin** 2-8-11 0 CharlesBishop(3) 6 63+
(Mick Channon) *dwlt: bhd: hdwy over 1f out: hung lft: str run fnl f: led nr fin* **8/1**

3 **2** *nk* **Just Marion (IRE)**[32] 1169 2-8-11 0 DeclanBates(3) 4 62
(David Evans) *sn rdn to chse ldr: led wl over 1f out: hrd rdn fnl f: ct nr fin* **11/10**[1]

0 **3** *1 3/4* **Nimble (IRE)**[23] 1349 2-9-0 0 LiamJones 7 56
(J S Moore) *sn pushed along in 5th: hdwy 2f out: hrd rdn over 1f out: kpt on same pce* **33/1**

**4** *3/4* **Chetan** 2-9-2 0 OisinMurphy(3) 1 58+
(Milton Bradley) *sn pushed along in 4th: lost pl 3f out: styd on wl fnl f* **33/1**

0 **5** *nk* **Jet Mate (IRE)**[27] 1259 2-9-5 0 (b[1]) MartinDwyer 2 57
(William Muir) *s.i.s: hdwy 3f out: one pce appr fnl f* **7/1**[3]

05 **6** *2 1/4* **Chester Deal**[11] 1571 2-9-2 0 MichaelJMMurphy(3) 3 49
(Jo Hughes) *prom tl outpcd fnl 2f* **7/2**[2]

0 **7** *6* **Majenski (IRE)**[11] 1571 2-9-5 0 FergusSweeney 5 27
(Jamie Osborne) *led at str pce tl wknd wl over 1f out: eased whn wl btn fnl f* **7/1**[3]

1m 5.18s (2.88) **Going Correction** +0.35s/f (Good) **7** Ran SP% **111.8**
Speed ratings (Par 92): **90,89,86,85,85 81,71**
CSF £16.56 TOTE £5.60: £3.30, £1.10; EX 18.80 Trifecta £138.60.
**Owner** M Channon **Bred** Mike Channon Bloodstock Ltd **Trained** West Ilsley, Berks

**FOCUS**
All races on inner line and distances as advertised. A briskly run opener, but the time was slow and they finished in a heap. Probably modest form.

## 1873 HARRINGTONS LETTINGS GRANDSTAND SPONSOR H'CAP 6f 209y
5:25 (5:26) (Class 5) (0-75,75) 4-Y-O+ **£2,587** (£770; £384; £192) **Stalls** Low

Form RPR

6653 **1** **Alice's Dancer (IRE)**[21] 1375 5-9-3 74 OisinMurphy(3) 5 85
(William Muir) *chsd ldr: led over 2f out: rdn clr ins fnl f: comf* **3/1**[1]

-464 **2** *3 1/4* **Great Expectations**[6] 1667 6-9-6 74 FergusSweeney 1 77
(J R Jenkins) *hld up in tch: chsd wnr 2f out: unable qck ins fnl f* **6/1**

-300 **3** *1* **Severiano (USA)**[18] 1440 4-8-8 62 (b) MartinLane 4 62
(Roger Varian) *in tch: rdn 3f out: chsd ldrs and hung lft over 1f out: one pce* **9/2**[3]

4056 **4** *3/4* **Jay Bee Blue**[16] 1490 5-9-7 75 (bt) JohnFahy 2 73
(Sean Curran) *dwlt: hld up in rr: effrt in centre and hrd rdn 2f out: styd on same pce* **6/1**

10-6 **5** *12* **Bountybeamadam**[41] 1026 4-9-2 **70**..........................(v[1]) MartinDwyer 3 37
(George Baker) *led tl over 2f out: wknd wl over 1f out* **16/1**

000- **6** *5* **Messila Star**[199] 7224 4-9-7 **75**..........................(t) ShaneKelly 7 29
(Jeremy Noseda) *in tch tl wknd 2f out* **4/1**[2]

1m 24.71s (1.61) **Going Correction** +0.35s/f (Good) **6** Ran SP% **97.6**
Speed ratings (Par 103): **104,100,99,98,84 78**
CSF £15.47 TOTE £4.40: £1.90, £3.30; EX 11.80 Trifecta £68.50.
**Owner** Perspicacious Punters Racing Club **Bred** Rathasker Stud **Trained** Lambourn, Berks

■ Polar Kite was withdrawn. Price at time of withdrawal 5/1. Rule 4 applies to all bets - deduct 15p in the pound.

**FOCUS**
This was ordinary for the grade and it proved plain sailing for the favourite. The time was modest.

## 1874 HARRINGTONSLETTINGS.CO.UK H'CAP — 1m 3f 196y

**5:55** (5:57) (Class 6) (0-60,60) 4-Y-O+ **£1,940** (£577; £288; £144) **Stalls** High

Form RPR

-014 **1** **Anjuna Beach (USA)**[29] 1215 4-9-6 **60**.......................... ShaneKelly 1 70+
(Gary Moore) *s.s: t.k.h in rr: hdwy 4f out: eased ins 3f out: led wl over 1f out: rdn clr ent fnl f* **6/1**[2]

030/ **2** *3¼* **Turbulent Priest**[537] 6948 6-8-5 **47**..........................(p) SimonPearce[(3)] 3 52
(Zoe Davison) *in rr: rdn and hdwy 2f out: styd on to take 2nd ins fnl f: nt trble wnr* **66/1**

000- **3** *2½* **Corn Maiden**[121] 8449 5-8-10 **56**.......................... LewisWalsh[(7)] 12 57
(Lydia Pearce) *towards rr: rdn and styd on fnl 2f: hung lft: nrest at fin* **5/1**[1]

0352 **4** *1½* **Herbalist**[18] 1453 4-9-0 **57**..........................(b) OisinMurphy[(3)] 11 55
(Sean Curran) *led tl wl over 1f out: hrd rdn: one pce* **6/1**[2]

540- **5** *4½* **Sweeping Rock (IRE)**[195] 7331 4-9-2 **56**..........................(t) MartinDwyer 9 47
(Marcus Tregoning) *chsd ldrs tl wknd 2f out* **12/1**

**6** *hd* **Crouching Harry (IRE)**[104] 5506 5-8-13 **52**..........................(p) MartinLane 8 43
(Anabel K Murphy) *hld up towards rr: hdwy 7f out: chsd ldrs over 3f out: wknd wl over 1f out* **16/1**

0-55 **7** *nk* **Lambert Pen (USA)**[19] 1428 4-8-5 **50**.......................... ShelleyBirkett[(5)] 5 40
(Peter Hiatt) *prom: lost pl 5f out: n.d after* **8/1**[3]

060- **8** *6* **Wedding Speech (IRE)**[224] 6522 4-9-2 **56**.......................... HayleyTurner 10 37
(James Fanshawe) *chsd ldr tl wknd over 2f out* **8/1**[3]

00-4 **9** *4* **Dorry K (IRE)**[27] 1263 5-9-2 **55**.......................... StevieDonohoe 6 29
(Jim Best) *chsd ldrs tl wknd 3f out* **6/1**[2]

030- **10** *3¼* **King's Road**[322] 3213 9-9-0 **53**..........................(t) LukeMorris 2 22
(Anabel K Murphy) *towards rr: mod effrt 3f out: sn wknd* **16/1**

066- **11** *10* **Two Sugars**[163] 6899 6-8-10 **49**.......................... LiamJones 4 2
(Laura Mongan) *a towards rr: bhd fnl 3f* **8/1**[3]

505 **12** *21* **Fleetwood Nix**[34] 1119 4-8-6 **46** oh1.......................... WilliamCarson 7
(Pat Phelan) *in tch: rdn and lost pl over 3f out: sn struggling* **33/1**

2m 36.75s (4.05) **Going Correction** +0.35s/f (Good)
**WFA** 4 from 5yo+ 1lb **12** Ran SP% **116.7**
Speed ratings (Par 101): **100,97,96,95,92 92,91,87,85,83 76,62**
CSF £322.10 CT £2116.84 TOTE £8.80: £3.10, £8.10, £2.90; EX 594.30 Trifecta £1582.90 Part won..
**Owner** C E Stedman **Bred** Daniel J Yates **Trained** Lower Beeding, W Sussex

**FOCUS**
A competitive, if low-grade handicap in which they got racing plenty soon enough. The winner rates back to his early best.

## 1875 STREAMLINE TAXIS BRIGHTON 202020 H'CAP — 1m 1f 209y

**6:25** (6:27) (Class 6) (0-65,63) 4-Y-O+ **£1,940** (£577; £288; £144) **Stalls** High

Form RPR

0-04 **1** **Choral Festival**[23] 1354 8-9-7 **63**.......................... WilliamCarson 7 72
(John Bridger) *hld up in 5th: smooth hdwy 4f out: led 3f out: rdn clr 1f out: edgd lft: styd on wl* **7/4**[1]

0200 **2** *2¼* **Litmus (USA)**[6] 1664 5-8-8 **50**..........................(b) HayleyTurner 8 54
(Simon Dow) *led 4f: led 4f out tl 3f out: kpt on u.p: hld by wnr fnl f* **12/1**

04-5 **3** *1¾* **Lindsay's Dream**[6] 1664 8-8-4 **49** oh4..........................(p) SimonPearce[(3)] 5 50
(Zoe Davison) *s.s: bhd: hdwy and hrd rdn 2f out: styd on same pce: nvr able to chal* **16/1**

1025 **4** *¾* **Attain**[18] 1450 5-9-1 **62**.......................... ShelleyBirkett[(5)] 1 62
(Julia Feilden) *prom: rdn over 2f out: one pce* **9/2**[3]

/00- **5** *3¼* **Indian Scout**[138] 8270 6-8-11 **53**..........................(p) MartinLane 2 46
(Anabel K Murphy) *chsd ldrs: rdn 3f out: wknd over 1f out* **5/1**

3116 **6** *13* **Dozy Joe**[18] 1454 6-9-5 **61**..........................(bt) LukeMorris 3 30
(Joseph Tuite) *hld up in 6th: hdwy and rdn 4f out: wknd over 2f out* **11/4**[2]

66-0 **7** *11* **Ella Motiva (IRE)**[18] 1453 4-8-2 **49** oh4.......................... NoelGarbutt[(5)] 6
(Mark Brisbourne) *prom: led 6f out tl 4f out: wknd 3f out* **33/1**

2m 6.93s (3.33) **Going Correction** +0.35s/f (Good) **7** Ran SP% **114.4**
Speed ratings (Par 101): **100,98,96,96,93 83,74**
CSF £24.20 CT £254.69 TOTE £2.90: £1.60, £4.70; EX 18.10 Trifecta £80.90.
**Owner** Mrs Liz Gardner **Bred** Cheveley Park Stud Ltd **Trained** Liphook, Hants

**FOCUS**
A pretty weak handicap, and not totally convincing form.

## 1876 HARRINGTONS LETTINGS BRIGHTON H'CAP — 7f 214y

**7:00** (7:00) (Class 5) (0-70,67) 4-Y-O+ **£2,587** (£770; £384; £192) **Stalls** Low

Form RPR

3005 **1** **Little Indian**[9] 1613 4-9-0 **60**.......................... FergusSweeney 7 68
(J R Jenkins) *chsd ldrs: chal 2f out: led 1f out: rdn to hold on fnl f* **9/2**[2]

6500 **2** *½* **Minimee**[6] 1668 4-8-6 **55**..........................(v) OisinMurphy[(3)] 2 62
(Phil McEntee) *chsd ldr: led 4f out tl 1f out: kpt on u.p* **8/1**

66-0 **3** *nk* **Loucal**[25] 1302 4-8-11 **57**..........................(b) AdamBeschizza 5 63
(Noel Quinlan) *led 4f: rdn and lost pl 2f out: styd on wl fnl f: clsng at fin* **10/1**

3552 **4** *3½* **Prince Of Burma (IRE)**[4] 1718 6-9-3 **66**..........................(v) DeclanBates[(3)] 3 64
(David Evans) *hld up in rr: hdwy in centre 2f out: hrd rdn over 1f out: no imp* **7/2**[1]

4234 **5** *3* **Skidby Mill (IRE)**[21] 1392 4-9-1 **61**.......................... LiamJones 4 52
(Laura Mongan) *s.i.s: plld hrd in rr: gd hdwy on ins rail 2f out: wknd 1f out* **13/2**

-424 **6** *2¼* **Tax Reform (IRE)**[49] 927 4-9-6 **66**..........................(b) RobertHavlin 6 52
(Mark Hoad) *hld up towards rr: effrt towards centre 2f out: sn wknd* **7/2**[1]

-366 **7** *¾* **Malaysian Boleh**[35] 1102 4-9-7 **67**.......................... LukeMorris 1 51
(Simon Dow) *prom tl wknd wl over 1f out* **6/1**[3]

1m 40.81s (4.81) **Going Correction** +0.35s/f (Good) **7** Ran SP% **110.4**
Speed ratings (Par 103): **89,88,88,84,81 79,78**
CSF £36.40 TOTE £5.60: £2.30, £3.20; EX 36.90 Trifecta £126.60.
**Owner** Two Little Indians **Bred** D R Tucker **Trained** Royston, Herts

**FOCUS**
It's unlikely that this took a great of winning but it served up the finish of the evening. The runner-up sets the standard.

## 1877 HARRINGTONS LETTINGS BRIGHTON FOR STUDENT ACCOMMODATION H'CAP — 6f 209y

**7:35** (7:35) (Class 6) (0-55,59) 4-Y-O+ **£1,940** (£577; £288; £144) **Stalls** Low

Form RPR

0062 **1** **Welsh Inlet (IRE)**[8] 1631 6-9-4 **50**.......................... WilliamCarson 7 65
(John Bridger) *prom: chsd ldr after 2f: led 2f out: edgd rt 1f out: drvn clr* **5/1**[3]

3231 **2** *3¾* **Pour La Victoire (IRE)**[6] 1666 4-9-13 **59** 6ex.......................... LukeMorris 11 64
(Tony Carroll) *trckd ldrs in 4th: drvn to chse wnr 1f out: no imp* **5/4**[1]

464- **3** *hd* **Elle Rebelle**[151] 8119 4-9-2 **48**.......................... ShaneKelly 9 53
(Mark Brisbourne) *hld up towards rr: rdn and hdwy 2f out: styd on* **10/1**

055- **4** *3¾* **Interakt**[121] 8449 7-9-2 **51**.......................... OisinMurphy[(3)] 3 46
(Joseph Tuite) *towards rr: swtchd to centre and effrt 3f out: hung lft 2f out: sme late hdwy* **9/2**[2]

-500 **5** *1* **Sweet Piccolo**[60] 798 4-8-8 **45**.......................... DavidKenny[(5)] 2 37
(Paddy Butler) *in tch: outpcd and lost pl 3f out: styd on same pce fnl f* **100/1**

40- **6** *2¾* **Perseverent Pete (USA)**[195] 7322 4-8-8 **45**.......................... EoinWalsh[(5)] 8 30
(Christine Dunnett) *chsd ldr 2f: prom tl wknd 2f out* **20/1**

0600 **7** *hd* **Homeboy (IRE)**[55] 864 6-8-6 **45**..........................(v) HollieDoyle[(7)] 1 30
(David Evans) *led tl 2f out: wknd 1f out* **10/1**

000- **8** *11* **Depden (IRE)**[236] 6156 6-8-13 **45**.......................... StevieDonohoe 6
(John Butler) *s.i.s: towards rr: drvn along 3f out: sn struggling* **25/1**

603- **9** *nk* **Fleeting Indian (IRE)**[165] 7929 5-8-13 **45**.......................... RobertHavlin 5
(Linda Jewell) *mid-div: rdn 3f out: sn wknd* **50/1**

0000 **10** *4½* **Jackie Love (IRE)**[21] 1387 6-8-6 **45**..........................(v) RhiainIngram[(7)] 10
(Roger Ingram) *v.s.a: a wl bhd* **25/1**

1m 24.92s (1.82) **Going Correction** +0.35s/f (Good) **10** Ran SP% **112.9**
Speed ratings (Par 101): **103,98,98,94,93 89,89,77,76,71**
CSF £10.65 CT £58.04 TOTE £6.80: £2.00, £1.10, £2.30; EX 13.40 Trifecta £71.10.
**Owner** J J Bridger **Bred** Patrick Gleeson **Trained** Liphook, Hants

**FOCUS**
A weak contest in which only a handful could be seriously fancied and it was those towards the head of the market that fared best. The winner is rated to a better view of her winter AW runs.

## 1878 FOLLOW @HARRINGTONSLETT ON TWITTER H'CAP — 5f 59y

**8:05** (8:05) (Class 5) (0-70,70) 4-Y-O+ **£2,587** (£770; £384; £192) **Stalls** Low

Form RPR

2-66 **1** **Ladweb**[28] 1244 4-9-2 **68**.......................... MichaelJMMurphy[(3)] 4 80
(John Gallagher) *mde all: hrd rdn wl over 1f out: hld on gamely fnl f* **7/1**

0116 **2** *¾* **Secret Millionaire (IRE)**[19] 1431 7-9-7 **70**.......................... LukeMorris 2 79
(Tony Carroll) *chsd ldrs: drvn to chal fnl f: r.o* **10/1**

00-3 **3** *1¼* **Storm Lightning**[19] 1431 5-9-7 **70**..........................(b) ShaneKelly 8 75
(Mark Brisbourne) *prom: hrd rdn over 1f out: kpt on: hld fnl 100yds* **6/1**[3]

20-3 **4** *1* **Indian Tinker**[9] 1618 5-9-1 **67**.......................... OisinMurphy[(3)] 1 69
(Robert Cowell) *in tch on ins rail: effrt 2f out: hrd rdn over 1f out: one pce* **7/4**[1]

-002 **5** *1¼* **Commandingpresence (USA)**[3] 1766 8-8-13 **62**.......................... WilliamCarson 3 59
(John Bridger) *hld up in 6th: effrt 2f out: no imp over 1f out* **4/1**[2]

3035 **6** *3¼* **Welease Bwian (IRE)**[44] 987 5-8-13 **69**.......................... AaronJones[(7)] 5 55
(Stuart Williams) *s.s: bhd: rdn over 2f out: passed btn horses fnl f* **7/1**

0505 **7** *2½* **Billy Red**[35] 1109 10-9-3 **66**..........................(b) FergusSweeney 9 43
(J R Jenkins) *w ldrs: hung bdly lft 2f out: sn wknd* **25/1**

4103 **8** *1¾* **Compton Prince**[44] 993 5-9-2 **65**..........................(b) SteveDrowne 7 36
(Milton Bradley) *in tch on outer tl hrd rdn and wknd 2f out* **20/1**

1m 3.64s (1.34) **Going Correction** +0.35s/f (Good) **8** Ran SP% **113.3**
Speed ratings (Par 103): **103,101,99,98,96 91,87,84**
CSF £71.86 CT £446.44 TOTE £11.60: £2.10, £1.90, £2.20; EX 72.10 Trifecta £250.40.
**Owner** The Juniper Racing Club & Andrew Bell **Bred** Adweb Ltd **Trained** Chastleton, Oxon

**FOCUS**
A competitive sprint finale. A length personal best from the winner.
T/Plt: £59.70 to a £1 stake. Pool of £45464.38 - 555.06 winning tickets. T/Qpdt: £29.80 to a £1 stake. Pool of £6155.51 - 152.84 winning tickets. LM

# [1482] PONTEFRACT (L-H)

### Wednesday, April 30

**OFFICIAL GOING: Good (good to firm in places; 8.2)**
Wind: almost nil Weather: fine

## 1879 WILLIAM HILL / BRITISH STALLION STUDS EBF MAIDEN STKS (BOBIS RACE) — 5f

**2:10** (2:11) (Class 4) 2-Y-O **£4,528** (£1,347; £673; £336) **Stalls** Low

Form RPR

**1** **Firgrove Bridge (IRE)** 2-9-5 0.......................... PaulMulrennan 6 77
(Kevin Ryan) *w ldr: led appr fnl f: hld on towards fin* **9/1**

**2** *½* **Zeela (IRE)** 2-9-0 0.......................... DuranFentiman 3 71+
(Tim Easterby) *trckd ldrs: effrt 2f out: styd on to take 2nd last 50yds* **3/1**[2]

63 **3** *1¼* **Red Connect**[14] 1504 2-9-5 0.......................... SilvestreDeSousa 2 71
(Alan McCabe) *led: hdd appr fnl f: wandered and fdd last 50yds* **5/2**[1]

**4** *4½* **Juventas** 2-8-11 0.......................... WilliamTwiston-Davies[(3)] 4 50
(Mick Channon) *t.k.h in rr: outpcd over 2f out: sme hdwy over 1f out: kpt on* **22/1**

**5** *¾* **Bobby's Flyer (IRE)** 2-9-5 0.......................... PhillipMakin 1 52
(Tim Easterby) *chsd ldrs: drvn over 2f out: edgd rt and wknd fnl f* **22/1**

**6** *nk* **Montefalcon (IRE)** 2-9-5 0.......................... TonyHamilton 9 51
(Richard Fahey) *dwlt: wnt rt after s: sn swtchd lft and t.k.h: hdwy over 2f out: nvr nr ldrs* **3/1**[2]

**7** *4½* **British Art** 2-9-5 0.......................... GrahamLee 7 35
(Paul Cole) *in rr: drvn over 2f out: sn lost pl* **6/1**[3]

**8** *9* **Luvlylynnthomas** 2-9-0 0.......................... PJMcDonald 8
(Micky Hammond) *chsd ldrs: lost pl over 2f out: sn bhd* **50/1**

1m 4.86s (1.56) **Going Correction** -0.05s/f (Good) **8** Ran SP% **113.5**
Speed ratings (Par 94): **85,84,82,75,73 73,66,51**
CSF £35.22 TOTE £9.80: £2.80, £1.10, £1.20; EX 42.30 Trifecta £254.70.
**Owner** Mrs Margaret Forsyth **Bred** T Jones **Trained** Hambleton, N Yorks

**FOCUS**
Jockeys involved in the first felt that the ground was good, a bit dead in places, but with no good to firm in it. The first three pulled clear in what was probably a fair maiden.

## 1880 TOTEPOOL SUPPORTS THE NRC / BREEDERS BACKING RACING EBF MAIDEN STKS — 1m 2f 6y
**2:45** (2:48) (Class 5) 3-Y-0 — **£3,881** (£1,155; £577; £288) **Stalls** Low

Form — RPR
02-3 **1** **Roseburg (IRE)**[21] 1395 3-9-5 83 ........ AndreaAtzeni 5 — 85+
(Luca Cumani) *trckd ldrs: 2nd 2f out: led appr fnl f: drvn clr: readily* **5/4**[1]
00- **2** *3 1/4* **Asteroidea**[221] 6643 3-8-11 0 ........ RossAtkinson(3) 4 — 73
(Pam Sly) *sn trcking ldrs: effrt over 2f out: nt clr run over 1f out: sn swtchd rt: styd on to take 2nd last 50yds* **100/1**
04- **3** *3/4* **Express Himself (IRE)**[187] 7502 3-9-5 0 ........ GrahamLee 9 — 77
(Ed McMahon) *s.s: t.k.h: sn trcking ldrs: 3rd 2f out: kpt on same pce fnl f* **7/2**[2]
62- **4** *4 1/2* **Swilken**[168] 7860 3-9-5 0 ........ BenCurtis 6 — 68
(Mark H Tompkins) *trckd ldrs: t.k.h: led over 8f out: hdd appr fnl f: wknd last 150yds* **25/1**
0-3 **5** *2* **Master Clockmaker (IRE)**[13] 1542 3-9-5 0 ........ PJMcDonald 3 — 65
(Ann Duffield) *in rr: hdwy to trck ldrs 6f out: wknd over 1f out* **14/1**
25-5 **6** *18* **Mambo Rhythm**[21] 1391 3-9-0 68 ........ FrannyNorton 7 — 25
(Mark Johnston) *led over 1f: chsd ldr: drvn over 4f out: wknd 2f out: sn bhd* **14/1**
**7** *56* **Montone (IRE)** 3-9-2 0 ........ (v[1]) RobertTart(3) 2
(Sir Michael Stoute) *s.i.s: sn drvn along in last: reminders over 7f out: lost tch 3f out: sn wl bhd: hopelessly t.o* **8/1**[3]

2m 13.13s (-0.57) **Going Correction** -0.05s/f (Good) — **7** Ran SP% **95.9**
Speed ratings (Par 98): **100,97,96,93,91 77,32**
CSF £75.31 TOTE £1.60: £1.20, £9.30; EX 73.00 Trifecta £238.40.
**Owner** Sheikh Mohammed Obaid Al Maktoum **Bred** Mrs Brid Cosgrove **Trained** Newmarket, Suffolk

■ Desert Snow was withdrawn. Price at time of withdrawal 9/2. Rule 4 applies to all bets - deduct 15p in the pound.

**FOCUS**
A fair maiden which was weakened by the withdrawal of Desert Snow. A brisk early pace soon appeared to steady. The winner ste the standard and the second was a big improver.

## 1881 BETFRED SUPPORTS THE NRC H'CAP — 1m 4y
**3:20** (3:20) (Class 5) (0-75,75) 4-Y-0+ — **£3,234** (£962; £481; £240) **Stalls** Low

Form — RPR
153- **1** **Correggio**[223] 6563 4-9-6 74 ........ PJMcDonald 3 — 80
(Micky Hammond) *chsd ldr: 2nd 2f out: styd on to ld last 50yds* **15/2**[3]
06-5 **2** *1/2* **Dakota Canyon (IRE)**[89] 410 5-8-13 67 ........ (b) TonyHamilton 6 — 72
(Richard Fahey) *chsd ldr: drvn over 2f out: kpt on to take 2nd nr fin* **11/1**
06-6 **3** *1* **Shamaheart (IRE)**[25] 1306 4-9-7 75 ........ (p) SilvestreDeSousa 4 — 78
(Geoffrey Harker) *led: qcknd pce over 2f out: hdd wl ins fnl f: no ex* **16/1**
6-22 **4** *nk* **Who's Shirl**[9] 1609 8-9-6 74 ........ PaulMulrennan 9 — 76+
(Chris Fairhurst) *hld up in rr: hdwy over 1f out: styd on last 100yds* **16/1**
006- **5** *shd* **St Paul De Vence (IRE)**[322] 3214 4-9-6 74 ........ RaulDaSilva 7 — 76
(Paul Cole) *chsd ldrs: drvn over 3f out: styd on last 100yds* **10/1**
2-12 **6** *2 1/4* **Icy Blue**[18] 1446 6-8-6 63 ........ (p) GeorgeChaloner(3) 5 — 59
(Richard Whitaker) *hld up in mid-div: t.k.h: effrt 2f out: hung lft and kpt on one pce* **9/1**
506- **7** *1 1/4* **Shadowtime**[218] 6721 9-9-5 73 ........ DaleSwift 8 — 67
(Tracy Waggott) *stdd s: t.k.h in rr: effrt and swtchd outside 2f out: nvr nr ldrs* **20/1**
23-0 **8** *2* **Duke Of Grazeon (IRE)**[18] 1446 4-9-1 69 ........ RoystonFfrench 1 — 58
(Mrs Ilka Gansera-Leveque) *hld up in mid-div: effrt over 2f out: wknd fnl f: struck into* **3/1**[2]
25-1 **9** *6* **Dark Ocean (IRE)**[22] 1356 4-9-4 72 ........ GrahamLee 2 — 47
(Jedd O'Keeffe) *chsd ldrs: drvn over 2f out: lost pl over 1f out* **2/1**[1]

1m 44.67s (-1.23) **Going Correction** -0.05s/f (Good) — **9** Ran SP% **114.0**
Speed ratings (Par 103): **104,103,102,102,102 99,98,96,90**
CSF £84.78 CT £1273.89 TOTE £8.90: £2.70, £4.60, £3.70; EX 100.30 Trifecta £1725.70.
**Owner** Forty Forty Twenty **Bred** Christopher & Annabelle Mason **Trained** Middleham Moor, N Yorks

**FOCUS**
A prominent pitch was important in this ordinary handicap, as they went no great gallop. A marginal best from the winner.

## 1882 LADBROKES MOBILE FILLIES' H'CAP — 1m 2f 6y
**3:55** (3:55) (Class 3) (0-90,87) 3-Y-0 **£9,337** (£2,796; £1,398; £699; £349) **Stalls** Low

Form — RPR
0-62 **1** **Maven**[13] 1539 6-9-3 83 ........ RachelRichardson(7) 2 — 92
(Tim Easterby) *w ldr: led over 4f out: clr over 1f out: drvn out* **4/1**[3]
0-1 **2** *2 1/4* **Saltwater Creek (IRE)**[19] 1427 3-8-0 76 ........ JamesSullivan 5 — 78
(Michael Bell) *t.k.h: hld up in last: hdwy over 2f out: wnt 2nd over 1f out: kpt on: nt rch wnr* **14/1**
01-0 **3** *13* **A Star In My Eye (IRE)**[18] 1444 4-9-8 81 ........ GrahamLee 1 — 61
(Kevin Ryan) *led: hdd over 4f out: drvn over 3f out: wknd fnl f* **11/4**[2]
330- **4** *6* **Lyric Ballad**[209] 6976 4-9-3 76 ........ AndreaAtzeni 4 — 45
(Hughie Morrison) *trckd ldng pair: stdd after 2f: hdwy to chse ldrs 4f out: drvn over 2f out: lost pl over 1f out* **6/1**
011- **5** *27* **Tender Emotion**[216] 6770 3-8-11 87 ........ SilvestreDeSousa 7
(Charlie Appleby) *hld up: t.k.h: hdwy to trck ldrs 4f out: drvn over 2f out: sn wknd: t.o whn eased ins fnl f* **6/4**[1]

2m 11.43s (-2.27) **Going Correction** -0.05s/f (Good)
**WFA** 3 from 4yo+ 17lb — **5** Ran SP% **107.6**
Speed ratings (Par 104): **107,105,94,90,68**
CSF £43.93 TOTE £4.90: £2.10, £3.40; EX 30.60 Trifecta £220.90.
**Owner** Mrs Jennifer E Pallister **Bred** Habton Farms **Trained** Great Habton, N Yorks

**FOCUS**
A fair fillies' handicap on paper, but questionable form with only two running their races. The race is rated cautiously around the winner.

## 1883 NORTHERN RACING COLLEGE H'CAP (BOBIS RACE) — 1m 2f 6y
**4:25** (4:25) (Class 4) (0-85,85) 3-Y-0 — **£6,469** (£1,925; £962; £481) **Stalls** Low

Form — RPR
11-3 **1** **Latenightrequest**[31] 1195 3-9-1 79 ........ TonyHamilton 3 — 88
(Richard Fahey) *trckd ldr: chal over 2f out: led over 1f out: drvn out* **6/1**
13-2 **2** *2* **Mr Gallivanter (IRE)**[31] 1195 3-9-4 82 ........ GrahamLee 2 — 87
(John Quinn) *dwlt: sn mid-div: hdwy to trck ldrs 5f out: drvn over 2f out: chsd wnr over 1f out: no imp* **5/2**[2]
2135 **3** *3 1/2* **God's Speed (IRE)**[19] 1419 3-9-6 84 ........ ChrisCatlin 6 — 83
(Rae Guest) *in last: swtchd lft after 1f: pushed along 6f out: outpcd over 2f out: kpt on to take 3rd last 100yds* **16/1**
421- **4** *5* **Dullingham**[205] 7061 3-9-7 85 ........ SilvestreDeSousa 5 — 74
(Charlie Appleby) *led: drvn over 2f out: hdd over 1f out: wknd fnl f* **13/8**[1]
5-12 **5** *2 1/2* **Filament Of Gold (USA)**[69] 670 3-8-12 76 ........ FrannyNorton 1 — 60
(Mark Johnston) *chsd ldng pair: pushed along 5f out: lost pl over 1f out* **5/1**[3]
4-1 **6** *11* **Champagne Rules**[22] 1357 3-9-3 81 ........ PaddyAspell 4 — 44
(Sharon Watt) *t.k.h: hdwy 6f out: sn trcking ldrs on outer: effrt over 2f out: sn hung bdly rt and ended up stands' side: wknd appr fnl f: bhd whn eased towards fin* **12/1**

2m 12.01s (-1.69) **Going Correction** -0.05s/f (Good) — **6** Ran SP% **111.2**
Speed ratings (Par 100): **104,102,99,95,93 84**
CSF £20.92 TOTE £5.60: £1.80, £1.80; EX 18.10 Trifecta £111.40.
**Owner** Middleham Park Racing XVI & Partner **Bred** Mrs S J Walker **Trained** Musley Bank, N Yorks

**FOCUS**
An interesting little handicap and for the grade, the pick of the C&D times. The first two home had been placed behind Rudi Five One at Doncaster a month ago and were closely matched here. The winner continues to progress.

## 1884 CORAL.CO.UK H'CAP — 6f
**5:00** (5:03) (Class 5) (0-75,75) 3-Y-0 — **£3,234** (£962; £481; £240) **Stalls** Low

Form — RPR
52-1 **1** **Shared Equity**[25] 1304 3-9-7 75 ........ GrahamLee 3 — 90
(Jedd O'Keeffe) *chsd ldrs: 2nd over 2f out: styd on to ld last 75yds: drvn out* **5/4**[1]
23-5 **2** *1 1/4* **Smidgen (IRE)**[21] 1379 3-8-12 66 ........ ChrisCatlin 6 — 77
(Ed de Giles) *led: hdd ins fnl f: no ex* **13/2**[3]
12-6 **3** *3 1/4* **Zain Zone (IRE)**[98] 279 3-9-7 75 ........ JamesSullivan 8 — 76
(Ruth Carr) *hld up in rr: hdwy on outer 2f out: styd on to take 3rd last 50yds* **33/1**
221 **4** *2 1/4* **Elusive George (IRE)**[23] 1347 3-9-5 73 ........ SilvestreDeSousa 9 — 67
(John Quinn) *trckd ldrs on outer: drvn over 2f out: fdd last 100yds* **7/2**[2]
60-0 **5** *4 1/2* **Foxy Clarets (IRE)**[22] 1358 3-9-7 75 ........ TonyHamilton 5 — 54
(Richard Fahey) *chsd ldr: drvn over 2f out: wknd last 150yds* **13/2**[3]
012- **6** *2 1/2* **Heroique (IRE)**[187] 7503 3-9-4 72 ........ DuranFentiman 4 — 43
(Tim Easterby) *chsd ldrs: outpcd over 2f out: wknd over 1f out* **11/1**
3-30 **7** *nk* **Steele Ranger**[14] 1513 3-8-9 70 ........ JordanNason(7) 7 — 40
(Peter Chapple-Hyam) *s.i.s: sn outpcd and detached in last: sme hdwy over 1f out: nvr on terms* **16/1**
-100 **8** *31* **Mon Petit Secret**[14] 1507 3-8-4 63 ........ (b[1]) ShaneGray(5) 1
(Kevin Ryan) *chsd ldrs: drvn over 2f out: sn lost pl: bhd whn eased ins fnl f: t.o* **33/1**

1m 16.17s (-0.73) **Going Correction** -0.05s/f (Good) — **8** Ran SP% **113.4**
Speed ratings (Par 98): **102,100,96,93,87 83,83,41**
CSF £9.84 CT £168.67 TOTE £2.00: £1.10, £2.00, £5.20; EX 10.10 Trifecta £118.70.
**Owner** Paul & Dale Chapman Racing **Bred** Trickledown Stud Limited **Trained** Middleham Moor, N Yorks

**FOCUS**
An ordinary sprint handicap. The winner is progressive, as is the second.

## 1885 GO RACING IN YORKSHIRE FUTURE STARS APPRENTICE H'CAP (ROUND 3) — 1m 2f 6y
**5:35** (5:38) (Class 5) (0-75,74) 4-Y-0+ — **£3,234** (£962; £481; £240) **Stalls** Low

Form — RPR
500- **1** **Ever Fortune (USA)**[20] 8047 5-8-13 69 ........ MeganCarberry(3) 2 — 78
(Brian Ellison) *trckd ldr: effrt over 2f out: chal over 1f out: rdr dropped rein: led narrowly jst ins fnl f: kpt on towards fin* **11/2**[3]
05-4 **2** *1/2* **Red Charmer (IRE)**[10] 1598 4-9-2 74 ........ RowanScott(5) 6 — 82
(Ann Duffield) *led: increased pce over 2f out: rdn and edgd rt over 1f out: hdd jst ins fnl f: no ex in clsng stages* **6/1**
006/ **3** *10* **Fisher**[46] 4210 5-8-12 65 ........ (t) JoeDoyle 8 — 54
(John Quinn) *chsd ldrs: drvn over 2f out: one pce* **13/8**[1]
24-1 **4** *2* **Pertuis (IRE)**[22] 1362 8-9-3 70 ........ MatthewHopkins 4 — 55
(Micky Hammond) *hld up in rr: hdwy over 3f out: drvn over 2f out: one pce* **7/1**
456- **5** *9* **Time Of My Life (IRE)**[61] 5185 5-8-12 68 ........ (t) LukeLeadbitter(3) 1 — 36
(Patrick Holmes) *sn chsng ldrs: drvn over 3f out: outpcd over 2f out: sn wknd* **5/1**[2]
211- **6** *hd* **Valentine's Gift**[194] 7346 6-8-6 62 ........ RachelRichardson(3) 3 — 30
(Neville Bycroft) *rrd s: in rr: bhd and drvn over 3f out: nvr on terms* **8/1**
050- **7** *18* **Jordaura**[122] 8436 8-8-10 68 ........ JordanHibberd(5) 9
(Alan Berry) *racd wd: chsd ldrs: lost pl after 3f: bhd fnl 3f: wl bhd whn eased in clsng stages* **50/1**

2m 12.01s (-1.69) **Going Correction** -0.05s/f (Good) — **7** Ran SP% **110.0**
Speed ratings (Par 103): **104,103,95,94,86 86,72**
CSF £34.82 CT £71.07 TOTE £6.30: £5.70, £2.90; EX 39.50 Trifecta £122.40.
**Owner** D Gilbert, M Lawrence, A Bruce **Bred** Lantern Hill Farm Llc **Trained** Norton, N Yorks

**FOCUS**
A very modest event run at a reasonable gallop, and the first two pulled well clear. The winner is rated back to his Flat best.
T/Plt: £324.40 to a £1 stake. Pool of £61306.81 - 137.95 winning tickets. T/Qpdt: £88.70 to a £1 stake. Pool of £2889.57 - 24.10 winning tickets. WG

# 1800 SOUTHWELL (L-H)
Wednesday, April 30

**OFFICIAL GOING: Standard**
Wind: Virtually nil Weather: Cloudy

## 1886 QUICKSILVERSLOTS MORE JACKPOTS MORE MACHINES H'CAP — 1m (F)
**1:50** (1:50) (Class 5) (0-75,75) 4-Y-0+ — **£2,587** (£770; £384; £192) **Stalls** Low

Form — RPR
-263 **1** **Mishrif (USA)**[29] 1222 8-9-0 73 ........ (v) ConnorBeasley(5) 4 — 83
(J R Jenkins) *trckd ldrs: hdwy over 2f out: chsd ldr over 1f out: rdn to chal ent fnl f: led last 75yds: styd on* **8/1**[3]
50-2 **2** *1 1/4* **Midaz**[28] 1245 4-8-12 66 ........ RobertHavlin 6 — 73
(Hughie Morrison) *sn cl up: led wl over 2f out: clr over 1f out: rdn and jnd ent fnl f: sn drvn: hdd & wknd last 75yds* **2/1**[1]
4423 **3** *7* **Royal Holiday (IRE)**[1] 1839 7-9-3 71 ........ (p) DanielTudhope 2 — 62
(Marjorie Fife) *led: pushed along 1/2-way and sn hdd: rdn wl over 2f out: sn one pce* **2/1**[1]
2-06 **4** *6* **Our Ivor**[80] 550 5-9-0 75 ........ AlistairRawlinson(7) 5 — 52
(Michael Appleby) *cl up: pushed along after 2f and sn lost pl: rdn over 3f out and sn outpcd* **3/1**[2]
1000 **5** *12* **Basingstoke (IRE)**[29] 1217 5-9-2 70 ........ TomEaves 1 — 20
(Simon Hodgson) *dwlt: a in rr* **50/1**

30-5 **6** *8* **Caledonia Prince**[35] [1113] 6-9-1 **74**..........................(bt) PhilipPrince(5) 3
(Jo Hughes) *cl up on outer: hdwy to ld briefly over 3f out: wd st and racd nr stands' rail: sn hdd & wknd* **14/1**

1m 44.61s (0.91) **Going Correction** +0.25s/f (Slow) **6** Ran SP% **111.4**
Speed ratings (Par 103): **105,103,96,90,78 70**
CSF £24.09 TOTE £11.50: £5.40, £1.50; EX 25.20 Trifecta £51.10.
**Owner** Mrs Wendy Jenkins **Bred** Mr & Mrs Theodore Kuster Et Al **Trained** Royston, Herts

**FOCUS**
Fences and bend into home straight 5yds inside and Golf Club bend 5yds outside line raced on April 16. A fair handicap for the grade, featuring a number of course specialists. The pace was solid. The winner is rated pretty much to his best since his 3yo days.

## 1887 QUICKSILVERSLOTS PLAY FROM 10P TO £2 H'CAP 5f (F)
**2:20** (2:20) (Class 6) (0-55,55) 4-Y-0+ **£1,940** (£577; £288; £144) **Stalls** High

Form RPR

6-55 **1** **Spring Bird**[10] [1602] 5-9-0 **48**.................................... AdrianNicholls 1 57
(David Nicholls) *mde all: rdn clr over 1f out: kpt on strly* **9/2**

5600 **2** *2 ½* **Cadeaux Pearl**[21] [1378] 6-9-7 **55**..................................(v) TomEaves 4 55
(Scott Dixon) *prom: rdn along over 2f out: drvn and kpt on same pce fnl f* **3/1**[2]

0006 **3** *1 ¼* **Upper Lambourn (IRE)**[29] [1228] 6-8-7 **46** oh1..............(t) JackDuern(5) 5 42
(Christopher Kellett) *chsd ldrs: rdn along and outpcd 1/2-way: styd on u.p appr fnl f: tk 3rd nr line* **12/1**

0510 **4** *½* **Spic 'n Span**[27] [1270] 9-9-4 **52**..................................(v) GrahamGibbons 3 46
(Ronald Harris) *dwlt and swtchd lft s: sn prom: chsd wnr 1/2-way: rdn 2f out: wknd fnl f* **4/1**[3]

5456 **5** *½* **China Excels**[11] [1584] 7-8-8 **49**..........................(b[1]) AlistairRawlinson(7) 2 41
(Mandy Rowland) *dwlt: wnt lft s: chsd ldrs on wd outside: rdn along 2f out: sn one pce* **9/4**[1]

045 **6** *1 ½* **Busy Bimbo (IRE)**[33] [1147] 5-8-11 **48** oh1 ow2............. SladeO'Hara(3) 6 35
(Alan Berry) *in tch: rdn along over 2f out: sn drvn and wknd* **33/1**

3564 **7** *1 ¼* **Lord Buffhead**[2] [1804] 5-8-8 **47**..................................(v) PhilipPrince(5) 7 29
(Richard Guest) *sn outpcd in rr: rdn along 1/2-way: n.d* **8/1**

6050 **8** *6* **Lexi's Beauty (IRE)**[68] [692] 4-8-9 **46** oh1............. MatthewLawson(3) 8 6
(Brian Baugh) *sn outpcd and a in rr* **33/1**

1m 1.97s (2.27) **Going Correction** +0.425s/f (Slow) **8** Ran SP% **118.6**
Speed ratings (Par 101): **98,94,92,91,90 88,86,76**
CSF £19.22 CT £152.41 TOTE £4.80: £1.80, £1.40, £4.20; EX 17.60 Trifecta £160.00.
**Owner** D G Clayton **Bred** D G Clayton **Trained** Sessay, N Yorks

**FOCUS**
A weak sprint handicap and few had convincing profiles. The winner built on her recent turf form.

## 1888 QUICKSILVERSLOTS PLAY £500 JACKPOT RAINBOW RICHES MAIDEN FILLIES' STKS 1m (F)
**2:55** (2:55) (Class 5) 3-Y-0+ **£2,587** (£770; £384; £192) **Stalls** Low

Form RPR

00-2 **1** **Dalmarella Dancer (IRE)**[19] [1427] 3-8-11 73.............. DanielTudhope 3 76+
(K R Burke) *trckd ldrs: hdwy on bit to ld 2f out: sn clr: shkn up ent fnl f: styd on: readily* **8/13**[1]

03- **2** *3 ½* **Miss Lucy Jane**[239] [6069] 3-8-11 0.................................... LeeTopliss 7 67
(Richard Fahey) *dwlt and bhd: pushed along and hdwy 1/2-way: wd st: rdn over 2f out: styd on to chse wnr ent fnl f: sn no imp* **4/1**[2]

00 **3** *12* **Puppet Theatre (IRE)**[39] [1069] 4-9-11 0........................ AdrianNicholls 4 43
(Mark Johnston) *cl up: rdn along to ld 3f out: hdd 2f out: sn drvn and one pce* **10/1**

03-3 **4** *4 ½* **Speedbird One**[47] [962] 3-8-11 65.................................... TomEaves 2 29
(James Given) *slt ld: rdn along and hdd 3f out: wknd over 2f out* **8/1**[3]

**5** *6* **Moonwood** 3-8-6 0................................................ JacobButterfield(5) 1 15
(Ollie Pears) *chsd ldrs on inner: rdn along over 3f out: swtchd rt and drvn over 2f out: sn wknd* **25/1**

**6** *7* **Lady Jamesway (IRE)** 3-8-11 0................................ RussKennemore 6
(Ann Duffield) *prom on outer: pushed along and hung rt over 3f out: sn rdn and wknd* **16/1**

**7** *10* **Ninny Noodle** 4-9-4 0................................................... DanielCremin(7) 5
(Miss Imogen Pickard) *s.i.s: green and a bhd* **50/1**

1m 45.39s (1.69) **Going Correction** +0.25s/f (Slow)
**WFA** 3 from 4yo 14lb **7** Ran SP% **113.8**
Speed ratings (Par 100): **101,97,85,81,75 68,58**
CSF £3.33 TOTE £1.30: £1.10, £2.90; EX 3.80 Trifecta £17.00.
**Owner** Dr M E Glaze & I Mcinnes **Bred** Old Carhue Stud **Trained** Middleham Moor, N Yorks

**FOCUS**
An uncompetitive fillies' maiden. There was little market confidence behind the newcomers and the favourite won easily. She's rated in line with her previous effort.

## 1889 IRISH EBF/QUICKSILVERSLOTS OPEN AFTER 10PM MEDIAN AUCTION MAIDEN STKS 5f (F)
**3:30** (3:30) (Class 5) 2-Y-0 **£2,911** (£866; £432; £216) **Stalls** High

Form RPR

2 **1** **Midterm Break (IRE)**[13] [1536] 2-9-5 0........................ GrahamGibbons 4 77+
(David Barron) *mde all: shkn up ent fnl f: styd on: readily* **1/3**[1]

**2** *1 ¾* **Rita's Boy (IRE)** 2-9-5 0.................................................. DanielTudhope 2 71+
(K R Burke) *s.i.s and bhd: hdwy wl over 1f out: styd on wl to take 2nd ins fnl f: bttr for r* **9/2**[2]

04 **3** *1 ½* **Rose Of Kiev (IRE)**[11] [1583] 2-9-0 0.............................. AdrianNicholls 5 59
(Mark Johnston) *cl up: rdn along 2f out: sn edgd lft and one pce ent fnl f* **10/1**[3]

**4** *1* **Diminutive (IRE)** 2-9-0 0..................................................... HarryBentley 1 56
(Jamie Osborne) *cl up: rdn along 2f out: drvn and one pce ent fnl f* **33/1**

**5** *16* **Tuebrook** 2-9-5 0................................................................ TomEaves 3 3
(Michael Easterby) *dwlt: t.k.h and sn trcking ldrs: rdn 2f out: swtchd rt wl over 1f out: sn wknd* **33/1**

**6** *7* **Pearlise (FR)** 2-8-7 0................................................ MatthewHopkins(7) 6
(Scott Dixon) *prom: rdn along over 2f out: sn wknd* **14/1**

1m 2.36s (2.66) **Going Correction** +0.425s/f (Slow) **6** Ran SP% **114.8**
Speed ratings (Par 92): **95,92,89,88,62 51**
CSF £2.42 TOTE £1.20: £1.10, £2.40; EX 2.30 Trifecta £5.40.
**Owner** Laurence O'Kane **Bred** J O'Connor **Trained** Maunby, N Yorks

**FOCUS**
An uncompetitive juvenile maiden and the winner was always in command.

## 1890 QUICKSILVERSLOTS £1 TO WIN £500 H'CAP 7f (F)
**4:05** (4:05) (Class 6) (0-60,59) 3-Y-0 **£1,940** (£577; £288; £144) **Stalls** Low

Form RPR

1426 **1** **It's All A Game**[7] [1648] 3-8-9 **52**..............................(b) ConnorBeasley(5) 1 65
(Richard Guest) *chsd ldrs: hdwy 3f out: cl up over 2f out: led wl over 1f out: rdn and edgd lft ent fnl f: drvn out* **3/1**[2]

56-0 **2** *2 ¾* **Sleet (IRE)**[13] [1542] 3-8-4 **45**.............................................(p) BillyCray(3) 5 51
(Michael Appleby) *trckd ldng pair: hdwy to chse ldr 3f out: cl up 2f out: sn rdn and ev ch tl drvn and no ex ins fnl f* **12/1**

6534 **3** *8* **Black Geronimo**[34] [1130] 3-9-1 **58**..............................(v) PhilipPrince(5) 3 43
(Roy Bowring) *n.m.r in rr after 1f and sn lost pl: bhd and rdn along 1/2-way: hdwy over 2f out: styd on u.p appr fnl f: tk modest 3rd towards fin* **9/2**[3]

6-40 **4** *1 ¼* **Picanight**[6] [1683] 3-8-2 **45**..........................................(b[1]) JoeyHaynes(5) 8 27
(Eve Johnson Houghton) *set str pce: rdn along 3f out: drvn 2f out: sn hdd & wknd* **6/1**

000- **5** *7* **McCarthy Mor (IRE)**[194] [7335] 3-9-7 **59**.................................... DavidNolan 7 23
(Richard Fahey) *trckd ldr: cl up 1/2-way: rdn along 3f out: sn wknd* **1/1**[1]

-6P0 **6** *3 ¾* **Volodina (IRE)**[14] [1503] 3-9-3 **55**..................................(v) PatrickMathers 4
(Alan McCabe) *a towards rr: outpcd and bhd fnl 3f* **20/1**

1m 32.8s (2.50) **Going Correction** +0.25s/f (Slow) **6** Ran SP% **119.9**
Speed ratings (Par 96): **95,91,82,81,73 69**
CSF £38.03 CT £164.57 TOTE £3.50: £2.20, £6.10; EX 26.00 Trifecta £48.60.
**Owner** Viscount Environmental Ltd **Bred** Mrs G Sainty **Trained** Wetherby, W Yorks

**FOCUS**
A low-grade 3yo handicap, run at a quick pace, which saw a late gamble go astray. The form is best rated around the winner.

## 1891 QUICKSILVERSLOTS PLAY YOUR FAVOURITE £500 JACKPOT H'CAP 1m 3f (F)
**4:35** (4:35) (Class 6) (0-60,59) 4-Y-0+ **£2,045** (£603; £302) **Stalls** Low

Form RPR

2443 **1** **Solarmaite**[15] [1496] 5-8-11 **54**..........................................(b) PhilipPrince(5) 1 69
(Roy Bowring) *mde all: rdn clr wl over 3f out: unchal* **11/4**[1]

0644 **2** *21* **Excellent News (IRE)**[18] [1453] 5-8-0 **45**........................ AdamMcLean(7) 5 24
(Tony Forbes) *trckd ldrs: hdwy on outer 1/2-way: chsd wnr 3f out and sn rdn: drvn and plugged on same pce fr over 2f out* **16/1**

055- **3** *1 ½* **Politbureau**[193] [7376] 7-8-8 **46** ow1............................... GrahamGibbons 4 23
(Michael Easterby) *prom: chsd wnr after 4f: rdn along over 3f out: drvn over 2f out: plugged on one pce* **4/1**[3]

025/ **4** *5* **Host The Band**[1055] [2871] 10-9-0 **55**................................ RossAtkinson(3) 6 23
(Tony Newcombe) *chsd ldrs on outer: rdn along over 4f out: sn outpcd* **12/1**

2664 **5** *4* **Kyllachykov (IRE)**[28] [1249] 6-8-12 **53**................................ JasonHart(3) 3 14
(Robin Bastiman) *chsd ldrs: pushed along 1/2-way: rdn 5f out: sn outpcd and bhd* **3/1**[2]

4205 **6** *2 ¾* **Troy Boy**[40] [1050] 4-8-4 **45**................................................ NeilFarley(3) 7
(Robin Bastiman) *a in rr* **7/1**

300- **7** *18* **Janie Runaway (IRE)**[303] [3900] 4-9-7 **59**........................ HarryBentley 2
(Brian Meehan) *prom on inner: rdn along over 4f out: sn wknd and bhd* **5/1**

2m 28.28s (0.28) **Going Correction** +0.25s/f (Slow) **7** Ran SP% **114.4**
Speed ratings (Par 101): **108,92,91,88,85 83,70**
CSF £44.75 CT £192.60 TOTE £2.60: £1.60, £9.00; EX 42.10 Trifecta £197.80.
**Owner** S R Bowring **Bred** S R Bowring **Trained** Edwinstowe, Notts

**FOCUS**
A low-grade middle-distance handicap, won in runaway style by the well-supported favourite in a fair time for the grade. Hard form to pin down.

## 1892 QUICKSILVERSLOTS FUN ON THE HIGH STREET H'CAP 6f (F)
**5:05** (5:06) (Class 5) (0-70,70) 4-Y-0+ **£2,587** (£770; £384; £192) **Stalls** Low

Form RPR

6022 **1** **Clubland (IRE)**[6] [1678] 5-9-1 **69**........................................ PhilipPrince(5) 9 79
(Roy Bowring) *trckd ldrs: smooth hdwy on outer and wd st: cl up 2f out: led 1 1/2f out: rdn ent fnl f: kpt on* **11/10**[1]

3231 **2** *1 ¼* **Spitfire**[15] [1497] 9-9-0 **70**..................................................(t) VictorSantos(7) 7 76
(J R Jenkins) *dwlt and towards rr: hdwy 2f out: sn rdn: styd on wl fnl f* **8/1**[3]

2304 **3** *nk* **Pull The Pin (IRE)**[4] [1739] 5-8-13 **62**............................(bt) PaulMulrennan 4 67
(Ann Stokell) *led: rdn along over 2f out: hdd 1 1/2f out: cl up whn rdr dropped reins ent fnl f: kpt on same pce* **7/2**[2]

6-54 **4** *1 ½* **Hazard Warning (IRE)**[41] [1030] 4-8-6 **62** ow2....(b) AlistairRawlinson(7) 3 62
(Mandy Rowland) *chsd ldrs: hdwy and cl up 1/2-way: rdn along over 2f out: drvn wl over 1f out and one pce appr fnl f* **14/1**

0100 **5** *2 ½* **All Right Now**[22] [1365] 7-8-5 **57** oh2 ow1................(bt) RossAtkinson(3) 1 49
(Tony Newcombe) *towards rr: hdwy on inner wl over 2f out: rdn wl over 1f out and no imp* **25/1**

6536 **6** *5* **Monnoyer**[35] [1115] 5-8-8 **57**..........................................(b) TomEaves 6 33
(Scott Dixon) *cl up: rdn wl over 2f out: sn drvn and wknd* **8/1**[3]

1515 **7** *1 ¾* **Interchoice Star**[54] [866] 9-8-7 **61**..................................(p) JoeyHaynes(5) 2 32
(Ray Peacock) *prom: rdn along wl over 2f out: sn wknd* **14/1**

6430 **8** *1 ¾* **Prince Of Passion (CAN)**[16] [1487] 6-8-10 **59**..................(v) DaleSwift 8 24
(Derek Shaw) *chsd ldrs: rdn along bef 1/2-way: sn outpcd* **10/1**

1m 18.07s (1.57) **Going Correction** +0.25s/f (Slow) **8** Ran SP% **118.3**
Speed ratings (Par 103): **99,97,96,94,91 84,82,80**
CSF £11.53 CT £25.83 TOTE £2.30: £1.10, £1.90, £1.40; EX 12.80 Trifecta £31.90.
**Owner** S R Bowring **Bred** Mrs Sharon Slattery **Trained** Edwinstowe, Notts

**FOCUS**
A moderate sprint handicap featuring mostly exposed performers. The pace was solid. The winner is rated close to his turf form.
T/Plt: £24.20 to a £1 stake. Pool of £43445.90 - 1309.44 winning tickets. T/Qpdt: £5.10 to a £1 stake. Pool of £3025.21 - 438.15 winning tickets. JR

# 1829 LINGFIELD (L-H)
### Thursday, May 1

**OFFICIAL GOING: Standard**
Wind: virtually nil Weather: showers

## 1893 RUDRIDGE LTD CLAIMING STKS 6f 1y(P)
**1:35** (1:35) (Class 6) 3-Y-0+ **£2,045** (£603; £302) **Stalls** Low

Form RPR

100- **1** **Aye Aye Digby (IRE)**[218] [6744] 9-9-10 80.............................. RichardHughes 1 85
(Patrick Chamings) *led tl over 4f out: chsd ldr after: rdn to chal over 1f out: led ins fnl f: drvn fnl 100yds: hld on* **5/4**[1]

2035 **2** *hd* **Kuanyao (IRE)**[7] [1678] 8-9-1 75...................................(b) DannyBrock(5) 4 80
(Lee Carter) *pressed ldr tl led over 4f out: wnt clr over 3f out: rdn and pressed over 1f out: hdd ins fnl f: rallied and styd on wl towards fin* **3/1**[2]

056- **3** *2 ½* **Noverre To Go (IRE)**[222] [6647] 8-9-8 81...............................(p) SteveDrowne 2 74
(Ronald Harris) *t.k.h: hld up in tch in midfield: wnt 3rd over 2f out: drvn and styd on same pce fr over 1f out* **9/2**[3]

6050 **4** 1 1/2 **Ceelo**10 1613 4-9-1 62 SimonPearce(3) 5 66
(Lydia Pearce) *taken down early: dwlt: hld up in tch in rr: effrt over 1f out: kpt on ins fnl f: nvr trbld ldrs* **33/1**

4641 **5** hd **Lujeanie**19 1448 8-9-6 74 ShaneKelly 6 67
(Peter Crate) *hld up in last pair: effrt in 4th but wd bnd 2f out: kpt on but no threat to ldrs fnl f* **8/1**

11-0 **6** 6 **Touch The Clouds**22 1396 3-8-9 78 LouisSteward(5) 3 49
(William Stone) *chsd ldrs: rdn 1/2-way and sn struggling: bhd over 1f out* **7/1**

1m 10.93s (-0.97) **Going Correction** -0.15s/f (Stan)
**WFA** 3 from 4yo+ 10lb **6** Ran SP% **114.2**
Speed ratings (Par 101): **100,99,96,94,94 86**
CSF £5.39 TOTE £2.10: £1.10, £3.30; EX 7.00 Trifecta £20.20.Kuanyao was claimed by Mr Conor Dore for £8,000.
**Owner** Trolley Action **Bred** G J King **Trained** Baughurst, Hants
■ Stewards' Enquiry : Danny Brock four-day ban: used whip above permitted level (May 16,18-20)

**FOCUS**
An ordinary claimer, dominated by the two market leaders.

## 1894 OYSTER PARTNERSHIP MEDIAN AUCTION MAIDEN STKS 1m 1y(P)
**2:05** (2:05) (Class 6) 3-Y-O £2,249 (£664; £332) **Stalls** Low

Form RPR

4- **1** **Reedcutter**190 7469 3-9-2 0 RobertTart(3) 2 82
(James Toller) *t.k.h: hld up in tch in last pair: hmpd over 5f out: wnt 4th 3f out: rdn and effrt on inner over 1f out: qcknd to ld ins fnl f: r.o strly: readily* **4/1**3

5 **2** 1 3/4 **Halation (IRE)**10 1612 3-9-0 0 MarcMonaghan(5) 5 78
(Marco Botti) *dwlt: t.k.h: hdwy to chse ldrs 6f out: upsides ldrs 3f out: rdn to ld but edgd lft over 1f out: hdd ins fnl f: outpcd by wnr but kpt on for clr 2nd* **11/4**2

**3** 2 1/2 **Cincinnati Girl (IRE)** 3-9-0 0 ShaneKelly 3 67
(Denis Coakley) *stdd after s: hld up in tch in rr: shkn up and effrt 2f out: rn green and edging lft whn swtchd rt 1f out: kpt on to go 3rd wl ins fnl f: no threat to ldrs* **16/1**

0 **4** 1 **Inspector Norse**19 1433 3-9-5 0 RichardHughes 6 70
(Sylvester Kirk) *led 6f out: jnd 3f out: rdn and hdd over 1f out: wknd ins fnl f* **6/1**

5 **5** 1 3/4 **Hoy Hoy (IRE)**19 1433 3-9-2 0 WilliamTwiston-Davies(3) 4 66
(Mick Channon) *led 7f out tl 6f out: chsd ldr after: ev ch 3f out: rdn and struggling to qckn whn squeezed for room and hmpd ent fnl f: sn wknd* **6/4**1

**6** 3 **Topaling** 3-9-0 0 JimmyFortune 1 54
(Mark H Tompkins) *t.k.h: led for 1f: midfield after: rdn over 2f out: dropped to last 2f out: sn wknd* **20/1**

1m 36.53s (-1.67) **Going Correction** -0.15s/f (Stan) **6** Ran SP% **111.6**
Speed ratings (Par 97): **102,100,97,96,95 92**
CSF £15.18 TOTE £5.00: £2.90, £1.80; EX 15.20 Trifecta £178.80.
**Owner** M E Wates **Bred** M E Wates **Trained** Newmarket, Suffolk

**FOCUS**
An ordinary maiden, but the winner did it nicely.

## 1895 PREMIER SHOWFREIGHT LTD H'CAP 1m 7f 169y(P)
**2:35** (2:35) (Class 6) (0-60,60) 4-Y-O+ £2,385 (£704; £352) **Stalls** Low

Form RPR

154U **1** **Graylyn Ruby (FR)**29 1242 9-8-6 52 KieranShoemark(7) 6 61
(Robert Eddery) *hld up off the pce in last trio: clsd and in tch 6f out: rdn and effrt on inner to chse ldr over 1f out: drvn to ld ins fnl f: hld on cl home* **9/2**3

4343 **2** hd **Bert The Alert**11 1242 6-9-0 60 CharlotteJenner(7) 5 68
(Laura Mongan) *stdd s: hld up off the pce in rr: clsd and in tch 6f out: rdn and effrt over 1f out: swtchd rt 1f out: str run ins fnl f: jst hld cl home* **7/2**1

0401 **3** 1 1/2 **Novel Dancer**28 1263 6-8-1 47 JennyPowell(7) 4 53
(Lydia Richards) *chsd clr ldng pair: clsd to trck ldrs 6f out: gng wl but n.m.r over 2f out: hdwy to ld ent fnl 2f: rdn over 1f out: hdd ins fnl f: outpcd fnl 100yds* **8/1**

0553 **4** 3 1/2 **Willow Island (IRE)**21 842 5-8-0 46 oh1 HollieDoyle(7) 3 48
(David Evans) *chsd ldr and clr of rivals: jnd ldr 12f out tl led 1/2-way: hdd and rdn ent fnl 2f: 3rd and no ex 1f out: wknd ins fnl f* **25/1**

-023 **5** 1/2 **Annaluna (IRE)**12 1574 5-9-2 55 (v) RichardHughes 7 56
(David Evans) *racd in midfield: clsd and wl in tch 6f out: swtchd rt and hdwy u.p to chal 2f out: 4th and btn 1f out: wknd fnl f* **4/1**2

0551 **6** nse **See And Be Seen**12 1574 4-9-3 59 (p) RenatoSouza 1 60
(Sylvester Kirk) *prom in main gp: clsd and chsd ldrs 6f out: rdn and unable qck 2f out: outpcd and btn over 1f out: wknd fnl f* **6/1**

5241 **7** 8 **Dr Finley (IRE)**29 1242 7-9-0 56 (v) SimonPearce(3) 2 48
(Lydia Pearce) *racd in midfield: rdn and n.m.r over 2f out: btn wl over 1f out: sn wknd* **5/1**

2-50 **8** nk **Rollin 'n Tumblin**57 842 10-8-11 50 JoeFanning 8 41
(Michael Attwater) *stdd s: racd in midfield: clsd and in tch 6f out: rdn and effrt over 2f out: wd and lost pl on bnd 2f out: sn wknd* **16/1**

0-66 **9** 18 **Supersticion**20 455 5-8-7 46 oh1 (v) HayleyTurner 9 16
(Michael Madgwick) *led and sn clr w rival: hdd 8f out but styd w ldr tl lost pl over 2f out: sn bhd* **50/1**

3m 23.9s (-1.80) **Going Correction** -0.15s/f (Stan)
**WFA** 4 from 5yo+ 3lb **9** Ran SP% **114.2**
Speed ratings (Par 101): **98,97,97,95,95 95,91,90,81**
CSF £20.38 CT £120.94 TOTE £8.40: £2.20, £1.30, £4.80; EX 27.80 Trifecta £247.20.
**Owner** Graham & Lynn Knight **Bred** Jonathan Jay **Trained** Newmarket, Suffolk
■ Stewards' Enquiry : Hollie Doyle two-day ban: careless riding (May 15-16)

**FOCUS**
A moderate handicap, but a fair pace with two soon scampering clear. This was a triumph for the 7lb claimers, who filled the first four places.

## 1896 H&V SERVICEPLAN FILLIES' H'CAP 6f 1y(P)
**3:05** (3:06) (Class 5) (0-70,68) 4-Y-O+ £3,234 (£962; £481; £240) **Stalls** Low

Form RPR

3-35 **1** **Clock Opera (IRE)**87 453 4-8-10 62 LouisSteward(5) 3 70
(William Stone) *wnt rt sn after s: chsd ldrs: rdn and effrt to chse ldr 1f out: styd on strly u.p to ld cl home* **14/1**

203- **2** nk **Pucon**191 7445 5-9-4 68 OisinMurphy(3) 1 75
(Roger Teal) *racd keenly: led: rdn over 1f out: drvn ins fnl f: kpt on: hdd and no ex cl home* **6/1**3

6-61 **3** 1 **Aeolian Blue**21 1405 4-9-3 64 ShaneKelly 6 68
(William Knight) *racd keenly: in tch in midfield: rdn 2f out: wdst bnd 2f out: hdwy and drvn to chse ldrs 1f out: wnt 3rd fnl 100yds: no imp after* **5/4**1

060- **4** 1 **Ada Lovelace**143 8216 4-8-13 63 MichaelJMMurphy(3) 2 64
(John Gallagher) *chsd ldrs and travelled wl: wnt 2nd but fnd little u.p over 1f out: one pce ins fnl f* **14/1**

0053 **5** 1/2 **Chevise (IRE)**21 1405 6-8-6 58 (b) RyanTate(5) 7 57
(Steve Woodman) *chsd ldrs: rdn and effrt ent fnl 2f: lost 2nd over 1f out: wknd ins fnl f* **8/1**

146- **6** 1 **Koharu**169 7861 4-9-5 66 (t) SteveDrowne 4 62
(Peter Makin) *hld up in tch in last trio: effrt over 1f out: kpt on but no real imp fnl f: nvr trbld ldrs* **25/1**

000- **7** shd **Silvee**182 7643 7-8-0 54 oh9 CamHardie(7) 8 50
(John Bridger) *in tch in rr: rdn over 4f out: kpt on ins fnl f: nvr trbld ldrs* **66/1**

545- **8** 1 1/2 **Emerald Sea**169 7861 4-9-5 66 TedDurcan 5 57
(Chris Wall) *stdd and short of room sn after s: hld up in tch in last pair: rdn and no hdwy wl over 1f out: nvr trbld ldrs* **9/4**2

1m 11.0s (-0.90) **Going Correction** -0.15s/f (Stan) **8** Ran SP% **119.3**
Speed ratings (Par 100): **100,99,98,96,96 94,94,92**
CSF £98.65 CT £185.17 TOTE £13.10: £2.90, £1.90, £1.10; EX 72.80 Trifecta £146.40.
**Owner** Caroline Scott & Shane Fairweather **Bred** Ms H W Topping **Trained** West Wickham, Cambs

**FOCUS**
Several of these were returning from absences. The start was a bit messy with the winner going out to her right after exiting the stalls.

## 1897 KC FACILITIES H'CAP (BOBIS RACE) 7f 1y(P)
**3:35** (3:35) (Class 4) (0-80,79) 3-Y-O £5,175 (£1,540; £769; £384) **Stalls** Low

Form RPR

041- **1** **Aertex (IRE)**191 7435 3-9-4 76 RichardHughes 5 84
(Richard Hannon) *t.k.h: midfield tl chsd ldng pair after 2f: effrt and wnt 2nd 2f out: rdn to ld 1f out: qcknd u.p and in command fnl 100yds: comf* **9/2**3

543- **2** 1 3/4 **Pure Amber (IRE)**182 7647 3-9-4 76 JimmyFortune 6 79
(Ismail Mohammed) *led for 2f: chsd ldr tl 2f out: rdn over 1f out: chsd clr wnr ins fnl f: kpt on but no imp fnl 100yds* **20/1**

220- **3** nk **Alisios (GR)**190 7471 3-9-6 78 FrankieDettori 1 80+
(Luca Cumani) *t.k.h: hld up wl in tch in midfield: rdn and effrt on inner over 1f out: kpt on same pce ins fnl f* **11/4**1

015- **4** 3/4 **Mezel**271 4988 3-9-5 77 PaulHanagan 9 77
(J W Hills) *hld up in tch in midfield: rdn and effrt 2f out: no imp tl styd on ins fnl f: no threat to wnr* **16/1**

22-0 **5** nk **Maraayill (IRE)**12 1586 3-8-13 76 MarcMonaghan(5) 3 75
(Marco Botti) *t.k.h: hld up in tch in midfield: hdwy between horses 1f out: kpt on u.p fnl f: no threat to wnr* **7/2**2

6-42 **6** 1/2 **Sir Guy Porteous (IRE)**11 1601 3-8-10 68 JoeFanning 8 66+
(Mark Johnston) *taken down early: t.k.h: chsd ldr tl led after 2f: rdn and edging rt wl over 1f out: hdd 1f out: wknd fnl 100yds* **7/1**

3123 **7** 1/2 **Jaahiez (USA)**24 1352 3-9-4 76 (p) WilliamBuick 7 73
(Roger Varian) *stdd after s: hld up in tch in last trio: swtchd rt and effrt over 1f out: kpt on ins fnl f: nvr threatened ldrs* **9/2**3

514- **8** nk **Wickhambrook (IRE)**192 7428 3-9-4 79 OisinMurphy(3) 2 75
(Ismail Mohammed) *t.k.h: hld up wl in tch in midfield: rdn and effrt over 1f out: no imp: wknd ins fnl f* **8/1**

1544 **9** 1 1/2 **Captain Myles (IRE)**62 785 3-9-5 77 (bt[1]) StevieDonohoe 4 69
(Tim Pitt) *stdd s: t.k.h: hld up in tch in rr: rdn and no hdwy over 1f out: nvr trbld ldrs* **33/1**

1m 23.7s (-1.10) **Going Correction** -0.15s/f (Stan) **9** Ran SP% **122.4**
Speed ratings (Par 101): **100,98,97,96,96 95,95,94,93**
CSF £93.05 CT £300.33 TOTE £6.10: £2.00, £4.40, £1.60; EX 87.20 Trifecta £571.50.
**Owner** Mrs James Wigan **Bred** Mrs James Wigan **Trained** East Everleigh, Wilts

**FOCUS**
A decent 3yo handicap and the form should stand up.

## 1898 CHARTPLAN H'CAP 1m 4f (P)
**4:05** (4:05) (Class 5) (0-70,70) 3-Y-O £3,234 (£962; £481; £240) **Stalls** Low

Form RPR

0-13 **1** **Right Of Appeal**23 1367 3-9-3 66 JoeFanning 2 73+
(Mark Johnston) *racd keenly: mde all: drvn over 1f out: hrd pressed ins fnl f: edging lft but hld on wl fnl 100yds: drvn out* **5/2**1

044- **2** 1/2 **Loving Your Work**164 7944 3-8-13 62 MartinDwyer 4 68
(George Baker) *t.k.h: in tch in midfield: hdwy ent fnl 2f: swtchd ins and rdn wl over 1f out: drvn and str chal jst ins fnl f: kpt on but hld towards fin* **25/1**

34-6 **3** 1 1/2 **Loch Ma Naire (IRE)**15 1508 3-9-6 69 (b[1]) RichardHughes 1 73
(Ed Dunlop) *chsd ldrs: wnt 2nd over 3f out tl over 1f out: styd on same pce u.p ins fnl f* **5/1**

50-0 **4** 3/4 **Lucky Jim**22 1401 3-9-4 67 GeorgeBaker 3 70+
(Chris Wall) *chsd wnr for 2f: in tch in midfield after: reminder over 4f out: 5th and drvn over 1f out: styd on ins fnl f: nvr gng pce to chal* **11/4**2

03-0 **5** 1 1/2 **Supachap**22 1401 3-9-2 65 JimmyFortune 5 65
(Hughie Morrison) *stdd s: t.k.h: hld up in tch in rr: clsd on inner over 2f out: rdn and effrt over 1f out: fnd little and no hdwy fnl f* **4/1**3

-550 **6** 4 1/2 **Son Of Feyan (IRE)**17 1494 3-9-0 66 [1] OisinMurphy(3) 7 59
(Roger Teal) *chsd wnr 10f out tl over 8f out: rdn and lost pl over 2f out: wknd over 1f out* **25/1**

01-0 **7** 2 **New Colours**22 1401 3-9-5 68 (b[1]) ShaneKelly 9 58
(Marcus Tregoning) *t.k.h: hld up in midfield: hdwy to chse wnr over 8f out tl over 3f out: losing pl whn short of room ent fnl 2f: wknd u.p over 1f out* **12/1**

066 **8** 14 **Bongo Beat**28 1258 3-9-3 66 PaulHanagan 6 34
(Michael Attwater) *stdd s: t.k.h: hld up in tch in last pair: rdn 4f out: lost tch 2f out* **12/1**

2m 30.21s (-2.79) **Going Correction** -0.15s/f (Stan) **8** Ran SP% **115.0**
Speed ratings (Par 99): **103,102,101,101,100 97,95,86**
CSF £63.20 CT £288.73 TOTE £2.90: £1.10, £2.70, £1.60; EX 34.30 Trifecta £138.50.
**Owner** Sheikh Hamdan bin Mohammed Al Maktoum **Bred** Lordship Stud **Trained** Middleham Moor, N Yorks

**FOCUS**
A modest middle-distance handicap for 3yos.

## 1899 CITY FIRE PROTECTION/CPFC STUDY CENTRE H'CAP 1m 2f (P)
**4:35** (4:35) (Class 5) (0-75,75) 4-Y-O+ £3,234 (£962; £481; £240) **Stalls** Low

Form RPR

650- **1** **Xinbama (IRE)**146 8179 5-9-2 70 FrankieDettori 11 79
(J W Hills) *hld up in rr: hdwy into midfield over 2f out: swtchd to outer over 1f out: str run to ld fnl 75yds: r.o wl* **8/1**

602- **2** *1* **Dandy (GER)**[228] 6428 5-8-11 **72** ........ RobHornby(7) 6 79
(Andrew Balding) *sn led: rdn over 1f out: edgd rt u.p ins fnl f: hdd and no ex fnl 75yds: kpt on to hold 2nd* **6/1**[3]

00-1 **3** *1 1/4* **Tilstarr (IRE)**[22] 1393 4-9-3 **74** ........ OisinMurphy(3) 4 79
(Roger Teal) *hld up in tch in last quartet: rdn and effrt wl over 1f out: r.o wl ins fnl f: snatched 3rd last stride: nt rch ldrs* **7/1**

4235 **4** *shd* **Aldeburgh**[27] 1281 5-8-12 **66** ........ RichardHughes 1 71
(Jim Old) *in tch in midfield: hdwy on inner to chse ldrs 4f out: rdn and effrt on inner over 1f out: styd on same pce ins fnl f: lost 3rd last stride* **5/1**[2]

62-6 **5** *1/2* **Aint Got A Scooby (IRE)**[24] 1351 4-9-0 **73** ........ RyanTate(5) 10 77
(Clive Cox) *t.k.h: hdwy to chse ldrs over 8f out: rdn to chse ldr 2f out: pressing ldr whn carried sltly rt ins fnl f: no ex and outpcd fnl 100yds* **6/1**[3]

106- **6** *hd* **Tafawuk (USA)**[336] 2808 5-9-4 **72** ........ WilliamBuick 3 75
(Roger Varian) *chsd ldr tl over 5f out: wl in tch but n.m.r ent fnl 2f: rdn and effrt over 1f out: nvr much room and kpt on same pce ins fnl f* **11/4**[1]

5145 **7** *1/2* **Lady Lunchalot (USA)**[13] 1553 4-9-7 **75** ........ LiamJones 9 77
(Laura Mongan) *rdn along early: in tch towards rr: hdwy on outer into midfield over 3f out: rdn over 1f out: styd on same pce ins fnl f* **10/1**

**8** *3/4* **Qasser (IRE)**[52] 3451 5-8-10 **69** ........ LouisSteward(5) 2 70
(Harry Whittington) *hld up in tch in midfield: effrt over 1f out: chsng ldrs but looked hld whn short of room: clipped heels and stmbld ins fnl f: no hdwy after* **25/1**

5-10 **9** *1 3/4* **Archie Rice (USA)**[102] 250 8-9-1 **72** ........ RobertTart(3) 8 70
(Tom Keddy) *s.i.s: hld up in tch in rr: effrt on inner over 1f out: no real imp: nvr trbld ldrs* **12/1**

0-06 **10** *nse* **Idol Deputy (FR)**[28] 1267 8-9-1 **74** ........(p) RachealKneller(5) 7 71
(James Bennett) *in tch in midfield: shuffled bk towards rr but stl in tch whn jostled and hmpd ent fnl 2f: no hdwy after* **25/1**

0/20 **11** *hd* **Pentameter**[17] 1491 5-8-8 **69** ........ CamHardie(7) 5 66
(John Butler) *t.k.h: chsd ldrs: wnt 2nd 6f out tl 2f out: no ex u.p over 1f out: wknd fnl f* **25/1**

2m 4.67s (-1.93) **Going Correction** -0.15s/f (Stan) **11** Ran SP% **123.8**
Speed ratings (Par 103): **101,100,99,99,98 98,98,97,96,96 95**
CSF £57.21 CT £355.63 TOTE £11.00: £3.00, £2.60, £2.40; EX 79.20 Trifecta £1163.70.
**Owner** Tony Waspe Partnership **Bred** P Heffernan **Trained** Upper Lambourn, Berks
■ Stewards' Enquiry : Rob Hornby three-day ban: careless riding (May 15-16,18)

**FOCUS**
An ordinary handicap and several were still within a length or so of each other entering the last furlong.
T/Plt: £60.80 to a £1 stake. Pool: £53,361.71 - 640.19 winning units. T/Qpdt: £11.50 to a £1 stake. Pool: £5996.60 - 384.85 winning units. SP

## 1604 REDCAR (L-H)
### Thursday, May 1

**OFFICIAL GOING: Soft (6.3)**
Wind: light half behind Weather: Cloudy

### 1900 HAPPY 10TH BIRTHDAY RACING UK MAIDEN AUCTION STKS 5f
**1:55** (1:55) (Class 6) 2-Y-O **£2,045** (£603; £302) **Stalls** Centre

Form RPR

0 **1** **Granny Alice**[14] 1528 2-9-0 0 ........ GrahamLee 6 70
(Noel Quinlan) *chsd ldrs: rdn to ld ins fnl f: kpt on* **11/10**[1]

0 **2** *1 1/4* **The Card Players (IRE)**[7] 1670 2-9-5 0 ........ DaleSwift 7 71
(Brian Ellison) *chsd ldrs: rdn and outpcd 1/2-way: kpt on fr over 1f out: wnt 2nd 110yds out* **6/1**[3]

6 **3** *1 1/2* **Compton River**[24] 1342 2-9-5 0 ........ PaulMulrennan 4 65
(Bryan Smart) *led narrowly: wandered u.p appr fnl f: hdd ins fnl f: no ex* **9/2**[2]

40 **4** *1/2* **Binky Blue (IRE)**[15] 1505 2-9-0 0 ........ BarryMcHugh 2 58
(Tony Coyle) *in tch: rdn 1/2-way: kpt on* **12/1**

**5** *2 1/2* **Ingleby Spring (IRE)** 2-9-0 0 ........ TonyHamilton 9 49+
(Richard Fahey) *dwlt: outpcd in rr tl kpt on fnl f* **10/1**

**6** *2 3/4* **Hell For Leather** 2-9-0 0 ........ RyanWhile(5) 5 44
(Bill Turner) *sn pushed along in midfield: wknd 1/2-way* **10/1**

**7** *nse* **Sunhill Lodge Lady** 2-9-0 0 ........ PJMcDonald 1 39
(Ann Duffield) *dwlt: sn outpcd towards rr: nvr threatened* **33/1**

0 **8** *1/2* **On Appro**[15] 1504 2-8-9 0 ........ AdamCarter(5) 8 37
(Tim Easterby) *w ldr: rdn 1/2-way: edgd rt over 1f out: wknd fnl f* **50/1**

1m 4.28s (5.68) **Going Correction** +1.125s/f (Soft) **8** Ran SP% **110.9**
Speed ratings (Par 91): **99,97,94,93,89 85,85,84**
CSF £7.48 TOTE £1.60: £1.10, £2.40, £1.70; EX 8.70 Trifecta £40.10.
**Owner** R Morris J Russell O Doyle J Murphy 1 **Bred** Brook Stud Bloodstock Ltd **Trained** Newmarket, Suffolk

**FOCUS**
Jockeys agreed the ground was riding soft, although Paul Mulrennan stressed "They are getting through it". Modest juvenile form. The time was 1.06secs faster than the following seller.

### 1901 ENJOY HOSPITALITY AT REDCAR RACECOURSE (S) STKS 5f
**2:25** (2:26) (Class 6) 2-Y-O **£2,045** (£603; £302) **Stalls** Centre

Form RPR

0 **1** **Tagtale (IRE)**[24] 1342 2-8-7 0 ........(b[1]) PatrickMathers 5 54+
(Richard Fahey) *chsd ldr: rdn 1/2-way: led ins fnl f: kpt on* **7/2**[2]

**2** *2 1/4* **Strategic Order (IRE)** 2-8-12 0 ........ GrahamLee 3 51
(Paul Midgley) *chsd ldr: rdn 1/2-way: kpt on* **6/1**

606 **3** *1 1/4* **Keep 'r Lit**[7] 1663 2-8-7 0 ........(v[1]) BenCurtis 2 41
(David Evans) *hld up in tch: rdn 2f out: kpt on: wnt 3rd towards fin* **10/1**

**4** *hd* **Fairweather Trader (IRE)** 2-8-12 0 ........(v[1]) PaulMulrennan 4 46
(Paul Midgley) *led: rdn 1/2-way: hdd ins fnl f: wknd* **33/1**

0 **5** *15* **Hard To Find (IRE)**[27] 1276 2-8-12 0 ........ GrahamGibbons 7
(David Evans) *sn outpcd in rr: a bhd* **20/1**

**6** *1 1/4* **Hemi Bossena** 2-8-3 0 ow1 ........ RyanWhile(5) 1
(Bill Turner) *wnt lft s: in tch tl wknd qckly 1/2-way* **11/8**[1]

0 **7** *11* **May One**[12] 1571 2-8-8 0 ow1 ........ SamHitchcott 6
(Mick Channon) *chsd ldrs: hung lft thrght: wknd 3f out: sn wl bhd* **11/2**[3]

1m 5.34s (6.74) **Going Correction** +1.125s/f (Soft) **7** Ran SP% **110.8**
Speed ratings (Par 91): **91,87,85,85,61 59,41**
CSF £22.87 TOTE £3.10: £2.20, £3.00; EX 33.90 Trifecta £312.70.Strategic Order was the subject of a friendly claim.
**Owner** Richard Fahey Ebor Racing Club Ltd **Bred** Sean O'Sullivan **Trained** Musley Bank, N Yorks
■ Stewards' Enquiry : Ben Curtis two-day ban: used whip above permitted level (May 15-16)

**FOCUS**
A weak juvenile seller, with the favourite flopping and three of the first four home wearing headgear for the first time. The time was 1.06secs slower than the opening maiden.

### 1902 CELEBRATE 10 YEARS WITH RACING UK ANYWHERE MAIDEN FILLIES' STKS 6f
**2:55** (2:56) (Class 5) 3-Y-O+ **£2,587** (£770; £384; £192) **Stalls** Centre

Form RPR

0 **1** **Election Night**[32] 1192 3-9-0 0 ........[1] PhillipMakin 7 71
(Tim Easterby) *hld up in tch: rdn and hdwy to chse ldr over 1f out: led jst ins fnl f: kpt on* **20/1**

6- **2** *3 1/4* **Secret Oasis**[274] 4886 3-9-0 0 ........ PaulMulrennan 2 61
(Bryan Smart) *dwlt: sn led: rdn over 2f out: hdd jst ins fnl f: no ex* **6/1**[2]

6 **3** *2* **Zaawia (IRE)**[20] 1422 3-9-0 0 ........ DaneO'Neill 8 55
(Ed Dunlop) *s.i.s: hld up: pushed along bef 1/2-way: rdn 2f out: one pce and nvr seriously threatened: wnt modest 3rd 110yds out* **1/3**[1]

65-3 **4** *1 3/4* **Miss Acclaimed (IRE)**[29] 1246 3-8-8 66 ow1 ........ MeganCarberry(7) 3 51
(Brian Ellison) *chsd ldr: rdn over 2f out: wknd fnl f* **8/1**[3]

**5** *7* **Lucky Times** 3-9-0 0 ........ DuranFentiman 4 29
(Mel Brittain) *chsd ldr: rdn over 2f out: wknd appr fnl f* **50/1**

06-6 **6** *3 1/2* **Lady Liz**[24] 1344 3-9-0 55 ........ AndrewElliott 1 19
(George Moore) *chsd ldrs tl wknd 1/2-way* **40/1**

1m 18.29s (6.49) **Going Correction** +1.125s/f (Soft) **6** Ran SP% **109.6**
Speed ratings (Par 100): **101,96,94,91,82 77**
CSF £122.47 TOTE £22.10: £8.60, £2.20; EX 141.40 Trifecta £159.20.
**Owner** J Shack **Bred** R G & T E Levin **Trained** Great Habton, N Yorks

**FOCUS**
Not form to get excited about, with red-hot favourite Zaawia labouring in the soft ground.

### 1903 REDCAR RACECOURSE CONFERENCE & WEDDING VENUE H'CAP 7f
**3:25** (3:25) (Class 4) (0-85,87) 3-Y-O+ **£6,469** (£1,925; £962; £481) **Stalls** Centre

Form RPR

-011 **1** **Victoire De Lyphar (IRE)**[2] 1839 7-10-2 **87** 12ex....(e) JamesSullivan 4 99
(Ruth Carr) *hld up: pushed along and gd hdwy 2f out: led ins fnl f: kpt on* **11/4**[2]

00-2 **2** *1 1/4* **Johnny Cavagin**[32] 1190 5-9-5 **76** ........(t) TomEaves 9 84
(Richard Guest) *hld up in tch: hdwy to chse ldr over 2f out: chal over 1f out: kpt on but comf hld by wnr fnl 110yds* **7/1**[3]

0010 **3** *1 1/4* **Piceno (IRE)**[9] 1630 6-9-0 **78** ........(p) MatthewHopkins(7) 10 83
(Scott Dixon) *led: rdn over 2f out: hdd ins fnl f: no ex* **18/1**

000- **4** *2 1/2* **Bachotheque (IRE)**[235] 6238 4-9-4 **75** ........ GrahamLee 1 74
(Tim Easterby) *racd keenly in tch: rdn over 1f out: sn one pce* **25/1**

0-02 **5** *2* **Dream Walker (FR)**[9] 1637 5-9-13 **84** ........ DaleSwift 7 77
(Brian Ellison) *hld up: rdn over 2f out: sn no imp on ldrs* **2/1**[1]

13-4 **6** *3* **Dubai Hills**[36] 1114 8-9-11 **82** ........ DanielTudhope 3 68
(David O'Meara) *chsd ldr: rdn over 2f out: wknd fnl f* **8/1**

0-00 **7** *3/4* **Rocket Ronnie (IRE)**[17] 1483 4-9-7 **78** ........ AdrianNicholls 5 62
(David Nicholls) *dwlt: hld up: rdn over 2f out: nvr threatened* **33/1**

62-0 **8** *3 1/4* **Torchlighter (IRE)**[20] 1420 3-9-2 **85** ........ FrannyNorton 2 56
(Mark Johnston) *prom: rdn 3f out: wknd over 1f out* **8/1**

00-0 **9** *13* **Xilerator (IRE)**[8] 1646 7-9-6 **77** ........ PaulQuinn 8 18
(David Nicholls) *dwlt: sn in tch racing keenly: rdn 3f out: sn wknd* **40/1**

40-5 **10** *12* **Penny Garcia**[29] 1247 4-9-5 **76** ........ DuranFentiman 6
(Tim Easterby) *chsd ldrs tl wknd over 2f out: eased* **28/1**

1m 31.17s (6.67) **Going Correction** +1.125s/f (Soft)
**WFA** 3 from 4yo+ 12lb **10** Ran SP% **112.7**
Speed ratings (Par 105): **106,104,103,100,98 94,93,90,75,61**
CSF £20.48 CT £288.69 TOTE £6.30: £1.30, £2.00, £6.50; EX 21.00 Trifecta £326.70.
**Owner** The Beer Stalkers & Ruth Carr **Bred** Mrs Monica Hackett **Trained** Huby, N Yorks

**FOCUS**
A fair handicap.

### 1904 RACINGUK.COM/ANYWHERE: 3 DEVICES, 1 PRICE H'CAP 1m 1f
**3:55** (3:55) (Class 5) (0-70,67) 3-Y-O **£2,587** (£770; £384; £192) **Stalls** Low

Form RPR

45-4 **1** **Innocent Touch (IRE)**[15] 1509 3-9-7 **67** ........ TonyHamilton 6 75+
(Richard Fahey) *pressed ldr: rdn over 2f out: led over 1f out: idled and briefly pressed ins fnl f: responded and a in command fnl 110yds* **9/4**[2]

00-4 **2** *1 1/4* **Aldreth**[9] 1632 3-8-11 **57** ........ GrahamGibbons 2 62
(Michael Easterby) *trckd ldng pair: rdn over 2f out: chal jst ins fnl f: kpt on but hld fnl 110yds* **6/1**[3]

0-1 **3** *2 1/4* **Deep Resolve (IRE)**[23] 1364 3-9-7 **67** ........ BenCurtis 1 67
(Alan Swinbank) *dwlt: sn led: rdn over 2f out: hdd over 1f out: sn no ex* **17/2**

32-4 **4** *1 1/2* **Spirit Or Soul (FR)**[22] 1395 3-9-7 **67** ........ LukeMorris 7 64
(Marco Botti) *chsd ldng pair: rdn 4f out: sn one pce: wknd fnl f* **6/5**[1]

36-6 **5** *18* **Sketch Map (IRE)**[24] 1346 3-9-3 **63** ........ RussKennemore 5 22
(Jedd O'Keeffe) *hld up: rdn over 3f out: sn btn* **10/1**

2m 1.2s (8.20) **Going Correction** +0.90s/f (Soft) **5** Ran SP% **110.1**
Speed ratings (Par 99): **99,97,95,94,78**
CSF £15.21 TOTE £4.60: £3.90, £2.40; EX 11.00 Trifecta £56.40.
**Owner** Nicholas Wrigley & Kevin Hart **Bred** B Kennedy **Trained** Musley Bank, N Yorks

**FOCUS**
This modest handicap was run at a steady pace, but it still looked hard work for the runners in the ground.

### 1905 WIN A VIP DAY @ REDCARRACING.CO.UK CLAIMING STKS 6f
**4:30** (4:31) (Class 6) 3-Y-O+ **£2,045** (£603; £302) **Stalls** Centre

Form RPR

60-0 **1** **Bunce (IRE)**[10] 1606 6-8-8 61 ........ GemmaTutty(7) 4 69
(Karen Tutty) *chsd ldrs: rdn over 2f out: kpt on to ld 50yds out* **16/1**

42-0 **2** *1/2* **Captain Royale (IRE)**[2] 1843 9-8-12 68 ........(p) ConnorBeasley(5) 5 69
(Tracy Waggott) *led: drvn and strly pressed fr over 1f out: hdd 50yds out* **4/1**[3]

06-5 **3** *3/4* **Betty Boo (IRE)**[15] 1503 4-8-7 39 ........ ShirleyTeasdale(5) 7 62
(Shaun Harris) *chsd ldrs: rdn and ev ch over 1f out: one pce fnl 110yds* **200/1**

0-44 **4** *nk* **Beckermet (IRE)**[10] 1610 12-9-4 71 ........ JamesSullivan 6 67
(Ruth Carr) *chsd ldrs: rdn over 2f out: one pce* **7/4**[1]

0-66 **5** *1 1/2* **Tajneed (IRE)**[14] 1537 11-9-3 74 ........ AdrianNicholls 3 62
(David Nicholls) *w ldr: rdn and outpcd 1/2-way: no threat after* **7/2**[2]

16-0 **6** *2 1/2* **Kylladdie**[19] 1440 7-9-6 72 ........(b) LukeMorris 1 57
(Steve Gollings) *chsd ldrs: rdn 1/2-way: wknd over 1f out* **5/1**

6520 **7** *22* **Britain (IRE)**[8] 1642 3-8-3 **53**............................(v) RaulDaSilva 2
(David C Griffiths) *rrd and slowly away: hld up: rdn 1/2-way: sn wknd: eased* **12/1**

1m 18.2s (6.40) **Going Correction** +1.125s/f (Soft)
**WFA** 3 from 4yo+ 10lb **7** Ran SP% **109.3**
Speed ratings (Par 101): **102,101,100,99,97 94,65**
CSF £71.56 TOTE £10.80: £5.20, £1.50; EX 78.00 Trifecta £1327.40.Bunce was claimed by Miss L. A. Perratt for £3,000.
**Owner** Thoroughbred Homes Ltd **Bred** John Doyle **Trained** Osmotherley, N Yorks

**FOCUS**
A couple of the key contenders failed to give their running in this claimer and the form is worth little, with the 39-rated Betty Boo, a 200-1 shot, beaten just over a length in third.

## 1906 DOWNLOAD NEW RACING UK IPAD APP H'CAP (STRAIGHT-MILE CHAMPIONSHIP QUALIFIER) 1m
5:05 (5:09) (Class 6) (0-60,63) 3-Y-O **£2,045** (£603; £302) **Stalls** Centre

Form RPR

0401 **1** **Sheriff Of Nawton (IRE)**[8] 1647 3-9-10 **63** 6ex.......... DanielTudhope 7 75+
(David O'Meara) *in tch: smooth hdwy over 2f out: led on bit over 1f out: nudged clr fnl f: easily* **5/4**[1]

05-5 **2** *2 ¾* **Trinity Star (IRE)**[8] 1648 3-9-1 **59**.......................... ConnorBeasley(5) 11 59
(Michael Dods) *hld up: rdn in rr over 3f out: kpt on fr over 1f out: wnt 2nd 50yds out: no ch w wnr* **7/2**[2]

00-5 **3** *1* **Petergate**[24] 1346 3-9-7 **60**.......................... BarryMcHugh 3 58
(Brian Rothwell) *hld up: rdn and hdwy over 2f out: chsd wnr over 1f out: one pce: lost 2nd 50yds out* **12/1**

-604 **4** *hd* **Sicilian Bay (IRE)**[26] 1303 3-8-10 **54**.................. ShirleyTeasdale(5) 10 52
(Paul Midgley) *midfield: hdwy over 2f out: rdn to chse ldrs over 1f out: one pce fnl f* **22/1**

0-50 **5** *6* **Elle West**[8] 1647 3-9-0 **60**.......................... AnnaHesketh(7) 1 44
(Michael Easterby) *prom: led over 2f out: hdd over 1f out: wknd fnl f* **40/1**

2306 **6** *2 ¼* **Needs The Run**[9] 1632 3-9-0 **53**..........................(v[1]) GrahamGibbons 13 32
(David Evans) *chsd ldrs: rdn over 2f out: wknd over 1f out* **25/1**

45-5 **7** *4* **Bearskin (IRE)**[10] 1611 3-9-7 **60**..........................(p) PJMcDonald 8 29
(Ann Duffield) *midfield: rdn 3f out: nvr threatened* **14/1**

00-3 **8** *2 ½* **Where's Tiger**[26] 1308 3-9-4 **57**.......................... PhillipMakin 16 21
(Jedd O'Keeffe) *s.i.s: hld up: rdn over 3f out: nvr threatened* **7/1**[3]

005- **9** *3 ¼* **Bridge Of Avon**[212] 6914 3-8-7 **46** oh1.......................... AndrewElliott 4 2
(Mel Brittain) *hld up: rdn in rr 1/2-way: nvr threatened* **100/1**

00-0 **10** *7* **Nu Form Fire (IRE)**[8] 1648 3-8-11 **50**.......................... LeeTopliss 9
(Nigel Tinkler) *trckd ldrs: rdn over 2f out: sn wknd* **66/1**

060- **11** *1 ½* **First Commandment**[195] 7341 3-8-9 **48**.......................... GrahamLee 14
(Tim Easterby) *midfield: rdn over 2f out: sn wknd* **20/1**

56-0 **12** *12* **Wilberfoss (IRE)**[26] 1308 3-9-4 **57**..........................(b[1]) TonyHamilton 12
(Mel Brittain) *hld up: a towards rr* **66/1**

3500 **13** *3* **This Charming Man (IRE)**[7] 1657 3-8-13 **52**..................(p) TomEaves 2
(Keith Dalgleish) *led: rdn whn hdd over 2f out: wknd* **33/1**

1m 46.99s (10.39) **Going Correction** +1.125s/f (Soft) **13** Ran SP% **115.8**
Speed ratings (Par 97): **93,90,89,89,83 80,76,74,71,64 62,50,47**
CSF £4.41 CT £35.41 TOTE £1.90: £1.10, £2.10, £3.50; EX 7.20 Trifecta £46.70.
**Owner** Direct Racing **Bred** Lawman Syndicate & Pipe View Stud **Trained** Nawton, N Yorks

**FOCUS**
A low-grade handicap that revolved around the favourite.
T/Plt: £983.50 to a £1 stake. Pool: £42,507.05 - 31.55 winning units. T/Qpdt: £305.50 to a £1 stake. Pool: £3344.20 - 8.10 winning units. AS

# 1502 SAINT-CLOUD (L-H)
Thursday, May 1

**OFFICIAL GOING: Turf: soft**

## 1907a PRIX GOUVERNANT (MAIDEN) (3YO) (TURF) 1m
12:15 (12:00) 3-Y-O **£6,666** (£2,666; £2,000; £1,333; £666)

RPR

**1** **Charlie's Angel (FR)**[229] 3-8-8 0.......................... RonanThomas 12 78
(H-F Devin, France) **19/2**

**2** *¾* **Netsuke (IRE)**[16] 3-8-13 0.......................... ChristopheSoumillon 2 81
(F Vermeulen, France) **8/5**[1]

**3** *nk* **Wikita (FR)**[149] 3-8-8 0.......................... TonyPiccone 3 75
(F Chappet, France) **223/10**

**4** *snk* **Boetie's Dream (IRE)**[16] 3-9-0 0.......................... ThierryJarnet 7 81
(P Bary, France) **14/5**[2]

**5** *¾* **Appiano (FR)**[54] 3-9-0 0..........................(b) MorganDelalande 10 79
(Y Barberot, France) **40/1**

**6** *nk* **Berrahri (IRE)**[133] 8354 3-9-4 0.......................... Pierre-CharlesBoudot 4 83
(John Best) *pressed ldr on outer: pushed along fr 2 1/2f out: rdn to chal over 1 1/2f out: grad fdd ins fnl f* **19/5**[3]

**7** *1 ¾* **Bombineta (FR)**[42] 3-8-8 0.......................... RaphaelMarchelli 9 69
(P Adda, France) **43/1**

**8** *1 ¾* **Sagal Nel Vento (SER)**[7] 3-8-11 0..........................(b) FabienLefebvre 1 68
(B Vidovic, Croatia) **82/1**

**9** *4* **Giny Queen (FR)**[56] 3-8-8 0.......................... AlexisBadel 11 55
(Mlle V Dissaux, France) **51/1**

**10** *hd* **All Valentine (FR)** 3-8-10 0.......................... TheoBachelot 6 57
(S Wattel, France) **63/10**

1m 44.27s (-3.23) **10** Ran SP% **121.0**
WIN (incl. 1 euro stake): 10.50. PLACES: 2.00, 1.50, 3.20. DF: 11.90. SF: 32.00.
**Owner** M Offenstadt & Mlle V Devin **Bred** S.F. Bloodstock Llc **Trained** France

## 1908a PRIX DU MUGUET (GROUP 2) (4YO+) (TURF) 1m
1:50 (12:00) 4-Y-O+ **£61,750** (£23,833; £11,375; £7,583; £3,791)

RPR

**1** **Sommerabend**[23] 1371 7-8-11 0.......................... GeraldMosse 8 116
(M Rulec, Germany) *a.p on outer: rdn to chse clr ldr over 1 1/2f out: grad reeled in ldr to ld 75yds out* **5/1**[3]

**2** *1 ¼* **Matorio (FR)**[32] 4-8-8 0.......................... FabriceVeron 7 110
(H-A Pantall, France) *t.k.h: hld up towards rr: swtchd outside and pushed along 2 1/2f out: styd on u.p appr 1f out: kpt on wl fnl f: nvr on terms w wnr* **18/1**

**3** *1* **Kokaltash (FR)**[23] 1371 4-8-11 0.......................... ChristopheSoumillon 4 111
(M Delzangles, France) *hld up towards rr: effrt and edgd rt over 1 1/2f out: styd on wl u.p fnl f: tk 3rd fnl stride* **9/4**[1]

**4** *nse* **Pinturicchio (IRE)**[42] 1037 6-8-11 0.......................... GregoryBenoist 9 111
(E Lellouche, France) *chsd ldrs on outer: outpcd and pushed along over 2f out: styd on u.p fnl f: lost 3rd fnl stride* **7/1**

**5** *hd* **Anodin (IRE)**[207] 7059 4-8-11 0.......................... FlavienPrat 5 110
(F Head, France) *led: kicked 3 l clr 2 1/2f out: rdn and rallied appr fnl f: hdd 75yds out: no ex* **14/1**

**6** *2 ½* **Fiesolana (IRE)**[201] 7190 5-8-11 0.......................... StephanePasquier 2 105
(W McCreery, Ire) *t.k.h: trckd ldrs between horses: 4th and rdn over 1 1/2f out: grad outpcd by ldrs fnl f* **6/1**

**7** *3 ½* **Amaron**[18] 1478 5-8-11 0.......................... FabienLefebvre 1 97
(Andreas Lowe, Germany) *trckd ldr on rail: pushed along to chse clr ldr appr 2f out: rdn and wknd fr 1 1/2f out* **7/2**[2]

**8** *½* **Pilote (IRE)**[23] 1371 4-8-11 0.......................... OlivierPeslier 6 95
(A Fabre, France) *hld up in rr: rdn and nt qckn 2f out: nvr in contention* **8/1**

**9** *¾* **Kenhope (FR)**[23] 1371 4-8-8 0..................(p) Christophe-PatriceLemaire 3 91
(H-A Pantall, France) *t.k.h: hld up towards rr: rdn and no imp fr 2f out: nvr a factor* **14/1**

1m 42.67s (-4.83) **9** Ran SP% **126.2**
WIN (incl. 1 euro stake): 6.20. PLACES: 2.00, 3.60, 1.70. DF: 42.70. SF: 76.50.
**Owner** Stall Am Alten Flies **Bred** Gestut Schlenderhan **Trained** Germany

# CHEPSTOW (L-H)
Friday, May 2

**OFFICIAL GOING: Soft (heavy in places; 4.0)**
Wind: slight across Weather: cloudy

## 1909 32RED ON THE APP STORE H'CAP 1m 4f 23y
1:45 (1:45) (Class 5) (0-75,75) 4-Y-O+ **£2,587** (£770; £384; £192) **Stalls** Low

Form RPR

130- **1** **One Pursuit (IRE)**[163] 7976 6-9-0 **75**.......................... JennyPowell(7) 3 95
(Brendan Powell) *trckd ldrs: led gng wl 3f out: sn pushed clr: easily* **8/1**

530- **2** *9* **Ivanhoe**[37] 6743 4-8-9 **63**.......................... DavidProbert 1 70
(Michael Blanshard) *in tch: hdwy over 3f out: wnt 2nd wl over 1f out: kpt on but no ch w easy wnr* **7/1**[3]

30-2 **3** *3* **Rosie Rebel**[27] 1307 4-9-6 **74**.......................... ChrisCatlin 9 76
(Rae Guest) *s.s: last but in tch: shkn up and gd hdwy over 3f out: wnt 3rd over 1f out: one pce and no further imp* **5/2**[1]

3011 **4** *2 ¼* **Geeaitch**[17] 1496 5-8-12 **66**.......................... RobertWinston 4 65
(Peter Hiatt) *hld up towards rr: hdwy over 4f out: rdn and outpcd by principals over 2f out: styd on fnl f: tk 4th post* **8/1**

-344 **5** *nk* **Modem**[25] 1355 4-8-13 **67**..........................(b) AndreaAtzeni 2 65
(Rod Millman) *led: brought field to centre of trck in home st: rdn and hdd 3f out: sn outpcd by wnr: lost 2nd wl over 1f out: wknd fnl f* **7/2**[2]

115- **6** *12* **Eton Rambler (USA)**[180] 6827 4-9-4 **72**..................(p) MartinDwyer 7 52
(George Baker) *in rr: rdn over 3f out: one pce and no imp on ldrs* **14/1**

231 **7** *2 ¼* **Time Square (FR)**[22] 1406 7-8-2 **61**.......................... JoeyHaynes(5) 10 38
(Tony Carroll) *pressed ldr: rdn over 3f out: wknd over 2f out* **10/1**

60-0 **8** *3* **Shades Of Silver**[25] 1355 4-8-8 **65**.......................... WilliamTwiston-Davies(3) 5 37
(Michael Scudamore) *s.i.s: sn rcvrd and chsd ldrs after 2f: hit rail and stmbld over 5f out: pushed along 3f out: sn wknd* **50/1**

000- **9** *42* **Sunny Future (IRE)**[194] 7396 8-9-4 **72**.......................... RichardHughes 8
(Malcolm Saunders) *in tch tl rdn and wknd 3f out: eased over 2f out: t.o* **10/1**

2m 49.86s (10.86) **Going Correction** +1.025s/f (Soft) **9** Ran SP% **112.3**
Speed ratings (Par 103): **104,98,96,94,94 86,84,82,54**
CSF £60.54 CT £179.24 TOTE £10.10: £3.90, £2.10, £1.10; EX 36.40 Trifecta £298.10.
**Owner** Nicholas J E Maher **Bred** Clougher Partnership **Trained** Upper Lambourn, Berks

**FOCUS**
After 6mm rain the previous day underfoot conditions were fairly testing. Just a steady pace before the winner made a race-winning move about 3f from home. The whole field came centre in the home straight. The winner impressed but the level is hard to gauge given the conditions.

## 1910 32RED CASINO FILLIES' H'CAP 1m 2f 36y
2:15 (2:15) (Class 5) (0-75,75) 4-Y-O+ **£2,587** (£770; £384; £192) **Stalls** Low

Form RPR

111- **1** **Calm Attitude (IRE)**[231] 6357 4-8-13 **67**.......................... ChrisCatlin 5 76
(Rae Guest) *hld up towards rr: hdwy over 5f out: rdn over 2f out: sn chsd ldr: led appr fnl f: styd on wl* **5/2**[2]

010- **2** *3 ½* **Laura Secord (CAN)**[220] 6735 4-9-3 **71**.......................... AndreaAtzeni 6 74
(Heather Main) *prom s: chsd ldr 4f out to 3f out: sn drvn and sltly outpcd by principals: kpt on to take 2nd nr fin* **8/1**

24-3 **3** *1 ½* **Play Street**[13] 1568 5-9-4 **75**.......................... MatthewLawson(3) 4 75
(Jonathan Portman) *led: rdn over 2f out: hdd appr fnl f: sn wknd: lost 2nd nr fin* **4/1**[3]

02- **4** *7* **Monopoli**[227] 6491 5-8-7 **61** oh1.......................... FergusSweeney 2 49
(John O'Shea) *hld up in tch: rdn to chse ldr 3f out: lost 2nd 2f out: sn wknd* **6/1**

150- **5** *12* **Our Phylli Vera (IRE)**[38] 7504 5-9-6 **74**.......................... RichardHughes 1 40
(Alan King) *taken to post early: trckd ldr to 4f out: wknd 3f out* **2/1**[1]

04-0 **6** *3* **Ashkalara**[92] 382 7-7-7 **61** oh6.......................... JimmyQuinn 3 22
(Stuart Howe) *hld up in rr: rdn over 4f out: bhd fnl 3f* **33/1**

2m 22.43s (11.83) **Going Correction** +1.025s/f (Soft) **6** Ran SP% **110.2**
Speed ratings (Par 100): **93,90,89,83,73 71**
CSF £20.99 TOTE £2.60: £1.40, £3.90; EX 17.20 Trifecta £67.00.
**Owner** The Calm Again Partnership **Bred** R N Auld **Trained** Newmarket, Suffolk

**FOCUS**
It paid to bide your time in this slowly run fillies' handicap. Questionable form.

## 1911 32RED.COM MAIDEN STKS 1m 2f 36y
2:50 (2:50) (Class 5) 3-Y-O+ **£3,234** (£962; £481; £240) **Stalls** Low

Form RPR

3- **1** **Melrose Abbey (IRE)**[205] 7128 3-8-7 0.......................... AndreaAtzeni 1 83
(Ralph Beckett) *trckd ldrs: pushed along over 3f out: sn led: strly pressed fnl 2f: drvn out ins fnl f to hold rival* **5/4**[1]

0- **2** *nk* **Nabatean (IRE)**[189] 7502 3-8-12 0.......................... DavidProbert 9 87
(Andrew Balding) *chsd ldrs: impr gng wl 3f out: pressed wnr over 2f out: ev ch ins fnl f: r.o: jst hld* **9/2**

3 **3** *3 ½* **Karraar**[13] 1582 3-8-12 0.......................... DaneO'Neill 5 81
(Richard Hannon) *mid-div: hdwy 3f out: sn rdn: kpt on but lacked the pce to chal ldng pair* **4/1**[3]

0- **4** *18* **Taws**[219] 6740 3-8-7 0 MartinLane 6 44
(Rod Millman) *in rr: rdn 4f out: outpcd by principals 3f out: styd on same pce to go mod 4th over 1f out* **66/1**

004 **5** *8* **Flamenco Flyer**[37] 1111 5-9-10 22 (p) ThomasBrown(3) 8 35
(Edward Bevan) *in rr: pushed along over 4f out: sn struggling in last: plugged on past btn rivals fnl 2f* **100/1**

00-2 **6** *4 1/2* **Arable**[32] 1208 3-8-12 80 RichardHughes 4 26
(Charles Hills) *trckd ldrs: rdn and ev ch 3f out: wknd qckly* **3/1**[2]

5- **7** *9* **Danz Star (IRE)**[249] 5811 3-8-12 0 SteveDrowne 3
(Malcolm Saunders) *s.s: towards rr: rdn over 3f out: sn wknd: t.o* **14/1**

4 **8** *9* **Medburn Cutler**[36] 1119 4-9-13 0 FergusSweeney 2
(George Baker) *led tl hdd 3f out: wknd qckly: t.o* **33/1**

2m 20.15s (9.55) **Going Correction** +1.025s/f (Soft)
**WFA** 3 from 4yo+ 15lb 8 Ran SP% **119.7**
Speed ratings (Par 103): **102,101,98,84,78 74,67,60**
CSF £7.94 TOTE £2.70: £1.10, £1.30, £1.10; EX 7.90 Trifecta £28.50.
**Owner** J H Richmond-Watson **Bred** Lawn Stud **Trained** Kimpton, Hants

**FOCUS**
Not a bad maiden with the first three home each lightly raced, unexposed types who finished a long way clear. The third and sixth set the standard.

## 1912 32RED VETERANS' H'CAP 5f 16y
**3:25** (3:25) (Class 5) (0-75,75) 6-Y-O+ **£2,587** (£770; £384; £192) **Stalls** Centre

Form RPR

00-0 **1** **Taurus Twins**[31] 1221 8-8-11 **65** (b) DaneO'Neill 7 75
(Richard Price) *a.p: led narrowly over 2f out tl hdd wl over 1f out: rallied ins fnl f: sn carried lft: led last strides* **10/1**

-664 **2** *shd* **Solemn**[4] 1787 9-8-11 **65** (v) DavidProbert 10 74
(Milton Bradley) *chsd ldrs: edgd lft u.p wl ins fnl f: led 50yds out tl last strides* **4/1**[2]

-035 **3** *1 3/4* **Monsieur Jamie**[11] 1618 6-9-7 **75** (v) AndreaAtzeni 2 78
(J R Jenkins) *chsd ldrs: led narrowly wl over 1f out: sn edgd lft u.p: hdd 50yds out: no ex* **7/2**[1]

3002 **4** *1 1/2* **Dark Lane**[10] 1639 8-8-0 **61** oh2 HollieDoyle(7) 1 58
(David Evans) *chsd ldrs: rdn over 2f out: carried lft ent fnl f: one pce after* **7/1**

400- **5** *1* **Italian Tom (IRE)**[136] 8321 7-9-7 **75** LiamJones 3 69
(Ronald Harris) *squeezed out s: bhd: rdn along over 3f out: hdwy on outer 2f out: no further prog fnl f* **12/1**

4-40 **6** *3 3/4* **Ginzan**[4] 1789 6-9-7 **75** RichardHughes 5 55
(Malcolm Saunders) *hld up: rdn over 2f out: swtchd lft over 1f out: one pce whn briefly short of room appr fnl f: eased whn hld 150yds out* **9/2**[3]

5414 **7** *1/2* **West Coast Dream**[21] 1431 7-8-13 **67** ChrisCatlin 9 45
(Roy Brotherton) *led tl over 2f out: wknd fnl f* **5/1**

6240 **8** *1 1/4* **Quality Art (USA)**[4] 1787 6-8-9 **63** SteveDrowne 8 37
(Simon Hodgson) *rdn 2f out: a towards rr* **16/1**

1m 3.41s (4.11) **Going Correction** +1.025s/f (Soft) 8 Ran SP% **112.2**
Speed ratings: **104,103,101,98,97 91,90,88**
CSF £47.86 CT £169.68 TOTE £13.10: £4.00, £1.50, £1.10; EX 66.40 Trifecta £371.00.
**Owner** G E Amey & G D Bailey **Bred** G E Amey **Trained** Ullingswick, H'fords

**FOCUS**
Some battle-hardened sprinters in this veterans' sprint handicap. The form is rated around the second.

## 1913 32RED.COM H'CAP (BOBIS RACE) 1m 14y
**3:55** (3:55) (Class 4) (0-80,80) 3-Y-O **£6,469** (£1,925; £962; £481) **Stalls** Centre

Form RPR

410- **1** **Flippant (IRE)**[209] 7016 3-9-1 **79** NathanAlison(5) 6 87
(William Haggas) *trckd ldrs: pushed along over 2f out: drvn ins fnl f: r.o wl to ld last strides* **6/1**

231- **2** *nk* **Tullia (IRE)**[200] 7243 3-9-1 **74** [1] AndreaAtzeni 5 81
(William Knight) *cl up: led after 1f tl over 1f out: rallied u.p to ld 100yds out: r.o: hdd last strides* **3/1**[1]

-150 **3** *1 3/4* **Can't Change It (IRE)**[58] 850 3-9-4 **77** FergusSweeney 7 80
(David Simcock) *trckd ldrs: rdn to ld over 1f out: hdd 100yds out: no ex* **12/1**

5362 **4** *4* **Boogangoo (IRE)**[23] 1400 3-9-0 **73** DavidProbert 1 67
(Grace Harris) *s.s: towards rr: rdn and hdwy over 2f out: sn outpcd by principals: kpt on same pce* **10/1**

01-5 **5** *8* **Hedge End (IRE)**[30] 1240 3-9-7 **80** RichardHughes 4 55
(Richard Hannon) *led 1f: trckd ldr: rdn over 2f out: wknd qckly over 1f out* **10/1**

35-0 **6** *nse* **Canova (IRE)**[13] 1586 3-8-10 **72** WilliamTwiston-Davies(3) 2 47
(Roger Charlton) *hld up towards rr: pushed along over 2f out: unable qck and no imp* **7/1**

14-6 **7** *1/2* **Star Code (IRE)**[25] 1350 3-9-5 **78** PatDobbs 3 52
(Richard Hannon) *hld up in tch: rdn over 2f out: wknd appr fnl f* **5/1**[3]

31-4 **8** *7* **Rock Of Dreams (IRE)**[16] 1507 3-9-2 **75** RobertWinston 8 33
(Charles Hills) *towards rr: hdwy over 3f out: rdn and unable qck 2f out: wknd fnl f* **4/1**[2]

1m 42.96s (6.76) **Going Correction** +1.025s/f (Soft) 8 Ran SP% **114.3**
Speed ratings (Par 101): **103,102,100,96,88 88,88,81**
CSF £24.35 CT £208.92 TOTE £6.70: £3.30, £1.40, £3.70; EX 40.80 Trifecta £213.80.
**Owner** Bernard Kantor **Bred** Wentworth Racing (pty) Ltd **Trained** Newmarket, Suffolk

**FOCUS**
The principals had this to themselves from some way out. The winner is entitled to do better still.

## 1914 32RED FREE £10 BONUS H'CAP 6f 16y
**4:30** (4:30) (Class 6) (0-65,65) 3-Y-O **£1,940** (£577; £288; £144) **Stalls** Centre

Form RPR

2614 **1** **Coiste Bodhar (IRE)**[11] 1611 3-8-10 **61** (p) NoraLooby(7) 5 66
(Joseph Tuite) *mde all: 3 l clr 3f out: reduced ld 1f out: rdn out and a holding rivals* **5/1**[3]

460- **2** *1* **Fantasy Justifier (IRE)**[226] 6517 3-9-7 **65** SteveDrowne 6 67
(Ronald Harris) *towards rr: rdn 3f out: sn swtchd lft and hdwy: chsd wnr over 1f out: kpt on u.p but a being hld* **14/1**

2026 **3** *1 1/4* **Intense Feeling (IRE)**[13] 1570 3-9-0 **61** DeclanBates(3) 8 59
(David Evans) *chsd ldrs: disp 2nd over 2f out tl over 1f out: kpt on u.p* **7/2**[2]

-555 **4** *5* **Miss Tweedy**[30] 1235 3-8-8 **52** AndreaAtzeni 4 35
(Rod Millman) *chsd ldrs: rdn over 2f out: one pce* **6/1**

50-6 **5** *shd* **Zafraaj**[13] 1569 3-9-2 **60** DavidProbert 3 43
(Ronald Harris) *prom: disp 2nd over 2f out tl over 1f out: sn wknd* **20/1**

0-06 **6** *10* **Oakley Dancer**[29] 1264 3-8-2 **51** oh6 JoeyHaynes(5) 9 4
(Tony Carroll) *chsd ldrs: began to hang lft and rdn over 3f out: lost 2nd over 2f out: grad wknd* **50/1**

550- **7** *34* **Connaught Water (IRE)**[240] 6111 3-8-8 **55** MatthewLawson(3) 7
(Jonathan Portman) *s.s: in rr: rdn over 3f out: no imp on ldrs: sn wknd: virtually p.u fnl f: t.o* **8/1**

-235 **8** *27* **La Napoule**[86] 486 3-9-4 **62** RichardHughes 1
(Richard Hannon) *in tch: rdn over 3f out: sn wknd: eased wl over 1f out: virtually p.u fnl f: t.o* **7/4**[1]

1m 16.92s (4.92) **Going Correction** +1.025s/f (Soft) 8 Ran SP% **114.0**
Speed ratings (Par 97): **104,102,101,94,94 80,35,**
CSF £69.67 CT £274.80 TOTE £7.20: £1.90, £5.40, £1.90; EX 64.90 Trifecta £205.70.
**Owner** Shefford Valley Racing **Bred** C Amerian **Trained** Great Shefford, Berks

**FOCUS**
The first three home had this to themselves from some way out. Weak form, the winner enjoying an uncontested lead.

## 1915 32REDPOKER.COM H'CAP (DIV I) 2m 49y
**5:00** (5:03) (Class 6) (0-65,65) 4-Y-O+ **£1,940** (£577; £288; £144) **Stalls** Low

Form RPR

605- **1** **Captain Sharpe**[29] 4238 6-9-3 **58** (t) MartinLane 1 65
(Bernard Llewellyn) *chsd ldrs: rdn to chal 4f out: styd on u.p in sustained duel to ld last stride* **14/1**

5-0 **2** *nse* **Cropley (IRE)**[34] 1167 5-9-5 **65** (p) GeorgeDowning(5) 2 72
(Ian Williams) *led: jnd 4f out: sn drvn: styd on and maintained slender ld in duel tl hdd last stride* **9/4**[2]

504- **3** *6* **Fuzzy Logic (IRE)**[36] 4938 5-8-5 **46** DavidProbert 8 47
(Bernard Llewellyn) *chsd ldrs: drvn 3f out: hung lft and no ex ins fnl f* **8/1**

651- **4** *16* **Red Four**[53] 7636 4-9-4 **62** (p) RichardHughes 4 50
(George Baker) *hld up in rr: hdwy 5f out: drvn over 3f out: sn one pce and no imp on ldng trio: wknd over 1f out* **5/4**[1]

660/ **5** *5* **Hector's House**[11] 4280 8-8-11 **55** MatthewCosham(3) 5 35
(Nikki Evans) *in rr: clsd 7f out: drvn along 5f out: outpcd and no ch w ldrs fnl 3f* **33/1**

00-0 **6** *21* **Studfarmer**[45] 289 4-8-10 **54** LiamJones 3 13
(John Panvert) *trckd ldr: rdn over 4f out: wknd 3f out: t.o* **50/1**

1011 **7** *7* **Newtown Cross (IRE)**[29] 1262 4-8-10 **61** CamHardie(7) 9 13
(Jimmy Fox) *mid-div: rdn 5f out: wknd 4f out: t.o* **6/1**[3]

4m 1.55s (22.65) **Going Correction** +1.025s/f (Soft)
**WFA** 4 from 5yo+ 3lb 7 Ran SP% **112.2**
Speed ratings (Par 101): **84,83,80,72,70 59,56**
CSF £44.08 CT £274.72 TOTE £14.40: £7.90, £1.30; EX 62.20 Trifecta £221.00.
**Owner** B J Llewellyn **Bred** Bumble Bloodstock & Mrs S Nicholls **Trained** Fochriw, Caerphilly
■ Stewards' Enquiry : George Downing seven-day ban: used whip above permitted level (May 16-22)

**FOCUS**
This very modest 2m handicap was run at a steady pace to past halfway. The first two had it to themselves head-to-head all the way up the home straight. The winner is rated to his form from this time last year.

## 1916 32REDPOKER.COM H'CAP (DIV II) 2m 49y
**5:35** (5:36) (Class 6) (0-65,62) 4-Y-O+ **£1,940** (£577; £288; £144) **Stalls** Low

Form RPR

6-35 **1** **Lac Sacre (FR)**[22] 400 5-8-7 **45** (bt) DavidProbert 3 55
(John Flint) *s.i.s: towards rr: hdwy over 6f out: trckd ldrs 4f out: drvn to ld ins fnl f: hld on wl* **5/4**[1]

130/ **2** *1* **Bute Street**[515] 7968 9-9-6 **58** DaneO'Neill 7 67
(Chris Gordon) *led 1f: sn reined bk and hld up: hdwy after 6f: led 5f out: rdn 2f out: hdd over 1f out: kpt on* **8/1**[3]

500- **3** *3/4* **Noor Al Haya (IRE)**[177] 7767 4-8-7 **55** CharlotteJenner(7) 1 63
(Mark Usher) *hld up in last: stdy hdwy 5f out: rdn and briefly outpcd by ldrs 3f out: styd on and ev ch 1f out: no ex fnl 100yds* **8/1**[3]

360- **4** *13* **Zarosa (IRE)**[199] 7280 5-9-3 **60** NoelGarbutt(5) 8 55
(John Berry) *mainly chsd ldr: rdn over 3f out: sn lost 2nd: wknd over 1f out* **5/1**[2]

/00- **5** *35* **Ponte Di Rosa**[169] 6736 6-8-11 **49** SteveDrowne 4 9
(Simon Hodgson) *chsd ldrs: rdn over 4f out: wknd over 3f out: t.o* **33/1**

532- **6** *1/2* **Hendry Trigger**[162] 6457 5-8-12 **55** DanielMuscutt(5) 5 15
(Bernard Llewellyn) *chsd ldrs: pushed along 1/2-way: drvn 5f out: wknd over 3f out: t.o* **10/1**

34-0 **7** *58* **Hypnotism**[8] 1664 4-8-4 **45** (p[1]) LiamJones 2
(Ronald Harris) *t.k.h in rr: drvn along 1/2-way: lost tch 6f out: wl t.o* **14/1**

160/ **8** *30* **Scripturist**[571] 6924 5-9-3 **55** (b) MartinLane 6
(Bernard Llewellyn) *led tl rdn and hdd 5f out: wknd rapidly: wl t.o* **16/1**

54- **9** *39* **Slipper Satin (IRE)**[61] 8366 4-9-2 **62** TobyAtkinson(5) 9
(Noel Quinlan) *chsd ldrs tl rdn and wknd over 6f out: wl t.o fnl 5f* **8/1**[3]

3m 59.31s (20.41) **Going Correction** +1.025s/f (Soft)
**WFA** 4 from 5yo+ 3lb 9 Ran SP% **119.0**
Speed ratings (Par 101): **89,88,88,81,64 63,34,19,**
CSF £12.62 CT £60.89 TOTE £1.90: £1.02, £4.20, £1.30; EX 15.50 Trifecta £92.50.
**Owner** L H & Mrs T Evans **Bred** Mlle Francoise Perree **Trained** Kenfig Hill, Bridgend

**FOCUS**
The pace was slightly more generous in part two of this very modest 2m handicap. There were just four in serious contention once in line for home and three almost upsides inside the final furlong. The winner was thrown in on his jumps form.
T/Plt: £76.30 to a £1 stake. Pool: £69,209.54 - 661.62 winning tickets. T/Qpdt: £10.30 to a £1 stake. Pool: £64,10.26 - 457.62 winning tickets. RL

# 1893 LINGFIELD (L-H)
Friday, May 2

**OFFICIAL GOING: Standard**
Wind: Moderate, half against Weather: Cloudy

## 1917 DOWNLOAD THE 888SPORT.COM MOBILE APP H'CAP 1m 1y(P)
**2:05** (2:05) (Class 6) (0-60,58) 4-Y-O+ **£2,726** (£805; £402) **Stalls** High

Form RPR

0263 **1** **Meddling**[36] 1131 4-9-2 **58** ShelleyBirkett(5) 9 65
(Julia Feilden) *mde all: rdn 2 l clr 2f out: jst hld on* **20/1**

2461 **2** *hd* **Olivers Mount**[23] 1387 4-9-4 **58** OisinMurphy(3) 4 64
(Ed Vaughan) *trckd ldrs: pushed along 3f out: prog and rdn over 1f out: wnt 2nd ins fnl f: clsd on wnr: jst failed* **5/2**[1]

3244 **3** *1/2* **Warbond**[35] 1141 6-9-6 **57** (v) GeorgeBaker 6 62+
(Michael Madgwick) *hld up in last pair: prog into midfield over 2f out but nt on terms w ldrs: r.o fnl f: tk 3rd nr fin and clsd on ldng pair* **7/2**[2]

6-24 **4** *3/4* **Carrera**[87] 467 4-9-4 **55** LiamKeniry 10 58
(Michael Blanshard) *prom: chsd wnr 1/2-way: rdn and no imp over 1f out: lost 2 pls ins fnl f* **8/1**[3]

1212 **5** *1* **Benandonner (USA)**[43] 1036 11-9-7 **58**................................ ShaneKelly 3 59
(Mike Murphy) *dwlt: t.k.h and hld up: prog on outer to chse ldrs over 2f out: nt qckn over 1f out: styd on ins fnl f* **8/1**[3]

0-00 **6** *1 1/4* **Lewamy (IRE)**[42] 1040 4-9-2 **53**................................ HayleyTurner 5 51
(John Best) *prom: chsd ldng pair over 3f out: rdn 2f out: wknd on inner fnl f* **33/1**

564- **7** *1 1/4* **Norwegian Reward (IRE)**[267] 5170 6-8-13 **50**................................ KierenFallon 1 45
(Michael Wigham) *dwlt: t.k.h in last pair: outpcd over 2f out: swtchd rt over 1f out: pushed along and kpt on: nvr involved* **7/2**[2]

5621 **8** *1 1/2* **Indian Violet (IRE)**[23] 1386 8-9-3 **54**................................(p) JimCrowley 7 46
(Zoe Davison) *t.k.h: hld up in rr: struggling over 2f out: no prog after* **10/1**

-050 **9** *1* **Titan Triumph**[27] 1302 10-9-5 **56**................................(t) RobertHavlin 2 45
(Michael Attwater) *mostly in midfield: outpcd and rdn whn bmpd over 2f out: n.d after* **33/1**

6-02 **10** *1 1/4* **Zammy**[23] 1387 5-8-12 **49**................................ FrannyNorton 8 35
(Michael Wigham) *chsd wnr to 1/2-way: sn lost pl: wknd over 2f out* **14/1**

1m 37.43s (-0.77) **Going Correction** -0.025s/f (Stan) **10** Ran SP% **121.6**
Speed ratings (Par 101): **102,101,101,100,99 98,97,95,94,93**
CSF £71.75 CT £233.10 TOTE £25.20: £6.80, £1.10, £1.60; EX 125.50 Trifecta £357.60.
**Owner** Good Company Partnership **Bred** G Strawbridge & London Thoroughbred Services Ltd **Trained** Exning, Suffolk

**FOCUS**
A moderate handicap.

## 1918 EVERGREEN (S) STKS 1m 1y(P)
**2:35** (2:39) (Class 6) 3-Y-O **£2,045** (£603; £302) **Stalls** High

Form RPR

4332 **1** **Clapperboard**[8] 1666 3-8-7 52................................(b) WilliamCarson 5 55
(Paul Fitzsimons) *led 1f: mostly trckd ldr: rdn to ld over 1f out: drvn and styd on wl* **5/1**[3]

0-60 **2** *1 1/4* **Dylan's Centenary**[23] 1389 3-8-12 64................................ FrederikTylicki 2 57
(Rod Millman) *dwlt: sn in midfield: prog 2f out: rdn to chse wnr 1f out: styd on but no imp* **2/1**[1]

3430 **3** *1/2* **Evacusafe Lady**[4] 1794 3-8-4 59................................(t) RyanPowell(3) 9 50
(John Ryan) *trckd ldrs: cl enough whn short of room briefly over 1f out: prog to go 3rd jst ins fnl f: styd on but unable to chal* **5/2**[2]

004- **4** *1 3/4* **Benoordenhout (IRE)**[240] 6095 3-8-12 40................................ JimmyFortune 3 51
(Jonathan Portman) *t.k.h: hld up towards rr: effrt over 2f out: rdn over 1f out: styd on to take 4th ins fnl f: n.d* **33/1**

6204 **5** *1 1/2* **Previous Acclaim (IRE)**[29] 1257 3-8-2 45................................ ShelleyBirkett(5) 7 43
(Julia Feilden) *led after 1f: shkn up and hdd over 1f out: wknd fnl f* **25/1**

0-00 **6** *shd* **Dover The Moon (IRE)**[10] 1632 3-8-5 60................................ GaryMahon(7) 6 48
(Sylvester Kirk) *prom: disp 2nd and rdn 2f out: outpcd over 1f out: fdd* **16/1**

04 **7** *3 1/4* **Nutbush**[9] 1645 3-8-7 0................................ SamHitchcott 1 35
(Mick Channon) *chsd ldrs: rdn 3f out: tried to cl on inner over 1f out: wknd qckly fnl f* **6/1**

**8** *5* **The Pocket Dot** 3-8-0 0................................ DanielCremin(7) 4 24
(Mick Channon) *a in rr: struggling over 3f out: sn bhd* **16/1**

**9** *1 3/4* **Jamie Lee's Girl** 3-8-7 0................................ RenatoSouza 10 20
(David Flood) *dwlt: t.k.h in rr: struggling fr 3f out: sn bhd* **16/1**

0- **10** *3/4* **Zigzag Hill**[184] 7630 3-8-4 0 ow2................................ RyanWhile(5) 8 20
(Bill Turner) *reluctant to enter stalls: dwlt: a in rr: struggling sn after 1/2-way* **66/1**

1m 38.56s (0.36) **Going Correction** -0.025s/f (Stan) **10** Ran SP% **118.8**
Speed ratings (Par 97): **97,95,95,93,92 91,88,83,81,81**
CSF £15.50 TOTE £3.90: £1.30, £1.40, £1.50; EX 19.90 Trifecta £66.50.There was no bid for the winner.
**Owner** Saxon Gate Bloodstock (Helene Moller) **Bred** Theakston Stud **Trained** Upper Lambourn, Berks

**FOCUS**
Nor form to dwell on.

## 1919 4TH BARRY GURR MEMORIAL H'CAP 1m 4f (P)
**3:10** (3:10) (Class 6) (0-65,65) 4-Y-O+ **£2,726** (£805; £402) **Stalls** Low

Form RPR

35-3 **1** **Atalanta Bay (IRE)**[117] 64 4-9-4 **62**................................ ShaneKelly 8 71+
(Marcus Tregoning) *hld up in midfield: rdn over 4f out: prog over 2f out: led over 1f out: styd on wl* **9/2**[2]

1433 **2** *2* **Standing Strong (IRE)**[27] 1302 6-9-4 **62**................................(p) LiamKeniry 2 67
(Zoe Davison) *hld up in rr gng wl: smooth prog over 2f out: brought to chal 1f out: rdn and fnd nil* **4/1**[1]

06-0 **3** *1/2* **Isdaal**[49] 380 7-8-7 **58**................................[1] JordanNason(7) 9 62
(Kevin Morgan) *hld up in rr: rapid prog to trck ldrs 4f out: rdn to ld over 2f out: hdd and one pce over 1f out* **25/1**

/006 **4** *3 1/2* **Swampfire (IRE)**[43] 1027 6-9-6 **64**................................(b) GeorgeBaker 11 62
(Gary Moore) *s.i.s and early reminder: prog to trck ldrs after 4f: rdn over 2f out: nt qckn wl over 1f out: plugged on* **10/1**

6036 **5** *1* **Understory (USA)**[27] 1302 7-9-5 **63**................................ HayleyTurner 1 60
(Tim McCarthy) *led 1f: trckd ldng pair: lost pl fr 3f out: rdn over 1f out: one pce* **7/1**

0020 **6** *nk* **Ice Tres**[30] 1249 5-8-8 **52**................................ PaulHanagan 10 48
(Rod Millman) *t.k.h: trckd ldr after 2f: led after 4f: clr w one rival at 1/2-way: hdd over 2f out: wknd over 1f out* **10/1**

2361 **7** *1 1/2* **Maison Brillet (IRE)**[30] 1232 7-9-3 **61**................................(p) RobertHavlin 6 55
(Clive Drew) *hld up in last: nvr on terms: rdn and plugged on fr over 1f out* **6/1**

56-4 **8** *3 1/2* **Freddy Q (IRE)**[29] 1262 5-9-4 **65**................................ OisinMurphy(3) 4 53
(Roger Teal) *led after 1f tl after 4f out: pressed ldr after and clr of rest 1/2-way: drvn 3f out: wknd 2f out* **5/1**[3]

**9** *10* **Chaparella (IRE)**[183] 4-9-2 **60**................................ FrannyNorton 7 32
(Mark Johnston) *rdn to hold midfield pl after 4f: wknd 4f out: sn bhd* **14/1**

430 **10** *1/2* **Candesta (USA)**[33] 1197 4-9-2 **65**................................ ShelleyBirkett(5) 5 37
(Julia Feilden) *a in rr: shoved along by 1/2-way: bhd fnl 3f* **12/1**

2m 31.08s (-1.92) **Going Correction** -0.025s/f (Stan) **10** Ran SP% **118.0**
Speed ratings (Par 101): **105,103,103,101,100 100,99,96,90,89**
CSF £23.20 CT £408.54 TOTE £4.60: £1.80, £1.70, £7.60; EX 16.00 Trifecta £507.30.
**Owner** Miss S Sharp **Bred** Manister House Stud **Trained** Whitsbury, Hants

**FOCUS**
An ordinary handicap.

## 1920 £88 IN FREE BETS AT 888SPORT.COM MAIDEN FILLIES' STKS 7f 1y(P)
**3:45** (3:48) (Class 5) 3-Y-O+ **£2,726** (£805; £402) **Stalls** Low

Form RPR

6 **1** **Etaab (USA)**[15] 1534 3-8-10 0................................ PaulHanagan 7 77+
(William Haggas) *mde virtually all: shkn up and asserted over 1f out: readily* **8/15**[1]

0 **2** *2 1/4* **Dorraar (IRE)**[15] 1534 3-8-10 0................................ JackMitchell 1 71
(Roger Varian) *dwlt: t.k.h and sn cl up: prog on inner over 2f out: chsd wnr jst over 1f out: styd on but no imp* **25/1**

**3** *nk* **Bragging (USA)** 3-8-10 0................................ JamesDoyle 3 70+
(Sir Michael Stoute) *wl in tch: pushed along over 2f out: prog over 1f out: wnt 3rd ins fnl f: styd on* **7/1**[3]

0- **4** *1 1/2* **Swiss Kiss**[329] 3057 3-8-10 0................................[1] WilliamBuick 5 66+
(John Gosden) *t.k.h: hld up: stl in last trio 2f out: rn green but styd on fnl f to take 4th nr fin* **6/1**[2]

50- **5** *nk* **Aristocratic Duty**[147] 8176 3-8-6 0 ow1................................ JoshBaudains(5) 10 66
(Sylvester Kirk) *t.k.h: pressed wnr after 1f to jst over 1f out: fdd* **50/1**

**6** *hd* **Sejel (IRE)** 3-8-10 0................................ RobertHavlin 13 66+
(John Gosden) *slowly away: hld up in last pair: prog on inner over 1f out: short of room briefly: pushed along and kpt on* **20/1**

**7** *1* **High Drama (IRE)** 3-8-10 0................................ LiamKeniry 9 62
(Andrew Balding) *dwlt: sn wl in tch: pushed along and steadily fdd fr over 1f out* **25/1**

**8** *1/2* **Triple Star** 3-8-10 0................................ JimCrowley 12 60+
(Hughie Morrison) *hld up in rr: sme prog and reminder over 1f out: no hdwy fnl f: nt disgracd* **20/1**

000- **9** *1 3/4* **Ellingham (IRE)**[267] 5199 3-8-10 0................................ AdamBeschizza 14 56?
(Christine Dunnett) *chsd wnr 1f: prom tl wknd 2f out* **100/1**

**10** *1/2* **Calamity Jane** 3-8-3 0................................ PatrickO'Donnell(7) 11 54
(Ralph Beckett) *hld up in last pair: nvr on terms* **25/1**

**11** *1 1/2* **Lizalia (FR)**[167] 3-8-5 62................................ PhilipPrince(5) 8 50
(Jo Hughes) *nvr beyond midfield: pushed along by 1/2-way: wknd 2f out* **66/1**

1m 25.35s (0.55) **Going Correction** -0.025s/f (Stan)
**WFA** 3 from 4yo 12lb **11** Ran SP% **117.5**
Speed ratings (Par 100): **95,92,92,90,90 89,88,88,86,85 83**
CSF £23.48 TOTE £1.40: £1.02, £5.70, £1.90; EX 18.30 Trifecta £121.00.
**Owner** Hamdan Al Maktoum **Bred** Shadwell Farm LLC **Trained** Newmarket, Suffolk

**FOCUS**
They bet 20-1 bar three in this fillies' maiden, but it was an interesting contest and a few of those in behind caught the eye.

## 1921 "BET AND WATCH" AT 888SPORT.COM H'CAP 6f 1y(P)
**4:15** (4:16) (Class 5) (0-75,75) 4-Y-O+ **£3,234** (£962; £481; £240) **Stalls** Low

Form RPR

4231 **1** **Desert Strike**[6] 1739 8-9-7 **75**................................(p) HayleyTurner 1 83
(Conor Dore) *mde all: shkn up wl over 1f out: drvn and kpt on wl fnl f* **4/1**[1]

2106 **2** *1* **Seek The Fair Land**[4] 1796 8-9-6 **74**................................(b) WilliamCarson 2 79
(Lee Carter) *cl up: chsd wnr 2f out: nt qckn over 1f out: styd on but a hld fnl f* **9/2**[2]

1131 **3** *hd* **Spellmaker**[51] 925 5-9-0 **73**................................ EoinWalsh(5) 5 77
(Tony Newcombe) *trckd ldrs: nt clr run briefly wl over 1f out: prog to dispute 2nd fnl f: kpt on but a hld* **4/1**[1]

1040 **4** *3/4* **Temple Road (IRE)**[8] 1678 6-9-6 **74**................................(p) RichardKingscote 8 76
(Milton Bradley) *stdd s: hld up in last pair: stl there 2f out: prog and n.m.r briefly over 1f out: disp 2nd fnl f: rdn and nt qckn* **12/1**

322 **5** *1 1/4* **Alnoomaas (IRE)**[23] 1388 5-9-0 **68**................................ JimmyFortune 6 66
(Luke Dace) *t.k.h: prom: nt qckn 2f out and lost pl: one pce fnl f* **5/1**[3]

2-50 **6** *nk* **Diamondhead (IRE)**[20] 1447 5-9-1 **72**................................ OisinMurphy(3) 4 69
(Ed de Giles) *sn drvn in last pair: nvr a factor but styd on fnl f* **5/1**[3]

5061 **7** *2 1/2* **Only Ten Per Cent (IRE)**[37] 1115 6-9-7 **75**................................(v) FrederikTylicki 3 64
(J R Jenkins) *awkward s: t.k.h and hld up: effrt on inner over 1f out: wknd fnl f* **12/1**

/0-4 **8** *3 1/4* **Pira Palace (IRE)**[29] 1266 4-9-4 **72**................................ JamesDoyle 7 50
(Jim Boyle) *chsd wnr to 2f out: wknd jst over 1f out* **33/1**

0-03 **9** *2 1/2* **Langley Vale**[35] 1144 5-9-6 **74**................................ SebSanders 9 44
(Roger Teal) *racd wd: in tch: rdn and wknd over 1f out* **6/1**

1m 10.94s (-0.96) **Going Correction** -0.025s/f (Stan) **9** Ran SP% **124.1**
Speed ratings (Par 103): **105,103,103,102,100 100,97,92,89**
CSF £24.04 CT £80.38 TOTE £5.90: £1.80, £1.40, £1.50; EX 34.80 Trifecta £130.30.
**Owner** Andrew Page **Bred** Mrs Mary Rowlands **Trained** Hubbert's Bridge, Lincs
■ Stewards' Enquiry : William Carson three-day ban: careless riding (May 16,18,19)
Hayley Turner two-day ban: careless riding (May 16,18)

**FOCUS**
A modest sprint handicap.

## 1922 "CASH IN EARLY" AT 888SPORT.COM H'CAP 5f 6y(P)
**4:45** (4:46) (Class 4) (0-85,83) 4-Y-O+ **£5,207** (£1,549; £774; £387) **Stalls** High

Form RPR

-015 **1** **Sandfrankskipsgo**[69] 719 5-9-5 **81**................................ GeorgeBaker 6 89
(Peter Crate) *chsd ldr: 2 l down 2f out: rdn to chal fnl f: kpt on to ld last strides* **8/1**

40-0 **2** *hd* **Royal Acquisition**[21] 1431 4-8-10 **72**................................[1] JimCrowley 2 79
(Robert Cowell) *fast away: led: 2 l clr 2f out: edgd rt u.p 1f out: kpt on but hdd last strides* **20/1**

204- **3** *nk* **Port Alfred**[206] 7112 4-9-6 **82**................................ WilliamBuick 4 88
(Charlie Appleby) *sn chsd ldng pair: rdn 2f out: clsd u.p fnl f: nvr quite got there* **5/4**[1]

0100 **4** *3 1/2* **Profile Star (IRE)**[3] 1843 5-8-12 **77**................................ OisinMurphy(3) 9 70
(Ann Stokell) *racd on outer: chsd ldrs: nt qckn 2f out: no imp fr over 1f out* **20/1**

211- **5** *shd* **Green Monkey**[255] 5620 4-9-0 **76**................................ ShaneKelly 8 69+
(James Fanshawe) *restless stalls: hld up in last pair: rdn and no prog 2f out: wl hld after* **7/2**[3]

-311 **6** *13* **Gregori (IRE)**[29] 1261 4-9-7 **83**................................(tp) JimmyFortune 5 29+
(Brian Meehan) *dwlt: hld up in last pair: trying to make prog whn impeded on inner wl over 1f out: allowed to coast home after* **5/2**[2]

58.31s (-0.49) **Going Correction** -0.025s/f (Stan) **6** Ran SP% **115.9**
Speed ratings (Par 105): **102,101,101,95,95 74**
CSF £129.20 CT £328.49 TOTE £11.30: £9.90, £9.00; EX 94.50 Trifecta £321.20.
**Owner** Peter Crate **Bred** Peter Crate **Trained** Newdigate, Surrey

**FOCUS**
A fair sprint handicap and they went quick.

## 1923 SHOVELSTRODE RACING STABLES H'CAP — 1m 2f (P)
5:20 (5:20) (Class 6) (0-60,59) 4-Y-0+ £2,726 (£805; £402) Stalls Low

Form RPR
2132 1 **Tijuca (IRE)**23 1385 5-9-6 58 FrederikTylicki 2 68+
(Ed de Giles) *hld up in 5th: quick move on inner to ld 1f out: shkn up and sn clr* 3/1[2]
3002 2 2½ **Daniel Thomas (IRE)**4 1819 12-8-9 50 (tp) OisinMurphy(3) 8 55
(Ann Stokell) *s.i.s and rousted to get gng: in tch: rdn 2f out: hung rt to nr side rail but styd on fnl f to take 2nd nr fin* 5/1[3]
432- 3 1 **Giantstepsahead (IRE)**237 6216 5-9-7 59 JackMitchell 4 62
(Denis Quinn) *t.k.h: prom: pressed ldr 3f out: upsides as wnr wnt by 1f out: outpcd and lost 2nd nr fin* 5/1[3]
00-0 4 1½ **Red Willow**112 116 8-8-8 46 ow1 (p) SamHitchcott 7 46
(John E Long) *led to 6f out: cl up: nt qckn 2f out: one pce after* 33/1
5050 5 nse **Copperwood**27 1302 9-9-5 57 (v) AmirQuinn 6 57
(Lee Carter) *t.k.h: trckd ldng trio: rdn and nt qckn wl over 1f out: one pce after* 8/1
00-1 6 2 **Overrider**49 964 4-9-5 57 (t) RenatoSouza 3 53
(Alastair Lidderdale) *tk fierce hold: pressed ldr: led 6f out: hdd & wknd 1f out* 10/1
400/ 7 12 **Teutonic Knight (IRE)**822 366 7-8-5 48 EoinWalsh(5) 9 21
(Tony Newcombe) *dwlt: hld up in last pair: detached bef 1/2-way and nt gng wl: wl bhd fnl 3f* 25/1
00/0 P **The Cash Generator (IRE)**44 1017 6-9-6 58 GeorgeBaker 5
(Ralph J Smith) *stdd s: t.k.h: hld up in last pair: lost action and p.u 1/2-way* 9/4[1]

2m 6.59s (-0.01) **Going Correction** -0.025s/f (Stan) 8 Ran SP% 116.1
Speed ratings (Par 101): **99,97,96,95,94 93,83,**
CSF £18.79 CT £72.42 TOTE £3.10: £1.10, £3.10, £1.90; EX 15.10 Trifecta £44.50.
**Owner** E B De Giles **Bred** M Kennelly **Trained** Ledbury, H'fords

**FOCUS**
A muddling race and pretty weak form.
T/Jkpt: Not won. T/Plt: £95.90 to a £1 stake. Pool: £81,178.22 - 617.72 winning tickets. T/Qpdt: £49.60 to a £1 stake. Pool: £5,242.84 - 78.10 winning tickets. JN

# 1596 MUSSELBURGH (R-H)
Friday, May 2

**OFFICIAL GOING: Good to soft (7.0)**
Wind: Breezy, half behind Weather: Cloudy, bright

## 1924 BRITISH STALLION STUDS EBF MAIDEN STKS (BOBIS RACE) — 5f
1:55 (1:55) (Class 4) 2-Y-0 £4,204 (£1,251; £625; £312) Stalls High

Form RPR
1 **Mambo Paradise** 2-9-0 0 JoeFanning 5 75+
(Mark Johnston) *dwlt: t.k.h and sn trcking ldrs: shkn up to ld 1f out: pushed clr: readily* 16/1
2 2 3 **Al Ghuwariyah (IRE)**15 1528 2-9-0 0 JamieSpencer 4 64
(Kevin Ryan) *led: rdn: edgd rt and hdd 1f out: kpt on same pce ins fnl f* 8/15[1]
3 hd **Winstanley (IRE)** 2-9-5 0 TonyHamilton 1 68
(Richard Fahey) *trckd ldr: rdn 2f out: kpt on same pce fnl f* 11/2[3]
4 2 **Secret Friend (IRE)** 2-9-0 0 DuranFentiman 2 56
(Tim Easterby) *chsd ldrs: effrt and rdn over 1f out: edgd rt and wknd ins fnl f* 4/1[2]

1m 1.4s (1.00) **Going Correction** +0.075s/f (Good) 4 Ran SP% 106.5
Speed ratings (Par 95): **95,90,89,86**
CSF £25.70 TOTE £9.50; EX 18.50 Trifecta £22.60.
**Owner** Around The World Partnership **Bred** Highclere Stud & Mr & Mrs G Middlebrook **Trained** Middleham Moor, N Yorks

**FOCUS**
The time for this maiden suggested the ground was as described, on the slow side of good. Quite a hot little race, with a likeable effort from the winner.

## 1925 RACING UK ANYWHERE AVAILABLE NOW H'CAP — 5f
2:25 (2:25) (Class 6) (0-65,62) 3-Y-0 £2,587 (£770; £384; £192) Stalls High

Form RPR
6-12 1 **Orient Class**8 1676 3-9-7 62 (v) GrahamLee 4 70+
(Paul Midgley) *trckd ldr: shkn up to ld over 1f out: qcknd clr ins fnl f: readily* 2/5[1]
0-60 2 2¾ **Dream Sika (IRE)**9 1642 3-8-10 51 JamesSullivan 2 48
(Ruth Carr) *led and sn crossed to stands' rail: rdn and hdd over 1f out: kpt on fnl f: no ch w wnr* 10/1[3]
0-20 3 ¾ **Roomie**20 1441 3-8-13 54 (b[1]) DuranFentiman 6 48
(Tim Easterby) *prom: sn pushed along: effrt and edgd rt over 1f out: kpt on same pce ins fnl f* 16/1
03-6 4 2½ **Sleeper Class**27 1304 3-9-5 60 GaryBartley 3 45
(Jim Goldie) *bhd and sn outpcd: rdn and hdwy over 1f out: no imp fnl f* 20/1
60-2 5 2½ **Straight Gin**23 1373 3-8-6 47 (tp) BarryMcHugh 1 23
(Alan Berry) *cl up on outside: rdn along 1/2-way: wknd over 1f out* 9/2[2]

1m 1.01s (0.61) **Going Correction** +0.075s/f (Good) 5 Ran SP% 109.3
Speed ratings (Par 97): **98,93,92,88,84**
CSF £5.22 TOTE £1.30: £1.10, £4.00; EX 5.90 Trifecta £27.90.
**Owner** Frank & Annette Brady **Bred** Frank Brady **Trained** Westow, N Yorks
■ Stewards' Enquiry : James Sullivan one-day ban: failed to ride to draw (May 16)

**FOCUS**
Not much of a race but the winner took another step forward.

## 1926 CORE OIL AND GAS H'CAP — 1m 1f
3:00 (3:00) (Class 4) (0-85,83) 4-Y-0+ £6,469 (£1,925; £962; £481) Stalls Low

Form RPR
35-1 1 **Hit The Jackpot (IRE)**8 1660 5-9-4 80 6ex DanielTudhope 3 92
(David O'Meara) *t.k.h: cl up: led over 2f out: rdn and edgd rt over 1f out: pushed out fnl f* 5/6[1]
-040 2 1¾ **San Cassiano (IRE)**6 1724 7-9-0 76 JamesSullivan 4 84
(Ruth Carr) *led to over 2f out: sn drvn along: rallied over 1f out: kpt on ins fnl f: nt rch wnr* 8/1[3]
-142 3 3 **Tenor (IRE)**8 1682 4-9-0 76 (t) JamieSpencer 6 77
(John Ryan) *prom: drvn along over 3f out: rallied and edgd rt over 1f out: one pce fnl f* 3/1[2]
20-0 4 2¾ **No Poppy (IRE)**25 1345 6-9-2 83 AdamCarter(5) 2 78
(Tim Easterby) *prom: effrt and rdn over 2f out: outpcd appr fnl f* 9/1
5130 5 37 **Thatchmaster (USA)**18 1483 4-8-12 74 JoeFanning 1
(Mark Johnston) *dwlt: bhd: struggling over 3f out: btn and eased fnl 2f* 11/1

1m 55.05s (1.15) **Going Correction** +0.30s/f (Good) 5 Ran SP% 109.0
Speed ratings (Par 105): **106,104,101,99,66**
CSF £7.95 TOTE £1.70: £1.02, £4.50; EX 8.70 Trifecta £23.30.
**Owner** Hambleton Racing Ltd XXX **Bred** Moyglare Stud Farm Ltd **Trained** Nawton, N Yorks

**FOCUS**
The form is rated around the runner-up, with the winner not far off last week's mark.

## 1927 WEATHERBYS PRIVATE BANKING H'CAP (BOBIS RACE) — 1m 1f
3:35 (3:35) (Class 3) (0-90,85) 3-Y-0 £7,762 (£2,310; £1,154) Stalls Low

Form RPR
142- 1 **Master Of Finance (IRE)**171 7846 3-9-1 79 JoeFanning 1 85
(Mark Johnston) *mde all: pushed along over 2f out: styd on strly fnl f* 7/4[2]
01-6 2 1¾ **Ventura Quest (USA)**14 1563 3-9-7 85 TonyHamilton 4 87
(Richard Fahey) *chsd ldr: effrt and ev ch over 2f out: rdn and edgd rt over 1f out: kpt on same pce ins fnl f* 4/5[1]
1420 3 3 **Frankthetank (IRE)**6 1723 3-8-9 73 TomEaves 2 69
(Keith Dalgleish) *stdd bhd ldrs: effrt and rdn over 2f out: no ex over 1f out* 6/1[3]

1m 58.05s (4.15) **Going Correction** +0.30s/f (Good) 3 Ran SP% 106.2
Speed ratings (Par 103): **93,91,88**
CSF £3.53 TOTE £3.20; EX 3.00 Trifecta £2.90.
**Owner** J David Abell & Markus Graff **Bred** Maddenstown Equine Enterprise Ltd **Trained** Middleham Moor, N Yorks

**FOCUS**
A disappointing turnout for this 0-90 handicap. All three of these had made all to win in the past, but a disputed lead in a three-runner race was always unlikely, and in the event Joe Fanning was given a free hand in front. The winner is rated in line with his 2yo form, but there are doubts.

## 1928 WEATHERBYS BANK H'CAP — 7f 30y
4:05 (4:08) (Class 3) (0-90,89) 4-Y-0+ £7,762 (£2,310; £1,154; £577) Stalls Low

Form RPR
0-03 1 **Just Paul (IRE)**11 1607 4-8-8 76 PJMcDonald 7 86+
(Philip Kirby) *hld up towards rr: effrt and hdwy whn nt clr run and swtchd rt over 1f out: swtchd lft and led ins fnl f: pushed out* 5/2[1]
40-0 2 1¾ **Majestic Moon (IRE)**14 1564 4-9-7 89 (b) DavidNolan 6 94
(Richard Fahey) *t.k.h: led and 3 l clr: rdn and hdd over 1f out: rallied to chse wnr ins fnl f: kpt on: no imp* 4/1[2]
4160 3 2¾ **Stonefield Flyer**14 1564 5-9-5 87 TomEaves 2 85
(Keith Dalgleish) *cl up: hdwy to ld over 1f out: rdn and hdd ins fnl f: sn no ex* 10/1
/0-4 4 1 **Grissom (IRE)**20 1442 8-9-3 85 DuranFentiman 1 80
(Tim Easterby) *trckd ldrs: effrt and rdn 2f out: kpt on same pce fnl f* 7/1
00-3 5 2 **Powerful Presence (IRE)**15 1537 8-9-0 82 DanielTudhope 5 72
(David O'Meara) *prom: effrt and drvn over 2f out: btn fnl f* 9/2[3]
02-0 6 4½ **Silver Rime (FR)**14 1564 9-9-5 87 PhillipMakin 4 66
(Linda Perratt) *hld up: rdn and outpcd over 2f out: n.d after* 25/1

1m 30.53s (1.53) **Going Correction** +0.30s/f (Good) 6 Ran SP% 92.2
Speed ratings (Par 107): **103,101,97,96,94 89**
CSF £8.20 TOTE £3.00: £1.30, £1.40; EX 8.70 Trifecta £48.00.
**Owner** Mr and Mrs Paul Chapman **Bred** Oghill House Stud **Trained** Middleham, N Yorks
■ Flexible Flyer (100-30) was withdrawn. Rule 4 applies to all bets. Deduction - 20p in the pound.

**FOCUS**
On paper there was a lot of pace in this race, and there was indeed a battle for the early lead, won by Majestic Moon. The winner continues to progress.

## 1929 THOMSONGRAY H'CAP — 1m 6f
4:40 (4:40) (Class 5) (0-70,73) 4-Y-0+ £3,234 (£962; £481; £240) Stalls Low

Form RPR
42-4 1 **Choisan (IRE)**33 1197 5-9-10 70 (tp) DuranFentiman 3 77
(Tim Easterby) *pressed ldr: drvn to ld over 1f out: edgd rt ins fnl f: r.o wl* 7/1
10-0 2 ¾ **Medieval Bishop (IRE)**27 1307 5-9-1 64 (p) JasonHart(3) 5 70
(Mark Walford) *trckd ldrs: effrt and edgd rt over 2f out: chsd wnr ins fnl f: r.o* 4/1[2]
360- 3 ½ **Mason Hindmarsh**254 5640 7-9-5 65 BarryMcHugh 2 70
(Karen McLintock) *led at stdy pce: qcknd over 2f out: hdd over 1f out: rallied: kpt on same pce ins fnl f* 10/1
000- 4 ½ **Aleksandar**202 7210 5-9-5 65 GrahamLee 8 70
(Jim Goldie) *in tch: rdn and outpcd over 3f out: rallied and swtchd rt over 1f out: styd on ins fnl f* 11/2[3]
335- 5 6 **La Bacouetteuse (FR)**202 6086 9-9-7 67 (b) JoeFanning 1 63
(Iain Jardine) *rrd and lost many l s: bhd: stdy hdwy on outside over 5f out: drvn and edgd rt over 2f out: no imp over 1f out* 11/1
4-01 6 ½ **Cavalieri (IRE)**9 1644 4-9-5 73 6ex EvaMoscrop(7) 7 69
(Philip Kirby) *t.k.h: hld up in midfield: pushed along and shortlived effrt over 2f out: btn over 1f out* 13/8[1]
021/ 7 1¾ **Cool Baranca (GER)**9 7102 8-8-3 54 ow3 EmmaSayer(5) 10 47
(Dianne Sayer) *bhd: outpcd over 5f out: rallied 2f out: kpt on: nvr able to chal* 20/1
426- 8 4½ **Schmooze (IRE)**277 4822 5-9-6 66 PJMcDonald 6 53
(Linda Perratt) *hld up: rdn and outpcd over 3f out: btn fnl 2f* 16/1
6-30 9 nk **Primary Route (IRE)**71 671 4-8-4 54 NeilFarley(3) 9 40
(Ian Semple) *prom: drvn over 3f out: wknd fr 2f out* 33/1

3m 12.39s (7.09) **Going Correction** +0.30s/f (Good)
**WFA** 4 from 5yo+ 1lb 9 Ran SP% 117.0
Speed ratings (Par 103): **91,90,90,90,86 86,85,82,82**
CSF £35.63 CT £283.51 TOTE £7.30: £2.50, £1.30, £4.60; EX 50.80 Trifecta £526.80.
**Owner** Taylor, Hebdon & Habton **Bred** David A Cahill **Trained** Great Habton, N Yorks

**FOCUS**
Very few got into this, as Mason Hindmarsh was allowed to dictate a steady pace out in front. The winner was entitled to win this on last year's best.

## 1930 BAILLIE GIFFORD H'CAP — 7f 30y
5:10 (5:10) (Class 6) (0-65,65) 4-Y-0+ £2,587 (£770; £384; £192) Stalls Low

Form RPR
5-61 1 **Alluring Star**9 1649 6-8-13 57 GrahamGibbons 4 68
(Michael Easterby) *pressed ldr: ev ch and rdn over 1f out: led wl ins fnl f: kpt on* 9/2[3]
25-3 2 hd **Clumber Place**27 1310 8-8-8 55 JasonHart(3) 9 65
(Shaun Harris) *led at ordinary gallop: rdn and hrd pressed over 1f out: hdd wl ins fnl f: kpt on* 20/1

-611 **3** 2 1/2 **Global Leader (IRE)**[4] 1813 4-9-3 61 12ex................ PatrickDonaghy 2 65
(Paul D'Arcy) *hld up in tchf: effrt and swtchd rt over 2f out: drifted rt over 1f out: kpt on ins fnl f: nt rch first two* **15/8**[1]

0-21 **4** 2 **Echo Of Lightning**[12] 1596 4-9-2 60 6ex........................... PaulPickard 3 58
(Brian Ellison) *hld up: rdn and effrt on outside over 2f out: kpt on fnl f: nvr able to chal* **2/1**[2]

6-04 **5** 3/4 **Funding Deficit (IRE)**[5] 1758 4-9-1 62......................... IanBrennan(3) 5 58
(Jim Goldie) *t.k.h: prom: effrt over 2f out: n.m.r briefly and hung rt over 1f out: sn btn* **20/1**

560- **6** 7 **Jebel Tara**[147] 8187 9-9-2 65.................................(bt) JacobButterfield(5) 1 43
(Alan Brown) *prom: drvn along and swtchd rt wl over 1f out: sn btn* **12/1**

0-02 **7** nk **Mowhoob**[12] 1596 4-8-13 57........................................... GrahamLee 8 34
(Jim Goldie) *hld up: rdn and outpcd over 2f out: hung rt and sn wknd* **12/1**

0/0- **8** 16 **Ebony Clarets**[182] 7669 5-8-13 57.........................................[1] PhillipMakin 6
(Linda Perratt) *s.i.s: bhd: struggling over 2f out: sn btn: t.o* **50/1**

1m 31.14s (2.14) **Going Correction** +0.30s/f (Good) **8** Ran SP% **113.2**
Speed ratings (Par 101): **99,98,95,93,92 84,84,66**
CSF £84.68 CT £224.25 TOTE £7.30: £3.10, £4.70, £1.10; EX 23.00 Trifecta £133.90.
**Owner** Jeff Hamer & Bernard Bargh **Bred** B Bargh **Trained** Sheriff Hutton, N Yorks

**FOCUS**
Just a modest handicap but there were a few in-form horses in the line-up. The time was relatively good with the winner rated similar to Catterick latest.
T/Plt: £308.00 to a £1 stake. Pool: £42,008.81 - 99.55 winning tickets. T/Qpdt: £18.90 to a £1 stake. Pool: £4,321.49 - 168.55 winning tickets. RY

1931 - 1933a (Foreign Racing) - See Raceform Interactive

## 1710 DONCASTER (L-H)

Saturday, May 3

**OFFICIAL GOING: Good to soft (soft in places; 7.6)**
Course railed out from 10f start to where Round joins straight, increasing distances on Round course by about 18yds.
Wind: Virtually nil Weather: Fine and dry

### 1934 POLONUS APPRENTICE H'CAP — 1m 4f
**5:15** (5:15) (Class 4) (0-85,85) 4-Y-0+ **£5,175** (£1,540; £769; £384) **Stalls** Low

Form RPR

143- **1** **Silk Sari**[183] 7659 4-9-0 85.................................. GianlucaSanna(7) 8 98
(Luca Cumani) *trckd ldrs: smooth hdwy 3f out: rdn to ld over 1f out: styd on* **15/8**[1]

220- **2** 2 3/4 **Astra Hall**[175] 7822 5-8-11 82.......................... PatrickO'Donnell(7) 7 90
(Ralph Beckett) *hld up towards rr: stdy hdwy on outer 3f out: rdn wl over 1f out: chsd wnr ins fnl f: no imp* **9/2**[2]

01- **3** 4 **Phosphorescence (IRE)**[142] 8260 4-9-0 81............ LouisSteward(3) 9 83
(Lady Cecil) *slt ld: pushed along over 3f out: rdn over 2f out: drvn and hdd over 1f out: grad wknd* **9/1**

130- **4** shd **Pernica**[252] 5743 4-8-9 73.................................................. RobertTart 6 74
(Lucy Wadham) *cl up: effrt 3f out: sn rdn along: drvn wl over 1f out: grad wknd* **12/1**

135- **5** 2 1/2 **Beat The Tide**[214] 6917 4-8-5 72.............................. ConnorBeasley(3) 10 69
(Michael Dods) *trckd ldrs: effrt over 3f out: rdn along wl over 2f out: drvn 2f out and sn wknd* **11/2**

000- **6** 2 1/4 **Warlu Way**[189] 7526 7-9-0 85....................................(t) DanielleMooney(7) 5 79
(Michael Easterby) *hld up in rr: hdwy over 2f out: sn rdn and n.d* **28/1**

115- **7** 1 1/4 **Dolphin Village (IRE)**[212] 6976 4-8-11 80............... SammyJoBell(5) 1 72
(Richard Fahey) *in tch: effrt on inner over 3f out: rdn along and nt much room over 2f out* **5/1**[3]

13-5 **8** 13 **Omnipresent**[9] 1659 4-9-1 79...................................... SamJames 3 50
(David O'Meara) *trckd ldrs on inner: pushed along over 3f out: rdn and edgd lft wl over 2f out: sn wknd* **11/1**

2m 34.49s (-0.41) **Going Correction** +0.125s/f (Good) **8** Ran SP% **114.5**
Speed ratings (Par 105): **106,104,101,101,99 98,97,88**
CSF £10.34 CT £59.15 TOTE £3.30: £2.30, £2.90, £2.50; EX 13.30 Trifecta £70.60.
**Owner** Fittocks Stud & Andrew Bengough **Bred** Fittocks Stud Ltd & Arrow Farm Stud **Trained** Newmarket, Suffolk
■ Stewards' Enquiry : Sam James nine-day ban: intentionally caused interference (May 17-24,26)

**FOCUS**
Course railed out from 1m2f start to where Round joins straight, increasing distances on Round course by about 18yds. After riding in the second race on the card, Seb Sanders disagreed with the official going, saying "It's good ground" and Graham Gibbons said "It's just on the easy side of good." A decent race for apprentices. The early pace was fairly sedate, but things picked up in the straight. The first three were unexposed/progressive.

### 1935 BARDI H'CAP — 1m 6f 132y
**5:45** (5:45) (Class 4) (0-85,84) 4-Y-0+ **£5,175** (£1,540; £769; £384) **Stalls** Low

Form RPR

00-6 **1** **Itlaaq**[15] 1562 8-9-7 81...................................(t) GrahamGibbons 4 90+
(Michael Easterby) *in tch: hdwy to trck ldrs over 3f out: swtchd rt and effrt over 2f out: rdn to chal and edgd lft wl over 1f out: sn led: clr ins fnl f* **6/1**[3]

234- **2** 3/4 **Lion Beacon**[212] 6978 4-9-7 83.......................................... SebSanders 6 89
(Amanda Perrett) *led: pushed along and jnd over 3f out: rdn along over 2f out: drvn and hdd over 1f out: kpt on u.p fnl f* **7/2**[1]

200- **3** 2 **Man Of Plenty**[183] 7660 5-9-10 84..............................(p) PaulMulrennan 8 87
(Ed Dunlop) *trckd ldr: cl up over 4f out: chal 3f out: rdn over 2f out: drvn whn n.m.r wl over 1f out: kpt on same pce* **9/1**

1333 **4** 3/4 **Bute Hall**[21] 1444 5-9-10 84............................................ JimmyQuinn 7 86
(David Thompson) *trckd ldrs: hdwy over 4f out: cl up wl over 2f out: rdn along whn n.m.r wl over 1f out: kpt on same pce* **7/1**

10-0 **5** 1/2 **Twelve Strings (IRE)**[13] 1599 5-9-5 82........................ RobertTart(3) 2 84
(Brian Ellison) *s.i.s and bhd: hdwy on outer wl over 2f out: sn rdn and styd on fnl f: nrst fin* **8/1**

213- **6** 2 1/2 **Perennial**[164] 7975 5-9-9 83........................................ DanielTudhope 1 82
(Philip Kirby) *trckd ldng pair on inner: effrt over 3f out: cl up and pushed along 2f out: rdn and n.m.r and squeezed out wl over 1f out: one pce after* **9/2**[2]

102- **7** shd **Snowy Dawn**[212] 6978 4-8-13 80................................. JackDuern(5) 9 78
(Andrew Hollinshead) *hld up towards rr: effrt and sme hdwy on outer over 3f out: rdn along wl over 2f out: no imp* **13/2**

120- **8** 3 **Duke Of Yorkshire**[203] 7210 4-8-9 71.......................... DuranFentiman 5 65
(Tim Easterby) *in tch: hdwy to trck ldrs over 4f out: pushed along 3f out: sn rdn and wknd 2f out* **14/1**

4/0- **9** 1/2 **Scots Gaelic (IRE)**[28] 7210 7-9-7 84.............................. IanBrennan(3) 3 78
(John Quinn) *in rr: reminders after 2f: rdn along 5f out: nvr a factor* **16/1**

3m 10.56s (3.16) **Going Correction** +0.125s/f (Good)
**WFA** 4 from 5yo+ 2lb **9** Ran SP% **114.2**
Speed ratings (Par 105): **96,95,94,94,93 92,92,90,90**
CSF £26.97 CT £187.36 TOTE £5.30: £2.30, £2.00, £2.50; EX 29.30 Trifecta £422.70.
**Owner** Mrs Jean Turpin **Bred** Shadwell Estate Company Limited **Trained** Sheriff Hutton, N Yorks

**FOCUS**
The pace generally held up here. The winner is rated in line with his latter 2013 form.

### 1936 ICE FRESH SEAFOOD MAIDEN STKS — 5f
**6:15** (6:16) (Class 5) 2-Y-O **£2,911** (£866; £432; £216) **Stalls** High

Form RPR

**1** **Natural Order (USA)** 2-9-5 0.................................... DanielTudhope 1 77+
(K R Burke) *dwlt: sn trcking ldrs on outer: hdwy 2f out: sn cl up: rdn to chal ent fnl f: led last 110yds: kpt on* **5/2**[1]

**2** hd **Flying Machine (IRE)** 2-9-5 0.................................... TonyHamilton 4 76+
(Richard Fahey) *led 1 1/2f: prom: rdn over 1f out: ev ch ins fnl tl no extyra towards fin* **4/1**[2]

0 **3** 1/2 **Union Rose**[14] 1571 2-9-5 0............................................ LiamJones 2 74
(Ronald Harris) *prom: led after 1 1/2f: rdn over 1f out: drvn ins fnl f: hdd and no ex last 100yds* **12/1**

**4** shd **Latch Onto Blue** 2-9-5 0.......................................... RobertWinston 8 74+
(Charles Hills) *trckd ldrs: hdwy over 2f out: effrt wl over 1f out: sn rdn and ev ch tl no ex wl ins fnl f* **7/1**[3]

**5** 1 **Power Play (IRE)** 2-9-5 0.............................................. SeanLevey 5 71+
(Richard Hannon) *prom: effrt over 2f out: rdn and ev ch over 1f out: kpt on same pce ins fnl f* **4/1**[2]

**6** 2 3/4 **Big Chill (IRE)** 2-9-5 0............................................... SebSanders 7 61+
(Charles Hills) *in tch: smooth hdwy to trck ldrs 2f out: effrt and nt clr run over 1f out: kpt on same pce after* **9/1**

**7** 3 3/4 **Toni's A Star** 2-9-0 0................................................ RaulDaSilva 6 42
(Paul Green) *dwlt: a towards rr* **25/1**

**8** 1 1/2 **Frosty Times (FR)** 2-9-5 0.......................................... DavidNolan 3 42
(Richard Fahey) *sn outpcd and a in rr* **12/1**

1m 0.83s (0.33) **Going Correction** -0.025s/f (Good) **8** Ran SP% **110.3**
Speed ratings (Par 93): **96,95,94,94,93 88,82,80**
CSF £11.47 TOTE £2.70: £1.10, £1.80, £2.50; EX 14.80 Trifecta £128.10.
**Owner** Hubert John Strecker **Bred** Chelston **Trained** Middleham Moor, N Yorks
■ Stewards' Enquiry : Liam Jones one-day ban: failed to ride to draw (May 18)

**FOCUS**
They finished in a heap in this maiden. There was plenty of promise on show and some of these will step forward.

### 1937 PESCAFRIA H'CAP (BOBIS RACE) — 7f
**6:45** (6:45) (Class 2) (0-105,91) 3-Y-O **£12,291** (£3,657; £1,827; £913) **Stalls** High

Form RPR

60-0 **1** **Azagal (IRE)**[17] 1515 3-9-5 89........................................ DavidAllan 7 96
(Tim Easterby) *hld up in rr: swtchd lft to outer wl over 2f out: str run fr wl over 1f out: rdn to ld ins fnl f: edgd rt and styd on* **15/2**

23-3 **2** 2 **Beau Nash (IRE)**[29] 1278 3-9-1 85.................................. SeanLevey 2 87
(Richard Hannon) *cl up: led over 2f out: rdn over 1f out: drvn and hdd ins fnl f: kpt on* **6/1**

-160 **3** 3 3/4 **Lady Frances**[15] 1555 3-9-2 89............................ MichaelJMMurphy(3) 6 81
(Mark Johnston) *trckd ldrs: hdwy over 2f out: rdn wl over 1f out: drvn and one pce fnl f* **11/1**

0-21 **4** 1 3/4 **Willy Brennan (IRE)**[37] 1126 3-8-8 85........................ JackGarritty(7) 3 73
(Andrew Balding) *t.k.h early: cl up: led over 3f out: rdn along and hdd over 2f out: grad wknd* **11/2**[3]

11-0 **5** 1 1/2 **Kenny The Captain (IRE)**[25] 1358 3-9-0 84............... DuranFentiman 1 68
(Tim Easterby) *trckd ldrs: hdwy on outer over 2f out: rdn to chal and edgd rt over 1f out: wknd ent fnl f* **13/2**

31-0 **6** 1 1/2 **Roachdale House (IRE)**[15] 1563 3-9-7 91........................ TonyHamilton 5 71
(Richard Fahey) *trckd ldrs: hdwy 3f out: rdn whn n.m.r 2f out: sn wknd* **2/1**[1]

01-0 **7** 18 **Scrutiny**[17] 1513 3-9-4 88.......................................(p) LiamJones 4 21
(William Haggas) *led: hdd over 3f out: sn rdn and wknd* **5/1**[2]

1m 26.01s (-0.29) **Going Correction** -0.025s/f (Good) **7** Ran SP% **113.1**
Speed ratings (Par 105): **100,97,93,91,89 88,67**
CSF £49.75 TOTE £9.50: £4.90, £3.40; EX 57.80 Trifecta £755.20.
**Owner** Roger Sidebottom **Bred** Robert Norton **Trained** Great Habton, N Yorks

**FOCUS**
A nice prize but a pretty poor race for the class, with the top-weight rated a full stone below the ceiling for the race. The winner is rated back to her seemingly flattered 2yo Group form.

### 1938 ARCTIC WARRIOR H'CAP — 6f
**7:15** (7:17) (Class 3) (0-90,87) 4-Y-0+ **£8,409** (£2,502; £1,250; £625) **Stalls** High

Form RPR

30-2 **1** **Right Touch**[16] 1537 4-9-4 84........................................ DavidNolan 6 94
(Richard Fahey) *trckd ldrs: hdwy 2f out: sn rdn: drvn to ld jst ins fnl f: kpt on wl* **4/1**[1]

4001 **2** 1/2 **Corporal Maddox**[9] 1667 7-9-7 87..............................(p) SteveDrowne 7 95
(Ronald Harris) *in rr: rdn along 1/2-way: gd hdwy over 1f out: styd on strly u.p fnl f* **20/1**

10-1 **3** nk **Mutafaakir (IRE)**[7] 1731 5-9-1 81.............................(p) JamesSullivan 5 88
(Ruth Carr) *t.k.h: trckd ldr: swtchd lft and hdwy over 2f out: led wl over 1f out: rdn ent fnl f: sn hdd and kpt on same pce towards fin* **9/2**[2]

4-04 **4** 1 1/2 **Singeur (IRE)**[17] 1506 7-9-4 87....................................... NeilFarley(3) 2 90
(Robin Bastiman) *dwlt and towards rr: stdy hdwy 1/2-way: rdn to chal wl over 1f out: drvn ent fnl f and kpt on same pce* **14/1**

0-05 **5** 1/2 **Mon Brav**[16] 1541 7-8-8 74.............................................. PaulPickard 11 75
(Brian Ellison) *hld up towards rr: gd hdwy on wd outside 2f out: sn cl up: rdn over 1f out: kpt on same pce fnl f* **12/1**

00-0 **6** 3/4 **Dark Castle**[16] 1537 5-9-2 82.......................................... PJMcDonald 1 81
(Micky Hammond) *trckd ldrs: effrt 2f out and sn rdn: drvn and one pce appr fnl f* **20/1**

10/0 **7** 1 1/4 **Englishman**[21] 1442 4-9-7 87.......................................... HarryBentley 13 82
(Charles Hills) *hld up in rr: gd hdwy over 2f out: rdn to chse ldrs over 1f out: sn cl up tl drvn and wknd fnl f* **14/1**

/00- **8** 2 **Lightnin Hopkins (IRE)**[197] 7358 4-9-5 85................. DanielTudhope 8 73
(David O'Meara) *chsd ldrs: rdn along over 2f out: grad wknd* **16/1**

5-60 **9** nk **Baby Strange**[19] 1484 10-8-11 84............................ AdamMcLean(7) 12 71+
(Derek Shaw) *dwlt and in rr: detached 1/2-way: hdwy whn nt clr run over 1f out: no ch after* **9/1**

304- **10** nse **Half A Billion (IRE)**[208] 7080 5-8-8 79..................... ConnorBeasley(5) 4 66
(Michael Dods) *prom: rdn along wl over 2f out: sn wknd* **7/1**[3]

00-0 **11** ½ **Sacrosanctus**[7] 1742 6-9-3 **83**.....................(p) TonyHamilton 3 69
(Scott Dixon) *led: rdn along over 2f out: hdd wl over 1f out and sn wknd*
**50/1**

52U- **12** 1 ½ **Hoofalong**[237] 6238 4-9-5 **85**.......................[1] PaulMulrennan 10 66
(Michael Easterby) *trckd ldrs on inner: rdn along wl over 2f out: sn wknd*
**4/1**[1]

1m 12.32s (-1.28) **Going Correction** -0.025s/f (Good) **12** Ran SP% **119.1**
Speed ratings (Par 107): **107,106,105,103,103 102,100,97,97,97 96,94**
CSF £88.52 CT £380.03 TOTE £5.20: £2.00, £4.60, £1.90; EX 91.60 Trifecta £261.40.
**Owner** Nicholas Wrigley & Kevin Hart **Bred** The Athenians **Trained** Musley Bank, N Yorks
**FOCUS**
In-form horses came to the fore here, the winner rated similar to his Ripon mark..

## 1939 SAMHERJI MAIDEN STKS 6f
7:45 (7:46) (Class 5) 3-4-Y-O £2,911 (£866; £432; £216) Stalls High

Form RPR

**1** **Run With Pride (IRE)** 4-9-12 0.......................... DaleSwift 9 85+
(Derek Shaw) *towards rr: hdwy on inner wl over 2f out: rdn to ld appr fnl f: styd on strly*
**33/1**

0-U2 **2** 2 ¼ **Naggers (IRE)**[19] 1486 3-9-2 0.......................... GrahamLee 7 73
(Paul Midgley) *trckd ldrs: pushed along and sltly outpcd wl over 1f out: sn rdn: styd on wl fnl f to take 2nd nr fin*
**8/1**[3]

222- **3** ¾ **Kommander Kirkup**[197] 7341 3-9-2 87.......................... PaulMulrennan 8 70
(Michael Dods) *trckd ldng pair: hdwy to ld wl over 2f out: rdn and edgd lft over 1f out: sn hdd and drvn: one pce*
**4/7**[1]

0 **4** 3 **Fujin**[9] 1671 3-9-2 0.......................... DuranFentiman 1 61
(Noel Wilson) *cl up: rdn along over 2f out: drvn over 1f out: grad wknd*
**66/1**

50- **5** hd **Oak Bluffs (IRE)**[237] 6234 3-9-2 0.......................... DavidNolan 4 60
(Richard Fahey) *in rr and sn pushed along: rdn and outpcd 1/2-way: hdwy over 1f out: styd on fnl f: nrst fin*
**14/1**

64 **6** ¾ **More Beau (USA)**[19] 1486 3-9-2 0.......................... PaddyAspell 5 58
(Ed Dunlop) *chsd ldrs: rdn along over 2f out: sn no imp*
**20/1**

3-54 **7** 1 ½ **Highland Acclaim (IRE)**[17] 1513 3-9-2 84.......................... DanielTudhope 3 53
(David O'Meara) *prom: rdn along 2f out: sn drvn and wknd over 1f out*
**5/2**[2]

**8** 2 **Yard Of Ale** 3-9-2 0.......................... JamesSullivan 2 47
(Kristin Stubbs) *s.i.s: a bhd*
**25/1**

6-4 **9** ½ **Best Tamayuz**[37] 1126 3-9-2 0.......................... PJMcDonald 6 45
(Scott Dixon) *slt ld: rdn along and hdd wl over 2f out: sn wknd*
**50/1**

1m 12.73s (-0.87) **Going Correction** -0.025s/f (Good)
**WFA** 3 from 4yo 10lb **9** Ran SP% **125.0**
Speed ratings (Par 103): **104,101,100,96,95 94,92,90,89**
CSF £276.33 TOTE £27.70: £6.80, £2.30, £1.10; EX 247.80 Trifecta £711.00.
**Owner** The Whiteman Partnership **Bred** Barouche Stud Ireland Ltd **Trained** Sproxton, Leics
**FOCUS**
The two form horses boasted ratings in the 80s, but one ran no sort of race and the other didn't fancy it, so this didn't take much winning. A nice debut from the winner, though.

## 1940 SEAGOLD H'CAP 6f 110y
8:15 (8:17) (Class 5) (0-75,75) 3-Y-O £2,587 (£770; £384; £192) Stalls High

Form RPR

052- **1** **Inyordreams**[183] 7662 3-9-6 **74**.......................... DaleSwift 9 81
(James Given) *mde all: rdn over 2f out: drvn over 1f out: styd on gamely fnl f*
**7/1**

20-0 **2** 1 ¾ **Supersta**[34] 1192 3-9-5 **73**.......................... LiamJones 10 75
(Ronald Harris) *dwlt and in rr: gd hdwy over 2f out: rdn to chse ldrs whn edgd lft jst over 1f out and again ins fnl f: kpt on wl towards fin*
**20/1**

321 **3** hd **Jaeger Train (IRE)**[53] 906 3-9-5 **73**.......................... DanielTudhope 8 74
(K R Burke) *hld up in tch: hdwy 2f out: sn rdn: chsd wnr ent fnl f: sn drvn: edgd lft and one pce*
**3/1**[1]

01-5 **4** 1 ½ **Honey Meadow**[26] 1350 3-9-2 **70**.......................... JimmyQuinn 5 67
(Robert Eddery) *in tch: effrt over 2f out: sn rdn: styd on fnl f*
**12/1**

431- **5** ½ **Look Here's Al**[203] 7200 3-9-4 **72**.......................... SebSanders 2 68
(Andrew Hollinshead) *hld up: hdwy 2f out: rdn to chse ldrs over 1f out: drvn and no imp fnl f*
**14/1**

53-1 **6** 1 ½ **Two Shades Of Grey (IRE)**[16] 1543 3-9-0 **68**.......................... TonyHamilton 6 60
(Richard Fahey) *chsd wnr: rdn along 2f out: drvn and wknd over 1f out*
**9/2**[3]

351- **7** ½ **Pennine Warrior**[179] 7756 3-9-7 **75**.......................... PaulMulrennan 4 65
(Scott Dixon) *trckd ldrs: effrt wl over 2f out: rdn along wl over 1f out: grad wknd*
**12/1**

2214 **8** 2 **Elusive George (IRE)**[3] 1884 3-8-12 **73**.......................... JoeDoyle[(7)] 7 58
(John Quinn) *chsd ldng pair: rdn along over 2f out: drvn and wknd over 1f out*
**4/1**[2]

21-0 **9** hd **Toboggan Star**[26] 1346 3-8-13 **67**.......................... PJMcDonald 1 51
(Ann Duffield) *in tch: effrt and sme hdwy on outer 3f out: rdn along over 2f out: sn wknd*
**16/1**

03-4 **10** 3 **Magnus Romeo**[30] 1258 3-8-13 **72**.......................... MarcMonaghan[(5)] 3 48
(Marco Botti) *towards rr: rdn along 1/2-way: sn btn*
**12/1**

1m 19.87s (-0.03) **Going Correction** -0.025s/f (Good) **10** Ran SP% **116.1**
Speed ratings (Par 99): **99,97,96,95,94 92,92,89,89,86**
CSF £134.69 CT £428.16 TOTE £7.60: £2.40, £5.40, £1.70; EX 185.60 Trifecta £1892.90 Part won..
**Owner** Bolton Grange **Bred** Exors Of The Late J Ellis **Trained** Willoughton, Lincs
■ Stewards' Enquiry : Jimmy Quinn caution: careless riding.
**FOCUS**
There looked to be plenty with chances here. The first three all raced on the stands' rail and the form is rated around the third and fourth.
T/Plt: £82.20 to a £1 stake. Pool: £54444.86 - 483.23 winning tickets T/Qpdt: £28.40 to a £1 stake. Pool: £6426.13 - 167.05 winning tickets JR

# GOODWOOD (R-H)
Saturday, May 3

**OFFICIAL GOING: Good to soft (6.6)**
First 2f of mile course dolled out 6yds increasing distances by about 12yds.
Wind: Almost nil Weather: Sunny

## 1941 BETFRED HISTORY MAKING £5 MILLION SCOOP6 TODAY STKS (H'CAP) 1m 6f
1:45 (1:45) (Class 5) (0-75,75) 4-Y-O+ £3,234 (£962; £481; £240) Stalls Low

Form RPR

1 **1** **Civil War (IRE)**[26] 1355 5-9-7 **72**.......................... GeorgeBaker 5 86+
(Gary Moore) *hld up in midfield: smooth prog on inner over 3f out: trckd ldr over 2f out: led over 1f out and stl gng easily: rdn and hung lft fnl f: hrd pressed last 75yds: fnd enough*
**11/8**[1]

21-5 **2** hd **Story Writer**[22] 1418 5-9-4 **69**.......................... AdamKirby 6 80
(William Knight) *hld up in midfield: pushed along 4f out: drvn and prog on outer 2f out: styd on to take 2nd ins fnl f: str chal last 75yds: jst hld nr fin*
**4/1**[2]

530/ **3** 2 **Kings Bayonet**[31] 5857 7-9-10 **75**.......................... HayleyTurner 12 83
(Alan King) *stdd s: hld up in last pair: stdy prog gng strly 3f out: nt clr run briefly over 2f out: clsd to dispute 2nd 1f out: hmpd sn after: kpt on* **20/1**

1202 **4** nk **Afro**[18] 1496 4-8-10 **65**.......................... (p) CharlesBishop[(3)] 14 73
(Peter Hedger) *trckd ldr after 1f: rdn 3f out: sn dropped to 3rd: kpt on to dispute 2nd again 1f out: hmpd sn after: no ex*
**14/1**

2315 **5** 3 **Poitin**[24] 1383 4-9-8 **74**.......................... RichardKingscote 7 78
(Harry Dunlop) *hld up towards rr: prog whn hmpd 3f out and again 2f out: no ch after but kpt on fnl f*
**16/1**

3202 **6** nk **Daring Indian**[7] 1743 6-8-10 **68**.......................... (p) JennyPowell[(7)] 2 71
(Tom Dascombe) *wl plcd bhd ldrs: pushed along fr 3f out: nt qckn 2f out: one pce after and nvr threatened*
**16/1**

/050 **7** 1 **Treasure The Ridge (IRE)**[26] 1355 5-8-13 **67**.......(b) OisinMurphy[(3)] 13 69
(Brett Johnson) *led after 100yds: rdn over 2f out: hdd & wknd over 1f out*
**12/1**[3]

000/ **8** 3 ½ **Pippa Greene**[17] 6808 10-9-7 **72**.......................... FergusSweeney 4 69
(Nicky Henderson) *hld up wl in rr: rdn and no prog wl over 2f out: n.d after*
**12/1**[3]

030/ **9** 3 ¼ **Dollar Bill**[22] 3592 5-9-3 **68**.......................... (tp) FrannyNorton 8 61
(Nick Gifford) *sn in last pair: nt gng wl fr 1/2-way: wl btn 3f out: modest late prog*
**18/1**

020 **10** 2 **Honourable Knight (IRE)**[4] 1849 6-8-11 **62** ow1.......... DaneO'Neill 9 52
(Mark Usher) *chsd ldrs on outer: rdn 3f out: no imp 2f out: wknd over 1f out*
**25/1**

-260 **11** 1 ¾ **Bramshill Lass**[47] 992 5-8-10 **61**.......................... RobertHavlin 1 48
(Amanda Perrett) *broke wl and led 100yds: stdd into 3rd: rdn and wknd wl over 2f out*
**25/1**

21-4 **12** 1 ½ **Admirable Duque (IRE)**[110] 158 8-9-2 **67**..........(b) MartinLane 3 52
(Dominic Ffrench Davis) *chsd ldng trio to wl over 2f out: sn wknd* **33/1**

0-16 **13** dist **Gentlemax (FR)**[59] 848 4-8-13 **65**.......................... (p) ShaneKelly 10
(Jim Boyle) *racd wd in midfield: dropped away 6f out: virtually p.u over 3f out: walked in*
**40/1**

3m 12.82s (9.22) **Going Correction** +0.60s/f (Yiel)
**WFA** 4 from 5yo+ 1lb **13** Ran SP% **119.0**
Speed ratings (Par 103): **97,96,95,95,93 93,93,91,89,88 87,86,**
CSF £5.54 CT £77.05 TOTE £2.60: £1.20, £1.80, £3.60; EX 7.20 Trifecta £42.90.
**Owner** Ashley Head **Bred** Grangemore Stud **Trained** Lower Beeding, W Sussex
■ Stewards' Enquiry : George Baker three-day ban: careless riding (May 18-20)
**FOCUS**
First 2f of 1m course dolled out 6yds increasing distances by about 12yds. They seemed to go a decent gallop here. The race lacked depth and the form is best rated around the second.

## 1942 BETFRED £5 MILLION SCOOP6 TODAY EBF STALLIONS DAISY WARWICK STKS (LISTED RACE) (F&M) 1m 4f
2:20 (2:20) (Class 1) 4-Y-O+ £23,680 (£8,956; £4,476; £2,236) Stalls High

Form RPR

63-3 **1** **Special Meaning**[15] 1562 4-9-0 93.......................... FrannyNorton 5 99
(Mark Johnston) *mde all: rdn over 2f out: edgd lft over 1f out: kpt on wl fnl f*
**9/2**[2]

2-51 **2** 1 **Noble Protector**[14] 1568 4-9-0 85.......................... ShelleyBirkett 3 97
(Stuart Kittow) *trckd ldrs: lost pl 1/2-way: prog again on outer 3f out: drvn to chse wnr 2f out: kpt on but hld ins fnl f*
**14/1**

21-2 **3** shd **Freedom's Light**[11] 1636 4-9-0 82.......................... RobertHavlin 1 97
(John Gosden) *hld up towards rr: prog whn n.m.r jst over 3f out: drvn to dispute 2nd 2f out: nt qckn over 1f out: kpt on*
**11/2**[3]

510- **4** 2 ½ **Waila**[196] 7365 4-9-0 108.......................... ShaneKelly 7 93
(Sir Michael Stoute) *hld up in rr: prog on outer whn edgd rt: nudged rival and slipped sltly over 3f out: sn chsd wnr: fnd little and lost 2nd 2f out: one pce after*
**9/4**[1]

312- **5** 9 **Toptempo**[233] 6336 5-9-0 77.......................... AdamKirby 8 79
(Mark H Tompkins) *dwlt: detached in last and pushed along at various times: nvr a factor but passed wkng rivals fnl 2f*
**33/1**

625- **6** 1 ¾ **Livia's Dream (IRE)**[157] 8062 5-9-0 92.......................... HayleyTurner 6 76
(Ed Walker) *hld up in rr: shkn up and no real prog 3f out: wl btn after* **10/1**

01-1 **7** 1 ¾ **Wall Of Sound**[16] 1539 4-9-0 95.......................... RichardKingscote 2 73
(Tom Dascombe) *chsd wnr to 3f out: sn wknd*
**9/2**[2]

1U0- **8** 12 **Bonanza Creek (IRE)**[175] 7822 4-9-0 86.......................... PatDobbs 9 54
(Luca Cumani) *trckd ldrs: pushed along whn squeezed out jst over 3f out: sn wknd: t.o*
**20/1**

0- **9** 10 **Magic Art (IRE)**[244] 6031 4-9-0 90.......................... DaneO'Neill 4 38
(Marco Botti) *chsd wnr to over 3f out: wkng whn short of room sn after: t.o*
**14/1**

2m 43.11s (4.71) **Going Correction** +0.60s/f (Yiel) **9** Ran SP% **112.6**
Speed ratings (Par 111): **108,107,107,105,99 98,97,89,82**
CSF £62.81 TOTE £4.50: £1.60, £3.70, £1.90; EX 61.80 Trifecta £294.80.
**Owner** Newsells Park Stud **Bred** Newsells Park Stud **Trained** Middleham Moor, N Yorks
■ Stewards' Enquiry : Shane Kelly two-day ban: careless riding (May 18-19)

**FOCUS**
A below-standard Listed contest, with the favourite below par. The first two are progressive.

## 1943 PLAY £5 MILLION SCOOP6 AT TOTEPOOL.COM STKS (H'CAP) 7f
2:55 (2:55) (Class 2) (0-100,98) 4-Y-0+ £19,407 (£5,775; £2,886; £1,443) Stalls Low

Form RPR
2302 1 **Absolutely So (IRE)**[35] 1172 4-8-12 92........................ OisinMurphy(3) 5 109+
(Andrew Balding) *treacked ldng trio: prog to ld over 2f out: in command over 1f out: rdn and r.o wl* 3/1[1]
20-0 2 3 1/4 **Jack's Revenge (IRE)**[35] 1165 6-9-3 94..................(bt) FergusSweeney 7 102
(George Baker) *hld up in 7th: waiting for room over 2f out: prog to chse wnr over 1f out: styd on but no imp* 6/1
1215 3 2 **George Guru**[15] 1558 7-9-7 98 ........................ RobertHavlin 1 101
(Michael Attwater) *hld up in 5th: waiting for room over 2f out: prog to take 3rd jst over 1f out: one pce and no imp after* 8/1
130- 4 3/4 **Czech It Out (IRE)**[275] 4922 4-8-6 86 oh2 ow2........ CharlesBishop(3) 3 87
(Amanda Perrett) *in tch in 6th: pushed along and sme prog on outer 3f out: nt qckn 2f out: one pce after* 20/1
404- 5 4 **The Confessor**[202] 7222 7-8-12 89........................ DaneO'Neill 2 79
(Henry Candy) *chsd ldng pair: lost pl wl over 2f out: in last pair and btn over 1f out* 4/1[2]
-053 6 3/4 **Newstead Abbey**[7] 1719 4-9-6 97........................ AdamKirby 4 86
(David Barron) *chsd ldr to over 2f out: chsd wnr to over 1f out: wknd* 5/1
02-0 7 hd **Magic City (IRE)**[21] 1437 5-9-6 97........................ PatDobbs 8 85
(Richard Hannon) *hld up in last: shkn up and no prog wl over 2f out* 9/2[3]
0004 8 1 1/4 **Clockmaker (IRE)**[43] 1041 8-9-0 91........................ HayleyTurner 6 76
(Conor Dore) *led: pushed along and hdd over 2f out: sn wknd* 20/1
1m 29.53s (2.53) **Going Correction** +0.60s/f (Yiel) 8 Ran SP% 114.8
Speed ratings (Par 109): **109,105,103,102,97 96,96,95**
CSF £21.49 CT £128.32 TOTE £3.90: £1.40, £2.10, £2.30; EX 22.90 Trifecta £88.00.
**Owner** Jackie & George Smith **Bred** L Mulryan **Trained** Kingsclere, Hants
**FOCUS**
A competitive little handicap and a smart effort from the winner. The form looks sound enough.

## 1944 FOLLOW SCOOP6 AT TOTEPOOLLIVEINFO.COM STKS (H'CAP) 5f
3:30 (3:30) (Class 3) (0-95,95) 4-Y-0+ £9,703 (£2,887; £1,443; £721) Stalls High

Form RPR
-450 1 **Pandar**[19] 1489 5-8-3 82........................ PhilipPrince(5) 6 89
(Milton Bradley) *trckd ldrs: pushed along fr 1/2-way: gap there and rdn to ld 1f out: styd on wl whn pressed last 100yds* 40/1
4-54 2 1 **Waseem Faris (IRE)**[16] 1541 5-8-0 81 oh3........ DanielCremin(7) 3 84
(Mick Channon) *hld up in last: stl there wl over 1f out: gd prog fnl f to chal last 100yds: styd on but no imp nr fin* 10/1
20-6 3 1 1/2 **Kyleakin Lass**[22] 1421 5-9-5 93........................ GeorgeBaker 9 91
(Jonathan Portman) *hld up in last trio: prog on outer over 1f out to chal ins fnl f: one pce last 100yds* 8/1
440- 4 2 1/2 **Long Awaited (IRE)**[279] 4800 6-9-5 93..................(b) AdamKirby 5 82
(David Barron) *trckd ldrs: gng wl whn nt clr run fr 2f out to jst over 1f out: limited rspnse whn in the clr fnl f* 9/2[3]
3050 5 1 1/4 **Jiroft (ITY)**[75] 644 7-9-1 89..................(p) RichardKingscote 7 74
(Robert Cowell) *s.i.s: hld up in last pair: rdn over 1f out: one pce and no great prog* 11/1
000- 6 hd **Ajjaadd (USA)**[136] 8334 8-9-7 95........................ PatDobbs 10 79
(Ted Powell) *settled towards rr on nr side: rdn over 1f out: one pce and no real prog* 8/1
-032 7 1 **Elusivity (IRE)**[10] 1650 6-9-0 88........................ ShaneKelly 2 68
(Peter Crate) *w ldrs towards outer tl wknd over 1f out* 4/1[2]
51-1 8 1/2 **Pal Of The Cat**[19] 1489 4-8-5 82..................(tp) OisinMurphy(3) 8 60
(Brian Gubby) *mde most towards nr side to 1f out: wknd* 7/2[1]
0000 9 7 **Tennessee Wildcat (IRE)**[10] 1650 4-9-2 90..................(p) RobertHavlin 1 43
(Robert Cowell) *racd on outer: w ldrs 3f: wknd qckly* 25/1
-333 10 1 **Fair Value (IRE)**[10] 1650 6-8-10 84........................ HayleyTurner 4 34
(Simon Dow) *w ldrs: upsides 2f out to jst over 1f out: edgd rt and wknd rapidly* 8/1
59.84s (-0.36) **Going Correction** +0.15s/f (Good) 10 Ran SP% 117.4
Speed ratings (Par 107): **108,106,104,100,98 97,96,95,84,82**
CSF £398.82 CT £3599.76 TOTE £51.00: £9.00, £3.20, £2.30; EX 395.20 Trifecta £2069.10 Part won..
**Owner** Dab Hand Racing **Bred** Miss F Vittadini **Trained** Sedbury, Gloucs
**FOCUS**
A competitive sprint run at a strong pace and that helped those coming from off the pace to take over in the final furlong. The form is rated around the runner-up.

## 1945 £5 MILLION SCOOP6 TODAY BRITISH STALLION STUDS EBF CONQUEROR STKS (LISTED RACE) (F&M) 1m
4:05 (4:07) (Class 1) 3-Y-0+
£22,684 (£8,600; £4,304; £2,144; £1,076; £540) Stalls Low

Form RPR
2-2 1 **Be My Gal**[22] 1423 3-8-8 0........................ HayleyTurner 1 104
(Roger Charlton) *dwlt: sn trckd ldrs in 5th: eased off rail 3f out and swtchd lft to wd outside over 2f out: rdn and prog after: led jst ins fnl f: drvn out* 6/1
114- 2 3/4 **Princess Loulou (IRE)**[175] 7822 4-9-7 93........................ DaneO'Neill 4 105
(Roger Varian) *trckd ldng pair: wnt 2nd over 2f out: rdn to ld over 1f out: hdd jst ins fnl f: styd on* 5/1[3]
114- 3 3/4 **Zibelina (IRE)**[245] 6000 4-9-7 109........................ MartinLane 7 103
(Charlie Appleby) *w.w in 6th: clsd on ldrs 2f out: tried to chal over 1f out: nt qckn but styd on fnl f* 3/1[2]
4022 4 3 3/4 **Askaud (IRE)**[7] 1728 6-9-7 95..................(p) RichardKingscote 3 95
(Scott Dixon) *led after 1f: rdn over 2f out: hdd over 1f out: steadily wknd* 8/1
421- 5 nk **Vanity Rules**[225] 6611 4-9-7 80........................ GeorgeBaker 5 94
(Ed Vaughan) *stdd s: plld hrd in last pair: shkn up 2f out: plugged on but nvr gng pce to threaten* 20/1
46-0 6 5 **Amulet**[21] 1437 4-9-7 86........................ ShaneKelly 9 83
(Eve Johnson Houghton) *led 1f: chsd ldr tl wl over 2f out: sn wknd* 14/1
54-5 7 3/4 **Maureen (IRE)**[35] 1163 4-9-7 107........................ PatDobbs 8 81
(Richard Hannon) *trckd ldng trio: rdn to cl over 2f out: wknd wl over 1f out* 5/2[1]
650- 8 8 **Aquatinta (GER)**[245] 6000 4-9-7 100........................ AdamKirby 2 62
(Clive Cox) *t.k.h: hld up in last pair: rdn and no prog over 2f out: wknd and t.o* 14/1
1m 43.15s (3.25) **Going Correction** +0.60s/f (Yiel)
**WFA** 3 from 4yo+ 13lb 8 Ran SP% 113.7
Speed ratings (Par 111): **107,106,105,101,101 96,95,87**
CSF £35.50 TOTE £5.90: £1.90, £1.70, £1.30; EX 31.70 Trifecta £114.50.
**Owner** D J Deer **Bred** D J And Mrs Deer **Trained** Beckhampton, Wilts
**FOCUS**
With the two standout horses on ratings underperforming to differing degrees, this might not have turned out to be the strongest of Listed contests. The winner has the clear potential to do better.

## 1946 BETFRED "RACING'S BIGGEST SUPPORTER" MEDIAN AUCTION MAIDEN STKS 7f
4:40 (4:41) (Class 5) 3-Y-0 £3,234 (£962; £481; £240) Stalls Low

Form RPR
0 1 **Temptress (IRE)**[22] 1422 3-9-0 0........................ PatDobbs 3 79
(Roger Charlton) *trckd ldng trio: shkn up wl over 1f out: clsd fnl f to ld last 100yds: pushed out* 8/1
2 2 3/4 **Between Wickets**[17] 1511 3-9-5 0........................ HayleyTurner 1 82
(Marcus Tregoning) *t.k.h: trckd ldr 2f and again jst over 2f out: sn rdn: clsd v grad u.p to ld ins fnl f: sn hdd and outpcd: hung lft nr fin* 8/11[1]
0- 3 1 1/2 **Skaters Waltz (IRE)**[251] 5790 3-9-5 0........................ ChrisCatlin 2 79
(Paul Cole) *dwlt: hld up in last pair: stl there wl over 1f out: drvn and prog to go 3rd fnl f: keeping on whn impeded nr fin* 12/1
5-4 4 2 1/2 **Foxford**[28] 1296 3-8-11 0........................ OisinMurphy(3) 5 67
(Patrick Chamings) *led: rdn over 2f out: racd quite awkwardly after: hdd & wknd ins fnl f* 20/1
5 2 1/4 **Greengage Summer** 3-8-11 0.................. WilliamTwiston-Davies(3) 4 61
(Mick Channon) *hld up in last: sme prog on outer 2f out: wknd jst over 1f out* 20/1
6 1 **Doctor Sardonicus** 3-9-5 0........................ MartinLane 6 63
(David Simcock) *hld up in 5th: shkn up over 2f out: no prog and btn over 1f out* 7/1[3]
7 5 **Field Force** 3-9-5 0........................ RobertHavlin 7 50
(Amanda Perrett) *dwlt: t.k.h: trckd ldr after 2f to jst over 2f out: wandered u.p and wknd* 5/1[2]
1m 33.28s (6.28) **Going Correction** +0.60s/f (Yiel) 7 Ran SP% 115.4
Speed ratings (Par 99): **88,87,85,82,80 78,73**
CSF £14.61 TOTE £7.60: £3.70, £1.10; EX 19.40 Trifecta £118.80.
**Owner** The Pyoneers **Bred** J Hanly, A Stroud And T Stewart **Trained** Beckhampton, Wilts
**FOCUS**
Some interesting newcomers on show and a decent form standard set by Between Wickets but all were brushed aside by the winner. The time was slow and the favourite is rated a bit off her debut form.

## 1947 TOTEPOOL.COM STKS (H'CAP) 1m 1f 192y
5:10 (5:11) (Class 5) (0-70,70) 3-Y-0 £3,234 (£962; £481; £240) Stalls Low

Form RPR
000- 1 **Arab Dawn**[192] 7460 3-9-3 66........................ GeorgeBaker 4 77+
(Hughie Morrison) *hld up in last pair: stdy prog gng wl fr 3f out: pushed along to chal 1f out: shkn up to ld narrowly 100yds out: shade cleverly* 3/1[1]
-541 2 nk **Cotton Club (IRE)**[14] 1588 3-9-0 70........................ PatMillman(7) 2 80
(Rod Millman) *trckd ldrers: prog over 2f out: rdn to ld wl over 1f out: hdd last 100yds: r.o but hld nr fin* 9/2[2]
-346 3 4 **Sherston**[24] 1389 3-9-3 66........................ FrannyNorton 7 68
(Mark Johnston) *led at mod pce: pushed along and hdd wl over 2f out: stl upsides on inner wl over 1f out: outpcd after* 8/1
0-00 4 3/4 **Lord Brantwood**[19] 1491 3-9-0 66.................. WilliamTwiston-Davies(3) 8 67
(Mick Channon) *prom: trckd ldr 6f out: led wl over 2f out: hdd wl over 1f out: outpcd* 25/1
55-2 5 1/2 **High Master (IRE)**[6] 1765 3-9-7 70........................ PatDobbs 5 70
(Richard Hannon) *trckd ldr to 6f out: styd cl up: rdn and rt on terms 2f out: outpcd after* 3/1[1]
-335 6 2 3/4 **Turnbury**[61] 828 3-9-3 66..................(t) MartinLane 3 60
(Robert Mills) *trckd ldrs: cl up jst over 2f out: sn rdn: wknd over 1f out* 33/1
640- 7 3 1/2 **Mabdhool (IRE)**[283] 4640 3-9-5 68........................ DaneO'Neill 1 56
(Marcus Tregoning) *dwlt: t.k.h: hld up in 7th: rdn over 2f out: no prog wl over 1f out: fdd* 7/1[3]
36-6 8 1 1/4 **Bognor (USA)**[14] 1588 3-8-12 64........................ OisinMurphy(3) 6 49
(Jo Hughes) *plld hrd: hld up in rr: rdn and no prog wl over 2f out: sn btn* 12/1
426 9 4 **Sparkling Ice (IRE)**[31] 1233 3-9-5 68........................ JohnFahy 10 46
(Eve Johnson Houghton) *w ldrs 2f: stdd and towards rr after 4f: rdn on outer wl over 2f out: wknd over 1f out* 16/1
01-5 10 12 **Dutchartcollector**[105] 236 3-9-1 64........................ FergusSweeney 9 19
(Gary Moore) *hld up in last pair: shkn up and wknd over 2f out: t.o* 12/1
2m 18.5s (10.40) **Going Correction** +0.60s/f (Yiel) 10 Ran SP% 119.8
Speed ratings (Par 99): **82,81,78,77,77 75,72,71,68,58**
CSF £16.92 CT £100.21 TOTE £4.20: £1.90, £1.80, £3.10; EX 23.30 Trifecta £196.40.
**Owner** Eason,Kerr-Dineen,Hughes,Edwards-Jones **Bred** Fittocks Stud **Trained** East Ilsley, Berks
**FOCUS**
Quite a few of these probably have more to offer further down the line. The first two did quite well to pull clear.
T/Plt: £113.60 to a £1 stake. Pool: £87252.04 - 560.61 winning tickets T/Qpdt: £26.70 to a £1 stake. Pool: £4347.70 - 120.30 winning tickets JN

# 1528 NEWMARKET (R-H)
Saturday, May 3

**OFFICIAL GOING: Good to firm (good in places; overall 7.9, stands' side 7.9, centre 8.0, far side 7.7)**
Stands side track used.
Wind: very light, half behind Weather: light cloud, bright spells, dry

## 1948 QATAR RACING SUFFOLK STKS (H'CAP) 1m 1f
2:05 (2:07) (Class 2) 3-Y-0+
£28,012 (£8,388; £4,194; £2,097; £1,048; £526) Stalls Centre

Form RPR
000- 1 **Niceofyoutotellme**[218] 6801 5-8-8 90........................ JimCrowley 6 103
(Ralph Beckett) *stdd s: hld up in tch towards rr: rdn and hdwy wl over 1f out: drvn to ld ins fnl f: hrd pressed fnl 75yds: hld on wl cl home* 10/1[3]
105- 2 nk **Ajmany (IRE)**[220] 6751 4-8-7 89..................(b) AndreaAtzeni 19 102
(Luca Cumani) *in tch in midfield: rdn and effrt 2f out: hdwy and edging rt over 1f out: str run to chal fnl 75yds: r.o but jst hld* 14/1
310- 3 1 3/4 **Bold Sniper**[273] 4984 4-9-3 99........................ RyanMoore 17 108+
(Sir Michael Stoute) *t.k.h: hld up in tch in rr: gd hdwy to chse ldrs and shifting rt jst over 1f out: styd on same pce fnl 100yds* 9/1[2]

66-5 **4** *2* **Trumpet Major (IRE)**[35] 1170 5-9-10 **106**................(t) RichardHughes 12 111
(Richard Hannon) *w ldr tl led 2f and gng best of ldng trio: rdn over 1f out: hdd ins fnl f: no ex and sn btn: wknd towards fin* **14/1**

15-5 **5** *3/4* **Farraj (IRE)**[42] 1068 5-9-6 **102**.................................... TomQueally 4 105
(Roger Varian) *lw: hld up in tch in midfield: effrt and nt clr run wl over 1f out: rdn and hdwy over 1f out: styd on wl ins fnl f: nt rch ldrs* **10/1**[3]

-664 **6** *1* **Circumvent**[14] 1578 7-8-2 **84**.................................(b) RaulDaSilva 13 85
(Paul Cole) *lw: t.k.h: led: hdd and rdn 2f out: kpt on and stl ev ch tl no ex and btn 1f out: wknd ins fnl f* **14/1**

600 **7** *1/2* **Burano (IRE)**[21] 1437 5-9-4 **100**.................................. JimmyFortune 11 100
(Brian Meehan) *hld up in tch in last quartet: effrt and nt clr run over 1f out: rdn and hdwy 1f out: styd on wl ins fnl f: nvr trbld ldrs* **14/1**

005- **8** *hd* **Directorship**[210] 7018 8-8-13 **95**....................................... LiamKeniry 15 95
(Patrick Chamings) *wl in tch in midfield: outpcd and lost pl 2f out: rallied u.p ent fnl f: styd on but no threat to ldrs fnl f* **25/1**

0550 **9** *hd* **Strictly Silver (IRE)**[56] 887 5-9-2 **98**...........................(v) KierenFallon 1 97
(Alan Bailey) *wl in tch in midfield: hdwy to join ldrs 4f out: ev ch and rdn over 2f out: no ex and btn 1f out: wknd ins fnl f* **25/1**

31-0 **10** *1/2* **Highland Duke (IRE)**[21] 1437 5-8-0 **87**............................ RyanTate[(5)] 16 85
(Clive Cox) *chsd ldrs: rdn and sltly hmpd 2f out: drvn and outpcd over 1f out: hld and one pce fnl f* **9/1**[2]

345- **11** *1* **Rock Choir**[210] 7020 4-8-12 **94**........................................ SebSanders 18 90
(William Haggas) *stdd s: hld up in tch in towards rr: rdn over 2f out: no imp: plugged on but no threat to ldrs fnl f* **7/1**[1]

40-0 **12** *1/2* **Lunar Deity**[26] 1351 5-8-0 **82** oh1...................................... NickyMackay 3 77
(Stuart Williams) *wl in tch in midfield: rdn and unable qck ent fnl 2f: drvn and btn over 1f out* **50/1**

045- **13** *shd* **Two For Two (IRE)**[204] 7172 6-9-3 **99**......................... SilvestreDeSousa 7 94
(David O'Meara) *t.k.h: chsd ldrs: rdn and lost pl over 1f out: wknd ins fnl f* **14/1**

1-13 **14** *1/2* **Big Baz (IRE)**[82] 559 4-8-3 **85**.................................... MartinDwyer 5 79
(William Muir) *hld up in tch towards rr: stl towards rr and n.m.r wl over 1f out: styd on fnl f: nvr trbld ldrs* **10/1**[3]

505- **15** *1/2* **Spifer (IRE)**[128] 8398 6-8-8 **90**...................................(p) AntonioFresu 14 83
(Marco Botti) *hld up in tch in midfield: lost pl and rdn over 2f out: towards rr and hrd drvn wl over 1f out: plugged on but n.d fnl f* **50/1**

4360 **16** *1/2* **Veeraya**[15] 1559 4-8-3 **85**..........................................(b) AdamBeschizza 2 77
(Julia Feilden) *wl in tch in midfield: rdn 3f out: sn struggling: wknd u.p wl over 1f out* **40/1**

05-2 **17** *3 1/2* **Roserrow**[24] 1399 5-8-10 **92**.............................................. DavidProbert 9 76
(Andrew Balding) *chsd ldrs tl over 2f out: sn u.p and struggling: bhd 1f out* **11/1**

34-2 **18** *1 1/2* **Stand My Ground (IRE)**[35] 1164 7-8-13 **95**............... JamieSpencer 10 76
(David O'Meara) *stdd s: t.k.h: hld up in tch in rr: effrt nrest far rail ent fnl 2f: no hdwy and btn over 1f out: eased fnl f* **12/1**

206- **19** *1 1/2* **Proud Chieftain**[133] 8386 6-9-1 **97**.................................... JamesDoyle 8 75
(Clifford Lines) *wl in tch in midfield: drvn and unable qck ent fnl 2f: wknd over 1f out: bhd ins fnl f* **20/1**

1m 52.4s (0.70) **Going Correction** +0.10s/f (Good) **19** Ran SP% **127.9**
Speed ratings (Par 109): **100,99,98,96,95 94,94,94,94,93 92,92,92,91,91 90,87,86,85**
CSF £137.26 CT £1360.36 TOTE £10.70: £2.60, £4.80, £2.30, £3.40; EX 268.60 Trifecta £3640.60.
**Owner** R Roberts **Bred** Minster Stud **Trained** Kimpton, Hants
■ Stewards' Enquiry : James Doyle Fine: £80, entered wrong stall.
Silvestre De Sousa Fine: £80, entered wrong stall.

**FOCUS**
Stands' side track used Stalls: Centre. A very good handicap and the action unfolded mainly down the middle of the track. The first three have progressive profiles.

## 1949 PEARL BLOODSTOCK PALACE HOUSE STKS (GROUP 3) 5f

**2:40** (2:41) (Class 1) 3-Y-O+

**£36,861** (£13,975; £6,994; £3,484; £1,748; £877) **Stalls** Centre

Form RPR

2-40 **1** **Sole Power**[35] 1179 7-9-2 **114**.............................................. RyanMoore 6 117
(Edward Lynam, Ire) *hld up in tch in midfield and travelled wl: effrt over 1f out: nt clr run and swtchd rt jst ins fnl f: rdn and qcknd readily to ld fnl 50yds: in command fin* **9/4**[1]

530- **2** *1/2* **Kingsgate Native (IRE)**[209] 7054 9-9-2 **112**.................. JimCrowley 9 115
(Robert Cowell) *t.k.h: chsd ldrs: rdn over 1f out: drvn ins fnl f: r.o wl u.p fnl 100yds to snatch 2nd cl home* **12/1**

312- **3** *hd* **Hot Streak (IRE)**[203] 7191 3-8-10 **112**............................ HarryBentley 3 113
(Kevin Ryan) *swtg: travelled strly: chsd ldrs: hdwy to join ldrs 2f out: ev ch and rdn over 1f out: led ins fnl f: hdd and no ex fnl 50yds: lost 2nd cl home* **7/1**[3]

0-15 **4** *nk* **Stepper Point**[15] 1557 5-9-2 **111**...................................(p) MartinDwyer 4 113
(William Muir) *pressed ldr: rdn and ev ch wl over 1f out: drvn and led 1f out: sn hdd: kpt on but no ex towards fin* **16/1**

210- **5** *1* **Moviesta (USA)**[253] 5726 4-9-2 **113**........................... PaulMulrennan 10 110
(Bryan Smart) *t.k.h: hld up towards rr: hdwy into midfield 1/2-way: rdn over 1f out: nt clr run and swtchd rt jst ins fnl f: pushed along and kpt on fnl 100yds: nvr trbld ldrs* **15/2**

310- **6** *nk* **Justineo**[209] 7054 5-9-2 **108**...........................................(b) AndreaAtzeni 8 109
(Roger Varian) *led: rdn wl over 1f out: hdd 1f out: no ex and btn fnl 100yds: wknd towards fin* **12/1**

6-14 **7** *nk* **Dinkum Diamond (IRE)**[16] 1531 6-9-2 **108**................ DavidProbert 12 108
(Henry Candy) *in tch in midfield: pushed along 3f out: drvn and sltly outpcd 2f out: rallied and hdwy 1f out: kpt on but no threat to ldrs ins fnl f* **16/1**

/3-1 **8** *3/4* **Pearl Secret**[24] 1397 5-9-2 **110**..................................... JamieSpencer 11 105
(David Barron) *lw: stdd s: t.k.h: hld up in rr: swtchd lft and effrt u.p wl over 1f out: drvn and no hdwy 1f out: wknd wl ins fnl f* **10/3**[2]

021- **9** *1/2* **Rocky Ground (IRE)**[221] 6719 4-9-2 **101**..................... FrankieDettori 2 103
(Roger Varian) *hld up in tch in last trio: rdn and effrt wl over 1f out: drvn and no hdwy 1f out: wknd ins fnl f* **20/1**

034- **10** *1 3/4* **Extortionist (IRE)**[210] 7011 3-8-7 **102**................... MickaelBarzalona 5 93
(Olly Stevens) *t.k.h: hld up in tch in last trio: rdn and effrt over 1f out: no hdwy: wknd ins fnl f* **33/1**

-542 **11** *50* **Iptisam**[42] 1066 5-9-2 **102**..............................................(p) LukeMorris 1
(James Tate) *in tch in midfield: rdn 1/2-way: sn drvn and struggling: lost tch over 1f out: heavily eased ins fnl f: t.o* **50/1**

58.74s (-0.36) **Going Correction** +0.10s/f (Good)
**WFA** 3 from 4yo+ 9lb **11** Ran SP% **114.9**
Speed ratings (Par 113): **106,105,104,104,102 102,101,100,99,97 17**
CSF £29.56 TOTE £2.90: £1.20, £4.30, £2.30; EX 28.00 Trifecta £194.10.
**Owner** Mrs S Power **Bred** G Russell **Trained** Dunshaughlin, Co Meath

**FOCUS**
An up-to-scratch Palace House, run at a frantic early pace. It saw plenty in with a chance a furlong out, but ultimately there was a repeat of last year's one-two. Similar form to last year.

## 1950 QATAR BLOODSTOCK JOCKEY CLUB STKS (GROUP 2) 1m 4f

**3:10** (3:13) (Class 1) 4-Y-O+

**£56,710** (£21,500; £10,760; £5,360; £2,690; £1,350) **Stalls** Centre

Form RPR

15-4 **1** **Gospel Choir**[16] 1533 5-9-0 **110**........................................ RyanMoore 6 115
(Sir Michael Stoute) *lw: hld up wl in tch in midfield: rdn and effrt to press ldrs 2f out: led wl over 1f out: styd on wl fnl f: rdn out* **6/1**[2]

131- **2** *2 1/4* **Pether's Moon (IRE)**[178] 7768 4-9-0 **106**..................... RichardHughes 9 112
(Richard Hannon) *chsd ldr tl 5f out: styd chsng ldrs: rdn and effrt to chse wnr wl over 1f out: styd on same pce ins fnl f* **10/1**

223- **3** *2* **Trading Leather (IRE)**[238] 6226 4-9-0 **120**.................. KevinManning 1 109
(J S Bolger, Ire) *lw: stdd s: plld hrd: hld up in last trio: rdn and effrt over 2f out: 5th and no imp over 1f out: kpt on ins fnl f to go 3rd fnl 75yds: no threat to ldrs* **4/6**[1]

31-0 **4** *1 1/4* **Renew (IRE)**[63] 811 4-9-0 **105**......................................... LukeMorris 7 107
(Marco Botti) *chsd ldrs: wnt 2nd 5f out: rdn wl over 2f out: drvn and lost 2nd wl over 1f out: outpcd and btn 1f out: wknd fnl 75yds* **25/1**

11-1 **5** *1 1/4* **Brass Ring**[28] 1299 4-9-0 **98**........................................... JamesDoyle 2 105
(John Gosden) *lw: led: rdn jst over 2f out: hdd wl over 1f out: flashed tail u.p and outpcd over 1f out: wknd ins fnl f* **15/2**[3]

300- **6** *1* **Havana Beat (IRE)**[231] 6393 4-9-0 **103**.......................... DavidProbert 3 103
(Andrew Balding) *stdd s: t.k.h: hld up in last pair: rdn and effrt 2f out: 6th and no prog u.p wl over 1f out: plugged on* **25/1**

130- **7** *5* **Times Up**[196] 7363 8-9-3 **112**.......................................... WilliamBuick 8 98
(Ed Dunlop) *in tch in midfield: rdn over 3f out: dropped to rr 2f out: sn outpcd and wl hld after* **33/1**

25-0 **8** *3 1/4* **Penglai Pavilion (USA)**[56] 900 4-9-0 **118**............. MickaelBarzalona 4 96
(Charlie Appleby) *stdd s: plld hrd: hld up in last pair: rdn and effrt wl over 2f out: no hdwy and btn 2f out: wknd* **8/1**

2m 33.03s (1.03) **Going Correction** +0.10s/f (Good) **8** Ran SP% **116.9**
Speed ratings (Par 115): **100,98,97,96,95 94,91,89**
CSF £61.85 TOTE £6.40: £1.60, £2.60, £1.10; EX 59.20 Trifecta £143.60.
**Owner** Cheveley Park Stud **Bred** Cheveley Park Stud Ltd **Trained** Newmarket, Suffolk

**FOCUS**
Probably not a great race for the grade with the favourite short of his best, but the winner is very progressive and the level od the form seems sound enough. The action unfolded middle to far side.

## 1951 QIPCO 2000 GUINEAS STKS (THE 206TH RUNNING) (BRITISH CHAMPIONS SERIES) (GROUP 1) (C&F) 1m

**3:50** (3:52) (Class 1) 3-Y-O

**£255,195** (£96,750; £48,420; £24,120; £12,105; £6,075) **Stalls** Centre

Form RPR

11-2 **1** **Night Of Thunder (IRE)**[21] 1436 3-9-0 **109**..................... KierenFallon 3 124
(Richard Hannon) *grad moved across to r far side: in tch in midfield overall: rdn, hdwy and shifting lft over 1f out: drvn and chal fnl 100yds: hung bdly lft across crse but r.o to ld cl home* **40/1**

11-1 **2** *1/2* **Kingman**[21] 1436 3-9-0 **118**................................................. JamesDoyle 1 123
(John Gosden) *lw: grad moved across to r far side: hld up towards rr: overall: rdn and effrt over 1f out: gd hdwy to ld 1f out: drvn ins fnl f: kpt on tl hdd and no ex towards fin* **6/4**[1]

1- **3** *hd* **Australia**[238] 6223 3-9-0 **117**........................................ JosephO'Brien 10 122+
(A P O'Brien, Ire) *lengthy: tall: racd centre tl swtchd to stands' side after 1f: wl in tch in midfield overall: rdn and w ldrs over 1f out: chsd overall ldr briefly jst ins fnl f: 3rd and kpt on u.p fnl 100yds* **5/2**[2]

11-1 **4** *2 1/4* **Shifting Power**[17] 1514 3-9-0 **107**............................... FrankieDettori 11 117
(Richard Hannon) *lw: racd in centre tl swtchd to stands' side after 1f: chsd ldrs overall: rdn and upsides gp ldr over 1f out: no ex and outpcd fnl 150yds: outpoced and n.m.r sn after: kpt on* **50/1**

3-1 **5** *3/4* **Charm Spirit (IRE)**[30] 1272 3-9-0 **113**.......................... OlivierPeslier 6 115
(F Head, France) *w'like: sweating: grad moved across to r far side: chsd gp ldr and prom overall: rdn wl over 1f out: no ex 1f out: kpt on same pce ins fnl f* **33/1**

12- **6** *1/2* **Noozhoh Canarias (SPA)**[34] 3-9-0 **116**............ ChristopheSoumillon 8 114
(Enrique Leon Penate, Spain) *athletic: overall ldr and grad moved across to far rail: rdn over 1f out: hdd 1f out: no ex: wknd fnl 100yds* **22/1**

11-1 **7** *shd* **Toormore (IRE)**[16] 1532 3-9-0 **122**............................ RichardHughes 14 114
(Richard Hannon) *racd stands' side thrght: led gp and prom overall: rdn and edgd rt over 1f out: lost gp ld jst ins fnl f: no ex and wknd fnl 75yds* **15/2**[3]

111- **8** *3/4* **Kingston Hill**[189] 7528 3-9-0 **120**...................................... AndreaAtzeni 4 112+
(Roger Varian) *lw: racd centre tl swtchd to stands' side after 1f: hld up in rr: rdn and effrt 2f out: sme hdwy into midfield whn edgd lft over 1f out: kpt on steadily ins fnl f: nvr trbld ldrs* **10/1**

311- **9** *hd* **War Command (USA)**[203] 7192 3-9-0 **119**...................... RyanMoore 9 112
(A P O'Brien, Ire) *racd centre tl swtchd to stands' side after 1f: rdn and effrt 2f out: drvn and no prog over 1f out: kpt on same pce fnl f* **8/1**

20-2 **10** *3/4* **The Grey Gatsby (IRE)**[16] 1532 3-9-0 **110**................... JamieSpencer 2 110
(Kevin Ryan) *grad moved across to far side: in tch in midfield overall: rdn 2f out: unable qck u.p and btn 1f out: wknd ins fnl f* **66/1**

4 **11** *3/4* **Bookrunner (USA)**[30] 1272 3-9-0 0........... Christophe-PatriceLemaire 5 108
(M Delzangles, France) *w'like: tall: grad moved across to far side: hld up towards rr overall: rdn and effrt over 1f out: no imp and unbalanced over 1f out: kpt on steadily ins fnl f: nvr trbld ldrs* **33/1**

51-0 **12** *11* **Master The World (IRE)**[17] 1516 3-9-0 **92**........................ LiamKeniry 7 83
(David Elsworth) *racd centre tl swtchd to stands' side after 1f: hld up in rr: rdn ent fnl 2f: sn btn: bhd over 1f out: eased wl ins fnl f* **100/1**

1-11 **13** *3/4* **Ertijaal (IRE)**[15] 1555 3-9-0 **105**...................................... PaulHanagan 12 81
(William Haggas) *swtg: racd centre tl swtchd to stands' side after 1f: stdd s: t.k.h: hld up in midfield overall: rdn wl over 1f out: wknd over 1f out: bhd fnl f: eased towards fin* **33/1**

131- **14** *1 1/4* **Outstrip**[183] 7688 3-9-0 **117**...................................... MickaelBarzalona 13 78
(Charlie Appleby) *swtg: racd stands' side thrght: hld up towards rr: effrt u.p and swtchd ent fnl 2f: no imp whn short of room over 1f out: wl btn after: eased ins fnl f* **25/1**

1m 36.61s (-1.99) **Going Correction** +0.10s/f (Good) **14** Ran SP% **124.4**
Speed ratings: **113,112,112,110,109 108,108,107,107,107 106,95,94,93**
CSF £99.15 CT £236.52 TOTE £23.00: £4.90, £1.20, £1.40; EX 160.00 Trifecta £778.90.
**Owner** Saeed Manana **Bred** Frank Dunne **Trained** East Everleigh, Wilts
■ A Classic winner in his first season for Richard Hannon junior.
■ Stewards' Enquiry : Joseph O'Brien two-day ban: used whip above permitted level (May 18-19)

**FOCUS**
The hottest 2000 Guineas for years on paper, with real strength in depth. However, it proved an unsatisfactory affair due to the field splitting into two groups, one towards the far rail and the other stands' side, with the stalls again down the middle. That made for a messy race. The time and overall form suggest the race was at least up to scratch despite the surprise winner and split field. Night Of Thunder improved the best part of a stone to reverse Greenham form with Kingman, who's rated to his Newbury mark.

## 1952 HARBOUR WATCH AT TWEENHILLS H'CAP (BOBIS RACE) 6f
4:25 (4:25) (Class 2) (0-100,92) 3-Y-O £12,938 (£3,850; £1,924; £962) Stalls Centre

Form RPR
1-02 1 **Nova Champ (IRE)**[12] 1615 3-8-2 73 oh1 (p) AndreaAtzeni 1 81
(Stuart Williams) *mde all: rdn over 1f out: pressed and drvn ins fnl f: styd on wl: drvn out* **16/1**
21- 2 ¾ **Stars Above Me**[222] 6697 3-9-3 88 JamesDoyle 6 93+
(Roger Charlton) *lw: hld up in tch in midfield: effrt and shifting rt over 1f out: chsd ldng pair 1f out: kpt on u.p ins fnl f: snatched 2nd last stride* **15/8**[1]
00-1 3 shd **Strategic Force (IRE)**[23] 1404 3-8-4 80 RyanTate(5) 10 85
(Clive Cox) *chsd ldng pair: rdn 2f out: chsd wnr and drvn over 1f out: styd on and pressing wnr ins fnl f: no imp towards fin: lost 2nd last stride* **20/1**
13-6 4 1½ **Eastern Impact (IRE)**[21] 1445 3-9-6 91 RyanMoore 12 91
(Richard Fahey) *hld up towards rr: pushed along and no hdwy on downhill run over 1f out: rdn and hdwy 1f out: styd on wl to chse ldng trio wl ins fnl f: nvr trbld ldrs* **8/1**
20-0 5 2 **Outer Space**[17] 1518 3-9-7 92 RichardHughes 2 86
(Jamie Osborne) *hld up in tch in last quartet: rdn and effrt wl over 1f out: no imp tl styd on ins fnl f: nvr gng pce to trble ldrs* **7/1**[3]
01-5 6 nse **Meritocracy (IRE)**[17] 1518 3-9-4 89 JamieSpencer 9 83
(Paul Cole) *stdd s: hld up in tch in rr: rdn and effrt over 1f out: drvn 1f out: kpt on ins fnl f: nvr gng pce to trble ldrs* **10/1**
25-5 7 ½ **Captain Midnight (IRE)**[37] 1136 3-8-12 83 SilvestreDeSousa 4 75
(David Brown) *chsd wnr: rdn jst over 2f out: drvn and lost 2nd over 1f out: wknd ins fnl f* **20/1**
21-1 8 hd **Perfect Alchemy (IRE)**[23] 1409 3-8-9 80 JimCrowley 5 71
(Ralph Beckett) *t.k.h: hld up in tch in midfield: rdn and effrt to chse ldrs over 1f out: no ex 1f out: wknd ins fnl f* **6/1**[2]
120- 9 nk **Tanseeb**[233] 6328 3-9-3 88 PaulHanagan 11 78
(Mark Johnston) *lw: t.k.h: hld up in tch in midfield: rdn and effrt over 1f out: no prog 1f out: wknd ins fnl f* **8/1**
00-0 10 ¾ **Diamond Lady**[12] 1614 3-8-10 81 FrederikTylicki 8 69
(William Stone) *stdd and awkward leaving stalls: hld up in tch in rr: effrt 2f out: sme hdwy u.p over 1f out: sn struggling and lost pl again: wknd ins fnl f* **40/1**
100- 11 4½ **Red Lady (IRE)**[198] 7329 3-8-12 83 JimmyFortune 3 57
(Brian Meehan) *in tch in midfield: effrt u.p wl over 1f out: lost pl and bhd 1f out: sn wknd* **16/1**

1m 13.57s (1.37) **Going Correction** +0.10s/f (Good) **11 Ran SP% 116.6**
Speed ratings (Par 105): **94,93,92,90,88 88,87,87,86,85 79**
CSF £44.80 CT £647.24 TOTE £20.90: £4.30, £1.40, £4.50; EX 77.60 Trifecta £1910.60 Part won..
**Owner** Qatar Racing Limited **Bred** Hyde Park Stud & Paddy Conney **Trained** Newmarket, Suffolk

**FOCUS**
This looked an ordinary race of its type with the top weight rated 8lb below the race ceiling. The winner hadn't really progressed at two.

## 1953 MAKFI NEWMARKET STKS (LISTED RACE) (C&G) 1m 2f
5:00 (5:01) (Class 1) 3-Y-O £22,684 (£8,600; £4,304; £2,144; £1,076; £540) Stalls Centre

Form RPR
5-24 1 **Barley Mow (IRE)**[17] 1516 3-9-0 107 RichardHughes 1 108
(Richard Hannon) *mde all: rdn and clr w runner-up whn edgd rt and bmpd rival 1f out: battled on wl u.p fnl f: rdn out* **14/1**
2-2 2 nk **Mutakayyef**[21] 1433 3-9-0 0 PaulHanagan 3 107
(William Haggas) *lw: chsd ldrs: wnt 2nd over 2f out: rdn to chal and clr w wnr over 1f out: carried rt and bmpd 1f out: kpt on wl but a hld ins fnl f* **8/1**[3]
110- 3 2 **Pinzolo**[189] 7528 3-9-0 97 MickaelBarzalona 2 104
(Charlie Appleby) *stdd s: t.k.h: hld up in tch in rr: effrt to chse ldng trio ent fnl 2f: hung rt over 1f out: swtchd lft ins fnl f: kpt on to go 3rd towards fin* **13/2**[2]
12-3 4 nk **Postponed (IRE)**[16] 1532 3-9-0 104 AndreaAtzeni 6 103
(Luca Cumani) *in tch in midfield: hdwy to chse ldrs over 2f out: cl 3rd and rdn wl over 1f out: sn outpcd by ldng pair: styd on same pce fnl f: lost 3rd towards fin* **15/8**[1]
1-1 5 9 **Cloudscape (IRE)**[16] 1535 3-9-0 95 WilliamBuick 7 86
(John Gosden) *t.k.h: hld up wl in tch in midfield: rdn over 2f out: 5th and btn 2f out: sn wknd* **15/8**[1]
136- 6 3¼ **Pupil (IRE)**[203] 7195 3-9-0 92 JimmyFortune 8 80
(Richard Hannon) *hld up in tch in last pair: rdn and short-lived effrt over 2f out: sn btn and no chwl over 1f out* **33/1**
43-0 7 2 **Sir Jack Layden**[35] 1178 3-9-0 105 FrankieDettori 4 76
(David Brown) *wl in tch in midfield: rdn wl over 2f out: drvn: 6th and struggling 2f out: sn wknd* **20/1**
311- 8 6 **Bremner**[226] 6545 3-9-0 95 (tp) RyanMoore 5 65
(Hugo Palmer) *chsd wnr tl over 2f out: sn lost pl and bhd 2f out* **16/1**

2m 4.89s (-0.91) **Going Correction** +0.10s/f (Good) 8 Ran SP% **114.3**
Speed ratings (Par 107): **107,106,105,104,97 95,93,88**
CSF £118.86 TOTE £11.60: £2.70, £2.40, £2.40; EX 82.90 Trifecta £833.10.
**Owner** Lady Rothschild **Bred** The Rt Hon Lord Rothschild **Trained** East Everleigh, Wilts
■ Stewards' Enquiry : Richard Hughes one-day ban: careless riding (May 18)

**FOCUS**
Usually an informative 3yo Listed contest, and this was more competitive than most renewals. They went a modest pace early, heading more towards the far side after half a mile, and it was probably no coincidence that the winner made all the running. Barley Mow is rated back to his best.

## 1954 QIPCO SUPPORTS RACING WELFARE H'CAP (BOBIS RACE) 1m
5:35 (5:36) (Class 2) (0-105,97) 3-Y-O £12,938 (£3,850; £1,924; £962) Stalls Centre

Form RPR
12-5 1 **Hors De Combat**[22] 1420 3-9-1 91 FrederikTylicki 7 99+
(James Fanshawe) *racd in centre: stdd s: hld up in tch in rr: rdn and effrt to chal 1f out: led ins fnl f: r.o wl: rdn out* **7/1**[3]
31 2 ¾ **Born In Bombay**[66] 748 3-8-8 84 DavidProbert 4 90+
(Andrew Balding) *athletic: racd in centre: t.k.h: hld up in tch in last pair: rdn and effrt to chal over 1f out: led ins fnl f: sn hdd: one pce towards fin* **7/2**[2]
00-5 3 ½ **Lyn Valley**[16] 1530 3-9-3 93 RyanMoore 6 98
(Mark Johnston) *racd in centre: led gp after 1f: chsd ldrs overall: rdn ent fnl 2f: ev ch ins fnl f: kpt on same pce fnl 100yds* **9/1**
4-1 4 2 **Yenhaab (IRE)**[16] 1542 3-8-9 85 JamieSpencer 3 85+
(William Haggas) *str: overall ldr and wnt to r far side sn after s: rdn wl over 1f out: hdd ins fnl f: wknd ins fnl f* **11/4**[1]
41-6 5 ½ **Golden Town (IRE)**[21] 1436 3-9-7 97 SilvestreDeSousa 2 96
(Saeed bin Suroor) *wnt to r far side sn after s: t.k.h: in tch in midfield overall: rdn to press ldr and wandered u.p over 1f out: wknd ins fnl f* **11/4**[1]
505- 6 1¼ **Ifwecan**[238] 6187 3-8-10 86 JoeFanning 1 82
(Mark Johnston) *wnt to r far side sn after s: chsd ldr tl wl over 1f out: no ex 1f out: wknd ins fnl f* **16/1**
211- 7 1 **Monsea (IRE)**[185] 7626 3-9-0 90 RichardHughes 5 84
(Richard Hannon) *racd centre: t.k.h: led gp for 1f: styd prom overall: rdn wl over 1f out: no ex 1f out: wknd ins fnl f* **7/1**[3]

1m 40.53s (1.93) **Going Correction** +0.10s/f (Good) **7 Ran SP% 116.4**
Speed ratings (Par 105): **94,93,92,90,90 89,88**
CSF £32.61 TOTE £9.00: £3.80, £2.30; EX 28.40 Trifecta £278.10.
**Owner** Chris Van Hoorn **Bred** Newsells Park Stud **Trained** Newmarket, Suffolk

**FOCUS**
Even in a seven-runner race the jockeys didn't fancy staying in one group, three of them going for the far rail and four staying up the middle, so another unsatisfactory race. The early pace was steady and the form is rated around the runner-up.
T/Jkpt: Not won. T/Plt: £150.00 to a £1 stake. Pool: £225959.53 - 1099.53 winning tickets
T/Qpdt: £26.10 to a £1 stake. Pool: £10190.73 - 288.15 winning tickets SP

# 1440 THIRSK (L-H)
Saturday, May 3

**OFFICIAL GOING: Good (good to firm in places; 9.3)**
Both bends dolled out adding 10yds to 7f and 1m races and circa 15yds to 12f races.
Wind: light 1/2 against Weather: fine and sunny

## 1955 TEN TO FOLLOW ENTRIES CLOSE NOON TODAY MAIDEN AUCTION STKS 5f
1:55 (1:57) (Class 5) 2-Y-O £3,234 (£962; £481; £240) Stalls High

Form RPR
1 **Captain Colby (USA)** 2-9-5 0 TomEaves 7 80+
(Kevin Ryan) *mde all: kpt on wl towards fin* **5/2**[2]
2 ¾ **Denton Dawn (IRE)** 2-8-9 0 ConnorBeasley(5) 4 72
(Michael Dods) *chsd ldrs: upsides and hung lft over 1f out: no ex clsng stages* **6/1**
52 3 3½ **Horsforth**[19] 1482 2-9-0 0 BarryMcHugh 10 60
(Tony Coyle) *chsd ldrs: 3rd over 1f out: kpt on same pce* **9/4**[1]
4 1¼ **Gold Pursuit** 2-9-5 0 BenCurtis 3 60
(Alan Swinbank) *chsd ldrs: fdd over 1f out* **20/1**
5 ¾ **Stanghow** 2-9-5 0 GrahamLee 1 58+
(Mel Brittain) *dwlt and carried lft s: swtchd rt after s: hdwy over 2f out: styd on fnl f* **25/1**
0 6 6 **Dragline**[26] 1342 2-9-5 0 DavidAllan 2 36
(Tim Easterby) *wnt lft s: sn chsng ldrs: drvn and hung lft over 2f out: edgd rt and wknd over 1f out* **14/1**
7 1½ **Billy Bond** 2-9-2 0 GeorgeChaloner(3) 8 31
(Richard Fahey) *wnt lft s: in rr and sn drvn along: nvr on terms* **5/1**[3]
8 1 **Rocco's Delight** 2-9-0 0 AdamCarter(5) 5 27
(John Wainwright) *s.s: sn swvd bdly lft: a bhd* **14/1**
9 1 **Rutland Panther** 2-9-5 0 SteveDrowne 6 23
(Ollie Pears) *dwlt: a in rr* **20/1**
10 2 **Related To Ewe (IRE)** 2-9-5 0 DuranFentiman 11 16
(Tim Easterby) *mid-div: sn drvn along: lost pl over 2f out* **33/1**

1m 1.0s (1.40) **Going Correction** +0.125s/f (Good) **10 Ran SP% 119.9**
Speed ratings (Par 93): **93,91,86,84,83 73,71,69,67,64**
CSF £17.53 TOTE £3.00: £1.10, £2.00, £1.20; EX 21.70 Trifecta £44.70.
**Owner** Mrs R G Hillen **Bred** Castleton Lyons & Kilboy Estate **Trained** Hambleton, N Yorks

**FOCUS**
Both bends dolled out adding 10yds to 7f and 1m races and circa 15yds to 1m4f races. Promising first efforts from the leading pair, who pulled nicely clear of a fair yardstick in the third. There's probably more to come from the winner.

## 1956 £5MILLION TOTESCOOP6 TODAY FILLIES' H'CAP 1m
2:25 (2:25) (Class 4) (0-85,85) 3-Y-O+ £4,851 (£1,443; £721; £360) Stalls Low

Form RPR
1-0 1 **Pelerin (IRE)**[17] 1515 3-8-6 81 MarcMonaghan(5) 9 93
(Marco Botti) *hld up in rr: swtchd lft after 1f: effrt over 3f out: hdwy on ins to ld over 1f out: drew clr* **8/1**
51- 2 3½ **Crowley's Law**[227] 6512 3-8-7 77 GrahamGibbons 6 81
(Tom Dascombe) *hld up in rr: hdwy over 4f out: sn trcking ldrs: nt clr run and swtchd rt 2f out: r.o to take 2nd ins fnl f* **11/8**[1]
431- 3 ½ **Annawi**[227] 6531 4-9-10 81 TedDurcan 2 87
(Henry Candy) *sn trcking ldr: effrt over 2f out: kpt on same pce appr fnl f* **6/1**[3]
20-1 4 ¾ **Flycatcher (IRE)**[17] 1507 3-8-5 75 PatrickMathers 4 76
(Richard Fahey) *sn chsng ldrs: drvn over 3f out: sn outpcd: kpt on wl fnl f* **11/2**[2]
25-4 5 hd **Zeyran (IRE)**[19] 1483 5-9-8 82 RobertTart(3) 8 86
(Hugo Palmer) *swtchd lft after s: mid-div: drvn 3f out: one pce* **6/1**[3]
0-00 6 3 **Lilac Lace (IRE)**[7] 1733 4-9-12 83 DuranFentiman 3 80
(Tim Easterby) *led: hdd over 1f out: wknd fnl 150yds* **16/1**
606- 7 5 **Oddysey (IRE)**[216] 6875 5-9-9 85 ConnorBeasley(5) 7 70
(Michael Dods) *chsd ldrs on outer: drvn over 3f out: wknd over 1f out* **11/1**

1m 39.72s (-0.38) **Going Correction** +0.125s/f (Good)
**WFA** 3 from 4yo+ 13lb **7 Ran SP% 111.4**
Speed ratings (Par 102): **106,102,102,101,101 98,93**
CSF £18.50 CT £69.19 TOTE £7.40: £3.20, £1.20; EX 20.50 Trifecta £123.70.
**Owner** Mr Bruni & Mr Somma **Bred** Rabbah Bloodstock Limited **Trained** Newmarket, Suffolk

**FOCUS**
This looked a tight handicap but it turned out to be anything but, with a most impressive winner. Better than average fillies' form.

## 1957 LIVE TOTESCOOP6 INFORMATION AT TOTEPOOL.COM H'CAP 7f
3:00 (3:00) (Class 4) (0-85,91) 4-Y-O+ £6,469 (£1,925; £962; £481) Stalls Low

Form RPR
0-60 **1** **Ruwaiyan (USA)**[83] [552] 5-9-1 **79**....(p) GrahamLee 12 95+
(James Tate) *hld up in rr: t.k.h: smooth hdwy on outside over 2f out: led on bit 1f out: wnt clr: smoothly* **14/1**
4435 **2** 3 ½ **Capaill Liath (IRE)**[26] [1345] 6-8-9 **78**....(p) ShaneGray(5) 4 84
(Kevin Ryan) *sn mid-div: hdwy over 2f out: sn chsng ldrs: swtchd outside over 1f out: styd on to take 2nd post* **15/2**[3]
40-0 **3** shd **Shahdaroba (IRE)**[21] [1442] 4-9-7 **85**.... PJMcDonald 10 91
(Micky Hammond) *in rr: effrt over 2f out: nt clr run over 1f out: edgd rt: styd on to take 3rd nr fin* **25/1**
36-1 **4** nk **Music In The Rain (IRE)**[10] [1646] 6-9-13 **91**.... DanielTudhope 8 96
(David O'Meara) *trckd ldrs: kpt on same pce fnl f* **7/4**[1]
-314 **5** ½ **Trade Secret**[9] [1672] 7-9-1 **79**.... DavidAllan 9 83
(Mel Brittain) *chsd ldrs: hdd appr fnl f: kpt on same pce* **10/1**
5-00 **6** 1 ½ **Fieldgunner Kirkup (GER)**[15] [1564] 6-8-12 **76**.... GrahamGibbons 2 76
(David Barron) *in tch: nt clr run over 2f out: kpt on fnl f* **11/1**
32-5 **7** 1 ½ **Talent Scout (IRE)**[19] [1483] 8-8-13 **84**.... GemmaTutty(7) 7 80
(Karen Tutty) *led: hdd appr fnl f: sn wknd* **7/1**[2]
0-00 **8** 1 ½ **Le Deluge (FR)**[13] [1598] 4-8-11 **75**.... JamesSullivan 14 67
(Michael Easterby) *chsd ldrs on outer: wknd over 1f out* **50/1**
0-62 **9** nk **Our Boy Jack (IRE)**[10] [1646] 5-8-13 **80**.... GeorgeChaloner(3) 13 71
(Richard Fahey) *sn chsng ldrs on outer: drvn over 4f out: fdd fnl f* **7/1**[2]
5-00 **10** ¾ **Al Muheer (IRE)**[10] [1646] 9-8-11 **78**....(p) JasonHart(3) 11 67
(Ruth Carr) *s.i.s: swtchd lft after s: sme hdwy on outside 2f out: nvr a factor* **11/1**
40-0 **11** 1 **Kingscroft (IRE)**[19] [1483] 6-8-12 **81**.... JacobButterfield(5) 1 68
(Michael Herrington) *s.i.s: a in rr* **33/1**
20-0 **12** 5 **Relight My Fire**[12] [1609] 4-8-10 **74**....(b) DuranFentiman 3 48
(Tim Easterby) *mid-div: hdwy on ins 3f out: lost pl over 1f out* **33/1**

1m 26.72s (-0.48) **Going Correction** +0.125s/f (Good) **12 Ran SP% 117.2**
Speed ratings (Par 105): **107,103,102,102,101 100,98,96,96,95 94,88**
CSF £110.39 CT £2648.10 TOTE £19.90: £3.70, £2.10, £7.80; EX 166.50 Trifecta £1537.20 Part won..
**Owner** Saeed Manana **Bred** Rabbah Bloodstock Llc **Trained** Newmarket, Suffolk
**FOCUS**
Another seemingly competitive handicap which ended up being very one-sided, the winner much improved back on turf. This rates another step up from him. There was a sound pace.

## 1958 TOTEPOOL THIRSK HUNT CUP (H'CAP) 1m
3:40 (3:40) (Class 2) (0-100,98) 4-Y-O+ £16,172 (£4,812; £2,405; £1,202) Stalls Low

Form RPR
0-60 **1** **Fort Bastion (IRE)**[7] [1719] 5-9-0 **91**.... JamesSullivan 9 100
(Ruth Carr) *in rr: hdwy on ins over 2f out: swtchd rt over 1f out: r.o to ld last 100yds* **9/1**
10-5 **2** ¾ **Ingleby Angel (IRE)**[7] [1721] 5-9-5 **96**.... DanielTudhope 12 103
(David O'Meara) *hld up in rr: gd hdwy over 1f out: styd on wl to take 2nd nr fin* **8/1**[3]
-531 **3** shd **Bold Prediction (IRE)**[7] [1744] 4-8-2 **84** 6h2.... JoeyHaynes(5) 7 91
(K R Burke) *chsd ldrs: upsides ins fnl f: no ex* **33/1**
00-0 **4** ½ **Osteopathic Remedy (IRE)**[21] [1442] 10-9-1 **92**.... TomEaves 6 98
(Michael Dods) *hld up in rr: gd hdwy over 1f out: styd on wl towards fin* **40/1**
5606 **5** nk **Joe Eile (IRE)**[10] [1646] 6-8-3 **87**.... JoeDoyle(7) 3 92
(John Quinn) *chsd ldrs: upsides ins fnl f: no ex* **50/1**
51-5 **6** ½ **Multi Bene**[24] [1399] 5-8-13 **90**.... GrahamLee 16 94
(Ed McMahon) *hld up on outer towards rr: hdwy 2f out: kpt on fnl f* **12/1**
0310 **7** ¾ **Robert The Painter (IRE)**[7] [1721] 6-9-4 **98**....(v) JulieBurke(3) 11 100
(David O'Meara) *w ldrs: led after 3f: clr over 3f out: wknd and hdd last 100yds* **14/1**
3535 **8** 1 **Showboating (IRE)**[10] [1646] 6-8-13 **90**....(vt) SeanLevey 10 90
(Alan McCabe) *s.i.s: in rr: hdwy on outside over 2f out: kpt on fnl f* **25/1**
5-41 **9** nk **Farlow (IRE)**[21] [1442] 6-8-13 **90**.... TonyHamilton 5 89
(Richard Fahey) *chsd ldrs: dropped midfield 4f out: hdwy 2f out: kpt on fnl f* **7/1**[2]
00-0 **10** 4 ½ **Norse Blues**[21] [1442] 6-9-3 **94**.... GrahamGibbons 4 83
(David Barron) *prom: drvn and outpcd over 3f out: lost pl over 1f out* **8/1**[3]
00-6 **11** 2 **Anderiego (IRE)**[7] [1733] 6-8-5 **85**.... SamJames(3) 8 69
(David O'Meara) *chsd ldrs: lost pl 2f out* **10/1**
11-5 **12** ¾ **Off Art**[35] [1165] 4-9-2 **93**.... DavidAllan 2 75
(Tim Easterby) *dwlt: stmbld sn after s: drvn into mid-div after 2f: nvr a factor: wknd fnl f* **9/4**[1]
30-3 **13** hd **Wannabe King**[10] [1646] 8-8-11 **88**....(p) PJMcDonald 13 70
(Geoffrey Harker) *mid-divivsion: drvn and lost pl 3f out* **33/1**
0-01 **14** nse **Trail Blaze (IRE)**[7] [1733] 5-8-11 **93**....(p) ShaneGray(5) 1 75
(Kevin Ryan) *led 3f: chsd ldrs: wknd over 1f out* **10/1**

1m 39.22s (-0.88) **Going Correction** +0.125s/f (Good) **14 Ran SP% 122.2**
Speed ratings (Par 109): **109,108,108,107,107 106,106,105,104,100 98,97,97,97**
CSF £76.95 CT £2297.79 TOTE £11.40: £3.30, £3.50, £8.90; EX 92.10 Trifecta £2309.00 Part won..
**Owner** Sprint Thoroughbred Racing **Bred** L White & D McGregor **Trained** Huby, N Yorks
**FOCUS**
A useful and competitive handicap. The leaders went off hard and three of the first four home came from off the pace. The winner's best run since he was a 3yo.

## 1959 TOTEPOOL HOME OF POOL BETTING MAIDEN STKS (BOBIS RACE) (DIV I) 7f
4:15 (4:17) (Class 4) 3-Y-O £4,851 (£1,443; £721; £360) Stalls Low

Form RPR
**1** **Royal Temptress (IRE)** 3-9-0 0.... BenCurtis 1 76
(Alan Swinbank) *s.s: gd hdwy on outside over 2f out: chsd ldr and edgd lft over 1f out: led last 150yds: styd on wl* **25/1**
220- **2** 1 ¾ **Dutch Breeze**[254] [5679] 3-9-5 83.... DavidAllan 4 76
(Tim Easterby) *trckd ldrs: led after 2f: hdd ins fnl f: no ex* **4/6**[1]
4 **3** ¾ **Lince Suertudo (FR)**[46] [1002] 3-9-5 0.... BarryMcHugh 2 74
(Tony Coyle) *hld up in mid-div: lost pl over 3f out: hdwy and swtchd rt 2f out: styd on to take 3rd 1f out: kpt on* **28/1**
**4** 3 ¼ **Dutch Descent (IRE)** 3-9-5 0.... GrahamGibbons 3 66
(David Barron) *chsd ldrs: fdd fnl f* **6/1**[3]
0 **5** 1 **Mendelita**[16] [1542] 3-8-11 0.... GeorgeChaloner(3) 10 58
(Richard Fahey) *chsd ldrs on outer: drvn and hung lft over 2f out: wknd fnl f* **12/1**
5 **6** 3 ¼ **Cape Karli (IRE)**[29] [1280] 3-9-0 0.... WilliamCarson 8 50
(Charles Hills) *s.i.s: in rr: drvn over 3f out: kpt on fnl f: nvr a factor* **7/2**[2]
00- **7** hd **Sleeping Star**[250] [5827] 3-9-0 0.... TomEaves 9 49
(Mel Brittain) *t.k.h: led 2f: chsd ldrs: wknd fnl f* **80/1**
0 **8** nse **Two B'S**[12] [1608] 3-8-12 0.... RachelRichardson(7) 6 54
(Tim Easterby) *s.i.s: hld up in rr: hdwy on outside over 4f out: sn chsng ldrs: wknd 2f out* **33/1**
**9** 5 **No Indication (IRE)** 3-9-5 0.... TedDurcan 7 41
(John Butler) *mid-div: hdwy 4f out: sn chsng ldrs: wknd over 1f out* **18/1**

1m 29.7s (2.50) **Going Correction** +0.125s/f (Good) **9 Ran SP% 120.9**
Speed ratings (Par 101): **90,88,87,83,82 78,78,78,72**
CSF £43.82 TOTE £17.60: £3.80, £1.10, £9.00; EX 85.60 Trifecta £977.40.
**Owner** Mrs Lizzy Wilson **Bred** K Molloy **Trained** Melsonby, N Yorks
**FOCUS**
An ordinary maiden run in a 20lb slower time than division II. Shaky form, rated around the runner-up.

## 1960 EXCLUSIVE TICKET GIVEAWAYS @TOTEPOOL MAIDEN STKS 1m 4f
4:50 (4:54) (Class 5) 3-Y-O+ £3,234 (£962; £481; £240) Stalls High

Form RPR
**1** **Tiger Lilly (IRE)** 3-8-4 0.... PatrickMathers 2 75+
(Richard Fahey) *chsd ldrs: nt clr run and swtchd rt over 2f out: 4 l 3rd 1f out: edgd lft and styd on wl to ld towards fin* **18/1**
4-6 **2** ¾ **Sternrubin (GER)**[21] [1438] 3-8-9 0.... GrahamLee 12 78
(Peter Chapple-Hyam) *sn trcking ldrs: t.k.h: 2nd over 3f out: styd on to take 2nd nr fin* **7/2**[2]
3 **3** ½ **Miss Crystal (IRE)**[99] [316] 3-8-4 0.... WilliamCarson 1 72
(Charles Hills) *led: t.k.h: drvn 2f out: hdd towards fin* **10/1**[3]
**4** 4 ½ **Chatham House Rule** 3-8-9 0.... PJMcDonald 5 70
(Michael Bell) *trckd ldrs: t.k.h: drvn over 2f out: one pce* **14/1**
3- **5** 1 ¼ **Tacticus (USA)**[157] [8066] 3-8-9 0.... TedDurcan 7 68
(Lady Cecil) *gave problems loading: half-rrd s: sn trcking ldrs: drvn 3f out: hung lft over 1f out: sn wknd* **4/5**[1]
0 **6** 2 **High Love (IRE)**[25] [1357] 3-8-4 0.... BarryMcHugh 6 60
(Tom Dascombe) *mid-div: drvn over 2f out: kpt on fnl f* **50/1**
32- **7** 1 ½ **Dan Emmett (USA)**[140] [8298] 4-10-0 0.... PaulPickard 3 64
(John Wainwright) *chsd ldrs: drvn 3f out: one pce* **16/1**
**8** 3 ½ **Saddlers Mot**[20] 10-9-2 0.... GemmaTutty(7) 11 54
(Karen Tutty) *s.i.s: hld up in rr: hdwy to chse ldrs over 4f out: wknd 2f out* **80/1**
**9** 1 **Fickle Feelings (IRE)** 3-8-4 0.... RoystonFfrench 9 50
(David Barron) *in rr: sme hdwy over 2f out: nvr a factor* **33/1**
0 **10** ½ **Yorkshire Monarch (IRE)**[12] [1608] 3-8-2 0.... RachelRichardson(7) 4 54
(Tim Easterby) *rr-div: sme hdwy over 2f out: wknd over 1f out* **66/1**
3 **11** 2 **First Move**[11] [1627] 4-9-11 0.... MichaelJMMurphy(3) 10 53
(Mark Johnston) *sn chsng ldrs: wknd 2f out* **11/1**
**12** 8 **Lacocodanza**[46] 5-9-2 0.... KieranSchofield(7) 13 35
(George Moore) *s.i.s: hdwy to chse ldrs over 4f out: lost pl over 3f out* **100/1**
**13** 1 ¼ **King's Prospect** 3-8-9 0.... PaulQuinn 8 36
(Tracy Waggott) *s.s: last whn rn v wd bnd after 2f: bhd fnl 3f* **100/1**

2m 41.26s (5.06) **Going Correction** +0.125s/f (Good)
**WFA** 3 from 4yo+ 19lb **13 Ran SP% 122.6**
Speed ratings (Par 103): **88,87,87,84,83 82,81,78,78,77 76,71,70**
CSF £81.91 TOTE £17.00: £3.60, £1.50, £2.80; EX 97.20 Trifecta £823.60.
**Owner** Sir Robert Ogden **Bred** Lynch Bages Ltd **Trained** Musley Bank, N Yorks
**FOCUS**
An ordinary maiden. The gallop looked pretty sedate, with the race not really beginning in earnest until the final 4f. The form is rated around the runner-up.

## 1961 COLLECT TOTEPOOL WINNINGS AT BETFRED SHOPS H'CAP 5f
5:20 (5:25) (Class 4) (0-85,85) 4-Y-O+ £6,469 (£1,925; £962; £481) Stalls High

Form RPR
-040 **1** **Lastchancelucas**[17] [1506] 4-8-11 **78**....(b) JasonHart(3) 11 88
(Declan Carroll) *racd stands' side: in rr: sn drvn along: hdwy over 1f out: styd on wl to ld fnl strides: 1st of 9 that gp* **10/1**[3]
0042 **2** ¾ **Tax Free (IRE)**[8] [1695] 12-9-5 **83**.... AdrianNicholls 3 90
(David Nicholls) *racd far side: chsd ldrs: led briefly wl ins fnl f: hdd last strides: 1st of 9 that gp* **18/1**
12-0 **3** ½ **Oldjoesaid**[58] [863] 10-8-13 **77**.... PhillipMakin 10 83
(Paul Midgley) *swtchd rt s and racd stands' side: in rr: swtchd rt to rail over 2f out: hdwy over 1f out: fin strly: 2nd of 9 that gp* **28/1**
00-2 **4** shd **Bronze Beau**[15] [1566] 7-8-9 **78**....(t) JacobButterfield(5) 18 83
(Kristin Stubbs) *racd stands' side: led that gp: kpt on same pce last 75yds: 3rd of 9 that gp* **12/1**
32-0 **5** shd **Tumblewind**[17] [1506] 4-9-3 **84**.... GeorgeChaloner(3) 5 89+
(Richard Whitaker) *overall ldr far side: hdd and no ex last 30yds: 2nd of 9 that gp* **16/1**
43-5 **6** 1 **Space Artist (IRE)**[15] [1566] 4-9-1 **79**.... RoystonFfrench 19 80
(Bryan Smart) *racd stands' side: w ldr: kpt on same pce fnl f: 4th of 9 that gp* **11/1**
20-0 **7** shd **Towbee**[16] [1538] 5-9-0 **78**.... BarryMcHugh 1 79
(Michael Easterby) *racd far side: sn outpcd: hdwy over 1f out: styd on ins fnl f: 3rd of 9 that gp* **50/1**
00-2 **8** 1 **Mayfield Girl (IRE)**[4] [1850] 4-8-11 **75**.... AndrewElliott 2 72
(Mel Brittain) *racd far side: chsd ldrs: one pce appr fnl f: 4th of 9 that gp* **20/1**
43-0 **9** nk **Holy Angel (IRE)**[21] [1440] 5-8-10 **74**....(e) TomEaves 16 70
(Tim Easterby) *s.i.s: racd stands' side: hdwy over 1f out: keeping on at fin: 5th of 9 that gp* **16/1**
30-6 **10** 1 ½ **Haajes**[58] [863] 10-8-8 **77**....(v) ShirleyTeasdale(5) 15 68
(Paul Midgley) *racd stands' side: chsd ldrs: drvn over 2f out: one pce: 6th of 9 that gp* **25/1**
0-51 **11** 2 ¼ **Silvanus (IRE)**[15] [1565] 9-9-3 **81**.... GrahamLee 12 64
(Paul Midgley) *racd stands' side: chsd ldrs: drvn over 2f out: wknd over 1f out: 7th of 9 that gp* **17/2**[2]
-144 **12** 2 ½ **Sleepy Blue Ocean**[8] [1695] 8-9-0 **78**....(p) TedDurcan 7 52
(John Balding) *racd far side: in rr: hdwy over 2f out: chsng ldrs over 1f out: lost pl and eased ins fnl f: 5th of 9 that gp* **25/1**
240- **13** 1 **Dusty Storm (IRE)**[207] [7112] 4-9-0 **78**.... SteveDrowne 4 48
(Ed McMahon) *racd far side: w ldrs: wknd fnl f: 6th of 9 that gp* **25/1**
66-0 **14** ½ **Arctic Feeling (IRE)**[17] [1506] 6-8-10 **81**.... JoshQuinn(7) 13 49
(Richard Fahey) *racd stands' side: in rr: nvr a factor: 8th of 9 that gp* **10/1**[3]

-521 **15** 1 3/4 **Red Baron (IRE)**[8] 1695 5-9-4 **85**.............................. NeilFarley(3) 14 55
(Eric Alston) *racd stands' side: w ldrs: rdn and hung bdly lft over 1f out: sn lost pl and eased: last of 9 that gp* **11/4**[1]
60-0 **16** *hd* **Captain Dunne (IRE)**[8] 1695 9-8-4 **75**............... RachelRichardson(7) 9 36
(Tim Easterby) *swtchd lft and racd far side: chsd ldrs: wknd 2f out: 7th of 9 that gp* **16/1**
1006 **17** 2 1/4 **Royal Bajan (USA)**[7] 1742 6-8-11 **75**........................(v) JamesSullivan 6 28
(James Given) *racd far side: chsd ldrs: wknd over 1f out: 8th of 9 that gp* **22/1**
00-0 **18** 1/2 **Bosun Breese**[8] 1695 9-9-1 **79**.............................. PJMcDonald 8 30
(Paul Midgley) *rrd s: racd far side: a bhd: last of 9 that gp* **33/1**
59.59s (-0.01) **Going Correction** +0.125s/f (Good) **18** Ran SP% **123.3**
Speed ratings (Par 105): **105,103,103,102,102 101,100,99,98,96 92,88,87,86,83 83,79,78**
CSF £158.08 CT £4960.92 TOTE £15.10: £4.20, £1.90, £7.60, £3.30; EX 332.60 Trifecta £1642.30 Part won..
**Owner** C H Stephenson & Partners **Bred** C H Stephenson **Trained** Sledmere, E Yorks
**FOCUS**
A fair sprint. Half the field headed over to the far side and there was little between the two groups throughout. The winner is rated to his best.

## 1962 TOTEPOOL HOME OF POOL BETTING MAIDEN STKS (BOBIS RACE) (DIV II) 7f
**5:50** (5:52) (Class 4) 3-Y-O **£4,851** (£1,443; £721; £360) **Stalls** Low

Form RPR
262- **1** **Rogue Wave (IRE)**[197] 7335 3-9-5 80.............................. GrahamLee 5 81
(Alan Jarvis) *led early: trckd ldr: led narrowly 2f out: fnd ex clsng stages* **5/2**[2]
**2** 1/2 **Foxcover (IRE)** 3-9-5 0.............................. LeeTopliss 6 79
(Richard Fahey) *mid-div: drvn over 3f out: hdwy on ins and upsides 2f out: no ex nr fin* **5/1**[3]
3-3 **3** 6 **Premium Pressure (USA)**[77] 626 3-9-5 0.............................. PhillipMakin 1 63
(David Barron) *sn led: rdn and hdd 2f out: wknd fnl f* **10/11**[1]
00- **4** 3 1/4 **Sooqaan**[203] 7209 3-9-5 0.............................. TomEaves 7 54
(Mel Brittain) *trckd ldrs on outer: effrt over 2f out: wknd appr fnl f* **25/1**
00 **5** 5 **Shades Of Silk**[52] 930 3-9-0 0.............................. DaleSwift 2 36
(James Given) *trckd ldrs: t.k.h: drvn and outpcd 4f out: wknd over 1f out* **40/1**
**6** 1 3/4 **Some Boy Lukey** 3-9-5 0.............................. StevieDonohoe 8 37
(David Thompson) *s.i.s: lost pl over 4f out: bhd fnl 2f* **16/1**
00 **7** 1 1/2 **To Begin**[16] 1542 3-9-0 0.............................. AdamCarter(5) 4 33
(Tim Easterby) *s.i.s: in rr: bhd fnl 2f* **20/1**
**8** 18 **Reeflex** 3-9-2 0.............................. JasonHart(3) 9
(Eric Alston) *hung bdly rt s: sn in rr: hung rt bnd over 3f out: bhd and eased over 1f out: t.o* **14/1**
1m 28.72s (1.52) **Going Correction** +0.125s/f (Good) **8** Ran SP% **121.2**
Speed ratings (Par 101): **96,95,88,84,79 77,75,54**
CSF £16.20 TOTE £2.40: £1.10, £1.80, £1.10; EX 13.10 Trifecta £28.00.
**Owner** Market Avenue Racing Club & Partners **Bred** Kevin Walsh **Trained** Twyford, Bucks
**FOCUS**
Just a fair maiden, the leading pair coming clear in the final 2f. It was 20lb faster than the first division and the winner is rated close to his mark.
T/Plt: £411.30 to a £1 stake. Pool: £56631.54 - 100.49 winning tickets T/Qpdt: £254.20 to a £1 stake. Pool: £3127.03 - 9.10 winning tickets WG

1963 - (Foreign Racing) - See Raceform Interactive

# 1931 CHURCHILL DOWNS (L-H)
Saturday, May 3
**OFFICIAL GOING: Dirt: fast; turf: firm**

## 1964a KENTUCKY DERBY PRESENTED BY YUM! BRANDS (GRADE 1) (3YO) (DIRT) 1m 2f (D)
**11:24** (12:00) 3-Y-O **£854,096** (£240,963; £120,481; £60,240; £36,144)

RPR
**1** **California Chrome (USA)**[28] 1330 3-9-0 0..............(b) VictorEspinoza 6 122+
(Art Sherman, U.S.A) **5/2**[1]
**2** 1 3/4 **Commanding Curve (USA)**[35] 1189 3-9-0 0........... SXBridgmohan 17 118
(Dallas Stewart, U.S.A) **38/1**
**3** 1 1/4 **Danza (USA)**[20] 3-9-0 0.............................. JBravo 5 115
(Todd Pletcher, U.S.A) **87/10**[3]
**4** 2 3/4 **Wicked Strong (USA)**[28] 1326 3-9-0 0.............................. RMaragh 20 110
(James Jerkens, U.S.A) **13/2**[2]
**5** *nse* **Samraat (USA)**[28] 1326 3-9-0 0.............................. JLOrtiz 7 109
(Richard Violette Jr, U.S.A) **167/10**
**6** 1/2 **Dance With Fate (USA)**[21] 1464 3-9-0 0.............................. CNakatani 12 108
(Peter Eurton, U.S.A) **16/1**
**7** 1/2 **Ride On Curlin (USA)**[20] 3-9-0 0.............................. CHBorel 19 113+
(William Gowan, U.S.A) **173/10**
**8** 3/4 **Medal Count (USA)**[21] 1464 3-9-0 0.............................. RAlbarado 14 106
(Dale Romans, U.S.A) **26/1**
**9** 1/2 **Chitu (USA)**[40] 3-9-0 0..............................(b) MartinAGarcia 13 105
(Bob Baffert, U.S.A) **26/1**
**10** *nk* **We Miss Artie (CAN)**[42] 3-9-0 0.............................. JJCastellano 8 104
(Todd Pletcher, U.S.A) **28/1**
**11** *hd* **General A Rod (USA)**[35] 1188 3-9-0 0..............................(b) JRosario 9 104
(Michael J Maker, U.S.A) **31/1**
**12** 3/4 **Intense Holiday (USA)**[35] 1189 3-9-0 0.............................. JRVelazquez 16 102
(Todd Pletcher, U.S.A) **141/10**
**13** 2 3/4 **Candy Boy (USA)**[28] 1330 3-9-0 0.............................. GaryStevens 18 97
(John W Sadler, U.S.A) **94/10**
**14** 4 1/4 **Uncle Sigh (USA)**[28] 1326 3-9-0 0..............................(b[1]) IOrtizJr 4 88
(Gary Contessa, U.S.A) **31/1**
**15** 1 1/4 **Tapiture (USA)**[20] 3-9-0 0.............................. RSantanaJr 15 86
(Steven Asmussen, U.S.A) **35/1**
**16** 6 1/4 **Harry's Holiday (USA)**[21] 1464 3-9-0 0..............................(b) CLanerie 3 73
(Michael J Maker, U.S.A) **44/1**
**17** 5 1/2 **Vinceremos (USA)**[21] 1464 3-9-0 0..............................(b) JRoccoJr 10 62
(Todd Pletcher, U.S.A) **50/1**
**18** *nk* **Wildcat Red (USA)**[35] 1188 3-9-0 0.............................. LSaez 11 62
(Jose Garoffalo, U.S.A) **186/10**
**19** 10 **Vicar's In Trouble (USA)**[35] 1189 3-9-0 0..............(b) RosieNapravnik 2 42
(Michael J Maker, U.S.A) **204/10**
2m 3.66s (2.47) **19** Ran SP% **121.9**
PARI-MUTUEL (all including 2 usd stake): WIN 7.00; PLACE (1-2) 5.60, 31.80; SHOW (1-2-3): 4.20, 15.40, 6.00; SF 340.00.
**Owner** Steven Coburn & Perry Martin **Bred** Perry Martin & Steve Coburn **Trained** USA

**FOCUS**
The final time was noticeably slow (winning Beyer of just 97 is reportedly the lowest for any Derby or Preakness winner since Andrew Beyer has been making figures), but it was a gusty day and perhaps the wind was a contributing factor. It looked a reasonable enough running of the Derby - the 140th - with the hot favourite followed home by some promising sorts.

# 1907 SAINT-CLOUD (L-H)
Saturday, May 3
**OFFICIAL GOING: Turf: soft**

## 1965a PRIX GREFFULHE (GROUP 2) (3YO COLTS & FILLIES) (TURF) 1m 2f
**6:15** (12:00) 3-Y-O **£61,750** (£23,833; £11,375; £7,583; £3,791)

RPR
**1** **Prince Gibraltar (FR)**[175] 7828 3-9-2 0.............. ChristopheSoumillon 1 113+
(J-C Rouget, France) *dwlt sltly and hld up in tch in last: gng best whn taken across to r alone against nr side rail over 1f out: rdn and r.o strly ins fnl f: led towards fin and qcknd clr w rdr easing down: impressive* **17/10**[2]
**2** 2 **Earnshaw (USA)**[30] 1272 3-9-2 0.............................. MaximeGuyon 5 108+
(A Fabre, France) *t.k.h early: trckd ldrs: rdn 2f out: edgd rt and nt qckn u.p: styd on and wnt 2nd post: no match for wnr* **31/10**[3]
**3** *nse* **Nolohay (IRE)**[31] 3-9-2 0.............................. OlivierPeslier 4 108
(C Laffon-Parias, France) *led: pushed along into st: rdn ent fnl f: styd on but hdd towards fin and readily outpcd by wnr: jst prevailed for 3rd post* **6/5**[1]
**4** *shd* **Golden Guepard (IRE)**[34] 1205 3-9-2 0............ Pierre-CharlesBoudot 3 108
(A Fabre, France) *pressed ldr on inner: pushed along 2f out: rdn ent fnl f: styd on and ev ch tl wnr qcknd by towards fin: jst lost out for 3rd post* **138/10**
**5** *nk* **Norse Prize (FR)**[34] 1205 3-9-2 0.............................. AlexisBadel 2 107
(Mme M Bollack-Badel, France) *in tch on inner: rdn 2f out: ev ch ent fnl f: styd on but nt pce of wnr towards fin and hld: dropped to last fnl strides* **119/10**
2m 13.56s (-2.44) **5** Ran SP% **121.4**
WIN (incl. 1 euro stake): 2.70. PLACES: 1.90, 2.20. SF: 9.40.
**Owner** Jean-Francois Gribomont **Bred** Jean-Francois Gribomont **Trained** Pau, France

# HAMILTON (R-H)
Sunday, May 4
**OFFICIAL GOING: Good to soft (soft in places; 7.3)**
All races over 1m and beyond increased in distance by 25yds due to rail realignment around the loop.
Wind: Light, half behind Weather: Overcast

## 1966 BEST ODDS GUARANTEED AT TOTEPOOL.COM H'CAP 5f 4y
**1:55** (1:55) (Class 5) (0-70,70) 4-Y-0+ **£3,881** (£1,155; £577; £288) **Stalls** Centre

Form RPR
0-66 **1** **Economic Crisis (IRE)**[7] 1758 5-8-13 **62**.............................. JamesSullivan 2 73
(Alan Berry) *taken early to post: cl up on outside: hdwy to ld 1f out: sn rdn: hld on wl towards fin* **8/1**[3]
13-0 **2** *hd* **Manatee Bay**[20] 1487 4-8-8 **57**.............................. JoeFanning 3 68
(David Nicholls) *dwlt: in tch: effrt and rdn over 1f out: styd on wl fnl f: jst hld* **5/2**[1]
0-06 **3** *hd* **Lothair (IRE)**[8] 1710 5-9-4 **67**.............................. BenCurtis 6 77
(Alan Swinbank) *led: rdn and hdd 1f out: rallied: hld towards fin* **5/2**[1]
0003 **4** 6 **Amenable (IRE)**[9] 1689 7-9-2 **68**..............(p) MichaelJMMurphy(3) 7 56
(Ann Stokell) *taken early to post: in tch: rdn over 2f out: edgd rt: no imp fr over 1f out* **9/2**[2]
10-0 **5** 1 1/4 **Chloe's Dream (IRE)**[7] 1759 4-8-10 **64**..............(p) GarryWhillans(5) 5 48
(Ian Semple) *chsd ldrs tl rdn and wknd over 1f out* **16/1**
000- **6** 2 **The Nifty Fox**[187] 7593 10-9-7 **70**..............................(p) PhillipMakin 8 47
(Tim Easterby) *hld up: pushed along wl over 1f out: sn n.d* **12/1**
00-6 **7** 6 **Findog**[16] 1566 4-9-1 **64**.............................. PaulMulrennan 4 19
(Linda Perratt) *t.k.h: cl up tl rdn and wknd wl over 1f out* **8/1**[3]
1m 1.18s (1.18) **Going Correction** +0.325s/f (Good) **7** Ran SP% **111.1**
Speed ratings (Par 103): **103,102,102,92,90 87,77**
CSF £26.73 CT £62.29 TOTE £12.90: £5.00, £3.20; EX 256.50.
**Owner** Mr & Mrs T Blane **Bred** Philip Hore Jnr **Trained** Cockerham, Lancs
**FOCUS**
The ground was on the soft side of good. Due to rail alignment on the loop races beyond a mile were run over 25yds further than the advertised distance. A weak sprint handicap and the first three finished well clear.

## 1967 BET TOTEEXACTA ON ALL RACES H'CAP 6f 5y
**2:30** (2:31) (Class 4) (0-80,80) 4-Y-0+ **£5,822** (£1,732; £865; £432) **Stalls** Centre

Form RPR
6-22 **1** **Khelman (IRE)**[8] 1710 4-9-0 **76**..............................(p) GeorgeChaloner(3) 9 84
(Richard Fahey) *midfield: drvn along thrght: hdwy u.p over 1f out: styd on wl to ld last stride* **11/4**[2]
346- **2** *shd* **Rasaman (IRE)**[181] 7731 10-9-5 **78**.............................. GrahamLee 7 86
(Jim Goldie) *prom: hdwy over 1f out: rdn to ld wl ins fnl f: hdd last stride* **20/1**
-100 **3** 1 **Klynch**[17] 1538 8-9-5 **78**..............................(b) JamesSullivan 8 83
(Ruth Carr) *led at decent gallop: 3 l clr over 1f out: sn rdn: hdd and no ex wl ins fnl f* **8/1**
00-4 **4** *hd* **Sunraider (IRE)**[25] 1375 7-9-2 **75**.............................. PaulMulrennan 6 79
(Paul Midgley) *hld up: rdn and hdwy over 1f out: kpt on wl fnl f: nrst fin* **10/1**
4-00 **5** 1 1/2 **Alexandrakollontai (IRE)**[16] 1566 4-8-5 **67**..............(b) JulieBurke(3) 4 66
(Alistair Whillans) *towards rr: rdn and hdwy 2f out: no imp ins fnl f* **20/1**
50-6 **6** 4 1/2 **Bonnie Charlie**[17] 1538 8-9-1 **74**.............................. PaulQuinn 5 59
(David Nicholls) *hld up: rdn over 2f out: hdwy over 1f out: kpt on fnl f: nvr able to chal* **28/1**
5-60 **7** 8 **Lady Ibrox**[16] 1565 4-9-7 **80**.............................. DaleSwift 2 39
(Alan Brown) *prom: drvn 1/2-way: wknd wl over 1f out* **28/1**
241- **8** 1 3/4 **Feel The Heat**[244] 6052 7-8-13 **72**..............................(v) RoystonFfrench 11 26
(Bryan Smart) *in tch: drvn along over 2f out: wknd wl over 1f out* **20/1**
21-2 **9** 9 **Be Lucky**[13] 1604 4-9-2 **75**.............................. GrahamGibbons 10
(Michael Easterby) *prom: drvn along 1/2-way: wknd 2f out* **6/1**[3]

120- **10** *13* **Shady McCoy (USA)**[226] 6586 4-9-7 **80**...................... RobertWinston 1
(David Barron) *dwlt: sn in tch: rdn over 2f out: sn lost pl: eased whn no ch over 1f out* **5/2**[1]

-504 **11** *3* **Bapak Chinta (USA)**[23] 1429 5-9-4 **77**........................... PhillipMakin 3
(Kevin Ryan) *slowly away: bhd and outpcd: shortlived effrt 1/2-way: hung rt and sn wknd* **20/1**

1m 13.52s (1.32) **Going Correction** +0.325s/f (Good) **11** Ran SP% **115.7**
Speed ratings (Par 105): **104,103,102,102,100 94,83,81,69,51 47**
CSF £61.92 CT £388.48 TOTE £5.80: £3.00, £4.20, £4.00; EX 303.70.
**Owner** S & G Clayton **Bred** Ogill House Stud & Jimmy Hyland **Trained** Musley Bank, N Yorks

**FOCUS**
A decent sprint handicap and the first five finished clear.

## 1968 EBF STALLIONS TANGERINE TREES CONDITIONS STKS (BOBIS RACE) 5f 4y
**3:00** (3:01) (Class 2) 3-Y-O **£16,172** (£4,812; £2,405; £1,202) **Stalls** Centre

Form RPR

24-1 **1** **Mecca's Angel (IRE)**[22] 1445 3-8-9 105..................... PaulMulrennan 1 107+
(Michael Dods) *chsd ldrs: shkn up and hdwy to ld wl over 1f out: qcknd clr: impressive* **10/11**[1]

06-1 **2** *8* **Eccleston**[9] 1700 3-9-0 96.............................................. SamJames 4 83
(David O'Meara) *in tch: pushed along over 2f out: hdwy to chse (clr) wnr ins fnl f: no imp* **2/1**[2]

4-03 **3** *1 1/4* **Meadway**[8] 1737 3-9-0 84........................................ GrahamLee 7 79
(Bryan Smart) *cl up: led after 2f: rdn and hdd wl over 1f out: sn one pce* **18/1**

2100 **4** *3/4* **Oriental Relation (IRE)**[16] 1555 3-9-0 87..................(b) JamesSullivan 5 76
(James Given) *cl up: drvn and hung rt 2f out: sn btn* **25/1**

011- **5** *nk* **Sandra's Diamond (IRE)**[197] 7370 3-8-9 79..................... TomEaves 2 70
(Keith Dalgleish) *led 2f: cl up: rdn and edgd rt 2f out: sn wknd* **20/1**

021- **6** *9* **Viva Verglas (IRE)**[190] 7545 3-9-3 96.........................(b) GrahamGibbons 6 46
(David Barron) *dwlt: hld up: rdn and hung rt over 2f out: sn btn* **9/1**[3]

1m 0.05s (0.05) **Going Correction** +0.325s/f (Good) **6** Ran SP% **109.6**
Speed ratings (Par 105): **112,99,97,96,95 81**
CSF £2.71 TOTE £2.20: £3.10, £2.20; EX 2.00.
**Owner** David T J Metcalfe **Bred** Yeomanstown Stud & Doc Bloodstock **Trained** Denton, Co Durham

**FOCUS**
A valuable 5f 3yo conditions event and a highly impressive winner. It's unlikely the form can be taken at face value.

## 1969 SODEXO OPEN MAIDEN STKS 1m 65y
**3:35** (3:37) (Class 5) 3-5-Y-O **£3,881** (£1,155; £577; £288) **Stalls** Low

Form RPR

5 **1** **Ayrad (IRE)**[18] 1517 3-9-1 0.............................................. GrahamLee 2 84+
(Roger Varian) *trcked lders: shaken up and hdwy to ld wl over 1f out: soon clr: easily* **2/5**[1]

3 **2** *4* **Molly Cat**[14] 1600 4-9-9 0.............................................. BenCurtis 3 71
(Alan Swinbank) *led after 1f, set ordinary gallop, rdn and hdd over 1f out, kpt on same pce fnl f* **6/1**[3]

**3** *8* **Another Lincolnday** 3-9-1 0.......................................... PhillipMakin 8 55
(David Barron) *s.i.s, held up, shkn up and hdwy over 3f out, chased clear ldng pair over 1f out, no imp* **20/1**

**4** *7* **Knight Of Glin** 3-9-1 0.............................................. GrahamGibbons 1 39
(David Barron) *hld up, stdy hdwy 4f out, rdn over 2f out, sn no imp* **12/1**

00-6 **5** *2 3/4* **Samoan (IRE)**[39] 1112 5-9-11 46...............................(b) SladeO'Hara(3) 5 35
(Alan Berry) *dwlt: sn prom: drvn and outpcd wl over 2f out: sn btn* **50/1**

2403 **6** *3* **Tarrafal (IRE)**[10] 1662 3-9-1 70.......................................... JoeFanning 4 25
(Mark Johnston) *pressed lder, drvn over 3f out, wknd wl over 1f out* **5/1**[2]

4 **7** *3/4* **Silver Craftsman (IRE)**[13] 1608 3-8-12 0.......... MichaelJMMurphy(3) 9 24
(Alan Swinbank) *bhd and sn pushed along: struggling over 3f out: never on terms* **14/1**

4- **8** *13* **Mystical King**[223] 6684 4-10-0 0.......................................... TomEaves 7
(Linda Perratt) *reluctant to enter stalls: towards rear: struggling over 4f out: sn beaten* **33/1**

1m 50.33s (1.93) **Going Correction** +0.45s/f (Yiel)
**WFA** 3 from 4yo+ 13lb **8** Ran SP% **126.4**
Speed ratings (Par 103): **108,104,96,89,86 83,82,69**
CSF £4.23 TOTE £2.30: £1.30, £1.10, £3.70; EX 3.70.
**Owner** Saleh Al Homaizi & Imad Al Sagar **Bred** Gerrardstown House Stud **Trained** Newmarket, Suffolk

**FOCUS**
A one-sided maiden with only the first two seriously involved in the latter stages.

## 1970 GINGER GROUSE H'CAP 1m 65y
**4:10** (4:11) (Class 5) (0-75,72) 4-Y-O+ **£4,528** (£1,347; £673; £336) **Stalls** Low

Form RPR

-540 **1** **Ted's Brother (IRE)**[13] 1610 6-9-0 68...................(e) ConnorBeasley(3) 3 79
(Richard Guest) *chsd clr ldng pair: hdwy to ld over 2f out: rdn and r.o wl fr over 1f out* **13/2**[2]

00-0 **2** *2* **Another For Joe**[14] 1598 6-8-13 64........................................ GrahamLee 4 70
(Jim Goldie) *prom, effrt and rdn over 2f out, chsd wnr ins fnl f, r.o* **12/1**

0-30 **3** *hd* **I'm Super Too (IRE)**[10] 1675 7-9-0 65................................ BenCurtis 7 71
(Alan Swinbank) *hld up: pushed along over 2f out: hdwy over 1f out: kpt on fnl f: nvr able to chal* **12/1**

2-46 **4** *shd* **Lord Franklin**[14] 1598 5-9-0 68........................................ JasonHart(3) 2 74
(Eric Alston) *led: rdn and edgd rt over 2f out: hdd over 1f out: kpt on same pce ins fnl f* **3/1**[1]

040- **5** *3/4* **Never Forever**[211] 7028 5-9-1 71...................................... GarryWhillans(5) 8 75
(Jim Goldie) *hld up: pushed along over 3f out: styd on fr 2f out: nrst fin* **16/1**

0323 **6** *3/4* **Kyllachy Star**[8] 1718 8-9-3 68.........................................(v) DavidNolan 12 70
(Richard Fahey) *midfield: drvn over 3f out: effrt over 1f out: no imp fnl f* **7/1**[3]

3-0 **7** *1/2* **Henpecked**[36] 1167 4-8-7 58 oh1...................................... PJMcDonald 10 59
(Alistair Whillans) *towards rr: rdn and outpcd over 4f out: rallied over 1f out: styd on: nvr able to chal* **12/1**

641- **8** *1 1/2* **Rioja Day (IRE)**[195] 7429 4-9-1 66.................................... GaryBartley 1 64
(Jim Goldie) *pressed ldr: rdn over 3f out: wknd over 1f out* **8/1**

622/ **9** *3 1/4* **Saved By The Bell (IRE)**[181] 4-9-1 69............................ SamJames(3) 6 59
(David O'Meara) *in tch: pushed along and outpcd over 2f out: sn btn* **13/2**[2]

4-00 **10** *6* **Staffhoss**[13] 1607 4-9-0 72.............................................. PaulaMuir(7) 9 48
(Mark Johnston) *bhd and sn pushed along: no imp fr 1/2-way* **33/1**

425- **11** *2 1/4* **Vittachi**[142] 8270 7-8-1 59.............................................. RowanScott(7) 13 30
(Alistair Whillans) *bhd and sn outpcd: nvr on terms* **25/1**

220- **12** *4* **Tectonic (IRE)**[206] 7152 5-9-5 70........................................(p) TomEaves 5 32
(Keith Dalgleish) *in tch: shkn up and edgd rt over 2f out: sn struggling* **9/1**

1m 50.51s (2.11) **Going Correction** +0.45s/f (Yiel) **12** Ran SP% **121.0**
Speed ratings (Par 103): **107,105,104,104,103 103,102,101,97,91 89,85**
CSF £83.98 CT £927.92 TOTE £9.00: £1.70, £2.40, £3.20; EX 90.80 Trifecta £28.40.
**Owner** Ontoawinner & Guest **Bred** T Counihan **Trained** Wetherby, W Yorks

**FOCUS**
A field of infrequent winners. The pace looked sound yet the first two raced prominently throughout.

## 1971 TOTEPOOL BUTTONHOOK H'CAP 1m 5f 9y
**4:45** (4:45) (Class 3) (0-95,92) 4-Y-O+ **£16,172** (£4,812; £2,405; £1,202) **Stalls** Low

Form RPR

0-52 **1** **Sirvino**[16] 1562 9-9-7 92.............................................. PhillipMakin 6 100
(David Barron) *hld up in tch: smooth hdwy over 2f out: led over 1f out: sn rdn: kpt on strly* **7/2**[2]

00-0 **2** *3* **O Ma Lad (IRE)**[22] 1444 6-8-9 83...................................... IanBrennan(3) 2 86
(John Quinn) *hld up bhd ldng gp: pushed along over 3f out: rallied to chse wnr over 1f out: kpt on: no imp* **9/4**[1]

00-2 **3** *1/2* **Categorical**[16] 1567 11-8-2 73...................................... JamesSullivan 7 75
(Keith Reveley) *hld up: pushed along and outpcd 4f out: rallied over 1f out: kpt on fnl f: nvr able to chal* **14/1**

02-3 **4** *1 1/4* **Pixie Cut (IRE)**[25] 1377 4-7-13 73 oh3.............................. JulieBurke(3) 5 73
(Alistair Whillans) *trckd ldr: rdn and outpcd 3f out: kpt on ins fnl f: no imp* **9/1**

00-1 **5** *1 3/4* **Jonny Delta**[16] 1562 7-8-11 82........................................ GrahamLee 3 80
(Jim Goldie) *hmpd s: sn prom: effrt and rdn over 2f out: edgd rt and wknd over 1f out* **7/2**[2]

05-0 **6** *4* **Linguine (FR)**[22] 1444 4-9-3 88.................................... PaulMulrennan 1 80
(Paul Midgley) *t.k.h: led: rdn over 2f out: hdd over 1f out: sn btn* **8/1**[3]

2640 **7** *16* **Aryal**[11] 1651 4-8-9 80.........................................................(b) JoeFanning 4 48
(Mark Johnston) *chsd ldrs: drvn and hung rt over 2f out: sn wknd: t.o* **8/1**[3]

2m 57.07s (3.17) **Going Correction** +0.45s/f (Yiel) **7** Ran SP% **114.1**
Speed ratings (Par 107): **108,106,105,105,104 101,91**
CSF £11.77 TOTE £4.40: £3.20, £1.70; EX 19.30.
**Owner** Theo Williams and Charles Mocatta **Bred** Allan W J Perry **Trained** Maunby, N Yorks

**FOCUS**
Not a strong handicap for a race carrying £25,000 prize-money. The pace was just steady until the final half-mile.

## 1972 CHRIS & JENNIFER FORTHCOMING WEDDING H'CAP 5f 4y
**5:20** (5:21) (Class 6) (0-60,58) 4-Y-O+ **£3,408** (£1,006; £503) **Stalls** Centre

Form RPR

456 **1** **Busy Bimbo (IRE)**[4] 1887 5-8-8 45..............................(b) PatrickMathers 3 53
(Alan Berry) *hld up: hdwy on far side over 1f out: rdn and led ins fnl f: kpt on strly* **40/1**

04-0 **2** *3/4* **Classy Anne**[7] 1758 4-8-5 45........................................ IanBrennan(3) 9 50
(Jim Goldie) *hld up: rdn and hdwy over 1f out: styd on to go 2nd towards fin: nt rch wnr* **10/1**

6162 **3** *1/2* **Roy's Legacy**[14] 1602 5-9-4 58.............................. MichaelJMMurphy(3) 6 62
(Shaun Harris) *n.m.r s: sn prom: rdn and ch 1f out: kpt on ins fnl f: hld towards fin* **5/1**[3]

045 **4** *3/4* **Captain Scooby**[30] 1282 8-8-9 49............................ ConnorBeasley(3) 10 50
(Richard Guest) *in tch: rdn and outpcd wl over 1f out: edgd rt and rallied fnl f: no imp* **9/4**[1]

-551 **5** *3/4* **Spring Bird**[4] 1887 5-8-10 54 6ex.................................... AnnaHesketh(7) 1 52
(David Nicholls) *in tch on outside: hdwy to ld over 1f out: edgd lft: hdd ins fnl f: sn outpcd* **11/4**[2]

00-0 **6** *1* **Pavers Star**[14] 1602 5-9-0 51..........................................(p) GrahamLee 11 46
(Noel Wilson) *racd jst away fr main gp towards stands' rail: spd to over 1f out: sn no ex* **22/1**

00-0 **7** *1 1/4* **Ichimoku**[122] 12 4-8-9 46..........................................(t) RoystonFfrench 8 36
(Bryan Smart) *mde most tl rdn and hdd over 1f out: wknd ins fnl f* **16/1**

01-0 **8** *1/2* **Tadalavil**[14] 1602 9-9-5 56.............................................. PhillipMakin 5 44
(Linda Perratt) *hld up bhd ldng gp: rdn over 2f out: sme late hdwy: nvr able to chal* **20/1**

0004 **9** *2 1/2* **Two Turtle Doves (IRE)**[25] 1378 8-8-13 55.......... ShirleyTeasdale(5) 4 34
(Michael Mullineaux) *prom tl rdn and wknd over 1f out* **8/1**

0005 **10** *2 1/4* **Amis Reunis**[19] 1497 5-8-1 45..................................(p) JordanHibberd(7) 2 16
(Alan Berry) *prom: drvn over 2f out: wknd over 1f out* **33/1**

554- **11** *1 1/2* **Rock Canyon (IRE)**[206] 7149 5-8-11 48................................ PJMcDonald 7 14
(Linda Perratt) *chsd ldrs: drvn along over 2f out: sn lost pl* **14/1**

1m 1.35s (1.35) **Going Correction** +0.325s/f (Good) **11** Ran SP% **121.3**
Speed ratings (Par 101): **102,100,100,98,97 96,94,93,89,85 83**
CSF £395.38 CT £2409.87 TOTE £25.00: £6.50, £1.80, £2.50; EX 396.00.
**Owner** Alan Berry **Bred** Tally-Ho Stud **Trained** Cockerham, Lancs
■ Stewards' Enquiry : Anna Hesketh two-day ban: careless riding (May 18-19)

**FOCUS**
A rock-bottom sprint handicap and a surprise winner to say the very least.
T/Plt: £98.60 to a £1 stake. Pool: £3866.75 - 28.60 wiing units. T/Qpdt: £49.20 to a £1 stake. Pool: £133.00 - 2.00 winning units. RY

# 1948 NEWMARKET (R-H)
Sunday, May 4

**OFFICIAL GOING: Good to firm (good in places) changing to good to firm after race 2 (2.40)**
Stands side track used.
Wind: medium, across Weather: dry and bright

## 1973 QIPCO SUPPORTING BRITISH RACING STKS (H'CAP) 1m 4f
**2:05** (2:05) (Class 2) (0-105,99) 4-Y-O+
**£28,012** (£8,388; £4,194; £2,097; £1,048; £526) **Stalls** Centre

Form RPR

/1-0 **1** **Mighty Yar (IRE)**[25] 1398 4-9-0 89.................................. RyanMoore 14 101+
(Lady Cecil) *lw: in tch in midfield: clsd to chse ldrs and nt clr run ent fnl f: swtchd lft jst ins fnl f: str run u.p fnl 150yds to ld towards fin* **5/1**[1]

14- **2** *1/2* **Miss Marjurie (IRE)**[211] 7022 4-8-6 81................................ LukeMorris 1 92
(Denis Coakley) *chsd ldrs: rdn and pressed ldng pair over 1f out: drvn to ld ins fnl f: kpt on wl tl hdd and no ex towards fin* **33/1**

210- **3** *2* **Amralah (IRE)**[204] 7196 4-9-3 92.................................... WilliamBuick 6 100
(Mick Channon) *chsd ldrs: rdn and ev ch wl over 1f out: led 1f out: sn hdd: no ex and outpcd fnl 100yds* **5/1**[1]

0-10 **4** *nk* **Salutation (IRE)**[11] 1653 4-9-6 **95**........................ SilvestreDeSousa 4 102
(Mark Johnston) *chsd ldr: rdn to ld over 2f out: drvn and hrd pressed over 1f out: hdd 1f out: no ex and outpcd fnl 100yds* **16/1**

55-1 **5** *½* **Lord Van Percy**[43] 1071 4-8-12 **90**........................ OisinMurphy(3) 7 97+
(Andrew Balding) *stdd s: hld up in tch in rr: effrt 2f out: rdn and hdwy over 1f out: chsd ldrs ins fnl f: kpt on* **13/2**[2]

252- **6** *3¼* **Cafe Society (FR)**[200] 7304 4-9-1 **90**........................ JamieSpencer 8 91
(David Simcock) *lw: stdd s: hld up in rr: pushed along 2f out: nt clr run wl over 1f out: hdwy ent fnl f: kpt on but no ch w ldrs* **5/1**[1]

126- **7** *nk* **Urban Dance (IRE)**[179] 7768 4-9-10 **99**........................ MickaelBarzalona 13 100
(Charlie Appleby) *t.k.h: hld up towards rr: hdwy into midfield 7f out: rdn and unable qck over 1f out: wknd fins inal f* **10/1**

4-45 **8** *½* **Bancnuanaheireann (IRE)**[16] 1559 7-9-9 **98**........................ TomQueally 5 98
(Michael Appleby) *hld up in tch in midfield: effrt u.p 2f out: drvn and no prog over 1f out: plugged on same pce fnl f* **20/1**

120- **9** *1* **Elhaame (IRE)**[205] 7174 4-9-7 **96**........................ AndreaAtzeni 11 94
(Luca Cumani) *lw: t.k.h early: wl in tch in midfield: rdn wl over 2f out: outpcd and btn 1f out: wknd ins fnl f* **8/1**[3]

3-30 **10** *3¾* **Centurius**[26] 1360 4-9-4 **93**........................(p) AdamKirby 9 85
(Marco Botti) *hld up in tch in last quartet: rdn and effrt jst over 2f out: no real hdwy: wknd 1f out* **16/1**

500- **11** *18* **Ray Ward (IRE)**[243] 6066 4-9-6 **95**........................ JamesDoyle 12 59
(David Simcock) *chsd ldrs: rdn 3f out: wknd u.p over 1f out: bhd and eased ins fnl f: t.o* **25/1**

412- **12** *8* **Asbaab (USA)**[241] 6144 4-9-7 **96**........................ PaulHanagan 10 47
(Brian Meehan) *led until over 2f out: sn rdn and no ex: btn over 1f out: eased ins fnl f: t.o* **20/1**

-521 **13** *11* **Viewpoint (IRE)**[16] 1553 5-9-10 **99**........................ RichardHughes 3 32
(Richard Hannon) *wl in tch in midfield:rdn and no hdwy over 2f out: wknd over 1f out: bhd and eased ins fnl f: t.o* **12/1**

000- **14** *42* **Buckland (IRE)**[280] 4796 6-9-6 **95**........................ FrederikTylicki 2
(Charlie Fellowes) *midfield tl dropped to rr 4f out: lost tch over 2f out: t.o and virtually p.u fr over 1f out* **66/1**

2m 31.23s (-0.77) **Going Correction** +0.075s/f (Good) **14** Ran SP% **120.8**
Speed ratings (Par 109): **105,104,103,103,102 100,100,100,99,96 84,79,72,44**
CSF £188.48 CT £880.56 TOTE £5.80: £3.00, £8.30, £2.70; EX 564.80.
**Owner** R A H Evans **Bred** Gerry Flannery Developments **Trained** Newmarket, Suffolk

**FOCUS**
This decent middle-distance handicap was run at a modest early tempo and steadied after half a mile until lifting seriously again at the eight-furlong marker. Solid form despite the surprise runner-up. Afterwards the jockeys were very much of the opinion that the ground had dried out since the previous day and was on the quick side.

## 1974 QATAR BLOODSTOCK DAHLIA STKS (GROUP 3) (F&M) 1m 1f
**2:40** (2:40) (Class 1) 4-Y-O+

**£36,861** (£13,975; £6,994; £3,484; £1,748; £877) **Stalls** Centre

Form RPR

20-4 **1** **Esoterique (IRE)**[26] 1371 4-9-0 109........................ MaximeGuyon 8 114
(A Fabre, France) *str: lw: trckd ldrs: upsides ldrs and stl on bit over 1f out: rdn and qckned to ld ent fnl f:edgd rt and r.o strly fnl f: a jst holding runner-up* **9/4**[2]

012- **2** *hd* **Integral**[218] 6837 4-9-0 115........................ RyanMoore 1 113
(Sir Michael Stoute) *stdd s: t.k.h: hld up in last pair:hdwy 1/2-way: rdn to press ldrs over 1f out: chal 1f out: drew clr w wnr and sustained duel fnl f: r.o wl:a jst hld* **7/4**[1]

225- **3** *3¼* **Gifted Girl (IRE)**[210] 7057 5-9-0 110........................ TomQueally 4 106
(Paul Cole) *lw: wl in tch in midfield: rdn and effrt over 2f out: drvn and ev ch over 1f out: sn outpcd by ldng pair: kpt on to hold 3rd ins fnl f* **7/1**[3]

01- **4** *nk* **Quaduna**[28] 4-9-3 104........................ WilliamBuick 7 108
(A Wohler, Germany) *w'like: led and set stdy : rdn and qcknd 3f out: drvn and hrd pressed over 1f out: hdd ent fnl f: sn outpcd by ldng pair: battling for 3rd fnl f: kpt on* **20/1**

34-2 **5** *2¼* **Odeliz (IRE)**[42] 1076 4-9-0 102........................ DanielTudhope 3 100
(K R Burke) *stdd s: t.k.h: hld up in rr: outpcd and rdn over 2f out: no ch but kpt on again ins fnl f* **15/2**

/30- **6** *nk* **Madame Defarge (IRE)**[338] 2842 4-9-0 90........................ FrankieDettori 6 100
(Michael Bell) *hld up in tch in last trio: outpcd u.p over 2f out: no theat to ldrs whn flashed tail u.p over 1f out* **20/1**

61-1 **7** *3½* **Zurigha (IRE)**[15] 1577 4-9-0 109........................ RichardHughes 5 92
(Richard Hannon) *t.k.h: chsd ldr tl 2f out: sn pushed along and btn on downhill run over 1f out: nt given and hrd time after and wknd ent fnl f: eased towards fin* **15/2**

1m 50.41s (-1.29) **Going Correction** +0.075s/f (Good) **7** Ran SP% **112.7**
Speed ratings (Par 113): **108,107,104,104,102 102,99**
CSF £6.38 TOTE £4.40: £2.90, £2.40; EX 9.60 Trifecta £37.80.
**Owner** Baron Edouard De Rothschild **Bred** Societe Civile De L'Ecurie De Meautry **Trained** Chantilly, France

**FOCUS**
Sectionals recorded that the gallop gradually cranked up throughout the race, with the quickest furlong being the second-last. Sir Michael Stoute has made a habit of winning this, sending out five of the previous seven winners, and he was represented by the highest rated runner in the field this time in Integral. A good renewal run at a steady early pace. Esoterique is rated back to her French Guineas level.

## 1975 HAVANA GOLD AT TWEENHILLS H'CAP 6f
**3:10** (3:10) (Class 2) 4-Y-O+

**£28,012** (£8,388; £4,194; £2,097; £1,048; £526) **Stalls** Centre

Form RPR

600- **1** **Goldream**[185] 7642 5-8-10 **90**........................(p) AndreaAtzeni 10 101
(Robert Cowell) *lw: racd centre to stands' side: inin tch in midfield: rdn and effrt to chal whn edgd lft over 1f out: led 1f out: kpt on wl: rdn out* **25/1**

-003 **2** *½* **Yeeoow (IRE)**[20] 1484 5-8-5 **90**........................ JoeyHaynes(5) 4 99
(K R Burke) *racd centre to far side: in tch in midfield overall: rdn and hdwy over 1f out: chsd wnr ins final furlong: r.o wl* **10/1**[3]

500- **3** *nk* **Ninjago**[212] 6990 4-9-7 **101**........................ RichardHughes 3 109
(Richard Hannon) *racd centre to far side: hld up in rr: swtchd lft and hdwy over 1f out: r.o wl ins fnl f: nt quite rch ldrs* **7/1**[1]

1251 **4** *½* **Alben Star (IRE)**[16] 1557 6-9-9 **103**........................ PaulHanagan 21 109+
(Richard Fahey) *racd centre to stands' side: hld up midfield: nt clr run and shuffled bk towards rr wl over 1f out: hdwy between horses ins fnl f: r.o strly: nt quite rch ldrs* **12/1**

0-56 **5** *nse* **Hadaj**[18] 1506 5-8-3 **83**........................ SilvestreDeSousa 6 89
(Ruth Carr) *racd centre to far side: chsd ldrs and proninent overall: rdn ent fnl 2f: kpt on but unable qck fnl 100yds* **12/1**

200- **6** *½* **Secretinthepark**[212] 6990 4-9-0 **94**........................ SteveDrowne 17 99
(Ed McMahon) *lw: racd centre to stands' side: in tch in midfield: short of room and hmpd over 1f out: sn swtchd rt: hdwy jst ins fnl f: styd on wl: nt rch ldrs* **12/1**

161- **7** *2* **Ashpan Sam**[203] 7222 5-9-3 **97**........................ RyanMoore 16 95
(John Spearing) *lw: racd centre to stands' side: pressed ldrs: rdn and ev ch 2f out: led over 1f out tl 1f out: wknd ins fnl f* **14/1**

2150 **8** *½* **Go Far**[8] 1742 4-7-11 **82** ow2........................(b) TimClark(5) 8 79
(Alan Bailey) *racd centre to far side: led gp and chsd ldrs overall: pressing overall ldr and rdn over 1f out: hung rt and wknd ins fnl f* **50/1**

132- **9** *hd* **Seeking Magic**[204] 7208 6-9-0 **99**........................(t) RyanTate(5) 18 95
(Clive Cox) *racd centre to stands' side: t.k.h: hld up in tch in midfield: effrt whn n.m.r on rail over 1f out: kpt on but no threat to ldrs fnl f* **9/1**[2]

0-01 **10** *hd* **Kimberella**[17] 1538 4-8-10 **90**........................ AdrianNicholls 12 85
(David Nicholls) *racd centre to stands' side: w overall ldr tl led 3f out: rdn and hdd over 1f out: short of room and hmpd ent fnl f: wknd fnl 100yds* **12/1**

305- **11** *½* **Out Do**[274] 4983 5-8-11 **91**........................ DanielTudhope 11 85
(David O'Meara) *racd centre to stands' side, in tch in midfield, effort 2f out, chased ldrs and edgd lft u.p over 1f out, wknd ins fnl f* **10/1**[3]

102- **12** *2¾* **Secondo (FR)**[238] 6238 4-8-13 **93**........................ JamesDoyle 7 78
(Roger Charlton) *racd centre to far side, in rr, rdn halfway, sme prog under pressure 2f out, no hdwy and beaten 1f out, weakened ins fnl furlong* **10/1**[3]

055- **13** *shd* **Pearl Acclaim (IRE)**[264] 5375 4-9-1 **95**........................(p) JamieSpencer 15 80
(Robert Cowell) *racd centre to stands' side: overall ldr tl 3f out: styd prom: losing pl u.p whn hmpd and swtchd rt over 1f out: btn and eased fnl 75yds* **25/1**

4-42 **14** *nk* **Jimmy Styles**[23] 1421 10-9-10 **104**........................(p) AdamKirby 20 88
(Clive Cox) *rd centre to stands' side: towards rr: effort and swtchd rt wl over 1f out: plugged on but no threat to lders final furlong* **16/1**

0005 **15** *1¾* **Swiss Cross**[5] 1862 7-8-8 **88**........................(t) LukeMorris 5 66
(Phil McEntee) *racd centre to far side: chsd gp ldr and tch overall: rdn 1/2-way: btn over 1f out: wknd ins fnl f* **33/1**

000- **16** *1* **Zanetto**[169] 7928 4-9-5 **102**........................ OisinMurphy(3) 14 77
(Andrew Balding) *racd centre to stands' side: sn niggled along in midfield: drvn over 2f oput: no prog: wknd over 1f out* **10/1**[3]

100- **17** *nse* **Crew Cut (IRE)**[197] 7368 6-8-5 **85**........................ NickyMackay 9 60
(Stuart Williams) *racd centre to stands' side: a towards rr: drvn over 1f out: nvr trbld ldrs* **33/1**

400- **18** *1¼* **Tamayuz Star (IRE)**[212] 6990 4-9-2 **96**........................ TomQueally 2 67
(George Margarson) *swtg: racd centre to far side: a towards rr overall: rdn 1/2-way: no imp: bhd 1f out* **20/1**

3320 **19** *4* **Hannahs Turn**[16] 1554 4-7-9 **80** oh2........................ NoelGarbutt(5) 13 38
(Chris Dwyer) *taken down early: racd centre to stands' side:chsd ldrs: rdn ent fnl 2f: sn struggling: wknd over 1f out: bhd fnl f* **50/1**

010- **20** *10* **Zero Money (IRE)**[232] 6391 8-9-4 **98**........................(b) FrankieDettori 19 24
(Hugo Palmer) *racd centre to stands' side: chsd ldrs tl rdn and btn 2f out: sn wknd: bhd and eased ins fnl f* **33/1**

6120 **21** *10* **Baddilini**[36] 1172 4-8-10 **90**........................(p) KierenFallon 1
(Alan Bailey) *racd centre to far side: a rr: lost tch 2f out: eased fnl f: t.o* **33/1**

1m 11.12s (-1.08) **Going Correction** +0.075s/f (Good) **21** Ran SP% **130.3**
Speed ratings (Par 109): **110,109,108,108,108 107,104,104,103,103 103,99,99,98,96 95,95,93,88,74 61**
CSF £247.86 CT £2006.19 TOTE £40.80: £10.90, £3.80, £2.30, £3.30; EX 365.40.
**Owner** J Sargeant & Mrs J Morley **Bred** Tsega Breeding Limited **Trained** Six Mile Bottom, Cambs

**FOCUS**
This extremely competitive sprint handicap had a classy look about it. There was no hanging about and the field were spread across the track, but most shunned the far side. The winner is basically rated to his best.

## 1976 QIPCO 1000 GUINEAS STKS (THE 201ST RUNNING) (BRITISH CHAMPIONS SERIES) (GROUP 1) (FILLIES) 1m
**3:50** (3:52) (Class 1) 3-Y-O

**£246,617** (£93,498; £46,792; £23,309; £11,698; £5,870) **Stalls** Centre

Form RPR

1-6 **1** **Miss France (IRE)**[31] 1273 3-9-0 112........................ MaximeGuyon 4 111
(A Fabre, France) *chsd ldrs: rdn and effrt wl over 1f out: drvn to chal 1f out: led ins fnl f: kpt on: rdn out* **7/1**[3]

124- **2** *nk* **Lightning Thunder**[204] 7194 3-9-0 110........................ HarryBentley 14 110
(Olly Stevens) *lw: in tch in midfield: effrt and swed lft over 1f out: drvn and edgd lft ins fnl f: edging bk rt but str run to chse wnr towards fin: nvr quite getting to wnr* **14/1**

3-11 **3** *½* **Ihtimal (IRE)**[66] 771 3-9-0 114........................ SilvestreDeSousa 3 109
(Saeed bin Suroor) *wl in tch in midfield: rdn and effrt 2f out: drvn over 1f out: styd on and pressing wnr fnl 100yds: lost 2nd and no ex towards fin* **7/1**[3]

02-5 **4** *¾* **Manderley (IRE)**[22] 1435 3-9-0 98........................ PatDobbs 5 107?
(Richard Hannon) *led: rdn ent fnl 2f: hrd pressed and drvn ent fnl f: hdd ins fnl f: no ex and outpcd towards fin* **100/1**

1-12 **5** *1½* **Euro Charline**[18] 1515 3-9-0 101........................ AdamKirby 12 104
(Marco Botti) *chsd ldrs: clsd to chse wnr ent fnl 2f: drvn and ev ch wl over 1f out tl jst ins fnl f: weakend fnl 75yds* **14/1**

01-3 **6** *1¼* **Majeyda (USA)**[18] 1515 3-9-0 101........................ MickaelBarzalona 8 101
(Charlie Appleby) *chsd ldr tl ent fnl 2f: sn drvn: unable qck over 1f out: wknd ins fnl f* **33/1**

312- **7** *nk* **Rizeena (IRE)**[219] 6798 3-9-0 113........................ RichardHughes 7 100
(Clive Brittain) *hld up wl in tch in midfield: rdn and effrt 2f out: drvn and unable qck over 1f out: styd on same pce fnl f: nvr gng pce to chal* **9/2**[2]

10-2 **8** *shd* **Vorda (FR)**[31] 1273 3-9-0 114........................ Christophe-PatriceLemaire 19 100
(P Sogorb, France) *stdd s: hld up in tch towards rr: plenty to do and rdn over 1f out: kpt on steadily ins fnl f: nvr gng pce to rch ldrs* **14/1**

10-1 **9** *1* **Sandiva (IRE)**[18] 1515 3-9-0 109........................ FrankieDettori 9 97
(Richard Fahey) *in toouch in midfield: rdn ent fnl 2f: outpcd u.p wl over 1f out: no threat to ldrs but rallied and kpt on again ins fnl f* **16/1**

65-4 **10** *½* **Lamar (IRE)**[18] 1515 3-9-0 96........................ LukeMorris 18 96
(James Tate) *hld up in tch in last pair: effrt u.p wl over 1f out: sme hdwy over 1f out: edgd rt u.p jst ins fnl f: onepced after* **100/1**

16-3 **11** *¾* **Joyeuse**[22] 1435 3-9-0 104........................ JamesDoyle 17 94
(Lady Cecil) *lw: stdd s: hld up in tch in last pair: swtchd rt and hdwy over 3f out: wl in tch and rdn 2f out: no prog and sn outpcd: wknd fnl f* **16/1**

512- **12** *nk* **Princess Noor (IRE)**[218] 6836 3-9-0 111........................(p) AndreaAtzeni 16 94
(Roger Varian) *broke wl: sn stdd and hld up in midfield: rdn and effrt 2f out: no prog: keeping on same pce whn carried rt jst ins fnl f* **25/1**

31-4 **13** 1 ½ **Lady Lara (IRE)**[22] 1435 3-9-0 100 KierenFallon 10 92
(Alan Jarvis) *stdd and jostling match leaving stalls: hld up towards rr: hmpd 1/2-way: rdn and effrt 2f out: no real imp: wl hld and eased towards fin* **40/1**

0-1 **14** 1 ½ **Bracelet (IRE)**[35] 1201 3-9-0 106 RyanMoore 2 86
(A P O'Brien, Ire) *leggy: in tch in midfield: rdn and effrt jst over 2f out: no prog and outpcd over 1f out: wknd 1f out* **11/1**

1- **15** 6 **Betimes**[137] 8332 3-9-0 86 WilliamBuick 11 72
(John Gosden) *w'like: stdd and jostling w rival leaving stalls: plld hrd: hld up in tch in midfield: rdn ent fnl 2f: sn btn: wknd over 1f out* **25/1**

611- **16** 13 **Lucky Kristale**[255] 5680 3-9-0 108 TomQueally 15 41
(George Margarson) *stdd s: plld hrd: hld up towards rr: hmpd and bmpd rival 1/2-way: shkn up and btn ent fnl 2f: sn btn and bhd: eased fnl f* **14/1**

13- **17** 1 **Tapestry (IRE)**[245] 6024 3-9-0 112 JosephO'Brien 6 38
(A P O'Brien, Ire) *leggy: chsd ldrs: rdn over 2f out: no rspnse and sn dropped out: eased fr over 1f out* **4/1**[1]

1m 37.4s (-1.20) **Going Correction** +0.075s/f (Good) **17** Ran SP% **125.0**
Speed ratings: **109,108,108,107,105 104,104,104,103,102 102,101,100,98,92 79,78**
CSF £98.21 CT £748.26 TOTE £6.50: £2.60, £4.20, £4.20; EX 158.30.
**Owner** Ballymore Thoroughbred Ltd **Bred** Dayton Investments Ltd **Trained** Chantilly, France
■ A full set of English Classics for Andre Fabre, and a first for Maxime Guyon.
■ Stewards' Enquiry : Harry Bentley two-day ban: used whip above permitted level (May 18-19)

**FOCUS**
A wide-open Guineas, reflected in the betting, and a case could be made for several in the line-up. They stayed in one group and the early gallop wasn't strong. It paid to race handily, highlighted by the leader, 100-1 shot Manderley, being able to hang on for fourth place. The Oh So Sharp Stakes, won by Miss France from Lightning Thunder, turned out to be the key piece of 2yo form. A good renewal on paper but Miss France's figure is a little below the race standard. The fourth is the key.

## 1977 MAKFI FUTURE STARS MAIDEN STKS (BOBIS RACE) 5f
**4:25** (4:26) (Class 4) 2-Y-O **£6,469** (£1,925; £962; £481) **Stalls** Centre

Form RPR

**1** **Elite Gardens (USA)** 2-9-0 0 KierenFallon 14 83+
(Saeed bin Suroor) *w'like: str: dwlt: in tch in midfield: pushed along and hdwy to chal over 1f out: led jst ins fnl f: hld on cl home* **8/1**

**2** shd **Aktabantay** 2-9-5 0 RyanMoore 15 88+
(Hugo Palmer) *lengthy: scope: s.i.s: in tch in rr: clsd and nt clr run over 1f out: hdwy and edging rt over 1f out: str run ins fnl f: chsd wnr wl ins fnl f: nt quite rch wnr* **5/1**[2]

**3** 2 **Symbolic Star (IRE)** 2-9-5 0 WilliamBuick 1 81+
(Charlie Appleby) *w'like: lengthy: swtchd lft after s: hld up in tch: rdn and effrt to chse ldrs over 1f out: chsd wnr fnl 150yds: no imp and lost 2nd wl ins fnl f* **16/1**

6 **4** 1 ½ **Brazen Spirit**[30] 1276 2-9-5 0 AdamKirby 10 75+
(Clive Cox) *leggy: led: rdn wl over 1f out: hdd 1f out: wknd ins fnl f* **8/1**

**5** ¾ **Shackled N Drawn (USA)** 2-9-5 0 (t) FrankieDettori 7 73
(Olly Stevens) *athletic: chsd ldrs: upsides ldr 2f out: rdn and ev ch over 1f out: led 1f out: sn hdd: wknd ins fnl f* **8/1**

**6** 1 ½ **Billyoakes (IRE)** 2-9-5 0 JamesDoyle 13 67+
(Mick Channon) *w'like: in tch in midfield: effrt: rn green on downhill run and no imp over 1f out: carried rt 1f out: kpt on same pce after* **14/1**

**7** 1 ¼ **Wet Sail (USA)** 2-9-5 0 FrederikTylicki 9 63
(Charlie Fellowes) *w'like: hld up in tch in midfield: rdn and unable qck over 1f out: wknd 1f out* **33/1**

**8** 2 ¼ **Barchan (USA)** 2-9-5 0 MickaelBarzalona 6 55
(Charlie Appleby) *w'like: scope: str: chsd ldrs: rdn and unable qck over 1f out: sn outpcd and btn: wknd fnl f* **3/1**[1]

**9** nk **Forcible** 2-9-5 0 JamieSpencer 4 54
(David Brown) *unf: scope: chsd ldr tl 2f out: sn rdn and btn: wknd 1f out* **10/1**

**10** 1 ¼ **Fit The Bill (IRE)** 2-9-5 0 LukeMorris 11 49
(James Tate) *leggy: sn pushed along towards rr: nvr trbld ldrs* **40/1**

**11** ¾ **Kassbaan** 2-9-5 0 AndreaAtzeni 3 46+
(Marco Botti) *str: hld up wl in tch in midfield: rdn ent fnl 2f: sn struggling and short of room wl over 1f out: wknd over 1f out* **11/2**[3]

**12** nk **Lightning Stride** 2-9-5 0 HarryBentley 8 45
(Brian Meehan) *unf: hld up in tch towards rr: rdn over 2f out: sn btn* **25/1**

**13** 4 **Alpine Affair** 2-9-5 0 JimmyFortune 5 31
(Brian Meehan) *w'like: dwlt: hld up in rr: rdn 2f out: sn btn and bhd over 1f out* **33/1**

**14** 9 **Sky Steps (IRE)** 2-9-0 0 DannyBrock(5) 12
(Philip McBride) *w'like: s.i.s: a bhd* **50/1**

1m 0.18s (1.08) **Going Correction** +0.075s/f (Good) **14** Ran SP% **126.2**
Speed ratings (Par 95): **94,93,90,88,87 84,82,79,78,76 75,74,68,54**
CSF £48.13 TOTE £7.70: £2.70, £3.30, £7.20; EX 66.30.
**Owner** Godolphin **Bred** Dr Catherine Wills **Trained** Newmarket, Suffolk

**FOCUS**
Very little previous form to go on here, but the one with a previous outing hit the frame and it rates a fair contest. They kept mid-track and went a sound pace, with two nicely clear at the finish. Some really good prospects on show.

## 1978 TWEENHILLS PRETTY POLLY STKS (LISTED RACE) (FILLIES) 1m 2f
**5:00** (5:00) (Class 1) 3-Y-O
**£22,684** (£8,600; £4,304; £2,144; £1,076; £540) **Stalls** Centre

Form RPR

1- **1** **Taghrooda**[225] 6643 3-9-0 89 PaulHanagan 5 105+
(John Gosden) *lengthy: lw: t.k.h: chsd ldrs: clsd to join ldrs over 2f out: rdn 2f out: led over 1f out: styd on strly and drew clr fnl f: impressive* **1/1**[1]

01- **2** 6 **Jordan Princess**[201] 7277 3-9-0 79 AndreaAtzeni 3 93
(Luca Cumani) *lengthy: tall: t.k.h: chsd ldr: clsd and upsides over 2f out: rdn to ld 2f out: hdd over 1f out: no ch w wnr fnl f: kpt on to hold 2nd* **13/2**[3]

116- **3** 1 ¼ **Sound Reflection (USA)**[219] 6798 3-9-0 100[1] MickaelBarzalona 2 91
(Charlie Appleby) *led: wnt clr 1/2-way tl jnd over 2f out: hdd and rdn 2f out: 3rd and no ch w wnr fnl f: kpt on* **4/1**[2]

010- **4** nk **Uchenna (IRE)**[219] 6798 3-9-0 87 RyanMoore 6 90
(David Simcock) *hld up in tch: clsd 3f out: rdn and outpcd 2f out: 4th and edging rt over 1f out: kpt on and pressing for placings ins fnl f: no ch w* **16/1**

- **5** 9 **Night Fever (IRE)** 3-9-0 0 WilliamBuick 4 72+
(John Gosden) *w'like: stdd s:t.k.h: hld up in last pair: clsd 3f out: rdn over 2f out: sn btn: wknd over 1f out: heavily eased ins fnl f* **8/1**

10- **6** 13 **Surcingle (USA)**[183] 7695 3-9-0 77 JamesDoyle 1 46
(Sir Michael Stoute) *stdd s: t.k.h: hld up in tch: clsd 3f out: rdn over 2f out: sn struggling: wknd over 1f out* **9/1**

2m 5.68s (-0.12) **Going Correction** +0.075s/f (Good) **6** Ran SP% **110.3**
Speed ratings (Par 104): **103,98,97,96,89 79**
CSF £7.73 TOTE £1.80: £1.50, £2.70; EX 8.30 Trifecta £47.30.
**Owner** Hamdan Al Maktoum **Bred** Shadwell Estate Company Limited **Trained** Newmarket, Suffolk

**FOCUS**
In recent years both Ouija Board and Talent have won this race on their way to Oaks glory, and with all six engaged at Epsom there was plenty of hope it would throw up another strong candidate. The impressive Taghrooda rates to the top end of the race averages.

## 1979 QATAR RACING H'CAP (BOBIS RACE) 1m 2f
**5:35** (5:35) (Class 2) (0-100,95) 3-Y-O
**£12,450** (£3,728; £1,864; £932; £466; £234) **Stalls** Centre

Form RPR

52-6 **1** **Zee Zeely**[26] 1357 3-8-5 79 (p) PaulHanagan 8 89+
(William Haggas) *lw: chsd ldrs tl rdn to ld 2f out: styd on wl u.p fnl f: rdn out* **8/1**

411- **2** ¾ **Miner's Lamp (IRE)**[208] 7107 3-9-7 95 MickaelBarzalona 3 103+
(Charlie Appleby) *stdd s: plld hrd: hld up in tch in rr: hdwy 2f out: sn drvn and chsd wnr: kpt on trying but a hld ins fnl f* **9/2**[2]

55-5 **3** 2 **Ganges (IRE)**[18] 1511 3-8-3 77 AndreaAtzeni 5 82
(James Toller) *lw: hld up wl in tch in midfield: rdn and effrt 2f out: drvn and hdwy to chse ldng pair 1f out: kpt on but nvr threatened ldrs* **5/1**[3]

40-1 **4** 2 ½ **Donny Rover (IRE)**[15] 1586 3-8-5 82 OisinMurphy(3) 6 82
(Michael Appleby) *lw: hld up in tch in midfield: effrt 2f out: chsd ldng pair and edging rt over 1f out: 4th and btn 1f out: wknd ins fnl f* **9/1**

1 **5** 2 ¼ **Lungarno Palace (USA)**[72] 696 3-8-8 82 LukeMorris 4 78
(Marco Botti) *lw: hld up in tch towards rr: rdn over 2f out: n.m.r 2f out: swtchd rt and hrd drvn wl over 1f out: no imp* **25/1**

31-2 **6** nk **Snow Trouble (USA)**[15] 1580 3-9-1 89 RyanMoore 1 84
(Marcus Tregoning) *hld up in tch in last trio: rdn over 2f out: drvn and no prog whn pushed rt wl over 1f out: wl hld after* **9/4**[1]

-241 **7** nse **Old Town Boy**[25] 1401 3-8-3 77 SilvestreDeSousa 7 72
(Philip McBride) *led tl hdd and rdn 2f out: sn outpcd and drvn: carried rt and btn over 1f out: wknd ins fnl f* **9/2**[2]

1-30 **8** 15 **Act Of Charity (IRE)**[84] 553 3-9-0 88 DavidProbert 2 61
(Gay Kelleway) *lw: pressed ldr tl rdn and unable qck ent fnl 2f: wknd u.p over 1f out: wl bhd and eased ins fnl f* **25/1**

2m 5.32s (-0.48) **Going Correction** +0.075s/f (Good) **8** Ran SP% **112.6**
Speed ratings (Par 105): **104,103,101,99,98 97,97,85**
CSF £42.39 CT £197.43 TOTE £9.70: £2.10, £2.00, £1.70; EX 52.80.
**Owner** Bernard Kantor **Bred** Meon Valley Stud **Trained** Newmarket, Suffolk
■ Stewards' Enquiry : Paul Hanagan four-day ban: used whip above permitted level (May 18-21)

**FOCUS**
There was an even pace on in this fair 3yo handicap and the form should work out. The first three are all improving.
T/Jkpt: Not won. T/Plt: £272.40 to a £1 stake. Pool: £36,538.29 - 97.90 winning units. T/Qpdt: £14.00 to a £1 stake. Pool: £727.40 - 38.20 winning units. SP

# SALISBURY (R-H)
Sunday, May 4

**OFFICIAL GOING: Soft (good to soft in places; 6.8)**
Wind: virtually nil Weather: sunny

## 1980 BETFRED "GOALS GALORE" MAIDEN STKS 6f
**1:45** (1:47) (Class 5) 3-Y-O+ **£3,234** (£962; £481; £240) **Stalls** Low

Form RPR

**1** **Lightning Moon (IRE)** 3-9-3 0 GeorgeBaker 5 87+
(Ed Walker) *pressed ldr: pushed into narrow advantage ent fnl f: rdn whn green fnl 120yds: kpt on* **5/1**[3]

6-0 **2** nk **Spring Fling**[17] 1534 3-8-12 0 DaneO'Neill 1 81
(Henry Candy) *led: rdn and narrowly hdd ent fnl f: rallied gamely fnl 120yds: kpt on* **11/4**[1]

62- **3** 5 **Bold Spirit**[279] 4827 3-9-3 0 SeanLevey 9 71
(Richard Hannon) *racd keenly: trckd ldng pair: rdn 2f out: kpt on but sn outpcd by front pair* **3/1**[2]

00-5 **4** 2 ¾ **Pashan Garh**[35] 1190 5-9-8 68 LouisSteward(5) 7 66
(Pat Eddery) *s.i.s: sn mid-div: rdn into 4th 2f out: kpt on but nvr gng pce to get on terms* **6/1**

4- **5** 3 ¼ **Diamonds A Dancing**[275] 3606 4-9-13 0 (p) RobertHavlin 6 56
(Brian Gubby) *in tch: rdn over 2f out: sn one pce* **66/1**

34-2 **6** 11 **Kuala Queen (IRE)**[15] 1569 3-8-12 70 JohnFahy 8 15
(Denis Coakley) *hld up towards rr: rdn over 2f out: nvr any imp: wknd over 1f out* **8/1**

60- **7** 5 **Dark Phantom (IRE)**[327] 3175 3-9-3 0 SebSanders 3 5
(Peter Makin) *trckd ldrs: rdn over 3f out: wknd over 1f out* **33/1**

000- **8** nk **Spirited Silver**[232] 6408 3-8-12 25 SamHitchcott 10
(John Bridger) *trckd ldrs: rdn 3f out: wknd 2f out* **250/1**

0-6 **9** 1 ¼ **Mercury Magic**[102] 284 3-9-3 0 (v[1]) JimCrowley 2
(Ralph Beckett) *chsd ldrs for 2f: sn drvn: wknd 2f out* **15/2**

**10** ¾ **Femme De Menage** 3-8-12 0 LiamKeniry 4
(Andrew Balding) *slwoly into stride: a towards rr* **16/1**

1m 17.22s (2.42) **Going Correction** +0.575s/f (Yiel)
**WFA** 3 from 4yo+ 10lb **10** Ran SP% **116.2**
Speed ratings (Par 103): **106,105,98,95,90 76,69,69,67,66**
CSF £19.02 TOTE £8.20: £2.90, £1.70, £2.30; EX 17.00.
**Owner** M Betamar **Bred** Michael Collins **Trained** Newmarket, Suffolk

**FOCUS**
Some likeable sorts in the parade-ring contested this maiden in which most of the runners had little or no experience. The first two should both have a good season, and there are likely to have been more winners behind them.

## 1981 BETFRED "CITY BOWL" H'CAP 1m 6f 21y
**2:20** (2:20) (Class 3) (0-95,93) 4-Y-O+
**£12,450** (£3,728; £1,864; £932; £466; £234)

Form RPR

112/ **1** **Whiplash Willie**[988] 5283 6-9-10 93 LiamKeniry 1 104
(Andrew Balding) *hld up: stdy prog fr over 3f out: chal over 1f out: led fnl 120yds: styd on wl: rdn out* **5/1**[3]

300- **2** 3/4 **Rockfella**253 5746 8-8-5 **74** oh1 .......... MartinDwyer 5 84
(Denis Coakley) *led after 2f: rdn 2f out: jnd over 1f out: hdd fnl 120yds: styd on but no ex* **9/1**

250- **3** 6 **Albert Bridge**69 7193 6-9-4 **87** .......... JimCrowley 6 89
(Ralph Beckett) *trckd ldrs: rdn to chse ldng pair over 3f out: styd on same pce fnl 2f* **5/2**1

03-4 **4** 3/4 **Spice Fair**25 1383 7-8-8 **77** .......... RobertHavlin 3 78
(Mark Usher) *hld up into uch: rdn into 4th over 2f out: nvr threatened ldrs: styd on same pce* **14/1**

3300 **5** 8 **Duchess Of Gazeley (IRE)**16 1556 4-9-1 **85** .......... JimmyQuinn 9 76
(Dean Ivory) *hld up in tch: shortof room and lost pl after 4f: pushed along on loop: rdn over 3f out: nvr threatened: wknd jst over 1f out* **9/1**

014- **6** 1 1/2 **Riptide**150 7064 8-8-10 **82** .......... (v) WilliamTwiston-Davies(3) 7 71
(Michael Scudamore) *led for 2f: w ldr: rdn over 3f out: wknd jst over 1f out* **25/1**

260- **7** 23 **Nicholascopernicus (IRE)**176 7823 5-9-9 **92** .......... GeorgeBaker 4 51
(Ed Walker) *hld up in tch: effrt 3f out: wknd 2f out: eased fnl f* **4/1**2

4-23 **8** 15 **Ridgeway Storm (IRE)**20 1491 4-8-9 **79** .......... FergusSweeney 2 18
(Alan King) *t.k.h: sn in tch: rdn over 3f out: wknd over 2f out: eased fnl f* **5/1**3

012/ **P** **Cunning Act**947 6499 6-9-6 **89** .......... StephenCraine 8
(Jonathan Portman) *hld up: struggling whn lost action and p.u over 3f out: fatally injured* **20/1**

3m 13.88s (6.48) **Going Correction** +0.675s/f (Yiel)
**WFA** 4 from 5yo+ 1lb **9** Ran SP% **117.2**
Speed ratings (Par 107): **108,107,104,103,99 98,85,76,**
CSF £49.90 CT £139.08 TOTE £5.50: £1.60, £2.60, £2.30; EX 139.60 Trifecta £40.40.
**Owner** J C & S R Hitchins **Bred** J C & S R Hitchins **Trained** Kingsclere, Hants

**FOCUS**
There was a decent turnout for this good prize. The early pace wasn't testing but it stepped up a notch after they joined the main course, 7f out. The winner looked ast least as good as ever.

## 1982 BETFRED "GOALS GALORE EXTRA" FILLIES' CONDITIONS STKS (BOBIS RACE) 5f
**2:50** (2:51) (Class 3) 2-Y-O **£6,792** (£2,021; £1,010; £505) **Stalls** Low

Form RPR

1 **1** **Tiggy Wiggy (IRE)**36 1169 2-9-0 0 .......... SeanLevey 3 88+
(Richard Hannon) *mde all but hrd pressed thrght tl asserted fnl 120yds: kpt on wl* **8/11**1

**2** 1 1/4 **Exentricity** 2-8-6 0 ow1 .......... WilliamTwiston-Davies(3) 2 79+
(Mick Channon) *little slowly away: chsd ldrs: rdn 2f out: kpt on to go 2nd fnl 100yds but a being hld* **14/1**

01 **3** 3 1/4 **Mylaporyours (IRE)**6 1788 2-8-6 0 .......... LouisSteward(5) 4 69
(Rod Millman) *prom tl sltly outpcd 2f out: kpt on ins fnl f to regain 3rd fnl strides* **15/2**3

21 **4** nk **Paddy Again (IRE)**27 1342 2-8-6 0 .......... RyanWhile(5) 1 68
(Bill Turner) *pressed wnr: rdn over 2f out: ev ch tl fdd fnl 120yds: lost 3rd fnl strides* **5/2**2

416 **5** 9 **Low Cut Affair (IRE)**10 1670 2-8-8 0 .......... DeclanBates(3) 6 35
(David Evans) *sn rdn along to chse ldrs: nvr gng pce to threaten: wknd ent fnl f* **20/1**

1m 4.21s (3.21) **Going Correction** +0.575s/f (Yiel) **5** Ran SP% **109.7**
Speed ratings (Par 94): **97,95,89,89,74**
CSF £11.93 TOTE £2.20: £1.60, £2.10; EX 8.70.
**Owner** Potensis Ltd & Ms Elaine Chivers **Bred** Cbs Bloodstock **Trained** East Everleigh, Wilts

**FOCUS**
Some speedy youngsters contested this, and the first two should win their fair share of races.

## 1983 BETFRED TV H'CAP (BOBIS RACE) 1m 1f 198y
**3:25** (3:25) (Class 4) (0-85,85) 3-Y-O **£4,851** (£1,443; £721; £360) **Stalls** Low

Form RPR

5-41 **1** **Black Schnapps (IRE)**9 1690 3-9-7 **85** .......... MartinDwyer 7 96
(William Muir) *trckd ldr: lft in ld on bnd 6f out: sn jnd: qcknd clr over 1f out: in command fnl f: readily* **15/8**1

364- **2** 5 **Template (IRE)**216 6896 3-8-8 **72** .......... RobertHavlin 3 73
(Amanda Perrett) *trckd ldr: lft prom briefly 6f out: rdn 2f out: kpt on but nt pce of ready wnr* **16/1**

021- **3** 2 1/4 **The Alamo (IRE)**195 7428 3-9-1 **79** .......... DaneO'Neill 4 76
(Richard Hannon) *trckd ldrs: rdn whn swtchd lft 2f out: kpt on but nt pce to get involved* **7/2**2

2-30 **4** 3/4 **Resolute**16 1563 3-9-2 **80** .......... GeorgeBaker 5 75
(Ed de Giles) *hld up bhd eladers: smooth hdwy 3f out: sn rdn in disp 2nd: fdd fnl 120yds: lost 3rd fnl strides* **6/1**

13- **5** nk **Cape Wrath**193 7468 3-9-6 **84** .......... SeanLevey 1 79
(Richard Hannon) *trckd ldrs: rdn 2f out: nt pce to threaten* **5/1**3

01-3 **6** 8 **Love Tangle (IRE)**20 1494 3-8-10 **74** .......... MartinLane 6 54
(Brian Meehan) *led tl rn v wd on bnd 6f out: sn bk upsides: rdn over 2f out: sn hld: wknd fnl f:* **5/1**3

2m 17.51s (7.61) **Going Correction** +0.675s/f (Yiel) **6** Ran SP% **110.5**
Speed ratings (Par 101): **96,92,90,89,89 82**
CSF £30.42 TOTE £3.00: £2.80, £5.30; EX 51.80.
**Owner** O'Mulloy, Collenette, Quaintance, Clark **Bred** J & J Waldron **Trained** Lambourn, Berks

**FOCUS**
Following a medium pace in this decent 3yo handicap, all the runners had a chance entering the last 3f but the winner then left them standing.

## 1984 BETFRED MOBILE LOTTO EBF STALLIONS MAIDEN STKS 1m 4f
**4:00** (4:01) (Class 5) 3-Y-O **£3,881** (£1,155; £577; £288) **Stalls** Low

Form RPR

3-0 **1** **Wrangler**18 1517 3-9-5 0 .......... SebSanders 1 96+
(William Haggas) *trckd ldrs: led 2f out: sn clr: v easily* **3/1**2

6 **2** 4 **Min Alemarat (IRE)**18 1517 3-9-0 0 .......... MarcMonaghan(5) 2 88
(Marco Botti) *hld up towards rr: rdn 3f out: hdwy whn swtchd lft 2f out: rn green and drifting lft over 1f out: styd on to chse wnr ent fnl f but no ch* **5/2**1

**3** 7 **The Corsican (IRE)** 3-9-5 0 .......... MartinLane 11 77
(David Simcock) *hld up towards rr: hdwy 3f out: rdn to chse wnr 2f out tl ent fnl f: no ex* **15/2**

0 **4** 5 **Catadupa**22 1438 3-8-11 0 .......... WilliamTwiston-Davies(3) 7 64
(Roger Charlton) *in tch: rdn over 2f out: styd on same pce* **16/1**

3-22 **5** 3 1/4 **Libeccio (FR)**26 1367 3-9-5 71 .......... LiamKeniry 4 64
(Andrew Balding) *led for 3f: trckd ldr tl rdn over 2f out: wknd jst over 1f out* **9/1**

23-3 **6** 8 **Carthage (IRE)**9 1690 3-9-5 78 .......... SeanLevey 9 51
(Richard Hannon) *trckd ldrs: rdn wl over 2f out: wknd over 1f out* **5/1**3

**7** 3/4 **Goldenrod** 3-9-5 0 .......... JimCrowley 8 50
(Ralph Beckett) *prom: led after 3f: wnt sltly wd on bnd 6f out: rdn and hdd 2f out: sn wknd* **7/1**

**8** 1 **Little Flo** 3-9-0 0 .......... RichardKingscote 5 43
(Brendan Powell) *slowly away: sn mid-div: rdn 3f out: wknd over 1f out* **40/1**

0 **9** 6 **Dark Days**22 1438 3-9-5 0 .......... (t) FergusSweeney 12 38
(Paul Cole) *s.i.s: towards rr: rdn 3f out: wknd 2f out* **33/1**

5-0 **10** 11 **Sweet Summer**15 1587 3-9-0 0 .......... StevieDonohoe 3 16
(John Holt) *in tch tl wknd over 3f out* **100/1**

**11** 4 1/2 **Fly A Kite** 3-9-5 0 .......... StephenCraine 10 14
(Jonathan Portman) *slwoly into stride: towards rr: hdwy after 4f to sit in tch on outer: rdn 5f out: wknd over 2f out* **33/1**

2m 42.6s (4.60) **Going Correction** +0.675s/f (Yiel) **11** Ran SP% **119.7**
Speed ratings (Par 99): **111,108,103,100,98 92,92,91,87,80 77**
CSF £10.92 TOTE £4.10: £1.80, £1.90, £4.60; EX 17.90.
**Owner** Highclere Thoroughbred Racing - Ashes **Bred** Palm Tree Thoroughbreds **Trained** Newmarket, Suffolk

**FOCUS**
There wasn't much experience on show, but most are late developers and a number have potential. The pace was good and the form should stand up.

## 1985 BETFRED FOLLOW US ON FACEBOOK FILLIES' H'CAP 6f 212y
**4:35** (4:35) (Class 3) (0-90,90) 3-Y-O+ **£7,762** (£2,310; £1,154; £577) **Stalls** Low

Form RPR

1-2 **1** **Tea Leaf (IRE)**17 1543 3-8-0 **74** .......... JimmyQuinn 7 86+
(Ralph Beckett) *awkward leaving stalls: trckd ldrs: pushed along whn nt clrest of runs over 2f out: led jst over 1f out: r.o strly: rdn clr* **11/4**1

120- **2** 3 **Musicora**184 7657 3-9-2 **90** .......... SeanLevey 3 94
(Richard Hannon) *hld up: hdwy 2f out: sn rdn: kpt on ins fnl f: wnt 2nd towards fin* **12/1**

04-5 **3** nk **Saucy Minx (IRE)**46 1020 4-9-4 **80** .......... JimCrowley 4 87
(Amanda Perrett) *prom: rdn to ld over 2f out: hdd jst over 1f out: kpt on same pce: lost 2nd towards fin* **11/2**

2-21 **4** 1 1/4 **Nakuti (IRE)**8 1725 3-8-9 **83** .......... LiamKeniry 1 83
(Sylvester Kirk) *hld up: smooth hdwy to join ldrs 2f out: sn rdn: kpt on same pce* **7/2**3

30-1 **5** 3/4 **Cay Dancer**8 1711 3-8-5 **79** .......... MartinDwyer 8 77
(Richard Hannon) *trckd ldrs: rdn 2f out: sn one pce* **3/1**2

303- **6** 3 3/4 **Sarangoo**202 7254 6-9-2 **78** .......... GeorgeBaker 5 70
(Malcolm Saunders) *led tl rdn over 2f out: sn hld: wknd fnl f* **14/1**

64-0 **7** 1 1/2 **Valen (IRE)**13 1614 3-8-7 **84** .......... WilliamTwiston-Davies(3) 6 68
(Michael Bell) *hld up: hdwy 3f out: effrt 2f out: wknd over 1f out* **10/1**

100- **8** 1 3/4 **Chutney (IRE)**234 6326 3-7-9 **76** .......... CamHardie(7) 2 56
(Richard Hannon) *trckd ldrs: struggling 3f out: wknd over 1f out* **16/1**

1m 31.89s (3.29) **Going Correction** +0.575s/f (Yiel)
**WFA** 3 from 4yo+ 12lb **8** Ran SP% **118.6**
Speed ratings (Par 104): **104,100,100,98,97 93,91,89**
CSF £37.72 CT £175.28 TOTE £2.60: £1.10, £3.70, £1.70; EX 68.90.
**Owner** McCalmont and Drew **Bred** Barbara Prendergast **Trained** Kimpton, Hants

**FOCUS**
In a good handicap for fillies and mares, the pace was only average but stamina was just as important as finishing speed.

## 1986 BETFRED MOBILE SPORTS LADY RIDERS' H'CAP (FOR LADY AMATEUR RIDERS) 6f 212y
**5:10** (5:10) (Class 6) (0-65,58) 4-Y-O+ **£2,495** (£774; £386; £193) **Stalls** Low

Form RPR

02-6 **1** **Who's That Chick (IRE)**10 1664 5-9-12 **56** .......... MissEllaSmith(7) 1 66
(Ralph J Smith) *slowly away: bhd: hdwy over 2f out: swtchd lft over 1f out: led jst over 1f out: a holding on* **6/1**3

3002 **2** nk **Sea Soldier (IRE)**33 1215 6-9-11 **55** .......... MissMWall(7) 9 64
(Andrew Balding) *bhd: hdwy 2f out: r.o strly fnl f: clsng on wnr at fin but nvr quite getting there* **7/2**2

2520 **3** 2 1/2 **Byrd In Hand (IRE)**46 1015 7-9-12 **49** .......... (b) MissADeniel 2 52+
(John Bridger) *trckd ldrs: led over 2f out: carried rt and hmpd by loose horse sn after: swtchd lft over 1f out: sn hdd: no ex* **8/1**

00-0 **4** 4 1/2 **Silvee**3 1896 7-9-5 **47** ow2 .......... MissLDempster(5) 10 38
(John Bridger) *towards rr: rdn and hdwy over 3f out: ch over 1f out: kpt on same pce* **14/1**

0203 **5** 1 **One Last Dream**6 1787 5-10-6 **57** .......... MissSBrotherton 3 45
(Ron Hodges) *led for 1f: chsd clr ldrs: rdn over 2f out: sn one pce* **9/4**1

0556 **6** 1 1/4 **Hinton Admiral**12 1631 10-9-7 **51** .......... MissMeganNicholls(7) 8 36
(Pat Eddery) *nvr bttr than mid-div* **20/1**

3320 **7** 1/2 **Catalyze**10 1668 6-10-2 **58** .......... (t) MissMBryant(5) 5 42
(Paddy Butler) *chsd ldrs: rdn whn lost pl over 2f out: nt a threat after* **16/1**

0250 **8** 1 1/4 **Ryedale Lass**80 586 6-9-2 **46** .......... (b) MissLWest(7) 7 26
(Geoffrey Deacon) *wnt bdly rt and bmpd s: hld up: swtchd rt over 1f out: nvr any imp* **16/1**

/ **9** 3/4 **Tamujin (IRE)**249 5908 6-9-8 **45** .......... MissEJJones 4 23
(Ken Cunningham-Brown) *mid-div: rdn 3f out: chsd ldrs 2f out: wknd ent fnl f* **33/1**

-060 **10** 21 **Camache Queen (IRE)**6 1804 6-9-12 **52** .......... (bt) MissCBoxall(3) 11
(Joseph Tuite) *led after 1f: edgd lft and hdd over 2f out: sn rdn: wknd over 1f out: t.o* **20/1**

55-4 **U** **Interakt**4 1877 7-9-11 **51** .......... (p) MissJoannaMason(3) 6
(Joseph Tuite) *bdly hmpd and uns rdr leaving stalls* **8/1**

1m 34.2s (5.60) **Going Correction** +0.575s/f (Yiel) **11** Ran SP% **120.4**
Speed ratings (Par 101): **91,90,87,82,81 80,79,78,77,53**
CSF £27.25 CT £176.51 TOTE £5.60: £1.40, £2.20, £2.70; EX 40.40.
**Owner** Piper, Churchill, Hirschfeld **Bred** T Hirschfeld **Trained** Epsom, Surrey
■ Stewards' Enquiry : Miss L Dempster three-day ban: weighed-in 2lb heavy (tbn)

**FOCUS**
In a typically modest race of its type, the pace was strong, setting it up for the hold-up runners. Neither of the two riders involved in the finish was vigorous, but they both rode good tactical races.
T/Plt: £18.60 to a £1 stake. Pool: £4068.14 - 159.57 winning units. T/Qpdt: £4.70 to a £1 stake. Pool: £135.10 - 20.90 winning units. TM

## 1619 COLOGNE (R-H)

Sunday, May 4

**OFFICIAL GOING: Turf: good**

### 2001a GERLING-PREIS (GROUP 2) (4YO+) (TURF) 1m 4f

**4:10** (12:00) 4-Y-0+

**£33,333** (£12,916; £5,416; £3,333; £2,083; £1,250)

RPR

1 **Ivanhowe (GER)**[301] 4103 4-9-3 0........ AdriedeVries 6 112
(Jean-Pierre Carvalho, Germany) **13/10**[1]

2 1 ½ **Night Wish (GER)**[28] 4-9-0 0........ SHellyn 7 107
(W Figge, Germany) **51/10**

3 nk **Destor (GER)**[213] 6987 4-9-0 0........ DennisSchiergen 9 106
(U Stech, Germany) **19/2**

4 nse **Iniciar (GER)**[24] 4-9-0 0........ FilipMinarik 3 106
(Jean-Pierre Carvalho, Germany) **29/10**[2]

5 1 ¾ **Daytona Bay**[217] 6887 4-8-10 0........ NRichter 4 99
(Ferdinand J Leve, Germany) **10/1**

6 shd **Sir Lando**[14] 7-9-0 0........ EPedroza 1 103
(Wido Neuroth, Norway) **112/10**

7 hd **Girolamo (GER)**[266] 5324 5-9-3 0........ DanielePorcu 5 106
(P Schiergen, Germany) **22/5**[3]

2m 30.09s (-2.81) **7 Ran SP% 130.8**
WIN (incl. 10 euro stake): 23. PLACES: 18, 20. SF: 108.
**Owner** Gestut Schlenderhan **Bred** Gestut Schlenderhan **Trained** Germany

## KYOTO (R-H)

Sunday, May 4

**OFFICIAL GOING: Turf: firm**

### 2002a TENNO SHO (SPRING) (GRADE 1) (4YO+) (TURF) 2m

**7:40** (12:00) 4-Y-0+ **£778,733** (£310,162; £192,360; £114,705; £75,705)

RPR

1 **Fenomeno (JPN)**[36] 5-9-2 0........ MasayoshiEbina 7 115
(Hirofumi Toda, Japan) **105/10**

2 nk **Win Variation (JPN)**[36] 6-9-2 0........ KoshiroTake 12 115
(Masahiro Matsunaga, Japan) **11/2**[3]

3 nse **Hokko Brave (JPN)**[36] 6-9-2 0........ HironobuTanabe 6 115+
(Yasutoshi Matsunaga, Japan) **101/1**

4 ½ **Kizuna (JPN)**[28] 4-9-2 0........ YutakaTake 14 117+
(Shozo Sasaki, Japan) **7/10**[1]

5 1 ½ **Tanino Epaulette (JPN)**[21] 7-9-2 0........ RyujiWada 9 113
(Akira Murayama, Japan) **168/1**

6 ½ **Fame Game (JPN)**[71] 4-9-2 0........ HiroshiKitamura 10 115
(Yoshitada Munakata, Japan) **91/1**

7 nk **Gold Ship (JPN)**[42] 5-9-2 0........(b) CraigAWilliams 8 112+
(Naosuke Sugai, Japan) **33/10**[2]

8 hd **Satono Noblesse (JPN)**[42] 4-9-2 0........ SuguruHamanaka 3 115
(Yasutoshi Ikee, Japan) **36/1**

9 ½ **Last Impact (JPN)**[36] 4-9-2 0........ YugaKawada 11 114
(Hiroyoshi Matsuda, Japan) **53/1**

10 2 ½ **Silent Melody (JPN)**[36] 7-9-2 0........(b) KenichiIkezoe 4 108
(Sakae Kunieda, Japan) **284/1**

11 nk **Admire Flight (JPN)**[36] 5-9-2 0........ YuichiFukunaga 2 108
(Mitsuru Hashida, Japan) **57/1**

12 nk **Ocean Blue (JPN)**[36] 6-9-2 0........(b) ShinjiFujita 13 108
(Yasutoshi Ikee, Japan) **178/1**

13 nk **Admire Rakti (JPN)**[42] 6-9-2 0........ HirofumiShii 15 107
(Tomoyuki Umeda, Japan) **88/1**

14 hd **Red Cadeaux**[36] 1183 8-9-2 0........ GeraldMosse 5 107
(Ed Dunlop) **86/1**

15 2 ½ **Hit The Target (JPN)**[42] 6-9-2 0........ YuichiKitamura 17 104
(Keiji Kato, Japan) **206/1**

16 2 ½ **Jaguar Mail (JPN)**[36] 10-9-2 0........(b) SyulshibashI 16 102
(Noriyuki Hori, Japan) **274/1**

17 1 ¾ **Desperado (JPN)**[77] 6-9-2 0........ NorihiroYokoyama 18 100
(Akio Adachi, Japan) **26/1**

18 9 **Asuka Kurichan (JPN)**[36] 7-9-2 0........ ShinichiroAkiyama 1 90
(Naosuke Sugai, Japan) **200/1**

3m 15.1s (195.10)
**WFA** 4 from 5yo+ 3lb **18 Ran SP% 123.3**
PARI-MUTUEL (all including 100 jpy stake): WIN 1150; SHOW 310, 220, 1470; DF 2080; SF 5670.

**Owner** Sunday Racing Co Ltd **Bred** Oiwake Farm **Trained** Japan

## SENONNES-POUANCE

Sunday, May 4

**OFFICIAL GOING: Turf: good to soft**

### 2003a PRIX DU DOCTEUR GUY JALLOT (MAIDEN) (3YO COLTS & GELDINGS) (TURF) 1m 2f 110y

**12:00** (12:00) 3-Y-0 **£5,000** (£2,000; £1,500; £1,000; £500)

RPR

1 **Monatorio (FR)** 3-9-2 0........ AntoineWerle 10 70
(H-A Pantall, France) **2/1**[1]

2 2 ½ **Diyoudar (FR)** 3-9-2 0........ IoritzMendizabal 16 65
(J-C Rouget, France) **5/2**[2]

3 hd **Bal D'Or (FR)** 3-9-2 0........ ChristopherGrosbois 15 65
(J Boisnard, France) **22/1**

4 2 ½ **Kerdelan (IRE)**[80] 600 3-9-2 0........ MathieuAndrouin 1 60
(P Monfort, France) **73/10**[3]

5 hd **Bofalco (IRE)**[79] 3-9-2 0........ TonyPiccone 11 60
(C Lotoux, France) **9/1**

6 2 **Lucilo (FR)** 3-9-2 0........ ArnaudBourgeais 13 56
(N Leenders, France) **78/10**

7 1 **Meeska Moska (FR)**[32] 3-9-2 0........ JeromeClaudic 4 54
(C Plisson, France) **44/1**

8 ½ **All Include (FR)**[194] 3-8-13 0........ JulienGuillochon(3) 12 53
(J Thibault, France) **48/1**

9 1 **Agrapart (FR)** 3-8-11 0........ BenjaminHubert 7 46
(Nick Williams) **62/1**

10 shd **Doctor De L'Aube (FR)**[38] 3-9-2 0........ AntoineSamson 6 51
(C Plisson, France) **34/1**

11 2 **Aquilleus** 3-8-11 0........ AlexandreRoussel 5 42
(G Henrot, France) **25/1**

12 2 ½ **Celtic Tune (FR)** 3-9-2 0........ JeromeCabre 8 42
(L Viel, France) **35/1**

13 1 **Martha's Stand (FR)** 3-9-2 0........ AdrienFouassier 3 40
(E Libaud, France) **24/1**

14 1 **Star De La Barre (FR)**[276] 3-8-13 0........ StephaneLaurent(3) 9 38
(C Plisson, France) **62/1**

P **P'Tit Milord (FR)** 3-8-11 0........ DavidFournier 2
(M Ortholan, France) **107/1**

2m 17.16s (137.16) **15 Ran SP% 121.5**
PARI-MUTUEL (all including 1 euro stake): WIN 3.00; PLACE 1.50, 1.80, 3.80; DF 4.80; SF 9.00.
**Owner** Patrick Chedeville **Bred** Earl Sylvain Le Goff, Mme F Bazin & P Chedeville **Trained** France

## 1785 SHA TIN (R-H)

Sunday, May 4

**OFFICIAL GOING: Turf: good**

### 2004a CHAMPIONS MILE (GROUP 1) (3YO+) (TURF) 1m

**9:35** (12:00) 3-Y-0+

**£532,710** (£205,607; £93,457; £52,959; £31,152; £18,691)

RPR

1 **Variety Club (SAF)**[36] 1176 6-9-0 0........ AntonMarcus 12 124+
(M F De Kock, South Africa) **116/10**

2 4 **Able Friend (AUS)**[28] 5-9-0 0........(p) JoaoMoreira 14 115
(J Moore, Hong Kong) **7/10**[1]

3 1 ¼ **Dan Excel (IRE)**[49] 6-9-0 0........(t) TommyBerry 7 112
(J Moore, Hong Kong) **10/1**[3]

4 shd **Glorious Days (AUS)**[105] 7-9-0 0........(b) KTeetan 8 112
(J Size, Hong Kong) **10/1**[3]

5 ¾ **Gold-Fun (IRE)**[49] 5-9-0 0........(b) DouglasWhyte 2 110
(R Gibson, Hong Kong) **16/5**[2]

6 1 ½ **Blazing Speed**[36] 1181 5-9-0 0........(t) NeilCallan 1 107
(A S Cruz, Hong Kong) **26/1**

7 1 **Gordon Lord Byron (IRE)**[22] 1468 6-9-0 0........ ZacPurton 13 104
(T Hogan, Ire) **48/1**

8 1 ¾ **Mshawish (USA)**[36] 1181 4-9-0 0........ UmbertoRispoli 6 100
(M Delzangles, France) **118/1**

9 ½ **Flame Hero (NZ)**[18] 5-9-0 0........ HughBowman 11 99
(L Ho, Hong Kong) **125/1**

10 nk **Meiner Lacrima (JPN)**[63] 6-9-0 0........ DaichiShibata 5 98
(Hiroyuki Uehara, Japan) **129/1**

11 nk **California Memory (USA)**[168] 8-9-0 0........ MatthewChadwick 10 98
(A S Cruz, Hong Kong) **52/1**

12 3 ¾ **Real Specialist (NZ)**[91] 7-9-0 0........(b) ODoleuze 3 89
(J Size, Hong Kong) **62/1**

13 2 **Helene Spirit (IRE)**[28] 7-9-0 0........(bt[1]) ASuborics 4 84
(C Fownes, Hong Kong) **97/1**

14 13 **Zaidan (USA)**[35] 6-9-0 0........(t) BrettPrebble 9 55
(A S Cruz, Hong Kong) **129/1**

1m 34.11s (-0.59) **14 Ran SP% 122.2**
PARI-MUTUEL (all including 10 hkd stake): WIN 126.00; PLACE 27.00, 11.00, 25.00; DF 119.00.
**Owner** Mrs Ingrid Jooste & Markus Jooste **Bred** Beaumont Stud **Trained** South Africa

**FOCUS**

On rain soaked ground, the pace was quick early before slowing on the bend: 24.17 (400m), 22.56 (800m), 23.94 (1200m, bend), 23.44 (finish).

## BELMONT PARK (L-H)

Thursday, May 1

**OFFICIAL GOING: Dirt: fast**

### 2005a ELUSIVE QUALITY STKS (CONDITIONS) (4YO+) (DIRT) 7f (D)

**9:57** (12:00) 4-Y-0+ **£36,144** (£12,048; £6,024; £3,012)

RPR

1 **Integrity (USA)**[250] 5781 4-8-10 0........ JJCastellano 2 106
(Chad C Brown, U.S.A) **17/20**[1]

2 3 **Tenango (USA)**[73] 4-8-8 0........ RAlvaradoJr 4 96
(David Jacobson, U.S.A) **9/4**[2]

3 4 ¼ **Cease (USA)**[103] 7-8-6 0........(b) CHVelasquez 3 83
(David Jacobson, U.S.A) **27/10**[3]

4 17 ¼ **Emkanaat**[78] 574 6-8-6 0........(b) ASolis 1 36
(Amy Weaver) **109/10**

1m 22.9s (0.87) **4 Ran SP% 120.3**
PARI-MUTUEL (all including 2 usd stake): WIN 3.70; PLACE (1-2) 2.20, 2.70; SF 7.20.
**Owner** Robert V LaPenta **Bred** Peter E Blum **Trained** USA

## MUNICH (L-H)
Thursday, May 1

**OFFICIAL GOING: Turf: good**

### 2006a SILBERNE PEITSCHE (GROUP 3) (3YO+) (TURF) 6f 110y
**3:40** (12:00) 3-Y-0+

**£26,666** (£9,166; £4,583; £2,500; £1,666; £1,250)

RPR

**1** **Amarillo (IRE)**[166] 7941 5-9-6 0 ........ DennisSchiergen 9 113
(P Schiergen, Germany) *w.w in midfield: gd hdwy on rail to ld 1 1/2f out: rdn and wnt 2 l clr appr fnl f: drvn out* **56/10**

**2** *1 1/2* **Guinnevre (IRE)**[246] 4-9-3 0 ........ EPedroza 5 106
(A Wohler, Germany) *disp 3rd on inner: chsd ldng gp fr 1/2-way: rdn to chal 2f out: styd on u.p fnl f: a wl hld by wnr* **43/10**[2]

**3** *nk* **Gracia Directa (GER)**[173] 7821 6-9-3 0 ........ OliverWilson 6 105
(D Moser, Germany) *disp 3rd on outer: chsd ldr fr 1/2-way: rdn to chal over 2f out: outpcd by wnr appr fnl f: kpt on u.p fr 1f out: no imp on wnr* **103/10**

**4** *1/2* **Baiadera (GER)**[210] 7-9-3 0 ........ MartinLane 4 104
(R Dzubasz, Germany) *t.k.h: chsd ldng trio: outpcd 2 1/2f out: rdn and styd on to chse ldrs over 1 1/2f out: kpt on at same pce fnl f* **247/10**

**5** *2* **Konig Concorde (GER)**[9] 1641 9-9-6 0 ........ (p) WPanov 10 101
(Christian Sprengel, Germany) *towards rr: rdn and effrt over 2f out: kpt on ins fnl f: nvr on terms w ldrs* **157/10**

**6** *3* **Smooth Operator (GER)**[25] 8-9-6 0 ........ (b) StefanieHofer 7 92
(Mario Hofer, Germany) *midfield: chsd ldrs over 2f out: sn rdn: wknd fnl f* **10/1**

**7** *hd* **Princess Bavaroise (FR)**[49] 944 3-8-5 0 ........ JimmyQuinn 1 85
(H-A Pantall, France) *t.k.h: led: rdn over 2f out: hdd 1 1/2f out: wknd ins fnl f* **53/10**[3]

**8** *3* **Opium Bullet** 3-8-8 0 ........ RobertHavlin 3 79
(Jozef Roszival, Hungary) *slow to stride: a towards rr* **109/10**

**9** *3* **High Duty**[18] 3-8-8 0 ........ DanielePorcu 2 70
(P Schiergen, Germany) *chsd ldr: rdn over 2 1/2f out: sn wknd* **9/5**[1]

**10** *1* **Birthday Prince (GER)**[25] 6-9-6 0 ........ (p) KClijmans 8 71
(Christian Sprengel, Germany) *s.s: hld up in rr: nvr a factor* **25/1**

1m 18.04s (-1.96)
**WFA** 3 from 4yo+ 10lb **10** Ran SP% **125.7**
WIN (incl. 10 euro stake): 66. PLACES: 20, 17, 25. SF: 242.
**Owner** Stall Nizza **Bred** Juergen Imm **Trained** Germany

## 1786 BATH (L-H)
Monday, May 5

**OFFICIAL GOING: Good (8.2)**
All races incorporating bottom bend increased in distance by 10yds.
Wind: mild breeze across Weather: cloudy

### 2007 32RED FREE £10 BONUS MEDIAN AUCTION MAIDEN STKS 5f 11y
**1:30** (1:34) (Class 5) 2-Y-0 **£2,587** (£770; £384; £192) **Stalls** Centre

Form RPR

6 **1** **Ivors Rebel**[16] 1575 2-9-5 0 ........ LiamKeniry 1 75
(David Elsworth) *mde all: pushed clr wl over 1f out: kpt on fnl f: rdn out* **9/1**

**2** *3/4* **Aevalon** 2-9-0 0 ........ JohnFahy 6 68
(Eve Johnson Houghton) *racd keenly: mid-div: pushed along and hdwy over 1f out: r.o fnl f: wnt 2nd fnl strides* **20/1**

53 **3** *hd* **Jersey Bull (IRE)**[16] 1571 2-9-5 0 ........ SamHitchcott 10 72
(Mick Channon) *wnt to s early: pressed wnr tl rdn 2f out: kpt on but sn hld: lost 2nd fnl strides* **3/1**[1]

35 **4** *nk* **Designate (IRE)**[16] 1575 2-9-5 0 ........ JamesDoyle 5 71
(Ralph Beckett) *trckd ldrs: rdn over 2f out: kpt on ins fnl f but nt pce to chal* **5/1**[3]

**5** *1 3/4* **Popeswood (IRE)** 2-9-5 0 ........ MartinDwyer 4 65+
(Mick Channon) *hmpd s: towards rr: pushed along over 2f out: kpt on fnl f: nvr trbld ldrs* **33/1**

4 **6** *1* **Arizona Snow**[9] 1741 2-9-5 0 ........ FrannyNorton 7 61
(Ronald Harris) *mid-div: rdn over 2f out: sn one pce* **20/1**

**7** *3/4* **Thumper (FR)** 2-9-5 0 ........ JamieSpencer 11 58
(Robert Cowell) *s.i.s: sn in tch: effrt to chse ldrs 2f out: rn green whn rdn ent fnl f: wknd* **4/1**[2]

**8** *1 1/4* **Clampdown** 2-9-5 0 ........ LukeMorris 2 54
(James Tate) *trckd ldrs: rdn 2f out: wknd fnl f* **10/1**

**9** *5* **Divine Law** 2-9-5 0 ........ RichardHughes 9 36
(Richard Hannon) *s.i.s: sn pushed along: a in rr* **3/1**[1]

0 **10** *1* **Air Of York (IRE)**[28] 1349 2-9-5 0 ........ DavidProbert 8 32
(Ronald Harris) *a towards rr* **66/1**

1m 3.29s (0.79) **Going Correction** -0.075s/f (Good) **10** Ran SP% **119.7**
Speed ratings (Par 93): **90,88,88,88,85 83,82,80,72,70**
CSF £174.63 TOTE £10.50: £3.30, £8.10, £2.00; EX 202.70 Trifecta £1601.30 Part won..
**Owner** Ivor Perry **Bred** Ghelardini Marco **Trained** Newmarket, Suffolk

**FOCUS**
All races incorporating bottom bend increased in distance by 10yds. There was an all-the-way winner of this maiden and the third adds some substance to the form.

### 2008 32RED ON THE APP STORE H'CAP 5f 11y
**2:00** (2:03) (Class 6) (0-60,56) 4-Y-0+ **£1,940** (£577; £288; £144) **Stalls** Centre

Form RPR

146- **1** **Beach Rhythm (USA)**[129] 8411 7-9-4 56 ........ DeclanBates(3) 2 72
(Jim Allen) *mde all: rdn over 1f out: kpt on wl fnl f* **16/1**

-606 **2** *2 3/4* **Molly Jones**[95] 384 5-8-10 45 ........ LiamKeniry 3 51
(Derek Haydn Jones) *chsd ldrs: rdn 2f out: sn chsng wnr: kpt on but a being hld* **20/1**

042 **3** *1* **Christopher Chua (IRE)**[67] 760 5-8-11 46 ........ JamieSpencer 10 48
(Michael Scudamore) *towards rr: swtchd to far rails in 1st f: pushed along and hdwy over 1f out: r.o ins fnl f: nt threat to wnr* **8/1**[2]

5333 **4** *nk* **Belle Bayardo (IRE)**[13] 1639 6-9-5 54 ........ RichardHughes 5 55
(Tony Carroll) *s.i.s: outpcd in rr: r.o ent fnl f: nvr threatened ldrs* **7/4**[1]

2206 **5** *2 3/4* **Diamond Vine (IRE)**[30] 1312 6-8-13 48 ........ (p) DavidProbert 4 39
(Ronald Harris) *nvr bttr than mid-div* **8/1**[2]

5660 **6** *2 1/4* **Little Choosey**[16] 1573 4-9-1 50 ........ MickaelBarzalona 1 33
(Anabel K Murphy) *chsd ldrs: rdn over 2f out: fdd fnl 120yds* **8/1**[2]

25-0 **7** *nse* **Maltease Ah**[25] 1405 5-9-6 55 ........ FergusSweeney 11 38
(Andrew Reid) *chsd ldrs: rdn over 2f out: wknd ent fnl f* **25/1**

1044 **8** *hd* **Volcanic Dust (IRE)**[32] 1270 6-8-12 54 ........ (t) LeroyLynch(7) 6 36
(Milton Bradley) *prom: rdn over 2f out: wknd ent fnl f* **16/1**

4130 **9** *3* **Outbid**[32] 1270 4-9-2 51 ........ LukeMorris 8 23
(Tony Carroll) *mid-div: rdn 3f out: nvr any imp: fdd fnl f* **14/1**

5104 **10** *3 1/4* **Spic 'n Span**[5] 1887 9-8-12 47 ........ (b) LiamJones 9 7
(Ronald Harris) *taken to s early: tried to duck under stalls and nrly uns rdr leaving s: nvr rcvrd: a in rr* **8/1**[2]

146- **11** *15* **Burnt Cream**[201] 7292 7-9-5 54 ........ (t) JamesDoyle 7
(Martin Bosley) *hld up towards rr: rdn over 2f out: nvr any imp: eased whn btn fnl f* **17/2**[3]

1m 1.97s (-0.53) **Going Correction** -0.075s/f (Good) **11** Ran SP% **118.4**
Speed ratings (Par 101): **101,96,95,94,90 86,86,86,81,76 52**
CSF £299.44 CT £2802.00 TOTE £17.10: £4.90, £5.70, £4.60; EX 329.00 Trifecta £719.20 Part won..
**Owner** J P Allen **Bred** Christoph Amerian **Trained** Stoodleigh, Devon

**FOCUS**
The winner scored under a positive ride in this low-grade handicap.

### 2009 32RED.COM H'CAP (BOBIS RACE) 1m 3f 144y
**2:35** (2:35) (Class 4) (0-80,79) 3-Y-0 **£5,112** (£1,509; £755) **Stalls** Low

Form RPR

32-2 **1** **Solidarity**[19] 1509 3-9-7 79 ........ MickaelBarzalona 1 86
(Charlie Appleby) *trckd ldr: chal over 2f out: led wl over 1f out: sn rdn: kpt on wl fnl f: rdn out* **15/8**[2]

5-01 **2** *1/2* **Good Value**[8] 1765 3-9-1 73 6ex ........ JamesDoyle 2 79
(Sir Michael Stoute) *trckd ldng pair: pushed along over 2f out: 1 l down whn rdn ent fnl f: kpt on but nt quite pce to mount serious chal* **8/11**[1]

44-1 **3** *1 3/4* **Opera Fan (FR)**[11] 1661 3-8-7 66 ........ FrannyNorton 3 69
(Mark Johnston) *led: jnd over 2f out: sn rdn: hdd wl over 1f out: kpt on same pce fnl f* **5/1**[3]

2m 34.44s (3.84) **Going Correction** +0.20s/f (Good) **3** Ran SP% **109.4**
Speed ratings (Par 101): **95,94,93**
CSF £3.76 TOTE £3.90; EX 3.90 Trifecta £5.20.
**Owner** Godolphin **Bred** Darley **Trained** Newmarket, Suffolk

**FOCUS**
They went a stop-start gallop in this interesting handicap and there was not much separating the three runners.

### 2010 32RED FILLIES' H'CAP 1m 3f 144y
**3:10** (3:10) (Class 3) (0-90,87) 4-Y-0+ **£7,439** (£2,213; £1,106; £553) **Stalls** Low

Form RPR

215- **1** **Debdebdeb**[254] 5764 4-9-6 86 ........ DavidProbert 1 98
(Andrew Balding) *led for 5f: trckd ldr: led 2f out: sn rdn: styd on strly to draw clr fnl f: rdn out* **11/4**[2]

21- **2** *6* **Norway Cross**[196] 7422 4-9-3 83 ........ RichardHughes 2 85
(Luca Cumani) *trckd ldrs: wnt cl 3rd over 2f out: rdn to dispute 2nd over 1f out: a being hld by wnr ins fnl f: no ex fnl 100yds* **6/5**[1]

/51- **3** *5* **Kalispell (IRE)**[192] 7504 4-9-7 87 ........ MickaelBarzalona 3 82
(Charlie Appleby) *trckd ldng pair: led after 5f: rdn and hdd 2f out: kpt on for disp 2nd tl no ex ins fnl f* **3/1**[3]

04-0 **4** *27* **Opera Box**[30] 1299 6-9-7 87 ........ JamesDoyle 4 34
(Marcus Tregoning) *trckd ldr for 5f: rdn in 3rd over 4f out: wknd 2f out* **7/1**

2m 30.64s (0.04) **Going Correction** +0.20s/f (Good) **4** Ran SP% **109.6**
Speed ratings (Par 104): **107,103,99,81**
CSF £6.59 TOTE £5.00; EX 7.10 Trifecta £10.70.
**Owner** C C Buckley **Bred** C C And Mrs D J Buckley **Trained** Kingsclere, Hants

**FOCUS**
They went a steady pace in this handicap but the winner scored with authority on her comeback.

### 2011 32RED CASINO H'CAP 2m 1f 34y
**3:45** (3:45) (Class 4) (0-85,84) 4-Y-0+ **£4,851** (£1,443; £721; £360) **Stalls** Centre

Form RPR

05-2 **1** **The Quarterjack**[7] 1791 5-8-5 65 oh2 ........ DavidProbert 7 73
(Ron Hodges) *trckd ldrs: rdn over 2f out: led over 1f out: styd on wl: rdn out* **7/2**[2]

-313 **2** *1 1/4* **Arty Campbell (IRE)**[24] 1418 4-8-12 75 ........ JamieSpencer 2 81
(Bernard Llewellyn) *trckd ldr: led wl over 2f out: rdn and hdd over 1f out: styd on same pce* **6/4**[1]

5134 **3** *3/4* **Sir Frank Morgan (IRE)**[15] 1599 4-8-7 70 ........ FrannyNorton 1 75
(Mark Johnston) *dictated stdy pce tl qcknd 5f out: rdn and hdd over 2f out: styd on to regain 3rd ins fnl f* **5/1**

-120 **4** *1/2* **Ordensritter (GER)**[35] 1213 6-9-1 75 ........ JohnFahy 4 79
(Chris Down) *trckd ldrs: rdn in cl 2nd over 2f out: no ex ins fnl f* **4/1**[3]

650- **5** *6* **Petaluma**[241] 6173 5-8-2 67 ........ KatiaScallan(5) 5 64
(Mick Channon) *racd keenly: hld up bhd ldrs: rdn over 2f out: nt pce to get involved: fdd fnl f* **14/1**

00/0 **6** *1 1/4* **Moon Trip**[24] 1418 5-9-0 74 ........ FergusSweeney 3 69?
(Geoffrey Deacon) *hld up but wl in tch: trckd ldrs 4f out: rdn wl over 2f out: fdd fnl f* **12/1**

4m 3.19s (11.29) **Going Correction** +0.20s/f (Good)
**WFA** 4 from 5yo+ 3lb **6** Ran SP% **113.2**
Speed ratings (Par 105): **81,80,80,79,77 76**
CSF £9.36 TOTE £4.40: £3.00, £1.70; EX 13.40 Trifecta £31.50.
**Owner** P E Axon **Bred** Cheveley Park Stud Ltd **Trained** Charlton Mackrell, Somerset

**FOCUS**
They went a very steady pace in this staying handicap and it developed into a sprint.

### 2012 32REDPOKER.COM H'CAP 1m 5y
**4:20** (4:21) (Class 4) (0-80,77) 4-Y-0+ **£4,851** (£1,443; £721; £360) **Stalls** Low

Form RPR

120- **1** **Harry Bosch**[275] 5004 4-9-7 77 ........ JamieSpencer 6 85
(Brian Meehan) *mde all: kpt on wl fnl f: rdn out* **4/1**[1]

-155 **2** *2* **Pick A Little**[10] 1689 6-8-10 66 ........ LukeMorris 7 69
(Michael Blake) *trckd wnr: rdn over 2f out: kpt on gamely for 2nd but hld by wnr fnl f* **16/1**

11-3 **3** *hd* **Scottish Glen**[121] 56 8-9-2 72 ........ DavidProbert 5 75
(Patrick Chamings) *mid-div: hdwy over 2f out: sn rdn to chse ldrs: kpt on same pce fnl f* **9/2**[2]

1205 **4** 2¼ **My Son Max**[9] 1710 6-9-1 **71** MickaelBarzalona 4 68
(Michael Blake) *dwlt: towards rr: hdwy over 2f out: sn rdn: styd on same pce: wnt 4th ins fnl f* **5/1**[3]

03-0 **5** 1¼ **Breakheart (IRE)**[7] 1796 7-8-12 **75** JackGarritty(7) 3 69
(Andrew Balding) *hld up: hdwy fr 3f out: rdn in 3rd 2f out: fdd ins fnl f* **8/1**

4353 **6** 2½ **Gracious George (IRE)**[11] 1682 4-8-11 **74** CamHardie(7) 8 63
(Jimmy Fox) *mid-div: nt clr run on rails over 3f out: rdn over 2f out: nt pce to get involved* **8/1**

-420 **7** 2¼ **Oratorio's Joy (IRE)**[87] 514 4-9-5 **75** FergusSweeney 1 59
(Jamie Osborne) *hld up: rdn over 2f out: nvr threatened* **8/1**

5-03 **8** 2 **Alpine Mist**[65] 800 4-8-9 **65** FrannyNorton 9 44
(Peter Makin) *trckd wnr tl rdn over 2f out: sn wknd* **9/1**

540- **9** 3¼ **Speedy Writer**[242] 6134 4-8-13 **74** AmyScott(5) 2 45
(Henry Candy) *hld up: rdn over 2f out: nvr threatened: wknd fnl f* **11/2**

1m 41.61s (0.81) **Going Correction** +0.20s/f (Good) **9** Ran SP% **119.4**
Speed ratings (Par 105): **103,101,100,98,97 94,92,90,87**
CSF £70.22 CT £304.54 TOTE £3.80: £1.70, £5.20, £1.70; EX 74.90 Trifecta £450.30.
**Owner** Michael Buckley **Bred** C J Murfitt **Trained** Manton, Wilts

**FOCUS**
The winner made all in this handicap and the hold-up performers couldn't land a major blow.

## 2013 32RED TOMB RAIDER SLOT CLASSIFIED STKS 1m 5y
**4:55** (4:56) (Class 5) 3-Y-O **£2,726** (£805; £402) **Stalls** Low

Form RPR

05-0 **1** **Gannicus**[26] 1400 3-9-0 67 LiamKeniry 3 74
(Brendan Powell) *hmpd s: trckd ldrs: rdn over 2f out: led ent fnl f: kpt on: drvn out* **7/1**

2335 **2** 2 **Handwoven (IRE)**[11] 1657 3-9-0 70 FrannyNorton 1 69
(Mark Johnston) *led: rdn and hdd over 2f out: rallied and ev ch ent fnl f: kpt on but sn no ex* **11/4**[2]

13-0 **3** ½ **Peacemaker (IRE)**[28] 1352 3-9-0 69 JohnFahy 6 68
(Eve Johnson Houghton) *s.i.s: sn chsng ldrs: rdn to ld over 2f out: hdd ent fnl f: no ex* **5/1**[3]

4-02 **4** 3¼ **Double Czech (IRE)**[7] 1786 3-9-0 66 DavidProbert 5 60
(Patrick Chamings) *hmpd s: trckd ldr: rdn and ev ch over 2f out: kpt on same pce fr over 1f out* **2/1**[1]

023- **5** hd **Avocadeau (IRE)**[151] 8164 3-9-0 68 MartinDwyer 7 60
(William Muir) *wnt lft s: in tch: pushed along over 3f out: rdn over 2f out: nvr threatened: kpt on same pce* **6/1**

-406 **6** 4 **Autopilot**[7] 1786 3-8-7 65 (b) JackGarritty(7) 4 51
(Anabel K Murphy) *hmpd s: in tch: rdn over 2f out: nt pce to chal: fdd ins fnl f* **10/1**

24-0 **7** 34 **Sydney James (IRE)**[8] 1765 3-9-0 68 SamHitchcott 2
(Dai Burchell) *sn pushed along in last: wknd 2f out: t.o* **25/1**

1m 41.74s (0.94) **Going Correction** +0.20s/f (Good) **7** Ran SP% **116.4**
Speed ratings (Par 99): **103,101,100,97,97 93,59**
CSF £27.44 TOTE £10.30: £5.20, £2.40; EX 37.00 Trifecta £262.40.
**Owner** Winterbeck Manor Stud **Bred** Winterbeck Manor Stud **Trained** Upper Lambourn, Berks

**FOCUS**
Most of the runners were closely matched on form in this classified stakes, but the unexposed winner scored with something in hand.
T/Plt: £860.70 to a £1 stake. Pool: £42,342.94 - 35.91 winning tickets. T/Qpdt: £29.60 to a £1 stake. Pool: £2,966.85 - 74.05 winning tickets. TM

# 1656 BEVERLEY (R-H)
## Monday, May 5

**OFFICIAL GOING: Good to firm (9.2)**
Wind: Moderate across Weather: Cloudy with sunny periods

## 2014 MAYDAY RACEDAY MEDIAN AUCTION MAIDEN STKS 5f
**2:05** (2:05) (Class 6) 2-Y-O **£2,264** (£673; £336; £168) **Stalls** Low

Form RPR

2 **1** **Clouds Rest**[16] 1583 2-9-0 0 TonyHamilton 1 79
(Richard Fahey) *qckly away and mde all: rdn and clr over 1f out: drvn ins fnl f: jst hld on* **5/6**[1]

**2** nse **Free Entry (IRE)** 2-9-0 0 PaulMulrennan 6 79+
(James Tate) *chsd wnr: rdn along 2f out: styd on wl u.p fnl f: jst failed* **17/2**

**3** 8 **Show Spirit** 2-8-9 0 ShaneGray(5) 8 50
(Kevin Ryan) *trckd ldrs on outer: hdwy 1/2-way: chsd ldng pair and rdn over 1f out: kpt on same pce* **7/1**[2]

**4** nk **Soie D'Leau** 2-9-5 0 TomEaves 2 54
(Kristin Stubbs) *in tch: swtchd lft to outer and hdwy 2f out: rdn to chse ldng pair ent fnl f: kpt on same pce* **20/1**

3 **5** 3 **Multiplier**[19] 1505 2-9-5 0 RoystonFfrench 7 43
(Kristin Stubbs) *towards rr: rdn along on outer 1/2-way: styd on appr fnl f: nrst fin* **14/1**

**6** nk **Autumn Revue** 2-9-0 0 RobertWinston 9 37
(Tim Easterby) *towards rr: rdn along over 2f out: styd on fnl f: nrst fin* **33/1**

0 **7** ½ **Monsieur Jimmy**[37] 1161 2-9-2 0 NeilFarley(3) 3 40
(Declan Carroll) *chsd ldrs: rdn along 2f out: sn wknd* **8/1**[3]

**8** ½ **Alfie Bond** 2-9-5 0 BarryMcHugh 4 38
(Brian Rothwell) *chsd ldrs: rdn along wl over 1f out: sn wknd* **50/1**

**9** 1¾ **Don't Tell Bertie** 2-9-0 0 JamesSullivan 10 27
(Tom Tate) *wnt bdly lft s: a bhd* **20/1**

**10** 4 **Penny Royale** 2-9-0 0 DavidAllan 5 13
(Tim Easterby) *s.i.s and a bhd* **12/1**

1m 3.56s (0.06) **Going Correction** -0.20s/f (Firm) **10** Ran SP% **117.5**
Speed ratings (Par 91): **91,90,78,77,72 72,71,70,67,61**
CSF £8.10 TOTE £1.60: £1.02, £2.90, £5.40; EX 10.60 Trifecta £59.50.
**Owner** Racegoers Club Owners Group **Bred** Whitsbury Manor Stud **Trained** Musley Bank, N Yorks

**FOCUS**
Very few got into this median auction maiden and the front two pulled well clear.

## 2015 STRAWBERRY SPRINT STKS (H'CAP) 5f
**2:40** (2:40) (Class 5) (0-75,76) 3-Y-O **£3,234** (£962; £481; £240) **Stalls** Low

Form RPR

065- **1** **Money Team (IRE)**[174] 7846 3-9-5 **73** GrahamGibbons 10 83
(David Barron) *in tch: hdwy over 1f out: swtchd rt and rdn ent fnl f: led last 100yds: kpt on* **8/1**[3]

241- **2** 1¼ **Rural Celebration**[251] 5857 3-9-6 **74** DanielTudhope 1 80
(David O'Meara) *prom: cl up bef 1/2-way: rdn to chal over 1f out: swtchd lft ent fnl f: sn drvn and kpt on same pce* **8/1**[3]

234- **3** 1½ **Gold Club**[223] 6718 3-9-1 **69** PaulMulrennan 7 69+
(Ed McMahon) *hld up in rr: gd hdwy wl over 1f out: nt clr run over 1f out: styd on strly ins fnl f: nrst fin* **11/1**

10-5 **4** nk **Distant Past**[23] 1445 3-9-6 **74** TomEaves 6 73
(Kevin Ryan) *sn led: rdn along wl over 1f out: drvn and edgd lft ent fnl f: hdd & wknd last 100yds* **11/2**[1]

1-44 **5** shd **Royal Warrior**[27] 1368 3-9-7 **75** BenCurtis 9 74
(Alan McCabe) *towards rr: hdwy 2f out: swtchd rt and rdn to chse ldrs over 1f out: kpt on fnl f* **33/1**

0113 **6** 1¼ **Dont Have It Then**[32] 1260 3-8-13 **67** RobertWinston 11 61+
(Willie Musson) *trckd ldrs: effrt and nt clr run wl over 1f out: rdn and styd on fnl f: nrst fin* **7/1**[2]

-216 **7** 2½ **Proclamationofwar**[26] 1396 3-8-12 **71** ShaneGray(5) 15 56
(Kevin Ryan) *chsd ldrs on wd outside: rdn along wl over 1f out: sn one pce* **14/1**

33-1 **8** ½ **Le Laitier (FR)**[14] 1611 3-9-1 **69** PJMcDonald 3 52
(Scott Dixon) *prom: rdn along 2f out: wknd appr fnl f* **11/2**[1]

250- **9** ¾ **Tweety Pie (IRE)**[236] 6295 3-8-12 **69** NeilFarley(3) 12 50
(Declan Carroll) *in tch: effrt and swtchd to outer 1/2-way: sn rdn along and wknd fr wl over 1f out* **16/1**

-405 **10** nse **Danfazi (IRE)**[11] 1676 3-8-13 **70** NataliaGemelova(3) 2 50
(Kristin Stubbs) *t.k.h: chsd ldrs: rdn along 2f out: wknd appr fnl f* **20/1**

505- **11** hd **Offshore Bond**[208] 7126 3-8-13 **67** GrahamLee 8 47
(Jedd O'Keeffe) *a towards rr* **22/1**

4-04 **12** ¾ **Tinsill**[11] 1676 3-8-6 **63** (v) JasonHart(3) 4 40
(Nigel Tinkler) *dwlt and towards rr: nt clr run on inner 2f out: n.d* **8/1**[3]

4-36 **13** nk **Camanche Grey (IRE)**[11] 1676 3-8-9 **63** AndrewElliott 5 39
(Ben Haslam) *prom: rdn along 2f out: sn wknd* **50/1**

0-31 **14** 1 **Lorimer's Lot (IRE)**[9] 1737 3-9-6 **74** DuranFentiman 14 46
(Mark Walford) *a towards rr* **10/1**

136- **15** hd **Jamboree Girl**[199] 7333 3-9-6 **74** PhillipMakin 16 46
(Tim Easterby) *dwlt and swtchd lft s: a towards rr* **16/1**

1m 2.39s (-1.11) **Going Correction** -0.20s/f (Firm) **15** Ran SP% **126.5**
Speed ratings (Par 99): **100,98,95,95,94 92,88,88,86,86 86,85,84,83,82**
CSF £70.96 CT £742.91 TOTE £11.40: £3.40, £2.40, £4.60; EX 72.50 Trifecta £1278.20.
**Owner** Hardisty Rolls II **Bred** Mrs Claire Doyle **Trained** Maunby, N Yorks

**FOCUS**
A wide-open sprint handicap.

## 2016 PETER WALFORD MEMORIAL H'CAP 1m 1f 207y
**3:15** (3:15) (Class 4) (0-80,80) 4-Y-O+ **£4,690** (£1,395; £697; £348) **Stalls** Low

Form RPR

2 **1** **Easter Sky (IRE)**[14] 1608 4-9-7 **80** DanielTudhope 9 94+
(David O'Meara) *prom: led after 2f: rdn clr over 1f out: kpt on strly* **5/1**[3]

2125 **2** 3¾ **Mr Red Clubs (IRE)**[13] 1637 5-9-3 **76** RobertWinston 10 83
(Michael Appleby) *hld up towards rr: hdwy into midfield 1/2-way: effrt on inner over 2f out: rdn to chse wnr over 1f out: sn drvn and no imp* **16/1**

00-1 **3** 1½ **Ever Fortune (USA)**[5] 1885 5-8-10 **69** DaleSwift 8 73
(Brian Ellison) *prom: chsd wnr wl over 2f out: rdn wl over 1f out and kpt on same pce* **3/1**[2]

160- **4** 2¾ **Woodacre**[199] 7346 7-8-4 **66** oh4 ConnorBeasley(3) 5 65
(Richard Whitaker) *sn trcking ldrs: hdwy to chse wnr after 4f: rdn along 3f out: drvn 2f out and grad wknd* **14/1**

P20- **5** ¾ **Allnecessaryforce (FR)**[198] 7369 4-9-3 **76** TonyHamilton 3 74
(Richard Fahey) *hld up in rr: effrt wl over 2f out: rdn and hdwy over 1f out: styd on fnl f: nrst fin* **14/1**

02-3 **6** nse **Moccasin (FR)**[23] 1451 5-9-6 **79** TomEaves 2 76
(Geoffrey Harker) *trckd ldrs: hdwy 3f out: rdn along 2f out: sn drvn and wknd* **12/1**

20-0 **7** hd **Prophesy (IRE)**[21] 1483 5-9-0 **76** NeilFarley(3) 7 73
(Tim Easterby) *hld up in rr: sme hdwy on outer over 2f out: sn rdn along and n.d* **12/1**

1-1 **8** ¾ **Grasped**[26] 1392 4-9-1 **74** GrahamLee 1 70
(Lady Cecil) *midfield: niggled along bef 1/2-way: rdn along 3f out: n.d* **7/4**[1]

46-5 **9** 15 **Magic Skyline (IRE)**[28] 1348 4-8-7 **66** oh4 BenCurtis 4 45
(Brian Ellison) *led 2f: prom: rdn along 4f out: wknd over 3f out: sn bhd* **40/1**

2m 3.12s (-3.88) **Going Correction** -0.275s/f (Firm) **9** Ran SP% **115.1**
Speed ratings (Par 105): **104,101,99,97,97 96,96,96,84**
CSF £79.79 CT £280.27 TOTE £7.80: £2.00, £3.60, £1.40; EX 56.40 Trifecta £324.70.
**Owner** Helmsley Bloodstock **Bred** M3 Elevage And Haras D'Etreham **Trained** Nawton, N Yorks

**FOCUS**
A fair handicap.

## 2017 SWAN INDUSTRIAL DRIVES H'CAP 1m 100y
**3:50** (3:50) (Class 4) (0-85,85) 4-Y-O+ **£6,469** (£1,925; £962; £481) **Stalls** Low

Form RPR

-645 **1** **Dubai Dynamo**[8] 1762 9-9-2 **80** PJMcDonald 7 89
(Ruth Carr) *hld up in rr: hdwy wl over 1f out: swtchd lft and rdn ent fnl f: styd on strly to ld nr fin* **4/1**[2]

06-0 **2** nk **Shadowtime**[5] 1881 9-8-9 **73** DaleSwift 4 81
(Tracy Waggott) *in tch: hdwy to chse ldrs over 3f out: effrt on inner 2f out: rdn to chal ent fnl f: squeezed through to ld 120yds out: drvn: hdd and no ex nr fin* **12/1**

10-2 **3** 1½ **Ingleby Symphony (IRE)**[8] 1762 4-8-7 **71** PatrickMathers 5 76
(Richard Fahey) *towards rr: pushed along over 3f out: hdwy on wd outside 2f out: rdn over 1f out: kpt on fnl f* **10/1**

40-0 **4** 1¾ **King Of The Danes**[18] 1539 4-9-5 **83** JoeFanning 6 84
(Mark Johnston) *cl up: rdn along over 2f out: ev ch tl drvn ent fnl f and wknd last 100yds* **5/1**[3]

0-05 **5** 2¾ **Zaitsev (IRE)**[15] 1598 4-8-9 **73** ow1 RobertWinston 2 67
(Ollie Pears) *led: pushed along and jnd over 2f out: rdn wl over 1f out: drvn ent fnl f: hdd & wknd last 120yds* **9/1**

00-3 **6** 1½ **Toto Skyllachy**[17] 1564 9-9-7 **85** DanielTudhope 8 76
(David O'Meara) *trckd ldrs: hdwy wl over 2f out: rdn over 1f out: drvn and wknd ent fnl f* **11/2**

0 **7** 3 **Bob**[21] 1483 4-9-0 **78** DavidAllan 9 62
(Les Eyre) *chsd ldrs: rdn along over 2f out: drvn and wknd over 1f out* **25/1**

33-4 **8** 1¼ **Woody Bay**[26] 1399 4-8-12 **76** GrahamLee 1 57
(James Given) *hld up: a towards rr* **3/1**[1]

21/0 **9** 8 **Engrossing**[14] 1607 5-8-11 **75** JamesSullivan 3 38
(Ruth Carr) *dwlt: a bhd* **40/1**

2314 **10** *38* **Silverware (USA)**30 1316 6-9-5 **83**................................ TomEaves 10
(Kristin Stubbs) *cl up on outer: rdn along wl over 3f out: sn wknd* **14/1**
1m 44.14s (-3.46) **Going Correction** -0.275s/f (Firm) **10** Ran SP% **116.8**
Speed ratings (Par 105): **106,105,104,102,99 98,95,93,85,47**
CSF £51.32 CT £451.23 TOTE £5.20: £1.70, £4.80, £2.80; EX 63.90 Trifecta £1630.30.
**Owner** The Bottom Liners **Bred** T K & Mrs P A Knox **Trained** Huby, N Yorks

**FOCUS**
A decent handicap and they went a good pace, with a few taking each other on early, but this suited the hold-up horses.

## 2018 BRIAN BROWN "OPEN ALL TURNSTILES" RETIREMENT H'CAP 1m 4f 16y
**4:25** (4:25) (Class 5) (0-75,69) 3-Y-O **£3,408** (£1,006; £503) **Stalls** Low

Form RPR
3-00 **1** **Full Day**19 1509 3-8-10 **69**................................ MeganCarberry(7) 3 72
(Brian Ellison) *trckd ldng pair on inner: effrt and n.m.r over 2f out: swtchd lft and rdn over 1f out: swtchd rt and hdwy on inner ent fnl f: drvn and styd on wl to ld nr line* **11/4**3

-530 **2** *shd* **Rookery (IRE)**13 1635 3-9-3 **69**................................ AdrianNicholls 1 71
(Mark Johnston) *led: rdn along and jnd wl over 2f out: drvn over 1f out: edgd lft ins fnl f: hdd nr line* **10/1**

-333 **3** *3* **Power Up**39 1135 3-9-2 **68**................................ JoeFanning 4 65
(Mark Johnston) *trckd ldng pair: hdwy on outer 3f out: chal 2f out and sn rdn: drvn and ev ch over 1f out tl wknd ins fnl f* **15/8**2

221- **4** *8* **Fair Flutter (IRE)**215 6946 3-9-2 **68**................................ TonyHamilton 2 52
(Richard Fahey) *trckd ldr: cl up over 3f out: rdn along over 2f out: sn btn* **13/8**1

2m 38.97s (-0.83) **Going Correction** -0.275s/f (Firm) **4** Ran SP% **108.6**
Speed ratings (Par 99): **91,90,88,83**
CSF £21.98 TOTE £4.60; EX 21.80 Trifecta £70.00.
**Owner** Dan Gilbert **Bred** W And R Barnett Ltd **Trained** Norton, N Yorks
■ Stewards' Enquiry : Adrian Nicholls two-day ban: used whip down the shoulder in the forehand (May 19-20)

**FOCUS**
A tight little 3yo handicap with just 1lb covering the four runners, none of whom had been over this trip before. They didn't go much of a pace until things quickened up coming to the last half-mile.

## 2019 RACING AGAIN ON TUESDAY 13 MAY H'CAP 7f 100y
**5:00** (5:01) (Class 5) (0-70,70) 4-Y-O+ **£3,234** (£962; £481; £240) **Stalls** Low

Form RPR
451 **1** **Real Tigress (IRE)**19 1510 5-9-0 **63**................................ DavidAllan 2 79+
(Les Eyre) *in tch on inner: smooth hdwy 2f out: led wl over 1f out: rdn clr appr fnl f: kpt on strly* **3/1**1

30-0 **2** *4* **Juvenal (IRE)**19 1503 5-9-5 **68**................................(p) TomEaves 10 73
(Geoffrey Harker) *dwlt and in rr: hdwy wl over 1f out: swtchd lft and rdn appr fnl f: fin strly* **25/1**

00-0 **3** *nk* **Day Of The Eagle (IRE)**23 1446 8-9-6 **69**................ GrahamGibbons 8 73
(Michael Easterby) *hld up towards rr: hdwy on inner over 2f out: rdn to chse ldrs whn hmpd ins fnl f: kpt on wl towards fin* **12/1**

5126 **4** *hd* **Ellaal**11 1675 5-9-0 **63**................................ JamesSullivan 1 67
(Ruth Carr) *trckd ldrs on inner: swtchd lft and effrt to chal 2f out: rdn over 1f out and ev ch whn n.m.r and sltly hmpd 1f out: sn drvn and kpt on same pce* **7/1**

-346 **5** *2 1/4* **Thrust Control (IRE)**12 1649 7-8-4 **56** oh9..........(p) ConnorBeasley(3) 6 54
(Tracy Waggott) *set str pce: rdn along and edgd lft wl over 1f out: sn drvn and hdd: edgd rt ins fnl f: sn wknd* **20/1**

40-2 **6** *1 1/4* **Mister Marcasite**6 1845 4-8-13 **62**................................ GrahamLee 3 57
(Mel Brittain) *chsd ldrs: rdn along wl over 2f out: n.m.r wl over 1f out: sn drvn and one pce appr fnl f* **4/1**2

3246 **7** *nk* **Silly Billy (IRE)**10 1689 6-8-7 **59**................................(p) JasonHart(3) 13 53
(John Balding) *midfield: effrt on outer over 2f out: sn rdn and no imp* **8/1**

5-00 **8** *shd* **Banovallum**26 1376 4-9-0 **70**................................ DanielleMooney(7) 7 64
(Michael Easterby) *midfield: hdwy ovr 2f out: rdn and nt clr run wl over 1f out: one pce after* **20/1**

0046 **9** *1/2* **Imperator Augustus (IRE)**63 817 6-8-10 **59**.......... PaulMulrennan 4 52
(Patrick Holmes) *chsd ldr: cl up on outer 3f out: rdn along over 2f out: drvn wl over 1f out and sn wknd* **6/1**3

36-6 **10** *2* **Shearian**14 1610 4-8-11 **60**................................ BarryMcHugh 9 48
(Tracy Waggott) *hld up towards rr: hdwy whn nt clr run and hmpd wl over 1f out: sn swtchd rt and rdn: no imp* **25/1**

2-12 **11** *nse* **Bond Artist (IRE)**52 964 5-8-4 **56** oh1................................ IanBrennan(3) 5 44
(Geoffrey Oldroyd) *dwlt and towards rr: effrt and sme hdwy on inner whn n.m.r wl over 1f out: n.d after* **9/1**

6062 **12** *2 3/4* **Mitchum**14 1606 5-8-9 **58** ow2................................ DaleSwift 12 39
(Ron Barr) *a towards rr* **20/1**

60-6 **13** *15* **Spithead**19 1503 4-8-8 **57**................................ PJMcDonald 11
(Mike Sowersby) *prom on outer: rdn along wl over 2f out: sn wknd* **40/1**

1m 31.73s (-2.07) **Going Correction** -0.275s/f (Firm) **13** Ran SP% **125.0**
Speed ratings (Par 103): **100,95,95,94,92 90,90,90,89,87 87,84,67**
CSF £93.29 CT £851.44 TOTE £3.90: £1.10, £8.80, £4.70; EX 101.10 Trifecta £1151.20.
**Owner** GIB Bloodstock Limited **Bred** Atacama Bloodstock Ltd **Trained** Catton, North Yorkshire

**FOCUS**
A modest handicap, but run at a decent pace and won with some authority by the favourite.

## 2020 WHITE RABBIT H'CAP 7f 100y
**5:30** (5:31) (Class 6) (0-65,65) 3-Y-O **£2,264** (£673; £336; £168) **Stalls** Low

Form RPR
0-02 **1** **Mariners Moon (IRE)**11 1657 3-9-7 **65**................................ DanielTudhope 4 79
(David O'Meara) *trckd ldrs on inner: swtchd lft over 2f out: effrt over 1f out: led ent fnl f: sn rdn clr* **15/8**1

4-30 **2** *6* **The Dukkerer (IRE)**25 1403 3-9-2 **60**................................ PaulMulrennan 5 59
(Garry Moss) *trckd ldrs: hdwy to chse ldr 2f out: sn rdn and ev ch: drvn and kpt on same pce fnl f* **7/1**2

3-36 **3** *1 1/4* **Lynngale**30 1308 3-8-11 **60**................................ JacobButterfield(5) 14 56
(Kristin Stubbs) *in tch: hdwy on outer to chse ldrs over 2f out: rdn wl over 1f out: kpt on u.p fnl f* **16/1**

6-42 **4** *hd* **Tamayuz Magic (IRE)**12 1648 3-9-3 **61**................(b) GrahamGibbons 9 56
(Michael Easterby) *in tch: hdwy 3f out: chsd ldrs 2f out: sn rdn and kpt on same pce ent fnl f* **8/1**3

2320 **5** *3/4* **Queenie's Home**14 1611 3-9-5 **63**................................ GrahamLee 10 57
(James Given) *hld up in rr: hdwy into midfield 1/2-way: rdn to chse ldrs whn n.m.r and swtchd rt ent fnl f: one pce after* **10/1**

66-0 **6** *hd* **China In My Hands**14 1611 3-9-2 **60**................................ JoeFanning 12 53
(James Bethell) *hld up in rr: hdwy into midfield 1/2-way: swtchd lft to outer and rdn 2f out: drvn and no imp appr fnl f* **16/1**

00-0 **7** *nk* **Moxey**16 1588 3-8-8 **52**................................1 PJMcDonald 1 44
(John Davies) *bhd: hdwy over 3f out: rdn wl over 1f out: styd on fnl f: nrst fin* **33/1**

00-6 **8** *1/2* **Bahamian C**21 1486 3-9-7 **65**................................(p) TonyHamilton 15 56
(Richard Fahey) *hld up in rr: hdwy 2f out: rdn over 1f out: styd on fnl f: nrst fin* **16/1**

4255 **9** *3 1/2* **Armelle (FR)**45 1048 3-8-1 **52**................................ MatthewHopkins(7) 11 34
(Scott Dixon) *led: rdn along 2f out: drvn over 1f out: hdd & wknd ent fnl f* **25/1**

66-4 **10** *3 1/2* **Maysville (IRE)**12 1647 3-8-8 **52**................................1 BarryMcHugh 3 26
(Tony Coyle) *a towards rr* **12/1**

04-0 **11** *nk* **Edward Elgar**23 1441 3-8-12 **56**................................ PaulQuinn 7 29
(Richard Whitaker) *a in rr* **33/1**

6-35 **12** *shd* **White Rose Runner**23 1441 3-9-6 **64**................................ DavidAllan 2 37
(Mel Brittain) *dwlt and in rr: hdwy 1/2-way: effrt on inner whn nt clr run 2f out: sn wknd* **7/1**2

0-44 **13** *3 3/4* **Soul Artist (IRE)**12 1648 3-8-8 **52**................................(b1) DuranFentiman 13 15
(Tim Easterby) *chsd ldr: rdn over 2f out: drvn wl over 1f out and sn wknd* **25/1**

60-0 **14** *3/4* **Snugfit Sam**14 1611 3-8-9 **53**................................ TomEaves 6 14
(John Quinn) *prom: rdn along over 3f out: sn wknd* **22/1**

1m 32.25s (-1.55) **Going Correction** -0.275s/f (Firm) **14** Ran SP% **123.2**
Speed ratings (Par 97): **97,90,88,88,87 87,87,86,82,78 78,78,73,72**
CSF £13.66 CT £172.53 TOTE £3.50: £1.60, £2.20, £5.80; EX 27.30 Trifecta £531.50.
**Owner** Stu, Mark, Ed Racing **Bred** Sarah McNicholas **Trained** Nawton, N Yorks

**FOCUS**
A moderate handicap, with only one of the 14 runners a previous winner. The favourite was different class.
T/Jkpt: £25,663.00 to a £1 stake. Pool: £54,217.66 - 1.50 winning units. T/Plt: £423.50 to a £1 stake. Pool: £64,277.14 - 110.79 winning units. T/Qpdt: £84.20 to a £1 stake. Pool: £3141.27 - 27.60 winning units. JR

# 1677 WARWICK (L-H)
## Monday, May 5

**OFFICIAL GOING: Good (good to soft in places; 6.3)**
Wind: Light half-behind Weather: Cloudy with sunny spells

## 2021 ART KITCHEN, WARWICK APPRENTICE H'CAP 1m 20y
**1:55** (1:56) (Class 6) (0-65,65) 4-Y-O+ **£1,940** (£577; £288; £144) **Stalls** Low

Form RPR
35-4 **1** **Balmoral Castle**35 1209 5-9-3 **64**................................ NedCurtis(3) 9 74+
(Jonathan Portman) *prom: lost pl 5f out: hdwy over 1f out: led ins fnl f: r.o* **6/1**

-350 **2** *1 3/4* **Living Leader**94 410 5-8-12 **61**................................ KieranShoemark(5) 8 67
(Grace Harris) *hld up: rdn over 3f out: hdwy over 2f out: chsd wnr ins fnl f: r.o* **14/1**

-361 **3** *1* **George Benjamin**97 367 7-8-13 **60**................(tp) AlistairRawlinson(3) 1 64
(Michael Appleby) *chsd ldrs: led over 2f out: rdn and hdd ins fnl f: styd on same pce* **9/2**2

00-2 **4** *3 3/4* **Specialty (IRE)**14 1613 4-9-4 **62**................................ TimClark 4 57
(Pam Sly) *led: rdn and hdd over 2f out: edgd rt fr over 1f out: wknd ins fnl f* **4/1**1

-000 **5** *1* **Admirable Art (IRE)**68 750 4-9-2 **60**................(p) MarcMonaghan 2 53
(Tony Carroll) *s.i.s: hld up: rdn over 1f out: nvr trbld ldrs* **8/1**

0-54 **6** *nse* **Kay Gee Be (IRE)**32 1268 10-9-2 **65**................................ JordanHibberd(5) 11 58
(Alan Berry) *mid-div: hdwy 5f out: rdn over 2f out: styd on same pce* **16/1**

04-4 **7** *hd* **Clary (IRE)**13 1631 4-8-7 **51**................................ DanielMuscutt 7 43
(James Unett) *chsd ldrs: rdn over 1f out: wknd ins fnl f* **25/1**

060- **8** *1* **Glasgon**230 6497 4-8-5 **54** ow2................................ LukeLeadbitter(5) 5 44
(Declan Carroll) *hld up: hdwy 1/2-way: rdn over 2f out: wknd fnl f* **11/2**3

00-4 **9** *1/2* **Hayek**30 1309 7-8-2 **51** oh1................................(b) RachelRichardson(5) 3 40
(Tim Easterby) *s.s: hld up: a in rr* **12/1**

50-0 **10** *shd* **Hawk Moth (IRE)**11 1664 6-8-9 **56**................................(b) RyanWhile(3) 6 44
(John Spearing) *hld up: rdn over 2f out: n.d* **22/1**

-235 **11** *1 1/2* **Candy Kitten**35 1209 4-9-7 **65**................................(p) DannyBrock 10 50
(Alastair Lidderdale) *chsd ldr tl rdn over 2f out: wknd over 1f out* **12/1**

1m 41.34s (0.34) **Going Correction** +0.10s/f (Good) **11** Ran SP% **115.1**
Speed ratings (Par 101): **102,100,99,95,94 94,94,93,92,92 91**
CSF £84.81 CT £419.65 TOTE £7.30: £2.30, £4.90, £2.00; EX 89.40 Trifecta £548.80.
**Owner** J G B Portman **Bred** Springcombe Park Stud **Trained** Upper Lambourn, Berks

**FOCUS**
A dry run up to the meeting saw the ground dry out to good to soft, good in places and there was a breeze behind the runners in the straight. Mainly exposed performers in a modest handicap run at an ordinary gallop. The field raced-centre-to stands' side in the straight and the first three finished clear.

## 2022 BRITISH STALLION STUDS EBF MAIDEN FILLIES' STKS (BOBIS RACE) 5f
**2:30** (2:32) (Class 5) 2-Y-O **£2,911** (£866; £432; £216) **Stalls** Low

Form RPR
6 **1** **Rise Up Lotus (IRE)**18 1528 2-9-0 0................................ PaulHanagan 9 70+
(Charles Hills) *s.i.s: plld hrd and sn trcking ldrs: rdn to ld 1f out: r.o* **2/1**1

3 **2** *1* **War Paint (IRE)**21 1482 2-9-0 0................................ RichardKingscote 6 66
(Tom Dascombe) *wnt rt s: sn led: rdn and hdd 1f out: styd on* **2/1**1

4 **3** *1/2* **Simply Magic (IRE)**16 1571 2-9-0 0................................ PatDobbs 2 65
(Richard Hannon) *trckd ldrs: rdn over 1f out: edgd rt: r.o* **7/1**2

0 **4** *1/2* **Tarando**18 1528 2-9-0 0................................ TomQueally 1 63+
(Michael Bell) *hld up: pushed along and hdwy over 1f out: r.o* **8/1**

**5** *2 1/2* **Clodovil Doll (IRE)** 2-9-0 0................................ JimmyQuinn 8 54+
(James Tate) *hmpd s: plld hrd and sn w ldr: rdn and ev ch over 1f out: wknd ins fnl f* **25/1**

**6** *1/2* **Zuzinia (IRE)** 2-8-11 0................................ WilliamTwiston-Davies(3) 5 52+
(Mick Channon) *hmpd s: sn prom: rdn over 1f out: no ex fnl f* **15/2**3

**7** *1/2* **Blue Burmese (IRE)** 2-9-0 0................................ JimmyFortune 4 50
(Mark Usher) *s.i.s: hld up: nvr on terms* **50/1**

0 **8** *1 3/4* **Karluk (IRE)**21 1488 2-9-0 0................................ DaneO'Neill 7 44
(Eve Johnson Houghton) *s.i.s: hld up: pushed along 1/2-way: wknd over 1f out* **25/1**

**9** *7* **Swift Susie** 2-8-7 0................................(b1) AaronJones(7) 3 19
(Stuart Williams) *hld up: a in rr: wknd wl over 1f out* **16/1**

1m 1.44s (1.84) **Going Correction** +0.10s/f (Good) **9** Ran SP% **117.6**
Speed ratings (Par 90): **89,87,86,85,81 81,80,77,66**
CSF £5.64 TOTE £2.50: £1.02, £1.10, £3.10; EX 6.80 Trifecta £26.30.
**Owner** Hamdan Al Maktoum **Bred** Tally-Ho Stud **Trained** Lambourn, Berks

**FOCUS**
No more than a fair fillies' maiden and one in which the gallop was reasonable. The field edged towards the stands' side in the last quarter mile.

## 2023 TURFTV H'CAP — 5f
**3:05** (3:10) (Class 6) (0-60,60) 3-Y-O — **£1,940** (£577; £288; £144) **Stalls** Low

Form — RPR

425- **1** **Where The Boys Are (IRE)**[157] [8090] 3-9-7 **60**............. PaulHanagan 3 — 68
(Ed McMahon) *a.p: shkn up over 1f out: led and hung lft ins fnl f: r.o* **11/4**[1]

550- **2** *1 3/4* **Red Forever**[179] [7789] 3-8-12 **54**.................................. SladeO'Hara(3) 11 — 56
(Alan Berry) *chsd ldrs: shkn up and hung lft fr over 1f out: sn ev ch: hmpd ins fnl f: styd on same pce* **12/1**

2303 **3** *2 1/2* **Narborough**[12] [1642] 3-9-3 **59**........................ WilliamTwiston-Davies(3) 2 — 52
(Mick Channon) *trckd ldrs: shkn up to ld over 1f out: hdd and no ex ins fnl f* **4/1**[2]

626- **4** *1* **Astral Rose**[147] [8222] 3-9-4 **57**............................... RichardKingscote 9 — 46
(Jonathan Portman) *led: rdn and hdd over 1f out: styng on same pce whn hmpd ins fnl f* **16/1**

46-2 **5** *hd* **Clear Focus (IRE)**[13] [1626] 3-8-0 **46** oh1..................(p) JennyPowell(7) 8 — 34
(Brendan Powell) *chsd ldrs: rdn over 1f out: no ex fnl f* **9/2**[3]

6644 **6** *1 1/4* **Brean Splash Susie**[13] [1626] 3-8-2 **46** oh1..................(b) RyanWhile(5) 4 — 30
(Bill Turner) *s.i.s: hld up: nvr trbld ldrs* **10/1**

0540 **7** *4* **Back On Baileys**[35] [1211] 3-8-7 **46**......................................... ChrisCatlin 1 — 15
(John Ryan) *s.i.s: outpcd* **20/1**

06-0 **8** *3/4* **Bashiba (IRE)**[14] [1611] 3-8-7 **46** oh1........................ SilvestreDeSousa 6 — 13
(Nigel Tinkler) *hld up: rdn over 1f out: sn wknd and eased* **6/1**

5450 **9** *3* **Luv U Honey**[12] [1647] 3-8-7 **46** oh1..................................... JimmyQuinn 5
(Brian Baugh) *hmpd sn after s: a in rr* **33/1**

-066 **10** *2* **Oakley Dancer**[3] [1914] 3-8-0 **46** oh1...............................(t) JoeDoyle(7) 10
(Tony Carroll) *chsd ldrs: sn pushed along: lost pl after 1f: n.d after* **33/1**

1m 0.37s (0.77) **Going Correction** +0.10s/f (Good) — **10** Ran SP% **112.4**
Speed ratings (Par 97): **97,94,90,88,88 86,79,78,73,70**
CSF £35.03 CT £131.51 TOTE £3.70: £1.80, £2.50, £1.60; EX 30.90 Trifecta £197.00.
**Owner** Philip Wilkins **Bred** Neville O'Byrne **Trained** Lichfield, Staffs
■ Stewards' Enquiry : Paul Hanagan two-day ban: careless riding (May 22-23)

**FOCUS**
Effectively a maiden handicap and the start was delayed as the subsequently withdrawn Little Briar Rose went down in the stalls. The gallop was sound, but those held up were at a disadvantage.

## 2024 QUANTUM MANUFACTURING FILLIES' H'CAP — 7f
**3:40** (3:42) (Class 5) (0-75,75) 3-Y-O+ — **£2,587** (£770; £384; £192) **Stalls** Low

Form — RPR

063- **1** **Ixelles Diamond (IRE)**[244] [6070] 3-8-9 **68**...................... PaulHanagan 4 — 72
(Richard Fahey) *hld up: pushed along 1/2-way: hdwy over 1f out: r.o u.p to ld post* **9/2**

4512 **2** *hd* **Serenity Spa**[26] [1392] 4-9-12 **73**................................ SilvestreDeSousa 6 — 80
(Tony Carroll) *trckd ldrs: led over 1f out: rdn and edgd rt ins fnl f: hdd post* **6/1**

0-31 **3** *3/4* **Broughtons Charm (IRE)**[33] [1247] 4-10-0 **75**.................. ChrisCatlin 2 — 80
(Willie Musson) *led 1f: trckd ldr tl led again 2f out: rdn and hdd over 1f out: styd on* **10/1**

1-20 **4** *3/4* **Bousatet (FR)**[14] [1607] 4-9-8 **74**.......................................... KevinStott(5) 5 — 77
(Kevin Ryan) *trckd ldrs: rdn over 1f out: styd on* **7/2**[2]

55-5 **5** *1/2* **Lulu The Zulu (IRE)**[18] [1537] 6-9-13 **74**............................ TomQueally 3 — 81+
(Michael Appleby) *stdd s: hld up: hdwy and edgd rt over 1f out: styng on whn nt clr run wl ins fnl f: nt rcvr* **11/4**[1]

6540 **6** *21* **Hold The Star**[13] [1631] 8-8-10 **62** oh16 ow1..................... AnnStokell(5) 7 — 9
(Ann Stokell) *s.s: outpcd* **100/1**

-122 **7** *25* **Chantrea (IRE)**[26] [1389] 3-8-13 **72**...............................(v[1]) AndreaAtzeni 1
(Lady Cecil) *led 6f out: rdn and hdd 2f out: sn wknd* **4/1**[3]

1m 25.96s (2.76) **Going Correction** +0.10s/f (Good)
**WFA** 3 from 4yo+ 12lb — **7** Ran SP% **111.4**
Speed ratings (Par 100): **88,87,86,86,85 61,32**
CSF £29.47 TOTE £5.00: £3.30, £3.90; EX 35.70 Trifecta £384.00.
**Owner** Miss Louise Tillett **Bred** Lynn Lodge Stud **Trained** Musley Bank, N Yorks

**FOCUS**
A fair fillies' handicap in which the gallop was reasonable and the field again migrated to the stands' side in the straight. The first five finished in a heap.

## 2025 BREEDERS BACKING RACING EBF MAIDEN STKS (DIV I) — 1m 20y
**4:15** (4:18) (Class 5) 3-Y-O+ — **£3,881** (£1,155; £577; £288) **Stalls** Low

Form — RPR

**1** **Sharp Volley (IRE)** 3-9-1 0........................................... AndreaAtzeni 3 — 78+
(Stuart Williams) *trckd ldrs: shkn up over 2f out: led and edgd lft ins fnl f: r.o wl* **10/1**

34-0 **2** *2 1/4* **Bon Voyage**[19] [1513] 3-9-1 92............................................. PatDobbs 7 — 73
(Richard Hannon) *trckd ldr: shkn up to ld over 1f out: rdn: edgd lft and hdd ins fnl f: styd on same pce* **6/5**[1]

00 **3** *1/2* **Semaral (IRE)**[14] [1612] 3-8-10 0....................................... TedDurcan 1 — 67
(Chris Wall) *trckd ldrs: shkn up and ev ch over 1f out: styd on same pce ins fnl f* **50/1**

0 **4** *2 1/4* **Saalib (USA)**[16] [1582] 3-9-1 0...............................(t[1]) PaulHanagan 5 — 66
(Brian Meehan) *led at stdy pce tl qcknd over 2f out: rdn and hdd over 1f out: no ex ins fnl f* **10/1**

0 **5** *1 3/4* **Scarlet Plum**[24] [1422] 3-8-10 0.................................... FrederikTylicki 2 — 57
(Roger Charlton) *s.i.s: sn prom: rdn over 2f out: styd on same pce fr over 1f out* **3/1**[2]

40 **6** *1* **Musical Theme**[14] [1616] 3-8-10 0....................................... PaddyAspell 9 — 55
(Willie Musson) *prom: rdn over 2f out: styd on same pce fr over 1f out* **66/1**

**7** *3/4* **Hooke's Law (IRE)** 3-9-1 0............................................ JimmyFortune 8 — 58
(Brian Meehan) *s.i.s: hld up: shakne up over 1f out: nvr nrr* **16/1**

2-0 **8** *1/2* **Gambol (FR)**[9] [1730] 4-10-0 0.......................................[1] DaneO'Neill 6 — 60
(J W Hills) *broke wl: sn stdd and lost pl: shkn up over 2f out: nt trble ldrs* **15/2**[3]

**9** *2 1/4* **Havana Girl (IRE)** 3-8-10 0.......................................... TomQueally 10 — 47
(Harry Dunlop) *hld up: a in rr* **20/1**

00 **10** *2 1/2* **Sound Of Life (IRE)**[26] [1395] 3-8-10 0............................ ChrisCatlin 4 — 41
(Rae Guest) *mid-div: shkn up over 2f out: sn outpcd* **66/1**

060 **11** *8* **Purana**[11] [1680] 3-8-10 0.........................................[1] SilvestreDeSousa 11 — 23
(Tony Carroll) *hld up: pushed along over 2f out: wknd over 1f out* **33/1**

1m 43.49s (2.49) **Going Correction** +0.10s/f (Good)
**WFA** 3 from 4yo 13lb — **11** Ran SP% **118.9**
Speed ratings (Par 103): **91,88,88,86,84 83,82,82,79,77 69**
CSF £22.06 TOTE £11.60: £4.60, £1.10, £15.60; EX 44.50 Trifecta £649.30.
**Owner** Champion Bloodstock Ltd **Bred** Yves Elliot **Trained** Newmarket, Suffolk

**FOCUS**
A variety of ability on show, and the pace was no more than fair.

## 2026 BREEDERS BACKING RACING EBF MAIDEN STKS (DIV II) — 1m 20y
**4:50** (4:54) (Class 5) 3-Y-O+ — **£3,881** (£1,155; £577; £288) **Stalls** Low

Form — RPR

3-5 **1** **Munaaser**[27] [1357] 3-9-1 0............................................... PaulHanagan 1 — 88+
(Sir Michael Stoute) *hld up in tch: shkn up to chse ldr over 1f out: r.o to ld wl ins fnl f: sn clr* **11/8**[1]

00- **2** *5* **Newton's Law (IRE)**[212] [7017] 3-9-1 0........................(t) JimmyFortune 3 — 75
(Brian Meehan) *led: clr 2f out: rdn and hdd wl ins fnl f: sn outpcd* **9/2**[3]

**3** *1/2* **Kleo (GR)** 3-8-10 0................................................ LemosdeSouza 5 — 69
(Luca Cumani) *hld up: hdwy over 1f out: r.o: nt rch ldrs* **20/1**

0-0 **4** *2 1/4* **Windy Citi**[14] [1612] 3-8-10 0.............................................. TedDurcan 9 — 64
(Chris Wall) *hld up: hdwy over 1f out: styd on same pce fnl f* **33/1**

6 **5** *2* **Emirati Spirit**[19] [1511] 3-9-1 0........................................ AndreaAtzeni 8 — 64
(Roger Varian) *trckd ldr 2f: remained handy: rdn over 2f out: wknd fnl f* **15/8**[2]

0-0 **6** *1 3/4* **Saxon Princess (IRE)**[16] [1582] 3-8-10 0..................... FrederikTylicki 2 — 55
(Roger Charlton) *s.s: hld up: nvr nrr* **20/1**

**7** *nse* **Cobham's Circus (IRE)** 3-8-8 0...................................... JoeDoyle(7) 4 — 60
(Marcus Tregoning) *s.i.s: hld up: pushed along over 2f out: n.d* **40/1**

0 **8** *7* **Ballyfarsoon (IRE)**[11] [1681] 3-9-1 0.................................. StevieDonohoe 7 — 44
(Ian Williams) *mid-div: rdn and wknd over 2f out* **100/1**

0-5 **9** *3* **Storm Rider (IRE)**[7] [1808] 3-9-1 0....................................... PatDobbs 6 — 37
(Richard Hannon) *hld up: a in rr: rdn and wknd over 2f out* **16/1**

6 **10** *6* **Nouvelle Ere**[11] [1681] 3-9-1 0................................. SilvestreDeSousa 10 — 23
(Tony Carroll) *racd wd to 1/2-way: prom: wnt 2nd 6f out tl rdn over 2f out: sn wknd* **50/1**

1m 40.82s (-0.18) **Going Correction** +0.10s/f (Good) — **10** Ran SP% **118.8**
Speed ratings (Par 103): **104,99,98,96,94 92,92,85,82,76**
CSF £7.66 TOTE £2.10: £1.10, £2.20, £4.70; EX 9.30 Trifecta £79.10.
**Owner** Hamdan Al Maktoum **Bred** Shadwell Estate Company Limited **Trained** Newmarket, Suffolk

**FOCUS**
An uncompetitive maiden in which the gallop was reasonable. The winner came down the centre and won with something in hand.

## 2027 RACINGUK.COM H'CAP (A LONDON MILE SERIES QUALIFIER) — 1m 20y
**5:25** (5:27) (Class 5) (0-70,70) 3-Y-O — **£2,587** (£770; £384; £192) **Stalls** Low

Form — RPR

21-3 **1** **Sahra Al Khadra**[26] [1389] 3-9-7 **70**..................................... PaulHanagan 4 — 76+
(Charles Hills) *plld hrd: trckd ldrs: wnt 2nd 6f out: rdn over 1f out: led wl ins fnl f: jst hld on* **10/11**[1]

34-3 **2** *nse* **Space Walker (IRE)**[25] [1404] 3-9-4 **67**............................... TomQueally 5 — 73
(Harry Dunlop) *s.i.s: sn rcvrd to ld at stdy pce: qcknd over 2f out: rdn over 1f out: hdd wl ins fnl f: r.o* **8/1**

56-2 **3** *1 3/4* **Mfiftythreedotcom (IRE)**[19] [1507] 3-9-6 **69**........................ DavidNolan 1 — 71
(Richard Fahey) *chsd ldr 2f: remained handy: rdn over 1f out: styd on same pce ins fnl f* **7/2**[2]

65-0 **4** *1* **Craftsmanship (FR)**[14] [1620] 3-9-6 **69**............................ AndreaAtzeni 2 — 69
(Robert Eddery) *hld up: rdn over 1f out: edgd lft ins fnl f: styd on same pce* **8/1**

21-3 **5** *1 3/4* **Bon Port**[116] [103] 3-9-0 **63**............................................. JimmyFortune 3 — 59
(Hughie Morrison) *hld up: rdn over 1f out: eased whn hld wl ins fnl f* **13/2**[3]

1m 44.09s (3.09) **Going Correction** +0.10s/f (Good) — **5** Ran SP% **110.2**
Speed ratings (Par 99): **88,87,86,85,83**
CSF £8.80 TOTE £1.20: £1.02, £5.00; EX 8.90 Trifecta £24.70.
**Owner** Hamdan Al Maktoum **Bred** Sheikh Hamdan Bin Maktoum Al Maktoum **Trained** Lambourn, Berks

**FOCUS**
A modest handicap in which the gallop was on the steady side and the bare form doesn't look reliable. The field came towards the stands' side.

## 2028 DINE IN THE 1707 RESTAURANT H'CAP — 1m 2f 202y
**5:55** (5:55) (Class 6) (0-60,60) 3-Y-O — **£1,940** (£577; £288; £144) **Stalls** Low

Form — RPR

5563 **1** **Jazri**[11] [1683] 3-9-4 **57**............................................... FrederikTylicki 1 — 62
(Milton Bradley) *s.i.s: jnd ldr after 1f: led over 8f out: rdn over 2f out: jst hld on* **5/1**[3]

50-4 **2** *shd* **Mister Uno (IRE)**[26] [1372] 3-8-9 **48**......................... SilvestreDeSousa 3 — 53
(Ann Duffield) *led over 2f: chsd wnr: rdn over 1f out: r.o* **7/2**[1]

**3** *4* **San Quentin (IRE)**[150] [8193] 3-8-7 **49**.......... WilliamTwiston-Davies(3) 5 — 47
(Tony Carroll) *hld up: hdwy u.p over 1f out: r.o: nrst fin* **11/1**

000- **4** *1/2* **King Calypso**[254] [5757] 3-8-0 **46** oh1..............................(v[1]) JoeDoyle(7) 6 — 43
(Denis Coakley) *plld hrd and prom: outpcd over 2f out: styd on wl ins fnl f* **4/1**[2]

30-0 **5** *nk* **Gold Class**[11] [1683] 3-9-4 **57**.........................................(b[1]) PaulHanagan 2 — 53
(Ed McMahon) *chsd ldrs: rdn over 2f out: no ex fnl f* **10/1**

3232 **6** *1 1/2* **Frederic Chopin**[52] [960] 3-9-7 **60**................................(t) AndreaAtzeni 8 — 53
(Stuart Williams) *prom: rdn and edgd lft over 1f out: no ex* **7/2**[1]

00-5 **7** *1/2* **Bed Bed**[46] [1032] 3-8-11 **50**...........................................(v[1]) TomQueally 7 — 43
(Michael Bell) *hld up in tch: racd keenly: rdn over 2f out: no ex fr over 1f out* **20/1**

606 **8** *2* **Radebe (USA)**[14] [1608] 3-8-4 **48**....................................(p) KevinStott(5) 9 — 37
(Kevin Ryan) *sn pushed along in rr: n.d* **10/1**

00-0 **9** *3 3/4* **Petale Noir**[38] [1143] 3-8-7 **46** oh1..................................... NickyMackay 4 — 28
(Jonathan Portman) *hmpd sn after s: wnt prom over 8f out: rdn over 2f out: wknd over 1f out* **40/1**

2m 24.15s (3.05) **Going Correction** +0.10s/f (Good) — **9** Ran SP% **114.8**
Speed ratings (Par 97): **92,91,89,88,88 87,86,85,82**
CSF £22.72 CT £183.06 TOTE £6.40: £1.90, £1.70, £1.50; EX 26.10 Trifecta £215.50.
**Owner** Dab Hand Racing **Bred** Broughton Bloodstock **Trained** Sedbury, Gloucs

**FOCUS**
A couple of unexposed sorts in a low-grade handicap. A steady gallop saw those held up at a disadvantage and the front two pulled clear.

T/Plt: £56.90 to a £1 stake. Pool: £52003.51 - 666.21 winning tickets T/Qpdt: £13.20 to a £1 stake. Pool: £3003.86 - 168.10 winning tickets CR



The Form Book, Raceform Ltd, Newbury, RG14 5SJ

## [1807]WINDSOR (R-H)

Monday, May 5

**OFFICIAL GOING: Good to soft (good in places; 6.6)**

Top bend dolled out 6yds adding 20yds to races of one mile and beyond.

Wind: Light across Weather: Sunny

### 2029 BET TOTEPLACEPOT APPRENTICE TRAINING SERIES H'CAP (PART OF THE RACING EXCELLENCE INITIATIVE) 6f

**2:25** (2:25) (Class 6) (0-65,64) 4-Y-0+ **£1,940** (£577; £288; £144) **Stalls** Low

Form RPR

1446 **1** **Catalinas Diamond (IRE)**[16] 1573 6-8-11 **54**..........(t) RobJFitzpatrick 6 62
(Pat Murphy) *hld up in rr: rdn and hdwy 2f out: led appr fnl f: edgd lft: kpt on* **8/1**

-014 **2** *3/4* **Encapsulated**[13] 1639 4-8-8 **58**..................................(p) RhiainIngram(7) 8 64
(Roger Ingram) *racd keenly hld up: wnt prom 1/2-way: rdn over 2f out: kpt on but a jst hld fnl f* **6/1**

-540 **3** *1/2* **Magical Rose (IRE)**[89] 496 4-9-4 **61**........................ JordanVaughan 5 65
(Conrad Allen) *midfield: pushed along 1/2-way: kpt on: wnt 3rd towards fin* **5/1**[3]

4244 **4** *1* **Pharoh Jake**[40] 1109 6-8-12 **58**..................................... CamHardie(3) 7 59
(John Bridger) *prom: led 1/2-way: sn rdn: hdd appr fnl f: no ex* **7/2**[1]

0004 **5** *3/4* **El Mirage (IRE)**[8] 1766 4-8-8 **56**..................................... PaulBooth(5) 2 54
(Dean Ivory) *hld up: rdn 1/2-way: ended up isolated towards stands' rail fnl 2f: nvr threatened ldrs* **10/1**

0140 **6** *2 1/2* **Foie Gras**[8] 1766 4-9-2 **64**........................................ ThomasHemsley(5) 1 54
(Chris Dwyer) *hld up: pushed along 1/2-way: nvr threatened* **12/1**

0-00 **7** *1/2* **Belinsky (IRE)**[93] 424 7-8-7 **50** oh3.............................. AdamMcLean 9 39
(Dean Ivory) *in tch on outer: rdn over 2f out: wknd fnl f* **33/1**

50-0 **8** *3* **Gaelic Wizard (IRE)**[93] 425 6-9-2 **59**.............................(p) PatMillman 3 38
(Dominic Ffrench Davis) *led: rdn whn hdd 1/2-way: sn wknd* **12/1**

4041 **9** *1* **Black Truffle (FR)**[8] 1766 4-8-7 **53** 6ex................(v) CharlotteJenner(3) 4 29
(Mark Usher) *racd keenly cl up: wknd fnl 2f* **9/2**[2]

1m 15.55s (2.55) **Going Correction** +0.175s/f (Good) 9 Ran SP% **109.9**

Speed ratings (Par 101): **90,89,88,87,86 82,82,78,76**

CSF £51.00 CT £246.51 TOTE £6.60: £1.80, £2.70, £2.50; EX 58.20 Trifecta £358.60.

**Owner** Briton International **Bred** Sean Gorman **Trained** East Garston, Berks

■ Stewards' Enquiry : Rob J Fitzpatrick two-day ban: used whip above permitted level (May 19-20)

**FOCUS**

Top bend dolled out 6yds, adding 20yds to races of one mile and beyond. A modest contest in which the majority drifted into the centre of the track up the straight.

### 2030 BET ON ALL UK RACING WITH TOTEPOOL H'CAP 6f

**3:00** (3:00) (Class 4) (0-85,84) 4-Y-0+ **£4,851** (£1,443; £541; £541) **Stalls** Low

Form RPR

00-0 **1** **Links Drive Lady**[21] 1492 6-9-6 **83**................................ WilliamBuick 9 91
(Dean Ivory) *prom: rdn over 2f out: upsides fr over 1f out: kpt on: led towards fin* **16/1**

534- **2** *nk* **Kinglami**[158] 8088 5-8-13 **79**...........................................(p) OisinMurphy(3) 4 86
(Brian Gubby) *prom: rdn to ld narrowly over 1f out: kpt on: hdd towards fin* **5/2**[2]

60-0 **3** *hd* **Midnight Rider (IRE)**[21] 1492 6-9-4 **81**.......................... GeorgeBaker 8 87
(Chris Wall) *hld up in tch: angled lft and gd hdwy over 1f out: kpt on u.p fnl f: jst hld* **9/2**[3]

0-50 **3** *dht* **Trader Jack**[11] 1672 5-9-3 **80**........................................ StephenCraine 5 86
(David Flood) *chsd ldrs: rdn over 2f out: kpt on: jst hld* **16/1**

0-26 **5** *1/2* **Marjong**[35] 1212 4-8-9 **77**..................................................[1] JackDuern(5) 3 82
(Simon Dow) *slowly away: rdn and hdwy on outer 2f out: kpt on* **7/1**

00-0 **6** *4 1/2* **Dominate**[21] 1492 4-9-7 **84**........................................... RyanMoore 6 74
(Richard Hannon) *led: rdn whn hdd over 1f out: wknd* **9/4**[1]

036- **7** *3 1/2* **Tidal's Baby**[203] 7254 5-9-2 **79**.................................... SteveDrowne 1 58
(Tony Carroll) *hld up: rdn over 2f out: sn btn* **16/1**

221- **8** *9* **Silverrica (IRE)**[313] 3678 4-8-9 **72**.................................. JimCrowley 7 22
(Malcolm Saunders) *racd keenly: chsd ldrs: wknd over 1f out: eased* **20/1**

1m 14.22s (1.22) **Going Correction** +0.175s/f (Good) 8 Ran SP% **112.4**

Speed ratings (Par 105): **98,97,97,97,96 90,86,74**

WIN: 14.00 Links Drive Lady; PL: .90 Midnight Rider, 4.70 Links Drive Lady, 2.10 Trader Jack, 1.10 Kinglami; EX: 63.80; CSF: 54.30; TC: 108.50, 334.77; TF: 329.50, 605.50;.

**Owner** It's Your Lucky Day **Bred** Peter Webb **Trained** Radlett, Herts

■ Stewards' Enquiry : Jack Duern two-day ban: used whip above permitted level (May 19-20)

**FOCUS**

There was a blanket finish to this sprint handicap.

### 2031 BET TOTEQUADPOT MEDIAN AUCTION MAIDEN STKS 1m 67y

**3:35** (3:35) (Class 5) 3-4-Y-0 **£2,587** (£770; £384; £192) **Stalls** Low

Form RPR

2- **1** **Takreym (IRE)**[202] 7270 3-9-1 0.......................................(b[1]) RyanMoore 1 83
(Roger Varian) *trckd ldr: rdn to ld 2f out: sn clr: easily* **8/13**[1]

**2** *7* **Chauvelin** 3-8-12 0............................................... OisinMurphy(3) 2 67
(Roger Charlton) *midfield: rdn and hdwy over 1f out: wnt 2nd 1f out: kpt on but no ch w wnr* **6/1**[2]

**3** *1 1/4* **Chantecler** 3-9-1 0................................................... RobertHavlin 5 64
(Hughie Morrison) *racd keenly: hld up in midfield: pushed along over 2f out: kpt on fnl f: wnt 3rd towards fin* **33/1**

556- **4** *1 1/4* **Persian Bolt (USA)**[201] 7296 3-8-10 74.......................... WilliamBuick 4 56
(Eve Johnson Houghton) *sn led: rdn whn hdd 2f out: edgd lft over 1f out: lost 2nd 1f out: grad wknd* **8/1**[3]

**5** *1 3/4* **Oskar Denarius (IRE)** 3-9-1 0........................................ ShaneKelly 6 57
(Marcus Tregoning) *slowly away: hld up: pushed along over 2f out: nvr threatened* **20/1**

0 **6** *1/2* **Sleeper**[23] 1433 3-8-10 0................................................ JimCrowley 7 51
(Ralph Beckett) *hld up: rdn over 3f out: sn btn* **10/1**

0- **7** *1 1/2* **Swanwick Shore (IRE)**[192] 7500 3-9-1 0......................... SeanLevey 3 53
(Richard Hannon) *in tch: rdn over 2f out: sn wknd* **10/1**

1m 45.5s (0.80) **Going Correction** +0.10s/f (Good) 7 Ran SP% **113.2**

Speed ratings (Par 103): **100,93,91,90,88 88,86**

CSF £4.68 TOTE £1.50: £1.10, £2.50; EX 5.10 Trifecta £59.10.

**Owner** Sheikh Ahmed Al Maktoum **Bred** John Fielding **Trained** Newmarket, Suffolk

**FOCUS**

This proved fairly straightforward for the odds-on favourite.

### 2032 BET TOTEEXACTA FILLIES' H'CAP 1m 67y

**4:10** (4:10) (Class 3) (0-95,88) 4-Y-0+ **£7,439** (£2,213; £1,106; £553) **Stalls** Low

Form RPR

2-11 **1** **Trixie Malone**[9] 1716 4-8-1 **73**..................................... JoeyHaynes(5) 4 82
(K R Burke) *mde all: rdn over 3f out: strly pressed fr over 1f out: hld on gamely* **11/10**[1]

1144 **2** *hd* **Fashion Line (IRE)**[17] 1554 4-9-2 **88**.......................... LouisSteward(5) 3 96
(Michael Bell) *trckd ldr: rdn to chal strly over 1f out: kpt on but a jst hld* **7/4**[2]

2114 **3** *1 3/4* **Waveguide (IRE)**[60] 857 5-8-3 **70**..................................... MartinLane 5 74
(David Simcock) *hld up in tch in 4th: rdn over 2f out: chsd ldng pair over 1f out: kpt on* **10/1**

020- **4** *21* **Beautiful View**[191] 7538 4-9-4 **85**..................................... RyanMoore 1 70
(Richard Hannon) *racd keenly: trckd ldr: rdn over 2f out: hung lft over 1f out: wknd and eased* **5/1**[3]

1m 45.4s (0.70) **Going Correction** +0.10s/f (Good) 4 Ran SP% **109.7**

Speed ratings (Par 104): **100,99,98,77**

CSF £3.37 TOTE £2.00; EX 3.30 Trifecta £8.50.

**Owner** Mrs Elaine M Burke **Bred** Llety Farms **Trained** Middleham Moor, N Yorks

**FOCUS**

A decent fillies' handicap, despite the small field.

### 2033 BET TOTESWINGER H'CAP 1m 2f 7y

**4:45** (4:45) (Class 4) (0-85,84) 4-Y-0+ **£4,851** (£1,443; £721; £360) **Stalls** Centre

Form RPR

0600 **1** **Presburg (IRE)**[17] 1556 5-9-3 **83**................................... OisinMurphy(3) 7 92
(Joseph Tuite) *hld up: rdn and hdwy over 2f out: led over 1f out: kpt on* **8/1**[3]

200- **2** *1* **Bobbyscot (IRE)**[233] 6405 7-8-9 **72**................................. RobertHavlin 4 79
(Mark Hoad) *hld up: rdn and hdwy over 1f out: kpt on: wnt 2nd towards fin* **16/1**

0-32 **3** *shd* **Starwatch**[7] 1810 7-8-10 **73**.......................................... WilliamCarson 2 80
(John Bridger) *w ldr: rdn to ld 2f out: hdd over 1f out: one pce: lost 2nd towards fin* **5/1**[2]

-250 **4** *hd* **Icebuster**[17] 1553 6-9-7 **84**........................................... GeorgeBaker 6 90
(Rod Millman) *s.i.s: hld up in rr: rdn 2f out: kpt on fnl f* **8/1**[3]

600- **5** *1* **One Pekan (IRE)**[200] 7330 4-9-4 **81**................................. RyanMoore 5 86
(Roger Varian) *trckd ldng pair: rdn and ev ch over 1f out: wknd fnl 75yds* **7/4**[1]

152- **6** *3 1/4* **Storm (IRE)**[159] 8060 4-8-8 **71**...................................... WilliamBuick 1 69
(Charles Hills) *trckd ldrs: rdn over 2f out: wknd ins fnl f* **5/1**[2]

3522 **7** *9* **Appease**[33] 1241 5-9-0 **77**...............................................(p) SeanLevey 3 58
(John Butler) *led: rdn over 3f out: hdd 2f out: wknd* **5/1**[2]

2m 8.56s (-0.14) **Going Correction** +0.10s/f (Good) 7 Ran SP% **114.5**

Speed ratings (Par 105): **104,103,103,102,102 99,92**

CSF £116.68 TOTE £10.30: £3.40, £6.60; EX 137.80 Trifecta £866.30.

**Owner** www.isehove.com **Bred** Limestone And Tara Studs **Trained** Great Shefford, Berks

**FOCUS**

Recent winning form was thin on the ground here and the form doesn't look anything special.

### 2034 BET TOTETRIFECTA H'CAP 1m 3f 135y

**5:20** (5:20) (Class 4) (0-85,82) 4-Y-0+ **£4,851** (£1,443; £721; £360) **Stalls** Centre

Form RPR

1-24 **1** **Flemish School**[8] 1770 4-9-6 **81**.....................................(p) WilliamBuick 1 95
(David Elsworth) *midfield: rdn over 2f out: hdwy to chal over 1f out: led jst ins fnl f: kpt on wl to go clr* **9/2**[2]

60-6 **2** *6* **Jupiter Storm**[21] 1493 5-9-2 **77**....................................... RyanMoore 3 81
(Gary Moore) *trckd ldr: led 3f out: sn rdn: drvn whn jnd over 1f out: edgd lft appr fnl f: hdd jst ins fnl f: hung lft and sn hld in 2nd* **6/4**[1]

226 **3** *3 1/2* **Echo Brava**[66] 784 4-9-2 **80**.................................. MichaelJMMurphy(3) 6 78
(Luke Dace) *in tch: rdn over 2f out: hdwy and ev ch 2f out: hld in 3rd fr appr fnl f* **6/1**[3]

30- **4** *1 1/4* **Meetings Man (IRE)**[164] 8004 7-8-11 **72**........................ SteveDrowne 7 68
(Ali Stronge) *hld up in tch: rdn over 2f out: one pce and nvr threatened* **16/1**

3062 **5** *2 1/2* **Uphold**[13] 1636 7-9-3 **81**...............................................(v) OisinMurphy(3) 2 73
(Gay Kelleway) *chsd ldr: rdn and ev ch 2f out: wknd appr fnl f* **6/1**[3]

10-0 **6** *6* **Ascendant**[26] 1383 8-9-5 **80**.........................................(v) JimCrowley 5 61
(Andrew Reid) *slowly away: hld up in rr: riidden over 3f out: nvr threatened* **20/1**

256- **7** *1/2* **Interior Minister**[48] 5448 4-9-7 **82**................................... GeorgeBaker 4 63
(Jonjo O'Neill) *hld up in rr: pushed along over 3f out: nvr threatened* **20/1**

-505 **8** *14* **Anton Chigurh**[7] 1811 5-9-5 **80**......................................(p) SeanLevey 9 37
(Brendan Powell) *led: rdn whn hdd 3f out: wknd* **8/1**

2m 28.61s (-0.89) **Going Correction** +0.10s/f (Good) 8 Ran SP% **113.3**

Speed ratings (Par 105): **106,102,99,98,97 93,92,83**

CSF £11.42 CT £38.74 TOTE £5.30: £2.00, £1.10, £2.10; EX 14.80 Trifecta £69.90.

**Owner** Mrs Barbara M Keller **Bred** Horizon Bloodstock Limited **Trained** Newmarket, Suffolk

**FOCUS**

Perhaps not the strongest of races for the grade.

### 2035 COLLECT TOTEPOOL WINNINGS AT BETFRED SHOPS H'CAP 5f 10y

**5:50** (5:53) (Class 5) (0-75,73) 3-Y-0 **£2,587** (£770; £384; £192) **Stalls** Low

Form RPR

1-53 **1** **Flashy Queen (IRE)**[11] 1669 3-9-4 **70**............................ SteveDrowne 1 76
(Joseph Tuite) *mde all: rdn 2f out: strly pressed over 1f out: kpt on wl and in command fnl 110yds* **6/1**

16-5 **2** *1 1/4* **Debt Settler (IRE)**[113] 149 3-9-1 **70**................... MichaelJMMurphy(3) 4 72
(Luke Dace) *in tch on outer: rdn and hdwy to chal strly over 1f out: one pce and hld in 2nd fnl 110yds* **16/1**

53-4 **3** *shd* **Groundworker (IRE)**[16] 1569 3-9-2 **68**............................ RyanMoore 5 69
(Sylvester Kirk) *s.i.s: hld up in rr: swtchd lft to wd outside 2f out: sn rdn and hdwy: kpt on fnl f* **5/1**[3]

44-2 **4** *3 1/4* **Captain Whoosh (IRE)**[16] 1585 3-9-6 **72**................. RichardKingscote 8 61
(Tom Dascombe) *w ldr: rdn 2f out: wknd appr fnl f* **5/4**[1]

34-3 **5** *1/2* **Broadway Ranger (IRE)**[16] 1569 3-9-4 **70**..................... WilliamBuick 7 58
(Charles Hills) *chsd ldng pair: rdn 2f out: wknd fnl f* **9/2**[2]

032- **6** *6* **By Rights**[196] 7426 3-8-4 **61**.......................................... JoeyHaynes(5) 3 27
(Tony Carroll) *chsd ldng pair: rdn 1/2-way: wknd over 1f out* **10/1**

234- 7 3/4 **Mr Dandy Man (IRE)**[257] 5648 3-9-7 73 ............................ LiamJones 2 36
(Ronald Harris) *racd keenly: chsd ldng pair: rdn 2f out: wknd over 1f out* **16/1**

1m 1.13s (0.83) **Going Correction** +0.175s/f (Good) 7 Ran SP% **114.4**
Speed ratings (Par 99): **100,98,97,92,91 82,81**
CSF £88.99 CT £513.71 TOTE £7.40: £2.30, £6.30; EX 60.50 Trifecta £274.00.
**Owner** B Woodward,P & A Burton & B & A Lampard **Bred** Stourbank Stud **Trained** Great Shefford, Berks

**FOCUS**
A modest sprint.
T/Plt: £323.40 to a £1 stake. Pool: £70997.84 - 160.22 winning tickets T/Qpdt: £171.60 to a £1 stake. Pool: £4129.01 - 17.80 winning tickets AS

2036 - 2039a (Foreign Racing) - See Raceform Interactive

## 1470 CURRAGH (R-H)

### Monday, May 5

**OFFICIAL GOING: Good to firm changing to good after race 6 (4:50)**

## 2040a HIGH CHAPARRAL EUROPEAN BREEDERS FUND MOORESBRIDGE STKS (GROUP 3) 1m 2f

**4:15** (4:15) 4-Y-0+ **£40,625** (£11,875; £5,625; £1,875)

RPR

1 **Magician (IRE)**[37] 1182 4-9-10 124 ............................ JosephO'Brien 1 117+
(A P O'Brien, Ire) *w.w in rr of quintet: stl plenty to do travelling wl 2f out: clsd on outer under hands and heels to chal in 3rd ins fnl f: rdn and sn on terms: led cl home* **2/13**[1]

2 nk **Parish Hall (IRE)**[9] 1750 5-9-6 110 ............................(t) KevinManning 3 112
(J S Bolger, Ire) *settled bhd ldrs in 4th: rdn and hdwy fr 3f out on outer to chal 1 1/2f out: led narrowly ent fnl f: sn strly pressed and edgd lft u.p: hdd cl home* **6/1**[2]

3 2 1/4 **Hall Of Mirrors (IRE)**[577] 6859 4-9-3 97 ............................ SeamieHeffernan 5 105
(A P O'Brien, Ire) *sn chsd ldrs in 3rd: clsr in 2nd into st and rdn to ld over 1 1/2f out: sn jnd and hdd ent fnl f: no ex u.p in 3rd nr fin: kpt on same pce* **16/1**

4 2 1/2 **Paene Magnus (IRE)**[199] 7361 5-9-3 102 ............................ RonanWhelan 4 100
(J S Bolger, Ire) *chsd ldr in 2nd tl dropped to 3rd into st: sn no imp u.p in rr: kpt on into mod 4th ins fnl f* **12/1**[3]

5 1 3/4 **Jazz Girl (IRE)**[16] 1592 6-9-0 95 ............................ ChrisHayes 2 93
(A Oliver, Ire) *led: over 1 l clr 1/2-way: rdn fr under 3f out and hdd over 1 1/2f out: sn no ex u.p in 4th: one pce ins fnl f and dropped to rr nr fin* **33/1**

2m 8.91s (-0.39) **Going Correction** +0.25s/f (Good) 5 Ran SP% **117.5**
Speed ratings: **111,110,108,106,105**
CSF £2.13 TOTE £1.10: £1.02, £1.60; DF 2.20 Trifecta £5.80.
**Owner** Michael Tabor & Derrick Smith & Mrs John Magnier **Bred** Absolutelyfabulous Syndicate **Trained** Cashel, Co Tipperary

**FOCUS**
The winner was below his best but was given a patient ride.

## 2042a CANFORD CLIFFS EUROPEAN BREEDERS FUND ATHASI STKS (GROUP 3) 7f

**5:25** (5:25) 3-Y-0+ **£40,625** (£11,875; £5,625; £1,875)

RPR

1 **Flying Jib**[204] 7226 3-8-11 106 ............................ KevinManning 7 103+
(D K Weld, Ire) *w.w: 9th 1/2-way: prog fr 2f out nr side into 2nd ent fnl f: clsd u.p to ld fnl 50yds: kpt on wl* **2/1**[1]

2 1/2 **Peace Burg (FR)**[185] 7685 4-10-0 111 ............................ JosephO'Brien 5 111
(A P O'Brien, Ire) *chsd ldrs: 3rd 1/2-way: rdn to ld 1 1/2f out: strly pressed u.p wl ins fnl f and hdd fnl 50yds: no ex* **8/1**

3 1 1/2 **Wannabe Better (IRE)**[22] 1473 4-9-9 105 ............................ WayneLordan 1 102
(T Stack, Ire) *hld up: 8th 1/2-way: prog to chse ldrs in 6th over 1f out: kpt on wl u.p into 3rd ins fnl f: nt trble principals* **9/4**[2]

4 1 3/4 **Tahaany (IRE)**[29] 1337 3-8-12 94 ow1 ............................ ChrisHayes 3 94
(D K Weld, Ire) *prom: settled bhd ldrs: 4th 1/2-way: tk clsr order far side over 1 1/2f out: sn no imp on ldrs u.p: kpt on same pce* **11/2**[3]

5 1/2 **Switcher (IRE)**[212] 7015 5-9-9 97 ............................ ConorHoban 8 96
(M Halford, Ire) *sn trckd ldr on nr side: cl 2nd 1/2-way: on terms over 2f out and sn led: rdn and hdd 1 1/2f out: no ex and dropped to 5th ins fnl f: kpt on one pce* **20/1**

6 shd **Chicago Girl (IRE)**[204] 7226 3-8-11 105 ............................ FergalLynch 10 92
(J P Murtagh, Ire) *dwlt sltly: chsd ldrs: 7th 1/2-way: tk clsr order bhd ldrs 2f out: sn pushed along and no ex u.p ent fnl f: kpt on one pce* **6/1**

7 1 3/4 **Morning Frost (IRE)**[29] 1333 4-9-9 103 ............................[1] ShaneFoley 4 91
(M Halford, Ire) *chsd ldrs: 5th 1/2-way: tk clsr order fr under 2f out: rdn in 3rd ent fnl f and no imp on ldrs: wknd* **33/1**

8 nk **Beyond Brilliance (IRE)**[9] 1747 3-8-11 80 ............................ AnaO'Brien 9 86
(A P O'Brien, Ire) *dwlt and racd towards rr: clsr in 6th 1/2-way: rdn and no ex over 1f out: kpt on one pce* **33/1**

9 3/4 **Lottie Dod (IRE)**[7] 1824 4-9-9 91 ............................ FMBerry 6 88
(Charles O'Brien, Ire) *hld up: last 1/2-way: rdn 2f out and sn no ex u.p: kpt on one pce fnl f* **33/1**

10 13 **Pianota (USA)** 3-8-11 ............................ RonanWhelan 2 49
(J S Bolger, Ire) *sn led: narrow advantage 1/2-way: pushed along and jnd over 2f out: sn hdd & wknd qckly: eased ins fnl f* **33/1**

1m 26.47s (-4.33) **Going Correction** -0.30s/f (Firm)
**WFA** 3 from 4yo+ 12lb 10 Ran SP% **121.4**
Speed ratings: **112,111,109,107,107 107,105,104,103,88**
CSF £18.45 TOTE £2.70: £1.30, £2.10, £1.10; DF 26.00 Trifecta £49.60.
**Owner** K Abdullah **Bred** Juddmonte Farms Ltd **Trained** Curragh, Co Kildare

**FOCUS**
The runner-up was back to her best on debut for Aidan O'Brien.

2041 - 2043a (Foreign Racing) - See Raceform Interactive

## 1872 BRIGHTON (L-H)

### Tuesday, May 6

**OFFICIAL GOING: Good changing to good (good to firm in places; 7.0) after race 1 (2.20)**
Rail dolled out from 6f to 2f increasing distances by 12yds.
Wind: Fresh; half against Weather: Sunny

## 2044 DONATELLO ITALIAN RESTAURANT MAIDEN STKS 5f 213y

**2:20** (2:21) (Class 5) 3-Y-0+ **£2,587** (£770; £384; £192) **Stalls** Centre

Form RPR

200- 1 **Iftaar (IRE)**[207] 7170 3-9-2 78 ............................ DaneO'Neill 4 76+
(Charles Hills) *mde all: rdn clr ins fnl 2f: eased nr fin* **4/5**[1]

625- 2 1 **A Legacy Of Love (IRE)**[159] 8083 3-8-11 74 ............................ RobertHavlin 2 62
(Amanda Perrett) *in tch: rdn to chse wnr over 2f out: kpt on fnl f: flattered by proximity to wnr* **15/8**[2]

620- 3 nk **Royal Brave (IRE)**[127] 8442 3-9-2 62 ............................ MartinDwyer 3 66
(William Muir) *chsd ldrs: kpt on same pce fnl 2f* **7/1**[3]

0- 4 12 **Staines Massive**[211] 7073 4-9-5 0 ............................[1] LewisWalsh(7) 1 31
(Jane Chapple-Hyam) *sn outpcd in rr: unbalanced on trck and effrt in centre over 3f out: wknd over 2f out* **20/1**

6463 5 4 1/2 **Bold Max**[8] 1802 3-8-13 46 ............................(p) RossAtkinson(3) 6 13
(Zoe Davison) *s.s: sn prom: wknd 2f out* **66/1**

6 1/2 **Spider Bay** 5-9-7 0 ............................ SteveDrowne 5 10
(Lydia Richards) *s.s: sn prom: wknd over 2f out* **66/1**

1m 11.3s (1.10) **Going Correction** +0.20s/f (Good)
**WFA** 3 from 4yo+ 10lb 6 Ran SP% **110.6**
Speed ratings (Par 103): **100,98,98,82,76 75**
CSF £2.40 TOTE £1.90: £1.10, £1.20; EX 3.30 Trifecta £5.10.
**Owner** Hamdan Al Maktoum **Bred** Cbs Bloodstock **Trained** Lambourn, Berks

**FOCUS**
Rail dolled out from 6f to 2f, increasing distances by 12yds. The opening contest was a fair small-field sprint maiden in which they went a decent gallop on ground officially described as good, with good to firm places added after this race.

## 2045 WINNER PLANT HIRE CLASSIFIED STKS 5f 213y

**2:50** (2:50) (Class 6) 3-Y-0+ **£1,940** (£577; £288; £144) **Stalls** Centre

Form RPR

0543 1 **Crystalized (IRE)**[7] 1833 3-8-9 52 ............................ FergusSweeney 5 52
(Dean Ivory) *hld up in 5th: qcknd to ld over 2f out: sn in control: rdn and styd on wl* **2/1**[1]

5005 2 1 3/4 **Sweet Piccolo**[6] 1877 4-9-0 35 ............................ DavidKenny(5) 3 49
(Paddy Butler) *hld up in rr: nt clr run over 2f out: rdn and hdwy over 1f out: styd on to take 2nd fnl 75yds* **20/1**

5543 3 2 1/4 **Jazz Bay**[14] 1626 3-8-9 45 ............................ SamHitchcott 1 39
(John Bridger) *chsd ldrs on rail: rdn to chse wnr over 2f out: one pce fnl f: lost 2nd fnl 75yds* **8/1**

000- 4 8 **Princess Cammie (IRE)**[196] 7443 4-8-12 48 ............................(p) CamHardie(7) 4 17
(John Bridger) *hld up in 6th: effrt in centre over 2f out: sn outpcd* **9/2**[3]

000- 5 9 **Paradise Child**[164] 8017 3-8-4 45 ............................ RyanWhile(5) 2
(Bill Turner) *led tl over 2f out: sn wknd* **14/1**

0605 6 2 1/4 **Sakhee'Ssquirrel**[12] 1666 3-8-6 45 ............................(b) RossAtkinson(3) 7
(Sean Curran) *pressed ldrs tl wknd 2f out* **6/1**

0-60 7 2 **Spring Lady**[13] 1647 3-8-9 45 ............................ MartinDwyer 6
(Alan Jarvis) *w ldr tl wknd 2f out* **7/2**[2]

1m 11.84s (1.64) **Going Correction** +0.20s/f (Good)
**WFA** 3 from 4yo 10lb 7 Ran SP% **110.6**
Speed ratings (Par 101): **97,94,91,81,69 66,63**
CSF £40.01 TOTE £2.90: £1.80, £7.00; EX 25.30 Trifecta £154.00.
**Owner** Tom Glynn **Bred** Brendan Holland And P Connell **Trained** Radlett, Herts

**FOCUS**
A moderate classified stakes. The winner has been rated around recent AW form.

## 2046 MAYO WYNNE BAXTER APPRENTICE H'CAP 1m 1f 209y

**3:20** (3:21) (Class 6) (0-65,61) 4-Y-0+ **£1,940** (£577; £288; £144) **Stalls** High

Form RPR

40-1 1 **Megalala (IRE)**[12] 1664 13-8-13 **56** ............................ CamHardie(3) 2 66
(John Bridger) *mde all: pushed along 4f out: clr over 2f out: styd on wl* **15/8**[2]

0432 2 3 1/2 **Salient**[7] 1835 10-8-0 **47** ............................ RhiainIngram(7) 4 50
(Michael Attwater) *chsd wnr: rdn over 3f out: one pce* **8/1**

2125 3 3/4 **Minstrels Gallery (IRE)**[15] 1617 5-9-7 **61** ............................(p) DanielCremin 1 63
(Lucy Wadham) *hld up in cl 3rd: effrt 3f out: one pce: b.b.v* **6/4**[1]

343/ 4 3/4 **Dark And Dangerous (IRE)**[16] 6567 6-9-1 **58** ............................ JennyPowell(3) 3 59
(Brendan Powell) *cl up in 4th: rdn 4f out: one pce* **6/1**[3]

0104 5 62 **Dazzling Valentine**[8] 1816 6-9-3 **60** ............................(v) DavidParkes(3) 6
(Alan Bailey) *reluctant to s and lost 25 l: a t.o* **12/1**

2m 4.92s (1.32) **Going Correction** +0.20s/f (Good) 5 Ran SP% **107.9**
Speed ratings (Par 101): **102,99,98,98,48**
CSF £15.20 TOTE £2.20: £1.10, £5.20; EX 11.60 Trifecta £23.90.
**Owner** Trevor Wallace **Bred** Joseph Gallagher **Trained** Liphook, Hants

**FOCUS**
A modest small-field handicap for apprentice riders in which they went an even gallop. The ages of the first two combined was 23.

## 2047 EBF STALLIONS BREEDING WINNERS FILLIES' H'CAP 1m 1f 209y

**3:50** (3:51) (Class 3) (0-90,90) 4-Y-0+ **£9,955** (£2,979; £1,489; £745) **Stalls** High

Form RPR

000- 1 **Boonga Roogeta**[220] 6838 5-9-4 **90** ............................ RosieJessop(3) 4 92
(Peter Charalambous) *led after 1f: set modest pce: qcknd over 2f out: narrow ld fnl f: jst prevailed* **11/4**[2]

0-56 2 nse **Yojojo (IRE)**[48] 1020 5-9-5 **88** ............................ KierenFallon 1 90
(Gay Kelleway) *hld up in cl 4th: effrt on ins rail 2f out: w wnr fnl f: r.o* **15/8**[1]

161- 3 1 1/4 **Familliarity**[244] 6098 4-8-11 **80** ............................ DaneO'Neill 2 80
(Roger Varian) *trckd ldrs in cl 3rd: sltly outpcd 2f out: rallied ins fnl f: one pce fnl 50yds* **15/8**[1]

433- 4 1 1/2 **Mu'Ajiza**[247] 6016 4-8-7 76 oh2 ............................ MartinLane 3 73
(Paul Midgley) *led 1f: trckd wnr after tl rdn and no ex over 1f out* **8/1**[3]

2m 7.03s (3.43) **Going Correction** +0.20s/f (Good) 4 Ran SP% **107.3**
Speed ratings (Par 104): **94,93,92,91**
CSF £8.11 TOTE £4.50; EX 7.40 Trifecta £15.10.
**Owner** pcracing.co.uk **Bred** Peter Charles **Trained** Newmarket, Suffolk

**FOCUS**
The feature race was a decent small-field fillies' handicap in which they went a steady gallop. The winner was rated to her best since this time last year.

## 2048 BRIGHTON AND HOVE BUSES H'CAP 6f 209y
4:20 (4:20) (Class 5) (0-75,74) 4-Y-O+ £2,587 (£770; £384; £192) Stalls Centre

Form RPR
4311 1 **Ishiamber**34 1230 4-9-7 74 MartinDwyer 4 86
(George Baker) *led 1f: trckd ldr: led 3f out: wnt 3 l clr 1f out: drvn out* 7/2[2]
-440 2 1 1/4 **Eastern Dragon (IRE)**68 757 4-8-10 68 JackDuern(5) 2 77
(Michael Scudamore) *trckd ldrs in 4th: rdn over 2f out: r.o fnl f: clsng at fin: a hld* 7/2[2]
13-4 3 nk **Jaladee**32 1281 4-9-6 73 JackMitchell 5 81
(Roger Varian) *cl up in 3rd: rdn and outpcd 2f out: rallied and r.o fnl f* 6/5[1]
06-0 4 4 1/2 **Eager To Bow (IRE)**31 1297 8-8-13 66 (p) LiamKeniry 1 62
(Patrick Chamings) *hld up in 5th: promising effrt on bridle and wnt 3rd 2f out: shkn up over 1f out: no rspnse* 5/1[3]
200- 5 15 **Assembly**148 8220 4-8-11 67 (b) JemmaMarshall(3) 6 24
(Pat Phelan) *stdd s: t.k.h: hdwy to ld after 1f: hdd 3f out: wknd over 2f out* 16/1

1m 23.76s (0.66) **Going Correction** +0.20s/f (Good) 5 Ran SP% 112.4
Speed ratings (Par 103): **104,102,102,97,79**
CSF £16.07 TOTE £3.10: £1.80, £2.70; EX 14.70 Trifecta £22.20.
**Owner** Mrs P Scott-Dunn **Bred** Patricia Ann Scott-Dunn **Trained** Manton, Wilts

**FOCUS**
A fair handicap in which they went a decent gallop. The winner continues to progress.

## 2049 BRIGHTON THISTLE HOTEL H'CAP 5f 213y
4:50 (4:52) (Class 5) (0-70,70) 3-Y-O £2,587 (£770; £384; £192) Stalls Centre

Form RPR
33-0 1 **Lady Horatia**19 1534 3-9-6 69 MartinDwyer 3 79
(William Muir) *chsd ldr: led 2f out: drvn clr 1f out: readily* 13/8[1]
24-6 2 6 **Baars Causeway (IRE)**26 1404 3-9-7 70 KierenFallon 5 61
(Alan Jarvis) *chsd ldng pair: wnt 2nd 1f out: no imp* 8/1[3]
22-1 3 1 1/2 **Skinny Love**108 232 3-9-7 70 (p) LiamKeniry 2 56
(Zoe Davison) *led tl 2f out: one pce appr fnl f* 14/1
555 4 2 1/2 **Spinning Cobblers**48 1018 3-9-2 65 DaneO'Neill 1 43
(Stuart Williams) *sn outpcd in rr: drvn along over 2f out: n.d* 8/1[3]
6141 5 1 **Coiste Bodhar (IRE)**4 1914 3-8-11 67 6ex (p) NoraLooby(7) 7 42
(Joseph Tuite) *wd: in tch tl hrd rdn and wknd over 2f out* 7/4[2]
40-4 6 3/4 **Kalon Brama (IRE)**15 1615 3-8-6 62 BradleyBosley(7) 4 34
(Peter Charalambous) *s.i.s: 5th most of way: wknd 2f out* 20/1

1m 11.06s (0.86) **Going Correction** +0.20s/f (Good) 6 Ran SP% 108.1
Speed ratings (Par 99): **102,94,92,88,87 86**
CSF £13.69 TOTE £2.70: £2.60, £3.50; EX 14.40 Trifecta £91.70.
**Owner** Muir Racing Partnership - Ascot **Bred** The Pocock Family **Trained** Lambourn, Berks

**FOCUS**
A modest 3yo handicap in which they went a strong pace.

## 2050 JAMES ROSS JEWELLERS (BRIGHTON) H'CAP 5f 59y
5:25 (5:25) (Class 4) (0-80,79) 4-Y-O+ £4,690 (£1,395; £697; £348) Stalls Centre

Form RPR
2156 1 **Hamoody (USA)**8 1803 10-8-12 73 ThomasBrown(3) 6 81
(Joseph Tuite) *chsd ldr: led over 1f out: rdn out* 6/1
6-50 2 3/4 **Sir Pedro**22 1490 5-9-4 76 DaneO'Neill 1 81
(Robert Cowell) *led tl over 1f out: kpt on u.p* 4/1[2]
0-30 3 nk **Secret Missile**22 1490 4-9-7 79 (b[1]) MartinDwyer 3 83
(William Muir) *in tch: rdn over 2f out: r.o fnl f* 4/1[2]
00-1 4 1 1/4 **Ruby's Day**19 1541 5-8-13 78 ClaireMurray(7) 4 78
(David Brown) *chsd ldrs: rdn over 2f out: one pce fnl f* 5/1[3]
55-4 5 3 1/4 **Whitecrest**7 1850 6-9-0 72 SamHitchcott 2 63
(John Spearing) *prom tl wknd 1f out: eased whn btn* 5/1[3]
3405 6 hd **Diamond Charlie (IRE)**13 1650 6-9-0 77 JackDuern(5) 5 65
(Simon Dow) *stdd s: hld up: shkn up in centre 2f out: sn btn* 10/3[1]

1m 2.83s (0.53) **Going Correction** +0.20s/f (Good) 6 Ran SP% 110.7
Speed ratings (Par 105): **103,101,101,99,94 93**
CSF £28.80 TOTE £8.40: £2.90, £3.90; EX 31.60 Trifecta £163.20.
**Owner** Andrew Liddiard **Bred** Ragged Mountain Farm **Trained** Great Shefford, Berks

**FOCUS**
A fair sprint handicap and they went a contested gallop.
T/Plt: £117.60 to a £1 stake. Pool: £45,191.88 - 280.29 winning units T/Qpdt: £56.70 to a £1 stake. Pool: £2,789.36 - 36.40 winning units LM

# 1642 CATTERICK (L-H)
### Tuesday, May 6

**OFFICIAL GOING: Good (good to soft in places; 7.6)**
Wind: fresh across Weather: sunny

## 2051 HAPPY 10TH BIRTHDAY RACING UK MAIDEN AUCTION STKS 5f
6:00 (6:01) (Class 6) 2-Y-O £2,385 (£704; £352) Stalls Low

Form RPR
6 1 **Appleberry (IRE)**22 1482 2-8-10 0 RobertWinston 6 78+
(Michael Appleby) *prom: rdn to ld over 1f out: kpt on* 5/1
4 2 1 1/2 **Make On Madam (IRE)**12 1656 2-8-8 0 DaleSwift 3 71
(Brian Ellison) *hld up: pushed along 1/2-way: hdwy on outer over 1f out: kpt on fnl f: wnt 2nd 75yds out* 11/4[1]
5 3 1 1/4 **Millar Rose (IRE)**12 1656 2-8-1 0 RobJFitzpatrick(7) 1 67
(K R Burke) *midfield: rdn and hdwy to chse wnr over 1f out: one pce fnl f: lost 2nd 75yds out* 9/2[3]
4 2 3/4 **Olivia Fallow (IRE)** 2-8-6 0 JamesSullivan 8 55+
(Paul Midgley) *wnt rt s: sn swtchd lft to inner: hld up in rr: pushed along 1/2-way: kpt on fnl f: nvr threatened ldrs* 16/1
0 5 1 1/2 **Diatomic (IRE)**29 1342 2-9-3 0 RichardKingscote 4 60
(Tom Dascombe) *chsd ldng pair: rdn 1/2-way: wknd fnl f* 33/1
6 2 **Atreus** 2-9-1 0 GrahamGibbons 2 51
(Michael Easterby) *slowly away: hld up: pushed along 1/2-way: nvr threatened* 50/1
3 7 1 1/2 **Magic Time (IRE)**12 1656 2-9-2 0 PJMcDonald 9 47
(Ann Duffield) *led: rdn whn hdd over 1f out: wknd* 6/1
4 8 10 **Alaskan Wing (IRE)**10 1732 2-9-5 0 BarryMcHugh 7
(Tony Coyle) *chsd ldng pair: wknd over 1f out* 4/1[2]

1m 1.56s (1.76) **Going Correction** +0.175s/f (Good) 8 Ran SP% 106.6
Speed ratings (Par 91): **92,89,87,83,80 77,75,59**
CSF £16.53 TOTE £8.90: £1.40, £1.70, £1.60; EX 20.00 Trifecta £112.90.
**Owner** Pryke Dixon Golding Appleby **Bred** Doc Bloodstock **Trained** Danethorpe, Notts

■ Smart Stepper was withdrawn. Price at time of withdrawal 12-1. Rule 4 applies to all bets - deduction 5p in the pound.

**FOCUS**
Although the course soaked up 7mm of overnight rain, a drying day saw the ground revert to good, good to soft in places before racing began and, although the winning rider said the surface was "lovely, good ground", the times suggested the ground was just on the soft side. A modest event in which the gallop was sound throughout.

## 2052 RACING UK ANYWHERE AVAILABLE NOW CLAIMING STKS 1m 3f 214y
6:30 (6:30) (Class 6) 4-Y-O+ £2,385 (£704; £352) Stalls Low

Form RPR
0-02 1 **War Poet**8 1816 7-8-13 80 TomEaves 1 79
(Brian Ellison) *hld up in tch: hdwy over 2f out: rdn to ld over 1f out: carried hd awkwardly u.p fnl f but a holding on* 5/4[1]
5-00 2 1 **Sherman McCoy**27 1377 8-8-10 71 RobertWinston 3 74
(Marjorie Fife) *led: rdn whn hdd over 1f out: briefly dropped to 3rd ins fnl f: kpt on to regain 2nd 50yds out* 4/1[3]
040- 3 1 1/4 **Ethics Girl (IRE)**234 6377 8-8-6 72 (t) FrannyNorton 8 68
(John Berry) *trckd ldr: rdn and briefly outpcd in 4th 2f out: rallied to chse wnr ins fnl f: no ex and lost 2nd 50yds out* 7/2[2]
40 4 2 1/2 **Safe Home (IRE)**10 1715 4-9-13 82 PhillipMakin 5 85
(John Quinn) *s.i.s: sn trckd ldr: rdn and ev ch 2f out: wknd appr fnl f* 13/2
026- 5 11 **Korngold**200 7342 6-8-7 54 JoeFanning 2 47
(Tracy Waggott) *racd keenly: hld up: rdn over 2f out: sn btn: eased fnl f* 10/1

2m 42.71s (3.81) **Going Correction** +0.10s/f (Good) 5 Ran SP% 109.1
Speed ratings (Par 101): **91,90,89,87,80**
CSF £6.38 TOTE £2.70: £1.20, £1.90; EX 8.10 Trifecta £15.00.Korngold was claimed by Mr Barry Leavy for £5,000
**Owner** M Kirby **Bred** Darley **Trained** Norton, N Yorks

**FOCUS**
A couple of useful sorts, but this wasn't a competitive race and a steady gallop means this form isn't reliable.

## 2053 BOOK NOW FOR 30TH MAY MAIDEN STKS 7f
7:00 (7:00) (Class 5) 3-Y-O+ £2,911 (£866; £432; £216) Stalls Low

Form RPR
2 1 **Lord Of The Nile (IRE)**19 1542 3-9-0 80 DanielTudhope 1 67+
(David O'Meara) *mde all: rdn over 1f out: briefly drvn ins fnl f: kpt on* 1/7[1]
50- 2 2 **Danzki (IRE)**242 6169 3-9-0 0 GrahamLee 5 62
(Gay Kelleway) *trckd ldr: rdn over 2f out: kpt on but a hld* 7/1[2]
500- 3 2 1/2 **Rokeby**220 6842 3-9-0 47 AndrewElliott 6 55
(George Moore) *in tch: rdn 3f out: one pce and hld in 3rd fr over 1f out* 33/1
6 4 3 1/2 **Navajo Dream**56 914 3-8-9 0 RobertWinston 4 41
(Michael Appleby) *hld up: rdn over 2f out: wnt modest 4th ins fnl f: nvr threatened* 10/1[3]
-4 5 1 1/2 **Haidees Reflection**9 1757 4-9-7 0 PJMcDonald 2 41
(Lucy Normile) *in tch: rdn over 3f out: wknd over 1f out* 66/1
403- 6 3 3/4 **Captain Rhyric**246 6050 5-9-12 47 LucyAlexander 7 36
(James Moffatt) *slowly away: hld up: a towards rr* 33/1
0 7 2 3/4 **Sirnita**10 1713 5-9-4 0 ConnorBeasley(3) 3 24
(Richard Guest) *midfield: rdn over 3f out: wknd 2f out* 33/1

1m 28.36s (1.36) **Going Correction** +0.10s/f (Good)
**WFA** 3 from 4yo+ 12lb 7 Ran SP% 119.4
Speed ratings (Par 103): **96,93,90,86,85 80,77**
CSF £2.09 TOTE £1.40: £1.10, £2.40; EX 2.60 Trifecta £26.50.
**Owner** Sir Robert Ogden **Bred** Magic Carpet Syndicate **Trained** Nawton, N Yorks

**FOCUS**
A very one-sided maiden on paper, but just a workmanlike success from the short-priced market leader. The gallop was an ordinary one and the proximity of the third holds down the form.

## 2054 YORKSHIRE-OUTDOORS.CO.UK ADVENTURE ACTIVITIES H'CAP 7f
7:30 (7:32) (Class 4) (0-80,80) 4-Y-O+ £6,469 (£1,925; £962; £481) Stalls Low

Form RPR
3430 1 **Conry (IRE)**10 1710 8-9-4 77 StevieDonohoe 1 87
(Ian Williams) *hld up: rdn and hdwy over 1f out: kpt on wl fnl f: led post* 6/1
0103 2 hd **Piceno (IRE)**5 1903 6-8-11 77 (p) MatthewHopkins(7) 11 86
(Scott Dixon) *w ldr: rdn to ld over 2f out: kpt on: hdd post* 9/2[2]
0-20 3 2 **Solar Spirit (IRE)**13 1646 9-9-1 77 IanBrennan(3) 6 81
(Tracy Waggott) *midfield: smooth hdwy over 2f out: rdn to chal appr fnl f: no ex and hld in 3rd fnl 110yds* 20/1
63-0 4 nk **Bartack (IRE)**22 1483 4-9-7 80 (v[1]) DanielTudhope 9 83
(David O'Meara) *chsd ldrs: rdn over 2f out: one pce* 15/2
/0-3 5 1 3/4 **Kosika (USA)**12 1667 4-9-0 73 JoeFanning 3 71
(Mark Johnston) *chsd ldrs: rdn over 2f out: no ex ins fnl f* 7/2[1]
3160 6 3/4 **Bogsnog (IRE)**14 1630 4-9-2 75 TomEaves 4 72
(Kristin Stubbs) *midfield: rdn over 2f out: one pce and nvr threatened ldrs* 25/1
5355 7 shd **Pearl Nation (USA)**14 1630 5-9-0 76 JasonHart(3) 2 72
(Brian Baugh) *hld up: rdn over 2f out: one pce and nvr threatened* 11/2[3]
0-00 8 7 **Snow Bay**29 1345 8-8-13 77 ShirleyTeasdale(5) 10 55
(Paul Midgley) *led narrowly: rdn whn hdd over 2f out: wknd over 1f out* 11/1
22-0 9 3 1/4 **Mishaal (IRE)**24 1447 4-8-13 72 BarryMcHugh 7 42
(Michael Herrington) *v.s.a and lost 15 l s: a bhd* 22/1
6-63 10 6 **Shamaheart (IRE)**6 1881 4-9-2 75 (v[1]) PJMcDonald 5 29
(Geoffrey Harker) *chsd ldrs: rdn over 2f out: wknd over 1f out* 10/1
000- 11 9 **Kerbaaj (USA)**256 5721 4-9-2 75 JamesSullivan 12 6
(Ruth Carr) *slowly away: hld up in rr: rdn over 3f out: sn btn* 28/1

1m 26.75s (-0.25) **Going Correction** +0.10s/f (Good) 11 Ran SP% 115.7
Speed ratings (Par 105): **105,104,102,102,100 99,99,91,87,80 70**
CSF £30.74 CT £516.09 TOTE £7.00: £2.40, £2.00, £5.50; EX 36.20 Trifecta £191.20.
**Owner** Ian Williams **Bred** Shay White **Trained** Portway, Worcs

**FOCUS**
Not many in-form types in a fair handicap. The gallop was sound throughout.

## 2055 GO RACING IN YORKSHIRE H'CAP 1m 7f 177y
8:00 (8:02) (Class 6) (0-65,69) 4-Y-O+ £2,726 (£805; £402) Stalls Low

Form RPR
50-4 1 **Miss Macnamara (IRE)**15 1605 5-9-5 60 PhillipMakin 15 74+
(Martin Todhunter) *midfield: smooth hdwy to trck ldr over 3f out: led 2f out: rdn clr: eased fnl 50yds* 11/1

5-02 **2** 3 1/2 **Cropley (IRE)**[4] 1915 5-9-5 **65**....(b) GeorgeDowning(5) 4 74
(Ian Williams) *w ldr tl led 9f out: drvn whn hdd 2f out: kpt on but no ch w wnr* **7/2**[1]
-030 **3** 8 **My Destination (IRE)**[15] 1605 5-9-0 **62**.... LukeLeadbitter(7) 8 61
(Declan Carroll) *hld up: rdn and hdwy on outer over 3f out: plugged on to go modest 3rd ins fnl f* **20/1**
0-01 **4** 2 3/4 **Dubara Reef (IRE)**[15] 1605 7-8-3 **51** ow2.... JordanNason(7) 7 47
(Paul Green) *led: hdd 9f out: remained prom: rdn 5f out: outpcd in 3rd over 2f out: wknd over 1f out* **9/2**[2]
452- **5** 2 1/2 **Beat The Shower**[166] 7099 8-9-4 **59**.... GrahamLee 12 52
(Peter Niven) *hld up in midfield: rdn over 3f out: sn no imp on ldrs* **10/1**
-606 **6** 2 3/4 **Voice From Above (IRE)**[12] 1674 5-8-2 **50**.... JackGarritty(7) 10 40
(Patrick Holmes) *hld up in midfield: rdn and brief hdwy over 3f out: sn no imp on ldrs* **33/1**
-031 **7** 1/2 **Dynastic**[8] 1806 5-9-7 **69** 6ex.... LauraBarry(7) 3 58
(Tony Coyle) *hld up: rdn over 3f out: nvr threatened* **12/1**
10-6 **8** 4 1/2 **El Massivo (IRE)**[31] 1307 4-9-4 **62**.... DaleSwift 11 46
(Brian Ellison) *slowly away: hld up: rdn over 3f out: nvr threatened* **7/1**[3]
00-2 **9** 2 **Al Furat (USA)**[13] 1644 6-9-4 **59**.... DavidAllan 6 40
(Ron Barr) *hld up: nvr threatened* **10/1**
50-2 **10** 3 1/4 **Waltz Darling (IRE)**[15] 1374 6-9-4 **59**.... TomEaves 13 37
(Keith Reveley) *chsd ldrs: rdn over 3f out: wknd over 2f out* **8/1**
00-4 **11** 9 **Patavium (IRE)**[14] 1374 11-8-12 **53**.... JamesSullivan 1 20
(Edwin Tuer) *chsd ldrs: rdn and lost pl over 3f out: sn btn* **28/1**
3045 **12** 2 1/2 **Stormy Morning**[18] 1567 8-8-9 **57**....(p) EvaMoscrop(7) 5 21
(Philip Kirby) *hld up: nvr threatened* **25/1**
/6-4 **13** 1 1/4 **Leroy Parker (IRE)**[18] 1567 6-9-7 **65**.... ConnorBeasley(3) 14 27
(Barry Murtagh) *in tch: rdn over 3f out: wknd 2f out* **33/1**
030- **14** 26 **Young Jay**[17] 7066 4-9-2 **60**.... JoeFanning 9
(Andrew Crook) *midfield: wknd over 3f out* **40/1**

3m 32.61s (0.61) **Going Correction** +0.10s/f (Good)
**WFA** 4 from 5yo+ 3lb **14 Ran SP% 118.6**
Speed ratings (Par 101): **102,100,96,94,93 92,92,89,88,87 82,81,80,67**
CSF £44.75 CT £780.15 TOTE £15.90: £4.00, £2.00, £6.50; EX 48.90 Trifecta £907.60.
**Owner** Javas Charvers **Bred** Airlie Stud **Trained** Orton, Cumbria
■ Stewards' Enquiry : Jordan Nason two-day ban: used whip above permitted level (May 20-21)

**FOCUS**
A modest handicap, but a reasonable gallop and the first two deserve credit for pulling clear in the straight.

## 2056 DON'T MISS SATURDAY 24TH MAY H'CAP 5f
**8:30** (8:32) (Class 5) (0-75,75) 4-Y-0+ **£3,067** (£905; £453) **Stalls** Low

Form RPR
0052 **1** **Keep It Dark**[7] 1843 5-9-2 **70**.... BarryMcHugh 5 84
(Tony Coyle) *mde all: pushed out fr over 1f out: firmly in command ins fnl f* **10/3**[1]
-051 **2** 2 1/2 **Boxing Shadows**[13] 1643 4-8-11 **65**.... DavidAllan 6 70
(Les Eyre) *chsd ldrs: rdn 1/2-way: chsd wnr appr fnl f: kpt on but comf hld* **10/3**[1]
-041 **3** hd **Fleurtille**[7] 1843 5-8-10 **67** 6ex.... ConnorBeasley(3) 7 71
(Robert Johnson) *hld up: rdn 1/2-way: kpt on fr over 1f out: wnt 3rd 110yds out* **5/1**[2]
1-02 **4** 1 **Windforpower (IRE)**[13] 1643 4-8-10 **64**....(p) JoeFanning 9 65
(Tracy Waggott) *midfield: rdn 1/2-way: kpt on* **12/1**
160- **5** 3/4 **Rock On Candy**[181] 7777 5-9-4 **72**.... TomEaves 1 70
(John Spearing) *prom: rdn 1/2-way: no ex fnl f* **10/1**[3]
1-56 **6** 3/4 **Thatcherite (IRE)**[13] 1643 6-9-1 **69**....(bt) StephenCraine 8 64
(Tony Coyle) *slowly away: sn pushed along in rr: minor late hdwy: nvr threatened* **14/1**
-624 **7** 1/2 **Beau Mistral (IRE)**[15] 1604 5-8-12 **73**.... JordanNason(7) 2 66
(Paul Green) *w ldr: rdn 1/2-way: wknd fnl f* **12/1**
20-0 **8** 1 3/4 **Ypres**[15] 1609 5-9-7 **75**.... GrahamLee 4 62
(Jason Ward) *hld up: nvr threatened* **20/1**
-000 **9** 3 3/4 **Mister Manannan (IRE)**[19] 1541 7-9-7 **75**....(p) AdrianNicholls 3 49
(David Nicholls) *chsd ldrs: rdn 1/2-way: wknd over 1f out* **22/1**
0400 **10** 1 **Lost In Paris (IRE)**[24] 1447 8-8-11 **72**.... LauraBarry(7) 11 42
(Tony Coyle) *midfield: rdn 1/2-way: wknd fnl f* **20/1**
0-05 **11** 1/2 **Chosen One (IRE)**[13] 1643 9-8-7 **61** oh1.... PJMcDonald 10 29
(Ruth Carr) *hld up: a towards rr* **12/1**

1m 0.15s (0.35) **Going Correction** +0.175s/f (Good) **11 Ran SP% 115.5**
Speed ratings (Par 103): **104,100,99,98,96 95,94,92,86,84 83**
CSF £12.82 CT £54.13 TOTE £4.00: £2.20, £2.20, £1.20; EX 19.70 Trifecta £69.20.
**Owner** N Hetherton **Bred** Heather Raw **Trained** Norton, N Yorks

**FOCUS**
A fair handicap in which the pace was sound, but a race in which it paid to be close to the pace.
T/Plt: £20.40 to a £1 stake. Pool: £58,590.08 - 2,091.43 winning units T/Qpdt: £8.70 to a £1 stake. Pool: £4,805.40 - 408.50 winning units AS

# 1793 KEMPTON (A.W) (R-H)
Tuesday, May 6

**OFFICIAL GOING: Standard**
Wind: Light; across Weather: Cloudy with sunny spells

## 2057 IRISH STALLION FARMS EBF MAIDEN STKS 5f (P)
**2:10** (2:11) (Class 5) 2-Y-0 **£2,911** (£866; £432; £216) **Stalls** Low

Form RPR
**1** **Merdon Castle (IRE)** 2-9-5 0.... LiamKeniry 3 79+
(David Elsworth) *a.p: shkn up over 1f out: r.o to ld nr fin* **7/1**[3]
3 **2** 3/4 **Colour Catcher**[17] 1575 2-9-5 0.... MickaelBarzalona 4 76
(Charlie Appleby) *led: hdd over 3f out: chsd ldr: rdn and ev ch ins fnl f: styd on* **10/11**[1]
2 **3** nk **Littlemissblakeney**[12] 1670 2-8-9 0.... NoelGarbutt(5) 1 70
(Hugo Palmer) *trckd ldr: racd keenly: led over 3f out: rdn and hdd nr fin* **7/1**[3]
4 **4** 2 3/4 **Jersey Belle**[9] 1764 2-8-11 0.... WilliamTwiston-Davies(3) 2 60
(Mick Channon) *trckd ldrs: nt clr run over 1f out: sn rdn: styd on same pce ins fnl f* **25/1**
**5** 4 **Foxtrot Knight** 2-9-5 0.... HarryBentley 5 51
(Olly Stevens) *hld up: rdn over 1f out: wknd fnl f* **20/1**
**6** 3/4 **Rasha (IRE)** 2-9-0 0.... WilliamBuick 7 43
(Roger Varian) *s.s: hdwy over 3f out: rdn and hung lft over 1f out: wknd fnl f* **7/2**[2]
0 **7** 2 1/2 **Now Say Boooom**[25] 1417 2-9-0 0.... LukeMorris 6 34
(Luke Dace) *dwlt and wnt lft s: hld up: rdn and wknd over 1f out* **66/1**

1m 2.0s (1.50) **Going Correction** +0.025s/f (Slow) **7 Ran SP% 109.7**
Speed ratings (Par 93): **89,87,87,82,76 75,71**
CSF £12.77 TOTE £7.20: £5.30, £1.02; EX 15.00 Trifecta £85.10.
**Owner** J C Smith **Bred** Littleton Stud **Trained** Newmarket, Suffolk

**FOCUS**
An interesting little maiden. The winner could prove quite a bit better than the bare form in future.

## 2058 PLAY ROULETTE & BLACKJACK AT BETVICTOR.COM H'CAP 7f (P)
**2:40** (2:40) (Class 5) (0-70,73) 3-Y-0 **£2,587** (£770; £384; £192) **Stalls** Low

Form RPR
43-1 **1** **Despot (IRE)**[9] 1769 3-9-10 **73** 6ex.... RyanMoore 5 80
(Charles Hills) *mde all: shkn up: edgd rt and wnt clr over 1f out: rdn out* **8/15**[1]
3555 **2** 1 1/4 **Penny's Boy**[8] 1786 3-9-5 **68**....(t) JamesDoyle 2 72
(Sylvester Kirk) *trckd ldrs: plld hrd: rdn over 2f out: edgd lft over 1f out: styd on to go 2nd wl ins fnl f* **25/1**
54-1 **3** 1 1/4 **Si Senor (IRE)**[36] 1214 3-9-6 **69**.... WilliamBuick 7 70
(Ed Vaughan) *a.p: chsd wnr 5f out: rdn over 2f out: styd on same pce ins fnl f* **11/4**[2]
015- **4** 1 1/2 **New Row**[188] 7626 3-9-4 **70**.... MichaelJMMurphy(3) 4 67
(William Jarvis) *hld up: rdn over 2f out: styd on ins fnl f: nt trble ldrs* **14/1**[3]
002- **5** 1 1/4 **Half Way**[257] 5675 3-9-0 **68**.... AmyScott(5) 8 62
(Henry Candy) *hld up: racd keenly: rdn over 1f out: kpt on ins fnl f: n.d* **25/1**
513- **6** 1/2 **Fiftyshadesfreed (IRE)**[153] 8147 3-9-6 **69**.... JimCrowley 1 61
(George Baker) *chsd ldrs: rdn over 2f out: no ex fnl f* **20/1**
450- **7** 2 **Orlando Star (CAN)**[224] 6731 3-9-1 **67**.... OisinMurphy(3) 9 54
(Roger Teal) *hld up: rdn over 2f out: n.d* **50/1**

1m 26.11s (0.11) **Going Correction** +0.025s/f (Slow) **7 Ran SP% 113.0**
Speed ratings (Par 99): **100,98,97,95,94 93,91**
CSF £21.44 CT £24.56 TOTE £1.40: £1.10, £10.30; EX 16.30 Trifecta £35.80.
**Owner** Hon Mrs Corbett, C Wright, Mrs B W Hills **Bred** Michael G Daly **Trained** Lambourn, Berks

**FOCUS**
This was all about the top weight and odds-on favourite.

## 2059 BETVICTOR.COM H'CAP 7f (P)
**3:10** (3:10) (Class 4) (0-80,85) 4-Y-0+ **£4,690** (£1,395; £697; £348) **Stalls** Low

Form RPR
2/5- **1** **Mac's Superstar (FR)**[371] 1908 4-9-3 **75**....[1] ShaneKelly 2 82+
(James Fanshawe) *hld up: rdn over 1f out: swtchd rt and r.o ins fnl f: led post* **5/1**
05-6 **2** nk **Glanely (IRE)**[97] 372 4-9-4 **76**.... RichardHughes 3 82
(Martyn Meade) *trckd ldrs: rdn to ld over 1f out: hdd post* **7/2**[1]
1321 **3** nk **Athletic**[12] 1668 5-9-0 **72**....(v) JimCrowley 8 77
(Andrew Reid) *gate did nt open properly: s.s: hld up: nt clr run and swtchd lft over 1f out: rdn and r.o ins fnl f* **4/1**[2]
-340 **4** nse **New Leyf (IRE)**[10] 1731 8-8-13 **71**....(b) SeanLevey 4 76
(Jeremy Gask) *trckd ldrs: rdn and ev ch fr over 1f out: unable qck nr fin* **16/1**
00-2 **5** 1 **Bayleyf (IRE)**[8] 1799 5-8-13 **71** ow1.... AmirQuinn 6 73
(Lee Carter) *dwlt: hdwy 5f out: rdn over 2f out: styd on* **6/1**
616 **6** 3 **The Happy Hammer (IRE)**[64] 825 8-8-4 **65**....(b) OisinMurphy(3) 9 60
(Eugene Stanford) *disp ld tl rdn over 1f out: no ex ins fnl f* **10/1**
-420 **7** 1/2 **Gold Beau (FR)**[15] 1610 4-8-11 **74**....(p) JacobButterfield(5) 7 67
(Kristin Stubbs) *disp ld tl rdn to ld over 1f out: sn hdd: no ex ins fnl f* **12/1**
3000 **8** 5 **Spin Artist (USA)**[16] 1598 4-9-4 **76**....(b[1]) SilvestreDeSousa 1 56
(Mark Johnston) *sn pushed along and prom: lost pl 5f out: rdn over 2f out: wknd fnl f* **9/2**[3]

1m 25.7s (-0.30) **Going Correction** +0.025s/f (Slow) **8 Ran SP% 114.0**
Speed ratings (Par 105): **102,101,101,101,100 96,96,90**
CSF £22.72 CT £76.36 TOTE £6.50: £2.20, £1.10, £1.50; EX 34.10 Trifecta £157.60.
**Owner** Michael McDonnell **Bred** Stowell Hill Ltd **Trained** Newmarket, Suffolk

**FOCUS**
An open handicap on paper, but the pace looked sound and although there were a bunch of horses close together at the finish, the form should stand up.

## 2060 DOWNLOAD THE BETVICTOR APP NOW H'CAP (LONDON MIDDLE DISTANCE QUALIFIER) (BOBIS RACE) 1m 3f (P)
**3:40** (3:40) (Class 3) (0-90,88) 3-Y-0
**£7,158** (£2,143; £1,071; £535; £267; £134) **Stalls** Low

Form RPR
212- **1** **Devilment**[195] 7471 3-9-0 **81**.... WilliamBuick 4 92
(Charlie Appleby) *chsd ldrs: rdn to ld over 1f out: styd on wl* **2/1**[1]
61- **2** 1 **Warrior Of Light (IRE)**[176] 7834 3-9-1 **82**.... TedDurcan 5 91
(David Lanigan) *prom: lost pl over 5f out: hdwy over 2f out: jnd wnr over 1f out: sn rdn: unable qck wl ins fnl f* **11/4**[2]
1-0 **3** 4 1/2 **Moontime**[13] 1652 3-9-7 **88**.... MickaelBarzalona 1 89
(Charlie Appleby) *broke wl: lost pl after 1f: hld up: rdn over 2f out: r.o to go 3rd ins fnl f: nvr trbld ldrs* **6/1**
012- **4** 3/4 **Elysian Prince**[167] 7979 3-8-11 **78**.... JimCrowley 2 78
(Paul Cole) *hld up: hdwy over 5f out: rdn over 2f out: styd on same pce fr over 1f out* **14/1**
511 **5** 3/4 **Fitzgerald (IRE)**[52] 975 3-9-4 **85**.... LukeMorris 7 84
(Marco Botti) *led: rdn and hdd over 1f out: wknd ins fnl f* **9/2**[3]
16-0 **6** 7 **Laugharne**[19] 1535 3-9-6 **87**.... JamesDoyle 8 73
(Roger Charlton) *chsd ldr tl rdn over 2f out: wknd over 1f out* **10/1**
044- **7** 6 **Inevitable**[204] 7252 3-8-4 **71**.... SilvestreDeSousa 6 46
(Mark Johnston) *s.i.s: sn prom: rdn over 4f out: wknd 2f out* **16/1**

2m 19.8s (-2.10) **Going Correction** +0.025s/f (Slow) **7 Ran SP% 114.1**
Speed ratings (Par 103): **108,107,104,103,102 97,93**
CSF £7.63 CT £26.43 TOTE £3.40: £1.30, £1.60; EX 12.30 Trifecta £54.90.
**Owner** Godolphin **Bred** Cliveden Stud **Trained** Newmarket, Suffolk

**FOCUS**
Some nicely bred 3yos here who should have bright futures, so an interesting race and it was run at an even pace. The form looks sound. Two pulled clear and both look smart, although the result might not be the same if they meet in the future.

## 2061 BREEDERS BACKING RACING EBF MAIDEN FILLIES' STKS (BOBIS RACE) 1m (P)
**4:10** (4:13) (Class 5) 3-Y-O **£3,881** (£1,155; £577; £288) **Stalls** Low

Form RPR

1 **Provenance** 3-9-0 0 RyanMoore 12 88+
(Sir Michael Stoute) *hld up in tch: shkn up to ld over 1f out: qcknd clr fnl f* **12/1**

4- 2 4 ½ **Award (IRE)**[203] 7260 3-9-0 0[1] WilliamBuick 6 77
(John Gosden) *chsd ldrs: nt clr run over 2f out: rdn and ev ch over 1f out: styd on same pce fnl f* **8/1**[3]

54- 3 1 ¼ **Baynunah (USA)**[181] 7764 3-9-0 0 HayleyTurner 14 74
(James Fanshawe) *led 1f: chsd ldr: led again wl over 1f out: sn rdn and hdd: no extera ins fnl f* **20/1**

4 ¾ **Colourful** 3-9-0 0 JamesDoyle 7 72
(Lady Cecil) *a.p: rdn over 2f out: no ex fnl f* **10/1**

5 shd **Lilly Junior** 3-9-0 0 SebSanders 11 72
(William Haggas) *hld up: rdn over 2f out: hdwy and hung rt over 1f out: kpt on* **20/1**

5 6 ¾ **Wojha (IRE)**[25] 1422 3-9-0 0 PaulHanagan 4 70
(William Haggas) *s.i.s: sn pushed along and prom: rdn over 2f out: no ex fnl f* **11/8**[1]

5-0 7 shd **Cadeaux Power**[19] 1530 3-9-0 0 SilvestreDeSousa 9 70
(Clive Brittain) *led after 1f: rdn and hdd wl over 1f out: wknd ins fnl f* **5/1**[2]

8 1 ¾ **Lady Brigid (IRE)** 3-9-0 0 TomQueally 5 66+
(Amanda Perrett) *s.i.s: hld up: hdwy and edgd rt over 2f out: wknd ins fnl f* **33/1**

9 2 ½ **Dubai Hadeia** 3-9-0 0 MickaelBarzalona 2 60
(Charlie Appleby) *dwlt: hld up: rdn over 2f out: sme hdwy over 1f out: wknd fnl f* **10/1**

10 2 ¼ **Capmonde (IRE)** 3-9-0 0 JimCrowley 13 54
(William Knight) *s.s: hld up: nvr nrr* **33/1**

11 ½ **Tarap (IRE)** 3-9-0 0 SeanLevey 10 53
(Richard Hannon) *prom: lost pl over 5f out: rdn 1/2-way: wknd over 2f out* **33/1**

00 12 hd **Scariff Hornet (IRE)**[9] 1768 3-8-9 0 JoshBaudains[(5)] 1 53
(Sylvester Kirk) *hld up: rdn over 2f out: a in rr* **66/1**

0 13 ¾ **Ascending Angel (IRE)**[9] 1768 3-9-0 0 RichardHughes 3 51
(Richard Hannon) *s.i.s: sn pushed along into mid-div: hdwy over 3f out: rdn and wknd over 1f out* **33/1**

0-0 14 2 ¾ **Magic Shoes (IRE)**[25] 1424 3-8-11 0 OisinMurphy[(3)] 8 44
(Roger Charlton) *hld up: pushed along over 2f out: a in rr* **33/1**

1m 40.24s (0.44) **Going Correction** +0.025s/f (Slow) **14** Ran SP% **121.5**
Speed ratings (Par 96): **98,93,92,91,91 90,90,88,86,84 83,83,82,79**
CSF £95.89 TOTE £13.00: £3.40, £3.20, £5.50; EX 94.90 Trifecta £665.30.
**Owner** Cheveley Park Stud **Bred** Cheveley Park Stud Ltd **Trained** Newmarket, Suffolk

**FOCUS**
A revealing fillies' maiden which appeared to throw up something quite special.

## 2062 DOWNLOAD THE BETVICTOR INSTABET APP JUBILEE H'CAP (LONDON MILE SERIES QUALIFIER) 1m (P)
**4:40** (4:41) (Class 3) (0-90,89) 4-Y-O+
**£7,158** (£2,143; £1,071; £535; £267; £134) **Stalls** Low

Form RPR

40-0 1 **Secret Art (IRE)**[24] 1437 4-9-3 85 GeorgeBaker 5 97
(William Knight) *hld up: hdwy over 1f out: shkn up to ld ins fnl f: qcknd clr* **7/1**

5112 2 4 ½ **High Time Too (IRE)**[18] 1554 4-9-2 84 RyanMoore 1 86
(Hugo Palmer) *trckd ldrs: racd keenly: shkn up to ld over 1f out: rdn and hdd ins fnl f: sn outpcd* **3/1**[1]

321- 3 ¾ **Don't Stare**[272] 5133 4-9-2 84 ShaneKelly 3 84+
(James Fanshawe) *s.i.s: hdwy over 6f out: shkn up and nt clr run over 1f out: styd on to go 3rd towards fin* **7/2**[2]

2442 4 hd **Nassau Storm**[31] 1301 5-9-2 84 WilliamBuick 6 84
(William Knight) *hld up: rdn over 2f out: styd on ins fnl f* **14/1**

0000 5 ½ **Loyalty**[17] 1578 7-8-10 85 (v) AdamMcLean[(7)] 7 84
(Derek Shaw) *s.i.s: hld up: hdwy over 1f out: n.m.r ins fnl f: kpt on* **25/1**

4110 6 1 ½ **Silverheels (IRE)**[18] 1558 5-9-3 85 (b) JimCrowley 2 80
(Paul Cole) *led early: chsd ldrs: rdn and ev ch wl over 1f out: no ex ins fnl f* **7/1**

2-13 7 hd **Bustopher (USA)**[7] 1834 4-9-6 88 MickaelBarzalona 4 83
(Charlie Appleby) *sn chsng ldr: rdn over 2f out: ev ch over 1f out: no ex ins fnl f* **3/1**[1]

40-1 8 1 ½ **Tobacco Road (IRE)**[29] 1351 4-9-7 89 RichardHughes 2 80
(Richard Hannon) *sn led: rdn and hdd over 1f out: wknd ins fnl f* **6/1**[3]

1m 38.58s (-1.22) **Going Correction** +0.025s/f (Slow) **8** Ran SP% **122.0**
Speed ratings (Par 107): **107,102,101,101,101 99,99,97**
CSF £30.37 CT £90.21 TOTE £8.30: £2.90, £1.10, £2.00; EX 38.50 Trifecta £192.50.
**Owner** Circuit Racing **Bred** Grange Stud **Trained** Patching, W Sussex

**FOCUS**
An open handicap which was run at an even pace.

## 2063 FOLLOW @BETVICTORRACING ON TWITTER H'CAP (BOBIS RACE) 1m (P)
**5:10** (5:11) (Class 4) (0-85,81) 3-Y-O **£4,690** (£1,395; £697; £348) **Stalls** Low

Form RPR

2-11 1 **Crystal Lake (IRE)**[19] 1540 3-9-7 81 JimCrowley 5 89+
(Ralph Beckett) *trckd ldr tl led over 2f out: rdn over 1f out: styd on gamely* **3/1**[2]

01-4 2 ½ **Royal Preserve**[27] 1381 3-9-0 74 DavidProbert 6 81
(Andrew Balding) *trckd ldrs: racd keenly: rdn over 1f out: r.o* **12/1**

1-5 3 shd **Billingsgate (IRE)**[11] 1690 3-9-6 80 MickaelBarzalona 4 87+
(Charlie Appleby) *s.i.s: hld up: pushed along and edgd rt over 2f out: hdwy over 1f out: r.o* **3/1**[2]

41- 4 ¾ **Kafeel (USA)**[187] 7647 3-9-4 78 PaulHanagan 8 83
(Roger Varian) *chsd ldrs: rdn to go 2nd over 1f out: unable qck wl ins fnl f* **7/1**[3]

01- 5 ¾ **Best Kept**[209] 7120 3-9-5 79 RyanMoore 10 82+
(Amanda Perrett) *hld up: rdn over 2f out: hdwy over 1f out: nt rch ldrs* **9/4**[1]

5-62 6 3 ¾ **Seaham**[27] 1381 3-9-3 77 JamesDoyle 7 72
(Rod Millman) *s.i.s: hld up: hdwy over 1f out: no ex fnl f* **40/1**

243- 7 2 ¾ **Adore**[201] 7326 3-8-7 67 HayleyTurner 2 55
(Sir Michael Stoute) *chsd ldrs: rdn over 2f out: wknd fnl f* **25/1**

35-0 8 1 ¾ **Dancealot**[19] 1530 3-9-7 81 LukeMorris 9 65
(Clive Brittain) *sn pushed along in rr: effrt over 2f out: wknd over 1f out* **33/1**

34-3 9 nse **Black Caesar (IRE)**[27] 1390 3-9-6 80 RichardHughes 1 64
(Richard Hannon) *hld up: rdn over 2f out: wknd over 1f out* **12/1**

105- 10 2 ½ **Ajig**[210] 7088 3-8-11 71 SilvestreDeSousa 3 49
(Eve Johnson Houghton) *led: rdn and hdd over 2f out: wknd fnl f* **66/1**

1m 39.84s (0.04) **Going Correction** +0.025s/f (Slow) **10** Ran SP% **119.4**
Speed ratings (Par 101): **100,99,99,98,97 94,91,89,89,87**
CSF £38.11 CT £119.36 TOTE £3.30: £1.50, £3.40, £2.10; EX 24.00 Trifecta £159.50.
**Owner** The Pickford Hill Partnership **Bred** B Holland, S Hillen & J Cullinan **Trained** Kimpton, Hants

**FOCUS**
A good-quality handicap featuring several horses who have plenty of potential for the future.
T/Plt: £50.00 to a £1 stake. Pool: £51,649.20 - 753.35 winning units T/Qpdt: £30.10 to a £1 stake. Pool: £3,243.51 - 79.70 winning units CR

# 2044 BRIGHTON (L-H)
Wednesday, May 7

**OFFICIAL GOING: Good to firm (7.4)**
Rail dolled out from 6f to 2f, increasing distances by 12yds.
Wind: Strong, half against Weather: Mainly cloudy

## 2064 GATWICK DIAMOND BUSINESS 60TH YEAR MAIDEN STKS 5f 59y
**2:05** (2:05) (Class 5) 2-Y-O **£2,587** (£770; £384; £192) **Stalls** Centre

Form RPR

2 1 **Dougal (IRE)**[9] 1807 2-9-5 0 RichardHughes 5 92+
(Richard Hannon) *trckd ldrs in 3rd: swtchd ins and led over 1f out: sn clr: easily* **2/7**[1]

2 2 5 **Brown Velvet**[15] 1633 2-9-0 0 (v) MartinDwyer 1 67
(Hugo Palmer) *sn led: hdd over 1f out: easily outpcd by wnr* **8/1**[3]

42 3 3 ¾ **Ar Colleen Aine**[10] 1764 2-8-11 0 WilliamTwiston-Davies[(3)] 3 54
(Mick Channon) *pressed ldr: rdn to chal 2f out: sn outpcd* **5/1**[2]

4 3 ½ **Marti Ella** 2-8-9 0 PhilipPrince[(5)] 2 41
(J S Moore) *s.s: bhd and rdn along in 4th: no hdwy fnl 2f* **100/1**

1m 5.04s (2.74) **Going Correction** +0.30s/f (Good) **4** Ran SP% **106.5**
Speed ratings (Par 93): **90,82,76,70**
CSF £3.05 TOTE £1.50; EX 2.00 Trifecta £2.60.
**Owner** Mrs J Wood **Bred** Ardrums House Stud **Trained** East Everleigh, Wilts

**FOCUS**
The ground had quickened up, no doubt aided by the strong wind, for the second day of Brighton's two-day May meeting. It was officially given as good to firm. The rails had been pushed out from the first day, adding 12yds to all race distances. The useful winner might do better still.

## 2065 GATWICK AIRPORT H'CAP 5f 213y
**2:35** (2:35) (Class 5) (0-75,74) 4-Y-O+ **£2,587** (£770; £384; £192) **Stalls** Centre

Form RPR

5064 1 **Clear Praise (USA)**[34] 1261 7-9-6 73 RichardHughes 1 81
(Simon Dow) *mde all: sn 3 l ahd at gd pce: edgd rt over 1f out: drvn along: a in control* **11/8**[1]

6412 2 ¾ **Top Cop**[11] 1739 5-9-2 74 (be) DCByrne[(5)] 5 80
(Ronald Harris) *t.k.h: chsd wnr: kpt on u.p fnl f: a hld* **11/8**[1]

030- 3 1 **Spiraea**[211] 7106 4-8-12 65 LukeMorris 4 67
(Mark Rimell) *sn pushed along in 3rd: hrd rdn and chal for 2nd over 1f out: unable qck fnl f* **8/1**[2]

043- 4 2 ¾ **Paradise Spectre**[259] 5645 7-8-11 64 (p) LiamKeniry 2 58
(Zoe Davison) *dwlt: hld up in rr: effrt 2f out: no imp over 1f out* **25/1**

-005 5 hd **Blazing Knight (IRE)**[13] 1667 4-9-3 70 (p) JimCrowley 3 63
(Chris Gordon) *hld up in 4th: rdn over 2f out: one pce* **12/1**[3]

1m 11.67s (1.47) **Going Correction** +0.30s/f (Good) **5** Ran SP% **106.9**
Speed ratings (Par 103): **102,101,99,96,95**
CSF £3.14 TOTE £2.40: £1.10, £1.10; EX 3.70 Trifecta £13.00.
**Owner** Racing Clear Partnership **Bred** Juddmonte Farms Inc **Trained** Epsom, Surrey

**FOCUS**
A modest sprint handicap where the winner made all. He's rated close to last year's turf best.

## 2066 T.M. LEWIN, SHIRTS, SUITS AND MORE CLASSIFIED STKS 1m 1f 209y
**3:05** (3:06) (Class 6) 3-Y-O+ **£1,940** (£577; £288; £144) **Stalls** High

Form RPR

-433 1 **Sandy Cove**[35] 1235 3-8-5 55[1] LukeMorris 3 60
(James Eustace) *chsd ldrs: wnt 2nd 2f out: drvn to ld ins fnl f: rdn out nr fin* **11/8**[1]

000- 2 1 **My Secret Dream (FR)**[203] 7293 3-8-5 50 HarryBentley 12 58
(Ron Hodges) *t.k.h in rr: rdn and hdwy in centre over 1f out: r.o to take 2nd fnl 100yds* **25/1**

100- 3 1 ¾ **Cherry Princess**[199] 7395 4-9-6 55 GeorgeBaker 6 56
(Stuart Williams) *led: brought field to stands' rail in st: hrd rdn and hdd ins fnl f: one pce* **6/1**[3]

-035 4 4 **Highly Likely (IRE)**[27] 1406 5-9-6 51 JimCrowley 7 48
(Steve Woodman) *t.k.h: chsd ldrs: one pce fnl 2f* **12/1**

004- 5 ½ **Zeteah**[174] 7873 4-9-3 44 WilliamTwiston-Davies[(3)] 9 47
(David Lanigan) *hld up towards rr: hdwy and hrd rdn in centre over 1f out: no ex fnl f* **8/1**

5234 6 nk **Petersboden**[49] 1016 5-9-6 51 FergusSweeney 4 47
(Michael Blanshard) *hld up towards rr: sme hdwy in centre 2f out: no ex fnl f* **5/1**[2]

000- 7 1 ½ **Estibdaad (IRE)**[154] 8160 4-8-13 55 (t) CamHardie[(7)] 5 44
(Paddy Butler) *chsd ldr: rdn over 2f out: sn lost pl* **16/1**

0-00 8 3 ¾ **Up Hill Battle's**[100] 355 3-8-5 48 FrankieMcDonald 10 36
(Daniel Mark Loughnane) *in rr: hdwy on outer over 3f out: hrd rdn over 2f out: sn wknd* **20/1**

0034 9 1 **Knight Charm**[8] 1854 4-9-1 52 DanielMuscutt[(5)] 11 35
(Gay Kelleway) *t.k.h in midfield: effrt 3f out: rdn whn n.m.r 2f out: n.d after* **16/1**

2m 8.13s (4.53) **Going Correction** +0.30s/f (Good)
**WFA** 3 from 4yo+ 15lb **9** Ran SP% **112.2**
Speed ratings (Par 101): **93,92,90,87,87 86,85,82,81**
CSF £40.60 TOTE £2.20: £1.20, £4.10, £1.70; EX 31.90 Trifecta £344.40.
**Owner** Blue Peter Racing 12 **Bred** D J And Mrs Deer **Trained** Newmarket, Suffolk

**FOCUS**
A weak contest and muddling form. The winner's latest AW run could be rated this high.

## 2067 STREAMLINE TAXIS BRIGHTON 202020 H'CAP 1m 3f 196y
3:35 (3:37) (Class 5) (0-70,70) 4-Y-O+ £2,587 (£770; £384; £192) Stalls High

Form RPR
-024 1 **Ssafa**[42] 1099 6-9-4 **67**.....(p) GeorgeBaker 4 76
(Alastair Lidderdale) *hld up in rr: hdwy on inner 4f out: effrt in centre and hung lft over 1f out: drvn to ld ins fnl f* **11/1[3]**
000- 2 2 1/4 **Highlife Dancer**[232] 6492 6-8-7 **59**..... CharlesBishop(3) 5 64
(Mick Channon) *broke wl: led: hrd rdn over 1f out: hdd ins fnl f: one pce* **16/1**
241- 3 1 3/4 **Uganda Glory (USA)**[170] 6257 4-9-2 **65**.....(v) PatCosgrave 9 67
(George Baker) *chsd ldr: rdn to chal over 2f out: no ex ins fnl f* **5/1[2]**
465/ 4 6 **Soundbyte**[635] 5038 9-8-0 **56**..... EilishMcCall(7) 7 48
(John Gallagher) *wd: hld up in 5th: rdn and struggling over 3f out: n.d after* **50/1**
3343 5 4 1/2 **Layline (IRE)**[11] 1743 7-9-1 **69**..... DanielMuscutt(5) 1 54
(Gay Kelleway) *chsd ldrs: rdn 3f out: sn wknd* **12/1**
6 68 **Nesterenko (GER)**[32] 5-8-9 **58**..... KierenFallon 6
(Nicky Henderson) *in tch: pushed along and dropped to rr over 4f out: bhd whn virtually p.u 3f out: fin lame* **1/2[1]**

2m 35.49s (2.79) **Going Correction** +0.30s/f (Good) 6 Ran SP% **107.2**
Speed ratings (Par 103): **102,100,99,95,92 47**
CSF £134.14 CT £855.71 TOTE £9.70: £4.10, £5.00; EX 50.30 Trifecta £129.60.
**Owner** The What A Mare Partnership **Bred** Newsells Park Stud **Trained** Lambourn, Berks

**FOCUS**
An uncompetitive handicap which looked to revolve around the favourite, but he finished lame. The runner-up is on a winnable mark.

## 2068 GATWICKDIAMONDBUSINESS.COM H'CAP 7f 214y
4:10 (4:10) (Class 4) (0-80,80) 3-Y-O+ £6,301 (£1,886; £943; £472) Stalls Centre

Form RPR
0-05 1 **Heavy Metal**[13] 1682 4-9-6 **79**..... KierenFallon 5 91
(Mark Johnston) *chsd ldr over 2f: dropped to last and struggling 4f out: rallied and led over 1f out: rdn clr: styd on wl* **7/1**
1-55 2 4 **Fleckerl (IRE)**[30] 1351 4-9-2 **75**..... MartinDwyer 4 78
(William Muir) *hld up in 3rd: chsd clr ldr over 5f out: clsd 2f out: briefly disp ld over 1f out: one pce* **6/4[1]**
-232 3 hd **Aqua Ardens (GER)**[13] 1667 6-9-3 **76**.....(t) RichardHughes 1 78
(George Baker) *hld up in 4th: wnt 3rd 4f out: rdn 3f out: styng on whn n.m.r on rail ins fnl f: one pce* **15/8[2]**
361- 4 9 **Take A Note**[233] 6475 5-9-7 **80**.....(v) JimCrowley 3 62
(Patrick Chamings) *led at str pce and sn 8 l clr: reduced ld 2f out: hdd & wknd over 1f out* **9/2[3]**

1m 38.06s (2.06) **Going Correction** +0.30s/f (Good)
**WFA** 3 from 4yo+ 13lb 4 Ran SP% **105.5**
Speed ratings (Par 105): **101,97,96,87**
CSF £17.07 TOTE £4.30; EX 12.60 Trifecta £21.00.
**Owner** Sheikh Hamdan bin Mohammed Al Maktoum **Bred** Darley **Trained** Middleham Moor, N Yorks

**FOCUS**
A disappointing turnout for this fair handicap, offering decent prize-money, but it saw a return to last season's best from the winner. The pace was strong.

## 2069 GATWICKAIRPORT.COM H'CAP 6f 209y
4:45 (4:45) (Class 6) (0-60,62) 4-Y-O+ £1,940 (£577; £288; £144) Stalls Centre

Form RPR
4616 1 **Darnathean**[16] 1613 5-9-6 **59**.....(p) SeanLevey 5 68
(Paul D'Arcy) *chsd ldrs: led over 1f out: rdn out* **5/2[2]**
2-61 2 2 1/2 **Who's That Chick (IRE)**[3] 1986 5-9-2 **62** 6ex..... DanielCremin(7) 4 65
(Ralph J Smith) *s.s: bhd: hdwy 2f out: edgd lft and nt clr run over 1f out: swtchd rt: r.o to take 2nd nr fin* **15/8[1]**
430 3 1/2 **For Shia And Lula (IRE)**[16] 1606 5-9-7 **60**.....(v[1]) ShaneKelly 3 61
(Daniel Mark Loughnane) *chsd ldrs: rdn to chal over 1f out: one pce fnl f* **5/1[3]**
006 4 1 **Laguna Belle**[41] 1119 4-8-7 **46** oh1..... AdamBeschizza 6 45
(Pat Phelan) *dwlt: bhd: rdn and styd on fnl 2f: nvr nrr* **33/1**
0500 5 hd **Claude Greenwood**[49] 1016 4-8-6 **50**.....(b) PhilipPrince(5) 1 48
(Linda Jewell) *led: hdd and n.m.r over 1f out: no ex fnl f* **16/1**
-656 6 5 **Thewestwalian (USA)**[13] 1668 6-8-7 **46** oh1..... ChrisCatlin 10 31
(Peter Hiatt) *prom tl wknd over 1f out* **14/1**
0040 7 2 **Little Red Nell (IRE)**[42] 1110 5-8-4 **46** oh1.....(p) MichaelJMMurphy(3) 8 26
(Martin Bosley) *hld up in 6th: rdn over 2f out: sn outpcd* **33/1**
6210 8 1 3/4 **Indian Violet (IRE)**[5] 1917 8-9-1 **54**.....(p) JimCrowley 2 29
(Zoe Davison) *bhd: effrt 2f out: wknd over 1f out* **8/1**
6000 9 6 **Ishisoba**[36] 1223 4-8-7 **46** oh1..... FrankieMcDonald 9 6
(Ronald Harris) *prom: hrd rdn 2f out: wknd over 1f out* **25/1**

1m 24.8s (1.70) **Going Correction** +0.30s/f (Good) 9 Ran SP% **113.4**
Speed ratings (Par 101): **102,99,98,97,97 91,89,87,80**
CSF £7.24 CT £19.53 TOTE £4.60: £1.10, £1.10, £1.90; EX 10.60 Trifecta £24.10.
**Owner** K Snell **Bred** K Snell **Trained** Newmarket, Suffolk
■ Stewards' Enquiry : Philip Prince two-day ban: failed to take all reasonable and permissable measures to obtain best possible placing (May 21-22)

**FOCUS**
A moderate race that didn't take much winning. The winner was on a good mark on last year's best form.

## 2070 GATWICK DIAMOND BUSINESS H'CAP 5f 59y
5:20 (5:20) (Class 5) (0-70,70) 4-Y-O+ £2,587 (£770; £384; £192) Stalls Centre

Form RPR
024- 1 **Dreams Of Glory**[245] 6096 6-9-3 **66**..... KierenFallon 3 78
(Ron Hodges) *mde all: c to stands' rail over 2f out: rdn clr ins fnl f: readily* **4/1[3]**
4531 2 2 1/4 **Picansort**[40] 1145 7-9-1 **64**.....(v) ShaneKelly 5 68
(Peter Crate) *s.s: wnt 4th over 3f out: drvn to press wnr 1f out: one pce* **9/4[2]**
400- 3 3 1/4 **Hit The Lights (IRE)**[223] 6771 4-8-13 **65**..... ThomasBrown(3) 1 58
(Patrick Chamings) *plld hrd early: chsd ldrs: hrd rdn over 1f out: no ex* **2/1[1]**
-034 4 hd **Danzoe (IRE)**[18] 1584 7-8-6 **60**..... EoinWalsh(5) 4 52
(Christine Dunnett) *in tch: rdn and outpcd 2f out: unable to chal* **10/1**
50-0 5 2 **Alpha Delta Whisky**[49] 1019 6-9-4 **70**.....(v) MichaelJMMurphy(3) 2 55
(John Gallagher) *sn chsng wnr: hrd rdn and lost 2nd 1f out: wknd fnl f* **6/1**
000- 6 7 **Magical Speedfit (IRE)**[284] 4746 9-8-12 **68**..... JordanVaughan(7) 7 29
(George Margarson) *outpcd: a last* **14/1**

1m 3.37s (1.07) **Going Correction** +0.30s/f (Good) 6 Ran SP% **114.1**
Speed ratings (Par 103): **103,99,94,93,90 79**
CSF £13.79 TOTE £5.70: £2.30, £1.10; EX 14.00 Trifecta £24.10.
**Owner** P E Axon **Bred** P E Axon **Trained** Charlton Mackrell, Somerset

**FOCUS**
A modest sprint and another all-the-way winner. This was a personal best.
T/Plt: £199.60 to a £1 stake. Pool: £51,204.09 - 187.23 winning units. T/Qpdt: £147.10 to a £1 stake. Pool: £3281.53 - 16.50 winning units. LM

# CHESTER (L-H)
Wednesday, May 7

**OFFICIAL GOING: Good (good to firm in places) changing to good after race 1 (1.45)**
Running rail on inside line and distances as advertised.
Wind: Fresh, half against Weather: Showers

## 2071 MANOR HOUSE STABLES LILY AGNES CONDITIONS STKS (BOBIS RACE) 5f 16y
1:45 (1:49) (Class 2) 2-Y-O £12,602 (£3,772; £1,886; £944; £470) Stalls Low

Form RPR
1 1 **Mukhmal (IRE)**[19] 1560 2-9-7 0..... PaulHanagan 10 96+
(Mark Johnston) *mde all: c over to ins rail over 3f out: rdn over 1f out: r.o and a looked in command* **6/1**
1 2 1 1/4 **Roudee**[20] 1536 2-9-1 0..... RichardKingscote 9 86
(Tom Dascombe) *edgy bef r: a.p: rdn over 1f out: def 2nd ins fnl f: kpt on towards fin: no real imp on wnr* **5/1[3]**
221 3 1/2 **Charlie's Star**[15] 1633 2-8-7 0..... FrannyNorton 3 76
(David Evans) *sn pushed along in midfield: rdn over 1f out: styd on ins fnl f: nrst fin: nvr gng pce to chal* **8/1**
5 4 1 1/4 **Casterbridge**[19] 1560 2-8-12 0..... JasonHart 8 77
(Eric Alston) *a.p: rdn 2f out: nt qckn over 1f out: kpt on ins fnl f tl no ex towards fin* **25/1**
41 5 3/4 **Elizabeth Flynn (IRE)**[11] 1741 2-8-10 0..... MartinLane 5 72
(K R Burke) *chsd ldrs: rdn and outpcd over 1f out: kpt on same pce ins fnl f* **25/1**
0 6 1/2 **Magical Memory (IRE)**[26] 1417 2-8-12 0..... WilliamBuick 7 72
(Charles Hills) *dwlt: outpcd and bhd: rdn and wanted to lug lft whn kpt on ins fnl f: nvr able to trble ldrs* **7/2[2]**
12 7 4 **Cheerio Sweetie (IRE)**[19] 1560 2-8-7 0..... JFEgan 1 53
(David Evans) *in tch: rdn and outpcd over 1f out: wl btn ins fnl f* **7/4[1]**
3 8 7 **Agadoo**[11] 1712 2-8-7 0.....[1] DavidProbert 4 27
(Shaun Harris) *a outpcd and bhd: nvr on terms* **25/1**
U **Saphira Silver (IRE)** 2-8-7 0..... MatthewCosham 2
(Nikki Evans) *rdr lost iron and uns jst after s* **100/1**

1m 1.53s (0.53) **Going Correction** +0.30s/f (Good) 9 Ran SP% **113.2**
Speed ratings (Par 99): **107,105,104,102,101 100,93,82,**
CSF £33.70 TOTE £5.40: £2.20, £2.20, £1.90; EX 33.40 Trifecta £114.30.
**Owner** Hamdan Al Maktoum **Bred** Pier House Stud & Martinstown **Trained** Middleham Moor, N Yorks

**FOCUS**
Running rail on inside line and distances as advertised. The official going had dried a touch to good, good to firm in places, but Jason Hart said "My fella was just getting his toe in" and Richard Kingscote said "It's good at the moment." The running rail was on the inside the whole way round. A fine effort by the winner and the level of the form is pretty solid.

## 2072 WEATHERBYS PRIVATE BANKING CHESHIRE OAKS (ROBERT SANGSTER MEMORIAL CUP) (LISTED RACE) (FILLIES) 1m 3f 79y
2:15 (2:19) (Class 1) 3-Y-O
£22,684 (£8,600; £4,304; £2,144; £1,076; £540) Stalls Low

Form RPR
4-11 1 **Anipa**[23] 1494 3-9-0 80..... AndreaAtzeni 2 96
(Roger Varian) *chsd ldrs: wnt 2nd 4f out: rdn to ld ins fnl f: kpt on wl towards fin* **16/1**
-211 2 1/2 **Secret Pursuit (IRE)**[28] 1400 3-9-0 79..... OisinMurphy 4 95
(Marcus Tregoning) *led: rdn over 1f out: hdd ins fnl f: stl ev ch: hld nr fin* **16/1**
1 3 1 1/2 **Bright Approach (IRE)**[26] 1423 3-9-0 88..... WilliamBuick 9 93+
(John Gosden) *hld up: pushed along 3f out: hdwy 2f out: chsd ldrs over 1f out: wnt 3rd fnl 150yds: styd on under hands and heels towards fin: nt trble front two* **5/2[2]**
221- 4 3 1/4 **Psychometry (FR)**[231] 6523 3-9-0 81..... RyanMoore 3 87
(Sir Michael Stoute) *in tch: pushed along to chse ldrs over 2f out: no real imp: one pce ins fnl f* **8/1[3]**
5 2 3/4 **Terrific (IRE)**[25] 1457 3-9-0 99.....(b) JosephO'Brien 5 82
(A P O'Brien, Ire) *midfield: pushed along 3f out: effrt to chse ldrs over 2f out but no imp: plugged on at one pce: nvr able to chal* **15/8[1]**
31 6 5 **Full Moon Fever (IRE)**[25] 1452 3-9-0 75..... GrahamLee 8 74
(Ed Walker) *hld up in rr: struggling 3f out: nvr able to trble ldrs* **66/1**
51- 7 7 **Lady Tyne**[193] 7533 3-9-0 90..... JamesDoyle 7 62
(Roger Charlton) *in tch: pushed along over 3f out: wknd over 2f out* **8/1[3]**
1-12 8 14 **Groovejet**[35] 1240 3-9-0 83..... PaulHanagan 6 38
(Peter Chapple-Hyam) *chsd ldr to 4f out: sn pushed along: wknd over 2f out* **33/1**
4-3 9 1 1/4 **Brown Diamond (IRE)**[25] 1433 3-9-0 0..... JamieSpencer 1 36
(Charles Hills) *missed break: hld up: pushed along over 3f out: wl adrift 2f out* **10/1**

2m 25.48s (0.68) **Going Correction** +0.30s/f (Good) 9 Ran SP% **110.9**
Speed ratings (Par 104): **109,108,107,105,103 99,94,84,83**
CSF £228.05 TOTE £16.60: £2.70, £4.40, £1.60; EX 127.70 Trifecta £555.90.
**Owner** Nurlan Bizakov **Bred** Hesmonds Stud Ltd **Trained** Newmarket, Suffolk

**FOCUS**
With the rain coming down the going was changed to good prior to this race. No winner of this has gone on to take the Oaks since 2007 when Light Shift did the double, but the 2011 winner Wonder Of Wonders only found one too good at Epsom afterwards. The forn pair are the likely key to the form, both improving from their handiacp wins.

## 2073 STANJAMES.COM CHESTER CUP (HERITAGE H'CAP) 2m 2f 147y
2:45 (2:53) (Class 2) 4-Y-0+
£74,700 (£22,368; £11,184; £5,592; £2,796; £1,404) Stalls High

Form RPR
52-3 **1** **Suegioo (FR)**[11] 1736 5-9-4 **93**..........(p) RyanMoore 4 103
(Marco Botti) *midfield: hdwy whn nt clr run on inner 2f out: wnt 2nd 1f out: coming to chal whn carried rt ins fnl f: styd on to ld towards fin* **10/1**

-441 **2** ½ **Angel Gabrial (IRE)**[11] 1735 5-9-2 **91** 3ex.......... JamieSpencer 11 100+
(Richard Fahey) *hld up in rr: pushed along over 3f out: sn gd hdwy on outer: led over 2f out: sn edgd lft onto rail: rdn to assert over 1f out: jinked bdly rt ins fnl f and carried wnr wd: hdd towards fin* **7/1[3]**

2343 **3** 3¾ **Communicator**[19] 1556 6-9-1 **93**.......... OisinMurphy(3) 2 98
(Andrew Balding) *racd keenly: hld up: rdn over 2f out: hdwy on outer over 1f out: styd on ins fnl f to take 3rd fnl 50yds: nt trble front two* **6/1[2]**

43-2 **4** ¾ **Mubaraza (IRE)**[11] 1735 5-9-5 **94**.......... PaulHanagan 5 98
(Ed Dunlop) *chsd ldrs: led briefly wl over 2f out: unable to go w ldr over 1f out: sn lost 2nd: kpt on same pce ins fnl f* **4/1[1]**

46-6 **5** 1½ **Glenard**[37] 1213 4-8-13 **92**.......... FrannyNorton 14 95
(Charles Hills) *s.i.s: sn in midfield: hdwy over 2f out: chsd ldrs on inner over 1f out: kpt on ins fnl f: one pce cl home* **12/1**

25-3 **6** *shd* **Shwaiman (IRE)**[18] 1581 4-9-4 **97**.......... FrederikTylicki 18 99
(James Fanshawe) *midfield: rdn and hdwy over 2f out: styd on ins fnl f: nt rch ldrs* **20/1**

033- **7** 1 **Duke Of Clarence (IRE)**[205] 7250 5-9-6 **95**.......... DavidNolan 8 96
(Richard Fahey) *chsd ldrs: effrt 3f out: kpt on ins fnl f: one pce fnl 100yds* **14/1**

306- **8** 3 **Brockwell**[194] 7496 5-9-1 **90**.......... RichardKingscote 13 88
(Tom Dascombe) *in tch: pushed along 5f out: rdn and outpcd over 2f out: kpt on but n.d ins fnl f* **16/1**

3-66 **9** 1 **Gabrial's King (IRE)**[28] 1398 5-9-2 **91**.......... AndreaAtzeni 9 88
(David Simcock) *midfield: effrt bhd ldrs 3f out: rdn and wknd over 2f out* **33/1**

300- **10** 3½ **Open Eagle (IRE)**[140] 8327 5-9-5 **94**..........[1] DanielTudhope 16 87
(David O'Meara) *chsd ldrs: rdn over 2f out: wknd over 1f out* **25/1**

620- **11** ½ **Mawaqeet (USA)**[246] 6066 5-9-4 **93**..........(b) GrahamLee 7 86
(Donald McCain) *hld up: rdn overt 2f out: nvr on terms* **14/1**

1-16 **12** 1 **White Nile (IRE)**[18] 1581 5-9-2 **91**.......... WilliamBuick 17 82
(Ed Dunlop) *hld up: pushed along and hdwy 3f out: rdn and wknd on outer wl over 2f out* **25/1**

0-32 **13** 3¼ **Clowance Estate (IRE)**[18] 1581 5-9-7 **96**..........(p) JamesDoyle 15 84
(Roger Charlton) *prom: w ldr 5f out: led 4f out: rdn and hdd wl over 2f out: wknd over 1f out: eased whn btn ins fnl f* **12/1**

623- **14** *shd* **Body Language (IRE)**[223] 6766 6-9-5 **94**..........(p) SilvestreDeSousa 6 82
(Ian Williams) *hld up: nt clr run over 3f out: rdn over 2f out: nvr on terms w ldrs* **14/1**

242- **15** 1 **Waterclock (IRE)**[207] 7193 5-9-2 **91**..........(p) TomQueally 19 78
(Jedd O'Keeffe) *hld up: rdn 3f out: nvr on terms* **22/1**

05-0 **16** 35 **Golden Bowl (FR)**[11] 1736 4-9-6 **99**.......... RobertWinston 10 47
(Ian Williams) *in tch: lost pl 5f out: rdn 3f out: bhd fnl 2f: t.o* **40/1**

400- **17** 69 **Montaser (IRE)**[235] 6385 5-9-10 **99**.......... JoeFanning 1
(David Simcock) *led: hdd 4f out: wknd qckly over 3f out: t.o* **20/1**

4m 7.85s (3.05) **Going Correction** +0.30s/f (Good)
**WFA** 4 from 5yo+ 4lb **17 Ran SP% 124.1**
Speed ratings (Par 109): **105,104,103,102,102 102,101,100,100,98 98,98,96,96,96 81,52**
CSF £71.66 CT £470.56 TOTE £9.80: £2.60, £2.30, £1.70, £1.80; EX 91.90 Trifecta £701.30.
**Owner** Dr Marwan Koukash **Bred** Rabbah Bloodstock Ltd **Trained** Newmarket, Suffolk
■ Stewards' Enquiry : Jamie Spencer four-day ban: careless riding (May 21-24)

**FOCUS**
Despite the distance, a low draw has still proved an advantage in this marathon handicap, with six of the previous ten winners being drawn in one of the lowest five stalls. That trend continued. The third is the initial guide to the form but this is rarely a race to be too literal about.

## 2074 STELLAR GROUP H'CAP 5f 16y
3:15 (3:23) (Class 2) (0-105,102) 4£16,762 (£4,715; £2,357; £1,180; £587) Stalls Low

Form RPR
503- **1** **Sir Maximilian (IRE)**[249] 5998 5-8-7 **88**.......... StevieDonohoe 4 101
(Tim Pitt) *hld up: hdwy 2f out: r.o to ld ins fnl f: won gng away* **7/1**

6413 **2** 2¾ **Caspian Prince (IRE)**[11] 1742 5-9-2 **97**..........(t) JamesDoyle 1 100
(Tony Carroll) *led: rdn over 1f out: hdd ins fnl f: unable to go w wnr after* **4/1[1]**

3036 **3** ½ **Ballista (IRE)**[19] 1557 6-9-6 **101**..........(p) RichardKingscote 7 102
(Tom Dascombe) *w ldr: rdn and ev ch over 1f out: nt qckn ins fnl f: styd on same pce* **5/1[3]**

3132 **4** ½ **Top Boy**[11] 1742 4-8-5 **86**..........(v) JoeFanning 2 85
(Derek Shaw) *towards rr: outpcd over 3f out: rdn and hdwy 1f out: styd on ins fnl f: nrst fin* **5/1[3]**

0-21 **5** 2¼ **Go Nani Go**[19] 1566 8-8-6 **87**.......... FrannyNorton 3 78
(Ed de Giles) *midfield: hdwy 2f out: kpt on inder press over 1f out: one pce fnl 100yds* **9/2[2]**

5210 **6** 2 **Red Baron (IRE)**[4] 1961 5-8-1 **85**..........(p) NeilFarley(3) 6 69
(Eric Alston) *chsd ldrs: rdn over 1f out: wknd ins fnl f* **9/1**

130- **7** *hd* **Noble Storm (USA)**[214] 7010 8-9-5 **100**.......... GrahamLee 8 83
(Ed McMahon) *chsd ldrs: effrt 2f out: wknd over 1f out* **20/1**

050- **8** *nk* **Confessional**[193] 7527 7-9-2 **97**..........(e) DavidAllan 9 79
(Tim Easterby) *midfield: rdn and outpcd 2f out: n.d after* **20/1**

-024 **9** 4 **Rusty Rocket (IRE)**[11] 1742 5-8-4 **85**.......... MartinLane 11 53
(Paul Green) *in tch: dropped to midfield after 1f: rdn and wknd wl over 1f out* **20/1**

060- **10** 2¼ **Swendab (IRE)**[225] 6719 6-8-5 **86**..........(v) DavidProbert 5 46
(John O'Shea) *midfield: sn pushed along: wknd over 1f out* **25/1**

00-0 **11** *hd* **Fitz Flyer (IRE)**[14] 1650 8-8-5 **86**..........(v) AdrianNicholls 12 45
(David Nicholls) *swtchd lft s: a outpcd and bhd* **40/1**

400- **12** 12 **Free Zone**[179] 7821 5-9-7 **102**.......... PaulMulrennan 15 18
(Bryan Smart) *swtchd lft s: a outpcd and bhd* **40/1**

1m 1.13s (0.13) **Going Correction** +0.30s/f (Good) **12 Ran SP% 117.0**
Speed ratings (Par 109): **110,105,104,104,100 97,96,96,90,86 86,66**
CSF £31.17 CT £155.11 TOTE £7.50: £3.30, £1.30, £1.40; EX 43.30 Trifecta £255.50.
**Owner** Paul Wildes **Bred** Holborn Trust Co **Trained** Market Drayton, Shropshire

**FOCUS**
The previous ten winners of this had been drawn 4626743723, so no surprise to see low draws dominating, but puzzling that there had been no winner from stall one. The form makes sense.

## 2075 BOODLES DIAMOND MAIDEN STKS (BOBIS RACE) 1m 2f 75y
3:50 (3:51) (Class 3) 3-Y-0 £9,056 (£2,695; £1,346; £673) Stalls High

Form RPR
5 **1** **Prince Of Stars**[20] 1529 3-9-5 0.......... WilliamBuick 8 85+
(John Gosden) *midfield: hdwy over 3f out: looked green: led over 1f out: r.o ins fnl f: a in control towards fin* **11/8[1]**

2-0 **2** 1 **Dursey Island (USA)**[25] 1433 3-9-5 0.......... RyanMoore 1 83+
(Richard Hannon) *hld up: hdwy wl over 1f out: wnt 2nd fnl 150yds: styd on: unable to chal wnr* **16/1**

53-6 **3** 2¾ **Glasgow Central**[18] 1582 3-9-5 72.......... RobertWinston 4 78
(Charles Hills) *trckd ldrs: rdn over 3f out: chal wl over 1f out: unable qck: kpt on ins fnl f but n.d to ldrs* **33/1**

4 **4** *nk* **Obstinate (IRE)**[54] 954 3-9-5 0.......... DavidProbert 2 77
(Andrew Balding) *led: rdn and hdd over 1f out: no ex fnl 100yds* **12/1**

- **5** 2½ **The Character (IRE)** 3-9-5 0.......... StephenCraine 10 72
(Tom Dascombe) *hld up: pushed along over 3f out: hdwy over 2f out to chse ldrs: one pce ins fnl f* **100/1**

6 **6** 3 **Race To Glory (FR)**[11] 1730 3-9-5 0.......... GrahamLee 9 67
(Roger Charlton) *dwlt: hld up: pushed along over 4f out: nvr able to trble ldrs* **25/1**

**7** 3¼ **Special Fighter (IRE)** 3-9-5 0.......... FrannyNorton 5 61
(Mark Johnston) *racd keenly: prom: rdn over 3f out: stl there 2f out: wknd over 1f out* **25/1**

3- **8** 4 **Ghosting (IRE)**[210] 7119 3-9-5 0..........(t[1]) RichardKingscote 6 53
(Tom Dascombe) *midfield tl rdn and wknd over 3f out* **4/1[2]**

0 **9** 3¼ **Computer (USA)**[20] 1529 3-9-5 0.......... JamesDoyle 7 47
(Charles Hills) *in tch: clsd on outer over 3f out: chalng over 2f out: wknd wl over 1f out* **10/1**

332- **10** 3 **Rangi Chase (IRE)**[208] 7175 3-9-5 77.......... JamieSpencer 11 41
(Richard Fahey) *prom: rdn whn chalng over 2f out: wknd wl over 1f out: eased whn btn ins fnl f* **6/1[3]**

06 **11** 21 **Enniscorthy Myles (USA)**[9] 1817 3-9-5 0.......... StevieDonohoe 3
(Tim Pitt) *hld up in rr: pushed along over 4f out: lft bhd over 3f out* **150/1**

2m 15.0s (3.80) **Going Correction** +0.30s/f (Good) **11 Ran SP% 111.3**
Speed ratings (Par 103): **96,95,93,92,90 88,85,82,79,77 60**
CSF £23.91 TOTE £2.20: £1.10, £3.40, £5.90; EX 20.60 Trifecta £131.20.
**Owner** Jaber Abdullah **Bred** Rabbah Bloodstock Limited **Trained** Newmarket, Suffolk

**FOCUS**
This is usually a good maiden, with seven of the previous ten winners being given an RPR in the 90s, and three of them going on to win in Group company, including King George winner Harbinger. This year's race didn't look up to that standard, with the third rated just 72, but the form has been rated on the positive side. The winner should live up to the race standard.

## 2076 STELLA ARTOIS CONDITIONS STKS 5f 16y
4:25 (4:25) (Class 3) 3-Y-0+ £10,350 (£3,080; £1,539; £769) Stalls Low

Form RPR
10-4 **1** **Swan Song**[18] 1572 5-8-13 94.......... DavidProbert 3 103
(Andrew Balding) *w ldr tl over 3f out: continued to r in 2nd: rdn over 1f out: led fnl 150yds: r.o* **5/1[3]**

-360 **2** 1 **Masamah (IRE)**[69] 769 8-9-4 102..........(p) JamieSpencer 4 104
(Marco Botti) *led: edgd over to ins rail over 3f out: rdn over 1f out: hdd fnl 150yds: hld nr fin* **5/1[3]**

1212 **3** 1½ **Trinityelitedotcom (IRE)**[19] 1557 4-9-4 103.......... RichardKingscote 6 99
(Tom Dascombe) *chsd ldrs: rdn and nt qckn over 1f out: styd on same pce ins fnl f* **3/1[2]**

5140 **4** ¾ **Addictive Dream (IRE)**[19] 1557 7-9-4 104.......... TonyHamilton 5 96
(David Nicholls) *chsd ldrs: rdn over 1f out: kpt on same pce ins fnl f* **20/1**

50-1 **5** 1 **Lucky Beggar (IRE)**[26] 1421 4-9-4 107.......... WilliamBuick 1 93+
(Charles Hills) *t.k.h to post: in rr: outpcd over 1f out: kpt on ins fnl f: nvr able to trble ldrs* **15/8[1]**

11-5 **6** *hd* **Da'Quonde (IRE)**[32] 1305 6-8-13 87.......... PaulMulrennan 10 87
(Bryan Smart) *midfield: rdn over 1f out: nvr able to chal* **33/1**

40-2 **7** *nk* **Borderlescott**[19] 1561 12-9-1 100.......... NeilFarley(3) 2 91
(Robin Bastiman) *midfield: pushed along and outpcd over 2f out: rdn and no imp over 1f out: nvr able to trble ldrs* **11/1**

-043 **8** 4½ **Inxile (IRE)**[19] 1561 9-9-4 96..........(p) AdrianNicholls 7 75
(David Nicholls) *hld up: rdn and outpcd over 2f out: nvr a threat* **50/1**

41-1 **9** 4½ **Foxy Music**[35] 1244 10-9-1 83.......... JasonHart(3) 11 59
(Eric Alston) *hld up: pushed along and outpcd over 2f out: bhd wl over 1f out* **66/1**

1m 1.32s (0.32) **Going Correction** +0.30s/f (Good) **9 Ran SP% 112.6**
Speed ratings (Par 107): **109,107,105,103,102 101,101,94,87**
CSF £28.23 TOTE £4.00: £1.50, £1.50, £2.20; EX 28.40 Trifecta £136.10.
**Owner** J C Smith **Bred** Littleton Stud **Trained** Kingsclere, Hants

**FOCUS**
There looked to be quite a bit of pace in this race, but as it turned out few got involved. The winner posted a personal best.

## 2077 DIABETES UK H'CAP (BOBIS RACE) 1m 4f 66y
5:00 (5:01) (Class 3) (0-90,87) 3-Y-0 £10,350 (£3,080; £1,539; £769) Stalls Low

Form RPR
35-1 **1** **Storm Force Ten**[36] 1220 3-8-13 **79**.......... DavidProbert 1 86
(Andrew Balding) *a.p: rdn over 1f out: r.o to ld ins fnl f: hld on wl cl home* **3/1[1]**

02-1 **2** *hd* **Captain Morley**[114] 167 3-8-13 **79**.......... JamieSpencer 9 85+
(David Simcock) *n.m.r after s: hld up in midfield: hdwy over 1f out: edgd rt and r.o ins fnl f: fin strly* **4/1[2]**

1310 **3** *hd* **Swivel**[19] 1563 3-9-7 **87**.......... JoeFanning 2 93
(Mark Johnston) *racd keenly: a.p: rdn to ld ent fnl f: sn hdd: continued to chal: r.o u.p: hld nr fin* **11/1**

4110 **4** 2½ **Maxie T**[20] 1530 3-8-11 **77**.......... FrannyNorton 12 79+
(Mark Johnston) *hld up: rdn over 2f out: hdwy over 1f out: styd on ins fnl f: nt rch ldrs* **12/1**

-513 **5** *nk* **Ujagar (IRE)**[21] 1508 3-8-11 **77**..........(b) RichardKingscote 8 79
(Tom Dascombe) *led: rdn over 1f out: hdd ent fnl f: fdd fnl 100yds* **20/1**

45-6 **6** 1 **Lovelocks (IRE)**[21] 1509 3-8-6 **72**..........[1] PaulHanagan 7 72
(Charles Hills) *midfield: pushed along over 3f out: kpt on and edgd lft ins fnl f: nt trble ldrs* **8/1**

461- **7** 2¼ **Istimraar (IRE)**[211] 7113 3-8-12 **78**.......... PhillipMakin 3 74
(Philip Kirby) *midfield: effrt over 2f out: one pce ins fnl f* **14/1**

54-1 **8** ¾ **Lady Yeats**[30] 1348 3-8-7 **73**.......... PJMcDonald 10 68
(George Moore) *in rr: rdn over 2f out: no imp* **11/1**

01 9 1 1/4 **Nam Hai (IRE)**[15] 1627 3-8-10 **76** ........................................ TomQueally 6 69
(Michael Bell) *in rr: pushed along 4f out: plugged on ins fnl f: nvr a threat* **25/1**

-211 10 5 **Anglo Irish**[27] 1407 3-9-2 **82** ........................................ WilliamBuick 4 67
(John Gosden) *in tch: rdn over 2f out: wknd over 1f out* **9/2[3]**

0230 11 5 **Whitby High Light**[74] 721 3-8-13 **79** ........................................ GrahamLee 11 56
(Andrew Hollinshead) *racd keenly: hld up: rdn and outpcd over 2f out: nvr a threat* **50/1**

2m 42.43s (3.93) **Going Correction** +0.30s/f (Good) **11** Ran SP% **115.9**
Speed ratings (Par 103): **98,97,97,96,95 95,93,93,92,89 85**
CSF £14.00 CT £115.09 TOTE £4.20: £1.20, £1.70, £2.40; EX 15.00 Trifecta £173.00.
**Owner** Robert Waley-Cohen **Bred** Upton Viva Stud **Trained** Kingsclere, Hants

**FOCUS**
They didn't go that quick early and it paid to race handily. This race can throw up a good horse, with future Pattern winners Lochbuie, Allied Powers and Brown Panther all successful over the past decade. The winner is progressing.
T/Jkpt: Not won. T/Plt: £68.70 to a £1 stake. Pool: £212,553.17 - 2256.22 winning units. T/Qpdt: £6.80 to a £1 stake. Pool: £13,982.21 - 1507.10 winning units. DO

# 2057 KEMPTON (A.W) (R-H)
## Wednesday, May 7

**OFFICIAL GOING: Standard**
Wind: Fresh, across (away from stands) Weather: Cloudy

## 2078 NEXT FIXTURE HERE ON 21.05.13 H'CAP — 1m (P)
**6:15** (6:15) (Class 6) (0-60,60) 3-Y-O — **£1,940** (£577; £288; £144) **Stalls** Low

Form RPR

0-00 1 **Plucky Dip**[13] 1683 3-8-8 **47** ........................................ RoystonFfrench 8 59
(John Ryan) *trckd ldr after 1f: led over 2f out: drvn and jnd jst over 1f out: kpt on gamely and a holding on nr fin* **25/1**

005- 2 nk **Stybba**[196] 7466 3-9-3 **56** ........................................ HarryBentley 9 67+
(Andrew Balding) *trckd ldng trio: prog over 2f out: jnd wnr jst over 1f out: nt qckn fnl f and jst hld nr fin* **5/4[1]**

02-2 3 3 1/4 **Choral Clan (IRE)**[28] 1384 3-9-7 **60** ........................................(t) JackMitchell 4 64
(Philip Mitchell) *led 150yds: trckd ldng pair after: chal over 2f out and w wnr: lost 2nd over 1f out: outpcd* **4/1[2]**

-615 4 3 3/4 **Prim And Proper**[13] 1683 3-9-2 **55** ........................................ SebSanders 10 50
(Brendan Powell) *racd wd: chsd ldrs: rdn over 2f out: wnt 4th over 1f out but wl outpcd: no hdwy after* **12/1**

40-3 5 1 1/4 **Nissaki Kasta**[13] 1684 3-9-6 **59** ........................................ JimmyFortune 2 51
(Hughie Morrison) *chsd ldrs: rdn into 4th 2f out: sn outpcd: wknd fnl f* **14/1**

00-0 6 1/2 **Rock Of Leon**[28] 1395 3-8-11 **50** ........................................(v[1]) LukeMorris 1 41
(Michael Bell) *pushed along leaving stalls: in rr and rn in snatches: rdn and no prog over 2f out: kpt on fnl f* **13/2[3]**

04-0 7 hd **Manor Way (IRE)**[37] 1214 3-9-7 **60** ........................................ RichardHughes 13 51
(Richard Hannon) *stdd s: hld up in rr: hanging whn shkn up over 2f out: no prog tl modest late hdwy* **10/1**

00-5 8 1/2 **Movie Magic**[10] 1769 3-8-7 **46** oh1 ........................................ WilliamCarson 7 36
(John Bridger) *nvr bttr than midfield: rdn and struggling over 2f out* **50/1**

42-3 9 3/4 **Sexy Secret**[8] 1855 3-9-6 **59** ........................................ RobertHavlin 14 47
(Lydia Pearce) *stdd s: hld up in last pair: pushed along and no prog over 2f out: reminder over 1f out: nvr in it* **25/1**

000- 10 1/2 **Moneypennie**[140] 8328 3-8-11 **55** ........................................ ShelleyBirkett(5) 11 42
(Marcus Tregoning) *hld up in rr: sme prog over 2f out: wknd wl over 1f out* **25/1**

-000 11 1 **French Accent**[69] 753 3-8-7 **46** oh1 ........................................ MartinDwyer 6 30
(John Best) *slowly away: a in last pair: shkn up and no prog over 2f out* **66/1**

6660 12 5 **Dark Tsarina (IRE)**[18] 1588 3-9-5 **58** ........................................(p) AdamKirby 5 31
(John Butler) *pushed up to ld after 150yds: hdd & wknd rapidly over 2f out* **33/1**

1m 40.66s (0.86) **Going Correction** 0.0s/f (Stan) **12** Ran SP% **119.2**
Speed ratings (Par 97): **95,94,91,87,86 85,85,85,84,84 83,78**
CSF £54.78 CT £170.89 TOTE £41.60: £10.50, £1.10, £1.90; EX 146.80 Trifecta £789.30.
**Owner** Byron, Lavallin & Donnison **Bred** Cheveley Park Stud Ltd **Trained** Newmarket, Suffolk

**FOCUS**
A modest but competitive 3yo handicap in which the pace held up. The winner got back to his standout 2yo run.

## 2079 BETBRIGHT MONEYBACK OFFERS H'CAP — 1m (P)
**6:45** (6:46) (Class 5) (0-75,74) 4-Y-O+ — **£2,587** (£770; £384; £192) **Stalls** Low

Form RPR

4-51 1 **Lawmans Thunder**[10] 1771 4-9-4 **71** 6ex ........................................ MickaelBarzalona 8 87
(Ismail Mohammed) *trckd ldng trio: smooth prog over 2f out: led wl over 1f out: easily drew clr fnl f* **5/6[1]**

3/32 2 4 1/2 **Rome**[9] 1796 4-9-7 **74** ........................................ GeorgeBaker 1 79
(Gary Moore) *led 2f: chsd ldr led over 2f out to wl over 1f out: no ch w wnr fnl f* **6/1[3]**

610- 3 1 **Dana's Present**[203] 7306 5-9-4 **71** ........................................ PatCosgrave 2 74
(George Baker) *hld up in 5th: prog over 2f out: chsd ldng pair over 1f out: kpt on same pce* **8/1**

304- 4 3/4 **Celestial Ray**[144] 8295 5-8-8 **61** ........................................ RobertHavlin 3 62
(Linda Jewell) *hld up in 6th: pushed along over 2f out: sn outpcd: rdn and styd on fnl f: nvr in it* **33/1**

0050 5 nse **Toymaker**[13] 1665 7-9-4 **71** ........................................ AdamKirby 4 72
(Phil McEntee) *trckd ldr 2f: styd cl up: rdn over 2f out: sn outpcd* **20/1**

10-6 6 nk **Barnmore**[9] 1799 6-8-12 **68** ........................................ CharlesBishop(3) 7 68
(Peter Hedger) *taken down early: heavily restrained after s: hld up in last trio: shkn up over 2f out: no prog tl rdn and kpt on fnl f* **16/1**

2030 7 6 **Steelriver (IRE)**[16] 1607 4-9-6 **73** ........................................(v[1]) TedDurcan 9 60
(James Bethell) *awkward s: rapid prog to ld after 2f: hdd over 2f out: hanging and wknd qckly* **11/2[2]**

3432 8 4 1/2 **Officer In Command (USA)**[35] 1236 8-9-2 **69** ........................................(p) LiamKeniry 5 45
(John Butler) *c out of stalls slowly: hld up in last pair: shkn up over 2f out: sn lft bhd* **33/1**

04-0 9 hd **Woolston Ferry (IRE)**[11] 1729 8-8-12 **65** ........................................ FergusSweeney 11 41
(Henry Candy) *heavily restrained after s: hld up in last pair: shkn up over 2f out: sn lft bhd* **25/1**

1m 39.36s (-0.44) **Going Correction** 0.0s/f (Stan) **9** Ran SP% **115.7**
Speed ratings (Par 103): **102,97,96,95,95 95,89,84,84**
CSF £5.79 CT £23.33 TOTE £1.60: £1.02, £2.80, £2.70; EX 5.70 Trifecta £30.00.
**Owner** Sheikh Juma Dalmook Al Maktoum **Bred** Foursome Thoroughbreds **Trained** Newmarket, Suffolk

**FOCUS**
A fair handicap, turned into a procession by the progressive winner who is clearly some way ahead of his mark.

## 2080 BETBRIGHT.COM H'CAP — 1m 3f (P)
**7:15** (7:15) (Class 6) (0-65,65) 3-Y-O — **£1,940** (£577; £288; £144) **Stalls** Low

Form RPR

05-1 1 **Nyanza (GER)**[9] 1793 3-9-6 **64** 6ex ........................................ RichardHughes 3 74+
(Alan King) *trckd ldng trio: pushed along to cl 2f out: shkn up to ld 1f out: narrow but decisive advantage after: readily* **5/2[2]**

0-61 2 nk **Next Stop**[35] 1235 3-9-5 **63** ........................................ AmirQuinn 2 72
(Lee Carter) *trckd ldr 2f and again 2f out: led briefly over 1f out: pressed wnr after and styd on but readily hld* **9/4[1]**

0-10 3 3 1/2 **Zanouska (USA)**[30] 1348 3-9-7 **65** ........................................ AdamKirby 4 68
(Mark Johnston) *led: rdn over 2f out: hdd and wandered sltly over 1f out: fdd fnl f* **16/1**

050- 4 4 1/2 **Deauville Dancer (IRE)**[188] 7646 3-9-6 **64** ........................................ GeorgeBaker 6 59
(Lady Herries) *trckd ldr after 2f: asked to chal over 2f out but hanging bdly: sn lost pl: wknd fnl f* **5/2[2]**

14-0 5 2 1/2 **Improvized**[23] 1494 3-9-5 **63** ........................................ MartinDwyer 5 53
(William Muir) *dwlt: hld up in last pair: pushed along over 3f out: no prog whn rdn over 2f out: wl btn after* **25/1**

0063 6 1/2 **Roman Riches**[9] 1793 3-9-0 **58** ........................................(b[1]) JimCrowley 1 48
(Gary Moore) *hld up in last pair: tried to make prog over 2f out: wknd over 1f out* **7/1[3]**

2m 21.51s (-0.39) **Going Correction** 0.0s/f (Stan) **6** Ran SP% **110.1**
Speed ratings (Par 97): **101,100,98,94,93 92**
CSF £8.20 TOTE £2.60: £1.60, £1.60; EX 7.30 Trifecta £28.30.
**Owner** Hunscote Stud **Bred** Gestut Ebbesloh **Trained** Barbury Castle, Wilts

**FOCUS**
A fair race for the grade, run in a relatively good time. The winner more than confirmed his good impression from C&D.

## 2081 BETBRIGHT MOBILE MEDIAN AUCTION MAIDEN STKS — 1m 3f (P)
**7:45** (7:46) (Class 5) 3-5-Y-O — **£2,587** (£770; £384; £192) **Stalls** Low

Form RPR

52 1 **Gallic Destiny (IRE)**[25] 1452 3-8-11 0 ........................................ LiamKeniry 1 76
(Andrew Balding) *disp ld 3f: trckd ldng pair after: clsd to chal 2f out: pressed new ldr fnl f: drvn to ld post* **11/4[2]**

2 nse **Perspicace** 3-8-8 0 ........................................ WilliamTwiston-Davies(3) 11 76+
(Roger Charlton) *hld up in last trio: gd prog fr over 2f out: rdn to ld narrowly 1f out: kpt on but hdd post* **7/1**

6 3 nk **Holberg Suite**[23] 1491 3-8-6 0 ........................................ NickyMackay 8 70
(John Gosden) *forced to r wd most of way: trckd ldng pair 7f out: nt qckn jst over 2f out: rallied over 1f out: tk 3rd fnl f and clsd on ldng pair fin* **7/2[3]**

022- 4 1 **Black Label**[226] 6688 3-8-11 74 ........................................ RichardHughes 2 75
(Harry Dunlop) *racd on outer most of way: disp ld 3f: stdd bk bhd ldrs: rdn and nt qckn over 2f out: rallied over 1f out: tk 4th fnl f: hld and eased cl home* **5/2[1]**

02-3 5 2 1/2 **Lisamour (IRE)**[9] 1795 3-8-6 0 ........................................ ChrisCatlin 7 64
(Paul Cole) *t.k.h early: trckd ldr over 7f out: rdn and nt qckn over 2f out: lost pl and fdd over 1f out* **8/1**

00- 6 1 **Severn Crossing**[217] 6954 3-8-11 0 ........................................ MartinDwyer 4 67
(William Muir) *prog to ld after 3f: rdn over 2f out: hdd & wknd 1f out* **50/1**

7 1 1/4 **Smageta** 3-8-6 0 ........................................ LukeMorris 9 60
(Marco Botti) *in tch in midfield: shkn up over 2f out: no imp on ldrs after but kpt on tl fdd fnl f* **10/1**

8 2 3/4 **Not Another Bill** 3-8-11 0 ........................................ SebSanders 5 60
(Chris Wall) *restless in stalls: towards rr: pushed along and no imp on ldrs over 2f out: wknd fnl f* **33/1**

00 9 1/2 **Abyaat (IRE)**[9] 1797 3-8-11 0 ........................................ PatDobbs 6 59
(Richard Hannon) *dwlt: hld up in last pair: shkn up and struggling 3f out: sn adrift: plugged on fnl f* **33/1**

0- 10 nk **Give Us A Reason**[203] 7298 4-9-6 0 ........................................ RobertTart(3) 10 55
(James Toller) *awkward s: a wl in rr: last and lost tch 3f out: kpt on fnl f* **33/1**

0-0 11 11 **Burmese Breeze**[29] 1357 3-8-11 0 ........................................ TedDurcan 3 39
(Chris Wall) *wl in tch tl wknd rapidly over 2f out: t.o* **50/1**

2m 23.55s (1.65) **Going Correction** 0.0s/f (Stan)
**WFA** 3 from 4yo 17lb **11** Ran SP% **122.9**
Speed ratings (Par 103): **94,93,93,93,91 90,89,87,87,86 78**
CSF £22.68 TOTE £3.70: £1.50, £2.40, £1.90; EX 23.00 Trifecta £157.50.
**Owner** Dr Philip Brown **Bred** Good Breeding **Trained** Kingsclere, Hants

**FOCUS**
A fair 3yo maiden which was steadily run. The winner stepped up a bit on previous promise.

## 2082 BETBRIGHT.COM MAIDEN FILLIES' STKS (BOBIS RACE) — 1m 4f (P)
**8:15** (8:15) (Class 5) 3-Y-O — **£2,587** (£770; £384; £192) **Stalls** Centre

Form RPR

52-3 1 **Tioga Pass**[9] 1809 3-9-0 73 ........................................ LukeMorris 1 80
(Paul Cole) *chsd ldng pair: racd awkwardly bnd after 3f and shoved along: frequently off the bridle after but styd in tch: drvn and r.o over 1f out: led last 100yds: won gng away* **8/1**

23- 2 1 3/4 **Sweeping Up**[217] 6949 3-9-0 0 ........................................ JimmyFortune 6 77
(Hughie Morrison) *trckd ldr: led over 6f out: rdn and jnd over 1f out: hdd and outpcd last 100yds* **3/1[2]**

0 3 3/4 **Every Time**[21] 1517 3-9-0 0 ........................................ LiamKeniry 2 76
(Andrew Balding) *trckd ldrs: wnt 2nd 6f out: rdn to chal and w ldr over 1f out: nt qckn and dropped to 3rd ins fnl f* **7/2[3]**

0 4 8 **Approaching Star (FR)**[26] 1424 3-9-0 0 ........................................ RichardHughes 3 63
(William Haggas) *led: stdd pce and hdd over 6f out: sn dropped to 3rd: pushed along over 2f out: steadily wknd* **15/8[1]**

4 5 1 1/2 **Affaire De Coeur**[16] 1616 3-9-0 0 ........................................ JimCrowley 4 61
(David Simcock) *s.s: t.k.h: hld up in last: gng wl enough 3f out: shkn up and fnd nil over 2f out: sn bhd* **6/1**

6 2 1/2 **Housewives Choice** 3-9-0 0 ........................................ TedDurcan 5 57
(James Bethell) *in tch in 5th: shkn up over 2f out: no prog and wknd over 1f out* **33/1**

2m 34.5s **Going Correction** 0.0s/f (Stan) **6** Ran SP% **110.3**
Speed ratings (Par 96): **100,98,98,93,92 90**
CSF £30.88 TOTE £7.70: £2.80, £2.10; EX 26.60 Trifecta £94.10.
**Owner** The Fairy Story Partnership **Bred** Deepwood Farm Stud **Trained** Whatcombe, Oxon

**FOCUS**
Nothing stood out on the figures in this open 3yo fillies' maiden. A muddliong sort of race and it's hard to be too positive about the form.

## 2083 BETBRIGHT - LIVE THE MOMENT H'CAP (BOBIS RACE) 6f (P)
**8:45** (8:46) (Class 4) (0-85,84) 3-Y-O **£4,690** (£1,395; £697; £348) **Stalls** Low

Form RPR

125- **1** **Banaadeer (IRE)**[259] 5656 3-9-5 **82** DaneO'Neill 2 88+
(Richard Hannon) *w.w in 7th: prog fr 2f out: rdn and sustained effrt to ld last 100yds: readily* **6/1**

040- **2** ¾ **Peterkin (IRE)**[182] 7771 3-9-4 **84** MichaelJMMurphy(3) 7 87
(Mark Johnston) *led after 1f: rdn over 1f out: kpt on but hdd and one pce last 100yds* **25/1**

140- **3** *nk* **Biography**[291] 4528 3-9-4 **81** RichardHughes 4 83
(Richard Hannon) *led 1f: sn dropped to 3rd: clsd on ldng pair over 1f out: shkn up and styd on fnl f but nvr quite pce to chal* **16/1**

32-3 **4** *nk* **Intermedium**[32] 1296 3-9-5 **82** MickaelBarzalona 3 83
(Charlie Appleby) *trckd ldr over 4f out: rdn and nt qckn fr 2f out: lost pl fnl f* **9/4**[1]

21-6 **5** *nk* **Quiet Warrior (IRE)**[21] 1518 3-9-5 **82** LukeMorris 5 82
(Marco Botti) *trckd ldng trio: shkn up and nt qckn 2f out: lost pl over 1f out: kpt on u.p fnl f* **4/1**[2]

150- **6** ½ **Smart Salute**[208] 7170 3-9-1 **78** JimCrowley 6 77
(Ed Walker) *in tch in 6th: shkn up on outer and no prog jst over 2f out: kpt on fnl f: nrst fin* **10/1**

31-0 **7** ¾ **Sleepy Sioux**[21] 1518 3-9-5 **82** LiamKeniry 1 78
(David Elsworth) *trckd ldrs in 5th: pushed along on inner 2f out: no imp whn reminder 1f out: one pce* **10/1**

-231 **8** 2 **Android (IRE)**[28] 1379 3-9-0 **77** AdamKirby 8 67+
(Clive Cox) *hld up in last pair: rdn 2f out: no prog and no imp on ldrs* **9/2**[3]

3-20 **9** 6 **Dark Leopard**[11] 1725 3-8-11 **74** JimmyFortune 9 45
(Roger Charlton) *awkward s and dropped into last fr wdst draw: hanging bnd 3f out: sn btn* **8/1**

1m 12.4s (-0.70) **Going Correction** 0.0s/f (Stan) **9** Ran SP% **122.3**
Speed ratings (Par 101): **104,103,102,102,101 101,100,97,89**
CSF £145.56 CT £2311.11 TOTE £9.70: £2.30, £7.90, £4.50; EX 202.40 Trifecta £2542.50 Part won..
**Owner** Hamdan Al Maktoum **Bred** Victor Stud And Brendan Cummins **Trained** East Everleigh, Wilts

**FOCUS**
A useful sprint handicap for 3yos in which the pace was solid throughout. The form has been given a bit of a chance.

## 2084 MIX BUSINESS WITH PLEASURE H'CAP 1m 4f (P)
**9:15** (9:16) (Class 6) (0-60,66) 4-Y-O+ **£1,940** (£577; £288; £144) **Stalls** Centre

Form RPR

3333 **1** **Lily Edge**[8] 1835 5-9-0 **53** (v) WilliamCarson 1 61
(John Bridger) *trckd ldr: drvn to ld 2f out: hld on wl fnl f* **14/1**

6644 **2** ½ **Mr Lando**[13] 1664 5-8-13 **57** RyanTate(5) 3 64
(Tony Carroll) *taken down early: racd keenly: led: set mod pce to 1/2-way: drvn and hdd 2f out: kpt on to press wnr after: jst hld nr fin* **4/1**[3]

056- **3** *nk* **Hallingham**[205] 7248 4-9-6 **59** JimCrowley 6 66
(Jonathan Portman) *hld up in 7th: rdn and prog over 2f out: chsd ldng pair jst over 1f out: kpt on fnl f: nvr quite got there* **14/1**

4205 **4** 1¼ **Ogaritmo**[18] 1574 5-9-4 **57** (t) DaneO'Neill 5 62
(Seamus Durack) *hld up in last trio: nt clr run on inner over 2f out: prog after: tried to cl on ldrs fr over 1f out: one pce last 150yds* **16/1**

-566 **5** 1 **If I Were A Boy (IRE)**[35] 1232 7-9-5 **58** (be) AdamKirby 10 61
(Dominic Ffrench Davis) *stdd s: hld up in last trio: pushed along and prog wl over 1f out: reminder and kpt on fnl f: nvr really threatened* **14/1**

130- **6** 1¾ **Mister Bob (GER)**[396] 1390 5-9-7 **60** (b[1]) TedDurcan 4 60
(James Bethell) *trckd ldng trio: rdn and nt qckn over 2f out: tried to cl again over 1f out: one pce fnl f: eased nr fin* **7/2**[2]

0141 **7** *nk* **Anjuna Beach (USA)**[7] 1874 4-9-13 **66** 6ex GeorgeBaker 8 66
(Gary Moore) *stdd s: hld up in detached last: stl there as r unfolded over 2f out: urged along and no ch after: kpt on fnl f* **9/4**[1]

0-00 **8** 4½ **Gung Ho (FR)**[49] 1012 5-8-9 **48** SteveDrowne 7 40
(Tony Newcombe) *trckd ldrs: rdn over 2f out: no imp over 1f out: wknd fnl f* **7/1**

26-0 **9** 1 **Party Palace**[35] 1232 10-8-7 **49** ow2 WilliamTwiston-Davies(3) 9 40
(Stuart Howe) *chsd ldrs in 6th: rdn and lost pl wl over 2f out: sn btn* **33/1**

3-06 **10** 12 **Roy Rocket (FR)**[34] 1263 4-8-7 **46** oh1 JimmyQuinn 2 18
(John Berry) *trckd ldr: rdn over 3f out: wknd rapidly over 2f out* **20/1**

2m 35.04s (0.54) **Going Correction** 0.0s/f (Stan) **10** Ran SP% **119.1**
Speed ratings (Par 101): **98,97,97,96,95 94,94,91,90,82**
CSF £70.86 CT £821.28 TOTE £11.10: £1.60, £2.40, £5.70; EX 56.90 Trifecta £1941.20 Part won..
**Owner** J J Bridger **Bred** W J Wyatt **Trained** Liphook, Hants

**FOCUS**
A moderate handicap in which the first two were always the front pair. The winner is rated up slightly on recent runs.
T/Plt: £142.00 to a £1 stake. Pool: £64,059.73 - 329.30 winning units. T/Qpdt: £52.90 to a £1 stake. Pool: £4489.29 - 62.76 winning units. JN

# 2071 CHESTER (L-H)
### Thursday, May 8

**OFFICIAL GOING: Soft (7.2)**
Rail moved out 3yds from 6f until 'drop in' at 1.5f. Consequently 14yds added to races 1, 2 &7, 20yds to race 3, 13yds to races 4 & 6 and 10yds to race 5.
Wind: Moderate, behind Weather: Wet

## 2085 IG H'CAP 1m 2f 75y
**1:45** (1:46) (Class 2) (0-105,105) 4£15,762 (£4,715; £2,357; £1,180; £587) **Stalls** High

Form RPR

-005 **1** **Tres Coronas (IRE)**[15] 1653 7-8-10 **94** GrahamGibbons 3 104
(David Barron) *midfield: hdwy over 1f out: led ins fnl f: drvn out and r.o towards fin* **11/2**[2]

-031 **2** 2 **Sennockian Star**[15] 1653 4-9-3 **101** (v) JoeFanning 11 107
(Mark Johnston) *in tch: checked sltly 2f out: rdn to ld over 1f out: hdd ins fnl f: styd on u.p but unable to go w wnr towards fin* **9/1**

4-21 **3** ½ **That's Plenty (IRE)**[20] 1564 5-8-9 **96** RonanWhelan(3) 2 101
(John Patrick Shanahan, Ire) *led for 1f: remained prom: rdn to chal over 1f out: nt qckn ins fnl f: kpt on u.p towards fin* **5/1**[1]

5-13 **4** 2¼ **Squire Osbaldeston (IRE)**[40] 1170 4-9-1 **99** RyanMoore 10 100
(Martyn Meade) *hld up: rdn and hdwy over 1f out: kpt on ins fnl f: one pce and no imp on ldrs towards fin* **10/1**

5500 **5** 4½ **Strictly Silver (IRE)**[5] 1948 5-9-0 **98** (v) KierenFallon 5 91
(Alan Bailey) *s.i.s: midfield: effrt on outer 2f out: chsd ldrs over 1f out: one pce ins fnl f* **7/1**

502- **6** *hd* **Wigmore Hall (IRE)**[223] 6800 7-9-7 **105** JamieSpencer 14 98
(Michael Bell) *s.s: in rr: rdn over 1f out: plugged on ins fnl f: nvr a threat* **18/1**

020- **7** *shd* **Gabrial The Great (IRE)**[152] 6838 5-8-12 **96** GrahamLee 1 88
(Donald McCain) *in tch: rdn 2f out: outpcd over 1f out: n.d after* **7/1**

3050 **8** 1 **Party Royal**[20] 1559 4-8-2 **86** oh1 SilvestreDeSousa 7 77
(Mark Johnston) *w ldr: led after 1f: pushed along 3f out: rdn and hdd over 2f out: stl ev ch over 1f out: wknd ins fnl f* **33/1**

260- **9** ½ **Makafeh**[239] 6308 4-8-7 **91** AndreaAtzeni 4 81
(Luca Cumani) *in tch: sn dropped to midfield: niggled along 5f out: rdn and wknd over 2f out* **7/1**

46-3 **10** 1¾ **Marcret (ITY)**[21] 1539 7-8-11 **95** DanielTudhope 9 82
(David O'Meara) *trckd ldrs: wnt 2nd wl over 7f out: led over 2f out: rdn and hdd over 1f out: wknd ins fnl f* **13/2**[3]

-300 **11** *nse* **Anaconda (FR)**[20] 1558 5-8-12 **96** RichardKingscote 12 82
(Tom Dascombe) *hld up: rdn over 2f out: nvr on terms* **20/1**

2m 13.49s (2.29) **Going Correction** +0.50s/f (Yiel) **11** Ran SP% **114.9**
Speed ratings (Par 109): **110,108,108,106,102 102,102,101,101,99 99**
CSF £53.01 CT £262.95 TOTE £6.60: £2.80, £2.10, £1.80; EX 39.40 Trifecta £191.80.
**Owner** D Pryde & J Cringan **Bred** Denis McDonnell **Trained** Maunby, N Yorks

**FOCUS**
At the overnight stage, the ground was given as good, but due to plenty of rain it was revised to soft by the time the runners jumped off for the opener. Rail moved out 3yds from 6f until 'drop in' at 1.5f. Consequently 14yds added to races 1, 2 & 7, 20yds to race 3, 13yds to races 4 & 6 and 10yds to race 5. This looked a competitive start to the day, and it saw the winner come from off the pace. A personal best from the winner with the runner-up to form.

## 2086 BETFAIR PRICE RUSH HUXLEY STKS (FOR THE TRADESMAN'S CUP) (GROUP 3) 1m 2f 75y
**2:15** (2:17) (Class 1) 4-Y-O+
**£34,026** (£12,900; £6,456; £3,216; £1,614; £810) **Stalls** High

Form RPR

4-21 **1** **Noble Mission**[13] 1697 5-9-3 115 JamesDoyle 8 123
(Lady Cecil) *led: hdd wl over 7f out: racd in 2nd pl tl regained ld over 5f out: kicked on over 2f out: sn rdn: styd on ins fnl f: a in control* **9/4**[1]

21-2 **2** 2¼ **Telescope (IRE)**[13] 1697 4-9-0 115 RyanMoore 7 116
(Sir Michael Stoute) *trckd ldrs: wnt 2nd over 4f out: chalng 3f out: sn rdn and nt qckn: hung lft ent fnl f whn no imp on wnr: kpt on same pce* **5/2**[2]

21-6 **3** 8 **Danadana (IRE)**[21] 1533 6-9-5 114 AndreaAtzeni 3 106
(Luca Cumani) *trckd ldrs: rdn 3f out: outpcd by ldrs over 2f out: no imp after* **12/1**

-612 **4** 9 **Gabrial's Kaka (IRE)**[12] 1721 4-9-0 103 JamieSpencer 1 84
(Richard Fahey) *in rr: pushed along 6f out: rdn 4f out and unable to go pce: wnt mod 4th 1f out: nvr a threat* **15/2**

1S0- **5** 1¼ **Ektihaam (IRE)**[285] 4745 5-9-0 115 PaulHanagan 4 81
(Roger Varian) *racd keenly: w ldr: led wl over 7f out: hdd over 5f out: rdn and wknd 3f out* **11/4**[3]

046 **6** 2½ **Edu Querido (BRZ)**[61] 902 5-9-0 108 MarcMonaghan 6 77
(Marco Botti) *hld up in rr: rdn and outpcd by ldrs whn wnt mod 4th 3f out: lost 4th over 2f out: bhd after* **33/1**

2m 13.11s (1.91) **Going Correction** +0.50s/f (Yiel) **6** Ran SP% **108.4**
Speed ratings (Par 113): **112,110,103,96,95 93**
CSF £7.57 TOTE £2.90: £1.50, £1.10; EX 5.10 Trifecta £21.10.
**Owner** K Abdullah **Bred** Juddmonte Farms Ltd **Trained** Newmarket, Suffolk

**FOCUS**
A couple of these were known to front-run and a good gallop was provided. The front pair pulled clear and Noble Mission confirmed he is better than ever.

## 2087 MBNA CHESTER VASE (GROUP 3) (C&G) 1m 4f 66y
**2:45** (2:46) (Class 1) 3-Y-O
**£42,532** (£16,125; £8,070; £4,020; £2,017; £1,012) **Stalls** Low

Form RPR

**1** **Orchestra (IRE)**[259] 5686 3-9-0 95 RyanMoore 2 112+
(A P O'Brien, Ire) *trckd ldrs: effrtlessly impr to ld on inner 2f out: 2 l clr over 1f out: rdn whn edgd rt and stl looked green wl ins fnl f: jst hld on* **3/1**[1]

31 **2** *nse* **Romsdal**[29] 1380 3-9-0 92 WilliamBuick 3 111
(John Gosden) *midfield: pushed along bhd ldrs 3f out: impr to take 2nd over 2 l down over 1f out: styd on wl towards fin: jst failed* **9/2**[2]

31-4 **3** 8 **Scotland (GER)**[27] 1419 3-9-0 95 JimCrowley 9 99
(Andrew Balding) *stdd s: hld up: pushed along and hdwy 2f out: rdn to chse ldrs over 1f out: no imp: one pce ins fnl f* **7/1**[3]

1-3 **4** 2¼ **Seagull Star**[21] 1530 3-9-0 97 GrahamLee 8 96
(William Haggas) *s.i.s: hld up: pushed along 2f out: hdwy for press over 1f out: edgd rt ent fnl f: no imp on ldrs* **9/2**[2]

15-3 **5** 5 **Stars Over The Sea (USA)**[15] 1652 3-9-0 99 FrannyNorton 6 88
(Mark Johnston) *led after 1f: rdn and hung rt over 2f out: sn hdd: wkng whn checked sltly ent fnl f* **10/1**

3-25 **6** 9 **Automated**[13] 1699 3-9-0 88 KierenFallon 1 75
(Clive Brittain) *racd keenly: led for 1f: chsd ldr: ev ch 3f out: rdn 2f out: wkng whn hung rt on bnd wl over 1f out* **14/1**

41-4 **7** 12 **Festival Theatre (IRE)**[28] 1407 3-9-0 84 ShaneKelly 7 57
(Sir Michael Stoute) *dwlt: hld up: pushed along over 3f out: lft bhd over 2f out* **33/1**

4 **8** 31 **Carlo Bugatti (IRE)**[26] 1458 3-9-0 0 (b[1]) JosephO'Brien 5 10
(A P O'Brien, Ire) *racd keenly: chsd ldrs: ev ch 3f out: rdn 2f out: sn wknd: t.o* **9/2**[2]

2m 42.05s (3.55) **Going Correction** +0.50s/f (Yiel) **8** Ran SP% **110.7**
Speed ratings (Par 109): **108,107,102,101,97 91,83,63**
CSF £15.38 TOTE £2.90: £1.10, £1.50, £3.90; EX 17.20 Trifecta £106.40.
**Owner** Mrs John Magnier & Michael Tabor & Derrick Smith **Bred** Storm Bloodstock **Trained** Cashel, Co Tipperary

**FOCUS**
It was difficult to know what to make of these before the off, but the race usually goes to an above-average type, exemplified by subsequent Derby winner Ruler Of The World's success last season, and this edition looks no different. The first two were clear and Orchestra looks like being among the better winners of the race. Big improvement from Romsdal.

## 2088 BOODLES DIAMOND H'CAP (BOBIS RACE) 7f 122y
3:15 (3:19) (Class 2) (0-100,90) 3-Y-O £15,752 (£4,715; £2,357; £1,180; £587) Stalls Low

Form RPR
35-5 1 **Legend Rising (IRE)**[17] 1614 3-9-3 86 RyanMoore 4 97
(Martyn Meade) *racd keenly: in tch: effrt over 1f out: led fnl 100yds: r.o* **6/1**
20-1 2 1 1/4 **Captain Bob (IRE)**[14] 1681 3-8-11 80 WilliamBuick 5 88
(Charles Hills) *racd keenly: led: hdd over 5f out: remained w ldr: regained ld wl over 1f out: edgd lft ins fnl f: hdd fnl 100yds: no ex fnl strides* **9/2[3]**
104- 3 2 **Hot Coffee (IRE)**[243] 6185 3-9-7 90 RichardKingscote 1 93
(Tom Dascombe) *bustled along s: racd keenly: in tch: sn trckd ldrs: pushed along over 2f out: rdn and chalng over 1f out: nt qckn ins fnl f: styd on same pce fnl 100yds* **15/2**
3-12 4 1 1/4 **Our Gabrial (IRE)**[105] 301 3-8-13 82 (b) JamieSpencer 3 82
(Richard Fahey) *missed break: rdn s: in rr: hdwy over 2f out: kpt on ins fnl f: unable to mount serious chal* **4/1[2]**
21- 5 3 **Erroneous (IRE)**[215] 7023 3-9-0 83 JimCrowley 7 75
(David Simcock) *prom: pushed along over 3f out: rdn and outpcd over 1f out: one pce ins fnl f* **7/2[1]**
1140 6 2 1/4 **Almargo (IRE)**[13] 1696 3-9-3 86 FrannyNorton 2 73
(Mark Johnston) *racd keenly: prom: led over 5f out: rdn and hdd wl over 1f out: wknd ins fnl f* **7/1**
1- 7 2 1/4 **Brian Noble**[245] 6127 3-8-10 79 GrahamLee 9 60
(Richard Fahey) *missed break: hld up: pushed along over 2f out: sn outpcd: nvr a threat* **6/1**
615- 8 2 **Edge (IRE)**[203] 7326 3-8-12 81 DavidProbert 6 57
(Bernard Llewellyn) *hld up: pushed along over 2f out: sn outpcd: nvr a threat* **20/1**

1m 36.9s (3.10) **Going Correction** +0.50s/f (Yiel) **8 Ran SP% 118.0**
Speed ratings (Par 105): **104,102,100,99,96 94,92,90**
CSF £34.22 CT £209.88 TOTE £5.70: £1.60, £2.00, £3.20; EX 28.70 Trifecta £429.20.
**Owner** David Caddy **Bred** Gus Roche **Trained** Newmarket, Suffolk

**FOCUS**
Quite a bit of interest in this handicap was lost when the unbeaten Muteela unshipped her jockey on the way to the start, having to be withdrawn, but it still left a decent race for the level. The winner is rated back to his best early 2yo form.

## 2089 T&L LEASING EBF STALLIONS MAIDEN STKS (BOBIS RACE) 5f 16y
3:50 (3:53) (Class 3) 2-Y-O £9,056 (£2,695; £1,346; £673) Stalls Low

Form RPR
3 1 **Ballymore Castle (IRE)**[27] 1417 2-9-5 0 RyanMoore 2 82+
(Richard Fahey) *bmpd s: in tch: pushed along 3f out: outpcd over 2f out: prog and hung lft ins fnl f: str run to burst through gap to ld towards fin* **5/6[1]**
04 2 3/4 **London Life (IRE)**[21] 1528 2-9-0 0 KierenFallon 5 74
(Tom Dascombe) *chsd ldrs: rdn over 1f out: chalng wl ins fnl f: kpt on but outpcd by wnr towards fin* **11/2[2]**
43 3 nse **Hell Of A Lord**[12] 1726 2-9-0 0 RyanWhile(5) 7 79
(Bill Turner) *chsd ldr: rdn over 1f out: led fnl 100yds: hdd and outpcd by wnr towards fin* **8/1[3]**
4 1 1/2 **Red Icon (IRE)** 2-9-5 0 FrannyNorton 6 74+
(Tom Dascombe) *bmpd s: trckd ldrs: rdn over 1f out: ev ch fnl 100yds: kpt on same pce towards fin* **16/1**
4 5 1 **Come Uppence**[34] 1276 2-9-5 0 JFEgan 1 70
(David Evans) *led: rdn and over 2 l clr over 1f out: hdd fnl 100yds: no ex towards fin* **10/1**
32 6 5 **Just Marion (IRE)**[8] 1872 2-8-11 0 (v[1]) DeclanBates(3) 10 47
(David Evans) *bhd and pushed along: kpt on u.p into midfield over 1f out: no imp on ldrs* **33/1**
7 3/4 **Billy Slater** 2-9-5 0 JamieSpencer 8 49+
(Richard Fahey) *missed break: outpcd and bhd: kpt on ins fnl f: nvr able to trble ldrs* **12/1**
42 8 4 1/2 **Macarthurs Park (IRE)**[14] 1663 2-9-0 0 RichardKingscote 9 28
(Tom Dascombe) *flashed tail several times: midfield: outpcd over 2f out: wl btn ins fnl f* **20/1**
0 9 3 **Toni's A Star**[5] 1936 2-9-0 0 JoeFanning 11 17
(Paul Green) *wnt rt s: bhd and outpcd: nvr on terms* **66/1**
10 9 **New Abbey Dancer (IRE)** 2-9-0 0 DavidProbert 13
(Gay Kelleway) *missed break and awkward s: bhd and outpcd: nvr on terms* **66/1**
0 11 39 **Wiggle**[33] 1314 2-9-0 0 StevieDonohoe 3
(Tim Pitt) *bmpd s: hld up: wl bhd fnl 2f* **25/1**

1m 4.89s (3.89) **Going Correction** +0.75s/f (Yiel) **11 Ran SP% 118.3**
Speed ratings (Par 97): **98,96,96,94,92 84,83,76,71,57**
CSF £5.15 TOTE £1.80: £1.10, £1.90, £3.30; EX 6.90 Trifecta £28.40.
**Owner** Sheikh Rashid Dalmook Al Maktoum **Bred** Mogeely Stud **Trained** Musley Bank, N Yorks

**FOCUS**
Most of these had previous experience, so this is probably just fair maiden form. The pace was very strong.

## 2090 BETFAIR CASH OUT H'CAP (BOBIS RACE) 6f 18y
4:25 (4:26) (Class 3) (0-90,87) 3-Y-O £10,350 (£3,080; £1,539; £769) Stalls Low

Form RPR
1-46 1 **The Hooded Claw (IRE)**[13] 1693 3-9-0 80 GrahamGibbons 9 91
(Tim Easterby) *a.p: led wl over 1f out: edgd lft ins fnl f: kpt on wl* **6/1**
0-65 2 3/4 **Kickboxer (IRE)**[13] 1700 3-8-12 81 WilliamTwiston-Davies(3) 7 90
(Mick Channon) *midfield: hdwy on inner 2f out: wnt 2nd over 1f out: chalng wnr ins fnl f: kpt on* **4/1[2]**
1-05 3 6 **Jazz (IRE)**[13] 1693 3-9-6 86 WilliamBuick 1 77
(Charles Hills) *trckd ldrs: rdn and chalng over 1f out: outpcd by front two ins fnl f* **9/4[1]**
61-4 4 2 1/4 **Exceeder**[57] 926 3-8-9 80 MarcMonaghan(5) 6 64
(Marco Botti) *midfield: rdn and outpcd over 2f out: styd on ins fnl f: nvr able to chal* **25/1**
1-16 5 3/4 **Thataboy (IRE)**[96] 429 3-8-11 77 (t) RichardKingscote 4 59
(Tom Dascombe) *led: rdn and hdd wl over 1f out: wknd ins fnl f* **25/1**
1-44 6 nk **Fiftyshadesofgrey (IRE)**[31] 1350 3-9-2 82 (t) JamesDoyle 13 63
(George Baker) *dwlt: hld up in rr: outpcd over 2f out: kpt on fnl f: nvr able to trble ldrs* **20/1**
421- 7 1 3/4 **Chorlton Manor (IRE)**[234] 6477 3-8-12 78 StevieDonohoe 12 54
(Tim Pitt) *trckd ldrs: effrt over 1f out: wknd ins fnl f* **25/1**
4-10 8 nk **Sacha Park (IRE)**[13] 1700 3-9-7 87 RyanMoore 3 62
(Richard Hannon) *hld up: struggling over 2f out: nvr a threat* **12/1**
310- 9 2 1/4 **Spiceupyourlife (IRE)**[209] 7170 3-8-7 73 DavidProbert 10 41
(Richard Fahey) *dwlt: hld up: outpcd over 2f out: nvr a threat* **33/1**
4230 10 2 1/2 **Outbacker (IRE)**[17] 1614 3-8-11 77 JoeFanning 8 38
(Mark Johnston) *midfield: hdwy to chse ldrs over 2f out: wknd over 1f out* **50/1**
12-0 11 1/2 **Pushkin Museum (IRE)**[13] 1700 3-9-2 82 [1] JamieSpencer 5 41
(Richard Fahey) *racd keenly: prom tl rdn and wknd wl over 1f out* **25/1**
3-40 12 140 **Quickaswecan**[22] 1513 3-9-1 81 FrannyNorton 2
(Mark Johnston) *a outpcd and bhd: t.o* **5/1[3]**

1m 19.55s (5.75) **Going Correction** +1.00s/f (Soft) **12 Ran SP% 114.5**
Speed ratings (Par 103): **101,100,92,89,88 87,85,84,81,78 77,**
CSF £26.30 CT £70.60 TOTE £10.30: £3.30, £3.00, £1.10; EX 34.30 Trifecta £193.30.
**Owner** April Fools **Bred** Newlands House Stud **Trained** Great Habton, N Yorks

**FOCUS**
A decent handicap that appeared to be run at a fair gallop. The first two, who looked well treated on standout 2yo runs, pulled clear.

## 2091 INVESTEC STRUCTURED PRODUCTS H'CAP 1m 2f 75y
5:00 (5:00) (Class 3) (0-90,90) 4-Y-O+ £10,350 (£3,080; £1,539; £769) Stalls High

Form RPR
50-2 1 **Stellar Express (IRE)**[24] 1483 5-9-1 84 AndrewMullen 6 95
(Michael Appleby) *mde all: rdn 2f out: over 2 l clr 1f out: styd on wl* **7/1**
200- 2 3 **Pilgrims Rest (IRE)**[307] 4028 5-9-2 85 StevieDonohoe 4 90
(Tim Pitt) *prom: rdn 3f out: wnt 2nd 2f out: over 2 l down 1f out: no imp on wnr ins fnl f* **40/1**
1220 3 3 1/4 **Tepmokea (IRE)**[26] 1444 8-9-1 84 (p) HayleyTurner 13 83
(Conor Dore) *chsd wnr after 2f: rdn 3f out: lost 2nd 2f out: one pce fr over 1f out* **16/1**
-111 4 7 **Memory Cloth**[12] 1724 7-8-12 81 DaleSwift 1 68
(Brian Ellison) *midfield: rdn over 3f out: rdn to chse ldrs over 2f out: one pce and no imp over 1f out: wl btn fnl f* **10/3[1]**
000- 5 4 **Red Seventy**[28] 4746 5-8-5 77 (p) WilliamTwiston-Davies(3) 2 56
(David Pipe) *hld up: hmpd ins first f: pushed along over 3f out: rdn and no imp over 2f out: nvr threatened* **11/2[3]**
0- 6 5 **Long Journey Home (IRE)**[13] 1708 6-9-7 90 (t) JosephO'Brien 7 60
(Daniel William O'Sullivan, Ire) *trckd ldrs tl rdn and wknd over 2f out* **12/1**
323- 7 7 **Buckstay (IRE)**[187] 7696 4-9-3 86 JimCrowley 8 44
(Peter Chapple-Hyam) *hld up: hdwy 4f out: chsd ldrs 3f out: sn rdn: wknd over 1f out* **5/1[2]**
5111 8 8 **Spes Nostra**[42] 1133 6-9-3 86 (b) GrahamGibbons 5 29
(David Barron) *hld up in rr: struggling 6f out: lost tch 3f out* **12/1**
00-5 9 2 3/4 **Cosmic Halo**[12] 1716 5-8-9 78 FrannyNorton 11 16
(Richard Fahey) *s.i.s: in rr: struggling 3f out: nvr a threat* **20/1**
10 1/2 **Dispour (IRE)**[12] 4-8-13 82 (b) GrahamLee 14 20
(Donald McCain) *missed break: midfield after 2f: rdn and wknd 4f out* **6/1**
0010 11 77 **Halfsin (IRE)**[70] 764 6-8-11 85 (t) MarcMonaghan(5) 3
(Marco Botti) *midfield: rdn over 4f out: wknd over 3f out: eased whn wl btn over 2f out: t.o* **16/1**

2m 19.57s (8.37) **Going Correction** +1.00s/f (Soft) **11 Ran SP% 116.3**
Speed ratings (Par 107): **106,103,101,95,92 88,82,76,74,73 12**
CSF £243.05 CT £4249.12 TOTE £6.90: £3.10, £6.20, £4.40; EX 158.80 Trifecta £1380.60.
**Owner** Dallas Racing **Bred** Adrian Purvis **Trained** Danethorpe, Notts

**FOCUS**
This doesn't look form to follow too closely, as the first three were in the leading trio throughout. The form is rated around the second.
T/Jkpt: £20,890.40 to a £1 stake. Pool: £29,423.12 - 1.00 winning tickets. T/Plt: £21.60 to a £1 stake. Pool: £203,917.10 - 6,872.17 winning tickets. T/Qpdt: £9.10 to £1 stake. Pool: £9,223.33 - 748.68 winning tickets. DO

# 1886 SOUTHWELL (L-H)
Thursday, May 8

**OFFICIAL GOING: Standard**
Wind: Light across Weather: Heavy grey cloud and rain showers

## 2092 QUICKSILVERSLOTS MORE JACKPOTS MORE MACHINES H'CAP 1m (F)
1:55 (1:55) (Class 6) (0-60,60) 4-Y-O+ £1,940 (£577; £288; £144) Stalls Low

Form RPR
1003 1 **Roger Thorpe**[10] 1800 5-9-2 60 JackDuern(5) 11 69
(Deborah Sanderson) *dwlt: hdwy to trck ldrs after 2f: wd st: effrt to chal over 2f out: rdn and slt ld wl over 1f out: edgd lft and hdd ent fnl f: sn drvn and kpt on gamely to ld again last 100yds* **5/1[2]**
2222 2 3/4 **General Tufto**[10] 1800 9-8-13 52 (b) MartinLane 9 59
(Charles Smith) *sn pushed along and outpcd in rr: rdn and hdwy on outer over 3f out: wd st: cl up over 2f out: rdn to chal wl over 1f out: slt ld ent fnl f: sn drvn: hdd and no ex last 100yds* **5/1[2]**
4431 3 4 **Solarmaite**[8] 1891 5-9-2 60 6ex (b) PhilipPrince(5) 5 58
(Roy Bowring) *cl up: led 1/2-way: pushed along and hdd 3f out: wd st: rdn over 2f out and ev ch tl drvn and one pce appr fnl f* **10/11[1]**
6664 4 9 **Refuse Colette (IRE)**[45] 1086 5-8-2 46 oh1 DannyBrock(5) 8 23
(Mick Quinn) *led: rdn and cl up 1/2-way: led again 3f out: styd nr inner rail and sn rdn: drvn and hdd wl over 1f out: grad wknd* **20/1**
030 5 1 3/4 **Chez Vrony**[16] 1631 8-8-8 47 (p) WilliamCarson 3 20
(Dave Morris) *in tch: hdwy to chse ldrs over 3f out: rdn along wl over 2f out: sn one pce* **20/1**
0-54 6 8 **Lenderking (IRE)**[10] 1805 6-8-3 49 oh1 ow3 (t) RobJFitzpatrick(7) 7 4
(Michael Chapman) *towards rr: rdn along wl over 3f out: sme hdwy fnl 2f: nvr a factor* **100/1**
00-0 7 2 1/4 **Bond Blade**[58] 910 6-8-0 46 oh1 [1] JordanVaughan(7) 10
(Suzzanne France) *a towards rr* **50/1**
4-60 8 2 1/4 **Limon Squeezy**[55] 964 5-8-2 46 oh1 JoeyHaynes(5) 2
(Mike Murphy) *chsd ldrs on inner: rdn along 3f out: sn wknd* **33/1**
0460 9 7 **Strandfield Bay (IRE)**[11] 1761 8-8-13 52 (bt[1]) PaulQuinn 6
(Sharon Watt) *chsd ldrs: rdn along wl over 3f out: sn wknd and bhd* **16/1**
0-00 10 4 1/2 **First Sargeant**[17] 1613 4-9-6 59 (b) PJMcDonald 1
(Geoffrey Harker) *dwlt: a in rr: bhd fnl 3f* **16/1**
3336 11 3 3/4 **Shamiana**[9] 1865 4-8-12 51 (b) MickaelBarzalona 4
(Daniel Kubler) *chsd ldrs: rdn along wl over 3f out: sn wknd* **10/1[3]**

1m 44.33s (0.63) **Going Correction** +0.20s/f (Slow) **11 Ran SP% 122.0**
Speed ratings (Par 101): **104,103,99,90,88 80,78,76,69,64 60**
CSF £29.81 CT £44.09 TOTE £4.20: £2.20, £1.40, £1.10; EX 32.80 Trifecta £58.40.
**Owner** J M Lacey **Bred** J M Lacey **Trained** Tickhill, S Yorks

■ Stewards' Enquiry : Danny Brock two-day ban: used whip above shoulder height (May 22-23)

**FOCUS**
A moderate handicap. The winner turned around a 7l beating by the runner-up latest.

## 2093 QUICKSILVERSLOTS PLAY FROM 10P TO £2 MAIDEN STKS 5f (F)
**2:25** (2:27) (Class 5) 3-Y-O+ **£2,587** (£770; £384; £192) **Stalls** High

Form RPR
3 **1** **Saakhen (IRE)**[14] 1671 3-9-3 83..............................(t) TonyHamilton 6 79
(Richard Fahey) *cl up: pushed along bef 1/2-way: rdn along over 2f out: drvn over 1f out: kpt on to ld last 150yds* **1/5**[1]

0- **2** *1 1/4* **Naivasha**[230] 6607 3-8-12 0..............................(e) MickaelBarzalona 8 69
(Robert Cowell) *racd nr stands' rail: cl up: led wl over 1f out and sn rdn: drvn and edgd lft ent fnl f: hdd and one pce last 150yds: rn w eye shield nt eye cover as declared* **10/1**[3]

0- **3** *7* **Templar Boy**[231] 6569 3-8-10 0.............................. VictorSantos(7) 1 48
(J R Jenkins) *in tch: rdn along 1/2-way: sn edgd lft to far rail: drvn and kpt on appr fnl f* **25/1**

**4** *6* **Bondi Beach Babe** 4-9-0 0.............................. JordanNason(7) 7 26
(James Turner) *racd nr stands' rail: s.i.s and bhd: rdn along bef 1/2-way: styd on fr over 1f out: tk modest 4th nr fin* **25/1**

**5** *nk* **Procurer (FR)** 3-9-3 0.............................. LukeMorris 3 26
(Scott Dixon) *sn led: rdn along over 2f out: hdd wl over 1f out: sn wknd* **8/1**[2]

5655 **6** *nse* **Jiminy**[31] 1343 4-9-9 46..............................(b) SladeO'Hara(3) 2 29
(Alan Berry) *prom: rdn along 1/2-way: sn wknd* **25/1**

0 **7** *24* **Tellatail**[17] 1612 4-9-5 0.............................. ThomasHemsley(7) 5
(Chris Dwyer) *sn outpcd and a bhd* **50/1**

1m 1.46s (1.76) **Going Correction** +0.40s/f (Slow)
**WFA** 3 from 4yo 9lb 7 Ran SP% **117.0**
Speed ratings (Par 103): **101,99,87,78,77 77,39**
CSF £3.13 TOTE £1.20: £1.10, £3.90; EX 4.30 Trifecta £37.80.
**Owner** Middleham Park Racing LXXI & Partner **Bred** Mr And Mrs B Firestone **Trained** Musley Bank, N Yorks

**FOCUS**
An uncompetitive maiden in which long odds-on backers would have got nervous. It remains to be seen what ability the winner retains.

## 2094 QUICKSILVERSLOTS PLAY £500 JACKPOT RAINBOW RICHES H'CAP 6f (F)
**2:55** (2:56) (Class 6) (0-55,61) 4-Y-O+ **£1,940** (£577; £288; £144) **Stalls** Low

Form RPR
5-21 **1** **Meshardal (GER)**[10] 1804 4-9-13 61 6ex.............................. JamesSullivan 9 71+
(Ruth Carr) *t.k.h: cl up: led after 2f: rdn over 1f out: kpt on wl u.p fnl f* **4/7**[1]

5020 **2** *1 1/2* **Novalist**[41] 1148 6-8-9 46..............................(b) JasonHart(3) 10 51
(Robin Bastiman) *midfield: hdwy and wd st: rdn to chse ldrs and edgd lft 2f out: drvn and edgd lft ent fnl f: sn chsng wnr: no imp towards fin* **16/1**

1-26 **3** *1/2* **Major Muscari (IRE)**[118] 121 6-9-0 53.............................. AdamCarter(5) 11 56
(Shaun Harris) *prom: cl up over 2f out: rdn to chal over 1f out: ev ch tl drvn and kpt on same pce ins fnl f* **8/1**[3]

0005 **4** *2 1/4* **Fairy Wing (IRE)**[10] 1804 7-9-1 54..............................(b) TimClark(5) 4 50
(Ann Stokell) *chsd ldrs: rdn along over 2f out: drvn and kpt on same pce appr fnl f* **25/1**

4260 **5** *1* **Masked Dance (IRE)**[33] 1309 7-9-3 51..............................(b) LukeMorris 6 44
(Scott Dixon) *chsd ldrs: effrt and cl up 1/2-way: rdn along over 2f out: sn drvn and one pce* **6/1**[2]

2312 **6** *1 1/2* **Doctor Hilary**[10] 1804 12-9-4 52..............................(v) RobertHavlin 1 40
(Mark Hoad) *towards rr: rdn along and wd st: sme hdwy over 2f out: sn drvn and no imp* **11/1**

00-6 **7** *3* **Evens And Odds (IRE)**[35] 1270 10-9-1 52.............................. SladeO'Hara(3) 2 31
(Peter Grayson) *chsd ldrs on inner: rdn along wl over 2f out: drvn and edgd rt over 1f out: sn wknd* **20/1**

6050 **8** *3/4* **Celestial Dawn**[9] 1838 5-9-2 50..............................(v[1]) MartinLane 5 26
(John Weymes) *s.i.s and a in rr* **25/1**

4600 **9** *2 3/4* **Durham Express (IRE)**[30] 1365 7-8-9 46 oh1......(b) ConnorBeasley(3) 8 13
(Colin Teague) *led 2f: cl up: rdn wl over 2f out: grad wknd* **50/1**

3360 **10** *2 1/2* **Partner's Gold (IRE)**[45] 1081 4-8-12 46 oh1..............(b) PatrickMathers 3 5
(Alan Berry) *dwlt: a in rr* **25/1**

046- **11** *1* **Copper To Gold**[198] 7454 5-8-9 46.............................. NeilFarley(3) 7 2
(Robin Bastiman) *swtchd rt to outer sn after s: a in rr* **33/1**

1m 17.76s (1.26) **Going Correction** +0.20s/f (Slow) 11 Ran SP% **124.5**
Speed ratings (Par 101): **99,97,96,93,92 90,86,85,81,78 76**
CSF £11.61 CT £51.85 TOTE £1.90: £1.10, £4.10, £2.30; EX 14.50 Trifecta £72.60.
**Owner** The Hollinbridge Partnership & Ruth Carr **Bred** Gestut Hofgut Heymann **Trained** Huby, N Yorks

**FOCUS**
A moderate sprint handicap won by another short-priced favourite. The winner was not as impressive as last week.

## 2095 QUICKSILVERSLOTS £1 TO WIN £500 MEDIAN AUCTION MAIDEN STKS 7f (F)
**3:25** (3:25) (Class 6) 3-4-Y-O **£1,940** (£577; £288; £144) **Stalls** Low

Form RPR
3 **1** **Glorious Star (IRE)**[23] 1498 4-9-12 0.............................. GeorgeBaker 1 73+
(Ed Walker) *mde all: qcknd wl over 1f out: rdn appr fnl f: kpt on strly* **2/1**[2]

5-3 **2** *2 1/2* **Interconnection**[10] 1817 3-9-0 0.............................. LukeMorris 4 62
(Ed Vaughan) *cl up on outer: niggled along 1/2-way: swtchd lft and rdn 2f out: chal over 1f out: ev ch tl drvn and kpt on same pce ins fnl f* **7/4**[1]

6-02 **3** *2 1/4* **Sleet (IRE)**[8] 1890 3-8-11 40..............................(v[1]) BillyCray(3) 2 56
(Michael Appleby) *cl up: rdn 2f out: ev ch tl drvn and one pce appr fnl f* **16/1**

00- **4** *3/4* **Quest Of Colour (IRE)**[222] 6828 3-8-9 0.............................. TonyHamilton 3 49
(Richard Fahey) *trckd ldrs on inner: pushed along wl over 2f out: rdn wl over 1f out: sn one pce* **16/1**

2 **5** *15* **Va Benny**[30] 1364 3-9-0 0.............................. FrederikTylicki 5 22
(J R Jenkins) *dwlt: rdn along in rr 1/2-way: sn outpcd and bhd whn eased over 1f out* **5/2**[3]

1m 31.27s (0.97) **Going Correction** +0.20s/f (Slow)
**WFA** 3 from 4yo 12lb 5 Ran SP% **110.0**
Speed ratings (Par 101): **102,99,96,95,78**
CSF £5.90 TOTE £2.50: £1.30, £1.10; EX 5.50 Trifecta £33.00.
**Owner** Ms A A Yap **Bred** Ballylinch Stud **Trained** Newmarket, Suffolk

**FOCUS**
A modest maiden with a 45-rated horse not beaten far into third, but the time was respectable. The winner is entitled to improve again.

## 2096 EBF STALLIONS BREEDING WINNERS /QUICKSILVERSLOTS AFTER 10PM FILLIES' H'CAP 5f (F)
**4:00** (4:00) (Class 4) (0-80,80) 4-Y-O+ **£6,469** (£1,925; £962; £481) **Stalls** High

Form RPR
4-63 **1** **Six Wives**[9] 1850 7-8-12 73..............................(p) MatthewHopkins(7) 1 81
(Scott Dixon) *sn led and clr: rdn over 1f out: kpt on wl* **2/1**[1]

1322 **2** *1 1/2* **Ray Of Joy**[23] 1500 8-9-4 72..............................(v) FrederikTylicki 4 74
(J R Jenkins) *chsd ldrs: rdn along wl over 1f out: kpt on fnl f: tk 2nd nr fin* **9/2**[3]

0533 **3** *nk* **Amosite**[12] 1739 8-9-1 72..............................(v) ConnorBeasley(3) 3 73
(J R Jenkins) *chsd wnr: hdwy wl over 1f out: sn rdn: drvn and one pce ins fnl f* **9/2**[3]

4111 **4** *3 1/2* **Megaleka**[11] 1759 4-9-7 80 6ex.............................. TimClark(5) 2 68
(Alan Bailey) *stmbld s: sn swtchd lft to outer and chsd ldrs: rdn along 2f out: drvn and btn over 1f out* **5/2**[2]

01-5 **5** *13* **Dark Opal (IRE)**[9] 1843 4-8-11 70.............................. JoeyHaynes(5) 5 12
(John Weymes) *sn rdn along and outpcd: bhd fnl 2f* **7/1**

1m 0.84s (1.14) **Going Correction** +0.40s/f (Slow) 5 Ran SP% **110.8**
Speed ratings (Par 102): **106,103,103,97,76**
CSF £11.23 TOTE £2.50: £1.90, £2.40; EX 12.30 Trifecta £28.40.
**Owner** Sexy Six Partnership **Bred** Cheveley Park Stud Ltd **Trained** Babworth, Notts

**FOCUS**
The order barely changed during this fillies' sprint handicap. The winner is rated back to his form from this time last year.

## 2097 QUICKSILVERSLOTS PLAY YOUR FAVOURITE £500 JACKPOT H'CAP 1m 6f (F)
**4:35** (4:35) (Class 5) (0-75,75) 4-Y-O+ **£2,587** (£770; £384; £192) **Stalls** Low

Form RPR
2363 **1** **Royal Marskell**[10] 1806 5-8-13 64.............................. TomEaves 2 74
(Alison Hutchinson) *hld up in tch: hdwy on inner 4f out: swtchd rt and effrt over 2f out: chal wl over 1f out: rdn to ld ent fnl f: drvn and kpt on wl towards fin* **14/1**

/11- **2** *2* **Mungo Park**[243] 6217 6-9-5 75.............................. DanielMuscutt(5) 1 82
(Gay Kelleway) *trckd ldrs: smooth hdwy 4f out: led wl over 2f out: rdn wl over 1f out: hdd and drvn ent fnl f: no ex last 100yds* **8/1**

0124 **3** *5* **Marina Ballerina**[10] 1806 6-8-9 65..............................(p) PhilipPrince(5) 7 65
(Roy Bowring) *led 5f: cl up: rdn along over 3f out: drvn over 2f out: grad wknd appr fnl f* **16/1**

2216 **4** *2* **Jacobs Son**[12] 1729 6-9-10 75.............................. TomQueally 6 72
(Michael Appleby) *hld up towards rr: rdn along and outpcd 4f out: plugged on u.p fnl 2f: n.d* **7/2**[2]

3-12 **5** *3/4* **Divea**[48] 1046 5-9-2 67.............................. WilliamCarson 5 63
(Anthony Carson) *t.k.h: trckd ldrs: hdwy and cl up 4f out: rdn along 3f out: drvn and wknd over 2f out* **5/1**[3]

212 **6** *shd* **Teajaybe (USA)**[30] 1366 6-9-9 74.............................. BenCurtis 9 70
(Chris Dwyer) *in tch: hdwy to trck ldrs 1/2-way: effrt on outer 3f out: rdn along over 2f out: sn drvn and btn* **11/10**[1]

5/60 **7** *32* **Switched Off**[12] 1729 9-9-0 65.............................. LukeMorris 3 16
(Kevin Frost) *cl up: led after 5f: rdn along 4f out: hdd wl over 2f out and sn wknd* **20/1**

/0-5 **8** *25* **Lady Amakhala**[30] 1366 6-9-2 67.............................. PJMcDonald 8
(George Moore) *in rr: pushed along after 4f: rdn along 1/2-way: sn bhd* **50/1**

3m 9.87s (1.57) **Going Correction** +0.20s/f (Slow) 8 Ran SP% **116.9**
Speed ratings (Par 103): **103,101,99,97,97 97,79,64**
CSF £121.61 CT £1819.41 TOTE £12.70: £5.00, £4.40, £4.60; EX 113.50 Trifecta £773.30.
**Owner** Miss Chantal Wootten **Bred** Miss V Woodward **Trained** Exning, Suffolk

**FOCUS**
An ordinary staying handicap which fell apart a bit. The winner winner rates a small personal best.

## 2098 QUICKSILVERSLOTS FUN ON THE HIGH STREET H'CAP 1m 3f (F)
**5:10** (5:10) (Class 5) (0-70,65) 3-Y-O **£2,587** (£770; £384; £192) **Stalls** Low

Form RPR
30-3 **1** **Cape Arrow**[10] 1792 3-8-13 57.............................. MartinLane 7 68+
(Paul Cole) *hld up in tch: pushed along over 4f out: rdn along and wd st: hdwy on outer to chal 2f out: led over 1f out: clr ins fnl f and kpt on strly* **9/4**[1]

2-00 **2** *3 1/4* **Master Dan**[9] 1847 3-9-4 65.............................. ConnorBeasley(3) 6 70
(James Given) *cl up: effrt over 3f out and sn led: rdn over 2f out: drvn and hdd over 1f out: kpt on same pce* **4/1**[3]

-232 **3** *4* **Hallouella**[49] 1032 3-9-5 63..............................(p) LukeMorris 3 61
(James Tate) *slt ld 1f: cl up: effrt 3f out: rdn over 2f out and ev ch tl drvn and one pce over 1f out* **5/1**

5-12 **4** *1/2* **Vosne Romanee**[9] 1840 3-8-8 52..............................(p) TomEaves 4 49
(Keith Dalgleish) *hld up in tch: hdwy over 3f out: swtchd lft and effrt wl over 2f out: sn rdn and ev ch: drvn over 1f out and sn wknd* **7/2**[2]

00-3 **5** *1/2* **Frosty The Snowman (IRE)**[17] 1608 3-9-6 64.............................. JamesSullivan 1 61
(Ruth Carr) *trckd ldrs on inner: hdwy over 3f out: rdn and cl up over 2f out: drvn and wknd over 1f out* **16/1**

6-30 **6** *6* **Zephyr**[16] 1635 3-9-0 65..............................(v[1]) RobJFitzpatrick(7) 2 51
(K R Burke) *awkward and reminders s: led after 1f: rdn along 4f out: hdd 3f out: drvn on inner and wknd fnl 2f* **5/1**

2m 31.64s (3.64) **Going Correction** +0.20s/f (Slow) 6 Ran SP% **112.2**
Speed ratings (Par 99): **94,91,88,88,88 83**
CSF £11.50 TOTE £3.50: £1.30, £3.20; EX 15.20 Trifecta £50.90.
**Owner** C Shiacolas **Bred** David John Brown **Trained** Whatcombe, Oxon

**FOCUS**
A modest 3yo handicap. The winner built on his Bath level.

T/Plt: £37.10 to a £1 stake. Pool: £43,107.50 - 846.95 winning tickets. T/Qpdt: £33.10 to a £1 stake. Pool: £3,299.72 - 73.60 winning tickets. JR

## [1782]LONGCHAMP (R-H)

Thursday, May 8

**OFFICIAL GOING: Turf: good to soft**

**2106a** **PRIX D'HEDOUVILLE (GROUP 3) (4YO+) (TURF)** **1m 4f**
**1:50** (12:00) 4-Y-O+ **£33,333** (£13,333; £10,000; £6,666; £3,333)

RPR

1 **Spiritjim (FR)**[21] 1552 4-8-10 0 ow1 ChristopheSoumillon 3 112
(P Bary, France) *led: shkn up whn jnd by eventual runner-up 2f out: rdn over 1f out: styd on strly and grad asserted again ins fnl f: in control towards fin: shade cosily* **21/10**[2]

2 ¾ **Meleagros (IRE)**[21] 1552 5-8-9 0 AdrienFouassier 4 109
(Alain Couetil, France) *midfield in tch on inner: hdwy into st: rdn to chal and jnd eventual wnr 2f out: styd on wl u.p but hdd ins fnl f and hld towards fin* **74/10**

3 2½ **Singing (FR)**[32] 1341 4-8-11 0 OlivierPeslier 5 107
(C Laffon-Parias, France) *t.k.h: midfield in tch on outer: pushed along 2f out: rdn and wnt 3rd ent fnl f: edgd rt u.p: styd on but nt pce of front pair and sn wl hld* **33/10**[3]

4 nk **Gosh (IRE)**[39] 4-8-8 0 Christophe-PatriceLemaire 6 104
(Mme Pia Brandt, France) *hld up in last pair: rdn 2f out: outpcd in last ent fnl f: styd on wl fnl 100yds and wnt 4th cl home: nvr nrr* **12/1**

5 ½ **Spirit's Revench (FR)**[14] 4-8-9 0 ThierryJarnet 1 104
(P Demercastel, France) *dwlt sltly and hld up in last: rdn 2f out: kpt on same pce and n.d* **202/10**

6 ½ **Au Revoir (IRE)**[21] 1552 4-8-9 0 MaximeGuyon 7 103
(A Fabre, France) *trckd ldr on outer: rdn and brief effrt to chal 2f out: sn outpcd by front pair: no ex and fdd ins fnl f* **19/10**[1]

7 1¼ **Tunkwa (FR)**[39] 1206 4-8-6 0 TheoBachelot 2 98
(D Sepulchre, France) *trckd ldr on inner: rdn and lost pl over 2f out: outpcd in 6th and btn whn sltly short of room ins fnl f: dropped to last sn after* **184/10**

2m 37.77s (7.37) **7** Ran SP% **119.5**
WIN (incl. 1 euro stake): 3.10. PLACES: 1.90, 3.10. SF: 21.20.
**Owner** Hspirit **Bred** Haras Des Sablonnets Et Al **Trained** Chantilly, France

## [1866]ASCOT (R-H)

Friday, May 9

**OFFICIAL GOING: Straight course - good; round course - good to soft (good in places; stands' side 7.3, centre 7.3, farside 7.2, round 7.2)**

Rail on Round course moved in 3yds from 12f to Home st, adding 9yds to Old Mile and 16yds to 2m race.

Wind: Light, against Weather: Fine but cloudy

**2107** **MILWARD PRINTING IRISH EBF MAIDEN FILLIES' STKS (BOBIS RACE)** **5f**
**5:35** (5:39) (Class 4) 2-Y-O **£5,175** (£1,540; £769; £384) **Stalls** High

Form RPR

1 **Dangerous Moonlite (IRE)** 2-9-0 0 RichardHughes 11 83+
(Richard Hannon) *mde virtually all: def advantage wl over 1f out: pushed out: readily* **7/1**

2 1 **Ajmal Ihsaas** 2-9-0 0 LukeMorris 12 79+
(Marco Botti) *towards rr: prog on nr side 2f out: rdn to chse wnr 1f out: styd on but unable to chal* **12/1**

3 1¾ **Falling Petals (IRE)** 2-9-0 0 RobertHavlin 14 73
(John Gosden) *w wnr to 2f out: lost 2nd and one pce 1f out* **13/2**[3]

4 1 **Golden Zephyr (IRE)** 2-9-0 0 PaulHanagan 13 70
(J W Hills) *t.k.h: hld up in midfield: pushed along wl over 1f out: kpt on same pce* **33/1**

5 nk **Showcard** 2-9-0 0 JimmyFortune 1 68+
(Gary Moore) *dwlt: sn detached in last: stl last over 1f out: gd prog fnl f: gng on at fin* **50/1**

6 nse **Crawford Avenue** 2-9-0 0 AdamKirby 4 68+
(Clive Cox) *difficult to load into stalls: dwlt: pushed along in rr: swtchd to outer and prog 1/2-way: rdn and kpt on one pce fr over 1f out* **12/1**

5 7 ½ **Belle Fille**[22] 1528 2-9-0 0 JimCrowley 9 66
(David Brown) *towards rr: pushed along and prog 2f out: no imp on ldrs fr 1f out* **4/1**[1]

8 3 **Hikayati (IRE)** 2-9-0 0 SebSanders 10 56
(William Haggas) *chsd ldrs: shkn up 2f out: hanging after and no prog: fdd fnl f* **8/1**

9 shd **Kinematic** 2-9-0 0 DavidProbert 8 55+
(Andrew Balding) *hld up in tch towards outer: nt clr run jst over 2f out and swtchd rt: rn green whn shkn up over 1f out: wknd* **8/1**

10 4½ **Arabian Queen (IRE)** 2-9-0 0 LiamKeniry 3 39+
(David Elsworth) *dwlt: rcvrd and prom on outer: wknd qckly over 1f out* **6/1**[2]

2 11 3¾ **Stinky Socks (IRE)**[20] 1571 2-9-0 0 WilliamBuick 2 26
(Charles Hills) *prom but sn pushed along: lost pl 1/2-way: sn wl btn* **4/1**[1]

1m 3.36s (2.86) **Going Correction** +0.30s/f (Good) **11** Ran SP% **122.6**
Speed ratings (Par 92): **89,87,84,83,82 82,81,76,76,69 63**
CSF £91.83 TOTE £5.70: £1.90, £2.60, £3.00; EX 112.30 Trifecta £472.00.
**Owner** Mrs J Wood **Bred** J K Thoroughbreds **Trained** East Everleigh, Wilts

**FOCUS**

Rail on Round course moved in 3yds from 1m4f to home straight, adding 9yds to Old Mile and 16yds to 2m race. The ground was drying out and the opener was run in a time 3.86sec outside the standard. This maiden was won a year ago by Rizeena, who went on to win in Group 1 company. Like the race's three earlier winners, she came here with a previous run under her belt, but this year's renewal was dominated by debutantes. It was dominated by those draw high too, the first four coming from the highest four stalls. Winners should come out of it.

**2108** **CENTERPLATE H'CAP** **2m**
**6:05** (6:06) (Class 3) (0-90,89) 4-Y-O+
**£7,470** (£2,236; £1,118; £559; £279; £140) **Stalls** Low

Form RPR

12-3 1 **Chocala (IRE)**[13] 1735 4-9-3 85 RichardHughes 5 94+
(Alan King) *hld up bhd ldng pair: clsd to go 2nd 2f out: rdn to ld jst ins fnl f: narrow but decisive advantage after: pushed out nr fin* **11/8**[1]

1343 2 nk **Sir Frank Morgan (IRE)**[4] 2011 4-8-2 70 JoeFanning 3 78
(Mark Johnston) *trckd ldr: led over 2f out: drvn and hdd jst ins fnl f: kpt on wl but a hld* **10/1**

001- 3 1½ **Sohar**[189] 7660 6-9-5 84 SebSanders 4 90
(James Toller) *hld up disputing 5th: pushed along whn pce lifted over 5f out: drvn and prog over 2f out: chsd ldng pair jst over 1f out: kpt on same pce* **7/2**[2]

5-05 4 1¾ **Albonny (IRE)**[14] 1692 5-8-5 70 LukeMorris 9 74
(Alan Jarvis) *hld up in 7th: rdn 3f out: kpt on u.p to take 4th fnl f: n.d* **33/1**

1310 5 ½ **Arr' Kid (USA)**[21] 1556 4-8-11 79 (b) TomEaves 7 82
(Keith Dalgleish) *led at generous pce early: tried to kick on over 5f out: hdd and nt qckn over 2f out: fdd* **16/1**

03-6 6 6 **Argent Knight**[30] 1383 4-9-7 89 (v) SteveDrowne 1 85
(William Jarvis) *trckd ldng pair: rdn wl over 2f out: wknd wl over 1f out* **10/1**

32-2 7 1 **Ashdown Lad**[10] 1849 5-8-12 77 PaulHanagan 6 72
(Tom Symonds) *hld up disputing 5th: rdn whn pce lifted over 5f out: no prog over 2f out: wknd* **9/1**

050- 8 ½ **Swinging Hawk (GER)**[132] 8429 8-8-10 80 ow1 (t) GeorgeDowning(5) 2 74
(Ian Williams) *hld up in last: lost tch whn pce lifted over 5f out: brought wd in st and shkn up: no prog* **8/1**[3]

3m 33.29s (4.29) **Going Correction** +0.45s/f (Yiel)
**WFA** 4 from 5yo+ 3lb **8** Ran SP% **112.4**
Speed ratings (Par 107): **107,106,106,105,104 101,101,101**
CSF £15.92 CT £40.05 TOTE £2.10: £1.10, £2.30, £1.60; EX 13.80 Trifecta £63.80.
**Owner** High 5 **Bred** Peter Harris **Trained** Barbury Castle, Wilts

**FOCUS**

The 2009 winner Judgethemoment went on to take the Ascot Stakes over an extra half-mile at the Royal Meeting. They went an ordinary pace in this fair staying handicap and the order barely changed until they had turned for home. The winner continues to progress and the form is rated at face value.

**2109** **ON 5 MAIDEN FILLIES' STKS** **1m 2f**
**6:40** (6:40) (Class 4) 3-Y-O+ **£5,175** (£1,540; £769; £384) **Stalls** Low

Form RPR

4 1 **Marsh Daisy**[28] 1423 3-8-12 0 JimmyFortune 8 88+
(Hughie Morrison) *trckd ldrs in 5th: shkn up over 2f out: prog to chse ldr over 1f out: led ins fnl f: edgd lft and jst hld on* **6/4**[1]

203- 2 shd **Toast Of The Town (IRE)**[301] 4257 4-9-13 84 WilliamBuick 5 89+
(John Gosden) *trckd ldr: led over 2f out: drifted lft u.p after: hdd ins fnl f: kpt on wl: jst failed* **5/1**[3]

3 1¾ **Wonderstruck (IRE)** 3-8-12 0 FrankieDettori 3 85+
(William Haggas) *trckd ldng pair: rdn over 2f out: tried to cl over 1f out: styd on same pce* **5/2**[2]

4 3 **Rewaaya (IRE)** 3-8-12 0 PaulHanagan 7 79+
(John Gosden) *dwlt: t.k.h early in last pair: prog jst over 2f out: hanging bdly and green whn shkn up over 1f out: kpt on fnl f* **9/1**

5 1¼ **Cabin Fever** 3-8-12 0 JimCrowley 11 76+
(Ralph Beckett) *trckd ldng pair: sing to be outpcd whn short of room briefly wl over 1f out: pushed along and one pce after: nt disgracd* **16/1**

4-0 6 1¼ **Intense Tango**[28] 1423 3-8-12 0 KierenFallon 1 74
(Alan Jarvis) *led: rdn and hdd over 2f out: wknd over 1f out* **33/1**

6 7 1¼ **Prairie Rose (GER)**[20] 1587 3-8-12 0 HarryBentley 9 71
(Olly Stevens) *v awkward s: mostly in last pair: rdn and sme prog 3f out: rn green and no hdwy 2f out* **25/1**

8 3½ **Quenelle** 3-8-12 0 SeanLevey 4 64
(Ed Dunlop) *nvr bttr than midfield: pushed along and steadily lft bhd fr over 2f out* **50/1**

9 3 **Pink Diamond** 3-8-12 0 JohnFahy 6 58
(Eve Johnson Houghton) *dwlt: a in rr: pushed along over 3f out: no prog and wl btn 2f out* **66/1**

0 10 10 **Cypress Point (FR)**[50] 1024 3-8-12 0 JimmyQuinn 10 38
(Ed Vaughan) *nbever bttr than midfield: shkn up and no prog over 2f out: wknd: t.o* **66/1**

0- 11 7 **Stars Aligned (IRE)**[205] 7295 3-8-12 0 RichardHughes 2 24
(Richard Hannon) *in tch in midfield: shkn up over 2f out: wknd over 1f out: eased and t.o* **16/1**

2m 10.2s (2.80) **Going Correction** +0.45s/f (Yiel)
**WFA** 3 from 4yo 15lb **11** Ran SP% **118.7**
Speed ratings (Par 102): **106,105,104,102,101 100,99,96,93,85 80**
CSF £9.22 TOTE £2.90: £1.10, £2.10, £1.60; EX 8.60 Trifecta £29.90.
**Owner** Sir Thomas Pilkington **Bred** Meon Valley Stud **Trained** East Ilsley, Berks
■ Stewards' Enquiry : William Buick four-day ban: used whip above permitted level (May 23,24,26,27)

**FOCUS**

An interesting fillies' maiden with a fine finish. The pace wasn't great. Decent form, the runner-up rated to the same mark as when second last year.

**2110** **MILES & MORRISON H'CAP** **6f**
**7:15** (7:17) (Class 3) (0-95,94) 4-Y-O+ **£7,762** (£1,732; £1,732; £577) **Stalls** Centre

Form RPR

3-35 1 **Blessington (IRE)**[25] 1492 4-9-0 87 (t) WilliamBuick 8 102
(John Gosden) *s.i.s: hld up in last pair: swtchd to wd outside jst over 2f out: gd prog after: swept into ld ins fnl f: sn clr* **5/1**[2]

2113 2 3¼ **Hillbilly Boy (IRE)**[13] 1734 4-9-0 87 AndreaAtzeni 15 92+
(Martin Smith) *led trio towards nr side and wl on terms: overall ldr over 2f out: dashed for home wl over 1f out: hdd and brushed aside ins fnl f* **4/1**[1]

0-32 2 dht **Red Refraction (IRE)**[22] 1538 4-8-8 81 SeanLevey 5 86+
(Richard Hannon) *hld up in rr: nowhere to go jst over 2f out and dropped to last: prog over 1f out: r.o wl fnl f to join runner-up on line* **14/1**

015- 4 2 **Milly's Gift**[225] 6768 4-9-1 88 AdamKirby 10 87
(Clive Cox) *hld up in midfield: prog 2f out: disp 2nd over 1f out: outpcd after* **14/1**

00-0 5 1 **Secret Witness**[40] 1193 8-9-7 94 (b) SteveDrowne 9 89
(Ronald Harris) *hld up in midfield: lost pl and in rr 2f out: prog over 1f out: kpt on fnl f but nvr a threat* **25/1**

040- 6 2¾ **Gabbiano**[223] 6831 5-8-12 88 RobertTart(3) 7 75
(Jeremy Gask) *n.m.r s: hld up wl in rr: promising prog over 2f out: hanging and fnd nil over 1f out: wknd fnl f* **14/1**

-503 7 shd **Trader Jack**[4] 2030 5-8-4 80 MichaelJMMurphy(3) 11 66
(David Flood) *dwlt: wl in rr: rdn over 2f out: modest prog over 1f out: nvr a threat* **8/1**

103- 8 1 **Shore Step (IRE)**[237] 6382 4-8-9 85 WilliamTwiston-Davies(3) 6 68
(Mick Channon) *prom gng strly: rdn 2f out: wknd jst over 1f out* **25/1**

520- **9** *3 ¼* **Fairway To Heaven (IRE)**[216] 7013 5-9-6 **93**............. FrankieDettori 13 66
(Michael Wigham) *dwlt: wl adrift of other pair that racd towards nr side: shkn up over 2f out: rchd midfield over 1f out: wknd fnl f* **8/1**

35-6 **10** *3* **Extrasolar**[13] 1731 4-8-11 **84**..............................................(t) JimCrowley 4 47
(Amanda Perrett) *nvr beyond in midfield: rdn and no prog wl over 1f out: wknd* **20/1**

3-22 **11** *1 ¼* **Joey's Destiny (IRE)**[25] 1492 4-9-2 **89**........................... PatCosgrave 1 48
(George Baker) *a towards rr: rdn and no prog over 2f out: wknd over 1f out* **13/2**[3]

00-4 **12** *1 ¼* **Clear Spring (IRE)**[13] 1734 6-9-6 **93**................................ TomEaves 3 48
(John Spearing) *chsd ldrs: rdn over 2f out: wknd over 1f out* **16/1**

010- **13** *hd* **Cruise Tothelimit (IRE)**[208] 7222 6-8-9 **82**................. PaulHanagan 12 36
(Ian Williams) *overall ldr 2f: styd prom tl wknd wl over 1f out* **40/1**

010- **14** *2 ¾* **B Fifty Two (IRE)**[223] 6831 5-9-1 **88**................................ SebSanders 17 34
(J W Hills) *chsd ldr in trio towards nr side: wknd 2f out* **25/1**

-221 **15** *11* **Firmdecisions (IRE)**[51] 1020 4-9-2 **89**..........................(v) KierenFallon 2
(Brett Johnson) *racd freely: overall ldr after 2f to over 2f out: wknd rapidly: t.o* **8/1**

1m 14.96s (0.46) **Going Correction** +0.30s/f (Good) **15** Ran SP% **128.0**
Speed ratings (Par 107): **108,103,103,101,99 96,95,94,90,86 84,82,82,78,64**
WIN: 5.90 Blessington; PL: 4.80 Red Refraction, 2.10 Hillbilly Boy, 2.40 Blessington; EX: 11.30, 52.50; CSF: 12.48, 36.19; TC: 142.11, 162.84; TF: 243.00, 497.60;.
**Owner** HRH Princess Haya Of Jordan **Bred** David John Brown **Trained** Newmarket, Suffolk

**FOCUS**
A competitive handicap in which the bulk of the field raced down the centre, with three of them racing more towards the stands' side. A clear personal best from the winner.

## 2111 PADDY POWER H'CAP (BOBIS RACE) 7f
**7:50** (7:50) (Class 2) (0-105,95) 3-Y-O **£19,407** (£5,775; £2,886; £1,443) **Stalls** Centre

Form RPR

4-03 **1** **Brazos (IRE)**[28] 1420 3-9-7 **95**................................ WilliamBuick 8 102
(Clive Brittain) *cl up: shkn up 2f out: clsd to ld jst over 1f out: rdn and styd on wl* **7/2**[1]

-023 **2** *1 ¼* **Wee Jean**[18] 1614 3-8-8 **85**........................ WilliamTwiston-Davies(3) 3 89
(Mick Channon) *w.w towards rr: prog over 2f out: rdn to chse wnr fnl f: styd on but no imp* **8/1**

0-30 **3** *1 ¼* **Mr Matthews (IRE)**[14] 1693 3-8-7 **81**................................ BenCurtis 7 82
(K R Burke) *hld up in rr: drvn and prog over 1f out: styd on fnl f to take 3rd last strides* **12/1**

1102 **4** *hd* **Crowdmania**[10] 1861 3-8-10 **84**........................................ JoeFanning 6 84
(Mark Johnston) *led: shkn up 2f out: hdd jst over 1f out: fdd* **6/1**[3]

2-13 **5** *nk* **Hagree (IRE)**[20] 1580 3-8-11 **85**...................................... AntonioFresu 10 84
(Marco Botti) *prom: urged along and nt qckn fr 2f out: kpt on again ins fnl f* **6/1**[3]

030- **6** *shd* **Mawfoor (IRE)**[225] 6765 3-9-6 **94**................................ PaulHanagan 9 93
(Brian Meehan) *hld up in tch: rdn and nt qckn jst over 2f out: sn outpcd: kpt on ins fnl f* **10/1**

2-45 **7** *1 ½* **Sir Robert Cheval**[21] 1555 3-9-7 **95**.................................. AdamKirby 1 90
(Marco Botti) *hld up in last: drvn and prog over 1f out: chsd ldrs ins fnl f: nvr on terms and fdd nr fin* **5/1**[2]

1503 **8** *8* **Can't Change It (IRE)**[7] 1913 3-8-3 **77**............................ LukeMorris 5 51
(David Simcock) *mostly chsd ldr to 2f out: sn wknd* **10/1**

25-0 **9** *3* **Cool Bahamian (IRE)**[21] 1563 3-9-0 **88**............................ JimCrowley 2 55
(Eve Johnson Houghton) *a towards rr on outer: wknd over 2f out* **16/1**

1603 **10** *1 ¾* **Lady Frances**[6] 1937 3-9-1 **89**...................................... RichardHughes 4 51
(Mark Johnston) *prom on outer: pushed along and wknd 2f out: eased ins fnl f* **12/1**

1m 29.81s (2.21) **Going Correction** +0.30s/f (Good) **10** Ran SP% **118.0**
Speed ratings (Par 105): **99,97,96,95,95 95,93,84,81,79**
CSF £32.30 CT £313.06 TOTE £4.10: £1.50, £2.60, £3.90; EX 29.60 Trifecta £1170.20.
**Owner** Saeed Manana **Bred** John O'Kelly Bloodstock Services **Trained** Newmarket, Suffolk

**FOCUS**
A valuable handicap, but not a particularly strong race for the grade with the topweights running off 10lb less than the permitted maximum. The 2012 winner Sovereign Debt was runner-up in last year's Lockinge. The form makes a fair bit of sense.

## 2112 PADDY POWER MOBILE APP H'CAP (BOBIS RACE) 1m (S)
**8:20** (8:21) (Class 4) (0-85,85) 3-Y-O £5,175 (£1,540; £769; £384) **Stalls** Centre

Form RPR

6-21 **1** **Zerfaal**[20] 1582 3-9-2 **80**.............................................. PaulHanagan 10 89+
(John Gosden) *hld up in tch: prog to trck ldr 2f: led over 1f out: hrd pressed fnl f: styd on wl* **3/1**[1]

631- **2** *nk* **Donncha (IRE)**[177] 7853 3-8-12 **76**.............................. AndreaAtzeni 11 84
(Robert Eddery) *wl in tch: prog 2f out: drvn to chse wnr jst over 1f out: str chal fnl f: styd on but a jst hld* **3/1**[1]

11-4 **3** *1 ¾* **Cricklewood Green (USA)**[14] 1696 3-9-5 **83**............. RichardHughes 2 87
(Richard Hannon) *settled in rr: pushed along 3f out: prog u.p wl over 1f out: kpt on wl fnl f to win battle for 3rd: nvr gng pce to chal* **5/1**[3]

61 **4** *nse* **Thanks Harry**[24] 1498 3-8-10 **74**................................... JimmyFortune 5 78
(Gary Moore) *hld up in rr: prog 2f out: rdn to chse ldng pair fnl f: styd on but no imp last 150yds: lost 3rd fnl strides* **20/1**

34-0 **5** *8* **Malachim Mist (IRE)**[35] 1279 3-9-5 **83**......................... FrankieDettori 3 68
(Richard Hannon) *hld up in last pair: rdn and prog on outer over 2f out: tried to cl on ldrs over 1f out: wknd fnl f* **20/1**

123- **6** *1* **Homestretch**[279] 4988 3-9-2 **80**...................................... WilliamBuick 6 63
(Mick Channon) *prom: rdn over 2f out: nt pce to chal over 1f out: wknd fnl f* **16/1**

3341 **7** *½* **Basil Berry**[13] 1714 3-9-1 **79**........................................ BenCurtis 4 61
(Chris Dwyer) *led at gd pce: rdn and hdd over 1f out: wknd* **16/1**

1-5 **8** *6* **Champagne Sydney (IRE)**[22] 1540 3-9-7 **85**.................... SeanLevey 1 53
(Richard Hannon) *towards rr: rdn wl over 2f out: sn wknd* **25/1**

0-13 **9** *1 ¾* **Grevillea (IRE)**[22] 1540 3-9-4 **85**................ WilliamTwiston-Davies(3) 7 49
(Mick Channon) *wl in tch: rdn over 2f out: wknd qckly wl over 1f out* **20/1**

01-2 **10** *8* **Secret Archive (USA)**[20] 1586 3-9-2 **80**........................ JimCrowley 8 26
(Ralph Beckett) *chsd ldr to over 2f out: wknd rapidly and eased* **4/1**[2]

43-6 **11** *10* **Berrahri (IRE)**[8] 1907 3-9-2 **80**...................................... FergusSweeney 9
(John Best) *racd freely: prom to 3f out: wknd rapidly: t.o* **33/1**

1m 43.32s (2.52) **Going Correction** +0.30s/f (Good) **11** Ran SP% **119.5**
Speed ratings (Par 101): **99,98,96,96,88 87,87,81,79,71 61**
CSF £10.92 CT £44.76 TOTE £3.80: £1.60, £2.20, £2.00; EX 16.40 Trifecta £58.50.
**Owner** Hamdan Al Maktoum **Bred** Shadwell Estate Company Limited **Trained** Newmarket, Suffolk

**FOCUS**
A fair handicap in which four came clear. Handicap debutants who won maidens last time came to the fore, and this could be form to follow. The winner and second came out of the two highest stalls.

T/Jkpt: Part won. £7100.00 to a £1 stake. Pool of £1000.00 - 0.50 winning units. T/Plt: £50.80 to a £1 stake. Pool of £136526.35 - 1961.47 winning tickets. T/Qpdt: £7.70 to a £1 stake. Pool of £8096.84 - 777.35 winning tickets. JN

# [2085]CHESTER (L-H)
Friday, May 9

**OFFICIAL GOING: Soft (7.2)**
Rail moved out a further 3yds from 6f to drop-in at 1.5f. 24yds added to races 1, 5 & 6, 26yds to race 2, 44yds to race 3, 20yds to race 4 and 38yds to race 7.
Wind: Moderate, against Weather: Fine

## 2113 SPORTINGBET.COM EARL GROSVENOR H'CAP 7f 122y
**1:45** (1:45) (Class 2) (0-105,103) 4-Y-O+ **£15,762** (£4,715; £2,357; £1,180; £587) **Stalls** Low

Form RPR

140- **1** **Here Comes When (IRE)**[324] 3455 4-8-10 **95**............ OisinMurphy(3) 1 111
(Andrew Balding) *racd keenly: in tch: swtchd rt and clsd over 4f out: rdn to ld over 1f out: styd on wl to draw clr ins fnl f* **2/1**[1]

31 **2** *5* **Abseil (USA)**[18] 1612 4-8-9 **91**........................................ RyanMoore 13 95+
(Sir Michael Stoute) *dwlt: hld up in rr: pushed along over 2f out: hdwy whn swtchd rt over 1f out: wnt 2nd ins fnl f: edgd rt and styd on: nt trble wnr* **9/2**[2]

100- **3** *2 ½* **Pacific Heights (IRE)**[216] 7014 5-8-13 **95**........................ DaleSwift 8 92
(Brian Ellison) *towards rr: hld up: rdn and hdwy whn nt clr run over 1f out: styd on ins fnl f: tk 3rd nr fin: nt trble front two* **10/1**

340- **4** *hd* **Laffan (IRE)**[150] 8231 5-8-8 **90**...................................... DavidAllan 14 87
(Tim Easterby) *midfield: rdn 2f out: hdwy over 1f out: kpt on ins fnl f: no imp on ldrs* **12/1**

1320 **5** *3 ¾* **Apostle (IRE)**[76] 715 5-8-8 **90**......................................(p) JoeFanning 6 77
(David Simcock) *prom: chalng 2f out: rdn over 1f out: btn ins fnl f* **25/1**

420- **6** *3 ¼* **Deauville Prince (FR)**[426] 953 4-9-0 **103**.................... JennyPowell(7) 3 82
(Tom Dascombe) *led: pressed 2f out: rdn and hdd over 1f out: wknd fnl f* **25/1**

1210 **7** *6* **Frontier Fighter**[21] 1558 6-8-12 **94**............................... DanielTudhope 4 58
(David O'Meara) *trckd ldrs: pushed along over 2f out: wknd over 1f out* **8/1**[3]

0-05 **8** *5* **Balty Boys (IRE)**[13] 1719 5-8-13 **95**.............................(p) BarryMcHugh 10 47
(Brian Ellison) *hmpd s: towards rr: rdn on outer and sme hdwy into midfield 3f out: sn lost pl: bhd fnl 2f* **8/1**[3]

60-5 **9** *10* **Pintura**[27] 1443 7-9-4 **100**...........................................(p) JamieSpencer 9 27
(Kevin Ryan) *pushed along early towards rr: rdn 2f out: nvr on terms* **10/1**

10-0 **10** *52* **Big Johnny D (IRE)**[13] 1719 5-9-0 **96**..................(b[1]) GrahamGibbons 2
(David Barron) *worked hrd to r w ldr tl checked in bhd over 5f out: wknd qckly over 4f out: lost tch 3f out: t.o* **17/2**

1m 38.63s (4.83) **Going Correction** +0.875s/f (Soft) **10** Ran SP% **117.8**
Speed ratings (Par 109): **110,105,102,102,98 95,89,84,74,22**
CSF £10.68 CT £71.68 TOTE £3.00: £1.30, £1.50, £3.40; EX 12.60 Trifecta £97.30.
**Owner** Mrs Fitri Hay **Bred** Old Carhue & Graeng Bloodstock **Trained** Kingsclere, Hants
■ Stewards' Enquiry : David Allan caution: careless riding.
Jenny Powell three-day ban: careless riding (May 23,24,26)

**FOCUS**
Rail moved out a further 3yds (6yds in total) from 6f until 'drop in' at 1.5f. Consequently 24yds added to races 1, 5 & 6, 26yds to race 2, 44yds to race 3, 20yds to race 4 and 38yds to race 7. Following the opener, Ryan Moore described the ground as "soft", while David Allan felt it was "very tacky". They avoided the rail in the straight, as was the case all afternoon. The right horses came to the fore in what was a decent handicap. The winner improved on the bare form of his C7D win last year.

## 2114 BETFAIR CASH OUT DEE STKS (LISTED RACE) (C&G) 1m 2f 75y
**2:15** (2:15) (Class 1) 3-Y-O
**£42,532** (£16,125; £8,070; £4,020; £2,017; £1,012) **Stalls** High

Form RPR

35-5 **1** **Kingfisher (IRE)**[27] 1458 3-9-0 98.............................. JosephO'Brien 3 101
(A P O'Brien, Ire) *trckd ldrs: effrt 2f out: wnt 2nd wl over 1f out: styd on ins fnl f: led towards fin* **11/4**[1]

-015 **2** *1* **Bow Creek (IRE)**[21] 1563 3-9-3 104.............................. FrannyNorton 5 102
(Mark Johnston) *racd keenly: w ldr: helped inrease pce over 4f out: led over 2f out: rdn and abt 3 l clr over 1f out: hrd pressed wl ins fnl f: worn down and no ex towards fin* **5/1**[3]

20-5 **3** *1* **Somewhat (USA)**[23] 1516 3-9-3 109................................ JoeFanning 7 100
(Mark Johnston) *in tch: lost pl over 4f out: struggling to go pce over 2f out: styd on u.p ins fnl f: tk 3rd fnl 150yds: nt quite get to ldrs* **11/4**[1]

0- **4** *1 ¾* **Century (IRE)**[195] 7528 3-9-0 0...................................... RyanMoore 2 94
(A P O'Brien, Ire) *hld up: niggled along whn pce increased over 4f out: u.p and gng nowhere over 2f out: styd on and wanted to lug lft ins fnl f: nvr able to trble ldrs* **3/1**[2]

6-21 **5** *shd* **Zampa Manos (USA)**[20] 1580 3-9-0 90.......................... OisinMurphy 4 94
(Andrew Balding) *led: increased pce over 4f out: rdn 3f out: hdd over 2f out: styd on same pce u.p fnl f* **10/1**

0 **6** *3 ¾* **Randwick (IRE)**[22] 1529 3-9-0 0................................... JamieSpencer 6 87
(Charles Hills) *hld up: hdwy 5f out: sn prom on outer: pushed along over 3f out: rdn and nt qckn 2f out: wknd 1f out* **14/1**

**7** *8* **Drummore Road (IRE)**[12] 1778 3-9-0 0........................... RonanWhelan 1 73
(John Patrick Shanahan, Ire) *missed break: in rr: rdn 3f out: no imp: nvr on terms* **50/1**

2m 20.49s (9.29) **Going Correction** +0.925s/f (Soft) **7** Ran SP% **112.7**
Speed ratings (Par 107): **99,98,97,96,95 92,86**
CSF £16.40 TOTE £3.50: £2.00, £3.80; EX 17.00 Trifecta £55.90.
**Owner** Derrick Smith & Mrs John Magnier & Michael Tabor **Bred** Whisperview Trading Ltd **Trained** Cashel, Co Tipperary
■ Stewards' Enquiry : Franny Norton one-day ban: careless riding (May 23)

**FOCUS**
An open edition of this race, which has lost its Group 3 status, and it proved quite a muddling affair, with the pace, which had been steady early on, suddenly lifting over 4f out and catching several of them out. It's hard to see any of these going on to make a serious impact at Epsom. This was a weak renewal and it didn't look strong form even for a Listed race.

## 2115 BOODLES DIAMOND ORMONDE STKS (GROUP 3) 1m 5f 89y
**2:45** (2:45) (Class 1) 4-Y-O+ **£42,532** (£16,125; £8,070; £4,020) **Stalls** Low

Form RPR

150- **1** **Brown Panther**[185] 7761 6-9-0 0.................................. RichardKingscote 6 117
(Tom Dascombe) *sluggish s: wnt 2nd after 1f: led over 3f out: tried to assert over 2f out: rdn 1f out: gamely kpt finding ex ins fnl f: styd on wl* **6/4**[2]

46-0 **2** 2¼ **Hillstar**[41] 1183 4-9-0 115 ... RyanMoore 3 114
(Sir Michael Stoute) *wore hood in paddock: trckd ldrs: wnt 2nd wl over 2f out: sn pushed along: rdn abt 2 l down and trying to chal over 1f out: no imp and kpt on same pce fnl 100yds* **4/5**[1]

3-66 **3** 16 **Banoffee (IRE)**[78] 682 4-8-11 100 ... OisinMurphy 4 87
(Hughie Morrison) *racd keenly: restrained after 1f: hld up in rr after: rdn 3f out: struggling to go pce after: wnt poor 3rd 2f out: no ch w front two* **10/1**[3]

340- **4** 17 **Jathabah (IRE)**[216] 7020 4-8-11 97 ... JamieSpencer 5 61
(Clive Brittain) *led: rdn and hdd over 3f out: wknd wl over 2f out* **25/1**

3m 5.96s (13.26) **Going Correction** +0.975s/f (Soft) 4 Ran SP% **108.5**
Speed ratings (Par 113): **98,96,86,76**
CSF £3.06 TOTE £3.50; EX 2.70 Trifecta £4.40.
**Owner** A Black & Owen Promotions Limited **Bred** Owen Promotions Ltd **Trained** Malpas, Cheshire

**FOCUS**
With two of the major players, Ernest Hemingway and Mount Athos, coming out on account of soft ground, this was left to look a straight match and the big two duly came clear. Brown Panther looked at least as good as ever.

## 2116 CRABBIE'S EBF STALLIONS H'CAP (BOBIS RACE) 5f 16y
3:15 (3:15) (Class 2) (0-105,96) 3-Y-O £15,752 (£4,715; £2,357; £1,180; £587) Stalls Low

Form RPR
61-2 **1** **Blithe Spirit**[27] 1445 3-8-11 **89** ... JasonHart(3) 4 97
(Eric Alston) *mde all: rdn to go clr over 1f out: r.o wl* **11/4**[2]

21-6 **2** 2¾ **Viva Verglas (IRE)**[5] 1968 3-9-7 **96** ... (b) GrahamGibbons 1 94
(David Barron) *dwlt and awkward at s: sn chsd ldrs: rdn to take 2nd over 1f out but unable to go w wnr: no imp fnl f* **5/1**[3]

10-0 **3** ½ **Ventura Mist**[23] 1518 3-9-7 **96** ... (p) DuranFentiman 3 92
(Tim Easterby) *dwlt: in rr: sn pushed along: rdn over 1f out: styd on ins fnl f: nvr able to chal* **8/1**

02-2 **4** hd **See The Sun**[31] 1358 3-9-1 **90** ... DavidAllan 7 85
(Tim Easterby) *in rr: effrt for press on outer wl over 1f out: styd on ins fnl f: nvr able to chal* **2/1**[1]

5 **5** 1 **Fine Cut (IRE)**[23] 1520 3-9-1 **90** ... (p) FMBerry 5 82
(T Stack, Ire) *in tch: sn niggled along: pushed along over 2f out: sn outpcd: no imp after* **13/2**

15-5 **6** 3½ **Fine 'n Dandy (IRE)**[30] 1397 3-9-6 **95** ... RichardKingscote 6 74
(Tom Dascombe) *chsd wnr tl rdn over 1f out: wknd fnl 150yds* **9/1**

1m 4.78s (3.78) **Going Correction** +1.025s/f (Soft) 6 Ran SP% **111.1**
Speed ratings (Par 105): **110,105,104,104,102 97**
CSF £16.24 TOTE £3.70: £1.60, £3.10; EX 14.30 Trifecta £64.00.
**Owner** Liam & Tony Ferguson **Bred** Liam & Tony Ferguson **Trained** Longton, Lancs

**FOCUS**
No hanging around here. Another personal best from the winner.

## 2117 BETFAIR PRICE RUSH H'CAP 7f 2y
3:50 (3:50) (Class 4) (0-85,85) 4-Y-O+ £7,762 (£2,310; £1,154; £577) Stalls Low

Form RPR
4544 **1** **Verse Of Love**[16] 1646 5-9-4 **82** ... JFEgan 4 93
(David Evans) *tried to get down in stalls and awkward s: displayed gd pce to r w ldr: led 4f out: rdn 2f out: asserted over 1f out: kpt on wl* **7/1**

0-44 **2** 2¼ **Grissom (IRE)**[7] 1928 8-9-7 **85** ... DavidAllan 10 90
(Tim Easterby) *midfield: hdwy over 3f out: wnt 2nd over 1f out: styd on for press ins fnl f: nt quite able to chal wnr* **8/1**

6-63 **3** 4½ **King Of Eden (IRE)**[15] 1672 8-8-13 **80** ... JasonHart(3) 2 74+
(Eric Alston) *rrd s and slowly away: bhd: rdn over 4f out: stl plenty to do 3f out: hdwy 2f out: styd on ins fnl f: tk 3rd fnl 150yds: nt rch ldrs* **9/2**[2]

11-2 **4** ½ **Dancing Cosmos (IRE)**[19] 1598 4-8-13 **80** ... RonanWhelan(3) 14 73
(John Patrick Shanahan, Ire) *chsd ldrs: rdn to take 2nd 2f out: lost 2nd over 1f out: no ex ins fnl f* **20/1**

1121 **5** 7 **Jubilee Brig**[28] 1429 4-9-2 **83** ... (v) OisinMurphy(3) 11 58
(Sean Curran) *pushed along most of way: towards rr: hung rt and kpt on ins fnl f: nvr able to trble ldrs* **8/1**

0005 **6** 3 **Dr Red Eye**[44] 1114 6-8-13 **84** ... (p) MatthewHopkins(7) 9 52
(Scott Dixon) *led: hdd 4f out: rdn and lost 2nd 2f out: wknd over 1f out* **5/1**[3]

120/ **7** 3¾ **Gabrial's Bounty (IRE)**[694] 3063 5-9-4 **82** ... RyanMoore 1 41
(Richard Fahey) *chsd ldrs: lost pl 3f out: n.d after* **11/4**[1]

00-0 **8** 7 **Lord Of The Dance (IRE)**[55] 977 8-9-7 **85** ... RichardKingscote 5 26
(Michael Mullineaux) *stdd s: hld up: rdn over 2f out: nvr a threat* **25/1**

2100 **9** ½ **Skytrain**[13] 1721 4-9-7 **85** ... FrannyNorton 6 25
(Mark Johnston) *towards rr: pushed along 5f out: outpcd 3f out: nvr on terms* **12/1**

14-4 **10** 2½ **Goldstorm**[13] 1744 6-9-4 **82** ... PaddyAspell 13 16
(Brian Baugh) *midfield: rdn 3f out: wknd 2f out* **33/1**

1m 32.86s (6.36) **Going Correction** +1.075s/f (Soft) 10 Ran SP% **115.5**
Speed ratings (Par 105): **106,103,98,97,89 86,82,74,73,70**
CSF £59.48 CT £287.17 TOTE £5.60: £2.90, £1.90, £2.40; EX 57.20 Trifecta £436.70.
**Owner** Wayne Clifford **Bred** Mrs S Clifford **Trained** Pandy, Monmouths
■ Stewards' Enquiry : J F Egan four-day ban: used whip above permitted level (May 23,24,26,27)

**FOCUS**
Few got into this from off the pace, despite it being run at a strong gallop. The winner is the key to the form.

## 2118 MERSEYRAIL DAY SAVER TICKET MAIDEN FILLIES' STKS (BOBIS RACE) 7f 2y
4:25 (4:26) (Class 4) 3-Y-O £7,762 (£2,310; £1,154; £577) Stalls Low

Form RPR
3- **1** **Destiny's Kitten (IRE)**[224] 6789 3-9-0 0 ... RichardKingscote 2 83
(Tom Dascombe) *prom: wnt 2nd over 2f out: led ins fnl f: r.o to draw clr fnl 100yds* **7/1**

5-3 **2** 3¾ **Sitting Pretty (IRE)**[49] 1045 3-9-0 0 ... FrannyNorton 7 73
(Tom Dascombe) *wnt lft s: led: rdn over 1f out: hdd ins fnl f: outpcd by wnr and no ch fnl 100yds* **25/1**

0-22 **3** 1¼ **Polar Eyes**[16] 1645 3-9-0 77 ... JamieSpencer 4 70
(Peter Chapple-Hyam) *hmpd s: chsd ldrs: rdn and outpcd over 2f out: kpt on ins fnl f: tk 3rd cl home: nvr able to chal* **4/1**[3]

0-43 **4** nk **Sighora (IRE)**[22] 1534 3-9-0 78 ... RyanMoore 5 69
(Ismail Mohammed) *hmpd s: sn chsd ldr: pushed along 3f out: rdn and lost 2nd over 2f out: outpcd over 1f out: kpt on same pce ins fnl f* **6/4**[1]

0 **5** 9 **Scillonian Sunset (IRE)**[28] 1422 3-8-11 0 ... OisinMurphy(3) 3 46
(Charles Hills) *hmpd s: towards rr: pushed along over 4f out: struggling over 2f out: nvr a threat* **7/1**

**6** hd **Tohaveandtohold** 3-9-0 0 ... JosephO'Brien 1 45
(William Haggas) *hld up: rdn over 3f out: struggling over 2f out: nvr a threat* **7/2**[2]

- **7** 39 **Weddings Off** 3-8-9 0 ... DanielMuscutt(5) 8
(Bernard Llewellyn) *sn wl bhd and outpcd: nvr on terms: t.o* **50/1**

1m 33.53s (7.03) **Going Correction** +1.125s/f (Soft) 7 Ran SP% **113.0**
Speed ratings (Par 98): **104,99,98,97,87 87,42**
CSF £139.84 TOTE £9.20: £5.00, £7.70; EX 66.20 Trifecta £324.10.
**Owner** Chasemore Farm **Bred** Shadwell Estate Company Limited **Trained** Malpas, Cheshire

**FOCUS**
A couple of the key contenders failed to give their running in what had looked a fair maiden, no more, and the form looks ordinary. The winner did it well enough but this looks a lesser renewal.

## 2119 LDF APPRENTICE H'CAP 1m 4f 66y
5:00 (5:00) (Class 4) (0-85,85) 4-Y-O+ £9,703 (£2,887; £1,443; £721) Stalls Low

Form RPR
-204 **1** **Gabrial's Star**[30] 1377 5-9-5 **82** ... (b) IanBrennan 12 93
(Richard Fahey) *in rr: rdn over 4f out: sn bk on bridle: hdwy to ld 3f out: rdn whn pressed over 1f out: styd on to draw away ins fnl 100yds* **4/1**[2]

14-1 **2** 2¾ **Running Deer (IRE)**[11] 1811 5-9-5 **85** 6ex ... LouisSteward(3) 5 92
(Eve Johnson Houghton) *in tch: effrt to chse wnr over 2f out: rdn to chal over 1f out: no ex ins fnl 100yds* **7/2**[1]

1- **3** 6 **Innsbruck**[155] 6566 4-9-1 **83** ... JoeDoyle(5) 7 81
(John Quinn) *s.i.s: hld up: rdn over 3f out: hdwy 2f out: wnt 3rd wl over 1f out: no imp on front two* **8/1**

1-30 **4** 12 **King Of Paradise (IRE)**[21] 1562 5-9-0 **77** ... JasonHart 2 57
(Eric Alston) *led: rdn over 3f out: sn hdd: wknd wl over 1f out* **9/2**[3]

0-41 **5** 4 **Licence To Till (USA)**[11] 1816 7-9-2 **84** 6ex ... JennyPowell(5) 1 58
(Tom Dascombe) *chsd ldr: ev ch 3f out: sn rdn and lost pl: wl btn over 1f out* **10/1**

16 **6** 1¾ **Future Security (IRE)**[63] 870 5-8-7 **75** ... DanielCremin(5) 3 46
(Anthony Middleton) *midfield: rdn over 3f out: sn lft bhd by ldrs* **10/1**

401- **7** 1½ **Ultimate**[20] 7369 8-8-9 **77** ... MeganCarberry(5) 11 46
(Brian Ellison) *midfield: rdn 4f out: sn wknd* **8/1**

1-42 **8** 26 **First Warning**[43] 1128 4-9-0 **77** ... (b) OisinMurphy 8 7
(Tim Pitt) *chsd ldrs: rdn over 4f out: wknd over 3f out: t.o* **9/1**

100- **9** 1½ **Palazzo Bianco**[321] 3560 6-9-0 **84** ... KevinLundie(7) 9 12
(Brian Ellison) *in rr: rdn over 7f out: lft bhd 6f out: t.o* **20/1**

2m 50.07s (11.57) **Going Correction** +1.175s/f (Soft) 9 Ran SP% **115.6**
Speed ratings (Par 105): **108,106,102,94,91 90,89,72,71**
CSF £18.45 CT £106.24 TOTE £5.70: £1.60, £1.40, £3.30; EX 16.70 Trifecta £108.50.
**Owner** Dr Marwan Koukash **Bred** Miss K Rausing **Trained** Musley Bank, N Yorks

**FOCUS**
The front pair drew clear in what was a decent apprentice handicap. A good pace was always likely with King Of Paradise in the field. A pace best from the winner.
T/Plt: £545.20 to a £1 stake. Pool: £175873.06 - 235.45 winning tickets T/Qpdt: £74.20 to a £1 stake. Pool: £8078.24 - 80.46 winning tickets DO

# [1917] LINGFIELD (L-H)
### Friday, May 9

**OFFICIAL GOING: Straight course - good (soft between 7f 140yds and 5f); round course - good (good to firm in places; straight 7.8, round 8.5); all-weather track - standard**
In order to try and combat draw bias, the stands' rail on the Straight course was moved in 5 metres from maximum width.
Wind: Strong, across towards stand Weather: Sunny spells

## 2120 LADBROKES CLASSIFIED STKS 1m 2f
2:05 (2:05) (Class 5) 3-Y-O £3,363 (£1,001; £500; £250) Stalls Low

Form RPR
1 **1** **Libran (IRE)**[19] 1597 3-9-0 72 ... BenCurtis 6 83+
(Alan Swinbank) *hld up in 4th: hdwy to ld 2f out: drvn out* **9/4**[2]

U41 **2** 1¼ **Maahir**[50] 1035 3-9-0 74 ... LukeMorris 3 80+
(Marco Botti) *chsd ldr: rdn to chal 2f out: kpt on u.p fnl f* **2/1**[1]

30-0 **3** 2½ **Dance Bid**[16] 1655 3-9-0 75 ... MickaelBarzalona 1 75
(Clive Brittain) *t.k.h in 5th: rdn over 2f out: styd on fr over 1f out* **16/1**

-233 **4** 2 **Shimba Hills**[17] 1635 3-8-11 75 ... WilliamTwiston-Davies(3) 5 71
(Mick Channon) *led tl 2f out: wknd jst over 1f out* **11/4**[3]

20-5 **5** ¾ **Lucky Visione**[17] 1635 3-9-0 74 ... AdamKirby 2 70
(Gay Kelleway) *broke wl: stdd bk to 3rd: effrt and hrd rdn 2f out: sn btn* **8/1**

2m 9.65s (-0.85) **Going Correction** -0.075s/f (Good) 5 Ran SP% **107.8**
Speed ratings (Par 99): **100,99,97,95,94**
CSF £6.82 TOTE £4.40: £1.40, £2.40; EX 8.90 Trifecta £70.50.
**Owner** Mrs J Porter **Bred** Roundhill Stud **Trained** Melsonby, N Yorks

**FOCUS**
The going was officially described as good, but soft between 5f and 7f 140y on the straight track and good to firm in places on the round course. In a bid to eliminate the straight course draw bias, the turf track had been narrowed with the stands' rail moved in five metres from the maximum width. As a result the safety factor for races on the straight course had been reduced from 18 to 12 and the stalls were positioned in the centre. The first race of the year on the turf track here was a modest affair and the pace looked ordinary, but the first two are both unexposed and have scope for further improvement.

## 2121 LADBROKES BET ON YOUR MOBILE FILLIES' H'CAP 7f 140y
2:35 (2:37) (Class 4) (0-80,80) 4-Y-O+ £6,469 (£1,925; £962; £481) Stalls Centre

Form RPR
20-4 **1** **Al Manaal**[13] 1716 4-9-4 **80** ... CharlesBishop(3) 2 87
(Mick Channon) *chsd ldrs: rdn to chal 1f out: led fnl 75yds: drvn out* **14/1**

4-53 **2** hd **Saucy Minx (IRE)**[5] 1985 4-9-7 **80** ... JimCrowley 6 86
(Amanda Perrett) *t.k.h: chsd ldr: led 2f out: hrd rdn and edgd lft 1f out: hdd fnl 75yds: r.o* **9/4**[1]

0-35 **3** 2 **Kosika (USA)**[3] 2054 4-9-0 73 ... AdamKirby 3 74
(Mark Johnston) *led on stands' rail: rdn and hdd 2f out: kpt on same pce* **3/1**[2]

5122 **4** ½ **Serenity Spa**[4] 2024 4-9-0 73 ... LukeMorris 1 73
(Tony Carroll) *hld up in 5th: rdn to chse ldrs 2f out: one pce* **7/2**[3]

6010 **5** 1½ **Bold Ring**[21] 1554 8-8-7 66 oh8 ... JimmyQuinn 5 62?
(Edward Creighton) *chsd ldrs: rdn and outpcd fnl 2f* **33/1**

354- **6** ¾ **Anya**[238] 6359 5-9-4 77 ... FergusSweeney 4 71
(Henry Candy) *hld up in rr: rdn over 2f out: btn wl over 1f out* **7/2**[3]

1m 32.54s (0.24) **Going Correction** +0.10s/f (Good) 6 Ran SP% **109.8**
Speed ratings (Par 102): **102,101,99,99,97 97**
CSF £43.74 TOTE £10.70: £3.40, £1.70; EX 32.80 Trifecta £136.70.
**Owner** M Channon **Bred** Darley **Trained** West Ilsley, Berks
■ Stewards' Enquiry : Charles Bishop two-day ban: used whip above permitted level (May 23-24)


The Form Book, Raceform Ltd, Newbury, RG14 5SJ

**FOCUS**
The field for this fair fillies' handicap wasn't really big enough to test the new track layout, but the jockeys wasted no time in heading for the stands' rail. The second sets the standard but the fifth limits the form.

## 2122 LADBROKES MOBILE H'CAP (BOBIS RACE) 6f
3:05 (3:06) (Class 4) (0-80,80) 3-Y-O £6,469 (£1,925; £962; £481) Stalls Centre

Form RPR

63-1 1 **Stomp**[32] 1350 3-9-6 **79**........................ GeorgeBaker 8 91
(Roger Charlton) *hld up towards rr: gd hdwy over 1f out: led ins fnl f: pushed out: readily* **5/2**[2]

1 2 1 ½ **Double Up**[67] 824 3-8-13 **72**........................ AndreaAtzeni 11 79
(Roger Varian) *chsd ldrs: led over 1f out: hrd rdn and hdd ins fnl f: unable qck* **7/4**[1]

36-1 3 2 **Costa Filey**[121] 82 3-9-1 **74**........................ JimmyQuinn 1 75
(Ed Vaughan) *hld up in rr: rdn and hdwy over 1f out: r.o fnl f* **66/1**

200- 4 1 ½ **Lady Lydia (IRE)**[288] 4682 3-9-4 **77**....................[1] SilvestreDeSousa 2 73
(Conrad Allen) *hld up towards rr: hdwy on far side 2f out: no ex fnl f* **25/1**

6-30 5 1 ¾ **Knockroon**[23] 1511 3-8-11 **70**........................ DavidProbert 9 61
(Andrew Balding) *disp ld at gd pce tl over 1f out: sn outpcd* **10/1**

134- 6 2 **Djinni (IRE)**[176] 7879 3-9-4 **77**........................ MickaelBarzalona 10 61
(Richard Hannon) *mid-div: rdn to chse ldrs 2f out: wknd fnl f* **10/1**

-252 7 2 ¼ **Amahoro**[20] 1570 3-9-4 **80**........................ WilliamTwiston-Davies(3) 7 57
(Mick Channon) *in tch: rdn to chse ldrs 2f out: wknd 1f out* **16/1**

5-1 8 ½ **Ashkari (IRE)**[20] 1569 3-9-7 **80**........................ AdamKirby 5 55
(Clive Cox) *prom: rdn over 2f out: wknd over 1f out* **9/2**[3]

214- 9 6 **Pensax Lad (IRE)**[140] 8364 3-9-2 **75**........................ SteveDrowne 6 31
(Ronald Harris) *disp ld at gd pce tl wknd over 1f out* **50/1**

1m 11.52s (0.32) **Going Correction** +0.10s/f (Good) 9 Ran SP% **114.5**
Speed ratings (Par 101): **101,99,96,94,92 89,86,85,77**
CSF £7.09 CT £210.52 TOTE £3.80: £1.30, £1.10, £4.20; EX 8.30 Trifecta £232.30.
**Owner** Lady Rothschild **Bred** The Rt Hon Lord Rothschild **Trained** Beckhampton, Wilts

**FOCUS**
A better test of the new track layout, but even though it's still early days the feeling is that the bias has been removed to a degree, despite stall 8 beating stall 11. Again the riders made for the nearside rail. This was a decent 3yo sprint handicap and we should be hearing much more of the first two. The form is rated on the positive side.

## 2123 LADBROKES DOWNLOAD THE APP H'CAP 5f
3:35 (3:35) (Class 3) (0-95,95) 4-Y-O+ £9,703 (£2,887; £1,443; £721) Stalls Centre

Form RPR

40-0 1 **Normal Equilibrium**[23] 1506 4-8-8 **85**........................(p) RobertTart(3) 5 96
(Robert Cowell) *chsd ldrs: styd on to ld wl ins fnl f: rdn out* **6/1**

F0-2 2 1 ¾ **Arctic Lynx (IRE)**[25] 1489 7-8-8 **82**........................ FrederikTylicki 4 87
(Robert Cowell) *chsd ldr: led 2f out: hdd and unable qck wl ins fnl f* **5/1**[3]

60-0 3 ½ **Jillnextdoor (IRE)**[20] 1572 4-8-13 **90**........................ WilliamTwiston-Davies(3) 6 93
(Mick Channon) *dwlt: hld up in rr: rdn and hdwy over 1f out: r.o fnl f* **10/1**

05-0 4 1 **Barnet Fair**[53] 991 6-9-5 **93**........................ AmirQuinn 3 92
(Lee Carter) *t.k.h in 5th: hdwy to chse ldrs jst ins fnl f: one pce fnl 100yds* **5/1**[3]

44-0 5 nk **Exceptionelle**[20] 1572 4-8-13 **87**........................ AndreaAtzeni 2 85
(Roger Varian) *dwlt: hld up in 6th: rdn over 2f out: styd on same pce: nvr able to chal* **11/4**[1]

34-4 6 1 ¾ **Pearl Blue (IRE)**[16] 1650 6-9-4 **92**........................ GeorgeBaker 1 84
(Chris Wall) *restless in stalls: chsd ldrs: rdn over 2f out: wknd ins fnl f* **3/1**[2]

000- 7 shd **Judge 'n Jury**[195] 7527 10-9-7 **95**........................(t) SteveDrowne 7 87
(Ronald Harris) *led on stands' rail tl 2f out: wknd ins fnl f* **12/1**

57.14s (-1.06) **Going Correction** 0.0s/f (Good) 7 Ran SP% **116.1**
Speed ratings (Par 107): **108,105,104,102,102 99,99**
CSF £36.62 TOTE £10.10: £5.90, £3.20; EX 49.80 Trifecta £325.00.
**Owner** T W Morley & Mrs J Morley **Bred** D R Tucker **Trained** Six Mile Bottom, Cambs

**FOCUS**
A small field for a decent prize in this 0-95 sprint handicap, which provided a 1-2 for trainer Robert Cowell. Again they came over to the nearside and few got into it. The winner is rated back to his early 3yo level.

## 2124 LADBROKES H'CAP (LADY AMATEUR RIDERS) 7f
4:10 (4:13) (Class 5) (0-75,74) 4-Y-O+ £3,300 (£1,023; £511; £256) Stalls Centre

Form RPR

400- 1 **Another Try (IRE)**[156] 8157 9-9-13 **66**........................ MissSBrotherton 6 74
(Alan Jarvis) *t.k.h to post: w ldr: led 3f out: rdn out* **5/2**[1]

00-0 2 2 ¼ **Jontleman (IRE)**[13] 1710 4-10-7 **74**........................ MissEJJones 7 76
(Mick Channon) *hld up in 5th: swtchd lft and effrt over 1f out: rdn to chal ent fnl f: unable qck* **4/1**[3]

040- 3 nk **Hernando Torres**[212] 7132 6-9-3 **61**........................(p) MrsRWilson(5) 8 62
(Michael Easterby) *hld up in 6th: hdwy and nt clr run over 1f out: swtchd lft: r.o* **7/2**[2]

4 1 ¾ **Victor's Bet (SPA)**[264] 5-10-0 **72**........................(t) MissEllaSmith(5) 4 69
(Ralph J Smith) *hld up in 4th: shkn up and lost pl 2f out: gng on again at fin* **16/1**

5434 5 shd **Shifting Star (IRE)**[12] 1771 9-9-8 **61**........................(bt) MissADeniel 2 58
(John Bridger) *slt ld tl 3f out: w ldrs tl wknd fnl f* **4/1**[3]

630- 6 ¾ **All Or Nothin (IRE)**[149] 8244 5-9-12 **70**........................ MissMBryant(5) 1 65
(Paddy Butler) *chsd ldrs tl wknd ins fnl f* **25/1**

43-4 7 2 ¼ **Paradise Spectre**[2] 2065 7-9-4 **64**........................(p) MissMBishop-Peck(7) 9 53
(Zoe Davison) *s.s: t.k.h in rr: swtchd wd to far side and hdwy over 2f out: wknd 1f out* **14/1**

0000 8 16 **Pelmanism**[13] 1710 7-9-3 **63**........................ MissAnne-SophieCrombez(7) 3 10
(Gay Kelleway) *s.s: a in rr: no ch fnl 3f* **14/1**

1m 25.6s (2.30) **Going Correction** +0.10s/f (Good) 8 Ran SP% **113.9**
Speed ratings (Par 103): **90,87,87,85,84 84,81,63**
CSF £12.56 CT £33.82 TOTE £3.00: £1.20, £1.20, £2.20; EX 13.90 Trifecta £59.40.
**Owner** The Twyford Partnership **Bred** Jarvis Associates **Trained** Twyford, Bucks

**FOCUS**
A modest lady amateurs' event in which they again came nearside. The winner has dropped 16lb in the past year and is rated to last year's best.

## 2125 LADBROKES MAIDEN FILLIES' STKS (BOBIS RACE) 6f 1y(P)
4:45 (4:48) (Class 5) 3-Y-O £3,363 (£1,001; £500; £250) Stalls Low

Form RPR

22-2 1 **Penny Drops**[13] 1713 3-9-0 **87**........................ SilvestreDeSousa 5 76+
(William Haggas) *w ldrs: led on bit over 1f out: cruised clr: easily* **4/7**[1]

4 2 2 ¾ **Backstage Gossip**[15] 1677 3-9-0 0........................ FergusSweeney 6 67+
(Hughie Morrison) *hld up in midfield: shkn up and hdwy over 1f out: r.o to take 2nd fnl strides* **14/1**

2-2 3 nk **Misstemper (IRE)**[29] 1404 3-9-0 0........................ JohnFahy 1 66
(Sean Curran) *led tl over 1f out: kpt on u.p: no ch w wnr: lost 2nd fnl strides* **12/1**[3]

00- 4 1 ½ **Katawi**[188] 7692 3-9-0 0........................[1] JackMitchell 8 61+
(Chris Wall) *towards rr: hdwy on inner ent st: one pce appr fnl f* **33/1**

5 5 shd **Champagne Charley**[13] 1713 3-9-0 0........................ AdamBeschizza 3 61
(Des Donovan) *chsd ldrs: rdn to press ldng pair wl over 1f out: no ex fnl f* **40/1**

3- 6 shd **Majestic Song**[185] 7737 3-8-11 0........................[1] RobertTart(3) 4 61+
(James Toller) *s.s: bhd: pushed along 3f out: wd into st: gd hdwy fnl f* **14/1**

0 7 3 ¼ **Solar Moon**[22] 1534 3-9-0 0........................ MickaelBarzalona 11 50+
(Charlie Appleby) *w ldrs on outer tl nt handle fnl bnd and wknd 2f out* **7/2**[2]

0- 8 ½ **Diamond Solitaire (IRE)**[350] 2625 3-9-0 0........................ KierenFallon 9 49
(Alan Jarvis) *in tch tl wknd over 1f out: eased whn btn ins fnl f* **16/1**

9 8 **Chufft** 3-8-7 0........................ CharlieBennett(7) 7 23
(Hughie Morrison) *dwlt: outpcd: a bhd* **33/1**

50 10 4 **Dorset Gift**[13] 1713 3-9-0 0........................ HayleyTurner 10 10
(Michael Bell) *outpcd towards rr: n.d fnl 3f* **66/1**

1m 10.85s (-1.05) **Going Correction** -0.10s/f (Stan) 10 Ran SP% **122.6**
Speed ratings (Par 96): **103,99,98,96,96 96,92,91,81,75**
CSF £11.81 TOTE £1.50: £1.02, £4.40, £2.80; EX 12.70 Trifecta £56.30.
**Owner** Mr & Mrs G Middlebrook **Bred** Mr & Mrs G Middlebrook **Trained** Newmarket, Suffolk

**FOCUS**
In order to try and combat draw bias the stands' rail on the Straight course was moved in 5metres from maximum width. They bet 12-1 bar two in this fillies' maiden and it proved straightforward for the hot favourite. Modest form, rated around the third.

## 2126 LADBROKES MAIDEN STKS 7f 1y(P)
5:20 (5:22) (Class 5) 3-Y-O+ £3,363 (£1,001; £500; £250) Stalls Low

Form RPR

-0 1 **Zman Awal (IRE)**[28] 1422 3-8-9 0........................ HayleyTurner 9 73+
(James Fanshawe) *trckd ldrs on outer: led over 1f out: rdn out* **8/1**[3]

323- 2 1 ½ **Mia San Triple**[218] 6974 3-8-9 **78**........................ FrederikTylicki 10 69
(Jeremy Noseda) *t.k.h: cl up on outer: rdn to press ldrs 2f out: one pce appr fnl f* **9/4**[2]

3 nk **Inkerman (IRE)**[276] 5118 4-9-12 **75**........................ FergusSweeney 1 77
(Jamie Osborne) *led: hrd rdn and hdd over 1f out: one pce* **8/1**[3]

4 2 ¾ **Winter Thunder** 3-9-0 0........................[1] SilvestreDeSousa 4 66+
(Saeed bin Suroor) *in tch: rdn and struggling to hold pl 3f out: styd on fnl f* **5/4**[1]

03 5 ½ **Southern Cross**[12] 1767 3-8-9 0........................ MickaelBarzalona 8 60
(Hughie Morrison) *mid-div: hdwy and carried hd awkwardly over 1f out: styd on* **14/1**

5 6 ½ **Crafty Business (IRE)**[10] 1831 3-9-0 0........................ AdamBeschizza 3 63
(Mark Hoad) *prom tl outpcd fnl 2f* **66/1**

2-5 7 ¾ **Garraun (IRE)**[15] 1677 3-8-9 0........................ ChrisCatlin 7 56
(Jeremy Noseda) *wd: towards rr: effrt on outer 2f out: no imp over 1f out* **16/1**

46 8 2 ¾ **Marweena (IRE)**[12] 1768 3-8-9 0........................ NickyMackay 2 49
(Michael Bell) *prom: hmpd on rail after 2f: wknd over 1f out* **33/1**

5 9 ½ **Haames (IRE)**[19] 1600 7-9-5 0........................ CamHardie(7) 5 57
(Kevin Morgan) *dwlt: a towards rr* **66/1**

5 10 1 ¾ **Monsieur Chabal**[10] 1830 3-8-9 0........................ RachealKneller(5) 11 48
(Jamie Osborne) *s.s: a bhd* **66/1**

11 shd **Royal College** 4-9-12 0........................ GeorgeBaker 12 52
(Gary Moore) *s.s: a bhd* **25/1**

12 ½ **Mumarasaat (USA)** 3-8-9 0........................ WilliamCarson 6 42
(Phil McEntee) *mid-div tl outpcd fnl 2f* **50/1**

4 13 ½ **Notgordonitsrodger (IRE)**[10] 1853 4-9-7 0........................ TobyAtkinson(5) 13 49
(Phil McEntee) *s.s: t.k.h in rr: shkn up 3f out: n.d after* **66/1**

1m 24.23s (-0.57) **Going Correction** -0.10s/f (Stan)
**WFA** 3 from 4yo+ 12lb 13 Ran SP% **124.7**
Speed ratings (Par 103): **99,97,96,93,93 92,91,88,88,86 85,85,84**
CSF £26.82 TOTE £10.30: £4.00, £1.20, £2.20; EX 50.50 Trifecta £252.30.
**Owner** Mohamed Obaida **Bred** Rabbah Bloodstock Limited **Trained** Newmarket, Suffolk
■ Stewards' Enquiry : Adam Beschizza two-day ban: careless riding (May 23-24)

**FOCUS**
An interesting maiden, though few could be seriously fancied. The form looks a bit shaky with the third looking the best guide.
T/Plt: £42.00 to a £1 stake. Pool: £56801.12 - 986.20 winning tickets T/Qpdt: £10.20 to a £1 stake. Pool: £4576.64 - 329.86 winning tickets LM

# 1844 NOTTINGHAM (L-H)
Friday, May 9

**OFFICIAL GOING: Good changing to good to soft after race 2 (5.45)**
Outer track used for first time this season and distances as advertised.
Wind: Moderate against Weather: Cloudy with sunny periods and showers

## 2127 32RED APPRENTICE H'CAP 6f 15y
5:15 (5:16) (Class 6) (0-60,59) 4-Y-O+ £1,940 (£577; £288; £144) Stalls High

Form RPR

-564 1 **Prigsnov Dancer (IRE)**[35] 1282 9-8-13 **56**........................ DavidParkes(5) 11 67
(Deborah Sanderson) *in tch stands' side: hdwy over 2f out: rdn to chse ldr over 1f out: led ins fnl f: sn clr* **16/1**

3054 2 4 **Consistant**[27] 1448 6-9-4 **56**........................ EoinWalsh 15 54
(Brian Baugh) *sltly hmpd s and in rr stands' side: hdwy nr stands' rail over 2f out: swtchd lft and rdn over 1f out: styd on wl fnl f: 2nd of 10 in gp* **10/1**[3]

0600 3 1 ¾ **Burnhope**[67] 826 5-9-4 **56**........................(p) DannyBrock 17 48
(Scott Dixon) *chsd ldng pair stands' side: hdwy 2f out: rdn over 1f out: sn one pce: 3rd of 10 in gp* **8/1**[1]

405 4 1 ½ **Avonmore Star**[20] 1584 6-9-3 **55**........................ MarcMonaghan 14 43
(Alan McCabe) *rrd and wnt rt s: bhd stands' side: rdn along 2f out: styd on wl fnl f: nrst fin: 4th of 10 in gp* **9/1**[2]

4130 5 2 **Guishan**[99] 383 4-9-4 **59**........................(p) AlistairRawlinson(3) 7 40+
(Michael Appleby) *hld up towards rr: hdwy on outer 2f out: sn rdn and styd on fnl f: nrst fin: 5th of 10 in gp* **8/1**[1]

5152 6 nk **Lucky Mark (IRE)**[35] 1282 5-8-11 **54**........................(v) BradleyBosley(5) 16 34
(Garry Moss) *chsd clr ldr stands' side: rdn along and hdwy wl over 1f out: drvn and wknd ent fnl f: 6th of 10 in gp* **12/1**

3402 7 ½ **Pearl Noir**[27] 1448 4-9-4 **59**........................(b) RobJFitzpatrick(3) 8 38
(Scott Dixon) *racd stands' side: overall ldr and sn clr: rdn wl over 1f out: drvn and hung lft ent fnl f: sn hdd & wknd 7th of 10 in gp* **14/1**

2362 **8** ½ **Hamis Al Bin (IRE)**[20] 1573 5-9-3 **58**.........................(t) RyanWhile(3) 10 35
(Milton Bradley) *a towards rr stands' side: 8th of 10 in gp* **8/1**[1]
-544 **9** *hd* **Hazard Warning (IRE)**[9] 1892 4-9-3 **55**.......................(b) NoelGarbutt 9 31
(Mandy Rowland) *chsd ldrs stands' side: rdn along over 2f out: sn drvn and wknd: 9th of 10 in gp* **25/1**
26-4 **10** ½ **Tiger's Home**[10] 1863 4-9-5 **57**......................... ShelleyBirkett 13 32
(Julia Feilden) *a towards rr stands' side: last of 10 in gp* **14/1**
6155 **11** *8* **Invigilator**[13] 1739 6-9-3 **58**.......................................(t) AdamMcLean(3) 6 7
(Derek Shaw) *chsd ldr far side: rdn along and outpcd 1/2-way: bhd whn edgd rt fnl 2f: 1st of 4 in gp* **8/1**[1]
-002 **12** 2½ **Dancing Maite**[20] 1584 9-9-3 **55**...................................(b) PhilipPrince 2
(Roy Bowring) *led far side gp: rdn along and outpcd fr 1/2-way: bhd whn edgd rt fnl 2f: 2nd of 4 in gp* **8/1**[1]
360- **13** ¾ **Ishi Honest**[205] 7315 4-9-1 **58**..............................(v[1]) CharlotteJenner(5) 5
(Mark Usher) *chsd ldr far side: rdn along 1/2-way and sn outpcd: bhd whn edgd rt fnl 2f: 2nd of 4 in gp* **16/1**
1453 **14** 1¼ **Sewn Up**[11] 1813 4-9-2 **54**...............................................(p) JackDuern 3
(Andrew Hollinshead) *chsd ldr far side: rdn along and outpcd 1/2-way: bhd whn swtchd rt fnl 2f: 4th of 4 in gp* **8/1**[1]

1m 14.43s (-0.27) **Going Correction** 0.0s/f (Good) **14** Ran SP% **122.4**
Speed ratings (Par 101): **101,95,93,91,88 88,87,86,86,86 75,72,71,69**
CSF £170.43 CT £1396.66 TOTE £24.50: £6.00, £5.40, £3.30; EX 313.10 Trifecta £1181.40 Part won. Pool of £1575.30 - 0.21 winning units..
**Owner** J M Lacey **Bred** Tom Radley **Trained** Tickhill, S Yorks

**FOCUS**
Outer track used for first time this season and distances as advertised. Patchy rain ahead of this ultra competitive, if low-grade sprint opener. Surprise improvement from the winner.

## 2128 32RED MEDIAN AUCTION MAIDEN FILLIES' STKS (BOBIS RACE) 5f 13y
**5:45** (5:45) (Class 5) 2-Y-O **£3,234** (£962; £481; £240) **Stalls** High

Form RPR
2 **1** **Polar Vortex (IRE)**[25] 1488 2-8-9 0.............................. RyanTate(5) 8 74
(Clive Cox) *slt ld: pushed along and jnd over 1f out: sn rdn: drvn and edgd lft wl ins fnl f: kpt on* **11/10**[1]
**2** *hd* **Parsley (IRE)** 2-9-0 0.............................................. TedDurcan 2 73+
(Richard Hannon) *sn cl up: effrt 2f out: chal over 1f out: rdn and edgd rt ent fnl f and ev ch tl sltly hmpd and no ex nr line* **11/4**[2]
**3** 2¼ **Lanai (IRE)** 2-9-0 0.............................................. TonyHamilton 1 65
(David Barron) *in tch on outer: hdwy 2f out: rdn to chse ldng pair and ev ch appr fnl f: kpt on same pce* **8/1**
6 **4** ½ **Alpha Spirit**[13] 1726 2-9-0 0.......................................... MartinLane 10 63
(Mick Channon) *cl up on inner: effrt over 2f out: rdn over 1f out: kpt on same pce fnl f* **11/1**
00 **5** 1¾ **Seamoor Secret**[20] 1571 2-8-11 0.......................... ConnorBeasley(3) 9 57
(Alex Hales) *chsd ldrs: rdn along wl over 1f out: one pce appr fnl f* **50/1**
**6** *2* **Gregoria (IRE)** 2-9-0 0.............................................. GrahamLee 3 50
(William Haggas) *trckd ldrs: hdwy 2f out: sn rdn and one pce appr fnl f* **7/1**[3]
03 **7** ½ **Lunar Knot**[17] 1633 2-9-0 0.......................................... TomQueally 6 48
(Alan McCabe) *sltly hmpd s: a towards rr* **25/1**
**8** *nse* **Sculptured (FR)** 2-8-9 0.......................................... PhilipPrince(5) 5 48
(Jo Hughes) *dwlt: a in rr* **100/1**
60 **9** *hd* **Multi Quest**[20] 1571 2-9-0 0.......................................... MartinDwyer 7 47
(Jo Hughes) *wnt rt s: a towards rr* **66/1**
6 **10** *17* **Pearlise (FR)**[9] 1889 2-8-9 0.................................. MarcMonaghan(5) 4
(Scott Dixon) *cl up: rdn along 1/2-way: sn wknd* **40/1**

1m 2.69s (1.19) **Going Correction** 0.0s/f (Good) **10** Ran SP% **117.0**
Speed ratings (Par 90): **90,89,86,85,82 79,78,78,78,50**
CSF £4.01 TOTE £2.10: £1.10, £1.10, £3.60; EX 7.00 Trifecta £30.00.
**Owner** Alan G Craddock **Bred** Chasemore Farm & Owen Promotions **Trained** Lambourn, Berks

**FOCUS**
Not many could be seriously fancied for this juvenile fillies' maiden and the finish was fought out by those at the head of the market. The form is rated to the race average, taking out last year's winner Sandiva.

## 2129 32RED CASINO MAIDEN FILLIES' STKS (BOBIS RACE) 1m 75y
**6:15** (6:17) (Class 5) 3-Y-O **£3,234** (£962; £481; £240) **Stalls** Centre

Form RPR
**1** **My Spirit (IRE)** 3-9-0 0.............................................. GrahamGibbons 1 79+
(William Haggas) *dwlt and towards rr: hdwy whn nt clr run wl over 2f out: swtchd rt wl over 1f out: rdn and str run ent fnl f: led nr fin* **7/1**[3]
0-5 **2** *1* **Heho**[20] 1582 3-9-0 0.............................................. TedDurcan 5 76
(Sir Michael Stoute) *led: rdn along 3f out: drvn over 1f out: kpt on gamely fnl f: hdd and no ex nr fin* **4/1**[2]
04- **3** ½ **Silver Mirage**[205] 7295 3-9-0 0......................................[1] TomQueally 4 74
(Michael Bell) *trckd ldrs: hdwy over 2f out: rdn to chse ldng pair over 1f out: drvn and ev ch ins fnl f: kpt on same pce towards fin* **16/1**
3-0 **4** *hd* **She's Gorgeous (IRE)**[30] 1394 3-9-0 0.......................... MartinLane 11 74
(James Fanshawe) *prom: hdwy over 3f out: cl up over 2f out: rdn to chal wl over 1f out: ev cvhance tl drvn and kpt on same pce ins fnl f* **10/1**
5- **5** 2¼ **Wahgah (USA)**[272] 5282 3-9-0 0.......................................... DaneO'Neill 2 69
(Saeed bin Suroor) *t.k.h: trckd ldng pair on inner: rdn along over 2f out: drvn over 1f out: wknd appr fnl f* **11/10**[1]
**6** 1¾ **Cape Mystery** 3-9-0 0.............................................. MartinDwyer 3 65
(Peter Chapple-Hyam) *dwlt and in rr: rdn along and hdwy 2f out: n.m.r over 1f out: sn no imp* **20/1**
**7** ½ **Pleasant Valley (IRE)** 3-9-0 0.......................................... PatDobbs 12 64
(Luca Cumani) *trckd ldr: effrt and cl up 3f out: sn rdn along and grad wknd fnl 2f* **16/1**
0-00 **8** *1* **Insight (IRE)**[15] 1681 3-9-0 0.......................................... SamHitchcott 9 61
(John Spearing) *s.i.s and in rr: hdwy on inner over 2f out and sn rdn along: n.m.r wl over 1f out and sn wknd* **100/1**
**9** *6* **Mystic Angel (IRE)** 3-9-0 0.......................................... StevieDonohoe 7 48
(William Muir) *towards rr: hdwy 1/2-way: effrt on outer to chse ldrs over 3f out: rdn along over 2f out and sn wknd* **100/1**
0-24 **10** 3½ **Molly Ahoy**[31] 1364 3-8-9 0.................................. MarcMonaghan(5) 10 40
(Alan McCabe) *in tch: hdwy on outer over 3f out: rdn to chse ldrs over 2f out: sn drvn and wknd* **100/1**

1m 48.74s (-0.26) **Going Correction** -0.20s/f (Firm) **10** Ran SP% **108.7**
Speed ratings (Par 96): **93,92,91,91,89 87,86,85,79,76**
CSF £31.51 TOTE £4.80: £1.60, £1.20, £2.30; EX 37.30 Trifecta £562.30.
**Owner** Miss Pat O'Kelly **Bred** Kilcarn Stud **Trained** Newmarket, Suffolk

**FOCUS**
Another maiden in which few could be considered, but the red-hot favourite failed to run up to expectations. Felwah, a stablemate of the winner, got upset in the stalls and had to be withdrawn. The form was slow but the form has been rated to the race standard.

## 2130 32RED FREE £10 BONUS FILLIES' H'CAP 1m 75y
**6:50** (6:51) (Class 5) (0-75,74) 3-Y-O **£2,726** (£805; £402) **Stalls** Centre

Form RPR
02-3 **1** **Stereo Love (FR)**[35] 1280 3-9-1 **73**.............................. RyanTate(5) 2 80
(Clive Cox) *trckd ldrs: hdwy wl over 2f out: rdn over 1f out: styd on ent fnl f: led last 100yds* **4/1**[2]
420- **2** 1¾ **Amaseena (IRE)**[188] 7695 3-9-6 **73**.......................... MartinDwyer 1 76
(Roger Varian) *trckd ldng pair: chsd ldr 3f out: rdn to ld over 1f out: drvn ins fnl f: hdd and no ex last 100yds* **2/1**[1]
3624 **3** *nk* **Boogangoo (IRE)**[7] 1913 3-9-6 **73**.......................... StevieDonohoe 5 75
(Grace Harris) *dwlt and in rr: hdwy on outer wl over 2f out: rdn wl over 1f out: kpt on u.p fnl f: nrst fin* **7/1**
0-12 **4** *nk* **Nimble Kimble**[13] 1711 3-9-6 **73**.......................... DaneO'Neill 10 74
(James Eustace) *trckd ldrs: hdwy 3f out: rdn 2f out: drvn ent fnl f and kpt on same pce* **5/1**[3]
451- **5** ¾ **Maiden Approach**[195] 7541 3-9-1 **68**.......................... TonyHamilton 3 68
(Richard Fahey) *dwlt and in rr: hdwy on inner 3f out: chsd ldrs 2f out: sn rdn and n.m.r wl over 1f out: kpt on same pce fnl f* **7/1**
13 **6** 1¾ **Bridie ffrench**[13] 1723 3-9-7 **74**.......................... SamHitchcott 7 70
(Mick Channon) *sn led: rdn along wl over 2f out: drvn and hdd over 1f out: sn wknd* **12/1**
224- **7** 1½ **Percy's Gal**[181] 7817 3-8-12 **72**.......................... GemmaTutty(7) 9 64
(Karen Tutty) *in tch: hdwy on outer 3f out: rdn to chse ldrs 2f out: sn drvn and wknd* **10/1**
100- **8** *8* **Baileys Forever**[175] 7892 3-9-1 **68**.......................... GrahamLee 6 42
(James Given) *t.k.h: cl up: rdn along over 3f out: sn wknd* **50/1**

1m 47.85s (-1.15) **Going Correction** -0.20s/f (Firm) **8** Ran SP% **113.7**
Speed ratings (Par 96): **97,95,94,94,93 92,90,82**
CSF £12.28 CT £52.52 TOTE £7.20: £2.40, £6.10, £1.40; EX 11.30 Trifecta £71.70.
**Owner** Al Asayl Bloodstock Ltd **Bred** Sheik Khalifa Bin Zayed Al Nahyan **Trained** Lambourn, Berks

**FOCUS**
A competitive fillies' handicap, run 18lb faster than the previous maiden. Sound form.

## 2131 32RED.COM H'CAP 1m 75y
**7:25** (7:26) (Class 4) (0-80,81) 4-Y-O+ **£5,175** (£1,540; £769; £384) **Stalls** Centre

Form RPR
11-3 **1** **Knight Owl**[32] 1345 4-9-7 **79**.......................... ShaneKelly 7 91+
(James Fanshawe) *trckd ldrs: smooth hdwy 3f out: cl up on bit wl over 1f out: shkn up to ld jst over 1f out: carried hd high and wandered ins fnl f: sn drvn and kpt on* **3/1**[2]
46-0 **2** *2* **Save The Bees**[32] 1345 6-8-13 **78**.......................... LukeLeadbitter(7) 6 84
(Declan Carroll) *cl up: led after 1f: rdn along and hdd over 3f out: drvn and outpcd wl over 1f out: styd on u.p fnl f* **10/1**
3-51 **3** ¾ **Self Employed**[72] 750 7-8-9 **70**.......................... ConnorBeasley(3) 4 74
(Garry Woodward) *hld up in tch: hdwy 3f out: rdn to chse ldrs wl over 1f out: drvn and kpt on same pce fnl f* **8/1**
321 **4** *nk* **Ishikawa (IRE)**[9] 1871 6-9-2 **81** 6ex.......................... RobJFitzpatrick(7) 3 85
(K R Burke) *led 1f: cl up: led again over 3f out: rdn 2f out: hdd and drvn over 1f out: sn wknd* **9/4**[1]
5402 **5** 1¾ **Docofthebay (IRE)**[13] 1717 10-8-8 **66**.......................... MartinDwyer 1 66
(Scott Dixon) *hld up in rr: hdwy 3f out: rdn over 2f out: sn no imp* **12/1**
01-4 **6** *11* **No Dominion (IRE)**[18] 1607 5-9-7 **79**.......................... GrahamLee 5 53
(James Given) *hld up in tch: effrt on outer wl over 2f out: sn rdn and btn* **9/2**[3]
611- **7** *1* **Cape Samba**[198] 7462 5-9-6 **78**.......................... TomQueally 2 50
(Ismail Mohammed) *trckd ldng pair on inner: rdn along 3f out: drvn 2f out and sn wknd* **8/1**

1m 46.35s (-2.65) **Going Correction** -0.20s/f (Firm) **7** Ran SP% **113.0**
Speed ratings (Par 105): **105,103,102,101,100 89,88**
CSF £31.15 TOTE £3.60: £1.30, £7.80; EX 36.10 Trifecta £589.30.
**Owner** Miss Annabelle Condon **Bred** Car Colston Hall Stud **Trained** Newmarket, Suffolk

**FOCUS**
This was a decent race for the grade. The runner-up helps with the standard.

## 2132 32RED ON THE APP STORE H'CAP 1m 6f 15y
**8:00** (8:01) (Class 5) (0-75,74) 3-Y-O **£2,587** (£770; £384; £192) **Stalls** Low

Form RPR
0-22 **1** **Norse Star (IRE)**[25] 1494 3-9-7 **74**.......................... PatDobbs 5 78
(Sylvester Kirk) *trckd ldng pair: hdwy 3f out: rdn to ld over 1f out: styd on wl fnl f* **5/6**[1]
4236 **2** *2* **Trafalgar Rock**[30] 1391 3-9-2 **69**.......................... FrannyNorton 2 69
(Mark Johnston) *cl up: led after 3f: pushed along and hdd 3f out: cl up: rdn and ev ch over 1f out: drvn and kpt on same pce fnl f* **6/1**[2]
4436 **3** ½ **Izbushka (IRE)**[67] 828 3-8-9 **62**..............................(t) StevieDonohoe 1 61
(Ian Williams) *trckd ldng pair on inner: pushed along over 3f out: rdn 2f out: drvn and kpt on same pce appr fnl f* **12/1**
0-40 **4** *hd* **Tactical Strike**[14] 1691 3-8-9 **67**..............................(t) NoelGarbutt(5) 3 66
(Hugo Palmer) *in tch: rdn along over 4f out: hdwy on outer wl over 2f out: drvn and one pce ent fnl f* **14/1**
10-5 **5** *2* **Running Wolf (IRE)**[23] 1508 3-9-0 **70**.......................... ConnorBeasley(3) 6 66
(Michael Dods) *led 3f: cl up: pushed along to ld 3f out: sn rdn: drvn and hdd wl over 1f out: wknd appr fnl f* **8/1**[3]
4360 **6** *nk* **Galaxy (IRE)**[17] 1635 3-8-13 **66**..............................(v) TomQueally 4 62
(Alan McCabe) *hld up: effrt 3f out: rdn along 2f out: n.d* **6/1**[2]

3m 10.58s (3.58) **Going Correction** -0.20s/f (Firm) **6** Ran SP% **108.6**
Speed ratings (Par 99): **81,79,79,79,78 78**
CSF £5.73 TOTE £1.40: £1.10, £2.60; EX 5.30 Trifecta £26.40.
**Owner** J C Smith **Bred** Littleton Stud **Trained** Upper Lambourn, Berks

**FOCUS**
A bunch finish off a steady pace, and it's unlikely this took much winning.

## 2133 32RED CASINO H'CAP 1m 2f 50y
**8:30** (8:31) (Class 5) (0-75,75) 3-Y-O **£2,587** (£770; £384; £192) **Stalls** Low

Form RPR
05-2 **1** **Insaany**[19] 1597 3-9-0 **68**.......................... DaneO'Neill 6 77
(Mark Johnston) *set stdy pce: qcknd 3f out: rdn clr wl over 1f out: kpt on strly ins fnl f* **6/1**
024- **2** 2¼ **Placidia (IRE)**[228] 6691 3-9-7 **75**.......................... TedDurcan 5 81
(David Lanigan) *trckd wnr: hdwy over 2f out: over 1f out: drvn and edgd rt ent fnl f: sn no imp* **4/1**[3]

60-0 **3** 1 1/4 **Ralphy Lad (IRE)**[32] 1346 3-9-2 **70** ........ TomQueally 2 71
(Alan Swinbank) *in rr: hdwy on outer over 3f out: rdn along 2f out: kpt on same pce appr fnl f* **14/1**

00-3 **4** 3/4 **Winter Spice (IRE)**[20] 1588 3-8-5 **64** ........ RyanTate(5) 7 64
(Clive Cox) *trckd ldng pair: chsd wnr 6f out: pushed along 3f out: rdn over 2f out: drvn and one pce appr fnl f* **5/2**[2]

00-5 **5** 1 3/4 **Unfinishedbusiness**[32] 1347 3-8-10 **64** ........ TonyHamilton 4 61
(Richard Fahey) *hld up: hdwy on outer over 4f out: chsd ldrs 3f out: rdn along 2f out: sn wknd* **16/1**

52-5 **6** 4 **Dorset Cream**[28] 1424 3-9-5 **73** ........ MartinLane 3 62
(Lady Cecil) *trckd ldrs: pushed along 3f out: rdn over 2f out and sn btn* **11/8**[1]

2m 17.84s (3.54) **Going Correction** -0.20s/f (Firm) **6** Ran SP% **117.5**
Speed ratings (Par 99): **77,75,74,73,72 69**
CSF £31.29 TOTE £4.90: £2.60, £3.20; EX 20.30 Trifecta £324.20.
**Owner** Hamdan Al Maktoum **Bred** Qatar Bloodstock Ltd **Trained** Middleham Moor, N Yorks

**FOCUS**
Plenty of potential in this finale but they went very steadily and it's difficult to be too enthusiastic. The 1-2 are bred to do better.
T/Plt: £98.10 to a £1 stake. Pool of £47769.50 - 355.22 winning tickets. T/Qpdt: £15.00 to £1 stake. Pool of £3681.23 - 181.50 winning tickets. JR

# 1732 RIPON (R-H)
## Friday, May 9

**OFFICIAL GOING: Good to soft (7.8)**
Rail on bend from back straight to home straight moved out 6yds increasing distances on Round course by 12yds.
Wind: Fairly strong, across Weather: Cloudy, bright

## 2134 SIS BRINGING BETTING TO LIFE MAIDEN AUCTION STKS 5f
**5:55** (5:55) (Class 5) 2-Y-O **£3,234** (£962; £481; £240) **Stalls** High

Form RPR

2 **1** **Cabbies Lou**[10] 1837 2-8-2 0 ........ JoeyHaynes(5) 3 64
(Noel Wilson) *chsd ldrs: drvn and outpcd over 2f out: rallied over 1f out: kpt on wl fnl f to ld towards fin* **10/3**[2]

5 **2** *nk* **Stanghow**[6] 1955 2-8-11 0 ........ PJMcDonald 4 67
(Mel Brittain) *led: rdn over 1f out: hung rt ins fnl f: kpt on: hdd towards fin* **11/4**[1]

0 **3** 2 **Pickle Lilly Pearl**[36] 1259 2-8-8 0 ........ RoystonFfrench 5 57
(David C Griffiths) *chsd ldr: effrt and drvn wl over 1f out: kpt on same pce ins fnl f* **33/1**

**4** 2 1/2 **Snow Cloud (IRE)** 2-8-4 0 ........ JulieBurke(3) 1 47
(David O'Meara) *in tch on outside: effrt and pushed along over 2f out: hung rt and no imp fr over 1f out* **11/4**[1]

4 **5** 1 **Fairweather Trader (IRE)**[8] 1901 2-8-11 0 ........ PaulMulrennan 2 47
(Paul Midgley) *chsd ldrs: drvn and outpcd over 2f out: n.d after* **14/1**

**6** 3/4 **Elevator Action (IRE)** 2-8-9 0 ........ GeorgeChaloner(3) 8 45+
(Richard Fahey) *rn green in rr: sn outpcd: kpt on fnl f: nvr on terms* **5/1**[3]

**7** 5 **Blazing Rose (IRE)** 2-8-5 0 ........ SamJames(3) 7 23
(David O'Meara) *s.i.s: sn wl bhd: no ch fr 1/2-way* **10/1**

1m 2.14s (2.14) **Going Correction** +0.075s/f (Good) **7** Ran SP% **111.8**
Speed ratings (Par 93): **85,84,81,77,75 74,66**
CSF £12.32 TOTE £2.40: £1.30, £3.70; EX 15.90 Trifecta £89.60.
**Owner** Glyn Budden **Bred** Lordship Stud **Trained** Middleham, N Yorks

**FOCUS**
Rail on bend from back straight to home straight moved out 6yds, increasing distances on Round course by 12yds. Just an ordinary maiden, with experience coming to the fore. The rating is in keeping with the race average.

## 2135 SIS LIVE (S) STKS 1m 1f 170y
**6:25** (6:25) (Class 6) 3-4-Y-O **£2,587** (£770; £384; £192) **Stalls** Low

Form RPR

10/0 **1** **Aseela (IRE)**[15] 1673 4-9-5 64 ........ AndrewElliott 1 55
(George Moore) *hld up towards rr: stdy hdwy over 2f out: effrt and rdn over 1f out: led ins fnl f: kpt on wl* **11/2**[2]

4-34 **2** 1 **Hello Sweetness**[10] 1852 3-8-4 46 ........ JamesSullivan 4 52?
(Jason Ward) *hld up in midfield: hdwy over 2f out: chsd wnr wl ins fnl f: r.o* **12/1**

-064 **3** *nk* **Ronya (IRE)**[20] 1588 3-7-13 59 ........ JoeyHaynes(5) 8 51
(K R Burke) *t.k.h: cl up: led over 2f out: rdn and hung rt over 1f out: hdd ins fnl f: kpt on same pce* **1/1**[1]

514- **4** 2 1/2 **Banreenahreenkah (IRE)**[16] 8093 4-9-2 58 ........ (t) GeorgeChaloner(3) 5 47
(Jennie Candlish) *t.k.h: led: rdn and hdd over 2f out: rallied: kpt on same pce ins fnl f* **6/1**[3]

040- **5** 8 **Card High (IRE)**[305] 4118 4-9-5 48 ........ KevinStott(5) 3 35
(Wilf Storey) *hld up in midfield: hdwy on outside to chse ldrs 3f out: rdn and wknd over 1f out* **66/1**

230- **6** 6 **Diddy Eric**[216] 7027 4-9-10 49 ........ PJMcDonald 10 23
(Micky Hammond) *hld up: rdn over 3f out: no imp fr 2f out* **14/1**

3442 **7** 2 1/4 **Bix (IRE)**[101] 363 4-9-7 44 ........ SladeO'Hara(3) 2 19
(Alan Berry) *missed break: bhd: shortlived effrt on ins wl over 2f out: sn btn* **40/1**

032- **8** 15 **Elusive Band (USA)**[247] 6114 4-9-10 59 ........ (p) PhillipMakin 7
(Bernard Llewellyn) *chsd ldrs: lost pl qckly 3f out: sn struggling* **13/2**

500- **9** 10 **Don't Tell**[16] 7343 4-8-12 41 ........ KieranSchofield(7) 9
(George Moore) *t.k.h: cl up tl rdn and wknd 3f out* **80/1**

2m 8.44s (3.04) **Going Correction** +0.25s/f (Good)
**WFA** 3 from 4yo 15lb **9** Ran SP% **112.5**
Speed ratings (Par 101): **97,96,95,93,87 82,80,68,60**
CSF £65.38 TOTE £3.50: £1.10, £2.30, £1.10; EX 107.00 Trifecta £170.40.There was no bid for the winner.
**Owner** Mrs Susan Moore **Bred** Gestut Sohrenhof **Trained** Middleham Moor, N Yorks

**FOCUS**
Decidedly modest fare in this seller, with the runner-up a doubt over the form.

## 2136 THEAKSTON OF MASHAM PARADISE ALE H'CAP 6f
**7:00** (7:02) (Class 4) (0-85,84) 4-Y-O+ **£4,851** (£1,443; £721; £360) **Stalls** High

Form RPR

6-04 **1** **Angus Og**[21] 1566 4-9-0 **82** ........ JoeyHaynes(5) 9 92
(K R Burke) *reluctant to enter stalls: prom: effrt and rdn over 2f out: hdwy and edgd rt over 1f out: led ins fnl f: kpt on wl* **16/1**

-565 **2** 1 1/2 **Hadaj**[5] 1975 5-9-1 **83** ........ KevinStott(5) 11 88+
(Ruth Carr) *hld up bhd ldng gp: rdn wl over 2f out: hdwy over 1f out: styd on to take 2nd nr fin: nt rch wnr* **7/4**[1]

6-53 **3** *nk* **Adam's Ale**[22] 1538 5-8-3 **71** ........ ShirleyTeasdale(5) 12 75
(Paul Midgley) *w ldr against stands' rail: rdn over 2f out: kpt on ins fnl f* **15/2**[3]

0-13 **4** 3/4 **Mutafaakir (IRE)**[6] 1938 5-9-4 **81** ........ (p) PJMcDonald 7 83
(Ruth Carr) *led: rdn 2f out: hdd ins fnl f: kpt on same pce* **11/4**[2]

40-4 **5** *nk* **Green Howard**[22] 1538 6-9-2 **82** ........ NeilFarley(3) 4 83
(Robin Bastiman) *towards rr: hdwy on outside 2f out: rdn and no imp over 1f out* **11/1**

6-03 **6** 3 1/2 **Teetotal (IRE)**[27] 1440 4-8-9 **72** ........ AndrewMullen 3 62
(Nigel Tinkler) *t.k.h: trckd ldrs: rdn over 2f out: wknd over 1f out* **22/1**

60-0 **7** 5 **Head Space (IRE)**[15] 1672 6-9-7 **84** ........ (p) JamesSullivan 10 58
(Ruth Carr) *stdd in rr: rdn and outpcd over 2f out: passed btn horses ins fnl f: nvr on terms* **14/1**

550- **8** 3/4 **Avon Breeze**[200] 7420 5-9-3 **80** ........ RobertWinston 8 51
(Richard Whitaker) *hld up bhd ldng gp: struggling over 2f out: sn btn* **10/1**

322- **9** 1/2 **Ambitious Icarus**[184] 7777 5-9-3 **80** ........ (e) RobbieFitzpatrick 1 50
(Richard Guest) *hld up in midfield on outside: stdy hdwy over 3f out: rdn and wknd 2f out* **20/1**

200- **10** 3/4 **Another Citizen (IRE)**[272] 5294 6-8-4 **74** ........ (b) RachelRichardson(7) 6 41
(Tim Easterby) *hld up in midfield: struggling over 2f out: sn btn* **40/1**

1m 12.46s (-0.54) **Going Correction** +0.075s/f (Good) **10** Ran SP% **116.3**
Speed ratings (Par 105): **106,104,103,102,102 97,90,89,89,88**
CSF £43.37 CT £227.13 TOTE £64.20: £11.10, £1.02, £1.10; EX 66.00 Trifecta £539.90.
**Owner** D Simpson & Mrs E Burke **Bred** Shane O'Sullivan **Trained** Middleham Moor, N Yorks

**FOCUS**
A fairly useful handicap. The pace soon looked sound. High draws looked best and the winner rates a small personal best.

## 2137 SIS TOP ATA DELIVERY H'CAP 1m 1f 170y
**7:35** (7:37) (Class 3) (0-90,89) 4-Y-O **£7,561** (£2,263; £1,131; £566; £282) **Stalls** Low

Form RPR

352- **1** **Flow (USA)**[209] 7211 4-9-4 **86** ........ (t) PhillipMakin 3 97+
(Lady Cecil) *trckd ldrs gng wl: smooth hdwy to ld over 1f out: edgd lft ins fnl f: rdn out* **2/1**[1]

0402 **2** 1 1/2 **San Cassiano (IRE)**[7] 1926 7-8-7 **75** ........ JamesSullivan 5 83
(Ruth Carr) *led at ordinary gallop: qcknd over 3f out: rdn and hdd over 1f out: rallied: one pce wl ins fnl f* **4/1**[2]

0-56 **3** 1/2 **Ardmay (IRE)**[22] 1539 5-8-11 **79** ........ (p) DanielTudhope 7 86
(Kevin Ryan) *in tch: effrt and rdn 2f out: edgd rt: kpt on same pce ins fnl f* **8/1**

14-4 **4** 6 **Off The Pulse**[113] 200 4-8-13 **81** ........ PaulMulrennan 10 76
(John Mackie) *t.k.h: chsd ldr: rdn over 2f out: wknd over 1f out* **20/1**

00-0 **5** *nse* **St Moritz (IRE)**[13] 1724 8-8-5 **76** ........ SamJames(3) 2 71
(David O'Meara) *dwlt: hld up towards rr: rdn and effrt on outside over 2f out: no imp over 1f out* **6/1**

5-04 **6** 3/4 **Amaze**[34] 1306 6-8-13 **81** ........ (p) BarryMcHugh 8 74
(Brian Ellison) *hld up towards rr: rdn over 3f out: edgd rt and no imp 2f out* **16/1**

0-06 **7** 6 **Las Verglas Star (IRE)**[13] 1715 6-8-10 **81** ........ GeorgeChaloner(3) 1 62
(Richard Fahey) *hld up: n.m.r bnd over 5f out: sn rdn along: struggling fr over 2f out* **5/1**[3]

020- **8** 20 **Muffin McLeay (IRE)**[300] 4280 6-9-7 **89** ........ AndrewMullen 4 29
(David Barron) *t.k.h in rr: checked bnd after 4f: sn rdn: lost tch fr 4f out: t.o* **16/1**

2m 5.95s (0.55) **Going Correction** +0.25s/f (Good) **8** Ran SP% **111.9**
Speed ratings (Par 107): **107,105,105,100,100 99,95,79**
CSF £9.45 CT £49.52 TOTE £2.10: £1.10, £1.60, £2.50; EX 10.80 Trifecta £41.30.
**Owner** Niarchos Family **Bred** Flaxman Holdings Ltd **Trained** Newmarket, Suffolk
■ Stewards' Enquiry : Sam James three-day ban: careless riding (May 27-29); four-day ban: failed to ride out for 4th (May 30-Jun 2)

**FOCUS**
A useful performance from the winner, who looks set for a fruitful campaign. The field soon become strung out once the leader quickened the tempo early in the straight. The form is rated around the runner-up's recent form.

## 2138 SIS DELIVERING CONTENT FOR DIGITAL PLATFORMS MAIDEN STKS 6f
**8:10** (8:12) (Class 5) 3-Y-O **£3,234** (£962; £481; £240) **Stalls** High

Form RPR

23-2 **1** **Galvanize**[12] 1757 3-9-5 86 ........ PaulMulrennan 2 85
(Kevin Ryan) *mde all: rdn over 1f out: hrd pressed fnl f: hld on wl towards fin* **11/4**[2]

0-22 **2** 1/2 **Soul Brother (IRE)**[15] 1671 3-9-5 84 ........ DuranFentiman 4 83
(Tim Easterby) *t.k.h: chsd wnr: effrt and rdn over 1f out: chal fnl f: kpt on: hld nr fin* **4/7**[1]

-540 **3** 5 **Highland Acclaim (IRE)**[6] 1939 3-9-5 84 ........ DanielTudhope 1 67
(David O'Meara) *awkward s: in tch: shkn up and effrt over 2f out: outpcd by first two fr over 1f out* **5/1**[3]

00- **4** 12 **Lunesdale Buddy**[252] 5970 3-9-2 0 ........ SladeO'Hara(3) 3 29
(Alan Berry) *cl up tl rdn and wknd fr over 2f out* **100/1**

1m 13.67s (0.67) **Going Correction** +0.075s/f (Good) **4** Ran SP% **108.0**
Speed ratings (Par 99): **98,97,90,74**
CSF £4.79 TOTE £3.70; EX 4.00 Trifecta £5.60.
**Owner** Matt & Lauren Morgan **Bred** Mrs Susan Field **Trained** Hambleton, N Yorks

**FOCUS**
Effectively a match but it didn't go the way the betting suggested. The front three had all shown form good enough to win the usual race of this type.

## 2139 SIS AT THE HEART OF RACING H'CAP 2m
**8:40** (8:42) (Class 5) (0-75,76) 4-Y-O+ **£3,234** (£962; £481; £240) **Stalls** Low

Form RPR

20-6 **1** **Rosairlie (IRE)**[30] 1374 6-9-10 **73** ........ PJMcDonald 10 85
(Micky Hammond) *hld up on ins: hdwy 3f out: rdn to ld appr fnl f: edgd rt: styd on strly* **10/1**

022- **2** 3 3/4 **Perfect Summer (IRE)**[203] 7342 4-9-4 **70** ........ PaulMulrennan 5 77
(Lady Cecil) *t.k.h: hld up in tch: smooth hdwy over 4f out: led over 2f out: edgd rt: rdn and hdd appr fnl f: kpt on same pce last 150yds* **5/4**[1]

-313 **3** 4 1/2 **Naburn**[21] 1567 6-9-7 **70** ........ RobertWinston 3 72
(Alan Swinbank) *t.k.h: in tch: rdn 3f out: edgd rt wl over 1f out: styd on to take 3rd towards fin* **13/2**[2]

2-41 **4** 1 1/4 **Choisan (IRE)**[7] 1929 5-9-13 **76** 6ex ........ (tp) DuranFentiman 6 76
(Tim Easterby) *cl up: led over 3f out to over 2f out: rallied: outpcd fnl f* **17/2**

00-0 **5** 3/4 **Petella**[18] 1605 8-7-13 **55**............ KieranSchofield(7) 2 54
(George Moore) *bhd: rdn 1/2-way: hdwy on outside over 4f out: cl up tl wknd appr fnl f* **28/1**

0 **6** 3 1/4 **Baccalaureate (FR)**[30] 1377 8-9-9 **72**............ DougieCostello 9 67
(Sue Smith) *hld up: rdn and effrt over 3f out: outpcd fnl 2f* **66/1**

5-02 **7** 8 **Jan Smuts (IRE)**[18] 1605 6-8-11 **65**............(tp) KevinStott(5) 4 51
(Wilf Storey) *hld up: rdn and effrt over 3f out: sn no imp: btn fnl 2f* **7/1**[3]

2-04 **8** 2 1/2 **Sergeant Pink (IRE)**[12] 1763 8-8-3 **57** ow3............(b) EmmaSayer(5) 1 40
(Dianne Sayer) *dwlt: sn cl up: rdn and wknd fr 3f out* **25/1**

1110 **9** nse **Travel (USA)**[14] 1692 4-9-4 **70**............ AdrianNicholls 7 53
(Mark Johnston) *led at ordinary gallop: rdn and hdd over 3f out: wknd 2f out* **8/1**

2-05 **10** 5 **Cowslip**[18] 1605 5-8-5 **54**............ AndrewElliott 11 31
(George Moore) *prom on outside: drvn over 5f out: wknd fr 4f out* **12/1**

3m 34.36s (2.56) **Going Correction** +0.25s/f (Good)
**WFA** 4 from 5yo+ 3lb **10** Ran SP% **117.5**
Speed ratings (Par 103): **103,101,98,98,97 96,92,91,90,88**
CSF £22.78 CT £93.20 TOTE £14.10: £3.30, £1.10, £3.00; EX 33.20 Trifecta £236.40.
**Owner** Late Night Drinkers & Wishful Thinkers **Bred** Airlie Stud **Trained** Middleham Moor, N Yorks

**FOCUS**
A fair staying event. The gallop looked modest until they quickened early in the straight. A personal best from the winner.
T/Plt: £46.10 to a £1 stake. Pool of £59522.48 - 941.83 winning tickets. T/Qpdt: £16.10 to a £1 stake. Pool of £4808.85 - 220.90 winning tickets. RY

2140 - 2141a (Foreign Racing) - See Raceform Interactive

# 2107 ASCOT (R-H)

Saturday, May 10

**OFFICIAL GOING: Good to soft changing to good to soft (soft in places) after race 1 (2.05)**
Rail on Round course moved in 3yds from 12f to Home straight, adding 12yds to 1m 4f races.
Wind: Strong, half against Weather: Showery

## 2142 LEO BANCROFT SIGNATURE HAIRCARE H'CAP 1m 4f
2:05 (2:05) (Class 3) (0-95,95) 4-Y-0+ **£8,409** (£2,502; £1,250; £625) **Stalls** Low

Form RPR

454- **1** **Al Saham**[221] 6927 5-9-3 **91**............ SilvestreDeSousa 5 105
(Saeed bin Suroor) *dwlt: plld hrd: sn in tch: led 3f out: hrd rdn over 1f out: hld on by diminishing margin* **8/1**[3]

511- **2** 1/2 **Hamelin (IRE)**[214] 7105 4-9-3 **91**............ RichardHughes 8 104+
(Lady Cecil) *hld up towards rr: hdwy 3f out: drvn to chse wnr over 1f out: clsd fnl f: nt quite able to get up* **9/4**[1]

100- **3** 7 **Rhombus (IRE)**[182] 7823 4-9-1 **89**............ TomQueally 4 91
(Ismail Mohammed) *t.k.h towards rr: hdwy 3f out: wnt 4th over 2f out: styd on same pce* **8/1**[3]

1- **4** 4 **Semeen**[288] 4720 5-9-2 **90**............ AdamKirby 1 85
(Luca Cumani) *chsd ldrs: wnt 2nd and hung rt wl over 2f out: wknd over 1f out* **8/1**[3]

0356 **5** 5 **Swing Alone (IRE)**[22] 1556 5-9-5 **93**............ LukeMorris 7 80
(Gay Kelleway) *bhd: rdn 5f out: n.d* **16/1**

0/0- **6** 5 **Aazif (IRE)**[24] 3685 5-8-9 **83**............(t) StevieDonohoe 6 62
(Ian Williams) *bhd: rdn over 5f out: nvr trbld ldrs* **33/1**

1110 **7** 10 **The Lock Master (IRE)**[22] 1553 7-8-13 **87**............ JamieSpencer 2 50
(Michael Appleby) *prom in chsng gp: rdn and clsd on ldng pair 4f out: wknd 3f out* **25/1**

11/0 **8** 18 **Restraint Of Trade (IRE)**[107] 305 4-9-7 **95**............(p) MartinLane 3 30
(Charlie Appleby) *chsd ldr: led after 3f and sn wnt 8 l clr at str pce: hdd over 3f out: wknd rapidly and eased* **10/1**

22-3 **9** 25 **Glorious Protector (IRE)**[35] 1299 4-9-1 **89**............ GeorgeBaker 9
(Ed Walker) *led 3f: chsd clr ldr and 8 l clr of rest: clsd and led briefly over 3f out: wknd qckly wl over 2f out: bled fr the nose* **11/4**[2]

2m 35.57s (3.07) **Going Correction** +0.475s/f (Yiel) **9** Ran SP% **112.5**
Speed ratings (Par 107): **108,107,103,100,97 93,87,75,58**
CSF £25.54 CT £148.89 TOTE £10.50: £2.50, £1.30, £2.80; EX 28.10 Trifecta £301.50.
**Owner** Godolphin **Bred** Darley **Trained** Newmarket, Suffolk

**FOCUS**
The rail on the round course had been moved in 3yds from 1m4f start to home straight, adding 12yds to 1m4f races. The ground had eased following 3mm of rain overnight. A good handicap that was run at a furious gallop, Martin Lane riding Restraint Of Trade as though it were a 5f race. The front pair drew clear. The form is a bit out of line with the winner's profile.

## 2143 CAREY GROUP BUCKHOUNDS STKS (LISTED RACE) 1m 4f
2:40 (2:40) (Class 1) 4-Y-0+
**£25,519** (£9,675; £4,842; £2,412; £1,210; £607) **Stalls** Low

Form RPR

22-2 **1** **Gatewood**[41] 1194 6-9-0 104............ FrankieDettori 3 109
(John Gosden) *chsd ldrs: wnt 2nd over 3f out: led 2f out: a jst holding runner-up: rdn out* **4/1**[1]

31-2 **2** 1/2 **Pether's Moon (IRE)**[7] 1950 4-9-3 110............ RichardHughes 2 111
(Richard Hannon) *hld up in midfield: lost pl over 5f out: rallied 3f out: str chal fnl 2f: jst hld* **4/1**[1]

03-1 **3** 1 3/4 **Elidor**[28] 1444 4-9-0 99............ WilliamTwiston-Davies 1 105
(Mick Channon) *trckd ldrs gng wl: rdn 2f out: kpt on same pce* **8/1**

66-4 **4** 1/2 **Continuum**[31] 1398 5-9-0 94............ LukeMorris 8 104
(Peter Hedger) *bhd: rdn over 3f out: styd on wl fnl 2f: nvr nrr* **33/1**

160- **5** 4 1/2 **Cap O'Rushes**[238] 6393 4-9-0 108............ SilvestreDeSousa 10 97
(Charlie Appleby) *led: sn wnt 3 l clr at gd pce: hdd 2f out: sn wknd* **7/1**

000- **6** 2 **Kelinni (IRE)**[182] 7827 6-9-0 106............[1] AdamKirby 9 94
(Marco Botti) *a stuck wd: towards rr: effrt 4f out: btn 3f out* **8/1**

12-0 **7** 4 **Harris Tweed**[10] 1869 7-9-0 112............(p) GeorgeBaker 6 87
(William Haggas) *chsd ldr tl over 3f out: wknd 2f out* **9/2**[2]

0-60 **8** 13 **Buckwheat**[70] 811 4-9-0 107............ MartinLane 7 67
(Charlie Appleby) *bhd: rdn along and mod effrt over 2f out: sn wknd* **16/1**

02-1 **9** 27 **Area Fifty One**[41] 1194 6-9-0 105............ JamieSpencer 4 23
(Nicky Henderson) *towards rr on outer: effrt 4f out: wknd 3f out* **6/1**[3]

2m 36.13s (3.63) **Going Correction** +0.475s/f (Yiel) **9** Ran SP% **116.0**
Speed ratings (Par 111): **106,105,104,104,101 99,97,88,70**
CSF £20.07 TOTE £4.70: £1.70, £1.50, £2.70; EX 19.50 Trifecta £123.40.
**Owner** O T I Racing & G Strawbridge **Bred** George Strawbridge **Trained** Newmarket, Suffolk

**FOCUS**
Solid Listed form. Silvestre de Sousa ensured the gallop was a decent one aboard the returning Cap O'Rushes, although the time was 8lb lower than the preceding handicap. The winner is rated to his British form since returning from Australia.

## 2144 SODEXO FILLIES' H'CAP 1m (S)
3:15 (3:16) (Class 2) 3-Y-0+ **£29,110** (£8,662; £4,329; £2,164) **Stalls** Centre

Form RPR

6-06 **1** **Amulet**[7] 1945 4-8-9 **84**............ ShaneKelly 6 93
(Eve Johnson Houghton) *mde all: edgd lft fnl f: hld on wl: drvn out* **15/2**

13-2 **2** nk **Ribbons**[21] 1577 4-9-6 **95**............ HayleyTurner 4 103
(James Fanshawe) *hld up in 6th: hdwy 3f out: wnt 2nd 2f out: drvn to press wnr fnl f: jst hld* **5/4**[1]

1/1- **3** 1 1/4 **Majestic Queen (IRE)**[15] 1703 4-9-5 **94**............ GaryCarroll 9 99
(Tracey Collins, Ire) *prom: rdn over 2f out: kpt on wl* **7/1**[3]

003- **4** 3 1/2 **Masarah (IRE)**[191] 7649 4-9-9 **98**............ RichardHughes 10 95
(Clive Brittain) *stdd s: hld up in detached last: shkn up and hdwy over 1f out: styd on* **14/1**

0-03 **5** 3 **Nurpur (IRE)**[13] 1762 4-8-10 **85**............ DanielTudhope 3 75
(David O'Meara) *hld up in 7th: hdwy and swtchd rt over 1f out: no ex fnl f* **16/1**

52-4 **6** 3 3/4 **Rasheeda**[10] 1868 3-8-0 **88** oh2............ LukeMorris 8 66
(Marco Botti) *sn prom: rdn over 2f out: wknd wl over 1f out* **7/1**[3]

126- **7** 8 **Dutch Rose (IRE)**[217] 7025 5-9-7 **99**............ SamJames(3) 2 62
(David O'Meara) *prom tl wknd 2f out* **20/1**

1442 **8** 1 3/4 **Fashion Line (IRE)**[5] 2032 4-8-8 **88**............ LouisSteward(5) 5 47
(Michael Bell) *prom tl wknd 2f out* **5/1**[2]

1m 46.91s (6.11) **Going Correction** +0.575s/f (Yiel)
**WFA** 3 from 4yo+ 13lb **8** Ran SP% **115.2**
Speed ratings (Par 96): **92,91,90,86,83 80,72,70**
CSF £17.48 CT £70.83 TOTE £8.70: £2.30, £1.30, £2.20; EX 24.20 Trifecta £198.20.
**Owner** Mrs Virginia Neale **Bred** Cherry Park Stud **Trained** Blewbury, Oxon

**FOCUS**
A useful fillies' handicap that was run at an ordinary gallop. They raced centre-field. The winner resumed her progress from last year.

## 2145 £7.5 MILLION TOTESCOOP6 VICTORIA CUP (HERITAGE H'CAP) 7f
3:50 (3:52) (Class 2) 4-Y-0+
**£62,250** (£18,640; £9,320; £4,660; £2,330; £1,170) **Stalls** Centre

Form RPR

5-05 **1** **Gabriel's Lad (IRE)**[14] 1728 5-9-8 **102**............ GeorgeBaker 25 114
(Denis Coakley) *towards rr stands' side: smooth hdwy 2f out: led ins fnl f: rdn out* **12/1**[3]

0-21 **2** 2 1/4 **Glen Moss (IRE)**[14] 1719 5-9-7 **101**............ SeanLevey 29 107
(David Brown) *racd stands' side: prom: led gp 2f out tl ins fnl f: unable qck* **16/1**

260- **3** 2 1/2 **Belgian Bill**[224] 6838 6-9-8 **102**............(tp) PatCosgrave 21 102
(George Baker) *in tch stands' side: effrt 2f out: one pce fnl f* **25/1**

01-3 **4** 1 1/4 **Ayaar (IRE)**[21] 1576 4-9-3 **97**............ FrankieDettori 23 93
(Luca Cumani) *in tch stands' side: styd on fnl 2f* **9/1**[1]

30-0 **5** 1/2 **Gramercy (IRE)**[14] 1719 7-8-13 **93**............(b) JamieSpencer 16 88
(David Simcock) *in rr stands' side: hdwy over 1f out: r.o* **20/1**

000- **6** nk **Pastoral Player**[196] 7540 7-9-6 **100**............ HayleyTurner 26 94
(Hughie Morrison) *towards rr stands' side: hdwy over 1f out: nvr nrr* **25/1**

56-0 **7** nk **Boots And Spurs**[42] 1164 5-8-7 **90**............(t) WilliamTwiston-Davies(3) 22 83
(Stuart Williams) *chsd ldrs stands' side: kpt on same pce fnl 2f* **20/1**

-420 **8** hd **Don't Call Me (IRE)**[14] 1721 7-9-1 **95**............(t) AdrianNicholls 17 88
(David Nicholls) *mid-div stands' side: styd on same pce fnl 2f* **14/1**

50-4 **9** 1 **Dont Bother Me (IRE)**[14] 1719 4-9-0 **99**............ MarcMonaghan(5) 18 89
(Marco Botti) *prom stands' side tl wknd over 1f out* **16/1**

-601 **10** 2 **Ruwaiyan (USA)**[7] 1957 5-8-9 **89**............(p) LukeMorris 5 74
(James Tate) *t.k.h: in rr far side: styd on fnl 2f: 1st of 9 in gp: no ch w stands' side* **16/1**

3120 **11** nk **Sound Advice**[14] 1721 5-8-10 **90**............ TomEaves 28 74
(Keith Dalgleish) *chsd ldr stands' side: led briefly over 2f out: sn wknd* **66/1**

2041 **12** hd **Georgian Bay (IRE)**[21] 1576 4-9-5 **99**............(v) AdamKirby 4 83
(K R Burke) *in tch far side: outpcd fnl 2f: 2nd of 9 in gp* **16/1**

0-23 **13** 1/2 **Brownsea Brink**[28] 1437 4-8-13 **93**............ RichardHughes 13 75
(Richard Hannon) *mid-div stands' side: rdn and btn 2f out* **9/1**[1]

0-66 **14** nse **Heaven's Guest (IRE)**[23] 1531 4-9-6 **103**............ GeorgeChaloner(3) 20 85
(Richard Fahey) *chsd ldrs stands' side: wknd over 1f out* **14/1**

15-4 **15** 1/2 **Redvers (IRE)**[16] 1679 6-9-4 **98**............(b) FrederikTylicki 8 79
(Ed Vaughan) *prom: jnd far side ldr over 1f out: wknd fnl f: 3rd of 9 in gp* **20/1**

4-11 **16** nse **Purcell (IRE)**[35] 1301 4-9-1 **98**............ OisinMurphy(3) 10 79
(Andrew Balding) *led far side gp: edgd lft over 1f out: wknd fnl f: no ch w stands' side: 4th of 9 in gp* **12/1**[3]

0-53 **17** 1 1/4 **Spiritual Star (IRE)**[49] 1070 5-8-11 **91**............ WilliamCarson 14 69
(Anthony Carson) *towards rr stands' side: n.d* **33/1**

000- **18** 2 **Excellent Guest**[203] 7364 7-9-1 **95**............ TomQueally 11 67
(George Margarson) *chsd ldr far side: btn whn carried lft over 1f out: sn wknd: 5th of 9 in gp* **20/1**

0336 **19** 4 1/2 **Bertiewhittle**[14] 1719 6-9-2 **103**............ JackGarritty(7) 2 64
(David Barron) *chsd ldrs far side: wknd 2f out: 6th of 9 in gp* **20/1**

100- **20** nk **Burn The Boats (IRE)**[209] 7227 5-8-12 **95**............ ColinKeane(3) 12 55
(G M Lyons, Ire) *in tch stands' side: wknd 2f out* **16/1**

0-02 **21** 3/4 **Louis The Pious**[14] 1719 6-9-5 **99**............ DanielTudhope 19 57
(David O'Meara) *chsd ldrs stands' side: wknd 2f out* **16/1**

03-1 **22** 4 **Flyman**[41] 1193 4-9-4 **98**............ TonyHamilton 3 46
(Richard Fahey) *prom far side: wknd 2f out: 7th of 9 in gp* **16/1**

33-5 **23** 4 1/2 **Loving Spirit**[21] 1578 6-9-2 **99**............ RobertTart(3) 7 35
(James Toller) *chsd ldrs far side: wknd over 2f out: 8th of 9 in gp* **10/1**[2]

-245 **24** 1 3/4 **Captain Ramius (IRE)**[14] 1734 8-9-5 **104**............ ShaneGray(5) 6 35
(Kevin Ryan) *rrd s: sn prom far side: wknd over 2f out: last of 9 in gp* **25/1**

0-06 **25** 3/4 **Dubawi Sound**[14] 1728 6-8-7 **92**............(b) LouisSteward(5) 27 21
(Hugo Palmer) *led stands' side gp tl wknd qckly over 2f out: sn bhd* **33/1**

1m 29.78s (2.18) **Going Correction** +0.575s/f (Yiel) **25** Ran SP% **141.7**
Speed ratings (Par 109): **110,107,104,103,102 102,101,101,100,98 97,97,97,97,96 96,94,92,87,87 86,81,76,74,73**
CSF £179.83 CT £4811.73 TOTE £16.60: £5.30, £5.40, £5.80, £2.60; EX 340.20 Trifecta £1748.10.
**Owner** Killoran Ennis Conway **Bred** Yeomanstown Stud **Trained** West Ilsley, Berks

**FOCUS**
A typically competitive edition of this race. They split into two, with the bigger group, stands' side, coming out well on top. The form is Listed grade at least.

## 2146 PLAY THE TOTESCOOP6 TODAY MAIDEN STKS (BOBIS RACE) 5f
**4:25** (4:25) (Class 3) 2-Y-O **£7,762** (£2,310; £1,154; £577) **Stalls** High

Form RPR
1 **Moonraker** 2-9-2 0 WilliamTwiston-Davies(3) 5 86+
(Mick Channon) *dwlt: sn in tch and gng wl: led 2f out: rdn to hold on fnl f* **9/2**[3]

2 *nk* **Mubtaghaa (IRE)** 2-9-5 0 PaulHanagan 4 85+
(William Haggas) *dwlt: hld up in rr: shkn up and hdwy over 1f out: r.o wl fnl f: clsng at fin* **6/1**

3 *hd* **Winslow (USA)** 2-9-5 0 SilvestreDeSousa 3 84
(Charlie Appleby) *rn green thrght: in tch: rdn and r.o fr over 1f out: clsng at fin* **8/1**

4 *2* **St Brelades Bay (IRE)** 2-9-5 0 SeanLevey 8 80+
(Richard Hannon) *hld up in rr: rdn 2f out: disputing 4th and running on whn sltly hmpd ins fnl f* **8/1**

5 *1 1/4* **Sunset Sail (IRE)** 2-9-5 0 RichardHughes 1 73
(Richard Hannon) *led and sn crossed to stands' rail: hdd 2f out: grad fdd* **7/2**[2]

4 6 *3 1/2* **The Paco Kid**[29] 1417 2-9-5 0 FrankieDettori 7 60
(Olly Stevens) *hld up in 6th: effrt 2f out: wknd over 1f out* **5/2**[1]

7 *hd* **Outback Ruler (IRE)** 2-9-5 0 AdamKirby 6 59
(Clive Cox) *prom tl hung rt and wknd over 1f out* **20/1**

8 *25* **Indescribable (IRE)** 2-9-5 0 FrannyNorton 2
(Mark Johnston) *chsd ldr tl hung rt and wknd qckly over 2f out: sn wl bhd* **16/1**

1m 4.01s (3.51) **Going Correction** +0.575s/f (Yiel) **8 Ran SP% 116.1**
Speed ratings (Par 97): **94,93,93,90,88 82,82,42**
CSF £32.03 TOTE £5.70: £1.80, £1.90, £2.30; EX 40.80 Trifecta £382.00.
**Owner** Christopher Wright & Miss Emily Asprey **Bred** Stratford Place Stud **Trained** West Ilsley, Berks

**FOCUS**
A race quite capable of throwing up a smart juvenile and there were several performances of note, but a guessy level of form. They raced stands' side

## 2147 ESPIRITO SANTO INVESTMENT BANK H'CAP 6f
**5:00** (5:01) (Class 4) (0-80,80) 4-Y-O+ **£6,469** (£1,925; £962; £481) **Stalls** Centre

Form RPR
631- 1 **Intrinsic**[220] 6940 4-9-7 80 RichardHughes 4 98+
(Robert Cowell) *hld up in rr and confidently rdn: gd hdwy over 1f out: led ins fnl f: pushed out* **10/1**

5030 2 *1 1/4* **Trader Jack**[1] 2110 5-9-4 80 RobertTart(3) 20 92
(David Flood) *hld up in rr: gd hdwy over 1f out: chsd wnr ins fnl f: kpt on* **7/1**[2]

11-3 3 *2 1/2* **Marmalady (IRE)**[26] 1490 4-9-7 80 GeorgeBaker 14 84
(Gary Moore) *trckd ldrs: rdn to ld briefly ins fnl f: one pce* **10/1**

4-06 4 *nk* **Triple Chocolate**[66] 843 4-8-13 72 JimmyQuinn 15 75
(Roger Ingram) *chsd ldrs: led over 1f out tl ins fnl f: no ex* **16/1**

30-0 5 *1 1/2* **Slip Sliding Away (IRE)**[26] 1492 7-9-7 80 AdamKirby 11 78
(Peter Hedger) *mid-div: rdn 2f out: kpt on fnl f* **16/1**

2-50 6 *3/4* **Vallarta (IRE)**[14] 1731 4-8-12 74 WilliamTwiston-Davies(3) 19 70
(Mick Channon) *hld up towards rr: hdwy and sltly hmpd over 1f out: nvr nrr* **16/1**

-026 7 *3/4* **Commanche**[16] 1678 5-9-4 77 SilvestreDeSousa 10 70
(Chris Dwyer) *in tch: rdn to chse ldr 2f out: wknd 1f out* **20/1**

34-2 8 *nk* **Kinglami**[5] 2030 5-9-3 79 OisinMurphy(3) 16 71+
(Brian Gubby) *hld up in midfield: hdwy whn no room and bdly squeezed over 1f out: nt rcvr* **4/1**[1]

1011 9 *1* **Multitask**[43] 1144 4-9-2 75 JamieSpencer 9 64
(Michael Madgwick) *in rr tl pushed along and sme hdwy fr over 1f out* **12/1**

06-5 10 *nk* **Lupo D'Oro (IRE)**[26] 1490 5-9-7 80 TomQueally 8 68
(John Best) *mid-div: effrt 2f out: wknd over 1f out* **25/1**

16-0 11 *2 1/4* **Gravitational (IRE)**[14] 1731 4-9-2 78 AshleyMorgan(3) 17 59+
(Chris Wall) *in tch: hmpd and lost pl wl over 1f out: nt rcvr* **12/1**

-656 12 *1 3/4* **Lionheart**[16] 1667 4-9-3 76 ShaneKelly 5 52
(Peter Crate) *stdd s: hld up towards rr: rdn over 1f out: nvr rchd ldrs* **25/1**

140- 13 *1 3/4* **Generalyse**[163] 8088 5-9-5 78 (b) HayleyTurner 22 48
(Ben De Haan) *chsd ldrs tl 2f out: btn whn n.m.r on stands' rail over 1f out* **25/1**

-120 14 *3/4* **Rambo Will**[26] 1490 6-8-9 71 NataliaGemelova(3) 3 39
(J R Jenkins) *w ldrs: racd alone in centre tl c across to join rest of field fr 1/2-way: wknd wl over 1f out* **25/1**

000- 15 *1 1/2* **Ask Dad**[12] 1822 4-8-10 76 (bt) MeganCarberry(7) 7 39
(Damian Joseph English, Ire) *prom: rdn and struggling to hold pl whn bmpd over 1f out: no ch after* **8/1**[3]

51-3 16 *1* **Prince Regal**[14] 1731 4-9-5 78 DanielTudhope 12 38
(Alan Jarvis) *chsd ldr tl wknd 2f out* **7/1**[2]

100- 17 *1* **Common Cents**[346] 2780 5-8-8 67 StevieDonohoe 21 23
(Ian Williams) *led tl wknd and edgd lft over 1f out* **25/1**

1421 18 *1 1/4* **Sweet Talking Guy (IRE)**[39] 1221 4-8-7 69 (t) SimonPearce(3) 1 21
(Lydia Pearce) *mid-div: rdn 3f out: sn btn: eased whn no ch over 1f out* **20/1**

1m 16.63s (2.13) **Going Correction** +0.575s/f (Yiel) **18 Ran SP% 136.1**
Speed ratings (Par 105): **108,106,103,102,100 99,98,98,96,96 93,91,88,87,85 84,83,81**
CSF £78.44 CT £751.42 TOTE £8.50: £2.30, £2.40, £2.10, £4.30; EX 119.00 Trifecta £499.80.
**Owner** Malih Lahej Al Basti **Bred** Cheveley Park Stud Ltd **Trained** Six Mile Bottom, Cambs

**FOCUS**
In a reaction to the earlier big-field handicap, everything wanted to race stands' side and racing room was at a premium nearest the rail. The race threw up quite a taking winner.
T/Jkpt: Not won. T/Plt: £268.30 to a £1 stake. Pool of £209239.06 - 569.10 winning units. T/Qpdt: £72.10 to a £1 stake. Pool of £13897.95 - 142.60 winning units. LM

# 1717 HAYDOCK (L-H)
Saturday, May 10

**OFFICIAL GOING: Soft (good to soft in places on flat course) changing to soft after race 2 (2:25)**
NH: Bends moved out 4m and distances increased by about 12yds per circuit.
Flat: All races on stands' side st. Dists on Rnd course increased by 43yds.
Wind: Fresh, half against Weather: Cloudy, heavy showers

## 2148 PERTEMPS NETWORK H'CAP (BOBIS RACE) 1m
**2:25** (2:26) (Class 3) (0-95,93) 3-Y-O **£8,086** (£2,406; £1,202; £601) **Stalls** Low

Form RPR
13-4 1 **Red Stargazer (IRE)**[16] 1658 3-9-4 90 GrahamGibbons 2 101
(David Barron) *in rr: niggled along 3f out: hdwy 2f out: wnt 2nd over 1f out: chalng ins fnl f: styd on to ld cl home* **14/1**

31-1 2 *nk* **Chatez (IRE)**[17] 1655 3-9-0 86 FergusSweeney 3 96+
(Alan King) *hld up: hdwy over 2f out: rdn to ld over 1f out: pressed ins fnl f: hdd cl home* **9/4**[1]

35-0 3 *3 3/4* **Stormardal (IRE)**[24] 1516 3-9-7 93 PaulMulrennan 5 94
(Ismail Mohammed) *led: rdn 2f out: hdd over 1f out: unable to go w front two fnl 100yds: styd on same pce* **14/1**

5-42 4 *shd* **Showpiece**[14] 1714 3-8-11 83 PatDobbs 7 84
(Richard Hannon) *s.i.s: hld up: hdwy over 2f out: rdn to chse ldrs over 1f out: kpt on ins fnl f: unable to mount serious chal* **7/1**

453- 5 *1 1/4* **Riverboat Springs (IRE)**[201] 7421 3-9-5 91 LiamKeniry 6 89
(Mick Channon) *chsd ldrs: rdn and outpcd over 2f out: kpt on ins fnl f: no imp* **25/1**

1 6 *hd* **Matalleb (USA)**[28] 1433 3-9-1 87 DaneO'Neill 1 85
(John Gosden) *s.i.s: racd keenly: hld up: hdwy 2f out: chsd ldrs over 1f out: no ex fnl 100yds* **7/2**[3]

50-6 7 *11* **Rising Breeze (FR)**[41] 1195 3-8-11 83 PhillipMakin 9 56
(K R Burke) *chsd ldr tl rdn over 2f out: wknd wl over 1f out* **40/1**

1 8 *3/4* **Active Spirit (IRE)**[26] 1486 3-9-0 86 KierenFallon 4 57
(Saeed bin Suroor) *chsd ldrs: pushed along over 3f out: wknd over 1f out* **5/2**[2]

1m 46.12s (2.42) **Going Correction** +0.425s/f (Yiel) **8 Ran SP% 113.7**
Speed ratings (Par 103): **104,103,99,99,98 98,87,86**
CSF £45.31 CT £460.94 TOTE £11.70: £2.40, £1.50, £2.60; EX 49.40 Trifecta £1001.30.
**Owner** Twinacre Nurseries Ltd **Bred** Maurice Burns **Trained** Maunby, N Yorks

**FOCUS**
All races on stands' side home straight and distances on Round course increased by 43yds. After riding in the first Flat race, Pat Dobbs said: "It's soft ground" and Dane O'Neill said: "It's soft, maybe a little slower." The official going on the Flat track was amended afterwards. An interesting 3yo handicap, but the once-raced maiden winners both disappointed. The runners came down the centre in the home straight. The winner showed his debut win didn't flatter him.

## 2149 PERTEMPS NETWORK CONDITIONS STKS 6f
**3:00** (3:00) (Class 2) 3-Y-O+
**£12,450** (£3,728; £1,864; £932; £466; £234) **Stalls** Centre

Form RPR
021- 1 **Intibaah**[218] 6990 4-9-0 108 DaneO'Neill 1 111
(Brian Meehan) *hld up in tch: clsd 2f out: wnt 2nd over 1f out: led fnl 150yds: r.o wl* **5/2**[1]

4-42 2 *1 1/4* **Annunciation**[26] 1484 4-9-0 103 PatDobbs 2 107
(Richard Hannon) *chsd ldr: rdn and lost 2nd over 1f out: nt qckn: stl ev ch whn n.m.r and snatched up 150yds out: styd on but no imp on wnr after* **4/1**[2]

-404 3 *nk* **Hawkeyethenoo (IRE)**[22] 1557 8-9-0 109 GaryBartley 7 106
(Jim Goldie) *hld up: swtchd lft and effrt over 1f out: styd on ins fnl f* **5/2**[1]

010- 4 *1* **Morache Music**[182] 7821 6-9-0 105 RobertHavlin 6 103+
(Peter Makin) *trckd ldrs: shkn up briefly over 1f out: sn nt clr run: denied run thrght fnl f: fin full of running* **7/1**[3]

22-2 5 *nse* **Mar Mar (IRE)**[16] 1679 4-8-9 96 (b) KierenFallon 4 98
(Saeed bin Suroor) *led: rdn over 1f out: hdd fnl 150yds: no ex* **7/1**[3]

60-0 6 *nse* **Mass Rally (IRE)**[42] 1163 7-9-0 107 (b) PaulMulrennan 5 103
(Michael Dods) *hld up in rr: rdn over 2f out: styd on ins fnl f: one pce towards fin* **8/1**

1m 15.67s (1.87) **Going Correction** +0.60s/f (Yiel) **6 Ran SP% 113.3**
Speed ratings (Par 109): **111,109,108,107,107 107**
CSF £12.97 TOTE £2.70: £1.70, £2.80; EX 13.30 Trifecta £34.60.
**Owner** Hamdan Al Maktoum **Bred** Shadwell Estate Company Limited **Trained** Manton, Wilts
■ Stewards' Enquiry : Dane O'Neill one-day ban: careless riding (May 24)

**FOCUS**
Bated Breath beat Society Rock in this conditions event three years ago. This edition was an unsatisfactory, messy race, with the runner-up and especially the fourth finding trouble after the field had come over to race on the stands' rail. The runner-up and fifth help with the standard.

## 2150 PERTEMPS NETWORK SPRING TROPHY STKS (LISTED RACE) 7f
**4:05** (4:05) (Class 1) 3-Y-O+ **£20,982** (£7,955; £3,981; £1,983) **Stalls** Low

Form RPR
2-13 1 **Breton Rock (IRE)**[14] 1728 4-9-7 107 FergusSweeney 7 113
(David Simcock) *hld up in rr: effrt 2f out: led over 1f out: hung lft ins fnl f: kpt on wl* **11/4**[2]

0-32 2 *1/2* **Custom Cut (IRE)**[27] 1473 5-9-7 108 DavidNolan 1 111
(David O'Meara) *led: rdn and hdd over 1f out: styd on u.p: rallied towards fin* **9/2**[3]

120- 3 *2* **Lockwood**[210] 7190 5-9-7 113 KierenFallon 3 106
(Saeed bin Suroor) *racd keenly: chsd ldrs: pushed along 2f out: ev ch ins fnl f: no ex fnl 75yds* **11/4**[2]

412- 4 *2 1/4* **Highland Colori (IRE)**[182] 7821 6-9-7 111 LiamKeniry 5 100
(Andrew Balding) *chsd ldr tl rdn 2f out: one pce fnl f* **7/4**[1]

1m 32.72s (2.02) **Going Correction** +0.425s/f (Yiel) **4 Ran SP% 107.9**
Speed ratings (Par 111): **105,104,102,99**
CSF £13.71 TOTE £4.40; EX 11.30 Trifecta £40.40.
**Owner** John Cook **Bred** George Kent **Trained** Newmarket, Suffolk

**FOCUS**
A disappointing turnout for this Listed prize, but still an interesting little race. The pace was reasonable and the runners came down the middle of the track once in line for home.The winner remains progressive.

## 2120 LINGFIELD (L-H)

Saturday, May 10

**OFFICIAL GOING: Good (good to soft in places; soft between 7f 140yds and 5f; str 6.4, rnd 8.2)**

In order to try and combat draw bias the stands rail on the Straight course was moved in 5metres from maximum width.

Wind: strong and gusty half behind Weather: dry and breezy, showers late afternoon

### 2151 BETFRED MONUMENTAL SCOOP6/BRITISH STALLION STUDS EBF MAIDEN STKS (BOBIS RACE) 5f

**1:45** (1:46) (Class 4) 2-Y-O £4,457 (£1,326; £662; £331) **Stalls** Centre

Form RPR

1 **Wild Tobacco** 2-9-5 0 SeanLevey 7 78+
(Richard Hannon) *rn green: racd keenly: mde all: drew clr w runner-up 2f out: rdn over 1f out: asserted ins fnl f: r.o wl* **3/1**[2]

042 2 1 ½ **King Crimson**[11] 1859 2-9-5 0 AndreaAtzeni 3 73
(Mick Channon) *plld hrd: chsd ldrs: chsd wnr after 2f: upsides and drew clr w wnr 2f out: drvn jst over 1f out: no ex and btn fnl 100yds* **5/1**[3]

3 1 ¾ **Primrose Valley** 2-9-0 0 TedDurcan 1 62+
(Ed Vaughan) *stdd and dropped in bhd after s: hld up in rr: pushed along and hdwy whn nt clr run and swtchd sharply lft 1f out: chsd clr ldng pair ins fnl f: styd on* **33/1**

4 ¾ **British Embassy (IRE)** 2-9-5 0 JimCrowley 5 64
(Eve Johnson Houghton) *dwlt: bustled along and early and sn in tch in midfield: outpcd by ldng pair and rdn 2f out: styd on same pce after* **8/1**

5 1 ½ **Town Crier (IRE)** 2-9-5 0 RyanMoore 6 62+
(William Haggas) *rn green: dwlt: in tch towards rr: rdn and outpcd ent fnl 2f: wl hld and keeping on same pce whn hmpd and stmbld 1f out: plugged on* **11/10**[1]

0 6 5 **Go Gently (IRE)**[33] 1349 2-9-5 0 PatCosgrave 4 41
(George Baker) *chsd ldr for 2f: lost pl u.p 1/2-way: bhd fnl f* **25/1**

7 nse **Next Generation (IRE)** 2-9-0 0 HarryBentley 2 35
(Olly Stevens) *rn green: dwlt: in tch towards rr: rdn 1/2-way: no hdwy: bhd fnl f* **16/1**

59.3s (1.10) **Going Correction** +0.10s/f (Good) 7 Ran SP% **113.1**
Speed ratings (Par 95): **95,92,89,88,86 78,78**
CSF £17.87 TOTE £4.40: £3.00, £1.90; EX 19.80 Trifecta £321.70.

**Owner** Rockcliffe Stud **Bred** Rockcliffe Stud **Trained** East Everleigh, Wilts

■ Stewards' Enquiry : Ted Durcan one-day ban: careless riding (May 24)

**FOCUS**

In order to try and combat draw bias the stands' rail on the straight course was moved in 5metres from maximum width. Following some rain the ground was officially good, good to soft in places on both the straight and round courses. As on the previous day, and in a bid to eliminate the straight course draw bias, the turf track had been narrowed with the stands' rail moved in five metres from the maximum width. As a result, the safety factor for races on the straight course had been reduced from 18 to 12 and the stalls were positioned in the centre. This seemed a fair 2yo maiden and the winner looks a nice type.

### 2152 BETFRED £7.5 MILLION SCOOP6 TODAY OAKS TRIAL STKS (LISTED RACE) (FILLIES) 1m 3f 106y

**2:20** (2:21) (Class 1) 3-Y-O

£22,684 (£8,600; £4,304; £2,144; £1,076; £540) **Stalls** High

Form RPR

03-1 1 **Honor Bound**[12] 1809 3-9-0 79 JoeFanning 2 91+
(Ralph Beckett) *t.k.h: hld up in tch in midfield: effrt towards inner ent fnl 2f: rdn to chal 1f out: led ins fnl f: hld on cl home* **12/1**

5-31 2 nse **Criteria (IRE)**[12] 1797 3-9-0 78 WilliamBuick 5 90
(John Gosden) *led for 2f: chsd ldr tl 8f out: styd handy: rdn to chal 2f out: drvn to ld ins fnl f: sn hdd but stl ev ch: rallied gamely towards fin: jst hld* **8/1**

3- 3 1 ¼ **Momentus (IRE)**[207] 7277 3-9-0 0 HarryBentley 4 88
(David Simcock) *stdd s: t.k.h: hld up in tch in last trio: hdwy towards inner and edgd lft over 1f out: chsd ldrs ins fnl f: no imp fnl 75yds* **14/1**

1 4 ¾ **Kallisha**[15] 1701 3-9-0 0 RichardKingscote 8 87
(Ralph Beckett) *in tch in midfield: clsd and nt clr run 2f out tl swtchd lft and clr run 1f out: styd on same pce u.p fnl 100yds* **8/1**

213- 5 ¾ **Island Remede**[189] 7695 3-9-0 87 PaulHanagan 11 86
(Ed Dunlop) *hld up in tch in last trio: rdn and effrt ent fnl 2f: no imp tl styd on u.p ins fnl f: nvr gng pce to threaten ldrs* **6/1**[3]

25-4 6 ½ **Mutatis Mutandis (IRE)**[15] 1690 3-9-0 79 AndreaAtzeni 7 85
(Ed Walker) *t.k.h: chsd ldrs: wnt 2nd 7f out tl rdn to ld 2f out: drvn and hdd ins fnl f: no ex and wknd fnl 75yds* **14/1**

232- 7 1 ¼ **Casual Smile**[231] 6643 3-9-0 89 DavidProbert 1 83
(Andrew Balding) *t.k.h: hld up wl in tch in midfield: rdn and chalng 2f out: no ex u.p and btn 1f out: wknd ins fnl f* **11/4**[1]

1 8 1 ¼ **Moonrise Landing (IRE)**[50] 1044 3-9-0 77 JimCrowley 6 81+
(Ralph Beckett) *wl in tch in midfield: rdn and unable qck ent fnl 2f: outpcd and lost pl wl over 1f out: pushed along and n.d fr over 1f out* **6/1**[3]

21-0 9 5 **Isabella Beeton**[17] 1655 3-9-0 68 TedDurcan 3 73?
(Pat Phelan) *stdd s: hld up in rr: rdn and effrt ent fnl 2f: no hdwy and btn over 1f out: wknd 1f out* **100/1**

1- 10 9 **Queen's Prize**[229] 6691 3-9-0 80 RyanMoore 10 59
(Sir Michael Stoute) *t.k.h: pressed ldr tl led 8f out: rdn and hdd 2f out: sn btn and dropped out: bhd fnl f* **4/1**[2]

2m 32.42s (0.92) **Going Correction** +0.15s/f (Good) 10 Ran SP% **119.5**
Speed ratings (Par 104): **102,101,101,100,99 99,98,97,94,87**
CSF £106.87 TOTE £16.70: £4.30, £2.60, £4.30; EX 139.90 Trifecta £1790.90 Part won..

**Owner** Ashley House Stud **Bred** Ashley House Stud **Trained** Kimpton, Hants

**FOCUS**

Four winners of the Lingfield Oaks Trial since 1992 had gone on to be successful at Epsom, the most recent being Midday in 2009. Although there were some nice fillies taking part this year, there wasn't that much covering the principals at the line and the feeling is that this isn't Oaks-winning form. In fact, it's substandard for this race, although the first fou r at least were unexposed.

### 2153 BETFRED.COM DERBY TRIAL STKS (LISTED RACE) (C&G) 1m 3f 106y

**2:55** (2:55) (Class 1) 3-Y-O

£56,710 (£21,500; £10,760; £5,360; £2,690; £1,350) **Stalls** High

Form RPR

10-2 1 **Snow Sky**[29] 1419 3-9-0 97 JimCrowley 7 109+
(Sir Michael Stoute) *chsd ldng trio: hdwy to join ldrs and gng wl over 2f out: led 2f out: sn rdn to readily assert and edgd lft: clr and in command 1f out: r.o wl: comf* **5/1**[3]

13-5 2 2 **Hartnell**[17] 1652 3-9-0 99 WilliamBuick 4 105
(Mark Johnston) *t.k.h: chsd ldrs: effrt on inner to chse ldr whn swtchd rt wl over 1f out: hung rt u.p and no imp ent fnl f: styd on same pce after* **12/1**

21-1 3 ½ **Sudden Wonder (IRE)**[23] 1530 3-9-0 105 MickaelBarzalona 6 104+
(Charlie Appleby) *midfield early: grad stdd bk and hld up in last trio after 2f: effrt u.p ent fnl 2f: wnt 3rd 1f out: kpt on u.p: no threat to wnr* **6/1**

4 2 **Blue Hussar (IRE)**[188] 7717 3-9-0 0 RyanMoore 3 101+
(A P O'Brien, Ire) *s.i.s: niggled along and detached in last: struggling to handle downhill run 4f out: swtchd rt and sme hdwy 2f out: swtchd lft and kpt on ins fnl f: nvr trbld ldrs* **7/2**[2]

10-4 5 1 ¼ **Signposted (IRE)**[17] 1652 3-9-0 99 DavidProbert 5 99
(Andrew Balding) *in tch in midfield: effrt u.p over 2f out: no imp: kpt on same pce fr over 1f out* **16/1**

21-4 6 1 ½ **Red Galileo**[15] 1699 3-9-0 92 AndreaAtzeni 2 97
(Ed Dunlop) *t.k.h: hld up in tch in last trio: rdn and effrt on inner ent fnl 2f: drvn and no hdwy over 1f out: nvr trbld ldrs* **20/1**

32-1 7 nse **Munjaz**[24] 1517 3-9-0 91 PaulHanagan 8 97
(John Gosden) *t.k.h: chsd ldr over 10f out tl unable qck u.p over 2f out: no ch w wnr and plugged on same pce fr over 1f out* **7/1**

16-3 8 2 ¾ **Double Bluff (IRE)**[29] 1419 3-9-0 97 JoeFanning 9 92
(Mark Johnston) *led tl drvn and hdd 2f out: sn outpcd and btn: wknd 1f out and wl hld whn n.m.r ins fnl f* **14/1**

14- 9 8 **Mekong River (IRE)**[182] 7828 3-9-3 110 (b) JosephO'Brien 1 82
(A P O'Brien, Ire) *hld up in tch in midfield: rdn and no rspnse over 2f out: lost pl and bhd over 1f out: eased ins fnl f* **3/1**[1]

2m 30.68s (-0.82) **Going Correction** +0.15s/f (Good) 9 Ran SP% **115.7**
Speed ratings (Par 107): **108,106,106,104,103 102,102,100,94**
CSF £62.82 TOTE £7.00: £2.80, £3.50, £1.30; EX 44.70 Trifecta £175.60.

**Owner** K Abdullah **Bred** Juddmonte Farms Ltd **Trained** Newmarket, Suffolk

**FOCUS**

Four winners of this race had gone on to Epsom glory since 1983, but not since High-Rise was successful in 1998. This looked a more solid trial than the fillies' version, though, with the winning time 1.74sec quicker. The form makes a fair bit of sense but this is not among the race's better runnings.

### 2154 WEATHERBYS "MY STABLE" H'CAP 1m 2f

**3:25** (3:26) (Class 2) (0-100,100) 4-Y-O+£14,231 (£4,235; £2,116; £1,058) **Stalls** Low

Form RPR

05-3 1 **Soviet Rock (IRE)**[17] 1653 4-8-13 **92** DavidProbert 7 101
(Andrew Balding) *chsd ldr tl led over 2f out: edgd lft u.p over 1f out: kpt on wl fnl f: rdn out* **7/4**[1]

065- 2 ½ **Blue Surf**[227] 6741 5-9-2 **95** RyanMoore 5 103
(Amanda Perrett) *hld up in midfield: effrt and n.m.r 2f out: hdwy over 1f out: kpt on wl u.p ins fnl f: wnt 2nd cl home* **4/1**[3]

310- 3 nk **Border Legend**[182] 7823 5-8-10 **89** JimCrowley 8 96
(Roger Charlton) *stdd s: hld up in last pair: clsd on inner over 2f out: chsd ldr and swtchd rt 1f out: kpt on same pce ins fnl f: lost 2nd cl home* **7/1**

110- 4 1 ½ **Ennistown**[196] 7526 4-9-7 **100** MickaelBarzalona 1 105
(Charlie Appleby) *t.k.h: hld up in midfield: effrt u.p ent fnl 2f: kpt on same pce ins fnl f* **8/1**

01/ 5 hd **Altruism (IRE)**[631] 5321 4-9-0 **93** WilliamBuick 2 97
(Charlie Appleby) *t.k.h: chsd ldrs: effrt to chse wnr ent fnl 2f tl 1f out: wknd ins fnl f* **14/1**

123- 6 11 **Ajman Bridge**[197] 7497 4-8-13 **92** AndreaAtzeni 3 75
(Luca Cumani) *chsd ldrs: rdn wl over 2f out: drvn and outpcd wl over 1f out: wknd fnl f* **7/2**[2]

3000 7 4 ½ **Luhaif**[33] 1351 4-8-7 **86** oh4 (b[1]) AdamBeschizza 6 61
(Julia Feilden) *racd keenly: led tl rdn and hdd over 2f out: sn btn: bhd over 1f out* **50/1**

0200 8 29 **Uramazin (IRE)**[22] 1559 8-9-2 **95** RichardKingscote 4 15
(Philip Hide) *taken down early: a in rr: bhd fnl 2f: t.o* **25/1**

2m 9.6s (-0.90) **Going Correction** +0.15s/f (Good) 8 Ran SP% **114.7**
Speed ratings (Par 109): **109,108,108,107,107 98,94,71**
CSF £8.95 CT £38.19 TOTE £2.80: £1.20, £2.10, £1.60; EX 10.80 Trifecta £31.40.

**Owner** Jackie & George Smith **Bred** Grangecon Stud **Trained** Kingsclere, Hants

**FOCUS**

A decent handicap in which they went an even gallop. The winner picked up on his 3yo progress.

### 2155 FOLLOW SCOOP6 AT TOTEPOOLLIVEINFO.COM CHARTWELL FILLIES' STKS (GROUP 3) 7f

**4:00** (4:01) (Class 1) 3-Y-O+

£34,026 (£12,900; £6,456; £3,216; £1,614; £810) **Stalls** Centre

Form RPR

3 1 **Emerald Star**[19] 1619 3-8-6 98 DanielePorcu 6 102
(P Schiergen, Germany) *chsd ldrs: rdn and effrt to ld 1f out: r.o wl: rdn out* **16/1**

166- 2 1 ½ **Veiled Intrigue**[196] 7537 3-8-6 94 DavidProbert 2 98
(Henry Candy) *bhd: rdn along 4f out: switching lft over 2f out: hdwy u.p 1f out: styd on wl to go 2nd towards fin: nvr threatened wnr* **33/1**

414- 3 hd **Annecdote**[240] 6327 4-9-4 107 RichardKingscote 5 107+
(Jonathan Portman) *hld up in tch in last pair: nt clr run wl over 1f out tl ins fnl f: r.o strly fnl 100yds: wnt 3rd last strides* **6/1**[3]

40-0 4 ½ **Pavlosk (USA)**[14] 1728 4-9-4 100 RyanMoore 8 100
(Sir Michael Stoute) *racd keenly: chsd ldr tl led 2f out: drvn and hdd 1f out: styd on same pce ins fnl f: lost 2 pls towards fin* **10/1**

02-4 5 ½ **Broadway Duchess (IRE)**[21] 1577 4-9-4 84 WilliamBuick 1 99
(Richard Hannon) *in tch in midfield: rdn and effrt u.p to chse ldrs ent fnl f: no ex fnl 100yds: wknd towards fin* **20/1**

4/0- **6** 1 1/2 **Melody Of Love**[357] 2452 4-9-4 97 MickaelBarzalona 11 95
(Brian Meehan) *chsd ldrs: rdn and swtchd lft wl over 1f out: styd on same pce and no hdwy fnl f* **33/1**

**7** *shd* **Dalayna (FR)**[37] 1274 4-9-4 98 ChristopheSoumillon 4 95
(A De Royer-Dupre, France) *hld up in tch in midfield: swtchd lft and effrt u.p over 1f out: no imp fnl f* **6/4**[1]

232- **8** 6 **Winning Express (IRE)**[217] 7021 4-9-4 105 JimCrowley 9 79
(Ed McMahon) *wl in tch in midfield: rdn and unable qck wl over 1f out: shuffled bk and btn ent fnl f: wknd* **7/4**[2]

040- **9** 3/4 **Valais Girl**[191] 7649 4-9-4 92 (p) HarryBentley 10 77
(Marcus Tregoning) *led tl 2f: sn rdn and outpcd: wknd ent fnl f* **50/1**

00-5 **10** *nk* **Senafe**[21] 1577 4-9-4 93 (p) AndreaAtzeni 3 77
(Marco Botti) *wl in tch in midfield: rdn to chse ldrs over 1f out: no ex and btn 1f out: wknd ins fnl f* **33/1**

1m 24.15s (0.85) **Going Correction** +0.40s/f (Good)
**WFA** 3 from 4yo 12lb **10** Ran SP% **121.2**
Speed ratings (Par 110): **111,109,109,108,107 106,106,99,98,98**
CSF £444.46 TOTE £16.90: £4.50, £7.70, £2.20; EX 596.60 Trifecta £1343.70.

**Owner** Stall Emerald **Bred** Newsells Park Stud **Trained** Germany

**FOCUS**
There were only two 3yos in this Group 3 fillies' contest and they filled the first two places. Probably just Listed-class form, rated around the fourth.

## 2156 BETFRED LIFE CHANGING SCOOP6 TODAY H'CAP 7f 140y
**4:35** (4:35) (Class 3) (0-95,88) 4-Y-O+ **£9,703** (£2,887; £1,443; £721) **Stalls** Centre

Form RPR

003- **1** **Dark Emerald (IRE)**[182] 6867 4-9-2 **83** RichardKingscote 4 91
(Brendan Powell) *mde all and sn crossed to r against stands' rail: rdn and fnd ex wl over 1f out: r.o wl: rdn out* **14/1**

65-1 **2** 1 3/4 **Whipper Snapper (IRE)**[12] 1796 4-9-1 **82** JimCrowley 8 86
(William Knight) *wl in tch in midfield: effrt u.p over 1f out: kpt on u.p ins fnl f: wnt 2nd last strides: no threat to wnr* **7/1**[3]

0000 **3** *hd* **Talented Kid**[14] 1721 5-9-4 **85** JoeFanning 7 88
(Mark Johnston) *taken down early: chsd wnr: rdn ent fnl 2f: drvn and styd on same pce ins fnl f* **10/1**

00-6 **4** *shd* **George Cinq**[21] 1578 4-9-5 **86** RyanMoore 2 89
(Michael Bell) *dwlt: hld up in tch towards rr: hdwy 3f out: drvn to chse ldrs over 1f out: wnt 2nd ins fnl f: kpt on same pce: lost 2 pls last strides* **4/1**[2]

00-6 **5** 2 3/4 **Good Authority (IRE)**[26] 1492 7-9-2 **86** ThomasBrown(3) 3 82
(Karen George) *hld up in tch in rr: switching lft and effrt 2f: edging lft u.p and no hdwy 1f out: wknd ins fnl f* **10/1**

0-31 **6** 1 1/4 **Yourartisonfire**[14] 1721 4-9-1 **87** (v) JoeyHaynes(5) 5 80
(K R Burke) *t.k.h: hld up in tch in midfield: rdn 2f out: drvn and no hdwy over 1f out: kpt on same pce fnl f: bled fr the nose* **11/10**[1]

10-6 **7** 6 **Vainglory (USA)**[11] 1862 10-9-0 **88** LewisWalsh(7) 6 66
(David Simcock) *in tch towards rr: dropped to rr 1/2-way: rdn and struggling 3f out: wknd over 1f out* **33/1**

104- **8** 1 1/2 **Footstepsintherain (IRE)**[199] 7464 4-9-3 **84** MickaelBarzalona 1 58
(David Dennis) *chsd ldrs: rdn 2f out: drvn and btn over 1f out: wknd fnl f* **16/1**

1m 34.09s (1.79) **Going Correction** +0.40s/f (Good) **8** Ran SP% **113.8**
Speed ratings (Par 107): **107,105,105,104,102 100,94,93**
CSF £105.96 CT £1042.19 TOTE £15.50: £3.30, £2.00, £3.80; EX 81.60 Trifecta £280.80.

**Owner** K Rhatigan **Bred** Olive O'Connor **Trained** Upper Lambourn, Berks

**FOCUS**
A good handicap, but another race where racing against the stands' rail was an advantage. Not the strongest form for the grade.

## 2157 TOTEPOOL.COM H'CAP 7f
**5:10** (5:11) (Class 4) (0-85,85) 4-Y-O+ **£6,469** (£1,925; £962; £481) **Stalls** Centre

Form RPR

-004 **1** **Born To Surprise**[35] 1301 5-9-7 **85** AmirQuinn 3 94
(Lee Carter) *hld up in tch and travelled strly: wnt 2nd wl over 1f out: drvn to ld 1f out: hrd pressed fnl 100yds: hld on wl: all out* **4/1**[3]

4642 **2** *shd* **Great Expectations**[10] 1873 6-8-8 **72** AdamBeschizza 5 80
(J R Jenkins) *dwlt: hld up in tch: rdn and effrt 2f out: hdwy u.p over 1f out: str chal fnl 100yds: r.o: jst hld* **6/1**

11-5 **3** 3 **Interception (IRE)**[22] 1554 4-9-5 **83** TedDurcan 8 83+
(David Lanigan) *in tch in midfield: stuck bhd rivals and switching lft whn hmpd over 1f out: in the clr and hdwy to go 3rd ins fnl f: no threat to ldrs: eased towards fin* **3/1**[2]

-010 **4** 1 1/4 **Upavon**[21] 1576 4-8-13 **77** MickaelBarzalona 2 74
(David Elsworth) *chsd ldrs: rdn ent fnl 2f: drvn and unable qck over 1f out: wknd ins fnl f* **10/1**

1062 **5** 1/2 **Seek The Fair Land**[8] 1921 8-8-2 **71** oh1 (b) NathanAlison(5) 1 67+
(Lee Carter) *led and crossed to r against stands' rail: rdn and hdd 1f out: wknd ins fnl f* **14/1**

00-0 **6** 3/4 **Freddy With A Y (IRE)**[26] 1492 4-8-8 **79** HectorCrouch(7) 9 73
(Gary Moore) *chsd ldr tl wl over 1f out: stuck bhd rival on rail after and shuffled bk: kpt on same pce and n.d fnl f* **14/1**

000- **7** 4 1/2 **Annina (IRE)**[189] 7699 4-9-5 **83** RyanMoore 6 65
(Henry Candy) *hld up in tch in last trio: effrt 2f out: sn btn: bhd fnl f* **2/1**[1]

00-0 **8** 32 **Snow King (USA)**[98] 426 4-9-4 **82** JohnFahy 4
(Ted Powell) *in tch in last trio: rdn and lost tch ent fnl 2f: t.o* **20/1**

1m 25.61s (2.31) **Going Correction** +0.40s/f (Good) **8** Ran SP% **119.8**
Speed ratings (Par 105): **102,101,98,97,96 95,90,53**
CSF £29.65 CT £83.66 TOTE £5.10: £1.80, £1.90, £1.40; EX 26.60 Trifecta £47.80.

**Owner** John Joseph Smith **Bred** Rabbah Bloodstock Limited **Trained** Epsom, Surrey

■ Stewards' Enquiry : Amir Quinn 24-day ban (eight days deferred for six weeks): excessive use of the whip (5th suspension within 6 mths) (May 23-Jun 8).

**FOCUS**
A fair handicap, but a bit of a muddling race. The winner is rated to last year's turf form.

T/Plt: £877.00 to a £1 stake. Pool: £75198.74 - 62.58 winning tickets T/Qpdt: £66.40 to a £1 stake. Pool: £7718.99 - 86.02 winning tickets SP

# 2127 NOTTINGHAM (L-H)
### Saturday, May 10

**OFFICIAL GOING: Good to soft (soft in places; 7.4)**
Outer track used and distances as advertised.
Wind: Strong against Weather: Cloudy

## 2158 THE MOST RELIABLE BET DG TAXIS MAIDEN STKS 6f 15y
**2:15** (2:15) (Class 5) 3-Y-O **£3,234** (£962; £481; £240) **Stalls** High

Form RPR

6- **1** **For Ayman**[191] 7638 3-9-5 0 SteveDrowne 3 72
(Seamus Durack) *trckd ldng pair: hdwy 2f out: swtchd lft to outer and chal over 1f out: rdn to ld ent fnl f: kpt on strly towards fin* **4/1**[3]

6- **2** 1 1/2 **Boy In The Bar**[225] 6790 3-9-5 0 RobertWinston 2 68
(David Barron) *qckly away and sn led on stands' rail: jnd 1/2-way: rdn along 2f out: drvn over 1f out: hdd ent fnl f: no ex last 100yds: edgd lft towards fin* **11/8**[1]

42 **3** *hd* **Bush Warrior (IRE)**[52] 1018 3-9-5 0 GrahamLee 6 67
(Robert Eddery) *trckd ldr: hdwy and cl uip 4f out: disp ld over 2f out: rdn wl over 1f out and ev ch: drvn and edgd rt ins fnl f: no ex last 100yds* **7/4**[2]

0-60 **4** 6 **Mercury Magic**[6] 1980 3-9-5 0 (b[1]) SebSanders 9 48
(Ralph Beckett) *reminders s: green and sn outpcd and bhd: sme hdwy wl over 1f out: kpt on fnl f: n.d* **10/1**

0 **5** 11 **Khelfan**[11] 1860 3-9-0 0 NickyMackay 8 8
(Martin Smith) *trckd ldng pair: rdn along over 2f out: sn wknd* **28/1**

1m 18.52s (3.82) **Going Correction** +0.125s/f (Good)
**WFA** 3 from 4yo 10lb **5** Ran SP% **111.0**
Speed ratings (Par 99): **79,77,76,68,54**
CSF £10.11 TOTE £4.50: £2.50, £1.40; EX 13.40 Trifecta £31.60.

**Owner** A A Byrne **Bred** Anthony Byrne **Trained** Baydon, Wilts

■ Stewards' Enquiry : Robert Winston caution: careless riding.

**FOCUS**
Outer track used and distances as advertised. A large number of non-runners due to the change in the ground. A weak opener, run in blustery conditions and in a slow time. The form is rated around the second and third.

## 2159 £7.5 MILLION TOTESCOOP6 SPRINT H'CAP (JOCKEY CLUB GRASSROOTS SPRINT SERIES QUALIFIER) 5f 13y
**2:45** (2:45) (Class 5) (0-75,75) 4-Y-O+ **£3,234** (£962; £481; £240) **Stalls** High

Form RPR

0-01 **1** **Taurus Twins**[8] 1912 8-9-2 **70** (b) RobertWinston 15 80
(Richard Price) *wnt lft s: sn led on stands' rail: rdn over 1f out: kpt on wl fnl f* **9/2**[2]

0- **2** 1 1/4 **Cardinal**[152] 8224 9-8-13 **67** SteveDrowne 17 72
(Robert Cowell) *hld up in tch: hdwy 2f out: effrt and n.m.r over 1f out: swtchd lft and rdn ent fnl f: chsd wnr and kpt on wl towards fin* **12/1**

0643 **3** 1 **Harrogate Fair**[11] 1843 4-8-7 **61** oh3 LiamJones 8 62
(Michael Squance) *towards rr: pushed along 1/2-way: hdwy wl over 1f out: n.m.r and swtchd lft appr fnl f: sn rdn and kpt on* **10/1**

545- **4** 1 3/4 **Oscars Journey**[311] 3956 4-9-2 **70** NickyMackay 9 65
(J R Jenkins) *trckd ldrs: hdwy 2f out: rdn ent fnl f: sn drvn and kpt on same pce* **14/1**

-004 **5** 3/4 **Exotic Guest**[11] 1843 4-8-10 **64** JamesSullivan 7 56
(Ruth Carr) *in rr: pushed along over 2f out: rdn wl over 1f out: swtchd lft and hdwy appr fnl f: kpt on: nrst fin* **8/1**

-622 **6** 3/4 **Point North (IRE)**[51] 1031 7-8-12 **69** (b) NeilFarley(3) 16 59
(John Balding) *cl up: effrt 2f out and sn ev ch: rdn over 1f out: wknd ent fnl f* **4/1**[1]

000- **7** 1 1/2 **Invincible Lad (IRE)**[192] 7633 10-9-0 **68** GrahamLee 3 52
(Ed McMahon) *cl up: rdn along wl over 1f out: wknd ent fnl f* **50/1**

35-0 **8** 2 **Rylee Mooch**[36] 1283 6-9-4 **75** (e[1]) ConnorBeasley(3) 11 52
(Richard Guest) *cl up: rdn along 2f out: drvn and wknd appr fnl f* **11/2**[3]

0335 **9** 3 1/4 **Beacon Tarn**[15] 1694 4-8-10 **67** (b) JasonHart(3) 4 32
(Eric Alston) *racd wd: chsd ldrs: rdn along 2f out: sn wknd* **14/1**

0353 **10** 3/4 **Monsieur Jamie**[8] 1912 6-9-7 **75** (v) JimmyFortune 13 38
(J R Jenkins) *hamperd s: sn rdn along and a in rr* **4/1**[1]

1m 1.57s (0.07) **Going Correction** +0.125s/f (Good) **10** Ran SP% **116.8**
Speed ratings (Par 103): **104,102,100,97,96 95,92,89,84,83**
CSF £57.38 CT £527.14 TOTE £5.20: £1.90, £2.70, £3.60; EX 63.70 Trifecta £768.60 Part won..

**Owner** G E Amey & G D Bailey **Bred** G E Amey **Trained** Ullingswick, H'fords

**FOCUS**
A competitive sprint handicap, despite some notable absentees and a smart front-running performance from the winner, who had the rail. The form is rated around around the second and third.

## 2160 THE SAFE BET DG TAXIS 01159500500 H'CAP 1m 6f 15y
**3:20** (3:20) (Class 4) (0-85,85) 4-Y-O+ **£6,469** (£1,925; £962; £481) **Stalls** Low

Form RPR

13-1 **1** **Hassle (IRE)**[11] 1848 5-9-5 **85** (p) RyanTate(5) 3 94+
(Clive Cox) *hld up in rr: smooth hdwy over 4f out: trckd ldrs 3f out: chal on bit 2f out: led over 1f out: sn rdn and hung bdly rt ins fnl f: kpt on* **9/4**[2]

34-0 **2** 1/2 **Bohemian Rhapsody (IRE)**[18] 784 5-9-10 **85** RobertWinston 2 91
(Seamus Durack) *hld up towards rr: hdwy over 4f out: chsd ldrs over 2f out: effrt whn nt clr run and swtchd lft over 1f out: sn rdn and ev ch ins fnl f: kpt on* **3/1**[3]

402/ **3** 2 1/2 **Local Hero (GER)**[20] 5333 7-9-8 **83** (b[1]) GrahamLee 8 86
(Steve Gollings) *trckd ldrs: hdwy to chse ldr 4f out: rdn along 2f out: drvn appr fnl f: kpt on same pce* **10/1**

0013 **4** 9 **Brigadoon**[16] 1659 7-9-9 **84** AndrewMullen 1 74
(Michael Appleby) *led: rdn along over 3f out: drvn and hdd wl over 1f out: sn wknd* **8/1**

520- **5** 1 1/2 **Zipp (IRE)**[177] 7890 4-9-6 **82** SebSanders 9 70
(Ralph Beckett) *cl up: rdn along over 3f out: wknd 2f out* **15/8**[1]

1333 **6** 21 **Lineman**[11] 1849 4-8-7 **69** JamesSullivan 4 27
(Andrew Hollinshead) *trckd ldrs: hdwy 4f out: rdn along over 3f out: wkng whn n.m.r and hmpd wl over 2f out: bhd after* **20/1**

3m 6.28s (-0.72) **Going Correction** +0.025s/f (Good)
**WFA** 4 from 5yo+ 1lb **6** Ran SP% **115.5**
Speed ratings (Par 105): **103,102,101,96,95 83**
CSF £9.86 CT £54.25 TOTE £2.20: £1.50, £2.70; EX 12.20 Trifecta £56.30.

**Owner** A D Spence **Bred** Cheval Court Stud **Trained** Lambourn, Berks

**FOCUS**
Another race hit by non-runners, but it served up an exciting finish. The winner looks capable of better.

## 2161 EBF STALLIONS WEATHERBYS BLOODSTOCK REPORTS KILVINGTON FILLIES' STKS (LISTED RACE) 6f 15y
3:55 (3:55) (Class 1) 3-Y-0+

£22,684 (£8,600; £4,304; £2,144; £1,076; £540) Stalls High

Form RPR
05-3 1 **Caledonia Lady**[21] 1572 5-9-3 98 LiamJones 7 105
(Jo Hughes) *hld up in tch: hdwy 2f out: chal ent fnl f: sn rdn: led last 100yds* **8/1**
523- 2 1 3/4 **Spinatrix**[182] 7821 6-9-3 107 (p) ConnorBeasley 5 99
(Michael Dods) *trckd ldr: cl up 4f out: led over 3f out: rdn over 1f out: hdd and no ex last 100yds* **7/4**[1]
16-0 3 3/4 **Body And Soul (IRE)**[14] 1734 4-9-3 100 DuranFentiman 6 97+
(Tim Easterby) *trckd ldrs: effrt whn nt clr run and hmpd wl over 1f out: sn swtchd lft and rdn: kpt on fnl f* **4/1**[3]
00-0 4 3 **Gladiatrix**[21] 1572 5-9-3 86 SebSanders 2 87+
(Rod Millman) *dwlt: hld up in rr: effrt whn hmpd wl over 1f out: sn swtchd lft and rdn: kpt on fnl f* **40/1**
3502 5 1 **Golden Amber (IRE)**[15] 1693 3-8-8 92 ow1 RobertWinston 3 82
(Dean Ivory) *trckd ldrs: rdn along over 2f out: swtchd rt wl over 1f out: sn drvn and btn* **17/2**
112- 6 2 **Artistic Jewel (IRE)**[238] 6414 5-9-3 107 GrahamLee 1 78
(Ed McMahon) *chsd ldrs on outer: rdn along over 2f: sn wknd* **11/4**[2]
-110 7 15 **Captain Secret**[22] 1555 3-8-7 95 AntonioFresu 10 27
(Marco Botti) *led: pushed along and hdd over 3f out: rdn over 2f out and sn wknd* **16/1**

1m 15.3s (0.60) **Going Correction** +0.125s/f (Good)
**WFA** 3 from 4yo+ 10lb 7 Ran SP% **113.0**
Speed ratings (Par 108): **101,98,97,93,92 89,69**
CSF £21.95 TOTE £8.10: £3.40, £1.60; EX 28.10 Trifecta £92.70.
**Owner** Isla & Colin Cage **Bred** Mrs I M Cage And C J Cage **Trained** Lambourn, Berks
■ Stewards' Enquiry : Robert Winston three-day ban: careless riding (May 24,26,27)

**FOCUS**
A messy affair and the form isn't taken too literally. The winner is rated back to her best.

## 2162 FAMILY FUN DAY SUNDAY 1ST JUNE H'CAP (JOCKEY CLUB GRASSROOTS MIDDLE DISTANCE SERIES QUALIFIER) 1m 2f 50y
4:30 (4:31) (Class 4) (0-80,80) 4-Y-0+ £6,469 (£1,925; £962; £481) Stalls Low

Form RPR
0-02 1 **Barren Brook**[11] 1842 7-9-1 74 BarryMcHugh 14 84
(Michael Easterby) *trckd ldrs: hdwy wl over 2f out: rdn over 1f out: styd on strly u.p fnl f to ld nr line* **20/1**
14-2 2 nk **Saigon City**[33] 1351 4-9-7 80 (b) LemosdeSouza 3 89+
(Luca Cumani) *trckd ldng pair on inner: hdwy 3f out: led wl over 1f out: rdn ins fnl f: hdd and no ex nr line* **3/1**[1]
32-4 3 1 1/4 **Raskova (USA)**[18] 1636 4-9-3 76 JimmyFortune 7 83
(William Jarvis) *in tch: hdwy on outer wl over 2f out: rdn to chse ldrs over 1f out: drvn and kpt on fnl f* **8/1**
2-06 4 1 3/4 **Hydrant**[27] 1113 8-9-2 78 ConnorBeasley(3) 13 82
(Richard Guest) *cl up: rdn along 3f out: drvn wl over 1f out: kpt on same pce fnl f* **25/1**
13-0 5 nk **Eurystheus (IRE)**[19] 1607 5-9-6 79 AndrewMullen 10 82
(Michael Appleby) *midfield: hdwy on outer 3f out: rdn along to chse ldrs 2f out: drvn and kpt on same pce ent fnl f* **8/1**
05/3 6 nk **Putra Eton (IRE)**[19] 1612 4-9-4 77 JackMitchell 12 80+
(Roger Varian) *hld up: hdwy on outer 3f out: sn pushed along: swtchd lft and rdn over 1f out: kpt on fnl f: nrst fin* **5/1**[3]
2551 7 2 1/2 **All The Winds (GER)**[18] 1628 9-8-11 70 (t) ChrisCatlin 5 68
(Shaun Lycett) *stmbld sn after s and bhd: hdwy on outer wl over 2f out: sn rdn and kpt on fnl f: nrst fin* **28/1**
2-34 8 nk **Handheld**[12] 1810 7-8-12 76 (p) ShelleyBirkett(5) 2 73
(Julia Feilden) *sn led: pushed along over 3f out: rdn over 2f out: hdd wl over 1f out: wknd fnl f* **4/1**[2]
60-0 9 1 **Artful Prince**[19] 1607 4-9-4 77 (b) GrahamLee 4 72
(James Given) *trckd ldrs: effrt 3f out: rdn along 2f out: grad wknd* **20/1**
0-00 10 shd **Destiny Blue (IRE)**[19] 1607 7-8-9 68 (p) SteveDrowne 11 63
(Brian Ellison) *a towards rr* **33/1**
0332 11 1/2 **Syncopate**[14] 1724 5-9-2 78 RossAtkinson(3) 1 72
(Pam Sly) *midfield: hdwy on inner and in tch 1/2-way: rdn along wl over 2f out: sn drvn and wknd* **6/1**
-060 12 3 1/2 **Idol Deputy (FR)**[9] 1899 8-8-8 72 (p) RachealKneller(5) 6 60
(James Bennett) *a towards rr* **66/1**
0-50 13 4 1/2 **Surround Sound**[19] 1607 4-8-8 67 DuranFentiman 8 46
(Tim Easterby) *a towards rr* **25/1**

2m 13.11s (-1.19) **Going Correction** +0.025s/f (Good) 13 Ran SP% **123.3**
Speed ratings (Par 105): **105,104,103,102,102 101,99,99,98,98 98,95,91**
CSF £76.98 CT £550.08 TOTE £34.50: £9.20, £1.30, £2.30; EX 160.60 Trifecta £1517.10 Part won..
**Owner** D Scott, Mrs E Wright & J Clark **Bred** David Allan **Trained** Sheriff Hutton, N Yorks
■ Stewards' Enquiry : Lemos de Souza three-day ban: used whip without giving gelding time to respond (May 24,26,27)

**FOCUS**
Arguably the most competitive race on the card. The winner is rated to last year's best.

## 2163 THE ODDS ON FAVOURITE DG TAXIS 01159500500 H'CAP 1m 75y
5:05 (5:06) (Class 5) (0-75,75) 3-Y-O £3,234 (£962; £481; £240) Stalls Centre

Form RPR
32-5 1 **Ice Slice (IRE)**[31] 1390 3-9-7 75 GrahamLee 5 82
(James Eustace) *hld up in rr: hdwy wl over 2f out: swtchd rt over 1f out: sn rdn and styd on strly fnl f to ld nr fin* **5/1**
0-03 2 1/2 **Aran Sky (IRE)**[11] 1858 3-8-4 65 RobJFitzpatrick(7) 4 71+
(K R Burke) *prom: hdwy to ld wl over 2f out: clr over 1f out: rdn ent fnl f: hdd and no ex nr fin* **4/1**[2]
652- 3 7 **Rolling Dice**[208] 7243 3-9-5 73 [1] SteveDrowne 8 63
(Dominic Ffrench Davis) *hld up: hdwy over 3f out: chsd ldrs 2f out: rdn to chse ldr appr fnl f: sn drvn and one pce* **8/1**
40-4 4 3 **Pipe Dream**[16] 1680 3-9-0 68 JimmyFortune 2 51
(Brian Meehan) *trckd ldrs: effrt wl over 2f out: sn rdn along and outpcd: plugged on fnl f* **10/1**
4-40 5 3 **Woodbridge**[41] 1192 3-8-10 64 SebSanders 1 40
(Richard Fahey) *t.k.h: led early: chsd clr ldr tl led briefly 3f out: sn hdd and rdn: drvn wl over 1f out and sn wknd* **9/2**[3]
2-42 6 1 3/4 **Tyrsal (IRE)**[12] 1794 3-8-4 65 KieranShoemark(7) 3 37
(Robert Eddery) *dwlt and towards rr: hdwy on inner and in tch 1/2-way: effrt to chse ldrs wl over 2f out: sn rdn and wknd wl over 1f out* **3/1**[1]
51- 7 8 **Bousfield**[177] 7883 3-8-13 70 NeilFarley(3) 7 24
(Declan Carroll) *a in rr* **9/1**
4-10 8 52 **Walta (IRE)**[21] 1585 3-8-8 67 (b) PhilipPrince(5) 6
(Roy Bowring) *plld hrd: rapid hdwy to ld after 1f and sn clr: set furious gallop tl wknd rapidly and hdd 3f out: sn wl bhd* **20/1**

1m 48.38s (-0.62) **Going Correction** +0.025s/f (Good) 8 Ran SP% **114.8**
Speed ratings (Par 99): **104,103,96,93,90 88,80,28**
CSF £25.42 CT £158.43 TOTE £5.40: £1.80, £1.80, £3.30; EX 28.10 Trifecta £177.70.
**Owner** The MacDougall Two **Bred** Kilfrush Stud **Trained** Newmarket, Suffolk

**FOCUS**
A furiously run handicap, and the time was good. The first pair were clear.

## 2164 SEE YOU ON TUESDAY 20TH MAY APPRENTICE TRAINING SERIES H'CAP (THE RACING EXCELLENCE INITIATIVE) 1m 75y
5:35 (5:35) (Class 6) (0-65,65) 4-Y-0+ £1,940 (£577; £288; £144) Stalls Centre

Form RPR
-611 1 **Alluring Star**[8] 1930 6-8-13 62 DanielleMooney(5) 7 71
(Michael Easterby) *chsd ldng pair on inner: hdwy over 2f out: chsd ldr over 1f out: sn rdn and styd on ins fnl f to ld last 100yds* **4/1**[2]
4312 2 1 **Polar Forest**[16] 1675 4-8-9 58 (e) KieranShoemark(5) 8 65
(Richard Guest) *chsd ldr: cl up 1/2-way: led 3f out: rdn wl over 1f out: drvn ent fnl f: hdd and no ex last 100yds* **13/2**
0063 3 nk **Last Minute Lisa (IRE)**[16] 1668 4-8-4 51 oh2 CamHardie(5) 9 57
(Sylvester Kirk) *trckd ldrs: hdwy over 3f out: rdn over 2f out: kpt on u.p fnl f* **5/1**[3]
3613 4 6 **George Benjamin**[5] 2021 7-9-2 60 (tp) AlistairRawlinson 11 52
(Michael Appleby) *midfield: hdwy over 4f out: rdn to chse ldrs over 2f out: drvn and no imp appr fnl f* **5/2**[1]
0000 5 3 3/4 **Pelmanism**[1] 2124 7-8-12 63 TomasHarrigan(7) 14 47
(Gay Kelleway) *towards rr: rdn along and hdwy 3f out: drvn and plugged on one pce fnl 2f: n.d* **25/1**
00-6 6 1 3/4 **Misty Pearl**[18] 1639 4-8-2 51 oh6 GaryMahon(5) 13 31
(Michael Appleby) *nvr bttr than midfield* **40/1**
6144 7 1/2 **Indus Valley (IRE)**[19] 1613 7-9-1 59 DanielCremin 5 37
(Des Donovan) *towards rr: sme hdwy over 3f out: sn rdn along and n.d* **17/2**
5131 8 hd **Sam Spade (IRE)**[12] 1800 4-9-5 63 (v) AdamMcLean 2 41
(Derek Shaw) *led: rdn along and hdd 3f out: sn drvn and wknd 2f out* **9/1**
6550 9 nk **Mr Chocolate Drop (IRE)**[20] 1596 10-8-2 51 oh5 (vt) PaulBooth(5) 12 28
(Mandy Rowland) *dwlt and in rr: sme hdwy on wd outside over 3f out: sn rdn and nvr a factor* **25/1**
02-0 10 14 **Khelac**[17] 1644 4-9-2 60 (v) MatthewHopkins 15 5
(Micky Hammond) *chsd ldrs: rdn along over 3f out: sn wknd* **16/1**

1m 48.6s (-0.40) **Going Correction** +0.025s/f (Good) 10 Ran SP% **115.1**
Speed ratings (Par 101): **103,102,101,95,91 90,89,89,89,75**
CSF £29.11 CT £132.02 TOTE £4.40: £2.00, £1.40, £2.80; EX 24.30 Trifecta £254.70.
**Owner** Jeff Hamer & Bernard Bargh **Bred** B Bargh **Trained** Sheriff Hutton, N Yorks

**FOCUS**
Some significant non-runners, but still a strong race for the grade. Few were involved and the winner is rated back to last year's best.
T/Plt: £89.80 to a £1 stake. Pool: £51318.44 - 416.94 winning tickets T/Qpdt: £19.80 to a £1 stake. Pool: £2981.28 - 111.25 winning tickets JR

# 1955 THIRSK (L-H)
## Saturday, May 10

**OFFICIAL GOING: Good to soft (soft in places) changing to soft after race 1 (5:40)**
Both bends dolled out adding 10yds to 7f and 1m races and circa 15yds to 12f races.
Wind: moderate 1/2 behind Weather: overcast, frequent showers 1st 3

## 2165 ABF THE SOLDIERS' CHARITY H'CAP 1m
5:40 (5:42) (Class 6) (0-60,60) 3-Y-O £2,726 (£805; £402) Stalls Low

Form RPR
00-4 1 **Sooqaan**[7] 1962 3-9-5 58 PJMcDonald 14 64
(Mel Brittain) *s.i.s: in rr: hdwy on outside over 2f out: chsng ldrs over 1f out: edgd rt ins fnl f: led post* **14/1**
-326 2 hd **Baltic Fire (IRE)**[16] 1657 3-9-7 60 PhillipMakin 7 65
(K R Burke) *in rr: hdwy on outer over 2f out: styd on to ld nr fin: hdd post* **7/2**[1]
4261 3 nk **It's All A Game**[10] 1890 3-9-1 57 (b) JasonHart(3) 11 61
(Richard Guest) *w ldrs: led over 2f out: hdd and no ex clsng stages* **8/1**
65-4 4 1 3/4 **Kalahari Kingdom (IRE)**[16] 1657 3-9-2 60 (p) SammyJoBell(5) 1 60
(Richard Fahey) *s.i.s: sn trcking ldrs: nt clr run over 2f out: styd on same pce fnl f* **5/1**[2]
306- 5 2 1/4 **Rockie Road (IRE)**[175] 7935 3-8-11 55 KevinStott(5) 6 50
(Paul Green) *in rr: sn drvn along: hdwy to chse ldrs over 3f out: one pce over 1f out* **18/1**
0-06 6 1 **Minionette (IRE)**[14] 1713 3-9-4 57 BenCurtis 3 50
(Alan Swinbank) *s.i.s: hdwy to chse ldrs over 2f out: fdd fnl f* **10/1**
33-3 7 nk **Another Royal**[19] 1611 3-9-5 58 (p) DavidAllan 5 50
(Tim Easterby) *w ldrs: led briefly 3f out: fdd fnl f* **13/2**[3]
1543 8 18 **Kraka Gym (IRE)**[16] 1657 3-9-7 60 (b) GrahamGibbons 4 10
(Michael Easterby) *hdwy to ld after 1f: hdd 3f out: wknd and eased over 1f out* **5/1**[2]
-053 9 hd **Marlismamma (FR)**[17] 1648 3-8-12 54 JulieBurke(3) 9 4
(David O'Meara) *rr-div: sme hdwy on outer 4f out: sn lost pl* **16/1**
2350 10 1/2 **Her Red Devil (IRE)**[21] 1588 3-9-2 55 LeeToplis 12 4
(Richard Fahey) *led 1f: chsd ldrs: lost pl over 1f out: eased ins fnl f* **16/1**
000- 11 2 **Shamouti (IRE)**[271] 5352 3-8-11 55 [1] JacobButterfield(5) 8
(Ollie Pears) *swtchd lft s: in rr: bhd fnl 2f* **40/1**

1m 49.6s (9.50) **Going Correction** +1.15s/f (Soft) 11 Ran SP% **115.2**
Speed ratings (Par 97): **98,97,97,95,93 92,92,74,74,73 71**
CSF £61.32 CT £435.58 TOTE £13.90: £6.30, £1.80, £3.10; EX 104.00 Trifecta £1514.70 Part won..
**Owner** David Horner **Bred** J A And Mrs Duffy **Trained** Warthill, N Yorks



The Form Book, Raceform Ltd, Newbury, RG14 5SJ

**FOCUS**
Both bends dolled out, adding 10yds to 7f and 1m races and circa 15yds to 1m4f races. A modest but competitive contest. The winner built on his latest maiden run.

## 2166 THIRSK RACECOURSE & CONFERENCE CENTRE (S) STKS 6f
**6:10** (6:11) (Class 6) 3-Y-O+ **£1,940** (£577; £288; £144) **Stalls** High

Form RPR
0-00 **1** **Bear Behind (IRE)**[28] 1442 5-9-6 93........................ GrahamGibbons 4 74
(Tom Dascombe) *swtchd rt after 1f: mde all stands' side: rdn over 1f out: styd on to forge clr last 100yds* **5/4**[1]
0-54 **2** 2 1/4 **Bond Club**[33] 1343 4-9-6 59........................(b) DavidAllan 2 67
(Geoffrey Oldroyd) *rr-div: sn drvn along: hdwy over 2f out: chsd wnr jst ins fnl f: no imp* **8/1**
35-0 **3** 2 1/4 **Mission Impossible**[11] 1838 9-9-6 58....................(p) PatrickMathers 11 60
(Tracy Waggott) *dwlt: hdwy over 2f out: n.m.r 1f out: kpt on to take 3rd nr fin* **12/1**
-444 **4** 3/4 **Beckermet (IRE)**[9] 1905 12-9-6 68........................ JamesSullivan 5 57
(Ruth Carr) *trckd ldrs: effrt over 2f out: kpt on same pce fnl f* **13/2**[3]
0236 **5** 1 1/2 **Greenhead High**[11] 1838 6-9-4 57....................(v) AnnaHesketh(7) 7 58
(David Nicholls) *trckd wnr: wknd fnl 150yds* **12/1**
6206 **6** 1 1/2 **Cape Of Hope (IRE)**[19] 1609 4-9-6 71........................ DavidNolan 10 48
(David O'Meara) *chsd ldrs on ins: outpcd over 3f out: hdwy over 2f out: one pce over 1f out* **7/2**[2]
350- **7** 4 1/2 **Angels Calling**[197] 7512 4-8-8 58........................ BTTreanor(7) 3 28
(K R Burke) *chsd ldrs: rdn over 2f out: wknd over 1f out* **25/1**
40-0 **8** 1/2 **Native Falls (IRE)**[23] 1543 3-8-10 62........................ BenCurtis 1 29
(Alan Swinbank) *swvd lft s: sn chsng ldrs on outside: wknd over 1f out* **33/1**
-600 **9** 2 **Tarrsille (IRE)**[11] 1838 8-9-6 57........................ PaulMulrennan 6 25
(Paul Midgley) *in rr: nvr on terms* **50/1**
500- **10** 16 **Rio Sands**[319] 3654 9-8-13 45........................ CaseyWilcox(7) 9
(Richard Whitaker) *s.i.s: bhd over 1f out: eased and t.o* **100/1**

1m 17.55s (4.85) **Going Correction** +1.05s/f (Soft)
**WFA** 3 from 4yo+ 10lb **10 Ran SP% 116.2**
Speed ratings (Par 101): **109,106,103,102,100 98,92,91,88,67**
CSF £11.89 TOTE £2.20: £1.10, £3.20, £3.60; EX 13.70 Trifecta £116.90.The winner was bought in £16,000.
**Owner** Bellman Black Marantelli Owen **Bred** Rory O'Brien **Trained** Malpas, Cheshire

**FOCUS**
This was far from straightforward for a horse miles clear on official ratings, and the form could be rated a length better.

## 2167 DICK PEACOCK SPRINT H'CAP 6f
**6:40** (6:40) (Class 5) (0-75,75) 4-Y-O+ **£3,234** (£962; £481; £240) **Stalls** High

Form RPR
-063 **1** **Lothair (IRE)**[6] 1966 5-8-13 **67**........................ BenCurtis 15 78
(Alan Swinbank) *wnt lft and bmpd s: mid-div: hdwy over 2f out: chsng ldrs over 1f out: styd on to ld towards fin* **7/2**[1]
130 **2** 3/4 **Layla's Hero (IRE)**[39] 1224 7-8-6 63....................(v) JasonHart(3) 12 71
(David Nicholls) *bmpd s: sn chsng ldrs: led over 1f out: hdd and no ex clsng stages* **9/1**
504- **3** hd **Master Bond**[132] 8439 5-9-5 73........................ DavidNolan 20 80
(David O'Meara) *in rr: hdwy 2f out: styd on to chse ldrs last 75yds: no ex* **5/1**[3]
20-2 **4** nk **Rothesay Chancer**[13] 1759 6-9-5 73........................ GaryBartley 9 79
(Jim Goldie) *in rr: hdwy over 2f out: carried lft over 1f out: chsng ldrs jst ins fnl f: kpt on* **25/1**
105- **5** 3 1/4 **Bosham**[251] 6018 4-9-0 68........................ GrahamGibbons 7 64
(Michael Easterby) *swtchd rt after s: led: hdd over 1f out: fdd jst ins fnl f* **16/1**
0063 **6** 1 1/4 **Lucky Dan (IRE)**[21] 1584 8-8-10 64........................ JamesSullivan 11 56
(Paul Green) *in rr: hdwy appr fnl f: styng on at fin* **33/1**
-666 **7** 1 **Majestic Manannan (IRE)**[23] 1541 5-9-0 68........................ RobertHavlin 6 57
(David Nicholls) *chsd ldr: drvn 2f out: fdd fnl f* **22/1**
50-0 **8** 1 **Noodles Blue Boy**[15] 1695 8-9-1 74........................ JacobButterfield(5) 18 60
(Ollie Pears) *in rr-div: hdwy 2f out: kpt on: nvr a factor* **40/1**
4-06 **9** nk **Opt Out**[13] 1759 4-8-11 65........................ PJMcDonald 19 50
(Alistair Whillans) *dwlt: in rr: hdwy over 2f out: carried lft over 1f out: nvr a factor* **22/1**
000- **10** 11 **Jamesbo's Girl**[245] 6208 4-9-4 72....................(p) PhillipMakin 8 21
(Philip Kirby) *mid-div: drvn over 2f out: sn btn: hung rt and eased ins fnl f* **8/1**
00-2 **11** 1 **Pastureyes**[28] 1447 4-8-4 63........................ TimClark(5) 5 9
(Scott Dixon) *w ldrs on outer: wknd over 1f out: eased whn bhd ins fnl f* **9/1**
0-00 **12** 1 1/2 **The Strig**[15] 1695 7-8-11 72....................(v) RachelRichardson(7) 10 13
(Nigel Tinkler) *hld up in mid-div: lost pl over 2f out: bhd whn eased ins fnl f* **50/1**
4512 **13** 1/2 **Bapak Bangsawan**[36] 1283 4-9-2 70........................ KierenFallon 17 25
(Kevin Ryan) *chsd ldrs: edgd rt over 1f out: sn wknd and eased* **4/1**[2]
32-0 **14** 4 **Sunny Side Up (IRE)**[28] 1440 5-8-10 71........................ GemmaTutty(7) 3
(Karen Tutty) *chsd ldrs on outside: lost pl 2f out: eased whn bhd ins fnl f* **25/1**

1m 18.39s (5.69) **Going Correction** +1.05s/f (Soft) **14 Ran SP% 119.6**
Speed ratings (Par 103): **104,103,102,102,98 96,95,93,93,78 77,75,74,69**
CSF £31.97 CT £160.52 TOTE £5.90: £2.20, £3.90, £1.90; EX 32.30 Trifecta £343.30.
**Owner** Mrs J Porter **Bred** Lynch Bages Ltd & Samac Ltd **Trained** Melsonby, N Yorks

**FOCUS**
The field stayed in one group towards the stands' side. The winner found a bit on his latest start.

## 2168 GT GROUP H'CAP 1m 4f
**7:10** (7:10) (Class 4) (0-80,80) 4-Y-O+ **£5,175** (£1,540; £769; £384) **Stalls** High

Form RPR
414- **1** **Aramist (IRE)**[208] 7242 4-9-0 73........................ BenCurtis 10 83
(Alan Swinbank) *sn trcking ldrs: t.k.h: cl 2nd over 8f out: led over 1f out: drvn out* **4/1**[2]
4-06 **2** 1 3/4 **Gran Maestro (USA)**[17] 1644 5-8-10 69....................(b) JamesSullivan 7 76
(Ruth Carr) *reluctant ldr: hdd over 8f out: chsd wnr appr fnl f: styd on same pce* **10/1**
-041 **3** 3/4 **Arizona John (IRE)**[16] 1659 9-9-5 78........................ RobertHavlin 14 84
(John Mackie) *hld up in rr: hdwy 5f out: sn chsng ldrs: 3rd 1f out: kpt on same pce* **18/1**
12 **4** 1 3/4 **Genius Boy**[16] 1660 4-8-12 71........................ PaulMulrennan 8 74
(James Tate) *trckd ldr: t.k.h: led over 8f out: qckd pce over 5f out: hdd over 1f out: kpt on one pce* **5/2**[1]
053- **5** 3 **Noble Alan (GER)**[166] 8041 11-9-4 80........................ IanBrennan(3) 11 78
(Nicky Richards) *hld up in rr: hdwy 4f out: drvn 3f out: nvr a threat* **4/1**[2]
4-14 **6** 1 1/2 **Pertuis (IRE)**[10] 1885 8-8-11 70........................ PJMcDonald 3 66
(Micky Hammond) *chsd ldrs: drvn over 3f out: wknd over 1f out* **16/1**
0-0 **7** 1/2 **Cloud Monkey (IRE)**[14] 1724 4-9-1 74........................[1] PhillipMakin 12 69
(Martin Todhunter) *stdd s: hld up in rr: sme hdwy 3f out: wknd over 1f out* **25/1**
-464 **8** 2 3/4 **Fujin Dancer (FR)**[16] 1659 9-9-3 76........................ PaulPickard 1 67
(Brian Ellison) *t.k.h: trckd ldrs: stdd to rr after 1f: drvn over 3f out: nvr a factor* **20/1**
404- **9** 9 **Eltheeb**[53] 4264 7-9-7 80........................ KierenFallon 9 56
(Philip Kirby) *trckd ldrs: drvn over 3f out: hung rt and lost pl 2f out: bhd whn eased ins fnl f* **6/1**[3]

2m 52.89s (16.69) **Going Correction** +1.15s/f (Soft) **9 Ran SP% 111.7**
Speed ratings (Par 105): **90,88,88,87,85 84,83,82,76**
CSF £41.33 CT £627.88 TOTE £5.20: £1.30, £3.10, £3.30; EX 40.40 Trifecta £425.50.
**Owner** Pam & Richard Ellis **Bred** Fiona Craig & S Couldridge **Trained** Melsonby, N Yorks

**FOCUS**
The early gallop wasn't strong, and it paid to be prominent. The second and third set the standard.

## 2169 CALVERTS CARPETS H'CAP 1m
**7:40** (7:41) (Class 5) (0-75,75) 4-Y-O+ **£3,234** (£962; £481; £240) **Stalls** Low

Form RPR
6-01 **1** **Eutropius (IRE)**[20] 1598 5-9-6 74........................ BenCurtis 18 84
(Alan Swinbank) *racd v wd: led 1f: chsd ldrs: led over 1f out: drvn out* **7/1**[3]
5-04 **2** 1 1/4 **The Osteopath (IRE)**[11] 1842 11-9-4 72........................ PJMcDonald 3 79
(John Davies) *in rr: hdwy over 2f out: styd on to take 2nd last 50yds* **16/1**
-025 **3** nk **Millkwood**[19] 1610 4-9-6 74........................[1] PhillipMakin 13 80
(John Davies) *in rr: hdwy on outer over 2f out: edgd rt over 1f out: styd on to take 3rd last 50yds* **20/1**
2551 **4** 2 1/2 **Repetition**[15] 1689 4-9-3 71........................ JamesSullivan 16 71
(Kristin Stubbs) *chsd ldrs: led briefly 2f out: fdd last 75yds* **14/1**
4233 **5** 3/4 **Royal Holiday (IRE)**[10] 1886 7-9-2 70....................(p) BarryMcHugh 11 69
(Marjorie Fife) *t.k.h: led after 1f: hdd 2f out: one pce* **14/1**
4511 **6** 3 1/2 **Real Tigress (IRE)**[5] 2019 5-9-1 69 6ex........................ DavidAllan 10 59
(Les Eyre) *in rr-div: hdwy and in tch after 2f: chsng ldrs over 2f out: wknd fnl f* **3/1**[1]
04-6 **7** 4 **Space War**[28] 1446 7-8-12 66........................ GrahamGibbons 17 47
(Michael Easterby) *mid-div: hdwy over 3f out: sn chsng ldrs: wknd over 1f out* **14/1**
0-33 **8** 4 **Steel Stockholder**[19] 1609 8-8-13 67........................ RobertWinston 12 39
(Mel Brittain) *chsd ldrs: drvn over 3f out: wknd over 1f out* **18/1**
03-1 **9** 3/4 **Flexible Flyer**[28] 1446 5-9-4 75....................(t) JasonHart(3) 14 45
(Mark Walford) *stdd s: t.k.h towards rr: hdwy 4f out: chsng ldrs on outside over 2f out: bmpd and wknd over 1f out* **4/1**[2]
1232 **10** 1 **My Single Malt (IRE)**[14] 1744 6-9-5 73....................(p) PaulMulrennan 1 41
(Julie Camacho) *mid-div: drvn over 3f out: wknd over 1f out* **14/1**
0-20 **11** 1 **Rio Cobolo (IRE)**[17] 1649 8-8-4 65....................(b) EvaMoscrop(7) 5 31
(Philip Kirby) *chsd ldrs: lost pl over 1f out* **33/1**
-000 **12** 2 1/2 **Le Deluge (FR)**[7] 1957 4-9-4 72........................ DavidNolan 4 32
(Michael Easterby) *chsd ldrs: lost pl over 1f out* **40/1**
010- **13** 3 1/2 **Spin Cast**[18] 7539 6-9-4 72........................ PaulPickard 9 24
(Brian Ellison) *s.i.s: a in rr* **40/1**
6-30 **14** 1 3/4 **Mystical Moment**[19] 1607 4-8-10 69........................ KevinStott(5) 8 17
(Edwin Tuer) *in tch: drvn 3f out: lost pl over 1f out* **28/1**
35-4 **15** 1 1/4 **Red Paladin (IRE)**[15] 1689 4-9-1 69....................(p) GrahamLee 2 14
(Kevin Ryan) *stmbld s: drvn along in rr: nvr on terms* **12/1**
100- **16** 9 **Dennis**[181] 6291 4-8-12 66........................ KierenFallon 6
(Tim Easterby) *chsd ldrs: drvn over 3f out: sn lost pl: bhd whn eased over 1f out* **25/1**
000- **17** 12 **Printmaker (IRE)**[182] 7824 6-8-11 65........................ DuranFentiman 7
(Tim Easterby) *mid-div: lost pl 4f out: bhd whn eased ins fnl f* **66/1**

1m 48.31s (8.21) **Going Correction** +1.15s/f (Soft) **17 Ran SP% 124.4**
Speed ratings (Par 103): **104,102,102,99,99 95,91,87,86,85 84,82,78,77,75 66,54**
CSF £107.65 CT £2235.64 TOTE £10.10: £2.70, £5.60, £4.30, £3.10; EX 169.30 Trifecta £1198.10 Part won..
**Owner** Andrew Sparks **Bred** Grangemore Stud **Trained** Melsonby, N Yorks

**FOCUS**
The whole field didn't want to know about the inside rail once in the home straight, and headed down the middle. The winner rates better than ever.

## 2170 THOMAS LORD DINE & VIEW RESTAURANT MAIDEN STKS 1m
**8:10** (8:11) (Class 5) 3-Y-O+ **£2,587** (£770; £384; £192) **Stalls** Low

Form RPR
4 **1** **Famous Kid (USA)**[23] 1529 3-9-0 0........................ KierenFallon 8 90+
(Saeed bin Suroor) *towards rr: sn pushed along: hdwy to chse ldrs 4f out: sn hrd drvn 3rd over 2f out: led over 1f out: edgd rt: styd on* **6/5**[1]
3-24 **2** 3 1/2 **Three Peaks**[21] 1587 3-9-0 80....................(p) RobertWinston 5 79
(Charles Hills) *led 1f: chsd ldr: led 3f out: hdd over 1f out: styd on same pce* **7/4**[2]
**3** 1 **Park Place**[232] 6615 4-9-13 0........................ GrahamLee 7 80
(Donald McCain) *trckd ldrs: t.k.h: stdd after 2f: 2nd over 2f out: kpt on same pce over 1f out* **4/1**[3]
00 **4** 10 **Two B'S**[7] 1959 3-9-0 0........................ DavidAllan 9 54
(Tim Easterby) *wnt rt s: in rr: sme hdwy over 2f out: kpt on to take poor 4th nr fin* **50/1**
**5** 1/2 **Showtime Star** 4-9-13 0........................ BenCurtis 11 56
(Alan Swinbank) *in rr: sme hdwy over 2f out: nvr on terms* **16/1**
**6** 1 3/4 **Spiritorio (IRE)** 3-8-11 0........................ MichaelJMMurphy(3) 2 49
(Mark Johnston) *mid-div and sn drvn along: outpcd and lost pl 5f out: sme hdwy over 2f out: nvr a factor* **12/1**
000- **7** 21 **Roc Fort**[203] 7372 5-9-13 35........................ PaulMulrennan 6
(James Moffatt) *t.k.h: trckd ldrs: lost pl over 4f out: bhd fnl 3f: t.o* **100/1**
00 **8** 14 **Sirnita**[4] 2053 5-9-5 0........................ ConnorBeasley(3) 3
(Richard Guest) *t.k.h: led after 1f: hdd 3f out: sn lost pl and bhd: eased ins fnl f* **100/1**
05- **9** 15 **Mrs Gorsky**[164] 8070 4-9-8 0........................ AndrewMullen 1
(Patrick Holmes) *chsd ldrs: lost pl over 4f out: wl bhd whn eased over 1f out: hopelessly t.o* **66/1**

1m 50.24s (10.14) **Going Correction** +1.15s/f (Soft)
**WFA** 3 from 4yo+ 13lb **9 Ran SP% 120.8**
Speed ratings (Par 103): **95,91,90,80,80 78,57,43,28**
CSF £3.75 TOTE £2.00: £1.10, £1.60, £1.70; EX 4.00 Trifecta £6.50.
**Owner** Godolphin **Bred** Darley **Trained** Newmarket, Suffolk

**FOCUS**
The market suggested only three would count, and so it proved. Ordinary form.

## 2171 "IRISH DAY" NEXT SATURDAY 17TH MAY H'CAP 7f
8:40 (8:40) (Class 6) (0-65,65) 4-Y-0+ £2,587 (£770; £384; £192) Stalls Low

Form RPR
3-06 1 **Lady Artiste (IRE)**14 1716 4-9-5 **63**.......... BenCurtis 3 78
(Alan Swinbank) *hld up in rr: hdwy on outside over 2f out: hung lft and led 1f out: drvn out* 8/1
441- 2 3 1/4 **Cara's Request (AUS)**236 6464 9-9-3 **64**.......... ConnorBeasley(3) 10 71
(Michael Dods) *chsd ldrs: led 3f out: hdd 1f out: no ex* 3/1[1]
0-60 3 1/2 **Mercers Row**17 1643 7-9-0 **65**.......... GemmaTutty(7) 2 70
(Karen Tutty) *hld up in rr: hdwy over 2f out: sn w ldrs: kpt on same pce fnl f* 20/1
-126 4 1/2 **Icy Blue**10 1881 6-9-2 **63**..........(p) GeorgeChaloner(3) 7 67
(Richard Whitaker) *sn drvn along: sn chsng ldrs: 2nd 2f out: kpt on same pce fnl f* 5/1[2]
144- 5 6 **Orpsie Boy (IRE)**156 8163 11-9-5 **63**.......... DaleSwift 14 51
(Ruth Carr) *s.i.s: in rr: sme hdwy over 2f out: edgd rt over 1f out: sn wknd* 12/1
0-30 6 1 1/4 **Secret City (IRE)**17 1649 8-9-1 **62**..........(b) JasonHart(3) 4 47
(Robin Bastiman) *chsd ldrs: drvn over 3f out: swtchd rt over 1f out: sn wknd* 9/1
0-43 7 8 **Lucky Lodge**19 1610 4-9-5 **63**..........(b) DavidAllan 13 27
(Mel Brittain) *mid-div on outer: hdwy to chse ldrs 4f out: weakwning whn sltly hmpd over 1f out* 11/2[3]
5-00 8 4 **Dream Ally (IRE)**17 1643 4-9-6 **64**.......... PJMcDonald 1 18
(Micky Hammond) *mid-div: lost pl over 2f out* 12/1
0040 9 4 1/2 **Bapak Muda (USA)**14 1717 4-9-7 **65**.......... KierenFallon 6 7
(Kevin Ryan) *chsd ldrs: sn drvn along: wknd over 1f out: eased ins fnl f* 8/1
0000 10 11 **Marcus Caesar (IRE)**17 1649 4-9-2 **60**..........(b1) JamesSullivan 8
(Ruth Carr) *set str pce: styd alone far side and hdd 3f out: sn lost pl and bhd: eased fnl f* 25/1
050- 11 18 **Clock On Tom**245 6214 4-9-3 **61**.......... GrahamGibbons 11
(Michael Easterby) *chsd ldrs on outside: hung rt and lost pl over 3f out: bhd whn eased over 1f out: t.o* 20/1

1m 34.47s (7.27) **Going Correction** +1.15s/f (Soft) 11 Ran SP% **118.0**
Speed ratings (Par 101): **104,100,99,99,92 90,81,77,72,59 38**
CSF £31.39 CT £482.53 TOTE £9.00: £3.70, £1.40, £7.30; EX 42.70 Trifecta £1178.90 Part won..
**Owner** Andrew Sparks **Bred** Lynch Bages, Samac Ltd & Longfield Stud **Trained** Melsonby, N Yorks

**FOCUS**
A modest handicap, that was run at a sound pace considering conditions. The winner rates better than ever for an in-form card.
T/Plt: £114.10 to a £1 stake. Pool: £66741.40 - 426.80 winning tickets T/Qpdt: £24.90 to a £1 stake. Pool: £6501.70 - 192.60 winning tickets WG

# 2021 WARWICK (L-H)
Saturday, May 10

**OFFICIAL GOING: Soft (5.3)**
Wind: Strong behind Weather: Showers

## 2172 EBFSTALLIONS.COM EBF MAIDEN STKS 5f
5:55 (5:56) (Class 5) 2-Y-0 £2,911 (£866; £432; £216) Stalls Low

Form RPR
1 **Bonnie Grey** 2-9-0 0.......... MartinLane 3 75+
(Rod Millman) *sn pushed along and prom: edgd rt over 1f out: led sn after: r.o wl* 16/1
5 2 2 1/4 **Power Play (IRE)**7 1936 2-9-5 0.......... SeanLevey 6 72
(Richard Hannon) *disp ld: bmpd over 1f out: sn rdn: and hdd: styd on same pce ins fnl f* 4/6[1]
3 3 1/2 **Perardua**14 1741 2-9-0 0.......... TonyHamilton 2 65
(Richard Fahey) *disp ld: rdn and edgd rt over 1f out: sn hdd: no ex ins fnl f* 7/2[2]
03 4 4 **Kidmeforever**12 1788 2-9-0 0.......... LukeMorris 8 51
(J S Moore) *chsd ldrs: rdn whn nt clr run over 1f out: wknd ins fnl f* 17/2
5 1 1/2 **Decisive Rebel** 2-9-5 0.......... LiamJones 5 50
(Jo Hughes) *s.s: outpcd: hdwy over 1f out: wknd fnl f* 16/1
6 8 **Honest Bob'S** 2-9-5 0.......... SamHitchcott 1 22
(Mick Channon) *s.s: outpcd* 8/1[3]
7 nse **Cerise Firth** 2-8-9 0.......... JackDuern(5) 4 16
(Steph Hollinshead) *s.s: outpcd* 33/1
4 8 2 **Storming Harry**12 1807 2-9-5 0.......... RoystonFfrench 7 14
(Robin Dickin) *prom: rdn 1/2-way: wknd wl over 1f out* 33/1

1m 1.44s (1.84) **Going Correction** +0.30s/f (Good) 8 Ran SP% **121.5**
Speed ratings (Par 93): **97,93,92,86,83 71,70,67**
CSF £29.13 TOTE £14.70: £4.00, £1.02, £1.80; EX 44.40 Trifecta £196.20.
**Owner** Howard Barton Stud **Bred** Redmyre Bloodstock & Tweenhills Stud **Trained** Kentisbeare, Devon

**FOCUS**
A shock here, but take nothing away from the winner who was impressive and is a filly of above average ability. The fifst three came clear.

## 2173 DINE IN THE 1707 RESTAURANT MAIDEN AUCTION STKS 5f 110y
6:25 (6:25) (Class 5) 2-Y-O £2,587 (£770; £384; £192) Stalls Low

Form RPR
2 1 **Doomah (IRE)**12 1788 2-8-13 0.......... FrankieDettori 8 75+
(Richard Hannon) *mde all: shkn up over 1f out: comf* 4/5[1]
0 2 1/2 **Blue Burmese (IRE)**5 2022 2-8-6 0.......... LukeMorris 6 66
(Mark Usher) *a.p: chsd wnr over 2f out: rdn and ev ch fr over 1f out: styd on* 10/1
3 6 **Only Joking** 2-8-10 0.......... MartinDwyer 11 51
(Hugo Palmer) *s.i.s and rn green in rr: hdwy over 2f out: wnt 3rd over 1f out: styd on same pce* 7/1[3]
4 2 1/4 **Buckleberry** 2-8-12 0.......... MatthewLawson(3) 2 48
(Jonathan Portman) *sn pushed along in rr: hdwy over 2f out: nvr nrr* 16/1
5 1 1/4 **Miss Van Gogh** 2-8-10 0.......... TonyHamilton 4 39
(Richard Fahey) *sn pushed along and prom: swtchd rt 2f out: sn wknd* 4/1[2]
4 6 2 **Chetan**10 1872 2-8-11 0.......... FrederikTylicki 10 33
(Milton Bradley) *trckd wnr: pushed along and lost 2nd over 2f out: wknd over 1f out* 7/1[3]
05 7 2 **Arousal**18 1633 2-8-8 0.......... LiamJones 13 24
(Michael Bell) *s.i.s: hdwy over 4f out: rdn and wknd over 1f out* 25/1
8 35 **Cap la Nna** 2-8-8 0.......... RoystonFfrench 5
(David C Griffiths) *hmpd s: sn pushed along towards rr: wknd 1/2-way* 25/1

1m 8.62s (2.72) **Going Correction** +0.45s/f (Yiel) 8 Ran SP% **123.2**
Speed ratings (Par 93): **99,98,90,87,85 83,80,33**
CSF £11.81 TOTE £1.90: £1.02, £2.50, £2.20; EX 11.80 Trifecta £77.20.
**Owner** Al Shaqab Racing **Bred** Churchtown House Stud **Trained** East Everleigh, Wilts

**FOCUS**
A heavily depleted field lined up for this 2yo maiden run in lashing rain. The front pair pulled clear and the form seems sound enough.

## 2174 SECOND TIME FOR CERTAIN H'CAP 6f
6:55 (6:56) (Class 6) (0-65,68) 4-Y-0+ £1,940 (£577; £288; £144) Stalls Low

Form RPR
215- 1 **Euroquip Boy (IRE)**215 7079 7-8-2 **51** oh1.......... NoelGarbutt(5) 4 63
(Michael Scudamore) *a.p: chsd ldr over 2f out: rdn to ld ins fnl f: edgd rt: styd on* 12/1
-201 2 3/4 **Whipphound**12 1787 6-9-10 **68**.......... LukeMorris 10 78
(Mark Brisbourne) *hld up: hdwy u.p over 1f out: chsd wnr ins fnl f: styd on* 10/3[1]
5150 3 2 3/4 **Interchoice Star**10 1892 9-8-9 **53**..........(p) MartinLane 17 55
(Ray Peacock) *chsd ldr tl led over 3f out: rdn and hdd ins fnl f: styd on same pce* 16/1
5-4U 4 1 **Interakt**6 1986 7-8-7 **51** oh1..........(p) DavidProbert 3 50
(Joseph Tuite) *mid-div: sn drvn along: hdwy u.p over 1f out: styd on same pce ins fnl f* 7/1
1200 5 1/2 **Divine Call**13 1766 7-9-3 **61**.......... LiamJones 15 58
(Milton Bradley) *s.i.s: hdwy u.p over 1f out: no ex ins fnl f* 13/2[3]
0024 6 1 3/4 **Dark Lane**8 1912 8-8-11 **60**.......... EoinWalsh(5) 13 52
(David Evans) *prom: rdn over 2f out: styd on same pce fr over 1f out* 6/1[2]
0-16 7 2 3/4 **Reginald Claude**92 511 6-8-9 **58**.......... RachealKneller(5) 7 42
(Mark Usher) *hld up: shkn up over 1f out: nvr nrr* 20/1
2006 8 1 1/4 **Climaxfortackle (IRE)**47 1080 6-9-1 **59**.......... TonyHamilton 2 39
(Derek Shaw) *s.i.s: hdwy u.p over 1f out: wknd fnl f* 16/1
6-02 9 1/2 **Addictive Nature (IRE)**12 1790 4-8-5 **54**.......... LouisSteward(5) 11 32
(John Gallagher) *chsd ldrs: rdn over 2f out: wknd over 1f out* 7/1
111 10 4 1/2 **Louis Vee (IRE)**78 693 6-9-2 **60**..........(t) ChrisCatlin 16 25
(Roy Brotherton) *led: hdd over 3f out: wknd wl over 1f out* 12/1
1415 11 7 **Dishy Guru**12 1787 5-9-7 **65**..........(b) LiamKeniry 5 9
(Michael Blanshard) *prom: pushed along over 2f out: wknd over 1f out* 15/2
605- 12 11 **Ozz**227 6753 5-9-0 **58**..........(bt) AntonioFresu 6
(James Unett) *mid-div: sn pushed along: lost pl over 3f out: sn bhd* 16/1

1m 14.95s (3.15) **Going Correction** +0.60s/f (Yiel) 12 Ran SP% **125.3**
Speed ratings (Par 101): **103,102,98,97,96 94,90,88,88,82 72,58**
CSF £54.77 CT £685.20 TOTE £20.20: £4.90, £1.70, £7.20; EX 77.10 Trifecta £1671.10 Part won..
**Owner** Ted Bennett **Bred** Gerard And Yvonne Kennedy **Trained** Bromsash, H'fords

**FOCUS**
A competitive sprint handicap in which plenty arrived in form. The winner was close to his 2012 reappearance form.

## 2175 NEW PEUGEOT 108 H'CAP 1m 7f 9y
7:25 (7:25) (Class 5) (0-75,74) 4-Y-0+ £2,587 (£770; £384; £192) Stalls Low

Form RPR
30-2 1 **Ivanhoe**8 1909 4-8-11 **63**.......... DavidProbert 4 71
(Michael Blanshard) *prom: lost pl over 6f out: hdwy over 2f out: chsd ldr over 1f out: styd on u.p to ld post* 11/8[1]
50-0 2 nse **Kashgar**29 1418 5-9-7 **71**.......... MartinLane 7 78
(Bernard Llewellyn) *chsd ldr 6f: wnt 2nd again over 6f out: led over 2f out: rdn over 1f out: hdd post* 8/1
35-4 3 3 1/2 **Nolecce**14 1740 7-7-12 **55** oh5.......... JackGarritty(7) 2 57
(Tony Forbes) *led 6f: chsd ldr tl over 6f out: remained handy: nt clr run over 1f out: styd on same pce ins fnl f* 11/1
-560 4 1 3/4 **Eshtyaaq**11 1848 7-9-3 **70**.......... DeclanBates(3) 6 70
(David Evans) *trckd ldrs: plld hrd: wnt 2nd 9f out: led over 7f out: rdn and hdd over 2f out: no ex fnl f* 8/1
0303 5 1 1/2 **My Destination (IRE)**4 2055 5-8-5 **62**.......... LukeLeadbitter(7) 3 60
(Declan Carroll) *hld up: hdwy over 4f out: rdn over 3f out: styd on same pce fr over 1f out* 3/1[2]
-254 6 hd **Kenny's Girl (IRE)**11 1848 4-8-8 **60**.......... MartinDwyer 8 58
(William Muir) *hld up: hdwy over 6f out: rdn over 2f out: no ex fr over 1f out* 9/2[3]

3m 34.69s (15.69) **Going Correction** +0.90s/f (Soft)
**WFA** 4 from 5yo+ 2lb 6 Ran SP% **115.8**
Speed ratings (Par 103): **94,93,92,91,90 90**
CSF £13.91 CT £88.25 TOTE £1.90: £1.20, £3.40; EX 16.10 Trifecta £47.90.
**Owner** The Lansdowners & N Price **Bred** Simon Balding **Trained** Upper Lambourn, Berks

**FOCUS**
With the defection of Wannabe Your Man this was a weak staying handicap. It's hard to be confident about this form.

## 2176 NEW CITROEN C1 H'CAP (BOBIS RACE) 7f
7:55 (7:55) (Class 4) (0-85,88) 3-Y-O £5,175 (£1,540; £769) Stalls Low

Form RPR
00-3 1 **Regiment**20 1601 3-8-10 **74**.......... TonyHamilton 5 85
(Richard Fahey) *chsd ldr: pushed along over 2f out: led over 1f out: styd on wl* 10/1[3]
-362 2 1 3/4 **Lincoln (IRE)**16 1658 3-9-1 **82**.......... WilliamTwiston-Davies(3) 1 88
(Mick Channon) *led: qcknd over 2f out: hdd over 1f out: styd on same pce ins fnl f* 7/2[2]
51- 3 1 3/4 **Sea Defence (USA)**190 7654 3-9-4 **82**.......... FrankieDettori 2 84
(Roger Charlton) *hld up: shkn up over 2f out: styd on same pce fnl f* 2/7[1]

1m 29.11s (5.91) **Going Correction** +0.90s/f (Soft) 3 Ran SP% **109.1**
Speed ratings (Par 101): **102,100,98**
CSF £31.50 TOTE £4.50; EX 15.40 Trifecta £9.70.
**Owner** T G & Mrs M E Holdcroft **Bred** Bearstone Stud **Trained** Musley Bank, N Yorks

**FOCUS**
Just the three runners lined up for this 3yo handicap and it went to the outsider. The time was reasonable but it;'s still hard to be confident about the form.

## 2177 CUT THE MUSTARD WITH MUSTARD PRESENTATIONS H'CAP 7f
8:25 (8:26) (Class 5) (0-75,75) 4-Y-0+ £2,587 (£770; £384; £192) Stalls Low

Form RPR
660- **1** **Exzachary**[200] 7452 4-8-9 70 HarryBurns(7) 2 79
(Jo Hughes) *hld up: hdwy over 2f out: chsd ldr over 1f out: led ins fnl f: pushed out* **16/1**
-313 **2** *hd* **Uncle Dermot (IRE)**[11] 1845 6-9-5 73 RichardKingscote 1 81
(Brendan Powell) *led 2f: chsd ldr tl led again 3f out: rdn and hdd ins fnl f: r.o* **11/8**[1]
14-5 **3** *5* **Barista (IRE)**[12] 1800 6-8-3 64 DanielCremin(7) 6 59
(Brian Forsey) *trckd ldrs: nt clr run over 2f out: rdn over 1f out: styd on same pce fnl f* **10/1**
5-12 **4** *nse* **Llewellyn**[19] 1610 6-9-4 75 NeilFarley(3) 5 70
(Declan Carroll) *trckd ldrs: rdn over 2f out: styd on same pce fnl f* **13/8**[2]
21-0 **5** *nk* **Kimbali (IRE)**[14] 1739 5-8-11 70 EoinWalsh(5) 8 64
(David Evans) *s.s: hld up: rdn and n.m.r over 1f out: nvr trbld ldrs* **5/1**[3]
000- **6** *14* **My Stroppy Poppy**[261] 5667 5-8-7 61 oh16 MartinLane 7 19
(Alan Phillips) *trckd ldr: plldhrd: led 5f out tl 3f out: rdn and wknd over 1f out* **25/1**

1m 29.74s (6.54) **Going Correction** +0.90s/f (Soft) **6** Ran SP% **115.7**
Speed ratings (Par 103): **98,97,92,92,91 75**
CSF £40.33 CT £246.51 TOTE £18.20: £6.50, £1.30; EX 62.90 Trifecta £241.80.
**Owner** Joseph Smith **Bred** Allseasons Bloodstock **Trained** Lambourn, Berks

**FOCUS**
An ordinary handicap, rated around the runner-up.
T/Plt: £120.10 to a £1 stake. Pool: £73449.23 - 446.16 winning tickets T/Qpdt: £73.70 to a £1 stake. Pool: £3337.89 - 33.50 winning tickets CR

2178 - 2184a (Foreign Racing) - See Raceform Interactive

# [1250]LEOPARDSTOWN (L-H)
Sunday, May 11

**OFFICIAL GOING: Yielding to soft**

## 2185a ARDGLEN AMETHYST STKS (GROUP 3) 1m
2:55 (2:56) 3-Y-0+ £33,854 (£9,895; £4,687; £1,562)

RPR
**1** **Mustajeeb**[260] 5774 3-8-10 110 PatSmullen 10 114+
(D K Weld, Ire) *hld up in tch: 6th 1/2-way: qcknd wl 1 1/2f out and clsd on outer to ld over 150yds out: rdn clr: comf* **5/2**[1]
**2** *2 1/2* **Brendan Brackan (IRE)**[64] 899 5-9-12 112 ColinKeane 8 114
(G M Lyons, Ire) *broke wl to ld tl sn settled bhd ldr: cl 2nd 1/2-way: rdn to ld 1 1/2f out: sn strly pressed and hdd u.p over 150yds out: no ch w wnr: kpt on same pce* **10/3**[2]
**3** *3 1/2* **One Spirit (IRE)**[246] 6224 6-9-6 100 GaryCarroll 5 100
(F Dunne, Ire) *chsd ldrs: rdn in 4th over 2f out and wnt 3rd u.p fnl 150yds: kpt on same pce: nt trble principals* **28/1**
**4** *3/4* **Pop Art (IRE)**[28] 1473 4-9-6 100 FMBerry 3 98
(Charles O'Brien, Ire) *hld up: 7th 1/2-way: rdn fr 2f out and sme hdwy on outer into mod 5th ins fnl f: kpt on towards fin: nvr trbld ldrs* **12/1**
**5** *hd* **Pearl Of Africa (IRE)**[80] 682 4-9-6 106 FergalLynch 6 98
(Edward Lynam, Ire) *hld up in tch: 5th 1/2-way: sme hdwy far side 1 1/2f out where nt clr run on inner: kpt on towards fin* **13/2**
**6** *1 3/4* **Penitent**[16] 1698 8-9-9 111 DanielTudhope 4 97
(David O'Meara) *sn led: narrow advantage 1/2-way: rdn and hdd 1 1/2f out: sn no ex u.p in 3rd: wknd* **9/2**[3]
**7** *1 1/2* **Qewy (IRE)**[39] 1252 4-9-9 107 DeclanMcDonogh 2 93
(John M Oxx, Ire) *sn chsd ldrs: 3rd 1/2-way: rdn into st and no imp on ldrs: wknd fr 1 1/2f out* **6/1**
**8** *18* **Leitir Mor (IRE)**[13] 1824 4-9-12 108 (p) KevinManning 1 55
(J S Bolger, Ire) *v.s.a and detached in rr: tk clsr order 1/2-way: rdn and no ex 2f out: wknd and eased* **12/1**

1m 42.64s (1.44) **Going Correction** +0.50s/f (Yiel)
**WFA** 3 from 4yo+ 13lb **8** Ran SP% **116.3**
Speed ratings: **112,109,106,105,105 103,101,83**
CSF £11.15 TOTE £2.30: £1.30, £1.60, £5.40; DF 12.20 Trifecta £462.20.
**Owner** Hamdan Al Maktoum **Bred** Shadwell Estate Company Limited **Trained** Curragh, Co Kildare

**FOCUS**
This had been won by Famous Name in three of the last four years and the Dermot Weld stable regained the winning habit. It was genuine Group 3 in terms of quality with the first two home rated 110 and 112. It was run a decent clip given the conditions. The front two pulled nicely clear of the remainder.

## 2186a DERRINSTOWN STUD 1,000 GUINEAS TRIAL (GROUP 3) (FILLIES) 1m
3:25 (3:25) 3-Y-0 £32,500 (£9,500; £4,500; £1,500)

RPR
**1** **Afternoon Sunlight (IRE)**[15] 1747 3-9-0 98 PatSmullen 2 101
(D K Weld, Ire) *mde all: narrow advantage 1/2-way: gng wl into st and extended ld fr 2f out: reduced advantage u.p wl ins fnl f: all out towards fin to jst hold on* **9/4**[1]
**2** *hd* **Palace (IRE)**[29] 1461 3-9-1 ow1 JosephO'Brien 6 101
(A P O'Brien, Ire) *dwlt sltly and w.w in rr: hdwy on outer to chse ldrs in cl 3rd bef 1/2-way: rdn in 2nd over 1 1/2f out and sn no imp on wnr: kpt on wl to strly press wnr towards fin: jst hld* **3/1**[3]
**3** *3/4* **Ballybacka Queen (IRE)**[226] 6798 3-9-0 99 SeamieHeffernan 9 99+
(P A Fahy, Ire) *hld up: last 1/2-way: rdn in rr over 1f out and r.o wl u.p towards fin into nvr nrr 3rd: nvr trbld ldrs* **20/1**
**4** *1/2* **Waltzing Matilda (IRE)**[39] 1250 3-9-0 WayneLordan 4 98
(T Stack, Ire) *towards rr: tk clsr order in 6th 1/2-way: pushed along into st and hung: wnt 4th between horses over 1f out: sn no imp on ldrs u.p in 3rd and dropped to 4th towards fin* **10/1**
**5** *1/2* **Booker**[28] 1471 3-9-0 92 FMBerry 5 97
(David Wachman, Ire) *chsd ldrs: 5th 1/2-way: pushed along into st and hdwy u.p into 3rd briefly ins fnl f: no imp on ldrs and dropped to 5th nr fin* **10/1**
**6** *2 1/2* **Harry's Princess (IRE)**[42] 1201 3-9-0 NGMcCullagh 7 91
(John M Oxx, Ire) *trckd ldr: cl 2nd 1/2-way: rdn 2f out and sn no imp u.p in 3rd: wknd fnl f* **10/1**

**7** *4 3/4* **Stars So Bright (IRE)**[25] 1523 3-9-0 DeclanMcDonogh 1 88+
(John M Oxx, Ire) *chsd ldrs: 4th 1/2-way: niggled along 3f out: n.m.r on inner 1 1/2f out and dropped to mod 6th ent fnl f: eased* **5/2**[2]

1m 43.84s (2.64) **Going Correction** +0.50s/f (Yiel) **7** Ran SP% **116.4**
Speed ratings: **106,105,105,104,104 101,96**
CSF £9.70 TOTE £3.00: £1.30, £1.80; DF 12.40 Trifecta £69.40.
**Owner** Moyglare Stud Farm **Bred** Moyglare Stud Farm Ltd **Trained** Curragh, Co Kildare

**FOCUS**
A top-notch renewal that exceeded recent years in terms of quality. The two non-runners would have been outsiders anyway and the seven that remained had all won previously. The winner set a sedate early gallop and her ability to quicken early in the home straight proved the winning move.

## 2187a DERRINSTOWN STUD DERBY TRIAL STKS (GROUP 3) 1m 2f
3:55 (3:55) 3-Y-0 £50,000 (£15,833; £7,500; £2,500; £1,666; £833)

RPR
**1** *hd* **Fascinating Rock (IRE)**[29] 1458 3-9-3 107 PatSmullen 5 110+
(D K Weld, Ire) *w.w in rr: hdwy on outer fr 1 1/2f out to go 2nd ins fnl f: styd on wl u.p towards fin where bmpd: jst failed: fin 2nd: awrdd the r* **1/1**[1]
**2** **Ebanoran (IRE)**[42] 1200 3-9-3 DeclanMcDonogh 7 110
(John M Oxx, Ire) *cl up and t.k.h early: clsd in 4th over 2f out: qcknd on outer to ld fr 1 1/2f out where wnt lft: all out u.p and wnt rt towards fin to jst hold on: fin 1st: disqualified and plcd 2nd* **8/1**[3]
**3** *2 1/2* **Geoffrey Chaucer (USA)**[224] 6884 3-9-6 112 JosephO'Brien 4 112+
(A P O'Brien, Ire) *hld up bhd ldrs in 4th: tk clsr order in 3rd over 4f out: hdwy between horses fr under 2f out into 2nd: sn short of room and checked briefly: rdn in 3rd ins fnl f and n.m.r bhd horses: eased* **7/4**[2]
**4** *2 1/2* **Answered**[29] 1458 3-9-3 103 KevinManning 8 100
(J S Bolger, Ire) *sn trckd ldrs: 3rd 1/2-way: rdn and no ex fr 2f out: kpt on one pce in 4th ins fnl f* **10/1**
**5** *2 3/4* **Highly Toxic (IRE)**[42] 1200 3-9-3 89 DannyGrant 1 95
(Patrick J Flynn, Ire) *trckd ldrs tl led after 1f: pushed along into st and hdd 1 1/2f out: no ex and dropped to 5th ins fnl f: kpt on one pce* **100/1**
**6** *4 1/2* **Altruistic (IRE)**[197] 7528 3-9-3 107 RichardHughes 6 86
(J P Murtagh, Ire) *led tl hdd after 1f: 2nd 1/2-way: pushed along into st and sn no ex u.p in 5th: wknd* **20/1**

2m 14.95s (6.75) **Going Correction** +0.15s/f (Good) **6** Ran SP% **112.3**
Speed ratings: **78,79,76,74,72 68**
CSF £10.08 TOTE £2.10: £1.10, £4.10; DF 10.40 Trifecta £32.00.
**Owner** Newtown Anner Stud Farm Ltd **Bred** Newtown Anner Stud **Trained** Curragh, Co Kildare
■ Stewards' Enquiry : Declan McDonogh two-day ban (reduced from 3 on appeal): careless riding (May 26, 29)

**FOCUS**
Sinndar (2000), Galileo (2001) and High Chaparral (2002) all won this before going on to Epsom glory and last year's winner Battle Of Marengo subsequently finished fourth behind Ruler Of The World. There was no Australia, who will head straight to the Derby from the Guineas, but it did contain three of the most promising 3yo colts on these shores and they filled the first three places. With no obvious pacesetter in the line-up from any of the top yards, there was a steady early gallop. It turned into a sprint finish and we were left with more questions than answers.

# [1779]CAPANNELLE (R-H)
Sunday, May 11

**OFFICIAL GOING: Turf: good**

## 2191a PREMIO PRESIDENTE DELLA REPUBBLICA GBI RACING (GROUP 1) (4YO+) (TURF) 1m 2f
3:50 (12:00) 4-Y-0+ £79,166 (£34,833; £19,000; £9,500)

RPR
**1** **Refuse To Bobbin (IRE)**[14] 4-9-2 0 DPerovic 6 105
(A Giorgi, Italy) *towards rr: hdwy over 2f out: rdn and r.o wl fnl f: led fnl stride* **57/1**
**2** *shd* **Biz The Nurse (IRE)**[203] 7414 4-9-2 0 AndreaAtzeni 8 105
(Stefano Botti, Italy) *trckd ldr: pushed along to hold pl over 2 1/2f out: rdn to chal between horses over 1f out: led ins fnl f: r.o u.p: hdd fnl stride* **3/5**[1]
**3** *nk* **Occhio Della Mente (IRE)**[21] 1603 7-9-2 0 (b) MircoDemuro 9 104
(E Botti, Italy) *trckd ldng pair on outer: rdn to chal 2f out: led 1 1/2f out: hdd ins fnl f: no ex* **47/10**[2]
**4** *hd* **Lodovico Il Moro (IRE)**[14] 4-9-2 0 AndreaMezzatesta 5 104
(L Riccardi, Italy) *trckd ldng pair on inner: rdn and ev ch 2f out: kpt on u.p fnl f but nt pce to chal* **47/10**
**5** *1/2* **Vedelago (IRE)**[189] 7724 5-9-2 0 MEsposito 4 103
(Stefano Botti, Italy) *hld up in rr: hdwy 2 1/2f out: styd on u.p fnl f: nvr on terms* **48/10**[3]
**6** *hd* **Orpello (IRE)**[21] 1603 5-9-2 0 (b) FabioBranca 7 103
(Stefano Botti, Italy) *led: hdd 1 1/2f out: kpt on at one pce u.p fnl f* **32/5**
**7** *nk* **Demeteor (ITY)**[35] 4-9-2 0 GMarcelli 3 102
(R Menichetti, Italy) *midfield on inner: rdn and nt qckn 2f out: kpt on u.p fnl f: nt pce to chal* **269/10**
**8** *nk* **Saint Bernard**[28] 5-9-2 0 GBietolini 2 101
(D Camuffo, Italy) *t.k.h: hld up in rr: hdwy to chse ldrs over 1 1/2f out: one pce fnl f* **104/10**
**9** *1 1/4* **Pattaya (ITY)**[14] 6-9-2 0 CFiocchi 1 99
(Stefano Botti, Italy) *towards rr: hdwy 2 1/2f out: rdn and effrt on outside appr fnl f: wknd fnl 150yds* **68/10**
**10** *7* **Mr Gotham**[35] 5-9-2 0 PBorrelli 10 85
(C Impelluso, Italy) *midfield on outer: rdn and wknd over 1 1/2f out* **217/10**

2m 3.78s (0.48) **10** Ran SP% **159.6**
WIN (incl. 1 euro stake): 58.00. PLACES: 7.45, 1.28, 1.93. DF: 246.01.
**Owner** Scuderia Chimax **Bred** Scuderia Chimax Srl **Trained** Italy

2106 **LONGCHAMP** (R-H)

Sunday, May 11

**OFFICIAL GOING: Turf: good to soft**

## 2192a PRIX DE L'ASSOCIATION LE RIRE MEDECIN (PRIX DU CHATEAU D'EAU) (CLAIMER) (4YO) (TURF) 1m 4f

**12:30** (12:30) 4-Y-O **£7,916** (£3,166; £2,375; £1,583; £791)

RPR

1 **Conceptuelle (FR)**[223] 4-9-1 0.......... ChristopheSoumillon 3 79
(C Lotoux, France) **18/5**[3]

2 1 ½ **Destiny Highway (FR)**[4] 4-8-11 0.......... (b) SylvainRuis 5 72
(Mlle M Henry, France) **52/1**

3 2 **Pegasus Bridge (FR)**[459] 543 4-8-9 0.......... (p) MickaelBerto(6) 7 73
(K Borgel, France) **149/10**

4 2 **Jebril (FR)**[238] 6435 4-9-1 0.......... IoritzMendizabal 9 70
(Jonathan Portman) *hld up towards rr: hdwy on outer fr 5f out and prom into st: rdn over 2f out: outpcd by ldrs over 1f out: styd on ins fnl f and tk wl hld 4th cl home* **175/10**

5 snk **Arthur The King (IRE)**[19] 4-9-4 0.......... MaximeGuyon 2 73
(N Bertran De Balanda, France) **31/10**[2]

6 ¾ **Albegna (GER)**[58] 4-8-8 0.......... UmbertoRispoli 6 61
(H Blume, Germany) **11/1**

7 snk **Kaabamix (FR)**[19] 4-8-11 0.......... FlavienPrat 11 64
(D Windrif, France) **27/10**[1]

8 2 **Gingka (FR)**[19] 4-8-11 0.......... (b) GregoryBenoist 8 61
(Mme P Butel, France) **41/5**

9 10 **River Prince (FR)**[10] 4-9-1 0.......... (p) AntoineHamelin 1 49
(P Adda, France) **45/1**

10 4 ½ **Promesse D'Ecouves (FR)**[210] 4-8-8 0.......... RaphaelMarchelli 4 35
(K Borgel, France) **83/1**

11 6 **Lowenthal (GER)**[96] 4-9-2 0.......... (b) FabriceVeron 10 33
(S Smrczek, Germany) **93/10**

2m 36.05s (5.65) 11 Ran SP% **119.0**
WIN (incl. 1 euro stake): 4.60. PLACES: 2.40, 9.50, 4.60. DF: 80.60. SF: 136.60.
**Owner** Michel Delaunay **Bred** J-L Pariente **Trained** France

## 2194a PRIX HOCQUART (GROUP 2) (3YO COLTS & FILLIES) (TURF) 1m 3f

**1:30** (1:29) 3-Y-O **£61,750** (£23,833; £11,375; £7,583; £3,791)

RPR

1 **Free Port Lux**[35] 1340 3-9-2 0.......... ThierryJarnet 6 114+
(F Head, France) *hld up in tch: swtchd to outer and hdwy 2f out: rdn to chal over 1f out: styd on and led ins fnl 150yds: pushed out and a holding runner-up towards fin* **3/1**[2]

2 ½ **Adelaide (IRE)**[197] 7551 3-9-2 0.......... RyanMoore 7 113+
(A P O'Brien, Ire) *trckd ldr on inner: rdn and hdwy on rail to chal ent fnl f: styd on wl for 2nd but hld by wnr towards fin* **5/2**[1]

3 2 **Gallante (IRE)**[20] 1621 3-9-2 0.......... Pierre-CharlesBoudot 4 110
(A Fabre, France) *led: rdn and strly pressed fr over 1f out: styd on but hdd ins fnl 150yds and dropped to 3rd: no ex* **9/1**

4 snk **Orbec (FR)**[28] 3-9-2 0.......... GregoryBenoist 3 109+
(J-C Rouget, France) *midfield in tch on outer: pushed along and ev ch 2f out: rdn and outpcd by ldrs ent fnl f: styd on: clsng on 3rd at fin but wl hld by front pair* **8/1**

5 ½ **Aventador (FR)**[20] 1621 3-9-2 0.......... RaphaelMarchelli 5 108
(T Castanheira, France) *stdd and hld up in last: pushed along and hdwy on outer fr 2f out: rdn over 1f out: hung rt u.p: styd on but nvr threatened* **12/1**

6 1 **Elliptique (IRE)**[35] 1340 3-9-2 0.......... MaximeGuyon 1 107
(A Fabre, France) *stdd and sn midfield in tch on inner: rdn and shuffled bk 2f out: outpcd in rr whn short of room and checked over 1f out: styd on towards fin but nt rcvr* **9/2**[3]

7 2 **Diaghan (FR)**[35] 1340 3-9-2 0.......... ChristopheSoumillon 2 103
(M Delzangles, France) *dwlt: qckly rcvrd and trckd ldr on outer: gng wl and ev ch 2f out: rdn over 1f out and fnd little: sn btn: fdd and dropped to last* **11/2**

2m 23.11s (3.21) **Going Correction** +0.45s/f (Yiel) 7 Ran SP% **115.9**
Speed ratings: **106,105,104,104,103 102,101**
WIN (incl. 1 euro stake): 3.80. PLACES: 2.00, 2.40. SF: 19.60.
**Owner** Olivier Thomas **Bred** Ecurie Des Monceaux **Trained** France

## 2195a POULE D'ESSAI DES POULICHES (PRIX LE PARISIEN) (GROUP 1) (3YO FILLIES) (TURF) 1m

**2:08** (2:10) 3-Y-O **£214,275** (£85,725; £42,862; £21,412; £10,725)

RPR

1 **Avenir Certain (FR)**[32] 3-9-0 0.......... GregoryBenoist 10 118+
(J-C Rouget, France) *hld up in midfield: swtchd lft and rdn 2f out: drifted rt u.p but r.o strly and led ent fnl f: qcknd clr: reduced advantage towards fin but in full control: impressive* **14/1**

2 1 ¼ **Veda (FR)**[20] 3-9-0 0.......... ChristopheSoumillon 15 115+
(A De Royer-Dupre, France) *hld up fr wd draw and sn last: smooth hdwy 2f out: rdn over 1f out: r.o and wnt 2nd ins fnl f: chsd wnr and clsd towards fin but a wl hld* **9/1**

3 2 ½ **Xcellence (FR)**[38] 1273 3-9-0 0.......... CristianDemuro 7 109
(F Doumen, France) *midfield: rdn 2f out: hdwy and ev ch tl outpcd by wnr ent fnl f: kpt on and jst hld on for 3rd* **6/1**[2]

4 shd **Bawina (IRE)**[42] 3-9-0 0.......... OlivierPeslier 9 109
(C Laffon-Parias, France) *t.k.h and trapped wd in midfield early: sn hld up towards rr on outer: bmpd as eventual wnr swtchd lft 2f out: sn rdn: r.o wl ins fnl f and almost snatched 3rd post: nvr able to chal* **6/1**[2]

5 1 **Stellar Path (FR)**[47] 1096 3-9-0 0.......... GeraldMosse 11 106
(X Thomas-Demeaulte, France) *t.k.h: hld up towards rr: disputing last whn bmpd 2f out: sn rdn: r.o ins fnl f and wnt 5th cl home: fin wl but nvr able to chal* **33/1**

6 ½ **This Time (FR)**[38] 1273 3-9-0 0.......... FabriceVeron 3 105
(H-A Pantall, France) *t.k.h early: midfield in tch: rdn and ev ch 2f out: kpt on but outpcd by wnr ent fnl f and sn hld: dropped to 6th cl home* **33/1**

7 1 **J Wonder (USA)**[29] 1435 3-9-0 0.......... Christophe-PatriceLemaire 1 103
(Brian Meehan) *t.k.h early: prom on inner: travelled strly to 2f out: pushed along to chal and led briefly over 1f out tl hdd ent fnl f: sn no ex and fdd* **8/1**

8 nk **Al Thakhira**[29] 1435 3-9-0 0.......... FrankieDettori 13 102
(Marco Botti) *hld up and sn towards rr on outer: rdn and disputing last whn sltly hmpd 2f out: kpt on and sme hdwy ins fnl f but nvr threatened* **16/1**

9 ¾ **Wonderfully (IRE)**[217] 7055 3-9-0 0.......... RyanMoore 14 101
(A P O'Brien, Ire) *pushed along to go forward and prom on outer early: midfield fr bef 1/2-way: pushed along whn bmpd as wnr swtchd lft 2f out: shuffled bk towards rr and sn last: kpt on wl towards fin and wnt 9th post: nt rcvr* **20/1**

10 shd **Indonesienne (IRE)**[28] 1480 3-9-0 0.......... FlavienPrat 2 100
(C Ferland, France) *pushed along to go forward and prom early: settled in midfield bef 1/2-way: pushed along 2f out: rdn and outpcd over 1f out: kpt on ins fnl f but wl hld* **7/1**[3]

11 hd **Queen Catrine (IRE)**[25] 1515 3-9-0 0.......... JamieSpencer 4 100
(Charles Hills) *broke wl and led: pushed along over 2f out: rdn and hdd over 1f out: no ex and btn ins fnl f: fdd* **20/1**

12 1 ½ **Lesstalk In Paris (IRE)**[28] 1480 3-9-0 0.......... IoritzMendizabal 8 96
(J-C Rouget, France) *t.k.h: midfield on inner: rdn 2f out: kpt on same pce tl no ex and btn ins fnl f: fdd and eased towards fin* **4/1**[1]

13 3 ½ **Ice Love (FR)**[38] 1273 3-9-0 0.......... RaphaelMarchelli 12 88
(T Castanheira, France) *dwlt sltly and hld up towards rr on inner: swtchd lft and rdn 2f out: sn outpcd and btn: n.d* **100/1**

14 2 **Straight Thinking (USA)**[28] 1480 3-9-0 0.......... MaximeGuyon 5 84
(A Fabre, France) *bobbled s but qckly rcvrd: trckd ldr: rdn and effrt to chal 2f out: no ex and lost pl over 1f out: sn btn and wknd: eased ins fnl f* **10/1**

15 7 **Mintaka (FR)**[19] 3-9-0 0.......... FreddyDiFede 16 68
(A De Royer-Dupre, France) *prom on wd outside: trckd ldr 5f out: rdn and brief effrt to chal 2f out: sn no ex and btn: wknd: eased ins fnl f* **150/1**

16 hd **Cape Factor (IRE)**[191] 7657 3-9-0 0.......... WilliamBuick 6 67
(Rae Guest) *broke wl and trckd ldr early: shuffled bk bef 1/2-way but remained prom: rdn over 2f out: no ex and btn over 1f out: eased ins fnl f* **33/1**

1m 39.95s (1.55) **Going Correction** +0.45s/f (Yiel) 16 Ran SP% **123.8**
Speed ratings: **110,108,106,106,105 104,103,103,102,102 102,100,97,95,88 88**
WIN (incl. 1 euro stake): 8.40. PLACES: 3.50, 3.30, 3.60. DF: 39.60. SF: 90.00.
**Owner** A Caro & G Augustin-Normand **Bred** Mme E Vidal **Trained** Pau, France

**FOCUS**
The ground was already soft and further rain not long after racing got under way would have only made the going more testing. This didn't exactly look a vintage edition of the race, and it was run at no more than an ordinary gallop, but two clearly very smart fillies came to the fore. The standard is set by the fifth, sixth and seventh.

## 2196a POULE D'ESSAI DES POULAINS (GROUP 1) (3YO COLTS) (TURF) 1m

**2:45** (2:49) 3-Y-O **£261,891** (£104,775; £52,387; £26,170; £13,108)

RPR

1 **Karakontie (JPN)**[28] 1481 3-9-2 0.......... StephanePasquier 1 117+
(J E Pease, France) *sn midfield in tch on inner: pushed along and hdwy on rail 2f out: rdn to chal over 1f out and led narrowly ent fnl f: r.o wl and a jst holding persistent runner-up* **6/4**[1]

2 nk **Prestige Vendome (FR)**[28] 1481 3-9-2 0.......... (p) ThierryThulliez 6 116
(N Clement, France) *trckd ldr on outer: led gng best 2f out: rdn and strly pressed fr over 1f out: narrowly hdd ent fnl f: kpt on wl u.p and battled bk gamely but a jst hld* **14/1**

3 1 ½ **Pornichet (FR)**[24] 3-9-2 0.......... GregoryBenoist 5 113
(N Clement, France) *t.k.h and restrained early: sn midfield on inner: rdn and hdwy on rail into 3rd over 1f out: kpt on wl ins fnl f but nt pce of front pair* **66/1**

4 hd **Muwaary**[30] 1420 3-9-2 0.......... PaulHanagan 2 112
(John Gosden) *t.k.h and led early: sn restrained and trckd ldr on inner: pushed along and sltly outpcd 2f out: rdn over 1f out: rallied u.p and r.o wl ins fnl f: almost snatched 3rd post* **7/1**

5 1 **Galiway**[28] 1481 3-9-2 0.......... OlivierPeslier 3 110
(A Fabre, France) *in tch on outer: pushed along over 2f out: rdn and outpcd by ldrs over 1f out: kpt on ins fnl f but wl hld* **5/1**[2]

6 ¾ **Kiram (FR)**[38] 1272 3-9-2 0.......... ChristopheSoumillon 14 108+
(J-C Rouget, France) *hld up towards rr: rdn 2f out: angled lft for clr run over 1f out: kpt on nicely under mostly hands and heels ins fnl f and wnt 6th towards fin: nvr nrr* **13/2**[3]

7 ½ **Giovanni Boldini (USA)**[43] 1178 3-9-2 0.......... RyanMoore 13 107+
(A P O'Brien, Ire) *midfield on outer: pushed along over 2f out: rdn and nt qckn over 1f out: kpt on same pce ins fnl f and dropped to 7th towards fin* **8/1**

8 1 **Salai (FR)**[47] 1095 3-9-2 0.......... Christophe-PatriceLemaire 11 105
(J-C Rouget, France) *t.k.h: hld up in midfield on outer: pushed along over 2f out: rdn over 1f out: kpt on same pce u.p and nvr threatened* **25/1**

9 2 **End Of Line**[16] 1696 3-9-2 0.......... HarryBentley 10 100
(Andrew Balding) *dwlt: hld up towards rr on inner: pushed along over 2f out: rdn and outpcd over 1f out: kpt on under hand ride and tk mod 9th fnl strides: nvr a factor* **25/1**

10 snk **Itoobeboss (IRE)**[4] 3-9-2 0.......... VincentVion 7 100?
(Rod Collet, France) *sn led: rdn whn hdd 2f out: sn no ex and btn: fdd: eased towards fin and dropped to 10th fnl strides* **200/1**

11 ½ **Zakhar Star (USA)**[15] 3-9-2 0.......... FabriceVeron 4 99
(A Savujev, Czech Republic) *dwlt sltly and hld up in midfield on inner: rdn over 2f out: sn towards rr and btn: n.d* **66/1**

12 dist **Lat Hawill (IRE)**[29] 1436 3-9-2 0.......... JamieSpencer 9
(Marco Botti) *dwlt and hld up in last: pushed along 3f out: no ex and btn over 1f out: eased and t.o* **10/1**

1m 41.06s (2.66) **Going Correction** +0.45s/f (Yiel) 12 Ran SP% **120.5**
Speed ratings: **104,103,102,102,101 100,99,98,96,96 96,**
WIN (incl. 1 euro stake): 2.10. PLACES: 1.20, 2.40, 6.60. DF: 9.30. SF: 17.70.
**Owner** Niarchos Family **Bred** Flaxman Holdings Limited **Trained** Chantilly, France

**FOCUS**
A race lacking depth and, as with the Pouliches, the pace was ordinary at best, little getting into it from behind. The tenth limits the form.

## 2197a PRIX DE SAINT-GEORGES (GROUP 3) (3YO+) (TURF) 5f (S)

**3:55** (4:01) 3-Y-O+ **£33,333** (£13,333; £10,000; £6,666; £3,333)

RPR

1 **Catcall (FR)**[43] 1179 5-9-2 0.......... OlivierPeslier 10 116+
(P Sogorb, France) *hld up in tch: rdn and hdwy fr 2f out: r.o strly and chal ent fnl f: sn led and qcknd clr: won easing down: v readily* **9/4**[1]

2 1 ½ **Signs Of Blessing (IRE)**[25] 1527 3-8-5 0.......... StephanePasquier 4 105
(F Rohaut, France) *hld up in tch: pushed along 2f out: chal over 1f out and sn led: r.o wl but hdd ins fnl f and readily outpcd by wnr: hld* **4/1**[2]



The Form Book, Raceform Ltd, Newbury, RG14 5SJ

3 ¾ **Stepper Point**[8] 1949 5-9-0 0........................(p) MartinDwyer 1 106+
(William Muir) *sn disputing ld on rail: rdn 2f out: hdd over 1f out: r.o but sn dropped to 3rd and hld* **7/1**

4 nk **Dibajj (FR)**[19] 1641 4-9-3 0........................ GeraldMosse 5 108+
(A De Royer-Dupre, France) *s.s and bhd early: pushed along to cl 1/2-way: rdn over 2f out: r.o and wnt 4th post: nvr nrr* **8/1**

5 shd **Mirza**[217] 7054 7-9-6 0........................(p) WilliamBuick 8 111
(Rae Guest) *chsd ldrs: cl 3rd and ev ch whn rdn 2f out: keeping on same pce whn sltly short of room briefly ins fnl f: hld after* **20/1**

6 1 **Kingsgate Choice (IRE)**[50] 1066 7-9-0 0........................ FrederikTylicki 3 101
(Ed de Giles) *in tch: rdn over 2f out: kpt on same pce and wnt 6th post: nvr able to chal* **20/1**

7 shd **Hamza (IRE)**[24] 1531 5-9-6 0........................(b) JamieSpencer 7 107
(Kevin Ryan) *pushed along to go forward and sn disputing ld on outer: rdn 2f out: hdd over 1f out: no ex and fdd ins fnl f: dropped to 7th post* **11/2**[3]

8 1 ½ **Graphic Guest**[32] 1397 4-8-10 0........................ HarryBentley 2 92
(Robert Cowell) *dwlt slt and pushed along early: in tch on inner: rdn over 2f out: outpcd and btn ins fnl f: nvr able to chal* **20/1**

9 2 **Riskit Fora Biskit (IRE)**[22] 1572 4-8-10 0........................ IoritzMendizabal 9 84
(Michael Bell) *chsd ldrs: rdn over 2f out: sn lost pl: outpcd and btn ent fnl f: eased fnl 100yds* **20/1**

10 snk **Smoothtalkinrascal (IRE)**[23] 1561 4-9-0 0........................ RyanMoore 6 88
(David O'Meara) *sn outpcd in rr: pushed along and hopelessly detached 1/2-way: sn rdn and btn: sme v mod late hdwy but nvr a factor* **9/1**

11 3 **Murcielago (GER)**[19] 1641 7-9-0 0........................(p) MaximeGuyon 11 77
(M Keller, Germany) *in tch on outer: rdn and lost pl 2f out: sn btn and wknd: eased and dropped to last ins fnl f* **20/1**

56.92s (0.62) **Going Correction** +0.45s/f (Yiel) **11 Ran SP% 123.6**
**WFA** 3 from 4yo+ 9lb
Speed ratings: **113,110,109,108,108 107,107,104,101,101 96**
WIN (incl. 1 euro stake): 3.60. PLACES: 1.50, 1.80, 2.70. DF: 5.60. SF: 10.80.
**Owner** Mme Gerard Samama **Bred** Dr Fernanad Krief **Trained** France

# 1934 DONCASTER (L-H)

Monday, May 12

**OFFICIAL GOING: Soft changing to heavy after race 3 (2.40)**
Wind: Virtually nil Weather: Cloudy with heavy showers and sunny periods

## 2198 AJA GENTLEMAN AMATEUR RIDERS' H'CAP 1m 4f

**1:40** (1:40) (Class 5) (0-70,67) 3-Y-O **£2,495** (£774; £386; £193) **Stalls Low**

Form RPR

0-03 1 **Newgate Queen**[13] 1840 3-10-4 57........................ MrKWood(7) 6 64
(Tony Coyle) *trckd ldng pair on outer: hdwy and cl up 4f out: led 3f out: rdn along 2f out: hdd ent fnl f: rallied wl to ld again towards fin* **15/2**[3]

0-13 2 hd **Deep Resolve (IRE)**[11] 1904 3-11-6 66........................ MrSWalker 3 72
(Alan Swinbank) *trckd ldrs: hdwy over 3f out: rdn wl over 1f out: slt ld ent fnl f: sn drvn: hdd and no ex towards fin* **13/8**[1]

000- 3 ¾ **That Be Grand**[244] 6271 3-10-2 53 oh8........................ MrGrahamCarson(5) 7 58
(Shaun Harris) *hld up in rr: hdwy on outer wl over 2f out: rdn to chse ldng pair over 1f out: edgd lft jst ins fnl f: no imp towards fin* **100/1**

04-0 4 6 **Come On Sunshine**[26] 1508 3-11-5 65........................[1] FreddieMitchell 5 61
(Brian Ellison) *cl up: rdn along over 3f out: drvn 2f out: sn one pce* **8/1**

53-5 5 1 **Blue Talisman (IRE)**[33] 1372 3-10-4 55........................(b) MrWEasterby(5) 2 49
(Tim Easterby) *t.k.h: trckd ldng pair on inner: pushed along over 3f out: rdn wl over 2f out: sn one pce* **10/1**

5-44 6 ½ **Lightning Shower (USA)**[14] 1812 3-11-7 67........................(p) MrMarioBaratti 4 61
(Marco Botti) *hld up in rr: effrt and sme hdwy 3f out: rdn 2f out: sn btn* **11/4**[2]

1305 7 17 **Enquiring**[14] 1792 3-10-6 57........................ MrAlexFerguson(5) 1 25
(Mark Johnston) *set stdy pce: pushed along and hdd 4f out: sn wknd* **8/1**

2m 55.81s (20.91) **Going Correction** +1.125s/f (Soft) **7 Ran SP% 108.8**
Speed ratings (Par 99): **75,74,74,70,69 69,58**
CSF £18.22 TOTE £8.30: £4.60, £1.10; EX 24.80 Trifecta £481.80.
**Owner** W P S Johnson **Bred** W P S Johnson **Trained** Norton, N Yorks
■ Stewards' Enquiry : Mr K Wood two-day ban: used whip above permitted level (May 27,31)

**FOCUS**
Rail moved out from 1m2f until Round course meets home straight, increasing distances on Round course by about 18yds. A modest amateur riders' event that became a war of attrition and the form looks questionable with the third horse officially rated just 30. The time was slow.

## 2199 BETDAQ THE SPORTS BETTING EXCHANGE FILLIES' H'CAP 1m 2f 60y

**2:10** (2:13) (Class 5) (0-70,69) 4-Y-O+ **£2,911** (£866; £432; £216) **Stalls Low**

Form RPR

4-60 1 **Martinas Delight (USA)**[16] 1729 4-9-3 65........................ DanielTudhope 14 75
(Alan Jarvis) *in tch on outer: hdwy over 4f out: cl up 3f out: rdn along 2f out: styd on to ld ins fnl f: kpt on strly* **14/1**

4-22 2 2 ¼ **Missy Wells**[14] 1805 4-8-9 60........................ JasonHart(3) 3 66
(Mark Walford) *chsd ldrs: rdn along 5f out and sn outpcd: hdwy over 2f out: styd on u.p appr fnl f: tk 2nd nr line* **9/2**[1]

654 3 nk **Dansili Dutch (IRE)**[26] 1510 5-8-5 60........................ JoshDoyle(7) 12 65+
(David O'Meara) *dwlt and in rr: gd hdwy on outer 4f out: led wl over 2f out: rdn along 2f out: drvn and edgd rt ent fnl f: sn hdd and kpt on same pce* **25/1**

0-30 4 4 ½ **Ana Shababiya (IRE)**[21] 1617 4-9-6 68........................ MickaelBarzalona 7 65
(Ismail Mohammed) *cl up: led after 2f: rdn along and hdd over 3f out: drvn over 2f out and sn one pce* **9/2**[1]

33-4 5 1 ½ **The Ducking Stool**[21] 1617 7-9-1 68........................ ShelleyBirkett(5) 9 63
(Julia Feilden) *chsd ldrs: hdwy and cl up over 4f out: rdn along and led briefly 3f out: sn hdd & wknd fnl 2f* **8/1**[3]

6-03 6 4 ½ **Isdaal**[10] 1919 7-8-2 57........................ KieranShoemark(7) 8 44
(Kevin Morgan) *hld up in rr: sme hdwy over 3f out: rdn along and plugged on fnl 2f: nvr nr ldrs* **11/1**

4331 7 shd **Sixties Queen**[16] 1745 4-8-2 55 oh1........................ NatashaEaton(5) 6 41
(Alan Bailey) *led 2f: cl up: rdn along 3f out: grad wknd fnl 2f* **9/1**

0-42 8 27 **Push Me (IRE)**[20] 1638 7-9-6 68........................ FrankieDettori 10 6
(Iain Jardine) *a in rr* **6/1**[2]

/06- 9 1 ¾ **Grand Liaison**[339] 3063 5-9-7 69........................ GrahamLee 4 4
(James Given) *in tch on inner: rdn along 4f out: sn wknd* **12/1**

2252 10 6 **Conserve (IRE)**[61] 935 4-9-6 68........................ JimmyQuinn 2
(Neil King) *chsd ldrs: rdn along wl over 3f out: sn wknd* **9/1**

2333 11 4 **Goldmadchen (GER)**[16] 1740 6-8-8 56........................ PaulHanagan 11
(James Given) *a in rr* **10/1**

2m 20.59s (11.19) **Going Correction** +1.125s/f (Soft) **11 Ran SP% 117.4**
Speed ratings (Par 100): **100,98,97,94,93 89,89,67,66,61 58**
CSF £75.87 CT £1583.72 TOTE £13.30: £4.00, £2.00, £5.10; EX 190.70 Trifecta £1456.50 Part won..
**Owner** T&J Partnership **Bred** Lerici Syndicate **Trained** Twyford, Bucks

**FOCUS**
A competitive fillies' handicap, despite the four absentees. The riders were inclined to spurn the inside rail once into the straight and they finished well spread out. The winner's best form since last summer.

## 2200 BETDAQ £25 NO LOSE BET MAIDEN STKS 5f 140y

**2:40** (2:43) (Class 5) 2-Y-O **£2,587** (£770; £384; £192) **Stalls High**

Form RPR

1 **Muhaarar** 2-9-5 0........................ PaulHanagan 6 86+
(Charles Hills) *in tch: hdwy over 2f out: chsd ldr over 1f out: rdn to ld ent fnl f: sn clr* **5/6**[1]

633 2 4 **Red Connect**[12] 1879 2-9-5 0........................ BenCurtis 2 71
(Alan McCabe) *led: rdn along and jnd over 1f out: hdd ent fnl f: kpt on same pce* **13/2**[3]

03 3 2 ½ **Union Rose**[9] 1936 2-9-5 0........................ GrahamLee 5 63
(Ronald Harris) *chsd ldr: rdn along 2f out: drvn and kpt on same pce appr fnl f* **5/1**[2]

4 3 ½ **Arch Enemy** 2-9-5 0........................ GrahamGibbons 3 51
(Michael Easterby) *trckd ldrs: hdwy to chse ldng pair wl over 1f out: sn rdn and wknd appr fnl f* **16/1**

5 1 ¼ **Invincible Zeb (IRE)** 2-9-5 0........................ SteveDrowne 4 47
(Ronald Harris) *dwlt: green and in rr tl sme late hdwy* **33/1**

6 6 **Oud Malakiy (IRE)** 2-9-0 0........................ DavidNolan 7 22
(Richard Fahey) *dwlt: a towards rr* **7/1**

7 8 **Rosie Crowe (IRE)** 2-9-0 0........................ SebSanders 8
(David C Griffiths) *chsd ldng pair: rdn along 1/2-way: sn wknd* **25/1**

1m 13.9s (5.10) **Going Correction** +0.85s/f (Soft) **7 Ran SP% 109.7**
Speed ratings (Par 93): **100,94,91,86,85 77,66**
CSF £6.11 TOTE £1.90: £1.20, £1.80; EX 6.80 Trifecta £21.60.
**Owner** Hamdan Al Maktoum **Bred** Shadwell Estate Company Limited **Trained** Lambourn, Berks

**FOCUS**
Not the most competitive of maidens and conditions would have been difficult for these 2yos, especially the newcomers, but the feeling is that we saw a nice type. The winner can rate good bit higher.

## 2201 BETDAQ NO PREMIUM CHARGE MAIDEN STKS 1m (S)

**3:15** (3:20) (Class 5) 3-Y-O **£2,587** (£770; £384; £192) **Stalls High**

Form RPR

5-02 1 **Speculative Bid (IRE)**[14] 1795 3-9-5 79........................ JamieSpencer 3 86
(David Elsworth) *trckd ldrs: smooth hdwy 3f out: cl up 2f out: sn led and pushed clr: readily* **3/1**[2]

0 2 4 **Fallen In Line (IRE)**[25] 1529 3-9-5 0........................ WilliamBuick 6 77
(John Gosden) *trckd ldrs: hdwy 3f out: rdn wl over 1f out: styd on fnl f: no ch w wnr* **7/2**[3]

0- 3 1 ½ **Epsom Hill (SWE)**[199] 7502 3-9-5 0........................ JimmyFortune 4 73
(Charlie Fellowes) *chsd ldr: hdwy over 2f out: rdn wl over 1f out: drvn and kpt on same pce appr fnl f* **40/1**

0-4 4 1 ¼ **Spirit Raiser (IRE)**[16] 1722 3-9-0 0........................ HayleyTurner 5 65
(James Fanshawe) *in tch: hdwy wl over 2f out: rdn along wl over 1f out: kpt on fnl f* **7/1**

0 5 3 ½ **I Am Not Here (IRE)**[30] 1433 3-9-5 0........................ GrahamLee 14 62
(Alan Jarvis) *in rr tl styd on fnl 2f: n.d* **40/1**

00 6 nk **Silver Duke (IRE)**[13] 1844 3-9-5 0........................ DanielTudhope 1 62
(Alan Jarvis) *in tch: pushed along 3f out: sn rdn and no imp* **10/1**

40- 7 1 ½ **Ehtifaal (IRE)**[226] 6829 3-9-5 0........................ PaulHanagan 7 58
(William Haggas) *led and sn clr: rdn along 3f out: jnd jst over 2f out: sn drvn and hdd: wknd wl over 1f out* **2/1**[1]

0 8 4 ½ **Deadline Day (IRE)**[14] 1808 3-9-5 0........................ JackMitchell 2 48
(Roger Varian) *a in rr* **20/1**

0 9 1 ½ **Injun Sands**[25] 1529 3-9-5 0........................ FrederikTylicki 11 44
(Jane Chapple-Hyam) *a towards rr* **100/1**

5 10 nk **Moonwood**[12] 1888 3-9-0 0........................ RobertWinston 8 39
(Ollie Pears) *hld up: hdwy on outer 1/2-way: chsd ldrs wl over 2f out: sn rdn and wknd* **100/1**

1m 47.02s (7.72) **Going Correction** +1.00s/f (Soft) **10 Ran SP% 113.8**
Speed ratings (Par 99): **101,97,95,94,90 90,88,84,82,82**
CSF £12.57 TOTE £4.10: £1.70, £1.50, £6.70; EX 14.90 Trifecta £325.00.
**Owner** K Quinn/ C Benham/ I Saunders **Bred** Summerhill Bloodstock **Trained** Newmarket, Suffolk
■ Tap Your Toes was withdrawn. Price at time of withdrawal 12/1. Rule 4 applies to all bets - deduction 5p in the pound.

**FOCUS**
The going was changed to heavy before this race. The withdrawal of a couple of the fancied contenders weakened this modest 3yo maiden still further. They raced up the centre. The winner more than confirmed his Kempton run.

## 2202 BETDAQ 3% COMMISSION H'CAP 7f

**3:50** (3:52) (Class 3) (0-95,93) 4-Y-O+ **£7,439** (£2,213; £1,106; £553) **Stalls High**

Form RPR

0/0- 1 **Best Of Order (IRE)**[218] 7-9-6 92........................ DavidNolan 6 103
(David O'Meara) *dwlt: in tch: hdwy 3f out: cl up 2f out: sn led: rdn and edgd rt ent fnl f: drvn and edgd lft last 100yds: styd on strly* **4/1**[2]

250- 2 2 ¼ **Personal Touch**[175] 7949 5-8-7 80........................ PatrickMathers 9 85
(Richard Fahey) *prom: effrt 2f: sn rdn and ev ch tl drvn and kpt on same pce fnl f* **5/1**[3]

100- 3 1 **Life Partner (IRE)**[220] 6993 4-9-7 93........................ MickaelBarzalona 4 95+
(Charlie Appleby) *dwlt and hld up towards rr: hdwy on outer 3f out: effrt 2f out: rdn to chal and ev ch over 1f out: drvn and one pce fnl f* **12/1**

404- 4 2 ¼ **Alejandro (IRE)**[210] 7241 5-9-2 88........................ DanielTudhope 7 85
(David O'Meara) *cl up: led after 2f: rdn along and hdd wl over 2f out: grad wknd appr fnl f* **6/1**

0-06 5 6 **Foxtrot Romeo (IRE)**[16] 1721 5-8-13 90........................ MarcMonaghan(5) 10 71
(Marco Botti) *chsd ldrs: rdn along 3f out: wknd over 2f out* **3/1**[1]

0012 6 4 ½ **Corporal Maddox**[9] 1938 7-9-3 89........................(p) SteveDrowne 1 58
(Ronald Harris) *dwlt and in rr: effrt and sme hdwy wl over 2f out: nvr a factor* **15/2**

310- 7 1 ¾ **Henry The Aviator (USA)**[289] 4743 4-9-2 88........................ FrannyNorton 5 53
(Mark Johnston) *chsd ldrs: rdn along 1/2-way: sn wknd* **7/1**

-001 8 20 **Tasrih (USA)**[14] 1803 5-8-12 84 ........................ BenCurtis 8
(Alan McCabe) *led 2f: cl up: rdn along wl over 2f out: sn wknd and bhd whn eased over 1f out* 10/1

1m 32.47s (6.17) **Going Correction** +1.00s/f (Soft) 8 Ran SP% **117.0**
Speed ratings (Par 107): **104,101,100,97,90 85,83,60**
CSF £24.93 CT £223.60 TOTE £4.90: £2.00, £3.90, £2.80; EX 34.00 Trifecta £262.00.
**Owner** Richard Walker **Bred** Ballygallon Stud Limited **Trained** Nawton, N Yorks

**FOCUS**
An interesting handicap in which the market proved spot-on. The form is rated around the runner-up.

## 2203 CASH OUT ON THE BETDAQ + APP H'CAP (BOBIS RACE) 1m (S)
**4:25** (4:25) (Class 4) (0-80,80) 3-Y-0 **£4,690** (£1,395; £697; £348) **Stalls** High

Form RPR
4324 1 **Lesha (IRE)**[19] 1655 3-9-0 73 ........................ JamieSpencer 7 79
(Kevin Ryan) *hld up: hdwy on outer 2f out: chal over 1f out: rdn to ld jst ins fnl f: drvn out* 3/1[2]

01-4 2 1 ½ **Gilbey's Mate**[23] 1586 3-9-6 79 ........................ WilliamBuick 2 82
(John Gosden) *t.k.h early: trckd ldng pair: smooth hdwy over 2f out: led over 1f out: sn rdn: hdd and drvn ins fnl f: kpt on same pce towards fin* 1/1[1]

-230 3 2 **Munfallet (IRE)**[25] 1530 3-9-7 80 ........................ SeanLevey 1 78
(David Brown) *dwlt: hld up in rr: hdwy over 2f out: swtchd lft and effrt wl over 1f out: sn rdn and kpt on same pce fnl f* 7/1

210- 4 2 ¼ **Mayfield Boy**[199] 7492 3-9-3 76 ........................ GrahamLee 3 69
(Mel Brittain) *set stdy pce: qcknd over 3f out: rdn along wl over 2f out: hdd and drvn wl over 1f out: wknd appr fnl f* 6/1[3]

004- 5 4 ½ **Western Sands (IRE)**[234] 6597 3-8-10 69 ........................ LeeTopliss 8 52
(Richard Fahey) *cl up: disp ld 3f out: rdn along over 2f out: sn wknd* 14/1

1m 49.05s (9.75) **Going Correction** +1.00s/f (Soft) 5 Ran SP% **108.5**
Speed ratings (Par 101): **91,89,87,85,80**
CSF £6.24 TOTE £7.20: £1.60, £1.10; EX 5.90 Trifecta £17.60.
**Owner** Mubarak Al Naemi **Bred** Michael Conlon **Trained** Hambleton, N Yorks

**FOCUS**
This fair 3yo handicap was weakened by the withdrawal of a couple horses who would have been at the head of the market. The remaining five runners went no pace early and it developed into a sprint. The winner rates a small personal best.

## 2204 BETDAQ SUPPORTING THE INJURED JOCKEYS FUND H'CAP (DIV I) 7f
**5:00** (5:00) (Class 5) (0-70,71) 3-Y-0 **£3,234** (£962; £481; £240) **Stalls** High

Form RPR
26-0 1 **Sakhalin Star (IRE)**[16] 1725 3-8-12 64 ........................ BillyCray[(3)] 2 73
(Richard Guest) *midfield: hdwy to chse ldrs 3f out: rdn wl over 1f out: chsd wnr and swtchd rt ins fnl f: drvn and styd on wl to ld on line* 50/1

44-5 2 *nse* **Twin Appeal (IRE)**[25] 1542 3-9-4 67 ........................ GrahamGibbons 11 76
(David Barron) *trckd ldrs: hdwy 3f out: cl up over 2f out: led wl over 1f out: rdn clr and edgd lft ent fnl f: hdd on line* 6/1[2]

0-53 3 5 **Petergate**[11] 1906 3-8-10 59 ........................ WilliamBuick 8 55
(Brian Rothwell) *towards rr: hdwy wl over 2f out: rdn over 1f out: styd on fnl f* 6/1[2]

52-3 4 1 ¾ **Lendal Bridge**[41] 1223 3-8-12 61 ........................ JimmyFortune 6 52
(Tony Coyle) *chsd ldr: hdwy 1/2-way: led briefly over 2f out: sn rdn and hdd wl over 1f out: drvn and one pce appr fnl f* 9/1[3]

-505 5 3 **Elle West**[11] 1906 3-8-2 58 ow1 ........................ AnnaHesketh[(7)] 13 42
(Michael Easterby) *hld up: hdwy 3f out: chsd ldrs 2f out: sn rdn and edgd lft over 1f out: sn no imp* 20/1

30-0 6 3 ½ **Miaplacidus (IRE)**[33] 1400 3-9-3 66 ........................ DavidNolan 12 41
(Richard Fahey) *in tch: hdwy 1/2-way: chsd ldrs over 2f out: sn rdn and wknd over 1f out* 25/1

00-0 7 2 ¼ **Oriental Dream (IRE)**[21] 1608 3-8-7 56 oh11 ...............[1] AndrewMullen 4 25
(Nigel Tinkler) *prom: rdn along 3f out: sn wknd* 80/1

55-0 8 7 **Street Boss (IRE)**[18] 1657 3-8-9 58 ........................ PaulHanagan 7 9
(Tim Easterby) *chsd ldrs: rdn along over 2f out: sn wknd* 14/1

-021 9 ¾ **Mariners Moon (IRE)**[7] 2020 3-9-8 71 6ex ........................ DanielTudhope 1 20
(David O'Meara) *in tch: effrt 3f out: sn rdn along and wknd* 1/1[1]

00-0 10 ¾ **Sleeping Star**[9] 1959 3-8-8 57 ........................ AndrewElliott 5 4
(Mel Brittain) *led: rdn along 3f out: hdd over 2f out and sn wknd* 66/1

1136 11 19 **Razin' Hell**[23] 1585 3-9-4 67 ........................ BenCurtis 10
(Alan McCabe) *a in rr: bhd fr 1/2-way* 16/1

1m 32.77s (6.47) **Going Correction** +1.00s/f (Soft) 11 Ran SP% **114.4**
Speed ratings (Par 99): **103,102,97,95,91 87,85,77,76,75 53**
CSF £312.27 CT £2126.03 TOTE £30.50: £7.50, £1.90, £2.20; EX 249.30 Trifecta £1588.90.
**Owner** Bamboozelem **Bred** Sig Massimo Parri **Trained** Wetherby, W Yorks

**FOCUS**
Only two of the 11 remaining runners in this modest handicap had been successful before, including the disappointing favourite. The winner wasn't an onbious improver.

## 2205 BETDAQ SUPPORTING THE INJURED JOCKEYS FUND H'CAP (DIV II) 7f
**5:35** (5:35) (Class 5) (0-70,70) 3-Y-0 **£3,234** (£962; £481; £240) **Stalls** High

Form RPR
20-6 1 **Bajan Rebel**[22] 1601 3-8-7 56 oh2 ........................ AndrewMullen 5 60
(Michael Easterby) *chsd ldr: effrt 2f out: sn rdn and ev ch: drvn ent fnl f: kpt on gamely to ld nr line* 12/1

46-6 2 *shd* **Irondale Express**[35] 1348 3-9-4 67 ........................ PaulHanagan 4 71
(Tony Coyle) *towards rr: smooth hdwy on inner 2f out: chal over 1f out: sn rdn and ev ch: drvn ins fnl f: jst failed* 6/1

00-5 3 ½ **McCarthy Mor (IRE)**[12] 1890 3-8-8 57 ........................ PatrickMathers 2 59+
(Richard Fahey) *trckd ldrs: hdwy on outer and cl up over 2f out: rdn to ld wl over 1f out: drvn and edgd lft ins fnl f: hung lft and hdd nr fin* 14/1

524- 4 2 ½ **Please Let Me Go**[229] 6755 3-8-11 60 ........................(e[1]) GrahamLee 3 56
(Julie Camacho) *in rr: hdwy wl over 2f out: rdn to chse ldrs over 1f out: kpt on same pce fnl f* 13/2

00-6 5 5 **We'll Shake Hands (FR)**[16] 1723 3-9-0 70 ........................ RobJFitzpatrick[(7)] 9 53
(K R Burke) *in tch: hdwy to chse ldrs over 2f out: sn rdn and no imp appr fnl f* 9/4[1]

02-0 6 *nk* **Sartori**[25] 1543 3-9-3 66 ........................ RobertWinston 11 48
(Marjorie Fife) *led: rdn along over 2f out: hdd wl over 1f out: sn wknd* 5/1[3]

0521 7 *nse* **Wildcat Lass (USA)**[14] 1802 3-9-7 70 ........................ DanielTudhope 7 52
(David O'Meara) *chsd ldrs: rdn along over 2f out: sn wknd* 9/2[2]

0-06 8 24 **Buckland Beau**[18] 1680 3-8-13 62 ........................ FrederikTylicki 12
(Charlie Fellowes) *chsd ldng pair: rdn along wl over 2f out: sn wknd* 10/1

1m 34.72s (8.42) **Going Correction** +1.00s/f (Soft) 8 Ran SP% **116.7**
Speed ratings (Par 99): **91,90,90,87,81 81,81,53**
CSF £83.13 CT £1030.17 TOTE £9.50: £2.90, £2.00, £4.30; EX 119.10 Trifecta £771.60 Part won..
**Owner** Julian Rooney Steve Hull Simon Chappell **Bred** Aldridge Racing Partnership **Trained** Sheriff Hutton, N Yorks

**FOCUS**
Again only two of these had won a race before. The winning time was almost two seconds slower than the first division, though the runners in this leg had the worst of the ground. The winner is rated back to her debut form.
T/Jkpt: Not won. T/Plt: £280.60 to a £1 stake. Pool: £75,200.91 - 195.62 winning units. T/Qpdt: £22.90 to a £1 stake. Pool: £5916.10 - 190.90 winning units. JR

# 2151 LINGFIELD (L-H)
### Monday, May 12

**OFFICIAL GOING: Standard**
Wind: Fresh half-behind Weather: Sunny spells

## 2206 QUICKSILVERSLOTS MORE JACKPOTS MORE MACHINES MAIDEN AUCTION FILLIES' STKS (BOBIS RACE) 5f 6y(P)
**1:50** (1:52) (Class 5) 2-Y-0 **£2,911** (£866; £432; £216) **Stalls** High

Form RPR
4 1 **Madamoiselle Bond**[20] 1633 2-8-2 0 ........................[1] NoelGarbutt[(5)] 6 69
(William Jarvis) *hld up: hdwy 1/2-way: rdn over 1f out: r.o to ld towards fin* 16/1

6 2 1 **River Spirit**[14] 1788 2-8-7 0 ........................ SamHitchcott 7 65
(Mick Channon) *trckd ldrs: rdn to ld ins fnl f: hdd towards fin* 12/1

4 3 2 ½ **Diminutive (IRE)**[12] 1889 2-8-7 0 ........................ HarryBentley 2 56
(Jamie Osborne) *led: rdn over 1f out: hdd and unable qck ins fnl f* 11/4[2]

4 1 **Miss Jonh (FR)** 2-8-9 0 ........................ NickyMackay 4 54
(Martyn Meade) *pushed along and sn in tch: rdn and ev ch fr over 1f out tl no ex ins fnl f* 25/1

3 5 ½ **Howlin'For You**[15] 1764 2-8-5 0 ........................ CamHardie[(7)] 1 56
(David Brown) *s.w ldr: rdn and ev ch over 1f out: no ex ins fnl f* 5/4[1]

6 8 **Queen Of The Scots** 2-8-12 0 ........................ SilvestreDeSousa 5 27
(Keith Dalgleish) *dwlt: outpcd* 4/1[3]

30 7 2 ½ **Sparbrook (IRE)**[28] 1488 2-8-10 0 ........................ MartinDwyer 3 16
(George Baker) *chsd ldrs: pushed along 1/2-way: wknd wl over 1f out* 8/1

59.7s (0.90) **Going Correction** -0.025s/f (Stan) 7 Ran SP% **119.6**
Speed ratings (Par 90): **91,89,85,83,83 70,66**
CSF £190.03 TOTE £21.80: £6.60, £5.50; EX 176.70 Trifecta £745.70.
**Owner** Miss S E Hall **Bred** Miss S E Hall **Trained** Newmarket, Suffolk

**FOCUS**
This fixture was switched from Wolverhampton. The BOBIS bonus was up for grabs in this maiden auction for 2yo fillies. The form is rated around the race average and the third.

## 2207 QUICKSILVERSLOTS PLAY FROM 10P TO £2 H'CAP 1m 5f (P)
**2:20** (2:20) (Class 5) (0-70,69) 4-Y-0+ **£2,911** (£866; £432; £216) **Stalls** Low

Form RPR
6- 1 **Markami (FR)**[41] 3129 4-9-7 69 ........................ LiamKeniry 6 78
(Johnny Farrelly) *prom: pushed along over 3f out: outpcd over 2f out: rallied u.p to chse ldr over 1f out: edgd lft ins fnl f: styd on to ld nr fin* 8/1[3]

4-63 2 *shd* **Miss Tiger Lily**[20] 1629 4-9-6 68 ........................(b[1]) LukeMorris 1 77
(Harry Dunlop) *led and sn clr tl c bk to field over 8f out: rdn clr again over 1f out: rdr dropped rein ins fnl f: hdd nr fin* 2/1[1]

214- 3 7 **Amantius**[181] 7847 5-9-6 68 ........................(b) StevieDonohoe 5 67
(Johnny Farrelly) *hld up: hdwy over 3f out: chsd ldr over 2f out tl rdn over 1f out: styd on same pce* 5/2[2]

-545 4 8 **Omotesando**[13] 1865 4-7-11 50 ........................ NoelGarbutt[(5)] 4 37
(Mark Brisbourne) *trckd ldr tl rdn over 3f out: sn wknd* 12/1

-500 5 4 **Rollin 'n Tumblin**[11] 1895 10-7-9 50 oh3 ........................ CamHardie[(7)] 2 31
(Michael Attwater) *hld up: rdn and wknd over 3f out* 12/1

4132 6 ¾ **Menelik (IRE)**[47] 1108 5-9-4 66 ........................(b) WilliamCarson 3 45
(Lee Carter) *trckd ldrs: rdn over 4f out: wknd 3f out* 5/2[2]

2m 44.61s (-1.39) **Going Correction** -0.025s/f (Stan) 6 Ran SP% **117.0**
Speed ratings (Par 103): **103,102,98,93,91 90**
CSF £25.71 TOTE £9.90: £4.20, £2.20; EX 23.60 Trifecta £79.80.
**Owner** P Tosh **Bred** Haras De Son Altesse L'Aga Khan S C E A **Trained** Bridgwater, Somerset

**FOCUS**
Not form to get too excited about. It's rated around the runner-up to last year's C&D level.

## 2208 QUICKSILVERSLOTS PLAY £500 JACKPOT RAINBOW RICHES H'CAP 6f 1y(P)
**2:55** (2:55) (Class 5) (0-70,70) 3-Y-0 **£2,911** (£866; £432; £216) **Stalls** Low

Form RPR
6-16 1 **Moonspring (IRE)**[13] 1832 3-8-13 62 ........................(e) AndreaAtzeni 3 66
(Robert Cowell) *trckd ldr: rdn over 2f out: led ins fnl f: r.o* 5/2[1]

43-4 2 ½ **Baltic Brave (IRE)**[18] 1669 3-9-5 68 ........................(t) RichardHughes 1 70+
(Hughie Morrison) *s.i.s: hld up: plld hrd: rdn over 2f out: r.o ins fnl f: wnt 2nd nr fin: nt rch wnr* 11/4[2]

3-50 3 *nk* **Kodafine (IRE)**[23] 1570 3-9-3 66 ........................ AdamKirby 5 67
(David Evans) *led: qcknd over 2f out: rdn over 1f out: hdd ins fnl f: styd on: lost 2nd nr fin* 16/1

6-52 4 1 ½ **Debt Settler (IRE)**[7] 2035 3-9-4 70 ........................ MichaelJMMurphy[(3)] 4 66
(Luke Dace) *hld up in tch: racd keenly: rdn and hung lft fr over 1f out: styd on same pce ins fnl f* 11/4[2]

2210 5 10 **Jolly Red Jeanz (IRE)**[13] 1851 3-9-1 64 ........................ DaneO'Neill 2 36
(J W Hills) *chsd ldrs: rdn over 2f out: wknd over 1f out: eased* 7/1[3]

53-5 6 1 ½ **Quantum Dot (IRE)**[39] 1260 3-9-7 70 ................(bt[1]) RichardKingscote 6 29
(Tom Dascombe) *s.i.s: hld up: plld hrd: rdn and wknd over 2f out* 7/1[3]

1m 12.39s (0.49) **Going Correction** -0.025s/f (Stan) 6 Ran SP% **112.8**
Speed ratings (Par 99): **95,94,93,91,78 76**
CSF £9.80 TOTE £4.20: £4.50, £1.10; EX 10.10 Trifecta £101.00.
**Owner** P Foster & Friends **Bred** R N Auld **Trained** Six Mile Bottom, Cambs

**FOCUS**
A modest 3yo handicap, rated around the third.

## 2209 QUICKSILVERSLOTS OPEN AFTER 10PM H'CAP 7f 1y(P)
**3:30** (3:31) (Class 6) (0-60,60) 3-Y-0 **£2,264** (£673; £336; £168) **Stalls** Low

Form RPR
0263 1 **Intense Feeling (IRE)**[10] 1914 3-9-3 56 ........................ AdamKirby 10 63
(David Evans) *set stdy pce tl rdn and qcknd over 2f out: clr over 1f out: styd on u.p* 6/1[2]

3321 2 3 **Clapperboard**[10] 1918 3-9-2 55 ........................(b) WilliamCarson 8 54
(Paul Fitzsimons) *trckd ldrs: plld hrd: wnt 2nd over 2f out: sn rdn and outpcd: styd on ins fnl f* 6/1[2]

356 **3** *1* **Trinity Lorraine (IRE)**59 960 3-8-9 **48**..............(b1) SilvestreDeSousa 4 44
(Alan Bailey) *hld up: hdwy over 4f out: outpcd 2f out: r.o ins fnl f* **8/1**3

030 **4** *3/4* **Flying By**13 1844 3-9-0 **53**..............(b1) ChrisCatlin 6 47
(Rae Guest) *hdwy to join wnr over 5f out tl rdn over 2f out: sn outpcd: kpt on ins fnl f* **16/1**

046- **5** *1 1/4* **Irene Hull (IRE)**208 7310 3-9-7 **60**.............. JimCrowley 11 51
(Garry Moss) *chsd ldrs: rdn over 2f out: styd on same pce fr over 1f out* **6/1**2

3334 **6** *1 1/4* **Role Reversal**31 1430 3-9-7 **60**.............. LukeMorris 7 48
(James Tate) *chsd ldrs: pushed along and lost pl 1/2-way: n.d after* **8/1**3

6-14 **7** *shd* **Speed Society**18 1683 3-9-7 **60**.............. PatCosgrave 2 48
(Jim Boyle) *mid-div: hdwy over 2f out: rdn over 1f out: no ex fnl f* **7/4**1

040 **8** *1 3/4* **Nutbush**10 1918 3-9-1 **57**.............. WilliamTwiston-Davies(3) 9 40
(Mick Channon) *hld up: rdn over 2f out: nvr on terms* **33/1**

536 **9** *1* **Feisty Dragon (IRE)**18 1684 3-8-7 **46** oh1.............. FergusSweeney 1 27
(Jamie Osborne) *hld up: rdn over 2f out: a in rr* **25/1**

-446 **10** *14* **Captain T**35 1343 3-8-2 **46**.............. NoelGarbutt(5) 3
(Richard Ford) *in tch: plld hrd: hmpd wl over 5f out: sn lost pl: wknd over 2f out* **50/1**

1m 24.85s (0.05) **Going Correction** -0.025s/f (Stan) **10** Ran SP% **116.1**
Speed ratings (Par 97): **98,94,93,92,91 89,89,87,86,70**
CSF £40.94 CT £297.20 TOTE £5.90: £2.20, £1.90, £1.60; EX 33.10 Trifecta £220.40.
**Owner** Mrs E Evans **Bred** R And Mrs R Hodgins **Trained** Pandy, Monmouths

**FOCUS**
Take the winner out and this was a weak 3yo handicap. The winner is rated close to her recent turf form.

## 2210 QUICKSILVERSLOTS £1 TO WIN £500 FILLIES' H'CAP 1m 1y(P)
**4:05** (4:05) (Class 5) (0-70,70) 3-Y-O **£3,881** (£1,155; £577; £288) **Stalls** High

Form RPR

02-4 **1** **Merry Me (IRE)**15 1765 3-9-7 **70**.............. JimCrowley 6 79
(Andrew Balding) *trckd ldrs: racd keenly: rdn to ld ins fnl f: r.o* **3/1**2

4-43 **2** *3/4* **Starlit Cantata**14 1794 3-9-2 **65**.............. RichardHughes 7 72
(Eve Johnson Houghton) *hld up: hdwy over 3f out: rdn to chse wnr ins fnl f: styd on* **9/4**1

304 **3** *2 1/4* **Nothing Special**25 1542 3-8-12 **61**.............. RichardKingscote 3 63
(Tom Dascombe) *w ldr tl led 6f out: rdn over 1f out: hdd and unable qck ins fnl f* **6/1**3

300- **4** *1* **Sequester**187 7763 3-9-2 **65**.............. TedDurcan 9 65
(David Lanigan) *trckd ldrs: wnt 2nd over 4f out: shkn up over 1f out: styd on same pce fnl f* **6/1**3

10-0 **5** *hd* **Maid In Rio (IRE)**25 1540 3-9-4 **67**.............. SilvestreDeSousa 1 66
(Mark Johnston) *led 2f: remained handy: pushed along over 4f out: rdn over 2f out: no ex fnl f* **25/1**

20-2 **6** *2 1/4* **Tunnel Tiger (IRE)**18 1684 3-8-11 **60**.............. AndreaAtzeni 8 54
(William Knight) *s.i.s: hld up: rdn over 2f out: styd on ins fnl f: nvr nrr* **8/1**

5260 **7** *1/2* **Stoneham**13 1847 3-8-10 **62**.............. WilliamTwiston-Davies(3) 2 55
(Mick Channon) *hld up: hdwy over 1f out: wknd fnl f* **25/1**

036- **8** *3* **Great Wave (IRE)**209 7277 3-9-7 **70**.............. FergusSweeney 4 56
(David Simcock) *prom: lost pl over 3f out: wknd over 1f out* **8/1**

544- **9** *16* **Sleeping Venus (IRE)**286 4861 3-8-12 **61**.............. PatCosgrave 5 10
(George Baker) *in rr: reminders over 4f out: drvn and wknd over 2f out: eased* **25/1**

1m 37.78s (-0.42) **Going Correction** -0.025s/f (Stan) **9** Ran SP% **118.1**
Speed ratings (Par 96): **101,100,98,97,96 94,94,91,75**
CSF £10.19 CT £35.69 TOTE £3.60: £1.20, £1.60, £3.10; EX 11.60 Trifecta £46.70.
**Owner** Mrs Fitri Hay **Bred** Mrs Fitriani Hay **Trained** Kingsclere, Hants

**FOCUS**
The front pair, the most interesting contenders, pulled clear in the end in this weakish handicap for 3yo fillies.

## 2211 QUICKSILVERSLOTS PLAY YOUR FAVOURITE £500 JACKPOT MEDIAN AUCTION MAIDEN STKS 1m 1y(P)
**4:40** (4:45) (Class 6) 3-5-Y-O **£2,264** (£673; £336; £168) **Stalls** High

Form RPR

502- **1** **Rasameel (USA)**219 7019 3-9-0 78.............. DaneO'Neill 1 86
(J W Hills) *mde all: pushed clr fr over 1f out: eased towards fin* **4/5**1

**2** *2 1/4* **Wrood (USA)** 3-8-9 0.............. ShaneKelly 2 76
(James Fanshawe) *s.i.s: hdwy over 6f out: chsd wnr over 2f out: styd on same pce fr over 1f out* **5/1**2

4- **3** *hd* **Steppe Daughter (IRE)**223 6922 3-8-9 0.............. LukeMorris 4 75
(Denis Coakley) *hld up: hdwy 3f out: rdn and r.o ins fnl f: nrst fin* **14/1**

4343 **4** *5* **Gratzie**19 1655 3-8-6 72.............. WilliamTwiston-Davies(3) 5 64
(Mick Channon) *chsd ldrs: rdn over 2f out: wknd fnl f* **5/1**2

0202 **5** *2 1/4* **Brownsville (USA)**14 1817 3-9-0 69..............(v1) SilvestreDeSousa 9 64
(Mark Johnston) *chsd ldr tl rdn over 2f out: wknd over 1f out* **7/1**3

0- **6** *1 3/4* **Chesil Beach**208 7310 3-8-9 0.............. LiamKeniry 3 55
(Andrew Balding) *prom: pushed along 1/2-way: wknd over 2f out* **33/1**

0 **7** *9* **Slunovrat (FR)**13 1844 3-9-0 0.............. TedDurcan 10 39
(David Menuisier) *s.i.s: a in rr: wknd 3f out* **66/1**

50 **8** *1 1/4* **Monsieur Chabal**3 2126 3-8-9 0.............. RachealKneller(5) 6 36
(Jamie Osborne) *hld up: racd keenly early: wknd over 3f out* **66/1**

**9** *8* **Lucky Stars** 4-9-3 0.............. TimClark(5) 7 16
(Gay Kelleway) *in rr whn hmpd and hung rt 7f out: rdn and wknd wl over 2f out* **100/1**

1m 36.72s (-1.48) **Going Correction** -0.025s/f (Stan)
**WFA** 3 from 4yo 13lb **9** Ran SP% **115.0**
Speed ratings (Par 101): **106,103,103,98,96 94,85,84,76**
CSF £5.08 TOTE £1.90: £1.10, £1.50, £3.40; EX 6.40 Trifecta £41.40.
**Owner** Hamdan Al Maktoum **Bred** Fifty Seven Farm Inc **Trained** Upper Lambourn, Berks

**FOCUS**
An interesting maiden with the front two places filled by well-bred sorts. The winne set the standard.

## 2212 QUICKSILVERSLOTS FUN ON THE HIGH STREET AMATEUR RIDERS' H'CAP 1m 4f (P)
**5:10** (5:10) (Class 6) (0-55,55) 4-Y-O+ **£2,183** (£677; £338; £169) **Stalls** Low

Form RPR

4013 **1** **Novel Dancer**11 1895 6-10-1 **47**.............. MrJHarding(5) 5 60
(Lydia Richards) *a.p: pushed along over 4f out: chsd ldr over 1f out: led and edgd lft ins fnl f: styd on* **11/4**1

0661 **2** *1/2* **Glennten**13 1836 5-10-7 **53**.............. MrWillPettis(5) 3 65
(Sean Curran) *led 3f: chsd ldr tl led again over 2f out: rdn over 1f out: hdd and n.m.r ins fnl f: styd on* **4/1**2

4252 **3** *3 1/2* **Magicalmysterytour (IRE)**39 1263 11-10-12 **53**.............. MrRBirkett 6 60
(Willie Musson) *s.i.s: hld up: hdwy over 2f out: styd on: nt rch ldrs* **11/4**1

-550 **4** *9* **Lambert Pen (USA)**12 1874 4-10-3 **49**.............. MissMEdden(5) 2 41
(Peter Hiatt) *chsd ldrs: rdn over 2f out: wknd ins fnl f* **6/1**3

00-0 **5** *1 3/4* **Estibdaad (IRE)**5 2066 4-10-9 **55**..............(t) MissMBryant(5) 7 44
(Paddy Butler) *hld up: hdwy 1/2-way: rdn over 2f out: wknd fnl f* **14/1**

2002 **6** *1/2* **Litmus (USA)**12 1875 5-10-9 **55**..............(b) MrGeorgeCrate(5) 9 44
(Simon Dow) *s.s and rel to r: hdwy and in tch 8f out: rdn over 2f out: sn wknd* **10/1**

0022 **7** *5* **Daniel Thomas (IRE)**10 1923 12-10-4 **52**..(tp) MissCharlotteCooper(7) 8 33
(Ann Stokell) *s.i.s: hld up: bhd 5f out: nvr on terms* **14/1**

00-0 **8** *4* **Anginola (IRE)**18 1664 5-10-11 **55**..............(v) MissHayleyMoore(3) 10 29
(Laura Mongan) *sn prom: racd keenly: led 9f out: rdn and hdd over 2f out: wknd over 1f out* **25/1**

00-0 **9** *10* **Market Puzzle (IRE)**13 1865 7-10-2 **46** oh1......(p) BeckyBrisbourne(3) 4
(Mark Brisbourne) *prom tl rdn and wknd over 2f out* **25/1**

2m 33.31s (0.31) **Going Correction** -0.025s/f (Stan) **9** Ran SP% **117.7**
Speed ratings (Par 101): **97,96,94,88,87 86,83,80,74**
CSF £14.13 CT £31.78 TOTE £2.80: £1.10, £1.80, £1.70; EX 17.50 Trifecta £32.90.
**Owner** Mrs Lydia Richards **Bred** The Queen **Trained** Funtington, W Sussex

**FOCUS**
A tight finish to this amateur riders' handicap. The first three were clear and the form is sound.
T/Plt: £344.10 to a £1 stake. Pool: £56,078.06 - 118.95 winning units. T/Qpdt: £7.60 to a £1 stake. Pool: £6568.36 - 633.32 winning units. CR

# 1924 MUSSELBURGH (R-H)
### Monday, May 12

**OFFICIAL GOING: Good (good to soft in places; 7.3)**
Wind: Breezy, half behind Weather: Cloudy

## 2213 WILLIAM HILL H'CAP (FOR AMATEUR RIDERS) 2m
**2:00** (2:00) (Class 6) (0-65,65) 4-Y-O+ **£2,495** (£774; £386; £193) **Stalls** Low

Form RPR

00-5 **1** **Anne's Valentino**33 1374 4-9-7 **50**.............. MrTHamilton(3) 7 57
(Malcolm Jefferson) *t.k.h: cl up: hdwy on outside to ld over 2f out: rdn and r.o wl fnl f* **18/1**

0-20 **2** *1* **Waltz Darling (IRE)**6 2055 6-10-3 **59**.............. PhillipDennis(5) 1 65
(Keith Reveley) *in tch: effrt and rdn far side over 2f out: chsd (centre) wnr ins fnl f: kpt on* **10/3**1

00-4 **3** *1/2* **Aleksandar**10 1929 5-10-7 **65**.............. MrsICGoldie(7) 11 70
(Jim Goldie) *led after 2f: rdn and styd far side ent st: hdd over 2f out: rallied: kpt on ins fnl f* **4/1**2

/30- **4** *hd* **Hunters Belt (IRE)**5 6942 10-10-3 **59**..............(vt) MissJWalton(5) 10 64
(George Bewley) *dwlt: hld up: hdwy and prom 1/2-way: effrt and ev ch in centre over 2f out: kpt on same pce ins fnl f* **11/1**

03-1 **5** *1/2* **Frosty Berry**18 1674 5-10-7 **65**.............. MrAFrench(7) 5 70
(Paul Midgley) *hld up: hdwy and in tch over 5f out: effrt in centre over 2f out: kpt on same pce ins fnl f* **4/1**2

006- **6** *8* **Grethel (IRE)**259 5052 10-9-2 **46** oh1.............. JasonNuttall(7) 6 41
(Alan Berry) *hld up: stdy hdwy far side over 3f out: rdn and no imp fr 2f out* **80/1**

50-2 **7** *2* **Vicky Valentine**15 1763 4-10-10 **64**.............. MrJHamilton 9 57
(Alistair Whillans) *hld up: drvn along over 5f out: no imp towards far side fr 3f out* **8/1**

-012 **8** *shd* **Royal Defence (IRE)**38 1284 8-10-4 **55**..............(t) MissSBrotherton 8 47
(Richard Ford) *hld up in tch: rdn centre over 3f out: edgd rt and wknd over 2f out* **9/2**3

6-50 **9** *19* **Magic Skyline (IRE)**7 2016 4-10-3 **62**.............. MrDCottle(5) 4 32
(Brian Ellison) *led 2f: prom: rdn centre over 3f out: struggling over 2f out* **12/1**

/00- **10** *8* **Mystified (IRE)**294 3709 11-9-4 **46** oh1..............(p) MrJohnWilley(5) 2 6
(Alan Berry) *in tch: rdn and struggling far side over 3f out: sn btn* **100/1**

000 **11** *54* **Miss Bella Rose**21 1608 7-9-4 **46** oh1.............. MrSBushby(5) 3
(Richard Guest) *sn bhd: struggling 1/2-way: lost tch centre fr over 3f out* **66/1**

3m 37.79s (4.29) **Going Correction** +0.275s/f (Good)
**WFA** 4 from 5yo+ 3lb **11** Ran SP% **117.4**
Speed ratings (Par 101): **100,99,99,99,98 94,93,93,84,80 53**
CSF £77.42 CT £297.96 TOTE £17.80: £4.60, £2.20, £1.40; EX 113.90 Trifecta £1433.70 Part won..
**Owner** The Magic Circle **Bred** Mr & Mrs P Nelson **Trained** Norton, N Yorks

**FOCUS**
Bottom bend moved out one metre and distances as advertised. A modest staying handicap, confined to amateur riders, run at a sound pace. The winner backed up her reappearance improvement.

## 2214 BRITISH STALLION STUDS EBF MEDIAN AUCTION STKS 5f
**2:30** (2:31) (Class 5) 2-Y-O **£3,234** (£962; £481; £240) **Stalls** High

Form RPR

5 **1** **Vimy Ridge**16 1726 2-9-5 0.............. TonyHamilton 2 81+
(Richard Fahey) *w ldrs on outside: rdn to ld over 1f out: hld on wl towards fin* **5/2**2

**2** *nk* **Pres Rapide (IRE)** 2-9-5 0.............. PhillipMakin 4 80+
(John Quinn) *t.k.h: trckd ldrs: rdn to press wnr ins fnl f: kpt on: hld towards fin* **2/1**1

**3** *3* **Dominic Cork** 2-9-5 0.............. KierenFallon 6 69
(Kevin Ryan) *led tl pushed along and hdd over 1f out: rallied: outpcd last 100yds: bttr for r* **3/1**3

**4** *2 1/2* **Oregon Gift** 2-9-5 0.............. JoeFanning 3 60
(Mark Johnston) *w ldrs: rn green and outpcd 2f out: no imp fnl f* **15/2**

56 **5** *4* **Reassert**16 1732 2-9-5 0.............. DavidAllan 5 46
(Tim Easterby) *in tch: rdn over 2f out: edgd rt over 1f out: sn btn* **14/1**

**6** *1/2* **Danot (IRE)** 2-9-5 0.............. TomEaves 1 44
(Keith Dalgleish) *in tch tl rdn and wknd over 1f out* **20/1**

**7** *3 1/2* **Shamkhani** 2-9-2 0.............. SladeO'Hara(3) 7 31
(Alan Berry) *missed break: bhd and outpcd: nvr on terms* **80/1**

1m 0.81s (0.41) **Going Correction** -0.10s/f (Good) **7** Ran SP% **111.3**
Speed ratings (Par 93): **92,91,86,82,76 75,69**
CSF £7.46 TOTE £2.80: £2.60, £1.50; EX 9.80 Trifecta £34.00.
**Owner** P Timmins & A Rhodes Haulage **Bred** Mrs Sheila Oakes **Trained** Musley Bank, N Yorks
■ Stewards' Enquiry : Kieren Fallon caution: careless riding

**FOCUS**
A modest juvenile maiden where two came nicely clear. There should be more to come from the winner.

## 2215 CMS H'CAP 1m
3:05 (3:05) (Class 5) (0-70,70) 4-Y-O+ £3,234 (£962; £481; £240) Stalls Low

Form RPR
30-0 **1** **Ralphy Boy (IRE)**[21] 1610 5-9-4 **67**........................ PJMcDonald 2 75
(Alistair Whillans) *trckd ldrs: led over 2f out: sn rdn: hld on wl fnl f* **7/1**[3]

023- **2** ¾ **Live Dangerously**[213] 7165 4-9-4 **67**........................(t) TomEaves 1 73
(Keith Dalgleish) *hld up in tch: rdn and outpcd wl over 2f out: rallied over 1f out: chsd wnr ins fnl f: kpt on* **14/1**

6522 **3** ½ **Outlaw Torn (IRE)**[18] 1673 5-8-13 **62**..................(e) RobbieFitzpatrick 5 67
(Richard Guest) *in tch on outside: pushed along over 3f out: rallied 2f out: kpt on ins fnl f: nrst fin* **6/1**[2]

0005 **4** ¾ **Mysterial**[13] 1839 4-9-1 **69**........................ KevinStott(5) 7 72
(Ruth Carr) *hld up and bhd: gd hdwy over 1f out: styd on strly ins fnl f: nvr able to chal* **22/1**

355- **5** *shd* **Dhaular Dhar (IRE)**[155] 5637 12-8-10 **59**........................ GaryBartley 6 62
(Jim Goldie) *hld up: pushed along over 2f out: hdwy and swtchd lft over 1f out: kpt on fnl f: hld nr fin* **18/1**

-214 **6** 2 **Echo Of Lightning**[10] 1930 4-8-10 **59**........................ DaleSwift 10 58+
(Brian Ellison) *led: rdn and hdd over 2f out: rallied: wknd ins fnl f* **15/8**[1]

0-60 **7** 1½ **Look On By**[18] 1673 4-8-4 **56** oh1........................ ConnorBeasley(3) 11 51
(Ruth Carr) *pressed ldr: drvn and ev ch over 2f out: no ex over 1f out* **16/1**

5 **8** *shd* **Alanos (IRE)**[15] 1760 5-9-7 **70**........................ PhillipMakin 3 65
(James Ewart) *sn pushed along in midfield: drvn 3f out: no imp fr 2f out* **28/1**

05-6 **9** 1 **Tanawar (IRE)**[18] 1673 4-8-13 **62**........................ JamesSullivan 12 65+
(Ruth Carr) *t.k.h: hld up in midfield on outside: outpcd 3f out: rallied whn nt clr run over 1f out: sn n.d* **8/1**

10-0 **10** *nk* **Checkpoint**[16] 1710 5-9-3 **66**........................ BarryMcHugh 4 58
(Tony Coyle) *trckd ldrs: effrt over 2f out: edgd rt: wknd fnl f* **12/1**

4051 **11** 1¼ **Ad Vitam (IRE)**[21] 1606 6-8-8 **57**........................(vt) RoystonFfrench 8 46
(David C Griffiths) *hld up: drvn and outpcd over 3f out: nvr on terms* **25/1**

60-6 **12** 6 **Jebel Tara**[10] 1930 9-9-0 **63**........................(bt) KierenFallon 9 38
(Alan Brown) *hld up: struggling over 2f out: eased whn no ch fr over 1f out* **14/1**

1m 42.79s (1.59) **Going Correction** +0.275s/f (Good) **12** Ran SP% **116.5**
Speed ratings (Par 103): **103,102,101,101,100 98,97,97,96,96 94,88**
CSF £96.30 CT £624.86 TOTE £8.50: £2.70, £4.60, £1.20; EX 67.60 Trifecta £618.70.
**Owner** Frank Lowe **Bred** Frank Lowe **Trained** Newmill-On-Slitrig, Borders

**FOCUS**
They went a decent pace in this modest handicap. The winner is rated to last year's form.

## 2216 EXCLUSIVE FREE BETS AT MONSTERBET.CO.UK H'CAP 1m 4f 100y
3:40 (3:40) (Class 5) (0-75,75) 4-Y-O+ £3,234 (£962; £481; £240) Stalls Low

Form RPR
50-5 **1** **Love Marmalade (IRE)**[24] 1562 4-9-7 **75**........................ PJMcDonald 4 84
(Alistair Whillans) *pressed ldr: led over 3f out: drvn 2f out: hld on wl fnl f* **3/1**[2]

0-63 **2** ½ **Merchant Of Medici**[18] 1675 7-8-0 **57**........................ NeilFarley(3) 7 65
(Micky Hammond) *in tch on ins: rdn over 2f out: hdwy to chse wnr ins fnl f: kpt on fin* **12/1**

43-0 **3** 2 **Corton Lad**[22] 1599 4-9-4 **72**........................(tp) TomEaves 6 77
(Keith Dalgleish) *trckd ldrs: effrt and chsd wnr over 2f out: one pce and lost 2nd ins fnl f* **9/1**[3]

-252 **4** *hd* **Fly Solo**[33] 1377 5-9-3 **71**........................ KierenFallon 10 76
(Alan Swinbank) *t.k.h: in midfield: effrt and pushed along over 2f out: no imp tl styd on wl fr over 1f out: nvr able to chal* **13/8**[1]

0103 **5** 1 **Magnolia Ridge (IRE)**[18] 1660 4-8-11 **70**..........(p) JacobButterfield(5) 12 73
(Kristin Stubbs) *prom: effrt and drvn over 3f out: one pce appr fnl f* **14/1**

23-6 **6** 2 **Latin Rebel (IRE)**[15] 1761 7-7-11 **58**........................ JackGarritty(7) 5 58
(Jim Goldie) *hld up: rdn along over 2f out: hdwy over 1f out: nt pce to chal* **16/1**

56-0 **7** 2¼ **Madrasa (IRE)**[19] 1644 6-9-0 **68**........................ PhillipMakin 3 64
(Keith Reveley) *hld up: rdn and outpcd 3f out: rallied over 1f out: nvr able to chal* **20/1**

4/0- **8** 1 **Phase Shift**[32] 2435 6-8-3 **57**........................(t) PaulPickard 2 52
(Brian Ellison) *s.v.s: bhd: hdwy to join gp 1/2-way: rdn over 3f out: no imp fr 2f out* **33/1**

52-0 **9** 3½ **Musikhani**[13] 1848 4-9-1 **69**........................ RoystonFfrench 1 58
(Philip Kirby) *led at stdy pce: rdn and hdd over 3f out: rallied: wknd over 1f out* **11/1**

10-6 **10** 2 **Grand Diamond (IRE)**[15] 1763 10-8-3 **60**........................ IanBrennan(3) 9 46
(Jim Goldie) *t.k.h: hld up towards rr: shortlived effrt over 2f out: sn btn* **33/1**

0 **11** 6 **Chaparella (IRE)**[10] 1919 4-8-3 **57**........................ JoeFanning 8 34
(Mark Johnston) *chsd ldrs tl rdn: edgd rt and wknd 2f out* **25/1**

/55- **12** 1½ **Ihtikar (USA)**[60] 1468 4-8-11 **68**........................ ConnorBeasley(3) 11 43
(Lucy Normile) *hld up on outside: struggling over 3f out: btn fnl 2f* **100/1**

2m 47.93s (5.93) **Going Correction** +0.275s/f (Good) **12** Ran SP% **117.2**
Speed ratings (Par 103): **91,90,89,89,88 87,85,85,82,81 77,76**
CSF £35.83 CT £294.56 TOTE £6.10: £2.30, £2.60, £2.70; EX 41.20 Trifecta £407.70.
**Owner** Akela Construction Ltd **Bred** Stonethorn Stud Farms Ltd **Trained** Newmill-On-Slitrig, Borders

**FOCUS**
A steadily run affair in which the winner was always handy. The winner built on a good effort in a better race here last time.

## 2217 RACINGUK.COM/ANYWHERE 3DEVICES, 1PRICE MAIDEN STKS 5f
4:15 (4:16) (Class 5) 3-Y-O+ £2,587 (£770; £384; £192) Stalls High

Form RPR
65-3 **1** **Noble Asset**[18] 1676 3-9-5 68........................ PhillipMakin 6 71
(John Quinn) *mde all: rdn over 1f out: kpt on wl fnl f* **2/1**[1]

66-6 **2** 2 **Margrets Gift**[25] 1543 3-9-0 65........................ DavidAllan 8 59
(Tim Easterby) *prom: effrt on outside over 1f out: chsd wnr ins fnl f: r.o* **7/2**[2]

04 **3** 1¾ **Fujin**[9] 1939 3-9-5 0........................ DuranFentiman 5 58
(Noel Wilson) *chsd wnr: rdn along 2f out: lost 2nd ins fnl f: kpt on same pce* **5/1**[3]

**4** 2¾ **Piccadilly Jim (IRE)** 3-9-5 0........................ TonyHamilton 1 48+
(Richard Fahey) *upset in stalls: dwlt: sn pushed along and rn green bhd ldng gp: effrt over 1f out: no imp fnl f* **7/2**[2]

05-0 **5** 1¼ **Spirit Of Alsace (IRE)**[15] 1758 3-9-0 60........................ KierenFallon 7 38
(Jim Goldie) *t.k.h: cl up tl rdn and no ex over 1f out* **7/1**

3 **6** 2 **Poetree In Motion**[15] 1757 3-9-0 0........................ TomEaves 4 31
(Keith Dalgleish) *bhd and detached: sme late hdwy: nvr on terms* **25/1**

**7** ¾ **Aphrilis (IRE)** 3-9-0 0........................ DaleSwift 2 28
(Brian Ellison) *in tch on outside: drvn and edgd rt 2f out: sn btn* **25/1**

59.92s (-0.48) **Going Correction** -0.10s/f (Good)
**WFA** 3 from 4yo 9lb **7** Ran SP% **114.6**
Speed ratings (Par 103): **99,95,93,88,86 83,82**
CSF £9.28 TOTE £2.60: £1.90, £2.60; EX 12.20 Trifecta £48.00.
**Owner** Caron & Paul Chapman **Bred** Horizon Bloodstock Limited **Trained** Settrington, N Yorks

**FOCUS**
A weak maiden, run at a fair pace. The form is rated around the winner.

## 2218 RACING UK ANYWHERE AVAILABLE NOW H'CAP 7f 30y
4:50 (4:52) (Class 5) (0-75,75) 3-Y-O £4,528 (£1,347; £673; £336) Stalls Low

Form RPR
-426 **1** **Sir Guy Porteous (IRE)**[11] 1897 3-9-4 **72**........................ JoeFanning 5 79
(Mark Johnston) *pressed ldr: led over 2f out: sn rdn: hld on wl fnl f* **7/2**[1]

2-63 **2** 1¾ **Zain Zone (IRE)**[12] 1884 3-9-7 **75**........................ JamesSullivan 6 77
(Ruth Carr) *reluctant to enter stalls: t.k.h in rr: stdy hdwy whn nt clr run over 1f out: effrt over 1f out: styd on to take 2nd nr fin: nt rch wnr* **4/1**[2]

123 **3** 1 **Beautiful Stranger (IRE)**[45] 1149 3-9-2 **70**..................(p) PhillipMakin 9 69
(Keith Dalgleish) *led to over 2f out: styd upsides to over 1f out: one pce ins fnl f: lost 2nd nr fin* **9/1**

04-1 **4** 3 **Cahal (IRE)**[19] 1648 3-8-5 **59**........................ RoystonFfrench 2 51
(David Nicholls) *trckd ldr: rdn and effrt over 2f out: edgd lft over 1f out: outpcd fnl f* **7/1**

140- **5** 1¼ **Penina (IRE)**[184] 7819 3-8-11 **65**........................ PaulPickard 7 53
(Brian Ellison) *in tch: rdn and outpcd over 2f out: n.d after* **11/1**

52-0 **6** ½ **Tancred (IRE)**[35] 1346 3-9-3 **71**........................ BarryMcHugh 3 58
(Tony Coyle) *in tch: rdn 3f out: no imp wl over 1f out* **6/1**[3]

3-55 **7** 1 **Imshivalla (IRE)**[16] 1711 3-9-4 **72**........................ TonyHamilton 8 56
(Richard Fahey) *hld up: hdwy on outside over 2f out: wknd over 1f out* **15/2**

4203 **8** 3½ **Frankthetank (IRE)**[10] 1927 3-9-2 **70**........................ TomEaves 1 45
(Keith Dalgleish) *prom: drvn over 3f out: wknd fnl 2f* **14/1**

22-6 **9** 12 **Madame Mirasol (IRE)**[26] 1507 3-9-4 **72**........................ KierenFallon 4 16
(Kevin Ryan) *s.i.s: t.k.h: hld up: effrt and rdn on outside over 2f out: sn btn* **10/1**

1m 31.16s (2.16) **Going Correction** +0.275s/f (Good) **9** Ran SP% **114.9**
Speed ratings (Par 99): **98,96,94,91,90 89,88,84,70**
CSF £17.33 CT £115.60 TOTE £4.90: £1.50, £1.20, £2.20; EX 20.00 Trifecta £193.10.
**Owner** Paul Dean **Bred** Rabbah Bloodstock Limited **Trained** Middleham Moor, N Yorks

**FOCUS**
Not a bad winning time. The winner is the type to cintinue to progress.

## 2219 RACING UK'S IPAD APP, BET & WATCH H'CAP 7f 30y
5:20 (5:21) (Class 6) (0-60,60) 4-Y-O+ £2,587 (£770; £384; £192) Stalls Low

Form RPR
0460 **1** **Imperator Augustus (IRE)**[7] 2019 6-8-13 **59**........................ JackGarritty(7) 12 70
(Patrick Holmes) *hld up towards rr: hdwy over 2f out: rdn to ld appr fnl f: kpt on strly* **13/2**

5405 **2** 2¾ **Cyflymder (IRE)**[22] 1596 8-8-11 **50**........................(b) RoystonFfrench 9 54
(David C Griffiths) *sn chsng ldr: led over 2f out: rdn and hdd appr fnl f: kpt on same pce* **10/1**

60-0 **3** 1 **Eastlands Lad (IRE)**[18] 1673 5-8-11 **50**........................ PJMcDonald 8 51
(Micky Hammond) *in tch: effrt and rdn over 2f out: edgd lft appr fnl f: kpt on same pce* **22/1**

0050 **4** 3½ **Amis Reunis**[8] 1972 5-8-7 **46** oh1........................(p) JamesSullivan 3 38
(Alan Berry) *hld up in midfield: hmpd over 5f out: rdn and effrt on outside 2f out: kpt on ins fnl f: no imp* **33/1**

0504 **5** 1¾ **Viking Warrior (IRE)**[19] 1649 7-8-11 **50**........................ DuranFentiman 10 38
(Shaun Harris) *hld up: rdn and hdwy on outside over 2f out: no imp fnl f* **18/1**

5-32 **6** ¾ **Clumber Place**[10] 1930 8-9-3 **59**........................ NeilFarley(3) 4 45
(Shaun Harris) *led: rdn and hdd over 2f out: rallied: wknd over 1f out* **7/2**[2]

6-34 **7** 1 **Iggy**[22] 1602 4-9-6 **59**........................(t) KierenFallon 11 42
(Michael Easterby) *t.k.h: cl up: edgd rt bnd over 5f out: rdn over 2f out: wknd over 1f out* **3/1**[1]

0-15 **8** 1 **Graceful Act**[18] 1673 6-9-4 **57**........................ DaleSwift 2 37
(Ron Barr) *hld up towards rr: drvn along over 2f out: no imp over 1f out* **4/1**[3]

06-0 **9** 6 **Fife Jo**[15] 1758 4-8-4 **46** oh1........................(v) IanBrennan(3) 6 11
(Jim Goldie) *in tch: drvn and outpcd over 2f out: sn btn* **25/1**

540 **10** *nk* **Seaside Rock (IRE)**[18] 1675 4-9-7 **60**........................(b) TomEaves 5 24
(Keith Dalgleish) *s.i.s: bhd: rdn on outside over 2f out: sn btn* **14/1**

/0-0 **11** ½ **Ebony Clarets**[10] 1930 5-8-12 **54**........................ ConnorBeasley(3) 1 17
(Linda Perratt) *hld up: drvn and outpcd wl over 2f out: nvr on terms* **50/1**

1-00 **12** 3 **Tadalavil**[8] 1972 9-9-3 **56**........................ PhillipMakin 7 11
(Linda Perratt) *t.k.h: prom: hmpd twice bnd over 5f out: rdn and wknd over 2f out* **33/1**

1m 30.76s (1.76) **Going Correction** +0.275s/f (Good) **12** Ran SP% **117.6**
Speed ratings (Par 101): **100,96,95,91,89 88,87,86,79,79 78,75**
CSF £64.77 CT £1353.25 TOTE £7.30: £2.00, £3.90, £9.40; EX 57.80 Trifecta £2422.40 Part won..
**Owner** Foulrice Park Racing Limited **Bred** Western Bloodstock **Trained** Middleham, N Yorks
■ Stewards' Enquiry : Kieren Fallon three-day ban: careless riding (May 26-28)

**FOCUS**
A weak handicap which was sound run. The winner's best form since last August.
T/Plt: £60.40 to a £1 stake. Pool: £48,966.97 - 591.39 winning tickets. T/Qpdt: £20.90 to a £1 stake. Pool: 4430.48 - 156.75 winning units. RY

## 2029 WINDSOR (R-H)

Monday, May 12

**OFFICIAL GOING: Good changing to soft after race 1 (5.50)**

Wind: Light, behind Weather: Changeable - heavy shower before racing and during race 1. Further rain race 5.

### 2220 DOWNLOAD THE UNIBET PRO APP MAIDEN FILLIES' STKS (BOBIS RACE) 5f 10y

5:50 (5:53) (Class 5) 2-Y-O £2,911 (£866; £432; £216) Stalls Low

Form RPR

0 1 **Cajoling (IRE)**[14] 1788 2-9-0 0 RichardKingscote 9 74
(Jonathan Portman) *trckd ldr to 1/2-way: sn pressed new ldr: reminder to ld jst over 1f out: pushed clr* **33/1**

2 2 3/4 **Russian Heroine** 2-9-0 0 RyanMoore 5 64
(Sir Michael Stoute) *trckd ldrs: nipped through to ld against rail 1/2-way: pushed along and hdd jst over 1f out: one pce* **11/10**[1]

3 1 3/4 **Rocking The Boat (IRE)** 2-9-0 0 JimCrowley 3 58
(Charles Hills) *hld up: clsd on ldrs over 2f out: chsd ldng pair over 1f out: swtchd lft and reminder: one pce after* **5/2**[2]

4 2 **Lady Kyllar** 2-9-0 0 TomQueally 6 51
(George Margarson) *t.k.h: in tch: shkn up 2f out: steadily fdd* **10/1**

0 5 nk **Lyfka**[16] 1726 2-8-11 0 OisinMurphy(3) 2 50
(J W Hills) *s.i.s: in tch: shkn up 2f out: steadily fdd* **14/1**

4 6 hd **Fujiano**[14] 1788 2-9-0 0 FergusSweeney 8 49
(Derek Haydn Jones) *led to 1/2-way: wknd over 1f out* **5/1**[3]

1m 2.46s (2.16) **Going Correction** +0.20s/f (Good) **6 Ran SP% 111.6**
Speed ratings (Par 90): **90,85,82,79,79 78**
CSF £70.09 TOTE £17.00: £6.10, £1.30; EX 98.20 Trifecta £501.00.
**Owner** Berkeley Racing **Bred** Stephanie Von Schilcher & David Powell **Trained** Upper Lambourn, Berks

**FOCUS**
The inner of the straight was dolled out 5yds at the 6f point and 2yds at the winning post. The top bend was dolled out 6yds from the normal configuration, adding 20yds to race distances at 1m-plus. This opening race was run in heavy rain and afterwards the ground was eased to an official description of soft. They stayed stands' side throughout the card. The form could be underrated.

### 2221 CANCER RESEARCH UK, CANCERRESEARCHUK.ORG MEDIAN AUCTION MAIDEN STKS 1m 2f 7y

6:20 (6:21) (Class 5) 3-5-Y-O £2,911 (£866; £432; £216) Stalls Centre

Form RPR

3- 1 **Purple Spectrum**[161] 8123 3-8-13 0 RyanMoore 13 81+
(William Haggas) *led after 3f: urged along fr 4f out: drvn over 2f out: jnd jst over 1f out: rdr dropped whip jst ins fnl f: fnd enough to assert nr fin* **15/8**[1]

2 3/4 **Lamorak (FR)** 3-8-13 0 RichardHughes 2 79+
(Hugo Palmer) *sn prom: clsd to trck wnr gng wl over 1f out: sn upsides: no ex last 100yds* **20/1**

42- 3 1 1/4 **Grand Meister**[216] 7089 3-8-13 0 TomQueally 4 77
(Michael Bell) *trckd ldrs: shkn up in 5th over 2f out: clsd to chse ldng pair jst over 1f out: kpt on same pce fnl f* **5/1**[3]

0 4 3 1/2 **High Church (IRE)**[23] 1582 3-8-10 0 OisinMurphy(3) 11 70
(Roger Charlton) *hld up wl in rr: pushed along and prog on outer fr 3f out: shkn up and one pce fnl 2f: nt disgrcd* **4/1**[2]

30 5 shd **Arcamante (ITY)**[23] 1587 3-8-13 0 (b) AntonioFresu 1 70
(Marco Botti) *towards rr: sme prog over 3f out: reminder and hung lft wl over 2f out: urged along and kpt on after* **50/1**

0 6 3 1/4 **Ophir**[14] 1809 3-8-13 0 MartinDwyer 12 64
(William Muir) *trckd wnr after 3f to over 2f out: steadily fdd u.p* **33/1**

7 1/2 **Sir Rosco** 3-8-13 0 AndreaAtzeni 14 63
(Sir Michael Stoute) *sn wl in rr: pushed along 3f out: kpt on steadily after: n.d* **14/1**

24 8 shd **Russian Remarque**[14] 1808 3-8-13 0 ShaneKelly 10 63
(Jonathan Portman) *led 3f: styd prom: chsd wnr over 2f out to wl over 1f out: wknd* **10/1**

0-0 9 hd **Daydreamer**[21] 1612 3-8-13 0 LiamJones 8 62
(William Haggas) *settled wl in rr: prog into midfield 3f out: reminders and no hdwy 2f out: kpt on fnl f* **33/1**

06 10 nk **Censorius**[13] 1844 3-8-6 0 BradleyBosley(7) 3 62
(Ed Walker) *dwlt: mostly in last: bmpd along fr 3f out: nvr a factor but styd on fnl f* **66/1**

00 11 8 **Dark Days**[8] 1984 3-8-13 0 (t) LukeMorris 9 47
(Paul Cole) *nvr beyond midfield: shkn up and struggling over 3f out: sn wknd* **66/1**

6- 12 2 3/4 **Norse Light**[187] 7774 3-8-13 0 JimCrowley 5 41
(Ralph Beckett) *settled wl in rr: pushed along and rdn to prog over 2f out* **9/1**

5-6 13 3/4 **Rapunzal**[14] 1808 3-8-8 0 FergusSweeney 7 35
(Henry Candy) *chsd ldrs: pushed along 3f out: sn wknd* **66/1**

14 2 1/2 **Prince Of Islay (IRE)** 3-8-13 0 [1] MartinLane 15 35
(Robert Mills) *pushed up to chse ldrs after 4f: rdn and wknd 3f out* **100/1**

15 8 **Its Not Me Its You** 3-8-13 0 SebSanders 6 20
(Brendan Powell) *rn green and a in rr: t.o* **50/1**

2m 9.66s (0.96) **Going Correction** +0.125s/f (Good) **15 Ran SP% 117.2**
Speed ratings (Par 103): **101,100,99,96,96 93,93,93,93,93 86,84,83,81,75**
CSF £46.49 TOTE £2.80: £1.40, £7.10, £2.50; EX 71.20 Trifecta £526.10.
**Owner** The Queen **Bred** The Queen **Trained** Newmarket, Suffolk

**FOCUS**
The bare form looks just ordinary.

### 2222 HAPPY RETIREMENT IN BRAZIL MICHAEL BUTLIN H'CAP (BOBIS RACE) 1m 2f 7y

6:50 (6:52) (Class 4) (0-80,80) 3-Y-O £5,498 (£1,636; £817; £408) Stalls Centre

Form RPR

0-64 1 **Stampede (IRE)**[14] 1795 3-9-1 74 RyanMoore 1 83+
(Sir Michael Stoute) *hld up in last pair: clsd on ldrs and pushed along over 2f out: led jst ins fnl f: only pushed along firmly to assert: readily* **2/1**[1]

1-00 2 1 1/4 **New Colours**[11] 1898 3-8-7 66 MartinDwyer 7 72
(Marcus Tregoning) *trckd ldrs: clsd over 3f out: rdn to ld over 2f out: wandered u.p and hdd jst ins fnl f: kpt on but no ch w wnr* **66/1**

12-5 3 3 1/4 **Meteoroid (USA)**[23] 1586 3-9-7 80 GeorgeBaker 6 80
(Lady Cecil) *trckd ldrs: shkn up to chal over 2f out: stl cl up jst over 1f out: fdd fnl f* **9/4**[2]

424- 4 3 1/2 **Be Seeing You**[182] 7835 3-8-11 73 OisinMurphy(3) 5 66
(Roger Charlton) *s.i.s: hld up in last pair: prog 3f out: pressed ldrs and drvn 2f out: wknd fnl f* **7/2**[3]

-131 5 nk **Right Of Appeal**[11] 1898 3-8-12 71 SilvestreDeSousa 2 64
(Mark Johnston) *in tch: pushed along over 3f out: dropped to last and btn over 2f out* **10/1**

0-50 6 1 3/4 **Filosofo (IRE)**[14] 1795 3-9-4 77 RichardHughes 4 66
(Richard Hannon) *trckd ldr: lft in ld over 3f out: hdd over 2f out: steadily wknd* **25/1**

1-22 U **Chinotto (IRE)**[73] 785 3-9-7 80 DavidProbert 8
(Andrew Balding) *mde most tl jinked and uns rdr over 3f out: slipped up while loose* **7/1**

2m 9.47s (0.77) **Going Correction** +0.125s/f (Good) **7 Ran SP% 113.3**
Speed ratings (Par 101): **101,100,97,94,94 92,**
CSF £96.52 CT £318.99 TOTE £3.10: £1.50, £8.30; EX 58.60 Trifecta £161.10.
**Owner** Highclere Thoroughbred Racing - Ashes **Bred** Camas Park Stud & Summerhill **Trained** Newmarket, Suffolk

### 2223 UNIBET.CO.UK ROYAL WINDSOR STKS (LISTED RACE) (C&G) 1m 67y

7:20 (7:20) (Class 1) 3-Y-O+ £20,982 (£7,955; £3,981; £1,983; £995) Stalls Low

Form RPR

0141 1 **Ocean Tempest**[12] 1870 5-9-6 115 AdamKirby 4 116
(John Ryan) *led 1f: led again 3f out: drvn wl over 1f out: styd on wl fnl f* **5/4**[1]

-234 2 3/4 **Fencing (USA)**[12] 1870 5-9-2 110 [1] RobertHavlin 1 110
(John Gosden) *stdd s: t.k.h: hld up in 4th: gng easily whn waiting for room 2f out: squeezed through to take 2nd ins fnl f: styd on but no ch to seriously chal* **3/1**[2]

10-6 3 1 1/2 **Fire Ship**[17] 1698 5-9-2 105 JimCrowley 5 107
(William Knight) *trckd ldrs: rdn to chse wnr over 2f out: no imp over 1f out: lost 2nd and one pce ins fnl f* **6/1**

10-0 4 3 **Baltic Knight (IRE)**[12] 1870 4-9-2 109 RichardHughes 6 100
(Richard Hannon) *hld up in last: shkn up over 2f out: wnt 4th and rdn over 1f out: no imp and eased last 100yds* **10/1**

310- 5 2 3/4 **Out Of Bounds (USA)**[212] 7206 5-9-2 108 SilvestreDeSousa 2 94
(Saeed bin Suroor) *racd freely: led after 1f to 3f out: steadily wknd fnl 2f* **11/2**[3]

1m 44.23s (-0.47) **Going Correction** +0.125s/f (Good) **5 Ran SP% 108.2**
Speed ratings (Par 111): **107,106,104,101,99**
CSF £4.98 TOTE £2.00: £1.10, £2.30; EX 5.30 Trifecta £11.50.
**Owner** W McLuskey & C Little **Bred** Old Mill Stud Ltd And Oomswell Ltd **Trained** Newmarket, Suffolk

### 2224 ANDREEA SMALEMBERG H'CAP 1m 67y

7:50 (7:50) (Class 5) (0-70,70) 3-Y-O £2,911 (£866; £432; £216) Stalls Low

Form RPR

145- 1 **Lady Marl**[243] 6311 3-9-1 64 RyanMoore 9 72
(Gary Moore) *t.k.h early: trckd ldng pair: rdn to ld over 1f out: styd on wl and clr fnl f* **5/1**[1]

360- 2 2 1/2 **Jersey Brown (IRE)**[256] 5926 3-8-11 63 WilliamTwiston-Davies(3) 14 69+
(Mick Channon) *hld up in last trio: stdy prog gng wl fr over 2f out: jst pushed along to take 2nd wl ins fnl f: no ch to threaten wnr* **7/1**[3]

063- 3 3/4 **Division Belle**[229] 6749 3-9-0 63 MartinDwyer 6 64
(William Muir) *t.k.h: hld up in midfield: shkn up over 2f out: reminders and prog over 1f out: kpt on to take 3rd last strides* **10/1**

02-0 4 nk **White Russian**[14] 1809 3-9-1 64 DaneO'Neill 4 64
(Henry Candy) *pressed ldr: led over 2f out: drvn and hdd over 1f out: no ch w wnr: one pce* **6/1**[2]

5-66 5 nse **Mendacious Harpy (IRE)**[16] 1725 3-9-7 70 (v[1]) PatCosgrave 3 70
(George Baker) *wl in tch: shkn up over 2f out: pressed for a pl and drvn 1f out: kpt on* **9/1**

20-0 6 3 **Llyrical**[16] 1725 3-8-13 62 LiamKeniry 2 55
(Derek Haydn Jones) *t.k.h: trckd ldng pair to 2f out: wknd jst over 1f out* **20/1**

55-5 7 3/4 **Pink Mirage (IRE)**[14] 1794 3-8-12 64 MatthewLawson(3) 8 56
(Jonathan Portman) *hld up towards rr: shkn up on outer over 2f out: no imp on ldrs fnl 2f* **10/1**

45-5 8 nk **Tubeanie (IRE)**[16] 1725 3-8-7 61 RyanTate(5) 12 52
(Clive Cox) *nvr bttr than midfield: pushed along and no imp on ldrs fnl 2f* **5/1**[1]

4-00 9 1 **Manor Way (IRE)**[5] 2078 3-8-4 60 (b[1]) CamHardie(7) 1 49
(Richard Hannon) *led to over 2f out: sn wknd* **12/1**

360- 10 1/2 **Capers Royal Star (FR)**[132] 8452 3-9-4 67 GeorgeBaker 7 54
(Alastair Lidderdale) *t.k.h: hld up in last trio: shkn up and no prog over 2f out: nvr involved* **14/1**

3150 11 6 **Plough Boy (IRE)**[33] 1401 3-8-12 61 ChrisCatlin 11 35
(Willie Musson) *hld up in last trio: shkn up and no prog over 2f out: sn wknd* **33/1**

00-0 12 16 **Kinloss**[33] 1389 3-9-1 64 RichardHughes 10
(Richard Hannon) *hld up in 8th: pushed along and wknd over 2f out: t.o* **14/1**

1m 46.62s (1.92) **Going Correction** +0.125s/f (Good) **12 Ran SP% 117.0**
Speed ratings (Par 99): **95,92,91,91,91 88,87,87,86,85 79,63**
CSF £38.68 CT £344.32 TOTE £5.10: £1.10, £2.70, £3.80; EX 40.90 Trifecta £486.60.
**Owner** Sir Eric Parker **Bred** Sir Eric Parker **Trained** Lower Beeding, W Sussex

**FOCUS**
Just a modest handicap.

### 2225 UNIBET OFFER DAILY JOCKEY & TRAINER SPECIALS H'CAP 1m 3f 135y

8:20 (8:20) (Class 5) (0-75,74) 3-Y-O £2,911 (£866; £432; £216) Stalls Centre

Form RPR

1 1 **Der Meister (IRE)**[21] 1616 3-9-4 74 OisinMurphy(3) 3 78+
(Andrew Balding) *s.i.s: sn trckd ldr: chal over 3f out and first one to be rdn: sustained effrt to ld jst ins fnl f: styd on* **6/4**[1]

64-2 2 1/2 **Template (IRE)**[8] 1983 3-9-5 72 RobertHavlin 4 75
(Amanda Perrett) *led at mod pce: awkward bnd 6f out to 5f out: tried to kick on 3f out: hdd and edgd lft jst ins fnl f: kpt on* **9/2**[3]

44-2 3 shd **Loving Your Work**[11] 1898 3-8-12 65 PatCosgrave 6 68
(George Baker) *hld up in last pair: clsd on ldrs over 2f out: chal and upsides fr over 1f out: hanging lft and nt qckn last 100yds* **7/1**

00-2 4 1 3/4 **Snow Conditions**[14] 1793 3-8-7 60 LiamKeniry 2 60
(Philip Hide) *hld up in last pair: tried to cl on ldrs over 2f out: rdn and nt qckn over 1f out* **8/1**

2332 **5** 1 1/2 **Yeah Baby (IRE)**[14] 1812 3-9-3 **70**.................................. RichardHughes 1 68
(Charles Hills) *trckd ldng pair: pushed along over 2f out: nt qckn whn shkn up briefly over 1f out: fdd* **11/4**[2]
2m 40.56s (11.06) **Going Correction** +0.125s/f (Good) **5** Ran SP% **108.5**
Speed ratings (Par 99): **68,67,67,66,65**
CSF £8.23 TOTE £2.60: £1.40, £2.90; EX 8.20 Trifecta £23.20.
**Owner** James/Michaelson/Greenwood 1 **Bred** Mrs C L Weld **Trained** Kingsclere, Hants

**FOCUS**
Just an ordinary handicap, but a likeable performance from the winner.
T/Plt: £8.60 to a £1 stake. Pool: £84,135.73 - 7115.27 winning units. T/Qpdt: £6.40 to a £1 stake. Pool: £7236.20 - 833.71 winning units. JN

## 1640 MAISONS-LAFFITTE (R-H)
Monday, May 12
**OFFICIAL GOING: Turf: very soft**

### 2226a PRIX TEXANITA (LISTED RACE) (3YO) (TURF) 5f 110y
2:20 (12:00) 3-Y-O **£22,916** (£9,166; £6,875; £4,583; £2,291)

RPR
**1** **Rangali**[26] 1527 3-8-11 0.......................................... FabriceVeron 7 106
(H-A Pantall, France) **101/10**
**2** 1 3/4 **Son Cesio (FR)**[26] 1527 3-8-11 0.......................................... MaximeGuyon 1 100
(H-A Pantall, France) **53/10**[3]
**3** 3/4 **Harlem Shake (IRE)**[16] 3-8-11 0.......................................... LManiezzi 2 97
(Marco Gasparini, Italy) **113/10**
**4** shd **Farmah (USA)**[26] 1527 3-8-8 0.......................... Francois-XavierBertras 9 94
(F Rohaut, France) **42/10**[2]
**5** 1 1/2 **Mecca's Angel (IRE)**[8] 1968 3-8-8 0.......................... PaulMulrennan 4 89
(Michael Dods) *t.k.h: w ldrs: pushed along between horses to hold pl over 1 1/2f out: grad lft bhd by ldrs fnl f* **2/1**[1]
**6** 2 1/2 **Elusive Pearl (FR)**[234] 3-8-8 0.......................................... FranckBlondel 6 81
(F Rossi, France) **214/10**
**7** 3 **Oeil De Tigre (FR)**[26] 1527 3-8-11 0.......................... UmbertoRispoli 8 74
(H-A Pantall, France) **166/10**
**8** 1 3/4 **Zygmunt (FR)**[39] 1272 3-9-2 0.......................................... AlexisBadel 5 73
(Mme M Bollack-Badel, France) **134/10**
**9** 3/4 **Gentle Breeze (IRE)**[45] 3-8-8 0.......................................... ThierryJarnet 3 63
(H-A Pantall, France) **94/10**
**10** 1 **Vedeux (IRE)**[26] 1527 3-8-11 0..........................(b[1]) MarcLerner 10 62
(C Lerner, France) **134/10**
1m 6.5s (-0.80) **10** Ran SP% **119.2**
WIN (incl. 1 euro stake): 11.10. PLACES: 2.80, 2.20, 3.70. DF: 21.40. SF: 56.70.
**Owner** Henri-Alex Pantall **Bred** Y Chabot And H A Pantall **Trained** France

## 2005 BELMONT PARK (L-H)
Friday, May 9
**OFFICIAL GOING: Turf: good**

### 2227a ALLOWANCE RACE (ALLOWANCE) (3YO+ FILLIES & MARES) (TURF) 1m 110y
9:26 (12:00) 3-Y-O+
**£27,831** (£9,277; £4,638; £2,319; £1,391; £463)

RPR
**1** **Wholelottashakin (USA)**[104] 5-8-12 0.......................................... JLezcano 4 95
(Thomas Bush, U.S.A) **43/20**[2]
**2** 1 1/4 **Tokyo Time (USA)**[371] 4-8-12 0..........................(b) JJCastellano 6 92
(Claude McGaughey III, U.S.A) **3/1**[3]
**3** 3 **Walk With An Angel**[56] 957 3-8-4 0.......................................... JBravo 7 90?
(Amy Weaver) *dwlt: w.w in rr: moved into 5th bef 1/2-way: shkn up and hdwy on rail 2f out: sn angled out: kpt on fnl f: nvr on terms w ldrs* **173/10**
**4** 1 1/2 **Swakopmund (USA)**[28] 5-8-1 0..........................(b) LMejias(7) 3 78
(Michael Hushion, U.S.A) **216/10**
**5** 1 1/4 **Ear D'Rhythm (USA)** 4-8-8 0..........................(b) CHVelasquez 1 76
(Rudy Rodriguez, U.S.A) **27/1**
**6** 2 1/2 **Balashkova (FR)**[244] 6229 4-8-12 0.......................................... JRVelazquez 2 74
(Chad C Brown, U.S.A) **8/5**[1]
**7** 1 3/4 **Fingers Crossed (USA)** 3-8-6 0.......................................... LSaez 5 76
(Kiaran McLaughlin, U.S.A) **77/10**
1m 44.26s (104.26)
**WFA** 3 from 4yo+ 13lb **7** Ran SP% **120.2**
PARI-MUTUEL (all including 2 usd stake): WIN 6.30; PLACE (1-2) 3.20, 3.90; SHOW (1-2-3): 2.40, 3.20, 4.60; SF 22.00.
**Owner** Parting Glass Racing **Bred** Mia Gallo **Trained** North America

## 2227 BELMONT PARK (L-H)
Sunday, May 11
**OFFICIAL GOING: Dirt: standard changing to fast, turf: good**

### 2228a MAN O' WAR STKS (GRADE 1) (4YO+) (TURF) 1m 3f (T)
10:43 (12:00) 4-Y-O+
**£144,578** (£48,192; £24,096; £12,048; £7,228; £4,819)

RPR
**1** **Imagining (USA)**[91] 6-8-9 0..........................(b) JRosario 2 112
(Claude McGaughey III, U.S.A) **13/4**[2]
**2** 3/4 **Real Solution (USA)**[43] 5-8-12 0.......................................... JJCastellano 6 114+
(Chad C Brown, U.S.A) **9/2**[3]
**3** 1/2 **Grandeur (IRE)**[23] 1559 5-8-9 0.......................................... JRLeparoux 1 110+
(Jeremy Noseda) **23/5**
**4** 2 3/4 **Frac Daddy (USA)**[22] 4-8-5 0.......................................... AGarcia 4 101
(Kenneth McPeek, U.S.A) **6/1**
**5** 1 1/2 **Vertiformer (USA)**[43] 7-8-3 0.......................................... JBravo 3 96
(Christophe Clement, U.S.A) **87/10**

**6** 3 3/4 **Amira's Prince (IRE)**[43] 5-8-9 0..........................(b) JRVelazquez 5 95
(William Mott, U.S.A) **9/5**[1]
2m 14.33s (-0.72) **6** Ran SP% **119.9**
PARI-MUTUEL (all including 2 usd stake): WIN 8.50; PLACE (1-2) 4.50, 5.00; SHOW (1-2-3): 2.90, 3.50, 4.00; SF 35.60.
**Owner** Phipps Stable **Bred** Phipps Stable **Trained** USA

## HOPPEGARTEN (R-H)
Sunday, May 11
**OFFICIAL GOING: Turf: good to soft**

### 2229a OLEANDER-RENNEN (GROUP 3) (4YO+) (TURF) 2m
4:20 (12:00) 4-Y-O+
**£26,666** (£9,166; £4,583; £2,500; £1,666; £1,250)

RPR
**1** **Altano (GER)**[196] 7566 8-9-6 0.......................................... EPedroza 7 116+
(A Wohler, Germany) *w.w in rr: last and pushed along over 2 1/2f out: gd hdwy on outer to chse ldrs under 2f out: rdn to ld 1 1/2f out: drvn out fnl f* **13/10**[1]
**2** 3 **Rock Of Romance (IRE)**[197] 7591 4-9-0 0.......................................... JBojko 8 110
(A Wohler, Germany) *trckd ldr on outer: rdn to ld wl over 2f out: hdd 1 1/2f out: kpt on at same pce u.p fnl f* **47/10**
**3** 4 **Technokrat (IRE)**[35] 6-8-11 0.......................................... KClijmans 6 99+
(S Smrczek, Germany) *towards rr: rdn and hdwy over 1 1/2f out: styd on wl fnl f: tk 3rd fnl stride: nvr nrr* **177/10**
**4** nse **Tres Rock Danon (FR)**[10] 8-8-11 0.......................................... AntonioFresu 2 99
(Gerald Geisler, Germany) *trckd ldr on inner: rdn and outpcd over 2f out: fdd ins fnl f: lost 3rd fnl stride* **42/10**[3]
**5** 16 **Lucarelli (GER)**[33] 1370 8-9-0 0..........................(b) NRichter 5 85
(Ferdinand J Leve, Germany) *led: hdd wl over 2f out: wknd appr fnl f* **14/1**
**6** nk **Stellato**[336] 4-8-11 0.......................................... WPanov 4 84
(Waldemar Hickst, Germany) *towards rr: rdn and no imp fr over 2f out* **26/1**
**7** 2 1/2 **Quinzieme Monarque (USA)**[35] 4-9-0 0.......................................... DanielePorcu 3 85
(P Schiergen, Germany) *midfield on outer: rdn 3f out: no real imp u.p fr over 2f out: wknd fnl 1 1/2f* **5/2**[2]
**8** 17 **Scouting (IRE)**[20] 4-8-8 0.......................................... MichaelCadeddu 1 60
(J Hirschberger, Germany) *midfield on inner: lost pl 2 1/2f out: sn wl btn* **215/10**
3m 30.6s (210.60)
**WFA** 4 from 6yo+ 3lb **8** Ran SP% **129.0**
WIN (incl. 10 euro stake): 23. PLACES: 13, 14, 25. SF: 80.
**Owner** Frau Dr I Hornig **Bred** Gestut Hof Ittlingen **Trained** Germany

## 2014 BEVERLEY (R-H)
Tuesday, May 13
**OFFICIAL GOING: Heavy (soft in places; 7.2)**
Wind: Moderate behind Weather: Cloudy with sunny periods

### 2230 GREAT BRITISH RACEDAY SATURDAY 24 MAY (S) STKS 5f
2:00 (2:00) (Class 6) 3-Y-O **£2,264** (£673; £336; £168) **Stalls** Low

Form RPR
006 **1** **Robbian**[39] 1277 3-8-11 33.......................................... RobbieFitzpatrick 1 54
(Charles Smith) *qckly away: mde all: rdn clr wl over 1f out: drvn out* **16/1**
0-00 **2** 2 3/4 **Nu Form Fire (IRE)**[12] 1906 3-8-11 45..........................[1] AndrewMullen 6 44
(Nigel Tinkler) *chsd ldrs: rdn along 1/2-way: drvn and styd on to chse wnr appr fnl f: no imp towards fin* **9/2**
000- **3** 2 **White Flag**[175] 7956 3-7-13 54.......................... RachelRichardson(7) 3 32
(Tim Easterby) *wnt sltly lft s: in rr: hdwy on inner 2f out: sn rdn and one pce appr fnl f* **4/1**[3]
1250 **4** 6 **El Duque**[22] 1606 3-8-11 64..........................(b[1]) RyanWhile(5) 2 20
(Bill Turner) *sn chsng wnr: cl up 1/2-way: rdn 2f out: sn drvn and wknd* **13/8**[1]
2202 **5** 13 **Under Approval**[15] 1801 3-8-11 62.......................................... DanielTudhope 7
(David O'Meara) *prom: rdn along bef 1/2-way: wknd 2f out and bhd whn eased fnl f* **11/4**[2]
1m 6.53s (3.03) **Going Correction** +0.50s/f (Yiel) **5** Ran SP% **108.8**
Speed ratings (Par 97): **95,90,87,77,57**
CSF £78.76 TOTE £21.80: £7.20, £2.60; EX 108.60 Trifecta £313.00.There was no bid for the winner.
**Owner** Rob Lewin **Bred** John Starbuck **Trained** Temple Bruer, Lincs

**FOCUS**
There was 5.5mm of rain overnight and the going was changed to heavy, soft in places. The outsider landed this ordinary seller and the market leaders filled the last two places. The form is rated around the reasonable time. Daniel Tudhope reported that the ground was very testing.

### 2231 RACING UK ON CHANNEL 432 MAIDEN STKS 5f
2:30 (2:32) (Class 5) 2-Y-O **£3,408** (£1,006; £503) **Stalls** Low

Form RPR
**1** **Northgate Lad (IRE)** 2-9-5 0.......................................... TomEaves 5 81
(Brian Ellison) *qckly away and mde all: rdn clr ent fnl f: kpt on wl towards fin* **9/1**
2 **2** 1/2 **Mattmu**[17] 1712 2-9-5 0.......................................... RobertWinston 6 79
(Tim Easterby) *sn trcking ldrs: effrt 2f out: swtchd lft over 1f out: rdn and edgd sltly lft ent fnl f: sn chsng wnr: styd on* **5/4**[1]
**3** 6 **Miami Carousel (IRE)** 2-9-5 0.......................................... PhillipMakin 7 57
(John Quinn) *chsd ldrs: rdn along 2f out: kpt on same pce* **16/1**
**4** 1/2 **Izzthatright (IRE)** 2-9-5 0.......................................... PaulMulrennan 9 56
(Nigel Tinkler) *bhd: hdwy on inner whn nt clr run wl over 1f out: sn rdn and styd on wl fnl f: nrst fin* **50/1**
00 **5** 1/2 **Monsieur Jimmy**[8] 2014 2-9-2 0.......................................... NeilFarley(3) 4 54
(Declan Carroll) *prom: rdn along 2f out: grad wknd* **20/1**
05 **6** 1 **Mountain Man**[17] 1712 2-9-5 0.......................................... GrahamGibbons 3 50
(Michael Easterby) *chsd ldrs: rdn along 2f out: sn edgd rt and wknd over 1f out* **7/1**[3]
4 **7** 3/4 **Bowson Fred**[25] 1560 2-9-5 0.......................................... JamesSullivan 8 48
(Michael Easterby) *sn chsng wnr: cl up 2f out: sn rdn and wknd ent fnl f* **9/2**[2]

0 **8** 1 ¼ **Rocco's Delight**[10] 1955 2-9-0 0 ........ AdamCarter(5) 10 43
(John Wainwright) *towards rr: sme hdwy over 2f out: sn rdn and n.d* **50/1**

**9** ½ **Triggers Broom (IRE)** 2-9-0 0 ........ TonyHamilton 1 36
(Richard Fahey) *trckd ldrs on inner: pushed along 1/2-way: rdn along wl over 1f out: sn btn* **8/1**

**10** 1 **Straightothepoint** 2-9-5 0 ........ RoystonFfrench 11 38
(Bryan Smart) *wnt lft s: a in rr* **33/1**

6 **11** nk **Celestial Dancer (FR)**[14] 1837 2-9-0 0 ........ AndrewMullen 2 32
(Michael Appleby) *towards rr: rdn along bef 1/2-way: nvr a factor* **22/1**

1m 7.04s (3.54) **Going Correction** +0.50s/f (Yiel) **11** Ran SP% **118.1**
Speed ratings (Par 93): **91,90,80,79,79 77,76,74,73,71 71**
CSF £19.75 TOTE £15.80: £4.40, £1.10, £4.50; EX 42.20 Trifecta £377.20.
**Owner** Mrs J A Martin **Bred** Frank Moynihan **Trained** Norton, N Yorks

**FOCUS**
They went a fair pace in this maiden and the first two pulled clear, showing a useful level of form.

## 2232 ANNIE OXTOBY MEMORIAL H'CAP (DIV I) 5f
**3:00** (3:01) (Class 5) (0-70,70) 4-Y-O+ **£3,234** (£962; £481; £240) **Stalls** Low

Form RPR

0034 **1** **Amenable (IRE)**[9] 1966 7-9-2 **68** ........(p) OisinMurphy(3) 5 76
(Ann Stokell) *dwlt and sn pushed along in rr: hdwy and swtchd lft to wd outside over 1f out: rdn and str run ins fnl f to ld nr fin* **13/2**[3]

40-0 **2** 1 **Lees Anthem**[14] 1838 7-8-7 **56** oh3 ........ PJMcDonald 1 60
(Mel Brittain) *sn led: rdn over 1f out: drvn clr ent fnl f: hdd and no ex nr fin* **10/1**

-024 **3** ¾ **Windforpower (IRE)**[7] 2056 4-9-1 **64** ........(p) JoeFanning 10 65
(Tracy Waggott) *chsd ldrs: rdn over 1f out: swtchd lft ent fnl f: sn drvn and styd on* **8/1**

1-55 **4** ¾ **Dark Opal (IRE)**[5] 2096 4-9-2 **70** ........ JoeyHaynes(5) 2 69
(John Weymes) *chsd ldrs: hdwy to chse wnr over 1f out: sn rdn and kpt on same pce* **6/1**[2]

5640 **5** 1 **Lord Buffhead**[13] 1887 5-8-4 **56** oh5 ........(p) BillyCray(3) 9 51
(Richard Guest) *towards rr: hdwy 2f out: rdn wl over 1f out: kpt on fnl f: nrst fin* **10/1**

4020 **6** 1 ½ **Pearl Noir**[4] 2127 4-8-10 **59** ........(b) GrahamLee 6 49
(Scott Dixon) *cl up: rdn wl over 1f out: grad wknd ent fnl f* **10/1**

0-33 **7** 4 ½ **Storm Lightning**[13] 1878 5-9-6 **69** ........(v[1]) GrahamGibbons 4 42
(Mark Brisbourne) *cl up: rdn along 2f out: drvn appr fnl f and sn wknd* **9/4**[1]

40-2 **8** 1 **Speightowns Kid (USA)**[15] 1814 6-8-13 **62** ........ TomEaves 3 32
(Michael Herrington) *chsd ldrs: rdn along over 2f out: sn wknd* **12/1**

06-0 **9** 1 ¾ **Lizzy's Dream**[23] 1602 6-8-4 **56** ........ NeilFarley(3) 8 20
(Robin Bastiman) *dwlt and swtchd rt s: a in rr* **14/1**

402- **10** nk **Wotalad**[154] 8235 4-8-6 **58** oh2 ow2 ........ GeorgeChaloner(3) 7 20
(Richard Whitaker) *a towards rr* **20/1**

1m 6.23s (2.73) **Going Correction** +0.50s/f (Yiel) **10** Ran SP% **115.9**
Speed ratings (Par 103): **98,96,95,94,92 90,82,81,78,77**
CSF £69.18 CT £540.66 TOTE £6.40: £2.40, £3.00, £2.20; EX 79.60 Trifecta £1169.70.
**Owner** Stephen Arnold **Bred** Michael Downey & Roalso Ltd **Trained** Lincoln, Lincolnshire
■ Stewards' Enquiry : Joey Haynes two-day ban: careless riding (May 27,29)

**FOCUS**
The pace was fairly strong in this handicap and the winner came from a long way back. The runner-up is on the best guide.

## 2233 ANNIE OXTOBY MEMORIAL H'CAP (DIV II) 5f
**3:30** (3:30) (Class 5) (0-70,70) 4-Y-O+ **£3,234** (£962; £481; £240) **Stalls** Low

Form RPR

-000 **1** **Banovallum**[8] 2019 4-9-7 **70** ........ GrahamGibbons 2 81
(Michael Easterby) *chsd ldrs on inner: gd hdwy wl over 1f out: rdn to ld ins fnl f: kpt on wl towards fin* **5/1**[3]

3-2 **2** 1 ¼ **Niceonemyson**[14] 1838 5-8-6 **60** ow1 ........ KevinStott(5) 5 67
(Christopher Wilson) *chsd ldrs: hdwy on outer over 1f out: sn rdn and styd on wl fnl f* **9/4**[1]

454 **3** 1 ¼ **Captain Scooby**[9] 1972 8-8-4 **56** oh7 ........ ConnorBeasley(3) 3 58
(Richard Guest) *in tch: hdwy wl over 1f out: rdn and styd on fnl f: nrst fin* **4/1**[2]

-060 **4** 3 ¾ **Balinka**[14] 1843 4-8-7 **56** oh4 ........ PJMcDonald 1 45
(Mel Brittain) *slt ld: rdn along wl over 1f out: drvn and edgd lft ent fnl f: sn hdd & wknd* **16/1**

00-0 **5** 1 ¾ **Choc'A'Moca (IRE)**[20] 1643 7-8-9 **58** ........(v) PaulMulrennan 10 40
(Paul Midgley) *cl up: effrt 2f out: rdn and ev ch over 1f out: wknd ent fnl f* **16/1**

1004 **6** nk **Profile Star (IRE)**[11] 1922 5-9-0 **66** ........ OisinMurphy(3) 9 47
(Ann Stokell) *dwlt and in rr: rdn along wl over 1f out: kpt on fnl f: nrst fin* **14/1**

2113 **7** 8 **Seamster**[57] 987 7-9-0 **63** ........(bt) GrahamLee 8 15
(Richard Ford) *cl up: chal 2f out: sn rdn and wknd over 1f out* **10/1**

-263 **8** ½ **Major Muscari (IRE)**[5] 2094 6-8-3 **57** oh3 ow1 ........(p) AdamCarter(5) 7 8
(Shaun Harris) *chsd ldrs: effrt on wd outside wl over 1f out: sn rdn and wknd* **12/1**

40-0 **9** 1 ¼ **One Kool Dude**[20] 1643 5-8-7 **56** oh2 ........ DuranFentiman 4 2
(Micky Hammond) *a in rr: bhd fr 1/2-way* **25/1**

314- **10** 3 **Poyle Vinnie**[143] 8384 4-9-1 **67** ........ RyanPowell(3) 6 2
(George Margarson) *dwlt and a in rr* **8/1**

1m 5.66s (2.16) **Going Correction** +0.50s/f (Yiel) **10** Ran SP% **117.6**
Speed ratings (Par 103): **102,100,98,92,89 88,75,75,73,68**
CSF £16.78 CT £49.92 TOTE £6.20: £1.70, £1.40, £1.60; EX 29.00 Trifecta £145.00.
**Owner** Brian Padgett & Dean Fielding **Bred** Whitsbury Manor Stud And Mrs M E Slade **Trained** Sheriff Hutton, N Yorks

**FOCUS**
The leaders went off hard in this handicap and it set up for the closers. It was the slightly faster division and the winner is rated back to his best.

## 2234 HAPPY BIRTHDAY GRAHAM ROBERTS H'CAP 1m 100y
**4:00** (4:00) (Class 4) (0-85,85) 4-Y-O+ **£6,469** (£1,925; £962; £481) **Stalls** Low

Form RPR

-056 **1** **Busatto (USA)**[15] 1811 4-8-12 **76** ........ JoeFanning 3 87
(Mark Johnston) *mde all: rdn clr over 1f out: styd on wl* **7/1**

51 **2** 2 ½ **Baraweez (IRE)**[16] 1762 4-9-1 **79** ........ DaleSwift 6 84
(Brian Ellison) *t.k.h: trckd ldrs: effrt 2f out: sn rdn along and sltly outpcd: styd on u.p fnl f: tk 2nd nr line* **6/4**[1]

-000 **3** nk **Al Muheer (IRE)**[10] 1957 9-8-9 **76** ........(p) JasonHart(3) 1 81
(Ruth Carr) *trckd wnr on inner: swtchd lft and hdwy to chal wl over 1f out: sn rdn: drvn and one pce fnl f: lost 2nd nr line* **15/2**

0-36 **4** 2 ¾ **Toto Skyllachy**[8] 2017 9-9-7 **85** ........ DanielTudhope 5 83
(David O'Meara) *awkward s and ct up in gate: slowly away and in rr: hdwy on outer wl over 1f out: sn rdn and kpt on fnl f* **13/2**[3]

5401 **5** nk **Ted's Brother (IRE)**[9] 1970 6-8-7 **74** 6ex ........(e) ConnorBeasley(3) 4 72
(Richard Guest) *hld up in tch: hdwy on outer over 2f out: rdn to chse ldrs over 1f out: wknd ent fnl f* **9/2**[2]

0-00 **6** 3 **Kingscroft (IRE)**[10] 1957 6-8-8 **77** ........(b[1]) JacobButterfield(5) 2 68
(Michael Herrington) *t.k.h: trckd ldrs: hdwy on inner over 2f out: rdn along over 1f out: sn btn* **25/1**

6-52 **7** 3 ¾ **Dakota Canyon (IRE)**[13] 1881 5-8-7 **71** oh2 ........(b) PatrickMathers 7 53
(Richard Fahey) *sn prom: rdn along over 2f out: sn wknd* **14/1**

53-1 **8** 2 ¾ **Correggio**[13] 1881 4-8-13 **77** ........ PJMcDonald 9 53
(Micky Hammond) *hld up: a towards rr* **9/1**

1m 50.24s (2.64) **Going Correction** +0.50s/f (Yiel) **8** Ran SP% **116.3**
Speed ratings (Par 105): **106,103,103,100,100 97,93,90**
CSF £18.29 CT £83.84 TOTE £8.70: £2.70, £1.10, £2.70; EX 22.60 Trifecta £225.80.
**Owner** Sheikh Hamdan bin Mohammed Al Maktoum **Bred** Palides Investments N V Inc **Trained** Middleham Moor, N Yorks

**FOCUS**
The winner made all in this fair handicap and is rated in line with last year's maiden win.

## 2235 COLIN HEPPLE - THE GAMBLER MEMORIAL H'CAP 1m 1f 207y
**4:30** (4:30) (Class 5) (0-70,71) 3-Y-O **£3,234** (£962; £481; £240) **Stalls** Low

Form RPR

11-3 **1** **Emerahldz (IRE)**[34] 1401 3-9-1 **65** ........ GeorgeChaloner(3) 3 72+
(Richard Fahey) *in rr: pushed along 3f out: rdn 2f out: styd on appr fnl f: drvn and kpt on gamely to ld last 100yds* **7/4**[1]

1 **2** ¾ **Barleycorn Lady (IRE)**[38] 1303 3-8-12 **62** ........ JasonHart(3) 2 67
(Mark Walford) *dwlt: hdwy to trck ldrs 4f out: rdn along 2f out: drvn to chal ent fnl f: ev ch tl no ex last 100yds* **7/2**[3]

63-4 **3** 1 **Stanarley Pic**[36] 1344 3-9-7 **68** ........ BenCurtis 8 72
(Alan Swinbank) *trckd ldrs: hdwy on outer to chse ldr 1/2-way: chal over 2f out and sn rdn: led over 1f out: drvn ins fnl f: hdd and no ex last 100yds* **5/2**[2]

5500 **4** nk **Eddiemaurice (IRE)**[14] 1847 3-9-4 **65** ........ RobbieFitzpatrick 6 68
(Richard Guest) *trckd ldrs: hdwy on outer over 2f out: rdn over 1f out: drvn and ev ch ent fnl f: one pce last 100yds* **7/1**

00-5 **5** 8 **Danzig In The Dark (IRE)**[20] 1645 3-8-11 **58** ........ DavidAllan 7 47
(Tim Easterby) *cl up: led after 2f: rdn along over 2f out: drvn and hdd over 1f out: sn wknd* **14/1**

0-40 **6** 1 ¾ **Tears And Rain (IRE)**[20] 1647 3-8-8 **55** ........ DuranFentiman 4 40
(Tim Easterby) *t.k.h: led 2f out: chsd ldrs: rdn along over 2f out: sn wknd* **25/1**

2m 14.96s (7.96) **Going Correction** +0.50s/f (Yiel) **6** Ran SP% **110.2**
Speed ratings (Par 99): **88,87,86,86,79 78**
CSF £7.87 CT £12.93 TOTE £2.50: £1.20, £4.00; EX 7.70 Trifecta £14.90.
**Owner** Mrs H Steel **Bred** D G Iceton **Trained** Musley Bank, N Yorks

**FOCUS**
They went a steady pace and there was not much separating the first four. It's hard to be confident about the form but the winner is progressive and the next two were unexposed.

## 2236 BEVERLEY DRIFTWOOD HORSE MAIDEN STKS 7f 100y
**5:00** (5:03) (Class 5) 3-Y-O **£3,234** (£962; £481; £240) **Stalls** Low

Form RPR

005- **1** **Jacbequick**[237] 6513 3-9-0 55 ........ JacobButterfield(5) 9 73
(Ollie Pears) *led 2f: cl up: rdn to chal 2f out: drvn over 1f out: kpt on to ld ins fnl f* **40/1**

30- **2** ¾ **Coin Broker (IRE)**[235] 6597 3-9-0 0 ........ DanielTudhope 7 66
(David O'Meara) *trckd ldrs: effrt wl over 1f out: sn rdn and styd on fnl f* **4/1**[3]

0- **3** 1 ¼ **Abbey Village (IRE)**[279] 5145 3-9-5 0 ........ DavidNolan 6 68
(Richard Fahey) *trckd ldrs: hdwy over 2f out: rdn over 1f out: kpt on fnl f: nrst fin* **11/4**[2]

3352 **4** ½ **Handwoven (IRE)**[8] 2013 3-9-5 70 ........ JoeFanning 4 67
(Mark Johnston) *cl up: led after 2f: rdn along 2f out: drvn over 1f out: hdd ins fnl f: one pce* **9/4**[1]

0- **5** 6 **Oscuro**[362] 2401 3-9-5 0 ........ DavidAllan 5 52
(Tim Easterby) *hld up towards rr: hdwy over 2f out: rdn wl over 1f out: n.d* **14/1**

45- **6** ¾ **Ofelia (IRE)**[294] 4610 3-9-0 0 ........ PaulPickard 1 45
(Brian Ellison) *in rr: effrt over 2f out: sn rdn and plugged on fnl f: n.d* **33/1**

03 **7** 2 ¼ **Dynamic Vision (IRE)**[14] 1831 3-9-5 0 ........ JackMitchell 3 44
(Roger Varian) *chsd ldrs: rdn along over 2f out: sn drvn and wknd* **11/4**[2]

00- **8** 9 **Major Rowan**[185] 7818 3-9-5 0 ........(b[1]) RoystonFfrench 8 22
(Bryan Smart) *a towards rr* **50/1**

0-0 **9** 21 **The Brockster**[63] 906 3-9-5 0 ........ GrahamLee 10
(Richard Ford) *wnt bdly lft s: in tch tl hung bdly lft and lost pl bnd at 1/2-way: sn bhd* **100/1**

1m 38.55s (4.75) **Going Correction** +0.50s/f (Yiel) **9** Ran SP% **119.1**
Speed ratings (Par 99): **92,91,89,89,82 81,78,68,44**
CSF £197.69 TOTE £18.10: £4.30, £2.10, £1.50; EX 110.20 Trifecta £750.40.
**Owner** Cherry Garth Racing **Bred** Russ Wake **Trained** Norton, N Yorks

**FOCUS**
There was a surprise result in this maiden. The time wasn't bad but the form is rated a little cautiously.

## 2237 BEVERLEY MIDDLE DISTANCE SERIES H'CAP 1m 4f 16y
**5:35** (5:35) (Class 6) (0-60,60) 3-Y-O **£2,264** (£673; £336; £168) **Stalls** Low

Form RPR

644- **1** **Dry Your Eyes (IRE)**[174] 7979 3-9-7 **60** ........ JoeFanning 1 73+
(Mark Johnston) *mde all: pushed along over 2f out: rdn clr over 1f out: readily* **5/1**[3]

-P01 **2** 5 **Sirpertan**[14] 1840 3-9-0 **56** ........ JasonHart(3) 2 59
(Mark Walford) *trckd ldng pair on inner: swtchd lft and effrt 2f out: sn rdn: drvn and edgd lft jst over 1f out: one pce* **2/1**[1]

04-0 **3** nk **Kashstaree**[24] 1588 3-8-9 **48** ........ GrahamGibbons 4 51
(David Barron) *hld up towards rr: hdwy 2f out: rdn and styng on whn hmpd jst over 1f out: kpt on u.p towards fin* **11/2**

-0-35 **4** 1 ¼ **Bentons Lad**[14] 1840 3-8-12 **51** ........ AndrewElliott 3 52
(George Moore) *trckd ldrs: effrt 2f out: sn rdn and kpt on one pce* **7/1**

0-42 **5** nk **Aldreth**[12] 1904 3-9-4 **57** ........ BarryMcHugh 9 58+
(Michael Easterby) *hld up in rr: hdwy over 2f out: rdn wl over 1f out: kpt on fnl f: nrst fin* **7/2**[2]

-036 **6** 1 **Casper Lee (IRE)**[19] 1661 3-8-9 **53** ........ JacobButterfield(5) 10 52
(Michael Herrington) *t.k.h: trckd wnr: effrt over 2f out: rdn along wl over 1f out: wknd ent fnl f* **16/1**

6-52 **7** *1 1/4* **Belle Peinture (FR)**[117] 198 3-8-6 **48** ow1............ GeorgeChaloner(3) 5 45
(Alan Lockwood) *trckd ldrs on inner: swtchd lft and effrt 2f out: sn rdn and wknd over 1f out* **16/1**
320 **8** *2 1/4* **Tortoise**[98] 480 3-8-4 **46**..............................(e1) BillyCray(3) 8 40
(Richard Guest) *hld up: a in rr* **33/1**
00-0 **9** *16* **Mystical Maze**[17] 1722 3-8-9 **48**.............................. PaulMulrennan 7 18
(Mark Brisbourne) *chsd ldrs: rdn along on outer 3f out: sn wknd* **33/1**
2m 52.87s (13.07) **Going Correction** +0.50s/f (Yiel) **9** Ran SP% **117.8**
Speed ratings (Par 97): **76,72,72,71,71 70,69,68,57**
CSF £15.74 CT £56.45 TOTE £6.30: £2.60, £1.20, £2.40; EX 18.90 Trifecta £109.80.
**Owner** D & G Mercer 1 **Bred** Floors Farming **Trained** Middleham Moor, N Yorks
**FOCUS**
There was a runaway front-running winner in this steadily-run handicap. She is rated back to her standout 2yo run.
T/Plt: £233.20 to a £1 stake. Pool of £71831.65 - 224.78 winning tickets. T/Qpdt: £15.10 to a £1 stake. Pool of £7320.87 - 357.30 winning tickets. JR

## 1827 CHANTILLY (R-H)
Tuesday, May 13
**OFFICIAL GOING: Polytrack: standard; turf: very soft**

### 2242a PRIX DE GUICHE (GROUP 3) (3YO COLTS) (TURF) 1m 1f
**1:20** (1:20) 3-Y-O **£33,333** (£13,333; £10,000; £6,666; £3,333)

RPR
**1** **Bodhi (FR)**[33] 3-9-2 0.............................. Jean-BernardEyquem 4 114+
(J-F Bernard, France) *trckd ldr on inner: shkn up and qcknd to ld ins fnl f: drvn clr: readily* **14/5**[2]
**2** *3* **Army Bulletin (IRE)**[21] 1640 3-9-2 0.............................. MaximeGuyon 2 108+
(A Fabre, France) *settled in rr: shkn up and swtchd outside over 1 1/2f out: styd on ins fnl f: tk 2nd cl home: nvr on terms w wnr* **17/10**[1]
**3** *1/2* **Calling Out (FR)**[18] 3-9-2 0.............................. AntoineHamelin 1 107
(J-P Gauvin, France) *led: rdn and hdd ins fnl f: kpt on at one pce: lost 2nd cl home* **68/10**
**4** *2* **Monoceros (USA)**[22] 3-9-2 0.............................. StephanePasquier 3 103
(P Bary, France) *disp 4th on inner: pushed along and nt qckn over 1 1/2f out: hrd rdn 1f out: kpt on on fnl f: nvr in contention* **59/10**
**5** *3* **No Mood**[19] 3-9-2 0.............................. OlivierPeslier 5 96
(C Laffon-Parias, France) *t.k.h: disp 4th on outer: lost pl 1 1/2f out: sn btn* **7/2**[3]
**6** *1* **Kenbest (FR)**[10] 3-9-2 0.............................. FabriceVeron 6 94
(H-A Pantall, France) *trckd ldr on outer: rowed along 2f out: wknd appr fnl f* **119/10**
1m 57.06s (5.96) **6** Ran SP% **120.6**
WIN (incl. 1 euro stake): 3.80. PLACES: 1.90, 1.70. SF: 11.30.
**Owner** Steeve Berland **Bred** S Berland & C Berland **Trained** France

## JAGERSRO (R-H)
Tuesday, May 13
**OFFICIAL GOING: Dirt: standard**

### 2244a LANWADES STUD JAGERSRO SPRINT (LISTED RACE) (DIRT) 6f (D)
**7:40** (7:40) 3-Y-O+ **£18,761** (£9,380; £4,502; £3,001; £1,876)

RPR
**1** **Let'sgoforit (IRE)**[229] 6-9-6.............................. CarlosLopez 3
(Bodil Hallencreutz, Sweden) **31/20**[1]
**1** *dht* **Over The Ocean (USA)**[222] 4-9-6.............................. RafaelSchistl 2
(Niels Petersen, Norway) **43/20**[2]
**3** *2* **Sir Freddie (USA)**[371] 2146 5-9-6.............................. ValmirDeAzeredo 9
(Fredrik Reuterskiold, Sweden) **152/10**
**4** *1* **Ikc Dragon Heart (USA)**[261] 4-9-6.............................. ShaneKarlsson 7
(Johan Reuterskiold, Sweden) **237/10**
**5** *hd* **Alcohuaz (CHI)**[229] 9-9-6.............................. ElioneChaves 8
(Lennart Reuterskiold Jr, Sweden) **98/10**[3]
**6** *3* **Beat Baby (IRE)**[45] 1179 7-9-6.............................. Per-AndersGraberg 1
(Niels Petersen, Norway) **15/1**
**7** *5* **Spykes Bay (USA)**[312] 4018 5-9-6.............................. JacobJohansen 6
(Vanja Sandrup, Sweden) **225/10**
**8** *nse* **Liber**[607] 6162 4-9-6.............................. OliverWilson 5
(Sir Mark Prescott Bt) **179/10**
1m 11.1s (71.10) **8** Ran SP% **106.2**
PARI-MUTUEL (all including 1sek stake): WIN 3.16; PLACE 3.05, 1.64, 4.42; SF 15.97.
**Owner** Atle Walgren & Lars Blyverket **Bred** Sun Valley Farm **Trained** Norway
**Owner** Bodil Hallencreutz & Barbro L Wehtje **Bred** Castlemartin Sky & Skymarc Farm **Trained** Sweden

### 2245a PRAMMS MEMORIAL (GROUP 3) (4YO+) (DIRT) 1m 143y(D)
**8:05** (12:00) 4-Y-O+ **£37,523** (£18,761; £9,005; £6,003; £3,752)

RPR
**1** **Avon Pearl**[66] 899 5-9-4 0..............................(b) JacobJohansen 10 105
(Rune Haugen, Norway) *towards rr on outer: hdwy to press two ldrs 2f out: rdn to ld appr fnl f: drvn out* **61/10**[3]
**2** *1 3/4* **Hurricane Red (IRE)**[240] 6453 4-9-4 0.............................. ElioneChaves 1 101
(Lennart Reuterskiold Jr, Sweden) *chsd ldng quartet: pushed along and outpcd 2 1/2f out: rallying whn checked and jockey stopped riding 2f out: hdwy on outside under 1 1/2f out: r.o u.p fnl f: nt rch wnr* **1/1**[1]
**3** *1 3/4* **Energia Dust (BRZ)**[436] 6-9-4 0.............................. ValmirDeAzeredo 2 97
(Fabricio Borges, Sweden) *disp ld on rail: led over 2f out: sn rdn: hdd appr fnl f: no ex u.p* **104/10**
**4** *1/2* **Funinthesand (IRE)**[23] 5-9-4 0.............................. CarlosLopez 7 96
(Wido Neuroth, Norway) *disp ld on outside: rdn and chsd ldr over 2f out: outpcd by front 2 appr fnl f: one pce u.p last 150yds* **208/10**
**5** *nk* **Plantagenet (SPA)**[73] 807 7-9-4 0.............................. Per-AndersGraberg 9 96
(Niels Petersen, Norway) *disp last on outer: in rr and rdn over 2 1/2f out: hdwy on outside to chse ldrs fnl bnd: one pce fr over 1f out* **19/5**[2]
**6** *1 1/2* **Berling (IRE)**[229] 6784 7-9-4 0.............................. OliverWilson 6 92
(Jessica Long, Sweden) *trckd ldng trio: scrubbed along over 1 1/2f out: btn whn squeezed out appr fnl f* **225/10**

**7** *2 1/2* **Global Thrill**[30] 1478 5-9-4 0.............................. MircoDemuro 8 87
(J Hirschberger, Germany) *disp last on inner hdwy 1/2-way: rdn and wknd fr 1 1/2f out* **101/10**
**8** *1/2* **Copper Canyon**[371] 2146 6-9-4 0.............................. ShaneKarlsson 3 86
(Vanja Sandrup, Sweden) *chsd ldng quartet: lost pl 1/2-way: sn btn* **39/1**
**9** *6* **Silver Ocean (USA)**[73] 809 6-9-4 0.............................. RafaelSchistl 5 72
(Niels Petersen, Norway) *disp ld between horses: scrubbed along and lost pl 2f out: sn wl btn* **97/10**
**10** *3/4* **Noble Citizen (USA)**[25] 1558 9-9-4 0..............................(b) MartinLane 4 71
(David Simcock) *towards rr on inner: pushed along to hold pl 2 1/2f out: sn rdn and no imp: wknd fnl 1 1/2f* **233/10**
1m 45.2s (105.20) **10** Ran SP% **127.5**
PARI-MUTUEL (all including 1sek stake): WIN 7.09; PLACE 1.76, 1.17, 1.94; SF 26.53.
**Owner** Jostein Jorgensen **Bred** Park Farm Racing **Trained** Norway

## 1909 CHEPSTOW (L-H)
Wednesday, May 14
**OFFICIAL GOING: Soft (good to soft in places; 4.7)**
Wind: slight against Weather: sunny spells

### 2246 32RED MAIDEN AUCTION STKS 5f 16y
**5:25** (5:26) (Class 5) 2-Y-O **£3,881** (£1,155; £577; £288) **Stalls** Centre

Form RPR
52 **1** **Be Bold**[25] 1575 2-9-0 0.............................. PatDobbs 4 82+
(Richard Hannon) *broke wl: mde all: pushed clr fnl f: easily* **1/3**[1]
0 **2** *4* **Cornwallville (IRE)**[46] 1161 2-8-12 0.............................. JohnFahy 5 63
(J S Moore) *s.i.s: rdn along to chse ldrs after 1f: drvn and wnt 2nd 1/2-way: outpcd by wnr fnl f* **7/1**[2]
46 **3** *3/4* **Chetan**[4] 2173 2-8-11 0.............................. DavidProbert 2 59
(Milton Bradley) *pressed ldr tl relegated to 3rd 1/2-way: kpt on same pce after* **8/1**[3]
**4** *5* **Go White Lightning (IRE)** 2-8-8 0.............................. MartinLane 1 38
(David Evans) *s.s: sn rdn along and outpcd in rr: modest late prog* **10/1**
**5** *10* **Fly Grazer (IRE)** 2-8-6 0.............................. LiamJones 3
(J S Moore) *chsd ldrs 1f: sn rdn along and outpcd in rr* **20/1**
1m 2.84s (3.54) **Going Correction** +0.45s/f (Yiel) **5** Ran SP% **112.5**
Speed ratings (Par 93): **89,82,81,73,57**
CSF £3.49 TOTE £1.20: £1.02, £4.70; EX 2.90 Trifecta £8.30.
**Owner** Mrs C O'Gorman & K T Ivory **Bred** Simon Balding **Trained** East Everleigh, Wilts
**FOCUS**
Jockeys reported the ground to be on the slow side of good. Little depth to this maiden.

### 2247 32RED.COM H'CAP 1m 4f 23y
**5:55** (5:57) (Class 6) (0-65,63) 3-Y-O **£1,940** (£577; £288; £144) **Stalls** Low

Form RPR
0-53 **1** **Kashmiri Sunset**[15] 1847 3-9-7 **63**.............................. ChrisCatlin 6 79+
(Ed de Giles) *hld up in last: hdwy to chse ldrs over 3f out: led over 1f out: idled ins fnl f: drvn out to hold on* **2/1**[2]
0-22 **2** *1/2* **Bold Runner**[16] 1792 3-9-6 **62**.............................. JohnFahy 2 76
(Sean Curran) *led 2f: trckd ldr to 1/2-way: chsd ldrs after: hanging lft and rdn fnl 4f: chsd wnr 1f out: r.o u.p* **7/2**[3]
00-1 **3** *5* **Gimme Five**[16] 1792 3-9-2 **58**.............................. FergusSweeney 7 64
(Alan King) *trckd ldr tl led after 2f: pushed along and hdd 3f out: one pce fnl 2f* **7/4**[1]
3 **4** *4 1/2* **San Quentin (IRE)**[9] 2028 3-8-7 **49**.............................. LukeMorris 3 48
(Tony Carroll) *trckd ldrs tl wnt 2nd 1/2-way: led 3f out and rdn along: hdd over 1f out: wknd fnl f* **14/1**
0-30 **5** *31* **Kaizen Factor**[16] 1792 3-8-13 **55**..............................(p) SeanLevey 4
(Rod Millman) *chsd ldrs: rdn and outpcd by ldrs whn hmpd over 3f out: sn bhd: t.o* **14/1**
2m 50.97s (11.97) **Going Correction** +0.60s/f (Yiel) **5** Ran SP% **105.3**
Speed ratings (Par 97): **84,83,80,77,56**
CSF £8.37 TOTE £2.00: £1.30, £2.80; EX 8.10 Trifecta £10.50.
**Owner** Jennifer & Alex Viall **Bred** K F Fallon **Trained** Ledbury, H'fords
■ Vera Lou was withdrawn. Price at time of withdrawal 25/1. Rule 4 does not apply.
■ Stewards' Enquiry : John Fahy eight-day ban: excessive use & careless riding (May 28-June 4)
**FOCUS**
A low-grade handicap, but it was dominated by the right horses. The winner was value for a bit extra.

### 2248 32RED H'CAP 1m 2f 36y
**6:25** (6:25) (Class 5) (0-75,75) 4-Y-O+ **£3,234** (£962; £481; £240) **Stalls** Low

Form RPR
00-2 **1** **Bobbyscot (IRE)**[9] 2033 7-9-4 **72**.............................. RobertHavlin 9 82
(Mark Hoad) *s.s: towards rr: hdwy 3f out: rdn 2f out: r.o u.p to ld fnl 50yds* **6/1**[2]
3630 **2** *1/2* **First Post (IRE)**[14] 1871 7-9-7 **75**.............................. HarryBentley 1 84
(Derek Haydn Jones) *chsd ldrs: rdn to ld over 2f out: r.o: hdd fnl 50yds* **6/1**[2]
6-1 **3** *2* **Stockhill Diva**[18] 1729 4-8-9 **63**.............................. LiamKeniry 7 68
(Brendan Powell) *hld up in tch: smooth hdwy 3f out: rdn to chse ldr over 1f out: one pce fnl f* **9/4**[1]
0-50 **4** *3 1/2* **Sheila's Buddy**[14] 1871 5-9-7 **75**.............................. JohnFahy 8 74
(J S Moore) *dwlt: in rr tl hdwy over 3f out: rdn 2f out: one pce* **7/1**[3]
1124 **5** *3 1/4* **Thane Of Cawdor (IRE)**[16] 1798 5-8-5 **62**.............................. OisinMurphy(3) 10 54
(Joseph Tuite) *trckd ldr: drvn over 2f out: sn ev ch: wknd appr fnl f* **11/1**
-564 **6** *1 1/4* **Angus Glens**[16] 1791 4-9-3 **71**..............................(v1) LukeMorris 4 61
(David Dennis) *t.k.h in midfield: drvn over 3f out: grad wknd* **7/1**[3]
000- **7** *1* **April Ciel**[152] 8270 5-8-11 **65**.............................. LiamJones 2 53
(Ronald Harris) *led tl over 2f out: wknd over 1f out* **16/1**
60-0 **8** *2* **Mombasa**[33] 1418 4-8-12 **66**.............................. DavidProbert 3 50
(Harry Dunlop) *chsd ldrs: rdn over 2f out: sn wknd* **16/1**
151- **9** *21* **Let Me In (IRE)**[194] 7666 4-8-11 **65**..............................(b1) MartinLane 5 9
(Bernard Llewellyn) *hld up: rdn over 4f out: wknd over 2f out: t.o* **12/1**
2m 15.44s (4.84) **Going Correction** +0.60s/f (Yiel) **9** Ran SP% **112.1**
Speed ratings (Par 103): **104,103,102,99,96 95,94,93,76**
CSF £40.16 CT £103.53 TOTE £9.10: £2.40, £2.30, £1.30; EX 40.50 Trifecta £227.70.
**Owner** Ian Tarbox **Bred** P Newman & Dr M Klay **Trained** Lewes, E Sussex

**FOCUS**
An ordinary handicap that was run at just an ordinary gallop. The winner is rated in line with last year's best form.

## 2249 32RED.COM CLASSIFIED STKS 6f 16y
6:55 (6:55) (Class 6) 3-Y-O £1,940 (£577; £288; £144) Stalls Centre

Form RPR
000- 1 **Comanchero (IRE)**[175] 7971 3-8-11 65 OisinMurphy(3) 1 61+
(Andrew Balding) *chsd ldrs: shkn up to ld over 2f out: drvn out to hold on ins fnl f* 13/8[2]
2350 2 hd **Bonjour Steve**[15] 1851 3-9-0 62 LukeMorris 5 60
(Richard Price) *s.i.s: sn trcking ldrs: rdn 1/2-way: hung lft over 1f out: r.o u.p ins fnl f: jst hld* 6/4[1]
0-65 3 ½ **Zafraaj**[12] 1914 3-9-0 57 DavidProbert 2 58
(Ronald Harris) *narrow ld tl rdn and hdd over 2f out: kpt on same pce u.p* 7/1[3]
00-2 4 1 **Yankee Red**[22] 1634 3-9-0 65 SteveDrowne 3 55
(John Best) *hld up in last: pushed along to cl 1/2-way: chsd ldrs over 1f out: no ex ins fnl f* 8/1
-404 5 6 **Picanight**[14] 1890 3-8-11 43 (b) MichaelJMMurphy(3) 4 36
(Eve Johnson Houghton) *cl up: rdn over 2f out: sn outpcd and lost tch* 14/1
1m 15.1s (3.10) **Going Correction** +0.45s/f (Yiel) 5 Ran SP% 108.4
Speed ratings (Par 97): **97,96,96,94,86**
CSF £4.27 TOTE £2.60: £1.50, £1.20; EX 3.10 Trifecta £13.70.
**Owner** Kennet Valley Thoroughbreds VII **Bred** Yeomanstown Stud **Trained** Kingsclere, Hants
■ Stewards' Enquiry : Luke Morris two-day ban: use of whip (28-29 May)

**FOCUS**
Weak form, with the first four separated by under 2l. The winner was entitled to take this.

## 2250 32REDPOKER.COM H'CAP 6f 16y
7:25 (7:28) (Class 5) (0-70,69) 4-Y-O+ £3,234 (£962; £481; £240) Stalls Centre

Form RPR
0-03 1 **Pettochside**[16] 1789 5-9-4 66 PatDobbs 12 78
(Chris Gordon) *hld up: rdn and hdwy 2f out: r.o to ld fnl 100yds* 11/2[3]
4461 2 ¾ **Catalinas Diamond (IRE)**[9] 2029 6-8-0 55 oh1 (t) RobJFitzpatrick(7) 10 65
(Pat Murphy) *towards rr: hdwy over 2f out: sn edgd rt: ev ch 1f out tl no ex nr fin* 8/1
-000 3 nk **New Decade**[32] 1448 5-9-0 65 (t) OisinMurphy(3) 1 74
(Milton Bradley) *chsd ldrs on outside: led 2f out: edgd rt u.p: hdd and no ex fnl 100yds* 25/1
2035 4 3½ **One Last Dream**[10] 1986 5-8-8 56 (b) DavidProbert 5 53
(Ron Hodges) *chsd ldrs: rdn over 2f out: one pce* 8/1
6652 5 ½ **Ostralegus**[19] 1689 4-8-12 63 MichaelJMMurphy(3) 11 59
(John Gallagher) *taken to post early: cl up tl led narrowly over 3f out: hdd 2f out: one pce fnl f* 4/1[2]
6642 6 2¾ **Solemn**[12] 1912 9-9-7 69 (v) LukeMorris 8 56
(Milton Bradley) *in tch: rdn and outpcd by ldrs over 2f out: styd on ins fnl f* 10/1
1005 7 ¾ **All Right Now**[14] 1892 7-8-7 55 oh1 (tp) MartinDwyer 6 40
(Tony Newcombe) *chsd ldrs: rdn over 2f out: wknd over 1f out* 16/1
-006 8 ½ **Ficelle (IRE)**[16] 1787 5-8-4 55 oh6 (p) MatthewCosham(3) 2 38
(Nikki Evans) *prom: rdn 3f out: wknd over 1f out* 33/1
5-00 9 ¾ **Verus Delicia (IRE)**[17] 1758 5-9-0 62 StephenCraine 4 43
(Daniel Mark Loughnane) *taken to post early: s.v.s: bhd: clsd on pack 1/2-way: rdn and hung lft over 1f out: nvr nr ldrs* 12/1
05-3 10 1¼ **Dream Catcher (FR)**[20] 1678 6-9-6 68 FergusSweeney 9 45
(Henry Candy) *led over 2f: rdn and wknd over 2f out* 3/1[1]
2330 11 hd **Thorpe Bay**[15] 1843 5-9-3 65 AndrewMullen 7 41
(Michael Appleby) *uns rdr and rn loose gng to post: s.s: sn in tch: rdn 1/2-way: wknd over 1f out* 12/1
1m 14.73s (2.73) **Going Correction** +0.45s/f (Yiel) 11 Ran SP% 119.8
Speed ratings (Par 103): **99,98,97,92,92 88,87,86,85,84 84**
CSF £50.11 CT £1042.58 TOTE £6.10: £2.20, £1.90, £6.60; EX 64.20 Trifecta £1453.50.
**Owner** David Henery **Bred** New Hall Stud **Trained** Morestead, Hants
■ Stewards' Enquiry : Pat Dobbs two-day ban: use of whip (28-29 May)

**FOCUS**
The first three drew a little way clear and the form looks reasonable for the level. The winner built on his Bath run.

## 2251 32RED ON THE APP STORE H'CAP 1m 14y
7:55 (7:57) (Class 5) (0-75,73) 4-Y-O+ £3,234 (£962; £481; £240) Stalls Centre

Form RPR
60-5 1 **Sweet Martoni**[15] 1846 4-8-9 64 OisinMurphy(3) 2 73
(William Knight) *led 3f: styd cl up tl led again 2f out: sn edgd rt u.p: r.o wl* 4/1[2]
040- 2 1¼ **Harwoods Star (IRE)**[168] 8072 4-8-9 61 RobertHavlin 4 67
(Amanda Perrett) *cl up: led after 3f to 2f out: rdn and kpt on wl* 12/1
06-0 3 nk **Granell (IRE)**[15] 1845 4-9-4 70 (p) JimmyFortune 10 75
(Brian Meehan) *towards rr: hdwy u.p 3f out: r.o ins fnl f* 7/1
00-0 4 2¼ **Tenbridge**[15] 1846 5-8-6 61 (v) RosieJessop(3) 11 61
(Derek Haydn Jones) *taken to post early: hld up in rr: hdwy over 3f out: pushed along 2f out: no ex fnl f* 6/1[3]
10-0 5 2 **Peak Storm**[98] 493 5-9-7 73 LukeMorris 6 69
(John O'Shea) *midfield: rdn and outpcd over 3f out: styd on again ins fnl f* 20/1
410- 6 1½ **Falcon's Reign (FR)**[186] 7824 5-9-0 73 AlistairRawlinson(7) 5 65
(Michael Appleby) *in tch: rdn over 2f out: one pce* 3/1[1]
00-0 7 3 **Secret Beau**[65] 294 4-9-5 71 LiamJones 7 56
(John Spearing) *midfield: rdn over 3f out: wknd over 1f out* 16/1
3354 8 1¾ **Raging Bear (USA)**[15] 1845 4-8-9 66 (p) DavidKenny(5) 3 47
(James Evans) *midfield: rdn over 2f out: grad wknd* 7/1
-064 9 3½ **Our Ivor**[14] 1886 5-9-4 70 AndrewMullen 8 43
(Michael Appleby) *chsd ldrs: rdn over 3f out: wknd over 2f out* 10/1
00-0 10 hd **Federal Blue (USA)**[16] 1789 4-9-4 70 DavidProbert 1 43
(Milton Bradley) *chsd ldrs: rdn over 3f out: sn wknd* 33/1
6-45 11 1¼ **Viva Vettori**[15] 1845 10-8-7 62 CharlesBishop(3) 9 32
(Brian Forsey) *dwlt: t.k.h in rr: rdn 3f out: no hdwy* 20/1
1m 38.98s (2.78) **Going Correction** +0.45s/f (Yiel) 11 Ran SP% 119.4
Speed ratings (Par 103): **104,102,102,100,98 96,93,91,88,88 87**
CSF £50.65 CT £337.95 TOTE £5.40: £1.20, £3.30, £3.00; EX 54.80 Trifecta £929.20.
**Owner** Lavell Willis **Bred** Mrs M Lavell **Trained** Patching, W Sussex

**FOCUS**
The 4yos dominated this handicap, which was run at a fair gallop. The front pair were always up there and the winner is rated to her best.

## 2252 32RED FREE £10 BONUS H'CAP 2m 49y
8:25 (8:25) (Class 6) (0-60,59) 4-Y-O+ £1,940 (£577; £288; £144) Stalls Low

Form RPR
6-04 1 **Taste The Wine (IRE)**[39] 460 8-9-6 58 (t) LukeMorris 7 68
(Bernard Llewellyn) *towards rr: rdn 4f out: hdwy 3f out: styd on wl fnl f to ld last strides* 14/1
00-3 2 hd **Noor Al Haya (IRE)**[12] 1916 4-8-8 56 CharlotteJenner(7) 11 65
(Mark Usher) *hld up in rr: clsd 1/2-way: chal on bit 2f out: rdn to take narrow ld ins fnl f: hdd last strides* 6/1[2]
-351 3 nk **Lac Sacre (FR)**[12] 1916 5-8-10 48 (bt) DavidProbert 10 57
(John Flint) *hld up in rr: stdy hdwy 4f out: led 2f out: sn rdn and jnd: hdd and nt qckn ins fnl f* 6/4[1]
/14- 4 3¼ **Princesse Fleur**[229] 5977 6-8-12 53 WilliamTwiston-Davies(3) 8 58
(Michael Scudamore) *midfield: hdwy 5f out: led narrowly 3f out: hdd 2f out: one pce* 8/1
05-1 5 10 **Captain Sharpe**[12] 1915 6-9-7 59 (t) MartinLane 6 52
(Bernard Llewellyn) *chsd ldrs: rdn 4f out: wknd over 1f out* 7/1[3]
363- 6 7 **Karl Marx (IRE)**[21] 2924 4-8-4 48 ow2 (b) OisinMurphy(3) 1 33
(Mark Gillard) *chsd ldr: led 4f out to 3f out: sn wknd* 14/1
352- 7 2 **Glens Wobbly**[226] 6895 6-8-8 46 FergusSweeney 13 28
(Jonathan Geake) *in rr: hdwy into midfield after 3f: rdn over 3f out: sn wknd* 16/1
60-0 8 1½ **Superciliary**[28] 380 5-9-6 58 PatDobbs 12 39
(Chris Gordon) *chsd ldrs rdn 3f out: wknd over 2f out* 16/1
-050 9 8 **Chief Executive (IRE)**[20] 1675 4-8-6 47 AndrewMullen 9 18
(Mandy Rowland) *a towards rr: rdn 4f out: wknd 3f out* 33/1
40-5 10 20 **Sweeping Rock (IRE)**[14] 1874 4-9-0 55 (t) HarryBentley 3 2
(Marcus Tregoning) *chsd ldrs tl rdn and wknd 4f out: t.o* 8/1
25/4 11 29 **Host The Band**[14] 1891 10-9-0 52 PatCosgrave 5
(Tony Newcombe) *t.k.h: chsd ldrs 2f: midfield after tl drvn and wknd over 4f out: t.o* 50/1
60/0 12 6 **Scripturist**[12] 1916 5-8-8 51 (b) DanielMuscutt(5) 4
(Bernard Llewellyn) *midfield tl dropped in rr 1/2-way: lost tch 6f out: t.o* 40/1
60/5 13 6 **Hector's House**[12] 1915 8-8-9 50 (p) MatthewCosham(3) 2
(Nikki Evans) *led: clr after 2f tl after 7f: rdn and hdd 4f out: wknd qckly: t.o* 66/1
3m 48.3s (9.40) **Going Correction** +0.60s/f (Yiel)
**WFA** 4 from 5yo+ 3lb 13 Ran SP% 122.9
Speed ratings (Par 101): **100,99,99,98,93 89,88,87,83,73 59,56,53**
CSF £97.10 CT £205.82 TOTE £13.70: £5.30, £2.50, £1.10; EX 96.10 Trifecta £403.10.
**Owner** Alan J Williams **Bred** Trevor Reilly **Trained** Fochriw, Caerphilly

**FOCUS**
Run at a fair gallop, the front three pulled away close home in this low-grade staying handicap. The form is taken at face value.
T/Plt: £32.50 to a £1 stake. Pool of £58710.19 - 1315.18 winning tickets. T/Qpdt: £12.70 to a £1 stake. Pool of £5697.15 - 329.95 winning tickets. RL

# YORK (L-H)
Wednesday, May 14

**OFFICIAL GOING: Soft (good to soft in places) changing to good to soft (soft in places) after race 4 (3.15)**
Wind: almost nil Weather: fine and sunny, warm

## 2253 STANJAMES.COM STKS (H'CAP) 1m 2f 88y
1:45 (1:45) (Class 2) (0-100,100) 4-Y-O+ £16,172 (£4,812; £2,405; £1,202) Stalls Low

Form RPR
1 1 **Clever Cookie**[19] 1691 6-8-9 88 GrahamLee 17 99+
(Peter Niven) *swtchd lft after s: hld up in rr: hdwy over 2f out: nt clr run over 1f out: styd on wl to ld towards fin* 7/1[2]
0051 2 ¾ **Tres Coronas (IRE)**[6] 2085 7-9-7 100 6ex GrahamGibbons 16 108
(David Barron) *mid-div: hdwy over 3f out: led over 1f out: hdd and no ex nr fin* 11/1
0-04 3 ¾ **Awake My Soul (IRE)**[18] 1736 5-8-12 91 DanielTudhope 8 98+
(David O'Meara) *trckd ldrs: upsides over 1f out: no ex last 75yds* 11/1
01-0 4 2½ **Pasaka Boy**[21] 1653 4-8-7 86 RichardKingscote 14 88
(Jonathan Portman) *chsd ldrs: drvn over 2f out: kpt on one pce over 1f out* 16/1
2/1- 5 hd **Rye House (IRE)**[362] 2431 5-9-5 98 RyanMoore 5 99+
(Sir Michael Stoute) *lw: mid-div: effrt over 2f out: n.m.r over 1f out: kpt on fnl f* 4/1[1]
10-0 6 hd **Silvery Moon (IRE)**[46] 1164 7-8-11 90 ow1 RobertWinston 7 91
(Tim Easterby) *lw: mid-div: hdwy over 2f out: kpt on same pce appr fnl f* 20/1
7 1½ **Tahira (GER)**[227] 4-9-5 98 PhillipMakin 2 98
(John Quinn) *mid-div: stdy hdwy over 2f out: keeping on whn nt clr run ins fnl f* 25/1
10-0 8 nk **Spirit Of The Law (IRE)**[18] 1715 5-8-7 86 oh1 PatrickMathers 11 84
(Richard Fahey) *prom: drvn over 3f out: sn w ldrs: wknd over 1f out* 20/1
130- 9 2 **Cashpoint**[186] 7823 9-8-7 86 oh2 SilvestreDeSousa 15 80
(Ian Williams) *prom: drvn over 3f out: chsng ldrs over 1f out: sn fdd* 33/1
-621 10 nk **Maven**[14] 1882 6-8-3 89 RachelRichardson(7) 12 82
(Tim Easterby) *chsd ldrs: wknd fnl f* 16/1
510- 11 ½ **Lahaag**[186] 7823 5-9-7 100 PaulHanagan 4 92
(John Gosden) *lw: hld up in rr: kpt on fnl 2f: nvr on terms* 8/1[3]
0-04 12 ½ **Hi There (IRE)**[21] 1653 5-9-0 98 SammyJoBell(5) 3 89
(Richard Fahey) *in rr: hdwy over 2f out: wknd appr fnl f* 10/1
-004 13 1¾ **Global Village (IRE)**[18] 1715 9-8-10 89 DaleSwift 1 77
(Brian Ellison) *s.i.s: sme hdwy over 3f out: wknd 2f out* 16/1
-410 14 2 **Sky Khan**[64] 887 5-8-5 87 (p) IanBrennan(3) 18 71
(John Wainwright) *trckd ldrs: effrt over 2f out: sn wknd* 40/1
0610 15 nk **Ansaab**[18] 1715 6-8-8 87 (t) BenCurtis 9 71
(Alan McCabe) *chsd ldr: led over 2f out: hdd over 1f out: sn lost pl* 33/1
R6-6 16 12 **King's Warrior (FR)**[21] 1653 7-8-9 93 ShelleyBirkett(5) 13 54
(Tom George) *s.s: a in rr: eased whn bhd fnl f* 20/1
00-3 17 2¼ **Storm King**[18] 1715 5-8-10 92 OisinMurphy(3) 10 49
(David C Griffiths) *led: hdd over 2f out: sn wknd: eased ins fnl f* 16/1

133- **18** *4 ½* **Grandorio (IRE)**237 6551 4-8-12 **91**............................ RichardHughes 6 39
(David O'Meara) *in rr: bhd whn eased fnl f* **11/1**

2m 9.51s (-2.99) **Going Correction** -0.05s/f (Good) **18** Ran SP% **127.7**
Speed ratings (Par 109): **109,108,107,105,105 105,104,104,102,102 101,101,100,98,98 88,86,83**
CSF £76.90 CT £865.95 TOTE £6.40: £2.10, £2.60, £3.60, £6.00; EX 83.90 Trifecta £2511.10 Part won. Pool of £3348.15 - 0.87 winning units..
**Owner** Francis Green Racing Ltd **Bred** Mrs J A Niven **Trained** Barton-le-Street, N Yorks

**FOCUS**
Running rail on inside line and distances on Round course reduced by 24yds. It was dry overnight but the going was still given as soft, good to soft in places. The time of the first seemed to suggest it was riding on the soft side of good, though, and jockeys reported it to be good to soft and tacky. Often a strong handicap and they went a good gallop. Solid form, with the winner capable of better.

## 2254 INFINITY TYRES STKS (H'CAP) 6f
**2:15** (2:17) (Class 2) (0-105,104) 4-Y-0+**£16,172** (£4,812; £2,405; £1,202) **Stalls** High

Form RPR

3-10 **1** **Aetna**28 1506 4-8-9 **92**.............................................. GrahamGibbons 20 106
(Michael Easterby) *hld up towards rr: stdy hdwy 2f out: chsd ldrs ent fnl f: n.m.r and sn swtchd rt: rdn to ld last 100yds: sn edgd lft and kpt on strly* **7/1**1

50-2 **2** *1 ¼* **Baccarat (IRE)**32 1443 5-9-3 **103**............................ GeorgeChaloner(3) 5 113
(Richard Fahey) *lw: trckd ldrs: hdwy and cl up over 2f out: rdn to ld wl over 1f out: drvn ent fnl f: hdd and no ex last 100yds* **7/1**1

00-5 **3** *nk* **Blaine**28 1506 4-8-12 **95**............................................. RichardHughes 19 104
(Kevin Ryan) *prom: effrt and cl up 2f out: rdn over 1f out: ev ch tl drvn and hld whn sltly hmpd wl ins fnl f* **9/1**3

-011 **4** *1* **Fast Shot**18 1734 6-8-7 **97**......................... RachelRichardson(7) 14 103+
(Tim Easterby) *midfield: hdwy over 2f out: rdn to chse ldrs whn n.m.r jst over 1f out: swtchd rt and kpt on fnl f* **14/1**

00-6 **5** *1 ¼* **Royal Rascal**30 1484 4-8-12 **95**................................... DavidAllan 12 97
(Tim Easterby) *chsd ldrs: rdn along 2f out: drvn and edgd lft jst over 1f out: kpt on same pce fnl f* **14/1**

06-3 **6** *¾* **Jamaican Bolt (IRE)**39 1305 6-8-10 **93**............... SilvestreDeSousa 9 92
(Geoffrey Oldroyd) *trckd ldrs: effrt over 2f out: rdn and ev ch over 1f out: edgd lft and one pce fnl f* **11/1**

-560 **7** *nse* **Regal Parade**18 1719 10-8-9 **92**..............................(t) FrederikTylicki 18 91
(Milton Bradley) *in tch on outer: hdwy to chse ldrs 2f out: rdn over 1f out: one pce fnl f* **25/1**

0-05 **8** *½* **Secret Witness**5 2110 8-8-11 **94**...........................(b) JamesDoyle 11 92
(Ronald Harris) *towards rr: hdwy 2f out: rdn over 1f out: kpt on fnl f* **16/1**

05-0 **9** *½* **Out Do**10 1975 5-8-8 **91**.............................................. KierenFallon 6 87+
(David O'Meara) *lw: midfield: hdwy over 2f out: effrt whn n.m.r and sltly hmpd over 1f out: one pce after* **16/1**

442- **10** *nk* **Picture Dealer**168 8064 5-8-6 **92**............................ SimonPearce(3) 17 87
(Lydia Pearce) *towards rr: hdwy wl over 1f out: sn rdn and kpt on fnl f: nrst fin* **20/1**

00-3 **11** *1* **Royal Rock**20 1679 10-9-5 **102**.................................... GeorgeBaker 15 94
(Chris Wall) *s.i.s: a towards rr* **40/1**

01-0 **12** *nk* **Valbchek (IRE)**26 1557 5-9-7 **104**..............................(b) RyanMoore 1 95
(Jeremy Noseda) *towards rr far side: hdwy to trck ldrs 1/2-way: rdn wl over 1f out: wknd appr fnl f* **20/1**

0032 **13** *hd* **Yeeoow (IRE)**10 1975 5-8-2 **90**.................................. JoeyHaynes(5) 8 80
(K R Burke) *chsd ldrs: pushed along 2f out: rdn and edgd lft over 1f out: sn wknd* **7/1**1

3-50 **14** *1 ¼* **Lancelot Du Lac (ITY)**26 1557 4-9-6 **103**...................... JimCrowley 16 89
(Dean Ivory) *a towards rr* **8/1**2

3-00 **15** *¾* **Colonel Mak**18 1734 7-8-6 **92**..................................... JasonHart(3) 10 76
(David Barron) *slt ld: hdd over 2f out and sn rdn along and grad wknd* **33/1**

0-40 **16** *5* **El Viento (FR)**18 1734 6-8-10 **93**..........................(v) PaulHanagan 4 61
(Richard Fahey) *cl up: led over 2f out: sn rdn and hdd wl over 1f out: sn wknd* **33/1**

200- **17** *2 ¼* **Whozthecat (IRE)**266 5651 7-8-9 **99**......................... LukeLeadbitter(7) 2 60
(Declan Carroll) *cl up on wd outside: disp ld 1/2-way: sn rdn along and wknd fnl 2f* **40/1**

523- **18** *hd* **Joe Packet**213 7222 7-8-7 **90**........................................ JoeFanning 7 50
(Jonathan Portman) *chsd ldrs: rdn along over 2f out: sn wknd* **33/1**

005- **19** *3 ½* **Summerinthecity (IRE)**228 6845 7-8-4 **90**.................. IanBrennan(3) 3 39
(Richard Fahey) *dwlt: a in rr* **16/1**

12-0 **20** *2 ¾* **Mezzotint (IRE)**46 1165 5-9-2 **99**................................ AndreaAtzeni 13 39
(Stuart Williams) *s.i.s: a bhd* **50/1**

1m 13.37s (1.47) **Going Correction** +0.50s/f (Yiel) **20** Ran SP% **127.0**
Speed ratings (Par 109): **110,108,107,106,104 103,103,103,102,102 100,100,100,98,97 90,87,87,82,79**
CSF £47.88 CT £471.05 TOTE £9.70: £2.90, £2.30, £2.40, £2.10; EX 77.60 Trifecta £988.60.
**Owner** B Padgett **Bred** Bearstone Stud **Trained** Sheriff Hutton, N Yorks

**FOCUS**
A competitive sprint handicap in which the field raced as one group up the centre of the track, but those drawn high held the edge. The pace was decent with a three-way battle for the early lead involving Whozthecat, El Viento and Colonel Mak. The form is rated on the positive side.

## 2255 TATTERSALLS MUSIDORA STKS (GROUP 3) (FILLIES) 1m 2f 88y
**2:45** (2:46) (Class 1) 3-Y-O

**£45,368** (£17,200; £8,608; £4,288; £2,152; £1,080) **Stalls** Low

Form RPR

1- **1** **Madame Chiang**204 7449 3-9-0 0.................................... KierenFallon 10 101
(David Simcock) *athletic: tall: lw: dwlt: in rr: drvn over 4f out: swtchd lft then rt over 1f out: styd on to ld last 50yds: drvn out* **8/1**

23-6 **2** *1 ¼* **Lily Rules (IRE)**28 1515 3-9-0 96.................................. BarryMcHugh 7 98
(Tony Coyle) *mid-div: smooth hdwy to ld 2f out: hdd and no ex wl ins fnl f* **7/1**

221- **3** *2 ½* **Regardez**201 7493 3-9-0 82.............................................. JimCrowley 6 93
(Ralph Beckett) *chsd ldr: drvn 3f out: upsides over 1f out: styd on same pce* **13/2**

42 **4** *1 ¼* **Nancy From Nairobi**19 1701 3-9-0 0.............. WilliamTwiston-Davies 9 91
(Mick Channon) *swtchd lft after s: in rr: hdwy on outer 3f out: kpt on one pce over 1f out* **25/1**

1-1 **5** *1* **Queen Of Ice**25 1579 3-9-0 93.......................................... SebSanders 5 89
(William Haggas) *t.k.h: trckd ldrs: drvn 3f out: one pce over 1f out* **5/1**2

1-31 **6** *2* **Latenightrequest**14 1883 3-9-0 86.................................... PaulHanagan 2 85
(Richard Fahey) *mid-div: drvn over 3f out: one pce fnl 2f* **7/1**

1- **7** *2 ½* **Cambridge**224 6949 3-9-0 84............................................. JamesDoyle 4 81
(Charles Hills) *str: lengthy: lw: t.k.h in mid-div: hdwy over 6f out: drvn over 2f out: wknd fnl f* **9/2**1

3-1 **8** *6* **Shama (IRE)**41 1258 3-9-0 82............................................ RyanMoore 3 69
(Sir Michael Stoute) *unf: scope: tall: led: qcknd pce over 5f out: hdd 2f out: sn wknd* **11/2**3

431- **9** *3 ¾* **Lady Heidi**205 7421 3-9-0 97...................................... SilvestreDeSousa 8 62
(Philip Kirby) *in rr: drvn over 5f out: lost pl 3f out: sn bhd* **7/1**

2m 11.04s (-1.46) **Going Correction** -0.05s/f (Good) **9** Ran SP% **116.0**
Speed ratings (Par 106): **103,102,100,99,98 96,94,89,86**
CSF £62.97 TOTE £9.20: £3.10, £2.30, £2.20; EX 71.70 Trifecta £785.80.
**Owner** Miss K Rausing **Bred** Miss K Rausing **Trained** Newmarket, Suffolk

**FOCUS**
Traditionally one of the strongest Oaks trials. They went a decent gallop, it was an advantage to be held up, and the time was 1.53sec slower than the opening handicap for older horses. This looked a lesser renewal, but the winner is at least unbeaten. The form is rated around the runner-up.

## 2256 DUKE OF YORK CLIPPER LOGISTICS STKS (GROUP 2) 6f
**3:15** (3:17) (Class 1) 3-Y-O+

**£56,710** (£21,500; £10,760; £5,360; £2,690; £1,350) **Stalls** High

Form RPR

0-02 **1** **Maarek**16 1824 7-9-13 114......................................... DeclanMcDonough 4 118
(Miss Evanna McCutcheon, Ire) *trckd ldrs: hdwy to chal over 1f out: rdn to ld jst ins fnl f and sn edgd rt: kpt on wl towards fin* **12/1**

11-5 **2** *½* **Astaire (IRE)**32 1436 3-9-3 114...................................... RichardHughes 2 113
(Kevin Ryan) *lw: cl up: rdn to ld wl over 1f out: drvn and edgd rt ent fnl f: sn hdd: kpt on u.p towards fin* **5/1**2

30-2 **3** *1 ½* **Es Que Love (IRE)**27 1531 5-9-8 108................................ AdamKirby 5 107
(Clive Cox) *lw: in tch: hdwy 2f out: rdn to chse ldng pair whn n.m.r and swtchd lft ins fnl f: sn drvn and kpt on same pce* **12/1**

0-06 **4** *nk* **Mass Rally (IRE)**4 2149 7-9-8 107..............................(b) PJMcDonald 3 106
(Michael Dods) *dwlt and in rr: hdwy on outer 2f out: rdn to chse ldrs over 1f out: kpt on same pce ins fnl f* **20/1**

4043 **5** *7* **Hawkeyethenoo (IRE)**4 2149 8-9-8 109............................ KierenFallon 9 83
(Jim Goldie) *towards rr: hdwy over 2f out: sn rdn and kpt on one pce* **11/1**

21-3 **6** *1 ¾* **Jack Dexter**46 1163 5-9-8 114.............................................. GrahamLee 1 78
(Jim Goldie) *in tch on outer: hdwy over 2f out: rdn along wl over 1f out: sn wknd* **4/1**1

04-5 **7** *5* **Heeraat (IRE)**26 1561 5-9-8 110...................................... PaulHanagan 7 62
(William Haggas) *led: pushed along wl over 2f out: rdn and hdd wl over 1f out: sn wknd* **12/1**

01-1 **8** *6* **Eton Rifles (IRE)**47 1207 9-9-8 107............................. GrahamGibbons 6 42
(Stuart Williams) *lw: chsd ldrs: rdn along 2f out: n.m.r and swtchd rt over 1f out: sn drvn and wknd* **10/1**

/31- **9** *6* **Boomerang Bob (IRE)**345 2936 5-9-8 104....................... SebSanders 10 23
(J W Hills) *dwlt: a in rr: bhd fr 1/2-way* **50/1**

-651 **10** *nk* **Ladies Are Forever**25 1572 6-9-5 108...............(b) SilvestreDeSousa 11 19
(Geoffrey Oldroyd) *chsd ldrs: rdn along over 2f out: sn wknd and bhd* **14/1**

6-03 **11** *7* **Body And Soul (IRE)**4 2161 4-9-5 100......................... DuranFentiman 13
(Tim Easterby) *chsd ldrs: rdn along over 2f out: sn wknd and bhd* **14/1**

10-5 **12** *½* **Moviesta (USA)**11 1949 4-9-8 113..................................... PaulMulrennan 8
(Bryan Smart) *lw: chsd ldrs: rdn along over 2f out: sn wknd and bhd* **7/1**3

1-05 **13** *2 ¼* **Tropics (USA)**27 1531 6-9-8 115..................................... RobertWinston 14
(Dean Ivory) *a in rr: rdn along 1/2-way: bhd fnl 2f* **17/2**

1m 13.53s (1.63) **Going Correction** +0.50s/f (Yiel)
**WFA** 3 from 4yo+ 10lb **13** Ran SP% **120.3**
Speed ratings (Par 115): **109,108,106,105,96 94,87,79,71,71 61,61,58**
CSF £71.41 TOTE £13.50: £4.20, £2.10, £4.20; EX 87.50 Trifecta £3538.20.
**Owner** Lisbunny Syndicate **Bred** New England Stud & P J & P M Vela **Trained** Fethard, Co Tipperary

**FOCUS**
This looked a decent Group 2 sprint beforehand and class came to the fore with the pair carrying Group 1 penalties fighting out the finish, but the time was 0.16sec slower than the earlier 0-105 handicap and it was strange to see the first four pull so far clear of the others. They raced centre to nearside. Maarek is rated in line with a better view of his form.

## 2257 CONUNDRUM HR CONSULTING STKS (H'CAP) (BOBIS RACE) 7f
**3:50** (3:54) (Class 3) (0-90,90) 3-Y-O **£12,938** (£3,850; £1,924; £962) **Stalls** Low

Form RPR

1 **1** **That Is The Spirit**45 1192 3-9-7 **90**................................ DanielTudhope 6 102+
(David O'Meara) *str: lengthy: lw: sn led: edgd rt fnl f: styd on wl* **5/2**1

62-2 **2** *1 ½* **Shot In The Sun (IRE)**27 1540 3-8-11 **80**........................ PaulHanagan 2 87
(Richard Fahey) *mid-div: hdwy over 2f out: styd on to take 2nd ins fnl f: no imp* **14/1**

52-1 **3** *2* **Inyordreams**11 1940 3-8-11 **80**......................................... DaleSwift 18 82
(James Given) *chsd ldrs: kpt on same pce fnl f* **33/1**

103- **4** *nk* **Tiger Twenty Two**235 6619 3-9-0 **86**..................... GeorgeChaloner(3) 4 87
(Richard Fahey) *chsd ldrs: drvn over 3f out: kpt on same pce over 1f out* **25/1**

2-00 **5** *2* **Torchlighter (IRE)**13 1903 3-9-0 **83**......................... SilvestreDeSousa 10 79
(Mark Johnston) *chsd ldrs: drvn 3f out: one pce fnl 2f* **40/1**

3-52 **6** *½* **Instant Attraction (IRE)**18 1725 3-8-13 **82**................. PaulMulrennan 16 77+
(Jedd O'Keeffe) *in rr: hdwy over 2f out: kpt on fnl f: nvr trbld ldrs* **33/1**

3562 **7** *2* **Bretherton**23 1614 3-9-0 **83**............................................(p) RyanMoore 19 72
(Richard Fahey) *in rr: styd on fnl 2f: nt rch ldrs* **14/1**

-21 **8** *½* **Provident Spirit**28 1511 3-9-4 **87**................................ WilliamBuick 5 75
(John Gosden) *lw: hld up in rr: hdwy over 2f out: nvr nr ldrs* **15/2**

U1- **9** *1 ½* **Idea (USA)**212 7251 3-8-10 **79**........................................ JamesDoyle 8 63
(Sir Michael Stoute) *lw: mid-div: effrt over 2f out: kpt on: nvr a factor* **4/1**2

23-0 **10** *5* **King Of Macedon (IRE)**37 1350 3-8-13 **82**......................... JoeFanning 7 53
(Mark Johnston) *in rr: sme hdwy over 2f out: nvr a factor* **33/1**

00-4 **11** *2 ¼* **Comino (IRE)**27 1540 3-8-11 **80**..................................... RichardHughes 9 45
(Kevin Ryan) *chsd ldrs: wknd over 1f out* **25/1**

220- **12** *2 ¾* **Makin The Rules (IRE)**215 7170 3-8-5 **77**................... IanBrennan(3) 15 35
(John Quinn) *hld up in mid-div: effrt over 2f out: nvr a factor* **33/1**

0-11 **13** *nk* **New Bidder**19 1693 3-9-4 **87**............................................. TomEaves 12 44
(Jedd O'Keeffe) *led early: chsd ldrs: wknd wl over 1f out* **25/1**

00-2 **14** *1 ¼* **Two Smart (IRE)**36 1361 3-8-10 **79**.............................. PhillipMakin 13 33
(K R Burke) *trckd ldrs: t.k.h: wknd 2f out* **28/1**

62-1 **15** *½* **Rogue Wave (IRE)**11 1962 3-8-11 **80**............................. GrahamLee 20 33
(Alan Jarvis) *a towards rr* **33/1**

1-21 **16** *6* **Tea Leaf (IRE)**10 1985 3-8-11 **80** 6ex.............................. JimCrowley 14 17
(Ralph Beckett) *mid-div: sme hdwy over 2f out: sn lost pl: eased in clsng stages* **6/1**3

41 **17** *18* **Slemy (IRE)**15 1831 3-8-13 **82**.................................... FrankieDettori 17
(Richard Hannon) *hld up in rr: sme hdwy stands' side 3f out: sn wknd: bhd whn eased fnl f: t.o* **20/1**

30-6 **18** *2* **Belayer (IRE)**[20] 1658 3-8-9 **78** KierenFallon 11
(Kevin Ryan) *chsd ldrs: sn drvn along: lost pl over 3f out: bhd whn eased over 1f out: t.o* **50/1**

1m 26.98s (1.68) **Going Correction** +0.40s/f (Good) **18** Ran SP% **126.8**
Speed ratings (Par 103): **106,104,102,101,99 98,96,95,94,88 85,82,82,81,80 73,53,50**
CSF £34.13 CT £1018.63 TOTE £3.30: £1.70, £2.70, £5.00, £3.70; EX 60.50 Trifecta £1146.20.
**Owner** F Gillespie **Bred** Cliveden Stud Ltd **Trained** Nawton, N Yorks

**FOCUS**
This looked a strong handicap on paper and it was won by a smart gelding. The form is rated on the positive side.

## 2258 BRITISH STALLION STUDS EBF NOVICE STKS (BOBIS RACE) 5f
**4:25** (4:26) (Class 3) 2-Y-O **£12,938** (£3,850; £1,924; £962) **Stalls** High

Form RPR
5 **1** **Mignolino (IRE)**[20] 1670 2-9-0 0 GrahamGibbons 3 83+
(David Barron) *w'like: str: cl up on outer: effrt to chal and edgd rt wl over 1f out: sn led: rdn and styd on wl fnl f* **5/1**[3]

123 **2** *1 ½* **Abscent Friends**[14] 1866 2-9-2 0 RyanWhile(5) 5 85
(Bill Turner) *cl up: pushed along 2f out: shkn up and n.m.r wl over 1f out: sn swtchd lft and rdn to chse wnr ins fnl f: drvn and no imp towards fin* **4/1**[2]

3 **3** *1 ¼* **Winstanley (IRE)**[12] 1924 2-9-0 0 RyanMoore 4 74+
(Richard Fahey) *athletic: sn pushed along and outpcd in rr: hdwy wl over 1f out: rdn and kpt on fnl f: nrst fin* **4/1**[2]

1 **4** *½* **Captain Colby (USA)**[11] 1955 2-9-4 0 TomEaves 6 76
(Kevin Ryan) *unf: sn led: rdn along 2f out: hdd wl over 1f out: drvn and wknd ent fnl f* **6/4**[1]

14 **5** *4 ½* **Magical Roundabout (IRE)**[14] 1866 2-9-7 0 RichardHughes 1 63+
(Richard Hannon) *cmpt: trckd ldrs: pushed along bef 1/2-way: rdn 2f out: btn over 1f out* **7/1**

1m 2.15s (2.85) **Going Correction** +0.50s/f (Yiel) **5** Ran SP% **109.2**
Speed ratings (Par 97): **97,94,92,91,84**
CSF £23.74 TOTE £7.00: £3.30, £2.50; EX 27.10 Trifecta £101.20.
**Owner** R G Toes **Bred** Knocklong House Stud **Trained** Maunby, N Yorks

**FOCUS**
Three of the five runners had won a race before.

## 2259 COOPERS MARQUEES STKS (H'CAP) 1m 4f
**5:00** (5:02) (Class 4) (0-85,85) 4-Y-0+ **£9,703** (£2,887; £1,443; £721) **Stalls** Centre

Form RPR
2305 **1** **Streets Of Newyork**[35] 1377 7-8-10 **74** RobertWinston 14 83
(Brian Ellison) *dwlt: in rr: drvn over 4f out: styd on to chse ldr over 1f out: led wl ins fnl f: hrd rdn: all out* **12/1**

00-2 **2** *shd* **Pilgrims Rest (IRE)**[6] 2091 5-9-7 **85** StevieDonohoe 12 94
(Tim Pitt) *lw: led: hdd last 50yds: rallied and jst denied* **20/1**

20-2 **3** *2 ½* **Astra Hall**[11] 1934 5-9-4 **82** JimCrowley 17 87+
(Ralph Beckett) *hld up in rr: hdwy and swtchd stands' side over 2f out: styd on to take 3rd in clsng stages* **15/2**[2]

2243 **4** *1 ¼* **Mica Mika (IRE)**[26] 1553 6-8-13 **77** (p) PaulHanagan 6 80
(Richard Fahey) *in tch: t.k.h: effrt 3f out: styd on same pce over 1f out* **10/1**

02/0 **5** *1 ½* **Deepsand (IRE)**[18] 1724 5-8-11 **75** GrahamLee 10 76
(Tim Easterby) *lw: hld up in mid-div: hdwy 3f out: nt clr run and swtchd rt 2f out: kpt on one* **20/1**

1-20 **6** *1* **Ebony Express**[21] 1653 5-9-5 **83** BenCurtis 16 82
(Alan Swinbank) *chsd ldrs: one pce fnl 2f* **15/2**[2]

-002 **7** *½* **Sherman McCoy**[8] 2052 8-8-2 **71** ShirleyTeasdale(5) 13 69
(Marjorie Fife) *trckd ldrs: effrt over 2f out: one pce* **25/1**

0-02 **8** *3 ¾* **O Ma Lad (IRE)**[10] 1971 6-9-2 **83** IanBrennan(3) 8 75
(John Quinn) *hld up in rr: hdwy over 3f out: wknd over 1f out* **9/1**[3]

254- **9** *5* **Good Speech (IRE)**[228] 6846 4-8-8 **72** AndrewElliott 3 56
(Tom Tate) *chsd ldrs: edgd lft and wknd appr fnl f* **25/1**

000- **10** *1 ½* **Crackentorp**[245] 6302 9-9-4 **82** DavidAllan 18 64
(Tim Easterby) *hld up in rr: t.k.h: nvr on terms* **14/1**

2041 **11** *2 ¼* **Gabrial's Star**[5] 2119 5-9-4 **82** (b) RyanMoore 2 60
(Richard Fahey) *mid-div: drvn 3f out: nvr a threat* **6/4**[1]

00-6 **12** *½* **Warlu Way**[11] 1934 7-9-5 **83** (t) GrahamGibbons 4 60
(Michael Easterby) *trckd ldrs: t.k.h: wknd 2f out* **20/1**

0-43 **13** *1* **Recession Proof (FR)**[36] 1366 8-8-8 **72** TomEaves 7 48
(John Quinn) *s.i.s: sn mid-div: reminders over 4f out: sn lost pl* **40/1**

1-00 **14** *3 ¼* **Bayan Kasirga (IRE)**[21] 1651 4-9-1 **84** SammyJoBell(5) 1 55
(Richard Fahey) *chsd ldrs: drvn over 4f out: lost pl over 2f out: eased whn bhd in clsng stages* **50/1**

00-0 **15** *11* **Ex Oriente (IRE)**[45] 1196 5-8-12 **76** (t) JamesDoyle 9 29
(Stuart Williams) *dwlt: swtchd wd and rapid hdwy to join ldr after 1f: lost pl 3f out: bhd whn hung bdly lft fnl f* **50/1**

2m 33.77s (0.57) **Going Correction** -0.05s/f (Good) **15** Ran SP% **125.3**
Speed ratings (Par 105): **96,95,94,93,92 91,91,88,85,84 83,82,82,79,72**
CSF £238.09 CT £1937.34 TOTE £17.00: £4.00, £5.20, £3.00; EX 406.40 Trifecta £4357.50.
**Owner** Koo's Racing Club **Bred** The Duke Of Devonshire **Trained** Norton, N Yorks
■ Stewards' Enquiry : Robert Winston four-day ban: use of whip (28-31 May)

**FOCUS**
They only went an ordinary pace in this fair handicap and again they came nearside after turning in. The market suggested this wasn't as competitive as the numbers would suggest. A personal best from the winner.
T/Jkpt: Not won. T/Plt: £1,860.60 to a £1 stake. Pool of £196742.48 - 77.18 winning tickets.
T/Qpdt: £360.00 to a £1 stake. Pool of £12893.15 - 26.50 winning tickets. WG

2260 - 2262a (Foreign Racing) - See Raceform Interactive

# 1820 NAAS (L-H)
Wednesday, May 14

**OFFICIAL GOING: Yielding to soft**

## 2263a IRISH STALLION FARMS EUROPEAN BREEDERS FUND BLUE WIND STKS (GROUP 3) (FILLIES) 1m 2f
**7:15** (7:15) 3-Y-0+ **£40,625** (£11,875; £5,625; £1,875)

RPR
**1** **Tarfasha (IRE)**[227] 6881 3-8-9 102 PatSmullen 10 109+
(D K Weld, Ire) *hld up in tch: 6th 1/2-way: clsr in 5th into st and gd hdwy on outer to ld fr under 2f out: rdn clr over 1f out and styd on wl: comf* **9/4**[2]

**2** *3 ¼* **We'll Go Walking (IRE)**[17] 1775 4-9-9 100 SeamieHeffernan 6 102
(J P Murtagh, Ire) *chsd ldrs: 3rd 1/2-way: rdn into 2nd over 1f out and sn no imp on wnr: kpt on same pce* **12/1**

**3** *3* **Dazzling (IRE)**[32] 1457 3-8-9 103 ColmO'Donoghue 4 96+
(A P O'Brien, Ire) *disp tl settled bhd ldr in cl 2nd after 2f: disp into st tl hdd fr under 2f out: sn no ex u.p in 3rd: kpt on same pce* **6/4**[1]

**4** *nk* **Morga (IRE)**[13] 1076 4-9-9 93 KevinManning 8 95
(Desmond McDonogh, Ire) *chsd ldrs: clsr in 4th 1/2-way: rdn and nt clr run between horses briefly under 3f out: no imp on ldrs in 5th 2f out: wnt mod 4th u.p over 1f out: kpt on* **14/1**

**5** *4 ½* **Tahaany (IRE)**[9] 2042 3-8-9 99 LeighRoche 7 86
(D K Weld, Ire) *disp tl led narrowly after 2f: disp into st tl hdd 2f out: sn no ex in 4th and dropped to 5th over 1f out: kpt on one pce* **14/1**

**6** *1 ¾* **Cristal Fashion (IRE)**[32] 1457 3-8-9 99 GaryCarroll 3 83
(G M Lyons, Ire) *chsd ldrs early: 7th 1/2-way: rdn into st and no imp on ldrs in 7th under 2f out: kpt on one pce into mod 6th ins fnl f* **6/1**[3]

**7** *1 ½* **Euphrasia (IRE)**[17] 1775 5-9-12 103 WayneLordan 2 83
(Joseph G Murphy, Ire) *chsd ldrs in 4th tl dropped to 5th 1/2-way: rdn in 6th into st and no imp on ldrs: dropped to mod 7th ins fnl f* **16/1**

**8** *12* **Achnaha (IRE)**[18] 1747 3-8-9 95 (p) ChrisHayes 1 56
(P D Deegan, Ire) *w.w towards rr: 8th 1/2-way: rdn into st and no imp: one pce fnl 2f* **20/1**

**9** *2 ¾* **Jazz Girl (IRE)**[9] 2040 6-9-9 95 ConnorKing 5 50
(A Oliver, Ire) *s.i.s and racd in rr: last 1/2-way: rdn into st and no imp: one pce fnl 2f* **33/1**

2m 14.34s (-1.26)
**WFA** 3 from 4yo+ 15lb **9** Ran SP% **119.7**
CSF £30.96 TOTE £4.90: £1.70, £3.60, £1.02; DF 24.20 Trifecta £153.00.
**Owner** Hamdan Al Maktoum **Bred** Rockfield Farm **Trained** Curragh, Co Kildare

**FOCUS**
Another Group 3 success for Dermot Weld following his hat-trick at the same level of competition at Leopardstown three days earlier. This was a race run at a good pace.

2264 - 2266a (Foreign Racing) - See Raceform Interactive

# 1965 SAINT-CLOUD (L-H)
Wednesday, May 14

**OFFICIAL GOING: Turf: soft**

## 2267a PRIX CLEOPATRE (GROUP 3) (3YO FILLIES) (TURF) 1m 2f 110y
**1:05** (1:05) 3-Y-0 **£33,333** (£13,333; £10,000; £6,666; £3,333)

RPR
**1** **Shamkala (FR)**[20] 3-8-10 0 ow1 ChristopheSoumillon 4 111+
(A De Royer-Dupre, France) *sn led and mde rest: gng best 2f out: qcknd over 1f out: pushed out to assert ins fnl f: eased towards fin: v easily* **2/5**[1]

**2** *¾* **Amour A Papa (FR)**[38] 1339 3-8-9 0 OlivierPeslier 5 107+
(J-Y Artu, France) *dwlt sltly: plld hrd: midfield in tch on outer: pushed along 2f out: rdn ent fnl f: styd on and wnt 2nd cl home: outclassed and flattered by proximity to wnr* **41/5**[3]

**3** *shd* **Hug And A Kiss (USA)**[29] 1502 3-8-9 0 Pierre-CharlesBoudot 6 107+
(A Fabre, France) *sn trcking ldr on outer: pushed along to try and chal 2f out: readily outpcd by wnr over 1f out: rdn ent fnl f: styd on but dropped to 3rd cl home: outclassed and flattered by proximity to wnr* **33/10**[2]

**4** *1 ½* **Bocaiuva (IRE)**[31] 1480 3-8-9 0 CristianDemuro 1 104
(F Chappet, France) *t.k.h: led early: restrained and sn hdd: trckd ldr on inner: pushed along and effrt to chal on rail 2f out: rdn and readily outpcd by wnr over 1f out: styd on for wl hld 4th* **139/10**

**5** *1 ¼* **Sinnamary (IRE)**[20] 3-8-9 0 JamieSpencer 2 101+
(M Delzangles, France) *hld up in last: pushed along 2f out: rdn and outpcd over 1f out: styd on but nvr a factor* **144/10**

**6** *4 ½* **My Jolie (IRE)**[29] 1502 3-8-9 0 MaximeGuyon 3 93
(A Fabre, France) *restrained early: sn settled in midfield in tch on inner: rdn 2f out: outpcd over 1f out: btn and dropped to last ins fnl f: eased towards fin* **224/10**

2m 26.03s (6.43) **6** Ran SP% **123.0**
WIN (incl. 1 euro stake): 1.40. PLACES: 1.10, 1.80. SF: 7.10.
**Owner** H H Aga Khan **Bred** His Highness The Aga Khan Studs Sc **Trained** Chantilly, France

# 1973 NEWMARKET (R-H)
Thursday, May 15

**OFFICIAL GOING: Good (7.1)**
Wind: virtually nil Weather: sunny and quite warm

## 2269 HOMESTORE AND SAFEPAC MAIDEN AUCTION STKS 6f
**5:25** (5:27) (Class 5) 2-Y-O **£3,234** (£962; £481; £240) **Stalls** Low

Form RPR
22 **1** **Realtra (IRE)**[19] 1732 2-8-8 0 PaulHanagan 9 80
(Richard Fahey) *chsd ldrs: rdn and effrt to ld over 1f out: styd on strly and asserted ins fnl f* **4/5**[1]

**2** *1 ¼* **Commander Patten (IRE)** 2-9-1 0 JoeFanning 7 83
(Alan Bailey) *in tch in midfield: clsd and pressed ldrs wl over 1f out: rdn and ev ch over 1f out: no ex fnl 100yds* **50/1**

**3** *1 ½* **Bazzana** 2-8-6 0 NickyMackay 4 70
(Martyn Meade) *hld up in tch in midfield: swtchd lft and effrt wl over 1f out: hdwy over 1f out: wnt 3rd ins fnl f: kpt on wl* **10/1**

3 **4** *3* **Celestial Vision (USA)**[26] 1583 2-9-3 0 RichardKingscote 5 72
(Tom Dascombe) *led: rdn and hrd pressed wl over 1f out: sn hdd: wknd ins fnl f* **7/2**[2]

0 **5** *1 ¼* **Forcible**[11] 1977 2-9-0 0 OisinMurphy(3) 2 68
(David Brown) *chsd ldrs: rdn and outpcd wl over 1f out: 5th and btn over 1f out: wknd ins fnl f* **7/1**[3]

**6** *½* **Ho Yam Lay** 2-8-10 0 TomQueally 11 60
(Michael Bell) *rn green: hld up in tch in last trio: effrt and sltly hmpd wl over 1f out: styd on steadily fnl f: nvr trbld ldrs* **20/1**

**7** *2 ¼* **York Express** 2-8-12 0 LukeMorris 1 55
(Ismail Mohammed) *s.i.s: t.k.h: hld up in tch in last trio: effrt wl over 1f out: swtchd lft over 1f out: plugged on: nvr trbld ldrs* **33/1**

0 **8** *3 ¼* **Framley Garth (IRE)**[29] 1512 2-8-13 0 LiamKeniry 6 46
(David Elsworth) *awkward leaving stalls: t.k.h: hld up in tch in last trio: rdn ent fnl 2f: wknd over 1f out* **14/1**

**9** *5* **This Is Too (IRE)** 2-8-6 0 LiamJones 3 24
(Alan Bailey) *pressed ldr: rdn 1/2-way: struggling u.p 2f out: sn wknd: bhd fnl f* **50/1**

1m 14.54s (2.34) **Going Correction** +0.225s/f (Good) **9** Ran SP% **117.7**
Speed ratings (Par 93): **93,91,89,85,83 83,80,75,69**
CSF £69.46 TOTE £1.60: £1.10, £6.20, £4.20; EX 45.70 Trifecta £390.40 Part won..

**Owner** Middleham Park Racing XC **Bred** Tom & Geraldine Molan **Trained** Musley Bank, N Yorks
**FOCUS**
Stands' side track used. Stalls far side except 1m4f: centre. Just an ordinary-looking maiden by this track's standards.

## 2270 CARRS BMW H'CAP — 1m 2f
5:55 (5:57) (Class 5) (0-75,74) 4-Y-0+ £3,881 (£1,155; £577; £288) Stalls Low

Form RPR
3420 1 **Chain Of Events**[23] [1636] 7-9-3 70 ........ GeorgeBaker 10 81
(Michael Wigham) *hld up in tch in midfield: clsd to chse ldrs 2f out: chsd ldr wl over 1f out: rdn to ld 1f out: r.o wl: rdn out* **8/1**[2]
-006 2 1 ½ **Tight Lipped (IRE)**[17] [1810] 5-9-1 71 ........ RosieJessop(3) 5 79
(James Eustace) *in tch in midfield: hdwy to press ldrs 3f out: rdn to ld over 1f out: hdd 1f out: styd on same pce ins fnl f* **8/1**[2]
2-65 3 ½ **Aint Got A Scooby (IRE)**[14] [1899] 4-9-1 73 ........ RyanTate(5) 14 80+
(Clive Cox) *hld up in tch in rr: hdwy over 1f out: r.o strly u.p ins fnl f: no threat to wnr* **10/1**[3]
06-5 4 2 ½ **St Paul De Vence (IRE)**[15] [1881] 4-9-6 73 ........ LukeMorris 8 75
(Paul Cole) *in tch in midfield: rdn 4f out: hdwy to ld 2f out: sn hrd drvn and hdd: btn 1f out: wknd ins fnl f* **8/1**[2]
00-0 5 ¾ **Laughing Jack**[23] [1636] 6-9-1 73 ........ GeorgeDowning(5) 15 74
(George Baker) *chsd ldr tl rdn and lost pl over 3f out: edging rt and rallied over 1f out: styd wl on ins fnl f: no threat to ldrs* **10/1**[3]
00-6 6 1 ¼ **Jonnie Skull (IRE)**[23] [1637] 8-9-5 72 ........(vt) JimmyQuinn 9 70
(Lydia Pearce) *chsd ldrs: rdn over 2f out: drvn and outpcd wl over 1f out: plugged on same pce fnl f* **33/1**
3066 7 1 ½ **Avidly**[26] [1568] 4-8-5 63 ........ ShelleyBirkett(5) 4 59
(Julia Feilden) *in tch in midfield: rdn and unable qck 2f out: no imp u.p fr over 1f out* **33/1**
0400 8 nk **Ocean Applause**[23] [1637] 4-8-12 72 ........(tp) JordonMcMurray(7) 19 67
(John Ryan) *in tch in midfield: rdn over 2f out: keeping on same pce whn short of room over 1f out: no imp fnl f* **33/1**
-353 9 4 **Chapter And Verse (IRE)**[47] [1175] 8-9-3 70 ........ ShaneKelly 1 57
(Mike Murphy) *hld up in tch in rr: hdwy ent fnl 2f: drvn and no hdwy over 1f out: wknd ins fnl f* **8/1**[2]
20/0 10 1 **Audacious**[20] [1689] 6-8-8 61 ........ MichaelStainton 12 47
(Charles Pogson) *chsd ldrs tl led over 3f out: rdn and hdd 2f out: sn struggling: wknd over 1f out* **50/1**
-550 11 4 **Special Mix**[46] [1196] 6-8-13 66 ........ TedDurcan 18 44
(Martin Smith) *hld up in tch in midfield: rdn and effrt over 2f out: no hdwy and btn whn nt clr run over 1f out: wknd fnl f* **25/1**
0131 12 1 ¼ **Eco Warrior**[17] [1791] 4-9-6 73 ........(b) JoeFanning 20 49
(J W Hills) *in tch in midfield: rdn 3f out: no hdwy: wknd wl over 1f out* **12/1**
02-2 13 4 ½ **Dandy (GER)**[14] [1899] 5-9-4 74 ........ OisinMurphy(3) 13 41
(Andrew Balding) *chsd ldrs: clsd to press ldrs and rdn over 2f out: fnd little and sn struggling wknd over 1f out: wl btn and eased wl ins fnl f* **6/1**[1]
2400 14 2 ¼ **Apache Glory (USA)**[57] [1022] 6-9-4 71 ........(p) StephenCraine 6 34
(John Stimpson) *taken down early: hld up in tch towards rr: rdn and effrt 3f out: no hdwy and wknd 2f out: wl bhd and eased ins fnl f* **22/1**
20-0 15 2 ¾ **Bison Grass**[44] [1216] 4-8-12 65 ........ PatrickDonaghy 3 23
(Giles Bravery) *hld up in tch in midfield: rdn and btn ent fnl 3f: bhd fnl 2f: eased wl ins fnl f* **25/1**
42-6 16 2 ½ **Shanti**[20] [1691] 4-9-5 72 ........ TomQueally 7 25
(Michael Bell) *t.k.h: hld up in tch towards rr: rdn 3f out: sn btn and bhd fnl 2f: eased ins fnl f: t.o* **16/1**
510- 17 5 **Lady Of Yue**[168] [8089] 4-8-10 63 ........ PaulHanagan 11 6
(Eugene Stanford) *led tl hdd and rdn over 3f out: sn lost pl: wl bhd and eased ins fnl f: t.o* **6/1**[1]
/200 18 3 ¾ **Pentameter**[14] [1899] 5-8-13 66 ........ LiamKeniry 2 2
(John Butler) *in tch towards rr: rdn over 3f out: sn btn: wl bhd and eased ins fnl f: t.o* **50/1**

2m 6.85s (1.05) **Going Correction** +0.225s/f (Good) **18 Ran SP% 129.6**
Speed ratings (Par 103): **104,102,102,100,99 98,97,97,94,93 90,89,85,83,81 79,75,72**
CSF £68.06 CT £669.58 TOTE £11.60: £2.70, £2.80, £3.10, £2.90; EX 66.70 Trifecta £707.70.
**Owner** P J Edwards **Bred** Bishop Wilton Stud **Trained** Newmarket, Suffolk
**FOCUS**
A wide-open handicap but run at a sound pace and they seemed to get racing quite a long way out. This matches the winner's old C&D best.

## 2271 JANE RUTHERFORD MEMORIAL EBF STALLIONS MAIDEN STKS (BOBIS RACE) — 1m 2f
6:25 (6:30) (Class 4) 3-Y-O £5,498 (£1,636; £817; £408) Stalls Low

Form RPR
6 1 **Tabreek (USA)**[28] [1529] 3-9-5 0 ........ PaulHanagan 11 86
(Richard Hannon) *chsd ldrs: clsd to join ldrs and clr in ldng quartet 2f out: rdn to ld wl over 1f out: sustained duel w rival fr over 1f out: r.o wl: rdn out* **9/4**[2]
43-2 2 nk **Venezia (IRE)**[29] [1517] 3-9-2 89 ........ OisinMurphy(3) 6 85
(Martyn Meade) *pressed ldr: rdn and ev ch ent fnl 2f: wnt clr w wnr and sustained duel fr over 1f out: r.o but a jst hld* **11/8**[1]
3 5 **Hatsaway (IRE)** 3-9-5 0 ........ LiamJones 1 76
(Clive Brittain) *pushed rt s: sn rcvrd and chsd ldrs: ev ch and clr in ldng quartet 2f out: sn rdn: 3rd and btn over 1f out: wknd ins fnl f but hung on to 3rd cl home* **25/1**
4 ½ **Igider (IRE)** 3-9-5 0 ........ AndreaAtzeni 5 75
(Roger Varian) *led and set stdy gallop: qcknd clr in ldng quartet ent fnl 2f: drvn and btn over 1f out: wknd ins fnl f* **14/1**
5 ½ **Gwafa (IRE)** 3-9-5 0 ........ LukeMorris 2 74
(Marco Botti) *ducked sharply rt leaving stalls: sn in tch in midfield: 5th and outpcd u.p 2f out: wl hld but plugged on fnl f* **33/1**
6 ½ **Kagami** 3-9-5 0 ........ ShaneKelly 14 73+
(Jeremy Noseda) *in tch in midfield: rdn and outpcd ent fnl 2f: no ch w ldrs but kpt on again ins fnl f* **33/1**
4- 7 ¾ **Shining Glitter (IRE)**[169] [8066] 3-9-0 0 ........ FrederikTylicki 16 66+
(James Fanshawe) *hld up in tch in last quartet: rdn over 2f out: outpcd and short of room 2f out: no ch but kpt on again ins fnl f* **16/1**
8 1 **Pas De Cheval (IRE)** 3-9-5 0 ........ RyanMoore 15 69+
(Sir Michael Stoute) *s.i.s and pushed along leaving stalls: hld up in tch in rr: outpcd over 2f out: pushed along and sme hdwy fnl f: nvr trbld ldrs* **9/1**[3]
9 nk **Aussie Andre** 3-9-5 0 ........ TomQueally 8 69+
(Jeremy Noseda) *hld up in tch in last quartet: rdn and struggling 3f out: n.d after: plugged on ins fnl f* **50/1**
0- 10 ½ **Mr Smith**[185] [7835] 3-9-5 0 ........ NickyMackay 9 68+
(John Gosden) *hld up in tch towards rr: rdn and outpcd over 2f out: n.d after: plugged on* **16/1**
00 11 1 ¾ **Flight Fight**[31] [1491] 3-9-5 0 ........ GeorgeBaker 3 64
(Chris Wall) *chsd ldrs: rdn and outpcd ent fnl 2f: wknd over 1f out: fdd ins fnl f* **66/1**
0- 12 1 ¼ **Secure Cloud (IRE)**[225] [6954] 3-9-5 0 ........ JoeFanning 12 62
(J W Hills) *hld up in tch in midfield: rdn and struggling over 2f out: sn outpcd and n.d fnl 2f* **66/1**
0 13 16 **Carnt Cash Sorry**[55] [1044] 3-9-5 0 ........(b[1]) JimmyQuinn 4 32
(Ed Vaughan) *in tch in midfield: rdn and outpcd over 2f out: wknd wl over 1f out: bhd and eased wl ins fnl f* **100/1**

2m 10.41s (4.61) **Going Correction** +0.225s/f (Good) **13 Ran SP% 117.0**
Speed ratings (Par 101): **90,89,85,85,84 84,83,83,82,82 81,80,67**
CSF £5.22 TOTE £2.50: £1.70, £1.10, £5.50; EX 7.10 Trifecta £91.70.
**Owner** Hamdan Al Maktoum **Bred** WinStar Farm LLC **Trained** East Everleigh, Wilts
**FOCUS**
This is often a good maiden and the 2014 version looks well up to scratch with the two leading form contenders settling down to scrap out a terrific finish and drawing clear of the rest. However, the time was modest.

## 2272 CHASSIS CAB DAF H'CAP — 1m 4f
7:00 (7:04) (Class 4) (0-85,87) 4-Y-0+ £6,469 (£1,925; £962; £481) Stalls Centre

Form RPR
21-2 1 **Certavi (IRE)**[47] [1175] 5-9-3 81 ........ LiamKeniry 5 92+
(Brendan Powell) *stdd s: hld up in tch in last pair: gd hdwy to trck ldrs 3f out: shkn up to chal and wnt lft jst ins fnl f: sn led and qcknd clr: readily* **10/1**
44-0 2 2 ¾ **Soul Intent (IRE)**[19] [1724] 4-8-10 74 ........ JoeFanning 14 81
(J W Hills) *hld up in tch in midfield: rdn and effrt over 2f out: led and edgd rt u.p over 1f out: hdd and pushed lft ins fnl f: sn outpcd but kpt on for clr 2nd* **14/1**
-243 3 1 ¼ **High Office**[25] [1599] 8-8-10 74 ........ PaulHanagan 8 79+
(Richard Fahey) *hld up in tch in midfield: nt clr run and shuffled bk to rr 3f out: swtchd lft and hdwy u.p over 1f out: styd on wl to go 3rd fnl 75yds: no ch w wnr* **6/1**[2]
30-1 4 2 **One Pursuit (IRE)**[13] [1909] 6-8-13 84 ........ JennyPowell(7) 3 86
(Brendan Powell) *chsd ldr tl led over 2f out: rdn and edgd lft wl over 1f out: hdd and carried rt over 1f out: outpcd whn squeezed for room ins fnl f: wknd fnl 100yds* **13/2**[3]
211/ 5 nk **Enthusiastic**[596] [6584] 6-9-7 85 ........ KierenFallon 2 86
(George Margarson) *hld up in tch in midfield: hdwy 3f out: rdn and unable qck ent fnl 2f: styd on same pce fr over 1f out* **8/1**
-241 6 2 ¾ **Flemish School**[10] [2034] 4-9-9 87 6ex ........(p) RyanMoore 9 84
(David Elsworth) *hld up in tch towards rr: hdwy 3f out: chsd ldrs and unable qck u.p wl over 1f out: wknd ins fnl f* **11/4**[1]
6366 7 ¾ **Thecornishcowboy**[17] [1798] 5-8-2 71 oh5 ........(t) ShelleyBirkett(5) 8 67
(John Ryan) *hld up in tch in midfield: nt clrest of runs ent fnl 2f: rdn and unable qck wl over 1f out: no imp after* **25/1**
521- 8 2 ¾ **Mallory Heights (IRE)**[162] [8159] 4-9-2 80 ........ AndreaAtzeni 1 71
(Luca Cumani) *chsd ldrs: rdn and unable qck over 2f out: wknd over 1f out* **8/1**
3504 9 nk **Outrageous Request**[16] [1849] 8-8-7 71 oh1 ........ LukeMorris 12 62
(William Stone) *hld up in tch towards rr: rdn and effrt over 2f out: no real imp: nvr trbld ldrs* **25/1**
0143 10 1 ¼ **Royal Alcor (IRE)**[51] [1091] 7-7-7 74 ow1 ........(t) OisinMurphy(3) 13 63
(Gay Kelleway) *stdd s: hld up in tch in rr: rdn and effrt ent fnl 2f: no hdwy and wknd over 1f out* **33/1**
005 11 hd **St Ignatius**[24] [1219] 7-8-2 71 oh1 ........(v) TimClark(5) 11 60
(Alan Bailey) *led: racd solo towards far side fr 10f out: rdn and hdd over 2f out: wknd u.p wl over 1f out* **40/1**
-242 12 2 ½ **Sporting Gold (IRE)**[21] [1659] 5-8-13 77 ........(b) TomQueally 15 62
(Roger Varian) *chsd ldrs: rdn over 2f out: struggling to qckn whn short of room and hmpd ent fnl 2f: sn wknd* **15/2**

2m 35.79s (3.79) **Going Correction** +0.225s/f (Good) **12 Ran SP% 117.1**
Speed ratings (Par 105): **96,94,93,92,91 89,89,87,87,86 86,84**
CSF £133.75 CT £918.30 TOTE £5.70: £3.30, £4.20, £2.70; EX 209.40 Trifecta £1800.60 Part won..
**Owner** Nigel M Davies **Bred** Anthony Jones **Trained** Upper Lambourn, Berks
**FOCUS**
The visual impression was that the overall gallop wasn't that strong. The winner continued his fine run, with a turf best from the runner-up.

## 2273 ORBITAL FOOD MACHINERY CLASSIFIED STKS — 1m 4f
7:35 (7:36) (Class 5) 3-Y-O £4,090 (£1,207; £604) Stalls Centre

Form RPR
34-2 1 **Sebastian Beach (IRE)**[16] [1844] 3-9-0 75 ........ RyanMoore 6 85
(Richard Hannon) *mde all: rdn 2f out: clr w rival ent fnl f: kpt on wl and a doing enough: rdn out* **5/2**[1]
1 2 nk **Luck Of The Game (USA)**[17] [1817] 3-9-0 71 ........ MartinLane 1 84
(David Simcock) *stdd s: hld up in tch in last: clsd to trck ldr over 2f out: rdn and ev ch over 1f out: kpt on but a jst hld fnl f* **4/1**[2]
44-1 3 7 **Cosette (IRE)**[17] [1812] 3-9-0 74 ........ DaneO'Neill 2 73
(Henry Candy) *t.k.h: chsd ldrs: rdn 3f out: outpcd 2f out: 3rd and wl hld fnl f: eased towards fin* **5/2**[1]
01-0 4 4 ½ **Crystal Pearl**[23] [1635] 3-9-0 74 ........ KierenFallon 3 66
(Mark H Tompkins) *t.k.h: hld up in tch in last pair: hdwy to press wnr 3f out tl over 2f out: rdn and btn over 1f out: wknd: eased towards fin* **15/2**[3]
0-52 5 18 **Pershing**[23] [1635] 3-9-0 74 ........ AndreaAtzeni 5 37
(Marco Botti) *chsd wnr tl 3f out: sn rdn and btn: wl bhd and eased ins fnl f* **4/1**[2]

2m 35.3s (3.30) **Going Correction** +0.225s/f (Good) **5 Ran SP% 108.9**
Speed ratings (Par 99): **98,97,93,90,78**
CSF £12.30 TOTE £3.10: £1.60, £2.40; EX 11.70 Trifecta £30.20.
**Owner** Justin Dowley & Michael Pescod **Bred** Conor Murphy & Rathmore Stud **Trained** East Everleigh, Wilts

**FOCUS**
A tight little classified event featuring unexposed three-year-olds and it produced a cracking finish. Only the first pair showed their form.

## 2274 PRECISION MARKETING GROUP GOLDEN GALLOP FILLIES' H'CAP (JC FLAT MIDDLE DISTANCE SERIES QUALIFIER) 1m
8:05 (8:06) (Class 5) (0-75,75) 3-Y-O £3,881 (£1,155; £577; £288) Stalls Low

Form RPR

35-2 **1** **Ghinia (IRE)**[19] 1723 3-9-1 **69**.................... AdamKirby 2 79+
(Pam Sly) *led for 2f: chsd ldr after tl rdn to ld over 1f out: rn green in front and edging lft 1f out: gng clr whn hung bdly lft ins fnl f: stened and r.o strly towards fin* **7/2**[2]

2-31 **2** *3* **Alquimia (IRE)**[19] 1723 3-9-6 **74**.................... PaulHanagan 3 77
(Richard Fahey) *chsd ldrs: rdn and effrt 2f out: styd on u.p to chse wnr fnl 150yds: no imp and one pce fnl 100yds* **7/2**[2]

02-0 **3** *nk* **Thatchereen (IRE)**[19] 1711 3-9-0 **68**.................... TomQueally 10 70+
(Michael Bell) *stdd s: hld up in rr: effrt 2f: styng on but stl plenty to do whn swtchd lft 1f out: styd on wl ins fnl f: snatched 3rd last strides: no ch w wnr* **33/1**

36-0 **4** *hd* **Cornish Path**[26] 1586 3-9-7 **75**.................... DaneO'Neill 8 77
(Henry Candy) *hld up in tch: hdwy u.p over 1f out: no threat to wnr but ev ch of 2nd ins fnl f: kpt on same pce fnl 100yds* **10/3**[1]

0-10 **5** *¾* **The Silver Kebaya (FR)**[20] 1690 3-9-4 **72**.................... RyanMoore 6 72
(Jeremy Noseda) *in tch: effrt u.p and chsd ldrs over 1f out: carried rt and no ex ins fnl f* **13/2**[3]

0-21 **6** *1* **Dalmarella Dancer (IRE)**[15] 1888 3-9-7 **75**.................... WilliamBuick 5 73+
(K R Burke) *stdd s: hld up in tch in last trio: swtchd to r nr far rail 1/2-way: hdwy u.p over 1f out: edgd lft and wknd fnl 100yds* **9/1**

0-15 **7** *1 ¾* **Platinum Pearl**[36] 1381 3-9-5 **73**.................... AndreaAtzeni 4 67
(Peter Chapple-Hyam) *in tch midfield: rdn and effrt over 2f out: chsd ldrs and unable qck u.p over 1f out: wknd ins fnl f* **16/1**

341- **8** *hd* **An Chulainn (IRE)**[189] 7790 3-9-5 **73**.................... JoeFanning 1 66
(Mark Johnston) *chsd ldrs: rdn and hld hd high over 1f out: wknd ins fnl f* **14/1**

0-46 **9** *1 ¼* **Kalon Brama (IRE)**[9] 2049 3-8-5 **62**.................... RosieJessop(3) 11 52
(Peter Charalambous) *t.k.h: chsd ldrs tl hdwy to ld 6f out: clr 1/2-way tl rdn and hdd over 1f out: lost 2nd fnl 150yds: fdd* **50/1**

3-63 **10** *nk* **Rocksee (IRE)**[16] 1832 3-9-0 **68**.................... RichardKingscote 7 58
(Tom Dascombe) *chsd ldrs: lost pl u.p 2f out: n.d fr over 1f out* **16/1**

2350 **11** *12* **La Napoule**[13] 1914 3-8-8 **62**.................... SeanLevey 9 24
(Richard Hannon) *stdd after s: hld up in last trio: rdn and effrt over 2f out: sn btn: bhd fnl f* **33/1**

1m 40.88s (2.28) **Going Correction** +0.225s/f (Good) **11 Ran SP% 117.1**
Speed ratings (Par 96): **97,94,93,93,92 91,90,89,88,88 76**
CSF £15.89 CT £351.55 TOTE £4.90: £1.80, £1.80, £6.60; EX 19.60 Trifecta £737.10.

**Owner** David L Bayliss **Bred** Pier House Stud **Trained** Thorney, Cambs

**FOCUS**
Some unexposed types open to progression in here. The winner reversed Haydock form with the runner-up, with the fourth and fifth setting the standard.

## 2275 REDBOURN ENGINEERING LTD H'CAP 5f
8:35 (8:37) (Class 4) (0-85,85) 4-Y-0+ £6,469 (£1,925; £962; £481) Stalls Low

Form RPR

0-00 **1** **Monumental Man**[20] 1695 5-9-0 **78**.................... (p) AdamKirby 5 87
(James Unett) *mde all: rdn over 1f out: hld on wl ins fnl f: drvn out* **14/1**

-510 **2** *½* **Silvanus (IRE)**[12] 1961 9-9-3 **81**.................... PaulHanagan 3 88
(Paul Midgley) *t.k.h: hld up in tch in midfield: rdn and effrt over 1f out: squeezed between horses to press wnr wl ins fnl f: r.o but hld towards fin* **12/1**

0/1- **3** *nse* **Foxy Forever (IRE)**[293] 4734 4-9-7 **85**.................... RichardKingscote 2 92+
(Michael Wigham) *stdd s: hld up in rr: clsd and nt clr run ent fnl f: swtchd lft ins fnl f: edgd lft u.p but r.o strly fnl 100yds: nt quite rch ldrs* **9/2**[1]

154- **4** *¾* **Angel Way (IRE)**[236] 6652 5-8-9 **73**.................... LukeMorris 11 77
(Mike Murphy) *travelled strly: chsd ldrs: wnt 2nd 2f out: rdn and effrt over 1f out: drvn and styd on same pce ins fnl f: lost 2 pls wl ins fnl f* **20/1**

06-0 **5** *1 ¼* **Rebecca Romero**[31] 1489 7-9-1 **79**.................... RyanMoore 4 79
(Denis Coakley) *outpcd towards rr: rdn and hdwy over 1f out: drvn and no imp ins fnl f* **7/1**[2]

10-0 **6** *¾* **Cincinnati Kit**[26] 1572 5-9-2 **80**.................... (t) AndreaAtzeni 7 77
(Stuart Williams) *in tch in midfield: effrt u.p over 1f out: keeping on same pce whn sltly hmpd ins fnl f: n.d after* **8/1**[3]

020- **7** *½* **Threes Grand**[156] 8232 4-8-8 **79**.................... MatthewHopkins(7) 9 74
(Scott Dixon) *chsd wnr tl 2f out: sn rdn and unable qck: hld and kpt on same pce ins fnl f* **33/1**

-502 **8** *hd* **Sir Pedro**[9] 2050 5-8-9 **76**.................... OisinMurphy(3) 8 71
(Robert Cowell) *chsd ldrs: rdn and effrt over 1f out: unable qck 1f out: wknd fnl 100yds* **7/1**[2]

123- **9** *1* **Asian Trader**[321] 3786 5-8-13 **84**.................... (t) GeorgiaCox(7) 1 75
(William Haggas) *stdd s: hld up off the pce in last trio: rdn and hdwy over 1f out: no hdwy 1f out: wknd ins fnl f* **11/1**

04-3 **10** *½* **Port Alfred**[13] 1922 4-9-6 **84**.................... WilliamBuick 6 73
(Charlie Appleby) *stdd s: hld up off the pce in rr: clsd into midfield 2f out: rdn and effrt over 1f out: no prog 1f out: wkng and nt clrest of runs ins fnl f* **9/2**[1]

11-5 **11** *14* **Green Monkey**[13] 1922 4-8-12 **76**.................... ShaneKelly 10 15
(James Fanshawe) *in tch in midfield: rdn and struggling 2f: bhd 1f out: sn wknd: eased towards fin* **7/1**[2]

1m 0.33s (1.23) **Going Correction** +0.225s/f (Good) **11 Ran SP% 115.4**
Speed ratings (Par 105): **99,98,98,96,94 93,92,92,91,90 67**
CSF £167.93 CT £881.53 TOTE £14.20: £4.10, £3.60, £2.20; EX 167.50 Trifecta £1483.90.

**Owner** R Milner & Partners **Bred** Christopher Chell **Trained** Tedsmore Hall, Shropshire

**FOCUS**
Quite a good little sprint, in which the pace held up. A length best from the winner.

T/Plt: £122.40 to a £1 stake. Pool: £81,129.95 - 483.53 winning units. T/Qpdt: £20.60 to a £1 stake. Pool: £6818.02 - 244.30 winning units. SP

# 1980 SALISBURY (R-H)
Thursday, May 15

**OFFICIAL GOING: Good to soft (good in places; 7.5)**
Wind: virtually nil Weather: sunny

## 2276 GLEBE FARM STUD MAIDEN STKS 5f
1:30 (1:31) (Class 5) 2-Y-O £3,234 (£962; £481; £240) Stalls High

Form RPR

4 **1** **Beacon**[19] 1712 2-9-5 0.................... RichardHughes 3 80+
(Richard Hannon) *trckd ldrs: nudged along early: nt clr run briefly 2f out: rdn and r.o wl ins fnl f: led fnl 20yds* **6/4**[1]

2 **2** *nk* **Fine Prince (IRE)**[38] 1349 2-9-5 0.................... JimmyFortune 1 79
(Robert Mills) *led for 1f: prom: led wl over 1f out: sn edgd sltly lft: rdn ent fnl f: kpt on: hdd fnl 20yds* **5/2**[2]

6 **3** *2* **Amber Crystal**[18] 1764 2-8-11 0.................... MichaelJMMurphy(3) 7 67
(John Gallagher) *led after 1f: rdn 2f out: rdr sn dropped whip and hdd: kpt on same pce fnl f* **66/1**

5 **4** *¾* **Popeswood (IRE)**[10] 2007 2-9-2 0.................... CharlesBishop(3) 6 69
(Mick Channon) *in tch: rdn 2f out: kpt on ins fnl f: wnt 4th nring fin* **7/1**[3]

**5** *½* **L'Etacq** 2-9-5 0.................... PatDobbs 5 67+
(Richard Hannon) *trckd ldrs: rdn to chal over 1f out: no ex ins fnl f* **9/1**

**6** *11* **Mister Arden (FR)** 2-9-5 0.................... AdamKirby 4 28
(Harry Dunlop) *in tch: outpcd over 3f out: wknd over 1f out* **28/1**

**7** *3 ¼* **El Campeon** 2-9-5 0.................... JamesDoyle 8 16
(Simon Dow) *s.i.s: sn outpcd in rr* **66/1**

**8** *nk* **Magic Round (IRE)** 2-9-0 0.................... RyanWhile(5) 2 15
(Bill Turner) *sn outpcd in rr* **16/1**

**9** *5* **Eileen Gray (IRE)** 2-9-0 0.................... WilliamBuick 9
(Charles Hills) *s.i.s: sn outpcd towards rr* **10/1**

1m 3.88s (2.88) **Going Correction** +0.50s/f (Yiel) **9 Ran SP% 112.5**
Speed ratings (Par 93): **96,95,92,91,90 72,67,67,59**
CSF £4.99 TOTE £2.10: £1.10, £1.50, £7.90; EX 6.40 Trifecta £98.40.

**Owner** Highclere Thoroughbred Racing (Albany) **Bred** J M Cole **Trained** East Everleigh, Wilts

**FOCUS**
The jockeys in the opener reported the ground to still be on the slow side. Those with previous experience filled the first four places in this ordinary maiden.

## 2277 BATHWICK TYRES EBF STALLIONS BREEDING WINNERS FILLIES' H'CAP (BOBIS RACE) 1m 1f 198y
2:00 (2:01) (Class 4) (0-85,83) 3-Y-O £7,762 (£2,310; £1,154; £577) Stalls Low

Form RPR

44-3 **1** **Crystal Nymph (IRE)**[16] 1846 3-8-10 **72**.................... RichardHughes 3 81+
(Richard Hannon) *hld up last: swtchd lft and stdy prog whn rdn jst over 2f out: kpt on wl to ld fnl 120yds: hld on wl* **8/1**

3-1 **2** *hd* **Melrose Abbey (IRE)**[13] 1911 3-9-2 **78**.................... RichardKingscote 8 86+
(Ralph Beckett) *in tch: nudged along on outer fr over 5f out: hdwy over 4f out: rdn for str chal over 2f out: led ent fnl f: kpt on whn hdd fnl 120yds: jst hld* **11/4**[1]

24-0 **3** *2 ¼* **Rosehill Artist (IRE)**[28] 1535 3-9-7 **83**.................... WilliamBuick 2 87
(Charles Hills) *led: rdn 2f out: hdd jst ins fnl f: no ex fnl 120yds* **7/1**

00-3 **4** *¾* **Mollasses**[43] 1240 3-8-8 **70**.................... MartinLane 5 73
(Jonathan Portman) *trckd ldrs: rdn 2f out: hung rt jst over 1f out: kpt on same pce* **9/1**

1-55 **5** *3 ½* **Hedge End (IRE)**[13] 1913 3-9-1 **77**.................... PatDobbs 1 73
(Richard Hannon) *hld up in tch: hdwy 3f out: sn rdn to chse ldrs: no ex ins fnl f* **25/1**

41-1 **6** *1 ¾* **Brown Eyed Honey**[36] 1381 3-9-3 **79**.................... AdamKirby 7 72
(William Haggas) *trckd ldr: chal 3f out: sn rdn: hld 2f out: fdd ins fnl f* **4/1**[2]

21-6 **7** *14* **Laurelita (IRE)**[51] 1096 3-9-6 **82**.................... PatCosgrave 4 48
(George Baker) *hld up: effrt to cl on ldrs 3f out: wknd over 1f out* **11/2**[3]

10-6 **8** *10* **Surcingle (USA)**[11] 1978 3-9-1 **77**.................... JamesDoyle 6 24
(Sir Michael Stoute) *off-fore shoe removed at s: trckd ldrs: rdn 3f out: wknd 2f out* **7/1**

2m 14.05s (4.15) **Going Correction** +0.50s/f (Yiel) **8 Ran SP% 112.0**
Speed ratings (Par 98): **103,102,101,100,97 96,85,77**
CSF £29.06 CT £161.11 TOTE £8.30: £2.60, £1.10, £1.90; EX 28.40 Trifecta £178.10.

**Owner** Mrs E Roberts **Bred** Joseph Broderick **Trained** East Everleigh, Wilts

**FOCUS**
Some unexposed and progressive fillies lined up for this handicap, but they went no pace early and it developed into a sprint. A personal best from the winner with the third and fourth setting the initial standard.

## 2278 SALLY-ANN FISHER WILL YOU MARRY ME H'CAP 6f
2:35 (2:35) (Class 5) (0-75,75) 3-Y-O £2,911 (£866; £432; £216) Stalls High

Form RPR

-341 **1** **Iseemist (IRE)**[21] 1669 3-9-1 **72**.................... MichaelJMMurphy(3) 10 81
(John Gallagher) *racd centre for 2f: a.p: led 2f out: r.o strly: rdn out* **9/1**

062- **2** *1 ¾* **Suitsus**[176] 7978 3-9-2 **70**.................... SteveDrowne 1 73
(Peter Makin) *racd stands' side: mid-div: sme prog whn nt clr run 2f out: hdwy to chse wnr ent fnl f: kpt on wout rching wnr* **20/1**

05-4 **3** *nk* **War Spirit**[47] 1173 3-9-2 **70**.................... RichardHughes 5 72
(Richard Hannon) *taken to s early: racd promly on stands' side: drifted lft fr over 1f out: sn rdn: kpt on ins fnl f but nvr gng pce to chal* **11/4**[1]

51-3 **4** *2 ¼* **Got To Dance**[36] 1381 3-9-7 **75**.................... SebSanders 3 70
(Ralph Beckett) *racd stands' side: carried rt s: towards rr: hdwy and nt clr run over 2f out: sn rdn: kpt on ent fnl f* **4/1**[2]

5-00 **5** *2 ¼* **Classic Pursuit**[26] 1570 3-9-1 **69**.................... JamesDoyle 14 57
(Ronald Harris) *racd centre for most of way: s.i.s: towards rr: rdn and hdwy 2f out but hanging rt: kpt on ins fnl f but n.d* **25/1**

-503 **6** *nk* **Kodafine (IRE)**[3] 2208 3-8-9 **66**.................... DeclanBates(3) 2 53
(David Evans) *racd stands' side: towards rr: rdn and hdwy over 2f out where nt clrest of runs: chsd ldrs over 1f out: no ex fnl f* **20/1**

56-4 **7** *1 ½* **Concrete Mac**[26] 1570 3-8-10 **71**.................... CharlieBennett(7) 15 53
(Hughie Morrison) *racd centre for 2f: chsd ldrs: rdn 3f out: one pce fnl 2f* **20/1**

1-34 **8** *2 ¼* **Invoke (IRE)**[17] 1818 3-9-4 **72**.................... WilliamBuick 9 47
(Michael Bell) *led centre gp tl jnd stands' side after 2f: rdn over 2f out: sn hdd: wknd over 1f out* **12/1**

35-2 **9** *1* **Perfect Pursuit**[127] 82 3-9-7 **75**.................... AdamKirby 4 46
(Clive Cox) *racd stands' side: wnt rt s: in tch: rdn over 2f out: nvr threatened: fdd fnl f* **11/1**

5-26 **10** *hd* **Touzr**[21] 1677 3-9-4 **72**....................(b[1]) SeanLevey 12 43
(Richard Hannon) *racd centre for 2f: mid-div: rdn 3f out: wknd over 1f out* **25/1**

102- **11** *2 1/2* **Go For Broke**[164] 8126 3-9-2 **70**.................... PatDobbs 7 33
(Richard Hannon) *racd stands' side: chsd ldrs: rdn over 2fg out: wknd over 1f out* **14/1**

3-50 **12** *7* **Telegraph (IRE)**[18] 1769 3-8-12 **66**....................(v[1]) DavidProbert 8 6
(Andrew Balding) *racd stands' side: s.i.s: sn mid-div: squeezed up 4f out: sn rdn: wknd over 1f out* **13/2[3]**

-146 **13** *2 3/4* **Monashka Bay (IRE)**[36] 1379 3-8-8 **62** oh1 ow1...... FergusSweeney 13
(Michael Blanshard) *racd centre for 2f: mid-div: rdn 3f out: wknd over 1f out* **66/1**

20-0 **14** *nse* **Stan Nineteen (IRE)**[17] 1786 3-8-4 **65**.................... CamHardie[(7)] 16
(Simon Hodgson) *racd centre for 2f: a towards rr* **50/1**

55-0 **15** *6* **Cadmium**[16] 1832 3-8-8 **62**.................... SilvestreDeSousa 6
(Harry Dunlop) *racd stands' side: mid-div tl outpcd 3f out: sn in rr* **40/1**

1m 17.69s (2.89) **Going Correction** +0.50s/f (Yiel) **15** Ran SP% **120.6**
Speed ratings (Par 99): **100,97,97,94,91 90,88,85,84,84 80,71,67,67,59**
CSF £180.19 CT £645.32 TOTE £9.00: £3.40, £6.20, £1.70; EX 297.60 Trifecta £2108.30.
**Owner** K Marsden **Bred** J P Lim,K Marsden & South Hatch Racing **Trained** Chastleton, Oxon

**FOCUS**
An ordinary 3yo sprint handicap. The field split early, though the two groups had merged after 2f. Another personal best from the winner.

## 2279 SMITH & WILLIAMSON MAIDEN FILLIES' STKS (DIV I) 1m 1f 198y
**3:05** (3:05) (Class 5) 3-Y-0+ **£3,234** (£962; £481; £240) **Stalls** Low

Form RPR

**1** **Hidden Gold (IRE)** 3-8-13 0....................[1] SilvestreDeSousa 4 85+
(Saeed bin Suroor) *mid-div: hdwy fr 3f out: led 2f out: sn wnt lft: kpt on wl ins fnl f: a holding on: pushed out* **7/1**

0- **2** *1* **Button Down**[190] 7763 3-8-13 0.................... JamesDoyle 5 83
(Lady Cecil) *trckd ldrs: rdn wl over 2f out: chsd wnr over 1f out: kpt on but a being hld fnl 120yds* **5/1**

6- **3** *3/4* **Some Site (IRE)**[205] 7450 3-8-13 0.................... MartinLane 10 82
(David Simcock) *hld up towards rr: rdn and stdy prog fr over 2f out: chsd ldrs over 1f out: styd on nicely ins fnl f* **4/1[2]**

6-2 **4** *7* **Shama's Song (IRE)**[16] 1841 3-8-13 0.................... RichardHughes 8 68
(Sir Michael Stoute) *trckd ldrs: rdn over 2f out: kpt on tl no ex fnl 120yds* **9/2[3]**

0-0 **5** *3/4* **Cinnilla**[33] 1438 3-8-13 0.................... SebSanders 6 67
(Ralph Beckett) *mid-div: rdn wl over 2f out: no imp tl kpt on ins fnl f* **10/1**

04 **6** *1 3/4* **Catadupa**[11] 1984 3-8-13 0.................... HayleyTurner 11 64
(Roger Charlton) *sn prom: led over 4f out: rdn and hdd 2f out: wknd ins fnl f* **12/1**

**7** *3 1/2* **Mikey Miss Daisy** 3-8-13 0.................... StevieDonohoe 2 57
(Martin Hill) *mid-div: rdn wl over 2f out: nvr any imp: fdd fnl f* **100/1**

**8** *2 1/4* **Too The Stars (IRE)** 3-8-13 0.................... WilliamBuick 9 53
(John Gosden) *s.i.s: towards rr: nudged along 5f out: hdwy into midfield 3f out: sn rdn: wknd over 1f out* **3/1[1]**

0 **9** *hd* **Hazel Brook**[20] 1691 5-10-0 0.................... FergusSweeney 7 53
(Mary Hambro) *mid-div: rdn 3f out: fdd fnl f* **100/1**

- **10** *2 3/4* **Perfect Romance**[204] 5-10-0 0.................... DavidProbert 1 48
(Patrick Chamings) *dwlt: a towards rr* **50/1**

**11** *2 3/4* **Tribulina** 3-8-8 0.................... MarcMonaghan[(5)] 12 42
(Marco Botti) *s.i.s: a towards rr* **33/1**

0 **12** *9* **Adaptability**[19] 1722 3-8-13 0.................... JimmyFortune 3 55
(Brian Meehan) *led tl over 4f out: chsd ldr: rdn over 3f out: wknd over 1f out* **40/1**

2m 14.46s (4.56) **Going Correction** +0.50s/f (Yiel)
**WFA** 3 from 5yo 15lb **12** Ran SP% **118.5**
Speed ratings (Par 100): **101,100,99,94,93 92,89,87,87,85 82,75**
CSF £41.15 TOTE £6.80: £3.20, £3.00, £1.40; EX 57.90 Trifecta £370.40.
**Owner** Godolphin **Bred** Darley **Trained** Newmarket, Suffolk

**FOCUS**
Some choicely bred fillies took part in this maiden. It was a stone+ slower than division II but the front three at least look up to race standard.

## 2280 SMITH & WILLIAMSON MAIDEN FILLIES' STKS (DIV II) 1m 1f 198y
**3:35** (3:35) (Class 5) 3-Y-0+ **£3,234** (£962; £481; £240) **Stalls** Low

Form RPR

**1** **Sultanina** 4-10-0 0....................[1] WilliamBuick 4 85+
(John Gosden) *racd green: sn pushed into midfield: lost pl and pushed along 5f out: stdy prog fr over 2f out: wnt 4th ent fnl f: styd on wl fnl 120yds to ld nring fin: rdn out* **9/2[3]**

**2** *nk* **Desert Snow** 3-8-13 0....................[1] SilvestreDeSousa 6 83+
(Saeed bin Suroor) *pushed along towards rr after 2f: stdy hdwy fr over 4f out: rdn 2f out: chsd ldr ent fnl f: led fnl 75yds: hdd nring fin* **4/1[2]**

60 **3** *2 1/4* **Prairie Rose (GER)**[6] 2109 3-8-13 0.................... HarryBentley 11 79
(Olly Stevens) *wnt lft s: sn led: rdn wl over 1f out: hdd fnl 75yds: no ex* **16/1**

43-2 **4** *2* **Cascading**[34] 1424 3-8-13 **78**.................... JimmyFortune 5 75
(Hughie Morrison) *trckd ldrs: rdn over 2f out: cl enough 3rd jst over 1f out: no ex fnl 120yds* **7/4[1]**

**5** *1 1/4* **Shadows Ofthenight (IRE)** 3-8-10 0.................... CharlesBishop[(3)] 8 73
(Mick Channon) *s.i.s: towards rr: midfield 3f out: sn rdn: kpt on ins fnl f but nvr gng pce to get involved* **33/1**

0-3 **6** *5* **What A Scorcher**[20] 1701 3-9-0 0 ow1.................... AdamKirby 1 64
(Clive Cox) *trckd ldrs tl outpcd over 2f out: kpt on again but no threat fnl f* **9/1**

0-5 **7** *4* **Hallbeck**[19] 1730 3-8-13 0.................... FergusSweeney 7 56
(Henry Candy) *trckd ldr: rdn over 2f out: lost 2nd over 1f out: sn wknd* **12/1**

0-4 **8** *shd* **Taws**[13] 1911 3-8-13 0.................... SteveDrowne 10 55
(Rod Millman) *s.i.s: sme late prog: mainly towards rr* **66/1**

5 **9** *2* **Double Dealites**[48] 1143 4-9-9 0.................... HarryPoulton[(5)] 3 53
(Jamie Poulton) *mid-div: rdn wl over 2f out: no imp: hung lft and wknd over 1f out* **66/1**

0 **10** *15* **Time Signal**[20] 1701 3-8-13 0.................... JamesDoyle 2 23
(Sir Michael Stoute) *mid-div tl lost pl 5f out: sn struggling in rr: wknd over 2f out* **6/1**

0 **11** *3 3/4* **Beauchamp Melba**[17] 1808 3-8-13 0.................... PatDobbs 9 16
(Paul Fitzsimons) *trckd ldrs tl over 4f out: sn bhd* **100/1**

2m 13.1s (3.20) **Going Correction** +0.50s/f (Yiel)
**WFA** 3 from 4yo 15lb **11** Ran SP% **119.3**
Speed ratings (Par 100): **107,106,104,103,102 98,95,95,93,81 78**
CSF £23.06 TOTE £4.80: £1.70, £1.80, £5.40; EX 29.60 Trifecta £247.70.
**Owner** Normandie Stud Ltd **Bred** Normandie Stud Ltd **Trained** Newmarket, Suffolk

**FOCUS**
A couple of newcomers, both sporting hoods, fought out the finish of this division for which the winning time was 1.36sec quicker than the first leg. Useful form, the fourth setting the standard.

## 2281 THE BOOT INN SHIPTON BELLINGER CLAIMING STKS 6f 212y
**4:10** (4:11) (Class 5) 3-Y-0 **£2,749** (£818; £408; £204) **Stalls** High

Form RPR

2631 **1** **Intense Feeling (IRE)**[3] 2209 3-7-9 61.................... NoelGarbutt[(5)] 3 61
(David Evans) *trckd ldrs: chal over 2f out: led wl over 1f out: kpt on wl: pushed out* **11/4[2]**

04 **2** *3/4* **Native Heart**[16] 1831 3-8-9 0.................... CharlesBishop[(3)] 8 71
(Mick Channon) *towards rr: rdn and hdwy but edging lft fr over 2f out: chsd wnr ent fnl f: kpt on* **14/1**

4546 **3** *4 1/2* **Honiton Lace**[21] 1683 3-8-8 55.................... SilvestreDeSousa 12 55
(J W Hills) *t.k.h early: struggling in rr over 3f out: hdwy 2f out: styd on to go 3rd ins fnl f: nvr trbld ldrs* **20/1**

532 **4** *1 1/2* **Dandys Perier (IRE)**[42] 1264 3-8-13 60.................... SteveDrowne 9 56
(Ronald Harris) *trckd ldr: rdn over 2f out: kpt on same pce* **22/1**

-500 **5** *1 1/2* **Vodka Time (IRE)**[68] 892 3-9-4 72.................... DeclanBates[(3)] 10 61
(David Evans) *in tch: swtchd lft 3f out: sn rdn: nt pce to get on terms* **14/1**

1415 **6** *1 1/2* **Coiste Bodhar (IRE)**[9] 2049 3-8-7 66....................(p) NoraLooby[(7)] 7 50
(Joseph Tuite) *wnt rt s: plld hrd: led: rdn 2f out: sn hdd: wknd fnl f* **10/1[3]**

4-30 **7** *1/2* **Black Caesar (IRE)**[9] 2063 3-9-7 80.................... RichardHughes 2 55
(Richard Hannon) *racd keenly: trckd ldrs: ev ch briefly 2f out: sn rdn and swtchd rt: hld 1f out: wknd fnl 120yds* **11/10[1]**

5554 **8** *1 1/2* **Miss Tweedy**[13] 1914 3-7-7 50....................(b[1]) CamHardie[(7)] 4 30
(Rod Millman) *chsd ldrs: rdn wl over 2f out: wknd jst over 1f out* **16/1**

0 **9** *17* **The Pocket Dot**[13] 1918 3-7-13 0.................... KatiaScallan[(5)] 14
(Mick Channon) *trckd ldrs for 3f: sn bhd: t.o* **50/1**

-006 **10** *nk* **Dover The Moon (IRE)**[13] 1918 3-8-0 50....................(b[1]) GaryMahon[(7)] 1
(Sylvester Kirk) *trckd ldrs: rdn 3f out: drifted bdly lft then rt whn btn fr over 2f out: t.o* **33/1**

1m 32.56s (3.96) **Going Correction** +0.50s/f (Yiel)
**WFA** 3 from 4yo 12lb **10** Ran SP% **116.6**
Speed ratings (Par 99): **97,96,91,89,87 85,85,83,64,63**
.Black Caesar was claimed by Mr P Hide for £12,000.\n\x\x Intense Feeling was claimed by Mr L. A. Carter for £4000.\n\x\x Native Heart was claimed by Mr J Osborne for £10,000.
**Owner** Mrs E Evans & C W Racing **Bred** R And Mrs R Hodgins **Trained** Pandy, Monmouths

**FOCUS**
A weak claimer with the favourite disappointing. The winner only needed to match her recent form.

## 2282 CGA RACING EXCELLENCE APPRENTICE H'CAP (WHIPS SHALL BE CARRIED BUT NOT USED) 6f 212y
**4:45** (4:45) (Class 5) (0-70,67) 4-Y-0+ **£2,911** (£866; £432; £216) **Stalls** High

Form RPR

0621 **1** **Welsh Inlet (IRE)**[15] 1877 6-8-8 **57**.................... CamHardie[(3)] 11 68
(John Bridger) *hld up: hdwy 2f out: kpt on wl to ld fnl 120yds: pushed out* **10/1**

0022 **2** *1/2* **Sea Soldier (IRE)**[11] 1986 6-8-4 **55**.................... KieranShoemark[(5)] 5 64
(Andrew Balding) *trckd ldrs: effrt 2f out: kpt on to press ldrs ins fnl f: hld nring fin* **5/2[1]**

2405 **3** *1 1/4* **Intomist (IRE)**[73] 817 5-9-7 **67**....................(p) DanielCremin 1 73
(Jim Boyle) *led: pushed along 2f out: kpt on tl no ex whn hdd fnl 120yds* **6/1[3]**

3302 **4** *2 3/4* **Bennelong**[18] 1771 8-8-8 **59**....................(b) PaigeBolton[(5)] 6 58
(Lee Carter) *chsd ldrs: kpt on same pce fnl 2f* **12/1**

113- **5** *3 3/4* **Be Royale**[159] 8199 4-9-2 **62**.................... AlistairRawlinson 12 51
(Michael Appleby) *chsd ldrs: one pce fnl 2f* **12/1**

3343 **6** *1/2* **West Leake (IRE)**[18] 1766 8-8-6 **57**.................... JoshQuinn[(5)] 8 45
(Paul Burgoyne) *towards rr: sme late prog: nvr a threat* **25/1**

2235 **7** *1 3/4* **Teen Ager (FR)**[17] 1799 10-8-4 **53** oh4....................(p) DavidParkes[(3)] 9 36
(Paul Burgoyne) *chsd ldrs tl wknd ent fnl f* **25/1**

0-13 **8** *1/2* **Burnt Fingers (IRE)**[19] 1716 4-9-6 **66**.................... PatMillman 7 48
(Rod Millman) *prom: pushed along over 2f out: wknd over 1f out* **11/4[2]**

45/0 **9** *5* **Stand Beside Me (IRE)**[26] 1573 7-8-5 **54**....................(t) JackGarritty[(3)] 4 23
(Tony Newcombe) *rrd leaving stalls: towards rr: effrt over 2f out: wknd over 1f out* **33/1**

0-13 **10** *13* **Secret Success**[18] 1771 4-9-5 **65**.................... JoeDoyle 10
(Paul Cole) *prom tl wknd over 2f out* **8/1**

1m 32.5s (3.90) **Going Correction** +0.50s/f (Yiel) **10** Ran SP% **115.7**
Speed ratings (Par 103): **97,96,95,91,87 87,85,84,78,63**
CSF £34.32 CT £171.66 TOTE £10.00: £3.40, £1.60, £2.30; EX 54.50 Trifecta £563.00.
**Owner** J J Bridger **Bred** Patrick Gleeson **Trained** Liphook, Hants

**FOCUS**
A modest apprentice handicap in which the winning time was only marginally quicker than the preceding 3yo claimer. The winner's best form for two years.
T/Plt: £234.30 to a £1 stake. Pool: £52,945.83 - 164.96 winning units. T/Qpdt: £105.60 to a £1 stake. Pool: £3667.56 - 25.70 winning units. TM

# 2253 YORK (L-H)
Thursday, May 15

**OFFICIAL GOING: Good to soft (good in places) changing to good (good to soft in places) after race 4 (3.15)**
Wind: Virtually nil Weather: Fine & dry

## 2283 BETFRED SUPPORTS JACK BERRY HOUSE STKS (H'CAP) 5f
**1:45** (1:48) (Class 2) (0-105,101) 4-Y-0+**£16,172** (£4,812; £2,405; £1,202) **Stalls** High

Form RPR

6060 **1** **Monsieur Joe (IRE)**[54] 1066 7-9-6 **100**.................... GrahamLee 4 111
(Paul Midgley) *hld up towards rr: hdwy 2f out: swtchd rt over 1f out: sn rdn: stayd on strly to ld last 75yds* **25/1**

0320 **2** *1* **Elusivity (IRE)**[12] 1944 6-8-8 **88**.................... ShaneKelly 12 95
(Peter Crate) *lw: in tch: hdwy 2f out: sn chsng ldrs: rdn to ld ent fnl f: sn drvn and edgd lft: hdd and no ex last 75yds* **14/1**

1324 **3** *nk* **Top Boy**[8] 2074 4-8-6 **86**....................(v) FrannyNorton 10 92
(Derek Shaw) *lw: hld up: hdwy 2f out: rdn to chse ldrs whn nt clr run ent fnl f: swtchd slt lft and styd on towards fin* **14/1**

61-0 **4** *3/4* **Ashpan Sam**[11] 1975 5-9-3 **97**.................... RyanMoore 11 100+
(John Spearing) *chsd ldrs: effrt wl over 1f out: sn rdn and edgd rt: drvn ent fnl f: kpt on* **11/2[1]**

-050 **5** *nk* **Secret Witness**[1] 2254 8-9-0 **94**....................(b) LukeMorris 5 96
(Ronald Harris) *chsd ldrs: rdn along wl over 1f out: styng on whn n.m.r and hmpd ent fnl f: kpt on wl towards fin* **16/1**

600- **6** 1/2 **Lady Gibraltar**[216] 7171 5-8-9 **89** IoritzMendizabal 6 89
(Alan Jarvis) *chsd ldr: hdwy 2f out: rdn and led briefly over 1f out: sn hdd and kpt on same pce* **33/1**

40-4 **7** 1 **Long Awaited (IRE)**[12] 1944 6-8-8 **91** (b) JasonHart(3) 2 88
(David Barron) *lw: hld up: hdwy 1/2-way: effrt wl over 1f out: rdn and n.m.r appr fnl f: kpt on same pce* **10/1**[3]

0-01 **8** 1/2 **Normal Equilibrium**[6] 2123 4-8-6 **91** 6ex (p) RyanTate(5) 8 86
(Robert Cowell) *in tch: hdwy wl over 1f out: sn rdn and n.m.r appr fnl f: kpt on same pce after* **10/1**[3]

0430 **9** 1 **Inxile (IRE)**[8] 2076 9-9-2 **96** (p) AdrianNicholls 7 87
(David Nicholls) *chsd ldr: rdn along 2f out: drvn over 1f out and grad wknd* **33/1**

51-6 **10** 3/4 **Best Trip (IRE)**[19] 1734 7-8-6 **86** PaulPickard 15 75
(Brian Ellison) *in tch: hdwy 2f out: sn rdn along and no imp ent fnl f* **12/1**

00-5 **11** 1 1/2 **Ballesteros**[34] 1421 5-9-4 **101** IanBrennan(3) 1 84
(Richard Fahey) *swtg: chsd ldrs: rdn along over 2f out: wknd over 1f out* **14/1**

0-00 **12** 1/2 **Ancient Cross**[19] 1734 10-9-3 **97** (t) JamesSullivan 9 79
(Michael Easterby) *dwlt and towards rr: hdwy 2f out: swtchd rt and rdn over 1f out: sn no imp* **22/1**

4501 **13** nk **Pandar**[12] 1944 5-8-0 **85** PhilipPrince(5) 13 65
(Milton Bradley) *in tch: rdn along 2f out: sn wknd* **16/1**

105- **14** 1 1/2 **Magical Macey (USA)**[243] 6391 7-9-7 **101** (b) GrahamGibbons 3 76
(David Barron) *swtg: led: rdn along 2f out: sn hdd and wkng whn hmpd appr fnl f* **12/1**

00-0 **15** 6 **Judge 'n Jury**[6] 2123 10-9-1 **95** (t) FrankieDettori 18 48
(Ronald Harris) *in tch: rdn along 2f out: sn wknd* **16/1**

0-30 **16** 7 **Doc Hay (USA)**[19] 1734 7-9-6 **100** DaleSwift 14 28
(Brian Ellison) *dwlt: a bhd* **33/1**

000- **17** 1 1/2 **Bogart**[215] 7208 5-9-6 **100** JamieSpencer 17 23
(Kevin Ryan) *lw: in tch: rdn along 2f out: sn wknd* **8/1**[2]

0-34 **18** 3 1/4 **Desert Law (IRE)**[84] 680 6-9-6 **100** KierenFallon 19 11
(Saeed bin Suroor) *towards rr: rdn along 1/2-way: sn bhd* **14/1**

0-63 **19** 13 **Kyleakin Lass**[12] 1944 5-8-12 **92** JimCrowley 20
(Jonathan Portman) *a in rr: bhd fnl 2f* **14/1**

1m 0.16s (0.86) **Going Correction** +0.40s/f (Good) **19** Ran SP% **128.1**
Speed ratings (Par 109): **109,107,106,105,105 104,102,102,100,99 96,96,95,93,83 72,69,64,43**
CSF £337.83 CT £5156.74 TOTE £33.80: £5.60, £4.30, £4.10, £1.80; EX 934.00 Trifecta £3773.00.
**Owner** Taylor's Bloodstock Ltd **Bred** Nicola And Eleanor Kent **Trained** Westow, N Yorks

**FOCUS**
Rail moved out 3m from 1m1f until entrance to home straight reducing distances on Round course by 17yds. Drying ground, described as "on the slower side of good" by riders in the first. The opening time was 2.66sec outside the standard. This competitive handicap was run at a frenetic pace, thanks to Magical Macey, who gave a tow to those racing near the middle of the track. In contrast, the group of seven who raced nearer the stands' rail (drawn 13 and higher) were never on terms and finished out the back. Their runs can be written off. The winner took advantage of a good mark and the second built on recent runs.

## 2284 "BETFRED £10 MILLION SCOOP6 THIS SATURDAY" MIDDLETON STKS (GROUP 2) (F&M) 1m 2f 88y
**2:15** (2:16) (Class 1) 4-Y-O+
**£56,710** (£21,500; £10,760; £5,360; £2,690; £1,350) **Stalls** Low

Form RPR

02-3 **1** **My Ambivalent (IRE)**[47] 1182 5-9-0 110 AndreaAtzeni 3 113
(Roger Varian) *set stdy pce: qcknd wl over 3f out: hdd jst over 2f out: cl up: rdn and edgd lft over 1f out: led again ent fnl f: sn edgd rt and drvn clr* **9/2**[2]

230- **2** 1 3/4 **Secret Gesture**[221] 7057 4-9-0 108 JamieSpencer 8 110
(Ralph Beckett) *trckd wnr: hdwy 3f out: slt ld over 2f out and sn rdn: carried sltly lft over 1f out: drvn and hdd ent fnl f: kpt on same pce* **9/2**[2]

4-25 **3** 1 **Odeliz (IRE)**[11] 1974 4-9-0 102 DanielTudhope 2 108
(K R Burke) *t.k.h: hld up in tch: hdwy over 2f out: chsd ldrs and swtchd rt over 1f out: sn rdn and kpt on same pce* **8/1**[3]

011- **4** 1 3/4 **Mango Diva**[235] 6674 4-9-0 106 RyanMoore 6 105
(Sir Michael Stoute) *hld up in rr: swtchd rt to outer and hdwy wl over 2f out: sn rdn and kpt on fnl f: nrst fin* **9/2**[2]

510- **5** 1/2 **The Lark**[200] 7566 4-9-2 107 TomQueally 1 106
(Michael Bell) *bit bkwd: trckd ldrs: hdwy on inner 3f out: cl up 2f out: rdn and ev ch over 1f out: wknd fnl f* **16/1**

263- **6** 1 **Thistle Bird**[221] 7057 6-9-0 114 FrankieDettori 4 102
(Roger Charlton) *lw: trckd ldrs: hdwy over 3f out: cl up over 2f out: sn rdn and wknd* **10/3**[1]

14-0 **7** 2 **Quiz Mistress**[33] 1434 6-9-0 105 IoritzMendizabal 5 98
(Hughie Morrison) *towards rr: effrt and sme hdwy over 3f out: rdn along wl over 2f out and sn wknd* **20/1**

25-3 **8** 5 **Gifted Girl (IRE)**[11] 1974 5-9-0 110 JimCrowley 7 89
(Paul Cole) *lw: hld up in tch: stdy hdwy on outer over 3f out and sn cl up: rdn 2f out and sn wknd* **8/1**[3]

2m 10.21s (-2.29) **Going Correction** +0.10s/f (Good) **8** Ran SP% **110.5**
Speed ratings (Par 115): **113,111,110,109,109 108,106,102**
CSF £23.25 TOTE £5.00: £1.70, £1.80, £2.00; EX 21.10 Trifecta £79.90.
**Owner** Ali Saeed **Bred** Darley **Trained** Newmarket, Suffolk

**FOCUS**
This looked a classy event, as a few of these had solid form at Group 1 level, but the winner was handed an easy time of it on the front end and then fought on in game style. A small personal best from Ambivalent.

## 2285 BETFRED DANTE STKS (GROUP 2) 1m 2f 88y
**2:45** (2:47) (Class 1) 3-Y-O
**£85,065** (£32,250; £16,140; £8,040; £4,035; £2,025) **Stalls** Low

Form RPR

0-20 **1** **The Grey Gatsby (IRE)**[12] 1951 3-9-0 108 RyanMoore 6 112
(Kevin Ryan) *chsd ldng pair: hdwy 3f out: cl up over 2f out: rdn to ld 1 1/2f out: hung rt appr fnl f: drvn and kpt on wl towards fin* **9/1**

3-1 **2** 3/4 **Arod (IRE)**[31] 1491 3-9-0 96 JamieSpencer 4 111
(Peter Chapple-Hyam) *athletic: leggy: hld up and bhd: hdwy over 3f out: chsd ldrs wl over 1f out: sn rdn and styng on whn n.m.r and swtchd lft ins fnl f: kpt on wl towards fin* **8/1**[3]

21-1 **3** 3/4 **True Story**[29] 1516 3-9-0 116 KierenFallon 3 110
(Saeed bin Suroor) *hld up: hdwy and niggled along 4f out: chsd ldrs wl over 2f out: rdn wl over 1f out: carried rt and hmpd jst ins fnl f: kpt on same pce* **8/13**[1]

5-1 **4** 1 1/2 **Odeon**[24] 1608 3-9-0 93 GrahamLee 5 106
(James Given) *unf: scope: led and sn clr: pushed along wl over 2f out: rdn and hdd 1 1/f out: kpt on u.p fnl f* **20/1**

121- **5** 3/4 **Bunker (IRE)**[277] 5313 3-9-0 107 FrankieDettori 2 105
(Richard Hannon) *lw: chsd clr ldr: tk clsr order over 2f out: rdn wl over 1f out: sn drvn and one pce appr fnl f* **9/2**[2]

2-2 **6** 3/4 **Saab Almanal**[26] 1587 3-9-0 0 ShaneKelly 1 104?
(James Fanshawe) *hld up in rr: pushed along and outpcd over 3f out: styd on wl appr fnl f: nrst fin* **50/1**

2m 8.99s (-3.51) **Going Correction** +0.10s/f (Good) **6** Ran SP% **107.9**
Speed ratings (Par 111): **118,117,116,115,115 114**
CSF £67.92 TOTE £8.40: £3.30, £2.60; EX 55.80 Trifecta £104.10.
**Owner** F Gillespie **Bred** M Parrish **Trained** Hambleton, N Yorks

**FOCUS**
A fascinating Dante on paper, although Kingston Hill (by the same sire as the winner) missed the race to wait for Epsom. The pace was sound and the time was 1.22sec quicker than that recorded by Ambivalent in the Middleton Stakes. However, the odds-on favourite was turned over in a rather messy finish, the six being covered by only four and a half lengths at the line, and the upshot was that this all cemented Australia's position at the head of the Derby market. It's hard to rate the form too highly and it comes out a little lower than the last couple of renewals. A length best from The Grey Gatsby.

## 2286 BETFRED HAMBLETON STKS (H'CAP) (LISTED RACE) 1m
**3:15** (3:18) (Class 1) (0-110,104) 4-Y-O+
**£22,684** (£8,600; £4,304; £2,144; £1,076; £540) **Stalls** Low

Form RPR

060- **1** **Navajo Chief**[229] 6834 7-9-0 **97** KierenFallon 1 106
(Alan Jarvis) *trckd ldng pair on inner: hdwy and cl up 2f out: rdn and ev ch over 1f out: drvn ins fnl f: styd on wl to ld nr fin* **15/2**[3]

-601 **2** shd **Fort Bastion (IRE)**[12] 1958 5-8-11 **94** JamesSullivan 4 103+
(Ruth Carr) *hld up: smooth hdwy over 2f out: rdn to ld over 1f out: drvn ins fnl f: hdd and no ex nr fin* **8/1**

000- **3** 1 1/4 **Prince Of Johanne (IRE)**[215] 7206 8-9-3 **100** (p) GrahamLee 3 106
(Tom Tate) *trckd ldrs: hdwy over 2f out: rdn over 1f out: kpt on wl u.p fnl f* **12/1**

4005 **4** 3/4 **Tales Of Grimm (USA)**[47] 1162 5-9-5 **102** TonyHamilton 8 106
(Richard Fahey) *hld up in rr: hdwy over 2f out: rdn over 1f out: drvn and kpt on fnl f: nrst fin* **25/1**

1553 **5** hd **Alfred Hutchinson**[27] 1558 6-8-7 **90** TomEaves 5 94
(Geoffrey Oldroyd) *trckd ldrs: effrt 2f out: nt clr run jst over 1f out: swtchd rt ins fnl f: rdn and styd on wl towards fin* **17/2**

0224 **6** nse **Askaud (IRE)**[12] 1945 6-8-12 **95** (p) FrederikTylicki 2 99
(Scott Dixon) *led: rdn along over 2f out: drvn and hdd over 1f out: grad wknd* **10/1**

3002 **7** shd **Spa's Dancer (IRE)**[33] 1437 7-9-1 **98** JimCrowley 9 101
(James Eustace) *lw: dwlt and in rr: hdwy on inner over 2f out: rdn to chse ldrs over 1f out: drvn and kpt on same pce ins fnl f* **11/2**[2]

0450 **8** 1 1/4 **Sweet Lightning**[19] 1721 9-9-0 **97** (t) DavidNolan 11 97
(David O'Meara) *hld up towards rr: effrt over 2f out: rdn along wl over 1f out: kpt on fnl f: nrst fin* **20/1**

0-52 **9** shd **Ingleby Angel (IRE)**[12] 1958 5-9-0 **97** DanielTudhope 6 97
(David O'Meara) *lw: t.k.h: chsd ldrs on outer: hdwy wl over 2f out: rdn along wl over 1f out: edgd lft and one pce appr fnl f* **15/2**[3]

000- **10** 6 **Fury**[208] 7368 6-8-12 **95** (p) RyanMoore 7 81
(William Haggas) *trckd ldr: cl up over 2f out: rdn wl over 1f out: wknd appr fnl f* **3/1**[1]

1-00 **11** 2 1/4 **Levitate**[15] 1870 6-9-7 **104** (v) PhillipMakin 10 85
(John Quinn) *t.k.h: chsd ldrs on outer: rdn along over 2f out: sn wknd* **25/1**

1m 37.7s (-1.30) **Going Correction** +0.10s/f (Good) **11** Ran SP% **114.8**
Speed ratings (Par 111): **110,109,108,107,107 107,107,106,106,100 97**
CSF £62.70 CT £514.99 TOTE £6.80: £2.60, £3.50, £4.00; EX 65.20 Trifecta £555.20.
**Owner** Geoffrey Bishop **Bred** Eurostrait Ltd **Trained** Twyford, Bucks

**FOCUS**
Some very useful types took their chance in a race that is one of 18 qualifiers for the Balmoral Handicap on QIPCO British Champions Day, which will be Europe's most valuable 1m handicap. The gallop seemed a fair one from the outset thanks to Askaud, despite a couple taking a keen hold. Straightforward form.

## 2287 BRITISH STALLION STUDS EBF CONDITIONS STKS (BOBIS RACE) 5f
**3:50** (3:50) (Class 2) 3-Y-O
**£22,641** (£6,737; £3,367; £1,683) **Stalls** High

Form RPR

150- **1** **Shamshon (IRE)**[195] 7688 3-9-7 0 FrankieDettori 2 109
(Richard Hannon) *cl up: led 1/2-way: rdn appr fnl f: kpt on* **9/1**

0-56 **2** 1 **One Chance (IRE)**[15] 1867 3-8-11 92 JamieSpencer 6 95
(John Butler) *stdd s and sn swtchd lft: hld up in rr: hdwy on wd outside wl over 1f out and ch ins fnl f: drvn and one pce towards fin* **22/1**

6-12 **3** 1 **Eccleston**[11] 1968 3-9-2 96 DanielTudhope 1 96
(David O'Meara) *lw: hld up in tch: hdwy 2f out: rdn over 1f out: kpt on same pce ins fnl f* **7/2**[2]

213- **4** 5 **Justice Day (IRE)**[215] 7191 3-9-5 108 RyanMoore 3 81
(David Elsworth) *cl up: rdn along 2f out: drvn over 1f out: wknd ent fnl f* **11/10**[1]

340- **5** 2 **Ambiance (IRE)**[244] 6347 3-9-7 103 AndreaAtzeni 5 76
(Roger Varian) *chsd ldrs: rdn along over 2f out: sn wknd* **5/1**[3]

10-2 **6** 8 **Hay Chewed (IRE)**[20] 1700 3-8-11 94 RobertHavlin 4 37
(Conrad Allen) *slt ld: hdd 1/2-way: sn rdn and wknd* **8/1**

1m 1.09s (1.79) **Going Correction** +0.40s/f (Good) **6** Ran SP% **112.0**
Speed ratings (Par 105): **101,99,97,89,86 73**
CSF £147.93 TOTE £7.20: £3.50, £5.20; EX 77.60 Trifecta £301.90.
**Owner** Al Shaqab Racing **Bred** Stonethorn Stud Farms Ltd **Trained** East Everleigh, Wilts

**FOCUS**
Some smart, not top-class, sprinters have taken this in the past. 2012 winner Pearl Secret finished third in the King's Stand the following season and Night Carnation, successful in 2011, was second in a Canadian Group 1 subsequently. Three came clear, with a smart effort from the winner.

## 2288 STRATFORD PLACE STUD CHRISELLIAM MEMORIAL EBF STALLIONS MAIDEN STKS (BOBIS RACE) 6f
**4:25** (4:27) (Class 3) 2-Y-O
**£12,938** (£3,850; £1,924; £962) **Stalls** High

Form RPR

**1** **Bossy Guest (IRE)** 2-9-2 0 WilliamTwiston-Davies(3) 1 84+
(Mick Channon) *str: hld up: smooth hdwy wl over 1f out: effrt whn nt clr run ent fnl f: sn rdn and styd on strly to ld nr fin* **5/1**[3]

2 *hd* **Mister Universe** 2-9-5 0 FrannyNorton 6 83+
(Mark Johnston) *athletic: lengthy: slt ld: rdn along wl over 1f out: drvn ent fnl f: kpt on: hdd and no ex nr line* **9/2**[2]

3 *1* **Silver Ranger** 2-9-5 0 RyanMoore 8 80
(Richard Hannon) *athletic: leggy: trckd ldrs: hdwy 1/2-way: cl up over 2f out: rdn to chal over 1f out: drvn and ev ch ins fnl f: no ex towards fin* **7/4**[1]

4 *1 3/4* **Gaudy (IRE)** 2-9-5 0 JamieSpencer 2 75
(Kevin Ryan) *leggy: prom: cl up 1/2-way: rdn and ev ch over 1f out: sn drvn and one pce ins fnl f* **9/2**[2]

5 *1/2* **Bonds Choice** 2-8-11 0 GeorgeChaloner(3) 4 69
(Richard Fahey) *angular: cl up: disp ld 1/2-way: rdn 2f out: drvn and wknd ent fnl f* **14/1**

6 *3 3/4* **Special Venture (IRE)** 2-9-5 0 RobertWinston 7 62
(Tim Easterby) *neat: dwlt: trckd ldrs: effrt and n.m.r over 1f out: rdn and wknd ins fnl f* **20/1**

7 *9* **Cisco Boy** 2-9-5 0 DavidAllan 3 35
(Tim Easterby) *w'like: str: wnt lft s: cl up on outer: rdn along wl over 2f out: sn wknd* **8/1**

8 *7* **Prince Rofan (IRE)** 2-9-5 0 DaleSwift 9 14
(Derek Shaw) *leggy: unf: chsd ldrs on outer: rdn along 1/2-way: outpcd fnl 2f* **40/1**

1m 15.98s (4.08) **Going Correction** +0.40s/f (Good) 8 Ran SP% **114.4**
Speed ratings (Par 97): **88,87,86,84,83 78,66,57**
CSF £27.71 TOTE £6.30: £1.70, £2.10, £1.20; EX 30.80 Trifecta £114.10.

**Owner** John Guest Racing **Bred** Dowager Countess Harrington **Trained** West Ilsley, Berks

**FOCUS**
The first 6f race in Britain for 2yos and none of these had run before. It remains to be seen how strong the form is.

## 2289 INVESTEC SPECIALIST BANK STKS (H'CAP) 2m 88y
**5:00** (5:01) (Class 3) (0-90,90) 4-Y-0+ **£12,938** (£3,850; £1,924; £962) **Stalls** Low

Form RPR

1145 1 **Villa Royale**[27] [1556] 5-9-10 **88** AndrewMullen 16 98
(Michael Appleby) *prom: led 3f out: rdn clr wl over 1f out: edgd lft fnl f: kpt on strly* **16/1**

00-0 2 *2* **Eagle Rock (IRE)**[27] [1562] 6-9-3 **81** (p) JamesSullivan 17 89
(Tom Tate) *lw: sn led: rdn along and hdd 3f out: chsd wnr: drvn wl over 1f out: kpt on fnl f* **16/1**

0-32 3 *nk* **Entihaa**[16] [1848] 6-8-13 **77** DavidAllan 3 85
(Alan Swinbank) *lw: midfield: hdwy 5f out: effrt to chse ldng pair wl over 2f out: sn rdn: drvn and kpt on fnl f* **10/1**

1-53 4 *1 1/2* **Mr Snoozy**[20] [1692] 5-8-13 **80** (p) JasonHart(3) 15 86
(Mark Walford) *chsd ldr: rdn along 4f out: sltly outpcd wl over 2f out: drvn and kpt on fnl f* **7/1**[2]

30-6 5 *2* **Dr Irv**[25] [1599] 5-8-12 **76** GrahamLee 5 79+
(Philip Kirby) *hld up towards rr: stdy hdwy over 3f out: chsd ldrs over 2f out: rdn and kpt on one pce fnl f* **16/1**

300- 6 *shd* **Suraj**[250] [6192] 5-9-12 **90** JamieSpencer 7 93
(Nicky Henderson) *hld up and bhd: hdwy 4f out: rdn along wl over 2f out: styd on u.p fnl f: nrst fin* **11/2**[1]

0/12 7 *shd* **Bob's World**[20] [1692] 5-8-12 **76** (tp) TomEaves 12 79
(Jennie Candlish) *midfield: hdwy and in tch 6f out: rdn along 3f out: chsd ldrs 2f out: sn drvn and one pce* **12/1**

16-3 8 *hd* **Calculated Risk**[37] [1359] 5-8-8 **75** IanBrennan(3) 2 78
(John Quinn) *lw: hld up: hdwy over 4f out: rdn along over 3f out: drvn wl over 1f out: kpt on one pce* **11/2**[1]

0-00 9 *1 3/4* **Moidore**[19] [1735] 5-9-6 **84** PhillipMakin 14 85
(John Quinn) *trckd ldrs: pushed along over 5f out: rdn over 3f out: grad wknd* **7/1**[2]

/10- 10 *1 1/4* **Hidden Justice (IRE)**[57] [2402] 5-9-3 **81** RobertWinston 11 80
(John Quinn) *hld up in rr: hdwy on outer over 3f out: swtchd lft and rdn over 2f out: n.d* **16/1**

0-00 11 *2 1/4* **Herostatus**[19] [1735] 7-9-0 **83** JoeyHaynes(5) 6 80
(Jason Ward) *hld up towards rr: hdwy on outer over 3f out: rdn to chse ldrs over 2f out: sn no imp* **50/1**

50-3 12 *4* **Albert Bridge**[11] [1981] 6-9-9 **87** JimCrowley 4 79
(Ralph Beckett) *midfield: effrt on inner over 3f out: rdn along over 2f out: sn btn* **9/1**[3]

000- 13 *4* **Nashville (IRE)**[209] [7338] 5-8-9 **76** (p) GeorgeChaloner(3) 13 63
(Richard Fahey) *chsd ldrs: rdn along over 4f out: wknd wl over 2f out* **33/1**

62/- 14 *2 1/2* **Cape Tribulation**[140] [7068] 10-9-1 **79** PJMcDonald 9 63
(Malcolm Jefferson) *midfield: hdwy on outer and in tch 7f out: rdn along 5f out: wknd over 3f out* **14/1**

52/0 15 *7* **Aviator (GER)**[33] [1444] 6-9-9 **87** GrahamGibbons 10 63
(James Eustace) *a towards rr* **33/1**

00-3 16 *6* **Man Of Plenty**[12] [1935] 5-9-5 **83** (p) FrankieDettori 1 51
(Ed Dunlop) *hld up: a towards rr* **16/1**

2400 17 *4* **Hunting Ground (USA)**[19] [1735] 4-8-12 **79** FrannyNorton 8 43
(Mark Johnston) *trckd ldrs on inner: pushed along 5f out: rdn along 4f out: sn wknd* **33/1**

3m 34.48s (-0.02) **Going Correction** +0.10s/f (Good)
**WFA** 4 from 5yo+ 3lb 17 Ran SP% **129.4**
Speed ratings (Par 107): **104,103,102,102,101 101,101,100,100,99 98,96,94,93,89 86,84**
CSF £258.26 CT £2717.95 TOTE £18.80: £4.50, £5.30, £3.00, £2.60; EX 430.50 Trifecta £3832.60 Part won..

**Owner** David Kuss & Tim Pakyurek **Bred** Lawn Stud **Trained** Danethorpe, Notts

**FOCUS**
Last year's race was won by Well Sharp, who added the Ascot Stakes at the Royal meeting. This was a competitive staying handicap, but few got into it off an ordinary gallop. The first two, and the fourth, emerged from the three highest stalls and were always prominent. The second and third set the standard.

T/Jkpt: Not won. T/Plt: £1473.10 to a £1 stake. Pool: £245,106.11 - 121.46 winning units. T/Qpdt: £198.90 to a £1 stake. Pool: 9953.90 - 37.05 winning units. JR

# LE CROISE-LAROCHE
Thursday, May 15

**OFFICIAL GOING: Turf: good to soft**

## 2290a PRIX DE MARQUETTE (MAIDEN) (3YO) (TURF) 1m 1f
**12:30** (12:00) 3-Y-O **£6,666** (£2,666; £2,000; £1,333; £666)

RPR

1 *1 3/4* **Silver Treasure (FR)**[28] [1551] 3-9-2 0 Pierre-CharlesBoudot 12 67
(Amy Weaver) *sn disputing ld fr wd draw: led on rail appr 1/2-way: rdn and lened over 1 1/2f out: hdd fnl 40yds: no ex: fin 2nd: plcd 1st* **17/10**[1]

2 *1 1/2* **Tucano (IRE)** 3-9-2 0 AnthonyCaramanolis 8 63
(N Clement, France) **14/5**[2]

3 *nse* **Cape Ice (IRE)**[203] 3-8-13 0 FlavienPrat 2 57
(F Head, France) **17/2**

4 **Shayboob (IRE)**[35] 3-8-8 0 Georges-AntoineAnselin(8) 1 67
(N Clement, France) **11/1**

5 *nse* **Wefeen (FR)**[24] [1620] 3-9-2 0 AntoineCoutier 9 60
(F Chappet, France) **20/1**

6 *nse* **Danseuse De Reve (IRE)**[337] 3-8-13 0 FabienLefebvre 10 57
(J E Hammond, France) **73/10**[3]

7 *nse* **Sakal** 3-8-8 0 UmbertoRispoli 13 52
(M Delzangles, France) **15/1**

8 *1* **Bombineta (FR)**[14] [1907] 3-8-13 0 RaphaelMarchelli 5 55
(P Adda, France) **52/1**

9 *1/2* **Baricella (FR)**[63] 3-8-13 0 FilipMinarik 11 54
(N Sauer, Germany) **29/1**

10 *hd* **Wachau (FR)**[203] 3-8-13 0 SHellyn 3 53
(K Demme, Germany) **65/1**

11 *1* **Lexa King's (FR)** 3-9-2 0 MarcLerner 6 54
(C Lerner, France) **15/1**

12 *3 1/2* **Kaniza (FR)**[35] 3-8-13 0 CristianDemuro 7 44
(Y Barberot, France) **60/1**

1m 55.9s (115.90) 12 Ran SP% **119.9**
WIN (incl. 1 euro stake): 2.70. PLACES: 1.30, 1.40, 1.80. DF: 4.80. SF: 6.80..
**Owner** Bringloe, Goddard, Hitchcock & Friends **Bred** Enrico Ciampi **Trained** Newmarket, Suffolk

# 1966 HAMILTON (R-H)
Friday, May 16

**OFFICIAL GOING: Good to soft (good in places; 7.3)**
Wind: Light, half behind Weather: Cloudy, bright

## 2291 IRISH STALLION FARMS EBF MAIDEN STKS 5f 4y
**5:55** (5:56) (Class 5) 2-Y-O **£3,881** (£1,155; £577; £288) **Stalls** High

Form RPR

6 1 **Billyoakes (IRE)**[12] [1977] 2-9-5 0 GrahamLee 5 81
(Mick Channon) *trckd ldrs: rdn over 1f out: rallied to ld ins fnl f: kpt on strly* **7/2**[3]

2 *1 1/4* **Denzille Lane (IRE)** 2-9-2 0 FrannyNorton 3 74+
(Mark Johnston) *cl up on outside: effrt and edgd lft over 1f out: led briefly ins fnl f: kpt on* **17/2**

2 3 *1 3/4* **Rita's Boy (IRE)**[16] [1889] 2-9-5 0 PJMcDonald 7 70
(K R Burke) *s.i.s: bhd and sn outpcd: plenty to do 1/2-way: gd hdwy fnl f: fin strly* **3/1**[2]

4 *1 1/4* **Spend A Penny (IRE)** 2-9-2 0 PhillipMakin 6 63
(John Quinn) *led against stands' rail: rdn over 1f out: hdd ins fnl f: sn outpcd* **7/4**[1]

5 *1 1/4* **Robben** 2-9-2 0 PaulMulrennan 2 58+
(Kevin Ryan) *rn green bhd ldng gp: pushed along and outpcd after 2f: hdwy over 1f out: nvr nr ldrs* **20/1**

6 *1 3/4* **Millgate** 2-9-2 0 LeeTopliss 4 52
(Richard Fahey) *chsd ldrs tl rdn and wknd over 1f out* **14/1**

7 *hd* **Just The Tip (IRE)** 2-8-11 0 TomEaves 1 46
(Keith Dalgleish) *t.k.h: prom: rdn over 2f out: wknd over 1f out* **16/1**

1m 1.94s (1.94) **Going Correction** +0.15s/f (Good) 7 Ran SP% **111.4**
Speed ratings (Par 93): **90,88,85,83,81 78,78**
CSF £30.65 TOTE £5.30: £1.90, £3.40; EX 31.50 Trifecta £156.70.
**Owner** Nick & Olga Dhandsa & John & Zoe Webster **Bred** Mrs M Cusack **Trained** West Ilsley, Berks

**FOCUS**
Rail realignment around the loop added 25yds to races on Round course. A race that threw up smart sprinter Spin Cycle in 2008, Woodcote winner Corporal Maddox in 2009, Norfolk Stakes winner Bapak Chinta in 2011 and Superlative Stakes winner Good Boy Lukey last year. However, it will be a surprise if this year's winner turns out as good. The gallop was sound. The winner left his debut effort behind.

## 2292 BILLY LESLIE OPEN MAIDEN STKS 1m 1f 36y
**6:30** (6:30) (Class 5) 3-Y-O+ **£3,234** (£962; £481; £240) **Stalls** Low

Form RPR

1 **Wee Frankie (IRE)** 3-9-0 0 PhillipMakin 5 83
(Keith Dalgleish) *trckd ldrs: effrt and rdn 2f out: led ins fnl f: styd on wl* **15/2**

63 2 *1 1/4* **Hesketh Bank**[20] [1738] 3-9-0 0 DavidNolan 7 80
(Richard Fahey) *t.k.h: led 1f: chsd ldr: rdn to ld over 2f out: edgd rt: hdd ins fnl f: kpt on* **2/1**[2]

-324 3 *5* **Clear Spell (IRE)**[104] [423] 3-9-0 69 PJMcDonald 4 69
(Alistair Whillans) *hld up in tch: effrt and rdn over 2f out: kpt on fnl f: nt pce to chal* **10/1**

6-22 4 *1 1/2* **Maracuja**[20] [1738] 3-8-9 74 FrannyNorton 1 61
(Mark Johnston) *t.k.h: led after 1f: rdn and hdd over 2f out: rallied: outpcd fnl f* **6/4**[1]

0- 5 *1/2* **Private Dancer**[233] [6754] 3-8-11 0 SamJames(3) 2 65
(Alan Swinbank) *t.k.h early: hld up in tch: pushed along over 2f out: sn outpcd: n.d after* **7/1**[3]

46 6 *4 1/2* **My Escapade (IRE)**[29] [1542] 3-8-9 0 RoystonFfrench 8 50
(Simon Waugh) *in tch: drvn and outpcd over 2f out: n.d after* **66/1**

7 *3 1/4* **Archie's Advice** 3-9-0 0 TomEaves 6 48
(Keith Dalgleish) *s.i.s: t.k.h in rr: rdn and carried hd high over 3f out: sn btn* **16/1**

8 21 **Bannock Town** 3-9-0 0 PaulMulrennan 3
(Linda Perratt) *s.i.s: hld up: struggling over 3f out: sn btn: t.o* **66/1**
2m 1.25s (1.55) **Going Correction** +0.20s/f (Good) **8 Ran SP% 115.6**
Speed ratings (Par 103): **101,99,95,94,93 89,86,68**
CSF £23.21 TOTE £7.60: £2.30, £1.30, £2.10; EX 26.10 Trifecta £156.80.
**Owner** Lamont Racing **Bred** Oak Lodge Bloodstock **Trained** Carluke, S Lanarks
**FOCUS**
A maiden that lacked strength in depth in which they went off quite quickly, but the leader slowed the pace after a couple of furlongs. The winner made a nice start.

## 2293 NAKED GROUSE SONS OF SCOTLAND H'CAP 1m 65y
7:00 (7:01) (Class 5) (0-75,75) 4-Y-O+ £4,090 (£1,207; £604) Stalls Low

Form RPR
-303 1 **I'm Super Too (IRE)**[12] 1970 7-8-8 **65** SamJames(3) 1 78+
(Alan Swinbank) *trckd ldrs: effrt over 2f out: rdn to ld over 1f out: styd on wl: eased nr fin* **6/1**[3]
5-10 2 3 ¾ **Dark Ocean (IRE)**[16] 1881 4-9-4 **72** GrahamLee 4 75
(Jedd O'Keeffe) *hld up bhd ldng gp: rdn over 2f out: effrt and hdwy over 1f out: chsd (clr) wnr ins fnl f: no imp* **10/1**
1264 3 2 **Ellaal**[11] 2019 5-8-9 **63** JamesSullivan 6 62
(Ruth Carr) *hld up: rdn along over 2f out: hdwy on outside over 1f out: kpt on fnl f: no imp* **11/1**
6111 4 1 **Alluring Star**[6] 2164 6-8-8 **62** GrahamGibbons 2 58
(Michael Easterby) *disp ld: drvn wl over 1f out: wknd ins fnl f* **9/4**[2]
2430 5 4 **Baltic Prince (IRE)**[25] 1610 4-8-8 **62** RaulDaSilva 5 49
(Paul Green) *slt ld to over 1f out: rdn and sn wknd* **25/1**
6645 6 4 ½ **Loud**[20] 1744 4-9-3 **71** FrannyNorton 7 48
(Mark Johnston) *hld up: rdn over 4f out: nvr on terms* **14/1**
0-00 7 6 **Act Your Shoe Size**[26] 1598 5-9-4 **72** TomEaves 8 35
(Keith Dalgleish) *hld up in tch on ins: struggling over 3f out: sn btn* **20/1**
5-42 8 3 ½ **Red Charmer (IRE)**[16] 1885 4-9-7 **75** PJMcDonald 3 30
(Ann Duffield) *cl up: rdn along over 2f out: wknd wl over 1f out* **2/1**[1]
1m 49.75s (1.35) **Going Correction** +0.20s/f (Good) **8 Ran SP% 111.1**
Speed ratings (Par 103): **101,97,95,94,90 85,79,76**
CSF £59.49 CT £624.14 TOTE £7.40: £2.80, £2.70, £2.20; EX 85.90 Trifecta £165.90.
**Owner** David C Young **Bred** Norelands Bloodstock, J Hanly & H Lascelles **Trained** Melsonby, N Yorks
**FOCUS**
A fair handicap comprising mainly exposed sorts but a race in which the two market leaders underperformed to varying degrees. The gallop was on the steady side and those held up were at a disadvantage. The winner is rated back to his form of this time last year.

## 2294 GINGER GROUSE BRAVEHEART STKS (H'CAP) (LISTED RACE) 1m 4f 17y
7:35 (7:36) (Class 1) (0-110,104) 4-Y-O+ £23,680 (£8,956; £4,476; £2,236) Stalls Low

Form RPR
540- 1 **Dare To Achieve**[251] 6186 4-9-0 **94** GrahamLee 7 104
(William Haggas) *t.k.h in midfield: hdwy to press ldr over 2f out: effrt and rdn over 1f out: led ins fnl f: styd on gamely* **7/2**[2]
0-35 2 nk **Rawaki (IRE)**[20] 1736 6-9-9 **103** ThomasBrown 9 112
(Andrew Balding) *hld up in tch: smooth hdwy over 3f out: led and carried hd high over 2f out: hung rt over 1f out: hdd ins fnl f: hld towards fin* **7/1**[3]
-521 3 5 **Sirvino**[12] 1971 9-9-1 **95** 3ex PhillipMakin 3 96
(David Barron) *hld up: rdn and hdwy over 2f out: kpt on fnl f: nt rch first two* **16/1**
23-0 4 ½ **Body Language (IRE)**[9] 2073 6-9-0 **94** (p) PJMcDonald 8 94+
(Ian Williams) *hld up: rdn and outpcd over 3f out: rallied over 1f out: kpt on fnl f* **33/1**
3-31 5 3 ¾ **Special Meaning**[13] 1942 4-8-13 **93** FrannyNorton 1 87
(Mark Johnston) *led at stdy gallop 4f: w ldr: drvn and ev ch over 3f out: no ex over 1f out* **7/2**[2]
313- 6 2 **Party Line**[268] 5655 5-8-11 **91** (v) JoeFanning 2 82
(Mark Johnston) *prom tl drvn and outpcd over 2f out: n.d after* **16/1**
0 7 6 **Valbucca (IRE)**[20] 1750 7-8-10 **90** oh1 (b) TomEaves 4 71
(Amy Weaver) *hld up: hdwy u.p over 3f out: wknd fr 2f out* **66/1**
4-12 8 10 **Clayton**[23] 1653 5-9-10 **104** PaulMulrennan 10 69
(Kevin Ryan) *t.k.h: chsd ldrs tl rdn and wknd over 2f out* **9/1**
3/ 9 14 **Bolingbroke (IRE)**[239] 5-9-3 **97** (t) KierenFallon 6 40
(Saeed bin Suroor) *t.k.h: chsd ldrs: hdwy to ld over 3f out: hdd over 2f out: sn struggling: eased whn btn appr fnl f* **5/2**[1]
303- 10 3 ¾ **Alta Lilea (IRE)**[246] 6329 4-9-6 **100** AdrianNicholls 5 37
(Mark Johnston) *pressed ldr: led after 4f to over 3f out: sn rdn and struggling: t.o* **25/1**
2m 37.92s (-0.68) **Going Correction** +0.20s/f (Good) **10 Ran SP% 115.6**
Speed ratings (Par 111): **110,109,106,106,103 102,98,91,82,79**
CSF £27.54 CT £345.34 TOTE £6.10: £2.10, £2.70, £3.90; EX 26.90 Trifecta £406.40.
**Owner** B Kantor & M Jooste **Bred** Hascombe & Valiant Stud & Amarvilas Bstk **Trained** Newmarket, Suffolk
■ Stewards' Enquiry : Thomas Brown two-day ban: used whip above permitted level (May 30-31)
**FOCUS**
A decent race for this Listed handicap in which the tempo was stepped up after a slowly-run first four furlongs and the first three all came from off the pace. The first two seem better than ever.

## 2295 FORD WINDOWS WILLIAM WALLACE H'CAP (BOBIS RACE) 6f 5y
8:05 (8:07) (Class 4) (0-85,85) 3-Y-O £6,469 (£1,925; £962; £481) Stalls High

Form RPR
13 1 **Divine (IRE)**[20] 1711 3-9-0 **78** GrahamLee 4 88+
(Mick Channon) *in tch: smooth hdwy over 2f out: rdn to ld ent fnl f: hld on wl* **4/1**[1]
20-1 2 ¾ **Red Pike (IRE)**[34] 1441 3-8-13 **77** PaulMulrennan 6 85+
(Bryan Smart) *led at decent gallop: rdn 2f out: hdd ent fnl f: kpt on: hld towards fin* **5/1**[3]
01 3 1 ½ **Election Night**[15] 1902 3-8-6 **70** DuranFentiman 5 73
(Tim Easterby) *hld up: rdn over 2f out: hdwy over 1f out: kpt on fnl f: nt rch first two* **16/1**
11-5 4 6 **Sandra's Diamond (IRE)**[12] 1968 3-9-1 **79** TomEaves 8 63
(Keith Dalgleish) *hld up in tch: rdn along 2f out: no imp fnl f* **11/1**
51-4 5 1 ½ **Lexington Abbey**[21] 1693 3-9-2 **85** ShaneGray(5) 9 64
(Kevin Ryan) *cl up: drvn over 2f out: wknd fnl f* **11/2**
13-0 6 1 ½ **Centre Haafhd**[21] 1693 3-8-13 **77** (b[1]) GrahamGibbons 3 51
(David Barron) *t.k.h: cl up: rdn and lost pl over 3f out: sme late hdwy past btn horses: nvr on terms* **9/2**[2]
026- 7 5 **Neighbother**[217] 7170 3-8-7 **71** PatrickMathers 1 29
(Richard Fahey) *checked s: hld up: rdn and hdwy on outside 1/2-way: wknd appr fnl f* **9/1**
05-6 8 2 ½ **Ifwecan**[13] 1954 3-9-6 **84** JoeFanning 7 34
(Mark Johnston) *cl up tl rdn and wknd wl over 1f out* **9/2**[2]
0-05 9 5 **De Repente (IRE)**[20] 1737 3-8-4 **68** RaulDaSilva 2
(Paul Green) *wnt rt s: sn cl up: drvn over 2f out: wknd over 1f out* **28/1**
1m 12.6s (0.40) **Going Correction** +0.15s/f (Good) **9 Ran SP% 116.1**
Speed ratings (Par 101): **103,102,100,92,90 88,81,78,71**
CSF £24.22 CT £288.48 TOTE £5.10: £2.00, £2.20, £3.40; EX 28.80 Trifecta £280.20.
**Owner** M Al-Qatami & K M Al-Mudhaf **Bred** Yeomanstown Stud **Trained** West Ilsley, Berks
**FOCUS**
A couple of unexposed sorts in a useful handicap. The gallop was sound throughout and the first three finished clear. The winner looks capable of better.

## 2296 FAMOUS GROUSE BANNOCKBURN H'CAP 6f 5y
8:40 (8:40) (Class 6) (0-65,65) 3-Y-O+ £2,385 (£704; £352) Stalls High

Form RPR
6210 1 **Orwellian**[65] 934 5-9-7 **58** PaulMulrennan 11 70
(Bryan Smart) *hld up: hdwy over 2f out: rdn to ld wl ins fnl f: kpt on wl* **28/1**
0451 2 ½ **Hab Reeh**[17] 1838 6-9-5 **56** JamesSullivan 9 66
(Ruth Carr) *t.k.h: in tch: hdwy to ld over 1f out: sn hrd pressed: hdd and no ex wl ins fnl f* **5/1**[2]
302 3 1 ½ **Layla's Hero (IRE)**[6] 2167 7-9-12 **63** (v) AdrianNicholls 1 68
(David Nicholls) *midfield on outside: drvn over 3f out: rallied to chal over 1f out to ins fnl f: no ex towards fin* **4/1**[1]
543 4 1 ½ **Captain Scooby**[3] 2233 8-8-12 **49** GrahamLee 2 49+
(Richard Guest) *hld up in midfield: stdy hdwy over 2f out: rdn over 1f out: one pce ins fnl f* **4/1**[1]
561 5 4 **Busy Bimbo (IRE)**[12] 1972 5-9-0 **51** 6ex (b) PatrickMathers 12 39
(Alan Berry) *prom: effrt and ev ch over 1f out: rdn and wknd last 100yds* **22/1**
6405 6 ½ **Lord Buffhead**[3] 2232 5-8-9 **51** (p) PhilipPrince(5) 13 37
(Richard Guest) *hld up in tch: drvn along over 1f out: btn ins fnl f* **9/1**
0-62 7 1 ¼ **See Clearly**[21] 1694 5-9-8 **59** (p) DuranFentiman 14 41
(Tim Easterby) *in tch: effrt and rdn over 2f out: btn ins fnl f* **8/1**[3]
6446 8 ½ **Ferdy (IRE)**[41] 1310 5-9-7 **58** RaulDaSilva 3 38
(Paul Green) *cl up: rdn and ev ch 2f out: sn no ex* **16/1**
645- 9 nk **Fabled City (USA)**[256] 6037 5-10-0 **65** TomEaves 7 44
(Keith Dalgleish) *mde most tl rdn and hdd over 1f out: sn btn* **12/1**
2-40 10 hd **Baltic Spirit (IRE)**[19] 1758 3-9-4 **64** JoeFanning 10 41
(Keith Dalgleish) *hld up: drvn along over 2f out: no imp over 1f out* **14/1**
646- 11 ¾ **M J Woodward**[230] 6855 5-9-8 **59** PJMcDonald 8 35
(Paul Green) *cl up: stmbld after 100yds: cl up tl rdn and wknd wl over 1f out* **33/1**
50-5 12 ¾ **Oak Bluffs (IRE)**[13] 1939 3-9-4 **64** LeeTopliss 5 36
(Richard Fahey) *hld up: drvn along and wandered over 2f out: sn n.d* **11/1**
-000 13 nk **Tadalavil**[4] 2219 9-9-0 **56** SammyJoBell(5) 4 29
(Linda Perratt) *t.k.h: in tch tl rdn and wknd over 2f out* **40/1**
0-53 14 6 **Cards**[20] 1713 4-9-10 **61** (p) PhillipMakin 6 15
(Kevin Ryan) *hld up: struggling over 2f out: sn btn* **22/1**
456- 15 23 **Thundering Cloud (IRE)**[182] 7892 3-9-0 **65** GarryWhillans(5) 15
(Simon Waugh) *bolted to post: bhd: lost tch 1/2-way: t.o* **33/1**
1m 13.19s (0.99) **Going Correction** +0.15s/f (Good)
**WFA** 3 from 4yo+ 9lb **15 Ran SP% 126.8**
Speed ratings (Par 101): **99,98,96,94,89 88,86,86,85,85 84,83,82,74,44**
CSF £161.01 CT £723.68 TOTE £31.60: £4.70, £3.00, £3.00; EX 282.20 Trifecta £710.60.
**Owner** B Smart **Bred** Mrs Fiona Denniff **Trained** Hambleton, N Yorks
**FOCUS**
A big field of mainly exposed sprinters featuring plenty of inconsistent and hard-to-win with sorts. The winner is getting back to his old best.

## 2297 VARIETY CLUB OF SCOTLAND H'CAP 5f 4y
9:10 (9:11) (Class 5) (0-75,75) 4-Y-O+ £3,557 (£1,058; £529; £264) Stalls High

Form RPR
-661 1 **Economic Crisis (IRE)**[12] 1966 5-8-13 **67** 6ex PaulMulrennan 6 77
(Alan Berry) *mde virtually all: rdn and r.o wl fr over 1f out* **7/1**
0-01 2 1 ¼ **Bunce (IRE)**[15] 1905 6-8-9 **63** PJMcDonald 9 69
(Linda Perratt) *hld up in tch: rdn and hdwy over 1f out: chsd wnr ins fnl f: r.o* **12/1**
0-60 3 1 **Haajes**[13] 1961 10-9-2 **75** (v) ShirleyTeasdale(5) 7 77
(Paul Midgley) *prom: effrt and rdn 2f out: kpt on ins fnl f* **13/2**[3]
6240 4 1 ¼ **Beau Mistral (IRE)**[10] 2056 5-9-5 **73** RaulDaSilva 8 70
(Paul Green) *w ldr: edgd rt and rdn over 1f out: kpt on same pce ins fnl f* **9/1**
3-02 5 ½ **Manatee Bay**[12] 1966 4-8-3 **57** AdrianNicholls 1 53
(David Nicholls) *in tch on outside: effrt and rdn over 2f out: edgd lft over 1f out: kpt on same pce* **7/4**[1]
044- 6 ½ **Gran Canaria Queen**[227] 6916 5-9-1 **69** DavidAllan 5 63
(Tim Easterby) *cl up tl rdn and no ex appr fnl f* **3/1**[2]
6213 7 5 **Red Cape (FR)**[18] 1814 11-8-8 **62** (b) JamesSullivan 3 38
(Ruth Carr) *t.k.h: prom tl rdn and wknd over 2f out* **8/1**
1m 0.19s (0.19) **Going Correction** +0.15s/f (Good) **7 Ran SP% 116.0**
Speed ratings (Par 103): **104,102,100,98,97 96,88**
CSF £84.41 CT £573.44 TOTE £9.50: £3.60, £5.30; EX 100.90 Trifecta £429.20.
**Owner** Mr & Mrs T Blane **Bred** Philip Hore Jnr **Trained** Cockerham, Lancs
**FOCUS**
Just a fair sprint for the grade but the pace wasn't particularly strong. The winner is getting back to her best.
T/Plt: £578.60 to a £1 stake. Pool: £68,838.24 - 86.84 winning units T/Qpdt: £72.60 to a £1 stake. Pool: £7,532.52 - 76.70 winning units. RY

# 1433 NEWBURY (L-H)
Friday, May 16

**OFFICIAL GOING: Good (7.2)**
Wind: very light breeze across Weather: sunny with some cloud

## 2298 AL BASTI EQUIWORLD MAIDEN STKS (BOBIS RACE) 6f 8y
1:30 (1:30) (Class 4) 2-Y-O £6,469 (£1,925; £962; £481) Stalls Centre

Form RPR
1 **Adaay (IRE)** 2-9-5 0 PaulHanagan 9 85+
(William Haggas) *trckd ldrs: sltly outpcd whn pushed along 2f out: str run ent fnl f: led fnl 120yds: readily* **3/1**[2]
2 ¾ **Kodi Bear (IRE)** 2-9-5 0 AdamKirby 16 83+
(Clive Cox) *trckd ldrs: rdn to ld and hanging lft fr over 1f out: hdd fnl 100yds: nt pce of wnr* **11/2**[3]

3 1 ¾ **Marcano (IRE)** 2-9-5 0 .... RobertHavlin 14 78+
(Rod Millman) *mid-div: rdn 2f out: hdwy over 1f out: r.o wl fnl f: wnt 3rd nring fin* **50/1**

4 hd **Among Angels** 2-9-5 0 .... JamieSpencer 10 77+
(Richard Hannon) *prom: rdn and ev ch briefly 2f out: disputing cl 3rd whn squeezed up ent fnl f: swtchd rt: kpt on fnl 100yds* **25/1**

5 nk **Aledaid (IRE)** 2-9-5 0 .... FrankieDettori 2 76+
(Richard Hannon) *mid-div: hdwy 2f out: rdn in clly disp 3rd over 1f out: edgd rt: nt pce to chal: no ex fnl 75yds* **9/4**[1]

6 1 **Goring (GER)** 2-9-5 0 .... JohnFahy 11 73
(Eve Johnson Houghton) *trckd ldrs: led 2f out: sn rdn: carried lft and hdd over 1f out: kpt on same pce ins fnl f* **66/1**

7 ¾ **Mustadeem (IRE)** 2-9-5 0 .... SilvestreDeSousa 15 71+
(Brian Meehan) *racd green: s.i.s: towards rr: pushed along 3f out: kpt on wl fr jst over 1f out: nvr threatened: improve* **20/1**

8 1 ½ **Captain Marmalade (IRE)** 2-9-5 0 .... GeorgeBaker 6 66+
(Roger Charlton) *hld up towards rr: swtchd lft and hdwy over 2f out: kpt on but nt pce to get on terms fnl f* **20/1**

9 1 ½ **Orlando Rogue (IRE)** 2-9-5 0 .... PatCosgrave 8 62
(George Baker) *wnt lft s: sn mid-div: rdn over 2f out: wknd over 1f out* **40/1**

0 10 ¾ **Alpine Affair**[12] 1977 2-9-5 0 .... StevieDonohoe 12 60
(Brian Meehan) *mid-div: rdn over 2f out: nvr any imp* **66/1**

11 1 ¼ **Pink Ribbon (IRE)** 2-9-0 0 .... JoshBaudains(5) 5 56
(Sylvester Kirk) *led: rdn and hdd 2f out: wknd fnl f* **150/1**

12 3 **Red Tornado (FR)** 2-9-5 0 .... LukeMorris 1 47
(Harry Dunlop) *chsd ldrs: rdn 3f out: grad fdd fr 2f out* **14/1**

13 ½ **Playboy Bay** 2-9-5 0 .... SamHitchcott 3 45
(Mick Channon) *mid-div: rdn 3f out: wknd fnl f* **66/1**

14 ¾ **Dutch Portrait** 2-9-5 0 .... DavidProbert 4 43
(Paul Cole) *a towards rr* **40/1**

15 ¾ **Western Playboy (IRE)** 2-9-2 0 .... RossAtkinson(3) 13 41
(Sylvester Kirk) *s.i.s: sn mid-div: rdn 3f out: wknd 2f out* **150/1**

16 2 ¾ **Silver Quay (IRE)** 2-9-5 0 .... RichardHughes 7 33
(Richard Hannon) *wnt lft s: racd green: a in rr* **13/2**

1m 13.73s (0.73) **Going Correction** +0.05s/f (Good) **16** Ran SP% **117.2**
Speed ratings (Par 95): **97,96,93,93,93 91,90,88,86,85 84,80,79,78,77 73**
CSF £17.06 TOTE £5.00: £2.10, £2.50, £9.30; EX 21.20 Trifecta £1001.50.
**Owner** Hamdan Al Maktoum **Bred** L Fox **Trained** Newmarket, Suffolk

**FOCUS**
Rail on back straight moved out, increasing distances on Round course by 22m. A maiden that invariably throws up some smart types and this year's renewal looks up to scratch and a rich source of future winners.

## 2299 SWETTENHAM STUD FILLIES' TRIAL STKS (LISTED RACE) 1m 2f 6y
**2:00** (2:00) (Class 1) 3-Y-O
**£20,982** (£7,955; £3,981; £1,983; £995; £499) **Stalls** Low

Form RPR
11-3 1 **Volume**[29] 1535 3-9-0 88 .... RichardHughes 5 103+
(Luca Cumani) *mde all: rdn whn strly pressed fr 2f out: battled on v bravely: asserting nr fin: game* **9/4**[1]

2 nk **Lahinch Classics (IRE)**[30] 1525 3-9-0 0 .... WayneLordan 3 102
(David Wachman, Ire) *trckd ldrs: str chal over 2f out gng wl: rdn over 1f out: couldn't quite edge ahd: ev ch fnl f: hld nring fin* **7/1**

1 3 2 **Hadaatha (IRE)**[29] 1534 3-9-0 83 .... PaulHanagan 4 99
(Roger Varian) *mid-div: hdwy 3f out: rdn to chse ldng pair 2f out: hld whn hung lft ent fnl f: kpt on same pce* **4/1**[2]

23-1 4 ¾ **Inchila**[35] 1424 3-9-0 83 .... JamieSpencer 6 97
(Peter Chapple-Hyam) *stdd s: last: smooth hdwy 3f out to trck ldrs: rdn whn swtchd lft in cl 4th ent fnl f: kpt on but nt pce to get on terms* **5/1**[3]

5-40 5 4 **Lamar (IRE)**[12] 1976 3-9-0 96 ....[1] LukeMorris 1 90
(James Tate) *little slowly away: mid-div: hdwy to trck ldrs 3f out: sn rdn: nt pce to threaten: no ex fnl f* **17/2**

16-3 6 ¾ **Sound Reflection (USA)**[12] 1978 3-9-0 100 .... SilvestreDeSousa 8 88
(Charlie Appleby) *racd keenly early: trckd wnr: chal over 2f out: sn rdn: 4th and hld whn edgd lft jst over 1f out: wknd fnl f* **8/1**

021- 7 2 ¼ **Likelihood (USA)**[263] 5812 3-9-0 80 ....[1] RobertHavlin 7 84
(John Gosden) *hld up in last pair: hdwy 3f out: sn rdn: nt pce to get involved: wknd jst over 1f out* **16/1**

4 8 15 **Grace And Favour**[21] 1701 3-9-0 0 .... DavidProbert 2 55
(Andrew Balding) *trckd ldrs: rdn over 3f out: wknd 2f out* **33/1**

2m 5.38s (-3.42) **Going Correction** -0.15s/f (Firm) **8** Ran SP% **110.4**
Speed ratings (Par 104): **107,106,105,104,101 100,98,86**
CSF £17.15 TOTE £3.30: £1.50, £2.20, £1.40; EX 16.40 Trifecta £79.90.
**Owner** S Stuckey **Bred** Stuart Stuckey **Trained** Newmarket, Suffolk

**FOCUS**
Not a race that usually has a bearing on the Oaks, although Eswarah won this in 2005, but this looked a decent renewal and the first four home are all progressive fillies. The winner should continue to impress.

## 2300 AL BASTI EQUIWORLD H'CAP (DIV I) 1m 2f 6y
**2:35** (2:35) (Class 5) (0-70,70) 4-Y-O+ **£3,234** (£962; £481; £240) **Stalls** Low

Form RPR
-041 1 **Choral Festival**[16] 1875 8-9-3 66 .... LukeMorris 6 72
(John Bridger) *mid-div: hdwy 3f out: pushed along to chal between horses jst over 1f out: hrd rdn to ld ins fnl f: kpt on gamely: drvn out* **11/2**[3]

5-41 2 nk **Balmoral Castle**[11] 2021 5-8-12 64 .... MatthewLawson(3) 4 69
(Jonathan Portman) *trckd ldrs: rdn over 2f out: led wl over 1f out: hrd pressed: hdd ins fnl f: kpt on: hld towards fin* **9/4**[1]

040- 3 ½ **Evervescent (IRE)**[234] 6720 5-9-7 70 .... PaulHanagan 3 74
(Graeme McPherson) *racd keenly: trckd ldr: rdn to ld wl over 2f out: hdd wl over 1f out: stl ev ch ent fnl f: kpt on but no ex fnl 120yds* **9/1**

3620 4 ¾ **Minstrel Lad**[25] 1617 6-8-4 56 .... SimonPearce(3) 1 59
(Lydia Pearce) *little slowly away: sn trcking ldrs: rdn and ev ch 2f out tl jst ins fnl f: kpt on but no ex fnl 120yds* **33/1**

0 5 2 **Qasser (IRE)**[15] 1899 5-9-0 68 .... RyanTate(5) 9 67
(Harry Whittington) *hld up: hdwy 3f out: nt clrest of runs whn rdn 2f out: swtchd lft over 1f out: styd on same pce fnl f* **8/1**

310 6 1 ½ **Time Square (FR)**[14] 1909 7-8-7 61 .... JoeyHaynes(5) 2 57
(Tony Carroll) *taken to s early: racd keenly: led: rdn and hdd wl over 2f out: kpt chsng ldrs: one pce fnl f* **12/1**

0-11 7 7 **Able Dash**[51] 1100 4-9-5 68 .... AdamKirby 5 51
(Michael Blake) *in tch: rdn over 3f out: nvr finding pce to get involved: wknd fnl f* **4/1**[2]

1130 8 nk **Masai Moon**[21] 1689 10-8-12 68 .... PatMillman(7) 8 50
(Rod Millman) *stdd sn after s: last: hdwy over 3f out: rdn over 2f out: nvr threatened: wknd fnl f* **28/1**

-346 9 6 **Golden Jubilee (USA)**[39] 1355 5-9-4 67 ....(v) StevieDonohoe 7 38
(Nigel Twiston-Davies) *in last trio whn pushed along over 4f out: rdn 3f out: nvr any imp: wknd over 1f out* **15/2**

2m 9.02s (0.22) **Going Correction** -0.15s/f (Firm) **9** Ran SP% **113.1**
Speed ratings (Par 103): **93,92,92,91,90 88,83,83,78**
CSF £17.85 CT £108.01 TOTE £7.00: £2.30, £1.50, £3.10; EX 15.80 Trifecta £101.80.
**Owner** Mrs Liz Gardner **Bred** Cheveley Park Stud Ltd **Trained** Liphook, Hants

**FOCUS**
The early pace looked only moderate in this run-of-the-mill handicap, but they got racing properly from the 3f pole. It's hard to rate the form too positively.

## 2301 AL BASTI EQUIWORLD H'CAP (DIV II) 1m 2f 6y
**3:05** (3:06) (Class 5) (0-70,70) 4-Y-O+ **£3,234** (£962; £481; £240) **Stalls** Low

Form RPR
22-2 1 **Kastini**[20] 1729 4-9-7 70 ....(v[1]) RichardHughes 3 81+
(Denis Coakley) *trckd ldrs: swtchd rt 2f out: qcknd up wl to ld ent fnl f: in command after: pushed out* **5/4**[1]

560- 2 nk **Fanzine**[282] 5125 4-9-5 68 .... GeorgeBaker 1 77
(Hughie Morrison) *mid-div: travelling wl but nt clr run over 2f out: swtchd rt: rdn and hdwy over 1f out: styd on ins fnl f: wnt 2nd fnl 75yds: nvr quite gng to rch wnr* **7/2**[2]

-443 3 1 ½ **The Firm (IRE)**[20] 1729 5-9-4 67 .... AdamKirby 8 73
(Daniel Mark Loughnane) *led: rdn wl over 2f out: hdd ent fnl f: sn hld: no ex fnl 75yds* **11/2**[3]

4230 4 2 **Reflect (IRE)**[11] 1729 6-9-3 66 ....(v) DaleSwift 9 68
(Derek Shaw) *hld up last: hdwy 2f out: sn rdn: styd on to go 4th ent fnl f: nvr threatening ldrs* **16/1**

2146 5 1 **Exclusive Waters (IRE)**[17] 1845 4-8-12 68 ....(b) CallumShepherd(7) 5 68
(Charles Hills) *plld hrd: hld up: hdwy on outer fr 5f out: trckd ldr 4f out: rdn over 2f out: styd on same pce fr over 1f out* **12/1**

25/0 6 3 ½ **Royal Mizar (SPA)**[19] 1771 4-8-8 62 .... DanielMuscutt(5) 7 56
(Alastair Lidderdale) *trckd ldr: rdn wl over 2f out: wknd fnl f* **66/1**

2245 7 2 ¼ **Shirazz**[20] 1740 5-8-10 59 ....(t) JamieSpencer 2 49
(Seamus Durack) *hld up: rdn wl over 2f out: nvr any imp* **15/2**

4046 8 1 ¾ **Innoko (FR)**[51] 1097 4-9-0 63 ....(t) DavidProbert 4 49
(Tony Carroll) *mid-div: rdn 3f out: wknd over 1f out* **33/1**

2m 9.06s (0.26) **Going Correction** -0.15s/f (Firm) **8** Ran SP% **111.8**
Speed ratings (Par 103): **92,91,90,88,88 85,83,82**
CSF £5.31 CT £15.94 TOTE £2.00: £1.10, £1.50, £2.00; EX 7.60 Trifecta £25.20.
**Owner** West Ilsley Racing **Bred** J W Ford **Trained** West Ilsley, Berks

**FOCUS**
A similar overall time to the first division and probably a similar standard of form, rated around the third.

## 2302 COOLMORE STUD FILLIES' CONDITIONS STKS (BOBIS RACE) 5f 34y
**3:35** (3:40) (Class 3) 2-Y-O
**£6,225** (£1,864; £932; £466; £233; £117) **Stalls** Centre

Form RPR
21 1 **Clouds Rest**[11] 2014 2-8-12 0 .... PaulHanagan 5 84
(Richard Fahey) *broke wl: mde all: kpt on wl fnl f: rdn out* **4/1**[3]

2 1 **Persun** 2-8-9 0 .... SamHitchcott 3 77+
(Mick Channon) *s.i.s: sn pushed along in last pair but in tch: hdwy fr over 1f out: r.o to chal for 2nd ins fnl f but a being hld by wnr* **25/1**

1 3 nse **Spirit Of Xian (IRE)**[29] 1528 2-9-1 0 .... RichardHughes 1 83
(Richard Hannon) *trckd ldrs: rdn to chse wnr over 1f out: kpt on but a being hld by wnr fnl f* **7/4**[1]

4 ¾ **Expensive Date** 2-8-9 0 .... LukeMorris 2 74+
(Paul Cole) *chsd ldrs: rdn over 2f out: kpt on but nt pce to chal fnl f* **14/1**

1 5 2 **Mambo Paradise**[14] 1924 2-9-1 0 .... SilvestreDeSousa 4 73
(Mark Johnston) *slowly away: in last pair but in tch: hdwy to trck ldrs 3f out: rdn over 1f out: nt pce to threaten* **15/8**[2]

415 6 6 **Elizabeth Flynn (IRE)**[9] 2071 2-8-10 0 .... JoeyHaynes(5) 7 52
(K R Burke) *trckd ldr: rdn 2f out: wknd ins fnl f* **12/1**

7 3 ¾ **Midnight Destiny (IRE)** 2-8-10 0 ow1 .... DaleSwift 6 33
(Derek Shaw) *wnt rt s: sn pushed along in tch: wknd ent fnl f* **40/1**

1m 1.17s (-0.23) **Going Correction** +0.05s/f (Good) **7** Ran SP% **111.8**
Speed ratings (Par 94): **103,101,101,100,96 87,81**
CSF £81.97 TOTE £5.50: £3.00, £6.10; EX 80.30 Trifecta £225.80.
**Owner** Racegoers Club Owners Group **Bred** Whitsbury Manor Stud **Trained** Musley Bank, N Yorks

**FOCUS**
A good little fillies' conditions race which was arguably won at the gates. The winner fits the race averages.

## 2303 JOHN SUNLEY MEMORIAL H'CAP (BOBIS RACE) 1m 3f 5y
**4:10** (4:11) (Class 4) (0-85,85) 3-Y-O **£4,690** (£1,395; £697; £348) **Stalls** Low

Form RPR
00-1 1 **Arab Dawn**[13] 1947 3-8-11 75 .... RichardHughes 5 87+
(Hughie Morrison) *hld up: hdwy on outer fr 5f out: rdn to chal whn bmpd jst over 1f out: led fnl 120yds: rdn out* **11/2**

21-1 2 ½ **Personal Opinion**[17] 1856 3-9-7 85 .... SilvestreDeSousa 2 96+
(Charlie Appleby) *in tch: nt clr run on rails 4f out tl swtchd rt to centre 3f out: sn rdn: hdwy over 1f out: drifting lft but running on wl fnl f: snatched 2nd fnl stride* **4/1**[3]

13-4 3 hd **Notarised**[47] 1195 3-8-12 76 .... PaulHanagan 7 87
(Mark Johnston) *led after 1f: rdn over 2f out: edgd rt and bmpd wnr jst over 1f out: hdd fnl 120yds: kpt on but no ex whn lost 2nd fnl stride* **7/2**[2]

31-4 4 4 ½ **Raven Ridge (IRE)**[29] 1535 3-9-7 85 .... JamieSpencer 1 88
(Michael Bell) *hld up in last pair: hdwy 3f out: rdn to chse ldng pair briefly over 1f out: nt pce to threaten: no ex fnl 120yds: jst hld on for 4th* **9/4**[1]

10-0 5 hd **Farquhar (IRE)**[21] 1702 3-9-4 82 .... RobertHavlin 3 85
(Peter Chapple-Hyam) *dwlt: last: tk clsr order 4f out: rdn over 2f out: sn one pce* **40/1**

1-0 6 3 **Mannaro (IRE)**[21] 1702 3-9-4 82 ....(b[1]) LukeMorris 8 79
(Marco Botti) *trckd ldrs: rdn to dispute 2nd 2f out: fdd ins fnl f* **20/1**

12-4 7 1 ¾ **Elysian Prince**[10] 2060 3-9-0 78 .... PatCosgrave 4 72
(Paul Cole) *in tch: tk clsr order over 3f out: effrt 2f out: nvr threatened: wknd fnl f* **20/1**

01- 8 1 ¼ **Hooded (USA)**[170] 8066 3-9-2 80 .... AdamKirby 6 72
(Roger Charlton) *led for 1f: trckd ldr tl rdn over 3f out: sn hld: wknd fnl f* **8/1**

2m 21.19s (-0.01) **Going Correction** -0.15s/f (Firm) **8** Ran SP% **111.5**
Speed ratings (Par 101): **94,93,93,90,90 87,86,85**
CSF £26.03 CT £84.76 TOTE £5.60: £1.50, £1.40, £1.30; EX 17.20 Trifecta £109.80.
**Owner** Eason,Kerr-Dineen,Hughes,Edwards-Jones **Bred** Fittocks Stud **Trained** East Ilsley, Berks


The Form Book, Raceform Ltd, Newbury, RG14 5SJ

**FOCUS**
A good little 3yo handicap featuring some horses with potential. The front three pulled clear and the form looks strong for the grade. The first three can all rate higher.

## 2304 BATHWICK TYRES CARNARVON STKS (LISTED RACE) 6f 8y
**4:45** (4:46) (Class 1) 3-Y-O

**£20,982** (£7,955; £3,981; £1,983; £995; £499) **Stalls** Centre

Form RPR
11-2 **1** **Musical Comedy**[16] 1867 3-9-0 106.............................. RichardHughes 2 106
(Richard Hannon) *travelled wl: trckd ldrs: led over 1f out: sn rdn: strly chal ins fnl f but holding on wl clsng stages* **7/2**[2]
01-3 **2** *hd* **Naadirr (IRE)**[30] 1513 3-9-0 92.............................. LukeMorris 1 105
(Marco Botti) *hld up: hdwy 2f out: sn rdn: str chal ins fnl f: kpt on wl* **14/1**
1330 **3** *3/4* **Major Crispies**[28] 1555 3-9-0 97.............................. RyanTate 4 103
(James Eustace) *disp ld: rdn 2f out: sn hdd: kpt on wl ins fnl f but a being hld by front pair* **25/1**
32-0 **4** *1 1/2* **Wind Fire (USA)**[30] 1515 3-8-12 99.............................. JamieSpencer 5 96
(David Brown) *in tch: tk clsr order 2f out: sn rdn: kpt on but nt pce to chal* **4/1**[3]
20-0 **5** *1 1/4* **No Leaf Clover (IRE)**[34] 1436 3-9-0 99.............................. DavidProbert 8 94
(Ollie Pears) *hld up: rdn 2f out: kpt on ins fnl f: nvr gng pce to threaten ldrs: snatched 5th fnl strides* **12/1**
11-2 **6** *nk* **Mushir**[30] 1514 3-9-3 101.............................. PaulHanagan 10 96
(Roger Varian) *hld up but in tch: swtchd rt 2f out: sn rdn: wnt hld 5th ent fnl f but nvr gng pce to get on terms: lost 5th fnl strides* **2/1**[1]
54-3 **7** *1 1/4* **Rufford (IRE)**[16] 1867 3-9-0 102.............................. AdamKirby 6 89
(Richard Fahey) *sn disputing ld: rdn 2f out: sn hdd: fdd ins fnl f* **15/2**
130- **8** *2 3/4* **Simple Magic (IRE)**[237] 6622 3-8-9 94.............................. RobertHavlin 7 75
(John Gosden) *dwlt: racd keenly and sn cl up: rdn for effrt 2f out: edgd rt and wkng whn hmpd briefly ins fnl f* **40/1**
U12- **9** *8* **Langavat (IRE)**[315] 4025 3-9-0 102.............................. SilvestreDeSousa 9 64
(Richard Hannon) *plld hrd: prom tl rdn 2f out: wknd ent fnl f* **16/1**

1m 12.14s (-0.86) **Going Correction** +0.05s/f (Good) **9** Ran SP% **113.8**
Speed ratings (Par 107): **107,106,105,103,102 101,100,96,85**
CSF £50.24 TOTE £4.40: £1.40, £4.10, £8.60; EX 25.10 Trifecta £478.20.
**Owner** The Queen **Bred** The Queen **Trained** East Everleigh, Wilts

**FOCUS**
A fairly open Listed contest but at the bottom end of the race averages.

## 2305 PERTEMPS NETWORK SHERIDAN MAINE APPRENTICE H'CAP 1m 4f 5y
**5:15** (5:16) (Class 5) (0-75,74) 4-Y-O+ **£3,234** (£962; £481; £240) **Stalls** Low

Form RPR
0-55 **1** **Barwick**[24] 1636 6-9-2 72.............................. CamHardie(3) 2 84
(Lady Herries) *s.i.s: sn in tch: trckd ldrs over 4f out: disp ld fr wl over 2f out: sn rdn: styd on wl fnl f: won on nod* **3/1**[2]
611- **2** *shd* **Mystery Drama**[25] 7543 4-9-6 73.............................. RobJFitzpatrick 5 85
(Alan King) *mid-div: hdwy 4f out: disp ld wl over 2f out: sn rdn: styd on wl fnl f: carried sltly lft: lost on nod* **3/1**[2]
300- **3** *7* **Discovery Bay**[58] 7369 6-9-4 71.............................. MeganCarberry 9 72
(Brian Ellison) *hld up: rdn over 2f out: no imp tl styd on ent fnl f: hung lft: wnt 3rd nring fin* **11/4**[1]
00-2 **4** *shd* **Highlife Dancer**[9] 2067 6-8-0 60 oh1.............................. PaddyPilley(7) 1 60
(Mick Channon) *racd keenly: led: rdn and hdd wl over 2f out: sn hld by front pair: kpt on same pce: lost 3rd fnl stride* **14/1**
52-6 **5** *1/2* **Storm (IRE)**[11] 2033 4-8-11 71.............................. JackBudge(7) 8 71
(Charles Hills) *trckd ldrs: rdn 3f out: styd on same pce fnl 2f* **12/1**
0024 **6** *nk* **Palus San Marco (IRE)**[18] 1811 5-9-4 71.............................. NedCurtis 11 70
(Tony Carroll) *s.i.s: bhd: hdwy over 4f out: rdn to chse ldrs 3f out: drifted to far side rails racing alone: no ex fnl f* **10/1**[3]
10-2 **7** *3/4* **Laura Secord (CAN)**[14] 1910 4-9-5 72.............................. GeorgeBuckell 3 70
(Heather Main) *trckd ldrs over 3f out: nt pce to threaten: no ex fnl f* **16/1**
1-40 **8** *1* **Admirable Duque (IRE)**[13] 1941 8-8-11 64.............................. (b) PatMillman 10 60
(Dominic Ffrench Davis) *hld up towards rr: rdn 3f out: nvr any imp* **25/1**
5201 **9** *2 3/4* **King Olav (UAE)**[50] 1120 9-9-4 71.............................. JordanVaughan 4 63
(Tony Carroll) *w ldr: tl rdn wl over 2f out: wknd over 1f out* **25/1**
0/0- **10** *1* **Bouggatti**[364] 2418 6-9-0 72.............................. GaryMahon(5) 6 62
(Lady Herries) *mid-div: hdwy on inner over 4f out: rdn wl over 2f out: wknd over 1f out* **33/1**

2m 36.14s (0.64) **Going Correction** -0.15s/f (Firm) **10** Ran SP% **116.6**
Speed ratings (Par 103): **91,90,86,86,85 85,85,84,82,82**
CSF £12.16 CT £26.93 TOTE £3.30: £1.10, £1.30, £1.50; EX 19.80 Trifecta £71.80.
**Owner** Seymour Bloodstock (uk) Ltd **Bred** Dullingham Park **Trained** Patching, W Sussex

**FOCUS**
An ordinary handicap to close, in which the first pair came clear.
T/Plt: £64.60 to a £1 stake. Pool: £70,339.16 - 793.70 winning units. T/Qpdt: £9.40 to a £1 stake. Pool: £4575.82 - 359.18 winning units. TM

# 2269 NEWMARKET (R-H)
### Friday, May 16
**OFFICIAL GOING: Good to firm (good in places; 7.2)**
Wind: virtually nil Weather: light cloud, quite warm

## 2306 CHEMTEST EBF STALLIONS MAIDEN FILLIES' STKS (BOBIS RACE) 6f
**2:25** (2:26) (Class 4) 2-Y-O **£4,528** (£1,347; £673; £336) **Stalls** High

Form RPR
4 **1** **Juventas**[16] 1879 2-8-11 0.............................. CharlesBishop(3) 6 77
(Mick Channon) *in tch in midfield: rdn and hdwy to chal over 1f out: drvn to ld ins fnl f: pricked ears in front but sn in command: r.o wl* **13/2**
**2** *1 1/2* **Dutch Party** 2-9-0 0.............................. SebSanders 1 73
(Richard Fahey) *chsd ldrs: rdn and effrt to chal wl over 1f out: ev ch after tl outpcd by wnr fnl 100yds: kpt on* **4/1**[2]
043 **3** *3/4* **Rose Of Kiev (IRE)**[16] 1889 2-9-0 0.............................. LiamJones 5 70
(Mark Johnston) *chsd ldr: rdn and ev ch whn wandered on downhill run wl over 1f out: drvn to ld jst ins fnl f: sn hdd and outpcd* **14/1**
**4** *1/2* **Ski Slope** 2-9-0 0.............................. PatDobbs 2 69+
(Richard Hannon) *dwlt: racd off the pce in last trio: rdn wl over 1f out: hdwy and switching rt ins fnl f: r.o wl: nt rch ldrs* **9/2**[3]
**5** *1 1/2* **Savoy Showgirl (IRE)** 2-9-0 0.............................. FrederikTylicki 7 64
(Michael Bell) *s.i.s: off the pce in last trio: hdwy into midfield 1/2-way: rdn 2f out: no imp tl kpt on steadily ins fnl f: nvr trbld ldrs* **14/1**
**6** *1/2* **Dubai Breeze (IRE)** 2-9-0 0.............................. JimmyFortune 8 63
(Clive Brittain) *t.k.h: pressed ldr tl dropped into midfield and swtchd lft after 1f: pushed along 1/2-way: styd on same pce fr over 1f out: eased towards fin* **16/1**
**7** *2* **True Course** 2-9-0 0.............................. MickaelBarzalona 9 57
(Charlie Appleby) *racd keenly: rdn wl over 1f out: drvn and hdd jst ins fnl f: btn whn rdr dropped whip sn after: wknd qckly and eased towards fin* **7/2**[1]
**8** *nk* **Khawaater** 2-9-0 0.............................. MartinDwyer 4 56+
(Roger Varian) *s.i.s: rn green and a in rr: rdn and no imp over 1f out* **9/2**[3]
**9** *2 1/4* **Celestine Abbey** 2-9-0 0.............................. AdamBeschizza 3 49
(Julia Feilden) *dwlt: a towards rr: rdn 1/2-way: n.d* **100/1**

1m 13.47s (1.27) **Going Correction** +0.05s/f (Good) **9** Ran SP% **112.1**
Speed ratings (Par 92): **93,91,90,89,87 86,84,83,80**
CSF £31.42 TOTE £7.40: £2.30, £2.30, £2.30; EX 32.20 Trifecta £337.00.
**Owner** Norman Court Stud **Bred** Norman Court Stud **Trained** West Ilsley, Berks

**FOCUS**
Stands' side track used. Stalls stands' side except 1m4f: centre. An interesting maiden in which the pace was solid throughout. Quite an ordinary race for the track.

## 2307 STREETS CHARTERED ACCOUNTANTS H'CAP 1m
**2:55** (2:56) (Class 5) (0-75,75) 3-Y-O **£3,881** (£1,155; £577; £288) **Stalls** High

Form RPR
046- **1** **All Talk N No Do (IRE)**[197] 7640 3-9-6 74.............................. FergusSweeney 8 80
(Seamus Durack) *bustled along to go prom sn after s: shuffled bk into midfield 5f out: effrt 2f out: hdwy u.p and swtchd rt jst over 1f out: led ins fnl f: r.o wl: rdn out* **6/1**[3]
53-4 **2** *3/4* **D'Avignon (USA)**[23] 1654 3-9-7 75.............................. (b[1]) NickyMackay 4 79
(John Gosden) *t.k.h: hdwy to ld and crossed to r against stands' rail: rdn 2f out: drvn over 1f out: hdd and one pce ins fnl f* **16/1**
50-3 **3** *nk* **After The Goldrush**[23] 1654 3-9-3 71.............................. PatDobbs 7 74
(Richard Hannon) *led tl hdd and sltly hmpd over 6f out: chsd ldrs after: ev ch and rdn wl over 1f out: sustained duel w rival tl one pce ins fnl f* **14/1**
60-4 **4** *3/4* **Ninety Minutes (IRE)**[20] 1725 3-9-1 69.............................. SteveDrowne 3 71
(John Best) *stdd s: hld up in tch: hdwy over 2f out: rdn and chsd ldng pair whn edgd lft over 1f out: styd on same pce ins fnl f* **12/1**
034- **5** *2 1/4* **Headlong (IRE)**[205] 7467 3-9-4 72.............................. JimmyFortune 9 68
(Brian Meehan) *hld up in last pair: effrt and swtchd sharply rt over 1f out: no imp 1f out: wknd ins fnl f* **7/1**
5-11 **6** *2* **Like A Prayer**[100] 492 3-9-0 68.............................. RichardKingscote 1 60
(Ralph Beckett) *t.k.h: chsd ldrs: rdn wl over 1f out: unable qck and struggling whn pushed rt and hmpd over 1f out: wknd ins fnl f* **7/4**[1]
5-01 **7** *1/2* **Gannicus**[11] 2013 3-9-5 73 6ex.............................. LiamKeniry 5 64
(Brendan Powell) *chsd ldrs: rdn and effrt 2f out: struggling whn pushed rt over 1f out: sn btn: wknd ins fnl f* **9/2**[2]
54-1 **8** *18* **Jeremos (IRE)**[58] 1008 3-9-6 74.............................. MickaelBarzalona 6 23
(Richard Hannon) *rdn along early: in tch towards rr: rdn and effrt over 2f out: wknd over 1f out: bhd and eased ins fnl f* **8/1**

1m 38.64s (0.04) **Going Correction** +0.05s/f (Good) **8** Ran SP% **112.7**
Speed ratings (Par 99): **101,100,99,99,96 94,94,76**
CSF £90.21 CT £1282.75 TOTE £8.00: £2.30, £2.70, £2.80; EX 102.80 Trifecta £666.30.
**Owner** Mrs Anne Cowley **Bred** John Kirby **Trained** Baydon, Wilts
■ Stewards' Enquiry : Nicky Mackay two-day ban: careless riding (May 30-31)

**FOCUS**
A fair 3yo handicap. The bare form is only ordinary.

## 2308 BARKER STOREY MATTHEWS NOVICE STKS (BOBIS RACE) 6f
**3:25** (3:27) (Class 4) 2-Y-O **£4,197** (£4,197; £962; £240; £240) **Stalls** High

Form RPR
21 **1** **Dougal (IRE)**[9] 2064 2-9-7 0.............................. PatDobbs 6 93
(Richard Hannon) *broke wl: mde all: rdn and qcknd over 1f out: sustained duel w rival after: r.o: jnd on post* **10/3**[2]
61 **1** *dht* **Justice Good (IRE)**[18] 1807 2-9-7 0.............................. LiamKeniry 3 93
(David Elsworth) *stdd s: hld up wl in tch: jnd ldr 2f out: rdn and qcknd clr w rival over 1f out: sustained duel w rival after: r.o: jnd ldr on post* **7/2**[3]
**3** *1 1/4* **Outlaw Country (IRE)** 2-9-0 0.............................. MartinLane 7 83+
(Charlie Appleby) *s.i.s: in tch in last trio: rdn and hdwy over 1f out: wnt 3rd and edgd lft ent fnl f: r.o wl* **8/1**
21 **4** *4 1/2* **Burtonwood**[27] 1583 2-9-7 0.............................. RichardKingscote 9 76
(Richard Fahey) *trckd ldrs: nt clr run over 2f out: gap opened and rdn over 1f out: no rspnse and sn struggling: wknd ins fnl f* **7/1**
1 **4** *dht* **Bronze Maquette (IRE)**[22] 1663 2-9-2 0.............................. JimmyFortune 5 71+
(Gary Moore) *in tch in midfield: rdn and effrt ent fnl 2f: outpcd and btn jst over 1f out: wknd fnl f* **11/4**[1]
**6** *1 1/4* **Black Granite (IRE)** 2-9-0 0.............................. SebSanders 1 65
(Jeremy Noseda) *s.i.s: in tch in rr: rdn 2f out: outpcd and btn over 1f out: wknd fnl f* **25/1**
**7** *1/2* **My Mate (IRE)** 2-9-0 0.............................. FrederikTylicki 4 64+
(Clive Brittain) *chsd ldr tl 2f out: sn rdn and unable qck: wknd fnl f* **33/1**
**8** *2* **Four Seasons (IRE)** 2-9-0 0.............................. MickaelBarzalona 2 58+
(Charlie Appleby) *s.i.s: in tch in last trio: rdn and effrt 2f out: running onto heels and shifted sharply rt over 1f out: no hdwy after: bhd ins fnl f* **8/1**

1m 13.72s (1.52) **Going Correction** +0.05s/f (Good) **8** Ran SP% **113.5**
Speed ratings (Par 95): **91,91,89,83,83 81,81,78**
WIN: 2.60 Dougal, 2.00 Justice Good; PL: 1.90 Dougal, 2.20 Outlaw Country, 1.60 Justice Good; EX: 10.20, 7.80; CSF: 7.60, 7.68; TC: ; TF: 77.30, 104.80;.
**Owner** Mrs J Wood **Bred** Ardrums House Stud **Trained** East Everleigh, Wilts
**Owner** Robert Ng **Bred** Mrs C Regalado-Gonzalez **Trained** Newmarket, Suffolk

**FOCUS**
A decent-looking novice event, made up of four last-time-out winners and four well-bred newcomers. Nothing between the reopposing dead-heaters.

## 2309 EDMONDSON HALL SOLICITORS & SPORTS LAWYERS H'CAP 1m 2f
**4:00** (4:01) (Class 3) (0-90,89) 4-Y-O+ **£9,056** (£2,695; £1,346; £673) **Stalls** High

Form RPR
150- **1** **Groundbreaking**[203] 7497 4-9-7 89.............................. MickaelBarzalona 10 106
(Charlie Appleby) *hld up in rr: stdy prog 4f out: led over 1f out and sn rdn clr: r.o wl: easily* **6/1**[3]
0-12 **2** *7* **Tigers Tale (IRE)**[27] 1578 5-9-6 88.............................. (v) LiamKeniry 1 92
(Roger Teal) *racd along in centre: overall ldr tl over 2f out: edging lft after: kpt on to go 2nd ins fnl f: no ch w wnr* **16/1**
06- **3** *1/2* **Double Discount (IRE)**[252] 6163 4-9-6 88.............................. RichardKingscote 2 91
(Tom Dascombe) *led nr side gp and prom overall: rdn over 2f out: no ch w wnr and kpt on same pce ins fnl f* **8/1**

224- **4** 1 1/2 **Velox**[259] 5944 4-9-6 **88** ... JimmyFortune 8 88
(Luca Cumani) *in tch in midfield: rdn and effrt to chse ldrs over 2f out: no ch w wnr 1f out: wknd ins fnl f* **7/2**[2]

-130 **5** nk **Big Baz (IRE)**[13] 1948 4-9-2 **84** ... MartinDwyer 5 84
(William Muir) *prom: led nr side gp 4f out: overall ldr over 2f out tl hdd over 1f out: sn brushed aside by wnr: wknd ins fnl f* **6/1**[3]

0-05 **6** 3 1/2 **Jacob Cats**[17] 1834 5-9-0 **82** ... KierenFox 7 75
(William Knight) *prom: rdn 5f out: wknd u.p wl over 1f out* **16/1**

11-2 **7** 20 **Gone Dutch**[34] 1439 4-9-3 **85** ... FrederikTylicki 9 40
(James Fanshawe) *hld up in tch in rr: rdn 4f out: btn 2f out: sn bhd: eased ins fnl f* **9/4**[1]

2504 **8** 2 **Icebuster**[11] 2033 6-9-2 **84** ... SteveDrowne 3 35
(Rod Millman) *stdd s: hld up in rr: rdn and short-lived effrt over 2f out: wl bhd and eased ins fnl f* **20/1**

-051 **9** 7 **Heavy Metal**[9] 2068 4-9-3 **85** 6ex ... LiamJones 4 23
(Mark Johnston) *chsd ldrs: rdn wl over 2f out: sn struggling and btn: wl bhd and eased ins fnl f* **16/1**

2m 3.45s (-2.35) **Going Correction** +0.05s/f (Good) **9 Ran SP% 115.1**
Speed ratings (Par 107): **111,105,105,103,103 100,84,83,77**
CSF £94.84 CT £771.16 TOTE £8.80: £2.20, £2.80, £2.50; EX 86.90 Trifecta £598.90.
**Owner** Godolphin **Bred** Highclere Stud **Trained** Newmarket, Suffolk

**FOCUS**
A good-quality handicap but not the strongest form for the grade.

## 2310 THE THREE BLACKBIRDS WOODDITTON FOR SALE MAIDEN FILLIES' STKS (BOBIS RACE) 1m 4f
**4:35** (4:39) (Class 4) 3-Y-O **£5,175** (£1,540; £769; £384) **Stalls** Centre

Form RPR

0 **1** **Seagull (IRE)**[27] 1587 3-9-0 0 ... SteveDrowne 7 82+
(John Gosden) *hld up in tch in midfield: clsd to chse ldr 3f out: rdn to ld over 1f out: in command and r.o wl ins fnl f* **6/1**[3]

2- **2** 3 **Swan Lakes (IRE)**[213] 7260 3-9-0 0 ... FergusSweeney 3 77
(David Simcock) *pressed ldr tl led over 3f out: rdn and hdd over 1f out: sn outpcd: kpt on to hold 2nd fnl f* **1/1**[1]

**3** 3/4 **Clear Mind** 3-9-0 0 ... NickyMackay 4 76
(John Gosden) *hld up in tch towards rr: clsd over 2f out: rdn and chsd ldrs over 1f out: no threat to wnr but battling for 2nd fnl f: kpt on* **12/1**

6-5 **4** 3 3/4 **Alphabetique**[35] 1427 3-9-0 0 ... JimmyFortune 2 70
(Peter Chapple-Hyam) *t.k.h: hld up in tch in midfield: hdwy to chse ldrs over 2f out: rdn and btn over 1f out: wknd fnl f* **20/1**

6 **5** 3/4 **Perfect Light (IRE)**[21] 1701 3-9-0 0 ... SebSanders 5 69
(William Haggas) *in tch in midfield: rdn 3f out: outpcd and btn over 1f out: wknd ins fnl f* **5/1**[2]

4 **6** 12 **Nusantara**[18] 1797 3-9-0 0 ... ChrisCatlin 9 50
(Paul Cole) *chsd ldrs: rdn over 2f out: sn struggling and btn 2f out: bhd and eased ins fnl f* **7/1**

06 **7** 1 1/4 **High Love (IRE)**[13] 1960 3-9-0 0 ... RichardKingscote 1 48
(Tom Dascombe) *chsd ldrs: rdn over 2f out: wknd wl over 1f out: bhd fnl f* **20/1**

6 **8** nk **Topaling**[15] 1894 3-9-0 0 ... MickaelBarzalona 6 47
(Mark H Tompkins) *stdd s: t.k.h: hld up in tch in rr: swtchd rt 4f out: rdn and btn over 2f out: bhd fnl f* **40/1**

0 **9** 17 **Little Flo**[12] 1984 3-8-7 0 ... JennyPowell(7) 8 20
(Brendan Powell) *led tl over 3f out: sn dropped out and bhd 2f out: t.o fnl f* **80/1**

2m 34.4s (2.40) **Going Correction** +0.05s/f (Good) **9 Ran SP% 114.3**
Speed ratings (Par 98): **94,92,91,89,88 80,79,79,68**
CSF £11.87 TOTE £6.40: £1.70, £1.10, £3.50; EX 14.60 Trifecta £166.90.
**Owner** Lady Rothschild **Bred** Mrs C L Weld **Trained** Newmarket, Suffolk

**FOCUS**
A fair 3yo fillies' maiden which matches up to the race average.

## 2311 NEWMARKETRACECOURSES.CO.UK H'CAP 1m
**5:05** (5:08) (Class 3) (0-95,90) 4-Y-0+ **£9,056** (£2,695; £1,346; £673) **Stalls** High

Form RPR

1423 **1** **Tenor (IRE)**[14] 1926 4-8-2 **78** ...(t) JoeDoyle(7) 2 86
(John Ryan) *w ldr: rdn ent fnl 2f: sustained duel w rival fr over 1f out: r.o u.p to ld last strides* **15/2**

6-30 **2** shd **Dance And Dance (IRE)**[48] 1164 8-9-6 **89** ... JimmyFortune 8 97
(Ed Vaughan) *led and set stdy gallop: rdn and qcknd wl over 1f out: sustained duel w wnr fr over 1f out: r.o wl tl hdd and no ex last strides* **6/1**[3]

40-1 **3** 1 **Angelic Upstart (IRE)**[43] 1267 6-8-5 **81** ... JackGarritty(7) 10 86
(Andrew Balding) *hld up wl in tch: rdn to chse ldrs and switching rt over 1f out: kpt on ins fnl f* **6/1**[3]

52-3 **4** 3/4 **Kakatosi**[17] 1862 7-9-0 **83** ... PatDobbs 4 87
(Mike Murphy) *hld up in tch in last pair: hdwy on stands' rail to chse ldrs 1f out: styd on same pce fnl 100yds* **12/1**

43-1 **5** 1 3/4 **Sir Mike**[24] 1637 5-9-7 **90** ... FrankieDettori 9 90
(Luca Cumani) *in tch in midfield: hdwy over 2f out: rdn to press ldrs over 1f out: no ex 1f out: wknd ins fnl f* **2/1**[1]

1064 **6** 3 1/2 **Tatting**[16] 1871 5-8-12 **81** ... LiamKeniry 1 73
(Chris Dwyer) *stdd s: hld up in tch in last pair: rdn and effrt wl over 1f out: no prog: nvr trbld ldrs* **33/1**

305- **7** 5 **Jodies Jem**[195] 7696 4-9-3 **86** ... SteveDrowne 6 66
(William Jarvis) *t.k.h: hld up wl in tch in midfield: rdn and unable qck 2f out: btn over 1f out: wknd fnl f* **8/1**

140- **8** 1 1/4 **Monsieur Rieussec**[245] 6356 4-8-13 **82** ... MickaelBarzalona 7 59
(Jonathan Portman) *t.k.h: hld up wl in tch in midfield: rdn and lost pl ent fnl 2f: wknd 1f out* **5/1**[2]

1-00 **9** 13 **Eurato (FR)**[20] 1715 4-8-13 **82** ... PaddyAspell 5 29
(Alan Jones) *pressed ldrs tl lost pl qckly ent fnl 2f: bhd fnl f* **100/1**

1m 37.43s (-1.17) **Going Correction** +0.05s/f (Good) **9 Ran SP% 113.1**
Speed ratings (Par 107): **107,106,105,105,103 99,94,93,80**
CSF £50.73 CT £288.35 TOTE £9.30: £2.90, £2.50, £2.30; EX 63.40 Trifecta £408.70.
**Owner** Kilco (International) Ltd **Bred** Epona Bloodstock Ltd And P A Byrne **Trained** Newmarket, Suffolk

**FOCUS**
A fair handicap. The 1-2 were always the front pair, with a small personal best from the winner.

## 2312 NEWMARKETEXPERIENCE.CO.UK RACING EXCELLENCE "HANDS AND HEELS" APPRENTICE SERIES H'CAP 6f
**5:40** (5:42) (Class 5) (0-75,75) 4-Y-O+ **£3,881** (£1,155; £577; £288) **Stalls** High

Form RPR

6-06 **1** **Kylladdie**[15] 1905 7-8-10 **69** ...(b) MichaelKenneally(5) 4 78
(Steve Gollings) *dwlt: rdn along thrght: struggling to go pce in rr: styd on over 1f out: led wl ins fnl f: r.o* **9/1**

411- **2** 3/4 **Honeymoon Express (IRE)**[264] 5800 4-9-2 **73**.(p) PatrickO'Donnell(3) 1 80
(Julia Feilden) *pressed ldrs: rdn to ld wl over 1f out: hdd ent fnl f: ev ch after: no ex towards fin* **7/1**

0356 **3** 1/2 **Welease Bwian (IRE)**[16] 1878 5-8-7 **66**....... NatalieHambling-Yates(5) 7 71+
(Stuart Williams) *hld up in tch in midfield: hdwy to chal wl over 1f out: rdn to ld ent fnl f: hdd wl ins fnl f: wknd cl home* **7/1**

-351 **4** 1 3/4 **Clock Opera (IRE)**[15] 1896 4-8-8 **65** ... KieranShoemark(3) 9 65
(William Stone) *t.k.h: pressed ldrs: rdn wl over 1f out: no ex ins fnl f: wknd fnl 75yds* **6/1**[3]

10-0 **5** 2 **Fossa**[22] 1678 4-8-13 **70** ... PaulBooth(3) 3 63
(Dean Ivory) *chsd ldrs: rdn and outpcd over 1f out: styd on same pce and no imp fnl f* **7/2**[1]

60-0 **6** 3 1/4 **Dominium (USA)**[20] 1731 7-9-7 **75** ...(b) DavidParkes 8 58
(Jeremy Gask) *s.i.s: hld up in tch in rr: hdwy over 1f out: no imp and wl hld whn nt clr run ins fnl f* **5/1**[2]

0610 **7** 1 **Only Ten Per Cent (IRE)**[14] 1921 6-9-2 **70**...............(v) LukeLeadbitter 6 50
(J R Jenkins) *t.k.h: hld up in midfield: effrt to press ldrs 2f out: rdn and unable qck over 1f out: fdd ins fnl f* **15/2**

0411 **8** 1 **Drawnfromthepast (IRE)**[37] 1388 9-8-8 **67**...............(p) CliffordLee(5) 2 44
(Ed Walker) *led: rdn and hdd wl over 1f out: btn ent fnl f: fdd* **7/1**

5040 **9** 18 **Waterloo Dock**[44] 1236 9-8-4 **61** oh16................(v) JonathanWillets(3) 5
(Mick Quinn) *bustled along to chse ldrs: lost pl and bhd 1/2-way: lost tch over 1f out* **100/1**

1m 13.01s (0.81) **Going Correction** +0.05s/f (Good) **9 Ran SP% 113.4**
Speed ratings (Par 103): **96,95,94,92,89 85,83,82,58**
CSF £68.98 CT £468.82 TOTE £15.00: £3.10, £2.80, £2.20; EX 110.20 Trifecta £1536.80.
**Owner** P S Walter **Bred** Horizon Bloodstock Limited **Trained** Scamblesby, Lincs
■ A winner on his first ride for Michael Kenneally.

**FOCUS**
A fair "hands and heels" handicap but not form to be confident about.
T/Plt: £356.30 to a £1 stake. Pool: £62,705.09 - 128.45 winning units. T/Qpdt: £33.70 to a £1 stake. Pool: £5271.41 - 115.60 winning units. SP

# 2283 YORK (L-H)
## Friday, May 16

**OFFICIAL GOING: Good (7.0)**
Wind: Light across Weather: Cloudy with sunny periods

## 2313 LANGLEYS SOLICITORS LLP EBF STALLIONS MARYGATE STKS (LISTED RACE) 5f
**1:45** (1:46) (Class 1) 2-Y-O
**£22,684** (£8,600; £4,304; £2,144; £1,076; £540) **Stalls** High

Form RPR

1 **1** **Patience Alexander (IRE)**[41] 1314 2-8-12 0 ... JimCrowley 11 97
(David Evans) *str: trckd ldrs: hdwy over 2f out: led over 1f out: rdn and kpt on wl fnl f* **5/1**

11 **2** 1/2 **Tiggy Wiggy (IRE)**[12] 1982 2-8-12 0 ... SeanLevey 10 95
(Richard Hannon) *leggy: trckd ldrs: hdwy halfway: led over 1f out: sn rdn: hdd and drvn ins fnl f: kpt on* **4/1**[2]

1 **3** 2 1/4 **Zuhoor Baynoona (IRE)**[17] 1859 2-8-12 0 ... RyanMoore 7 87
(Richard Fahey) *lengthy: tall: trckd ldrs: hdwy 2f out: sn rdn and ev ch tl wknd ent fnl f* **7/2**[1]

61 **4** nk **Appleberry (IRE)**[10] 2051 2-8-12 0 ... AndrewMullen 2 86
(Michael Appleby) *athletic: leggy: chsd ldrs: rdn along over 2f out: swtchd lft: drvn and sltly outpcd over 1f out: kpt on wl fnl f* **33/1**

1 **5** nse **Don't Tell Annie**[32] 1482 2-8-12 0 ... DavidAllan 8 86
(Tim Easterby) *w'like: str: midfield: pushed along 1/2-way: rdn wl over 1f out: kpt on fnl f: nrst fin* **8/1**

21 **6** 3/4 **Sarista (IRE)**[20] 1732 2-8-12 0 ... RobertWinston 1 83
(David Barron) *leggy: t.k.h: led: rdn along and hdd over 1f out: wknd fnl f* **9/2**[3]

2 **7** 3 1/2 **Exentricity**[12] 1982 2-8-12 0 ... WilliamTwiston-Davies 4 74+
(Mick Channon) *athletic: dwlt and in rr: hdwy and in tch over 2f out: rdn and wknd over 1f out* **10/1**

01 **8** 1/2 **Granny Alice**[15] 1900 2-8-12 0 ... AndreaAtzeni 6 69
(Noel Quinlan) *chsd ldrs: rdn along wl over 1f out: sn wknd* **25/1**

61 **9** 10 **Ko Cache (IRE)**[22] 1670 2-8-12 0 ... TomEaves 3 33
(Keith Dalgleish) *w'like: cl up: rdn 2f out: sn wknd* **50/1**

01 **10** 1/2 **Lazy Days In Loule (IRE)**[30] 1505 2-8-12 0 ... DuranFentiman 5 31
(Noel Wilson) *unf: scope: cl up: rdn along over 2f out: sn wknd* **50/1**

43 **11** 2 1/2 **Magic Florence (IRE)**[28] 1560 2-8-12 0 ... GrahamLee 13 22
(James Given) *cmpt: in rr: outpcd and bhd fr 1/2-way* **20/1**

32 **12** 2 3/4 **War Paint (IRE)**[11] 2022 2-8-12 0 ... KierenFallon 9 12
(Tom Dascombe) *w'like: lengthy: in rr: outpcd and bhd fr 1/2-way* **20/1**

03 **13** 1/2 **Pickle Lilly Pearl**[7] 2134 2-8-12 0 ... RoystonFfrench 12 10
(David C Griffiths) *leggy: in rr: outpcd and bhd fr 1/2-way* **100/1**

59.78s (0.48) **Going Correction** -0.05s/f (Good) **13 Ran SP% 118.5**
Speed ratings (Par 101): **94,93,89,89,89 87,82,81,65,64 60,56,55**
CSF £23.26 TOTE £6.10: £2.30, £1.70, £1.70; EX 28.30 Trifecta £128.50.
**Owner** Noel O'Callaghan **Bred** Mountarmstrong Stud **Trained** Pandy, Monmouths

**FOCUS**
Rail moved out 3m from 1m1f until entrance to home straight, reducing distances on Round course by 17yds. This race is in danger of being stripped of its Listed status, but it has gone to some useful fillies in its short history. Gilded (2006) and Ceiling Kitty (2012) went on to win the Queen Mary at Ascot as did Langs Lash, runner-up here in 2008. Misheer, who won this in 2009, was second in the Ascot race before taking the Cherry Hinton at Newmarket. The pace was quick and the time dipped inside a minute. The form pair came to the fore, pulling away late on. The form makes sense and matches the race average.

## 2314 SPORTINGBET.COM JORVIK STKS (H'CAP) 1m 4f
2:15 (2:15) (Class 2) (0-105,97) 4-Y-O+
**£31,125** (£9,320; £4,660; £2,330; £1,165; £585) **Stalls** Centre

Form RPR
2-11 **1** **Arab Spring (IRE)**[20] 1715 4-9-9 **96**................................... RyanMoore 3 106+
(Sir Michael Stoute) *lw: trckd ldrs: smooth hdwy over 3f out: cl up over 2f out: led wl over 1f out: rdn clr ent fnl f: drvn out* **13/8**[1]

33-0 **2** ½ **Duke Of Clarence (IRE)**[9] 2073 5-9-8 **95**......................(p) DavidNolan 1 104+
(Richard Fahey) *trckd ldrs: pushed along 3f out and sn sltly outpcd: rdn wl over 1f out: styd on strly u.p to chal wl ins fnl f: kpt on* **14/1**

0-61 **3** 2¼ **Itlaaq**[13] 1935 8-8-11 **84**.......................................(t) GrahamGibbons 5 90
(Michael Easterby) *lw: trckd ldrs: hdwy on outer 3f out: sn cl up: rdn 2f out and ev ch tl drvn and kpt on same pce ins fnl f* **12/1**

3334 **4** ½ **Bute Hall**[13] 1935 5-8-10 **83**.................................. JimmyQuinn 7 88
(David Thompson) *led: hdd 1/2-way: cl up: rdn along over 2f out: drvn over 1f out: kpt on same pce fnl f* **25/1**

44-6 **5** ½ **Saptapadi (IRE)**[20] 1735 8-9-1 **88**.................................(t) PaulPickard 11 92
(Brian Ellison) *hld up in rr: effrt and nt clr run 2f out: swtchd lft and rdn over 1f out: styd on fnl f: nrst fin* **12/1**

10-3 **6** ½ **Amralah (IRE)**[12] 1973 4-9-5 **92**.............................. WilliamBuick 13 95
(Mick Channon) *lw: trckd ldr: led 1/2-way: rdn along 3f out: hdd wl over 1f out: sn drvn and grad wknd* **5/1**[3]

-006 **7** 1¾ **Media Hype**[20] 1736 7-9-2 **89**.......................................(v) JimCrowley 9 90
(K R Burke) *hld up: hdwy on outer to chse ldrs 3f out: rdn along over 2f out: sn drvn and no imp* **25/1**

0-32 **8** 1½ **Chancery (USA)**[20] 1736 6-9-10 **97**........................... DanielTudhope 12 95
(David O'Meara) *lw: hld up: effrt and sme hdwy 3f out: rdn along 2f out: sn no imp* **9/2**[2]

2220 **9** 2 **Kashmir Peak (IRE)**[41] 784 5-9-1 **91**..........................[1] IanBrennan(3) 8 86
(John Quinn) *hld up: nvr bttr than midfield* **33/1**

00-0 **10** nk **Ardlui (IRE)**[20] 1735 6-9-6 **93**.....................................(b[1]) DavidAllan 2 88
(Tim Easterby) *swtg: chsd ldrs: rdn along wl over 2f out: sn drvn and wknd* **66/1**

**11** 1 **Shalaman (IRE)**[27] 1592 5-8-5 **81**.....................................(tp) OisinMurphy(3) 10 74
(Denis Gerard Hogan, Ire) *dwlt: a towards rr* **12/1**

2m 31.85s (-1.35) **Going Correction** -0.175s/f (Firm) **11 Ran SP% 114.8**
Speed ratings (Par 109): **97,96,95,94,94 94,93,92,90,90 89**
CSF £25.60 CT £208.55 TOTE £2.50: £1.10, £3.30, £2.80; EX 29.40 Trifecta £300.70.
**Owner** Ballymacoll Stud **Bred** Ballymacoll Stud Farm Ltd **Trained** Newmarket, Suffolk

**FOCUS**
Most of these are pretty exposed, but the exception was the winner who continues to progress. The time was relatively slow.

## 2315 SKY BET YORKSHIRE CUP (BRITISH CHAMPIONS SERIES) (GROUP 2) 1m 6f
2:45 (2:47) (Class 1) 4-Y-O+
**£79,394** (£30,100; £15,064; £7,504; £3,766; £1,890) **Stalls** Low

Form RPR
5-41 **1** **Gospel Choir**[13] 1950 5-9-0 115................................ RyanMoore 2 116
(Sir Michael Stoute) *trckd ldrs: hdwy 2f out: rdn to ld ent fnl f: sn drvn and hld on gamely towards fin* **7/2**[1]

21-1 **2** nk **Tac De Boistron (FR)**[16] 1869 7-9-4 117.......................... AndreaAtzeni 4 119
(Marco Botti) *lw: hld up in rr: hdwy over 3f out: swtchd rt 2f out: rdn and styd on to chal ins fnl f: ev ch tl drvn and no ex nr fin* **4/1**[2]

210- **3** ½ **Tiger Cliff (IRE)**[216] 7193 5-9-0 104.............................. TomQueally 6 114
(Alan King) *hld up towards rr: stdy hdwy over 3f out: rdn 2f out and sn ev ch: drvn ent fnl f and kpt on same pce towards fin* **10/1**

1F1- **4** 2½ **Seal Of Approval**[209] 7365 5-9-1 116............................ HayleyTurner 9 112
(James Fanshawe) *t.k.h: trckd ldrs: hdwy 3f out: ev ch 2f out: sn rdn and kpt on same pce appr fnl f* **10/1**

50-3 **5** ½ **High Jinx (IRE)**[37] 1398 6-9-0 107................................. ShaneKelly 12 110
(James Fanshawe) *hld up towards rr: hdwy 3f out: rdn along 2f out: kpt on appr fnl f: nrst fin* **14/1**

120- **6** nk **Ahzeemah (IRE)**[209] 7363 5-9-0 112...............................(p) KierenFallon 13 110
(Saeed bin Suroor) *trckd ldrs: hdwy 3f out: cl up 2f out: rdn to ld briefly over 1f out: drvn and hdd ent fnl f: sn wknd* **8/1**[3]

411- **7** ½ **Camborne**[237] 6636 6-9-0 114......................................(p) WilliamBuick 10 109
(John Gosden) *hld up and bhd: stdy hdwy on wd outside over 2f out: rdn wl over 1f out: kpt on fnl f* **9/1**

050- **8** ½ **Glen's Diamond**[243] 6453 6-9-0 109.............................. TonyHamilton 8 108
(Richard Fahey) *set stdy pce: pushed along and qcknd over 4f out: rdn 3f out: hdd 2f out: sn drvn and grad wknd* **16/1**

/1-5 **9** 1 **Khione**[34] 1434 5-8-11 105......................................... JoeFanning 7 104
(Luca Cumani) *lw: chsd ldrs: pushed along over 3f out: rdn over 2f out and grad wknd* **16/1**

64-5 **10** 1¼ **Repeater**[37] 1398 5-9-0 104........................................ DanielTudhope 1 105
(David O'Meara) *hld up: a towards rr* **33/1**

21-1 **11** 3½ **Cubanita**[34] 1434 5-8-11 111......................................... JimCrowley 3 97
(Ralph Beckett) *swtg: hld up in tch: gd hdwy on wd outside 3f out: led 2f out: sn rdn and hdd over 1f out: wknd fnl f* **10/1**

5-00 **12** 1¼ **Penglai Pavilion (USA)**[13] 1950 4-9-0 117....................... JamesDoyle 11 98
(Charlie Appleby) *lw: prom: rdn along 3f out: wknd over 2f out* **25/1**

3m 0.36s (0.16) **Going Correction** -0.175s/f (Firm) **12 Ran SP% 115.8**
Speed ratings (Par 115): **92,91,91,90,89 89,89,89,88,87 85,85**
CSF £16.50 TOTE £4.50: £1.90, £2.20, £2.80; EX 15.00 Trifecta £144.40.
**Owner** Cheveley Park Stud **Bred** Cheveley Park Stud Ltd **Trained** Newmarket, Suffolk

**FOCUS**
A good edition of this Group 2 event, with a larger field than usual. The pace was modest, though, the field stacking down the back, and there were half a dozen in line across the track heading down to the final furlong, the runners having come down the centre in the straight. The form makes sense.

## 2316 IRISH CHAMPIONS WEEKEND FILLIES' STKS (REGISTERED AS THE MICHAEL SEELY MEMORIAL STAKES) (LISTED) 1m
3:15 (3:24) (Class 1) 3-Y-O
**£22,684** (£8,600; £4,304; £2,144; £1,076; £540) **Stalls** Low

Form RPR
40-5 **1** **Lustrous**[16] 1868 3-9-0 93.......................................... AndreaAtzeni 12 102
(Richard Hannon) *led: hdd over 3f out: cl up: pushed along 2f out: rdn over 1f out: drvn ins fnl f and kpt on wl to ld nr fin* **20/1**

514- **2** nk **Radiator**[231] 6795 3-9-0 97........................................... JamesDoyle 3 101
(Sir Michael Stoute) *t.k.h early: trckd ldrs: hdwy over 2f out: sn cl up: chal over 1f out: rdn to ld ins fnl f: sn drvn: hdd and no ex nr fin* **9/2**[2]

1-40 **3** ½ **Lady Lara (IRE)**[12] 1976 3-9-0 100................................ KierenFallon 1 100
(Alan Jarvis) *trckd ldrs: hdwy 3f out: chal 2f out: rdn to ld wl over 1f out: drvn and hdd ins fnl f: kpt on* **4/1**[1]

11-6 **4** ¾ **Dutch Courage**[34] 1435 3-9-0 93................................... RyanMoore 9 98
(Richard Fahey) *midfield: hdwy 3f out: rdn along wl over 1f out: chsd ldrs appr fnl f: sn drvn and kpt on same pce* **8/1**

1 **5** 1 **Belle De Lawers**[20] 1722 3-9-0 84.................................. JoeFanning 8 96+
(James Bethell) *hld up towards rr: hdwy over 2f out: sn rdn and styd on appr fnl f: nrst fin* **10/1**

1-01 **6** ½ **Pelerin (IRE)**[13] 1956 3-9-0 89................................... MarcMonaghan 5 95
(Marco Botti) *midfield: hdwy and in tch 3f out: rdn 2f out: sn chsng ldrs: drvn and no imp fnl f* **15/2**[3]

46-2 **7** 3¾ **Midnite Angel (IRE)**[27] 1579 3-9-0 92..........................(b[1]) SeanLevey 2 86
(Richard Hannon) *hld up towards rr: hdwy over 2f out: sn rdn and no imp appr fnl f* **16/1**

1-0 **8** ¾ **Folk Melody (IRE)**[30] 1515 3-9-0 95................................[1] WilliamBuick 7 84
(Charlie Appleby) *hld up towards rr: hdwy over 2f out: sn rdn n.d* **8/1**

220- **9** nk **Qawaasem (IRE)**[245] 6350 3-9-0 100.............................. TomQueally 10 84
(Charles Hills) *prom: rdn along 3f out: wknd 2f out* **16/1**

22-1 **10** 2¾ **Adhwaa**[16] 1868 3-9-0 92.......................................... DaneO'Neill 14 77
(J W Hills) *lw: dwlt: a towards rr* **9/1**

0-1 **11** ¾ **Nirva (IRE)**[42] 1280 3-9-0 80...................................... JimCrowley 4 76
(Ralph Beckett) *nvr bttr than midfield* **25/1**

13-0 **12** hd **Dutch Romance**[34] 1435 3-9-0 93................................. RobertWinston 13 75
(Charles Hills) *chsd ldrs on outer: wd st and led over 3f out: sn rdn: hdd wl over 1f out and sn wknd* **40/1**

0-01 **13** 2 **Azagal (IRE)**[13] 1937 3-9-0 97.................................... DavidAllan 6 71
(Tim Easterby) *lw: a towards rr* **12/1**

03-4 **14** 22 **Gracie Hart**[19] 1767 3-9-0 69.................................... PhilipPrince 11 20
(Jo Hughes) *chsd ldrs: rdn along wl over 2f out: sn wknd* **100/1**

1m 37.61s (-1.39) **Going Correction** -0.175s/f (Firm) **14 Ran SP% 122.8**
Speed ratings (Par 104): **99,98,98,97,96 95,92,91,91,88 87,87,85,63**
CSF £107.38 TOTE £33.60: £7.60, £2.40, £2.00; EX 197.20 Trifecta £2120.50.
**Owner** Mrs P Good **Bred** Mrs P Good **Trained** East Everleigh, Wilts

**FOCUS**
This looked a wide-open Listed race, but they didn't go much of a pace and finished in a bit of a heap. A step up from the winner with the next two close to form.

## 2317 RALPH RAPER MEMORIAL STKS (H'CAP) (BOBIS RACE) 5f
3:50 (3:53) (Class 3) (0-90,90) 3-Y-O **£12,938** (£3,850; £1,924; £962) **Stalls** High

Form RPR
2-1 **1** **G Force (IRE)**[22] 1671 3-9-4 **87**................................ DanielTudhope 8 107+
(David O'Meara) *str: wnt lft s: hld up: smooth hdwy 2f out: swtchd rt and shkn up over 1f out: stroing run ent fnl f: led last 100yds and sn clr* **9/4**[1]

31- **2** 2½ **Speed Hawk (USA)**[185] 7844 3-9-1 **84**........................... AndreaAtzeni 2 95
(Robert Cowell) *trckd ldrs: hdwy on wd outside and cl up over 2f out: rdn to ld wl over 1f out: hdd last 100yds: kpt on: no ch w wnr* **14/1**

-652 **3** 2 **Kickboxer (IRE)**[8] 2090 3-8-9 **81**.................... WilliamTwiston-Davies(3) 9 85
(Mick Channon) *trckd ldrs: hdwy 2f out and sn pushed along: rdn over 1f out: styd on fnl f: nrst fin* **8/1**[2]

1151 **4** nk **Scarborough (IRE)**[17] 1851 3-8-9 **78**.......................... AndrewMullen 12 81
(Michael Appleby) *cl up: led 1/2-way: rdn and hdd wl over 1f out: sn drvn and one pce* **20/1**

0-41 **5** 2¼ **Skye's The Limit**[27] 1585 3-8-8 **77**.......................... TonyHamilton 1 72
(Richard Fahey) *prom: rdn along 2f out: grad wknd appr fnl f* **16/1**

20-2 **6** 4½ **Dutch Breeze**[13] 1959 3-8-11 **80**............................... DavidAllan 11 59
(Tim Easterby) *chsd ldrs: rdn along over 2f out: sn wknd* **25/1**

0-31 **7** nk **One Boy (IRE)**[22] 1676 3-8-13 **85**.......................... ConnorBeasley(3) 6 63
(Michael Dods) *wnt rt s: midfield: hdwy to chse ldrs 2f out: sn rdn and one pce* **25/1**

120- **8** hd **Grecian (IRE)**[287] 4948 3-8-11 **83**.......................... OisinMurphy(3) 15 60
(Paul Cole) *in tch: hdwy over 2f out: sn rdn and no imp appr fnl f* **14/1**

36-0 **9** 1¼ **Jamboree Girl**[11] 2015 3-8-7 **76** oh2............................ AndrewElliott 5 48
(Tim Easterby) *prom: rdn along over 2f out: sn drvn and wknd* **66/1**

2-21 **10** ½ **Piazon**[25] 1615 3-8-13 **85**............................... MichaelJMMurphy(3) 10 56+
(Michael Bell) *in tch: hdwy whn nt clr run wl over 1f out and again ent fnl f: n.d* **8/1**[2]

-033 **11** 2 **Meadway**[12] 1968 3-9-1 **84**....................................... WilliamBuick 13 47
(Bryan Smart) *chsd ldrs: rdn along over 2f out: sn wknd* **25/1**

1-14 **12** ¾ **Signore Piccolo**[20] 1737 3-8-8 **80**............................ JasonHart(3) 20 41
(Eric Alston) *led: rdn along and hdd 1/2-way: sn wknd* **12/1**[3]

1-06 **13** 3¼ **Flying Bear (IRE)**[21] 1700 3-8-7 **76**............................ HarryBentley 17 25
(Jeremy Gask) *dwlt: a in rr* **16/1**

1 **14** nk **Dinneratmidnight**[22] 1677 3-8-12 **81**.............................. JimCrowley 3 29
(Ralph Beckett) *neat: in tch: rdn along 1/2-way: sn outpcd* **14/1**

52-0 **15** 2¼ **Hatha Hooh**[30] 1513 3-8-13 **82**..................................... TomQueally 4 22
(Ismail Mohammed) *lw: chsd ldrs: rdn along over 2f out: sn wknd* **50/1**

10-4 **16** hd **Canyari (IRE)**[42] 1278 3-9-2 **88**......................... GeorgeChaloner(3) 7 27
(Richard Fahey) *hmpd s: a towards rr* **12/1**[3]

0-05 **17** 3 **Outer Space**[13] 1952 3-9-7 **90**..................................... JamesDoyle 16 18
(Jamie Osborne) *dwlt: a in rr* **25/1**

1004 **18** 4 **Oriental Relation (IRE)**[12] 1968 3-9-1 **87**..................(b) IanBrennan(3) 18
(James Given) *iin tch: rdn along bef 1/2-way: sn outpcd* **50/1**

4660 **19** 6 **Scruffy Tramp (IRE)**[21] 1700 3-8-13 **82**.......................(b) RyanMoore 19
(Alan Bailey) *dwlt: a bhd* **33/1**

58.66s (-0.64) **Going Correction** -0.05s/f (Good) **19 Ran SP% 128.6**
Speed ratings (Par 103): **103,99,95,95,91 84,84,83,81,80 77,76,71,70,67 66,62,55,46**
CSF £32.20 CT £242.58 TOTE £3.20: £1.20, £3.90, £2.60, £2.30; EX 38.50 Trifecta £462.60.
**Owner** Middleham Park Racing XVIII & Partner **Bred** Kildaragh Stud & Twelve Oaks Stud Est **Trained** Nawton, N Yorks

**FOCUS**
Strong handicap form, which should pay to follow. Some up-and-coming sprinters have won this event in recent seasons, notably subsequent Group performers Moviesta (last year), Hamish McGonagall and Hoof It, and on this evidence the winner could well be another in similar vein. The second was unexposed too.

## 2318 EBF STALLIONS BREEDING WINNERS RIPLEYCOLLECTION.COM FILLIES' (H'CAP) 7f
**4:25** (4:25) (Class 3) (0-90,88) 4-Y-0+ **£12,938** (£3,850; £1,924; £962) **Stalls** Low

Form RPR
54-5 **1** **Dusky Queen (IRE)**[34] 1442 4-9-5 **86**.............................. RyanMoore 10 94
(Richard Fahey) *hld up towards rr: hdwy 3f out: trckd ldrs 2f out: rdn to chse ldr over 1f out: led ins fnl f: drvn and hld on wl towards fin* **11/4**[1]
-550 **2** *nk* **Subtle Knife**[44] 1234 5-8-11 **78**.................................. PatrickDonaghy 11 85
(Giles Bravery) *in rr: detached and pushed along 3f out: hdwy on wd outside wl over 1f out: rdn to chse ldrs ent fnl f: sn drvn and kpt on towards fin* **33/1**
6531 **3** *nse* **Alice's Dancer (IRE)**[16] 1873 5-8-9 **79**........................ OisinMurphy(3) 3 86
(William Muir) *hld up: effrt and nt clr run 2f out: sn swtchd rt and rdn: styd on ent fnl f: sn drvn and kpt on wl towards fin* **10/1**
-313 **4** *nk* **Broughtons Charm (IRE)**[11] 2024 4-8-8 **75**............... RobertWinston 2 81+
(Willie Musson) *trckd ldr: led wl over 2f out: rdn over 1f out: hdd jst ins fnl f: sn drvn and no ex last 100yds* **9/1**
30-0 **5** *1 ¼* **Misplaced Fortune**[20] 1734 9-9-3 **87**..........................(v) JasonHart(3) 8 90
(Nigel Tinkler) *in rr: pushed along 1/2-way: rdn over 2f out: hdwy on outer over 1f out: styd on fnl f: nrst fin* **20/1**
600- **6** *1 ¼* **Audacia (IRE)**[208] 7404 4-9-3 **84**.................................. WilliamBuick 4 84
(Hugo Palmer) *trckd ldrs: effrt 2f out: rdn and n.m.r over 1f out: nt clr run and swtchd lft ent fnl f: kpt on towards fin* **8/1**
06-1 **7** *2 ½* **Patrona Ciana (FR)**[19] 1760 4-8-13 **80**........................ DanielTudhope 1 73
(David O'Meara) *trckd ldrs: hdwy 3f out: rdn to chse ldr 2f out: drvn and one pce appr fnl f* **12/1**
-044 **8** *1 ½* **Coincidently**[19] 1762 4-8-2 **74**........................................... TimClark(5) 7 63
(Alan Bailey) *in tch: hdwy to chse ldrs over 2f out: sn rdn and wknd over 1f out* **20/1**
-006 **9** *1* **Lilac Lace (IRE)**[13] 1956 4-9-0 **81**..................................... DavidAllan 6 68
(Tim Easterby) *trckd ldng pair: hdwy and cl up 3f out: rdn along over 2f out: wknd over 1f out* **15/2**[3]
40-2 **10** *8* **Tight Fit**[20] 1731 4-9-7 **88**............................................... DaneO'Neill 9 54
(Henry Candy) *lw: hld up in tch: effrt and sme hdwy 3f out: rdn over 2f out and sn wknd* **3/1**[2]
20-4 **11** *5* **Beautiful View**[11] 2032 4-9-4 **85**...................................... SeanLevey 5 38
(Richard Hannon) *lw: sn led: pushed along and hdd wl over 2f out: sn rdn and wknd* **33/1**

1m 24.71s (-0.59) **Going Correction** +0.025s/f (Good) **11** Ran SP% **116.7**
Speed ratings (Par 104): **104,103,103,103,101 100,97,95,94,85 79**
CSF £103.86 CT £803.58 TOTE £3.30: £1.40, £8.60, £2.90; EX 110.60 Trifecta £1082.70.
**Owner** Mrs H Steel **Bred** Paul Hyland **Trained** Musley Bank, N Yorks
■ Stewards' Enquiry : Patrick Donaghy four-day ban: used whip above permitted level (May 30-Jun 2)
Robert Winston four-day ban: used whip above permitted level (Jun 1-4)

**FOCUS**
They went a good gallop here and the first two were at the back of the field turning into the straight. The booking of Ryan Moore suggested a big run was expected from the winner. Ordinary fillies' form.

## 2319 RACING AT YORK YORKRACECOURSETIPS.CO.UK (H'CAP) (BOBIS RACE) 1m 4f
**5:00** (5:00) (Class 4) (0-80,80) 3-Y-O **£9,703** (£2,887; £1,443; £721) **Stalls** Centre

Form RPR
14-5 **1** **Adventure Seeker (IRE)**[30] 1509 3-9-5 **78**..................... JimCrowley 4 92
(Ed Vaughan) *hld up towards rr: gd hdwy 3f out: trckd ldrs wl over 1f out: effrt whn nt clr run over 1f out: swtchd lft and rdn to ld ins fnl f: styd on strly* **12/1**
0-01 **2** *2 ¼* **Penhill**[17] 1847 3-9-0 **73**................................................... TedDurcan 5 83
(James Bethell) *trckd ldrs: smooth hdwy 4f out: n.m.r over 2f out: led wl over 1f out: sn rdn: hdd ins fnl f: kpt on* **16/1**
31-2 **3** *3 ½* **Latin Charm (IRE)**[21] 1690 3-9-3 **76**........................(p) AndreaAtzeni 14 80
(Marco Botti) *hld up towards rr: hdwy over 3f out: rdn along whn n.m.r 2f out: hmpd over 1f out: swtchd rt ins fnl f and kpt on wl towards fin* **5/2**[1]
1-33 **4** *hd* **Rite To Reign**[20] 1727 3-9-3 **76**..................................... JamesDoyle 7 80
(Philip McBride) *lw: trckd ldrs: hdwy and cl up 4f out: rdn along wl over 2f out: drvn and edgd lft over 1f out: sn one pce* **8/1**
5-41 **5** *shd* **Innocent Touch (IRE)**[15] 1904 3-8-11 **70**..................... TonyHamilton 9 74
(Richard Fahey) *in tch: hdwy on outer 3f out: rdn along to chse ldrs 2f out: sn drvn: edgd lft and one pce* **12/1**
56-4 **6** *2 ¾* **Mairise**[24] 1635 3-8-13 **72**.............................................. RyanMoore 15 71
(Sir Michael Stoute) *lengthy: led: jnd and pushed along 4f out: rdn 3f out: drvn 2f out: sn hdd & wknd* **7/2**[2]
0463 **7** *1* **Flying Cape (IRE)**[17] 1856 3-8-12 **71**............................ ShaneKelly 2 69
(Andrew Hollinshead) *prom: trckd ldr 5f out: cl up 4f out: rdn along 3f out: grad wknd* **66/1**
525- **8** *nk* **Stout Cortez**[178] 7955 3-8-6 **68**........................... MichaelJMMurphy(3) 13 65
(Mark Johnston) *lw: t.k.h: prom: rdn along 5f out: wknd over 3f out* **33/1**
0-53 **9** *1 ¾* **Sellingallthetime (IRE)**[22] 1661 3-8-7 **66**................. AndrewMullen 3 61
(Michael Appleby) *hld up towards rr: sme hdwy over 3f out: rdn along wl over 2f out: n.d* **16/1**
216 **10** *4* **Belfilo (IRE)**[35] 1419 3-9-2 **78**..................................... OisinMurphy(3) 10 66
(Andrew Balding) *hld up towards rr: sme hdwy 4f out: rdn along 3f out: nvr a factor* **7/1**[3]
13-0 **11** *¾* **Shirocco Passion**[39] 1346 3-8-11 **70**............................ BarryMcHugh 6 57
(Tony Coyle) *a towards rr* **33/1**
4-04 **12** *3 ¾* **In Vino Veritas (IRE)**[22] 1661 3-8-7 **66**........................ JimmyQuinn 11 47
(Ann Duffield) *lw: a towards rr* **50/1**
2415 **13** *9* **Zamra (IRE)**[22] 1661 3-9-1 **74**.....................................(p) DanielTudhope 8 41
(David O'Meara) *hld up: a in rr* **20/1**
5302 **14** *5* **Rookery (IRE)**[11] 2018 3-8-10 **69**................................ DaneO'Neill 1 28
(Mark Johnston) *towards rr: sme hdwy into midfield 1/2-way: rdn along 4f out: sn wknd* **25/1**
10 **15** *22* **Votary (IRE)**[21] 1690 3-9-7 **80**...................................(b¹) WilliamBuick 16
(John Gosden) *trckd ldrs: rdn along 4f out: sn wknd* **14/1**

2m 30.54s (-2.66) **Going Correction** -0.175s/f (Firm) **15** Ran SP% **126.2**
Speed ratings (Par 101): **101,99,97,97,96 95,94,94,93,90 89,87,81,78,63**
CSF £185.13 CT £646.43 TOTE £13.40: £3.70, £5.10, £1.50; EX 261.50 Trifecta £800.70.
**Owner** Hamed Rashed Bin Ghadayer **Bred** Runnymede Farm Inc And Catesby W Clay **Trained** Newmarket, Suffolk

**FOCUS**
They didn't go a strong pace in this decent handicap. Again the field came down the middle once in the home straight. The form is rated around the fourth and fifth.
T/Jkpt: Not won. T/Plt: £16.00 to a £1 stake. Pool: £233,565.84 - 11,496.44 winning units.
T/Qpdt: £8.40 to a £1 stake. Pool: £11,640.87 - 1019.06 winning units. JR

2320 - 2326a (Foreign Racing) - See Raceform Interactive

# 2198 DONCASTER (L-H)
Saturday, May 17

**OFFICIAL GOING: Good (8.0)**
Wind: Moderate against Weather: Fine and dry

## 2327 CROWNHOTEL-BAWTRY.COM APPRENTICE H'CAP 1m 4f
**5:25** (5:27) (Class 5) (0-70,71) 4-Y-0+ **£3,067** (£905; £453) **Stalls** Low

Form RPR
22-2 **1** **Perfect Summer (IRE)**[8] 2139 4-9-5 **71**..................... LouisSteward(3) 18 84+
(Lady Cecil) *hld up towards rr: stdy hdwy 1/2-way: str run on outer to ld wl over 2f out: rdn over 1f out: styd on wl fnl f* **11/4**[1]
22/0 **2** *1 ¼* **Saved By The Bell (IRE)**[13] 1970 4-9-5 **68**..................... JulieBurke 13 79+
(David O'Meara) *hld up towards rr: hdwy over 2f out: swtchd lft and rdn over 1f out: styd on strly fnl f: nt rch wnr* **12/1**
-062 **3** *¾* **Gran Maestro (USA)**[7] 2168 5-9-4 **70**........................(b) KevinStott(3) 11 80
(Ruth Carr) *in tch: hdwy to trck ldrs over 4f out: effrt 3f out: rdn to chal 2f out and ev ch tl drvn ent fnl f and kpt on same pce* **9/1**[3]
6126 **4** *3 ½* **Noguchi (IRE)**[39] 1366 9-9-2 **70**........................(b) JordanVaughan(5) 9 74
(George Margarson) *midfield whn hmpd and lost pl after 1f: bhd: hdwy wl over 2f out: rdn along wl over 1f out: kpt on fnl f: nrst fin* **33/1**
2-34 **5** *½* **Pixie Cut (IRE)**[13] 1971 4-9-2 **70**......................... RobJFitzpatrick(5) 19 74+
(Alistair Whillans) *hld up in rr: hdwy on inner wl over 2f out: nt clr run and swtchd rt over 1f out: rdn and styd on wl fnl f: nrst fin* **7/1**[2]
3523 **6** *hd* **Star Of Namibia (IRE)**[61] 1000 4-8-9 **61**........................(v) TimClark(3) 3 64
(Michael Mullineaux) *chsd ldrs: rdn along 3f out: drvn 2f out: grad wknd appr fnl f* **20/1**
2442 **7** *1 ¾* **Yasir (USA)**[25] 1629 6-9-0 **66**....................................(p) DavidKenny(3) 10 66
(Conor Dore) *bhd: hdwy on outer over 2f out: sn rdn and kpt on fnl f: n.d* **25/1**
6-30 **8** *nk* **Keep Calm**[21] 1729 4-8-11 **65**......................................... JoeDoyle(5) 6 65
(John Mackie) *chsd ldrs: rdn along 3f out: drvn 2f out: grad wknd* **33/1**
4501 **9** *nk* **Cabuchon (GER)**[12] 2599 7-8-11 **60**.............................. DeclanBates 16 60
(David Evans) *hld up towards rr: hdwy over 4f out: rdn along on outer to chse ldrs 2f out: sn drvn and no imp appr fnl f* **25/1**
06/3 **10** *2 ½* **Fisher**[17] 1885 5-8-10 **62**........................................... MarcMonaghan(3) 20 58
(John Quinn) *midfield whn hmpd and lost pl after 1f: towards rr: hdwy on outer over 3f out: rdn along over 2f: no imp appr fnl f* **12/1**
0-60 **11** *1* **El Massivo (IRE)**[11] 2055 4-8-6 **60**.......................... MeganCarberry(5) 8 54
(Brian Ellison) *midfield whn hung bdly rt after 1f: hld up: hdwy on inner 5f out: rdn along to chse ldrs 4f out: wknd over 2f out* **9/1**[3]
112- **12** *1 ¼* **Blue Top**[190] 7151 5-8-13 **62**.....................................(p) GeorgeChaloner 2 54
(Mark Walford) *midfield: hdwy on inner to chse ldrs over 4f out: rdn along 3f out: drvn and grad wknd fnl 2f* **12/1**
11-6 **13** *2 ¾* **Valentine's Gift**[17] 1885 6-8-8 **62**.................... RachelRichardson(5) 4 50
(Neville Bycroft) *midfield: effrt and nt clr run wl over 2f out: rdn and n.m.r over 1f out: n.d* **25/1**
56-5 **14** *nse* **Time Of My Life (IRE)**[17] 1885 5-8-9 **63**....................... JackGarritty(5) 7 50
(Patrick Holmes) *in tch: effrt to chse ldrs over 4f out: rdn along 3f out: wknd 2f out* **20/1**
224- **15** *4* **El Bravo**[286] 5031 8-9-0 **70**........................................... AlexHopkinson(7) 15 51
(Shaun Harris) *chsd ldng pair: rdn along wl over 3f out: wknd over 2f out* **25/1**
450- **16** *½* **Frank's Folly (IRE)**[214] 7278 5-9-0 **63**............................ NeilFarley 12 43
(Mark Walford) *midfield whn hmpd and lost pl after 1f: towards rr: sme hdwy 1/2-way: rdn along in midfield 4f out: n.d* **20/1**
30-0 **17** *21* **Hurry Home Poppa (IRE)**[23] 1660 4-8-13 **65**........... DannyBrock(3) 14 12
(John Mackie) *sn cl up: led over 4f out: rdn along over 3f out: hdd & wknd wl over 2f out* **33/1**
5/0- **18** *14* **Travis County (IRE)**[165] 7498 5-8-5 **61**........................ KevinLundie(7) 5
(Brian Ellison) *set str pce: rdn along 4f out: sn hdd & wknd qckly wl over 3f out* **33/1**

2m 34.93s (0.03) **Going Correction** +0.10s/f (Good) **18** Ran SP% **123.7**
Speed ratings (Par 103): **103,102,101,99,99 98,97,97,97,95 94,94,92,92,89 89,75,65**
CSF £28.98 CT £262.10 TOTE £3.90: £1.60, £3.30, £2.80, £6.80; EX 37.10 Trifecta £247.30.
**Owner** G Schoeningh **Bred** John O'Connor **Trained** Newmarket, Suffolk
■ Stewards' Enquiry : Megan Carberry two-day ban: careless riding (May 31-Jun 1)

**FOCUS**
In a competitive race of its type, they went a good gallop and the first three set a decent standard for apprentice company. The form is rated around the third.

## 2328 ROBINSONS OF BAWTRY MAIDEN AUCTION STKS 5f
**5:55** (5:56) (Class 5) 2-Y-O **£2,911** (£866; £432; £216) **Stalls** Low

Form RPR
2 **1** **Haxby (IRE)**[21] 1726 2-9-4 0.......................................... TomQueally 5 82+
(Roger Varian) *trckd ldrs: hdwy to chse ldr 1/2-way: rdn to ld wl over 1f out: clr ent fnl f: readily* **10/11**[1]
0 **2** *1 ¾* **Bahamian Sunrise**[21] 1732 2-8-8 0........................ GeorgeChaloner(3) 3 68
(Richard Fahey) *chsd ldr: rdn along 2f out: kpt on same pce u.p fnl f* **10/1**
4 **3** *nse* **Indian Keys**[18] 1837 2-8-5 0........................................... KevinStott(5) 6 67
(Kevin Ryan) *hld up in rr: swtchd rt and hdwy over 2f out: rdn over 1f out: styd on wl fnl f: nrst fin* **8/1**
**4** *nk* **Prince Bonnaire** 2-8-13 0................................................ PhillipMakin 1 68
(David Brown) *trckd ldrs: cl up over 2f out: rdn along over 1f out: kpt on same pce fnl f* **11/4**[2]
04 **5** *4 ½* **Toytown (IRE)**[39] 1363 2-8-8 0..................................... AdamMcLean(7) 4 54
(Derek Shaw) *towards rr: pushed along and outpcd 1/2-way: rdn and hdwy over 1f out: kpt on fnl f* **16/1**
52 **6** *2 ¼* **Stanghow**[8] 2134 2-8-11 0.......................................... DuranFentiman 9 42
(Mel Brittain) *led: rdn along over 2f out: hdd wl over 1f out and sn wknd* **7/1**[3]
**7** *8* **Freeze The Secret (IRE)** 2-8-6 0.................................. DavidProbert 2 8
(David C Griffiths) *chsd ldr: rdn along 2f out: sn wknd* **28/1**
0 **8** *1 ½* **Areion (IRE)**[19] 1788 2-8-10 0....................................... PhilipPrince(5) 8 3
(J S Moore) *a in rr: rdn along 1/2-way: sn outpcd and bhd* **33/1**

1m 0.76s (0.26) **Going Correction** +0.025s/f (Good) **8** Ran SP% **124.0**
Speed ratings (Par 93): **98,95,95,94,87 83,71,68**
CSF £13.55 TOTE £1.80: £1.10, £2.90, £2.50; EX 12.50 Trifecta £87.00.
**Owner** The Haxby Partnership **Bred** John Malone **Trained** Newmarket, Suffolk

**FOCUS**
A routine 2yo maiden for the course with a clear-cut winner, rated up slightly from his debut.

## 2329 CHINA ROSE OF BAWTRY MEDIAN AUCTION MAIDEN STKS 6f
6:25 (6:27) (Class 5) 3-4-Y-O £2,911 (£866; £432; £216) Stalls Low

Form RPR
1 **Ella's Delight (IRE)**[34] 1471 4-9-7 0 PhillipMakin 6 69+
(Martin Todhunter) *trckd ldrs: hdwy over 2f out: rdn to chal ent fnl f: drvn and kpt on to ld nr line* 4/1[2]
4-35 2 shd **Broadway Ranger (IRE)**[12] 2035 3-9-3 69 RobertWinston 8 72
(Charles Hills) *led: rdn wl over 1f out: jnd and drvn ent fnl f: hdd and no ex nr line* 13/2
3 4 **Dancing Angel** 3-8-12 0 TomQueally 5 54
(James Eustace) *s.i.s: green and sn outpcd in rr: hdwy wl over 2f out: kpt on fnl f: nrst fin* 8/1
4 4 nk **Bondi Beach Babe**[9] 2093 4-9-0 0 JordanNason[(7)] 4 55
(James Turner) *in rr: green and rdn along 1/2-way: hdwy 2f out: swtchd rt and drvn wl over 1f out: edgd rt and styd on wl fnl f: nrst fin* 20/1
4-2 5 1 3/4 **Serata Di Gala (FR)**[18] 1853 3-8-7 0 DanielMuscutt[(5)] 2 48
(Marco Botti) *t.k.h: in tch: hdwy to trck ldrs 1/2-way: rdn over 2f out: wknd over 1f out* 9/2[3]
5-22 6 3 1/2 **Royal Connoisseur (IRE)**[19] 1802 3-9-3 76 DavidNolan 3 41
(Richard Fahey) *chsd ldr: rdn along over 2f out: drvn and wknd wl over 1f out* 3/1[1]
60 7 8 **Nouvelle Ere**[12] 2026 3-9-3 0 DavidProbert 9 16
(Tony Carroll) *in tch: hdwy to chse ldrs 1/2-way: sn rdn along and wknd over 2f out* 28/1
040- 8 5 **He's My Boy (IRE)**[178] 7978 3-9-3 69 [1] FrederikTylicki 7
(James Fanshawe) *chsd ldrs: rdn along wl over 2f out: sn wknd* 9/2[3]
0 9 shd **Jay Gee Speedfit (IRE)**[26] 1612 3-8-10 0 (t) JordanVaughan[(7)] 1
(George Margarson) *chsd ldrs: rdn along 1/2-way: sn wknd* 33/1

1m 14.33s (0.73) **Going Correction** +0.025s/f (Good)
**WFA** 3 from 4yo 9lb **9 Ran SP% 117.0**
Speed ratings (Par 103): **96,95,90,90,87 83,72,65,65**
CSF £29.73 TOTE £4.70: £1.90, £1.80, £2.80; EX 27.50 Trifecta £129.50.
**Owner** Mr & Mrs Ian Hall **Bred** John Cullinan **Trained** Orton, Cumbria

**FOCUS**
A mixture of late-developing types and more experienced performers. The former, including the winner, are of most interest. The runner-up is the key to the form.

## 2330 FINE & COUNTRY BAWTRY H'CAP (BOBIS RACE) 1m (R)
7:00 (7:01) (Class 3) (0-95,89) 3-Y-O £8,409 (£2,502; £1,250; £625) Stalls Low

Form RPR
1- 1 **Spark Plug (IRE)**[245] 6378 3-9-4 86 TomQueally 2 95+
(Brian Meehan) *trckd ldng pair: hdwy 3f and sn cl up: led 2f out: rdn appr fnl f: edgd rt nr fin: kpt on* 5/1[2]
65-6 2 nk **Free Code (IRE)**[26] 1614 3-9-7 89 PaulMulrennan 6 96
(James Tate) *trckd ldrs: hdwy 3f out: rdn to chse wnr wl over 1f out: drvn ins fnl f: kpt on wl towards fin* 10/1
2-1 3 3 1/4 **Man Of Harlech**[19] 1808 3-9-4 86 DavidProbert 5 86
(Andrew Balding) *t.k.h: trckd ldr: hdwy and slt ld 3f out: sn rdn and hdd 2f out: drvn and wknd over 1f out* 8/11[1]
1-5 4 1 1/2 **Announcement**[59] 1013 3-8-7 75 [1] StevieDonohoe 3 71
(Ian Williams) *dwlt and in rr: hdwy 3f out: rdn to chse ldrs over 2f out: sn no imp* 8/1
00-0 5 7 **Lanark (IRE)**[30] 1530 3-9-7 89 FrannyNorton 4 69
(Mark Johnston) *led: pushed along 4f out: rdn and hdd 3f out: sn wknd* 11/2[3]

1m 41.45s (1.75) **Going Correction** +0.10s/f (Good) **5 Ran SP% 110.2**
Speed ratings (Par 103): **95,94,91,89,82**
CSF £45.22 TOTE £3.90: £1.90, £4.10; EX 26.10 Trifecta £43.60.
**Owner** J L Day **Bred** Airlie Stud **Trained** Manton, Wilts

**FOCUS**
The pace was weak, turning this decent 1m race into a sprint. No depth to the race.

## 2331 CAVIARS OF BAWTRY FILLIES' H'CAP 1m 2f 60y
7:30 (7:30) (Class 3) (0-95,91) 4-Y-O+ £7,762 (£2,310; £1,154; £577) Stalls Low

Form RPR
24-2 1 **Cosseted**[21] 1716 4-8-8 78 ShaneKelly 1 94+
(James Fanshawe) *trckd ldrs: smooth hdwy on outer over 3f out: cl up over 2f out and led 2f out: rdn clr over 1f out: kpt on* 5/2[2]
12- 2 3 1/2 **Sea Meets Sky (FR)**[350] 2859 4-9-5 89 PhillipMakin 6 98+
(Lady Cecil) *trckd ldng pair: effrt and nt clr run on inner fr 3f out to wl over 1f out: swtchd rt and rdn to chse wnr appr fnl f: sn drvn and no imp* 7/4[1]
122- 3 3 1/4 **Missed Call (IRE)**[274] 5496 4-9-1 85 DavidProbert 2 88
(Martyn Meade) *hld up in rr: hdwy on outer wl over 2f out: sn chsng wnr: rdn wl over 1f out and kpt on one pce* 3/1[3]
0-0 4 6 **Magic Art (IRE)**[14] 1942 4-8-13 88 [1] MarcMonaghan[(5)] 3 80
(Marco Botti) *in rr: pushed along over 3f out: rdn along wl over 2f out: n.d* 25/1
00-1 5 2 1/4 **Boonga Roogeta**[11] 2047 5-9-4 91 RosieJessop[(3)] 4 78
(Peter Charalambous) *led: pushed along over 4f out: rdn over 3f out: hdd 2f out and sn wknd* 8/1
0-04 6 3 **No Poppy (IRE)**[15] 1926 6-8-6 81 AdamCarter[(5)] 5 63
(Tim Easterby) *trckd ldrs: hdwy to trck ldr after 2f: cl up over 4f out: rdn along 3f out: drvn over 2f out and sn wknd* 14/1

2m 11.74s (2.34) **Going Correction** +0.10s/f (Good) **6 Ran SP% 111.6**
Speed ratings (Par 104): **94,91,88,83,82 79**
CSF £7.20 TOTE £3.40: £1.90, £1.60; EX 7.90 Trifecta £12.50.
**Owner** Cheveley Park Stud **Bred** Cheveley Park Stud Ltd **Trained** Newmarket, Suffolk

**FOCUS**
This was a mid-range handicap in which there was an ordinary gallop that finally increased 3f out. Interesting form.

## 2332 INCOGNITO'S DRESSY DAMES H'CAP 6f
8:05 (8:07) (Class 4) (0-80,80) 4-Y-O+ £5,175 (£1,540; £769; £384) Stalls Low

Form RPR
65-4 1 **Duke Cosimo**[30] 1537 4-9-5 78 (b[1]) GrahamGibbons 14 89
(David Barron) *dwlt and towards rr: hdwy wl over 1f out: rdn to chse ldrs ent fnl f: styd on strly to ld last 40yds* 10/1[3]
0260 2 1/2 **Commanche**[7] 2147 5-9-2 75 BenCurtis 17 85
(Chris Dwyer) *in tch: hdwy 2f out: rdn to chse ldr jst over 1f out: led wl ins fnl f: drvn: hdd and no ex last 40yds* 10/1[3]
24-0 3 1 1/2 **Time And Place**[23] 1672 4-9-2 78 GeorgeChaloner[(3)] 18 83
(Richard Fahey) *racd wd: slt ld: rdn along wl over 1f out: drvn and hdd wl ins fnl f: kpt on same pce* 8/1[2]
-055 4 1/2 **Mon Brav**[14] 1938 7-9-0 73 RobertWinston 11 76
(Brian Ellison) *dwlt and towards rr: hdwy 2f out: sn rdn and styd on wl fnl f: nrst fin* 8/1[2]
26-2 5 2 1/2 **Willbeme**[30] 1541 6-8-6 72 MeganCarberry[(7)] 15 67
(Neville Bycroft) *prom: cl up over 2f out: rdn wl over 1f out and ev ch tl drvn and wknd ent fnl f* 10/1[3]
-005 6 1 1/4 **Alexandrakollontai (IRE)**[13] 1967 4-8-4 66 (b) JulieBurke[(3)] 19 57
(Alistair Whillans) *racd wd: towards rr: hdwy 2f out: sn rdn and styd on fnl f: nrst fin* 33/1
-322 7 2 **Orbit The Moon (IRE)**[18] 1839 6-9-1 77 (tp) ConnorBeasley[(3)] 2 62+
(Michael Dods) *prom: effrt 2f out: sn rdn and wknd appr fnl f* 5/1[1]
0-03 8 3/4 **Meandmyshadow**[22] 1694 6-8-7 66 FrannyNorton 7 49
(Alan Brown) *disp ld 3f: rdn along wl over 2f out: wknd wl over 1f out* 20/1
0-44 9 hd **Sunraider (IRE)**[13] 1967 7-9-2 75 PaulMulrennan 4 57+
(Paul Midgley) *hld up in rr: sme hdwy whn nt clr run over 1f out: sn swtchd rt and rdn: n.d* 10/1[3]
6103 10 1/2 **Expose**[30] 1541 6-8-12 78 AlistairRawlinson[(7)] 13 58
(Michael Appleby) *midfield: rdn along 2f out: no hdwy* 10/1[3]
46-2 11 1 **Rasaman (IRE)**[13] 1967 10-9-7 80 GrahamLee 5 57
(Jim Goldie) *in tch: hdwy 2f out: swtchd lft and rdn over 1f out: sn btn* 12/1
3145 12 1/2 **Trade Secret**[14] 1957 7-9-6 79 DavidAllan 6 55
(Mel Brittain) *dwlt and towards rr: sme hdwy 2f out: n.m.r wl over 1f out: n.d* 16/1
1003 13 1 **Klynch**[13] 1967 8-9-5 78 (b) JamesSullivan 10 50
(Ruth Carr) *nvr bttr than midfield* 14/1
56-0 14 1 1/2 **Enderby Spirit (GR)**[23] 1672 8-9-2 75 (t) PaddyAspell 1 43
(Bryan Smart) *chsd ldrs on outer: rdn along 2f out: sn wknd* 28/1
00-4 15 2 3/4 **Bachotheque (IRE)**[16] 1903 4-9-0 73 PhillipMakin 12 32
(Tim Easterby) *midfield: rdn along over 2f out: sn wknd* 14/1
20- 16 1 1/2 **Eland Ally**[224] 7030 6-8-13 72 AndrewElliott 9 26
(Tom Tate) *cl up: rdn along 1/2-way: sn wknd* 25/1
0-00 17 1/2 **Towbee**[14] 1961 5-9-4 77 BarryMcHugh 8 29
(Michael Easterby) *dwlt: a in rr* 20/1

1m 12.91s (-0.69) **Going Correction** +0.025s/f (Good) **17 Ran SP% 131.0**
Speed ratings (Par 105): **105,104,102,101,98 96,94,93,92,92 90,90,88,86,83 81,80**
CSF £105.94 CT £591.43 TOTE £9.70: £2.60, £3.50, £3.00, £2.50; EX 114.10 Trifecta £258.70.
**Owner** Mrs Christine Barron **Bred** Cheveley Park Stud Ltd **Trained** Maunby, N Yorks

**FOCUS**
A solid pace in this sprint gave the late finishers, including the winner, every chance. The principals raced on the outside of the main group.

## 2333 WALSH WEST H'CAP (BOBIS RACE) 7f
8:35 (8:37) (Class 4) (0-85,82) 3-Y-O £5,175 (£1,540; £769; £384) Stalls Low

Form RPR
3410 1 **Basil Berry**[8] 2112 3-9-4 79 BenCurtis 1 85
(Chris Dwyer) *cl up: led 3f out: rdn wl over 1f out: drvn ins fnl f: jst hld on* 8/1
020- 2 hd **Wilde Inspiration (IRE)**[220] 7120 3-8-11 72 PaulMulrennan 11 79+
(Julie Camacho) *hld up: smooth hdwy 2f out: chsd ldrs and nt clr run over 1f out: sn swtchd rt and rdn ent fnl f: fin strly: jst failed* 33/1
5-50 3 shd **Captain Midnight (IRE)**[14] 1952 3-9-3 81 ConnorBeasley[(3)] 6 86
(David Brown) *hld up in tch: hdwy 1/2-way: trckd ldrs 2f out: rdn to chse wnr over 1f out: drvn and styd on wl fnl f: jst failed* 16/1
21-3 4 1 3/4 **Finn Class (IRE)**[29] 1563 3-9-7 82 TomQueally 4 82
(Michael Bell) *hld up in tch: hdwy 3f out: rdn to chse ldrs over 2f out: drvn and kpt on same pce fnl f* 2/1[1]
30-0 5 nk **Xanthos**[30] 1540 3-9-5 80 GrahamLee 2 80
(Ed Walker) *chsd ldrs: rdn along 2f out: drvn and kpt on same pce fnl f* 16/1
1-65 6 3 **Quiet Warrior (IRE)**[10] 2083 3-9-2 82 MarcMonaghan[(5)] 3 74
(Marco Botti) *chsd ldrs: rdn along wl over 2f out: sn drvn and wknd* 8/1
1 7 1/2 **Rekdhat (IRE)**[20] 1768 3-9-4 79 JackMitchell 5 70
(Roger Varian) *chsd ldrs: rdn along 2f out: grad wknd* 7/1[3]
0520 8 hd **Intermath (IRE)**[28] 1586 3-9-1 79 DeclanBates[(3)] 7 69
(David Evans) *trckd ldrs: rdn over 2f out: sn drvn and wknd* 14/1
15-4 9 3 1/2 **Mezel**[16] 1897 3-9-2 77 DaneO'Neill 9 58
(J W Hills) *hld up in rr: hdwy on wd outside over 2f out: rdn to chse ldrs wl over 1f out: sn wknd* 13/2[2]
032- 10 7 **Syros (IRE)**[213] 7302 3-9-5 80 (v[1]) GrahamGibbons 10 43
(Michael Easterby) *chsd ldrs: rdn along 1/2-way: sn wknd* 10/1
00- 11 7 **Disclosure**[218] 7170 3-8-13 74 DavidAllan 8 19
(Les Eyre) *led: rdn along 1/2-way: sn hdd & wknd* 16/1

1m 26.34s (0.04) **Going Correction** +0.025s/f (Good) **11 Ran SP% 117.7**
Speed ratings (Par 101): **100,99,99,97,97 93,93,93,89,81 73**
CSF £237.32 CT £4129.76 TOTE £9.40: £2.60, £6.70, £4.60; EX 277.30 Trifecta £1371.00 Part won. Pool of £1828.03 - 0.65 winning units..
**Owner** Strawberry Fields Stud **Bred** Strawberry Fields Stud **Trained** Newmarket, Suffolk

**FOCUS**
The pace was solid, as can always be expected when the winner is in the line-up. A personal best from him.
T/Plt: £131.40 to a £1 stake. Pool of £79581.41 - 441.85 winning tickets. T/Qpdt: £51.40 to a £1 stake. Pool of £6292.90 - 90.50 winning tickets. JR

# 2298 NEWBURY (L-H)
Saturday, May 17

**OFFICIAL GOING: Good to firm (good in places)**
Wind: Light, against Weather: Fine and warm

## 2334 BETFRED PLAY £10 MILLION SCOOP6 TODAY EBF STALLIONS MAIDEN STKS (BOBIS RACE) 1m 2f 6y
1:30 (1:30) (Class 4) 3-Y-O £6,469 (£1,925; £962; £481) Stalls Low

Form RPR
3 1 **Connecticut**[31] 1517 3-9-5 0 AndreaAtzeni 15 88+
(Luca Cumani) *prom: jnd ldr over 4f out: led 3f out: rdn out: a holding runner-up* 3/1[2]
3 2 3/4 **Smiling Stranger (IRE)**[19] 1797 3-9-2 0 OisinMurphy[(3)] 2 86
(Andrew Balding) *led tl 3f out: pressed wnr after: kpt on wl: jst hld* 12/1
3- 3 2 1/4 **Mange All**[206] 7469 3-9-5 0 LiamJones 9 82
(William Haggas) *chsd ldrs: hung lft and nt clr run 2f out: hrd rdn over 1f out: styd on same pce* 11/4[1]

33 **4** ½ **Karraar**[15] 1911 3-9-5 0 PaulHanagan 8 81
(Richard Hannon) *mid-div on outer: hung lft and lost pl 3f out: rallied and r.o fnl f* **20/1**
**5** *hd* **Obsidian (USA)** 3-9-5 0 FrankieDettori 7 81+
(John Gosden) *s.s: hld up in rr: swtchd outside and effrt over 2f out: r.o fnl f: nrest at fin* **10/1**
3 **6** 1 **Moohaarib (IRE)**[28] 1587 3-9-5 0 LukeMorris 10 79
(Marco Botti) *mid-div: hdwy 3f out: no ex over 1f out* **7/1**[3]
**7** ¾ **New Story** 3-9-5 0 JamieSpencer 14 77+
(Ismail Mohammed) *s.i.s: plld hrd in rr: nt clr run over 2f out: rdn and r.o fr over 1f out: nvr nrr* **33/1**
**8** *nk* **Rembrandt Van Rijn (IRE)** 3-9-5 0 TedDurcan 3 77
(David Lanigan) *in tch on rail: rdn to chse ldrs 2f out: fdd fnl f* **40/1**
**9** 1 ¾ **Astronereus (IRE)** 3-9-5 0 RichardHughes 13 73
(Amanda Perrett) *plld hrd: prom tl wknd over 1f out* **16/1**
0- **10** 2 **Rochambeau (IRE)**[253] 6168 3-9-5 0 JamesDoyle 12 70
(Roger Charlton) *towards rr: rdn over 2f out: n.d* **66/1**
**11** 1 ¼ **Molly On The Shore** 3-8-7 0 PatrickO'Donnell(7) 16 62+
(Ralph Beckett) *t.k.h: towards rr: mod effrt on rail 3f out: nvr trbld ldrs* **50/1**
**12** ¾ **Rideonastar (IRE)** 3-9-5 0 JimCrowley 11 66+
(Ralph Beckett) *a towards rr* **16/1**
**13** 1 **Kamalaya** 3-8-12 0 CamHardie(7) 6 64
(Richard Hannon) *mid-div tl wknd over 2f out* **80/1**
3-5 **14** *nk* **Tacticus (USA)**[14] 1960 3-9-5 0 RyanMoore 1 63
(Lady Cecil) *prom on rail tl hrd rdn and wknd over 2f out* **8/1**
6-2 **15** *shd* **Moshe (IRE)**[24] 1654 3-9-5 0 JimmyFortune 4 63
(Hughie Morrison) *plld hrd: in tch tl wknd 3f out* **28/1**
**16** 18 **Beaver Creek** 3-9-5 0 RichardKingscote 5 29
(Ralph J Smith) *mid-div tl wknd 3f out: t.o* **80/1**

2m 6.31s (-2.49) **Going Correction** -0.10s/f (Good) **16 Ran SP% 123.3**
Speed ratings (Par 101): **105,104,102,102,102 101,100,100,99,97 96,95,95,94,94 80**
CSF £37.03 TOTE £3.60: £1.70, £3.40, £1.50; EX 44.90 Trifecta £221.30.
**Owner** Sheikh Mohammed Obaid Al Maktoum **Bred** Whatton Manor Stud **Trained** Newmarket, Suffolk

**FOCUS**
Rail on back straight moved out, increasing distances on Round course by 22m. A beautiful, sunny day saw the going updated to good, good to firm in places prior to racing. This opening maiden is usually a decent affair, taken in the past decade by subsequent Melbourne Cup winner Fiorente and last year by Remote, who went on to Group 3 success at Royal Ascot. There was a solid pace on early, before it steadied nearing halfway and suited those racing handy, but it should produce plenty of future winners. Improvement from the first two.

## 2335 JLT ASTON PARK STKS (LISTED RACE) 1m 5f 61y
**2:05** (2:05) (Class 1) 4-Y-0+
**£20,982** (£7,955; £3,981; £1,983; £995; £499) **Stalls** Low

Form RPR
0-30 **1** **Mount Athos (IRE)**[49] 1182 7-9-0 113 JamieSpencer 3 113+
(Marco Botti) *settled in 4th and gng wl: led 2f out: drvn clr over 1f out: styd on* **7/2**[2]
154- **2** 1 **Forgotten Voice (IRE)**[189] 7827 9-9-0 110 FrankieDettori 9 111
(Nicky Henderson) *dwlt: hld up in rr: hdwy and nt clr run wl over 1f out: swtchd lft: r.o to snatch 2nd on line* **5/1**[3]
55-0 **3** *nse* **First Mohican**[30] 1533 6-9-0 105 RichardHughes 2 110
(Alan King) *dwlt: t.k.h: sn prom: outpcd over 2f out: edgd rt and rallied to chse wnr over 1f out: kpt on: lost 2nd on line* **11/1**
56-0 **4** 3 ¼ **Elkaayed (USA)**[30] 1533 4-9-0 105 PaulHanagan 1 106
(Roger Varian) *prom: pressed ldr 1m out: ev ch over 2f out: wknd over 1f out* **18/1**
1-15 **5** ½ **Brass Ring**[14] 1950 4-9-0 103 JamesDoyle 7 105
(John Gosden) *dwlt: hld up in 5th: rdn 3f out: styd on same pce: unable to chal* **8/1**
13-4 **6** *hd* **Sky Hunter**[22] 1697 4-9-0 114 KierenFallon 8 105
(Saeed bin Suroor) *hld up in 6th: niggled along 5f out: effrt in centre over 2f out: no imp over 1f out* **13/2**
13-1 **7** 11 **Battalion (IRE)**[21] 1736 4-9-0 110 RyanMoore 4 97
(William Haggas) *led tl 2f out: wknd and eased over 1f out* **15/8**[1]

2m 48.72s (-3.28) **Going Correction** -0.10s/f (Good) **7 Ran SP% 111.7**
Speed ratings (Par 111): **106,105,105,103,103 102,96**
CSF £20.16 TOTE £4.20: £2.60, £2.70; EX 20.20 Trifecta £178.10.
**Owner** Dr Marwan Koukash **Bred** David Magnier And Cobra Bloodstock **Trained** Newmarket, Suffolk
■ Stewards' Enquiry : Jamie Spencer two-day ban: used whip above permitted level (May 31-Jun 1)

**FOCUS**
A classy race by Listed standards. It was run at a sound pace, but with two of the market leaders failing to fire the form is a little muddling. A solid renewal.

## 2336 BETFRED ASTRONOMICAL £10 MILLION SCOOP6 TODAY H'CAP 7f (S)
**2:40** (2:40) (Class 2) (0-105,105) 4-Y-0+
**£18,675** (£5,592; £2,796; £1,398; £699; £351) **Stalls** Centre

Form RPR
0000 **1** **Chil The Kite**[56] 1068 5-9-6 104 GeorgeBaker 3 115
(Hughie Morrison) *stdd s: hld up in rr: rapid hdwy 2f out: led ins fnl f: pushed out* **8/1**
063- **2** 2 **Fort Knox**[223] 7051 4-9-6 104 RyanMoore 7 111+
(Charlie Appleby) *hld up towards rr: nt clr run 1f out: swtchd rt: fin strly: snatched 2nd fnl strides* **8/1**
-025 **3** ½ **Dream Walker (FR)**[16] 1903 5-8-4 88 WilliamCarson 1 92
(Brian Ellison) *in tch: rdn 2f out: r.o fnl f* **16/1**
00-0 **4** 1 **Monsieur Chevalier (IRE)**[33] 1492 7-8-5 89 FrannyNorton 14 90
(P J O'Gorman) *mid-div: sltly outpcd over 2f out: effrt and n.m.r 1f out: r.o ins fnl f* **7/1**[3]
00-0 **5** *hd* **Bronze Angel (IRE)**[35] 1437 5-8-11 95 (b) HayleyTurner 11 96
(Marcus Tregoning) *prom: led over 2f out: rdn and hdd ins fnl f: wknd fnl 75yds* **4/1**[1]
0302 **6** *hd* **Trader Jack**[7] 2147 5-8-2 86 oh2 NickyMackay 4 86
(David Flood) *towards rr: hdwy over 2f out: kpt on u.p fnl f* **10/1**
-340 **7** 1 ¼ **Sir Reginald**[21] 1719 6-8-9 93 PaulHanagan 5 90
(Richard Fahey) *hmpd s: stdd bk into midfield: effrt and no room over 1f out: unable to chal* **7/1**[3]
642 **8** 1 ¼ **Tellovoi (IRE)**[18] 1862 6-8-9 93 (v) JamesDoyle 10 87
(Ann Stokell) *led after 1f tl over 2f out: wknd fnl f* **8/1**
1-40 **9** 8 **Set The Trend**[21] 1719 8-9-1 99 LukeMorris 9 72
(David Dennis) *chsd ldrs: hrd rdn 2f out: sn wknd* **40/1**
20- **10** 4 **Indignant**[198] 7649 4-9-0 98 RichardHughes 6 61
(Richard Hannon) *stmbld and nrly uns rdr leaving stalls: led 1f: prom tl wknd over 1f out* **6/1**[2]
-060 **P** **Kenny Powers**[21] 1719 5-8-13 97 (vt) RichardKingscote 13
(Tom Dascombe) *mid-div: outpcd 3f out: in rr whn broke down and p.u over 2f out: fatally injured* **16/1**

1m 24.87s (-0.83) **Going Correction** +0.15s/f (Good) **11 Ran SP% 115.9**
Speed ratings (Par 109): **110,107,107,106,105 105,104,102,93,88**
CSF £69.52 CT £1018.61 TOTE £8.00: £2.80, £2.80, £4.50; EX 81.50 Trifecta £1848.10.
**Owner** Hazel Lawrence & Graham Doyle **Bred** Whitsbury Manor Stud & Pigeon House Stud **Trained** East Ilsley, Berks

**FOCUS**
This competitive handicap proved a decent test as the runners chased a solid pace down the middle of the track. The top weights dominated with smart runs.

## 2337 BETFRED LONDON GOLD CUP (H'CAP) (BOBIS RACE) 1m 2f 6y
**3:15** (3:15) (Class 2) (0-105,92) 3-Y-0
**£15,562** (£4,660; £2,330; £1,165; £582; £292) **Stalls** Low

Form RPR
2-1 **1** **Cannock Chase (USA)**[40] 1353 3-9-4 89 RyanMoore 7 106+
(Sir Michael Stoute) *stdd s: hld up in rr: hdwy to ld 1f out: drvn out* **11/4**[1]
1-21 **2** 1 ¼ **Windshear**[22] 1702 3-9-6 91 RichardHughes 8 105
(Richard Hannon) *hld up in 6th: hdwy over 1f out: chsd wnr fnl f: kpt on* **11/4**[1]
16-2 **3** ¾ **Extra Noble**[29] 1563 3-9-7 92 JimCrowley 1 105
(Ralph Beckett) *hld up in 5th: hdwy to press ldrs over 1f out: kpt on fnl f* **8/1**[3]
1 **4** 1 **Satellite (IRE)**[21] 1738 3-9-1 86 FrankieDettori 3 97+
(William Haggas) *sn led: racd freely and sn clr: 10 l ahd 1/2-way: reduced ld 3f out: hld on wl tl hdd and no ex 1f out* **4/1**[2]
1-12 **5** 2 **Collaboration**[22] 1702 3-8-8 82 (t) OisinMurphy(3) 5 89
(Andrew Balding) *prom in chsng gp: wnt 2nd 4f out: pressed ldr over 2f out tl wknd 1f out* **8/1**[3]
42-1 **6** 2 ½ **Master Of Finance (IRE)**[15] 1927 3-8-12 83 KierenFallon 2 85
(Mark Johnston) *prom in chsng gp: outpcd 3f out: tried to rally and swtchd lft over 1f out: sn wknd* **14/1**
-126 **7** 1 ¼ **Arantes**[24] 1652 3-9-0 88 WilliamTwiston-Davies(3) 4 88
(Mick Channon) *stdd s: hld up in rr: effrt on rail 2f out: sn wknd* **40/1**
- **8** 3 ¼ **Aussie Valentine (IRE)**[30] 1549 3-9-6 91 ChrisHayes 6 85
(P D Deegan, Ire) *chsd ldrs: clsd and ev ch over 2f out: wknd over 1f out* **12/1**

2m 6.8s (-2.00) **Going Correction** -0.10s/f (Good) **8 Ran SP% 112.4**
Speed ratings (Par 105): **104,103,102,101,100 98,97,94**
CSF £9.80 CT £50.70 TOTE £3.20: £1.20, £1.40, £3.00; EX 8.40 Trifecta £56.70.
**Owner** Saeed Suhail **Bred** Hascombe Stud **Trained** Newmarket, Suffolk

**FOCUS**
A 3yo handicap with a rich history, having provided an excellent source of future Group winners. Monterosso went on to land the Dubai World Cup, triple Group 1 winner Al Kazeem prevailed in 2011, and Hillstar tasted Royal Ascot success despite being touched off last season. It was a compelling edition this year and there was a sound pace on. Hot form, with the first four likely ahead of their marks.

## 2338 JLT LOCKINGE STKS (BRITISH CHAMPIONS SERIES) (GROUP 1) 1m (S)
**3:50** (3:52) (Class 1) 4-Y-0+
**£121,359** (£46,010; £23,026; £11,470; £5,756; £2,889) **Stalls** Centre

Form RPR
210- **1** **Olympic Glory (IRE)**[196] 7714 4-9-0 125 (b) FrankieDettori 3 125+
(Richard Hannon) *hld up in 6th: hdwy 2f out: led and qcknd clr over 1f out: rdn out* **11/8**[1]
0-21 **2** 2 ¼ **Tullius (IRE)**[22] 1698 6-9-0 117 RyanMoore 2 119
(Andrew Balding) *hld up in rr: hdwy over 1f out: chsd wnr fnl f: kpt on: no imp* **9/2**[2]
04- **3** 1 ¾ **Verrazano (USA)**[168] 4-9-0 117 JosephO'Brien 5 114
(A P O'Brien, Ire) *hld up towards rr: hdwy and hrd rdn over 1f out: styd on same pce fnl f* **7/1**
00-2 **4** ½ **Chopin (GER)**[34] 1478 4-9-0 115 JamieSpencer 6 113
(A Wohler, Germany) *in tch: rdn to press ldrs whn distracted by rival's whip over 1f out: sn btn* **15/2**
0305 **5** 2 ½ **Empire Storm (GER)**[22] 1697 7-9-0 107 (t) KierenFallon 4 107
(Michael Attwater) *chsd ldrs: disp ld over 2f out tl wknd over 1f out* **66/1**
12-4 **6** 1 **Top Notch Tonto (IRE)**[22] 1698 4-9-0 118 DaleSwift 1 105
(Brian Ellison) *prom: disp ld over 2f out tl wknd over 1f out* **16/1**
41-1 **7** 8 **Sruthan (IRE)**[34] 1473 4-9-0 111 ChrisHayes 8 86
(P D Deegan, Ire) *chsd ldrs tl hrd rdn and wknd 2f out* **16/1**
52-2 **8** 6 **Montiridge (IRE)**[22] 1698 4-9-0 115 RichardHughes 7 71
(Richard Hannon) *led tl over 2f out: wknd wl over 1f out* **5/1**[3]

1m 36.98s (-2.72) **Going Correction** +0.15s/f (Good) **8 Ran SP% 114.5**
Speed ratings (Par 117): **119,116,115,114,112 111,103,97**
CSF £7.72 TOTE £2.50: £1.20, £1.90, £2.00; EX 8.70 Trifecta £46.10.
**Owner** Al Shaqab Racing **Bred** Denis McDonnell **Trained** East Everleigh, Wilts

**FOCUS**
This wasn't the most competitive Lockinge by any means. It was contested at a messy pace, with the field merging nearer the stands' side around halfway, and turned into a dash for home around 2f out. The reliable runner-up rates the best guide for the form, with Olympic Glory not required to be at his best.

## 2339 JLT ASIA MAIDEN STKS (BOBIS RACE) 7f (S)
**4:25** (4:28) (Class 4) 3-Y-0
**£6,469** (£1,925; £962; £481) **Stalls** Centre

Form RPR
0-3 **1** **Skaters Waltz (IRE)**[14] 1946 3-9-5 0 LukeMorris 8 84
(Paul Cole) *prom: rdn over 2f out: r.o u.p to ld fnl 100yds* **11/1**
**2** *nk* **Telefono** 3-9-5 0 JamesDoyle 9 83
(Amanda Perrett) *hld up towards rr: hdwy 2f out: pressed wnr fnl 75yds: jst hld* **16/1**
22 **3** *nk* **Between Wickets**[14] 1946 3-9-5 0 HayleyTurner 5 82
(Marcus Tregoning) *led: rdn and hdd jst over 1f out: kpt on wl* **8/1**
4-02 **4** *hd* **Bon Voyage**[12] 2025 3-9-5 88 RichardHughes 4 81
(Richard Hannon) *prom: hrd rdn over 1f out: kpt on* **5/2**[1]
**5** *nk* **Polybius** 3-9-5 0 TedDurcan 3 81+
(David Lanigan) *dwlt: t.k.h: sn in midfield: hdwy 2f out: led jst over 1f out tl fnl 100yds: no ex* **33/1**
**6** 1 ¾ **Telmeyd** 3-9-5 0 PaulHanagan 10 76
(William Haggas) *towards rr: effrt and in tch over 1f out: no imp fnl f* **7/1**[3]

3- **7** 1 1/4 **Dianora**[254] 6140 3-9-0 0 RyanMoore 13 68
(Sir Michael Stoute) *towards rr: effrt and hrd rdn over 1f out: unable to chal* **11/4**[2]

5 **8** 1 1/4 **Greengage Summer**[14] 1946 3-8-11 0 WilliamTwiston-Davies(3) 12 65
(Mick Channon) *bhd: rdn 3f out: late hdwy* **33/1**

0 **9** 2 **Cobham's Circus (IRE)**[12] 2026 3-9-0 0 ShelleyBirkett(5) 14 64
(Marcus Tregoning) *bhd: rdn over 2f out: n.d* **50/1**

4 **10** hd **Dreaming Brave**[93] 588 3-9-5 0 JimCrowley 6 64
(Amanda Perrett) *mid-div: rdn over 2f out: sn outpcd* **28/1**

**11** 1 **Jailawi (IRE)** 3-9-5 0 JamieSpencer 1 61
(Ismail Mohammed) *in tch tl hrd rdn and wknd 2f out* **14/1**

**12** 1 1/2 **Marydale** 3-8-11 0 OisinMurphy(3) 2 52
(Henry Candy) *prom tl wknd over 1f out* **33/1**

0 **13** 16 **Distant Shadow**[38] 1395 3-9-0 0 SteveDrowne 16 11
(Chris Wall) *plld hrd: sn pressing ldr: wknd qckly over 2f out* **66/1**

5 **14** 29 **Lindart (ITY)**[81] 739 3-9-5 0 KierenFallon 11
(Richard Hannon) *towards rr: rdn over 3f out: sn wl bhd* **16/1**

1m 26.49s (0.79) **Going Correction** +0.15s/f (Good) **14** Ran SP% **121.3**
Speed ratings (Par 101): **101,100,100,100,99 97,96,94,92,92 91,89,71,38**
CSF £165.46 TOTE £13.70: £3.10, £4.30, £2.40; EX 97.10 Trifecta £481.30.
**Owner** Sir George Meyrick **Bred** Patrick A Cluskey **Trained** Whatcombe, Oxon

**FOCUS**
A fair 3yo maiden. There field came together mid-track after a furlong or so and there was an average pace on, resulting in a bunched finish. The third and fourth set the standard.

## 2340 FOLLOW SCOOP6 AT TOTEPOOLLIVEINFO.COM FILLIES' H'CAP (BOBIS RACE) 7f (S)
**5:00** (5:02) (Class 4) (0-85,85) 3-Y-O **£4,690** (£1,395; £697; £348) **Stalls** Centre

Form RPR

41-1 **1** **Aertex (IRE)**[16] 1897 3-9-4 82 RichardHughes 10 93+
(Richard Hannon) *hld up in rr of midfield: gd hdwy over 1f out: led ins fnl f: rdn out* **11/2**[3]

1- **2** 3/4 **Token Of Love**[221] 7103 3-8-13 77 RyanMoore 8 85
(William Haggas) *towards rr: hdwy 2f out: chsd wnr ins fnl f: r.o* **7/4**[1]

42-0 **3** 3/4 **Venus Grace**[30] 1534 3-8-10 74 JimCrowley 9 80
(Ralph Beckett) *dwlt: in rr: rdn and hdwy fnl 2f: gng on wl at fin* **25/1**

0-15 **4** 1/2 **Cay Dancer**[13] 1985 3-8-8 79 CamHardie(7) 13 84
(Richard Hannon) *mid-div: hdwy over 1f out: styd on fnl f* **25/1**

13- **5** nk **Dutch S**[204] 7503 3-8-13 77 AdamKirby 14 81
(Clive Cox) *prom: hrd rdn over 1f out: kpt on* **8/1**

136 **6** 1 **Bridie ffrench**[8] 2130 3-8-7 73 ow1 WilliamTwiston-Davies(3) 6 75
(Mick Channon) *prom: hrd rdn over 1f out: one pce* **25/1**

221- **7** 3/4 **Stepping Out (IRE)**[341] 3148 3-9-4 82 RichardKingscote 4 81
(Tom Dascombe) *led: hrd rdn and hdd ins fnl f: wknd fnl 100yds* **12/1**

03-0 **8** 1/2 **Baby Bush (IRE)**[36] 1420 3-9-2 80 JamieSpencer 12 78
(Richard Hannon) *bhd: rdn 3f out: styd on fnl f* **20/1**

015- **9** 2 3/4 **Arranger (IRE)**[247] 6326 3-8-11 75 PaulHanagan 5 66
(Martyn Meade) *mid-div: rdn and no hdwy fnl 2f* **16/1**

231- **10** 4 1/2 **Tides Reach (IRE)**[228] 6923 3-8-5 72 OisinMurphy(3) 1 51
(Roger Charlton) *in rr: drvn along 3f out: sn bhd* **16/1**

3-1 **11** 1 3/4 **Angelic Air**[20] 1767 3-9-7 85 JamesDoyle 2 60
(John Gosden) *in tch: effrt and hung bdly lft fr over 2f out: wknd over 1f out* **9/2**[2]

00-0 **12** 1 **Red Lady (IRE)**[14] 1952 3-9-0 78 KierenFallon 15 50
(Brian Meehan) *racd alone on stands' rail: prom tl hrd rdn and wknd over 1f out* **33/1**

001- **13** 25 **Heavens Edge**[282] 5174 3-9-5 83 LukeMorris 3
(Christopher Mason) *prom tl wknd 3f out: bhd and eased fnl 2f* **40/1**

1m 25.21s (-0.49) **Going Correction** +0.15s/f (Good) **13** Ran SP% **122.2**
Speed ratings (Par 98): **108,107,106,105,105 104,103,102,99,94 92,91,62**
CSF £14.44 CT £233.99 TOTE £6.00: £2.30, £1.30, £7.40; EX 21.80 Trifecta £239.00.
**Owner** Mrs James Wigan **Bred** Mrs James Wigan **Trained** East Everleigh, Wilts

**FOCUS**
This good-quality fillies' handicap is always a competitive event. All bar one of the runners kept to the middle of the track early, but they got spread right across from halfway and it was a fairly messy race. Good fillies' form, rated on the positive side.
T/Jkpt: £28,710.10 to a £1 stake. Pool of £60655.16 - 1.50 winning tickets. T/Plt: £114.00 to a £1 stake. Pool of £130992.86 - 838.29 winning tickets. T/Qpdt: £28.50 to a £1 stake. Pool of £9966.39 - 258.48 winning tickets. LM

# 2306 NEWMARKET (R-H)
## Saturday, May 17

**OFFICIAL GOING: Good to firm (7.8)**
Wind: Light half-behind Weather: Sunny spells

## 2341 JOE BREEN AND SARAH MORRIS MEMORIAL H'CAP 7f
**1:45** (1:46) (Class 4) (0-80,78) 4-Y-O+ **£5,175** (£1,540; £769; £384) **Stalls** High

Form RPR

00-0 **1** **Front Page News**[43] 1275 4-9-0 71 FrederikTylicki 10 82
(Robert Eddery) *a.p: rdn over 1f out: led ins fnl f: edgd rt: r.o* **20/1**

2013 **2** 2 **Shaolin (IRE)**[19] 1796 4-9-7 78 (t) DaneO'Neill 7 84
(Seamus Durack) *hld up: hdwy over 2f out: rdn over 1f out: r.o* **5/1**[2]

3503 **3** 3/4 **Sheikh The Reins (IRE)**[26] 1613 5-8-9 66 (v) RobertHavlin 2 70
(John Best) *chsd ldrs: led 1/2-way: rdn over 1f out: hdd and unable qck ins fnl f* **11/1**

0111 **4** nk **Until Midnight (IRE)**[19] 1799 4-8-10 67 MartinDwyer 11 70
(Eugene Stanford) *s.i.s: nt clr run over 6f out: hld up: rdn over 1f out: r.o ins fnl f: nvr nrr* **10/1**

0-04 **5** 3/4 **Jack Of Diamonds (IRE)**[18] 1834 5-9-3 74 (v[1]) MickaelBarzalona 3 75
(Roger Teal) *chsd ldrs: rdn over 2f out: styd on same pce fnl f* **9/2**[1]

520- **6** nk **Evident (IRE)**[207] 7436 4-9-7 78 WilliamBuick 8 78
(Jeremy Noseda) *prom: lost pl over 4f out: rdn and swtchd rt over 1f out: styd on towards fin* **8/1**

-000 **7** nk **Staffhoss**[13] 1970 4-8-10 67 JoeFanning 6 67
(Mark Johnston) *chsd ldrs: rdn over 2f out: styd on same pce fnl f* **11/1**

-055 **8** nk **Zaitsev (IRE)**[12] 2017 4-9-1 72 SilvestreDeSousa 12 71
(Ollie Pears) *led to 1/2-way: remained handy: rdn over 1f out: sn ev ch: wknd wl ins fnl f* **6/1**[3]

46-0 **9** 3/4 **Duke Of Destiny (IRE)**[18] 1845 5-8-7 71 (p) CliffordLee(7) 5 68
(Ed Walker) *s.i.s: sn pushed along in rr: kpt on ins fnl f: nvr on terms* **33/1**

3025 **10** 1 1/2 **Smokethatthunders (IRE)**[35] 1451 4-9-3 74 (t[1]) StevieDonohoe 9 67
(Tim Pitt) *chsd ldrs: rdn over 2f out: wknd ins fnl f* **16/1**

2110 **11** 1 1/2 **Presumido (IRE)**[19] 1796 4-8-11 73 JackDuern(5) 4 62
(Simon Dow) *hld up: rdn over 1f out: n.d* **12/1**

0053 **12** 1 3/4 **Illustrious Prince (IRE)**[21] 1710 7-9-2 73 (p) GrahamLee 1 57
(Julie Camacho) *hld up: rdn over 3f out: wknd over 1f out* **8/1**

1m 24.71s (-0.69) **Going Correction** -0.15s/f (Firm) **12** Ran SP% **118.4**
Speed ratings (Par 105): **97,94,93,93,92 92,91,91,90,89 87,85**
CSF £117.14 CT £1198.31 TOTE £25.90: £6.50, £2.10, £4.10; EX 175.40 Trifecta £704.00.
**Owner** Gurnett, Rayment & Anderson **Bred** Helen Plumbly And Wendy Balding **Trained** Newmarket, Suffolk

**FOCUS**
Stands' side track used. Stalls stands' side except 1m4f &1m6f: centre. The ground continued to dry out and was changed to good to firm all round before racing. The jockeys in the opener described conditions as "quick with no jar" and "fast". The first race was a fair handicap, run at a solid pace, but with a surprise result. The winner is rated in line a better view of last year's form.

## 2342 TRICONNEX H'CAP 1m 6f
**2:20** (2:22) (Class 2) (0-105,100) 4-Y-O+
**£18,675** (£5,592; £2,796; £1,398; £699; £351) **Stalls** Centre

Form RPR

5-15 **1** **Lord Van Percy**[13] 1973 4-8-10 89 DavidProbert 9 101+
(Andrew Balding) *hld up: styd far side: hdwy 4f out: rdn to ld and edgd lft over 1f out: styd on wl: 1st of 4 in gp* **11/4**[1]

1500 **2** 3 1/4 **Blue Wave (IRE)**[21] 1736 4-9-3 96 JoeFanning 6 103
(Mark Johnston) *w ldr tl wnt centre and led that gp 10f out: led overall over 2f out: rdn and hdd over 1f out: edgd rt and no ex ins fnl f: 1st of 5 in gp* **14/1**

245- **3** 3/4 **Tropical Beat**[233] 6766 6-9-4 97 WilliamBuick 3 103
(David O'Meara) *hld up: wnt centre 10f out: hdwy over 2f out: sn rdn: edgd rt and kpt on ins fnl f: 2nd of 5 in gp* **9/2**[3]

30-0 **4** 2 **Highland Castle**[20] 1770 6-8-12 91 MartinLane 7 94
(Brian Meehan) *hld up: plld hrd: hdwy over 10f out: styd far side: trckd ldr over 5f out: led overall over 4f out: rdn and hdd over 2f out: styd on same pce fnl f: 2nd of 4 in gp* **9/1**

21-2 **5** 1 3/4 **Dark Ranger**[20] 1770 8-8-4 83 JimmyQuinn 2 84
(Tim Pitt) *chsd ldrs: styd far side: wnt 2nd over 3f out: sn rdn: edgd lft over 1f out: no ex fnl f: 3rd of 4 in gp* **14/1**

00-0 **6** 10 **Palazzo Bianco**[8] 2119 6-8-3 82 PaoloSirigu 4 69
(Brian Ellison) *overall ldr: styd far side: hdd over 4f out: rdn and wknd over 2f out: last of 4 in gp* **25/1**

21-0 **7** 5 **De Rigueur**[21] 1736 6-8-11 95 (tp) MarcMonaghan(5) 5 75
(Marco Botti) *hld up: wnt centre 10f out: hdwy over 4f out: rdn over 2f out: sn wknd: 3rd of 5 in gp* **11/2**

032- **8** 19 **Expert Fighter (USA)**[203] 7542 5-9-0 93 SilvestreDeSousa 8 46
(Saeed bin Suroor) *hld up: plld hrd: hdwy and wnt centre 10f out: chsd ldr over 5f out tl rdn over 3f out: wknd wl over 1f out: 4th of 5 in gp* **7/2**[2]

00P **9** 77 **Thecornishcockney**[47] 1213 5-9-7 100 (bt) StevieDonohoe 1
(John Ryan) *chsd ldrs: wnt centre and lft 2nd 10f out tl rdn over 5f out: wknd over 4f out: last of 5 in gp* **33/1**

3m 0.01s (3.01) **Going Correction** -0.15s/f (Firm) **9** Ran SP% **112.6**
Speed ratings (Par 109): **85,83,82,81,80 74,72,61,17**
CSF £41.50 CT £166.10 TOTE £3.40: £1.40, £3.90, £1.80; EX 38.00 Trifecta £144.60.
**Owner** Mrs L E Ramsden & Richard Morecombe **Bred** Mr & Mrs A E Pakenham **Trained** Kingsclere, Hants

**FOCUS**
This decent staying handicap has been won by some nice sorts in recent years, including the 2012 winner Mount Athos who has been successful in Group company since, while last year's winner Tiger Cliff went on to win the Ebor. This year's edition was something of a messy race thanks to an ordinary gallop and a difference of opinion on reaching the straight, with four staying against the far rail and the other five coming up the centre. The result suggested there was no great advantage to either group, but the winner looks progressive. A 5lb best from the winner.

## 2343 TAMDOWN KING CHARLES II STKS (LISTED RACE) 7f
**2:55** (2:55) (Class 1) 3-Y-O
**£20,982** (£7,955; £3,981; £1,983; £995; £499) **Stalls** High

Form RPR

320- **1** **Coulsty (IRE)**[247] 6328 3-9-0 97 SeanLevey 5 106
(Richard Hannon) *racd centre tl gps merged over 4f out: mde virtually all: rdn over 1f out: styd on gamely* **16/1**

16-2 **2** 1/2 **Toofi (FR)**[31] 1513 3-9-0 98 TomQueally 4 104
(Roger Varian) *racd centre tl gps merged over 4f out: w wnr: rdn over 1f out: styd on* **9/2**[3]

21-0 **3** shd **Windfast (IRE)**[35] 1436 3-9-0 97 DaneO'Neill 9 104
(Brian Meehan) *led stands' side duo tl gps merged over 4f out: chsd ldrs: rdn and ev ch fr over 1f out: styd on* **11/1**

33-5 **4** nse **Parbold (IRE)**[31] 1514 3-9-0 111 FrederikTylicki 10 104+
(Richard Fahey) *racd in centre tl gps merged over 4f out: a.p: rdn over 1f out: nt clr run ins fnl f: r.o towards fin* **3/1**[1]

11-0 **5** 1 1/2 **Complicit (IRE)**[29] 1555 3-9-0 95 SilvestreDeSousa 8 100
(Paul Cole) *racd centre tl gps merged over 4f out: hld up: outpcd 1/2-way: r.o ins fnl f: nt rch ldrs* **20/1**

12-3 **6** 1 **Aeolus**[31] 1514 3-9-0 102 GrahamLee 2 97+
(Ed McMahon) *racd in centre tl gps merged over 4f out: hld up in tch: rdn over 1f out: no ex ins fnl f* **7/2**[2]

-106 **7** nk **Alutiq (IRE)**[29] 1555 3-8-9 93 MartinLane 7 92
(Eve Johnson Houghton) *racd centre tl gps merged over 4f out: sn prom: rdn over 2f out: edgd lft and styd on same pce fnl f* **25/1**

01-6 **8** 2 **Miracle Of Medinah**[31] 1514 3-9-7 104 LiamKeniry 3 98
(Mark Usher) *racd centre tl gps merged over 4f out: chsd ldrs: rdn over 2f out: wknd ins fnl f* **25/1**

01- **9** 7 **Gamesome (FR)**[274] 5494 3-9-0 98 HarryBentley 11 73
(Olly Stevens) *racd stands' side tl gps merged over 4f out: plld hrd and sn trcking ldr: rdn over 1f out: sn wknd* **14/1**

25-0 **10** 9 **Dorothy B (IRE)**[31] 1515 3-8-9 107 WilliamBuick 6 45
(John Gosden) *racd centre tl gps merged over 4f out: a in rr: bhd fr 1/2-way* **5/1**

1m 23.72s (-1.68) **Going Correction** -0.15s/f (Firm) **10** Ran SP% **115.4**
Speed ratings (Par 107): **103,102,102,102,100 99,99,96,88,78**
CSF £83.60 TOTE £16.70: £4.20, £1.90, £3.80; EX 138.00 Trifecta £1645.40 Part won. Pool of £2193.98 - 0.16 winning units..
**Owner** Lord Vestey **Bred** Peter & Sarah Fortune **Trained** East Everleigh, Wilts

**FOCUS**
A tight Listed event with little covering the front four at the line. All bar Windfast and Gamesome raced away from the nearside rail early, though the field had joined into one group before reaching the 4f pole. A bit below the race standard.

## 2344 CORAL.CO.UK SPRINT TROPHY (H'CAP) (BOBIS RACE) 6f
**3:30** (3:33) (Class 2) (0-105,101) 3-Y-O

**£28,012** (£8,388; £4,194; £2,097; £1,048; £526) **Stalls** High

Form RPR
3-64 **1** **Eastern Impact (IRE)**[14] 1952 3-8-11 **91**........................ FrederikTylicki 8 101
(Richard Fahey) *a.p: rdn to chse ldr over 1f out: r.o to ld wl ins fnl f* **14/1**

12-1 **2** *3/4* **Fear Or Favour (IRE)**[28] 1570 3-8-0 **85** ow1.................. RyanTate(5) 10 93
(Clive Cox) *mid-div: swtchd rt and hdwy over 1f out: sn rdn: r.o* **11/2**[3]

3-11 **3** *nse* **Stomp**[8] 2122 3-8-2 **87**........................................ JoeyHaynes(5) 11 95
(Roger Charlton) *hld up: pushed along and hdwy over 1f out: r.o* **3/1**[1]

40-2 **4** *nk* **Peterkin (IRE)**[10] 2083 3-8-5 **85**................................ JoeFanning 7 92
(Mark Johnston) *led: shkn up over 1f out: hdd and unable qck wl ins fnl f* **25/1**

13-4 **5** *3/4* **Charles Molson**[22] 1700 3-8-10 **90**............................ DaneO'Neill 12 94
(Henry Candy) *hld up: nt clr run over 1f out: r.o ins fnl f: nt rch ldrs* **14/1**

-525 **6** *1 1/2* **Expert (IRE)**[17] 1867 3-9-7 **101**................................. SeanLevey 6 101
(Richard Hannon) *prom: chsd ldr 1/2-way tl rdn over 1f out: no ex ins fnl f* **8/1**

-021 **7** *3* **Nova Champ (IRE)**[14] 1952 3-8-1 **81** oh2 ow1............(p) AndreaAtzeni 9 71
(Stuart Williams) *chsd ldr to 1/2-way: rdn over 2f out: edgd rt and no ex fnl f* **12/1**

10-3 **8** *1 1/2* **Deeds Not Words (IRE)**[35] 1445 3-8-9 **92**............... CharlesBishop(3) 1 77+
(Mick Channon) *prom: rdn over 2f out: wknd fnl f* **10/1**

4-43 **9** *1/2* **Master Of Suspense**[23] 1677 3-8-0 **80** oh1.................... JimmyQuinn 4 64
(Peter Chapple-Hyam) *hld up: rdn over 2f out: wknd fnl f* **22/1**

21-2 **10** *3/4* **Stars Above Me**[14] 1952 3-8-11 **91**.............................. WilliamBuick 5 72+
(Roger Charlton) *s.i.s: hld up: hdwy over 2f out: rdn and edgd lft wl over 1f out: sn wknd* **5/1**[2]

1-56 **11** *3 1/2* **Meritocracy (IRE)**[14] 1952 3-8-7 **87**........................... ChrisCatlin 2 57+
(Paul Cole) *hld up: effrt over 2f out: wknd over 1f out* **25/1**

446- **12** *5* **Sleeper King (IRE)**[246] 6347 3-9-7 **101**........................ GrahamLee 3 55+
(Kevin Ryan) *hld up in tch: rdn over 2f out: hmpd and wknd wl over 1f out* **14/1**

1m 10.52s (-1.68) **Going Correction** -0.15s/f (Firm) **12** Ran SP% **117.0**
Speed ratings (Par 105): **105,104,103,103,102 100,96,94,93,92 88,81**
CSF £85.90 CT £295.20 TOTE £16.50: £3.60, £2.20, £1.70; EX 89.20 Trifecta £553.90.
**Owner** Exors of the late D W Barker **Bred** Airlie Stud **Trained** Musley Bank, N Yorks

**FOCUS**
A hot 3yo sprint handicap that has been won by subsequent Group-race winners Resplendent Glory, Genki, Ancien Regime and Mince within the past ten years. It's debatable whether the race will produce anything of their calibre this year, especially with the draw playing such a big part (those berthed towards the stands' side were at a major advantage), but the race should produce winners. The form has been given a bit of a chance.

## 2345 TAMDOWN FAIRWAY STKS (LISTED RACE) 1m 2f
**4:05** (4:07) (Class 1) 3-Y-O **£20,982** (£7,955; £3,981; £1,983; £995) **Stalls** High

Form RPR
10-3 **1** **Pinzolo**[14] 1953 3-9-3 104........................................ SilvestreDeSousa 3 104
(Charlie Appleby) *led: hdd over 2f out: sn rdn: rallied to ld over 1f out: styd on wl* **5/4**[1]

3-33 **2** *2* **Master Carpenter (IRE)**[22] 1699 3-9-3 103.................... AndreaAtzeni 4 100
(Rod Millman) *s.s: hld up: hdwy over 2f out: rdn to chse wnr fnl f: styd on same pce towards fin* **7/2**[2]

3-36 **3** *1/2* **Truth Or Dare**[22] 1699 3-9-3 104.................................... MartinDwyer 1 99
(Richard Hannon) *sn trcking wnr: lost 2nd over 3f out: rdn and outpcd over 1f out: r.o towards fin* **8/1**

44-0 **4** *1 1/4* **Hunters Creek (IRE)**[30] 1530 3-9-3 94........................... WilliamBuick 2 97
(John Gosden) *trckd ldrs: plld hrd: wnt 2nd over 3f out: led over 2f out: rdn and hdd over 1f out: no ex ins fnl f* **5/1**[3]

1 **5** *4 1/2* **Sloane Avenue (USA)**[98] 536 3-9-3 92............................. GrahamLee 5 88
(Jeremy Noseda) *prom: pushed along over 3f out: wknd over 1f out* **6/1**

2m 5.64s (-0.16) **Going Correction** -0.15s/f (Firm) **5** Ran SP% **108.7**
Speed ratings (Par 107): **94,92,92,91,87**
CSF £5.65 TOTE £1.80: £1.40, £1.70; EX 4.30 Trifecta £15.50.
**Owner** Godolphin **Bred** Fittocks Stud **Trained** Newmarket, Suffolk

**FOCUS**
This Listed event has been won by some big names in the past ten years, including the subsequent domestic Group 1 winners David Junior and Lucarno, together with the international Grade 1 winners Red Rocks and Green Moon. The quintet raced up the nearside rail throughout and the pace looked ordinary until it quickened coming to the last 3f. The form is in line with the recent race standard.

## 2346 TAMDOWN MAIDEN STKS (BOBIS RACE) 1m
**4:40** (4:42) (Class 4) 3-Y-O **£5,175** (£1,540; £769; £384) **Stalls** High

Form RPR
23- **1** **Yuften**[232] 6799 3-9-5 0............................................. AndreaAtzeni 6 97+
(William Haggas) *chsd ldr tl shkn up to ld and edgd lft over 1f out: r.o wl* **10/11**[1]

00-2 **2** *7* **Newton's Law (IRE)**[12] 2026 3-9-5 73....................(t) SilvestreDeSousa 2 78
(Brian Meehan) *led: rdn and hdd whn hmpd over 1f out: wknd ins fnl f* **9/1**

02-3 **3** *nk* **Mr Greenspan (USA)**[47] 1208 3-9-5 77............................ SeanLevey 8 77
(Richard Hannon) *chsd ldrs: pushed along over 3f out: rdn and swtchd rt 2f out: styd on same pce fr over 1f out* **12/1**

4 **4** *1/2* **Kinshasa**[33] 1491 3-9-5 0........................................ LemosdeSouza 1 76+
(Luca Cumani) *hld up: hdwy over 2f out: styd on same pce fr over 1f out* **9/2**[2]

02 **5** *hd* **Red Velour**[18] 1831 3-9-0 0......................................... WilliamBuick 3 70
(Jeremy Noseda) *prom: rdn over 2f out: styd on same pce fr over 1f out* **8/1**[3]

04 **6** *3* **Saalib (USA)**[12] 2025 3-9-5 0.....................................(t) DaneO'Neill 9 68
(Brian Meehan) *prom: rdn over 2f out: wknd over 1f out* **25/1**

0- **7** *1* **Beakers N Num Nums (IRE)**[212] 7327 3-9-5 0.............. GrahamLee 12 66
(William Jarvis) *hld up: pushed along 1/2-way: nvr on terms* **50/1**

0 **8** *shd* **Margaret's Mission (IRE)**[30] 1534 3-9-0 0.................(t) ChrisCatlin 7 60
(Jeremy Noseda) *mid-div: pushed along over 3f out: sn outpcd* **16/1**

**9** *20* **Prince Ballygowen** 3-9-5 0...................................... SamHitchcott 10 17
(Clifford Lines) *s.i.s: rn green and a in rr: wknd over 3f out* **66/1**

**10** *1* **Medallero (USA)** 3-9-5 0...................................... MickaelBarzalona 5 15
(Clive Brittain) *hld up: pushed along over 5f out: wknd over 3f out* **25/1**

40 **11** *9* **Gaelic O'Reagan**[21] 1730 3-9-5 0.................................... JimmyQuinn 11
(Robert Eddery) *dwlt: a in rr: wknd over 3f out* **66/1**

1m 37.4s (-1.20) **Going Correction** -0.15s/f (Firm) **11** Ran SP% **117.9**
Speed ratings (Par 101): **100,93,92,92,92 89,88,87,67,66 57**
CSF £9.60 TOTE £2.00: £1.10, £2.80, £2.80; EX 12.60 Trifecta £75.10.
**Owner** Saleh Al Homaizi & Imad Al Sagar **Bred** Saleh Al Homaizi & Imad Al Sagar **Trained** Newmarket, Suffolk
■ Stewards' Enquiry : Andrea Atzeni one-day ban: careless riding (May 31)

**FOCUS**
The favourite had won this maiden for the past eight years and that sequence never looked like being broken in a race lacking depth. The winner looks among the better winners of this race.

## 2347 TAMDOWN GROUP H'CAP (BOBIS RACE) 1m 4f
**5:15** (5:17) (Class 3) (0-95,98) 3-Y-O **£9,703** (£2,887; £1,443; £721) **Stalls** Centre

Form RPR
11-2 **1** **Miner's Lamp (IRE)**[13] 1979 3-9-10 **98**............................ WilliamBuick 2 109+
(Charlie Appleby) *chsd ldrs: led 10f out: shkn up over 1f out: rdn and edgd lft ins fnl f: styd on* **5/2**[1]

2-1 **2** *1/2* **Alex My Boy (IRE)**[27] 1600 3-8-9 **83**............................... JoeFanning 6 93
(Mark Johnston) *a.p: pushed along over 2f out: rdn to chse wnr ins fnl f: r.o* **5/1**[3]

0-31 **3** *1 1/4* **Talmada (USA)**[21] 1720 3-9-2 **90**................................. AndreaAtzeni 4 98
(Roger Varian) *chsd ldr 2f: remained handy: wnt 2nd again over 7f out: rdn over 2f out: styd on same pce ins fnl f* **5/2**[1]

3-22 **4** *6* **Cape Caster (IRE)**[21] 1730 3-8-8 **82**.......................... SilvestreDeSousa 5 81
(Ralph Beckett) *hld up: plld hrd: hdwy over 3f out: sn rdn: styd on same pce appr fnl f* **4/1**[2]

-115 **5** *5* **Rudi Five One (FR)**[30] 1535 3-8-8 **82**............................ JimmyQuinn 3 73
(Robert Eddery) *hld up: rdn over 3f out: wknd over 1f out* **11/1**

6-10 **6** *7* **Rock 'N' Roll Star**[31] 1516 3-8-6 **80**............................. RobertHavlin 7 59
(Peter Chapple-Hyam) *s.s: hld up: rdn and wknd over 2f out* **25/1**

21-3 **7** *11* **The Alamo (IRE)**[13] 1983 3-8-5 **79**.............................. MickaelBarzalona 1 41
(Richard Hannon) *led 2f: chsd ldr tl over 7f out: rdn over 4f out: wknd over 2f out* **14/1**

2m 31.65s (-0.35) **Going Correction** -0.15s/f (Firm) **7** Ran SP% **112.7**
Speed ratings (Par 103): **95,94,93,89,86 81,74**
CSF £14.96 TOTE £2.50: £1.90, £2.70; EX 15.60 Trifecta £26.80.
**Owner** Godolphin **Bred** Mrs C L Weld **Trained** Newmarket, Suffolk

**FOCUS**
An interesting 3yo middle-distance handicap, but the pace was ordinary and the winner dictated things. The seven runners came up the middle of the track in the straight. A smart effort from the winner.
T/Plt: £120.80 to a £1 stake. Pool of £94519.50 - 570.95 winning tickets. T/Qpdt: £15.50 to a £1 stake. Pool of £8103.21 - 385.30 winning tickets. CR

# 2165 THIRSK (L-H)
Saturday, May 17

**OFFICIAL GOING: Good (good to soft in places; 8.8)**
Wind: Breezy, half behind Weather: Sunny, hot

## 2348 IRISH STALLION FARMS EBF MAIDEN FILLIES' STKS (BOBIS RACE) (DIV I) 5f
**2:15** (2:17) (Class 4) 2-Y-O **£4,204** (£1,251; £625; £312) **Stalls** High

Form RPR
**1** **Harry's Dancer (IRE)** 2-8-11 0................................. IanBrennan(3) 2 83+
(John Quinn) *t.k.h: cl up on outside: led gng wl over 1f out: qcknd clr fnl f: readily* **14/1**

2 **2** *5* **Zeela (IRE)**[17] 1879 2-9-0 0....................................... DavidAllan 4 65
(Tim Easterby) *cl up: effrt and ev ch over 1f out: kpt on fnl f: no ch w ready wnr* **13/8**[1]

5 **3** *nk* **Clodovil Doll (IRE)**[12] 2022 2-9-0 0............................. PaulMulrennan 5 64
(James Tate) *hld up in tch: effrt and shkn up over 1f out: kpt on fnl f: nvr able to chal* **10/1**

**4** *3/4* **Mystic And Artist** 2-9-0 0........................................ DanielTudhope 1 61+
(K R Burke) *bhd and sn outpcd: hdwy over 1f out: kpt on fnl f: nvr rchd ldrs* **6/1**[3]

**5** *1/2* **Pastoral Girl** 2-9-0 0.............................................. JamesSullivan 9 59
(James Given) *t.k.h: trckd ldrs: effrt and edgd lft over 1f out: one pce fnl f* **20/1**

0 **6** *7* **Featsdontfailmenow**[19] 1788 2-8-9 0........................ ShirleyTeasdale(5) 6 34
(Lisa Williamson) *led against stands' rail: rdn and hdd over 1f out: wknd fnl f* **100/1**

**7** *1 3/4* **Secret Of Dubai** 2-9-0 0........................................... PaulPickard 7 28
(Brian Ellison) *s.i.s: bhd and outpcd: nvr on terms* **50/1**

**8** *1* **Ventura Shadow** 2-9-0 0............................................ TonyHamilton 3 24
(Richard Fahey) *noisy in paddock: bhd and outpcd: nvr on terms* **9/1**

**9** *1 1/4* **Bacall** 2-9-0 0........................................................ TomEaves 8 20
(Kevin Ryan) *plld hrd: cl up: rdn over 1f out: wknd fnl f* **11/4**[2]

1m 0.06s (0.46) **Going Correction** +0.15s/f (Good) **9** Ran SP% **112.5**
Speed ratings (Par 92): **102,94,93,92,91 80,77,75,73**
CSF £35.95 TOTE £16.30: £3.40, £1.10, £3.10; EX 41.00 Trifecta £1119.00 Part won. Pool of £1492.11 - 0.85 winning units..
**Owner** T G S Wood **Bred** Mrs Adelaide Doran **Trained** Settrington, N Yorks

**FOCUS**
Home bend dolled out about 7yds, adding 16yds to races on Round course. An impressive performance from the winner on debut in what was an ordinary maiden overall.

## 2349 IRISH STALLION FARMS EBF MAIDEN FILLIES' STKS (BOBIS RACE) (DIV II) 5f
**2:50** (2:51) (Class 4) 2-Y-O **£4,204** (£1,251; £625; £312) **Stalls** High

Form RPR
**1** **Secret Liaison (IRE)** 2-9-0 0.................................... PaulMulrennan 9 73+
(James Tate) *mde all: rdn over 1f out: drifted lft last 100yds: kpt on wl* **7/4**[1]

**2** *1/2* **Lily Moreton (IRE)** 2-8-11 0....................................... JasonHart(3) 8 71
(Noel Wilson) *w wnr: rdn 2f out: hung lft ins fnl f: kpt on: hld nr fin* **8/1**

04 **3** *1 3/4* **Tarando**[12] 2022 2-8-9 0.......................................... LouisSteward(5) 2 65
(Michael Bell) *trckd ldrs on outside: effrt and rdn over 1f out: kpt on same pce ins fnl f* **4/1**[3]

**4** *2 3/4* **Elizabeth Ernest** 2-8-11 0......................................... GeorgeChaloner(3) 7 55
(Richard Fahey) *trckd ldrs: effrt and rdn 2f out: outpcd fnl f* **6/1**

4 **5** *5* **Secret Friend (IRE)**[15] 1924 2-9-0 0............................. DuranFentiman 1 37
(Tim Easterby) *in tch: drvn over 2f out: wknd fnl f* **10/3**[2]



The Form Book, Raceform Ltd, Newbury, RG14 5SJ

6 7 **Fazenda's Girl** 2-9-0 0 GrahamGibbons 5 12
(Michael Easterby) *missed break: rn green in rr: nvr on terms* 20/1

7 2 1/2 **Sparkling Sapphire** 2-9-0 0 PaulQuinn 6 3
(Richard Whitaker) *reluctant to enter stalls: bhd and sn outpcd: no ch fr 1/2-way* 25/1

1m 1.32s (1.72) **Going Correction** +0.15s/f (Good) 7 Ran SP% 113.4
Speed ratings (Par 92): **92,91,88,84,76 64,60**
CSF £16.50 TOTE £2.60: £1.40, £3.30; EX 24.20 Trifecta £138.30.
**Owner** Sheikh Rashid Dalmook Al Maktoum **Bred** Liam Foley **Trained** Newmarket, Suffolk

**FOCUS**
Just an ordinary maiden in all probability. The time was a second and a half slower than the first division.

## 2350 HAPPY BIRTHDAY MIKE WOOD H'CAP 5f
3:25 (3:26) (Class 4) (0-85,85) 4-Y-O+ £4,690 (£1,395; £697; £348) Stalls High

Form RPR

2-05 1 **Tumblewind**[14] 1961 4-9-3 **84** GeorgeChaloner(3) 14 95
(Richard Whitaker) *trckd ldrs: effrt and rdn over 1f out: led ins fnl f: kpt on wl* 6/1[2]

0-24 2 1 1/2 **Bronze Beau**[14] 1961 7-8-9 **78** (t) JacobButterfield(5) 7 84
(Kristin Stubbs) *slt ld: rdn 2f out: hdd ins fnl f: kpt on: hld nr fin* 16/1

60-6 3 3/4 **Imperial Legend (IRE)**[24] 1650 5-9-7 **85** (p) PaulMulrennan 15 88
(David Nicholls) *prom: effrt whn n.m.r over 1f out: kpt on ins fnl f* 9/1[3]

0422 4 3/4 **Tax Free (IRE)**[14] 1961 12-9-6 **84** AdrianNicholls 2 85+
(David Nicholls) *prom: effrt and rdn over 2f out: kpt on same pce fnl f* 10/1

0401 5 3/4 **Lastchancelucas**[14] 1961 4-9-1 **82** (b) JasonHart(3) 13 80
(Declan Carroll) *sn pushed along towards rr: rdn and hdwy over 1f out: kpt on: nrst fin* 7/2[1]

62- 6 nse **Alaskan Bullet (IRE)**[380] 1964 5-9-0 **78** TomEaves 10 76
(Brian Ellison) *plld hrd in rr: rdn and hdwy over 1f out: kpt on fnl f: n.d* 25/1

1-30 7 1/2 **Prince Regal**[7] 2147 4-8-13 **77** BenCurtis 11 73
(Alan Jarvis) *prom: effrt and drvn over 1f out: edgd lft: outpcd ins fnl f* 6/1[2]

2-03 8 hd **Oldjoesaid**[14] 1961 10-8-13 **77** PhillipMakin 1 72
(Paul Midgley) *hld up in midfield: stdy hdwy 2f out: sn rdn: no imp fnl f* 14/1

0/0 9 1 1/2 **Blue Bullet (IRE)**[22] 965 4-8-7 **71** oh1 PaulPickard 4 61
(Brian Ellison) *bhd: pushed along over 2f out: nvr able to chal* 33/1

22-0 10 shd **Ambitious Icarus**[8] 2136 5-9-1 **79** (e) RobbieFitzpatrick 8 68
(Richard Guest) *taken early to post: hld up: rdn and swtchd lft over 1f out: n.d* 20/1

0521 11 hd **Keep It Dark**[11] 2056 5-9-1 **79** BarryMcHugh 9 68
(Tony Coyle) *dwlt: bhd: rdn over 2f out: nvr rchd ldrs* 9/1[3]

0-04 12 1/2 **First In Command (IRE)**[19] 1789 9-9-0 **78** ow1 (t) StephenCraine 12 65
(Daniel Mark Loughnane) *hld up in midfield: shortlived effrt 2f out: sn btn* 50/1

-631 13 nk **Six Wives**[9] 2096 7-8-4 **75** (p) MatthewHopkins(7) 5 61
(Scott Dixon) *disp ld and clr of rest: rdn 2f out: wknd ins fnl f* 20/1

3-60 14 5 **Go Go Green (IRE)**[22] 1695 8-8-7 **71** oh2 GaryBartley 6 39
(Jim Goldie) *bhd: rdn along over 2f out: nvr on terms* 28/1

2U-0 15 1 1/4 **Hoofalong**[19] 1938 4-9-6 **84** JamesSullivan 3 47
(Michael Easterby) *hld up: rdn over 2f out: btn over 1f out: b.b.v* 14/1

59.48s (-0.12) **Going Correction** +0.15s/f (Good) 15 Ran SP% 120.8
Speed ratings (Par 105): **106,103,102,101,100 99,99,98,96,96 95,95,94,86,84**
CSF £88.34 CT £886.91 TOTE £7.50: £2.50, £4.70, £3.60; EX 109.40 Trifecta £972.20.
**Owner** Nice Day Out Partnership **Bred** Hellwood Stud Farm **Trained** Scarcroft, W Yorks

**FOCUS**
An above average sprint. They went hard up front, courtesy of habitual pacesetter Bronze Beau, but not many actually threatened to get competitive.

## 2351 MARION GIBSON BROWN MEMORIAL H'CAP 1m
4:00 (4:00) (Class 4) (0-85,83) 4-Y-O+ £4,690 (£1,395; £697; £348) Stalls Low

Form RPR

21-0 1 **Llanarmon Lad (IRE)**[21] 1724 5-9-4 **80** PaulPickard 6 91
(Brian Ellison) *in tch: hdwy to ld over 1f out: hrd pressed ins fnl f: kpt on wl towards fin* 16/1

30-1 2 1 1/4 **Escape To Glory (USA)**[26] 1610 6-9-5 **81** PaulMulrennan 14 89
(Michael Dods) *hld up: stdy hdwy whn nt clr run over 2f out to over 1f out: effrt and ev ch ins fnl f: hld nr fin* 10/1

4352 3 1 1/2 **Capaill Liath (IRE)**[14] 1957 6-8-12 **79** (p) ShaneGray(5) 7 84
(Kevin Ryan) *t.k.h: hld up in midfield: effrt on outside over 1f out: kpt on ins fnl f* 14/1

06-0 4 shd **Oddysey (IRE)**[14] 1956 5-9-7 **83** TomEaves 11 87
(Michael Dods) *hld up: hdwy whn nt clr run wl over 1f out: rdn and kpt on ins fnl f* 50/1

6-02 5 nse **Save The Bees**[8] 2131 6-8-13 **78** JasonHart(3) 12 82
(Declan Carroll) *w ldr: led over 2f out to over 1f out: kpt on same pce ins fnl f* 10/1

-001 6 hd **Justonefortheroad**[31] 1503 8-8-8 **75** (b) SammyJoBell(5) 10 79
(Richard Fahey) *hld up towards rr: pushed along and hdwy over 1f out: kpt on ins fnl f: nrst fin* 14/1

-011 7 2 1/2 **Eutropius (IRE)**[7] 2169 5-9-4 **80** BenCurtis 5 78
(Alan Swinbank) *hld up in midfield: effrt and pushed along over 2f out: outpcd fnl f* 3/1[1]

0054 8 1 **Mysterial**[5] 2215 4-8-7 **69** PJMcDonald 2 65
(Ruth Carr) *hld up in midfield on ins: rdn and outpcd over 2f out: kpt on fnl f: n.d* 7/1[2]

1032 9 1/2 **Piceno (IRE)**[11] 2054 6-8-11 **80** (p) MatthewHopkins(7) 13 75
(Scott Dixon) *cl up tl rdn and wknd over 1f out* 25/1

-533 10 2 **Lord Aeryn (IRE)**[21] 1733 7-9-7 **83** (p) TonyHamilton 1 73
(Richard Fahey) *prom: effrt and drvn over 2f out: wknd fnl f* 7/1[2]

0003 11 3/4 **Al Muheer (IRE)**[4] 2234 9-9-0 **76** (b) JamesSullivan 3 64
(Ruth Carr) *missed break: hld up: hdwy on outside over 2f out: hung lft and sn no imp* 8/1[3]

-000 12 1/2 **Rocket Ronnie (IRE)**[16] 1903 4-9-0 **76** AdrianNicholls 4 63
(David Nicholls) *bhd: drvn over 2f out: sn btn* 25/1

05-1 13 4 1/2 **Celtic Sixpence (IRE)**[18] 1845 6-9-1 **77** MichaelStainton 8 54
(Nick Kent) *t.k.h: led to over 2f out: wknd wl over 1f out* 16/1

50-0 14 2 3/4 **Blighty (IRE)**[20] 1762 4-9-3 **79** DanielTudhope 9 49
(David O'Meara) *in tch on outside: effrt and rdn over 2f out: wknd over 1f out* 14/1

1m 41.19s (1.09) **Going Correction** +0.30s/f (Good) 14 Ran SP% 120.7
Speed ratings (Par 105): **106,104,103,103,103 102,100,99,98,96 96,95,91,88**
CSF £165.29 CT £2364.29 TOTE £18.90: £5.20, £3.90, £4.00; EX 266.50 Trifecta £1173.70 Part won. Pool of £1564.99 - 0.01 winning units..
**Owner** Middleham Park Racing XLIII & Partner **Bred** Miss Sarah Thompson **Trained** Norton, N Yorks

**FOCUS**
A fairly useful handicap which was soundly run.

## 2352 MARKET CROSS JEWELLERS H'CAP 6f
4:35 (4:35) (Class 3) (0-90,90) 4-Y-O+ £7,439 (£2,213; £1,106; £553) Stalls High

Form RPR

0312 1 **Barkston Ash**[21] 1734 6-9-3 **89** (p) JasonHart(3) 8 104
(Eric Alston) *prom: drvn over 2f out: hdwy to ld ins fnl f: kpt on strly* 7/1[3]

06-4 2 3 1/4 **Robot Boy (IRE)**[33] 1492 4-9-4 **87** GrahamGibbons 2 92+
(David Barron) *in tch on outside: hdwy to ld over 1f out: sn rdn and edgd rt: hdd ins fnl f: one pce* 7/2[1]

040- 3 1 1/4 **Lewisham**[236] 6692 4-9-1 **84** AdrianNicholls 1 85
(David Nicholls) *bhd: gd hdwy on outside 2f out: chsng ldrs whn edgd rt ins fnl f: kpt on same pce* 40/1

000- 4 2 **Bop It**[204] 7495 5-9-3 **86** DanielTudhope 9 81
(David O'Meara) *hld up in tch: rdn and hdwy 2f out: no imp fnl f* 12/1

6-00 5 1 1/2 **Arctic Feeling (IRE)**[14] 1961 6-8-10 **79** TonyHamilton 11 69
(Richard Fahey) *bhd: rdn over 2f out: hdwy over 1f out: no imp fnl f* 16/1

-134 6 shd **Mutafaakir (IRE)**[8] 2136 5-8-13 **82** (p) JamesSullivan 5 71
(Ruth Carr) *led to over 1f out: rdn and wknd ins fnl f* 8/1

00-0 7 2 1/4 **Polski Max**[49] 1172 4-9-2 **90** SammyJoBell(5) 12 72+
(Richard Fahey) *hld up against stands' rail: effrt whn no room over 1f out: nt rcvr* 14/1

6-11 8 nk **My Name Is Rio (IRE)**[23] 1672 4-8-12 **81** PaulMulrennan 3 62
(Michael Dods) *trckd ldrs: effrt and rdn whn short of room briefly wl over 1f out: btn fnl f* 4/1[2]

15-1 9 8 **Apricot Sky**[23] 1678 4-9-2 **85** FergusSweeney 6 41
(Henry Candy) *t.k.h: in tch: effrt and rdn 2f out: wknd fnl f* 7/1[3]

3-56 10 2 1/4 **Space Artist (IRE)**[14] 1961 4-8-9 **78** RoystonFfrench 7 27
(Bryan Smart) *chsd ldrs: drvn over 2f out: wknd wl over 1f out* 33/1

1-02 11 nk **Chooseday (IRE)**[31] 1506 5-9-6 **89** (p) TomEaves 10 37
(Kevin Ryan) *cl up tl rdn and wknd wl over 1f out* 10/1

1m 12.52s (-0.18) **Going Correction** +0.15s/f (Good) 11 Ran SP% 113.0
Speed ratings (Par 107): **107,102,101,98,96 96,93,92,82,79 78**
CSF £30.34 CT £922.18 TOTE £6.70: £2.40, £1.50, £6.10; EX 37.40 Trifecta £1195.70 Part won. Pool of £1594.35 - 0.87 winning units..
**Owner** The Selebians **Bred** Jonathan Shack **Trained** Longton, Lancs

**FOCUS**
This tunred out to be a one-sided sprint.

## 2353 WEATHERBYS PRIVATE BANKING H'CAP 5f
5:10 (5:10) (Class 2) (0-100,100) 4-Y-O+ £12,938 (£3,850; £1,924; £962) Stalls High

Form RPR

30-0 1 **Noble Storm (USA)**[10] 2074 8-9-3 **99** JasonHart(3) 3 109
(Ed McMahon) *mde all: rdn and edgd rt ins fnl f: kpt on strly* 16/1

55-0 2 2 3/4 **Pearl Acclaim (IRE)**[13] 1975 4-8-11 **93** (p) RobertTart(3) 9 93
(Robert Cowell) *trckd ldrs: effrt and wnt 2nd over 1f out: edgd rt ins fnl f: kpt on same pce* 11/2[3]

1-56 3 3/4 **Da'Quonde (IRE)**[10] 2076 6-8-8 **87** PaulMulrennan 2 84
(Bryan Smart) *trckd ldrs on outside: effrt and rdn over 1f out: kpt on same pce ins fnl f* 11/1

50-0 4 1 1/4 **Confessional**[10] 2074 7-9-2 **95** (e) DavidAllan 1 88
(Tim Easterby) *midfield on outside: effrt and drvn over 2f out: rallied over 1f out: kpt on same pce fnl f* 20/1

10-0 5 1 3/4 **Hopes N Dreams (IRE)**[21] 1734 6-9-4 **97** BarryMcHugh 8 84
(Kevin Ryan) *taken early to post: in midfield: drvn along 1/2-way: no imp fr over 1f out* 20/1

-010 6 1/2 **Kimberella**[13] 1975 4-8-11 **90** AdrianNicholls 11 75
(David Nicholls) *cl up: rdn 1/2-way: no ex over 1f out* 13/8[1]

0/0- 7 3/4 **Waffle (IRE)**[478] 365 8-8-11 **97** PaulMcGiff(7) 7 79
(David Barron) *bhd and outpcd: sme hdwy over 1f out: nvr able to chal* 22/1

40-0 8 3 **Cosmic Chatter**[21] 1734 4-9-3 **96** GrahamGibbons 6 67
(David Barron) *towards rr: drvn 1/2-way: nvr on terms* 5/1[2]

10- 9 1 **Lover Man (IRE)**[238] 6623 5-9-7 **100** (t) TomEaves 10 68
(Keith Dalgleish) *trckd ldrs tl rdn and wknd over 1f out* 10/1

-300 10 1 **Doc Hay (USA)**[2] 2283 7-9-7 **100** PaulPickard 4 64
(Brian Ellison) *missed break and sn wl bhd: nvr on terms* 25/1

6/1- 11 4 **Ziggy Lee**[315] 4047 8-8-2 **86** ShaneGray(5) 5 36
(Geoffrey Harker) *anticipated s and missed break: bhd and sn outpcd: nvr on terms* 25/1

59.15s (-0.45) **Going Correction** +0.15s/f (Good) 11 Ran SP% 115.0
Speed ratings (Par 109): **109,104,103,101,98 97,96,91,90,88 82**
CSF £90.85 CT £1030.17 TOTE £12.60: £3.10, £1.90, £2.90; EX 138.50 Trifecta £548.40.
**Owner** Mrs R L Bedding **Bred** Brereton C Jones **Trained** Lichfield, Staffs

**FOCUS**
A decent sprint but few ever got competitive, the winner showing that he's still capable of smart form at the age of eight.

## 2354 YORKSHIRE OUTDOORS ADVENTURE EXPERIENCES MAIDEN STKS 1m 4f
5:45 (5:45) (Class 5) 3-Y-O+ £2,587 (£770; £384; £192) Stalls High

Form RPR

2 1 **Air Pilot**[22] 1691 5-10-0 0 GrahamGibbons 13 85+
(Ralph Beckett) *t.k.h early: prom: smooth hdwy to ld 2f out: rdn fnl f: kpt on: all out* 5/4[1]

44- 2 nse **Ruwasi**[194] 7732 3-8-11 0 DanielTudhope 9 84+
(James Tate) *hld up in midfield: effrt and hdwy 2f out: kpt on wl fnl f: jst failed* 6/1[3]

3 3 3 3/4 **Miss Tree**[18] 1841 3-8-3 0 IanBrennan(3) 5 73
(John Quinn) *led tl rdn and hdd 2f out: kpt on same pce fnl f* 14/1

0 4 3 1/2 **Rocket Ship**[19] 1809 3-8-11 0 ShaneKelly 3 72
(Sir Michael Stoute) *t.k.h early: cl up: effrt and rdn over 2f out: outpcd wl over 1f out* 6/1[3]

0 5 2 3/4 **Saddlers Mot**[14] 1960 10-9-2 0 GemmaTutty(7) 15 64?
(Karen Tutty) *hld up in midfield: effrt and pushed along 3f out: no imp fr 2f out* 66/1

5 6 9 **Mount Shamsan**[56] 1069 4-10-0 0 SebSanders 4 61
(William Haggas) *plld hrd: chsd ldrs: rdn and hung lft over 2f out: wknd wl over 1f out* 3/1[2]

5 7 nk **Ronald Gee (IRE)**[22] 1691 7-10-0 0 GaryBartley 6 54
(Jim Goldie) *prom: drvn and outpcd over 3f out: n.d after* 66/1

004- 8 4 1/2 **Acquaint (IRE)**[170] 8086 3-8-6 64 PaulPickard 11 41
(John Wainwright) *hld up: rdn over 3f out: nvr rchd ldrs* 33/1

0 **9** *1 1/4* **Lacocodanza**[14] 1960 5-9-9 0 AndrewElliott 14 40
(George Moore) *s.i.s: bhd: rdn over 3f out: nvr on terms* **100/1**

40 **10** *1 1/4* **Silver Craftsman (IRE)**[13] 1969 3-8-11 0 BenCurtis 7 42
(Alan Swinbank) *hld up: struggling over 3f out: sn n.d* **25/1**

0 **11** *2* **Fickle Feelings (IRE)**[14] 1960 3-8-6 0 RoystonFfrench 8 34
(David Barron) *hld up: pushed along 3f out: btn fnl 2f* **50/1**

00 **12** *1 1/2* **Yorkshire Monarch (IRE)**[14] 1960 3-8-8 0 JasonHart(3) 2 36
(Tim Easterby) *trckd ldrs tl rdn and wknd over 2f out* **66/1**

0 **13** *2 3/4* **Notaprayer**[40] 1344 3-8-11 0 (b[1]) DavidAllan 1 32
(Tim Easterby) *midfield: rdn and outpcd over 4f out: sn btn* **50/1**

**14** *30* **Brookes Boy (IRE)** 3-8-11 0 TomEaves 12
(Michael Dods) *s.i.s: bhd: lost tch 1/2-way: no ch whn rn v wd bnd over 3f out: t.o* **33/1**

2m 39.96s (3.76) **Going Correction** +0.30s/f (Good)
**WFA** 3 from 4yo+ 17lb **14** Ran SP% **123.8**
Speed ratings (Par 103): **99,98,96,94,92 86,86,83,82,81 80,79,77,57**
CSF £9.18 TOTE £2.50: £1.20, £1.60, £3.60; EX 9.50 Trifecta £81.00.
**Owner** Lady Cobham **Bred** Lady Cobham **Trained** Kimpton, Hants

**FOCUS**
Fairly useful efforts from the leading pair in a maiden which lacked depth. The field was well strung out in behind.

## 2355 DON'T MISS "CHAMPAGNE TUESDAY" 17TH JUNE H'CAP 1m
**6:20** (6:23) (Class 6) (0-65,65) 3-Y-O **£2,587** (£770; £384; £192) **Stalls** Low

Form RPR

00-5 **1** **Dutch Lady**[24] 1647 3-8-7 **51** PatrickMathers 14 61
(John Holt) *hld up in midfield: gd hdwy on outside over 2f out: edgd lft and led appr fnl f: hld on wl towards fin* **50/1**

14-4 **2** *1/2* **Starlight Serenade**[21] 1711 3-9-7 **65** SebSanders 7 74
(Ralph Beckett) *hld up on outside: hdwy over 2f out: edgd lft and ev ch ins fnl f: hld nr fin* **3/1**[1]

-424 **3** *3 1/4* **Tamayuz Magic (IRE)**[12] 2020 3-9-2 **60** (b) DanielTudhope 13 61
(Michael Easterby) *trckd ldrs: effrt over 2f out: ch appr fnl f: one pce last 150yds* **9/1**

5-44 **4** *1 1/4* **Kalahari Kingdom (IRE)**[7] 2165 3-9-2 **60** (p) TonyHamilton 4 59
(Richard Fahey) *unruly bef s: hld up in midfield: rdn over 2f out: hdwy and hung lft over 1f out: no imp fnl f* **7/2**[2]

2613 **5** *1* **It's All A Game**[7] 2165 3-8-11 **58** (b) JasonHart(3) 2 54
(Richard Guest) *hld up in midfield: rdn over 2f out: one pce fr over 1f out* **4/1**[3]

0310 **6** *nk* **Uplifted (IRE)**[23] 1657 3-8-13 **62** (b) ShaneGray(5) 8 58
(Kevin Ryan) *slt ld tl rdn and hdd appr fnl f: sn outpcd* **16/1**

003- **7** *nk* **Bertha Burnett (IRE)**[249] 6284 3-8-9 **53** JamesSullivan 5 48
(Brian Rothwell) *hld up: stdy hdwy over 2f out: pushed along over 1f out: kpt on: nvr nrr* **50/1**

0-00 **8** *hd* **Green Zone (IRE)**[23] 1657 3-9-4 **62** (p) AdrianNicholls 16 56
(Nigel Tinkler) *cl up: chal over 3f out to appr fnl f: sn no ex* **28/1**

00-0 **9** *9* **Weisse Girl**[18] 1847 3-8-8 **52** MichaelStainton 3 26
(Nick Kent) *midfield: drvn over 3f out: hung both ways on outside over 2f out: sn btn* **50/1**

-363 **10** *3/4* **Lynngale**[12] 2020 3-8-11 **60** JacobButterfield(5) 1 32
(Kristin Stubbs) *hld up in midfield: drvn and outpcd over 2f out: sn btn* **16/1**

6-65 **11** *1/2* **Sketch Map (IRE)**[16] 1904 3-9-1 **59** RussKennemore 9 30
(Jedd O'Keeffe) *prom: rdn and outpcd over 2f out: sn btn* **25/1**

040- **12** *nk* **Prostate Awareness (IRE)**[213] 7309 3-9-5 **63** PaddyAspell 15 33
(Patrick Holmes) *bhd: rdn along 1/2-way: nvr on terms* **16/1**

00-5 **13** *2* **Highway Pursuit**[40] 1344 3-8-12 **56** TomEaves 6 21
(George Moore) *dwlt: sn rdn along: no ch fr 3f out* **33/1**

6-66 **14** *19* **Lady Liz**[16] 1902 3-8-7 **51** AndrewElliott 11
(George Moore) *bhd: struggling 1/2-way: nvr on terms* **33/1**

004- **15** *2 3/4* **Slingsby**[197] 7662 3-8-13 **57** (b[1]) GrahamGibbons 17
(Michael Easterby) *t.k.h: prom tl rdn and wknd over 2f out* **10/1**

306- **16** *22* **Arabian Sunset (IRE)**[209] 7394 3-8-9 **53** RoystonFfrench 10
(Simon Waugh) *midfield: struggling 1/2-way: sn lost tch: t.o* **40/1**

1m 43.22s (3.12) **Going Correction** +0.30s/f (Good) **16** Ran SP% **125.5**
Speed ratings (Par 97): **96,95,92,91,90 89,89,89,80,79 78,78,76,57,54 32**
CSF £193.56 CT £1551.60 TOTE £64.80: £9.00, £1.30, £2.00, £1.60; EX 632.00 Trifecta £1404.20 Part won. Pool of £1872.38 - 0.01 winning units..Always Resolute was withdrawn. Price at time of withdrawal 28/1. Rule 4 does not apply.
**Owner** David Botterill & John Guest **Bred** D R Botterill **Trained** Peckleton, Leics

**FOCUS**
A run-of-the-mill handicap which was run at a sound pace.
T/Plt: £515.20 to a £1 stake. Pool of £77605.21 - 109.96 winning tickets. T/Qpdt: £337.00 to a £1 stake. Pool of £4144.84 - 9.10 winning tickets. RY

2356 - (Foreign Racing) - See Raceform Interactive

# PIMLICO (L-H)
Saturday, May 17

**OFFICIAL GOING: Dirt: fast; turf: good**

## 2357a PREAKNESS STKS (GRADE 1) (3YO) (DIRT) 1m 1f 110y(D)
**11:18** (12:00) 3-Y-O **£542,168** (£180,722; £99,397; £54,216; £27,108)

RPR

**1** **California Chrome (USA)**[14] 1964 3-9-0 0 (b) VictorEspinoza 3 125+
(Art Sherman, U.S.A) **1/2**[1]

**2** *1 1/2* **Ride On Curlin (USA)**[14] 1964 3-9-0 0 JRosario 10 121
(William Gowan, U.S.A) **103/10**[3]

**3** *6 1/2* **Social Inclusion (USA)**[42] 1326 3-9-0 0 (b) LContreras 8 108
(Manuel J Azpurua, U.S.A) **53/10**[2]

**4** *hd* **General A Rod (USA)**[14] 1964 3-9-0 0 (b) JJCastellano 2 108
(Michael J Maker, U.S.A) **201/10**

**5** *4 1/4* **Ring Weekend (USA)**[42] 3-9-0 0 (b) AGarcia 4 99
(H Graham Motion, U.S.A) **30/1**

**6** *1 3/4* **Pablo Del Monte (USA)**[35] 1464 3-9-0 0 JASanchez 9 95
(Wesley A Ward, U.S.A) **34/1**

**7** *1 3/4* **Dynamic Impact (USA)**[28] 3-9-0 0 MMena 1 92
(Mark Casse, Canada) **222/10**

**8** *nse* **Kid Cruz (USA)**[28] 3-9-0 0 (b) JPimentel 7 92
(Linda Rice, U.S.A) **123/10**

**9** *5* **Bayern (USA)**[20] 3-9-0 0 RosieNapravnik 5 81
(Bob Baffert, U.S.A) **129/10**

**10** *10* **Ria Antonia (USA)**[15] 1933 3-8-9 0 CHBorel 6 56
(Thomas Amoss, U.S.A) **189/10**

1m 54.84s (-0.75) **10** Ran SP% **126.3**
PARI-MUTUEL (all including 2 usd stake): WIN 3.00; PLACE (1-2) 3.00, 5.60; SHOW (1-2-3) 2.40, 3.80, 3.40; SF 18.20.
**Owner** Steven Coburn & Perry Martin **Bred** Perry Martin & Steve Coburn **Trained** USA

**FOCUS**
The second leg of the American Triple Crown and a race that set the record straight in many ways, for although some questioned the value of the Kentucky Derby form due to a slow winning time, there were no such doubts here as this was the co-fastest winning time for the Preakness since Curlin in 2007. The split times were (2f) 23.56, (4f) 46.85, (6f) 1.11.06 and (1m) 1.35.65.

# 2134 RIPON (R-H)
Sunday, May 18

**OFFICIAL GOING: Good (8.1)**
Wind: Breezy, half behind Weather: Sunny, warm

## 2358 WOODEN SPOON, THE CHILDREN'S CHARITY OF RUGBY MAIDEN STKS (DIV I) 6f
**2:10** (2:13) (Class 5) 2-Y-O **£3,234** (£962; £481; £240) **Stalls** High

Form RPR

**1** **Via Via (IRE)** 2-9-5 0 KierenFallon 6 82+
(Clive Brittain) *midfield: pushed along 1/2-way: hdwy and rdn over 1f out: led last 75yds: eased nr fin: cosily* **5/1**[3]

6 **2** *nk* **Roossey (IRE)**[22] 1712 2-9-5 0 LiamJones 2 81
(William Haggas) *prom: rdn along over 2f out: hdwy to ld over 1f out: hdd last 75yds: kpt on but a hld by cosy wnr* **7/4**[1]

23 **3** *8* **Kylach Me If U Can**[22] 1732 2-9-5 0 TomEaves 10 57
(Kevin Ryan) *led at decent gallop: rdn and hdd over 1f out: sn outpcd by first two* **3/1**[2]

**4** *3* **Snoway** 2-9-0 0 BarryMcHugh 3 43
(Tony Coyle) *dwlt: bhd and sn pushed along: hdwy over 1f out: kpt on: nvr able to chal* **66/1**

0 **5** *1/2* **Mister York**[32] 1505 2-9-5 0 DavidAllan 5 46
(Mel Brittain) *galloped rdrless to post: cl up tl rdn and wknd wl over 1f out* **25/1**

0 **6** *4* **Don't Tell Bertie**[13] 2014 2-9-0 0 JamesSullivan 9 29
(Tom Tate) *noisy in paddock and uns rdr at s: bhd and rn green: rdn along over 3f out: n.d* **20/1**

**7** *2* **Douglas Bank (IRE)** 2-9-5 0 DavidNolan 7 28
(Richard Fahey) *dwlt: sn pushed along towards rr: no imp fr 1/2-way* **8/1**

**8** *2* **Sakhee's Return** 2-9-5 0 DuranFentiman 8 22
(Tim Easterby) *s.i.s: bhd and outpcd: nvr on terms* **25/1**

**9** *1 1/2* **Ripon Rose** 2-9-0 0 PaulMulrennan 1 13
(Paul Midgley) *sn cl up on outside: rdn and wknd over 2f out* **28/1**

**10** *8* **Chollima** 2-9-5 0 GrahamGibbons 4
(Tim Easterby) *s.i.s: bhd and outpcd: no ch fr 1/2-way* **16/1**

1m 12.24s (-0.76) **Going Correction** -0.325s/f (Firm) **10** Ran SP% **112.4**
Speed ratings (Par 93): **92,91,80,76,76 70,68,65,63,52**
CSF £12.71 TOTE £7.20: £2.10, £1.10, £1.60; EX 15.20 Trifecta £53.80.
**Owner** Saeed Manana **Bred** Kenilworth House Stud **Trained** Newmarket, Suffolk

**FOCUS**
Rail on bend from back straight to home straight moved out 6yds, increasing distances on Round course by about 12yds. The going was good following watering and the jockeys said it was as described or "just on the easy side". The first division of the juvenile maiden developed into a match in the closing stages.

## 2359 WOODEN SPOON, THE CHILDREN'S CHARITY OF RUGBY MAIDEN STKS (DIV II) 6f
**2:40** (2:43) (Class 5) 2-Y-O **£3,234** (£962; £481; £240) **Stalls** High

Form RPR

533 **1** **Jersey Bull (IRE)**[13] 2007 2-9-2 0 WilliamTwiston-Davies(3) 3 74
(Mick Channon) *mde all: pushed along over 2f out: clr whn rdr dropped whip over 1f out: kpt on wl fnl f* **11/2**[3]

2 **2** *1/2* **Flying Machine (IRE)**[15] 1936 2-9-5 0 TonyHamilton 4 73+
(Richard Fahey) *dwlt: sn pushed along in midfield: effrt whn n.m.r 1/2-way: rallied to chse wnr ins fnl f: clsng at fin* **1/1**[1]

**3** *3 1/2* **Secret Brief (IRE)** 2-9-5 0 JoeFanning 9 62+
(Mark Johnston) *noisy in paddock: cl up tl hmpd and lost grnd over 4f out: rallied to chse wnr 2f out: sn edgd lft: kpt on same pce fnl f: bttr for r* **11/4**[2]

**4** *3/4* **Star Ascending (IRE)** 2-9-5 0 DaleSwift 8 60+
(Brian Ellison) *bhd and pushed along: hdwy on outside 2f out: kpt on fnl f: no imp* **66/1**

**5** *2 1/4* **Lucilla Aurelius (IRE)** 2-9-0 0 BarryMcHugh 2 48+
(Tony Coyle) *s.i.s: bhd and pushed along: drvn over 2f out: no imp over 1f out* **50/1**

5 **6** *1* **Mr Shekells**[19] 1859 2-9-5 0 GrahamGibbons 5 50
(Philip McBride) *upset in stalls: prom: drvn and outpcd over 2f out: n.d after* **20/1**

5 **7** *3 1/2* **Bobby's Flyer (IRE)**[18] 1879 2-9-5 0 DavidAllan 6 40
(Tim Easterby) *pressed wnr: drvn over 2f out: n.m.r wl over 1f out: sn btn* **14/1**

**8** *5* **Mr Christopher (IRE)** 2-9-5 0 DuranFentiman 7 25
(Noel Wilson) *s.i.s: bhd and green: no ch fr 1/2-way* **25/1**

326 **9** *7* **Just Marion (IRE)**[10] 2089 2-9-0 0 (v) StevieDonohoe 1
(David Evans) *bhd: drvn along over 3f out: btn fnl 2f* **18/1**

1m 13.2s (0.20) **Going Correction** -0.325s/f (Firm) **9** Ran SP% **116.0**
Speed ratings (Par 93): **85,84,79,78,75 74,69,63,53**
CSF £11.15 TOTE £6.30: £1.60, £1.02, £1.60; EX 10.20 Trifecta £35.40.
**Owner** Lakedale **Bred** Rathasker Stud **Trained** West Ilsley, Berks

**FOCUS**
The second leg of the maiden was run nearly a second slower (hand timing) than the first.

## 2360 PREMEX SERVICES STIRRING YORKSHIRE CHILDREN'S SMILES CHARITY (S) STKS 6f
**3:10** (3:10) (Class 6) 2-Y-O **£3,234** (£962; £481; £240) **Stalls** High

Form RPR

6 **1** **Honest Bob'S**[8] 2172 2-8-11 0 WilliamTwiston-Davies(3) 7 70+
(Mick Channon) *trckd ldrs against stands' rail: hdwy to ld over 1f out: pushed clr fnl f: readily* **5/2**[1]

034 **2** *6* **Kidmeforever**[8] 2172 2-8-4 0 PhilipPrince(5) 2 47
(J S Moore) *w ldr: rdn and upsides over 1f out: sn one pce* **4/1**[3]

6 **3** 3/4 **Hell For Leather**17 1900 2-8-9 0..............(v1) RyanWhile(5) 1 50
(Bill Turner) hung rt thrght: cl up tl rdn and outpcd over 1f out 7/1
50 **4** 1 1/4 **Reet Petite (IRE)**24 1656 2-8-6 0..............(p) ConnorBeasley(3) 5 41
(Michael Dods) wnt rt s: t.k.h: in tch: rdn over 1f out: sn outpcd 7/22
0 **5** nse **Rutland Panther**15 1955 2-8-9 0.............. JacobButterfield(5) 3 46
(Ollie Pears) led tl rdn and hdd over 1f out: sn no ex 10/1
01 **6** 5 **Tagtale (IRE)**17 1901 2-9-0 0..............(b) PatrickMathers 4 31
(Richard Fahey) blkd s: prom: drvn over 2f out: sn wknd 4/13
1m 13.29s (0.29) **Going Correction** -0.325s/f (Firm) **6** Ran SP% **112.4**
Speed ratings (Par 91): **85,77,76,74,74 67**
CSF £12.76 TOTE £4.10: £1.10, £2.90; EX 13.30 Trifecta £69.50.The winner was sold to Yvonne Lowe for £15,000. Rutland Pather was claimed by Declan Carroll for £6,000.
**Owner** P Trant **Bred** Norman Court Stud & Mike Channon B/S Ltd **Trained** West Ilsley, Berks
**FOCUS**
This juvenile seller was run slower than the two legs of the maiden that preceded it.

## 2361 C. B. HUTCHINSON MEMORIAL CHALLENGE CUP (FILLIES' H'CAP) 6f
**3:40** (3:40) (Class 3) (0-95,91) 3-Y-O- **£8,191** (£2,451; £1,225; £613; £305) **Stalls High**

Form RPR
25-0 **1** **Love Island**22 1734 5-9-11 91.............. GeorgeChaloner(3) 7 103
(Richard Whitaker) cl up: led wl over 1f out: rdn and hld on wl fnl f 4/12
52-1 **2** 3/4 **Bondesire**32 1506 4-9-13 90.............. DanielTudhope 3 100
(David O'Meara) led and sn crossed to stands' rail: rdn and hdd wl over 1f out: rallied: kpt on: hld towards fin 11/81
1141 **3** 1 1/4 **Iffranesia (FR)**19 1850 4-9-0 77..............(p) GrahamLee 8 83
(Robert Cowell) trckd ldrs: effrt and edgd rt over 1f out: kpt on same pce ins fnl f 6/13
105- **4** 3 3/4 **Augusta Ada**266 5787 3-8-7 79.............. PaulMulrennan 5 71
(Ollie Pears) hld up: n.m.r over 2f out: effrt and rdn over 1f out: kpt on fnl f: nt pce to chal 12/1
0-20 **5** 2 **Mayfield Girl (IRE)**15 1961 4-9-0 77.............. PJMcDonald 4 64
(Mel Brittain) cl up on outside: rdn over 2f out: wknd fnl f 10/1
0-00 **6** 1 3/4 **Khalice**23 1693 3-8-0 77.............. SammyJoBell(5) 2 57
(Richard Fahey) s.i.s: hld up in tch on outside: effrt over 2f out: wknd over 1f out 7/1
-150 **7** 3 3/4 **Burren View Lady (IRE)**30 1554 4-9-4 81..............(e) DavidAllan 6 51
(Tim Easterby) prom: drvn along over 2f out: wknd over 1f out 16/1
1m 10.38s (-2.62) **Going Correction** -0.325s/f (Firm)
**WFA** 3 from 4yo+ 9lb **7** Ran SP% **111.6**
Speed ratings (Par 104): **104,103,101,96,93 91,86**
CSF £9.41 CT £29.88 TOTE £8.60: £2.40, £1.40; EX 13.30 Trifecta £64.50.
**Owner** J Barry Pemberton & R M Whitaker **Bred** Hellwood Farm And J B Pemberton **Trained** Scarcroft, W Yorks
**FOCUS**
A decent fillies' handicap in which the top weights fought out the finish. The time was 1.86secs faster than the quickest of the three juvenile races that preceded it.

## 2362 RIPON, YORKSHIRE'S GARDEN RACECOURSE H'CAP 1m
**4:10** (4:11) (Class 2) (0-105,99) 4-Y-O+
**£15,562** (£4,660; £2,330; £1,165; £582; £292) **Stalls Low**

Form RPR
1 **1** **Capo Rosso (IRE)**43 1316 4-8-12 90.............. RichardKingscote 11 100
(Tom Dascombe) mde all: rdn and qcknd over 1f out: hld on wl fnl f 15/23
5313 **2** 1/2 **Bold Prediction (IRE)**15 1958 4-8-2 85.............. JoeyHaynes(5) 4 94
(K R Burke) chsd ldrs: effrt and wnt 2nd over 1f out: kpt on fnl f: hld towards fin 9/1
6451 **3** 1 1/4 **Dubai Dynamo**13 2017 9-8-6 84.............. PJMcDonald 1 90
(Ruth Carr) hld up: stdy hdwy and weaved through over 2f out: effrt over 1f out: kpt on fnl f: nt rch first two 8/1
45-0 **4** 4 **Two For Two (IRE)**15 1948 6-9-7 99.............. DanielTudhope 10 96
(David O'Meara) hld up and bhd: hdwy on outside over 2f out: sn rdn: kpt on fnl f: no imp 8/1
0-04 **5** 1/2 **King Of The Danes**13 2017 4-8-4 82.............. JoeFanning 5 78
(Mark Johnston) hld up: hdwy on outside 3f out: rdn and no imp over 1f out 14/1
6065 **6** 2 **Joe Eile (IRE)**15 1958 6-8-2 87.............. JoeDoyle(7) 12 78
(John Quinn) s.i.s: t.k.h in rr: rdn and effrt over 2f out: nvr able to chal 25/1
-010 **7** 1 1/2 **Trail Blaze (IRE)**15 1958 5-8-10 93..............(p) ShaneGray(5) 6 81
(Kevin Ryan) pressed wnr: rdn over 2f out: wknd over 1f out 20/1
0-00 **8** 3 1/4 **Norse Blues**15 1958 6-9-0 92.............. GrahamGibbons 9 72
(David Barron) t.k.h: prom: drvn over 2f out: wknd over 1f out 16/1
4-11 **9** 1/2 **Manchestar**27 1607 4-8-4 82.............. PatrickMathers 3 61
(Richard Fahey) taken early to post: t.k.h: in tch: rdn over 2f out: sn lost pl 7/21
0500 **10** 2 **Party Royal**10 2085 4-8-5 83.............. FrannyNorton 2 57
(Mark Johnston) t.k.h in midfield: struggling over 2f out: sn btn 16/1
00-2 **11** hd **Yeager (USA)**19 1834 4-9-3 95.............. GrahamLee 7 69
(Jeremy Noseda) hld up: rdn wl over 2f out: fnd little and sn btn 4/12
0-04 **12** shd **Osteopathic Remedy (IRE)**15 1958 10-8-11 92.... ConnorBeasley(3) 8 66
(Michael Dods) hld up: shortlived effrt on outside 3f out: sn btn 12/1
1m 38.2s (-3.20) **Going Correction** -0.325s/f (Firm) **12** Ran SP% **120.9**
Speed ratings (Par 109): **103,102,101,97,96 94,93,90,89,87 87,87**
CSF £74.99 CT £572.31 TOTE £11.90: £2.50, £2.50, £3.30; EX 81.50 Trifecta £718.00.
**Owner** Deva Racing Red Clubs Partnership **Bred** Michael Wiley **Trained** Malpas, Cheshire
**FOCUS**
Decent prize-money for this feature race and it produced a competitive contest.

## 2363 MIDDLEHAM TRAINERS ASSOCIATION H'CAP (BOBIS RACE) 1m 1f 170y
**4:40** (4:40) (Class 4) (0-80,79) 3-Y-O **£6,301** (£1,886; £943; £472; £235) **Stalls Low**

Form RPR
2410 **1** **Old Town Boy**14 1979 3-9-5 77.............. GrahamGibbons 1 88
(Philip McBride) t.k.h: prom: effrt and rdn over 2f out: led ins fnl f: kpt on wl 11/41
14-5 **2** 3/4 **New Street (IRE)**19 1861 3-9-2 74.............. DavidNolan 2 83
(Richard Fahey) hld up: stdy hdwy over 3f out: rdn to ld over 1f out: hdd and edgd rt ins fnl f: kpt on: hld nr fin 7/22
21 **3** 5 **Lord Of The Nile (IRE)**12 2053 3-9-7 79.............. DanielTudhope 6 78
(David O'Meara) t.k.h: pressed ldr: led 1/2-way: rdn and hdd over 1f out: sn outpcd by first two 5/1
05-1 **4** 1 1/2 **Dalaki (IRE)**24 1657 3-8-12 70.............. KierenFallon 7 66
(Clive Brittain) sn towards rr: rdn and hdwy on outside 3f out: edgd rt and outpcd wl over 1f out 4/13
-301 **5** 5 **Solo Hunter**20 1786 3-8-13 71..............(v) StevieDonohoe 4 56
(David Evans) led to 1/2-way: cl up: rdn and wknd 2f out 25/1
60-5 **6** 1 1/4 **Mustadrik (USA)**39 1401 3-8-7 65 oh1.............. JoeFanning 8 48
(J W Hills) in tch: drvn and outpcd over 2f out: n.d after 12/1
2-20 **7** 19 **Passionate Affair (IRE)**39 1391 3-9-0 72..........(tp) RichardKingscote 5 16
(Tom Dascombe) prom: drvn and outpcd over 3f out: sn btn 20/1
0-32 **8** 10 **Notebook**24 1662 3-9-3 75..............(p) LiamJones 3
(William Haggas) bhd: lost tch 1/2-way: sn btn 7/1
2m 1.2s (-4.20) **Going Correction** -0.325s/f (Firm) **8** Ran SP% **114.4**
Speed ratings (Par 101): **103,102,98,97,93 92,77,69**
CSF £12.49 CT £44.44 TOTE £4.20: £1.80, £1.30, £1.70; EX 19.30 Trifecta £156.90.
**Owner** Richard Wilson (Hertfordshire) **Bred** Wood Farm Stud (Waresley) **Trained** Newmarket, Suffolk
**FOCUS**
A fair but competitive-looking 3yo handicap that was fought out by the market leaders.

## 2364 BARRY TAYLOR MEMORIAL H'CAP 5f
**5:10** (5:10) (Class 5) (0-75,75) 4-Y-O+ **£4,528** (£1,347; £673; £336) **Stalls High**

Form RPR
2-02 **1** **Captain Royale (IRE)**17 1905 9-8-13 67..............(p) DaleSwift 2 76
(Tracy Waggott) prom: hdwy to ld 1f out: rdn and kpt on wl 22/1
0-34 **2** 1 1/4 **Indian Tinker**18 1878 5-8-13 67.............. GrahamLee 10 72
(Robert Cowell) chsd ldr: effrt and ev ch 1f out: kpt on same pce last 75yds 8/1
-533 **3** 3/4 **Adam's Ale**9 2136 5-9-3 71.............. PaulMulrennan 7 77+
(Paul Midgley) midfield: rdn over 1f out: effrt and disputing 4th pl whn bdly hmpd ent fnl f: kpt on wl under hands and heels riding towards fin: unlucky 9/41
00-1 **4** 3/4 **Shillito**34 1487 4-8-10 64.............. BarryMcHugh 6 63
(Tony Coyle) prom: effrt and rdn over 1f out: kpt on same pce fnl f 12/1
-566 **5** hd **Thatcherite (IRE)**12 2056 6-9-0 68..............(t) StephenCraine 12 66+
(Tony Coyle) dwlt: hld up: rdn and swtchd rt 1f out: kpt on: nvr able to chal 14/1
-603 **6** 2 1/2 **Haajes**2 2297 10-9-2 75..............(v) ShirleyTeasdale(5) 3 64
(Paul Midgley) bhd on outside: effrt u.p 1/2-way: no imp over 1f out 11/1
0512 **7** nse **Boxing Shadows**12 2056 4-8-12 66.............. KierenFallon 4 55
(Les Eyre) t.k.h: hld up: rdn whn n.m.r briefly over 1f out: sme late hdwy: n.d 5/12
-211 **8** 2 1/2 **Come On Dave (IRE)**20 1814 5-9-7 75.............. AdrianNicholls 9 55
(David Nicholls) walked early to post: led at decent gallop: rdn: edgd rt and hdd 1f out: sn edgd lft and wknd 10/1
3-00 **9** 1 **Holy Angel (IRE)**15 1961 5-9-5 73..............(e) RobertWinston 8 50
(Tim Easterby) missed break: bhd and outpcd: rdn and hung rt over 2f out: nvr rchd ldrs 15/23
0-00 **10** nk **Noodles Blue Boy**8 2167 8-8-13 72.............. JacobButterfield(5) 5 48
(Ollie Pears) bhd: drvn along 1/2-way: nvr on terms 16/1
5-00 **11** 2 **Rylee Mooch**8 2159 6-9-1 72..............(e) BillyCray(3) 11 40
(Richard Guest) prom: drvn over 2f out: disputing 4th pl and one pce whn bdly hmpd ent fnl f: nt rcvr 16/1
58.0s (-2.00) **Going Correction** -0.325s/f (Firm) **11** Ran SP% **118.2**
Speed ratings (Par 103): **103,101,99,98,98 94,94,90,88,88 84**
CSF £189.25 CT £574.12 TOTE £22.70: £4.70, £3.10, £1.70; EX 166.30 Trifecta £1445.20 Part won. Pool: £1,927.06 - 0.85 winning units..
**Owner** H Conlon **Bred** Skymarc Farm Inc **Trained** Spennymoor, Co Durham
**FOCUS**
Another competitive if ordinary sprint with a couple of hard-luck stories.

## 2365 SIS LIVE MAIDEN STKS 1m 1f
**5:40** (5:41) (Class 5) 3-Y-O **£3,234** (£962; £481; £240) **Stalls Low**

Form RPR
2-3 **1** **Art Of War (IRE)**39 1394 3-9-5 0.............. RichardKingscote 7 91
(Tom Dascombe) hld up in tch: stdy hdwy over 3f out: effrt and drvn 2f out: styd on wl fnl f to ld towards fin 5/41
5-6 **2** shd **Almashooqa (USA)**37 1424 3-9-0 0.............. DaneO'Neill 8 86
(Roger Varian) pressed ldr: rdn wl over 2f out: led over 1f out: edgd rt: kpt on wl fnl f: hdd towards fin 9/42
52-6 **3** 7 **Makruma**37 1423 3-9-0 80.............. GrahamGibbons 4 73
(J W Hills) led at ordinary gallop: rdn and hdd over 1f out: sn outpcd by first two 4/13
05 **4** 5 **Mendelita**15 1959 3-9-0 0.............. TonyHamilton 3 62+
(Richard Fahey) t.k.h: hld up in tch: effrt whn nt clr run and swtchd lft over 2f out: sn no imp 25/1
0- **5** 1 1/2 **Walk Like A Giant**223 7061 3-9-5 0.............. JamesSullivan 2 61
(Tom Tate) chsd ldrs: rdn 3f out: outpcd fr 2f out 28/1
**6** 3 1/4 **Yawail** 3-9-0 0.............. BarryMcHugh 5 49
(Brian Rothwell) s.i.s: hld up: rdn along 3f out: btn fnl 2f 50/1
**7** 3 3/4 **Lacerta** 3-9-5 0.............. PJMcDonald 6 46
(Micky Hammond) s.i.s: hld up: rdn over 3f out: sn btn 50/1
0 **8** 3 **Special Fighter (IRE)**11 2075 3-9-5 0.............. JoeFanning 9 39
(Mark Johnston) chsd ldrs tl rdn: hung rt and wknd over 2f out 8/1
1m 52.71s (-1.99) **Going Correction** -0.325s/f (Firm) **8** Ran SP% **117.5**
Speed ratings (Par 99): **95,94,88,84,82 80,74,76**
CSF £4.28 TOTE £2.20: £1.10, £1.60, £1.70; EX 3.80 Trifecta £12.90.
**Owner** David Ward & Laurence Bellman **Bred** Irish National Stud **Trained** Malpas, Cheshire
**FOCUS**
A fair maiden.
T/Jkpt: Not won. T/Plt: £25.30 to a £1 stake. Pool: £102,591.17. 2,954.02 winning tickets.
T/Qpdt: £25.40 to a £1 stake. Pool: £4,752.91. 138.30 winning tickets. RY

# 1455 NAVAN (L-H)
Sunday, May 18
**OFFICIAL GOING: Good to firm changing to good after race 1 (2:05)**

## 2370a COOLMORE VINTAGE CROP STKS (GROUP 3) 1m 6f
**4:05** (4:05) 4-Y-O+ **£35,208** (£10,291; £4,875; £1,625)

RPR
**1** **Leading Light (IRE)**224 7058 4-9-8 118..............(p) JosephO'Brien 3 121+
(A P O'Brien, Ire) chsd ldr in 3rd tl prog into 2nd 2f out: styd on wl to ld ent fnl f: sn drew clr 1/11
**2** 3 **Royal Diamond (IRE)**211 7363 8-9-6 114.............. NGMcCullagh 4 115
(J P Murtagh, Ire) t.k.h and sn clr ldr: kpt to far side in st and styd on wl tl hdd ent fnl f: sn no ch w wnr 7/13

**3** ½ **Pale Mimosa (IRE)**[211] 7363 5-9-0 109 .............................. PatSmullen 2 108
(D K Weld, Ire) *chsd clr ldr in 2nd tl dropped to 3rd 2f out: kpt on same pce ins fnl f* **2/1**[2]

**4** 8½ **Sir Ector (USA)**[22] 1750 7-9-3 103 ..................................(b) ChrisHayes 5 99
(J J Lambe, Ire) *racd in 4th: rdn along under 4f out: nt qckn over 2f out: sn one pce* **16/1**

**5** hd **Leah Claire (IRE)**[28] 6886 8-9-0 101 .............................. DannyGrant 7 96
(W McCreery, Ire) *hld up in rr tl kpt on fr under 2f out: nt trble principals* **50/1**

**6** 6 **Saddler's Rock (IRE)**[50] 1177 6-9-3 110 ........................ WayneLordan 6 91
(John M Oxx, Ire) *racd in 5th tl pushed along 4f out and sn no imp: dropped to rr 2f out* **10/1**

3m 3.89s (-11.11) **6** Ran SP% **112.8**
CSF £9.03 TOTE £2.00: £1.02, £2.60; DF 7.60 Trifecta £7.20.
**Owner** Derrick Smith & Mrs John Magnier & Michael Tabor **Bred** Lynch-Bages Ltd **Trained** Cashel, Co Tipperary

**FOCUS**
The first running of this race as a Group 3 having been elevated from Listed level. It certainly warranted that status given the strength of the field with last year's St Leger winner, the 2012 Irish St Leger winner and a filly rated 109 locking horns. It was a contest that could potentially shape the landscape for the staying events later in the summer.

2371 - 2373a (Foreign Racing) - See Raceform Interactive

# 2191 CAPANNELLE (R-H)
## Sunday, May 18

**OFFICIAL GOING: Turf: good**

## 2374a PREMIO CARLO D'ALESSIO (GROUP 3) (4YO+) (TURF) 1m 4f
**2:05** (12:00) 4-Y-O+ **£23,333** (£10,266; £5,600; £2,800)

RPR

**1** **Orsino (GER)**[196] 7724 7-8-9 0 ...................................... MircoDemuro 9 106
(R Rohne, Germany) *mde all: qckd clr appr fnl f: r.o: v comf* **23/20**[1]

**2** 3 **Keshiro (IRE)**[42] 4-8-9 0 ...................................... CristianDemuro 1 101
(Stefano Botti, Italy) *trckd ldng pair: 4th and travelling wl enough 1/2-way: gd prog to chse ldr fr 2f out: kpt on ins fnl f: nt pce of wnr* **16/5**[2]

**3** ¾ **Wild Wolf (IRE)**[189] 5-8-9 0 ...............................(b) UmbertoRispoli 7 100
(Stefano Botti, Italy) *hld up in rr: hdwy over 2f out: styd on ins fnl f: nvr on terms w ldrs* **43/5**

**4** 1¼ **Pattaya (ITY)**[7] 2191 6-8-9 0 ...................................... AndreaAtzeni 3 98
(Stefano Botti, Italy) *midfield: tk clsr order over 2f out: kpt on u.p fnl f: nt pce to chal* **16/5**[2]

**5** 2½ **Principiante**[189] 4-8-9 0 ...................................... LManiezzi 5 94
(Marco Gasparini, Italy) *midfield: rdn and nt qckn ent fnl 2f: one pce fr over 1f out* **103/10**

**6** 2½ **Frankenstein**[42] 7-8-9 0 ...................................... FrankieDettori 8 90
(B Grizzetti, Italy) *settled towards rr: rdn 3f out: brief effrt over 1 1/2f out: sn btn: eased ins fnl 150yds* **7/2**[3]

**7** 5 **Storming Loose**[28] 1603 7-8-9 0 ...................................... DarioVargiu 6 82
(B Grizzetti, Italy) *towards rr: rdn and no real imp fr 2f out: nvr in contention* **19/2**

**8** 8 **Demeteor (ITY)**[7] 2191 4-8-9 0 ...................................... GMarcelli 4 69
(R Menichetti, Italy) *prom: disp 2nd on outer at 1/2-way: rdn to chse ldr 3f out: sn btn and wknd ins fnl 2f: eased fnl 150yds* **84/10**

**9** nk **Futuro Anteriore (IRE)**[126] 4-8-9 0 ...................................... GFormica 2 69
(L la Strina, Italy) *tk a t.k.h: trckd ldr: rdn and nt qckn fr 3f out: one pce tl wknd over 1f out* **55/1**

2m 28.03s (0.83) **9** Ran SP% **157.6**
WIN (incl. 1 euro stake): 2.16. PLACES: 1.38, 2.20, 2.40. DF: 8.36.
**Owner** Kurt Fekonja **Bred** Gestut Moenchhof **Trained** Germany

## 2375a PREMIO TUDINI (GROUP 3) (3YO+) (TURF) 6f
**3:50** (12:00) 3-Y-O+ **£23,333** (£10,266; £5,600; £2,800)

RPR

**1** **Omaticaya (IRE)**[35] 1477 3-8-2 0 ...................................... GFois 7 99
(V Fazio, Italy) *mde all: drvn clr ent fnl f: a holding runner-up readily* **39/10**[1]

**2** nk **Rosendhal (IRE)**[13] 7-9-4 0 ...................................... SSulas 16 107
(G Botti, France) *chsd ldrs on outer: wnt after wnr ent fnl f: kpt on wl u.p but a hld* **22/5**[2]

**3** 1¼ **Pride And Joy (IRE)**[140] 5-9-0 0 ...................................... DPerovic 15 99
(Riccardo Santini, Italy) *midfield on outer: hdwy over 1 1/2f out: chsd ldrs ent fnl f: r.o u.p: nvr quite on terms* **99/10**

**4** ½ **Elettrotreno (IRE)**[22] 4-9-2 0 ...................................... DarioVargiu 6 99
(A Giorgi, Italy) *a.p on rail: rdn sn after 1/2-way: styd on u.p fnl f: jst missed 3rd* **68/10**

**5** nk **Bettolle (ITY)**[35] 1477 5-8-10 0 ...................................... StefanoLandi 10 92
(Silvia Casati, Italy) *w.w in tch: rdn and short of room 2f out: swtchd ins and styd on fnl f: nt pce to chal* **128/10**

**6** nk **Clorofilla (IRE)**[35] 1477 4-9-1 0 ...................................... LManiezzi 11 96
(Marco Gasparini, Italy) *chsd ldrs: 2nd and ev ch appr 1f out: fdd u.p ins fnl f* **29/4**

**7** nk **Art Of Dreams (FR)**[22] 5-9-0 0 ...................................... FrankieDettori 4 95
(B Grizzetti, Italy) *hld up towards rr: sme hdwy fnl f: nvr trbld ldrs* **61/10**

**8** 2 **Gordol Du Mes (USA)**[266] 5806 4-9-0 0 ...................................... GBietolini 2 88
(Gianluca Bietolini, Italy) *towards rr: rdn and sme hdwy fr 1 1/2f out: nvr trbld ldrs* **183/10**

**9** 1 **Le Vie Infinite (IRE)**[364] 2491 7-9-0 0 ...................................... MircoDemuro 9 85
(R Brogi, Italy) *a towards rr: no real imp fnl 2f* **462/100**[3]

**10** ½ **Axa Reim (IRE)**[401] 5-9-0 0 ...................................... CDiNapoli 13 83
(F Boccardelli, Italy) *chsd ldrs: rdn and wknd fr over 1 1/2f out* **80/1**

**11** 2½ **Mord (ITY)** 3-8-5 0 ...................................... CristianDemuro 5 73
(E Botti, Italy) *midfield: rdn and shortlived effrt 2f out: sn btn* **61/10**

**12** 2 **Eldo River (IRE)**[22] 5-9-0 0 ...................................(b) PBorrelli 14 69
(Luigi Biagetti, Italy) *prom on outer: rdn and nt qckn 2f out: sn wknd* **174/10**

**13** hd **Universo Star (IRE)**[35] 1477 4-8-10 0 ...................................... MEsposito 3 64
(A Marcialis, Italy) *a among bkmarkers: rdn and btn fr 2f out* **6/1**

**14** 2½ **Chiara Wells (IRE)**[22] 5-8-10 0 ...................................... SBasile 8 56
(A Floris, Italy) *midfield: rdn and no hdwy 1/2-way: bhd fr 2f out* **40/1**

**15** 3 **Ridge Racer (ITY)** 3-8-7 0 ...................................... CFiocchi 12 51
(A Peraino, Italy) *a towards rr: no imp fr 1/2-way* **61/10**

1m 7.96s (-2.34)
**WFA** 3 from 4yo+ 9lb **15** Ran SP% **168.9**
WIN (incl. 1 euro stake): 4.88. PLACES: 2.49, 2.08, 4.26. DF: 33.89.
**Owner** Manila Illuminati **Bred** Epona Bloodstock Ltd **Trained** Italy

## 2376a DERBY ITALIANO (GROUP 2) (3YO COLTS & FILLIES) (TURF) 1m 3f
**5:10** (12:00) 3-Y-O **£291,666** (£128,333; £70,000; £35,000)

RPR

**1** **Dylan Mouth (IRE)**[28] 3-9-2 0 ...................................... FabioBranca 5 111
(Stefano Botti, Italy) *disp 3rd on inner: chsd ldrs 2f out: r.o wl u.p fnl f: led 50yds out: won gng away* **21/10**[1]

**2** 1½ **Autre Qualite (IRE)**[21] 3-9-2 0 ...................................... AndreaAtzeni 7 108
(Stefano Botti, Italy) *led: set decent pce: kicked clr over 2f out: r.o fnl f: hdd last 50yds: no ex* **21/10**[1]

**3** 2 **Oil Of England (GER)**[17] 3-9-2 0 ...................................... ThierryThulliez 9 104
(M Figge, Germany) *trckd ldr: rdn and no imp fr 2f out: kpt on u.p fnl f to hold 3rd* **61/10**

**4** ½ **Steaming Kitten (USA)**[21] 3-9-2 0 ...................................... GBietolini 1 104
(Gianluca Bietolini, Italy) *disp 6th on inner: swtchd outside and hdwy 2 1/2f out: styd on u.p fnl f: nt pce to chal* **61/10**

**5** ¾ **Dark Sea (IRE)**[26] 1640 3-9-2 0 ...................................... CristianDemuro 11 102
(G Botti, France) *midfield: rdn and briefly short of room 2f out: styd on wl u.p fnl f: nrest at fin* **59/10**

**6** ½ **Bertinoro (IRE)**[198] 7678 3-9-2 0 ...................................... CFiocchi 4 101
(Stefano Botti, Italy) *midfield on inner: rdn to chse ldng gp 1 1/2f out: kpt on ins fnl f: nt pce to trble ldrs* **189/10**

**7** 1½ **Salford Secret (IRE)**[21] 1779 3-9-2 0 ...................................... DPerovic 10 99
(Riccardo Santini, Italy) *hld up in midfield: rdn and kpt on fnl f: nt pce to trble ldrs* **48/10**[3]

**8** 3 **Hoovergetthekeys (USA)**[21] 1779 3-9-2 0 ...................................... MircoDemuro 14 93
(M Narduzzi, Italy) *hld up in rr: hdwy 2 1/2f out: sn rdn: btn appr fnl f* **111/10**

**9** 2 **Collateral Risk (IRE)**[21] 1779 3-9-2 0 ...................................... UmbertoRispoli 6 90
(Stefano Botti, Italy) *disp 6th on inner: rdn and effrt between horses 2f out: sn btn* **21/10**[1]

**10** ¾ **Grey Greezly (FR)**[21] 1779 3-9-2 0 ...................................... DarioVargiu 8 88
(B Grizzetti, Italy) *disp 3rd on outer: lost pl 2 1/2f out: sn btn* **224/10**

**11** hd **Svatantra**[21] 3-9-2 0 ...................................... AntonioFresu 2 88
(L Riccardi, Italy) *a among bkmarkers: nvr in contention* **47/1**

**12** hd **Sopran Nicolo (IRE)** 3-9-2 0 ...................................... FrankieDettori 15 87
(B Grizzetti, Italy) *w.w in tch: 5th: rdn and no imp 3 1/2f out: sn btn* **289/100**[2]

**13** 1¼ **Alegro (ITY)**[28] 3-9-2 0 ...................................... MEsposito 3 85
(Stefano Botti, Italy) *w.w towards rr: no imp fnl 2f* **90/1**

**14** nk **Slowpoke (IRE)**[42] 3-9-2 0 ...................................... FrancescoDettori 13 85
(L Riccardi, Italy) *a towards rr: nvr figured* **47/1**

**15** 5 **Ratmansky (ITY)**[198] 7678 3-9-2 0 ...................................... SDiana 12 76
(F Camici, Italy) *hld up towards rr: rdn and btn over 2f out*

2m 17.63s (137.63) **15** Ran SP% **205.2**
WIN (incl. 1 euro stake): 3.09 (Dylan Mouth combined with Autre Qualite & Collateral Risk)PLACES: 1.82, 3.33, 2.56. DF: 25.00.
**Owner** Scuderia Effevi SRL **Bred** Azienda Agricola Mariano **Trained** Italy

# 2001 COLOGNE (R-H)
## Sunday, May 18

**OFFICIAL GOING: Turf: good**

## 2377a MEHL MULHENS-RENNEN - GERMAN 2000 GUINEAS (GROUP 2) (3YO COLTS & FILLIES) (TURF) 1m
**4:20** (12:00) 3-Y-O **£83,333** (£25,000; £10,833; £5,833; £2,500)

RPR

**1** **Lucky Lion**[21] 1781 3-9-2 0 ...................................... IoritzMendizabal 2 110
(Andreas Lowe, Germany) *midfield on inner: prog to ld 3f out: rdn and 2 l clr appr fnl f: drvn clr: readily* **19/10**[2]

**2** 1½ **Nordico (GER)**[21] 1781 3-9-2 0 ...................................... FrederikTylicki 4 106
(Mario Hofer, Germany) *w.w in midfield: hdwy to chse ldr over 2f out: kpt on u.p fnl f but readily outpcd by wnr* **43/5**

**3** 2½ **Stillman (FR)**[21] 1781 3-9-2 0 ...................................... EddyHardouin 5 101
(Mario Hofer, Germany) *w.w towards rr: hdwy on inner over 2 1/2f out: 3rd and styng on u.p 1 1/2f out: one pce fnl f* **171/10**

**4** nk **Andoyas (GER)**[21] 1781 3-9-2 0 ...................................... OlivierPeslier 8 100
(J Hirschberger, Germany) *chsd ldrs on outer: carried v wd fnl bnd into st and relegated to last: hrd rdn and hdwy on outer over 1 1/2f out: styd on u.p fnl f: nt rch ldrs* **8/5**[1]

**5** nse **Cordite (IRE)**[32] 1516 3-9-2 0 ...................................... AndrewMullen 1 100
(Michael Appleby) *led on rail: c v wd and hdd fnl bnd 3f out: 5th and rallied whn rousted along over 2f out: no imp fnl f and lost 4th cl home* **14/1**

**6** 3½ **Kerosin (GER)**[21] 1781 3-9-2 0 ...................................... FilipMinarik 6 92
(Jean-Pierre Carvalho, Germany) *midfield: rdn and no imp over 2f out: sn btn* **63/10**[3]

**7** 2 **Sahand (IRE)**[21] 3-9-2 0 ...................................... MartinLane 9 87
(J Hirschberger, Germany) *towards rr: rdn and effrt over 2f out: sn btn* **45/1**

**8** nse **Wilshire Boulevard (IRE)**[22] 3-9-2 0 ...................................... OliverWilson 3 87
(Bettina Andersen, Denmark) *t.k.h: chsd ldr on inner: rdn and nt qckn 2f out: wknd wl over 1f out* **94/10**

**9** 7 **Rock Of Cashel (GER)**[21] 1781 3-9-2 0 ...................................... MSuerland 10 71
(Frau Erika Mader, Germany) *a towards rr: nvr got into the r* **224/10**

**10** shd **Nadelwald**[21] 1781 3-9-2 0 ...................................... AHelfenbein 7 71
(P Schiergen, Germany) *chsd ldr: carried v wd fnl bnd into st: nt rcvr* **169/10**

1m 35.17s (-3.22) **10** Ran SP% **130.9**
WIN (incl. 10 euro stake): 29.PLACES: 14, 21, 35. SF: 142.
**Owner** Gestut Winterhauch **Bred** Stall Parthenaue **Trained** Germany



The Form Book, Raceform Ltd, Newbury, RG14 5SJ

# KRANJI (L-H)

Sunday, May 18

**OFFICIAL GOING: Turf: good**

## 2378a KRISFLYER INTERNATIONAL SPRINT (GROUP 1) (3YO+) (TURF) 6f

12:50 (12:00) 3-Y-O+

**£272,727** (£96,889; £49,043; £23,923; £9,569; £4,784)

RPR

1 **Lucky Nine (IRE)**21 7-9-0 0 BrettPrebble 1 121
(C Fownes, Hong Kong) *chsd ldrs on inner: pushed along and angled rt for clr run 2f out: rdn to chal over 1f out: led ent fnl f: edgd lft to rail u.p but r.o strly and asserted: v readily* **11/5**2

2 2 1/2 **Emperor Max (AUS)**21 5-9-0 0 (b) ZacPurton 4 113
(S Gray, Singapore) *sn pressing ldr on outer: w ldr gng wl 2f out: rdn over 1f out: hdd ent fnl f: r.o wl for 2nd but readily outpcd by wnr* **58/10**

3 2 1/4 **Zac Spirit (AUS)**21 5-9-0 0 AlanMunro 2 106
(Cliff Brown, Singapore) *chsd ldrs on outer: rdn 2f out: cl up and ev ch over 1f out: readily outpcd by wnr ins fnl f: kpt on for wl hld 3rd* **13/5**3

4 1 1/4 **Captain Obvious (AUS)**44 9-9-0 0 (t) OChavez 7 102
(Hai Wang Tan, Singapore) *broke wl and led on rail: rdn over 1f out and hdd ent fnl f: no ex and fdd* **48/1**

5 nk **Sterling City (AUS)**50 1180 6-9-0 0 JoaoMoreira 9 101
(J Moore, Hong Kong) *pushed along to go forward but unable to go early gallop: niggled along in midfield on outer: rdn into st: nt qckn u.p: kpt on same pce and nvr able to chal* **7/5**1

6 1 1/2 **El Padrino (NZ)**21 6-9-0 0 (bt) DannyBeasley 6 96
(Hai Wang Tan, Singapore) *sltly slow to stride and pushed along in rr: detached 1/2-way: rdn and stl last whn fanned wd into st: kpt on and sme late hdwy to go 6th cl home but nvr a factor* **30/1**

7 3/4 **Slew Of Lode (ARG)**21 5-9-0 0 (t) JohnPowell 3 94
(Patrick Shaw, Singapore) *towards rr on inner: rdn over 2f out: swtchd off rail into st: sn outpcd and btn: nvr a factor* **32/1**

8 nk **Goal Keeper (AUS)**21 6-9-0 0 BVorster 5 93
(T Kieser, Singapore) *midfield on inner: ct on heels and restrained after 2f: rdn into st: outpcd and btn ent fnl f: fdd* **57/1**

9 6 **Balmont Mast (IRE)**50 1180 6-9-0 0 (t) ColmO'Donoghue 8 73
(Edward Lynam, Ire) *towards rr on outer: rdn 1/2-way: outpcd and btn in st: dropped to last over 1f out: eased ins fnl f: nvr a factor* **62/1**

1m 8.15s (68.15) **9 Ran SP% 127.0**
PARI-MUTUEL (including 5 sgd stakes): WIN 16.00; PLACE 7.00, 10.00, 8.00; (including 2 sgd stakes): DF 22.00.
**Owner** Dr Chang Fuk To & Maria Chang Lee Ming Shum **Bred** Darley **Trained** Hong Kong

## 2379a SINGAPORE AIRLINES INTERNATIONAL CUP (GROUP 1) (3YO+) (TURF) 1m 2f

1:40 (12:00) 3-Y-O+

**£818,181** (£290,669; £147,129; £71,770; £28,708; £14,354)

RPR

1 **Dan Excel (IRE)**14 2004 6-9-0 0 (p) TommyBerry 1 119
(J Moore, Hong Kong) *pushed along to hold early position and trckd ldr on inner: clsd 4f out: angled off rail and rdn to chal 2f out: led jst over 1f out: styd on strly and asserted: v readily* **48/10**3

2 1 3/4 **Smoking Sun (USA)**21 1783 5-9-0 0 (b) StephanePasquier 11 116+
(P Bary, France) *hld up towards rr on outer: rdn over 2f out: styd on steadily in st and wnt 2nd ins fnl 100yds: no ch w wnr but nrst fin* **102/10**

3 1 1/2 **Military Attack (IRE)**21 1785 6-9-0 0 JoaoMoreira 10 113
(J Moore, Hong Kong) *pushed along early: sn midfield: clsd on outer into st: rdn 2f out: styd on same pce u.p and nvr able to chal* **4/5**1

4 2 **Tokei Halo (JPN)**50 1181 5-9-0 0 HirofumiShii 9 109
(Hisashi Shimizu, Japan) *sn led and crossed to rail: 5 l clr 1/2-way: clsd down 4f out: rdn and hdd over 1f out: sn no ex: fdd and lost 2 pls ins fnl 120yds* **4/1**2

5 1 1/4 **Side Glance**50 1183 7-9-0 0 JamieSpencer 7 106
(Andrew Balding) *sltly slow to stride and hld up in last: stl in rr whn fanned to outer and rdn 2f out: styd on and tk nvr nrr 5th fnl strides* **102/10**

6 nk **Si Sage (FR)**64 4-9-0 0 (t) DFlores 4 105
(Darrell Vienna, U.S.A) *hld up in midfield on outer: effrt to improve on wd outside fr 4f out: rdn 2f out: styd on same pce in st and nvr threatened* **30/1**

7 nk **Mull Of Killough (IRE)**31 1533 8-9-0 0 DamienOliver 3 105
(Jane Chapple-Hyam) *hld up in midfield on inner: angled out and rdn over 2f out: styd on same pce u.p in st and nvr able to chal* **29/1**

8 2 1/4 **Limario (GER)**50 1176 4-9-0 0 PatDobbs 12 100
(Doug Watson, UAE) *midfield in tch on outer: rdn over 2f out: hung lft u.p: no ex and btn ins fnl f: fdd* **47/1**

9 1 1/4 **Johnny Guitar (ARG)**21 5-9-0 0 BVorster 6 98
(Patrick Shaw, Singapore) *midfield in tch on inner: swtchd off rail and rdn over 2f out: hung lft bk to rail u.p over 1f out: no ex and btn ins fnl f: fdd* **30/1**

10 2 1/2 **City Lad (NZ)**21 6-9-0 0 KBSoo 8 93
(D Koh, Singapore) *t.k.h: hld up towards rr on inner: rdn over 2f out: outpcd and btn in st: nvr a factor* **106/1**

11 1 3/4 **Tropaios**21 5-9-0 0 ZacPurton 5 89
(M Freedman, Singapore) *midfield on inner: rdn 2f out: outpcd whn short of room on rail over 1f out: sn no ex and btn: wknd* **32/1**

12 1/2 **Wild Geese**21 5-9-0 0 (e) KA'isisuhairi 2 88
(S Burridge, Singapore) *broke wl and led early: trckd ldr on outer once hdd: rdn and lost pl over 2f out: sn btn: wknd and dropped to last* **28/1**

1m 59.07s (119.07) **12 Ran SP% 129.9**
PARI-MUTUEL (including 5 sgd stakes): WIN 29.00; PLACE 7.00, 14.00, 6.00; (including 2 sgd stakes): DF 82.00.
**Owner** David Philip Boehm **Bred** John Connaughton **Trained** Hong Kong

1725 # LEICESTER (R-H)

Monday, May 19

**OFFICIAL GOING: Good to firm (8.2)**
Wind: Light across Weather: Fine

## 2380 LEICESTERSHIRE AND RUTLAND HIGH SHERIFFS EBF STALLIONS MAIDEN STKS (BOBIS RACE) 5f 2y

6:15 (6:15) (Class 4) 2-Y-O **£4,528** (£1,347; £673; £336) **Stalls High**

Form RPR

0 1 **Lightning Stride**15 1977 2-9-5 0 JamieSpencer 5 82+
(Brian Meehan) *led 1f: chsd ldrs: rdn to ld wl ins fnl f: edgd rt: r.o* **10/1**

5 2 1 **Town Crier (IRE)**9 2151 2-9-5 0 RyanMoore 1 78
(William Haggas) *w ldr: led 4f out: rdn and hdd over 1f out: rallied to ld ins fnl f: sn hdd and unable qck* **5/4**1

3 3/4 **Fuwairt (IRE)** 2-9-5 0 FrankieDettori 3 77+
(Richard Hannon) *w ldrs: shkn up to ld over 1f out: hdd ins fnl f: hmpd sn after: styd on same pce* **7/2**3

4 1 1/4 **Belvoir Diva** 2-9-0 0 TedDurcan 4 66+
(Chris Wall) *hld up: hdwy over 1f out: styd on* **50/1**

5 2 3/4 **Offshore** 2-9-5 0 RichardKingscote 8 61
(James Tate) *rn green and hung rt in rr: rdn and r.o ins fnl f: nvr nrr* **14/1**

6 1/2 **Invincible Gold (IRE)** 2-9-5 0 DaneO'Neill 6 60
(Ed Walker) *prom: pushed along 1/2-way: styd on same pce appr fnl f* **3/1**2

05 7 11 **Jet Mate (IRE)**19 1872 2-9-5 0 (b) MartinDwyer 2 20
(William Muir) *prom: pushed along 1/2-way: sn wknd* **33/1**

59.91s (-0.09) **Going Correction** -0.25s/f (Firm) **7 Ran SP% 112.3**
Speed ratings (Par 95): **90,88,87,85,80 80,62**
CSF £22.27 TOTE £8.60: £4.00, £1.90; EX 21.20 Trifecta £73.20.
**Owner** Qatar Racing Limited **Bred** Newsells Park Stud **Trained** Manton, Wilts

**FOCUS**
False rail from top of hill on the back straight to the winning post increased distances on Round course by about 17yds. After a scorching day the ground was officially described as good to firm (watered) prior to the first race. The winner of the opening maiden for 2yos usually verges on Listed class with Smoothtalkinrascal being the standout in recent years. The winner left his debut nehind and the front four are the ones to concentrate on.

## 2381 LEICESTERSHIRE CARES (S) STKS 1m 60y

6:45 (6:48) (Class 6) 3-Y-O+ **£1,940** (£577; £288; £144) **Stalls Low**

Form RPR

0250 1 **Swift Cedar (IRE)**47 1234 4-9-7 76 (p) DaneO'Neill 10 68
(Jeremy Gask) *hld up: hdwy 2f out: rdn to ld and edgd rt ins fnl f: r.o* **11/4**1

1-05 2 1 3/4 **Kimbali (IRE)**9 2177 5-9-7 69 AdamKirby 3 64
(David Evans) *s.s: hld up: hdwy over 2f out: rdn over 1f out: ev ch ins fnl f: styd on same pce* **6/1**2

14-4 3 2 **Banreenahreenkah (IRE)**10 2135 4-9-2 56 (t) TomQueally 1 54
(Jennie Candlish) *led: rdn over 2f out: hdd and unable qck ins fnl f* **10/1**

4045 4 nk **Prime Exhibit**56 1083 9-9-7 69 (t) EoinWalsh(5) 7 64
(Daniel Mark Loughnane) *hld up: hdwy over 3f out: rdn over 2f out: styd on same pce fnl f* **8/1**

-5P4 5 3/4 **Botanist**21 1800 7-9-0 42 AlexHopkinson(7) 5 57
(Shaun Harris) *trckd ldrs: wnt 2nd over 5f out: rdn and ev ch over 1f out: no ex ins fnl f* **50/1**

4514 6 9 **Duly Acclaimed (IRE)**47 1239 3-7-11 57 CamHardie(7) 4 28
(J S Moore) *chsd ldr 3f: remained handy: rdn and ev ch over 1f out: wknd ins fnl f* **20/1**

050- 7 1 **Carazam (IRE)**246 6435 7-9-7 65 JamieSpencer 6 43
(Bernard Llewellyn) *prom: rdn over 2f out: wknd and eased fnl f* **7/1**3

030- 8 5 **Violet Plum**224 7071 4-8-9 50 CharlotteJenner(7) 9 18
(Laura Mongan) *chsd ldrs: rdn over 2f out: wknd over 1f out* **33/1**

9 3 **Franklin Nights** 4-9-7 0 SamHitchcott 2 16
(Polly Gundry) *s.i.s: hld up: rdn and wknd over 2f out* **50/1**

1m 44.52s (-0.58) **Going Correction** -0.025s/f (Good)
**WFA** 3 from 4yo+ 12lb **9 Ran SP% 85.3**
Speed ratings (Par 101): **101,99,97,96,96 87,86,81,78**
CSF £8.82 TOTE £3.50: £1.40, £1.50, £2.30; EX 11.70 Trifecta £57.40.Swift Cedar was bought by David Evans for 7000gns.
**Owner** Guy Carstairs & Hawk Racing **Bred** Carlingford Breeding Syndicate **Trained** Sutton Veny, Wilts

■ Stevie Thunder was withdrawn. Price at time of withdrawal 7-4. Rule 4 applies to all bets - deduction 35p in the pound.

**FOCUS**
Drama prior to this seller as the favourite Stevie Thunder refused to go into the stalls. Drama exiting the stalls also with Kimbali giving away several lengths after standing still as they opened. Weakish selling form.

## 2382 FORBES CHARITABLE FOUNDATION DESIGN FOR LIFE H'CAP 1m 1f 218y

7:15 (7:15) (Class 4) (0-80,82) 4-Y-O+ **£4,690** (£1,395; £697; £348) **Stalls Low**

Form RPR

0561 1 **Busatto (USA)**6 2234 4-9-9 **82** 6ex FrannyNorton 1 98
(Mark Johnston) *mde virtually all: qcknd over 3f out: rdn clr fnl f* **5/2**1

30-0 2 4 1/2 **Ogbourne Downs**42 1351 4-9-6 **79** RyanMoore 6 86
(Charles Hills) *hld up in tch: rdn over 2f out: chsd wnr fnl f: styd on same pce* **5/2**1

-642 3 2 **Perfect Cracker**61 1022 6-8-11 **75** RyanTate(5) 3 78
(Clive Cox) *trckd ldrs: plld hrd: wnt 2nd 2f out: sn rdn: no ex fnl f* **7/2**2

2334 4 7 **Arlecchino (IRE)**23 1724 4-8-10 **69** (b) TomQueally 2 59
(Ed McMahon) *chsd wnr tl rdn 2f out: wknd fnl f* **7/2**2

110- 5 14 **Bold Duke**219 7211 6-9-2 80 EoinWalsh(5) 4 43
(Edward Bevan) *hld up: pushed along and wknd over 2f out* **10/1**3

2m 5.96s (-1.94) **Going Correction** -0.025s/f (Good) **5 Ran SP% 110.7**
Speed ratings (Par 105): **106,102,100,95,84**
CSF £9.03 TOTE £3.90: £1.30, £1.60; EX 9.60 Trifecta £35.60.
**Owner** Sheikh Hamdan bin Mohammed Al Maktoum **Bred** Palides Investments N V Inc **Trained** Middleham Moor, N Yorks

**FOCUS**
A depleted field for this 1m2f handicap which saw an impressive winner. The form is rated around the runner-up.

## 2383 LEICESTERSHIRE ESTATE AGENTS WARNING ZONE H'CAP (BOBIS RACE) 7f 9y
**7:45** (7:46) (Class 4) (0-80,79) 3-Y-O **£4,690** (£1,395; £697; £348) **Stalls** High

Form RPR
10-0 **1** **Extremity (IRE)**[38] 1420 3-9-6 **78** MartinDwyer 2 87+
(Hugo Palmer) *trckd ldrs: plld hrd: wnt 2nd over 2f out: shkn up to ld over 1f out: edgd lft: pushed out* **9/4**[1]
14- **2** *1* **Bold Lass (IRE)**[208] 7463 3-9-4 **76** TedDurcan 6 82
(David Lanigan) *hld up in tch: plld hrd: rdn over 1f out: r.o* **9/2**[3]
23-6 **3** *shd* **Homestretch**[10] 2112 3-9-7 **79** DaneO'Neill 4 85
(Mick Channon) *led at stdy pce tl qcknd 1/2-way: rdn and hdd over 1f out: styd on* **7/1**
6-64 **4** *1 3/4* **Know Your Name**[23] 1723 3-9-0 **72** (v) AdamKirby 9 73
(David Evans) *hld up: rdn over 2f out: hdwy over 1f out: no imp ins fnl f* **14/1**
214- **5** *6* **Peak Royale**[228] 6972 3-9-5 **77** RyanMoore 5 63
(Richard Hannon) *trckd ldr tl rdn over 2f out: wknd fnl f* **3/1**[2]
336- **6** *1/2* **Royal Connection**[205] 7533 3-8-6 **71** CamHardie(7) 7 56
(Richard Hannon) *hld up: plld hrd: rdn over 2f out: wknd fnl f* **25/1**
1- **7** *3 1/4* **Continental Drift (USA)**[215] 7294 3-9-5 **77** FrankieDettori 8 53
(Roger Charlton) *trckd ldrs: racd keenly: rdn over 2f out: wknd over 1f out* **6/1**
1-0 **8** *3 1/2* **Don't**[40] 1381 3-9-2 **74** LemosdeSouza 1 41
(Luca Cumani) *plld hrd and prom: rdn over 2f out: wknd over 1f out* **25/1**

1m 24.12s (-2.08) **Going Correction** -0.25s/f (Firm) **8** Ran SP% **115.1**
Speed ratings (Par 101): **101,99,99,97,90 90,86,82**
CSF £12.82 CT £58.38 TOTE £3.80: £1.40, £2.60, £2.80; EX 15.10 Trifecta £28.60.
**Owner** Kremlin Cottage II **Bred** B Holland, S Hillen & J Cullinan **Trained** Newmarket, Suffolk

**FOCUS**
A fascinating handicap, the form of which should be followed. The favourite was successful for the sixth year in a row. The winner gave the impression he was better than the bare form.

## 2384 WATLING JCB RABI SUPPORTING FARMING FAMILIES MAIDEN STKS 5f 218y
**8:15** (8:20) (Class 5) 3-Y-O **£3,067** (£905; £453) **Stalls** High

Form RPR
44-2 **1** **Byron's Gold**[25] 1677 3-8-9 **72** RyanTate(5) 4 75
(Ben De Haan) *racd centre: led that pair: rdn to ld overall 1f out: r.o* **12/1**
05- **2** *1* **Major Jack**[278] 5399 3-9-5 0 AdamKirby 2 77
(Roger Charlton) *s.i.s: sn trcking wnr in centre: rdn and ev ch 1f out: styd on* **3/1**[3]
3-3 **3** *nk* **Al Senad**[35] 1486 3-9-5 0 JamieSpencer 6 76
(Peter Chapple-Hyam) *plld hrd: overall ldr stands' side: hung rt 2f out: sn rdn: hdd 1f out: styd on u.p* **6/1**
22-0 **4** *3* **Alys Love**[37] 1435 3-9-0 **82** MartinDwyer 5 61
(William Muir) *chsd ldr stands' side: rdn over 2f out: styd on same pce fnl f* **2/1**[1]
3-6 **5** *2* **Majestic Song**[10] 2125 3-8-11 0 RobertTart(3) 7 55
(James Toller) *racd stands' side: prom: rdn and edgd rt over 2f out: no ex fnl f* **16/1**
0- **6** *14* **Humour (IRE)**[368] 2401 3-9-5 0 DaneO'Neill 8 15
(Roger Varian) *s.i.s: sn chsng ldrs stands' side: rdn over 2f out: edgd rt and wknd wl over 1f out* **9/4**[2]
**7** *2 1/2* **Ach Alannah (IRE)** 3-9-0 0 StevieDonohoe 1
(James Unett) *s.s: racd stands' side: a in rr: wknd over 2f out* **66/1**

1m 11.4s (-1.60) **Going Correction** -0.25s/f (Firm) **7** Ran SP% **118.5**
Speed ratings (Par 99): **100,98,98,94,91 72,69**
CSF £50.28 TOTE £11.40: £4.90, £2.00; EX 66.00 Trifecta £204.70.
**Owner** Mrs D Vaughan **Bred** Mrs D Vaughan **Trained** Lambourn, Berks

**FOCUS**
No more than a fair 3yo sprint maiden, with the favourite disappointing. The winner backed up her Warwick run.

## 2385 HARLEY STAPLES CANCER TRUST H'CAP 1m 3f 183y
**8:45** (8:46) (Class 5) (0-70,69) 3-Y-O **£3,234** (£962; £481; £240) **Stalls** Low

Form RPR
-113 **1** **Jarlath**[21] 1812 3-9-0 **62** RyanMoore 2 72+
(Seamus Mullins) *led: hdd 9f out: chsd ldr tl led again over 2f out: rdn over 1f out: styd on* **6/4**[1]
4-50 **2** *1 1/2* **The Kid**[30] 1588 3-9-2 **64** (t) RichardKingscote 7 71
(Tom Dascombe) *a.p: rdn to chse wnr over 1f out: styd on* **11/4**[2]
5-56 **3** *2 1/4* **Mambo Rhythm**[19] 1880 3-9-2 **64** FrannyNorton 5 67
(Mark Johnston) *chsd ldrs: rdn over 2f out: styd on same pce fnl f* **7/1**
63-4 **4** *3* **Bajan Beauty (IRE)**[34] 1498 3-9-7 **69** JamieSpencer 4 67
(Charles Hills) *s.i.s and hmpd s: hld up: hdwy over 2f out: rdn over 1f out: no ex fnl f* **14/1**
23-5 **5** *2 3/4* **Avocadeau (IRE)**[14] 2013 3-9-4 **66** MartinDwyer 3 60
(William Muir) *prom: rdn over 2f out: sn outpcd* **16/1**
4363 **6** *nk* **Izbushka (IRE)**[10] 2132 3-9-0 **62** (vt) StevieDonohoe 1 55
(Ian Williams) *sn drvn along to chse ldrs: led 9f out: hung lft over 5f out: rdn and hdd over 2f out: wknd fnl f* **14/1**
-004 **7** *1 1/2* **Lord Brantwood**[16] 1947 3-9-1 **66** WilliamTwiston-Davies(3) 8 57
(Mick Channon) *hld up: hdwy over 2f out: rdn: hung rt and wknd over 1f out* **6/1**[3]

2m 34.83s (0.93) **Going Correction** -0.025s/f (Good) **7** Ran SP% **112.7**
Speed ratings (Par 99): **95,94,92,90,88 88,87**
CSF £5.52 CT £19.75 TOTE £1.70: £1.80, £2.30; EX 5.80 Trifecta £42.80.
**Owner** Phoenix Bloodstock **Bred** D & C Bloodstock **Trained** Wilsford-Cum-Lake, Wilts

**FOCUS**
A weak 3yo handicap and a comfortable winner, who resumed his progress.

T/Plt: £51.20 to a £1 stake. Pool: £68,041.76 - 969.27 winning units. T/Qpdt: £34.20 to a £1 stake. Pool: £5747.51 - 124.00 winning units. CR

# 1900 REDCAR (L-H)
### Monday, May 19

**OFFICIAL GOING: Good to firm (good in places; 8.6)**
Wind: light 1/2 behind Weather: fine

## 2386 FOLLOW REDCARRACING ON FACEBOOK AND TWITTER MEDIAN AUCTION MAIDEN STKS 6f
**2:20** (2:21) (Class 5) 2-Y-O **£2,587** (£770; £384; £192) **Stalls** Centre

Form RPR
**1** **Prophesize** 2-9-5 0 PatCosgrave 5 80+
(Noel Quinlan) *trckd ldrs: led over 1f out: edgd rt ins fnl f: styd on strly: readily* **11/2**[3]
**2** *2 3/4* **Caprior Bere (FR)** 2-9-5 0 PhillipMakin 12 71
(K R Burke) *w ldrs: styd on same pce fnl f: no imp* **11/4**[1]
5 **3** *3/4* **Ythan Waters**[33] 1505 2-9-5 0 RoystonFfrench 14 69
(Bryan Smart) *s.i.s: sn chsng ldrs: kpt on wl fnl f* **9/1**
**4** *1 1/4* **Seeking Approval (IRE)** 2-9-0 0 TomEaves 8 60+
(Kevin Ryan) *dwlt: hdwy over 2f out: swtchd lft ins fnl f: gng on at fin* **14/1**
**5** *hd* **Alderaan (IRE)** 2-9-0 0 BarryMcHugh 1 60
(Tony Coyle) *led: hdd over 1f out: wknd ins fnl f* **18/1**
**6** *3 3/4* **Birkdale Boy (IRE)** 2-9-5 0 TonyHamilton 2 53+
(Richard Fahey) *s.i.s: hdwy 2f out: kpt on ins fnl f* **20/1**
**7** *1 1/4* **Groor** 2-9-5 0 GrahamLee 10 50
(James Tate) *mid-div: effrt over 2f out: nvr a threat* **5/1**[2]
4 **8** *3/4* **Soie D'Leau**[14] 2014 2-9-0 0 JacobButterfield(5) 6 47
(Kristin Stubbs) *prom: efoort over 2f out: wknd over 1f out* **14/1**
0 **9** *1* **Frosty Times (FR)**[16] 1936 2-9-2 0 GeorgeChaloner(3) 3 44
(Richard Fahey) *mid-div: effrt over 2f out: nvr nr ldrs* **33/1**
0 **10** *3/4* **Blazing Rose (IRE)**[10] 2134 2-9-0 0 DanielTudhope 9 37
(David O'Meara) *chsd ldrs: drvn over 2f out: sn wknd* **40/1**
**11** *1/2* **Bushranger Bay (IRE)** 2-9-5 0 DavidAllan 11 41+
(Tim Easterby) *in rr: sn drvn along: nvr on terms* **100/1**
**12** *5* **Doctor Watson** 2-9-5 0 JamesSullivan 13 26
(Tom Tate) *outpcd and a in rr* **80/1**
0 **13** *1/2* **Sparkle Girl**[33] 1505 2-9-0 0 DuranFentiman 15 19
(Tim Easterby) *s.s: reminders after 2f: a bhd* **100/1**
**14** *1/2* **Pencaitland** 2-8-11 0 NeilFarley(3) 4 18
(Noel Wilson) *w ldrs: lost pl 2f out* **40/1**
4 **15** *5* **Pomme De Terre (IRE)**[33] 1505 2-9-5 0 PaulMulrennan 7 8
(Michael Dods) *chsd ldrs: outpcd and lost pl over 3f out: bhd whn eased clsng stages* **6/1**

1m 12.25s (0.45) **Going Correction** +0.075s/f (Good) **15** Ran SP% **117.4**
Speed ratings (Par 93): **100,96,95,93,93 88,86,85,84,83 82,76,75,74,68**
CSF £19.27 TOTE £10.60: £9.70, £1.80, £2.90; EX 22.00 Trifecta £408.70.
**Owner** Miss M A Quinlan **Bred** Mrs P A Cave **Trained** Newmarket, Suffolk

**FOCUS**
A modest juvenile maiden in which they went a decent gallop on ground officially described as good to firm, good in places on a sunny afternoon. The form can't be rated much higher.

## 2387 RACING UK ON CHANNEL 432 H'CAP (DIV I) 5f
**2:50** (2:52) (Class 6) (0-60,60) 3-Y-O **£1,940** (£577; £288; £144) **Stalls** Centre

Form RPR
0-34 **1** **Storyline (IRE)**[25] 1671 3-9-5 **58** DavidAllan 2 71
(Tim Easterby) *mde all: edgd lft fnl f: styd on wl* **9/2**[2]
260- **2** *2 1/4* **Scoreline**[223] 7094 3-9-7 **60** DanielTudhope 10 65
(David O'Meara) *chsd ldrs: edgd lft and kpt on to take 2nd ins fnl f* **7/1**[3]
6-00 **3** *1 3/4* **Bashiba (IRE)**[14] 2023 3-8-7 **46** oh1 AdrianNicholls 8 45
(Nigel Tinkler) *mid-div: hdwy to chse ldrs over 2f out: kpt on same pce ins fnl f* **33/1**
**4** *nk* **Ever Yours (IRE)**[52] 1154 3-8-13 **52** (b[1]) GrahamLee 6 50
(John Joseph Murphy, Ire) *chsd ldrs: drvn over 2f out: outpcd over 1f out: kpt on towards fin* **9/2**[2]
-002 **5** *hd* **Nu Form Fire (IRE)**[6] 2230 3-8-7 **46** oh1 JamesSullivan 11 43
(Nigel Tinkler) *in rr: kpt on fnl f: nt rch ldrs* **10/1**
15-5 **6** *1 1/2* **Kiss From A Rose**[20] 1851 3-9-7 **60** ChrisCatlin 9 51
(Rae Guest) *dwlt and n.m.r sn after s: hdwy and hung lft over 2f out: sn chsng ldrs: one pce* **3/1**[1]
00-0 **7** *nk* **Classical Diva**[40] 1373 3-9-0 **56** JasonHart(3) 12 46
(Declan Carroll) *stdd s: hdwy over 2f out: kpt on fnl f* **14/1**
066- **8** *1* **Wolfwood**[195] 7755 3-8-8 **47** PJMcDonald 3 34
(John Davies) *dwlt: in rr: sme hdwy over 1f out: swtchd lft ins fnl f: nvr a factor* **25/1**
6040 **9** *shd* **La Paiva (FR)**[28] 1611 3-8-7 **46** oh1 (p) LukeMorris 1 32
(Scott Dixon) *w ldrs: wknd over 1f out* **22/1**
000- **10** *2 1/4* **Shikari**[210] 7419 3-8-13 **55** NeilFarley(3) 7 33
(Robin Bastiman) *wnt rt s: outpcd and a in rr* **33/1**
-006 **11** *nk* **Kinkohyo**[28] 1611 3-8-12 **51** (p) PaulMulrennan 4 28
(Bryan Smart) *chsd ldrs: wknd appr fnl f* **22/1**
066- **12** *1 3/4* **Lomond Lassie**[264] 5877 3-9-4 **57** TomEaves 5 28
(Keith Dalgleish) *chsd ldrs: lost pl over 1f out* **16/1**

58.27s (-0.33) **Going Correction** +0.075s/f (Good) **12** Ran SP% **113.9**
Speed ratings (Par 97): **105,101,98,98,97 95,94,93,93,89 89,86**
CSF £31.68 CT £918.19 TOTE £5.20: £1.30, £2.40, £12.80; EX 31.80 Trifecta £1402.60.
**Owner** Miss Yvonne Jacques **Bred** Tally-Ho Stud **Trained** Great Habton, N Yorks

**FOCUS**
The first division of a moderate 3yo sprint handicap. It was the quicker of the two and the form is rated slightly positively.

## 2388 RACING UK ON CHANNEL 432 H'CAP (DIV II) 5f
**3:20** (3:21) (Class 6) (0-60,60) 3-Y-O **£1,940** (£577; £288; £144) **Stalls** Centre

Form RPR
-040 **1** **Tinsill**[14] 2015 3-9-7 **60** PaulMulrennan 5 66
(Nigel Tinkler) *mid-div: lost pl and reminders over 2f out: hdwy and swtchd lft over 1f out: styd on to ld towards fin* **10/3**[1]
605- **2** *nk* **Raise A Billion**[223] 7094 3-8-7 **46** oh1 PatrickMathers 2 51
(Alan Berry) *chsd ldrs: outpcd and lost pl over 2f out: hdwy over 1f out: led briefly wl ins fnl f: no ex* **25/1**
50-5 **3** *1/2* **Reet Thicknstrong**[25] 1671 3-9-4 **57** RoystonFfrench 7 60
(Bryan Smart) *led: edgd lft and hdd wl ins fnl f: no ex* **13/2**
0-30 **4** *1/2* **Lady Mai (IRE)**[28] 1611 3-9-2 **55** TonyHamilton 6 56
(Richard Fahey) *chsd ldrs: kpt on same pce last 150yds* **11/2**[3]
3161 **5** *1/2* **Biscuiteer**[27] 1626 3-9-7 **60** (b) LukeMorris 11 59
(Scott Dixon) *chsd ldrs: kpt on ins fnl f* **12/1**

56-6 6 ½ **Singing Star (IRE)**[37] 1441 3-8-11 **50** DavidAllan 9 47
(Mel Brittain) *in mid-div: hdwy over 2f out: kpt on at same pce whn hmpd ins last 50yds* **8/1**
5400 7 ½ **Back On Baileys**[14] 2023 3-8-7 **46** oh1 ChrisCatlin 10 42
(John Ryan) *s.i.s: hdwy over 1f out: kpt on: nvr rchd ldrs* **40/1**
-203 8 2 **Roomie**[17] 1925 3-9-0 **53** (b) DuranFentiman 8 41
(Tim Easterby) *chsd ldrs: drvn over 2f out: one pce over 1f out* **16/1**
0-45 9 ¾ **Rostrum Farewell**[44] 1315 3-9-5 **58** AndrewElliott 3 44
(David Brown) *chsd ldrs: outpcd 2f out: no threat after* **13/2**
-602 10 1 **Dream Sika (IRE)**[17] 1925 3-8-12 **51** JamesSullivan 1 33
(Ruth Carr) *wnt lft s: t.k.h: sn w ldrs: wknd over 1f out* **9/2**[2]
4460 11 7 **Captain T**[7] 2209 3-8-7 **46** PJMcDonald 4
(Richard Ford) *mid-div: lost pl 3f out: sn bhd* **66/1**

58.91s (0.31) **Going Correction** +0.075s/f (Good) 11 Ran SP% **115.8**
Speed ratings (Par 97): **100,99,98,97,97 96,95,92,91,89 78**
CSF £91.29 CT £529.76 TOTE £3.50: £1.10, £10.20, £3.60; EX 112.10 Trifecta £1353.10.
**Owner** Crawford Society 1 **Bred** L T Roberts **Trained** Langton, N Yorks
■ Stewards' Enquiry : Royston Ffrench one-day ban: careless riding (Jun 2)

**FOCUS**
The second division of a moderate 3yo sprint handicap where it paid to be more conservatively ridden with the pace collapsing up ahead. It was the slower division and the winner probably ran only similar to this year's form.

## 2389 VOLTIGEUR RESTAURANT £11.95 TWO COURSE SPECIAL MAIDEN FILLIES' STKS — 7f
**3:50** (3:53) (Class 5) 3-Y-O+ **£2,726** (£805; £402) **Stalls** Centre

Form RPR
1 **Cool Music (IRE)** 4-9-4 0 RobertDodsworth(7) 1 74
(Mel Brittain) *w ldrs: styd on to ld ins fnl f: hld on towards fin* **100/1**
2 ½ **Gotcha** 3-9-0 0 PJMcDonald 2 69
(James Bethell) *dwlt: hdwy over 3f out: chsng ldrs over 2f out: swtchd rt over 1f out: styd on wl towards fin* **10/1**
524- 3 1 **My Inspiration (IRE)**[220] 7173 3-9-0 77 DavidAllan 5 66
(Tim Easterby) *led: hdd ins fnl f: kpt on same pce* **11/2**[2]
3 4 9 **Moonvoy**[32] 1529 3-9-0 0 SebSanders 7 43
(Jeremy Noseda) *chsd ldrs: drvn over 2f out: wknd appr fnl f* **4/9**[1]
003 5 3 ½ **Puppet Theatre (IRE)**[19] 1888 4-9-11 0 DanielTudhope 12 38+
(David O'Meara) *trckd ldrs: effrt over 2f out: wknd over 1f out* **8/1**[3]
00-0 6 nse **Magical Mischief**[44] 1303 4-9-11 23 MichaelStainton 10 37
(Chris Fairhurst) *chsd ldrs: drvn over 3f out: wknd over 1f out* **200/1**
0 7 7 **Mossy Marie (IRE)**[25] 1671 3-8-11 0 JasonHart(3) 4 15
(Eric Alston) *stmbld and wnt rt s: t.k.h: mid-div and drvn over 3f out: wknd over 2f out* **25/1**
0 8 1 **Cavallo Bella**[37] 1441 3-9-0 0 GrahamGibbons 15 13
(David Barron) *hld up in mid-div: effrt over 2f out: sn wknd* **22/1**
05-0 9 1 ½ **Mrs Gorsky**[9] 2170 4-9-4 41 JackGarritty(7) 13 13
(Patrick Holmes) *in rr: nvr on terms* **100/1**
10 1 ½ **Kaytom** 3-8-9 AdamCarter(5) 11 5
(John Wainwright) *s.i.s: nvr on terms* **100/1**
0 11 2 **Cool Reception**[91] 645 3-8-9 0 JacobButterfield(5) 3
(Ollie Pears) *w ldrs: rdn and wknd over 2f out* **66/1**
12 3 ¾ **Escaping Midge (IRE)** 3-9-0 0 DuranFentiman 9
(Tim Easterby) *s.s: nvr on terms* **40/1**
0-0 13 1 ¾ **Kalani's Diamond**[35] 1486 4-9-11 0 (t) PaulMulrennan 6
(Bryan Smart) *chsd ldrs: lost pl over 2f out* **66/1**
14 2 ½ **City Zip** 4-9-11 0 LukeMorris 8
(Alan McCabe) *in rr: reminders over 3f out: bhd fnl 2f* **33/1**
4 15 31 **La Brava**[21] 1790 4-9-6 0 ShirleyTeasdale(5) 16
(Lisa Williamson) *wnt rt s: a bhd: virtually p.u over 1f out: hopelessly t.o* **100/1**

1m 25.38s (0.88) **Going Correction** +0.075s/f (Good)
**WFA** 3 from 4yo 11lb 15 Ran SP% **125.9**
Speed ratings (Par 100): **97,96,95,85,81 80,72,71,70,68 66,61,59,56,21**
CSF £921.33 TOTE £74.70: £18.20, £3.40, £1.70; EX 1508.70 Trifecta £2966.10.
**Owner** Mel Brittain **Bred** Mrs D M Solomon **Trained** Warthill, N Yorks
■ Stewards' Enquiry : Robert Dodsworth caution: careless riding.

**FOCUS**
A fair fillies' maiden in which they went an honest gallop. There was no depth to the race, the first three finishing clear.

## 2390 HAPPY 10TH BIRTHDAY RACING UK H'CAP — 5f
**4:20** (4:24) (Class 3) (0-90,87) 3-Y-O+
**£7,158** (£2,143; £1,071; £535; £267; £134) **Stalls** Centre

Form RPR
5003 1 **Another Wise Kid (IRE)**[24] 1695 6-9-11 **86** GrahamLee 11 94
(Paul Midgley) *in rr: hdwy 2f out: edgd lft and styd on fnl f: led nr fin* **5/1**[2]
50-0 2 nk **Avon Breeze**[10] 2136 5-9-4 **79** RussKennemore 2 86
(Richard Whitaker) *dwlt: sn chsng ldrs: led over 1f out: hdd and no ex clsng stages* **10/1**
-044 3 nse **Singeur (IRE)**[16] 1938 7-9-9 **87** NeilFarley(3) 8 94
(Robin Bastiman) *in rr: styd on strly fnl f: fin wl* **8/1**
046- 4 1 **Jack Luey**[206] 7507 7-9-10 **85** DavidAllan 4 88
(Tim Easterby) *chsd ldrs: kpt on same pce last 150yds* **12/1**
0505 5 ½ **Jiroft (ITY)**[16] 1944 7-9-9 **87** (p) RobertTart(3) 3 88
(Robert Cowell) *led: hdd over 1f out: edeged rt jst ins fnl f: kpt on same pce* **11/2**[3]
5210 6 ½ **Keep It Dark**[2] 2350 5-9-4 **79** BarryMcHugh 1 79
(Tony Coyle) *racd virtually alone far side: w ldrs: carried hd high: fdd last 50yds* **4/1**[1]
0000 7 ½ **Tennessee Wildcat (IRE)**[16] 1944 4-9-12 **87** (v[1]) GrahamGibbons 7 85
(Robert Cowell) *in rr: rdn and hung lft over 2f out: kpt on fnl f* **25/1**
1-10 8 1 **Foxy Music**[12] 2076 10-9-5 **83** JasonHart(3) 10 77
(Eric Alston) *racd virtually alone stands' side: chsd ldrs: one pce over 1f out* **25/1**
36-6 9 ¾ **Corncockle**[127] 149 3-8-11 **80** DanielTudhope 6 68
(David O'Meara) *sn chsng ldrs: one pce fnl 2f: sltly hmpd jst ins fnl f* **25/1**
130- 10 ½ **Bondi Beach Boy**[241] 6586 5-8-13 **81** JordanNason(7) 5 71
(James Turner) *chsd ldrs: fading whn sltly hmpd jst ins fnl f* **13/2**
00- 11 46 **Stone Of Folca**[254] 6189 6-9-12 **87** LukeMorris 9
(John Best) *stmbld s: towards rr: heavily eased over 2f out: virtually p.u: hopelessly t.o* **7/1**

57.98s (-0.62) **Going Correction** +0.075s/f (Good)
**WFA** 3 from 4yo+ 8lb 11 Ran SP% **117.3**
Speed ratings (Par 107): **107,106,106,104,104 103,102,100,99,98 25**
CSF £52.62 CT £394.50 TOTE £6.70: £2.40, £3.70, £2.50; EX 70.30 Trifecta £664.40.
**Owner** Michael Ng **Bred** Paul Kavanagh **Trained** Westow, N Yorks

**FOCUS**
The feature race on the card was a decent sprint handicap. Straightforward form.

## 2391 DOWNLOAD NEW RACING UK IPAD APP H'CAP (STRAIGHT-MILE CHAMPIONSHIP QUALIFIER) — 1m
**4:50** (4:52) (Class 5) (0-75,75) 3-Y-O **£2,587** (£770; £384; £192) **Stalls** Centre

Form RPR
0-60 1 **Golden Spear**[23] 1725 3-9-3 **71** (p) PatCosgrave 1 82
(Noel Quinlan) *hld up in rr: t.k.h early: hdwy 2f out: edgd rt and led appr fnl f: wnt clr: readily* **6/1**[3]
4011 2 3 ½ **Sheriff Of Nawton (IRE)**[18] 1906 3-9-5 **73** DanielTudhope 2 76
(David O'Meara) *trckd ldng pair: effrt over 2f out: upsides over 1f out: edgd lft and kpt on same pce* **4/6**[1]
-323 3 3 **Truancy (IRE)**[94] 604 3-9-2 **70** PhillipMakin 6 66
(K R Burke) *led: hdd wl over 1f out: one pce* **9/1**
6-01 4 3 **Sakhalin Star (IRE)**[7] 2204 3-8-13 **70** 6ex BillyCray(3) 3 59
(Richard Guest) *fly-jmpd s: t.k.h in rr: effrt over 2f out: wknd over 1f out* **9/1**
310 5 shd **Dubawi Light**[45] 1279 3-9-7 **75** PaulMulrennan 4 64
(James Tate) *trckd ldr: led wl over 1f out: hdd & wknd appr fnl f* **5/1**[2]

1m 37.82s (1.22) **Going Correction** +0.075s/f (Good) 5 Ran SP% **110.9**
Speed ratings (Par 99): **96,92,89,86,86**
CSF £10.76 TOTE £9.10: £3.50, £1.02; EX 16.60 Trifecta £63.50.
**Owner** Newtown Anner Stud Farm Ltd **Bred** D P And Mrs J A Martin **Trained** Newmarket, Suffolk

**FOCUS**
A fair small-field 3yo handicap, but some doubts over the field. The winner is rated back to his standout previous run.

## 2392 LADIES' DAY ON SATURDAY 21ST JUNE MEDIAN AUCTION MAIDEN STKS — 1m
**5:20** (5:24) (Class 6) 3-5-Y-O **£2,045** (£603; £302) **Stalls** Centre

Form RPR
52 1 **Halation (IRE)**[18] 1894 3-9-1 0 LukeMorris 3 79
(Marco Botti) *mid-div: hdwy to trck ldrs over 3f out: chal over 2f out: edgd lft and styd on fnl f: led last 75yds* **15/8**[2]
4 2 1 ¼ **Discreetly**[20] 1844 3-8-10 0 MickaelBarzalona 10 71
(Hughie Morrison) *trckd ldrs: led over 2f out: rdn and edgd lft over 1f out: hdd and no ex wl ins fnl f* **5/4**[1]
5 3 3 ¼ **Sleeping Apache (IRE)**[35] 1486 4-9-13 0 PhillipMakin 9 72
(Philip Kirby) *hld up in mid-div: hdwy 3f out: chsng ldng pair over 1f out: kpt on one pce* **12/1**[3]
4 ¾ **Far Ranging (USA)** 3-8-10 0 BarryMcHugh 5 62
(Julie Camacho) *s.s: hdwy 3f out: sn chsng ldrs: edgd lft and one pce over 1f out* **50/1**
5 14 **Wild Hill Boy** 4-9-13 0 PaulMulrennan 2 38
(David C Griffiths) *in rr: hdwy over 3f out: lost pl over 1f out* **33/1**
6 6 2 ¾ **Some Boy Lukey**[16] 1962 3-9-1 0 GrahamLee 8 28
(David Thompson) *led: hdd over 2f out: sn lost pl* **25/1**
4 7 3 ½ **Knight Of Glin**[15] 1969 3-8-8 0 PaulMcGiff(7) 11 20
(David Barron) *w ldr: edgd lft and lost pl over 2f out* **20/1**
8 7 **Beaulie** 4-9-8 0 TomEaves 6
(Keith Reveley) *s.s: detached in last and hung lft thrght: wl bhd fnl 3f* **33/1**
-060 9 4 **Application**[104] 480 3-9-1 38 (p) RoystonFfrench 7
(Bryan Smart) *chsd ldrs: reminders 4f out: sn lost pl and bhd* **100/1**

1m 38.13s (1.53) **Going Correction** +0.075s/f (Good)
**WFA** 3 from 4yo 12lb 9 Ran SP% **104.4**
Speed ratings (Par 101): **95,93,90,89,75 73,69,62,58**
CSF £3.30 TOTE £2.50: £1.10, £1.20, £2.00; EX 3.70 Trifecta £15.40.
**Owner** Al Asayl Bloodstock Ltd **Bred** Sheikh Sultan Bin Khalifa Al Nayhan **Trained** Newmarket, Suffolk
■ Rule 4 of 15p in the pound applies to all bets; Withdrawn: Lucky Shadow

**FOCUS**
A modest maiden in which the winner built a bit on previous efforts.

## 2393 CELEBRATE 10 YEARS WITH RACING UK ANYWHERE H'CAP — 1m 2f
**5:50** (5:54) (Class 6) (0-80,59) 3-Y-O **£2,045** (£603; £302) **Stalls** Low

Form RPR
5-52 1 **Trinity Star (IRE)**[18] 1906 3-9-7 **59** (p) PaulMulrennan 14 64+
(Michael Dods) *hld up towards rr: hdwy on outer over 5f out: trcking ldrs over 3f out: led over 1f out: edgd lft: drvn out* **11/4**[1]
0-30 2 ¾ **Where's Tiger**[18] 1906 3-9-3 **55** PhillipMakin 15 59
(Jedd O'Keeffe) *hld up in rr: hdwy on outer over 5f out: chsng ldrs over 2f out: edgd lft and styd on to take 2nd towards fin* **10/1**
0-36 3 1 ½ **Nam Ma Prow**[20] 1840 3-8-13 **51** (p) AndrewElliott 11 52
(Simon West) *led 1f: w ldrs: led over 2f out: hdd over 1f out: kpt on same pce* **50/1**
0643 4 1 **Ronya (IRE)**[10] 2135 3-9-6 **58** DanielTudhope 7 59
(K R Burke) *in rr: hdwy on ins over 3f out: sn trcking ldrs: nt clr run and swtchd rt jst ins fnl f: styng on at fin* **9/2**[2]
605- 5 nk **Moving Waves (IRE)**[264] 5893 3-9-3 **55** RobertWinston 5 54
(Ollie Pears) *chsd ldrs: upsides over 2f out: keeping on same pce whn hmpd over 1f out* **10/1**
-124 6 nk **Vosne Romanee**[11] 2098 3-9-6 **58** (p) TomEaves 12 56
(Keith Dalgleish) *t.k.h in midfield: hdwy over 3f out: sn chsng ldrs: one pce over 1f out* **10/1**
0366 7 1 ¾ **Casper Lee (IRE)**[6] 2237 3-8-10 **53** JacobButterfield(5) 2 48
(Michael Herrington) *hld up in rr: hdwy on ins over 3f out: upsides over 2f out: wknd last 75yds* **16/1**
6044 8 nk **Sicilian Bay (IRE)**[18] 1906 3-9-1 **53** GrahamLee 4 47
(Paul Midgley) *chsd ldrs: one pce fnl 2f* **5/1**[3]
5640 9 6 **Marphilly (IRE)**[21] 1794 3-8-12 **50** LukeMorris 1 33
(John Best) *s.i.s: hdwy on inner to ld after 1f: hdd over 2f out: wknd over 1f out* **16/1**
5-30 10 2 ¼ **Gee Sharp**[81] 753 3-9-3 **55** JamesSullivan 9 33
(Julie Camacho) *s.i.s: t.k.h in rr: drvn over 4f out: nt clr run over 2f out: sn wknd* **40/1**
200 11 3 ½ **Tortoise**[6] 2237 3-8-5 **46** (b) BillyCray(3) 6 18
(Richard Guest) *dwlt: in rr: hdwy on ins 4f out: sn trcking ldrs: lost pl over 2f out* **40/1**
-342 12 1 ¾ **Hello Sweetness**[10] 2135 3-9-3 **55** DuranFentiman 8 23
(Jason Ward) *w ldrs: lost pl over 3f out* **16/1**
0-05 13 5 **Gold Class**[14] 2028 3-9-4 **56** (b) RoystonFfrench 10 15
(Ed McMahon) *hld up in rr: sme hdwy and hung lft over 2f out: sn wknd* **22/1**

2m 8.56s (1.46) **Going Correction** +0.075s/f (Good) 13 Ran SP% **117.6**
Speed ratings (Par 97): **97,96,95,94,94 93,92,92,87,85 82,81,77**
CSF £29.70 CT £1127.14 TOTE £4.10: £1.30, £4.10, £13.50; EX 40.30 Trifecta £840.50.

**Owner** Trinity Racing **Bred** Ms Natalie Cleary **Trained** Denton, Co Durham
■ Stewards' Enquiry : Paul Mulrennan two-day ban: used whip above permitted level (Jun 2-3)
**FOCUS**
The concluding contest was a moderate 3yo handicap. Improvement from the first two in their Newcastle meeting.
T/Jkpt: Not won. T/Plt: £284.30 to a £1 stake. Pool: £65,431.14 - 167.95 winning units. T/Qpdt: £48.10 to a £1 stake. Pool: £5057.89 - 117.80 winning units. WG

## 2092 SOUTHWELL (L-H)
Monday, May 19

**OFFICIAL GOING: Standard**
Wind: Moderate against Weather: Cloudy with sunny periods but warm

### 2394 QUICKSILVERSLOTS MORE JACKPOTS MORE MACHINES AMATEUR RIDERS' CLASSIFIED CLAIMING STKS 1m 6f (F)
**2:30** (2:30) (Class 6) 4-Y-0+ **£1,975** (£607; £303) **Stalls** Low

Form RPR
0310 1 **Dynastic**13 2055 5-10-5 69 MrKWood(5) 7 76
(Tony Coyle) *hld up in tch: hdwy over 3f out: wd st: rdn to ld wl over 1f out: drvn and kpt on wl fnl f* **3/1**3
3435 2 1 ¾ **Layline (IRE)**12 2067 7-11-0 75 MrSWalker 1 78
(Gay Kelleway) *trckd ldrs: hdwy 3f out: cl up 2f out: rdn and ev ch over 1f out: drvn: edgd lft and one pce ins fnl f* **8/1**
6516 3 1 ¾ **Incendo**27 1828 8-10-8 72 (t) MissSBrotherton 5 69
(Ian Williams) *trckd ldrs: hdwy 3f out: chsd ldrs 2f out: rdn to chse ldng pair over 1f out: drvn ent fnl f: kpt on same pce* **7/4**1
2126 4 3 ¼ **Teajaybe (USA)**11 2097 6-11-0 74 MrRBirkett 4 71
(Chris Dwyer) *trckd ldrs: hdwy 3f out: cl up 2f out: sn rdn and ev ch: drvn over 1f out: wknd ent fnl f* **9/4**2
-460 5 2 ½ **Tight Knit (USA)**33 1503 4-9-9 60 (b) PhillipDennis(5) 3 53
(John Weymes) *hld up in rr: swtchd to outer 7f out: hdwy to ld 5f out: rdn along over 2f out: hdd wl over 1f out and sn wknd* **20/1**
3506 6 8 **Joyful Motive**21 1806 5-10-6 47 MissLWilson(5) 6 53
(Michael Chapman) *chsd clr ldr: pushed along over 5f out: sn lost pl and bhd fnl 3f* **25/1**
00 7 42 **Big City Boy (IRE)**46 1263 6-9-7 37 MissEmmaJack(7) 2
(Phil McEntee) *plld hrd: set stdy pce: wnt clr after 3f: jnd and pushed along over 5f out: sn hdd: wknd qckly 3f out: sn bhd* **50/1**
3m 19.65s (11.35) **Going Correction** +0.25s/f (Slow) **7** Ran SP% **113.8**
Speed ratings (Par 101): **77,76,75,73,71 67,43**
CSF £25.54 TOTE £3.40: £1.40, £3.20; EX 25.10 Trifecta £62.80.
**Owner** Michael Anthony O'Donnell **Bred** Castleton Lyons & Kilboy Estate **Trained** Norton, N Yorks
**FOCUS**
A moderate amateur riders' staying event in which the pace didn't quicken appreciably until past halfway. The winner is accorded a personal best.

### 2395 QUICKSILVERSLOTS PLAY FROM 10P TO £2 MAIDEN AUCTION STKS 5f (F)
**3:00** (3:00) (Class 5) 2-Y-0 **£2,587** (£770; £384; £192) **Stalls** High

Form RPR
2 1 **Mecca's Mirage (IRE)**25 1656 2-8-6 0 ConnorBeasley(3) 3 70
(Michael Dods) *trckd ldrs: cl up 2f out: rdn to ld wl over 1f out: hdd and drvn ins fnl f: edgd lft and rallied u.p to ld again towards fin* **9/4**2
2 nk **Quint (IRE)** 2-8-9 0 DavidProbert 1 69+
(Martyn Meade) *s.i.s and bhd: pushed along bef 1/2-way: gd hdwy on wd outside over 1f out: rdn and slt ld ins fnl f: hdd and no ex towards fin* **8/1**
3 2 ½ **Grosmont** 2-9-3 0 DaleSwift 8 68
(James Given) *prom: rdn along and sltly outpcd over 2f out: kpt on fnl f* **20/1**
00 4 2 ½ **On Appro**18 1900 2-7-13 0 RachelRichardson(5) 2 48
(Tim Easterby) *led: rdn along over 2f out: hdd wl over 1f out: grad wknd* **50/1**
6 5 nk **Mount Isa (IRE)**46 1259 2-9-0 0 LiamJones 7 55
(J S Moore) *chsd ldrs: rdn along and outpcd 1/2-way: swtchd lft to wd outside wl over 1f out: kpt on fnl f* **25/1**
43 6 2 ¾ **Diminutive (IRE)**7 2206 2-8-6 0 JohnFahy 5 37
(Jamie Osborne) *chsd ldrs: rdn along over 2f out: wknd wl over 1f out* **10/1**
6332 7 ½ **Red Connect**7 2200 2-9-3 0 BenCurtis 4 46
(Alan McCabe) *cl up: effrt over 2f out and ev ch: rdn wl over 1f out: sn drvn and wknd* **6/4**1
8 6 **Indian Champ** 2-8-9 0 (b1) ShaneGray(5) 6 22+
(Kevin Ryan) *dwlt: hdwy nr stands' rails and in tch 1/2-way: sn rdn and wknd* **7/1**3
1m 3.01s (3.31) **Going Correction** +0.50s/f (Slow) **8** Ran SP% **114.0**
Speed ratings (Par 93): **93,92,88,84,84 79,78,69**
CSF £19.84 TOTE £3.60: £1.30, £3.00, £6.20; EX 20.60 Trifecta £156.90.
**Owner** David T J Metcalfe **Bred** Miss S Von Schilcher **Trained** Denton, Co Durham
**FOCUS**
A pretty modest maiden auction in which the main action unfolded down the centre of the track. The winner looks a nursery type.

### 2396 QUICKSILVERSLOTS PLAY £500 JACKPOT RAINBOW RICHES H'CAP 1m 3f (F)
**3:30** (3:30) (Class 6) (0-55,55) 4-Y-0+ **£2,045** (£603; £302) **Stalls** Low

Form RPR
-450 1 **Kingaroo (IRE)**81 759 8-8-9 46 oh1 ConnorBeasley(3) 6 56
(Garry Woodward) *prom: pushed along 5f out: rdn and lost pl 4f out: swtchd to outer and wd st: hdwy 2f out: styd on wl u.p appr fnl f: led nr fin* **16/1**
-053 2 nk **K Lightning (IRE)**22 1761 4-9-2 50 JimmyQuinn 9 59
(Sarah Humphrey) *trckd ldrs: smooth hdwy over 3f out: cl up on bit 2f out: shkn up to ld 1 1/2f out: sn rdn: drvn and edgd lft ins fnl f: hdd and no ex nr fin* **4/1**2
642 3 3 **Brown Pete (IRE)**20 1865 6-8-11 48 DeclanBates(3) 4 52
(Ann Stokell) *hld up: hdwy over 3f out: chsd ldrs 2f out: sn rdn and kpt on same pce fnl f* **5/1**3
0-0 4 1 ¼ **With Hindsight (IRE)**39 1408 6-8-11 52 JoeDoyle(7) 10 54
(John Spearing) *hld up in rr: hdwy on inner and in tch 1/2-way: trckd ldrs 4f out: effrt 3f out: rdn 2f out: sn drvn and one pce ent fnl f* **3/1**1
0200 5 hd **Mazij**37 1453 6-9-1 49 LiamJones 11 51
(Peter Hiatt) *slt ld: rdn along and hdd 3f out: cl up: drvn 2f out and grad wknd appr fnl f* **8/1**
26-5 6 4 ½ **Korngold**13 2052 6-9-3 54 IanBrennan(3) 13 48
(Barry Leavy) *prom: pushed along on outer 5f out: rdn and outpcd wl over 3f out* **7/1**
065- 7 ½ **Bullseye Babe**219 7204 4-9-0 48 DavidProbert 1 41
(Mark Usher) *trckd ldrs: effrt 3f out: rdn along over 2f out: sn wknd* **25/1**
6442 8 1 ½ **Excellent News (IRE)**19 1891 5-8-5 46 oh1 AdamMcLean(7) 8 36
(Tony Forbes) *prom: cl up 1/2-way: slt ld 3f out: rdn along over 2f out: hdd 1 1/2f out and sn wknd* **14/1**
55-3 9 8 **Politbureau**19 1891 7-8-5 46 oh1 DanielleMooney(7) 5 23
(Michael Easterby) *hld up: a towards rr* **12/1**
0/0- 10 1 ½ **Swords**256 6130 12-8-7 46 oh1 EoinWalsh(5) 7 20
(Ray Peacock) *rrd s and v.s.a: a bhd* **50/1**
30/2 11 30 **Turbulent Priest**19 1874 6-8-10 47 (tp) SimonPearce(3) 3
(Zoe Davison) *towards rr: hdwy and in tch 1/2-way: rdn along 4f out: sn outpcd* **10/1**
2m 31.83s (3.83) **Going Correction** +0.25s/f (Slow) **11** Ran SP% **120.4**
Speed ratings (Par 101): **96,95,93,92,92 89,88,87,82,80 59**
CSF £80.98 CT £380.26 TOTE £19.10: £4.20, £2.40, £2.40; EX 95.00 Trifecta £468.80.
**Owner** Mrs Elisabeth Cash **Bred** Kevin Walsh **Trained** Bolham, Notts
**FOCUS**
A moderate handicap and very much a race of changing fortunes. The form is rated around the third to his turf latest.

### 2397 QUICKSILVERSLOTS OPEN AFTER 10PM H'CAP 6f (F)
**4:00** (4:00) (Class 6) (0-60,60) 3-Y-0 **£1,940** (£577; £288; £144) **Stalls** Low

Form RPR
005 1 **Shades Of Silk**16 1962 3-8-4 46 oh1 ConnorBeasley(3) 5 57
(James Given) *trckd ldrs: swtchd rt to outer 1/2-way: hdwy to chal 2f out: rdn to ld wl over 1f out: drvn and kpt on strly fnl f* **8/1**
64-4 2 2 ¾ **Injaz**32 1543 3-9-2 60 ShaneGray(5) 6 62
(Kevin Ryan) *cl up: rdn along over 2f out: drvn to chse wnr ins fnl f: no imp* **11/4**1
2404 3 ½ **Meebo (IRE)**20 1860 3-9-5 58 PaoloSirigu 4 58
(J R Jenkins) *chsd ldrs: hdwy on inner and cl up over 2f out: rdn wl over 1f out: drvn and one pce ent fnl f* **8/1**
-023 4 2 ¾ **Sleet (IRE)**11 2095 3-9-2 55 (v) RobbieFitzpatrick 8 47
(Michael Appleby) *s.i.s and in rr: rdn along and wd st: plugged on u.p fnl 2f: n.d* **3/1**2
50-4 5 ¾ **Traditionelle**37 1441 3-9-5 58 DavidNolan 9 47
(Tim Easterby) *cl up on outer: hdwy to ld over 2f out: sn rdn: hdd wl over 1f out: sn drvn and wknd appr fnl f* **7/1**
32-6 6 8 **By Rights**14 2035 3-9-2 60 1 JoeyHaynes(5) 2 24
(Tony Carroll) *t.k.h: in tch: hdwy 1/2-way: chsd ldrs over 2f out: sn rdn and wknd* **20/1**
4635 7 hd **Bold Max**13 2044 3-8-7 46 (p) LiamJones 3 9
(Zoe Davison) *a towards rr* **20/1**
-302 8 1 ½ **Febrayer Star (IRE)**20 1833 3-8-12 51 (v) FrederikTylicki 7 9
(Robert Cowell) *slt ld: rdn along and hdd over 2f out: wknd wl over 1f out* **5/1**3
00-0 9 6 **Ellingham (IRE)**17 1920 3-9-7 60 AdamBeschizza 1
(Christine Dunnett) *a in rr* **33/1**
1m 17.99s (1.49) **Going Correction** +0.25s/f (Slow) **9** Ran SP% **115.5**
Speed ratings (Par 97): **100,96,95,92,91 80,80,78,70**
CSF £29.56 CT £184.64 TOTE £9.40: £2.30, £1.90, £1.40; EX 54.90 Trifecta £324.70.
**Owner** The Cool Silk Partnership **Bred** Mrs F S Williams **Trained** Willoughton, Lincs
**FOCUS**
A moderate 3yo sprint handicap, contested by nine maidens. It resulted in a hat-trick for apprentice Connor Beasley. The winner was showing her first real form.

### 2398 QUICKSILVERSLOTS £1 TO WIN £500 FILLIES' H'CAP 6f (F)
**4:30** (4:30) (Class 4) (0-80,80) 4-Y-0+ **£4,690** (£1,395; £697; £348) **Stalls** Low

Form RPR
1352 1 **Abi Scarlet (IRE)**34 1497 5-8-9 75 CharlieBennett(7) 1 84
(Hughie Morrison) *chsd ldrs on inner: pushed along and hdwy over 2f out: rdn over 1f out: led ins fnl f: styd on strly* **11/4**2
5333 2 3 ¼ **Amosite**11 2096 8-8-10 72 (v) ConnorBeasley(3) 3 71
(J R Jenkins) *led 1f: cl up: wd st: rdn to ld wl over 1f out: drvn and hdd ins fnl f: one pce* **5/1**3
-600 3 2 ¼ **Lady Ibrox**15 1967 4-9-5 78 (tp) DaleSwift 2 69
(Alan Brown) *cl up: led after 1f: rdn along wl over 2f out: hdd wl over 1f out: sn drvn and wknd appr fnl f* **14/1**
1305 4 3 **Guishan**10 2127 4-8-7 66 oh9 (p) AndrewMullen 5 48
(Michael Appleby) *cl up: rdn along and ev ch wl over 2f out: drvn wl over 1f out and sn wknd* **7/1**
6-10 5 4 ½ **Patrona Ciana (FR)**3 2318 4-9-7 80 DavidNolan 4 47
(David O'Meara) *in rr: hdwy and wd st: rdn to chse ldrs over 2f out: sn drvn and wknd* **11/10**1
1m 17.21s (0.71) **Going Correction** +0.25s/f (Slow) **5** Ran SP% **110.1**
Speed ratings (Par 102): **105,100,97,93,87**
CSF £16.06 TOTE £2.80: £1.40, £2.50; EX 8.80 Trifecta £48.50.
**Owner** H Morrison **Bred** Henry O'Callaghan **Trained** East Ilsley, Berks
**FOCUS**
A weak fillies' sprint handicap for the grade and a strong pace thanks to a disputed lead. The winner is rated to this year's best.

### 2399 QUICKSILVERSLOTS PLAY YOUR FAVOURITE £500 JACKPOT H'CAP 1m (F)
**5:00** (5:00) (Class 6) (0-65,65) 4-Y-0+ **£1,940** (£577; £288; £144) **Stalls** Low

Form RPR
1310 1 **Sam Spade (IRE)**9 2164 4-9-5 63 (v) DaleSwift 6 74
(Derek Shaw) *trckd ldrs: swtchd rt and hdwy over 3f out: sn cl up: led 2f out and sn rdn: drvn ent fnl f: kpt on strly towards fin* **7/2**1
2222 2 2 ¼ **General Tufto**11 2092 9-8-6 55 (b) JoeyHaynes(5) 9 61
(Charles Smith) *midfield: hdwy over 3f out: chsd ldrs wl over 2f out: chal wl over 1f out: sn rdn and ev ch tl drvn ins fnl f and kpt on same pce* **5/1**2
5005 3 2 ½ **Warfare**20 1842 5-9-1 64 KevinStott(5) 4 64
(Kevin Ryan) *in tch: hdwy over 3f out: chsd ldrs 2f out: rdn to chse ldng pair over 1f out: drvn and no imp fnl f* **7/2**1
0-00 4 1 **Habeshia**60 1023 4-8-9 53 (v) JohnFahy 12 51
(John Best) *prom on wd outside: cl up after 3f: disp ld 1/2-way: led 3f out: sn rdn: hdd 2f out: sn drvn and kpt on one pce* **14/1**
3400 5 ¾ **Sutton Sid**25 1675 4-9-4 62 (v) AndrewMullen 2 58
(John Balding) *bhd: rdn along and hdwy on inner over 2f out: styd on appr fnl f: nrst fin* **20/1**
0000 6 1 **Spirit Rider (USA)**27 1638 4-8-13 57 PatrickDonaghy 8 51
(Giles Bravery) *s.i.s and bhd tl styd on fnl 2f: nrst fin* **14/1**

0-6 **7** 5 **Perseverent Pete (USA)**19 1877 4-8-7 **51** oh6.......... AdamBeschizza 7 33
(Christine Dunnett) *chsd ldrs: rdn along over 3f out: sn wknd* **12/1**
0-60 **8** ½ **Jebel Tara**7 2215 9-8-11 **58**..................................(bt) ConnorBeasley(3) 11 39
(Alan Brown) *in tch on wd outside: hdwy and wd st: rdn to chse ldrs 2f out: edgd lft and wknd over 1f out* **8/1**3
2136 **9** 5 **On The Cusp (IRE)**34 1496 7-9-3 **64**..........................(b) DeclanBates(3) 5 34
(Ann Stokell) *led 3f: chsd ldrs: rdn along over 3f out and sn wknd* **12/1**
0/2- **10** 5 **Silvala Dance**336 3405 4-8-7 **51** oh1..................................... LiamJones 10 9
(Chris Wall) *chsd ldrs: slt ld after 3f: rdn along and hdd 3f out: sn wknd* **10/1**
0005 **11** 22 **Basingstoke (IRE)**19 1886 5-9-7 **65**................................ JimmyQuinn 3
(Simon Hodgson) *a in rr: bhd fnl 3f* **20/1**
600- **12** 8 **Silvas Romana (IRE)**206 7515 5-8-13 **57**.......................... PaulQuinn 1
(Mark Brisbourne) *towards rr: rdn along on inner 1/2-way: sn bhd* **25/1**

1m 45.24s (1.54) **Going Correction** +0.25s/f (Slow) **12** Ran SP% **123.4**
Speed ratings (Par 101): **102,99,97,96,95 94,89,89,84,79 57,49**
CSF £20.72 CT £69.14 TOTE £6.50: £1.80, £1.80, £1.10; EX 19.00 Trifecta £71.00.
**Owner** The Warren Partnership **Bred** Newhall Ltd **Trained** Sproxton, Leics

**FOCUS**
A moderate handicap. A personal best from the winner.

## 2400 QUICKSILVERSLOTS FUN ON THE HIGH STREET H'CAP 7f (F)
5:30 (5:30) (Class 5) (0-75,74) 4-Y-0+ **£2,587** (£770; £384; £192) **Stalls** Low

Form RPR
5514 **1** **Repetition**9 2169 4-9-7 **74**........................................ DaleSwift 3 88
(Kristin Stubbs) *trckd ldr: hdwy to ld over 2f out: rdn clr appr fnl f: styd on strly* **4/1**3
0312 **2** 4½ **Sakash**27 1630 4-9-5 **72**........................................ FrederikTylicki 1 74
(J R Jenkins) *trckd ldrs on inner: hdwy 3f out: chsd wnr wl over 1f out and sn rdn: drvn ent fnl f and no imp* **2/1**1
1552 **3** 3¾ **Pick A Little**14 2012 6-8-13 **66**.................................... LiamJones 5 59
(Michael Blake) *chsd ldrs: hdwy on outer wl over 2f out: rdn to chse ldng pair over 1f out: sn drvn and one pce* **12/1**
5422 **4** ¾ **Sofias Number One (USA)**68 929 6-9-1 **73**..........(b) PhilipPrince(5) 4 64
(Roy Bowring) *sn outpcd and wl bhd after 2f: hdwy 2f out: styd on strly appr fnl f: nrst fin* **11/4**2
3003 **5** ¾ **Severiano (USA)**19 1873 4-8-7 **60**...........................(v1) BenCurtis 6 49
(Alan McCabe) *sn outpcd and drvn along in rr after 1 1/2f: hdwy on outer over 2f out: styd on u.p fr over 1f out: nrst fin* **8/1**
6530 **6** ¾ **Tartan Trip**28 1609 7-9-3 **70**................................(v) AndrewMullen 2 57
(Michael Appleby) *chsd ldng pair on outer: rdn along 3f out: drvn 2f out: sn wknd* **7/1**
5056 **7** 7 **Pabusar**27 1630 6-8-11 **67**..........................DeclanBates(3) 7 36
(Ann Stokell) *led: rdn along 3f out: hdd over 2f out and sn wknd* **33/1**

1m 30.58s (0.28) **Going Correction** +0.25s/f (Slow) **7** Ran SP% **114.2**
Speed ratings (Par 103): **108,102,98,97,96 96,88**
CSF £12.43 TOTE £4.40: £2.60, £1.50; EX 23.50 Trifecta £162.80.
**Owner** The B P J Partnership **Bred** G Reed **Trained** Norton, N Yorks

**FOCUS**
An ordinary handicap, run at a decent pace. The winner took his form to a new high.
T/Plt: £61.30 to a £1 stake. Pool: £58,643.79 - 697.27 winning units. T/Qpdt: £8.30 to a £1 stake. Pool: £5198.08 - 460.50 winning units. JR

# 2220 WINDSOR (R-H)
Monday, May 19

**OFFICIAL GOING: Good to firm (8.7)**
Wind: Almost nil Weather: Fine, very warm

## 2401 DOWNLOAD THE UNIBET PRO APP CLAIMING STKS 6f
6:05 (6:05) (Class 5) 3-Y-0+ **£2,587** (£770; £384; £192) **Stalls** Low

Form RPR
1561 **1** **Hamoody (USA)**13 2050 10-9-2 77.................................. OisinMurphy(3) 1 78
(Joseph Tuite) *taken down early: led 1f: w ldr tl led again 2f out: edgd lft but in command fnl f: drvn out* **5/2**1
263 **2** 2 **Ocean Legend (IRE)**60 1026 9-9-1 62............................ LiamKeniry 9 68
(Tony Carroll) *hld up: prog gng wl on outer over 2f out: rdn to chse wnr jst over 1f out: nt qckn and nvr able to chal* **6/1**
3404 **3** ¾ **New Leyf (IRE)**13 2059 8-9-5 68..........................(b) SeanLevey 7 69
(Jeremy Gask) *in tch: pushed along bef 1/2-way: no prog over 2f out: styd on fr over 1f out to take 3rd ins fnl f* **5/1**
6600 **4** 2¼ **Scruffy Tramp (IRE)**3 2317 3-8-10 82....................(p) NatashaEaton(5) 4 65
(Alan Bailey) *s.i.s: sn chsd ldrs: cl enough 2f out: sn rdn and nt qckn: wl hld whn rdr dropped whip jst ins fnl f* **9/2**3
0352 **5** 1¼ **Kuanyao (IRE)**18 1893 8-9-5 74...........................(b) HayleyTurner 3 58
(Conor Dore) *taken down early: t.k.h: led after 1f to 2f out: sn rdn: wknd over 1f out* **3/1**2
03-0 **6** 2¼ **Fleeting Indian (IRE)**19 1877 5-8-8 41......................... DanielCremin(7) 5 47
(Linda Jewell) *a towards rr: rdn and no prog over 2f out* **100/1**
4-5 **7** 2½ **Diamonds A Dancing**15 1980 4-9-2 0..........................(p) JimCrowley 2 40
(Brian Gubby) *a towards rr: shkn up and no prog over 2f out* **20/1**
010/ **8** 2¼ **Medal Of Valour (JPN)**57 7130 6-9-0 67..............(t) SilvestreDeSousa 8 31
(Mark Gillard) *chsd ldrs: lost pl qckly 1/2-way: in rr after: eased fnl f* **33/1**

1m 12.37s (-0.63) **Going Correction** -0.175s/f (Firm)
**WFA** 3 from 4yo+ 9lb **8** Ran SP% **111.4**
Speed ratings (Par 103): **97,94,93,90,88 85,82,79**
CSF £16.86 TOTE £3.10: £1.10, £2.60, £2.10; EX 17.10 Trifecta £58.50.
**Owner** Andrew Liddiard **Bred** Ragged Mountain Farm **Trained** Great Shefford, Berks

**FOCUS**
Top bend dolled out 9yds from normal configuration, adding 35yds to races of one mile and beyond. Inner of straight dolled out 5yds at 6f and 2yds at winning post. A moderate claimer which has been rated cautiously.

## 2402 EBF BRITISH STALLION STUDS MAIDEN FILLIES' STKS (BOBIS RACE) 5f 10y
6:35 (6:37) (Class 5) 2-Y-0 **£2,911** (£866; £432; £216) **Stalls** Low

Form RPR
0 **1** **Arabian Queen (IRE)**10 2107 2-9-0 0.............................. LiamKeniry 7 79+
(David Elsworth) *trckd ldrs: shkn up wl over 1f out: clsd to chal fnl f: drvn to ld last 75yds* **4/1**3
**2** ½ **Al Fareej (IRE)** 2-9-0 0.............................. SilvestreDeSousa 6 77+
(James Tate) *chsd ldrs: pushed along and prog to go 2nd 1/2-way: rdn to ld over 1f out: kpt on but hdd last 75yds* **8/1**
**3** 1½ **Paint The Star (IRE)** 2-9-0 0.............................. RichardHughes 9 72+
(Richard Hannon) *disp 2nd pl to 1/2-way: styd wl in tch: clsd jst over 1f out: shkn up to chal ins fnl f: nt qckn* **5/2**1
34 **4** ¾ **No One Knows**25 1670 2-9-0 0.............................. WilliamBuick 1 69
(J W Hills) *off the pce in midfield: shkn up over 2f out: hanging lft over 1f out: styd on fnl f: nrst fin* **8/1**
**5** 1¼ **Zeb Un Nisa** 2-9-0 0.............................. JamesDoyle 11 65+
(Roger Charlton) *led and gd spd fr wdst draw to r against nr side rail: shkn up and hdd over 1f out: wknd fnl f* **14/1**
**6** 1¼ **Jimmy's Girl (IRE)** 2-9-0 0.............................. JimCrowley 4 60
(Richard Hannon) *dwlt: sn in midfield but off the pce: prog on outer 2f out: pushed along and rn green over 1f out: steadily fdd* **16/1**
**7** 8 **Papier** 2-9-0 0.............................. SeanLevey 3 31
(Richard Hannon) *dwlt: rn green in rr: nvr on terms* **25/1**
**8** 1 **Surrey Pink (FR)** 2-9-0 0.............................. SteveDrowne 8 28
(William Muir) *a in rr: no ch fnl 2f* **33/1**
6 **9** 13 **Rasha (IRE)**13 2057 2-9-0 0.............................. AndreaAtzeni 2
(Roger Varian) *disp 2nd pl to 1/2-way: wknd qckly and eased: t.o* **7/2**2
00 **10** 4½ **Now Say Boooom**13 2057 2-9-0 0.............................. FergusSweeney 10
(Luke Dace) *s.i.s: sn struggling in last: t.o* **66/1**

1m 0.12s (-0.18) **Going Correction** -0.175s/f (Firm) **10** Ran SP% **113.8**
Speed ratings (Par 90): **94,93,90,89,87 85,72,71,50,43**
CSF £34.42 TOTE £4.20: £1.60, £2.10, £1.70; EX 51.10 Trifecta £132.70.
**Owner** J C Smith **Bred** Littleton Stud **Trained** Newmarket, Suffolk

**FOCUS**
This had the look of a good fillies' maiden. The winner showed notable improvement.

## 2403 WEATHERBYS PRIVATE BANKING NOVICE STKS (BOBIS RACE) 5f 10y
7:05 (7:05) (Class 2) 2-Y-0 **£9,703** (£2,887; £1,443; £721) **Stalls** Low

Form RPR
1 **1** **Kool Kompany (IRE)**23 1726 2-9-4 0.............................. RichardHughes 5 91+
(Richard Hannon) *sn led and crossed to nr side rail: jnd 2f out: shkn up over 1f out: firmly pushed out fnl f and a holding on* **8/11**1
1 **2** ½ **Merdon Castle (IRE)**13 2057 2-9-7 0.............................. LiamKeniry 4 92
(David Elsworth) *best away but sn hdd: pressed wnr: upsides fr 2f out: drvn 1f out: styd on wl but a jst hld* **11/4**2
14 **3** 4½ **Bronze Maquette (IRE)**3 2308 2-9-2 0.............................. WilliamBuick 3 71
(Gary Moore) *chsd ldng pair: pushed along 2f out and in tch: lft bhd fnl f* **8/1**3
41 **4** ¾ **Madamoiselle Bond**7 2206 2-8-13 0.............................. JimCrowley 2 65
(William Jarvis) *chsd ldng pair: pushed along 2f out and in tch: lft bhd fnl f* **33/1**
214 **5** 12 **Paddy Again (IRE)**15 1982 2-8-13 0.............................. RyanWhile 1 22
(Bill Turner) *outpcd and a detached in last* **10/1**

59.87s (-0.43) **Going Correction** -0.175s/f (Firm) **5** Ran SP% **107.7**
Speed ratings (Par 99): **96,95,88,86,67**
CSF £2.76 TOTE £1.60: £1.10, £2.80; EX 3.10 Trifecta £8.20.
**Owner** Middleham Park Racing LXXXVI **Bred** Miss Imelda O'Shaughnessy **Trained** East Everleigh, Wilts

**FOCUS**
All five of these were previous winners and the front two, who had the race to themselves late on, were both bidding to follow up debut victories. The winner is the type to find another few lengths next time. The time was 0.25secs quicker than the preceding fillies' maiden.

## 2404 NEW HORSERACING ODDS AT UNIBET.CO.UK MAIDEN FILLIES' STKS 1m 67y
7:35 (7:36) (Class 5) 3-Y-0+ **£2,587** (£770; £384; £192) **Stalls** Low

Form RPR
3 **1** **Bragging (USA)**17 1920 3-9-0 0.............................. JamesDoyle 4 83+
(Sir Michael Stoute) *trckd ldng trio: pushed along and clsd fr over 2f out: led jst over 1f out: shkn up and wl in command fnl f* **7/4**1
**2** 2 **Hoop Of Colour (USA)** 3-9-0 0.............................. RichardHughes 3 77+
(Lady Cecil) *trckd ldrs in 5th: pushed along over 2f out: no imp tl styd on fr over 1f out: tk 2nd nr fin* **7/1**
4-2 **3** ½ **Award (IRE)**13 2061 3-9-0 0.............................. WilliamBuick 2 76
(John Gosden) *trckd ldr 3f: racd in 3rd after: pushed along 3f out: clsd and tried to chal over 1f out: shkn up and kpt on same pce* **9/2**2
6-4 **4** 1¾ **Darting**22 1768 3-8-11 0.............................. OisinMurphy(3) 11 72
(Andrew Balding) *t.k.h: led: rdn and hdd jst over 1f out: fdd fnl f* **20/1**
3 **5** 1½ **Kleo (GR)**14 2026 3-8-7 0.............................. GianlucaSanna(7) 14 69
(Luca Cumani) *trckd ldr after 3f: urged along furiously to try to chal jst over 2f out: steadily wknd jst over 1f out* **10/1**
3 **6** 1 **Cincinnati Girl (IRE)**18 1894 3-9-0 0.............................. ShaneKelly 5 66
(Denis Coakley) *chsd ldrs in 6th: nt on terms and pushed along over 2f out: no real imp but kpt on steadily* **16/1**
02 **7** shd **Dorraar (IRE)**17 1920 3-9-0 0..............................1 AndreaAtzeni 6 66
(Roger Varian) *off the pce in 8th whn awkward bnd 5f out and shoved along: nvr on terms after: styd on fr over 1f out* **5/1**3
**8** 4½ **Champs D'Or** 3-8-9 0.............................. MarcMonaghan(5) 1 56
(Marco Botti) *sn off the pce in abt 9th: shkn up and sme prog wl over 2f out: no hdwy over 1f out: fdd* **33/1**
20- **9** shd **Heartstrings**297 4702 3-9-0 0.............................. SilvestreDeSousa 7 55
(Mick Channon) *towards rr and off the pce: pushed along and sme prog 3f out: no hdwy 2f out: fdd* **14/1**
**10** 4½ **Statsminister** 3-9-0 0.............................. FergusSweeney 10 45
(Luke Dace) *s.i.s: rn green and a wl in rr: modest late prog* **100/1**
5/3 **11** 1½ **Sandaura (IRE)**22 1768 4-9-12 0.............................. SteveDrowne 8 45
(Clive Cox) *in tch in midfield: 7th 1/2-way: pushed along wl over 2f out: sn wknd: eased* **33/1**
**12** 2¼ **Greatday Allweek (IRE)**165 5-9-5 0.............................. GaryMahon(7) 13 39
(Seamus Mullins) *dwlt: a wl in rr: shkn up and no prog over 2f out* **100/1**
**13** 1 **Artistic Muse (IRE)** 3-9-0 0.............................. JimCrowley 9 34
(J W Hills) *restless in stalls: s.s: a in last pair: no ch over 2f out* **66/1**
45- **14** 1¾ **Ametrine (IRE)**198 7693 3-8-9 0.............................. NoelGarbutt(5) 12 30
(William Jarvis) *dwlt: a wl in rr: pushed along and no prog 1/2-way* **66/1**

1m 42.01s (-2.69) **Going Correction** -0.175s/f (Firm)
**WFA** 3 from 4yo+ 12lb **14** Ran SP% **121.0**
Speed ratings (Par 100): **106,104,103,101,100 99,99,94,94,90 88,86,85,83**
CSF £13.79 TOTE £2.90: £1.10, £2.60, £1.80; EX 15.10 Trifecta £47.30.
**Owner** K Abdullah **Bred** Juddmonte Farms Inc **Trained** Newmarket, Suffolk

**FOCUS**
Sir Michael Stoute was winning this fillies' maiden for the fifth time in the past decade. Fair form, the winner looking a nice type.

## 2405 UNIBET OFFER DAILY JOCKEY & TRAINER SPECIALS H'CAP — 1m 3f 135y
**8:05** (8:05) (Class 3) (0-95,94) 4-Y-O+ — **£7,439** (£2,213; £1,106; £553) **Stalls** Centre

Form — RPR

52-6 **1** **Cafe Society (FR)**[15] [1973] 4-9-3 **90** ........ JimCrowley 9 — 101
(David Simcock) *hld up in 4th: clsd fr 3f out gng wl: led wl over 1f out: pushed out: comf* **1/1**[1]

1145 **2** 2 ¼ **Modernism**[94] [611] 5-9-1 **88** ........ AndreaAtzeni 3 — 95
(David Simcock) *racd keenly: led: pushed along 3f out: hdd wl over 1f out: kpt on to hold on for 2nd but no ch w wnr* **20/1**

200- **3** nk **Kuda Huraa (IRE)**[59] [2648] 6-8-13 **86** ........ RichardHughes 7 — 92
(Alan King) *swtg: trckd ldng pair: cl up 2f out but wnr already gone by: drvn to chal for 2nd fnl f: kpt on* **8/1**[3]

0-15 **4** 4 ½ **Jakey (IRE)**[26] [1651] 4-8-8 **81** ........ FergusSweeney 5 — 80
(Pat Phelan) *hld up in last: pushed along over 2f out: reminder and kpt on fnl f to take 4th nr fin: nvr involved* **8/1**[3]

4160 **5** ½ **Commissar**[31] [1553] 5-8-9 **82** ........ (t) JamesDoyle 4 — 80
(Ian Williams) *awkward s: hld up in 5th: rdn over 2f out: no imp on ldrs over 1f out: fdd* **16/1**

112- **6** ½ **Ballinderry Boy**[199] [7660] 4-9-4 **94** ........ OisinMurphy[(3)] 2 — 91
(Andrew Balding) *chsd ldr: pushed along 3f out: lost 2nd jst over 2f out: steadily fdd* **3/1**[2]

2000 **7** 10 **Uramazin (IRE)**[9] [2154] 8-9-1 **88** ........ LiamKeniry 8 — 68
(Philip Hide) *taken down early: dwlt: hld up in 6th: drvn and no prog over 2f out: wknd wl over 1f out* **25/1**

2m 28.38s (-1.12) **Going Correction** -0.175s/f (Firm) — **7** Ran SP% **111.7**
Speed ratings (Par 107): **96,94,94,91,90 90,83**
CSF £23.26 CT £105.61 TOTE £1.60: £1.10, £7.80; EX 21.10 Trifecta £85.80.
**Owner** S Bamber J Barnett & M Caine **Bred** Haras Du Quesnay **Trained** Newmarket, Suffolk

**FOCUS**
A fair handicap where it paid to race handy. The form is rated around the second and third.

## 2406 SIS H'CAP (BOBIS RACE) — 5f 10y
**8:35** (8:37) (Class 4) (0-80,80) 3-Y-O — **£4,851** (£1,443; £721; £360) **Stalls** Low

Form — RPR

1-00 **1** **Sleepy Sioux**[12] [2083] 3-9-7 **80** ........ (p) SilvestreDeSousa 7 — 94
(David Elsworth) *fractious bef s: wl in tch: prog 2f out: rdn to ld jst over 1f out: r.o wl* **3/1**[1]

3-43 **2** 2 ¼ **Groundworker (IRE)**[14] [2035] 3-8-10 **69** ........ RichardHughes 4 — 75
(Sylvester Kirk) *hld up in rr: prog jst over 2f out: rdn over 1f out: styd on to take 2nd ins fnl f: no threat to wnr* **6/1**[2]

-314 **3** ¾ **Searchlight**[30] [1585] 3-9-2 **75** ........ JamesDoyle 1 — 78
(Kevin Ryan) *trckd ldrs: clsd against nr side rail to ld over 1f out: hung lft and sn hdd: nt qckn fnl f* **3/1**[1]

126 **4** 2 **Fuel Injection**[23] [1737] 3-8-8 **67** ........ (p) ShaneKelly 5 — 63
(Paul Midgley) *mde most: rdn and hdd over 1f out: fdd fnl f* **12/1**

35-5 **5** nk **Finflash (IRE)**[28] [1615] 3-9-3 **76** ........ WilliamBuick 2 — 71
(Mick Channon) *outpcd and detached in last: rdn and styd on fr over 1f out: nrst fin* **11/1**[3]

34-0 **6** 5 **Mr Dandy Man (IRE)**[14] [2035] 3-8-12 **71** ........ SteveDrowne 8 — 48
(Ronald Harris) *w ldr to 2f out: sn wknd* **20/1**

-531 **7** 3 ¾ **Flashy Queen (IRE)**[14] [2035] 3-8-13 **75** ........ OisinMurphy[(3)] 6 — 38
(Joseph Tuite) *w ldrs 1f: lost pl and struggling by 1/2-way: sn btn* **3/1**[1]

1-06 **8** hd **Touch The Clouds**[18] [1893] 3-9-3 **76** ........ (tp) JimCrowley 3 — 39
(William Stone) *in tch in rr: rdn 1/2-way: sn struggling and btn* **25/1**

59.3s (-1.00) **Going Correction** -0.175s/f (Firm) — **8** Ran SP% **113.9**
Speed ratings (Par 101): **101,97,96,93,92 84,78,78**
CSF £21.55 CT £57.61 TOTE £3.40: £1.10, £1.50, £1.80; EX 21.80 Trifecta £122.00.
**Owner** Ten Green Bottles I **Bred** New Hall Stud **Trained** Newmarket, Suffolk

**FOCUS**
An ordinary 3yo sprint handicap. The winner stepped up on her 2yo form.
T/Plt: £4.60 to a £1 stake. Pool: £85,716.24 - 13,355.50 winning units. T/Qpdt: £2.00 to a £1 stake. Pool: £6646.75 - 2415.30 winning units. JN

# [2267] SAINT-CLOUD (L-H)
### Monday, May 19

**OFFICIAL GOING: Turf: good**

## 2411a PRIX SICARELLE (MAIDEN) (3YO FILLIES) (TURF) — 1m 4f
**11:45** (12:00) 3-Y-O — **£10,416** (£4,166; £3,125; £2,083; £1,041)

RPR

**1** **Isabella Liberty (FR)**[53] [1139] 3-9-0 0 ........ IoritzMendizabal 1 — 81+
(Robert Eddery) *mde all: set stdy gallop: shkn up and lened 2 1/2f out: kpt on wl fnl f: won a shade cosily* **23/5**[2]

**2** ½ **Lupin Violet (IRE)**[32] 3-9-0 0 ........ ThierryJarnet 4 — 80
(J E Pease, France) **2/5**[1]

**3** 1 ½ **Mauny (FR)**[35] 3-9-0 0 ........ FabienLefebvre 3 — 78
(Mlle A Voraz, France) **58/10**[3]

**4** 1 ¼ **Artiste Lady (FR)**[23] 3-8-10 0 ........ CesarPasserat[(4)] 2 — 76
(Mme C Head-Maarek, France) **161/10**

**5** ¾ **Autignac (FR)**[69] 3-9-0 0 ........ AlexandreRoussel 6 — 74
(Mlle S-V Tarrou, France) **13/1**

**6** 9 **Dark Black Diamond (FR)** 3-8-10 0 ........ MlleAmelieFoulon[(4)] 7 — 60
(Mlle S-V Tarrou, France) **31/1**

2m 39.62s (-0.78) — **6** Ran SP% **120.1**
WIN (incl. 1 euro stake): 5.60. PLACES: 1.30, 1.10. SF: 11.40.
**Owner** E Phillips & Mrs M Matthews **Bred** Eduard Mordukhovitch **Trained** Newmarket, Suffolk

# [2007] BATH (L-H)
### Tuesday, May 20

**OFFICIAL GOING: Firm (10.2)**
Wind: mild breeze Weather: showers

## 2413 MERLIN STOVES/BRITISH STALLION STUDS EBF MAIDEN STKS — 5f 161y
**2:10** (2:11) (Class 5) 2-Y-O — **£3,067** (£905; £453) **Stalls** Centre

Form — RPR

22 **1** **Brown Velvet**[13] [2064] 2-9-0 0 ........ (v) MartinDwyer 1 — 68
(Hugo Palmer) *trckd ldr: rdn 2f out: kpt on ins fnl f: led fnl strides* **5/1**[3]

03 **2** shd **Arlecchino's Leap**[22] [1807] 2-9-5 0 ........ (v[1]) DavidProbert 4 — 73
(Mark Usher) *led: rdn over 1f out: kpt on but no ex whn hdd fnl strides* **16/1**

0 **3** 2 **Kassbaan**[16] [1977] 2-9-0 0 ........ MarcMonaghan[(5)] 8 — 66+
(Marco Botti) *awkward and wnt rt s: racd keenly: trckd ldng pair: rdn wl over 1f out: nt pce to chal: wnt 3rd fnl strides* **11/4**[2]

02 **4** ½ **Kibaar**[20] [1866] 2-9-5 0 ........ DaneO'Neill 6 — 64
(J W Hills) *racd keeny in tch: rdn 2f out: nt pce to get on terms: kpt on same pce fnl f: lost 3rd fnl strides* **1/2**[1]

0 **5** 6 **Verchild Lad (IRE)**[46] [1276] 2-9-5 0 ........ LiamKeniry 9 — 45
(David Evans) *hld up: rdn over 2f out: nvr gng pce to get on terms* **40/1**

5 **6** ½ **Invincible Zeb (IRE)**[8] [2200] 2-9-5 0 ........ LiamJones 7 — 43
(Ronald Harris) *squeezed out s: sn pushed along in tch: wknd fnl f* **16/1**

0 **7** 1 ¾ **Sculptured (FR)**[11] [2128] 2-8-9 0 ........ PhilipPrince[(5)] 5 — 32
(Jo Hughes) *hld up: rdn over 2f out: nvr threatened: wknd fnl f* **33/1**

U **8** 19 **Saphira Silver (IRE)**[13] [2071] 2-8-11 0 ........ MatthewCosham[(3)] 2
(Nikki Evans) *in tch: rdn over 3f out: wknd 2f out* **66/1**

1m 10.88s (-0.32) **Going Correction** -0.05s/f (Good) — **8** Ran SP% **128.6**
Speed ratings (Par 93): **100,99,97,96,88 87,85,60**
CSF £83.53 TOTE £6.00: £1.40, £2.80, £2.20; EX 47.40 Trifecta £172.50.
**Owner** Carmichael Humber **Bred** D R Botterill **Trained** Newmarket, Suffolk

**FOCUS**
Races incorporating bottom bend increased in distance by about 10yds. Very few ever got into this maiden and it paid to be right on the pace. With the two market leaders beating themselves to a degree, it remains to be seen what the form amounts to but there is no doubting the attitude of the front pair. The form is rated at the lower end of the race averages.

## 2414 WYE VALLEY DEMOLITION LTD H'CAP — 5f 161y
**2:40** (2:42) (Class 5) (0-75,74) 4-Y-O+ — **£2,587** (£770; £384; £192) **Stalls** Centre

Form — RPR

-506 **1** **Diamondhead (IRE)**[18] [1921] 5-9-7 **74** ........ PatCosgrave 12 — 82
(Ed de Giles) *sn pushed along in mid-div: hdwy on far rail fr wl over 1f out: r.o to ld fnl 120yds: hld on wl: drvn out* **15/2**[2]

0564 **2** nk **Jay Bee Blue**[20] [1873] 5-9-5 **72** ........ (bt) DaneO'Neill 5 — 79
(Sean Curran) *s.i.s: bhd: swtchd rt and hdwy fr 2f out: r.o wl fnl f: wnt cl 2nd nring fin* **10/1**

24-1 **3** nk **Dreams Of Glory**[13] [2070] 6-9-5 **72** ........ HarryBentley 3 — 78
(Ron Hodges) *a.p: led narrowly 2f out: sn rdn: hdd fnl 120yds: no ex whn lost 2nd nring fin* **6/1**[1]

-406 **4** 2 **Ginzan**[18] [1912] 6-9-5 **72** ........ RobertWinston 8 — 71
(Malcolm Saunders) *in tch: rdn over 2f out: hung rt whn chalng jst over 1f out: no ex ins fnl f* **10/1**

3620 **5** 1 **Hamis Al Bin (IRE)**[11] [2127] 5-8-2 **60** oh2 ........ (t) RyanTate[(5)] 2 — 56
(Milton Bradley) *towards rr: stdy prog fr 2f out: kpt on ins fnl f: nt rch ldrs* **14/1**

43-5 **6** nk **Edged Out**[22] [1789] 4-9-5 **72** ........ DavidProbert 14 — 67
(Christopher Mason) *mid-div on outer: hdwy 3f out: rdn to chse ldrs 2f out: kpt on same pce fnl f* **14/1**

54-2 **7** shd **Bilash**[120] [259] 7-8-13 **66** ........ PatDobbs 11 — 61
(Andrew Hollinshead) *mid-div: rdn 2f out: hdwy over 1f out: kpt on same pce fnl f* **12/1**

306- **8** 1 **Howyadoingnotsobad (IRE)**[210] [7445] 6-9-0 **72** ........ RyanWhile[(5)] 4 — 63
(Bill Turner) *led tl 2f out: sn rdn and ev ch tl no ex jst ins fnl f* **16/1**

0-04 **9** nse **Panther Patrol (IRE)**[26] [1678] 4-9-0 **67** ........ (v) JohnFahy 15 — 58
(Eve Johnson Houghton) *in tch: trcking ldrs whn nt clr run 2f out: sn rdn: trying to mount chal whn squeezed out jst over 1f out: no ch after* **8/1**[3]

65-6 **10** 3 ¼ **Alcando (IRE)**[22] [1789] 4-9-1 **68** ........ RoystonFfrench 6 — 49
(Denis Coakley) *trckd ldrs: rdn over 2f out: wknd fnl f* **9/1**

4122 **11** 3 ¾ **Top Cop**[13] [2065] 5-9-7 **74** ........ (be) LiamJones 16 — 42
(Ronald Harris) *chsd ldrs: rdn over 2f out: wknd over 1f out* **10/1**

0404 **12** 1 ¼ **Temple Road (IRE)**[18] [1921] 6-9-0 **72** ........ (p) DCByrne[(5)] 9 — 36
(Milton Bradley) *s.i.s: bhd: hdwy 3f out: sn rdn: wknd ent fnl f* **33/1**

455- **13** 7 **Comptonspirit**[258] [6096] 10-8-11 **67** ........ MatthewLawson[(3)] 7 — 8
(Brian Baugh) *a towards rr* **33/1**

0110 **14** 8 **Multitask**[10] [2147] 4-9-5 **72** ........ LiamKeniry 13
(Michael Madgwick) *s.i.s: pushed along and hdwy into midfield 3f out: wknd 2f out* **6/1**[1]

200- **15** 23 **Wooden King (IRE)**[178] [8029] 9-9-6 **73** ........ MartinDwyer 1
(Malcolm Saunders) *s.i.s: a bhd: virtually p.u fnl 2f* **25/1**

1m 10.16s (-1.04) **Going Correction** -0.05s/f (Good) — **15** Ran SP% **125.4**
Speed ratings (Par 103): **104,103,103,100,99 98,98,97,97,92 87,86,76,66,35**
CSF £81.96 CT £498.90 TOTE £8.10: £3.40, £4.70, £2.00; EX 115.20 Trifecta £1911.10 Part won..
**Owner** Mrs Beverley Smith **Bred** J Joyce **Trained** Ledbury, H'fords
■ Stewards' Enquiry : Pat Cosgrave four-day ban: used whip above permitted level (Jun 3-5,8)
Dane O'Neill two-day ban: used whip above permitted level (Jun 3-4)

**FOCUS**
It started to rain before this contest. A wide-open sprint handicap with several still holding every chance inside the last furlong. Straightforward, ordinary form.

## 2415 BLACKMORE BUILDING CONTRACTORS FILLIES' H'CAP — 1m 5y
**3:10** (3:10) (Class 5) (0-75,75) 4-Y-O+ — **£2,587** (£770; £384; £192) **Stalls** Low

Form — RPR

-353 **1** **Kosika (USA)**[11] [2121] 4-9-1 **72** ........ MichaelJMMurphy[(3)] 5 — 82
(Mark Johnston) *mde all: pushed clr over 1f out: styd on strly fnl f: comf* **2/1**[2]

5-35 **2** 4 **Starlight Symphony (IRE)**[22] [1796] 4-9-7 **75** ........ (b) PatDobbs 3 — 76
(Eve Johnson Houghton) *trckd ldng pair: rdn over 2f out: nvr threatened wnr but kpt on same pce to snatch 2nd fnl 75yds* **7/4**[1]

33-0 **3** hd **Dark Amber**[43] [1354] 4-8-13 **67** ........ LiamKeniry 6 — 67
(Brendan Powell) *pressed wnr: rdn 2f out: sn hld: kpt on same pce fnl f: lost 2nd narrowly fnl 75yds* **3/1**[3]

600- 4 3 1/4 **Precision Five**[165] 8179 5-8-7 **68**..........(p) DavidParkes(7) 1 61
(Jeremy Gask) *trckd ldng trio: effrt u.p over 2f out: one pce fnl f* **13/2**
1m 39.81s (-0.99) **Going Correction** -0.05s/f (Good) **4** Ran SP% **108.0**
Speed ratings (Par 100): **102,98,97,94**
CSF £5.83 TOTE £1.90; EX 4.10 Trifecta £6.50.
**Owner** Sheikh Hamdan bin Mohammed Al Maktoum **Bred** Betz Thoroughbred Et Al **Trained** Middleham Moor, N Yorks

**FOCUS**
This ordinary fillies' handicap was hit by three non-runners. The winner had an easy lead.

## 2416 32RED ON THE APP STORE H'CAP 1m 5y
**3:40** (3:42) (Class 6) (0-60,59) 3-Y-O **£1,940** (£577; £288; £144) **Stalls** Low

Form RPR
0-40 **1** **Caledonia Laird**[49] 1223 3-9-1 **53**.......... MartinDwyer 13 62
(Jo Hughes) *in tch: trckd ldrs over 3f out: sn swtchd rt and rdn: styd on ent fnl f: led fnl 100yds: rdn out* **16/1**
-001 **2** 3/4 **Plucky Dip**[13] 2078 3-9-2 **54**.......... RoystonFfrench 3 62
(John Ryan) *disp ld: rdn and strly pressed fr over 2f out: kpt on gamely tl no ex whn hdd fnl 100yds* **8/1**[3]
6154 **3** nk **Prim And Proper**[13] 2078 3-9-2 **54**.......... RobertWinston 7 61
(Brendan Powell) *a.p: rdn for str chal fr over 2f out: ev ch fnl f: kpt on but no ex nring fin* **8/1**[3]
500- **4** 3 1/4 **Bishop Wulstan (IRE)**[190] 7835 3-9-2 **54**.......... ASandesh 1 54
(Richard Hannon) *mid-div on rails: rdn wl over 2f out: no imp tl styd on ent fnl f: wnt 4th nring fin* **12/1**
0-06 **5** 1/2 **Saxon Princess (IRE)**[15] 2026 3-9-2 **54**.......... DaneO'Neill 2 52
(Roger Charlton) *disp ld tl rdn over 2f out: sn hld by ldr: kpt on same pce: lost 4th nring fin* **5/2**[1]
0-26 **6** 1 1/2 **Tunnel Tiger (IRE)**[8] 2210 3-9-7 **59**..........[1] HarryBentley 5 54
(William Knight) *trckd ldrs: rdn over 2f out: nvr threatened: kpt on same pce* **5/1**[2]
04-4 **7** 1 **Benoordenhout (IRE)**[18] 1918 3-8-11 **49**.......... PatDobbs 4 42+
(Jonathan Portman) *racd keenly in mid-div: rdn over 2f out: no imp* **20/1**
000- **8** 1/2 **Maid Of Tuscany (IRE)**[237] 6739 3-8-12 **57**.......... CharlotteJenner(7) 11 48+
(Mark Usher) *slipped leaving stalls: bhd: styd on far rail wout much room fr jst over 1f out but nvr threatening* **16/1**
660- **9** 1/2 **Jersey Cream (IRE)**[237] 6749 3-9-6 **58**.......... DougieCostello 10 48
(Gary Moore) *mid-div: rdn over 2f out: nvr any imp* **14/1**
-140 **10** 3 1/4 **Lucky Dottie**[48] 1235 3-8-8 **46**.......... FrankieMcDonald 6 29
(Pat Phelan) *unruly at s and in stalls: mid-div whn squeezed up and lost pl after 1f: nvr a threat* **25/1**
00-0 **11** 6 **Moneypennie**[13] 2078 3-8-9 **52**.......... KatiaScallan(5) 14 21
(Marcus Tregoning) *mid-div: rn v wd on bnd over 5f out: rdn wl over 2f out: wknd over 1f out* **20/1**
4403 **12** 1/2 **Synonym (ITY)**[21] 1829 3-8-12 **50**.......... LiamJones 15 18
(J W Hills) *sn swtchd lft: rdn over 3f out: a towards rr* **33/1**
-000 **13** 2 **Manor Way (IRE)**[8] 2224 3-8-13 **58**.......... CamHardie(7) 9 21
(Richard Hannon) *s.i.s: rdn wl over 2f out: a towards rr* **10/1**
50-0 **14** 2 1/4 **Reflection**[26] 1683 3-8-7 **45**.......... JohnFahy 12
(Brian Baugh) *rdn wl over 2f out: a towards rr* **50/1**
0040 **15** 20 **Spin For A Harp (IRE)**[41] 1384 3-9-3 **55**.......... DavidProbert 8
(David Dennis) *mid-div: rdn over 3f out: wknd 2f out: eased fnl f* **66/1**
1m 41.69s (0.89) **Going Correction** -0.05s/f (Good) **15** Ran SP% **122.4**
Speed ratings (Par 97): **93,92,91,88,88 86,85,85,84,81 75,74,72,70,50**
CSF £130.13 CT £1144.37 TOTE £17.70: £4.30, £2.20, £3.30; EX 243.00 Trifecta £3234.70 Part won..
**Owner** Isla & Colin Cage **Bred** Mrs I M Cage And C J Cage **Trained** Lambourn, Berks

**FOCUS**
A moderate 3yo handicap, run in a time 1.88sec slower than the older fillies' in the preceding contest, and another race in which few got involved from behind. Pretty ordinary form, judged around the second and third.

## 2417 32RED.COM H'CAP 1m 2f 46y
**4:10** (4:10) (Class 5) (0-70,67) 3-Y-O **£2,726** (£805; £402) **Stalls** Low

Form RPR
30-1 **1** **Aurelia Cotta (IRE)**[26] 1684 3-9-2 **62**.......... RobertWinston 1 73
(Charles Hills) *racd keenly: mde all: pushed clr over 1f out: readily* **10/1**
634- **2** 4 **Armourer (IRE)**[155] 8312 3-9-6 **66**.......... MartinDwyer 7 69
(William Muir) *trckd wnr: rdn 3f out: nvr quite able to mount chal after: kpt on same pce* **8/1**
40-0 **3** nk **Mabdhool (IRE)**[17] 1947 3-9-6 **66**.......... DaneO'Neill 2 68
(Marcus Tregoning) *s.i.s: sn trcking ldrs: rdn over 3f out: nvr threatened wnr: kpt on same pce fnl 2f* **4/1**[2]
65-3 **4** 3 3/4 **Spectator**[22] 1786 3-9-6 **66**.......... DavidProbert 6 61
(Andrew Balding) *hld up: pushed along and sme prog over 2f out: sn rdn: little imp on ldrs but wnt 4th ent fnl f* **5/4**[1]
00-4 **5** 1 3/4 **Sweetheart Abbey**[22] 1793 3-9-0 **60**.......... HarryBentley 3 52
(William Knight) *hld up in tch: pushed along over 4f out: rdn 3f out: sn one pce* **6/1**[3]
2-23 **6** 3 1/4 **Choral Clan (IRE)**[13] 2078 3-8-13 **59**..........(t) JackMitchell 4 45
(Philip Mitchell) *trckd ldrs: rdn 3f out: nvr threatened: wknd ent fnl f* **12/1**
55-0 **7** 4 **Classic Mission**[22] 1786 3-9-4 **67**.......... MatthewLawson(3) 8 45
(Jonathan Portman) *trckd ldrs: rdn over 3f out: hung lft and wknd over 1f out* **20/1**
100- **8** 3/4 **Oyster (IRE)**[276] 5536 3-9-4 **64**.......... LiamJones 5 41
(Nick Littmoden) *s.i.s: rdn over 4f out: a last* **25/1**
2m 11.58s (0.58) **Going Correction** -0.05s/f (Good) **8** Ran SP% **115.2**
Speed ratings (Par 99): **95,91,91,88,87 84,81,80**
CSF £86.66 CT £375.48 TOTE £7.60: £1.50, £3.30, £2.30; EX 90.00 Trifecta £453.30.
**Owner** Decadent Racing II **Bred** W J Kennedy **Trained** Lambourn, Berks

**FOCUS**
A modest 3yo handicap and yet another race in which nothing got involved from off the pace. The winner improved again on her Warwick win.

## 2418 32RED FREE £10 BONUS MEDIAN AUCTION MAIDEN STKS 1m 2f 46y
**4:40** (4:42) (Class 6) 3-5-Y-O **£1,940** (£577; £288; £144) **Stalls** Low

Form RPR
3-2 **1** **Royal Warranty**[21] 1830 3-8-7 **0**.......... DavidProbert 4 69+
(Andrew Balding) *mid-div: pushed along over 3f out: hdwy over 2f out: rdn to ld ent fnl f: styd on: rdn out* **3/1**[2]
0-0 **2** 1 **Swanwick Shore (IRE)**[15] 2031 3-8-12 **0**.......... PatDobbs 5 72
(Richard Hannon) *trckd ldr: led 2f out: sn drvn: hdd ent fnl f: kpt on but hld fnl 100yds* **20/1**
62-2 **3** hd **Artful Rogue (IRE)**[136] 50 3-8-12 **71**.......... PatCosgrave 10 72
(Amanda Perrett) *trckd ldrs: rdn and ev ch fr 2f out: kpt on ins fnl f but hld by wnr fnl 120yds* **5/1**[3]
3-63 **4** 1/2 **Glasgow Central**[13] 2075 3-8-12 **76**.......... RobertWinston 6 71
(Charles Hills) *trckd ldrs: rdn over 3f out: tending to hang lft whn swtchd rt over 1f out: kpt on ins fnl f* **7/4**[1]
5- **5** 1 3/4 **Haleo**[155] 8312 3-8-12 **0**.......... DaneO'Neill 13 68
(William Muir) *hld up towards rr: rdn 3f out: hdwy over 2f out: kpt on nicley ins fnl f wout ever threatening* **50/1**
**6** 1 3/4 **Pendley Legacy** 3-8-7 **0**.......... JohnFahy 11 59+
(Clive Cox) *s.i.s: settled in last: hdwy over 2f out: styd on fnl f: nvr threatened ldrs* **14/1**
4-0 **7** 2 **Pink And Black (IRE)**[39] 1423 3-8-7 **0**.......... MartinDwyer 3 56
(William Muir) *led: rdn and hdd 2f out: sn wknd* **8/1**
**8** 1 **Bowberry** 3-8-2 **0**.......... RyanTate(5) 8 54
(Clive Cox) *hld up towards rr: rdn 3f out: nvr any danger but styd on wl fnl f* **25/1**
00 **9** 6 **Mountain Dew**[31] 1582 3-8-0 **0**.......... PatrickO'Donnell(7) 2 42
(Ralph Beckett) *trckd ldrs: rdn 3f out: sn wknd* **28/1**
0-23 **10** 1 1/4 **Dynamic Ranger (USA)**[76] 839 3-8-12 **75**.......... DougieCostello 1 45
(Gary Moore) *mid-div: rdn 3f out: wknd over 1f out* **16/1**
0 **11** 8 **Its Not Me Its You**[8] 2221 3-8-12 **0**.......... JackMitchell 12 30
(Brendan Powell) *mid-div: rdn over 2f out: sn wknd* **100/1**
0 **12** 17 **Jamie Lee's Girl**[18] 1918 3-8-7 **0**.......... LiamJones 9
(David Flood) *racd keenly: hld up: rdn over 3f out: wknd over 2f out* **100/1**
2m 11.33s (0.33) **Going Correction** -0.05s/f (Good) **12** Ran SP% **117.7**
Speed ratings (Par 101): **96,95,95,94,93 91,90,89,84,83 77,63**
CSF £68.47 TOTE £4.40: £2.00, £5.00, £1.90; EX 91.70 Trifecta £523.10.
**Owner** Sir Gordon Brunton **Bred** Sir Gordon Brunton **Trained** Kingsclere, Hants

**FOCUS**
An ordinary maiden, though the winning time was 0.25sec quicker than the preceding handicap. Although those that raced handily were again favoured, the winner came from a bit further back. It's doubtful the winner had to improve on her bare AW form.

## 2419 FOSTER REFRIGERATOR FILLIES' H'CAP 1m 5f 22y
**5:10** (5:10) (Class 5) (0-70,70) 4-Y-O+ **£2,726** (£805; £402) **Stalls** High

Form RPR
30-3 **1** **Happy Families**[41] 1393 4-8-13 **62**.......... DaneO'Neill 2 72
(Heather Main) *mde all: set str pce: clr over 3f out: sn shkn up: wl in command fr 2f out: easily* **7/2**[2]
2054 **2** 6 **Ogaritmo**[13] 2084 5-8-7 **56** oh3..........(t) LiamJones 7 57
(Alex Hales) *slowly away: last tl clsd on ldrs over 7f out: rdn into 3rd over 3f out: styd on to chse wnr over 1f out but nvr any ch* **8/1**
445- **3** 3 **Bernisdale**[232] 1974 6-9-1 **64**.......... DavidProbert 6 61
(John Flint) *prom for 3f: trckd ldng pair tl rdn to chse wnr 3f out: sn hld: lost 2nd over 1f out: kpt on same pce* **8/1**
220 **4** 8 **Neston Grace**[13] 1491 6-9-7 **70**.......... RobertWinston 4 55
(Simon Hodgson) *little slowly away: hld up: pushed along and hdwy to cl on ldrs 6f out: rdn over 3f out: sn wnt 4th but nvr gng pce to get involved* **5/1**[3]
-632 **5** 26 **Miss Tiger Lily**[8] 2207 4-9-5 **68**..........(b) PatDobbs 3 14
(Harry Dunlop) *sn chsng wnr: rdn 4f out: qckly btn: wknd wl over 2f out* **11/10**[1]
6054 **6** 34 **Pembroke Pride**[50] 1210 4-8-7 **56** oh8.......... JohnFahy 1
(Philip Hide) *hld up 4th: clsd on ldrs over 7f out: struggling in last 5f out: sn wknd: t.o* **25/1**
2m 49.67s (-2.33) **Going Correction** -0.05s/f (Good) **6** Ran SP% **112.6**
Speed ratings (Par 100): **105,101,99,94,78 57**
CSF £30.02 TOTE £4.70: £3.10, £3.00; EX 28.10 Trifecta £103.60.
**Owner** K Mercer & Wetumpka Racing **Bred** Usk Valley Stud **Trained** Kingston Lisle, Oxon

**FOCUS**
A modest fillies' handicap with half the field going off like scalded cats early and normally that would be suicidal, but with the track riding the way it was two of the three ended up finishing first and third. The winner is rated back to her early form.
T/Jkpt: Not won. T/Plt: £209.20 to a £1 stake. Pool: £73,440.17 - 256.21 winning tickets. T/Qpdt: £38.20 to a £1 stake. Pool: £5,513.90 - 106.60 winning tickets. TM

# 1837 NEWCASTLE (L-H)
Tuesday, May 20

**OFFICIAL GOING: Good (7.3)**
Wind: Almost nil Weather: Overcast

## 2420 JOHN SMITHS MAIDEN STKS 5f
**2:20** (2:20) (Class 5) 3-Y-O **£2,587** (£770; £384; £192) **Stalls** Centre

Form RPR
-222 **1** **Soul Brother (IRE)**[11] 2138 3-9-5 **84**.......... DavidAllan 2 90+
(Tim Easterby) *mde all: shkn up and qcknd clr over 1f out: easily* **1/12**[1]
6 **2** 9 **Carnamoney**[26] 1671 3-9-5 **0**.......... GrahamGibbons 5 61
(David Barron) *dwlt: t.k.h in tch: hdwy to chse wnr 2f out: sn rdn and hung lft: one pce* **13/2**[2]
5 **3** 2 3/4 **Lucky Times**[19] 1902 3-9-0 **0**.......... SilvestreDeSousa 3 43
(Mel Brittain) *chsd wnr to 2f out: sn drvn and outpcd* **20/1**
0- **4** 2 1/2 **Panzi Potter Too**[328] 3681 3-8-11 **0**..........(b[1]) ConnorBeasley(3) 1 34
(Michael Dods) *t.k.h: cl up tl hung lft and wknd over 2f out* **25/1**
**5** 3 **Patron Of Explores (USA)** 3-9-5 **0**.......... DanielTudhope 4 28
(Patrick Holmes) *in tch: drvn and outpcd 1/2-way: sn btn* **16/1**[3]
59.79s (-1.31) **Going Correction** -0.075s/f (Good) **5** Ran SP% **120.2**
Speed ratings (Par 99): **107,92,88,84,79**
CSF £1.91 TOTE £1.10, £2.10; EX 1.80 Trifecta £6.40.
**Owner** C H Stevens **Bred** Michael Downey & Roalso Ltd **Trained** Great Habton, N Yorks

**FOCUS**
After a dry night the going was good. A desperately uncompetitive maiden, the winner scoring as entitled.

## 2421 BILLS QUATRE-VINGT FILLIES' H'CAP 5f
**2:50** (2:52) (Class 5) (0-70,69) 3-Y-O+ **£2,587** (£770; £384; £192) **Stalls** Centre

Form RPR
451- **1** **Adiator**[214] 7345 6-8-13 **61**.......... AdamCarter(5) 5 71+
(Neville Bycroft) *trckd ldrs: effrt and rdn wl over 1f out: led last 50yds: kpt on wl* **9/2**[2]
006- **2** nk **Flighty Clarets (IRE)**[217] 7282 4-9-2 **64**.......... SammyJoBell(5) 4 73
(Richard Fahey) *chsd ldr: led and rdn over 1f out: hdd and no ex last 50yds* **8/1**
0413 **3** 1/2 **Fleurtille**[14] 2056 5-9-11 **68**.......... PJMcDonald 2 75
(Robert Johnson) *mounted on crse and taken early to post: dwlt: bhd: effrt over 2f out: kpt on fnl f: nvr able to chal* **4/1**[1]

0604 **4** *1 ¾* **Balinka**[7] 2233 4-8-12 **55** oh3 DavidAllan 7 56
(Mel Brittain) *led tl rdn and hdd over 1f out: kpt on same pce ins fnl f* **12/1**

022- **5** *½* **Madagascar Moll (IRE)**[229] 6967 3-9-4 **69** DanielTudhope 3 65
(David O'Meara) *trckd ldrs: effrt and pushed along 2f out: kpt on same pce fnl f* **10/1**

22-0 **6** *hd* **Dartrix**[38] 1440 5-9-9 **69** ConnorBeasley(3) 6 67
(Michael Dods) *mounted on crse and taken early to post: towards rr: rdn and hdwy wl over 1f out: kpt on fnl f: no imp* **4/1**[1]

-554 **7** *2 ¼* **Dark Opal (IRE)**[7] 2232 4-9-12 **69** GrahamLee 1 59
(John Weymes) *towards rr: rdn and edgd lft over 2f out: short-lived effrt over 1f out: sn no imp* **7/1**[3]

-000 **8** *1* **Sunrise Dance**[21] 1839 5-9-9 **69** JasonHart(3) 10 56
(Robert Johnson) *towards rr: drvn and struggling wl over 1f out: sn btn* **16/1**

424- **9** *10* **Classy Lassy (IRE)**[252] 6284 3-9-3 **68** TomEaves 9 16
(Brian Ellison) *hld up towards rr: struggling over 2f out: sn btn: t.o* **20/1**

1m 0.35s (-0.75) **Going Correction** -0.075s/f (Good)
**WFA** 3 from 4yo+ 8lb **9** Ran SP% **109.2**
Speed ratings (Par 100): **103,102,101,98,98 97,94,92,76**
CSF £36.50 CT £139.95 TOTE £9.10: £2.40, £5.60, £1.50; EX 63.20 Trifecta £436.20.
**Owner** N Bycroft **Bred** Mickley Stud & C J Whiston **Trained** Norton, N Yorks

**FOCUS**
The pace was honest for this fillies' sprint handicap. The winner is entitled to do better again.

## 2422 FOSTERS MAIDEN STKS — 1m 2f 32y
**3:20** (3:21) (Class 5) 3-Y-O — **£2,587** (£770; £384; £192) **Stalls** Centre

Form RPR

0 **1** **Comedy King (IRE)**[24] 1730 3-9-5 0 AndreaAtzeni 10 85+
(Luca Cumani) *in tch: plld out and smooth hdwy to ld 2f out: rdn and hrd pressed fnl f: kpt on strly* **9/2**[3]

**2** *½* **Fullaah (IRE)** 3-9-0 0 SilvestreDeSousa 8 79+
(Saeed bin Suroor) *hld up: pushed along and rn green over 4f out: gd hdwy on outside fr 2f out: ev ch ins fnl f: hld towards fin: improve* **10/3**[1]

**3** *¾* **Potent Embrace (USA)** 3-9-0 0 FrannyNorton 6 78
(Mark Johnston) *t.k.h early: midfield on outside: stdy hdwy over 2f out: chsd wnr over 1f out to ins fnl f: hld towards fin* **28/1**

**4** *2 ¾* **Stonecutter (IRE)** 3-9-5 0 PaddyAspell 3 77
(Marco Botti) *hld up: pushed along on outside over 2f out: hdwy over 1f out: kpt on strly fnl f: nrst fin* **8/1**

5 **5** *2 ¼* **Lilly Junior**[14] 2061 3-9-0 0 DanielTudhope 7 68
(William Haggas) *trckd ldrs: effrt gng wl whn n.m.r briefly over 1f out: sn rdn and edgd lft: wknd ins fnl f* **5/1**

- **6** *1 ½* **Galactic Heroine** 3-9-0 0 GrahamLee 5 65
(James Given) *in tch: drvn and outpcd 3f out: rallied over 1f out: kpt on fnl f: nt pce to chal* **28/1**

022- **7** *1 ¼* **Empress Ali (IRE)**[217] 7277 3-9-0 73 JamesSullivan 11 63
(Tom Tate) *cl up: rdn and ev ch 2f out: wknd fnl f* **6/1**

4 **8** *1* **Chatham House Rule**[17] 1960 3-9-5 0 TomQueally 4 66
(Michael Bell) *led: rdn and hdd 2f out: wknd appr fnl f* **4/1**[2]

3 **9** *5* **Another Lincolnday**[16] 1969 3-9-5 0 GrahamGibbons 9 57
(David Barron) *hld up: pushed along over 3f out: nvr on terms* **20/1**

0 **10** *2 ¼* **King's Prospect**[17] 1960 3-9-2 0 ConnorBeasley(3) 2 52
(Tracy Waggott) *hld up: rdn and effrt over 2f out: no imp: wknd wl over 1f out* **100/1**

**11** *7* **Drinks For Losers (IRE)** 3-9-5 0 TomEaves 1 39
(Ian Semple) *in tch: drvn and struggling 3f out: btn fnl 2f* **100/1**

2m 10.44s (-1.46) **Going Correction** -0.075s/f (Good) **11** Ran SP% **117.0**
Speed ratings (Par 99): **102,101,101,98,97 95,94,94,90,88 82**
CSF £18.91 TOTE £5.70: £1.70, £1.70, £7.30; EX 24.70 Trifecta £568.90.
**Owner** Sheikh Mohammed Obaid Al Maktoum **Bred** Floors Farming & The Duke Of Devonshire **Trained** Newmarket, Suffolk

**FOCUS**
Some well-bred newcomers in this maiden, which was run at a decent pace. The principals look useful and the time was fast, so a positive view has been taken of the form.

## 2423 BULMERS H'CAP — 1m 2f 32y
**3:50** (3:50) (Class 4) (0-85,84) 4-Y-O+ — **£4,690** (£1,395; £697; £348) **Stalls** Centre

Form RPR

400- **1** **Muharrer**[163] 6750 5-9-0 **80** ConnorBeasley(3) 6 92
(Michael Dods) *t.k.h: hld up on ins: gd hdwy to ld over 1f out: rdn and flashed tail ins fnl f: kpt on wl* **4/1**[1]

1114 **2** *2 ½* **Memory Cloth**[12] 2091 7-8-11 **81** MeganCarberry(7) 7 88
(Brian Ellison) *hld up in tch: effrt on outside over 2f out: chsd wnr ins fnl f: kpt on* **4/1**[1]

**3** *½* **Shouranour (IRE)**[285] 5210 4-9-0 **77** DanielTudhope 8 83
(David O'Meara) *prom: rdn and hdwy to ld over 2f out: hdd over 1f out: kpt on same pce ins fnl f* **12/1**

-064 **4** *1 ¼* **Hydrant**[10] 2162 8-9-0 **77** PhillipMakin 1 81
(Richard Guest) *trckd ldrs: effrt and rdn 2f out: kpt on same pce fnl f* **16/1**

-304 **5** *½* **King Of Paradise (IRE)**[11] 2119 5-8-10 **76** JasonHart(3) 3 79
(Eric Alston) *dwlt: t.k.h in rr: hdwy over 1f out: kpt on fnl f: nvr rchd ldrs* **6/1**[2]

4022 **6** *2 ½* **San Cassiano (IRE)**[11] 2137 7-8-13 **76** JamesSullivan 10 74
(Ruth Carr) *sn led: rdn and hdd over 2f out: wkng whn n.m.r briefly over 1f out* **7/1**

2-36 **7** *1 ¼* **Moccasin (FR)**[15] 2016 5-9-0 **77** PJMcDonald 12 73
(Geoffrey Harker) *hld up: rdn 3f out: styd on fnl f: nvr able to chal* **11/1**

5-10 **8** *nk* **Swehan (IRE)**[30] 1598 4-9-1 **78** TomEaves 9 73
(Kevin Ryan) *early ldr: sn chsd ldr: hdwy and ev ch over 2f out: rdn: edgd lft and wknd over 1f out* **25/1**

20-0 **9** *1* **Muffin McLeay (IRE)**[11] 2137 6-9-7 **84** GrahamGibbons 11 77
(David Barron) *hld up: shkn up over 2f out: nvr nr ldrs* **14/1**

323- **10** *1 ½* **Rex Whistler (IRE)**[197] 7734 4-8-10 **73** GrahamLee 5 64
(Julie Camacho) *t.k.h in midfield: drvn and outpcd over 2f out: sn btn* **13/2**[3]

250/ **11** *14* **Vito Volterra (IRE)**[571] 7366 7-9-6 **83** MichaelStainton 2 47
(Michael Smith) *midfield: struggling 3f out: sn btn: t.o* **25/1**

2m 10.93s (-0.97) **Going Correction** -0.075s/f (Good) **11** Ran SP% **116.4**
Speed ratings (Par 105): **100,98,97,96,96 94,93,92,92,90 79**
CSF £18.64 CT £172.16 TOTE £6.90: £1.70, £2.00, £4.60; EX 21.40 Trifecta £204.80.
**Owner** Andrew Tinkler **Bred** Shadwell Estate Company Limited **Trained** Denton, Co Durham

**FOCUS**
An open handicap run at a steady pace, and 20lb slower than the previous maiden. The winner is rated in line with his better 2013 form.

## 2424 STRONGBOW H'CAP — 2m 19y
**4:20** (4:21) (Class 5) (0-70,70) 4-Y-O+ — **£2,587** (£770; £384; £192) **Stalls** Low

Form RPR

-020 **1** **Jan Smuts (IRE)**[11] 2139 6-9-4 **64** (tp) GrahamLee 9 72
(Wilf Storey) *hld up bhd ldng gp: effrt and rdn over 2f out: led and jnd last 75yds: jst hld on* **7/1**

6-06 **2** *nse* **Summerlea (IRE)**[29] 1605 8-8-2 **51** oh5 (v[1]) NeilFarley(3) 8 59
(Micky Hammond) *hld up: hdwy on outside over 2f out: effrt and disp ld last 75yds: kpt on: jst failed* **16/1**

35-5 **3** *¾* **Beat The Tide**[17] 1934 4-9-5 **70** ConnorBeasley(3) 7 77
(Michael Dods) *t.k.h: hld up: hdwy to ld over 1f out: rdn and hdd last 75yds: nt qckn* **6/4**[1]

60-3 **4** *6* **Mason Hindmarsh**[18] 1929 7-9-6 **66** BarryMcHugh 10 66
(Karen McLintock) *led 6f: chsd ldr: drvn to ld briefly over 1f out: wknd ins fnl f* **9/1**

45-0 **5** *4* **Authentication**[29] 1605 5-8-5 **51** oh1 SilvestreDeSousa 5 46
(Mel Brittain) *t.k.h: cl up on outside: hdwy to ld after 6f: rdn and hdd over 1f out: sn btn* **6/1**[3]

60-4 **6** *5* **Zarosa (IRE)**[18] 1916 5-8-8 **59** NoelGarbutt(5) 2 48
(John Berry) *trckd ldrs: effrt and rdn over 2f out: wknd over 1f out* **5/1**[2]

-040 **7** *13* **Sergeant Pink (IRE)**[11] 2139 8-8-3 **54** ow2 EmmaSayer(5) 1 27
(Dianne Sayer) *cl up: drvn and outpcd over 2f out: sn btn* **25/1**

32-0 **8** *4* **Dan Emmett (USA)**[17] 1960 4-9-2 **67** IanBrennan(3) 4 36
(John Wainwright) *in tch: drvn and outpcd over 4f out: struggling fnl 3f* **10/1**

550- **9** *7* **Turjuman (USA)**[358] 2720 9-8-6 **52** oh4 ow1 AndrewElliott 6 12
(Simon West) *hld up: struggling over 3f out: sn btn* **80/1**

3m 36.63s (-2.77) **Going Correction** -0.075s/f (Good)
**WFA** 4 from 5yo+ 2lb **9** Ran SP% **113.5**
Speed ratings (Par 103): **103,102,102,99,97 95,88,86,83**
CSF £108.28 CT £253.38 TOTE £7.80: £2.10, £2.40, £1.30; EX 100.50 Trifecta £385.80.
**Owner** H S Hutchinson & W Storey **Bred** Tipper House Stud **Trained** Muggleswick, Co Durham
■ Stewards' Enquiry : Neil Farley four-day ban: used whip above permitted level (Jun 3-5,8)

**FOCUS**
An honest pace for this staying handicap. The first three came clear and the winner is rated to his penultimate form.

## 2425 BROWN ALE H'CAP — 7f
**4:50** (4:50) (Class 3) (0-90,90) 4-Y-O+ — **£7,439** (£2,213; £1,106; £553) **Stalls** Centre

Form RPR

650- **1** **King Torus (IRE)**[221] 7176 6-9-1 **84** JamesSullivan 1 92
(Ruth Carr) *cl up: led over 1f out: rdn and edgd rt ins fnl f: hld on wl* **25/1**

0-04 **2** *hd* **Zacynthus (IRE)**[28] 1637 6-8-13 **82** GrahamLee 2 89
(Michael Bell) *t.k.h: in tch: effrt and rdn over 1f out: kpt on wl fnl f: jst hld* **8/1**

-410 **3** *nk* **Farlow (IRE)**[17] 1958 6-9-7 **90** (p) TonyHamilton 9 96
(Richard Fahey) *trckd ldrs: effrt and drvn over 2f out: rallied and ev ch ins fnl f: hld cl home* **2/1**[1]

0-02 **4** *5* **Azrur (IRE)**[32] 1564 4-9-3 **86** AndrewElliott 4 79
(David Brown) *cl up: rdn and ev ch over 1f out: wknd ins fnl f* **13/2**

1000 **5** *nse* **Skytrain**[11] 2117 4-8-13 **82** FrannyNorton 8 75
(Mark Johnston) *dwlt: bhd and pushed along: hdwy u.p over 2f out: kpt on fnl f: no imp* **20/1**

-006 **6** *1* **Fieldgunner Kirkup (GER)**[17] 1957 6-8-7 **76** GrahamGibbons 6 66
(David Barron) *hld up: pushed along over 2f out: no imp fr over 1f out* **10/1**

00-0 **7** *2 ¾* **Lightnin Hopkins (IRE)**[17] 1938 4-9-0 **83** (p) DanielTudhope 7 66
(David O'Meara) *led at ordinary gallop: rdn and hdd over 1f out: sn btn* **16/1**

3- **8** *¾* **Dual Mac**[291] 4968 7-8-7 **76** oh2 BarryMcHugh 5 57
(Neville Bycroft) *plld hrd: chsd ldrs tl rdn and wknd over 1f out* **40/1**

-633 **9** *3 ½* **King Of Eden (IRE)**[11] 2117 8-8-11 **80** (b) DavidAllan 3 52
(Eric Alston) *dwlt: sn in tch: rdn over 2f out: wknd over 1f out* **11/2**[3]

-255 **10** *nk* **Lazarus Bell**[24] 1733 4-9-0 **83** (b[1]) SilvestreDeSousa 10 54
(Alan Brown) *plld hrd: hld up: struggling over 2f out: sn btn* **5/1**[2]

1m 25.97s (-1.83) **Going Correction** -0.075s/f (Good) **10** Ran SP% **115.8**
Speed ratings (Par 107): **107,106,106,100,100 99,96,95,91,91**
CSF £207.28 CT £600.98 TOTE £26.90: £5.60, £2.30, £1.60; EX 326.40 Trifecta £1895.70.
**Owner** Sprint Thoroughbred Racing **Bred** Whisperview Trading Ltd **Trained** Huby, N Yorks
■ Stewards' Enquiry : James Sullivan caution: careless riding.

**FOCUS**
A competitive handicap run at a fair pace. The front three finished clear.

## 2426 KRONENBOURG H'CAP (DIV I) — 1m 3y(S)
**5:20** (5:20) (Class 6) (0-60,60) 4-Y-O+ — **£1,940** (£577; £288; £144) **Stalls** Centre

Form RPR

5404 **1** **Run Fat Lass Run**[21] 1857 4-9-7 **60** PhillipMakin 9 69
(Philip Kirby) *in tch: effrt and rdn over 1f out: led ins fnl f: hld on wl towards fin* **8/1**

20-0 **2** *nk* **Byron's Dream**[25] 1689 4-9-4 **57** RussKennemore 5 65
(Jedd O'Keeffe) *hld up in tch: rdn and hdwy over 1f out: chsd wnr ins fnl f: kpt on: hld nr fin* **12/1**

543 **3** *nk* **Dansili Dutch (IRE)**[8] 2199 5-9-0 **60** JoshDoyle(7) 11 67
(David O'Meara) *hld up: rdn and hdwy over 1f out: kpt on ins fnl f: nrst fin* **7/2**[1]

35-0 **4** *1 ¼* **Seldom (IRE)**[26] 1673 8-9-4 **57** DavidAllan 10 61
(Mel Brittain) *led: rdn over 1f out: hdd ins fnl f: kpt on same pce* **13/2**[3]

/00- **5** *½* **Spokesperson (USA)**[227] 7027 6-8-4 **46** oh1 (p) NeilFarley(3) 2 49
(Frederick Watson) *in tch: drvn and sltly outpcd over 2f out: rallied fnl f: r.o* **80/1**

50-0 **6** *¾* **Monthly Medal**[26] 1675 11-8-9 **48** ow2 (t) GrahamLee 3 49
(Wilf Storey) *hld up: rdn and hdwy over 1f out: kpt on fnl f: no imp* **14/1**

63-6 **7** *3* **Midnight Warrior**[30] 1596 4-8-6 **50** ShirleyTeasdale(5) 8 44
(Ron Barr) *t.k.h: prom tl rdn and wknd over 1f out* **9/2**[2]

000- **8** *¾* **Eium Mac**[252] 6276 5-8-7 **51** AdamCarter(5) 6 44
(Neville Bycroft) *dwlt: sn cl up: ev ch tl rdn and wknd over 1f out* **16/1**

0-00 **9** *2 ¼* **Bitusa (USA)**[29] 1608 4-8-2 **48** GemmaTutty(7) 4 35
(Karen Tutty) *dwlt: hld up: rdn over 2f out: sn btn* **8/1**

-600 **10** *6* **Look On By**[8] 2215 4-9-2 **55** JamesSullivan 7 29
(Ruth Carr) *t.k.h: cl up tl rdn and wknd over 1f out* **15/2**

0200 **11** *3* **Daneside (IRE)**[108] 425 7-8-8 **47**...[1] AndrewElliott 12 14
(Simon West) *in tch: lost pl over 2f out: sn struggling* **14/1**

1m 41.54s (-1.86) **Going Correction** -0.075s/f (Good) **11** Ran SP% **115.9**
Speed ratings (Par 101): **106,105,105,104,103 102,99,99,96,90 87**
CSF £98.44 CT £405.55 TOTE £13.20: £3.90, £4.10, £1.40; EX 113.40 Trifecta £389.70.
**Owner** S C B Limited **Bred** Mrs C R Philipson & Mrs H G Lascelles **Trained** Middleham, N Yorks

**FOCUS**
A modest handicap run at a steady pace, but it was slightly faster than division II. Straightforward form.

## 2427 KRONENBOURG H'CAP (DIV II) 1m 3y(S)
**5:50** (5:50) (Class 6) (0-60,60) 4-Y-0+ **£1,940** (£577; £288; £144) **Stalls** Centre

Form RPR
3122 **1** **Polar Forest**[10] 2164 4-9-2 **58**...(e) ConnorBeasley(3) 1 71
(Richard Guest) *t.k.h: hld up in tch: smooth hdwy to ld over 1f out: shkn up and qckng clr ins fnl f: eased nr fin* **6/4**[1]

6-60 **2** *4 1/2* **Shearian**[15] 2019 4-9-7 **60**... BarryMcHugh 9 62
(Tracy Waggott) *hld up in tch: smooth hdwy over 2f out: rdn over 1f out: chsd wnr ins fnl f: no imp* **7/1**[3]

-150 **3** *hd* **Graceful Act**[8] 2219 6-8-13 **57**... NoelGarbutt(5) 6 58
(Ron Barr) *cl up: effrt and ev ch over 1f out: kpt on same pce ins fnl f* **10/1**

-000 **4** *1* **Delores Rocket**[21] 1846 4-9-2 **60**...(p) ShaneGray(5) 2 59
(Kevin Ryan) *prom: drvn over 2f out: kpt on same pce fnl f* **12/1**

0-40 **5** *1/2* **Hayek**[15] 2021 7-8-1 **47**...(b) RachelRichardson(7) 11 45
(Tim Easterby) *led: rdn and hdd over 1f out: no ex ins fnl f* **18/1**

00-0 **6** *1/2* **Liliargh (IRE)**[45] 1310 5-8-10 **49**...(v[1]) AndrewElliott 5 46
(Ben Haslam) *hld up: rdn and hdwy 2f out: no imp fnl f* **12/1**

40-5 **7** *5* **Card High (IRE)**[11] 2135 4-8-9 **48**... GrahamLee 10 33
(Wilf Storey) *t.k.h: cl up tl rdn and wknd wl over 1f out* **20/1**

45-3 **8** *1/2* **Mysterious Wonder**[27] 1649 4-9-4 **57**... RussKennemore 8 41
(Philip Kirby) *t.k.h: hld up: effrt over 2f out: nvr able to chal* **6/1**[2]

-004 **9** *2 1/2* **Taxiformissbyron**[30] 1596 4-8-12 **51**...(p) TomEaves 7 29
(Iain Jardine) *in tch: drvn over 2f out: wknd over 1f out* **10/1**

600- **10** *7* **Edas**[251] 6297 12-8-10 **52**... JasonHart(3) 4 14
(Thomas Cuthbert) *hld up: rdn along over 2f out: sn btn* **33/1**

00-0 **11** *13* **Roc Fort**[10] 2170 5-8-7 **46** oh1...(t) RaulDaSilva 3
(James Moffatt) *hld up towards rr: struggling over 3f out: sn btn* **66/1**

1m 42.01s (-1.39) **Going Correction** -0.075s/f (Good) **11** Ran SP% **114.8**
Speed ratings (Par 101): **103,98,98,97,96 96,91,90,88,81 68**
CSF £11.32 CT £79.07 TOTE £2.40: £1.10, £2.60, £1.90; EX 15.60 Trifecta £85.00.
**Owner** Maze Rattan Limited **Bred** Worksop Manor Stud **Trained** Wetherby, W Yorks

**FOCUS**
A steadily run modest handicap, run 0.47sec slower than division II. This has to rate a personal best from the winner.
T/Plt: £41.90 to a £1 stake. Pool: £65,770.05 - 1145.17 winning tickets. T/Qpdt: £9.90 to a £1 stake. Pool: £5,266.40 - 392.30 winning tickets. RY

# 2158 NOTTINGHAM (L-H)
### Tuesday, May 20

**OFFICIAL GOING: Good (good to firm in places; 8.5) changing to good to firm after race 2 (2.30)**
Wind: Virtually nil Weather: Cloudy with sunny periods

## 2428 EBF STALLIONS HAPPY 10TH BIRTHDAY RACING UK MAIDEN STKS 6f 15y
**2:00** (2:00) (Class 5) 2-Y-0 **£3,234** (£962; £481; £240) **Stalls** High

Form RPR
5 **1** **Dr No**[31] 1583 2-9-5 0... RichardHughes 5 89+
(Richard Hannon) *prom on wd outside: hdwy and cl up 1/2-way: rdn to ld jst over 1f out: edgd rt and kpt on strly fnl f* **10/1**[3]

2 **2** *1 3/4* **Aktabantay**[16] 1977 2-9-5 0... RyanMoore 8 84
(Hugo Palmer) *racd nr stands' rail: slt ld: pushed along and hdd over 1f out: sn rdn and hung lft ins fnl f: one pce* **1/4**[1]

**3** *1 3/4* **Star Citizen** 2-9-5 0... WilliamBuick 7 79+
(Charlie Appleby) *prom: pushed along over 2f out: rdn over 1f out: kpt on same pce fnl f* **16/1**

**4** *2 3/4* **Final Decision** 2-9-5 0... KierenFallon 1 70+
(Saeed bin Suroor) *t.k.h: trckd ldrs: cl up 1/2-way: rdn along 2f out: wknd over 1f out* **7/1**[2]

**5** *1 1/4* **Gideon Jukes** 2-9-2 0... GeorgeChaloner(3) 9 67
(Richard Fahey) *towards rr: hdwy 2f out: swtchd lft over 1f out: kpt on fnl f* **50/1**

**6** *3/4* **Skygazer (IRE)** 2-9-5 0... MartinLane 3 64
(Charlie Appleby) *dwlt and a in rr: rdn along and green 2f out: hung rt over 1f out* **50/1**

**7** *1* **Cotai Glory** 2-9-5 0... JamesDoyle 4 61+
(Charles Hills) *dwlt: plld hrd and sn chsng ldrs: cl up over 2f out: sn rdn: rn green and wknd* **50/1**

1m 13.0s (-1.70) **Going Correction** -0.40s/f (Firm) **7** Ran SP% **113.4**
Speed ratings (Par 93): **95,92,90,86,85 84,82**
CSF £12.96 TOTE £7.40: £3.00, £1.10; EX 14.10 Trifecta £42.30.
**Owner** Denford Stud **Bred** Denford Stud Ltd **Trained** East Everleigh, Wilts

**FOCUS**
Outer course used. Rail moved out 2yds on back straight and home bend increased distances on Round course by about 12yds. This looked quite a useful little maiden with Aktabantay setting a high standard on his first run and some big yards represented by newcomers. The winner is likely to rate higher.

## 2429 DOWNLOAD NEW RACING UK IPAD APP H'CAP (JOCKEY CLUB GRASSROOTS FLAT SPRINT SERIES QUALIFIER) 6f 15y
**2:30** (2:31) (Class 5) (0-75,75) 3-Y-0 **£2,587** (£770; £384; £192) **Stalls** High

Form RPR
5440 **1** **Captain Myles (IRE)**[19] 1897 3-9-6 **74**...(b) StevieDonohoe 15 82
(Tim Pitt) *racd alone stands' rail: sn led: clr 1/2-way: rdn wl over 1f out: drvn ins fnl f: jst hld on* **16/1**

401- **2** *nk* **Souville**[190] 7837 3-9-7 **75**... WilliamBuick 1 82+
(Chris Wall) *racd towards far side: in tch: gd hdwy over 2f out: rdn and ev ch whn hung rt ent fnl f: sn drvn and kpt on* **16/1**

-630 **3** *1* **Jive**[21] 1832 3-9-0 **68**... RichardHughes 12 72
(Richard Hannon) *trckd towards stands' side: in rr: hdwy over 2f out: rdn over 1f out: styd on to chal ins fnl f: one pce towards fin* **7/1**[2]

-144 **4** *3 1/4* **Exceeding Power**[118] 279 3-9-6 **74**... JoeFanning 2 68
(Martin Bosley) *racd towards far side: trckd ldrs: hdwy over 2f out: rdn wl over 1f out: kpt on same pce fnl f* **33/1**

34-3 **5** *shd* **Gold Club**[15] 2015 3-9-1 **69**... PaulMulrennan 4 62
(Ed McMahon) *racd towards far side: chsd ldrs: rdn along wl over 1f out: kpt on same pce* **5/1**[1]

3-16 **6** *1 3/4* **Two Shades Of Grey (IRE)**[17] 1940 3-9-0 **68**... RyanMoore 8 56
(Richard Fahey) *racd centre: midfield: sme hdwy over 2f out: sn rdn and kpt on one pce: nvr nr ldrs* **5/1**[1]

03-6 **7** *3/4* **Straits Of Malacca**[22] 1818 3-8-13 **67**... JamesDoyle 13 52
(Kevin Ryan) *racd towards stands' side: chsd wnr: rdn along 2f out: grad wknd* **8/1**[3]

0-30 **8** *1 3/4* **Why Not Now**[23] 1769 3-8-2 **61** oh1... JoeyHaynes(5) 14 41
(Roger Charlton) *racd towards stands' side: in rr tl sme late hdwy* **25/1**

11 **9** *3/4* **Red Primo (IRE)**[22] 1801 3-9-5 **73**... KierenFallon 6 50
(Alan McCabe) *racd towards centre: chsd ldrs: rdn along 2f out: grad wknd* **7/1**[2]

3-10 **10** *1 1/4* **Le Laitier (FR)**[15] 2015 3-9-1 **69**... LukeMorris 7 42
(Scott Dixon) *nvr bttr than midfield* **25/1**

325- **11** *nk* **Cincuenta Pasos (IRE)**[152] 8342 3-9-5 **73**... SteveDrowne 11 45
(Joseph Tuite) *dwlt and in rr: hdwy to chse ldrs 1/2-way: rdn over 2f out and sn wknd* **7/1**[2]

2200 **12** *nk* **Aspirant**[22] 1818 3-9-7 **75**...(t) DaleSwift 10 46
(Brian Ellison) *midfield: rdn along 1/2-way: n.d* **25/1**

-046 **13** *2 3/4* **Pendo**[23] 1769 3-8-8 **67**... DanielMuscutt(5) 5 30
(Alastair Lidderdale) *racd towards far side: prom: rdn along 1/2-way: sn wknd and bhd* **100/1**

31-5 **14** *19* **Look Here's Al**[17] 1940 3-9-3 **71**... AdamKirby 9
(Andrew Hollinshead) *racd towards stands' side: in tch: rdn along 1/2-way: sn lost pl and bhd* **10/1**

2-30 **15** *5* **Quincel**[24] 1723 3-8-11 **65**...(vt[1]) RichardKingscote 3
(Tom Dascombe) *racd towards far side: a in rr: bhd fnl 2f* **25/1**

1m 12.47s (-2.23) **Going Correction** -0.40s/f (Firm) **15** Ran SP% **122.1**
Speed ratings (Par 99): **98,97,96,91,91 89,88,86,85,83 83,82,79,53,47**
CSF £233.55 CT £2011.87 TOTE £26.60, £7.30, £2.40; EX 379.00 Trifecta £2561.80 Part won..
**Owner** Paul Wildes **Bred** Burgage Stud And Partners **Trained** Market Drayton, Shropshire

**FOCUS**
A wide-open 3yo sprint handicap. The winner grabbed the rail and the third helps with the standard.

## 2430 PHS GROUP H'CAP 2m 9y
**3:00** (3:00) (Class 5) (0-75,75) 4-Y-0+ **£2,587** (£770; £384; £192) **Stalls** Low

Form RPR
455- **1** **Hallstatt (IRE)**[295] 4838 8-9-0 **65**...(t) PaulMulrennan 2 73
(John Mackie) *trckd ldrs on inner: hdwy to chse ldng pair 3f out: swtchd rt and rdn to chal over 1f out: led ent fnl f: styd on wl towards fin* **6/1**[3]

3432 **2** *2* **Sir Frank Morgan (IRE)**[11] 2108 4-9-6 **73**... JoeFanning 5 79
(Mark Johnston) *trckd ldr: hdwy and cl up 3f out: led over 2f out: rdn and jnd over 1f out: hdd ent fnl f: sn drvn and kpt on same pce* **5/4**[1]

04-6 **3** *10* **Pearl Spice (IRE)**[21] 1849 4-9-8 **75**...(b) StevieDonohoe 6 69
(Tim Pitt) *sn led: rdn along over 3f out: hdd over 2f out: sn drvn and one pce* **3/1**[2]

644- **4** *2 1/2* **Epic Storm (IRE)**[89] 8309 6-8-5 **61**...(t) TimClark(5) 7 52
(Martin Keighley) *hld up and bhd: sme hdwy over 4f out: rdn along 3f out: sn btn* **25/1**

3155 **5** *43* **Poitin**[17] 1941 4-9-6 **73**... RichardKingscote 3 12
(Harry Dunlop) *chsd ldrs: rdn along over 5f out: sn outpcd and bhd fnl 3f* **3/1**[2]

3m 27.39s (-7.11) **Going Correction** -0.75s/f (Hard) course record
**WFA** 4 from 6yo+ 2lb **5** Ran SP% **112.6**
Speed ratings (Par 103): **87,86,81,79,58**
CSF £14.46 TOTE £8.10: £3.00, £1.10; EX 22.50 Trifecta £54.20.
**Owner** NSU Leisure & Mrs Carolyn Seymour **Bred** Darley **Trained** Church Broughton , Derbys

**FOCUS**
A modest contest run at a decent gallop (although the overall time was quite slow). The winner rates to last year's form.

## 2431 PHS WATERLOGIC FILLIES' H'CAP (BOBIS RACE) 1m 2f 50y
**3:30** (3:30) (Class 4) (0-80,80) 3-Y-0 **£6,469** (£1,925; £962; £481) **Stalls** Low

Form RPR
-141 **1** **Thurayaat**[28] 1635 3-9-5 **78**... JamesDoyle 2 85
(Roger Varian) *set stdy pce: qcknd over 3f out: pushed along over 2f out: rdn wl over 1f out: hdd appr fnl f: sn drvn and rallied gamely on inner to ld again nr fin* **3/1**[2]

00-5 **2** *nk* **Bureau (IRE)**[27] 1655 3-9-1 **74**... JoeFanning 8 80
(Mark Johnston) *trckd wnr: hdwy and cl up 3f out: rdn wl over 1f out: slt ld appr fnl f: sn drvn: hdd and no ex nr fin* **10/1**

1-0 **3** *1 1/2* **Kind Invitation**[20] 1868 3-9-7 **80**... WilliamBuick 6 83
(Charlie Appleby) *trckd ldng pair: pushed along over 2f out: rdn wl over 1f out: drvn and one pce appr fnl f* **12/1**

0-52 **4** *3 3/4* **Heho**[11] 2129 3-9-1 **74**... RyanMoore 1 70
(Sir Michael Stoute) *trckd ldrs on inner: swtchd rt and hdwy 3f out: rdn 2f out: drvn wl over 1f out and sn btn* **6/4**[1]

33-1 **5** *1* **Passing By**[55] 1107 3-9-4 **77**... RichardHughes 4 71
(Richard Hannon) *stdd s: t.k.h and hld up in rr: sme hdwy 2f out: nvr a factor* **7/1**

22-3 **6** *1/2* **Song Of Norway**[24] 1722 3-9-4 **77**... SteveDrowne 5 70
(Peter Makin) *stdd s: t.k.h and hld up in rr: swtchd rt and hdwy 3f out: rdn over 2f out: sn no imp* **6/1**[3]

540- **7** *15* **Crown Pleasure (IRE)**[199] 7695 3-8-12 **71**... KierenFallon 7 48
(Clive Brittain) *chsd ldrs on outer: rdn along 3f out: drvn over 2f out and sn wknd* **20/1**

2m 10.39s (-3.91) **Going Correction** -0.75s/f (Hard) **7** Ran SP% **113.3**
Speed ratings (Par 98): **85,84,83,80,79 79,67**
CSF £31.37 CT £311.37 TOTE £3.60: £2.30, £4.20; EX 32.00 Trifecta £242.70.
**Owner** Hamdan Al Maktoum **Bred** Shadwell Estate Company Limited **Trained** Newmarket, Suffolk

**FOCUS**
Some promising three-year-olds with the potential to be rated higher in the future. The first four raced in that order and the form isn't rated too positively.

## 2432 PHS WASHROOMS MAIDEN STKS 1m 75y
**4:00** (4:00) (Class 5) 3-Y-O **£3,234** (£962; £481; £240) **Stalls** Centre

Form RPR
63- **1** **Wannabe Yours (IRE)**[207] 7494 3-9-5 0........................ WilliamBuick 11 96+
(John Gosden) *hld up towards rr: swtchd rt and hdwy wl over 2f out: sn chsng ldrs: rdn to chse ldr jst ins fnl f: drvn and styd on strly to ld nr line* **6/4**[1]
-2 **2** *shd* **Lacan (IRE)**[41] 1395 3-9-5 0........................ AdamKirby 2 92
(Clive Cox) *led: shkn up over 2f out: rdn clr over 1f out: drvn ins fnl f: hdd nr fin* **5/2**[2]
0-26 **3** *5* **Arable**[18] 1911 3-9-5 80........................ JamesDoyle 8 80
(Charles Hills) *trckd ldr: cl up 3f out: rdn along 2f out: drvn over 1f out and sn one pce* **9/1**
6- **4** *1* **Alketios (GR)**[277] 5472 3-8-12 0........................ GianlucaSanna(7) 4 78
(Luca Cumani) *chsd ldng pair: hdwy on inner 3f out: chsd ldr wl over 1f out: sn rdn and one pce ent fnl f* **6/1**[3]
**5** *1* **Moholoholo (IRE)** 3-9-5 0........................ RichardHughes 7 76
(Hugo Palmer) *chsd ldrs: pushed along over 2f out: sn rdn and kpt on one pce* **20/1**
0 **6** *3 ¾* **Incredible Fresh (IRE)**[22] 1795 3-9-5 0........................ HayleyTurner 10 67
(James Fanshawe) *hld up: hdwy on outer 3f out: rdn along 2f out: sn drvn and btn* **25/1**
0 **7** *¾* **Zynah (IRE)**[23] 1768 3-9-0 0........................ KierenFallon 12 60
(Saeed bin Suroor) *trckd ldrs: hdwy 3f out: rdn along to chse ldrs 2f out: grad wknd appr fnl f* **14/1**
00- **8** *4 ½* **Wannabe Magic**[217] 7277 3-9-0 0........................ RichardKingscote 1 50
(Geoffrey Deacon) *chsd ldrs: rdn along 3f out: sn drvn and wknd* **100/1**
05 **9** *2* **Scarlet Plum**[15] 2025 3-9-0 0........................ MartinLane 6 45
(Roger Charlton) *a towards rr* **20/1**
64 **10** *1* **Navajo Dream**[14] 2053 3-9-0 0........................ RobbieFitzpatrick 3 43
(Michael Appleby) *dwlt: a towards rr* **50/1**
5 **11** *3 ½* **Mr Soprano**[83] 748 3-9-5 0........................ SaleemGolam 9 40
(Stuart Williams) *a in rr* **50/1**
0- **12** *7* **Archduchess**[209] 7466 3-9-0 0........................ ChrisCatlin 5 19
(Rae Guest) *a towards rr: rdn along 1/2-way: bhd fnl 4f* **100/1**

1m 44.33s (-4.67) **Going Correction** -0.75s/f (Hard) **12 Ran SP% 118.8**
Speed ratings (Par 99): **93,92,87,86,85 82,81,76,74,73 70,63**
CSF £4.77 TOTE £4.10: £1.50, £1.10, £3.20; EX 7.50 Trifecta £27.60.
**Owner** Normandie Stud Ltd **Bred** Normandie Stud Ltd **Trained** Newmarket, Suffolk
**FOCUS**
A steadily run maiden, and just fair form behind the first two, who pulled clear.

## 2433 PHS TREADSMART CLASSIFIED STKS 1m 75y
**4:30** (4:31) (Class 5) 3-Y-O **£2,587** (£770; £384; £192) **Stalls** Centre

Form RPR
-223 **1** **Rough Courte (IRE)**[21] 1844 3-8-11 68........................ CharlesBishop(3) 6 76
(Mick Channon) *mde all: rdn along wl over 2f out: drvn and edgd rt jst over 1f out: kpt on gamely u.p fnl f* **7/1**[3]
50-3 **2** *1 ¼* **Tower Power**[136] 50 3-9-0 67........................ JamesDoyle 1 73
(Ismail Mohammed) *trckd ldrs: effrt and edgd rt over 2f out: rdn and nt clr run over 1f out: swtchd rt and rdn ent fnl f: styd on wl towards fin* **20/1**
605- **3** *¾* **Rainbow Rock (IRE)**[222] 7146 3-9-0 70........................ JoeFanning 2 71
(Mark Johnston) *trckd ldrs: hdwy over 3f out: rdn to chal and edgd lft 2f out: drvn and ev ch whn rdr dropped whip ent fnl f: kpt on same pce towards fin* **5/4**[1]
5-25 **4** *½* **High Master (IRE)**[17] 1947 3-9-0 70........................(b[1]) RichardHughes 9 70
(Richard Hannon) *hld up: hdwy on inner 3f out: chsd ldrs 2f out: sn rdn and n.m.r ent fnl f: kpt on same pce* **5/1**[2]
63-1 **5** *6* **Ixelles Diamond (IRE)**[15] 2024 3-8-11 70........................ GeorgeChaloner(3) 3 56
(Richard Fahey) *dwlt and towards rr: hdwy 3f out: chsd ldrs over 2f out: sn rdn and no imp* **8/1**
54-3 **6** *3* **Baynunah (USA)**[14] 2061 3-9-0 69........................ HayleyTurner 4 49
(James Fanshawe) *hld up: hdwy on wd outside 3f out: rdn along to chse ldrs 2f out: sn no imp* **5/1**[2]
300- **7** *17* **Red Tide (IRE)**[194] 7782 3-9-0 68........................(p) MickaelBarzalona 7 10
(Alan McCabe) *a towards rr: bhd fnl 3f* **20/1**
05-0 **8** *2* **Ajig**[14] 2063 3-9-0 69........................ AdamKirby 10 6
(Eve Johnson Houghton) *chsd ldrs: rdn along 3f out: drvn over 2f out: sn wknd* **33/1**
35-4 **9** *2 ¼* **Weekend Getaway (IRE)**[39] 1427 3-9-0 70........................ KierenFallon 11
(Clive Brittain) *trckd ldrs: hdwy and cl up 1/2-way: rdn along 3f out: wkng whn squeezed out and hmpd wl over 1f out: bhd after* **15/8**

1m 43.2s (-5.80) **Going Correction** -0.75s/f (Hard) course record **9 Ran SP% 119.7**
Speed ratings (Par 99): **99,97,97,96,90 87,70,68,66**
CSF £137.42 TOTE £5.50: £1.50, £4.80, £1.50; EX 183.60 Trifecta £1112.70.
**Owner** Billy Parish **Bred** Futoo Club **Trained** West Ilsley, Berks
**FOCUS**
Some lightly-raced three-year-olds on show in this classified event and the front four finished clear, so the form might not turn out to be too bad. The winner is rated back to his latter 2yo form.

## 2434 CELEBRATE 10 YEARS WITH RACINGUK ANYWHERE H'CAP 5f 13y
**5:00** (5:00) (Class 5) (0-75,75) 4-Y-O+ **£2,587** (£770; £384; £192) **Stalls** High

Form RPR
-661 **1** **Ladweb**[20] 1878 4-9-0 73........................ LouisSteward(5) 11 82
(John Gallagher) *trckd ldrs: hdwy 2f out: rdn and n.m.r ent fnl f: squeezed through and kpt on wl to ld last 50yds* **3/1**[1]
3250 **2** *½* **Moorhouse Lad**[25] 1695 11-9-7 75........................ AdamKirby 1 82
(Garry Moss) *cl up: rdn wl over 1f out: ev ch tl drvn ins fnl f and no ex towards fin* **6/1**
6023 **3** *nk* **Tyfos**[27] 1643 9-9-1 69........................(p) KierenFallon 2 75
(Brian Baugh) *slt ld: rdn along and edgd rt wl over 1f out: drvn ent fnl f: hdd and no ex last 50yds* **9/2**[3]
6031 **4** *5* **Dawn Catcher**[31] 1584 4-9-0 68........................ HayleyTurner 9 56
(Geoffrey Deacon) *cl up: rdn along 2f out: grad wknd* **4/1**[2]
110- **5** *1 ¼* **Emjayem**[232] 6900 4-9-5 73........................ PaulMulrennan 7 56
(Ed McMahon) *awkward and dwlt s: in rr: hdwy wl over 1f out: rdn and kpt on fnl f: nrst fin* **7/1**
4140 **6** *2 ¼* **West Coast Dream**[18] 1912 7-8-10 67........................ DeclanBates(3) 10 42
(Roy Brotherton) *cl up: rdn along 1/2-way: sn wknd* **9/1**
640 **7** *7* **Sir Geoffrey (IRE)**[33] 1541 8-8-4 65........................(p) MatthewHopkins(7) 3 15
(Scott Dixon) *chsd ldrs: rdn along over 2f out: sn wknd* **16/1**
000- **8** *18* **Irish Boy (IRE)**[224] 7106 6-8-7 66........................(tp) EoinWalsh(5) 8
(Christine Dunnett) *sn rdn along and a outpcd: bhd fr 1/2-way* **14/1**

58.89s (-2.61) **Going Correction** -0.40s/f (Firm) **8 Ran SP% 112.5**
Speed ratings (Par 103): **104,103,102,94,92 89,77,49**
CSF £20.54 CT £78.39 TOTE £4.20: £1.70, £2.90, £1.60; EX 22.40 Trifecta £99.70.
**Owner** The Juniper Racing Club & Andrew Bell **Bred** Adweb Ltd **Trained** Chastleton, Oxon
**FOCUS**
A strongly run sprint in which the first three pulled a long way clear. The winner is generally progressive.
T/Plt: £79.10 to a £1 stake. Pool: £42,673.78 - 393.63 winning tickets. T/Qpdt: £13.60 to a £1 stake. Pool: £4,403.32 - 239.40 winning tickets. JR

2172

# WARWICK (L-H)
### Tuesday, May 20

**OFFICIAL GOING: Good to firm (8.1) (abandoned after race 2 (6.15) due to unsafe ground)**
Wind: Light behind Weather: Showers

## 2435 CELEBRATING 307 YEARS OF WARWICK RACECOURSE H'CAP 6f
**5:45** (5:45) (Class 6) (0-60,59) 4-Y-O+ **£2,264** (£673; £336; £168) **Stalls** Low

Form RPR
0060 **1** **Climaxfortackle (IRE)**[10] 2174 6-9-5 57........................ JimCrowley 11 70
(Derek Shaw) *hld up: pushed along over 2f out: hdwy over 1f out: led wl ins fnl f: r.o* **25/1**
334 **2** *½* **Belle Bayardo (IRE)**[15] 2008 6-9-2 54........................ LukeMorris 4 65
(Tony Carroll) *stmbld s and s.i.s: hdwy over 4f out: rdn over 1f out: ev ch ins fnl f: styd on* **9/2**[3]
60-4 **3** *1 ½* **Ada Lovelace**[19] 1896 4-9-4 59........................ MichaelJMMurphy(3) 2 65
(John Gallagher) *chsd ldrs: hmpd over 1f out: sn rdn: styd on: wnt 3rd nr fin* **14/1**
4010 **4** *nk* **Red Invader (IRE)**[26] 1668 4-9-5 57........................ JamieSpencer 9 62
(Charles Hills) *led: rdn and hung rt fr over 1f out: hdd ins fnl f: nt run on* **7/2**[2]
4530 **5** *1 ¼* **Sewn Up**[11] 2127 4-8-13 51........................(tp[1]) LiamKeniry 3 52
(Andrew Hollinshead) *hld up: hdwy over 1f out: sn rdn: styd on same pce ins fnl f* **14/1**
5566 **6** *1 ¼* **Hinton Admiral**[16] 1986 10-8-6 49........................ JoeyHaynes(5) 15 46
(Pat Eddery) *s.i.s: sn pushed along in rr: hdwy and nt clr run over 1f out: sn rdn: styd on same pce ins fnl f* **40/1**
1503 **7** *hd* **Interchoice Star**[10] 2174 9-8-11 52........................(p) OisinMurphy(3) 17 49
(Ray Peacock) *prom: chsd ldr 4f out: rdn and hmpd over 1f out: no ex ins fnl f* **12/1**
2010 **8** *½* **Glastonberry**[32] 1554 6-9-5 57........................ FergusSweeney 13 52
(Geoffrey Deacon) *hld up: nt clr run fr over 1f out: nvr trbld ldrs* **8/1**
3362 **9** *nk* **Haadeeth**[15] 2598 7-9-0 59........................(t) HollieDoyle(7) 12 53
(David Evans) *prom: rdn over 1f out: no ex fnl f* **11/1**
15-1 **10** *1 ¼* **Euroquip Boy (IRE)**[10] 2174 7-9-1 56........................ WilliamTwiston-Davies(3) 1 46
(Michael Scudamore) *chsd ldr 2f: remained handy: shkn up over 1f out: wknd ins fnl f* **3/1**[1]
620- **11** *6* **Rat Catcher (IRE)**[283] 5265 4-9-5 57........................(p) SamHitchcott 5 28
(Lisa Williamson) *sn pushed along in rr: bhd fr 1/2-way* **50/1**
060 **12** *½* **Spray Tan**[78] 819 4-9-5 57........................ StevieDonohoe 14 26
(Tony Carroll) *hld up: wknd 2f out* **25/1**
0-00 **S** **Artful Lady (IRE)**[95] 603 5-9-0 59........................ JordanVaughan(7) 10
(George Margarson) *sn pushed along in rr: slipped up wl over 2f out: fatally injured* **22/1**

1m 11.61s (-0.19) **Going Correction** 0.0s/f (Good) **13 Ran SP% 122.3**
Speed ratings (Par 101): **101,100,98,97,96 94,94,93,93,91 83,82,**
CSF £132.02 CT £1743.61 TOTE £31.60: £11.50, £2.80, £5.90; EX 213.70 Trifecta £2081.40 Part won..
**Owner** Shakespeare Racing **Bred** Pat Fullam **Trained** Sproxton, Leics
**FOCUS**
The ground was officially described as good to firm prior to this seven-race card. The opener was run in heavy rain. The winner is rated in line with her winter AW form.

## 2436 BRITISH STALLION STUDS EBF MAIDEN FILLIES' STKS (BOBIS RACE) 6f
**6:15** (6:35) (Class 5) 2-Y-O **£2,911** (£866; £432; £216) **Stalls** Low

Form RPR
0 **1** **Gold Waltz**[33] 1528 2-9-0 0........................ JimCrowley 6 63
(Ralph Beckett) *mde all: rdn over 1f out: jst hld on* **11/2**
0 **2** *nk* **Mary McPhee**[33] 1528 2-9-0 0........................ JamieSpencer 7 62
(Charles Hills) *a.p: rdn to chse wnr over 1f out: r.o* **7/4**[1]
**3** *1 ¼* **Dancing Moon (IRE)** 2-8-11 0........................ WilliamTwiston-Davies(3) 4 58+
(Mick Channon) *a.p: pushed along and swtchd lft over 1f out: r.o* **3/1**[2]
005 **4** *½* **Seamoor Secret**[11] 2128 2-8-11 0........................ OisinMurphy(3) 8 57
(Alex Hales) *sn outpcd: hdwy over 1f out: r.o: nt rch ldrs* **16/1**
40 **5** *3 ½* **As A Dream (IRE)**[31] 1571 2-9-0 0........................ SamHitchcott 2 46
(David Evans) *chsd ldrs: rdn 1/2-way: no ex fnl f* **16/1**
05 **6** *1 ¼* **Kodestiny (IRE)**[23] 1764 2-9-0 0........................ LiamKeniry 1 43
(Ismail Mohammed) *w wnr tl rdn over 1f out: wknd ins fnl f* **18/1**
**7** *2 ½* **Lady Zodiac (IRE)** 2-9-0 0........................ StevieDonohoe 5 35
(Tim Pitt) *s.i.s: outpcd* **25/1**
**8** *28* **Steel Blaze** 2-8-11 0........................ MatthewCosham(3) 3
(Nikki Evans) *prom: drvn along 1/2-way: wknd 2f out: sn hung rt* **66/1**
3 **9** *18* **Show Spirit**[15] 2014 2-9-0 0........................ RichardHughes 9
(Kevin Ryan) *chsd ldrs: pushed along over 2f out: wknd and eased over 1f out* **5/1**[3]

1m 12.96s (1.16) **Going Correction** 0.0s/f (Good) **9 Ran SP% 115.8**
Speed ratings (Par 90): **92,91,89,89,84 82,79,42,18**
CSF £15.55 TOTE £7.70: £2.00, £1.30, £2.10; EX 21.20 Trifecta £68.30.
**Owner** Sutong Pan **Bred** David Jamison Bloodstock **Trained** Kimpton, Hants



The Form Book, Raceform Ltd, Newbury, RG14 5SJ

**FOCUS**
They didn't seem to go that quick in this maiden fillies' race for 2yos, which was run on slippery ground, and the racing didn't begin until 2f out. Modest form.

## 2437 THE BEAUCHAMP FAMILY, EARLS OF WARWICK H'CAP 6f
() (Class 4) (0-80,) 4-Y-O+ £

## 2438 CELEBRATING 1100 YEARS OVER 1100 METRES H'CAP 5f
() (Class 6) (0-65,) 3-Y-O £

## 2439 WARWICK, 914-2014 H'CAP 1m 2f 202y
() (Class 5) (0-65,) 4-Y-O+ £

## 2440 WARWICK LADIES DAY FRIDAY 4TH JULY MAIDEN STKS 7f
() (Class 5) 3-Y-O £

## 2441 WARWICK GENTLEMEN'S DAY THURSDAY 10TH JULY H'CAP 1m 7f 9y
() (Class 5) (0-65,) 4-Y-O+ £

T/Plt: £5.20 to a £1 stake. Pool: £65,052.32 - 9008.35 winning tickets. CR

# 1859 YARMOUTH (L-H)
Tuesday, May 20

**OFFICIAL GOING: Good to firm (7.5)**
Wind: light, half against Weather: light rain races 1&2, overcast after

## 2442 YOUR WEDDING AT GREAT YARMOUTH RACECOURSE MAIDEN STKS 7f 3y
5:30 (5:33) (Class 5) 3-Y-O+ £2,587 (£770; £384; £192) Stalls Centre

Form RPR
40 **1** **Royal Seal**[24] 1722 3-8-10 0 RyanMoore 1 88
(Sir Michael Stoute) *travelled strly: chsd ldrs tl led 1/2-way: readily wnt clr ent fnl 2f: r.o wl: easily* 4/1[3]
**2** 3 ½ **Elizona** 3-8-10 0 FrederikTylicki 2 79
(James Fanshawe) *stdd s: hld up in last quartet: hdwy 1/2-way: wnt modest 5th 2f out: kpt on to chse clr wnr fnl 150yds: r.o wl for clr 2nd: no ch w wnr* 8/1
0-4 **3** 3 **Swiss Kiss**[18] 1920 3-8-10 0 RobertHavlin 8 71
(John Gosden) *chsd ldr tl 1/2-way: chsd wnr after: rdn and outpcd by wnr ent fnl 2f: no imp after: lost 2nd ins fnl f* 3/1[2]
0- **4** 3 ¾ **Tolmias (GR)**[284] 5244 3-9-1 0 LemosdeSouza 14 66
(Luca Cumani) *stdd s: t.k.h: hld up in last quartet: hdwy 3f out: modest 4th and rdn 2f out: no imp: wknd ins fnl f* 11/4[1]
**5** 1 ½ **Distant High** 3-8-10 0 TedDurcan 15 58
(Rae Guest) *s.i.s: hld up in last quartet: sme hdwy 2f out: n.d but kpt on steadily ins fnl f* 66/1
**6** shd **Role Player** 4-9-12 0 SebSanders 7 66
(Michael Bell) *jostled sn after leaving stalls: in tch in midfield: rdn 4f out: outpcd 1/2-way: n.d but kpt on again ins fnl f* 20/1
0-3 **7** hd **Bishan Bedi (IRE)**[129] 142 3-9-1 0 StephenCraine 12 62
(William Jarvis) *t.k.h: hld up in tch in midfield: swtchd lft and sme hdwy over 2f out: no imp 2f out: wl hld whn flashed tail u.p ins fnl f* 20/1
0 **8** 1 ¾ **Captain George (IRE)**[26] 1681 3-9-1 0 ShaneKelly 6 57
(James Fanshawe) *in tch in midfield: bmpd and pushed lft 3f out: sn rdn and outpcd: no ch fnl 2f* 25/1
6 **9** 4 **Tohaveandtohold**[11] 2118 3-8-10 0 AndrewMullen 11 42
(William Haggas) *in tch in midfield: rdn 4f out: lost pl and struggling 1/2-way: no ch but plugged on past btn horses fnl f* 12/1
0 **10** 1 **Mumarasaat (USA)**[11] 2126 3-8-10 0 WilliamCarson 3 39
(Phil McEntee) *a towards rr: n.d* 100/1
0-4 **11** 1 ¾ **Staines Massive**[14] 2044 4-9-9 0 RobertTart(3) 4 44
(Jane Chapple-Hyam) *in tch in midfield: rdn and struggling 1/2-way: no ch fnl 2f* 100/1
**12** ¾ **Quasqazah** 3-9-1 0 SeanLevey 13 38
(Roger Varian) *in tch in midfield: rdn and struggling whn bmpd and pushed lft 3f out: sn btn and no ch fnl 2f* 16/1
64- **13** 10 **Ellen May**[194] 7781 4-9-7 0 J-PGuillambert 9 11
(Nick Littmoden) *t.k.h: chsd ldrs tl 3f out: sn dropped out: wl bhd fnl f: t.o* 33/1
/0 **14** 7 **Beauchamp Bella**[92] 642 4-9-0 0 (b[1]) JoeDoyle(7) 5
(Paul Fitzsimons) *led tl 1/2-way: losing pl qckly whn ducked lft 3f out: t.o fnl f* 66/1
0- **R** **Gentlemen**[188] 7852 3-9-1 0 PatrickDonaghy 16
(Phil McEntee) *ref to r: tk no part* 100/1

1m 25.96s (-0.64) **Going Correction** +0.125s/f (Good)
**WFA** 3 from 4yo 11lb 15 Ran SP% 118.6
Speed ratings (Par 103): **108,104,100,96,94 94,94,92,87,86 84,83,72,64,**
CSF £32.14 TOTE £4.60: £1.70, £4.20, £1.40; EX 46.00 Trifecta £220.90.
**Owner** Cheveley Park Stud **Bred** Cheveley Park Stud Ltd **Trained** Newmarket, Suffolk

**FOCUS**
Plenty of unexposed types on show, but the winner had been soundly beaten in two previous attempts, so the form looks ordinary. It's been rated at face value. However, the strong pace makes the form reliable at this level and there will be future winners further down the field, mainly in handicaps.

## 2443 INJURED JOCKEYS FUND H'CAP 1m 2f 21y
6:00 (6:00) (Class 6) (0-60,60) 4-Y-O+ £1,940 (£577; £288; £144) Stalls Low

Form RPR
32-3 **1** **Giantstepsahead (IRE)**[18] 1923 5-9-5 58 SebSanders 6 71
(Denis Quinn) *mde virtually all: rdn and wnt clr 2f out: in command over 1f out: r.o wl: eased towards fin* 5/2[1]
460- **2** 3 ¼ **Hamble**[156] 7981 5-8-13 52 PatrickDonaghy 10 59
(Giles Bravery) *chsd clr ldrs: clsd over 3f out: rdn to chse wnr ent fnl 2f: kpt on but no imp* 11/4[2]
10 **3** nk **Appyjack**[41] 1387 6-8-9 51 RobertTart(3) 4 57+
(Tony Carroll) *stdd s: hld up off the pce in rr: effrt but stl plenty to do wl over 2f out: hdwy u.p over 1f out: battling for 2nd fnl 75yds: no ch w wnr* 6/1
200- **4** 3 **Red Catkin**[150] 8388 4-9-3 59 RyanPowell(3) 5 59
(George Margarson) *stdd after s: hld up off the pce in last trio: rdn and stl plenty to do over 3f out: hdwy over 1f out: plugged on same pce ins fnl f* 7/1
004- **5** 3 **Barnaby Brook (CAN)**[187] 7877 4-9-0 53 J-PGuillambert 1 48
(Nick Littmoden) *chsd clr ldrs: 4th and off the pce whn rdn 4f out: no real imp* 14/1
460- **6** nk **Lincolnrose (IRE)**[157] 8293 4-8-9 48 AndrewMullen 8 42
(Michael Appleby) *sn bustled along to press wnr: clr w wnr 7f out: rdn and unable qck in 3rd 2f out: btn over 1f out: wknd fnl f* 9/2[3]
06-0 **7** 2 ½ **Mastered (IRE)**[55] 1105 4-8-7 46 oh1 WilliamCarson 3 35
(John Best) *racd off the pce in last trio: rdn over 3f out: no imp* 50/1

2m 7.69s (-2.81) **Going Correction** -0.15s/f (Firm) 7 Ran SP% 108.8
Speed ratings (Par 101): **105,102,102,99,97 97,95**
CSF £8.62 CT £30.61 TOTE £4.10: £1.60, £2.20; EX 9.40 Trifecta £30.10.
**Owner** K Hills **Bred** Darragh O'Reilly **Trained** Newmarket, Suffolk

**FOCUS**
In a moderate handicap, the winner disputed or led all the way at a furious pace. The runner-up is the best guide.

## 2444 SNELLINGS OF NORFOLK 60TH ANNIVERSARY H'CAP 1m 2f 21y
6:30 (6:30) (Class 5) (0-75,75) 4-Y-O+ £2,587 (£770; £384; £192) Stalls Low

Form RPR
5-20 **1** **Silver Alliance**[28] 1636 6-9-0 73 (p) ShelleyBirkett(5) 7 82
(Julia Feilden) *hld up in tch: clsd to trck ldrs over 2f out: rdn to chal 1f out: led fnl 100yds: r.o wl and asserted towards fin* 8/1
4000 **2** ¾ **Ocean Applause**[5] 2270 4-8-11 72 (tp) JoeDoyle(7) 4 79
(John Ryan) *hld up in tch in midfield: rdn and effrt to chse ldrs 2f out: sn on u.p: wnt 2nd cl home* 7/1
4-66 **3** nk **Enriching (USA)**[80] 801 6-8-11 65 RyanMoore 1 71
(Nick Littmoden) *led tl 6f out: styd w ldr tl led again over 2f out: drvn and hdd over 1f out: led again ins fnl f: hdd fnl 100yds: no ex: lost 2nd cl home* 4/1[2]
231- **4** 1 **It Must Be Faith**[193] 7802 4-9-5 73 AndrewMullen 5 78
(Michael Appleby) *hld up in tch in midfield: hdwy to chse ldr over 2f out: sn rdn to chal: drvn to ld over 1f out: hdd ins fnl f: wknd towards fin* 9/2[3]
3656 **5** 3 **Gabrial The Terror (IRE)**[29] 1617 4-8-6 67 GeorgeBuckell(7) 6 66
(David Simcock) *hld up in tch in rr: rdn and effrt on inner ent fnl 2f: no imp fnl f* 6/1
236- **6** 11 **Forward March**[308] 4384 4-9-7 75 J-PGuillambert 3 53
(Nick Littmoden) *t.k.h: chsd ldr for 1f: grad stdd bk and last 4f out: rdn over 2f out: wknd over 1f out* 20/1
-12 **7** ½ **Ela Gog La Mou**[21] 1864 5-8-4 61 oh1 RosieJessop(3) 2 38
(Peter Charalambous) *dwlt and bustled along early: chsd ldr and t.k.h after 1f: led 1/2-way: hdd over 2f out: sn btn: wknd over 1f out* 9/4[1]

2m 8.74s (-1.76) **Going Correction** -0.15s/f (Firm) 7 Ran SP% 111.6
Speed ratings (Par 103): **101,100,100,99,96 88,87**
CSF £58.21 TOTE £14.80, £4.00; EX 61.60 Trifecta £259.80.
**Owner** In It To Win Partnership **Bred** Peter Harris **Trained** Exning, Suffolk

**FOCUS**
A fair handicap run at a good pace. There was a bunch finish and the winner is running as well as ever.

## 2445 MOULTON NURSERIES AT ACLE H'CAP 1m 3f 101y
7:00 (7:00) (Class 5) (0-75,75) 4-Y-O+ £2,587 (£770; £384; £192) Stalls Low

Form RPR
113- **1** **Nullarbor Sky (IRE)**[243] 6574 4-9-2 70 (p) RyanMoore 4 84+
(Lucy Wadham) *chsd ldr tl led 3f out: rdn and qcknd clr 2f out: in n.d over 1f out: r.o strly: easily* 5/2[1]
06-6 **2** 6 **Tafawuk (USA)**[19] 1899 5-9-4 72 FrederikTylicki 2 76
(Roger Varian) *chsd ldrs: rdn wl over 2f out: chsd clr wnr over 1f out: kpt on for clr 2nd but no imp on wnr* 6/1[3]
3660 **3** 1 ½ **Thecornishcowboy**[5] 2272 5-8-5 66 (tp) JoeDoyle(7) 6 67
(John Ryan) *stdd s: hld up in tch in rr: hdwy on outer 4f out: chsd wnr over 2f out: sn rdn and outpcd by wnr: lost 2nd over 1f out: plugged on* 8/1
3-45 **4** nk **The Ducking Stool**[8] 2199 7-8-9 68 ShelleyBirkett(5) 1 68
(Julia Feilden) *s.i.s: hld up in tch in last trio: nt clr run on inner 3f out: rdn 2f out: swtchd rt over 1f out: styd on ins fnl f: no ch w wnr* 6/1[3]
0-15 **5** 1 ¾ **Emulating (IRE)**[24] 1724 4-9-6 74 ShaneKelly 5 72
(James Fanshawe) *hld up in tch in midfield: rdn and unable qck whn short of room jst over 2f out: wknd over 1f out* 3/1[2]
26-4 **6** 2 ½ **Gabrial The Duke (IRE)**[28] 1628 4-9-3 71 (p) SebSanders 7 64
(David Simcock) *hld up in tch in last trio: rdn and effrt over 2f out: no imp: wl hld over 1f out* 8/1
066- **7** 4 **Colinca's Lad (IRE)**[188] 7857 12-9-4 75 RosieJessop(3) 3 61
(Peter Charalambous) *led: hdd and rdn 3f out: sn struggling: wknd wl over 1f out: bhd fnl f* 8/1

2m 25.17s (-3.53) **Going Correction** -0.15s/f (Firm) 7 Ran SP% 115.5
Speed ratings (Par 103): **106,101,100,100,99 97,94**
CSF £18.30 TOTE £2.70: £1.80, £5.20; EX 17.70 Trifecta £233.90.
**Owner** Tim Wood **Bred** Vincent Hannon **Trained** Newmarket, Suffolk

**FOCUS**
The pace in this middling handicap was ordinary until quickening at halfway. With the much-improved winner turning it into a procession from what should prove to have been a lenient mark, her rivals probably ran better than appeared to be the case. The second and third are rated to their marks.

## 2446 NORWICH AIRPORT H'CAP 5f 43y
7:30 (7:30) (Class 4) (0-85,85) 4-Y-O+ £4,690 (£1,395; £697; £348) Stalls Centre

Form RPR
-320 **1** **Peace Seeker**[27] 1650 6-9-7 85 (t) WilliamCarson 3 94
(Anthony Carson) *mde all: rdn and edgd lft over 1f out: edgd bk rt ins fnl f: r.o wl: rdn out* 11/4[2]
1-50 **2** 2 **Green Monkey**[5] 2275 4-8-12 76 ShaneKelly 2 78
(James Fanshawe) *in tch: clsd over 1f out: wnt 2nd and swtchd lft jst ins fnl f: sn rdn 2nd but no imp and styd on same pce* 4/1
0-22 **3** 4 **Arctic Lynx (IRE)**[11] 2123 7-9-1 82 RobertTart(3) 1 69
(Robert Cowell) *chsd wnr: rdn over 1f out: unable qck and lost 2nd jst ins fnl f: wknd fnl 75yds* 15/8[1]
4200 **4** 3 ¾ **Ubetterbegood (ARG)**[24] 1742 6-9-1 79 (p) RyanMoore 4 53
(Robert Cowell) *stdd after s: t.k.h: hld up in tch: rdn and effrt wl over 1f out: wknd fnl f* 3/1[3]

1m 2.5s (-0.20) **Going Correction** +0.125s/f (Good) 4 Ran SP% 106.4
Speed ratings (Par 105): **106,102,96,90**
CSF £12.50 TOTE £3.20; EX 10.80 Trifecta £12.80.
**Owner** Hugh & Mindi Byrne **Bred** C J Mills **Trained** Newmarket, Suffolk

**FOCUS**
These were decent sprinters, and the pace was good despite the lack of runners. The winner is rated to his AW best.

## 2447 AKS SKIPS H'CAP 7f 3y
**8:00** (8:00) (Class 5) (0-70,69) 3-Y-O **£2,587** (£770; £384; £192) **Stalls** Centre

Form RPR
5-52 **1** **Relation Alexander (IRE)**[23] 1769 3-9-5 **67** SeanLevey 5 75
(Paul D'Arcy) *chsd ldr: rdn to ld over 1f out: in command and r.o wl ins fnl f: rdn out* **7/2**[3]

400 **2** 2 ¼ **Clever Miss**[21] 1832 3-9-5 **67** (v[1]) FrederikTylicki 2 69
(Alan McCabe) *led tl rdn and hdd over 1f out: styd on same pce u.p fnl f* **12/1**

466- **3** 1 **Hoon (IRE)**[219] 7218 3-9-7 **69** [1] ShaneKelly 1 69
(Rae Guest) *chsd ldng pair: rdn wl over 1f out: unable qck and btn 1f out: no threat to wnr but kpt on again fnl 100yds* **2/1**[2]

-336 **4** 1 ½ **Seven Lucky Seven**[26] 1669 3-8-13 **61** (p) JimmyQuinn 3 57
(Nick Littmoden) *t.k.h: hld up in tch: rdn and effrt 2f out: 4th and no imp fr wl over 1f out* **20/1**

02-5 **5** 4 **Pastoral Witness**[40] 1404 3-9-4 **66** TedDurcan 4 51
(Clive Brittain) *stdd s: hld up in tch in rr: swtchd lft and effrt over 2f out: no imp: wknd over 1f out* **14/1**

05-0 **6** 6 **Sahara Desert (IRE)**[41] 1401 3-9-3 **65** (v[1]) RyanMoore 6 35
(Sir Michael Stoute) *t.k.h: hld up in tch in midfield: rdn ent fnl 2f: sn btn: bhd over 1f out* **15/8**[1]

1m 26.91s (0.31) **Going Correction** +0.125s/f (Good) **6 Ran SP% 109.5**
Speed ratings (Par 99): **103,100,99,97,93 86**
CSF £38.63 TOTE £4.10: £2.00, £3.30; EX 53.60 Trifecta £183.70.
**Owner** K Snell **Bred** Gerry Flannery Developments **Trained** Newmarket, Suffolk

**FOCUS**
A routine handicap in which they were soon going a solid pace. Not much depth to this but the winner rates a personal best.

## 2448 FACEBOOK AT GREAT YARMOUTH FILLIES' H'CAP 7f 3y
**8:30** (8:30) (Class 5) (0-75,74) 4-Y-O+ **£2,587** (£770; £384; £192) **Stalls** Centre

Form RPR
5-21 **1** **Meet Me Halfway**[21] 1863 4-9-3 **73** AshleyMorgan(3) 6 87+
(Chris Wall) *racd centre to nrside: hld up in tch in midfield: rdn to chal over 1f out: led ins fnl f: r.o wl* **9/2**[3]

5-55 **2** 2 **Lulu The Zulu (IRE)**[15] 2024 6-9-7 **74** AndrewMullen 3 83
(Michael Appleby) *racd centre to far side: plld hrd early: chsd ldrs: rdn to ld over 1f out: hdd and styd on same pce ins fnl f* **15/8**[1]

1224 **3** 2 ½ **Serenity Spa**[11] 2121 4-9-7 **74** RyanMoore 1 77
(Tony Carroll) *racd centre to far side: led: rdn 2f out: hdd over 1f out: no ex and outpcd ins fnl f* **9/4**[2]

5403 **4** shd **Magical Rose (IRE)**[15] 2029 4-8-8 **61** FrederikTylicki 5 63
(Conrad Allen) *racd centre to nrside: chsd ldr: rdn 2f out: unable qck over 1f out: plugged on same pce fnl f* **6/1**

030- **5** 7 **Olney Lass**[199] 7699 7-9-0 **70** SimonPearce(3) 4 54
(Lydia Pearce) *racd centre to far side: in tch in last pair: rdn and effrt 2f out: unable qck over 1f out: wknd fnl f* **33/1**

50-3 **6** 6 **Gift Of Silence**[21] 1863 5-8-13 **66** SeanLevey 2 34
(John Berry) *racd centre to far side: in tch in rr: rdn 2f out: sn btn: bhd fnl f* **12/1**

1m 26.33s (-0.27) **Going Correction** +0.125s/f (Good) **6 Ran SP% 108.7**
Speed ratings (Par 100): **106,103,100,100,92 85**
CSF £12.50 TOTE £5.50: £2.30, £2.10; EX 11.00 Trifecta £36.10.
**Owner** Des Thurlby **Bred** Stratford Place Stud And Watership Down **Trained** Newmarket, Suffolk

**FOCUS**
The pace was ordinary and that meant a dash to the line in the last 3f. The winner is progressing well now.
T/Plt: £898.80 to a £1 stake. Pool: £67,658.26 - 54.95 winning tickets. T/Qpdt: £391.00 to a £1 stake. Pool: £5,199.55 - 9.84 winning tickets. SP

# 1757 AYR (L-H)
### Wednesday, May 21

**OFFICIAL GOING: Good to soft (soft in places; 8.3)**
Wind: Fresh, half against Weather: Sunny, warm

## 2450 EBF STALLIONS RACING UK 10TH ANNIVERSARY MAIDEN STKS (BOBIS RACE) 6f
**1:50** (1:51) (Class 4) 2-Y-O **£4,204** (£1,251; £625; £312) **Stalls** High

Form RPR
**1** **The Wow Signal (IRE)** 2-9-5 0 PhillipMakin 5 92+
(John Quinn) *mde all against stands' rail: pushed clr fr over 1f out: readily* **5/2**[2]

**2** 9 **Doc Charm** 2-9-5 0 TomEaves 1 68
(Keith Dalgleish) *noisy and green in paddock: in tch: swtchd to stands' rail sn after s: effrt and chsd wnr over 1f out: kpt on but no imp* **14/1**

**3** 11 **Jungle Cat (IRE)** 2-9-5 0 JoeFanning 2 32
(Mark Johnston) *cl up: rdn over 2f out: wknd over 1f out* **12/5**[1]

**4** 6 **Al Rayyan (IRE)** 2-9-5 0 PaulMulrennan 4 14
(Kevin Ryan) *noisy and green in paddock: cl up: rdn 1/2-way: wknd 2f out* **9/2**

**5** 4 ½ **Poolstock** 2-9-5 0 DanielTudhope 3
(K R Burke) *prom: smooth hdwy over 2f out: rdn and wknd over 1f out: eased whn btn ins fnl f* **3/1**[3]

1m 17.95s (5.55) **Going Correction** +0.675s/f (Yiel) **5 Ran SP% 107.8**
Speed ratings (Par 95): **90,78,63,55,49**
CSF £29.03 TOTE £3.40: £1.50, £6.00; EX 42.00 Trifecta £109.20.
**Owner** Ross Harmon **Bred** Mrs T Stack **Trained** Settrington, N Yorks

**FOCUS**
Home straight inside rail moved in 8m, stands' rail normal position. Home bend out 2m added 6yds to races on Round course. The stalls were placed on the stands' side and they finished well strung out. All debutants for this interesting sprint maiden, run in a time 7.95 seconds slower than Racing Post standard (marginally quicker than the 6f handicap which followed).

## 2451 RACING UK ANYWHERE AVAILABLE NOW H'CAP (DIV I) 6f
**2:20** (2:20) (Class 6) (0-60,60) 4-Y-O+ **£1,940** (£577; £288; £144) **Stalls** High

Form RPR
06-5 **1** **Goninodaethat**[24] 1758 6-9-0 **53** GaryBartley 5 61
(Jim Goldie) *trckd ldrs: drvn to ld over 1f out: hrd pressed wl ins fnl f: hld on gamely* **5/1**[3]

54-0 **2** hd **Rock Canyon (IRE)**[17] 1972 5-8-8 **47** PJMcDonald 6 54
(Linda Perratt) *in tch: drvn and outpcd 1/2-way: rallied over 1f out: chal wl ins fnl f: jst hld* **14/1**

6061 **3** 2 **Fathom Five (IRE)**[29] 1639 10-8-3 **49** JoshQuinn(7) 9 50
(Shaun Harris) *cl up: rdn and led 1/2-way: hdd over 1f out: kpt on same pce ins fnl f* **11/4**[1]

06/3 **4** ½ **New Lease Of Life**[24] 1758 5-9-3 **56** GrahamLee 2 55
(Jim Goldie) *hld up: pushed along over 2f out: hdwy over 1f out: kpt on fnl f: no imp* **11/2**

-306 **5** nk **Secret City (IRE)**[11] 2171 8-9-4 **60** (b) JasonHart(3) 10 58
(Robin Bastiman) *in tch: drvn and outpcd over 3f out: rallied over 1f out: kpt on: nt gng pce to chal* **3/1**[2]

0500 **6** 1 ¾ **Celestial Dawn**[13] 2094 5-8-9 **48** (t) PaulMulrennan 8 41
(John Weymes) *dwlt: hld up: drvn along over 2f out: sme hdwy over 1f out: n.d* **13/2**

0000 **7** 27 **Marcus Caesar (IRE)**[11] 2171 4-9-5 **58** (b) JamesSullivan 7
(Ruth Carr) *t.k.h: led to 1/2-way: lost tch fr 2f out: t.o* **12/1**

1m 18.32s (5.92) **Going Correction** +0.675s/f (Yiel) **7 Ran SP% 111.4**
Speed ratings (Par 101): **87,86,84,83,83 80,44**
CSF £64.13 CT £223.18 TOTE £6.20: £2.40, £4.80; EX 48.90 Trifecta £258.40.
**Owner** G E Adams & J S Goldie **Bred** W G H Barrons **Trained** Uplawmoor, E Renfrews

**FOCUS**
They raced stands' side and went hard early in this lowly sprint, but it was the slower division. The winner basically ran to form.

## 2452 RACING UK ANYWHERE AVAILABLE NOW H'CAP (DIV II) 6f
**2:50** (2:50) (Class 6) (0-60,59) 4-Y-O+ **£1,940** (£577; £288; £144) **Stalls** High

Form RPR
-504 **1** **Monel**[22] 1838 6-8-13 **51** GrahamLee 9 66+
(Jim Goldie) *prom: nt clr run fr over 2f out tl 1f out: qcknd to ld ins fnl f: pushed clr* **7/2**[2]

4512 **2** 3 ¼ **Hab Reeh**[5] 2296 6-9-4 **56** JamesSullivan 8 61
(Ruth Carr) *cl up: led over 1f out to ins fnl f: kpt on: nt gng pce of wnr* **2/1**[1]

-060 **3** ½ **Senora Lobo (IRE)**[68] 963 4-8-2 **45** (p) ShirleyTeasdale(5) 7 48
(Lisa Williamson) *chsd ldrs: drvn and ev ch over 1f out to ins fnl f: one pce* **40/1**

0202 **4** ¾ **Novalist**[13] 2094 6-8-6 **47** (b) JasonHart(3) 11 48
(Robin Bastiman) *led against stands' rail: rdn and hdd over 1f out: kpt on same pce fnl f* **11/2**[3]

6-00 **5** 6 **Fife Jo**[9] 2219 4-8-4 **45** (v) IanBrennan(3) 5 26
(Jim Goldie) *hld up: stdy hdwy to chse ldrs wl over 1f out: wknd fnl f* **20/1**

6-00 **6** 2 **Saxonette**[24] 1758 6-8-12 **50** PJMcDonald 6 25
(Linda Perratt) *hld up bhd ldng gp: rdn and edgd lft 2f out: sn btn* **16/1**

20-0 **7** 1 **Black Douglas**[22] 1838 5-9-5 **57** TomEaves 3 29
(Jim Goldie) *dwlt: hld up: stdy hdwy over 2f out: n.m.r briefly wl over 1f out: sn rdn and btn* **14/1**

3 **8** 8 **Times In Anatefka (IRE)**[27] 1688 4-9-2 **54** (t[1]) StevieDonohoe 4
(Adrian Brendan Joyce, Ire) *t.k.h: cl up: rdn over 2f out: sn struggling* **11/2**[3]

0004 **9** 11 **Great Demeanor (USA)**[24] 1760 4-9-2 **59** (b) EmmaSayer(5) 1
(Dianne Sayer) *racd wd of stands' side gp: cl up tl rdn and wknd over 2f out* **14/1**

1m 17.22s (4.82) **Going Correction** +0.675s/f (Yiel) **9 Ran SP% 112.7**
Speed ratings (Par 101): **94,89,89,88,80 77,76,65,50**
CSF £10.56 CT £225.27 TOTE £6.80: £1.80, £1.10, £9.30; EX 13.40 Trifecta £356.60.
**Owner** Johnnie Delta Racing **Bred** Frank Brady And Brian Scanlon **Trained** Uplawmoor, E Renfrews

**FOCUS**
The second division of this lowly sprint handicap was run in a marginally quicker time. Again they came up the stands rail. The winner looks back to his 3yo level.

## 2453 HAMILTON BROTHERS AND KUBOTA H'CAP 7f 50y
**3:20** (3:20) (Class 4) (0-85,85) 4-Y-O+ **£5,175** (£1,540; £769; £384) **Stalls** High

Form RPR
3132 **1** **Uncle Dermot (IRE)**[11] 2177 6-8-11 **75** GrahamLee 6 91
(Brendan Powell) *mde all: qcknd clr over 2f out: kpt on strly: unchal* **10/3**[2]

540- **2** 8 **George Rooke (IRE)**[170] 8127 4-8-13 **77** TomEaves 5 72
(Keith Dalgleish) *t.k.h: sn chsng wnr: rdn over 2f out: sn one pce* **7/1**

2-06 **3** 4 **Silver Rime (FR)**[19] 1928 9-9-7 **85** PhillipMakin 3 70
(Linda Perratt) *hld up: rdn and hdwy over 2f out: no imp fr over 1f out* **22/1**

655- **4** 3 ½ **Balducci**[170] 8122 7-9-7 **85** DanielTudhope 1 61
(David O'Meara) *prom: drvn along 3f out: outpcd fnl 2f* **9/2**

333- **5** shd **Tatlisu (IRE)**[207] 7531 4-9-6 **84** TonyHamilton 2 59
(Richard Fahey) *t.k.h: trckd ldrs: rdn over 2f out: sn outpcd* **7/2**[3]

00-6 **6** 9 **Order Of Service**[24] 1762 4-8-8 **72** GaryBartley 4 24
(Jim Goldie) *hld up on ins: shortlived effrt over 2f out: sn btn* **18/1**

0003 **7** 11 **Talented Kid**[11] 2156 5-9-7 **85** JoeFanning 7 8
(Mark Johnston) *in tch: drvn and struggling 3f out: sn btn: eased whn no ch over 1f out* **3/1**[1]

1m 34.85s (1.45) **Going Correction** +0.375s/f (Good) **7 Ran SP% 110.6**
Speed ratings (Par 105): **106,96,92,88,88 77,65**
CSF £24.61 CT £411.43 TOTE £3.10: £1.80, £4.60; EX 31.30 Trifecta £305.90.
**Owner** K Rhatigan **Bred** Ballyhane Stud **Trained** Upper Lambourn, Berks

**FOCUS**
They went a reasonable pace for the conditions in this fair handicap and the winner showed useful form.

## 2454 RACING UK IPAD APP RACINGUK.COM/MOBILE H'CAP (£15,000 BETFAIR SCOTTISH MILE QUALIFIER) 1m
**3:50** (3:50) (Class 5) (0-70,69) 4-Y-O+ **£3,234** (£962; £481; £240) **Stalls** Low

Form RPR
4-22 **1** **True Pleasure (IRE)**[76] 853 7-9-5 **67** PJMcDonald 6 78
(James Bethell) *hld up in tch: hdwy to ld over 2f out: rdn and edgd lft over 1f out: drvn out fnl f* **5/2**[1]

0-60 **2** 2 ½ **Spavento (IRE)**[30] 1607 8-9-4 **69** JasonHart(3) 2 74
(Eric Alston) *hld up: effrt and swtchd rt over 2f out: chsd wnr wl over 1f out: edgd rt: kpt on same pce ins fnl f* **3/1**[2]

0-00 **3** 6 **Ebony Clarets**[9] 2219 5-8-4 **55** oh1 ConnorBeasley(3) 1 46
(Linda Perratt) *cl up: effrt and ev ch over 2f out: outpcd by first two fr over 1f out* **28/1**

50-0 **4** 2 ¼ **Angels Calling**[11] 2166 4-8-3 **56** JoeyHaynes(5) 4 42
(K R Burke) *cl up: drvn over 2f out: wknd over 1f out* **13/2**

0/05 **5** 4 **La Danza**[25] 1718 4-8-7 **60** ShirleyTeasdale(5) 5 37
(Lisa Williamson) *t.k.h: cl up on outside tl rdn and wknd 2f out* **11/1**

310- **6** *9* **Natures Law (IRE)**[209] 7489 4-9-1 **63** TomEaves 8 19
(Keith Dalgleish) *t.k.h: led at ordinary gallop: rdn and hdd over 2f out: sn btn* **9/2**[3]
20-2 **7** *3* **Thorntoun Lady (USA)**[24] 1760 4-9-7 **69** GrahamLee 7 18
(Jim Goldie) *hld up: rdn on outside wl over 2f out: sn btn* **5/1**
1m 47.34s (3.54) **Going Correction** +0.375s/f (Good) **7** Ran SP% **113.5**
Speed ratings (Par 103): **97,94,88,86,82 73,70**
CSF £10.07 CT £160.39 TOTE £3.20: £1.40, £2.60; EX 12.80 Trifecta £143.40.
**Owner** Clarendon Thoroughbred Racing **Bred** Michael O'Mahony **Trained** Middleham Moor, N Yorks

**FOCUS**
The pace was ordinary for this modest handicap. The form looks solid enough, rated around the runner-up.

## 2455 WATCH ON 3 DEVICES RACINGUK.COM/ANYWHERE H'CAP (£15,000 BETFAIR SCOTTISH STAYERS QUALIFIER) 1m 7f
**4:20** (4:20) (Class 6) (0-60,58) 4-Y-O+ **£1,940** (£577; £288; £144) **Stalls** Low

Form RPR
6-65 **1** **Father Shine (IRE)**[28] 1197 11-9-0 **51** DuranFentiman 3 58
(Shaun Harris) *chsd ldrs: drvn and outpcd over 2f out: rallied over 1f out: led ins fnl f: styd on wl* **14/1**
21/0 **2** *2 1/4* **Cool Baranca (GER)**[19] 1929 8-8-9 **51** EmmaSayer(5) 2 55
(Dianne Sayer) *bhd: gd hdwy on outside to ld over 1f out: hdd ins fnl f: kpt on same pce* **8/1**
00-5 **3** *3/4* **Forrest Flyer (IRE)**[24] 1763 10-9-6 **57** PhillipMakin 9 60
(Jim Goldie) *chsd ldr: drvn to chal over 2f out: kpt on same pce ins fnl f* **10/3**[2]
-426 **4** *3 3/4* **Funky Munky**[13] 640 9-9-0 **51** (p) PJMcDonald 6 49
(Alistair Whillans) *led: rdn and hdd over 2f out: rallied: outpcd ins fnl f* **9/2**[3]
3-66 **5** *6* **Latin Rebel (IRE)**[9] 2216 7-9-7 **58** GrahamLee 4 48
(Jim Goldie) *t.k.h: prom: stdy hdwy over 4f out: drvn and ev ch over 2f out: wknd fnl f* **9/4**[1]
0-44 **6** *13* **Brabazon (IRE)**[49] 1242 11-8-13 **55** (b) ShaneGray(5) 5 28
(Emmet Michael Butterly, Ire) *hld up in tch: drvn and struggling over 2f out: sn btn* **33/1**
**7** *14* **Coach Bombay (IRE)**[26] 1709 6-9-3 **54** (tp) StevieDonohoe 1 9
(Adrian Brendan Joyce, Ire) *prom: effrt and rdn 3f out: wknd 2f out* **7/1**
4605 **8** *27* **Tight Knit (USA)**[2] 2394 4-8-10 **53** (b) JoeyHaynes(5) 8
(John Weymes) *hld up: drvn and struggling 3f out: sn btn: t.o* **12/1**
3m 37.86s (17.46) **Going Correction** +0.375s/f (Good)
**WFA** 4 from 5yo+ 1lb **8** Ran SP% **112.9**
Speed ratings (Par 101): **68,66,66,64,61 54,46,32**
CSF £116.21 CT £463.04 TOTE £15.40: £4.10, £3.30, £1.02; EX 108.00 Trifecta £530.70.
**Owner** Mrs Anna Kenny **Bred** C Kenneally **Trained** Carburton, Notts

**FOCUS**
A moderate staying handicap run at a weak early pace. It turned into a sprint with 4f to run, and then a slog. The form is rated cautiously given the conditions.

## 2456 NAIRN BROWN 50TH ANNIVERSARY H'CAP 5f
**4:50** (4:50) (Class 3) (0-90,85) 4-Y-O+ **£7,762** (£2,310; £1,154; £577) **Stalls** High

Form RPR
-011 **1** **Taurus Twins**[11] 2159 8-8-11 **75** (b) JoeFanning 11 84
(Richard Price) *mde all against stands' rail: rdn and hrd pressed over 1f out: kpt on wl fnl f: eased cl home* **9/2**[2]
6-20 **2** *nk* **Rasaman (IRE)**[4] 2332 10-9-2 **80** GrahamLee 7 88
(Jim Goldie) *hld up: no room tl gap appeared appr fnl f: kpt on strly under hands and heels: jst hld* **8/1**
44-0 **3** *1 1/2* **Gowanharry (IRE)**[22] 1850 5-8-8 **75** ConnorBeasley(3) 10 78
(Michael Dods) *cl up: rdn to chal over 1f out to ins fnl f: hld towards fin* **7/1**[3]
0-24 **4** *1 3/4* **Rothesay Chancer**[11] 2167 6-8-6 **73** IanBrennan(3) 5 69
(Jim Goldie) *in tch: rdn and hung lft over 1f out: kpt on same pce ins fnl f* **10/1**
600 **5** *hd* **Go Go Green (IRE)**[4] 2350 8-7-12 **69** JackGarritty(7) 1 65
(Jim Goldie) *dwlt: hld up: effrt whn n.m.r briefly over 1f out: kpt on ins fnl f* **20/1**
1114 **6** *3 1/2* **Megaleka**[13] 2096 4-9-2 **85** TimClark(5) 8 68
(Alan Bailey) *in tch on outside: rdn over 2f out: no ex over 1f out* **7/1**[3]
44-0 **7** *1/2* **L'Ami Louis (IRE)**[33] 1565 6-8-12 **81** GarryWhillans(5) 9 62
(Ian Semple) *dwlt: t.k.h and sn prom against stands' rail: rdn and outpcd wl over 1f out: sn btn* **22/1**
0-34 **8** *2* **Jinky**[24] 1759 6-8-6 **70** PJMcDonald 6 44
(Linda Perratt) *hld up: rdn along over 2f out: nvr on terms* **12/1**
0-66 **9** *4* **Bonnie Charlie**[17] 1967 8-8-8 **72** PaulQuinn 4 32
(David Nicholls) *taken early to post: prom: drvn over 2f out: wknd wl over 1f out* **14/1**
0-63 **10** *7* **Imperial Legend (IRE)**[4] 2350 5-9-7 **85** (p) PaulMulrennan 2 19
(David Nicholls) *sn chsng wnr: rdn over 2f out: wkng whn hmpd over 1f out* **5/2**[1]
1m 1.94s (2.54) **Going Correction** +0.675s/f (Yiel) **10** Ran SP% **115.4**
Speed ratings (Par 107): **106,105,103,100,100 94,93,90,84,72**
CSF £39.95 CT £248.73 TOTE £6.00, £2.20, £1.90; EX 39.10 Trifecta £290.00.
**Owner** G E Amey & G D Bailey **Bred** G E Amey **Trained** Ullingswick, H'fords

**FOCUS**
As it had been all afternoon, the stands' rail was the place. The winner was still a length off his form of this time last year.

## 2457 RACING UK ANDROID APP RACINGUK.COM/MOBILE APPRENTICE H'CAP 1m 1f 20y
**5:20** (5:20) (Class 6) (0-60,59) 4-Y-O+ **£1,940** (£577; £288; £144) **Stalls** Low

Form RPR
063- **1** **Remember Rocky**[232] 6921 5-8-9 **47** (p) MeganCarberry 2 57
(Lucy Normile) *chsd ldr: rdn to ld over 1f out: pushed clr fnl f* **9/2**[2]
00-0 **2** *6* **Gadobout Dancer**[24] 1761 7-8-7 **45** LauraBarry 1 42
(Keith Dalgleish) *in tch: effrt whn n.m.r and swtchd lft over 1f out: sn chsng wnr: kpt on fnl f: no imp* **8/1**[3]
453- **3** *1 1/4* **Testa Rossa (IRE)**[208] 7515 4-9-7 **59** JackGarritty 6 48
(Jim Goldie) *hld up in tch: effrt and drvn over 2f out: one pce fr over 1f out: fin 4th: plcd 3rd* **7/2**[1]
0-00 **4** *1 3/4* **Cheeky Wee Red**[27] 1673 6-8-5 **48** (t) RowanScott(5) 8 33
(Alistair Whillans) *t.k.h: in tch: effrt and rdn over 2f out: no ex over 1f out: fin 5th: plcd 4th* **20/1**
000- **5** *1/2* **Inniscastle Boy**[138] 7238 5-8-0 **45** RachaelGrant(7) 9 29
(Jim Goldie) *s.i.s: bhd: struggling over 3f out: hdwy over 1f out: kpt on: no imp: fin 6th: plcd 5th* **20/1**
40-4 **6** *3/4* **Gabrial The Thug (FR)**[22] 1864 4-9-4 **56** SammyJoBell 3 39
(Richard Fahey) *t.k.h: cl up: effrt and ch over 2f out: wknd over 1f out: fin 7th: plcd 6th* **7/2**[1]
0-02 **7** *hd* **Jumbo Prado (USA)**[8] 1745 5-9-7 **59** (p) JoeDoyle 5 42
(John Stimpson) *s.i.s: bhd: struggling over 2f out: n.d after: fin 8th: plcd 7th* **12/1**
3310 **D** *2 1/4* **Sixties Queen**[9] 2199 4-8-9 **54** KevinLundie(5) 10 46?
(Alan Bailey) *t.k.h: led and sddle sn slipped: lost weight cloth over 5f out: sddle slipped bk over 2f out: hdd over 1f out: sn one pce: fin 3rd: disqualified and plcd last* **7/2**[1]
2m 4.39s (6.89) **Going Correction** +0.375s/f (Good) **8** Ran SP% **113.2**
Speed ratings (Par 101): **84,78,75,74,73 72,72,76**
CSF £38.97 CT £137.73 TOTE £6.80: £1.70, £2.70; EX 53.00 Trifecta £380.10.
**Owner** Byrne Racing **Bred** Cherry Park Stud **Trained** Duncrievie, Perth & Kinross

**FOCUS**
A moderate apprentices' handicap and the pace was very ordinary in the testing ground. The winner is rated back to his 3yo form.
T/Plt: £443.30 to a £1 stake. Pool: £55873.41 - 92.00 winning tickets T/Qpdt: £13.00 to a £1 stake. Pool: £5408.73 - 307.61 winning tickets RY

# 2078 KEMPTON (A.W) (R-H)
Wednesday, May 21

**OFFICIAL GOING: Standard**
Wind: Moderate, half behind Weather: Cloudy

## 2458 KEMPTON FOR WEDDINGS MEDIAN AUCTION MAIDEN STKS 5f (P)
**5:50** (5:54) (Class 6) 2-Y-O **£1,940** (£577; £288; £144) **Stalls** Low

Form RPR
23 **1** **Littlemissblakeney**[15] 2057 2-8-9 0 NoelGarbutt(5) 1 85+
(Hugo Palmer) *nipped through on inner to join ldrs over 3f out: led 1/2-way: drew clr wl over 1f out: pushed out* **8/1**
33 **2** *3 3/4* **Harry Hurricane**[35] 1512 2-9-5 0 PatCosgrave 3 77
(George Baker) *awkward s: in tch: prog 1/2-way: rdn to chse wnr over 1f out: styd on but no imp* **10/11**[1]
**3** *3* **When Will It End (IRE)** 2-9-5 0 RichardHughes 2 66+
(Richard Hannon) *slowly away: mostly in last tl 2f out: kpt on fr over 1f out to take 3rd ins fnl f: n.d* **5/2**[2]
0 **4** *1* **Zebs Lad (IRE)**[44] 1349 2-9-5 0 LiamJones 4 62
(Ronald Harris) *led: hanging bnd after 1f: hdd 1/2-way: hanging again over 1f out: sn wknd* **33/1**
0 **5** *nk* **Thumper (FR)**[16] 2007 2-9-5 0 HarryBentley 5 61
(Robert Cowell) *w ldr for 2f: outpcd 2f out: no ch after* **6/1**[3]
44 **6** *2* **Jersey Belle**[15] 2057 2-8-11 0 WilliamTwiston-Davies(3) 6 49
(Mick Channon) *awkward to load into stalls: w ldrs 1f: wd on bnd sn after: dropped to rr and wl btn 2f out* **20/1**
1m 0.11s (-0.39) **Going Correction** -0.125s/f (Stan) **6** Ran SP% **114.1**
Speed ratings (Par 91): **98,92,87,85,85 81**
CSF £16.31 TOTE £7.40: £3.30, £1.10; EX 15.70 Trifecta £31.60.
**Owner** The Walled Garden Partnership **Bred** Tobias B P Coles **Trained** Newmarket, Suffolk

**FOCUS**
Not the strongest of juvenile maidens with those that had already run only showing solid, rather than spectacular form. The pace was fairly steady and the winning time was a second outside of standard.

## 2459 CASH OUT ON THE BETDAQ APP H'CAP 5f (P)
**6:20** (6:20) (Class 6) (0-65,64) 4-Y-O+ **£1,940** (£577; £288; £144) **Stalls** Low

Form RPR
004- **1** **Lager Time (IRE)**[190] 7848 4-9-6 **63** AdamKirby 1 74
(David Evans) *trckd ldng pair: clsd gng wl to ld over 1f out: sn rdn: clr ins fnl f: drvn out* **13/8**[1]
-613 **2** *1 3/4* **Aeolian Blue**[20] 1896 4-9-7 **64** ShaneKelly 6 69
(William Knight) *chsd ldng trio: rdn 1/2-way: styd on fr over 1f out to take 2nd last 100yds: unable to chal* **5/1**[3]
3126 **3** *1 1/4* **Bubbly Bailey**[43] 1369 4-8-12 **55** (v) FrederikTylicki 4 56
(J R Jenkins) *wnt lft s but led: drvn and hdd over 1f out: one pce* **2/1**[2]
-000 **4** *nk* **Belinsky (IRE)**[16] 2029 7-8-9 **52** JimmyQuinn 3 51
(Dean Ivory) *hld up in last and sn wl adrift of ldrs: prog wl over 1f out: rdn and kpt on fnl f: no ch* **25/1**
2444 **5** *1 1/4* **Pharoh Jake**[16] 2029 6-9-5 **62** WilliamCarson 7 57
(John Bridger) *trapped out wd: in tch: rdn over 2f out: nt qckn over 1f out: one pce* **14/1**
3043 **6** *3 3/4* **Pull The Pin (IRE)**[21] 1892 5-9-2 **62** (bt) OisinMurphy(3) 8 43
(Ann Stokell) *spd fr wd draw to press ldr: nt qckn 2f out and sn lost 2nd: wknd fnl f* **10/1**
0030 **7** *1 3/4* **Brandywell Boy (IRE)**[97] 586 11-8-7 **50** oh5 RoystonFfrench 2 25
(Dominic Ffrench Davis) *a in last trio: struggling fr 2f out* **50/1**
2400 **8** *2 3/4* **Quality Art (USA)**[19] 1912 6-9-4 **61** SteveDrowne 5 26
(Simon Hodgson) *dwlt and impeded s: a in last trio: nvr a factor* **20/1**
59.42s (-1.08) **Going Correction** -0.125s/f (Stan) **8** Ran SP% **114.4**
Speed ratings (Par 101): **103,100,98,97,95 89,86,82**
CSF £10.07 CT £16.59 TOTE £3.80, £1.20, £1.20; EX 14.60 Trifecta £31.10.
**Owner** Mrs E Evans **Bred** Polish Belle Partnership **Trained** Pandy, Monmouths

**FOCUS**
A modest handicap where the money got it spot on.

## 2460 BRITISH STALLION STUDS EBF MAIDEN FILLIES' STKS (BOBIS RACE) 6f (P)
**6:50** (6:51) (Class 5) 2-Y-O **£2,911** (£866; £432; £216) **Stalls** Low

Form RPR
**1** **Cursory Glance (USA)** 2-9-0 0 AndreaAtzeni 5 76+
(Roger Varian) *awkward to load into stalls: chsd ldng trio: shkn up over 2f out: clsd on wd outer over 1f out: rdn to ld ins fnl f: styd on* **5/2**[1]
0 **2** *1* **No Delusion (USA)**[34] 1528 2-9-0 0 WilliamBuick 2 71
(Charlie Appleby) *chsd ldrs in 5th: prog fr 2f out: rdn and styd on to take 2nd last 50yds: unable to chal* **7/2**[3]
**3** *3/4* **One Moment** 2-8-11 0 OisinMurphy(3) 4 69
(Robert Cowell) *led: veered lft jst over 2f out: kpt on: hdd and one pce ins fnl f* **10/1**
64 **4** *1* **Alpha Spirit**[12] 2128 2-8-11 0 WilliamTwiston-Davies(3) 9 66
(Mick Channon) *trckd ldr: tried to chal over 2f out: carried lft sn after: nt qckn and hld 1f out: fdd* **16/1**
3 **5** *1 1/4* **Only Joking**[11] 2173 2-9-0 0 MartinDwyer 8 62
(Hugo Palmer) *off the pce in 7th: shkn up and prog 2f out: tk 5th over 1f out: kpt on but n.d* **7/1**

64 **6** *8* **Tommys Geal**[27] 1663 2-9-0 0 ........ LukeMorris 6 38
(Michael Madgwick) *chsd ldrs: rdn and no prog over 2f out: wknd qckly over 1f out* **50/1**

**7** *1* **Calypso Beat (USA)** 2-9-0 0 ........[1] TomQueally 7 35
(Kevin Ryan) *rn green in last pair: a bhd* **10/1**

**8** *3* **Conjuring (IRE)** 2-9-0 0 ........ ShaneKelly 3 26
(Mike Murphy) *slowly away: rn green in last pair: a bhd* **33/1**

**9** *1* **Larch (IRE)** 2-9-0 0 ........ RichardHughes 1 23
(Richard Hannon) *trckd ldng pair: nudged along and lost pl 2f out: wknd and eased* **3/1**[2]

1m 13.0s (-0.10) **Going Correction** -0.125s/f (Stan) **9 Ran SP% 117.3**
Speed ratings (Par 90): **95,93,92,91,89 79,77,73,72**
CSF £11.65 TOTE £4.40: £2.40, £1.10, £3.20; EX 12.50 Trifecta £88.40.
**Owner** Merry Fox Stud Limited **Bred** Merry Fox Stud Limited **Trained** Newmarket, Suffolk
■ Stewards' Enquiry : Andrea Atzeni one-day ban: careless riding (Jun 4)

**FOCUS**
Roger Varian had taken this race in the past two seasons with Exceptionelle and the classy Princess Noor and he looks to have another above-average filly in his care in the shape of the winner. She was value for a bit extra.

## 2461 BETDAQ - SPORTS BETTING EXCHANGE H'CAP (LONDON MIDDLE DISTANCE SERIES QUALIFIER) 1m 3f (P)
7:20 (7:20) (Class 3) (0-95,95) 4-Y-0+
**£7,158** (£2,143; £1,071; £535; £267; £134) **Stalls** Low

Form RPR

32-5 **1** **Magic Hurricane (IRE)**[25] 1715 4-8-9 **83** ........ FrederikTylicki 4 94+
(James Fanshawe) *trckd ldng pair: rdn and clsd fr 2f out: led 1f out: pushed firmly clr* **11/4**[1]

16-2 **2** *2 ¼* **Jazz Master**[25] 1715 4-8-12 **86** ........ AndreaAtzeni 8 93+
(Luca Cumani) *trckd ldrs: outpcd and rdn over 2f out: styd on fr over 1f out to take 2nd nr fin* **7/2**[2]

2-1 **3** *½* **Economy**[50] 1218 4-8-9 **83** ........ JamesDoyle 12 89
(Sir Michael Stoute) *trckd ldr: rdn to chal over 2f out: sn nt qckn: hld whn lost 2nd and hmpd 1f out: kpt on* **6/1**

602- **4** *hd* **Zain Eagle**[187] 7906 4-9-7 **95** ........ RichardHughes 9 101
(Robert Cowell) *led: pressed and rdn over 2f out: hanging lft over 1f out: sn hdd and nt qckn* **5/1**[3]

3-03 **5** *¾* **Noble Gift**[21] 1871 4-8-9 **83** ........ JimCrowley 1 87+
(William Knight) *mounted on crse: hld up in 10th: pushed along 4f out: rdn and prog fr 2f out but no ch: kpt on fnl f: nrst fin* **7/1**

-300 **6** *½* **Centurius**[17] 1973 4-8-11 **90** ........(p) MarcMonaghan(5) 3 93
(Marco Botti) *trckd ldrs: rdn and outpcd over 2f out: kpt on fr over 1f out: no threat to ldrs* **16/1**

05-0 **7** *4* **Spifer (IRE)**[18] 1948 6-9-0 **88** ........(p) AntonioFresu 2 84
(Marco Botti) *hld up towards rr: urged along on inner and outpcd over 2f out: no imp after* **16/1**

3565 **8** *1 ¼* **Swing Alone (IRE)**[11] 2142 5-9-5 **93** ........ LukeMorris 11 87
(Gay Kelleway) *mounted outside paddock: hld up towards rr: rdn and outpcd over 2f out: no ch after* **16/1**

016- **9** *¾* **Azrag (USA)**[207] 7542 6-8-12 **86** ........(p) RobertHavlin 10 79
(Michael Attwater) *taken down early and walked to post: w.w in midfield: rdn and outpcd over 2f out: no ch after* **33/1**

0/0- **10** *1* **Rosslyn Castle**[29] 2052 5-8-9 **88** ........ LouisSteward(5) 5 79
(Philip McBride) *stdd s: hld up in last: outpcd and shkn up over 2f out: nvr in it* **50/1**

050- **11** *48* **Apache (IRE)**[337] 3423 6-8-12 **86** ........ PatCosgrave 6
(Jane Chapple-Hyam) *mounted outside paddock: chsd ldrs: pushed along over 3f out: wknd over 2f out: t.o: lame* **20/1**

2m 18.4s (-3.50) **Going Correction** -0.125s/f (Stan) **11 Ran SP% 119.7**
Speed ratings (Par 107): **107,105,105,104,104 103,101,100,99,98 63**
CSF £12.18 CT £54.28 TOTE £4.90: £1.80, £2.00, £2.40; EX 12.90 Trifecta £65.30.
**Owner** Dragon Gate **Bred** Pat & Eoghan Grogan **Trained** Newmarket, Suffolk

**FOCUS**
A good, competitive race which the market got spot on. The pace was true and the time was decent.

## 2462 BETDAQ NO PREMIUM CHARGE H'CAP (LONDON MILE SERIES QUALIFIER) 1m (P)
7:50 (7:50) (Class 4) (0-85,85) 4-Y-0+ **£4,690** (£1,395; £697; £348) **Stalls** Low

Form RPR

-511 **1** **Lawmans Thunder**[14] 2079 4-9-5 **83** ........ TomQueally 7 99
(Ismail Mohammed) *trckd ldrs: prog to ld over 1f out: pushed along and drew clr: v readily* **13/8**[1]

0005 **2** *4* **Loyalty**[15] 2062 7-9-0 **85** ........(v) AdamMcLean(7) 2 91
(Derek Shaw) *trckd ldng pair: tried to chal on inner 2f out: hanging and nt qckn over 1f out: urged along to take 2nd ins fnl f: no ch w wnr* **12/1**

34-0 **3** *¾* **Pleasure Bent**[25] 1724 4-9-2 **80** ........ AndreaAtzeni 1 84
(Luca Cumani) *led: kicked on over 2f out: hdd over 1f out: outpcd and lost 2nd fnl f: kpt on* **5/1**[3]

513 **4** *hd* **Self Employed**[12] 2131 7-8-7 **71** oh1 ........ LukeMorris 4 75
(Garry Woodward) *hld up towards rr: prog on inner 2f out: chal for a pl fnl f: no room nr fin* **16/1**

1106 **5** *1 ¼* **Silverheels (IRE)**[15] 2062 5-9-2 **85** ........(b) LouisSteward(5) 9 86
(Paul Cole) *hld up towards rr: shkn up over 2f out: kpt on fr over 1f out to take 5th ins fnl f: n.d* **16/1**

0-06 **6** *2 ¼* **Freddy With A Y (IRE)**[11] 2157 4-8-13 **77** ........ JimCrowley 3 72
(Gary Moore) *chsd ldr: rdn and nt qckn over 2f out: sn lost 2nd and btn* **25/1**

226- **7** *2* **Twenty One Choice (IRE)**[234] 6883 5-9-4 **85** ........ OisinMurphy(3) 8 76
(Ed de Giles) *trckd ldrs on outer: edgd rt and shkn up over 2f out: nt qckn and sn btn* **11/4**[2]

062- **8** *1 ½* **Silver Dixie (USA)**[154] 8336 4-9-4 **82** ........ AdamKirby 5 69
(Peter Hedger) *hld up in last: no prog 2f out: nvr in it* **7/1**

5220 **9** *1 ½* **Appease**[16] 2033 5-8-13 **77** ........(p) RichardHughes 6 60
(John Butler) *hld up in last pair: pushed along over 2f out: no prog* **10/1**

456- **10** *3 ¼* **Plover**[256] 6188 4-9-7 **85** ........[1] KierenFallon 10 61
(Michael Attwater) *racd wdst thrght: towards rr: rdn and no prog over 2f out* **33/1**

1m 38.41s (-1.39) **Going Correction** -0.125s/f (Stan) **10 Ran SP% 129.3**
Speed ratings (Par 105): **101,97,96,96,94 92,90,89,87,84**
CSF £27.28 CT £95.07 TOTE £3.90: £1.70, £4.50, £1.70; EX 26.80 Trifecta £136.60.
**Owner** Sheikh Juma Dalmook Al Maktoum **Bred** Foursome Thoroughbreds **Trained** Newmarket, Suffolk

**FOCUS**
A fair handicap turned into a procession by the winner.

## 2463 VISIT AND DINE IN THE PANORAMIC H'CAP 7f (P)
8:20 (8:20) (Class 6) (0-65,65) 4-Y-0+ **£1,940** (£577; £288; £144) **Stalls** Low

Form RPR

4345 **1** **Shifting Star (IRE)**[12] 2124 9-9-2 **60** ........(vt) WilliamCarson 8 67
(John Bridger) *prom: drvn over 2f out: chsd ldr over 1f out: styd on fnl f to ld last 50yds* **16/1**

0-02 **2** *nk* **Mrs Warren**[27] 1668 4-9-4 **62** ........ PatCosgrave 10 68
(George Baker) *hld up towards rr on outer: rdn over 2f out: prog over 1f out: clsd w others fnl f: styd on to take 2nd last strides* **16/1**

P-20 **3** *hd* **Substantivo (IRE)**[26] 1689 4-9-2 **60** ........ KierenFallon 7 66+
(Alan Jarvis) *trckd ldrs in 5th: shkn up over 2f out: prog whn nt clr run and lost pl over 1f out: styd on again fnl f: fin best* **7/1**[3]

5636 **4** *hd* **Meridius (IRE)**[24] 1766 4-9-5 **63** ........(p) JamesDoyle 1 68
(Nick Littmoden) *led: kicked on over 2f out: drvn over 1f out: hdd last 50yds: lost 2 pls fnl strides* **20/1**

4050 **5** *hd* **Greensward**[44] 1354 8-9-6 **64** ........(p) HayleyTurner 9 69
(Conor Dore) *prom: rdn over 2f out: clsd grad fr over 1f out: kpt on but nvr quite pce to chal* **11/1**

0511 **6** *1* **Exceedexpectations (IRE)**[46] 1312 5-9-3 **61** ........(v) AmirQuinn 5 63
(Lee Carter) *hld up in 8th: prog jst over 2f out: rdn to chse ldrs over 1f out: one pce last 100yds* **12/1**

04-4 **7** *½* **Celestial Ray**[14] 2079 5-9-2 **60** ........ RobertHavlin 13 61
(Linda Jewell) *racd on outer in midfield: rdn over 2f out: nt qckn and sn lost pl: kpt on fr jst over 1f out: n.d* **14/1**

634- **8** *nk* **Uprise**[163] 8220 5-9-2 **63** ........ RyanPowell(3) 4 63
(George Margarson) *hld up in last trio: shakern up over 2f out: sme prog over 1f out: rdn and kpt on fnl f: nrst fin* **14/1**

3-23 **9** *1* **Victorian Number (FR)**[113] 366 6-9-6 **64** ........ GeorgeBaker 3 61
(Geoffrey Deacon) *trckd ldrs disputing 6th: shkn up on inner over 2f out: nt qckn w ldrs over 1f out: wl hld after* **5/1**[2]

1406 **10** *nse* **Foie Gras**[16] 2029 4-9-6 **64** ........ LukeMorris 6 61
(Chris Dwyer) *mostly in last trio: rdn 3f out: no prog tl kpt on fnl f* **33/1**

-350 **11** *¾* **Princess Spirit**[33] 1554 5-9-2 **60** ........(p) JimCrowley 11 55
(Edward Creighton) *hld up in last trio: jst pushed along fr 2f out: no real prog: nvr involved* **7/1**[3]

6161 **12** *1 ¼* **Darnathean**[14] 2069 5-9-6 **64** ........(p) RichardHughes 2 56
(Paul D'Arcy) *hld up towards rr: pushed along on inner over 2f out: no prog over 1f out: wknd* **9/2**[1]

6324 **13** *2 ¼* **Colour My World**[25] 1717 4-9-2 **60** ........(b) AdamKirby 14 46
(Ed McMahon) *pressed ldr: hrd rdn over 2f out: lost 2nd and wknd qckly over 1f out* **7/1**[3]

1m 25.72s (-0.28) **Going Correction** -0.125s/f (Stan) **13 Ran SP% 121.2**
Speed ratings (Par 101): **96,95,95,95,94 93,93,92,91,91 90,89,86**
CSF £253.47 CT £1967.26 TOTE £20.00: £4.40, £3.50, £3.40; EX 362.80 Trifecta £1646.00 Part won..
**Owner** Night Shadow Syndicate **Bred** Hardys Of Kilkeel Ltd **Trained** Liphook, Hants

**FOCUS**
Most of these could be given a chance in this weak handicap and it resulted in a real bunched finish.

## 2464 BETDAQ £25 NO LOSE FREE BET APPRENTICE H'CAP 1m 3f (P)
8:50 (8:50) (Class 5) (0-70,68) 4-Y-0+ **£2,587** (£770; £384; £192) **Stalls** Low

Form RPR

5012 **1** **Nelson Quay (IRE)**[27] 1664 4-9-2 **68** ........ DavidParkes(5) 8 76
(Jeremy Gask) *trckd ldrs: clsd w others to chal 2f out: rdn to ld jst over 1f out: hld on nr fin* **7/1**

6442 **2** *hd* **Mr Lando**[14] 2084 5-8-12 **59** ........ RyanTate 2 67
(Tony Carroll) *t.k.h: trckd ldng trio: clsd to chal 2f out: nt qckn over 1f out: styd on to take 2nd ins fnl f: clsd on wnr at fin* **9/2**[1]

0-11 **3** *2 ½* **Megalala (IRE)**[15] 2046 13-8-11 **63** ........ CamHardie(5) 7 66
(John Bridger) *led at decent pce: rdn over 2f out: hdd and one pce jst over 1f out* **8/1**

3024 **4** *shd* **Bennelong**[6] 2282 8-8-7 **59** ........(b) CharlotteJenner(5) 4 62
(Lee Carter) *t.k.h: hld up in rr: nt clr run over 2f out and swtchd rt: swtchd rt wl over 1f out: tried to cl on ldrs but one pce fnl f* **6/1**[3]

00-3 **5** *4* **Tingo In The Tale (IRE)**[23] 1798 5-9-2 **66** ........ JordanVaughan(3) 3 62
(David Arbuthnot) *chsd ldr after 3f to 2f out: wknd fnl f* **5/1**[2]

-023 **6** *¾* **Mcbirney (USA)**[23] 1815 7-8-12 **66** ........ JessicaWestgate(7) 6 60
(Paul D'Arcy) *hld up and detached in last pair early: in tch after 4f: prog arnd field bnd 4f out to go prom over 2f out: wknd over 1f out* **9/1**

00- **7** *nk* **Evergreen Forest (IRE)**[216] 6377 6-9-2 **63** ........ LouisSteward 9 57
(Natalie Lloyd-Beavis) *nvr bttr than midfield: no prog over 2f out: btn over 1f out* **20/1**

3106 **8** *2 ½* **Time Square (FR)**[5] 2300 7-9-0 **61** ........ MarcMonaghan 1 50
(Tony Carroll) *chsd ldr 3f: prom tl wknd over 2f out* **9/2**[1]

4320 **9** *25* **Officer In Command (USA)**[14] 2079 8-8-13 **67** ........(p) GeorgiaCox(7) 5 11
(John Butler) *s.s: in tch in rr tl wknd over 4f out: t.o* **25/1**

0-45 **U** **Oetzi**[22] 1848 6-9-3 **64** ........ JackDuern 10
(Alan Jarvis) *propped in stalls and uns rdr as they opened* **10/1**

2m 20.03s (-1.87) **Going Correction** -0.125s/f (Stan) **10 Ran SP% 118.6**
Speed ratings (Par 103): **101,100,99,98,96 95,95,93,75,**
CSF £39.27 CT £262.38 TOTE £9.10: £3.40, £2.00, £2.80; EX 56.80 Trifecta £217.00.
**Owner** S T Brankin **Bred** Albert Conneally **Trained** Sutton Veny, Wilts

**FOCUS**
A typically weak apprentice handicap which was further weakened when Oetzi got rid of his jockey before the stalls opened.
T/Jkpt: £23,671.50 to a £1 stake. Pool: £66,680.55 - 2.00 winning tickets T/Plt: £44.40 to a £1 stake. Pool: £77061.05 - 1264.30 winning tickets T/Qpdt: £28.50 to a £1 stake. Pool: £6358.9 - 164.70 winning tickets JN

2206 **LINGFIELD (L-H)**
Wednesday, May 21

**OFFICIAL GOING: Turf course - good to firm changing to good to firm (firm in places) after race 1 (2:00); all-weather - standard**
Wind: light to meduim, half against Weather: dry, overcast

## 2465 DAILY MAIL H'CAP — 1m 3f 106y
**2:00** (2:00) (Class 6) (0-60,60) 4-Y-0+ £2,385 (£704; £352) **Stalls High**

Form RPR
222- 1 **Men Don't Cry (IRE)**179 8031 5-9-2 58 ... OisinMurphy(3) 7 65+
(Ed de Giles) *chsd ldng trio: effrt and rdn to ld 2f out: drvn and forged ahd over 1f out: idling in front ins fnl f: a jst holding on* 2/1[1]
3-6 2 shd **Neuilly**30 1622 7-9-7 60 ... GeorgeBaker 5 66
(Gary Moore) *stdd s: hld up in midfield: rdn and effrt on outer over 1f out: chsd wnr ins fnl f: r.o and grad clsd: nt quite rch wnr* 6/1[3]
5010 3 3/4 **Cabuchon (GER)**4 2327 7-9-7 60 ...(t) AdamKirby 1 65
(David Evans) *broke wl: sn settled in bk and hld up in midfield: hdwy ent fnl 2f: chsd ldrs and drvn 1f out: styd on same pce fnl 100yds* 7/2[2]
22-3 4 1 1/2 **Zinnobar**22 1865 4-8-10 49 ... RichardKingscote 3 52
(Jonathan Portman) *chsd ldr: rdn and ev ch 2f out: drvn and unable qck over 1f out: lost 2nd ins fnl f: wknd towards fin* 7/1
43/4 5 1 1/4 **Dark And Dangerous (IRE)**15 2046 6-8-11 57 ... JennyPowell(7) 2 58
(Brendan Powell) *bustled along leaving stalls: sn led: hdd after 1f: chsd ldrs after: n.m.r and rdn 2f out: unable qck u.p over 1f out: wknd ins fnl f* 14/1
0332 6 1 **Abigails Angel**22 1836 7-8-4 50 ow2 ... DavidParkes(7) 10 49
(Brett Johnson) *hld up off the pce in last trio: rdn and effrt on inner over 2f out: rdn over 1f out: kpt on but nvr gng pce to rch ldrs* 10/1
6600 7 4 1/2 **Bell'Arte (IRE)**14 842 4-8-9 48 ...(p) LiamJones 8 40
(Laura Mongan) *stdd s: hld up off the pce in rr: rdn 4f out: plugged on fnl 2f: n.d* 50/1
0-64 8 9 **Booktheband (IRE)**65 989 4-8-10 49 ... RichardHughes 9 26
(Clive Brittain) *led after 1f: hdd 2f out: sn btn and eased fr 1f out* 8/1
/04- 9 1/2 **Unidexter (IRE)**10 3219 4-8-9 48 ... ChrisCatlin 4 25
(Sheena West) *stdd after s: hld up off the pce in last pair: rdn 4f out: no prog: n.d* 25/1

2m 34.42s (2.92) **Going Correction** -0.025s/f (Good) 9 Ran SP% 115.0
Speed ratings (Par 101): **88,87,87,86,85 84,81,74,74**
CSF £14.34 CT £39.32 TOTE £2.40: £1.10, £1.70, £1.90; EX 16.30 Trifecta £51.50.
**Owner** Clarke, King & Lewis **Bred** Ecurie Des Monceaux **Trained** Ledbury, H'fords

**FOCUS**
Few would argue with the result of this modest opener. Muddling form which is difficult to be confident about.

## 2466 TELEGRAPH MAIDEN STKS — 1m 3f 106y
**2:30** (2:31) (Class 5) 3-Y-0+ £2,726 (£805; £402) **Stalls High**

Form RPR
64-3 1 **Gold Approach**40 1427 3-8-6 73 ... SilvestreDeSousa 7 83
(William Haggas) *chsd ldr: rdn to chal and clr w rival wl over 2f out: drvn to ld over 1f out: styd on wl and drew clr fnl f* 5/1[3]
022- 2 5 **Pack Leader (IRE)**238 6740 3-8-11 89 ...(p) RichardHughes 6 80
(Amanda Perrett) *in tch in midfield on outer: clsd to chse ldrs 5f out: rdn and outpcd by ldng pair wl over 2f out: wnt 3rd 2f out: no ch w wnr but plugged on to go 2nd wl ins fnl f* 1/1[1]
62- 3 1 **Conquerant**186 7936 3-8-11 0 ... WilliamBuick 1 78
(Charlie Appleby) *led: rdn and clr w wnr wl over 1f out: btn 1f out: wknd ins fnl f: lost 2nd towards fin* 3/1[2]
5-5 4 3 3/4 **Micras**23 1809 3-8-3 0 ... OisinMurphy(3) 3 67
(Andrew Balding) *in tch towards rr: struggling on downhill run and lost grnd 4f out: modest 6th 3f out: styd on fnl 2f: no threat to ldrs* 8/1
4 5 4 1/2 **Sixties Love**22 1830 3-8-7 0 ow1 ... MickaelBarzalona 4 61
(Simon Dow) *chsd ldrs: 3rd and outpcd u.p wl over 1f out: wknd over 1f out* 16/1
0- 6 1/2 **Hiorne Tower (FR)**163 8213 3-8-11 0 ... HayleyTurner 9 64
(John Best) *stdd s: hld up in tch in rr: outpcd on downhill run 4f out: rdn and hung lft 3f out: no ch after* 66/1
7 3 3/4 **Exclusive Contract (IRE)** 3-8-7 0 ow1 ... FergusSweeney 5 54
(Jamie Osborne) *chsd ldr for 1f: in tch tl rdn and struggling 3f out: sn wknd* 33/1
0- 8 41 **I'm Lucy (IRE)**174 8084 3-8-7 0 ow1 ... SaleemGolam 2
(Linda Jewell) *in tch in midfield: dropped towards rr 5f out: lost tch 3f out: t.o* 100/1

2m 30.2s (-1.30) **Going Correction** -0.025s/f (Good)
**WFA** 3 from 7yo 15lb 8 Ran SP% 114.1
Speed ratings (Par 103): **103,99,98,95,92 92,89,59**
CSF £10.37 TOTE £4.60: £1.70, £1.10, £1.10; EX 11.90 Trifecta £29.60.
**Owner** Jaber Abdullah **Bred** Rabbah Bloodstock Limited **Trained** Newmarket, Suffolk

**FOCUS**
This was sound run and the winner improved for the set up in trip.

## 2467 NFRN H'CAP — 1m 3f 106y
**3:00** (3:01) (Class 5) (0-70,70) 4-Y-0+ £3,234 (£962; £481) **Stalls High**

Form RPR
5-24 1 **Manomine**65 990 5-9-3 68 ... RichardHughes 1 77
(Clive Brittain) *mde all: pressed 4f out tl 2f out: hrd pressed and drvn over 1f out: sustained duel w rival after: fnd ex and definate advantage wl ins fnl f: r.o* 6/4[1]
510- 2 hd **Silk Train**201 7659 4-9-2 70 ... OisinMurphy(3) 2 78
(David Simcock) *stdd s: hld up in last: 6 l down over 3f out: rdn over 2f out: hdwy to chse wnr 2f out sn drvn and ev ch over 1f out: r.o but no ex and hld wl ins fnl f* 7/4[2]
1264 3 7 **Noguchi (IRE)**4 2327 9-9-5 70 ...(b) TomQueally 4 66
(George Margarson) *chsd wnr: clsd and pressing wnr 4f out tl outpcd u.p and dropped to 3rd 2f out: wknd over 1f out* 9/4[3]

2m 35.78s (4.28) **Going Correction** -0.025s/f (Good) 3 Ran SP% 107.1
Speed ratings (Par 103): **83,82,77**
CSF £4.27 TOTE £2.30; EX 4.10 Trifecta £3.60.
**Owner** Mrs C E Brittain **Bred** C R Mason **Trained** Newmarket, Suffolk

**FOCUS**
Tactics played a huge part in the outcome of this weak, muddling three-runner handicap. The winner is rated to form.

## 2468 MENZIES DISTRIBUTION H'CAP — 1m 6f
**3:30** (3:30) (Class 5) (0-70,75) 4-Y-0+ £3,234 (£962; £481; £240) **Stalls High**

Form RPR
663/ 1 **Dovils Date**26 5789 5-9-7 70 ... DavidProbert 1 82+
(Tim Vaughan) *mde all: rdn over 2f out: forged ahd ent fnl f: stormed clr and r.o strly fnl f: readily* 5/2[1]
3610 2 6 **Maison Brillet (IRE)**19 1919 7-8-12 61 ...(p) RobertHavlin 8 64
(Clive Drew) *in tch in midfield: rdn over 3f out: no imp: no ch w wnr but styd on u.p fnl f: wnt 2nd nr fin* 16/1
200 3 nk **Honourable Knight (IRE)**18 1941 6-8-10 59 ... SilvestreDeSousa 2 62
(Mark Usher) *chsd wnr: rdn and ev ch over 2f out tl no ex ent fnl f: outpcd by wnr and one pce fnl f: lost 2nd nr fin* 9/2[2]
0123 4 1 1/2 **Keep Kicking (IRE)**61 1043 7-9-7 70 ... JimCrowley 7 71
(Simon Dow) *stdd s: t.k.h: hld up in tch in last pair: rdn and effrt on inner over 2f out: rdn and no hdwy over 1f out* 5/1[3]
3631 5 1 3/4 **Royal Marskell**13 2097 5-9-3 66 ... RichardHughes 4 64
(Alison Hutchinson) *chsd ldrs: rdn and sltly outpcd over 1f out: keeping on same pce whn hmpd and swtchd lft over 1f out: wl hld fnl f* 5/2[1]
3432 P **Bert The Alert**20 1895 6-8-1 57 ... CharlotteJenner(7) 5
(Laura Mongan) *stdd s: hld up in tch in rr: rdn and hdwy on outer over 3f out: 3rd keeping on same pce whn lost action and p.u jst over 1f out: fatally injured* 6/1

3m 14.74s (4.74) **Going Correction** -0.025s/f (Good) 6 Ran SP% 112.2
Speed ratings (Par 103): **85,81,81,80,79**
CSF £40.79 CT £168.88 TOTE £3.60: £1.80, £4.80; EX 54.80 Trifecta £341.50.
**Owner** Itsfuninit **Bred** Cranford Stud **Trained** Aberthin, Vale of Glamorgan

**FOCUS**
Modest staying form but a ready winner.

## 2469 NEWS UK CLAIMING STKS — 7f 1y(P)
**4:00** (4:04) (Class 6) 3-Y-0+ £2,249 (£664; £332) **Stalls Low**

Form RPR
0625 1 **Seek The Fair Land**11 2157 8-9-3 75 ...(b) NathanAlison(5) 9 69
(Lee Carter) *t.k.h: chsd ldr tl 1/2-way: styd chsng ldrs: rdn 2f out: drvn and ev ch ins fnl f: r.o u.p to ld towards fin* 5/1[3]
3212 2 3/4 **Clapperboard**9 2209 3-8-2 55 ...(b) WilliamCarson 6 54
(Paul Fitzsimons) *led and set stdy gallop tl hdd 1/2-way: chsd ldr after: rdn 2f out: drvn and ev ch over 1f out: led ins fnl f: hdd and no ex towards fin* 10/1
1604 3 1/2 **Dividend Dan (IRE)**23 1813 4-9-2 55 ... ShaneKelly 5 60
(Mike Murphy) *t.k.h: chsd ldrs tl led 1/2-way and qcknd gallop: rdn 2f out: hrd drvn wl over 1f out: hdd ins fnl f: styd on same pce fnl 100yds* 33/1
2345 4 2 **Skidby Mill (IRE)**21 1876 4-8-11 59 ... LiamJones 3 50
(Laura Mongan) *in tch in midfield: effrt on inner and drvn to press ldrs over 1f out: wknd fnl 75yds* 12/1
3523 5 1 1/2 **Capaill Liath (IRE)**4 2351 6-9-7 79 ...(p) RichardHughes 7 56
(Kevin Ryan) *in tch in midfield: pushed along 1/2-way: drvn and no hdwy wl over 1f out: styd on same pce after* 10/11[1]
23-3 6 2 1/2 **Cash Is King**139 19 4-9-3 65 ...(v[1]) J-PGuillambert 1 45
(Nick Littmoden) *rrd as stalls opened and s.i.s: in tch in rr of main gp: rdn over 2f out: no imp and styd on same pce fr over 1f out* 12/1
0 7 11 **Leftrightleftright (IRE)**39 1433 3-8-7 0 ... LukeMorris 4 14
(Luke Dace) *stdd s: t.k.h: hld up in tch in rr of main gp: rdn 3f out: wknd 2f out: wl bhd fnl f* 50/1
-052 8 17 **Kimbali (IRE)**2 2381 5-9-2 69 ... AdamKirby 8
(David Evans) *rel to r and set off 100yds bhd: nvr clsd and t.o thrght* 4/1[2]

1m 24.43s (-0.37) **Going Correction** +0.10s/f (Slow)
**WFA** 3 from 4yo+ 11lb 8 Ran SP% 118.4
Speed ratings (Par 101): **106,105,104,102,100 97,85,65**
CSF £55.02 TOTE £4.80: £1.10, £2.50, £5.30; EX 34.70 Trifecta £1447.60.
**Owner** John Joseph Smith **Bred** Raimon Bloodstock **Trained** Epsom, Surrey

**FOCUS**
Some enigmatic characters on show here. The second and third set the limited standard.

## 2470 CITIPOST LTD FILLIES' H'CAP — 6f 1y(P)
**4:30** (4:32) (Class 5) (0-70,70) 3-Y-0 £3,234 (£962; £481; £240) **Stalls Low**

Form RPR
21 1 **Dreams Of Reality**40 1430 3-9-7 70 ... RichardKingscote 8 76+
(Tom Dascombe) *hld up in tch: hdwy on outer bnd 2f out: rdn and effrt ent fnl f: qcknd u.p ins fnl f to ld fnl 75yds: sn in command: r.o wl* 7/1
2212 2 1 1/4 **Hustle Bustle (IRE)**39 1449 3-8-13 67 ... MarcMonaghan(5) 4 69
(David Brown) *led: rdn 2f out: hrd pressed and drvn over 1f out: kpt on wl tl hdd and outpcd by wnr fnl 75yds* 5/1[3]
16-5 3 nk **Value (IRE)**64 1006 3-9-2 65 ... DavidProbert 7 66
(Gay Kelleway) *chsd ldrs: wnt 2nd 1/2-way: rdn and ev ch 2f out: hrd drvn 1f out: no ex and outpcd by wnr fnl 75yds* 25/1
003- 4 3/4 **Trillian Astra (IRE)**189 7859 3-8-12 61 ... SteveDrowne 2 60
(Clive Cox) *chsd ldr tl 1/2-way: chsd ldrs after: drvn and ev ch ent fnl f: kpt on tl no ex fnl 75yds* 20/1
40-1 5 1/2 **Frangipanni (IRE)**22 1833 3-9-3 66 ... JamesDoyle 6 63+
(Roger Charlton) *short of room leaving stalls and s.i.s: hld up towards rr: rdn and effrt over 1f out: no imp tl styd on strly ins fnl f: nvr trbld ldrs* 5/2[1]
-340 6 3/4 **Caminel (IRE)**42 1379 3-8-11 60 ... LiamKeniry 10 55
(Jeremy Gask) *s.i.s: in rr: rdn over 2f out: styd on wl ins fnl f: nvr trbld ldrs* 25/1
50-5 7 nse **Aristocratic Duty**19 1920 3-9-0 68 ... JoshBaudains(5) 11 62
(Sylvester Kirk) *stdd and dropped in bhd after s: hld up in rr: effrt over 1f out: squeezed between horses and kpt on ins fnl f: nvr trbld ldrs* 20/1
-464 8 1 **Poetic Choice**24 1769 3-9-5 68 ... GeorgeBaker 3 59
(Nick Littmoden) *hld up in tch in midfield: effrt towards inner over 1f out: sme hdwy 1f out: kpt on same pce and no imp fnl 150yds* 4/1[2]
50-0 9 hd **Nelson's Pride**30 1611 3-8-12 61 ...(b[1]) TomQueally 9 52
(Kevin Ryan) *chsd ldng trio: rdn ent fnl 2f: outpcd and lost pl jst over 1f out: kpt on same pce fnl f* 33/1
54-3 10 3/4 **Shushu Sugartown (IRE)**28 1645 3-9-7 70 ... SilvestreDeSousa 5 58
(Ian Williams) *in tch in midfield: rdn and unable qck over 1f out: wknd ins fnl f* 10/1
234 11 1 **Blacke Forest**62 1024 3-9-1 64 ... MartinDwyer 1 49
(William Muir) *in tch towards rr: rdn and effrt on inner over 1f out: no imp: nvr trbld ldrs* 8/1

1m 12.53s (0.63) **Going Correction** +0.10s/f (Slow) 11 Ran SP% 118.1
Speed ratings (Par 96): **99,97,96,95,95 94,94,92,92,91 90**
CSF £38.72 CT £837.32 TOTE £10.30: £3.50, £1.70, £5.30; EX 27.90 Trifecta £727.20.

**Owner** John A Duffy **Bred** J A And Mrs Duffy **Trained** Malpas, Cheshire
**FOCUS**
A devilishly competitive handicap. The third lends a bit of doubt to the form.

## 2471 SMITHS NEWS H'CAP — 1m 1y(P)
**5:00** (5:00) (Class 5) (0-75,72) 4-Y-0+ **£3,234** (£962; £481; £240) **Stalls** High

Form RPR
4343 **1** **Run It Twice (IRE)**$^{42}$ 1388 4-9-2 **67**............(b) JamesDoyle 6 76
(David Evans) *in tch in midfield: effrt on inner to chal over 1f out: hrd drvn 1f out: led wl ins fnl f: r.o: drvn out* **9/2**$^{1}$
0-52 **2** *shd* **George Baker (IRE)**$^{30}$ 1623 7-8-10 **68**............ ChrisMeehan$^{(7)}$ 3 76
(George Baker) *chsd ldrs: rdn to chal over 1f out: drvn to ld 1f out: r.o wl u.p tl hdd and no ex wl ins fnl f* **7/1**$^{3}$
1226 **3** *1 1/4* **Nubar Boy**$^{25}$ 1717 7-8-11 **69**............(p) CharlotteJenner$^{(7)}$ 11 74
(Ian Williams) *racd keenly: led: rdn and hrd pressed over 1f out: hdd 1f out: kpt on tl no ex and btn fnl 75yds* **8/1**
25 **4** *1/2* **Alnoomaas (IRE)**$^{19}$ 1921 5-9-2 **67**............ LukeMorris 8 71
(Luke Dace) *in tch in midfield: effrt on inner and drvn to chal 1f out: no ex and btn whn n.m.r wl ins fnl f* **7/1**$^{3}$
4006 **5** *1 3/4* **Red Dragon (IRE)**$^{23}$ 1791 4-9-3 **68**............ FergusSweeney 7 68
(Michael Blanshard) *broke wl: stdd and chsd ldrs: rdn and lost pl whn wd bnd 2f out: rallied and kpt on ins fnl f* **9/2**$^{1}$
3660 **6** *shd* **Malaysian Boleh**$^{21}$ 1876 4-9-6 **71**............ HayleyTurner 1 70
(Simon Dow) *stdd after s: hld up in tch in last trio: rdn and hdwy over 1f out: kpt on u.p ins fnl f: nvr trbld ldrs* **8/1**
030 **7** *1/2* **Alpine Mist**$^{16}$ 2012 4-9-0 **65**............ SebSanders 10 63
(Peter Makin) *chsd ldr tl wl over 1f out: sn drvn and outpcd: no threat to ldrs and kpt on same pce fnl f* **12/1**
4 **8** *1 1/2* **Victor's Bet (SPA)**$^{12}$ 2124 5-9-7 **72**............ RichardKingscote 9 67
(Ralph J Smith) *in tch in midfield: rdn and no hdwy over 1f out: outpcd and btn 1f out: eased wl ins fnl f* **10/1**
1446 **9** *hd* **Club House (IRE)**$^{49}$ 1234 4-9-7 **72**............ RobertHavlin 2 66
(Robert Mills) *hld up in last trio: pushed along over 1f out: no real imp: nvr trbld ldrs* **5/1**$^{2}$
40-5 **10** *3 1/2* **Tevez**$^{46}$ 1317 9-9-7 **72**............(p) AdamBeschizza 5 58
(Des Donovan) *s.i.s: a last: rdn over 2f out: no prog* **16/1**

1m 38.3s (0.10) **Going Correction** +0.10s/f (Slow) **10** Ran SP% **122.9**
Speed ratings (Par 103): **103,102,101,101,99 99,98,97,97,93**
CSF £38.26 CT £259.21 TOTE £4.90: £1.70, £4.50, £3.00; EX 33.80 Trifecta £498.80.
**Owner** Shropshire Wolves 4 **Bred** Yeomanstown Stud **Trained** Pandy, Monmouths
**FOCUS**
Modest form. The winner is rated back to his best.
T/Plt: £133.30 to a £1 stake. Pool: £67463.73 - 369.41 winning tickets T/Qpdt: £82.10 to a £1 stake. Pool: £4240.89 - 38.20 winning tickets SP

# 2450 AYR (L-H)
### Thursday, May 22
**OFFICIAL GOING: Good to soft (8.6)**
Wind: Breezy, half behind Weather: Overcast

## 2472 COCA-COLA/BRITISH STALLION STUDS EBF MAIDEN STKS (BOBIS RACE) — 5f
**1:50** (1:50) (Class 4) 2-Y-O **£4,204** (£1,251; £625; £312) **Stalls** Centre

Form RPR
54 **1** **Casterbridge**$^{15}$ 2071 2-9-2 0............ JasonHart$^{(3)}$ 4 79
(Eric Alston) *mde all: rdn wl over 1f out: hld on wl fnl f* **6/4**$^{1}$
2 **2** *1/2* **Denton Dawn (IRE)**$^{19}$ 1955 2-8-11 0............ ConnorBeasley$^{(3)}$ 2 72
(Michael Dods) *prom: effrt and chsd wnr over 1f out: kpt on fnl f: hld towards fin* **15/8**$^{2}$
**3** *12* **Westhoughton** 2-9-5 0............ DanielTudhope 1 34
(K R Burke) *prom: rdn and outpcd wl over 1f out: tk modest 3rd ins fnl f: no imp* **8/1**
**4** *9* **Soft Love (IRE)** 2-9-0 0............ PaulMulrennan 3
(Kevin Ryan) *chsd wnr tl rdn and wknd over 1f out* **7/2**$^{3}$

1m 1.9s (2.50) **Going Correction** +0.375s/f (Good) **4** Ran SP% **108.1**
Speed ratings (Par 95): **95,94,75,60**
CSF £4.59 TOTE £2.40; EX 4.30 Trifecta £9.80.
**Owner** Liam & Tony Ferguson **Bred** Liam & Tony Ferguson **Trained** Longton, Lancs
**FOCUS**
Home straight inside rail moved in 8m, stands' rail normal position. Home bend out 2m added 6yds to races on Round course. The home bend and straight were moved out adding approximately six yards to races of 7f or further. A decent maiden, despite the small field, that was dominated by those with experience. It's hard to rate the form any higher.

## 2473 WHYTE & MACKAY H'CAP — 5f
**2:20** (2:22) (Class 6) (0-65,65) 4-Y-0+ **£1,940** (£577; £288; £144) **Stalls** Centre

Form RPR
4-02 **1** **Classy Anne**$^{18}$ 1972 4-7-9 **46**............ JackGarritty$^{(7)}$ 6 61
(Jim Goldie) *cl up centre: led after 2f: rdn and kpt on wl fnl f* **9/1**
-012 **2** *1 1/4* **Bunce (IRE)**$^{6}$ 2297 6-9-5 **63**............ GrahamLee 9 73
(Linda Perratt) *cl up: effrt and chsd wnr over 2f out: rdn over 1f out: edgd lft ins fnl f: kpt on same pce towards fin* **9/2**$^{2}$
4-02 **3** *3 1/4* **Rock Canyon (IRE)**$^{1}$ 2451 5-8-1 **48** ow1............ NeilFarley$^{(3)}$ 11 46
(Linda Perratt) *prom: rdn over 2f out: outpcd over 1f out: kpt on ins fnl f: nt rch first two* **11/1**
4400 **4** *nk* **I'll Be Good**$^{43}$ 1378 5-8-13 **60**............(t) SladeO'Hara$^{(3)}$ 10 57
(Alan Berry) *hld up: stdy hdwy over 2f out: hung lft over 1f out: kpt on fnl f: nvr rchd ldrs* **14/1**
5260 **5** *1/2* **Commandable (AUS)**$^{25}$ 1758 10-8-9 **53**............(p) TomEaves 14 48
(Ian Semple) *cl up: swtchd to stands' rail w one other after 1f: rdn over 2f out: edgd lft and one pce fnl f* **12/1**
434 **6** *1/2* **Captain Scooby**$^{6}$ 2296 8-8-1 **48**............ ConnorBeasley$^{(3)}$ 5 42
(Richard Guest) *bhd and drvn along: hdwy over 1f out: kpt on: nvr able to chal* **3/1**$^{1}$
0045 **7** *3 3/4* **Exotic Guest**$^{12}$ 2159 4-9-5 **63**............ JamesSullivan 7 43
(Ruth Carr) *chsd ldrs tl rdn and wknd over 1f out* **13/2**$^{3}$
4056 **8** *1 1/4* **Lord Buffhead**$^{6}$ 2296 5-8-4 **51**............(v) IanBrennan$^{(3)}$ 1 27
(Richard Guest) *led 2f in centre: drvn and struggling 2f out: sn btn* **11/1**
-060 **9** *1* **Opt Out**$^{12}$ 2167 4-9-5 **63**............ PJMcDonald 3 35
(Alistair Whillans) *hld up: drvn on outside over 2f out: nvr on terms* **12/1**
-660 **10** *4* **Auntie Mildred (IRE)**$^{91}$ 676 4-8-1 **48**............ JulieBurke$^{(3)}$ 13 6
(David O'Meara) *bmpd s: tacked over to r stands' side after 1f: hld up: rdn and struggling over 2f out: sn btn* **25/1**
0-06 **11** *8* **Pavers Star**$^{18}$ 1972 5-8-5 **49**............(p) DuranFentiman 8
(Noel Wilson) *dwlt: bhd and drvn along: no ch fr 1/2-way* **28/1**

1m 0.92s (1.52) **Going Correction** +0.375s/f (Good) **11** Ran SP% **112.5**
Speed ratings (Par 101): **102,100,94,94,93 92,86,84,83,76 63**
CSF £47.02 CT £458.58 TOTE £9.90: £3.30, £2.00, £3.70; EX 49.00 Trifecta £262.50.
**Owner** The Vital Sparks **Bred** Jonayro Investments **Trained** Uplawmoor, E Renfrews
**FOCUS**
An open sprint handicap run at a fair pace. The principals raced towards the centre and few got involved. The winer built on her latest personal best.

## 2474 JACK DANIELS H'CAP (£15,000 BETFAIR SCOTTISH SPRINT SERIES FINAL QUALIFIER) — 6f
**2:50** (2:51) (Class 5) (0-75,75) 3-Y-O **£3,234** (£962; £481; £240) **Stalls** Centre

Form RPR
3-64 **1** **Sleeper Class**$^{20}$ 1925 3-8-0 **61** oh4............ JackGarritty$^{(7)}$ 3 70+
(Jim Goldie) *in tch: hdwy to ld over 1f out: sn rdn and hrd pressed: edgd lft ins fnl f: hld on wl towards fin* **8/1**
0-05 **2** *hd* **Foxy Clarets (IRE)**$^{22}$ 1884 3-9-4 **72**............(b$^{1}$) TonyHamilton 6 80
(Richard Fahey) *pressed ldr: rdn and disp ld over 1f out: edgd lft ins fnl f: kpt on: hld nr fin* **2/1**$^{1}$
5-05 **3** *4* **Spirit Of Alsace (IRE)**$^{10}$ 2217 3-8-4 **61** oh1............ IanBrennan$^{(3)}$ 2 56
(Jim Goldie) *rrd s: bhd: hdwy and in tch over 2f out: rdn: hung lft and carried hd high over 1f out: tk 3rd ins fnl f: no ch w first two* **14/1**
006- **4** *6* **Pavers Bounty**$^{328}$ 3766 3-8-11 **65**............ DuranFentiman 5 41
(Noel Wilson) *led tl rdn and hdd over 1f out: wknd ins fnl f* **9/1**
200- **5** *3 1/4* **Mount Cheiron (USA)**$^{216}$ 7340 3-8-4 **63** oh1 ow2....... EmmaSayer$^{(5)}$ 7 29
(Dianne Sayer) *in tch: drvn and outpcd wl over 2f out: sn btn* **8/1**
0-20 **6** *29* **False Witness (IRE)**$^{35}$ 1543 3-8-7 **68**............ AnnaHesketh$^{(7)}$ 1
(David Nicholls) *fly-jmpd s: bhd: lost tch after 2f: t.o* **5/1**$^{3}$
2300 **7** *17* **Outbacker (IRE)**$^{14}$ 2090 3-9-7 **75**............ JoeFanning 4
(Mark Johnston) *chsd ldrs to 1/2-way: sn struggling: lost tch fnl 2f: t.o* **4/1**$^{2}$

1m 16.79s (4.39) **Going Correction** +0.375s/f (Good) **7** Ran SP% **108.9**
Speed ratings (Par 99): **85,84,79,71,67 28,5**
CSF £22.11 TOTE £10.00: £2.90, £1.80; EX 33.50 Trifecta £121.90.
**Owner** Frank Brady **Bred** Jonayro Investments **Trained** Uplawmoor, E Renfrews
**FOCUS**
A weak contest for the grade with the field again racing up the centre. The time was slow and the form is rated around the runner-up.

## 2475 GLENFIDDICH H'CAP (DIV I) — 1m 2f
**3:25** (3:25) (Class 6) (0-60,60) 4-Y-0+ **£1,940** (£577; £288; £144) **Stalls** Low

Form RPR
3-00 **1** **Henpecked**$^{18}$ 1970 4-9-3 **56**............ PJMcDonald 2 67+
(Alistair Whillans) *hld up in tch: hdwy on ins over 2f out: rdn to ld over 1f out: keeping on whn pricked ears: idled and hung rt nr fin* **4/1**$^{1}$
2056 **2** *1 1/4* **Troy Boy**$^{22}$ 1891 4-8-4 **46** oh1............ NeilFarley$^{(3)}$ 4 53
(Robin Bastiman) *led at ordinary gallop: rdn over 2f out: hdd over 1f out: kpt on ins fnl f* **80/1**
0031 **3** *nse* **Call Of Duty (IRE)**$^{25}$ 1761 9-8-7 **51**............(b) EmmaSayer$^{(5)}$ 12 58
(Dianne Sayer) *s.i.s: hld up: hdwy on outside 2f out: kpt on fnl f: nrst fin* **9/1**$^{3}$
64-4 **4** *4* **Kolonel Kirkup**$^{28}$ 1675 4-9-2 **58**............(p) ConnorBeasley$^{(3)}$ 11 57
(Michael Dods) *t.k.h: prom on outside: smooth hdwy over 2f out: rdn and hung lft over 1f out: sn no ex* **4/1**$^{1}$
3103 **5** *1 1/2* **Sixties Queen**$^{1}$ 2457 4-9-1 **54**............ JoeFanning 7 51
(Alan Bailey) *in tch: effrt and rdn over 2f out: edgd lft wl over 1f out: sn btn* **6/1**$^{2}$
304- **6** *1 1/4* **Wolf Heart (IRE)**$^{366}$ 2536 6-8-9 **48**............ PaulMulrennan 8 42
(Lucy Normile) *hld up: rdn and outpcd over 3f out: rallied whn nt clr run over 2f out: shkn up and styd on steadily fnl f: nvr nrr* **20/1**
55-5 **7** *6* **Dhaular Dhar (IRE)**$^{10}$ 2215 12-9-6 **59**............ GaryBartley 9 42
(Jim Goldie) *hld up: rdn 3f out: hdwy over 1f out: nvr on terms* **14/1**
1264 **8** *1/2* **Kyle Of Bute**$^{78}$ 838 8-8-7 **53**............ JackGarritty$^{(7)}$ 5 35
(Richard Ford) *midfield: drvn and outpcd over 2f out: sn btn* **28/1**
5454 **9** *4 1/2* **Omotesando**$^{10}$ 2207 4-8-6 **50**............ NoelGarbutt$^{(5)}$ 6 23
(Mark Brisbourne) *hld up in midfield on ins: struggling over 2f out: sn btn* **50/1**
000- **10** *2 1/2* **Titus Bolt (IRE)**$^{12}$ 7239 5-9-7 **60**............ GrahamLee 13 29
(Jim Goldie) *cl up tl rdn: edgd lft and wknd qckly over 2f out* **4/1**$^{1}$
0-02 **11** *8* **Gadobout Dancer**$^{1}$ 2457 7-8-8 **47** oh1 ow1............ TomEaves 10
(Keith Dalgleish) *rdr lost iron briefly leaving stall: hld up on outside: drvn over 3f out: wknd over 2f out* **12/1**
63-0 **12** *8* **Joshua The First**$^{32}$ 1596 5-9-0 **58**............ GarryWhillans$^{(5)}$ 1
(Ian Semple) *t.k.h: cl up tl rdn: hung lft and wknd over 2f out* **16/1**

2m 16.02s (4.02) **Going Correction** +0.225s/f (Good) **12** Ran SP% **115.9**
Speed ratings (Par 101): **92,91,90,87,86 85,80,80,76,74 68,61**
CSF £381.96 CT £2706.11 TOTE £3.20: £1.60, £10.10, £2.80; EX 386.70 Trifecta £2086.90 Part won..
**Owner** Eildon Hill Racing **Bred** T Hirschfeld **Trained** Newmill-On-Slitrig, Borders
**FOCUS**
Plenty of pace for this modest contest. A similar time to the runner-up, and the winner is a bit better than the bare form.

## 2476 GLENFIDDICH H'CAP (DIV II) — 1m 2f
**4:00** (4:00) (Class 6) (0-60,64) 4-Y-0+ **£1,940** (£577; £288; £144) **Stalls** Low

Form RPR
3340 **1** **Rockweiller**$^{16}$ 1644 7-8-9 **50**............ JasonHart$^{(3)}$ 4 65+
(Shaun Harris) *cl up: led over 3f out: rdn clr over 1f out: eased last 75yds* **11/2**
25- **2** *3 1/4* **Ptolomeos**$^{145}$ 5142 11-8-3 **46**............ ShirleyTeasdale$^{(5)}$ 6 53
(Sean Regan) *hld up: rdn and hdwy over 2f out: chsd (clr) wnr ins fnl f: kpt on: no imp* **40/1**
40-2 **3** *1 3/4* **Eilean Mor**$^{25}$ 1761 6-8-5 **48**............ NoelGarbutt$^{(5)}$ 10 52
(R Mike Smith) *t.k.h: cl up: ev ch over 3f out to over 1f out: kpt on same pce fnl f* **9/2**$^{3}$
34/5 **4** *2 1/4* **Snooker (GER)**$^{25}$ 1761 8-9-2 **54**............ TonyHamilton 12 53
(Rose Dobbin) *hld up on outside: stdy hdwy and in tch over 2f out: sn rdn: one pce fr over 1f out* **11/1**
0/60 **5** *3/4* **Frontline Phantom (IRE)**$^{31}$ 1617 7-9-4 **56**............ DanielTudhope 1 54
(K R Burke) *chsd ldrs: effrt and drvn over 2f out: outpcd over 1f out* **4/1**$^{2}$
33-0 **6** *5* **Uncle Brit**$^{47}$ 1307 8-9-7 **59**............ PJMcDonald 5 47
(Malcolm Jefferson) *hld up on ins: drvn over 2f out: sn no imp* **7/2**$^{1}$
30-6 **7** *10* **Mister Bob (GER)**$^{15}$ 2084 5-9-5 **57**............(b) GrahamLee 8 26
(James Bethell) *hld up: hdwy and in tch over 3f out: hung lft and wknd over 2f out* **6/1**

00-0 **8** 2 1/2 **Amazing Blue Sky**[28] 1675 8-8-13 **51**........................... JamesSullivan 2 16
(Ruth Carr) *led to over 3f out: rdn and wknd over 2f out* **14/1**
00-0 **9** 29 **Euston Square**[28] 1675 8-9-1 **58**........................... GarryWhillans(5) 11
(Alistair Whillans) *s.v.s and wl bhd: hdwy to tag on to bk of gp 1/2-way: rdn over 4f out: hung lft and lost tch over 2f out* **16/1**
000- **10** 69 **Hayley**[262] 6049 4-8-4 **45**........................... IanBrennan(3) 7
(Jim Goldie) *hld up: drvn and struggling over 3f out: sn lost tch: t.o* **66/1**
2m 16.16s (4.16) **Going Correction** +0.225s/f (Good) **10** Ran SP% **114.9**
Speed ratings (Par 101): **92,89,88,86,85 81,73,71,48,**
CSF £189.47 CT £1068.01 TOTE £5.80: £2.70, £8.00, £1.70; EX 192.90 Trifecta £2184.40.
**Owner** S A Harris **Bred** Exors Of The Late Mrs E A Hankinson **Trained** Carburton, Notts
**FOCUS**
A modest handicap run at a fair pace, and in a similar time to division I. Comparable form.

## 2477 MAGNERS CIDER H'CAP (£15,000 BETFAIR SCOTTISH MILE SERIES FINAL QUALIFIER) 1m
**4:35** (4:35) (Class 5) (0-75,75) 4-Y-O+ **£3,234** (£962; £481; £240) **Stalls** Low

Form RPR
0-02 **1** **Another For Joe**[18] 1970 6-8-10 **64**........................... GrahamLee 8 79
(Jim Goldie) *trckd ldr: led over 2f out: rdn clr over 1f out: kpt on strly* **7/2**[2]
50 **2** 6 **Alanos (IRE)**[10] 2215 5-9-2 **70**........................... PaulMulrennan 9 71
(James Ewart) *prom: effrt and drvn over 2f out: chsd (clr) wnr over 1f out: no imp* **25/1**
40-5 **3** 1/2 **Never Forever**[18] 1970 5-8-12 **71**........................... GarryWhillans(5) 6 71
(Jim Goldie) *in tch: outpcd and hung lft over 2f out: rallied fnl f: kpt on wl* **11/2**[3]
-042 **4** 1 3/4 **The Osteopath (IRE)**[12] 2169 11-9-7 **75**........................... PJMcDonald 7 71
(John Davies) *hld up: pushed along over 2f out: hdwy over 1f out: kpt on: nvr able to chal* **11/2**[3]
0-23 **5** hd **Ingleby Symphony (IRE)**[17] 2017 4-9-4 **72**........................... TonyHamilton 5 68
(Richard Fahey) *prom: drvn and outpcd over 2f out: rallied over 1f out: no imp* **9/4**[1]
41-0 **6** 2 1/2 **Rioja Day (IRE)**[18] 1970 4-8-12 **66**........................... GaryBartley 10 56
(Jim Goldie) *led tl rdn and hdd over 2f out: wknd ins fnl f* **7/1**
145- **7** 4 **Rasselas (IRE)**[219] 7283 7-8-4 **65**........................... AnnaHesketh(7) 4 46
(David Nicholls) *t.k.h in rr: pushed along 3f out: nvr able to chal* **20/1**
06-6 **8** 7 **Good Boy Jackson**[25] 1760 6-8-8 **67**........................... NoelGarbutt(5) 3 32
(R Mike Smith) *hld up on ins: struggling over 3f out: sn btn* **20/1**
214/ **9** 2 **Mazeppa**[689] 3695 4-9-1 **69**........................... TomEaves 11 29
(Keith Dalgleish) *t.k.h: hld up on outside: rdn and edgd lft over 2f out: wknd wl over 1f out* **12/1**
1m 45.42s (1.62) **Going Correction** +0.225s/f (Good) **9** Ran SP% **117.3**
Speed ratings (Par 103): **100,94,93,91,91 89,85,78,76**
CSF £90.01 CT £478.61 TOTE £5.10: £1.30, £5.90, £2.20; EX 87.90 Trifecta £1499.10.
**Owner** Mr & Mrs Gordon Grant & J S Goldie **Bred** G Merkel **Trained** Uplawmoor, E Renfrews
**FOCUS**
An honest pace for this fair handicap. The winner is rated back to last year's level.

## 2478 SMIRNOFF GOLD H'CAP 1m
**5:10** (5:10) (Class 3) (0-95,95) 4-Y-O+ **£7,762** (£2,310; £1,154; £577) **Stalls** Low

Form RPR
1321 **1** **Uncle Dermot (IRE)**[1] 2453 6-8-4 **81** 6ex........................... ConnorBeasley(3) 8 92
(Brendan Powell) *mde all: qcknd clr over 2f out: kpt on wl fnl f: unchal* **3/1**[2]
063- **2** 1 3/4 **Le Chat D'Or**[204] 7632 6-8-8 **82**...........................(bt) PaulMulrennan 3 89
(Michael Dods) *hld up in last pl: swtchd rt and effrt over 2f out: chsd (clr) wnr and hung lft over 1f out: kpt on fnl f: no further imp last 75yds* **13/2**
4513 **3** 7 **Dubai Dynamo**[4] 2362 9-8-10 **84**........................... PJMcDonald 2 75
(Ruth Carr) *hld up: rdn over 2f out: hdwy on ins over 1f out: no imp* **5/1**[3]
-063 **4** 3 **Silver Rime (FR)**[1] 2453 9-8-11 **85**........................... GrahamLee 4 69
(Linda Perratt) *hld up in tch: effrt whn n.m.r briefly over 2f out: sn rdn and no imp fr over 1f out* **25/1**
6-30 **5** 4 **Marcret (ITY)**[14] 2085 7-9-7 **95**........................... DanielTudhope 7 70
(David O'Meara) *t.k.h: in tch: drvn over 2f out: btn wl over 1f out* **13/2**
1200 **6** 5 **Sound Advice**[12] 2145 5-9-0 **88**........................... TomEaves 6 51
(Keith Dalgleish) *chsd wnr: drvn over 2f out: wknd over 1f out* **14/1**
5611 **7** 15 **Busatto (USA)**[3] 2382 4-9-0 **88** 12ex........................... JoeFanning 1 17
(Mark Johnston) *chsd ldrs: drvn along over 3f out: wknd over 2f out: lost tch over 1f out: t.o* **9/4**[1]
1m 43.96s (0.16) **Going Correction** +0.225s/f (Good) **7** Ran SP% **109.6**
Speed ratings (Par 107): **108,106,99,96,92 87,72**
CSF £20.56 CT £84.69 TOTE £3.80: £1.20, £4.60; EX 22.10 Trifecta £111.90.
**Owner** K Rhatigan **Bred** Ballyhane Stud **Trained** Upper Lambourn, Berks
**FOCUS**
A decent handicap run at a sound pace. The winner, successful for the second time in 24 hours, is better than ever.

## 2479 CALEDONIA BEST H'CAP 7f 50y
**5:45** (5:45) (Class 6) (0-60,57) 4-Y-O+ **£1,940** (£577; £288; £144) **Stalls** High

Form RPR
5440 **1** **Ellies Image**[56] 1138 7-8-6 **45**........................... ConnorBeasley(3) 8 58
(Richard Ford) *hld up in last pl: gd hdwy on outside 2f out: led ins fnl f: sn clr* **18/1**
0043 **2** 3 1/4 **Hellbender (IRE)**[37] 1499 8-8-12 **51**........................... JasonHart(3) 9 56
(Shaun Harris) *cl up: rdn to ld over 1f out: edgd lft and hdd ins fnl f: kpt on same pce* **4/1**[2]
5041 **3** 1 1/4 **Monel**[1] 2452 6-9-7 **57** 6ex........................... GrahamLee 2 59
(Jim Goldie) *hld up in tch: rdn over 2f out: hdwy and edgd lft over 1f out: sn chsng ldrs: kpt on same pce ins fnl f* **11/8**[1]
2463 **4** 1 1/4 **Medam**[56] 1123 5-9-1 **54**........................... NeilFarley(3) 10 53
(Shaun Harris) *flyj. s: cl up: led over 2f out to over 1f out: kpt on same pce fnl f* **10/1**
0504 **5** 1 1/4 **Amis Reunis**[10] 2219 5-8-9 **45**...........................(p) JamesSullivan 7 40
(Alan Berry) *t.k.h: trckd ldrs: drvn over 2f out: no ex over 1f out* **18/1**
0400 **6** 1/2 **High On The Hog (IRE)**[69] 963 6-8-5 **46**........................... NoelGarbutt(5) 6 40
(Mark Brisbourne) *hld up: hdwy 3f out: sn rdn: kpt on same pce fr over 1f out* **28/1**
0-00 **7** 2 1/4 **Black Douglas**[1] 2452 5-9-7 **57**........................... TomEaves 5 45
(Jim Goldie) *midfield: outpcd and edgd lft over 2f out: n.d after* **14/1**
46-0 **8** nk **Copper To Gold**[14] 2094 5-8-9 **45**........................... DuranFentiman 1 32
(Robin Bastiman) *led tl rdn and hdd over 2f out: wknd over 1f out* **40/1**
64-3 **9** nk **Elle Rebelle**[22] 1877 4-8-12 **48**........................... PaulMulrennan 4 35
(Mark Brisbourne) *dwlt: hld up: rdn over 2f out: sn btn* **13/2**[3]

-005 **10** 14 **Fife Jo**[1] 2452 4-8-6 **45**...........................(v) IanBrennan(3) 3
(Jim Goldie) *hld up: rdn over 2f out: hung lft and sn wknd* **12/1**
1m 36.51s (3.11) **Going Correction** +0.225s/f (Good) **10** Ran SP% **115.3**
Speed ratings (Par 101): **91,87,85,84,83 82,79,79,79,63**
CSF £87.87 CT £171.25 TOTE £23.30: £4.60, £2.30, £1.10; EX 132.90 Trifecta £730.10.
**Owner** J H Chrimes **Bred** Miss S M Potts **Trained** Garstang, Lancs
**FOCUS**
The pace was strong for this moderate handicap. It's hard to be confident about this weak form.
T/Plt: £357.90 to a £1 stake. Pool: £55,497.00 - 113.17 winning tickets. T/Qpdt: £97.80 to a £1 stake. Pool: £4,489.91 - 33.95 winning tickets. RY

# 1941 GOODWOOD (R-H)
### Thursday, May 22

**OFFICIAL GOING: Soft**
Wind: Moderate; across (away from stands) Weather: Rain before racing; mostly fine

## 2480 IRISH STALLION FARMS EBF MAIDEN STKS (BOBIS RACE) 6f
**2:10** (2:11) (Class 4) 2-Y-O **£3,881** (£1,155; £577; £288) **Stalls** High

Form RPR
5 **1** **Portamento (IRE)**[36] 1512 2-9-5 0........................... WilliamBuick 2 90+
(Charlie Appleby) *mde all and racd against nr side rail: drew clr wl over 1f out: easily* **9/4**[2]
**2** 4 **Estidhkaar (IRE)** 2-9-5 0........................... DaneO'Neill 7 75+
(Richard Hannon) *athletic: str: s.i.s: swtchd to outer and in tch: shkn up and outpcd 2f out: styd on to take 2nd ins fnl f: no ch w wnr* **5/4**[1]
**3** 2 3/4 **Tansfeeq** 2-9-5 0........................... FrankieDettori 3 67+
(J W Hills) *rn green: in tch: shkn up and outpcd 2f out: kpt on to take 3rd wl ins fnl f* **14/1**
**4** 1 **Secret Journey (IRE)** 2-9-5 0........................... PatDobbs 1 64+
(Hughie Morrison) *pressed wnr: lft bhd fr 2f out: wknd fnl f* **25/1**
**5** 3 **Emef Rock (IRE)** 2-9-2 0........................... WilliamTwiston-Davies(3) 8 55
(Mick Channon) *leggy: tall: hld up in tch: shkn up over 2f out: sn wl outpcd: fdd* **14/1**
**6** 1 1/4 **Quintus Cerialis (IRE)** 2-9-5 0........................... AdamKirby 4 51
(Clive Cox) *chsd ldng pair to over 2f out: wknd and hung rt over 1f out* **25/1**
**7** 6 **Pinter** 2-9-5 0........................... RyanMoore 9 33
(Charlie Appleby) *w'like: s.s: rn green and a last: jst in tch after 2f: sn btn* **5/1**[3]
1m 15.55s (3.35) **Going Correction** +0.425s/f (Yiel) **7** Ran SP% **112.9**
Speed ratings (Par 95): **94,88,85,83,79 78,70**
CSF £5.27 TOTE £2.60: £1.90, £1.70; EX 6.70 Trifecta £44.70.
**Owner** Godolphin **Bred** Darley **Trained** Newmarket, Suffolk
**FOCUS**
First 2f of 1m course dolled out 5yds, top bend out 3yds. Lower bend out 5yds from 6f to 2f in straight increasing distances on Round course by 15yds. After a morning of heavy rain conditions had changed to soft before racing got underway, and this opener was run around 6sec slower than standard. The winner impressed and reached a very useful level.

## 2481 WRIGHT JOINERY COMPANY STKS (H'CAP) (BOBIS RACE) 1m 1f
**2:40** (2:42) (Class 4) (0-85,85) 3-Y-O
**£6,225** (£1,864; £932; £466; £233; £117) **Stalls** Low

Form RPR
3015 **1** **Solo Hunter**[4] 2363 3-8-7 **71**........................... FrannyNorton 11 77
(David Evans) *settled in last trio: clsd on ldrs and drvn 2f out: styd on wl between rivals to ld last 100yds: sn clr* **25/1**
61-4 **2** 1 1/4 **Gothic**[27] 1702 3-9-5 **83**........................... RyanMoore 3 89+
(Sir Michael Stoute) *hld up in midfield: cl up bhd ldrs fr 3f out but nowhere to go: lost pl 2f out: renewed effrt over 1f out: styd on to take 2nd last stride* **4/1**[2]
3-33 **3** hd **Loving Home**[26] 1730 3-9-2 **80**........................... WilliamBuick 1 83
(John Gosden) *trckd ldng pair: squeezed through to ld over 2f out: drvn and hrd pressed after: hdd last 100yds: lost 2nd post* **9/2**[3]
20-6 **4** nse **Raise Your Gaze**[33] 1586 3-8-13 **77**........................... SteveDrowne 6 80
(Clive Cox) *led 100yds: restrained bhd ldrs: clsd to chal 2f out: nt qckn over 1f out: kpt on again nr fin and nrly snatched 3rd* **16/1**
01-5 **5** 1 **Best Kept**[16] 2063 3-9-1 **79**........................... AndreaAtzeni 13 80
(Amanda Perrett) *str: lw: racd on outer in midfield: pushed along 1/2-way: prog to chal and upsides 2f out: edgd lft and nt qckn over 1f out: one pce after* **7/2**[1]
0-14 **6** 3 1/4 **Donny Rover (IRE)**[18] 1979 3-9-4 **82**........................... AndrewMullen 7 77
(Michael Appleby) *lw: s.i.s: mostly in last trio: rdn over 2f out: nt qckn and n.d but plugged on fr over 1f out* **10/1**
134 **7** 3 3/4 **Officer Drivel (IRE)**[23] 1856 3-8-7 **71**........................... LukeMorris 2 58
(Luke Dace) *hld up in last trio: rdn 2f out: no prog over 1f out: wknd* **33/1**
16-0 **8** 3/4 **Top Of The Glas (IRE)**[27] 1690 3-8-13 **77**........................... DaneO'Neill 8 63
(Alan Jarvis) *trckd ldr after 1f: chal over 2f out: wknd over 1f out: eased* **25/1**
12-3 **9** 1 1/2 **Emef Diamond**[33] 1586 3-8-13 **80**........................... WilliamTwiston-Davies(3) 10 63
(Mick Channon) *led after 100yds: hdd over 2f out: wknd wl over 1f out* **8/1**
4-21 **10** 19 **Fast Delivery**[23] 1853 3-9-6 **84**........................... SilvestreDeSousa 4 29
(Saeed bin Suroor) *lw: t.k.h: hld up in midfield: wknd over 2f out: t.o* **5/1**
2m 1.4s (5.10) **Going Correction** +0.675s/f (Yiel) **10** Ran SP% **113.8**
Speed ratings (Par 101): **104,102,102,102,101 98,95,94,93,76**
CSF £117.90 CT £556.24 TOTE £28.40: £6.10, £1.60, £2.00; EX 194.80 Trifecta £1214.00.
**Owner** Wayne Clifford **Bred** Willie Musson Racing Ltd **Trained** Pandy, Monmouths
**FOCUS**
This open handicap didn't appear to be run at a particularly strong gallop, but it still looked hard work in the closing stages and the overall time was 10sec slower than standard, a proper soft-ground time. A surprise winner but the form makes some sense.

## 2482 WEATHERBYS SPORTS PUBLISHING STKS (H'CAP) 2m
**3:15** (3:15) (Class 4) (0-85,85) 4-Y-O+ **£6,469** (£1,925; £962; £481) **Stalls** Low

Form RPR
1-52 **1** **Story Writer**[19] 1941 5-8-11 **72**........................... AndreaAtzeni 5 85
(William Knight) *prom: steadily lost pl fr 7f out and wl in rr over 4f out: prog on outer over 3f out to chal over 2f out: w ldr and clr of rest after: drvn fnl f: led last 75yds* **9/2**[2]
0-02 **2** nk **Kashgar**[12] 2175 5-8-12 **73**........................... MartinLane 13 85
(Bernard Llewellyn) *prog into midfield after 3f: dropped to rr 5f out: hdwy on outer over 3f out to ld over 2f out: gd battle w wnr after and clr of rest: hdd last 75yds* **20/1**

34-2 **3** *6* **Lion Beacon**[19] 1935 4-9-7 **84** RyanMoore 7 89
(Amanda Perrett) *lw: trckd ldrs: rdn to chal 3f out: hanging and could nt qckn sn after: modest 3rd fnl 2f and no imp on ldng pair* **7/2**[1]
06-1 **4** *1 ½* **Presto Volante (IRE)**[25] 1770 6-9-10 **85** (p) JamesDoyle 12 88
(Amanda Perrett) *settled towards rr: in last quartet 4f out: swtchd to outer and rdn 3f out: kpt on but no threat to ldng pair* **7/1**[3]
54-2 **5** *4* **Our Folly**[41] 1418 6-8-13 **74** (t) TomQueally 10 72
(Stuart Kittow) *dwlt: wl in rr: prog on inner whn chopped off 4f out and dropped to rr: tried to make hdwy over 2f out: no ch w ldrs* **7/1**[3]
-054 **6** *4* **Albonny (IRE)**[13] 2108 5-8-8 **69** LukeMorris 2 62
(Alan Jarvis) *hld up towards rr: prog to trck ldrs 5f out: rdn to dispute 2nd 3f out: wknd 2f out* **14/1**
1204 **7** *¾* **Ordensritter (GER)**[17] 2011 6-9-0 **75** AdamKirby 1 68
(Chris Down) *prom: led 4f out and kicked for home: hdd over 2f out: sn wknd* **14/1**
3132 **8** *8* **Arty Campbell (IRE)**[17] 2011 4-9-0 **77** RobertHavlin 8 60
(Bernard Llewellyn) *hld up in rr: gng wl whn nt clr run over 3f out: sn rdn: sme prog over 2f out: wknd qckly sn after* **16/1**
14-6 **9** *2 ¼* **Riptide**[18] 1981 8-9-2 **80** (v) WilliamTwiston-Davies(3) 4 60
(Michael Scudamore) *settled in last pair: rdn 4f out: struggling after: passed wkng rivals fnl f* **33/1**
0-10 **10** *¾* **New Youmzain (FR)**[27] 1692 5-9-5 **80** AndrewMullen 11 59
(Michael Appleby) *pressed ldr after 6f: rdn 6f out: led 5f out to 4f out: sn wknd* **16/1**
5604 **11** *½* **Eshtyaaq**[12] 2175 7-8-7 **68** FrannyNorton 3 47
(David Evans) *trckd ldrs: cl up 4f out: sn rdn: wknd wl over 2f out* **25/1**
263 **12** *4 ½* **Echo Brava**[17] 2034 4-9-1 **78** RichardHughes 9 51
(Luke Dace) *dwlt: in tch in midfield: prog on inner 4f out: cl up 3f out: pushed along and wknd over 2f out: eased* **12/1**
210/ **13** *47* **Figaro**[36] 3625 6-9-8 **83** (t) DavidProbert 6
(Tim Vaughan) *mde most to 5f out: wknd qckly over 3f out: eased and wl t.o* **12/1**

3m 37.3s (8.30) **Going Correction** +0.675s/f (Yiel)
**WFA** 4 from 5yo+ 2lb **13** Ran SP% **117.4**
Speed ratings (Par 105): **106,105,102,102,100 98,97,93,92,92 91,89,66**
CSF £93.88 CT £353.01 TOTE £5.30: £1.80, £6.10, £2.00; EX 125.30 Trifecta £852.00.
**Owner** The Pheasant Rew Partnership **Bred** Oakhill Stud **Trained** Patching, W Sussex

**FOCUS**
A real war of attrition and a time, 16secs slower than standard, more often associated with a national hunt race. The strongest stayers came to the fore to fight it out and the form isn't rated literally.

## 2483 WINNEREVENTS.COM H'CAP 7f
3:50 (3:50) (Class 2) (0-100,100) 4-Y-O+ **£16,172** (£4,812; £2,405; £1,202) **Stalls** Low

Form RPR
12-2 **1** **Russian Realm**[22] 1871 4-8-9 **88** RyanMoore 3 102+
(Sir Michael Stoute) *lw: hld up in 5th: shkn up and prog over 2f out: led jst over 1f out: styd on strly* **5/4**[1]
2153 **2** *2 ½* **George Guru**[19] 1943 7-9-3 **96** RobertHavlin 7 103
(Michael Attwater) *trckd ldng trio: rdn to chse ldrs over 2f out: kpt on fr over 1f out to take 2nd ins fnl f: no ch w wnr* **8/1**
3-01 **3** *1 ½* **So Beloved**[23] 1834 4-9-0 **93** JamesDoyle 2 96
(Roger Charlton) *lw: trckd ldr: led main gp towards nr side in st and sn overall ldr: hld together tl hdd and rdn jst over 1f out: no rspnse* **7/1**[3]
2-00 **4** *1 ½* **Magic City (IRE)**[19] 1943 5-9-2 **95** RichardHughes 5 94
(Richard Hannon) *stdd s: hld up in last pair: prog to chse ldrs over 2f out: sn rdn: one pce after* **5/1**[2]
11-4 **5** *4* **Mabait**[23] 1862 8-8-9 **95** GeorgeBuckell(7) 1 84
(David Simcock) *hld up in last pair: shkn up and no prog 3f out: no ch after* **16/1**
5441 **6** *3 ¾* **Verse Of Love**[13] 2117 5-8-8 **87** JimCrowley 4 66
(David Evans) *led: initially styd far side in st and sn hdd: rdn 3f out: wknd* **8/1**
024- **7** *10* **Equity Risk (USA)**[257] 6208 4-8-12 **91** FrankieDettori 6 44
(Kevin Ryan) *chsd ldng pair: drvn and nt qckn wl over 2f out: wknd rapidly wl over 1f out: eased and t.o* **10/1**

1m 30.27s (3.27) **Going Correction** +0.675s/f (Yiel) **7** Ran SP% **110.8**
Speed ratings (Par 109): **108,105,103,101,97 92,81**
CSF £11.14 CT £46.84 TOTE £2.20: £1.10, £3.70; EX 10.70 Trifecta £80.00.
**Owner** Cheveley Park Stud **Bred** Cheveley Park Stud Ltd **Trained** Newmarket, Suffolk

**FOCUS**
A sound gallop to this contest and most of the riders elected to come down the middle in the straight, suggesting the far rail was not the place be. The winner can rate higher than this.

## 2484 BIBENDUM HEIGHT OF FASHION STKS (LISTED RACE) (FILLIES) 1m 1f 192y
4:25 (4:25) (Class 1) 3-Y-O **£23,680** (£8,956; £4,476; £2,236) **Stalls** Low

Form RPR
41 **1** **Marsh Daisy**[13] 2109 3-9-0 87 PatDobbs 7 105+
(Hughie Morrison) *w.w in 5th: prog and brought to r against nr side rail in st: led 2f out and swiftly in command: rdn over 1f out: pushed out fnl f: readily* **7/1**[3]
32-2 **2** *2* **Eastern Belle**[35] 1534 3-9-0 78 WilliamBuick 2 101
(John Gosden) *lw: hld up in 4th: prog in centre over 2f out: chsd wnr over 1f out: hrd rdn and styd on but no imp fnl f* **8/1**
21-4 **3** *7* **Psychometry (FR)**[15] 2072 3-9-0 88 RyanMoore 3 88
(Sir Michael Stoute) *hld up in 6th: rdn and prog to take 3rd over 1f out: lost grnd on ldng pair after* **9/2**[2]
6-14 **4** *2* **Emaratiya Ana (IRE)**[35] 1530 3-9-0 90 TomQueally 6 84
(Roger Varian) *lw: trckd ldng pair: clsd 3f out: rdn over 2f out: sn lft bhd and btn* **16/1**
2112 **5** *1 ¾* **Secret Pursuit (IRE)**[15] 2072 3-9-0 96 HayleyTurner 8 81
(Marcus Tregoning) *racd freely: led and clr: 6 l up after 4f: c bk to field 3f out: hdd & wknd 2f out* **5/2**[1]
10-4 **6** *3 ½* **Uchenna (IRE)**[18] 1978 3-9-0 87 JimCrowley 5 74
(David Simcock) *hld up in last: pushed along 4f out: rdn and wknd jst over 2f out* **10/1**
01-2 **7** *1 ¼* **Jordan Princess**[18] 1978 3-9-0 89 AndreaAtzeni 1 72
(Luca Cumani) *lw: chsd clr ldr: clsd 3f out: sn rdn: wknd wl over 1f out* **5/2**[1]

2m 11.59s (3.49) **Going Correction** +0.675s/f (Yiel) **7** Ran SP% **113.9**
Speed ratings (Par 104): **113,111,105,104,102 100,99**
CSF £59.22 TOTE £7.70: £3.20, £4.20; EX 83.80 Trifecta £373.30.
**Owner** Sir Thomas Pilkington **Bred** Meon Valley Stud **Trained** East Ilsley, Berks

**FOCUS**
This is normally a notable marker in the pecking order of some of the better fillies around and most of these have big future engagement. The first pair were clear and the form looks at the top end of the race standard.

## 2485 BREEDERS BACKING RACING EBF MAIDEN STKS 1m 3f
5:00 (5:00) (Class 5) 3-Y-O **£3,881** (£1,155; £577; £288) **Stalls** High

Form RPR
6-2 **1** **Black Shadow**[24] 1809 3-9-5 0 TomQueally 5 95
(Amanda Perrett) *athletic: lw: mde all: led field to nr side in st and racd against rail fr 2f out: sn rdn: styd on stoutly* **9/4**[1]
0 **2** *3 ½* **Altaayil (IRE)**[33] 1587 3-9-5 0 MickaelBarzalona 3 88
(Sir Michael Stoute) *w'like: scope: hld up in 4th: chsd ldng pair 3f out: sn rdn: styd on to take 2nd over 1f out: nvr able to threaten wnr* **11/4**[2]
06 **3** *3 ¾* **Randwick (IRE)**[13] 2114 3-9-5 0 RobertWinston 1 82
(Charles Hills) *trckd ldng pair: chsd wnr 1/2-way: rdn wl over 2f out: cl enough but hld wl over 1f out: sn lost 2nd and one pce* **7/2**[3]
3- **4** *7* **Skilled**[232] 6953 3-9-5 0 JamesDoyle 6 70
(Roger Charlton) *lw: dwlt: hld up in detached last: nvr on terms: rdn to go 4th over 2f out: no hdwy after* **11/4**[2]
**5** *37* **Pennine Panther** 3-9-5 0 FergusSweeney 2 7
(Henry Candy) *chsd wnr to 1/2-way: wknd 3f out: t.o* **25/1**

2m 33.8s (7.30) **Going Correction** +0.675s/f (Yiel) **5** Ran SP% **110.2**
Speed ratings (Par 99): **100,97,94,89,62**
CSF £8.74 TOTE £2.40: £1.20, £2.40; EX 8.50 Trifecta £24.50.
**Owner** A D Spence **Bred** Minster Stud And Mrs H Dalgety **Trained** Pulborough, W Sussex

**FOCUS**
A reasonable maiden but the slowest time performance (per furlong) of the card so far. The winner built on his reappearance effort.

## 2486 TJ GROUP APPRENTICE STKS (H'CAP) 6f
5:35 (5:36) (Class 5) (0-70,74) 4-Y-O+ **£3,234** (£962; £481; £240) **Stalls** High

Form RPR
4402 **1** **Eastern Dragon (IRE)**[16] 2048 4-9-7 **69** JackDuern 5 79+
(Michael Scudamore) *settled in rr: prog on wd outside over 2f out: drvn to ld jst over 1f out: styd on wl* **6/1**[2]
2351 **2** *1 ¾* **Heartsong (IRE)**[27] 1694 5-9-6 **68** LouisSteward 6 71
(John Gallagher) *trckd ldrs: led 2f out: hdd jst over 1f out: outpcd but hld on for 2nd* **7/1**[3]
0025 **3** *hd* **Commandingpresence (USA)**[22] 1878 8-8-10 **61** RyanWhile(3) 4 64
(John Bridger) *w ldr: led 4f out to 2f out: nt qckn over 1f out: styd on same pce fnl f* **14/1**
0055 **4** *hd* **Blazing Knight (IRE)**[15] 2065 4-9-5 **67** (b) TimClark 10 69
(Chris Gordon) *trckd ldrs: rdn 2f out: styd on fnl f to press plcd horses nr fin* **33/1**
0-04 **5** *nk* **Silvee**[18] 1986 7-8-2 **55** oh10 CamHardie(5) 3 56
(John Bridger) *sn pushed along in rr: prog u.p over 1f out: styd on fnl f: nrst fin* **33/1**
4053 **6** *2* **Intomist (IRE)**[7] 2282 5-9-2 **67** (p) DanielCremin(3) 1 62
(Jim Boyle) *pressed ldrs: upsides 2f out: nt qckn over 1f out: wknd last 150yds* **4/1**[1]
0341 **7** *3 ¾* **Amenable (IRE)**[9] 2232 7-9-12 **74** 6ex (p) MarcMonaghan 9 57
(Ann Stokell) *n.m.r s: sn detached in last: no ch fr 1/2-way: kpt on past wkng rivals fr over 1f out* **20/1**
2-20 **8** *hd* **Shirley's Pride**[31] 1604 4-9-4 **69** (t) AlistairRawlinson(3) 7 51
(Michael Appleby) *chsd ldrs: swtchd lft and rdn 2f out: wknd over 1f out* **8/1**
0535 **9** *2 ¾* **Chevise (IRE)**[21] 1896 6-8-4 **55** (b) RobJFitzpatrick(3) 8 28
(Steve Woodman) *awkward s but led: hdd after 2f: wknd towards nr side wl over 1f out* **8/1**
46-6 **10** *1 ½* **Koharu**[21] 1896 4-9-4 **66** (t) JoeyHaynes 12 34
(Peter Makin) *racd against nr side rail: in tch: nt clr run over 2f out: sn wknd* **16/1**

1m 14.05s (1.85) **Going Correction** +0.425s/f (Yiel) **10** Ran SP% **92.2**
Speed ratings (Par 103): **104,101,101,101,100 98,93,92,89,87**
CSF £27.86 CT £232.79 TOTE £6.00: £1.90, £2.10, £3.80; EX 27.70 Trifecta £235.00.
**Owner** JCG Chua & CK Ong **Bred** James Mahon **Trained** Bromsash, H'fords
■ Rule 4 of 25p in the pound applies to all bets; Withdrawn: Perfect Muse

**FOCUS**
A modest handicap but notably those who raced closest to the stands rail were well beaten off and the action unfolded down the centre. A small personal best from the winner.
T/Jkpt: Not won. T/Plt: £145.60 to a £1 stake. Pool: £108,912.51 - 545.75 winning tickets.
T/Qpdt: £44.00 to a £1 stake. Pool: £5,866.85 - 98.58 winning tickets. JN

# 2276 SALISBURY (R-H)
### Thursday, May 22

**OFFICIAL GOING: Soft (6.7)**
Wind: virtually nil Weather: sunny periods with showers

## 2487 IRISH STALLION FARMS EBF BATHWICK TYRES MAIDEN STKS (BOBIS RACE) 5f
6:05 (6:05) (Class 4) 2-Y-O **£4,204** (£1,251; £625; £312) **Stalls** Low

Form RPR
**1** **Percy Alleline** 2-9-5 0 RichardKingscote 4 85+
(Ralph Beckett) *chsd ldrs: little green and pushed along early: disp 2f out: led fnl 120yds: kpt on wl: pushed out* **9/2**[3]
5 **2** *1 ¼* **Sunset Sail (IRE)**[12] 2146 2-9-5 0 RichardHughes 3 80+
(Richard Hannon) *trckd ldrs: nudged way out to chal 2f out: sn disputing: rdn ent fnl f: hdd fnl 120yds: sn hld* **4/5**[1]
4 **3** *6* **British Embassy (IRE)**[12] 2151 2-9-5 0 ShaneKelly 5 58
(Eve Johnson Houghton) *disp ld: rdn 2f out: hdd jst over 1f out: wknd ins fnl f* **10/1**
64 **4** *12* **Brazen Spirit**[18] 1977 2-9-5 0 (p) SteveDrowne 1 15
(Clive Cox) *disp ld tl rdn over 2f out: wknd over 1f out* **3/1**[2]

1m 4.12s (3.12) **Going Correction** +0.725s/f (Yiel) **4** Ran SP% **107.8**
Speed ratings (Par 95): **104,102,92,73**
CSF £8.69 TOTE £6.60; EX 10.20 Trifecta £17.30.
**Owner** Jeremy Gompertz & Mrs Ralph Beckett **Bred** Stowell Hill Ltd **Trained** Kimpton, Hants


The Form Book, Raceform Ltd, Newbury, RG14 5SJ

**FOCUS**
Rail erected 8yds off permanent far side rail throughout the last 6.5f. A fair little maiden. The winner overcame her inexperience and the second can rate higher too.

## 2488 BATHWICK TYRES ANDOVER H'CAP — 6f
6:40 (6:40) (Class 6) (0-65,65) 4-Y-O+ £2,587 (£770; £384; £192) Stalls Low

Form — RPR

30-3 **1** **Spiraea**[15] 2065 4-9-6 **64** RichardHughes 12 — 73
*(Mark Rimell) hld up: hdwy 3f out: rdn for str chal fr 2f out: kpt on wl: won on nod* **6/1**

0003 **2** *shd* **New Decade**[8] 2250 5-9-4 **65** (t) OisinMurphy(3) 10 — 74
*(Milton Bradley) trckd ldrs: led 3f out: rdn whn hrd pressed fr 2f out: kpt on wl: lost on nod* **3/1**[2]

/444 **3** *4 1/2* **Picc Of Burgau**[33] 1573 4-9-0 **58** HayleyTurner 4 — 54
*(Geoffrey Deacon) led tl 3f out: prom: rdn over 2f out: edgd lft over 1f out: no ex ent fnl f* **5/1**[3]

5-00 **4** *1* **Captain Kendall (IRE)**[24] 1799 5-9-3 **64** MichaelJMMurphy(3) 8 — 57
*(Harry Chisman) trckd ldrs: rdn over 2f out: kpt on same pce fnl f* **14/1**

0504 **5** *7* **Ceelo**[21] 1893 4-9-1 **62** SimonPearce(3) 6 — 34
*(Lydia Pearce) taken to s early: trckd ldrs: rdn over 2f out: nvr quite able to chal: wknd ent fnl f* **15/2**

026- **6** *1* **Logans Lad (IRE)**[216] 7354 4-9-4 **62** (t) FrankieMcDonald 9 — 31
*(Daniel Mark Loughnane) hld up: pushed along over 4f out: rdn over 3f out: nvr threatened: wknd ent fnl f* **18/1**

0142 **7** *6* **Encapsulated**[17] 2029 4-9-1 **59** (p) RobertHavlin 1 — 10
*(Roger Ingram) racd keenly trcking ldr: rdn for short-lived effrt 2f out: sn wknd* **2/1**[1]

1m 18.82s (4.02) **Going Correction** +0.725s/f (Yiel) 7 Ran SP% **113.0**
Speed ratings (Par 101): **102,101,95,94,85 83,75**
CSF £23.71 CT £95.70 TOTE £8.50: £3.60, £3.30; EX 19.40 Trifecta £147.40.
**Owner** Mark Rimell **Bred** Coln Valley Stud **Trained** Leafield, Oxon

**FOCUS**
A moderate sprint handicap, decimated by non-runners. They went just an average pace and the first pair dominated from the furlong marker. The winner's best previous run came on her debut over C&D.

## 2489 BATHWICK TYRES MAIDEN FILLIES' STKS — 6f
7:15 (7:17) (Class 5) 3-Y-O+ £3,234 (£962; £481; £240) Stalls Low

Form — RPR

42 **1** **Backstage Gossip**[13] 2125 3-9-0 0 RobertHavlin 1 — 71
*(Hughie Morrison) a.p: led after 1f tl after 2f: led over 2f out: rdn clr fnl f: r.o wl* **5/2**[1]

**2** *2* **Inis Airc (IRE)** 3-9-0 0 MickaelBarzalona 11 — 65
*(Sylvester Kirk) prom: led after 2f tl rdn over 2f out: kpt on but nt pce of wnr fnl f* **9/1**

**3** *3 1/2* **Lunarian** 3-9-0 0 JamesDoyle 3 — 53
*(Mick Channon) led for 1f: chsd ldrs: rdn wl over 2f out: sn hld by front pair: kpt on same pce* **5/1**[3]

**4** *1 1/4* **Belletriste (FR)** 3-9-0 0 RichardHughes 8 — 49+
*(Sylvester Kirk) stdd s: towards rr nt clr run whn carried lft over 2f out: swtchd rt over 1f out: r.o fnl f: wnt 4th nring fin* **9/2**[2]

**5** *nk* **Lead A Merry Dance** 3-8-9 0 JoshBaudains(5) 9 — 48
*(Sylvester Kirk) mid-div: rdn to chse ldrs over 2f out: kpt on same pce fnl f: lost 4th nring fin* **25/1**

**6** *2 1/2* **Silken Poppy** 3-8-11 0 ThomasBrown(3) 6 — 40+
*(Patrick Chamings) wnt rt s: sn mid-div: rdn whn swtchd rt over 2f out: nvr threatened* **22/1**

6 **7** *3/4* **Byrae**[25] 1767 4-9-9 0 SamHitchcott 12 — 40
*(Polly Gundry) mid-div: hdwy to chse ldrs u.p 3f out: wknd ent fnl f* **25/1**

**8** *hd* **Smile For Me (IRE)** 3-8-11 0[1] OisinMurphy(3) 14 — 37
*(Harry Dunlop) unsettled in stalls and awkward away: in rr: midfield 1/2-way: sn rdn: no further imp* **10/1**

**9** *hd* **Goddess Of Gloom** 3-9-0 0 ShaneKelly 5 — 37
*(Peter Chapple-Hyam) a towards rr* **8/1**

**10** *2 3/4* **Petite Fille** 3-8-7 0 DavidParkes(7) 4 — 28
*(Jeremy Gask) chsd ldrs: rdn 3f out: wknd over 1f out* **33/1**

**11** *5* **Sterling Kate** 3-9-0 0 MartinDwyer 10 — 12
*(Roger Ingram) mid-div: rdn over 3f out: sn btn* **25/1**

**12** *2 1/2* **The French Grey (FR)** 3-9-0 0 HarryBentley 7 — 4
*(Ron Hodges) outpcd after 2f: sn in rr* **33/1**

**13** *21* **Phantom Spirit** 3-9-0 0 PatCosgrave 2
*(George Baker) dwlt: hdwy into midfield after 2f: rdn 3f out: sn wknd: t.o* **14/1**

1m 19.1s (4.30) **Going Correction** +0.725s/f (Yiel)
**WFA** 3 from 4yo 9lb 13 Ran SP% **122.1**
Speed ratings (Par 100): **100,97,92,91,90 87,86,86,85,82 75,72,44**
CSF £24.00 TOTE £3.50: £1.10, £3.60, £2.60; EX 32.60 Trifecta £200.40.
**Owner** Runs In The Family **Bred** Mrs A Plummer **Trained** East Ilsley, Berks

**FOCUS**
This looked a modest fillies' maiden. There was a sound pace on and they finished pretty strung out. The winner stepped up on her modest serious standard.

## 2490 BATHWICK TYRES SALISBURY H'CAP — 1m 6f 21y
7:50 (7:51) (Class 4) (0-85,82) 4-Y-O+ £6,469 (£1,925; £962; £481)

Form — RPR

5-21 **1** **The Quarterjack**[17] 2011 5-8-5 **69** OisinMurphy(3) 5 — 77
*(Ron Hodges) cl up: tk clsr order 3f out: sn rdn: swtched rt and styd on ent fnl f: chal fnl 120yds: led line* **7/2**[3]

0-21 **2** *shd* **Ivanhoe**[12] 2175 4-8-5 **66** HayleyTurner 2 — 74
*(Michael Blanshard) trckd ldrs: chal over 2f out: sn rdn: drifted lft over 1f out: led jst ins fnl f: styd on: hdd line* **7/1**

0-23 **3** *3/4* **Rosie Rebel**[20] 1909 4-8-13 **74** ChrisCatlin 4 — 81
*(Rae Guest) racd keenly: cl up: rdn 3f out: hdwy jst over 1f out: styd on wl to go 3rd fnl 120yds* **13/2**

26-3 **4** *2 3/4* **Opera Buff**[24] 1811 5-9-5 **80** (p) MickaelBarzalona 3 — 83
*(Sean Curran) led: rdn over 2f out: rdr dropped whip ent fnl f: sn hdd: no ex* **3/1**[2]

44-2 **5** *2 1/4* **Burnham**[38] 1493 5-9-4 **79** (p) RichardHughes 8 — 79
*(Hughie Morrison) hld up: hdwy to trck ldr 5f out: outpcd 3f out: styd on again into cl 5th ent fnl f: wknd fnl 120yds* **2/1**[1]

030- **6** *4 1/2* **Saborido (USA)**[243] 6646 8-9-7 **82** RobertHavlin 9 — 76
*(Amanda Perrett) hld up: rdn 3f out: nvr threatened: wknd jst over 1f out* **25/1**

000- **7** *3* **Ermyn Lodge**[295] 4873 8-8-11 **75** (vt) JemmaMarshall(3) 7 — 64
*(Pat Phelan) trckd ldr: rdn 3f out: wknd over 1f out* **33/1**

3m 22.68s (15.28) **Going Correction** +0.825s/f (Soft) 7 Ran SP% **113.2**
Speed ratings (Par 105): **89,88,88,86,85 83,81**
CSF £27.09 CT £93.10 TOTE £4.80: £2.20, £3.20; EX 19.10 Trifecta £92.50.
**Owner** P E Axon **Bred** Cheveley Park Stud Ltd **Trained** Charlton Mackrell, Somerset

**FOCUS**
A modest staying handicap. The winner is rated back to last year's form.

## 2491 BATHWICK TYRES BOURNEMOUTH H'CAP — 1m 4f
8:20 (8:20) (Class 6) (0-65,69) 3-Y-O £2,587 (£770; £384; £192) Stalls Low

Form — RPR

-222 **1** **Bold Runner**[8] 2247 3-9-4 **62** MickaelBarzalona 2 — 79
*(Sean Curran) mid-div: trckd ldrs after 3f: led wl over 2f out: styd on strly and in command fr over 1f out: rdn out* **11/4**[2]

-531 **2** *2 1/2* **Kashmiri Sunset**[8] 2247 3-9-11 **69** 6ex ChrisCatlin 10 — 82
*(Ed de Giles) sn pushed along towards rr: stdy prog fr 3f out: sn drvn: styd on fnl f: wnt 2nd fnl 120yds: a being hld by wnr* **11/4**[2]

00-0 **3** *10* **Lochalsh (IRE)**[23] 1830 3-8-12 **59** OisinMurphy(3) 11 — 58
*(William Knight) trckd ldrsled 3f out tl wl over 2f out: sn rdn: kpt chsng wnr tl wknd fnl 120yds* **33/1**

44-1 **4** *15* **Dry Your Eyes (IRE)**[9] 2237 3-9-5 **66** 6ex MichaelJMMurphy(3) 5 — 44
*(Mark Johnston) led tl rdn 3f out: wknd jst over 1f out* **5/2**[1]

000- **5** *3 3/4* **Haines**[248] 6460 3-8-5 **52** oh1 ow1 ThomasBrown(3) 9 — 25
*(Brett Johnson) trckd ldrs: briefly chal over 3f out: sn rdn and hld: wknd jst over 1f out* **25/1**

0-50 **6** *2* **Assoluta (IRE)**[24] 1793 3-8-11 **55** RenatoSouza 7 — 25
*(Sylvester Kirk) towards rr: hdwy over 3f out: sn rdn: nvr threatened: wknd over 1f out* **33/1**

0-00 **7** *1/2* **Magic Shoes (IRE)**[16] 2061 3-8-13 **57** JamesDoyle 4 — 26
*(Roger Charlton) mid-div: rdn over 3f out: sn btn* **14/1**[3]

5-65 **8** *3/4* **Softly She Treads (IRE)**[24] 1812 3-9-1 **62** JemmaMarshall(3) 12 — 30
*(Pat Phelan) mid-div: rdn over 3f out: nvr thretaned: wknd over 1f out* **25/1**

00-2 **9** *2 3/4* **My Secret Dream (FR)**[15] 2066 3-8-12 **56** HarryBentley 8 — 20
*(Ron Hodges) racd keenly: hld up towards rr: effrt to cl on outer over 3f out: sn hung rt u.p: wknd over 1f out* **14/1**[3]

000 **10** *19* **Abyaat (IRE)**[15] 2081 3-9-7 **65** RichardHughes 1 — 3
*(Richard Hannon) trckd ldr: rdn 3f out: wknd 2f out: eased* **14/1**[3]

2m 47.93s (9.93) **Going Correction** +0.825s/f (Soft) 10 Ran SP% **115.5**
Speed ratings (Par 97): **99,97,90,80,78 76,76,76,74,61**
CSF £10.14 CT £191.83 TOTE £3.90: £1.50, £1.20, £5.50; EX 12.70 Trifecta £198.40.
**Owner** Bob Cooper & Val Dean **Bred** Natton House Thoroughbreds & Mark Woodall **Trained** Hatford, Oxon

**FOCUS**
They were strung out in this moderate 3yo handicap. The first two were clear and came out similar at the revised weights to Chepstow.

## 2492 BATHWICK TYRES FERNDOWN CLASSIFIED STKS — 1m 1f 198y
8:50 (8:51) (Class 5) 3-Y-O £2,911 (£866; £432; £216) Stalls Low

Form — RPR

2-35 **1** **Lisamour (IRE)**[15] 2081 3-8-9 70 LouisSteward(5) 6 — 82
*(Paul Cole) mde all: drifted lft whn rdn 2f out: styd on gamely: hld on but jst enough in hand clsng stages* **16/1**

05-3 **2** *hd* **Curbyourenthusiasm (IRE)**[24] 1808 3-9-0 69 MartinDwyer 2 — 81+
*(David Simcock) s.i.s: towards rr but in tch: pushed along over 4f out: rdn 3f out: sn chsng wnr: edgd lft ent fnl f: fin strly fnl 75yds: jst failed* **2/1**[1]

60-2 **3** *8* **Gavlar**[23] 1847 3-8-11 67 OisinMurphy(3) 1 — 66
*(William Knight) in tch: hdwy 3f out: sn rdn to chse ldng pair: styd on same pce* **2/1**[1]

40-6 **4** *5* **Travis Bickle (IRE)**[87] 731 3-9-0 68 RichardHughes 3 — 57
*(Sylvester Kirk) in tch: effrt 3f out: fdd ent fnl f* **16/1**

5-40 **5** *3 1/4* **Kisanji**[40] 1438 3-9-0 69 JamesDoyle 8 — 51
*(Mick Channon) hld up in tch: hdwy 3f out: sn rdn: wknd over 1f out* **13/2**[3]

30-6 **6** *9* **Seek A Star (USA)**[26] 1722 3-9-0 69 MickaelBarzalona 9 — 35
*(Luca Cumani) trckd wnr: rdn 3f out: wknd over 1f out* **11/2**[2]

-223 **7** *3 3/4* **Speechday (IRE)**[92] 660 3-8-9 70 MarcMonaghan(5) 10 — 28
*(Marco Botti) trckd ldrs: rdn 3f out: sn hld: wknd over 1f out* **20/1**

2m 20.4s (10.50) **Going Correction** +0.825s/f (Soft) 7 Ran SP% **111.9**
Speed ratings (Par 99): **91,90,84,80,77 70,67**
CSF £46.38 TOTE £12.00: £5.80, £2.70; EX 57.20 Trifecta £179.10.
**Owner** Frank Stella **Bred** Anthony Rafferty **Trained** Whatcombe, Oxon

**FOCUS**
They went a fair enough pace in this 3yo classified race and the centre of the home straight was again favoured. The first two were clear.
T/Plt: £332.20 to a £1 stake. Pool: £46,369.58 - 101.87 winning tickets. T/Qpdt: £13.20 to a £1 stake. Pool: £6,940.36 - 386.98 winning tickets. TM

# 1696 SANDOWN (R-H)
### Thursday, May 22

**OFFICIAL GOING: Good to soft changing to soft after race 4 (7.35)**
Wind: light, across Weather: dry after heavy shower before racing

## 2493 DYNAMYX BRITISH STALLION STUDS EBF MAIDEN FILLIES' STKS (BOBIS RACE) — 5f 6y
5:55 (5:58) (Class 5) 2-Y-O £3,881 (£1,155; £577; £288) Stalls Low

Form — RPR

**1** **Dame Liberty (IRE)** 2-9-0 0 PatDobbs 1 — 78+
*(Richard Hannon) led and set stdy gallop: rdn and hdd ent fnl f: rallied to ld again ins fnl f: in command fnl 75yds: r.o wl* **16/1**

2 **2** *1 1/4* **Russian Heroine**[10] 2220 2-9-0 0 RyanMoore 3 — 73
*(Sir Michael Stoute) dwlt: sn rcvrd: t.k.h and trckd ldrs: swtchd lft and effrt over 1f out: drvn and styd wl on ins fnl f: snatched 2nd last stride* **11/8**[1]

**3** *hd* **Blue Aegean** 2-9-0 0 WilliamBuick 4 — 72+
*(Charlie Appleby) chsd ldrs: clsd to press wnr over 1f out: rdn to ld ent fnl f: rn green and wandered in front: sn hdd and unable qck: outpcd fnl 100yds and lost 2nd last stride* **7/2**[2]

6 **4** *1 1/2* **Zuzinia (IRE)**[17] 2022 2-8-11 0 WilliamTwiston-Davies(3) 6 — 67
*(Mick Channon) rn green: s.i.s: sn rcvrd and in tch in rr: swtchd lft and pushed along over 1f out: kpt on steadily ins fnl f: nvr trbld ldrs* **9/1**

**5** *shd* **Looking Good** 2-9-0 0 SilvestreDeSousa 5 — 67
*(David Brown) rn green: s.i.s: sn bustled along in last pair: styd on steadily ins fnl f: nvr trbld ldrs* **13/2**

2 **6** *4 1/2* **Aevalon**[17] 2007 2-9-0 0 JohnFahy 2 50
(Eve Johnson Houghton) *chsd ldr tl over 1f out: losing pl and btn whn rn green and wandered 1f out: wknd fnl 150yds* **5/1**[3]

1m 4.38s (2.78) **Going Correction** +0.375s/f (Good) 6 Ran SP% **110.2**
Speed ratings (Par 90): **92,90,89,87,87 79**
CSF £37.47 TOTE £16.00: £7.90, £1.10; EX 37.80 Trifecta £191.40.
**Owner** Michael Cohen & Adam Victor **Bred** R Morecombe **Trained** East Everleigh, Wilts

**FOCUS**
Sprint track at full width. Back straight and home bend on outside configuration. Home straight railed out 4yds and distances on Round course increased by 10yds. A decent fillies' maiden that has thrown up subsequent Queen Mary heroine Maqaasid and Albany winner Jewel In The Sand in recent seasons and the latter's yard was represented by the Dame Liberty, who was surprisingly the outsider of the field. The winner enjoyed agood trip on the rail and matches the race standard.

## 2494 MEZZANINE INTERNATIONAL H'CAP (BOBIS RACE) 1m 6f
**6:25** (6:25) (Class 4) (0-85,81) 3-Y-O **£5,175** (£1,540; £769; £384) **Stalls** Low

Form RPR

53-5 **1** **Vent De Force**[24] 1797 3-8-12 **72** WilliamBuick 3 80
(Hughie Morrison) *hld up in tch in last pair: swtchd lft and hdwy over 1f out: str run to ld ins fnl f: styd on strly and gng away at fin: readily* **7/2**[1]

4222 **2** *2* **New Tarabela**[32] 1600 3-9-3 **77** LukeMorris 2 83
(James Tate) *dwlt and rdn along early: in tch in last pair: rdn and hdwy over 2f out: ev ch over 1f out: led 1f out: hdd ins fnl f: sn outpcd by wnr but kpt on for 2nd* **8/1**

0-42 **3** *1 1/4* **Alzammaar (USA)**[30] 1627 3-8-13 **73** DaneO'Neill 8 77
(Charles Hills) *dwlt and rdn along early: rdn and hdwy over 2f out: ev ch over 1f out: edgd rt and styd on same pce fnl 100yds* **33/1**

1104 **4** *2* **Maxie T**[15] 2077 3-9-3 **77** SilvestreDeSousa 5 78
(Mark Johnston) *led: rdn and qcknd over 3f out: hdd and drvn over 2f out: kpt on tl no ex 1f out: kpt on same pce fnl f* **9/2**[3]

1-65 **5** *3* **Poker Gold (FR)**[38] 1494 3-8-11 **71** (t) LiamJones 7 68
(Heather Main) *hld up wl in tch in midfield: rdn and hdwy to chse ldr 3f out: led over 2f out: drvn and hrd pressed over 1f out: hdd 1f out: wknd ins fnl f* **25/1**

4-53 **6** *2 1/2* **Norab (GER)**[26] 1720 3-9-1 **75** AndreaAtzeni 1 68
(Marco Botti) *chsd ldr for 3f: styd chsng ldrs: rdn ent fnl 3f: drvn and struggling 2f out: wknd jst over 1f out* **4/1**[2]

-221 **7** *3 3/4* **Norse Star (IRE)**[13] 2132 3-9-7 **81** PatDobbs 4 69
(Sylvester Kirk) *hld up in tch in midfield: nt clr run 3f out tl 2f out: sn rdn and no imp: wknd ent fnl f* **5/1**

4-22 **8** *5* **Template (IRE)**[10] 2225 3-8-12 **72** RyanMoore 6 53
(Amanda Perrett) *chsd ldrs tl wnt 2nd 11f out tl 3f out: lost pl u.p ent fnl 2f: bhd fnl f* **6/1**

3m 12.31s (7.81) **Going Correction** +0.55s/f (Yiel) 8 Ran SP% **109.3**
Speed ratings (Par 101): **99,97,97,96,94 92,90,87**
CSF £28.81 CT £705.70 TOTE £4.20: £1.50, £2.10, £3.50; EX 30.30 Trifecta £830.70 Part won..
**Owner** The Fairy Story Partnership **Bred** Deepwood Farm Stud **Trained** East Ilsley, Berks

**FOCUS**
A 3yo staying handicap in which the order did not change until the straight, but the first three were the last trio turning in. A clear personal best from the winner.

## 2495 WATERLOO H'CAP (BOBIS RACE) 1m 14y
**7:00** (7:00) (Class 4) (0-85,84) 3-Y-O **£5,175** (£1,540; £769; £384) **Stalls** Low

Form RPR

4-1 **1** **Reedcutter**[21] 1894 3-9-0 **80** RobertTart(3) 6 87
(James Toller) *t.k.h: hld up in tch: hdwy to chse ldr 5f out tl led 2f out: clr and edgd lft 1f out: in command and r.o wl fnl f: rdn out* **7/1**[3]

1 **2** *1* **Cape Icon**[23] 1844 3-9-3 **80** AdamKirby 2 85+
(Clive Cox) *stdd s: t.k.h: hld up in tch in rr: rdn 3f out: hdwy u.p to go 3rd and edgd rt over 1f out: wnt 2nd wl ins fnl f: styd on* **9/4**[2]

1 **3** *3/4* **Provenance**[16] 2061 3-9-7 **84** RyanMoore 4 87
(Sir Michael Stoute) *t.k.h: chsd ldr for 2f: styd handy: effrt to press wnr 2f out: rdn and struggling to qckn whn swtchd rt 1f out: styd on same pce and lost 2nd wl ins fnl f* **5/6**[1]

13-5 **4** *7* **Cape Wrath**[18] 1983 3-9-5 **82** PatDobbs 1 69
(Richard Hannon) *t.k.h: chsd ldrs: wnt 2nd 6f out tl 5f out: rdn ent fnl 2f: sn outpcd: wknd over 1f out* **16/1**

1-00 **5** *9* **Westminster (IRE)**[31] 1614 3-9-5 **82** (p) WilliamBuick 5 48
(John Gosden) *led at stdy gallop tl hdd and rdn 2f out: sn btn: wl bhd fnl f* **20/1**

1m 48.69s (5.39) **Going Correction** +0.55s/f (Yiel) 5 Ran SP% **108.5**
Speed ratings (Par 101): **95,94,93,86,77**
CSF £22.26 TOTE £6.20: £3.80, £2.40; EX 19.40 Trifecta £33.00.
**Owner** M E Wates **Bred** M E Wates **Trained** Newmarket, Suffolk

**FOCUS**
An interesting 3yo handicap featuring several unexposed types and the first three came clear. The winner improved again.

## 2496 SURBITON H'CAP (BOBIS RACE) 1m 2f 7y
**7:35** (7:35) (Class 3) (0-90,88) 3-Y-O **£7,762** (£2,310; £1,154; £577) **Stalls** Low

Form RPR

1-3 **1** **Elite Army**[27] 1702 3-9-5 **86** KierenFallon 2 96+
(Saeed bin Suroor) *t.k.h early: hld up in tch in midfield: trcking ldrs and nt clr run 2f out: rdn and qcknd between horses to ld jst ins fnl f: r.o wl: readily* **9/4**[1]

012- **2** *2 1/2* **Gold Trail (IRE)**[225] 7129 3-9-7 **88** WilliamBuick 8 93
(Charlie Appleby) *chsd ldrs: jnd ldr 3f out tl led over 2f out: hrd pressed and rdn 2f out: hdd ins fnl f: styd on same pce after* **15/2**

3-51 **3** *1* **Munaaser**[17] 2026 3-9-1 **82** DaneO'Neill 6 85
(Sir Michael Stoute) *hld up in tch in midfield: hdwy to press ldr ent fnl 2f: drvn and ev ch over 1f out: no ex jst ins fnl f: styd on same pce after* **11/4**[2]

441- **4** *1/2* **Master Dancer**[227] 7069 3-8-8 **75** LiamKeniry 5 77
(Philip Hide) *t.k.h: hld up in tch in last pair: hdwy to chse ldrs and rdn 2f out: drvn and no ex 1f out: styd on same pce after* **33/1**

61-2 **5** *2 1/2* **Warrior Of Light (IRE)**[16] 2060 3-9-7 **88** TedDurcan 4 85
(David Lanigan) *chsd ldr tl 3f out: nt clr run and shuffled bk over 2f out: swtchd lft and sme hdwy over 1f out: n.d but kpt on fnl f* **7/2**[3]

1-43 **6** *2 3/4* **Cricklewood Green (USA)**[13] 2112 3-9-2 **83** RyanMoore 1 75
(Richard Hannon) *hld up in toouch in rr: rdn ent fnl 2f: swtchd lft and no imp over 1f out: wknd ins fnl f* **5/1**

4-41 **7** *9* **Sayed Youmzain**[23] 1841 3-9-1 **82** AdamKirby 7 57
(Marco Botti) *led tl hdd and rdn over 2f out: sn struggling: bhd 1f out* **14/1**

2m 15.02s (4.52) **Going Correction** +0.55s/f (Yiel) 7 Ran SP% **117.7**
Speed ratings (Par 103): **103,101,100,99,97 95,88**
CSF £20.81 CT £48.86 TOTE £3.30: £2.80, £4.00; EX 20.50 Trifecta £81.70.
**Owner** Godolphin **Bred** Darley **Trained** Newmarket, Suffolk

**FOCUS**
There was more rain before this race and the going was changed to soft. Another good 3yo handicap and a one-two for Godolphin. The form could prove to be very decent, with the winner sure to rate higher.

## 2497 BREEDERS BACK RACING EBF MAIDEN STKS 1m 2f 7y
**8:10** (8:12) (Class 5) 3-4-Y-O **£3,881** (£1,155; £577; £288) **Stalls** Low

Form RPR

2-22 **1** **Mutakayyef**[19] 1953 3-8-12 **107** DaneO'Neill 4 86+
(William Haggas) *chsd ldr for 1f: chsd ldrs tl wnt 2nd again 5f out: clr w ldr 3f out: led over 2f out: drew wl clr over 1f out: r.o wl: easily* **1/4**[1]

0- **2** *7* **Green Light**[223] 7175 3-8-12 0 JimCrowley 7 72
(Ralph Beckett) *stdd s: hld up in rr: swtchd lft and pushed along over 2f out: nudged along and hdwy over 1f out: wnt 2nd wl ins fnl f: no ch w wnr* **8/1**

0 **3** *3/4* **Mawaseel**[35] 1529 3-8-12 0 TedDurcan 1 71
(J W Hills) *dwlt: sn rcvrd and chsd ldrs after 1f: 3rd and outpcd 3f out: no ch after but kpt on fnl f* **14/1**

**4** *nk* **Savant (IRE)** 3-8-12 0 RyanMoore 8 70
(Sir Michael Stoute) *chsd ldrs for 1f: stdd and in tch in midfield after: rdn over 2f out: no ch w wnr but kpt on ins fnl f* **7/1**[3]

0 **5** *nk* **Do Wah Diddy Diddy**[33] 1587 3-8-12 0 LukeMorris 6 70
(Clive Cox) *hld up in last pair: rdn over 2f out: sn outpcd: no ch but rallied and swtchd rt ins fnl f: kpt on* **25/1**

**6** *1/2* **Bold Arial** 3-8-7 0 JohnFahy 9 64
(Eve Johnson Houghton) *led for 1f: chsd ldr tl 5f out: 4th and outpcd u.p 3f out: no ch w wnr after: keeping on whn bmpd ins fnl f* **25/1**

03 **7** *3/4* **Every Time**[15] 2082 3-8-7 0 DavidProbert 3 62
(Andrew Balding) *chsd ldrs: wnt 2nd after 1f out tl led 8f out: wnt clr w wnr 3f out: hdd over 2f out: wl btn but stl 2nd 1f out: lost 2nd and fdd wl ins fnl f* **6/1**[2]

40 **8** *14* **Medburn Cutler**[20] 1911 4-9-12 0 FergusSweeney 5 42
(George Baker) *hld up in tch in midfield: rdn and btn over 2f out: sn lost tch* **33/1**

2m 16.83s (6.33) **Going Correction** +0.55s/f (Yiel)
**WFA** 3 from 4yo 14lb 8 Ran SP% **135.2**
Speed ratings (Par 103): **96,90,89,89,89 88,88,77**
CSF £4.96 TOTE £1.20: £1.02, £3.10, £2.80; EX 6.60 Trifecta £54.50.
**Owner** Hamdan Al Maktoum **Bred** Cheveley Park Stud Ltd **Trained** Newmarket, Suffolk

**FOCUS**
The easy winner didn't need to approach his Listed form.

## 2498 FOXWARREN FILLIES' H'CAP 1m 1f
**8:40** (8:40) (Class 5) (0-75,74) 3-Y-O+ **£3,234** (£962; £481; £240) **Stalls** Low

Form RPR

56-1 **1** **Lady Tiana**[23] 1846 3-9-0 **73** LukeMorris 1 82
(Lucy Wadham) *t.k.h: chsd ldr after 1f: rdn to ld over 1f out: asserting whn edgd rt u.p 1f out: kpt on wl: rdn out* **11/4**[2]

621- **2** *1 1/2* **Gay Marriage (IRE)**[167] 8175 3-9-0 **73** WilliamBuick 2 79
(John Gosden) *led: rdn and hdd over 1f out: no ex and styd on same pce fnl f* **4/1**[3]

0-13 **3** *1 3/4* **Tilstarr (IRE)**[21] 1899 4-10-0 **74** AndreaAtzeni 9 78
(Roger Teal) *taken down early: chsd ldr for 1f: in tch tl lost pl and rdn over 2f out: rallied and kpt on ins fnl f: snatched 3rd last strides* **7/1**

23-2 **4** *hd* **Lady Guinevere**[23] 1846 4-9-7 **67** RyanMoore 7 71
(Stuart Williams) *awkward leaving stalls and slowly awy: steadily rcvrd and chsd ldrs 6f out: rdn and effrt wl over 1f out: styd on same pce fnl f: lost 3rd last strides* **15/8**[1]

600- **5** *1* **Beep**[187] 7922 4-8-10 **63** NedCurtis(7) 3 64
(Lydia Richards) *t.k.h: hld up in tch in midfield: nt clr run 2f out: rdn and hdwy between horses over 1f out: kpt on same pce ins fnl f* **50/1**

005- **6** *2* **Ballyshonagh**[190] 7864 4-9-4 **64** TedDurcan 5 61
(Chris Wall) *in tch in midfield: rdn and outpcd 2f out: rallied and kpt on ins fnl f: no threat to ldrs* **20/1**

3-50 **7** *7* **Chrissycross (IRE)**[119] 300 5-9-0 **60** (v) RobertWinston 10 43
(Roger Teal) *hld up in tch in rr: effrt on inner over 2f out: no prog over 1f out: wknd fnl f* **16/1**

1-00 **8** *3* **Isabella Beeton**[12] 2152 3-8-9 **68** FergusSweeney 8 42+
(Pat Phelan) *t.k.h: hld up in tch: swtchd rt and effrt over 2f out: no prog and btn over 1f out: sn wknd* **12/1**

2m 1.16s (5.46) **Going Correction** +0.55s/f (Yiel)
**WFA** 3 from 4yo+ 13lb 8 Ran SP% **114.2**
Speed ratings (Par 100): **97,95,94,93,93 91,85,82**
CSF £14.21 CT £68.67 TOTE £3.90: £1.40, £1.30, £2.60; EX 15.50 Trifecta £87.50.
**Owner** The FOPS **Bred** Mr & Mrs A E Pakenham **Trained** Newmarket, Suffolk
■ Stewards' Enquiry : Ned Curtis two-day ban; careless riding (5th,8th June)

**FOCUS**
An ordinary fillies' handicap. The winner improved again from Nottingham.
T/Plt: £68.50 to a £1 stake. Pool: £66,846.99 - 711.58 winning tickets. T/Qpdt: £9.70 to a £1 stake. Pool: £5,168.12 - 390.90 winning tickets. SP

# 2480 GOODWOOD (R-H)
## Friday, May 23

**OFFICIAL GOING: Good to soft changing to soft after race 2 (2.50)**
Wind: Brisk, across (away from stands) Weather: Overcast with showers

## 2499 SPITFIRE MAIDEN AUCTION STKS 5f
**2:20** (2:21) (Class 5) 2-Y-O **£3,234** (£962; £481; £240) **Stalls** High

Form RPR

2 **1** **Parsley (IRE)**[14] 2128 2-8-10 0 RichardHughes 3 82+
(Richard Hannon) *trckd ldng pair: clsd 2f out: led over 1f out: pushed clr: comf* **6/4**[1]

**2** *3 1/4* **Little Palaver** 2-8-6 0 RyanTate(5) 6 70+
(Clive Cox) *w.w in rr and off the pce: pushed along and prog wl over 1f out: styd on to take 2nd last 100yds: no ch w wnr* **25/1**

**3** *1/2* **Step To The Shears** 2-9-3 0 PatDobbs 4 75+
(Richard Hannon) *racd against nr side rail: chsd ldng trio but nt on terms: shkn up 2f out: kpt on fr over 1f out to take 3rd nr fin* **4/1**[3]

45 **4** *1* **Come Uppence**[15] 2089 2-8-13 0 JamesDoyle 8 67
(David Evans) *led: edgd rt over 1f out: sn hdd: wknd ins fnl f* **3/1**[2]

**5** *5* **Rockaroundtheclock (IRE)** 2-9-1 0 LukeMorris 1 51
(Paul Cole) *hanging rt s and rn green: off the pce in 5th: clsd after 2f: urged along over 2f out: no imp over 1f out: fdd* **5/1**

6 **6** 1 1/4 **Itsindebag**[39] 1488 2-8-6 0 ... LiamJones 2 37
(J S Moore) *s.s: pushed along and in tch after 2f: rdn over 2f out: no hdwy over 1f out: fdd* **16/1**

5 **7** 2 1/2 **Foxtrot Knight**[17] 2057 2-9-3 0 ... DavidProbert 5 39
(Olly Stevens) *w ldr to 2f out: wknd qckly over 1f out* **16/1**

**8** 2 3/4 **Just Because** 2-8-6 0 ... JenniferFerguson(7) 7 26
(Edward Creighton) *dwlt: a in last pair and bhd* **66/1**

1m 0.79s (0.59) **Going Correction** -0.05s/f (Good) **8** Ran SP% **118.8**
Speed ratings (Par 93): **93,87,87,85,77 75,71,67**
CSF £46.72 TOTE £2.10: £1.10, £4.70, £2.30; EX 37.90 Trifecta £187.50.
**Owner** De La Warr Racing **Bred** Thomas Hassett **Trained** East Everleigh, Wilts

**FOCUS**
First 2f of 1m course dolled out 5yds, top bend out 3yds. Lower bend out 5yds from 6f to 2f in straight increasing distances on Round course by 15yds. Some speedy types on show, and the winner did it well.

## 2500 REHEAT STKS (H'CAP) 7f
**2:50** (2:51) (Class 4) (0-85,84) 4-Y-O+ **£6,469** (£1,925; £962; £481) **Stalls** Low

Form RPR

-322 **1** **Red Refraction (IRE)**[14] 2110 4-9-5 **82** ... RichardHughes 7 92
(Richard Hannon) *trckd ldrs: shkn up over 2f out: clsd u.p 1f out: styd on to ld last strides* **7/4**[1]

30-4 **2** shd **Czech It Out (IRE)**[20] 1943 4-9-5 **82** ... JamesDoyle 4 91
(Amanda Perrett) *chsd ldrs: shkn up 3f out: prog to chse ldr jst over 2f out: drvn to ld 1f out: hdd last strides* **6/1**

520- **3** 1 1/2 **Related**[231] 6993 4-9-5 **82** ... FergusSweeney 2 87
(David Simcock) *led: tk field towards nr side in st: rdn 2f out: hdd and one pce 1f out* **7/2**[2]

20-6 **4** 1 1/2 **Good Luck Charm**[23] 1871 5-9-5 **82** ... RyanMoore 6 83
(Gary Moore) *hld up in last: rdn and cl up 2f out: tried to chal over 1f out: fdd ins fnl f* **4/1**[3]

503- **5** nk **Lord Ofthe Shadows (IRE)**[233] 6956 5-9-6 **83** ... PatDobbs 3 83
(Richard Hannon) *chsd ldr: rdn and lost 2nd jst over 2f out: stl in tch but hld whn rdr dropped whip 1f out: one pce* **8/1**

-246 **6** 7 **Atlantis Crossing (IRE)**[24] 1834 5-8-13 **76** ... PatCosgrave 1 58
(Jim Boyle) *trckd ldng pair: rdn over 2f out: wknd over 1f out* **16/1**

1m 32.99s (5.99) **Going Correction** +0.625s/f (Yiel) **6** Ran SP% **109.9**
Speed ratings (Par 105): **90,89,88,86,86 78**
CSF £12.10 CT £29.48 TOTE £2.50: £1.50, £2.20; EX 11.70 Trifecta £34.60.
**Owner** Middleham Park Racing IV & James Pak **Bred** Tally-Ho Stud **Trained** East Everleigh, Wilts
■ Stewards' Enquiry : James Doyle two-day ban: used whip above permitted level (Jun 8-9)

**FOCUS**
A competitive race, despite a couple of a notable absentees, and it produced a thrilling last-gasp victory for the well-supported winner. However the time was modest. The winner is rated in line with the better view of his 3yo form.

## 2501 GOODWOOD FLYING SCHOOL FILLIES' (H'CAP) 1m 4f
**3:25** (3:26) (Class 3) (0-90,90) 3-Y-O+ **£9,703** (£2,887; £1,443; £721) **Stalls** High

Form RPR

2-31 **1** **Tioga Pass**[16] 2082 3-8-0 **79** oh1 ... LukeMorris 5 91
(Paul Cole) *in tch: pushed along briefly over 4f out: prog over 3f out: led 2f out: sn drvn: forged clr fnl f* **11/4**[3]

015- **2** 6 **Sula Two**[231] 6992 7-9-5 **86** ... (t) PhilipPrince(5) 1 89
(Liam Corcoran) *hld up in last: prog to chse ldr 7f out to over 2f out: edgd rt u.p sn after: kpt on to take 2nd again ins fnl f: lost more grnd on wnr after* **8/1**

4-12 **3** 2 1/2 **Running Deer (IRE)**[14] 2119 5-9-5 **86** ... LouisSteward(5) 6 85
(Eve Johnson Houghton) *led: tk field towards nr side in st: rdn and hdd 2f out: no ch w wnr 1f out: fdd* **5/2**[2]

/0U- **4** 1 3/4 **Tantalising (IRE)**[201] 7723 6-9-7 **83** ...[1] JamesDoyle 2 80
(Martyn Meade) *wl in tch: disp 2nd 5f out to over 3f out: shkn up and no rspnse: wl btn fnl 2f* **8/1**

00-0 **5** 4 1/2 **Rosaceous**[27] 1716 4-9-2 **78** ... (p) SteveDrowne 7 67
(Daniel Kubler) *cl up: n.m.r against rail over 8f out: nvr gng wl after: last and rdn 1/2-way: struggling over 3f out* **20/1**

51-3 **6** 34 **Kalispell (IRE)**[18] 2010 4-9-10 **86** ... RyanMoore 3 21
(Charlie Appleby) *trckd ldr to 7f out: rdn and wknd qckly over 3f out: t.o and eased over 1f out* **7/4**[1]

2m 47.02s (8.62) **Going Correction** +0.625s/f (Yiel)
**WFA** 3 from 4yo+ 17lb **6** Ran SP% **118.6**
Speed ratings (Par 104): **96,92,90,89,86 63**
CSF £25.54 TOTE £4.00: £2.40, £3.00; EX 18.60 Trifecta £49.60.
**Owner** The Fairy Story Partnership **Bred** Deepwood Farm Stud **Trained** Whatcombe, Oxon

**FOCUS**
The official going was changed to soft from good to soft prior to this fillies' handicap. The form is taken at something like face value.

## 2502 CASCO EBF STALLIONS COCKED HAT STKS (LISTED RACE) (C&G) 1m 3f
**4:00** (4:00) (Class 1) 3-Y-O **£22,684** (£8,600; £4,304; £2,144; £1,076) **Stalls** High

Form RPR

2-2 **1** **Observational**[36] 1530 3-9-0 0 ... JamesDoyle 4 105+
(Roger Charlton) *chsd ldr to wl over 2f out: sn drvn: angled rt jst over 2f out: clsd u.p to ld last 100yds: styd on* **2/1**[1]

1-2 **2** nk **Marzocco (USA)**[30] 1652 3-9-0 100 ... RyanMoore 6 104+
(John Gosden) *hld up in 4th: shkn up 3f out: rdn whn nudged by wnr jst over 2f out: clsd to take 2nd last 75yds: jst hld* **2/1**[1]

0-45 **3** 1/2 **Signposted (IRE)**[13] 2153 3-9-0 99 ... DavidProbert 3 103
(Andrew Balding) *led: brought field to nr side in st and racd against rail: drvn and jnd wl over 1f out: hdd and no ex last 100yds* **8/1**[3]

-241 **4** hd **Barley Mow (IRE)**[20] 1953 3-9-3 109 ... RichardHughes 1 106
(Richard Hannon) *trckd ldng pair: wnt 2nd wl over 2f out and looked to be gng best: chal and upsides wl over 1f out: drvn and nt qckn fnl f: lost pl last 100yds* **11/4**[2]

1-26 **5** 17 **Snow Trouble (USA)**[19] 1979 3-9-0 89 ... (tp) MartinDwyer 5 84
(Marcus Tregoning) *rel to r and reminders to get gng: in tch after 3f: rdn and strugging whn shied away fr rival 2f out: wknd and eased* **20/1**

2m 35.2s (8.70) **Going Correction** +0.625s/f (Yiel) **5** Ran SP% **109.2**
Speed ratings (Par 107): **93,92,92,92,79**
CSF £6.16 TOTE £2.70: £1.60, £1.70; EX 6.00 Trifecta £26.90.
**Owner** Seasons Holidays **Bred** Highclere Stud **Trained** Beckhampton, Wilts
■ Stewards' Enquiry : James Doyle one-day ban: careless riding (Jun 10)

**FOCUS**
Only one Epsom Derby entry in the line-up and with the first four home separated by less than a length, it's unlikely we've seen any superstars of the future. The third is the key to the form with the fourth emerging as best at the weights.

## 2503 IBA STKS (H'CAP) 6f
**4:35** (4:35) (Class 2) (0-105,99) 3-Y-O+
**£15,562** (£4,660; £2,330; £1,165; £582; £292) **Stalls** High

Form RPR

31-1 **1** **Intrinsic**[13] 2147 4-9-4 **89** ... RichardHughes 13 103+
(Robert Cowell) *hld up in chsng gp: rdn jst over 2f out: chsd clr ldr over 1f out: hung lft fnl f to nr side rail: r.o to ld post* **9/4**[1]

1-04 **2** hd **Ashpan Sam**[8] 2283 5-9-12 **97** ... RyanMoore 4 110
(John Spearing) *led and clr: rdn 2f out: stl 3 l clr 1f out: edgd rt u.p: hdd post* **3/1**[2]

3-1 **3** 1 1/4 **Watchable**[26] 1757 4-9-10 **95** ... DanielTudhope 14 104+
(David O'Meara) *led pair on nr side rail: rdn 2f out: styd on fnl f: hld whn intimidated nr fin* **12/1**

22-1 **4** 1 3/4 **Desert Command**[25] 1789 4-8-13 **84** ... DavidProbert 3 87
(Andrew Balding) *chsd ldr ldr to over 1f out: one pce* **7/1**[3]

0-05 **5** 3 **Gramercy (IRE)**[13] 2145 7-9-8 **93** ... (b) FergusSweeney 11 87
(David Simcock) *hld up towards rr and off the pce: shkn up over 1f out: kpt on fnl f: nvr involved* **9/1**

00-0 **6** 3/4 **Crew Cut (IRE)**[19] 1975 6-8-13 **84** ... AndreaAtzeni 8 75
(Stuart Williams) *prom in chsng gp: rdn over 2f out: wknd over 1f out* **12/1**

00-6 **7** hd **Ajjaadd (USA)**[20] 1944 8-9-8 **93** ... GeorgeBaker 9 84
(Ted Powell) *hld up in rr and off the pce: prog on outer over 2f out: rdn over 1f out: wknd fnl f* **16/1**

000- **7** dht **Humidor (IRE)**[216] 7364 7-9-13 **98** ... (tp) PatCosgrave 15 89
(George Baker) *taken down early: dwlt: hld up in last and wl off the pce: no ch whn rdn over 1f out: mod late prog: nvr involved* **25/1**

23-0 **9** 1/2 **Joe Packet**[9] 2254 7-9-5 **90** ... LukeMorris 16 79
(Jonathan Portman) *towards rr and off the pce: rdn over 2f out: no prog over 1f out: fdd* **25/1**

-542 **10** 2 1/2 **Waseem Faris (IRE)**[20] 1944 5-8-3 **81** ... DanielCremin(7) 17 62
(Mick Channon) *free to post: t.k.h: hld up and racd towards nr side rail: rdn and no prog 2f out: edgd rt fnl f* **12/1**

1m 13.6s (1.40) **Going Correction** +0.175s/f (Good) **10** Ran SP% **114.9**
Speed ratings (Par 109): **97,96,95,92,88 87,87,87,86,83**
CSF £8.63 CT £63.31 TOTE £2.80: £1.20, £1.50, £2.70; EX 9.20 Trifecta £55.20.
**Owner** Malih Lahej Al Basti **Bred** Cheveley Park Stud Ltd **Trained** Six Mile Bottom, Cambs

**FOCUS**
This was decimated by non-runners but there was no shortage of drama in this decent handicap. The winner can do better still.

## 2504 GOODWOOD AERO CLUB FILLIES' STKS (H'CAP) (BOBIS RACE) 1m
**5:10** (5:10) (Class 4) (0-80,80) 3-Y-O
**£6,225** (£1,864; £932; £466; £233; £117) **Stalls** Low

Form RPR

4-42 **1** **Starlight Serenade**[6] 2355 3-8-7 **66** oh1 ... MartinDwyer 6 75
(Ralph Beckett) *trckd ldng trio: prog and pushed into ld 2f out: shkn up over 1f out: styd on: readily* **3/1**[2]

2-31 **2** 1 1/2 **Stereo Love (FR)**[14] 2130 3-8-13 **77** ... RyanTate(5) 5 83
(Clive Cox) *hld up in 5th: clsd over 2f out: sn rdn: chsd wnr jst over 1f out: one pce u.p* **11/4**[1]

31-2 **3** 1 1/4 **Tullia (IRE)**[21] 1913 3-9-4 **77** ... AndreaAtzeni 10 80
(William Knight) *led: pressed 1/2-way: hdd 2f out: styd cl up but nt qckn and lost 2nd jst over 1f out* **7/2**[3]

30-1 **4** 3/4 **Cameo Tiara (IRE)**[51] 1233 3-9-7 **80** ... RichardHughes 8 81
(Richard Hannon) *prom: moved up to chal 1/2-way: shkn up and lost 2nd over 2f out: nt qckn after* **10/1**

21- **5** 3 3/4 **Dynaglow (USA)**[237] 6821 3-9-5 **78** ...[1] RobertHavlin 4 71
(John Gosden) *chsd ldr to 1/2-way: rdn over 2f out: steadily fdd* **9/2**

43-0 **6** 13 **Adore**[17] 2063 3-8-8 **67** ... (v[1]) RyanMoore 3 30
(Sir Michael Stoute) *dwlt: hld up in last: rdn and no rspnse 3f out: sn bhd: t.o* **8/1**

1m 44.68s (4.78) **Going Correction** +0.625s/f (Yiel) **6** Ran SP% **112.3**
Speed ratings (Par 98): **101,99,98,97,93 80**
CSF £11.67 CT £28.32 TOTE £3.80: £1.50, £2.30; EX 14.10 Trifecta £42.60.
**Owner** Melody Racing **Bred** Melody Bloodstock **Trained** Kimpton, Hants

**FOCUS**
Another race hit hard by withdrawals but there were still some progressive fillies on show. The form makes a fair bit of sense despite the ground.

## 2505 TURFTV FOR BETTING SHOPS STKS (H'CAP) 5f
**5:45** (5:45) (Class 5) (0-70,70) 3-Y-O **£3,234** (£962; £481; £240) **Stalls** High

Form RPR

-432 **1** **Groundworker (IRE)**[4] 2406 3-9-6 **69** ... RyanMoore 6 76
(Sylvester Kirk) *trckd ldrs: clsd 2f out: rdn to ld over 1f out: r.o wl* **6/4**[1]

16-1 **2** 1 1/4 **Gulland Rock**[30] 1642 3-9-3 **66** ... MartinDwyer 9 68
(William Muir) *w ldrs: rdn and nt qckn wl over 1f out: styd on again fnl f to take 2nd nr fin* **5/1**[2]

3114 **3** nk **The Dandy Yank (IRE)**[94] 650 3-9-7 **70** ... RichardHughes 5 71
(Jamie Osborne) *mde most: rdn and hdd over 1f out: one pce and lost 2nd nr fin* **8/1**

5433 **4** 1 1/2 **Jazz Bay**[17] 2045 3-8-9 **58** oh11 ow2 ... SamHitchcott 1 54
(John Bridger) *cl up: effrt to chal on wd outside 2f out: nt qckn over 1f out: fdd* **33/1**

3033 **5** 1/2 **Narborough**[18] 2023 3-8-7 **59** ... CharlesBishop(3) 8 53
(Mick Channon) *awkward s: hld up in last pair: sme prog and shkn up over 1f out: kpt on but nt pce to threaten* **7/1**

00-0 **6** 3 1/4 **Spirited Silver**[19] 1980 3-8-0 **56** oh11 ... CamHardie(7) 7 38
(John Bridger) *chsd ldrs: rdn 2f out: no prog and btn over 1f out: fdd* **66/1**

004- **7** 2 **Lucky Surprise**[276] 5609 3-9-2 **65** ... SteveDrowne 4 40
(Jeremy Gask) *mostly in last pair: outpcd 1/2-way: pushed along and no imp over 1f out* **14/1**

4222 **8** 1 3/4 **Katja**[42] 1430 3-8-13 **62** ... JamesDoyle 3 31
(J W Hills) *racd freely: disp ld to 1/2-way: wknd over 1f out: eased ins fnl f* **6/1**[3]

26-4 **9** 9 **Astral Rose**[18] 2023 3-8-7 **56** oh1 ... (b) LukeMorris 10
(Jonathan Portman) *in tch: rdn 2f out: wknd qckly over 1f out: t.o* **14/1**

1m 1.17s (0.97) **Going Correction** +0.175s/f (Good) **9** Ran SP% **112.3**
Speed ratings (Par 99): **99,97,96,94,93 88,84,82,67**
CSF £8.58 CT £43.42 TOTE £2.20: £1.10, £2.30, £2.80; EX 11.10 Trifecta £40.70.
**Owner** Deauville Daze Partnership **Bred** Knockainey Stud **Trained** Upper Lambourn, Berks

**FOCUS**
A low-key finale, and the fourth and sixth are doubts over the form. The winner seems to be improving.
T/Plt: £35.90 to a £1 stake. Pool: £107,167.48 - 2178.67 winning units. T/Qpdt: £11.80 to a £1 stake. Pool: £5,211.69 - 326.00 winning units. JN

# 2148 HAYDOCK (L-H)
Friday, May 23

**OFFICIAL GOING: Firm (good to firm in places; 9.8) changing to good after race 1 (2.00)**
Wind: Strong behind Weather: Cloudy

## 2506 PHS GROUP H'CAP (JOCKEY CLUB GRASSROOTS FLAT MIDDLE DISTANCE SERIES QUALIFIER) 1m 2f 95y
**2:00** (2:01) (Class 5) (0-75,75) 3-Y-O **£3,234** (£962; £481; £240) **Stalls** High

Form RPR
5-21 1 **Insaany**[14] 2133 3-9-7 **75** PaulHanagan 4 83
(Mark Johnston) *set stdy pce: qcknd over 3f out: pushed along over 2f out: sn jnd and rdn: drvn fnl f and hld on gamely* **6/1[2]**
5412 2 *nk* **Cotton Club (IRE)**[20] 1947 3-9-0 **75** PatMillman(7) 9 82+
(Rod Millman) *hld up in rr: hdwy on outer over 2f out: rdn over 1f out: str run ins fnl f: edgd lft nr fin and jst failed* **7/1[3]**
12 3 *shd* **Luck Of The Game (USA)**[8] 2273 3-9-0 **71** OisinMurphy(3) 6 78
(David Simcock) *trckd wnr: niggled along 3f out: pushed along and cl up 2f out: sn rdn to chal: drvn and edgd lft ent fnl f: ev ch tl no ex towards fin* **8/11[1]**
2-64 4 1 ¾ **Damascene**[24] 1861 3-9-6 **74** FrankieDettori 11 78
(Marco Botti) *hld up in rr: rapid hdwy on outer over 3f out: chsd ldng pair over 2f out: rdn wl over 1f out: kpt on same pce fnl f* **8/1**
424 5 4 ½ **All Reddy**[27] 1738 3-9-3 **71** RichardKingscote 1 66
(Tom Dascombe) *hld up towards rr: hdwy 3f out: rdn along and sltly outpcd 2f out: n.m.r over 1f out: kpt on fnl f* **20/1**
30-3 6 5 **Testing (FR)**[41] 1452 3-9-1 **69** FrannyNorton 3 55
(Mark Johnston) *plld hrd: chsd ldng pair: rdn along over 3f out: wknd over 2f out* **20/1**
50- 7 1 ¼ **Dream And Search (GER)**[205] 7626 3-9-4 **72** (t) HarryBentley 10 56
(Charles Hills) *chsd ldrs: rdn along over 3f out: sn wknd* **16/1**
250- 8 4 ½ **Crakehall Lad (IRE)**[226] 7129 3-8-13 **67** BenCurtis 2 42
(Alan Swinbank) *hld up in rr: rdn along over 3f out and sn bhd* **22/1**

2m 14.74s (-0.76) **Going Correction** -0.40s/f (Firm) 8 Ran SP% **115.6**
Speed ratings (Par 99): **87,86,86,85,81 77,76,73**
CSF £45.54 CT £65.11 TOTE £5.10: £1.80, £1.90, £1.10; EX 23.60 Trifecta £33.80.
**Owner** Hamdan Al Maktoum **Bred** Qatar Bloodstock Ltd **Trained** Middleham Moor, N Yorks

**FOCUS**
All races on Inner home straight and distances on Round course reduced by 5yds. Despite 6.5mm of rain in the 24 hours prior to racing, the ground was reported to have quickened up overnight to firm, good to firm in places (from good to firm), despite the GoingStick suggesting otherwise. However, there was a heavy shower during the opening race and the going was changed to good immediately afterwards, meaning the clerk's original assessment was well out. Such mixed messages puts punters at a real disadvantage. The winner made all and improved again.

## 2507 EBF STALLIONS PHS WASHROOMS MAIDEN STKS 6f
**2:30** (2:31) (Class 5) 2-Y-O **£3,234** (£962; £481; £240) **Stalls** Centre

Form RPR
3 1 **Winslow (USA)**[13] 2146 2-9-5 0 SilvestreDeSousa 1 89+
(Charlie Appleby) *cl up: led 1/2-way: rdn over 1f out: drvn and egded lft ins fnl f: styd on strly towards fin* **10/11[1]**
2 2 ½ **Baitha Alga (IRE)** 2-9-5 0 FrankieDettori 8 82+
(Richard Hannon) *trckd ldrs: hdwy 2f out: chal wl over 1f out: rdn and ev ch ent fnl f: kpt on same pce last 100yds* **8/1**
3 1 **Ustinov** 2-9-5 0 MartinLane 6 79+
(Brian Meehan) *dwlt and hld up towards rr: hdwy 1/2-way: swtchd lft and effrt to chse ldrs 2f out: rdn to chal over 1f out: ev ch tl drvn and one pce wl ins fnl f* **25/1**
4 3 ¾ **Marmalad (IRE)** 2-9-5 0 RichardKingscote 9 67+
(Tom Dascombe) *cl up: rdn along wl over 2f out: grad wknd appr fnl f* **9/1**
5 1 **Revolutionist (IRE)** 2-9-5 0 FrannyNorton 10 64+
(Mark Johnston) *wnt rt s: green and towards rr: hdwy 2f out: kpt on fnl f* **6/1[2]**
6 *nk* **Markaz (IRE)** 2-9-5 0 PaulHanagan 2 63+
(J W Hills) *in tch: pushed along: green and sltly outpcd 1/2-way: hdwy on wd outside to chse ldrs 2f out: rdn wl over 1f out: grad wknd* **11/1**
7 2 ¾ **Red Flute** 2-9-5 0 BenCurtis 7 55
(Alan McCabe) *chsd ldrs: rdn along wl over 2f out: sn wknd* **66/1**
8 ¾ **Medrano** 2-9-5 0 PaulMulrennan 4 53
(David Brown) *dwlt: a in rr* **33/1**
433 9 *nse* **Hell Of A Lord**[15] 2089 2-9-0 0 RyanWhile(5) 5 53
(Bill Turner) *slt ld: hdd 1/2-way: sn rdn along and wknd* **7/1[3]**

1m 13.08s (-0.72) **Going Correction** -0.10s/f (Good) 9 Ran SP% **116.9**
Speed ratings (Par 93): **100,96,95,90,89 88,84,83,83**
CSF £9.00 TOTE £1.80: £1.10, £2.00, £5.60; EX 10.10 Trifecta £106.70.
**Owner** Godolphin **Bred** Clearsky Farms **Trained** Newmarket, Suffolk

**FOCUS**
Probably not a bad maiden, and the form is rated on the positive side. Winners should come out of this.

## 2508 PHS WATERLOGIC CLASSIFIED STKS 6f
**3:05** (3:05) (Class 4) 3-Y-O **£6,469** (£1,925; £962; £481) **Stalls** Centre

Form RPR
0-12 1 **Red Pike (IRE)**[7] 2295 3-9-0 77 PaulMulrennan 3 86
(Bryan Smart) *mde virtually all: rdn appr fnl f: edgd lft last 100yds: kpt on wl* **5/6[1]**
00-1 2 1 ½ **Iftaar (IRE)**[17] 2044 3-9-0 78 PaulHanagan 2 81
(Charles Hills) *trckd ldr: hdwy wl over 1f out: rdn to chal and ch ent fnl f: sn drvn and kpt on same pce* **11/4[2]**
2520 3 *nk* **Amahoro**[14] 2122 3-8-11 79 WilliamTwiston-Davies(3) 6 80
(Mick Channon) *trckd ldng pair: hdwy wl over 1f out: rdn ent fnl f: kpt on same pced* **4/1[3]**
-445 4 62 **Royal Warrior**[18] 2015 3-8-7 74 CallumShepherd(7) 4
(Alan McCabe) *virtually ref to r and a wl t.o* **20/1**

1m 12.96s (-0.84) **Going Correction** -0.10s/f (Good) 4 Ran SP% **106.0**
Speed ratings (Par 101): **101,99,98,15**
CSF £3.22 TOTE £2.00; EX 3.20 Trifecta £3.60.
**Owner** Sir A Ferguson, P Deal & G Lowe **Bred** Mrs M Marnane **Trained** Hambleton, N Yorks

**FOCUS**
Effectively just three runners after Royal Warrior blotted his copybook by refusing to come out of the stalls, so not form to go overboard about. The time was relatively slow and the winner improved again.

## 2509 IJF 50TH ANNIVERSARY H'CAP 1m 2f 95y
**3:40** (3:40) (Class 5) (0-70,70) 4-Y-O+ **£3,234** (£962; £481; £240) **Stalls** High

Form RPR
-464 1 **Lord Franklin**[19] 1970 5-9-1 **67** JasonHart(3) 4 76+
(Eric Alston) *trckd ldr: shkn up over 2f out: rdn wl over 1f out: styd on to chal ins fnl f: led last 60yds: idled nr line* **85/40[1]**
10-1 2 ¾ **Hussar Ballad (USA)**[29] 1675 5-8-12 **61** DavidAllan 10 68
(Mel Brittain) *led: pushed clr 3f out: rdn over 1f out: drvn and jnd ins fnl f: hdd and no ex last 60yds* **6/1[3]**
324 3 ½ **Coillte Cailin (IRE)**[88] 735 4-9-2 **65** StephenCraine 6 71
(Daniel Mark Loughnane) *hld up towards rr: hdwy and swtchd lft to inner 2f out: rdn to chse ldng pair ent fnl f: sn n.m.r and swtchd rt: kpt on towards fin* **14/1**
2-41 4 4 **Taro Tywod (IRE)**[24] 1864 5-8-13 **67** JackDuern(5) 9 65
(Mark Brisbourne) *trckd ldrs: hdwy over 2f out: rdn wl over 1f out: no imp fnl f* **6/1[3]**
-546 5 *shd* **Kay Gee Be (IRE)**[18] 2021 10-8-11 **63** ow1 SladeO'Hara(3) 11 61
(Alan Berry) *chsd ldr: rdn along wl over 2f out: drvn wl over 1f out: grad wknd* **14/1**
4/ 6 *nse* **Rockabilly Riot (IRE)**[14] 4189 4-9-2 **65** PJMcDonald 5 63
(Martin Todhunter) *midfield: sme hdwy over 2f out: swtchd rt to outer and rdn over 1f out: styd on: nrst fin* **5/1[2]**
1035 7 2 ¼ **Magnolia Ridge (IRE)**[11] 2216 4-9-2 **70** (p) JacobButterfield(5) 3 63
(Kristin Stubbs) *trckd ldrs on inner: rdn along and hld whn sltly hmpd 2f out: sn wknd* **5/1[2]**
0-00 8 11 **Thistleandtworoses (USA)**[27] 1717 4-9-4 **67** DavidNolan 1 40
(David O'Meara) *hld up: a in rr: rdn along 3f out: nvr a factor* **16/1**

2m 12.99s (-2.51) **Going Correction** -0.40s/f (Firm) 8 Ran SP% **113.1**
Speed ratings (Par 103): **94,93,93,89,89 89,87,79**
CSF £14.79 CT £138.97 TOTE £3.10: £1.10, £1.80, £2.50; EX 15.50 Trifecta £230.70.
**Owner** Liam & Tony Ferguson **Bred** Tony Ferguson & Liam Ferguson **Trained** Longton, Lancs

**FOCUS**
A modest handicap featuring mainly exposed types, none of whom stood out as being particularly well handicapped. The winner ran as well as ever.

## 2510 PHS TREADSMART H'CAP (BOBIS RACE) 1m
**4:15** (4:16) (Class 4) (0-80,80) 3-Y-O **£6,469** (£1,925; £962; £481) **Stalls** Low

Form RPR
51-2 1 **Crowley's Law**[20] 1956 3-9-5 **78** RichardKingscote 11 98+
(Tom Dascombe) *trckd ldrs: smooth hdwy 3f out: led over 2f out: rdn clr over 1f out: styd on strly* **9/4[1]**
1- 2 4 ½ **Tanqeya (IRE)**[213] 7442 3-9-4 **77** PaulHanagan 9 86
(Richard Hannon) *in rr and sn pushed along: six l bhd after 2f: rdn along wl over 2f out: hdwy wl over 1f out: styd on wl fnl f: tk 2nd nr fin* **6/1[3]**
34-5 3 ½ **Majorities**[24] 1844 3-8-12 **71** MartinLane 3 79
(Brian Meehan) *trckd ldr whn carried lft bnd after 2f: prom: rdn to chse wnr over 1f out: drvn and kpt on one pce ins fnl f: lost 2nd nr fin* **14/1**
1-42 4 5 **Royal Preserve**[17] 2063 3-9-0 **76** OisinMurphy(3) 7 73
(Andrew Balding) *hld up in rr: gd hdwy on outer over 2f out: rdn appr fnl f: sn drvn and one pce* **4/1[2]**
231- 5 4 ½ **Tea In Transvaal (IRE)**[221] 7244 3-9-6 **79** JimCrowley 8 65
(Richard Hannon) *midfield: hdwy and in tch over 2f out: sn rdn and no imp* **10/1**
1- 6 1 ¼ **Dutch Rifle**[147] 8415 3-9-6 **79** PaulMulrennan 2 62
(James Tate) *hld up in tch: hdwy on outer 3f out: rdn along to chse ldrs 2f out: sn btn* **15/2**
2303 7 *nse* **Munfallet (IRE)**[11] 2203 3-9-7 **80** [1] PJMcDonald 10 63
(David Brown) *swtchd lft s and hld up in rr: sme hdwy on inner wl over 2f out: sn rdn along and n.d* **33/1**
43-2 8 3 ¾ **Pure Amber (IRE)**[22] 1897 3-9-4 **77** StevieDonohoe 6 52
(Ismail Mohammed) *chsd ldr: edgd lft bnd after 2f: rdn along 3f out: sn wknd* **12/1**
0-1 9 ¾ **Battle Command (USA)**[29] 1680 3-9-6 **79** FrankieDettori 5 52
(Peter Chapple-Hyam) *led: rdn along over 3f out: hdd wl over 2f out: sn wknd* **16/1**
0-11 10 1 **Arrowzone**[46] 1346 3-9-0 **76** BillyCray(3) 1 47
(Garry Moss) *cl up on inner whn hmpd bnd after 2f: chsd ldrs: rdn along whn n.m.r and hmpd over 2f out: bhd after* **14/1**

1m 40.13s (-3.57) **Going Correction** -0.40s/f (Firm) 10 Ran SP% **115.8**
Speed ratings (Par 101): **101,96,96,91,86 85,85,81,80,79**
CSF £15.65 CT £156.67 TOTE £2.90: £1.10, £2.50, £5.50; EX 19.20 Trifecta £296.10.
**Owner** Paul Crowley & Co **Bred** Middle Park Stud Ltd **Trained** Malpas, Cheshire

**FOCUS**
A good 3yo handicap that produced by far and away the best time performance of the afternoon to this point. The first three were clear and the winner will rate much higher than this level.

## 2511 PHS GROUP MAIDEN STKS 1m
**4:50** (4:53) (Class 5) 3-Y-O+ **£3,234** (£962; £481; £240) **Stalls** Low

Form RPR
0 1 **Hooke's Law (IRE)**[18] 2025 3-9-2 0 StevieDonohoe 7 76+
(Brian Meehan) *hld up towards rr: gd hdwy on outer wl over 1f out: str run ent fnl f: led last 75yds* **14/1**
0-0 2 2 ½ **Mantonize (USA)**[34] 1582 3-9-2 0 MartinLane 9 71
(Brian Meehan) *trckd ldrs: hdwy over 3f out: chal 2f out: rdn and slt ld ent fnl f: drvn: hdd and no ex last 75yds* **8/1**
3- 3 ¾ **Aragosta**[368] 2519 4-9-9 0 HayleyTurner 14 67
(James Fanshawe) *trckd ldr: cl up 1/2-way: slt ld 3f out: rdn along 2f out: hdd ent fnl f: kpt on same pce* **9/4[1]**
4 *shd* **Laftah (IRE)** 3-8-11 0 PaulMulrennan 5 64+
(Roger Varian) *t.k.h: trckd ldrs on inner: effrt 2f out and sn nt clr run: n.m.r and nt clr run over 1f out: swtchd rt ins fnl f: kpt on towards fin* **7/2[2]**
6 5 1 ½ **Cape Mystery**[14] 2129 3-8-11 0 JimCrowley 6 60
(Peter Chapple-Hyam) *t.k.h: in tch: hdwy over 2f out: rdn along over 1f out: kpt on one pce fnl f* **13/2[3]**
6 12 **Pindora (GER)** 3-8-11 0 PJMcDonald 8 33
(Noel Quinlan) *a towards rr: rdn along 3f out: sn outpcd* **25/1**
04/ 7 14 **Hollydanfaye**[591] 6954 4-9-9 0 RaulDaSilva 13
(Paul Green) *set stdy pce: rdn along 4f out: hdd 3f out: wknd 2f out* **50/1**

1m 44.32s (0.62) **Going Correction** -0.40s/f (Firm)
**WFA** 3 from 4yo+ 12lb 7 Ran SP% **89.9**
Speed ratings (Par 103): **80,77,76,76,75 63,49**
CSF £68.20 TOTE £12.40: £4.90, £2.50; EX 37.60 Trifecta £239.60.

**Owner** The Pony Club & Partner **Bred** Airlie Stud **Trained** Manton, Wilts
■ Rule 4 of 25p in the pound applies to all bets; Withdrawn: Potentate
**FOCUS**
A greatly reduced field thanks to the changes in the going, and Potentate was a further absentee after refusing to go in the stalls. The time was slow. The first two both stepped up on their previous maiden form.
T/Jkpt: £4,032.30 to a £1 stake Pool: £19,877.94 - 3.50 winning units. T/Plt: £242.10 to a £1 stake. Pool: £82,357.30 - 248.23 winning units. T/Qpdt: £239.90 to a £1 stake. Pool: £4214.67 - 13.00 winning units. JR

# 2213 MUSSELBURGH (R-H)

Friday, May 23

**OFFICIAL GOING: Good to firm (good in places; 7.9)**
Wind: Fresh, half behind Weather: Cloudy

## 2512 MCQUAY HIGH EFFICIENCY CLASSIC AMATEUR RIDERS' H'CAP — 1m 5f
6:10 (6:10) (Class 6) (0-65,65) 4-Y-O+ — £2,495 (£774; £386; £193) — Stalls Low

Form — RPR

45-4 **1** **Rocky Two (IRE)**[29] 1674 4-9-8 **50** ... PhillipDennis(5) 6 — 60
(Philip Kirby) *t.k.h early: hld up in tch: smooth hdwy on outside to ld over 1f out: pushed out ins fnl f* — 9/4[1]

4212 **2** *1* **Ballyheigue (IRE)**[18] 2595 5-10-1 **57** ... (p) MissHHeal(5) 1 — 65
(Liam Corcoran) *chsd clr ldr: hdwy and ev ch over 1f out: kpt on fnl f: hld nr fin* — 9/4[1]

30-4 **3** *3 ¾* **Hunters Belt (IRE)**[11] 2213 10-10-3 **59** ... (vt) MissJWalton(5) 4 — 61
(George Bewley) *hld up and bhd: effrt and pushed along over 2f out: pushed along and no imp over 1f out* — 7/2[2]

0-60 **4** *3 ½* **Grand Diamond (IRE)**[11] 2216 10-10-2 **60** ... MrsICGoldie(7) 3 — 57
(Jim Goldie) *hld up: rdn along over 2f out: no imp fr over 1f out* — 12/1

000- **5** *¾* **Rare Coincidence**[87] 5267 13-9-2 **46** oh1 ... (t) JasonNuttall(7) 7 — 42
(Alan Berry) *led and sn wl clr: rdn over 3f out: hdd over 1f out: sn btn* — 50/1

10-0 **6** *hd* **Golden Future**[32] 1605 11-10-2 **56** ... MrTHamilton(3) 2 — 52
(Peter Niven) *chsd ldrs: drvn and outpcd over 2f out: sn n.d* — 9/2[3]

2m 52.6s (0.60) **Going Correction** -0.15s/f (Firm) — **6** Ran SP% **111.6**
Speed ratings (Par 101): **92,91,89,86,86 86**
CSF £7.40 TOTE £3.50: £2.20, £1.20; EX 9.60 Trifecta £18.10.
**Owner** Geoff & Sandra Turnbull **Bred** Her Diamond Necklace **Trained** Middleham, N Yorks
**FOCUS**
Back straight and bottom bend returned to innermost position and distances as advertised. An ordinary handicap. Leader Rare Coincidence went off hard and was ignored by the rest of the field to some extent, with the overall pace fair.

## 2513 CANACCORD GENUITY MAIDEN STKS (BOBIS RACE) — 5f
6:40 (6:40) (Class 4) 2-Y-O — £3,881 (£1,155; £577; £288) — Stalls High

Form — RPR

**1** **Elusive Epona (USA)** 2-9-0 0 ... TonyHamilton 4 — 72+
(Richard Fahey) *trckd ldrs: effrt and swtchd rt over 1f out: led last 100yds: rdn out* — 7/4[1]

3 **2** *¾* **Lanai (IRE)**[14] 2128 2-9-0 0 ... GrahamGibbons 2 — 69
(David Barron) *cl up: rdn to ld 1f out: hung rt and hdd last 100yds: rallied: hld towards fin* — 9/4[2]

3 **3** *1 ½* **Dominic Cork**[11] 2214 2-9-5 0 ... GrahamLee 3 — 69
(Kevin Ryan) *cl up: led briefly over 1f out: kpt on same pce ins fnl f* — 10/3[3]

**4** *4* **Charles Messier** 2-9-5 0 ... RoystonFfrench 1 — 55
(Bryan Smart) *wnt rt s: rn green in rr: sme hdwy over 1f out: nvr able to chal* — 18/1

55 **5** *3 ¼* **Bahamian Art**[24] 1837 2-9-0 0 ... JoeFanning 5 — 38
(Mark Johnston) *t.k.h: led to over 1f out: sn wknd* — 5/1

59.29s (-1.11) **Going Correction** -0.325s/f (Firm) — **5** Ran SP% **112.1**
Speed ratings (Par 95): **95,93,91,85,79**
CSF £6.14 TOTE £3.50: £2.40, £2.10; EX 5.70 Trifecta £18.30.
**Owner** Middleham Park Racing XLVII & Partner **Bred** WinStar Farm LLC **Trained** Musley Bank, N Yorks
**FOCUS**
A promising effort from the winner on her debut to see off a couple who'd already shown a fair level of ability. There's surely more to come from the winner.

## 2514 NAIRNS OATCAKES H'CAP — 5f
7:10 (7:10) (Class 6) (0-65,63) 4-Y-O+ — £2,587 (£770; £384; £192) — Stalls High

Form — RPR

1623 **1** **Roy's Legacy**[19] 1972 5-9-2 **58** ... DaleSwift 12 — 68
(Shaun Harris) *mde all: drvn over 1f out: hld on wl fnl f* — 7/2[1]

5515 **2** *½* **Spring Bird**[19] 1972 5-8-13 **55** ... GrahamGibbons 3 — 64
(David Nicholls) *cl up: effrt and chsd wnr over 1f out: kpt on fnl f: hld nr fin* — 13/2[2]

320- **3** *1 ¼* **See Vermont**[262] 6088 6-8-3 **48** ... NeilFarley(3) 13 — 52
(Robin Bastiman) *pressed ldr to over 1f out: kpt on same pce ins fnl f* — 16/1

0000 **4** *nk* **Tadalavil**[7] 2296 9-8-8 **55** ... SammyJoBell(5) 7 — 58
(Linda Perratt) *hld up: pushed along and hdwy over 1f out: kpt on fnl f: nrst fin* — 25/1

615 **5** *¾* **Busy Bimbo (IRE)**[7] 2296 5-8-7 **49** ... (b) RoystonFfrench 8 — 49
(Alan Berry) *prom: effrt and rdn 2f out: kpt on same pce fnl f* — 16/1

0-00 **6** *½* **Here Now And Why (IRE)**[33] 1602 7-9-0 **56** ... GrahamLee 11 — 54
(Philip Kirby) *prom: drvn along over 2f out: one pce appr fnl f* — 7/2[1]

0560 **7** *nk* **Lord Buffhead**[1] 2473 5-8-6 **51** ... (v) GeorgeChaloner(3) 1 — 48
(Richard Guest) *bhd on outside: hdwy 1/2-way: rdn and no imp over 1f out* — 12/1

000- **8** *1 ½* **Hellolini**[221] 7236 4-8-6 **48** ow1 ... BarryMcHugh 9 — 40
(Robin Bastiman) *dwlt: hld up bhd ldng gp: drvn along 1/2-way: nvr able to chal* — 33/1

0-60 **9** *1 ½* **Findog**[19] 1966 4-9-3 **62** ... ConnorBeasley(3) 4 — 49
(Linda Perratt) *bhd: struggling 1/2-way: sme late hdwy to pass btn horses: nvr on terms* — 7/1[3]

0-05 **10** *¾* **Chloe's Dream (IRE)**[19] 1966 4-9-6 **62** ... TomEaves 2 — 46
(Ian Semple) *chsd ldrs tl rdn and wknd over 1f out* — 20/1

0600 **11** *1* **Opt Out**[1] 2473 4-9-2 **63** ... GarryWhillans(5) 6 — 43
(Alistair Whillans) *missed break: sn wl bhd: nvr on terms* — 13/2[2]

50-0 **12** *5* **Arch Walker (IRE)**[24] 1843 7-8-12 **54** ... DuranFentiman 5 — 16
(John Weymes) *hld up bhd ldng gp on outside: rdn over 2f out: wknd wl over 1f out* — 22/1

58.52s (-1.88) **Going Correction** -0.325s/f (Firm) — **12** Ran SP% **119.0**
Speed ratings (Par 101): **102,101,99,98,97 96,96,93,91,90 88,80**
CSF £24.69 CT £330.47 TOTE £4.30: £2.10, £2.50, £6.20; EX 28.30 Trifecta £176.30.
**Owner** P Birley,S Mohammed,S Rowley,K Blackwell **Bred** A Christou **Trained** Carburton, Notts
**FOCUS**
A run-of-the-mill sprint which few ever threatened to get into.

## 2515 BELMONT WALLYFORD H'CAP — 1m 6f
7:40 (7:40) (Class 5) (0-75,74) 4-Y-O+ — £5,175 (£1,540; £769; £384) — Stalls Low

Form — RPR

0-43 **1** **Aleksandar**[11] 2213 5-8-12 **65** ... GrahamLee 1 — 74
(Jim Goldie) *mde all at ordinary gallop: stdd 1/2-way: pushed along over 3f out: styd on strly fnl f* — 9/4[1]

660- **2** *2* **Merchant Of Dubai**[142] 7193 9-9-5 **72** ... GaryBartley 2 — 78
(Jim Goldie) *trckd ldrs: drvn over 2f out: rallied to chse wnr ins fnl f: kpt on* — 10/1

00-3 **3** *1* **Discovery Bay**[7] 2305 6-8-11 **71** ... (p) MeganCarberry(7) 10 — 76
(Brian Ellison) *t.k.h: hld up: smooth hdwy on outside to chse wnr over 1f out: sn rdn: lost 2nd and no ex ins fnl f* — 3/1[2]

0-02 **4** *1 ½* **Medieval Bishop (IRE)**[21] 1929 5-8-13 **66** ... (p) GrahamGibbons 6 — 69
(Mark Walford) *prom: flashed tail twice after 4f: drvn and outpcd over 5f out: rallied over 3f out: kpt on same pce fr 2f out* — 9/2[3]

56-3 **5** *7* **Geanie Mac (IRE)**[26] 1763 5-8-2 **58** ... (p) ConnorBeasley(3) 3 — 51
(Linda Perratt) *t.k.h: hld up in tch: effrt and drvn on outside over 2f out: no imp over 1f out* — 16/1

25-0 **6** *nk* **Vittachi**[19] 1970 7-8-6 **59** ... BarryMcHugh 7 — 52
(Alistair Whillans) *t.k.h: hld up: hdwy and prom 1/2-way: wnt 2nd over 2f out: outpcd whn n.m.r briefly over 1f out: sn btn* — 20/1

1100 **7** *3* **Travel (USA)**[14] 2139 4-8-13 **66** ... JoeFanning 4 — 54
(Mark Johnston) *pressed wnr tl lost pl over 2f out: sn struggling* — 9/1

0-23 **8** *nk* **Categorical**[19] 1971 11-9-6 **73** ... TomEaves 11 — 61
(Keith Reveley) *hld up and bhd: struggling 3f out: nvr on terms* — 9/1

3m 1.51s (-3.79) **Going Correction** -0.15s/f (Firm) — **8** Ran SP% **113.7**
Speed ratings (Par 103): **104,102,102,101,97 97,95,95**
CSF £25.46 CT £67.72 TOTE £2.80: £1.10, £3.20, £1.70; EX 30.30 Trifecta £276.70.
**Owner** Mrs M Craig **Bred** Fittocks Stud Ltd **Trained** Uplawmoor, E Renfrews
**FOCUS**
A fair handicap. The winner made all, his rider steadying the tempo in the back straight before winding it up again from 4f out.

## 2516 CENTRAL TAXIS MAIDEN STKS — 7f 30y
8:10 (8:12) (Class 5) 3-Y-O+ — £3,234 (£962; £481; £240) — Stalls Low

Form — RPR

-020 **1** **Mowhoob**[21] 1930 4-10-0 57 ... GrahamLee 1 — 74
(Jim Goldie) *mde all at modest gallop: qcknd clr after 3f: rdn and styd on wl fnl 2f: unchal* — 9/1

0- **2** *2 ¾* **Protected**[230] 7019 3-8-12 0 ... HarryPoulton(5) 6 — 63
(James Tate) *plld hrd: chsd ldrs: rdn over 2f out: effrt and carried hd high over 1f out: kpt on fnl f to take 2nd cl home: nt rch wnr* — 2/1[1]

3524 **3** *nk* **Handwoven (IRE)**[10] 2236 3-9-3 69 ... JoeFanning 3 — 62
(Mark Johnston) *dwlt: prom: effrt and chsd wnr over 3f out: rdn and edgd rt over 1f out: no ex ins fnl f: lost 2nd cl home* — 2/1[1]

52- **4** *8* **Thorntoun Care**[225] 7146 3-9-3 0 ... GaryBartley 7 — 41
(Jim Goldie) *hld up: drvn and outpcd over 3f out: kpt on fnl f: nvr able to chal* — 12/1

50-2 **5** *nk* **Danzki (IRE)**[17] 2053 3-9-3 62 ... GrahamGibbons 4 — 40
(Gay Kelleway) *chsd wnr to over 3f out: sn rdn and wknd over 2f out* — 11/2[2]

52-3 **6** *1 ¾* **Princess Rose**[45] 1361 3-8-9 66 ... ConnorBeasley(3) 2 — 31
(John Weymes) *hld up in tch: struggling wl over 2f out: sn btn* — 6/1[3]

1m 28.58s (-0.42) **Going Correction** -0.15s/f (Firm)
**WFA** 3 from 4yo 11lb — **6** Ran SP% **114.0**
Speed ratings (Par 103): **96,92,92,83,83 81**
CSF £28.10 TOTE £9.50: £3.30, £2.00; EX 40.20 Trifecta £243.30.
**Owner** Johnnie Delta Racing **Bred** Scuderia Archi Romani **Trained** Uplawmoor, E Renfrews
**FOCUS**
A weak maiden, the winner getting off the mark at the 20th time of asking.

## 2517 TURCAN CONNELL H'CAP — 7f 30y
8:40 (8:42) (Class 5) (0-70,70) 3-Y-O — £3,881 (£1,155; £577; £288) — Stalls Low

Form — RPR

4-52 **1** **Twin Appeal (IRE)**[11] 2204 3-9-4 **67** ... GrahamGibbons 10 — 75
(David Barron) *in tch: drvn along and edgd rt over 2f out: hdwy over 1f out: led ins fnl f: kpt on strly* — 11/8[1]

1233 **2** *2 ¼* **Beautiful Stranger (IRE)**[11] 2218 3-9-7 **70** ... (p) TomEaves 3 — 72
(Keith Dalgleish) *t.k.h early: pressed ldr and clr of rest over 4f out: drvn and led over 1f out: edgd rt and hdd ins fnl f: one pce* — 6/1[3]

2160 **3** *½* **Proclamationofwar**[18] 2015 3-9-6 **69** ... GrahamLee 4 — 70
(Kevin Ryan) *in tch: effrt and rdn 2f out: kpt on ins fnl f: nrst fin* — 6/1[3]

66-0 **4** *nk* **Lomond Lassie**[4] 2387 3-8-8 **57** ... BarryMcHugh 6 — 57
(Keith Dalgleish) *midfield: drvn along over 2f out: rallied appr fnl f: kpt on: nvr able to chal* — 20/1

4-14 **5** *1 ¼* **Cahal (IRE)**[11] 2218 3-8-10 **59** ... RoystonFfrench 1 — 56
(David Nicholls) *led and clr w runner-up fr over 4f out: hdd over 1f out: no ex whn edgd rt ins fnl f* — 10/1

5-34 **6** *1 ½* **Miss Acclaimed (IRE)**[22] 1902 3-8-13 **62** ... (p) DaleSwift 2 — 55
(Brian Ellison) *t.k.h early: prom: drvn along over 2f out: rallied: no ex over 1f out* — 16/1

6-06 **7** *1 ¼* **China In My Hands**[18] 2020 3-8-6 **58** ... ConnorBeasley(3) 8 — 48
(James Bethell) *unruly bef s: t.k.h in rr: drvn along on outside over 2f out: no imp* — 4/1[2]

400- **8** *6* **Mitcd (IRE)**[240] 6755 3-8-11 **60** ... TonyHamilton 5 — 34
(Richard Fahey) *towards rr: drvn and outpcd over 3f out: nvr on terms* — 25/1

5350 **9** *5* **Torridon**[30] 1648 3-8-4 **53** ... JoeFanning 9 — 14
(Mark Johnston) *hld up: struggling over 3f out: btn fnl 2f* — 25/1

000- **10** *3 ¾* **Connexion Francais**[188] 7934 3-7-9 **51** oh6 ... [1] JoeDoyle(7) 7
(Tim Etherington) *s.i.s: bhd: struggling 1/2-way: nvr on terms* — 40/1

1m 28.63s (-0.37) **Going Correction** -0.15s/f (Firm) — **10** Ran SP% **120.5**
Speed ratings (Par 99): **96,93,92,92,91 89,87,81,75,71**
CSF £9.92 CT £41.00 TOTE £2.30: £1.10, £2.20, £1.90; EX 10.00 Trifecta £40.90.
**Owner** Twinacre Nurseries Ltd **Bred** Glashare House Stud **Trained** Maunby, N Yorks

**FOCUS**
A comfortable win in the end for the favourite, who was 5lb well in compared to his future mark. The leaders went off hard, finally coming back to the field late on.

## 2518 GORDON AND HALLIDAY FLOORING H'CAP — 1m
9:10 (9:11) (Class 6) (0-65,64) 4-Y-O+ £2,587 (£770; £384; £192) Stalls Low

Form RPR
5223 1 **Outlaw Torn (IRE)**[11] 2215 5-9-2 62 (e) ConnorBeasley(3) 2 71
(Richard Guest) *chsd ldrs: rdn over 2f out: led 1f out: kpt on wl fnl f* 13/8[1]
00-4 2 1 1/2 **Nelson's Bay**[29] 1673 5-9-5 62 GrahamLee 3 68
(Wilf Storey) *hld up in tch on ins: rdn over 2f out: hdwy over 1f out: chsd wnr last 50yds: kpt on* 4/1[2]
5-04 3 1 1/4 **Camerooney**[32] 1609 11-9-7 64 (p) BarryMcHugh 5 67
(Marjorie Fife) *led: rdn over 2f out: hdd 1f out: kpt on same pce: lost 2nd last 50yds* 8/1
-045 4 3 1/2 **Funding Deficit (IRE)**[21] 1930 4-9-5 62 GaryBartley 4 57
(Jim Goldie) *w ldr: rdn and edgd rt fr over 2f out: wknd last 100yds* 8/1
123- 5 5 **Lil Sophella (IRE)**[225] 7153 5-8-8 58 JackGarritty(7) 1 41
(Patrick Holmes) *missed break: bhd: rdn and effrt on outside over 2f out: hung rt and sn wknd* 11/2[3]
0-00 6 nk **Cono Zur (FR)**[27] 1718 7-9-6 63 TomEaves 6 45
(Ruth Carr) *chsd ldrs: rdn wl over 2f out: edgd lft: wknd over 1f out* 7/1
664- 7 21 **Conjuror's Bluff**[262] 6083 6-8-4 50 oh3 (p) NeilFarley(3) 7
(Frederick Watson) *hld up in tch: struggling over 2f out: lost tch over 1f out* 16/1

1m 39.72s (-1.48) **Going Correction** -0.15s/f (Firm) 7 Ran SP% **114.1**
Speed ratings (Par 101): **101,99,98,94,89 89,68**
CSF £8.18 TOTE £2.00: £1.10, £3.50; EX 8.50 Trifecta £40.40.
**Owner** James S Kennerley **Bred** Derek Veitch & Rory O'Brien **Trained** Wetherby, W Yorks

**FOCUS**
A modest handicap which was truly run.
T/Plt: £12.60 to a £1 stake. Pool: £61,520.19 - 3548.40 wining units. T/Qpdt: £9.00 to a £1 stake. Pool: £4867.54 - 397.00 winning units. RY

# 1879 PONTEFRACT (L-H)
Friday, May 23

**OFFICIAL GOING: Good to soft (good in places) changing to soft after race 2 (7.00)**
Wind: moderate 1/2 against Weather: changeable, showers

## 2519 HEART BREAKFAST H'CAP — 1m 4y
6:30 (6:30) (Class 5) (0-75,75) 4-Y-O+ £3,234 (£962; £481; £240) Stalls Low

Form RPR
210- 1 **Border Bandit (USA)**[220] 7283 6-8-8 65 (p) IanBrennan(3) 6 74
(Tracy Waggott) *led 1f: chsd ldrs: styd on to ld last 100yds: hld on* 12/1
-266 2 3/4 **No Win No Fee**[112] 406 4-8-10 64 AndrewMullen 10 71
(Michael Appleby) *sn trcking ldrs: drvn over 2f out: tk 2nd last 75yds: no ex* 14/1
6-40 3 3/4 **Fazza**[27] 1733 7-9-2 75 KevinStott(5) 4 81
(Edwin Tuer) *s.i.s: hdwy over 2f out: swtchd rt 1f out: styd on wl to take 3rd last 50yds* 10/3[1]
3031 4 3 **I'm Super Too (IRE)**[7] 2293 7-9-2 70 6ex BenCurtis 1 69
(Alan Swinbank) *hld up on inner: nt clr run over 2f out tl swtchd rt over 1f out: kpt on: nt rch ldrs* 9/2[3]
0340 5 nse **Toga Tiger (IRE)**[41] 1439 7-9-7 75 DavidNolan 2 74
(Jeremy Gask) *strated slowly: t.k.h detached in last: effrt over 2f out: hdwy on outside over 1f out: nvr nr ldrs* 11/2
600- 6 1/2 **Gala Casino Star (IRE)**[246] 6563 9-8-9 70 (p) JordanNason(7) 11 67
(Deborah Sanderson) *chsd ldrs: wknd fnl 150yds* 20/1
-630 7 3/4 **Shamaheart (IRE)**[17] 2054 4-9-7 75 (p) SilvestreDeSousa 8 71
(Geoffrey Harker) *led after 1f: hdd & wknd last 100yds* 20/1
0-01 8 6 **Charles De Mille**[29] 1673 6-8-8 62 AndrewElliott 9 44
(George Moore) *mid-div: effrt over 3f out: nt clr run 1f out: edgd lft and sn wknd* 14/1
0151 9 2 **Cravat**[27] 1717 5-9-6 74 FrederikTylicki 3 51
(Ed de Giles) *sn drvn along in rr: lost pl over 1f out* 7/2[2]
120- 10 3 1/2 **The Blue Banana (IRE)**[217] 7346 5-8-11 65 (b) JamesSullivan 5 34
(Edwin Tuer) *chsd ldrs: drvn over 2f out: lost pl over 2f out* 25/1

1m 48.39s (2.49) **Going Correction** +0.425s/f (Yiel) 10 Ran SP% **113.3**
Speed ratings (Par 103): **104,103,102,99,99 98,98,92,90,86**
CSF £155.94 CT £699.78 TOTE £11.20: £3.50, £5.10, £1.10; EX 160.80 Trifecta £970.70.
**Owner** Elsa Crankshaw Gordon Allan **Bred** Darley **Trained** Spennymoor, Co Durham
■ Stewards' Enquiry : Ian Brennan two-day ban: used whip in incorrect place (Jun 8-9)

**FOCUS**
Temporary rail throughout last 6f, sited 15ft from permanent rail and all distances increased by about 12yds. After the first both Ben Curtis and Freddie Tylicki said the ground was on the soft side of good. A modest handicap in which the pace soon slowed before picking up again turning in. It proved difficult to make up ground from the rear. A personal best from the winner.

## 2520 CONSTANT SECURITY SERVING YORKSHIRE RACECOURSES H'CAP — 1m 4f 8y
7:00 (7:00) (Class 4) (0-80,80) 4-Y-O+ £5,175 (£1,540; £769; £384) Stalls Low

Form RPR
14-1 1 **Aramist (IRE)**[13] 2168 4-9-4 77 BenCurtis 2 85
(Alan Swinbank) *sn chsng ldrs: pushed along 6f out: led 2f out: jst hld on* 5/2[1]
0413 2 nse **Arizona John (IRE)**[13] 2168 9-9-5 78 FrannyNorton 6 86
(John Mackie) *hld up in mid-div: swtchd ins over 3f out: sn chsng ldrs: swtchd rt and rdr drpped whip: styd on strly wl ins fnl f: jst hld* 8/1
414- 3 1 1/2 **Embsay Crag**[31] 8130 8-9-2 75 RussKennemore 9 81
(Philip Kirby) *s.i.s: hdwy on outer over 2f out: styd on fnl f: tk 3rd nr fin* 25/1
0-00 4 2 **Prophesy (IRE)**[18] 2016 5-8-12 74 JasonHart(3) 10 76
(Tim Easterby) *hld up in rr: hdwy over 3f out: upsides 2f out: wknd clsng stages* 14/1
00-1 5 1 **Arthurs Secret**[54] 1197 4-9-0 73 RobertWinston 3 74
(John Quinn) *trckd ldrs: shkn up over 5f out: one pce appr fnl f* 11/4[2]
6352 6 20 **Flying Power**[57] 1133 6-9-0 73 PaddyAspell 1 42
(John Norton) *led after 2f: hdd 2f out: sn wknd and eased: t.o* 18/1
332- 7 26 **Sioux Chieftain (IRE)**[206] 7596 4-9-7 80 AndrewMullen 11 7
(Michael Appleby) *chsd ldrs: drvn over 3f out: lost pl 2f out: sn bhd and eased: t.o* 5/1[3]
2122 8 58 **Wilhana (IRE)**[25] 1811 4-9-2 78 RossAtkinson(3) 5
(Pam Sly) *led 2f: drvn over 5f out: lost pl over 2f out: sn eased and t.o: eventually fin* 9/1
9 41 **Dabuki (FR)**[226] 4-9-2 75 PJMcDonald 7
(Geoffrey Harker) *in rr: drvn over 3f out: sn lost pl and wl bhd: hopelessly t.o over 2f out: eventually fin* 33/1

2m 44.76s (3.96) **Going Correction** +0.425s/f (Yiel) 9 Ran SP% **111.7**
Speed ratings (Par 105): **103,102,101,100,99 86,69,30,3**
CSF £22.01 CT £389.76 TOTE £3.50: £1.90, £2.50, £5.00; EX 24.20 Trifecta £138.10.
**Owner** Pam & Richard Ellis **Bred** Fiona Craig & S Couldridge **Trained** Melsonby, N Yorks

**FOCUS**
Heavy rain fell before and during this ordinary handicap. The pace was brisk and those who disputed it - Flying Power, Sioux Chieftain and Wilhana - were beaten miles. The first two come out similar to the weights as their Thirsk meeting.

## 2521 EBF STALLIONS YOUNGSTERS CONDITIONS STKS (BOBIS RACE) — 6f
7:30 (7:31) (Class 2) 2-Y-O £11,205 (£3,355; £1,677; £838; £419) Stalls Low

Form RPR
1 1 **Bond's Girl**[29] 1656 2-8-7 0 PatrickMathers 2 86
(Richard Fahey) *led over 1f: chsd ldr: drvn over 2f out: led 1f out: kpt on wl* 10/1[3]
1 2 1 1/2 **Kasb (IRE)**[42] 1417 2-8-12 0 PaulHanagan 1 87
(John Gosden) *dwlt: hdwy to ld over 4f out: drvn over 1f out: sn hdd: kpt on same pce* 4/9[1]
1 3 1 1/2 **Buccaneers Vault (IRE)**[37] 1504 2-8-12 0 PaulMulrennan 4 82
(Michael Dods) *trckd ldrs: effrt over 2f out: styd on same pce fnl f* 7/2[2]
013 4 2 **Mylaporyours (IRE)**[19] 1982 2-8-7 0 MartinLane 3 71
(Rod Millman) *stdd s: t.k.h in last: effrt 2f out: hung rt fnl f: kpt on last 75yds* 20/1
21 5 10 **Cabbies Lou**[14] 2134 2-8-7 0 JoeyHaynes 5 41
(Noel Wilson) *chsd ldrs: drvn over 2f out: wknd over 1f out: eased clsng stages* 25/1

1m 21.96s (5.06) **Going Correction** +0.75s/f (Yiel) 5 Ran SP% **109.2**
Speed ratings (Par 99): **96,94,92,89,76**
CSF £15.14 TOTE £10.60: £4.70, £1.10; EX 17.60 Trifecta £49.10.
**Owner** Crown Select **Bred** David Holgate **Trained** Musley Bank, N Yorks

**FOCUS**
The official ground description was changed to soft before this event. This is often a decent little race with former winners Hellvelyn going on to take the Coventry and Tony James the Gimcrack, while Group-winning juveniles Caspar Netscher and Red Duke have been beaten here. The form fits fits and could be worth a few pounds more.

## 2522 CONSTANT SECURITY SERVICES H'CAP — 6f
8:00 (8:00) (Class 4) (0-85,82) 4-Y-O+ £6,469 (£1,925; £962; £481) Stalls Low

Form RPR
036 1 **Teetotal (IRE)**[14] 2136 4-8-10 71 SilvestreDeSousa 2 82
(Nigel Tinkler) *dwlt: hld up in rr: drvn over 2f out: swtchd to wd outside over 1f out: edgd lft and styd on wl to ld last 100yds* 3/1[1]
0-05 2 2 1/4 **Line Of Reason (IRE)**[29] 1672 4-9-5 80 PaulHanagan 1 84
(Paul Midgley) *hld up in rr: hdwy over 2f out: nt clr run on ins over 1f out: led 1f out: hdd and no ex ins fnl f* 10/3[2]
6-00 3 nk **Gravitational (IRE)**[13] 2147 4-8-13 77 AshleyMorgan(3) 3 80
(Chris Wall) *trckd ldrs: nt clr run over 2f out: edgd lft 1f out: styd on same pce* 11/2[3]
-203 4 1 1/4 **Solar Spirit (IRE)**[17] 2054 9-8-13 77 IanBrennan(3) 4 76
(Tracy Waggott) *hld up in rr: hdwy over 2f out: styd on ins fnl f* 7/1
0-00 5 4 **Relight My Fire**[20] 1957 4-8-11 72 (b) DavidAllan 6 58
(Tim Easterby) *chsd ldrs: led over 2f out: hdd 1f out: sn edgd rt and wknd* 20/1
0631 6 4 **Lothair (IRE)**[13] 2167 5-8-10 71 BenCurtis 10 44
(Alan Swinbank) *chsd ldrs: rdn over 2f out: wkng whn sltly hmpd jst ins fnl f* 11/2[3]
0-00 7 2 1/4 **Head Space (IRE)**[14] 2136 6-9-7 82 (p) JamesSullivan 7 48
(Ruth Carr) *chsd ldrs on outer: rdn over 1f out: sn wknd* 10/1
20-0 8 3 1/2 **Springinmystep (IRE)**[27] 1731 5-9-7 82 FrederikTylicki 9 37
(Ed de Giles) *led: hdd over 2f out: wknd appr fnl f* 16/1
41-0 9 43 **Feel The Heat**[19] 1967 7-8-11 72 (v) PaulMulrennan 5
(Bryan Smart) *chsd ldrs: lost pl over 2f out: sn bhd and eased: hopelessly t.o* 16/1

1m 20.41s (3.51) **Going Correction** +0.75s/f (Yiel) 9 Ran SP% **117.0**
Speed ratings (Par 105): **106,103,102,100,95 90,87,82,25**
CSF £13.30 CT £52.17 TOTE £3.30: £1.80, £2.10, £1.30; EX 14.90 Trifecta £74.40.
**Owner** Raybould & Scott **Bred** T Jones **Trained** Langton, N Yorks
■ Stewards' Enquiry : David Allan one-day ban: careless riding (Jun 8)

**FOCUS**
They didn't go a frantic gallop in this fair handicap but it was the pick of the three C&D times. The winner goes well here.

## 2523 ALAMO BUSINESS SYSTEMS FILLIES' H'CAP — 1m 2f 6y
8:30 (8:31) (Class 5) (0-70,68) 3-Y-O+ £3,881 (£1,155; £577; £288) Stalls Low

Form RPR
53-2 1 **Lunar Spirit**[29] 1661 3-9-0 68 [1] JimCrowley 6 78
(Ralph Beckett) *hld up and sn in rr: t.k.h: hdwy on outer over 3f out: w ldr over 2f out: edgd rt and kpt on to ld ins fnl f* 9/2[2]
-222 2 2 1/2 **Missy Wells**[11] 2199 4-9-3 60 (p) JasonHart(3) 7 66
(Mark Walford) *chsd ldr: drvn over 4f out: led over 2f out: hdd ins fnl f: eased whn hld towards fin* 9/2[2]
3 4 **Mornin' Gorgeous**[220] 7289 4-9-8 62 PJMcDonald 3 60
(Micky Hammond) *in rr: effrt over 2f out: kpt on to take modest 3rd last 100yds* 8/1
03-2 4 2 **Miss Lucy Jane**[23] 1888 3-8-11 65 PaulHanagan 4 59
(Richard Fahey) *chsd ldrs: one pce over 1f out* 4/1[1]
1321 5 4 **Tijuca (IRE)**[21] 1923 5-9-3 57 FrederikTylicki 5 44
(Ed de Giles) *dwlt: hld up in rr: hdwy over 3f out: chsng ldng pair on ins over 2f out: wknd fnl f* 6/1
3333 6 13 **Power Up**[18] 2018 3-9-0 68 SilvestreDeSousa 1 29
(Mark Johnston) *led: clr after 3f: hdd over 2f out: sn wknd: bhd whn eased ins fnl f* 11/2[3]
655- 7 3/4 **Chortle**[213] 7449 3-8-13 67 MartinLane 8 27
(Charlie Appleby) *hld up in rr: drvn over 3f out: sme hdwy over 2f out: wknd over 1f out: eased whn bhd clsng stages* 6/1

2m 20.43s (6.73) **Going Correction** +0.75s/f (Yiel)
**WFA** 3 from 4yo+ 14lb 7 Ran SP% **111.4**
Speed ratings (Par 100): **103,101,97,96,93 82,82**
CSF £23.54 CT £151.08 TOTE £5.90: £3.20, £2.40; EX 28.60 Trifecta £646.80.
**Owner** Mr and Mrs David Aykroyd **Bred** Mr & Mrs David Aykroyd **Trained** Kimpton, Hants

**FOCUS**
A reasonable race for the grade and a personal best from the winner. The first two came widest down the home straight.

## 2524 WEST YORKSHIRE FESTIVAL NIGHT 9TH JUNE MAIDEN STKS 6f
9:00 (9:00) (Class 5) 3-Y-O £3,881 (£1,155; £577; £288) Stalls Low

Form RPR
6-2 1 **Boy In The Bar**[13] 2158 3-9-5 0 (b[1]) RobertWinston 5 77
(David Barron) *w ldrs on outer: t.k.h: hung bdly lft and led over 1f out: drvn out* **11/4**[1]
2 2 ½ **Eternitys Gate** 3-9-5 0 JimCrowley 2 69
(Peter Chapple-Hyam) *dwlt: sn chsng ldrs: drvn over 2f out: sn sltly outpcd: kpt on and 2nd 1f out: no imp* **10/3**[2]
66- 3 2 ¼ **Mr Win (IRE)**[225] 7155 3-9-2 0 AshleyMorgan(3) 6 62
(Chris Wall) *trckd ldrs: stdd after 1f: outpcd over 2f out: hdwy on ins over 1f out: kpt on to take 3rd jst ins fnl f* **7/2**[3]
46-0 4 4 **Henke (IRE)**[29] 1657 3-9-5 58 AdrianNicholls 4 49
(Nigel Tinkler) *t.k.h: led hdd over 2f out: hmpd over 1f out: wknd fnl f* **14/1**
20- 5 2 ½ **In Focus (IRE)**[342] 3350 3-9-5 0 BenCurtis 1 41
(Alan Swinbank) *s.i.s: hld up in rr: outpcd over 2f out: bhd over 1f out* **6/1**
23-0 6 ¾ **Lord Clyde**[29] 1671 3-9-5 75 PatrickMathers 3 39
(Richard Fahey) *dwlt: sn w ldrs: led over 2f out: edgd rt and hdd over 1f out: wknd fnl f* **9/2**
60- 7 3 ¼ **Llandanwg**[197] 7779 3-9-0 0 PaulMulrennan 7 23
(Bryan Smart) *sn chsng ldrs: lost pl over 2f out: sn bhd* **33/1**
1m 21.68s (4.78) **Going Correction** +0.75s/f (Yiel) 7 Ran SP% **114.0**
Speed ratings (Par 99): **98,94,91,86,83 82,77**
CSF £12.10 TOTE £3.20: £2.30, £2.30; EX 9.20 Trifecta £35.10.
**Owner** S Rudolf **Bred** Brinkley Stud S R L **Trained** Maunby, N Yorks
**FOCUS**
Modest maiden form, with doubts over some of these. Improvement from the winner in blinkers.
T/Plt: £35.60 to a £1 stake. Pool: £81,672.88 - 1670.68 winning units. T/Qpdt: £6.40 to a £1 stake. Pool: £7113.92 - 229.20 winning units. WG

# 2442 YARMOUTH (L-H)
Friday, May 23

**OFFICIAL GOING: Good to soft (6.1)**
Wind: Bright and breezy

## 2525 MOUGHTON ENGINEERING MEDIAN AUCTION MAIDEN STKS 6f 3y
2:10 (2:12) (Class 6) 3-5-Y-O £2,264 (£673; £336; £168) Stalls Centre

Form RPR
454- 1 **Johara (IRE)**[222] 7218 3-8-12 69 TedDurcan 2 82+
(Chris Wall) *chsd ldrs: wnt 2nd over 2f out: pushed along to ld over 1f out: clr fnl f: eased towards fin: v easily* **5/4**[1]
4-25 2 2 **Serata Di Gala (FR)**[6] 2329 3-8-7 0 MarcMonaghan(5) 4 69
(Marco Botti) *taken down early: led: rdn and hdd over 1f out: no ch w wnr but kpt on for clr 2nd fnl f* **3/1**[2]
3 13 **Vecheka (IRE)** 3-9-3 0 [1] LiamKeniry 8 32
(Andrew Balding) *awkward leaving stalls and v.s.a: rn green in rr: pushed along and styd on past btn over 1f out: wnt modest 3rd jst ins fnl f: nvr trbld ldrs* **9/2**[3]
P 4 3 **Smart Life**[123] 254 3-9-3 0 (b[1]) JimmyQuinn 6 23
(Robert Eddery) *racd in midfield: rdn and struggling 1/2-way: no ch fnl 2f: wnt modest 4th ins fnl f* **12/1**
5 ¾ **Scafell Pike** 3-9-0 0 RobertTart(3) 9 20
(Dr Jon Scargill) *s.i.s: rn green and rdn along in rr: no ch but passed btn horses ins fnl f* **16/1**
0 6 2 ¼ **Happy Jack (IRE)**[31] 1634 3-9-3 0 TomQueally 3 13
(Michael Wigham) *hld up in rr: struggling 1/2-way: no ch over 2f out* **16/1**
05 7 1 ¼ **Khelfan**[13] 2158 3-8-12 0 NickyMackay 7
(Martin Smith) *chsd ldrs: rdn and struggling over 2f out: modest 3rd wl over 1f out: no hdwy: wknd ins fnl f* **33/1**
060 8 6 **Jalusive (IRE)**[32] 1612 5-9-7 44 ShelleyBirkett(5) 1
(Christine Dunnett) *chsd ldr tl over 2f out: fdd over 1f out: t.o ins fnl f* **66/1**
0-R 9 99 **Gentlemen**[3] 2442 3-8-12 0 [1] DannyBrock(5) 5
(Phil McEntee) *taken down early: virtually ref to r: eventually set off as rivals were at 1/2-way* **50/1**
1m 15.99s (1.59) **Going Correction** +0.325s/f (Good)
**WFA** 3 from 5yo 9lb 9 Ran SP% **113.5**
Speed ratings (Par 101): **102,99,82,78,77 74,72,64,**
CSF £4.80 TOTE £2.40: £1.10, £1.10, £2.10; EX 5.70 Trifecta £14.80.
**Owner** Mrs Claude Lilley **Bred** Tribesmen Syndicate **Trained** Newmarket, Suffolk
**FOCUS**
A drying day and the going was upgraded to good to soft prior to the opener. This was a very weak maiden and the market got it spot on.

## 2526 NORFOLK CHAMBER OF COMMERCE H'CAP 7f 3y
2:40 (2:41) (Class 6) (0-60,60) 3-Y-O £1,940 (£577; £288; £144) Stalls Centre

Form RPR
66-5 1 **Strike A Light**[29] 1681 3-9-0 53 ChrisCatlin 4 58+
(Rae Guest) *hld up in tch: hdwy 1/2-way: rdn to chse ldr over 1f out: led 1f out: forged ahd ins fnl f: kpt on: rdn out* **7/2**[1]
400- 2 nk **Blue Bounty**[213] 7451 3-9-7 60 TedDurcan 8 64+
(Mark H Tompkins) *t.k.h: hld up in tch in midfield: clsng whn nt clr run: snatched up and swtchd lft over 1f out: switching bk rt and stl n.m.r ins fnl f: gap opened and r.o strly fnl 100yds: wnt 2nd cl home* **5/1**[3]
2-30 3 ½ **Sexy Secret**[16] 2078 3-9-1 57 SimonPearce(3) 6 60
(Lydia Pearce) *in tch in midfield: rdn and effrt 2f out: led jst over 1f out: hdd ent fnl f: sltly outpcd 150yds out: rallied and kpt on again towards fin* **16/1**
0-40 4 ¾ **Starlite Jewel**[24] 1860 3-8-12 51 TomQueally 3 52
(George Margarson) *stdd s: t.k.h: hld up in tch in rr: clsd to chse ldrs whn hmpd and stmbld jst over 2f out: swtchd lft over 1f out: drvn to chse ldr 1f out: no ex fnl 100yds: lost 2 pls cl home* **20/1**
6-25 5 3 **Clear Focus (IRE)**[18] 2023 3-8-7 46 oh1 JackMitchell 7 39
(Brendan Powell) *t.k.h: chsd ldrs: wnt 2nd ent fnl 2f: rdn to ld over 1f out: sn hdd: wknd ins fnl f* **8/1**
3500 6 4 ½ **Maro**[31] 1626 3-8-0 46 oh1 (v) AdamMcLean(7) 9 27
(Derek Shaw) *led tl rdn and hdd over 1f out: btn 1f out: wknd ins fnl f* **66/1**
4043 7 1 **Meebo (IRE)**[4] 2397 3-9-5 58 KierenFallon 1 37
(J R Jenkins) *chsd ldrs: rdn and unable qck over 1f out: wknd fnl f* **4/1**[2]
000- 8 6 **No Second Thoughts (IRE)**[234] 6922 3-8-4 46 oh1 (p) RyanPowell(3) 11 9
(Michael Squance) *in tch in midfield: dropped towards rr and rdn over 2f out: sn struggling: wknd over 1f out* **50/1**
-465 9 1 ½ **Water For Life**[29] 1684 3-8-4 46 (p) RobertTart(3) 2 5
(Dave Morris) *in tch towards rr: hdwy 1/2-way: rdn and no hdwy ent fnl 2f: wknd over 1f out* **4/1**[2]
-026 10 ½ **Keep To The Beat**[112] 411 3-9-2 60 ShaneGray(5) 5 18
(Kevin Ryan) *chsd ldr tl ent fnl 2f: sn dropped out u.p: bhd fnl f* **14/1**
0060 11 14 **Appellez Baileys (FR)**[29] 1684 3-8-9 48 (p[1]) LiamKeniry 10
(Chris Dwyer) *dwlt: sn pushed and qckly rcvrd and chsd ldrs: wknd over 2f out: t.o fnl f* **22/1**
1m 29.73s (3.13) **Going Correction** +0.325s/f (Good) 11 Ran SP% **115.1**
Speed ratings (Par 97): **95,94,94,93,89 84,83,76,74,74 58**
CSF £19.74 CT £245.05 TOTE £2.90: £1.80, £1.90, £3.40; EX 31.10 Trifecta £947.70.
**Owner** Trevor Benton **Bred** Cheveley Park Stud Ltd **Trained** Newmarket, Suffolk
**FOCUS**
This ordinary 3yo handicap looked wide open. Once again the centre of the track was favoured and they got sorted out from the furlong marker.

## 2527 GOLD AND SILVER EXCHANGE H'CAP 7f 3y
3:15 (3:15) (Class 5) (0-75,73) 4-Y-O+ £2,587 (£770; £384; £192) Stalls Centre

Form RPR
44-6 1 **Comrade Bond**[130] 161 6-9-4 70 (p) TedDurcan 3 77
(Mark H Tompkins) *racd in centre: hld up in tch in rr: effrt to chal over 1f out: rdn to ld 1f out: kpt on u.p: drvn out* **2/1**[1]
-305 2 ½ **Afkar (IRE)**[81] 825 6-9-5 71 MickaelBarzalona 8 77
(Clive Brittain) *racd in centre: overall ldr tl over 5f out: chsd ldr tl rdn to ld again over 1f out: hdd 1f out: kpt on u.p: unable qck fnl 75yds* **5/2**[2]
31 3 nse **Glorious Star (IRE)**[15] 2095 4-9-6 72 TomQueally 5 78
(Ed Walker) *racd in centre: chsd ldr tl over 5f out: styd chsng ldrs: rdn and ev ch over 1f out: drvn and kpt on same pce ins fnl f* **10/3**[3]
4-06 4 22 **Two No Bids (IRE)**[24] 1864 4-8-7 64 (be) DannyBrock(5) 7 13
(Phil McEntee) *s.i.s: swtchd rt to r solo against stands' rail: racd freely: hdwy to ld over 5f out: rdn and hdd over 1f out: sn btn: bhd and eased ins fnl f* **4/1**
1m 28.6s (2.00) **Going Correction** +0.325s/f (Good) 4 Ran SP% **105.0**
Speed ratings (Par 103): **101,100,100,75**
CSF £6.74 TOTE £2.70; EX 6.90 Trifecta £15.50.
**Owner** Raceworld **Bred** Misses Wright, Lightowler And King **Trained** Newmarket, Suffolk
**FOCUS**
A moderate little handicap and a bunched three-way finish.

## 2528 TRAFALGAR RESTAURANT AT GREAT YARMOUTH RACECOURSE FILLIES' H'CAP 1m 3y
3:50 (3:50) (Class 4) (0-85,82) 4-Y-O+ £4,690 (£1,395; £697) Stalls Centre

Form RPR
1143 1 **Waveguide (IRE)**[18] 2032 5-8-2 70 LewisWalsh(7) 3 80
(David Simcock) *trckd rivals: rdn and effrt ent fnl 2f: led over 1f out: forged ahd ins fnl f: styd on: rdn out* **4/1**[3]
-532 2 2 **Saucy Minx (IRE)**[14] 2121 4-9-7 82 (b) SebSanders 4 87
(Amanda Perrett) *led tl over 4f out: chsd ldr: rdn and ev ch over 1f out: no ex and btn ins fnl f: wknd towards fin* **2/1**[2]
5-45 3 1 ¼ **Zeyran (IRE)**[20] 1956 5-9-2 80 RobertTart(3) 2 82
(Hugo Palmer) *t.k.h: w ldr tl led over 4f out: rdn over 2f out: hdd over 1f out and sn outpcd: plugged on same pce fnl f* **10/11**[1]
1m 43.26s (2.66) **Going Correction** +0.325s/f (Good) 3 Ran SP% **105.7**
Speed ratings (Par 102): **99,97,95**
CSF £10.64 TOTE £3.80; EX 6.70 Trifecta £6.20.
**Owner** Tick Tock Partnership **Bred** T Darcy & Vincent McCarthy **Trained** Newmarket, Suffolk
■ Stewards' Enquiry : Lewis Walsh two-day ban: used whip in incorrect place (Jun 8-9)
**FOCUS**
There was a fair enough pace on in this modest little fillies' handicap.

## 2529 JOHN KEMP 4 X 4 OF NORFOLK H'CAP 1m 3y
4:25 (4:25) (Class 5) (0-70,68) 4-Y-O+ £2,587 (£770; £384; £192) Stalls Centre

Form RPR
00-5 1 **Hot Mustard**[31] 1638 4-8-11 58 TomQueally 3 66
(Michael Bell) *stdd after s: hld up in tch in last pair: swtchd lft and hdwy 2f out: rdn to chal 1f out: led and edgd rt ins fnl f: styd on: rdn out* **10/1**
0-24 2 ¾ **Specialty (IRE)**[18] 2021 4-9-1 62 LiamKeniry 2 68
(Pam Sly) *t.k.h: led tl 1/2-way: styd chsng ldrs: rdn to ld again over 1f out: hdd and styd on same pce ins fnl f* **7/2**[3]
5524 3 nk **Prince Of Burma (IRE)**[23] 1876 6-9-2 66 (v) DeclanBates(3) 1 72
(David Evans) *v.s.a: in tch in rr: hdwy to chse ldrs and rdn 2f out: nt clr run over 1f out: swtchd lft ins fnl f: styd on same pce fnl 100yds* **12/1**
3311 4 2 ½ **Kasbhom**[32] 1613 4-9-7 68 (tp) WilliamCarson 5 68
(Anthony Carson) *t.k.h: chsd ldr tl 1/2-way: styd prom: rdn to ld 2f out: edgd lft and hdd over 1f out: wknd ins fnl f* **3/1**[1]
0-45 5 2 **Keep The Secret**[26] 1771 4-9-1 62 TedDurcan 7 59
(William Knight) *taken down early: in tch in midfield: rdn and effrt against stands' rail over 1f out: no imp and btn ins fnl f: eased wl ins fnl f* **3/1**[1]
4001 6 4 ½ **My Manekineko**[31] 1638 5-9-2 63 KierenFallon 4 50
(J R Jenkins) *in tch in midfield: hdwy to ld 1/2-way: rdn and hdd 2f out: losing pl whn hmpd over 1f out: wknd 1f out* **10/3**[2]
1m 42.49s (1.89) **Going Correction** +0.325s/f (Good) 6 Ran SP% **112.1**
Speed ratings (Par 103): **103,102,101,99,97 92**
CSF £44.13 TOTE £10.30: £4.90, £2.80; EX 60.30 Trifecta £365.50.
**Owner** Mrs G Rowland-Clark **Bred** Mrs F A Veasey **Trained** Newmarket, Suffolk
**FOCUS**
A tight handicap. Two came stands' side away from the centre quartet before they merged nearing 2f out and it produced a bunched finish.

## 2530 HOLIDAYS ON NORFOLK BROADS H'CAP (BOBIS RACE) 1m 3f 101y
5:00 (5:00) (Class 4) (0-85,84) 3-Y-O £4,690 (£1,395; £697) Stalls Low

Form RPR
3-43 1 **Notarised**[7] 2303 3-8-10 76 MichaelJMMurphy(3) 2 87
(Mark Johnston) *trckd rivals: wnt 2nd 5f out: upsides ldr and gng best 2f out: rdn to ld over 1f out: rdn clr ins fnl f: r.o wl: readily* **11/10**[1]
2-21 2 5 **Solidarity**[18] 2009 3-9-7 84 MickaelBarzalona 3 86
(Charlie Appleby) *led: rdn over 2f out: drvn and hdd over 1f out: no ex and btn ins fnl f: wknd fnl 100yds* **2/1**[2]

521 3 23 **Gallic Destiny (IRE)**16 2081 3-8-13 76 ........ LiamKeniry 4 48
(Andrew Balding) *chsd ldr tl 5f out: rdn over 3f out: sn struggling and btn: wl bhd and eased ins fnl f* 11/4[3]

2m 28.12s (-0.58) **Going Correction** 0.0s/f (Good) 3 Ran SP% **107.6**
Speed ratings (Par 101): **102,98,81**
CSF £3.51 TOTE £1.80; EX 3.60 Trifecta £3.40.
**Owner** Hugh Hart **Bred** Mrs P Hart **Trained** Middleham Moor, N Yorks

**FOCUS**
This fair 3yo handicap was anything but tactical as they went a solid pace.

## 2531 CONFERENCES AT GREAT YARMOUTH RACECOURSE H'CAP 1m 6f 17y
5:35 (5:35) (Class 6) (0-60,60) 4-Y-O+ £1,940 (£577; £288; £144) Stalls High

Form RPR

0-61 1 **Camelopardalis**24 1865 5-9-1 59 ........ DannyBrock(5) 5 70+
(Philip McBride) *chsd ldr tl led 6f out: clr 5f out: rdn ent fnl 2f: stl 3 l clr and drvn 1f out: a hoding on: rdn out* 2/1[1]

-330 2 1 **Ice Apple**85 759 6-8-5 47 ........ MichaelJMMurphy(3) 6 53
(John E Long) *racd in last pair: rdn and effrt to go 3rd over 2f out: kpt on u.p fnl f: wnt 2nd nr fin: nvr getting to wnr* 4/1[3]

0022 3 ½ **Hazzaat (IRE)**27 1740 4-9-7 60 ........ JimmyQuinn 7 65
(Neil King) *stdd s: hld up in last pair: hdwy 4f out: chsd clr wnr over 2f out: rdn 2f out: kpt on u.p fnl f: lost 2nd nr fin* 5/1

2410 4 3¼ **Dr Finley (IRE)**22 1895 7-9-0 56 ........ (v) SimonPearce(3) 2 57
(Lydia Pearce) *chsd ldrs: drvn 3f out: 4th and looked wl hld over 1f out: plugged on fnl f* 8/1

5534 5 2¾ **Willow Island (IRE)**16 1895 5-8-4 46 oh1 ........ (t) DeclanBates(3) 8 43
(David Evans) *in tch in midfield: rdn 4f out: no prog after: wl hld over 1f out* 20/1

30/2 6 2¼ **Bute Street**21 1916 9-9-7 60 ........ LiamKeniry 4 54
(Chris Gordon) *led tl 6f out: rdn 3f out: lost 2nd and btn over 1f out: bhd 1f out* 11/4[2]

3m 8.62s (1.02) **Going Correction** 0.0s/f (Good) 6 Ran SP% **112.5**
Speed ratings (Par 101): **97,96,96,94,92 91**
CSF £10.41 CT £33.32 TOTE £3.30: £2.00, £1.50; EX 10.00 Trifecta £45.70.
**Owner** Budgett, Fleming, Hamilton **Bred** Miss Harriet Budgett **Trained** Newmarket, Suffolk

**FOCUS**
A weak staying handicap run at a proper gallop.
T/Plt: £297.70 to a £1 stake. Pool: £65,380.39 - 160.28 winning units. T/Qpdt: £119.40 to a £1 stake. Pool: £3728.21 - 23.10 winning units. SP

2532 - 2539a (Foreign Racing) - See Raceform Interactive

# 2230 BEVERLEY (R-H)
Saturday, May 24

**OFFICIAL GOING: Good to soft**
Wind: Moderate behind Weather: Heavy cloud and rain

## 2540 VERY BRITISH SING SONG AFTER RACING H'CAP 1m 1f 207y
2:00 (2:00) (Class 5) (0-75,75) 4-Y-O+ £3,408 (£1,006; £503) Stalls Low

Form RPR

00-5 1 **Maybeme**30 1660 8-8-10 64 ........ (p) AndrewElliott 6 78
(Neville Bycroft) *hld up and bhd: swtchd lft to outer and gd hdwy over 2f out: rdn over 1f out: styng on whn edgd rt jst over 1f out: led ins fnl f: sn clr* 14/1

41-5 2 4½ **Thankyou Very Much**25 1857 4-8-6 63 ........ RobertTart(3) 2 68
(James Bethell) *towards rr whn n.m.r and sltly hmpd sn after s: in rr tl hdwy on inner over 2f out: rdn to chse ldr over 1f out: drvn and kpt on fnl f* 9/2[2]

124 3 ¾ **Genius Boy**14 2168 4-9-3 71 ........ PaulMulrennan 4 75
(James Tate) *set stdy pce: qcknd over 4f out: pushed clr wl over 2f out: rdn wl over 1f out: hdd ins fnl f: sn one pce* 13/8[1]

0-00 4 7 **Artful Prince**14 2162 4-9-7 75 ........ (b) TonyHamilton 1 66
(James Given) *in tch: hdwy 4f out: rdn along on outer 2f out: drvn and one pce whn n.m.r appr fnl f* 10/1

26-5 5 4 **Brockfield**67 1003 8-8-11 65 ........ DavidAllan 5 48
(Mel Brittain) *trckd ldrs: hdwy to chse ldr 3f out: rdn 2f out: sn drvn and grad wknd* 8/1

44-0 6 ¾ **Saint Thomas (IRE)**30 1660 7-8-13 67 ........ PaddyAspell 7 49
(John Mackie) *trckd ldrs: hdwy 3f out: rdn along over 2f out: sn drvn and wknd over 1f out* 7/1[3]

0/0- 7 nk **Quite Sparky**365 2615 7-8-6 65 ........ JacobButterfield(5) 3 46
(Mike Sowersby) *in tch on inner: pushed along over 4f out: rdn 3f out: sn wknd* 66/1

10-0 8 3½ **Spin Cast**14 2169 6-9-3 71 ........ PaulPickard 10 45
(Brian Ellison) *hld up: a towards rr* 16/1

-211 9 34 **Dubai Celebration**58 1134 6-9-5 73 ........ LiamKeniry 9
(Julie Camacho) *prom: cl up 1/2-way: rdn along over 3f out and sn wknd* 12/1

1305 10 11 **Thatchmaster (USA)**22 1926 4-9-3 71 ........ SilvestreDeSousa 8
(Mark Johnston) *in tch: rdn along over 4f out: sn wknd* 12/1

2m 8.12s (1.12) **Going Correction** +0.225s/f (Good) 10 Ran SP% **118.4**
Speed ratings (Par 103): **104,100,99,94,91 90,90,87,60,51**
CSF £77.20 CT £161.41 TOTE £18.70: £3.70, £1.50, £1.80; EX 120.80 Trifecta £1064.60.
**Owner** Mrs J Dickinson **Bred** Harts Farm And Stud **Trained** Norton, N Yorks

**FOCUS**
Rail around bottom bend moved to fresh and distances on Round course increased by 21yds. The opening contest was a fair handicap for older horses in which they went an honest gallop on good to soft ground. Improvement from the winner, the form taken at something like face value.

## 2541 COTTINGHAM PARKS GOLF AND LEISURE CLUB MEDIAN AUCTION MAIDEN STKS 5f
2:30 (2:30) (Class 5) 2-Y-O £3,234 (£962; £481; £240) Stalls Low

Form RPR

1 **Diamond Creek (IRE)** 2-9-0 0 ........ TonyHamilton 1 77+
(Richard Fahey) *mde most: rdn over 1f out: green and edgd lft ins fnl f: kpt on wl towards fin* 4/1[1]

42 2 nk **Make On Madam (IRE)**18 2051 2-9-0 0 ........ TomEaves 2 76
(Brian Ellison) *a cl up: effrt to chal over 1f out and sn rdn: drvn ins fnl f: kpt on wl towards fin: jst hld* 4/1[1]

3 4½ **Studio Star** 2-9-0 0 ........ JacobButterfield(5) 4 64
(Ollie Pears) *trckd ldrs on inner: hdwy 2f out: sn rdn: chsd ldng pair ent fnl f: kpt on* 25/1

4 4 1½ **Izzthatright (IRE)**11 2231 2-9-0 0 ........ ShelleyBirkett(5) 5 59
(Nigel Tinkler) *in tch: pushed along and hdwy 2f out: sn rdn and kpt on fnl f* 8/1[3]

0 5 1½ **Clampdown**19 2007 2-9-5 0 ........ PaulMulrennan 6 54
(James Tate) *chsd ldng pair: cl up 1/2-way: rdn along wl over 1f out and grad wknd* 9/1

6 1¾ **Tachophobia** 2-9-5 0 ........ ChrisCatlin 9 47+
(Richard Fahey) *towards rr: pushed along and green 1/2-way: styd on appr fnl f* 10/1

7 1¾ **Pillar Box (IRE)** 2-9-5 0 ........ LiamKeniry 8 41
(William Haggas) *chsd ldrs on outer: rdn along 1/2-way: wknd wl over 1f out* 5/1[2]

6 8 4 **Fazenda's Girl**7 2349 2-9-0 0 ........ DavidAllan 7 22
(Michael Easterby) *a towards rr* 33/1

9 2 **Jubilee Spirit** 2-9-2 0 ........ RobertTart(3) 10 19+
(Geoffrey Oldroyd) *wnt lft s: a bhd* 25/1

10 3¾ **Yorkie Talkie (IRE)** 2-9-5 0 ........ SilvestreDeSousa 3 6
(Mark Johnston) *chsd ldrs: rdn along 1/2-way: sn wknd* 4/1[1]

1m 5.41s (1.91) **Going Correction** +0.175s/f (Good) 10 Ran SP% **117.5**
Speed ratings (Par 93): **91,90,83,80,78 75,72,66,63,57**
CSF £19.50 TOTE £5.90: £1.70, £1.70, £4.50; EX 21.30 Trifecta £585.20.
**Owner** Middleham Park Racing CVII & Partner **Bred** Oliver Donlon **Trained** Musley Bank, N Yorks

**FOCUS**
A modest juvenile sprint maiden, but the winner and the form in general are likely to rate higher.

## 2542 HAPPY BIRTHDAY GRAHAM HALLETT FILLIES' H'CAP 5f
3:05 (3:05) (Class 5) (0-75,72) 4-Y-O+ £3,234 (£962; £481; £240) Stalls Low

Form RPR

6-25 1 **Willbeme**7 2332 6-9-6 71 ........ SilvestreDeSousa 2 88
(Neville Bycroft) *chsd ldr on inner: smooth hdwy to chal 2f out: sn led: rdn clr ent fnl f: kpt on strly* 1/1[1]

-223 2 5 **Barbs Princess**110 453 4-9-6 71 ........ ChrisCatlin 5 70
(Charles Hills) *chsd ldrs: rdn along and sltly outpcd 1/2-way: hdwy wl over 1f out: styd on u.p to take 2nd ins fnl f: no ch w wnr* 8/1

6310 3 4 **Six Wives**7 2350 7-9-0 72 ........ (p) MatthewHopkins(7) 6 57
(Scott Dixon) *led: rdn along 2f out: sn hdd and drvn: wknd appr fnl f* 13/2[3]

3410 4 shd **Dodina (IRE)**25 1843 4-9-2 67 ........ (p) TomEaves 7 51
(Brian Ellison) *chsd ldrs: rdn 2f out: drvn wl over 1f out and sn one pce* 9/1

35-6 5 ½ **Ingenti**25 1843 6-8-11 67 ........ KevinStott(5) 8 49
(Christopher Wilson) *hld up in tch: effrt and sme hdwy 2f out: sn rdn: kpt on fnl f: n.d* 9/2[2]

6-31 6 ½ **Foreign Rhythm (IRE)**33 1604 9-8-13 64 ........ PaulMulrennan 4 45
(Ron Barr) *a towards rr* 14/1

340- 7 6 **Charlemagne Diva**177 8082 4-8-5 59 ........ BillyCray(3) 3 18
(Richard Guest) *chsd ldr: rdn along 1/2-way: sn wknd* 25/1

1m 3.91s (0.41) **Going Correction** +0.175s/f (Good) 7 Ran SP% **113.1**
Speed ratings (Par 100): **103,95,88,88,87 86,77**
CSF £9.66 CT £34.64 TOTE £1.80: £1.50, £3.10; EX 8.50 Trifecta £27.40.
**Owner** P D Burrow **Bred** Mrs J M Russell **Trained** Norton, N Yorks

**FOCUS**
Only fillies' form, and little depth to this. The winner seems back to her best.

## 2543 BRIAN YEARDLEY CONTINENTAL TWO YEAR OLD TROPHY CONDITIONS STKS (C&G) (BOBIS RACE) 5f
3:40 (3:40) (Class 2) 2-Y-O
£9,337 (£2,796; £1,398; £699; £349; £175) Stalls Low

Form RPR

21 1 **Midterm Break (IRE)**24 1889 2-9-0 0 ........ DavidAllan 4 88+
(David Barron) *cl up: chal over 2f out: rdn to ld wl over 1f out: clr ins fnl f: kpt on* 11/4[1]

51 2 2 **Vimy Ridge**12 2214 2-9-0 0 ........ TonyHamilton 5 81+
(Richard Fahey) *sn rdn along outpcd in rr: hdwy wl over 1f out: rdn and styd on wl fnl f: nrst fin* 7/1

1 3 ½ **Sea Wolf (IRE)**28 1712 2-9-2 0 ........ LiamKeniry 6 81
(Michael Dods) *sn rdn along and outpcd in rr: hdwy 2f out: rdn to chse ldng pair over 1f out: kpt on fnl f: nrst fin* 10/1

1 4 3¼ **Northgate Lad (IRE)**11 2231 2-9-2 0 ........ TomEaves 1 69
(Brian Ellison) *led: jnd and rdn over 2f out: hdd wl over 1f out: sn drvn and wknd* 7/2[2]

1 5 1½ **Firgrove Bridge (IRE)**24 1879 2-9-2 0 ........ PaulMulrennan 2 64
(Kevin Ryan) *chsd ldrs: rdn along over 2f out: drvn and wknd wl over 1f out* 11/2[3]

2 6 7 **Denzille Lane (IRE)**8 2291 2-8-12 0 ........ SilvestreDeSousa 3 35
(Mark Johnston) *prom: rdn along 1/2-way: sn wknd* 7/2[2]

5331 7 4½ **Jersey Bull (IRE)**6 2359 2-9-2 0 ........ SamHitchcott 7 23
(Mick Channon) *in tch: rdn along bef 1/2-way: sn outpcd and bhd* 14/1

1m 3.87s (0.37) **Going Correction** +0.175s/f (Good) 7 Ran SP% **114.8**
Speed ratings (Par 99): **104,100,100,94,92 81,74**
CSF £22.60 TOTE £4.20: £3.30, £3.10; EX 22.10 Trifecta £150.50.
**Owner** Laurence O'Kane **Bred** J O'Connor **Trained** Maunby, N Yorks

**FOCUS**
The feature race on the card, and the form is rated up to the race average. The first two are capable of better.

## 2544 BRITISH STALLION STUDS BRANTINGHAM EBF CONDITIONS STKS (BOBIS RACE) 1m 100y
4:15 (4:15) (Class 4) 3-Y-O £6,225 (£1,864; £932; £466) Stalls Low

Form RPR

1024 1 **Crowdmania**15 2111 3-8-12 86 ........ PaulMulrennan 2 91
(Mark Johnston) *mde all: rdn clr over 2f out: drvn and styd on strly fnl f* 7/1[3]

1 2 2¼ **Basem**37 1529 3-9-1 0 ........ SilvestreDeSousa 1 89
(Saeed bin Suroor) *dwlt sltly: sn trcking ldng pair: hdwy to chse wnr over 2f out: rdn and edgd rt over 1f out: sn drvn and no imp fnl f* 4/9[1]

5-6 3 3¾ **Surety (IRE)**33 1612 3-8-12 0 ........ ChrisCatlin 5 77?
(Clive Brittain) *trckd ldrs: pushed along over 3f out: rdn along over 2f out: sn one pce* 28/1

1163 4 1 **Pool House**36 1555 3-8-12 99 ........ LiamKeniry 4 75
(Andrew Balding) *trckd wnr: pushed along 3f out: rdn over 2f out: sn drvn and wknd* 11/4[2]

1m 49.17s (1.57) **Going Correction** +0.225s/f (Good) 4 Ran SP% **111.9**
Speed ratings (Par 101): **101,98,95,94**
CSF £11.41 TOTE £8.20; EX 16.00 Trifecta £42.40.
**Owner** Sheikh Hamdan bin Mohammed Al Maktoum **Bred** Car Colston Hall Stud **Trained** Middleham Moor, N Yorks

**FOCUS**
A decent small-field 3yo conditions stakes in which they went a steady gallop. The form is rated around the winner, who made all.

## 2545 VERY BRITISH RACEDAY STKS (H'CAP) 7f 100y
4:50 (4:50) (Class 5) (0-70,70) 3-Y-O £3,234 (£962; £481; £240) Stalls Low

Form RPR
10-0 1 **Spiceupyourlife (IRE)**[16] 2090 3-9-7 **70** TonyHamilton 5 81
(Richard Fahey) *hld up in rr: hdwy over 2f out: swtchd lft wl over 1f out: sn rdn to chse ldr over 1f out: led ins fnl f: kpt on strly* **11/4**[2]
40-5 2 2 3/4 **Penina (IRE)**[12] 2218 3-9-1 **64** PaulPickard 3 68
(Brian Ellison) *led: rdn along 2f out: drvn over 1f out: hdd ins fnl f: kpt on same pce* **5/1**[3]
0-41 3 7 **Sooqaan**[14] 2165 3-8-12 **61** DavidAllan 1 48
(Mel Brittain) *trckd ldrs: hdwy on inner over 2f out: rdn wl over 1f out: sn one pce* **7/4**[1]
0530 4 7 **Marlismamma (FR)**[14] 2165 3-8-4 **56** oh4 (v) JulieBurke(3) 4 25
(David O'Meara) *chsd ldr: rdn along wl over 2f out: drvn wl over 1f out: sn wknd* **11/1**
4036 5 3 1/4 **Tarrafal (IRE)**[20] 1969 3-9-2 **65** SilvestreDeSousa 6 26
(Mark Johnston) *towards rr: effrt on outer wl over 2f out: sn rdn and nvr a factor* **7/1**
253 6 12 **Sleipnir**[66] 1008 3-9-7 **70** (b[1]) LiamKeniry 8
(Philip Hide) *chsd ldng pair on outer: rdn along wl over 2f out: sn wknd* **6/1**

1m 36.56s (2.76) **Going Correction** +0.225s/f (Good) **6 Ran SP% 114.8**
Speed ratings (Par 99): **93,89,81,73,70 56**
CSF £17.17 CT £29.57 TOTE £5.60: £2.70, £4.40; EX 17.00 Trifecta £64.00.
**Owner** Diamond Racing Ltd **Bred** Kildaragh Stud **Trained** Musley Bank, N Yorks

**FOCUS**
A modest 3yo handicap in which they went an honest gallop. The form is rated around the runner-up.

## 2546 RACING UK ON SKY 432 H'CAP 1m 100y
5:25 (5:25) (Class 5) (0-70,68) 4-Y-0+ £3,234 (£962; £481; £240) Stalls Low

Form RPR
2643 1 **Ellaal**[8] 2293 5-9-1 **62** PaulMulrennan 7 71
(Ruth Carr) *trckd ldrs: hdwy 2f out: rdn over 1f out: chal ent fnl f: drvn to ld last 100yds: kpt on* **8/1**
5543 2 1 1/4 **Ewell Place (IRE)**[28] 1717 5-9-3 **64** DavidNolan 3 70
(Richard Fahey) *led: pushed along over 2f out: rdn wl over 1f out: drvn ent fnl f: hdd and no ex last 100yds* **11/4**[1]
140- 3 hd **Joyful Sound (IRE)**[322] 4052 6-8-11 **58** PaulPickard 4 63
(Brian Ellison) *in rr: gd hdwy on outer 2f out: rdn to chse ldrs over 1f out: drvn to chal and ev ch whn hung rt wl ins fnl f: one pce after* **7/1**[3]
0031 4 1 1/4 **Roger Thorpe**[16] 2092 5-8-11 **65** DavidParkes(7) 10 67
(Deborah Sanderson) *hld up towards rr: hdwy over 2f out: rdn to chse ldrs appr fnl f: drvn and no imp towards fin* **16/1**
4-60 5 3 1/4 **Space War**[14] 2169 7-9-3 **64** SamHitchcott 1 59
(Michael Easterby) *trckd ldrs on inner: effrt 2f out: nt clr run over 1f out and again ent fnl f: wknd towards fin* **10/1**
00-0 6 2 1/2 **Kuwait Star**[28] 1718 5-9-6 **67** TonyHamilton 8 56
(Michael Herrington) *prom: rdn along 2f out: drvn and wknd appr fnl f* **20/1**
1264 7 3/4 **Icy Blue**[14] 2171 6-8-10 **62** (p) JacobButterfield(5) 11 50
(Richard Whitaker) *in tch: hdwy to chse ldrs 2f out: sn rdn and wknd appr fnl f* **9/1**
0-02 8 1 3/4 **Juvenal (IRE)**[19] 2019 5-9-7 **68** (p) TomEaves 6 52
(Geoffrey Harker) *dwlt: a towards rr* **7/1**[3]
5-04 9 shd **Seldom (IRE)**[4] 2426 8-8-10 **57** DavidAllan 2 40
(Mel Brittain) *hld up towards rr: hdwy over 2f out: rdn along wl over 1f out: n.d* **10/1**
006- 10 7 **Last Destination (IRE)**[309] 4469 6-8-2 **54** oh6 ShelleyBirkett(5) 9 21
(Nigel Tinkler) *a towards rr* **28/1**
4025 11 47 **Docofthebay (IRE)**[15] 2131 10-9-4 **65** SilvestreDeSousa 5
(Scott Dixon) *chsd ldr: rdn along wl over 2f out: sn lost pl and bhd whn virtually p.u fnl f: dismntd after line* **6/1**[2]

1m 50.0s (2.40) **Going Correction** +0.225s/f (Good) **11 Ran SP% 119.3**
Speed ratings (Par 103): **97,95,95,94,91 88,87,86,85,78 31**
CSF £30.68 CT £167.25 TOTE £7.50: £3.20, £1.40, £2.50; EX 49.10 Trifecta £174.80.
**Owner** The Bottom Liners & Paul Saxton **Bred** W And R Barnett Ltd **Trained** Huby, N Yorks

**FOCUS**
The concluding contest was a modest handicap for older horses in which there was a contested early lead. The winner's best form so far for this yard.
T/Plt: £593.00 to a £1 stake. Pool of £34262.26 - 42.17 winning tickets. T/Qpdt: £162.00 to a £1 stake. Pool of £2746.67 - 12.54 winning tickets. JR

# 2051 CATTERICK (L-H)
Saturday, May 24

**OFFICIAL GOING: Good to soft (soft in places) changing to soft (good to soft in places) after race 1 (2.15)**
Wind: Fresh, across Weather: Wet

## 2547 £15MILLION TOTESCOOP6 TODAY CLASSIFIED CLAIMING STKS 1m 3f 214y
2:15 (2:16) (Class 6) 4-Y-0+ £2,726 (£805; £402) Stalls Low

Form RPR
5163 1 **Incendo**[5] 2394 8-8-13 72 (v) PJMcDonald 3 71
(Ian Williams) *s.i.s: hld up in tch: hdwy over 2f out: rdn to chse ldr appr fnl f: kpt on to ld 75yds out* **5/2**[3]
0-13 2 1 1/4 **Ever Fortune (USA)**[19] 2016 5-8-10 72 MeganCarberry(7) 7 73
(Brian Ellison) *trckd ldr: rdn over 2f out: led over 1f out: hdd 75yds out: no ex* **2/1**[1]
0623 3 1 1/2 **Gran Maestro (USA)**[7] 2327 5-9-7 70 (b) JamesSullivan 5 76
(Ruth Carr) *led: rdn whn hdd over 1f out: keeping on and 3/4 l down in dispute of 2nd whn sltly short of room on rail 100yds out: nt rcvr* **9/4**[2]
40-3 4 hd **Ethics Girl (IRE)**[18] 2052 8-8-12 70 (t) RoystonFfrench 6 65
(John Berry) *trckd ldr: rdn and outpcd over 2f out: plugged on fnl f* **6/1**

2m 43.5s (4.60) **Going Correction** +0.50s/f (Yiel) **4 Ran SP% 107.0**
Speed ratings (Par 101): **104,103,102,102**
CSF £7.64 TOTE £2.90; EX 9.00 Trifecta £12.10.
**Owner** Ian Williams **Bred** London Thoroughbred Services Ltd **Trained** Portway, Worcs
■ Stewards' Enquiry : Megan Carberry one-day ban: careless riding (Jun 8)

**FOCUS**
The ground was changed to soft, good to soft in places after the opener. Just the four remained after the defections and it was run at a steady gallop. The third is the key to the level.

## 2548 TOTESCOOP6 THE £2 LIFE CHANGING BET H'CAP 7f
2:50 (2:51) (Class 3) (0-90,90) 4-Y-0+ £12,938 (£3,850; £1,924; £962) Stalls Low

Form RPR
4301 1 **Conry (IRE)**[18] 2054 8-8-12 **81** StevieDonohoe 3 90
(Ian Williams) *hld up: rdn over 2f out: hdwy over 1f out: r.o wl: led towards fin* **17/2**
40-4 2 hd **Laffan (IRE)**[15] 2113 5-9-0 **90** RachelRichardson(7) 6 98
(Tim Easterby) *midfield: rdn and hdwy over 2f out: led ins fnl f: kpt on: hdd towards fin* **8/1**[3]
0-45 3 3/4 **Green Howard**[15] 2136 6-8-9 **81** NeilFarley(3) 8 88
(Robin Bastiman) *dwlt: sn in midfield: rdn over 3f out: chsd ldrs over 1f out: kpt on* **6/1**[1]
04-4 4 1 1/4 **Alejandro (IRE)**[12] 2202 5-9-4 **87** DavidNolan 4 90
(David O'Meara) *chsd ldrs: rdn over 3f out: kpt on* **11/1**
0656 5 shd **Joe Eile (IRE)**[6] 2362 6-8-11 **87** JoeDoyle(7) 7 90
(John Quinn) *midfield: rdn and hdwy on outer 2f out: ev ch ins fnl f: wknd fnl 50yds* **17/2**
440- 6 1/2 **Mujazif (IRE)**[223] 7223 4-9-6 **89** BarryMcHugh 13 91
(David Nicholls) *hld up: rdn over 2f out: kpt on fnl f: nrst fin* **33/1**
5652 7 1 1/2 **Hadaj**[15] 2136 5-8-8 **84** JackGarritty(7) 11 82
(Ruth Carr) *hld up: rdn and sme hdwy whn sltly short of room jst ins fnl f: kpt on but no ch after* **15/2**[2]
0040 8 hd **Clockmaker (IRE)**[21] 1943 8-9-6 **89** [1] JamesSullivan 15 86
(Conor Dore) *hld up: rdn over 2f out: kpt on fnl f: nvr threatened* **25/1**
5350 9 1 1/2 **Showboating (IRE)**[21] 1958 6-9-6 **89** (tp) StephenCraine 12 82
(Alan McCabe) *dwlt: hld up: nvr threatened* **10/1**
0056 10 1 1/4 **Dr Red Eye**[15] 2117 6-8-13 **82** (p) AndrewMullen 2 72
(Scott Dixon) *led for 1f: trckd ldr: rdn to ld again over 1f out: hdd ins fnl f: wknd* **12/1**
0-30 11 3/4 **Wannabe King**[21] 1958 8-9-5 **88** (v) PJMcDonald 9 76
(Geoffrey Harker) *chsd ldrs: rdn 3f out: ev ch over 1f out: wknd ins fnl f* **33/1**
0-00 12 3 3/4 **Evanescent (IRE)**[31] 1646 5-8-8 **80** IanBrennan(3) 14 58
(John Quinn) *led after 1f: rdn over 2f out: hdd over 1f out: wknd* **50/1**
-031 13 nse **Just Paul (IRE)**[22] 1928 4-8-12 **81** RussKennemore 5 59
(Philip Kirby) *midfield on inner: rdn over 2f out: wknd over 1f out* **6/1**[1]
-620 P **Our Boy Jack (IRE)**[21] 1957 5-8-8 **80** (p) GeorgeChaloner(3) 10
(Richard Fahey) *chsd ldrs: rdn and lost pl 4f out: sn wknd and eased: p.u over 1f out* **16/1**

1m 29.66s (2.66) **Going Correction** +0.575s/f (Yiel) **14 Ran SP% 115.2**
Speed ratings (Par 107): **107,106,105,104,104 103,102,101,100,98 97,93,93,**
CSF £69.19 CT £440.88 TOTE £8.90: £2.50, £2.70, £2.50; EX 86.20 Trifecta £218.80.
**Owner** Hickesh Parmar **Bred** Shay White **Trained** Portway, Worcs
■ Stewards' Enquiry : Joe Doyle four-day ban: used whip above permitted level (Jun 8-10 & one-day remedial training).

**FOCUS**
A competitive handicap that was run at a good gallop and set up for the closers. The form makes a fair bit of sense.

## 2549 FOLLOW SCOOP6 AT TOTEPOOLLIVEINFO.COM H'CAP 7f
3:25 (3:25) (Class 4) (0-80,80) 4-Y-0+ £6,817 (£2,013; £1,007) Stalls Low

Form RPR
0-22 1 **Johnny Cavagin**[23] 1903 5-9-5 **78** (t) StevieDonohoe 10 91
(Richard Guest) *dwlt: hld up: smooth hdwy on outer fr over 2f out: led appr fnl f: rdn clr* **9/2**[2]
0-35 2 3 3/4 **Powerful Presence (IRE)**[22] 1928 8-9-7 **80** DavidNolan 14 84
(David O'Meara) *chsd ldrs: rdn and ev ch over 1f out: kpt on but no ch w wnr fnl f* **12/1**
4444 3 1 1/4 **Beckermet (IRE)**[14] 2166 12-8-7 **66** oh1 JamesSullivan 8 66
(Ruth Carr) *hld up: rdn over 3f out: kpt on fr over 1f out: wnt 3rd nr fin* **20/1**
-221 4 1/2 **Khelman (IRE)**[20] 1967 4-9-2 **78** (p) GeorgeChaloner(3) 2 77
(Richard Fahey) *chsd ldrs: rdn 3f out: one pce fnl f: lost 3rd nr fin* **4/1**[1]
2034 5 1 1/2 **Solar Spirit (IRE)**[1] 2522 9-9-1 **77** IanBrennan(3) 3 72
(Tracy Waggott) *midfield: smooth hdwy over 2f out: n.m.r and swtchd rt over 1f out: sn rdn and no imp* **17/2**
0253 6 3/4 **Millkwood**[14] 2169 4-9-4 **77** (p[1]) PJMcDonald 4 70
(John Davies) *dwlt: hld up: rdn over 3f out: kpt on fnl f: nvr threatened* **11/2**[3]
0320 7 hd **Piceno (IRE)**[7] 2351 6-9-7 **80** (p) AndrewMullen 1 73
(Scott Dixon) *led narrowly: rdn over 2f out: hdd appr fnl f: wknd* **12/1**
5-10 8 nk **Celtic Sixpence (IRE)**[7] 2351 6-9-4 **77** (p) MichaelStainton 13 69
(Nick Kent) *w ldr: rdn over 2f out: wknd fnl f* **33/1**
0-03 9 1 3/4 **Day Of The Eagle (IRE)**[19] 2019 8-8-10 **69** BarryMcHugh 6 56
(Michael Easterby) *midfield: rdn and outpcd over 3f out: nvr threatened* **9/1**
-000 10 2 1/2 **Snow Bay**[18] 2054 8-8-11 **75** ShirleyTeasdale(5) 11 56
(Paul Midgley) *slowly away: sn in midfield on outer: rdn over 2f out: wknd over 1f out* **28/1**
-300 11 shd **Mystical Moment**[14] 2169 4-8-3 **67** (p) ShaneGray(5) 12 48
(Edwin Tuer) *hld up: rdn over 3f out: nvr threatened* **28/1**
1606 12 3 1/4 **Bogsnog (IRE)**[18] 2054 4-9-0 **73** RoystonFfrench 9 45
(Kristin Stubbs) *chsd ldrs: wknd over 1f out* **33/1**

1m 29.97s (2.97) **Going Correction** +0.575s/f (Yiel) **12 Ran SP% 119.3**
Speed ratings (Par 105): **106,101,100,99,98 97,96,96,94,91 91,87**
CSF £53.42 CT £993.74 TOTE £6.60: £1.70, £4.30, £4.30; EX 73.10 Trifecta £965.10.
**Owner** A Bell **Bred** A Bell **Trained** Wetherby, W Yorks

**FOCUS**
Another open handicap run at a decent gallop. The form is perhaps worth a bit more at face value.

## 2550 TOTEEXACTA PICK THE 1 2 H'CAP 1m 7f 177y
4:00 (4:00) (Class 5) (0-70,67) 4-Y-0+ £3,234 (£962; £481; £240) Stalls Low

Form RPR
0-41 1 **Miss Macnamara (IRE)**[18] 2055 5-9-10 **67** PJMcDonald 4 78+
(Martin Todhunter) *in tch: smooth hdwy 3f out: led over 1f out: pushed clr fnl f* **11/10**[1]
1/02 2 3 **Cool Baranca (GER)**[3] 2455 8-8-3 **51** EmmaSayer(5) 7 57
(Dianne Sayer) *hld up in rr: rdn and hdwy over 2f out: wnt 2nd ins fnl f: kpt on but no ch w wnr* **7/1**[3]
-062 3 1/2 **Summerlea (IRE)**[4] 2424 8-8-2 **48** oh2 (b) NeilFarley(3) 5 53
(Micky Hammond) *hld up in tch: rdn over 2f out: kpt on* **11/4**[2]

4220 **4** 2 3/4 **Carlanda (FR)**[60] 1091 4-9-7 **66**....[1] AndrewMullen 8 68
(Michael Appleby) *slowly away: sn trckd ldr: led 4f out: rdn whn hdd over 1f out: wknd ins fnl f* **9/1**

6-00 **5** 6 **Madrasa (IRE)**[12] 2216 6-9-10 **67**.... JamesSullivan 3 62
(Keith Reveley) *trckd ldrs: pushed along 4f out: wknd over 1f out* **10/1**

00 **6** 26 **Chaparella (IRE)**[12] 2216 4-8-6 **54**.... MichaelJMMurphy(3) 6 18
(Mark Johnston) *led: hdd 4f out: wknd over 2f out* **20/1**

3m 49.11s (17.11) **Going Correction** +0.65s/f (Yiel)
**WFA** 4 from 5yo+ 2lb **6** Ran SP% **110.6**
Speed ratings (Par 103): **83,81,81,79,76 63**
CSF £9.22 CT £15.79 TOTE £1.70: £1.10, £6.60; EX 8.30 Trifecta £13.30.

**Owner** Javas Charvers **Bred** Airlie Stud **Trained** Orton, Cumbria

**FOCUS**
A weak staying handicap that was run at a steady gallop through the early stages. The winner built on her latest C&D win.

## 2551 BET ON ALL UK RACING WITH TOTEPOOL MEDIAN AUCTION MAIDEN STKS 5f
**4:35** (4:36) (Class 6) 3-Y-O **£2,726** (£805; £402) **Stalls** Low

Form RPR

0-2 **1** **Naivasha**[16] 2093 3-8-11 0....[1] MichaelJMMurphy(3) 4 67+
(Robert Cowell) *mde all: pushed out fnl f: a in command* **11/8**[1]

53 **2** 1 1/4 **Lucky Times**[4] 2420 3-9-0 0.... PJMcDonald 6 63
(Mel Brittain) *chsd ldr: rdn 2f out: kpt on but a hld* **12/1**

5-26 **3** 6 **Chuckamental**[99] 608 3-9-5 58....(t) RoystonFfrench 2 46
(Bryan Smart) *chsd ldng pair: outpcd 1/2-way: no threat after* **9/2**[3]

00-4 **4** 1 **Lunesdale Buddy**[15] 2138 3-9-2 37.... SladeO'Hara(3) 3 42
(Alan Berry) *chsd ldng pair: outpcd 1/2-way: no threat after* **100/1**

00- **5** 5 **My Boy Bob**[316] 4259 3-9-5 0.... LeeTopliss 5 24
(Richard Fahey) *dwlt: sn outpcd towards rr: nvr threatened* **11/4**[2]

**6** 13 **Aqueous (IRE)** 3-9-0 0.... JimmyQuinn 7
(James Tate) *s.i.s: a bhd* **7/1**

1m 3.82s (4.02) **Going Correction** +0.65s/f (Yiel) **6** Ran SP% **108.1**
Speed ratings (Par 97): **93,91,81,79,71 51**
CSF £17.36 TOTE £2.00: £1.10, £5.00; EX 14.70 Trifecta £39.70.

**Owner** Lowther Racing **Bred** Lowther Racing **Trained** Six Mile Bottom, Cambs

**FOCUS**
A typically weak 3yo sprint, with no depth.

## 2552 COLLECT TOTEPOOL WINNINGS AT BETFRED SHOPS H'CAP 5f 212y
**5:10** (5:10) (Class 5) (0-75,76) 4-Y-O+ **£3,234** (£962; £481; £240) **Stalls** Low

Form RPR

1006 **1** **Take The Lead**[39] 1500 4-8-3 **64**.... AnnaHesketh(7) 4 73
(David Nicholls) *mde all: rdn over 2f out: kpt on: pressed fnl 75yds but a jst holding on* **25/1**

-211 **2** nk **Meshardal (GER)**[16] 2094 4-8-13 **67**.... JamesSullivan 6 75
(Ruth Carr) *trckd ldr: rdn over 2f out: kpt on but a jst hld* **9/2**[3]

4133 **3** 3/4 **Fleurtille**[4] 2421 5-9-0 **68**.... LeeTopliss 3 74
(Robert Johnson) *dwlt: sn in tch: rdn to chse ldrs over 1f out: kpt on* **11/4**[1]

5-03 **4** 2 3/4 **Mission Impossible**[14] 2166 9-8-4 **61** oh3....(p) IanBrennan(3) 1 58
(Tracy Waggott) *hld up: rdn and sme hdwy over 2f out: kpt on: nvr threatened ldrs* **13/2**

0243 **5** 1/2 **Windforpower (IRE)**[11] 2232 4-8-9 **63**....(p) RoystonFfrench 9 58
(Tracy Waggott) *midfield: rdn over 2f out: one pce* **8/1**

0001 **6** 1 3/4 **Banovallum**[11] 2233 4-9-1 **76**.... DanielleMooney(7) 5 66
(Michael Easterby) *hld up: rdn over 2f out: nvr threatened* **4/1**[2]

2-00 **7** nk **Sunny Side Up (IRE)**[14] 2167 5-8-7 **68**.... GemmaTutty(7) 10 57
(Karen Tutty) *racd keenly: hld up: rdn over 2f out: nvr threatened* **22/1**

2130 **8** 7 **Red Cape (FR)**[8] 2297 11-8-7 **61** oh1....(b) PJMcDonald 11 27
(Ruth Carr) *midfield on outer: wknd 2f out* **12/1**

3300 **9** 5 **Thorpe Bay**[10] 2250 5-8-9 **63**....(v[1]) AndrewMullen 7 13
(Michael Appleby) *slowly away: hld up: rdn over 2f out: sn wknd* **12/1**

1m 17.45s (3.85) **Going Correction** +0.725s/f (Yiel) **9** Ran SP% **112.9**
Speed ratings (Par 103): **103,102,101,97,97 94,94,85,78**
CSF £131.01 CT £416.33 TOTE £32.60: £6.90, £1.10, £2.40; EX 183.70 Trifecta £627.30.

**Owner** David Nicholls Racing Club **Bred** Lady Whent **Trained** Sessay, N Yorks

**FOCUS**
Moderate sprinting form. The first two are rated to their AW form.

## 2553 TOTETRIFECTA PICK THE 1 2 3 MEDIAN AUCTION MAIDEN FILLIES' STKS 5f 212y
**5:45** (5:46) (Class 6) 3-4-Y-O **£2,726** (£805; £402) **Stalls** Low

Form RPR

5-32 **1** **Sitting Pretty (IRE)**[15] 2118 3-9-0 77.... StephenCraine 7 73
(Tom Dascombe) *mde all: rdn over 2f out: carried hd high but c clr* **2/7**[1]

24-6 **2** 6 **Goadby**[42] 1449 3-9-0 58.... JimmyQuinn 5 54
(John Holt) *chsd ldr: rdn over 2f out: sn no ch w wnr* **4/1**[2]

403- **3** 10 **Penny Pursuits**[235] 6915 3-8-11 53.... SladeO'Hara(3) 2 22
(Alan Berry) *sn outpcd towards rr: nvr threatened: wnt remote 3rd post* **16/1**[3]

4-50 **4** 1/2 **Lady Dancer (IRE)**[31] 1647 3-9-0 30....(b) PJMcDonald 6 20
(George Moore) *chsd ldr: rdn over 2f out: wknd over 1f out* **33/1**

**5** 5 **Blue Jacket (USA)** 3-8-9 0.... EmmaSayer(5) 1 4
(Dianne Sayer) *slowly away: a wl bhd* **20/1**

1m 18.63s (5.03) **Going Correction** +0.725s/f (Yiel)
**WFA** 3 from 4yo 9lb **5** Ran SP% **111.3**
Speed ratings (Par 98): **95,87,73,73,66**
CSF £1.85 TOTE £1.20: £1.10, £1.80; EX 1.80 Trifecta £4.80.

**Owner** N & S Mather,Owen Promotions,I Flanagan **Bred** S F Bloodstock **Trained** Malpas, Cheshire

**FOCUS**
Little depth to this sprint maiden which was 10lb slower than the previous handicap. The jury's out as to what the winner achieved.

T/Plt: £168.30 to a £1 stake. Pool of £39765.80 - 172.39 winning tickets. T/Qpdt: £9.70 to a £1 stake. Pool of £2999.50 - 227.99 winning tickets. AS

# [2499] GOODWOOD (R-H)
Saturday, May 24

**OFFICIAL GOING: Soft (6.3)**
Wind: Moderate, across (away from stands) Weather: Fine but cloudy

## 2554 32RED CASINO STKS (REGISTERED AS THE FESTIVAL STAKES) (LISTED RACE) 1m 1f 192y
**1:50** (1:50) (Class 1) 4-Y-O+
**£22,684** (£8,600; £4,304; £2,144; £1,076; £540) **Stalls** Low

Form RPR

2-23 **1** **French Navy**[24] 1870 6-9-0 112.... AdamKirby 4 113
(Charlie Appleby) *hld up in 6th: styd far side in st: clsd on ldrs 2f out: hrd rdn to ld ins fnl f: styd on* **2/1**[1]

2-12 **2** 1/2 **Windhoek**[63] 1068 4-9-0 106.... KierenFallon 1 112
(Saeed bin Suroor) *trckd ldng pair: styd far side in st: rdn to ld jst over 2f out: hdd ins fnl f: styd on but a hld* **3/1**[3]

211- **3** 1 1/2 **Nabucco**[203] 7697 5-9-3 109.... RobertHavlin 7 112
(John Gosden) *trckd ldr: led quartet in centre of crse over 3f out: drvn over 2f out: tried to cl on ldng pair over 1f out: one pce fnl f* **11/4**[2]

0-04 **4** 1 1/2 **Baltic Knight (IRE)**[12] 2223 4-9-0 105.... PatDobbs 2 106
(Richard Hannon) *led: styd far side in st: rdn and hdd jst over 2f out: one pce after* **12/1**

40-0 **5** 2 1/2 **Auction (IRE)**[35] 1577 4-8-9 96....(p) DaneO'Neill 5 97
(Ed Dunlop) *hld up in last: racd in centre in st: modest prog 2f out: limited rspnse u.p after* **40/1**

-006 **6** 1 1/4 **Starboard**[86] 773 5-9-0 100.... MartinLane 6 99
(David Simcock) *hld up in tch: racd in centre in st: rdn over 2f out: wknd over 1f out* **20/1**

2-00 **7** 22 **Quick Wit**[77] 902 7-9-0 107....(p) AhmedAjtebi 9 57
(Saeed bin Suroor) *t.k.h: hld up in tch: racd in centre in st: wknd over 2f out: eased and t.o* **9/1**

2m 14.7s (6.60) **Going Correction** +0.625s/f (Yiel) **7** Ran SP% **109.9**
Speed ratings (Par 111): **98,97,96,95,93 92,74**
CSF £7.52 TOTE £2.50: £1.60, £1.80; EX 7.10 Trifecta £15.10.

**Owner** Godolphin **Bred** Darley **Trained** Newmarket, Suffolk

■ Stewards' Enquiry : Adam Kirby two-day ban: used whip in incorrect place (Jun 8-9)

**FOCUS**
First 2f of 1m course dolled out 5yds. The first 2f of the Mile course was dolled out 5yds and the ground was confirmed as being soft by the jockeys following the opener. This looked a Listed event with a bit of depth, but the field split into a couple of small groups turning into the home straight, and racing closer to the inside rail seemed best. The winner was the form pick and is rated close to his best.

## 2555 32RED STKS (REGISTERED AS THE TAPSTER STAKES) (LISTED RACE) 1m 4f
**2:20** (2:20) (Class 1) 4-Y-O+ **£23,680** (£8,956; £4,476; £2,236) **Stalls** Centre

Form RPR

2-21 **1** **Gatewood**[14] 2143 6-9-3 104.... FrankieDettori 2 107
(John Gosden) *hld up in last: clsd over 3f out: pushed into ld 2f out: edgd rt sn after: shkn up and continued to edge rt 1f out: styd on and in command after* **4/7**[1]

00-0 **2** 3/4 **Mirsaale**[63] 1068 4-9-0 100....(p) KierenFallon 4 103
(James Tate) *led: rdn 3f out: hdd 2f out: hld whn tightened up 1f out: styd on* **10/1**

00-6 **3** 3/4 **Kelinni (IRE)**[14] 2143 6-9-0 103.... LukeMorris 1 102
(Marco Botti) *hld up in 3rd: clsd 4f out: rdn to chal over 2f out: nt qckn whn carried rt wl over 1f out: kpt on fnl f* **5/1**[3]

65-2 **4** 1 **Blue Surf**[14] 2154 5-9-0 97.... RobertHavlin 3 102
(Amanda Perrett) *trckd ldr: rdn to chal over 2f out: cl up but looked hld whn bdly squeezed out over 1f out: kpt on nr fin* **9/2**[2]

2m 48.77s (10.37) **Going Correction** +0.625s/f (Yiel) **4** Ran SP% **107.6**
Speed ratings (Par 111): **90,89,89,88**
CSF £6.58 TOTE £1.40; EX 5.90 Trifecta £17.70.

**Owner** O T I Racing & G Strawbridge **Bred** George Strawbridge **Trained** Newmarket, Suffolk

■ Stewards' Enquiry : Frankie Dettori 1st incident: one-day ban: careless riding (Jun 8); 2nd; three-day ban: careless riding (Jun 9-11)

**FOCUS**
From a form perspective, it's unlikely this result means a great deal as it developed into a sprint down the home straight and there was trouble in the closing stages. There are doubts over the form and the winner is the best guide.

## 2556 32RED.COM STKS (H'CAP) (BOBIS RACE) 7f
**2:55** (2:57) (Class 2) 3-Y-O **£32,345** (£9,625; £4,810; £2,405) **Stalls** Low

Form RPR

0232 **1** **Wee Jean**[15] 2111 3-8-2 **88**.... LukeMorris 6 97
(Mick Channon) *trckd ldrs in 6th: rdn over 2f out: squeezed through over 1f out: chal on inner fnl f: sustained effrt to ld nr fin* **8/1**[3]

2-21 **2** hd **Penny Drops**[15] 2125 3-8-1 **87**.... LiamJones 4 95
(William Haggas) *trckd ldrs: prog 2f out: rdn to ld over 1f out: hrd pressed after: kpt on but hdd nr fin* **6/1**[2]

3-32 **3** hd **Beau Nash (IRE)**[21] 1937 3-7-9 **88**.... CamHardie(7) 10 96
(Richard Hannon) *trckd ldrs: clsd on outer 2f out: rdn to chal over 1f out: nt qckn and hld nr fin* **6/1**[2]

-214 **4** 3 **Nakuti (IRE)**[20] 1985 3-7-9 **86** oh3.... NoelGarbutt(5) 9 86
(Sylvester Kirk) *hld up towards rr: waiting for room 3f out: drvn and sme prog over 1f out: kpt on but nt pce to threaten* **14/1**

-214 **5** 1 1/2 **Willy Brennan (IRE)**[21] 1937 3-8-0 **86** oh1.... DavidProbert 1 82
(Andrew Balding) *led: rdn over 2f out: hdd over 1f out: wknd fnl f* **12/1**

16-0 **6** 3/4 **Supplicant**[42] 1436 3-9-5 **105**.... KierenFallon 3 99+
(Richard Fahey) *t.k.h: hld up in last pair: waiting for room 3f out: eased to outer wl over 1f out: limited prog and n.d* **3/1**[1]

6030 **7** 2 1/4 **Lady Frances**[15] 2111 3-8-0 **86** oh1.... FrannyNorton 7 74
(Mark Johnston) *trckd ldr to 2f out: steadily wknd* **33/1**

0141 **8** 1 **Mick's Yer Man**[24] 1867 3-9-2 107.... RyanWhile(5) 11 93
(Bill Turner) *hld up towards rr: rdn on outer over 2f out: no prog and btn wl over 1f out* **8/1**[3]

103- **9** 11 **Wahaab (IRE)**[263] 6064 3-8-5 **91**.... MartinLane 8 48
(Richard Hannon) *dropped in fr wd draw and hld up last: pushed along and no prog 3f out: sn bhd: t.o* **6/1**[2]

2557-2562

2120 **10** *hd* **Harwoods Volante (IRE)**[36] 1555 3-8-6 **92**.................... RobertHavlin 2 49
(Amanda Perrett) *rrd s: sn chsd ldng pair: wknd rapidly 2f out: t.o* **10/1**
1m 30.13s (3.13) **Going Correction** +0.625s/f (Yiel) **10** Ran SP% **116.5**
Speed ratings (Par 105): **107,106,106,103,101 100,97,96,84,84**
CSF £55.34 CT £317.62 TOTE £8.40: £2.30, £2.30, £2.70; EX 45.90 Trifecta £206.50.
**Owner** B Robe **Bred** Mickley Stud & B Robe **Trained** West Ilsley, Berks

**FOCUS**
A competitive handicap ran at what appeared to be an even gallop, but plenty found trouble in running. The form is rated as standard.

## 2557 EBFSTALLIONS.COM MAIDEN FILLIES STKS (BOBIS RACE) 6f
**3:30** (3:30) (Class 5) 2-Y-O **£5,175** (£1,540; £769; £384) **Stalls** High

Form RPR
5 **1** **Showcard**[15] 2107 2-9-0 0............................ AdamKirby 8 74
(Gary Moore) *best away: led against nr side rail: rdn 2f out: sn hdd: rallied strly under firm pushing fnl f to ld last strides* **10/3**[3]
20 **2** *hd* **Exentricity**[8] 2313 2-8-11 0............................ WilliamTwiston-Davies(3) 4 73
(Mick Channon) *pressed ldr: shkn up to ld wl over 1f out: drvn fnl f: hdd last strides* **11/8**[1]
**3** *3* **Crystal Malt (IRE)** 2-9-0 0............................ PatDobbs 3 64
(Richard Hannon) *dwlt: in tch in last: shkn up and outpcd 2f out: kpt on fnl f to take 3rd nr fin* **6/1**
**4** *1* **Carrot Top** 2-9-0 0............................ DaneO'Neill 2 61
(Ralph Beckett) *dwlt: sn chsd ldng pair: rdn 2f out: fdd jst over 1f out* **11/4**[2]
**5** *2 1/4* **Lady Marita (IRE)** 2-8-9 0............................ PhilipPrince(5) 6 54
(J S Moore) *dwlt: hld up in tch: shkn up and outpcd 2f out: n.d after* **20/1**
1m 16.83s (4.63) **Going Correction** +0.625s/f (Yiel) **5** Ran SP% **110.9**
Speed ratings (Par 93): **94,93,89,88,85**
CSF £8.47 TOTE £4.60: £2.30, £1.30; EX 7.60 Trifecta £25.00.
**Owner** Sir Eric Parker **Bred** Sir Eric Parker **Trained** Lower Beeding, W Sussex

**FOCUS**
An ordinary maiden, with the two who had previous experience dominating. The form is rated at the lower end of the race averages.

## 2558 MARK NORMAN BIRTHDAY CELEBRATION STKS (H'CAP) 1m 6f
**4:05** (4:05) (Class 2) (0-105,98) 4-Y-O+ **£16,172** (£4,812; £2,405; £1,202) **Stalls** Low

Form RPR
6/30 **1** **Ted Spread**[34] 803 7-8-12 **89**............................(t) LukeMorris 7 98
(Suzy Smith) *trckd ldr over 10f out: led jst over 2f out: sn jnd again and drvn: fine duel after: forced ahd last strides* **7/1**
15-1 **2** *hd* **Debdebdeb**[19] 2010 4-8-13 **90**............................ DavidProbert 10 98
(Andrew Balding) *sn led: shkn up and hdd jst over 2f out: sn w wnr again: great battle fnl 2f: jst hdd last strides* **11/8**[1]
016- **3** *2* **Totalize**[105] 7723 5-8-10 **87**............................ WilliamCarson 3 92
(Brian Ellison) *hld up in last pair: rdn 4f out: cl enough over 2f out: nt qckn after: kpt on to take 3rd nr fin* **11/2**[3]
/0-1 **4** *nk* **Christopher Wren (USA)**[28] 1493 7-8-12 **89**................ FrannyNorton 5 94
(Nick Gifford) *hld up in last pair: prog to chse ldng pair over 2f out: sn rdn and nt qckn: lost 3rd nr fin* **7/1**
630- **5** *14* **Eshtiaal (USA)**[239] 6793 4-9-4 **95**............................(bt) DaneO'Neill 4 85
(Brian Meehan) *chsd ldng pair over 10f out: rdn 4f out: cl enough over 2f out: wknd and eased wl over 1f out: t.o* **7/1**
4/ **P** **Dildar (IRE)**[34] 2521 6-9-4 **95**............................ KierenFallon 6
(Paul Nicholls) *trckd ldr tl broke down and p.u over 10f out: fatally injured* **5/1**[2]
3m 12.98s (9.38) **Going Correction** +0.625s/f (Yiel) **6** Ran SP% **111.7**
Speed ratings (Par 109): **98,97,96,96,88**
CSF £17.02 CT £55.52 TOTE £8.50: £3.90, £1.40; EX 24.10 Trifecta £86.40.
**Owner** False Nose 'N Glasses Partnership **Bred** Pollards Stables **Trained** Lewes, E Sussex

**FOCUS**
Quite a few non-runners weakened this field a bit and it paid to race handy.

## 2559 ALLANS OF PETWORTH STKS (H'CAP) 6f
**4:40** (4:40) (Class 4) (0-80,83) 6-Y-O+ **£6,469** (£1,925; £962; £481) **Stalls** High

Form RPR
0-05 **1** **Slip Sliding Away (IRE)**[14] 2147 7-9-7 **79**.................... AdamKirby 6 91
(Peter Hedger) *stdd s: hld up in last: prog to chse ldr over 1f out: rdn to ld ins fnl f: edgd lft but styd on strly* **7/4**[1]
0554 **2** *1 1/4* **Mon Brav**[7] 2332 7-9-0 **72**............................ MartinLane 2 80
(Brian Ellison) *trckd ldrs: prog to ld wl over 1f out: hdd ins fnl f: styd on but readily hld* **2/1**[2]
00-5 **3** *7* **Italian Tom (IRE)**[22] 1912 7-9-1 **73**............................ LukeMorris 10 59
(Ronald Harris) *trckd ldrs: rdn over 2f out: nt qckn and easily lft bhd fr over 1f out* **9/1**
03-6 **4** *1 3/4* **Sarangoo**[20] 1985 6-9-0 **77**............................(p) RyanWhile(5) 5 57
(Malcolm Saunders) *pressed ldr: no room against rail 4f out and swtchd rt: led over 2f out: hdd wl over 1f out: sn wknd* **8/1**
00-1 **5** *11* **Aye Aye Digby (IRE)**[23] 1893 9-9-5 **77**............................ DaneO'Neill 3 22
(Patrick Chamings) *sn led: hdd over 2f out: wknd: t.o* **9/2**[3]
1m 15.03s (2.83) **Going Correction** +0.625s/f (Yiel) **5** Ran SP% **109.0**
Speed ratings: **106,104,95,92,78**
CSF £5.42 TOTE £2.70: £1.20, £1.40; EX 5.30 Trifecta £18.10.
**Owner** Simon Holt, Mary Boylan, Wendy Mole **Bred** S Holt & A C Beggan & R J Beggan **Trained** Dogmersfield, Hampshire

**FOCUS**
A race decimated by non-runners was taken in good style by the winner. who has a good record here.

## 2560 MARY HOW TRUST MAIDEN FILLIES' STKS (BOBIS RACE) 7f
**5:15** (5:16) (Class 5) 3-Y-O
**£3,112** (£932; £466; £233; £116; £58) **Stalls** High

Form RPR
**1** **Buredyma** 3-9-0 0............................ FrankieDettori 11 76+
(William Haggas) *edgd lft s: wl off the pce in last: pushed along 1/2-way: gd prog on outer over 2f out: clsd to chal 1f out: encouraged along and led nr fin* **7/2**[2]
0 **2** *1/2* **Lady Brigid (IRE)**[18] 2061 3-9-0 0............................ PatDobbs 6 74
(Amanda Perrett) *trckd ldr and clr of rest: clsd to ld wl over 1f out: sn hrd pressed: kpt on but hdd nr fin* **11/2**[3]
0 **3** *shd* **Palerma**[43] 1422 3-8-11 0............................ WilliamTwiston-Davies(3) 9 74
(Mick Channon) *hld up in 4th: clsd on ldrs over 2f out: rdn to chal jst over 1f out: nt qckn ins fnl f: styd on nr fin* **3/1**[1]
0- **4** *nk* **Tiptree Lace**[296] 4921 3-9-0 0............................ KierenFallon 3 73
(William Knight) *trckd clr ldng pair: clsd then swtchd lft jst over 2f out: chsd ldr over 1f out and sn chalng: nt qckn last 100yds* **7/1**
**5** *1 3/4* **Felwah** 3-8-9 0............................ NathanAlison(5) 2 68
(William Haggas) *mounted on crse: hld up in 5th: clsd over 2f out on inner: chsd ldrs over 1f out: one pce after* **8/1**
**6** *6* **First Embrace (IRE)** 3-9-0 0............................ RobertHavlin 5 53
(William Jarvis) *sltly awkward s: hld up in 6th: clsng w others whn n.m.r jst over 2f out: wknd over 1f out* **12/1**
0 **7** *7* **Calamity Jane**[22] 1920 3-8-7 0............................ PatrickO'Donnell(7) 10 35
(Ralph Beckett) *racd freely: led and clr: hdd & wknd rapidly wl over 1f out* **8/1**
46- **U** **Nibbling (IRE)**[228] 7103 3-9-0 0............................(b[1]) MartinLane 13
(Paul Cole) *fractious preliminaries: veered violently lft leaving stalls and sn uns rdr* **9/1**
1m 31.96s (4.96) **Going Correction** +0.625s/f (Yiel) **8** Ran SP% **115.0**
Speed ratings (Par 96): **96,95,95,94,92 86,78,**
CSF £23.22 TOTE £2.80: £1.10, £2.00, £1.50; EX 15.70 Trifecta £34.50.
**Owner** Saleh Al Homaizi & Imad Al Sagar **Bred** Pantile Stud **Trained** Newmarket, Suffolk

**FOCUS**
It's probably best to presume this is modest form, but it fits the race average.
T/Plt: £9.90 to a £1 stake.Pool: £69,679.16 - 5,118.59 winning tickets. T/Qpdt: £5.80 to a £1 stake.Pool: £5,561.86 - 700.75 winning tickets. JN

# 2506 HAYDOCK (L-H)
Saturday, May 24

**OFFICIAL GOING: Good changing to good to soft after race 1 (1.35) changing to soft after race 2 (2.05)**
Wind: Fresh, behind Weather: Rain

## 2561 BETFRED EDWARD WALLIS STKS (H'CAP) 2m 45y
**1:35** (1:36) (Class 2) (0-110,99) 4-Y-O+ **£16,172** (£4,812; £2,405; £1,202) **Stalls** Low

Form RPR
-224 **1** **Noble Silk**[35] 1581 5-8-13 **91**............................(p) OisinMurphy(3) 7 101
(Lucy Wadham) *hld up: hdwy 3f out: led wl over 1f out: sn edgd lft: styd on wl: in command after* **10/1**
60-0 **2** *2* **Nearly Caught (IRE)**[42] 1434 4-9-8 **99**............................ GeorgeBaker 5 106
(Hughie Morrison) *hld up: hdwy for press over 1f out: styd on ins fnl f: tk 2nd towards fin: nt rch wnr* **8/1**
-323 **3** *3/4* **Entihaa**[9] 2289 6-8-5 **80** oh1............................ BenCurtis 2 86
(Alan Swinbank) *prom: rdn to ld over 2f out: hdd wl over 1f out: styd on same pce ins fnl f: lost 2nd towards fin* **8/1**
06-0 **4** *3* **Brockwell**[17] 2073 5-8-13 **88**............................ RichardKingscote 8 90
(Tom Dascombe) *in tch: rdn and outpcd over 2f out: styd on ins fnl f: nvr able to chal* **7/2**[1]
11/0 **5** *1 1/2* **Huff And Puff**[19] 1735 7-8-10 **85**............................ JimCrowley 9 86
(Venetia Williams) *prom: rdn to chal 2f out: one pce ins fnl f* **12/1**
1-15 **6** *3 1/2* **Esteaming**[28] 1735 4-9-2 **93**............................ GrahamGibbons 12 89
(David Barron) *midfield: effrt to chse ldrs over 2f out: no imp over 1f out: wknd fnl 110yds* **6/1**[3]
0-15 **7** *2 1/4* **Jonny Delta**[20] 1971 7-8-4 **82**............................ ConnorBeasley(3) 1 76
(Jim Goldie) *s.s: in rr: rdn over 2f out: nvr on terms* **12/1**
3-66 **8** *7* **Argent Knight**[15] 2108 4-8-11 **88**............................(b[1]) SteveDrowne 13 73
(William Jarvis) *pushed along and swtchd lft jst after s: hld up: struggling in rr over 3f out: eased whn wl btn fnl f* **25/1**
6-65 **9** *9* **Glenard**[17] 2073 4-9-1 **92**............................ RyanMoore 11 67
(Charles Hills) *led at stdy pce: incresed tempo over 3f out: rdn and hdd over 2f out: wknd over 1f out: eased whn wl btn fnl f* **9/2**[2]
03-2 **10** *2 1/2* **Masquerading (IRE)**[45] 1383 4-8-11 **88**............................ GrahamLee 10 60
(Jonjo O'Neill) *hld up: rdn over 2f out: struggling after: nvr a danger* **14/1**
1-60 **11** *8* **Theology**[84] 803 7-9-4 **93**............................ FrederikTylicki 6 55
(Steve Gollings) *prom tl rdn and wknd over 2f out* **50/1**
3m 37.45s (3.15) **Going Correction** +0.425s/f (Yiel)
**WFA** 4 from 5yo+ 2lb **11** Ran SP% **113.9**
Speed ratings (Par 109): **109,108,107,106,105 103,102,99,94,93 89**
CSF £84.80 CT £672.52 TOTE £11.10: £3.60, £3.80, £2.50; EX 109.60 Trifecta £1874.80.
**Owner** The FOPS **Bred** Mr & Mrs A E Pakenham **Trained** Newmarket, Suffolk
■ Stewards' Enquiry : Ryan Moore two-day ban: improper riding (Jun 8-9)

**FOCUS**
All races on stands' side home straight and races on Round course increased by 50yds. A reasonable staying handicap in which the pace didn't look strong. The winner rates a personal best.

## 2562 BETFRED SCOOP6 £15 MILLION TODAY H'CAP 6f
**2:05** (2:07) (Class 3) (0-90,97) 4-Y-O+ **£9,703** (£2,887; £1,443; £721) **Stalls** Centre

Form RPR
-001 **1** **Bear Behind (IRE)**[14] 2166 5-9-5 **88**............................ RichardKingscote 7 99
(Tom Dascombe) *racd far side: mde all: rdn over 1f out: r.o ins fnl f and in control: 1st of 10 in gp* **16/1**
03-0 **2** *1 3/4* **Shore Step (IRE)**[15] 2110 4-9-1 **84**............................ GrahamLee 8 89
(Mick Channon) *racd far side: a.p: rdn and nt qckn over 1f out: kpt on but no real imp on wnr ins fnl f: 2nd of 10 in gp* **12/1**
3121 **3** *shd* **Barkston Ash**[7] 2352 6-9-11 **97**............................(p) JasonHart(3) 16 102+
(Eric Alston) *led small gp on stands' side: rdn wl over 2f out: styd on u.p ins fnl f: hld cl home: 1st of 3 in gp* **11/2**[2]
-442 **4** *nse* **Grissom (IRE)**[15] 2117 8-9-2 **85**............................ DuranFentiman 3 90
(Tim Easterby) *racd far side: chsd ldrs: rdn over 2f out: kpt on ins fnl f: nt pce to chal wnr: 3rd of 10 in gp* **12/1**
3026 **5** *nk* **Trader Jack**[7] 2336 5-9-1 **84**............................ RyanMoore 10 88+
(David Flood) *racd far side: in rr: hdwy over 1f out: styd on towards fin wout mounting serious chal: 4th of 10 in gp* **7/1**[3]
1 **6** *3/4* **Run With Pride (IRE)**[21] 1939 4-8-11 **80**............................ DaleSwift 6 81
(Derek Shaw) *racd far side: midfield: rdn over 2f out: hdwy to chse ldrs over 1f out: one pce fnl 75yds: 5th of 10 in gp* **15/2**
10-0 **7** *1 3/4* **Cruise Tothelimit (IRE)**[15] 2110 6-8-8 **80**............................ OisinMurphy(3) 5 76
(Ian Williams) *racd far side: chsd ldrs: rdn over 1f out: no ex fnl 100yds: 6th of 10 in gp* **25/1**
5-00 **8** *1 1/2* **Out Do**[10] 2254 5-9-7 **90**............................ DanielTudhope 14 81
(David O'Meara) *racd stands' side: hld up: effrt 2f out: wnt 2nd in gp wl over 1f out: sn tried to chal: nt qckn ins fnl f: no ex whn eased fnl 100yds: 2nd of 3 in gp* **5/1**[1]
500 **9** *hd* **Go Far**[20] 1975 4-8-6 **80**............................(b) TimClark(5) 2 70
(Alan Bailey) *racd far side: in tch: lost pl over 4f out: pushed along and outpcd after: 7th of 10 in gp* **22/1**

0-00 **10** *1* **Polski Max**[7] 2352 4-9-0 **88** SammyJoBell(5) 11 75
(Richard Fahey) *racd far side: in tch: rdn over 2f out: wknd over 1f out: 8th of 10 in gp* **15/2**

-600 **11** *½* **Baby Strange**[21] 1938 10-8-13 **82** JoeFanning 4 67
(Derek Shaw) *s.i.s: racd far side: hld up: pushed along over 2f out: no imp: 9th of 10 in gp* **14/1**

0104 **12** *¾* **Upavon**[14] 2157 4-8-7 **76** oh1 MickaelBarzalona 9 59
(David Elsworth) *racd far side: hld up: pushed along 1/2-way: rdn 2f out: no imp: 10th of 10 in gp* **16/1**

3-50 **13** *8* **Al Mukhdam**[36] 1564 4-8-13 **82** PatCosgrave 12 39
(Ed de Giles) *racd stands' side: w gp ldr: rdn 2f out: wknd over 1f out: 3rd of 3 in gp* **12/1**

1m 13.72s (-0.08) **Going Correction** +0.225s/f (Good) **13** Ran SP% **117.8**
Speed ratings (Par 107): **109,106,106,106,106 105,102,100,100,99 98,97,86**
CSF £193.05 CT £1236.91 TOTE £14.40: £3.60, £3.10, £2.40; EX 220.40 Trifecta £1147.10.

**Owner** Bellman Black Marantelli Owen **Bred** Rory O'Brien **Trained** Malpas, Cheshire

■ Stewards' Enquiry : Jason Hart two-day ban: used whip above permitted level (Jun 8-9)

**FOCUS**
It continued to rain heavily and the going was changed to soft following this race. Three horses raced stands' side and the pace held up well. The winner is rated back to his best since early last year.

## 2563 BETFRED.COM TEMPLE STKS (BRITISH CHAMPIONS SERIES) (GROUP 2) 5f

**2:40** (2:41) (Class 1) 3-Y-0+

**£56,710** (£21,500; £10,760; £5,360; £2,690; £1,350) **Stalls** Centre

Form RPR

12-3 **1** **Hot Streak (IRE)**[21] 1949 3-8-10 115 OisinMurphy 7 116
(Kevin Ryan) *mde all: shkn up over 1f out: rdn ins fnl f: r.o: a doing enough nr fin* **9/4**[1]

3-10 **2** *½* **Pearl Secret**[21] 1949 5-9-4 110 RyanMoore 1 117
(David Barron) *midfield: hdwy on rail over 1f out: sn wnt 2nd: styd on ins fnl f: clsd on wnr nr fin: nvr gng to get there* **10/3**[2]

30-2 **3** *3* **Kingsgate Native (IRE)**[21] 1949 9-9-4 112 JimCrowley 5 106
(Robert Cowell) *in tch: effrt over 2f out: rdn and nt qckn over 1f out: sn outpcd by ldrs: kpt on to take 3rd towards fin: no imp on front two* **8/1**

13-4 **4** *nk* **Justice Day (IRE)**[9] 2287 3-8-10 108 MickaelBarzalona 3 102
(David Elsworth) *in tch: effrt to chal over 1f out: styd on same pce ins fnl f* **14/1**

1-36 **5** *hd* **Jack Dexter**[10] 2256 5-9-4 113 GrahamLee 6 104
(Jim Goldie) *hld up towards rr: nt clr run fr over 1f out: sn pushed along but nvr a clr passage: styd on towards fin* **6/1**[3]

10-6 **6** *2* **Justineo**[21] 1949 5-9-4 108 (b) AndreaAtzeni 2 97
(Roger Varian) *w wnr tl rdn over 1f out: wknd ins fnl f* **11/1**

10-5 **7** *¾* **Mirza**[13] 2197 7-9-4 109 (p) SebSanders 10 95
(Rae Guest) *chsd ldrs: rdn 2f out: sn hung lft: btn over 1f out* **9/1**

0435 **8** *5* **Hawkeyethenoo (IRE)**[10] 2256 8-9-4 107 GaryBartley 4 77
(Jim Goldie) *hld up: outpcd and lft bhd over 1f out: nvr on terms* **14/1**

-010 **9** *4½* **Smoothtalkinrascal (IRE)**[13] 2197 4-9-4 104 (v) DanielTudhope 8 60
(David O'Meara) *hld up: rdn over 2f out: outpcd over 1f out* **25/1**

1m 0.15s (-0.65) **Going Correction** +0.225s/f (Good)
**WFA** 3 from 4yo+ 8lb **9** Ran SP% **114.8**
Speed ratings (Par 115): **114,113,108,107,107 104,103,95,88**
CSF £9.51 TOTE £3.10: £1.20, £1.40, £2.50; EX 10.30 Trifecta £39.90.

**Owner** Qatar Racing Limited **Bred** Barry Noonan **Trained** Hambleton, N Yorks

**FOCUS**
A one-two for Qatar Racing. Not the strongest of renewals, the ground a factor, but the first two were clear. Hot Streak has the potential to do better still.

## 2564 BETFRED MIND BLOWING SCOOP6 TODAY EBF STALLIONS STKS (LISTED RACE) (FILLIES) 6f

**3:10** (3:11) (Class 1) 3-Y-0+

**£26,653** (£10,105; £5,057; £2,519; £1,264; £634) **Stalls** Centre

Form RPR

6-30 **1** **Joyeuse**[20] 1976 3-8-12 101 RyanMoore 8 107
(Lady Cecil) *hld up towards rr: hdwy over 2f out: sn swtchd lft: led 1f out: rdn and r.o ins fnl f: in command towards fin* **3/1**[1]

100- **2** *1¼* **Gathering Power (IRE)**[26] 1822 4-9-3 93 MickaelBarzalona 5 101
(Edward Lynam, Ire) *hld up: hdwy over 2f out: rdn to ld over 1f out: hdd 1f out: styd on u.p ins fnl f: one pce and hld cl home* **8/1**

31 **3** *4½* **Perfect Blessings (IRE)**[28] 1713 3-8-8 95 SteveDrowne 6 85
(Clive Cox) *a.p: led under 2f out: sn hdd: styd on same pce and unable to go w front two ins fnl f* **11/2**[3]

0-20 **4** *2* **Graphic Guest**[13] 2197 4-9-3 93 JimCrowley 3 80
(Robert Cowell) *chsd ldrs: rdn over 1f out: styd on same pce ins fnl f* **16/1**

130- **5** *hd* **Hallelujah**[196] 7821 6-9-7 103 (t) HayleyTurner 7 84
(James Fanshawe) *midfield: pushed along and outpcd over 3f out: kpt on ins fnl f wout troubling ldrs* **8/1**

23-2 **6** *2* **Spinatrix**[14] 2161 6-9-3 105 (p) ConnorBeasley 14 73
(Michael Dods) *chsd ldrs: rdn 2f out: one pce ins fnl f* **10/3**[2]

0-04 **7** *¾* **Gladiatrix**[14] 2161 5-9-3 87 SebSanders 12 71
(Rod Millman) *midfield: rdn over 2f out: btn 1f out* **33/1**

0-03 **8** *1* **Jillnextdoor (IRE)**[15] 2123 4-9-3 90 PaulHanagan 9 68
(Mick Channon) *bhd: rdn over 2f out: no imp* **25/1**

1-21 **9** *1¼* **Blithe Spirit**[15] 2116 3-8-8 97 JasonHart 10 62
(Eric Alston) *led: rdn and hdd under 2f out: wknd over 1f out* **9/1**

00-3 **10** *shd* **Gracia Directa (GER)**[23] 2006 6-9-3 102 DanielePorcu 1 63
(D Moser, Germany) *prom: rdn over 2f out: sn wknd* **12/1**

1m 14.63s (0.83) **Going Correction** +0.225s/f (Good)
**WFA** 3 from 4yo+ 9lb **10** Ran SP% **116.0**
Speed ratings (Par 108): **103,101,95,92,92 89,88,87,85,85**
CSF £27.42 TOTE £3.50: £1.70, £2.60, £2.20; EX 27.50 Trifecta £109.40.

**Owner** K Abdullah **Bred** Juddmonte Farms Ltd **Trained** Newmarket, Suffolk

**FOCUS**
An interesting fillies' Listed event run at a strong-looking gallop, and again the action took place middle to far side. The race is rated up to standard but the first two were the only ones to show their form.

## 2565 BETFRED MOBILE CASINO SILVER BOWL STKS (H'CAP) (BOBIS RACE) 1m

**3:45** (3:47) (Class 2) 3-Y-O

**£43,575** (£13,048; £6,524; £3,262; £1,631; £819) **Stalls** Low

Form RPR

1-12 **1** **Chatez (IRE)**[14] 2148 3-9-2 **91** FergusSweeney 6 102
(Alan King) *hld up: hdwy 2f out: rdn to ld 1f out: styd on: kpt on and a doing enough towards home* **7/1**[3]

41-2 **2** *½* **Zarwaan**[43] 1420 3-9-6 **95** PaulHanagan 11 105
(Ed Dunlop) *hld up: pushed along briefly on bnd over 5f out: in rr: hdwy on outer over 1f out: wnt 2nd fnl 100yds: styd on u.p towards fin: nvr quite getting there* **8/1**

16-3 **3** *1¾* **First Flight (IRE)**[29] 1696 3-9-1 **90** AndreaAtzeni 8 96
(Saeed bin Suroor) *racd keenly: sn dropped into midfield: hdwy 3f out: rdn to chal over 1f out: stl ev ch ins fnl f: kpt on same pce fnl 100yds* **7/1**[3]

04-3 **4** *1¼* **Hot Coffee (IRE)**[16] 2088 3-9-1 **90** RichardKingscote 16 93
(Tom Dascombe) *prom: effrt to chal 2f out: stl there u.p over 1f out: n.m.r briefly ins fnl f: kpt on same pce fnl 100yds* **20/1**

-130 **5** *½* **Grevillea (IRE)**[15] 2112 3-8-9 **84** MartinDwyer 14 86
(Mick Channon) *hld up: hdwy over 2f out: rdn over 1f out: kpt on ins fnl f: nvr avble to chal* **33/1**

41-1 **6** *½* **Bilimbi (IRE)**[36] 1563 3-9-1 **90** RyanMoore 1 91
(William Haggas) *w ldr: rdn over 2f out: sn led: hdd 1f out: fdd fnl 100yds* **5/2**[1]

216- **7** *1¾* **Braidley (IRE)**[245] 6619 3-8-13 **88** TedDurcan 7 85
(James Bethell) *trckd ldrs: rdn over 2f out: wknd over 1f out* **20/1**

0-53 **8** *1* **Lyn Valley**[21] 1954 3-9-6 **95** JoeFanning 10 89
(Mark Johnston) *racd keenly: led: rdn over 2f out: sn hdd: wknd over 1f out* **8/1**

14-1 **9** *1¼* **What About Carlo (FR)**[29] 1696 3-9-5 **94** GrahamLee 3 86
(Eve Johnson Houghton) *chsd ldrs: ev ch 3f out: rdn 2f out: wknd over 1f out* **7/2**[2]

53-5 **10** *2* **Riverboat Springs (IRE)**[14] 2148 3-9-0 **89** DanielTudhope 12 76
(Mick Channon) *hld up: rdn 2f out: no imp* **25/1**

2-22 **11** *4* **Shot In The Sun (IRE)**[10] 2257 3-8-9 **84** PatrickMathers 2 62
(Richard Fahey) *midfield: pushed along over 5f out: rdn and no imp over 2f out: wknd over 1f out* **16/1**

3-41 **12** *1¼* **Red Stargazer (IRE)**[14] 2148 3-9-7 **96** GrahamGibbons 9 71
(David Barron) *midfield: lost pl 5f out: rdn whn bhd over 2f out: wl btn* **14/1**

30-6 **13** *4½* **Mawfoor (IRE)**[15] 2111 3-9-5 **94** TomQueally 5 58
(Brian Meehan) *hld up: hdwy into midfield over 4f out: rdn over 2f out: sn wknd* **25/1**

1m 47.77s (4.07) **Going Correction** +0.425s/f (Yiel) **13** Ran SP% **130.7**
Speed ratings (Par 105): **96,95,93,92,92 91,89,88,87,85 81,80,75**
CSF £63.34 CT £425.97 TOTE £8.30: £2.20, £3.40, £3.50; EX 56.90 Trifecta £561.90.

**Owner** Mrs Peter Andrews **Bred** Colin Kennedy **Trained** Barbury Castle, Wilts

**FOCUS**
A typically strong renewal of this valuable 3yo handicap. The ground was clearly a factor but the form is still rated on the positive side. The winner progressed again.

## 2566 FOLLOW THE SCOOP6 AT TOTEPOOLLIVEINFO.COM H'CAP (BOBIS RACE) 1m 3f 200y

**4:20** (4:20) (Class 2) (0-100,95) 3-Y-O

**£15,562** (£4,660; £2,330; £1,165; £582; £292) **Stalls** Centre

Form RPR

3-01 **1** **Wrangler**[20] 1984 3-9-1 **89** RyanMoore 2 93+
(William Haggas) *prom: effrt 2f out: wnt sltly lft and led fnl 110yds: styd on wl and edgd rt cl home* **11/10**[1]

2-12 **2** *½* **Montaly**[28] 1727 3-8-9 **86** OisinMurphy(3) 8 90
(Andrew Balding) *hld up: tk clsr order to chse ldrs 9f out: effrt 2f out: str chal and led briefly ins fnl f: kpt on wl: hld cl home* **4/1**[3]

-411 **3** *1* **Black Schnapps (IRE)**[20] 1983 3-9-6 **94** MartinDwyer 7 96
(William Muir) *hld up: rdn over 1f out: styd on ins fnl f: gng on at fin* **15/2**

103- **4** *1¼* **Fire Fighting (IRE)**[234] 6935 3-9-4 **92** JoeFanning 1 92
(Mark Johnston) *led: rdn whn pressed over 1f out: hdd ins fnl f: no ex fnl 75yds* **20/1**

31-1 **5** *4½* **Fun Mac (GER)**[28] 1727 3-8-9 **83** MickaelBarzalona 4 76
(Hughie Morrison) *racd keenly: prom: stdd after 2f: rdn 2f out: wknd ins fnl f* **7/2**[2]

1-03 **6** *3* **Moontime**[18] 2060 3-9-0 **88** PaulHanagan 6 76
(Charlie Appleby) *prom: pushed along over 2f out: wknd over 1f out* **14/1**

2m 43.42s (9.62) **Going Correction** +0.425s/f (Yiel) **6** Ran SP% **113.0**
Speed ratings (Par 105): **84,83,83,82,79 77**
CSF £5.93 CT £20.75 TOTE £2.10: £1.30, £3.00; EX 6.30 Trifecta £23.90.

**Owner** Highclere Thoroughbred Racing - Ashes **Bred** Palm Tree Thoroughbreds **Trained** Newmarket, Suffolk

**FOCUS**
A race won by Opinion Poll (2009) and Brown Panther (2011), who both progressed into high-class stayers. They went steady early and some of these were keen. The runners came up the middle in the straight. Useful form, but a tight finish compromises the level to some extent.

## 2567 BETFRED DOWNLOAD THE APP H'CAP (BOBIS RACE) 7f

**4:55** (4:56) (Class 3) (0-95,95) 3-Y-O **£9,703** (£2,887; £1,443; £721) **Stalls** Low

Form RPR

5620 **1** **Bretherton**[10] 2257 3-8-9 **83** (b) GrahamLee 4 91
(Richard Fahey) *hld up: hdwy 2f out: wnt 2nd 1f out: edgd rt ins fnl f: styd on to ld ins fnl 75yds: in control fnl strides* **9/1**

3622 **2** *½* **Lincoln (IRE)**[14] 2176 3-8-8 **82** MartinDwyer 9 89
(Mick Channon) *led: rdn over 1f out: edgd rt ins fnl f: hdd ins fnl 75yds: no ex fnl strides* **9/2**[3]

2-1 **3** *3¼* **Takreym (IRE)**[19] 2031 3-8-8 **82** (b) AndreaAtzeni 2 81
(Roger Varian) *chsd ldr: rdn over 1f out: lost 2nd 1f out: no ex fnl 100yds* **2/1**[1]

-303 **4** *6* **Mr Matthews (IRE)**[15] 2111 3-8-7 **81** BenCurtis 8 64
(K R Burke) *hld up: rdn 2f out: no imp over 1f out* **15/2**

3-1 **5** *3* **Destiny's Kitten (IRE)**[15] 2118 3-8-11 **85** RichardKingscote 1 60
(Tom Dascombe) *in tch: bmpd 4f out: rdn 2f out: wknd over 1f out* **7/1**

04-6 **6** *5* **Art Official (IRE)**[29] 1696 3-8-13 **87**.................................. RyanMoore 6 49
(Richard Hannon) *racd keenly: chsd ldrs: pushed along over 2f out: rdn and wknd over 1f out* **5/2**[2]

1m 32.56s (1.86) **Going Correction** +0.425s/f (Yiel) **6** Ran SP% **114.4**
Speed ratings (Par 103): **106,105,101,94,91 85**
CSF £49.06 CT £113.43 TOTE £13.80: £5.70, £2.90; EX 70.50 Trifecta £282.20.
**Owner** David W Armstrong **Bred** J & Mrs S Davis **Trained** Musley Bank, N Yorks

**FOCUS**
They raced middle to stands' side in the straight. The winner is rated back to his standout Southwell win.
T/Jkpt: Not won. T/Plt: £154.00 to a £1 stake. Pool: £131,039.65 - 621.0 winning tickets. T/Qpdt: £8.70 to a £1 stake. Pool: £9,952.77 - 845.84 winning tickets. DO

2568 - (Foreign Racing) - See Raceform Interactive

## [2036]CURRAGH (R-H)
Saturday, May 24

**OFFICIAL GOING: Straight course - soft to heavy; round course - soft**

### 2569a COLD MOVE EUROPEAN BREEDERS FUND MARBLE HILL STKS (LISTED RACE) 5f
**2:15** (2:15) 2-Y-O **£28,437** (£8,312; £3,937; £1,312)

RPR

**1** **Cappella Sansevero**[10] 2261 2-9-3 ..................................... GaryCarroll 6 101
(G M Lyons, Ire) *w.w in 4th tl prog under 2f out: chsd clr ldr in 2nd over 1f out: styd on wl to ld fnl 150yds: sn pushed clr: comf* **4/6**[1]

**2** *3 ¼* **Sors (IRE)**[48] 1331 2-9-3 ..................................... DeclanMcDonogh 2 89
(Andrew Slattery, Ire) *sn rdn along in rr: remote 5th over 1f out: styd on wl u.str.p into 2nd clsng stages: nt trble wnr* **11/4**[2]

**3** *3 ¼* **Primo Uomo (IRE)**[13] 2184 2-9-3 ..................................... PatSmullen 5 78
(Gerard O'Leary, Ire) *chsd ldr in 3rd tl prog to chse clr ldr in 2nd 1/2-way: rdn and no imp in 3rd 1f out: kpt on one pce* **10/1**

**4** *½* **Coto (IRE)**[26] 1823 2-8-12 ..................................... ColinKeane 1 71
(M J Tynan, Ire) *broke smartly and sn led: 4 l clr after 1/2-way: advantage reduced 1f out and hdd fnl 150yds: sn no match for wnr and dropped to 4th cl home* **7/1**[3]

**5** *12* **Blackbriar**[6] 2368 2-8-12 ..................................... WayneLordan 4 28
(T Stack, Ire) *trckd ldr in 2nd: dropped to 3rd 1/2-way: sn rdn and dropped to rr: eased fnl f* **33/1**

1m 4.69s (1.79) **Going Correction** +0.60s/f (Yiel) **5** Ran SP% **111.2**
Speed ratings: **109,103,98,97,78**
CSF £2.80 TOTE £1.50: £1.02, £1.50; DF 3.20 Trifecta £7.50.
**Owner** Sean Jones **Bred** Genesis Green Stud Ltd **Trained** Dunsany, Co Meath

**FOCUS**
The inevitable withdrawal of The Great War due to the deteriorating ground conditions turned this from an intriguing Listed contest into a disappointing one. That said, the winner needed to be good to win in the manner he did, given that he had fully 6l to make up 2f out, and still managed to win convincingly.

### 2570a WEATHERBYS IRELAND GREENLANDS STKS (GROUP 3) 6f
**2:45** (2:45) 3-Y-O+ **£35,208** (£10,291; £4,875; £1,625)

RPR

**1** **Slade Power (IRE)**[167] 8209 5-10-0 115.............................. WayneLordan 2 122+
(Edward Lynam, Ire) *sn trckd ldrs in 3rd: travelled best to cl in 2nd under 2f out: led 1f out and sn pushed clr: styd on wl* **5/2**[2]

**2** *2* **Maarek**[10] 2256 7-10-0 115.............................. DeclanMcDonogh 3 116
(Miss Evanna McCutcheon, Ire) *w.w: prog but rdn along in 4th over 1f out: styd on wl into 2nd fnl 150yds: nt trble wnr* **11/8**[1]

**3** *1 ¾* **An Saighdiur (IRE)**[26] 1824 7-9-9 106.............................. BillyLee 5 105
(Andrew Slattery, Ire) *smartly away and led tl hdd 1f out: sn no match for wnr and dropped to 3rd: kpt on same pce* **20/1**

**4** *½* **Viztoria (IRE)**[217] 7364 4-9-11 111.............................. PatSmullen 1 105
(Edward Lynam, Ire) *hld up in rr: 4th whn nt qckn 1f out: kpt on same pce ins fnl f* **5/1**[3]

**5** *6 ½* **Focus On Venice (IRE)**[19] 2038 3-9-0 104.............................. KevinManning 4 81
(J S Bolger, Ire) *chsd ldr in 2nd tl rdn along 2f out: sn wknd* **12/1**

**6** *19* **Darwin (USA)**[251] 6440 4-9-12 114.............................. JosephO'Brien 6 25
(A P O'Brien, Ire) *hld up on stands' side: 4th 1/2-way: no imp and dropped to rr 2f out: sn eased* **7/1**

1m 17.15s (1.65) **Going Correction** +0.60s/f (Yiel)
**WFA** 3 from 4yo+ 9lb **6** Ran SP% **112.3**
Speed ratings: **113,110,108,107,98 73**
CSF £6.35 TOTE £3.20: £1.80, £1.40; DF 6.90 Trifecta £60.00.
**Owner** Mrs S Power **Bred** Mrs S Power **Trained** Dunshaughlin, Co Meath

**FOCUS**
Quality fare. A Group 3 in name but the runner-up is already a Group 1 winner and it was arguably the sprint with most substance run so far this season. The pace was solid from the outset thanks to An Saighdiur and the winner made a real statement of intent.

### 2571a TATTERSALLS IRISH 2,000 GUINEAS (GROUP 1) (ENTIRE COLTS & FILLIES) 1m
**3:20** (3:21) 3-Y-O
**£145,000** (£47,500; £22,500; £7,500; £5,000; £2,500)

RPR

**1** **Kingman**[21] 1951 3-9-0 119.............................. JamesDoyle 1 126+
(John Gosden) *w.w in mid-div tl tk clsr order 2f out in 4th towards outer: travelled wl to ld 1f out and sn qcknd clr: comf* **4/5**[1]

**2** *5* **Shifting Power**[21] 1951 3-9-0 114.............................. RichardHughes 6 115
(Richard Hannon) *sn led: rdn to briefly extend advantage 2f out: strly rdn and hdd 1f out: sn no match for wnr: kpt on same pce* **7/1**[3]

**3** *2* **Mustajeeb**[13] 2185 3-9-0 114.............................. PatSmullen 2 110
(D K Weld, Ire) *trckd ldrs: 3rd 1/2-way: rdn along briefly in 2nd appr fnl f: sn dropped to 3rd and no imp: kpt on one pce* **4/1**[2]

**4** *6* **Johann Strauss**[8] 2320 3-9-0 104.............................. JosephO'Brien 13 96
(A P O'Brien, Ire) *hld up towards inner tl prog to chse ldrs under 2f out: no imp in 4th ent fnl f: kpt on one pce* **12/1**

**5** *2 ¾* **Big Time (IRE)**[286] 5319 3-9-0 114.............................. ShaneFoley 5 90
(John Joseph Murphy, Ire) *racd in mid-div: rdn along over 2f out: no imp in 6th appr fnl f: kpt on one pce* **14/1**

**6** *2* **Great White Eagle (USA)**[19] 2038 3-9-0 106.......... SeamieHeffernan 7 85
(A P O'Brien, Ire) *trckd ldr in cl 2nd tl rdn and nt qckn under 2f out: no imp in 5th appr fnl f* **20/1**

**7** *2 ¾* **Michaelmas (USA)**[19] 2038 3-9-0 105.............................. ColmO'Donoghue 12 79
(A P O'Brien, Ire) *trckd ldrs in 4th tl rdn and nt qckn 2f out: sn no ex* **20/1**

**8** *hd* **Dolce N Karama (IRE)**[86] 770 3-9-0 102.............................. RonanWhelan 4 78
(John Patrick Shanahan, Ire) *hld up: rdn along under 3f out: wnt 8th 2f out: kpt on one pce* **100/1**

**9** *1 ½* **Davids Park**[11] 2238 3-9-0 95.............................. (b[1]) WayneLordan 14 75
(John Joseph Murphy, Ire) *a in rr: no threat over 2f out* **100/1**

**10** *3 ¾* **Fountain Of Youth (IRE)**[19] 2038 3-9-0 100.............................. FMBerry 11 66
(A P O'Brien, Ire) *t.k.h early and trckd ldrs: rdn 3f out: sn no imp and wknd* **50/1**

**11** *96* **Obliterator (IRE)**[38] 1516 3-9-0 109.............................. (p) JamieSpencer 9
(G M Lyons, Ire) *hld up: bit keen early on: rdn along 1/2-way: dropped to rr over 2f out and sn eased* **12/1**

1m 47.29s (1.29) **Going Correction** +0.375s/f (Good) **11** Ran SP% **123.6**
Speed ratings: **108,103,101,95,92 90,87,87,85,82**
CSF £7.29 CT £17.51 TOTE £2.30: £1.02, £1.50, £1.20; DF 6.80 Trifecta £13.90.
**Owner** K Abdullah **Bred** Juddmonte Farms Ltd **Trained** Newmarket, Suffolk

**FOCUS**
The winner was strong to the line and rest strung out. The time was, however, slower than a handicap later on the card. There wasn't much depth with War Command a late defection, but Kingman ranks up with the best winners of this race in the last decade.

### 2572a LANWADES STUD STKS (GROUP 3) (F&M) 1m
**3:55** (3:57) 4-Y-O+ **£33,854** (£9,895; £4,687; £1,562)

RPR

**1** **Purr Along**[239] 6796 4-9-0 106.............................. JamieSpencer 4 111
(J P Murtagh, Ire) *hld up in rr tl gd prog on outer over 1f out: travelled wl to ld ins fnl f: kpt on wl clsng stages* **20/1**

**2** *½* **Fiesolana (IRE)**[23] 1908 5-9-5 114.............................. BillyLee 12 115
(W McCreery, Ire) *trckd ldrs: travelled wl to join issue 1f out: sn hdd by wnr: rallied wl but hld cl home* **4/1**[2]

**3** *1 ½* **Princess Loulou (IRE)**[21] 1945 4-9-0 95.............................. JamesDoyle 3 106
(Roger Varian) *trckd ldrs in 3rd: on terms under 2f out and sn led briefly: hdd and dropped to 4th ins fnl f: kpt on same pce into 3rd clsng stages* **7/1**[3]

**4** *½* **Big Break**[202] 7719 4-9-0 106.............................. PatSmullen 2 105
(D K Weld, Ire) *racd in mid-div tl tk clsr order 2f out: sn pressed ldr in 2nd tl no ex ins fnl f and dropped to 4th* **4/1**[2]

**5** *2 ¾* **Pearl Of Africa (IRE)**[13] 2185 4-9-0 106.............................. HarryBentley 7 99
(Edward Lynam, Ire) *racd in mid-div tl prog whn short of room and swtchd rt over 1f out: kpt on into 5th ent fnl f: sn no imp on ldrs* **14/1**

**6** *1 ¼* **Alive Alive Oh**[41] 1474 4-9-0 106.............................. FMBerry 13 96
(T Stack, Ire) *racd in mid-div tl tk clsr order on stands' side 3f out: rdn along in 5th appr fnl f: sn no imp* **7/1**[3]

**7** *4 ½* **Mizzava (IRE)**[27] 1775 4-9-0 105.............................. ShaneFoley 5 86
(M Halford, Ire) *hld up towards rr: rdn along over 2f out: no imp ent fnl f: kpt on one pce* **25/1**

**8** *nk* **Pop Art (IRE)**[13] 2185 4-9-0 98.............................. RichardHughes 14 85
(Charles O'Brien, Ire) *hld up towards rr: sme prog under 2f out: no imp 1f out* **16/1**

**9** *1 ¾* **Switcher (IRE)**[19] 2042 5-9-0 97.............................. (p) ConorHoban 8 81
(M Halford, Ire) *sn led: c centre trck bef 1/2-way: hdd under 2f out and sn no ex: wknd* **50/1**

**10** *6* **Peace Burg (FR)**[19] 2042 4-9-5 111.............................. JosephO'Brien 6 72
(A P O'Brien, Ire) *racd in mid-div tl prog to trck ldrs in 3rd whn squeezed for room under 2f out: sn no ex* **7/2**[1]

**11** *5 ½* **Tobann (IRE)**[27] 1775 4-9-0 99.............................. (t) KevinManning 11 55
(J S Bolger, Ire) *hld up towards stands' side: rdn 2f out and sn no imp* **33/1**

**12** *4 ¼* **Wannabe Better (IRE)**[19] 2042 4-9-0 104.............................. WayneLordan 1 45
(T Stack, Ire) *hld up on far side: rdn and no imp under 2f out* **10/1**

**13** *½* **One Spirit (IRE)**[13] 2185 6-9-0 100.............................. NGMcCullagh 9 44
(F Dunne, Ire) *t.k.h and trckd ldr in 2nd tl wknd qckly over 2f out* **33/1**

**14** *15* **Izola**[27] 1775 4-9-0 90.............................. SeamieHeffernan 10 9
(Miss Evanna McCutcheon, Ire) *t.k.h early and chsd ldrs tl nt qckn under 3f out and sn dropped to rr* **100/1**

1m 47.55s (1.55) **Going Correction** +0.375s/f (Good) **14** Ran SP% **126.3**
Speed ratings: **107,106,105,104,101 100,96,95,93,87 82,78,77,62**
CSF £98.91 TOTE £27.90: £5.80, £1.90, £2.30; DF 210.80 Trifecta £1344.20.
**Owner** Qatar Racing Ltd & Newsells Park Stud **Bred** Moyns Park Estate And Stud Ltd **Trained** Coolaghknock Glebe,Co Kildare

**FOCUS**
Just as they did 2,000 Guineas, they neglected the far rail in favour of crossing to the stands' side in the home straight but they were spread out all over the track in the closing stages. Plenty swung for home travelling well within themselves but the winner was last off the bridle and prevailed with a shade more in hand that the winning margin suggested.

## [2568]CURRAGH (R-H)
Sunday, May 25

**OFFICIAL GOING: Straight course - heavy; round course - soft**

### 2579a AIRLIE STUD GALLINULE STKS (GROUP 3) 1m 2f
**2:45** (2:47) 3-Y-O **£35,208** (£10,291; £4,875; £1,625)

RPR

**1** **Adelaide (IRE)**[14] 2194 3-9-3.............................. JosephO'Brien 1 110+
(A P O'Brien, Ire) *chsd ldrs in mod 3rd: tk clsr order fr 1/2-way: clsd into st and led on outer gng best over 1f out: rdn clr ins fnl f: comf* **4/6**[1]

**2** *3* **Mekong River (IRE)**[15] 2153 3-9-3 110.................(b) SeamieHeffernan 7 104
(A P O'Brien, Ire) *led and sn clr: reduced advantage fr 1/2-way: rdn into st and hdd narrowly fr 2f out: no imp on wnr u.p in 3rd over 1f out: kpt on again into 2nd ins fnl 100yds: nt trble wnr* **7/1**[3]

**3** *½* **Boqa (IRE)**[38] 1548 3-9-3 89.............................. (t) WayneLordan 5 103
(T Stack, Ire) *chsd ldr in mod 2nd: tk clsr order fr 1/2-way: clsd on outer to ld narrowly fr 2f out: sn strly pressed and hdd over 1f out: no imp on wnr in 2nd ins fnl and dropped to 3rd ins fnl 100yds* **25/1**

**4** *4 ¾* **Renaissance Art (USA)**[329] 3867 3-9-3 94.................(t) KevinManning 3 94
(J S Bolger, Ire) *w.w in rr: tk clsr order bhd ldrs in 4th fr after 1/2-way: rdn on outer over 2f out and no imp on ldrs: kpt on one pce* **11/1**

**5** *4 ½* **Blue Hussar (IRE)**[15] 2153 3-9-3.............................. RyanMoore 6 85
(A P O'Brien, Ire) *hld up in mod 4th: tk clsr order fr 1/2-way: pushed along in rr over 3f out and no imp into st: one pce fnl 2f* **11/4**[2]

2m 16.79s (7.49) **Going Correction** +0.60s/f (Yiel) **5** Ran SP% **111.3**
Speed ratings: **94,91,91,87,83**
CSF £6.21 TOTE £1.60: £1.02, £2.70; DF 5.90 Trifecta £39.60.
**Owner** Derrick Smith & Mrs John Magnier & Michael Tabor **Bred** Elletelle Syndicate **Trained** Cashel, Co Tipperary

**FOCUS**
A race Aidan O'Brien often wins, and Adelaide did it with a bit to spare.

## 2580a TATTERSALLS GOLD CUP (GROUP 1) — 1m 2f 110y
3:20 (3:20) 4-Y-0+ **£108,500** (£33,250; £15,750; £5,250; £1,750)

RPR

1 **Noble Mission**[17] 2086 5-9-3 117 ........ JamesDoyle 3 112+
(Lady Cecil) *sn led: over 1 l clr 1/2-way: extended advantage gng wl appr st and wnt wl clr 2f out: rdn and reduced advantage wl ins fnl f: kpt on* **Evs**[1]

2 1 1/4 **Magician (IRE)**[20] 2040 4-9-3 124 ........ JosephO'Brien 5 109+
(A P O'Brien, Ire) *w.w: tk clsr order in 3rd after 3f: wnt mod 2nd over 3f out: rdn into st and no imp on wnr 2f out: clsd on wnr disputing 2nd u.p wl ins fnl f: wnt 2nd fnl strides: a hld* **Evs**[1]

3 hd **Euphrasia (IRE)**[11] 2263 5-9-0 100 ........ GaryCarroll 6 106
(Joseph G Murphy, Ire) *prom: sn settled bhd ldrs in 3rd: dropped to 4th after 3f: rdn into mod 3rd 3f out: clsd on wnr u.p disputing 2nd wl ins fnl f: dropped to 3rd fnl strides: a hld* **50/1**

4 21 **Einsteins Folly (IRE)**[21] 1991 4-9-3 99 ........(p) RonanWhelan 7 68
(J S Bolger, Ire) *w.w in rr: last 1/2-way: rdn in mod 4th fr 3f out and no imp u.p: one pce fnl 2f* **33/1**[3]

5 28 **Hall Of Mirrors (IRE)**[20] 2040 4-9-3 106 ........(v[1]) SeamieHeffernan 4 13
(A P O'Brien, Ire) *sn chsd ldr in 2nd: rdn appr st and sn no ex u.p: dropped to rr 3f out: eased fr over 2f out* **16/1**[2]

2m 21.71s (1.71) **Going Correction** +0.60s/f (Yiel) 5 Ran SP% **110.8**
Speed ratings: **117,116,115,100,80**
CSF £2.20 TOTE £1.60: £1.02, £1.02; DF 2.40 Trifecta £15.30.
**Owner** K Abdullah **Bred** Juddmonte Farms Ltd **Trained** Newmarket, Suffolk

**FOCUS**
A rather disappointing feel to this year's renewal given that Al Kazeem fought off Camelot in the race 12 months previously. The winner, revitalised by the switch to trailblazing tactics this season, again made all and looked likely to route the field early in the home straight. The fact that a mare rated 100 got within a head of Magician raises serious question marks about the form.

## 2581a ETIHAD AIRWAYS IRISH 1,000 GUINEAS (GROUP 1) (FILLIES) — 1m
3:55 (3:55) 3-Y-0
**£145,000** (£47,500; £22,500; £7,500; £5,000; £2,500)

RPR

1 **Marvellous (IRE)**[56] 1201 3-9-0 ........ RyanMoore 11 117+
(A P O'Brien, Ire) *dwlt sltly and w.w towards rr: last 1/2-way: pushed along in 9th 3f out and clsd u.p on outer to chal in 2nd ins fnl f: led ins fnl 150yds and sn edgd rt: styd on wl* **10/1**

2 3 **Lightning Thunder**[21] 1976 3-9-0 111 ........ HarryBentley 1 110
(Olly Stevens) *chsd ldrs: 5th 1/2-way: clsr in 4th 3f out: clsd on outer fr 2f out to ld u.p over 1f out: sn strly pressed and hdd ins fnl 150yds: no ex* **10/3**[1]

3 4 1/4 **Vote Often**[63] 1076 3-9-0 104 ........ JamesDoyle 9 100
(D K Weld, Ire) *chsd ldrs: 2nd 1/2-way: rdn fr 2f out and outpcd in 4th over 1f out: kpt on u.p into mod 3rd nr fin* **4/1**[2]

4 1/2 **Avenue Gabriel**[56] 1201 3-9-0 103 ........ ChrisHayes 5 99
(P D Deegan, Ire) *chsd ldrs: 3rd 1/2-way: rdn to ld over 2f out: strly pressed u.p and hdd over 1f out: sn no ex in 3rd and dropped to mod 4th nr fin* **16/1**

5 1 1/4 **Palace (IRE)**[14] 2186 3-9-1 102 ow1 ........ JosephO'Brien 6 96
(A P O'Brien, Ire) *dwlt sltly: hld up: 8th 1/2-way: rdn over 2f out and no imp on ldrs in 7th ent fnl f: kpt on u.p into mod 5th ins fnl 150yds* **6/1**[3]

6 4 1/2 **Tested**[21] 1987 3-9-0 ........ PatSmullen 12 86
(D K Weld, Ire) *in tch: 6th 1/2-way: rdn 2f out on outer and sn no ex u.p in 5th: dropped to mod 6th ins fnl 150yds* **6/1**[3]

7 nk **Queen Of Power (IRE)**[28] 1772 3-9-0 98 ........ FergalLynch 2 85
(M D O'Callaghan, Ire) *hld up: 9th 1/2-way: dropped to rr 3f out: sme hdwy far side u.p over 2f out: kpt on one pce into mod 7th ins fnl 150yds* **20/1**

8 6 1/2 **Heart Focus (IRE)**[311] 4462 3-9-0 100 ........(b[1]) KevinManning 4 73
(J S Bolger, Ire) *towards rr: 10th 1/2-way: rdn 3f out and sn swtchd rt in rr: mod 10th over 1f out: kpt on one pce* **33/1**

9 hd **Wonderfully (IRE)**[14] 2195 3-9-0 105 ........ SeamieHeffernan 7 70
(A P O'Brien, Ire) *sn led: rdn and hdd over 2f out: wknd: eased ins fnl f* **14/1**

10 2 **Ballybacka Queen (IRE)**[14] 2186 3-9-0 100 ........ FMBerry 10 65
(P A Fahy, Ire) *on toes befhand: chsd ldrs: 4th 1/2-way: sn pushed along in 5th and wknd qckly u.p fr 3f out* **10/1**

11 1 1/4 **Al Thakhira**[14] 2195 3-9-0 103 ........ RichardHughes 3 62
(Marco Botti) *in tch: 7th 1/2-way: hdwy between horses to chse ldrs in 4th 1 1/2f out: rdn and no ex: wknd and eased ins fnl f* **6/1**[3]

1m 45.52s (-0.48) **Going Correction** +0.20s/f (Good) 11 Ran SP% **124.4**
Speed ratings: **110,107,102,102,101 96,96,89,89,87 86**
CSF £45.92 CT £166.05 TOTE £12.00: £3.20, £1.30, £1.70; DF 64.00 Trifecta £626.30.
**Owner** Derrick Smith & Mrs John Magnier & Michael Tabor **Bred** You'resothrilling Syndicate **Trained** Cashel, Co Tipperary

**FOCUS**
The second set the standard and seemed to run her race. The had been beaten in Group 3 company on her previous start.

2582 - 2583a (Foreign Racing) - See Raceform Interactive

# 1478 DUSSELDORF (R-H)
Sunday, May 25

**OFFICIAL GOING: Turf: good**

## 2584a GERMAN 1000 GUINEAS (GROUP 2) (3YO FILLIES) (TURF) — 1m
3:25 (12:00) 3-Y-0
**£58,333** (£23,333; £11,666; £5,833; £2,916; £2,083)

RPR

1 **Ajaxana (GER)**[34] 1619 3-9-2 0 ........ AnthonyCrastus 4 108
(Waldemar Hickst, Germany) *mde all: rdn whn chal under 2f out: virtually jnd on inner 1f out: rallied and r.o u.p: asserted fnl 50yds* **6/4**[1]

2 3/4 **Indian Rainbow (IRE)**[24] 3-9-2 0 ........ JBojko 3 107
(Andreas Lowe, Germany) *trckd ldr on inner: rdn to chal on ins under 2f out: n.m.r but virtually upsides ldr 1f out: r.o u.p: no ex fnl 50yds* **111/10**

3 nse **Diamond Dove (GER)**[217] 7406 3-9-2 0 ........ AndreBest 7 106
(Andreas Lowe, Germany) *chsd ldng trio: rdn and nt qckn 1 1/2f out: styd on wl u.p fnl f: jst missed 2nd* **77/10**

4 3/4 **Evita Peron**[25] 1868 3-9-2 0 ........ JimCrowley 6 105+
(Ralph Beckett) *wnt rt leaving stalls: w.w in midfield: rdn ins fnl 2f: effrt on outside 1 1/2f out: styd on u.p fnl f: nt pce to chal* **53/10**[3]

5 3/4 **Ninas Terz (GER)**[24] 3-9-2 0 ........ FilipMinarik 8 103
(P Schiergen, Germany) *trckd ldr on outer: hrd rdn and nt qckn over 1 1/2f out: grad outpcd by ldrs ins fnl f* **61/10**

6 1 1/2 **Artwork Genie (IRE)**[24] 3-9-2 0 ........ AdriedeVries 2 100
(Jean-Pierre Carvalho, Germany) *trckd ldng gp: rdn to chse first four fr 2f out: sn no imp: one pce fnl f* **7/2**[2]

7 2 **Feodora (GER)**[21] 3-9-2 0 ........ MartinLane 5 95+
(Frau R Weissmeier, Germany) *dwlt and sltly impeded leaving stalls: hld up towards rr: rdn and swtchd outside 2f out: styd on u.p fnl f: nrest at fin* **169/10**

8 1 1/2 **Turfmaid (GER)**[34] 1619 3-9-2 0 ........ SHellyn 9 93
(J Hirschberger, Germany) *towards rr: rdn and no imp over 2f out: sn btn* **34/1**

9 1/2 **Wild Step (GER)**[34] 1619 3-9-2 0 ........ AHelfenbein 11 90+
(Markus Klug, Germany) *in rr: rdn and swtchd outside over 2f out: no real hdwy and nvr in contention* **156/10**

10 1 1/2 **Filaga (FR)**[24] 3-9-2 0 ........ MSuerland 1 87
(M Figge, Germany) *towards rr on inner: rdn and btn fr over 2f out* **31/1**

11 nk **Oriental Magic (GER)**[24] 3-9-2 0 ........ MichaelCadeddu 10 86
(J Hirschberger, Germany) *midfield on outer: rdn and wknd fnl 2f* **37/1**

1m 37.67s (-3.49) 11 Ran SP% **132.2**
WIN (incl. 10 euro stake): 25. PLACES: 15, 28, 26. SF: 378.
**Owner** Stall Lucky Owner **Bred** Klaus Hofmann **Trained** Germany

2585 - (Foreign Racing) - See Raceform Interactive

# 2449 LONGCHAMP (R-H)
Sunday, May 25

**OFFICIAL GOING: Turf: soft**

## 2586a POUR MOI COOLMORE PRIX SAINT-ALARY (GROUP 1) (3YO FILLIES) (TURF) — 1m 2f
2:45 (2:47) 3-Y-0 **£119,041** (£47,625; £23,812; £11,895; £5,958)

RPR

1 3 **Vazira (FR)**[28] 1782 3-9-0 0 ........ ChristopheSoumillon 6 108+
(A De Royer-Dupre, France) *bucked leaving stalls and dwlt: sn rcvrd and hld up towards rr: pushed along and hdwy 2f out: rdn over 1f out: styd on and wnt 2nd ins fnl f: chsd wnr but no imp and wl hld* **5/4**[1]

2 3 **Bereni Ka (FR)**[40] 1502 3-9-0 0 ........ ThierryThulliez 8 102
(Y Gourraud, France) *dropped in fr wdst draw and hld up: sn last: pushed along and hdwy fr 2f out: rdn over 1f out: styd on and tk 3rd towards fin: nvr nrr* **25/1**

3 1/2 **Lady Penko (FR)**[30] 3-9-0 0 ........ StephanePasquier 1 101
(C Delcher-Sanchez, France) *dwlt sltly: pushed along to rcvr and sn led: rdn over 2f out: hdd over 1f out: no ex ins fnl f and dropped to 4th towards fin* **11/1**

4 1 1/4 **Stormyra (FR)**[40] 1502 3-9-0 0 ........ UmbertoRispoli 4 99
(J-P Gallorini, France) *t.k.h: hld up in midfield on inner: swtchd lft and rdn into st: styd on same pce fr over 1f out and sn wl hld* **14/1**

5 3/4 **Chocolatier (FR)**[28] 1782 3-9-0 0 ........ Christophe-PatriceLemaire 2 97
(M Delzangles, France) *trckd ldr early: sn midfield in tch on inner: rdn 2f out: styd on same pce fr over 1f out and sn wl hld* **33/1**

6 20 **Goldy Espony (FR)**[40] 1502 3-9-0 0 ........ FabriceVeron 3 57
(H-A Pantall, France) *trckd ldr on outer: restrained bhd ldng pair 1/2-way: rdn and ev ch into st: no ex and btn over 1f out: fdd and eased* **6/1**[3]

7 1 3/4 **Green Speed (FR)**[40] 1502 3-9-0 0 ........ AlexisBadel 7 54
(Mme M Bollack-Badel, France) *midfield on outer: hdwy to trck ldr 1/2-way: pushed along and brief effrt to chal into st: shuffled bk to rr 2f and sn btn: eased* **33/1**

D **We Are (IRE)**[24] 3-9-0 0 ........ ThierryJarnet 5 114
(F Head, France) *t.k.h: sn midfield on outer: clsd gng strly into st: shkn up to chal 2f out: rdn to ld over 1f out: styd on strly and asserted ins fnl f: pushed out towards fin: comf* **2/1**[2]

2m 8.45s (4.45) **Going Correction** +0.725s/f (Yiel) 8 Ran SP% **116.8**
Speed ratings: **108,106,105,104,104 88,86,111**
WIN (incl. 1 euro stake): 2.70. PLACES: 1.40, 1.30, 2.90. DF: 3.00. SF: 5.70.
**Owner** H H Aga Khan **Bred** Haras De Son Altesse L'Aga Khan Scea **Trained** Chantilly, France

**FOCUS**
A race that is essentially a trial for the Diane, but is a Group 1 in its own right and two classy fillies' came clear. Strong form.

## 2587a PRIX D'ISPAHAN (GROUP 1) (4YO+) (TURF) — 1m 1f 55y
3:15 (3:17) 4-Y-0+ **£119,041** (£47,625; £23,812; £11,895; £5,958)

RPR

1 **Cirrus Des Aigles (FR)**[28] 1783 8-9-2 0 ........ ChristopheSoumillon 1 122+
(Mme C Barande-Barbe, France) *broke wl and mde all: pushed along and qcknd 2f out: r.o strly and asserted under mostly hands and heels ins fnl f: comf* **4/7**[1]

2 1 1/2 **Anodin (IRE)**[24] 1908 4-9-2 0 ........ OlivierPeslier 3 118
(F Head, France) *t.k.h: trckd ldr on outer: pushed along 2f out: rdn over 1f out: r.o and wnt 2nd wl ins fnl f: nt pce of wnr* **33/1**

3 1 1/4 **Pollyana (IRE)**[232] 7047 5-8-13 0 ........ FabienLefebvre 4 112
(J E Hammond, France) *restrained early and hld up towards rr on inner: pushed along into st: 4th whn rdn ent fnl f: r.o and wnt 3rd towards fin: nt pce to chal* **25/1**[3]

4 3/4 **Olympic Glory (IRE)**[8] 2338 4-9-2 0 ........(b) FrankieDettori 2 114+
(Richard Hannon) *dwlt sltly but qckly rcvrd: trckd ldr on inner: rdn 2f out: kpt on but sn hld by wnr: no ex and fdd ins fnl 100yds* **15/8**[2]

5 1/2 **Neatico (GER)**[42] 1478 7-9-2 0 ........ ThierryThulliez 6 113
(P Schiergen, Germany) *midfield: rdn 2f out: sn outpcd: styd on but nvr threatened* **25/1**[3]

6 snk **Matorio (FR)**[24] 1908 4-8-13 0 ........ FabriceVeron 5 109
(H-A Pantall, France) *hld up in last: pushed along 3f out: rdn and outpcd over 1f out: styd but nvr threatened* **33/1**

1m 57.98s (2.68) **Going Correction** +0.725s/f (Yiel) 6 Ran SP% **112.0**
Speed ratings: **117,115,114,113,113 113**
WIN (incl. 1 euro stake): 1.60. PLACES: 1.10, 1.90. SF: 9.50.
**Owner** Jean-Claude-Alain Dupouy **Bred** M Yvon Lelimouzin & M Benoit Deschamps **Trained** France

**FOCUS**
The big duel between Cirrus Des Aigles and Olympic Glory failed to materialise.

## 2588a PRIX VICOMTESSE VIGIER (GROUP 2) (4YO+) (TURF) 1m 7f 110y
3:55 (3:56) 4-Y-0+ £61,750 (£23,833; £11,375; £7,583; £3,791)

RPR

1 **Fly With Me (FR)**[28] 1784 4-8-11 0............................(p) MaximeGuyon 4 116+
(E Libaud, France) *led 2f: trckd ldr on outer once hdd: pushed along in cl 2nd 3f out: rdn and sltly outpcd by ldr over 2f out: rallied u.p and styd on strly to chal ins fnl f: led on hd bob post* **11/2**[3]

2 nse **Goldtara (FR)**[28] 1784 6-8-8 0..................... Christophe-PatriceLemaire 8 111
(A Lyon, France) *midfield early: led after 2f: gng best whn pushed along 2f out: rdn over 1f out: strly pressed ins fnl f: styd on gamely u.p but jst lost out on hd bob post* **14/1**

3 1 ¼ **Terrubi (IRE)**[28] 1784 4-8-11 0........................................ ThierryJarnet 2 115+
(P Bary, France) *sn midfield in tch on outer: pushed along over 2f out: rdn over 1f out: styd on and wnt 3rd ins fnl f: nt pce of front pair* **3/1**[2]

4 2 ½ **Montclair (IRE)**[28] 1784 4-8-11 0........................ Pierre-CharlesBoudot 1 112
(A Fabre, France) *restrained and sn in midfield on inner: pushed along 3f out: rdn 2f out: styd on but nt pce to chal* **5/2**[1]

5 hd **Ebiyza (IRE)**[28] 1784 4-8-10 0........................... ChristopheSoumillon 3 110
(A De Royer-Dupre, France) *w ldr 2f: trckd ldr on inner whn hdd: rdn 2f out: edgd lft over 1f out: styd on but nt pce of ldrs and sn hld* **7/1**

6 nk **Solow**[22] 4-8-11 0........................................................ OlivierPeslier 6 111
(F Head, France) *restrained and hld up towards rr: pushed along in last 3f out: rdn 2f out: swtchd rt over 1f out: styd on but nt pce to chal and sn wl hld* **13/2**

7 4 **Times Up**[22] 1950 8-9-0 0............................................... GeraldMosse 5 107
(Ed Dunlop) *t.k.h: hld up and a towards rr: pushed along 3f out: rdn and outpcd 2f out: hung rt u.p: eased whn btn ins fnl f: nvr a factor* **8/1**

8 10 **Les Beaufs (FR)**[28] 1784 5-8-11 0.............................. JulienGuillochon 7 92
(Mme V Seignoux, France) *hld up in rr on inner: hdwy into midfield 3f out: rdn over 2f out: sn outpcd and btn: dropped to last again over 1f out: eased* **14/1**

3m 32.22s (10.72) **Going Correction** +0.725s/f (Yiel)
**WFA** 4 from 5yo+ 1lb 8 Ran SP% **119.2**
Speed ratings: **102,101,101,100,100 99,97,92**
WIN (incl. 1 euro stake): 5.90. PLACES: 2.00, 4.40, 1.80. DF: 63.40. SF: 97.50.
**Owner** Jean Luck **Bred** Sca Haras De La Barbottiere **Trained** France

# 1603 SAN SIRO (R-H)
Sunday, May 25

**OFFICIAL GOING: Turf: good**

## 2589a PREMIO CARLO VITTADINI (GROUP 2) (3YO+) (TURF) 1m
3:25 (12:00) 3-Y-0+ £39,583 (£17,416; £9,500; £4,750)

RPR

1 **Priore Philip (ITY)**[28] 1779 3-8-11 0............................ CristianDemuro 4 108
(Stefano Botti, Italy) *w.w in midfield: hdwy on outer 2 1/2f out: shkn up to chal appr fnl f: drvn and r.o to ld cl home* **154/100**[1]

2 nk **Verdetto Finale**[28] 4-9-5 0........................................ MircoDemuro 5 106
(R Biondi, Italy) *led: hdd over 3f out: shkn up and rallied to regain ld 2 1/2f out: rdn and r.o whn chal appr fnl f: hdd cl home: no ex* **155/10**

3 3 **Passaggio (ITY)**[14] 6-9-5 0................................................ CFiocchi 3 99
(A Cascio, Italy) *t.k.h in midfield: sltly outpcd and rdn 2 1/2f out: swtchd outside and styd on u.p fr over 1f out: nvr on terms w first two* **51/1**

4 1 ¾ **Vola E Va**[21] 5-9-5 0........................................................ DarioVargiu 7 95
(B Grizzetti, Italy) *towards rr: rdn and prog 2f out: kpt on u.p fnl f: nt pce to chal* **153/10**

5 nse **Porsenna (IRE)**[42] 4-9-5 0.............................................. AndreaAtzeni 8 95
(Stefano Botti, Italy) *towards rr: tk clsr order over 1 1/2f out: kpt on ins fnl f: jst missed 4th: nvr in contention* **89/10**

6 nse **Vedelago (IRE)**[14] 2191 5-9-5 0.................................... MEsposito 9 95
(Stefano Botti, Italy) *missed break: hld up towards rr: rdn and outpcd 2f out: kpt on ins fnl f: nvr nrr* **14/5**[2]

7 5 **Summer Fall (USA)**[204] 5-9-2 0..................................... FabioBranca 1 80
(B Grizzetti, Italy) *broke out of stalls bef s: towards rr: sme hdwy on ins over 2f out: sn btn* **175/10**

8 ½ **Nabucco (GER)**[21] 4-9-5 0............................................... DPerovic 6 82
(R Rohne, Germany) *trckd ldr on outer: led over 3f out: hdd 2 1/2f out: wknd fnl 2f* **67/20**[3]

9 5 **Saint Bernard**[14] 2191 5-9-7 0........................................ GBietolini 2 73
(D Camuffo, Italy) *chsd ldng pair: rdn and wknd fr over 1 1/2f out* **57/10**

1m 35.1s (-7.00)
**WFA** 3 from 4yo+ 12lb 9 Ran SP% **133.2**
WIN (incl. 1 euro stake): 2.53. PLACES> 1.57, 3.39, 9.08. DF: 20.99.
**Owner** Scuderia Ste Ma **Bred** Azienda Agricola Luciani Loreto **Trained** Italy

## 2590a OAKS D'ITALIA (GROUP 2) (3YO FILLIES) (TURF) 1m 3f
4:10 (12:00) 3-Y-O £154,166 (£67,833; £37,000; £18,500)

RPR

1 **Final Score (IRE)**[35] 3-8-11 0......................................... FabioBranca 12 99
(Stefano Botti, Italy) *trckd ldr on outer: hrd rdn to chal fr 1 1/2f out: led narrowly appr fnl f: r.o gamely under driving fr 1f out: asserted fnl 50yds* **10/11**[1]

2 ½ **Scighera**[21] 3-8-11 0........................................................ AndreaAtzeni 8 98
(Stefano Botti, Italy) *led: pushed along and upped tempo 3f out: hdd over 2f out: sn rallied u.p: kpt on wl fnl f: nvr quite getting bk up* **68/10**

3 1 ½ **So Many Shots (IRE)**[21] 3-8-11 0................................. CristianDemuro 9 95
(Stefano Botti, Italy) *w.w in 5th: chal outside three rivals appr fnl f: kpt on u.p: outpcd by first two fnl 100yds* **71/20**[2]

4 ½ **Finidaprest (IRE)**[28] 1780 3-8-11 0..................................... IRossi 3 95
(B Grizzetti, Italy) *trckd ldng pair on inner: rdn to ld over 2f out: hdd appr fnl f: sn one pce and no ex fnl 100yds* **68/10**

5 snk **Elektrum (IRE)**[27] 3-8-11 0.......................................... KierenFallon 2 94
(G Botti, France) *t.k.h: w.w in tch between horses: rdn and chsd ldrs appr fnl f: kpt on u.p fnl f: nt pce to chal* **101/20**[3]

6 ½ **Vallecupa (ITY)**[21] 3-8-11 0............................................ DPerovic 10 93
(D Zarroli, Italy) *hld up towards rr: hdwy on ins over 2f out: kpt on u.p fnl f: nvr on terms w ldrs* **158/10**

7 shd **Donna Prassede (ITY)**[28] 1780 3-8-11 0............................ CFiocchi 1 93
(Stefano Botti, Italy) *w.w in tch on inner: rdn and outpcd 2f out: kpt on u.p fr 1f out: nt pce to chal* **34/1**

8 2 ½ **Vague Nouvelle (IRE)**[28] 1780 3-8-11 0...................... MircoDemuro 11 89
(R Biondi, Italy) *t.k.h: hld up in rr: hdwy 3f out: cl 6th and rdn over 2f out: hld pl tl wknd fnl f: eased* **25/4**

9 8 **Lady Dutch**[28] 1780 3-8-11 0............................................ DarioVargiu 6 74
(B Grizzetti, Italy) *w.w in midfield: scrubbed along and no imp over 2 1/2f out: sn btn: eased fnl f* **155/10**

10 shd **Nauka (GER)**[24] 3-8-11 0................................................ MartinSeidl 7 74
(Markus Klug, Germany) *w.w in tch on outer: pushed along to hold pl over 4f out: lost pl 2 1/2f out and sn btn: eased fnl f* **177/10**

11 3 ½ **Daring Life (IRE)** 3-8-11 0.......................................(b) MEsposito 5 68
(Gabriele Miliani, Italy) *hld up towards rr: rdn and no imp over 2 1/2f out: sn btn* **36/1**

12 1 ½ **Hurrimera (ITY)**[28] 1780 3-8-11 0..................................... LManiezzi 4 65
(R Menichetti, Italy) *chsd ldrs: rdn and wknd fr 3f out* **119/1**

2m 14.5s (-4.10) 12 Ran SP% **154.1**
WIN (incl. 1 euro stake): 1.91. PLACES: 1.18, 1.89, 1.44. DF: 17.00.
**Owner** Scuderia Effevi SRL **Bred** Razza Del Velino Srl **Trained** Italy

# 1622 LES LANDES
Sunday, May 25

**OFFICIAL GOING: Turf: good to soft**

## 2591a CHANNEL ISLAND RACING AND HUNT CLUB H'CAP SPRINT 5f 100y
3:05 (3:05) (0-60,) 3-Y-O+ £955 (£340; £205)

RPR

1 **Purley Queen (IRE)**[176] 8119 5-10-12 ................................. MrFTett 2 58
(Mrs C Gilbert, Jersey) **2/1**[1]

2 6 **Country Blue (FR)**[20] 2598 5-10-2.......................(p) ThomasGarner 4 28
(Mrs A Malzard, Jersey) **9/2**[2]

3 nse **Thrtypointstothree (IRE)**[20] 2598 3-10-11.......... MatthewCosham 1 42
(Nikki Evans) **11/2**[3]

4 3 ½ **Lively Little Lady**[34] 1623 4-8-12 ........................ JenniferFerguson 3
(Mrs A Corson, Jersey) **12/1**

1m 10.0s (1.00)
**WFA** 3 from 4yo+ 8lb 4 Ran SP% **74.6**

**Owner** Manor Farm Racing **Bred** Mark & Pippa Hackett **Trained** Jersey

## 2592a BLOODSTOCK ADVISORY SERVICE JERSEY GUINEAS 1m 100y
3:45 (3:45) 3-Y-O+ £1,760 (£650; £390)

RPR

1 **Ancient Greece**[34] 1624 7-10-5 ..........................(t) MattieBatchelor 4 58
(George Baker) **4/11**[1]

2 2 **First Cat**[34] 1623 7-10-5 ........................................... MichaelStainton 6 54
(K Kukk, Jersey) **4/1**[2]

3 4 ½ **Spanish Bounty**[34] 1623 9-10-5 ..................................... ThomasGarner 3 44
(Mrs A Malzard, Jersey) **4/1**[2]

4 8 **Mr Opulence**[34] 1622 5-9-9 ..........................................(b) MrRHodson 5 17
(T Le Brocq, Jersey) **8/1**

5 hd **Fast Freddie**[20] 2597 10-10-5 .......................................(p) MrPCollington 2 26
(Mrs A Corson, Jersey) **4/1**[2]

6 20 **Buaiteoir (FR)**[80] 858 8-10-5 ..................................... MatthewCosham 1
(Nikki Evans) **9/1**

7 15 **Esprit De Midas**[34] 1623 8-10-5 ....................................... JoshBaudains 7
(K Kukk, Jersey) **6/1**[3]

1m 52.0s (112.00) 7 Ran SP% **168.7**

**Owner** Inkin, Inkin, Byng, Baker & Partners **Bred** Darley **Trained** Manton, Wilts

## 2593a LIBERATION BREWERY H'CAP 1m 4f
4:15 (4:15) 3-Y-O+ £1,460 (£525; £315)

RPR

1 **I'm Harry**[20] 2599 5-10-12 ...........................................(vt) MattieBatchelor 2 70
(George Baker) **4/6**[1]

2 2 ½ **River Du Nord (FR)**[34] 1622 7-9-0 ................................ JemmaMarshall 3 40
(Sue Gardner) **4/1**[3]

3 10 **King Kenny**[34] 1624 9-8-12 ....................................... JenniferFerguson 6 22
(Mrs A Corson, Jersey) **11/2**

4 6 **Steely**[34] 1624 6-10-6 ................................................. MichaelStainton 1 34
(K Kukk, Jersey) **3/1**[2]

5 ¾ **Sweet Liberta (IRE)**[343] 5-10-9 .......................................... MrRHodson 4 36
(T Le Brocq, Jersey) **4/1**[3]

6 8 **Reve De Gosse (FR)**[141] 4-10-7 ...................................(b) ThomasGarner 5 21
(Mrs A Malzard, Jersey) **13/2**

2m 47.0s (-3.00) 6 Ran SP% **153.7**

**Owner** Wickfield Stud And Hartshill Stud **Bred** Wickfield Stud And Hartshill Stud **Trained** Manton, Wilts

## 2594a CHANNEL ISLAND RACING AND HUNT CLUB H'CAP 1m 1f
4:50 (4:50) (0-55,) 3-Y-O+ £955 (£340; £205)

RPR

1 **Midnight Sequel**[34] 1622 5-10-12 ............................(p) MattieBatchelor 2 60
(Neil Mulholland) **7/4**[1]

2 ½ **Grey Panel (FR)**[34] 1625 6-9-10 ......................................... MrRHodson 1 43
(T Le Brocq, Jersey) **5/2**[3]

3 3 ½ **Pas D'Action**[20] 2597 6-10-3 ...................................... ThomasGarner 6 43
(Mrs A Malzard, Jersey) **5/1**

4 nse **Up In Flames (IRE)**[222] 7266 5-10-7 .................................. OllieGarner 3 46
(Martin Keighley) **2/1**[2]

5 2 **Lady Petrus**[34] 1622 9-8-11 oh8 ow6.......................... MichaelStainton 11 18
(K Kukk, Jersey) **14/1**

6 2 **Rocquaine (IRE)**[20] 2599 5-8-5 ..............................(p) JemmaMarshall 9 8
(Mrs A Malzard, Jersey) **18/1**

7 1 **Jackpot**[34] 1625 4-9-6 ................................................... MatthewCosham 10 21
(Mrs A Malzard, Jersey) **10/3**

8 *dist* **Athania (IRE)**[34] 1625 8-9-2 ....(p) MrPCollington 8
(Mrs A Corson, Jersey) **12/1**
9 *dist* **Frankkie M (JER)**[331] 4-8-11 ow1.... JoshBaudains 5
(Mrs A Corson, Jersey) **18/1**
F **Rebel Woman**[34] 1625 8-9-2 .... JenniferFerguson 4
(Mrs A Corson, Jersey) **5/1**
2m 2.0s (122.00) **10** Ran SP% **179.6**

**Owner** Dajam Ltd **Bred** M Burbidge **Trained** Limpley Stoke, Wilts

# L'ANCRESSE

Monday, May 5

**OFFICIAL GOING: Good (good to soft in places)**

## 2595a BETWAY BAILIWICK CUP (H'CAP) 1m 6f

**2:15** (2:15) 3-Y-O+ **£1,800** (£750; £450)

RPR
1 **Omega Omega**[62] 831 5-9-7 ....(b) PhilipPrince
(Liam Corcoran) **8/1**
2 *hd* **Ballyheigue (IRE)**[17] 1567 5-10-6 ....(p) MissHHeal
(Liam Corcoran) **1/1**[1]
3 *nk* **Scribe (IRE)**[21] 1485 6-10-8 ....(vt) RichardEvans
(David Evans) **5/4**[2]
4 *8* **Candelita**[22] 4938 7-10-12 .... MrJamesHughes
(Jo Hughes) **3/1**[3]
5 *15* **Reach Out**[14] 1018 6-9-12 .... JemmaMarshall
(Mrs A Malzard, Jersey) **10/1**
ms **5** Ran SP% **139.6**

**Owner** John W Ford **Bred** J Ford & Peter J Skinner **Trained** Lovington, Somerset

## 2596a BOB FROOME & SONS H'CAP 1m 2f

**2:50** (2:50) 3-Y-O+ **£1,800** (£750; £450)

RPR
1 **One Way Or Another (AUS)**[30] 1311 11-10-0 ....(t) RichardEvans 62
(David Evans) **6/4**[1]
2 *1* **The Bay Bandit**[14] 1050 7-9-7 ....(p) MattieBatchelor 53
(Neil Mulholland) **5/2**[2]
3 *2* **Beck's Bolero (IRE)**[14] 1624 8-9-4 ....(p) JenniferFerguson 46
(Mrs A Corson, Jersey) **6/1**
4 **Do More Business (IRE)**[9] 1745 7-9-10 ....(vt) PhilipPrince
(Liam Corcoran) **5/2**[2]
5 **Citizen Kaine (IRE)**[34] 1220 3-10-0 .... JosephineGordon
(Jo Hughes) **9/2**[3]
6 **Illegale (IRE)**[6] 1836 8-8-13 .... MatthewCosham
(Nikki Evans) **10/1**
2m 12.0s (132.00)
**WFA** 3 from 7yo+ 15lb **6** Ran SP% **138.7**

**Owner** Mrs E Evans **Bred** Segenho Stud **Trained** Pandy, Monmouths

## 2597a RAVENSCROFT CHANNEL ISLAND H'CAP 1m

**3:25** (3:25) (0-70,) 3-Y-O+ **£3,100** (£1,200; £700)

RPR
1 **Hail Promenader (IRE)**[41] 1087 8-10-12 ....(tp) PhilipPrince 67
(Anthony Carson) **5/4**[1]
2 *2* **The Mongoose**[12] 1649 6-10-7 ....(t) RichardEvans 57
(David Evans) **5/4**[1]
3 *hd* **Fast Freddie**[14] 1623 10-9-6 ....(p) JenniferFerguson 42
(Mrs A Corson, Jersey) **6/1**
4 *hd* **Pas D'Action**[14] 1623 6-9-7 .... JemmaMarshall 42
(Mrs A Malzard, Jersey) **2/1**[2]
5 *10* **Flying Giant (IRE)**[7] 1819 4-10-1 .... MrJamesHughes 27
(Jo Hughes) **9/2**[3]
1m 47.0s (107.00) **5** Ran SP% **154.7**

**Owner** Richard Prince **Bred** Rathbarry Stud **Trained** Newmarket, Suffolk

## 2598a HUNSCOTE STUD H'CAP 6f

**4:00** (4:00) 3-Y-O+ **£1,800** (£750; £450)

RPR
1 **Style And Panache (IRE)**[579] 6788 6-9-6 .... PhilipPrince 55
(R Storp, Germany) **5/1**[3]
2 *7* **Haadeeth**[26] 1388 7-10-9 .... RichardEvans 50
(David Evans) **1/1**[1]
3 *nk* **Kersivay**[252] 7143 8-10-12 .... JenniferFerguson 52
(Mrs A Malzard, Jersey) **10/1**
4 *6* **Novabridge**[54] 921 6-10-12 .... MattieBatchelor 33
(Neil Mulholland) **11/4**[2]
5 **Country Blue (FR)**[14] 1623 5-9-11 .... JemmaMarshall
(Mrs A Malzard, Jersey) **8/1**
6 **Homeboy (IRE)**[5] 1877 6-10-0 ow6.... MrJamesHughes
(David Evans) **8/1**
7 **Chester'slittlegem (IRE)**[7] 1787 5-10-2 .... JosephineGordon
(Jo Hughes) **11/2**
8 **Thrtypointstothree (IRE)**[197] 7393 3-10-8 .... MatthewCosham
(Nikki Evans) **7/1**
1m 11.0s (71.00)
**WFA** 3 from 5yo+ 10lb **8** Ran SP% **152.5**

**Owner** Bernward Weber **Bred** Rathasker Stud **Trained** Germany

## 2599a IN MEMORY OF THE LATE IAN MONACHAN H'CAP 1m 4f

**4:35** (4:35) (0-70,) 3-Y-O+ **£1,800** (£750; £450)

RPR
1 **Cabuchon (GER)**[16] 1574 7-10-7 .... RichardEvans 65
(David Evans) **10/11**[1]

2 *1* **I'm Harry**[14] 1622 5-10-12 ....(vt) MattieBatchelor 68
(George Baker) **6/4**[2]
3 *½* **Nice Story (IRE)**[345] 2651 4-9-12 .... MrJamesHughes 53
(R Storp, Germany) **7/2**[3]
4 **Rocquaine (IRE)**[14] 1625 5-8-5 .... JenniferFerguson
(Mrs A Malzard, Jersey) **12/1**
5 **Constanzina (FR)**[14] 1624 5-10-4 .... JemmaMarshall
(Mrs A Malzard, Jersey) **14/1**
2m 41.0s (161.00) **5** Ran SP% **129.0**

**Owner** Mrs E Evans **Bred** Gestut Schlenderhan **Trained** Pandy, Monmouths

# CARLISLE (R-H)

Monday, May 26

**OFFICIAL GOING: Good (good to soft in places between 1m 1f & 7f)**
Wind: Breezy, half behind Weather: Cloudy

## 2601 EBF STALLIONS IJF 50TH ANNIVERSARY MAIDEN STKS 5f

**2:10** (2:10) (Class 5) 2-Y-O **£3,234** (£962; £481; £240) **Stalls** Low

Form RPR
1 **Likely (GER)** 2-9-0 0.... HarryBentley 5 93+
(David Barron) *trckd ldrs: smooth hdwy to ld over 1f out: shkn up and qcknd clr fnl f: readily* **11/8**[1]
22 2 *5* **Mattmu**[13] 2231 2-9-5 0.... DavidAllan 7 76
(Tim Easterby) *pressed ldr: led appr 2f out: sn rdn: hdd over 1f out: no ch w ready wnr* **15/8**[2]
3 *9* **Ocean Sheridan (IRE)** 2-9-2 0.... ConnorBeasley(3) 6 44
(Michael Dods) *midfield: pushed along whn checked over 2f out: sn rdn: kpt on fnl f: no ch w first two* **12/1**
4 *1 ¼* **Lady Desire (IRE)** 2-9-0 0.... TomEaves 3 34+
(Keith Dalgleish) *s.i.s: rn green in rr: hdwy over 1f out: hung lft ins fnl f: nrst fin* **50/1**
5 5 *¾* **Robben**[10] 2291 2-9-5 0.... PaulMulrennan 10 36
(Kevin Ryan) *sn pushed along towards rr: drvn along 1/2-way: edgd rt over 1f out: no imp* **20/1**
6 *hd* **Don Ricardo (IRE)** 2-9-5 0.... TonyHamilton 4 36
(Richard Fahey) *bhd and sn pushed along: sme late hdwy: nvr on terms* **9/1**[3]
7 *nse* **Miss Mullberry** 2-9-0 0.... DanielTudhope 1 31+
(David O'Meara) *t.k.h: led to appr 2f out: rdn and wknd fnl f* **16/1**
8 *2 ¼* **Twin Turbo (IRE)** 2-9-5 0.... JoeFanning 8 27
(Mark Johnston) *midfield: drvn and rn green over 2f out: wknd over 1f out* **10/1**
00 9 *3 ½* **Toni's A Star**[18] 2089 2-9-0 0.... RaulDaSilva 9 10
(Paul Green) *prom: drvn along 1/2-way: wknd wl over 1f out* **100/1**
1m 1.41s (0.61) **Going Correction** +0.20s/f (Good) **9** Ran SP% **117.3**
Speed ratings (Par 93): **103,95,80,78,77 77,77,73,67**
CSF £4.09 TOTE £2.30: £1.10, £1.20, £3.50; EX 4.40 Trifecta £49.90.
**Owner** Qatar Racing Limited **Bred** Stiftung Gestut Fahrhof **Trained** Maunby, N Yorks

**FOCUS**
Following 8mm of rain in the preceding 24 hours, the ground eased from good to firm, good in places to good, good to soft in places (between 1m1f and 7f starts). The jockeys reported the ground to be on the soft side of good. A couple of interesting newcomers on paper, but an impressive debut display from a potentially smart sort. The runner-up is rated to his debut form. The gallop was sound and the first two pulled clear. The winner looks a smart recruit and probable Ascot material, with the second rated to his mark.

## 2602 GET £50 FREE BETS WITH APOLLOBET.COM H'CAP 5f 193y

**2:40** (2:42) (Class 4) (0-80,78) 4-Y-O+ **£6,469** (£1,925; £962; £481) **Stalls** Low

Form RPR
0-40 1 **Bachotheque (IRE)**[9] 2332 4-8-13 **70**....[1] DavidAllan 10 80
(Tim Easterby) *pressed ldr: drvn over 2f out: led wl ins fnl f: kpt on wl* **17/2**
421- 2 *½* **Circuitous**[248] 6586 6-9-7 **78**....(v) TomEaves 8 86
(Keith Dalgleish) *led against ins rail: rdn over 2f out: hdd wl ins fnl f: hld nr fin* **6/1**[2]
-440 3 *2* **Sunraider (IRE)**[9] 2332 7-9-3 **74**.... PaulMulrennan 3 76+
(Paul Midgley) *stdd s: sn niggled in rr: stdy hdwy and weaved through fr over 1f out: shkn up and styd on wl fnl f to take 3rd nr fin: nvr nrr* **13/2**[3]
0030 4 *hd* **Klynch**[9] 2332 8-9-6 **77**....(b) JamesSullivan 11 78
(Ruth Carr) *midfield: effrt and rdn over 2f out: hung rt over 1f out: kpt on same pce ins fnl f* **9/1**
2404 5 *1 ¾* **Beau Mistral (IRE)**[10] 2297 5-9-0 **71**.... RaulDaSilva 2 66
(Paul Green) *chsd ldrs: drvn along over 2f out: kpt on same pce appr fnl f* **16/1**
0-00 6 *3 ½* **Ypres**[20] 2056 5-9-2 **73**.... HarryBentley 6 57
(Jason Ward) *prom: rdn along over 2f out: outpcd appr fnl f* **28/1**
4200 7 *hd* **Gold Beau (FR)**[20] 2059 4-9-2 **73**....(p) DaleSwift 5 57
(Kristin Stubbs) *towards rr: rdn and effrt against ins rail 2f out: no imp fnl f* **14/1**
10-0 8 *1 ¼* **Just The Tonic**[32] 1672 7-9-5 **76**.... DanielTudhope 1 56
(Marjorie Fife) *dwlt: bhd and pushed along: sme hdwy fnl f: nvr on terms* **25/1**
3220 9 *¾* **Orbit The Moon (IRE)**[9] 2332 6-9-1 **75**....(tp) ConnorBeasley(3) 13 52
(Michael Dods) *midfield on wd outside: drvn over 2f out: edgd rt and no ex over 1f out* **10/3**[1]
400- 10 *1 ¾* **Sound Amigo (IRE)**[291] 5183 6-9-3 **74**.... BarryMcHugh 12 46
(Ollie Pears) *prom: rdn over 2f out: hung rt and wknd over 1f out* **50/1**
00-0 11 *2 ½* **Medici Time**[39] 1541 9-8-11 **68**....(v) TonyHamilton 14 32
(Tim Easterby) *s.i.s: bhd on outside: rdn over 2f out: nvr on terms* **33/1**
0-02 12 *nk* **Diamond Blue**[29] 1758 6-8-7 **64**....(p) PatrickMathers 7 27
(Richard Fahey) *sn drvn along in rr: hdwy u.p on outside over 2f out: sn btn* **8/1**
-124 13 *2 ¼* **Llewellyn**[16] 2177 6-9-1 **75**....(b[1]) NeilFarley(3) 9 30
(Declan Carroll) *t.k.h: trckd ldrs tl rdn and wknd over 1f out* **17/2**
50-0 14 *nk* **Red Explorer (USA)**[144] 20 4-9-1 **75**.... MichaelJMMurphy(3) 4 29
(Ann Stokell) *towards rr against ins rail: struggling over 2f out: sn btn* **25/1**
1m 14.05s (0.35) **Going Correction** +0.20s/f (Good) **14** Ran SP% **121.5**
Speed ratings (Par 105): **105,104,101,101,99 94,94,92,91,89 85,85,82,82**
CSF £56.16 CT £371.42 TOTE £11.10: £3.20, £1.30, £3.10; EX 92.90 Trifecta £793.40.
**Owner** Richard Taylor & Philip Hebdon **Bred** Tally-Ho Stud **Trained** Great Habton, N Yorks


The Form Book, Raceform Ltd, Newbury, RG14 5SJ

**FOCUS**
This looked a competitive sprint, but few featured as the first two were the first two throughout. The pace held up through the card. The winner built on his penultimate promise.

## 2603 FOLLOW @APOLLOBET ON TWITTER AND FACEBOOOK H'CAP 7f 200y
**3:15** (3:15) (Class 4) (0-80,80) 4-Y-O+ **£6,469** (£1,925; £962; £481) **Stalls** Low

Form RPR
1-00 **1** **Johnno**[42] 1483 5-9-4 **77** AdrianNicholls 2 86
(David Nicholls) *led after 1f: mde rest at ordinary gallop: rdn 2f out: kpt on wl fnl f* **5/1**[3]
5-10 **2** ¾ **Kiwi Bay**[35] 1607 9-9-5 **78** PaulMulrennan 1 85
(Michael Dods) *trckd ldrs: effrt and rdn 2f out: chsd wnr ins fnl f: r.o: hld nr fin* **12/1**
3-04 **3** 1 ¾ **Bartack (IRE)**[20] 2054 4-9-7 **80**(v) DanielTudhope 7 83
(David O'Meara) *t.k.h: trckd ldrs: rdn and wnt 2nd over 2f out to ins fnl f: kpt on same pce* **9/2**[2]
3-01 **4** 1 ¼ **Hakuna Matata**[27] 1842 7-9-3 **79**(b) ConnorBeasley(3) 10 79+
(Michael Dods) *s.i.s: hld up: gd hdwy on outside 2f out: hung rt and no ex ins fnl f* **7/2**[1]
6-02 **5** ½ **Shadowtime**[21] 2017 9-9-3 **76** DaleSwift 6 75
(Tracy Waggott) *midfield: effrt and rdn over 2f out: outpcd fnl f* **14/1**
0030 **6** *shd* **Al Muheer (IRE)**[9] 2351 9-9-3 **76**(p) JamesSullivan 8 75
(Ruth Carr) *hld up: effrt over 2f out: n.m.r briefly over 1f out: sn rdn and drifted rt: kpt on fnl f: no imp* **8/1**
40-0 **7** 5 **Argaki (IRE)**[30] 1724 4-9-5 **78** TomEaves 9 65
(Keith Dalgleish) *t.k.h: in tch: drvn and outpcd 2f out: sn btn* **33/1**
1-20 **8** 1 **Sword Of The Lord**[26] 1871 4-9-4 **77** BarryMcHugh 3 62
(George Margarson) *hmpd sn after s: in rr: rdn over 2f out: nvr able to chal* **9/2**[2]
0-01 **9** 3 ¼ **Ralphy Boy (IRE)**[14] 2215 5-8-13 **72** TonyHamilton 11 50
(Alistair Whillans) *plld hrd: led 1f: chsd wnr to over 2f out: sn wknd* **8/1**
000 **10** 10 **Spin Artist (USA)**[20] 2059 4-9-0 **73** JoeFanning 5 28
(Mark Johnston) *hld up on ins: struggling over 2f out: sn btn* **16/1**

1m 40.14s (0.14) **Going Correction** +0.15s/f (Good) **10 Ran SP% 120.7**
Speed ratings (Par 105): **105,104,102,101,100 100,95,94,91,81**
CSF £65.73 CT £301.14 TOTE £7.00: £3.00, £4.00, £1.60; EX 115.50 Trifecta £1120.70.
**Owner** Alan Zheng **Bred** Gestut Sohrenhof **Trained** Sessay, N Yorks

**FOCUS**
A fair handicap in which the ordinary gallop suited those racing close to the pace.

## 2604 EBF STALLIONS DOWNLOAD THE APOLLOBET APP FILLIES' H'CAP 7f 200y
**3:50** (3:50) (Class 4) (0-85,84) 3-Y-O+ **£6,469** (£1,925; £962; £481) **Stalls** Low

Form RPR
-061 **1** **Lady Artiste (IRE)**[16] 2171 4-9-0 **70** DavidAllan 7 78
(Alan Swinbank) *in tch: effrt and rdn over 1f out: led wl ins fnl f: r.o* **5/2**[1]
-224 **2** *nk* **Who's Shirl**[20] 1881 8-9-4 **74** MichaelStainton 6 81
(Chris Fairhurst) *trckd ldrs on outside: hdwy to ld 1f out: sn rdn and hung rt: hdd wl ins fnl f: r.o* **7/1**
6-23 **3** 2 ¼ **Simply Shining (IRE)**[27] 1842 4-9-4 **74** TonyHamilton 1 76
(Richard Fahey) *t.k.h: led at modest gallop: rdn and hdd 1f out: kpt on same pce* **5/2**[1]
-046 **4** *nk* **No Poppy (IRE)**[9] 2331 6-9-8 **78** TomEaves 2 79
(Tim Easterby) *trckd ldrs: effrt and rdn over 2f out: n.m.r briefly over 1f out and ins fnl f: one pce* **5/1**[3]
116- **5** 11 **Top Dollar**[205] 7695 3-9-0 **82** PaulMulrennan 3 63
(James Tate) *plld hrd: pressed ldr: rdn over 2f out: wknd appr fnl f* **3/1**[2]

1m 41.67s (1.67) **Going Correction** +0.15s/f (Good)
**WFA** 3 from 4yo+ 12lb **5 Ran SP% 111.3**
Speed ratings (Par 102): **97,96,94,94,83**
CSF £19.33 TOTE £3.10: £2.90, £2.60; EX 21.70 Trifecta £41.40.
**Owner** Andrew Sparks **Bred** Lynch Bages, Samac Ltd & Longfield Stud **Trained** Melsonby, N Yorks

**FOCUS**
A steady gallop for this fillies' handicap. The winner built on her Thirsk win.

## 2605 APOLLOBET HORSE RACING BEST ODDS GUARANTEED H'CAP 6f 192y
**4:20** (4:20) (Class 5) (0-70,65) 4-Y-O+ **£4,204** (£1,251; £625; £312) **Stalls** Low

Form RPR
-603 **1** **Mercers Row**[16] 2171 7-9-0 **65** GemmaTutty(7) 5 74
(Karen Tutty) *t.k.h: hld up in tch: effrt and rdn over 1f out: led wl ins fnl f: r.o* **7/1**[3]
1114 **2** ½ **Alluring Star**[10] 2293 6-9-7 **65** JamesSullivan 1 72
(Michael Easterby) *pressed ldr: rdn to ld over 1f out: hdd wl ins fnl f: kpt on same pce* **15/8**[2]
5-50 **3** 1 ¾ **Running Reef (IRE)**[35] 1609 5-9-6 **64** BarryMcHugh 6 67
(Tracy Waggott) *trckd ldrs: effrt and rdn over 1f out: kpt on same pce ins fnl f* **9/1**
0400 **4** *shd* **Bapak Muda (USA)**[16] 2171 4-9-0 **63**(b[1]) KevinStott(5) 2 66
(Kevin Ryan) *t.k.h: led at modest gallop: qcknd 3f out: hdd over 1f out: one pce fnl f* **14/1**
4-0 **5** 1 **Janaab (IRE)**[30] 1718 4-9-7 **65**(t[1]) DavidAllan 7 65
(Tim Easterby) *t.k.h: hld up in tch: effrt whn n.m.r over 2f out: hung rt: kpt on same pce fnl f* **9/1**
4601 **6** ½ **Imperator Augustus (IRE)**[14] 2219 6-9-0 **65** JackGarritty(7) 8 64
(Patrick Holmes) *t.k.h: hld up: stdy hdwy on outside over 2f out: rdn over 1f out: outpcd fnl f* **13/8**[1]

1m 28.67s (1.57) **Going Correction** +0.15s/f (Good) **6 Ran SP% 112.0**
Speed ratings (Par 103): **97,96,94,94,93 92**
CSF £20.54 CT £118.07 TOTE £9.30: £3.20, £1.30; EX 20.60 Trifecta £80.00.
**Owner** K Fitzsimons **Bred** Heather Raw **Trained** Osmotherley, N Yorks

**FOCUS**
A modest handicap in which the steady gallop to the home turn saw several fail to settle and the field finished in a bit of a heap. Not the strongest for the grade.

## 2606 APOLLOBET ENHANCED DAILY RACING SPECIALS H'CAP 5f
**4:50** (4:50) (Class 5) (0-70,73) 3-Y-O+ **£3,881** (£1,155; £577; £288) **Stalls** Low

Form RPR
46-0 **1** **M J Woodward**[10] 2296 5-8-6 **57** JackGarritty(7) 8 65
(Paul Green) *cl up far side: rdn to ld 1f out: edgd rt and hld on wl towards fin: 1st of 9 in gp* **33/1**
5665 **2** *nse* **Thatcherite (IRE)**[8] 2364 6-9-10 **68**(t) StephenCraine 7 76
(Tony Coyle) *in tch far side: effrt and rdn over 1f out: edgd rt and kpt on wl towards fin: jst hld: 2nd of 9 in gp* **17/2**
5120 **3** ¾ **Bapak Bangsawan**[16] 2167 4-9-10 **68** DanielTudhope 5 74
(Kevin Ryan) *led far side: rdn and hdd 1f out: 3rd and one pce whn hmpd towards fin: 3rd of 9 in gp* **7/1**[3]
2012 **4** ¾ **Whipphound**[16] 2174 6-9-9 **70** MichaelJMMurphy(3) 6 74
(Mark Brisbourne) *prom far side: effrt and rdn over 1f out: keeping on same pce whn hmpd towards fin: 4th of 9 in gp* **4/1**[1]
-021 **5** ½ **Captain Royale (IRE)**[8] 2364 9-10-1 **73** 6ex(p) DaleSwift 16 74+
(Tracy Waggott) *bhd stands' side gp: rdn and hdwy 2f out: led that gp ins fnl f: nt rch far side: 1st of 6 in gp* **11/1**
325- **6** *hd* **Red Cobra (IRE)**[199] 7807 4-9-0 **58** TonyHamilton 4 60
(Tim Easterby) *trckd far side ldrs: effrt and rdn over 1f out: one pce whn bdly hmpd wl ins fnl f: 5th of 9 in gp* **33/1**
-025 **7** ½ **Manatee Bay**[10] 2297 4-9-3 **61**(p) JoeFanning 1 61
(David Nicholls) *missed break and wnt lft s: bhd far side: effrt and hdwy over 1f out: one pce whn hmpd wl ins fnl f: 6th of 9 in gp* **15/2**
3-22 **8** *hd* **Niceonemyson**[13] 2233 5-8-13 **62** KevinStott(5) 2 60
(Christopher Wilson) *hld up in midfield far side: effrt over 1f out: keeping on but no imp whn hmpd wl ins fnl f: 7th of 9 in gp* **6/1**[2]
0-05 **9** 1 ¼ **Choc'A'Moca (IRE)**[13] 2233 7-8-12 **56**(v) PaulMulrennan 11 49
(Paul Midgley) *chsd stands' side ldr: rdn to ld that gp over 1f out to ins fnl f: kpt on same pce: 2nd of 6 in gp* **16/1**
0-14 **10** 2 ½ **Shillito**[8] 2364 4-9-6 **64** BarryMcHugh 12 48
(Tony Coyle) *in tch stands' side gp: effrt and rdn wl over 1f out: no imp ins fnl f: 3rd of 6 in gp* **10/1**
00-6 **11** *nk* **The Nifty Fox**[22] 1966 10-9-10 **68**(p) JamesSullivan 3 51
(Tim Easterby) *in tch far side: drvn and outpcd over 1f out: n.d after: 8th of 9 in gp* **25/1**
1130 **12** 2 ¼ **Seamster**[13] 2233 7-8-13 **60**(bt) ConnorBeasley(3) 13 35
(Richard Ford) *led stands' side gp: rdn and hdd over 1f out: sn btn: 4th of 6 in gp* **20/1**
04-3 **13** 1 ¼ **Salvatore Fury (IRE)**[29] 1759 4-9-9 **67**(p) TomEaves 15 38
(Keith Dalgleish) *in tch stands' side bunch: drvn over 2f out: outpcd fr over 1f out: 5th of 6 in gp* **11/1**
-000 **14** *nse* **The Strig**[16] 2167 7-9-11 **69**(v) HarryBentley 10 39
(Nigel Tinkler) *hld up in tch stands' side: drvn over 2f out: wknd over 1f out: last of 6 in gp* **50/1**
400- **15** 19 **Evie Jay (IRE)**[191] 7935 3-8-10 **62** RaulDaSilva 9
(Paul Green) *in tch on outside of far side gp: rdn 1/2-way: lost tch over 1f out: last of 9 in gp* **33/1**

1m 2.04s (1.24) **Going Correction** +0.20s/f (Good)
**WFA** 3 from 4yo+ 8lb **15 Ran SP% 120.1**
Speed ratings (Par 103): **98,97,96,95,94 94,93,93,91,87 86,83,81,81,50**
CSF £276.76 CT £2214.75 TOTE £42.10: £12.10, £4.10, £2.70; EX 429.90 Trifecta £1181.20 Part won..
**Owner** Paul Green (Oaklea) **Bred** Paul Green **Trained** Lydiate, Merseyside

■ Stewards' Enquiry : Stephen Craine three-day ban: careless riding (Jun 9-11)

Jack Garritty three-day ban: careless riding (Jun 9-11)

**FOCUS**
Mainly exposed sorts in this sprint handicap in which they split into two groups, with ten going the shortest route on the far side. That group held the call. The surprise winner is rated back to his old turf mark.

## 2607 LIVE IN PLAY BETTING WITH APOLLOBET.COM H'CAP 1m 1f 61y
**5:20** (5:20) (Class 5) (0-70,70) 4-Y-O+ **£2,587** (£770; £384; £192) **Stalls** Low

Form RPR
34-0 **1** **Valantino Oyster (IRE)**[32] 1674 7-8-9 58(p) DaleSwift 10 67
(Tracy Waggott) *mde all: clr w one other 4f out: rdn 2f out: styd on gamely fnl f* **18/1**
-520 **2** 1 **Dakota Canyon (IRE)**[13] 2234 5-9-6 69(p) TonyHamilton 12 76
(Richard Fahey) *prom: rdn over 3f out: rallied and hung rt over 1f out: sn chsng wnr: kpt on ins fnl f* **10/1**
014- **3** 1 **Pat's Legacy (USA)**[213] 7515 8-9-0 63 DanielTudhope 4 68
(Marjorie Fife) *plld hrd early: hld up: hdwy and prom over 1f out: rdn and kpt on ins fnl f* **10/1**
-160 **4** 2 ¼ **Samoset**[41] 1496 4-8-7 56 oh1 DavidAllan 3 56
(Alan Swinbank) *hld up: rdn and outpcd over 3f out: rallied over 1f out: kpt on wl fnl f* **18/1**
0540 **5** ¾ **Mysterial**[9] 2351 4-9-1 69 KevinStott(5) 8 68+
(Ruth Carr) *s.i.s: hld up: hdwy on outside and in tch over 1f out: outpcd ins fnl f* **11/2**[3]
23-5 **6** 1 **Mash Potato (IRE)**[48] 1362 4-9-4 70(p) ConnorBeasley(3) 5 66
(Michael Dods) *chsd ldrs: drvn along over 3f out: rallied wl over 1f out: outpcd fnl f* **2/1**[1]
00-0 **7** 6 **Printmaker (IRE)**[16] 2169 6-8-9 58 PaulMulrennan 11 42
(Tim Easterby) *pressed ldr: clr of rest 4f out: rdn over 2f out: wknd over 1f out* **25/1**
20-0 **8** 6 **Tectonic (IRE)**[22] 1970 5-9-6 69(p) TomEaves 2 40
(Keith Dalgleish) *hld up on ins: drvn along over 2f out: btn over 1f out* **10/1**
0000 **9** 3 ½ **Staffhoss**[9] 2341 4-9-2 65 JoeFanning 7 29
(Mark Johnston) *hld up: drvn and outpcd 4f out: n.d after* **9/2**[2]
2245 **10** *hd* **Gabrial's Hope (FR)**[32] 1675 5-8-7 56 oh4 BarryMcHugh 9 19
(Tracy Waggott) *plld hrd: in tch tl rdn and wknd 2f out* **12/1**

1m 58.96s (1.36) **Going Correction** +0.15s/f (Good) **10 Ran SP% 116.2**
Speed ratings (Par 103): **99,98,97,95,94 93,88,83,79,79**
CSF £185.22 CT £1906.84 TOTE £10.80: £3.10, £2.90, £2.20; EX 107.40 Trifecta £1309.90.
**Owner** Steve Sawley **Bred** Des Vere Hunt Farm Co And Jack Ronan **Trained** Spennymoor, Co Durham

**FOCUS**
There were a few disappointing sorts in this handicap, which was run at a good gallop. The form is rated around the runner-up.

T/Jkpt: Not won. T/Plt: £410.80 to a £1 stake. Pool: £89483.05 - 159.00 winning tickets T/Qpdt: £132.60 to a £1 stake. Pool: £4249.84 - 23.70 winning tickets RY

# 2380 LEICESTER (R-H)

Monday, May 26

**OFFICIAL GOING: Good to soft (soft in places) changing to soft after race 3 (3:20)**

Wind: Almost nil Weather: Light rain

## 2608 BET TOTEPLACEPOT FILLIES' H'CAP 7f 9y

**2:15** (2:15) (Class 4) (0-80,78) 4-Y-O+ **£6,301** (£1,886; £943; £472; £235) **Stalls** High

Form RPR

2016 **1** **Fanoos**[38] [1554] 5-9-7 **78**..........................(p) RichardKingscote 1 89
(Dr Jon Scargill) *hld up: racd keenly: hdwy 1/2-way: rdn to ld ins fnl f: r.o* **9/4**[2]

-111 **2** *2* **Trixie Malone**[21] [2032] 4-9-0 **76**.......................... JoeyHaynes(5) 7 82
(K R Burke) *w ldr tl led over 2f out: rdn over 1f out: hdd ins fnl f: no ex towards fin* **85/40**[1]

3134 **3** *½* **Broughtons Charm (IRE)**[10] [2318] 4-9-4 **75**.......................... ChrisCatlin 6 80
(Willie Musson) *hld up in tch: racd keenly: jnd ldr over 2f out: rdn over 1f out: styd on same pce ins fnl f* **7/2**[3]

3531 **4** *7* **Kosika (USA)**[6] [2415] 4-9-7 **78** 6ex.......................... FrannyNorton 4 65
(Mark Johnston) *led over 4f: rdn and wknd over 1f out* **5/1**

3200 **5** *6* **Hannahs Turn**[22] [1975] 4-9-4 **75**.......................... DaneO'Neill 3 46
(Chris Dwyer) *rrd and lost many l s: nvr on terms* **20/1**

215- **6** *1* **Dutch Mistress**[326] [3983] 5-8-11 **68**.......................... LukeMorris 5 36
(James Unett) *chsd ldrs: rdn over 2f out: sn wknd* **16/1**

1m 28.37s (2.17) **Going Correction** +0.30s/f (Good) 6 Ran SP% **112.3**
Speed ratings (Par 102): **99,96,96,88,81 80**
CSF £7.47 TOTE £3.90: £2.30, £1.80; EX 11.70 Trifecta £37.60.
**Owner** Theme Tune Partnership **Bred** Miss Otis Partnership **Trained** Newmarket, Suffolk

**FOCUS**
A fair fillies' handicap with the front four all of some interest. The winner built on her AW form.

## 2609 DOWNLOAD THE TOTEPOOL LIVE INFO APP (S) STKS 1m 1f 218y

**2:45** (2:45) (Class 6) 3-5-Y-O **£2,045** (£603; £302) **Stalls** Low

Form RPR

2-4 **1** **Monopoli**[24] [1910] 5-9-2 57..........................(p) LukeMorris 4 62
(John O'Shea) *hld up: hdwy to chse ldr over 2f out: sn rdn: styd on u.p to ld wl ins fnl f* **11/4**[2]

4-43 **2** *½* **Banreenahreenkah (IRE)**[7] [2381] 4-9-2 56..........................(t) TomQueally 8 61
(Jennie Candlish) *sn led: rdn over 1f out: hdd and unable qck wl ins fnl f* **3/1**[3]

120 **3** *19* **Chanceuse**[28] [1793] 3-8-7 56.......................... MartinDwyer 3 29
(Gay Kelleway) *chsd ldrs: rdn over 3f out: wknd over 1f out* **7/1**

0004 **4** *1* **Admirals Walk (IRE)**[32] [1666] 4-9-2 44.......................... JoshBaudains(5) 1 28
(Barry Brennan) *hld up: hdwy 1/2-way: rdn over 2f out: wknd over 1f out* **33/1**

5530 **5** *2* **Another Journey**[95] [672] 5-9-4 40.......................... WilliamTwiston-Davies(3) 6 24
(Lisa Williamson) *hld up: rdn and wknd over 2f out* **66/1**

366 **6** *shd* **Remix (IRE)**[61] [1099] 5-8-11 57.......................... GeorgeDowning(5) 2 19
(Ian Williams) *sn pushed along in rr: swtchd lft 8f out: hdwy over 2f out: wknd over 1f out* **2/1**[1]

-005 **7** *2½* **Berkeley Street (USA)**[27] [1836] 4-9-7 53..........................(b[1]) FrannyNorton 5 19
(Jane Chapple-Hyam) *chsd ldr tl rdn over 2f out: wknd over 1f out* **12/1**

2m 14.81s (6.91) **Going Correction** +0.725s/f (Yiel)
**WFA** 3 from 4yo+ 14lb 7 Ran SP% **109.6**
Speed ratings (Par 101): **101,100,85,84,83 82,80**
CSF £10.43 TOTE £3.60: £2.10, £1.70; EX 6.40 Trifecta £29.60.The winner was sold to Austin Darton for 5,500gns. Banreenahreenkah was claimed by Mr Paul Fitzsimons for £7,000.
**Owner** The Cross Racing Club **Bred** M H Dixon **Trained** Elton, Gloucs

**FOCUS**
A weak seller and the front two pulled miles clear. The winner is rated around last year's form.

## 2610 BET TOTEQUADPOT H'CAP 1m 1f 218y

**3:20** (3:20) (Class 5) (0-70,70) 4-Y-O+ **£3,881** (£1,155; £577; £288) **Stalls** Low

Form RPR

6204 **1** **Minstrel Lad**[10] [2300] 6-8-4 **56** oh1.......................... SimonPearce(3) 7 71
(Lydia Pearce) *s.i.s: hdwy to chse ldrs 8f out: shkn up to ld over 2f out: clr fnl f: easily* **10/1**

6-03 **2** *7* **Granell (IRE)**[12] [2251] 4-9-7 **70**..........................(p) DaneO'Neill 6 72
(Brian Meehan) *hld up: rdn over 2f out: hdwy: nt clr run and swtchd lft over 1f out: wnt 2nd ins fnl f: no ch w wnr* **9/4**[1]

0-20 **3** *3¾* **Zafranagar (IRE)**[30] [1729] 9-9-1 **69**.......................... GeorgeDowning(5) 2 64
(Ian Williams) *trckd ldrs: nt clr run and swtchd lft over 2f out: sn rdn: styd on same pce fr over 1f out* **3/1**[2]

06-0 **4** *hd* **Grand Liaison**[14] [2199] 5-9-3 **66**.......................... PaulHanagan 5 60
(James Given) *trckd ldr: rdn and ev ch over 2f out: edgd rt and no ex fnl f* **20/1**

4433 **5** *3* **The Firm (IRE)**[10] [2301] 5-9-4 **67**.......................... LukeMorris 8 55
(Daniel Mark Loughnane) *led: rdn and hdd over 2f out: wknd fnl f* **4/1**

2-10 **6** *2¾* **Grey Blue (IRE)**[28] [1798] 4-9-5 **68**.......................... TomQueally 1 51
(Nicky Henderson) *hld up: rdn over 2f out: wknd over 1f out* **7/2**[3]

2m 16.72s (8.82) **Going Correction** +0.725s/f (Yiel) 6 Ran SP% **111.8**
Speed ratings (Par 103): **93,87,84,84,81 79**
CSF £32.58 CT £84.19 TOTE £8.80: £4.90, £1.60; EX 45.20 Trifecta £215.40.
**Owner** S & M Supplies (Aylsham) Ltd **Bred** Theresa Fitsall **Trained** Newmarket, Suffolk

**FOCUS**
A fair handicap run at a steady pace. The form is rated cautiously.

## 2611 FOLLOW @TOTEPOOL ON TWITTER H'CAP (BOBIS RACE) 5f 218y

**3:55** (3:55) (Class 4) (0-85,85) 3-Y-O **£6,469** (£1,925; £962; £481) **Stalls** High

Form RPR

6523 **1** **Kickboxer (IRE)**[10] [2317] 3-9-4 **85**.......................... WilliamTwiston-Davies(3) 3 95
(Mick Channon) *hld up: hdwy over 2f out: led over 1f out: r.o* **5/2**[2]

2-1 **2** *1½* **Golden Steps (FR)**[34] [1634] 3-9-2 **85**..........................[1] MarcMonaghan(5) 5 90
(Marco Botti) *s.i.s: hld up: rdn over 1f out: hung lft and r.o ins fnl f: wnt 2nd post: nt rch wnr* **7/1**

3-01 **3** *hd* **Lady Horatia**[20] [2049] 3-9-2 **80**.......................... MartinDwyer 7 85
(William Muir) *trckd ldrs: racd keenly: rdn over 1f out: styd on* **8/1**

46-6 **4** *½* **Munjally**[28] [1795] 3-8-12 **76**.......................... DaneO'Neill 1 79
(Richard Hannon) *led: rdn and hdd over 1f out: styd on same pce ins fnl f* **7/1**

41-3 **5** *nse* **Greeb**[40] [1518] 3-9-5 **83**.......................... PaulHanagan 6 86
(Charles Hills) *trckd ldrs: pushed along over 2f out: styd on* **9/4**[1]

5-10 **6** *5* **Ashkari (IRE)**[17] [2122] 3-8-11 **80**.......................... RyanTate(5) 2 67
(Clive Cox) *trckd ldrs: rdn over 1f out: wknd fnl f* **13/2**[3]

1m 14.38s (1.38) **Going Correction** +0.30s/f (Good) 6 Ran SP% **108.8**
Speed ratings (Par 101): **102,100,99,99,99 92**
CSF £18.37 CT £105.95 TOTE £3.10: £2.50, £3.50; EX 23.00 Trifecta £68.60.
**Owner** Living Legend Racing Partnership 1 **Bred** Rathasker Stud **Trained** West Ilsley, Berks

**FOCUS**
A useful 3yo handicap. The winner is rated back to his 2yo best.

## 2612 BET TOTETRIFECTA MEDIAN AUCTION MAIDEN STKS 5f 2y

**4:25** (4:25) (Class 5) 2-Y-O **£3,234** (£962; £481; £240) **Stalls** High

Form RPR

**1** **Jane's Memory (IRE)** 2-9-0 0.......................... MartinDwyer 2 71+
(Rae Guest) *a.p: shkn up to ld ins fnl f: edgd lft: r.o* **5/1**[3]

**2** *¾* **Tigrilla (IRE)** 2-9-0 0.......................... FrederikTylicki 9 68+
(Roger Varian) *chsd ldrs: rdn over 1f out: ev ch and edgd rt ins fnl f: styd on same pce* **5/1**[3]

**3** *hd* **Burning The Clocks (IRE)** 2-9-5 0.......................... DaneO'Neill 4 73+
(Peter Chapple-Hyam) *hld up in tch: rdn: edgd rt and ev ch ins fnl f: unable qck towards fin* **7/2**[2]

**4** *5* **Crosse Fire** 2-9-5 0.......................... LukeMorris 7 55
(Scott Dixon) *prom: chsd ldr over 3f out: rdn over 1f out: wknd ins fnl f* **20/1**

**5** *1¼* **Native Charmer** 2-9-2 0.......................... WilliamTwiston-Davies(3) 8 50
(Ed McMahon) *sn pushed along in rr: hung rt 1/2-way: n.d* **8/1**

3 **6** *¾* **Rocking The Boat (IRE)**[14] [2220] 2-9-0 0.......................... PaulHanagan 5 42
(Charles Hills) *led: rdn over 1f out: hdd & wknd ins fnl f* **7/4**[1]

**7** *9* **Happy Pursuit** 2-9-0 0.......................... SaleemGolam 3 10
(Stuart Williams) *s.i.s: a in rr: wknd 1/2-way* **20/1**

**8** *3½* **Cool Choice** 2-9-5 0.......................... J-PGuillambert 1 2
(Nick Littmoden) *chsd ldr tl pushed along over 3f out: wknd 1/2-way* **33/1**

1m 3.31s (3.31) **Going Correction** +0.30s/f (Good) 8 Ran SP% **115.5**
Speed ratings (Par 93): **85,83,83,75,73 72,57,52**
CSF £29.42 TOTE £7.50: £1.30, £1.50, £2.90; EX 29.00 Trifecta £144.20.
**Owner** O T Lury **Bred** Knocklong House Stud **Trained** Newmarket, Suffolk

**FOCUS**
An interesting maiden that should produce winners, but the nare form is at the lower end of the race average.

## 2613 BET TOTEEXACTA BREEDERS BACKING RACING EBF MAIDEN FILLIES' STKS 1m 3f 183y

**4:55** (4:56) (Class 5) 3-Y-O+ **£3,881** (£1,155; £577; £288) **Stalls** Low

Form RPR

4 **1** **Rewaaya (IRE)**[17] [2109] 3-8-10 0.......................... PaulHanagan 4 87+
(John Gosden) *s.i.s: sn rcvrd to ld: flashed tail at times: pushed clr fnl 2f: easily* **4/7**[1]

0 **2** *9* **Quenelle**[17] [2109] 3-8-10 0.......................... SebSanders 11 69
(Ed Dunlop) *a.p: rdn to chse wnr over 2f out: sn outpcd* **8/1**

0 **3** *½* **Strawberry Martini**[31] [1701] 3-8-10 0.......................... MartinDwyer 3 68
(William Muir) *s.i.s: hld up: rdn over 3f out: hdwy to go 3rd over 1f out: nvr trbld ldrs* **25/1**

5 **4** *hd* **Shadows Ofthenight (IRE)**[11] [2280] 3-8-7 0 WilliamTwiston-Davies(3) 5 68
(Mick Channon) *hld up: pushed along over 5f out: hung rt and styd on appr fnl f: nvr nrr* **7/2**[2]

00 **5** *7* **Hazel Brook**[11] [2279] 5-9-8 0.......................... RyanTate(5) 8 58
(Mary Hambro) *chsd wnr: rdn over 4f out: lost 2nd over 2f out: wknd wl over 1f out* **50/1**

50 **6** *19* **Sawwala**[28] [1797] 4-9-13 0.......................... FrederikTylicki 2 27
(J R Jenkins) *chsd ldrs: rdn over 4f out: wknd over 3f out* **33/1**

26 **7** *1¼* **Amourita (IRE)**[47] [1380] 3-8-7 0.......................... MatthewLawson(3) 9 24
(Jonathan Portman) *s.i.s: hld up: rdn over 4f out: wknd 3f out* **25/1**

**8** *33* **Love D'Oro (USA)** 3-8-10 0.......................... FrannyNorton 1
(Mark Johnston) *sn pushed along and prom: n.m.r and lost pl over 10f out: bhd fnl 8f* **5/1**[3]

2m 41.37s (7.47) **Going Correction** +0.725s/f (Yiel)
**WFA** 3 from 4yo+ 17lb 8 Ran SP% **126.2**
Speed ratings (Par 100): **104,98,97,97,92 80,79,57**
CSF £7.27 TOTE £1.50: £1.10, £1.90, £6.20; EX 5.90 Trifecta £69.60.
**Owner** Hamdan Al Maktoum **Bred** Shadwell Estate Company Limited **Trained** Newmarket, Suffolk

**FOCUS**
This maiden was weakened by the withdrawal of Wonderstruck who had finished ahead of the winner on her debut at Ascot. The first two both improved on their debuts efforts behind Marsh Dasiy.

## 2614 COLLECT TOTEPOOL WINNINGS AT BETFRED SHOPS APPRENTICE H'CAP 1m 3f 183y

**5:25** (5:25) (Class 6) (0-60,60) 4-Y-O+ **£2,726** (£805; £402) **Stalls** Low

Form RPR

0-24 **1** **Highlife Dancer**[10] [2305] 6-9-0 **60**.......................... PaddyPilley(7) 9 69
(Mick Channon) *chsd ldr tl led over 9f out: rdn and hung lft fr over 1f out: styd on* **9/2**[3]

3/45 **2** *3* **Dark And Dangerous (IRE)**[5] [2465] 6-9-4 **57**..........(v) JoshBaudains 10 61
(Brendan Powell) *chsd ldrs: wnt 2nd over 6f out: rdn over 2f out: styd on same pce ins fnl f* **11/4**[1]

00-3 **3** *2½* **Corn Maiden**[26] [1874] 5-8-13 **55**.......................... LewisWalsh(3) 11 55
(Lydia Pearce) *hld up: hdwy over 2f out: rdn over 1f out: styd on same pce fnl f* **9/2**[3]

6 **4** *2¾* **Crouching Harry (IRE)**[26] [1874] 5-8-12 **51**..........................(p) JoeDoyle 3 47
(Anabel K Murphy) *hld up: hdwy over 3f out: rdn over 2f out: no ex fnl f* **9/1**

5504 **5** *nk* **Lambert Pen (USA)**[14] [2212] 4-8-4 **48**.......................... RobHornby(5) 2 43
(Peter Hiatt) *led: hdd over 9f out: chsd wnr tl over 6f out: remained handy: rdn over 2f out: no ex fnl f* **12/1**

2523 **6** *2½* **Magicalmysterytour (IRE)**[14] [2212] 11-8-8 **52**.......................... JoshQuinn(5) 7 43
(Willie Musson) *s.i.s: hld up: rdn over 1f out: nvr on terms* **7/2**[2]

434- **7** *4½* **Now What**[318] [4238] 7-9-4 **57**.......................... NedCurtis 6 41
(Jonathan Portman) *prom: rdn over 2f out: sn wknd* **14/1**

30-0 **8** *1¼* **King's Road**[26] [1874] 9-8-12 **51**..........................(t) PatMillman 4 33
(Anabel K Murphy) *hld up: rdn and edgd rt over 2f out: wknd over 1f out* **25/1**

0053 **9** *16* **Stamp Duty (IRE)**[32] [1674] 6-8-7 **46**.......................... JordanVaughan 8 2
(Suzzanne France) *hld up: rdn over 3f out: sn wknd* **14/1**

2m 42.62s (8.72) **Going Correction** +0.725s/f (Yiel) 9 Ran SP% **120.1**
Speed ratings (Par 101): **99,97,95,93,93 91,88,87,77**
CSF £18.09 CT £60.32 TOTE £6.50: £2.80, £1.90, £1.30; EX 17.40 Trifecta £62.80.

**Owner** The Highlife Racing Club **Bred** Imperial & Mike Channon Bloodstock Ltd **Trained** West Ilsley, Berks
■ Paddy Pilley's first winner under rules.
**FOCUS**
A modest but competitive apprentice handicap. The time was relatively modest.
T/Plt: £23.90 to a £1 stake. Pool: £77048.55 - 2351.85 winning tickets T/Qpdt: £9.70 to a £1 stake. Pool: £5850.82 - 442.88 winning tickets CR

# 2386 REDCAR (L-H)
## Monday, May 26

**OFFICIAL GOING: Good to soft (soft in places, 7.6)**
Wind: Virtually nil Weather: Cloudy

## 2615 RACING UK ANYWHERE AVAILABLE NOW MAIDEN AUCTION STKS — 5f
2:35 (2:37) (Class 5) 2-Y-O **£2,726** (£805; £402) **Stalls** Centre

Form / RPR

4 **1** **Prince Bonnaire**[9] 2328 2-8-13 0 ... GrahamLee 10 82+
(David Brown) *prom: pushed along to ld 2f out: rdn clr fnl 110yds* **7/4**[1]

**2** 3 **Eye Glass (IRE)** 2-8-8 0 ... DuranFentiman 6 66
(Tim Easterby) *w ldr: rdn 2f out: kpt on but no ch w wnr ins fnl f* **25/1**

00 **3** 2 3/4 **Bahango (IRE)**[32] 1670 2-8-13 0 ... BenCurtis 11 61
(Kristin Stubbs) *chsd ldrs: rdn 1/2-way: kpt on to go 3rd ins fnl f* **16/1**

5 **4** 1 1/4 **Ingleby Spring (IRE)**[25] 1900 2-8-2 0 ... SammyJoBell(5) 8 51+
(Richard Fahey) *led narrowly: pushed along whn hdd 2f out: grad wknd* **11/2**[3]

**5** 1 1/4 **Pryers Princess** 2-8-5 0 ... JasonHart(3) 5 47+
(Michael Herrington) *in tch: rdn 2f out: one pce and no imp on ldrs* **9/2**[2]

**6** 1/2 **Denton Carnival (IRE)** 2-8-11 0 ... AndrewMullen 7 48+
(Michael Dods) *s.i.s: sn pushed along in rr: kpt on ins fnl f* **12/1**

**7** 3/4 **Dad's Girl** 2-8-3 0 ... IanBrennan(3) 1 41
(Ollie Pears) *s.i.s and swtchd rt: sn in tch racing keenly: rdn and rn green over 1f out: wknd fnl 110yds* **8/1**

6 **8** 1 1/2 **Astrea**[32] 1656 2-8-6 0 ... SilvestreDeSousa 9 35
(Nigel Tinkler) *racd keenly: hld up in tch: rdn 1/2-way: sn struggling* **12/1**

0 **9** 3 1/4 **This Is Too (IRE)**[11] 2269 2-8-1 0 ... NoelGarbutt(5) 2 23
(Alan Bailey) *midfield: wknd 1/2-way* **66/1**

**10** 7 **Ubedizzy (IRE)** 2-8-11 0 ... GrahamGibbons 3 3
(Noel Wilson) *chsd ldrs: hung lft and wknd fr 1/2-way* **12/1**

1m 0.79s (2.19) **Going Correction** +0.45s/f (Yiel) **10** Ran SP% **115.3**
Speed ratings (Par 93): **100,95,90,88,86 86,84,82,77,66**
CSF £54.19 TOTE £2.30: £1.10, £4.40, £4.20; EX 27.60 Trifecta £412.40.
**Owner** D A West **Bred** Mrs K E Collie **Trained** Averham Park, Notts
**FOCUS**
A modest 2yo maiden. The third and fourth support the level of the form.

## 2616 CONGRATULATIONS GOLDEN TICKET WINNER SARAH BEAUMONT MAIDEN H'CAP (DIV I) — 1m 6f 19y
3:05 (3:06) (Class 6) (0-65,65) 3-Y-O **£2,045** (£603; £302) **Stalls** Low

Form / RPR

3-55 **1** **Blue Talisman (IRE)**[14] 2198 3-8-10 **54** ... (b) DuranFentiman 1 64
(Tim Easterby) *led for 2f: trckd ldr: rdn to ld over 2f out: styd on wl and drew clr fr over 1f out* **14/1**

00-6 **2** 4 1/2 **Kirkman (IRE)**[30] 1738 3-8-12 **56** ... PJMcDonald 3 59
(James Bethell) *hld up: hdwy on inner over 3f out: sn chsd ldrs: kpt on: wnt 2nd 75yds out* **20/1**

-563 **3** 3/4 **Mambo Rhythm**[7] 2385 3-9-6 **64** ... SilvestreDeSousa 5 66
(Mark Johnston) *prom: led after 2f: rdn 4f out: hdd over 2f out: one pce: lost 2nd 75yds out* **2/1**[1]

0-04 **4** hd **Olymnia**[31] 1691 3-9-3 **61** ... AndreaAtzeni 8 63
(Robert Eddery) *hld up in midfield: hdwy over 5f out: angled to outer over 3f out: sn rdn and one pce* **7/2**[2]

3606 **5** 6 **Galaxy (IRE)**[17] 2132 3-9-7 **65** ... (v) BenCurtis 2 59
(Alan McCabe) *midfield: rdn and hdwy to chse ldrs 3f out: wknd fnl f* **10/1**

-306 **6** 4 **Zephyr**[18] 2098 3-9-4 **62** ... GrahamLee 7 50
(K R Burke) *hld up: rdn over 3f out: sn btn* **20/1**

-354 **7** 1 1/2 **Bentons Lad**[13] 2237 3-8-7 **51** ... AndrewElliott 11 37
(George Moore) *trckd ldrs: rdn over 3f out: wknd over 2f out* **7/1**

4-03 **8** 1 3/4 **Kashstaree**[13] 2237 3-8-6 **50** ... RoystonFfrench 6 33
(David Barron) *midfield: rdn over 3f out: sn wknd* **11/2**[3]

04-0 **9** 7 **Acquaint (IRE)**[9] 2354 3-9-2 **60** ... PaulPickard 4 34
(John Wainwright) *hld up: nvr threatened* **40/1**

-520 **10** 9 **Belle Peinture (FR)**[13] 2237 3-7-12 **47** ow1 ... SammyJoBell(5) 9 8
(Alan Lockwood) *hld up in midfield: rdn over 3f out: sn wknd* **33/1**

0-00 **11** 20 **Tawan**[27] 1840 3-7-11 **46** oh1 ... (p) NoelGarbutt(5) 10
(Brian Rothwell) *chsd ldrs: wknd 4f out* **100/1**

3m 12.07s (7.37) **Going Correction** +0.45s/f (Yiel) **11** Ran SP% **115.1**
Speed ratings (Par 97): **96,93,93,92,89 87,86,85,81,76 64**
CSF £259.42 CT £799.60 TOTE £11.80: £4.70, £5.70, £1.10; EX 179.30 Trifecta £1315.80.
**Owner** Ambrose Turnbull **Bred** Mark & Pippa Hackett **Trained** Great Habton, N Yorks
**FOCUS**
A typically weak maiden handicap. The pace was fair and the winner improved.

## 2617 MARKET CROSS JEWELLERS H'CAP (BOBIS RACE) — 1m 2f
3:40 (3:41) (Class 4) (0-85,85) 3-Y-O **£5,175** (£1,540; £769; £384) **Stalls** Low

Form / RPR

34-1 **1** **Al Busayyir (IRE)**[40] 1509 3-9-2 **80** ... AndreaAtzeni 4 91
(Marco Botti) *mde all: pushed along 3f out: rdn and jnd over 1f out: kpt on wl and a holding on fnl 110yds* **5/2**[2]

11 **2** nk **Libran (IRE)**[17] 2120 3-9-1 **79** ... BenCurtis 2 89
(Alan Swinbank) *s.i.s: hld up: smooth hdwy 3f out: rdn and upsides over 1f out: kpt on wl but a jst hld fnl 110yds* **7/1**

4-52 **3** 6 **New Street (IRE)**[8] 2363 3-8-7 **74** ... GeorgeChaloner(3) 1 73
(Richard Fahey) *trckd ldr: rdn over 3f out: one pce and hld in 3rd fr wl over 1f out* **4/1**[3]

-641 **4** 6 **Stampede (IRE)**[14] 2222 3-9-3 **81** ... RyanMoore 6 69
(Sir Michael Stoute) *dwlt: hld up: in tch: rdn over 3f out: wknd over 1f out* **6/4**[1]

21-4 **5** 7 **Dullingham**[26] 1883 3-9-7 **85** ... MickaelBarzalona 3 59
(Charlie Appleby) *hld up in tch: hdwy 3f out: rdn over 2f out: wknd over 1f out* **14/1**

2025 **6** 8 **Brownsville (USA)**[14] 2211 3-8-8 **72** ... SilvestreDeSousa 5 31
(Mark Johnston) *trckd ldr: rdn over 3f out: sn wknd* **40/1**

2m 11.55s (4.45) **Going Correction** +0.45s/f (Yiel) **6** Ran SP% **110.2**
Speed ratings (Par 101): **100,99,94,90,84 78**
CSF £18.89 TOTE £4.40: £1.60, £2.50; EX 16.80 Trifecta £33.40.
**Owner** Mubarak Al Naemi **Bred** Jim Halligan **Trained** Newmarket, Suffolk
**FOCUS**
A decent 3-y-o handicap and solid form. Off sensible fractions, they came up the centre of the track, a protracted battle ensued and the front two drew clear. There's a chance the form is worth more at face value.

## 2618 HAPPY 10TH BIRTHDAY RACING UK ZETLAND GOLD CUP (H'CAP) — 1m 2f
4:15 (4:15) (Class 2) (0-105,102) 3-Y-O+ **£16,172** (£4,812; £2,405; £1,202) **Stalls** Low

Form / RPR

30-0 **1** **Cashpoint**[12] 2253 9-8-4 **83** ... ShaneGray(5) 2 94
(Ian Williams) *trckd ldr: rdn to ld narrowly over 2f out: edgd rt ins fnl f: hld on towards fin* **20/1**

0020 **2** nk **Spa's Dancer (IRE)**[11] 2286 7-9-9 **97** ... GrahamLee 3 107
(James Eustace) *hld up: stdy hdwy fr over 2f out: rdn to chal strly ins fnl f: carried hd bit awkwardly and a jst hld fnl 50yds* **9/1**

0-06 **3** 3 1/4 **Silvery Moon (IRE)**[12] 2253 7-8-12 **89** ... JasonHart(3) 6 93
(Tim Easterby) *dwlt: sn rcvrd to trck ldrs racing keenly: rdn and ev ch 2f out: one pce and hld in 3rd ins fnl f* **5/1**[2]

6302 **4** 2 1/4 **Stepping Ahead (FR)**[48] 1360 4-9-11 **99** ... BenCurtis 8 99
(K R Burke) *led: rdn whn hdd over 2f out: sn outpcd and dropped to 4th: plugged on fnl f* **10/1**

00-2 **5** nk **Ginger Jack**[30] 1733 7-9-0 **88** ... PJMcDonald 4 87
(Geoffrey Harker) *in tch: rdn over 2f out: one pce and nt rch ldrs* **16/1**

-010 **6** 3 1/2 **Whispering Warrior (IRE)**[58] 1165 5-9-6 **94** ... ShaneKelly 1 86
(David Simcock) *midfield: rdn and hdwy to chse ldrs 2f out: wknd appr fnl f* **10/1**

6210 **7** 6 **Maven**[12] 2253 6-8-7 **88** ... RachelRichardson(7) 5 69
(Tim Easterby) *racd keenly in tch: rdn over 2f out: wknd over 1f out* **25/1**

4100 **8** 4 **Sky Khan**[12] 2253 5-8-6 **83** oh1 ... IanBrennan(3) 12 56
(John Wainwright) *prom: rdn over 3f out: wknd over 2f out* **66/1**

10-4 **9** 1 **Ennistown**[16] 2154 4-9-12 **100** ... MickaelBarzalona 10 71
(Charlie Appleby) *hld up: rdn and sme hdwy 3f out: wknd over 1f out* **7/1**[3]

0312 **10** 13 **Sennockian Star**[18] 2085 4-10-0 **102** ... (v) SilvestreDeSousa 7 49
(Mark Johnston) *midfield: rdn over 4f out: sn wknd* **9/2**[1]

5005 **11** 7 **Strictly Silver (IRE)**[18] 2085 5-9-6 **94** ... (v) GrahamGibbons 11 27
(Alan Bailey) *hld up in midfield: rdn over 3f out: sn wknd* **16/1**

05-2 **12** 21 **Ajmany (IRE)**[23] 1948 4-9-7 **95** ... (b) AndreaAtzeni 9
(Luca Cumani) *midfield: rdn 4f out: sn btn and eased* **9/2**[1]

2m 8.96s (1.86) **Going Correction** +0.45s/f (Yiel) **12** Ran SP% **115.6**
Speed ratings (Par 109): **110,109,107,105,105 102,97,94,93,83 77,60**
CSF £182.56 CT £1049.13 TOTE £21.90: £7.80, £4.40, £1.60; EX 327.70 Trifecta £2502.30 Part won. Pool: £3,336.51 - 0.83 winning units..
**Owner** Macable Partnership **Bred** Stowell Park Stud **Trained** Portway, Worcs
**FOCUS**
Often a well-contested handicap and this renewal looked as competitive as it has been in recent times. Ten of the previous 11 winners of the Zetland Gold Cup were officially rated between 91 and 98, but for the second year running it went to a lower-rated gelding. He produced a personal best at the afe of nine. The pace was ordinary.

## 2619 WIN A VIP DAY OUT @ REDCARRACING.CO.UK MEDIAN AUCTION MAIDEN STKS — 6f
4:45 (4:47) (Class 5) 3-Y-O **£2,587** (£770; £384; £192) **Stalls** Centre

Form / RPR

-U22 **1** **Naggers (IRE)**[23] 1939 3-9-5 74 ... GrahamLee 7 80
(Paul Midgley) *trckd ldr: led over 1f out: nudged clr: easily* **4/6**[1]

5 **2** 10 **Procurer (FR)**[18] 2093 3-8-12 0 ... MatthewHopkins(7) 4 48
(Scott Dixon) *led: rdn whn hdd over 1f out: sn no ch w wnr* **25/1**

05- **3** 3/4 **Ty Cobb (IRE)**[220] 7341 3-9-2 0 ... IanBrennan(3) 2 46
(John Quinn) *in tch: rdn over 2f out: sn one pce and hld in 3rd* **7/1**[3]

6-50 **4** 5 **Spinner Lane**[32] 1671 3-8-11 48 ... GeorgeChaloner(3) 1 25
(Richard Whitaker) *chsd ldr: rdn 1/2-way: wknd over 1f out* **33/1**

6-2 **P** **Secret Oasis**[25] 1902 3-9-0 0 ... RoystonFfrench 3
(Bryan Smart) *hld up: rdn over 3f out: p.u sharply and dismntd over 1f out* **5/2**[2]

1m 14.85s (3.05) **Going Correction** +0.45s/f (Yiel) **5** Ran SP% **107.8**
Speed ratings (Par 99): **97,83,82,76,**
CSF £17.40 TOTE £1.60: £1.10, £11.00; EX 13.80 Trifecta £40.60.
**Owner** Taylor's Bloodstock Ltd **Bred** Azienda Agricola Rosati Colarieti **Trained** Westow, N Yorks
**FOCUS**
A weak 3yo maiden in which the winner was left with little to beat.

## 2620 COME RACING AGAIN TOMORROW H'CAP — 1m 6f 19y
5:15 (5:15) (Class 6) (0-65,65) 4-Y-O+ **£1,940** (£577; £288; £144) **Stalls** Low

Form / RPR

0-51 **1** **Anne's Valentino**[14] 2213 4-8-8 **52** ... PJMcDonald 10 62+
(Malcolm Jefferson) *trckd ldr: led 3f out: sn rdn: strly pressed ins fnl f: hld on wl* **4/1**[2]

0-05 **2** 1 1/4 **Petella**[17] 2139 8-8-3 **54** ... (p) KieranSchofield(7) 4 62
(George Moore) *hld up in rr: rdn over 4f out: stl last 3f out: gd hdwy on outer fr over 2f out: chal strly ins fnl f: edgd lft 110yds out: one pce and hld fnl 50yds*

4420 **3** 1 1/4 **Yasir (USA)**[9] 2327 6-9-7 **65** ... (p) DavidNolan 5 71
(Conor Dore) *midfield: rdn over 3f out: hdwy over 2f out: chsd ldr over 1f out: kpt on* **7/1**[3]

52-5 **4** 1 1/4 **Beat The Shower**[20] 2055 8-9-0 **58** ... GrahamLee 9 62
(Peter Niven) *hld up: hdwy 3f out: n.m.r over 2f out and swtchd towards outer: styd on fnl f: wnt 4th towards fin* **8/1**

655- **5** 1/2 **Amir Pasha (UAE)**[13] 7375 9-8-4 **48** ... (b) SilvestreDeSousa 2 52
(Micky Hammond) *hld up in midfield: rdn and hdwy 3f out: chsd ldr 2f out: no ex fnl 110yds: lost 4th towards fin* **8/1**

12-0 **6** 1 3/4 **Blue Top**[9] 2327 5-9-0 **61** ... (p) JasonHart(3) 3 62
(Mark Walford) *slowly away: hld up: rdn over 4f out: hdwy to chse ldr 2f out: wknd ins fnl f* **11/4**[1]

6066 **7** 4 1/2 **Voice From Above (IRE)**[20] 2055 5-8-3 **47** ... AndrewMullen 12 42
(Patrick Holmes) *hld up: rdn over 3f out: nvr threatened* **25/1**

4-11 **8** 1 1/2 **Precision Strike**[30] 1740 4-9-0 **63** ... (v) PhilipPrince(5) 11 56
(Richard Guest) *trckd ldr towards outer: rdn over 3f out: wknd over 1f out* **10/1**

0-40 **9** 5 **Patavium (IRE)**[20] 2055 11-8-1 **50** ... (b[1]) ShaneGray(5) 7 36
(Edwin Tuer) *led: rdn whn hdd 3f out: sn wknd* **33/1**

22-5 **10** *6* **Tobrata**[32] 1674 8-8-12 **56** ............ DuranFentiman 1 33
(Mel Brittain) *trckd ldr: rdn over 3f out: wknd fnl 2f* **8/1**

0450 **11** *42* **Stormy Morning**[20] 2055 8-8-11 **55** ............(p) RussKennemore 6
(Philip Kirby) *midfield: rdn over 4f out: wknd over 2f out: eased* **25/1**

3m 10.48s (5.78) **Going Correction** +0.45s/f (Yiel) 11 Ran SP% **118.1**
Speed ratings (Par 101): **101,100,99,98,98 97,95,94,91,87 63**
CSF £64.67 CT £440.29 TOTE £7.50: £1.60, £3.90, £2.20; EX 101.80 Trifecta £512.20.
**Owner** The Magic Circle **Bred** Mr & Mrs P Nelson **Trained** Norton, N Yorks

**FOCUS**
They went a fair gallop in this very modest staying handicap. The winner built on her Musselburgh win.

## 2621 CONGRATULATIONS GOLDEN TICKET WINNER SARAH BEAUMONT MAIDEN H'CAP (DIV II) 1m 6f 19y
**5:45** (5:46) (Class 6) (0-65,65) 3-Y-O **£2,045** (£603; £302) **Stalls** Low

Form RPR

00-3 **1** **That Be Grand**[14] 2198 3-8-6 **53** ............ JasonHart(3) 7 63
(Shaun Harris) *midfield: hdwy over 4f out: led over 3f out: sn rdn: styd on wl* **5/1**[2]

560- **2** *3 ½* **Chivers (IRE)**[257] 6299 3-8-13 **57** ............ PJMcDonald 6 62
(Tim Easterby) *hld up in midfield: hdwy over 3f out: rdn to chse wnr over 2f out: styd on but a hld* **7/2**[1]

2323 **3** *4* **Halllouella**[18] 2098 3-9-4 **62** ............(p) GrahamLee 4 61
(James Tate) *led narrowly: rdn whn hdd over 3f out: plugged on* **13/2**[3]

000 **4** *4* **To Begin**[23] 1962 3-8-4 **48** ............ DuranFentiman 2 41
(Tim Easterby) *hld up: rdn over 3f out: hdwy into modest 4th over 1f out: no further imp ins fnl f* **10/1**

0-00 **5** *1 ½* **Telegraphy (USA)**[31] 1701 3-9-4 **62** ............ GrahamGibbons 10 53
(Ed Dunlop) *midfield: rdn 4f out: sme hdwy whn bmpd 3f out: no imp after: wknd ins fnl f* **7/2**[1]

-002 **6** *shd* **Master Dan**[18] 2098 3-9-3 **61** ............(p) DavidNolan 5 52
(James Given) *in tch: rdn over 3f out: wknd over 1f out* **15/2**

5-00 **7** *10* **Sweet Summer**[22] 1984 3-7-11 **46** oh1 ............ NoelGarbutt(5) 9 23
(John Holt) *w ldr: rdn over 4f out: wknd over 2f out* **28/1**

6600 **8** *12* **Dark Tsarina (IRE)**[19] 2078 3-8-11 **55** ............ AndreaAtzeni 3 15
(John Butler) *hld up: pushed along over 4f out: nvr threatened* **25/1**

4254 **9** *19* **Mary Le Bow**[55] 1220 3-9-7 **65** ............(p) PaddyAspell 8
(Lucy Wadham) *trckd ldrs: rdn 4f out: wknd over 2f out* **13/2**[3]

3m 13.44s (8.74) **Going Correction** +0.45s/f (Yiel) 9 Ran SP% **115.9**
Speed ratings (Par 97): **93,91,88,86,85 85,79,72,62**
CSF £22.97 CT £115.18 TOTE £5.90: £2.40, £2.60, £1.60; EX 19.20 Trifecta £108.40.
**Owner** C A Harris & Peter Dawson **Bred** Kassala Limited **Trained** Carburton, Notts

**FOCUS**
They finished well strung out in this second division of the 3yo maiden handicap. It was the slower time and the winner came from the same Doncaster handicap as the division I winner.
T/Plt: £193.90 to a £1 stake. Pool: £70,819.74 - 266.51 winning tickets. T/Qpdt: £77.80 to a £1 stake. Pool: £4,207.56 - 40.00 winning tickets. AS

# 2401 WINDSOR (R-H)
## Monday, May 26

**OFFICIAL GOING: Soft (6.9)**
Wind: virtually nil Weather: rain Rails: Top bend dolled out 9yds from normal configuration adding 35yds to races of one mile and beyond. Inner of Straight dolled out 10yds at 6f and 4yds at Winning Post

## 2622 LADBROKES MAIDEN AUCTION STKS (DIV I) 6f
**2:00** (2:01) (Class 5) 2-Y-O **£2,911** (£866; £432; £216) **Stalls** Low

Form RPR

3 **1** **Bazzana**[11] 2269 2-8-6 0 ............ DavidProbert 1 83
(Martyn Meade) *stdd s: chsd ldng pair and a travelling wl: led ent fnl 2f: drew wl clr over 1f out: r.o wl: v easily* **4/5**[1]

4 **2** *10* **Buckleberry**[16] 2173 2-8-13 0 ............ JimCrowley 3 60
(Jonathan Portman) *racd in midfield: rdn over 2f out: 4th and no ch w wnr over 1f out: styd on to go modest 2nd fnl 75yds* **10/1**[3]

0 **3** *1 ¼* **Divine Law**[21] 2007 2-9-1 0 ............ RichardHughes 9 58
(Richard Hannon) *racd in midfield: rdn over 2f out: chsd clr wnr over 1f out: no imp and lost 2nd fnl 75yds* **5/1**[2]

6 **4** *2 ¾* **Ho Yam Lay**[11] 2269 2-8-8 0 ............ HayleyTurner 4 43
(Michael Bell) *t.k.h: chsd ldr tl jst over 2f out: lost 2nd and wl btn over 1f out: wknd ins fnl f* **5/1**[2]

**5** *1 ½* **Orobas (IRE)** 2-9-4 0 ............ GeorgeBaker 2 49
(Harry Whittington) *hld up in last pair: rdn and modest hdwy ent fnl f: n.d* **12/1**

0 **6** *2 ¼* **Endislie (IRE)**[58] 1161 2-8-11 0 ............ LiamJones 5 35
(J S Moore) *sn towards rr: rdn 4f out: n.d* **25/1**

**7** *1* **Gavarnie Encore** 2-8-11 0 ............ LiamKeniry 11 32
(Michael Blanshard) *s.i.s: rcvrd and in midfield over 4f out: rdn and struggling fnl 2f: wknd over 1f out* **33/1**

0 **8** *hd* **El Campeon**[11] 2276 2-9-1 0 ............ JimmyQuinn 6 35
(Simon Dow) *a in rr: rdn 1/2-way: n.d* **50/1**

0 **9** *1 ¾* **Overstone Lass (IRE)**[30] 1732 2-8-7 0 ow1 ............ JohnFahy 7 22
(John Spearing) *t.k.h: in midfield early: dropped to rr 4f out: rdn and wl btn over 2f out: wknd* **100/1**

00 **10** *7* **Majenski (IRE)**[26] 1872 2-8-13 0 ............ RachealKneller(5) 10 12
(Jamie Osborne) *racd freely: led and clr tl hdes ent fnl 2f: sn btn: fdd over 1f out* **50/1**

1m 15.84s (2.84) **Going Correction** +0.65s/f (Yiel) 10 Ran SP% **117.4**
Speed ratings (Par 93): **107,93,92,88,86 83,82,81,79,70**
CSF £9.87 TOTE £1.70: £1.10, £2.30, £2.00; EX 10.20 Trifecta £28.90.
**Owner** The Below Reeve Partnership **Bred** Mrs J A Cornwell **Trained** Newmarket, Suffolk

**FOCUS**
Top bend dolled out 9yds from normal configuration adding 35yds to races of one mile and beyond. Inner of straight dolled out 10yds at 6f and 4yds at winning post. Testing conditions after a lot of rain fell on the track in the previous 24 hours. The winner is clearly very promising but the bare form is limited.

## 2623 LADBROKES MAIDEN AUCTION STKS (DIV II) 6f
**2:30** (2:30) (Class 5) 2-Y-O **£2,911** (£866; £432; £216) **Stalls** Low

Form RPR

4 **1** **Among Angels**[10] 2298 2-9-4 0 ............ RichardHughes 3 78+
(Richard Hannon) *hld up in tch in midfield: shuffled bk into last trio 1/2-way: rdn and hdwy wl over 1f out: led ent fnl f: styd on and gng away at fin* **1/2**[1]

00 **2** *2 ¼* **Well Fleeced**[40] 1504 2-8-11 0 ............ JohnFahy 10 64
(J S Moore) *dwlt: sn rcvrd and in tch in midfield: rdn and effrt to ld wl over 1f out: hdd ent fnl f: one pce fnl 150yds* **10/1**

0 **3** *1 ¼* **Outback Ruler (IRE)**[16] 2146 2-9-4 0 ............ AdamKirby 2 68
(Clive Cox) *chsd ldrs: rdn and ev ch wl over 1f out tl no ex ent fnl f: styd on same pce after* **5/1**[2]

65 **4** *2* **Mount Isa (IRE)**[7] 2395 2-8-11 0 ............ LiamJones 7 55
(J S Moore) *in tch in midfield: effrt and clsd to press ldrs whn squeezed and hmpd 2f out: edgd lft u.p and one pce fnl f* **25/1**

**5** *½* **Cape Cay** 2-8-10 0 ............ JimCrowley 4 52
(Ralph Beckett) *s.i.s: in tch in rr: hdwy 1/2-way: chsd ldrs and rdn wl over 1f out: no ex and btn 1f out: plugged on same pce fnl f* **6/1**[3]

00 **6** *2 ½* **Ciaras Cookie (IRE)**[30] 1741 2-8-3 0 ............ DeclanBates(3) 5 41
(David Evans) *led: edgd lft u.p 2f out: sn hdd and btn: wknd over 1f out* **50/1**

**7** *1* **Bakht A Rawan (IRE)** 2-9-1 0 ............ LiamKeniry 1 47
(Mark Usher) *in tch in last trio: sme hdwy 1/2-way: rdn and btn 2f out: wknd over 1f out* **16/1**

0 **8** *18* **Royal Street**[45] 1417 2-9-1 0 ............ WilliamCarson 9
(Seamus Durack) *t.k.h: chsd ldr tl over 2f out: sn dropped out: wl bhd fnl f* **20/1**

1m 16.87s (3.87) **Going Correction** +0.65s/f (Yiel) 8 Ran SP% **123.2**
Speed ratings (Par 93): **100,97,95,92,92 88,87,63**
CSF £7.75 TOTE £1.60: £1.10, £2.30, £1.50; EX 8.80 Trifecta £38.70.
**Owner** Pineapple Stud **Bred** The Pineapple Stud Ltd **Trained** East Everleigh, Wilts

**FOCUS**
Probably an ordinary race for the track.

## 2624 LADBROKES H'CAP 1m 67y
**3:00** (3:01) (Class 5) (0-75,74) 3-Y-O **£2,911** (£866; £432; £216) **Stalls** Low

Form RPR

4-32 **1** **Space Walker (IRE)**[21] 2027 3-9-3 **70** ............ AdamKirby 2 80
(Harry Dunlop) *sn led and mde rest: set stdy gallo tl rdn and qcknd over 2f out: clr and edgd lft u.p ins fnl f: styd on: rdn out* **7/1**[3]

60-2 **2** *2* **Jersey Brown (IRE)**[14] 2224 3-8-10 **66** ............ CharlesBishop(3) 10 71+
(Mick Channon) *v.s.a: in tch in rr: hdwy and sltly impeded 2f out: styd on to chse wnr 1f out: edgd lft and and no imp fnl f* **5/1**[2]

0-33 **3** *2 ½* **After The Goldrush**[10] 2307 3-9-4 **71** ............ RichardHughes 7 70
(Richard Hannon) *in tch in midfield: rdn and effrt over 2f out: awkward hd carriage but hdwy to chse wnr over 1f out tl 1f out: wknd ins fnl f* **8/1**

6243 **4** *nk* **Boogangoo (IRE)**[17] 2130 3-9-6 **73** ............ StevieDonohoe 9 72
(Grace Harris) *in tch in last trio: hdwy u.p over 1f out: styd on fnl f and pressing for 3rd cl home: no threat to wnr* **10/1**

614 **5** *2 ¼* **Thanks Harry**[17] 2112 3-9-7 **74** ............ GeorgeBaker 11 67+
(Gary Moore) *hld up in tch in midfield: effrt jst over 2f out: drvn and no imp over 1f out: wl hld and plugged on same pce fnl f* **5/2**[1]

-024 **6** *hd* **Double Czech (IRE)**[21] 2013 3-9-2 **69** ............ DavidProbert 6 62
(Patrick Chamings) *broke wl: sn stdd to chse ldrs: rdn jst over 2f out: keeping on same pce whn n.m.r over 1f out: one pce and wl hld fnl f* **14/1**

53-3 **7** *nse* **What A Dandy (IRE)**[123] 291 3-9-1 **68** ............ PatCosgrave 1 61
(Jim Boyle) *t.k.h: chsd ldrs: rdn and effrt over 2f out: hung lft and btn over 1f out: one pce and wl hld fnl f* **50/1**

34-5 **8** *10* **Headlong (IRE)**[10] 2307 3-9-3 **70** ............(v[1]) MartinLane 5 40
(Brian Meehan) *t.k.h: chsd ldr: rdn over 2f out: lost 2nd wl over 1f out: sn btn: wl bhd and eased wl ins fnl f* **8/1**

3624 **9** *nse* **Fruit Pastille**[27] 1846 3-9-0 **67** ............[1] PatDobbs 12 37
(Hughie Morrison) *in tch in midfield: rdn over 2f out: sn struggling: wl bhd and eased wl ins fnl f* **8/1**

15-4 **10** *9* **New Row**[20] 2058 3-9-3 **70** ............ RobertHavlin 8 19
(William Jarvis) *plld hrd: hld up in tch in last trio: rdn over 2f out: lost tch over 1f out: eased ins fnl f* **16/1**

1m 49.96s (5.26) **Going Correction** +0.65s/f (Yiel) 10 Ran SP% **114.7**
Speed ratings (Par 99): **99,97,94,94,91 91,91,81,81,72**
CSF £41.19 CT £292.73 TOTE £7.10: £1.90, £2.50, £2.30; EX 40.40 Trifecta £172.00.
**Owner** Carter,Craig-Wood,Drake,Gehring,Lewis **Bred** S F Bloodstock **Trained** Lambourn, Berks
■ Stewards' Enquiry : Pat Cosgrave caution: careless riding.

**FOCUS**
An open handicap in which they all pretty much ended up on the far side in the straight. The winner had the run of things but this looks a step up.

## 2625 LADBROKES MAIDEN STKS 5f 10y
**3:35** (3:36) (Class 5) 3-Y-0+ **£2,911** (£866; £432; £216) **Stalls** Low

Form RPR

463- **1** **High On Life**[252] 6477 3-9-4 73 ............ RichardHughes 5 73
(Jamie Osborne) *mde all: pushed along and asserting whn hung rt over 1f out: drew clr fnl f: easily* **11/10**[1]

6446 **2** *4 ½* **Brean Splash Susie**[21] 2023 3-8-8 44 ............ RyanWhile(5) 2 52
(Bill Turner) *chsd wnr: drvn and unable qck over 1f out: no ch w wnr but battled on to hold 2nd fnl f* **50/1**

55 **3** *1 ¼* **Champagne Charley**[17] 2125 3-8-13 0 ............ AdamBeschizza 4 47
(Des Donovan) *hld up in tch in last pair: hdwy to chse ldrs and n.m.r 2f out: drvn and unable qck over 1f out: kpt on same pce fnl f* **5/1**[3]

0- **4** *½* **See No Ships**[248] 6589 3-8-13 0 ............ DavidProbert 3 46
(Mark Usher) *stdd s: t.k.h: in tch in rr: effrt wl over 1f out: swtchd lft 1f out: no ch w wnr and one pce ins fnl f* **12/1**

5 **5** *hd* **Dubawi Coast**[37] 1569 3-8-13 0 ............ JimCrowley 6 45
(James Tate) *trckd ldrs: rdn 2f out: unable qck and btn ent fnl f: kpt on same pce fnl f* **2/1**[2]

0 **6** *10* **Royal College**[17] 2126 4-9-5 0 ............ HectorCrouch(7) 7 17
(Gary Moore) *s.i.s: sn rdn along: hdwy into midfield after 1f: struggling 1/2-way: bhd over 1f out* **20/1**

1m 3.07s (2.77) **Going Correction** +0.65s/f (Yiel)
**WFA** 3 from 4yo 8lb 6 Ran SP% **112.0**
Speed ratings (Par 103): **103,95,93,93,92 76**
CSF £48.19 TOTE £1.80: £1.10, £8.40; EX 26.80 Trifecta £81.40.
**Owner** Michael Buckley **Bred** Moyns Park Estate And Stud Ltd **Trained** Upper Lambourn, Berks

**FOCUS**
A weak maiden, with the runner-up rated just 44. The winner did not need to improve.

## 2626 DOWNLOAD THE NEW LADBROKES APP H'CAP (BOBIS RACE) 5f 10y
**4:10** (4:10) (Class 4) (0-85,85) 3-Y-O **£5,822** (£1,732; £865; £432) **Stalls** Low

Form RPR

-210 **1** **Piazon**[10] 2317 3-9-2 **85** ............ LouisSteward(5) 3 93
(Michael Bell) *taken down early: pressed ldr: ev ch and carried lft over 1f out: sn rdn to ld: r.o wl: rdn out* **3/1**[2]

5203 **2** 1 1/4 **Amahoro**[3] 2508 3-8-12 **79** CharlesBishop(3) 2 83
(Mick Channon) *taken down early: hld up in tch: hdwy u.p and swtchd lft over 1f out: chsd wnr ins fnl f: styd on but no imp* **7/1**

20-0 **3** 1 3/4 **Grecian (IRE)**[10] 2317 3-9-0 **81** (t) OisinMurphy(3) 5 78
(Paul Cole) *in tch: hdwy u.p over 1f out: wnt 3rd ins fnl f: styd on same pce after* **9/2**[3]

-053 **4** 2 1/2 **Jazz (IRE)**[18] 2090 3-9-7 **85** RichardHughes 1 73
(Charles Hills) *led and racd against stands' rail: rdn and hung lft over 1f out: sn hdd: lost 2nd and wknd ins fnl f* **11/4**[1]

2122 **5** 1 **Taquka (IRE)**[30] 1737 3-9-4 **82** JimCrowley 6 67
(Ralph Beckett) *dwlt: in tch in rr: rdn over 2f out: no real imp: nvr threatened ldrs* **6/1**

016- **6** 2 1/4 **Hopefilly (IRE)**[201] 7771 3-9-2 **80** HayleyTurner 8 57
(Ed Walker) *racd along in centre: chsd ldrs: rdn 2f out: sn struggling and btn 1f out: wknd fnl f* **25/1**

0-30 **7** 2 **Desert Ace (IRE)**[31] 1700 3-9-7 **85** (p) AdamKirby 4 54
(Clive Cox) *in tch in midfield: rdn over 2f out: struggling and btn over 1f out: wknd fnl f* **8/1**

1m 3.06s (2.76) **Going Correction** +0.65s/f (Yiel) **7 Ran SP% 111.6**
Speed ratings (Par 101): **103,101,98,94,92 89,85**
CSF £22.70 CT £89.67 TOTE £3.30: £1.90, £5.40; EX 25.10 Trifecta £163.90.
**Owner** R P B Michaelson **Bred** Peter Baldwin **Trained** Newmarket, Suffolk

**FOCUS**
This looked quite a good little sprint on paper and although conditions weren't ideal for a few of these, the winner looks a sprinter on the upgrade and worth following. The runner-up helps set the standard.

## 2627 BET NOW WITH THE LADBROKES APP H'CAP — 1m 2f 7y
4:40 (4:40) (Class 4) (0-85,85) 4-Y-O+ £5,822 (£1,732; £865; £432) Stalls Low

Form RPR

-323 **1** **Starwatch**[21] 2033 7-8-9 **73** WilliamCarson 5 82
(John Bridger) *led tl 1/2-way: chsd ldr tl rdn to ld again ent fnl 2f: edgd lft u.p fnl f: hld on wl: drvn out* **7/1**[3]

-504 **2** 1 1/4 **Sheila's Buddy**[12] 2248 5-8-10 **74** RichardHughes 7 81
(J S Moore) *stdd s: hld up in rr: rdn and hdwy 2f out: drvn to chse ldrs 1f out: kpt on to go 2nd towards fin* **8/1**

4-22 **3** shd **Saigon City**[16] 2162 4-9-5 **83** (b) AdamKirby 11 89
(Luca Cumani) *hld up in tch in midfield: hdwy and edging rt over 2f out: pressing wnr fr 2f out: rdn 1f out: carried lft but fnd little for press: btn fnl 50yds: lost 2nd towards fin* **2/1**[1]

04-3 **4** 2 **Number One London (IRE)**[28] 1810 4-8-13 **77** (p) StevieDonohoe 3 80
(Brian Meehan) *chsd ldrs: bmpd over 2f out: rdn and unable qck 2f out: kpt on again ins fnl f* **7/1**[3]

6001 **5** hd **Presburg (IRE)**[21] 2033 5-9-4 **85** OisinMurphy(3) 6 87
(Joseph Tuite) *hld up in tch in last trio: hdwy and nt clr run over 1f out: sn swtchd lft and effrt u.p: styd on same pce ins fnl f* **5/1**[2]

5-35 **6** 3/4 **Nave (USA)**[113] 450 7-8-7 **71** oh2 MartinLane 4 72
(David Simcock) *in tch in midfield: n.m.r 2f out: rdn and effrt over 1f out: no imp and one pce fnl f* **25/1**

2203 **7** hd **Tepmokea (IRE)**[18] 2091 8-9-3 **81** (p) HayleyTurner 1 81
(Conor Dore) *chsd ldr tl led 1/2-way: rdn and hdd 2f out: btn ent fnl f: wknd ins fnl f* **8/1**

106- **8** 22 **Couloir Extreme (IRE)**[167] 6136 4-8-12 **76** PatDobbs 10 35
(Gary Moore) *wl in tch in midfield: rdn and lost pl over 2f out: wl bhd and eased ins fnl f: t.o* **25/1**

500 **9** 1 1/4 **Ruzeiz (USA)**[68] 1014 5-8-10 **77** CharlesBishop(3) 8 33
(Peter Hedger) *t.k.h: hld up in tch in midfield: rdn and effrt over 2f out: struggling and btn 2f: wl bhd and eased ins fnl f: t.o* **10/1**

6040 **10** 3 **Tinshu (IRE)**[38] 1559 8-9-2 **80** (p) LiamKeniry 9 31
(Derek Haydn Jones) *hld up wl in tch: rdn jst over 2f out: sn btn: wl bhd and eased ins fnl f: t.o* **25/1**

2m 13.66s (4.96) **Going Correction** +0.65s/f (Yiel) **10 Ran SP% 117.9**
Speed ratings (Par 105): **106,105,104,103,103 102,102,84,83,81**
CSF £60.81 CT £151.38 TOTE £8.80: £2.30, £2.60, £1.60; EX 36.30 Trifecta £188.80.
**Owner** J J Bridger **Bred** Mrs J A Chapman **Trained** Liphook, Hants

**FOCUS**
A competitive handicap run at a sound gallop. The winner rates up a length on recent C&D runs.

## 2628 LADBROKES FILLIES' H'CAP — 1m 3f 135y
5:10 (5:10) (Class 5) (0-75,74) 4-Y-O+ £2,911 (£866; £432; £216) Stalls Centre

Form RPR

10-0 **1** **Lady Of Yue**[11] 2270 4-8-7 **63** ow1 RobertTart(3) 10 76
(Eugene Stanford) *hld up in tch in last pair: hdwy in centre over 2f out: rdn to chse ldrs over 1f out: led ins fnl f: styd on wl: rdn out* **8/1**

30-4 **2** 3 3/4 **Pernica**[23] 1934 4-9-4 **71** (p) DavidProbert 9 78
(Lucy Wadham) *in tch in midfield: clsd to trck ldrs and racing in centre 3f out: rdn and ev ch over 1f out: led 1f out: sn hdd and no ex: plugged on* **7/2**[1]

2-24 **3** 1 3/4 **Tracks Of My Tears**[45] 1426 4-8-5 **61** RyanPowell(3) 6 65+
(Giles Bravery) *in tch in midfield: lost pl whn hmpd and dropped to last 6f out: detached and rdn over 3f out: racing in centre over 2f out: hdwy over 1f out: styd on wl: no threat to wnr* **20/1**

30-4 **4** 1 **Lyric Ballad**[26] 1882 4-9-7 **74** RichardHughes 8 77
(Hughie Morrison) *led for 2f: in tch after: racing in centre and effrt over 2f out: drvn to ld over 1f out: hdd 1f out: wknd ins fnl f* **8/1**

41-3 **5** 2 **Uganda Glory (USA)**[19] 2067 4-8-12 **65** (v) PatCosgrave 5 64
(George Baker) *dwlt: sn rdn and hdwy to ld after 2f: styd against stands' rail and rdn over 2f out: hdd over 1f out: wknd and hung lft fnl f* **6/1**[3]

0411 **6** 1 1/2 **Choral Festival**[10] 2300 8-9-1 **68** WilliamCarson 7 65
(John Bridger) *t.k.h: chsd ldrs: wnt 2nd and styd towards stands' side 3f out: drvn and btn over 1f out: edgd lft and wknd fnl f* **9/2**[2]

1522 **7** 6 **Sian Gwalia**[28] 1815 4-9-3 **70** MartinLane 4 57
(David Simcock) *hld up in rr: hdwy towards centre over 2f out: rdn and btn over 1f out: eased wl ins fnl f* **14/1**

32-4 **8** 35 **Kingston Eucalypt**[47] 1393 4-9-5 **72** LiamKeniry 11 3
(David Elsworth) *in tch towards rr: rdn and c towards centre over 2f out: btn 2f out: sn lost tch: t.o and virtually p.u ins fnl f* **10/1**

2-65 **9** 18 **Storm (IRE)**[10] 2305 4-9-0 **70** OisinMurphy(3) 3
(Charles Hills) *t.k.h: chsd ldr after 2f tl 3f out: sn dropped out: t.o and eased ins fnl f* **7/1**

2546 **10** 3/4 **Kenny's Girl (IRE)**[16] 2175 4-8-4 **57** (bt[1]) HayleyTurner 2
(William Muir) *chsd ldrs: rdn 7f out: lost pl u.p 6f out: lost tch 3f: t.o and eased ins fnl f* **16/1**

2m 37.13s (7.63) **Going Correction** +0.65s/f (Yiel) **10 Ran SP% 115.8**
Speed ratings (Par 100): **100,97,96,95,94 93,89,66,54,53**
CSF £35.89 CT £546.44 TOTE £9.90: £3.40, £1.80, £4.50; EX 61.10 Trifecta £644.40.
**Owner** Mrs Janice Quy **Bred** Mrs J M Quy **Trained** Newmarket, Suffolk

■ Stewards' Enquiry : Robert Tart trainer said, regarding apparent improvement in form, that the filly was better suited by the soft ground and the longer trip.

**FOCUS**
They went hard and this turned into a war of attrition in the straight. The form is rated around the runner-up.

## 2629 THIS IS THE LADBROKES LIFE H'CAP — 6f
5:40 (5:41) (Class 4) (0-85,85) 4-Y-O+ £5,822 (£1,732; £865; £432) Stalls Low

Form RPR

0-01 **1** **Links Drive Lady**[21] 2030 6-9-7 **85** RichardHughes 8 94
(Dean Ivory) *stdd s: hld up in tch in last trio: hdwy 2f out: racing against far rail and ev ch 1f out: rdn to ld ins fnl f: hrd pressed fnl 75yds: r.o and hld on wl* **9/2**[3]

0/00 **2** shd **Englishman**[23] 1938 4-9-7 **85** JimCrowley 2 94
(Charles Hills) *hld up in tch in last trio: swtchd and effrt over 1f out: edging lft but hdwy to chal ins fnl f: r.o wl: jst hld* **6/1**

3644 **3** 1 1/4 **O'Gorman**[42] 1490 5-9-2 **80** LiamKeniry 4 85
(Gary Brown) *s.i.s: hld up in rr: effrt and forced to switch sharply rt over 1f out: str run u.p ins fnl f: nt rch ldrs* **12/1**

064 **4** 1/2 **Triple Chocolate**[16] 2147 4-8-8 **72** JimmyQuinn 1 75
(Roger Ingram) *in tch in midfield: rdn and effrt to chse ldrs 1f out: nt clrest of runs ins fnl f: kpt on* **7/2**[2]

0-03 **5** 2 **Midnight Rider (IRE)**[21] 2030 6-9-3 **81** GeorgeBaker 9 81
(Chris Wall) *chsd ldrs: rdn to ld over 1f out: drvn and hdd ins fnl f: styng on same pce and btn whn hmpd ins fnl f: wknd towards fin* **11/4**[1]

232 **6** 1 1/4 **Vincentti (IRE)**[28] 1789 4-9-2 **80** DavidProbert 5 73
(Ronald Harris) *t.k.h: chsd ldr: rdn wl over 2f out: struggling to qckn and losing pl whn short of room and hmpd jst over 1f out: wknd ins fnl f* **6/1**

6-50 **7** nk **Lupo D'Oro (IRE)**[16] 2147 5-9-0 **78** SteveDrowne 6 70
(John Best) *in tch in midfield: swtchd lft and effrt u.p over 1f out: keeping on same pce whn short of room and hmpd 1f out: wknd ins fnl f* **14/1**

4004 **8** 1/2 **I'll Be Good**[4] 2473 5-8-7 **74** oh11 ow3 (t) SladeO'Hara(3) 7 64
(Alan Berry) *led tl rdn and hdd over 1f out: wknd ins fnl f* **25/1**

1m 16.37s (3.37) **Going Correction** +0.65s/f (Yiel) **8 Ran SP% 113.8**
Speed ratings (Par 105): **103,102,101,100,97 96,95,95**
CSF £31.17 CT £302.05 TOTE £5.20: £1.50, £2.80, £2.90; EX 20.80 Trifecta £266.80.
**Owner** It's Your Lucky Day **Bred** Peter Webb **Trained** Radlett, Herts
■ Stewards' Enquiry : Jim Crowley two-day ban: careless riding (Jun 9-10)

**FOCUS**
This looks reasonable form for the grade, the winner back to her best. The first four came from the rear.

T/Plt: £18.10 to a £1 stake. Pool: £93,358.67 - 3760.53 winning tickets T/Qpdt: £20.70 to a £1 stake. Pool: £5,006.75 - 178.40 winning tickets SP

# 2411 SAINT-CLOUD (L-H)
Friday, May 23

**OFFICIAL GOING: Turf: good to soft**

## 2630a PRIX GYGES (MAIDEN) (UNRACED 3YO COLTS & GELDINGS) (TURF) — 7f
1:20 (12:00) 3-Y-O £10,416 (£4,166; £3,125; £2,083; £1,041)

RPR

**1** **Castagnou (IRE)** 3-9-2 0 Christophe-PatriceLemaire 5 88
(P Bary, France) **23/10**[2]

**2** 2 **Magistrat (IRE)** 3-9-2 0 AdrienFouassier 1 83
(Alain Couetil, France) **49/10**[3]

**3** 1/2 **Muzaahim (IRE)** 3-9-2 0 AurelienLemaitre 6 81
(F Head, France) **58/10**

**4** 1/2 **Always Ready (FR)** 3-9-2 0 GeraldMosse 3 80
(C Bresson, France) **199/10**

**5** 3/4 **Kalidjar (FR)** 3-9-2 0 ChristopheSoumillon 4 78
(M Delzangles, France) **13/10**[1]

**6** 3 **Dominandros (FR)** 3-9-2 0 MaximeGuyon 2 70
(Gay Kelleway) **9/1**

1m 34.18s (1.98) **6 Ran SP% 120.2**
WIN (incl. 1 euro stake): 3.30. Places: 1.80, 2.10. SF: 13.10..
**Owner** Ecurie Jean-Louis Bouchard **Bred** J Hayoz **Trained** Chantilly, France

## 2631a PRIX CORRIDA (GROUP 2) (4YO+ FILLIES & MARES) (TURF) — 1m 2f 110y
2:20 (12:00) 4-Y-O+ £61,750 (£23,833; £9,479; £9,479; £3,791)

RPR

**1** **Siljan's Saga (FR)**[25] 1827 4-8-9 0 Pierre-CharlesBoudot 12 110
(J-P Gauvin, France) *hld up in midfield: pushed along and clsd 2f out: rdn and hung lft over 1f out: chal ent fnl f and sn led: styd on strly and asserted: readily* **104/10**

**2** 2 1/2 **Vally Jem (FR)**[25] 1827 5-8-9 0 (p) IoritzMendizabal 10 105
(D Sepulchre, France) *dwlt and hld up towards rr: rdn 2f out: styd on steadily and wnt 2nd post: nt pce of wnr* **43/1**

**3** nse **Nymphea (IRE)**[166] 8208 5-9-2 0 DanielePorcu 1 112
(P Schiergen, Germany) *led: rdn and hdd over 1f out: rallied u.p and styd on gamely but nt pce of wnr* **13/1**

**3** dht **Daksha (FR)**[25] 1827 4-8-11 0 ThierryThulliez 5 107
(Waldemar Hickst, Germany) *prom: pushed along to chal and w ldrs over 1f out: outpcd by wnr ins fnl f: styd on* **78/10**

**5** shd **Baltic Baroness (GER)**[26] 1783 4-8-9 0 MaximeGuyon 2 105
(A Fabre, France) *midfield on inner: rdn 2f out: short of room on rail and swtchd rt ent fnl f: nt clr run again 120yds out: styd on wl towards fin but nvr able to chal* **48/10**[3]

**6** snk **Entree**[25] 1827 4-8-10 0 ow1 ChristopheSoumillon 11 106
(P Bary, France) *trckd ldr: pushed along to chal 2f out: rdn to ld over 1f out: hdd ins fnl f and readily outpcd by wnr: no ex and lost 4 pls fnl 75yds* **41/10**[2]

**7** 1 **Star Lahib (IRE)**[32] 5-8-9 0 EPedroza 13 103
(A Wohler, Germany) *dwlt sltly but qckly rcvrd: midfield in tch on outer: rdn over 2f out: outpcd over 1f out: styd on* **26/1**

**8** nk **Gaga A (URU)**[25] 1827 5-8-9 0 GregoryBenoist 6 102
(D Smaga, France) *midfield: pushed along over 2f out: rdn and outpcd over 1f out: styd on* **30/1**

**9** nse **Ipswich (IRE)**[25] 1827 4-8-9 0 GeraldMosse 3 102
(A De Royer-Dupre, France) *prom on inner: pushed along over 2f out: rdn over 1f out: styng on whn nt clr run ins fnl f: swtchd lft and again short of room towards fin: nt rcvr* **181/10**

10 1 1/2 **Ferevia (IRE)**[286] 5297 4-8-9 0........................ Christophe-PatriceLemaire 8 99
(C Laffon-Parias, France) *hld up towards rr: pushed along over 2f out: rdn and outpcd over 1f out: nt clr run ent fnl f: wl hld after: nvr threatened* **33/1**

11 1/2 **No News (FR)**[25] 1827 4-8-9 0........................ ThomasMessina 9 98
(X Nakkachdji, France) *dwlt sltly and hld up in last: rdn over 2f out: outpcd over 1f out and sn btn: nvr a factor* **136/10**

12 2 **Fate (FR)**[23] 5-8-9 0........................ StephanePasquier 7 94
(A De Royer-Dupre, France) *hld up in last pair: rdn over 2f out: outpcd and dropped to last over 1f out: sn btn: nvr a factor* **11/5**[1]

2m 16.19s (-3.41) **12** Ran SP% **119.6**
WIN (incl. 1 euro stake): 11.40. Places: 3.40, 8.00, 2.00, 3.00. DF: 162.00. SF: 312.00..
**Owner** E Palluat De Besset & E Tassin **Bred** Mme P Ouvry **Trained** France

# 2608 LEICESTER (R-H)
Tuesday, May 27

**OFFICIAL GOING: Heavy (soft in places; 5.5)**
Wind: Light against Weather: Raining

## 2637 ABBEY PARK H'CAP — 5f 2y
**2:30** (2:31) (Class 5) (0-75,75) 4-Y-0+ **£3,234** (£962; £481; £240) **Stalls** High

| Form | | | | RPR |
|---|---|---|---|---|
| 6433 | 1 | | **Harrogate Fair**[17] 2159 4-8-7 **61** oh2........................(p) LukeMorris 2 <br>(Michael Squance) *a.p: pushed along over 2f out: led wl over 1f out: rdn clr fnl f* **5/2**[1] | 74 |
| -000 | 2 | 4 1/2 | **Towbee**[10] 2332 5-9-7 **75**........................ PaulHanagan 8 <br>(Michael Easterby) *chsd ldrs: rdn over 2f out: styd on same pce fnl f* **5/2**[1] | 72 |
| 2 | 3 | 3/4 | **Cardinal**[17] 2159 9-9-0 **68**........................ TomEaves 5 <br>(Robert Cowell) *trckd ldr: rdn and ev ch over 1f out: no ex ins fnl f* **9/2**[3] | 62 |
| 0046 | 4 | 2 1/4 | **Profile Star (IRE)**[14] 2233 5-8-7 **64**........................ OisinMurphy(3) 4 <br>(Ann Stokell) *hld up: rdn over 2f out: hdwy over 1f out: wknd ins fnl f* **14/1** | 50 |
| 1200 | 5 | hd | **Rambo Will**[17] 2147 6-8-11 **68**........................ NataliaGemelova(3) 3 <br>(J R Jenkins) *led over 3f: wknd ins fnl f* **4/1**[2] | 53 |
| 5-45 | 6 | 2 3/4 | **Whitecrest**[21] 2050 6-9-2 **70**........................ ChrisCatlin 7 <br>(John Spearing) *hld up: rdn over 1f out: nt clr run ins fnl f: nvr on terms* **10/1** | 45 |
| 0-00 | 7 | 12 | **Sophie's Beau (USA)**[38] 1584 7-8-1 **62** oh9 ow1(bt) MichaelKenneally(7) 1 <br>(Michael Chapman) *s.s: sn pushed along in rr: bhd fr 1/2-way* **50/1** | |

1m 4.69s (4.69) **Going Correction** +1.05s/f (Soft) **7** Ran SP% **113.0**
Speed ratings (Par 103): **104,96,95,92,91 87,68**
CSF £8.58 CT £24.90 TOTE £4.40: £2.40, £1.40; EX 10.70 Trifecta £27.40.
**Owner** Miss K Squance **Bred** Kevin Daniel Crabb **Trained** Newmarket, Suffolk

**FOCUS**
Luke Morris described the ground as "heavy and very testing". A modest sprint, in which they raced stands' side. The winner is rated to his AW best.

## 2638 STATHERN CLAIMING STKS — 7f 9y
**3:00** (3:00) (Class 5) 3-Y-O **£2,587** (£770; £384; £192) **Stalls** High

| Form | | | | RPR |
|---|---|---|---|---|
| 042 | 1 | | **Native Heart**[12] 2281 3-8-11 68........................ RachealKneller(5) 1 <br>(Jamie Osborne) *trckd ldr tl led over 4f out: rdn clr fr over 1f out* **3/1**[2] | 74 |
| -626 | 2 | 14 | **Seaham**[21] 2063 3-9-11 73........................[1] PaulHanagan 2 <br>(Rod Millman) *hld up: hdwy 1/2-way: rdn over 2f out: wknd fnl f* **11/4**[1] | 47 |
| 3660 | 3 | 3 1/4 | **Casper Lee (IRE)**[8] 2393 3-8-5 52........................(v) JohnFahy 6 <br>(Michael Herrington) *hld up: hdwy over 2f out: sn rdn: wknd fnl f* **16/1** | 18 |
| 5036 | 4 | 2 | **Kodafine (IRE)**[12] 2278 3-7-9 64........................ NoelGarbutt(5) 5 <br>(David Evans) *prom: chsd wnr 3f out: rdn and wknd over 1f out* **9/2** | 8 |
| U604 | 5 | 4 | **Sand Stormer (IRE)**[28] 1829 3-8-4 55........................ OisinMurphy(3) 9 <br>(William Muir) *chsd ldrs tl rdn and wknd over 2f out* **33/1** | 5 |
| 0-60 | 6 | 2 1/4 | **Belayer (IRE)**[13] 2257 3-8-11 75........................ TomEaves 7 <br>(Kevin Ryan) *prom: rdn 1/2-way: hung rt and wknd over 2f out* **4/1**[3] | 3 |
| 1-14 | 7 | 8 | **Slinky McVelvet**[124] 301 3-8-10 72........................ AndrewMullen 4 <br>(Garry Moss) *led: hdd over 4f out: rdn: hung rt and wknd over 2f out* **5/1** | |

1m 32.06s (5.86) **Going Correction** +1.05s/f (Soft) **7** Ran SP% **115.3**
Speed ratings (Par 99): **108,92,88,86,81 78,69**
CSF £11.94 TOTE £2.80: £1.30, £3.20; EX 11.90 Trifecta £138.30.The winner was claimed by Phil McEntee for £13,000.
**Owner** Homecroft Wealth Racing & Partner **Bred** R W K Lewis **Trained** Upper Lambourn, Berks

**FOCUS**
Not much of a claimer and it produced an authoritative winner, the only one to run her race.

## 2639 CORONATION FILLIES' H'CAP (BOBIS RACE) — 7f 9y
**3:30** (3:30) (Class 4) (0-85,82) 3-Y-O **£4,690** (£1,395; £697; £348) **Stalls** High

| Form | | | | RPR |
|---|---|---|---|---|
| 1366 | 1 | | **Bridie ffrench**[10] 2340 3-8-8 **72**........................ WilliamTwiston-Davies(3) 6 <br>(Mick Channon) *s.i.s and hmpd s: hld up: hdwy over 2f out: led and edgd lft over 1f out: rdn out* **9/2** | 78 |
| 310- | 2 | 1 1/4 | **Meeting Waters**[241] 6839 3-9-5 **80**........................ PaulHanagan 3 <br>(William Haggas) *led: sn edgd lft: rdn and hdd over 1f out: styd on same pce ins fnl f* **7/2**[2] | 83 |
| 56-4 | 3 | nk | **Persian Bolt (USA)**[22] 2031 3-8-11 **72**........................ JohnFahy 1 <br>(Eve Johnson Houghton) *chsd ldrs: rdn and ev ch over 1f out: styd on same pce ins fnl f* **20/1** | 74 |
| 0-10 | 4 | 1 1/2 | **Nirva (IRE)**[11] 2316 3-9-5 **80**........................ RichardKingscote 4 <br>(Ralph Beckett) *prom: pushed along and lost pl 1/2-way: rdn and hdwy over 1f out: styd on same pce ins fnl f* **4/1**[3] | 78 |
| 41-0 | 5 | 5 | **An Chulainn (IRE)**[12] 2274 3-8-11 **72**........................ SilvestreDeSousa 5 <br>(Mark Johnston) *hmpd s: hld up: hdwy 1/2-way: rdn whn nt clr run over 1f out: wknd ins fnl f* **8/1** | 57 |
| 306 | 6 | 4 | **Stosur (IRE)**[27] 1868 3-9-7 **82**........................(p) LukeMorris 7 <br>(Gay Kelleway) *prom: pushed along 1/2-way: rdn and wknd over 1f out* **8/1** | 57 |
| 01-0 | 7 | 1 3/4 | **Miss Lillie**[41] 1515 3-9-4 **82**........................ OisinMurphy(3) 2 <br>(Roger Teal) *chsd ldrs: rdn over 2f out: wknd over 1f out* **11/4**[1] | 52 |

1m 34.02s (7.82) **Going Correction** +1.05s/f (Soft) **7** Ran SP% **114.1**
Speed ratings (Par 98): **97,95,95,93,87 83,81**
CSF £20.46 TOTE £10.00: £3.40, £2.40; EX 19.90 Trifecta £207.30.
**Owner** Anne & Steve Fisher **Bred** Wansdyke Farms Limited **Trained** West Ilsley, Berks

**FOCUS**
Quite a competitive handicap, in which they again raced stands' side. Deterorating ground, but still a slow time. The winner was up slightly on her efforts this year.

## 2640 BROCK HILL H'CAP — 1m 3f 183y
**4:00** (4:00) (Class 5) (0-75,75) 4-Y-0+ **£3,234** (£962; £481) **Stalls** Low

| Form | | | | RPR |
|---|---|---|---|---|
| 30/3 | 1 | | **Kings Bayonet**[24] 1941 7-9-6 **75**........................ HayleyTurner 3 <br>(Alan King) *hld up: smooth hdwy to ld on bit over 2f out: sn clr: easily* **4/5**[1] | 87 |
| 4000 | 2 | 17 | **Hunting Ground (USA)**[12] 2289 4-9-5 **74**........................ SilvestreDeSousa 2 <br>(Mark Johnston) *led: pushed along 4f out: rdn and hdd over 2f out: sn wknd* **9/2**[3] | 59 |
| 60-2 | 3 | 42 | **Warrigal (IRE)**[29] 1798 4-9-2 **71**........................ PaulHanagan 1 <br>(Jeremy Noseda) *trckd ldr: rdn over 2f out: sn wknd and eased* **2/1**[2] | |

2m 52.97s (19.07) **Going Correction** +1.475s/f (Soft) **3** Ran SP% **107.1**
Speed ratings (Par 103): **95,83,55**
CSF £4.25 TOTE £1.60; EX 4.50 Trifecta £4.40.
**Owner** W H Ponsonby **Bred** Mickley Stud & C J Whiston **Trained** Barbury Castle, Wilts

**FOCUS**
Just the three runners and two of them completely failed to handle the ground, resulting in a wide-margin victory for the favourite. It's hard to be too positive about the form.

## 2641 BRITISH STALLION STUDS EBF MAIDEN FILLIES' STKS (BOBIS RACE) — 5f 2y
**4:30** (4:30) (Class 4) 2-Y-O **£4,528** (£1,347; £673) **Stalls** High

| Form | | | | RPR |
|---|---|---|---|---|
| 042 | 1 | | **London Life (IRE)**[19] 2089 2-9-0 0........................ RichardKingscote 2 <br>(Tom Dascombe) *mde all: shkn up over 1f out: rdn out* **7/4**[2] | 77 |
| 2 | 2 | 2 1/4 | **Persun**[11] 2302 2-8-11 0........................ WilliamTwiston-Davies(3) 3 <br>(Mick Channon) *s.i.s: sn rcvrd to trck wnr: rdn over 1f out: styd on same pce ins fnl f* **1/2**[1] | 69 |
| 0 | 3 | 3 3/4 | **Midnight Destiny (IRE)**[11] 2302 2-9-0 0........................ DaleSwift 6 <br>(Derek Shaw) *chsd ldrs: pushed along 1/2-way: rdn over 1f out: no ex fnl f* **25/1**[3] | 55 |

1m 6.3s (6.30) **Going Correction** +1.05s/f (Soft) **3** Ran SP% **106.9**
Speed ratings (Par 92): **91,87,81**
CSF £3.08 TOTE £1.90; EX 3.30 Trifecta £3.00.
**Owner** P Bamford & C McKee **Bred** Olive O'Connor **Trained** Malpas, Cheshire

**FOCUS**
Just the three remaining runners and the winner scored readily. It's possible this rating underestimates her.

## 2642 BRITISH STALLION STUDS EBF MAIDEN STKS (BOBIS RACE) — 5f 218y
**5:00** (5:00) (Class 4) 2-Y-O **£4,528** (£1,347; £673; £336) **Stalls** High

| Form | | | | RPR |
|---|---|---|---|---|
| 0 | 1 | | **Four Seasons (IRE)**[11] 2308 2-9-5 0........................ MickaelBarzalona 5 <br>(Charlie Appleby) *s.i.s: plld hrd and hdwy over 4f out: led over 2f out: rdn clr fr over 1f out* **4/1**[2] | 84 |
| | 2 | 2 1/2 | **Classic Collection** 2-9-5 0........................ PaulHanagan 8 <br>(Saeed bin Suroor) *sn outpcd: hdwy over 1f out: r.o to go 2nd wl ins fnl f: no ch w wnr* **6/1** | 77+ |
| 6 | 3 | 2 1/2 | **Goring (GER)**[11] 2298 2-9-5 0........................ JohnFahy 2 <br>(Eve Johnson Houghton) *w ldrs: led 1/2-way: hdd over 2f out: wknd ins fnl f* **5/1**[3] | 69 |
| | 4 | 2 1/4 | **Azraff (IRE)** 2-9-5 0........................ LukeMorris 10 <br>(Marco Botti) *prom: shkn up over 2f out: wknd fnl f* **12/1** | 62 |
| 0 | 5 | 5 | **Smugglers Lane (IRE)**[49] 1363 2-9-2 0........................ DeclanBates(3) 7 <br>(David Evans) *in tch: sn pushed along in rr: wknd over 2f out* **33/1** | 47 |
| 3 | 6 | 2 1/4 | **Silver Ranger**[12] 2288 2-9-5 0........................ SeanLevey 11 <br>(Richard Hannon) *led to 1/2-way: wknd and eased wl over 1f out* **5/6**[1] | 41 |
| 05 | 7 | 3 | **Josie Joe**[49] 1363 2-9-0 0........................ AndrewMullen 4 <br>(David Evans) *w ldrs tl rdn 1/2-way: wknd over 2f out* **33/1** | 27 |
| | 8 | 20 | **Cupulation** 2-9-5 0........................ TomEaves 9 <br>(Amy Weaver) *s.i.s: hld up: wknd over 2f out* **50/1** | |

1m 18.91s (5.91) **Going Correction** +1.05s/f (Soft) **8** Ran SP% **121.0**
Speed ratings (Par 95): **102,98,95,92,85 82,78,52**
CSF £29.33 TOTE £5.90: £1.70, £2.40, £1.40; EX 32.40 Trifecta £161.30.
**Owner** Godolphin **Bred** Michael E Wates **Trained** Newmarket, Suffolk

**FOCUS**
This maiden saw a one-two for Godolphin. It's usually a very strong race, but in the ground the form is a bit below the usual level.

## 2643 OADBY H'CAP — 1m 1f 218y
**5:30** (5:30) (Class 6) (0-65,65) 3-Y-O **£1,940** (£577; £288; £144) **Stalls** Low

| Form | | | | RPR |
|---|---|---|---|---|
| 06-4 | 1 | | **Allergic Reaction (IRE)**[29] 1794 3-8-10 **57**........................ OisinMurphy(3) 7 <br>(William Knight) *mde virtually all: qcknd over 3f out: rdn over 1f out: hung lft ins fnl f: styd on* **5/2**[1] | 65 |
| 20-4 | 2 | 3/4 | **Gift Of Rain (IRE)**[28] 1858 3-9-7 **65**........................ PaulHanagan 2 <br>(Ed Dunlop) *broke wl: sn stdd and lost pl: hdwy over 2f out: rdn to chse wnr over 1f out: running on whn hmpd wl ins fnl f* **4/1**[3] | 73+ |
| 5631 | 3 | 4 | **Jazri**[22] 2028 3-9-5 **63**........................ FrederikTylicki 1 <br>(Milton Bradley) *a.p: chsd wnr over 2f out tl rdn over 1f out: no ex ins fnl f* **6/1** | 62 |
| -604 | 4 | 1 1/2 | **Mercury Magic**[17] 2158 3-9-2 **60**........................[1] RichardKingscote 8 <br>(Ralph Beckett) *chsd ldrs: rdn over 2f out: edgd rt and no ex fnl f* **10/1** | 57 |
| 4-05 | 5 | 1 3/4 | **Improvized**[20] 2080 3-9-2 **60**........................(t) LukeMorris 3 <br>(William Muir) *hld up: rdn over 3f out: hdwy over 2f out: wknd fnl f* **3/1**[2] | 53 |
| 3-34 | 6 | 1/2 | **Speedbird One**[27] 1888 3-9-2 **63**........................ ThomasBrown(3) 5 <br>(James Given) *chsd wnr over 7f: rdn over 1f out: wknd fnl f* **12/1** | 55 |
| 0-00 | 7 | 2 1/2 | **Haaffa Sovereign**[102] 607 3-8-0 **51** oh6........(b[1]) JordanVaughan(7) 6 <br>(George Margarson) *chsd ldrs: rdn over 2f out: wknd fnl f* **33/1** | 39 |
| 3205 | 8 | 28 | **Queenie's Home**[22] 2020 3-9-3 **61**........................ TomEaves 4 <br>(James Given) *hld up: rdn and wknd over 2f out* **10/1** | |

2m 23.05s (15.15) **Going Correction** +1.475s/f (Soft) **8** Ran SP% **116.7**
Speed ratings (Par 97): **98,97,94,93,91 91,89,66**
CSF £13.12 CT £53.98 TOTE £3.40: £1.40, £1.80, £1.50; EX 10.70 Trifecta £97.10.
**Owner** Four Men & A Dream Partnership **Bred** Worksop Manor Stud **Trained** Patching, W Sussex
■ Stewards' Enquiry : Oisin Murphy three-day ban: careless riding (Jun 10-12)

**FOCUS**
Run at a steady gallop, Allergic Reaction made all, but Gift Of Rain may well have triumphed had the winner not run across him close home. The placings remained the same following a Stewards' inquiry. A personal best from the winner.
T/Plt: £235.10 to a £1 stake. Pool: £61,652.20 - 191.40 winning tickets. T/Qpdt: £56.00 to a £1 stake. Pool: £3,814.75 - 50.40 winning tickets. CR



The Form Book, Raceform Ltd, Newbury, RG14 5SJ

## 2465 LINGFIELD (L-H)

Tuesday, May 27

**OFFICIAL GOING: Standard**

Wind: Moderate, across towards stand Weather: Damp

### 2644 BRITISH STALLION STUDS EBF MAIDEN FILLIES' STKS (BOBIS RACE) 6f 1y(P)

2:10 (2:12) (Class 5) 2-Y-O £3,067 (£905; £453) Stalls Low

| Form | | | | RPR |
|---|---|---|---|---|
| | 1 | | **Peace And War (USA)** 2-9-0 0 HarryBentley 5 (Olly Stevens) *dwlt: in tch on outer: effrt 2f out: rdn to ld ins fnl f: a jst holding runner-up* 11/10[1] | 73+ |
| 0 | 2 | ½ | **Khawaater**[11] 2306 2-9-0 0 [1] JimCrowley 6 (Roger Varian) *t.k.h: pressed ldr: led over 1f out tl ins fnl f: kpt on* 5/2[2] | 69 |
| 0 | 3 | 7 | **Surrey Pink (FR)**[8] 2402 2-9-0 0 JamesDoyle 2 (William Muir) *led tl wknd over 1f out* 12/1 | 48 |
| | 4 | 5 | **Winter Queen** 2-9-0 0 MartinLane 3 (Charlie Appleby) *dwlt: in tch: rdn over 2f out: sn outpcd* 7/2[3] | 33 |
| | 5 | 7 | **Perfect Concord** 2-9-0 0 DavidProbert 4 (Michael Blanshard) *t.k.h: cl up tl wknd wl over 1f out* 20/1 | 12 |
| | 6 | 9 | **Pixie** 2-9-0 0 [1] StevieDonohoe 1 (Ian Williams) *in tch: wknd 3f out: sn bhd* 66/1 | |

1m 11.91s (0.01) **Going Correction** -0.075s/f (Stan) 6 Ran SP% 112.4

Speed ratings (Par 90): **96,95,86,79,70 58**

CSF £4.10 TOTE £2.30: £1.10, £2.50; EX 4.90 Trifecta £19.10.

**Owner** Sheikh Suhaim Al Thani/QRL/M Al Kubaisi **Bred** Sally J Anderson **Trained** Chiddingfold, Surrey

**FOCUS**

Only six runners, but some nicely bred and/or expensive purchases took part so the form will probably work out. However its not the easiest form to pin down.

### 2645 DOWNLOAD THE 888SPORT.COM MOBILE APP H'CAP 5f 6y(P)

2:40 (2:42) (Class 4) (0-80,80) 4-Y-O+ £5,175 (£1,540; £769; £384) Stalls High

| Form | | | | RPR |
|---|---|---|---|---|
| 03-2 | 1 | | **Pucon**[26] 1896 5-8-11 70 JamesDoyle 5 (Roger Teal) *mde all: drvn along fnl f: hld on wl* 16/1 | 78 |
| 311- | 2 | 1 | **Oh So Sassy**[217] 7445 4-9-7 80 GeorgeBaker 8 (Chris Wall) *t.k.h: trckd ldrs on outer: rdn over 1f out: r.o to take 2nd fnl stride* 3/1[2] | 84+ |
| -303 | 3 | nse | **Secret Missile**[21] 2050 4-9-7 80 (b) DavidProbert 9 (William Muir) *dwlt: towards rr: hrd rdn over 1f out: gd hdwy fnl f* 10/1 | 84 |
| 2330 | 4 | nse | **Ask The Guru**[43] 1489 4-8-4 70 (v) CamHardie(7) 6 (Michael Attwater) *prom: rdn 2f out: chsd wnr 1f out: kpt on: lost 2nd fnl stride* 25/1 | 74 |
| 1-33 | 5 | nk | **Marmalady (IRE)**[17] 2147 4-9-7 80 AdamKirby 4 (Gary Moore) *in tch: drvn to chse ldrs fnl f: kpt on* 6/4[1] | 83 |
| 5-55 | 6 | 1 | **Jungle Bay**[31] 1731 7-9-3 76 (b) LiamJones 7 (Jane Chapple-Hyam) *mid-div on outer: effrt over 1f out: hrd rdn and one pce ins fnl f* 7/1[3] | 75 |
| 2311 | 7 | nk | **Desert Strike**[25] 1921 8-9-1 79 (p) LouisSteward(5) 10 (Conor Dore) *wd: hld up in rr: shkn up and r.o fr over 1f out: gng on at fin* 16/1 | 77 |
| 06-0 | 8 | 1¼ | **Howyadoingnotsobad (IRE)**[7] 2414 6-8-8 72 RyanWhile(5) 2 (Bill Turner) *chsd wnr tl wknd 1f out* 25/1 | 66 |
| 36-0 | 9 | 2¾ | **Tidal's Baby**[22] 2030 5-9-5 78 MartinLane 3 (Tony Carroll) *s.s: a in rr* 33/1 | 62 |
| 0-02 | 10 | 9 | **Royal Acquisition**[25] 1922 4-9-2 75 JimCrowley 1 (Robert Cowell) *mid-div on rail tl wknd wl over 1f out* 12/1 | 26 |

58.05s (-0.75) **Going Correction** -0.075s/f (Stan) 10 Ran SP% 116.7

Speed ratings (Par 105): **103,101,101,101,100 99,98,96,92,77**

CSF £62.72 CT £521.25 TOTE £18.10: £4.20, £1.90, £2.90; EX 52.30 Trifecta £888.10.

**Owner** J A Redmond **Bred** J Redmond **Trained** Ashtead, Surrey

**FOCUS**

A decent sprint handicap, but they bet 7-1 bar two suggesting it wasn't thought as competitive as it looked. Very few ever got into it. This rates a length best from the winner.

### 2646 BERNARD CORK BIRTHDAY H'CAP 1m 1y(P)

3:10 (3:13) (Class 6) (0-65,65) 4-Y-O+ £2,726 (£805; £402) Stalls High

| Form | | | | RPR |
|---|---|---|---|---|
| 1555 | 1 | | **Fearless Lad (IRE)**[29] 1798 4-9-3 61 (t) GeorgeBaker 1 (John Best) *hld up in rr: gd hdwy over 1f out: r.o to ld ins fnl f: rdn out* 7/1[3] | 70 |
| 3500 | 2 | 1½ | **Princess Spirit**[6] 2463 5-9-2 60 (p) JimCrowley 10 (Edward Creighton) *t.k.h towards rr: hdwy over 2f out: hrd rdn over 1f out: styd on to take 2nd nr fin* 8/1 | 66 |
| 166 | 3 | ½ | **The Happy Hammer (IRE)**[21] 2059 8-9-3 64 (b) RobertTart(3) 12 (Eugene Stanford) *prom: wnt 2nd over 2f out: drvn to chal 1f out: one pce ins fnl f* 7/1[3] | 68 |
| -130 | 4 | nk | **Secret Success**[12] 2282 4-9-1 64 (t) DuilioDaSilva(5) 2 (Paul Cole) *chsd ldr: led over 2f out tl ins fnl f: no ex* 5/1[2] | 68 |
| 4246 | 5 | hd | **Tax Reform (IRE)**[27] 1876 4-9-1 64 (b) LouisSteward(5) 3 (Mark Hoad) *sn chsng ldrs: sltly outpcd 2f out: styng on again at fin* 14/1 | 67 |
| 4612 | 6 | 1 | **Olivers Mount**[25] 1917 4-8-8 59 CamHardie(7) 11 (Ed Vaughan) *chsd ldrs: hrd rdn over 1f out: one pce* 7/2[1] | 60 |
| 1440 | 7 | nk | **Indus Valley (IRE)**[17] 2164 7-9-1 59 AdamBeschizza 5 (Des Donovan) *t.k.h in midfield: rdn and styd on same pce fnl 2f: no imp* 25/1 | 59 |
| 3166 | 8 | 3 | **Divine Rule (IRE)**[30] 1771 6-9-2 60 (p) LiamJones 7 (Laura Mongan) *s.s: hld up in rr: rdn wl over 1f out: n.d* 20/1 | 53 |
| -005 | 9 | 2¼ | **Keene's Pointe**[33] 1665 4-9-6 64 [1] JamesDoyle 9 (J W Hills) *a towards rr: drvn along and nt trble ldrs fnl 2f* 10/1 | 52 |
| | 10 | 2½ | **Settle For Red (IRE)**[130] 226 4-9-7 65 HarryBentley 4 (Jeremy Gask) *chsd ldrs early: lost pl and in midfield after 2f: outpcd in rr fnl 3f* 8/1 | 47 |
| 0105 | 11 | 2 | **Bold Ring**[18] 2121 8-9-0 58 JimmyQuinn 6 (Edward Creighton) *t.k.h: prom: hmpd after 2f: wknd 3f out* 25/1 | 36 |
| 1326 | 12 | 12 | **Menelik (IRE)**[15] 2207 5-9-7 65 (b) AdamKirby 8 (Lee Carter) *s.i.s and rdn early: sn led: hdd over 2f out: sn wknd* 7/1[3] | 15 |

1m 36.76s (-1.44) **Going Correction** -0.075s/f (Stan) 12 Ran SP% 126.8

Speed ratings (Par 101): **104,102,102,101,101 100,100,97,94,92 90,78**

CSF £64.96 CT £421.42 TOTE £7.70: £3.00, £3.30, £2.60; EX 105.50 Trifecta £860.40.

**Owner** Mrs Jackie Jones **Bred** Brittas House Stud & Lynch Bages & Samac **Trained** Hucking, Kent

■ Stewards' Enquiry : Duilio Da Silva one-day ban: careless riding (Jun 10)

**FOCUS**

A moderate handicap, run at a strong pace thanks to Menelik, who was given an attacking ride on this drop back in trip, but he merely ended up running himself into the ground. The first two came from the rear and the third helpd with the standard.

### 2647 "CASH IN EARLY" AT 888SPORT.COM H'CAP 7f 1y(P)

3:40 (3:43) (Class 5) (0-70,70) 3-Y-O £3,234 (£962; £481; £240) Stalls Low

| Form | | | | RPR |
|---|---|---|---|---|
| 5-41 | 1 | | **Syrian Pearl**[28] 1832 3-8-12 64 AshleyMorgan(3) 3 (Chris Wall) *mde all: drvn 3 l clr 1f out: rdn to hold on nr fin* 12/1 | 72 |
| 3-42 | 2 | nk | **Baltic Brave (IRE)**[15] 2208 3-9-7 70 (t) GeorgeBaker 13 (Hughie Morrison) *stdd s and dropped in: hld up in last: gd hdwy on rail over 1f out: fin wl: wnt 2nd and clsng at fin* 5/1[3] | 77+ |
| 63-5 | 3 | 1 | **Goodwood Storm**[28] 1832 3-9-6 69 JimCrowley 7 (William Knight) *hld up in 5th: drvn to chse wnr wl over 1f out: kpt on: lost 2nd fnl 50yds* 9/4[1] | 73 |
| 13-6 | 4 | ¾ | **Fiftyshadesfreed (IRE)**[21] 2058 3-9-5 68 (p) PatCosgrave 4 (George Baker) *dwlt: towards rr: rdn and hdwy over 1f out: styd on fnl f* 12/1 | 70 |
| 5552 | 5 | ½ | **Penny's Boy**[21] 2058 3-9-7 70 (t) JamesDoyle 12 (Sylvester Kirk) *wd in midfield: effrt 2f out: rdn and kpt on fnl f* 4/1[2] | 71 |
| 640- | 6 | nk | **Dream Impossible (IRE)**[238] 6923 3-8-7 56 oh1 FrannyNorton 11 (Peter Makin) *mid-div: effrt and hrd rdn over 1f out: styd on same pce* 50/1 | 56 |
| 6311 | 7 | 1½ | **Intense Feeling (IRE)**[12] 2281 3-8-8 62 NathanAlison(5) 1 (Lee Carter) *prom: hrd rdn over 1f out: wknd fnl f* 8/1 | 58 |
| 0-44 | 8 | 1¾ | **Pipe Dream**[17] 2163 3-9-4 67 StevieDonohoe 2 (Brian Meehan) *dwlt: sn in midfield: rdn 3f out: no imp* 33/1 | 59 |
| 1460 | 9 | 1 | **Monashka Bay (IRE)**[12] 2278 3-8-10 59 DavidProbert 10 (Michael Blanshard) *chsd ldrs tl wknd 2f out* 66/1 | 48 |
| 00-5 | 10 | 1¾ | **Bowsers Bold**[33] 1669 3-8-8 62 ShelleyBirkett(5) 9 (Marcus Tregoning) *dwlt: t.k.h: in rr on outer: rdn over 2f out: nvr nr ldrs* 14/1 | 47 |
| -060 | 11 | shd | **Buckland Beau**[15] 2205 3-8-11 60 MartinLane 6 (Charlie Fellowes) *mid-div: outpcd 3f out: n.d towards rr whn n.m.r and eased over 1f out* 33/1 | 52 |
| 0-00 | 12 | hd | **Palace Princess (FR)**[28] 1847 3-9-3 66 AdamKirby 8 (Ed Dunlop) *chsd wnr tl wl over 1f out: sn wknd and eased* 33/1 | 50 |
| 65-0 | 13 | hd | **Calrissian (IRE)**[31] 1725 3-9-4 70 RobertTart(3) 5 (K R Burke) *a bhd* 16/1 | 53 |

1m 24.07s (-0.73) **Going Correction** -0.075s/f (Stan) 13 Ran SP% 118.8

Speed ratings (Par 99): **101,100,99,98,98 97,96,94,92,90 90,90,90**

CSF £68.36 CT £194.86 TOTE £12.80: £3.30, £1.50, £1.30; EX 57.00 Trifecta £250.40.

**Owner** The Clodhoppers **Bred** Jeremy Green And Sons **Trained** Newmarket, Suffolk

**FOCUS**

A modest 3yo handicap in which the winner had things go her way, whereas they didn't for the runner-up. Fair form for the grade.

### 2648 £88 IN FREE BETS AT 888SPORT.COM H'CAP 6f 1y(P)

4:10 (4:12) (Class 5) (0-70,70) 4-Y-O+ £2,587 (£770; £384; £192) Stalls Low

| Form | | | | RPR |
|---|---|---|---|---|
| 414- | 1 | | **Clearing**[318] 4283 4-9-0 63 PatCosgrave 11 (Jim Boyle) *mde all: rdn clr over 1f out: qcknd wl: comf* 14/1 | 76 |
| 0132 | 2 | 3¼ | **Johnny Splash (IRE)**[55] 1238 5-8-6 58 (v) RobertTart(3) 6 (Roger Teal) *chsd wnr: rdn 2f out: one pce appr fnl f* 3/1[1] | 61 |
| 0410 | 3 | 1 | **Black Truffle (FR)**[22] 2029 4-8-9 58 (v) DavidProbert 5 (Mark Usher) *a chsng ldrs: rdn and btn over 1f out* 4/1[2] | 57 |
| 3436 | 4 | hd | **West Leake (IRE)**[12] 2282 8-8-8 57 (p) JimmyQuinn 4 (Paul Burgoyne) *t.k.h in rr: rdn and r.o fnl 2f: nrest at fin* 5/1[3] | 56+ |
| 30-6 | 5 | shd | **All Or Nothin (IRE)**[18] 2124 5-8-9 63 DavidKenny(5) 7 (Paddy Butler) *prom: rdn 2f out: btn over 1f out* 16/1 | 61 |
| 6-00 | 6 | 2½ | **Trending (IRE)**[29] 1787 5-8-7 63 (tp) DavidParkes(7) 2 (Jeremy Gask) *mid-div: outpcd over 2f out: n.d after* 16/1 | 53 |
| 264- | 7 | ½ | **Compton Albion (IRE)**[248] 6651 4-8-7 56 oh3 HarryBentley 3 (Jeremy Gask) *t.k.h in midfield: rdn and btn 2f out* 16/1 | 45 |
| | 8 | ½ | **Salvado (IRE)**[186] 8011 4-9-7 70 AdamKirby 8 (Tony Carroll) *dwlt: plld hrd early: pushed along 2f out: a bhd* 4/1[2] | 57 |
| -160 | 9 | shd | **Reginald Claude**[17] 2174 6-8-2 58 CharlotteJenner(7) 1 (Mark Usher) *a towards rr* 6/1 | 45 |

1m 11.31s (-0.59) **Going Correction** -0.075s/f (Stan) 9 Ran SP% 120.3

Speed ratings (Par 103): **100,95,94,94,93 90,89,89,89**

CSF £58.32 CT £210.34 TOTE £12.10: £2.90, £1.80, £2.00; EX 37.40 Trifecta £181.50.

**Owner** The Paddock Space Partnership **Bred** Paddock Space **Trained** Epsom, Surrey

**FOCUS**

Another modest handicap and another all-the-way winner in a race where again very few got into it. The winner rates a personal best.

### 2649 NECK REFUNDS AT 888SPORT.COM MAIDEN FILLIES' STKS (DIV I) 1m 2f (P)

4:40 (4:41) (Class 5) 3-Y-O+ £2,760 (£611; £611) Stalls Low

| Form | | | | RPR |
|---|---|---|---|---|
| 5-5 | 1 | | **Wahgah (USA)**[18] 2129 3-8-10 [1] HarryBentley 10 (Saeed bin Suroor) *t.k.h: cl up in 4th: rdn over 2f out: pressed ldrs ins fnl f: r.o to ld on line* 7/1[3] | 81 |
| 4 | 2 | hd | **Colourful**[21] 2061 3-8-10 JamesDoyle 1 (Lady Cecil) *led: hrd rdn and edgd rt ins fnl f: jst ct* 7/1[3] | 80 |
| 03-2 | 2 | dht | **Toast Of The Town (IRE)**[18] 2109 4-9-10 84 (p) NickyMackay 2 (John Gosden) *prom: drvn to chal ins fnl f: r.o* 8/11[1] | 81 |
| 6- | 4 | 4½ | **Carnevale**[194] 7875 3-8-10 JimCrowley 8 (Ralph Beckett) *prom tl wknd over 1f out* 5/1[2] | 71 |
| 2 | 5 | 1¾ | **Elpida (USA)**[60] 1143 3-8-10 PatCosgrave 5 (David Simcock) *rrd s: towards rr: rdn over 2f out: sme late hdwy* 25/1 | 68 |
| | 6 | 2½ | **Lola Montez (IRE)** 3-8-10 [1] TedDurcan 6 (David Lanigan) *in tch tl rdn and btn over 2f out* 66/1 | 63 |
| 0- | 7 | ¾ | **Aurora Borealis (IRE)**[214] 7493 3-8-10 LiamKeniry 9 (Ed Dunlop) *towards rr: effrt 3f out: sn outpcd* 25/1 | 62 |
| 60 | 8 | 7 | **Topaling**[11] 2310 3-8-7 AshleyMorgan(3) 3 (Mark H Tompkins) *a bhd* 66/1 | 49 |
| 2- | 9 | 1¾ | **Sibling Honour**[202] 7764 3-8-10 AhmedAjtebi 4 (Charlie Appleby) *plld hrd: a bhd* 7/1[3] | 45 |
| | 10 | 25 | **Romantic Link** 3-8-10 LiamJones 7 (Luke Dace) *in tch: rdn 4f out: wknd 3f out* 100/1 | |

2m 5.75s (-0.85) **Going Correction** -0.075s/f (Stan)

**WFA** 3 from 4yo 14lb 10 Ran SP% 123.7

Speed ratings (Par 100): **100,99,99,96,94 92,92,86,85,65**

WIN: 7.90 Wahgah; PL: 1.10 Toast Of The Town, 1.70 Colourful, 2.20 Wahgah; EX: 9.20, 15.40; CSF: 6.56, 27.95; TC: ; TF: 36.80, 51.10;.

**Owner** Godolphin **Bred** Shadwell Farm LLC **Trained** Newmarket, Suffolk

**FOCUS**

Some interesting fillies took part in this maiden and it produced a thrilling three-way finish. Pace held up and the winner rates a personal best.

## 2650 NECK REFUNDS AT 888SPORT.COM MAIDEN FILLIES' STKS (DIV II) — 1m 2f (P)

**5:10** (5:16) (Class 5) 3-Y-O+ — **£2,760** (£815; £407) **Stalls** Low

Form — RPR

24-2 **1** **Placidia (IRE)**[18] 2133 3-8-10 78 ........ TedDurcan 2 — 86
(David Lanigan) *trckd ldrs: led and qcknd clr over 1f out: pushed out* **11/4**[2]

**2** 2 ½ **Scallop** 3-8-10 ........ JamesDoyle 9 — 81
(Sir Michael Stoute) *hld up towards rr: rdn over 2f out: late hdwy to take 2nd fnl 75yds* **8/1**

**3** nk **Dream Child (IRE)** 3-8-10 ........ MartinLane 4 — 80
(Charlie Appleby) *prom: wnt 2nd 6f out: led briefly wl over 1f out: sn outpcd by wnr: lost 2nd fnl 75yds* **16/1**

-5 **4** 2 ¼ **Allegria (IRE)**[32] 1701 3-8-10 ........ NickyMackay 3 — 76
(John Gosden) *hld up in 5th: rdn over 2f out: styd on same pce* **4/1**[3]

3 **5** 2 **Potent Embrace (USA)**[7] 2422 3-8-10 ........ FrannyNorton 6 — 72
(Mark Johnston) *led tl wl over 1f out: sn wknd* **7/4**[1]

**6** ¾ **Westerly** 3-8-10 ........ LiamJones 10 — 71
(William Haggas) *rn green in rr: outpcd and lost tch 3f out: n.d after* **50/1**

35 **7** 10 **Dream Big (IRE)**[48] 1380 3-8-10 ........ JimCrowley 1 — 52
(Jo Crowley) *prom tl wknd and eased over 2f out* **33/1**

2m 5.25s (-1.35) **Going Correction** -0.075s/f (Stan)
**WFA** 3 from 4yo 14lb — **7 Ran SP% 104.9**
Speed ratings (Par 100): **102,100,99,97,96 95,87**
CSF £20.12 TOTE £3.20: £1.90, £2.60; EX 21.20 Trifecta £103.60.
**Owner** B E Nielsen **Bred** Bjorn Nielsen **Trained** Upper Lambourn, Berks
■ Rule 4 of 10p in the pound applies to all bets; Withdrawn: Bikini Island

**FOCUS**

Despite the smaller field, reduced further when Bikini Island was withdrawn after getting upset in the stalls, the winning time was half a second quicker than the first division. The winner is rated in line with her Nottingham run.

## 2651 STUART RUSHWORTH'S 50 YEARS H'CAP — 1m 5f (P)

**5:40** (5:41) (Class 5) (0-75,75) 4-Y-O+ — **£3,234** (£962; £481; £240) **Stalls** Low

Form — RPR

30-4 **1** **Meetings Man (IRE)**[22] 2034 7-9-3 71 ........(p) AdamKirby 1 — 81
(Ali Stronge) *in tch: swtchd outside 3f out: led and kicked clr over 2f out: hrd rdn over 1f out: wl in control fnl f* **4/1**[2]

1143 **2** 3 ½ **Munsarim (IRE)**[62] 1108 7-8-12 73 ........(b) CharlotteJenner(7) 3 — 77
(Lee Carter) *s.s: hld up in rr: rdn and hdwy over 1f out: styd on to take 2nd fnl 75yds* **9/2**[3]

0241 **3** ¾ **Ssafa**[20] 2067 6-9-3 71 ........(p) GeorgeBaker 5 — 74
(Alastair Lidderdale) *cl up in 3rd: drvn to chse wnr over 1f out: one pce: lost 2nd fnl 75yds* **9/2**[3]

0244 **4** ¾ **Bennelong**[6] 2464 8-8-2 61 oh2 ........(v) NathanAlison(5) 2 — 63
(Lee Carter) *t.k.h in 5th: hdwy on outer to chse ldrs 2f out: one pce* **10/1**

4352 **5** 2 **Layline (IRE)**[8] 2394 7-9-2 75 ........ DanielMuscutt(5) 4 — 74
(Gay Kelleway) *led tl over 2f out: wknd jst over 1f out: btn whn n.m.r ins fnl f* **12/1**

12-5 **6** 6 **Grayswood**[34] 1644 4-9-4 72 ........(p) JamesDoyle 7 — 62
(William Muir) *pressed ldr: rdn and outpcd over 2f out: wknd over 1f out* **7/4**[1]

2m 46.01s (0.01) **Going Correction** -0.075s/f (Stan) — **6 Ran SP% 109.5**
Speed ratings (Par 103): **96,93,93,92,91 88**
CSF £20.77 TOTE £4.00: £2.20, £2.80; EX 31.10 Trifecta £143.90.
**Owner** Mrs Bettine Evans **Bred** Hakan Keles **Trained** Eastbury, Berks

**FOCUS**

An ordinary handicap and not much of a test at the trip as they went no pace early. Rather muddling form.
T/Plt: £58.70 to a £1 stake. Pool: £65,633.86 - 816.18 winning tickets. T/Qpdt: £14.50 to a £1 stake. Pool: £5,692.10 - 289.5 winning tickets. LM

# 2615 REDCAR (L-H)

### Tuesday, May 27

**OFFICIAL GOING: Good to soft (soft in places; 7.6)**

Wind: light against Weather: Cloudy, drizzle on and off after race 3

## 2652 IRISH STALLION FARMS EBF MEDIAN AUCTION MAIDEN FILLIES' STKS (BOBIS RACE) — 6f

**2:20** (2:21) (Class 5) 2-Y-O — **£2,911** (£866; £432; £216) **Stalls** Centre

Form — RPR

**1** **Russian Punch** 2-9-0 0 ........ GrahamLee 4 — 70+
(James Given) *in tch: pushed along and rn green over 1f out: bmpd whn gng for gap appr fnl f: gd hdwy sn after: led ins fnl f: kpt on wl to go clr* **9/2**[3]

**2** 2 ¾ **Cumbrianna** 2-9-0 0 ........ PaulMulrennan 1 — 62+
(Bryan Smart) *dwlt: sn led: rdn 2f out: hdd ins fnl f: one pce and no ch w wnr* **11/1**

**3** nk **Flatcapper (IRE)** 2-9-0 0 ........ TonyHamilton 5 — 61+
(Richard Fahey) *w ldr: rdn over 2f out: one pce fnl f* **7/4**[1]

**4** nse **Caltra Colleen** 2-9-0 0 ........ SamHitchcott 7 — 61+
(Mick Channon) *chsd ldrs: rdn 2f out: one pce fnl f* **15/8**[2]

**5** 1 **Diracan (IRE)** 2-9-0 0 ........ J-PGuillambert 2 — 58
(Nick Littmoden) *hld up in tch: rdn over 2f out: one pce fnl f* **16/1**

0 **6** 1 ½ **Cerise Firth**[17] 2172 2-8-9 0 ........ JackDuern(5) 3 — 53
(Steph Hollinshead) *hld up in tch: pushed along over 2f out: nvr threatened* **33/1**

**7** 6 **Just No Rules** 2-9-0 0 ........ BarryMcHugh 6 — 35
(Tony Coyle) *prom: rdn over 2f out: edgd lft appr fnl f: sn wknd* **18/1**

1m 17.94s (6.14) **Going Correction** +0.575s/f (Yiel) — **7 Ran SP% 111.7**
Speed ratings (Par 90): **82,78,77,77,76 74,66**
CSF £48.19 TOTE £4.90: £2.50, £3.90; EX 39.90 Trifecta £108.20.
**Owner** Lovely Bubbly Racing **Bred** Mrs Deborah O'Brien **Trained** Willoughton, Lincs

**FOCUS**

A moderate opener, run on tacky ground. With little to go on the form has been rated as average.

## 2653 HAPPY 10TH BIRTHDAY RACING UK (S) STKS — 7f

**2:50** (2:50) (Class 6) 3-5-Y-O — **£2,045** (£603; £302) **Stalls** Centre

Form — RPR

3-23 **1** **Mitchell**[28] 1838 4-9-4 56 ........(p) ConnorBeasley(3) 7 — 60
(David Thompson) *hld up in tch: rdn over 2f out: stl only 5th appr fnl f: kpt on to ld 75yds out* **3/1**[2]

0620 **2** 1 ¼ **Mitchum**[22] 2019 5-9-2 55 ........(v) ShirleyTeasdale(5) 8 — 57
(Ron Barr) *hld up in tch: rdn and hdwy to chse ldrs over 1f out: kpt on: swtchd lft 75yds out: wnt 2nd nr fin* **14/1**

02-0 **3** nk **Kalithea**[49] 1365 4-9-2 55 ........(e) BarryMcHugh 6 — 51
(Julie Camacho) *hld up in tch: rdn and gd hdwy 2f out: led ins fnl f: hdd fnl 75yds: no ex and lost 2nd nr fin* **14/1**

2066 **4** 2 ¼ **Cape Of Hope (IRE)**[17] 2166 4-9-7 68 ........ AdrianNicholls 9 — 50
(David Nicholls) *chsd ldrs: rdn over 2f out: one pce* **6/1**

-542 **5** ¾ **Bond Club**[17] 2166 4-9-7 60 ........(b) DavidAllan 5 — 48
(Geoffrey Oldroyd) *prom: led 4f out: rdn over 2f out: hdd ins fnl f: wknd* **5/2**[1]

-043 **6** 8 **Red Shadow**[110] 502 5-9-2 47 ........(p) GrahamGibbons 1 — 22
(Alan Brown) *led: hdd 4f out: wknd fnl 2f* **40/1**

-634 **7** hd **Plunder**[105] 565 4-9-4 61 ........(p) SladeO'Hara(3) 3 — 27
(Alan Berry) *chsd ldrs: wknd over 2f out* **16/1**

-060 **8** 1 ¼ **Hard Core Debt**[31] 1710 4-9-0 70 ........(t) MeganCarberry(7) 4 — 24
(Brian Ellison) *v.s.a: hld up: rdn 1/2-way: nvr threatened* **4/1**[3]

0 **9** 1 ¼ **Beaulie**[8] 2392 4-8-11 0 ........ EmmaSayer(5) 2 — 15
(Keith Reveley) *sn pushed along in rr: a bhd* **100/1**

1m 31.77s (7.27) **Going Correction** +0.575s/f (Yiel) — **9 Ran SP% 110.5**
Speed ratings (Par 101): **81,79,79,76,75 66,66,65,63**
CSF £41.03 TOTE £4.70: £1.30, £6.20, £4.90; EX 41.50 Trifecta £431.90.There was no bid for the winner.
**Owner** Alan Sayers **Bred** Conor J C Parsons & Brian M Parsons **Trained** Bolam, Co Durham

**FOCUS**

Low-grade stuff with doubts over some of the better-in ones. The form is rated around the first two.

## 2654 WIN A VIP DAY OUT @ REDCARRACING.CO.UK H'CAP — 1m 1f

**3:20** (3:21) (Class 5) (0-75,75) 4-Y-O+ — **£2,587** (£770; £384; £192) **Stalls** Low

Form — RPR

0-05 **1** **St Moritz (IRE)**[18] 2137 8-9-4 72 ........(v[1]) DanielTudhope 2 — 91+
(David O'Meara) *led: hdd over 7f out: remained prom: led again over 2f out: sn rdn clr: eased fnl 50yds* **3/1**[2]

-620 **2** 8 **Bling King**[33] 1660 5-9-7 75 ........(p) PJMcDonald 8 — 76
(Geoffrey Harker) *midfield: rdn over 3f out: kpt on to go 2nd ins fnl f: no ch w easy wnr* **8/1**

1/00 **3** nk **Engrossing**[22] 2017 5-9-2 70 ........(e[1]) JamesSullivan 3 — 70
(Ruth Carr) *hld up in rr: rdn over 3f out: kpt on fr over 1f out: wnt 3rd 50yds out* **40/1**

000- **4** 1 ¼ **Yorksters Prince (IRE)**[221] 7346 7-8-2 61 oh4 ....(p) ShirleyTeasdale(5) 6 — 59
(Marjorie Fife) *prom: led over 7f out: rdn whn hdd over 2f out: sn no ch w wnr: no ex and lost 2 pls ins fnl f* **33/1**

600- **5** hd **Rex Romanorum (IRE)**[202] 7772 6-8-9 63 ........ DuranFentiman 4 — 60
(Patrick Holmes) *hld up: rdn over 3f out: kpt on ins fnl f: nvr threatened* **28/1**

0-20 **6** 1 ½ **Al Furat (USA)**[21] 2055 6-8-7 61 oh4 ........(v[1]) PaulPickard 9 — 55
(Ron Barr) *dwlt: hld up: rdn over 3f out: nvr threatened* **16/1**

0-12 **7** ¾ **Hussar Ballad (USA)**[4] 2509 5-8-7 61 ........ DavidAllan 1 — 54
(Mel Brittain) *trckd ldrs: rdn over 3f out: wknd appr fnl f* **2/1**[1]

3-40 **8** 1 ¾ **Woody Bay**[22] 2017 4-9-6 74 ........ GrahamLee 7 — 63
(James Given) *dwlt: sn in midfield: rdn over 3f out: wknd over 1f out* **5/1**[3]

0-50 **9** ½ **Wyldfire (IRE)**[33] 1660 4-8-9 63 ........ PaulMulrennan 5 — 51
(Ruth Carr) *trckd ldrs: rdn over 3f out: wknd over 1f out* **8/1**

1m 57.85s (4.85) **Going Correction** +0.65s/f (Yiel) — **9 Ran SP% 111.9**
Speed ratings (Par 103): **104,96,96,95,95 94,93,91,91**
CSF £25.63 CT £775.68 TOTE £4.30: £1.60, £1.70, £8.20; EX 18.50 Trifecta £478.40.
**Owner** Billy Hughes **Bred** Newsells Park Stud **Trained** Nawton, N Yorks

**FOCUS**

A number of these had contested races at a significantly higher level earlier in their careers. The winner is rated close to last summer's form.

## 2655 RACINGUK.COM/ANYWHERE: 3DEVICES, 1PRICE MEDIAN AUCTION MAIDEN STKS — 1m 2f

**3:50** (3:52) (Class 5) 3-5-Y-O — **£2,587** (£770; £384; £192) **Stalls** Low

Form — RPR

**1** **Harmonic Lady** 4-9-9 0 ........ DavidAllan 9 — 62+
(Mel Brittain) *s.i.s: hld up: pushed along and hdwy over 3f out: chsd ldr over 1f out: led fnl 100yds: kpt on* **50/1**

2 **2** 1 ½ **Lamorak (FR)**[15] 2221 3-9-0 0 ........ GrahamLee 1 — 63
(Hugo Palmer) *racd keenly: trckd ldrs: led gng wl over 2f out: rdn over 1f out: drvn and one pce fnl f: hdd fnl 100yds* **8/15**[1]

2300 **3** 2 ¼ **Whitby High Light**[20] 2077 3-8-9 76 ........ JackDuern(5) 2 — 58
(Andrew Hollinshead) *midfield: rdn over 3f out: hdwy to chse ldr over 1f out: one pce fnl f* **8/1**[3]

00-4 **4** 1 ¼ **Barbara Elizabeth**[28] 1840 3-8-9 45 ........ BarryMcHugh 6 — 51?
(Tony Coyle) *led: hdd over 3f out: sn rdn: plugged on* **25/1**

050 **5** 2 ¾ **Mary's Prayer**[81] 871 3-8-9 51 ........ PatrickMathers 8 — 46
(John Holt) *prom: rdn to ld over 3f out: hdd over 2f out: remained cl up tl wknd fnl f* **50/1**

0-5 **6** 7 **Private Dancer**[11] 2292 3-9-0 0 ........ BenCurtis 7 — 37
(Alan Swinbank) *racd keenly: trckd ldrs: rdn over 3f out: sn wknd* **8/1**[3]

340- **7** 2 **Sound Of Summer (IRE)**[227] 7202 3-8-9 73 ........ GrahamGibbons 5 — 29
(Charles Hills) *trckd ldrs: rdn over 3f out: sn wknd* **5/1**[2]

5- **8** 10 **Cassie Jem**[201] 7791 4-9-9 0 ........ PaulMulrennan 4 — 11
(David C Griffiths) *midfield: rdn over 3f out: wknd over 2f out* **25/1**

0 **9** 89 **Goldfellow**[35] 1634 3-8-7 0 ........ JordanNason(7) 10
(Peter Chapple-Hyam) *slowly away: hld up: rdn over 5f out: sn struggling: t.o* **25/1**

2m 14.39s (7.29) **Going Correction** +0.65s/f (Yiel)
**WFA** 3 from 4yo 14lb — **9 Ran SP% 119.6**
Speed ratings (Par 103): **96,94,93,92,89 84,82,74,3**
CSF £79.40 TOTE £37.00: £7.60, £1.10, £2.10; EX 194.10 Trifecta £1756.30.
**Owner** Mel Brittain **Bred** Northgate Lodge Stud Ltd **Trained** Warthill, N Yorks

**FOCUS**
This developed into a slog and, with the odds-on favourite barely able to raise a leg in the final 100 yards, it was rather weak. No fluke from the winner though.

## 2656 FOLLOW REDCARRACING ON FACEBOOK & TWITTER H'CAP 5f
**4:20** (4:20) (Class 4) (0-85,85) 4-Y-O+ **£6,469** (£1,925; £962; £481) **Stalls** Centre

Form RPR
2106 **1** **Keep It Dark**[8] 2390 5-9-0 **78** BarryMcHugh 2 87
(Tony Coyle) *racd isolated far side: mde all: hld together over 1f out: rdn and carried hd high ins fnl f: jst hld on* **7/1**
0-02 **2** *nse* **Avon Breeze**[8] 2390 5-9-1 **79** RussKennemore 9 88
(Richard Whitaker) *trckd ldr: rdn 2f out: wnt 2nd over 1f out: kpt on wl: jst failed* **6/1**[2]
46-4 **3** *1 1/4* **Jack Luey**[8] 2390 7-9-7 **85** DavidAllan 5 90
(Tim Easterby) *midfield: rdn 1/2-way: kpt on fnl f* **7/2**[1]
-030 **4** *shd* **Oldjoesaid**[10] 2350 10-8-13 **77** PJMcDonald 1 81
(Paul Midgley) *hld up: rdn 1/2-way: kpt on fnl f* **13/2**[3]
30-0 **5** *3 3/4* **Bondi Beach Boy**[8] 2390 5-8-10 **81** JordanNason[(7)] 7 72
(James Turner) *dwlt: hld up: rdn 1/2-way: minor late hdwy: nvr threatened* **12/1**
-242 **6** *1* **Bronze Beau**[10] 2350 7-8-10 **79** (t) JacobButterfield[(5)] 6 66
(Kristin Stubbs) *w ldr: rdn 1/2-way: wknd fnl f* **7/1**
4224 **7** *1* **Tax Free (IRE)**[10] 2350 12-9-5 **83** AdrianNicholls 3 66
(David Nicholls) *prom: rdn over 2f out: wknd fnl f* **13/2**[3]
550- **8** *1* **Bispham Green**[246] 6699 4-9-1 **79** DanielTudhope 4 59
(David O'Meara) *prom: rdn 1/2-way: wknd fnl f* **8/1**
251- **9** *3/4* **Tom Sawyer**[194] 7887 6-8-6 **73** (b) ConnorBeasley[(3)] 8 50
(Julie Camacho) *hld up: nvr threatened* **20/1**
1m 0.69s (2.09) **Going Correction** +0.575s/f (Yiel) **9 Ran SP% 111.7**
Speed ratings (Par 105): **106,105,103,103,97 96,94,92,91**
CSF £46.33 CT £170.12 TOTE £6.10: £2.00, £2.20, £1.90; EX 37.60 Trifecta £169.70.
**Owner** N Hetherton **Bred** Heather Raw **Trained** Norton, N Yorks

**FOCUS**
The feature brought up the closest finish of the afternoon. The form is rated through the runner-up.

## 2657 CELEBRATE 10 YEARS WITH RACING UK ANYWHERE H'CAP 6f
**4:50** (4:52) (Class 5) (0-70,69) 3-Y-O **£2,587** (£770; £384; £192) **Stalls** Centre

Form RPR
646 **1** **More Beau (USA)**[24] 1939 3-9-0 **62** PaddyAspell 9 73+
(Ed Dunlop) *hld up: smooth hdwy over 2f out: pushed along to ld 1f out: sn rdn: edgd lft: kpt on wl* **10/1**
6-62 **2** *3 1/4* **Margrets Gift**[15] 2217 3-9-2 **64** DavidAllan 2 65
(Tim Easterby) *prom: rdn over 2f out: kpt on but no ch w wnr ins fnl f* **9/1**
2-34 **3** *1 1/2* **Lendal Bridge**[15] 2204 3-8-11 **59** BarryMcHugh 8 55
(Tony Coyle) *in tch: rdn over 2f out: kpt on* **4/1**[2]
1-54 **4** *hd* **Honey Meadow**[24] 1940 3-9-0 **69** KieranShoemark[(7)] 4 65
(Robert Eddery) *midfield: rdn 1/2-way: hdwy to chse ldrs over 1f out: kpt on* **7/2**[1]
30-5 **5** *nk* **Smart Alec (IRE)**[42] 1498 3-8-11 **59** BenCurtis 6 54
(Alan Swinbank) *hld up: pushed along and outpcd 1/2-way: kpt on fr over 1f out: nrst fin* **13/2**[3]
0-00 **6** *1/2* **Sleeping Star**[15] 2204 3-8-7 **55** oh1 PJMcDonald 3 48
(Mel Brittain) *dwlt: hld up: rdn 1/2-way: sme hdwy over 1f out: one pce fnl f* **50/1**
50-0 **7** *2 3/4* **Tweety Pie (IRE)**[22] 2015 3-9-2 **67** NeilFarley[(3)] 1 51
(Declan Carroll) *led: rdn whn hdd 1f out: wknd* **25/1**
0-05 **8** *2* **St Paul'S (IRE)**[105] 564 3-8-9 **57** (b[1]) PaulMulrennan 5 35
(David C Griffiths) *midfield: rdn 1/2-way: sn btn* **25/1**
00-2 **9** *3* **Tell Me When**[36] 1611 3-8-8 **56** JamesSullivan 13 24
(Brian Rothwell) *hld up: rdn 1/2-way: nvr threatened* **10/1**
00-0 **10** *8* **Baileys Forever**[18] 2130 3-9-0 **65** (b[1]) ConnorBeasley[(3)] 15 8
(James Given) *slowly away: hld up: nvr threatened* **20/1**
-540 **11** *1* **Sandsman's Girl (IRE)**[116] 401 3-9-5 **67** (b) GrahamLee 14 6
(James Given) *chsd ldrs: wknd over 1f out* **25/1**
26-0 **12** *19* **Neighbother**[11] 2295 3-9-7 **69** (b[1]) TonyHamilton 12
(Richard Fahey) *prom: rdn over 2f out: wknd over 1f out: eased* **13/2**[3]
1m 15.84s (4.04) **Going Correction** +0.575s/f (Yiel) **12 Ran SP% 115.3**
Speed ratings (Par 99): **96,91,89,89,89 88,84,82,78,67 66,40**
CSF £87.14 CT £428.54 TOTE £14.90: £4.40, £2.30, £1.70; EX 93.00 Trifecta £480.50.
**Owner** Robert Ng **Bred** Nursery Place **Trained** Newmarket, Suffolk

**FOCUS**
A modest handicap with the unexposed winner a big improver.

## 2658 VOLTIGEUR RESTAURANT 2 COURSES FOR £11.95 AMATEUR RIDERS' MAIDEN H'CAP 6f
**5:20** (5:26) (Class 6) (0-65,62) 4-Y-O+ **£1,975** (£607; £303) **Stalls** Centre

Form RPR
-655 **1** **Absolute Bearing (IRE)**[87] 799 5-9-9 **48** oh3 MissLWilson[(5)] 12 54
(Tim Etherington) *hld up in rr: stl plenty to do 2f out: kpt on to ld fnl 75yds* **11/2**
0500 **2** *nk* **Lexi's Beauty (IRE)**[27] 1887 4-10-0 **48** oh3 MissSBrotherton 1 53
(Brian Baugh) *midfield: rdn 1/2-way: kpt on: ev ch fnl 110yds: jst hld* **25/1**
0-60 **3** *2 1/4* **Perfect Words (IRE)**[37] 1596 4-10-4 **57** MissNHayes[(5)] 3 55+
(Marjorie Fife) *led narrowly: rdn and edgd rt fr 2f out: hdd fnl 75yds: wknd* **4/1**[2]
3-60 **4** *1 1/4* **Midnight Warrior**[7] 2426 4-9-11 **50** [1] PhillipDennis[(5)] 10 44
(Ron Barr) *sn outpcd in rr: kpt on fnl f: nrst fin* **11/4**[1]
00-0 **5** *1/2* **Eium Mac**[7] 2426 5-10-3 **51** MissCWalton 5 43
(Neville Bycroft) *midfield: rdn and outpcd 1/2-way: kpt on fnl f: nvr threatened* **5/1**[3]
0/40 **6** *nk* **Spowarticus**[77] 918 5-9-9 **48** (v[1]) MrKLocking[(5)] 4 39
(Scott Dixon) *w ldr: rdn over 2f out: hung rt fr over 1f out: wknd ins fnl f* **16/1**
353- **7** *1/2* **Karate Queen**[300] 4891 9-10-0 **48** oh2 (p) MrJHamilton 11 38
(Ron Barr) *hld up: sn outpcd: nvr threatened* **8/1**
600- **8** *7* **Finn Mac**[283] 5515 4-9-10 **51** MrPHardy[(7)] 7 18
(John Norton) *hld up: outpcd 1/2-way: nvr threatened* **50/1**
0-00 **9** *2 1/4* **Jack Barker**[34] 1649 5-9-9 **50** oh3 ow2 MrRAsquith[(7)] 9 10
(Robin Bastiman) *chsd ldrs: wknd over 2f out* **20/1**
62-6 **10** *1/2* **Moss Hill**[140] 77 5-10-4 **52** (t) MrWHogg 6 10
(Jason Ward) *chsd ldrs: wknd over 1f out* **14/1**
556 **11** *7* **Jiminy**[19] 2093 4-9-7 **48** oh3 (p) JasonNuttall[(7)] 8
(Alan Berry) *midfield: wknd 1/2-way* **16/1**
1m 18.04s (6.24) **Going Correction** +0.575s/f (Yiel) **11 Ran SP% 118.8**
Speed ratings (Par 101): **81,80,77,75,75 74,74,64,61,61 51**
CSF £138.23 CT £622.99 TOTE £9.40: £2.20, £3.80, £3.00; EX 194.20 Trifecta £1585.30.
**Owner** Tim Etherington **Bred** Ballyhane Stud **Trained** Norton, N Yorks

**FOCUS**
Not for the first time in an amateur contest this season, they went a suicidal early pace and that played into the hands of the winner. The form is shaky but has been taken at face value.
T/Jkpt: Not won. T/Plt: £408.90 to a £1 stake. Pool: £73,089.55 - 130.46 winning tickets. T/Qpdt: £13.50 to a £1 stake. Pool: £5,969.82 - 325.05 winning tickets. AS

2659 - (Foreign Racing) - See Raceform Interactive

# 2540 BEVERLEY (R-H)
Wednesday, May 28

**2660 Meeting Abandoned** - Waterlogged in places.

# 2246 CHEPSTOW (L-H)
Wednesday, May 28

**OFFICIAL GOING: Soft (5.2)**
Wind: Light; half behind Weather: Overcast; light rain from Race 4

## 2666 32RED ON THE APP STORE/IRISH EBF MAIDEN STKS 5f 16y
**2:00** (2:01) (Class 5) 2-Y-O **£2,911** (£866; £432; £216) **Stalls** Centre

Form RPR
4 **1** **Majestic Hero (IRE)**[32] 1726 2-9-5 0 DavidProbert 6 79+
(Ronald Harris) *pressed ldr: pushed along and ev ch 2f out: rdn to ld ent fnl f: styd on wl and drew clr fnl 100yds* **7/4**[1]
53 **2** *3 3/4* **Clodovil Doll (IRE)**[11] 2348 2-9-0 0 JimCrowley 1 61
(James Tate) *led: rdn 2f out: drvn and hdd ent fnl f: wknd fnl 100yds* **7/4**[1]
**3** *3* **Boann (IRE)** 2-9-0 0 LiamJones 5 50
(J S Moore) *chsd ldng trio: pushed along by ldng pair wl over 1f out: wnt 3rd over 1f out: kpt on same pce fnl f* **50/1**
**4** *3 3/4* **Nona Blu** 2-9-5 0 LukeMorris 2 41+
(Harry Dunlop) *chsd ldng pair: rdn 1/2-way: 3rd and outpcd wl over 1f out: wknd ins fnl f* **4/1**[2]
**5** *1/2* **Abba Zabba (IRE)** 2-9-5 0 AdamKirby 3 39
(David Evans) *broke okay but sn dropped to last pair and outpcd: n.d* **20/1**
**6** *2 1/4* **Wink Oliver** 2-9-2 0 WilliamTwiston-Davies[(3)] 4 31
(Mick Channon) *s.i.s: a outpcd in rr: nvr on terms* **8/1**[3]
1m 2.71s (3.41) **Going Correction** +0.50s/f (Yiel) **6 Ran SP% 110.6**
Speed ratings (Par 93): **92,86,81,75,74 70**
CSF £4.71 TOTE £3.00: £3.20, £1.50; EX 5.30 Trifecta £62.80.
**Owner** Mrs Jackie Jarrett & Ridge House Stables **Bred** Mrs Diane Williams **Trained** Earlswood, Monmouths

**FOCUS**
David Probert described the ground as "testing enough", while Jim Crowley agreed with the official description of soft. A modest juvenile maiden that was dominated by the two with previous experience, unsurprisingly given the testing conditions. Improvement from the winner.

## 2667 32RED.COM MAIDEN STKS 6f 16y
**2:30** (2:32) (Class 5) 3-Y-O+ **£2,587** (£770; £384; £192) **Stalls** Centre

Form RPR
626- **1** **Minty Jones**[175] 8146 5-9-7 48 (v) TimClark[(5)] 7 60
(Michael Mullineaux) *mde all: wnt clr after 2f: stl clr and rdn over 1f out: edgd lft ins fnl f: a holding on: rdn out* **25/1**
**2** *1 1/2* **Debit** 3-9-3 0 AdamKirby 1 54+
(Clive Cox) *chsd ldrs: outpcd 1/2-way: rallied and wnt 4th 1f out: styd on strly to go 2nd fnl 50yds: nvr gng to rch wnr* **11/4**[2]
55 **3** *2* **Hoy Hoy (IRE)**[27] 1894 3-9-0 0 WilliamTwiston-Davies[(3)] 9 48
(Mick Channon) *chsd ldrs: outpcd 1/2-way: rdn and effrt to chse clr wnr wl over 1f out: nvr gng to rch wnr but kpt on ins fnl f: lost 2nd fnl 50yds* **6/4**[1]
60 **4** *shd* **Lucky Clover**[39] 1569 3-8-7 0 RyanWhile[(5)] 8 42
(Malcolm Saunders) *w wnr for 1f: chsd ldrs after: hanging lft 2f out: pushed along and styd on ins fnl f: no threat to wnr* **33/1**
**5** *5* **Crazy Train**[35] 5-9-0 0 DavidParkes[(7)] 2 29
(Keiran Burke) *midfield: outpcd 1/2-way: n.d after: plugged on fnl f* **50/1**
**6** *1/2* **Avon Scent** 4-9-4 0 OisinMurphy[(3)] 10 28
(Christopher Mason) *s.i.s: a in rr: outpcd 1/2-way: plugged on fnl f: n.d* **14/1**
6-05 **7** *1/2* **Lady Rain**[103] 610 5-9-7 42 LiamJones 11 26
(Ronald Harris) *stdd s: hld up towards rr: outpcd 1/2-way: n.d after: plugged on fnl f* **50/1**
-460 **8** *1 1/4* **Harlequin Jinks**[83] 855 3-8-12 37 RobertHavlin 6 20
(Mark Usher) *midfield: dropped to rr and losing tch 1/2-way: sltly hmpd over 1f out: styd on ins fnl f: n.d* **100/1**
-500 **9** *2* **Telegraph (IRE)**[13] 2278 3-9-3 63 (v) DavidProbert 4 19
(Andrew Balding) *chsd ldrs: wnt 2nd after 1f out tl wl over 1f out: 5th and btn 1f out: fdd ins fnl f* **3/1**[3]
**10** *43* **Sunsational Girl**[11] 5-9-7 0 ChrisCatlin 5
(Dai Burchell) *s.i.s: immediately outpcd and sn t.o* **66/1**
0- **S** **Rowlestone Express**[215] 7500 3-8-12 0 LiamKeniry 3
(Tony Carroll) *midfield: outpcd 1/2-way: wl hld whn slipped up over 1f out* **20/1**
1m 16.01s (4.01) **Going Correction** +0.50s/f (Yiel)
**WFA** 3 from 4yo+ 9lb **11 Ran SP% 116.3**
Speed ratings (Par 103): **93,91,88,88,81 80,80,78,75,18**
CSF £89.57 TOTE £28.50: £7.90, £1.10, £1.10; EX 170.50 Trifecta £272.10.
**Owner** P Clacher **Bred** Mr & Mrs A Jones **Trained** Alpraham, Cheshire

**FOCUS**
A bit of a turn-up in this weak 3yo-plus sprint maiden, with an exposed 48-rated 5yo making all. The time was ordinary.

## 2668 32RED FREE £10 BONUS H'CAP 6f 16y
**3:00** (3:12) (Class 6) (0-65,62) 3-Y-O **£1,940** (£577; £288; £144) **Stalls** Centre

Form RPR
**1** **Lady Ranger (IRE)**[5] 2533 3-8-0 **48** SeanCorby[(7)] 2 60+
(Adrian Paul Keatley, Ire) *hld up in midfield: clsd to join ldrs and stl on bridle over 1f out: led 1f out: pushed along and readily asserted ins fnl f: easily* **2/1**[1]
3502 **2** *2 3/4* **Bonjour Steve**[14] 2249 3-9-7 **62** (p) LukeMorris 6 63
(Richard Price) *stdd s: hld up: pushed along over 2f out: rdn to ld over 1f out: hdd 1f out: no ch w wnr but hld on for 2nd fnl f* **11/4**[2]

00-0 **3** *nk* **Trigger Park (IRE)**[134] 173 3-8-9 **55** DCByrne(5) 3 55
(Ronald Harris) *in tch in midfield: chsd ldng pair over 4f out: drvn and effrt to press ldrs over 1f out: 3rd and styd on same pce ins fnl f* **20/1**

0-00 **4** *2* **Eugenic**[49] 1384 3-8-13 **54** SteveDrowne 1 48
(Rod Millman) *racd in last pair: switching rt towards stands' rail over 2f out: pushed along and hdwy over 1f out: rdn: edgd lft and no imp fnl f* **16/1**

0400 **5** *1 1/4* **Nutbush**[16] 2209 3-8-10 **54** WilliamTwiston-Davies(3) 7 44
(Mick Channon) *stdd and dropped in bhd after s: hld up in rr: rdn and struggling 1/2-way: swtchd lft and kpt on ins fnl f: n.d* **14/1**

-255 **6** *2 1/2* **Clear Focus (IRE)**[5] 2526 3-8-4 **48** oh3 OisinMurphy(3) 4 30
(Brendan Powell) *chsd ldrs for over 1f out: rdn and struggling in midfield 1/2-way: no threat to ldrs after* **3/1**[3]

-653 **7** *hd* **Zafraaj**[14] 2249 3-9-5 **60** (b[1]) DavidProbert 5 41
(Ronald Harris) *led: rdn and hdd over 1f out: btn 1f out: wknd ins fnl f* **10/1**

1m 15.29s (3.29) **Going Correction** +0.50s/f (Yiel) 7 Ran SP% **111.4**
Speed ratings (Par 97): **98,94,93,91,89 86,86**
CSF £7.25 TOTE £2.80: £1.70, £1.80; EX 9.20 Trifecta £95.40.
**Owner** Adrian Paul Keatley **Bred** Knocklong House Stud **Trained** Dunlavin, Co. Kildare

**FOCUS**
Racing was allowed to continue following a track inspection, prompted by the fall of a runner in the previous race. They went off hard in this sprint, considering the conditions, and the race set up perfectly for the winner. The form is rated around the second.

## 2669 32RED CASINO H'CAP — 7f 16y
3:30 (3:44) (Class 5) (0-70,69) 4-Y-O+ — £2,587 (£770; £384; £192) Stalls Centre

Form — RPR

4021 **1** **Eastern Dragon (IRE)**[6] 2486 4-9-2 **69** JackDuern(5) 7 79
(Michael Scudamore) *in tch in midfield: hdwy to chse ldrs 2f out: rdn and ev ch over 1f out: led fnl 75yds: r.o wl: rdn out* **15/8**[1]

0005 **2** *nk* **Admirable Art (IRE)**[23] 2021 4-8-5 **58** (p) DanielMuscutt(5) 9 67
(Tony Carroll) *hld up in tch towards rr: clsd over 2f out: jnd ldrs over 1f out: rdn to ld 1f out: hdd fnl 75yds: r.o but hld towards fin* **16/1**

0-65 **3** *nk* **Bountybeamadam**[28] 1873 4-9-5 **67** (p) PatCosgrave 2 75
(George Baker) *chsd ldr and crossed to racd nr stands' rail: rdn to ld 2f out: drvn and hdd 1f out ev ch fnl f: unable qck cl home* **33/1**

0-40 **4** *7* **Bajan Story**[31] 1771 5-8-7 **55** oh10 DavidProbert 3 45
(Michael Blanshard) *chsd ldrs: drvn and pressing ldrs wl over 1f out: unable qck and btn 1f out: wknd ins fnl f* **66/1**

0-00 **5** *2* **Secret Beau**[14] 2251 4-9-7 **69** AdamKirby 10 54
(John Spearing) *in tch in midfield: rdn 2f out: sn outpcd and btn: wknd over 1f out* **8/1**

0-54 **6** *1 1/4* **Pashan Garh**[24] 1980 5-9-2 **67** OisinMurphy(3) 6 49
(Pat Eddery) *s.i.s and hmpd sn after s: hld up in rr of main gp: swtchd lft and effrt 2f out: no imp and wl btn 1f out* **7/1**

440 **7** *nk* **Dimitar (USA)**[30] 1799 5-9-5 **67** StephenCraine 5 48
(Johnny Farrelly) *hld up in rr of main gp: pushed along and effrt 2f out: no prog: nvr trbld ldrs* **33/1**

0-22 **8** *nk* **Midaz**[28] 1886 4-9-4 **66** RobertHavlin 4 46
(Hughie Morrison) *chsd ldrs: rdn and struggling ent fnl 2f: btn over 1f out: wknd fnl f* **5/1**[3]

340- **9** *3* **The Name Is Frank**[258] 6323 9-8-2 **55** oh8 (t) PhilipPrince(5) 11 27
(Mark Gillard) *chsd ldrs tl lost pl 1/2-way: bhd over 1f out* **100/1**

0000 **10** *hd* **Decision By One**[107] 562 5-8-6 **57** DeclanBates(3) 1 29
(David Evans) *led tl 2f out: 5th and wkng over 1f out: fdd ins fnl f* **50/1**

450- **11** *2 1/4* **Lady Bayside**[189] 7970 6-9-7 **69** LukeMorris 12 35
(Malcolm Saunders) *in tch in midfield: rdn and struggling 3f out: wknd 2f out* **14/1**

0-04 **12** *2* **Tenbridge**[14] 2251 5-8-9 **60** (v) RosieJessop(3) 8 21
(Derek Haydn Jones) *s.i.s: a bhd* **4/1**[2]

1m 27.66s (4.46) **Going Correction** +0.50s/f (Yiel) 12 Ran SP% **117.9**
Speed ratings (Par 103): **94,93,93,85,83 81,81,80,77,77 74,72**
CSF £35.54 CT £779.90 TOTE £3.10: £1.20, £4.10, £6.00; EX 36.50 Trifecta £415.60.
**Owner** JCG Chua & CK Ong **Bred** James Mahon **Trained** Bromsash, H'fords
■ Stewards' Enquiry : Daniel Muscutt four-day ban: used whip above permitted level (Jun 11-14)

**FOCUS**
There was little between the first three, who pulled clear in what was a modest handicap. The winner rates similar to his Goodwood win.

## 2670 32RED H'CAP — 1m 4f 23y
4:05 (4:07) (Class 4) (0-80,80) 4-Y-O+ — £4,690 (£1,395; £697; £348) Stalls Low

Form — RPR

6-56 **1** **Aldborough (IRE)**[30] 1809 4-8-11 **70** (p) JimCrowley 4 79
(Ralph Beckett) *chsd ldr tl led over 3f out: kpt on wl fnl f: rdn out* **11/4**[2]

3445 **2** *1 1/2* **Modem**[26] 1909 4-8-4 **66** (b) OisinMurphy(3) 1 72
(Rod Millman) *t.k.h: chsd ldng pair: wnt 2nd 3f out: drvn and pressing wnr over 1f out: styd on same pce ins fnl f* **7/2**[3]

4313 **3** *1 1/4* **Back Burner (IRE)**[30] 1816 6-9-6 **79** DavidProbert 7 83
(Dai Burchell) *stdd s: in tch in last pair: rdn and effrt 3f out: 3rd and styd on same pce fr over 1f out* **6/1**

11-1 **4** *5* **Calm Attitude (IRE)**[26] 1910 4-9-3 **76** ChrisCatlin 5 72
(Rae Guest) *stdd s: in tch in last pair: effrt 3f out: 4th and no imp over 1f out: eased towards fin* **5/2**[1]

10-5 **5** *3 3/4* **Bold Duke**[9] 2382 6-9-4 **80** ThomasBrown(3) 6 70
(Edward Bevan) *t.k.h: hld up in tch in midfield: rdn and effrt 3f out: no imp 2f out: wknd over 1f out* **16/1**

00-1 **6** *18* **Conquestadim**[30] 1798 4-8-12 **71** RobertHavlin 2 32
(Hughie Morrison) *led tl over 3f out: sn rdn and lost pl: bhd over 1f out: eased wl ins fnl f* **6/1**

2m 53.11s (14.11) **Going Correction** +1.025s/f (Soft) 6 Ran SP% **111.9**
Speed ratings (Par 105): **93,92,91,87,85 73**
CSF £12.65 TOTE £5.50: £2.30, £2.50; EX 13.30 Trifecta £50.30.
**Owner** Mr and Mrs David Aykroyd **Bred** Mr & Mrs David Aykroyd **Trained** Kimpton, Hants

**FOCUS**
Run at a steady pace, this fair handicap was won by the least exposed runner in the field. Modest form for the grade.

## 2671 32REDPOKER.COM H'CAP — 1m 2f 36y
4:40 (4:43) (Class 5) (0-70,70) 3-Y-O — £2,587 (£770; £384; £192) Stalls Low

Form — RPR

5-34 **1** **Spectator**[8] 2417 3-9-2 **66** (p) DavidProbert 2 72
(Andrew Balding) *chsd ldrs: hdwy to chse clr ldr 3f out: rdn and 3 l down 2f out: styd on and grad clsd: led wl ins fnl f: rdn out* **2/1**[1]

4-63 **2** *1/2* **Loch Ma Naire (IRE)**[27] 1898 3-9-6 **70** (b) AdamKirby 4 75
(Ed Dunlop) *t.k.h: chsd ldr tl led 1/2-way: stl travelling wl 3f out: rdn and 3 l clr 2f: grad worn down: hdd and no ex wl ins fnl f* **3/1**[3]

-002 **3** *3 1/4* **New Colours**[16] 2222 3-9-4 **68** MartinDwyer 1 67
(Marcus Tregoning) *t.k.h: led tl 1/2-way: chsd ldr tl 3f out: styd on same pce fnl 2f* **9/4**[2]

206 **4** *3/4* **Drifter (IRE)**[29] 1830 3-9-2 **66** StephenCraine 5 63
(Tom Dascombe) *taken down early: stdd s: hld up in rr: rdn over 3f out: battling for 3rd but no threat to ldng pair over 1f out: one pce fnl f* **11/1**

3434 **5** *5* **Gratzie**[16] 2211 3-9-2 **69** WilliamTwiston-Davies(3) 3 57
(Mick Channon) *in tch: rdn and unable qck over 3f out: drvn and btn 2f out: bhd fnl f* **6/1**

2m 22.17s (11.57) **Going Correction** +1.025s/f (Soft) 5 Ran SP% **111.7**
Speed ratings (Par 99): **94,93,91,90,86**
CSF £8.47 TOTE £2.90: £2.10, £2.10; EX 8.60 Trifecta £23.10.
**Owner** Kingsclere Racing Club **Bred** Kingsclere Stud **Trained** Kingsclere, Hants

**FOCUS**
A modset handicap that saw the front pair pull clear. Small personal bests from the first two.

## 2672 32REDBINGO.COM H'CAP — 1m 2f 36y
5:15 (5:15) (Class 6) (0-65,65) 4-Y-O+ — £1,940 (£577; £288; £144) Stalls Low

Form — RPR

260- **1** **Belle Park**[217] 7458 7-8-1 **52** KieranShoemark(7) 8 64+
(Victor Dartnall) *hld up towards rr: swtchd rt and hdwy over 3f out: trcking ldrs over 1f out: shkn up to ld 1f out: sn rdn and qcknd clr: r.o wl* **5/1**[1]

300- **2** *1 3/4* **Urban Space**[219] 7433 8-8-5 **52** (t) RossAtkinson(3) 3 61
(John Flint) *hld up in midfield: rdn and effrt 2f out: 5th and drvn over 1f out: styd on strly ins fnl f to go 2nd towards fin* **12/1**

506- **3** *1* **Pandorica**[246] 6435 6-9-2 **65** (p) DanielMuscutt(5) 9 72
(Bernard Llewellyn) *in tch in midfield: hdwy to join ldrs 2f out: drvn and ev ch over 1f out tl jst ins fnl f: chsd wnr and one pce fnl 150yds: lost 2nd towards fin* **5/1**[1]

0460 **4** *5* **Innoko (FR)**[12] 2301 4-9-0 **61** (t) WilliamTwiston-Davies(3) 11 59
(Tony Carroll) *chsd ldrs: led 2f out: sn drvn and hdd over 1f out: wknd ins fnl f* **14/1**

1245 **5** *1* **Thane Of Cawdor (IRE)**[14] 2248 5-9-0 **61** OisinMurphy(3) 12 57
(Joseph Tuite) *stdd s: hld up in rr: gd hdwy on outer over 3f out: rdn to chal 2f out: led over 1f out tl hdd 1f out: wknd ins fnl f* **7/1**[2]

0245 **6** *nk* **Fair Comment**[29] 1835 4-8-10 **54** RobertHavlin 1 56+
(Michael Blanshard) *t.k.h: hld up wl in tch in midfield: travelling wl but stuck bhd rivals and shuffled wl bk over 2f out: swtchd lft and wnt modest 6th over 1f out: no ch but styd on fnl f* **14/1**

04-4 **7** *9* **Petrify**[30] 1815 4-8-11 **55** ChrisCatlin 6 33
(Bernard Llewellyn) *hld up in rr: hdwy over 3f out: drvn and no hdwy wl over 2f out: wknd wl over 1f out* **8/1**[3]

0-06 **8** *1/2* **Studfarmer**[26] 1915 4-8-4 **51** oh2 DeclanBates(3) 4 28
(John Panvert) *chsd ldr tl 7f out: chsd ldrs after tl wknd u.p 2f out* **50/1**

56-3 **9** *5* **Hallingham**[21] 2084 4-8-13 **60** MatthewLawson(3) 5 27
(Jonathan Portman) *hld up in tch: rdn and effrt over 2f out: struggling and btn 2f out: sn wknd* **8/1**[3]

6355 **10** *3/4* **Xclusive**[64] 1087 4-9-1 **59** DavidProbert 14 25
(Ronald Harris) *chsd ldrs tl wnt 2nd 7f out: rdn to ld 2f out: sn hdd and btn: wknd* **8/1**[3]

643- **11** *11* **Priestley's Reward (IRE)**[347] 3319 5-9-2 **60** (p) RaulDaSilva 10 5
(Alan Phillips) *led: rdn over 3f out: hdd over 2f out and sn dropped out: bhd fnl f: t.o* **16/1**

32-0 **12** *6* **Elusive Band (USA)**[19] 2135 4-8-6 **55** (p) PhilipPrince(5) 13
(Bernard Llewellyn) *wl in tch in midfield: rdn and lost pl over 2f out: t.o* **20/1**

51-0 **13** *102* **Let Me In (IRE)**[14] 2248 4-8-13 **64** (v) DavidParkes(7) 7
(Bernard Llewellyn) *a towards rr: dropped to last 1/2-way: lost tch 4f out: t.o* **20/1**

2m 20.23s (9.63) **Going Correction** +1.025s/f (Soft) 13 Ran SP% **117.6**
Speed ratings (Par 101): **102,100,99,95,95 94,87,87,83,82 73,68,**
CSF £63.25 CT £318.04 TOTE £5.70: £1.80, £4.60, £2.20; EX 91.90 Trifecta £479.60.
**Owner** V R A Dartnall **Bred** C A Green **Trained** Brayford, Devon

**FOCUS**
Lowly handicap form, but competitive for the grade. The winner looked better than ever.
T/Plt: £11.60 to a £1 stake. Pool: £72,422.24 - 4,539.05 winning units T/Qpdt: £7.70 to a £1 stake. Pool: £4,873.73 - 467.60 winning units SP

# 2291 HAMILTON (R-H)
### Wednesday, May 28

**OFFICIAL GOING: Good (8.1)**
Wind: Breezy; half against Weather: Overcast Rails: Rail realignment around the loop decreased distances on Round course by about 50yds

## 2673 MANDORA MAIDEN AUCTION STKS — 6f 5y
2:10 (2:13) (Class 6) 2-Y-O — £2,587 (£770; £384; £192) Stalls High

Form — RPR

35 **1** **Multiplier**[23] 2014 2-8-11 0 JamesSullivan 2 70
(Kristin Stubbs) *chsd ldrs: drvn and outpcd over 2f out: rallied over 1f out: led ins fnl f: kpt on wl* **6/1**[3]

43 **2** *1 3/4* **Indian Keys**[11] 2328 2-8-7 0 KevinStott(5) 4 66
(Kevin Ryan) *dwlt: hld up in tch: stdy hdwy 1/2-way: effrt and ev ch ins fnl f: edgd lft: kpt on: hld towards fin* **8/11**[1]

05 **3** *1 1/4* **Diatomic (IRE)**[22] 2051 2-8-8 0 JennyPowell(7) 3 65
(Tom Dascombe) *led: rdn over 1f out: hdd ins fnl f: kpt on same pce* **12/1**

0 **4** *2 1/4* **Sudest (IRE)**[41] 1536 2-8-10 0 ShaneGray(5) 6 61
(Kevin Ryan) *bhd and sn drvn along: hdwy over 2f out: kpt on same pce ins fnl f* **11/1**

5 **5** *1* **Decisive Rebel**[18] 2172 2-8-11 0 JoeFanning 1 51
(Jo Hughes) *w ldr: rdn over 2f out: wknd ins fnl f* **9/2**[2]

00 **6** *1 3/4* **Blazing Rose (IRE)**[9] 2386 2-8-7 0 JulieBurke(3) 5 45
(David O'Meara) *prom: outpcd and hung rt wl over 2f out: n.d after* **66/1**

1m 14.45s (2.25) **Going Correction** +0.10s/f (Good) 6 Ran SP% **107.9**
Speed ratings (Par 91): **89,86,85,82,80 78**
CSF £10.02 TOTE £5.90: £2.90, £1.10; EX 12.90 Trifecta £41.50.
**Owner** Chester Racing Club Ltd **Bred** Chester Racing Club Ltd **Trained** Norton, N Yorks
■ Stewards' Enquiry : Jenny Powell two-day ban: careless riding (Jun 11-12)



The Form Book, Raceform Ltd, Newbury, RG14 5SJ

**FOCUS**
Rail realignment around the loop decreased distances on Round course by about 50yds. With just 1mm of overnight rain this was expected to be around the best going domestically of the week. This looked an ordinary juvenile maiden and the first five all held a chance of sorts approaching the final furlong. Probably form to be a bit wary of.

## 2674 HAPPY 10TH BIRTHDAY RACING UK H'CAP 1m 1f 36y
**2:40** (2:40) (Class 6) (0-60,64) 3-Y-O+ **£2,045** (£603; £302) **Stalls** Low

Form RPR
63-1 **1** **Remember Rocky**[7] 2457 5-8-9 **48** ow1................(p) MeganCarberry[(7)] 7 57
(Lucy Normile) *prom: effrt and rdn over 2f out: hdwy and edgd rt fr over 1f out: led last 50yds: kpt on* **3/1**[1]
-004 **2** *hd* **Raamz (IRE)**[63] 1097 7-9-7 **53**................................ JoeFanning 5 62
(Kevin Morgan) *t.k.h: trckd ldr: led over 2f out: sn rdn and edgd rt: hdd last 50yds: kpt on* **7/1**
5-50 **3** *1 ½* **Dhaular Dhar (IRE)**[6] 2475 12-9-10 **59**........................ GaryBartley[(3)] 12 64
(Jim Goldie) *hld up: rdn over 2f out: hdwy and prom over 1f out: edgd rt: kpt on ins fnl f* **20/1**
30-6 **4** *½* **Diddy Eric**[19] 2135 4-9-2 **48**.............................................(b[1]) GrahamLee 9 52
(Micky Hammond) *s.i.s: hld up: rdn and hdwy 2f out: kpt on same pce ins fnl f* **25/1**
423 **5** *3 ¼* **Brown Pete (IRE)**[9] 2396 6-8-11 **48**........................ ShirleyTeasdale[(5)] 6 46
(Ann Stokell) *midfield: effrt and rdn 3f out: no imp over 1f out* **8/1**
0324 **6** *¾* **Incurs Four Faults**[34] 1684 3-8-12 **57**................................ TomEaves 1 51
(Keith Dalgleish) *plld hrd early: trckd ldrs: effrt and rdn over 2f out: wknd fnl f* **4/1**[2]
215- **7** *5* **Galilee Chapel (IRE)**[172] 8199 5-8-12 **47**........................ JasonHart[(3)] 4 32
(Alistair Whillans) *midfield: drvn and outpcd wl over 2f out: sn btn* **12/1**
00-0 **8** *shd* **Persian Peril**[128] 253 10-10-0 **60**........................................ BenCurtis 11 45
(Alan Swinbank) *missed break: bhd: struggling 1/2-way: rallied to pass btn rivals fnl f: nvr on terms* **12/1**
3106 **9** *4* **Uplifted (IRE)**[11] 2355 3-9-1 **60**..................................(b) PaulMulrennan 8 35
(Kevin Ryan) *led: rdn and hdd over 2f out: wknd over 1f out* **6/1**[3]
46-0 **10** *2* **Noosa Sound**[34] 1674 4-9-0 **46**..................................(t) RoystonFfrench 10 19
(John Davies) *midfield on outside: hdwy and prom over 2f out: rdn and wknd wl over 1f out* **16/1**

1m 59.38s (-0.32) **Going Correction** 0.0s/f (Good)
**WFA** 3 from 4yo+ 13lb **10** Ran SP% **112.8**
Speed ratings (Par 101): **101,100,99,99,96 95,91,90,87,85**
CSF £23.27 CT £348.68 TOTE £3.70: £1.10, £2.70, £7.20; EX 29.60 Trifecta £568.10.
**Owner** Byrne Racing **Bred** Cherry Park Stud **Trained** Duncrievie, Perth & Kinross

**FOCUS**
A weak handicap, run at a sound pace. The form looks sound enough.

## 2675 AVON GORGE H'CAP 5f 4y
**3:10** (3:13) (Class 6) (0-65,64) 3-Y-O+ **£2,045** (£603; £302) **Stalls** Centre

Form RPR
05-2 **1** **Raise A Billion**[9] 2388 3-8-1 **45**............................ PatrickMathers 1 56
(Alan Berry) *hld up in tch: hdwy to ld over 1f out: rdn out fnl f* **17/2**
60-2 **2** *1 ½* **Scoreline**[9] 2387 3-9-2 **60**...................................... DanielTudhope 7 65
(David O'Meara) *chsd ldrs: led over 2f out to over 1f out: kpt on u.p fnl f: nt rch wnr* **3/1**[1]
6/0 **3** *nk* **Incomparable**[78] 908 9-8-5 **48**...........................(p) MatthewHopkins[(7)] 8 55
(Scott Dixon) *prom: drvn and effrt over 1f out: kpt on ins fnl f* **66/1**
-023 **4** *¾* **Rock Canyon (IRE)**[6] 2473 5-8-6 **47**............................ KevinStott[(5)] 10 51
(Linda Perratt) *hld up bhd ldng gp: rdn and hung lft wl over 1f out: kpt on ins fnl f* **7/2**[2]
-050 **5** *5* **Chloe's Dream (IRE)**[5] 2514 4-9-7 **62**....................(p) GarryWhillans[(5)] 9 48
(Ian Semple) *hld up bhd ldng gp: effrt whn n.m.r briefly over 2f out: rdn and no imp over 1f out* **14/1**
56-6 **6** *nk* **Ballarina**[37] 1604 8-9-5 **58**........................................ JasonHart[(3)] 5 43
(Eric Alston) *t.k.h: cl up: chal over 2f out to over 1f out: wknd ins fnl f* **12/1**
6/34 **7** *1 ¾* **New Lease Of Life**[7] 2451 5-9-6 **56**................................ GrahamLee 6 35
(Jim Goldie) *t.k.h early: in tch: rdn and outpcd over 2f out: n.d after* **9/2**[3]
1615 **8** *nk* **Biscuiteer**[9] 2388 3-9-2 **60**........................................(b) TomEaves 3 35
(Scott Dixon) *led to over 2f out: rdn and wknd over 1f out* **16/1**
-600 **9** *2 ¼* **Findog**[5] 2514 4-9-9 **62**...................................... ConnorBeasley[(3)] 4 32
(Linda Perratt) *unruly bef s: s.i.s: a outpcd and bhd* **13/2**

1m 0.18s (0.18) **Going Correction** +0.10s/f (Good)
**WFA** 3 from 4yo+ 8lb **9** Ran SP% **111.0**
Speed ratings (Par 101): **102,99,99,97,89 89,86,86,82**
CSF £32.25 CT £1528.91 TOTE £7.30: £2.80, £1.70, £5.80; EX 30.00 Trifecta £2141.80.
**Owner** T Blane, F Flynn, H Rocks & M Rocks **Bred** Bearstone Stud **Trained** Cockerham, Lancs

**FOCUS**
This moderate sprint handicap saw the first four dominate the finish. The winner is just getting his act together.

## 2676 CADZOW CASTLE FILLIES' H'CAP 1m 65y
**3:40** (3:40) (Class 5) (0-70,69) 3-Y-O+ **£3,234** (£962; £481; £240) **Stalls** Low

Form RPR
-420 **1** **Push Me (IRE)**[16] 2199 7-9-13 **68**...................................... GrahamLee 1 76
(Iain Jardine) *hld up in midfield: stdy hdwy over 1f out: pushed along and styd on wl fnl f to ld towards fin* **6/1**[3]
0004 **2** *½* **Delores Rocket**[8] 2427 4-9-0 **60**..................................(p) ShaneGray[(5)] 2 67
(Kevin Ryan) *led: rdn and hrd pressed fr 2f out: kpt on fnl f: hdd and no ex towards fin* **8/1**
43-0 **3** *hd* **Pigeon Pie**[98] 667 3-8-13 **66**...................................... JoeFanning 4 69
(Mark Johnston) *pressed ldr: effrt and ev ch fr 2f out: kpt on fnl f: one pce towards fin* **8/1**
433 **4** *½* **Dansili Dutch (IRE)**[8] 2426 5-8-13 **61**............................ JoshDoyle[(7)] 6 67+
(David O'Meara) *hld up bhd ldng gp: effrt whn nt clr run over 2f out to over 1f out: kpt on fnl f: nrst fin* **9/2**[2]
-602 **5** *2* **Spavento (IRE)**[7] 2454 8-9-11 **69**...................................... JasonHart[(3)] 9 69
(Eric Alston) *t.k.h: hld up bhd ldng gp: hdwy on outside 3f out: sn edgd rt: one pce fnl f* **7/2**[1]
561- **6** *3* **Neuf Des Coeurs**[241] 6873 3-8-10 **63**................................ TomEaves 7 53
(Keith Dalgleish) *chsd ldrs: drvn and outpcd over 2f out: rallied over 1f out: no imp fnl f* **11/1**
-005 **7** *shd* **Cheeky Wee Red**[7] 2457 6-8-9 **50** oh2......................(t) PaulMulrennan 8 43
(Alistair Whillans) *hld up: rdn wl over 2f out: kpt on fnl f: nvr able to chal* **33/1**
3043 **8** *½* **Nothing Special**[16] 2210 3-8-1 **61**................................ JennyPowell[(7)] 10 52
(Tom Dascombe) *prom on outside: rdn and edgd rt 2f out: wknd ins fnl f: eased whn btn* **7/1**
10-6 **9** *4* **Natures Law (IRE)**[7] 2454 4-9-5 **63**............................ ConnorBeasley[(3)] 3 45
(Keith Dalgleish) *t.k.h: trckd ldrs tl rdn and wknd over 2f out* **9/1**
-003 **10** *¾* **Ebony Clarets**[7] 2454 5-8-6 **50**...................................... IanBrennan[(3)] 5 30
(Linda Perratt) *hld up: drvn and outpcd wl over 2f out: sn btn* **20/1**

1m 49.23s (0.83) **Going Correction** 0.0s/f (Good)
**WFA** 3 from 4yo+ 12lb **10** Ran SP% **115.4**
Speed ratings (Par 100): **95,94,94,93,91 88,88,88,84,83**
CSF £52.73 CT £305.14 TOTE £6.10: £2.50, £2.90, £3.00; EX 56.00 Trifecta £342.90.
**Owner** Alex and Janet Card **Bred** Mrs Dolores Gleeson **Trained** Bonchester Bridge, Borders

**FOCUS**
An ordinary fillies' handicap, run at an uneven pace. The winner is rated to form.

## 2677 DUKES BRIDGE H'CAP (QUALIFIER FOR THE £15,000 BETFAIR SCOTTISH SPRINT SERIES FINAL) 6f 5y
**4:15** (4:16) (Class 5) (0-75,74) 4-Y-O+ **£3,881** (£1,155; £577; £288) **Stalls** High

Form RPR
0056 **1** **Alexandrakollontai (IRE)**[11] 2332 4-8-9 **65**................(b) JulieBurke[(3)] 4 74
(Alistair Whillans) *hld up: rdn and gd hdwy over 1f out: kpt on wl fnl f to ld cl home* **8/1**[3]
2112 **2** *shd* **Meshardal (GER)**[4] 2552 4-9-0 **67**............................ JamesSullivan 12 76
(Ruth Carr) *t.k.h: in tch: gd hdwy to ld wl over 1f out: sn rdn and edgd rt: kpt on fnl f: edgd lft and hdd cl home* **5/1**[1]
6611 **3** *1 ¼* **Economic Crisis (IRE)**[12] 2297 5-9-5 **72**.................... PaulMulrennan 6 77
(Alan Berry) *rrd s: bhd: hdwy and swtchd lft over 1f out: kpt on wl to take 3rd cl home: nt rch first two* **10/1**
3410 **4** *nk* **Amenable (IRE)**[6] 2486 7-8-13 **71**....................(p) ShirleyTeasdale[(5)] 3 75
(Ann Stokell) *cl up: disp ld wl over 1f out: one pce ins fnl f: lost 3rd towards fin* **33/1**
6316 **5** *1 ¾* **Lothair (IRE)**[5] 2522 5-9-4 **71**...................................... BenCurtis 13 69
(Alan Swinbank) *hld up in midfield: outpcd over 2f out: rallied fnl f: nvr able to chal* **8/1**[3]
0122 **6** *1* **Bunce (IRE)**[6] 2473 6-8-4 **64**...................................... JackGarritty[(7)] 2 59
(Linda Perratt) *hld up in midfield: effrt and rdn 2f out: no ex ins fnl f* **8/1**[3]
2-06 **7** *shd* **Dartrix**[8] 2421 5-8-13 **69**...................................... ConnorBeasley[(3)] 8 64
(Michael Dods) *towards rr: rdn and hdwy over 1f out: no imp fnl f* **12/1**
0-00 **8** *½* **Baron Run**[46] 1447 4-8-10 **70**............................ RobJFitzpatrick[(7)] 11 63
(K R Burke) *cl up: ev ch over 2f out to over 1f out: outpcd fnl f* **7/1**[2]
0-00 **9** *1 ¼* **One Kool Dude**[15] 2233 5-8-2 **55** oh2............................ PatrickMathers 14 44
(Micky Hammond) *bhd: drvn and outpcd 1/2-way: sme late hdwy: nvr on terms* **66/1**
-340 **10** *nk* **Jinky**[7] 2456 6-9-3 **70**...................................... JoeFanning 7 58
(Linda Perratt) *towards rr: sn pushed along: shortlived effrt 1/2-way: nvr rchd ldrs* **14/1**
003 **11** *1 ½* **Al Khan (IRE)**[43] 1497 5-9-2 **74**............................ JacobButterfield[(5)] 1 57
(Ollie Pears) *bhd: drvn along wl over 2f out: nvr able to chal* **12/1**
0-3 **12** *2 ½* **Jumbo Steps (IRE)**[31] 1760 7-9-4 **71**................................ GrahamLee 9 46
(Jim Goldie) *cl up tl rdn and wknd wl over 1f out* **9/1**
4-30 **13** *¾* **Salvatore Fury (IRE)**[2] 2606 4-9-0 **67**..............................(p) TomEaves 5 40
(Keith Dalgleish) *in tch: rdn and edgd lft wl over 1f out: sn wknd* **16/1**
0-20 **14** *hd* **Pastureyes**[18] 2167 4-8-3 **63**............................ MatthewHopkins[(7)] 10 35
(Scott Dixon) *led at decent gallop: rdn and hdd wl over 1f out: sn btn* **25/1**

1m 12.19s (-0.01) **Going Correction** +0.10s/f (Good) **14** Ran SP% **117.8**
Speed ratings (Par 103): **104,103,102,101,99 98,98,97,95,95 93,89,88,88**
CSF £45.91 CT £421.01 TOTE £11.30: £3.30, £2.00, £3.40; EX 71.60 Trifecta £743.20.
**Owner** Chris Spark & William Orr **Bred** Sean O'Sullivan **Trained** Newmill-On-Slitrig, Borders

**FOCUS**
A wide-open looking sprint handicap. The form looks straightforward.

## 2678 ORBISTON H'CAP (QUALIFIER FOR THE £15,000 BETFAIR SCOTTISH STAYERS SERIES FINAL) 1m 4f 17y
**4:50** (4:53) (Class 5) (0-70,70) 4-Y-O+ **£3,881** (£1,155; £577; £288) **Stalls** Low

Form RPR
2/02 **1** **Saved By The Bell (IRE)**[11] 2327 4-9-6 **69**.................. DanielTudhope 3 81+
(David O'Meara) *prom: shkn up and gd hdwy to ld over 1f out: qcknd clr fnl f: easily* **6/4**[1]
056- **2** *2 ½* **Northside Prince (IRE)**[160] 8353 8-9-4 **67**............................ BenCurtis 5 72
(Alan Swinbank) *hld up: rdn and hdwy over 1f out: chsd wnr wl ins fnl f: no imp* **9/2**[3]
30-1 **3** *1* **A Southside Boy (GER)**[31] 1763 6-9-3 **66**........................ GrahamLee 1 69
(Jim Goldie) *t.k.h: led at ordinary gallop: rdn and hdd over 1f out: kpt on same pce fnl f* **6/1**
-345 **4** *1 ½* **Pixie Cut (IRE)**[11] 2327 4-9-7 **70**............................ PaulMulrennan 7 71
(Alistair Whillans) *trckd ldr: rdn over 2f out: no ex over 1f out* **10/3**[2]
-036 **5** *2* **Isdaal**[16] 2199 7-8-7 **56**...................................... JoeFanning 6 54
(Kevin Morgan) *prom: effrt and rdn over 2f out: no imp over 1f out* **14/1**
600- **6** *10* **Spieta (IRE)**[229] 7169 4-8-11 **63**............................ IanBrennan[(3)] 2 45
(John Quinn) *t.k.h: cl up tl edgd rt and wknd wl over 1f out* **12/1**
600/ **7** *7* **Momkinzain (USA)**[20] 4097 7-9-7 **70**..............................(p) TomEaves 4 41
(Lucinda Russell) *hld up towards rr: struggling 3f out: btn fnl 2f* **66/1**

2m 38.97s (0.37) **Going Correction** 0.0s/f (Good) **7** Ran SP% **111.4**
Speed ratings (Par 103): **98,96,95,94,93 86,82**
CSF £8.09 TOTE £2.50: £1.50, £4.10; EX 13.30 Trifecta £57.20.
**Owner** J Blackburn & A Turton **Bred** Dowager Countess Harrington **Trained** Nawton, N Yorks

**FOCUS**
This modest handicap was run at a solid pace and the form should work out. The winner built on his Doncaster latest.

## 2679 BOOK NOW FOR THE SAINTS AND SINNERS H'CAP 1m 3f 16y
**5:25** (5:25) (Class 6) (0-65,64) 3-Y-O **£2,045** (£603; £302) **Stalls** Low

Form RPR
-103 **1** **Zanouska (USA)**[21] 2080 3-9-7 **64**...................................... JoeFanning 4 70
(Mark Johnston) *mde all at stdy gallop: hrd pressed over 2f out: asserted over 1f out: kpt on strly fnl f* **9/2**
-032 **2** *3 ¾* **Company Secretary (USA)**[29] 1852 3-9-2 **59**..............(b) GrahamLee 5 59
(Jo Hughes) *pressed ldr: hdwy to chal over 2f out to over 1f out: kpt on same pce ins fnl f* **3/1**[2]
3066 **3** *shd* **Zephyr**[2] 2616 3-8-12 **62**...................................... RobJFitzpatrick[(7)] 1 61
(K R Burke) *hld up in tch: outpcd and hung lft wl over 1f out: kpt on fnl f: nvr able to chal* **7/2**[3]
-066 **4** *hd* **Minionette (IRE)**[18] 2165 3-8-12 **55**................................ BenCurtis 3 54
(Alan Swinbank) *t.k.h: prom: drvn and outpcd over 2f out: kpt on ins fnl f* **11/8**[1]
00-0 **5** *shd* **Shamouti (IRE)**[18] 2165 3-8-4 **50**............................ IanBrennan[(3)] 2 49
(Ollie Pears) *trckd ldrs: rdn and edgd lft over 2f out: hung rt over 1f out: sn no ex* **33/1**

2m 28.38s (2.78) **Going Correction** 0.0s/f (Good) **5** Ran SP% **110.5**
Speed ratings (Par 97): **89,86,86,86,85**
CSF £18.05 TOTE £4.50: £2.00, £1.70; EX 4.90 Trifecta £16.70.

**Owner** Nabil Mourad **Bred** Rabbah Bloodstock Llc **Trained** Middleham Moor, N Yorks
■ Stewards' Enquiry : Ben Curtis two-day ban: used whip above permitted level (Jun 11-12)
**FOCUS**
A moderate 3yo handicap. The form is taken at face value.
T/Plt: £110.20 to a £1 stake. Pool: £70,429.26 - 466.28 winning units T/Qpdt: £52.70 to a £1 stake. Pool: £3,999.86 - 56.16 winning units RY

## 2458 KEMPTON (A.W) (R-H)
Wednesday, May 28

**OFFICIAL GOING: Standard**
Wind: Almost nil Weather: Overcast

### 2680 GOFFS LONDON SALE - KEMPTON-BREEZE/KENSINGTON-SALE 16.06.14 MAIDEN AUCTION STKS 6f (P)
**5:45** (5:45) (Class 5) 2-Y-O **£2,587** (£770; £384; £192) **Stalls** Low

Form RPR
00 1 **Areion (IRE)**[11] 2328 2-8-6 ....................(b[1]) LiamJones 1 59
(J S Moore) *chsd ldrs: rdn over 2f out: disp ld fnl f: jst prevailed* **50/1**
2 nse **Red Touch (USA)** 2-9-2 .................... SilvestreDeSousa 6 69+
(Alan McCabe) *hld up in 5th: rdn and rn green over 2f out: hdwy 1f out: r.o wl fnl f: nt quite able to get up* **11/4[2]**
36 3 hd **Basil The Great**[42] 1505 2-8-12 .................... RichardKingscote 5 64
(Tom Dascombe) *led tl over 2f out: led wl over 1f out tl disp ld fnl f: jst lost out in cl fin* **5/2[1]**
0 4 3 ½ **Lady Zodiac (IRE)**[8] 2436 2-8-10 .................... StevieDonohoe 4 52
(Tim Pitt) *chsd ldrs: rdn over 2f out: chal over 1f out tl no ex ins fnl f* **14/1**
5 1 ¼ **Ms Eboracum (IRE)** 2-8-6 .................... JimmyQuinn 2 44
(Edward Creighton) *s.s: hld up in 6th: rdn over 2f out: sme hdwy over 1f out: no imp* **33/1**
6 ½ **Vegas Rebel (IRE)** 2-9-2 .................... JamieSpencer 3 52
(Peter Chapple-Hyam) *dwlt: sn pushed along and rn green in rr: hung rt in st: n.d* **7/2[3]**
6 7 2 **Mister Arden (FR)**[13] 2276 2-9-0 .................... TomQueally 7 44
(Harry Dunlop) *chsd ldr: slt ld over 2f out tl wl over 1f out: n.m.r: sn wknd* **8/1**
8 6 **Mullionheir** 2-9-0 .................... SteveDrowne 8 26+
(John Best) *swvd lft s: a wl outpcd in last pl* **7/1**

1m 14.15s (1.05) **Going Correction** +0.075s/f (Slow) **8 Ran SP% 112.6**
Speed ratings (Par 93): **96,95,95,91,89 88,86,78**
CSF £179.21 TOTE £25.30: £5.10, £1.10, £1.60; EX 274.10 Trifecta £1659.60.
**Owner** The Bottom Liners & J S Moore **Bred** Tribes Man Syndicate **Trained** Upper Lambourn, Berks
■ Stewards' Enquiry : Richard Kingscote two-day ban: careless riding (June 11-12)
**FOCUS**
This didn't take a lot of winning but it produced an exciting finish. The winner was showing her first real form.

### 2681 IRISH NIGHT ON 09.07.14 MAIDEN STKS (DIV I) 7f (P)
**6:15** (6:18) (Class 5) 3-Y-0+ **£2,587** (£770; £384; £192) **Stalls** Low

Form RPR
6 1 **Role Player**[8] 2442 4-10-0 .................... TomQueally 4 84
(Michael Bell) *free to post: t.k.h: trckd ldrs: led ins fnl f: drvn out* **16/1**
6 2 nk **Doctor Sardonicus**[25] 1946 3-9-3 .................... JamieSpencer 1 79
(David Simcock) *t.k.h: led: hrd rdn and hdd ins fnl f: r.o* **14/1**
2- 3 nk **Oh Star (USA)**[247] 6690 3-8-12 .................... WilliamBuick 9 73
(John Gosden) *prom: drvn to chal 1f out: ev ch fnl f: r.o* **6/5[1]**
0 4 3 ¼ **Field Force**[25] 1946 3-9-3 ....................[1] JamesDoyle 5 70+
(Amanda Perrett) *hld up towards rr: rdn over 2f out: hung lft: gd late hdwy* **9/1**
0/ 5 1 ½ **Koala Bear**[630] 5943 4-9-9 .................... HayleyTurner 11 65+
(James Fanshawe) *in tch: rdn over 2f out: kpt on fnl furlong* **8/1[3]**
6 ¾ **Daisy's Secret** 3-8-12 .................... PatCosgrave 10 59+
(George Baker) *reluctant to enter stalls: plld hrd in midfield: rdn over 2f out: styd on fnl f* **66/1**
7 nk **Franco's Secret** 3-9-0 .................... CharlesBishop(3) 13 63+
(Peter Hedger) *dwlt: rn green towards rr: pushed along and styd on steadily fnl 2f: nvr nrr* **66/1**
00- 8 nk **Stapleford Lad**[160] 8342 3-9-3 .................... KierenFox 12 62
(Stuart Williams) *mid-div: effrt over 2f out: no imp over 1f out* **100/1**
5 9 2 ¼ **Miss Moppet**[31] 1768 3-8-12 .................... RichardHughes 14 51+
(Hughie Morrison) *t.k.h: trckd ldr tl hung rt and wknd 2f out* **20/1**
02 10 1 ¼ **Triple Chief (IRE)**[34] 1681 3-9-3 .................... FrederikTylicki 8 53
(Rod Millman) *towards rr: rdn and sme hdwy over 1f out: wknd fnl f* **7/2[2]**
0-0 11 ¾ **Venus Marina**[29] 1844 3-8-9 .................... AshleyMorgan(3) 6 46
(Chris Wall) *stdd s: plld hrd in last pl: shkn up over 2f out: nvr nr ldrs* **66/1**
6-5 12 1 ¼ **Inheritance**[31] 1767 3-8-12 .................... ShaneKelly 2 43
(Sir Michael Stoute) *chsd ldrs: rdn 2f out: wknd over 1f out* **10/1**
00 13 2 ¼ **Mumarasaat (USA)**[8] 2442 3-8-12 .................... LukeMorris 3 37
(Phil McEntee) *in tch tl wknd 2f out* **100/1**
0 14 2 ¾ **Femme De Menage**[24] 1980 3-8-12 .................... SteveDrowne 7 30
(Andrew Balding) *missed break and wnt rt s: a bhd: no ch fnl 2f* **66/1**

1m 26.35s (0.35) **Going Correction** +0.075s/f (Slow)
**WFA** 3 from 4yo 11lb **14 Ran SP% 123.1**
Speed ratings (Par 103): **101,100,100,96,94 94,93,93,90,89 88,87,84,81**
CSF £220.93 TOTE £23.00: £5.00, £3.70, £1.10; EX 396.30 Trifecta £2147.40 Part won..
**Owner** Sheikh Marwan Al Maktoum **Bred** Darley **Trained** Newmarket, Suffolk
**FOCUS**
A suspicion that many of these were types for the future as opposed to the now and that seemed to play out in the race itself as a trio drew well clear. The form is rated around the third.

### 2682 IRISH NIGHT ON 09.07.14 MAIDEN STKS (DIV II) 7f (P)
**6:45** (6:49) (Class 5) 3-Y-0+ **£2,587** (£770; £384; £192) **Stalls** Low

Form RPR
1 **Knavery (USA)** 3-9-3 .................... JamieSpencer 1 92
(Roger Varian) *chsd clr ldng pair: shkn up over 2f out: led over 1f out: rdn clr: comf* **6/1**
4- 2 3 ½ **Amber Isle (USA)**[337] 3664 3-8-12 .................... JamesDoyle 6 78
(Roger Charlton) *led at gd pce: rdn and hdd over 1f out: sn outpcd by wnr* **7/2[3]**
6 3 3 ¼ **Sejel (IRE)**[26] 1920 3-8-12 .................... DaneO'Neill 4 70
(John Gosden) *chsd ldr at gd pce: rdn over 2f out: btn over 1f out* **5/2[2]**
4 nk **Inflection (IRE)** 3-8-7 ....................(t) NoelGarbutt(5) 11 69+
(Hugo Palmer) *dwlt: towards rr on outer: hdwy over 2f out: chsd ldrs over 1f out: one pce* **50/1**
254- 5 1 ½ **Whaleweigh Station**[304] 4816 3-9-3 98.................... RichardKingscote 12 70
(Tom Dascombe) *off the pce in midfield: rdn and sme hdwy 2f out: no imp* **7/4[1]**
00 6 2 ¼ **Its Not Me Its You**[8] 2418 3-9-3 .................... JackMitchell 3 64?
(Brendan Powell) *mainly 5th tl outpcd 2f out: kpt on fnl f* **100/1**
0- 7 hd **Fiftyshadesdarker (IRE)**[152] 8415 3-9-3 ....................(t) PatCosgrave 2 64
(George Baker) *travelled wl on rail in midfield: sme hdwy 2f out: shkn up and fdd over 1f out* **20/1**
56 8 nk **Crafty Business (IRE)**[19] 2126 3-9-3 .................... AdamBeschizza 8 63
(Mark Hoad) *mod 6th tl rdn and btn over 2f out* **66/1**
3 9 ¾ **Chantecler**[23] 2031 3-9-3 .................... RichardHughes 5 61
(Hughie Morrison) *stdd s: t.k.h: sn chsng ldrs: wknd over 1f out* **12/1**
40 10 2 ¾ **Notgordonitsrodger (IRE)**[19] 2126 4-10-0 .................... LukeMorris 13 58
(Phil McEntee) *bhd: sltly hmpd over 2f out: nvr trbld ldrs* **100/1**
0- 11 ½ **Danglydontask**[263] 6184 3-9-3 ....................(b[1]) PaddyAspell 10 52
(David Arbuthnot) *bhd: rdn 3f out: nvr nr ldrs* **100/1**
00 12 ¾ **Jay Gee Speedfit (IRE)**[11] 2329 3-9-3 ....................(t) TomQueally 9 50
(George Margarson) *t.k.h in midfield on outer: hung rt and n.m.r over 2f out: n.d after* **66/1**
13 nk **Purple Spot** 3-8-12 ....................[1] FrederikTylicki 7 45
(Rod Millman) *a bhd* **66/1**
00 14 2 ½ **Distant Shadow**[11] 2339 3-8-12 .................... TedDurcan 14 38
(Chris Wall) *stdd s and swtchd to ins rail: a bhd* **100/1**

1m 25.85s (-0.15) **Going Correction** +0.075s/f (Slow)
**WFA** 3 from 4yo 11lb **14 Ran SP% 124.3**
Speed ratings (Par 103): **103,99,95,94,93 90,90,90,89,86 85,84,84,81**
CSF £27.65 TOTE £7.30: £4.20, £1.40, £2.20; EX 29.10 Trifecta £165.70.
**Owner** Qatar Racing Limited **Bred** W S Farish & Michael H Cline **Trained** Newmarket, Suffolk
**FOCUS**
This was stronger than the first division and the time was 0.5sec quicker. The first three were always prominent and the form is rated around the second and third.

### 2683 VISIT AND DINE IN THE PANORAMIC H'CAP 2m (P)
**7:15** (7:17) (Class 5) (0-70,70) 4-Y-0+ **£2,587** (£770; £384; £192) **Stalls** Low

Form RPR
2340 1 **Arashi**[49] 1374 8-9-1 61....................(v) TomQueally 7 70+
(Derek Shaw) *t.k.h in rr: smooth hdwy on outer 3f out: disp ld 2f out: led on bit over 1f out: rdn clr* **4/1[2]**
20-0 2 2 ¼ **Jezza**[47] 1418 8-9-5 65....................(bt) RichardHughes 5 71
(Karen George) *stdd s: hld up in rr: rapid hdwy on inner to dispute ld 2f out: outpcd by wnr over 1f out* **5/1[3]**
030- 3 1 **Money Talks**[17] 4634 4-9-3 65 .................... FergusSweeney 8 70
(Michael Madgwick) *in tch: rdn to chse ldrs over 1f out: styd on same pce* **14/1**
4-52 4 ¾ **Montjess (IRE)**[72] 992 4-9-8 70....................(p) LiamJones 6 74
(Laura Mongan) *chsd ldrs: pushed along 6f out: rdn and one pce fnl 2f* **7/2[1]**
0110 5 4 ½ **Newtown Cross (IRE)**[26] 1915 4-8-4 59.................... CamHardie(7) 1 58
(Jimmy Fox) *prom tl hrd rdn and wknd 2f out* **7/2[1]**
/0-0 6 7 **Bouggatti**[12] 2305 6-9-8 68.................... PatCosgrave 2 58
(Lady Herries) *in tch: pushed along 6f out: wknd over 2f out* **14/1**
0/06 7 7 **Moon Trip**[23] 2011 5-9-9 69.................... SilvestreDeSousa 3 51
(Geoffrey Deacon) *sn led: set modest pce: rdn and wknd 2f out* **8/1**
2600 8 2 ¾ **Bramshill Lass**[25] 1941 5-9-9 69....................(b) JimCrowley 9 47
(Amanda Perrett) *pressed ldr tl wknd 2f out* **8/1**

3m 31.55s (1.45) **Going Correction** +0.075s/f (Slow)
**WFA** 4 from 5yo+ 2lb **8 Ran SP% 116.7**
Speed ratings (Par 103): **99,97,97,97,94 91,87,86**
CSF £24.85 CT £255.43 TOTE £4.60: £1.50, £1.50, £4.60; EX 25.10 Trifecta £315.20.
**Owner** Philip Derbyshire **Bred** Wyck Hall Stud Ltd **Trained** Sproxton, Leics
**FOCUS**
They went very steadily in this staying handicap. The winner is rated back to his best.

### 2684 BETDAQ £25 NO LOSE FREE BET H'CAP 7f (P)
**7:45** (7:46) (Class 4) (0-80,79) 4-Y-0+ **£4,690** (£1,395; £697; £348) **Stalls** Low

Form RPR
5-44 1 **Accession (IRE)**[30] 1796 5-9-7 79.................... MartinLane 8 88
(Charlie Fellowes) *trckd ldr: drvn to ld ins fnl f: hld on wl* **16/1**
/322 2 ½ **Rome**[21] 2079 4-9-4 76.................... GeorgeBaker 7 83
(Gary Moore) *led: rdn wl over 1f out: hdd ins fnl f: kpt on* **5/2[2]**
1100 3 1 ¼ **Multitask**[8] 2414 4-9-3 75.................... WilliamBuick 3 79
(Michael Madgwick) *prom: rdn over 1f out: one pce* **9/1**
0-65 4 ¾ **Good Authority (IRE)**[18] 2156 7-9-2 74.................... RichardHughes 1 76+
(Karen George) *dwlt: hld up in rr: shkn up and hdwy over 1f out: fin wl* **15/8[1]**
3536 5 shd **Gracious George (IRE)**[23] 2012 4-9-0 72....................(p) JimCrowley 2 74
(Jimmy Fox) *in tch: effrt and rdn over 1f out: styd on same pce* **11/2**
/5-1 6 nse **Mac's Superstar (FR)**[22] 2059 4-9-5 77.................... ShaneKelly 4 79
(James Fanshawe) *stdd s: hld up towards rr: effrt on inner 2f out: no imp* **4/1[3]**
4043 7 hd **New Leyf (IRE)**[9] 2401 8-8-13 71....................(b) SteveDrowne 5 72
(Jeremy Gask) *plld hrd in 5th: cajoled along and no hdwy fnl 2f* **20/1**
00-1 8 1 **Another Try (IRE)**[19] 2124 9-8-13 71.................... LukeMorris 6 69
(K R Burke) *chsd ldrs: rdn over 2f out: wknd over 1f out* **16/1**
0- 9 3 **Dougal Philps**[147] 1168 5-9-6 78.................... DaneO'Neill 10 68
(Jeremy Gask) *stdd s: plld hrd in rr: rdn over 2f out: sn outpcd* **25/1**

1m 26.16s (0.16) **Going Correction** +0.075s/f (Slow) **9 Ran SP% 129.1**
Speed ratings (Par 105): **102,101,100,99,99 98,98,97,94**
CSF £62.81 CT £416.84 TOTE £17.60: £4.50, £2.00, £3.10; EX 86.90 Trifecta £2288.70 Part won..
**Owner** Lady De Ramsey **Bred** Corduff Stud Ltd **Trained** Newmarket, Suffolk
**FOCUS**
This tactically run handicap was dominated by the two pacesetters. It's hard to be too positive given the lack of pace.

### 2685 BETDAQ SUPPORTING THE INJURED JOCKEYS FUND H'CAP (MIDDLE DISTANCE SERIES QUALIFIER) (BOBIS RACE) 1m 3f (P)
**8:15** (8:17) (Class 4) (0-80,80) 3-Y-O **£4,690** (£1,395; £697; £348) **Stalls** Low

Form RPR
0-11 1 **Arab Dawn**[12] 2303 3-9-7 80.................... RichardHughes 10 90
(Hughie Morrison) *trckd ldrs: led on bit 2f out: shkn up over 1f out: pushed out: a holding runner-up* **9/4[1]**
-012 2 ¾ **Good Value**[23] 2009 3-9-5 78.................... JamesDoyle 5 86
(Sir Michael Stoute) *in tch: drvn to press wnr 1f out: kpt on: a hld* **9/4[1]**

114- 3 nse **Anglophile**217 7471 3-9-7 **80**........ MartinLane 3 88
(Charlie Appleby) *dwlt: hld up towards rr: hrd rdn over 2f out: hdwy over 1f out: r.o* **14/1**

42-3 4 3 **Grand Meister**16 2221 3-9-3 **76**........ TomQueally 2 79
(Michael Bell) *hld up in 6th: hdwy and hrd rdn 2f out: no ex fnl f* **7/1**3

21-0 5 1 1/4 **Likelihood (USA)**12 2299 3-9-7 **80**........ RobertHavlin 8 81
(John Gosden) *led: hung lft and rn sltly wd into bk st: hdd 2f out: wknd 1f out* **25/1**

413- 6 2 **Tucson Arizona**153 8397 3-9-3 **76**........ WilliamCarson 7 73
(Anthony Carson) *towards rr: rdn and hdwy wl over 1f out: sn wknd* **33/1**

26-2 7 3/4 **Ultimate Act**49 1401 3-8-12 **71**........ JamieSpencer 9 67+
(Seamus Mullins) *stdd s and t.k.h: bhd: rdn 4f out: nvr rchd ldrs* **6/1**2

316 8 4 1/2 **Full Moon Fever (IRE)**21 2072 3-9-2 **75**........ NickyMackay 1 63
(Ed Walker) *chsd ldrs tl wknd wl over 1f out* **12/1**

0-32 9 17 **Classic Devotion (USA)**30 1797 3-9-7 **80**........ WilliamBuick 6 37
(Charlie Appleby) *trckd ldr tl lost action and wknd qckly 2f out: bhd whn virtually p.u fnl f* **8/1**

-125 10 12 **Filament Of Gold (USA)**28 1883 3-9-3 **76**........ SilvestreDeSousa 4 12
(Mark Johnston) *towards rr: n.m.r and rdn 7f out: swtchd outside: wknd 3f out: sn wl bhd* **25/1**

2m 18.94s (-2.96) **Going Correction** +0.075s/f (Slow) **10** Ran SP% **124.4**
Speed ratings (Par 101): **113,112,112,110,109 107,107,104,91,82**
CSF £7.13 CT £60.27 TOTE £4.50: £1.70, £1.30, £3.40; EX 9.80 Trifecta £112.70.
**Owner** Eason,Kerr-Dineen,Hughes,Edwards-Jones **Bred** Fittocks Stud **Trained** East Ilsley, Berks

**FOCUS**
A stop/start messy affair, but hard to fault the performance of the winner. The form makes a fair bit of sense.

## 2686 BETDAQ - THE SPORTS BETTING EXCHANGE H'CAP 6f (P)
**8:45** (8:46) (Class 5) (0-70,70) 3-Y-O **£2,587** (£770; £384; £192) **Stalls** Low

Form RPR

-161 1 **Moonspring (IRE)**16 2208 3-9-3 **66**........(e) AndreaAtzeni 2 75
(Robert Cowell) *chsd ldr: led over 1f out: rdn clr and r.o wl fnl f: readily* **7/4**1

-252 2 3 **Serata Di Gala (FR)**5 2525 3-9-3 **70**........ MarcMonaghan(5) 1 69
(Marco Botti) *led tl over 1f out: unable qck* **5/2**2

4-62 3 2 1/4 **Baars Causeway (IRE)**22 2049 3-9-6 **69**........ LukeMorris 4 61
(K R Burke) *chsd ldrs: rdn over 2f out: one pce* **5/1**3

565- 4 nk **Pelagian (USA)**244 6776 3-8-0 **56** oh1........ CamHardie(7) 6 47
(Michael Attwater) *dwlt: t.k.h in 5th: outpcd and struggling 2f out: styd on fnl f* **33/1**

40-0 5 nk **He's My Boy (IRE)**11 2329 3-9-4 **67**........ FrederikTylicki 3 57
(James Fanshawe) *cl up in 3rd: rdn to chal 2f out: wknd 1f out* **8/1**

4553 6 1 3/4 **Artemis (IRE)**55 1264 3-8-11 **60**........ MartinDwyer 5 44
(Conrad Allen) *stdd s: plld hrd in rr: effrt over 2f out: btn over 1f out* **12/1**

1m 12.8s (-0.30) **Going Correction** +0.075s/f (Slow) **6** Ran SP% **103.3**
Speed ratings (Par 99): **105,101,98,97,97 94**
CSF £5.22 TOTE £2.00: £1.70, £1.20; EX 4.00 Trifecta £13.40.
**Owner** P Foster & Friends **Bred** R N Auld **Trained** Six Mile Bottom, Cambs
■ Hipz was withdrawn. Price at time of withdrawal 12-1. Rule 4 applies to all bets - deduction 5p in the pound.

**FOCUS**
A fair race for the grade and a fluent success from the improving winner. The runner-up helps set the standard.

## 2687 BETDAQ NO PREMIUM CHARGE H'CAP (LONDON MILE SERIES QUALIFIER) 1m (P)
**9:15** (9:15) (Class 5) (0-75,75) 4-Y-O+ **£2,587** (£770; £384; £192) **Stalls** Low

Form RPR

0-66 1 **Barnmore**21 2079 6-8-9 **66**........ CharlesBishop(3) 4 75
(Peter Hedger) *t.k.h in midfield on rail: hdwy 2f out: led over 1f out: rdn out* **25/1**

430- 2 2 **Rouge Nuage (IRE)**321 4214 4-9-4 **72**........ MartinDwyer 1 76
(Conrad Allen) *led: rdn and hdd over 1f out: unable qck* **7/1**3

6-54 3 shd **St Paul De Vence (IRE)**13 2270 4-9-4 **72**........(b1) LukeMorris 6 76
(Paul Cole) *chsd ldr: hrd rdn and outpcd 2f out: rallied and r.o fnl f* **11/8**1

-156 4 1/2 **Wilfred Pickles (IRE)**61 1142 8-9-3 **71**........(p) DaneO'Neill 10 74
(Jo Crowley) *in tch: rdn 2f out: styd on fnl f* **25/1**

0-05 5 nk **Fossa**12 2312 4-9-5 **73**........ JimCrowley 3 75
(Dean Ivory) *t.k.h: prom: rdn over 2f out: one pce* **16/1**

44-5 6 nk **Top Set (IRE)**30 1810 4-9-0 **73**........(b1) MarcMonaghan(5) 9 74
(Marco Botti) *chsd ldrs: rdn over 2f out: one pce* **5/1**2

1003 7 1/2 **Whitby Jet (IRE)**34 1665 6-9-5 **73**........ WilliamCarson 5 73
(Ed Vaughan) *towards rr: rdn 2f out: nvr able to chal* **14/1**

2-04 8 1 1/4 **Aomen Rock**30 1799 4-9-0 **68**........1 HayleyTurner 7 65
(James Fanshawe) *in tch tl outpcd fnl 2f* **5/1**2

2306 9 hd **Daring Dragon**32 1739 4-9-3 **71**........(b) GeorgeBaker 2 68
(Ed Walker) *s.s: t.k.h in rr: hdwy 2f out: wknd fnl f* **16/1**

00-4 10 27 **Hilali (IRE)**139 101 5-9-7 **75**........ TedDurcan 8
(Gary Brown) *a towards rr: wl bhd fnl 3f* **33/1**

1m 40.55s (0.75) **Going Correction** +0.075s/f (Slow) **10** Ran SP% **117.0**
Speed ratings (Par 103): **99,97,96,96,96 95,95,94,93,66**
CSF £188.02 CT £423.24 TOTE £22.70: £6.20, £1.80, £1.50; EX 182.70 Trifecta £853.80.
**Owner** P C F Racing Ltd **Bred** J J Whelan **Trained** Dogmersfield, Hampshire

**FOCUS**
An unsatisfactory slow pace and that provoked another upset on the card. The runner-up helps set the standard.
T/Jkpt: Not won. T/Plt: £51.90 to a £1 stake. Pool: £99,037.47 - 1,390.98 winning units T/Qpdt: £21.70 to a £1 stake. Pool: £13,026.12 - 442.30 winning units LM

# 2413 BATH (L-H)
## Thursday, May 29

**OFFICIAL GOING: Good to soft (soft in places; 6.4)**
Wind: light, half behind Weather: bright spells and heavy showers Rails: Races incorporating bottom bend increased in distance by about 10yds

## 2688 32REDPOKER.COM H'CAP (DIV I) 1m 5y
**2:00** (2:00) (Class 6) (0-65,64) 3-Y-O **£1,940** (£577; £288; £144) **Stalls** Low

Form RPR

2325 1 **Khee Society**30 1847 3-9-5 **62**........1 GeorgeBaker 8 68
(David Evans) *stdd s: hld up in last: prog over 1f out: rdn and chsd ldrs 1f out: led fnl 50yds: styd on* **5/2**1

0-55 2 1 1/4 **Mister Mayday (IRE)**32 1765 3-9-4 **61**........(v1) PatCosgrave 9 64
(George Baker) *taken down early: restless in stalls: towards rr: hdwy over 2f out: rdn to chal over 1f out: led ins fnl f: hdd and outpcd fnl 50yds* **17/2**

3643 3 nk **Indira**64 1098 3-9-1 **61**........ OisinMurphy(3) 5 63
(John Berry) *wl in tch in midfield: lost pl and rdn 3f out: swtchd rt 2f out: rallied u.p 1f out: styd on* **5/1**3

5-03 4 3/4 **Sweet Cherry (IRE)**30 1854 3-8-7 **50**........ RobertHavlin 11 51
(Peter Makin) *in tch in midfield: rdn and effrt to chal 2f out: drvn to ld over 1f out: hdd ins fnl f: no ex* **25/1**

0-56 5 1/2 **Mustadrik (USA)**11 2363 3-9-7 **64**........ DaneO'Neill 12 63
(J W Hills) *chsd ldrs: effrt u.p but unable qck 2f out: styd on same pce ins fnl f* **4/1**2

00-0 6 2 1/4 **Borough Belle**32 1767 3-8-7 **55**........ AmyScott(5) 6 49
(Henry Candy) *sn led: hdd after 2f: chsd ldr tl rdn to ld again over 2f out: hdd over 1f out: wknd ins fnl f* **20/1**

4260 7 2 1/4 **Sparkling Ice (IRE)**26 1947 3-9-7 **64**........ ShaneKelly 13 53
(Eve Johnson Houghton) *stdd and dropped in bhd after s: hld up in last pair: rdn over 2f out: no imp tl styd on ins fnl f: nvr trbld ldrs* **14/1**

0-50 8 nk **Movie Magic**22 2078 3-8-7 **50** oh5........ WilliamCarson 10 38
(John Bridger) *t.k.h: chsd ldrs: rdn ent fnl 2f: unable qck: wknd fnl f* **50/1**

4066 9 1 1/2 **Autopilot**24 2013 3-9-2 **59**........(b) HarryBentley 7 44
(Anabel K Murphy) *stdd bk sn after s: hld up towards rr: rdn and effrt on outer over 2f out: no real imp: no threat to ldrs fnl f* **12/1**

050- 10 3/4 **Excedo Praecedo**195 7893 3-9-3 **60**........1 JimCrowley 1 43
(Amanda Perrett) *t.k.h: sn chsng ldr: led 6f out tl rdn and hdd over 2f out: wknd jst over 1f out* **14/1**

000 11 18 **Scariff Hornet (IRE)**23 2061 3-9-6 **63**........ RichardHughes 4 5
(Sylvester Kirk) *broke wl and led early: stdd but t.k.h and hld up in tch: rdn and btn ent fnl 2f: wl bhd and eased ins fnl f* **14/1**

-560 12 4 **Confiture**49 1403 3-8-12 **55**........ DavidProbert 2
(Michael Blanshard) *in tch in midfield: rdn and struggling over 2f out: sn wknd: wl bhd and eased ins fnl f* **20/1**

1m 45.37s (4.57) **Going Correction** +0.475s/f (Yiel) **12** Ran SP% **118.0**
Speed ratings (Par 97): **96,94,94,93,93 90,88,88,86,86 68,64**
CSF £22.91 CT £101.07 TOTE £3.20: £1.10, £2.50, £2.30; EX 24.20 Trifecta £101.60.
**Owner** Wayne Clifford **Bred** Mrs S Clifford **Trained** Pandy, Monmouths

**FOCUS**
Races incorporating bottom bend increased in distance by about 10yds. After 3mm of rain overnight, the ground had eased to good to soft, soft in places. A moderate handicap and testing conditions. The winner is rated back to his early best.

## 2689 AVON VALLEY CLEANING H'CAP 1m 5y
**2:30** (2:31) (Class 6) (0-60,60) 4-Y-O+ **£1,940** (£577; £288; £144) **Stalls** Low

Form RPR

1236 1 **Zed Candy Girl**71 1015 4-8-8 **47** oh1 ow1........(p) SamHitchcott 5 58
(Dai Burchell) *wl in tch in midfield: rdn and effrt ent fnl 2f: drvn to ld 1f out: r.o wl u.p and forged ahd fnl 100yds* **22/1**

2125 2 1 **Benandonner (USA)**27 1917 11-8-12 **51**........ ShaneKelly 12 60
(Mike Murphy) *hld up in tch in midfield: rdn and effrt 2f out: ev ch 1f out: r.o but outpcd by wnr fnl 100yds* **15/2**3

0633 3 3 **Last Minute Lisa (IRE)**19 2164 4-8-11 **50**........ RichardHughes 13 52
(Sylvester Kirk) *hld up in tch in midfield: hdwy on inner over 2f out: rdn and fnd nil over 1f out: drvn ins fnl f: kpt on to go 3rd towards fin* **3/1**1

5506 4 1/2 **Nifty Kier**35 1666 5-8-7 **49**........ OisinMurphy(3) 10 50
(Phil McEntee) *stdd s: hld up in tch towards rr: rdn and hdwy wl over 1f out: drvn and no ex 1f out: outpcd fnl f* **20/1**

-244 5 hd **Carrera**27 1917 4-9-2 **55**........ JimCrowley 3 55
(Michael Blanshard) *wl in tch in midfield: hdd to ld over 2f out: drvn and hdd 1f out: wknd and lost 2 pls wl ins fnl f* **8/1**

4-06 6 1 **Ashkalara**27 1910 7-8-13 **52**........ HarryBentley 15 50
(Stuart Howe) *hld up in tch towards rr: rdn and hdwy ent fnl 2f: drvn and no imp 1f out: wknd ins fnl f* **20/1**

-045 7 nk **Silvee**7 2486 7-8-7 **46** oh1........ WilliamCarson 9 44
(John Bridger) *in tch in midfield: lost pl and in rr of main gp whn rdn 4f out: swtchd rt over 2f out: n.d but styd on ins fnl f* **7/1**2

30 8 2 3/4 **Delightful Sleep**73 998 6-9-1 **57**........ DeclanBates(3) 16 48
(David Evans) *in tch in midfield: clsd on outer and travelling wl over 2f out: rdn over 1f out: sn btn: wknd ins fnl f* **12/1**

214- 9 4 1/2 **Squirrel Wood (IRE)**162 8329 6-9-4 **57**........ GeorgeBaker 7 38
(Mary Hambro) *hld up wl in tch in midfield: switching lft but nt clrest of runs 2f out: sn btn: wknd over 1f out* **10/1**

4563 10 shd **Devote Myself (IRE)**31 1819 5-8-9 **48**........(bt) DavidProbert 4 29
(John Flint) *chsd ldr tl 5f out: drvn and unable qck over 2f out: wknd over 1f out* **8/1**

-004 11 1/2 **Habeshia**10 2399 4-9-0 **53**........(v) RobertHavlin 14 32
(John Best) *wl in tch in midfield: rdn and unable qck over 2f out: wknd over 1f out* **10/1**

00-4 12 15 **Princess Cammie (IRE)**23 2045 4-8-0 **46** oh1........(p) CamHardie(7) 2
(John Bridger) *stdd s: t.k.h: sn dashed up to chse ldrs: sddle slipped and led whn edgd rt bnd 5f out: rdn and hdd over 2f out: sn wknd: bhd 1f out* **25/1**

500- 13 31 **Bridge Builder**336 3731 4-9-4 **60**........(b1) CharlesBishop(3) 8
(Peter Hedger) *stdd s: hld up in rr: detached and rdn over 4f out: no rspnse and sn lost tch: t.o and virtually p.u ins fnl f* **16/1**

0000 14 1/2 **Tingle Tangle (USA)**90 783 4-8-7 **46** oh1........ JimmyQuinn 1
(Tony Carroll) *t.k.h: led tl hdd and pushed rt bnd 5f out: chsd ldr tl wknd qckly over 2f out: t.o and virtually p.u ins fnl f* **33/1**

1m 44.32s (3.52) **Going Correction** +0.475s/f (Yiel) **14** Ran SP% **123.9**
Speed ratings (Par 101): **101,100,97,96,96 95,95,92,87,87 87,72,41,40**
CSF £173.41 CT £670.45 TOTE £27.90: £5.60, £2.40, £1.80; EX 139.90 Trifecta £1156.80.
**Owner** Robert Emmanuel **Bred** H H L Bloodstock **Trained** Briery Hill, Blaenau Gwent

**FOCUS**
Another moderate handicap, this time for older horses. The winner stepped up on her AW form.

## 2690 32RED £10 BONUS MAIDEN STKS 1m 5y
**3:00** (3:02) (Class 5) 3-Y-O+ **£2,587** (£770; £384; £192) **Stalls** Low

Form RPR

1 **Agent Murphy** 3-9-2 0........ MartinLane 12 86+
(Brian Meehan) *in tch in midfield on outer: rdn over 2f out: hdwy to chse ldrs 1f out: edgd lft but sn chalng: styd on wl to ld towards fin* **33/1**

2 2 hd **Principle Equation (IRE)**31 1808 3-8-11 0........ JimCrowley 10 81
(Ralph Beckett) *chsd ldrs: rdn to chse ldr 2f out: drvn and ev ch ent fnl f: led fnl 100yds: kpt on tl hdd and no ex towards fin* **11/10**1

3 1 3/4 **New Identity (IRE)** 3-9-2 0........ PatCosgrave 4 82
(Denis Coakley) *in tch in midfield: rdn and effrt ent fnl 2f: swtchd rt 1f out: kpt on ins fnl f: snatched 3rd last strides* **33/1**

522 **4** *nk* **Late Night Mark (IRE)**[52] 1353 3-9-2 80 ......................... GeorgeBaker 3 81
(Charles Hills) *led: rdn ent fnl 2f: drvn and hrd pressed 1f out: hdd fnl f: styd on same pce after* **5/1**[3]

-024 **5** *1 ½* **Bon Voyage**[12] 2339 3-9-2 84 ......................... RichardHughes 11 78
(Richard Hannon) *hld up in tch towards rr: hdwy over 3f out: drvn and effrt to chse ldrs over 1f out: no imp and one pce ins fnl f* **5/2**[2]

0 **6** *¾* **High Drama (IRE)**[27] 1920 3-8-11 0 ......................... DavidProbert 6 71
(Andrew Balding) *wl in tch: rdn 2f out: shifting rt and unable qck ent fnl f: styd on same pce fnl f* **16/1**

06 **7** *7* **Ophir**[17] 2221 3-9-2 0 ......................... MartinDwyer 8 60
(William Muir) *t.k.h: chsd ldr tl 2f out: drvn and btn over 1f out: wknd fnl f* **33/1**

0 **8** *½* **Triple Star**[27] 1920 3-8-11 0 ......................... RobertHavlin 2 54
(Hughie Morrison) *chsd ldrs: rdn jst over 2f out: outpcd and btn over 1f out: wknd fnl f* **33/1**

**9** *hd* **Vilaz** 3-9-2 0 ......................... DaneO'Neill 14 58
(Brian Meehan) *s.i.s: in tch in last pair: rdn ent fnl 2f: no imp and sn btn: plugged on fnl f* **28/1**

**10** *hd* **Soundtrack (IRE)** 3-8-13 0 ......................... OisinMurphy(3) 7 58
(William Knight) *s.i.s: hld up in tch in last pair: rdn over 2f out: no prog and wl hld over 1f out* **25/1**

0 **11** *6* **Tarap (IRE)**[23] 2061 3-8-11 0 ......................... KieranO'Neill 9 39
(Richard Hannon) *in tch in midfield: rdn 3f out: sn struggling and lost pl: bhd fnl f* **66/1**

00 **12** *12* **Beauchamp Melba**[14] 2280 3-8-11 0 .........................(b[1]) WilliamCarson 1 11
(Paul Fitzsimons) *in tch in midfield: rdn and lost pl 1/2-way: t.o over 1f out* **100/1**

60 **13** *6* **Byrae**[7] 2489 4-9-9 0 ......................... SamHitchcott 5
(Polly Gundry) *t.k.h: in tch in midfield: rdn and lost pl 3f out: t.o fnl f* **100/1**

1m 45.04s (4.24) **Going Correction** +0.475s/f (Yiel)
**WFA** 3 from 4yo 12lb **13** Ran SP% **121.3**
Speed ratings (Par 103): **97,96,95,94,93 92,85,85,84,84 78,66,60**
CSF £68.71 TOTE £31.10: £6.00, £1.10, £11.80; EX 98.00 Trifecta £723.90.
**Owner** W A Harrison-Allan **Bred** Wellsummers Stud **Trained** Manton, Wilts

**FOCUS**
There was heavy rain before this maiden. They bet 16-1 bar three which shows how uncompetitive the race was, but it produced a shock result. The time was modest but the principals showed fair form.

## 2691 32RED.COM H'CAP 5f 161y
**3:30** (3:38) (Class 5) (0-75,79) 4-Y-0+ **£2,587** (£770; £384; £192) **Stalls** Centre

Form RPR

6611 **1** **Ladweb**[9] 2434 4-9-6 79 6ex ......................... JoeyHaynes(5) 2 93
(John Gallagher) *chsd ldr tl led jst over 2f out: edgd rt but rdn clr over 1f out: in command and styd on wl fnl f* **6/1**[3]

0032 **2** *2 ½* **New Decade**[7] 2488 5-8-10 67 .........................(t) OisinMurphy(3) 6 73
(Milton Bradley) *chsd ldrs: rdn to chse clr wnr wl over 1f out: no imp but kpt on for clr 2nd* **10/3**[2]

5642 **3** *1 ½* **Jay Bee Blue**[9] 2414 5-9-4 72 .........................(bt) DaneO'Neill 5 73+
(Sean Curran) *s.i.s: clsd and in tch in rr 4f out: hdwy between horses over 1f out: wnt 3rd jst ins fnl f: kpt on: nvr trbld ldrs* **11/4**[1]

0000 **4** *2* **Bainne (IRE)**[31] 1789 4-9-7 75 ......................... SteveDrowne 4 69
(Jeremy Gask) *chsd ldrs: rdn over 2f out: outpcd and btn over 1f out: plugged on same pce again ins fnl f* **14/1**

1100 **5** *1 ¼* **Presumido (IRE)**[12] 2341 4-9-4 72 ......................... RichardHughes 12 62
(Simon Dow) *stdd s: hld up in tch towards rr: swtchd rt and effrt over 1f out: kpt on same pce fnl f* **10/1**

1220 **6** *1 ¼* **Top Cop**[9] 2414 5-9-1 74 .........................(p) DCByrne(5) 7 60
(Ronald Harris) *in tch in midfield: rdn over 2f out: sn struggling and outpcd wl over 1f out: wl hld fnl f* **10/1**

3150 **7** *¾* **New Rich**[58] 1221 4-8-8 62 .........................(p) ShaneKelly 10 46
(Eve Johnson Houghton) *hld up in tch towards rr: rdn: nt clr run and looking to switch rt 2f out: wl hld whn swtchd lft and hmpd jst ins fnl f: nvr trbld ldrs* **20/1**

6426 **8** *hd* **Solemn**[15] 2250 9-8-13 67 .........................(v) DavidProbert 3 50
(Milton Bradley) *led tl jst over 2f out: sn drvn: 3rd and outpcd over 1f out: wknd ins fnl f* **9/1**

0150 **9** *1 ¾* **Time Medicean**[35] 1678 8-9-2 70 ......................... WilliamCarson 11 47
(Tony Carroll) *in tch in midfield on outer: rdn ent fnl 2f: no hdwy and sn struggling: wknd over 1f out* **28/1**

20-0 **10** *19* **Saga Lout**[77] 938 4-8-9 63 .........................(p) JimmyQuinn 1
(Ray Peacock) *t.k.h: hld up towards rr: rdn and no rspnse over 2f out: lost tch over 1f out: t.o and eased ins fnl f* **66/1**

1m 15.5s (4.30) **Going Correction** +0.65s/f (Yiel) **10** Ran SP% **108.6**
Speed ratings (Par 103): **97,93,91,89,87 85,84,84,82,56**
CSF £22.85 CT £57.48 TOTE £7.00: £2.10, £1.80, £1.40; EX 23.90 Trifecta £45.00.
**Owner** The Juniper Racing Club & Andrew Bell **Bred** Adweb Ltd **Trained** Chastleton, Oxon
■ Rule 4 of 5p in the pound applies to all bets; Withdrawn: Lager Time

**FOCUS**
An ordinary sprint handicap in which the pace held up on worsening ground. The winner improved again.

## 2692 32RED MAIDEN AUCTION STKS 5f 11y
**4:00** (4:04) (Class 5) 2-Y-0 **£2,587** (£770; £384; £192) **Stalls** Centre

Form RPR

033 **1** **Union Rose**[17] 2200 2-9-5 0 ......................... LiamJones 1 88+
(Ronald Harris) *nt best away but sn pushed up to ld: mde rest: rdn clr ent fnl 2f: wl clr 1f out: rdn out* **9/4**[2]

6 **2** *7* **Jimmy's Girl (IRE)**[10] 2402 2-9-0 0 ......................... SeanLevey 6 58
(Richard Hannon) *chsd wnr rdn and outpcd ent fnl 2f: no ch w wnr but plugged on to hold 2nd fnl f* **4/1**[3]

**3** *1* **Maesmor Magic (IRE)** 2-9-0 0 ......................... DavidProbert 3 54
(Martyn Meade) *racd in midfield: rdn 1/2-way: no ch w wnr fnl 2f: plugged on to go 3rd ins fnl f* **16/1**

**4** *¾* **Indaria** 2-8-11 0 ......................... OisinMurphy(3) 5 52
(Rod Millman) *dwlt: rn green in midfield: chsd ldng pair over 3f out: rdn and outpcd over 2f out: no ch w wnr and one pce fnl 2f* **14/1**

62 **5** *7* **River Spirit**[17] 2206 2-9-0 0 ......................... SamHitchcott 9 26
(Mick Channon) *hld up in midfield: rdn and outpcd 3f out: sn struggling: no ch fnl 2f: wl bhd fnl f* **7/1**

**6** *8* **Emilys Girl (IRE)** 2-8-9 0 ......................... DCByrne(5) 7
(Ronald Harris) *slowly to stride: rn green and immediately outpcd in last: t.o* **33/1**

**7** *¾* **Star Pursuits** 2-9-0 0 ......................... PatCosgrave 4
(Noel Quinlan) *dwlt: sn rcvrd to r in midfield: rdn and struggling 3f out: sn btn: wl bhd 1f out: eased ins fnl f* **7/4**[1]

1m 5.44s (2.94) **Going Correction** +0.65s/f (Yiel) **7** Ran SP% **115.1**
Speed ratings (Par 93): **102,90,89,88,76 64,62**
CSF £11.94 TOTE £3.10: £2.60, £1.90; EX 11.50 Trifecta £90.00.
**Owner** Adrian Evans **Bred** Home Farm **Trained** Earlswood, Monmouths

**FOCUS**
One colt against six fillies in this modest maiden auction, in which previous experience proved key. The order didn't change that much during the contest. Improved form from the winner, but no depth to the race.

## 2693 32RED ON THE APP STORE H'CAP 1m 3f 144y
**4:30** (4:32) (Class 5) (0-70,70) 4-Y-0+ **£2,587** (£770; £384; £192) **Stalls** Low

Form RPR

4623 **1** **Ivor's Princess**[31] 1791 5-9-1 64 .........................(b) SeanLevey 5 74+
(Rod Millman) *in tch in midfield: rdn and hdwy to ld over 2f out: clr and idling ins fnl f: a holding on* **7/1**

045- **2** *½* **Shades Of Grey**[215] 7539 7-8-11 65 ......................... RyanTate(5) 6 72
(Clive Cox) *in tch in last pair: rdn and effrt to chse ldrs 3f out: chsd clr wnr 2f out: no real imp tl clsd on idling wnr fnl 100yds: nvr getting to wnr* **2/1**[1]

15-6 **3** *4* **Eton Rambler (USA)**[27] 1909 4-9-7 70 .........................(p) PatCosgrave 3 71
(George Baker) *in tch in midfield: rdn 4f out: hdwy to chse ldng pair 2f out: styd on same pce fr over 1f out: eased towards fin* **4/1**[2]

00-0 **4** *16* **April Ciel**[15] 2248 5-9-1 64 .........................(p) LiamJones 1 39
(Ronald Harris) *t.k.h: led tl rdn and hdd over 2f out: sn outpcd and btn: 4th and fdd fnl f* **9/2**[3]

3331 **5** *7* **Lily Edge**[22] 2084 5-8-7 56 .........................(v) WilliamCarson 4 20
(John Bridger) *chsd ldng pair: wnt 2nd 6f out tl over 2f out: sn lost pl u.p: wl bhd over 1f out* **8/1**

0004 **6** *13* **Wild Desert (FR)**[57] 1231 9-8-13 62 ......................... JimmyQuinn 2 5
(Tony Carroll) *chsd ldr tl 6f out: rdn and btn 3f out: wl bhd fnl 2f: t.o* **14/1**

544- **7** *4 ½* **Sir Tyto (IRE)**[171] 8225 6-8-8 57 .........................(p) SteveDrowne 7
(Peter Makin) *in tch in midfield: rdn and lost pl over 5f out: lost tch 4f out: t.o and eased fnl 2f* **10/1**

1045 **8** *28* **Dazzling Valentine**[23] 2046 6-8-6 60 .........................(v) NatashaEaton(5) 9
(Alan Bailey) *stdd s: hld up in rr: lost tch 4f out: t.o and eased fnl 2f* **16/1**

2m 37.4s (6.80) **Going Correction** +0.65s/f (Yiel) **8** Ran SP% **116.8**
Speed ratings (Par 103): **103,102,100,89,84 76,73,54**
CSF £21.94 CT £65.08 TOTE £5.40: £1.30, £1.50, £2.00; EX 19.40 Trifecta £83.40.
**Owner** P G Gibbins & Ivor Perry **Bred** The Three Point Partnership **Trained** Kentisbeare, Devon

**FOCUS**
The softening conditions took their toll on the runners in this ordinary handicap, with the field finishing well spread out. The winner was value for a bit extra but the form is tricky to pin down.

## 2694 32RED CASINO H'CAP 1m 2f 46y
**5:00** (5:02) (Class 6) (0-55,55) 3-Y-O **£1,940** (£577; £288; £144) **Stalls** Low

Form RPR

-600 **1** **Graphene**[31] 1793 3-9-7 55 .........................[1] SeanLevey 15 61
(Rod Millman) *hld up towards rr: hdwy whn swtchd rt and slipped bnd wl over 3f out: hdwy to ld over 1f out: hung rt ins fnl f: styd on: rdn out* **17/2**

3-00 **2** *1 ½* **Solent Lad (USA)**[114] 480 3-8-12 46 .........................(p) JimmyQuinn 1 49
(Robert Eddery) *hld up in midfield: rdn and effrt 3f out: swtchd rt over 1f out: styd on u.p to chse wnr ins fnl f: kpt on* **16/1**

00-4 **3** *3 ¼* **King Calypso**[24] 2028 3-8-9 46 oh1 .........................(v) OisinMurphy(3) 4 43
(Denis Coakley) *in tch in midfield: hdwy u.p to press ldrs 2f out: chsd wnr over 1f out: plugged on same pce and lost 2nd ins fnl f* **10/3**[1]

-000 **4** *nk* **Up Hill Battle's**[22] 2066 3-8-12 46 ......................... FrankieMcDonald 14 42
(Daniel Mark Loughnane) *in tch in midfield: rdn and effrt over 2f out: styd on and battling for 2nd over 1f out: no ex and one pce fnl f* **25/1**

0000 **5** *2 ½* **French Accent**[22] 2078 3-8-12 46 oh1 ......................... SteveDrowne 10 38
(John Best) *hld up in rr: hdwy over 3f out: rdn and effrt over 2f out: chsd ldrs over 1f out: no imp: wknd ins fnl f* **33/1**

4-40 **6** *nse* **Benoordenhout (IRE)**[9] 2416 3-9-1 49 ......................... LiamJones 13 41
(Jonathan Portman) *chsd ldrs: rdn to ld over 2f out: hung lft and hdd over 1f out: wknd fnl f* **9/1**

34 **7** *6* **San Quentin (IRE)**[15] 2247 3-8-10 49 ......................... RyanTate(5) 3 29
(Tony Carroll) *in tch in midfield: rdn over 3f out: hdwy u.p over 2f out: no prog and btn over 1f out: wknd fnl f* **7/2**[2]

0-00 **8** *11* **Redlorryyellowlorry (IRE)**[57] 1235 3-8-12 46 .........................(t) PatCosgrave 7 5
(George Baker) *chsd ldrs: rdn over 4f out: drvn and stl cl enough 2f out: struggling whn pushed lft over 1f out: sn wknd* **25/1**

0-05 **9** *¾* **Satin Waters**[31] 1793 3-8-12 46 oh1 .........................(b) ShaneKelly 9 4
(Eve Johnson Houghton) *led: drvn and hdd over 2f out: sn btn and wknd over 1f out* **7/1**[3]

342 **10** *10* **Flying Author (IRE)**[57] 1239 3-8-9 48 .........................(tp) RachealKneller(5) 8
(Phil McEntee) *chsd ldr tl lost pl u.p over 2f out: sn btn: wknd and wl bhd fnl f: t.o* **7/1**[3]

00-0 **11** *hd* **Squaw King**[31] 1792 3-9-5 53 .........................(b[1]) DaneO'Neill 2
(Eve Johnson Houghton) *dwlt: sn bustled along and hdwy to chse ldrs after 2f: drvn and btn 3f out: sn wknd: bhd fnl f: t.o* **20/1**

-650 **12** *12* **Confucius Legend (IRE)**[31] 1812 3-9-7 55 .........................(b[1]) WilliamCarson 16
(Jim Boyle) *chsd ldrs: rdn and losing pl 4f out: t.o 2f out: eased fnl f* **40/1**

0400 **13** *27* **Abdication**[31] 1808 3-9-7 55 .........................(p) RobertHavlin 6
(Gary Moore) *a in rr: lost tch over 3f out: wl t.o and eased fnl 2f* **33/1**

-406 **14** *nk* **Ormer**[64] 1098 3-8-9 46 oh1 ......................... DeclanBates(3) 11
(David Evans) *a towards rr: lost tch over 3f out: wl t.o and eased fnl 2f* **40/1**

600- **15** *4* **Divine Bay**[219] 7441 3-8-12 46 oh1 ......................... SamHitchcott 5
(Gary Moore) *stdd s: a in rr: lost tch over 3f out: wl t.o and eased fnl 2f* **20/1**

2m 23.05s (12.05) **Going Correction** +1.125s/f (Soft) **15** Ran SP% **124.7**
Speed ratings (Par 97): **96,94,92,91,89 89,85,76,75,67 67,57,36,36,32**
CSF £125.09 CT £552.46 TOTE £9.70: £3.00, £3.90, £2.50; EX 169.80 Trifecta £779.70.
**Owner** The Graphene Partnership **Bred** Usk Valley Stud **Trained** Kentisbeare, Devon

**FOCUS**
It rained heavily again before this moderate handicap in which all 15 runners came into it as maidens. The majority of the field made for the centre of the track up the home straight. The form is rated cautiously.

## 2695 32REDPOKER.COM H'CAP (DIV II) 1m 5y
5:30 (5:30) (Class 6) (0-65,64) 3-Y-O £1,940 (£577; £288; £144) Stalls Low

Form RPR

-030 1 **Sweet Alibi (IRE)**[50] 1400 3-9-0 **62**................................ PhilipPrince(5) 8 66
(J S Moore) *hld up in midfield: stl plenty to do and rdn over 2f out: c towards centre and hdwy 2f out: wnt 3rd 1f out: styd on wl to ld towards fin* **14/1**

2600 2 *nk* **Stoneham**[17] 2210 3-9-0 **60**................................ CharlesBishop(3) 3 63
(Mick Channon) *led: rdn and clr w rival over 2f out: hdd over 1f out: battled on gamely and led again ins fnl f: hdd and no ex towards fin* **12/1**

-401 3 *2 1/4* **Caledonia Laird**[9] 2416 3-9-2 **59** 6ex................................ LiamJones 2 57+
(Jo Hughes) *t.k.h: hld up wl in tch: wnt 2nd 5f out: rdn and wnt clr w ldr over 2f out: led over 1f out: wandered rt and hdd ins fnl f: wknd towards fin* **8/1**

0-35 4 *3* **Nissaki Kasta**[22] 2078 3-9-1 **58**................................ RobertHavlin 4 49
(Hughie Morrison) *chsd ldr tl 5f out: 3rd and outpcd u.p over 2f out: 4th and plugged on same pce fnl f* **12/1**

63-3 5 *6* **Division Belle**[17] 2224 3-9-6 **63**................................ MartinDwyer 9 40
(William Muir) *stdd and dropped in after s: in rr early: hdwy into midfield 1/2-way: 4th and outpcd over 2f out: wknd wl over 1f out* **7/2**[2]

5463 6 *6* **Honiton Lace**[14] 2281 3-8-9 **55**................................ OisinMurphy(3) 10 18
(J W Hills) *plld hrd: hld up towards rr: dropped to last over 4f out: c towards centre and effrt over 2f out: no imp and wl btn fnl 2f* **5/1**[3]

1543 7 *nk* **Prim And Proper**[9] 2416 3-8-12 **55** ow1................................ SebSanders 11 18
(Brendan Powell) *hld up in last pair: c towards centre and effrt 3f out: no real imp: wknd and wl btn fnl 2f* **9/4**[1]

1-50 8 *7* **Dutchartcollector**[26] 1947 3-9-4 **61**................................(p) SeanLevey 12 8
(Gary Moore) *dwlt: sn bustled along: hdwy into midfield after 2f: rdn and lost pl 5f out: c towards centre and wknd u.p over 2f out: eased fnl f* **10/1**

563 9 *4* **Trinity Lorraine (IRE)**[17] 2209 3-8-7 **50** oh3...........(b) RoystonFfrench 5
(Alan Bailey) *in tch in midfield: rdn and losing pl over 3f out: sn wl bhd: t.o and eased ins fnl f* **20/1**

0-00 10 *1/2* **Stan Nineteen (IRE)**[14] 2278 3-9-5 **62**................................ SteveDrowne 7
(Simon Hodgson) *hld up in midfield: c towards centre and struggling over 2f out: sn bhd: t.o and eased ins fnl f* **40/1**

1m 50.04s (9.24) **Going Correction** +1.125s/f (Soft) **10** Ran SP% **119.1**
Speed ratings (Par 97): **98,97,95,92,86 80,80,73,69,68**
CSF £173.39 CT £1473.51 TOTE £14.10: £2.90, £4.80, £3.00; EX 124.30 Trifecta £1979.70.
**Owner** G V March & J S Moore **Bred** Patrick F Kelly And M J Foley **Trained** Upper Lambourn, Berks

**FOCUS**
The field fanned right out on reaching the home straight and they finished very tired. The winning time was 4.67sec slower than the first division, though conditions had deteriorated markedly in the meantime. The winner was back to her early 2yo form.
T/Jkpt: Not won. T/Plt: £13.20 to a £1 stake. Pool of £97222.35 - 5348.58 winning tickets.
T/Qpdt: £5.80 to a £1 stake. Pool of £5136.10 - 646.06 winning tickets. SP

# 2561 HAYDOCK (L-H)
Thursday, May 29

**OFFICIAL GOING: Soft**
Wind: Fresh, half behind Weather: Overcast Rails: All races on Inner home straight and distances on Round course increased by 1yd

## 2696 80'S MUSIC NIGHT HERE 21ST JUNE MAIDEN STKS 1m 3f 200y
2:20 (2:21) (Class 5) 3-Y-O+ £2,587 (£770; £384; £192) Stalls Centre

Form RPR

62 1 **Min Alemarat (IRE)**[25] 1984 3-8-11 0................................ JamieSpencer 4 93+
(Marco Botti) *chsd ldrs: rdn to take 2nd over 3f out: led 2f out: drew clr over 1f out: styd on wl: eased cl home* **2/5**[1]

04 2 *7* **Rocket Ship**[12] 2354 3-8-11 0................................ GrahamLee 5 80
(Sir Michael Stoute) *in tch: pushed along to go pce over 3f out: rdn wl over 2f out: styd on u.p over 1f out: sn wnt 2nd: no ch w wnr* **14/1**

66 3 *1 1/4* **Race To Glory (FR)**[22] 2075 3-8-8 0............ WilliamTwiston-Davies(3) 1 78
(Roger Charlton) *dwlt: hld up: pushed along to chse ldrs over 2f out: wnt 2nd over 1f out: no imp on wnr: sn lost 2nd: one pce ins fnl f* **16/1**

36- 4 *6* **Fine Vintage (FR)**[158] 8389 3-8-8 0................................ MichaelJMMurphy(3) 7 68
(Mark Johnston) *racd keenly: led: sn abt 5 l clr: hdd over 3f out: sn rdn: wknd wl over 1f out* **12/1**[3]

50 5 *10* **Ronald Gee (IRE)**[12] 2354 7-9-11 0................................ GaryBartley(3) 3 53
(Jim Goldie) *hld up in rr: pushed along on outer wl over 3f out: sn no imp: lft bhd ent fnl 2f* **66/1**

62-3 6 *1 1/4* **Conquerant**[8] 2466 3-8-11 0................................ WilliamBuick 6 59
(Charlie Appleby) *racd keenly: sn chsd ldr: led over 3f out: rdn and hung lft over 2f out: sn hdd: wknd over 1f out: eased whn wl btn ins fnl f* **9/2**[2]

0 7 *31* **Ninny Noodle**[29] 1888 4-9-9 0................................ StevieDonohoe 2
(Miss Imogen Pickard) *in tch: rdn and wknd qckly under 4f out: t.o* **100/1**

2m 35.27s (1.47) **Going Correction** +0.15s/f (Good)
**WFA** 3 from 4yo+ 17lb **7** Ran SP% **112.3**
Speed ratings (Par 103): **101,96,95,91,84 84,63**
CSF £7.59 TOTE £1.30: £1.10, £2.60; EX 6.00 Trifecta £26.70.
**Owner** Ahmad Abdulla Al Shaikh **Bred** Barronstown Stud **Trained** Newmarket, Suffolk

**FOCUS**
All races on Inner home straight and distances on Round course increased by 1yd. The opening contest on a six-race card was a good middle-distance maiden in which they went a proper gallop on soft ground. The form is rated slightly positively.

## 2697 BRITISH STALLION STUDS EBF MAIDEN FILLIES' STKS (BOBIS RACE) 6f
2:50 (2:51) (Class 5) 2-Y-O £2,911 (£866; £432; £216) Stalls Centre

Form RPR

5 1 **Savoy Showgirl (IRE)**[13] 2306 2-9-0 0................................ WilliamBuick 1 77+
(Michael Bell) *mde all: rdn whn pressed over 1f out: pushed out and kpt on wl towards fin* **7/2**[2]

2 *3/4* **Malabar** 2-8-11 0................................ WilliamTwiston-Davies(3) 2 75+
(Mick Channon) *trckd ldrs: effrt whn nt clr run over 1f out: n.m.r ins fnl f: styd on to take 2nd nr fin* **11/4**[1]

0 3 *1/2* **York Express**[14] 2269 2-9-0 0................................ MickaelBarzalona 3 73
(Ismail Mohammed) *a.p: rdn to chal fr over 1f out: no ex and lost 2nd nr fin* **8/1**

4 *nse* **Fruity (IRE)** 2-9-0 0................................ JamieSpencer 6 73+
(Clive Cox) *w wnr: pushed along 2f out: rdn and nt qckn over 1f out: kpt on towards fin* **11/4**[1]

5 *3/4* **Abbey Angel (IRE)** 2-9-0 0................................ TonyHamilton 7 71+
(Richard Fahey) *dwlt: racd keenly: hld up in tch: pushed along 2f out: green and wanted to lug lft fr over 1f out: chsd ldrs and kpt on same pce ins fnl f* **11/2**[3]

6 *3 1/4* **Liberal Angel (FR)** 2-9-0 0................................ DanielTudhope 5 61
(K R Burke) *hld up: rdn over 1f out: no imp: wl btn fnl 100yds* **7/1**

1m 16.73s (2.93) **Going Correction** +0.15s/f (Good) **6** Ran SP% **114.6**
Speed ratings (Par 90): **86,85,84,84,83 78**
CSF £13.94 TOTE £4.20: £2.60, £2.70; EX 15.70 Trifecta £55.40.
**Owner** Miss Emily Asprey & Christopher Wright **Bred** Hyde Park Stud & Lisglen **Trained** Newmarket, Suffolk

**FOCUS**
A fair juvenile fillies' maiden in which they went an honest gallop. No more than fair form, the field finishing bunched.

## 2698 HAPPY 10TH BIRTHDAY RACING UK MAIDEN STKS 6f
3:20 (3:21) (Class 5) 2-Y-O £2,587 (£770; £384; £192) Stalls Centre

Form RPR

4 1 **Red Icon (IRE)**[21] 2089 2-9-5 0................................ HayleyTurner 1 86
(Tom Dascombe) *mde virtually all: rdn and edgd rt ins fnl f: styd on wl* **6/5**[1]

2 *2 1/4* **Intiwin (IRE)** 2-9-5 0................................ TonyHamilton 9 79+
(Richard Fahey) *s.v.s and lost over 6 l: in tch after 1f: pushed along over 2f out: rdn and styd on to take 2nd ins fnl f: no real imp on wnr* **9/1**

3 *3/4* **Grigolo** 2-9-5 0................................ GrahamLee 2 77+
(Mark Johnston) *w wnr: rdn and nt qckn over 1f out: lost 2nd ins fnl f: kpt on same pce fnl 100yds* **7/1**[3]

4 *4 1/2* **Brando** 2-9-5 0................................ JamieSpencer 7 64+
(Kevin Ryan) *chsd ldrs: rdn 2f out: no imp over 1f out: one pce and btn fnl f* **7/4**[2]

5 *15* **Roman De Brut (IRE)** 2-9-5 0................................ StevieDonohoe 6 19
(Ian Williams) *in tch early: outpcd fr 1/2-way: wl btn* **33/1**

6 *2 1/4* **Red Stripes (USA)** 2-9-5 0................................ TomEaves 8 12
(Michael Mullineaux) *s.s: a bhd and outpcd: nvr on terms* **33/1**

1m 15.66s (1.86) **Going Correction** +0.15s/f (Good) **6** Ran SP% **110.2**
Speed ratings (Par 93): **93,90,89,83,63 60**
CSF £12.35 TOTE £2.00: £1.30, £4.30; EX 12.70 Trifecta £31.90.
**Owner** True Reds **Bred** Gigginstown House Stud **Trained** Malpas, Cheshire

**FOCUS**
A fair juvenile maiden in which they went a decent gallop. The form could conceivably be a bit better or worse than rated.

## 2699 ROA OWNERS JACKPOT H'CAP 1m
3:50 (3:52) (Class 3) (0-90,90) 4-Y-O+ £8,086 (£2,406; £1,202; £601) Stalls Low

Form RPR

4-44 1 **Off The Pulse**[20] 2137 4-8-8 **77**................................ BenCurtis 10 87
(John Mackie) *midfield: hdwy 3f out: rdn over 2f out: edgd lft fr over 1f out: styd on ins fnl f to ld towards fin* **12/1**

-000 2 *3/4* **Chosen Character (IRE)**[33] 1721 6-8-12 **88**........(vt) JennyPowell(7) 12 96
(Tom Dascombe) *led: c over to inner rail after 1f: rdn over 2f out: hdd and hld towards fin* **11/2**[3]

6100 3 *1 1/2* **Ansaab**[15] 2253 6-9-3 **86**................................(t) MickaelBarzalona 8 91
(Alan McCabe) *chsd ldrs: rdn over 2f out: sn trying to chal: ev ch ins fnl f: one pce towards fin* **5/1**[2]

0-60 4 *2 1/4* **Anderiego (IRE)**[26] 1958 6-8-13 **82**................................(v[1]) DanielTudhope 5 82
(David O'Meara) *hld up: rdn over 2f out: hdwy over 1f out: kpt on ins fnl f: nt rch ldrs* **7/1**

-563 5 *1* **Ardmay (IRE)**[20] 2137 5-8-10 **79**................................(p) JamieSpencer 1 77
(Kevin Ryan) *racd keenly on outer: chsd ldr tl 3f out: sn outpcd: kpt on u.p ins fnl f: no imp* **7/2**[1]

2550 6 *1 3/4* **Lazarus Bell**[9] 2425 4-8-9 **83**................................ JacobButterfield(5) 4 77
(Alan Brown) *s.i.s: bustled along to sn trck ldrs: rdn and tried to chal over 2f out: fdd ins fnl f* **11/1**

0-00 7 *3* **Lord Of The Dance (IRE)**[20] 2117 8-9-0 **83**................................ TomEaves 9 70
(Michael Mullineaux) *hld up in rr: effrt and hdwy over 2f out: sn chsd ldrs: no imp fnl f and btn* **28/1**

-000 8 *2 1/4* **Eurato (FR)**[13] 2311 4-8-8 **77**................................ PaddyAspell 3 58
(Alan Jones) *midfield: rdn and hdwy 3f out: nt rch ldrs: wknd over 1f out* **66/1**

5330 9 *6* **Lord Aeryn (IRE)**[12] 2351 7-8-13 **82**................................ TonyHamilton 6 50
(Richard Fahey) *restless in stalls: midfield: rdn 2f out: wknd fnl f* **11/2**[3]

421- 10 *5* **Autun (USA)**[252] 6559 4-8-11 **87**................................ MeganCarberry(7) 11 43
(Brian Ellison) *racd wout a hind shoe: unruly bef r: hld up: rdn over 2f out: no imp over 1f out: wl btn* **13/2**

1m 43.46s (-0.24) **Going Correction** +0.15s/f (Good) **10** Ran SP% **116.5**
Speed ratings (Par 107): **107,106,104,102,101 99,96,94,88,83**
CSF £76.58 CT £379.13 TOTE £13.80: £3.10, £1.80, £2.50; EX 120.20 Trifecta £605.40.
**Owner** G B Maher **Bred** Mrs V E Hughes **Trained** Church Broughton , Derbys

**FOCUS**
A decent handicap for older horses in which they went a proper gallop. The winner is rated to his AW best.

## 2700 RACING UK 10TH ANNIVERSARY H'CAP 1m 3f 200y
4:20 (4:21) (Class 4) (0-85,84) 4-Y-O+ £5,175 (£1,540; £769; £384) Stalls Centre

Form RPR

0-14 1 **One Pursuit (IRE)**[14] 2272 6-9-0 **84**................................ JennyPowell(7) 7 96+
(Brendan Powell) *chsd ldrs: wnt 2nd 4f out: rdn to ld over 2f out: drew clr over 1f out: styd on wl: comf* **4/1**[2]

20-5 2 *2 3/4* **Allnecessaryforce (FR)**[24] 2016 4-8-12 **75**................................ TonyHamilton 6 82
(Richard Fahey) *hld up: hdwy over 3f out: rdn 2f out: styd on ins fnl f: tk 2nd fnl 75yds: no ch w wnr* **14/1**

11-2 3 *1 1/4* **Mystery Drama**[13] 2305 4-9-0 **77**................................ FergusSweeney 8 82
(Alan King) *midfield: hdwy over 3f out: rdn to chse ldrs over 2f out: wnt 2nd 1f out: no imp on wnr: lost 2nd and no ex fnl 75yds* **5/1**[3]

01-3 4 *1 1/2* **Phosphorescence (IRE)**[26] 1934 4-8-11 **79**................................ LouisSteward(5) 2 82
(Lady Cecil) *led: rdn and hdd over 2f out: lost 2nd 1f out: one pce after* **6/1**

060- 5 *2 1/4* **Rock A Doodle Doo (IRE)**[62] 4512 7-8-12 **75**........(p) JamesSullivan 1 74
(Sally Hall) *hld up: pushed along over 3f out: rdn over 2f out: sn chsd ldrs: one pce fnl f* **33/1**

21-2 **6** *1 3/4* **Norway Cross**[24] 2010 4-9-6 **83** WilliamBuick 9 79
(Luca Cumani) *hld up: rdn over 3f out: nvr able to trble ldrs* **2/1**[1]
11/5 **7** *6* **Enthusiastic**[14] 2272 6-9-7 **84** KierenFallon 3 71
(George Margarson) *hld up: hdwy into midfield 7f out: impr to chse ldrs 4f out: sn rdn: wknd 2f out* **7/1**
1100 **8** *3 1/2* **The Lock Master (IRE)**[19] 2142 7-9-5 **82** AndrewMullen 11 63
(Michael Appleby) *chsd ldrs: lost pl over 5f out: rdn over 4f out: bhd fnl 3f* **25/1**
0625 **9** *2 1/4* **Uphold**[24] 2034 7-9-3 **80** (v) AndrewElliott 10 57
(Gay Kelleway) *chsd ldr to 4f out: rdn and wknd over 3f out* **20/1**

2m 34.94s (1.14) **Going Correction** +0.15s/f (Good) **9** Ran SP% **115.0**
Speed ratings (Par 105): **102,100,99,98,96 95,91,89,87**
CSF £55.17 CT £285.25 TOTE £4.00: £1.30, £3.60, £1.70; EX 64.00 Trifecta £282.00.
**Owner** Nicholas J E Maher **Bred** Clougher Partnership **Trained** Upper Lambourn, Berks

**FOCUS**
A good middle-distance handicap for older horses. The winner more than confirmed his Chepstow romp.

## 2701 HAPPY 60TH BIRTHDAY MAURICE CROOKS H'CAP (FOR LADY AMATEUR RIDERS) 1m 3f 200y
**4:50** (4:50) (Class 5) (0-70,70) 4-Y-0+ **£2,495** (£774; £386; £193) **Stalls** Centre

Form RPR
24-6 **1** **Aldwick Bay (IRE)**[33] 1724 6-9-12 **68** MissCAGreenway(7) 10 79
(Tom Dascombe) *plld hrd: sn prom: led over 9f out: rdn over 1f out: styd on wl and in command fnl f: eased cl home* **9/4**[1]
0-20 **2** *3 3/4* **Vicky Valentine**[17] 2213 4-10-0 **63** MissJCoward 6 68
(Alistair Whillans) *prom: lost pl 4f out: hdwy 2f out: styd on to take 2nd cl home: no ch w wnr* **4/1**[2]
-632 **3** *nk* **Merchant Of Medici**[17] 2216 7-9-11 **60** MissCWalton 11 65
(Micky Hammond) *hld up: in tch over 9f out: clsd over 2f out: wnt 2nd jst over 1f out: no imp on wnr: no ex and lost 2nd cl home* **4/1**[2]
660- **4** *3 1/4* **Dancing Primo**[263] 6239 8-9-13 **65** BeckyBrisbourne(3) 3 64
(Mark Brisbourne) *stdd s: hld up: hdwy over 4f out: wnt 2nd over 3f out: rdn over 2f out: no imp on wnr over 1f out: sn lost 2nd: no ex ins fnl f* **8/1**[3]
00-0 **5** *3/4* **Edas**[9] 2427 12-9-4 **56** oh4 [1] MissHCuthbert(3) 5 54
(Thomas Cuthbert) *hld up: hdwy 4f out: rdn to chse ldrs over 2f out: wknd over 1f out* **40/1**
000- **6** *1/2* **Queen's Estate (GER)**[297] 5048 5-9-6 **60** MissJoeyEllis(5) 8 57
(Miss Joey Ellis) *prom tl wknd over 1f out* **16/1**
-000 **7** *10* **Flag Of Glory**[118] 405 7-9-5 **59** MissMEdden(5) 2 40
(Peter Hiatt) *led: hdd over 9f out: remained prom: rdn over 3f out: wknd over 2f out* **16/1**
50-0 **8** *7* **Jordaura**[29] 1885 8-9-11 **63** MissJRRichards(3) 9 33
(Alan Berry) *hld up: pushed along 4f out: nvr a threat* **11/1**
340/ **9** *22* **Snow Dancer (IRE)**[669] 4621 10-10-6 **69** MissEJJones 7 4
(John David Riches) *midfield: lost pl over 4f out: lft bhd over 2f out: eased whn btn ins fnl f* **16/1**
1430 **10** *27* **Royal Alcor (IRE)**[14] 2272 7-10-0 **70** ....(t) MissAnne-SophieCrombez(7) 1
(Gay Kelleway) *chsd ldrs tl wknd over 4f out: t.o fnl 3f* **14/1**

2m 37.98s (4.18) **Going Correction** +0.15s/f (Good) **10** Ran SP% **117.0**
Speed ratings (Par 103): **92,89,89,87,86 86,79,74,60,42**
CSF £10.99 CT £33.88 TOTE £5.10: £1.40, £1.80, £1.90; EX 11.10 Trifecta £31.20.
**Owner** R Greenway **Bred** Ailesbury Bloodstock **Trained** Malpas, Cheshire

**FOCUS**
A modest handicap. The winner is rated back to the level of last summer's form.
T/Plt: £35.20 to a £1 stake. Pool of £62233.79 - 1288.57 winning tickets. T/Qpdt: £14.30 to a £1 stake. Pool of £4028.35 - 207.64 winning tickets. DO

# 2493 SANDOWN (R-H)
### Thursday, May 29

**OFFICIAL GOING: Soft (heavy in places; sprint 5.3, round 5.4)**
Wind: Almost nil Weather: Fine but cloudy, shower before race 4 Rails: Track at innermost configuration and distances as advertised

## 2702 CANTOR FITZGERALD RESEARCH H'CAP (JOCKEY CLUB GRASSROOTS FLAT MIDDLE DISTANCE SERIES QUALIFIER) 1m 2f 7y
**6:10** (6:10) (Class 5) (0-75,75) 4-Y-0+ **£3,234** (£962; £481; £240) **Stalls** Low

Form RPR
4201 **1** **Chain Of Events**[14] 2270 7-9-7 **75** JamesDoyle 1 87
(Michael Wigham) *trckd ldng pair: pushed into ld wl over 1f out: drvn and pressed sn after: styd on wl* **7/2**[2]
2-21 **2** *3/4* **Kastini**[13] 2301 4-9-6 **74** (v) AndreaAtzeni 5 84
(Denis Coakley) *hld up in midfield: smooth prog jst over 2f out: chal over 1f out and gng much bttr than wnr: rdn and nt qckn fnl f: kpt on but hld after* **2/1**[1]
300- **3** *3 3/4* **Nordic Quest (IRE)**[24] 7220 5-9-2 **70** TomQueally 3 72
(Nicky Henderson) *dwlt: hld up in last pair: waiting for room 3f out: rdn and prog 2f out: tk 3rd fnl f: no imp on ldng pair* **6/1**
-203 **4** *2 3/4* **Zafranagar (IRE)**[3] 2610 9-8-12 **71** ow2 GeorgeDowning(5) 4 68
(Ian Williams) *hld up in last pair: shkn up 3f out: kpt on one pce fnl 2f: n.d* **9/1**
16-6 **5** *1 1/4* **Dellbuoy**[118] 405 5-8-12 **66** TedDurcan 2 61
(Pat Phelan) *dwlt: t.k.h in midfield: rdn 3f out: nt qckn 2f out: fdd fnl f* **25/1**
3412 **6** *1 3/4* **Cathedral**[51] 1362 5-9-7 **75** RyanMoore 6 67
(Ed de Giles) *led: brought field to nr side rail in st: rdn and pressed 3f out: hdd wl over 1f out: wknd* **4/1**[3]
2312 **7** *4 1/2* **Gaelic Silver (FR)**[35] 1665 8-8-11 **72** HectorCrouch(7) 8 55
(Gary Moore) *t.k.h: trckd ldng pair: tried to chal against rail 3f out but nowhere to go: hanging and wknd 2f out* **20/1**
2-10 **8** *4 1/2* **Indian Trifone (IRE)**[30] 1845 4-9-3 **71** GeorgeBaker 7 45
(Ed Walker) *pressed ldr: chal jst over 3f out: wknd qckly 2f out* **16/1**

2m 15.6s (5.10) **Going Correction** +0.625s/f (Yiel) **8** Ran SP% **114.3**
Speed ratings (Par 103): **104,103,100,98,97 95,92,88**
CSF £10.92 CT £39.14 TOTE £5.10: £1.90, £1.10, £2.70; EX 11.80 Trifecta £50.10.
**Owner** P J Edwards **Bred** Bishop Wilton Stud **Trained** Newmarket, Suffolk

**FOCUS**
Tom Queally felt the ground was "very soft", while James Doyle described it as "hard work". The rail was at its innermost configuration and the distances were as advertised. They predictably came stands' side in the straight, given the conditions, in what was an average handicap dominated by the market leaders. The pace was a steady one. The winner was back to his best.

## 2703 CANTOR FITZGERALD EQUITIES NATIONAL STKS (LISTED RACE) 5f 6y
**6:40** (6:42) (Class 1) 2-Y-O
**£14,744** (£5,590; £2,797; £1,393; £699; £351) **Stalls** Low

Form RPR
112 **1** **Tiggy Wiggy (IRE)**[13] 2313 2-8-9 **0** RichardHughes 2 104+
(Richard Hannon) *racd against far rail: trckd ldng pair: eased out 2f out: clsd and pushed into ld jst ins fnl f: bounded clr* **3/1**[2]
1 **2** *3 3/4* **Cock Of The North**[61] 1161 2-9-0 **0** FrederikTylicki 1 94
(Scott Dixon) *dwlt: racd against far rail: in last trio tl rdn and prog 2f out: kpt on fnl f to take 2nd nr fin: no ch w wnr* **2/1**[1]
12 **3** *1* **Roudee**[22] 2071 2-9-0 **0** RichardKingscote 5 90
(Tom Dascombe) *led and racd against far rail: rdn 2f out: hdd jst ins fnl f: no ch w wnr: lost 2nd nr fin* **6/1**
1 **4** *4* **Bonnie Grey**[19] 2172 2-8-9 **0** MartinLane 4 71
(Rod Millman) *racd wdst of all: mostly in last trio and pushed along: outpcd fr 2f out: kpt on fnl f: nt disgracd* **10/1**
1 **5** *1 1/4* **Via Via (IRE)**[11] 2358 2-9-0 **0** RyanMoore 6 72
(Clive Brittain) *green to post: sn pushed along in last pair: outpcd fr 2f out: kpt on fnl f: no ch* **4/1**[3]
011 **6** *6* **Escalating**[29] 1866 2-9-0 **0** JamesDoyle 7 50
(Pat Eddery) *pressed ldr: rdn over 2f out: wknd qckly over 1f out* **14/1**
01 **7** *14* **Cajoling (IRE)**[17] 2220 2-8-9 **0** JamieSpencer 3
(Jonathan Portman) *chsd ldrs: rdn after 2f: wknd qckly 2f out: t.o* **28/1**

1m 3.92s (2.32) **Going Correction** +0.50s/f (Yiel) **7** Ran SP% **111.8**
Speed ratings (Par 101): **101,95,93,87,85 75,53**
CSF £8.98 TOTE £3.20: £1.40, £2.30; EX 7.90 Trifecta £36.70.
**Owner** Potensis Ltd & Ms Elaine Chivers **Bred** Cbs Bloodstock **Trained** East Everleigh, Wilts

■ Stewards' Enquiry : Frederik Tylicki two-day ban: used whip down the shoulder in the forehand (Jun 12-13)

**FOCUS**
A race capable of throwing some really smart sprinting juveniles, the form may not be worth a great deal, with a number appearing to struggle on the ground. The first three raced on the rail for most of the race. The winner impressed and can rate a bit higher.

## 2704 CANTOR FITZGERALD HENRY II STKS (GROUP 3) 2m 78y
**7:15** (7:15) (Class 1) 4-Y-O+
**£35,443** (£13,437; £6,725; £3,350; £1,681; £843) **Stalls** Centre

Form RPR
50-1 **1** **Brown Panther**[20] 2115 6-9-4 **115** RichardKingscote 5 118
(Tom Dascombe) *t.k.h early: trckd ldr 3f: cl up in 3rd after: shkn up over 2f out: led over 1f out: drvn clr: decisively* **2/1**[1]
0-35 **2** *3 1/2* **High Jinx (IRE)**[13] 2315 6-9-2 **108** JamesDoyle 3 112
(James Fanshawe) *trckd ldng trio: rdn 4f out: lost pl and struggling 3f out: rallied 2f out: styd on to take 2nd fnl f: no ch w wnr* **8/1**[3]
12/1 **3** *1 1/4* **Whiplash Willie**[25] 1981 6-9-2 **99** DavidProbert 12 110
(Andrew Balding) *hld up in last quartet: rdn over 3f out: no prog tl styd on fr over 1f out to take 3rd last 75yds* **16/1**
43-0 **4** *3/4* **Girolamo (GER)**[25] 2001 5-9-2 **112** RichardHughes 7 109
(P Schiergen, Germany) *led: brought most of field to nr side in st: hdd over 1f out: one pce* **8/1**[3]
10-3 **5** *1/2* **Tiger Cliff (IRE)**[13] 2315 5-9-2 **112** TomQueally 10 109
(Alan King) *settled in midfield: rdn and prog to chse ldng trio wl over 1f out: no hdwy after* **5/1**[2]
30-0 **6** *1/2* **Seismos (IRE)**[61] 1177 6-9-2 **115** AndreaAtzeni 2 108
(Marco Botti) *chsd ldrs: disputing 4th whn styd alone far side in st: lost no grnd on rivals but nvr quite on terms after* **14/1**
16-3 **7** *shd* **Oriental Fox (GER)**[29] 1869 6-9-2 **105** JoeFanning 9 108
(Mark Johnston) *mostly in last quartet: rdn over 3f out: no prog 2f out: plugged on fnl f* **25/1**
64-2 **8** *3/4* **El Salvador (IRE)**[33] 1750 5-9-2 **106** (p) RyanMoore 11 107
(A P O'Brien, Ire) *trckd ldr after 3f: rdn to chal 3f out: nt qckn 2f out: steadily wknd* **8/1**[3]
**9** *nk* **Menorah (IRE)**[33] 9-9-2 **0** KierenFallon 6 107
(Philip Hobbs) *s.s and pushed along early: prog fr rr into midfield 6f out: drvn and outpcd over 3f out: sn last: kpt on again fnl f* **20/1**
11-0 **10** *1 1/2* **Camborne**[13] 2315 6-9-4 **113** (p) WilliamBuick 8 107
(John Gosden) *dwlt: settled in last: rdn 3f out: modest prog 2f out: no hdwy over 1f out: fdd* **8/1**[3]
46-0 **11** *16* **Biographer**[50] 1398 5-9-2 **107** (b[1]) TedDurcan 1 92
(David Lanigan) *settled in midfield: rdn 3f out: sn wknd: t.o* **25/1**

3m 47.94s (9.24) **Going Correction** +0.625s/f (Yiel) **11** Ran SP% **119.4**
Speed ratings (Par 113): **101,99,98,98,98 97,97,97,97,96 88**
CSF £18.21 TOTE £3.10: £1.30, £2.70, £4.40; EX 22.10 Trifecta £479.40.
**Owner** A Black & Owen Promotions Limited **Bred** Owen Promotions Ltd **Trained** Malpas, Cheshire

**FOCUS**
Run at a steady gallop early, this staying contest had looked more open than the market suggested. Brown Panther is rated around his best previous figures and could be better than ever.

## 2705 CANTOR FITZGERALD BRIGADIER GERARD STKS (GROUP 3) 1m 2f 7y
**7:50** (7:52) (Class 1) 4-Y-O+ **£35,443** (£13,437; £6,725) **Stalls** Low

Form RPR
001- **1** **Sharestan (IRE)**[250] 6620 6-9-0 **111** KierenFallon 5 113
(Saeed bin Suroor) *hld up bhd ldr tl led after 4f: jnd 3f out: rdn to assert over 1f out: jnd again last strides: won on the nod* **5/6**[1]
1360 **2** *nse* **Sheikhzayedroad**[61] 1177 5-9-0 **108** [1] MartinLane 3 113
(David Simcock) *t.k.h: hld up in 3rd: urged along fr 3f out: rallied over 1f out: tk 2nd ins fnl f: jnd wnr last strides: jst pipped* **5/1**[3]
2-46 **3** *2 3/4* **Top Notch Tonto (IRE)**[12] 2338 4-9-3 **115** DaleSwift 4 111
(Brian Ellison) *led at mod pce for 4f: pressed wnr after: upsides fr 3f out to wl over 1f out: nt qckn and lost 2nd ins fnl f* **15/8**[2]

2m 23.46s (12.96) **Going Correction** +0.625s/f (Yiel) **3** Ran SP% **106.0**
Speed ratings (Par 113): **73,72,70**
CSF £4.58 TOTE £1.70; EX 3.00 Trifecta £4.80.
**Owner** Godolphin **Bred** His Highness The Aga Khan's Studs S C **Trained** Newmarket, Suffolk

**FOCUS**
The testing ground resulted in the two classiest runners, Hillstar and Remote, being non-runners, so it was left to look a weak and disappointing edition of the race. Top Notch Tonto took them along at a dawdling early gallop, but his stamina still didn't last, and the other pair drew clear late on. The runner-up is the best guide to the form.

## 2706 CANTOR FITZGERALD CORPORATE FINANCE HERON STKS (LISTED RACE) 1m 14y
**8:20** (8:20) (Class 1) 3-Y-O **£20,982** (£7,955; £3,981; £1,983; £995) **Stalls** Low

Form RPR
-332 1 **Master Carpenter (IRE)**[12] 2345 3-9-0 100 RyanMoore 5 103
(Rod Millman) *s.s: off the pce in last tl styd on inner bnd 5f out as rest charted wd crse: led over 4f out as a result: jnd 3f out: rdn and drew rt away over 1f out* **3/1**[3]
1- 2 7 **Indy (IRE)**[201] 7818 3-9-0 95 GrahamGibbons 3 87
(David Barron) *t.k.h: trckd ldr: tk wd crse bnd 5f out and lost pl: tk 2nd again 2f out and cl enough: sn rdn and easily lft bhd* **9/4**[2]
1-20 3 1 3/4 **End Of Line**[18] 2196 3-9-0 98 JamieSpencer 1 83
(Andrew Balding) *hld up in 4th: tk wd crse bnd 5f out: rdn wl over 2f out: no imp and easily lft bhd fr over 1f out* **15/8**[1]
0 4 3 3/4 **Nonno Giulio (IRE)**[36] 1652 3-9-0 0 WilliamBuick 2 74
(John Gosden) *racd freely: led and clr: steered v wd bnd 5f out and sn hdd: jnd wnr 3f out tl over 2f out: fdd* **25/1**
1-4 5 1 1/4 **Patentar (FR)**[42] 1532 3-9-0 99 (t) AndreaAtzeni 4 71
(Marco Botti) *hld up in 4th: wd bnd 5f out: rdn 3f out: no prog and wl btn over 1f out* **5/1**

1m 49.24s (5.94) **Going Correction** +0.625s/f (Yiel) **5 Ran SP% 111.1**
Speed ratings (Par 107): **95,88,86,82,81**
CSF £10.24 TOTE £3.50: £1.70, £1.90; EX 12.40 Trifecta £27.30.
**Owner** Links Partnership/Cheveley Park Stud **Bred** Naiff Sa & Newtown Stud **Trained** Kentisbeare, Devon

**FOCUS**
Quite a messy race, with outsider Nonno Giulio leading them wide down the far side and into the straight, and the time was slow. The winner was very much suited by the way the race panned out.

## 2707 CANTOR FITZGERALD WHITSUN CUP H'CAP 1m 14y
**8:50** (8:51) (Class 3) (0-95,95) 4-Y-O+ **£8,086** (£2,406; £1,202; £601) **Stalls** Low

Form RPR
214 1 **Ishikawa (IRE)**[20] 2131 6-8-0 81 RobJFitzpatrick(7) 8 91
(K R Burke) *t.k.h: trckd ldr: led 5f out: dashed for home over 3f out and sn clr: drvn 2f out: ld dwindled but nvr gng to be ct: eased last strides* **5/2**[1]
0253 2 1/2 **Dream Walker (FR)**[12] 2336 5-9-0 88 DaleSwift 6 97
(Brian Ellison) *t.k.h: hld up in 5th: rdn over 2f out: prog to go 2nd 1f out: clsd on wnr fin but a hld* **5/1**[3]
0-64 3 3 **George Cinq**[19] 2156 4-8-12 86 JamieSpencer 11 88
(Michael Bell) *trckd ldng pair: chsd clr wnr over 2f out: no great imp: lost 2nd and one pce fnl f* **6/1**
05-0 4 3/4 **Jodies Jem**[13] 2311 4-8-11 85 JoeFanning 4 85
(William Jarvis) *trckd ldng trio: rdn to dispute 2nd over 2f out to over 1f out: one pce after* **11/1**
16-0 5 1 **Tinghir (IRE)**[47] 1437 4-9-6 94 (p) TedDurcan 1 92
(David Lanigan) *hld up in last trio: shkn up wl over 2f out: kpt on to take 5th ins fnl f: no ch* **11/1**
0-01 6 1/2 **Secret Art (IRE)**[23] 2062 4-9-6 94 GeorgeBaker 7 91
(William Knight) *stdd s: hld up in last trio: rdn and nt qckn 2f out: kpt on one pce after: no ch* **4/1**[2]
0-10 7 7 **Tobacco Road (IRE)**[23] 2062 4-9-1 89 RichardHughes 9 70
(Richard Hannon) *led 3f: chsd wnr to over 2f out: wknd* **6/1**
0410 8 2 1/4 **Myboyalfie (USA)**[29] 1871 7-8-13 87 FrederikTylicki 3 63
(J R Jenkins) *hld up in 6th: rdn 3f out: no prog and wl btn fnl 2f* **16/1**
014- 9 1 1/4 **Common Touch (IRE)**[189] 7991 6-9-7 95 ChrisCatlin 2 68
(Willie Musson) *awkward s: hld up in last: pushed along over 2f out: no prog and nvr involved* **33/1**

1m 46.52s (3.22) **Going Correction** +0.625s/f (Yiel) **9 Ran SP% 119.3**
Speed ratings (Par 107): **108,107,104,103,102 102,95,93,91**
CSF £15.76 CT £69.82 TOTE £4.10: £1.80, £2.20, £2.20; EX 20.00 Trifecta £84.80.
**Owner** Tim Dykes **Bred** Ken Carroll **Trained** Middleham Moor, N Yorks

**FOCUS**
A fair handicap, in which it paid to race handy. The winner rates to his AW best.
T/Plt: £17.00 to a £1 stake. Pool of £114520.30 - 4893.72 winning tickets. T/Qpdt: £10.60 to a £1 stake. Pool of £7705.21 - 536.30 winning tickets. JN

# BADEN-BADEN (L-H)
Thursday, May 29

**OFFICIAL GOING: Turf: good**

## 2715a BADENER MEILE (GROUP 3) (3YO+) (TURF) 1m
**3:50** (12:00) 3-Y-O+
**£26,666** (£9,166; £4,583; £2,500; £1,666; £1,250)

RPR
1 **Red Dubawi (IRE)**[105] 593 6-9-0 0 EddyHardouin 8 107
(Frau Erika Mader, Germany) *hld up in rr: pushed along and hdwy 2f out: rdn and r.o to ld ent fnl f: drvn out and a holding runner-up fnl 100yds* **248/10**
2 1 1/2 **Peace At Last (IRE)**[25] 4-9-6 0 FabriceVeron 3 110+
(H-A Pantall, France) *hld up towards rr: pushed along and hdwy on wd outside under 2f out: r.o u.p to chse eventual wnr fr 1f out: kpt on u.p but a hld by wnr* **51/10**
3 3/4 **Gereon (GER)**[25] 6-9-6 0 AdriedeVries 1 108
(C Zschache, Germany) *wnt lft leaving stalls: trckd ldr: led 2 1/2f out: hdd ent fnl f: no ex* **9/2**[3]
4 2 **Calyxa**[25] 4-8-13 0 NRichter 4 96
(Ferdinand J Leve, Germany) *prom leaving stalls but sn w.w in midfield: lost pl sn after 1/2-way: pushed along but short of room 2 1/2f out: rdn to chse ldrs 1 1/2f out: one pce fnl f* **21/10**[2]
5 1 1/2 **More Than Sotka (FR)**[26] 4-8-10 0 AntoineHamelin 9 90
(Matthieu Palussiere, France) *hld up towards rr: moved into midfield after 2 1/2f: rdn and rdn 2f out: kpt on u.p fnl f: nt pce to trble ldrs* **189/10**
6 1 3/4 **Point Blank (GER)**[25] 6-9-0 0 (p) StefanieHofer 5 90
(Mario Hofer, Germany) *led: hdd 2 1/2f out: grad dropped away* **133/10**
7 hd **Ocean Tempest**[17] 2223 5-9-2 0 EPedroza 7 91
(John Ryan) *prom on outer: rdn over 2f out but nt qckn: grad dropped away fr over 1f out* **8/5**[1]
8 2 **King's Hall**[26] 6-9-0 0 (p) DanielePorcu 2 85
(M Figge, Germany) *prom bhd ldng pair: sn hld up in midfield: nvr in contention* **27/1**
9 2 1/2 **Global Thrill**[16] 2245 5-9-2 0 (b) CristianDemuro 6 81
(J Hirschberger, Germany) *wnt lft leaving stalls: trckd ldr: rdn to chse ldr over 2f out: sn wknd* **167/10**

1m 38.11s (-1.00) **9 Ran SP% 130.4**
WIN (incl. 10 euro stake): 258. PLACES: 43, 21, 19. SF: 1698.
**Owner** Zalim Bifov **Bred** Haras Des Sablonnets **Trained** Germany

# 2064 BRIGHTON (L-H)
Friday, May 30

**OFFICIAL GOING: Good (good to soft in places; 6.5)**
Wind: medium, behind Weather: overcast, brightening up Rails: All races on inner line and distances as advertised

## 2716 SIMON VANCE 70TH BIRTHDAY MAIDEN FILLIES' STKS (BOBIS RACE) 5f 59y
**1:50** (1:50) (Class 5) 2-Y-O **£2,587** (£770; £384; £192) **Stalls** Low

Form RPR
4 1 **Expensive Date**[14] 2302 2-9-0 0 LukeMorris 2 74+
(Paul Cole) *led: sn stdd and chsd ldr: rdn over 2f out: edging lft but hdwy to ld fnl 150yds: sn in command but idling in front: drvn out* **8/11**[1]
63 2 2 1/2 **Amber Crystal**[15] 2276 2-8-11 0 MichaelJMMurphy(3) 5 65
(John Gallagher) *sn led: stl travelling strly 2f out: rdn over 1f out: hdd fnl 150yds: one pce and btn whn swtchd rt wl ins fnl f* **9/2**[3]
6 3 2 3/4 **Gregoria (IRE)**[21] 2128 2-9-0 0 LiamJones 3 55
(William Haggas) *chsd ldng pair: rdn and unable qck over 2f out: kpt on same pce fnl 2f* **11/4**[2]
66 4 1 1/4 **Itsindebag**[7] 2499 2-8-9 0 PhilipPrince(5) 1 51
(J S Moore) *s.i.s: sn rcvrd and in tch in rr: swtchd rt and effrt in centre over 2f out: sn outpcd and wl btn over 1f out* **25/1**

1m 3.38s (1.08) **Going Correction** 0.0s/f (Good) **4 Ran SP% 106.6**
Speed ratings (Par 90): **91,87,82,80**
CSF £4.22 TOTE £1.30; EX 3.30 Trifecta £3.80.
**Owner** Chris Wright,Holly Wright,Chloe Forsyth **Bred** Stratford Place Stud **Trained** Whatcombe, Oxon

**FOCUS**
All races on inner line and distances as advertised. Following a dry night the ground had quickened up a touch and was given as good, good to soft in places (from good to soft). The GoingStick read 6.5. The winner ran close to her debut mark in this modest event.

## 2717 FROSTS4CARS.CO.UK H'CAP 5f 213y
**2:20** (2:20) (Class 5) (0-75,75) 3-Y-O **£2,587** (£770; £384; £192) **Stalls** Low

Form RPR
4454 1 **Royal Warrior**[7] 2508 3-9-2 74 OisinMurphy(3) 6 81
(Alan McCabe) *sn led and crossed to inner rail: set stdy gallop: rdn and qcknd ent fnl 2f: edgd rt over 1f out: in command and r.o wl fnl f* **16/1**
4-23 2 1 1/2 **Three Cliffs**[77] 954 3-9-3 75 RossAtkinson(3) 4 77
(Roger Varian) *wl in tch in midfield: rdn and effrt 2f out: styd on u.p ins fnl f: wnt 2nd towards fin: nvr threatened wnr* **6/1**[3]
2403 3 1/2 **Spreadable (IRE)**[32] 1818 3-9-2 71 (b) LukeMorris 1 72
(Nick Littmoden) *stdd after s: t.k.h: trckd ldrs: rdn and effrt 2f out: drvn over 1f out: chsd wnr wl ins fnl f: no imp: lost 2nd towards fin* **10/1**
-625 4 3/4 **Minley**[32] 1818 3-9-5 74 PatCosgrave 2 72
(Charlie Fellowes) *led briefly: sn stdd to chse wnr: rdn ent 2f out: styd on same pce and lost 2 pls wl ins fnl f* **5/2**[2]
1-34 5 3 3/4 **Got To Dance**[15] 2278 3-9-5 74 JamesDoyle 5 60
(Ralph Beckett) *in tch in last pair: rdn and effrt 2f out: edgd lft and no imp over 1f out: wknd ins fnl f* **5/4**[1]
14-0 6 3 3/4 **Pensax Lad (IRE)**[21] 2122 3-9-3 72 SteveDrowne 3 46
(Ronald Harris) *stdd s: t.k.h: hld up in tch in rr: swtchd lft and effrt nrest inner over 1f out: no prog and btn 1f out: wknd fnl f* **12/1**

1m 10.75s (0.55) **Going Correction** 0.0s/f (Good) **6 Ran SP% 110.0**
Speed ratings (Par 99): **96,94,93,92,87 82**
CSF £99.32 TOTE £17.40: £5.20, £1.70; EX 139.40 Trifecta £152.60.
**Owner** A J McCabe **Bred** A S Denniff **Trained** Averham Park, Notts

**FOCUS**
Just 4lb separated the top weight from bottom weight in this tight little handicap. This rates a personal best from the winner.

## 2718 BRIGHTONANDHOVEBUSES.CO.UK H'CAP 5f 213y
**2:55** (2:55) (Class 4) (0-80,79) 4-Y-O+ **£4,690** (£1,395; £697; £348) **Stalls** Low

Form RPR
534- 1 **Daylight**[242] 6900 4-9-1 76 (t[1]) OisinMurphy(3) 7 85+
(Andrew Balding) *taken down early: chsd ldng trio and clr of field: rdn and ev ch whn carried rt over 1f out: led 1f out: edging bk lft u.p but styd on wl fnl f* **5/1**[3]
0004 2 3/4 **Naabegha**[34] 1731 7-9-6 78 (p) PatCosgrave 5 84
(Alan McCabe) *taken down early: stdd s: hld up off the pce in last trio: rdn and gd hdwy towards inner over 1f out: pressing wnr ins fnl f: no ex and hld towards fin* **9/2**[2]
30-5 3 1 1/4 **Olney Lass**[10] 2448 7-8-9 70 SimonPearce(3) 4 72
(Lydia Pearce) *racd off the pce in midfield: hdwy u.p over 1f out: chsd ldrs and styd on same pce ins fnl f* **12/1**
6-3 4 3/4 **Noverre To Go (IRE)**[29] 1893 8-9-7 79 (p) SteveDrowne 8 79
(Ronald Harris) *stdd s: t.k.h: hld up off the pce in last trio: swtchd lft and hdwy over 1f out: styd on wl to snatch 4th last strides* **10/1**
-031 5 hd **Pettochside**[16] 2250 5-8-13 71 PatDobbs 3 70
(Chris Gordon) *racd off pce in midfield: rdn and hdwy over 1f out: chsd ldrs and styd on same pce ins fnl f: lost 4th last strides* **7/2**[1]
4-13 6 4 1/2 **Dreams Of Glory**[10] 2414 6-9-0 72 DavidProbert 11 57
(Ron Hodges) *led: rdn 2f out: edgd rt over 1f out: hdd 1f out: wknd* **5/1**[3]
4056 7 2 1/4 **Diamond Charlie (IRE)**[24] 2050 6-9-2 74 HayleyTurner 9 52
(Simon Dow) *chsd ldrs: hdwy to join ldr 4f out tl drvn and btn ent fnl f: wknd* **12/1**
0054 8 2 **Decent Fella (IRE)**[31] 1839 8-8-8 69 (p) MichaelJMMurphy(3) 6 40
(Ann Stokell) *v.s.a: wl off the pce in rr: n.d* **25/1**

00-5 **9** *11* **Assembly**[24] 2048 4-8-9 **67** ........................ FergusSweeney 10 3
(Pat Phelan) *racd off the pce in midfield: effrt u.p over 2f out: sn struggling: wknd over 1f out: wl bhd and eased ins fnl f* **33/1**

0641 **10** *23* **Clear Praise (USA)**[23] 2065 7-8-13 **76** ........................ JackDuern(5) 2
(Simon Dow) *taken down early: w ldr for 2f: chsd ldrs tl lost pl qckly over 2f out: t.o and heavily eased fnl 100yds: b.b.v* **8/1**

1m 9.44s (-0.76) **Going Correction** 0.0s/f (Good) **10** Ran SP% **116.1**
Speed ratings (Par 105): **105,104,102,101,101 95,92,89,74,44**
CSF £27.67 CT £256.90 TOTE £6.00: £2.30, £2.30, £3.70; EX 30.70 Trifecta £278.00.
**Owner** Kennet Valley Thoroughbreds V **Bred** Bearstone Stud And T Herbert Jackson **Trained** Kingsclere, Hants

**FOCUS**
The handicapper knows where he stands with most of these. It was sound run and the winner could build on this.

## 2719 SD2FESTIVAL.CO.UK H'CAP 1m 3f 196y
**3:30** (3:30) (Class 5) (0-75,75) 3-Y-O £2,587 (£770; £384; £192) **Stalls** High

Form RPR

021- **1** **Tears Of The Sun**[161] 8362 3-9-6 **74** ........................ HarryBentley 3 82+
(Roger Varian) *chsd ldrs: clsd to join ldrs and travelling best 2f out: shkn up to ld 1f out: sn rdn and readily qcknd clr: pushed out towards fin* **12/1**

41-6 **2** *nk* **Oasis Fantasy (IRE)**[35] 1702 3-9-3 **74** ........................ OisinMurphy(3) 5 81
(Ed Dunlop) *in tch in midfield: chsng ldrs and nt clr run over 1f out: gap opened and hdwy to chse clr wnr ins fnl f: r.o wl to press wnr towards fin: a hld* **3/1**[2]

0-31 **3** *3* **Cape Arrow**[22] 2098 3-8-10 **64** ........................ LukeMorris 1 66
(Paul Cole) *hld up in tch in last pair: rdn and effrt on inner ent fnl 2f: outpcd over 1f out: styd on to go 3rd ins fnl f: no imp* **7/2**[3]

1-36 **4** *2* **Love Tangle (IRE)**[26] 1983 3-9-6 **74** ........................ HayleyTurner 4 73
(Brian Meehan) *led and set stdy gallop: rdn and qcknd over 2f out: hdd ent fnl f: sn outpcd and btn: wknd ins fnl f* **10/1**

4-13 **5** *3 3/4* **Opera Fan (FR)**[25] 2009 3-8-9 **66** ........................ MichaelJMMurphy(3) 6 59
(Mark Johnston) *chsd ldr: rdn and ev ch 2f out: unable qck and btn 1f out: sn wknd* **7/1**

0-55 **6** *32* **Lucky Visione**[21] 2120 3-9-5 **73** ........................ DavidProbert 2
(Gay Kelleway) *hld up in tch in last pair: rdn and effrt over 2f out: sn struggling and btn: t.o and virtually p.u fnl f* **20/1**

115- **7** *12* **Jelly Fish**[219] 7471 3-9-7 **75** ........................[1] JamesDoyle 7
(Amanda Perrett) *in tch in midfield: drvn and no rspnse 3f out: btn 2f out and sn wl bhd: t.o and virtually p.u fnl f* **2/1**[1]

2m 34.07s (1.37) **Going Correction** 0.0s/f (Good) **7** Ran SP% **114.6**
Speed ratings (Par 99): **95,94,92,91,88 67,59**
CSF £48.10 TOTE £10.20: £4.20, £2.40; EX 61.80 Trifecta £185.20.
**Owner** Qatar Racing Limited **Bred** Dr Bridget Drew & John Burke **Trained** Newmarket, Suffolk

**FOCUS**
An interesting 3yo handicap run at a steady pace. Improvement from the winner.

## 2720 BRIGHTON AND HOVE STREAMLINE TAXIS H'CAP 1m 1f 209y
**4:05** (4:05) (Class 6) (0-60,59) 4-Y-0+ £1,940 (£577; £288; £144) **Stalls** High

Form RPR

0022 **1** **Auden (USA)**[64] 1129 6-9-6 **58** ........................(v) PatDobbs 6 72
(J R Jenkins) *in tch in midfield: c to r nr stands' rail over 2f out: hdwy to chal 2f out: rdn to ld over 1f out: rdn clr fnl f: readily* **5/1**[2]

0026 **2** *4* **Litmus (USA)**[18] 2212 5-8-11 **49** ........................(b) HayleyTurner 1 55
(Simon Dow) *taken down early: sn led: rdn and styd centre over 2f out: rdn and hdd 2f out: 3rd and one pce 1f out: kpt on to go 2nd again fnl 75yds* **8/1**

4110 **3** *3* **Cataria Girl (USA)**[58] 1232 5-9-2 **59** ........................(t[1]) ShelleyBirkett(5) 4 59
(Marcus Tregoning) *hld up in tch in last trio: rdn and hdwy nrest inner rail 2f out: chsd ldrs and no imp 1f out: plugged on to go 3rd last stride* **10/1**

3524 **4** *shd* **Herbalist**[23] 1874 4-9-4 **56** ........................(v) JamesDoyle 5 56
(Sean Curran) *led early: chsd ldr tl 6f out: c to r on stands' rail and rdn to ld again 2f out: hdd over 1f out: drvn and btn fnl 150yds: wknd and lost 2 pls fnl 75yds* **5/1**[2]

000/ **5** *1 1/4* **Just Duchess**[624] 6156 4-8-7 **45** ........................ DavidProbert 11 43
(Michael Blanshard) *hld up in tch in last quartet: c to r nr stands' rail and rdn ent fnl 2f: no imp tl styd on ins fnl f: no ch w wnr* **28/1**

6566 **6** *2 1/2* **Thewestwalian (USA)**[23] 2069 6-8-7 **45** ........................ SamHitchcott 3 38
(Peter Hiatt) *t.k.h: hld up in tch in last quartet: rdn and effrt in centre ent fnl 2f: no imp: wknd 1f out* **33/1**

3201 **7** *4* **Katmai River (IRE)**[32] 1819 7-8-10 **55** ........................ CharlotteJenner(7) 2 40
(Mark Usher) *in tch in midfield: styd centre to far side over 2f out: btn ent fnl f: fdd ins fnl f* **7/1**[3]

4322 **8** *2* **Salient**[24] 2046 10-8-11 **49** ........................ KierenFox 10 31
(Michael Attwater) *t.k.h: wl in tch in midfield: c centre to stands' side over 2f out: no ex u.p 2f out: wknd over 1f out* **10/1**

0121 **9** *3* **Nelson Quay (IRE)**[9] 2464 4-9-0 **59** ........................ DavidParkes(7) 12 35
(Jeremy Gask) *chsd ldrs: wnt 2nd 6f out: jnd ldr 5f out: rdn and c centre over 2f out: no ex and btn 2f out: wknd over 1f out* **11/4**[1]

2450 **10** *24* **Shirazz**[14] 2301 5-9-4 **56** ........................(t) FergusSweeney 8
(Seamus Durack) *hld up in rr: styd centre and rdn over 2f out: sn btn and lost tch: t.o and eased fnl f* **16/1**

2m 3.51s (-0.09) **Going Correction** 0.0s/f (Good) **10** Ran SP% **114.1**
Speed ratings (Par 101): **100,96,94,94,93 91,88,86,84,64**
CSF £43.64 CT £383.12 TOTE £6.80: £2.60, £3.50, £2.50; EX 52.80 Trifecta £281.00.
**Owner** Miss Caroline A Jenkins **Bred** Darley **Trained** Royston, Herts

**FOCUS**
A low-grade handicap and not much solid form to go on. The winner is rated back to the level of his Southwell win.

## 2721 WINNER PLANT HIRE H'CAP 7f 214y
**4:40** (4:40) (Class 5) (0-70,68) 4-Y-0+ £2,587 (£770; £384; £192) **Stalls** Low

Form RPR

632 **1** **Ocean Legend (IRE)**[11] 2401 9-8-10 **62** ........................ RyanTate(5) 1 73
(Tony Carroll) *hld up in rr: swtchd rt and effrt in centre over 2f out: gd hdwy to chal and edging lft over 1f out: led fnl 150yds: r.o wl* **6/1**

15-0 **2** *2 1/4* **Imperial Glance**[56] 1281 4-9-4 **68** ........................[1] OisinMurphy(3) 6 74
(Andrew Balding) *dwlt: t.k.h: hld up in tch: hdwy to press ldr 5f out: drvn ent fnl 2f: led over 1f out: hdd and one pce fnl 150yds* **11/4**[1]

5523 **3** *2* **Pick A Little**[11] 2400 6-9-5 **66** ........................ LukeMorris 3 67
(Michael Blake) *chsd ldr tl 5f out: rdn and outpcd ent fnl 2f: rallied u.p and styd on again ins fnl f: wnt 3rd last strides* **12/1**

00-4 **4** *hd* **Siouxperhero (IRE)**[36] 1665 5-9-7 **68** ........................(p) JamesDoyle 2 69
(William Muir) *hld up in tch in last trio: rdn and effrt on inner rail ent fnl 2f: chsd ldrs and styd on same pce ins fnl f: lost 3rd last strides* **8/1**

211- **5** *hd* **Sonnetation (IRE)**[204] 7784 4-9-1 **62** ........................ PatCosgrave 5 62
(Jim Boyle) *led: jnd 5f out: rdn ent fnl 2f: hdd over 1f out: no ex and outpcd jst ins fnl f: kpt on same pce after* **10/1**

1610 **6** *1 3/4* **Darnathean**[9] 2463 5-9-3 **64** ........................(p) SeanLevey 4 60
(Paul D'Arcy) *t.k.h: chsd ldrs tl settled bk in midfield but stl keen after 2f: rdn and unable qck over 1f out: wknd ins fnl f* **9/2**[3]

0254 **7** *14* **Attain**[30] 1875 5-8-9 **61** ........................(p) ShelleyBirkett(5) 8 25
(Julia Feilden) *chsd ldrs: rdn ent fnl 2f: outpcd and btn over 1f out: sn wknd* **12/1**

00-3 **8** *34* **Orders From Rome (IRE)**[32] 1799 5-9-1 **62** ........................ SteveDrowne 7
(Charlie Fellowes) *in tch in last trio: rdn and effrt whn pushed rt and hmpd over 2f out: sn wl btn: t.o and virtually p.u ins fnl f* **4/1**[2]

1m 35.75s (-0.25) **Going Correction** 0.0s/f (Good) **8** Ran SP% **114.7**
Speed ratings (Par 103): **101,98,96,96,96 94,80,46**
CSF £22.98 CT £193.33 TOTE £6.80: £1.90, £1.20, £3.70; EX 28.90 Trifecta £321.10.
**Owner** W McLuskey **Bred** Mark Commins **Trained** Cropthorne, Worcs
■ Stewards' Enquiry : Ryan Tate 1st incident: two-day ban: careless riding (Jun 13-14); (2nd) one-day ban: careless riding (Jun 15)

**FOCUS**
Modest form, but sound enough.

## 2722 HARRINGTONS LETTINGS H'CAP (DIV I) 6f 209y
**5:15** (5:15) (Class 6) (0-55,55) 4-Y-O+ £1,940 (£577; £288; £144) **Stalls** Low

Form RPR

342 **1** **Belle Bayardo (IRE)**[10] 2435 6-9-6 **54** ........................ LukeMorris 10 64
(Tony Carroll) *chsd ldrs: effrt u.p to ld over 1f out: sn hrd pressed: drvn and forged ahd ins fnl f: styd on* **9/2**[3]

0060 **2** *1* **Fairy Mist (IRE)**[36] 1668 7-8-12 **46** oh1 ........................(b) SeanLevey 4 53
(John Bridger) *t.k.h: hld up in tch towards rr: rdn and hdwy over 1f out: str chal u.p 1f out: no ex and one pce fnl 100yds* **16/1**

1242 **3** *3 3/4* **Bladewood Girl**[31] 1863 6-9-6 **54** ........................ PatDobbs 3 51
(J R Jenkins) *in tch in midfield: drvn and edgd lft 1f out: kpt on same pce ins fnl f to go 3rd towards fin* **4/1**[2]

/0 **4** *1 1/4* **Tamujin (IRE)**[26] 1986 6-8-12 **46** oh1 ........................ SamHitchcott 8 40
(Ken Cunningham-Brown) *hld up in tch towards rr: effrt u.p wl over 1f out: no imp 1f out: kpt on same pce and wnt 4th last stride* **66/1**

5005 **5** *shd* **Claude Greenwood**[23] 2069 4-8-10 **47** ........................(b) CharlesBishop(3) 9 41
(Linda Jewell) *chsd ldr tl led 5f out: rdn ent fnl 2f: drvn and hdd over 1f out: 3rd and btn ins fnl f: wknd and lost 2 pls towards fin* **8/1**

-4U4 **6** *1* **Interakt**[20] 2174 7-8-12 **49** ........................(b) OisinMurphy(3) 2 43
(Joseph Tuite) *wl in tch in midfield: rdn ent fnl 2f: outpcd and hrd drvn over 1f out: swtchd and rallied ins fnl f: keeping but no ch whn nt clr run and eased towards fin* **7/2**[1]

000 **7** *2 1/4* **Ghostwing**[90] 799 7-8-13 **52** ........................ RyanTate(5) 7 37
(Ralph J Smith) *led tl 5f out: styd chsng ldr: drvn and ev ch over 1f out: no ex and btn 1f out: wknd ins fnl f* **12/1**

5434 **8** *1 1/2* **Claude Monet (BRZ)**[31] 1836 5-9-0 **48** ........................ HayleyTurner 11 29
(Simon Dow) *hit front of stalls early and missed break: rcvrd and in midfield after 2f: rdn 2f out: sn btn* **10/1**

5623 **9** *1 1/4* **Greek Islands (IRE)**[31] 1836 6-9-0 **55** ........................ MichaelKenneally(7) 1 33
(Edward Creighton) *awkward leaving stalls and slowly away: hld up in rr: effrt and edgd rt 2f out: no hdwy and sn wl btn* **14/1**

0354 **10** *5* **One Last Dream**[16] 2250 5-9-7 **55** ........................(b) DavidProbert 6 20
(Ron Hodges) *t.k.h: hld up in tch in midfield: dropped towards rr 4f out: rdn over 2f out: sn btn* **6/1**

1m 22.7s (-0.40) **Going Correction** 0.0s/f (Good) **10** Ran SP% **116.6**
Speed ratings (Par 101): **102,100,96,95,95 93,91,89,88,82**
CSF £73.59 CT £319.74 TOTE £4.90: £1.90, £4.80, £2.10; EX 99.70 Trifecta £732.60.
**Owner** Richard Ward **Bred** L Mulryan **Trained** Cropthorne, Worcs

**FOCUS**
Modest form, with the runner-up 4lb out of the handicap.

## 2723 HARRINGTONS LETTINGS H'CAP (DIV II) 6f 209y
**5:45** (5:45) (Class 6) (0-55,55) 4-Y-0+ £1,940 (£577; £288; £144) **Stalls** Low

Form RPR

5655 **1** **Perfect Pastime**[36] 1668 6-9-7 **55** ........................(b) PatCosgrave 2 64
(Jim Boyle) *hld up in tch: hdwy to trck ldrs 2f out: swtchd rt and rdn to chal 1f out: led ins fnl f: styd on wl* **9/2**[2]

5203 **2** *3/4* **Byrd In Hand (IRE)**[26] 1986 7-9-1 **49** ........................(v) SeanLevey 6 56+
(John Bridger) *dwlt: rcvrd to ld after 1f: rdn ent fnl 2f: hdd and styd on same pce ins fnl f* **11/4**[1]

2500 **3** *2 3/4* **Ryedale Lass**[26] 1986 6-8-5 **46** oh1 ........................(b) PaddyPilley(7) 8 46
(Geoffrey Deacon) *in tch in midfield: effrt u.p over 1f out: wnt 3rd but no threat to ldng pair ins fnl f: kpt on* **20/1**

3326 **4** *2* **Abigails Angel**[9] 2465 7-8-7 **48** ........................ DavidParkes(7) 9 43
(Brett Johnson) *s.i.s: bhd: hdwy u.p over 1f out: styng on whn rdn dropped whip ins fnl f: kpt on: nvr trbld ldrs* **6/1**

00-6 **5** *2* **Alberto**[32] 1819 4-8-5 **46** oh1 ........................ CharlotteJenner(7) 10 36
(Alastair Lidderdale) *in toouch towards rr: effrt in centre over 2f out: no imp tl plugged on ins fnl f: nvr trbld ldrs* **28/1**

6-40 **6** *nk* **Tiger's Home**[21] 2127 4-9-2 **55** ........................ ShelleyBirkett(5) 1 44
(Julia Feilden) *led for 1f: chsd ldr: rdn 2f out: no ex jst ins fnl f: sn wknd* **10/1**

3-06 **7** *3 1/4* **Fleeting Indian (IRE)**[11] 2401 5-8-12 **46** oh1 ........................ SaleemGolam 3 26
(Linda Jewell) *chsd ldrs: effrt and n.m.r on inner over 1f out: wknd and wnt rt ins fnl f* **33/1**

0052 **8** *3* **Sweet Piccolo**[24] 2045 4-8-8 **47** ow1 ........................ DavidKenny(5) 7 19
(Paddy Butler) *chsd ldrs: rdn and unable qck 2f out: wknd ent fnl f* **12/1**

0054 **9** *1 1/4* **Fairy Wing (IRE)**[22] 2094 7-9-1 **52** ........................(b) OisinMurphy(3) 5 21
(Ann Stokell) *stdd s: t.k.h: hld up in tch: rdn and no hdwy 2f out: wknd and edgd lft over 1f out* **7/1**

3620 **10** *2 1/2* **Where's Reiley (USA)**[41] 1573 8-9-6 **54** ........................(p) SebSanders 11 17
(Michael Attwater) *chsd ldrs: rdn and struggling 2f out: wknd jst over 1f out* **5/1**[3]

1m 23.92s (0.82) **Going Correction** 0.0s/f (Good) **10** Ran SP% **116.2**
Speed ratings (Par 101): **95,94,91,88,86 86,82,78,77,74**
CSF £16.80 CT £230.14 TOTE £7.20: £2.10, £1.40, £4.90; EX 21.30 Trifecta £311.30.
**Owner** The Paddock Space Partnership 2 **Bred** R G & T E Levin **Trained** Epsom, Surrey
■ Stewards' Enquiry : Paddy Pilley two-day ban: used whip above permitted level (Jun 13-14)

**FOCUS**
The time was 1.22sec slower than the first division. The early pace was stronger but as a result they finished slower. The winner is rated to his winter AW form.
T/Plt: £323.50 to a £1 stake. Pool: £60,557.67 - 136.65 winning tickets T/Qpdt: £44.40 to a £1 stake. Pool: £6,632.13 - 10.50 winning tickets SP

## [2547] CATTERICK (L-H)

Friday, May 30

**OFFICIAL GOING: Soft (6.5)**

Wind: Virtually nil Weather: Cloudy

### 2724 YORKSHIRE-OUTDOORS.CO.UK ADVENTURE ACTIVITIES APPRENTICE H'CAP — 5f

**6:40** (6:41) (Class 6) (0-60,58) 4-Y-O+ — **£2,385** (£704; £352) **Stalls** Low

Form — RPR

0613 **1** **Fathom Five (IRE)**[9] 2451 10-8-7 **49**.................................. JoshQuinn(5) 5 60
(Shaun Harris) *mde all: rdn over 1f out: edgd rt ins fnl f: kpt on wl towards fin* **15/2**[3]

2630 **2** *1* **Major Muscari (IRE)**[17] 2233 6-8-9 **53**..................(p) AlexHopkinson(7) 1 60
(Shaun Harris) *dwlt and towards rr: gd hdwy to trck ldrs 1/2-way: swtchd rt and effrt wl over 1f out: chal and edgd lft ent fnl f: rdn and ev ch whn edgd lft again ins fnl f: kpt on same pce* **14/1**

2365 **3** *2 1/2* **Greenhead High**[20] 2166 6-8-13 **55**..........................(v) AnnaHesketh(5) 4 53
(David Nicholls) *chsd ldng pair: rdn along 2f out: one pce ent fnl f* **5/2**[1]

020- **4** *2* **Nine Before Ten (IRE)**[358] 3026 6-8-8 **50**.............(t) RobJFitzpatrick(5) 3 41
(Deborah Sanderson) *chsd ldrs: rdn along 2f out: wknd appr fnl f* **14/1**

-050 **5** *2 3/4* **Chosen One (IRE)**[24] 2056 9-9-4 **58**.............................. GemmaTutty(3) 2 39
(Ruth Carr) *cl up on inner: rdn along 2f out: grad wknd appr fnl f* **14/1**

630 **6** *2 3/4* **Give Us A Belle (IRE)**[41] 1584 5-9-3 **57**....................(vt) NoelGarbutt(3) 6 28
(Christine Dunnett) *midfield: hdwy on wd outside and in tch 1/2-way: rdn along 2f out: sn no imp* **17/2**

0000 **7** *1 1/4* **Newbury Street**[39] 1606 7-8-3 **45**...............................(b[1]) JackGarritty(5) 8 12
(Patrick Holmes) *chsd ldrs: rdn along over 2f out: sn wknd* **33/1**

0-00 **8** *1* **Ichimoku**[26] 1972 4-8-4 **46**..........................................(t) KevinLundie(5) 11 9
(Bryan Smart) *nvr nr ldrs* **10/1**

5600 **9** *hd* **Lord Buffhead**[7] 2514 5-8-13 **50**...............................(v) JacobButterfield 7 12
(Richard Guest) *in tch: rdn along 2f out: sn no hdwy* **8/1**

0-50 **10** *1 1/4* **Card High (IRE)**[10] 2427 4-8-11 **48**................................. EmmaSayer 10 6
(Wilf Storey) *sn outpcd and a in rr* **33/1**

6044 **11** *2 1/2* **Balinka**[10] 2421 4-8-10 **52**....................................... RobertDodsworth(5) 13 1
(Mel Brittain) *chsd ldrs on wd outside: rdn along over 2f out and sn wknd* **7/1**[2]

0-00 **12** *5* **Roc Fort**[10] 2427 5-8-8 **45**.............................................. ShaneGray 9
(James Moffatt) *sn outpcd and a bhd* **100/1**

/00- **13** *4 1/2* **Koolgreycat (IRE)**[358] 3026 5-8-11 **53**.............................. BTTreanor(5) 12
(Noel Wilson) *dwlt: a outpcd and bhd* **40/1**

1m 2.34s (2.54) **Going Correction** +0.55s/f (Yiel) **13** Ran SP% **112.9**

Speed ratings (Par 101): **101,99,95,92,87 83,81,79,79,77 73,65,58**

CSF £99.06 CT £292.41 TOTE £6.90: £2.80, £4.30, £1.10; EX 32.30 Trifecta £125.90.

**Owner** Nottinghamshire Racing **Bred** Eamonn Connolly **Trained** Carburton, Notts

**FOCUS**

A modest handicap, confined to apprentice riders, run at a sound pace. The five lowest drawn runners were in control throughout. The winner built a bit on his Yarmouth win.

### 2725 IRISH STALLION FARMS EBF MAIDEN FILLIES' STKS (BOBIS RACE) — 5f

**7:10** (7:14) (Class 5) 2-Y-O — **£3,067** (£905; £453) **Stalls** Low

Form — RPR

33 **1** **Perardua**[20] 2172 2-8-11 0.................................. GeorgeChaloner(3) 6 70
(Richard Fahey) *trckd ldrs: smooth hdwy 1/2-way: led over 1f out: sn rdn and hung bdly rt ins fnl f: kpt on* **5/2**[2]

5 **2** *1/2* **Alderaan (IRE)**[11] 2386 2-9-0 0........................................ BarryMcHugh 3 68
(Tony Coyle) *chsd ldrs: pushed along and sltly outpcd 2f out: sn rdn and styd on wl fnl f* **15/8**[1]

2 **3** *1* **Lily Moreton (IRE)**[13] 2349 2-9-0 0............................. DuranFentiman 8 65
(Noel Wilson) *slt ld: rdn and hdd over 1f out: kpt on same pce fnl f* **5/1**[3]

**4** *1 1/2* **Pearl's Azinger (IRE)** 2-9-0 0....................................... GrahamGibbons 9 60+
(David Barron) *swtchd lft s: trckd ldrs: hdwy wl over 1f out: styng on ins fnl f whn n.m.r on inner and eased towards fin* **12/1**

0 **5** *3/4* **Ripon Rose**[12] 2358 2-9-0 0.............................................. DavidNolan 4 57
(Paul Midgley) *dwlt: green and bhd: hdwy 2f out: kpt on fnl f: nrst fin* **40/1**

53 **6** *5* **Millar Rose (IRE)**[24] 2051 2-8-7 0.............................. RobJFitzpatrick(7) 1 39
(K R Burke) *cl up on inner: rdn along wl over 1f out: grad wknd* **13/2**

**7** *1 3/4* **Cafe Cortado (IRE)** 2-9-0 0................................................ BenCurtis 7 32
(K R Burke) *green: sn outpcd and a in rr* **25/1**

0 **8** *1* **Luvlylynnthomas**[30] 1879 2-9-0 0.......................................... AdrianNicholls 5 29
(Micky Hammond) *towards rr: rdn along and outpcd fr 1/2-way* **100/1**

056 **9** *2 3/4* **Kodestiny (IRE)**[10] 2436 2-8-9 0...................................... JoeyHaynes(5) 10 19
(Ismail Mohammed) *chsd ldrs on wd outside: rdn along bef 1/2-way: sn wknd* **25/1**

1m 2.88s (3.08) **Going Correction** +0.55s/f (Yiel) **9** Ran SP% **112.2**

Speed ratings (Par 90): **97,96,94,92,91 83,80,78,74**

CSF £7.07 TOTE £3.30: £1.60, £1.10, £1.30; EX 10.40 Trifecta £26.50.

**Owner** Diamond Racing Ltd **Bred** Diamond Racing Ltd **Trained** Musley Bank, N Yorks

**FOCUS**

They went a sound pace for this fillies' maiden but the time was ordinary. The form is too.

### 2726 GORDON WILLIAM COLEMAN (S) STKS — 5f 212y

**7:40** (7:40) (Class 6) 3-4-Y-O — **£2,385** (£704; £352) **Stalls** Low

Form — RPR

6-53 **1** **Betty Boo (IRE)**[29] 1905 4-8-7 50................................... AlexHopkinson(7) 3 67
(Shaun Harris) *cl up: effrt to ld ent fnl f: sn clr* **10/1**

01-4 **2** *5* **Next Door (IRE)**[35] 1694 4-9-6 69......................................... GrahamGibbons 2 57
(David Barron) *rdn along sn after s and sn slt ld: rdn along over 2f out: drvn and hdd ent fnl f: sn one pce* **6/5**[1]

500- **3** *3 1/4* **A J Cook (IRE)**[213] 7598 4-9-6 59.................................. ShirleyTeasdale(5) 4 52
(Ron Barr) *sltly hmpd s: hld up: hdwy 2f out: sn rdn and no imp appr fnl f* **22/1**

0-04 **4** *nk* **Angels Calling**[9] 2454 4-9-1 56........................................ JoeyHaynes(5) 6 46
(K R Burke) *chsd ldng pair: rdn along 2f out: sn hung bdly rt and btn over 1f out* **15/2**[3]

-504 **5** *2 1/2* **Lady Dancer (IRE)**[6] 2553 3-7-12 30............................(b) KieranSchofield(7) 1 30
(George Moore) *chsd ldrs: rdn along over 2f out: sn wknd* **80/1**

0664 **6** *1 1/4* **Cape Of Hope (IRE)**[3] 2653 4-9-11 68................................ AdrianNicholls 7 39
(David Nicholls) *trckd ldrs on outer: lost pl bef 1/2-way: rdn along and sme hdwy over 2f out: sn drvn and btn* **15/8**[2]

1m 17.04s (3.44) **Going Correction** +0.65s/f (Yiel)

**WFA** 3 from 4yo 9lb **6** Ran SP% **106.7**

Speed ratings (Par 101): **103,96,92,91,88 86**

CSF £20.47 TOTE £10.30: £6.70, £1.02; EX 26.20 Trifecta £171.60.The winner was bought in 14,000gns.

**Owner** Andy Elton **Bred** Bryan Ryan **Trained** Carburton, Notts

**FOCUS**

The pace was honest for this weak seller. Again those drawn low dominated. The winner confirmed her Redcar form.

### 2727 ANNE AND TONY'S 30TH WEDDING ANNIVERSARY H'CAP — 5f

**8:10** (8:10) (Class 4) (0-80,84) 3-Y-O+ — **£6,469** (£1,925; £962; £481) **Stalls** Low

Form — RPR

41-2 **1** **Rural Celebration**[25] 2015 3-9-0 **76**.................................. DanielTudhope 2 89
(David O'Meara) *trckd ldng pair: swtchd rt and smooth hdwy to ld wl over 1f out: clr ent fnl f: readily* **11/4**[2]

000- **2** *3* **Tango Sky (IRE)**[265] 6209 5-9-6 **74**...................................... DavidNolan 4 79
(Richard Fahey) *in tch: hdwy 2f out: sn rdn and kpt on to chse wnr ent fnl f: sn no imp* **20/1**

2-00 **3** *1 1/2* **Ambitious Icarus**[13] 2350 5-9-6 **77**........................(e) ConnorBeasley(3) 7 77
(Richard Guest) *towards rr: hdwy 2f out: sn rdn and n.m.r over 1f out: kpt on: nrst fin* **12/1**

0/00 **4** *1/2* **Blue Bullet (IRE)**[13] 2350 4-9-1 **69**...................................... PaulPickard 1 67
(Brian Ellison) *in rr: bhd 1/2-way: hdwy over 1f out: sn rdn and styd on fnl f: nrst fin* **25/1**

60-5 **5** *1/2* **Rock On Candy**[24] 2056 5-9-3 **71**............................................ ChrisCatlin 9 67
(John Spearing) *dwlt and in rr: hdwy wl over 1f out: n.m.r ent fnl f: kpt on: nrst fin* **7/1**

0-00 **6** *3/4* **Bosun Breese**[27] 1961 9-9-9 **77**...................................... PaulMulrennan 10 70
(Paul Midgley) *qckly away: slt ld and set str pce: rdn 2f out: sn hdd & wknd appr fnl f* **33/1**

-310 **7** *1 1/4* **Lorimer's Lot (IRE)**[25] 2015 3-8-12 **74**............................ DuranFentiman 8 60
(Mark Walford) *chsd ldrs on outer: rdn along 2f out: sn drvn and btn over 1f out* **12/1**

1061 **8** *1* **Keep It Dark**[3] 2656 5-10-2 **84** 6ex................................... BarryMcHugh 5 69
(Tony Coyle) *chsd ldrs: rdn along 1/2-way: sn carried hd high and wknd* **2/1**[1]

2426 **9** *4* **Bronze Beau**[3] 2656 7-9-6 **79**...............................(tp) JacobButterfield(5) 6 50
(Kristin Stubbs) *disp ld at str pce: rdn along 2f out: sn wknd* **13/2**[3]

1m 1.7s (1.90) **Going Correction** +0.55s/f (Yiel)

**WFA** 3 from 4yo+ 8lb **9** Ran SP% **112.8**

Speed ratings (Par 105): **106,101,98,98,97 96,94,92,86**

CSF £56.67 CT £567.33 TOTE £3.00: £1.30, £5.30, £3.60; EX 56.80 Trifecta £643.00.

**Owner** Hambleton Racing Ltd - Two Chances **Bred** J A And M A Knox **Trained** Nawton, N Yorks

**FOCUS**

A fair handicap run at a decent pace. A solid personal best from the winner, but little depth to the race.

### 2728 LESLIE PETCH H'CAP (A QUALIFIER FOR THE 2014 CATTERICK TWELVE FURLONG SERIES FINAL) — 1m 3f 214y

**8:45** (8:45) (Class 5) (0-75,75) 3-Y-O+ — **£3,881** (£1,155; £577; £288) **Stalls** Low

Form — RPR

2524 **1** **Fly Solo**[18] 2216 5-9-10 **71**........................................................ BenCurtis 8 79
(Alan Swinbank) *trckd ldng pair: hdwy and cl up 3f out: led wl over 1f out: jnd and drvn ins fnl f: edgd lft: kpt on wl towards fin* **7/2**[1]

2/05 **2** *1/2* **Deepsand (IRE)**[16] 2259 5-9-13 **74**..................................(p) DavidAllan 6 81
(Tim Easterby) *hld up: hdwy wl over 2f out: swtchd lft and rdn over 1f out: chal ins fnl f: ev ch tl drvn and no ex towards fin* **6/1**

0-00 **3** *1 3/4* **Cloud Monkey (IRE)**[20] 2168 4-9-9 **70**............................ PJMcDonald 4 74
(Martin Todhunter) *hld up in rr: hdwy over 2f out: rdn wl over 1f out: styd on fnl f: nrst fin* **11/1**

352- **4** *1/2* **Fair Loch**[49] 8092 6-9-9 **75**............................................... JoeyHaynes(5) 7 79
(K R Burke) *hld up: hdwy on outer over 4f out: effrt to chal over 2f out: sn rdn and ev ch tl drvn and one pce ent fnl f* **6/1**

643- **5** *nk* **Poetic Verse**[163] 7118 4-9-6 **70**..................................... IanBrennan(3) 3 73
(John Quinn) *trckd ldrs on inner: rdn along wl over 2f out: drvn over 1f out and grad wknd* **16/1**

2-03 **6** *2 3/4* **Tinseltown**[17] 1644 8-9-5 **66**............................................ BarryMcHugh 2 65
(Brian Rothwell) *chsd ldr: rdn along over 3f out: wknd over 2f out* **18/1**

1315 **7** *2 3/4* **Right Of Appeal**[18] 2222 3-8-7 **71**....................................... JoeFanning 1 64
(Mark Johnston) *led: rdn along over 3f out: drvn over 2f out: hdd wl over 1f out and sn wknd* **9/2**[3]

6-05 **8** *2 1/2* **Zeus Magic**[43] 1539 4-9-13 **74**...................................... GrahamGibbons 5 64
(Brian Ellison) *dwlt and in rr: sme hdwy on inner 4f out: rdn along and lost pl over 3f out: sn bhd* **4/1**[2]

-016 **9** *25* **Cavalieri (IRE)**[28] 1929 4-9-3 **71**.................................. EvaMoscrop(7) 9 21
(Philip Kirby) *chsd ldrs on outer: rdn along 4f out: wknd 3f out* **12/1**

2m 47.0s (8.10) **Going Correction** +0.65s/f (Yiel)

**WFA** 3 from 4yo+ 17lb **9** Ran SP% **116.1**

Speed ratings (Par 103): **99,98,97,97,96 95,93,91,74**

CSF £24.91 CT £209.44 TOTE £4.60: £1.10, £3.40, £3.20; EX 32.20 Trifecta £170.40.

**Owner** Guy Reed Racing **Bred** G Reed **Trained** Melsonby, N Yorks

**FOCUS**

This was competitive enough for the grade, but the field finished relatively bunched.

### 2729 ELLERY HILL RATING RELATED MAIDEN STKS — 7f

**9:15** (9:17) (Class 6) 3-Y-O+ — **£2,385** (£704; £352) **Stalls** Low

Form — RPR

0-06 **1** **Miaplacidus (IRE)**[18] 2204 3-9-0 63.................................... DavidNolan 9 58
(Richard Fahey) *trckd ldrs: hdwy 3f out: led 2f out: sn rdn: drvn ins fnl f and kpt on wl towards fin* **10/3**[2]

06-5 **2** *1* **Rockie Road (IRE)**[20] 2165 3-9-0 53.................................. RaulDaSilva 6 55
(Paul Green) *trckd ldrs on inner: hdwy over 2f out: rdn over 1f out: ev ch ins fnl f: sn drvn and kpt on same pce towards fin* **7/2**[3]

-660 **3** *1 1/4* **Lady Liz**[13] 2355 3-9-0 48...........................................(b[1]) AndrewElliott 4 52
(George Moore) *hld up towards rr: swtchd rt to outer and hdwy wl over 1f out: styd on fnl f: nrst fin* **25/1**

00-3 **4** *1 1/2* **Rokeby**[24] 2053 3-9-0 52.................................................. PJMcDonald 10 48
(George Moore) *trckd ldrs: hdwy on outer over 2f out: sn cl up: rdn and ev ch over 1f out: sn edgd rt and wknd ent fnl f* **8/1**

0-00 **5** *1* **Emily Davison (IRE)**[37] 1647 3-8-7 50............................ GemmaTutty(7) 2 45
(Karen Tutty) *led: rdn along 3f out: hdd 2f out and sn wknd* **16/1**

464 **6** *5* **Tashbeeh (IRE)**[84] 871 3-8-9 65......................................... EmmaSayer(5) 3 32
(Dianne Sayer) *s.i.s: in rr and detached 1/2-way: sme hdwy 2f out: nvr a factor* **9/1**

3-00 **7** *2 3/4* **Miss Sophisticated**[36] 1657 3-9-0 62............................. GrahamGibbons 7 25
(David Barron) *cl up: rdn along wl over 2f out: sn wknd* **3/1**[1]

023- **8** *3/4* **Maillot Jaune (IRE)**[175] 8180 4-9-4 50.............................. JackGarritty(7) 1 27
(Patrick Holmes) *a towards rr* **16/1**

004- **9** *2 3/4* **Rosie Hall (IRE)**[288] [5425] 4-9-11 46 ........ DavidAllan 8 20
(Les Eyre) *cl up: rdn along 3f out: sn drvn and wknd 2f out* **10/1**

1m 32.21s (5.21) **Going Correction** +0.65s/f (Yiel)
**WFA** 3 from 4yo 11lb **9** Ran SP% **116.1**
Speed ratings (Par 101): **96,94,93,91,90 84,81,80,77**
CSF £15.57 TOTE £5.00: £1.50, £1.10, £8.90; EX 17.30 Trifecta £523.20.
**Owner** Mrs H Steel **Bred** Oghill House Stud & Jimmy Hyland **Trained** Musley Bank, N Yorks

**FOCUS**
This 0-65 maiden was run at a fair pace. Moderate form, rated cautiously.
T/Plt: £17.10 to a £1 stake. Pool: £64,458.36 - 2,744.58 winning tickets. T/Qpdt: £13.20 to a £1 stake. Pool: £4,142.54 - 230.90 winning tickets. JR

## 2696 HAYDOCK (L-H)
### Friday, May 30

**OFFICIAL GOING: Soft (good to soft in places) changing to good to soft after race 2 (7.00)**
Wind: almost nil Weather: fine Rails: All races on Inner home straight and distances on Round course increased by 1yd

### 2730 BETDAQ HAYDOCK PARK APPRENTICE TRAINING SERIES H'CAP (PART OF THE RACING EXCELLENCE INITIATIVE) 1m 2f 95y
**6:30** (6:30) (Class 5) (0-70,73) 4-Y-O+ **£2,587** (£770; £384) **Stalls** Low

Form RPR
6233 **1** **Gran Maestro (USA)**[6] [2547] 5-9-7 **70** ........(v[1]) KevinStott 1 79
(Ruth Carr) *trckd ldr: chal on bit over 2f out: shkn up to ld over 1f out: styd on wl: eased nr fin* **6/4**[1]

4641 **2** *2 1/4* **Lord Franklin**[7] [2509] 5-9-7 **73** 6ex ........ LukeLeadbitter(3) 7 78
(Eric Alston) *set v stdy pce: shkn up 2f out: sn hdd: kpt on same pce* **9/4**[3]

21 **3** *23* **Polar Forest**[10] [2427] 4-9-1 **64** 6ex ........(e) AlistairRawlinson 3 28
(Richard Guest) *rrd s: hld up in last: drvn over 2f out: lost pl over 1f out: sn bhd: eased towards fin* **15/8**[2]

2m 20.27s (4.77) **Going Correction** -0.175s/f (Firm) **3** Ran SP% **105.6**
Speed ratings (Par 103): **73,71,52**
CSF £4.74 TOTE £2.50; EX 4.70 Trifecta £10.90.
**Owner** Paul Saxton & The Bottom Liners **Bred** Darley **Trained** Huby, N Yorks

**FOCUS**
All races on Inner home straight and distances on Round course increased by 1yd. This modest apprentice riders' handicap was hit by non-runners, but still featured a pair of last-time-out scorers and the previous year's winner. It proved tactical from the start. The form is rated around the winner's last couple of runs.

### 2731 HALLIWELL JONES BMW I3 BECOME ELECTRIC EBF STALLIONS MAIDEN STKS 5f
**7:00** (7:01) (Class 5) 2-Y-O **£2,911** (£866; £432; £216) **Stalls** Centre

Form RPR
**1** **Snap Shots (IRE)** 2-9-5 0 ........ RichardKingscote 1 86+
(Tom Dascombe) *led: edgd rt appr fnl f: hdd narrowly jst ins fnl f: kpt on wl clsng stages* **15/8**[2]

**2** *3/4* **Maljaa** 2-9-5 0 ........ DaneO'Neill 7 84+
(Roger Varian) *trckd ldrs: smooth hdwy over 1f out: led briefly jst ins fnl f: no ex clsng stages* **11/10**[1]

**3** *1 1/2* **Pallister** 2-9-5 0 ........ FrannyNorton 6 78+
(Mark Johnston) *chsd ldrs: upsides over 2f out: sn drvn: styd on same pce fnl f* **15/2**[3]

**4** *3* **Doctor Kehoe** 2-9-5 0 ........ TonyHamilton 4 68+
(Richard Fahey) *s.s: in rr: drvn and sme hdwy over 2f out: sn outpcd kpt on fnl f* **14/1**

0 **5** *1 1/4* **Straightothepoint**[17] [2231] 2-9-5 0 ........ RoystonFfrench 5 63
(Bryan Smart) *trckd ldr: upsides over 2f out: wkng whn sltly hmpd appr fnl f* **25/1**

**6** *2 3/4* **Savannah Beau** 2-9-0 0 ........ GrahamLee 3 48
(Marjorie Fife) *dwlt: t.k.h in rr: hdwy over 2f out: lost pl over 1f out* **20/1**

1m 1.81s (1.01) **Going Correction** +0.175s/f (Good) **6** Ran SP% **109.4**
Speed ratings (Par 93): **98,96,94,89,87 83**
CSF £4.03 TOTE £2.10: £1.30, £1.40; EX 3.90 Trifecta £10.60.
**Owner** True Reds **Bred** Tally-Ho Stud **Trained** Malpas, Cheshire

**FOCUS**
A decent 2yo maiden and the form is rated round the race average.

### 2732 HALLIWELL JONES FOR APPROVED USED CARS H'CAP 6f
**7:30** (7:32) (Class 4) (0-85,84) 4-Y-O+ **£6,469** (£1,925; £962; £481) **Stalls** Centre

Form RPR
005 **1** **Go Go Green (IRE)**[9] [2456] 8-8-2 **70** oh2 ........ SammyJoBell(5) 9 78
(Jim Goldie) *s.s: swtchd lft after s: hdwy to trck ldrs over 2f out: styd on fnl f: led nr fin* **11/1**

0-00 **2** *nk* **Cruise Tothelimit (IRE)**[6] [2562] 6-9-3 **80** ........ RichardHughes 10 87
(Ian Williams) *sn trcking ldrs: c stands' side over 1f out: upsides ins fnl f: no ex nr fin* **9/2**[2]

-005 **3** *shd* **Arctic Feeling (IRE)**[13] [2352] 6-9-0 **77** ........(b[1]) TonyHamilton 1 84
(Richard Fahey) *trckd ldrs on outer: led over 1f out: hdd and no ex cl home* **16/1**

0-06 **4** *2 1/2* **Dark Castle**[27] [1938] 5-9-4 **81** ........ MichaelStainton 5 80
(Micky Hammond) *dwlt: hld up: effrt over 2f out: one pce fnl f* **14/1**

10/6 **5** *1* **Bond Fastrac**[55] [1305] 7-9-0 **80** ........ RobertTart(3) 8 75
(Geoffrey Oldroyd) *dwlt: hld up in rr: hdwy stands' side over 2f out: one pce over 1f out* **7/1**

-100 **6** *1 1/2* **Foxy Music**[11] [2390] 10-9-6 **83** ........ GrahamLee 2 74
(Eric Alston) *led: hdd over 1f out: wknd fnl 150yds* **25/1**

4015 **7** *hd* **Lastchancelucas**[13] [2350] 4-9-2 **82** ........(b) JasonHart(3) 7 72
(Declan Carroll) *t.k.h in rr: edgd rt over 2f out: nvr a factor* **11/2**

0240 **8** *8* **Rusty Rocket (IRE)**[23] [2074] 5-9-2 **84** ........ KevinStott(5) 4 48
(Paul Green) *chsd ldrs: drvn over 2f out: lost pl over 1f out: eased whn bhd clsng stages* **3/1**[1]

-300 **9** *1 1/4* **Prince Regal**[13] [2350] 4-8-13 **76** ........ KierenFallon 6 36
(K R Burke) *chsd ldrs: drvn over 2f out: lost pl over 1f out: eased whn bhd clsng stages* **5/1**[3]

1m 13.91s (0.11) **Going Correction** +0.175s/f (Good) **9** Ran SP% **112.5**
Speed ratings (Par 105): **106,105,105,102,100 98,98,87,86**
CSF £58.05 CT £796.37 TOTE £15.90: £5.00, £2.10, £4.50; EX 73.50 Trifecta £615.60 Part won..
**Owner** Johnnie Delta Racing **Bred** Edmond And Richard Kent **Trained** Uplawmoor, E Renfrews
■ Stewards' Enquiry : Sammy Jo Bell two-day ban: used whip above permitted level (Jun 13-14)

**FOCUS**
There was no hanging about in this modest sprint handicap and the form looks fair with the principals coming nicely clear. Just about the winner's best run for two years.

### 2733 HALLIWELL JONES FOR LOW RATE FINANCE MAIDEN STKS 1m
**8:00** (8:03) (Class 5) 3-Y-O+ **£2,587** (£770; £384; £192) **Stalls** Low

Form RPR
0-3 **1** **Abbey Village (IRE)**[17] [2236] 3-9-2 0 ........ GrahamLee 1 86
(Richard Fahey) *wnt lft s: trckd ldrs: effrt over 2f out: led over 1f out: kpt on wl* **8/1**

56 **2** *1* **Mount Shamsan**[13] [2354] 4-10-0 0 ........ KierenFallon 9 87
(William Haggas) *trckd ldr: drvn over 2f out: styd on same pce last 100yds* **5/1**[3]

2- **3** *1 1/2* **Outlawed**[174] [8201] 3-9-2 0 ........ GeorgeBaker 4 80
(Ed Walker) *swtchd lft after s: mid-div: hdwy on inner to chse ldrs over 2f out: kpt on same pce fnl f* **7/4**[1]

-242 **4** *1 1/2* **Three Peaks**[20] [2170] 3-9-2 80 ........(p) RichardHughes 3 77
(Charles Hills) *trckd ldrs: effrt over 1f out: one pce* **3/1**[2]

**5** *nk* **Above The Rest (IRE)** 3-9-2 0 ........ DaneO'Neill 8 76
(K R Burke) *mid-div: effrt over 3f out: kpt on same pce over 1f out* **14/1**

6-2 **6** *1* **L'Importante**[69] [1069] 3-9-2 0 ........[1] PaddyAspell 2 74
(Marco Botti) *led: hdd over 1f out: wknd last 75yds* **7/1**

3- **7** *5* **Malraaj**[319] [4337] 3-8-11 0 ........ SammyJoBell(5) 5 63
(Richard Fahey) *mid-div: lost pl 6f out: drvn and sme hdwy over 3f out: lost pl wl over 1f out* **33/1**

50 **8** *1* **Haames (IRE)**[21] [2126] 7-9-7 0 ........ JordanNason(7) 6 63
(Kevin Morgan) *hld up in rr: effrt over 3f out: wknd 2f out* **66/1**

**9** *29* **Meeson** 3-8-13 0 ........ JasonHart(3) 7
(Violet M Jordan) *s.i.s: in rr: drvn 4f out: hung rt and sn bhd: t.o* **80/1**

1m 44.82s (1.12) **Going Correction** -0.175s/f (Firm)
**WFA** 3 from 4yo+ 12lb **9** Ran SP% **114.0**
Speed ratings (Par 103): **87,86,84,83,82 81,76,75,46**
CSF £46.65 TOTE £7.20: £2.10, £2.10, £1.20; EX 54.60 Trifecta £209.40.
**Owner** David W Armstrong **Bred** Laundry Cottage Stud Farm **Trained** Musley Bank, N Yorks

**FOCUS**
Not a bad maiden, but the time was slow. The form is taken at face value. Plenty were in with a chance near the two-furlong marker although they got sorted out from there.

### 2734 HALLIWELL JONES FOR 5 YEARS SERVICING H'CAP (BOBIS RACE) 7f
**8:35** (8:40) (Class 4) (0-80,80) 3-Y-O **£5,175** (£1,540; £769; £384) **Stalls** Low

Form RPR
01-3 **1** **You're Fired (IRE)**[35] [1693] 3-9-5 **78** ........ JimCrowley 4 91+
(K R Burke) *hld up in rr: hdwy on ins 3f out: nt clr run fr over 2f out tl swtchd outside over 1f out: styd on wl fnl f: led nr fin* **9/4**[1]

0-31 **2** *nk* **Regiment**[20] [2176] 3-9-5 **78** ........ TonyHamilton 6 87
(Richard Fahey) *trckd ldrs: effrt over 2f out: led over 1f out: hdd and no ex nr fin* **9/2**[2]

14-0 **3** *3 1/4* **Wickhambrook (IRE)**[29] [1897] 3-9-4 **77** ........ KierenFallon 5 78
(Ismail Mohammed) *hld up in rr: t.k.h: hdwy on outer 3f out: chsng ldrs over 1f out: kpt on one pce* **7/1**

3-00 **4** *1 1/4* **King Of Macedon (IRE)**[16] [2257] 3-9-7 **80** ........ FrannyNorton 7 78
(Mark Johnston) *chsd ldrs: drvn over 2f out: kpt on ins fnl f: tk 4th nr fin* **7/1**

-210 **5** *shd* **Excellent Royale (IRE)**[41] [1586] 3-8-13 **72** ........ RichardHughes 2 69
(Charles Hills) *led: hdd over 1f out: fdd fnl 75yds* **14/1**

0-05 **6** *2 1/4* **Xanthos**[13] [2333] 3-9-6 **79** ........ GrahamLee 1 71
(Ed Walker) *trckd ldrs: effrt over 2f out: wknd fnl f* **5/1**[3]

1m 29.25s (-1.45) **Going Correction** -0.175s/f (Firm) **6** Ran SP% **97.3**
Speed ratings (Par 101): **101,100,96,95,95 92**
CSF £9.09 CT £32.61 TOTE £2.00: £1.20, £2.10; EX 9.00 Trifecta £31.30.
**Owner** Market Avenue Racing Club & Partners **Bred** Shefford Valley Stud **Trained** Middleham Moor, N Yorks
■ Zain Zone (5-1) was withdrawn. Rule 4 applies to all bets. Deduction - 15p in the pound.

**FOCUS**
This fair 3yo handicap was run at a sound enough pace and two drew clear near the finish. The best time on the card.

### 2735 VANESSA ROGERS H'CAP 1m 3f 200y
**9:05** (9:07) (Class 5) (0-70,68) 3-Y-O **£2,587** (£770; £384; £192) **Stalls** Centre

Form RPR
0-05 **1** **Maid In Rio (IRE)**[18] [2210] 3-9-4 **65** ........ FrannyNorton 10 73
(Mark Johnston) *mid-div: hdwy 7f out: chsng ldrs over 2f out: led appr fnl f: styd on wl: readily* **25/1**

1-31 **2** *1 3/4* **Emerahldz (IRE)**[17] [2235] 3-9-6 **67** ........ TonyHamilton 9 72
(Richard Fahey) *trckd ldrs: chal 3f out: led briefly over 1f out: styd on same pce* **4/1**[2]

0-05 **3** *1/2* **Cinnilla**[15] [2279] 3-9-5 **66** ........(b[1]) JimCrowley 11 70
(Ralph Beckett) *stdd s: hld up in rr: hdwy over 3f out: 3rd over 1f out: kpt on* **7/1**

0-13 **4** *3 3/4* **Gimme Five**[16] [2247] 3-8-11 **58** ........ RichardHughes 8 56+
(Alan King) *trckd ldrs early: sn hld up in mid-div: hdwy and nt clr run over 2f out: one pce over 1f out* **9/4**[1]

05-0 **5** *nse* **Kinema (IRE)**[41] [1582] 3-9-7 **68** ........ GeorgeBaker 6 66
(Ed Walker) *stdd sn after s: hld up in rr: hdwy over 2f out: kpt on same pce fnl f* **14/1**

0-00 **6** *3/4* **Daydreamer**[18] [2221] 3-9-6 **67** ........ DaneO'Neill 1 64+
(William Haggas) *chsd ldrs: nt clr run over 2f out: one pce appr fnl f* **5/1**[3]

20-0 **7** *nk* **Craggaknock**[43] [1542] 3-9-4 **65** ........ GrahamLee 2 61
(Mark Walford) *hld up in mid-div: hdwy over 2f out: nt clr run over 1f out: one pce* **20/1**

P012 **8** *5* **Sirpertan**[17] [2237] 3-8-8 **58** ........ JasonHart(3) 5 52
(Mark Walford) *hld up in rr: drvn and hdwy over 2f out: nt clr run over 1f out: wknd and eased fnl f* **9/1**

3636 **9** *7* **Izbushka (IRE)**[11] [2385] 3-9-1 **62** ........ StevieDonohoe 3 39
(Ian Williams) *led: hdd over 2f out: lost pl over 1f out: eased whn bhd ins fnl f* **25/1**

34-2 **10** *9* **Armourer (IRE)**[10] [2417] 3-9-5 **66** ........ KierenFallon 7 29
(William Muir) *trckd ldr: led over 4f out: hdd over 1f out: sn wknd and eased* **10/1**

2m 36.14s (2.34) **Going Correction** -0.175s/f (Firm) **10** Ran SP% **118.1**
Speed ratings (Par 99): **85,83,83,81,80 80,80,76,72,66**
CSF £121.69 CT £792.88 TOTE £17.60: £4.40, £1.40, £2.80; EX 130.90 Trifecta £841.40 Part won..
**Owner** The New Fairyhouse Partnership **Bred** Miss Susan Bates And Suzannah Dwyer **Trained** Middleham Moor, N Yorks

**FOCUS**
A modest 3yo handicap in which the majority still held a chance of sorts 2f out. The winner was back to the level of her standout 2yo run.
T/Plt: £85.60 to a £1 stake. Pool: £67,697.01 - 576.94 winning tickets. T/Qpdt: £23.70 to a £1 stake. Pool: £5,505.02 - 171.76 winning tickets. WG

## 2420 NEWCASTLE (L-H)
Friday, May 30

**OFFICIAL GOING: Soft (5.6)**
Wind: Light, half behind Weather: Overcast

### 2736 LAFARGE TARMAC ULTIMATE/BRITISH STALLION STUDS EBF MAIDEN STKS (BOBIS RACE) 6f
**2:10** (2:10) (Class 4) 2-Y-O **£4,075** (£1,212; £606; £303) **Stalls** Centre

Form RPR
**1** **Dragon King (IRE)** 2-9-5 0 PaulMulrennan 3 72+
(Michael Dods) *in tch: effrt 2f out: led ins fnl f: edgd rt u.p and hld on wl nr fin* **11/8**[1]
**2** *3/4* **Split The Atom (IRE)**[32] 1820 2-9-2 0 RonanWhelan(3) 1 70
(John Patrick Shanahan, Ire) *t.k.h: led: rdn over 2f out: edgd lft over 1f out: hdd ins fnl f: one pce whn carried rt nr fin* **4/1**[2]
**3** *3/4* **Danny O'Ruairc (IRE)** 2-9-5 0 TomEaves 4 68
(James Moffatt) *missed break: bhd: gd hdwy and drifted both ways fr over 1f out: fin strly: improve* **33/1**
**4** *nk* **Our Kylie (IRE)** 2-9-0 0 BarryMcHugh 8 62
(Tony Coyle) *missed break: hld up: hdwy over 1f out: kpt on ins fnl f: nrst fin* **12/1**
**5** *3 1/4* **Subversive (IRE)** 2-9-5 0 JoeFanning 7 57
(Mark Johnston) *wnt rt s: sn trcking ldrs: rdn and edgd lft over 1f out: wknd ins fnl f: bttr for r* **9/2**[3]
**6** *3* **Sandgate** 2-9-5 0 TonyHamilton 2 48
(Richard Fahey) *green in preliminaries: disp ld to over 2f out: rdn and wknd over 1f out* **15/2**
6 **7** *2 1/4* **Autumn Revue**[25] 2014 2-9-0 0 DuranFentiman 5 36
(Tim Easterby) *t.k.h: prom: rdn and outpcd over 2f out: btn over 1f out* **14/1**
0 **8** *2* **Shamkhani**[18] 2214 2-9-2 0 SladeO'Hara(3) 6 35
(Alan Berry) *dwlt: hld up in tch: struggling over 2f out: sn btn* **80/1**
1m 18.29s (3.69) **Going Correction** +0.30s/f (Good) **8** Ran SP% **110.6**
Speed ratings (Par 95): **87,86,85,84,80 76,73,70**
CSF £6.37 TOTE £2.40: £1.10, £1.70, £5.50; EX 7.70 Trifecta £108.50.
**Owner** Mr & Mrs Paul Gaffney **Bred** Mountarmstrong Stud **Trained** Denton, Co Durham
■ Stewards' Enquiry : Paul Mulrennan one-day ban: careless riding (Jun 13)
**FOCUS**
Soft but drying ground and the opening time was 6.29sec outside standard. This was no more than a fair maiden. The winner can better the bare form.

### 2737 MITIE MAIDEN STKS 7f
**2:40** (2:41) (Class 5) 3-Y-O **£2,587** (£770; £384; £192) **Stalls** Low

Form RPR
20-2 **1** **Wilde Inspiration (IRE)**[13] 2333 3-9-5 76 PaulMulrennan 14 81+
(Julie Camacho) *in tch: hdwy over 2f out: rdn and led appr fnl f: kpt on wl* **3/1**[1]
24-0 **2** *1 1/4* **Percy's Gal**[21] 2130 3-8-7 70 GemmaTutty(7) 4 72
(Karen Tutty) *t.k.h: led: rdn over 2f out: hdd appr fnl f: rallied: one pce ins fnl f* **5/1**[3]
43 **3** *3 3/4* **Lince Suertudo (FR)**[27] 1959 3-9-5 0 DaleSwift 1 67
(Brian Ellison) *in tch: effrt and rdn 2f out: outpcd fnl f* **8/1**
**4** *1 1/2* **Dancin Alpha** 3-9-5 0 BenCurtis 11 63+
(Alan Swinbank) *dwlt: rn green in rr: hdwy over 1f out: kpt on fnl f: improve* **25/1**
0 **5** *1 1/4* **Yard Of Ale**[27] 1939 3-9-5 0 GrahamGibbons 12 60
(Kristin Stubbs) *hld up bhd ldng gp: effrt and rdn over 2f out: edgd lft and no imp over 1f out* **66/1**
5 **6** *1 1/2* **Queens Park (FR)**[55] 1303 3-9-0 0 PJMcDonald 10 51
(John Davies) *prom: drvn over 2f out: edgd lft over 1f out: sn outpcd* **33/1**
**7** *3* **Mr McLaren** 3-9-5 0 DanielTudhope 6 48+
(David O'Meara) *dwlt: bhd: rdn and rn green after 2f: hdwy over 1f out: nvr rchd ldrs* **20/1**
**8** *2* **Saltire (IRE)**[16] 2266 3-8-11 0 RonanWhelan(3) 7 38
(John Patrick Shanahan, Ire) *t.k.h: cl up tl rdn and wknd 2f out* **50/1**
5 **9** *3 3/4* **Patron Of Explores (USA)**[10] 2420 3-9-5 0 AndrewMullen 9 33
(Patrick Holmes) *trckd ldrs tl rdn and wknd over 2f out* **66/1**
4- **10** *3 1/2* **Saranta**[237] 7023 3-9-0 0 TonyHamilton 5 19
(Richard Fahey) *hld up bhd ldng gp: drvn over 2f out: sn btn* **7/2**[2]
2-06 **11** *5* **Tancred (IRE)**[18] 2218 3-9-5 69 (b[1]) BarryMcHugh 2 11
(Tony Coyle) *early reminders: towards rr on outside: effrt 1/2-way: wknd fnl 2f* **10/1**
006 **12** *1 3/4* **Silver Duke (IRE)**[18] 2201 3-8-12 72 RobJFitzpatrick(7) 3 7
(K R Burke) *dwlt: bhd and sn struggling: btn over 2f out* **7/1**
1m 29.65s (1.85) **Going Correction** +0.30s/f (Good) **12** Ran SP% **113.1**
Speed ratings (Par 99): **101,99,95,93,92 90,87,84,80,76 70,68**
CSF £15.88 TOTE £3.20: £1.40, £3.00, £1.90; EX 16.60 Trifecta £73.60.
**Owner** Judy & Richard Peck **Bred** Pier House Stud **Trained** Norton, N Yorks
**FOCUS**
The first two finished clear in this ordinary maiden. The form is rated around the runner-up.

### 2738 AIS OFFSHORE TRAINING H'CAP 1m 4f 93y
**3:15** (3:16) (Class 6) (0-60,60) 4-Y-O+ **£1,940** (£577; £288; £144) **Stalls** High

Form RPR
5-02 **1** **Kathlatino**[36] 1674 7-9-2 55 (v) DuranFentiman 4 64
(Micky Hammond) *hld up in tch: rdn and outpcd over 2f out: rallied over 1f out: led wl ins fnl f: styd on* **10/1**
3035 **2** *3/4* **My Destination (IRE)**[20] 2175 5-9-4 60 (b) JasonHart(3) 13 68
(Declan Carroll) *hld up in midfield: stdy hdwy over 3f out: rdn to ld over 1f out: hdd wl ins fnl f: no ex* **4/1**[2]
5-30 **3** *hd* **Politbureau**[11] 2396 7-8-7 46 oh1 (b) BarryMcHugh 15 53
(Michael Easterby) *hld up in tch: smooth hdwy to ld over 3f out: rdn and edgd lft over 2f out: hdd over 1f out: rallied and ev ch ins fnl f: hld nr fin* **14/1**
0-00 **4** *3* **Amazing Blue Sky**[8] 2476 8-8-12 51 PJMcDonald 5 54
(Ruth Carr) *hld up on ins: rdn and hdwy 2f out: kpt on fnl f: nt rch first three* **10/1**
5500 **5** *shd* **Rainford Glory (IRE)**[102] 643 4-9-2 55 (p) DavidNolan 3 58
(Richard Fahey) *hld up in midfield: rdn over 2f out: hdwy over 1f out: kpt on ins fnl f* **16/1**
040- **6** *2* **District Attorney (IRE)**[17] 5882 5-8-8 47 MichaelStainton 9 46
(Chris Fairhurst) *hld up: hdwy and prom over 3f out: rdn and outpcd over 1f out* **25/1**
6-55 **7** *1* **Bold And Free**[47] 831 4-9-4 57 StevieDonohoe 8 55
(David Thompson) *hld up in tch: effrt and cl up 3f out: no ex over 1f out* **20/1**
03-6 **8** *11* **Captain Rhyric**[24] 2053 5-8-8 47 JoeFanning 10 27
(James Moffatt) *hld up: drvn over 3f out: nvr able to chal* **22/1**
0-65 **9** *3/4* **Samoan (IRE)**[26] 1969 5-8-7 46 oh1 PatrickMathers 12 25
(Alan Berry) *hld up: struggling over 3f out: n.d after* **25/1**
00-0 **10** *8* **Comical**[36] 1675 5-8-11 50 BenCurtis 11 16
(George Moore) *w ldr: ev ch tl rdn and wknd over 2f out* **10/1**
05-0 **11** *6* **Slip Of A Girl (IRE)**[142] 81 4-8-0 46 JackGarritty(7) 16 3
(Patrick Holmes) *bhd: struggling 4f out: nvr on terms* **33/1**
5-05 **12** *4 1/2* **Authentication**[10] 2424 5-8-11 50 DavidAllan 14
(Mel Brittain) *t.k.h: chsd ldrs tl rdn and wknd 3f out* **7/2**[1]
555- **13** *12* **Yorkshireman (IRE)**[278] 5791 4-9-7 60 PaddyAspell 6
(Lynn Siddall) *hld up in midfield: struggling over 3f out: sn btn* **20/1**
50-0 **14** *29* **Frank's Folly (IRE)**[13] 2327 5-9-7 60 (p) GrahamGibbons 1
(Mark Walford) *slt ld to over 3f out: sn rdn and wknd* **6/1**[3]
5-00 **15** *59* **Mrs Gorsky**[11] 2389 4-8-7 46 oh1 AndrewMullen 7
(Patrick Holmes) *hld up: struggling over 4f out: sn lost tch: t.o* **100/1**
2m 50.24s (4.64) **Going Correction** +0.30s/f (Good) **15** Ran SP% **121.8**
Speed ratings (Par 101): **96,95,95,93,93 91,91,83,83,78 74,71,63,43,4**
CSF £45.61 CT £579.68 TOTE £5.50: £2.50, £2.10, £3.90; EX 23.20 Trifecta £61.30.
**Owner** 50/50 Racing Club **Bred** Mrs Jayce Haley **Trained** Middleham Moor, N Yorks
**FOCUS**
A low-grade handicap run at a fair gallop. The form is rated around the runner-up.

### 2739 O'BRIEN WASTE RECYLING SOLUTIONS H'CAP 2m 19y
**3:50** (3:50) (Class 4) (0-85,83) 4-Y-O+ **£4,690** (£1,395; £697; £348) **Stalls** High

Form RPR
-000 **1** **Moidore**[15] 2289 5-9-7 83 IanBrennan(3) 11 92
(John Quinn) *hld up on outside: smooth hdwy and cl up whn outpcd over 2f out: rallied to ld ins fnl f: styd on wl* **9/2**[2]
00-0 **2** *1/2* **Nashville (IRE)**[15] 2289 5-9-1 74 DavidNolan 7 82
(Richard Fahey) *hld up: hdwy to ld over 2f out: sn rdn: edgd rt and hdd ins fnl f: kpt on* **50/1**
0-61 **3** *1 1/4* **Rosairlie (IRE)**[21] 2139 6-9-5 78 PJMcDonald 3 85
(Micky Hammond) *hld up: hdwy and ev ch over 2f out: sn rdn: one pce ins fnl f* **9/2**[2]
-534 **4** *1 3/4* **Mr Snoozy**[15] 2289 5-9-4 80 (p) JasonHart(3) 6 85
(Mark Walford) *midfield: hdwy on outside and cl up over 2f out: sn rdn: kpt on same pce fnl f* **11/4**[1]
2/-0 **5** *2 1/2* **Cape Tribulation**[15] 2289 10-9-2 75 DanielTudhope 8 77
(Malcolm Jefferson) *hld up in tch: stdy hdwy over 4f out: edgd lft and ev ch over 2f out: outpcd over 1f out* **14/1**
0546 **6** *8* **Albonny (IRE)**[8] 2482 5-8-3 69 RobJFitzpatrick(7) 4 61
(K R Burke) *hld up: rdn over 3f out: no imp fr 2f out* **12/1**
000/ **7** *shd* **Nafaath (IRE)**[542] 7522 8-9-1 77 ConnorBeasley(3) 1 69
(Donald McCain) *hld up in tch: rdn over 3f out: outpcd fnl 2f* **16/1**
3105 **8** *7* **Arr' Kid (USA)**[21] 2108 4-9-2 77 (b) GrahamGibbons 10 61
(Keith Dalgleish) *s.i.s: hdwy to ld after 1f: sn clr: rdn over 3f out: hdd & wknd over 2f out* **12/1**
-230 **9** *2* **Categorical**[7] 2515 11-8-9 73 EmmaSayer(5) 9 54
(Keith Reveley) *s.i.s: hld up: rdn over 4f out: nvr on terms* **25/1**
0-30 **10** *75* **Man Of Plenty**[15] 2289 5-9-9 82 (b) PaulMulrennan 2
(Ed Dunlop) *led 1f: chsd clr ldr: rdn over 4f out: wknd wl over 2f out: virtually p.u fnl f* **16/1**
4322 **11** *23* **Sir Frank Morgan (IRE)**[10] 2430 4-8-12 73 JoeFanning 5
(Mark Johnston) *chsd clr ldrs: drvn and struggling over 4f out: sn btn: t.o* **11/2**[3]
3m 41.68s (2.28) **Going Correction** +0.30s/f (Good)
**WFA** 4 from 5yo+ 2lb **11** Ran SP% **118.0**
Speed ratings (Par 105): **106,105,105,104,103 99,98,95,94,56 45**
CSF £198.18 CT £1077.75 TOTE £7.00: £1.60, £10.90, £2.30; EX 203.60 Trifecta £2854.90 Part won..
**Owner** Estio Pinnacle Racing **Bred** The Queen **Trained** Settrington, N Yorks
■ Stewards' Enquiry : David Nolan one-day ban: careless riding (Jun 13)
**FOCUS**
A decent staying handicap in which Arr' Kid was clear for a while, setting quite a gallop. The principals came from off the pace and raced down the middle of the track in the home straight. Five of the field, including four of the first five, had met in Villa Royale's race at York earlier in the month. The winner is rated in line with his latter form.

### 2740 KNIGHT FRANK CUP FILLIES' H'CAP 1m 3y(S)
**4:25** (4:25) (Class 5) (0-75,75) 3-Y-O **£2,587** (£770; £384; £192) **Stalls** Low

Form RPR
-223 **1** **Polar Eyes**[21] 2118 3-9-0 75 JordanNason(7) 6 84
(Peter Chapple-Hyam) *dwlt: t.k.h: in tch: swtchd rt and hdwy to ld over 2f out: pushed out fnl f* **9/1**
51-5 **2** *2 1/4* **Maiden Approach**[21] 2130 3-8-10 67 GeorgeChaloner(3) 1 71
(Richard Fahey) *t.k.h: cl up: ev ch over 2f out to over 1f out: kpt on fnl f: nt rch wnr* **5/1**[3]
6-62 **3** *2 1/2* **Irondale Express**[18] 2205 3-9-1 69 BarryMcHugh 2 67
(Tony Coyle) *hld up: effrt and pushed along 2f out: kpt on ins fnl f* **16/1**
2-03 **4** *3/4* **Thatchereen (IRE)**[15] 2274 3-8-9 68 LouisSteward(5) 5 65
(Michael Bell) *hld up in tch: stdy hdwy over 2f out: sn rdn and edgd lft: no imp fr over 1f out* **3/1**[1]
-216 **5** *1 3/4* **Dalmarella Dancer (IRE)**[15] 2274 3-9-2 75 JoeyHaynes(5) 7 68
(K R Burke) *cl up: ev ch over 2f out: no ex over 1f out* **8/1**
30-2 **6** *10* **Coin Broker (IRE)**[17] 2236 3-9-0 68 DanielTudhope 3 38
(David O'Meara) *led: rdn and hdd over 2f out: wknd over 1f out* **4/1**[2]
051- **7** *13* **L'Artiste (IRE)**[289] 5379 3-8-13 70 IanBrennan(3) 4 10
(John Quinn) *hld up: rdn and outpcd wl over 2f out: sn btn* **20/1**
4-4 **8** *7* **Tiffany Bay (IRE)**[26] 1999 3-9-2 73 RonanWhelan(3) 8
(John Patrick Shanahan, Ire) *t.k.h: cl up tl rdn and wknd over 2f out* **12/1**
64-6 **9** *10* **Lady Red Oak**[31] 1846 3-8-11 65 (p) GrahamGibbons 9
(Tom Dascombe) *prom tl drvn and wknd over 2f out* **7/1**
1m 45.15s (1.75) **Going Correction** +0.30s/f (Good) **9** Ran SP% **113.6**
Speed ratings (Par 96): **103,100,98,97,95 85,72,65,55**
CSF £52.60 CT £714.27 TOTE £8.50: £2.70, £1.60, £3.60; EX 59.30 Trifecta £380.70.
**Owner** The Illusionists **Bred** Societa Agricola Gem Srl **Trained** Newmarket, Suffolk

**FOCUS**
They didn't go a strong pace in this fillies' handicap, and the form looks very ordinary. Not a race to be too positive about.

## 2741 NRG FAVOURITES IN RECRUITMENT NRGPLC.COM H'CAP (DIV I) 1m 3y(S)
5:00 (5:01) (Class 6) (0-60,59) 3-Y-O £1,940 (£577; £288; £144) Stalls Low

Form RPR
000 1 **Tortoise**11 2393 3-8-4 45 (b) ConnorBeasley(3) 1 58
(Richard Guest) *taken early to post: prom: hdwy to ld over 2f out: pushed clr over 1f out: comf* **9/1**
1246 2 4 ½ **Vosne Romanee**11 2393 3-9-6 58 (p) JoeFanning 3 61
(Keith Dalgleish) *t.k.h: hld up: smooth hdwy to press wnr over 2f out: rdn and hd high over 1f out: one pce fnl f* **5/2**1
0-51 3 ½ **Dutch Lady**13 2355 3-9-7 59 StevieDonohoe 6 61
(John Holt) *t.k.h: hld up: drvn and hung lft over 2f out: styd on fnl f: nvr able to chal* **3/1**2
5304 4 4 ½ **Marlismamma (FR)**6 2545 3-8-11 52 JulieBurke(3) 9 44
(David O'Meara) *t.k.h: prom: rdn over 2f out: wknd over 1f out* **13/2**
-300 5 ¾ **Gee Sharp**11 2393 3-9-3 55 (b1) BarryMcHugh 2 45
(Julie Camacho) *led at ordinary gallop: rdn and hdd over 2f out: wknd over 1f out* **12/1**
0-00 6 2 ½ **Oriental Dream (IRE)**18 2204 3-8-7 45 AndrewMullen 7 29
(Nigel Tinkler) *cl up tl rdn and wknd over 2f out* **25/1**
45-6 7 1 ½ **Ofelia (IRE)**17 2236 3-8-12 50 DaleSwift 8 31
(Brian Ellison) *dwlt: hld up bhd ldng gp: rdn over 3f out: wknd over 2f out* **5/1**3
464- 8 3 ¼ **Winter Picnic (IRE)**234 7111 3-9-1 53 DuranFentiman 4 26
(Tim Easterby) *cl up: rdn and ev ch over 2f out: wknd wl over 1f out* **10/1**

1m 47.07s (3.67) **Going Correction** +0.30s/f (Good) 8 Ran SP% **114.2**
Speed ratings (Par 97): **93,88,88,83,82 80,78,75**
CSF £31.77 CT £85.30 TOTE £8.90: £3.50, £1.10, £1.30; EX 53.10 Trifecta £170.80.
**Owner** Available For Sale Or Lease **Bred** Ellis Stud And Bellow Hill Stud **Trained** Wetherby, W Yorks

**FOCUS**
A decidedly moderate event, run at a steady initial gallop, and the slower division by two seconds. They finished strung out behind the winner. Probably not form to be too literal about.

## 2742 NRG FAVOURITES IN RECRUITMENT NRGPLC.COM H'CAP (DIV II) 1m 3y(S)
5:35 (5:35) (Class 6) (0-60,59) 3-Y-O £1,940 (£577; £288; £144) Stalls Low

Form RPR
6135 1 **It's All A Game**13 2355 3-9-2 57 (b) ConnorBeasley(3) 2 65
(Richard Guest) *taken early to post: trckd ldrs: rdn over 2f out: led over 1f out: kpt on strly* **11/4**2
-000 2 3 ¼ **Green Zone (IRE)**13 2355 3-9-7 59 (p) AndrewMullen 5 60
(Nigel Tinkler) *bhd: drvn along over 3f out: rallied and hung lft 2f out: chsd (clr) wnr ins fnl f: r.o* **8/1**
0440 3 3 ¾ **Sicilian Bay (IRE)**11 2393 3-9-1 53 PaulMulrennan 9 45
(Paul Midgley) *trckd ldrs: hdwy and ev ch over 2f out: sn rdn and edgd lft: wnt 2nd briefly ins fnl f: one pce* **5/1**3
00-5 4 2 ¼ **Halloween Moon**38 1632 3-8-2 45 ShirleyTeasdale(5) 7 32
(James Bethell) *t.k.h: cl up: rdn and outpcd over 2f out: rallied over 1f out: sn no imp* **16/1**
00-4 5 nse **Notts So Blue**32 1801 3-8-8 46 DaleSwift 1 33
(Shaun Harris) *led: rdn and hrd pressed over 2f out: hdd over 1f out: sn btn* **40/1**
-023 6 1 ¾ **Bourbon Prince**31 1852 3-8-10 53 LouisSteward(5) 4 36
(Michael Bell) *hld up in tch: rdn and hung lft over 2f out: sn outpcd* **2/1**1
00-0 7 3 ½ **Skinny Latte**37 1648 3-8-7 45 PatrickMathers 3 20
(Micky Hammond) *hld up bhd ldng gp: drvn along 3f out: btn fnl 2f* **50/1**
044- 8 9 **Modify**192 7956 3-9-3 55 DanielTudhope 8 9
(David O'Meara) *hld up: rdn along over 3f out: wknd over 2f out* **12/1**
0-00 9 32 **Moxey**25 2020 3-8-12 50 PJMcDonald 6
(John Davies) *bhd: struggling over 3f out: sn btn: t.o* **14/1**

1m 45.02s (1.62) **Going Correction** +0.30s/f (Good) 9 Ran SP% **112.4**
Speed ratings (Par 97): **103,99,96,93,93 91,88,79,47**
CSF £24.23 CT £103.34 TOTE £4.30: £1.60, £3.30, £1.90; EX 24.00 Trifecta £134.40.
**Owner** Viscount Environmental Ltd **Bred** Mrs G Sainty **Trained** Wetherby, W Yorks

**FOCUS**
This was another weak race, but it was the quicker of the two divisions by two seconds. Doubts over the field, but improvement from the winner.

## 2743 TSG IT & TELECOMS H'CAP 5f
6:05 (6:06) (Class 5) (0-70,69) 4-Y-O+ £2,587 (£770; £384; £192) Stalls Centre

Form RPR
4331 1 **Harrogate Fair**3 2637 4-9-3 65 6ex (p) JoeFanning 2 74
(Michael Squance) *in tch: shkn up and hdwy to ld appr fnl f: edgd lft: pushed out* **4/5**1
2435 2 ¾ **Windforpower (IRE)**6 2552 4-9-1 63 (p) PaulPickard 3 69
(Tracy Waggott) *t.k.h: cl up: effrt and rdn over 1f out: chsd wnr ins fnl f: r.o* **13/2**3
0-02 3 1 **Lees Anthem**17 2232 7-8-8 56 DavidAllan 7 59
(Mel Brittain) *t.k.h: led: rdn and hdd appr fnl f: rallied: one pce and lost 2nd ins fnl f* **4/1**2
0-00 4 1 ½ **Tuibama (IRE)**37 1643 5-8-9 57 (p) DaleSwift 5 54
(Tracy Waggott) *t.k.h: cl up: rdn wl over 1f out: kpt on same pce fnl f* **8/1**
0000 5 7 **Sunrise Dance**10 2421 5-9-4 69 ConnorBeasley(3) 4 41
(Robert Johnson) *in tch: outpcd after 2f: sn n.d* **16/1**

1m 2.13s (1.03) **Going Correction** +0.30s/f (Good) 5 Ran SP% **105.9**
Speed ratings (Par 103): **103,101,100,97,86**
CSF £5.82 TOTE £1.40: £1.10, £2.90; EX 6.00 Trifecta £9.80.
**Owner** Miss K Squance **Bred** Kevin Daniel Crabb **Trained** Newmarket, Suffolk

**FOCUS**
A modest little handicap, rated around the second and third.
T/Jkpt: £92,476.50 to a £1 stake. Pool: £846,615.90 - 6.50 winning tickets T/Plt: £65.70 to a £1 stake. Pool: £108,428.10 - 1204.63 winning tickets T/Qpdt: £27.60 to a £1 stake. Pool: £6,621.68 - 177.40 winning tickets RY

# 2341 NEWMARKET (R-H)
Friday, May 30

**OFFICIAL GOING: Soft changing to good to soft after race 2 (2.30)**
Wind: Light across Weather: Overcast Rails: First meeting of year on July Course. Far side track used. Stalls Far side except 10f &12: Centre

## 2744 COUNTRYSIDE ALLIANCE FOUNDATION EBF STALLIONS MAIDEN FILLIES' STKS (BOBIS RACE) 6f
2:00 (2:01) (Class 4) 2-Y-O £4,528 (£1,347; £673; £336) Stalls Low

Form RPR
1 **Bitter Lake (USA)** 2-9-0 0 MickaelBarzalona 9 83+
(Charlie Appleby) *hld up: swtchd rt and hdwy over 1f out: r.o to ld wl ins fnl f* **7/1**
0 2 1 ¼ **Kinematic**21 2107 2-9-0 0 RichardHughes 8 77
(Andrew Balding) *led: qcknd over 2f out: rdn over 1f out: hdd wl ins fnl f* **4/1**2
5 3 2 ¼ **Looking Good**8 2493 2-9-0 0 JamieSpencer 6 70
(David Brown) *trckd ldr: rdn over 2f out: styd on same pce fnl f* **4/1**2
4 ½ **Hound Music** 2-9-0 0 ShaneKelly 4 69
(Jonathan Portman) *s.i.s: hld up: pushed along 1/2-way: hmpd over 1f out: r.o ins fnl f: nrst fin* **100/1**
5 ¾ **Hoorayforhollywood** 2-9-0 0 JimCrowley 1 66
(Sir Michael Stoute) *hld up: shkn up and hdwy over 2f out: styd on same pce fnl f* **12/1**
6 hd **Lashkaal** 2-9-0 0 PaulHanagan 3 66
(John Gosden) *s.i.s: sn pushed along and rn green in rr: r.o ins fnl f: nvr nrr* **10/3**1
7 1 **Stone Roses (IRE)** 2-9-0 0 TomQueally 2 63
(Michael Bell) *trckd ldrs: rdn over 2f out: edgd rt over 1f out: wknd ins fnl f* **14/1**
8 hd **Nancy Astor** 2-9-0 0 WilliamBuick 5 62
(John Gosden) *s.i.s: sn prom: pushed along 2f out: wknd ins fnl f* **9/2**3
9 3 ¾ **Assault On Rome (IRE)** 2-9-0 0 KierenFallon 7 51
(Mark Johnston) *chsd ldrs: pushed along 1/2-way: wknd over 1f out* **20/1**

1m 16.45s (3.95) **Going Correction** +0.575s/f (Yiel) 9 Ran SP% **113.9**
Speed ratings (Par 92): **96,94,91,90,89 89,88,87,82**
CSF £34.61 TOTE £8.00: £3.50, £1.60, £1.90; EX 35.40 Trifecta £139.70.
**Owner** Godolphin **Bred** Darley **Trained** Newmarket, Suffolk
■ Stewards' Enquiry : Mickael Barzalona one-day ban: careless riding (Jun 13)

**FOCUS**
First meeting of year on July Course. Far side track used. Stalls far side except 1m2f &1m4f: centre. Following a dry night, the going remained officially soft, though a couple of the jockeys in the first race thought it was more good to soft. An interesting fillies' maiden to start the card and we should be hearing plenty more of a few of these. The winner impressed. They raced far side.

## 2745 COUNTRYSIDE ALLIANCE EBF STALLIONS FILLIES' H'CAP (BOBIS RACE) 6f
2:30 (2:31) (Class 4) (0-85,85) 3-Y-O £6,469 (£1,925; £962; £481) Stalls Low

Form RPR
3-00 1 **Baby Bush (IRE)**13 2340 3-8-13 77 RichardHughes 12 84
(Richard Hannon) *hld up: hdwy over 1f out: rdn and r.o to ld wl ins fnl f* **9/2**1
6303 2 ¾ **Jive**10 2429 3-8-4 68 KieranO'Neill 3 73
(Richard Hannon) *chsd ldrs: rdn to ld over 1f out: hdd and unable qck wl ins fnl f* **12/1**
15-0 3 ½ **Arranger (IRE)**13 2340 3-8-9 73 RobertHavlin 6 76
(Martyn Meade) *hld up: shkn up over 1f out: r.o to go 3rd post* **8/1**
00-4 4 hd **Lady Lydia (IRE)**21 2122 3-8-11 75 JimmyQuinn 5 78
(Conrad Allen) *s.i.s: hld up: hdwy 2f out: sn rdn and edgd lft: styd on* **16/1**
61-4 5 1 ¾ **Terhaab (USA)**50 1409 3-8-12 76 1 PaulHanagan 7 73
(John Gosden) *plld hrd and prom: rdn over 1f out: styd on same pce ins fnl f* **12/1**
4-00 6 ¾ **Valen (IRE)**26 1985 3-9-2 80 TomQueally 8 75
(Michael Bell) *hld up: rdn over 1f out: styd on ins fnl f: nvr nrr* **8/1**
11- 7 ½ **Pull The Plug (IRE)**290 5366 3-9-2 83 NeilFarley(3) 11 76
(Declan Carroll) *led: hdd over 4f out: chsd ldr: rdn over 2f out: no ex fnl f* **16/1**
13-2 8 ½ **Miss Atomic Bomb**32 1818 3-8-13 82 MarcMonaghan(5) 13 74
(Marco Botti) *chsd ldrs: rdn over 1f out: no ex fnl f* **7/1**3
1-10 9 ½ **Perfect Alchemy (IRE)**27 1952 3-9-1 79 JimCrowley 10 69
(Ralph Beckett) *hld up: hdwy over 1f out: wknd ins fnl f* **13/2**2
021- 10 1 ¾ **Much Promise**206 7737 3-9-2 80 WilliamBuick 1 64
(John Gosden) *s.i.s: plld hrd and sn prom: rdn over 1f out: wknd fnl f* **9/2**1
01 11 9 **Little Shambles**37 1645 3-9-0 78 KierenFallon 2 34
(Mark Johnston) *w ldr tl led over 4f out: rdn: edgd lft and hdd over 1f out: wknd fnl f* **14/1**

1m 15.38s (2.88) **Going Correction** +0.575s/f (Yiel) 11 Ran SP% **118.2**
Speed ratings (Par 98): **103,102,101,101,98 97,97,96,95,93 81**
CSF £60.44 CT £431.70 TOTE £5.10: £1.70, £3.40, £4.00; EX 85.30 Trifecta £475.70.
**Owner** Malih Lahej Al Basti **Bred** Edward And Mrs S Hannigan **Trained** East Everleigh, Wilts

**FOCUS**
A competitive fillies' sprint handicap in which they raced down the centre. It resulted in a 1-2 for trainer Richard Hannon. Ordinary form.

## 2746 LLOYDS BANK COMMERCIAL MAIDEN STKS 1m 4f
3:05 (3:06) (Class 5) 3-Y-O £5,175 (£1,540; £769; £384) Stalls Centre

Form RPR
3 1 **Wonderstruck (IRE)**21 2109 3-9-0 0 FrankieDettori 8 90+
(William Haggas) *hld up: hdwy over 2f out: rdn to ld and hung rt 1f out: styd on* **11/4**2
0- 2 ¾ **Forever Now**200 7834 3-9-5 0 WilliamBuick 4 93
(John Gosden) *chsd ldr: rdn and ev ch whn hmpd 1f out: styd on* **8/1**
334 3 3 **Karraar**13 2334 3-9-5 77 PaulHanagan 7 89
(Richard Hannon) *led: rdn over 2f out: sn hung rt: hung lft and hdd 1f out: sn hung rt again: no ex and hung lft wl ins fnl f* **12/1**
3 4 2 ¼ **Hatsaway (IRE)**15 2271 3-9-5 0 RichardHughes 6 85
(Clive Brittain) *hld up: hdwy over 2f out: rdn over 1f out: no ex fnl f* **14/1**
2-26 5 1 **Saab Almanal**15 2285 3-9-5 103 TomQueally 10 83
(James Fanshawe) *hld up: hdwy u.p over 1f out: no ex ins fnl f* **7/4**1
6 4 ½ **Hydrogen** 3-9-5 0 JamieSpencer 3 76
(Peter Chapple-Hyam) *hld up: hdwy over 2f out: shkn up and wknd over 1f out* **4/1**3

00 **7** *2 ½* **Injun Sands**[18] 2201 3-9-5 0............................ FrederikTylicki 9 72
(Jane Chapple-Hyam) *s.i.s: hld up: rdn over 2f out: wknd over 1f out*
**200/1**

0 **8** *4* **Rideonastar (IRE)**[13] 2334 3-9-5 0............................ JimCrowley 5 66
(Ralph Beckett) *prom: rdn over 3f out: wknd over 2f out* **33/1**

0-0 **9** *7* **Mr Smith**[15] 2271 3-9-5 0............................ KierenFallon 2 55
(John Gosden) *prom: rdn over 3f out: wknd over 2f out* **40/1**

2m 40.24s (7.34) **Going Correction** +0.75s/f (Yiel) 9 Ran SP% **114.4**
Speed ratings (Par 99): **105,104,102,101,100 97,95,93,88**
CSF £24.50 TOTE £3.00: £1.10, £2.10, £2.60; EX 31.80 Trifecta £199.00.
**Owner** Lael Stable **Bred** Lael Stables **Trained** Newmarket, Suffolk

**FOCUS**
The ground was change to good to soft before this race. A fascinating 3yo maiden featuring some very interesting types, but they didn't go much of a pace. The runners made for the centre of the track after turning in. Not the form it might have been, with the favourite disappointing, and the winner didn't need to improve on her debut effort.

## 2747 LLOYDS BANK CARDNET H'CAP 7f
**3:40** (3:40) (Class 3) (0-95,95) 4-Y-0+ **£9,056** (£2,695; £1,346; £673) **Stalls** Low

Form RPR

1132 **1** **Hillbilly Boy (IRE)**[21] 2110 4-9-0 **88**............................ AndreaAtzeni 3 103
(Martin Smith) *trckd ldr tl led over 1f out: shkn up and c clr ins fnl f: comf*
**2/1**[1]

00-3 **2** *5* **Life Partner (IRE)**[18] 2202 4-9-5 **93**............................ WilliamBuick 1 95
(Charlie Appleby) *s.s: hld up: plld hrd: hdwy 1/2-way: rdn over 1f out: styd on same pce: wnt 2nd wl ins fnl f* **7/1**

0-02 **3** *¾* **Majestic Moon (IRE)**[28] 1928 4-9-1 **89**............................ PaulHanagan 2 89
(Richard Fahey) *sn led: rdn and hdd over 1f out: no ex ins fnl f* **4/1**[2]

0111 **4** *5* **Victoire De Lyphar (IRE)**[29] 1903 7-9-7 **95**..............(e) JamesSullivan 4 82
(Ruth Carr) *trckd ldrs: rdn over 1f out: wknd fnl f: b.b.v* **5/1**[3]

0-60 **5** *14* **Pearl Ice**[34] 1734 6-9-3 **91**............................ TedDurcan 7 42
(Charlie Fellowes) *slipped s: hld up: rdn over 2f out: sn wknd* **33/1**

-530 **6** *3* **Spiritual Star (IRE)**[20] 2145 5-9-2 **90**............................ WilliamCarson 5 33
(Anthony Carson) *hld up: rdn and wknd over 2f out* **16/1**

00-0 **7** *22* **Tamayuz Star (IRE)**[26] 1975 4-9-7 **95**............................ TomQueally 6
(George Margarson) *chsd ldrs tl rdn and wknd over 2f out* **14/1**

0-42 **8** *42* **Czech It Out (IRE)**[7] 2500 4-8-8 **82**............................ JimCrowley 8
(Amanda Perrett) *hld up: rdn and hung lft 1/2-way: sn eased: fin lame*
**11/2**

1m 26.42s (0.72) **Going Correction** +0.325s/f (Good) 8 Ran SP% **113.4**
Speed ratings (Par 107): **108,102,101,95,79 76,51,3**
CSF £16.41 CT £50.46 TOTE £2.70: £1.40, £1.80, £1.30; EX 13.20 Trifecta £34.70.
**Owner** Macguire's Bloodstock Ltd **Bred** Tipper House Stud **Trained** Newmarket, Suffolk

**FOCUS**
This looked a decent handicap beforehand, but it proved a strange race as they finished spread out across Newmarket Heath and perhaps the drying ground caught out a few. The winner took his form to a new high.

## 2748 LLOYDS BANK COMMERCIAL SUPPORTING YOUR BUSINESS H'CAP (BOBIS RACE) 1m 2f
**4:15** (4:17) (Class 3) (0-95,95) 3-Y-O **£9,056** (£2,695; £1,346; £673) **Stalls** Centre

Form RPR

12-6 **1** **Top Tug (IRE)**[43] 1535 3-8-10 **84**............................ ShaneKelly 3 96
(Sir Michael Stoute) *chsd ldr tl rdn over 2f out: wnt 2nd again over 1f out: r.o to ld wl ins fnl f* **4/1**[2]

1-15 **2** *¾* **Cloudscape (IRE)**[27] 1953 3-9-7 **95**..............(t) WilliamBuick 7 106
(John Gosden) *trckd ldrs: racd keenly: wnt 2nd over 2f out: led over 1f out: sn edgd rioht: rdn and hdd wl ins fnl f* **7/4**[1]

5-03 **3** *7* **Stormardal (IRE)**[20] 2148 3-9-4 **92**............................ TomQueally 5 90
(Ismail Mohammed) *led: rdn and hdd over 1f out: nt clr run sn after: wknd ins fnl f* **6/1**

12-1 **4** *½* **Devilment**[24] 2060 3-9-2 **90**............................ MickaelBarzalona 6 87
(Charlie Appleby) *hld up: hdwy over 2f out: sn rdn: no ex fnl f* **11/2**[3]

11-0 **5** *nk* **Bremner**[27] 1953 3-9-7 **95**..............(tp) MartinDwyer 4 91
(Hugo Palmer) *prom: plld hrd: n.m.r: stdd and lost pl after 1f: hdwy over 3f out: rdn over 2f out: styd on same pce fr over 1f out* **25/1**

41 **6** *5* **Famous Kid (USA)**[20] 2170 3-9-3 **91**............................ KierenFallon 1 78
(Saeed bin Suroor) *unruly in stalls: prom: pushed along over 3f out: hung lft and wknd over 1f out* **7/1**

51 **7** *4* **Barye**[105] 607 3-8-2 **76**............................ MartinLane 2 55
(David Simcock) *hld up: swtchd lft over 3f out: rdn and wknd over 1f out*
**7/1**

2m 12.25s (6.75) **Going Correction** +0.75s/f (Yiel) 7 Ran SP% **114.9**
Speed ratings (Par 103): **103,102,96,96,96 92,88**
CSF £11.56 TOTE £5.40: £2.60, £1.70; EX 15.00 Trifecta £76.40.
**Owner** Mrs Denis Haynes **Bred** Wretham Stud **Trained** Newmarket, Suffolk

**FOCUS**
A decent 3yo handicap in which the first two home had contested the traditionally warm 3yo handicap at the Craven meeting and their domination here further boosted the form of that contest. The winner improved the best part of a stone. They didn't go much of a pace early.

## 2749 LEX AUTOLEASE CLASSIFIED STKS 1m
**4:50** (4:50) (Class 5) 3-Y-O **£3,881** (£1,155; £577; £288) **Stalls** Low

Form RPR

10-4 **1** **Mayfield Boy**[18] 2203 3-9-0 75............................ KierenFallon 3 79
(Mel Brittain) *sn led: edgd rt over 3f out: pushed along and hdd over 2f out: rallied to ld nr fin* **7/1**

0-14 **2** *nse* **Flycatcher (IRE)**[27] 1956 3-9-0 75............................ PaulHanagan 2 79
(Richard Fahey) *chsd wnr after 1f tl shkn up to ld over 2f out: rdn over 1f out: edgd lft ins fnl f: hdd nr fin* **9/4**[1]

3-04 **3** *1 ¼* **She's Gorgeous (IRE)**[21] 2129 3-9-0 73............................ FrederikTylicki 6 76
(James Fanshawe) *a.p: rdn over 2f out: styd on u.p* **9/2**[3]

240 **4** *2* **Russian Remarque**[18] 2221 3-9-0 74............................ TomQueally 4 72
(Jonathan Portman) *led early: chsd ldrs: rdn and ev ch over 1f out: wknd wl ins fnl f* **14/1**

1-3 **5** *1 ¼* **Argot**[34] 1725 3-9-0 73............................ WilliamCarson 5 69
(Anthony Carson) *s.i.s: sn prom: rdn over 2f out: styd on same pce fr over 1f out* **5/2**[2]

34-6 **6** *36* **Djinni (IRE)**[21] 2122 3-9-0 75............................ RichardHughes 1
(Richard Hannon) *hld up: shkn up over 2f out: wknd and eased over 1f out* **7/1**

1m 43.93s (3.93) **Going Correction** +0.325s/f (Good) 6 Ran SP% **109.2**
Speed ratings (Par 99): **93,92,91,89,88 52**
CSF £21.86 TOTE £8.00: £3.60, £1.60; EX 25.80 Trifecta £89.10.
**Owner** Mel Brittain **Bred** D J And Mrs Deer **Trained** Warthill, N Yorks

**FOCUS**
A tight little classified event with just 2lb covering the six horses. In a race not run at a searching gallop, the field started out up the centre of the track before moving towards the nearside after halfway, while the front pair edged back to the middle through the latter stages. The winner stepped up on his 2yo maiden win.

## 2750 LLOYDS BANK COMMERCIAL EAST ENGLAND FILLIES' H'CAP 1m 2f
**5:25** (5:25) (Class 5) (0-75,74) 4-Y-0+ **£4,090** (£1,207; £604) **Stalls** Centre

Form RPR

530- **1** **Trulee Scrumptious**[177] 8148 5-8-2 **55** oh5..............(v) JimmyQuinn 3 65
(Peter Charalambous) *mde all: rdn over 1f out: edgd rt ins fnl f: styd on*
**15/2**

010- **2** *1* **Magique (IRE)**[213] 7608 4-9-7 **74**............................ WilliamBuick 1 82
(Jeremy Noseda) *wnt rt s: hld up: hdwy over 2f out: rdn over 1f out: r.o to go 2nd wl ins fnl f: nt rch wnr* **7/2**[2]

-133 **3** *2 ¾* **Tilstarr (IRE)**[8] 2498 4-9-7 **74**............................ RichardHughes 2 77
(Roger Teal) *hld up: hdwy over 2f out: sn rdn: chsd wnr and swtchd lft ins fnl f: no ex towards fin* **15/8**[1]

3-03 **4** *2* **Dark Amber**[10] 2415 4-9-0 **67**............................ KierenFallon 8 66
(Brendan Powell) *s.i.s: hld up: pushed along and hdwy over 2f out: sn outpcd: r.o towards fin* **9/2**[3]

4200 **5** *½* **Oratorio's Joy (IRE)**[25] 2012 4-9-7 **74**............................ WilliamCarson 5 72
(Jamie Osborne) *chsd wnr: rdn: edgd lft and ev ch over 1f out: wknd ins fnl f* **15/2**

6-05 **6** *14* **Super Cookie**[31] 1864 4-8-9 **62**..............(p) AndreaAtzeni 7 34
(Noel Quinlan) *chsd ldrs tl rdn and wknd over 2f out* **12/1**

3443 **7** *2 ¼* **The Blue Dog (IRE)**[70] 1046 7-8-1 **61**............................ JoeDoyle(7) 6 28
(Phil McEntee) *hld up: rdn and wknd over 2f out* **16/1**

2m 11.93s (6.43) **Going Correction** +0.75s/f (Yiel) 7 Ran SP% **112.3**
Speed ratings (Par 100): **104,103,101,99,99 87,86**
CSF £32.54 CT £68.64 TOTE £10.30: £5.30, £3.10; EX 34.30 Trifecta £169.40.
**Owner** pcracing.co.uk **Bred** Dxb Bloodstock Ltd **Trained** Newmarket, Suffolk

**FOCUS**
An ordinary fillies' handicap and another strange race in some ways, as three of the runners were soon well clear of the other four, but the leading trio included the winner so they couldn't have gone off too quick. The winner confirmed some seemingly flattering runs last year.
T/Plt: £160.60 to a £1 stake. Pool: £101,276.08 - 460.28 winning tickets T/Qpdt: £14.40 to a £1 stake. Pool: £6,907.17 - 354.91 winning tickets CR

2751 - 2754a (Foreign Racing) - See Raceform Interactive

# 2226 MAISONS-LAFFITTE (R-H)
Friday, May 30

**OFFICIAL GOING: Turf: very soft**

## 2755a PRIX KEFALIN (MAIDEN) (2YO) (TURF) 6f (S)
**1:20** (12:00) 2-Y-0 **£10,416** (£4,166; £3,125; £2,083; £1,041)

RPR

**1** **Kenouska (FR)**[34] 2-8-13 0............................ FabriceVeron 4 92
(H-A Pantall, France) **53/10**[2]

**2** *7* **Redlake (FR)** 2-9-2 0............................ AlexandreGavilan 5 74
(D Guillemin, France) **17/2**

**3** *1 ¼* **Rose Doloise (FR)**[14] 2-8-13 0............................ RonanThomas 1 68
(A Bonin, France) **68/10**[3]

**4** *nk* **Princesse Savoie** 2-8-9 0............................ ThierryJarnet 3 63
(J Bertran De Balanda, France) **13/1**

**5** *3* **Cornwallville (IRE)**[16] 2246 2-9-2 0............................ IoritzMendizabal 12 61
(J S Moore) *midfield: rdn and ev ch 2f out: outpcd by easy wnr fr over 1f out: no ex and fdd ins fnl f* **9/1**

**6** *2* **Celestial House**[22] 2-9-2 0............................ ThierryThulliez 8 55
(N Clement, France) **13/10**[1]

**7** *hd* **Maui (FR)** 2-8-9 0............................ FranckBlondel 7 47
(Mlle V Dissaux, France) **63/1**

**8** *2* **Monsieur Royal (FR)**[13] 2-9-2 0..............(p) AnthonyBernard 6 48
(C Plisson, France) **15/1**

**9** *1 ½* **Alexandra Dancer (FR)**[38] 2-8-7 0.......... MllePaulineDominois(6) 2 41
(J-P Delaporte, France) **50/1**

**10** *¾* **Sioux Dakota (FR)**[14] 2-9-2 0............................ TheoBachelot 9 41
(L Baudron, France) **65/1**

**11** *nk* **Something Lucky (IRE)** 2-8-13 0............................ TonyPiccone 10 37
(Matthieu Palussiere, France) **13/1**

**12** *7* **Fulki (FR)** 2-8-13 0............................ EddyHardouin 11 16
(J Heloury, France) **37/1**

1m 14.8s (1.40) 12 Ran SP% **120.9**
WIN (incl. 1 euro stake): 6.30. PLACES: 2.10, 2.30, 2.10. DF: 18.00. SF: 62.50.
**Owner** Guy Pariente **Bred** Guy Pariente Holding **Trained** France

# 2113 CHESTER (L-H)
Saturday, May 31

**OFFICIAL GOING: Good to soft (soft in places; 6.9)**
Wind: Almost nil Weather: Sunny Rails: Entire length of running rail moved out 3-9yds. Races 1, 2, 3, &4 increased in distance by 37yds, race 5 by 69yds, race 6 by 60yds and race 7 by 41yds

## 2756 ONE COST / EBF STALLIONS MAIDEN STKS (BOBIS RACE) 6f 18y
**2:00** (2:01) (Class 4) 2-Y-0 **£7,762** (£2,310; £1,154; £577) **Stalls** Low

Form RPR

2 **1** **Baitha Alga (IRE)**[8] 2507 2-9-5 0............................ SeanLevey 2 84+
(Richard Hannon) *broke wl: chsd ldrs: effrt on inner whn nt clr run and snatched up over 1f out: sn swtchd rt: r.o to ld ins fnl f: pushed out: comf*
**8/11**[1]

**2** *1 ¾* **Cymro (IRE)** 2-9-2 0............................ OisinMurphy(3) 3 73+
(Tom Dascombe) *chsd ldrs: pushed along over 4f out: outpcd 2f out: styd on ins fnl 100yds: tk 2nd towards fin: no ch w wnr* **4/1**[2]

54 **3** *hd* **Popeswood (IRE)**[16] 2276 2-9-2 0.......... WilliamTwiston-Davies(3) 6 72
(Mick Channon) *hld up: effrt and hdwy on outer over 2f out: sn chsd ldrs: styd on ins fnl f: one pce fnl strides* **10/1**

0 **4** *¾* **Billy Slater**[23] 2089 2-9-5 0............................ TomEaves 1 70+
(Richard Fahey) *towards rr: pushed along and struggling to go pce over 4f out: prog wl ins fnl f: styd on: nt pce to chal* **5/1**[3]

5 ½ **Anonymous John (IRE)** 2-9-5 0 AdamKirby 4 68
(David Evans) *chsd ldr: rdn whn chalng over 1f out: sn led: hdd ins fnl f: sn outpcd by wnr: lost 2nd and no ex towards fin* **14/1**

0 6 1 ¼ **Indescribable (IRE)**[21] 2146 2-9-5 0 JoeFanning 7 65
(Mark Johnston) *led: rdn over 1f out: sn hdd: wknd fnl 100yds* **22/1**

05 7 27 **Verchild Lad (IRE)**[11] 2413 2-9-5 0 PaulMulrennan 5
(David Evans) *a bhd: outpcd over 4f out: lft bhd over 1f out: nvr on terms* **66/1**

1m 21.44s (7.64) **Going Correction** +0.975s/f (Soft) 7 Ran SP% **116.2**
Speed ratings (Par 95): **88,85,85,84,83 82,46**
CSF £4.15 TOTE £1.50: £1.02, £3.20; EX 5.20 Trifecta £18.50.
**Owner** Al Shaqab Racing **Bred** Ms Theresa Killen **Trained** East Everleigh, Wilts

**FOCUS**
The entire length of the running rail had been moved out by between 3 and 9 yards, so the actual race distances measured: 6f 55y (+37y), 7f 39y (+37y), 1m 2f 116y (+41y), 1m 4f 126y (+60y), 1m 5f 158y (+69y). The winner didn't need to improve.

## 2757 APPLETISER FILLIES' H'CAP 6f 18y
**2:30** (2:32) (Class 3) (0-95,95) 4-Y-O+ **£13,584** (£4,042; £2,020; £1,010) **Stalls** Low

Form RPR

2-12 1 **Bondesire**[13] 2361 4-9-1 **92** JulieBurke(3) 4 101
(David O'Meara) *mde all: tacked across to inner rail after 1f: rdn abt 3 l clr over 1f out: kpt on wl towards fin* **7/2**[2]

0-65 2 1 ¼ **Royal Rascal**[17] 2254 4-9-6 **94** TomEaves 1 99
(Tim Easterby) *chsd ldrs: rdn 2f out: wnt 2nd over 1f out and abt 3 l down: styd on ins fnl f: nt quite able to get to wnr* **3/1**[1]

5-01 3 1 **Love Island**[13] 2361 5-9-4 **95** ConnorBeasley(3) 8 97+
(Richard Whitaker) *hld up: pushed along over 2f out: nt clr run and swtchd rt over 1f out: hdwy ins fnl f: styd on towards fin: nt quite rch ldrs* **13/2**

2005 4 3 ½ **Hannahs Turn**[5] 2608 4-8-7 **81** oh6 JoeFanning 3 72
(Chris Dwyer) *hmpd after 1f: chsd ldr: rdn and lost 2nd over 1f out: one pce ins fnl f* **20/1**

400- 5 nk **Califante**[106] 618 4-8-5 **82** oh6 ow1 OisinMurphy(3) 2 72
(T Hogan, Ire) *midfield: pushed along over 2f out: rdn over 1f out: no imp* **11/2**[3]

-030 6 3 **Jillnextdoor (IRE)**[7] 2564 4-8-13 **90** WilliamTwiston-Davies(3) 5 70
(Mick Channon) *in rr: rdn wl over 1f out: nvr a threat* **12/1**

15-4 7 3 **Milly's Gift**[22] 2110 4-9-0 **88** AdamKirby 7 58
(Clive Cox) *hld up: rdn 2f out: sn struggling: nvr a threat: lame* **3/1**[1]

0-40 8 nk **Beautiful View**[15] 2318 4-8-8 **82** oh1 ow1 SeanLevey 6 51
(Richard Hannon) *chsd ldrs: pushed along over 2f out: rdn and wknd over 1f out* **20/1**

1m 19.24s (5.44) **Going Correction** +0.975s/f (Soft) 8 Ran SP% **118.2**
Speed ratings (Par 104): **102,100,99,94,93 89,85,85**
CSF £15.04 CT £63.76 TOTE £4.70: £1.40, £1.60, £2.50; EX 20.70 Trifecta £56.00.
**Owner** Geoff & Sandra Turnbull **Bred** A C M Spalding **Trained** Nawton, N Yorks
■ Stewards' Enquiry : Julie Burke two-day ban: failed to ride to draw (Jun 14-15)

**FOCUS**
A decent fillies' handicap. They didn't go much of a pace early on but the form makes sense.

## 2758 MATTHEW CLARK H'CAP 7f 2y
**3:05** (3:05) (Class 2) (0-105,100) 4-Y-O+**£29,110** (£8,662; £4,329; £2,164) **Stalls** Low

Form RPR

00-3 1 **Pacific Heights (IRE)**[22] 2113 5-9-2 **95** DaleSwift 1 106
(Brian Ellison) *in tch: effrt over 1f out: rdn to ld ins fnl f: r.o wl and in command fnl 75yds* **7/2**[2]

3205 2 1 ¾ **Apostle (IRE)**[22] 2113 5-8-7 **89** WilliamTwiston-Davies(3) 8 95
(David Simcock) *midfield: pushed along over 4f out: hdwy 2f out: chalng ins fnl f: nt qckn and outpcd by wnr fnl 75yds* **33/1**

-305 3 1 **Marcret (ITY)**[9] 2478 7-9-0 **93** StevieDonohoe 7 96
(David O'Meara) *hld up: hdwy 2f out: swtchd rt over 1f out: styd on ins fnl f: nt rch ldrs* **20/1**

0536 4 ½ **Newstead Abbey**[28] 1943 4-9-4 **97** TomEaves 6 99
(David Barron) *led for 1f: trckd ldrs: rdn to ld over 1f out: hdd ins fnl f: styd on same pce fnl 100yds* **14/1**

0-42 5 1 **Laffan (IRE)**[7] 2548 5-8-7 **93** RachelRichardson(7) 9 93
(Tim Easterby) *in tch: bmpd after nrly 1f: effrt and tried to chal over 1f out: sltly short of room ins fnl f: no ex fnl 100yds* **8/1**[3]

3100 6 1 **Robert The Painter (IRE)**[28] 1958 6-9-1 **97** (v) JulieBurke(3) 10 94
(David O'Meara) *midfield: pushed along and outpcd 4f out: kpt on ins fnl f: nvr able to trble ldrs* **12/1**

-000 7 1 ¼ **Norse Blues**[13] 2362 6-8-11 **90** PaulMulrennan 13 84
(David Barron) *bhd: pushed along and hdwy over 1f out: kpt on ins fnl f: nvr trbld ldrs* **33/1**

420 8 ½ **Tellovoi (IRE)**[14] 2336 6-9-0 **93** (v) SeanLevey 3 85
(Ann Stokell) *led after 1f: rdn and hdd over 1f out: wknd fnl 150yds* **10/1**

-110 9 3 ¾ **Purcell (IRE)**[21] 2145 4-9-1 **97** OisinMurphy(3) 2 80
(Andrew Balding) *prom: rdn whn chalng over 1f out: n.m.r whn wkng ins fnl f* **15/8**[1]

-055 10 2 ¼ **Gramercy (IRE)**[8] 2503 7-8-12 **91** (be) ChrisCatlin 4 68
(David Simcock) *hld up: pushed along over 2f out: nvr on terms* **10/1**

20-6 11 28 **Deauville Prince (FR)**[22] 2113 4-9-0 **100** JennyPowell(7) 5 4
(Tom Dascombe) *prom: wnt sltly rt and bmpd after nrly 1f: rdn and wknd 2f out* **16/1**

-400 12 ¾ **Set The Trend**[14] 2336 8-9-4 **97** (v) SebSanders 12
(David Dennis) *midfield: rdn 4f out: wknd over 2f out* **33/1**

0000 13 16 **Forest Edge (IRE)**[47] 1484 5-9-0 **93** ow1 (v[1]) AdamKirby 11
(David Evans) *midfield: pushed along over 4f out: wknd over 2f out* **25/1**

1m 31.61s (5.11) **Going Correction** +0.975s/f (Soft) 13 Ran SP% **124.0**
Speed ratings (Par 109): **109,107,105,105,104 103,101,101,96,94 62,61,43**
CSF £129.27 CT £2089.69 TOTE £5.70: £1.60, £7.00, £4.60; EX 163.90 Trifecta £807.80 Part won. Pool: £1,077.17 - 0.60 winning tickets..
**Owner** A Barnes **Bred** Smythson **Trained** Norton, N Yorks

**FOCUS**
A competitive handicap, but not the strongest for the grade.

## 2759 J2O PEAR MAIDEN STKS (BOBIS RACE) 6f 18y
**3:40** (3:41) (Class 4) 3-Y-O **£7,762** (£2,310; £1,154; £577) **Stalls** Low

Form RPR

6 1 **Telmeyd**[14] 2339 3-9-5 0 SebSanders 5 94
(William Haggas) *trckd ldr: led 2f out: rdn over 1f out: r.o wl to draw clr ins fnl f: sn edgd rt: eased cl home* **1/1**[1]

24-3 2 5 **My Inspiration (IRE)**[12] 2389 3-9-0 75 PaulMulrennan 3 73
(Tim Easterby) *sn led: pushed along and hdd 2f out: no ch w wnr ins fnl f* **4/1**[3]

-352 3 9 **Broadway Ranger (IRE)**[14] 2329 3-9-2 72 OisinMurphy(3) 2 49
(Charles Hills) *broke wl: led early: sn stdd: hld up bhd ldrs: pushed along and outpcd 3f out: kpt on to take 3rd 1f out: no ch w front two* **2/1**[2]

50-2 4 2 ½ **Red Forever**[26] 2023 3-9-2 54 SladeO'Hara(3) 4 41
(Alan Berry) *plld hrd: trckd ldrs: rdn 3f out: outpcd over 2f out: sn no ch: lost 3rd 1f out: wl btn* **12/1**

0 5 7 **Ach Alannah (IRE)**[12] 2384 3-9-0 0 StevieDonohoe 1 14
(James Unett) *sed awkwardly and slowly away: a bhd: outpcd over 2f out: nvr on terms* **28/1**

1m 19.34s (5.54) **Going Correction** +0.975s/f (Soft) 5 Ran SP% **114.5**
Speed ratings (Par 101): **102,95,83,80,70**
CSF £5.84 TOTE £2.40: £1.10, £1.80; EX 4.30 Trifecta £6.70.
**Owner** Sheikh Ahmed Al Maktoum **Bred** Cheveley Park Stud Ltd **Trained** Newmarket, Suffolk

**FOCUS**
An ordinary maiden, lacking depth, but the winner impressed in a relatively fast time.

## 2760 KOZEL H'CAP 1m 5f 89y
**4:15** (4:15) (Class 3) (0-90,90) 4-Y-O+ **£13,584** (£4,042; £2,020; £1,010) **Stalls** Low

Form RPR

3/6- 1 **Swnymor (IRE)**[45] 7823 5-8-11 **83** IanBrennan(3) 3 96+
(John Quinn) *hld up: impr into midfield over 7f out: smooth hdwy over 3f out: led on bit wl over 1f out: effrtlessly drew clr ins fnl f: v easily* **5/1**[2]

-660 2 2 ¾ **Gabrial's King (IRE)**[24] 2073 5-9-6 **89** ChrisCatlin 8 94
(David Simcock) *hld up: rdn 3f out: hdwy u.p over 2f out: styd on to take 2nd nr fin: no ch w wnr* **20/1**

50-0 3 nk **Swinging Hawk (GER)**[22] 2108 8-8-4 **76** ConnorBeasley(3) 5 81
(Ian Williams) *s.s: bhd: pushed along over 2f out: hdwy on outer over 1f out: styd on ins fnl f: gng on at fin: no ch w wnr* **8/1**

53-5 4 shd **Noble Alan (GER)**[21] 2168 11-8-7 **79** OisinMurphy(3) 2 83
(Nicky Richards) *trckd ldrs: wnt 2nd over 4f out: rdn to ld 3f out: hdd wl over 1f out: no ch w wnr fnl f: lost 2nd nr fin* **6/1**[3]

0-23 5 2 **Astra Hall**[17] 2259 5-9-1 **84** SebSanders 4 85
(Ralph Beckett) *trckd ldrs: rdn over 3f out: stl chsng ldrs u.p over 1f out but no imp: wknd ins fnl f* **5/1**[2]

3-11 6 1 ¾ **Hassle (IRE)**[21] 2160 5-9-6 **89** (p) AdamKirby 10 88
(Clive Cox) *hld up: rdn 5f out: hdwy into midfield over 2f out: no imp: one pce fnl f* **3/1**[1]

0-22 7 4 ½ **Pilgrims Rest (IRE)**[17] 2259 5-9-7 **90** StevieDonohoe 7 82
(Tim Pitt) *led: rdn and hdd 3f out: stl chsng ldrs u.p but no imp over 1f out: wknd fnl f* **8/1**

0410 8 1 ¼ **Gabrial's Star**[17] 2259 5-9-3 **86** (b) TomEaves 1 76
(Richard Fahey) *midfield: hdwy over 3f out: rdn over 2f out: sn wknd* **7/1**

-000 9 119 **Bayan Kasirga (IRE)**[17] 2259 4-8-12 **81** PaulMulrennan 6
(Richard Fahey) *w ldr: rdn 6f out: lost 2nd over 4f out: wknd over 3f out: t.o* **25/1**

0002 10 15 **Hunting Ground (USA)**[4] 2640 4-8-5 **74** JoeFanning 9
(Mark Johnston) *trckd ldrs: lost pl over 7f out: bhd over 4f out: t.o* **20/1**

3m 4.1s (11.40) **Going Correction** +0.975s/f (Soft) 10 Ran SP% **120.7**
Speed ratings (Par 107): **103,101,101,101,99 98,95,95, ,**
CSF £104.34 CT £801.08 TOTE £8.20: £3.00, £5.50, £4.20; EX 124.70 Trifecta £1185.30.
**Owner** Carl Hinchy **Bred** Easton Park Stud **Trained** Settrington, N Yorks

**FOCUS**
This looked quite competitive on paper but the winner scored with tons in hand, value for more like 6l.

## 2761 RUSSIAN STANDARD VODKA H'CAP (BOBIS RACE) 1m 4f 66y
**4:50** (4:50) (Class 4) (0-85,85) 3-Y-O **£7,762** (£2,310; £1,154; £577) **Stalls** Low

Form RPR

2-12 1 **Captain Morley**[24] 2077 3-9-5 **83** AdamKirby 4 95+
(David Simcock) *midfield: hdwy to ld 4f out: rdn to assert 2f out: kpt on gamely and a doing enough towards fin* **11/4**[2]

4101 2 ¾ **Old Town Boy**[13] 2363 3-9-7 **85** SeanLevey 2 95
(Philip McBride) *chsd ldrs: rdn over 4f out: wnt 2nd jst over 1f out: styd on ins fnl f: clsd on wnr clsng stages* **7/2**[3]

1260 3 2 ½ **Arantes**[14] 2337 3-9-1 **82** WilliamTwiston-Davies(3) 8 88
(Mick Channon) *midfield: hdwy over 4f out: wnt 2nd over 3f out: sn chalng: rdn over 2f out: no imp on wnr over 1f out: sn lost 2nd: styd on same pce ins fnl f* **16/1**

5-11 4 11 **Storm Force Ten**[24] 2077 3-9-3 **84** OisinMurphy(3) 1 72
(Andrew Balding) *prom: rdn 3f out: stl chsng ldrs u.p 2f out but no imp: wknd over 1f out* **5/2**[1]

6-12 5 9 **Late Shipment**[52] 1372 3-8-12 **76** PaulMulrennan 10 50
(Mark Johnston) *hld up: rdn over 4f out: effrt over 3f out: no imp: wknd over 2f out* **14/1**

0151 6 11 **Solo Hunter**[9] 2481 3-8-10 **74** TomEaves 6 30
(David Evans) *hld up in rr: nvr nr ldrs: rdn and struggling over 2f out: nvr a threat* **25/1**

3-1 7 15 **Purple Spectrum**[19] 2221 3-9-2 **80** SebSanders 5 12
(William Haggas) *rdn s: chsd ldr: rdn 6f out: lost 2nd and wknd over 3f out* **6/1**

4-14 8 3 ½ **Dry Your Eyes (IRE)**[9] 2491 3-8-7 **71** oh1 RoystonFfrench 3
(Mark Johnston) *led: rdn and hdd 4f out: sn wknd* **33/1**

5-11 9 37 **Piton**[65] 1124 3-8-13 **77** JoeFanning 7
(Mark Johnston) *midfield tl rdn and wknd over 4f out: t.o* **11/1**

2m 49.55s (11.05) **Going Correction** +0.975s/f (Soft) 9 Ran SP% **119.4**
Speed ratings (Par 101): **102,101,99,92,86 79,69,66,42**
CSF £13.43 CT £131.54 TOTE £3.80: £1.10, £2.40, £5.80; EX 18.90 Trifecta £262.10.
**Owner** Dr Marwan Koukash **Bred** Miss K Rausing **Trained** Newmarket, Suffolk

**FOCUS**
There was a good gallop on here, they finished well strung out and the form looks solid. The winner reversed C&D latest with the favourite.

## 2762 APEROL SPRITZ H'CAP 1m 2f 75y
**5:25** (5:26) (Class 4) (0-85,85) 4-Y-O+ **£7,762** (£2,310; £1,154; £577) **Stalls** High

Form RPR

-060 1 **Las Verglas Star (IRE)**[22] 2137 6-9-1 **79** PaulMulrennan 9 87
(Richard Fahey) *hld up: nt clr run whn hdwy over 1f out: r.o ins fnl f: led fnl 75yds: in control cl home* **8/1**

0644 2 ½ **Hydrant**[11] 2423 8-8-9 **76** ConnorBeasley(3) 7 83
(Richard Guest) *in tch: rdn to take 2nd wl over 1f out: chalng wl ins fnl f: hld by wnr cl home* **10/1**

0005 3 1 **Skytrain**[11] 2425 4-9-3 **81** JoeFanning 1 86
(Mark Johnston) *led: rdn over 1f out: hrd pressed ins fnl f: hdd fnl 75yds: no ex cl home* **7/1**[3]

00-0 **4** 2 ¼ **Dolphin Rock**[47] 1483 7-8-11 **75**........................ DaleSwift 2 76
(Brian Ellison) *handy: rdn and nt qckn 2f out: styd on to chse ldrs ins fnl f: kpt on same pce fnl 100yds* **11/2**[2]

0646 **5** ½ **Tatting**[15] 2311 5-9-0 **78**........................ AdamKirby 6 78
(Chris Dwyer) *racd keenly in midfield: rdn over 1f out: one pce fnl 100yds* **11/1**

24-0 **6** 1 ¼ **El Bravo**[14] 2327 8-8-4 **71** oh3........................ NeilFarley(3) 11 69
(Shaun Harris) *midfield: pushed along over 4f out: hdwy on outer over 3f out: rdn over 2f out: stl chsng ldrs over 1f out: no ex ins fnl f* **22/1**

6-46 **7** 3 **Gabrial The Duke (IRE)**[11] 2445 4-8-7 **71** oh2..............(b[1]) ChrisCatlin 5 63
(David Simcock) *s.i.s and faltered early: in rr: struggling over 2f out: nvr able to trble ldrs* **20/1**

1-46 **8** 1 ¼ **No Dominion (IRE)**[22] 2131 5-9-1 **79**........................ TomEaves 8 68
(James Given) *racd keenly in midfield: rdn and wknd over 1f out* **20/1**

213- **9** nk **Empress Adelaide**[230] 7223 4-9-7 **85**........................ SebSanders 4 74
(William Haggas) *chsd ldrs: rdn over 2f out: wknd over 1f out* **6/5**[1]

0510 **10** hd **Heavy Metal**[15] 2309 4-9-7 **85**........................ RoystonFfrench 10 73
(Mark Johnston) *hld up: rdn over 2f out: no imp* **20/1**

0100 **11** 7 **Halfsin (IRE)**[23] 2091 6-9-3 **81**........................(t) PaoloSirigu 3 56
(Marco Botti) *racd keenly: chsd ldr: rdn and lost 2nd wl over 1f out: wknd ins fnl f* **22/1**

2m 21.86s (10.66) **Going Correction** +0.975s/f (Soft) **11 Ran SP% 124.9**
Speed ratings (Par 105): **96,95,94,93,92 91,89,88,87,87 82**
CSF £81.24 CT £596.88 TOTE £12.10: £2.50, £3.10, £2.50; EX 82.20 Trifecta £745.50.
**Owner** CBWS Partnership **Bred** Brendan Holland And P Connell **Trained** Musley Bank, N Yorks

**FOCUS**
A fair handicap. The winner is rated back to his turf best.
T/Plt: £84.10 to a £1 stake. Pool: £53,310.99 - 462.69 winning tickets. T/Qpdt: £39.20 to a £1 stake. Pool: £3,620.73 - 68.30 winning tickets. DO

## 2730 HAYDOCK (L-H)
### Saturday, May 31

**OFFICIAL GOING: Good to soft (good in places; 7.4)**
Wind: light 1/2 against Weather: fine and sunny Rails: All races on Stands side home straight and races on Round course increased by 57yds

### 2763 HAYDOCK-PARK.CO.UK H'CAP 1m
**1:30** (1:30) (Class 4) (0-80,80) 4-Y-0+ **£5,175** (£1,540; £769; £384) **Stalls** Low

Form RPR

3-46 **1** **Dubai Hills**[30] 1903 8-9-7 **80**........................ DanielTudhope 11 96
(David O'Meara) *led 1f: chsd ldr: led 3f out: drvn clr over 1f out* **4/1**[2]

122- **2** 4 **Extraterrestrial**[234] 7130 10-9-2 **75**........................ FrankieDettori 5 82
(Richard Fahey) *hld up in mid-div: stdy hdwy over 2f out: chsd wnr over 1f out: no imp* **13/2**[3]

00 **3** 3 ¾ **Bob**[26] 2017 4-9-2 **75**........................ TomQueally 10 73
(Les Eyre) *stdd s: t.k.h in rr: effrt and swtchd outside over 2f out: kpt on to take modest 3rd last 100yds* **14/1**

3-05 **4** ¾ **Eurystheus (IRE)**[21] 2162 5-9-5 **78**........................ AndrewMullen 6 75
(Michael Appleby) *dwlt: sn drvn along: hdwy over 5f out: kpt on to take modest 4th last 100yds* **11/4**[1]

0016 **5** 1 ½ **Justonefortheroad**[14] 2351 8-9-2 **75**........................(b) PatSmullen 4 68
(Richard Fahey) *trckd ldrs: drvn over 3f out: one pce fnl 2f* **4/1**[2]

6330 **6** hd **King Of Eden (IRE)**[11] 2425 8-9-2 **78**........................ JasonHart(3) 1 71
(Eric Alston) *led after 1f: hdd 3f out: one pce fnl 2f* **11/1**

60-1 **7** 4 **Exzachary**[21] 2177 4-8-8 **74**........................ HarryBurns(7) 9 58
(Jo Hughes) *stdd s: hld up in rr: sme hdwy on outside over 2f out: edgd rt: nvr a factor* **15/2**

-200 **8** ½ **Rio Cobolo (IRE)**[21] 2169 8-8-7 **66** oh4........................ PJMcDonald 8 48
(Philip Kirby) *sn mid-div: drvn 3f out: edgd lft and lost pl over 1f out* **25/1**

064/ **9** 15 **Take It To The Max**[594] 7083 7-9-7 **80**........................ AndrewElliott 7 28
(George Moore) *chsd ldrs: pushed along over 5f out: lost pl 2f out: bhd whn eased ins fnl f* **40/1**

1m 44.82s (1.12) **Going Correction** +0.275s/f (Good) **9 Ran SP% 113.0**
Speed ratings (Par 105): **105,101,97,96,95 94,90,90,75**
CSF £29.46 CT £327.85 TOTE £5.00: £1.80, £1.50, £2.90; EX 34.60 Trifecta £443.80.
**Owner** Mrs F Denniff **Bred** A S Denniff **Trained** Nawton, N Yorks

**FOCUS**
All races on stands' side home straight and races on Round course increased by 57yds. The ground was drying out and was now officially good to soft, good in places. The winning rider described conditions as "tacky". A fair handicap to start, but not that many ever got into it. The winner was back to last year's turf form.

### 2764 PINNACLE STKS (GROUP 3) (F&M) 1m 3f 200y
**2:05** (2:05) (Class 1) 4-Y-0+
**£35,727** (£13,545; £6,778; £3,376; £1,694; £850) **Stalls** High

Form RPR

1 **1** **Sultanina**[16] 2280 4-9-0 85........................ WilliamBuick 7 107
(John Gosden) *s.i.s: effrt over 3f out: styd on and 2nd over 1f out: kpt on wl to ld post* **10/1**

1-23 **2** shd **Freedom's Light**[28] 1942 4-9-0 90........................ FrankieDettori 1 106
(John Gosden) *trckd ldrs: drvn and sltly outpcd 3f out: styd on to ld wl over 1f out: hdd post* **9/1**

43-1 **3** ½ **Silk Sari**[28] 1934 4-9-0 93........................ DavidProbert 3 105
(Luca Cumani) *mid-div: hdwy over 2f out: styd on to take 3rd last 75yds: kpt on wl* **7/1**[3]

4-00 **4** ½ **Quiz Mistress**[16] 2284 6-9-0 104........................ DanielTudhope 4 104
(Hughie Morrison) *dwlt: hld up in rr: swtchd outside 2f out: styd on to take 4th last 75yds: kpt on* **16/1**

-315 **5** 3 **Special Meaning**[15] 2294 4-9-0 93........................ FrannyNorton 8 99
(Mark Johnston) *led: hdd over 2f out: fdd last 100yds* **16/1**

21-4 **6** 4 ½ **Astonishing (IRE)**[49] 1434 4-9-0 109........................ RichardHughes 6 92
(Sir Michael Stoute) *trckd ldr: upsides 4f out: led briefly over 2f out: wknd fnl f* **11/4**[1]

1-10 **7** ½ **Cubanita**[15] 2315 5-9-3 111........................ JimCrowley 5 94
(Ralph Beckett) *trckd ldrs: upsides 3f out: led briefly 2f out: wknd fnl f* **7/2**[2]

-504 **8** nse **Moment In Time (IRE)**[63] 1177 5-9-0 104........................ MartinLane 10 91
(David Simcock) *s.i.s: hld up in rr: effrt over 3f out: chsng ldrs on outer over 2f out: wknd over 1f out* **8/1**

1-50 **9** 1 ¾ **Khione**[15] 2315 5-9-0 104........................ KierenFallon 11 88
(Luca Cumani) *trckd ldrs: drvn over 4f out: lost pl over 2f out* **9/1**

30-6 **10** 4 ½ **Madame Defarge (IRE)**[27] 1974 4-9-0 95........................[1] TomQueally 2 81
(Michael Bell) *t.k.h early: sn mid-div: effrt over 3f out: lost pl over 1f out* **25/1**

055- **11** 9 **Hollowina**[214] 7596 4-9-0 76........................ PatSmullen 9 67
(David Brown) *chsd ldrs: lost pl over 2f out: sn bhd* **66/1**

2m 34.39s (0.59) **Going Correction** +0.275s/f (Good) **11 Ran SP% 118.7**
Speed ratings (Par 113): **109,108,108,108,106 103,102,102,101,98 92**
CSF £97.76 TOTE £10.70: £2.90, £3.00, £3.20; EX 54.70 Trifecta £232.50.
**Owner** Normandie Stud Ltd **Bred** Normandie Stud Ltd **Trained** Newmarket, Suffolk

**FOCUS**
A fascinating Group 3 and although the pace seemed ordinary, it resulted in a thrilling finish between the two John Gosden-trained fillies. The form is best rated around the fourth and fifth.

### 2765 TIMEFORM JURY STKS (REGISTERED AS THE JOHN OF GAUNT STAKES) (GROUP 3) 7f
**2:40** (2:41) (Class 1) 4-Y-0+
**£35,727** (£13,545; £6,778; £3,376; £1,694; £850) **Stalls** Low

Form RPR

-036 **1** **Penitent**[20] 2185 8-9-0 109........................ DanielTudhope 3 114
(David O'Meara) *trckd ldr: led over 2f out: styd on gamely fnl f: all out* **33/1**

-131 **2** shd **Breton Rock (IRE)**[21] 2150 4-9-0 109........................ MartinLane 2 113+
(David Simcock) *in rr: drvn 3f out: swtchd lft 1f out: chsd wnr last 100yds: jst failed* **6/1**[3]

15-1 **3** 2 ¼ **Eton Forever (IRE)**[35] 1728 7-9-0 112........................ FrankieDettori 9 107
(Roger Varian) *hld up towards rr: hdwy over 3f out: upsides over 1f out: kpt on same pce last 100yds* **4/1**[2]

63-5 **4** nk **Garswood**[36] 1698 4-9-0 117........................ PatSmullen 5 106
(Richard Fahey) *chsd ldrs: effrt over 2f out: sn sltly outpcd: kpt on to take 4th last 50yds* **11/4**[1]

40-1 **5** ¾ **Here Comes When (IRE)**[22] 2113 4-9-0 106........................ JimCrowley 1 104
(Andrew Balding) *mid-div: effrt over 2f out: sn chsng ldrs: one pce over 1f out: 5th last 50yds* **4/1**[2]

3055 **6** 1 ¾ **Empire Storm (GER)**[14] 2338 7-9-0 107........................(t) TomQueally 6 100
(Michael Attwater) *led: hdd over 2f out: wknd last 100yds* **50/1**

341- **7** 2 ¼ **Tawhid**[253] 6595 4-9-0 111........................(p) KierenFallon 7 94
(Saeed bin Suroor) *dwlt: hdwy over 3f out: upsides over 2f out: wknd fnl 150yds* **9/1**

-322 **8** 4 **Custom Cut (IRE)**[21] 2150 5-9-0 108........................ WilliamBuick 8 84
(David O'Meara) *chsd ldrs on outer: drvn over 3f out: wknd over 1f out: sn eased* **12/1**

20-1 **9** 2 ½ **Amarillo (IRE)**[30] 2006 5-9-3 112........................ RichardHughes 4 80
(P Schiergen, Germany) *hld up in rr: effrt over 3f out: wknd and eased 1f out* **6/1**[3]

1m 31.31s (0.61) **Going Correction** +0.275s/f (Good) **9 Ran SP% 117.8**
Speed ratings (Par 113): **107,106,104,103,103 101,98,93,91**
CSF £223.48 TOTE £22.80: £4.20, £2.40, £1.90; EX 198.20 Trifecta £1580.00.
**Owner** Middleham Park Racing XVII **Bred** Cheveley Park Stud Ltd **Trained** Nawton, N Yorks

**FOCUS**
They went an even pace in this Group 3, which produced a surprise winner in Penitent, who's rated back to last year's form.

### 2766 WINNING EXPRESS ACHILLES STKS (LISTED RACE) 5f
**3:15** (3:17) (Class 1) 3-Y-0+
**£20,982** (£7,955; £3,981; £1,983; £995; £499) **Stalls** High

Form RPR

10-3 **1** **Steps (IRE)**[50] 1421 6-9-8 105........................(b) KierenFallon 5 112
(Roger Varian) *trckd ldrs: effrt and 2nd 1f out: styd on to ld towards fin* **6/1**

1-10 **2** nk **Eton Rifles (IRE)**[17] 2256 9-9-8 107........................ PatSmullen 1 111
(Stuart Williams) *trckd ldr: led appr fnl f: hdd and no ex clsng stages* **7/1**

-563 **3** 2 **Da'Quonde (IRE)**[14] 2353 6-8-13 86........................ RoystonFfrench 4 95
(Bryan Smart) *in rr: swtchd lft 2f out: styd on and 3rd 1f out: kpt on same pce* **33/1**

040- **4** 1 ¼ **Move In Time**[322] 4275 6-9-4 105........................ DanielTudhope 10 96
(David O'Meara) *trckd ldrs: kpt on same pce appr fnl f* **9/2**[3]

0-04 **5** nk **Confessional**[14] 2353 7-9-4 94........................(e) PJMcDonald 9 94
(Tim Easterby) *trckd ldrs: drvn 2f out: one pce over 1f out* **16/1**

-140 **6** ½ **Dinkum Diamond (IRE)**[28] 1949 6-9-8 107........................ TomQueally 3 97
(Henry Candy) *mid-div on outer: effrt over 2f out: sn chsng ldrs: one pce appr fnl f* **10/1**

022- **7** 1 **York Glory (USA)**[252] 6639 6-9-4 109........................(b) RichardHughes 7 89
(Kevin Ryan) *dwlt: hld up in rr: effrt whn nt clr run 1f out: wknd fnl 50yds* **7/2**[2]

0-01 **8** 1 ½ **Noble Storm (USA)**[14] 2353 8-9-4 105........................ JasonHart 8 84
(Ed McMahon) *led: drvn over 2f out: rdr lost whip over 1f out: sn hdd & wknd* **9/1**

0-41 **9** 5 **Swan Song**[24] 2076 5-8-13 100........................ DavidProbert 2 61
(Andrew Balding) *hood removed v late: dwlt: sn chsng ldrs: drvn over 2f out: lost pl over 1f out* **11/4**[1]

1m 0.87s (0.07) **Going Correction** +0.275s/f (Good) **9 Ran SP% 121.8**
Speed ratings (Par 111): **110,109,106,104,103 103,101,99,91**
CSF £50.19 TOTE £5.40: £2.40, £2.30, £5.50; EX 43.60 Trifecta £1152.80.
**Owner** Michael Hill **Bred** Eamon Beston **Trained** Newmarket, Suffolk

**FOCUS**
A decent Listed sprint in which the runners stayed towards the nearside of the track. The form makes sense.

### 2767 NEW TIMEFORM FLAGS SANDY LANE STKS (LISTED RACE) 6f
**3:50** (3:51) (Class 1) 3-Y-O
**£20,982** (£7,955; £3,981; £1,983; £995; £499) **Stalls** High

Form RPR

2-36 **1** **Aeolus**[14] 2343 3-9-0 101........................ RichardHughes 6 109
(Ed McMahon) *hld up: stdy hdwy 2f out: shkn up to ld 1f out: hung lft and drvn clr* **3/1**[2]

1-0 **2** 2 ¾ **Betimes**[27] 1976 3-8-9 86........................ WilliamBuick 4 95
(John Gosden) *t.k.h: trckd ldrs: styd on fnl f: tk 2nd nr fin* **15/2**

3-54 **3** ¾ **Parbold (IRE)**[14] 2343 3-9-0 109........................ PatSmullen 8 98
(Richard Fahey) *led: edgd lft over 2f out: hung bdly lft and hdd 1f out: kpt on same pce* **5/4**[1]

50-1 **4** nk **Shamshon (IRE)**[16] 2287 3-9-3 106........................ FrankieDettori 1 100
(Richard Hannon) *w ldrs on outside: drvn over 1f out: kpt on same pce* **5/1**[3]

0-05 **5** 6 **No Leaf Clover (IRE)**[15] 2304 3-9-0 97........................ DavidProbert 3 78
(Ollie Pears) *w ldrs: drvn over 2f out: wknd 1f out* **14/1**

140- **6** *3¾* **Bahamian Heights**[253] 6584 3-9-0 96........................(b) FrannyNorton 2 66
(Clive Brittain) *w ldrs: wknd over 1f out* **25/1**

00-1 **7** *15* **Ben Hall (IRE)**[92] 778 3-9-0 100.......................... KierenFallon 7 18
(Mike Murphy) *wnt rt s: in rr: rdn 2f out: sn lost pl: eased whn bhd* **20/1**

1m 14.22s (0.42) **Going Correction** +0.275s/f (Good) **7** Ran SP% **113.2**
Speed ratings (Par 107): **108,104,103,102,94 89,69**
CSF £24.75 TOTE £4.50: £2.50, £2.90; EX 25.40 Trifecta £77.70.
**Owner** Andrew Buxton **Bred** Andrew Buxton **Trained** Lichfield, Staffs

**FOCUS**
They finished well spread out in this Listed 3yo sprint and the winner was impressive. The time was relatively slow and this is tricky form to pin down.

## 2768 RACING UK ANYWHERE AVAILABLE NOW H'CAP (BOBIS RACE) 6f
**4:25** (4:27) (Class 4) (0-85,84) 3-Y-O **£6,469** (£1,925; £962; £481) **Stalls** High

Form RPR

1 **1** **Lightning Moon (IRE)**[27] 1980 3-9-5 82.......................... WilliamBuick 1 103
(Ed Walker) *trckd ldrs: smooth hdwy and upsides 2f out: led over 1f out: shkn up and qcknd clr: impressive* **11/10**[1]

1-0 **2** *6* **Pennine Warrior**[28] 1940 3-8-10 73........................(p) RichardHughes 4 75
(Scott Dixon) *dwlt: drvn and outpcd over 3f out: swtchd lft and hdwy on outside over 2f out: 2nd 1f out: no ch w wnr* **14/1**

0-00 **3** *3¼* **Red Lady (IRE)**[14] 2340 3-8-13 76................................(p[1]) KierenFallon 2 68
(Brian Meehan) *led: hdd over 1f out: kpt on one pce* **10/1**

1-45 **4** *¾* **Lexington Abbey**[15] 2295 3-9-7 84.......................... PatSmullen 8 73
(Kevin Ryan) *t.k.h: trckd ldrs stands' side: one pce over 1f out* **11/2**[3]

6-53 **5** *1¼* **Value (IRE)**[10] 2470 3-8-7 70.......................... DavidProbert 7 55
(Gay Kelleway) *chsd ldrs towards stands' side: one pce over 1f out* **20/1**

00-0 **6** *nk* **Disclosure**[14] 2333 3-8-9 72..........................[1] MartinLane 3 56
(Les Eyre) *w ldr: fdd fnl f* **25/1**

-415 **7** *2* **Skye's The Limit**[15] 2317 3-8-13 76.......................... PatrickMathers 5 54
(Richard Fahey) *dwlt: sn chsng ldrs: lost pl over 1f out* **9/2**[2]

0-20 **8** *5* **Two Smart (IRE)**[17] 2257 3-9-1 78.......................... DanielTudhope 6 40
(K R Burke) *dwlt: sn trcking ldrs: drvn over 2f out: sn lost pl* **17/2**

1m 13.79s (-0.01) **Going Correction** +0.275s/f (Good) **8** Ran SP% **116.1**
Speed ratings (Par 101): **111,103,98,97,96 95,92,86**
CSF £19.56 CT £108.75 TOTE £2.10: £1.10, £2.80, £3.10; EX 14.40 Trifecta £93.10.
**Owner** M Betamar **Bred** Michael Collins **Trained** Newmarket, Suffolk

**FOCUS**
A one-sided handicap, run in a time 0.43sec quicker than the preceding Listed race and the winner proved different class. A positive view has been taken of the winner.

## 2769 DOWNLOAD NEW RACINGUK IPAD APP H'CAP (BOBIS RACE) 1m 2f 95y
**5:00** (5:00) (Class 4) (0-80,80) 3-Y-O **£6,469** (£1,925; £962; £481) **Stalls** High

Form RPR

0-05 **1** **Farquhar (IRE)**[15] 2303 3-9-7 80.......................... FrankieDettori 8 95+
(Peter Chapple-Hyam) *stdd s: t.k.h: hld up in detached last: stdy hdwy over 2f out: sn swtchd outside: 2nd over 1f out: led jst ins fnl f: wnt clr: v readily* **2/1**[1]

23-4 **2** *4* **Early Morning (IRE)**[35] 1730 3-9-4 77.......................... WilliamBuick 1 84
(Harry Dunlop) *pushed along to ld after 1f: hdd last 150yds: no ch w wnr* **9/2**[3]

02-0 **3** *1* **Classical Art (IRE)**[33] 1795 3-9-0 73.......................... KierenFallon 2 78
(Roger Varian) *mid-div: drvn and hdwy 3f out: kpt on to take 3rd last 100yds* **8/1**

3243 **4** *¾* **Clear Spell (IRE)**[15] 2292 3-8-10 69.......................... PJMcDonald 7 73
(Alistair Whillans) *in rr: pushed along and hdwy over 3f out: kpt on to take 4th nr fin* **25/1**

-243 **5** *½* **Samtu (IRE)**[89] 828 3-8-12 71.......................... MartinLane 5 74
(Clive Brittain) *led 1f: drvn over 3f out: one pce over 1f out* **16/1**

2334 **6** *6* **Shimba Hills**[22] 2120 3-8-12 74.......................... CharlesBishop(3) 3 66
(Mick Channon) *t.k.h: chsd ldrs: lost pl over 1f out* **11/2**

0-12 **7** *6* **Saltwater Creek (IRE)**[31] 1882 3-9-4 77.......................... TomQueally 6 57
(Michael Bell) *mid-div: effrt over 3f out: lost pl 2f out: eased whn bhd* **4/1**[2]

61-0 **8** *7* **Istimraar (IRE)**[24] 2077 3-9-3 76.......................... DanielTudhope 4 43
(Philip Kirby) *trckd ldrs: drvn over 3f out: lost pl 2f out: eased whn bhd* **12/1**

2m 15.5s **Going Correction** +0.275s/f (Good) **8** Ran SP% **115.4**
Speed ratings (Par 101): **111,107,107,106,106 101,96,90**
CSF £11.27 CT £58.47 TOTE £2.60: £1.30, £1.50, £2.60; EX 12.50 Trifecta £89.40.
**Owner** T Elliott & P Cunningham **Bred** D G Iceton **Trained** Newmarket, Suffolk

**FOCUS**
They went a decent early pace in this and it was another handicap won by a horse well ahead of his mark. He provided another boost to the Newbury race won by Arab Dawn.
T/Plt: £830.40 to a £1 stake. Pool: £148,259.41 - 130.32 winning tickets. T/Qpdt: £31.60 to a £1 stake. Pool: £11,418.05 - 267.09 winning tickets. WG

# 2334 NEWBURY (L-H)
### Saturday, May 31

**OFFICIAL GOING: Good to soft**
Wind: virtually nil Weather: overcast Rails: Rail moved in since last meeting and distances as advertised

## 2770 AL BASTI EQUIWORLD AMATEUR RIDERS' H'CAP 1m 2f 6y
**6:10** (6:10) (Class 5) (0-70,69) 4-Y-O+ **£3,119** (£967; £483; £242) **Stalls** Low

Form RPR

65-4 **1** **Jebril (FR)**[20] 2192 4-10-7 67.......................... MrJHarding(5) 7 82
(Jonathan Portman) *led tl over 5f out: led 4f out: clr over 2f out: in command after: pushed out* **4/1**[2]

0033 **2** *7* **Jewelled**[86] 857 8-10-9 69.......................... MissEllaSmith(5) 2 71
(Ralph J Smith) *s.i.s: sn keen in mid-div: swtchd rt and hdwy 4f out: chsd wnr 3f out: nvr got on terms: styd on same pce* **9/1**

2356 **3** *1½* **Polydamos**[66] 1100 5-9-9 55 oh5.......................... MissMeganNicholls(5) 8 54
(Tony Carroll) *racd keenly: trckd ldrs: disp 2nd fr 4f out: hld fr over 2f out: no ex ins fnl f* **25/1**

13-4 **4** *4* **Candelita**[26] 2595 7-10-1 63..........................[1] MrStanSheppard(7) 6 54
(Matt Sheppard) *hld up towards rr: hdwy fr over 4f out: rdn into 4th 3f out: no further imp on ldrs* **10/1**

006- **5** *1* **Young Dottie**[189] 8020 8-10-7 67.......................... MissLDempster(5) 11 56
(Pat Phelan) *hld up bhd: stdy prog fr 2f out: styd on fnl f: nvr any danger to ldrs* **12/1**

214 **6** *nk* **Supa Seeker (USA)**[33] 1819 8-10-0 55 oh4.......................... MissSBrotherton 9 44
(Tony Carroll) *racd keenly in tch: rdn 3f out: nvr threatened: one pce fnl 2f* **8/1**

40-3 **7** *3¾* **Hernando Torres**[22] 2124 6-10-1 61.......................... MrsRWilson(5) 3 43
(Michael Easterby) *nvr bttr than mid-div* **5/1**[3]

/452 **8** *11* **Dark And Dangerous (IRE)**[5] 2614 6-10-1 56..........(v) MissEJJones 4 17
(Brendan Powell) *racd keenly: trckd ldrs tl wknd over 3f out* **7/2**[1]

0-60 **9** *1¼* **Kilburn**[129] 281 10-9-7 55 oh8..........................(vt[1]) MissNicolaCurrie(7) 12 13
(Alastair Lidderdale) *kpt wd: racd keenly: led after 5f tl 4f out: sn wknd* **40/1**

2211 **10** *8* **Hail Promenader (IRE)**[26] 2597 8-10-3 65..........(t) MissLMager(7) 10 8
(Anthony Carson) *racd keenly: trckd ldrs tl wknd over 3f out* **16/1**

54- **11** *9* **Pahente**[436] 1097 6-10-5 63..........................(p) MissJoannaMason(3) 1
(Tony Carroll) *a bhd* **25/1**

2m 13.0s (4.20) **Going Correction** +0.325s/f (Good) **11** Ran SP% **112.8**
Speed ratings (Par 103): **96,90,89,86,85 84,81,73,72,65 58**
CSF £37.18 CT £782.62 TOTE £5.30: £2.20, £4.10, £3.30; EX 33.30 Trifecta £850.60.
**Owner** J G B Portman **Bred** Mme Heather Murat **Trained** Upper Lambourn, Berks
■ Stewards' Enquiry : Miss L Dempster ten-day ban: failed to take all reasonable and permissable measures to obtain best possible placing (tbn)

**FOCUS**
Rail moved in since last meeting and distances as advertised. A moderate handicap, confined to lady amatuer riders.

## 2771 RELYON CLEANING NEWBURY MAIDEN AUCTION FILLIES' STKS (BOBIS RACE) 6f 8y
**6:40** (6:48) (Class 5) 2-Y-O **£3,234** (£962; £481; £240) **Stalls** Low

Form RPR

**1** **Sleepy Dust (IRE)** 2-8-5 0.......................... JoshBaudains(5) 14 79+
(Sylvester Kirk) *s.i.s: racd green towards rr: hdwy but hanging lft fr over 2f out: led ent fnl f: r.o wl* **33/1**

**2** *2¼* **Free To Love** 2-8-13 0.......................... SteveDrowne 8 75+
(Charles Hills) *s.i.s: mid-div: hdwy over 2f out: rdn and ch jst over 1f out: kpt on same pce* **16/1**

**3** *1¼* **Secret Spirit** 2-8-8 0.......................... RyanTate(5) 2 72+
(Clive Cox) *mid-div: rdn over 2f out: styd on fnl f: wnt 3rd fnl 120yds* **9/1**

**4** *2* **Gilded Lace** 2-8-1.......................... PhilipPrince(5) 13 59
(J S Moore) *chsd ldrs: rdn and ev ch 2f out: sn outpcd: hld after but kpt on again ins fnl f* **50/1**

0342 **5** *nk* **Kidmeforever**[13] 2360 2-7-13.......................... RobHornby(7) 11 58
(J S Moore) *led: rdn wheh hrd pressed fr 2f out: hdd ent fnl f: sn no ex* **25/1**

**6** *7* **Baronessa (IRE)** 2-8-13.......................... RichardHughes 10 44+
(Richard Hannon) *s.i.s: towards rr: sme minor late prog: nvr a threat* **5/2**[1]

**7** *2¼* **Birdie Must Fly** 2-8-6 0.......................... KieranO'Neill 9 30
(Jimmy Fox) *little slowly away: sn trcking ldrs: rdn over 2f out: wknd over 1f out* **7/1**

**8** *½* **White Vin Jan** 2-8-10 0.......................... PatCosgrave 6 32
(Michael Bell) *chsd ldrs: rdn over 2f out: wknd over 1f out* **16/1**

02 **9** *1¼* **Blue Burmese (IRE)**[21] 2173 2-8-6.......................... MartinDwyer 5 25
(Mark Usher) *prom: rdn over 2f out: wknd jst over 1f out: eased* **11/2**[3]

**10** *1¼* **Mistral** 2-8-2 0 ow1.......................... ShelleyBirkett(5) 12 22
(Steph Hollinshead) *s.i.s: a towards rr* **100/1**

**11** *1* **Paco's Dream** 2-8-8 0..........................[1] HarryBentley 7 20
(Harry Dunlop) *s.i.s: a towards rr* **25/1**

**12** *shd* **Royal Razalma (IRE)** 2-8-5 0.......................... MatthewLawson(3) 3 20
(Jonathan Portman) *s.i.s: mid-div: hdwy 3f out: effrt over 2f out: wknd over 1f out* **14/1**

**13** *2¾* **Azure Amour (IRE)** 2-8-10 0.......................... JimCrowley 1 13
(Ralph Beckett) *mid-div: rdn over 2f out: wknd over 1f out* **4/1**[2]

**14** *½* **Magic Mac** 2-8-6.......................... FrankieMcDonald 4 8
(Hughie Morrison) *racd keenly: trckd ldrs: rdn over 3f out: wknd over 2f out* **33/1**

1m 18.01s (5.01) **Going Correction** +0.60s/f (Yiel) **14** Ran SP% **121.4**
Speed ratings (Par 90): **90,87,85,82,82 72,69,69,67,65 64,64,60,60**
CSF £472.80 TOTE £23.40: £8.00, £4.20, £3.10; EX 457.30 Trifecta £2115.10 Part won..
**Owner** Malih Lahej Al Basti **Bred** Holborn Trust Co **Trained** Upper Lambourn, Berks
■ Stewards' Enquiry : Rob Hornby four-day ban: failed to ride out for 4th (Jun 14-16,22)

**FOCUS**
A modest fillies' maiden.

## 2772 BATHWICK TYRES H'CAP 1m 7y(R)
**7:10** (7:17) (Class 4) (0-85,88) 4-Y-O+ **£4,690** (£1,395; £697; £348) **Stalls** Low

Form RPR

45-4 **1** **Ree's Rascal (IRE)**[26] 1241 6-8-13 82.......................... NathanAlison(5) 8 96
(Jim Boyle) *hld up towards rr: swtchd rt 3f out: hdwy sn after: rdn 2f out: hanging lft whn ldng ent fnl f: styd on strly to assert: rdn out* **10/1**

23-0 **2** *3¾* **Buckstay (IRE)**[23] 2091 4-9-4 82.......................... JimCrowley 3 88
(Peter Chapple-Hyam) *mid-div: hdwy 3f out: rdn and ev ch 2f out: tl squeezed up on rails ent fnl f: hld after but kpt on to regain 2nd fnl stride* **7/1**[3]

6302 **3** *hd* **First Post (IRE)**[17] 2248 7-8-13 77.......................... HarryBentley 2 83
(Derek Haydn Jones) *trckd ldrs: led 3f out: rdn 2f out: hdd whn squeezed up ent fnl f: jinked sltly rt fnl 120yds: briefly lost momentum: lost 2nd fnl stride* **10/1**

1-31 **4** *2¼* **Knight Owl**[22] 2131 4-9-7 85.......................... ShaneKelly 9 85
(James Fanshawe) *mid-div: hdwy 3f out: sn rdn to chse ldrs: styd on same pce fnl 2f* **7/2**[1]

31-3 **5** *1¾* **Annawi**[28] 1956 4-9-3 81.......................... FergusSweeney 4 77
(Henry Candy) *mid-div: hdwy 4f out: chal 3f out: rdn 2f out: kpt on same pce fr over 1f out* **8/1**

2466 **6** *1¼* **Atlantis Crossing (IRE)**[8] 2500 5-8-8 72.......................... WilliamCarson 5 65
(Jim Boyle) *mid-div: rdn over 2f out: styd on same pce* **50/1**

3211 **7** *1½* **Uncle Dermot (IRE)**[9] 2478 6-9-5 88.......................... RyanTate(5) 1 77
(Brendan Powell) *awkward away: sn trcking ldrs: rdn over 2f out: hld in 8th whn hmpd over 1f out* **5/1**[2]

660- **8** *½* **Mazaaher**[228] 7275 4-8-9 73.......................... RobertHavlin 11 61
(J W Hills) *hld up towards rr: rdn 3f out: nvr any real imp on ldrs* **33/1**

2323 **9** *2½* **Aqua Ardens (GER)**[24] 2068 6-8-12 76..........................(t) PatCosgrave 6 58
(George Baker) *hld up towards rr: rdn over 2f out: nvr any imp* **25/1**

10-6 **10** *hd* **Falcon's Reign (FR)**[17] 2251 5-8-8 72.......................... AndrewMullen 12 54
(Michael Appleby) *trckd ldrs: rdn w ch over 2f out: wknd over 1f out* **33/1**

1305 **11** *18* **Big Baz (IRE)**[15] 2309 4-9-3 81.......................... MartinDwyer 10 22
(William Muir) *pressed ldr: led after 2f: rdn and hdd 3f out: wknd over 1f out* **5/1**[2]

20-1 **12** 3/4 **Harry Bosch**[26] 2012 4-9-4 **82**........................ RichardHughes 7 21
(Brian Meehan) *racd freely: led for over 2f: trckd ldr: rdn 3f out: sn wknd: eased whn btn* **8/1**

1m 39.88s (1.18) **Going Correction** +0.325s/f (Good) **12** Ran SP% **120.1**
Speed ratings (Par 105): **107,103,103,100,99 97,96,95,93,93 75,74**
CSF £76.99 CT £739.65 TOTE £12.60: £3.70, £2.60, £3.90; EX 106.00 Trifecta £1131.70.
**Owner** Walter Hayford **Bred** Pier House Stud **Trained** Epsom, Surrey
■ Stewards' Enquiry : Nathan Alison one-day ban: careless riding (Jun 14)

**FOCUS**
A fair handicap.

## 2773 BATHWICK TYRES MAIDEN STKS — 1m 2f 6y
**7:40** (7:46) (Class 5) 3-Y-O — **£3,234** (£962; £481; £240) **Stalls** Low

Form RPR

2- **1** **Second Step (IRE)**[214] 7607 3-9-5 0........................ ShaneKelly 8 79+
(Luca Cumani) *in tch: trckd ldrs over 2f out: led jst over 1f out: briefly rdn: a holding on fnl 120yds: pushed out* **3/1**[1]

4 **2** 1/2 **Igider (IRE)**[16] 2271 3-9-5 0........................ AndreaAtzeni 4 78
(Roger Varian) *trckd ldrs: rdn over 2f out: kpt on ins fnl f: a being jst hld by wnr fnl 120yds: snatched 2nd fnl strides* **9/2**[3]

6-0 **3** *shd* **Norse Light**[19] 2221 3-9-5 0........................ HarryBentley 1 78
(Ralph Beckett) *led: rdn and hdd over 2f out: rallied wl to hold ev ch ent fnl f: kpt on but hld fnl 120yds: lost 2nd fnl strides* **33/1**

**4** 1/2 **Kings Fete** 3-9-5 0........................ JamesDoyle 3 77+
(Sir Michael Stoute) *hld up towards rr: rdn wl over 2f out: hdwy but hanging lft fr over 1f out: styd on ins fnl f: snatched 4th fnl strides* **12/1**

5 **5** 1/2 **Fastnet Red**[54] 1353 3-9-5 0........................ RobertHavlin 6 76
(John Gosden) *in tch: rdn 3f out: hdwy but hanging lft over 1f out: styd on ins fnl f* **7/2**[2]

**6** *nse* **Jonny Rae** 3-9-5 0........................ MartinDwyer 12 76
(Andrew Balding) *mid-div: rdn over 2f out: hdwy over 1f out: styng on and would have fin v cl but nt clr run fnl 120yds* **25/1**

45- **7** 4 **Yaakooum (IRE)**[260] 6355 3-9-5 0........................ KieranO'Neill 13 68
(Richard Hannon) *hld up twards rr: pushed along over 4f out: styd on fnl f: nvr trbld ldrs* **20/1**

2-02 **8** 1 **Dursey Island (USA)**[24] 2075 3-9-5 81........................ RichardHughes 10 67
(Richard Hannon) *pressed ldr: led over 2f out: sn rdn: hdd jst over 1f out: wknd fnl 120yds* **5/1**

6- **9** 3/4 **Cinnamon Spice**[218] 7500 3-9-5 0........................ PatCosgrave 7 65
(Harry Dunlop) *mid-div: hdwy 4f out: rdn over 2f out: fdd ent fnl f* **50/1**

50 **10** 2 **Greengage Summer**[14] 2339 3-9-0 0........................ SamHitchcott 16 56
(Mick Channon) *s.i.s: a towards rr* **33/1**

05 **11** 3 **Do Wah Diddy Diddy**[9] 2497 3-9-5 0........................ SteveDrowne 9 56
(Clive Cox) *mid-div tl wknd 2f out* **33/1**

00 **12** *nk* **Little Flo**[15] 2310 3-8-9 0........................ RyanTate[(5)] 14 50
(Brendan Powell) *mid-div: rdn 3f out: wknd ent fnl f* **100/1**

0 **13** 2 3/4 **Goldenrod**[27] 1984 3-9-5 0........................ JimCrowley 2 50
(Ralph Beckett) *racd keenly: trckd ldrs: rdn over 2f out: wknd over 1f out* **12/1**

**14** 59 **Dukes Den** 3-9-0 0........................ JoshBaudains[(5)] 11
(Sylvester Kirk) *cantered loose befhand: s.i.s: racd green: a towards rr: tailing off whn veered rt over 1f out* **66/1**

2m 13.32s (4.52) **Going Correction** +0.325s/f (Good) **14** Ran SP% **119.3**
Speed ratings (Par 99): **94,93,93,93,92 92,89,88,88,86 84,83,81,34**
CSF £14.98 TOTE £5.60: £2.20, £2.40, £9.00; EX 19.20 Trifecta £675.60.
**Owner** Merry Fox Stud Limited **Bred** Merry Fox Stud Limited **Trained** Newmarket, Suffolk

**FOCUS**
The pace was modest for this fair 3yo maiden.

## 2774 AL BASTI EQUIWORLD H'CAP — 1m 5f 61y
**8:10** (8:13) (Class 5) (0-75,77) 4-Y-O+ — **£3,234** (£962; £481; £240) **Stalls** Low

Form RPR

2024 **1** **Afro**[28] 1941 4-8-10 **65**........................(p) CharlesBishop[(3)] 10 74
(Peter Hedger) *w ldr for 2f: trckd ldrs: led wl over 2f out: sn rdn: strly chal over 1f out: hld on wl ins fnl f: drvn out* **5/1**[3]

3-41 **2** 1/2 **Wannabe Your Man**[32] 1849 4-9-7 **73**........................ AndreaAtzeni 5 81
(Roger Varian) *mid-div: pushed along and hdwy over 3f out: rdn to chse wnr wl over 1f out: edgd lft: hld by wnr ins fnl f but kpt on to go cl 2nd nr fin* **6/4**[1]

6226 **3** *nk* **My Lord**[66] 1108 6-9-1 **67**........................ RichardHughes 8 74
(Luke Dace) *stdd in rr sn after s: smooth hdwy fr over 3f out: swtchd lft 2f out: sn rdn for str chal: hld fnl 120yds: lost 2nd fnl strides* **16/1**

5516 **4** 12 **See And Be Seen**[30] 1895 4-8-7 **59** oh1........................(p) MartinDwyer 6 49
(Sylvester Kirk) *led for 2f: pressed ldr tl rdn 3f out: kpt on same pce fnl 2f* **25/1**

2413 **5** 3 3/4 **Ssafa**[4] 2651 6-9-5 **71**........................(p) JamesDoyle 7 55
(Alastair Lidderdale) *led after 2f: rdn and hdd wl over 2f out: kpt chsng ldrs tl fdd ins fnl f* **10/1**

-400 **6** 5 **Admirable Duque (IRE)**[15] 2305 8-8-10 **62**........................(p) JimCrowley 3 39
(Dominic Ffrench Davis) *hld up towards rr: rdn over 2f out: styd on but nvr finding the pce to get involved* **16/1**

1264 **7** 18 **Teajaybe (USA)**[12] 2394 6-9-1 **72**........................(p) MarcMonaghan[(5)] 2 22
(Chris Dwyer) *trckd ldrs: rdn 4f out: wknd 2f out* **25/1**

400- **8** 8 **Laser Blazer**[26] 8159 6-9-6 **72**........................ FergusSweeney 4 10
(Alan King) *in tch: rdn over 3f out: nvr threatened: wknd 2f out* **9/2**[2]

32-0 **9** 8 **Red Pilgrim (IRE)**[33] 1810 4-9-4 **73**........................(t) RobertTart[(3)] 1
(James Toller) *s.i.s: in last trio: rdn over 4f out: nvr any imp: wknd 2f out* **15/2**

2m 56.69s (4.69) **Going Correction** +0.325s/f (Good) **9** Ran SP% **115.2**
Speed ratings (Par 103): **98,97,97,90,87 84,73,68,63**
CSF £12.83 CT £107.21 TOTE £6.60: £1.80, £1.40, £2.90; EX 16.60 Trifecta £172.50.
**Owner** P C F Racing Ltd **Bred** The Lavington Stud **Trained** Dogmersfield, Hampshire

**FOCUS**
A modest staying handicap where the principals came clear.

## 2775 PREMIER FOOD COURTS FILLIES' H'CAP — 7f (S)
**8:40** (8:41) (Class 5) (0-75,70) 3-Y-O+ — **£3,234** (£962; £481; £240) **Stalls** Low

Form RPR

3513 **1** **Pretty Bubbles**[32] 1857 5-9-12 **68**........................ FrederikTylicki 11 78
(J R Jenkins) *trckd ldr: led over 1f out: sn rdn: r.o wl fnl f: readily* **7/1**

36-6 **2** 2 **Royal Connection**[12] 2383 3-9-3 **70**........................ RichardHughes 5 71
(Richard Hannon) *stdd s: hdwy 2f out: sn rdn: r.o wl fnl f: wnt 2nd fnl strides: no ch w wnr* **11/2**[3]

-130 **3** *hd* **Burnt Fingers (IRE)**[16] 2282 4-9-10 **66**........................ AndreaAtzeni 9 70
(Rod Millman) *mid-div: rdn wl over 2f out: no imp tl r.o ent fnl f: wnt 2nd fnl 100yds but no ch w wnr: lost 2nd fnl strides* **7/2**[1]

13-5 **4** 1 1/2 **Be Royale**[16] 2282 4-9-6 **62**........................ AndrewMullen 3 62
(Michael Appleby) *racd freely: led: rdn whn hdd over 1f out: no ex ins fnl f* **12/1**

-040 **5** *shd* **Tenbridge**[3] 2669 5-9-1 **60**........................(v) RosieJessop[(3)] 8 60
(Derek Haydn Jones) *trckd ldrs: rdn and ev ch over 2f out: hld over 1f out: no ex ins fnl f* **8/1**

6211 **6** 1 3/4 **Welsh Inlet (IRE)**[16] 2282 6-9-5 **61**........................ WilliamCarson 4 57
(John Bridger) *trckd ldrs: rdn over 2f out: sn one pce* **9/2**[2]

010- **7** 1 **It's Taboo**[254] 6564 4-9-13 **69**........................ SteveDrowne 1 62
(Mark Usher) *hld up: rdn over 2f out: nt pce to get involved* **16/1**

3342 **8** 1 **Two In The Pink (IRE)**[65] 1123 4-9-5 **61**........................ JamesDoyle 10 51
(Ralph J Smith) *hld up: rdn over 2f out: nvr any imp* **16/1**

-000 **9** 3 1/2 **Insight (IRE)**[22] 2129 3-8-4 **62**........................ PhilipPrince[(5)] 7 39
(John Spearing) *in tch: rdn over 2f out: wknd over 1f out* **25/1**

0-50 **10** 7 **Aristocratic Duty**[10] 2470 3-8-8 **66**........................ JoshBaudains[(5)] 2 25
(Sylvester Kirk) *chsd ldrs tl wknd 2f out* **10/1**

531- **11** 1 **Tregereth (IRE)**[289] 5447 4-9-2 **61**........................ MatthewLawson[(3)] 6 21
(Jonathan Portman) *trckd ldrs: rdn over 2f out: sn wknd* **25/1**

1m 29.24s (3.54) **Going Correction** +0.60s/f (Yiel)
**WFA** 3 from 4yo+ 11lb **11** Ran SP% **115.6**
Speed ratings (Par 100): **103,100,100,98,98 96,95,94,90,82 81**
CSF £44.51 CT £158.49 TOTE £5.10: £1.30, £2.40, £1.60; EX 55.00 Trifecta £282.70.
**Owner** Mark Goldstein **Bred** Southill Stud **Trained** Royston, Herts

**FOCUS**
An ordinary fillies' handicap.
T/Plt: £909.50 to a £1 stake. Pool: £78,504 - 63.00 winning tickets T/Qpdt: £23.40 to a £1 stake. Pool: £8,136 - 257.05 winning tickets TM

# 2744 NEWMARKET (R-H)
Saturday, May 31

**OFFICIAL GOING: Good (6.3)**
Wind: virtually nil Weather: dry, bright spells Rails: Far side track used. Stalls Far side except 10f, 12f, &14f: Centre

## 2776 L-3.CO SUPPORTING THE AHT EBF STALLIONS MAIDEN STKS (BOBIS RACE) (DIV I) — 6f
**1:55** (1:56) (Class 4) 2-Y-O — **£4,528** (£1,347; £673; £336) **Stalls** Low

Form RPR

**1** **Peacock** 2-9-5 0........................ RyanMoore 1 85+
(Richard Hannon) *stdd after s: chsd ldrs: swtchd lft and effrt to chal over 1f out: drew clr w rival 1f out: led fnl 100yds: styd on wl: rdn out* **7/2**[2]

2 **2** 1/2 **Commander Patten (IRE)**[16] 2269 2-9-5 0........................ AndreaAtzeni 10 83
(Alan Bailey) *chsd ldr tl led ent fnl 2f: hrd pressed and drvn over 1f out: drew clr w wnr 1f out: hdd and kpt on same pce fnl 100yds* **7/2**[2]

**3** 1 3/4 **Epithet (IRE)** 2-9-5 0........................ JamesDoyle 7 78+
(Charlie Appleby) *in tch in last trio: nt clrest of run wl over 1f out: swtchd lft and effrt ent fnl 2f: str run ins fnl f to go 3rd fnl 50yds: nvr gng to rch ldng pair* **6/1**[3]

**4** 1/2 **Richard Pankhurst** 2-9-5 0........................ RobertHavlin 9 76+
(John Gosden) *chsd ldrs: rdn and effrt over 1f out: 3rd and unable qck jst over 1f out: kpt on same pce after: lost 3rd fnl 50yds* **5/2**[1]

**5** 1 1/4 **Arc Cara (ITY)** 2-9-5 0........................ RichardKingscote 5 73
(Ralph Beckett) *awkward leaving stalls: t.k.h: sn in tch in midfield: rdn and hdwy over 1f out: battling for 3rd but outpcd by ldng pair 1f out: wknd fnl 75yds* **20/1**

**6** 1 **Steady Major (IRE)** 2-9-5 0........................ PatCosgrave 2 70+
(David Simcock) *s.i.s: sn rcvrd and in tch in rr: rdn and hdwy over 1f out: styd on same pce ins fnl f* **33/1**

**7** 3/4 **Shaakis (IRE)** 2-9-5 0........................ PaulHanagan 3 67
(Marcus Tregoning) *in tch in midfield: rdn and outpcd over 1f out: styd on same pce and no threat to ldrs fnl f* **16/1**

**8** 3/4 **Faithful Creek (IRE)** 2-9-5 0........................ DaneO'Neill 11 65
(Brian Meehan) *in tch in midfield: rdn 2f out: outpcd over 1f out: no imp and one pce fnl f* **20/1**

**9** 3 1/4 **Dark Profit (IRE)** 2-9-5 0........................ GeorgeBaker 8 55
(Charles Hills) *stdd s: hld up in rr: swtchd lft and effrt wl over 1f out: no prog: wknd fnl f* **8/1**

00 **10** 2 **Framley Garth (IRE)**[16] 2269 2-9-5 0........................ WilliamCarson 6 49
(David Elsworth) *broke qckly: t.k.h: led at stdy gallop tl hdd and rdn ent fnl 2f: lost pl and bhd 1f out: wknd* **100/1**

1m 15.2s (2.70) **Going Correction** +0.175s/f (Good) **10** Ran SP% **117.8**
Speed ratings (Par 95): **89,88,86,85,83 82,81,80,76,73**
CSF £15.70 TOTE £4.20: £1.90, £1.80, £1.80; EX 16.60 Trifecta £45.10.
**Owner** The Queen **Bred** The Queen **Trained** East Everleigh, Wilts

**FOCUS**
Far side track used. Stalls far side except 1m2f, 1m4f, &1m6f: centre. The ground had dried out from its overnight description as soft. The time for the opener was nearly two seconds quicker than the second division. Group colts Havana Gold and Jallota have won this maiden in the last couple of years. The runners raced near to the stands' side, and the first pair came clear before the pack closed on them late. The form is rated around the runner-up.

## 2777 L-3.CO SUPPORTING THE AHT EBF STALLIONS MAIDEN STKS (BOBIS RACE) (DIV II) — 6f
**2:25** (2:29) (Class 4) 2-Y-O — **£4,528** (£1,347; £673; £336) **Stalls** Low

Form RPR

**1** **Justice Well** 2-9-5 0........................ WilliamCarson 7 84+
(David Elsworth) *hld up wl in tch in midfield: effrt and rn green wl over 1f out: gd hdwy 1f out: chsd clr wnr ins fnl f: r.o strly fnl 100yds to ld towards fin* **12/1**

**2** 1/2 **Burnt Sugar (IRE)** 2-9-5 0........................ PatDobbs 8 83+
(Richard Hannon) *w ldr tl led 1/2-way: rdn over 1f out: gng clr but edging lft fr 1f out: kpt on but worn down and hdd towards fin* **7/2**[2]

**3** 2 **Disegno (IRE)** 2-9-5 0........................ RyanMoore 4 77+
(Sir Michael Stoute) *in tch towards rr: effrt: rn green and flashed tail 2f out: no imp tl hdwy jst ins fnl f: styd on to go 3rd fnl 75yds: gng on fin* **4/1**[3]

**4** 1 3/4 **Speedy Move (IRE)** 2-9-5 0........................ LiamJones 3 71
(Ismail Mohammed) *led at v stdy gallop tl hdd 1/2-way: rdn over 2f out: outpcd u.p and edgd rt jst over 1f out: no threat to ldrs but kpt on again ins fnl f* **25/1**

5 nk **Alakhtal (IRE)** 2-9-5 0 PaulHanagan 10 70
(Charles Hills) *stdd s: t.k.h: hld up wl in tch in midfield: hdwy to chse ldr over 2f out: rdn and ev ch over 1f out: unable qck 1f out: wknd ins fnl f* **13/2**

6 nk **Beauchamp Ace** 2-9-5 0 RichardKingscote 5 70+
(Paul Fitzsimons) *in tch in midfield: effrt 2f out: outpcd and bhd whn hmpd jst over 1f out: no threat to ldrs but styd on ins fnl f* **66/1**

6 7 2 **Skygazer (IRE)**[11] 2428 2-9-5 0 JamesDoyle 9 63
(Charlie Appleby) *t.k.h: chsd ldrs: rdn 2f out: sn outpcd and lost pl: no threat to ldrs and one pce fnl f* **8/1**

8 3/4 **Scutum (IRE)** 2-9-5 0 MartinDwyer 6 61
(Brian Meehan) *stdd s: t.k.h: hld up in tch in last trio: effrt and shifted lft 2f out: no prog and wl hld 1f out* **16/1**

9 4 **Heartbreak Hero** 2-9-5 0 AndreaAtzeni 2 49
(William Haggas) *s.i.s: rn green and hld up in tch in rr: effrt 2f out: no hdwy: wknd 1f out* **9/4**[1]

1m 17.17s (4.67) **Going Correction** +0.175s/f (Good) **9** Ran SP% **116.3**
Speed ratings (Par 95): **75,74,71,69,68 68,65,64,59**
CSF £54.26 TOTE £13.70: £2.90, £1.70, £1.70; EX 68.80 Trifecta £364.90.
**Owner** Robert Ng **Bred** Usk Valley Stud **Trained** Newmarket, Suffolk

**FOCUS**
The slower division by two seconds, but still a pretty good maiden. Unlike the first, the runners raced towards the far rail.

## 2778 BETFAIR SUPPORTING THE ANIMAL HEALTH TRUST H'CAP 6f
**3:00** (3:01) (Class 2) (0-105,100) 3-Y-O+**£19,407** (£5,775; £2,886; £1,443) **Stalls** Low

Form RPR

522- 1 **Rene Mathis (GER)**[245] 6826 4-9-3 **89** DavidNolan 5 101
(Richard Fahey) *chsd ldr: rdn to ld ent fnl f: sustained battle w rival fnl f: styd on wl rdn out* **10/1**

100- 2 nk **Hoodna (IRE)**[196] 7928 4-9-10 **96** [1] HarryBentley 13 107
(Saeed bin Suroor) *wl in tch in midfield: swtchd lft and effrt to chal ent fnl f: ev ch and sustained battled w wnr fnl f: r.o: a hld* **20/1**

0-40 3 2 **Dont Bother Me (IRE)**[21] 2145 4-9-12 **98** (p) RyanMoore 9 103+
(Marco Botti) *stdd s: hld up in tch: rdn over 1f out: hdwy whn carried rt jst ins fnl f: styd on wl to go 3rd towards fin* **9/2**[1]

00-1 4 1/2 **Goldream**[27] 1975 5-9-9 **95** (p) AndreaAtzeni 12 98
(Robert Cowell) *chsd ldrs: rdn and pressing ldrs whn carried lft and sltly hmpd 1f out: styd on same pce after* **5/1**[2]

6520 5 nk **Hadaj**[7] 2548 5-8-12 **84** (p) JamesSullivan 6 86
(Ruth Carr) *chsd ldrs: rdn 2f out: drvn and unable qck over 1f out: kpt on same pce ins fnl f* **6/1**[3]

0-06 6 3 **Dominate**[26] 2030 4-8-10 **82** PatDobbs 2 74
(Richard Hannon) *stdd s: hld up in tch towards rr: effrt 2f out: sme hdwy and swtchd rt 1f out: styd on: nvr trbld ldrs* **10/1**

42-0 7 1/2 **Picture Dealer**[17] 2254 5-9-2 **91** SimonPearce(3) 7 82
(Lydia Pearce) *hld up in tch in rr: effrt wl over 1f out: no imp tl styd on and nt clr run ins fnl f: swtchd lft and kpt on fnl 100yds: nvr trbld ldrs* **15/2**

00-0 8 nk **Zanetto**[27] 1975 4-10-0 **100** MartinDwyer 1 90
(Andrew Balding) *dwlt: sn in tch in midfield: effrt and unable qck 2f out: plugged on same pce fnl f* **14/1**

0-24 9 1 1/2 **Peterkin (IRE)**[14] 2344 3-8-5 **86** LiamJones 11 69
(Mark Johnston) *racd freely: led tl edgd lft and hdd ent fnl f: sn wknd* **12/1**

5600 10 1 1/4 **Regal Parade**[17] 2254 10-8-13 **90** (t) PhilipPrince(5) 8 71
(Milton Bradley) *in tch in midfield: rdn and over 2f out: outpcd and btn over 1f out* **16/1**

000- 11 1/2 **Burwaaz**[224] 7366 5-9-9 **95** DaneO'Neill 10 74
(Ed Dunlop) *chsd ldrs: effrt 2f out: rdn and unable qck over 1f out: btn whn short of room and hmpd ins fnl f: eased towards fin* **14/1**

0- 12 nk **Secret Asset (IRE)**[245] 6830 9-9-7 **98** DavidKenny(5) 4 77
(Jane Chapple-Hyam) *stdd s: hld up in tch towards rr: rdn and effrt whn nt clr run and swtchd rt over 1f out: no prog after* **33/1**

20-0 13 6 **Tanseeb**[28] 1952 3-8-6 **87** PaulHanagan 3 44
(Mark Johnston) *stdd s: hld up in rr: rdn and no hdwy wl over 1f out: wknd ins fnl f: eased towards fin* **16/1**

1m 12.07s (-0.43) **Going Correction** +0.175s/f (Good)
**WFA** 3 from 4yo+ 9lb **13** Ran SP% **119.6**
Speed ratings (Par 109): **109,108,105,105,104 100,100,99,97,96 95,95,87**
CSF £194.62 CT £1067.33 TOTE £9.20: £2.80, £6.40, £2.30; EX 261.70 Trifecta £1176.00.
**Owner** Dr Marwan Koukash **Bred** Stall 5-Stars **Trained** Musley Bank, N Yorks

**FOCUS**
A decent sprint handicap in which the runners raced down the centre of the track. It proved difficult to get involved from the rear. A personal best from the winner.

## 2779 JOHN SUNLEY MEMORIAL LEVY BOARD H'CAP 1m 4f
**3:35** (3:36) (Class 2) (0-105,102) 4-Y-O+**£32,345** (£9,625; £4,810; £2,405) **Stalls** Centre

Form RPR

1-00 1 **De Rigueur**[14] 2342 6-9-1 **93** (tp) AndreaAtzeni 3 101+
(Marco Botti) *stdd s: hld up in rr: effrt and nt clr run ent fnl f: squeezed between horses and edgd lft u.p jst ins fnl f: str run fnl 100yds to ld nr fin* **25/1**

3-02 2 nk **Duke Of Clarence (IRE)**[15] 2314 5-9-7 **99** (p) DavidNolan 10 106
(Richard Fahey) *chsd ldrs: rdn and ev ch over 1f out: led and wandered lft jst ins fnl f: kpt on u.p tl hdd and no ex nr fin* **14/1**

1452 3 3/4 **Modernism**[12] 2405 5-8-10 **88** RichardKingscote 11 94
(David Simcock) *chsd ldr: led 2f out: hung rt over 1f out: edging bk lft and hdd jst ins fnl f: kpt on same pce after* **28/1**

062- 4 nk **Dashing Star**[280] 5764 4-9-7 **99** DaneO'Neill 14 104
(David Elsworth) *taken down early: racd keenly: led: racd against stands' rail fr 8f out: hdd 2f out: kpt on u.p: unable qck fnl 100yds* **12/1**

00-6 5 1/2 **Havana Beat (IRE)**[28] 1950 4-9-10 **102** MartinDwyer 7 106
(Andrew Balding) *t.k.h: hld up in tch towards rr: rdn and effrt wl over 1f out: swtchd lft over 1f out: kpt on u.p ins fnl f: nvr gng pce to rch ldrs* **16/1**

12- 6 shd **Plutocracy (IRE)**[259] 6380 4-9-0 **92** TedDurcan 6 96+
(David Lanigan) *in tch in midfield: hdwy over 2f out: chsd ldrs and rdn wl over 1f out: no ex and one pce fnl 100yds* **10/1**[3]

1-01 7 shd **Mighty Yar (IRE)**[27] 1973 4-9-2 **94** JamesDoyle 13 98
(Lady Cecil) *wl in tch in midfield: rdn 3f out: drvn over 1f out: styd on u.p ins fnl f: nvr gng pce to chal* **15/8**[1]

400- 8 hd **Macbeth (IRE)**[222] 4394 5-8-10 **95** AlistairRawlinson(7) 9 99
(Michael Appleby) *in tch in midfield: rdn and effrt 2f out: hdwy u.p to chse ldrs ins fnl f: styd on same pce fnl 100yds* **33/1**

00-0 9 1 1/4 **Ray Ward (IRE)**[27] 1973 4-8-13 **91** PatCosgrave 1 93
(David Simcock) *hld up in tch in midfield: rdn and effrt 2f out: keeping on whn pushed lft jst ins fnl f: styd on same pce after* **25/1**

2416 10 1/2 **Flemish School**[16] 2272 4-8-12 **90** (p) WilliamCarson 4 91
(David Elsworth) *hld up towards rr: c to r against stands' rail fr 8f out: hdwy to chse ldrs 5f out: rdn and effrt 2f out: keeping on same pce whn pushed lft jst ins fnl f* **25/1**

/1-5 11 9 **Rye House (IRE)**[17] 2253 5-9-6 **98** RyanMoore 5 84
(Sir Michael Stoute) *wl in tch in midfield: rdn over 2f out: unable qck and btn ent fnl f: sn wknd* **5/2**[2]

40-4 12 13 **Jathabah (IRE)**[22] 2115 4-9-4 **96** PatDobbs 12 62
(Clive Brittain) *chsd ldrs: rdn over 2f out: lost pl and bhd jst over 1f out: sn wknd: eased wl ins fnl f* **50/1**

10-0 13 hd **Lahaag**[17] 2253 5-9-7 **99** PaulHanagan 8 64
(John Gosden) *wl in tch in midfield: rdn jst over 2f out: lost pl and bhd jst over 1f out: wknd fnl f: eased wl ins fnl f* **10/1**[3]

/5-0 14 1 3/4 **Romeo Montague**[34] 1770 6-8-11 **89** PaddyAspell 2 52
(Ed Dunlop) *t.k.h: hld up in tch in rr: rdn 2f out: wknd jst over 1f out: bhd and eased wl ins fnl f* **66/1**

2m 35.43s (2.53) **Going Correction** +0.35s/f (Good) **14** Ran SP% **123.2**
Speed ratings (Par 109): **105,104,104,104,103 103,103,103,102,102 96,87,87,86**
CSF £329.46 CT £9501.63 TOTE £33.00: £6.20, £3.60, £5.40; EX 366.80 Trifecta £4085.60.
**Owner** N A Jackson **Bred** Cheveley Park Stud Ltd **Trained** Newmarket, Suffolk

**FOCUS**
A valuable and competitive handicap, but the pace wasn't especially strong and they finished in a heap with the first ten separated by under four lengths. Most of the field raced down the middle, with two staying on the stands' rail in the long home straight. Ordinary form for the level, with the market leaders disappointing.

## 2780 LADBROKES CHARITABLE TRUST MAIDEN FILLIES' STKS (BOBIS RACE) 7f
**4:05** (4:09) (Class 5) 3-Y-O **£3,881** (£1,155; £577; £288) **Stalls** Low

Form RPR

1 **Swift Campaign (IRE)** 3-9-0 0 TedDurcan 4 86
(John Gosden) *hld up in tch towards rr: hdwy over 2f out: chsd ldrs and rdn 1f out: flashed tail but r.o strly fnl 50yds to ld last strides* **40/1**

- 2 nk **Belle D'Or (USA)** 3-9-0 0 RobertHavlin 3 85
(John Gosden) *t.k.h: hld up in midfield: hdwy to chse ldrs 3f out: rdn and ev ch over 1f out: led 1f out: kpt on wl u.p tl hdd and no ex last strides* **4/1**[2]

6- 3 2 1/2 **Spellbind**[337] 3781 3-9-0 0 JamesDoyle 14 79
(Charlie Appleby) *hld up in tch in rr: swtchd lft and hdwy 2f out: ev ch 1f out: no ex and btn fnl 75yds: wknd towards fin* **5/1**[3]

4 1 3/4 **Free Rein** 3-9-0 0 RichardKingscote 12 74
(Ralph Beckett) *t.k.h: hld up wl in tch in midfield: rdn to chse ldrs 2f out: outpcd u.p 1f out: no threat to ldrs but plugged on to go 4th nr fin* **11/1**

3- 5 1/2 **Water Queen**[253] 6594 3-9-0 0 RyanMoore 9 73
(William Haggas) *restless in stalls: t.k.h: w ldr tl led 4f out: rdn wl over 1f out: hdd 1f out: no ex and sn btn: wknd fnl 75yds and lost 4th nr fin* **13/8**[1]

6 3/4 **Venturous Spirit (IRE)** 3-9-0 0 NickyMackay 11 71
(John Gosden) *hld up in tch in rr: rdn over 2f out: hdwy and swtchd lft 1f out: styng on wl ins fnl f: nvr trbld ldrs* **25/1**

7 nk **Roly Tricks** 3-9-0 0 HarryBentley 7 70
(Olly Stevens) *hld up in tch in midfield: rdn over 2f out: outpcd and btn over 1f out: styd on same pce fnl f* **66/1**

63 8 2 3/4 **Zaawia (IRE)**[30] 1902 3-9-0 0 PaulHanagan 10 63
(Ed Dunlop) *in tch in midfield: rdn and effrt ent fnl 2f: no hdwy u.p over 1f out: wknd ins fnl f* **8/1**

9 1/2 **Sensible Way (USA)** 3-9-0 0 PatDobbs 2 62
(Richard Hannon) *rn green and sn dropped to rr: rdn 3f out: hung lft and no hdwy 2f out: styd on ins fnl f: nvr trbld ldrs* **20/1**

0 10 hd **Capmonde (IRE)**[25] 2061 3-9-0 0 AndreaAtzeni 13 61
(William Knight) *in tch in midfield: rdn and effrt jst over 2f out: no prog and btn over 1f out: wknd ins fnl f* **33/1**

00 11 shd **Swiss Lait**[34] 1767 3-9-0 0 DaneO'Neill 6 61
(David Elsworth) *s.i.s: t.k.h: hld up in tch in midfield: rdn 2f out: sn outpcd and btn: wknd fnl f* **66/1**

60 12 3 1/4 **Tohaveandtohold**[11] 2442 3-9-0 0 LiamJones 5 53
(William Haggas) *t.k.h: chsd ldrs: rdn ent fnl 2f: sn struggling and lost pl: wknd 1f out* **33/1**

13 4 1/2 **Remy** 3-9-0 0 J-PGuillambert 8 41
(Nick Littmoden) *in tch in midfield: rdn and no hdwy ent fnl 2f: lost pl and bhd 1f out* **66/1**

0 14 3/4 **Goddess Of Gloom**[9] 2489 3-9-0 0 MartinDwyer 1 39
(Peter Chapple-Hyam) *t.k.h: led for 3f: losing pl whn hung rt ent fnl 2f: wknd and bhd 1f out: fdd* **40/1**

00 15 7 **Solar Moon**[22] 2125 3-9-0 0 AhmedAjtebi 15 42
(Charlie Appleby) *chsd ldrs: rdn and wandered u.p wl over 1f out: btn jst over 1f out: fdd fnl f* **25/1**

1m 27.45s (1.75) **Going Correction** +0.175s/f (Good) **15** Ran SP% **121.4**
Speed ratings (Par 96): **97,96,93,91,91 90,90,86,86,86 85,82,77,76,68**
CSF £184.31 TOTE £44.70: £10.50, £1.90, £1.70; EX 148.90 Trifecta £3377.00 Part won. Pool: £4,502.76 - 0.58 winning tickets..
**Owner** Sheikh Juma Dalmook Al Maktoum **Bred** Glending Bloodstock **Trained** Newmarket, Suffolk

**FOCUS**
Some well-bred fillies contested this interesting maiden. The bare form is just fair, but winners should emerge from the race. John Gosden saddled three debutantes and was rewarded with a 1-2.

## 2781 BETSI GOLDEN MILE H'CAP (BOBIS RACE) 1m
**4:40** (4:43) (Class 3) (0-90,90) 3-Y-O **£9,703** (£2,887; £1,443; £721) **Stalls** Low

Form RPR

1-1 1 **Muteela**[37] 1658 3-9-4 **87** DaneO'Neill 1 101
(Mark Johnston) *mde all: rdn 2f out: hrd pressed and battled on gamely u.p fnl f: drvn out* **12/1**

1- 2 1/2 **Pretzel (IRE)**[220] 7467 3-9-0 **83** AndreaAtzeni 3 96+
(Roger Varian) *chsd wnr thrght: rdn and effrt 2f out: pressing wnr whn hung lft 1f out: stl pressing wnr and racing on far rail fnl 100yds: hld towards fin* **7/2**[1]

-111 3 3 3/4 **Crystal Lake (IRE)**[25] 2063 3-9-2 **85** RichardKingscote 10 89
(Ralph Beckett) *hld up in touch in midfield: effrt u.p 2f out: chsd clr ldng pair 1f out: styd on but no imp* **10/1**[3]

-526 4 1/2 **Instant Attraction (IRE)**[17] 2257 3-8-13 **82** RussKennemore 6 85
(Jedd O'Keeffe) *hld up in tch in midfield: rdn 3f out: styd and sme hdwy over 1f out: no threat to ldrs but kpt on fnl f* **40/1**

-021 **5** 3 1/4 **Speculative Bid (IRE)**[19] 2201 3-8-8 **82** JoeyHaynes(5) 5 77
(David Elsworth) *stdd s: t.k.h: hdwy into midfield after 1f: chsd ldrs 1/2-way: rdn 2f out: 3rd and outpcd over 1f out: wknd ins fnl f* **12/1**

46-1 **6** 1/2 **All Talk N No Do (IRE)**[15] 2307 3-8-8 **77** TedDurcan 7 71
(Seamus Durack) *chsd ldrs: rdn ent fnl 2f: outpcd and btn over 1f out: wknd fnl f* **20/1**

140- **7** 1 1/2 **Remember**[210] 7695 3-9-7 **90** PatDobbs 9 81
(Richard Hannon) *t.k.h: in tch in midfield: rdn 2f out: sn struggling and btn over 1f out: wknd fnl f* **33/1**

2-51 **8** 3/4 **Ice Slice (IRE)**[21] 2163 3-8-12 **81** PaddyAspell 8 70
(James Eustace) *hld up in tch in last trio: rdn ent fnl 2f: sn outpcd and btn: no ch but plugged on fnl f* **20/1**

-513 **9** 3 1/4 **Munaaser**[9] 2496 3-8-13 **82** RyanMoore 2 64
(Sir Michael Stoute) *hld up in tch in last trio: effrt u.p jst over 2f out: drvn and btn over 1f out: wknd fnl f* **5/1**[2]

-211 **10** 19 **Zerfaal**[22] 2112 3-9-2 **85** PaulHanagan 12 23
(John Gosden) *hld up in towards rr: rdn 2f out: sn drvn and btn: bhd and eased wl ins fnl f* **7/2**[1]

10 **11** 42 **Equitable**[32] 1861 3-8-9 **78** ow1 (t) JamesDoyle 4
(Lady Cecil) *chsd ldrs tl lost pl qckly 3f out: t.o and eased fnl f* **20/1**

1m 39.24s (-0.76) **Going Correction** +0.175s/f (Good) **11 Ran SP% 105.3**
Speed ratings (Par 103): **110,109,105,105,102 101,100,99,96,77 35**
CSF £38.23 CT £284.45 TOTE £14.10: £4.30, £1.60, £2.80; EX 62.30 Trifecta £576.00.
**Owner** Hamdan Al Maktoum **Bred** Shadwell Estate Company Limited **Trained** Middleham Moor, N Yorks

■ Glorious Empire was withdrawn. Price at time of withdrawal 11-2. Rule 4 applies to all bets - deduction 15p in the pound.

**FOCUS**
A warm handicap, although it was weakened a little when Glorious Empire declined to enter the stalls. The first two filled the same positions throughout and the winner continues to progress.

## 2782 MARGARET GIFFEN MEMORIAL H'CAP 1m 6f 175y
**5:15** (5:17) (Class 4) (0-85,85) 4-Y-O+ **£7,762** (£2,310; £1,154; £577) **Stalls** Centre

Form RPR

100- **1** **Poyle Thomas**[231] 7193 5-9-8 **83** RichardKingscote 9 95+
(Ralph Beckett) *hld up in midfield: clsd on ldrs and swtchd rt over 2f out: rdn to ld jst over 1f out: styd on wl* **7/1**[3]

01-3 **2** 1 3/4 **Sohar**[22] 2108 6-9-10 **85** GeorgeBaker 1 94
(James Toller) *hld up in rr: clsd on ldrs and swtchd rt over 2f out: rdn and ev ch over 1f out: no ex and btn fnl 100yds* **9/2**[2]

0-02 **3** 5 **Eagle Rock (IRE)**[16] 2289 6-9-8 **83** (p) JamesSullivan 5 85
(Tom Tate) *chsd clr ldr: clsd and led over 3f out: drvn over 2f out: hdd jst over 1f out: wknd ins fnl f* **12/1**

0U-4 **4** nk **Tantalising (IRE)**[8] 2501 6-9-4 **79** PaulHanagan 6 81
(Martyn Meade) *chsd ldrs: clsd and ev ch over 3f out: rdn over 2f out: no ex ent fnl f: plugged on same pce after* **16/1**

0-14 **5** 6 **Red Runaway**[38] 1651 4-9-5 **81** DaneO'Neill 2 74
(Ed Dunlop) *hld up in midfield: clsd and wl in tch over 3f out: rdn over 2f out: wknd over 1f out* **14/1**

4-23 **6** 6 **Lion Beacon**[9] 2482 4-9-8 **84** PatDobbs 3 69
(Amanda Perrett) *chsd ldrs: clsd over 3f out: sn rdn: wknd wl over 1f out* **8/1**

010/ **7** 23 **Gifted Leader (USA)**[40] 6690 9-9-2 **82** (tp) GeorgeDowning(5) 7 35
(Ian Williams) *led and sn wl clr hdd over 3f out: sn dropped out: t.o fnl f* **20/1**

12-5 **8** 6 **Toptempo**[28] 1942 5-9-2 **77** TedDurcan 8 21
(Mark H Tompkins) *hld up in last trio: clsd and in tch 3f out: sn rdn and btn: t.o* **25/1**

2-21 **9** 20 **Perfect Summer (IRE)**[14] 2327 4-9-0 **76** RyanMoore 4
(Lady Cecil) *t.k.h: hld up in last trio: clsd and rdn over 3f out: sn btn: t.o over 1f out* **5/4**[1]

3m 11.36s (2.96) **Going Correction** +0.35s/f (Good)
**WFA** 4 from 5yo+ 1lb **9 Ran SP% 115.1**
Speed ratings (Par 105): **106,105,102,102,99 95,83,80,69**
CSF £38.37 CT £373.41 TOTE £7.90: £2.20, £2.00, £3.60; EX 45.80 Trifecta £463.50.
**Owner** Cecil And Miss Alison Wiggins **Bred** Miss Alison Wiggins **Trained** Kimpton, Hants

**FOCUS**
They went a decent pace in this fair handicap, as Gifted Leader, who ran too free according to George Downing, opened up a clear advantage. The runner-up is the best guide.

## 2783 OFQUEST OFFICE FURNITURE SUPPORTING AHT H'CAP 1m 2f
**5:45** (5:46) (Class 3) (0-95,92) 4-Y-O+ **£9,703** (£2,887; £1,443; £721) **Stalls** Centre

Form RPR

11-4 **1** **Stomachion (IRE)**[49] 1444 4-8-13 **84** RyanMoore 1 94
(Sir Michael Stoute) *stdd after s: hld up in midfield: switching lft and hdwy over 1f out: chalng and hanging lft ins fnl f: led fnl 75yds: styd on wl* **3/1**[1]

4-21 **2** 1 **Cosseted**[14] 2331 4-9-1 **86** DaneO'Neill 9 94
(James Fanshawe) *hld up in tch in rr: hdwy wl over 1f out: drvn and ev ch ins fnl f: styd on to snatch 2nd last stride* **7/2**[2]

10-3 **3** shd **Border Legend**[21] 2154 5-9-6 **91** GeorgeBaker 6 99
(Roger Charlton) *led tl 1/2-way: rdn and clsd on ldr over 1f out: drvn to ld 1f out: hdd fnl 75yds: kpt on same pce and lost 2nd last stride* **6/1**[3]

52-1 **4** 1/2 **Flow (USA)**[22] 2137 4-9-7 **92** (t) TedDurcan 3 99
(Lady Cecil) *chsd ldrs: rdn and effrt 2f out: chal u.p 1f out: styd on same pce fnl 100yds* **3/1**[1]

1111 **5** 5 **Top Diktat**[33] 1810 6-9-4 **89** PatDobbs 5 87
(Gary Moore) *hld up in tch in rr: rdn and effrt 2f out: no imp and btn 1f out: outpcd fnl f* **11/1**

550- **6** 1 1/2 **Art Scholar (IRE)**[301] 4979 7-8-11 **89** AlistairRawlinson(7) 4 84
(Michael Appleby) *stdd and dropped in after s: t.k.h: hld up in tch: effrt u.p 2f out: wknd 1f out* **14/1**

2-43 **7** 1/2 **Raskova (USA)**[21] 2162 4-8-1 **77** (b[1]) NoelGarbutt(5) 2 71
(William Jarvis) *stdd s and slowly away: t.k.h: hld up in rr: hdwy into midfield after 2f: led and stl nt settled over 3f out: sn clr tl rdn and hdd jst over 1f out: fdd ins fnl f* **14/1**

325- **8** 1 **Bantam (IRE)**[212] 7650 4-9-6 **91** PaddyAspell 8 83
(Ed Dunlop) *in tch in midfield: nt clr run: shuffled bk to rr and hmpd 2f out: no prog after* **33/1**

-562 **9** 44 **Yojojo (IRE)**[25] 2047 5-9-3 **88** PaulHanagan 7
(Gay Kelleway) *chsd ldr: c centre and racd alone 8f out: overall ldr 1/2-way tl over 3f out: hung rt and wknd 2f out: eased fr over 1f out: t.o* **16/1**

2m 10.52s (5.02) **Going Correction** +0.35s/f (Good) **9 Ran SP% 117.0**
Speed ratings (Par 107): **93,92,92,91,87 86,86,85,50**
CSF £13.82 CT £59.08 TOTE £4.60: £1.80, £1.60, £2.20; EX 15.70 Trifecta £104.90.
**Owner** Niarchos Family **Bred** Niarchos Family **Trained** Newmarket, Suffolk

**FOCUS**
A decent handicap, and form that should pay to follow. All except Yojojo raced on the stands' side in the straight, but the first four, who finished clear, ended up near the far rail.
T/Jkpt: Not won. T/Plt: £605.20 to a £1 stake. Pool: £112038.56 - 135.13 winning tickets T/Qpdt: £270.40 to a £1 stake. Pool: £7657.24 - 20.95 winning tickets SP

# 2313 YORK (L-H)
### Saturday, May 31

**OFFICIAL GOING: Good to soft (overall 6.1, home straight: far side 6.1, centre 5.8, stands' side 5.9)**
Wind: Moderate half against Weather: Cloudy Rails: Rail moved onto fresh ground from 9f to entrance to home straight and distances on Round course reduced by 24yds

## 2784 ONE MARKETING COMMUNICATIONS STKS (H'CAP) 7f
**1:50** (1:50) (Class 2) (0-112,105) 3-Y-O+ **£16,172** (£4,812; £2,405; £1,202) **Stalls** Low

Form RPR

26-0 **1** **Dutch Rose (IRE)**[21] 2144 5-9-2 **98** LukeMorris 1 105
(David O'Meara) *cl up on inner: led over 4f out: pushed clr wl over 2f out: rdn over 1f out: jnd and drvn ins fnl f: kpt on gamely towards fin* **9/1**

1-06 **2** 3/4 **Sirius Prospect (USA)**[31] 1870 6-9-9 **105** GrahamLee 4 110
(Dean Ivory) *trckd ldrs: hdwy wl over 2f out: rdn to chal over 1f out: ev ch ins fnl f: drvn and no ex nr fin* **3/1**[1]

0-10 **3** 1 1/2 **Brae Hill (IRE)**[35] 1721 8-9-2 **98** FrederikTylicki 5 99
(Richard Fahey) *cl up on outer: effrt over 2f out: rdn and ev ch over 1f out: drvn and kpt on same pce ins fnl f* **9/1**

/0-1 **4** 1/2 **Best Of Order (IRE)**[19] 2202 7-8-13 **98** RonanWhelan(3) 6 98
(David O'Meara) *chsd ldrs on inner: pushed along 3f out: rdn over 2f out: drvn and kpt on fnl f* **9/2**[3]

5535 **5** hd **Alfred Hutchinson**[16] 2286 6-8-13 **98** RobertTart(3) 8 97
(Geoffrey Oldroyd) *hld up in rr: hdwy over 2f out: effrt and n.m.r over 1f out: sn swtchd rt and rdn: kpt on fnl f: nrst fin* **4/1**[2]

3360 **6** 1 **Bertiewhittle**[21] 2145 6-9-6 **102** GrahamGibbons 7 103+
(David Barron) *dwlt: hld up in rr: hdwy over 2f out: effrt and n.m.r over 1f out: sn rdn and kpt on same pce* **5/1**

-050 **7** 3 3/4 **Balty Boys (IRE)**[22] 2113 5-9-2 **98** (b) BarryMcHugh 3 85
(Brian Ellison) *awkward s: sn pushed along to ld after 150yds: hdd over 4f out: cl up tl rdn wl over 1f out and grad wknd* **12/1**

0-50 **8** 6 **Pintura**[22] 2113 7-9-2 **98** TonyHamilton 2 69
(Kevin Ryan) *trckd ldrs: pushed along over 2f out: sn rdn and wknd* **16/1**

1m 26.44s (1.14) **Going Correction** +0.425s/f (Yiel) **8 Ran SP% 113.4**
Speed ratings (Par 109): **110,109,107,106,106 105,101,94**
CSF £35.63 CT £254.22 TOTE £8.10: £2.10, £1.70, £2.60; EX 22.30 Trifecta £268.50.
**Owner** Favourites Racing XXIV **Bred** Joseph Kennedy **Trained** Nawton, N Yorks

**FOCUS**
Rail moved onto fresh ground from 1m1f to entrance to home straight and distances on Round course reduced by 24yds. A good quality seven-race card got underway with a high-class limited handicap in which they went a proper gallop on good to soft ground. The pack come over to race towards the stands' side rail in the home straight. Fout of the field, including the winner, were out of the handicap.

## 2785 STOWE FAMILY LAW LLP GRAND CUP (LISTED RACE) 1m 6f
**2:20** (2:23) (Class 1) 4-Y-O+
**£15,642** (£15,642; £4,304; £2,144; £1,076; £540) **Stalls** Low

Form RPR

0405 **1** **Ralston Road (IRE)**[63] 1177 4-9-0 107 RonanWhelan 4 110
(John Patrick Shanahan, Ire) *t.k.h: hld up in midfield: smooth hdwy 4f out: led 2f out: sn rdn: drvn and hdd wl ins fnl f: rallied gamely nr line* **12/1**

11 **1** dht **Clever Cookie**[17] 2253 6-9-0 96 GrahamLee 7 110
(Peter Niven) *hld up in rr: smooth hdwy over 2f out: nt clr run over 1f out: swtchd rt and effrt ent fnl f: sn chal: rdn to take slt ld last 100yds: sn drvn: egded lft and jnd nr line* **3/1**[1]

5-36 **3** 1 3/4 **Shwaiman (IRE)**[24] 2073 4-9-0 97 TonyHamilton 10 108
(James Fanshawe) *trckd ldrs: hdwy 3f out: sn cl up: rdn and ev ch ent fnl f: drvn and hld whn n.m.r nr fin* **12/1**

-352 **4** 1 3/4 **Rawaki (IRE)**[15] 2294 6-9-0 108 HayleyTurner 3 105
(Andrew Balding) *prom: effrt 3f out: rdn wl over 1f out: kpt on fnl f* **11/2**[3]

1-00 **5** 2 1/4 **Statutory (IRE)**[91] 811 4-9-0 100 FrederikTylicki 9 102
(Saeed bin Suroor) *hld up: hdwy over 5f out: rdn along wl over 2f out: kpt on u.p fnl f: nrst fin* **8/1**

4-50 **6** hd **Repeater**[15] 2315 5-9-0 104 LukeMorris 8 102
(David O'Meara) *hld up in rr: hdwy over 3f out: rdn over 1f out: kpt on fnl f: nrst fin* **12/1**

1-04 **7** shd **Renew (IRE)**[28] 1950 4-9-3 105 AntonioFresu 12 105
(Marco Botti) *prom: trckd ldr after 4f: rdn along 3f out: drvn over 1f out: grad wknd* **16/1**

5-03 **8** 3 3/4 **First Mohican**[14] 2335 6-9-0 108 FergusSweeney 2 96
(Alan King) *in tch on inner: smooth hdwy 4f out: cl up over 2f out and sn ev ch: rdn over 1f out: wknd fnl f* **9/2**[2]

5213 **9** 9 **Sirvino**[15] 2294 9-9-0 96 GrahamGibbons 6 84
(David Barron) *hld up in rr: effrt and rdn wl over 2f out: n.d* **16/1**

03-0 **10** 3 **Alta Lilea (IRE)**[15] 2294 4-8-9 98 AdrianNicholls 13 74
(Mark Johnston) *set stdy pce: pushed along and qcknd 3f out: sn rdn and hdd 2f out: sn wknd* **33/1**

13-6 **11** 1 1/2 **Party Line**[15] 2294 5-8-9 89 (v) MichaelJMMurphy 1 72
(Mark Johnston) *prom on inner: effrt over 3f out: sn rdn along and wknd* **33/1**

60-5 **12** 36 **Cap O'Rushes**[21] 2143 4-9-0 108 MickaelBarzalona 11 27
(Charlie Appleby) *in tch on outer: rdn along wl over 3f out: sn wknd and bhd whn eased over 1f out* **11/1**

3m 3.14s (2.94) **Going Correction** +0.10s/f (Good) **12 Ran SP% 118.7**
Speed ratings (Par 111): **95,95,94,93,91 91,91,89,84,82 81,61**
WIN: 7.50 Ralston Road, 1.70 Clever Cookie; PL: 4.50 Ralston Road, 1.50 Clever Cookie, 3.60 Shwaiman; EX: 20.40, 32.20; CSF: 20.42, 23.97; TC: ; TF: 257.80, 505.60;.
**Owner** Francis Green Racing Ltd **Bred** Mrs J A Niven **Trained** Barton-le-Street, N Yorks
**Owner** Thistle Bloodstock Limited **Bred** Thistle Bloodstock Ltd **Trained** Kells, Co Kilkenny
■ Stewards' Enquiry : Antonio Fresu seven-day ban: used whip above permitted level without giving colt time to respond (Jun 14-20)

**FOCUS**
A quality Listed staying contest which was won in 2011 by Times Up, who went on to Lonsdale and Doncaster Cup success in Group 2 company the following year. Ralston Road is rated around his better 3yo form, with Clever Cookie improving again.

## 2786 BETBRIGHT TROPHY (H'CAP) 5f
2:50 (2:53) (Class 2) (0-105,105) 3-Y-O+
£31,125 (£9,320; £4,660; £2,330; £1,165; £585) Stalls High

Form | | | | RPR

3243 **1** **Top Boy**[16] 2283 4-7-13 **87**............(v) AdamMcLean(7) 8 96
(Derek Shaw) *towards rr: hdwy whn nt clr run and hmpd over 1f out: swtchd lft and rdn whn n.m.r ent fnl f: swtchd rt wl ins fnl f and fin strly to ld nr line* **12/1**

-030 **2** *nk* **Body And Soul (IRE)**[17] 2256 4-9-5 **100**............ DuranFentiman 1 108
(Tim Easterby) *chsd ldrs: hdwy 2f out: swtchd rt and rdn jst over 1f out: chsd ldr and styd on to ld last 100yds: hdd and no ex nr fin* **17/2**[2]

0505 **3** *nse* **Secret Witness**[16] 2283 8-8-11 **92**............(b) BenCurtis 7 100
(Ronald Harris) *towards rr: hdwy 2f out: chsd ldrs over 1f out: sn swtchd lft and rdn: ev ch ins fnl f: no ex towards fin* **14/1**

-010 **4** *½* **Normal Equilibrium**[16] 2283 4-8-6 **90**............(p) MichaelJMMurphy(3) 11 96
(Robert Cowell) *in tch: rdn along and hdwy wl over 1f out: sn swtchd lft: drvn and kpt on fnl f: nrst fin* **12/1**

0443 **5** *nk* **Singeur (IRE)**[12] 2390 7-8-5 **89**............ NeilFarley(3) 12 94
(Robin Bastiman) *chsd ldrs: hdwy wl over 1f out: sn rdn and kpt on fnl f* **20/1**

-400 **6** *½* **El Viento (FR)**[17] 2254 6-8-5 **91**............(b) SammyJoBell(5) 16 94
(Richard Fahey) *in rr: hdwy wl over 1f out: swtchd lft and rdn ent fnl f: kpt on: nrst fin* **28/1**

0601 **7** *1 ¼* **Monsieur Joe (IRE)**[16] 2283 7-9-10 **105**............ GrahamLee 13 104
(Paul Midgley) *towards rr: hdwy 2f out: swtchd lft and effrt whn n.m.r over 1f out: rdn and kpt on fnl f* **17/2**[2]

-000 **8** *1 ½* **Ancient Cross**[16] 2283 10-9-0 **95**............(t) BarryMcHugh 4 88
(Michael Easterby) *hmpd sn after s and towards rr: rdn and hdwy appr fnl f: kpt on: nrst fin* **25/1**

5020 **9** *½* **Racy**[44] 1531 7-9-5 **100**............(p) FrederikTylicki 17 91
(Brian Ellison) *hld up: hdwy on outer 2f out: rdn to chse ldrs over 1f out: sn drvn and no imp* **14/1**

1300 **10** *hd* **Even Stevens**[43] 1557 6-8-2 **90**............(v) MatthewHopkins(7) 10 81
(Scott Dixon) *sn led and clr at str pce: rdn and edgd lft over 1f out: hdd wl ins fnl f and wknd qckly* **25/1**

-051 **11** *nk* **Tumblewind**[14] 2350 4-8-6 **90**............ GeorgeChaloner(3) 14 80
(Richard Whitaker) *prom: chsd clr ldr over 2f out: rdn wl over 1f out: grad wknd fnl f* **16/1**

6-36 **12** *¾* **Jamaican Bolt (IRE)**[17] 2254 6-8-8 **92**............ RobertTart(3) 19 79
(Geoffrey Oldroyd) *towards rr: hdwy on outer 2f out: sn rdn and n.d* **9/1**[3]

2514 **13** *½* **Alben Star (IRE)**[27] 1975 6-9-9 **104**............ TonyHamilton 2 89
(Richard Fahey) *a towards rr* **6/1**[1]

05-0 **14** *1* **Magical Macey (USA)**[16] 2283 7-9-5 **100**............(b) GrahamGibbons 5 82
(David Barron) *prom: rdn wl over 1f out: wknd appr fnl f* **11/1**

0-40 **15** *2* **Long Awaited (IRE)**[16] 2283 6-8-8 **89**............(b) HayleyTurner 18 63
(David Barron) *a towards rr* **11/1**

0111 **16** *2* **Taurus Twins**[10] 2456 8-8-0 **81**............(b) RaulDaSilva 6 48
(Richard Price) *chsd clr ldr: rdn along 2f out: sn wknd* **16/1**

3602 **17** *¾* **Masamah (IRE)**[24] 2076 8-9-7 **102**............(p) LukeMorris 15 66
(Marco Botti) *midfield: rdn along 1/2-way: sn wknd* **14/1**

4300 **18** *5* **Inxile (IRE)**[16] 2283 9-8-12 **93**............(p) AdrianNicholls 9 39
(David Nicholls) *s.i.s: a bhd* **40/1**

1m 0.28s (0.98) **Going Correction** +0.45s/f (Yiel) **18 Ran SP% 127.5**
Speed ratings (Par 109): **110,109,109,108,108 107,105,102,102,101 101,100,99,97,94 91,90,82**
CSF £106.71 CT £1480.65 TOTE £13.50: £2.60, £3.00, £3.90, £4.50; EX 152.20 Trifecta £3343.40.
**Owner** Brian Johnson (Northamptonshire) **Bred** Mrs C R Philipson & Mrs H G Lascelles **Trained** Sproxton, Leics
■ Stewards' Enquiry : Ben Curtis two-day ban: used whip above permitted level (Jun 14-15)

**FOCUS**
A high-class sprint handicap in which Even Stevens set a blistering pace up the centre of the course before drifting towards the far rail where the serious action unfolded. The winner found a bit on his recent form.

## 2787 IRISH CHAMPIONS WEEKEND STKS (H'CAP) 1m 4f
3:25 (3:25) (Class 3) (0-90,90) 4-Y-O+ £9,703 (£2,887; £1,443; £721) Stalls Centre

Form | | | | RPR

300- **1** **Wadi Al Hattawi (IRE)**[266] 6186 4-9-5 **88**............(p) FrederikTylicki 17 101+
(Saeed bin Suroor) *in tch: smooth hdwy 4f out: led over 2f out: sn rdn clr: edgd lft and drvn out towards fin* **8/1**[3]

2433 **2** *1 ¼* **High Office**[16] 2272 8-8-2 **76** oh1............ SammyJoBell(5) 11 84
(Richard Fahey) *trckd ldrs: hdwy 3f out: rdn to chse wnr wl over 1f out: kpt on fnl f* **14/1**

0-52 **3** *1 ¾* **Allnecessaryforce (FR)**[2] 2700 4-8-7 **76** oh1............ TonyHamilton 6 81
(Richard Fahey) *hld up towards rr: hdwy over 3f out: chsd ldrs 2f out: sn rdn and kpt on same pce fnl f* **14/1**

02/3 **4** *1 ¼* **Local Hero (GER)**[21] 2160 7-8-13 **82**............(b) MickaelBarzalona 3 85
(Steve Gollings) *hld up in midfield: hdwy on inner over 3f out: rdn along 2f out: drvn and kpt on same pce appr fnl f* **9/1**

3344 **5** *1 ½* **Bute Hall**[15] 2314 5-9-0 **83**............ JimmyQuinn 2 84
(David Thompson) *led 3f: prom: rdn along wl over 2f out: drvn and one pce fr over 1f out* **16/1**

33-0 **6** *nse* **Grandorio (IRE)**[17] 2253 4-9-3 **89**............[1] RonanWhelan(3) 12 90
(David O'Meara) *hld up towards rr: hdwy 3f out: rdn along 2f out: kpt on same pce* **14/1**

3051 **7** *1* **Streets Of Newyork**[17] 2259 7-8-8 **80**............ RobertTart(3) 10 79
(Brian Ellison) *hld up towards rr: hdwy 3f out: rdn along 2f out: sn no imp* **6/1**[1]

-613 **8** *hd* **Itlaaq**[15] 2314 8-9-2 **85**............(t) GrahamGibbons 5 84
(Michael Easterby) *hld up towards rr: sme hdwy over 2f out: sn rdn and no imp fnl f* **10/1**

60-0 **9** *½* **Nicholascopernicus (IRE)**[27] 1981 5-9-7 **90**............ GrahamLee 8 88
(Ed Walker) *hld up: hdwy 3f out: sn rdn along and no imp fr wl over 1f out* **10/1**

026- **10** *½* **Rio's Rosanna (IRE)**[191] 7990 7-9-1 **87**............ GeorgeChaloner(3) 16 84
(Richard Whitaker) *hld up towards rr: effrt and sme hdwy 3f out: rdn along 2f out: n.d* **16/1**

0-60 **11** *6* **Warlu Way**[17] 2259 7-8-12 **81**............ BarryMcHugh 14 68
(Michael Easterby) *s.i.s: a in rr* **40/1**

61- **12** *2* **Great Fighter**[219] 7488 4-9-2 **85**............ HayleyTurner 4 69
(Saeed bin Suroor) *chsd ldrs: rdn along over 3f out: wknd over 2f out* **8/1**[3]

213- **13** *5* **Endless Credit (IRE)**[315] 4537 4-9-3 **86**............ LukeMorris 15 62
(Luca Cumani) *prom: led after 3f: rdn along 3f out: hdd over 2f out and sn wknd* **7/1**[2]

00-0 **14** *7* **Crackentorp**[17] 2259 9-8-10 **79**............ DavidAllan 13 44
(Tim Easterby) *chsd ldrs: rdn along over 3f out: sn wknd* **16/1**

-206 **15** *23* **Ebony Express**[17] 2259 5-8-13 **82**............ BenCurtis 9 10
(Alan Swinbank) *chsd ldrs: rdn along over 3f out: sn wknd* **14/1**

2m 32.17s (-1.03) **Going Correction** +0.10s/f (Good) **15 Ran SP% 123.9**
Speed ratings (Par 107): **107,106,105,104,103 103,102,102,102,101 97,96,93,88,73**
CSF £118.04 CT £1566.74 TOTE £9.40: £3.50, £4.60, £4.90; EX 152.70 Trifecta £1506.00 Part won. Pool: £2,008.12 - 0.40 winning tickets..
**Owner** Godolphin **Bred** Darley **Trained** Newmarket, Suffolk

**FOCUS**
A decent middle-distance handicap in which there was a contested gallop. The winner rates a bit better than the bare form.

## 2788 YORKSHIRE REGIMENT EBF STALLIONS MEDIAN AUCTION MAIDEN STKS (BOBIS RACE) 6f
4:00 (4:02) (Class 3) 2-Y-O £7,439 (£2,213; £1,106; £553) Stalls High

Form | | | | RPR

2 **1** **Mister Universe**[16] 2288 2-9-5 0............ GrahamLee 1 89+
(Mark Johnston) *mde all: pushed clr wl over 1f out: shkn up ins fnl f: edgd lft and kpt on* **11/10**[1]

**2** *¾* **Home Cummins (IRE)** 2-9-0 0............ TonyHamilton 5 82+
(Richard Fahey) *in tch on outer: hdwy over 2f out: chsd wnr whn green and edgd lft over 1f out: styd on wl fnl f* **4/1**[2]

4 **3** *8* **Arch Enemy**[19] 2200 2-9-5 0............ GrahamGibbons 2 63
(Michael Easterby) *in rr: hdwy 2f out: sn rdn and kpt on fnl f* **9/1**

6 **4** *1 ½* **Upward Trend (IRE)**[45] 1504 2-9-5 0............ DavidAllan 4 59
(Tim Easterby) *in rr: pushed along over 2f out: sn rdn and kpt on fnl f* **11/1**

**5** *½* **Muradif (IRE)** 2-9-5 0............ MickaelBarzalona 8 57
(William Haggas) *trckd ldrs: effrt on outer 2f out: sn rdn: green and edgd lft: wknd ent fnl f* **6/1**[3]

5 **6** *1 ½* **Bonds Choice**[16] 2288 2-8-11 0............ GeorgeChaloner(3) 7 48
(Richard Fahey) *cl up: rdn along over 2f out: grad wknd* **8/1**

0 **7** *1* **Penny Royale**[26] 2014 2-9-0 0............ DuranFentiman 6 45
(Tim Easterby) *chsd ldng pair: rdn along wl over 2f out: sn wknd* **33/1**

1m 15.27s (3.37) **Going Correction** +0.45s/f (Yiel) **7 Ran SP% 114.3**
Speed ratings (Par 97): **95,94,83,81,80 78,77**
CSF £5.69 TOTE £2.00: £1.30, £2.30; EX 5.70 Trifecta £36.80.
**Owner** Abdulla Al Mansoori **Bred** Car Colston Hall Stud **Trained** Middleham Moor, N Yorks

**FOCUS**
A good juvenile maiden in which the first two pulled clear to show very useful form.

## 2789 INFINITY TYRES EBF STALLIONS MAIDEN STKS (BOBIS RACE) 6f
4:35 (4:35) (Class 4) 3-Y-O £8,086 (£2,406; £1,202; £601) Stalls High

Form | | | | RPR

234- **1** **Blurred Vision**[231] 7207 3-9-5 84............ GrahamGibbons 2 85
(William Jarvis) *trckd ldr: hdwy to chal over 1f out: sn rdn: led and edgd lft ins fnl f: kpt on* **4/5**[1]

0-26 **2** *2* **Dutch Breeze**[15] 2317 3-9-5 78............ DavidAllan 4 79
(Tim Easterby) *led: rdn along 2f out: drvn and hdd ins fnl f: kpt on same pce towards fin* **2/1**[2]

4 **3** *6* **Piccadilly Jim (IRE)**[19] 2217 3-9-5 0............ TonyHamilton 1 60
(Richard Fahey) *chsd ldng pair: rdn along 2f out: sn outpcd* **12/1**

0 **4** *9* **Quasqazah**[11] 2442 3-9-5 0............ GrahamLee 3 31
(Roger Varian) *s.i.s and green: a outpcd and bhd* **10/1**[3]

1m 13.25s (1.35) **Going Correction** +0.45s/f (Yiel) **4 Ran SP% 105.7**
Speed ratings (Par 101): **109,106,98,86**
CSF £2.48 TOTE £1.60; EX 2.30 Trifecta £3.40.
**Owner** Clive Washbourn & Nigel T Gadsby **Bred** R F And S D Knipe **Trained** Newmarket, Suffolk

**FOCUS**
A good small-field 3yo sprint maiden in which they went a proper gallop. The first two were close to their marks.

## 2790 JOHN WRIGHT ELECTRICAL GENTLEMAN AMATEUR RIDERS' STKS (H'CAP) 1m 2f 88y
5:10 (5:10) (Class 4) (0-80,79) 4-Y-O+ £6,239 (£1,935; £967; £484) Stalls Low

Form | | | | RPR

0226 **1** **San Cassiano (IRE)**[11] 2423 7-10-13 **76**............ MrRColley(5) 11 84
(Ruth Carr) *set stdy pce: pushed along wl over 2f out: rdn wl over 1f out: drvn ins fnl f: kpt on wl towards fin* **11/1**

0314 **2** *½* **I'm Super Too (IRE)**[8] 2519 7-10-9 **72**............ MrORJSangster(5) 1 79
(Alan Swinbank) *hld up in rr: hdwy wl over 2f out: rdn to chse ldrs over 1f out: kpt on fnl f* **8/1**

-021 **3** *¾* **War Poet**[25] 2052 7-11-7 **79**............ MrSWalker 10 85
(Brian Ellison) *hld up: stdy hdwy 3f out: trckd ldrs 2f out: effrt to chal over 1f out: sn rdn and ev ch whn edgd repeatedly lft ins fnl f: no imp towards fin* **11/4**[1]

-046 **4** *1 ½* **Amaze**[22] 2137 6-10-13 **76**............(p) MrAlexFerguson(5) 3 79
(Brian Ellison) *trckd ldrs: hdwy over 2f out: rdn wl over 1f out: kpt on same pce fnl f* **13/2**

2434 **5** *shd* **Mica Mika (IRE)**[17] 2259 6-11-5 **77**............(v) MrJHamilton 7 80
(Richard Fahey) *trckd wnr: hdwy 3f out: chal 2f out: sn rdn and ev ch tl drvn and wknd ins fnl f* **11/2**[3]

6033 **6** *3 ½* **Karaka Jack**[35] 1724 7-11-5 **77**............ MrHAABannister 2 73
(David Nicholls) *trckd ldrs: hdwy 3f out: rdn along 2f out: n.m.r over 1f out and sn one pce* **5/1**[2]

065- **7** *1 ¼* **Christmas Light**[231] 7211 7-11-0 **77**............ MrDCottle(5) 5 71
(Brian Ellison) *hld up in rr: sme hdwy over 2f out: sn rdn and no imp fnl f* **12/1**

4/6- **8** *hd* **Only Orsenfoolsies**[420] 1391 5-10-13 **71**............ MrWHogg 4 64
(Micky Hammond) *trckd ldng pair: rdn along 3f out: wknd 2f out* **20/1**

060- **9** *2 ¾* **Next Edition (IRE)**[155] 8416 6-11-2 **79**............ PhillipDennis(5) 9 67
(Philip Kirby) *in tch on wd outside: rdn along 3f out: sn wknd* **14/1**

33-4 **10** *hd* **Mu'Ajiza**[25] 2047 4-10-8 **73**............ MrAFrench(7) 6 61
(Paul Midgley) *in tch: hdwy on outer over 3f out: rdn to chse ldrs over 2f out: edgd rt and wknd over 1f out* **25/1**

/0-0 **11** *2 ½* **Travis County (IRE)**[14] 2327 5-10-2 **65** oh7............ MrJohnWilley(5) 8 48
(Brian Ellison) *a in rr* **33/1**

2m 12.42s (-0.08) **Going Correction** +0.10s/f (Good) **11 Ran SP% 117.4**
Speed ratings (Par 105): **104,103,103,101,101 98,97,97,95,95 93**
CSF £93.56 CT £313.59 TOTE £13.80: £3.30, £2.30, £1.50; EX 146.30 Trifecta £745.40.
**Owner** S Jackson, L Shaw, Mrs R Carr **Bred** Peter Savill **Trained** Huby, N Yorks
■ Stewards' Enquiry : Mr R Colley four-day ban: used whip above permitted level (tbn)

**FOCUS**
A fair handicap restricted to gentlemen amateur riders in which they went an even gallop. The winner is rated to form.
T/Plt: £208.40 to a £1 stake. Pool: £181,564.51 - 635.82 winning tickets. T/Qpdt: £40.10 to a £1 stake. Pool: £8,113.98 - 149.38 winning tickets. JR

2791 - 2798a (Foreign Racing) - See Raceform Interactive

## 2585 LONGCHAMP (R-H)
Saturday, May 31

**OFFICIAL GOING: Turf: soft**

### 2799a PRIX DU PALAIS-ROYAL (GROUP 3) (3YO+) (TURF) 7f
1:30 (12:00) 3-Y-O+ £33,333 (£13,333; £10,000; £6,666; £3,333)

RPR

1 **American Devil (FR)**55 5-9-4 0 Pierre-CharlesBoudot 4 111
(E Libaud, France) *a.p: pushed along to qckn and clsd on ldr ent fnl f: sn led: r.o strly and asserted: comf* 13/5[1]

2 1 ½ **Sommerabend**30 [1908] 7-9-8 0 GeraldMosse 7 111
(M Rulec, Germany) *sn trcking ldr on outer: pushed along to chal over 1f out and led ent fnl f: r.o but sn hdd: no ex and hld* 16/5[2]

3 nk **Bamiyan (FR)**39 [1641] 4-9-4 0 ThierryJarnet 2 106
(T Lemer, France) *midfield in tch on inner: pushed along over 1f out: rdn and swtchd lft ins fnl f: r.o and wnt 3rd cl home: fin strly but nvr able to chal* 188/10

4 ¾ **Complimentor (IRE)**18 4-9-4 0 MaximeGuyon 6 104
(X Thomas-Demeaulte, France) *plld hrd: midfield in tch on outer: pushed along over 1f out: rdn ins fnl f: r.o and wnt 4th cl home: nt pce to chal* 134/10

5 nk **Thawaany (IRE)**246 [6819] 4-9-1 0 OlivierPeslier 3 100
(F Head, France) *sn led: pushed along 2f out: strly pressed over 1f out and hdd ent fnl f: kpt on tl no ex fnl 100yds: fdd and lost 2 pls cl home* 18/5[3]

6 nk **High Duty**30 [2006] 3-8-7 0 UmbertoRispoli 1 98
(P Schiergen, Germany) *led early: prom on inner once hdd: pushed along 2f out: rdn in 4th ent fnl f: kpt on same pce and sn dropped to 6th and hld* 26/1

7 2 **Aksil (FR)**18 4-9-1 0 ValentinGambart 5 94
(M Boutin, France) *hld up in last trio: pushed along and hdwy fr 2f out: rdn over 1f out: kpt on same pce ins fnl f and nvr threatened* 26/1

8 ¾ **Sunny (FR)**39 [1641] 5-9-4 0 ChristopheSoumillon 8 95
(J-C Rouget, France) *hld up in midfield: pushed along 2f out: sn outpcd: kpt on under hand ride fnl f but nvr threatened* 77/10

9 ¾ **Desert Blanc**211 [7685] 6-9-6 0 GregoryBenoist 9 95
(C Baillet, France) *t.k.h: restrained fr wd draw and hld up in last pair: pushed along in last 2f out: rdn and outpcd ent fnl f: kpt on but nvr a factor* 37/1

10 1 ½ **Imperiator**58 [1272] 3-8-7 0 FranckBlondel 10 85
(P Decouz, France) *stdd fr wdst draw and hld up in last: pushed along 2f out: rdn and outpcd ent fnl f: sn dropped to last again and btn: nvr a factor* 66/10

1m 22.53s (1.83)
**WFA** 3 from 4yo+ 11lb 10 Ran SP% 120.0
WIN (incl. 1 euro stake): 3.60. PLACES: 1.60, 1.50, 3.10. DF: 7.40. SF: 15.00.
**Owner** Ecurie Haras de Quetieville **Bred** Ecurie Haras De Quetieville **Trained** France

## 2428 NOTTINGHAM (L-H)
Sunday, June 1

**OFFICIAL GOING: Soft (good to soft in places) changing to good to soft (soft in places) after race 2 (2.45)**
Wind: Light across Weather: Cloudy with sunny spells

### 2800 BRITISH STALLION STUDS EBF MAIDEN STKS 5f 13y
2:15 (2:15) (Class 5) 2-Y-O £3,881 (£1,155; £577; £288) Stalls High

Form RPR

2 1 **Mubtaghaa (IRE)**22 [2146] 2-9-5 0 DaneO'Neill 4 77+
(William Haggas) *s.i.s and hmpd s: hld up: hdwy 1/2-way: rdn to chse ldr over 1f out: r.o to ld wl ins fnl f* 4/11[1]

3 2 ¾ **One Moment**11 [2460] 2-8-11 0 OisinMurphy(3) 6 69
(Robert Cowell) *led 4f out: rdn and hdd wl ins fnl f: styd on same pce* 10/1[3]

0 3 ¾ **Grazed Knees (IRE)**36 [1726] 2-9-5 0 SeanLevey 2 72
(David Brown) *prom: nt clr run over 1f out: styd on same pce ins fnl f* 25/1

4 3 **Little Belter (IRE)** 2-9-5 0 RichardKingscote 3 61
(Tom Dascombe) *edgd rt s: chsd ldr pushed along 1/2-way: lost 2nd over 1f out: no ex fnl f* 25/1

5 2 ¾ **Speed Machine (IRE)** 2-9-5 0 LukeMorris 1 51
(Paul Cole) *led 1f: chsd ldrs: rdn 1/2-way: wknd over 1f out* 50/1

6 3 ½ **Emirates Challenge (IRE)** 2-9-0 0 KierenFallon 5 33
(Saeed bin Suroor) *s.i.s: hld up: shkn and wknd over 1f out* 5/1[2]

1m 1.94s (0.44) **Going Correction** +0.05s/f (Good) 6 Ran SP% 108.7
Speed ratings (Par 93): **98,96,95,90,86 80**
CSF £4.28 TOTE £1.40: £1.10, £2.90; EX 3.80 Trifecta £12.00.
**Owner** Hamdan Al Maktoum **Bred** Minch & Fullbury Bloodstock **Trained** Newmarket, Suffolk

**FOCUS**
Outer course used and distances as advertised. Potentially a reasonable maiden in which the pace was decent, enhancing the performance of the winner. He probably only had to match his debut form.

### 2801 DOWNLOAD NEW RACING UK IPAD APP H'CAP 1m 6f 15y
2:45 (2:46) (Class 5) (0-70,70) 4-Y-O+ £3,234 (£962; £481; £240) Stalls Low

Form RPR

5236 1 **Magicalmysterytour (IRE)**6 [2614] 11-8-3 52 LukeMorris 2 61
(Willie Musson) *hld up: hdwy over 3f out: rdn to chse ldr over 1f out: edgd lft and styd on to ld wl ins fnl f* 8/1[3]

5-43 2 1 ¾ **Nolecce**22 [2175] 7-7-11 53 JackGarritty(7) 5 60+
(Tony Forbes) *chsd ldrs: led over 4f out: rdn over 1f out: hdd wl ins fnl f* 8/1[3]

50-5 3 nk **Petaluma**27 [2011] 5-8-13 65 WilliamTwiston-Davies(3) 10 71
(Mick Channon) *hld up: hdwy u.p over 2f out: edgd lft and styd on ins fnl f: nt rch ldrs* 10/1

-300 4 5 **Keep Calm**15 [2327] 4-9-0 63 KierenFallon 6 62
(John Mackie) *hld up in tch: rdn over 2f out: styd on same pce fnl f* 6/1[1]

65/4 5 1 **Soundbyte**25 [2067] 9-8-2 51 AndrewMullen 9 49
(John Gallagher) *s.i.s: sn pushed along in rr: styd on appr fnl f: nvr nrr* 16/1

20-0 6 nk **Duke Of Yorkshire**29 [1935] 4-9-7 70 DavidAllan 4 67
(Tim Easterby) *prom: rdn over 3f out: wknd fnl f* 15/2[2]

0-00 7 ½ **Shades Of Silver**30 [1909] 4-8-12 61 PaulMulrennan 12 58
(Michael Scudamore) *sn chsng ldr: rdn and ev ch over 3f out: hung lft over 2f out: wknd over 1f out* 16/1

6315 8 2 ¼ **Royal Marskell**11 [2468] 5-9-3 66 TomEaves 1 59
(Alison Hutchinson) *hld up: hdwy over 4f out: rdn and wknd over 2f out* 8/1[3]

222- 9 6 **Mr Plod**345 [1794] 9-8-4 53 HayleyTurner 7 38
(Andrew Reid) *hld up: nt clr run over 4f out: nvr on terms* 16/1

2-00 10 17 **Musikhani**20 [2216] 4-9-0 66 OisinMurphy(3) 11 27
(Philip Kirby) *hld up: rdn over 5f out: wknd over 3f out: eased fnl f* 8/1[3]

-014 11 6 **Dubara Reef (IRE)**26 [2055] 7-8-2 51 oh2 RaulDaSilva 3 4
(Paul Green) *led: hung rt over 5f out: hdd over 4f out: rdn and wknd over 2f out* 6/1[1]

4501 12 14 **Kingaroo (IRE)**13 [2396] 8-8-0 52 oh1 ow1 ConnorBeasley(3) 8
(Garry Woodward) *prom: rdn over 6f out: wknd over 3f out: eased* 25/1

3m 6.55s (-0.45) **Going Correction** -0.175s/f (Firm) 12 Ran SP% 115.4
Speed ratings (Par 103): **94,93,92,89,89 89,88,87,84,74 71,63**
CSF £68.66 CT £648.31 TOTE £7.80: £3.10, £3.40, £2.70; EX 53.40 Trifecta £2068.90 Part won..
**Owner** Broughton Thermal Insulation **Bred** Premier Bloodstock **Trained** Newmarket, Suffolk

**FOCUS**
The pace was good, making this a solid test of stamina. The winner is rated in line with his recent AW form.

### 2802 SPORTS NIGHT ON TUESDAY 17TH JUNE H'CAP 5f 13y
3:15 (3:17) (Class 6) (0-65,65) 3-Y-O £2,587 (£770; £384; £192) Stalls High

Form RPR

2-66 1 **By Rights**13 [2397] 3-8-8 57 JoeyHaynes(5) 8 63
(Tony Carroll) *chsd ldrs: led over 3f out: rdn and hung lft fr over 1f out: styd on* 14/1

0335 2 ½ **Narborough**9 [2505] 3-8-10 57 WilliamTwiston-Davies(3) 12 61
(Mick Channon) *hld up: hdwy over 1f out: rdn ins fnl f: kpt on* 7/1[3]

532 3 ¾ **Lucky Times**8 [2551] 3-9-0 58 PJMcDonald 1 60+
(Mel Brittain) *chsd ldrs: rdn and ev ch fr over 1f out: unable qck towards fin* 10/1

0401 4 1 ¾ **Tinsill**13 [2388] 3-9-6 64 PaulMulrennan 10 59
(Nigel Tinkler) *prom: rdn over 1f out: styd on* 8/1

0-45 5 nse **Traditionelle**13 [2397] 3-8-12 56 TomEaves 11 51
(Tim Easterby) *prom: nt clr run and lost pl 2f out: edgd lft and r.o ins fnl f* 7/1[3]

-442 6 2 ¼ **Fredricka**39 [1642] 3-9-5 63 AndrewMullen 3 50
(Garry Moss) *s.i.s: hdwy 1/2-way: rdn over 1f out: wknd ins fnl f* 12/1

-304 7 3 ½ **Lady Mai (IRE)**13 [2388] 3-8-11 55 TonyHamilton 14 29
(Richard Fahey) *chsd ldrs: rdn 1/2-way: wknd over 1f out* 5/1[2]

224 8 2 ¼ **Argent Touch**75 [1005] 3-9-6 64 DaleSwift 6 30
(Derek Shaw) *s.i.s: hld up: rdn 1/2-way: wknd over 1f out* 16/1

53-0 9 2 **Little Briar Rose**33 [1851] 3-8-10 57 [1] RobertTart(3) 5 16
(John Spearing) *hood removed late and s.i.s: hld up: rdn 1/2-way: wknd over 1f out* 33/1

2-23 10 6 **Misstemper (IRE)**23 [2125] 3-9-3 64 OisinMurphy(3) 2
(Sean Curran) *sn prom: rdn 1/2-way: wknd over 1f out* 7/2[1]

043 11 shd **Fujin**20 [2217] 3-9-7 65 DuranFentiman 4 2
(Noel Wilson) *chsd ldrs: rdn over 1f out: sn wknd* 14/1

00-5 12 1 ½ **Paradise Child**26 [2045] 3-8-2 46 oh1 LukeMorris 7
(Bill Turner) *led: hdd over 3f out: rdn and wknd wl over 1f out* 50/1

006- 13 5 **Paparima (IRE)**296 [5225] 3-8-2 46 oh1 (v[1]) RaulDaSilva 9
(Paul Green) *s.i.s: hdwy 1/2-way: rdn and wknd wl over 1f out* 66/1

1m 1.79s (0.29) **Going Correction** +0.05s/f (Good) 13 Ran SP% 117.4
Speed ratings (Par 97): **99,98,97,94,94 90,84,81,78,68 68,65,57**
CSF £106.14 CT £1066.54 TOTE £18.30: £6.10, £2.30, £2.30; EX 130.40 Trifecta £1682.80 Part won..
**Owner** Last Day Racing Partnership **Bred** Grove Farm Stud **Trained** Cropthorne, Worcs

**FOCUS**
A modest sprint handicap in which a number were lightly raced and can improve a bit. The field initially split into two groups, one in the middle and one on the stands' side, but the result suggests there was no advantage to either bunch. The winner was back towards the best of his 2yo form.

### 2803 RACING UK ANYWHERE H'CAP 5f 13y
3:45 (3:46) (Class 3) (0-95,91) 4-Y-O+ £9,703 (£2,887; £1,443; £721) Stalls High

Form RPR

23-0 1 **Asian Trader**17 [2275] 5-8-5 82 StephanieJoannides(7) 9 95+
(William Haggas) *hld up: nt clr run over 1f out: swtchd lft and hdwy sn after: r.o to ld wl ins fnl f* 8/1[3]

0-00 2 ¾ **Judge 'n Jury**17 [2283] 10-9-4 91 (t) OisinMurphy(3) 5 98
(Ronald Harris) *led: rdn over 1f out: hdd and unable qck wl ins fnl f* 8/1[3]

/1-0 3 1 **Ziggy Lee**15 [2353] 8-9-1 85 PJMcDonald 1 89
(Geoffrey Harker) *w ldr: rdn over 1f out: no ex towards fin* 33/1

3201 4 ¾ **Peace Seeker**12 [2446] 6-9-6 90 (t) WilliamCarson 7 91
(Anthony Carson) *chsd ldrs: rdn over 1f out: styd on same pce ins fnl f* 8/1[3]

4-46 5 nk **Pearl Blue (IRE)**23 [2123] 6-9-6 90 GeorgeBaker 11 90
(Chris Wall) *hld up and bhd: swtchd lft 1/2-way: shkn up over 1f out: rdn and styd on ins fnl f: nt trble ldrs* 11/4[1]

-630 6 ½ **Kyleakin Lass**17 [2283] 5-9-6 90 (b[1]) RichardHughes 8 88
(Jonathan Portman) *hld up: nt clr run over 1f out: r.o towards fin: nvr nrr* 6/1[2]

1146 7 1 **Megaleka**11 [2456] 4-8-9 84 TimClark(5) 6 79
(Alan Bailey) *s.i.s: sn mid-div: rdn over 1f out: no ex fnl f* 12/1

-003 8 shd **Ambitious Icarus**2 [2727] 5-8-4 77 (e) ConnorBeasley(3) 2 71
(Richard Guest) *s.i.s: sn chsng ldrs: rdn over 1f out: styd on same pce* 11/4[1]

0-00 9 1 ¾ **Steel Rain**34 [1789] 6-8-5 75 LukeMorris 3 63
(Nikki Evans) *chsd ldrs: rdn 1/2-way: wknd fnl f* 25/1

1m 0.83s (-0.67) **Going Correction** +0.05s/f (Good) 9 Ran SP% 115.4
Speed ratings (Par 107): **107,105,104,103,102 101,100,99,97**
CSF £69.96 CT £2000.99 TOTE £9.60: £3.00, £3.70, £4.20; EX 124.50 Trifecta £954.80.
**Owner** Somerville Lodge Limited **Bred** Mike Smith **Trained** Newmarket, Suffolk

**FOCUS**
There were some useful sprinters in this handicap, and the winner is progressive. The pace held up well.

## 2804 CARIBBEAN PARTY NIGHT SATURDAY 5TH JULY MAIDEN FILLIES' STKS (BOBIS RACE) 1m 75y
4:15 (4:18) (Class 5) 3-Y-O £3,881 (£1,155; £577; £288) Stalls Centre

Form RPR
2-54 1 **Manderley (IRE)**[28] 1976 3-9-0 109 RichardHughes 1 82+
(Richard Hannon) *mde all: shkn up over 1f out: comf* 1/3[1]
3 2 ½ **Maid Of The Glens (IRE)**[42] 1597 3-9-0 0 TedDurcan 5 79
(John Patrick Shanahan, Ire) *a.p: chsd wnr 1/2-way: rdn over 2f out: styd on same pce fnl f* 10/1[3]
0- 3 2¾ **Spirit Of Winning**[155] 8425 3-9-0 0 RobertHavlin 3 76+
(John Gosden) *s.i.s: hld up: nt clr run over 2f out: swtchd rt and hdwy over 1f out: wnt 3rd ins fnl f: nt trble ldrs* 10/1[3]
-40 4 1¾ **Ski Lift**[36] 1722 3-9-0 0 JamesDoyle 4 69
(John Gosden) *chsd wnr to 1/2-way: remained handy: rdn over 2f out: styd on same pce fnl f* 5/1[2]
00 5 ¾ **Adaptability**[17] 2279 3-9-0 0 SeanLevey 10 67
(Brian Meehan) *prom: rdn over 3f out: no ex fnl f* 33/1
0 6 6 **Mystic Angel (IRE)**[23] 2129 3-9-0 0 StevieDonohoe 8 53
(William Muir) *hld up: hdwy over 3f out: wknd over 1f out* 50/1
7 1 **Queen's Dream (IRE)** 3-9-0 0 JackMitchell 2 51
(Roger Varian) *s.i.s: hdwy 7f out: rdn and wknd 2f out* 12/1
8 1½ **Eloquence** 3-9-0 0 RichardKingscote 7 47
(Tom Dascombe) *hld up: wknd 2f out* 20/1
9 5 **Wilful Minx (FR)** 3-9-0 0 JamesSullivan 6 36
(James Given) *plld hrd and prom: stdd and lost pl after 1f: wknd 3f out* 33/1

1m 48.42s (-0.58) **Going Correction** -0.175s/f (Firm) 9 Ran SP% **130.2**
Speed ratings (Par 96): **95,94,91,90,89 83,82,80,75**
CSF £6.29 TOTE £1.30: £1.02, £2.20, £2.80; EX 6.20 Trifecta £28.90.
**Owner** Mrs J Wood **Bred** Rathasker Stud **Trained** East Everleigh, Wilts

**FOCUS**
In an above-average maiden, the classy winner made all at a medium early gallop, with Hughes gradually turning the screw on his rivals in the home straight. The winner did not need to match her Guineas form.

## 2805 WATCH RACING UK ON SKY CHANNEL 432 H'CAP 1m 75y
4:45 (4:49) (Class 5) (0-70,70) 3-Y-O £3,234 (£962; £481; £240) Stalls Centre

Form RPR
5-04 1 **Craftsmanship (FR)**[27] 2027 3-9-5 68 (p) FrederikTylicki 12 78
(Robert Eddery) *hld up: hdwy over 2f out: rdn to chse ldr over 1f out: hung lft and led ins fnl f: r.o* 8/1
-420 2 2¼ **Suni Dancer**[43] 1588 3-8-2 51 oh2 RaulDaSilva 4 56
(Paul Green) *chsd ldrs: led over 3f out: rdn over 1f out: hdd and unable qck ins fnl f* 20/1
-014 3 ½ **Sakhalin Star (IRE)**[13] 2391 3-9-4 70 BillyCray(3) 14 74
(Richard Guest) *hld up: hdwy u.p over 1f out: hung lft ins fnl f: styd on* 20/1
530- 4 1 **Go Sakhee**[204] 7818 3-9-7 70 DaneO'Neill 2 72
(Roger Varian) *trckd ldrs: rdn over 2f out: no ex ins fnl f* 13/2[3]
-630 5 2¾ **Rocksee (IRE)**[17] 2274 3-9-5 68 RichardKingscote 5 63
(Tom Dascombe) *prom: hmpd and lost pl after 1f: hdwy over 5f out: rdn over 2f out: styng on same pce whn nt clr run ins fnl f* 14/1
0-04 6 ¾ **Windy Citi**[27] 2026 3-8-13 62 TedDurcan 13 56
(Chris Wall) *hld up: hdwy over 2f out: rdn over 1f out: wknd ins fnl f* 6/1[2]
-032 7 nk **Aran Sky (IRE)**[22] 2163 3-9-2 70 JoeyHaynes(5) 8 63
(K R Burke) *trckd ldrs: plld hrd: rdn over 2f out: wknd over 1f out* 3/1[1]
-405 8 ½ **Kisanji**[10] 2492 3-9-1 67 CharlesBishop(3) 11 59
(Mick Channon) *led after 1f: hdd over 3f out: sn rdn: wknd fnl f* 12/1
5004 9 1¼ **Eddiemaurice (IRE)**[19] 2235 3-8-11 63 ConnorBeasley(3) 10 52
(Richard Guest) *hld up in tch: plld hrd: rdn to chse ldr over 2f out tl wknd over 1f out* 6/1[2]
2312 10 1½ **Cascadia (IRE)**[81] 931 3-8-7 56 JamesSullivan 7 41
(Alison Hutchinson) *led 1f: chsd ldr to 1/2-way: rdn and wknd wl over 1f out* 14/1
406 11 hd **Musical Theme**[27] 2025 3-8-10 59 StevieDonohoe 9 44
(Willie Musson) *hld up: rdn over 2f out: a in rr* 25/1
3-40 12 34 **Magnus Romeo**[29] 1940 3-9-7 70 (t) LukeMorris 3
(Marco Botti) *hld up: rdn 1/2-way: wknd 3f out: eased* 20/1

1m 47.61s (-1.39) **Going Correction** -0.175s/f (Firm) 12 Ran SP% **117.2**
Speed ratings (Par 99): **99,96,96,95,92 91,91,90,89,88 88,54**
CSF £160.43 CT £3107.65 TOTE £9.20: £2.90, £5.70, £5.20; EX 280.10 Trifecta £2132.90.
**Owner** Trisha Keane & Julia Rayment **Bred** Haras Du Logis Saint Germain **Trained** Newmarket, Suffolk

■ Bousfield was withdrawn. Price at time of withdrawal 25-1. Rule 4 does not apply.

**FOCUS**
This was a routine handicap, run at an ordinary pace, but the best of the winner is probably yet to come now he has headgear to help him. The form seems sound.

## 2806 NEW RACING UK ANYWHERE AVAILABLE NOW H'CAP 1m 2f 50y
5:15 (5:16) (Class 6) (0-65,67) 4-Y-O+ £2,587 (£770; £384; £192) Stalls Low

Form RPR
1 **Kalahari (IRE)**[399] 5-9-1 59 (p) FrederikTylicki 14 72+
(Lucy Wadham) *hld up: hdwy over 2f out: led 1f out: edgd lft: pushed out* 15/8[1]
5-2 2 2 **Ptolomeos**[10] 2476 11-7-11 46 ShirleyTeasdale(5) 6 53
(Sean Regan) *prom: outpcd over 3f out: r.o ins fnl f* 14/1
-000 3 ½ **First Sargeant**[24] 2092 4-8-11 55 (p) PJMcDonald 3 61
(Geoffrey Harker) *hld up: hdwy over 1f out: edgd lft and styd on ins fnl f* 25/1
2030 4 nk **Amtired**[38] 1674 8-8-6 50 (b) BarryMcHugh 10 55
(Marjorie Fife) *chsd ldrs: nt clr run 3f out: led over 1f out: hung lft: hdd 1f out: styd on same pce* 20/1
5500 5 hd **Mr Chocolate Drop (IRE)**[22] 2164 10-8-2 46 (t) DuranFentiman 8 51
(Mandy Rowland) *hld up: plld hrd: hdwy and nt clr run over 1f out: swtchd rt ins fnl f: r.o towards fin: nvr able to chal* 50/1
4005 6 1¾ **Sutton Sid**[13] 2399 4-8-13 60 (b) OisinMurphy(3) 13 62
(John Balding) *prom: led over 2f out tl rdn and hdd over 1f out: no ex ins fnl f* 10/1
60-6 7 2¾ **Lincolnrose (IRE)**[12] 2443 4-8-3 47 AndrewMullen 11 44
(Michael Appleby) *led: rdn and hdd over 2f out: wknd ins fnl f* 20/1

3243 8 ¾ **Coillte Cailin (IRE)**[9] 2509 4-9-9 67 StephenCraine 5 62
(Daniel Mark Loughnane) *hld up: hdwy over 3f out: rdn over 1f out: wknd fnl f* 10/1
3502 9 ¾ **Living Leader**[27] 2021 5-8-10 61 KieranShoemark(7) 2 55
(Grace Harris) *hld up: rdn over 2f out: wknd over 1f out* 5/1[2]
2304 10 1 **Reflect (IRE)**[16] 2301 6-9-6 64 (v) DaleSwift 12 56
(Derek Shaw) *s.i.s: hld up: n.d* 16/1
6-55 11 9 **Brockfield**[8] 2540 8-9-5 63 (v[1]) DavidAllan 7 38
(Mel Brittain) *trckd ldr: rdn and ev ch over 2f out: wknd fnl f* 6/1[3]
2110 12 17 **John Potts**[53] 1385 9-8-5 52 ow3 JasonHart(3) 4
(Brian Baugh) *chsd ldrs tl wknd over 2f out* 16/1

2m 14.0s (-0.30) **Going Correction** -0.175s/f (Firm) 12 Ran SP% **117.7**
Speed ratings (Par 101): **94,92,92,91,91 90,88,87,86,86 78,65**
CSF £29.14 CT £510.69 TOTE £4.50: £1.90, £4.90, £5.60; EX 34.80 Trifecta £1589.70.
**Owner** J Gill/ H Spiller/ G Waterhouse **Bred** Summerhill Bloodstock **Trained** Newmarket, Suffolk

**FOCUS**
This was a moderate race run at just a medium gallop, but the winner is of some interest. He's value for a bit extra.
T/Jkpt: Not won. T/Plt: £1176.10 to a £1 stake. Pool: £99,969.32 - 62.05 winning units. T/Qpdt: £289.90 to a £1 stake. Pool: £7092.88 - 18.10 winning units. CR

# 2715 BADEN-BADEN (L-H)
Sunday, June 1

**OFFICIAL GOING: Turf: good**

## 2815a GROSSER PREIS DER BADISCHEN UNTERNEHMER (GROUP 2) (4YO+) (TURF) 1m 3f
3:50 (12:00) 4-Y-O+
£33,333 (£12,916; £5,416; £3,333; £2,083; £1,250)

RPR
1 **Almandin (GER)**[35] 4-9-0 0 FilipMinarik 8 112+
(Jean-Pierre Carvalho, Germany) *w.w towards rr: hdwy to chse ldrs over 2f out: rdn and r.o u.p to ld over 1f out: drvn clr fnl f: readily* 138/10
2 ¾ **Protectionist (GER)**[42] 4-9-0 0 EPedroza 1 111
(A Wohler, Germany) *towards rr on inner: shkn up 2 1/2f out: styd on appr 1f out: r.o u.p ins fnl f: nvr quite on terms w wnr* 33/10[2]
3 2½ **Lucky Speed (IRE)**[329] 4103 4-9-6 0 AdriedeVries 7 113+
(P Schiergen, Germany) *w.w in midfield: rdn 2 1/2f out: no imp on ldrs: hrd rdn and styd on ins fnl f: nvr rchd ldrs: bttr for r* 11/5[1]
4 ¾ **Polish Vulcano (GER)**[42] 6-9-0 0 JBojko 4 105
(H-J Groschel, Germany) *midfield early: sn chsng ldng pair on inner: wnt in pursuit of ldr 2f out: sn rdn and nt qckn: plugged on at one pce fnl f* 217/10
5 2½ **Night Wish (GER)**[28] 2001 4-9-0 0 SHellyn 5 101+
(W Figge, Germany) *towards rr on outer: c wd fnl bnd and rdn 2f out: plugged on fr over 1f out: nvr in contention* 23/5
6 hd **Vif Monsieur (GER)**[224] 7407 4-9-0 0 KClijmans 9 100+
(S Smrczek, Germany) *sn led: hdd after 2f and pressed ldr on outer: led again over 4 1/2f out: kicked 3 l clr 2 1/2f out: rdn and hdd over 1f out: wknd fnl f* 74/10
7 nk **Quinzieme Monarque (USA)**[21] 2229 4-9-0 0 DanielePorcu 2 100
(P Schiergen, Germany) *hld up in last: rdn and no imp over 2f out: plugged on at same pce u.p fnl f: nvr threatened* 206/10
8 11 **Adriana (GER)**[34] 1827 6-8-10 0 AHelfenbein 6 76+
(Markus Klug, Germany) *trckd ldr on inner: led after 2f: hdd over 4 1/2f out: wknd ins fnl 2f* 132/10
9 ¾ **Feuerblitz (GER)**[42] 5-9-6 0 CristianDemuro 10 85
(M Figge, Germany) *chsd ldng pair on outer: rdn and nt qckn over 2f out: sn outpcd by ldrs: wknd fnl f* 7/2[3]

2m 17.67s (-1.60) 9 Ran SP% **129.3**
WIN (incl. 10 euro stake): 148. PLACES: 29, 17, 16. SF: 868.
**Owner** Gestut Schlenderhan **Bred** Gestut Schlenderhan **Trained** Germany

# 2242 CHANTILLY (R-H)
Sunday, June 1

**OFFICIAL GOING: Turf: good**

## 2816a PRIX DE ROYAUMONT (EQUIDIA LIVE) (GROUP 3) (3YO FILLIES) (TURF) 1m 4f
1:20 (12:00) 3-Y-O £33,333 (£13,333; £10,000; £6,666; £3,333)

RPR
1 **Savanne (IRE)**[34] 3-9-0 0 Pierre-CharlesBoudot 4 107+
(A Fabre, France) *mde all: 1 l in front and gng best whn shkn up over 1f out: sn qcknd clr: pushed out fnl f: comf* 14/1
2 1¼ **Ball Dancing (USA)**[21] 2193 3-9-0 0 (b) AntoineHamelin 2 104+
(Mme Pia Brandt, France) *t.k.h: trckd ldr on inner: pushed along 2f out: rdn over 1f out: kpt on and wnt 2nd ins fnl f: chsd wnr but no real imp and hld* 9/4[2]
3 1¾ **Zarshana (IRE)**[21] 2193 3-9-0 0 ChristopheSoumillon 3 101
(A De Royer-Dupre, France) *trckd ldr on outer: pushed along in 2nd over 1f out: rdn and outpcd by wnr ent fnl f: sn dropped to 3rd: kpt on but wl hld* 4/1[3]
4 ¾ **Delivery**[29] 3-9-0 0 MaximeGuyon 6 100
(A Fabre, France) *t.k.h and restrained early: midfield in tch: pushed along over 1f out: rdn and nt qckn ent fnl f: kpt on same pce and nvr able to chal* 5/4[1]
5 1¼ **Whim**[21] 2193 3-9-0 0 (b) ThierryJarnet 1 98
(F Head, France) *hld up in tch in last pair on inner: waiting for run fr 2f out: tl angled lft jst over 1f out: rdn and kpt on wout threatening fnl f* 18/1
6 1¼ **Great Virtues (IRE)**[24] 3-9-0 0 MickaelBarzalona 5 96
(A Fabre, France) *hld up in tch in last pair on outer: rdn over 1f out: sn outpcd: kpt on but nvr threatened* 16/1

2m 32.89s (1.89) **Going Correction** +0.05s/f (Good) 6 Ran SP% **113.0**
Speed ratings: **95,94,93,92,91 90**
WIN (incl. 1 euro stake): 14.40. PLACES: 5.40, 1.90. SF: 43.10.
**Owner** Gestut Ammerland **Bred** Ammerland Verwaltung Gmbh **Trained** Chantilly, France

## 2817a PRIX DE SANDRINGHAM (GROUP 2) (3YO FILLIES) (TURF) 1m
2:30 (12:00) 3-Y-O £61,750 (£23,833; £11,375; £7,583; £3,791)

RPR

1 **Fintry (IRE)**[19] 2243 3-8-11 0 MaximeGuyon 1 111+
(A Fabre, France) *pressed ldr on rail: led over 2f out: drvn 3 l clr appr fnl f: a in control fnl f: comf* 11/4[2]

2 *1 1/4* **La Hoguette (FR)**[37] 3-8-11 0 GregoryBenoist 7 108+
(J-C Rouget, France) *w.w in rr: gd prog over 1 1/2f out: r.o fnl f: nvr on terms w wnr* 11/1

3 *hd* **Kenzadargent (FR)**[35] 1782 3-8-11 0 IoritzMendizabal 3 108
(J-C Rouget, France) *midfield on inner: rdn to chse ldr over 1f out: kpt on fnl f: nt pce to chal* 10/1[3]

4 *2 1/2* **Stormyra (FR)**[7] 2586 3-8-11 0 OlivierPeslier 4 102
(J-P Gallorini, France) *towards rr: hrd rdn to cl on ldng gp fr 2f out: one pce fnl f* 16/1

5 *shd* **Stellar Path (FR)**[21] 2195 3-8-11 0 GeraldMosse 6 102
(X Thomas-Demeaulte, France) *towards rr on outer: hdwy 1 1/2f out: styd on ins fnl f: nrest at fin* 10/1[3]

6 *hd* **Veda (FR)**[21] 2195 3-8-11 0 ChristopheSoumillon 8 101
(A De Royer-Dupre, France) *t.k.h: cl up on outer early: sn restrained towards rr: swtchd outside and hdwy over 1 1/2f out: short-lived effrt whn shkn up appr 1f out: sn no further imp and plugged on at one pce fnl f* 8/11[1]

7 *8* **Zavallya (FR)**[19] 2243 3-8-11 0 FreddyDiFede 5 83
(A De Royer-Dupre, France) *led: hdd over 2f out: wknd fnl f* 66/1

8 *snk* **Raphinae**[20] 3-8-11 0 FabriceVeron 2 82
(H-A Pantall, France) *cl up in 3rd: rdn to chse ldrs over 1 1/2f out: sn outpcd and wknd ins fnl f* 33/1

1m 35.16s (-2.84) **Going Correction** +0.05s/f (Good) 8 Ran SP% **121.4**
Speed ratings: **116,114,114,112,111 111,103,103**
WIN (incl. 1 euro stake): 3.60 (Fintry coupled with Raphinae). PLACES: 1.80, 2.90, 3.10. DF: 16.50. SF: 30.70.
**Owner** Godolphin SNC **Bred** Darley **Trained** Chantilly, France

## 2818a PRIX DU JOCKEY CLUB (GROUP 1) (3YO COLTS & FILLIES) (TURF) 1m 2f 110y
3:15 (12:00) 3-Y-O £714,250 (£285,750; £142,875; £71,375; £35,750)

RPR

1 **The Grey Gatsby (IRE)**[17] 2285 3-9-2 0 RyanMoore 6 119
(Kevin Ryan) *sn midfield on inner: angled off rail into st: pushed along and clsd 2f out: swtchd rt again and rdn to chal over 1f out: led jst ins fnl f and qcknd clr: styd on strly: readily* 12/1

2 *3* **Shamkiyr (FR)**[29] 3-9-2 0 ChristopheSoumillon 2 113
(A De Royer-Dupre, France) *sn prom: rdn to chal 2f out and sn led: strly pressed fr over 1f out: hdd jst ins fnl f and readily outpcd by wnr: styd on for wl hld 2nd* 13/2[3]

3 *snk* **Prince Gibraltar (FR)**[29] 1965 3-9-2 0 GeraldMosse 9 113+
(J-C Rouget, France) *t.k.h: dwlt and hld up in rr: last 1/2-way: pushed along to improve whn checked briefly jst ins fnl 2f: rdn over 1f out: swtchd lft ins fnl f: styd on strly and wnt 3rd cl home: nrst fin* 2/1[1]

4 *1/2* **Wild Chief (GER)**[63] 1205 3-9-2 0 FabienLefebvre 10 112
(J Hirschberger, Germany) *hld up and sn towards rr on inner: rdn and hdwy on rail over 2f out: swtchd lft to outer over 1f out: styd on wl but nt quite pce to chal and hld fnl f* 66/1

5 *hd* **Gonna Run (FR)**[38] 3-9-2 0 Pierre-CharlesBoudot 3 111
(J-C Rouget, France) *t.k.h: dwlt sltly and towards rr early: sn midfield: pushed along and clsd 2f out: rdn to chal over 1f out: w ldrs ent fnl f: sn outpcd by wnr: styd on but lost 2 pls towards fin* 11/1

6 *1 3/4* **Mr Pommeroy (FR)**[56] 1340 3-9-2 0 FabriceVeron 5 108
(H-A Pantall, France) *w ldrs early: led after 3f: rdn and strly pressed 2f out: sn hdd: outpcd fnl f but styd on for wl hld 6th* 40/1

7 *snk* **Aventador (FR)**[21] 2194 3-9-2 0 (p) RaphaelMarchelli 4 108
(T Castanheira, France) *dwlt sltly and pushed along towards rr early: midfield in tch on inner fr bef 1/2-way: rdn 2f out: cl up on rail and ev ch over 1f out: outpcd ent fnl f: styd on for wl hld 7th* 66/1

8 *1* **Karakontie (JPN)**[21] 2196 3-9-2 0 StephanePasquier 15 106
(J E Pease, France) *hld up in midfield on outer: pushed along over 2f out: rdn over 1f out: styd on but nvr able to chal and nt given hrd time once hld ins fnl f* 6/1[2]

9 *1 3/4* **Galiway**[21] 2196 3-9-2 0 OlivierPeslier 13 102
(A Fabre, France) *hmpd sn after s: shuffled bk and hld up in rr on outer: rdn over 2f out: styd on but nvr able to chal and nt given hrd time once hld ins fnl f* 14/1

10 *1 1/2* **Prestige Vendome (FR)**[21] 2196 3-9-2 0 (p) ThierryThulliez 16 99
(N Clement, France) *w ldrs early: trckd ldr after 3f: pushed along to chal 2f out: rdn and outpcd whn short of room over 1f out: sn no ex and btn: wknd fnl f* 16/1

11 *3 1/2* **Ayrad (IRE)**[28] 1969 3-9-2 0 AndreaAtzeni 7 93
(Roger Varian) *dwlt: pushed along to rcvr and sn prom: shuffled bk into midfield bef 1/2-way: pushed along 3f out: rdn and outpcd over 1f out: bhd and btn fnl f* 33/1

12 *4* **Master's Spirit (IRE)**[18] 3-9-2 0 IoritzMendizabal 11 85
(P Demercastel, France) *t.k.h: dwlt sltly: hld up in midfield: rdn over 2f out: outpcd and btn fnl f: fdd and eased* 100/1

13 *1 3/4* **Earnshaw (USA)**[29] 1965 3-9-2 0 MaximeGuyon 8 81
(A Fabre, France) *midfield: rdn over 2f out: outpcd over 1f out: sn btn: eased fnl f* 16/1

14 *3* **Free Port Lux**[21] 2194 3-9-2 0 ThierryJarnet 12 76
(F Head, France) *settled in midfield on outer: pushed along over 2f out: shuffled bk to rr and last over 1f out: sn btn: eased fnl f* 7/1

15 *1 1/2* **Nolohay (IRE)**[29] 1965 3-9-2 0 PaulHanagan 14 73
(C Laffon-Parias, France) *t.k.h: dwlt sltly and pushed along to rcvr: sn w ldrs: restrained after 2f but remained prom on outer: rdn and brief effrt 2f out: no ex and btn over 1f out: wknd and eased* 16/1

16 *10* **Stillman (FR)**[14] 2377 3-9-2 0 (b[1]) EddyHardouin 1 53
(Mario Hofer, Germany) *sn trcking ldr on inner: cl up and ev ch 3f out: rdn and wknd qckly 2f out: last and wl btn ent fnl f: eased* 66/1

2m 5.58s (-3.22) **Going Correction** +0.05s/f (Good) 16 Ran SP% **124.6**
Speed ratings: **113,110,110,110,110 108,108,108,106,105 103,100,99,96,95 88**
WIN (incl. 1 euro stake): 19.90. PLACES: 4.10, 2.10, 1.50. DF: 51.00. SF: 136.50.
**Owner** F Gillespie **Bred** M Parrish **Trained** Hambleton, N Yorks

**FOCUS**
The tenth running of the French Derby since the distance of the race was reduced in 2005, which incidentally was also the last time the race went to an overseas challenger. The early pace looked solid enough which might explain how the winner, third and fourth were able to come from well back.

## 2819a GRAND PRIX DE CHANTILLY (GROUP 2) (4YO+) (TURF) 1m 4f
4:00 (12:00) 4-Y-O+ £61,750 (£23,833; £11,375; £7,583; £3,791)

RPR

1 **Spiritjim (FR)**[24] 2106 4-8-11 0 ChristopheSoumillon 8 113
(P Bary, France) *sn led and mde rest: pushed along whn chal 2f out: rdn and qcknd over 1f out: styd on wl fnl f: strly pressed by runner-up towards fin but a jst doing enough: shade cosily* 11/4[2]

2 *hd* **Now We Can**[64] 1177 5-8-11 0 ThierryThulliez 3 113
(N Clement, France) *midfield in tch on outer: pushed along 2f out: rdn and wnt 2nd over 1f out: styd on wl and clsd to press wnr towards fin but a jst hld* 6/1[3]

3 *1 1/2* **Norse King (FR)**[35] 1783 5-9-2 0 AlexisBadel 6 116
(Mme M Bollack-Badel, France) *hld up towards rr on outer: pushed along over 2f out: rdn and wnt 3rd over 1f out: ev ch ent fnl f: styd on but nt pce of front pair* 11/4[2]

4 *nk* **Chalnetta (FR)**[45] 1552 4-8-8 0 FlavienPrat 1 107
(C Ferland, France) *trckd ldr on inner: rdn and outpcd over 1f out: rallied u.p and styd on wl fnl f but nvr able to chal* 14/1

5 *1 1/4* **Bathyrhon (GER)**[23] 2140 4-8-11 0 MaximeGuyon 5 108
(Mme Pia Brandt, France) *hld up in rr on inner: last of remainder 1/2-way: rdn over 2f out: sn outpcd: styd on and wnt 5th ins fnl f but nvr threatened* 20/1

6 *snk* **Ivanhowe (GER)**[28] 2001 4-9-2 0 GeraldMosse 4 113
(Jean-Pierre Carvalho, Germany) *t.k.h: dwlt sltly but qckly rcvrd: midfield on inner: pushed along and nt qckn 2f out: rdn over 1f out: styd on fnl f and nt pce to chal* 5/2[1]

7 *1 3/4* **Orion Love**[37] 4-8-8 0 (p) FabriceVeron 2 102
(H-A Pantall, France) *t.k.h: trckd ldr on outer: pushed along to chal 2f out: rdn and outpcd by wnr over 1f out: sn no ex and btn: fdd and dropped to last fnl f* 33/1

P **Going Somewhere (BRZ)**[35] 1784 5-8-11 0 GregoryBenoist 7
(D Smaga, France) *a in rr: eased as if smething amiss after 3f and qckly p.u* 14/1

2m 29.32s (-1.68) **Going Correction** +0.05s/f (Good) 8 Ran SP% **117.2**
Speed ratings: **107,106,105,105,104 104,103,**
WIN (incl. 1 euro stake): 3.10. PLACES: 1.30, 1.50, 1.30. DF: 8.20. SF: 12.70.
**Owner** Hspirit **Bred** Haras Des Sablonnets Et Al **Trained** Chantilly, France

## 2820a PRIX DU GROS-CHENE (GROUP 2) (3YO+) (TURF) 5f
4:35 (12:00) 3-Y-O+ £61,750 (£23,833; £11,375; £7,583; £3,791)

RPR

1 **Rangali**[20] 2226 3-8-9 0 FabriceVeron 2 118+
(H-A Pantall, France) *w.w in tch: rdn to chal 1 1/2f out: qcknd to ld appr 1f out: drvn clr ins fnl f: readily* 10/1

2 *2* **Catcall (FR)**[21] 2197 5-9-2 0 OlivierPeslier 3 114+
(P Sogorb, France) *hld up in rr: rdn and hdwy over 1 1/2f out: r.o ins fnl f: nvr on terms w wnr* 8/11[1]

3 *3/4* **Dibajj (FR)**[21] 2197 4-8-13 0 GeraldMosse 6 108
(A De Royer-Dupre, France) *t.k.h: hld up in rr: pushed along 2f out: rdn and styd on between horses fnl f: nrest at fin* 9/2[2]

4 *hd* **Stepper Point**[21] 2197 5-9-2 0 (p) MartinDwyer 1 111
(William Muir) *a.p on rail: led over 2f out: hdd appr fnl f: no ex* 15/2[3]

5 *2* **Lucky Beggar (IRE)**[25] 2076 4-9-2 0 ChristopheSoumillon 4 103
(Charles Hills) *chsd ldr towards rails: rdn to chal over 1 1/2f out: wknd ins fnl f* 12/1

6 *1* **Justineo**[8] 2563 5-9-2 0 (b) AndreaAtzeni 5 100
(Roger Varian) *broke wl and led on his own in centre of trck: hdd over 2f out: wknd fnl f* 12/1

57.32s (-0.98) **Going Correction** +0.05s/f (Good)
**WFA** 3 from 4yo+ 7lb 6 Ran SP% **112.3**
Speed ratings: **109,105,104,104,101 99**
WIN (incl. 1 euro stake): 7.30. PLACES: 2.00, 1.30. SF: 17.30.
**Owner** Henri-Alex Pantall **Bred** Y Chabot And H A Pantall **Trained** France

## 2821a PRIX DE LUZARCHES (PRIX NETWORKGALOP.COM) (CONDITIONS) (4YO) (TURF) 1m 2f
5:10 (12:00) 4-Y-O £11,666 (£4,666; £3,500; £2,333; £1,166)

RPR

1 **Commute**[35] 4-8-9 0 AlexisBadel 8 93
(D Smaga, France) 178/10

2 *3/4* **Cheyenne Home (USA)**[56] 4-9-5 0 ChristopheSoumillon 2 102
(P Bary, France) 9/5[1]

3 *1* **Spirit's Revench (FR)**[24] 2106 4-9-5 0 ThierryJarnet 4 100
(P Demercastel, France) 33/10[2]

4 *shd* **Filly Medi (FR)**[37] 4-9-2 0 StephanePasquier 6 96
(C Delcher-Sanchez, France) 13/2[3]

5 *1 3/4* **Chancelier (FR)**[179] 4-9-2 0 GregoryBenoist 9 93
(J-C Rouget, France) 10/1

6 *3/4* **Star System (IRE)**[32] 4-8-13 0 Pierre-CharlesBoudot 10 88
(Frau R Weissmeier, Germany) 9/1

7 *2 1/2* **Cellalando (FR)**[56] 4-8-13 0 (p) MaximeGuyon 3 83
(J E Pease, France) 13/1

8 *1/2* **Mister Smart (FR)**[32] 4-8-13 0 EddyHardouin 5 82
(D Darlix, France) 20/1

9 *6* **Lemon Pearl**[213] 7650 4-8-13 0 CesarPasserat[(3)] 1 73
(Mme C Head-Maarek, France) 25/1

10 *2* **Bonanza Creek (IRE)**[29] 1942 4-8-13 0 FranckBlondel 7 66
(Luca Cumani) *dwlt sltly and pushed along in rr early: stdy hdwy on outer and led after 4f: pushed along and hdd 2f out: sn btn and wknd: dropped to last whn short of room on rail jst over 1f out: eased fnl f* 11/1

2m 1.9s (-2.90) 10 Ran SP% **120.8**
WIN (incl. 1 euro stake): 18.80. PLACES: 3.00, 1.30, 1.60. DF: 24.50. SF: 84.70.
**Owner** Mme Marie-Joelle Goetschy **Bred** Juddmonte Farms Ltd **Trained** Lamorlaye, France

2822 - (Foreign Racing) - See Raceform Interactive

# 2601 CARLISLE (R-H)

Monday, June 2

**OFFICIAL GOING: Good (good to firm in places; 7.5)**

Wind: Light, half against Weather: Overcast

## 2823 APOLLOBET £50 FREE BETS APPRENTICE TRAINING SERIES H'CAP (THE RACING EXCELLENCE INITIATIVE) 7f 200y

6:15 (6:15) (Class 5) (0-75,75) 4-Y-0+ £2,587 (£770; £384; £192) Stalls Low

Form RPR

4041 1 **Run Fat Lass Run**[13] 2426 4-9-2 **65** ................................ EvaMoscrop 3 72+
(Philip Kirby) *hld up in tch: rdn whn n.m.r over 2f out: swtchd lft and hdwy over 1f out: led ent fnl f: kpt on wl* **7/1**

5432 2 *nk* **Ewell Place (IRE)**[9] 2546 5-9-1 **64** ................(p) SammyJoBell 4 70
(Richard Fahey) *led at stdy pce: rdn over 1f out: hdd ent fnl f: rallied: hld nr fin* **11/8**[1]

0 3 1 ¼ **Buzz Law (IRE)**[43] 1596 6-8-8 **57** ............................(v[1]) RobJFitzpatrick 6 60
(K R Burke) *t.k.h: hld up in tch: hdwy on outside 2f out: edgd rt and kpt on wl fnl f: nt rch first two* **6/1**[3]

40-P 4 1 ½ **Pivotman**[55] 1362 6-9-2 **70** ......................................(t) DanielleMooney[(5)] 7 70
(Michael Easterby) *s.i.s: t.k.h and sn prom: effrt and rdn over 2f out: edgd rt and kpt on same pce ins fnl f* **9/1**

00-5 5 *hd* **Califante**[2] 2757 4-9-7 **75** ........................ KatherineSO'Brien[(5)] 1 74
(T Hogan, Ire) *cl up: effrt and rdn wl over 1f out: kpt on same pce fnl f* **4/1**[2]

0-00 6 ¾ **Tectonic (IRE)**[7] 2607 5-9-6 **69** ................................(p) MeganCarberry 2 66
(Keith Dalgleish) *plld hrd: cl up: effrt and pushed along 2f out: outpcd ins fnl f* **17/2**

1m 41.06s (1.06) **Going Correction** -0.15s/f (Firm) **6** Ran SP% **109.4**
Speed ratings (Par 103): **88,87,86,84,84 84**
CSF £16.32 TOTE £5.50: £3.80, £1.10; EX 13.80 Trifecta £106.60.

**Owner** S C B Limited **Bred** Mrs C R Philipson & Mrs H G Lascelles **Trained** Middleham, N Yorks

**FOCUS**
Old Stable bend moved out 1yd and races on Round course increased by 2yds. A race lacking any strength or depth. The runner-up is the best guide.

## 2824 APOLLOBET BEST ODDS GUARANTEED MEDIAN AUCTION MAIDEN STKS 5f

6:45 (6:46) (Class 5) 2-Y-O £2,587 (£770; £384; £192) Stalls Low

Form RPR

1 **Effusive** 2-9-0 0 ........................................ SilvestreDeSousa 2 79+
(William Haggas) *hld up bhd ldng gp: plld out and rn green 2f out: gd hdwy and edgd rt to ld last 75yds: pushed out* **11/4**[2]

2 2 *nk* **Free Entry (IRE)**[28] 2014 2-9-0 0 ........................ PaulMulrennan 8 77
(James Tate) *led and sn crossed to ins rail: rdn 2f out: hdd last 75yds: kpt on: hld nr fin* **10/11**[1]

3 3 3 ¾ **Miami Carousel (IRE)**[20] 2231 2-9-2 0 ................... IanBrennan[(3)] 9 68
(John Quinn) *t.k.h: pressed ldr: rdn along 2f out: outpcd by first two fnl f* **20/1**

4 ½ **Heaven's Secret (IRE)** 2-9-5 0 ................................ TonyHamilton 3 67
(Richard Fahey) *dwlt: sn in tch: effrt and rdn 2f out: kpt on same pce fnl f* **12/1**

40 5 1 **Soie D'Leau**[14] 2386 2-9-5 0 ........................................ TomEaves 6 63
(Kristin Stubbs) *cl up: effrt and rdn 2f out: outpcd ent fnl f* **66/1**

6 *hd* **Shortmile Lady (IRE)** 2-8-11 0 .......................... ConnorBeasley[(3)] 4 57+
(Michael Dods) *hld up in tch: rdn and swtchd rt wl over 1f out: sn no imp* **10/1**[3]

63 7 ½ **Compton River**[32] 1900 2-9-5 0 ................................ RoystonFfrench 5 60
(Bryan Smart) *t.k.h: cl up: rdn and edgd rt wl over 1f out: btn ins fnl f* **10/1**[3]

45 8 4 **Fairweather Trader (IRE)**[24] 2134 2-9-5 0 ..................... PJMcDonald 7 46
(Paul Midgley) *s.i.s: bhd and outpcd: nvr on terms* **80/1**

9 2 **Little Lady Katie (IRE)** 2-9-0 0 ................................ DanielTudhope 1 34
(K R Burke) *dwlt: outpcd and bhd: nvr on terms* **25/1**

1m 1.33s (0.53) **Going Correction** -0.15s/f (Firm) **9** Ran SP% **116.3**
Speed ratings (Par 93): **89,88,82,81,80 79,79,72,69**
CSF £5.45 TOTE £4.40: £1.40, £1.02, £3.50; EX 7.40 Trifecta £69.50.

**Owner** Cheveley Park Stud **Bred** Cheveley Park Stud Ltd **Trained** Newmarket, Suffolk

**FOCUS**
This was a hugely promising start to the career of Effusive, but the time was fairly slow.

## 2825 APOLLOBET ENHANCED RACING SPECIALS H'CAP (JOCKEY CLUB GRASSROOTS FLAT SPRINT SERIES QUALIFIER) 5f 193y

7:15 (7:15) (Class 4) (0-80,80) 4-Y-O+ £5,175 (£1,540; £769; £384) Stalls Low

Form RPR

4403 1 **Sunraider (IRE)**[7] 2602 7-9-1 **74** ................................ PaulMulrennan 7 84
(Paul Midgley) *trckd ldrs: effrt whn n.m.r briefly wl over 1f out: kpt on to ld last 50yds: r.o* **3/1**[2]

-005 2 1 ¼ **Relight My Fire**[10] 2522 4-8-11 **70** ................................(b) DavidAllan 9 76
(Tim Easterby) *pressed ldr: rdn and led over 1f out: hdd wl ins fnl f: no ex* **25/1**

225- 3 1 **Rich Again (IRE)**[255] 6603 5-8-5 **64** ................................ JoeFanning 1 67
(James Bethell) *hld up in tch on ins: hdwy and swtchd lft wl over 1f out: kpt on ins fnl f* **11/1**

2-00 4 *shd* **Mishaal (IRE)**[27] 2054 4-8-12 **71** ................................(b[1]) BarryMcHugh 2 73
(Michael Herrington) *s.i.s: hld up: rdn 2f out: kpt on fnl f: nvr able to chal* **25/1**

-000 5 1 ½ **Head Space (IRE)**[10] 2522 6-9-6 **79** ................................(p) JamesSullivan 4 77
(Ruth Carr) *t.k.h: hld up in tch: effrt and pushed along 2f out: no imp fnl f* **18/1**

0304 6 1 **Klynch**[7] 2602 8-9-1 **77** ................................(b) JasonHart[(3)] 10 71
(Ruth Carr) *trckd ldrs: rdn and hung rt wl over 1f out: outpcd fnl f* **9/2**[3]

21-2 7 4 ½ **Circuitous**[7] 2602 6-9-5 **78** ................................(v) TomEaves 3 58
(Keith Dalgleish) *led: rdn and hdd over 1f out: wknd fnl f* **7/4**[1]

62-6 8 6 **Alaskan Bullet (IRE)**[16] 2350 5-9-3 **76** ................... SilvestreDeSousa 6 37
(Brian Ellison) *taken early to post: plld hrd: hld up: rdn over 2f out: wknd over 1f out: eased whn btn fnl f* **7/1**

1m 11.93s (-1.77) **Going Correction** -0.15s/f (Firm) **8** Ran SP% **113.3**
Speed ratings (Par 105): **105,103,102,101,99 98,92,84**
CSF £68.87 CT £721.58 TOTE £4.60: £1.50, £4.20, £2.70; EX 59.50 Trifecta £1149.70.

**Owner** David Mann **Bred** Lodge Park Stud **Trained** Westow, N Yorks

**FOCUS**
This was sound run. The winner is rated close to last year's best.

## 2826 APOLLOBET FREE DOWNLOAD APP FILLIES' H'CAP (JOCKEY CLUB GRASSROOTS MIDDLE DISTANCE QUALIFIER) 1m 1f 61y

7:45 (7:45) (Class 3) (0-90,88) 3-Y-O+ £8,086 (£2,406; £1,202; £601) Stalls Low

Form RPR

1 1 **My Spirit (IRE)**[24] 2129 3-8-5 **77** ................................ SilvestreDeSousa 3 89+
(William Haggas) *t.k.h: hld up in tch: shkn up and gd hdwy to ld over 1f out: pushed out fnl f: eased cl home: comf* **1/2**[1]

2100 2 1 **Maven**[7] 2618 6-9-7 **88** ................................ RachelRichardson[(7)] 1 93
(Tim Easterby) *t.k.h: led: rdn and hdd over 1f out: rallied: one pce last 100yds* **6/1**[2]

316- 3 11 **Mitchelton (FR)**[220] 7503 3-8-9 **81** ................................ JoeFanning 5 61
(Mark Johnston) *cl up tl rdn and dropped by first two fr over 1f out* **15/2**[3]

6025 4 2 ¼ **Spavento (IRE)**[5] 2676 8-8-6 **69** ................................ JasonHart[(3)] 2 46
(Eric Alston) *cl up: drvn along wl over 2f out: wknd over 1f out* **9/1**

0-50 5 12 **Cosmic Halo**[25] 2091 5-9-3 **77** ................................ TonyHamilton 4 29
(Richard Fahey) *blindfold slow to remove and dwlt: hld up: rdn and struggling over 3f out: sn btn* **25/1**

1m 55.07s (-2.53) **Going Correction** -0.15s/f (Firm)
**WFA** 3 from 5yo+ 12lb **5** Ran SP% **106.6**
Speed ratings (Par 104): **105,104,94,92,81**
CSF £3.55 TOTE £1.90: £1.20, £1.20; EX 3.00 Trifecta £13.60.

**Owner** Miss Pat O'Kelly **Bred** Kilcarn Stud **Trained** Newmarket, Suffolk

**FOCUS**
Plain sailing for the well related winner. The first pair were clear and the runner-up sets the standard.

## 2827 APOLLOBET IN PLAY BETTING H'CAP (BOBIS RACE) 7f 200y

8:15 (8:16) (Class 4) (0-80,78) 3-Y-O £5,175 (£1,540; £769; £384) Stalls Low

Form RPR

50-1 1 **Arabian Comet (IRE)**[34] 1858 3-9-5 **76** ................... SilvestreDeSousa 4 95
(William Haggas) *dwlt: hld up in tch: pushed along over 3f out: gd hdwy on outside 2f out: led ins fnl f: sn clr* **10/3**[3]

4261 2 5 **Sir Guy Porteous (IRE)**[21] 2218 3-9-7 **78** ........................ JoeFanning 6 86
(Mark Johnston) *t.k.h early: cl up: led over 2f out: rdn and edgd rt over 1f out: hdd ins fnl f: sn one pce* **5/2**[1]

-110 3 3 ¼ **Arrowzone**[10] 2510 3-9-5 **76** ................................ PaulMulrennan 5 76
(Garry Moss) *in tch: effrt and drvn over 2f out: kpt on same pce fr over 1f out* **3/1**[2]

326- 4 1 ¾ **Porthos Du Vallon**[231] 7237 3-8-10 **67** ................................ TomEaves 1 63
(Keith Dalgleish) *t.k.h: led to over 2f out: rdn and outpcd fr over 1f out* **28/1**

0210 5 4 **Mariners Moon (IRE)**[21] 2204 3-9-6 **77** ........................ DanielTudhope 3 67
(David O'Meara) *prom: drvn and edgd lft 2f out: sn wknd: eased whn btn ins fnl f* **3/1**[2]

04-5 6 6 **Western Sands (IRE)**[21] 2203 3-8-11 **68** ........................ TonyHamilton 2 41
(Richard Fahey) *cl up tl rdn and wknd over 3f out* **20/1**

1m 38.6s (-1.40) **Going Correction** -0.15s/f (Firm) **6** Ran SP% **109.9**
Speed ratings (Par 101): **101,96,92,91,87 81**
CSF £11.53 TOTE £4.20: £1.40, £1.80; EX 8.90 Trifecta £18.50.

**Owner** Abdulla Al Mansoori **Bred** Darley **Trained** Newmarket, Suffolk

**FOCUS**
A fair race for the grade/track. It developed into a proper test at this trip and it required a strong staying performance. The winner took another big step forward.

## 2828 APOLLOBET FOLLOW ON TWITTER AND FACEBOOK H'CAP 6f 192y

8:45 (8:45) (Class 5) (0-70,70) 3-Y-O £2,587 (£770; £384; £192) Stalls Low

Form RPR

0-65 1 **We'll Shake Hands (FR)**[21] 2205 3-9-5 **68** ................... DanielTudhope 4 74
(K R Burke) *mde all: drvn along 2f out: hld on gamely fnl f* **9/2**[2]

-533 2 1 ¼ **Petergate**[21] 2204 3-8-9 **58** ................................(p) BarryMcHugh 1 61
(Brian Rothwell) *trckd ldrs: effrt and rdn over 1f out: chsd wnr ins fnl f: kpt on* **5/1**[3]

0-61 3 ½ **Bajan Rebel**[21] 2205 3-8-10 **59** ................................ JamesSullivan 3 61
(Michael Easterby) *pressed wnr: drvn over 2f out: one pce and lost 2nd ins fnl f* **7/1**

2332 4 1 **Beautiful Stranger (IRE)**[10] 2517 3-9-7 **70** ................(p) TomEaves 6 69
(Keith Dalgleish) *t.k.h: in tch: rdn along 2f out: kpt on ins fnl f* **4/1**[1]

2-60 5 ¾ **Madame Mirasol (IRE)**[21] 2218 3-9-1 **69** ................(p) KevinStott[(5)] 10 66
(Kevin Ryan) *trckd ldrs: drvn over 2f out: no ex ins fnl f* **8/1**

3-30 6 ½ **Another Royal**[23] 2165 3-8-8 **57** ................................(b) DuranFentiman 5 53
(Tim Easterby) *t.k.h: hld up in tch: drvn and effrt whn hung rt over 1f out: no imp fnl f* **13/2**

24-4 7 *shd* **Please Let Me Go**[21] 2205 3-8-10 **59** ........................[1] PaulMulrennan 2 55
(Julie Camacho) *hld up on ins: effrt whn n.m.r briefly appr fnl f: no imp last 150yds* **9/1**

00-5 8 1 **Mount Cheiron (USA)**[11] 2474 3-8-5 **59** ........................ EmmaSayer[(5)] 9 52
(Dianne Sayer) *plld hrd: hld up: rdn and edgd rt over 1f out: sn no imp* **33/1**

40-0 9 1 ¼ **Miguela McGuire**[58] 1308 3-8-2 **54** oh2 ow3 ...................[1] NeilFarley[(3)] 7 44
(Eric Alston) *dwlt: plld hrd in rr: drvn along over 2f out: no imp over 1f out* **40/1**

00-0 10 3 ¼ **Lazy Sioux**[37] 1713 3-8-4 **53** ................................ PJMcDonald 8 34
(Philip Kirby) *hld up: rdn and hdwy on outside over 2f out: wknd over 1f out* **16/1**

1m 27.44s (0.34) **Going Correction** -0.10s/f (Good) **10** Ran SP% **113.1**
Speed ratings (Par 99): **94,92,92,90,90 89,89,88,86,83**
CSF £26.37 CT £135.74 TOTE £5.80: £2.50, £2.00, £3.50; EX 32.90 Trifecta £198.80.

**Owner** Market Avenue Racing Club & Mrs E Burke **Bred** Eric Puerari **Trained** Middleham Moor, N Yorks

**FOCUS**
Modest form. The pace was ordinary and the principals were always prominent. The winer is rated back to his maiden win.

T/Plt: £24.10 to a £1 stake. Pool of £62149.99- 1875.53 winning units. T/Qpdt: £13.40 to a £1 stake. Pool of £4547.52 - 250.90 winning units. RY

[2666]**CHEPSTOW** (L-H)

Monday, June 2

**OFFICIAL GOING: Soft (heavy in places)**

Wind: mild breeze against Weather: light showers

## 2829 32RED ON THE APP STORE MEDIAN AUCTION MAIDEN STKS 6f 16y
**2:00** (2:00) (Class 5) 2-Y-O £2,587 (£770; £384; £192) **Stalls Centre**

Form RPR

3 1 **Fuwairt (IRE)**[14] 2380 2-9-5 0 FrankieDettori 3 78+
(Richard Hannon) *hld up bhd ldrs: smooth hdwy over 2f out: led over 1f out: pushed clr: eased nring fin* **4/11**[1]

2 *nk* **Jaganory (IRE)** 2-9-5 0 MartinLane 1 71+
(David Evans) *trckd ldr tl outpcd 2f out: r.o again ins fnl f: snatched 2nd fnl stride* **16/1**

0 3 *shd* **Red Tornado (FR)**[17] 2298 2-9-5 0 DaneO'Neill 4 72
(Harry Dunlop) *trckd ldrs: rdn to chal 2f out tl wnr wnt on over 1f out: kpt on but sn hld: sltly hmpd nring fin: lost 2nd fnl strides* **8/1**[3]

56 4 *½* **Invincible Zeb (IRE)**[13] 2413 2-9-5 0 SteveDrowne 6 69
(Ronald Harris) *led: rdn whn jnd 2f out: hdd over 1f out: kpt on tl no ex fnl 100yds* **33/1**

5 5 *7* **Gamesters Lad**[37] 1732 2-9-5 0 StephenCraine 2 48
(Tom Dascombe) *trckd ldrs: rdn 2f out: sn one pce* **7/1**[2]

6 *9* **Indian Joe** 2-9-5 0 LiamJones 5 21
(J S Moore) *chsd ldrs: rdn over 2f out: wknd ent fnl f* **14/1**

1m 17.36s (5.36) **Going Correction** +0.70s/f (Yiel) **6 Ran SP% 112.4**
Speed ratings (Par 93): **92,91,91,90,81 69**
CSF £8.15 TOTE £1.10: £1.10, £6.80; EX 6.90 Trifecta £27.40.

**Owner** Al Shaqab Racing **Bred** Tommy Burns **Trained** East Everleigh, Wilts

**FOCUS**
This meeting had to pass two inspections owing to waterlogged patches. Unsurprisingly, they took things steady in this ordinary-looking juvenile maiden and there was a bunch finish. The winner was value for at least 6l.

## 2830 32RED CASINO H'CAP (DIV I) 5f 16y
**2:30** (2:31) (Class 6) (0-55,55) 4-Y-O+ £1,940 (£577; £288; £144) **Stalls Centre**

Form RPR

6131 1 **Fathom Five (IRE)**[3] 2724 10-8-8 49 JoshQuinn(7) 9 62
(Shaun Harris) *trckd ldrs: rdn to ld over 1f out: r.o wl fnl 100yds: rdn out* **7/4**[1]

4346 2 *1* **Captain Scooby**[11] 2473 8-8-10 49 PhilipPrince(5) 5 58
(Richard Guest) *chsd ldrs: rdn over 2f out: r.o wl to go 2nd jst ins fnl f: hld towards fin* **4/1**[2]

1040 3 *2* **Spic 'n Span**[28] 2008 9-8-12 46 (p[1]) SteveDrowne 3 48
(Ronald Harris) *trckd ldr: rdn to chal 2f out: kpt on same pce fnl f* **14/1**

1263 4 *½* **Bubbly Bailey**[12] 2459 4-9-4 52 (v) AdamBeschizza 4 52
(J R Jenkins) *led: rdn whn jnd 2f out: hdd over 1f out: no ex fnl 75yds* **6/1**[3]

20-0 5 *hd* **First Rebellion**[35] 1787 5-9-2 55 (b) RyanTate(5) 7 54
(Tony Carroll) *nt fluent leaving stalls: chsd ldrs: rdn over 2f out: nt gng pce to get on terms but kpt on fnl f* **10/1**

6062 6 *shd* **Molly Jones**[28] 2008 5-8-12 46 oh1 DaneO'Neill 10 45
(Derek Haydn Jones) *sn pushed along bhd ldrs: rdn over 2f out: no imp tl r.o ent fnl f* **8/1**

7 *2½* **To The Sky (IRE)**[26] 2900 6-9-2 50 (p) LukeMorris 1 40
(John O'Shea) *taken to s early: carried lft s: sn outpcd in rr: styd on wl fnl f but nvr any danger* **12/1**

5556 8 *1* **Methaaly (IRE)**[81] 937 11-8-9 48 TimClark(5) 2 34
(Michael Mullineaux) *wnt lft s: in last pair sltly detached: rdn over 2f out: sn hung lft: nvr any imp* **20/1**

0006 9 *1½* **Homeboy (IRE)**[28] 2598 6-8-5 46 oh1 (b) HollieDoyle(7) 6 27
(David Evans) *chsd ldrs: rdn over 2f out: wknd ent fnl f* **25/1**

1m 2.08s (2.78) **Going Correction** +0.70s/f (Yiel) **9 Ran SP% 113.8**
Speed ratings (Par 101): **105,103,100,99,99 98,94,93,90**
CSF £8.32 CT £71.26 TOTE £2.90: £1.10, £1.30, £4.70; EX 8.00 Trifecta £75.70.

**Owner** Nottinghamshire Racing **Bred** Eamonn Connolly **Trained** Carburton, Notts

**FOCUS**
A moderate sprint handicap. The winner is rated in line with last year's Flat form.

## 2831 32RED CASINO H'CAP (DIV II) 5f 16y
**3:05** (3:05) (Class 6) (0-55,53) 4-Y-O+ £1,940 (£577; £288; £144) **Stalls Centre**

Form RPR

0-00 1 **Night Trade (IRE)**[143] 121 7-9-1 52 (p) DCByrne(5) 8 61
(Ronald Harris) *in last pair: rdn and hdwy fr wl over 1f out: r.o wl to ld nring fin: rdn out* **16/1**

423 2 *nk* **Christopher Chua (IRE)**[28] 2008 5-8-11 46 WilliamTwiston-Davies(3) 2 54
(Michael Scudamore) *trckd ldr: rdn over 1f out: sn looking to hang lft: kpt on but no ex whn hdd nring fin* **3/1**[1]

0603 3 *2¼* **Senora Lobo (IRE)**[12] 2452 4-8-8 45 (p) ShirleyTeasdale(5) 5 45
(Lisa Williamson) *trckd ldr: rdn over 1f out: kpt on same pce ins fnl f* **7/1**

2065 4 *¾* **Diamond Vine (IRE)**[28] 2008 6-9-1 47 (p) SteveDrowne 9 44
(Ronald Harris) *trckd ldrs: rdn over 2f out: kpt on same pce: regained 4th fnl strides* **7/1**

000- 5 *nk* **Gracie's Games**[223] 7454 8-8-13 45 (b) SamHitchcott 3 41
(John Spearing) *led: rdn wl over 1f out: no ex whn hdd fnl 120yds* **16/1**

1300 6 *1¾* **Outbid**[28] 2008 4-9-3 49 LukeMorris 1 39
(Tony Carroll) *trckd ldrs: rdn over 1f out: nt pce to chal: fdd fnl 120yds* **8/1**

0040 7 *¾* **Two Turtle Doves (IRE)**[29] 1972 8-9-2 53 TimClark(5) 6 40
(Michael Mullineaux) *trckd ldrs: rdn over 1f out: sn hld: fdd fnl 120yds* **4/1**[3]

6000 8 *4½* **Lord Buffhead**[3] 2724 5-8-12 49 (vp) PhilipPrince(5) 7 20
(Richard Guest) *taken to s early: sn outpcd in rr: a in last* **7/2**[2]

1m 2.29s (2.99) **Going Correction** +0.70s/f (Yiel) **8 Ran SP% 115.1**
Speed ratings (Par 101): **104,103,99,98,98 95,94,87**
CSF £64.27 CT £380.22 TOTE £22.90: £4.90, £1.30, £2.30; EX 95.40 Trifecta £804.90.

**Owner** Alan & Adam Darlow, A Darlow Productions **Bred** John Foley **Trained** Earlswood, Monmouths

**FOCUS**
A slightly slower time than the first division but a slightly weaker race. The form is taken at face value.

## 2832 32RED.COM MAIDEN AUCTION STKS 7f 16y
**3:40** (3:44) (Class 5) 3-Y-O £2,587 (£770; £384) **Stalls Centre**

Form RPR

1 **Strawberriesncream (IRE)** 3-8-10 0 ChrisCatlin 1 67
(Rae Guest) *slowly away: led after 1f: jnd over 3f out: rdn fnl f: kpt on wl to assert fnl 120yds* **4/6**[1]

5-0 2 *2¼* **Danz Star (IRE)**[31] 1911 3-8-13 0 PatCosgrave 5 64
(Malcolm Saunders) *led for 1f: trckd wnr: chal over 3f out: rdn over 1f out: ev ch ent fnl f: no ex fnl 120yds* **4/1**[3]

3 *7* **Dunn's River (FR)** 3-9-1 0 FergusSweeney 2 52
(Jamie Osborne) *slowly away: trckd ldrs: rdn wl over 1f out: nvr gng pce to chal: wknd fnl f* **5/2**[2]

1m 28.31s (5.11) **Going Correction** +0.70s/f (Yiel) **3 Ran SP% 108.6**
Speed ratings (Par 99): **98,95,87**
CSF £3.53 TOTE £1.70; EX 2.90 Trifecta £3.80.

**Owner** Ballymore Downunder Syndicate **Bred** Rathbarry Stud **Trained** Newmarket, Suffolk

**FOCUS**
A weak maiden run in a slow time, 1.26secs slower than the following Class 4 handicap. What the winner achieved is unclear.

## 2833 32RED H'CAP 7f 16y
**4:10** (4:11) (Class 4) (0-85,84) 3-Y-O+ £6,469 (£1,925; £962; £481) **Stalls Centre**

Form RPR

5030 1 **Can't Change It (IRE)**[24] 2111 3-8-10 76 FergusSweeney 5 77
(David Simcock) *hld up: hdwy 2f out: sn rdn: r.o fnl f: led fnl strides* **3/1**[1]

-546 2 *shd* **Pashan Garh**[5] 2669 5-8-11 67 PatCosgrave 6 71
(Pat Eddery) *prom: led 4f out: rdn 2f out: kpt on but drifted lft fnl f: hdd fnl strides* **6/1**

03-0 3 *1* **Soaring Spirits (IRE)**[149] 56 4-9-9 79 (b) JimmyQuinn 8 80
(Dean Ivory) *trckd ldrs: rdn wl over 1f out: nt quite pce to chal: kpt on fnl f* **10/1**

6422 4 *2* **Great Expectations**[23] 2157 6-9-7 77 AdamBeschizza 1 73
(J R Jenkins) *racd keenly: trckd ldrs: rdn 2f out: kpt on same pce* **9/2**[2]

0-05 5 *nse* **Peak Storm**[19] 2251 5-9-1 71 (p) LukeMorris 4 67
(John O'Shea) *uns rdr gng to s but sn ct: trckd ldrs: rdn 2f out: sn hld: kpt on fnl 120yds* **6/1**

250- 6 *1¾* **Amadeus Wolfe Tone (IRE)**[291] 5437 5-10-0 84 (p) DaneO'Neill 7 76
(Jamie Osborne) *hld up: rdn 2f out: nvr any imp* **8/1**

0-10 7 *6* **Exzachary**[2] 2763 4-8-11 74 HarryBurns(7) 3 50
(Jo Hughes) *hld up: hdwy over 2f out: sn rdn in clly disp 3rd: wknd over 1f out* **5/1**[3]

15-0 8 *7* **Edge (IRE)**[25] 2088 3-8-12 78 (p) MartinLane 2 32
(Bernard Llewellyn) *led tl narrowly hdd 4f out: pressed ldr tl rdn over 2f out: sn wknd* **12/1**

1m 27.05s (3.85) **Going Correction** +0.70s/f (Yiel)
**WFA** 3 from 4yo+ 10lb **8 Ran SP% 116.3**
Speed ratings (Par 105): **106,105,104,102,102 100,93,85**
CSF £21.72 CT £160.04 TOTE £4.10: £1.20, £2.60, £3.60; EX 23.10 Trifecta £254.50.

**Owner** Mrs Fitri Hay **Bred** Peter & Hugh McCutcheon **Trained** Newmarket, Suffolk

**FOCUS**
Just an ordinary-looking handicap for the grade. The form is rated around the runner-up and third.

## 2834 32RED.COM H'CAP 1m 2f 36y
**4:45** (4:46) (Class 5) (0-70,70) 4-Y-O+ £2,587 (£770; £384; £192) **Stalls Low**

Form RPR

06-3 1 **Pandorica**[5] 2672 6-8-11 65 (p) DanielMuscutt(5) 4 74
(Bernard Llewellyn) *trckd ldrs: chal over 3f out: led wl over 2f out: rdn clr fnl f: comf* **7/4**[1]

2034 2 *3* **Zafranagar (IRE)**[4] 2702 9-9-1 69 GeorgeDowning(5) 5 72
(Ian Williams) *hld up bhd ldrs: pushed along over 4f out: rdn and stdy prog fr over 2f out: wnt 2nd over 1f out: styd on but no threat to wnr* **2/1**[2]

/10- 3 *3¼* **Acapulco Bay**[26] 3953 10-8-3 52 (p) LukeMorris 2 49
(Dai Burchell) *racd keenly: disp ld tl clr ldr after 2f: rdn and hdd wl over 2f out: styd on same pce fnl f* **8/1**

-000 4 *shd* **Greyemkay**[34] 1865 6-7-12 54 oh6 ow3 GaryMahon(7) 1 51?
(Richard Price) *disp ld for 2f: trckd ldr: rdn to dispute cl 3rd over 2f out: styd on same pce fnl f* **12/1**

4-40 5 *1¼* **Petrify**[5] 2672 4-8-6 55 MartinLane 6 50
(Bernard Llewellyn) *hld up bhd ldrs: rdn wl over 2f out: disputing cl 3rd over 1f out tl no ex fnl 120yds* **4/1**[3]

2m 16.34s (5.74) **Going Correction** +0.70s/f (Yiel) **5 Ran SP% 108.5**
Speed ratings (Par 103): **105,102,100,99,98**
CSF £5.37 TOTE £2.00: £1.40, £1.60; EX 6.30 Trifecta £13.80.

**Owner** Alex James **Bred** Ambersham Stud **Trained** Fochriw, Caerphilly

**FOCUS**
Very modest form, the winner rated to her best in the past year.

## 2835 32RED FREE £10 BONUS H'CAP 1m 4f 23y
**5:15** (5:16) (Class 5) (0-75,77) 4-Y-O+ £2,587 (£770; £384; £192) **Stalls Low**

Form RPR

3213 1 **Rocky Elsom (USA)**[21] 1628 7-9-2 67 (t) SaleemGolam 5 76
(Sophie Leech) *trckd ldng trio: pushed along and hdwy 3f out: led 2f out: styd on strly: pushed out* **11/4**[2]

/00- 2 *3½* **King Zeal (IRE)**[8] 7275 10-8-12 68 ow1 (t) GeorgeDowning(5) 2 71
(Barry Leavy) *little slowly away: sn trcking ldr: rdn to ld 3f out: hdd 2f out: styd on same pce fnl f* **8/1**[3]

0-41 3 *2½* **Meetings Man (IRE)**[6] 2651 7-9-12 77 6ex (p) SteveDrowne 1 76
(Ali Stronge) *racd keenly: trckd ldr: rdn 3f out: styd on same pce fnl 2f* **11/4**[2]

0-24 4 *25* **Yul Finegold (IRE)**[35] 1791 4-9-7 72 PatCosgrave 4 56
(George Baker) *led: rdn whn hdd 3f out: btn 2f out: eased fnl f* **5/4**[1]

2m 46.93s (7.93) **Going Correction** +0.70s/f (Yiel) **4 Ran SP% 108.9**
Speed ratings (Par 103): **101,98,97,80**
CSF £19.46 TOTE £3.00; EX 15.70 Trifecta £28.80.

**Owner** C J Leech **Bred** Michael Ryan **Trained** Elton, Gloucs

**FOCUS**
This race fell apart and the form was weak. The winner is rated in line with his recent AW form.

## 2836 32REDPOKER.COM H'CAP 1m 4f 23y
5:45 (6:10) (Class 6) (0-55,54) 4-Y-0+ £1,940 (£577; £288; £144) Stalls Low

Form RPR
440/ 1 **Lady Percy (IRE)**611 6690 5-8-10 50 CharlotteJenner(7) 12 60
(Mark Usher) *mde virtually all: rdn 2f out: strly chal and hld on v gamely thrght fnl f: all out* 16/1

40- 2 hd **Captain Oats (IRE)**269 6153 11-8-12 50 RachealKneller(5) 14 59
(Pam Ford) *s.i.s: towards rr: stdy prog on outer fr over 4f out: trckd ldrs 2f out: pushed along ent fnl f: styd on wl fnl 100yds: jst failed* 50/1

000/ 3 nk **Cappielow Park**22 8075 5-9-0 47 (p) PatCosgrave 17 55
(Ali Stronge) *trckd ldrs: rdn for str chal fr 2f out: ev ch thrght fnl f: kpt on* 5/4[1]

46-0 4 2 1/2 **Ninepointsixthree**94 115 4-9-2 49 (p) LukeMorris 13 53
(John O'Shea) *mid-div: rdn and hdwy 3f out to chse ldrs: styd on same pce fnl f* 14/1

64 5 1/2 **Crouching Harry (IRE)**7 2614 5-8-13 51 (p) LouisSteward(5) 9 54
(Anabel K Murphy) *mid-div: hdwy 4f out: rdn 3f out to chse ldrs: kpt on same pce fnl f* 7/1[2]

32-6 6 2 3/4 **Hendry Trigger**31 1916 5-9-5 52 (p) MartinLane 15 51
(Bernard Llewellyn) *trckd ldrs: rdn 3f out: one pce fnl 2f* 25/1

2-43 7 1/2 **Descaro (USA)**22 580 8-9-2 54 (p) DCByrne(5) 1 52
(John O'Shea) *sn prom: rdn 3f out: one pce fnl 2f* 20/1

0-44 8 shd **Kozmina Bay**9 640 5-8-9 47 (b) DanielMuscutt(5) 10 45
(Bernard Llewellyn) *in tch: rdn over 4f out: nvr quite threatened: one pce fnl 2f* 10/1[3]

0532 9 1 3/4 **K Lightning (IRE)**14 2396 4-8-13 53 GeorgeBuckell(7) 5 48+
(Sarah Humphrey) *hld up towards rr: hdwy over 3f out: sn rdn: chsd ldrs 2f out: fdd ent fnl f* 7/1[2]

63-6 10 7 **Karl Marx (IRE)**19 2252 4-8-8 46 (b) PhilipPrince(5) 4 30
(Mark Gillard) *mid-div tl wknd 3f out* 25/1

0/20 11 3 1/4 **Turbulent Priest**14 2396 6-8-11 47 (p) SimonPearce(3) 6 26
(Zoe Davison) *a towards rr* 25/1

0006 12 1 1/4 **Illegale (IRE)**28 2596 8-8-9 45 (bt) MatthewCosham(3) 3 22
(Nikki Evans) *s.i.s: towards rr: hdwy on outer fr 6f out: short-lived effrt over 3f out: wknd qckly* 66/1

6-56 13 5 **Korngold**14 2396 6-9-0 52 GeorgeDowning(5) 7 21
(Barry Leavy) *mid-div tl wknd 3f out* 14/1

2-34 14 16 **Zinnobar**12 2465 4-9-1 48 SamHitchcott 2
(Jonathan Portman) *prom tl 6f out: in tch: effrt over 3f out: sn wknd* 14/1

2m 48.66s (9.66) **Going Correction** +0.70s/f (Yiel) **14** Ran SP% **124.2**
Speed ratings (Par 101): **95,94,94,93,92 90,90,90,89,84 82,81,78,67**
CSF £680.14 CT £1730.13 TOTE £19.70: £6.20, £9.50, £1.70; EX 543.60 Trifecta £3036.30 Part won..
**Owner** Ushers Court **Bred** Garry Chong **Trained** Upper Lambourn, Berks

**FOCUS**
Another moderate contest, with little depth. The winner is rated close to his old best.
T/Plt: £9.60 to a £1 stake. Pool of £58006.55 - 4407.73 winning tickets. T/Qpdt: £7.90 to a £1 stake. Pool of £3489.03 - 326.10 winning tickets. TM

# 2637 LEICESTER (R-H)
Monday, June 2

**OFFICIAL GOING: Soft (good to soft in places; 5.9)**
Wind: Light half-behind Weather: Cloudy with sunny spells

## 2837 PYTCHLEY MAIDEN STKS 5f 218y
2:15 (2:15) (Class 5) 2-Y-0 £3,234 (£962; £481; £240) Stalls High

Form RPR
3 1 **Star Citizen**13 2428 2-9-5 0 WilliamBuick 5 88+
(Charlie Appleby) *trckd ldr: shkn up to ld over 1f out: r.o wl* 4/5[1]

05 2 4 1/2 **Thumper (FR)**12 2458 2-9-5 0 JamieSpencer 4 71
(Robert Cowell) *led: rdn and hdd over 1f out: styd on same pce* 16/1

3 1/2 **Critical Risk (IRE)** 2-9-5 0 JimmyFortune 6 72+
(Brian Meehan) *s.i.s: hld up: hdwy over 1f out: r.o: nt rch ldrs* 8/1[3]

4 1 1/2 **Mumford** 2-9-5 0 RyanMoore 2 65+
(Richard Hannon) *s.i.s: sn prom: shkn up over 2f out: styd on same pce fr over 1f out* 9/4[2]

00 5 3 3/4 **Frosty Times (FR)**14 2386 2-9-2 0 GeorgeChaloner(3) 7 54
(Richard Fahey) *prom tl rdn and wknd over 1f out* 50/1

05 6 6 **Smugglers Lane (IRE)**6 2642 2-9-5 0 AdamKirby 1 36
(David Evans) *sn pushed along in rr: wknd over 2f out* 25/1

0 7 3 **Douglas Bank (IRE)**15 2358 2-9-5 0 PaulHanagan 3 27
(Richard Fahey) *chsd ldrs tl rdn and wknd over 1f out* 20/1

1m 14.46s (1.46) **Going Correction** +0.20s/f (Good) **7** Ran SP% **113.9**
Speed ratings (Par 93): **98,92,91,89,84 76,72**
CSF £15.69 TOTE £1.90: £1.30, £5.00; EX 11.30 Trifecta £50.70.
**Owner** Godolphin **Bred** P E Barrett **Trained** Newmarket, Suffolk

**FOCUS**
The ground had dried out slightly from that forecast and was described as soft, good to soft in places. A couple of the riders in the opener described conditions as "on the easy side" and "holding". Things proved very straightforward for the warm favourite in this uncompetitive maiden. This is usually a very good race and a positve view has been taken of the form.

## 2838 HICKLING (S) STKS 5f 218y
2:45 (2:47) (Class 6) 3-5-Y-0 £2,045 (£603; £302) Stalls High

Form RPR
5425 1 **Bond Club**6 2653 4-9-2 60 (b) RobertTart(3) 3 70
(Geoffrey Oldroyd) *hld up: hdwy over 2f out: led over 1f out: edgd rt and rdn clr: eased nr fin* 9/4[2]

60-0 2 3 3/4 **Ishi Honest**24 2127 4-9-0 56 JimmyFortune 1 53
(Mark Usher) *chsd ldrs: led wl over 1f out: sn rdn and hdd: no ex ins fnl f* 12/1[3]

5400 3 shd **Sandsman's Girl (IRE)**6 2657 3-8-6 67 (b) FrannyNorton 6 51
(James Given) *chsd ldrs: rdn over 2f out: styd on same pce fnl f* 20/1

5020 4 1 3/4 **Sir Pedro**18 2275 5-9-5 77 GrahamLee 10 52
(Robert Cowell) *upset by rival in stalls: chsd ldrs: led over 3f out: rdn and hdd wl over 1f out: wknd ins fnl f* 11/8[1]

000- 5 1/2 **Blue Clumber**15 7454 4-8-7 48 AlexHopkinson(7) 5 45
(Shaun Harris) *led: hdd over 3f out: outpcd over 2f out: styd on ins fnl f* 25/1

0-50 6 1 1/2 **Go Charlie**44 1569 3-8-11 50 BenCurtis 7 44
(Ronald Harris) *hld up: hdwy over 3f out: sn rdn: wknd over 1f out* 50/1

0060 7 11 **Ficelle (IRE)**19 2250 5-9-0 49 (p) GrahamGibbons 8 5
(Nikki Evans) *chsd ldrs: rdn over 2f out: wknd over 1f out* 25/1

P4 8 12 **Smart Life**10 2525 3-8-4 0 (b) KieranShoemark(7) 4
(Robert Eddery) *s.i.s: sn pushed along in rr: bhd fr 1/2-way* 33/1

1m 13.67s (0.67) **Going Correction** +0.20s/f (Good)
**WFA** 3 from 4yo+ 8lb **8** Ran SP% **97.9**
Speed ratings (Par 101): **103,98,97,95,94 92,78,62**
CSF £15.89 TOTE £3.30: £1.10, £2.50, £2.80; EX 16.60 Trifecta £162.30.There was no bid for the winner.
**Owner** R C Bond **Bred** R C Bond **Trained** Brawby, N Yorks
■ Rule 4 of 20p in the pound applies to all bets; Withdrawn: Vodka Time

**FOCUS**
A moderate and uncompetitive seller. The form is rated around the winner to his best.

## 2839 BELVOIR CASTLE H'CAP (BOBIS RACE) 1m 1f 218y
3:20 (3:20) (Class 4) (0-85,84) 3-Y-0 £4,690 (£1,395; £697; £348) Stalls Low

Form RPR
14-3 1 **Anglophile**5 2685 3-9-3 80 WilliamBuick 3 93+
(Charlie Appleby) *mde all: shkn up over 2f out: styd on wl: eased nr fin* 15/8[1]

4-16 2 5 **Champagne Rules**33 1883 3-9-3 80 PaddyAspell 4 83
(Sharon Watt) *hld up: hdwy over 3f out: chsd wnr 2f out: sn rdn: hung rt and no ex ins fnl f* 25/1

-341 3 2 1/4 **Spectator**5 2671 3-8-2 72 6ex (p) KieranShoemark(7) 5 71
(Andrew Balding) *sn trcking ldrs: rdn and hung rt over 3f out: styd on same pce fr over 1f out* 4/1[3]

-212 4 3/4 **Solidarity**10 2530 3-9-7 84 MickaelBarzalona 7 82
(Charlie Appleby) *chsd wnr tl rdn 2f out: no ex fnl f* 3/1[2]

-124 5 8 **Our Gabrial (IRE)**25 2088 3-9-5 82 (v1) JamieSpencer 1 64
(Richard Fahey) *s.i.s: hld up: rdn over 2f out: sn hung rt and wknd* 4/1[3]

5200 6 19 **Intermath (IRE)**16 2333 3-9-0 77 AdamKirby 2 23
(David Evans) *prom: n.m.r over 3f out: wknd over 2f out* 14/1

2m 12.04s (4.14) **Going Correction** +0.475s/f (Yiel) **6** Ran SP% **110.3**
Speed ratings (Par 101): **102,98,96,95,89 74**
CSF £42.68 TOTE £2.10: £1.20, £9.10; EX 52.80 Trifecta £207.10.
**Owner** Godolphin **Bred** Darley **Trained** Newmarket, Suffolk

**FOCUS**
A decent 3yo handicap, but the pace looked ordinary and the winner had it all his own way. The form is rateda round the third.

## 2840 CHARNWOOD FOREST FILLIES' CONDITIONS STKS 7f 9y
3:55 (3:55) (Class 3) 3-Y-0+ £7,470 (£2,236; £1,118; £559; £279) Stalls High

Form RPR
1-21 1 **Crowley's Law**10 2510 3-8-7 89 RichardKingscote 5 102
(Tom Dascombe) *mde all: qcknd over 2f out: shkn up and edgd lft ins fnl f: r.o* 11/10[1]

20-2 2 2 1/4 **Musicora**29 1985 3-8-7 92 SeanLevey 1 95
(Richard Hannon) *hld up: hdwy over 1f out: r.o to go 2nd nr fin: nt trble wnr* 20/1

14 3 1 **Danehill Revival**33 1867 3-8-8 95 ow1 RyanMoore 2 93
(William Haggas) *trckd wnr: pushed along over 2f out: styd on same pce ins fnl f* 11/4[2]

2246 4 2 1/2 **Askaud (IRE)**18 2286 6-8-6 94 (p) MatthewHopkins(7) 3 86
(Scott Dixon) *chsd ldrs: rdn over 2f out: sn outpcd: r.o towards fin* 9/2[3]

133/ 5 1 1/2 **Desert Blossom (IRE)**597 7052 4-8-13 101 WilliamBuick 4 82
(Charlie Appleby) *hld up in tch: plld hrd: shkn up over 1f out: wknd ins fnl f* 8/1

1m 28.26s (2.06) **Going Correction** +0.20s/f (Good)
**WFA** 3 from 4yo+ 10lb **5** Ran SP% **108.3**
Speed ratings (Par 104): **96,93,92,89,87**
CSF £21.03 TOTE £1.90: £1.10, £4.00; EX 14.10 Trifecta £36.20.
**Owner** Paul Crowley & Co **Bred** Middle Park Stud Ltd **Trained** Malpas, Cheshire

**FOCUS**
An interesting fillies' conditions event, but it was another race in which the winner was allowed to dictatee.

## 2841 SHARNFORD H'CAP 7f 9y
4:25 (4:26) (Class 5) (0-75,74) 4-Y-0+ £3,234 (£962; £481; £240) Stalls High

Form RPR
1 **Sophisticated Heir (IRE)**61 1253 4-9-6 73 DavidNolan 4 81+
(David O'Meara) *chsd ldr tl led over 2f out: rdn and hung rt over 1f out: hdd ins fnl f: rallied to ld post* 5/2[1]

0066 2 hd **Fieldgunner Kirkup (GER)**13 2425 6-9-7 74 GrahamGibbons 2 81
(David Barron) *led over 4f: sn rdn: led again ins fnl f: sn hung rt: hdd post* 4/1[2]

2054 3 hd **My Son Max**28 2012 6-9-2 69 [1] RichardKingscote 1 75
(Michael Blake) *hld up: pushed along 1/2-way: hdwy over 2f out: rdn and ev ch ins fnl f: carried rt towards fin: r.o* 6/1[3]

0530 4 1 3/4 **Illustrious Prince (IRE)**16 2341 7-9-6 73 (p) GrahamLee 5 75
(Julie Camacho) *a.p: rdn and ev ch over 1f out: styng on same pce whn nt clr run wl ins fnl f* 14/1

6525 5 5 **Ostralegus**19 2250 4-8-7 63 MichaelJMMurphy(3) 7 52
(John Gallagher) *prom: racd keenly: rdn and hung rt over 1f out: wknd ins fnl f* 7/1

3101 6 3 **Sam Spade (IRE)**14 2399 4-9-0 67 (v) DaleSwift 6 48
(Derek Shaw) *chsd ldrs: rdn over 2f out: wknd wl over 1f out* 12/1

3236 7 5 **Kyllachy Star**29 1970 8-9-0 67 (v) JamieSpencer 3 35
(Richard Fahey) *hld up: rdn 1/2-way: wknd over 2f out* 4/1[2]

1m 26.84s (0.64) **Going Correction** +0.20s/f (Good) **7** Ran SP% **109.7**
Speed ratings (Par 103): **104,103,103,101,95 92,86**
CSF £11.47 TOTE £4.30: £2.20, £2.40; EX 16.60 Trifecta £48.40.
**Owner** Colne Valley Racing **Bred** J S Bolger & John Corcoran **Trained** Nawton, N Yorks

**FOCUS**
A modest handicap, but a thrilling finish. The winner could rate a bit higher on early Irish form.

## 2842 BREEDERS BACKING RACING EBF MAIDEN STKS 1m 60y
5:00 (5:01) (Class 5) 3-Y-0 £4,528 (£1,347; £673; £336) Stalls Low

Form RPR
56 1 **Wojha (IRE)**27 2061 3-9-0 0 PaulHanagan 6 75
(William Haggas) *mde all: rdn over 1f out: styd on wl* 5/2[2]

03-4 2 3/4 **Hanno (USA)**51 1433 3-9-5 79 RyanMoore 3 78
(Ed Dunlop) *trckd wnr: shkn up over 2f out: rdn over 1f out: nt qckn towards fin* 8/13[1]

0 3 11 **Fresh Kingdom (IRE)**42 1612 3-9-5 0 HayleyTurner 7 53
(James Fanshawe) *chsd ldrs: pushed along 5f out: outpcd fr over 3f out* 16/1

00 **4** *4 1/2* **Deadline Day (IRE)**[21] 2201 3-9-5 JackMitchell 1 42
(Roger Varian) *s.i.s: sn in tch: outpcd 1/2-way: n.d after* **33/1**
**5** *2* **Opus Too (IRE)** 3-9-0 0 ShelleyBirkett(5) 5 38
(Julia Feilden) *sn pushed along in rr: bhd fr 1/2-way* **100/1**
**6** *6* **Tap Your Toes (IRE)** 3-9-5 0 LemosdeSouza 2 24
(Luca Cumani) *s.i.s: sn prom: wknd over 2f out* **8/1**[3]
1m 49.24s (4.14) **Going Correction** +0.475s/f (Yiel) **6** Ran SP% **111.4**
Speed ratings (Par 99): **98,97,86,81,79 73**
CSF £4.29 TOTE £2.90: £2.10, £1.10; EX 5.60 Trifecta £18.60.
**Owner** Hamdan Al Maktoum **Bred** Shadwell Estate Company Limited **Trained** Newmarket, Suffolk

**FOCUS**
An uncompetitive maiden, but quite a battle between the two market leaders, who finished clear. The winner was up a bit on her Kempton form.

## 2843 SWANNINGTON H'CAP (DIV I) 7f 9y
**5:30** (5:31) (Class 6) (0-60,60) 4-Y-0+ **£1,940** (£577; £288; £144) **Stalls** High

Form RPR
3240 **1** **Colour My World**[12] 2463 4-9-5 **58** (b) FrannyNorton 6 68
(Ed McMahon) *mde all: shkn up over 1f out: styd on wl* **5/1**[3]
122- **2** *2 3/4* **Pink Lips**[312] 4689 6-9-6 **59** FrederikTylicki 8 62
(J R Jenkins) *prom: lost pl over 4f out: sn pushed along: hdwy u.p over 1f out: styd on to go 2nd nr fin: nt trble wnr* **2/1**[1]
-620 **3** *3/4* **Alfresco**[68] 1105 10-9-1 **54** (b) GrahamLee 3 55
(Martin Bosley) *plld hrd and prom: wnt 2nd over 2f out: rdn over 1f out: styd on same pce ins fnl f* **12/1**
203- **4** *6* **Crossley**[181] 8141 5-9-1 **57** RobertTart(3) 9 42
(Geoffrey Oldroyd) *s.i.s: hld up: hdwy u.p over 1f out: wknd ins fnl f* **4/1**[2]
-305 **5** *2 3/4* **McCool Bannanas**[37] 1717 6-9-3 **56** (v[1]) AdamKirby 7 34
(James Unett) *trckd ldrs: rdn over 2f out: wknd fnl f* **14/1**
0050 **6** *10* **Berkeley Street (USA)**[7] 2609 4-9-0 **53** (b) MickaelBarzalona 4 5
(Jane Chapple-Hyam) *s.i.s: sn rcvrd to chse wnr tl rdn over 2f out: wknd over 1f out* **16/1**
4034 **7** *2* **Magical Rose (IRE)**[13] 2448 4-9-0 **60** JordanVaughan(7) 5 7
(Conrad Allen) *hld up in tch: rdn 1/2-way: wknd 2f out* **4/1**[2]
350- **8** *36* **Douglas Pasha (IRE)**[374] 2613 4-8-10 **54** NathanAlison(5) 2
(Martin Smith) *prom: rdn over 4f out: wknd 1/2-way* **33/1**
1m 27.27s (1.07) **Going Correction** +0.20s/f (Good) **8** Ran SP% **113.2**
Speed ratings (Par 101): **101,97,97,90,87 75,73,32**
CSF £15.09 CT £112.40 TOTE £6.60: £1.90, £1.10, £3.10; EX 9.40 Trifecta £178.30.
**Owner** Philip Wilkins **Bred** Miss K Rausing **Trained** Lichfield, Staffs

**FOCUS**
A moderate handicap and another race in which the winner was gifted a soft lead. He is rated to form.

## 2844 SWANNINGTON H'CAP (DIV II) 7f 9y
**6:05** (6:05) (Class 6) (0-60,59) 4-Y-0+ **£1,940** (£577; £288; £144) **Stalls** High

Form RPR
5P45 **1** **Botanist**[14] 2381 7-8-8 **46** BenCurtis 2 54
(Shaun Harris) *trckd ldrs: plld hrd: rdn to ld over 1f out: edgd rt: r.o* **7/2**[3]
4006 **2** *1 1/4* **High On The Hog (IRE)**[11] 2479 6-8-2 **45** NoelGarbutt(5) 7 50
(Mark Brisbourne) *plld hrd and prom: led over 2f out: rdn: edgd rt and hdd over 1f out: styd on same pce ins fnl f* **20/1**
300 **3** *shd* **Delightful Sleep**[4] 2689 6-9-5 **57** AdamKirby 3 61
(David Evans) *a.p: rdn over 1f out: edgd rt: r.o* **3/1**[2]
5-10 **4** *3 1/2* **True Spirit**[118] 467 4-8-11 **56** JoeDoyle(7) 6 51
(Paul D'Arcy) *chsd ldr: ev ch over 2f out: sn rdn: no ex fnl f* **7/1**
0112 **5** *3* **Khajaaly (IRE)**[79] 979 7-9-7 **59** (vt) AndrewMullen 4 47
(Michael Appleby) *hld up: hdwy 2f out: sn rdn: wknd fnl f* **15/8**[1]
000- **6** *4* **Hazza The Jazza**[188] 8042 4-8-10 **55** MelissaThompson(7) 9 32
(Richard Guest) *hld up: racd keenly: hung rt and wknd over 1f out* **20/1**
00-0 **7** *19* **Ptolemy**[143] 126 5-9-2 **54** FrederikTylicki 5
(David Barron) *led over 4f: rdn and wknd wl over 1f out* **12/1**
1m 27.29s (1.09) **Going Correction** +0.20s/f (Good) **7** Ran SP% **111.7**
Speed ratings (Par 101): **101,99,99,95,92 87,65**
CSF £61.18 CT £227.81 TOTE £9.30: £3.00, £5.40; EX 34.90 Trifecta £176.50.
**Owner** N Blencowe, R Booth, D Cooper, M Lenton **Bred** Cheveley Park Stud Ltd **Trained** Carburton, Notts

**FOCUS**
The winning time was only fractionally slower than the first division. The form is rated a bit cautiously.
T/Plt: £43.70 to a £1 stake. Pool of £61857.74 - 1031.93 winning tickets. T/Qpdt: £6.40 to a £1 stake. Pool of £4719.67 - 542.50 winning tickets. CR

# 2622 WINDSOR (R-H)
Monday, June 2

**OFFICIAL GOING: Good**
Wind: Almost nil Weather: Overcast, warm

## 2845 EBF STALLIONS NOVICE STKS (BOBIS RACE) 5f 10y
**6:00** (6:00) (Class 4) 2-Y-0 **£6,469** (£1,925; £962; £481) **Stalls** Low

Form RPR
611 **1** **Justice Good (IRE)**[17] 2308 2-9-9 0 JoeyHaynes(5) 1 100
(David Elsworth) *w ldr: led 1/2-way: hrd pressed after: drvn and kpt on wl fnl f* **4/1**[3]
**2** *1/2* **Smaih (GER)** 2-9-0 0 FrankieDettori 6 84+
(Richard Hannon) *s.i.s: pushed along in last early: prog on outer fr 1/2-way: rdn to chal and upsides fnl f: no ex nr fin* **8/1**
21 **3** *1/2* **Haxby (IRE)**[16] 2328 2-9-4 0 AndreaAtzeni 5 86
(Roger Varian) *free to post: w ldrs: upsides and drvn over 1f out: nt qckn last 100yds* **9/4**[2]
1 **4** *nse* **Percy Alleline**[11] 2487 2-9-7 0 JimCrowley 2 90
(Ralph Beckett) *w ldrs 2f: sn pushed along and lost pl: rallied over 1f out: hanging but kpt on fnl f: one pce nr fin* **2/1**[1]
21 **5** *nk* **Doomah (IRE)**[23] 2173 2-8-13 0 RichardHughes 4 80
(Richard Hannon) *in tch in 5th: shkn up against nr side rail 2f: tried to cl on ldrs 1f out: kpt on but nvr quite able to chal* **10/1**
1232 **6** *5* **Abscent Friends**[19] 2258 2-9-2 0 RyanWhile(5) 3 70
(Bill Turner) *racd freely: led to 1/2-way: losing pl whn short of room wl over 1f out: wknd* **16/1**
1m 0.09s (-0.21) **Going Correction** 0.0s/f (Good) **6** Ran SP% **110.2**
Speed ratings (Par 95): **101,100,99,99,98 90**
CSF £32.57 TOTE £6.40: £2.40, £3.20; EX 36.70 Trifecta £186.10.
**Owner** Robert Ng **Bred** Mrs C Regalado-Gonzalez **Trained** Newmarket, Suffolk

**FOCUS**
Top bend dolled out 12yds from normal configuration adding 47yds to races of one mile and beyond. Inner of straight dolled out 14yds at 6f and 6yds at winning post. The going had dried out to good. This novice stakes has thrown up some smart sorts in recent years, including the Prix Morny and Middle Park winner Dutch Art. There were some potentially smart types in this year's contest and it produced a close finish. A very useful effort from the winner.

## 2846 ROYAL WINDSOR RACECOURSE MONDAY CLUB NIGHT MAIDEN STKS 6f
**6:30** (6:32) (Class 5) 3-Y-0+ **£2,587** (£770; £384; £192) **Stalls** Low

Form RPR
5 **1** **Polybius**[16] 2339 3-9-4 0 TedDurcan 10 88+
(David Lanigan) *trckd ldrs on outer: prog to ld wl over 1f out: sn clr: comf* **5/4**[1]
62-3 **2** *3* **Bold Spirit**[29] 1980 3-9-4 73 RichardHughes 2 73
(Richard Hannon) *trckd ldng pair: pushed along to dispute 2nd 2f out: wnr sn wnt by: stl pushed along and styd on to take 2nd ins fnl f* **15/8**[2]
2 **3** *1/2* **Eternitys Gate**[10] 2524 3-9-4 0 JimCrowley 1 71
(Peter Chapple-Hyam) *led and r against nr side rail: rdn 2f out: sn hdd: one pce and lost 2nd ins fnl f* **8/1**[3]
0- **4** *4 1/2* **Maymyo (IRE)**[271] 6110 3-9-4 0 JamesDoyle 5 57
(Sylvester Kirk) *in tch in midfield: rdn jst over 2f out: sn outpcd: plugged on* **33/1**
0- **5** *nk* **Loot**[250] 6754 3-8-13 0 RyanWhile(5) 8 56?
(Bill Turner) *chsd ldr to 2f out: steadily wknd* **66/1**
3 **6** *3 3/4* **Dancing Angel**[16] 2329 3-8-13 0 TomQueally 3 39
(James Eustace) *t.k.h: hld up: in tch 2f out: sn shkn up and wknd* **12/1**
3- **7** *1 3/4* **Celestial Knight**[228] 7328 3-9-4 0 ShaneKelly 4 38
(James Fanshawe) *a towards rr: shkn up and no prog over 2f out: wl btn after* **8/1**[3]
0 **8** *1 3/4* **Petite Fille**[11] 2489 3-8-6 0 DavidParkes(7) 9 28
(Jeremy Gask) *stdd s: t.k.h: hld up in rr: nvr any prog* **100/1**
6 **9** *2 3/4* **Spider Bay**[27] 2044 5-9-7 0 RobertHavlin 6 21
(Lydia Richards) *a in rr: rdn and struggling over 2f out* **100/1**
5 **10** *11* **Crazy Train**[5] 2667 5-9-7 0 DavidProbert 7
(Keiran Burke) *chsd ldrs 2f: sn lost pl u.p: t.o* **66/1**
1m 12.66s (-0.34) **Going Correction** 0.0s/f (Good)
**WFA** 3 from 5yo 8lb **10** Ran SP% **117.0**
Speed ratings (Par 103): **102,98,97,91,90 85,83,81,77,62**
CSF £3.69 TOTE £2.70: £1.10, £1.10, £2.40; EX 4.60 Trifecta £13.60.
**Owner** Niarchos Family **Bred** Niarchos Family **Trained** Upper Lambourn, Berks

**FOCUS**
A number of lightly raced types in this sprint maiden. There wasn't much depth, but the winner impressed and the form makes sense.

## 2847 DAILY UNIBET EARLY PRICES FROM 9AM H'CAP 1m 67y
**7:00** (7:10) (Class 5) (0-75,72) 3-Y-O **£2,587** (£770; £384; £192) **Stalls** Low

Form RPR
-333 **1** **After The Goldrush**[7] 2624 3-9-6 **71** (b[1]) RichardHughes 3 78
(Richard Hannon) *mde all: wound pce up fr 1/2-way: drvn wl over 1f out: styd on wl and in command after* **5/1**
0-64 **2** *1 1/2* **Light Of Asia (IRE)**[35] 1817 3-9-2 **67** PaddyAspell 4 71
(Ed Dunlop) *in tch: prog wl over 2f out: rdn and styd on fr over 1f out to take 2nd ins fnl f: no real threat to wnr* **20/1**
0-22 **3** *1 1/4* **Jersey Brown (IRE)**[7] 2624 3-8-12 **66** WilliamTwiston-Davies(3) 7 67
(Mick Channon) *trckd wnr: tried to chal jst over 2f out: nt qckn over 1f out: hld after: lost 2nd ins fnl f* **2/1**[1]
025 **4** *1/2* **Red Velour**[16] 2346 3-9-7 **72** JamesDoyle 2 72
(Jeremy Noseda) *trckd ldng pair: nt qckn and outpcd over 2f out: one pce and no imp after* **3/1**[2]
-116 **5** *3/4* **Like A Prayer**[17] 2307 3-9-3 **68** JimCrowley 9 66
(Ralph Beckett) *hld up in last pair: sme prog on outer over 2f out: reminder over 1f out: kpt on same pce after: nvr really threatened* **9/2**[3]
46-6 **6** *3* **Charlie Wells (IRE)**[36] 1765 3-9-2 **67** TomQueally 1 58
(Eve Johnson Houghton) *s.s: mostly in last pair: rdn over 2f out: no imp on ldrs* **14/1**
0-23 **7** *2 1/4* **Royal Encounter**[118] 477 3-9-2 **67** JimmyQuinn 5 53
(Ed Vaughan) *chsd ldrs: rdn 3f out: sn lost pl and btn* **12/1**
50-0 **8** *12* **Orlando Star (CAN)**[27] 2058 3-8-11 **65** OisinMurphy(3) 8 24
(Roger Teal) *t.k.h: in tch tl wknd 3f out: t.o* **25/1**
1m 46.17s (1.47) **Going Correction** +0.125s/f (Good) **8** Ran SP% **116.1**
Speed ratings (Par 99): **97,95,94,93,93 90,87,75**
CSF £95.25 CT £263.81 TOTE £5.60: £1.40, £4.80, £1.10; EX 123.50 Trifecta £389.20.
**Owner** The Gold Rush Partnership **Bred** The Pocock Family **Trained** East Everleigh, Wilts
■ Ixelles Diamond was withdrawn. Price at time of withdrawal 8/1. Rule 4 applies to bets struck prior to withdrawal but not to SP bets. Deduct 10p in the pound. New market formed.
■ Stewards' Enquiry : Paddy Aspell two-day ban: used whip down shoulder in the forehand (Jun 16,22)

**FOCUS**
A modest 3yo handicap but an all-the way winner, who's rated up 4lb.

## 2848 WEATHERBYS PRIVATE BANKING LEISURE STKS (LISTED RACE) 6f
**7:30** (7:35) (Class 1) 3-Y-O+ **£20,982** (£7,955; £3,981; £1,983; £995; £499) **Stalls** Low

Form RPR
21-0 **1** **Rocky Ground (IRE)**[30] 1949 4-9-0 103 AndreaAtzeni 1 114
(Roger Varian) *hld up in 9th: rdn and prog fr 2f out: clsd on ldrs 1f out: led 100yds out: sn clr: slipped up after fin* **16/1**
120- **2** *2* **Rex Imperator**[268] 6193 5-9-0 110 FrankieDettori 2 107+
(William Haggas) *w.w in last quartet: stl there 2f out: shkn up over 1f out: gd prog fnl f: tk 2nd last strides: too much to do* **7/1**[3]
33-4 **3** *hd* **Professor**[37] 1728 4-9-0 108 SeanLevey 15 107+
(Richard Hannon) *chsd ldrs on outer: outpcd and struggling in rr sn after 1/2-way: rdn over 1f out: styd on to take 3rd post* **8/1**
3-44 **4** *hd* **Justice Day (IRE)**[9] 2563 3-8-6 108 OisinMurphy 10 104
(David Elsworth) *prom: chsd ldr 1/2-way: drvn over 2f out: clsd to ld jst ins fnl f: hdd last 100yds: lost 2 pls nr fin* **9/1**
12-4 **5** *3/4* **Highland Colori (IRE)**[23] 2150 6-9-0 111 DavidProbert 7 104
(Andrew Balding) *chsd ldr to 1/2-way: styd prom: rdn over 2f out: one pce fr over 1f out* **8/1**
02-1 **6** *1/2* **Music Master**[39] 1679 4-9-0 108 DaneO'Neill 12 102
(Henry Candy) *led at str pce: hdd and fdd jst ins fnl f* **4/1**[1]
10-4 **7** *nk* **Morache Music**[23] 2149 6-9-0 105 JimmyFortune 6 101
(Peter Makin) *hld up in last quartet: stl there 2f out: n.m.r against rail sn after: styd on fnl f: nrst fin* **20/1**

-500 **8** *nk* **Lancelot Du Lac (ITY)**[19] 2254 4-9-0 102 .......... JimCrowley 11 100
(Dean Ivory) *racd on own out wd: prom: nt qckn 2f out: nvr quite on terms after* **16/1**

254- **9** *shd* **Minalisa**[240] 7021 5-8-9 100 .......... ChrisCatlin 5 95
(Rae Guest) *chsd ldrs: drvn over 2f out: nt qckn over 1f out: one pce after: lost pls nr fin* **33/1**

2-20 **10** *shd* **Montiridge (IRE)**[16] 2338 4-9-0 114 .......... RichardHughes 4 99+
(Richard Hannon) *hld up in last quartet: swtchd lft and shkn up 1f out: styd on quite takingly but no ch* **9/2**[2]

0030 **11** *1 1/4* **Hitchens (IRE)**[46] 1531 9-9-0 102 .......... GrahamGibbons 9 95
(David Barron) *nvr beyond midfield: no prog u.p 2f out: wknd* **33/1**

31-0 **12** *3/4* **Boomerang Bob (IRE)**[19] 2256 5-9-0 100 .......... SebSanders 13 93
(J W Hills) *s.i.s: sn in tch in midfield on outer: rdn 2f out: steadily wknd* **25/1**

1-00 **13** *1 3/4* **Valbchek (IRE)**[19] 2254 5-9-4 100 .......... (b) ShaneKelly 14 91
(Jeremy Noseda) *s.i.s: swtchd fr wd draw and hld up in last quartet: shkn up and no prog over 1f out* **50/1**

30-6 **14** *99* **March**[44] 1572 4-8-9 99 .......... SteveDrowne 3
(Robert Cowell) *virtually ref to r: allowed to amble home* **16/1**

1m 11.17s (-1.83) **Going Correction** 0.0s/f (Good)
**WFA** 3 from 4yo+ 8lb **14 Ran SP% 117.0**
Speed ratings (Par 111): **112,109,109,108,107 107,106,106,106,106 104,103,101,**
CSF £113.89 TOTE £18.90: £4.60, £2.60, £2.90; EX 120.80 Trifecta £2147.30.
**Owner** Clipper Logistics & Cheveley Park Stud **Bred** Messrs Mark Hanly & James Hanly **Trained** Newmarket, Suffolk

**FOCUS**
A big field for this Listed sprint and the draw played its part, with the first two, who were drawn against the rails, coming from off the pace to fill the first two places. A personal best from the winner.

## 2849 UNIBET BY PLAYERS FOR PLAYERS H'CAP 6f

**8:00** (8:02) (Class 3) (0-95,95) 4-Y-O+ **£7,439** (£2,213; £1,106; £553) **Stalls** Low

Form RPR

0-40 **1** **Clear Spring (IRE)**[24] 2110 6-9-5 **93** .......... LiamJones 5 103
(John Spearing) *chsd clr ldr: rdn 2f out: clsd to ld 1f out: edgd rt fnl f: styd on wl* **9/2**[2]

10-0 **2** *2* **B Fifty Two (IRE)**[24] 2110 5-8-13 **87** .......... (bt) FrankieDettori 2 93
(J W Hills) *led and clr against nr side rail: rdn 2f out: hdd 1f out: hld whn short of room ins fnl f: hld on for 2nd* **16/1**

-002 **3** *shd* **Cruise Tothelimit (IRE)**[3] 2732 6-7-13 **78** .......... JoeyHaynes(5) 8 82
(Ian Williams) *t.k.h: chsd ldrs: rdn 2f out: styd on fnl f to press for 2nd nr fin* **9/2**[2]

3-00 **4** *1* **Joe Packet**[10] 2503 7-8-13 **87** .......... JimCrowley 7 87
(Jonathan Portman) *chsd ldrs: short of room briefly 1/2-way: kpt on fr over 1f out but nvr gng pce to chal* **7/1**[3]

0041 **5** *2* **Born To Surprise**[23] 2157 5-9-3 **91** .......... StevieDonohoe 10 85
(Lee Carter) *s.i.s: towards rr: rdn 2f out: one pce and no imp on ldrs* **10/1**

30-1 **6** *nk* **Huntsmans Close**[49] 1492 4-9-0 **88** .......... JamesDoyle 4 81
(Roger Charlton) *chsd ldrs but nvr on terms: rdn 2f out: no hdwy* **3/1**[1]

/0-0 **7** *1* **Waffle (IRE)**[16] 2353 8-9-7 **95** .......... RichardHughes 6 85
(David Barron) *hld up in last pair: jst pushed along fr 2f out: no prog and nvr involved* **10/1**

0644 **8** *hd* **Triple Chocolate**[7] 2629 4-8-2 **76** oh4 .......... JimmyQuinn 3 65
(Roger Ingram) *s.i.s: chsd ldrs: lost pl and rdn over 2f out: no prog and btn over 1f out* **7/1**[3]

2220 **9** *1* **Mac's Power (IRE)**[63] 1212 8-8-4 **78** .......... ChrisCatlin 9 64
(Willie Musson) *hld up in last pair: jst pushed along fr 2f out: nvr involved: eased last strides* **33/1**

1m 11.66s (-1.34) **Going Correction** 0.0s/f (Good) **9 Ran SP% 113.4**
Speed ratings (Par 107): **108,105,105,103,101 100,99,99,97**
CSF £71.10 CT £341.85 TOTE £5.20: £1.70, £4.00, £2.00; EX 81.60 Trifecta £388.80.
**Owner** H James **Bred** Rocal Bloodstock **Trained** Kinnersley, Worcs

**FOCUS**
A decent sprint handicap run just under half a second slower than the preceding Listed race. Nothing came from off the pace this time. Another step up from the winner.

## 2850 MAINSTONE CELEBRATION MAIDEN AUCTION STKS 1m 2f 7y

**8:30** (8:31) (Class 5) 3-Y-O **£2,587** (£770; £384; £192) **Stalls** Centre

Form RPR

-224 **1** **Cape Caster (IRE)**[16] 2347 3-9-4 80 .......... JimCrowley 7 83+
(Ralph Beckett) *trckd ldng trio: prog to chse clr ldr 2f out: drvn and clsd fr over 1f out: styd on to ld last strides* **1/1**[1]

36 **2** *hd* **Cincinnati Girl (IRE)**[14] 2404 3-8-4 0 ow1 .......... OisinMurphy(3) 12 72
(Denis Coakley) *led: kicked on 3f out and sn clr: drvn over 1f out: kpt on but collared last strides* **7/2**[2]

22-4 **3** *7* **Black Label**[26] 2081 3-9-1 74 .......... TomQueally 9 66
(Harry Dunlop) *mostly chsd ldr to 2f out: easily outpcd but clung on for 3rd u.p* **10/1**[3]

06- **4** *1/2* **Scoppio Del Carro**[207] 7780 3-9-1 0 .......... (t) DavidProbert 6 65+
(Andrew Balding) *hld up in midfield: pushed along over 2f out: prog wl over 1f out: shkn up to press for 3rd fnl f* **16/1**

0 **5** *1 1/2* **Pink Diamond**[24] 2109 3-8-8 0 .......... JimmyQuinn 3 56
(Eve Johnson Houghton) *chsd ldrs in 5th: rdn 3f out: tried to press for a pl over 1f out: one pce fnl f* **16/1**

0-0 **6** *2 3/4* **Rochambeau (IRE)**[16] 2334 3-9-4 0 .......... JamesDoyle 11 60+
(Roger Charlton) *hld up in last quartet: pushed along fr 3f out: nvr involved but kpt on fnl 2f: possible improver* **12/1**

0- **7** *shd* **Sheer Poetry (IRE)**[244] 6922 3-8-9 0 ow1 .......... (e[1]) ShaneKelly 8 51
(Mike Murphy) *hld up and a abt same pl: pushed along and one pce fr over 2f out* **66/1**

0-0 **8** *1/2* **Beakers N Num Nums (IRE)**[16] 2346 3-8-13 0 .......... GrahamGibbons 1 54
(William Jarvis) *t.k.h early: hld up in last quartet: pushed along fr 3f out: nvr involved but kpt on: possible improver* **25/1**

5-5 **9** *2* **Haleo**[13] 2418 3-8-13 0 .......... RichardHughes 5 50
(William Muir) *wl in tch in 6th: no prog whn shkn up over 2f out: eased ins fnl f* **14/1**

6 **10** *6* **Pindora (GER)**[10] 2511 3-8-8 0 .......... AdamBeschizza 2 34
(Noel Quinlan) *s.s: hld up in last pair: rdn 1/2-way: effrt on outer 4f out: no prog* **66/1**

-600 **11** *8* **Storm Of Choice**[54] 1382 3-8-11 36 .......... RobertHavlin 10 22
(Michael Attwater) *chsd ldng pair to 3f out: wknd qckly* **100/1**

0- **P** **Fennann**[220] 7494 3-8-11 0 .......... (p) TedDurcan 4
(Anna Newton-Smith) *hld up in last pair: hung bdly lft and rn off the crse 5f out: p.u* **100/1**

2m 11.36s (2.66) **Going Correction** +0.125s/f (Good) **12 Ran SP% 116.2**
Speed ratings (Par 99): **94,93,88,87,86 84,84,83,82,77 71,**
CSF £4.02 TOTE £1.90: £1.10, £1.90, £2.50; EX 5.60 Trifecta £26.70.

**Owner** D P Barrie & D Redhead **Bred** Eimear Mulhern **Trained** Kimpton, Hants

**FOCUS**
Maidens on this track are quite often interesting affairs featuring unexposed types, but this was relatively uncompetitive and the market leaders came right away from the rest in the last two furlongs. The winner looked a bit better than the bare form.

## 2851 FITZROY CHARITY H'CAP 1m 3f 135y

**9:00** (9:00) (Class 4) (0-80,80) 4-Y-O+ **£4,851** (£1,443; £721; £360) **Stalls** Centre

Form RPR

0-62 **1** **Jupiter Storm**[28] 2034 5-9-3 **77** .......... (p) GeorgeBaker 3 88
(Gary Moore) *mde all: clr after 4f: drvn 2f out: hanging lft but styd on: unchal* **7/4**[1]

601- **2** *8* **Ronaldinho (IRE)**[37] 7248 4-9-6 **80** .......... RichardHughes 2 77
(Alan King) *chsd wnr but lfty bhd after 4f: pushed along 4f out and sn dropped to 3rd: drvn into 2nd again over 2f out: no imp* **2/1**[2]

2420 **3** *1 1/2* **Sporting Gold (IRE)**[18] 2272 5-9-3 **77** .......... (b) TomQueally 5 72
(Roger Varian) *trckd ldng pair: rdn to chse wnr over 3f out: no imp and lost 2nd over 2f out: one pce* **5/1**[3]

1605 **4** *1* **Commissar**[14] 2405 5-9-5 **79** .......... (t) JamesDoyle 6 72
(Ian Williams) *hld up in 5th: rdn over 3f out: tried to make inroads over 2f out: no hdwy over 1f out* **6/1**

-116 **5** *13* **Swift Blade (IRE)**[62] 1219 6-9-2 **76** .......... TedDurcan 1 53
(Lady Herries) *hld up in last: pushed along 4f out: no prog 3f out: wknd over 1f out: t.o* **14/1**

/00- **6** *7* **Starfield**[15] 3157 5-9-6 **80** .......... SteveDrowne 4 44
(Seamus Mullins) *hld up in 4th: rdn 4f out: sn wknd: eased and t.o fnl f* **66/1**

2m 29.41s (-0.09) **Going Correction** +0.125s/f (Good) **6 Ran SP% 108.8**
Speed ratings (Par 105): **105,99,98,98,89 84**
CSF £5.14 TOTE £2.60: £1.70, £1.70; EX 5.60 Trifecta £16.40.
**Owner** Heart Of The South Racing **Bred** Breeding Capital, Watership Down, Farish **Trained** Lower Beeding, W Sussex

**FOCUS**
A competitive middle-distance handicap on paper, with only 4lb covering them, but in truth a one-horse race. Not form to get carried away with.
T/Jkpt: £19,541.30 to a £1 stake. Pool of £41284.57 - 1.50 winning tickets. T/Plt: £113.40 to a £1 stake. Pool of £136454.72 - 878.10 winning tickets. T/Qpdt: £21.00 to a £1 stake. Pool of £13457.34 - 474.20 winning tickets. JN

# 2260 NAAS (L-H)

### Monday, June 2

**OFFICIAL GOING: Good to yielding**

## 2855a ALFRED NOBEL ROCHESTOWN (C & G) STKS (LISTED RACE) 6f

**4:00** (4:01) 2-Y-O **£32,500** (£9,500; £4,500; £1,500)

RPR

**1** **Kool Kompany (IRE)**[14] 2403 2-9-3 .......... PatDobbs 8 101
(Richard Hannon) *t.k.h early and sn led: jnd 2f out: rallied gamely fnl f: jst hld on* **7/2**[2]

**2** *hd* **Toscanini (IRE)**[19] 2261 2-9-3 .......... ShaneFoley 2 101
(M Halford, Ire) *trckd ldr in cl 2nd: on terms 2f out: styd on wl fnl f: jst hld* **7/1**[3]

**3** *3/4* **War Envoy (USA)**[35] 1820 2-9-3 .......... JosephO'Brien 3 98
(A P O'Brien, Ire) *trckd ldrs: 3rd 1/2-way: almost on terms under 2f out: sn rdn and edgd rt ins fnl f where no imp on ldng pair: kpt on* **8/15**[1]

**4** *2 3/4* **Kasbah (IRE)**[35] 1820 2-9-3 .......... PatSmullen 9 90
(J P Murtagh, Ire) *hld up: rdn along in 4th 1f out and sn no imp on ldrs: kpt on same pce* **25/1**

**5** *nse* **I Will Excel (IRE)** 2-9-3 .......... FergalLynch 5 90+
(M D O'Callaghan, Ire) *hld up in rr tl prog 2f out: nt qckn appr fnl f: kpt on again cl home wout troubling ldrs* **33/1**

**6** *1* **Bwana (IRE)**[28] 2036 2-9-3 .......... DeclanMcDonogh 1 87
(P J Prendergast, Ire) *w.w on far side: rdn along over 2f out: nt qckn 1f out: sn one pce* **20/1**

**7** *3/4* **Intense Style (IRE)**[8] 2577 2-9-3 .......... KevinManning 6 85
(J S Bolger, Ire) *hld up: nt qckn under 2f out: sn one pce* **14/1**

**8** *2* **Sors (IRE)**[9] 2569 2-9-3 .......... WayneLordan 7 79
(Andrew Slattery, Ire) *trckd ldrs in 3rd tl rdn 2f out and sn wknd* **16/1**

1m 11.29s (-1.91) **8 Ran SP% 124.1**
CSF £29.72 TOTE £5.30: £1.40, £2.20, £1.02; DF 23.70 Trifecta £83.00.
**Owner** Middleham Park Racing LXXXVI **Bred** Miss Imelda O'Shaughnessy **Trained** East Everleigh, Wilts

**FOCUS**
Stubbs won this last year before being sent off favourite for the Coventry Stakes and this looked an up-to-scratch renewal. Four of the eight runners had tasted success and the odds-on favourite brought a big reputation, emphasised by his strength in the market. It produced a thrilling finish and a brave winner. The compressed finish holds down the form.

## 2856a COOLMORE STUD EUROPEAN BREEDERS FUND FILLIES' SPRINT STKS (LISTED RACE) 6f

**4:30** (4:31) 2-Y-O **£31,145** (£9,104; £4,312; £1,437)

RPR

**1** **Beach Belle**[71] 1073 2-9-0 .......... ChrisHayes 3 97+
(Kevin Prendergast, Ire) *hld up in rr: niggled along to take clsr order 2f out: styd on strly on outer to ld fnl 100yds* **15/8**[1]

**2** *3/4* **Realtra (IRE)**[18] 2269 2-9-0 .......... KevinManning 5 95
(Richard Fahey) *trckd ldr in 2nd tl led briefly ins fnl f: hdd fnl 100yds and no match for wnr: kpt on* **7/1**

**3** *1* **Stormfly (IRE)**[51] 1456 2-9-0 .......... PatSmullen 2 92
(D K Weld, Ire) *hld up towards rr: last 2f out: kpt on wl ins fnl f: nrst fin* **11/1**

**4** *shd* **Spirit Of Xian (IRE)**[17] 2302 2-9-0 .......... PatDobbs 8 91
(Richard Hannon) *sn led: pressed fr 2f out: hdd ins fnl f: kpt on one pce* **4/1**[3]

**5** *1* **Newsletter (IRE)**[50] 1470 2-9-0 .......... ShaneFoley 6 88
(K J Condon, Ire) *hld up: prog briefly in 3rd 1f out: no imp whn short of room on inner fnl 100yds* **10/3**[2]

**6** *1* **Red Ivy (IRE)**[9] 2568 2-9-0 .......... FMBerry 4 85
(P D Deegan, Ire) *chsd ldrs in 4th towards inner: rdn along and nt qckn whn short of room over 1f out: sn no ex* **20/1**

**7** *1 1/4* **She's A Pistol (IRE)**[19] 2260 2-9-0 .......... DeclanMcDonogh 7 82
(P J Prendergast, Ire) *t.k.h and trckd ldrs in 3rd tl wknd qckly appr fnl f* **9/1**

1m 12.37s (-0.83) **7 Ran SP% 113.5**
CSF £15.48 TOTE £3.10: £2.20, £3.10; DF 12.70 Trifecta £104.70.



The Form Book, Raceform Ltd, Newbury, RG14 5SJ

**Owner** Lady O'Reilly **Bred** Castlemartin Sky & Skymarc Farm **Trained** Friarstown, Co Kildare

**FOCUS**

They crawled through the early stages of this which makes the performance of the winner, who swept from last to first down the outside, all the more admirable. She could prove to be a top-notch filly, but the bare form is limited with the time not quick.

2857 - 2858a (Foreign Racing) - See Raceform Interactive

## 2716 BRIGHTON (L-H)

Tuesday, June 3

**OFFICIAL GOING: Good to firm (good in places; 7.0)**

Wind: Moderate, half against Weather: Cloudy

### 2859 BRITISH STALLION STUDS EBF MAIDEN STKS — 5f 213y

**2:10** (2:11) (Class 5) 2-Y-O — **£2,911** (£866; £432; £216) **Stalls Low**

Form — RPR

3 **1** **When Will It End (IRE)**[13] 2458 2-9-5 0 RichardHughes 6 73+
(Richard Hannon) *chsd ldrs: led ins fnl f: drvn out* **7/2**[2]

**2** *nk* **The Dapper Tapper (IRE)** 2-9-5 0 ShaneKelly 2 72
(Eve Johnson Houghton) *dwlt: sn in tch: rdn 2f out: led 1f out tl ins fnl f: kpt on* **16/1**

43 **3** *1 1/2* **Simply Magic (IRE)**[29] 2022 2-9-0 0 SeanLevey 7 63
(Richard Hannon) *chsd ldr: led briefly over 1f out: one pce fnl f* **8/1**

5 **4** *1* **Offshore**[15] 2380 2-9-5 0 AdamKirby 4 65
(James Tate) *in tch: outpcd 2f out: rallied and r.o fnl f* **5/1**[3]

0 **5** *1/2* **Barchan (USA)**[30] 1977 2-9-5 0 (t) MartinLane 1 63
(Charlie Appleby) *led tl over 1f out: no ex fnl f* **6/4**[1]

0 **6** *nse* **Western Playboy (IRE)**[18] 2298 2-9-5 0 JimCrowley 5 63
(Sylvester Kirk) *prom: nt clr run 2f out: no imp fnl f* **20/1**

0 **7** *nk* **Pinter**[12] 2480 2-9-5 0 AhmedAjtebi 8 62+
(Charlie Appleby) *towards rr: rdn over 2f out: styng on at fin* **8/1**

6 **8** *2 3/4* **Wink Oliver**[6] 2666 2-9-2 0 WilliamTwiston-Davies(3) 9 54
(Mick Channon) *stdd in last pl s: bhd: rdn over 2f out: n.d* **50/1**

**9** *11* **Lady Ballantrae (IRE)** 2-9-0 0 HayleyTurner 3 16
(Simon Dow) *dwlt: towards rr: n.m.r over 4f out: rdn 3f out: wknd 2f out* **66/1**

1m 12.08s (1.88) **Going Correction** +0.25s/f (Good) **9 Ran SP% 115.2**

Speed ratings (Par 93): **97,96,94,93,92 92,92,88,73**

CSF £55.11 TOTE £4.70: £1.60, £4.90, £1.70; EX 77.70 Trifecta £368.70.

**Owner** Michael Buckley **Bred** Mountarmstrong Stud **Trained** East Everleigh, Wilts

**FOCUS**

Rail dolled out from 4.5f to 2.5f. Sean Levey described the going as "good, lovely ground". There was a rather bunched finish to this juvenile maiden. Fair form, the winner an improver.

### 2860 T M LEWIN, SHIRTS, SUITS AND MORE H'CAP — 6f 209y

**2:40** (2:40) (Class 6) (0-60,59) 3-Y-O — **£1,940** (£577; £288; £144) **Stalls Low**

Form — RPR

2122 **1** **Clapperboard**[13] 2469 3-9-3 55 (b) WilliamCarson 5 61
(Paul Fitzsimons) *mde all: qcknd clr over 2f out: hrd rdn over 1f out: drvn to hold on fnl 100yds* **5/2**[2]

5-50 **2** *1/2* **Tubeanie (IRE)**[22] 2224 3-9-7 59 AdamKirby 2 63
(Clive Cox) *chsd ldrs: wnt 4 l 2nd over 2f out: drvn to cl on wnr fnl f: jst hld* **2/1**[1]

6350 **3** *2 1/2* **Bold Max**[15] 2397 3-8-7 45 (b) LiamJones 3 43
(Zoe Davison) *stdd in rr s: styd on u.p fnl 2f: nt rch ldrs* **50/1**

00-4 **4** *1/2* **Bishop Wulstan (IRE)**[14] 2416 3-9-1 53 ASandesh 10 50+
(Richard Hannon) *hld up in rr: rdn 3f out: styd on fr over 1f out* **4/1**[3]

40-0 **5** *5* **Morgans Bluff**[64] 1211 3-8-7 48 OisinMurphy(3) 1 32
(Pat Phelan) *chsd ldrs: rdn 3f out: wknd wl over 1f out* **14/1**

0060 **6** *5* **Dover The Moon (IRE)**[19] 2281 3-8-10 48 (t) SeanLevey 4 19
(Sylvester Kirk) *in tch: rdn over 2f out: wknd wl over 1f out: eased whn btn ins fnl f* **16/1**

3-50 **7** *2 1/2* **Dancing Sal (IRE)**[130] 311 3-9-7 59 RichardHughes 7 23
(Brett Johnson) *chsd wnr tl over 2f out: wknd wl over 1f out: eased whn btn ins fnl f* **5/1**

1m 25.38s (2.28) **Going Correction** +0.25s/f (Good) **7 Ran SP% 113.1**

Speed ratings (Par 97): **96,95,92,92,86 80,77**

CSF £7.74 CT £181.03 TOTE £3.10: £1.80, £1.60; EX 8.20 Trifecta £146.70.

**Owner** Saxon Gate Bloodstock (Helene Moller) **Bred** Theakston Stud **Trained** Upper Lambourn, Berks

■ Stewards' Enquiry : Adam Kirby two-day ban: used whip above permitted level (Jun 22-23)

**FOCUS**

The right horses came to the fore in what was a moderate handicap. The winner is rated back to something like her best.

### 2861 JANES' SOLICITORS FILLIES' H'CAP — 6f 209y

**3:10** (3:10) (Class 4) (0-85,83) 4-Y-O+ — **£4,690** (£1,395; £697; £348) **Stalls Low**

Form — RPR

5322 **1** **Saucy Minx (IRE)**[11] 2528 4-9-4 81 (b) JimCrowley 4 89
(Amanda Perrett) *hld up in 4th: hrd rdn and hdwy over 1f out: edgd lft: styd on to ld nr fin* **4/1**[3]

1-53 **2** *1/2* **Interception (IRE)**[24] 2157 4-9-6 83 TedDurcan 1 90
(David Lanigan) *cl up in 3rd: led wl over 1f out: edgd rt 1f out: rdn fnl f: ct nr fin: b.b.v* **6/4**[1]

5313 **3** *1 3/4* **Alice's Dancer (IRE)**[18] 2318 5-9-0 80 OisinMurphy(3) 3 82
(William Muir) *plld hrd: chsd ldr tl 2f out: hrd rdn: one pce* **5/2**[2]

5502 **4** *nk* **Subtle Knife**[18] 2318 5-9-2 79 PatrickDonaghy 2 80
(Giles Bravery) *sn detached in last: rdn over 2f out: stl last but styng on whn nt clr run ins fnl f: swtchd rt: gng on at fin* **15/2**

0-41 **5** *3/4* **Al Manaal**[25] 2121 4-9-2 82 WilliamTwiston-Davies(3) 5 81
(Mick Channon) *led tl wl over 1f out: no ex ins fnl f* **9/1**

1m 25.39s (2.29) **Going Correction** +0.25s/f (Good) **5 Ran SP% 110.3**

Speed ratings (Par 102): **96,95,93,93,92**

CSF £10.52 TOTE £5.70: £3.00, £1.10; EX 12.90 Trifecta £29.50.

**Owner** Mr & Mrs F Cotton, Mr & Mrs P Conway **Bred** Summerhill & J Osborne **Trained** Pulborough, W Sussex

**FOCUS**

A fair handicap for the grade but a muddling race and a relatively slow time. A small personal best from the winner.

### 2862 LOTHBURY INVESTMENT MANAGEMENT H'CAP — 1m 1f 209y

**3:40** (3:40) (Class 5) (0-75,74) 4-Y-O+ — **£2,587** (£770; £384; £192) **Stalls High**

Form — RPR

2-21 **1** **Ifan (IRE)**[52] 1454 6-8-13 71 DanielMuscutt(5) 8 78
(Tim Vaughan) *mde virtually all: hld on gamely u.p fnl 2f* **11/4**[2]

1510 **2** *hd* **Cravat**[11] 2519 5-9-4 74 OisinMurphy(3) 3 80
(Ed de Giles) *t.k.h: prom: jnd ldr 2f out and sustained chal: kpt on wl: jst hld* **7/1**[3]

40-3 **3** *1/2* **Evervescent (IRE)**[18] 2300 5-9-3 70 AdamKirby 7 75
(Graeme McPherson) *hld up in rr: hdwy to chse ldrs over 1f out: hung lft: styd on* **7/1**[3]

3120 **4** *1* **Gaelic Silver (FR)**[5] 2702 8-8-12 72 HectorCrouch(7) 4 75
(Gary Moore) *in tch: drvn to press ldrs over 1f out: kpt on same pce* **12/1**

2444 **5** *1 3/4* **Bennelong**[7] 2651 8-8-0 60 oh1 (v) CharlotteJenner(7) 2 62
(Lee Carter) *t.k.h in rr: swtchd lft and hdwy over 1f out: in tch and styng on whn hmpd and snatched up ins fnl f: nt rcvr* **16/1**

450 **6** *nse* **Lady Lunchalot (USA)**[33] 1899 4-9-7 74 LiamJones 5 74
(Laura Mongan) *chsd ldrs: outpcd 2f out: styng on again at fin* **14/1**

4332 **7** *1/2* **Standing Strong (IRE)**[32] 1919 6-8-9 62 (p) JimCrowley 1 61
(Zoe Davison) *hld up in 6th: rdn and hdwy 2f out: no ex 1f out* **10/1**

-653 **8** *3* **Aint Got A Scooby (IRE)**[19] 2270 4-9-2 74 (p) RyanTate(5) 6 67
(Clive Cox) *chsd ldr: n.m.r and hit rail over 4f out: rallied 2f out: hung lft and hit rail over 1f out: sn wknd: fatally injured* **9/4**[1]

2m 6.12s (2.52) **Going Correction** +0.25s/f (Good) **8 Ran SP% 111.8**

Speed ratings (Par 103): **99,98,98,97,96 96,95,93**

CSF £21.22 CT £117.92 TOTE £3.70: £1.30, £2.60, £1.70; EX 21.60 Trifecta £84.90.

**Owner** WRB Racing 61 and Derek & Jean Clee **Bred** Dr John Waldron **Trained** Aberthin, Vale of Glamorgan

■ Stewards' Enquiry : Daniel Muscutt four-day ban: used whip above permitted level (Jun 22-25)

**FOCUS**

A modest handicap that saw a thoroughly game performance the winner, who rates a length personal best.

### 2863 BRIGHTON & HOVE STREAMLINE TAXIS H'CAP — 1m 1f 209y

**4:10** (4:10) (Class 6) (0-60,63) 4-Y-O+ — **£1,940** (£577; £288; £144) **Stalls High**

Form — RPR

-000 **1** **Gung Ho (FR)**[27] 2084 5-8-10 46 MartinLane 4 57
(Tony Newcombe) *prom: wnt 4 l 2nd over 2f out: clsd on ldr over 1f out: led ins fnl f: pushed out* **8/1**

0262 **2** *1 1/2* **Litmus (USA)**[4] 2720 5-8-13 49 (b) HayleyTurner 9 57
(Simon Dow) *led after 1f and sn clr: 5 l ahd 1/2-way: drvn along fnl 2f: hdd ins fnl f: no ex* **11/4**[2]

2346 **3** *2 3/4* **Petersboden**[27] 2066 5-9-0 50 FergusSweeney 3 53
(Michael Blanshard) *hld up in 6th: rdn and hdwy over 1f out: styd on fnl f* **10/1**

15 **4** *3/4* **Stanlow**[98] 737 4-9-6 56 (v) StephenCraine 7 58
(Daniel Mark Loughnane) *hld up in 5th: rdn to chse ldrs 2f out: one pce* **7/1**[3]

2-41 **5** *7* **Monopoli**[8] 2609 5-9-13 63 6ex (p) RichardHughes 2 51
(Chris Dwyer) *chsd ldrs: rdn over 3f out: wknd wl over 1f out* **2/1**[1]

6-50 **6** *2 1/4* **Chella Thriller (SPA)**[27] 1354 5-9-7 57 (b) GeorgeBaker 5 41
(Alastair Lidderdale) *a bhd* **10/1**

0354 **7** *6* **Highly Likely (IRE)**[27] 2066 5-8-13 49 JimCrowley 1 22
(Steve Woodman) *led 1f: chsd ldr after tl over 2f out: sn wknd* **8/1**

2m 6.14s (2.54) **Going Correction** +0.25s/f (Good) **7 Ran SP% 112.9**

Speed ratings (Par 101): **99,97,95,95,89 87,82**

CSF £29.49 CT £222.56 TOTE £13.00: £5.60, £1.80; EX 48.40 Trifecta £281.90.

**Owner** A T Owen **Bred** Mrs Kim Sundgren **Trained** Yarnscombe, Devon

**FOCUS**

Low-grade handicap form. The winner's best form since his British debut.

### 2864 SAGA HOLIDAYS H'CAP — 7f 214y

**4:40** (4:40) (Class 6) (0-60,59) 4-Y-O+ — **£1,940** (£433; £433; £144) **Stalls Low**

Form — RPR

333 **1** **Last Minute Lisa (IRE)**[5] 2689 4-8-12 50 RichardHughes 5 59
(Sylvester Kirk) *t.k.h: in tch: effrt and gng wl 2f out: qcknd to ld ins fnl f* **2/1**[1]

0450 **2** *1* **Silvee**[5] 2689 7-8-11 49 (p) WilliamCarson 1 56
(John Bridger) *led 3f: led jst over 1f out tl ins fnl f: unable qck* **16/1**

3200 **2** *dht* **Lutine Charlie (IRE)**[37] 1771 7-8-12 53 OisinMurphy(3) 2 60
(Pat Eddery) *chsd ldr: led after 3f tl jst over 1f out: one pce* **8/1**[3]

4-40 **4** *1* **Celestial Ray**[13] 2463 5-9-7 59 RobertHavlin 3 64
(Linda Jewell) *dwlt: sn prom: rdn and one pce fnl 2f* **16/1**

3301 **5** *1 1/2* **One Way Or Another (AUS)**[29] 2596 11-9-6 58 (t) AdamKirby 11 59
(David Evans) *towards rr: rdn and hdwy over 1f out: styd on* **10/1**

6-03 **6** *hd* **Loucal**[34] 1876 4-9-0 57 (b) TobyAtkinson(5) 9 58
(Noel Quinlan) *chsd ldrs: rdn and one pce fnl 2f* **5/1**[2]

4303 **7** *2* **For Shia And Lula (IRE)**[27] 2069 5-9-7 59 (v) ShaneKelly 4 55
(Daniel Mark Loughnane) *bhd: mod effrt over 1f out: no imp fnl f* **8/1**[3]

1660 **8** *3/4* **Divine Rule (IRE)**[7] 2646 6-8-8 53 (p) CharlotteJenner(7) 13 47
(Laura Mongan) *towards rr and wd: rdn over 2f out: n.d* **25/1**

6-56 **9** *3/4* **Gypsy Rider**[90] 846 5-9-0 52 JimCrowley 10 45
(Roger Curtis) *t.k.h in midfield: outpcd 2f out: sn btn* **11/1**

0-60 **10** *6* **Breezealong Riley**[37] 1767 5-8-7 45 LiamJones 12 24
(Zoe Davison) *mid-div tl wknd over 2f out* **100/1**

00-0 **11** *dist* **My Gigi**[131] 295 4-9-6 58 GeorgeBaker 8
(Gary Moore) *ref to r: completed crse in own time* **8/1**[3]

1m 38.77s (2.77) **Going Correction** +0.25s/f (Good) **11 Ran SP% 117.4**

Speed ratings (Par 101): **96,95,95,94,92 92,90,89,88,82**

WIN: 2.30 Last Minute Lisa; PL: 1.30 Last Minute Lisa, 2.60 Lutine Charlie, 5.00 Silvee; EX: 21.30, 9.00; CSF: 9.17, 19.34; TC: 102.02, 109.33; TF: 150.00, 174.20;.

**Owner** Gerry Dolan **Bred** Geoffrey Croke **Trained** Upper Lambourn, Berks

**FOCUS**

A race that set up well for the winner. Pace held up well.

### 2865 CATERING SERVICES INTERNATIONAL H'CAP — 5f 59y

**5:10** (5:10) (Class 5) (0-70,68) 4-Y-O+ — **£2,587** (£770; £384; £192) **Stalls Low**

Form — RPR

-330 **1** **Storm Lightning**[21] 2232 5-9-7 68 GeorgeBaker 8 78
(Mark Brisbourne) *bhd: hdwy over 1f out: r.o to ld ins fnl f* **4/1**[3]

3563 **2** *1 1/4* **Welease Bwian (IRE)**[18] 2312 5-8-12 66 AaronJones(7) 3 72
(Stuart Williams) *in tch: clsd on ldrs 2f out: slt ld 1f out tl hdd and outpcd ins fnl f* **8/1**

5312 **3** *1 1/4* **Picansort**[27] 2070 7-9-3 64 (b) ShaneKelly 4 65
(Peter Crate) *chsd ldrs: led 2f out tl 1f out: one pce* **3/1**[2]

0322 **4** *2 1/4* **New Decade**[5] 2691 5-9-3 67 (t) OisinMurphy(3) 6 60
(Milton Bradley) *towards rr: effrt and hrd rdn wl over 1f out: no imp* **11/4**[1]

4445 **5** *7* **Pharoh Jake**[13] 2459 6-8-9 56 WilliamCarson 2 25
(John Bridger) *prom tl hrd rdn and wknd over 1f out* **8/1**

000 **6** *7* **Dorback**[62] 1238 7-9-1 62 (bt[1]) AdamKirby 5 6
(Tony Newcombe) *w ldrs: led over 3f out tl 2f out: wknd over 1f out* **5/1**

5050 **7** 3 3/4 **Billy Red**[34] 1878 10-9-3 **64**........(b) FergusSweeney 1
(J R Jenkins) *led over 1f: w ldrs tl wknd wl over 1f out* **25/1**
1m 3.13s (0.83) **Going Correction** +0.25s/f (Good) **7** Ran SP% **114.4**
Speed ratings (Par 103): **103,101,99,95,84 73,67**
CSF £35.01 CT £108.11 TOTE £4.90: £2.40, £4.30; EX 34.70 Trifecta £141.30.
**Owner** Law Abiding Citizens **Bred** New England Stud And Partners **Trained** Great Ness, Shropshire
**FOCUS**
No hanging around here. The winner is rated back to something like his best.
T/Plt: £64.00 to a £1 stake. Pool: £85,573.7 - 974.91 winning tickets. T/Qpdt: £19.40 to a £1 stake. Pool: £5,390.33 - 205.10 winning tickets. LM

# 2358 RIPON (R-H)
## Tuesday, June 3

**OFFICIAL GOING: Good (good to soft in places; 7.6)**
Wind: Light half behind Weather: Cloudy

## 2866 BRITISH STALLION STUDS EBF MAIDEN STKS 5f
**2:25** (2:27) (Class 5) 2-Y-0 **£3,881** (£1,155; £577; £288) **Stalls** High

Form RPR
**1** **Angelic Lord (IRE)** 2-9-5 0........ RichardKingscote 8 82+
(Tom Dascombe) *sn cl up: effrt to chal wl over 1f out: rdn to ld wl ins fnl f: kpt on* **13/8**[1]
2 **2** *nse* **Al Fareej (IRE)**[15] 2402 2-9-0 0........ GrahamLee 1 77
(James Tate) *cl up: effrt wl over 1f out: rdn to ld ent fnl f: hdd wl ins fnl f: rallied towards fin: jst hld* **15/8**[2]
**3** 1 1/4 **Adulation (IRE)** 2-9-0 0........ GrahamGibbons 2 73+
(William Haggas) *led: pushed along 2f out: rdn over 1f out: hdd ent fnl f: kpt on same pce* **7/2**[3]
**4** 1 1/2 **Flicka's Boy** 2-9-5 0........ BarryMcHugh 3 72
(Tony Coyle) *cl up on outer: rdn along 2f out: wknd ent fnl f* **14/1**
**5** *nk* **Proud Of You (IRE)** 2-9-5 0........ AndrewMullen 9 71
(Nigel Tinkler) *chsd ldrs: rdn along and outpcd bef 1/2-way: styd on appr fnl f* **16/1**
0 **6** 1/2 **Ventura Shadow**[17] 2348 2-9-0 0........ TonyHamilton 5 64+
(Richard Fahey) *prom: rdn along over 2f out: sn one pce* **33/1**
**7** *10* **Cheeky Chapman** 2-9-5 0........ TomEaves 6 33
(Clive Mulhall) *s.i.s: a outpcd and bhd* **66/1**
1m 2.19s (2.19) **Going Correction** +0.325s/f (Good) **7** Ran SP% **112.1**
Speed ratings (Par 93): **95,94,92,90,90 89,73**
CSF £4.71 TOTE £2.20: £1.10, £1.50; EX 4.40 Trifecta £10.60.
**Owner** The Mad March Hares **Bred** Joe Fogarty **Trained** Malpas, Cheshire
**FOCUS**
Rail on inner most position and distances as advertised. A couple of well-bred newcomers were taking on a rival who had shown a useful level of form on debut and a race to take a positive view of.

## 2867 FOLLOW @RIPONRACES ON TWITTER H'CAP 1m 1f 170y
**2:55** (2:56) (Class 5) (0-70,70) 3-Y-0 **£3,234** (£962; £481; £240) **Stalls** Low

Form RPR
0-32 **1** **Tower Power**[14] 2433 3-9-7 **70**........ GrahamLee 2 79
(Ismail Mohammed) *led 1f: trckd ldr: hdwy to chal 3f out: rdn along 2f out: drvn ent fnl f: kpt on to ld last 100yds* **5/2**[1]
-425 **2** 1 1/2 **Aldreth**[21] 2237 3-8-8 **57**........(p) GrahamGibbons 7 63
(Michael Easterby) *pushed along s and led after 1f: jnd 3f out and sn rdn along: drvn over 1f out: hdd and no ex last 100yds* **6/1**[3]
-363 **3** 3/4 **Nam Ma Prow**[15] 2393 3-8-2 **51**........(p) DuranFentiman 3 55
(Simon West) *trckd ldrs: hdwy to chse ldng pair over 2f out: rdn over 1f out: kpt on u.p fnl f* **20/1**
3233 **4** *5* **Truancy (IRE)**[15] 2391 3-9-6 **69**........ DanielTudhope 10 63
(K R Burke) *in tch: hdwy to chse ldrs 3f out: rdn along 2f out: sn one pce* **7/1**
00-0 **5** 1 3/4 **Mitcd (IRE)**[11] 2517 3-8-6 **58**........ GeorgeChaloner(3) 9 48
(Richard Fahey) *midfield: effrt and sme hdwy wl over 2f out: sn rdn along and nvr nr ldrs* **25/1**
05-5 **6** *3* **Moving Waves (IRE)**[15] 2393 3-8-1 **53**........ IanBrennan(3) 1 37
(Ollie Pears) *t.k.h early: in tch on inner: pushed along 4f out: rdn 3f out: sn btn* **9/1**
30-4 **7** 2 3/4 **Special Miss**[141] 167 3-9-5 **68**........ LukeMorris 5 46
(Marco Botti) *towards rr: sme hdwy 3f out: rdn along over 2f out: nvr a factor* **7/1**
-000 **8** *15* **Tawan**[8] 2616 3-8-1 **53** oh6 ow2........(p) ConnorBeasley(3) 12
(Brian Rothwell) *prom: rdn along 4f out: sn wknd* **100/1**
222 **9** *shd* **Watersmeet**[75] 1035 3-9-7 **70**........ JoeFanning 8 17
(Mark Johnston) *cl up: rdn along over 3f out: sn wknd* **7/2**[2]
0-50 **10** *nk* **Highway Pursuit**[17] 2355 3-7-12 **54**........ KieranSchofield(7) 6
(George Moore) *s.i.s: a in rr* **50/1**
040- **11** *30* **Bar Shy**[266] 6284 3-8-7 **56**........ DavidAllan 11
(Tim Easterby) *a in rr: bhd fnl 3f* **11/1**
2m 7.51s (2.11) **Going Correction** +0.125s/f (Good) **11** Ran SP% **120.0**
Speed ratings (Par 99): **96,94,94,90,88 86,84,72,72,71 47**
CSF £17.67 CT £251.72 TOTE £3.50: £1.10, £2.70, £6.40; EX 19.10 Trifecta £282.80.
**Owner** Abdulla Al Mansoori **Bred** Sir Eric Parker **Trained** Newmarket, Suffolk
**FOCUS**
A run-of-the-mill 3yo handicap in which only a few appealed as being open to improvement beforehand. Not much got into it from the rear, but that may have been more a result of the best horses racing prominently rather than any pace bias. The form seems sound enough amongst the placers.

## 2868 RIPONBET OUR PROFITS STAY IN RACING H'CAP 1m 1f 170y
**3:25** (3:25) (Class 4) (0-85,85) 4-Y-0+ **£5,175** (£1,540; £769; £384) **Stalls** Low

Form RPR
-051 **1** **St Moritz (IRE)**[7] 2654 8-9-0 **78** 6ex........(v) DanielTudhope 1 93+
(David O'Meara) *mde all: eased clr over 2f out: readily* **8/13**[1]
0-44 **2** 2 3/4 **King Of The Celts (IRE)**[40] 1660 6-7-12 **69**........ RachelRichardson(7) 6 75
(Tim Easterby) *a chsng wnr: rdn along 2f out: drvn and no imp appr fnl f* **14/1**[3]
0-51 **3** *nk* **Maybeme**[10] 2540 8-8-7 **71**........(p) AndrewElliott 4 76
(Neville Bycroft) *trckd ldrs: hdwy to chse ldng pair 3f out: rdn 2f out: drvn and kpt on same pce fnl f* **8/1**[2]
3045 **4** *4* **King Of Paradise (IRE)**[14] 2423 5-8-8 **75**........ JasonHart(3) 7 72
(Eric Alston) *hld up: effrt on outer wl over 2f out: sn rdn and no imp* **8/1**[2]
-360 **5** *nk* **Moccasin (FR)**[14] 2423 5-8-10 **74**........ PJMcDonald 2 71
(Geoffrey Harker) *hld up in rr: effrt 3f out: sn rdn along: n.d* **8/1**[2]
1100 **6** *12* **Life And Times (USA)**[45] 1578 6-9-7 **85**........ JoeFanning 3 57
(Mark Johnston) *trckd ldng pair: rdn along over 3f out: sn wknd* **18/1**
2m 5.87s (0.47) **Going Correction** +0.125s/f (Good) **6** Ran SP% **107.2**
Speed ratings (Par 105): **103,100,100,97,97 87**
CSF £9.28 TOTE £1.10: £1.30, £4.20; EX 9.80 Trifecta £37.20.
**Owner** Billy Hughes **Bred** Newsells Park Stud **Trained** Nawton, N Yorks
**FOCUS**
A handicap featuring a hotpot, who'll still be well treated on old form.

## 2869 WILMOT-SMITH MEMORIAL H'CAP 1m
**3:55** (3:56) (Class 3) (0-95,95) 4-Y-0 **£7,561** (£2,263; £1,131; £566; £282) **Stalls** Low

Form RPR
50-1 **1** **King Torus (IRE)**[14] 2425 6-8-12 **86**........ JamesSullivan 4 96
(Ruth Carr) *in tch: hdwy 3f out: effrt over 1f out: rdn to chse ldr ent fnl f: styd on u.p to ld nr fin* **12/1**
3132 **2** *nk* **Bold Prediction (IRE)**[16] 2362 4-8-9 **88**........ JoeyHaynes(5) 1 97
(K R Burke) *led: pushed along 2f out: rdn over 1f out: drvn ins fnl f: hdd and no ex nr fin* **5/2**[2]
5-11 **3** 1 3/4 **Hit The Jackpot (IRE)**[32] 1926 5-8-13 **87**........ DanielTudhope 2 92
(David O'Meara) *cl up: rdn along over 2f out: ev ch tl drvn and one pce ent fnl f* **9/4**[1]
5133 **4** *nse* **Dubai Dynamo**[12] 2478 9-8-10 **84**........ PJMcDonald 9 89
(Ruth Carr) *hld up in rr: hdwy on outer wl over 2f out: rdn to chse ldrs over 1f out: kpt on same pce fnl f* **6/1**[3]
0-03 **5** 1 3/4 **Shahdaroba (IRE)**[31] 1957 4-8-12 **86**........ GrahamLee 6 87
(Micky Hammond) *hld up towards rr: pushed along 3f out: rdn 2f out: kpt on fnl f: nrst fin* **8/1**
605- **6** 3/4 **Suits Me**[249] 6792 11-9-1 **89**........ PhillipMakin 3 88
(David Barron) *trckd ldrs on inner: hdwy over 3f out: rdn along over 2f out: wknd over 1f out* **11/1**
-040 **7** *6* **Osteopathic Remedy (IRE)**[16] 2362 10-8-13 **90**........ ConnorBeasley(3) 5 75
(Michael Dods) *trckd ldng pair: rdn along over 3f out: wknd over 2f out* **9/1**
505- **8** *6* **Smarty Socks (IRE)**[271] 6129 10-9-0 **95**........ JoshDoyle(7) 7 67
(David O'Meara) *dwlt: a in rr* **33/1**
1m 40.72s (-0.68) **Going Correction** +0.125s/f (Good) **8** Ran SP% **113.7**
Speed ratings (Par 107): **108,107,105,105,104 103,97,91**
CSF £41.81 CT £93.88 TOTE £10.70: £2.70, £1.60, £1.30; EX 42.20 Trifecta £99.00.
**Owner** Sprint Thoroughbred Racing **Bred** Whisperview Trading Ltd **Trained** Huby, N Yorks
**FOCUS**
The feature event on the card and a cracking finish with the winner wearing down the runner-up late on in a race run at a solid gallop. The winner is getting a bit closer to his old form.

## 2870 INJURED JOCKEYS FUND 50TH ANNIVERSARY CELEBRATION H'CAP 6f
**4:25** (4:29) (Class 5) (0-70,70) 3-Y-0 **£3,234** (£962; £481; £240) **Stalls** High

Form RPR
363- **1** **Thornaby Princess**[279] 5883 3-8-11 **60**........ RussKennemore 12 69
(Marjorie Fife) *trckd ldrs: swtchd lft and hdwy to ld appr fnl f: sn rdn and kpt on strly* **22/1**
60-2 **2** 1 1/2 **Fantasy Justifier (IRE)**[32] 1914 3-9-4 **67**........ BenCurtis 6 71
(Ronald Harris) *hld up towards rr: hdwy on outer over 2f out: rdn over 1f out: styd on to chse wnr ins fnl f: no imp* **9/2**[3]
013 **3** *nk* **Election Night**[18] 2295 3-9-7 **70**........ PhillipMakin 5 73
(Tim Easterby) *trckd ldrs: effrt 2f out: sn rdn: kpt on same pce fnl f* **13/8**[1]
4-42 **4** 1 1/4 **Injaz**[15] 2397 3-8-9 **63**........ KevinStott(5) 10 62
(Kevin Ryan) *sn cl up: led 2f out and sn rdn: drvn and hdd appr fnl f: one pce* **7/2**[2]
22-5 **5** *5* **Madagascar Moll (IRE)**[14] 2421 3-9-5 **68**........ DanielTudhope 7 51
(David O'Meara) *cl up: rdn along 2f out: grad wknd* **15/2**
00-0 **6** 3/4 **Shikari**[15] 2387 3-8-3 **52**........ DuranFentiman 8 33
(Robin Bastiman) *led: rdn along over 2f out: sn hdd & wknd over 1f out* **66/1**
2-36 **7** *hd* **Princess Rose**[11] 2516 3-8-13 **62**........(b) LukeMorris 9 42
(John Weymes) *chsd ldrs: rdn along over 2f out: sn drvn and wknd* **16/1**
-263 **8** 1 1/2 **Chuckamental**[10] 2551 3-8-7 **56**........(t) RoystonFfrench 13 31
(Bryan Smart) *nvr bttr than midfield* **25/1**
24-0 **9** 1/2 **Classy Lassy (IRE)**[14] 2421 3-9-3 **66**........ PaulPickard 1 40
(Brian Ellison) *carried rt s: a in rr* **33/1**
00-0 **10** *5* **Locky Taylor (IRE)**[50] 1486 3-9-2 **65**........ TomEaves 2 23
(Kevin Ryan) *wnt bdly rt s: a in rr* **28/1**
1m 14.98s (1.98) **Going Correction** +0.325s/f (Good) **10** Ran SP% **112.2**
Speed ratings (Par 99): **99,97,96,94,88 87,87,85,84,77**
CSF £109.38 CT £260.20 TOTE £25.70: £5.00, £1.80, £1.40; EX 96.80 Trifecta £353.10.
**Owner** The Fallen Angels **Bred** Dave Scott **Trained** Stillington, N Yorks
**FOCUS**
A modest sprint handicap, but the placed horses looked progressive going into the race and the winner produced a much-improved performance on her handicap debut. Sound form.

## 2871 SIS LIVE MAIDEN STKS 1m
**4:55** (4:56) (Class 5) 3-Y-0 **£3,234** (£962; £481; £240) **Stalls** Low

Form RPR
36 **1** **Moohaarib (IRE)**[17] 2334 3-9-5 0........ LukeMorris 1 83+
(Marco Botti) *trckd ldng pair: hdwy 3f out: led over 2f out: rdn clr and edgd rt ent fnl f: styd on* **1/2**[1]
0 **2** 2 3/4 **Gang Warfare**[45] 1582 3-9-5 0........ HarryBentley 6 74
(Olly Stevens) *cl up: rdn wl over 2f out: drvn and sltly outpcd over 1f out: rallied towards fin* **20/1**
4 **3** *nk* **Miyachiku**[64] 1208 3-9-5 0........ GrahamLee 8 73
(Ed Dunlop) *hld up in tch: hdwy over 3f out: swtchd rt and rdn over 1f out: chsd wnr ins fnl f: sn drvn and one pce* **11/2**[3]
32-0 **4** *5* **Rangi Chase (IRE)**[27] 2075 3-9-5 77........ DavidNolan 7 62
(Richard Fahey) *chsd ldrs: hdwy on outer 3f out: rdn wl over 1f out: sn btn* **7/2**[2]
50 **5** 1 3/4 **Moonwood**[22] 2201 3-8-9 0........ JacobButterfield(5) 2 52
(Ollie Pears) *in tch: hdwy over 3f out: rdn to chse ldrs over 2f out: sn one pce* **100/1**
0 **6** 3 1/4 **Escaping Midge (IRE)**[15] 2389 3-9-0 0........ DuranFentiman 4 45
(Tim Easterby) *t.k.h: slt ld at stdy pce: pushed along 3f out: rdn and hdd over 2f out: sn wknd* **100/1**
**7** 3 1/4 **Pepperello** 3-9-5 0........[1] JamesSullivan 9 43
(Tim Etherington) *sn pushed along and green in rr: bhd fr 1/2-way* **66/1**
1m 46.22s (4.82) **Going Correction** +0.125s/f (Good) **7** Ran SP% **112.5**
Speed ratings (Par 99): **80,77,76,71,70 66,63**
CSF £14.18 TOTE £1.30: £1.10, £7.80; EX 11.30 Trifecta £36.20.
**Owner** Sheikh Mohammed Bin Khalifa Al Maktoum **Bred** Watership Down Stud **Trained** Newmarket, Suffolk

**FOCUS**
An uncompetitive maiden run at a very steady pace early on. The winner is only rated back to his debut form.

## 2872 LADIES DAY 19TH JUNE BOOK NOW H'CAP 1m 4f 10y
5:30 (5:32) (Class 5) (0-70,75) 4-Y-O+ £3,234 (£962; £481; £240) Stalls Low

Form RPR
/021 1 **Saved By The Bell (IRE)**[6] 2678 4-9-13 **75** 6ex......... DanielTudhope 10 87+
(David O'Meara) *trckd ldrs: hdwy over 3f out: led over 2f out: sn jnd: drn and hdd briefly over 1f out: rallied to ld again ent fnl f: kpt on strly* **8/11**[1]
-146 2 2¾ **Pertuis (IRE)**[24] 2168 8-8-13 **68**..........................(p) MeganCarberry(7) 7 77
(Micky Hammond) *trckd ldrs: hdwy and cl up 3f out: rdn to chal 2f out: slt ld over 1f out: hdd ent fnl f and kpt on same pce* **14/1**
0-00 3 1¾ **Hurry Home Poppa (IRE)**[17] 2327 4-9-0 **62**................ FrannyNorton 9 67
(John Mackie) *hld up in rr: hdwy on outer over 2f out: rdn over 1f out: kpt on fnl f: nrst fin* **25/1**
-004 4 ½ **Amazing Blue Sky**[4] 2738 8-8-2 **50** oh1...................... JamesSullivan 6 56
(Ruth Carr) *hld up towards rr: hdwy on inner 3f out: effrt and n.m.r 2f out: rdn over 1f out: kpt on fnl f: nrst fin* **10/1**[3]
/00- 5 ¾ **Tropical Bachelor (IRE)**[17] 6632 8-8-2 **50**.................. AndrewMullen 5 53
(Brian Baugh) *in tch: hdwy to chse ldrs 3f out: rdn along over 2f out: grad wknd* **80/1**
1-40 6 3 **Gold Chain (IRE)**[10] 1510 4-8-12 **65**........................ EmmaSayer(5) 1 63
(Dianne Sayer) *cl up: rdn along over 3f out: wknd over 2f out* **16/1**
53-0 7 4 **Triple Eight (IRE)**[33] 1167 6-9-7 **69**.......................(b) RussKennemore 4 61
(Philip Kirby) *hld up: effrt and hdwy over 3f out: rdn along to chse ldrs over 2f out: sn wknd* **20/1**
0350 8 2 **Magnolia Ridge (IRE)**[11] 2509 4-9-6 **68**..........................(p) BenCurtis 3 57
(Kristin Stubbs) *trckd ldrs on inner: rdn along 3f out: wknd 2f out* **14/1**
1-60 9 2½ **Valentine's Gift**[17] 2327 6-8-6 **61**........................ RachelRichardson(7) 2 46
(Neville Bycroft) *hld up in rr: effrt and sme hdwy on outer 3f out: sn rdn and wknd* **25/1**
2222 10 1¼ **Missy Wells**[11] 2523 4-8-11 **62**.............................(p) JasonHart(3) 8 45
(Mark Walford) *led: rdn along over 3f out: hdd over 2f out and sn wknd* **4/1**[2]

2m 38.72s (2.02) **Going Correction** +0.125s/f (Good) 10 Ran SP% **119.9**
Speed ratings (Par 103): **98,96,95,94,94 92,89,88,86,85**
CSF £13.07 CT £160.69 TOTE £1.60: £1.10, £3.10, £6.10; EX 10.80 Trifecta £168.70.
**Owner** J Blackburn & A Turton **Bred** Dowager Countess Harrington **Trained** Nawton, N Yorks
■ Stewards' Enquiry : Emma Sayer two-day ban: careless riding (Jun 22-23)

**FOCUS**
Another one-sided betting market, which was run at a good pace. The winner can do better and the form is rated around the runner-up.
T/Plt: £5.10 to a £1 stake. Pool: £84,083.60 - 11,918.95 winning tickets. T/Qpdt: £2.60 to a £1 stake. Pool: £4,973.79 - 1,404.80 winning tickets. JR

# 2525 YARMOUTH (L-H)
Tuesday, June 3

**OFFICIAL GOING: Good to firm (7.4)**
Wind: light to medium, across Weather: overcast

## 2873 EBF STALLIONS / 4 HEAD NOVICE STKS (BOBIS RACE) 6f 3y
5:25 (5:25) (Class 4) 2-Y-O £6,301 (£1,886; £943; £472; £235) Stalls Centre

Form RPR
1 1 **Adaay (IRE)**[18] 2298 2-9-7 0.......................................... PaulHanagan 5 98+
(William Haggas) *stdd after s: t.k.h: hld up wl in tch: effrt to ld 2f out: rdn hands and heels over 1f out: asserted ins fnl f: r.o wl: comf* **5/6**[1]
1 2 ¾ **Mind Of Madness (IRE)**[48] 1512 2-9-7 0........................ JamieSpencer 6 95
(David Brown) *stdd s: hld up in tch in rr: hdwy to join ldr 2f out: sn rdn: unable qck and btn ins fnl f: kpt on same pce fnl 100yds* **5/4**[2]
1 3 3¼ **Natural Order (USA)**[31] 1936 2-9-7 0........................ WilliamBuick 1 85
(K R Burke) *t.k.h: chsd ldng pair: rdn and effrt 2f out: 3rd and outpcd over 1f out: kpt on same pce and wl hld after* **20/1**[3]
3320 4 5 **Red Connect**[15] 2395 2-9-0 0.......................................... TomQueally 4 62
(Alan McCabe) *led tl 2f out: sn rdn and struggling: wknd over 1f out* **50/1**
5 2¼ **Sallabeh** 2-8-9 0.......................................... KierenFallon 3 49
(George Margarson) *t.k.h: chsd ldr: pushed along 1/2-way: sn lost pl: wknd over 1f out* **33/1**

1m 14.36s (-0.04) **Going Correction** -0.025s/f (Good) 5 Ran SP% **108.7**
Speed ratings (Par 95): **99,98,93,87,84**
CSF £2.03 TOTE £1.60: £1.10, £1.10; EX 2.20 Trifecta £4.60.
**Owner** Hamdan Al Maktoum **Bred** L Fox **Trained** Newmarket, Suffolk

**FOCUS**
Previous winners of this novice stakes had gone on to make their mark at a much higher level and it would be foolish to believe this year's renewal will prove any different. The winner is a likely type for Ascot.

## 2874 IBULEVE H'CAP 1m 3f 101y
5:55 (5:55) (Class 6) (0-60,60) 4-Y-O+ £1,940 (£577; £288; £144) Stalls Low

Form RPR
0-33 1 **Corn Maiden**[8] 2614 5-9-2 **55**.......................................... KierenFallon 8 67
(Lydia Pearce) *hld up in tch: hdwy to chse ldr and travelling strly wl over 2f out: led jst over 1f out: rdn and drew clr fnl f: readily* **3/1**[2]
-241 2 4 **Highlife Dancer**[8] 2614 6-9-4 **60**.......................... CharlesBishop(3) 7 65
(Mick Channon) *chsd ldr tl led 3f out: rdn and clr w wnr 2f out: hdd jst over 1f out: no ch w wnr fnl f: kpt on to hold 2nd* **6/4**[1]
-325 3 1¼ **Bethan**[69] 1117 5-9-0 **58**..........................................(p) ShelleyBirkett(5) 5 61
(Julia Feilden) *chsd ldrs: 3rd and drvn 2f out: styd on same pce after* **7/1**
00-4 4 8 **Red Catkin**[14] 2443 4-9-5 **58**.......................................... TomQueally 3 48
(George Margarson) *hld up in tch in rr: effrt 3f out: 4th and hld whn unbalanced over 1f out: wl btn after* **10/1**
4235 5 3¾ **Brown Pete (IRE)**[6] 2674 6-8-6 **48**..................(tp) MichaelJMMurphy(3) 4 32
(Ann Stokell) *stdd s: hld up in tch in rr: hdwy into midfield 7f out: clsd to chse ldrs 3f out: sn rdn and no rspnse: wknd 2f out* **4/1**[3]
6-00 6 34 **Mastered (IRE)**[14] 2443 4-8-7 **46** oh1........................ SilvestreDeSousa 1
(John Best) *led tl 3f out: sn lost pl u.p and btn: t.o fnl f* **50/1**

2m 27.61s (-1.09) **Going Correction** -0.025s/f (Good) 6 Ran SP% **108.6**
Speed ratings (Par 101): **102,99,98,92,89 64**
CSF £7.36 CT £22.49 TOTE £3.70: £2.00, £1.40; EX 7.20 Trifecta £28.10.
**Owner** Ms Johanna McHugh **Bred** G B Turnbull Ltd **Trained** Newmarket, Suffolk

**FOCUS**
They went a sound pace, in a fair time for the grade. The winner reversed Leicester form with the favourite.

## 2875 AEROPAK H'CAP 1m 2f 21y
6:25 (6:25) (Class 6) (0-55,61) 4-Y-O+ £1,940 (£577; £288; £144) Stalls Low

Form RPR
05-4 1 **Elizabeth Coffee (IRE)**[16] 1761 6-8-13 **47**.................... JamieSpencer 2 58
(John Weymes) *chsd ldrs: clsd and ev ch over 2f out: rdn to ld wl over 1f out: hrd drvn and styd on fnl f* **4/1**[2]
2041 2 ½ **Minstrel Lad**[8] 2610 6-9-10 **61** 6ex........................ SimonPearce(3) 11 71
(Lydia Pearce) *stdd s: hld up in tch in last pair: clsd 3f out: swtchd rt and effrt over 1f out: chsd ldrs and drvn 1f out: ra on to press wnr wl ins fnl f: r.o but hld towards fin* **11/4**[1]
/605 3 ¾ **Frontline Phantom (IRE)**[12] 2476 7-8-12 **53**.............. PeterSword(7) 13 61
(K R Burke) *hld up in tch but styd wd of rivals in bk st: hdwy and rdn 2f out: chsd wnr 1f out: kpt on but unable qck: lost 2nd wl ins fnl f* **6/1**
1035 4 6 **Sixties Queen**[12] 2475 4-9-5 **53**.......................... KierenFallon 10 50
(Alan Bailey) *t.k.h early: hld up in tch in midfield: rdn over 3f out: chsd ldrs and drvn over 1f out: wknd fnl f* **8/1**
0562 5 ¾ **Troy Boy**[12] 2475 4-8-12 **46**.......................... SilvestreDeSousa 4 42
(Robin Bastiman) *chsd ldr: rdn and ev ch over 3f out: drvn and no ex over 1f out: wknd fnl f* **5/1**[3]
-60 6 ½ **Perseverent Pete (USA)**[15] 2399 4-8-12 **46** oh1....... AdamBeschizza 6 41
(Christine Dunnett) *led: rdn and hrd pressed over 2f out: hdd and unable qck u.p wl over 1f out: wknd fnl f* **33/1**
4040 7 hd **Entrapping**[62] 1232 4-9-2 **53**.......................... MichaelJMMurphy(3) 9 47
(John E Long) *hld up in tch in rr: clsd 4f out: rdn and no hdwy 2f out: wknd ent fnl f* **8/1**
-640 8 7 **Booktheband (IRE)**[13] 2465 4-9-1 **49**.................... MickaelBarzalona 12 30
(Clive Brittain) *wl in tch in midfield: nt clr run 3f out: rdn over 2f out: sn btn: wknd over 1f out* **16/1**
001- 9 1¼ **Impertinent**[28] 7440 4-8-9 **48**.......................... ShelleyBirkett(5) 1 27
(Noel Quinlan) *chsd ldrs: nt clr run on inner 3f out: wknd over 1f out* **20/1**

2m 9.64s (-0.86) **Going Correction** -0.025s/f (Good) 9 Ran SP% **113.4**
Speed ratings (Par 101): **102,101,101,96,95 95,95,89,88**
CSF £15.10 CT £63.62 TOTE £5.20: £1.80, £1.30, £2.20; EX 14.00 Trifecta £100.70.
**Owner** Highmoor Racing 4 & Tag Racing **Bred** David Carey **Trained** Middleham Moor, N Yorks

**FOCUS**
An ordinary handicap and painful viewing for supporters of the well backed runner-up. The first three were clear and the winner is rated to last year's turf best.

## 2876 DIOMED DEVELOPMENT H'CAP 1m 3y
6:55 (6:55) (Class 4) (0-80,80) 4-Y-O+ £4,690 (£1,395; £697; £348) Stalls Centre

Form RPR
1243 1 **Genius Boy**[10] 2540 4-8-12 **71**.......................... KierenFallon 1 85+
(James Tate) *in tch in midfield: hdwy to ld ent fnl 2f: rdn and qcknd clr over 1f out: rdn out: comf* **3/1**[1]
00-5 2 3 **One Pekan (IRE)**[29] 2033 4-9-7 **80**.......................... JamieSpencer 7 87
(Roger Varian) *stdd s: hld up in tch in rr: nt clr run over 2f out: gap opened and hdd over 1f out: chsd clr wnr jst over 1f out: r.o but no imp* **7/2**[2]
0062 3 3¼ **Tight Lipped (IRE)**[19] 2270 5-8-11 **73**.................. RosieJessop(3) 3 73
(James Eustace) *t.k.h: chsd ldr: rdn and chsd wnr wl over 1f out tl jst over 1f out: wl outpcd but kpt on for 3rd fnl f* **4/1**[3]
-340 4 2 **Handheld**[24] 2162 7-8-11 **75**..........................(p) ShelleyBirkett(5) 5 70
(Julia Feilden) *chsd ldrs tl led wl over 2f out: hdd and rdn ent fnl 2f: outpcd over 1f out: wknd fnl f* **6/1**
20-6 5 nk **Evident (IRE)**[17] 2341 4-9-4 **77**.......................... WilliamBuick 2 71
(Jeremy Noseda) *hld up in tch in last pair: swtchd lft and effrt over 2f out: 5th and no hdwy over 1f out: wknd ins fnl f* **7/1**
-140 6 ½ **Secular Society**[34] 1871 4-9-6 **79**.......................... PaulHanagan 8 72
(George Baker) *hld up in tch in midfield: rdn and effrt wl over 1f out: sn no hdwy: wknd fnl f* **33/1**
3052 7 5 **Afkar (IRE)**[11] 2527 6-8-12 **71**.......................... RyanMoore 4 53
(Clive Brittain) *t.k.h: hld up in tch in midfield: rdn 2f out: sn btn and wknd over 1f out* **10/1**
0-66 8 1¼ **Jonnie Skull (IRE)**[19] 2270 8-8-8 **70**..................(vt) SimonPearce(3) 6 49
(Lydia Pearce) *led tl wl over 2f out: sn lost pl: bhd over 1f out* **20/1**

1m 39.28s (-1.32) **Going Correction** -0.025s/f (Good) 8 Ran SP% **110.8**
Speed ratings (Par 105): **105,102,98,96,96 95,90,89**
CSF £12.70 CT £38.99 TOTE £3.80: £2.10, £1.60, £1.10; EX 14.40 Trifecta £51.10.
**Owner** Sheikh Juma Dalmook Al Maktoum **Bred** Meon Valley Stud **Trained** Newmarket, Suffolk

**FOCUS**
A competitive handicap on paper was turned into a procession by the winner. It's not hard to see him foing better.

## 2877 FREEDERM MAIDEN STKS 1m 3y
7:30 (7:31) (Class 5) 3-Y-O+ £3,072 (£914; £456; £228) Stalls Centre

Form RPR
1 **Wistar** 3-9-3 0.......................................... WilliamBuick 1 81+
(Luca Cumani) *in tch in midfield: rdn 1/2-way: hdwy to chse ldng trio over 1f out: wnt 3rd ins fnl f: str run fnl 100yds to ld nr fin* **5/2**[2]
4 2 nk **Taqneen (IRE)**[35] 1841 3-9-3 0.......................................... PaulHanagan 7 80
(Ed Dunlop) *chsd ldr tl led wl over 1f out: sn rdn: hdd jst ins fnl f: led again fnl 100yds tl hdd and no ex nr fin* **10/1**
6-3 3 shd **Zilber (GER)**[48] 1511 3-9-3 0.......................................... JamieSpencer 8 80
(Ed Dunlop) *chsd ldng trio: clsd to join ldrs 2f out: rdn and ev ch over 1f out: led jst ins fnl f: nt qckn and hdd fnl 100yds: one pce towards fin* **7/4**[1]
00- 4 3¼ **Boboli Gardens**[230] 7311 4-10-0 0......................[1] MickaelBarzalona 5 75?
(Mrs Ilka Gansera-Leveque) *pushed lft s: chsd ldrs: rdn 2f out: 3rd and no ex ent fnl f: wknd fnl 150yds* **100/1**
00 5 1½ **Margaret's Mission (IRE)**[17] 2346 3-8-12 0...............(t) SebSanders 11 64+
(Jeremy Noseda) *hld up in last quartet: rdn and hdwy over 2f out: no imp on ldrs over 1f out: kpt on* **10/1**
0- 6 hd **Matravers**[251] 6739 3-9-3 0.......................................... RyanMoore 3 68+
(Sir Michael Stoute) *hld up towards rr: rdn and hdwy over 2f out: no threat to ldrs but kpt on ins fnl f* **7/2**[3]
0- 7 7 **Almax**[206] 7817 3-9-3 0.......................................... TomQueally 6 51
(Michael Bell) *stdd and wnt lft s: hld up in midfield: rdn and short-lived effrt wl over 1f out: sn wknd* **33/1**
0- 8 ¾ **Perspicacity**[259] 6500 3-8-5 0.......................... VictorSantos(7) 2 45
(J R Jenkins) *led tl wl over 1f out: 5th and btn over 1f out: fdd ins fnl f* **150/1**

9 *10* **Mantou (IRE)** 3-9-3 0 KierenFallon 4 26
(Michael Bell) *bmpd s: a towards rr: rdn over 2f out: no hdwy: wknd over 1f out* **25/1**

25 **10** *8* **Va Benny**[26] 2095 3-9-3 0 PaoloSirigu 10 6
(J R Jenkins) *t.k.h: hld up in tch: rdn and struggling 3f: bhd over 1f out* **66/1**

**11** *8* **Arryzona** 3-9-3 0 AdamBeschizza 9
(Christine Dunnett) *s.i.s: a bhd and sn pushed along: lost tch 3f out: t.o* **100/1**

1m 40.72s (0.12) **Going Correction** -0.025s/f (Good)
**WFA** 3 from 4yo 11lb 11 Ran SP% **116.3**
Speed ratings (Par 103): **98,97,97,94,92 92,85,84,74,66 58**
CSF £26.02 TOTE £3.20: £1.10, £3.60, £1.30; EX 21.00 Trifecta £101.80.
**Owner** Sheikh Mohammed Obaid Al Maktoum **Bred** Stilvi Compania Financiera Sa **Trained** Newmarket, Suffolk

**FOCUS**
Not much depth to this and the time was relatively slow, but that apart the form looks fair.

## 2878 ADIOS H'CAP 1m 3y
**8:00** (8:00) (Class 6) (0-60,60) 3-Y-O £2,264 (£673; £336; £168) **Stalls** Centre

Form RPR
4250 **1** **Choice Of Destiny**[52] 1449 3-9-2 **60** DannyBrock(5) 11 69
(Philip McBride) *stdd s: hld up in rr: gd hdwy 2f out: rdn to chal and clr w ldr 1f out: led ins fnl f: r.o wl: drvn out* **20/1**

0012 **2** *1 ½* **Plucky Dip**[14] 2416 3-9-5 **58** KierenFallon 7 64
(John Ryan) *chsd ldr for 2f: styd chsng ldr tl wnt 2nd again over 2f out: rdn to ld wl over 1f out: clr w wnr and drvn 1f out: hdd and styd in same pce ins fnl f* **9/2**[3]

6002 **3** *6* **Stoneham**[5] 2695 3-9-4 **60** CharlesBishop(3) 2 52
(Mick Channon) *t.k.h: led tl rdn and hdd wl over 1f out: 3rd and outpcd 1f out: no ch w ldng pair: battled on to hold 3rd fnl f* **4/1**[2]

6-51 **4** *hd* **Strike A Light**[11] 2526 3-9-4 **57** ChrisCatlin 1 49
(Rae Guest) *t.k.h: hld up in tch in midfield: hdwy and rdn to chse ldrs 2f out: no ch w ldng pair and battling for 3rd 1f out: kpt on* **3/1**[1]

-303 **5** *1 ½* **Sexy Secret**[11] 2526 3-9-3 **59** SimonPearce(3) 3 47
(Lydia Pearce) *chsd ldrs: rdn and effrt ent fnl 2f: outpcd and btn over 1f out: plugged on same pce after* **10/1**

6400 **6** *1 ¾* **Marphilly (IRE)**[15] 2393 3-8-8 **47** JimmyQuinn 8 31
(John Best) *t.k.h: hld up in tch in midfield: rdn over 3f out: sme hdwy to go modest 6th over 1f out: no prog after* **33/1**

4650 **7** *1 ¾* **Water For Life**[11] 2526 3-8-7 **46** oh1 JackMitchell 5 26
(Dave Morris) *in tch in midfield: effrt u.p over 2f out: outpcd and btn wl over 1f out: sn wknd* **33/1**

5006 **8** *¾* **Maro**[11] 2526 3-8-0 **46** oh1 (v) AdamMcLean(7) 9 25
(Derek Shaw) *chsd ldrs: rdn over 2f out: sn drvn and btn: wknd over 1f out* **100/1**

46-5 **9** *4* **Irene Hull (IRE)**[22] 2209 3-9-5 **58** TomQueally 10 27
(Garry Moss) *restless in stalls: s.i.s: hld up in tch in rr: rdn 3f out: no hdwy: wl btn over 1f out* **10/1**

630 **10** *8* **Trinity Lorraine (IRE)**[5] 2695 3-8-3 **47** (b) TimClark(5) 4
(Alan Bailey) *dwlt and bustled along early: hdwy to chse ldr 6f out tl over 2f out: sn rdn and struggling: wknd over 1f out* **28/1**

0-53 **11** *shd* **McCarthy Mor (IRE)**[22] 2205 3-9-5 **58** PaulHanagan 14 9
(Richard Fahey) *restless in stalls: s.i.s: a towards rr: rdn and no hdwy 3f out: bhd over 1f out* **6/1**

54-3 **12** *13* **Jayeff Herring (IRE)**[148] 71 3-8-9 **55** MichaelKenneally(7) 6
(Michael Bell) *in tch in midfield: lost pl 1/2-way: rdn and struggling over 3f out: lost tch wl over 1f out: t.o* **14/1**

1m 40.72s (0.12) **Going Correction** -0.025s/f (Good) 12 Ran SP% **117.4**
Speed ratings (Par 97): **98,96,90,90,88 87,85,84,80,72 72,59**
CSF £103.19 CT £450.53 TOTE £32.10: £6.70, £2.00, £1.10; EX 201.90 Trifecta £700.50.
**Owner** Four Winds Racing Partnership **Bred** Wood Farm Stud (Waresley) **Trained** Newmarket, Suffolk

**FOCUS**
The pick of the three C&D times relative to the grade. The winner is rated in line with her March Wolverhampton form.

## 2879 BAZUKA H'CAP 7f 3y
**8:30** (8:31) (Class 5) (0-75,75) 3-Y-O £2,911 (£866; £432; £216) **Stalls** Centre

Form RPR
-422 **1** **Baltic Brave (IRE)**[7] 2647 3-9-2 **70** (t) RyanMoore 2 81
(Hughie Morrison) *in tch in midfield: hdwy to chse ldrs 2f out: rdn to ld jst over 1f out: r.o wl: rdn out* **5/4**[1]

2-05 **2** *1 ½* **Maraayill (IRE)**[33] 1897 3-9-7 **75** (tp) PaoloSirigu 5 82
(Marco Botti) *hld up in tch in rr: hdwy 2f out: rdn over 1f out: chsd wnr jst ins fnl f: r.o but a hld* **3/1**[2]

5-63 **3** *1 ¾* **Surety (IRE)**[10] 2544 3-9-7 **75** MickaelBarzalona 3 77
(Clive Brittain) *chsd ldrs: wnt 2nd 4f out: rdn and ev ch wl over 1f out tl ent fnl f: styd on same pce fnl 150yds* **8/1**

-444 **4** *1 ½* **Kalahari Kingdom (IRE)**[17] 2355 3-8-5 **59** (p) PaulHanagan 1 58
(Richard Fahey) *led: rdn ent fnl 2f: hdd jst over 1f out: wknd fnl f* **4/1**[3]

130- **5** *2 ¼* **Chess Valley**[255] 6644 3-9-6 **74** ChrisCatlin 6 67
(Rae Guest) *stdd s: hld up in tch in last pair: effrt and swtchd rt over 1f out: no prog: wknd ins fnl f* **12/1**

0325 **6** *1 ½* **Happydoingnothing**[42] 1634 3-8-8 **62** AdamBeschizza 7 51
(Christine Dunnett) *chsd ldr tl 4f out: styd chsng ldrs tl lost pl u.p 2f out: n.d and one pce fr over 1f out* **66/1**

6004 **7** *29* **Scruffy Tramp (IRE)**[15] 2401 3-9-7 **75** (v) KierenFallon 4
(Alan Bailey) *in tch in midfield: rdn and effrt ent 2f out: btn over 1f out: bhd and heavily eased ins fnl f: t.o* **20/1**

1m 26.43s (-0.17) **Going Correction** -0.025s/f (Good) 7 Ran SP% **114.5**
Speed ratings (Par 99): **99,97,95,93,91 89,56**
CSF £5.20 CT £19.50 TOTE £1.90: £1.10, £2.20; EX 6.20 Trifecta £20.40.
**Owner** The Brave Partnership **Bred** Tally-Ho Stud **Trained** East Ilsley, Berks

**FOCUS**
The form looks sound, the winner up a length on his latest form.

T/Plt: £5.20 to a £1 stake. Pool: £71,773.00 - 9,908.43 winning tickets. T/Qpdt: £4.90 to a £1 stake. Pool: £6,717.00 - 1,006.16 winning tickets. SP

# 2680 KEMPTON (A.W) (R-H)
Wednesday, June 4

**OFFICIAL GOING: Standard**
Wind: Moderate, half against Weather: Fine becoming very overcast with heavy showers from race 4

## 2881 £500 FREE BETS AT BETDAQ MAIDEN STKS 1m 2f (P)
**6:00** (6:03) (Class 5) 3-Y-O £2,587 (£770; £384; £192) **Stalls** Low

Form RPR
44 **1** **Kinshasa**[18] 2346 3-9-5 0 LemosdeSouza 12 83+
(Luca Cumani) *dwlt: t.k.h: trckd ldrs: clsd fr 2f out: shkn up and r.o to ld last 150yds: pushed out* **7/2**[1]

0- **2** *1 ¼* **Dalmatia (IRE)**[320] 4491 3-9-0 0 ShaneKelly 1 75
(Sir Michael Stoute) *trckd ldng pair: shkn up 2f out: clsd to chal 1f out: styd on but readily hld last 100yds* **20/1**

0- **3** *1 ¾* **Bombardment (USA)**[271] 6168 3-9-5 0 MickaelBarzalona 9 76
(Charlie Appleby) *trckd ldr: led after 4f: rdn over 2f out: hdd over 1f out: outpcd* **20/1**

44 **4** *shd* **Obstinate (IRE)**[28] 2075 3-9-5 0 JimCrowley 2 76
(Andrew Balding) *led: stdd and hdd after 4f: trckd ldr tl rdn to ld over 1f out: hdd last 150yds: fdd* **8/1**[3]

00- **5** *¾* **Attenzione (IRE)**[167] 8340 3-9-5 0 (t) LukeMorris 6 75
(Marco Botti) *wl in tch: chsd ldng quartet over 3f out: shkn up over 2f out: kpt on one pce fr over 1f out* **33/1**

**6** *½* **Fighting Back** 3-9-5 0 TomQueally 11 76+
(Amanda Perrett) *slowly away: rn green in rr: in danger of losing tch 6f out and pushed along: prog over 2f out: shkn up over 1f out: keeping on whn rn out of room nr fin* **20/1**

0- **7** *1 ¾* **Mutaraadif (USA)**[224] 7469 3-9-5 0 FrederikTylicki 10 70
(Roger Varian) *in tch: pushed along 3f out: lft bhd fr 2f out: plugged on nr fin* **9/2**[2]

0 **8** *8* **Fine Tune (IRE)**[48] 1529 3-9-5 0 WilliamBuick 7 55
(John Gosden) *nvr beyond midfield: no prog 3f out: wknd 2f out* **10/1**

0 **9** *7* **Statsminister**[16] 2404 3-9-0 0 SteveDrowne 8 37
(Luke Dace) *s.i.s: rn green and a wl in rr* **66/1**

**10** *13* **Beauchamp Kite** 3-9-5 0 FergusSweeney 4 17
(Paul Fitzsimons) *prom 4f: sn lost pl: t.o 2f out* **66/1**

**11** *30* **Highplains Drifter (IRE)** 3-9-5 0 TedDurcan 3
(David Lanigan) *slowly away: rn green and a in last pair: wl t.o over 2f out* **25/1**

2m 7.72s (-0.28) **Going Correction** 0.0s/f (Stan) 11 Ran SP% **84.7**
Speed ratings (Par 99): **101,100,98,98,97 97,96,89,84,73 49**
CSF £32.12 TOTE £2.60: £1.20, £3.90, £4.00; EX 44.10 Trifecta £895.00.
**Owner** Fittocks Stud **Bred** Fittocks Stud Ltd **Trained** Newmarket, Suffolk
■ The first winner in Britain for Brazilian rider Lemos de Souza.
■ Rule 4 of 40p in the pound applies to all bets; Withdrawn: Winter Thunder

**FOCUS**
Some good stables represented in what could turn out to be be a fair maiden. However, it was weakened significantly when favourite Winter Thunder was withdrawn after appearing to get stuck in the stalls.

## 2882 BETDAQ £25 NO LOSE FREE BET H'CAP (JOCKEY CLUB GRASSROOTS FLAT MIDDLE DISTANCE SERIES QUALIFIER) 1m 2f (P)
**6:30** (6:31) (Class 4) (0-80,80) 4-Y-O+ £4,690 (£1,395; £697; £348) **Stalls** Low

Form RPR
66-0 **1** **Qanan**[43] 1636 5-9-0 **73** TedDurcan 4 88
(Chris Wall) *trckd ldng pair: wnt 2nd 4f out: led wl over 1f out and sn rdn clr: styd on* **9/2**[2]

50-1 **2** *2 ¾* **Xinbama (IRE)**[34] 1899 5-9-3 **76** KierenFallon 3 85
(B W Hills) *settled towards rr: pushed along briefly 1/2-way: rdn and prog 2f out: clr wnr 1f out: styd on wl but no ch to threaten* **5/1**[3]

-543 **3** *4 ½* **St Paul De Vence (IRE)**[7] 2687 4-8-13 **72** (b) LukeMorris 7 72
(Paul Cole) *settled towards rr: rdn wl over 2f out: styd on u.p fr over 1f out to take 3rd last 100yds* **3/1**[1]

2-20 **4** *2* **Dandy (GER)**[20] 2270 5-8-12 **74** OisinMurphy(3) 5 70
(Andrew Balding) *led 4f: chsd ldr to 4f out: cl up 2f out: hanging and nt qckn over 1f out: fdd* **10/1**

30-2 **5** *nk* **Rouge Nuage (IRE)**[7] 2687 4-8-13 **72** MartinDwyer 6 68
(Conrad Allen) *trckd ldr: led after 4f: rdn and hdd wl over 1f out: wknd fnl f* **10/1**

62-0 **6** *1 ¼* **Silver Dixie (USA)**[14] 2462 4-9-4 **80** CharlesBishop(3) 2 73
(Peter Hedger) *t.k.h: trckd ldng pair: lost pl over 3f out: shkn up and no prog fr 2f out: fdd* **7/1**

302- **7** *1* **Little Buxted (USA)**[196] 7970 4-9-3 **76** SteveDrowne 8 68
(Robert Mills) *stdd s: hld up in last pair: pushed along on outer on bnd 3f out: no prog: nvr in it* **10/1**

000- **8** *nk* **Takeitfromalady (IRE)**[226] 7431 5-8-8 **72** (b) LouisSteward(5) 1 63
(Lee Carter) *hld up in last pair: rdn and outpcd over 3f out: no prog after* **5/1**[3]

2m 6.1s (-1.90) **Going Correction** 0.0s/f (Stan) 8 Ran SP% **116.3**
Speed ratings (Par 105): **107,104,101,99,99 98,97,97**
CSF £27.72 CT £77.97 TOTE £4.70: £1.60, £2.80, £1.50; EX 45.00 Trifecta £159.00.
**Owner** Alan & Jill Smith **Bred** Genesis Green Stud Ltd **Trained** Newmarket, Suffolk

**FOCUS**
A wide-open fair handicap where a feasible case could have been made for any of the eight. They went a second and half quicker than the opening maiden.

## 2883 GOFFS LONDON SALE - KEMPTON-BREEZE/KENSINGTON-SALE 16.06.14 MEDIAN AUCTION MAIDEN STKS 1m (P)
**7:00** (7:04) (Class 6) 3-5-Y-O £1,940 (£577; £288; £144) **Stalls** Low

Form RPR
360- **1** **Amood (IRE)**[231] 7308 3-9-3 75 WilliamBuick 11 83
(Charles Hills) *trckd ldr: led wl over 2f out: drvn and kpt on fr over 1f out* **7/1**[2]

2 **2** *½* **Telefono**[18] 2339 3-9-3 0 PatDobbs 8 82
(Amanda Perrett) *trckd ldrs: shkn up over 2f out: prog to chse wnr wl over 1f out: styd on but nt qckn and a hld* **8/13**[1]

6- **3** *3 ¾* **Swordbearer**[246] 6922 3-9-3 0 FrederikTylicki 3 73
(James Fanshawe) *in tch in midfield: rdn and prog over 2f out: tk 3rd over 1f out: no imp on ldng pair after* **16/1**



The Form Book, Raceform Ltd, Newbury, RG14 5SJ

4 2¾ **Crown Of Aragon** 3-9-3 0 ShaneKelly 9 66+
(Denis Coakley) *settled in midfield: rdn over 2f out: styd on fnl 2f to take 4th last 50yds* **25/1**

62-4 5 2½ **Swilken**[35] 1880 3-9-3 72 TedDurcan 7 60
(Mark H Tompkins) *led to wl over 2f out: steadily wknd wl over 1f out* **7/1**[2]

0- 6 2¾ **Footsieonehundred (IRE)**[168] 8328 3-8-5 0 JackGilligan(7) 2 49
(Patrick Gilligan) *trckd ldrs: pushed along and fdd fnl 2f* **66/1**

00- 7 1½ **Pacific Trip**[254] 6689 3-8-10 0 JonathanWilletts(7) 5 50+
(Andrew Balding) *in tch in midfield: pushed along and nt qckn fr 3f out: steadily fdd* **66/1**

8 nk **Varsovian** 4-10-0 0 FergusSweeney 10 52
(Dean Ivory) *wl in rr: rdn whn bdly hmpd over 2f out: no ch after: plugged on* **14/1**[3]

00- 9 1½ **Key To Your Heart**[231] 7310 3-8-12 0 (t) MickaelBarzalona 14 41
(Hughie Morrison) *settled in rr: rdn and lost tch over 2f out: lost shoe and fin lame* **33/1**

00-6 10 6 **Severn Crossing**[28] 2081 3-9-3 67 MartinDwyer 13 31
(William Muir) *chsd ldng pair to over 2f out: hung lft and wknd* **25/1**

- 11 33 **Peace Palace** 3-8-12 0 LukeMorris 12
(Harry Dunlop) *wl in rr: rdn whn hmpd over 2f out: allowed to coast home* **50/1**

40 F **Dreaming Brave**[18] 2339 3-9-3 0 JimCrowley 1
(Amanda Perrett) *in tch in 9th: pushed along firmly whn clipped heels and fell over 2f out* **16/1**

00 U **Slunovrat (FR)**[23] 2211 3-9-3 0 MartinLane 6
(David Menuisier) *a in rr: rdn whn bdly hmpd and uns rdr over 2f out* **66/1**

0 U **Prince Ballygowen**[18] 2346 3-9-3 0 SamHitchcott 4
(Clifford Lines) *a in rr: u.p whn bdly hmpd and uns rdr over 2f out* **100/1**

1m 39.17s (-0.63) **Going Correction** 0.0s/f (Stan)
**WFA** 3 from 4yo 11lb 14 Ran SP% 123.4
Speed ratings (Par 101): **103,102,98,96,93 90,89,88,87,81 48,,,**
CSF £11.39 TOTE £10.20: £2.30, £1.02, £5.00; EX 15.20 Trifecta £150.70.
**Owner** Hamdan Al Maktoum **Bred** Shadwell Estate Company Limited **Trained** Lambourn, Berks
■ Stewards' Enquiry : Jonathan Willetts seven-day ban: careless riding (Jun 18-24)

**FOCUS**
A race marred by an awful incident in the home straight where Dreaming Brave clipped heels, came down and severely hampered both Prince Ballygowen and Slunovrat who both unshipped their jockeys. Remarkably both the horses and jockeys got to their feet.

## 2884 CASH OUT ON THE BETDAQ + APP H'CAP 7f (P)
**7:30** (7:34) (Class 5) (0-70,70) 4-Y-O+ £2,587 (£770; £384; £192) Stalls Low

Form RPR

5033 1 **Sheikh The Reins (IRE)**[18] 2341 5-9-3 66 (v) RobertHavlin 1 75
(John Best) *trckd ldrs: rdn 2f out: prog to go 2nd jst ins fnl f: str chal after: led last strides* **8/1**[3]

6113 2 hd **Global Leader (IRE)**[33] 1930 4-9-1 64 PatrickDonaghy 5 74+
(Paul D'Arcy) *trckd ldr 3f: styd prom: rdn to ld on inner wl over 1f out: hit rail after: kpt on u.p: hdd last strides* **7/4**[1]

3451 3 1¼ **Shifting Star (IRE)**[14] 2463 9-8-13 62 (vt) WilliamCarson 13 67
(John Bridger) *prom: trckd ldr after 3f: hrd rdn and nt qckn over 2f out: sn lost pl: kpt on again fnl f to take 3rd last stride* **25/1**

5-60 4 nse **Alcando (IRE)**[15] 2414 4-9-2 65 ShaneKelly 8 70
(Denis Coakley) *led: drvn and hdd wl over 1f out: lost 2nd jst ins fnl f: one pce* **16/1**

5-40 5 nk **Light Rose (IRE)**[39] 1731 4-9-7 70 LukeMorris 7 74
(Jeremy Gask) *prom on outer: rdn over 2f out: hanging rt and nt qckn over 1f out: kpt on* **8/1**[3]

043- 6 ½ **Black Dave (IRE)**[182] 8158 4-9-4 67 AdamKirby 12 70+
(David Evans) *sltly awkward s: towards rr: rdn and prog jst over 2f out: tried to cl on ldrs over 1f out: kpt on but nvr quite able to chal* **4/1**[2]

003- 7 nk **Galatian**[205] 7836 7-8-12 68 PatMillman(7) 6 70
(Rod Millman) *stdd s: hld up towards rr: pushed along over 2f out: sme prog and swtchd lft 1f out: styd on: nrst fin* **16/1**

4-50 8 3¼ **Diamonds A Dancing**[16] 2401 4-8-5 54 [1] JimmyQuinn 14 48
(Brian Gubby) *chsd ldrs on outer: rdn and struggling over 2f out: sn btn* **50/1**

0-50 9 ¾ **Tevez**[14] 2471 9-9-4 70 (p) OisinMurphy(3) 2 62
(Des Donovan) *a in rr: rdn and no prog over 2f out: no ch after* **33/1**

5210 10 1¼ **Spirit Of Gondree (IRE)**[53] 1454 6-9-3 66 (b) DavidProbert 10 55
(Milton Bradley) *stdd s: hld up wl in rr: no ch whn drvn over 1f out: nvr in it* **25/1**

0554 11 ½ **Blazing Knight (IRE)**[13] 2486 4-9-4 67 (b) PatDobbs 9 54
(Chris Gordon) *nvr beyond midfield on outer: rdn and struggling over 2f out: sn wknd* **20/1**

0050 12 2 **Basingstoke (IRE)**[16] 2399 5-8-13 62 SteveDrowne 3 44
(Simon Hodgson) *nvr beyond midfield: rdn and no prog over 2f out: wl btn after* **50/1**

40-6 13 4½ **Lucky Di**[151] 52 4-9-2 68 CharlesBishop(3) 11 38
(Peter Hedger) *rrd bdly s: a in last quartet: no prog over 2f out: wknd* **10/1**

1m 26.31s (0.31) **Going Correction** 0.0s/f (Stan) 13 Ran SP% 118.8
Speed ratings (Par 103): **98,97,96,96,95 95,95,91,90,89 88,86,81**
CSF £20.56 CT £355.66 TOTE £7.90: £2.60, £1.70, £3.30; EX 29.10 Trifecta £307.70.
**Owner** Curtis, Malt & Williams **Bred** M Enright **Trained** Hucking, Kent

**FOCUS**
A modest handicap.

## 2885 DUBLIN LEGENDS 09.07.14 H'CAP 2m (P)
**8:00** (8:02) (Class 6) (0-65,67) 4-Y-O+ £1,940 (£577; £288; £144) Stalls Low

Form RPR

3401 1 **Arashi**[7] 2683 8-9-12 67 6ex (v) TomQueally 3 76+
(Derek Shaw) *hld up towards rr: nt clr run briefly over 2f out: gd prog to chse clr ldr 1f out: styd on wl to ld nr fin: shade cleverly* **7/4**[1]

512- 2 ½ **Speed Steed (IRE)**[27] 4655 7-9-1 61 (v) DanielMuscutt(5) 11 68
(Tim Vaughan) *trckd ldr after 2f: led over 2f out and sn at least 2 l clr: drvn over 1f out: hdd and outpcd nr fin* **12/1**

6102 3 2 **Maison Brillet (IRE)**[14] 2468 7-9-6 61 (p) RobertHavlin 9 66
(Clive Drew) *trckd ldrs: rdn and nt qckn over 2f out: kpt on to take 3rd fnl f: nt gng pce to threaten* **10/1**

1336 4 1¼ **Uncle Bernie (IRE)**[39] 1740 4-8-13 55 (p) JimmyQuinn 6 58
(Andrew Hollinshead) *stdd s: hld up in last pair in slowly run contest: prog on inner over 2f out: kpt on same pce fr over 1f out* **7/1**[3]

4203 5 ¾ **Yasir (USA)**[9] 2620 6-9-10 65 (p) HayleyTurner 5 67
(Conor Dore) *led at v modest pce: kicked on over 3f out: hdd and nt qckn over 2f out: wknd fnl f* **9/2**[2]

5345 6 1 **Willow Island (IRE)**[12] 2531 5-7-12 46 oh1 HollieDoyle(7) 4 47
(David Evans) *hld up in midfield: outpcd over 2f out: urged along and one pce after* **20/1**

2003 7 ½ **Honourable Knight (IRE)**[14] 2468 6-9-8 63 DavidProbert 1 63
(Mark Usher) *trckd ldrs: rdn and nt qckn wl over 2f out: no imp after: fdd* **9/2**[2]

5-06 8 2½ **The Absent Mare**[21] 992 6-9-4 59 GeorgeBaker 10 56
(Robin Dickin) *stdd s: hld up in last pair in slowly run contest: shkn up over 2f out: nvr involved* **16/1**

/54- 9 6 **Faith Jicaro (IRE)**[182] 4365 7-8-0 48 ow2 CallumShepherd(7) 12 38
(John Groucott) *trckd ldr 2f: styd prom: nt qckn over 2f out: wknd over 1f out* **25/1**

0-40 10 7 **Rhinestone Rebel (IRE)**[43] 455 8-8-6 47 [1] WilliamCarson 2 29
(Peter Hiatt) *stdd s: hld up in rr: rdn as sn as pce lifted over 3f out: sn btn* **50/1**

65-0 11 52 **Bullseye Babe**[16] 2396 4-8-5 47 LukeMorris 8
(Mark Usher) *plld hrd: hld up in midfield: stl v keen and virtually rn off the crse on bnd over 4f out: t.o after* **33/1**

3m 39.97s (9.87) **Going Correction** 0.0s/f (Stan)
**WFA** 4 from 5yo+ 1lb 11 Ran SP% 121.4
Speed ratings (Par 101): **75,74,73,73,72 72,72,70,67,64 38**
CSF £25.52 CT £175.39 TOTE £2.90: £1.10, £3.00, £4.00; EX 29.70 Trifecta £147.60.
**Owner** Philip Derbyshire **Bred** Wyck Hall Stud Ltd **Trained** Sproxton, Leics

**FOCUS**
This was uncompetitive fare and they went no pace whatsoever.

## 2886 BETDAQ SUPPORTING THE INJURED JOCKEYS FUND H'CAP 6f (P)
**8:30** (8:31) (Class 5) (0-70,72) 3-Y-O £2,587 (£770; £384; £192) Stalls Low

Form RPR

1611 1 **Moonspring (IRE)**[7] 2686 3-9-6 72 6ex (e) OisinMurphy(3) 8 78
(Robert Cowell) *pressed ldr: upsides fr over 2f out: sn drvn: narrow ld ins fnl f: jst hld on* **11/4**[1]

1136 2 nse **Dont Have It Then**[30] 2015 3-9-3 66 ChrisCatlin 6 72
(Willie Musson) *chsd ldrs: rdn 2f out: clsd grad 1f out: styd on wl nr fin: jst pipped* **5/1**

03-4 3 nk **Trillian Astra (IRE)**[14] 2470 3-8-6 60 (p) RyanTate(5) 7 65
(Clive Cox) *mde most: jnd over 2f out: gd battle w wnr tl no ex and lost 2nd nr fin* **16/1**

054- 4 ¾ **Tahchee**[189] 8061 3-8-10 59 FrederikTylicki 3 61+
(James Fanshawe) *trckd ldng pair: rdn 2f out: tried to chal fr over 1f out: nt qckn ins fnl f* **7/2**[2]

-005 5 1 **Classic Pursuit**[20] 2278 3-9-4 67 LukeMorris 5 66
(Ronald Harris) *hld up in last pair: in trble once kick for home sed over 2f out: drvn over 1f out: styd on fnl f: nrst fin* **18/1**

25-0 6 nk **Cincuenta Pasos (IRE)**[15] 2429 3-9-7 70 SteveDrowne 1 68
(Joseph Tuite) *hld up towards rr: tried to cl on ldrs 2f out: nt qckn over 1f out: no imp after* **5/1**

-534 7 1 **Inciting Incident (IRE)**[36] 1851 3-9-6 69 (b) TedDurcan 4 64
(Ed McMahon) *t.k.h: hld up towards rr: rdn 2f out: hanging and nt qckn over 1f out: no* **14/1**

0364 8 ¾ **Kodafine (IRE)**[8] 2638 3-9-4 67 AdamKirby 10 60
(David Evans) *chsd ldrs: rdn 2f out: hanging and nt qckn over 1f out: fdd fnl f* **25/1**

0-24 9 3 **Yankee Red**[21] 2249 3-9-0 63 (v[1]) WilliamCarson 2 46
(John Best) *hld up in last pair: pushed along over 2f out: limited prog and drifted to far rail over 1f out: wknd* **25/1**

6-1 10 8 **For Ayman**[25] 2158 3-9-7 70 GeorgeBaker 11 28
(Seamus Durack) *chsd ldrs on outer to 1/2-way: sn dropped away: t.o* **9/2**[3]

1m 13.09s (-0.01) **Going Correction** 0.0s/f (Stan) 10 Ran SP% 125.9
Speed ratings (Par 99): **100,99,99,98,97 96,95,94,90,79**
CSF £18.44 CT £192.68 TOTE £3.30: £1.30, £3.00, £4.90; EX 29.50 Trifecta £218.20.
**Owner** P Foster & Friends **Bred** R N Auld **Trained** Six Mile Bottom, Cambs

**FOCUS**
A bunched finish but this looks okay form for the grade.

## 2887 IRISH NIGHT AT KEMPTON 09.07.14 H'CAP 6f (P)
**9:00** (9:00) (Class 6) (0-65,65) 4-Y-O+ £1,940 (£577; £288; £144) Stalls Low

Form RPR

0-53 1 **Italian Tom (IRE)**[11] 2559 7-9-7 65 LukeMorris 8 75
(Ronald Harris) *racd wd in midfield: pushed along bef 1/2-way: drvn 2f out: clsd on outer to ld 1f out: sn clr* **9/2**[2]

3-40 2 1¼ **Paradise Spectre**[26] 2124 7-9-4 62 (p) RobertHavlin 6 68+
(Zoe Davison) *hld up in rr: prog whn nt clr run on inner over 1f out: styd on to take 2nd ins fnl f: no ch to chal* **33/1**

-000 3 1¼ **Gung Ho Jack**[64] 1221 5-9-3 61 GeorgeBaker 10 63+
(John Best) *hld up wl in rr and off the pce: prog whn nt clr run on inner over 1f out: styd on fnl f to take 3rd nr fin* **20/1**

6132 4 ½ **Aeolian Blue**[14] 2459 4-9-6 64 [1] ShaneKelly 5 64
(William Knight) *in tch in midfield: prog 2f out: drvn and nt qckn jst over 1f out whn cl enough: one pce after* **7/2**[1]

3620 5 shd **Haadeeth**[15] 2435 7-9-5 63 (t) AdamKirby 4 63
(David Evans) *chsd clr ldr: drvn over 2f out: kpt on to chal 1f out: nt qckn after* **8/1**

45-0 6 nk **Emerald Sea**[34] 1896 4-9-5 63 (p) TedDurcan 7 62
(Chris Wall) *towards rr: shkn up over 2f out: kpt on fr over 1f out but nvr gng pce to threaten* **12/1**

5045 7 1 **Ceelo**[13] 2488 4-8-13 60 (b[1]) SimonPearce(3) 2 56
(Lydia Pearce) *led and clr: stl clr 2f out: edgd rt over 1f out: hdd and fdd 1f out* **16/1**

2005 8 hd **Divine Call**[25] 2174 7-9-6 64 LiamJones 9 59
(Milton Bradley) *hld up in last trio and wl off the pce: pushed along over 2f out: reminder over 1f out: kpt on but nvr involved* **14/1**

5116 9 hd **Exceedexpectations (IRE)**[14] 2463 5-9-3 61 (p) StevieDonohoe 12 56
(Lee Carter) *hld up in last pair and wl off the pce: shkn up over 2f out: kpt on fnl f: no ch* **14/1**

30 10 shd **Compton Prince**[35] 1878 5-9-6 64 (b) DavidProbert 1 58
(Milton Bradley) *chsd clr ldr: gng strly 2f out: rdn to chal jst over 1f out: sn wknd rapidly* **14/1**[3]

1500 11 ¾ **New Rich**[6] 2691 4-8-13 62 (p) GeorgeDowning(5) 3 54+
(Eve Johnson Houghton) *in tch in midfield: prog 2f out: trying to chal on inner whn hmpd over 1f out: nt rcvr and eased* **7/1**

6364 **12** *6* **Meridius (IRE)**[14] 2463 4-9-5 **63**....(p) KierenFallon 11 36
(Nick Littmoden) *chsd clr ldr: drvn and wknd over 2f out* **6/1**[3]

1m 12.91s (-0.19) **Going Correction** 0.0s/f (Stan) 12 Ran SP% **119.6**
Speed ratings (Par 101): **101,99,97,97,96 96,95,94,94,94 93,85**
CSF £142.80 CT £2706.92 TOTE £7.10: £1.90, £4.70, £5.40; EX 209.00 Trifecta £1194.30 Part won..
**Owner** S & A Mares **Bred** Tom Radley **Trained** Earlswood, Monmouths
■ Stewards' Enquiry : Luke Morris two-day ban: used whip above permitted level (Jun 22-23)
George Downing one-day ban: careless riding (Jun 22)

**FOCUS**
A low-grade sprint handicap but only 5lb covered the runners and it was competitive enough. The leaders went quick and the pace collapsed, setting it up for finishers and causing trouble in running for quite a few of these.
T/Jkpt: Not won. T/Plt: £5.40 to a £1 stake. Pool: £74274.55 - 9998.05 winning tickets T/Qpdt: £3.80 to a £1 stake. Pool: £5611.54 - 1077.75 winning tickets JN

# 2800 NOTTINGHAM (L-H)
Wednesday, June 4

**OFFICIAL GOING: Soft**
Wind: Light across Weather: Rain clearing

## 2888 BET TOTEJACKPOT IRISH STALLION FARMS EBF MAIDEN FILLIES' STKS (BOBIS RACE) 5f 13y
**2:20** (2:21) (Class 5) 2-Y-0 **£3,234** (£962; £481; £240) **Stalls** High

Form RPR
3 **1** **Blue Aegean**[13] 2493 2-9-0 0.... WilliamBuick 8 85+
(Charlie Appleby) *mde virtually all: shkn up and clr fnl f: comf* **7/4**[1]
**2** *2 3/4* **Osaila (IRE)** 2-9-0 0.... FrankieDettori 10 75+
(Richard Hannon) *hld up: hdwy to go 2nd over 1f out: styd on: no ch w wnr* **7/4**[1]
**3** *4* **Three Robins** 2-9-0 0.... RichardHughes 4 61+
(Richard Hannon) *racd alone in centre: chsd ldrs: pushed along 1/2-way: styd on same pce fr over 1f out* **7/1**[3]
46 **4** *3/4* **Fujiano**[23] 2220 2-9-0 0.... SteveDrowne 12 58+
(Derek Haydn Jones) *hld up: styd on ins fnl f: nvr nrr* **25/1**
**5** *nk* **Strategise (IRE)** 2-9-0 0.... StephenCraine 3 57+
(Tom Dascombe) *hld up: pushed along 1/2-way: styng on whn nt clr run fr over 1f out: nt trble ldrs* **25/1**
**6** *3/4* **Zifena** 2-9-0 0.... MartinLane 2 54
(Eve Johnson Houghton) *s.i.s: sn chsng ldrs: pushed along and edgd lft wl over 1f out: wknd fnl f* **33/1**
3 **7** *2 3/4* **Dancing Moon (IRE)**[15] 2436 2-8-11 0.... WilliamTwiston-Davies(3) 9 44
(Mick Channon) *chsd ldrs: pushed along 1/2-way: wknd over 1f out* **5/1**[2]
**8** *1* **Heavenlyfriendship** 2-8-7 0.... JennyPowell(7) 1 41
(Brendan Powell) *swtchd to r w main gp wl over 3f out: in tch: wknd over 1f out* **50/1**
**9** *12* **Supreme Belle (IRE)** 2-9-0 0.... DaleSwift 11
(Derek Shaw) *s.i.s: outpcd* **50/1**

1m 2.91s (1.41) **Going Correction** +0.275s/f (Good) 9 Ran SP% **116.4**
Speed ratings (Par 90): **99,94,88,87,86 85,80,79,60**
CSF £4.52 TOTE £2.50: £1.80, £1.10, £1.20; EX 6.60 Trifecta £20.00.
**Owner** Godolphin **Bred** Mr & Mrs G Middlebrook **Trained** Newmarket, Suffolk
■ Stewards' Enquiry : William Buick one-day ban: failed to ride to draw (Jun 22)

**FOCUS**
Outer track used and rail moved out 4m around whole course and distances increased by 24yds on Round course. Jockeys were in agreement that the ground was riding 'soft'. All bar Three Robins came stands' side in what looked a fair juvenile maiden. The winner built on her debut promise.

## 2889 TOTEEXACTA PICK THE 1, 2 H'CAP 5f 13y
**2:50** (2:50) (Class 5) (0-75,74) 3-Y-0 **£2,587** (£770; £384; £192) **Stalls** High

Form RPR
5310 **1** **Flashy Queen (IRE)**[16] 2406 3-9-7 **74**.... SteveDrowne 1 80
(Joseph Tuite) *w ldrs: led over 1f out: edgd rt: rdn out* **7/1**
-060 **2** *3/4* **Touch The Clouds**[16] 2406 3-8-12 **72**.... KieranShoemark(7) 6 76
(William Stone) *led 1f: chsd ldrs: rdn and ev ch over 1f out: styd on* **20/1**
264 **3** *3/4* **Fuel Injection**[16] 2406 3-8-12 **65**....(p) GrahamLee 2 66
(Paul Midgley) *hmpd s: hld up in tch: rdn over 1f out: no ex nr fin* **8/1**
1143 **4** *1* **The Dandy Yank (IRE)**[12] 2505 3-9-3 **70**.... RichardHughes 7 67
(Jamie Osborne) *w ldrs: steaided and lost pl after 1f: rdn and hdwy 1f out: no ex wl ins fnl f* **9/2**[2]
4-13 **5** *1 1/4* **Dynamo Walt (IRE)**[36] 1851 3-9-1 **68**....(v) DaleSwift 4 61
(Derek Shaw) *chsd ldrs: rdn over 1f out: no ex ins fnl f* **5/1**[3]
10-2 **6** *5* **Rozene (IRE)**[36] 1851 3-9-3 **70**.... GrahamGibbons 3 45
(David Barron) *s.i.s: rcvrd to ld after 1f: rdn and hdd over 1f out: wknd fnl f* **5/4**[1]
1-00 **7** *1* **Hickster (IRE)**[39] 1725 3-8-4 **62**....(v) PhilipPrince(5) 5 33
(Roy Bowring) *chsd ldrs tl rdn and wknd over 1f out* **20/1**

1m 2.96s (1.46) **Going Correction** +0.275s/f (Good) 7 Ran SP% **112.4**
Speed ratings (Par 99): **99,97,96,95,93 85,83**
CSF £117.72 TOTE £12.60: £3.40, £8.70; EX 92.00 Trifecta £487.30.
**Owner** B Woodward,P & A Burton & B & A Lampard **Bred** Stourbank Stud **Trained** Great Shefford, Berks

**FOCUS**
An open sprint, despite it being a fairly small field. The favourite disappointed but this was a personal best from the winner.

## 2890 TOTEQUADPOT FOUR PLACES IN FOUR RACES H'CAP 6f 15y
**3:20** (3:20) (Class 5) (0-75,75) 4-Y-0+ **£3,234** (£962; £481; £240) **Stalls** High

Form RPR
3512 **1** **Heartsong (IRE)**[13] 2486 5-8-9 **68**.... LouisSteward(5) 2 76
(John Gallagher) *a.p: led over 1f out: sn rdn: jst hld on* **9/2**[2]
00-4 **2** *shd* **Tagula Night (IRE)**[137] 233 8-9-6 **74**....(t) RichardHughes 4 82
(Dean Ivory) *mid-div: hdwy u.p over 1f out: r.o: jst failed* **9/2**[2]
1420 **3** *3/4* **Rigolleto (IRE)**[41] 1678 6-9-2 **70**....[1] PaulHanagan 7 75
(Anabel K Murphy) *chsd ldrs: shkn up to ld 2f out: sn hdd: styd on* **6/1**[3]
-004 **4** *2 1/4* **Captain Kendall (IRE)**[13] 2488 5-8-5 **62**.... MichaelJMMurphy(3) 6 60
(Harry Chisman) *hld up: pushed along 1/2-way: nt clr run 1f out: r.o: nt trble ldrs* **12/1**
0221 **5** *2* **Clubland (IRE)**[35] 1892 5-9-0 **73**.... PhilipPrince(5) 12 65
(Roy Bowring) *chsd ldrs: rdn over 1f out: no ex ins fnl f* **5/2**[1]
0-50 **6** *1 1/2* **Penny Garcia**[34] 1903 4-9-6 **74**.... DuranFentiman 8 61
(Tim Easterby) *chsd ldrs: rdn over 2f out: wknd ins fnl f* **10/1**

350- **7** *nk* **Going French (IRE)**[236] 7164 7-8-11 **65**.... PaddyAspell 1 51
(Grace Harris) *sn led: rdn and hdd 2f out: wknd fnl f* **16/1**
016- **8** *nk* **Queen Hermione (IRE)**[292] 5498 6-8-1 **62**....(vt) AdamMcLean(7) 5 47
(Derek Shaw) *s.i.s: sn pushed along in rr: nvr on terms* **8/1**
00-0 **9** *7* **Invincible Lad (IRE)**[25] 2159 10-8-11 **65**.... GrahamLee 3 28
(Ed McMahon) *chsd ldr to 1/2-way: wknd over 1f out* **25/1**

1m 17.22s (2.52) **Going Correction** +0.275s/f (Good) 9 Ran SP% **116.8**
Speed ratings (Par 103): **94,93,92,89,87 85,84,84,75**
CSF £25.42 CT £123.77 TOTE £5.30: £1.90, £1.40, £2.20; EX 24.20 Trifecta £111.40.
**Owner** Colin Rashbrook **Bred** Gerry And John Rowley **Trained** Chastleton, Oxon
■ Stewards' Enquiry : Richard Hughes two-day ban: used whip above permitted level (Jun 22-23)

**FOCUS**
Modest sprinting form. The winner found a bit on recent runs.

## 2891 TOTEPOOL HOME OF POOL BETTING H'CAP 1m 75y
**3:50** (3:50) (Class 2) (0-112,111) 3-Y-O+**£16,172** (£4,812; £2,405; £1,202) **Stalls** Centre

Form RPR
0500 **1** **Balty Boys (IRE)**[4] 2784 5-9-1 **98**....(b) PaulPickard 2 103
(Brian Ellison) *sn pushed along to ld: mde rest: clr 6f out: shkn up over 2f out: rdn ins fnl f: jst hld on* **8/1**
6/30 **2** *nk* **Artigiano (USA)**[118] 508 4-9-8 **105**.... RichardHughes 1 109
(Charlie Appleby) *sn chsng ldrs: wnt 2nd 3f out: rdn and hung lft fr over 1f out: r.o towards fin* **5/1**[3]
5-04 **3** *2 1/2* **Two For Two (IRE)**[17] 2362 6-9-1 **98**.... DanielTudhope 7 97
(David O'Meara) *chsd wnr whn wnt clr after 2f: rdn and lost 2nd 3f out: no ex ins fnl f* **7/4**[2]
6012 **4** *1 3/4* **Fort Bastion (IRE)**[20] 2286 5-9-1 **98**.... JamesSullivan 4 93
(Ruth Carr) *hld up: rdn over 2f out: styd on same pce ins fnl f* **6/4**[1]
023- **5** *13* **Beaumont's Party (IRE)**[160] 7775 7-9-1 **98**.... DaleSwift 6 63
(Brian Ellison) *hld up: outpcd fr 1/2-way* **16/1**

1m 49.07s (0.07) **Going Correction** +0.275s/f (Good) 5 Ran SP% **110.0**
Speed ratings (Par 109): **110,109,107,105,92**
CSF £44.10 TOTE £8.90: £3.80, £2.40; EX 35.20 Trifecta £135.30.
**Owner** Koo's Racing Club, Carr & Jacobs **Bred** Lynn Lodge Stud **Trained** Norton, N Yorks
■ Stewards' Enquiry : Paul Pickard two-day ban: used whip above permitted level (Jun 22-23)

**FOCUS**
With Remote a non-runner due to the ground, this had a more open look to it, despite what the betting suggested, and it turned into a strange contest, with Balty Boys establishing a clear lead under a positive ride and holding on nicely in the closing stages. It's not clear whether the form will prove reliable.

## 2892 TRY A TOTETRIFECTA TODAY EBF STALLIONS FILLIES' H'CAP (BOBIS RACE) 1m 75y
**4:20** (4:20) (Class 4) (0-85,84) 3-Y-O **£6,469** (£1,925; £962; £481) **Stalls** Centre

Form RPR
0421 **1** **Native Heart**[8] 2638 3-8-11 **74** 6ex.... DanielTudhope 3 85
(Phil McEntee) *mde all: clr 5f out: pushed along over 2f out: styd on wl* **4/1**[3]
31 **2** *2* **Bragging (USA)**[16] 2404 3-9-5 **82**.... JamesDoyle 2 88
(Sir Michael Stoute) *trckd wnr: rdn over 2f out: no imp ins fnl f* **6/4**[1]
10-6 **3** *8* **Hala Hala (IRE)**[64] 1225 3-9-1 **78**.... JamieSpencer 5 66
(Michael Bell) *plld hrd and prom: rdn over 2f out: styd on same pce* **33/1**
1305 **4** *1/2* **Grevillea (IRE)**[11] 2565 3-9-4 **84**.... WilliamTwiston-Davies(3) 7 71
(Mick Channon) *s.i.s: hld up: hdwy over 2f out: sn rdn: styd on same pce* **5/1**
15- **5** *10* **Boadicee**[258] 6572 3-9-1 **78**.... ChrisCatlin 4 42
(Rae Guest) *s.i.s: hld up: pushed along over 3f out: wknd over 2f out* **14/1**
31-5 **6** *10* **Tea In Transvaal (IRE)**[12] 2510 3-9-2 **79**.... RichardHughes 8 20
(Richard Hannon) *trckd ldrs: rdn over 3f out: wknd over 2f out* **11/4**[2]

1m 49.97s (0.97) **Going Correction** +0.275s/f (Good) 6 Ran SP% **112.9**
Speed ratings (Par 98): **106,104,96,95,85 75**
CSF £10.61 CT £163.87 TOTE £5.20: £2.00, £2.40; EX 13.00 Trifecta £130.30.
**Owner** Henry R Nothhaft **Bred** R W K Lewis **Trained** Newmarket, Suffolk

**FOCUS**
Another race that saw an all-the-way winner. The first pair were clear and the form has been given a bit of a chance.

## 2893 BET ON ALL UK RACING WITH TOTEPOOL H'CAP 1m 6f 15y
**4:50** (4:50) (Class 5) (0-70,69) 3-Y-O **£2,587** (£770; £384; £192) **Stalls** Low

Form RPR
0-40 **1** **Taws**[20] 2280 3-8-2 **57**.... CamHardie(7) 2 66+
(Rod Millman) *hld up: pushed along over 5f out: nt clr run over 3f out: hdwy over 2f out: rdn to ld 1f out: edgd lft: styd on* **9/2**[2]
-502 **2** *1 1/2* **The Kid**[16] 2385 3-8-12 **67**....(tp) JennyPowell(7) 6 74+
(Tom Dascombe) *hld up: hdwy over 2f out: n.m.r ins fnl f: styd on* **5/1**[3]
25-0 **3** *2 1/4* **Stout Cortez**[19] 2319 3-9-1 **66**.... MichaelJMMurphy(3) 4 70
(Mark Johnston) *sn led: rdn and hdd 1f out: styd on same pce* **5/1**[3]
-551 **4** *4* **Blue Talisman (IRE)**[9] 2616 3-8-12 **60** 6ex....(b) DuranFentiman 1 58
(Tim Easterby) *chsd ldrs: rdn and ev ch over 1f out: no ex ins fnl f* **9/2**[2]
0-04 **5** *9* **Lucky Jim**[34] 1898 3-9-5 **67**.... SebSanders 7 53
(Chris Wall) *prom: chsd ldr after 2f: rdn and ev ch over 2f out: wknd over 1f out* **10/1**
-404 **6** *14* **Tactical Strike**[26] 2132 3-8-13 **66**....(bt[1]) NoelGarbutt(5) 5 32
(Hugo Palmer) *s.i.s: sn pushed along in rr: hdwy over 6f out: rdn over 4f out: wknd 3f out* **16/1**
1131 **7** *19* **Jarlath**[16] 2385 3-9-6 **68**.... RichardHughes 3 7
(Seamus Mullins) *trckd ldrs: rdn over 4f out: wknd over 2f out: eased* **5/2**[1]

3m 16.46s (9.46) **Going Correction** +0.275s/f (Good) 7 Ran SP% **113.2**
Speed ratings (Par 99): **83,82,80,78,73 65,54**
CSF £26.42 CT £115.02 TOTE £7.40: £2.30, £2.70; EX 35.50 Trifecta £129.10.
**Owner** R K Arrowsmith **Bred** Harts Farm Stud **Trained** Kentisbeare, Devon

**FOCUS**
An interesting handicap, and the winner can do a bit better. It was run at a fair clip considering the trip and conditions, and those held up early came to the fore late on.

## 2894 FOLLOW @TOTEPOOL ON TWITTER "HANDS AND HEELS" APPRENTICE SERIES H'CAP (EXCELLENCE INITAITIVE) 1m 2f 50y
**5:20** (5:20) (Class 6) (0-65,65) 4-Y-O+ **£1,940** (£577; £288; £144) **Stalls** Low

Form RPR
603 **1** **Thecornishcowboy**[15] 2445 5-9-3 **64**....(t) JordonMcMurray(3) 5 78
(John Ryan) *hld up: hdwy over 2f out: led over 1f out: pushed clr fnl f* **5/1**[3]
0314 **2** *7* **Roger Thorpe**[11] 2546 5-9-7 **65**.... DavidParkes 6 66
(Deborah Sanderson) *s.i.s: plld hrd and rcvrd to ld after 1f: pushed along over 2f out: hdd over 1f out: no ex* **10/1**

-611 **3** *nk* **Camelopardalis**[12] [2531] 5-9-4 **62** PatrickO'Donnell 3 63
(Philip McBride) *chsd ldr: hmpd 6f out: pushed along and ev ch over 2f out: no ex fnl f* **5/4**[1]

3401 **4** *2½* **Rockweiller**[13] [2476] 7-8-11 **58** AlexHopkinson(3) 7 54
(Shaun Harris) *chsd ldrs: pushed along over 4f out: wknd fnl f* **11/4**[2]

05- **5** *18* **Skyfire**[222] [7498] 7-9-5 **63** (p) KevinLundie 2 27
(Nick Kent) *led 1f: chsd ldrs: pushed along over 3f out: wknd over 2f out* **10/1**

00-5 **6** *3¼* **Indian Scout**[35] [1875] 6-8-7 **51** (p) LewisWalsh 1 9
(Anabel K Murphy) *hld up: pushed along and bhd fr 1/2-way* **12/1**

2m 19.19s (4.89) **Going Correction** +0.275s/f (Good) **6** Ran SP% **113.7**
Speed ratings (Par 101): **91,85,85,83,68 66**
CSF £50.35 TOTE £5.30: £2.40, £3.20; EX 31.80 Trifecta £118.30.
**Owner** C Letcher & J Ryan **Bred** Hadi Al Tajir **Trained** Newmarket, Suffolk

**FOCUS**
Stamina kicked in late here, in what was a low-grade handicap. The winner is rated in line with this year's form.
T/Plt: £658.80 to a £1 stake. Pool: £65234.49 - 72.27 winning tickets T/Qpdt: £61.50 to a £1 stake. Pool: £4508.31 - 54.2 winning tickets CR

## 2866 RIPON (R-H)
### Wednesday, June 4

**OFFICIAL GOING: Heavy**
Wind: light 1/2 against Weather: overcast

### 2895 BRITISH STALLION STUDS EBF MAIDEN STKS 6f
**6:40** (6:42) (Class 5) 2-Y-O **£3,881** (£1,155; £577; £288) **Stalls** High

Form RPR
**1** **Geordie George (IRE)** 2-9-5 0 PhillipMakin 1 81+
(John Quinn) *hld up in rr: stdy hdwy over 2f out: swtchd rt appr fnl f: led last 150yds: drew clr* **10/1**[3]

4 **2** *5* **Marmalad (IRE)**[12] [2507] 2-9-5 0 RichardKingscote 2 66
(Tom Dascombe) *w ldrs: led over 3f out: hdd jst ins fnl f: no ex* **7/4**[1]

0 **3** *2¼* **Cisco Boy**[20] [2288] 2-9-5 0 DavidAllan 4 59
(Tim Easterby) *w ldrs: kpt on same pce fnl f* **18/1**

6 **4** *3* **Special Venture (IRE)**[20] [2288] 2-9-5 0 PaulMulrennan 5 53+
(Tim Easterby) *hmpd s: in rr: swtchd lft over 4f out: nt clr run and swtchd rt over 1f out: kpt on steadily* **8/1**[2]

0 **5** *12* **Triggers Broom (IRE)**[22] [2231] 2-9-0 0 TonyHamilton 8
(Richard Fahey) *wnt rt s: chsd ldrs: outpcd and lost pl over 3f out* **16/1**

0 **6** *2¾* **Secret Of Dubai**[18] [2348] 2-9-0 0 DaleSwift 7
(Brian Ellison) *carried lft s: sn chsng ldrs on outer: drvn over 2f out: sn wknd* **40/1**

**7** *2* **Flying Grange** 2-9-5 0 GrahamGibbons 11
(Tim Easterby) *s.i.s: in rr: bhd fnl 2f* **25/1**

0 **8** *1¼* **Sparkling Sapphire**[18] [2349] 2-9-0 0 PaulQuinn 9
(Richard Whitaker) *led tl over 3f out: lost pl over 1f out* **66/1**

1m 18.55s (5.55) **Going Correction** +0.725s/f (Yiel) **8** Ran SP% **75.5**
Speed ratings (Par 93): **92,85,82,78,62 58,56,54**
CSF £11.91 TOTE £5.70: £2.30, £1.10, £3.10; EX 12.70 Trifecta £116.10.
**Owner** Fletcher, Outhart, Moran & Maddison **Bred** Azienda Agricola Rosati Colarieti **Trained** Settrington, N Yorks
■ Rule 4 of 40p in the pound applies to all bets; Withdrawn: Revolutionist

**FOCUS**
Rail on inner most position and distances as advertised. The meeting had to survive an afternoon inspection, but 13mm of rain resulted in heavy going. There was no GoingStick reading. This was a real test in the conditions, confirmed by a time, 8.25sec slower than standard. The form is given a token rating through the runner-up.

### 2896 EURA AUDIT UK H'CAP 1m
**7:10** (7:10) (Class 5) (0-70,67) 3-Y-O **£3,234** (£962; £481; £240) **Stalls** Low

Form RPR
4243 **1** **Tamayuz Magic (IRE)**[18] [2355] 3-9-0 **60** (b) GrahamGibbons 2 64
(Michael Easterby) *trckd ldr: led over 6f out: clr over 1f out: eased nr fin* **5/6**[1]

500- **2** *3* **Mighty Missile (IRE)**[222] [7494] 3-9-2 **62** JamesSullivan 6 58
(Tom Tate) *trckd ldrs: drvn and wl outpcd over 4f out: hdwy over 2f out: swtchd rt appr fnl f: sn chsng wnr* **5/2**[2]

040- **3** *3¼* **Ice Mayden**[197] [7955] 3-8-9 **55** RoystonFfrench 5 44
(Bryan Smart) *trckd ldrs: 2nd over 2f out: rdn over 1f out: sn fdd* **5/1**[3]

66-0 **4** *11* **Wolfwood**[16] [2387] 3-7-9 **48** oh3 JackGarritty(7) 1 11
(John Davies) *t.k.h: led: hdd over 6f out: drvn 3f out: wknd wl over 1f out* **9/1**

1m 47.6s (6.20) **Going Correction** +0.725s/f (Yiel) **4** Ran SP% **109.8**
Speed ratings (Par 99): **98,95,91,80**
CSF £3.24 TOTE £1.70; EX 3.10 Trifecta £4.70.
**Owner** W H & Mrs J A Tinning **Bred** Eimear Mulhern **Trained** Sheriff Hutton, N Yorks

**FOCUS**
Not a strong race in the absence of four of those initially declared. The winner was the only one to show their form on the ground in all probability.

### 2897 RIPON FARM SERVICES H'CAP (BOBIS RACE) 6f
**7:40** (7:42) (Class 4) (0-85,84) 3-Y-O **£5,175** (£1,540; £769; £384) **Stalls** High

Form RPR
1-21 **1** **Rural Celebration**[5] [2727] 3-9-5 **82** 6ex DanielTudhope 10 92+
(David O'Meara) *led over 1f: nt clr run over 2f out tl swtchd rt over 1f out: led 1f out: hld on towards fin* **1/1**[1]

12-6 **2** *¾* **Heroique (IRE)**[35] [1884] 3-8-9 **72** (e) DuranFentiman 3 77
(Tim Easterby) *chsd ldr: led over 4f out: hdd 1f out: kpt on towards fin* **16/1**

416- **3** *3¼* **Withernsea (IRE)**[368] [2877] 3-9-2 **82** GeorgeChaloner(3) 2 77
(Richard Fahey) *sn chsng ldrs: drvn over 2f out: kpt on same pce fnl f* **14/1**

6-21 **4** *hd* **Boy In The Bar**[12] [2524] 3-8-12 **75** AndrewMullen 6 69
(David Barron) *in rr: drvn over 3f out: hdwy over 2f out: kpt on: nvr a threat* **7/2**[2]

0330 **5** *2¾* **Meadway**[19] [2317] 3-9-5 **82** PaulMulrennan 8 67
(Bryan Smart) *trckd ldrs: effrt 2f out: wknd fnl 100yds* **10/1**

-310 **6** *2¼* **One Boy (IRE)**[19] [2317] 3-9-4 **84** ConnorBeasley(3) 9 62
(Michael Dods) *in rr: drvn and hdwy on ins over 2f out: wknd over 1f out* **9/2**[3]

32-0 **7** *2* **Syros (IRE)**[18] [2333] 3-8-7 **77** DanielleMooney(7) 1 49
(Michael Easterby) *chsd ldrs on outer: drvn over 3f out: sn outpcd: wknd 2f out* **33/1**

1m 17.69s (4.69) **Going Correction** +0.725s/f (Yiel) **7** Ran SP% **115.0**
Speed ratings (Par 101): **97,96,91,91,87 84,82**
CSF £20.29 CT £148.09 TOTE £1.70: £1.10, £5.80; EX 19.50 Trifecta £186.30.
**Owner** Hambleton Racing Ltd - Two Chances **Bred** J A And M A Knox **Trained** Nawton, N Yorks

**FOCUS**
A good performance from the winner, who gave the impression he was better than the bare form.

### 2898 DIRECTORS CUP (HANDICAP STKS) 6f
**8:10** (8:10) (Class 3) (0-95,95) 4-Y-O **£7,561** (£2,263; £1,131; £566; £282) **Stalls** High

Form RPR
-000 **1** **Colonel Mak**[21] [2254] 7-8-13 **90** JasonHart(3) 8 102
(David Barron) *mde all: styd on wl ins fnl f* **14/1**

0011 **2** *1¾* **Bear Behind (IRE)**[11] [2562] 5-9-5 **93** RichardKingscote 3 99
(Tom Dascombe) *chsd ldrs: kpt on same pce fnl f* **11/4**[2]

0-00 **3** *nse* **Cosmic Chatter**[18] [2353] 4-9-5 **93** AndrewMullen 7 99
(David Barron) *sn chsng ldrs: drvn 3f out: styd on fnl f* **25/1**

3-13 **4** *½* **Watchable**[12] [2503] 4-9-7 **95** DanielTudhope 9 99+
(David O'Meara) *chsd ldrs: drvn to chse wnr 1f out: hung lft and wknd nr fin: sddle slipped* **2/1**[1]

1-10 **5** *3¼* **Tarooq (USA)**[47] [1557] 8-8-12 **86** GrahamGibbons 6 80
(David Barron) *in rr: reminders after 1f: sme hdwy over 2f out: eased ins fnl f* **7/1**

-041 **6** *2¾* **Angus Og**[26] [2136] 4-8-8 **87** JoeyHaynes(5) 10 72
(K R Burke) *s.s: hdwy over 2f out: wknd over 1f out* **5/1**[3]

1346 **7** *6* **Mutafaakir (IRE)**[18] [2352] 5-8-7 **81** (p) JamesSullivan 2 47
(Ruth Carr) *racd wd: t.k.h and hung rt: sme hdwy over 2f out: lost pl over 1f out* **11/2**

1m 16.06s (3.06) **Going Correction** +0.725s/f (Yiel) **7** Ran SP% **115.1**
Speed ratings (Par 107): **108,105,105,104,100 96,88**
CSF £53.10 CT £974.92 TOTE £15.20: £7.90, £1.70; EX 70.60 Trifecta £666.70.
**Owner** Norton Common Farm Racing,O'Kane,Murphy **Bred** Peter Baldwin **Trained** Maunby, N Yorks

**FOCUS**
Not a bad sprint handicap. The form is rated at face value, with the winner close to last year's best.

### 2899 SIS LIVE MAIDEN STKS 1m 1f 170y
**8:40** (8:41) (Class 5) 3-Y-O+ **£3,234** (£962; £481; £240) **Stalls** Low

Form RPR
22-0 **1** **Empress Ali (IRE)**[15] [2422] 3-8-9 73 JamesSullivan 3 74
(Tom Tate) *mde all: edgd lft ins fnl f: hld on gamely* **2/1**[2]

0- **2** *1¼* **Spiritoftheunion**[225] [7442] 3-8-9 0 JoeFanning 7 71
(Michael Bell) *trckd wnr: chal 3f out: styd on same pce ins fnl f* **6/1**[3]

0-3 **3** *1* **Epsom Hill (SWE)**[23] [2201] 3-9-0 0 FrankieDettori 8 74
(Charlie Fellowes) *hld up in mid-div: drvn and hdwy over 3f out: sn chsng ldng pair: hung rt over 1f out: kpt on same pce* **5/4**[1]

00 **4** *8* **Fickle Feelings (IRE)**[18] [2354] 3-8-9 0 GrahamGibbons 1 53
(David Barron) *chsd ldrs: drvn over 3f out: wknd over 1f out* **14/1**

6 **5** *2* **Housewives Choice**[28] [2082] 3-8-9 0 PJMcDonald 5 49
(James Bethell) *dwlt: mid-div: hdwy over 4f out: chsng ldrs 3f out: edgd lft and wknd over 1f out* **10/1**

/00- **6** *31* **Billy Redpath**[352] [3398] 6-9-10 31 [1] JasonHart(3) 2
(Frederick Watson) *s.i.s: t.k.h in rr: lost pl 4f out: bhd whn eased over 1f out: t.o* **100/1**

0-5 **7** *4½* **Oscuro**[22] [2236] 3-9-0 0 DavidAllan 9
(Tim Easterby) *chsd ldrs: drvn over 4f out: lost pl 3f out: sn bhd: t.o* **16/1**

**8** *11* **King Couture (IRE)** 3-9-0 0 BarryMcHugh 6
(Michael Easterby) *sed vefy slowly: in rr: bhd fnl 4f: t.o* **33/1**

2m 12.4s (7.00) **Going Correction** +0.725s/f (Yiel)
**WFA** 3 from 6yo 13lb **8** Ran SP% **117.6**
Speed ratings (Par 103): **101,100,99,92,91 66,62,54**
CSF £15.17 TOTE £3.50: £1.20, £2.20, £1.10; EX 17.80 Trifecta £31.50.
**Owner** T T Racing **Bred** Denis McDonnell **Trained** Tadcaster, N Yorks

**FOCUS**
Not a strong maiden. The first two held the same positions throughout and the winner is rated back to her 2yo form.

### 2900 LADIES DAY 19TH JUNE BOOK NOW H'CAP 2m
**9:10** (9:10) (Class 5) (0-75,73) 4-Y-O+ **£3,234** (£962; £481; £240) **Stalls** Low

Form RPR
502- **1** **Rayadour (IRE)**[43] [5052] 5-9-2 **65** (p) TomEaves 8 66
(Micky Hammond) *led 1f: led over 11f out: increased pce over 5f out: jnd over 3f out: hld on gamely fnl f* **6/1**[3]

0/2- **2** *nk* **Rumble Of Thunder (IRE)**[19] [2860] 8-9-8 **71** RussKennemore 6 72
(Philip Kirby) *trckd ldrs: chal over 3f out: ev ch fnl f: no ex whn n.m.r nr fin* **4/5**[1]

-050 **3** *shd* **Cowslip**[26] [2139] 5-7-12 **54** oh3 KieranSchofield(7) 7 55
(George Moore) *hld up in rr: hdwy 8f out: pushed along over 5f out: chsng ldrs over 2f out: styd on wl last 50yds* **7/1**

-414 **4** *shd* **Choisan (IRE)**[26] [2139] 5-9-10 **73** (tp) DuranFentiman 9 74
(Tim Easterby) *led after 1f: hdd over 11f out: drvn 4f out: rallied and edgd lft 2f out: ev ch fnl f: no ex nr fin* **10/3**[2]

636- **5** *3* **Spiekeroog**[13] [8004] 8-8-12 **61** DaleSwift 2 58
(Alan Brown) *hld up in rr: effrt over 3f out: chsng ldrs 2f out: one pce* **25/1**

3m 56.67s (24.87) **Going Correction** +0.725s/f (Yiel) **5** Ran SP% **109.3**
Speed ratings (Par 103): **66,65,65,65,64**
CSF £11.29 TOTE £5.30: £1.70, £1.30; EX 11.40 Trifecta £27.20.
**Owner** Straightline Construction Ltd **Bred** His Highness The Aga Khan's Studs S C **Trained** Middleham Moor, N Yorks

**FOCUS**
Unsurprisingly, given the conditions, they took things quite steadily early on. The first four finished in a heap and the form is hard to rate positively.
T/Plt: £8.10 to a £1 stake. Pool: £78,654 - 7,064.24 winning tickets T/Qpdt: £5.20 to a £1 stake. Pool: £5,081 - 721.66 winning tickets WG

# 2394 SOUTHWELL (L-H)

Wednesday, June 4

**OFFICIAL GOING: Standard**

Wind: Light across Weather: Cloudy

## 2901 NEWARK FESTIVAL 2014 H'CAP — 7f (F)

**2:30** (2:31) (Class 6) (0-65,65) 4-Y-O+ — **£1,940** (£577; £288; £144) **Stalls** Low

Form — RPR

40-1 **1** **Putin (IRE)**[130] 339 6-8-13 **62**....(bt) RachealKneller(5) 2 — 76
(Phil McEntee) *mde all: rdn along 2f out: drvn ins fnl f and kpt on strly* **8/1**

6644 **2** *4* **Refuse Colette (IRE)**[27] 2092 5-8-2 **46** oh1.... PaoloSirigu 7 — 50
(Mick Quinn) *chsd ldrs: pushed along 3f out: rdn over 2f out: styd on to chse wnr whn edgd lft ent fnl f: sn drvn and no imp* **12/1**

-230 **3** *1 ¾* **Victorian Number (FR)**[14] 2463 6-9-6 **64**.... HayleyTurner 1 — 63
(Geoffrey Deacon) *chsd ldrs: cl up 1/2-way: rdn along over 2f out: drvn over 1f out and sn one pce* **7/4**[1]

4060 **4** *3 ½* **Foie Gras**[14] 2463 4-9-4 **62**.... BenCurtis 4 — 52
(Chris Dwyer) *in tch: hdwy on outer and wd st: rdn along 2f out: drvn over 1f out and no imp* **7/1**

33-6 **5** *2 ½* **Tony Hollis**[153] 18 6-8-4 **48**....(vt¹) AndrewMullen 10 — 31
(Michael Appleby) *prom on outer: rdn along over 2f out: drvn wl over 1f out and sn wknd* **5/1**[3]

3200 **6** *6* **Officer In Command (USA)**[14] 2464 8-8-12 **63**....(p) GeorgiaCox(7) 3 — 31
(John Butler) *dwlt and sltly hmpd s: a in rr* **16/1**

-046 **7** *1 ½* **Blazeofenchantment (USA)**[72] 1082 4-9-2 **65**.... AdamCarter(5) 8 — 29
(John Wainwright) *s.i.s: sn swtchd lft to inner: hld up and bhd: tenderly rdn and nvr a factor* **4/1**[2]

00-0 **8** *3 ¼* **Frognal (IRE)**[40] 1689 8-8-12 **61**....(bt) ShirleyTeasdale(5) 9 — 17
(Ann Stokell) *chsd ldrs: rdn along over 2f out and sn wknd* **25/1**

265- **9** *4* **Chosen Forever**[320] 4504 9-9-4 **62**.... RussKennemore 6 — 7
(Lee James) *chsd ldrs: rdn along 1/2-way: sn wknd* **25/1**

1m 28.71s (-1.59) **Going Correction** -0.175s/f (Stan) — **9** Ran SP% **117.9**

Speed ratings (Par 101): **102,97,95,91,88 81,80,76,71**

CSF £100.34 CT £243.22 TOTE £7.80: £1.90, £4.50, £1.10; EX 158.00 Trifecta £627.70.

**Owner** Steve Jakes **Bred** D Llewelyn & J Runeckles **Trained** Newmarket, Suffolk

■ Stewards' Enquiry : Adam Carter matter referred: guilty of intentionally failing to ensure gelding ran on its merits.

**FOCUS**

The pace was sound for this handicap and the field finished strung out.

## 2902 CONNIE WHITE MEMORIAL MAIDEN STKS — 7f (F)

**3:00** (3:10) (Class 5) 3-Y-O+ — **£2,587** (£770; £384; £192) **Stalls** Low

Form — RPR

4-30 **1** **Yagheer (IRE)**[44] 1614 3-9-3 75.... JackMitchell 2 — 78+
(Roger Varian) *t.k.h: led 2f: cl up tl led again 1/2-way: jnd and rdn 2f out: drvn ent fnl f: kpt on* **11/10**[1]

3 **2** *1 ¼* **Inkerman (IRE)**[26] 2126 4-9-13 75.... JimmyFortune 4 — 77
(Jamie Osborne) *trckd ldng pair: hdwy 3f out: sn chsng wnr: rdn to chal 2f out and ev ch tl drvn and one pce ins fnl f* **5/4**[2]

0-0 **3** *7* **Solid Justice (IRE)**[48] 1542 3-9-3 0.... AndrewElliott 7 — 55
(Jason Ward) *towards rr: hdwy wl over 2f out: sn rdn: kpt on one pce: tk mod 3rd ins fnl f* **20/1**

-240 **4** *2 ½* **Molly Ahoy**[26] 2129 3-8-12 65.... AndrewMullen 5 — 43
(Alan McCabe) *chsd ldrs: hdwy to chse ldng pair wl over 2f out: sn rdn: drvn wl over 1f out and sn outpcd* **8/1**[3]

0 **5** *19* **City Zip**[16] 2389 4-9-5 0....(v¹) BillyCray(3) 1
(Alan McCabe) *cl up on inner: led after 2f: rdn along and hdd 1/2-way: wknd over 2f out* **33/1**

0 **6** *hd* **Shadow Of The Day**[44] 1608 7-9-13 0.... RussKennemore 8
(Lee James) *s.i.s: pushed along and sn chsng ldrs: rdn bef 1/2-way: sn outpcd and bhd* **33/1**

1m 28.83s (-1.47) **Going Correction** -0.175s/f (Stan)

**WFA** 3 from 4yo+ 10lb — **6** Ran SP% **113.8**

Speed ratings (Par 103): **101,99,91,88,67 66**

CSF £2.75 TOTE £2.10: £1.10, £1.10; EX 2.90 Trifecta £19.60.

**Owner** Sheikh Ahmed Al Maktoum **Bred** Castlemartin Sky & Skymarc Farm **Trained** Newmarket, Suffolk

**FOCUS**

In a race that was run at a fair gallop, the market principals were in command a long way out.

## 2903 32RED FREE £10 BONUS MAIDEN STKS — 6f (F)

**3:30** (3:35) (Class 5) 2-Y-O — **£2,587** (£770; £384; £192) **Stalls** Low

Form — RPR

26 **1** **Denzille Lane (IRE)**[11] 2543 2-9-5 0.... JoeFanning 5 — 80+
(Mark Johnston) *mde all: jnd and rdn over 2f out: hung bdly lft jst over 1f out: kpt on strly and clr ins fnl f* **5/6**[1]

3 **2** *6* **Grosmont**[16] 2395 2-9-5 0.... TomEaves 3 — 62
(James Given) *cl up: effrt over 2f out: rdn and ch whn hmpd and swtchd rt over 1f out: one pce after* **7/4**[2]

00 **3** *3 ¼* **Rocco's Delight**[22] 2231 2-9-0 0.... AdamCarter(5) 6 — 52
(John Wainwright) *dwlt and towards rr: hdwy on outer 1/2-way: rdn along over 2f out: kpt on: no ch w ldng pair* **50/1**

**4** *4* **Cheeco** 2-9-5 0.... PJMcDonald 1 — 40+
(Ruth Carr) *s.i.s: green and bhd: hdwy over 2f out: kpt on appr fnl f* **33/1**

030 **5** *5* **Lunar Knot**[26] 2128 2-9-0 0....(v¹) BenCurtis 2 — 20
(Alan McCabe) *dwlt: a towards rr* **25/1**

**6** *16* **Artic Promise** 2-9-5 0.... JimmyFortune 4
(Brian Meehan) *chsd ldng pair: rdn along 1/2-way: wknd 2f out* **8/1**[3]

1m 16.63s (0.13) **Going Correction** -0.175s/f (Stan) — **6** Ran SP% **110.8**

Speed ratings (Par 93): **92,84,79,74,67 46**

CSF £2.39 TOTE £1.60: £1.10, £1.10; EX 2.50 Trifecta £23.50.

**Owner** Sheikh Hamdan bin Mohammed Al Maktoum **Bred** Mountarmstrong Stud **Trained** Middleham Moor, N Yorks

**FOCUS**

An uncompetitive maiden run at a sound pace.

## 2904 32RED TOMB RAIDER SLOT CLAIMING STKS — 1m 4f (F)

**4:00** (4:00) (Class 5) 3-Y-O+ — **£2,726** (£805; £402) **Stalls** Low

Form — RPR

3-50 **1** **Omnipresent**[32] 1934 4-9-13 79.... DavidNolan 1 — 84
(David O'Meara) *led 1 1/2f: cl up: led again over 3f out: rdn 2f out: drvn ins fnl f and kpt on wl towards fin* **7/1**

3101 **2** *1 ½* **Dynastic**[16] 2394 5-9-5 72.... LauraBarry(7) 5 — 81
(Tony Coyle) *trckd ldrs: hdwy 4f out: chsd wnr over 2f out: sn rdn to chal and ev ch tl drvn ent fnl f and one pce* **3/1**[2]

2643 **3** *7* **Noguchi (IRE)**[14] 2467 9-9-2 73....(b) JordanVaughan(7) 3 — 66
(George Margarson) *trckd ldrs: hdwy over 4f out: effrt to chse wnr 3f out: sn cl up: rdn 2f out and grad wknd over 1f out* **11/2**[3]

05 **4** *12* **Saddlers Mot**[13] 2354 10-8-12 0.... GemmaTutty(7) 2 — 43
(Karen Tutty) *in rr: detached and swtchd wd after 1 1/2f: hdwy on outer to take clsr order 1/2-way: rdn along over 3f out: n.d* **50/1**

2112 **5** *nk* **Stand Guard**[50] 1495 10-9-12 82.... StevieDonohoe 6 — 50
(John Butler) *hld up in tch: pushed along 4f out: sn lost pl and wd in st: sn rdn along btn* **5/4**[1]

21-3 **6** *1 ½* **Rock Of Ages**[153] 14 5-9-10 60....(b) LiamJones 8 — 45
(Michael Murphy) *rdn along to ld after 1 1/2f: pushed along over 4f out: rdn over 3f out: sn hdd & wknd* **10/1**

36-6 **7** *13* **Forward March**[15] 2444 4-9-11 72.... J-PGuillambert 7 — 26
(Nick Littmoden) *chsd ldr: pushed along 5f out: rdn 4f out: sn lost pl and bhd* **25/1**

2m 38.99s (-2.01) **Going Correction** -0.175s/f (Stan) — **7** Ran SP% **112.2**

Speed ratings (Par 103): **99,98,93,85,85 84,75**

CSF £27.18 TOTE £7.30: £4.10, £1.30; EX 27.80 Trifecta £152.70.Ominpresent was claimed by R M H Cowell for £15,000.

**Owner** Middleham Park Racing XXXVIII **Bred** Juddmonte Farms Ltd **Trained** Nawton, N Yorks

**FOCUS**

They went a steady pace for this decent claimer.

## 2905 32RED CASINO H'CAP — 7f (F)

**4:30** (4:30) (Class 4) (0-80,80) 4-Y-O+ — **£4,690** (£1,395; £697; £348) **Stalls** Low

Form — RPR

-210 **1** **Two Moons**[51] 1483 4-9-2 **75**.... BarryMcHugh 5 — 84+
(Tony Coyle) *dwlt and in rr: hdwy 3f out: chal wl over 1f out: rdn and slt ld jst ins fnl f: drvn and hld on wl towards fin* **2/1**[1]

3200 **2** *hd* **Piceno (IRE)**[11] 2549 6-8-9 **75**....(p) MatthewHopkins(7) 4 — 83
(Scott Dixon) *cl up: led wl over 2f out: jnd and rdn 2f out: drvn and hdd jst ins fnl f: rallied wl u.p nr fin* **8/1**

5141 **3** *nse* **Repetition**[16] 2400 4-9-7 **80**.... TomEaves 1 — 88
(Kristin Stubbs) *chsd ldng pair: hdwy over 2f out: rdn to chal over 1f out: drvn ent fnl f and ev ch tl no ex nr fin* **4/1**[2]

-450 **4** *¾* **Intrepid (IRE)**[39] 1739 4-8-12 **71**.... StevieDonohoe 8 — 77
(Ian Williams) *racd wd: towards rr: hdwy on wd outside over 3f out: wd st: chsd ldrs 2f out and sn rdn: styd on wl u.p fnl f: nrst fin* **10/1**

3521 **5** *9* **Abi Scarlet (IRE)**[16] 2398 5-9-0 **80**.... CharlieBennett(7) 6 — 63
(Hughie Morrison) *chsd ldrs: rdn along 3f out: one pce fnl 2f* **6/1**

0560 **6** *5* **Pabusar**[16] 2400 6-8-0 **64**.... ShirleyTeasdale(5) 3 — 34
(Ann Stokell) *led: rdn along over 3f out: hdd wl over 2f out: sn wknd* **33/1**

2335 **7** *3 ¾* **Royal Holiday (IRE)**[25] 2169 7-8-10 **69**....(p) RussKennemore 2 — 29
(Marjorie Fife) *in tch and sn chsd along: rdn over 3f out: sn edgd lft to inner and wknd* **9/2**[3]

4-61 **8** *3* **Comrade Bond**[12] 2527 6-8-13 **72**....(p) BenCurtis 7 — 24
(Mark H Tompkins) *chsd ldrs on outer: rdn along 3f out: sn wknd* **14/1**

1m 28.55s (-1.75) **Going Correction** -0.175s/f (Stan) — **8** Ran SP% **115.6**

Speed ratings (Par 105): **103,102,102,101,91 85,81,78**

CSF £19.33 CT £59.75 TOTE £3.10: £1.70, £2.50, £1.30; EX 23.20 Trifecta £82.10.

**Owner** B Dunn **Bred** Mrs M L Parry & P M Steele-Mortimer **Trained** Norton, N Yorks

■ Stewards' Enquiry : Matthew Hopkins four-day ban: used whip above permitted level (Jun 22-25)

**FOCUS**

A fair handicap, run at a sound pace.

## 2906 32RED CLASSIFIED (S) STKS — 7f (F)

**5:00** (5:00) (Class 6) 3-Y-O — **£2,045** (£603; £302) **Stalls** Low

Form — RPR

2030 **1** **Frankthetank (IRE)**[23] 2218 3-9-4 73....(p) TomEaves 6 — 73
(Keith Dalgleish) *trckd ldr: effrt and cl up over 2f out: led wl over 1f out and sn rdn: drvn ins fnl f: hld on wl towards fin* **10/11**[1]

02 **2** *hd* **Black Vale (IRE)**[36] 1829 3-8-13 64....(t) DannyBrock(5) 1 — 72
(Phil McEntee) *set str pce: rdn along and jnd over 2f out: hdd wl over 1f out: drvn ins fnl f: rallied wl and ev ch tl no ex nr fin* **7/1**[3]

2050 **3** *1 ¼* **Queenie's Home**[8] 2643 3-9-4 72.... GrahamLee 2 — 69
(James Given) *in tch: hdwy on inner 1/2-way: rdn to chse ldng pair wl over 1f out: drvn and kpt on fnl f: nrst fin* **2/1**[2]

0234 **4** *6* **Sleet (IRE)**[16] 2397 3-8-9 54....(v) BillyCray(3) 4 — 47
(Michael Appleby) *dwlt and in rr: hdwy on inner 3f out: rdn over 2f out: kpt on one pce* **12/1**

6-40 **5** *5* **Maysville (IRE)**[30] 2020 3-8-12 50.... BarryMcHugh 5 — 34
(Tony Coyle) *chsd ldrs: rdn along 3f out: sn wknd* **33/1**

-005 **6** *½* **Emily Davison (IRE)**[5] 2729 3-8-5 50.... GemmaTutty(7) 3 — 33
(Karen Tutty) *chsd ldng pair: rdn along 1/2-way: wknd over 2f out* **50/1**

1m 29.12s (-1.18) **Going Correction** -0.175s/f (Stan) — **6** Ran SP% **110.8**

Speed ratings (Par 97): **99,98,97,90,84 84**

CSF £7.96 TOTE £2.20: £2.10, £1.90; EX 6.60 Trifecta £12.90.The winner was bought in for 6,750gns.

**Owner** Raymond McNeill **Bred** Burgage Stud **Trained** Carluke, S Lanarks

■ Stewards' Enquiry : Danny Brock four-day ban: used whip above permitted level (Jun 22-25)

**FOCUS**

The pace was honest for this uncompetitive seller, with the prominent runners always in command.

## 2907 32RED.COM H'CAP — 6f (F)

**5:30** (5:31) (Class 6) (0-60,59) 4-Y-O+ — **£1,940** (£577; £288; £144) **Stalls** Low

Form — RPR

4104 **1** **Amenable (IRE)**[7] 2677 7-9-2 **59**....(p) ShirleyTeasdale(5) 8 — 75
(Ann Stokell) *chsd ldrs: hdwy 1/2-way: wd in st: rdn to ld 1 1/2f out: clr ins fnl f: kpt on* **9/2**[2]

2024 **2** *4* **Novalist**[14] 2452 6-8-6 **47**....(b) JasonHart(3) 7 — 50
(Robin Bastiman) *qckly away and led: hdd after 1f: chsd ldr: rdn 2f out: drvn over 1f out: kpt on u.p fnl f* **9/2**[2]

0206 **3** *2 ½* **Pearl Noir**[22] 2232 4-9-0 **59**....(b) MatthewHopkins(7) 2 — 54
(Scott Dixon) *chsd ldr: led on inner after 1f: rdn over 2f out: hdd 1 1/2f out: sn drvn and kpt on same pce* **7/1**

5203 **4** *hd* **Flow Chart (IRE)**[37] 1804 7-8-8 **46**.... JoeFanning 4 — 41
(Peter Grayson) *chsd ldrs on inner: hdwy over 2f out: sn rdn and kpt on one pce fr over 1f out* **8/1**

0063 **5** *½* **Upper Lambourn (IRE)**[35] 1887 6-8-2 **46** oh1....(t) JackDuern(5) 5 — 38
(Christopher Kellett) *towards rr: wd st: hdwy 2f out: sn rdn and kpt on appr fnl f: nrst fin* **12/1**

0402 **6** 1 3/4 **Coach Montana (IRE)**[79] 996 5-8-8 **46**................(b) AdamBeschizza 10 33
(Christine Dunnett) *in tch: wd st: rdn along over 2f out: sn no imp* **7/2**[1]
3126 **7** 4 1/2 **Doctor Hilary**[27] 2094 12-9-0 **52**....................................(v) PaddyAspell 3 25
(Mark Hoad) *stmbld s: a in rr* **16/1**
2000 **8** 3/4 **Daneside (IRE)**[15] 2426 7-8-7 **46** oh1..........................(e[1]) AndrewElliott 9 16
(Simon West) *a in rr* **25/1**
00 **9** *hd* **Confidential Creek**[45] 1602 4-9-1 **58**..................(e[1]) JacobButterfield(5) 6 28
(Ollie Pears) *chsd ldrs: rdn wl over 1f out: wknd qckly appr fnl f* **6/1**[3]
00-0 **10** *nk* **Depden (IRE)**[35] 1877 6-8-8 **47** oh1 ow1...................[1] StevieDonohoe 11 15
(John Butler) *s.i.s: a bhd* **25/1**
1m 15.42s (-1.08) **Going Correction** -0.175s/f (Stan) **10** Ran SP% **117.7**
Speed ratings (Par 101): **100,94,91,91,90 88,82,81,80,80**
CSF £25.39 CT £141.87 TOTE £4.90: £1.80, £1.70, £3.00; EX 25.90 Trifecta £132.00.
**Owner** Stephen Arnold **Bred** Michael Downey & Roalso Ltd **Trained** Lincoln, Lincolnshire
**FOCUS**
A modest handicap run at a fair pace. The prominent runners were always in control.
T/Plt: £18.10 to a £1 stake. Pool: £60,259.55 - 2,418.04 winning tickets T/Qpdt: £8.60 to a £1 stake. Pool: £3,180.85 - 273.14 winning tickets JR

2908 - (Foreign Racing) - See Raceform Interactive

## 2673 HAMILTON (R-H)
### Thursday, June 5

**OFFICIAL GOING: Good to soft (good in places) changing to good to soft after race 2 (2.30)**
Wind: fine Weather: slight across

## 2909 LANARKSHIRE CHAMBER OF COMMERCE APPRENTICE H'CAP (ROUND 1 OF THE HAMILTON PARK APPRENTICE SERIES) 5f 4y
**2:00** (2:01) (Class 6) (0-65,60) 4-Y-0+ **£2,045** (£603; £302) **Stalls** Centre

Form RPR
-021 **1** **Classy Anne**[14] 2473 4-8-13 **52**...................................... JackGarritty(5) 6 72
(Jim Goldie) *trckd ldr: led over 1f out: pushed clr fnl f: readily* **5/2**[2]
0234 **2** 4 **Rock Canyon (IRE)**[8] 2675 5-9-2 **50**.............................. ConnorBeasley 1 56
(Linda Perratt) *hld up: hdwy on outside over 1f out: chsd (clr) wnr ins fnl f: kpt on: no imp* **12/1**
6302 **3** 1 1/4 **Major Muscari (IRE)**[6] 2724 6-9-5 **53**.........................(p) JasonHart 2 55
(Shaun Harris) *dwlt and fly-jmpd s: bhd tl hdwy over 1f out: kpt on fnl f: nrst fin* **9/4**[1]
6155 **4** 1/2 **Busy Bimbo (IRE)**[13] 2514 5-8-8 **49**.......................(b) JordanHibberd(7) 8 49
(Alan Berry) *hld up bhd ldng gp: pushed along over 2f out: hdwy fnl f: nvr rchd ldrs* **18/1**
3653 **5** 1/2 **Greenhead High**[6] 2724 6-9-0 **55**............................(v) AnnaHesketh(7) 4 53
(David Nicholls) *led to over 1f out: edgd lft and wknd ins fnl f* **4/1**[3]
0004 **6** 1/2 **Tadalavil**[13] 2514 9-9-1 **54**...................................... SammyJoBell(5) 3 50
(Linda Perratt) *prom: rdn over 2f out: outpcd fnl f* **20/1**
-000 **7** 1 **Black Douglas**[14] 2479 5-9-2 **55**.................................. MeganCarberry(5) 7 48
(Jim Goldie) *midfield: pushed along over 2f out: no imp whn n.m.r over 1f out: hung rt and sn btn* **16/1**
0050 **8** 2 1/2 **Fife Jo**[14] 2479 4-8-11 **45**........................................(b[1]) IanBrennan 11 29
(Jim Goldie) *prom: drvn over 2f out: wknd over 1f out* **50/1**
04/0 **9** *nk* **Hollydanfaye**[13] 2511 4-9-1 **52**.................................... KevinStott(3) 10 34
(Paul Green) *towards rr: drvn along over 2f out: sn btn* **80/1**
601- **10** 2 1/2 **Fol Hollow (IRE)**[248] 6903 9-9-5 **60**.............................. BTTreanor(7) 9 33
(Stuart Coltherd) *chsd ldrs: rdn along over 2f out: wknd over 1f out* **25/1**
1m 1.8s (1.80) **Going Correction** +0.40s/f (Good) **10** Ran SP% **110.0**
Speed ratings (Par 101): **101,94,92,91,91 90,88,84,84,80**
CSF £28.71 CT £69.46 TOTE £3.80: £1.30, £2.70, £1.10; EX 29.60 Trifecta £87.80.
**Owner** The Vital Sparks **Bred** Jonayro Investments **Trained** Uplawmoor, E Renfrews
■ Stewards' Enquiry : Anna Hesketh two-day ban: careless riding (Jun 22-23)
**FOCUS**
Rail realignment around the loop reduced distance by about 25yds on Round course. The ground was changed to good to soft, good in places from good, good to firm in places following 9mm of rain overnight. It was further amended following the second race to just good to soft. This was nothing more than a moderate event. The winner showed significant improvement.

## 2910 GRIFFITHS & ARMOUR OPEN MAIDEN STKS 6f 5y
**2:30** (2:30) (Class 5) 3-Y-0+ **£3,234** (£962; £481; £240) **Stalls** High

Form RPR
0 **1** **Mr McLaren**[6] 2737 3-9-5 0........................................ DavidNolan 5 81+
(David O'Meara) *trckd ldrs: smooth hdwy to ld over 1f out: rdn and edgd lft ins fnl f: kpt on strly* **2/1**[2]
-622 **2** 3 1/2 **Margrets Gift**[9] 2657 3-9-0 64...................................... DavidAllan 6 62
(Tim Easterby) *cl up: effrt and chsd wnr over 1f out: kpt on ins fnl f: nt pce of wnr* **4/5**[1]
00 **3** 4 1/2 **Mossy Marie (IRE)**[17] 2389 3-8-11 0.............................. JasonHart(3) 4 48
(Eric Alston) *t.k.h: led to over 1f out: wknd ins fnl f* **25/1**
0-25 **4** 1 3/4 **Straight Gin**[34] 1925 3-9-5 47........................................(t) GrahamLee 1 47
(Alan Berry) *prom: effrt and rdn 2f out: wknd fnl f* **8/1**[3]
36 **5** 1 1/2 **Poetree In Motion**[24] 2217 3-9-0 0.................................. TomEaves 2 37
(Keith Dalgleish) *hld up in tch: rdn over 2f out: wknd over 1f out* **18/1**
**6** 7 **Charedal** 6-9-8 0................................................(b[1]) PJMcDonald 3 17
(Iain Jardine) *s.v.s: bhd: drvn and struggling 1/2-way: nvr on terms* **80/1**
1m 15.2s (3.00) **Going Correction** +0.40s/f (Good)
**WFA** 3 from 4yo+ 8lb **6** Ran SP% **110.3**
Speed ratings (Par 103): **96,91,85,83,81 71**
CSF £3.76 TOTE £2.70: £1.10, £1.10; EX 4.80 Trifecta £35.70.
**Owner** Middleham Park Racing LXIV & Partner **Bred** R J Cornelius **Trained** Nawton, N Yorks
**FOCUS**
A maiden lacking depth, but the winner improved considerably from his debut.

## 2911 ALEX FERGUSSON MEMORIAL H'CAP (QUALIFIER FOR THE £15,000 BETFAIR SCOTTISH MILE SERIES FINAL) 1m 65y
**3:00** (3:00) (Class 6) (0-65,63) 4-Y-0+ **£1,940** (£577; £288; £144) **Stalls** Low

Form RPR
-043 **1** **Camerooney**[13] 2518 11-9-2 **63**.............................(p) NathanAlison(5) 6 75
(Marjorie Fife) *mde all at stdy pce: qcknd over 2f out: edgd lft and styd on wl fnl f: unchal* **5/2**[1]
23-5 **2** 2 1/2 **Lil Sophella (IRE)**[13] 2518 5-8-8 **57**...........................[1] JackGarritty(5) 3 62
(Patrick Holmes) *hld up bhd ldng gp: hdwy on outside to chse wnr over 1f out: edgd rt and kpt on ins fnl f: nt pce to chal* **13/2**[3]
-503 **3** *hd* **Dhaular Dhar (IRE)**[8] 2674 12-8-13 **58**........................ GaryBartley(3) 2 63
(Jim Goldie) *hld up: rdn and hdwy 2f out: disp 2nd pl ins fnl f: kpt on: hld nr fin* **13/2**[3]
4334 **4** 3/4 **Dansili Dutch (IRE)**[8] 2676 5-8-13 **62**........................... JoshDoyle(7) 1 65
(David O'Meara) *hld up in tch: hdwy to chse wnr over 2f out: wandered u.p and lost 2nd over 1f out: sn one pce* **11/4**[2]
66-0 **5** 2 **Eastward Ho**[42] 1673 6-9-5 **61**.................................... TonyHamilton 5 59
(Michael Herrington) *hld up in tch: rdn and outpcd over 2f out: plugged on fnl f: no imp* **16/1**
0030 **6** 1 1/4 **Ebony Clarets**[8] 2676 5-8-5 **50**................................ ConnorBeasley(3) 10 45
(Linda Perratt) *prom: drvn over 3f out: outpcd fnl 2f* **40/1**
5465 **7** 1 3/4 **Kay Gee Be (IRE)**[13] 2509 10-9-3 **59**............................ PaulMulrennan 8 50
(Alan Berry) *trckd wnr: rdn over 3f out: outpcd over 2f out: n.d after* **7/1**
3-00 **8** 7 **Joshua The First**[14] 2475 5-8-9 **56**........................... GarryWhillans(5) 11 31
(Ian Semple) *bhd: struggling 1/2-way: sme hdwy over 1f out: nvr on terms* **25/1**
0-06 **9** 1 **Liliargh (IRE)**[16] 2427 5-8-5 **47**..................................(v) AndrewElliott 9 20
(Ben Haslam) *prom on outside: rdn over 2f out: edgd rt and sn wknd* **16/1**
1m 51.24s (2.84) **Going Correction** +0.30s/f (Good) **9** Ran SP% **112.5**
Speed ratings (Par 101): **97,94,94,93,91 90,88,81,80**
CSF £18.59 CT £92.11 TOTE £3.30: £1.30, £2.10, £2.20; EX 22.20 Trifecta £131.70.
**Owner** Mrs Jean Stapleton **Bred** Miss Dianne Hill **Trained** Stillington, N Yorks
**FOCUS**
A few of these rated much higher in their prime, but this was just a moderate event. Slight improvement from the winner.

## 2912 WEATHERBYS PRIVATE BANKING HAMILTONIAN H'CAP 1m 1f 36y
**3:30** (3:30) (Class 4) (0-80,80) 4-Y-0+ **£6,469** (£1,925; £962; £481) **Stalls** Low

Form RPR
-045 **1** **King Of The Danes**[18] 2362 4-9-7 **80**............................ FrannyNorton 3 89
(Mark Johnston) *trckd ldr: led over 2f out: rdn and edgd lft over 1f out: hld on wl fnl f* **4/1**[3]
5202 **2** *nk* **Dakota Canyon (IRE)**[10] 2607 5-8-10 **69**...................(p) TonyHamilton 5 77
(Richard Fahey) *hld up: rdn and outpcd over 3f out: rallied on outside over 1f out: kpt on to take 2nd towards fin: r.o* **11/1**
0-53 **3** 3/4 **Never Forever**[14] 2477 5-8-4 **70**................................ JackGarritty(7) 4 76
(Jim Goldie) *hld up: hdwy on outside over 2f out: pressed wnr over 1f out: no ex and lost 2nd towards fin* **10/1**
6412 **4** 3 1/4 **Lord Franklin**[6] 2730 5-8-10 **72**................................ JasonHart(3) 2 72
(Eric Alston) *led: rdn and hdd over 2f out: outpcd over 1f out* **7/2**[2]
6431 **5** 3/4 **Ellaal**[12] 2546 5-8-6 **65**............................................ JamesSullivan 6 63
(Ruth Carr) *hld up in tch: drvn and outpcd over 2f out: n.d after* **11/1**
3 **6** *nk* **Shouranour (IRE)**[16] 2423 4-9-4 **77**.............................. DavidNolan 7 74
(David O'Meara) *prom: effrt and rdn over 2f out: no ex appr fnl f* **5/1**
-021 **7** 1 **Another For Joe**[14] 2477 6-9-2 **75**............................... GrahamLee 1 70
(Jim Goldie) *trckd ldrs: rdn whn n.m.r over 2f out: wknd over 1f out* **3/1**[1]
2m 1.13s (1.43) **Going Correction** +0.30s/f (Good) **7** Ran SP% **109.6**
Speed ratings (Par 105): **105,104,104,101,100 100,99**
CSF £41.45 TOTE £4.00: £3.10, £4.50; EX 41.20 Trifecta £565.00.
**Owner** Newsells Park Stud **Bred** Newsells Park Stud **Trained** Middleham Moor, N Yorks
**FOCUS**
This was the classiest race on the card, and it was run at a solid gallop from the outset. The winner's best form since winning at Goodwood last year.

## 2913 OGILVIE COMMUNICATIONS H'CAP 1m 3f 16y
**4:00** (4:00) (Class 6) (0-65,63) 4-Y-0+ **£2,045** (£603; £302) **Stalls** Low

Form RPR
30-0 **1** **Operateur (IRE)**[42] 1674 6-8-10 **52**.............................. AndrewElliott 5 60
(Ben Haslam) *trckd ldrs: rdn to ld over 1f out: styd on strly fnl f* **6/1**[3]
0313 **2** 2 **Call Of Duty (IRE)**[14] 2475 9-8-4 **51**.........................(b) EmmaSayer(5) 6 55
(Dianne Sayer) *hld up: rdn and hdwy 3f out: chsng ldrs whn hung rt over 1f out: rallied and chsd wnr ins fnl f: r.o* **2/1**[1]
3-60 **3** 1 1/4 **Captain Rhyric**[6] 2738 5-8-5 **47**................................ PJMcDonald 1 49
(James Moffatt) *led: rdn over 2f out: hdd over 1f out: one pce and lost 2nd ins fnl f* **9/1**
00 **4** 11 **Jordaura**[7] 2701 8-9-4 **63**........................................ SladeO'Hara(3) 4 45
(Alan Berry) *dwlt: hld up in tch: rdn and outpcd 3f out: n.d after* **6/1**[3]
005- **5** 8 **Perci French**[251] 6806 4-8-0 **45**................................ JulieBurke(3) 2 13
(David O'Meara) *t.k.h: pressed ldr tl rdn and wknd fr 2f out* **15/2**
435- **6** 5 **War Lord (IRE)**[75] 5789 4-9-6 **62**................................ PaulMulrennan 3 21
(Philip Kirby) *hld up: drvn along over 3f out: wknd over 2f out* **3/1**[2]
2m 33.82s (8.22) **Going Correction** +0.30s/f (Good) **6** Ran SP% **108.7**
Speed ratings (Par 101): **82,80,79,71,65 62**
CSF £17.26 TOTE £7.40: £2.50, £1.20; EX 23.60 Trifecta £130.00.
**Owner** Mrs Alison Royston & Mrs C Barclay **Bred** Razza Pallorsi **Trained** Middleham Moor, N Yorks
**FOCUS**
The early pace wasn't too bad, but it slowed down before quickening again heading to the final 5f. Muddling, weak form.

## 2914 WEATHERBYS BANK H'CAP (QUALIFIER FOR THE £15,000 BETFAIR SCOTTISH SPRINT SERIES FINAL) 6f 5y
**4:30** (4:33) (Class 5) (0-70,70) 4-Y-0+ **£3,408** (£1,006; £503) **Stalls** High

Form RPR
340- **1** **Mandalay King (IRE)**[276] 6052 9-8-12 **66**................ ShirleyTeasdale(5) 3 75
(Marjorie Fife) *in tch: hdwy on outside to ld wl over 1f out: rdn and drifted lft ins fnl f: r.o wl* **11/1**
5122 **2** 3/4 **Hab Reeh**[15] 2452 6-8-10 **59**...................................... JamesSullivan 6 66
(Ruth Carr) *in tch: hdwy on outside to chse wnr fnl f: kpt on but a hld* **11/2**[3]
2101 **3** 1 1/4 **Orwellian**[20] 2296 5-9-1 **64**...................................... PaulMulrennan 9 67+
(Bryan Smart) *dwlt: bhd tl rdn and hdwy over 1f out: kpt on fnl f: nrst fin* **9/2**[1]
1226 **4** *nk* **Bunce (IRE)**[8] 2677 6-9-2 **65**.................................... GrahamLee 8 67
(Linda Perratt) *in tch: drvn along 2f out: kpt on same pce fnl f* **11/2**[3]
0-00 **5** 2 1/2 **Medici Time**[10] 2602 9-9-5 **68**..............................(v) TonyHamilton 13 62+
(Tim Easterby) *s.i.s: hld up: smooth hdwy to chse wnr briefly over 1f out: sn pushed along: one pce fnl f* **33/1**
1-06 **6** 1 **Rioja Day (IRE)**[14] 2477 4-8-12 **64**............................ GaryBartley(3) 10 54
(Jim Goldie) *cl up: drvn over 2f out: no ex fr over 1f out* **15/2**
023 **7** 1/2 **Layla's Hero (IRE)**[20] 2296 7-9-2 **65**.......................(v) AdrianNicholls 1 57
(David Nicholls) *hld up: drvn and outpcd after 2f: rallied over 1f out: no imp whn n.m.r briefly ins fnl f: one pce* **5/1**[2]
6-51 **8** 1 **Goninodaethat**[15] 2451 6-8-1 **57**................................ JackGarritty(7) 2 43
(Jim Goldie) *t.k.h: cl up tl rdn and wknd over 1f out* **14/1**
0-60 **9** 3 1/2 **Evens And Odds (IRE)**[28] 2094 10-8-7 **56**.................... DavidAllan 5 30
(Peter Grayson) *towards rr: drvn after 2f: nvr able to chal* **40/1**
4305 **10** *nk* **Baltic Prince (IRE)**[20] 2293 4-8-11 **60**........................ RaulDaSilva 4 33
(Paul Green) *cl up tl rdn and wknd fr 2f out* **16/1**

06-2 **11** *6* **Flighty Clarets (IRE)**[16] 2421 4-8-13 **67**.................. SammyJoBell(5) 11 21
(Richard Fahey) *t.k.h: slt ld to wl over 1f out: sn wknd* **9/1**

1m 14.67s (2.47) **Going Correction** +0.40s/f (Good) **11** Ran SP% **113.6**
Speed ratings (Par 103): **99,98,96,95,92 91,90,89,84,84 76**
CSF £68.03 CT £320.02 TOTE £10.60: £3.20, £2.40, £1.70; EX 75.00 Trifecta £631.00.
**Owner** R W Fife **Bred** Forenaghts Stud And Dermot Cantillon **Trained** Stillington, N Yorks

**FOCUS**
A competitive-looking sprint for mainly modest types, it was run at a strong pace. Interestingly, the first two came with their runs from towards the centre of the track. The winner is rated in line with last year's form.

## 2915 LIB (LADIES IN BUSINESS) LUNCH H'CAP 1m 5f 9y
**5:00** (5:00) (Class 6) (0-65,63) 4-Y-0+ **£2,385** (£704; £352) **Stalls** Low

Form RPR

0660 **1** **Voice From Above (IRE)**[10] 2620 5-7-12 **47**.............(p) JackGarritty(7) 5 56
(Patrick Holmes) *mde all: pushed along and qcknd clr 2f out: kpt on fnl f: unchal* **6/1**

-665 **2** *3¼* **Latin Rebel (IRE)**[15] 2455 7-8-13 **55**.......................... GrahamLee 6 59
(Jim Goldie) *t.k.h early: hld up in tch: niggled along 1/2-way: rdn and outpcd 3f out: rallied over 1f out: styd on to take 2nd wl ins fnl f: nt rch wnr* **9/2**[3]

4/6 **3** *nk* **Rockabilly Riot (IRE)**[13] 2509 4-9-7 **63**.......................... PJMcDonald 2 67
(Martin Todhunter) *trckd ldrs: effrt and disp 2nd pl over 1f out to wl ins fnl f: kpt on same pce* **5/1**

5-41 **4** *shd* **Rocky Two (IRE)**[13] 2512 4-9-0 **56**.......................... PaulMulrennan 4 60
(Philip Kirby) *t.k.h: prom: effrt and chsd wnr over 2f out to wl ins fnl f: one pce* **14/5**[1]

4-44 **5** *2¾* **Kolonel Kirkup**[14] 2475 4-8-13 **58**.......................(b) ConnorBeasley(3) 8 58
(Michael Dods) *hld up: rdn over 3f out: hdwy wl over 1f out: no imp fnl f* **3/1**[2]

006 **6** *6* **Chaparella (IRE)**[12] 2550 4-8-7 **49**.......................... FrannyNorton 3 40
(Mark Johnston) *chsd wnr: rdn over 3f out: edgd rt and wknd wl over 1f out* **22/1**

4/4- **7** *5* **Endeavor**[42] 3287 9-8-3 **50** ow2.......................... EmmaSayer(5) 1 33
(Dianne Sayer) *s.v.s: bhd: shortlived effrt on outside 3f out: btn over 1f out* **22/1**

6-40 **8** *20* **Leroy Parker (IRE)**[30] 2055 6-9-4 **60**..........................(b) TomEaves 7 13
(Barry Murtagh) *hld up in tch: drvn and struggling over 3f out: lost tch over 2f out: t.o* **28/1**

3m 1.01s (7.11) **Going Correction** +0.30s/f (Good) **8** Ran SP% **112.6**
Speed ratings (Par 101): **90,88,87,87,86 82,79,66**
CSF £31.51 CT £143.47 TOTE £8.00: £1.90, £2.00, £1.30; EX 36.90 Trifecta £279.30.
**Owner** Grange Park Racing **Bred** Mrs L Vaughan **Trained** Middleham, N Yorks

T/Plt: £33.00 to a £1 stake. Pool: £62,476.33 - 1381.23 winning units. T/Qpdt: £23.60 to a £1 stake. Pool: £2806.22 - 87.90 winning units. RY

# 2881 KEMPTON (A.W) (R-H)
### Thursday, June 5

**OFFICIAL GOING: Standard**
Wind: light, across Weather: dry

## 2916 DUBLIN LEGENDS HERE ON 09.07.14 APPRENTICE H'CAP 1m 4f (P)
**5:40** (5:40) (Class 6) (0-65,70) 4-Y-0+ **£1,940** (£577; £288; £144) **Stalls** Centre

Form RPR

0131 **1** **Novel Dancer**[24] 2212 6-8-4 **50**.......................... JennyPowell(3) 5 61
(Lydia Richards) *hld up in tch towards rr: hdwy 4f out: rdn to chal and wnt clr w wnr 2f out: led ins fnl f: styd on wl* **4/1**[3]

233- **2** *hd* **Dumbfounded (FR)**[211] 7767 6-9-3 **63**.......................... CamHardie(3) 9 73
(Lady Herries) *chsd ldrs: hdwy to join ldr and travelling strly 3f out: led over 2f out: wnt clr w wnr 2f out: drvn over 1f out: hdd ins fnl f: styd on but a jst hld fnl 100yds* **5/2**[1]

00-0 **3** *4½* **Evergreen Forest (IRE)**[15] 2464 6-9-1 **61**...............(b) DavidParkes(3) 6 64
(Natalie Lloyd-Beavis) *hld up in tch in midfield: hdwy to chse ldrs and rdn ent fnl 2f: wnt 3rd jst over 1f out: kpt on but no imp* **14/1**

2250 **4** *½* **Elegant Ophelia**[40] 1729 5-8-11 **59**..........................(t) PaulBooth(5) 2 61
(Dean Ivory) *wl in tch in midfield: effrt to go 3rd and drvn 2f out: sn outpcd by ldng pair: lost 3rd and one pce fr jst over 1f out* **10/1**

-200 **5** *7* **Our Golden Girl**[94] 821 4-8-9 **52**..........................(b) JoshBaudains 11 43
(Shaun Lycett) *s.i.s: hld up in tch in last pair: rdn over 3f out: c wd st: styd on steadily fnl 2f: nvr trbld ldrs* **20/1**

6-64 **6** *¾* **Gravitate**[71] 1100 5-9-0 **62**..........................(t) RobHornby(5) 8 52
(Paul Webber) *chsd ldrs: rdn ent fnl 2f: sn outpcd and btn: wknd over 1f out* **7/2**[2]

033- **7** *8* **Green Earth (IRE)**[262] 6458 7-8-11 **59**.......................... SophieRalston(5) 12 36
(Pat Phelan) *hld up in rr: rdn over 3f out: no ch but plugged on past btn horses fr over 1f out* **16/1**

350- **8** *4* **Bridge That Gap**[365] 2982 6-8-13 **63**.......................... RhiainIngram(7) 3 34
(Roger Ingram) *t.k.h: chsd ldrs: wd and lost pl bnd 3f out: wknd over 2f out* **20/1**

0050 **9** *11* **Shirataki (IRE)**[38] 1798 6-9-0 **57**..........................(t) PatMillman 1 10
(Peter Hiatt) *in tch in midfield: rdn and effrt over 2f out: sn btn: wl bhd fnl f: t.o* **8/1**

0/0- **10** *7* **Bull Market (IRE)**[271] 6217 11-8-2 **45**.......................... RyanWhile 4
(Alan Jones) *s.i.s: hld up in rr: rdn 4f out: lost tch wl over 2f out: t.o fnl f: b.b.v* **20/1**

00/0 **11** *1½* **Osgood**[9] 405 7-8-10 **60**..........................(v) HectorCrouch(7) 10
(Gary Moore) *t.k.h: pressed ldr tl led 6f out: hdd wl over 2f out: sn dropped out: t.o fnl f* **14/1**

2m 33.26s (-1.24) **Going Correction** -0.05s/f (Stan) **11** Ran SP% **124.5**
Speed ratings (Par 101): **102,101,98,98,93 93,88,85,78,73 72**
CSF £14.87 CT £125.19 TOTE £3.80: £2.10, £1.70, £4.00; EX 16.00 Trifecta £410.60.
**Owner** Mrs Lydia Richards **Bred** The Queen **Trained** Funtington, W Sussex

**FOCUS**
A moderate handicap, confined to apprentice riders. It was run at an average pace and the first pair dominated the finish. The winner is rated in line with his better recent form.

## 2917 FOLLOW @BETVICTORRACING ON TWITTER MAIDEN STKS 1m 4f (P)
**6:10** (6:11) (Class 5) 3-Y-0+ **£2,587** (£770; £384; £192) **Stalls** Centre

Form RPR

3 **1** **The Corsican (IRE)**[32] 1984 3-8-13 0.......................... FergusSweeney 12 83
(David Simcock) *chsd ldr: rdn to chal ent fnl 2f: led 1f out: styd on wl and a doing enough: rdn out* **8/1**[3]

2 **2** *½* **Desert Snow**[21] 2280 3-8-8 0.......................... KierenFallon 5 77
(Saeed bin Suroor) *chsd ldrs: rdn and effrt ent fnl 2f: hrd drvn and wandered rt and lft ins fnl f: styd on to go 2nd wl ins fnl f: nvr quite getting to wnr* **4/6**[1]

30 **3** *1½* **Saarrem (USA)**[41] 1691 3-8-13 0.......................... DaneO'Neill 9 80
(John Gosden) *led: rdn ent fnl 2f: hdd 1f out: styd on same pce after: 3rd and hld whn eased towards fin* **4/1**[2]

0 **4** *4½* **Fort Berkeley (IRE)**[54] 1438 3-8-13 0.......................... FrankieDettori 4 72
(Paul Cole) *hld up in midfield: pushed along over 2f out: 6th and no ch w ldng trio over 1f out: kpt on into 4th ins fnl f* **50/1**

0 **5** *¾* **Sir Rosco**[24] 2221 3-8-13 0.......................... RyanMoore 11 71
(Sir Michael Stoute) *in tch in midfield: rdn and effrt over 2f out: sn outpcd: 5th and no ch w ldng trio over 1f out: plugged on* **8/1**[3]

**6** *¾* **New Reaction** 3-8-13 0.......................... PatDobbs 8 70
(Amanda Perrett) *chsd ldng trio: rdn ent fnl 2f: sn outpcd and wl btn 4th over 1f out: plugged on and lost 2 pls ins fnl f* **33/1**

**7** *5* **Uncle Muf (USA)**[61] 4-10-0 0.......................... MartinDwyer 6 62
(Ali Stronge) *in tch in midfield: rdn and effrt over 2f out: drvn and outpcd ent fnl 2f: sn wknd* **25/1**

40 **8** *6* **Bergan (GER)**[54] 1438 3-8-10 0.......................... WilliamTwiston-Davies(3) 14 52
(Mick Channon) *stdd s and dropped in bhd: in tch in rr: rdn and lost tch over 2f out* **50/1**

**9** *6* **Canadian Diamond (IRE)**[28] 5024 7-10-0 0.......................... LiamJones 3 43
(Brendan Powell) *s.i.s: t.k.h: hld up in tch in last quartet: hdwy into midfield 4f out: rdn over 2f out: sn wl btn* **25/1**

6-0 **10** *4½* **Lara Lipton (IRE)**[50] 1517 3-8-1 0.......................... LewisWalsh(7) 2 31
(Jane Chapple-Hyam) *a towards rr: rdn 3f out: sn lost tch* **100/1**

**11** *44* **Planet Rock** 3-8-6 0.......................... DavidParkes(7) 7
(Keiran Burke) *in tch in midfield: lost pl 4f out: t.o over 2f out* **100/1**

0-0 **12** *41* **I'm Lucy (IRE)**[15] 2466 3-8-8 0.......................... SaleemGolam 1
(Linda Jewell) *sn dropped to last: rdn 4f out: lost tch and t.o fnl 3f* **100/1**

2m 35.14s (0.64) **Going Correction** -0.05s/f (Stan)
**WFA** 3 from 4yo+ 15lb **12** Ran SP% **119.7**
Speed ratings (Par 103): **95,94,93,90,90 89,86,82,78,75 46,18**
CSF £13.45 TOTE £12.20: £1.90, £1.10, £1.60; EX 20.70 Trifecta £47.10.
**Owner** Mrs Fitri Hay **Bred** Mrs Fitriani Hay **Trained** Newmarket, Suffolk

**FOCUS**
Not a bad maiden. The first three were always prominent and there's a bit of doubt about how literal this form will prove.

## 2918 IRISH STALLION FARMS EBF MAIDEN FILLIES' STKS (BOBIS RACE) 6f (P)
**6:45** (6:49) (Class 5) 2-Y-O **£2,911** (£866; £432; £216) **Stalls** Low

Form RPR

**1** **Accipiter** 2-8-11 0.......................... AshleyMorgan(3) 8 85+
(Chris Wall) *chsd ldr: jnd ldr and travelling strly 2f out: pushed into ld ent fnl 1f: r.o strly and drew wl clr fnl f: readily* **33/1**

**2** *3¾* **Panda Spirit (USA)** 2-9-0 0.......................... RyanMoore 5 74+
(Sir Michael Stoute) *chsd ldng trio: rdn and effrt ent fnl 2f: chsd clr wnr ins fnl f: styd on for clr 2nd: no threat to wnr* **9/2**[3]

4 **3** *2¼* **Golden Zephyr (IRE)**[27] 2107 2-9-0 0.......................... JimmyFortune 7 67
(B W Hills) *led: rdn and jnd 2f out: hdd and immediately outpcd 1f out: lost 2nd and wknd ins fnl f* **9/4**[1]

**4** *1½* **Shagah (IRE)** 2-9-0 0.......................... FrankieDettori 6 63+
(Richard Hannon) *s.i.s: hld up towards rr: swtchd lft and effrt over 2f out: no threat to wnr but kpt on steadily fr over 1f out* **5/2**[2]

**5** *1¼* **Anastazia** 2-9-0 0.......................... SeanLevey 4 59+
(Paul D'Arcy) *chsd ldng pair: rdn and effrt ent fnl 2f: drvn and btn over 1f out: wknd fnl f* **50/1**

**6** *1¾* **All My Love (IRE)** 2-9-0 0.......................... PatDobbs 2 54
(Richard Hannon) *s.i.s: rn green towards rr: rdn and effrt over 2f out: sn struggling: wknd over 1f out* **12/1**

**7** *½* **Rathaath (IRE)** 2-9-0 0.......................... DaneO'Neill 11 52
(Brian Meehan) *s.i.s: rn green: sn in tch in midfield: effrt jst over 2f out: hung rt and no imp over 1f out: wknd fnl f* **16/1**

**8** *7* **Astrelle (IRE)** 2-9-0 0.......................... LukeMorris 3 31
(Marco Botti) *in tch in midfield: rdn jst over 2f out: sn struggling and outpcd: wknd wl over 1f out* **9/1**

**9** *2¾* **Goolagong Girl (IRE)** 2-9-0 0.......................... LiamJones 1 23+
(Jane Chapple-Hyam) *rn green: awkward leaving stalls and slowly away: a bhd: lost tch over 2f out* **50/1**

1m 13.19s (0.09) **Going Correction** -0.05s/f (Stan) **9** Ran SP% **108.0**
Speed ratings (Par 90): **97,92,89,87,85 83,82,73,69**
CSF £147.30 TOTE £30.90: £10.90, £2.20, £1.20; EX 346.00 Trifecta £736.80.
**Owner** Follow The Flag Partnership **Bred** The Lavington Stud **Trained** Newmarket, Suffolk
■ Primrose Valley was withdrawn. Price at time of withdrawal 8-1. Rule 4 applies to all bets - deduction 10p in the pound.

**FOCUS**
An interesting 2yo fillies' maiden, rated around the third. This is usually a good race and the winner impressed.

## 2919 DOWNLOAD THE BETVICTOR APP NOW H'CAP 6f (P)
**7:20** (7:20) (Class 4) (0-85,85) 4-Y-O+ **£4,690** (£1,395; £697; £348) **Stalls** Low

Form RPR

0132 **1** **Shaolin (IRE)**[19] 2341 4-9-2 **80**..........................(t) GeorgeBaker 2 89+
(Seamus Durack) *t.k.hs: chsd ldr for over 1f: styd chsng ldng pair: effrt on inner to chal 1f out: r.o wl to ld fnl 50yds* **3/1**[1]

3110 **2** *½* **Desert Strike**[9] 2645 8-9-1 **79**..........................(p) HayleyTurner 11 86
(Conor Dore) *taken down early: led: hrd pressed and rdn 2f out: drvn and battled on wl over 1f out: hdd and no ex fnl 50yds* **20/1**

000 **3** *¾* **Go Far**[12] 2562 4-9-0 **78**..........................(b) SilvestreDeSousa 9 83
(Alan Bailey) *chsd ldrs: wnt 2nd over 4f out: rdn and ev ch 2f out: kpt on u.p: no ex wl ins fnl f* **8/1**

5600 **4** *1¾* **Novellen Lad (IRE)**[52] 1492 9-9-2 **80**.......................... KierenFallon 4 79
(Willie Musson) *in tch in midfield: rdn over 2f out: outpcd 2f out: rallied and styd on ins fnl f: no threat to ldrs* **16/1**

-116 **5** *½* **Ex Ex**[110] 628 4-9-1 **79**.......................... LukeMorris 8 76
(Nick Littmoden) *in tch in last trio: rdn wl over 2f out: hdwy u.p over 1f out: styd on fnl f: no threat to ldrs* **10/1**

100 **6** *nk* **Light From Mars**[40] 1731 9-9-6 **84**..........................(p) LiamJones 12 80
(Ronald Harris) *stdd s: hld up in rr: rdn and effrt 2f out: hdwy over 1f out: styd on u.p fnl f: nvr threatened ldrs* **20/1**

215 **7** *hd* **Jubilee Brig**[27] 2117 4-9-5 **83**..........................(v) AdamKirby 5 79
(Sean Curran) *hld up in tch in last trio: effrt and n.m.r over 1f out: hdwy ins fnl f: styd on u.p fnl 150yds: nvr trbld ldrs* **4/1**[2]

4-20 **8** 1/2 **Kinglami**26 2147 5-8-13 80 OisinMurphy(3) 7 74
(Brian Gubby) *in tch in midfield: effrt but outpcd by ldrs 2f out: no imp over 1f out: styd on same pce fnl f* 4/1[2]

000- **9** 1 1/4 **Tommy's Secret**292 5537 4-9-7 85 PatDobbs 3 75
(Jane Chapple-Hyam) *chsd ldrs: rdn and unable qck ent fnl 2f: outpcd and btn over 1f out: wknd ins fnl f* 20/1

-34 **10** 1 1/2 **Noverre To Go (IRE)**6 2718 8-9-1 79 (p) SteveDrowne 1 64
(Ronald Harris) *dwlt: sn rcvrd and in tch in midfield: rdn and effrt ent fnl 2f: no hdwy and btn over 1f out: wknd fnl f* 6/1[3]

1m 12.28s (-0.82) **Going Correction** -0.05s/f (Stan) **10** Ran SP% **119.7**
Speed ratings (Par 105): **103,102,101,99,98 97,97,97,95,93**
CSF £70.44 CT £442.21 TOTE £3.30: £1.20, £4.70, £2.30; EX 41.40 Trifecta £513.10.
**Owner** P A Deal **Bred** Joe Fogarty **Trained** Baydon, Wilts

**FOCUS**
A competitive-looking sprint handicap but those racing handy always held sway. The runner-up is the key.

## 2920 DOWNLOAD THE BETVICTOR INSTABET APP H'CAP — 2m (P)
7:55 (7:56) (Class 4) (0-85,85) 4-Y-0+ £4,690 (£1,395; £697; £348) Stalls Low

Form RPR

3-44 **1** **Spice Fair**32 1981 7-9-0 75 SeanLevey 1 83
(Mark Usher) *t.k.h: wl in tch midfield: rdn and effrt over 2f out: clsd u.p over 1f out: styd on wl to ld towards fin* 5/1[1]

6-34 **2** nk **Opera Buff**14 2490 5-9-1 76 (p) JamesDoyle 4 83
(Sean Curran) *led and set stdy gallop: rdn and qcknd over 2f out: drvn and hrd pressed ins fnl f: hdd and no ex towards fin* 5/1[1]

/00- **3** shd **Courtesy Call (IRE)**33 5288 5-9-10 85 TomQueally 6 92
(Nicky Henderson) *wl in tch in midfield: rdn and effrt to chse ldr 2f out: clsd u.p over 1f out: ev ch ins fnl f: no ex cl home* 14/1[3]

1000 **4** nk **Travel (USA)**13 2515 4-9-0 76 SilvestreDeSousa 7 83
(Mark Johnston) *hld up in tch in midfield: rdn and gd hdwy over 1f out: ev ch wl ins fnl f: no imp cl home* 14/1[3]

30-6 **5** 3 1/4 **Saborido (USA)**14 2490 8-9-3 78 PatDobbs 10 81
(Amanda Perrett) *hld up in tch in last pair: hdwy u.p over 1f out: styd on to go 4th towards fin: nvr threatened ldrs* 8/1[2]

1-25 **6** 1/2 **Dark Ranger**19 2342 8-9-8 83 StevieDonohoe 11 86
(Tim Pitt) *hld up in tch towards rr: rdn and plenty to do over 2f out: swtchd lft over 1f out: styd on fnl f: nvr threatened ldrs* 8/1[2]

05-3 **7** nk **Softsong (FR)**26 591 6-9-10 85 AdamKirby 8 87
(James Evans) *chsd ldr: rdn over 2f out: btn ent fnl f: wknd fnl 150yds* 14/1[3]

4-25 **8** 1/2 **Burnham**14 2490 5-9-3 78 (p) JimmyFortune 9 80
(Hughie Morrison) *wl in tch in midfield: rdn and unable qck over 2f out: styd on same pacve and no threat to ldrs fnl f* 5/1[1]

630- **9** 4 **Uriah Heep (FR)**31 6750 5-9-2 77 FergusSweeney 3 74
(Alan King) *t.k.h: hld up in tch in last quartet: effrt over 2f out: sn outpcd: wknd over 1f out* 16/1

0/03 **10** 1/2 **Storm Hawk (IRE)**39 1770 7-8-9 73 (v) OisinMurphy(3) 5 69
(Pat Eddery) *awkward leaving stalls and v.s.a: effrt over 2f out: no real imp: nvr trbld ldrs* 16/1

6-1 **11** 20 **Markami (FR)**24 2207 4-8-10 72 (p) SamHitchcott 2 44
(Johnny Farrelly) *chsd ldrs: rdn and btn over 2f out: wknd wl over 1f out: bhd and eased ins fnl f* 5/1[1]

0050 **12** 3 **St Ignatius**21 2272 7-8-5 71 (v) NatashaEaton(5) 12 40
(Alan Bailey) *chsd ldrs: rdn and lost pl 3f out: wl bhd and eased ins fnl f* 33/1

3m 31.32s (1.22) **Going Correction** -0.05s/f (Stan)
**WFA** 4 from 5yo+ 1lb **12** Ran SP% **123.6**
Speed ratings (Par 105): **94,93,93,93,92 91,91,91,89,89 79,77**
CSF £29.71 CT £340.70 TOTE £7.70: £1.30, £2.60, £4.90; EX 43.20 Trifecta £368.10.
**Owner** Saxon House Racing **Bred** Mrs D Hughes **Trained** Upper Lambourn, Berks

**FOCUS**
A modest staying handicap that was wide open. The pace finally wound up around half a mile from home. The winner is rated close to last year's best.

## 2921 BETVICTOR.COM H'CAP (BOBIS RACE) — 7f (P)
8:30 (8:31) (Class 3) (0-90,89) 3-Y-0
£7,158 (£2,143; £1,071; £535; £267; £134) Stalls Low

Form RPR

U1-0 **1** **Idea (USA)**22 2257 3-8-11 79 JamesDoyle 3 93+
(Sir Michael Stoute) *t.k.h: chsd ldrs: rdn and qcknd to ld over 1f out: sn clr and r.o strly: readily* 11/8[1]

0-01 **2** 2 1/2 **Extremity (IRE)**17 2383 3-9-0 82 MartinDwyer 4 89+
(Hugo Palmer) *wl in tch in midfield: hdwy over 1f out: chsd clr wnr fnl 150yds: r.o wl but no threat to wnr* 11/4[2]

06-6 **3** 2 1/4 **Championship (IRE)**47 1580 3-9-7 89 PatDobbs 8 90
(Richard Hannon) *stdd s: hld up in tch in rr: rdn and gd hdwy on inner jst over 1f out: r.o to go 3rd nr fin: nvr trbld ldrs* 25/1

-005 **4** nk **Westminster (IRE)**14 2495 3-9-0 82 (b1) WilliamBuick 1 82
(John Gosden) *t.k.h: chsd ldr for 3f: rdn over 2f out: chsd clr wnr 1f out : no imp: lost 2 pls fnl 150yds* 20/1

5-00 **5** nk **Cool Bahamian (IRE)**27 2111 3-8-12 85 GeorgeDowning(5) 11 84
(Eve Johnson Houghton) *hld up in tch in last trio: rdn and stl plenty to do wl over 1f out: swtchd rt 1f out: styd on u.p ins fnl f: nvr trbld ldrs* 50/1

50-6 **6** 1 1/2 **Smart Salute**29 2083 3-8-9 77 (p) HayleyTurner 7 72
(Ed Walker) *wnt sharply rt leaving stalls:chsd ldrs: rdn ent fnl 2f: unable qck over 1f out: wknd ins fnl f* 16/1

3-21 **7** 3/4 **Bowie Boy (IRE)**112 588 3-8-13 81 RichardKingscote 5 74
(Ralph Beckett) *wl in tch in midfield: rdn and outpcd ent fnl 2f: kpt on but no threat to ldrs ins fnl f* 8/1[3]

001- **8** 3/4 **Constantine**202 7892 3-8-13 81 SeanLevey 6 72+
(Richard Hannon) *hmpd s: hld up towards rr: effrt ent fnl 2f: nop real imp: nvr trbld ldrs* 25/1

0-31 **9** 1 3/4 **Skaters Waltz (IRE)**19 2339 3-9-2 84 LukeMorris 2 79+
(Paul Cole) *in tch in midfield: effrt u.p ent fnl 2f: drvn and pressing for placings whn short of room and bdly hmpd ent fnl f: no ch after: eased wl ins fnl f* 12/1

-135 **10** hd **Hagree (IRE)**27 2111 3-9-3 85 MartinHarley 9 71
(Marco Botti) *led tl rdn and hdd over 1f out: sn outpcd and btn: wknd fnl f* 8/1[3]

1m 24.8s (-1.20) **Going Correction** -0.05s/f (Stan) **10** Ran SP% **119.0**
Speed ratings (Par 103): **104,101,98,98,97 96,95,94,92,92**
CSF £4.90 CT £64.54 TOTE £3.00: £1.80, £1.30, £7.50; EX 8.00 Trifecta £84.90.
**Owner** K Abdullah **Bred** Juddmonte Farms Inc **Trained** Newmarket, Suffolk

**FOCUS**
This good-quality 3yo handicap was run at a sound enough pace and the form looks solid as it was a good winning time. Improvement from the first two.

## 2922 £25 FREE BET AT BETVICTOR.COM H'CAP (LONDON MILE SERIES QUALIFIER) — 1m (P)
9:00 (9:01) (Class 4) (0-85,85) 4-Y-0+ £4,690 (£1,395; £697; £348) Stalls Low

Form RPR

610- **1** **Suehail**160 8416 5-9-0 78 PatDobbs 11 88
(Robert Cowell) *hld up in last trio: rdn and gd hdwy over 1f out: str chal ins fnl f: led fnl 50yds: r.o wl: drvn out* 33/1

1065 **2** 1/2 **Silverheels (IRE)**15 2462 5-9-6 84 LukeMorris 5 93
(Paul Cole) *hld up off the pce in midfield: rdn and gd hdwy on inner 2f out: led fnl 100yds: r.o wl but hdd and hld fnl 50yds* 20/1

-045 **3** 3 **Jack Of Diamonds (IRE)**19 2341 5-9-4 82 1 JamesDoyle 6 84
(Roger Teal) *hld up off the pce in midfield: hdwy u.p over 1f out: r.o wl to snatch 3rd last strides* 8/1

21-3 **4** hd **Don't Stare**30 2062 4-9-6 84 FrederikTylicki 4 86+
(James Fanshawe) *chsd ldrs: rdn to ld 2f out: drvn and hdd fnl 100yds: wknd towards fin* 5/2[1]

03-5 **5** shd **Lord Ofthe Shadows (IRE)**13 2500 5-8-9 80 CamHardie(7) 7 81
(Richard Hannon) *in tch in midfield: rdn and effrt ent fnl 2f out: styd on wl u.p ins fnl f* 14/1

5-12 **6** 1 1/2 **Whipper Snapper (IRE)**26 2156 4-9-1 82 OisinMurphy(3) 1 80
(William Knight) *in tch in midfield: effrt u.p towards inner 2f out: styd on same pce fnl f* 4/1[3]

3234 **7** 1 1/4 **Greyfriarschorista**38 1803 7-9-6 84 WilliamCarson 2 79
(Tom Keddy) *hld up off the pce in midfield: rdn and effrt over 2f out: styd on but no threat to ldrs* 25/1

0010 **8** 2 3/4 **Tasrih (USA)**24 2202 5-9-6 84 BenCurtis 8 73
(Alan McCabe) *led tl hdd 2f out: sn rdn and no ex: wknd jst over 1f out* 16/1

231- **9** 1/2 **Bouclier (IRE)**181 8180 4-9-2 80 AndreaAtzeni 13 68+
(Luca Cumani) *chsd ldr tl jst over 2f out: sn rdn and unable qck: wknd jst over 1f out* 7/2[2]

0052 **10** 2 1/4 **Loyalty**15 2462 7-9-0 85 (v) AdamMcLean(7) 9 67
(Derek Shaw) *wl in tch in midfield: rdn: wd and lost pl bnd 3f out: n.d after* 16/1

6334 **11** 1 3/4 **Rakaan (IRE)**104 689 7-8-10 81 JennyPowell(7) 12 59
(Brendan Powell) *s.i.s: hld up in rr: nvr dnagerous* 33/1

1600 **12** 1 1/2 **The Great Gabrial**45 1607 5-9-3 81 (p) TomQueally 3 56
(Alan McCabe) *hld up wl in tch in midfield: rdn and no hdwy jst over 1f out: wknd over 1f out* 33/1

135- **13** 1 3/4 **Al Jamal**260 6531 4-9-4 82 SeanLevey 10 53
(Jeremy Gask) *stdd after s: hld up in last trio: rdn and no hdwy 2f out: bhd fnl f* 16/1

1m 37.36s (-2.44) **Going Correction** -0.05s/f (Stan) **13** Ran SP% **123.7**
Speed ratings (Par 105): **110,109,106,106,106 104,103,100,100,97 96,94,92**
CSF £574.24 CT £5858.08 TOTE £57.70: £15.50, £4.10, £2.70; EX 762.50 Trifecta £1224.90 Part won..
**Owner** Malih Lahej Al Basti **Bred** Malih Al Basti **Trained** Six Mile Bottom, Cambs

**FOCUS**
There was no hanging about early on in this fair handicap and it was set up for the closers. The winner matched his old best.
T/Jkpt: Not won. T/Plt: £26.80 to a £1 stake. Pool: £71,292.96 - 1940.69 winning units. T/Qpdt: £23.90 to a £1 stake. Pool: 5738.40 - 177.20 winning units. SP

# 2644 LINGFIELD (L-H)
Thursday, June 5

**OFFICIAL GOING: Turf - good (7.5); all-weather - standard**
Wind: Moderate, half behind Weather: Fine but cloudy

## 2923 32RED FREE £10 BONUS H'CAP — 1m 3f 106y
2:10 (2:10) (Class 6) (0-55,55) 4-Y-0+ £2,590 (£764; £382) Stalls High

Form RPR

60-2 **1** **Hamble**16 2443 5-9-4 52 PatrickDonaghy 8 63
(Giles Bravery) *t.k.h: hld up in rr: smooth prog on outer over 3f out: led over 2f out: shkn up and wl in command 1f out: pushed out after* 7/1[2]

365- **2** 1 3/4 **Halling's Wish**221 5500 4-9-4 52 GeorgeBaker 1 59
(Gary Moore) *trckd ldng pair: rdn over 2f out: chsd wnr over 1f out: styd on but no imp* 11/4[1]

2456 **3** 2 **Fair Comment**8 2672 4-9-6 54 DavidProbert 10 58
(Michael Blanshard) *trckd ldrs: drvn and cl up over 2f out: kpt on one pce fnl 2f* 8/1[3]

52-0 **4** nk **Glens Wobbly**22 2252 6-8-7 46 oh1 RyanTate(5) 12 50
(Jonathan Geake) *trckd ldng trio: rdn over 2f out: kpt on same pce fnl 2f: unable to chal* 7/1[2]

400 **5** 1 1/4 **Medburn Cutler**14 2497 4-9-6 54 FergusSweeney 11 56
(George Baker) *in tch in midfield: rdn over 2f out: kpt on fr over 1f out: n.d* 25/1

/200 **6** 3 1/4 **Turbulent Priest**3 2836 6-8-10 47 (p) SimonPearce(3) 14 43
(Zoe Davison) *hld up in last trio: shuffled along 3f out: styd on steadily fnl 2f: reminder over 1f out: nvr involved* 33/1

2005 **7** hd **Mazij**17 2396 6-8-13 47 WilliamCarson 7 43
(Peter Hiatt) *led 1f: chsd ldr: drvn and upsides over 2f out: wknd over 1f out* 10/1

3264 **8** nk **Abigails Angel**6 2723 7-8-5 46 DavidParkes(7) 3 42
(Brett Johnson) *dwlt: hld up towards rr: effrt u.p over 2f out: hanging lft but plugged on* 8/1[3]

-53 **9** 5 **Lindsay's Dream**36 1875 8-8-12 46 oh1 (p) LukeMorris 2 34
(Zoe Davison) *wl plcd bhd ldrs: drvn over 2f out: wknd over 1f out* 16/1

00-3 **10** 1 3/4 **Cherry Princess**29 2066 4-9-0 55 AaronJones(7) 13 40
(Stuart Williams) *led after 1f to over 2f out: wknd* 16/1

5064 **11** 8 **Nifty Kier**7 2689 5-9-1 49 AdamKirby 5 21
(Phil McEntee) *hld up in last trio: rdn and no prog 3f out: sn bhd* 10/1

0-06 **12** 16 **Capetown Kid**37 1835 4-8-13 47 DaneO'Neill 9
(Sylvester Kirk) *nvr bttr than midfield: pushed along over 4f out: wknd over 3f out: t.o* 16/1

5-00 **13** 11 **Ctappers**45 656 5-8-12 46 oh1 SamHitchcott 4
(Michael Madgwick) *immediately drvn in last: t.o over 3f out* 50/1

2m 33.19s (1.69) **Going Correction** +0.175s/f (Good) **13** Ran SP% **118.5**
Speed ratings (Par 101): **100,98,97,97,96 93,93,93,89,88 82,71,63**
CSF £25.76 CT £161.57 TOTE £5.60: £1.60, £1.60, £2.70; EX 18.40 Trifecta £68.50.
**Owner** Hoofbeats Racing Club **Bred** C A Cyzer **Trained** Newmarket, Suffolk

**FOCUS**
The ground on the turf track was officially described as good and the rider of the runner-up described conditions as "nice ground, but a bit dead in places." A moderate handicap and they didn't go much of a pace. The winner is rated back to last year's form at least.

## 2924 HINDWOODS MAIDEN STKS (DIV I) 1m 3f 106y
**2:40** (2:44) (Class 5) 3-Y-0+ £2,726 (£805; £402) **Stalls** High

Form RPR

**1** **Arabian Revolution** 3-8-12 0 SilvestreDeSousa 2 86+
(Saeed bin Suroor) *trckd ldr: shkn up 3f out: clsd to ld wl over 1f out: styd on strly* **2/1**[1]

63 **2** 3¼ **Holberg Suite**[29] 2081 3-8-7 0 WilliamBuick 4 76
(John Gosden) *sn chsd ldng pair: shkn up 3f out: styd on fnl 2f to take 2nd last 100yds: no threat to wnr* **3/1**[2]

426- **3** ¾ **Dalgig**[254] 6738 4-9-12 77 JamieSpencer 1 80
(Jamie Osborne) *fast away: led and steered wd crse: drvn over 2f out: hdd and one pce wl over 1f out: lost 2nd last 100yds* **8/1**[3]

6 **4** 9 **Kagami**[21] 2271 3-8-12 0 JamesDoyle 10 66+
(Jeremy Noseda) *hld up in 7th: prog 1/2-way: outpcd and drvn 3f out: tk modest 4th 2f out: no imp after* **2/1**[1]

0-6 **5** 2 **Hiorne Tower (FR)**[15] 2466 3-8-12 0 HayleyTurner 5 62
(John Best) *hld up in midfield: shkn up and outpcd 3f out: kpt on one pce after: nt disgracd* **16/1**

0 **6** 16 **Greatday Allweek (IRE)**[17] 2404 5-9-0 0 GaryMahon(7) 7 32
(Seamus Mullins) *sn wl in rr: jst in tch over 4f out: wknd over 3f out* **100/1**

0 **7** ¾ **Prince Of Islay (IRE)**[24] 2221 3-8-12 0 JimmyFortune 3 36
(Robert Mills) *chsd ldng trio: rdn 1/2-way: wknd over 2f out* **100/1**

0-0 **8** 2 **Give Us A Reason**[29] 2081 4-9-4 0 [1] RobertTart(3) 11 27
(James Toller) *restless in stalls: a wl in rr: lost tch 4f out: wl bhd after* **100/1**

**9** 2¼ **Nancy** 3-8-7 0 MickaelBarzalona 6 24
(Mark H Tompkins) *uns rdr on way to s: slowly away: jst in tch in rr tl rdn and wknd over 3f out* **33/1**

0-0 **10** 34 **Archduchess**[16] 2432 3-8-7 0 ChrisCatlin 9
(Rae Guest) *sn dropped to rr and nt gng wl: t.o sn after 1/2-way* **100/1**

2m 32.34s (0.84) **Going Correction** +0.175s/f (Good)
**WFA** 3 from 4yo+ 14lb 10 Ran SP% **115.6**
Speed ratings (Par 103): **103,100,100,93,92 80,79,78,76,52**
CSF £8.20 TOTE £3.00: £1.10, £1.10, £2.40; EX 8.80 Trifecta £38.10.
**Owner** Godolphin **Bred** Darley **Trained** Newmarket, Suffolk
■ Stewards' Enquiry : Gary Mahon two-day ban: used whip above permitted level (Jun 22-23)

**FOCUS**
Not many ever got into this maiden. The winning time was 0.85sec quicker than the opening handicap, but 20lb slower than the second division. The form is rated around the third.

## 2925 HINDWOODS MAIDEN STKS (DIV II) 1m 3f 106y
**3:10** (3:13) (Class 5) 3-Y-0+ £2,726 (£805; £402) **Stalls** High

Form RPR

0-2 **1** **Nabatean (IRE)**[34] 1911 3-8-12 0 DavidProbert 6 82+
(Andrew Balding) *trckd ldrs: wnt 3rd over 4f out and 2nd over 2f out gng strly: pushed into ld over 1f out: sn rdn: kpt on* **5/4**[1]

6-20 **2** 3¼ **Ultimate Act**[8] 2685 3-8-12 71 JamieSpencer 3 78
(Seamus Mullins) *led: hrd rdn over 3f out: hdd over 1f out: kpt on tl hld and eased last 75yds* **7/2**[3]

0 **3** 14 **Lisanor**[62] 1280 3-8-7 0 WilliamBuick 9 49
(John Gosden) *s.s: sn in tch: shkn up 1/2-way: outpcd over 4f out: plugged on to take modest 3rd nr fin* **7/1**

23-2 **4** 1 **Sweeping Up**[29] 2082 3-8-7 75 MickaelBarzalona 8 48
(Hughie Morrison) *prom: trckd ldr 1/2-way: poised to chal over 3f out: sn rdn and nt qckn: lost 2nd and wknd over 2f out* **9/4**[2]

**5** 14 **Welcometothejungle**[30] 6-9-7 0 (t) DaneO'Neill 7 25
(Keiran Burke) *chsd ldr to 1/2-way: sn pushed along: wknd 4f out* **25/1**

00 **6** 41 **Carnt Cash Sorry**[21] 2271 3-8-12 0 JimmyQuinn 4
(Ed Vaughan) *chsd ldrs: awkward bnd 7f out and rdn: lost tch over 4f out: wknd rapidly over 2f out: wl t.o* **100/1**

**7** 10 **Red Inferno (IRE)** 3-8-5 0 JackGilligan(7) 2
(Miss Joey Ellis) *s.s: a wl t.o* **66/1**

-0 **8** 8 **Perfect Romance**[21] 2279 5-9-7 0 AdamKirby 1
(Patrick Chamings) *s.v.s: a wl t.o* **66/1**

2m 30.34s (-1.16) **Going Correction** +0.175s/f (Good)
**WFA** 3 from 4yo+ 14lb 8 Ran SP% **117.8**
Speed ratings (Par 103): **111,108,98,97,87 57,50,44**
CSF £6.28 TOTE £2.30: £1.10, £1.30, £2.50; EX 7.60 Trifecta £31.50.
**Owner** Lord Blyth **Bred** Lord Blyth **Trained** Kingsclere, Hants

**FOCUS**
This looked the stronger division beforehand and it was confirmed with the winning time exactly two seconds faster than the first leg. The runner-up is the key to the form.

## 2926 CW ENERGY H'CAP 1m 3f 106y
**3:40** (3:41) (Class 6) (0-60,60) 3-Y-0 £2,726 (£805; £402) **Stalls** High

Form RPR

0636 **1** **Roman Riches**[29] 2080 3-9-7 60 (v[1]) GeorgeBaker 1 64
(Gary Moore) *hld up in last trio: stl only 12th over 4f out: rdn and prog on outer over 3f out: clsd over 1f out: styd on to ld last 100yds: drvn out* **14/1**

00-0 **2** nk **Maid Of Tuscany (IRE)**[16] 2416 3-8-11 57 CharlotteJenner(7) 12 60
(Mark Usher) *hld up wl in rr: only 13th over 4f out: prog on inner fr 3f out: rdn 2f out: styd on fnl f to take 2nd last stride* **20/1**

0-03 **3** nse **Lochalsh (IRE)**[14] 2491 3-9-3 59 OisinMurphy(3) 14 62
(William Knight) *prom: trckd ldr 8f out to 6f out: styd handy: drvn 3f out: led over 1f out: hdd last 100yds: lost 2nd fnl stride* **6/1**[2]

000 **4** ¾ **Sound Of Life (IRE)**[31] 2025 3-8-8 47 (p) ChrisCatlin 8 49
(Rae Guest) *prog on outer fr midfield to chse ldr 6f out: drvn 3f out: upsides 2f out: kpt on but nt qckn fnl f* **16/1**

000 **5** 2½ **Dark Days**[24] 2221 3-9-5 58 (t) LukeMorris 6 56
(Paul Cole) *urged along early and wl in rr: shkn up at 1/2-way: effrt u.p over 3f out: kpt on fnl 2f: nvr gng pce to threaten* **7/2**[1]

00-4 **6** ¾ **Norse Legend**[38] 1792 3-8-9 48 RichardKingscote 4 45
(Daniel Kubler) *led 1f: styd prom: drvn 3f out: tried to chal 2f out: steadily fdd over 1f out* **7/1**[3]

2326 **7** 3 **Frederic Chopin**[31] 2028 3-9-7 60 (t) SeanLevey 2 54
(Stuart Williams) *wl in tch bhd ldrs: rdn 3f out: trying to cl whn nt clr run over 1f out: one pce after* **7/1**[3]

0-24 **8** ½ **Snow Conditions**[24] 2225 3-9-7 60 AdamKirby 13 51
(Philip Hide) *led after 1f: rdn 3f out: hdd 2f out: wknd over 1f out* **7/1**[3]

55-0 **9** 10 **Ede's The Business**[138] 236 3-8-13 55 JemmaMarshall(3) 5 30
(Pat Phelan) *wl in tch: lost pl and pushed along 5f out: no hdwy 3f out: wknd* **33/1**

00-5 **10** 2¾ **Coastal Storm**[57] 1382 3-9-4 57 JimmyFortune 9 28
(Hughie Morrison) *wl in rr: prog on wd outside 5f out: chsd ldrs over 3f out: hrd rdn and wknd 2f out: eased* **6/1**[2]

00-5 **11** 10 **Haines**[14] 2491 3-8-11 50 DavidProbert 11 5
(Brett Johnson) *trckd ldrs tl rdn and wknd qckly 4f out: t.o* **28/1**

05-6 **12** 4 **Vera Lou (IRE)**[77] 1029 3-8-12 51 (b[1]) FrederikTylicki 7
(Pat Eddery) *chsd ldrs: wknd 4f out: eased 2f out: t.o* **33/1**

000- **13** 5 **Lingfield Lupus (IRE)**[232] 7301 3-8-11 50 (v[1]) SteveDrowne 10
(John Best) *dropped to last and drvn over 6f out: t.o over 4f out* **50/1**

0-06 **14** 16 **Astrovirtue**[38] 1793 3-9-1 54 MickaelBarzalona 3
(Mark H Tompkins) *a towards rr: wknd over 3f out: wl t.o* **14/1**

2m 34.16s (2.66) **Going Correction** +0.175s/f (Good) 14 Ran SP% **123.6**
Speed ratings (Par 97): **97,96,96,96,94 93,91,91,84,82 74,71,68,56**
CSF £278.13 CT £1875.72 TOTE £13.00: £5.50, £6.10, £3.00; EX 371.70 Trifecta £1137.80.
**Owner** Five Star Racing Group & Partners **Bred** Northmore Stud **Trained** Lower Beeding, W Sussex

**FOCUS**
All 14 of these 3yos were maidens going into this moderate handicap. Despite the pace not looking strong (the time was much the slowest of the four races over the trip), the first two home came from last and last-but-one. The winner improved in the visor.

## 2927 32RED TOMB RAIDER SLOT H'CAP 1m 1f
**4:10** (4:11) (Class 6) (0-60,60) 3-Y-0 £2,726 (£805; £402) **Stalls** Low

Form RPR

0-50 **1** **Storm Rider (IRE)**[31] 2026 3-9-3 56 PatDobbs 2 70
(Richard Hannon) *trckd ldng pair: reminder over 4f out: sn in 2nd: led on inner over 3f out: scooted clr over 2f out: in n.d after: pushed out* **6/1**[3]

500- **2** 5 **Daisy Boy (IRE)**[208] 7818 3-9-7 60 JamesDoyle 9 64+
(Stuart Williams) *hld up in 8th: rdn and prog over 2f out: wnt 2nd fnl f: kpt on but no ch w wnr* **5/2**[1]

45-0 **3** 1¼ **Ametrine (IRE)**[17] 2404 3-9-7 60 SteveDrowne 1 61
(William Jarvis) *chsd ldrs in 5th: rdn over 2f out: chsd clr wnr 2f out to 1f out: one pce* **25/1**

4-60 **4** shd **Lifejacket (IRE)**[37] 1844 3-9-6 59 AdamKirby 11 60+
(Ed Dunlop) *hld up in 9th: pushed along 3f out: prog on inner fr 2f out: styd on fnl f: nrly snatched 3rd* **5/1**[2]

-650 **5** 1¾ **Softly She Treads (IRE)**[14] 2491 3-9-5 58 (v[1]) TomQueally 10 55
(Pat Phelan) *hld up in 7th: rdn and tried to cl on chsng pack over 2f out: ch of a pl over 1f out: one pce after* **8/1**

-506 **6** 1½ **Assoluta (IRE)**[14] 2491 3-8-13 52 JimmyFortune 13 46
(Sylvester Kirk) *hld up in 10th: rdn 3f out: limited prog tl kpt on fr over 1f out: nrst fin* **16/1**

0-06 **7** 2 **Rock Of Leon**[29] 2078 3-8-9 48 JamieSpencer 12 43
(Michael Bell) *hld up in last trio: shkn up over 3f out: sme prog fr 2f out: hanging and nvr rchd ldrs: eased last 75yds* **7/1**

0-45 **8** 1 **Sweetheart Abbey**[16] 2417 3-9-7 60 AndreaAtzeni 4 48
(William Knight) *led after 1f: wd bnd over 3f out and hdd: wknd 2f out* **7/1**

50-0 **9** 1 **Excedo Praecedo**[7] 2688 3-9-7 60 GeorgeBaker 14 46
(Amanda Perrett) *dropped in fr wd draw and hld up in last pair: shkn up on outer 3f out: hanging but kpt on fnl 2f: no ch* **12/1**

00-0 **10** 17 **No Second Thoughts (IRE)**[13] 2526 3-8-0 46 oh1(p) MichaelKenneally(7) 6
(Michael Squance) *lost tch after 4f: sn t.o* **50/1**

0-00 **11** 1¾ **Charlies Mate**[38] 1794 3-8-11 50 (v[1]) HayleyTurner 5
(John Best) *chsd ldrs to over 3f out: sn wknd and eased: t.o* **33/1**

500 **12** ½ **Monsieur Chabal**[24] 2211 3-9-5 58 FergusSweeney 8 3
(Jamie Osborne) *mostly chsd ldng trio to over 2f out: wknd and eased: t.o* **33/1**

00-0 **13** 2¼ **Macnamara**[57] 1380 3-8-7 46 oh1 (b[1]) LukeMorris 7
(Harry Dunlop) *led 1f: chsd ldr to 4f out: sn wknd: t.o* **33/1**

1m 58.06s (1.46) **Going Correction** +0.175s/f (Good) 13 Ran SP% **123.8**
Speed ratings (Par 97): **100,95,94,94,92 91,89,88,87,72 71,70,68**
CSF £21.16 CT £379.94 TOTE £7.20: £2.60, £1.20, £7.50; EX 29.90 Trifecta £778.40.
**Owner** Carmichael Humber **Bred** Barronstown Stud **Trained** East Everleigh, Wilts

**FOCUS**
Another 3yo handicap contested exclusively by maidens. It was sound run and was an interesting race for the grade, with the front four unexposed. The winner is entitled to be better than this.

## 2928 32RED CASINO MEDIAN AUCTION MAIDEN STKS 6f 1y(P)
**4:40** (4:42) (Class 5) 2-Y-0 £2,726 (£805; £402) **Stalls** Low

Form RPR

4 **1** **Ski Slope**[20] 2306 2-9-0 0 PatDobbs 10 83+
(Richard Hannon) *trckd clr ldng pair: clsd to ld over 2f out: sn clr: comf* **5/4**[1]

**2** 4½ **Secret Lightning (FR)** 2-9-0 0 JamesDoyle 11 68
(Sylvester Kirk) *chsd clr ldng quartet: prog 2f out: styd on to take 2nd last 75yds: no ch w wnr* **7/1**[3]

**3** ½ **Golden Wedding (IRE)** 2-9-5 0 TomQueally 6 71
(Eve Johnson Houghton) *s.s: wl off the pce in 9th early: pushed along and prog fr 1/2-way: styd on steadily fr over 1f out to take 3rd nr fin* **16/1**

**4** 1 **Godric** 2-9-5 0 HayleyTurner 9 68
(Tom Dascombe) *chsd clr ldr: clsd to chal over 2f out but wnr wnt past: in 2nd after tl fdd last 75yds* **16/1**

**5** ¾ **Euthenia** 2-8-11 0 CharlesBishop(3) 4 61
(Mick Channon) *bmpd s: wl off the pce in 7th: shkn up and prog 2f out: styd on fnl f: nrst fin* **33/1**

446 **6** nk **Jersey Belle**[15] 2458 2-8-11 0 WilliamTwiston-Davies(3) 8 60
(Mick Channon) *chsd clr ldng trio: rdn over 2f out: one pce and nvr able to threaten* **33/1**

363 **7** 1¼ **Basil The Great**[8] 2680 2-9-5 0 (v[1]) RichardKingscote 3 61+
(Tom Dascombe) *wnt rt s: led and clr: hdd over 2f out: steadily wknd* **3/1**[2]

**8** 2¼ **Feeling Easy (IRE)** 2-9-0 0 AndreaAtzeni 5 49
(Robert Eddery) *carried rt s: pushed along in 6th and nt on terms w ldrs: tried to cl 2f out: wknd over 1f out* **7/1**[3]

**9** 3¼ **Bombay Mix** 2-9-0 0 [1] FrederikTylicki 12 40
(Charlie Fellowes) *slowly away: long way adrift in last early: kpt on fr over 2f out: nvr a factor but nt totally disgracd* **100/1**

**10** 8 **St Paul's Square (IRE)** 2-9-5 0 FergusSweeney 1 21
(Jamie Osborne) *s.s: outpcd and a wl bhd* **33/1**

**11** shd **Tilly Range (IRE)** 2-8-11 0 DeclanBates(3) 7 15
(David Evans) *carried rt s: a wl bhd* **66/1**

6063 **12** 3¼ **Keep 'r Lit**[35] 1901 2-9-0 0.................................................(vt) AdamKirby 2
(David Evans) *outpcd and a wl adrift* **50/1**
1m 12.02s (0.12) **Going Correction** -0.10s/f (Stan) **12** Ran SP% **119.5**
Speed ratings (Par 93): **95,89,88,87,86 85,83,80,76,65 65,61**
CSF £10.45 TOTE £2.50: £1.60, £1.60, £5.00; EX 12.80 Trifecta £115.60.
**Owner** Cheveley Park Stud **Bred** Cheveley Park Stud Ltd **Trained** East Everleigh, Wilts

**FOCUS**
A slightly messy 2yo maiden with Basil The Great swerving out to his right exiting the stalls, causing problems with a few of his rivals including Feeling Easy and Tilly Range, whose efforts can be forgiven to a degree. The winner was in a completely different league. The sixth and the time offer some perspective on the form.

## 2929 32RED FILLIES' H'CAP 7f 1y(P)
5:10 (5:13) (Class 5) (0-75,75) 3-Y-O **£3,234** (£962; £481; £240) **Stalls** Low

Form RPR
25-2 **1** **A Legacy Of Love (IRE)**[30] 2044 3-9-4 **72**.......................... GeorgeBaker 3 78
(Amanda Perrett) *t.k.h early: cl up: led wl over 1f out: drvn fnl f: jnd nr fin: won on the nod* **12/1**
501- **2** *nse* **Jacquotte Delahaye**[198] 7960 3-9-4 **75**....................(b) OisinMurphy(3) 1 80
(David Brown) *hld up in 7th: prog on inner over 2f out: chsd wnr fnl f: drvn and upsides last strides: jst pipped* **14/1**
-124 **3** *1* **Nimble Kimble**[27] 2130 3-9-0 **73**.......................................... RyanTate(5) 6 75
(James Eustace) *trckd ldng pair: rdn and cl up over 1f out: nt qckn but kpt on* **3/1**[2]
5-20 **4** 1¼ **Perfect Pursuit**[21] 2278 3-9-0 **68**.......................................... AdamKirby 4 67
(Clive Cox) *trckd ldr: wd bnd 2f out: nt qckn and lost 2nd: kpt on same pce fnl f* **50/1**
3-02 **5** 1¾ **Shasta Daisy**[39] 1768 3-9-7 **75**.......................................... JamesDoyle 9 69
(Lady Cecil) *racd wd: chsd ldrs: shoved along wl over 2f out: wdst bnd 2f out: no prog after* **7/1**[3]
2-03 **6** ¾ **Venus Grace**[19] 2340 3-9-7 **75**.......................................... RichardKingscote 2 68
(Ralph Beckett) *hld up in 6th: rdn and no prog over 2f out: no imp after* **11/10**[1]
002 **7** *nse* **Clever Miss**[16] 2447 3-9-1 **69**..........................(v) FrederikTylicki 5 61
(Alan McCabe) *led: wd bnd 2f out and sn hdd: fdd and eased ins fnl f* **25/1**
**8** *nk* **Trikala (IRE)**[244] 7003 3-9-3 **71**..........................................[1] LukeMorris 8 63
(Marco Botti) *fractious gng to post: pushed along in rr 4f out: nvr on terms w ldrs* **20/1**
3000 **9** *1* **Outbacker (IRE)**[14] 2474 3-9-7 **75**.......................................... SilvestreDeSousa 7 64
(Mark Johnston) *dwlt: t.k.h early in last: pushed along bef 1/2-way: nvr on terms* **16/1**
1m 24.14s (-0.66) **Going Correction** -0.10s/f (Stan) **9** Ran SP% **115.9**
Speed ratings (Par 96): **99,98,97,96,94 93,93,93,91**
CSF £158.86 CT £639.67 TOTE £11.60: £3.50, £3.20, £1.60; EX 68.60 Trifecta £973.30.
**Owner** Mrs Brenda Karn-Smith **Bred** Rabbah Bloodstock Limited **Trained** Pulborough, W Sussex

**FOCUS**
An ordinary fillies' handicap, but a very tight finish. The third helps set the standard.

## 2930 32RED.COM H'CAP 1m 1y(P)
5:45 (5:46) (Class 5) (0-70,70) 4-Y-O+ **£3,234** (£962; £481; £240) **Stalls** High

Form RPR
1304 **1** **Secret Success**[9] 2646 4-9-1 **64**..............................(t) SilvestreDeSousa 2 79
(Paul Cole) *mde all at decent pce: sent for home over 2f out: drvn clr over 1f out: unchal* **7/2**[2]
11-5 **2** *2* **Sonnetation (IRE)**[6] 2721 4-8-13 **62**.......................................... WilliamCarson 9 70
(Jim Boyle) *chsd wnr: rdn and nt qckn over 2f out: kpt on fr over 1f out: nvr able to chal* **8/1**
3431 **3** ½ **Run It Twice (IRE)**[15] 2471 4-9-7 **70**..................................(b) AdamKirby 1 77
(David Evans) *chsd ldrs in 5th: rdn 3f out: prog to take 3rd 1f out: kpt on and nrst fin* **8/1**
0505 **4** 1¾ **Greensward**[15] 2463 8-9-1 **64**.............................................(v[1]) HayleyTurner 7 67
(Conor Dore) *trckd ldng pair: shkn up and nt qckn over 2f out: lost 3rd 1f out: one pce* **16/1**
2443 **5** *2* **Warbond**[34] 1917 6-8-8 **57**..................................................(v) SamHitchcott 4 55
(Michael Madgwick) *hld up in 7th: outpcd fr 3f out: drvn into 5th over 1f out: kpt on but no ch* **25/1**
0-51 **6** *3* **Sweet Martoni**[22] 2251 4-9-4 **70**.......................................... OisinMurphy(3) 8 61
(William Knight) *chsd ldng trio: rdn over 2f out: lost pl and btn wl over 1f out* **9/2**[3]
6-00 **7** 1¼ **Duke Of Destiny (IRE)**[19] 2341 5-9-6 **69**..........................(b[1]) GeorgeBaker 6 58
(Ed Walker) *s.i.s: hld up in 8th: coaxed along and no prog whn wd bnd 2f out: nvr a factor* **2/1**[1]
0-00 **8** *hd* **Bison Grass**[21] 2270 4-8-13 **62**.......................................... PatrickDonaghy 10 50
(Giles Bravery) *dwlt: mostly in last: struggling sn after 1/2-way: nvr a factor* **33/1**
5551 **9** ½ **Fearless Lad (IRE)**[9] 2646 4-9-4 **67** 6ex..............................(t) JamesDoyle 3 54
(John Best) *dwlt: hld up in 6th: rdn over 3f out: no prog and btn 2f out* **7/1**
1m 36.77s (-1.43) **Going Correction** -0.10s/f (Stan) **9** Ran SP% **121.1**
Speed ratings (Par 103): **103,101,100,98,96 93,92,92,91**
CSF £33.43 CT £216.77 TOTE £3.80: £1.70, £2.60, £2.60; EX 33.70 Trifecta £341.00.
**Owner** P F I Cole Ltd **Bred** Ray Bailey **Trained** Whatcombe, Oxon

**FOCUS**
A modest handicap and a strange race, in that the order barely changed. The winner looked to set a good pace.
T/Plt: £67.00 to a £1 stake. Pool: £70,365.77 - 765.90 winning units. T/Qpdt: £37.00 to a £1 stake. Pool: £4,142.98 - 82.70 winning units. JN

# 2901 SOUTHWELL (L-H)
Thursday, June 5

**OFFICIAL GOING: Standard**
Wind: Fresh behind Weather: Overcast

## 2931 32RED FREE £10 BONUS H'CAP 6f (F)
2:20 (2:21) (Class 6) (0-60,57) 3-Y-O **£2,102** (£625; £312; £156) **Stalls** Low

Form RPR
0051 **1** **Shades Of Silk**[17] 2397 3-9-3 **53**.......................................... DaleSwift 8 59+
(James Given) *racd wd: w ldrs tl lost pl over 4f out: pushed along and hdwy 2f out: led over 1f out: sn rdn and edgd lft: styd on* **8/11**[1]
0430 **2** *1* **Meebo (IRE)**[13] 2526 3-9-7 **57**..............................(vt) JoeFanning 4 60
(J R Jenkins) *disp ld tl wnt on over 2f out: rdn and hdd over 1f out: n.m.r ins fnl f: no ex nr fin* **9/2**[2]
6603 **3** *hd* **Casper Lee (IRE)**[9] 2638 3-8-10 **51**..........................(b) JacobButterfield(5) 2 53
(Michael Herrington) *pushed along early in rr: hdwy 1/2-way: rdn and ev ch over 1f out: hung lft ins fnl f: no ex towards fin* **16/1**
5-44 **4** *11* **Sylvan Spirit (IRE)**[110] 622 3-9-3 **53**.......................................... RobertWinston 7 20
(Roger Teal) *chsd ldrs: rdn over 2f out: wknd fnl f* **12/1**
00-4 **5** *nk* **Golly Miss Molly**[37] 1833 3-9-0 **50**.......................................... DanielTudhope 1 16
(Jeremy Gask) *in rr: rdn over 2f out: wknd over 1f out* **20/1**
006- **6** *nk* **Hoof's So Lucky**[240] 7096 3-8-11 **47**.......................................... GrahamGibbons 6 12
(Michael Easterby) *sn pushed along to chse ldrs: rdn over 2f out: wknd over 1f out* **7/1**[3]
4000 **7** *1* **Back On Baileys**[17] 2388 3-8-6 **45**.......................................... RyanPowell(3) 3 7
(John Ryan) *w ldrs: rdn over 2f out: wknd over 1f out* **25/1**
004- **8** *6* **Spider Lily**[252] 6776 3-9-0 **50**.......................................... SebSanders 5
(Peter Makin) *sn pushed along to dispute ld: rdn over 2f out: sn wknd* **16/1**
1m 16.53s (0.03) **Going Correction** -0.175s/f (Stan) **8** Ran SP% **116.7**
Speed ratings (Par 97): **92,90,90,75,75 74,73,65**
CSF £4.38 CT £28.56 TOTE £1.40: £1.02, £1.40, £4.20; EX 3.90 Trifecta £26.20.
**Owner** The Cool Silk Partnership **Bred** Mrs F S Williams **Trained** Willoughton, Lincs

**FOCUS**
A weak 3yo sprint handicap and the first three finished well clear. The winner gave the runner-up a similar beating to C&D latest.

## 2932 32RED TOMB RAIDER SLOT MAIDEN STKS 5f (F)
2:50 (2:51) (Class 5) 3-Y-O **£2,749** (£818; £408; £204) **Stalls** High

Form RPR
0-22 **1** **Scoreline**[8] 2675 3-9-5 60.......................................... DanielTudhope 1 74
(David O'Meara) *w ldr tl led 2f out: rdn and edgd lft ins fnl f: jst hld on* **11/10**[1]
224- **2** *shd* **Epic Voyage (USA)**[190] 8067 3-9-5 84.......................................... PaulPickard 3 73
(Brian Ellison) *sn outpcd: hdwy u.p over 1f out: sn hung lft and chsd wnr: ev ch ins fnl f: nt run on* **7/4**[2]
3-06 **3** *4* **Lord Clyde**[13] 2524 3-9-5 70.......................................... PatrickMathers 8 58
(Richard Fahey) *chsd ldrs: rdn 1/2-way: no ex fnl f* **20/1**
0-3 **4** *7* **Templar Boy**[28] 2093 3-8-12 0.......................................... VictorSantos(7) 7 33
(J R Jenkins) *sn outpcd* **20/1**
506 **5** ½ **Go Charlie**[3] 2838 3-9-5 50.......................................... BenCurtis 6 31
(Ronald Harris) *s.i.s: outpcd* **33/1**
0-53 **6** 3¼ **Reet Thicknstrong**[17] 2388 3-9-0 58.......................................... RoystonFfrench 2 15
(Bryan Smart) *sn led: hdd 3f out: rdn and wknd over 1f out* **6/1**[3]
58.63s (-1.07) **Going Correction** -0.275s/f (Stan) **6** Ran SP% **110.7**
Speed ratings (Par 99): **97,96,90,79,78 73**
CSF £3.09 TOTE £2.10: £1.30, £1.90; EX 4.50 Trifecta £13.00.
**Owner** K Nicholson & Partners **Bred** Mickley Stud **Trained** Nawton, N Yorks

**FOCUS**
A weak 3yo sprint maiden and official ratings went out of the window. Shaky form, but the time wasn't too bad.

## 2933 SOUTHWELL CLAIMING STKS 5f (F)
3:20 (3:21) (Class 6) 3-Y-O+ **£2,102** (£625; £312; £156) **Stalls** High

Form RPR
1-00 **1** **Baytown Kestrel**[54] 1445 3-9-2 80..............................(p) RobertWinston 4 85
(Brian Ellison) *led 4f out: rdn and edgd lft over 1f out: styd on* **14/1**
6100 **2** 1½ **Only Ten Per Cent (IRE)**[20] 2312 6-9-4 75..............................(v) JoeFanning 3 78
(J R Jenkins) *a.p: chsd wnr over 1f out: styd on same pce ins fnl f* **5/1**[2]
611 **3** 1¾ **Hamoody (USA)**[17] 2401 10-9-2 77.......................................... LouisSteward(5) 8 74+
(Joseph Tuite) *broke wl: sn lost pl and bhd: hdwy over 1f out: rdn and hung lft ins fnl f: eased whn hld nr fin* **7/1**[3]
525 **4** *1* **Kuanyao (IRE)**[17] 2401 8-9-6 74..............................(b) PhillipMakin 2 70
(Conor Dore) *chsd ldrs: rdn 1/2-way: styd on same pce fnl f* **16/1**
6145 **5** 1¼ **Muhdiq (USA)**[40] 1742 5-10-0 83.......................................... ShaneKelly 5 73
(Mike Murphy) *s.i.s: hdwy over 3f out: rdn over 1f out: styd on same pce* **5/2**[1]
1006 **6** *hd* **Foxy Music**[6] 2732 10-8-13 81.......................................... GrahamGibbons 7 57
(Eric Alston) *led 1f: chsd ldrs: drvn along 1/2-way: styd on same pce fr over 1f out* **5/2**[1]
0-20 **7** ½ **Speightowns Kid (USA)**[23] 2232 6-8-12 67.......... JacobButterfield(5) 6 60
(Michael Herrington) *prom: drvn along 1/2-way: sn outpcd: styd on ins fnl f* **33/1**
2110 **8** 1¾ **Come On Dave (IRE)**[18] 2364 5-9-2 70.......................................... RoystonFfrench 10 52
(David Nicholls) *prom: chsd wnr 1/2-way tl rdn over 1f out: wknd fnl f* **12/1**
0-00 **9** ¾ **Red Explorer (USA)**[10] 2602 4-8-13 68..............................(t) AnnStokell(5) 1 52
(Ann Stokell) *prom: pushed along and lost pl 4f out: n.d after* **33/1**
1300 **10** 2½ **Electric Qatar**[52] 1487 5-9-4 69..............................(p) BarryMcHugh 11 43
(Alan McCabe) *s.i.s: sn outpcd: bhd whn hung lft over 1f out* **20/1**
-040 **11** ¾ **First In Command (IRE)**[19] 2350 9-9-6 75..............................(t) StephenCraine 9 42
(Daniel Mark Loughnane) *broke wl enough: sn outpcd* **25/1**
57.93s (-1.77) **Going Correction** -0.275s/f (Stan)
**WFA** 3 from 4yo+ 7lb **11** Ran SP% **121.0**
Speed ratings (Par 101): **103,100,97,96,94 93,93,90,89,85 83**
CSF £81.64 TOTE £19.90: £3.70, £3.30, £1.70; EX 164.30 Trifecta £795.70.Muhdiq was claimed by Ed De Giles for £18,000; Foxy Music was claimed by Tony Coyle for £3,000.
**Owner** The Acorn Partnership **Bred** R F And S D Knipe **Trained** Norton, N Yorks

**FOCUS**
A good claimer, and the winner is rated at least as good as ever. The action was middle-to-far side and the first two dominated from some way out.

## 2934 32RED CASINO H'CAP 1m 4f (F)
3:50 (3:51) (Class 5) (0-75,71) 3-Y-O **£2,749** (£818; £408; £204) **Stalls** Low

Form RPR
-530 **1** **Sellingallthetime (IRE)**[20] 2319 3-8-8 **65**..........................(p) AlistairRawlinson(7) 3 77
(Michael Appleby) *trckd ldrs: plld hrd: wnt upsides over 4f out: led over 3f out: clr fnl 2f: easily* **7/2**[2]
1031 **2** *9* **Zanouska (USA)**[8] 2679 3-9-6 **70** 6ex.......................................... JoeFanning 2 68
(Mark Johnston) *led: rdn and hdd over 3f out: sn outpcd* **8/1**
-225 **3** *4* **Libeccio (FR)**[32] 1984 3-9-4 **71**..........................................[1] ThomasBrown(3) 5 63
(Andrew Balding) *s.i.s: hdwy to chse ldr over 10f out tl over 4f out: sn rdn: wknd over 2f out* **9/2**[3]
-132 **4** *3* **Deep Resolve (IRE)**[24] 2198 3-9-3 **67**.......................................... BenCurtis 1 54
(Alan Swinbank) *trckd ldrs: reminder 5f out: rdn and wknd over 2f out* **5/2**[1]
-313 **5** *1* **Cape Arrow**[6] 2719 3-8-9 **64**.......................................... LouisSteward(5) 4 49
(Paul Cole) *prom: lost pl after 1f: reminder over 4f out: rdn and wknd over 2f out* **5/2**[1]
2m 37.61s (-3.39) **Going Correction** -0.175s/f (Stan) **5** Ran SP% **108.7**
Speed ratings (Par 99): **104,98,95,93,92**
CSF £27.23 TOTE £6.20: £3.40, £2.90; EX 29.50 Trifecta £116.60.

**Owner** Robin Oliver **Bred** Roundhill Stud **Trained** Danethorpe, Notts
**FOCUS**
What looked beforehand a tricky 3yo handicap turned out to be a two-horse race and it produced a facile winner. The pace was sound and the form is rated around the runner-up.

## 2935 32RED.COM H'CAP 1m 3f (F)
4:20 (4:20) (Class 5) (0-75,74) 4-Y-0+ £2,749 (£818; £408; £204) Stalls Low

Form RPR
2164 1 **Jacobs Son**[28] 2097 6-9-7 **74**......... AndrewMullen 3 84+
(Michael Appleby) *chsd ldrs: drvn along 5f out: led wl over 2f out: rdn clr and hung lft over 1f out: eased ins fnl f* **9/4**[2]
00-5 2 6 **Master Of Song**[65] 1227 7-8-0 **58** ow1.........(p) PhilipPrince(5) 4 56
(Roy Bowring) *chsd ldr tl hmpd 10f out: remained handy: rdn over 4f out: styng on same pce whn wnt 2nd over 1f out* **7/1**
0-60 3 3 **Mister Bob (GER)**[14] 2476 5-8-4 **57**.........(b) JoeFanning 5 50
(James Bethell) *s.i.s: rcvrd to chse ldr 10f out: led 3f out: sn rdn and hdd: hung lft and wknd over 1f out* **7/2**[3]
4313 4 1 3/4 **Solarmaite**[28] 2092 5-8-9 **65**.........(b) BillyCray(3) 6 55
(Roy Bowring) *led: rdn and hdd 3f out: wknd wl over 1f out* **7/4**[1]
-005 5 6 **Layla's Boy**[83] 959 7-8-0 **56** oh7 ow1.........(b) RyanPowell(3) 2 36
(Simon West) *hld up and bhd: rdn over 4f out: nvr on terms* **50/1**
-500 6 22 **Chrissycross (IRE)**[14] 2498 5-9-5 **72**.........(v) RobertWinston 1 14
(Roger Teal) *dwlt: outpcd: hdwy 4f out: rdn and wknd over 2f out: eased* **14/1**

2m 23.66s (-4.34) **Going Correction** -0.175s/f (Stan) 6 Ran SP% **110.5**
Speed ratings (Par 103): **108,103,101,100,95 79**
CSF £17.23 TOTE £2.80: £1.40, £5.40; EX 18.70 Trifecta £68.80.
**Owner** The Rain Dancers **Bred** Stowell Park Stud **Trained** Danethorpe, Notts
■ Stewards' Enquiry : Billy Cray one-day ban: careless riding (Jun 22)
**FOCUS**
Another open-looking handicap which rather fell apart. The form can't be taken too literally as it's not obvious where the winner found improvement from.

## 2936 32RED H'CAP (BOBIS RACE) 1m (F)
4:50 (4:51) (Class 4) (0-80,79) 3-Y-O £4,851 (£1,443; £721; £360) Stalls Low

Form RPR
6-60 1 **Bognor (USA)**[33] 1947 3-8-7 **65** oh3......... AndrewMullen 8 73
(Michael Appleby) *chsd ldrs tl led over 2f out: rdn and hung lft fr over 1f out: jst hld on* **7/2**[3]
05-3 2 hd **Rainbow Rock (IRE)**[16] 2433 3-8-12 **70**......... JoeFanning 5 77
(Mark Johnston) *chsd ldrs: pushed along 3f out: rdn and ev ch ins fnl f: styd on* **7/4**[1]
5210 3 2 3/4 **Wildcat Lass (USA)**[24] 2205 3-8-11 **69** ow1......... DanielTudhope 6 71
(David O'Meara) *chsd ldrs: rdn and lost pl 1/2-way: hdwy 3f out: rdn and ev ch over 1f out: styng on same pce whn n.m.r wl ins fnl f: eased* **10/1**
1-60 4 4 **Grandest**[37] 1861 3-9-7 **79**......... RobertHavlin 3 70
(John Gosden) *trckd ldrs: led over 3f out tl over 2f out: sn rdn: styd on same pce appr fnl f* **5/2**[2]
-140 5 8 **Slinky McVelvet**[9] 2638 3-9-0 **72**......... PhillipMakin 7 45
(Garry Moss) *sn pushed along in rr: hdwy 6f out: lost pl over 4f out: rdn and wknd over 2f out* **25/1**
2-40 6 1 **Elysian Prince**[20] 2303 3-8-13 **76**......... LouisSteward(5) 1 47
(Paul Cole) *hld up: hdwy 5f out: rdn and wknd over 2f out* **10/1**
2000 7 4 **Aspirant**[16] 2429 3-9-6 **78**.........(t) BenCurtis 2 40
(Brian Ellison) *led over 4f: rdn and wknd wl over 1f out* **33/1**
3-03 8 3/4 **Peacemaker (IRE)**[31] 2013 3-8-10 **68**......... JohnFahy 4 28
(Eve Johnson Houghton) *s.s: a wl bhd* **20/1**

1m 41.91s (-1.79) **Going Correction** -0.175s/f (Stan) 8 Ran SP% **116.9**
Speed ratings (Par 101): **101,100,98,94,86 85,81,80**
CSF £10.08 CT £54.98 TOTE £5.70: £2.10, £1.10, £2.50; EX 14.60 Trifecta £63.80.
**Owner** 21C Telecom.co.uk **Bred** Klawervlei Stud (pty) Ltd **Trained** Danethorpe, Notts
■ Stewards' Enquiry : Joe Fanning four-day ban: used whip above permitted level (Jun 22-25)
**FOCUS**
A modest handicap. A clear personal best for the winner, giving his new yard a treble.

## 2937 GREEN FEE OFFERS AT SOUTHWELLGOLFCLUB.COM H'CAP 1m (F)
5:20 (5:20) (Class 6) (0-60,59) 4-Y-0+ £2,102 (£625; £312; £156) Stalls Low

Form RPR
56 1 **Alhaban (IRE)**[76] 1040 8-9-6 **58**.........(p) BenCurtis 7 66
(Ronald Harris) *chsd ldrs: led over 2f out: rdn and hung lft ins fnl f: styd on* **12/1**
2222 2 1/2 **General Tufto**[17] 2399 9-9-0 **55**.........(b) MichaelJMMurphy(3) 3 62
(Charles Smith) *hld up: hdwy 2f out: rdn to chse wnr fnl f: kpt on* **9/4**[2]
4420 3 2 3/4 **Excellent News (IRE)**[17] 2396 5-8-0 **45**.........(p) AdamMcLean(7) 1 46
(Tony Forbes) *led 1f: chsd ldr: rdn and ev ch over 2f out: styd on same pce fnl f* **14/1**
0000 4 nk **Daneside (IRE)**[1] 2907 7-8-7 **45**.........(v) PaulPickard 10 45
(Simon West) *hld up: hdwy over 2f out: rdn over 1f out: styd on same pce ins fnl f* **16/1**
0035 5 3/4 **Puppet Theatre (IRE)**[17] 2389 4-8-5 **46** ow1......... SamJames(3) 8 44
(David O'Meara) *s.i.s: hld up: hdwy over 2f out: rdn over 1f out: styd on same pce ins fnl f* **6/1**[3]
00-0 6 4 **Bridge Valley**[147] 100 7-8-4 **45**.........(be) BillyCray(3) 6 34
(Chris Bealby) *s.i.s: hld up: rdn over 3f out: n.d* **50/1**
00-3 7 nk **Pim Street (USA)**[147] 105 4-9-7 **59**......... DanielTudhope 5 47
(David O'Meara) *chsd ldrs: led over 3f out: hdd over 2f out: wknd fnl f* **5/4**[1]
560- 8 3 1/4 **Rosy Ryan (IRE)**[268] 6276 4-8-8 **46** ow1......... GrahamGibbons 4 27
(Tina Jackson) *prom: rdn 1/2-way: wknd over 1f out* **50/1**
04-0 9 1 1/2 **Rosie Hall (IRE)**[6] 2729 4-8-8 **46**.........[1] RoystonFfrench 9 23
(Les Eyre) *prom: pushed along 1/2-way: wknd over 2f out* **20/1**
145- 10 68 **Throwing Roses**[258] 6600 4-8-12 **50**......... PaddyAspell 2
(John Weymes) *led 7f out: hdd over 3f out: sn rdn and wknd* **20/1**

1m 43.81s (0.11) **Going Correction** -0.175s/f (Stan) 10 Ran SP% **123.2**
Speed ratings (Par 101): **92,91,88,88,87 83,83,80,78,10**
CSF £40.34 CT £415.96 TOTE £10.10: £2.70, £1.10, £2.80; EX 49.50 Trifecta £504.00.
**Owner** Ridge House Stables Ltd **Bred** Eimear Mulhern **Trained** Earlswood, Monmouths
**FOCUS**
A weak handicap run in a relatively slow time. Enough doubts over the field not to be too positive.
T/Plt: £75.80 to a £1 stake. Pool: £57,845.78 - 556.70 winning units. T/Qpdt: £31.20 to a £1 stake. Pool: £2901.57 - 68.72 winning units. CR

# [2688]BATH (L-H)
Friday, June 6

**OFFICIAL GOING: Good (7.3)**
Wind: quite strong half-behind Weather: sunny with cloudy periods

## 2942 BATH ALES GRAZE BAR AND CHOP HOUSE H'CAP 1m 5f 22y
5:50 (5:50) (Class 6) (0-60,60) 4-Y-0+ £1,940 (£577; £288; £144) Stalls High

Form RPR
2-04 1 **Glens Wobbly**[1] 2923 6-8-2 **46** oh1......... RyanTate(5) 14 58
(Jonathan Geake) *trckd ldrs: rdn to ld over 2f out: clr ent fnl f: styd on strly* **7/2**[2]
006- 2 5 **Walter De La Mare (IRE)**[46] 8302 7-8-0 **46** oh1......... JackGarritty(7) 7 51
(Anabel K Murphy) *fly-leapt leaving stalls: towards rr: hdwy over 2f out: sn rdn: styd on wl ent fnl f: sn chsng wnr but a being hld* **20/1**
3513 3 shd **Lac Sacre (FR)**[13] 2252 5-8-11 **50**.........(bt) LukeMorris 4 54
(John Flint) *mid-div: rdn and hdwy wl over 2f out: sn chsng ldrs: styd on wout ever threatening wnr* **9/4**[1]
3302 4 3/4 **Ice Apple**[14] 2531 6-8-4 **48**......... PhilipPrince(5) 3 51+
(John E Long) *mid-div: rdn over 2f out: no imp tl styd on strly fnl f: wnt 4th towards fin* **12/1**
5 1 1/4 **Quadriller (FR)**[29] 7-9-4 **60**.........(t) WilliamTwiston-Davies(3) 10 61+
(Philip Hobbs) *trckd ldrs: stirrup leather broke over 5f out: sn rdn along: styd on to dispute 3rd over 1f out: no ex ins fnl f* **14/1**
4-36 6 3/4 **Rowlestone Lass**[127] 380 4-8-10 **49**......... GrahamLee 11 49
(Richard Price) *s.i.s: sn mid-div on outer: rdn wl over 2f out: styd on same pce* **16/1**
2412 7 nk **Highlife Dancer**[3] 2874 6-9-0 **60**......... DanielCremin(7) 9 60
(Mick Channon) *disp ld most of way tl rdn and hdd by wnr over 2f out: hld in 2nd over 1f out: edgd lft: fdd ins fnl f* **4/1**[3]
333- 8 1 **Thundering Home**[12] 3412 7-9-2 **55**......... HayleyTurner 1 53
(Richard Mitchell) *chsd ldrs: rdn wl over 2f out: styng on at same pce in disp 3rd whn short of room 1f out: no ch after* **11/1**
0315 9 2 1/2 **Well Owd Mon**[39] 1815 4-8-11 **57**......... RobHornby(7) 13 52
(Andrew Hollinshead) *mainly towards rr: sme minor late prog: n.d* **20/1**
00-0 10 1/2 **Bondi Mist (IRE)**[60] 1355 5-9-3 **56**.........(v) FergusSweeney 8 50
(Jonathan Geake) *disp ld tl rdn and hdd over 2f out: kpt chsng ldng pair tl short of room ent fnl f: fdd fnl 120yds* **40/1**
0/-0 11 1 1/2 **Agapanthus (GER)**[29] 68 9-8-2 **46** oh1.........(p) RyanWhile(5) 6 38
(Neil Mulholland) *slowly away and hmpd: a towards rr* **33/1**
062- 12 19 **Youm Jamil (USA)**[290] 4036 7-8-4 **50**......... HollieDoyle(7) 2 13
(Tony Carroll) *rrd leaving stalls: towards rr: effrt to cl 2f out: little imp: wknd 1f out* **40/1**
00/0 13 dist **Teutonic Knight (IRE)**[35] 1923 7-8-9 **48**.........(t) SeanLevey 12
(Tony Newcombe) *mid-div tl dropped to rr qckly over 4f out: virtually p.u sn after* **66/1**

2m 52.91s (0.91) **Going Correction** +0.10s/f (Good) 13 Ran SP% **120.4**
Speed ratings (Par 101): **101,97,97,97,96 96,95,95,93,93 92,80,**
CSF £80.15 CT £194.19 TOTE £5.40: £1.70, £6.70, £1.40; EX 74.60 Trifecta £686.30.
**Owner** Glen Symes **Bred** H J Manners **Trained** Marlborough, Wilts
**FOCUS**
Races incorporating bottom bend increased in distance by about 10yds. There may have been plenty of runners in this opener but it was very moderate. This rates a personal best from the winner.

## 2943 BATH ALES GEM FILLIES' H'CAP 5f 11y
6:20 (6:20) (Class 5) (0-70,70) 3-Y-O £2,587 (£770; £384; £192) Stalls Centre

Form RPR
0-21 1 **Naivasha**[13] 2551 3-9-3 **66**......... RichardHughes 4 81+
(Robert Cowell) *mde all at str pce: clr fnl f: readily* **2/1**[1]
5-62 2 2 3/4 **Vodka Chaser (IRE)**[38] 1860 3-8-6 **60**......... PhilipPrince(5) 8 62
(Alison Hutchinson) *in tch: outpcd 3f out: hdwy 2f out: r.o wl fnl f: wnt 2nd fnl 75yds: nvr threatening wnr* **14/1**
0-53 3 shd **Wedgewood Estates**[100] 745 3-8-2 **56**......... RyanTate(5) 5 58
(Tony Carroll) *outpcd in last: hdwy over 1f out: sn swtchd rt: r.o wl: nrly snatched 2nd fnl stride* **20/1**
25-1 4 nk **Where The Boys Are (IRE)**[32] 2023 3-9-2 **65**......... GrahamLee 3 66
(Ed McMahon) *chsd wnr: rdn over 2f out: nt pce to get on terms: kpt on but lost 2 pls fnl 75yds* **7/2**[2]
110- 5 1 1/4 **Gower Princess**[207] 7837 3-9-3 **66**......... LukeMorris 1 63
(Ronald Harris) *chsd wnr: rdn 2f out: nt pce to get on terms: no ex fnl 120yds* **25/1**
-340 6 1 3/4 **Invoke (IRE)**[22] 2278 3-9-2 **70**......... LouisSteward(5) 7 60
(Michael Bell) *chsd wnr: rdn over 2f out: sn hung rt: btn over 1f out* **2/1**[1]
-210 7 2 1/2 **Crazee Diamond**[58] 1379 3-9-2 **68**......... WilliamTwiston-Davies(3) 2 49
(Mick Channon) *travelled wl bhd ldrs: trckd wnr in disp 2nd 3f out: rdn wl over 1f out: fnd little: wknd ins fnl f* **8/1**[3]

1m 1.63s (-0.87) **Going Correction** -0.175s/f (Firm) 7 Ran SP% **115.3**
Speed ratings (Par 96): **99,94,94,93,91 89,85**
CSF £32.66 CT £437.97 TOTE £2.70: £1.70, £5.40; EX 25.90 Trifecta £230.20.
**Owner** Lowther Racing **Bred** Lowther Racing **Trained** Six Mile Bottom, Cambs
**FOCUS**
A modest handicap but the winner made all in a good time. She's a bit better than the bare form.

## 2944 BATH ALES HOP POLE EBF STALLIONS MAIDEN STKS 5f 11y
6:50 (6:51) (Class 5) 2-Y-O £2,911 (£866; £432; £216) Stalls Centre

Form RPR
5 1 **Zeb Un Nisa**[18] 2402 2-9-0 0......... GrahamLee 3 84+
(Roger Charlton) *mde all: rdn clr fnl f: r.o wl: readily* **2/1**[1]
2 5 **La Cuesta (IRE)** 2-9-0 0......... FergusSweeney 11 66+
(Jamie Osborne) *mid-div: hdwy on outer over 3f out to dispute 3rd: rdn into 2nd jst over 1f out: edgd lft: kpt on but no ch w wnr* **12/1**
4 3 2 **Secret Journey (IRE)**[15] 2480 2-9-5 0......... GeorgeBaker 9 64
(Hughie Morrison) *chsd ldrs: sltly outpcd over 2f out: kpt on again ins fnl f* **9/2**[3]
52 4 3/4 **Don Sigfredo (IRE)**[41] 1741 2-9-5 0......... HayleyTurner 14 61
(Tom Dascombe) *sn trcking wnr: rdn over 2f out: nt pce to chal: no ex ins fnl f* **7/1**
5 5 1/2 **Emef Rock (IRE)**[15] 2480 2-9-2 0......... WilliamTwiston-Davies(3) 4 59
(Mick Channon) *in tch: rdn over 2f out: kpt on same pce fnl f* **16/1**
6 4 **Guilty (IRE)** 2-9-5 0......... RichardHughes 2 45+
(Richard Hannon) *sn pushed along in tch: rdn 2f out: nvr threatened: fdd ins fnl f* **5/2**[2]

04 **7** 2 **Zebs Lad (IRE)**[16] 2458 2-9-5 0 LukeMorris 10 38
(Ronald Harris) *nvr bttr than mid-div* 33/1

63 **8** 4 **Hell For Leather**[19] 2360 2-9-0 0 (v) RyanWhile(5) 6 23
(Bill Turner) *chsd wnr tl rdn over 2f out: wknd over 1f out* 50/1

06 **9** 3/4 **Is She Any Good (IRE)**[41] 1741 2-8-7 0 HollieDoyle(7) 13 16
(David Evans) *mid-div: rdn over 2f out: wknd over 1f out* 50/1

06 **10** hd **Clever Love (FR)**[48] 1571 2-9-0 0 LouisSteward(5) 1 20
(Jo Hughes) *s.i.s: a towards rr* 50/1

**11** 1/2 **Lady Charlie** 2-8-9 0 PhilipPrince(5) 7 13
(Jo Hughes) *s.i.s: sn outpcd: a towards rr* 66/1

5 **12** 2 **Abba Zabba (IRE)**[9] 2666 2-9-2 0 DeclanBates(3) 5 11
(David Evans) *sn outpcd: a towards rr* 66/1

**13** 2 **Trixy** 2-9-0 0 LiamJones 8
(Jo Hughes) *mid-div: sn pushed along: wknd 2f out* 66/1

**14** 25 **Blencathra** 2-8-12 0 HarryBurns(7) 12
(Jo Hughes) *s.i.s: a bhd: t.o* 100/1

1m 1.83s (-0.67) **Going Correction** -0.175s/f (Firm) **14** Ran SP% **120.5**
Speed ratings (Par 93): **98,90,86,85,84 78,75,68,67,67 66,63,60,20**
CSF £27.31 TOTE £3.30: £1.40, £3.80, £1.50; EX 32.60 Trifecta £135.00.
**Owner** A E Oppenheimer **Bred** Hascombe And Valiant Studs **Trained** Beckhampton, Wilts

**FOCUS**
The winner dominated in a fair time.

## 2945 BATH ALES SUMMER'S HARE H'CAP 5f 161y
7:25 (7:26) (Class 4) (0-80,80) 3-Y-O+ £4,690 (£1,395; £697; £348) Stalls Centre

Form RPR

3111 **1** **Ishiamber**[31] 2048 4-10-0 80 PatCosgrave 8 93
(George Baker) *trckd ldrs: led over 1f out: r.o strly: rdn out* 7/1

0124 **2** 1 1/2 **Whipphound**[11] 2606 6-9-4 70 GeorgeBaker 3 78
(Mark Brisbourne) *in tch: hdwy 2f out: sn rdn: chsd wnr ent fnl f: kpt on but a being hld* 4/1[2]

4064 **3** 1 1/2 **Ginzan**[17] 2414 6-9-0 71 RyanWhile(5) 1 74
(Malcolm Saunders) *led: rdn and hdd over 1f out: lost 2nd ent fnl f: kpt on same pce* 12/1

6-05 **4** hd **Rebecca Romero**[22] 2275 7-9-11 77 RichardHughes 5 79
(Denis Coakley) *hld up: hdwy over 1f out: sn rdn: kpt on same pce fnl f* 9/2[3]

353- **5** nk **Angelito**[199] 7959 5-9-10 76 GrahamLee 7 77
(Ed McMahon) *hld up in tch: rdn over 2f out: no imp tl r.o ins fnl f* 28/1

-506 **6** shd **Vallarta (IRE)**[27] 2147 4-9-4 73 WilliamTwiston-Davies(3) 9 74+
(Mick Channon) *hld up last but in tch: pushed along whn nt clr run over 1f out: swtchd lft: r.o but nvr any ch* 7/2[1]

326 **7** 1 **Vincentti (IRE)**[11] 2629 4-10-0 80 SteveDrowne 4 78
(Ronald Harris) *prom: rdn 2f out: sn hld: no ex ins fnl f* 16/1

2310 **8** 1 3/4 **Android (IRE)**[30] 2083 3-9-3 77 LukeMorris 6 67
(Clive Cox) *mid-div: rdn over 2f out: running on whn nt clr run and snatched up fnl 140yds* 12/1

-165 **9** nse **Thataboy (IRE)**[29] 2090 3-9-1 75 (t) HayleyTurner 2 65
(Tom Dascombe) *in tch: rdn over 2f out: nt pce to get on terms: fdd ins fnl f* 16/1

1m 10.86s (-0.34) **Going Correction** -0.175s/f (Firm)
**WFA** 3 from 4yo+ 8lb **9** Ran SP% **113.4**
Speed ratings (Par 105): **95,93,91,90,90 90,88,86,86**
CSF £34.45 CT £331.37 TOTE £5.80: £1.80, £1.50, £3.10; EX 31.40 Trifecta £250.60.
**Owner** Mrs P Scott-Dunn **Bred** Patricia Ann Scott-Dunn **Trained** Manton, Wilts

**FOCUS**
A hotly contested feature, with little in the way of early pace on offer. Another clear best from the winner, with the runner-up rated to his recent best.

## 2946 BATH ALES SPECIAL PALE ALE MAIDEN FILLIES' STKS 5f 161y
8:00 (8:08) (Class 5) 3-Y-O+ £2,587 (£770; £384; £192) Stalls Centre

Form RPR

432- **1** **Sunrise Star**[285] 5797 3-9-0 85 SeanLevey 5 88
(Lady Cecil) *a.p: led wl over 2f out: qcknd clr over 1f out: v easily* 4/7[1]

5 **2** 8 **Lead A Merry Dance**[15] 2489 3-9-0 0 GrahamLee 1 62
(Sylvester Kirk) *hld up: hdwy whn nt clr run 2f out: sn swtchd rt: r.o ent fnl f: wnt 2nd fnl 120yds: nvr any ch w easy wnr* 16/1

4 **3** 1 1/2 **Belletriste (FR)**[15] 2489 3-9-0 0 RichardHughes 2 57
(Sylvester Kirk) *taken to s early: mid-div: hdwy over 2f out: rdn to chse wnr over 1f out but nvr any ch: no ex whn lost 2nd fnl 120yds* 9/2[2]

2-5 **4** 2 1/2 **Twilight Angel**[148] 94 6-9-8 0 PatCosgrave 11 50
(Pat Eddery) *led tl rdn and hdd wl over 2f out: sn hld by wnr: lost 2nd over 1f out: no ex ins fnl f* 28/1

**5** 1 1/4 **Nora Batty** 3-8-9 0 RyanWhile(5) 7 44
(Bill Turner) *mid-div on outer: rdn and sme prog wl over 2f out: kpt on but nvr gng pce to get involved* 18/1

0- **6** 1/2 **Findhorn Magic**[209] 7817 3-9-0 0 SteveDrowne 3 43
(Peter Makin) *trckd ldrs: rdn whn nt clr run 2f out: hung bdly lft after: no further imp* 33/1

6 **7** nk **Silken Poppy**[15] 2489 3-8-11 0 ThomasBrown(3) 8 42
(Patrick Chamings) *trckd ldrs: rdn over 2f out: wknd ent fnl f* 40/1

0-4 **8** 3/4 **See No Ships**[11] 2625 3-9-0 0 LukeMorris 4 39
(Mark Usher) *cl up untl lost pl u.p over 2f out: nt a danger after* 40/1

3 **9** 3 1/2 **Lunarian**[15] 2489 3-8-11 0 WilliamTwiston-Davies(3) 6 28
(Mick Channon) *mid-div: rdn wl over 2f out: nvr any imp: wknd fnl f* 6/1[3]

0-54 **10** 9 **Perrydot (IRE)**[62] 1298 3-9-0 55 FergusSweeney 12
(Jo Crowley) *trckd ldrs: rdn over 2f out: wknd over 1f out* 66/1

60- **11** 1/2 **Posh Bounty**[396] 2068 3-8-9 0 ow2 ChrisMeehan(7) 9
(Carroll Gray) *unruly stalls: slowly away: a towards rr* 100/1

**12** 8 **Deja Bougg** 3-8-11 0 RobertTart(3) 10
(Michael Blake) *rn v green: v.s.a: a bhd* 25/1

1m 11.4s (0.20) **Going Correction** -0.175s/f (Firm)
**WFA** 3 from 6yo 8lb **12** Ran SP% **124.9**
Speed ratings (Par 100): **91,80,78,75,73 72,72,71,66,54 53,43**
CSF £13.16 TOTE £1.40: £1.10, £4.80, £1.50; EX 15.20 Trifecta £50.10.
**Owner** Lady Bamford **Bred** Moulton Stud **Trained** Newmarket, Suffolk

**FOCUS**
The winner won easily, but only as she was entitled to and the placed level is a bit shaky.

## 2947 BATH ALES SALAMANDER H'CAP 1m 2f 46y
8:30 (8:39) (Class 5) (0-70,70) 4-Y-O+ £2,587 (£770; £384; £192) Stalls Low

Form RPR

6-13 **1** **Stockhill Diva**[23] 2248 4-9-0 63 GrahamLee 13 77+
(Brendan Powell) *mid-div on outer: stdy prog fr over 2f out: rdn over 1f out: styd on strly fnl f: led fnl 20yds* 5/2[2]

-414 **2** 3/4 **Taro Tywod (IRE)**[14] 2509 5-9-4 67 RichardHughes 10 75
(Mark Brisbourne) *trckd ldr: led over 1f out: sn rdn: styd on but no ex whn hdd fnl 20yds* 9/1

0-04 **3** 3/4 **April Ciel**[8] 2693 5-9-1 64 (p) LukeMorris 11 71
(Ronald Harris) *led: rdn and hdd over 1f out: kpt on but no ex* 20/1

2331 **4** 2 3/4 **Gran Maestro (USA)**[7] 2730 5-9-2 70 (v) KevinStott(5) 5 71
(Ruth Carr) *mid-div: hdwy 3f out: sn rdn to chse ldrs: styd on same pce fnl 2f* 9/4[1]

34-0 **5** 2 1/2 **Foxhaven**[149] 85 12-9-4 70 (v) ThomasBrown(3) 12 67
(Patrick Chamings) *trckd ldrs: rdn over 2f out: sn one pce* 33/1

-315 **6** 1 1/4 **Adiynara (IRE)**[31] 1210 6-9-7 70 (p) GeorgeBaker 1 64
(Neil Mulholland) *mid-div: hdwy wl over 2f out: sn rdn to chse ldrs: nt pce to get on terms* 25/1

00-2 **7** nk **Urban Space**[9] 2672 8-8-3 52 (t) HayleyTurner 3 46
(John Flint) *trckd ldrs: rdn over 2f out: sn one pce* 6/1[3]

056- **8** 2 1/4 **Unison (IRE)**[217] 7656 4-9-5 68 SteveDrowne 7 57
(Peter Makin) *in tch: rdn wl over 2f out: wknd ent fnl f* 25/1

6-40 **9** 2 1/2 **Freddy Q (IRE)**[35] 1919 5-9-0 63 PatCosgrave 9 48
(Tony Newcombe) *a towards rr* 16/1

5243 **10** 1 1/2 **Prince Of Burma (IRE)**[14] 2529 6-9-0 66 (b) DeclanBates(3) 4 48
(David Evans) *slowly away: a towards rr* 20/1

00-4 **11** 2 **Precision Five**[17] 2415 5-9-4 67 (p) FergusSweeney 6 45
(Jeremy Gask) *fly-leapt leaving stalls: a towards rr* 20/1

210- **12** 1/2 **Bold Cross (IRE)**[249] 6898 11-9-4 70 RobertTart(3) 8 47
(Edward Bevan) *mid-div: rdn over 2f out: wknd over 1f out* 33/1

0-00 **13** 7 **Federal Blue (USA)**[23] 2251 4-9-4 67 (t) LiamJones 2 31
(Milton Bradley) *t.k.h towards rr: rdn into midfield 4f out: wknd 2f out* 66/1

2m 14.2s (3.20) **Going Correction** +0.10s/f (Good) **13** Ran SP% **118.9**
Speed ratings (Par 103): **91,90,89,87,85 84,84,82,80,79 77,77,71**
CSF £21.56 CT £376.61 TOTE £3.20: £1.20, £2.60, £3.70; EX 25.70 Trifecta £458.00.
**Owner** Mrs M Fairbairn & E Gadsden **Bred** Mrs M Fairbairn And E Gadsden **Trained** Upper Lambourn, Berks

**FOCUS**
This was run at an early crawl. The winner is potentially a fair bit better than the bare form.

## 2948 BATH ALES BREWERY CLASSIFIED STKS 1m 2f 46y
9:00 (9:00) (Class 6) 3-Y-O £2,045 (£603; £302) Stalls Low

Form RPR

3-55 **1** **Avocadeau (IRE)**[18] 2385 3-9-0 64 (p) MartinDwyer 6 68
(William Muir) *trckd ldr: led wl over 2f out: kpt on wl fnl f: rdn out* 7/1

0-64 **2** 3 1/4 **Travis Bickle (IRE)**[15] 2492 3-9-0 65 RichardHughes 3 62
(Sylvester Kirk) *trckd ldrs: hanging lft and reminder 6f out: rdn wl over 3f out: chsd wnr 2f out: kpt on same pce fnl f* 9/2[2]

60-0 **3** nk **Capers Royal Star (FR)**[25] 2224 3-9-0 65 LukeMorris 4 61
(Alastair Lidderdale) *hld up last but wl in tch: rdn over 2f out: sn disputing 2nd: kpt on same pce fnl f* 10/1

0040 **4** 18 **Lord Brantwood**[18] 2385 3-8-11 64 WilliamTwiston-Davies(3) 2 27
(Mick Channon) *led tl rdn wl over 2f out: wknd wl over 1f out* 6/1[3]

0-42 **5** 46 **Gift Of Rain (IRE)**[10] 2643 3-9-0 65 GrahamLee 1
(Ed Dunlop) *trckd ldrs tl wknd rapidly wl over 2f out: virtually p.u* 4/5[1]

2m 13.65s (2.65) **Going Correction** +0.10s/f (Good) **5** Ran SP% **109.6**
Speed ratings (Par 97): **93,90,90,75,38**
CSF £35.84 TOTE £6.90: £2.60, £2.20; EX 28.00 Trifecta £91.50.
**Owner** John O'Mulloy **Bred** Wiji Bloodstock & Ceka Ltd **Trained** Lambourn, Berks

**FOCUS**
A poor finale, with the favourite running no race. The winner is rated to form.
T/Plt: £37.00 to a £1 stake. Pool: £73,845.12 - 1,453.68 winning tickets T/Qpdt: £9.40 to a £1 stake. Pool: £7,630.12 - 595.92 winning tickets TM

# 2724 CATTERICK (L-H)
Friday, June 6

**OFFICIAL GOING: Soft (good to soft in places; 7.2)**
Wind: Moderate behind Weather: Warm sunshine

## 2949 BRITISH STALLION STUDS EBF MAIDEN STKS 5f
1:45 (1:45) (Class 5) 2-Y-O £2,911 (£866; £432; £216) Stalls Low

Form RPR

4 **1** **Pearl's Azinger (IRE)**[7] 2725 2-9-0 0 PhillipMakin 2 70+
(David Barron) *trckd ldr: cl up 1/2-way: led wl over 1f out: rdn ins fnl f: kpt on* 4/7[1]

**2** 2 1/4 **Fullon Clarets** 2-9-5 0 TonyHamilton 3 65+
(Richard Fahey) *chsd ldng pair: hdwy 2f out: rdn to chse wnr appr fnl f: kpt on same pce* 13/2[3]

6 **3** 4 1/2 **Atreus**[31] 2051 2-9-5 0 JamesSullivan 6 49
(Michael Easterby) *dwlt and green in rr: hdwy 2f out: styd on fnl f: nrst fin* 33/1

05 **4** 1 1/4 **Ripon Rose**[7] 2725 2-9-0 0 PaulMulrennan 5 40
(Paul Midgley) *chsd ldrs: rdn along 2f out: sn drvn and wknd over 1f out* 12/1

60 **5** 12 **Pearlise (FR)**[28] 2128 2-8-7 0 MatthewHopkins(7) 4
(Scott Dixon) *chsd ldrs: rdn along bef 1/2-way: sn outpcd and bhd* 100/1

**6** 8 **Grey Zeb (IRE)** 2-9-5 0 TomEaves 1 +
(Keith Dalgleish) *qckly away and led: jnd 1/2-way: rdn and hdd wl over 1f out: sn wknd and eased* 4/1[2]

1m 1.8s (2.00) **Going Correction** +0.275s/f (Good) **6** Ran SP% **108.6**
Speed ratings (Par 93): **95,91,84,82,63 50**
CSF £4.50 TOTE £1.90: £1.10, £2.60; EX 6.10 Trifecta £22.30.
**Owner** A F O'Callaghan **Bred** G Flannery Developments **Trained** Maunby, N Yorks

**FOCUS**
A weak maiden, favourite backers having few worrying moments. The time, race average and the third help set the level.

## 2950 YORKSHIRE-OUTDOORS.CO.UK (S) STKS 1m 5f 175y
2:20 (2:20) (Class 6) 4-Y-O+ £2,385 (£704; £352) Stalls Low

Form RPR

0020 **1** **Sherman McCoy**[23] 2259 8-8-12 68 RobertWinston 4 73
(Marjorie Fife) *trckd wnr: led 1/2-way: rdn along 3f out: styd on and clr fnl 2f* 1/4[1]

006- **2** 8 **English Summer**[272] 6217 7-8-9 75 (t) IanBrennan(3) 6 62
(Patrick Morris) *trckd ldng pair: cl up 1/2-way: chal 5f out: rdn along 3f out: drvn 2f out and sn one pce* 7/2[2]

4/0- **3** 44 **Born To Shine (USA)**[319] 2041 6-8-12 0 ..................... PaulPickard 1
(Tracy Waggott) *set stdy pce: awkward bnd after 5f: hdd 1/2-way and sn pushed along: rdn over 4f out and sn outpcd: wl bhd in poor 3rd fnl 3f* **16/1**[3]

650 **4** 3 **Samoan (IRE)**[7] 2738 5-8-12 42 ..................... (b) PatrickMathers 7
(Alan Berry) *awkward s: a in rr: wl outpcd fnl 4f* **66/1**

3m 7.62s (4.02) **Going Correction** +0.375s/f (Good) **4** Ran SP% **109.6**
Speed ratings (Par 101): **103,98,73,71**
CSF £1.51 TOTE £1.30; EX 1.90 Trifecta £2.20.There was no bid for the winner.
**Owner** T W Fife **Bred** Horizon Bloodstock Limited **Trained** Stillington, N Yorks

**FOCUS**
A glut of non-runners meant this provided a very good opportunity for the winner in this weak seller. He is rated to his recent best.

## 2951 LIONWELD KENNEDY H'CAP 5f
**2:55** (2:56) (Class 5) (0-70,69) 3-Y-O+ **£2,911** (£866; £432; £216) **Stalls** Low

Form RPR

00 **1** **Sir Geoffrey (IRE)**[17] 2434 8-8-12 **62** ..................... (p) MatthewHopkins(7) 7 73
(Scott Dixon) *mde all: rdn over 1f out: kpt on strly* **22/1**

0040 **2** 1 **I'll Be Good**[11] 2629 5-8-13 **59** ..................... (t) SladeO'Hara(3) 2 66
(Alan Berry) *hld up in tch: hdwy on inner 2f out: rdn to chse wnr ins fnl f: kpt on* **9/1**

4352 **3** 1 1/4 **Windforpower (IRE)**[7] 2743 4-9-5 **62** ..................... (p) PaulPickard 1 65
(Tracy Waggott) *prom: effrt 2f out: rdn to chse wnr appr fnl f: sn drvn and no imp towards fin* **9/4**[1]

2-55 **4** 2 **Madagascar Moll (IRE)**[3] 2870 3-9-1 **68** ..................... JulieBurke(3) 5 60
(David O'Meara) *in tch: pushed along over 2f out: rdn wl over 1f out: kpt on fnl f: nrst fin* **13/2**[3]

45-4 **5** nk **Oscars Journey**[27] 2159 4-9-11 **68** ..................... FrederikTylicki 3 62
(J R Jenkins) *chsd ldrs: rdn along 2f out: sn one pce* **3/1**[2]

-660 **6** nse **Bonnie Charlie**[16] 2456 8-9-12 **69** ..................... PaulQuinn 4 63
(David Nicholls) *in rr: rdn along 2f out: sme late hdwy* **15/2**

0061 **7** shd **Take The Lead**[13] 2552 4-9-4 **68** ..................... AnnaHesketh(7) 8 62
(David Nicholls) *cl up: disp ld 1/2-way: rdn along wl over 1f out: wknd appr fnl f* **15/2**

-400 **8** 1 3/4 **Baltic Spirit (IRE)**[21] 2296 3-8-12 **62** ..................... 1 TomEaves 9 46
(Keith Dalgleish) *towards rr: rdn along bef 1/2-way: sn outpcd* **20/1**

1m 0.7s (0.90) **Going Correction** +0.275s/f (Good)
**WFA** 3 from 4yo+ 7lb **8** Ran SP% **111.7**
Speed ratings (Par 103): **103,101,99,96,95 95,95,92**
CSF £193.43 CT £625.78 TOTE £24.90: £4.00, £3.00, £1.60; EX 215.30 Trifecta £892.10.
**Owner** General Sir Geoffrey Howlett **Bred** P Rabbitte **Trained** Babworth, Notts
■ Stewards' Enquiry : Matthew Hopkins 21-day ban (of which seven have been referred: used whip with excessive frequency (Jun 20-21, 28-30, Jul 1-9) (fifth offence in the past six months)

**FOCUS**
A modest sprint. The winner's best turf form since July 2012.

## 2952 RACINGUK.COM MAIDEN STKS 1m 3f 214y
**3:30** (3:30) (Class 5) 3-Y-O+ **£3,234** (£962; £481; £240) **Stalls** Low

Form RPR

44-2 **1** **Ruwasi**[20] 2354 3-8-13 80 ..................... PaulMulrennan 5 83
(James Tate) *hld up: hdwy on outer 1/2-way: trckd ldr over 4f out: rdn along wl over 2f out: drvn over 1f out: styd on to chal ent fnl f: led last 100yds* **2/5**[1]

33 **2** 1 **Miss Tree**[20] 2354 3-8-5 0 ..................... IanBrennan(3) 4 76
(John Quinn) *trckd ldrs: hdwy 1/2-way and sn cl up: led over 4f out: rdn clr wl over 2f out: drvn over 1f out: hdd and no ex last 100yds* **7/2**[2]

**3** 15 **Wor Lass**[12] 6-9-9 0 ..................... DavidAllan 7 52
(Iain Jardine) *prom: trckd ldr after 1f: rdn along 5f out: outpcd and lost pl 4f out: styd on to take poor 3rd over 1f out* **28/1**

00 **4** 7 **Lacocodanza**[20] 2354 5-9-2 0 ..................... KieranSchofield(7) 3 41
(George Moore) *dwlt and bhd: hdwy over 3f out: sn rdn along and plugged on one pce* **100/1**

0 **5** 3 1/4 **Archie's Advice**[21] 2292 3-8-13 0 ..................... TomEaves 2 41
(Keith Dalgleish) *prom: led after 1f: pushed along 1/2-way: hdd over 4f out and sn rdn along: drvn and outpcd over 3f out* **40/1**

66 **6** 5 **Some Boy Lukey**[18] 2392 3-8-13 0 ..................... StevieDonohoe 1 33
(David Thompson) *chsd ldrs: rdn along over 4f out: drvn over 3f out: sn wknd* **66/1**

356- **7** 40 **Street Artist (IRE)**[323] 4447 4-10-0 76 ..................... AdrianNicholls 6
(David Nicholls) *led 1f: prom: rdn along over 5f out: wknd 4f out: sn bhd* **10/1**[3]

2m 41.45s (2.55) **Going Correction** +0.375s/f (Good)
**WFA** 3 from 4yo+ 15lb **7** Ran SP% **111.1**
Speed ratings (Par 103): **106,105,95,90,88 85,58**
CSF £1.87 TOTE £1.60: £1.10, £1.40; EX 2.40 Trifecta £11.60.
**Owner** Saeed Manana **Bred** Highbury Terrace Owners Club **Trained** Newmarket, Suffolk

**FOCUS**
Another weak maiden, the leading pair finishing well clear. The winner made harder work of beating the second than at Thirsk latest.

## 2953 PIN POINT RECRUITMENT H'CAP 5f 212y
**4:10** (4:11) (Class 4) (0-85,83) 4-Y-O+ **£6,469** (£1,925; £962; £481) **Stalls** Low

Form RPR

5542 **1** **Mon Brav**[13] 2559 7-8-10 **72** ..................... DaleSwift 5 84
(Brian Ellison) *in rr and sn pushed along: rdn 2f out: drvn and hdwy over 1f out: str run ins fnl f to ld nr fin* **3/1**[2]

-352 **2** 1 1/4 **Powerful Presence (IRE)**[13] 2549 8-9-4 **80** ..................... DavidNolan 6 88
(David O'Meara) *trckd ldrs: hdwy 2f out: rdn to chal over 1f out: drvn to ld ins fnl f: hdd and no ex towards fin* **11/4**[1]

0345 **3** 1 1/2 **Solar Spirit (IRE)**[13] 2549 9-8-13 **75** ..................... RobertWinston 8 78
(Tracy Waggott) *hld up towards rr: gd hdwy over 2f out: rdn to ld jst over 1f out: drvn and hdd ins fnl f: kpt on same pce* **13/2**[3]

-000 **4** 2 1/2 **Holy Angel (IRE)**[19] 2364 5-8-10 **72** ..................... (e) DavidAllan 4 67+
(Tim Easterby) *hld up in rr: hdwy on inner 2f out: nt clr run over 1f out and again jst ins fnl f: swtchd rt and kpt on towards fin* **11/1**

1500 **5** nk **Burren View Lady (IRE)**[19] 2361 4-8-6 **75** ..................... RachelRichardson(7) 2 69+
(Tim Easterby) *trckd ldrs: effrt 2f out: sn rdn and one pce appr fnl f* **18/1**

0-00 **6** hd **Lightnin Hopkins (IRE)**[17] 2425 4-9-1 **80** ..................... (p) SamJames(3) 9 73
(David O'Meara) *trckd ldrs on outer: effrt 2f out: sn rdn and no imp appr fnl f* **16/1**

2240 **7** 2 1/2 **Tax Free (IRE)**[10] 2656 12-9-7 **83** ..................... AdrianNicholls 3 68
(David Nicholls) *led: rdn along and hdd 2f out: sn wknd* **14/1**

00-2 **8** 3/4 **Tango Sky (IRE)**[7] 2727 5-8-12 **74** ..................... TomEaves 1 57
(Richard Fahey) *trckd ldrs on inner: effrt over 2f out: sn rdn and wknd over 1f out* **17/2**

-500 **9** 1 1/4 **Al Mukhdam**[13] 2562 4-9-0 **79** ..................... ConnorBeasley(3) 7 58
(Ed de Giles) *chsd ldr: rdn to ld 2f out: drvn and hdd over 1f out: sn wknd* **7/1**

1m 14.89s (1.29) **Going Correction** +0.375s/f (Good) **9** Ran SP% **114.2**
Speed ratings (Par 105): **106,104,102,99,98 98,95,94,92**
CSF £11.53 CT £48.10 TOTE £4.80: £1.50, £1.10, £3.20; EX 13.80 Trifecta £54.10.
**Owner** Koo's Racing Club **Bred** J D Graham **Trained** Norton, N Yorks

**FOCUS**
A fairly useful handicap which was soundly run. The winner was still a length off last year's best.

## 2954 EBF STALLIONS BREEDING WINNERS FILLIES' H'CAP 7f
**4:40** (4:40) (Class 4) (0-80,79) 4-Y-O+ **£6,817** (£2,013; £1,007) **Stalls** Low

Form RPR

-221 **1** **True Pleasure (IRE)**[16] 2454 7-9-0 **72** ..................... PJMcDonald 4 86
(James Bethell) *hld up: smooth hdwy to trck ldng pair 1/2-way: effrt and swtchd rt 2f out: chal wl over 1f out: rdn to ld appr fnl f: sn clr and styd on wl* **15/8**[1]

60-0 **2** 5 **Gladsome**[39] 1813 6-8-0 **61** oh3 ow1 ..................... ConnorBeasley(3) 6 62
(Michael Herrington) *in rr: pushed along 1/2-way: hdwy on outer 2f out: sn rdn and styd on wl fnl f: tk 2nd nr line* **28/1**

-100 **3** 1/2 **Celtic Sixpence (IRE)**[13] 2549 6-8-11 **76** ..................... MeganCarberry(7) 2 76
(Nick Kent) *slt ld: hdd 1/2-way: cl up: rdn along wl over 1f out: styd on ins fnl f: edgd lft and lost 2nd nr line* **9/2**[3]

1503 **4** 1 3/4 **Graceful Act**[17] 2427 6-7-11 **60** oh4 ..................... (p) ShirleyTeasdale(5) 3 55
(Ron Barr) *chsd ldrs: n.m.r and pushed along 1/2-way: rdn 2f out: sn drvn and wknd* **13/2**

0060 **5** nk **Lilac Lace (IRE)**[21] 2318 4-9-7 **79** ..................... DuranFentiman 1 73
(Tim Easterby) *cl up on inner: led 1/2-way: rdn and edgd lft 2f out: hdd and drvn appr fnl f: sn wknd* **9/4**[2]

3000 **6** 3 **Mystical Moment**[13] 2549 4-8-6 **64** ..................... (p) JamesSullivan 5 51
(Edwin Tuer) *chsd ldrs: rdn along over 2f out: sn drvn and wknd* **17/2**

1m 28.75s (1.75) **Going Correction** +0.375s/f (Good) **6** Ran SP% **111.0**
Speed ratings (Par 102): **105,99,98,96,96 92**
CSF £45.07 CT £240.21 TOTE £2.40: £1.10, £12.60; EX 41.20 Trifecta £207.70.
**Owner** Clarendon Thoroughbred Racing **Bred** Michael O'Mahony **Trained** Middleham Moor, N Yorks

**FOCUS**
A weak handicap, particularly for the money, but the winner is clearly in the form of her life at present. The runner-up was out of the handicap.

## 2955 PARK AND CYCLE AT CATTERICK RACECOURSE H'CAP 5f 212y
**5:10** (5:10) (Class 6) (0-65,65) 3-Y-O+ **£2,385** (£704; £352) **Stalls** Low

Form RPR

6002 **1** **Cadeaux Pearl**[37] 1887 6-9-2 **55** ..................... 1 FrederikTylicki 4 67
(Scott Dixon) *trckd ldrs on inner: hdwy 2f out: rdn to chse ldr over 1f out: led ins fnl f: kpt on wl towards fin* **11/1**

-034 **2** 1/2 **Mission Impossible**[13] 2552 9-9-5 **58** ..................... (p) RobertWinston 8 68
(Tracy Waggott) *trckd ldrs: hdwy 2f out: rdn over 1f out: drvn and kpt on fnl f* **6/1**[2]

-531 **3** hd **Betty Boo (IRE)**[7] 2726 4-8-10 **56** 6ex ..................... AlexHopkinson(7) 6 65+
(Shaun Harris) *midfield: sddle slipped and edgd rt bnd at 1/2-way: hdwy to chse ldrs whn n.m.r over 1f out: swtchd rt and styd on wl towards fin* **7/2**[1]

5641 **4** 1 1/2 **Prigsnov Dancer (IRE)**[28] 2127 9-9-3 **63** ..................... DavidParkes(7) 9 67
(Deborah Sanderson) *midfield: hdwy on wd outside 2f out: rdn to chse ldrs over 1f out: kpt on same pce fnl f* **17/2**

0250 **5** hd **Manatee Bay**[11] 2606 4-9-8 **61** ..................... (p) AdrianNicholls 7 64
(David Nicholls) *towards rr: hdwy 2f out: swtchd rt and rdn over 1f out: kpt on fnl f: nrst fin* **15/2**

-030 **6** 1/2 **Meandmyshadow**[20] 2332 6-9-11 **64** ..................... DaleSwift 5 65
(Alan Brown) *sn chsng clr ldr: rdn along and hdwy 2f out: drvn and one pce appr fnl f* **9/1**

-603 **7** nk **Perfect Words (IRE)**[10] 2658 4-8-13 **57** ..................... (b[1]) ShirleyTeasdale(5) 1 57
(Marjorie Fife) *led and sn clr: rdn wl over 1f out: hdd ins fnl f and sn wknd* **7/1**[3]

0-50 **8** 2 1/4 **Oak Bluffs (IRE)**[21] 2296 3-9-1 **62** ..................... TonyHamilton 3 52
(Richard Fahey) *towards rr: sme hdwy 2f out: sn rdn and n.d* **16/1**

406- **9** 1 **Abraham Monro**[254] 6760 4-9-2 **55** ..................... JamesSullivan 2 44
(Ruth Carr) *a towards rr* **20/1**

-620 **10** 3 3/4 **See Clearly**[21] 2296 5-9-6 **59** ..................... (b) DuranFentiman 10 34
(Tim Easterby) *chsd ldrs: rdn along 2f out: sn drvn and wknd* **16/1**

0-00 **11** 3/4 **Almanack**[55] 1446 4-9-7 **65** ..................... (p) ShaneGray(5) 12 37
(Ian Williams) *a in rr* **14/1**

20-4 **12** 1 **Nine Before Ten (IRE)**[7] 2724 6-8-5 **51** oh1 ..................... (t) RobJFitzpatrick(7) 11 20
(Deborah Sanderson) *dwlt: a in rr* **20/1**

1m 15.92s (2.32) **Going Correction** +0.375s/f (Good)
**WFA** 3 from 4yo+ 8lb **12** Ran SP% **117.6**
Speed ratings (Par 101): **99,98,98,96,95 95,94,91,90,85 84,83**
CSF £75.03 CT £279.63 TOTE £11.90: £4.50, £2.50, £2.00; EX 69.60 Trifecta £611.50.
**Owner** P J Dixon & Partners **Bred** Catridge Farm Stud Ltd **Trained** Babworth, Notts

**FOCUS**
A run-of-the-mill contest which was run at a good pace. The form is rated around the runner-up.
T/Plt: £6.70 to a £1 stake. Pool: £36241.38 - 3891.91 winning tickets T/Qpdt: £4.00 to a £1 stake. Pool: £2303.32 - 425.34 winning tickets JR

# 1650 EPSOM (L-H)
Friday, June 6

**OFFICIAL GOING: Good (overall 7.5; home straight: stands' side 7.4, far side 7.1)**
Wind: light to medium, half behind Weather: dry and bright

## 2956 PRINCESS ELIZABETH STKS (SPONSORED BY INVESTEC) (GROUP 3) (F&M) 1m 114y
**1:35** (1:37) (Class 1) 3-Y-O+
**£39,697** (£15,050; £7,532; £3,752; £1,883; £945) **Stalls** Low

Form RPR

63-6 **1** **Thistle Bird**[22] 2284 6-9-6 114 ..................... JamesDoyle 6 108
(Roger Charlton) *hld up in tch in midfield: 7th st: rdn and hdwy wl over 1f out: str run to ld 1f out: edgd lft but r.o wl fnl f* **7/2**[2]

-253 **2** 1 **Odeliz (IRE)**[22] 2284 4-9-6 106 ..................... DanielTudhope 2 105
(K R Burke) *in tch in midfield: 5th st: rdn and effrt 2f out: hdwy to ld ent fnl f: sn hdd: edgd lft and outpcd by wnr ins fnl f: kpt on* **5/1**[3]

06-5 **3** *nk* **Just The Judge (IRE)**[50] 1533 4-9-6 110 ...... JamieSpencer 3 105
(Charles Hills) *hld up in tch in midfield: 6th st: switching out rt 2f out: hdwy ent fnl f: wnt 3rd ins fnl f: r.o wl but no threat to wnr* **10/3**[1]

03-4 **4** *2* **Masarah (IRE)**[27] 2144 4-9-6 98 ...... KierenFallon 7 100
(Clive Brittain) *t.k.h: chsd ldr tl led after 1f: rdn over 2f out: hdd ent fnl f: no ex and outpcd fnl 150yds* **25/1**

11-4 **5** *3/4* **Mango Diva**[22] 2284 4-9-9 106 ...... RyanMoore 1 101
(Sir Michael Stoute) *chsd ldrs: 4th st: nvr enough room on inner fr over 2f out tl gap opened ins fnl f: styd on but nvr able to chal* **7/2**[2]

20-0 **6** *3/4* **Butterfly McQueen (USA)**[69] 1162 4-9-6 97 ...... DavidProbert 8 97
(Andrew Balding) *chsd ldrs: 3rd st: effrt u.p to press ldr 2f out: unable qck over 1f out: wknd ins fnl f* **20/1**

1-10 **7** *1* **Zurigha (IRE)**[33] 1974 4-9-6 107 ...... RichardHughes 4 94
(Richard Hannon) *hld up in tch in last trio: 8th st: effrt 2f out: no imp u.p over 1f out: styd on same pce fnl f* **8/1**

00-6 **8** *1/2* **Audacia (IRE)**[21] 2318 4-9-6 84 ...... FrankieDettori 10 93
(Hugo Palmer) *stdd s and dropped in bhd: hld up in tch: 9th st: effrt u.p entering fnl 2f: no imp: nvr trbld ldrs* **50/1**

-061 **9** *shd* **Amulet**[27] 2144 4-9-6 89 ...... ShaneKelly 5 93
(Eve Johnson Houghton) *led for 1f: chsd ldr: 2nd st: rdn and effrt to press ldr over 2f out: no ex and btn over 1f out: wknd ins fnl f* **14/1**

/0-6 **10** *6* **Melody Of Love**[27] 2155 4-9-6 95 ...... JimmyFortune 9 79
(Brian Meehan) *s.i.s: hld up in rr: 10th st: rdn and no hdwy jst over 2f out: n.d* **66/1**

1m 42.65s (-3.45) **Going Correction** -0.15s/f (Firm) **10** Ran SP% **114.0**
Speed ratings (Par 113): **109,108,107,106,105 104,103,103,103,97**
CSF £20.03 TOTE £4.10: £1.80, £1.90, £1.40; EX 23.20 Trifecta £91.50.
**Owner** Lady Rothschild **Bred** The Rt Hon Lord Rothschild **Trained** Beckhampton, Wilts

**FOCUS**
Rail dolled out up to 6yds from 1m to winning post and distances on Round course increased by 17yds. This was a competitive Group 3 for fillies and there was a sound pace on. Solid form for the division. The fourth is the key, with Thistle Bird 4lb off last year's winning mark.

## 2957 INVESTEC WEALTH & INVESTMENT H'CAP — 1m 2f 18y
**2:10** (2:17) (Class 2) 4-Y-0+

**£31,125** (£9,320; £4,660; £2,330; £1,165; £585) **Stalls** Low

Form RPR

5-55 **1** **Farraaj (IRE)**[34] 1948 5-9-8 **102** ...... AndreaAtzeni 5 118
(Roger Varian) *chsd clr ldng pair: clsd smoothly to ld 2f out: sn rdn and clr w runner-up: asserted jst ins fnl f: r.o strly: readily* **13/2**[2]

21 **2** *2 1/2* **Air Pilot**[20] 2354 5-8-3 **83** ...... JimmyQuinn 10 94
(Ralph Beckett) *chsd ldng trio: clsd to press wnr 2f out: sn clr w wnr and rdn: no ex and btn jst ins fnl f: r.o same pce for clr 2nd* **8/1**[3]

-644 **3** *7* **Clon Brulee (IRE)**[106] 681 5-9-5 **99** ...... KierenFallon 6 97
(Saeed bin Suroor) *hld up in midfield: rdn and effrt over 2f out: outpcd by ldng pair 2f out: styd on to go modest 3rd ent fnl f: kpt on but no imp* **8/1**[3]

-020 **4** *3/4* **Gworn**[41] 1733 4-8-10 **90** ...... PaulHanagan 2 86
(Ed Dunlop) *hld up in midfield: outpcd by ldng pair 2f out: no threat to ldrs after: kpt on ins fnl f* **14/1**

0536 **5** *nk* **Aussie Reigns (IRE)**[49] 1559 4-9-7 **104** ...... OisinMurphy(3) 9 100
(William Knight) *hld up in last quartet: rdn and effrt ent fnl 2f: sn outpcd by ldng pair: no ch but kpt on ins fnl f* **20/1**

-040 **6** *1* **Hi There (IRE)**[23] 2253 5-9-4 **98** ...... RyanMoore 3 92+
(Richard Fahey) *hld up in last quartet: effrt on inner over 2f out: outpcd by ldng pair and swtchd rt wl over 1f out: wl hld and kpt on same pce after* **8/1**[3]

0-60 **7** *nse* **Charles Camoin (IRE)**[44] 1653 6-8-9 **88** ow1 ...... JamieSpencer 11 83
(Sylvester Kirk) *hld up in last quartet: effrt jst over 2f out: sn outpcd by ldng pair: stl 10th and hanging lft ent fnl f: styd on fnl 150yds: nvr trbld ldrs* **8/1**[3]

60-0 **8** *nse* **Resurge (IRE)**[44] 1653 9-8-10 **90** ...... (t) TomQueally 12 84
(Stuart Kittow) *s.i.s: sn rcvrd and in tch in midfield: rdn over 2f out: sn outpcd by ldng pair: n.d and plugged on same pce fnl 2f* **12/1**

0512 **9** *1 1/2* **Tres Coronas (IRE)**[23] 2253 7-9-10 **104** ...... GrahamGibbons 7 95
(David Barron) *s.i.s: bhd: rdn jst over 2f out: no hdwy and stl last ent fnl f: styd on fnl 150yds: nvr trbld ldrs* **9/1**

5-31 **10** *1/2* **Soviet Rock (IRE)**[27] 2154 4-9-3 **97** ...... DavidProbert 8 87
(Andrew Balding) *w ldr: led 7f out and sn wnt clr w rival: rdn and hdd 2f out: sn outpcd and btn: lost modest 3rd ent fnl f: wknd fnl 150yds* **5/1**[1]

-104 **11** *2 1/2* **Salutation (IRE)**[33] 1973 4-8-12 **95** ...... MichaelJMMurphy(3) 4 80
(Mark Johnston) *led tl 7f out: sn wnt clr and styd pressing ldr tl rdn and outpcd 2f out: wl btn 4th over 1f out: wknd fnl f* **20/1**

3120 **12** *4 1/2* **Sennockian Star**[11] 2618 4-9-8 **102** ...... (v) SilvestreDeSousa 1 79
(Mark Johnston) *spread a plate at s: in tch in midfield: rdn and struggling over 2f out: outpcd and wl btn over 1f out: bhd fnl f* **10/1**

2m 4.35s (-5.35) **Going Correction** -0.15s/f (Firm) **12** Ran SP% **117.4**
Speed ratings (Par 109): **115,113,107,106,106 105,105,105,104,104 102,98**
CSF £57.19 CT £418.71 TOTE £7.50: £2.60, £2.60, £3.10; EX 72.80 Trifecta £413.40.
**Owner** Sheikh Ahmed Al Maktoum **Bred** Darley **Trained** Newmarket, Suffolk

**FOCUS**
They went a good gallop here and the time was almost a second faster than standard. Few got involved and the first two finished clear. The winner is probably up to Group 2 level.

## 2958 INVESTEC DIOMED STKS (GROUP 3) — 1m 114y
**2:45** (2:49) (Class 1) 3-Y-0+

**£39,697** (£15,050; £7,532; £3,752; £1,883; £945) **Stalls** Low

Form RPR

-231 **1** **French Navy**[13] 2554 6-9-5 112 ...... AdamKirby 1 117
(Charlie Appleby) *s.i.s: in rr: dream run on inner and hdwy to chse ldrs 2f out: swtchd rt and wnt between rivals over 1f out: led 1f out: r.o strly and drew clr fnl 100yds* **13/2**

5-12 **2** *2 1/4* **Graphic (IRE)**[37] 1870 5-9-5 114 ...... (p) RyanMoore 5 112
(William Haggas) *sn bustled up to chse ldr: rdn 3f out: chalng whn nudged rt over 1f out: chsd wnr jst ins fnl f: r.o same pce* **9/4**[1]

-122 **3** *1* **Windhoek**[13] 2554 4-9-5 108 ...... KierenFallon 3 110
(Saeed bin Suroor) *in tch in last pair: effrt on outer wl over 2f out: hdwy u.p to chse ldrs over 1f out: styd on same pce to go 3rd wl ins fnl f* **3/1**[3]

-062 **4** *3/4* **Highland Knight (IRE)**[49] 1558 7-9-8 108 ...... (t) DavidProbert 7 111
(Andrew Balding) *led: rdn 2f out: hdd 1f out: 3rd and btn ins fnl f: lost 3rd and wknd towards fin* **14/1**

306- **5** *1 1/4* **Gregorian (IRE)**[230] 7366 5-9-5 116 ...... WilliamBuick 6 105
(John Gosden) *chsd ldrs: clsd and stl looked to be travelling wl enough 2f out: rdn and unable qck over 1f out: btn and edgd lft ins fnl f* **11/4**[2]

0466 **6** *2 1/2* **Edu Querido (BRZ)**[29] 2086 5-9-5 108 ...... (p) AndreaAtzeni 4 99
(Marco Botti) *stdd after s: hld up in tch in midfield: rdn and outpcd 2f out: styd on same pce and wl hld after* **33/1**

0361 **7** *1/2* **Penitent**[6] 2765 8-9-8 109 ...... DanielTudhope 2 103
(David O'Meara) *wl in tch in midfield: rdn and effrt over 2f out: btn over 1f out: wknd ins fnl f* **12/1**

1m 41.71s (-4.39) **Going Correction** -0.15s/f (Firm) **7** Ran SP% **113.1**
Speed ratings (Par 113): **113,111,110,109,108 106,105**
CSF £21.06 TOTE £7.00: £2.60, £1.90; EX 21.90 Trifecta £49.70.
**Owner** Godolphin **Bred** Darley **Trained** Newmarket, Suffolk

**FOCUS**
A fair event for the class and it was run at a solid pace, although only 10lb faster than the following handicap. The form makes sense with the winner better than ever at face value.

## 2959 INVESTEC MILE H'CAP — 1m 114y
**3:20** (3:21) (Class 2) (0-105,96) 4-Y-0+

**£21,787** (£6,524; £3,262; £1,631; £815; £409) **Stalls** Low

Form RPR

312 **1** **Abseil (USA)**[28] 2113 4-9-3 **92** ...... JamesDoyle 2 102+
(Sir Michael Stoute) *t.k.h: chsd ldrs: gng wl ent fnl 2f: jnd ldrs and effrt over 1f out: immediately wnt lft: rdn to ld and wnt further lft ins fnl f: in command fnl 75yds* **5/2**[1]

1-01 **2** *1/2* **Llanarmon Lad (IRE)**[20] 2351 5-8-11 **86** ...... KierenFallon 13 94+
(Brian Ellison) *hld up off the pce towards rr: rdn and stl plenty to do 2f out: edging lft and hdwy 1f out: str run ins fnl f to chse wnr towards fin: nvr quite getting to wnr* **14/1**

50-0 **3** *1 1/4* **Red Avenger (USA)**[44] 1653 4-9-7 **96** ...... WilliamBuick 1 104+
(Ed Dunlop) *in tch in midfiield: rdn and swtchd lft 2f out: gd hdwy to ld over 1f out: hdd ins fnl f: stl ev ch but keeping on same pce whn bdly hmpd wl ins fnl f: nt rcvr and lost 2nd sn after* **16/1**

00-0 **4** *hd* **Fury**[22] 2286 6-9-3 **92** ...... (p) RyanMoore 15 97
(William Haggas) *hld up towards rr: switching out rt over 2f out: stl plenty to do but hdwy jst over 1f out: nt clrest of runs jst ins fnl f: r.o strly u.p fnl 150yds: nt rch ldrs* **8/1**[3]

4103 **5** *1/2* **Farlow (IRE)**[17] 2425 6-9-1 **90** ...... PaulHanagan 3 94
(Richard Fahey) *in tch in midfield: effrt ent fnl 2f: hdwy jst over 1f out: styd on wl and edgd lft u.p ins fnl f: nt rch ldrs* **10/1**

-302 **6** *nk* **Dance And Dance (IRE)**[21] 2311 8-9-2 **91** ...... JimmyFortune 11 94
(Ed Vaughan) *s.i.s: wl off the pce in rr: hdwy u.p on inner wl over 1f out: nt clr run and swtchd rt and bmpd rivals wl ins fnl f: r.o: nt rch ldrs* **7/1**[2]

24-4 **7** *shd* **Velox**[21] 2309 4-8-12 **87** ...... AndreaAtzeni 8 95+
(Luca Cumani) *in tch in midfield: hdwy on inner to chal over 1f out: stl ev ch but keeping on same pce whn short of room, hit rail and bdly hmpd ins fnl f: nt rcvr* **12/1**

0-13 **8** *1 1/4* **Angelic Upstart (IRE)**[21] 2311 6-8-3 **81** ...... OisinMurphy(3) 14 82
(Andrew Balding) *in tch in midfield: rdn and effrt over 2f out: keeping on same pce whn nt clr run and hmpd jst ins fnl f: n.m.r again wl ins fnl f: kpt on* **10/1**

0100 **9** *1/2* **Trail Blaze (IRE)**[19] 2362 5-9-3 **92** ...... (b) JamieSpencer 16 91
(Kevin Ryan) *led: rdn ent fnl 2f: edgd rt wl over 1f out: hdd over 1f out: no ex and btn whn hmpd wl ins fnl f: eased towards fin* **50/1**

6110 **10** *1/2* **Busatto (USA)**[15] 2478 4-9-1 **90** ...... JoeFanning 9 89
(Mark Johnston) *in tch in midfield: rdn and effrt to chse ldrs 2f out: unable qck 1f out: hld whn bmpd and hmpd wl ins fnl f* **25/1**

0-00 **11** *nk* **Spirit Of The Law (IRE)**[23] 2253 5-8-6 **84** ...... (p) GeorgeChaloner(3) 4 81
(Richard Fahey) *in tch in midfield: effrt ent fnl 2f: drvn and keeping on but no threat to ldrs whn nt clr run wl ins fnl f* **14/1**

2200 **12** *2* **Brocklebank (IRE)**[38] 1834 5-8-5 **85** ...... JackDuern(5) 7 78
(Simon Dow) *hld up wl off the pce in rr: rdn and effrt over 1f out: sme hdwy fnl f: nvr trbld ldrs* **33/1**

-122 **13** *hd* **Tigers Tale (IRE)**[21] 2309 5-8-13 **88** ...... (v) RichardHughes 6 83
(Roger Teal) *chsd ldr: rdn and chal 2f out: no ex ent fnl f: btn whn nt clr run ins fnl f: eased towards fin* **14/1**

-056 **14** *nse* **Jacob Cats**[21] 2309 5-8-3 **78** ...... (v[1]) JimmyQuinn 12 70
(William Knight) *hld up off the pce in last quartet: rdn and effrt 2f out: no imp tl kpt on ins fnl f: nvr trbld ldrs* **33/1**

0-60 **15** *nse* **Vainglory (USA)**[27] 2156 10-8-10 **85** ...... MartinLane 10 77
(David Simcock) *hld up off the pce in last quartet: rdn and effrt towards inner 2f out: kpt on ins fnl f: nvr trbld ldrs* **14/1**

10-0 **16** *4 1/2* **Henry The Aviator (USA)**[25] 2202 4-8-13 **88** ...... SilvestreDeSousa 5 70
(Mark Johnston) *chsd ldrs tl lost pl over 2f out: bhd fnl f* **25/1**

1m 42.35s (-3.75) **Going Correction** -0.15s/f (Firm) **16** Ran SP% **126.1**
Speed ratings (Par 109): **110,109,108,108,107 107,107,106,105,105 105,103,103,103,103 99**
CSF £39.08 CT £513.97 TOTE £3.10: £1.30, £3.00, £4.10, £2.80; EX 41.50 Trifecta £850.80.
**Owner** K Abdullah **Bred** Juddmonte Farms Inc **Trained** Newmarket, Suffolk
■ Stewards' Enquiry : Jimmy Fortune one-day ban: careless riding (Jun 22)

**FOCUS**
They went a good pace in this thanks to habitual front-runner Trail Blaze, and it was the pick of the C&D times relative to the grade. The winner can do better still.

## 2960 INVESTEC OAKS (IN MEMORY OF SIR HENRY CECIL) (GROUP 1) (FILLIES) — 1m 4f 10y
**4:00** (4:05) (Class 1) 3-Y-O

**£297,727** (£112,875; £56,490; £28,140; £14,122; £7,087) **Stalls** Centre

Form RPR

1-1 **1** **Taghrooda**[33] 1978 3-9-0 103 ...... PaulHanagan 9 118+
(John Gosden) *travelled strly: in tch in midfield: clsd on ldrs and sltly hmpd 4f out: 4th st: chsd ldr 3f out: rdn to ld 2f out: r.o strly and drew clr ent fnl f: impressive* **5/1**[3]

3-1 **2** *3 3/4* **Tarfasha (IRE)**[23] 2263 3-9-0 109 ...... PatSmullen 10 111
(D K Weld, Ire) *in tch in midfield: hdwy and 5th st: 3rd and drvn over 1f out: no ch w wnr but battling for 2nd fnl f: kpt on to go 2nd last stride* **9/2**[2]

1-31 **3** *nse* **Volume**[21] 2299 3-9-0 98 ...... RichardHughes 17 111
(Luca Cumani) *chsd ldrs: wnt 2nd after 2f: sn led: rdn and hdd 2f out: unbalanced and chsd wnr jst over 1f out: no ch w wnr and kpt on same pce fnl f: lost 2nd last stride* **9/1**

3-14 **4** *nk* **Inchila**[21] 2299 3-9-0 92 ...... JamieSpencer 6 112+
(Peter Chapple-Hyam) *stdd and dropped in bhd after s: hld up in rr: 14th st: swtchd lft and hdwy over 2f out: 4th and styng on whn nt clr run and swtchd lft 1f out: kpt on: no ch w wnr* **40/1**

-113 **5** *1/2* **Ihtimal (IRE)**[33] 1976 3-9-0 110 ...... KierenFallon 7 110
(Saeed bin Suroor) *hld up in midfield: 13th st: c wdst and effrt hdwy 2f out: 5th wl over 1f out: styd on wl ins fnl f: no ch w wnr* **8/1**

61 **6** *4 1/2* **Marvellous (IRE)**[12] 2581 3-9-0 116 ............ JosephO'Brien 2 103
(A P O'Brien, Ire) *hld up in midfield: 8th st: drvn and no prog jst over 2f out: 6th and wl btn over 1f out* **4/1**[1]

25 **7** *shd* **Palace (IRE)**[12] 2581 3-9-0 102 ............ RyanMoore 3 103
(A P O'Brien, Ire) *hld up in last quartet: hdwy on inner and 11th st: swtchd rt and drvn over 2f out: no prog wl over 1f out: plugged on* **16/1**

3-3 **8** *1 1/2* **Momentus (IRE)**[27] 2152 3-9-0 0 ............ HarryBentley 8 100
(David Simcock) *hld up in midfield: 9th st: rdn and no prog over 2f out: wl hld and plugged on same pce fnl 2f* **50/1**

3-62 **9** *3/4* **Lily Rules (IRE)**[23] 2255 3-9-0 96 ............ BarryMcHugh 11 99
(Tony Coyle) *hld up in last quartet: 15th st: effrt and hmpd 3f out: styd on and hdwy past btn horses over 1f out: nvr trbld ldrs* **33/1**

1-1 **10** *3 1/2* **Madame Chiang**[23] 2255 3-9-0 100 ............ WilliamBuick 1 93
(David Simcock) *t.k.h early: hld up in midfield: 12th st: rdn 3f out: no imp: past btn horses over 1f out: nvr trbld ldrs* **9/1**

13-5 **11** *3 3/4* **Island Remede**[27] 2152 3-9-0 89 ............ JamesDoyle 14 87
(Ed Dunlop) *hld up in last quartet: 16th st: swtchd lft and effrt over 2f out: no prog: wl btn over 1f out* **100/1**

21-3 **12** *2 3/4* **Regardez**[23] 2255 3-9-0 92 ............ RichardKingscote 13 83
(Ralph Beckett) *led tl over 9f out: chsd ldr tl 7f out: 6th and losing pl st: wknd over 2f out: bhd over 1f out* **40/1**

411 **13** *1/2* **Marsh Daisy**[15] 2484 3-9-0 104 ............ JimmyFortune 5 82
(Hughie Morrison) *in tch in midfield: 7th st: 5th and outpcd u.p 2f out: wknd over 1f out: eased fnl f* **16/1**

3 **14** *8* **Dazzling (IRE)**[23] 2263 3-9-0 103 ............ SeamieHeffernan 4 69
(A P O'Brien, Ire) *chsd ldrs: wnt 2nd 7f out tl lost 2nd and unbalanced 3f out: sn wknd: wl bhd fnl f* **33/1**

-111 **15** *4 1/2* **Anipa**[30] 2072 3-9-0 98 ............ AndreaAtzeni 16 62
(Roger Varian) *chsd ldrs: shifted rt on downhill run 4f out: 3rd st: sn rdn and wknd over 2f out: t.o fnl f* **33/1**

3-11 **16** *hd* **Honor Bound**[27] 2152 3-9-0 94 ............[1] JimCrowley 15 62
(Ralph Beckett) *hld up in last quartet: 17th st: pushed along and btn 3f out: sn bhd: t.o fnl f* **33/1**

311- **17** *1 1/2* **Amazing Maria (IRE)**[286] 5737 3-9-0 105 ............ FrankieDettori 12 60
(Ed Dunlop) *hld up in midfield: 10th st: sn wknd and bhd: t.o 1f out* **16/1**

2m 34.89s (-4.01) **Going Correction** -0.15s/f (Firm) **17 Ran SP% 123.2**
Speed ratings (Par 110): **107,104,104,104,103 100,100,99,99,97 94,92,92,87,84 83,82**
CSF £26.03 CT £204.48 TOTE £5.80: £2.10, £2.40, £3.20; EX 23.70 Trifecta £290.10.
**Owner** Hamdan Al Maktoum **Bred** Shadwell Estate Company Limited **Trained** Newmarket, Suffolk

**FOCUS**
The Oaks this year looked most competitive with the winner of the Irish 1000 Guineas winner lining up, along with the third from Newmarket last month, and four fillies were supplemented (three trial winners). They appeared to go a sound pace, but not for the first time on the afternoon racing handily proved a definite advantage. The pre-race standard wasn't great, but Taghrooda impressed and rates a bit better than the standard winner, with the form looking fairly sound.

## 2961 INVESTEC SURREY STKS (LISTED RACE) 7f
**4:45** (4:45) (Class 1) 3-Y-O **£22,684** (£8,600; £4,304; £2,144; £1,076) **Stalls** Low

Form RPR

11 **1** **That Is The Spirit**[23] 2257 3-9-0 99 ............ DanielTudhope 6 105+
(David O'Meara) *mde all: rdn over 1f out: looked in command fnl 100yds: pushed along hands and heels after and jst lasted home* **11/10**[1]

-543 **2** *nse* **Parbold (IRE)**[6] 2767 3-9-0 109 ............[1] RyanMoore 2 104+
(Richard Fahey) *chsd ldng pair: rdn but nvr enough room on inner fr over 1f out: wnt 2nd jst ins fnl f: swtchd rt and r.o strly u.p fnl 100yds: jst failed* **13/8**[2]

-212 **3** *2 1/2* **Penny Drops**[13] 2556 3-8-9 90 ............ SilvestreDeSousa 4 92
(William Haggas) *t.k.h: hld up in tch in last pair: rdn and effrt 2f out: styd on same pce ins fnl f* **6/1**[3]

1-60 **4** *1* **Miracle Of Medinah**[20] 2343 3-9-6 102 ............ DavidProbert 5 100
(Mark Usher) *chsd wnr: rdn ent fnl 2f: no ex and lost 2nd jst ins fnl f: wknd wl ins fnl f* **20/1**

3-32 **5** *8* **Silver Treasure (FR)**[22] 2290 3-9-0 97 ............[1] KierenFallon 3 74
(Amy Weaver) *ponied to s: hld up in tch in rr: rdn over 2f out: sn struggling: wknd over 1f out* **25/1**

1m 21.58s (-1.72) **Going Correction** -0.15s/f (Firm) **5 Ran SP% 108.6**
Speed ratings (Par 107): **103,102,100,98,89**
CSF £3.02 TOTE £2.00: £1.10, £1.30; EX 3.50 Trifecta £6.10.
**Owner** F Gillespie **Bred** Cliveden Stud Ltd **Trained** Nawton, N Yorks

**FOCUS**
The winner only stepped up a little on his handicap form but should rate higher. The form is the best guide.

## 2962 INVESTEC ASSET MANAGEMENT H'CAP (BOBIS RACE) 7f
**5:20** (5:21) (Class 2) (0-100,95) 3-Y-O
**£15,562** (£4,660; £2,330; £1,165; £582; £292) **Stalls** Low

Form RPR

1406 **1** **Almargo (IRE)**[29] 2088 3-8-9 83 ............ SilvestreDeSousa 4 96
(Mark Johnston) *mde all: rdn 2f out: clr over 1f out: kpt on u.p and a holding on: rdn out* **7/1**

41-4 **2** *1 3/4* **Kafeel (USA)**[31] 2063 3-8-4 78 ............ PaulHanagan 5 86
(Roger Varian) *hld up in midfield: rdn and effrt ent fnl 2f: wnt 3rd ins fnl f: styd on wl to chse wnr towards fin: nvr gng to rch wnr* **9/2**[1]

100- **3** *1/2* **Suzi's Connoisseur**[231] 7333 3-9-2 95 ............ NoelGarbutt[(5)] 6 102
(Hugo Palmer) *dwlt and short of room sn after s: rdn and effrt on inner 3f out: hdwy to go 3rd over 1f out: chsd clr wnr fnl 150yds: kpt on but lost 2nd towards fin* **33/1**

-220 **4** *shd* **Shot In The Sun (IRE)**[13] 2565 3-8-7 84 ............ GeorgeChaloner[(3)] 9 90+
(Richard Fahey) *hld up in last quartet: rdn and plenty to do 2f out: hdwy on outer 1f out: r.o strly ins fnl f: nt rch ldrs* **6/1**[3]

2144 **5** *hd* **Nakuti (IRE)**[13] 2556 3-8-9 83 ............ JamieSpencer 2 90+
(Sylvester Kirk) *hld up in midfield: rdn and effrt ent fnl 2f: hdwy 1f out: styd on wl ins fnl f: nt rch ldrs* **8/1**

24-6 **6** *1 1/4* **Mime Dance**[44] 1655 3-8-2 76 oh1 ............ DavidProbert 10 79
(Andrew Balding) *hld up in midfield: rdn over 2f out: hdwy jst over 1f out: styd on ins fnl f: nvr trbld ldrs* **7/1**

-005 **7** *nk* **Torchlighter (IRE)**[23] 2257 3-8-9 83 ............ MartinLane 3 85
(Mark Johnston) *in tch in midfield: effrt u.p 2f out: no prog and edgd lft over 1f out: kpt on but no threat to ldrs ins fnl f* **12/1**

6222 **8** *1 1/2* **Lincoln (IRE)**[13] 2567 3-8-11 85 ............ MartinDwyer 13 83
(Mick Channon) *taken down early: chsd wnr: rdn and unable qck ent fnl 2f: outpcd and btn over 1f out: lost 2nd fnl 150yds: wknd* **5/1**[2]

4-66 **9** *2 3/4* **Art Official (IRE)**[13] 2567 3-8-11 85 ............ WilliamBuick 1 76
(Richard Hannon) *chsd ldrs: rdn ent fnl 2f: drvn and outpcd over 1f out: wknd fnl f* **8/1**

0210 **10** *1* **Nova Champ (IRE)**[20] 2344 3-8-4 78 ............(p) HarryBentley 11 66
(Stuart Williams) *chsd ldrs early: rdn and lost pl 2f out: wl hld whn nt clr run ins fnl f: eased towards fin* **20/1**

-100 **11** *nk* **Sacha Park (IRE)**[29] 2090 3-8-10 84 ............ KieranO'Neill 14 71
(Richard Hannon) *s.i.s: hld up in rr: rdn and no hdwy over 2f out: n.d but plugged on fnl f* **33/1**

6201 **12** *1 3/4* **Bretherton**[13] 2567 3-9-0 88 ............(b) DanielTudhope 12 71
(Richard Fahey) *chsd ldrs: rdn and unable qck ent fnl 2f: btn over 1f out: wkng whn short of room ins fnl f: eased wl ins fnl f* **14/1**

3-60 **13** *4* **Berrahri (IRE)**[28] 2112 3-8-3 77 oh1 ow1 ............ RoystonFfrench 15 49
(John Best) *taken down early: s.i.s: a bhd* **66/1**

1m 20.77s (-2.53) **Going Correction** -0.15s/f (Firm) **13 Ran SP% 122.9**
Speed ratings (Par 105): **108,106,105,105,105 103,103,101,98,97 96,94,90**
CSF £38.41 CT £1003.67 TOTE £8.60: £3.20, £1.90, £8.20; EX 48.60 Trifecta £1078.60.
**Owner** Sheikh Hamdan bin Mohammed Al Maktoum **Bred** Mountarmstrong Stud **Trained** Middleham Moor, N Yorks

**FOCUS**
A competitive handicap on paper, but they all struggled to land a blow on the winner, who made all. He was back to something like his best.
T/Jkpt: £7,281.70 to a £1 stake. Pool: £56408.10 - 5.50 winning tickets T/Plt: £27.10 to a £1 stake. Pool: £284453.00 - 7654.87 winning tickets T/Qpdt: £7.70 to a £1 stake. Pool: £13818.38 - 1313.41 winning tickets SP

# 2554 GOODWOOD (R-H)
### Friday, June 6

**OFFICIAL GOING: Good (7.4)**
Wind: Fresh, across away from stands Weather: Fine and warm

## 2963 R. L. FREEMANTLE ELECTRICAL LTD AMATEUR RIDERS' STKS (H'CAP) 1m 1f
**6:00** (6:03) (Class 5) (0-70,74) 4-Y-O+ **£3,119** (£967; £483; £242) **Stalls** Low

Form RPR

-412 **1** **Balmoral Castle**[21] 2300 5-10-9 68 ............ MrJHarding[(3)] 5 79
(Jonathan Portman) *hld up towards rr: hdwy over 2f out: led over 1f out: drvn out* **5/2**[1]

0-03 **2** *1/2* **City Ground (USA)**[55] 1450 7-10-6 62 ............ MissSBrotherton 4 70
(Michael Easterby) *led tl over 1f out: kpt on wl u.p* **14/1**

-612 **3** *1/2* **Who's That Chick (IRE)**[30] 2069 5-10-1 62 ............ MissEllaSmith[(5)] 2 69
(Ralph J Smith) *t.k.h towards rr: r.o fnl 2f: nrest at fin* **10/1**

5020 **4** *nk* **Living Leader**[5] 2806 5-10-0 61 ............ SeanBowen[(5)] 6 67
(Grace Harris) *bhd: hrd rdn 2f out: r.o fr over 1f out: nvr nrr* **7/1**

4-61 **5** *1 1/2* **Aldwick Bay (IRE)**[8] 2701 6-10-13 74 6ex ............ MissCAGreenway[(5)] 10 77
(Tom Dascombe) *hld up in rr: hdwy and nt clr run over 2f out: drvn and kpt on same pce whn clr wl over 1f out* **3/1**[2]

3655 **6** *3* **Lady Sylvia**[65] 1230 5-10-7 66 ............ MissHayleyMoore[(3)] 8 63
(Joseph Tuite) *chsd ldrs: effrt 3f out: wknd over 1f out* **20/1**

0236 **7** *3 1/4* **Mcbirney (USA)**[16] 2464 7-10-4 65 ............ MrsRWilson[(5)] 11 55
(Paul D'Arcy) *mid-div on outer: hdwy 3f out: wknd over 1f out* **14/1**

620- **8** *4* **Hyperlink (IRE)**[212] 7778 5-10-7 68 ............ MrAlexFerguson[(5)] 3 50
(Michael Bell) *chsd ldrs tl wknd wl over 1f out* **14/1**

0-53 **9** *26* **Automotive**[38] 1864 6-10-5 61 ............ MrRBirkett 7
(Julia Feilden) *prom: chal 3f out: wknd wl over 1f out* **6/1**[3]

002- **10** *1 3/4* **Dreamy Ciara**[227] 7443 4-9-10 59 ............ MissKARandall[(7)] 1
(Raymond York) *stmbld s: chsd ldr 4f: wknd 3f out: sn bhd* **66/1**

1m 57.68s (1.38) **Going Correction** -0.125s/f (Firm) **10 Ran SP% 114.9**
Speed ratings (Par 103): **88,87,87,86,85 82,79,76,53,51**
CSF £43.88 CT £343.91 TOTE £3.40: £1.50, £4.20, £2.30; EX 33.40 Trifecta £396.00.
**Owner** J G B Portman **Bred** Springcombe Park Stud **Trained** Upper Lambourn, Berks
■ Stewards' Enquiry : Miss K A Randall five-day ban: used whip when out of contention (Jun 23,26,30,Jul 5,6)
Sean Bowen two-day ban: used whip above permitted level (Jun 23,25)

**FOCUS**
First 2f of 1m course dolled out 5yds. A modest amateurs' handicap run at an ordinary pace. The winner looked a bit better than the bare form.

## 2964 ADVANCED RESOURCE MANAGERS EBF STALLIONS MAIDEN STKS 6f
**6:35** (6:35) (Class 5) 2-Y-O **£3,234** (£962; £481; £240) **Stalls** High

Form RPR

3 **1** **Jungle Cat (IRE)**[16] 2450 2-9-5 ............ JoeFanning 5 90+
(Mark Johnston) *pressed ldr: led 2f out: hld on wl whn chal over 1f out: rdn out* **5/1**[2]

**2** *2* **Sixty (IRE)** 2-9-5 ............ MickaelBarzalona 2 84+
(Richard Hannon) *in tch: wnt prom wd of others in centre 2f out: kpt on same pce fnl f* **14/1**[3]

5 **3** *1* **Aledaid (IRE)**[21] 2298 2-9-5 ............ FrankieDettori 13 81
(Richard Hannon) *chsd ldrs on rail: chal over 1f out: no ex ins fnl f* **8/15**[1]

**4** *4 1/2* **Geological (IRE)** 2-9-5 ............ PatDobbs 8 68+
(Richard Hannon) *in tch: effrt over 2f out: one pce appr fnl f* **14/1**[3]

**5** *2* **Harlequin Striker (IRE)** 2-9-5 ............ TomQueally 1 62+
(Mick Channon) *mid-div: rdn 3f out: nvr able to chal* **25/1**

**6** *1 1/4* **Able Mate** 2-9-5 ............ AdamKirby 12 58+
(Clive Cox) *led tl 2f out: wknd over 1f out* **14/1**[3]

**7** *3 1/4* **Kingsbridge** 2-9-5 ............ SebSanders 11 48+
(Rod Millman) *prom tl lost pl 3f out* **50/1**

**8** *1 1/4* **Best Endeavour** 2-9-5 ............ RichardKingscote 7 44
(William Muir) *a mid-div: rdn and btn over 2f out* **50/1**

**9** *1* **Maraakib (IRE)** 2-9-5 ............ DaneO'Neill 3 41
(Brian Meehan) *dwlt and bhd: rdn 3f out: nvr trbld ldrs* **14/1**[3]

**10** *1/2* **Chilworth Bells** 2-9-2 ............ CharlesBishop[(3)] 6 40
(Mick Channon) *dwlt and outpcd in rr: nvr nr ldrs* **33/1**

0 **11** *nse* **Pink Ribbon (IRE)**[21] 2298 2-9-0 ............ JoshBaudains[(5)] 9 40
(Sylvester Kirk) *dwlt: towards rr: rdn 3f out: n.d after* **33/1**

**12** *3 3/4* **Foylesideview (IRE)** 2-9-5 ............ ShaneKelly 10 28
(Luke Dace) *mid-div: wknd 3f out: sn bhd* **100/1**

1m 10.63s (-1.57) **Going Correction** -0.225s/f (Firm) **12 Ran SP% 123.2**
Speed ratings (Par 93): **101,98,97,91,88 86,82,80,79,78 78,73**
CSF £70.06 TOTE £4.50: £1.60, £4.30, £1.10; EX 91.90 Trifecta £308.00.
**Owner** Sheikh Hamdan bin Mohammed Al Maktoum **Bred** Darley **Trained** Middleham Moor, N Yorks

**FOCUS**
An interesting maiden that has thrown up Group 1 winners Dubawi and Olympic Glory in the last ten years, and it looked a good race again. The Hannon yard had won five of the last six renewals, and its trio all made the frame behind the winner, who left his debut well behind.

## 2965 EBF STALLIONS BREEDING WINNERS FILLIES' STKS (H'CAP) 6f
**7:10** (7:10) (Class 3) (0-90,91) 3-Y-O+ **£9,056** (£2,695; £1,346; £673) **Stalls** High

Form RPR
21-0 1 **Stepping Out (IRE)**[20] 2340 3-8-12 **80**.................... RichardKingscote 5 93+
(Tom Dascombe) *mde all: hld on wl fnl 2f: rdn out and in control nr fin* **9/4**[1]
131 2 *nk* **Divine (IRE)**[21] 2295 3-9-3 **85**................................ TomQueally 9 97+
(Mick Channon) *chsd ldrs: rdn to chal ins fnl f: r.o: jst hld* **4/1**[2]
114- 3 2 ½ **Our Queenie (IRE)**[307] 4988 3-9-5 **87**........................ PatDobbs 2 91
(Richard Hannon) *towards rr: rdn and hdwy over 1f out: kpt on fnl f* **6/1**
3411 4 *nk* **Iseemist (IRE)**[22] 2278 3-8-7 **78**................ MichaelJMurphy(3) 8 81
(John Gallagher) *chsd ldrs: one pce appr fnl f* **5/1**[3]
-265 5 2 **Marjong**[32] 2030 4-9-3 **77**.................................. SebSanders 7 76
(Simon Dow) *s.s: bhd: swtchd rt and styd on fr over 1f out: nt rch ldrs* **8/1**
-011 6 *hd* **Links Drive Lady**[11] 2629 6-10-3 **91** 6ex..................... KierenFallon 6 92
(Dean Ivory) *mid-div: rdn whn hmpd wl over 1f out: nt rcvr* **12/1**
-040 7 1 **Gladiatrix**[13] 2564 5-9-6 **87**.................................. PatMillman(7) 3 82
(Rod Millman) *in tch tl wknd over 1f out* **25/1**
14-1 8 12 **Clearing**[10] 2648 4-8-9 **69** 6ex oh2........................ JoeFanning 1 25
(Jim Boyle) *w ldr tl 2f out: wknd qckly over 1f out* **14/1**
005- 9 16 **Fire Blaze (IRE)**[279] 5994 3-9-6 **88**.......................... MickaelBarzalona 4
(Charlie Appleby) *stdd s: t.k.h: sn chsng ldrs: wknd qckly 2f out* **16/1**
1m 10.12s (-2.08) **Going Correction** -0.225s/f (Firm)
**WFA** 3 from 4yo+ 8lb **9** Ran SP% **116.9**
Speed ratings (Par 104): **104,103,100,99,97 96,95,79,58**
CSF £11.26 CT £47.72 TOTE £3.50: £1.40, £1.50, £2.40; EX 15.10 Trifecta £98.30.
**Owner** Attenborough Bellman Ingram Lowe **Bred** Glending Bloodstock **Trained** Malpas, Cheshire
■ Stewards' Enquiry : Tom Queally one-day ban: careless riding (Jun 22)

**FOCUS**
A good fillies' handicap, dominated by 3yos. The winner is rated in line with her Brighton form last year.

## 2966 MAZDA JINBA ITTAI STKS (H'CAP) 1m 4f
**7:45** (7:45) (Class 5) (0-75,74) 4-Y-O+ **£3,234** (£962; £481; £240) **Stalls** High

Form RPR
0-05 1 **Laughing Jack**[22] 2270 6-9-0 **72**.................... GeorgeDowning(5) 4 81
(George Baker) *prom: led after 4f and wnt 4 l clr: c bk to others and hrd rdn 2f out: styd on wl* **9/4**[2]
5510 2 3 ¾ **All The Winds (GER)**[27] 2162 9-9-1 **68**.................(t) AdamKirby 6 71
(Shaun Lycett) *hld up in rr: rdn and hdwy over 1f out: chsd wnr fnl f: one pce* **8/1**
6-62 3 ½ **Tafawuk (USA)**[17] 2445 5-9-5 **72**........................ AndreaAtzeni 5 74
(Roger Varian) *prom: chal 3f out: one pce appr fnl f* **7/4**[1]
-032 4 7 **Granell (IRE)**[11] 2610 4-9-3 **70**..........................(p[1]) TomQueally 3 61
(Brian Meehan) *hld up in 5th: effrt 3f out: drvn along 2f out: sn outpcd* **7/2**[3]
3/0- 5 3 **Asker (IRE)**[12] 6992 6-8-12 **72**....................(b) CharlotteJenner(7) 2 58
(Zoe Davison) *in tch tl wknd 2f out* **33/1**
321/ 6 48 **North Cape (USA)**[703] 6283 8-9-7 **74**........................ JohnFahy 1
(Alastair Lidderdale) *led 4f: cl up tl wknd qckly 3f out: sn wl bhd* **10/1**
2m 38.96s (0.56) **Going Correction** -0.125s/f (Firm) **6** Ran SP% **112.5**
Speed ratings (Par 103): **93,90,90,85,83 51**
CSF £19.92 TOTE £2.80: £1.90, £2.60; EX 17.80 Trifecta £64.00.
**Owner** Paul Downing **Bred** Sir Thomas Pilkington **Trained** Manton, Wilts
■ Stewards' Enquiry : George Downing two-day ban: careless riding (Jun 23-24)

**FOCUS**
A fair handicap with the whole field closely matched on paper. The early pace was steady and the winner made most. His best form since last summer.

## 2967 LEVY RESTAURANTS MAIDEN FILLIES' STKS 1m
**8:15** (8:19) (Class 5) 3-Y-O+ **£3,234** (£962; £481; £240) **Stalls** Low

Form RPR
0 1 **Sensible Way (USA)**[6] 2780 3-9-0 0........................ PatDobbs 1 82
(Richard Hannon) *chsd ldr: led ins fnl f: drvn out* **20/1**
40-2 2 *shd* **Joys Of Spring (IRE)**[46] 1612 3-9-0 74.................. AndreaAtzeni 6 81
(Luca Cumani) *in tch: effrt over 2f out: chal fnl 100yds: r.o* **9/4**[1]
603 3 1 ¼ **Prairie Rose (GER)**[22] 2280 3-9-0 78........................ HarryBentley 8 78
(Olly Stevens) *led: 5 l clr 1/2-way: rdn over 2f out: hdd and no ex ins fnl f* **7/2**[2]
6- 4 ¾ **Muhawalah (IRE)**[246] 6973 3-9-0 0........................ DaneO'Neill 4 76
(Roger Varian) *in tch: hrd rdn over 2f out: styd on wl fnl f* **9/2**[3]
02 5 2 ¾ **Lady Brigid (IRE)**[13] 2560 3-9-0 0........................ TomQueally 2 70
(Amanda Perrett) *in tch: effrt over 2f out: styd on same pce* **8/1**
6 2 ½ **Elysian Fields (GR)** 3-9-0 0........................ SebSanders 5 64
(Amanda Perrett) *s.i.s: towards rr: rdn and sme hdwy 2f out: nvr able to chal* **16/1**
05- 7 5 **Mumtaza**[267] 6340 3-9-0 0........................ JoeFanning 11 53
(Richard Hannon) *bhd: rdn over 2f out: nvr trbld ldrs* **33/1**
0 8 2 ½ **Champs D'Or**[18] 2404 3-9-0 0........................ AdamKirby 9 47
(Marco Botti) *a towards rr* **25/1**
5 9 3 ¾ **Chindeni**[87] 914 3-9-0 0........................ RichardKingscote 7 38
(Ed Vaughan) *mid-div tl wknd 3f out* **50/1**
42 10 7 **Discreetly**[16] 2392 3-9-0 0........................ MickaelBarzalona 3 22
(Hughie Morrison) *prom tl wknd 3f out* **8/1**
0-4 11 2 ½ **Tiptree Lace**[13] 2560 3-9-0 0........................ KierenFallon 10 16
(William Knight) *a bhd* **12/1**
1m 38.28s (-1.62) **Going Correction** -0.125s/f (Firm) **11** Ran SP% **120.5**
Speed ratings (Par 100): **103,102,101,100,98 95,90,88,84,77 74**
CSF £64.73 TOTE £27.40: £5.20, £1.40, £1.90; EX 93.20 Trifecta £476.00.
**Owner** Malih Lahej Al Basti **Bred** Malih Al Basti **Trained** East Everleigh, Wilts

**FOCUS**
Some well-bred types in this 3yo fillies' maiden, but the ratings of the placed horses suggest this was just a fair contest. The form is rated around the third and fifth.

## 2968 CHASE & STATUS H'CAP 1m
**8:45** (8:51) (Class 4) (0-80,80) 3-Y-O **£5,175** (£1,540; £769; £384) **Stalls** Low

Form RPR
02-4 1 **Rapid Advance**[48] 1582 3-9-5 78........................ ShaneKelly 4 85+
(Sir Michael Stoute) *prom: rdn to ld 1f out: hld on wl* **9/2**[3]
3-63 2 *nk* **Homestretch**[18] 2383 3-9-7 80........................ MickaelBarzalona 5 85
(Mick Channon) *t.k.h: in tch: led over 2f out tl 1f out: kpt on wl* **4/1**[2]
-555 3 ½ **Hedge End (IRE)**[22] 2277 3-9-1 74........................ PatDobbs 11 78
(Richard Hannon) *mid-div on outer: hrd rdn and hdwy over 1f out: styd on wl fnl f* **20/1**
-601 4 *nse* **Golden Spear**[18] 2391 3-9-5 78........................(p) AdamKirby 2 82
(Noel Quinlan) *bhd: rdn and hdwy in centre over 1f out: nrest at fin* **13/2**
1-55 5 2 ½ **Best Kept**[15] 2481 3-9-5 78........................ SebSanders 3 76
(Amanda Perrett) *mid-div on rail: rdn and lost pl 3f out: styd on again fnl f* **9/4**[1]
01- 6 ½ **Strait Run (IRE)**[224] 7500 3-9-0 80........................ CamHardie(7) 1 77
(Richard Hannon) *hld up in rr: rdn over 2f out: styd on fnl f* **10/1**
14-0 7 ½ **Miss Buckshot (IRE)**[49] 1563 3-9-7 80........................ ChrisCatlin 8 76
(Rae Guest) *towards rr: rdn over 2f out: stying on at fin* **20/1**
6-01 8 ¾ **Zambeasy**[39] 1794 3-8-11 70........................ RichardKingscote 9 64
(Philip Hide) *led tl 3f out: wknd over 1f out* **25/1**
20-3 9 1 ¾ **Alisios (GR)**[36] 1897 3-9-5 78........................ AndreaAtzeni 10 68
(Luca Cumani) *chsd ldrs tl wknd over 1f out* **10/1**
031- 10 5 **Raajis (IRE)**[264] 6426 3-9-4 77........................ DaneO'Neill 7 56
(Richard Hannon) *chsd ldr: led 3f out tl over 2f out: wknd wl over 1f out* **20/1**
1m 38.66s (-1.24) **Going Correction** -0.125s/f (Firm) **10** Ran SP% **118.6**
Speed ratings (Par 101): **101,100,100,100,97 96,95,94,89**
CSF £21.82 CT £338.61 TOTE £5.60: £2.60, £2.10, £1.80; EX 26.40 Trifecta £320.40.
**Owner** Saeed Suhail **Bred** Newsells Park Stud **Trained** Newmarket, Suffolk

**FOCUS**
A competitive handicap and a close finish. The time was 0.38secs slower than the preceding fillies' maiden and the form looks sound. The winner should be capable of better.
T/Plt: £35.50 to a £1 stake. Pool: £69,904.82 - 1,434.56 winning tickets T/Qpdt: £14.90 to a £1 stake. Pool: £6,272.51 - 310.70 winning tickets LM

2969 - 2975a (Foreign Racing) - See Raceform Interactive

# 1139 COMPIEGNE (L-H)
Friday, June 6

**OFFICIAL GOING: Turf: soft**

## 2976a PRIX DE DRESLINCOURT (CLAIMER) (2YO) (TURF) 7f
**1:20** (12:00) 2-Y-O **£7,916** (£3,166; £2,375; £1,583; £791)

RPR
1 **Voila Baileys (FR)**[73] 1094 2-9-1 0........................ TheoBachelot 9 63
(W Walton, France) **43/10**[2]
2 2 ½ **Gentledor (FR)** 2-9-1 0........................ FabriceVeron 8 56
(C Baillet, France) **207/10**
3 *shd* **Melchope (FR)** 2-9-1 0........................ CristianDemuro 5 56
(E J O'Neill, France) **30/1**
4 *nk* **Princesse Rebelle (FR)**[7] 2-9-1 0........................ MaximeGuyon 1 55
(M Nigge, France) **2/1**[1]
5 1 ¾ **Endislie (IRE)**[11] 2622 2-8-11 0........................(b[1]) SoufyaneMoulin(4) 10 50
(J S Moore) *dwlt sltly and hld up towards rr: pushed along 3f out: rdn 2f out: kpt on u.p but nt pce to chal* **99/10**
6 1 ¾ **Marlinda (FR)**[53] 2-9-1 0........................ Christophe-PatriceLemaire 6 46
(C Boutin, France) **53/10**[3]
7 3 ½ **Meshavita (FR)**[41] 2-8-11 0........................(b) UmbertoRispoli 4 33
(M Pimbonnet, France) **11/1**
8 ¾ **Loose Cannon (FR)** 2-9-1 0........................ AntoineHamelin 11 35
(Matthieu Palussiere, France) **155/10**
9 4 **Kisgreen (FR)** 2-8-11 0........................(b) GregoryBenoist 2 20
(C Baillet, France) **43/10**[2]
10 15 **Stevie Marvelous (IRE)** 2-8-11 0........................(b[1]) JimmyTastayre 7
(C Boutin, France) **64/1**
1m 27.19s (87.19) **10** Ran SP% **119.9**
WIN (incl. 1 euro stake): 5.30. PLACES: 2.10, 5.50, 7.50. DF: 50.00. SF: 77.90.
**Owner** G R Bailey Ltd (Baileys Horse Feeds) **Bred** P Venner **Trained** France

## 2978a PRIX D'ACTEON (CLAIMER) (3YO FILLIES) (TURF) 1m 2f
**3:50** (12:00) 3-Y-O **£7,916** (£3,166; £2,375; £1,583; £791)

RPR
1 **Finglass (IRE)**[14] 3-8-2 0........................ PierreBazire(7) 10 66
(P Bary, France) **28/1**
2 ½ **Cresselia (FR)**[65] 3-8-13 0........................ DelphineSantiago 7 69
(S Smrczek, Germany) **68/10**
3 1 ¾ **Madame Cecile (ITY)**[9] 3-8-13 0........................(p) CristianDemuro 12 66
(G Botti, France) **16/5**[1]
4 *snk* **Zashka (FR)**[23] 3-8-13 0........................ GregoryBenoist 11 65
(J-P Gallorini, France) **84/10**
5 2 ½ **Rakmanova (IRE)** 3-8-9 0........................ ThomasMessina 13 56
(C Martinon, France) **39/1**
6 ½ **Lingreville (FR)**[125] 436 3-8-7 0........................ NicolasLarenaudie(6) 17 59
(J-M Lefebvre, France) **153/10**
7 *nk* **Noctuelle (FR)**[46] 3-8-8 0........................(p) Georges-AntoineAnselin(6) 5 60
(N Caullery, France) **53/10**[2]
8 *nse* **Mary Is Back (FR)**[32] 3-9-2 0........................ Christophe-PatriceLemaire 15 62
(C Boutin, France) **26/1**
9 1 ¼ **Miss Rafael (FR)**[30] 3-8-13 0........................ TheoBachelot 8 56
(S Wattel, France) **56/10**[3]
10 2 ½ **Bolivia Sport (FR)**[428] 3-8-9 0........................ StephaneLaurent 9 47
(P Chevillard, France) **126/10**
11 1 ½ **Celesteen (IRE)**[21] 3-8-3 0........................(b) PaoloLamotte(6) 14 44
(C Lerner, France) **90/1**
12 1 ¼ **Dabayin (FR)**[23] 3-8-5 0........................ GuillaumeAmbrosioni(8) 3 46
(M Boutin, France) **26/1**
13 4 **Serrella (FR)**[65] 3-8-13 0........................(b[1]) CesarPasserat(3) 4 41
(J Van Handenhove, France) **84/1**
14 *snk* **Sparkel D'Hermeray (FR)**[247] 6961 3-9-2 0........................ AlexisBadel 1 40
(Mme C De La Soudiere-Niault, France) **31/1**
15 10 **Greve Generale**[274] 3-9-2 0........................(p) JimmyTastayre 6 20
(C Boutin, France) **65/1**
16 *nk* **Lady Knight (IRE)**[38] 1847 3-8-6 0........................(b[1]) SoufyaneMoulin(3) 2 13
(J S Moore) *led: rdn and hdd over 2f out: sn no ex and btn: wknd and eased* **205/10**
17 12 **Cheyne Walk (SWI)**[25] 3-8-9 0........................ AnthonyCrastus 18
(Mme B Suter, France) **43/1**
2m 8.1s (128.10) **17** Ran SP% **119.0**
WIN (incl. 1 euro stake): 28.90. PLACES: 6.60, 2.50, 1.90. DF: 144.50. SF: 354.10.
**Owner** Laghi France **Bred** M Solbiati **Trained** Chantilly, France

2977 - 2978a (Foreign Racing) - See Raceform Interactive

# [2327]DONCASTER (L-H)

Saturday, June 7

**OFFICIAL GOING: Soft (7.1)**

Wind: Light half against Weather: Heavy cloud and showers

## 2979 LADBROKES BRITISH STALLIONS EBF MAIDEN FILLIES' STKS (BOBIS RACE) 6f 110y

**2:00** (2:01) (Class 5) 2-Y-O £3,234 (£962; £481; £240) **Stalls** High

Form RPR

0 **1** **Assault On Rome (IRE)**[8] 2744 2-9-0 0 AdrianNicholls 1 74
(Mark Johnston) *mde all: rdn over 1f out: edgd lft ent fnl f: sn jnd and drvn: kpt on gamely towards fin* **16/1**

**2** *hd* **Turning Times (IRE)** 2-9-0 0 AhmedAjtebi 4 73+
(Charlie Appleby) *dwlt and towards rr: gd hdwy on outer 3f out: chsd ldrs 2f out: rdn to chal jst over 1f out: drvn and ev ch ins fnl f: no ex nr fin* **13/2**

**3** *4* **Liberty Sky (IRE)** 2-9-0 0 PaulHanagan 6 62+
(Richard Fahey) *midfield: green and sn pushed along: rdn along and outpcd over 2f out: styd on appr fnl f: nrst fin* **5/2**[2]

30 **4** *½* **Agadoo**[31] 2071 2-9-0 0 PaddyAspell 2 61
(Shaun Harris) *chsd ldr: rdn along over 2f out: grad wknd appr fnl f* **14/1**

**5** *1 ¾* **Candle Of The Sea (IRE)** 2-9-0 0 HarryBentley 9 56+
(Ed Vaughan) *in tch: effrt on wd outside over 2f out: sn rdn and no imp* **18/1**

**6** *hd* **Hangon Harriet** 2-8-11 0 RossAtkinson(3) 10 56
(Pam Sly) *trckd ldng pair: rdn along over 2f out: grad wknd* **50/1**

0 **7** *nk* **True Course**[22] 2306 2-9-0 0 MartinLane 3 55+
(Charlie Appleby) *trckd ldrs: hdwy 1/2-way: rdn and ev ch wl over 1f out: hld whn n.m.r and swtchd rt ent fnl f: sn wknd* **2/1**[1]

**8** *1* **Aqlette** 2-9-0 0 LukeMorris 8 52
(Marco Botti) *chsd ldrs: rdn along over 2f out: sn wknd* **5/1**[3]

**9** *nk* **Molly Approve (IRE)** 2-9-0 0 BarryMcHugh 7 51
(Tony Coyle) *dwlt: a in rr* **28/1**

1m 24.42s (4.52) **Going Correction** +0.40s/f (Good) **9 Ran SP% 115.1**
Speed ratings (Par 90): **90,89,85,84,82 82,82,80,80**
CSF £115.42 TOTE £17.00: £3.00, £2.20, £1.60; EX 150.50 Trifecta £446.50 Part won..
**Owner** Mrs Christine E Budden **Bred** Christine E Budden & Partners **Trained** Middleham Moor, N Yorks

**FOCUS**
Round course railed out from 1m2f to where it joins the Straight and distances on Round course increased in distance by 18yds. History suggests this winner will go on to contest Listed races, but the early pace looked ordinary and it paid to be prominent. Not an easy race to rate. Jockeys who rode in the first reported the ground as 'soft' and 'hard work'.

## 2980 DOWNLOAD THE NEW LADBROKES APP H'CAP 1m 6f 132y

**2:35** (2:35) (Class 5) (0-70,70) 4-Y-O+ £3,234 (£962; £481; £240) **Stalls** Low

Form RPR

-110 **1** **Precision Strike**[12] 2620 4-8-11 **60** (v) RobertWinston 4 71+
(Richard Guest) *hld up in rr: hdwy 1/2-way: tk clsr order 5f out: trckd clr ldr wl over 2f out: shkn up to ld ent fnl f: readily* **9/2**[3]

66-0 **2** *2 ¾* **Colinca's Lad (IRE)**[18] 2445 12-9-4 **70** RosieJessop(3) 3 75
(Peter Charalambous) *led and sn clr: pushed along 3f out: rdn wl over 1f out: hdd ent fnl f: kpt on same pce* **7/2**[2]

0-60 **3** *16* **Pertemps Networks**[78] 641 10-9-0 **70** DanielleMooney(7) 1 55
(Michael Easterby) *hld up: in rr 1/2-way: rdn along and poor 5th 3f out: styd on fnl 2f: tk remote 3rd ins fnl f* **16/1**

-052 **4** *½* **Petella**[12] 2620 8-8-0 **56** (p) KieranSchofield(7) 6 40
(George Moore) *s.i.s and sn pushed along: bhd tl hdwy over 4f out: rdn and plugged on to chse ldng pair 2f out: drvn and lost remote 3rd ins fnl f* **7/2**[2]

0-06 **5** *23* **Duke Of Yorkshire**[6] 2801 4-9-7 **70** PaulMulrennan 2 24
(Tim Easterby) *sn chsng clr ldr: tk clsr order over 4f out: pushed along 3f out: rdn wl over 2f out and sn wknd* **3/1**[1]

-125 **6** *85* **Divea**[30] 2097 5-8-11 **67** CamHardie(7) 5
(Anthony Carson) *chsd ldng pair: pushed along 1/2-way: sn lost pl and bhd: t.o fnl 3f* **9/2**[3]

3m 23.49s (16.09) **Going Correction** +0.775s/f (Yiel) **6 Ran SP% 111.7**
Speed ratings (Par 103): **88,86,78,77,65 20**
CSF £20.17 TOTE £5.50: £2.20, £2.70; EX 25.10 Trifecta £96.20.
**Owner** Resdev **Bred** Mickley Stud **Trained** Wetherby, W Yorks

**FOCUS**
This was run at a strong-looking gallop considering the conditions/field size. The winner is rated to his AW best, but there are doubts.

## 2981 BET WITH THE LADBROKES APP H'CAP 1m 4f

**3:10** (3:10) (Class 4) (0-85,93) 4-Y-O+ £5,175 (£1,540; £769; £384) **Stalls** Low

Form RPR

5-06 **1** **Linguine (FR)**[34] 1971 4-9-7 **85** PaulMulrennan 7 95
(Paul Midgley) *led 4f: trckd ldr tl led again wl over 2f out: rdn wl over 1f out: drvn ins fnl f and kpt on wl* **7/1**

2030 **2** *2* **Tepmokea (IRE)**[12] 2627 8-9-1 **79** (p) HayleyTurner 8 85
(Conor Dore) *trckd ldr tl led after 4f: pushed along and hdd wl over 2f out: rdn wl over 1f out: rallied ins fnl f: drvn and no imp towards fin* **5/1**[3]

-141 **3** *¾* **One Pursuit (IRE)**[9] 2700 6-9-8 **93** JennyPowell(7) 3 98
(Brendan Powell) *trckd ldrs: hdwy 3f out: rdn to chse wnr over 1f out: drvn and kpt on same pce fnl f* **7/4**[1]

1-3 **4** *3* **Innsbruck**[29] 2119 4-9-2 **83** IanBrennan(3) 9 83
(John Quinn) *trckd ldrs: hdwy over 4f out: rdn along wl over 2f out: drvn over 1f out and sn no imp* **3/1**[2]

0-55 **5** *6* **Bold Duke**[10] 2670 6-8-7 **74** ThomasBrown(3) 2 64
(Edward Bevan) *t.k.h: trckd ldrs 3f: shuffled bk and towards rr 1/2-way: sme hdwy wl over 2f out: sn rdn and n.d* **14/1**

2/00 **6** *1 ¼* **Aviator (GER)**[23] 2289 6-9-4 **82** (b) LukeMorris 6 70
(James Eustace) *trckd ldrs: hdwy to chse ldng pair bef 1/2-way: rdn along over 3f out: sn wknd* **12/1**

4640 **7** *2* **Fujin Dancer (FR)**[28] 2168 9-8-10 **74** PaulPickard 1 59
(Brian Ellison) *hld up: a in rr* **20/1**

0-00 **8** *17* **Muffin McLeay (IRE)**[18] 2423 6-9-6 **84** AndrewMullen 4 42
(David Barron) *a in rr: rdn along over 3f out: sn bhd* **20/1**

2m 41.57s (6.67) **Going Correction** +0.775s/f (Yiel) **8 Ran SP% 114.4**
Speed ratings (Par 105): **108,106,106,104,100 99,98,86**
CSF £41.75 CT £86.71 TOTE £8.80: £3.70, £1.90, £1.10; EX 40.90 Trifecta £132.60.
**Owner** Mrs Anne Cowley **Bred** Rupert Plersch **Trained** Westow, N Yorks

**FOCUS**
A useful contest, in which it paid to race handy. The winner is rated back to his best.

## 2982 LADBROKES CLASSIFIED STKS 1m 2f 60y

**3:45** (3:45) (Class 3) 3-Y-O £8,409 (£2,502; £1,250; £625) **Stalls** Low

Form RPR

2-31 **1** **Roseburg (IRE)**[38] 1880 3-9-3 88 LukeMorris 2 104
(Luca Cumani) *trckd ldng pair: hdwy 3f out: led jst over 2f out: rdn and edgd lft over 1f out: drvn and hung lft jst ins fnl f: jst hld on* **5/1**[3]

14 **2** *shd* **Satellite (IRE)**[21] 2337 3-9-3 87 [1] ShaneKelly 1 102
(William Haggas) *hld up in rr: hdwy over 3f out: effrt on outer to chse wnr wl over 1f out: sn rdn: carried hd high and hung lft ent fnl f: sn swtchd rt and drvn to chal last 100yds: jst hld* **11/8**[1]

12-2 **3** *9* **Gold Trail (IRE)**[16] 2496 3-9-3 90 MartinLane 5 85
(Charlie Appleby) *trckd ldr: hdwy and cl up 3f out: rdn 2f out: drvn and outpcd appr fnl f* **11/4**[2]

03-4 **4** *10* **Fire Fighting (IRE)**[14] 2566 3-9-3 90 AdrianNicholls 6 66
(Mark Johnston) *led: rdn along 3f out: hdd over 2f out and sn wknd* **13/2**

1 **5** *20* **Zaeemah (IRE)**[49] 1587 3-9-0 90 HarryBentley 3 40
(Saeed bin Suroor) *trckd ldrs: effrt over 3f out: sn rdn and wknd* **8/1**

2m 16.48s (7.08) **Going Correction** +0.775s/f (Yiel) **5 Ran SP% 109.9**
Speed ratings (Par 103): **102,101,94,86,70**
CSF £12.38 TOTE £5.20: £2.50, £1.10; EX 11.90 Trifecta £23.40.
**Owner** Sheikh Mohammed Obaid Al Maktoum **Bred** Mrs Brid Cosgrove **Trained** Newmarket, Suffolk

**FOCUS**
Plenty of these looked capable of more improvement, and two came clear. They were the only ones to show their form, but the winner is a nice type.

## 2983 LADBROKES H'CAP (BOBIS RACE) 1m (S)

**4:45** (4:45) (Class 2) (0-105,102) 3-Y-O £12,938 (£3,850; £1,924; £962) **Stalls** High

Form RPR

63-1 **1** **Wannabe Yours (IRE)**[18] 2432 3-8-3 **84** NickyMackay 4 105
(John Gosden) *trckd ldr: hdwy 3f out and sn led: rdn clr over 1f out: easily* **2/1**[1]

16-0 **2** *9* **Braidley (IRE)**[14] 2565 3-8-7 **88** TedDurcan 2 93
(James Bethell) *hld up: hdwy on outer wl over 2f out: rdn to chse wnr wl over 1f out: sn no imp* **11/2**

-010 **3** *6* **Azagal (IRE)**[22] 2316 3-9-1 **96** PaulMulrennan 1 83
(Tim Easterby) *hld up in rr: hdwy on inner and nt clr run 2f out and again over 1f out: swtchd lft ent fnl f: kpt on: no ch w ldng pair* **12/1**

11-0 **4** *2 ½* **Monsea (IRE)**[35] 1954 3-8-9 **90** SeanLevey 3 71
(Richard Hannon) *trckd ldng pair: effrt 3f out: rdn along 2f out: wl hld whn edgd rt over 1f out* **9/1**

12 **5** *2 ¾* **Cape Icon**[16] 2495 3-8-2 **83** oh1 LukeMorris 5 57
(Clive Cox) *led: pushed along 1/2-way: rdn 3f out: sn hdd and drvn: wknd fnl 2f* **10/3**[2]

1-40 **6** *63* **Lat Hawill (IRE)**[27] 2196 3-9-7 **102** HarryBentley 7
(Marco Botti) *trckd ldng pair: stmbld after 1f: rdn along wl over 2f out: sn wknd and bhd whn eased over 1f out* **7/2**[3]

1m 44.37s (5.07) **Going Correction** +0.875s/f (Soft) **6 Ran SP% 111.7**
Speed ratings (Par 105): **109,100,94,91,88 25**
CSF £13.25 TOTE £2.20: £1.40, £2.40; EX 11.30 Trifecta £73.50.
**Owner** Normandie Stud Ltd **Bred** Normandie Stud Ltd **Trained** Newmarket, Suffolk

**FOCUS**
Some decent horses have won this race in the past, including Remote in 2013. Tricky form to pin down, the testing ground a big factor, but the winner is rated up a stone on his maiden win.

## 2984 DOWNLOAD THE LADBROKES APP H'CAP 7f

**5:20** (5:21) (Class 2) (0-105,97) 4-Y-O+ £12,938 (£3,850; £1,924; £962) **Stalls** High

Form RPR

3221 **1** **Red Refraction (IRE)**[15] 2500 4-8-3 **86** CamHardie(7) 1 95
(Richard Hannon) *prom: chsd ldr over 2f out: rdn to chal ent fnl f: drvn and kpt on wl to ld last 50yds* **3/1**[2]

3400 **2** *½* **Sir Reginald**[21] 2336 6-9-2 **92** PaulHanagan 10 99
(Richard Fahey) *hld up in rr: hdwy over 1f out: sn rdn and styd on strly fnl f* **4/1**[3]

0550 **3** *nk* **Gramercy (IRE)**[7] 2758 7-8-13 **89** (b) HarryBentley 6 95
(David Simcock) *led: rdn wl over 1f out: drvn ins fnl f: edgd lft wl ins fnl f: hdd and no ex last 50yds* **6/1**

6-00 **4** *nk* **Boots And Spurs**[28] 2145 5-8-13 **89** (t) LukeMorris 3 94
(Stuart Williams) *trckd ldrs: pushed along over 2f out and sn sltly outpcd: rdn over 1f out: styd on fnl f: nrst fin* **5/2**[1]

0-50 **5** *2 ¼* **Senafe**[28] 2155 4-8-9 **90** (p) MarcMonaghan(5) 7 89
(Marco Botti) *trckd ldrs: hdwy 3f out: rdn along 2f out: drvn appr fnl f and kpt on same pce* **16/1**

522- **6** *7* **Modern Tutor**[232] 7337 5-9-0 **93** ThomasBrown(3) 4 74
(Andrew Balding) *prom: chsd ldr after 3f: rdn along 2f out: sn drvn and wknd over 1f out* **11/2**

1/5- **7** *6* **Mezmaar**[392] 2257 5-9-7 **97** [1] ShaneKelly 8 62
(Kevin Morgan) *dwlt: hld up: a in rr* **33/1**

1m 30.71s (4.41) **Going Correction** +0.875s/f (Soft) **7 Ran SP% 112.1**
Speed ratings (Par 109): **109,108,108,107,105 97,90**
CSF £14.75 CT £65.08 TOTE £3.70: £2.40, £1.30; EX 14.20 Trifecta £71.20.
**Owner** Middleham Park Racing IV & James Pak **Bred** Tally-Ho Stud **Trained** East Everleigh, Wilts

**FOCUS**
A really decent race of its type that produced a tight finish in the testing ground.

## 2985 LADBROKES MAIDEN STKS 5f

**5:50** (5:53) (Class 5) 3-Y-O+ £3,234 (£962; £481; £240) **Stalls** High

Form RPR

5-43 **1** **War Spirit**[23] 2278 3-9-5 71 SeanLevey 2 69
(Richard Hannon) *mde all: rdn and qcknd appr fnl f: kpt on wl u.p towards fin* **11/10**[1]

0-24 **2** *1* **Red Forever**[7] 2759 3-9-2 54 SladeO'Hara(3) 3 65
(Alan Berry) *a chsng wnr: rdn wl over 1f out: kpt on wl u.p fnl f* **14/1**

0/5 **3** *nk* **Koala Bear**[10] 2681 4-9-7 0 HayleyTurner 5 62
(James Fanshawe) *dwlt and hld up towards rr: hdwy 1/2-way: chsd ldrs wl over 1f out: sn rdn and kpt on same pce fnl f* **7/2**[2]

23-4 **4** *3 ¾* **Alpine Flower (IRE)**[42] 1713 3-9-0 75 PaulHanagan 6 45
(Tim Easterby) *in rr: hdwy wl over 1f out: sn rdn and kpt on fnl f: nrst fin* **7/2**[2]

**5** *¾* **Linda's Sister** 4-9-4 0 IanBrennan(3) 4 46
(John Quinn) *in tch: pushed along and green 2f out: sn rdn and kpt on fnl f* **11/1**[3]

44 **6** *nk* **Bondi Beach Babe**[21] 2329 4-9-4 0 .......................... GeorgeChaloner(3) 1 45
(James Turner) *chsd ldng pair: rdn wl over 1f out: wknd appr fnl f* **12/1**

6- **7** *15* **Jenny Twigg**[197] 8003 4-9-7 0 ..................................... MichaelStainton 7
(Chris Fairhurst) *sn outpcd and a in rr* **40/1**

1m 3.13s (2.63) **Going Correction** +0.65s/f (Yiel)
**WFA** 3 from 4yo 7lb **7** Ran SP% **117.2**
Speed ratings (Par 103): **104,102,101,95,94 94,70**
CSF £20.27 TOTE £2.00: £1.30, £3.90; EX 15.70 Trifecta £64.40.
**Owner** Mohamed Saeed Al Shahi **Bred** Biddestone Stud Ltd **Trained** East Everleigh, Wilts

**FOCUS**
Not form to go overboard about. The runner-up is the key and the winner didn't need to match his best.
T/Plt: £64.70 to a £1 stake. Pool: £72,090.43 - 813.35 winning units T/Qpdt: £5.20 to a £1 stake. Pool: £4,828.30 - 682.00 winning units JR

## 2956 EPSOM (L-H)
### Saturday, June 7

**OFFICIAL GOING: Good (good to soft in places) changing to good after race 2 (2.05)**
Wind: Light; half behind Weather: Overcast; bright spells

## 2986 INVESTEC OUT OF ORDINARY STKS (H'CAP) (BOBIS RACE) 1m 2f 18y
**1:35** (1:36) (Class 2) (0-105,99) 3-Y-O
**£31,125** (£9,320; £4,660; £2,330; £1,165; £585) **Stalls** Low

Form RPR

4-10 **1** **What About Carlo (FR)**[14] 2565 3-9-2 **94** ..................... JimmyFortune 6 103
(Eve Johnson Houghton) *hld up in tch in midfield: rdn and effrt 2f out: gd hdwy over 1f out: led jst ins fnl f: edging lft but sn in command: r.o strly* **9/1**

6-21 **2** *2* **Black Shadow**[16] 2485 3-9-1 **93** ........................................ TomQueally 3 98
(Amanda Perrett) *t.k.h: hld up wl in tch in midfield: rdn and effrt wl over 1f out: hdwy and ev ch 1f out: carried lft and unable qck ins fnl f: kpt on* **7/1**[3]

3-15 **3** *nk* **Hymenaios (IRE)**[43] 1702 3-8-8 **86** ........................................ RichardHughes 5 90
(Richard Hannon) *stdd s: hld up in tch in last trio: rdn and effrt 2f out: swtchd rt over 1f out: r.o strly ins fnl f: no threat to wnr* **5/1**[1]

4-14 **4** *hd* **Yenhaab (IRE)**[35] 1954 3-8-6 **84** ........................................ DavidProbert 7 89+
(William Haggas) *hld up in tch in midfield: effrt and drvn 2f out: edging lft and sltly hmpd over 1f out: rallied and r.o wl ins fnl f: no threat to wnr* **7/1**[3]

-530 **5** *1 ¾* **Lyn Valley**[14] 2565 3-9-3 **95** ........................................ AdamKirby 11 96
(Mark Johnston) *chsd ldr: rdn to chal 3f out: drvn to ld 2f out: hdd jst ins fnl f: unable qck and short of room sn after: wknd and lost 2 pls fnl 75yds* **20/1**

5-35 **6** *hd* **Stars Over The Sea (USA)**[30] 2087 3-9-7 **99** .................... KierenFallon 4 99+
(Mark Johnston) *awkward leaving stalls and s.i.s: hld up in rr: effrt on outer 2f out: hdwy and rdn 1f out: styd on but nvr gng to rch ldrs* **10/1**

6-12 **7** *1 ½* **Galizzi (USA)**[39] 1856 3-8-6 **84** ............................(v[1]) MickaelBarzalona 2 81
(Michael Bell) *t.k.h: chsd ldrs: rdn and effrt ent fnl 2f: no ex and btn over 1f out: wknd ins fnl f* **15/2**

10-1 **8** *hd* **Flippant (IRE)**[36] 1913 3-8-0 **83** ........................................ NathanAlison(5) 10 80
(William Haggas) *hld up in last quartet: c wdst and effrt 3f out: no imp 2f out: btn and sltly hmpd over 1f out: edging lft and one pce fnl f* **7/1**[3]

4-11 **9** *1 ¼* **Al Busayyir (IRE)**[12] 2617 3-8-10 **88** .................................. AndreaAtzeni 8 83
(Marco Botti) *chsd ldrs: rdn and effrt over 2f out: struggling and losing pl whn short of room and hmpd over 1f out: wl hld fnl f* **11/2**[2]

-215 **10** *2 ½* **Zampa Manos (USA)**[29] 2114 3-9-1 **96** ........................ OisinMurphy(3) 9 86
(Andrew Balding) *led: jnd 3f out: rdn and hdd 2f out: btn over 1f out: wknd fnl f* **20/1**

6-30 **11** *6* **Double Bluff (IRE)**[28] 2153 3-9-5 **97** ........................ SilvestreDeSousa 1 76
(Mark Johnston) *in tch in midfield: hmpd after 1f out: rdn and lost pl over 2f out: bhd over 1f out* **11/1**

2m 6.82s (-2.88) **Going Correction** -0.10s/f (Good) **11** Ran SP% **118.3**
Speed ratings (Par 105): **107,105,105,105,103 103,102,102,101,99 94**
CSF £71.12 CT £350.48 TOTE £10.90: £3.60, £2.30, £1.80; EX 78.80 Trifecta £684.00.
**Owner** Anthony Pye-Jeary **Bred** Earl Haras Du Logis & J Ince **Trained** Blewbury, Oxon

**FOCUS**
Track at inner (Derby) configuration and distances as advertised. The likes of Lailani (2002), Stage Gift (2006), Conduit (2008) and Dandino (2010) all landed this before winning in Group company, the first two named also successful at the top level. This was sound run and is good form which makes a fair bit of sense.

## 2987 INVESTEC WOODCOTE STKS (LISTED RACE) 6f
**2:05** (2:06) (Class 1) 2-Y-O
**£22,684** (£8,600; £4,304; £2,144; £1,076; £540) **Stalls** High

Form RPR

21 **1** **Baitha Alga (IRE)**[7] 2756 2-9-0 0 ........................................ FrankieDettori 1 97+
(Richard Hannon) *racd keenly: led for 1f: chsd ldr after: rdn to ld over 1f out: clr and in command whn drvn 1f out: r.o wl* **15/8**[1]

31 **2** *2* **Ballymore Castle (IRE)**[30] 2089 2-9-0 0 ............................ RyanMoore 8 90
(Richard Fahey) *broke wl enough: sltly hmpd and dropped to rr after 1f: struggling on downhill run and detached last after: swtchd rt and effrt 2f out: hdwy over 1f out: chsd clr wnr fnl 75yds: r.o* **10/3**[2]

41 **3** *¾* **Red Icon (IRE)**[9] 2698 2-9-0 0 ........................................ RichardKingscote 9 88
(Tom Dascombe) *in tch: rdn and effrt 2f out: hdwy over 1f out: styd on to chse clr wnr ins fnl f: lost 2nd fnl 75yds: kpt on* **9/2**[3]

214 **4** *2* **Burtonwood**[22] 2308 2-9-0 0 ........................................ AdamKirby 7 82
(Richard Fahey) *chsd ldrs: effrt u.p over 2f out: chsd ldng pair and drvn 2f out: kpt on same pce u.p fr over 1f out* **16/1**

01 **5** *1 ¼* **Lightning Stride**[19] 2380 2-9-0 0 ........................................ JamieSpencer 5 78
(Brian Meehan) *chsd ldrs: effrt and drvn jst over 2f out: unable qck and lost pl wl over 1f out: n.d and kpt on same pce fnl f* **8/1**

15 **6** *¾* **Mambo Paradise**[22] 2302 2-8-9 0 .................................. SilvestreDeSousa 4 71
(Mark Johnston) *s.i.s: rcvrd to ld after 1f out: rdn ent fnl 2f: drvn and hdd over 1f out: sn outpcd by wnr: lost 2nd and fdd fnl 100yds* **10/1**

22 **7** *nk* **Fine Prince (IRE)**[23] 2276 2-9-0 0 ........................................ JimmyFortune 3 78
(Robert Mills) *t.k.h: hld up in last pair: effrt on inner but nt handling trck fr 3f out: no prog: eased ins fnl f* **14/1**

202 **8** *½* **Exentricity**[14] 2557 2-8-9 0 ........................................ WilliamTwiston-Davies 6 68
(Mick Channon) *in tch in midfield: rdn and effrt over 2f out: struggling and losing pl whn short of room over 1f out: bhd after* **16/1**

1m 9.63s (0.23) **Going Correction** -0.10s/f (Good) **8** Ran SP% **114.7**
Speed ratings (Par 101): **94,91,90,87,86 85,84,83**
CSF £8.13 TOTE £2.30: £1.10, £1.60, £2.00; EX 6.40 Trifecta £25.40.
**Owner** Al Shaqab Racing **Bred** Ms Theresa Killen **Trained** East Everleigh, Wilts

**FOCUS**
Run at a good gallop, the two at the head of the market came to the fore and the form looks solid. However it was probably an ordinary renewal.

## 2988 INVESTEC CORONATION CUP (IN COMMEMORATION OF ST NICHOLAS ABBEY) (GROUP 1) 1m 4f 10y
**2:40** (2:43) (Class 1) 4-Y-O+
**£218,900** (£82,990; £41,533; £20,689; £10,383; £5,211) **Stalls** Centre

Form RPR

-211 **1** **Cirrus Des Aigles (FR)**[13] 2587 8-9-0 123 .......... ChristopheSoumillon 7 125
(Mme C Barande-Barbe, France) *hld up in midfield: 4th st: clsd smoothly to press ldr ent fnl 2f: shkn up to ld over 1f out: r.o strly u.p and in command fnl f* **10/11**[1]

140- **2** *2* **Flintshire**[244] 7058 4-9-0 120 ........................................ MaximeGuyon 5 121
(A Fabre, France) *hld up in tch in midfield: 5th and pushed along st: rdn and effrt over 2f out: drvn and hdwy to chse wnr 1f out: r.o but a hld* **4/1**[2]

2-31 **3** *2 ¼* **My Ambivalent (IRE)**[23] 2284 5-8-11 112 ........................ AndreaAtzeni 6 114
(Roger Varian) *ponied to s and taken down early: led: rdn and hdd over 1f out: 3rd and btn whn sltly hmpd jst ins fnl f: one pce* **13/2**[3]

2-24 **4** *3 ¼* **Empoli (GER)**[70] 1182 4-9-0 116 ........................................ AdriedeVries 1 112
(P Schiergen, Germany) *chsd ldr tl 8f out: 3rd st: n.m.r over 2f out: rdn 2f out: outpcd and btn over 1f out: wknd fnl f* **12/1**

023- **5** *3* **Talent**[231] 7365 4-8-11 114 ........................................ JimCrowley 8 104
(Ralph Beckett) *stdd s: hld up in last pair: 6th and clsd on ldrs st: rdn ent fnl 2f: sn btn* **9/1**

00-1 **6** *1 ½* **Beacon Lady**[45] 1651 5-8-11 96 ........................................ OisinMurphy 3 102
(William Knight) *taken down early: stdd s: hld up in detached last: 7th st: rdn and effrt 2f out: no imp* **40/1**

-605 **7** *8* **Joshua Tree (IRE)**[41] 1783 7-9-0 112 ........................................ RyanMoore 4 92
(Ed Dunlop) *chsd ldrs: wnt 2nd 8f out: 2nd in st: rdn over 3f out: lost 2nd ent fnl 2f: wknd over 1f out* **16/1**

2m 34.86s (-4.04) **Going Correction** -0.10s/f (Good) **7** Ran SP% **111.7**
Speed ratings (Par 117): **109,107,106,104,102 101,95**
CSF £4.47 TOTE £1.80: £1.20, £2.00; EX 4.70 Trifecta £14.90.
**Owner** Jean-Claude-Alain Dupouy **Bred** M Yvon Lelimouzin & M Benoit Deschamps **Trained** France

**FOCUS**
This year's Coronation Cup was run in commemoration of St Nicholas Abbey, who had won the last three runnings, and it went to a similarly popular type. Ruler Of The World was ruled out with a muscle injury. Straightforward form with the first three close to their marks.

## 2989 INVESTEC SPECIALIST BANK "DASH" (HERITAGE H'CAP) 5f
**3:15** (3:18) (Class 2) 3-Y-O+
**£62,250** (£18,640; £9,320; £4,660; £2,330; £1,170) **Stalls** High

Form RPR

4132 **1** **Caspian Prince (IRE)**[31] 2074 5-9-0 **97** ..........................(t) AdamKirby 14 106
(Tony Carroll) *sn led and crossed to r nr stands' rail: rdn and edgd lft over 1f out: hdd ent fnl f: battled bk gamely to ld again ins fnl f: hld on: all out* **9/1**[3]

32-0 **2** *hd* **Seeking Magic**[34] 1975 6-8-11 **99** ..............................(t) RyanTate(5) 17 107
(Clive Cox) *in tch in midfield: rdn and effrt over 1f out: clsng on ldrs and forced to switch lft ins fnl f: str run fnl 100yds: nt quite rch wnr* **7/1**[2]

1404 **3** *nk* **Addictive Dream (IRE)**[31] 2076 7-9-5 **102** .......... MickaelBarzalona 12 109
(David Nicholls) *chsd ldrs: rdn and chal over 1f out: drvn to ld ent fnl f: hdd ins fnl f: r.o wl but no ex cl home* **25/1**

0-31 **4** *hd* **Steps (IRE)**[7] 2766 6-9-12 **109** 4ex ..............................(b) KierenFallon 13 115+
(Roger Varian) *s.i.s: bhd: sme hdwy and sltly hmpd 2f out: switching rt over 1f out: wnt between rivals and hdwy 1f out: r.o v strly fnl 100yds: nt quite rch ldrs* **6/1**[1]

-410 **5** *½* **Swan Song**[7] 2766 5-9-3 **100** ........................................ DavidProbert 15 105
(Andrew Balding) *broke best: sn hdd and chsd ldr for over 1f out: chsd ldrs after: rdn and effrt over 1f out: kpt on wl ins fnl f: n.m.r nr fin* **10/1**

5-04 **6** *1* **Barnet Fair**[29] 2123 6-8-4 **92** ........................................ LouisSteward(5) 2 93+
(Lee Carter) *taken down early: hld up in midfield: rdn: swtchd lft to centre and hdwy over 2f out: styd on fnl f: nt rch ldrs* **25/1**

6010 **7** *hd* **Monsieur Joe (IRE)**[7] 2786 7-9-7 **104** 4ex ........................ TomQueally 9 104
(Paul Midgley) *in tch in midfield: pushed along 1/2-way: hdwy u.p jst over 1f out: styd on fnl f: nt rch ldrs* **12/1**

0100 **8** *nk* **Taajub (IRE)**[45] 1650 7-8-7 **90** ........................................ RichardKingscote 19 89
(Peter Crate) *towards rr: effrt u.p over 1f out: sme hdwy whn jostled 1f out: styd on ins fnl f: no threat to ldrs* **16/1**

210- **9** *¾* **New Fforest**[245] 7010 4-8-7 **93** ........................................ OisinMurphy(3) 7 90
(Andrew Balding) *dwlt: pushed along towards rr: hdwy into midfield 1/2-way: drvn over 1f out: kpt on ins fnl f: no threat to ldrs* **16/1**

-002 **10** *nse* **Judge 'n Jury**[6] 2803 10-8-9 **92** ..............................(t) SteveDrowne 1 88
(Ronald Harris) *taken down early: racd alone in centre: chsd ldrs: rdn over 1f out: drvn and btn 1f out: wknd ins fnl f* **33/1**

0100 **11** *nk* **Smoothtalkinrascal (IRE)**[14] 2563 4-9-9 **106** ........... DanielTudhope 18 101+
(David O'Meara) *taken down early: racd in last trio: nt clr run 2f out: swtchd lft and rdn jst ins fnl f: styd on: nvr trbld ldrs* **10/1**

03-4 **12** *nk* **Tangerine Trees**[50] 1561 9-9-2 **99** ..............................(v) RoystonFrench 11 93
(Bryan Smart) *in tch in midfield: effrt u.p 2f out: drvn: edgd lft and no ex ent fnl f: wknd fnl 150yds* **20/1**

00-6 **13** *¾* **Lady Gibraltar**[23] 2283 5-8-1 **89** ..............................(v) JoeyHaynes(5) 5 81
(Timothy Jarvis) *in tch in midfield: rdn and unable qck over 1f out: wknd ins fnl f* **16/1**

3202 **14** *½* **Elusivity (IRE)**[23] 2283 6-8-5 **88** ........................................ JimmyQuinn 6 78
(Peter Crate) *t.k.h: hld up in tch in midfield: rdn and effrt over 1f out: no imp 1f out: styd on same pce fnl f* **10/1**

0200 **15** *shd* **Racy**[7] 2786 7-9-3 **100** ..............................(p) FrederikTylicki 3 89
(Brian Ellison) *dwlt: sn bustled along towards rr: hdwy and swtchd lft ins fnl f: kpt on: nvr trbld ldrs* **25/1**

0-50 **16** *½* **Ballesteros**[23] 2283 5-9-4 **101** ........................................ JimCrowley 16 89
(Richard Fahey) *a towards rr: shkn and jst over 1f out: pushed along and kpt on ins fnl f: n.d* **20/1**

3000 **17** *¾* **Even Stevens**[7] 2786 6-8-0 **90** ..............................(v) MatthewHopkins(7) 20 75
(Scott Dixon) *nt best away and swtchd lft sn after s: sn chsng ldrs: wnt 2nd over 3f out tl over 1f out: wknd ins fnl f* **10/1**

0-05 **18** *nse* **Hopes N Dreams (IRE)**[21] 2353 6-8-9 **97** ........................ ShaneGray(5) 4 82
(Kevin Ryan) *taken down early: s.i.s: a bhd* **33/1**

00-0 **19** 1 1/2 **Free Zone**[31] 2074 5-9-0 100 RobertTart(3) 10 79
(Robert Cowell) *wl in tch in midfield: rdn 2f out: losing pl whn short of room 1f out: wknd fnl f* **25/1**

54.75s (-0.95) **Going Correction** +0.10s/f (Good) **19** Ran SP% **129.3**
Speed ratings (Par 109): **111,110,110,109,109 107,107,106,105,105 104,104,103,102,102 101,100,100,97**
CSF £64.98 CT £1561.96 TOTE £9.30: £2.70, £2.70, £6.00, £2.10; EX 85.00 Trifecta £2597.30.
**Owner** Stephen Louch **Bred** Ballygallon Stud Limited **Trained** Cropthorne, Worcs

**FOCUS**
This was always going to be fast and furious and the second and fourth will feel they could have won on another day. Surprisingly, though, there was very little trouble in behind. The winner is up a length on his previous C&D win.

## 2990 INVESTEC DERBY (GROUP 1) (ENTIRE COLTS & FILLIES) 1m 4f 10y
**4:00** (4:07) (Class 1) 3-Y-O

**£782,598** (£296,700; £148,488; £73,968; £37,122; £18,630) **Stalls** Centre

Form RPR

1-3 **1** **Australia**[35] 1951 3-9-0 119 JosephO'Brien 12 125
(A P O'Brien, Ire) *hld up in midfield: 8th st: smooth hdwy to press ldrs ent fnl 2f: rdn to ld over 1f out: styd on u.p fnl f and a holding runner-up: rdn out* **11/8**[1]

11-0 **2** 1 1/4 **Kingston Hill**[35] 1951 3-9-0 118 AndreaAtzeni 2 123
(Roger Varian) *chsd ldrs: 3rd st: clsd on ldrs 3f out: rdn to ld ent fnl 2f: drvn and hdd over 1f out: kpt on trying but a hld fnl f* **15/2**[2]

312 **3** 3 1/4 **Romsdal**[30] 2087 3-9-0 107 RichardHughes 11 118
(John Gosden) *wl in tch in midfield: 5th st: rdn and effrt to chse ldrs 2f out: 3rd and outpcd by ldng pair over 1f out: clr 3rd and kpt on same pce fnl f* **20/1**

3-12 **4** 3 3/4 **Arod (IRE)**[23] 2285 3-9-0 108 JamieSpencer 3 112
(Peter Chapple-Hyam) *hld up in midfield: 7th st: effrt u.p and switching rt over 2f out: wnt modest 4th wl over 1f out: kpt on but no imp* **20/1**

1-46 **5** 1 1/4 **Red Galileo**[28] 2153 3-9-0 95 OisinMurphy 8 110
(Ed Dunlop) *stdd s: hld up in rr: 16th st: rdn and effrt on outer ent fnl 2f: hdwy past btn horses over 1f out: styd on: wl fnl f: no threat to ldrs* **100/1**

1-11 **6** hd **Western Hymn**[43] 1699 3-9-0 104 WilliamBuick 13 110
(John Gosden) *t.k.h: hld up in midfield: short of room and jostled downhill run over 4f out: 10th st: effrt and struggling to handle trck 3f out: no prog tl hdwy 1f out: styd on ins fnl f: nvr trbld ldrs* **10/1**

1-13 **7** 3/4 **True Story**[23] 2285 3-9-0 114 KierenFallon 1 108
(Saeed bin Suroor) *wnt lft and awkward leaving stall: sn bustled along: hdwy to chse ldrs after 2f but a niggled along: 4th st: rdn: shifting rt over 2f out: sn outpcd: 5th and wl hld whn edgd lft over 1f out* **8/1**[3]

12 **8** 1 **Fascinating Rock (IRE)**[27] 2187 3-9-0 113 PatSmullen 15 107
(D K Weld, Ire) *hld up towards rr: hdwy on outer and barging match w rival over 4f out: 11th st: effrt u.p wl over 2f out: no prog 2f out: wl hld after* **12/1**

31 **9** 1 1/2 **Ebanoran (IRE)**[27] 2187 3-9-0 113 DeclanMcDonogh 6 104
(John M Oxx, Ire) *hld up wl in tch in midfield: 6th st: effrt u.p wl over 2f out: drvn and outpcd 2f out: sn wl btn* **12/1**

5-51 **10** 2 **Kingfisher (IRE)**[29] 2114 3-9-0 105 ColmO'Donoghue 16 101
(A P O'Brien, Ire) *chsd ldr: virtually upsides and 2nd st: sn drvn and ev ch tl outpcd and btn 2f out: wknd over 1f out: fdd and eased wl ins fnl f* **50/1**

51-2 **11** 1 1/4 **Impulsive Moment (IRE)**[43] 1699 3-9-0 97 DavidProbert 5 99
(Andrew Balding) *s.i.s: towards rr: effrt on inner and 12th st: drvn and no hdwy over 2f out: wknd wl over 1f out* **50/1**

1 **12** 1 1/2 **Orchestra (IRE)**[30] 2087 3-9-0 110 SeamieHeffernan 14 97
(A P O'Brien, Ire) *stdd after s: t.k.h: hld up towards rr: hmpd after 2f: hmpd again on downhill run over 4f out: 14th st: rdn and nt handle trck 3f out: sn bhd* **16/1**

21-1 **13** 1 1/4 **Our Channel (USA)**[45] 1652 3-9-0 101 SilvestreDeSousa 10 95
(William Haggas) *led: rdn 3f out: drvn and hdd ent fnl 2f: sn outpcd and btn: wknd over 1f out: fdd fnl f* **50/1**

0-31 **14** 10 **Pinzolo**[21] 2345 3-9-0 104 JamesDoyle 4 79
(Charlie Appleby) *hld up in midfield: 9th st: sn rdn and btn: wl bhd and eased ins fnl f* **40/1**

1-13 **15** 1/2 **Sudden Wonder (IRE)**[28] 2153 3-9-0 105 KevinManning 9 78
(Charlie Appleby) *bustled along leaving stalls: chsd ldrs: nt handle downhill run and lost pl over 4f out: 15th st: lost tch 2f out: wl bhd and eased ins fnl f* **66/1**

1-3 **16** 61 **Geoffrey Chaucer (USA)**[27] 2187 3-9-0 112 RyanMoore 7
(A P O'Brien, Ire) *hld up in midfield: rdn over 4f out: losing pl and 13th st: last and eased 2f out: t.o* **10/1**

2m 33.63s (-5.27) **Going Correction** -0.10s/f (Good) **16** Ran SP% **124.8**
Speed ratings (Par 113): **113,112,110,107,106 106,106,105,104,103 102,101,100,93,93 52**
CSF £10.87 CT £159.50 TOTE £2.30: £1.20, £2.80, £4.60; EX 15.50 Trifecta £292.60.
**Owner** D Smith/Mrs J Magnier/M Tabor/T Ah Khing **Bred** Stanley Estate And Stud Co **Trained** Cashel, Co Tipperary

■ Aidan O'Brien becomes the first trainer to complete a Derby hat-trick.

**FOCUS**
Victory for Australia saw Aidan O'Brien become the first trainer to complete a Derby hat-trick - it was his fifth win in the race overall - and this was a record sixth owners' success for Michael Tabor and Sue Magnier. The true worth of this form will be revealed in due course, but the 'right' horse won in a time over a second quicker than both the Coronation Cup and older-horse handicap, and the front two, who represented the red-hot 2,000 Guineas form, were clear of the others. The form is solid with Australia improving from Newmarket. So did Kingston Hill.

## 2991 INVESTEC ZEBRA STKS (H'CAP) 1m 4f 10y
**4:50** (4:51) (Class 2) (0-100,100) 4-Y-O+

**£18,675** (£5,592; £2,796; £1,398; £699; £351) **Stalls** Centre

Form RPR

4-2 **1** **Miss Marjurie (IRE)**[34] 1973 4-8-4 86 ow2 OisinMurphy(3) 5 98+
(Denis Coakley) *hld up in midfield: hdwy to chse ldr ent fnl 3f: rdn to ld over 2f out: qckned clr 2f out: styd on wl: rdn out* **7/1**[3]

1-41 **2** 2 1/2 **Stomachion (IRE)**[7] 2783 4-8-10 89 RyanMoore 2 97+
(Sir Michael Stoute) *hld up in tch towards rr: rdn and hdwy over 2f out: 3rd 2f out: chsd wnr ins fnl f: styd on but nvr a threat to wnr* **7/2**[1]

5-24 **3** 1/2 **Blue Surf**[14] 2555 5-9-4 97 PatDobbs 8 104
(Amanda Perrett) *hld up in tch in midfield: effrt and edging lft over 2f out: chsd clr wnr 2f out: no imp: lost 2nd ins fnl f: kpt on but no threat to wnr* **14/1**

1-04 **4** 3 1/4 **Pasaka Boy**[24] 2253 4-8-7 86 RichardKingscote 4 88
(Jonathan Portman) *s.i.s: hld up in last trio: hdwy and swtchd lft over 2f out: wnt 4th wl over 1f out: kpt on but no real imp* **10/1**

0-14 **5** hd **Christopher Wren (USA)**[14] 2558 7-8-9 88 AndreaAtzeni 13 89
(Nick Gifford) *stdd after s: hld up in rr: effrt on outer 2f out: hdwy over 1f out: battling for 4th and kpt on fnl f: nvr trbld ldrs* **20/1**

4-65 **6** 3 3/4 **Saptapadi (IRE)**[22] 2314 8-8-8 87 (t) SilvestreDeSousa 12 88
(Brian Ellison) *hld up in last trio: effrt and nt clr run and hmpd over 1f out: no ch but kpt on ins fnl f* **12/1**

40-1 **7** 2 **Dare To Achieve**[22] 2294 4-9-7 100 JamesDoyle 10 92
(William Haggas) *hld up towards rr: drvn and effrt jst over 2f out: no imp and wknd over 1f out* **9/2**[2]

0-01 **8** 7 **Cashpoint**[12] 2618 9-8-6 90 ShaneGray(5) 14 71
(Ian Williams) *hld up in toouch on outer: hdwy 5f out: rdn and no prog 2f out: edgd lft and btn over 1f out: wknd* **16/1**

00-0 **9** 1 1/4 **Open Eagle (IRE)**[31] 2073 5-9-0 93 DanielTudhope 16 72
(David O'Meara) *in toouch in midfield: hdwy to chse ldrs 8f out: rdn and struggling whn short of room and pushed lft over 2f out: wknd over 1f out* **16/1**

0-63 **10** 1 3/4 **Kelinni (IRE)**[14] 2555 6-9-6 99 (p) FrankieDettori 11 75
(Marco Botti) *t.k.h: led for over 1f: stdd bk and hld up wl in tch in midfield: rdn and btn 2f out: wknd and edgd lft over 1f out: eased wl ins fnl f* **10/1**

1-00 **11** 6 **Rossetti**[45] 1651 6-8-2 81 oh5 (p) DavidProbert 1 48
(Gary Moore) *chsd ldrs tl hdwy to ld over 10f out: rdn and hdd over 2f out: sn outpcd and btn: wknd over 1f out: eased wl ins fnl f* **66/1**

0-02 **12** 2 3/4 **Mirsaale**[14] 2555 4-9-7 100 (p) KierenFallon 6 62
(James Tate) *awkward leaving stalls and s.i.s: in tch in midfield: lost pl 4f out: bhd and rdn 3f out: sn btn: t.o fnl f* **14/1**

00-5 **13** 2 3/4 **Red Seventy**[30] 2091 5-7-12 84 oh6 ow3 (p) KieranShoemark(7) 7 42
(David Pipe) *in tch in midfield: lost pl and drvn 3f out: sn btn: t.o ins fnl f* **66/1**

00-3 **14** 1 1/4 **Kuda Huraa (IRE)**[19] 2405 6-8-7 86 FergusSweeney 3 42
(Alan King) *t.k.h: chsd ldr after 2f tl over 3f out: sn dropped out: t.o ins fnl f* **20/1**

5002 **P** **Blue Wave (IRE)**[21] 2342 4-9-4 97 AdamKirby 15
(Mark Johnston) *in toouch in midfield: hdwy to chse ldrs 8f out: rdn and dropped out over 3f out: bhd 2f out: sn eased and p.u ins fnl f* **14/1**

2m 34.87s (-4.03) **Going Correction** -0.10s/f (Good) **15** Ran SP% **123.1**
Speed ratings (Par 109): **109,107,107,104,104 102,100,96,95,94 90,88,86,85,**
CSF £30.93 CT £345.61 TOTE £6.90: £2.80, £1.50, £5.10; EX 40.20 Trifecta £666.00.
**Owner** Chris Van Hoorn **Bred** Coleman Bloodstock Limited **Trained** West Ilsley, Berks

**FOCUS**
A race where it paid to sit handily, with the pace no more than fair. The winner progressed from his good reappearance.

## 2992 VOYAGE BY INVESTEC STKS (H'CAP) 6f
**5:25** (5:28) (Class 2) (0-100,100) 4-Y-O+

**£18,675** (£5,592; £2,796; £1,398; £699; £351) **Stalls** High

Form RPR

-042 **1** **Ashpan Sam**[15] 2503 5-9-7 100 RyanMoore 6 111
(John Spearing) *mde all: rdn and edgd lft u.p over 1f out: clr ins fnl f: styd on wl: rdn out* **7/2**[1]

0050 **2** 1 1/2 **Swiss Cross**[34] 1975 7-8-6 85 (bt) SilvestreDeSousa 2 91
(Phil McEntee) *chsd ldrs: rdn over 2f out: kpt on u.p fnl f: wnt 2nd ins fnl f: no imp* **12/1**

6000 **3** 3/4 **Regal Parade**[7] 2778 10-8-8 87 (t) FrederikTylicki 4 91+
(Milton Bradley) *racd in midfield: lost pl and carried rt over 3f out: bhd tl hdwy u.p over 1f out: r.o strly ins fnl f: nvr gng to rch wnr* **33/1**

0104 **4** 3/4 **Normal Equilibrium**[7] 2786 4-8-12 91 (p) JimCrowley 1 93
(Robert Cowell) *chsd ldrs: effrt on inner to chse wnr wl over 1f out: short of room and sltly hmpd over 1f out: styd on same pce and lost 2 pls ins fnl f* **7/1**[2]

2-14 **5** hd **Desert Command**[15] 2503 4-8-5 84 DavidProbert 11 85
(Andrew Balding) *chsd ldr tl wl over 1f out: unable qck u.p over 1f out: styd on same pce ins fnl f* **15/2**[3]

-121 **6** 1 1/4 **Bondesire**[7] 2757 4-9-3 96 DanielTudhope 15 93
(David O'Meara) *chsd ldrs: rdn ent fnl 2f: outpcd and btn ent fnl f: plugged on same pce after* **8/1**

0-06 **7** nk **Crew Cut (IRE)**[15] 2503 6-8-3 82 AndreaAtzeni 9 78
(Stuart Williams) *racd off the pce towards rr: plenty to do and hdwy u.p over 1f out: styd on wl ins fnl f: nvr trbld ldrs* **33/1**

-004 **8** nk **Joe Packet**[5] 2849 7-8-8 87 RichardKingscote 13 82
(Jonathan Portman) *in tch in midfield: rdn and effrt ent fnl 2f: drvn and no imp over 1f out: styd on same pce fnl f* **14/1**

6000 **9** hd **Baby Strange**[14] 2562 10-7-11 81 oh2 ow2 AdamMcLean(7) 5 77
(Derek Shaw) *s.i.s: sn bhd: rdn over 2f out: hdwy but stl plenty to do ent fnl f: swtchd lft fnl 150yds: r.o strly: nt rch ldrs* **20/1**

40-3 **10** 2 **Lewisham**[21] 2352 4-8-5 84 MickaelBarzalona 3 72
(David Nicholls) *in tch in midfield: rdn and effrt over 2f out: no imp and sltly hmpd 2f out: styd on same pce and no imp after* **15/2**[3]

3000 **11** 3/4 **Doc Hay (USA)**[21] 2353 7-9-4 97 DaleSwift 8 83
(Brian Ellison) *s.i.s: sme hdwy but stl plenty to do whn hung rt 3f out: sme hdwy u.p 1f out: nvr trbld ldrs* **25/1**

0053 **12** nk **Arctic Feeling (IRE)**[8] 2732 6-8-2 81 oh2 (v[1]) JimmyQuinn 14 66
(Richard Fahey) *s.i.s: sn bhd and nt handle downhill run: rdn and edging lft 2f out: sme hdwy over 1f out: nvr trbld ldrs* **11/1**

-020 **13** 1/2 **Chooseday (IRE)**[21] 2352 5-8-10 89 (p) JamieSpencer 16 72
(Kevin Ryan) *stdd s: hld up off the pce in rr: rdn and stl plenty to do over 1f out: no hdwy: n.d* **25/1**

5010 **14** 1/2 **Pandar**[23] 2283 5-8-1 85 JoeyHaynes(5) 10 66
(Milton Bradley) *wl in tch in midfield: swtchd rt and struggling u.p 2f out: wknd ent fnl f* **16/1**

5-60 **15** hd **Extrasolar**[29] 2110 4-7-12 84 ow2 (t) KieranShoemark(7) 7 65
(Amanda Perrett) *in tch in midfield: effrt u.p and edging lft over 1f out: wknd ins fnl f* **40/1**

1-60 **16** 1 1/4 **Best Trip (IRE)**[23] 2283 7-8-6 88 ow3 RobertTart(3) 17 65
(Brian Ellison) *in tch in midfield: drvn and no hdwy 2f out: wknd ins fnl f* **14/1**

1m 7.5s (-1.90) **Going Correction** -0.10s/f (Good) **16** Ran SP% **125.4**
Speed ratings (Par 109): **108,106,105,104,103 102,101,101,101,98 97,96,96,95,95 93**
CSF £44.04 CT £895.87 TOTE £3.70: £1.60, £3.90, £6.20, £2.50; EX 74.50 Trifecta £1305.60.
**Owner** Advantage Chemicals Holdings Ltd **Bred** Advantage Chemicals Holdings Ltd **Trained** Kinnersley, Worcs

**FOCUS**
Few got into this decent sprint. The winner continued his fine run.
T/Jkpt: £17,750.00 to a £1 stake. Pool: £25,000.00 - 1.00 winning unit T/Plt: £18.20 to a £1 stake. Pool: £389,523.84 - 15,607.72 winning units T/Qpdt: £5.60 to a £1 stake. Pool: £19,873.20 - 2,592.44 winning units SP



The Form Book, Raceform Ltd, Newbury, RG14 5SJ

# [2923]LINGFIELD (L-H)

Saturday, June 7

**OFFICIAL GOING: Turf - good; all-weather - standard**

Wind: Fresh; half-behind Weather: Fine

## 2993 HEART FM 97.5 FM MAIDEN AUCTION STKS 5f

5:55 (5:57) (Class 5) 2-Y-0 £2,726 (£805; £402) Stalls Centre

Form RPR

625 1 **River Spirit**[9] 2692 2-8-6 0 SamHitchcott 5 65
(Mick Channon) *chsd ldrs: swtchd lft over 1f out: rdn to ld ins fnl f: r.o* 10/1[3]

032 2 1 ¾ **Arlecchino's Leap**[18] 2413 2-9-0 0 (v) DaneO'Neill 1 67
(Mark Usher) *disp ld tl wnt on 1/2-way: rdn: hung rt and hdd ins fnl f: styd on same pce* 4/7[1]

3 2 ½ **Ocean Crystal** 2-8-3 0 RyanPowell(3) 6 50+
(John Ryan) *in rr: pushed along hal;fway: n.m.r and r.o ins fnl f: wnt 3rd post: nrst fin* 20/1

4 nk **Icandi** 2-8-7 0 KieranO'Neill 7 50
(Tom Dascombe) *s.i.s: hdwy 1/2-way: rdn over 1f out: styd on same pce* 4/1[2]

60 5 nse **Mister Arden (FR)**[10] 2680 2-8-13 0 TomQueally 4 56
(Harry Dunlop) *disp ld to 1/2-way: rdn over 1f out: nt clr run and hit rails ins fnl f: no ex* 12/1

6 12 **Lady Of Illusion** 2-7-13 0 CharlotteJenner(7) 3 6
(Mark Usher) *plld hrd and prom: lost pl after 1f: wknd 1/2-way* 25/1

58.93s (0.73) **Going Correction** -0.05s/f (Good) 6 Ran SP% **109.0**
Speed ratings (Par 93): **92,89,85,84,84 65**
CSF £15.49 TOTE £5.60: £2.40, £1.10; EX 14.00 Trifecta £96.50.
**Owner** Lord Ilsley Racing (Shrewton Syndicate) **Bred** Darren Hudson-Wood **Trained** West Ilsley, Berks

**FOCUS**
A warm, sunny evening with a fresh breeze, half behind the runners. A total of 5mm of rain fell in the morning and the ground rode as advertised. Two colts against four fillies in a modest maiden auction, and experience proved key. The winner rates a minor best.

## 2994 TBA NEXT GENERATION CLUB FILLIES' H'CAP 5f

6:25 (6:25) (Class 5) (0-70,68) 3-Y-0+ £3,234 (£962; £481; £240) Stalls Centre

Form RPR

-456 1 **Whitecrest**[11] 2637 6-9-11 **68** WilliamTwiston-Davies(3) 10 76
(John Spearing) *mid-div: pushed along and hdwy over 1f out: rdn to ld wl ins fnl f: jst hld on* 7/1[3]

22-2 2 nse **Perfect Muse**[40] 1787 4-9-10 **64** AdamKirby 1 72+
(Clive Cox) *hld up: nt clr run over 1f out: swtchd lft and r.o wl ins fnl f: jst failed* 2/1[1]

350- 3 hd **Monarch Maid**[220] 7623 3-9-1 **62** ChrisCatlin 11 66
(Peter Hiatt) *led: rdn over 1f out: hdd wl ins fnl f* 20/1

13 4 1 ½ **Skinny Love**[32] 2049 3-9-7 **68** (p) AdamBeschizza 6 66
(Zoe Davison) *a.p: rdn over 1f out: styd on same pce ins fnl f* 14/1

0314 5 hd **Dawn Catcher**[18] 2434 4-9-13 **67** GeorgeBaker 9 68
(Geoffrey Deacon) *chsd ldr: shkn up over 1f out: styng on same pce whn hmpd towards fin* 3/1[2]

0045 6 nk **El Mirage (IRE)**[33] 2029 4-9-0 **54** DaneO'Neill 7 54
(Dean Ivory) *hld up: nt clr run over 1f out: r.o: nt trble ldrs* 7/1[3]

0-40 7 3 **Princess Cammie (IRE)**[9] 2689 4-8-6 **49** oh4 (p) RyanPowell(3) 5 38
(John Bridger) *s.i.s: hdwy 1/2-way: rdn over 1f out: wknd ins fnl f* 50/1

0253 8 ½ **Commandingpresence (USA)**[16] 2486 8-9-7 **61** WilliamCarson 2 48
(John Bridger) *mid-div: hdwy 1/2-way: rdn over 1f out: wknd ins fnl f* 7/1[3]

64-0 9 1 **Ellen May**[18] 2442 4-9-1 **55** J-PGuillambert 3 38
(Nick Littmoden) *chsd ldrs: rdn over 1f out: wknd fnl f* 25/1

57.17s (-1.03) **Going Correction** -0.05s/f (Good)
**WFA** 3 from 4yo+ 7lb 9 Ran SP% **113.1**
Speed ratings (Par 100): **106,105,105,103,102 102,97,96,95**
CSF £20.51 CT £267.36 TOTE £9.80: £2.40, £1.20, £3.80; EX 22.40 Trifecta £227.60.
**Owner** G M Eales **Bred** J Spearing And Kate Ive **Trained** Kinnersley, Worcs

**FOCUS**
A modest fillies' sprint in which they spread across the track and a desperately tight finish. The winner is rated in line with her best form from last summer.

## 2995 INVICTA BUILDING SERVICES H'CAP 6f

6:55 (6:55) (Class 4) (0-85,81) 4-Y-0+ £5,854 (£1,742; £870; £435) Stalls Centre

Form RPR

34-1 1 **Daylight**[8] 2718 4-9-4 **81** (t) OisinMurphy(3) 4 90+
(Andrew Balding) *hld up in tch: rdn to ld ins fnl f: r.o* 6/4[1]

205- 2 hd **Tidentime (USA)**[198] 7992 5-9-2 **79** WilliamTwiston-Davies(3) 1 87
(Mick Channon) *hld up: hdwy over 1f out: rdn to chse wnr wl ins fnl f: r.o* 5/1[3]

40-0 3 1 ¼ **Generalyse**[28] 2147 5-9-3 **77** (b) AdamKirby 6 81
(Ben De Haan) *trckd ldr tl rdn to ld over 1f out: hdd ins fnl f: styd on* 8/1

6251 4 2 ½ **Seek The Fair Land**[17] 2469 8-8-5 **70** (b) NathanAlison(5) 7 66
(Lee Carter) *led: rdn and hdd over 1f out: styd on same pce fnl f* 14/1

0042 5 ½ **Naabegha**[8] 2718 7-9-6 **80** (p) PatCosgrave 8 74
(Alan McCabe) *trckd ldrs: plld hrd: rdn over 1f out: styd on same pce fnl f* 7/2[2]

0050 6 4 ½ **Piscean (USA)**[49] 1576 9-9-1 **75** (b) WilliamCarson 2 55
(Tom Keddy) *s.s: hld up: outpcd over 2f out: n.d after* 12/1

1003 7 ¾ **Multitask**[10] 2684 4-8-4 **69** LouisSteward(5) 5 47
(Michael Madgwick) *trckd ldrs: racd keenly: rdn and ev ch over 1f out: hung rt and wknd ins fnl f* 14/1

1m 10.07s (-1.13) **Going Correction** -0.05s/f (Good) 7 Ran SP% **111.0**
Speed ratings (Par 105): **105,104,103,99,99 93,92**
CSF £8.69 CT £41.19 TOTE £2.40: £1.20, £3.40; EX 9.10 Trifecta £32.70.
**Owner** Kennet Valley Thoroughbreds V **Bred** Bearstone Stud And T Herbert Jackson **Trained** Kingsclere, Hants

**FOCUS**
Not particularly competitive and there are some doubts over the form. The winner built on his Brighton run.

## 2996 BUTTERFLIES AND BOWS VENUE DECORATION MAIDEN STKS 7f

7:25 (7:30) (Class 5) 3-Y-0 £2,726 (£805; £402) Stalls Centre

Form RPR

1 **Invincible Fresh (IRE)** 3-9-5 0 FrederikTylicki 8 91
(James Fanshawe) *s.i.s: hdwy over 4f out: shkn up to ld 1f out: r.o wl* 20/1

0 2 3 ¼ **Jailawi (IRE)**[21] 2339 3-9-5 0 MickaelBarzalona 2 82
(Ismail Mohammed) *hld up: pushed along 1/2-way: hdwy over 1f out: r.o: no ch w wnr* 33/1

0-22 3 2 ¾ **Newton's Law (IRE)**[21] 2346 3-9-5 77 (t) PatDobbs 6 75
(Brian Meehan) *led: hdd 1f out: no ex* 7/4[1]

424- 4 nk **Hesbaan (IRE)**[241] 7120 3-9-5 77 DaneO'Neill 5 74
(Marcus Tregoning) *chsd ldrs: rdn over 1f out: styng on same pce whn hmpd ins fnl f* 4/1[3]

0 5 3 ¾ **Roly Tricks**[7] 2780 3-8-11 0 OisinMurphy(3) 4 59
(Olly Stevens) *chsd ldr: rdn over 2f out: ev ch over 1f out: wknd ins fnl f* 14/1

00 6 ¾ **Cobham's Circus (IRE)**[21] 2339 3-9-0 0 KatiaScallan(5) 10 62
(Marcus Tregoning) *hld up: pushed along 1/2-way: swtchd lft over 2f out: wknd over 1f out* 50/1

7 1 ¾ **Blue Army** 3-9-5 0 SilvestreDeSousa 1 57+
(Saeed bin Suroor) *chsd ldrs: rdn over 2f out: edgd lft: ev ch over 1f out: wknd ins fnl f* 3/1[2]

0-4 8 11 **Tolmias (GR)**[18] 2442 3-9-5 0 LemosdeSouza 7 27
(Luca Cumani) *prom: rdn over 2f out: wkng whn hmpd ins fnl f* 16/1

0-5 9 12 **Crafty Exit**[44] 1680 3-9-5 0 AdamKirby 11
(William Knight) *sn pushed along in rr: bhd fnl 4f* 7/1

10 5 **Byronegetonefree** 3-9-5 0 SamHitchcott 3
(John E Long) *s.s: outpcd* 100/1

0 F **No Indication (IRE)**[35] 1959 3-9-5 0 TomQueally 9
(John Butler) *chsd ldrs: rdn and ev ch whn broke down and fell ins fnl f: fatally injured* 66/1

1m 22.0s (-1.30) **Going Correction** -0.05s/f (Good) 11 Ran SP% **118.6**
Speed ratings (Par 99): **105,101,98,97,93 92,90,78,64,58**
CSF £513.29 TOTE £29.50: £7.20, £6.80, £1.10; EX 312.40 Trifecta £948.40.
**Owner** Cheng Wai Tao **Bred** Roundhill Stud **Trained** Newmarket, Suffolk

**FOCUS**
While this did not take a lot of winning, it was an eventful 3yo maiden with No Indication coming to challenge the eventual winner, only to break down inside the final 1f. The form is unconvincing and has been rated modestly.

## 2997 "7TH SHAREN BLAQUIERE CELEBRATE A LIFE" (S) STKS 1m 4f (P)

7:55 (7:56) (Class 6) 3-Y-0 £2,385 (£704; £352) Stalls Low

Form RPR

0-6 1 **Chesil Beach**[26] 2211 3-8-0 0 RobHornby(7) 5 59
(Andrew Balding) *chsd ldr over 10f out tl 1/2-way: remained handy: wnt 2nd again over 2f out: led wl ins fnl f: jst hld on* 8/1[3]

-200 2 hd **Passionate Affair (IRE)**[20] 2363 3-8-12 72 (t) RichardKingscote 4 64
(Tom Dascombe) *hld up in tch: rdn over 1f out: r.o: jst failed* 5/4[1]

000 3 6 **Beauchamp Melba**[9] 2690 3-8-7 28 (p) WilliamCarson 3 49
(Paul Fitzsimons) *led after 1f: rdn over 2f out: hdd and no ex wl ins fnl f* 66/1

-050 4 1 ¼ **Satin Waters**[9] 2694 3-8-7 45 (b) JohnFahy 1 47
(Eve Johnson Houghton) *led 1f: chsd ldrs: wnt 2nd 1/2-way tl rdn over 2f out: no ex fnl f* 25/1

5 4 ½ **Sir Woodgate** 3-8-12 0 JimmyQuinn 6 45
(Edward Creighton) *s.s: hld up: rdn over 3f out: sn outpcd: kpt on towards fin* 33/1

035 6 nk **Moriond (USA)**[56] 1452 3-8-9 60 OisinMurphy(3) 2 44
(David Simcock) *chsd ldrs: rdn over 3f out: wknd over 1f out* 3/1[2]

6626 7 10 **No Refund (IRE)**[40] 1794 3-8-12 64 StevieDonohoe 7 28
(Lee Carter) *s.s: hld up: rdn over 2f out: sn wknd* 3/1[2]

2m 34.4s (1.40) **Going Correction** -0.05s/f (Stan) 7 Ran SP% **113.8**
Speed ratings (Par 97): **93,92,88,88,85 84,78**
CSF £18.46 TOTE £9.50: £2.60, £1.50; EX 25.20 Trifecta £941.40.There was no bid for the winner. No Refund was claimed by Mr Martin Smith for £6,000
**Owner** Kingsclere Racing Club **Bred** Kingsclere Stud **Trained** Kingsclere, Hants

**FOCUS**
The pace was well below standard and the complexion of the race changed in the last 1f. Shaky form.

## 2998 HICKSTEAD DERBY MEETING 25TH-29TH JUNE H'CAP 1m 2f (P)

8:25 (8:29) (Class 5) (0-70,70) 3-Y-0 £3,234 (£962; £481; £240) Stalls Low

Form RPR

-432 1 **Starlit Cantata**[26] 2210 3-9-5 **68** JohnFahy 10 73
(Eve Johnson Houghton) *chsd ldrs: rdn over 1f out: r.o to ld wl ins fnl f* 12/1

00-0 2 ½ **Oyster (IRE)**[18] 2417 3-8-12 **61** J-PGuillambert 7 65
(Nick Littmoden) *pushed along in rr early: hdwy over 4f out: swtchd rt over 1f out: r.o wl* 66/1

00-0 3 hd **Emaad (USA)**[52] 1509 3-9-4 **67** MickaelBarzalona 9 70
(Mark Johnston) *led: rdn clr over 1f out: hdd and unable qck wl ins fnl f* 5/2[1]

0-03 4 hd **Mabdhool (IRE)**[18] 2417 3-9-3 **66** DaneO'Neill 5 69
(Marcus Tregoning) *s.i.s: hdwy 6f out: rdn over 1f out: r.o* 8/1[3]

060- 5 shd **Cape Summit**[187] 8124 3-9-6 **69** AdamKirby 2 72+
(Ed Dunlop) *s.i.s: hld up: rdn and swtchd rt over 1f out: r.o wl ins fnl f: nt rch ldrs* 9/2[2]

3430 6 ½ **Masterpaver**[46] 1635 3-9-3 **69** (v) OisinMurphy(3) 6 71
(Alan Bailey) *mid-div: lost pl over 4f out: hdwy over 1f out: r.o* 8/1[3]

4245 7 2 **All Reddy**[15] 2506 3-9-7 **70** RichardKingscote 13 68
(Tom Dascombe) *chsd ldr 4f: wnt 2nd again 2 out: sn rdn: no ex ins fnl f* 8/1[3]

-140 8 ¾ **Barbary (IRE)**[58] 1403 3-8-12 **61** FrederikTylicki 11 58
(Charlie Fellowes) *hld up: hdwy over 6f out: rdn over 2f out: no ex fnl f* 16/1

4333 9 nk **Needless Shouting (IRE)**[47] 1616 3-9-1 **67** WilliamTwiston-Davies(3) 1 63
(Mick Channon) *prom: lost pl over 7f out: hdwy over 1f out: no ex ins fnl f* 10/1

302 10 1 ¼ **Goleador (USA)**[39] 1858 3-8-8 **62** (p) DanielMuscutt(5) 3 56
(Marco Botti) *chsd ldrs: rdn over 2f out: wknd ins fnl f* 25/1

045- 11 ½ **Ragged Robbin (FR)**[187] 8132 3-9-0 **63** (t) JimmyQuinn 14 56
(David Lanigan) *hld up: rdn over 1f out: nvr on terms* 20/1

046 12 ½ **Saalib (USA)**[21] 2346 3-9-7 **70** (t) PatCosgrave 4 62
(Brian Meehan) *hld up: rdn over 2f out: wknd over 1f out* 25/1

3336 13 shd **Power Up**[15] 2523 3-9-4 **67** SilvestreDeSousa 8 59
(Mark Johnston) *prom: chsd ldr 6f out tl rdn 2f out: wknd and eased fnl f* 14/1

2m 5.27s (-1.33) **Going Correction** -0.05s/f (Stan) 13 Ran SP% **123.4**
Speed ratings (Par 99): **103,102,102,102,102 101,100,99,99,98 97,97,97**
CSF £669.15 CT £2615.97 TOTE £9.90: £2.40, £10.20, £2.20; EX 1084.20 TRIFECTA Not won..
**Owner** Mrs Heather Raw **Bred** Heather Raw **Trained** Blewbury, Oxon

**FOCUS**
The pace was fair for this modest but competitive handicap. The winner built on recent form.

**2999** **BURRIDGE.CO.UK AMATEUR RIDERS' H'CAP** **1m 2f (P)**
() (Class 6) (0-60,) 4-Y-O+ £

T/Plt: £8.80 to a £1 stake. Pool: £55,197.57 - 4,559.93 winning units T/Qpdt: £5.80 to a £1 stake. Pool: £7,645.37 - 966.90 winning units CR

# 2512 MUSSELBURGH (R-H)
Saturday, June 7

**OFFICIAL GOING: Good (good to soft in places; 7.7) changing to soft after race 5 (4.30)**
Wind: Fresh across Weather: Cloudy; rain after 3rd

**3000** **BET TOTEPLACEPOT H'CAP** **7f 30y**
**1:50** (1:52) (Class 5) (0-70,73) 4-Y-O+ **£5,175** (£1,540; £769; £384) **Stalls** Low

Form RPR
41-2 **1** **Cara's Request (AUS)**[28] 2171 9-8-12 **64**.............. ConnorBeasley(3) 9 79
(Michael Dods) *mde all: clr 4f out: rdn over 2f out: kpt on wl* **5/2**[1]
0432 **2** *5* **Hellbender (IRE)**[16] 2479 8-8-2 **51**.............................. DuranFentiman 5 53
(Shaun Harris) *in tch in 3rd: rdn over 3f out: wnt 2nd over 1f out: one pce and no threat wnr* **11/1**
0201 **3** *1 1/4* **Mowhoob**[15] 2516 4-9-4 **67**................................................ GrahamLee 6 66
(Jim Goldie) *chsd ldr: rdn over 2f out: lost 2nd over 1f out: no ex fnl f* **8/1**
121- **4** *1 1/2* **Big Storm Coming**[200] 7953 4-8-13 **69**.................. MeganCarberry(7) 1 64
(Brian Ellison) *midfield on inner: rdn over 3f out: one pce and nvr threatened* **5/1**[3]
6016 **5** *shd* **Imperator Augustus (IRE)**[12] 2605 6-8-9 **65**.............[1] JackGarritty(7) 7 60
(Patrick Holmes) *s.i.s: hld up: bhd tl kpt on fnl f* **7/1**
44-5 **6** *1 1/2* **Orpsie Boy (IRE)**[28] 2171 11-8-11 **63**.............................. JasonHart(3) 10 54
(Ruth Carr) *dwlt: hld up: rdn over 3f out: nvr threatened* **22/1**
45-0 **7** *2 1/4* **Fabled City (USA)**[22] 2296 5-9-0 **63**................................(t) TomEaves 2 48
(Keith Dalgleish) *midfield: rdn over 3f out: wknd fnl f* **17/2**
0611 **8** *3 1/4* **Lady Artiste (IRE)**[12] 2604 4-9-10 **73**................................ BenCurtis 3 49
(Alan Swinbank) *dwlt: racd keenly hld up: rdn over 3f out: sn btn* **7/2**[2]
6551 **9** *13* **Absolute Bearing (IRE)**[11] 2658 5-8-2 **51** oh2............ JamesSullivan 4
(Tim Etherington) *dwlt: hld up in rr: a wl bhd* **22/1**

1m 28.01s (-0.99) **Going Correction** -0.025s/f (Good) **9** Ran **SP% 118.6**
Speed ratings (Par 103): **104,98,96,95,95 93,90,87,72**
CSF £32.59 CT £191.82 TOTE £3.30: £1.50, £2.80, £2.50; EX 28.20 Trifecta £130.10.
**Owner** Denton Hall Racing Ltd **Bred** S Aitken **Trained** Denton, Co Durham

**FOCUS**
Home and back straight at widest position and all distances as advertised. The track had escaped any pre-racing rain and the going was on the dead side of good. The first four were always prominent, with the winner dominating. The form is rated around the second.

**3001** **TOTEPOOL EBF STALLIONS.COM EDINBURGH CASTLE STKS CONDITIONS (BOBIS RACE)** **5f**
**2:20** (2:21) (Class 2) 2-Y-O
**£15,562** (£4,660; £2,330; £1,165; £582; £292) **Stalls** High

Form RPR
610 **1** **Ko Cache (IRE)**[22] 2313 2-8-10 **0**.......................................... TomEaves 1 85
(Keith Dalgleish) *wnt rt s: prom on outer: rdn 1/2-way: kpt on to ld towards fin* **33/1**
15 **2** *nk* **Don't Tell Annie**[22] 2313 2-8-10 **0**.................................. DavidAllan 4 84
(Tim Easterby) *w ldr: led 1/2-way: rdn 2f out: kpt on: hdd towards fin* **11/4**[2]
512 **3** *1* **Vimy Ridge**[14] 2543 2-8-12 **0**.......................................... TonyHamilton 6 82+
(Richard Fahey) *trckd ldrs: n.m.r over 1f out tl ins fnl f: kpt on* **3/1**[3]
41 **4** *1 3/4* **Prince Bonnaire**[12] 2615 2-8-12 **0**...................................... GrahamLee 3 76+
(David Brown) *chsd ldrs: rdn over 1f out: hmpd whn trying to squeeze through v narrow gap between ldng pair ins fnl f: one pce after* **5/2**[1]
51 **5** *3* **Mignolino (IRE)**[24] 2258 2-9-1 **0**................................ GrahamGibbons 2 68
(David Barron) *dwlt: hld up: pushed along 1/2-way: nvr threatened: eased fnl 50yds* **7/2**
1 **6** *2* **Diamond Creek (IRE)**[14] 2541 2-8-7 **0**......................... PatrickMathers 5 60
(Richard Fahey) *racd keenly: hdd 1/2-way: sn rdn: lost pl and looked btn whn hmpd ins fnl f: eased* **8/1**

59.33s (-1.07) **Going Correction** -0.225s/f (Firm) **6** Ran **SP% 116.5**
Speed ratings (Par 99): **99,98,96,94,89 86**
CSF £126.12 TOTE £20.80: £9.80, £2.60; EX 153.20 Trifecta £749.20.
**Owner** Straightline Construction Ltd **Bred** Tally-Ho Stud **Trained** Carluke, S Lanarks
■ Stewards' Enquiry : Tom Eaves caution: careless riding.

**FOCUS**
A Class 2 juvenile event that has given Royal Ascot pointers in the past, but this looked a fairly ordinary renewal. All six runners were previous winners but the outcome was hard to predict and it was quite messy.

**3002** **BET TOTEQUADPOT H'CAP (BOBIS RACE)** **1m**
**2:55** (2:56) (Class 4) (0-85,82) 3-Y-O **£8,086** (£2,406; £1,202; £601) **Stalls** Low

Form RPR
5-60 **1** **Ifwecan**[22] 2295 3-9-6 **81**............................................ FrannyNorton 2 94
(Mark Johnston) *mde all: t.k.h early: rdn over 2f out: kpt on wl to draw clr fnl f* **16/1**
-004 **2** *5* **King Of Macedon (IRE)**[8] 2734 3-9-3 **78**............................ JoeFanning 1 79
(Mark Johnston) *trckd ldr: rdn over 2f out: kpt on one pce: wnt 2nd towards fin* **8/1**
-521 **3** *1/2* **Twin Appeal (IRE)**[15] 2517 3-8-12 **73**........................ GrahamGibbons 6 73
(David Barron) *trckd ldrs: rdn over 2f out: chsd ldr over 1f out: edgd lft ins fnl f: no ex and lost 2nd towards fin* **9/4**[1]
1-34 **4** *1 3/4* **Finn Class (IRE)**[21] 2333 3-9-7 **82**................................. PJMcDonald 4 78
(Michael Bell) *hld up: rdn and hdwy over 2f out: one pce fr over 1f out* **11/4**[2]
3324 **5** *2 1/4* **Beautiful Stranger (IRE)**[5] 2828 3-8-9 **70**.....................(p) TomEaves 3 61
(Keith Dalgleish) *midfield: rdn and hdwy on outer over 2f out: wknd ins fnl f* **10/1**
213 **6** *2 1/4* **Lord Of The Nile (IRE)**[20] 2363 3-9-1 **79**....................... SamJames(3) 5 64
(David O'Meara) *trckd ldr: moved up to press ldr over 3f out: drvn over 2f out: wknd over 1f out* **10/3**[3]
340- **7** *9* **The Grumpy Gnome (IRE)**[212] 7782 3-8-5 **66**........(p) PatrickMathers 8 31
(Richard Fahey) *s.i.s: hld up: nvr threatened* **20/1**
601- **8** *7* **Giant Samurai (USA)**[204] 7902 3-9-0 **75**.............................. PhillipMakin 7 24
(John Quinn) *hld up: rdn over 3f out: sn wknd* **25/1**

1m 39.37s (-1.83) **Going Correction** -0.025s/f (Good) **8** Ran **SP% 115.2**
Speed ratings (Par 101): **108,103,102,100,98 96,87,80**
CSF £136.45 CT £406.42 TOTE £18.40: £4.90, £2.80, £1.10; EX 56.90 Trifecta £364.80.
**Owner** Douglas Livingston **Bred** P T Tellwright **Trained** Middleham Moor, N Yorks

**FOCUS**
What looked a competitive and open 3yo handicap was turned into a procession. The winner was still not back to his 2yo best.

**3003** **TOTESCOOP6 EDINBURGH CUP H'CAP STKS (BOBIS RACE)** **1m 4f 100y**
**3:30** (3:30) (Class 3) (0-95,90) 3-Y-O
**£37,350** (£11,184; £5,592; £2,796; £1,398; £702) **Stalls** Centre

Form RPR
632 **1** **Hesketh Bank**[22] 2292 3-8-7 **76**.............................. PJMcDonald 1 87
(Richard Fahey) *trckd ldr: rdn over 2f out: wandered u.p fnl f: kpt on to ld towards fin* **33/1**
2-16 **2** *nk* **Master Of Finance (IRE)**[21] 2337 3-9-0 **83**.................. JoeFanning 3 94
(Mark Johnston) *led: rdn over 2f out: kpt on: hdd towards fin* **8/1**
-415 **3** *3* **Innocent Touch (IRE)**[22] 2319 3-8-1 **70**.............. PatrickMathers 9 76+
(Richard Fahey) *dwlt: sn midfield: rdn and hdwy on outer over 2f out: kpt on: wnt 3rd ins fnl f* **16/1**
-001 **4** *2* **Full Day**[33] 2018 3-8-2 **71**............................................ JamesSullivan 4 74
(Brian Ellison) *in tch: rdn over 3f out: one pce* **40/1**
33-1 **5** *1 3/4* **Blue Atlantic (USA)**[52] 1508 3-8-8 **77**......................... FrannyNorton 7 77
(Mark Johnston) *racd keenly: trckd ldr: rdn over 2f out: carried appr fnl f: wknd ins fnl f* **20/1**
3-22 **6** *nk* **Mr Gallivanter (IRE)**[38] 1883 3-8-13 **82**............................ PhillipMakin 2 82
(John Quinn) *midfield: rdn over 3f out: one pce and nvr threatened* **9/1**
2-12 **7** *nk* **Alex My Boy (IRE)**[21] 2347 3-9-4 **87**................................. GrahamLee 13 86+
(Mark Johnston) *hld up: wnt a little in snatches: rdn over 3f out: drvn and stl last over 2f out: kpt on fnl f* **7/2**[1]
112 **8** *1 1/4* **Libran (IRE)**[12] 2617 3-9-2 **85**.......................................... BenCurtis 11 82+
(Alan Swinbank) *s.i.s: hld up in rr: rdn over 3f out: nvr threatened* **7/1**
-431 **9** *nse* **Notarised**[15] 2530 3-8-13 **82**...................................... RussKennemore 10 79
(Mark Johnston) *in tch: rdn over 3f out: wknd ins fnl f* **8/1**
12-0 **10** *2 1/4* **Trip To Paris (IRE)**[45] 1652 3-9-5 **88**.............................(b) SebSanders 14 82
(Ed Dunlop) *hld up towards outer: rdn over 3f out: nvr threatened* **20/1**
3103 **11** *5* **Swivel**[31] 2077 3-9-4 **90**................................... MichaelJMMurphy(3) 12 76
(Mark Johnston) *hld up in midfield: rdn over 3f out: sn wknd* **20/1**
-125 **12** *1 1/2* **Collaboration**[21] 2337 3-8-6 **82**...................................(t) JackGarritty(7) 6 66
(Andrew Balding) *in tch: rdn over 3f out: sn wknd* **6/1**[3]
1-23 **13** *4* **Latin Charm (IRE)**[22] 2319 3-8-8 **77**..................................(p) PaoloSirigu 5 54
(Marco Botti) *hld up: rdn over 3f out: a bhd* **4/1**[2]

2m 44.4s (2.40) **Going Correction** +0.275s/f (Good) **13** Ran **SP% 126.8**
Speed ratings (Par 103): **103,102,100,99,98 98,97,97,95 92,91,88**
CSF £278.72 CT £4411.62 TOTE £36.20: £9.60, £3.80, £6.20; EX 755.90 Trifecta £1963.70 Part won..
**Owner** David W Armstrong **Bred** Glebe Stud And Partners **Trained** Musley Bank, N Yorks

**FOCUS**
The rain had arrived ahead of this valuable and fiercely competitive 3yo handicap, The first two were in the first three throughout. The winner is progressing well.

**3004** **BET TOTEEXACTA H'CAP** **1m 4f 100y**
**4:30** (4:30) (Class 4) (0-80,79) 4-Y-O+ **£8,086** (£2,406; £1,202; £601) **Stalls** Centre

Form RPR
10-0 **1** **Dance King**[51] 1539 4-9-1 **73**............................................ DavidAllan 7 82
(Tim Easterby) *mde all: rdn and pressed over 2f out: kpt on and a in command fnl f* **20/1**
56-2 **2** *1 1/4* **Northside Prince (IRE)**[10] 2678 8-8-9 **67**............................ BenCurtis 4 73
(Alan Swinbank) *hld up: rdn and hdwy on outer over 2f out: kpt on fnl f: wnt 2nd post* **5/1**
3-03 **3** *shd* **Corton Lad**[26] 2216 4-8-11 **72**......................................(tp) JasonHart(3) 8 78
(Keith Dalgleish) *prom: rdn over 3f out: pressed ldr fr over 2f out: wandered and a hld ins fnl f: lost 2nd post* **9/2**[3]
-132 **4** *1 3/4* **Ever Fortune (USA)**[14] 2547 5-8-9 **72**.................. SammyJoBell(5) 1 75
(Brian Ellison) *midfield: rdn over 3f out: plugged on* **7/2**[2]
6400 **5** *2 3/4* **Aryal**[34] 1971 4-9-5 **77**...........................................(b) FrannyNorton 5 76
(Mark Johnston) *trckd ldrs: rdn over 3f out: wknd over 1f out* **11/1**
0-51 **6** *13* **Love Marmalade (IRE)**[26] 2216 4-9-7 **79**......................... PJMcDonald 2 58
(Alistair Whillans) *hld up: rdn over 3f out: wknd fnl 2f* **11/4**[1]
022- **7** *12* **Hero's Story**[228] 7434 4-7-9 **60** oh1................................ JackGarritty(7) 3 20
(Jim Goldie) *hld up: rdn over 3f out: sn wknd* **12/1**
01-0 **8** *11* **Ultimate**[29] 2119 8-8-11 **76**....................................... MeganCarberry(7) 6 19
(Brian Ellison) *prom: rdn over 5f out: sn wknd* **8/1**

2m 47.69s (5.69) **Going Correction** +0.45s/f (Yiel) **8** Ran **SP% 115.6**
Speed ratings (Par 105): **99,98,98,96,95 86,78,71**
CSF £117.57 CT £540.22 TOTE £11.20: £3.80, £2.30, £1.40; EX 98.80 Trifecta £312.40.
**Owner** Ambrose Turnbull **Bred** Meon Valley Stud **Trained** Great Habton, N Yorks

**FOCUS**
The rain continued to fall and the time suggested the ground had eased. A modest handicap with another front-running winner. The form is rated around the second and third.

**3005** **TOTEPOOL SUPPORTING THE SPORT YOU LOVE H'CAP** **1m 1f**
**5:05** (5:05) (Class 4) (0-80,80) 4-Y-O+ **£8,086** (£2,406; £1,202; £601) **Stalls** Low

Form RPR
-043 **1** **Bartack (IRE)**[12] 2603 4-9-4 **80**......................................(v) SamJames(3) 3 90
(David O'Meara) *led: hdd 6f out: racd in clr 2nd: led again over 1f out: rdn and kpt on* **10/3**[2]
0110 **2** *3* **Eutropius (IRE)**[21] 2351 5-9-6 **79**........................................ BenCurtis 2 82
(Alan Swinbank) *hld up in 3rd: rdn to chse clr ldng pair over 3f out: kpt on to go 2nd ins fnl f: no ch of rching wnr* **1/1**[1]
0000 **3** *3 3/4* **Staffhoss**[12] 2607 4-8-3 **62**............................................ FrannyNorton 7 57
(Mark Johnston) *hld up: rdn over 3f out: plugged on: wnt 3rd post* **9/1**
0600 **4** *shd* **Hard Core Debt**[11] 2653 4-7-13 **65**...............................(p) JoeDoyle(7) 6 60
(Brian Ellison) *slowly away: racd keenly and plld way to front over 6f out: rdn whn hdd over 1f out: wknd and lost 2 more pls ins fnl f* **16/1**
4201 **5** *8* **Push Me (IRE)**[10] 2676 7-8-11 **70**........................................ GrahamLee 4 47
(Iain Jardine) *hld up: rdn over 3f out: sn btn* **11/2**[3]
0254 **6** *2 3/4* **Spavento (IRE)**[5] 2826 8-8-7 **69**.................................. JasonHart(3) 5 40
(Eric Alston) *hld up: rdn over 3f out: sn btn* **17/2**

1m 56.61s (2.71) **Going Correction** +0.45s/f (Yiel) **6** Ran **SP% 114.9**
Speed ratings (Par 105): **105,102,99,98,91 89**
CSF £7.33 TOTE £3.90: £3.30, £1.20; EX 9.40 Trifecta £60.70.
**Owner** Ebor Racing Club III **Bred** Alberto Panetta **Trained** Nawton, N Yorks

**FOCUS**
After persistent rain the ground was changed to soft ahead of this quite valuable but modest handicap. The two pacesetters turned for home with a clear advantage. The winner might have improved but it's hard to be confident.

## 3006 BET TOTETRIFECTA H'CAP — 5f
5:40 (5:41) (Class 4) (0-85,85) 4-Y-0+ £8,086 (£2,406; £1,202; £601) Stalls High

| Form | | | | RPR |
|---|---|---|---|---|
| -244 | 1 | | **Rothesay Chancer**[17] 2456 6-8-9 **73** ow1 GrahamLee 1 (Jim Goldie) *hld up: rdn and hdwy 1/2-way: r.o to ld 110yds out: jst hld on* **10/3**[1] | 81 |
| 4-03 | 2 | nse | **Gowanharry (IRE)**[17] 2456 5-8-8 **75** (tp) ConnorBeasley(3) 7 (Michael Dods) *chsd ldng pair: rdn 1/2-way: carried rt and sltly short of room bef squeezing through gap 110yds out: kpt on jst failed* **7/2**[2] | 84+ |
| 340- | 3 | nk | **Lexington Place**[260] 6583 4-9-0 **81** SamJames(3) 3 (David O'Meara) *chsd ldng pair: rdn 2f out: led 1f out: drvn and edgd rt ins fnl f: hdd 110yds out: kpt on* **10/1** | 88 |
| 0051 | 4 | 1 | **Go Go Green (IRE)**[8] 2732 8-8-4 **73** SammyJoBell(5) 8 (Jim Goldie) *s.i.s: hld up: pushed along 1/2-way: hdwy over 1f out: kpt on fnl f* **7/1** | 76 |
| 26-5 | 5 | nk | **Jofranka**[39] 1850 4-8-12 **76** GrahamGibbons 5 (David Barron) *midfield: rdn 2f out: n.m.r jst ins fnl f: keeping on in cl 4th whn hmpd 110yds out: nt rcvr* **15/2** | 80 |
| 0-30 | 6 | 1 | **Jumbo Steps (IRE)**[10] 2677 7-7-13 **70** JackGarritty(7) 9 (Jim Goldie) *hld up: rdn 1/2-way: kpt on fnl f: nvr threatened* **8/1** | 69 |
| 2106 | 7 | 2 ½ | **Red Baron (IRE)**[31] 2074 5-9-4 **85** NeilFarley(3) 4 (Eric Alston) *led narrowly: rdn 1/2-way: hdd 1f out: wknd* **5/1**[3] | 75 |
| 0-00 | 8 | 1 ¼ | **Captain Dunne (IRE)**[35] 1961 9-8-8 **72** DavidAllan 6 (Tim Easterby) *w ldr: rdn 1/2-way: wknd fnl f* **16/1** | 57 |
| 0-60 | 9 | 3 | **The Nifty Fox**[12] 2606 10-8-2 **66** oh1 (p) PaulQuinn 2 (Tim Easterby) *dwlt: hld up: a towards rr* **12/1** | 40 |

1m 1.69s (1.29) **Going Correction** +0.425s/f (Yiel) **9 Ran SP% 120.0**
Speed ratings (Par 105): **106,105,105,103,103 101,97,95,90**
CSF £15.90 CT £108.32 TOTE £4.00: £1.90, £2.20, £2.90; EX 16.80 Trifecta £225.20.
**Owner** The McMaster Springford Partnership **Bred** Mrs S R Kennedy **Trained** Uplawmoor, E Renfrews

**FOCUS**
A tight finish to this competitive sprint handicap where racing room was at a premium in the closing stages. The winner's best run since winning this last year.
T/Plt: £640.10 to a £1 stake. Pool: £65,581.44 - 74.79 winning units T/Qpdt: £104.90 to a £1 stake. Pool: £3,785.31 - 26.70 winning units AS

# 2736 NEWCASTLE (L-H)
Saturday, June 7

**3007 Meeting Abandoned -** Heavy rain left areas of unsafe ground
Wind: Almost nil Weather: Overcast, heavy rain

# 2228 BELMONT PARK (L-H)
Saturday, June 7

**OFFICIAL GOING: Dirt: fast; turf: firm**

## 3025a KNOB CREEK MANHATTAN STKS (GRADE 1) (4YO+) (TURF) — 1m 2f (T)
10:45 (12:00) 4-Y-0+
£322,289 (£111,445; £60,240; £39,156; £24,096; £18,072)

| | | | RPR |
|---|---|---|---|
| 1 | | **Real Solution (USA)**[27] 2228 5-8-10 0 JJCastellano 8 (Chad C Brown, U.S.A) **11/2** | 116 |
| 2 | 1 ¼ | **Kaigun (CAN)**[35] 1963 4-8-2 0 AGarcia 9 (Mark Casse, Canada) **164/10** | 106 |
| 3 | 1 | **Seek Again (USA)**[35] 1963 4-8-6 0 JRosario 6 (William Mott, U.S.A) | 108 |
| 4 | nk | **Grandeur (IRE)**[27] 2228 5-8-10 0 GaryStevens 4 (Jeremy Noseda) **39/10**[2] | 111+ |
| 5 | ½ | **Five Iron (USA)**[35] 4-8-6 0 LSaez 7 (Brian A Lynch, Canada) **161/10** | 106 |
| 6 | 1 ¾ | **Imagining (USA)**[27] 2228 6-8-10 0 (b) JRVelazquez 1 (Claude McGaughey III, U.S.A) **51/10**[3] | 106 |
| 7 | ½ | **Boisterous (USA)**[35] 1963 7-8-10 0 CNakatani 5 (Todd Pletcher, U.S.A) **147/10** | 105 |
| 8 | 1 | **Rookie Sensation (USA)**[42] 4-8-4 0 (b) MESmith 3 (John Shirreffs, U.S.A) **74/10** | 97 |
| 9 | 6 ½ | **Hey Leroy (USA)**[21] 4-8-5 0 ow1 ASolis 2 (Manuel J Azpurua, U.S.A) **166/10** | 85 |
| 10 | hd | **Chamois (USA)**[21] 4-8-3 0 ow1 (b) JBravo 10 (Christophe Clement, U.S.A) **28/1** | 83 |

(Seek Again SP: **5/2**[1])

1m 59.27s (-2.02) **10 Ran SP% 119.8**
PARI-MUTUEL (all including 2 usd stake): WIN 13.00; PLACE (1-2) 6.80, 14.20; SHOW (1-2-3) 4.30, 8.20, 3.40; SF 186.00.
**Owner** Kenneth L & Sarah K Ramsey **Bred** Kenneth L Ramsey & Sarah K Ramsey **Trained** USA

## 3026a BELMONT STKS (GRADE 1) (3YO) (DIRT) — 1m 4f (D)
11:52 (12:00) 3-Y-0
£481,927 (£168,674; £90,361; £48,192; £48,192; £27,108)

| | | | RPR |
|---|---|---|---|
| 1 | | **Tonalist (USA)**[28] 3-9-0 0 (b) JRosario 11 (Christophe Clement, U.S.A) **92/10** | 119 |
| 2 | hd | **Commissioner (USA)**[28] 3-9-0 0 (b) JJCastellano 8 (Todd Pletcher, U.S.A) **28/1** | 119 |
| 3 | 1 | **Medal Count (USA)**[35] 1964 3-9-0 0 RAlbarado 1 (Dale Romans, U.S.A) **248/10** | 117 |
| 4 | ¾ | **California Chrome (USA)**[21] 2357 3-9-0 0 (b) VictorEspinoza 2 (Art Sherman, U.S.A) **17/20**[1] | 116 |
| 4 | dht | **Wicked Strong (USA)**[35] 1964 3-9-0 0 RMaragh 9 (James Jerkens, U.S.A) **53/10**[2] | 116 |
| 6 | 2 ¼ | **Samraat (USA)**[35] 1964 3-9-0 0 JLOrtiz 7 (Richard Violette Jr, U.S.A) **195/10** | 112 |
| 7 | 1 ¼ | **General A Rod (USA)**[21] 2357 3-9-0 0 (b) RosieNapravnik 10 (Michael J Maker, U.S.A) **34/1** | 110 |
| 8 | 4 ¾ | **Matterhorn (USA)**[28] 3-9-0 0 (b) JBravo 3 (Todd Pletcher, U.S.A) **41/1** | 103 |
| 9 | 2 ¾ | **Commanding Curve (USA)**[35] 1964 3-9-0 0 SXBridgmohan 4 (Dallas Stewart, U.S.A) **89/10** | 98 |
| 10 | dist | **Matuszak (USA)**[49] 3-9-0 0 (b) MESmith 6 (William Mott, U.S.A) **35/1** | |
| 11 | dist | **Ride On Curlin (USA)**[21] 2357 3-9-0 0 JRVelazquez 5 (William Gowan, U.S.A) **83/10**[3] | |

2m 28.52s (-0.44) **11 Ran SP% 120.8**
PARI-MUTUEL (all including 2 usd stake): WIN 20.40; PLACE (1-2) 9.60, 23.20; SHOW (1-2-3) 7.00, 13.20, 13.20; SF 348.00.
**Owner** Robert S Evans **Bred** Woodslane Farm **Trained** USA

**FOCUS**
California Chrome failed in his bid to become the first Triple Crown winner since Affirmed in 1978. The form is rated towards the bottom end of the race averages.

# 2816 CHANTILLY (R-H)
Saturday, June 7

**OFFICIAL GOING: Turf: good; polytrack: standard**

## 3027a PRIX LA FLECHE (LISTED RACE) (2YO) (TURF) — 5f
5:30 (12:00) 2-Y-0 £22,916 (£9,166; £6,875; £4,583; £2,291)

| | | | RPR |
|---|---|---|---|
| 1 | | **El Suizo (FR)**[25] 2-9-2 0 FabriceVeron 5 (H-A Pantall, France) **4/5**[1] | 101 |
| 2 | nk | **Jane's Memory (IRE)**[12] 2612 2-8-13 0 MartinDwyer 1 (Rae Guest) *t.k.h: hld up in midfield: rdn to chse ldrs over 1 1/2f: led appr fnl f: sn pressed by eventual wnr: r.o u.str.p: hdd cl home: no ex* **124/10** | 97 |
| 3 | 2 | **Preciously (FR)**[38] 2-8-13 0 ChristopheSoumillon 3 (D Guillemin, France) **27/10**[2] | 90 |
| 4 | 1 ¼ | **Dikta Del Mar (SPA)**[37] 2-8-13 0 BFayosMartin 4 (T Martins, Spain) **176/10** | 85 |
| 5 | 1 ¼ | **Lostinparadise**[9] 2-8-13 0 OlivierPeslier 6 (Matthieu Palussiere, France) **27/1** | 81 |
| 6 | ½ | **Pierre Precieuse (FR)**[22] 2-8-13 0 SebastienMaillot 2 (E Caroux, France) **233/10** | 79 |
| 7 | 1 | **Country Gorl (FR)**[22] 2-8-13 0 GregoryBenoist 7 (P Sogorb, France) **114/10**[3] | 77+ |
| 8 | snk | **Lifeisforliving (FR)**[38] 2-8-13 0 AntoineHamelin 8 (Matthieu Palussiere, France) **204/10** | 75 |
| 9 | 3 | **Hesat (FR)**[25] 2-8-13 0 (p) Christophe-PatriceLemaire 9 (M Boutin, France) **173/10** | 64 |

58.23s (-0.07) **9 Ran SP% 121.3**
WIN (incl. 1 euro stake): 1.80. PLACES: 1.10, 1.60, 1.20. DF: 9.70. SF: 12.20.
**Owner** Peter Rechsteiner **Bred** P Rechsteiner **Trained** France

## 3028a PRIX PAUL DE MOUSSAC (GROUP 3) (3YO COLTS & GELDINGS) (TURF) — 1m
6:00 (12:00) 3-Y-0 £33,333 (£13,333; £10,000; £6,666; £3,333)

| | | | RPR |
|---|---|---|---|
| 1 | | **Charm Spirit (IRE)**[35] 1951 3-8-13 0 OlivierPeslier 5 (F Head, France) *mde all: pushed along and qcknd 2f out: rdn and 2 l clr ent fnl f: kpt on: diminishing advantage towards fin but in control: cosily* **7/10**[1] | 114 |
| 2 | ¾ | **Salai (FR)**[27] 2196 3-8-10 0 ChristopheSoumillon 2 (J-C Rouget, France) *dwlt sltly: hld up in tch: rdn and bmpd rival over 1f out: wnt 2nd ent fnl f: kpt on and clsng on wnr towards fin but a hld* **41/10**[2] | 110+ |
| 3 | ¾ | **Army Bulletin (IRE)**[25] 2242 3-8-10 0 MaximeGuyon 1 (A Fabre, France) *t.k.h: hld up in tch: last 1/2-way: pushed along 2f out: rdn ent fnl f and sn wnt 3rd: kpt on and clsng at fin but nvr able to chal* **43/10**[3] | 108+ |
| 4 | 3 | **Chameur (FR)**[19] 2412 3-8-10 0 AlexisBadel 4 (Mme M Bollack-Badel, France) *trckd ldr on outer: pushed along and effrt to chal 2f out: sn outpcd by wnr: bmpd over 1f out and lost 2nd ent fnl f: no ex and fdd* **68/10** | 101 |
| 5 | 5 | **Abendwind (GER)**[27] 3-8-10 0 UmbertoRispoli 3 (Waldemar Hickst, Germany) *trckd ldr on inner: pushed along 2f out: rdn and outpcd over 1f out: last and btn ent fnl f: eased* **74/10** | 90 |

1m 35.82s (-2.18) **5 Ran SP% 122.0**
WIN (incl. 1 euro stake): 1.70. PLACES: 1.20, 1.80. SF: 5.30.
**Owner** H H Sheikh Abdulla Bin Khalifa Al Thani **Bred** Ecurie Des Monceaux **Trained** France

## 3029a PRIX DU BOIS BOURDON (PRIX GROUPE CPN) (CLAIMER) (2YO) (TURF) — 6f
6:30 (12:00) 2-Y-0 £11,250 (£4,500; £3,375; £2,250; £1,125)

| | | | RPR |
|---|---|---|---|
| 1 | | **Cornwallville (IRE)**[8] 2755 2-8-11 0 IoritzMendizabal 4 (J S Moore) *t.k.h: restrained bhd ldng trio: rdn to chal 1f out: r.o u.p fnl f: led cl home* **19/5**[3] | 72 |
| 2 | hd | **Seradora (FR)**[59] 1402 2-8-8 0 CristianDemuro 7 (E J O'Neill, France) **93/10** | 68 |
| 3 | snk | **Oui Monsieur (FR)**[21] 2-9-4 0 (p) AurelienLemaitre 3 (Robert Collet, France) **164/10** | 78 |
| 4 | ½ | **Bowmore (SPA)**[46] 2-8-11 0 ThierryJarnet 2 (J Heloury, France) **37/10**[2] | 69 |
| 5 | 2 | **Belle Du Jour (FR)**[8] 2-8-11 0 Christophe-PatriceLemaire 1 (M Boutin, France) **5/2**[1] | 63 |
| 6 | snk | **Little Mask (FR)**[8] 2-8-13 0 AntoineHamelin 6 (M Boutin, France) **19/5**[3] | 65 |
| 7 | hd | **Qoosine (FR)**[18] 2-9-1 0 StephanePasquier 8 (Rod Collet, France) **134/10** | 66 |
| 8 | 5 | **Prince D'Aumone (FR)**[21] 2-8-7 0 NathanKasztelan(8) 9 (S Jesus, France) **57/1** | 51 |
| 9 | 6 | **Kroaz (FR)** 2-8-8 0 EddyHardouin 5 (J Heloury, France) **27/1** | 26 |

1m 12.63s (1.23) **9 Ran SP% 119.2**
WIN (incl. 1 euro stake): 4.80. PLACES: 2.20, 3.00, 4.40. DF: 17.10. SF: 36.60.
**Owner** J S Moore & Partner **Bred** Corrin Stud & Blackwater Bloodstock Ltd **Trained** Upper Lambourn, Berks

## 3030a PRIX HAMPTON (LISTED RACE) (3YO+) (TURF) 5f
**7:00** (12:00) 3-Y-O+ **£21,666** (£8,666; £6,500; £4,333; £2,166)

RPR

1 **Son Cesio (FR)**[26] 2226 3-8-9 0 ........ FabriceVeron 2 98
(H-A Pantall, France) **7/5**[1]

2 *snk* **Mirza**[14] 2563 7-9-8 0 ........ (p) MartinDwyer 8 106
(Rae Guest) *hld up in tch on outer: led 1 1/2f out: sn rdn and hdd ent fnl f: rallied gamely and had jst regained ld whn ct by wnr fnl strides* **11/2**[3]

3 *shd* **Quirinus**[10] 7-9-2 0 ........ Christophe-PatriceLemaire 9 100
(M Boutin, France) **73/10**

4 *1 3/4* **Bajan Tryst (USA)**[33] 8-9-2 0 ........ UmbertoRispoli 4 94
(J-V Toux, France) **43/5**

5 *1* **Abu Sidra (FR)**[91] 898 5-9-2 0 ........ ChristopheSoumillon 1 90
(J-F Bernard, France) **13/5**[2]

6 *snk* **So Long Malpic (FR)**[118] 7-9-2 0 ........ OlivierPeslier 5 90
(T Lemer, France) **179/10**

7 *2* **Victory Laurel (IRE)**[265] 6445 4-9-2 0 ........ (p) ThierryThulliez 3 82
(Robert Cowell) *led: rdn and hdd 1 1/2f out: wknd fnl f* **17/1**

8 *1 1/4* **Princess Bavaroise (FR)**[37] 2006 3-8-9 0 ........ AntoineWerle 6 75
(H-A Pantall, France) **34/1**

57.91s (-0.39)
**WFA** 3 from 4yo+ 7lb **8 Ran SP% 121.0**
WIN (incl. 1 euro stake): 2.40. PLACES: 1.20, 1.60, 1.80. DF: 6.50. SF: 9.80.
**Owner** Yves Borotra **Bred** Y Borotra **Trained** France

# 2963 GOODWOOD (R-H)
Sunday, June 8

**OFFICIAL GOING: Good (7.6)**
Wind: Light, half against Weather: Fine, warm

## 3031 INJURED JOCKEYS FUND OAKSEY HOUSE MAIDEN STKS 1m 1f 192y
**2:25** (2:25) (Class 5) 3-Y-O+ **£3,234** (£962; £481; £240) **Stalls** Low

Form RPR

22-2 1 **Pack Leader (IRE)**[18] 2466 3-9-0 88 ........ RichardKingscote 7 83
(Amanda Perrett) *mde all: dictated stdy pce tl sent on 3f out: 2 l clr and rdn over 1f out: hung lft ins fnl f: ld dwindled nr fin but nvr in serious danger* **3/1**[2]

0 2 *3/4* **Astronereus (IRE)**[22] 2334 3-9-0 0 ........ PatDobbs 4 81
(Amanda Perrett) *hld up in 5th: rdn and prog to chse wnr wl over 1f out: clsd fnl f but nvr able to chal* **6/1**

3-36 3 *nk* **Carthage (IRE)**[35] 1984 3-9-0 78 ........ RichardHughes 5 80
(Richard Hannon) *hld up in 4th: rdn and prog 2f out: disp 2nd jst over 1f out: clsd on wnr but nvr able to chal* **7/2**[3]

6-44 4 *nk* **Rydan (IRE)**[41] 1809 3-9-0 80 ........ JimmyFortune 2 79
(Robert Mills) *hld up in last pair: stl last whn swtchd out wd over 2f out: rapid prog to dispute 2nd jst ins fnl f: drvn and nt qckn after* **9/4**[1]

0-2 5 *4 1/2* **Green Light**[17] 2497 3-9-0 0 ........ JimCrowley 8 71
(Ralph Beckett) *hld up in last pair: prog on outer 2f out: drvn and nt qckn over 1f out: wknd* **5/1**

0 6 *1 1/2* **Nelson Of The Nile**[41] 1809 3-9-0 0 ........ ShaneKelly 6 68?
(Jonathan Portman) *trckd wnr after 3f: rdn over 2f out: lost 2nd and wknd wl over 1f out* **100/1**

0-53 7 *3 1/2* **Hurricane Harry**[102] 748 3-8-11 0 ........ OisinMurphy(3) 1 61
(William Knight) *trckd wnr 3f: styd prom tl wknd 3f out* **50/1**

2m 11.42s (3.32) **Going Correction** +0.10s/f (Good)
**WFA** 3 from 4yo 13lb **7 Ran SP% 111.9**
Speed ratings (Par 103): **90,89,89,88,85 84,81**
CSF £20.18 TOTE £3.10: £1.80, £4.10; EX 22.00 Trifecta £66.30.
**Owner** George Materna **Bred** Diomed Bloodstock Ltd **Trained** Pulborough, W Sussex

**FOCUS**
First 2f of 1m course dolled out 5yds. A fair maiden with the form making a fair bit of sense.

## 3032 INJURED JOCKEYS FUND JACK BERRY HOUSE STKS (H'CAP) 1m 3f
**3:00** (3:00) (Class 5) (0-75,78) 4-Y-O+ **£3,234** (£962; £481; £240) **Stalls** Low

Form RPR

-241 1 **Manomine**[18] 2467 5-9-3 69 ........ RichardHughes 2 81
(Clive Brittain) *chsd clr ldr 3f: stdd to trck rivals: clsd 2f out: plld out over 1f out: pushed into ld jst ins fnl f: shkn up and sn clr* **5/2**[1]

-256 2 *4* **Emman Bee (IRE)**[102] 747 5-8-6 61 ........ MichaelJMMurphy(3) 3 66
(Luke Dace) *hld up in 4th: trckd ldng pair 5f out: clsd to ld over 2f out: drvn wl over 1f out: hdd and outpcd jst ins fnl f* **8/1**

5646 3 *3* **Angus Glens**[25] 2248 4-9-3 69 ........ (p) KierenFallon 4 69
(David Dennis) *chsd clr ldr after 3f: rdn and lost 2nd 3f out: stl on terms over 1f out: nt qckn and one pce after* **7/2**[3]

00-5 4 *4 1/2* **Beep**[17] 2498 4-8-2 61 ........ JennyPowell(7) 1 53
(Lydia Richards) *hld up in last pair: pushed along 6f out: effrt u.p 3f out: fdd over 2f out* **14/1**

-244 5 *1* **Yul Finegold (IRE)**[6] 2835 4-9-6 72 ........ (v[1]) FergusSweeney 6 62
(George Baker) *led and clr: rdn and hdd over 2f out: steadily wknd* **3/1**[2]

55-0 6 *47* **Greylami (IRE)**[102] 744 9-9-7 73 ........ SteveDrowne 7
(Clive Cox) *hld up in last pair: pushed along 6f out: lost tch 4f out: t.o and virtually p.u* **9/2**

2m 27.31s (0.81) **Going Correction** +0.10s/f (Good) **6 Ran SP% 111.8**
Speed ratings (Par 103): **101,98,95,92,91 57**
CSF £22.13 CT £67.58 TOTE £2.10: £1.20, £4.00; EX 16.10 Trifecta £64.80.
**Owner** Mrs C E Brittain **Bred** C R Mason **Trained** Newmarket, Suffolk

**FOCUS**
A modest handicap run at a fair gallop. This rates a personal best from the winner, but there were doubts over the field.

## 3033 VETERANS' STKS (H'CAP) 5f
**3:30** (3:31) (Class 4) (0-85,85) 6-Y-O+ **£6,469** (£1,925; £962; £481) **Stalls** High

Form RPR

0500 1 **Doctor Parkes**[70] 1193 8-9-3 81 ........ HarryBentley 3 92
(Stuart Williams) *trckd ldrs: shkn up on wd outside over 2f out: prog to ld 1f out: rdn out: jst hld on* **7/1**[2]

-051 2 *shd* **Slip Sliding Away (IRE)**[15] 2559 7-9-1 82 ........ OisinMurphy(3) 1 93+
(Peter Hedger) *s.i.s: hld up and sn outpcd: rdn over 1f out: str prog fnl f: clsd on wnr rapidly nr fin: jst failed* **6/4**[1]

162 3 *3/4* **Secret Millionaire (IRE)**[39] 1878 7-8-5 72 ........ MichaelJMMurphy(3) 8 80
(Tony Carroll) *w.w towards rr: swtchd lft 2f out: rdn over 1f out: prog after: styd on wl fnl f but nt as strly as runner-up* **10/1**

3330 4 *1 1/4* **Fair Value (IRE)**[36] 1944 6-9-4 82 ........[1] RichardHughes 7 85
(Simon Dow) *trckd ldrs: waiting for room fr 2f out: rdn whn in the clr fnl f: nt qckn* **8/1**[3]

0-05 5 *3/4* **Alpha Delta Whisky**[32] 2070 6-7-13 68 ........ (v) JoeyHaynes(5) 2 68
(John Gallagher) *sn chsd ldr: rdn to ld briefly jst over 1f out: fdd fnl f* **14/1**

3103 6 *1 1/4* **Six Wives**[15] 2542 7-7-13 70 ........ (p) MatthewHopkins(7) 5 66
(Scott Dixon) *mde most to jst over 1f out: fdd* **14/1**

254 7 *3/4* **Kuanyao (IRE)**[3] 2933 8-8-10 74 ........ (b) HayleyTurner 6 67
(Conor Dore) *sn pushed along in last trio: a struggling: passed wkng rivals fnl f* **20/1**

46-1 8 *1* **Beach Rhythm (USA)**[34] 2008 7-7-9 66 oh2 ........ JackGarritty(7) 10 56
(Jim Allen) *cl up: shkn up over 2f out: steadily wknd over 1f out* **10/1**

1-03 9 *shd* **Ziggy Lee**[7] 2803 8-9-7 85 ........ PJMcDonald 12 74
(Geoffrey Harker) *taken down early: fractious bef s: prom: shkn up 1/2-way: steadily wknd over 1f out* **12/1**

2502 10 *1* **Moorhouse Lad**[19] 2434 11-8-13 77 ........ (p) DavidProbert 11 63
(Garry Moss) *prom: shkn up 1/2-way: steadily wknd over 1f out* **12/1**

60-0 11 *7* **Swendab (IRE)**[32] 2074 6-9-2 85 ........ (v) MarcMonaghan(5) 9 45
(John O'Shea) *dwlt: nvr gng wl and a struggling: t.o* **33/1**

57.96s (-2.24) **Going Correction** -0.275s/f (Firm) **11 Ran SP% 118.2**
Speed ratings: **106,105,104,102,101 99,98,96,96,94 83**
CSF £17.87 CT £111.02 TOTE £10.30: £2.70, £1.30, £2.30; EX 22.70 Trifecta £335.90.
**Owner** Mrs S Mason & Partners **Bred** Joseph Heler **Trained** Newmarket, Suffolk

■ Stewards' Enquiry : Harry Bentley two-day ban: used whip above permitted level (Jun 22-23)

**FOCUS**
They raced centre to stands' side in this decent veterans' sprint handicap that set up for the closers. The form looks sound enough.

## 3034 INJURED JOCKEYS FUND 50TH ANNIVERSARY STKS (H'CAP) 2m
**4:05** (4:05) (Class 3) (0-90,90) 4-Y-O+ **£9,703** (£2,887; £1,443; £721) **Stalls** Low

Form RPR

4-34 1 **Number One London (IRE)**[13] 2627 4-8-9 76 ........ (p) MartinDwyer 12 86
(Brian Meehan) *t.k.h: trckd ldr: led 3f out gng strly: pressed and shkn up 2f out: rdn and kpt on fnl f* **12/1**

-022 2 *1 1/4* **Kashgar**[17] 2482 5-8-11 77 ........ MartinLane 3 85
(Bernard Llewellyn) *hld up towards rr: progrwess over 5f out: rdn 3f out: chsd wnr jst over 2f out and edgd rt: chal over 1f out: nt qckn and hld fnl f* **9/1**[3]

00-3 3 *1 1/4* **Rhombus (IRE)**[29] 2142 4-9-7 88 ........ MartinHarley 11 95
(Ismail Mohammed) *stdd s: hld up and last to 5f out: prog after: clsng on ldrs whn n.m.r briefly 2f out: drvn and one pce over 1f out* **5/1**[1]

6602 4 *1 1/2* **Gabrial's King (IRE)**[8] 2760 5-9-6 89 ........ WilliamTwiston-Davies(3) 7 94
(David Simcock) *stdd s: hld up in last trio: prog 3f out: sn rdn: tried to cl over 1f out but hanging and nt qckn: tk 4th fnl f: one pce* **9/1**[3]

6-14 5 *1 1/2* **Presto Volante (IRE)**[17] 2482 6-9-5 85 ........ (p) RichardHughes 1 88
(Amanda Perrett) *wl plcd bhd ldrs: rdn and nt qckn over 2f out: nt clr run briefly sn after: kpt on same pce fr over 1f out* **8/1**[2]

0-4 6 *1* **Teak (IRE)**[44] 1692 7-8-8 74 ........ StevieDonohoe 4 76
(Ian Williams) *chsd ldng pair to over 2f out: steadily fdd u.p over 1f out* **20/1**

-521 7 *shd* **Story Writer**[17] 2482 5-8-11 77 ........ KierenFallon 2 79
(William Knight) *wl plcd bhd ldrs: pushed along over 4f out: lost pl over 3f out: n.d after* **5/1**[1]

0-06 8 *1* **Palazzo Bianco**[22] 2342 6-9-0 80 ........ (p) DaleSwift 8 80
(Brian Ellison) *led: rdn and hdd 3f out: steadily fdd fnl 2f* **10/1**

2-20 9 *1/2* **Ashdown Lad**[30] 2108 5-8-11 77 ........ (p) JimmyFortune 9 77
(Tom Symonds) *bustled up to go prom and chsd ldng trio after 2f: rdn over 3f out: cl u ewhern n.m.r briefly 2f out: steadily fdd* **33/1**

-160 10 *1/2* **White Nile (IRE)**[32] 2073 5-9-7 90 ........ (t) OisinMurphy(3) 6 89
(Ed Dunlop) *t.k.h: hld up in last trio: prog on inner over 3f out: shkn up and swtchd lft over 2f out: steadily fdd* **5/1**[1]

-211 11 *9* **The Quarterjack**[17] 2490 5-8-7 73 ........ DavidProbert 10 61
(Ron Hodges) *nvr bttr than midfield: rdn and struggling over 3f out: sn lost tch* **12/1**

1234 12 *2* **Keep Kicking (IRE)**[18] 2468 7-8-5 71 oh2 ........ HarryBentley 13 57
(Simon Dow) *a towards rr: last and struggling over 4f out: sn no ch* **50/1**

15-2 13 *21* **Sula Two**[16] 2501 7-9-1 86 ........ (t) PhilipPrince(5) 5 47
(Liam Corcoran) *a towards rr: pushed along 6f out: wknd 4f out: t.o* **16/1**

3m 29.81s (0.81) **Going Correction** +0.10s/f (Good)
**WFA** 4 from 5yo+ 1lb **13 Ran SP% 121.1**
Speed ratings (Par 107): **101,100,99,99,98 97,97,97,96,96 92,91,80**
CSF £115.45 CT £622.09 TOTE £14.30: £4.90, £3.50, £2.30; EX 161.90 Trifecta £1964.30.
**Owner** Stewart Jones **Bred** Irish National Stud **Trained** Manton, Wilts

**FOCUS**
The pace slowed before halfway in this staying event. They finished in a relative bunch and the form may not prove all that reliable.

## 3035 GOODWOOD (S) STKS 1m
**4:35** (4:35) (Class 4) 3-Y-O+ **£6,469** (£1,925; £962; £481) **Stalls** Low

Form RPR

-415 1 **Licence To Till (USA)**[30] 2119 7-9-4 81 ........ JennyPowell(7) 6 71
(Tom Dascombe) *mde most: stretched away fr 3f out: edgd lft fnl 2f but clr and in n.d: rdn out* **6/4**[1]

10/0 2 *5* **Medal Of Valour (JPN)**[20] 2401 6-9-6 60 ........ (tp) DaneO'Neill 7 55
(Mark Gillard) *racd wd: in tch: rdn 3f out: kpt on u.p to take 2nd 1f out: no ch w wnr* **33/1**

0 3 *3/4* **To The Sky (IRE)**[6] 2830 6-9-1 50 ........ (p) MarcMonaghan(5) 2 53
(John O'Shea) *s.s: hld up in last: rdn 3f out: kpt on fr over 1f out to take 3rd nr fin* **20/1**[3]

0055 4 *1/2* **Claude Greenwood**[9] 2722 4-8-13 46 ........ (b) CamHardie(7) 1 52
(Linda Jewell) *hld up in rr: rdn 3f out: plugged on fr over 1f out to press for 3rd nr fin* **25/1**

-000 5 *1 1/4* **Destiny Blue (IRE)**[29] 2162 7-9-6 65 ........ (p) DaleSwift 3 49
(Brian Ellison) *trckd ldrs: rdn and nt qckn wl over 2f out: wnt 2nd briefly jst over 1f out: wknd last 150yds* **5/1**[2]

0165 6 *2 1/4* **Justonefortheroad**[8] 2763 8-9-8 74 ........ (v[1]) GeorgeChaloner(3) 4 49
(Richard Fahey) *t.k.h: hld up in tch: n.m.r after 3f: rdn 3f out: no prog and wl btn 2f out* **6/4**[1]

060 **7** *1 1/4* **Studfarmer**[11] 2672 4-9-3 47......................................(p) OisinMurphy(3) 5 41
(John Panvert) *mostly chsd wnr: lft bhd over 2f out: lost 2nd and wknd jst over 1f out* **28/1**

1m 41.05s (1.15) **Going Correction** +0.10s/f (Good) **7** Ran SP% **111.7**
Speed ratings (Par 105): **98,93,92,91,90 88,87**
CSF £58.27 TOTE £2.10: £1.20, £4.20; EX 20.40 Trifecta £172.00.The winner was bought in for £8,000.
**Owner** T Dascombe **Bred** John Hettinger **Trained** Malpas, Cheshire

**FOCUS**
This weak seller looked a match at the weights, and with the other joint favourite not running his race the winner had little to beat.

## 3036 IJF JOHN WOODMAN STKS (H'CAP) 7f
**5:10** (5:11) (Class 3) (0-90,90) 3-Y-O+ **£9,703** (£2,887; £1,443; £721) **Stalls** Low

Form RPR

0400 **1** **Clockmaker (IRE)**[15] 2548 8-9-11 **87**........................... HayleyTurner 1 99
(Conor Dore) *led: clr over 4f out: c bk to field and hdd 2f out: pushed into ld again jst over 1f out: sn jnd: drvn and fnd more to hold on wl* **10/1**

6010 **2** *nk* **Ruwaiyan (USA)**[29] 2145 5-9-13 **89**...........................(p) RichardHughes 2 100+
(James Tate) *stdd s: t.k.h: hld up In rr: smooth prog fr 1/2-way: brought to chal fnl f and sn upsides: styd on but nt qckn whn rdn last 100yds* **2/1**[1]

03-1 **3** *2 3/4* **Dark Emerald (IRE)**[29] 2156 4-9-11 **87**........................... KierenFallon 7 91
(Brendan Powell) *pushed along to chse ldrs: drvn 2f out: styd on to take 3rd last 100yds* **8/1**[3]

055- **4** *1 3/4* **Democretes**[207] 7856 5-10-0 **90**........................... MartinHarley 8 89
(John Butler) *trckd wnr: clsd to ld 2f out: hdd jst over 1f out: outpcd fnl f* **16/1**

0-00 **5** *1/2* **Lunar Deity**[36] 1948 5-9-4 **80**........................... HarryBentley 9 78
(Stuart Williams) *hld up wl in rr: shkn up over 2f out: prog over 1f out: kpt on but nt pce to threaten* **16/1**

0/1- **6** *1/2* **Obliterelght (IRE)**[159] 8455 5-9-9 **85**........................... MartinDwyer 3 82
(William Knight) *chsd ldng pair: rdn 2f out: wknd jst over 1f out* **12/1**

26-0 **7** *1 1/2* **Twenty One Choice (IRE)**[18] 2462 5-9-5 **84**........... OisinMurphy(3) 11 77
(Ed de Giles) *a in midfield: rdn 2f out and swtchd sltly lft: no prog over 1f out* **8/1**[3]

0160 **8** *1 1/4* **Forceful Appeal (USA)**[64] 1301 6-9-7 **86**...... WilliamTwiston-Davies(3) 4 76
(Simon Dow) *hld up wl in rr: rdn on inner 2f out: limited prog over 1f out: no hdwy after* **25/1**

04-5 **9** *1 1/4* **The Confessor**[36] 1943 7-9-12 **88**........................... DaneO'Neill 12 74
(Henry Candy) *chsd ldng trio: rdn 2f out: wknd jst over 1f out* **7/1**[2]

0-64 **10** *1 1/4* **Good Luck Charm**[16] 2500 5-9-4 **80**........................... PatDobbs 10 63
(Gary Moore) *hld up wl in rr: gng bttr than many whn nt clr run briefly 2f out: no prog and reminder fnl f: nvr involved* **10/1**

04-0 **11** *1* **Footstepsintherain (IRE)**[29] 2156 4-9-6 **82**............. FergusSweeney 6 63
(David Dennis) *hld up wl in rr: shkn up 2f out: no prog over 1f out: fdd fnl f* **40/1**

5306 **12** *1 1/4* **Spiritual Star (IRE)**[9] 2747 5-9-7 **88**........................... PhilipPrince(5) 16 65
(Anthony Carson) *chsd ldrs: rdn over 2f out: no prog: wknd over 1f out: eased fnl f* **33/1**

0-01 **13** *1 1/2* **Front Page News**[22] 2341 4-9-2 **78**........................... FrederikTylicki 15 51
(Robert Eddery) *a towards rr: wknd 2f out* **14/1**

1m 26.42s (-0.58) **Going Correction** +0.10s/f (Good) **13** Ran SP% **121.6**
Speed ratings (Par 107): **107,106,103,101,100 100,98,97,95,94 93,91,90**
CSF £30.20 CT £178.80 TOTE £13.50: £4.20, £1.70, £1.80; EX 45.00 Trifecta £409.30.
**Owner** CHP Consulting **Bred** Lemongrove Stud & Brendan Arthur **Trained** Hubbert's Bridge, Lincs
■ Realize (20-1) was withdrawn. Rule 4 does not apply.

**FOCUS**
Another race on the card where the winner made all, but it was a little different this time. The third is the best guide.

## 3037 SUNDAY SCHOOL STKS (H'CAP) 7f
**5:40** (5:44) (Class 5) (0-70,70) 3-Y-O **£3,234** (£962; £481; £240) **Stalls** Low

Form RPR

-405 **1** **Woodbridge**[29] 2163 3-8-9 **61**........................... GeorgeChaloner(3) 3 69
(Richard Fahey) *mde all: rdn 2f out: styd on strly fnl f* **12/1**

00-2 **2** *2 1/4* **Blue Bounty**[16] 2526 3-9-0 **63**........................... TedDurcan 1 65
(Mark H Tompkins) *trckd ldng pair: wnt 2nd wl over 1f out: sn rdn and nt qckn: wl hld after* **9/2**[1]

5525 **3** *nk* **Penny's Boy**[12] 2647 3-9-7 **70**...........................(t) PatDobbs 2 71
(Sylvester Kirk) *trckd ldng quartet: rdn 2f out: clsd to dispute 2nd fnl f: kpt on same pce* **11/2**[2]

64-0 **4** *nk* **Faure Island**[43] 1725 3-9-6 **69**........................... DaneO'Neill 11 69+
(Henry Candy) *trckd ldng trio: rdn on outer 2f out: nt qckn over 1f out: kpt on fnl f: nvr able to chal* **12/1**

-266 **5** *shd* **Tunnel Tiger (IRE)**[19] 2416 3-8-6 **58**........................... OisinMurphy(3) 7 58
(William Knight) *chsd wnr to wl over 1f out: styd on same pce fnl f* **16/1**

66-3 **6** *shd* **Mr Win (IRE)**[16] 2524 3-8-13 **65**........................... AshleyMorgan(3) 10 69+
(Chris Wall) *dwlt: hld up in rr: shkn up whn hmpd wl over 1f out: no ch after but r.o wl fnl f: nrst fin* **8/1**

-665 **7** *1* **Mendacious Harpy (IRE)**[27] 2224 3-9-6 **69**...........(v) FergusSweeney 4 66
(George Baker) *hld up in midfield: prog on inner 2f out: drvn to dispute 2nd 1f out: wknd last 150yds* **9/1**

64-3 **8** *nk* **Glebe Spirit (IRE)**[42] 1769 3-9-3 **66**........................... RichardHughes 14 62
(Richard Hannon) *s.i.s: hld up in midfield: rdn 2f out: kpt on same pce: n.d* **7/1**

0-20 **9** *hd* **My Secret Dream (FR)**[17] 2491 3-8-7 **56**........................... DavidProbert 9 52
(Ron Hodges) *hld up in midfield: rdn and edgd lft 2f out: nt qckn over 1f out: one pce after* **33/1**

02-0 **10** *5* **Go For Broke**[24] 2278 3-8-13 **69**........................... CamHardie(7) 13 52
(Richard Hannon) *hld up in rr: rdn whn hmpd wl over 1f out: no ch after* **20/1**

-223 **11** *5* **Jersey Brown (IRE)**[6] 2847 3-9-2 **68**........... WilliamTwiston-Davies(3) 6 38
(Mick Channon) *racd wd: in tch: rdn and no rspnse 2f out: wknd qckly and eased fnl f* **6/1**[3]

00-3 **12** *1/2* **Tete Orange**[40] 1860 3-8-4 **53**........................... HarryBentley 5 22
(Stuart Williams) *chsd ldrs on outer: lost pl and edgd rt 2f out: wknd qckly* **16/1**

0-23 **13** *65* **Shrewd Bob (IRE)**[60] 1379 3-9-4 **67**........................... JimmyQuinn 12
(Robert Eddery) *moved poorly to post: s.i.s: shoved along and no repsonse: eased after 1/2-way: virtually p.u* **33/1**

1m 27.79s (0.79) **Going Correction** +0.10s/f (Good) **13** Ran SP% **119.3**
Speed ratings (Par 99): **99,96,96,95,95 95,94,94,93,88 82,81,7**
CSF £63.81 CT £276.40 TOTE £17.70: £6.20, £2.40, £2.70; EX 111.60 Trifecta £636.80.
**Owner** R A Fahey **Bred** Mrs Alison Swinburn & Genesis Green Stud **Trained** Musley Bank, N Yorks

**FOCUS**
Little got into this. The winner stepped up on his previous best, which was on the AW.

T/Jkpt: Not won. T/Plt: £70.00 to a £1 stake. Pool: £128,046.00 - 1,333.96 winning tickets.
T/Qpdt: £15.90 to a £1 stake. Pool: £8,689.00 - 402.50 winning tickets. JN

# 2229 HOPPEGARTEN (R-H)
Sunday, June 8

**OFFICIAL GOING: Turf: good**

## 3046a DIANA-TRIAL (GROUP 2) (3YO FILLIES) (TURF) 1m 2f
**4:10** (12:00) 3-Y-O
**£33,333** (£12,916; £5,416; £3,333; £2,083; £1,250)

RPR

**1** **Longina (GER)**[56] 3-9-2 0........................... AdrieDeVries 7 100+
(P Schiergen, Germany) *sn led and mde rest: pushed along and qcknd fr 2f out: 2 l advantage ent fnl f: rdn and styd on wl: readily* **53/10**[2]

**2** *1 1/2* **Weltmacht**[56] 3-9-2 0........................... AHelfenbein 2 97
(Markus Klug, Germany) *led early: trckd ldr on inner once hdd: rdn over 2f out: outpcd by wnr over 1f out: styd on wl fnl f but hld* **3/5**[1]

**3** *hd* **Kamellata (FR)**[44] 3-9-2 0........................... FabriceVeron 9 97+
(H-A Pantall, France) *hld up in rr: hdwy on outer fr 2f out: rdn over 1f out: styd on wl fnl f but nvr able to chal* **6/1**[3]

**4** *nk* **Papagena Star (IRE)**[48] 1619 3-9-2 0........................... MartinSeidl 5 96
(Markus Klug, Germany) *midfield on inner: pushed along into st: rdn over 2f out: sn outpcd by wnr: styd on wl fnl f but nvr able to chal* **183/10**

**5** *3/4* **Ardeola (GER)** 3-9-2 0........................... FilipMinarik 10 95
(Jean-Pierre Carvalho, Germany) *hld up and sn towards rr on inner: angled out and pushed along over 2f out: rdn whn nt clrest of runs over 1f out: swtchd rt ent fnl f: styd on wl but nvr able to chal* **229/10**

**6** *1* **Turmalina (GER)**[231] 7406 3-9-2 0........................... SHellyn 6 93
(J Hirschberger, Germany) *midfield in tch on outer: ct on heels first turn: rdn 2f out: hdwy and disputing 2nd ent fnl f: kpt on tl no ex and fdd towards fin* **211/10**

**7** *1 1/2* **Pitrella (GER)** 3-9-2 0........................... DennisSchiergen 1 90
(U Stech, Germany) *hld up in rr: rdn over 2f out: sn outpcd: swtchd lft and bmpd rival ent fnl f: styd on but nvr threatened* **63/10**

**8** *3/4* **Veligandu (GER)**[231] 7406 3-9-2 0........................... APietsch 3 88
(R Dzubasz, Germany) *sn trcking ldr on outer: pushed along and effrt to chal into st: rdn and no ex over 1f out: fdd fnl f* **185/10**

**9** *4* **Danza Classica (GER)**[231] 7406 3-9-2 0........................... JBojko 8 80
(Waldemar Hickst, Germany) *hld up in midfield: rdn over 2f out: outpcd and btn whn bmpd ent fnl f: eased fnl 120yds* **39/1**

2m 2.3s (-4.40) **9** Ran SP% **127.9**
WIN (incl. 10 euro stake): 63. PLACES: 13, 11, 14. SF: 146.
**Owner** Gestut Ittlingen **Bred** Gestut Hof Ittlingen **Trained** Germany

# 2589 SAN SIRO (R-H)
Sunday, June 8

**OFFICIAL GOING: Turf: good**

## 3047a GRAN PREMIO DI MILANO (GROUP 1) (3YO+) (TURF) 1m 4f
**4:30** (12:00) 3-Y-O+ **£79,166** (£34,833; £19,000; £9,500)

RPR

**1** **Benvenue (IRE)**[28] 5-9-7 0........................... FBossa 6 109
(R Biondi, Italy) *hld up in midfield: travelling wl but short of room 2f out: hrd rdn whn gap appeared and styd on appr 1f out: r.o u.p fnl f: led cl home* **67/1**

**2** *nk* **Orsino (GER)**[21] 2374 7-9-7 0........................... MircoDemuro 3 109
(R Rohne, Germany) *pressed ldr: led after 2f: shkn up and wnt 3 l clr 2f out: r.o u.p fnl f: hdd cl home* **23/10**[2]

**3** *1* **Biz The Nurse (IRE)**[28] 2191 4-9-7 0........................... AndreaAtzeni 7 107
(Stefano Botti, Italy) *settled in midfield on outer: rdn and no immediate imp 2 1/2f out: kpt on u.p fr over 1f out: nt pce to chal* **13/20**[1]

**4** *2* **Steaming Kitten (USA)**[21] 2376 3-8-6 0........................... GBietolini 4 104
(Gianluca Bietolini, Italy) *w.w in midfield: rdn on outer over 2f out: no immediate imp: styd on ins fnl f: nrest at fin* **41/5**

**5** *1 1/2* **Awake My Soul (IRE)**[25] 2253 5-9-7 0........................... DanielTudhope 2 102
(David O'Meara) *trckd ldrs: rdn to chse ldr fr 2f out: one pce u.p fnl f* **15/2**

**6** *1 1/4* **Demeteor (ITY)**[21] 2374 4-9-7 0........................... GMarcelli 8 100
(R Menichetti, Italy) *hld up towards rr: rdn and nt qckn over 2f out: styd on u.p fnl f: nvr trbld ldrs* **73/1**

**7** *7* **Wild Wolf (IRE)**[21] 2374 5-9-7 0...........................(b) CristianDemuro 5 89
(Stefano Botti, Italy) *t.k.h: chsd ldr on outer: rdn and wknd ins fnl 1 1/2f* **76/10**

**8** *12* **Orpello (IRE)**[28] 2191 5-9-7 0...........................(b) FabioBranca 1 69
(Stefano Botti, Italy) *led: hdd after 2f: chsd ldr on inner: rdn and nt qckn over 2f out: btn and eased over 1 1/2f out* **76/10**

**9** *3* **Occhio Della Mente (IRE)**[28] 2191 7-9-7 0..........(b) UmbertoRispoli 11 65
(E Botti, Italy) *in rr: rdn and no imp 4f out: wl bhd fnl 2f* **69/10**[3]

**10** *7* **Lodovico Il Moro (IRE)**[28] 2191 4-9-7 0........................... DPerovic 10 53
(L Riccardi, Italy) *towards rr: bhd and no prog u.p fr 3 1/2f out: lost tch fr 2f out* **69/10**[3]

2m 26.4s (-5.10)
**WFA** 3 from 4yo+ 15lb **10** Ran SP% **164.9**
WIN (incl. 1 euro stake): 67.79. PLACES: 4.77, 1.42, 1.11. DF: 602.27.
**Owner** Incolinx **Bred** Curtasse S A S **Trained** Italy

# 2591 LES LANDES
Saturday, June 7

**OFFICIAL GOING: Good**

## 3048a GRACELAND H'CAP 2m
**8:20** (8:20) 3-Y-O+ **£950** (£345; £205)

RPR

**1** **Sworn Mammy (GER)**[1124] 7-8-10........................... PhilipPrince 5 48
(R Storp, Germany) **5/2**[2]

| | | | | |
|---|---|---|---|---|
| 2 | 15 | **Landolino (FR)**[13] 9-10-12 (Mrs C Gilbert, Jersey) 1/2[1] | MrFTett 2 | 62 |
| 3 | 8 | **River Du Nord (FR)**[13] 2593 7-9-8 (Sue Gardner) 5/2[2] | JemmaMarshall 3 | 35 |
| 4 | 5 | **Bollin Fergus**[13] 1622 10-8-5 (Mrs A Corson, Jersey) 17/2[3] | ShelleyBirkett 1 | 13 |
| 5 | 10 | **Constanzina (FR)**[13] 2599 5-10-7 (Mrs A Malzard, Jersey) 9/1 | ThomasGarner 4 | 32 |

3m 48.0s (228.00) **5** Ran SP% **144.3**

**Owner** Bernward Weber **Bred** Gestut Wittekindshof **Trained** Germany

## 2472 AYR (L-H)

Monday, June 9

**OFFICIAL GOING: Soft (8.3)**

Wind: Almost nil Weather: Overcast; raining

### 3049 EBF / SCOTTISH SUN RACEDAY 21ST JUNE MAIDEN STKS 6f

**2:30** (2:35) (Class 5) 2-Y-O **£2,911** (£866; £432; £216) **Stalls** Low

| Form | | | | | RPR |
|---|---|---|---|---|---|
| 2 | 1 | | **Doc Charm**[19] 2450 2-9-5 0 (Keith Dalgleish) *trckd ldrs gng wl: smooth hdwy to ld over 1f out: rdn clr* 1/1[1] | TomEaves 7 | 80+ |
| | 2 | 6 | **Blackfoot Brave (IRE)** 2-9-5 0 (Michael Dods) *s.i.s: bhd and green: hdwy over 1f out: chsd (clr) wnr ins fnl f: kpt on: no imp* 5/2[2] | PaulMulrennan 3 | 62+ |
| 6 | 3 | 1 ½ | **Big McIntosh (IRE)**[54] 1512 2-9-5 0 (John Ryan) *chsd ldrs: pushed along 1/2-way: rallied to dispute 2nd pl briefly ins fnl f: one pce* 5/1[3] | (t) GrahamLee 1 | 56 |
| 003 | 4 | 1 ¾ | **Bahango (IRE)**[14] 2615 2-9-5 0 (Kristin Stubbs) *t.k.h: led: rdn and hdd over 1f out: sn no ex* 7/1 | (b[1]) BenCurtis 2 | 50 |
| | 5 | ½ | **Go On Chas** 2-9-0 0 (Ian Semple) *pressed ldr: rdn over 2f out: no ex over 1f out* 40/1 | GarryWhillans(5) 8 | 49 |

1m 18.43s (6.03) **Going Correction** +0.85s/f (Soft) **5** Ran SP% **110.2**

Speed ratings (Par 93): **93,85,83,80,80**

CSF £3.75 TOTE £1.70: £1.40, £2.10; EX 4.00 Trifecta £10.20.

**Owner** Prestige Thoroughbred Racing II **Bred** Bishopswood Bloodstock & Trickledown Stud **Trained** Carluke, S Lanarks

**FOCUS**

After morning rain the going was eased to soft. Three withdrawals took plenty of interest out of this maiden.

### 3050 HAPPY 40TH BIRTHDAY ZOE HEANEY H'CAP 1m

**3:00** (3:01) (Class 4) (0-85,85) 3-Y-O+ **£5,175** (£1,540; £769; £384) **Stalls** Low

| Form | | | | | RPR |
|---|---|---|---|---|---|
| 63-2 | 1 | | **Le Chat D'Or**[18] 2478 6-10-0 85 (Michael Dods) *s.i.s: hld up: smooth hdwy over 2f out: pushed along and led over 1f out: kpt on strly fnl f* 3/1[1] | (bt) PaulMulrennan 5 | 96 |
| -441 | 2 | 2 ¼ | **Off The Pulse**[11] 2699 4-9-11 82 (John Mackie) *hld up on outside: hdwy to chal over 2f out to over 1f out: kpt on fnl f: nt pce of wnr* 5/1[3] | BenCurtis 10 | 88 |
| 0210 | 3 | 1 ¼ | **Another For Joe**[4] 2912 6-9-4 75 (Jim Goldie) *t.k.h: hld up in tch: hdwy to ld over 2f out to over 1f out: kpt on same pce fnl f* 6/1 | GrahamLee 9 | 78 |
| -643 | 4 | 5 | **George Cinq**[11] 2707 4-10-0 85 (Michael Bell) *dwlt: hld up bhd ldng gp: effrt and angled to outside 2f out: sn rdn and edgd lft: no imp fnl f* 7/2[2] | PaulHanagan 6 | 77 |
| 0-66 | 5 | 2 ¾ | **Order Of Service**[19] 2453 4-8-9 69 (Jim Goldie) *t.k.h: in tch: effrt and rdn over 2f out: edgd lft over 1f out: sn wknd* 28/1 | GaryBartley(3) 4 | 54 |
| 4231 | 6 | 3 | **Tenor (IRE)**[24] 2311 4-9-10 81 (John Ryan) *cl up: drvn and outpcd over 2f out: n.d after* 13/2 | (t) RoystonFfrench 3 | 59 |
| 506- | 7 | 10 | **Declamation (IRE)**[228] 7487 4-9-1 72 (Alistair Whillans) *led at ordinary gallop: rdn and hdd over 2f out: sn wknd* 16/1 | PJMcDonald 1 | 27 |
| 0053 | 8 | 3 ½ | **Skytrain**[9] 2762 4-9-12 83 (Mark Johnston) *trckd ldrs tl rdn and wknd over 2f out* 11/1 | FrannyNorton 11 | 30 |

1m 48.28s (4.48) **Going Correction** +0.70s/f (Yiel)

**WFA** 3 from 4yo+ 11lb **8** Ran SP% **109.2**

Speed ratings (Par 105): **105,102,101,96,93 90,80,77**

CSF £16.45 CT £74.16 TOTE £3.20: £1.50, £1.60, £1.70; EX 17.20 Trifecta £115.40.

**Owner** Dr Anne J F Gillespie **Bred** Dr A Gillespie **Trained** Denton, Co Durham

**FOCUS**

A competitive handicap run at a sensible pace in the conditions.

### 3051 RACINGUK.COM/FREETRIAL H'CAP (QUALIFIER FOR £15,000 BETFAIR SCOTTISH STAYERS FINAL) 1m 5f 13y

**3:30** (3:32) (Class 6) (0-65,65) 4-Y-O+ **£1,940** (£577; £288; £144) **Stalls** Low

| Form | | | | | RPR |
|---|---|---|---|---|---|
| 6/ | 1 | | **Lysino (GER)**[119] 5-9-7 65 (Keith Dalgleish) *t.k.h: chsd ldrs: lft in ld over 4f out: drvn over 2f out: styd on strly* 11/4[2] | TomEaves 3 | 83+ |
| 006- | 2 | 8 | **Tropenfeuer (FR)**[12] 3709 7-8-2 46 (Dianne Sayer) *chsd ldrs: ev ch over 4f out: rdn over 3f out: kpt on same pce fnl 2f* 5/2[1] | JamesSullivan 5 | 53 |
| -604 | 3 | 7 | **Grand Diamond (IRE)**[17] 2512 10-8-10 57 (Jim Goldie) *hld up in last pl: hdwy to chse clr ldng pair over 2f out: sn no imp* 11/1 | GaryBartley(3) 4 | 53 |
| 000- | 4 | ½ | **Sendiym (FR)**[12] 6290 7-8-5 54 (Dianne Sayer) *hld up in tch: rdn along 3f out: no imp fr 2f out* 25/1 | (p) EmmaSayer(5) 7 | 49 |
| 606/ | 5 | nk | **Laybach (IRE)**[15] 5761 10-7-11 46 oh1 (Jim Goldie) *hld up in tch: drvn and outpcd wl over 2f out: n.d after* 50/1 | SammyJoBell(5) 8 | 40 |
| 0120 | 6 | 25 | **Royal Defence (IRE)**[28] 2213 8-8-10 54 (Richard Ford) *chsd clr ldr: clsd 1/2-way: outpcd over 3f out: hung lft over 2f out: sn btn and eased: t.o* 13/2[3] | (t) PaulHanagan 2 | 11 |
| 0-53 | P | | **Forrest Flyer (IRE)**[19] 2455 10-8-13 57 (Jim Goldie) *led and clr to 1/2-way: pushed along and jst in front whn p.u over 4f out: sn dismntd: lame* 5/2[1] | GrahamLee 6 | |

3m 9.06s (15.06) **Going Correction** +0.70s/f (Yiel) **7** Ran SP% **111.3**

Speed ratings (Par 101): **81,76,71,71,71 55,**

CSF £9.49 CT £59.15 TOTE £4.50: £2.20, £1.50; EX 10.70 Trifecta £61.20.

**Owner** Straightline Construction Ltd **Bred** Gestut Hof Ittlingen **Trained** Carluke, S Lanarks

**FOCUS**

The pace was sound for this modest contest.

### 3052 JACQUI MALONEY 60TH BIRTHDAY CELEBRATION H'CAP 1m 2f

**4:00** (4:05) (Class 6) (0-65,64) 4-Y-O+ **£2,045** (£603; £302) **Stalls** Low

| Form | | | | | RPR |
|---|---|---|---|---|---|
| 031 | 1 | | **Thecornishcowboy**[5] 2894 5-9-7 64 (John Ryan) *hld up bhd ldng gp: smooth hdwy over 2f out: shkn up to ld ins fnl f: kpt on wl towards fin* 11/8[1] | (t) GrahamLee 6 | 74+ |
| 500- | 2 | 1 | **Thackeray**[215] 7778 7-8-12 55 (Chris Fairhurst) *hld up: rdn and hung lft over 2f out: gd hdwy over 1f out: styd on wl to take 2nd cl home: nt rch wnr* 80/1 | MichaelStainton 10 | 63 |
| 4014 | 3 | ½ | **Rockweiller**[5] 2894 7-8-12 58 (Shaun Harris) *led: rdn over 2f out: hdd ins fnl f: kpt on same pce: lost 2nd towards fin* 5/1[3] | JasonHart(3) 4 | 65 |
| 0044 | 4 | 2 ¼ | **Amazing Blue Sky**[6] 2872 8-8-7 50 (Ruth Carr) *in tch: effrt and drvn over 2f out: no ex over 1f out* 15/2 | JamesSullivan 1 | 53 |
| 00-6 | 5 | 9 | **Inniscastle Boy**[19] 2457 5-7-11 45 (Jim Goldie) *hld up: rdn and hdwy over 2f out: edgd lft over 1f out: sn no imp* 40/1 | (b) SammyJoBell(5) 3 | 31 |
| -300 | 6 | 4 ½ | **Primary Route (IRE)**[38] 1929 4-8-9 52 ow2 (Keith Dalgleish) *t.k.h early: prom: rdn over 3f out: wknd over 2f out* 33/1 | TomEaves 9 | 29 |
| -500 | 7 | 5 | **Wyldfire (IRE)**[13] 2654 4-9-3 60 (Ruth Carr) *taken early to post: hld up in tch: struggling wl over 2f out: sn btn* 20/1 | PaulMulrennan 2 | 28 |
| 060- | 8 | 14 | **Indian Giver**[233] 7379 6-8-3 53 (John David Riches) *w ldr to over 2f out: sn rdn and wknd* 40/1 | GaryMahon(7) 8 | |
| 001 | 9 | 97 | **Henpecked**[18] 2475 4-9-3 60 (Alistair Whillans) *hld up: rdn along 1/2-way: lost tch fr 3f out: eased* 5/2[2] | PJMcDonald 11 | |

2m 19.78s (7.78) **Going Correction** +0.80s/f (Soft) **9** Ran SP% **112.9**

Speed ratings (Par 101): **100,99,98,97,89 86,82,71,**

CSF £149.42 CT £445.53 TOTE £2.10: £1.10, £13.50, £2.40; EX 129.80 Trifecta £731.90.

**Owner** C Letcher & J Ryan **Bred** Hadi Al Tajir **Trained** Newmarket, Suffolk

■ Stewards' Enquiry : Michael Stainton two-day ban: used whip above permitted level (Jun 23-24)

**FOCUS**

This modest handicap was delayed as Rockweiller had to be re-shod.

### 3053 RACING UK FREE 1 MONTH TRIAL H'CAP (DIV I) 7f 50y

**4:30** (4:30) (Class 6) (0-65,70) 3-Y-O+ **£2,045** (£603; £302) **Stalls** High

| Form | | | | | RPR |
|---|---|---|---|---|---|
| 0413 | 1 | | **Monel**[18] 2479 6-9-8 59 (Jim Goldie) *t.k.h: hld up in tch: smooth hdwy and poised to chal over 1f out: shkn up to ld ins fnl f: kpt on wl* 5/1[3] | GrahamLee 7 | 70 |
| 001 | 2 | ¾ | **Tortoise**[10] 2741 3-8-6 53 (Richard Guest) *pressed ldr: drvn over 3f out: rallied and led over 2f out to ins fnl f: kpt on: hld nr fin* 17/2 | (b) BenCurtis 5 | 57 |
| 4443 | 3 | 3 ¼ | **Beckermet (IRE)**[16] 2549 12-10-0 65 (Ruth Carr) *led to over 2f out: rallied and ev ch over 1f out: kpt on same pce fnl f* 7/2[2] | JamesSullivan 9 | 65 |
| 4401 | 4 | nse | **Ellies Image**[18] 2479 7-9-0 51 (Richard Ford) *s.i.s: hld up: pushed along and hdwy over 2f out: drvn over 1f out: one pce fnl f* 5/1[3] | PaulHanagan 10 | 50 |
| 2462 | 5 | 1 ½ | **Vosne Romanee**[10] 2741 3-8-7 57 (Keith Dalgleish) *t.k.h: trckd ldrs: effrt and rdn over 2f out: outpcd fnl f* 7/2[2] | (b[1]) JasonHart(3) 11 | 49 |
| 3246 | 6 | 2 ¼ | **Incurs Four Faults**[12] 2674 3-8-9 56 (Keith Dalgleish) *dwlt: t.k.h and sn chsng ldrs: effrt and drvn over 2f out: wknd ent fnl f* 10/3[1] | TomEaves 1 | 42 |

1m 38.32s (4.92) **Going Correction** +0.80s/f (Soft)

**WFA** 3 from 4yo+ 10lb **6** Ran SP% **111.4**

Speed ratings (Par 101): **103,102,98,98,96 94**

CSF £43.06 CT £162.07 TOTE £5.60: £3.50, £2.90; EX 32.60 Trifecta £246.40.

**Owner** Johnnie Delta Racing **Bred** Frank Brady And Brian Scanlon **Trained** Uplawmoor, E Renfrews

**FOCUS**

They went a sound pace for this handicap.

### 3054 RACING UK FREE 1 MONTH TRIAL H'CAP (DIV II) 7f 50y

**5:00** (5:00) (Class 6) (0-65,65) 3-Y-O+ **£2,045** (£603; £302) **Stalls** High

| Form | | | | | RPR |
|---|---|---|---|---|---|
| -510 | 1 | | **Goninodaethat**[4] 2914 6-9-6 57 (Jim Goldie) *t.k.h: led and clr to over 2f out: rdn and hdd over 1f out: rallied and regained ld ins fnl f: gamely* 8/1 | GrahamLee 2 | 66 |
| 5045 | 2 | 1 | **Viking Warrior (IRE)**[28] 2219 7-8-11 48 (Shaun Harris) *hld up: hdwy over 2f out: led and hung lft over 1f out: hdd ins fnl f: no ex towards fin* 4/1[2] | BenCurtis 4 | 54 |
| 1351 | 3 | 2 | **It's All A Game**[10] 2742 3-9-2 63 (Richard Guest) *trckd ldrs: effrt and drvn over 2f out: kpt on same pce appr fnl f* 5/2[1] | (b) PaulHanagan 10 | 60 |
| 6-04 | 4 | 1 ¾ | **Lomond Lassie**[17] 2517 3-8-7 57 (Keith Dalgleish) *hld up bhd ldng gp: rdn and effrt over 2f out: no imp over 1f out* 7/1 | JasonHart(3) 5 | 50 |
| 14/0 | 5 | 1 ½ | **Mazeppa**[18] 2477 4-10-0 65 (Keith Dalgleish) *hld up: rdn and hdwy over 2f out: edgd lft and no imp over 1f out* 18/1 | TomEaves 7 | 58 |
| -066 | 6 | 1 ¾ | **Rioja Day (IRE)**[4] 2914 4-9-10 64 (Jim Goldie) *hld up: rdn and effrt over 2f out: no imp fr wl over 1f out* 11/2[3] | (b) GaryBartley(3) 11 | 52 |
| -600 | 7 | ½ | **Jebel Tara**[21] 2399 9-9-11 62 (Alan Brown) *hld up: rdn and outpcd over 3f out: sme late hdwy: nvr on terms* 22/1 | (bt) DaleSwift 3 | 49 |
| 15-0 | 8 | 2 | **Galilee Chapel (IRE)**[12] 2674 5-8-2 46 oh1 (Alistair Whillans) *hld up towards rr: drvn along over 2f out: sn no imp* 28/1 | RowanScott(7) 9 | 28 |
| 03-3 | 9 | 33 | **Penny Pursuits**[16] 2553 3-8-5 52 (Alan Berry) *chsd wnr to over 2f out: sn rdn and wknd: t.o* 50/1 | JamesSullivan 6 | |
| 64-0 | 10 | 2 ¼ | **Twenty Roses (IRE)**[41] 1847 3-8-9 56 (Ed Walker) *in tch: drvn and outpcd 3f out: sn btn: t.o* 8/1 | PaulMulrennan 8 | |

1m 38.87s (5.47) **Going Correction** +0.80s/f (Soft)

**WFA** 3 from 4yo+ 10lb **10** Ran SP% **113.7**

Speed ratings (Par 101): **100,98,96,94,92 90,90,88,50,47**

CSF £38.27 CT £105.06 TOTE £9.40: £3.60, £1.80, £1.40; EX 55.30 Trifecta £179.20.

**Owner** G E Adams & J S Goldie **Bred** W G H Barrons **Trained** Uplawmoor, E Renfrews

**FOCUS**
A modest handicap run at a fierce pace.

## 3055 RACING UK ANYWHERE AVAILABLE NOW H'CAP 1m 2f
5:30 (5:34) (Class 3) (0-95,90) 3-Y-O+ £7,762 (£2,310; £1,154; £577) Stalls Low

Form RPR
2261 1 **San Cassiano (IRE)**[9] 2790 7-9-5 **81**............ JamesSullivan 5 89
(Ruth Carr) *mde all at stdy pce: rdn over 2f out: kpt on wl fnl f* **5/1**[3]
0464 2 1 3/4 **Amaze**[9] 2790 6-8-13 **75**............(p) DaleSwift 7 80
(Brian Ellison) *reluctant to enter stalls: dwlt: hld up in tch: rdn over 3f out: hung lft and hdwy to chse (clr) wnr over 1f out: kpt on ins fnl f* **2/1**[2]
4420 3 8 **Fashion Line (IRE)**[30] 2144 4-9-11 **90**............ IanBrennan(3) 2 80
(Michael Bell) *trckd ldrs: effrt and rdn over 2f out: carried lft over 1f out: sn no imp* **13/2**
00- 4 1 1/4 **Pulpitarian (USA)**[33] 3345 6-9-7 **83**............(b) GrahamLee 1 71
(Lucinda Russell) *prom: drvn and outpcd over 2f out: n.d after* **28/1**
-211 5 15 **Insaany**[17] 2506 3-8-5 **80**............ PaulHanagan 3 55
(Mark Johnston) *t.k.h early: chsd wnr: effrt and rdn 3f out: edgd lft: one pce and lost 2nd whn blkd over 1f out: sn btn and eased* **11/8**[1]

2m 22.43s (10.43) **Going Correction** +0.90s/f (Soft)
**WFA** 3 from 4yo+ 13lb 5 Ran SP% **108.9**
Speed ratings (Par 107): **94,92,86,85,73**
CSF £15.04 TOTE £5.00: £2.60, £1.70; EX 15.80 Trifecta £59.00.
**Owner** S Jackson, L Shaw, Mrs R Carr **Bred** Peter Savill **Trained** Huby, N Yorks

**FOCUS**
A decent handicap run at a steady pace.

## 3056 MONTH'S FREE TRIAL RACING UK ANYWHERE APPRENTICE H'CAP 1m
6:00 (6:00) (Class 6) (0-60,60) 4-Y-O+ £1,940 (£577; £288; £144) Stalls Low

Form RPR
1 **Carraroe Flyer (IRE)**[9] 2795 4-8-0 **46** oh1............(p) JoshDoyle(7) 6 55
(Adrian Paul Keatley, Ire) *hld up in tch: smooth hdwy over 2f out: led appr fnl f: pushed out* **9/2**[2]
0306 2 2 1/2 **Ebony Clarets**[4] 2911 5-8-3 **47**............ RowanScott(5) 5 50
(Linda Perratt) *hld up in tch: rdn over 2f out: rallied and chsd wnr ins fnl f: kpt on same pce* **12/1**
0-23 3 3 3/4 **Eilean Mor**[18] 2476 6-8-4 **48**............ KevinLundie(5) 3 42
(R Mike Smith) *pressed ldr: led briefly over 1f out: outpcd ins fnl f* **3/1**[1]
-020 4 1 **Gadobout Dancer**[18] 2475 7-8-7 **46** oh1............ RachelRichardson 7 38
(Keith Dalgleish) *prom: effrt and ch over 1f out: no ex fnl f* **14/1**
-006 5 1 **Cono Zur (FR)**[17] 2518 7-9-4 **60**............ DanielleMooney(3) 1 50
(Ruth Carr) *led tl rdn and hdd over 1f out: sn outpcd* **9/1**
53-4 6 3/4 **Testa Rossa (IRE)**[19] 2457 4-8-12 **58**............ RachaelGrant(7) 9 46
(Jim Goldie) *hld up: rdn and outpcd over 3f out: sme late hdwy: nvr on terms* **7/1**[3]
0-51 7 1 1/4 **Hot Mustard**[17] 2529 4-9-2 **60**............ MichaelKenneally(5) 2 45
(Michael Bell) *dwlt: hld up: drvn and outpcd over 2f out: edgd rt and sn no imp* **3/1**[1]
6340 8 3 1/4 **Plunder**[13] 2653 4-9-0 **58**............ JordanHibberd(5) 8 36
(Alan Berry) *in tch: rdn over 3f out: wknd over 2f out* **18/1**
0/0- 9 82 **Forzarzi (IRE)**[523] 24 10-8-7 **49**............ GaryMahon(3) 4
(John David Riches) *cl up tl rdn and wknd fr 3f out: lost tch fnl 2f: t.o* **80/1**

1m 50.7s (6.90) **Going Correction** +0.90s/f (Soft) 9 Ran SP% **111.5**
Speed ratings (Par 101): **101,98,94,93,92 92,90,87,5**
CSF £53.92 CT £181.49 TOTE £5.30: £1.50, £4.30, £1.30; EX 47.50 Trifecta £297.70.
**Owner** Liffeydale Syndicate **Bred** Sean Murphy **Trained** Dunlavin, Co. Kildare
■ Stewards' Enquiry : Kevin Lundie two-day ban: careless riding (Jun 23-24)

**FOCUS**
A moderate handicap, confined to apprentice riders, run at a fair pace.
T/Plt: £43.80 to a £1 stake. Pool: £68,226.46 - 1,134.79 winning units T/Qpdt: £17.50 to a £1 stake. Pool: £4,218.47 - 177.65 winning units RY

# 2519 PONTEFRACT (L-H)
Monday, June 9
**3057 Meeting Abandoned** - waterlogged

# 2845 WINDSOR (R-H)
Monday, June 9
**OFFICIAL GOING: Good to firm (8.4)**
Wind: Almost nil Weather: Overcast, humid; raining race 6

## 3063 EBF STALLIONS MAIDEN STKS 6f
6:20 (6:20) (Class 5) 2-Y-O £2,911 (£866; £432; £216) Stalls Low

Form RPR
1 **Son Of Africa** 2-9-5 0............ DaneO'Neill 6 80+
(Henry Candy) *pressed ldr: led over 2f out: shkn up and pressed fnl f: pushed out nr fin* **25/1**
2 3/4 **Lady Moscou (IRE)** 2-9-0 0............ KierenFallon 11 73
(James Tate) *sn chsd ldng pair: pushed along 1/2-way: rdn to go 2nd over 1f out: chal fnl f: styd on but readily hld* **50/1**
3 1 1/2 **War Alert (USA)** 2-9-0 0............ JamieSpencer 1 68
(David Brown) *trckd ldrs: pushed along over 2f out: wnt 3rd 1f out and swtchd lft: kpt on same pce* **1/1**[1]
4 1 1/4 **Mistamel (IRE)** 2-9-5 0............ TomQueally 4 70
(Eve Johnson Houghton) *dwlt: last early: pushed along 1/2-way: shkn up and styd on steadily fnl 2f: nrst fin* **12/1**[3]
0 4 dht **Orlando Rogue (IRE)**[24] 2298 2-9-5 0............ PatCosgrave 2 70
(George Baker) *in tch: pushed along and nt on terms w ldrs 1/2-way: styd on and shkn up briefly 1f out: nrst fin* **20/1**
644 6 1 1/2 **Alpha Spirit**[19] 2460 2-8-11 0............ WilliamTwiston-Davies(3) 5 60
(Mick Channon) *led to over 2f out: lost 2nd and fdd over 1f out* **16/1**
7 2 3/4 **Lwah (IRE)** 2-9-5 0............ RichardHughes 8 57
(Richard Hannon) *t.k.h: hld up bhd ldrs: pushed along 1/2-way: no prog 2f out: fdd and eased* **7/4**[2]
8 12 **Red Tycoon (IRE)** 2-9-5 0............ WilliamBuick 9 21
(Ed Dunlop) *a in rr: pushed along and no prog 1/2-way: t.o* **16/1**
0 9 7 **Striking Stone**[44] 1726 2-9-0 0............ PhilipPrince(5) 7
(Jo Hughes) *s.i.s: rn green in rr: nvr a factor: t.o* **100/1**

1m 13.16s (0.16) **Going Correction** -0.35s/f (Firm) 9 Ran SP% **117.4**
Speed ratings (Par 93): **84,83,81,79,79 77,73,57,48**
CSF £843.68 TOTE £18.30: £5.50, £7.70, £1.10; EX 633.80 Trifecta £1076.30.
**Owner** One Too Many Partners **Bred** Mrs P A Clark **Trained** Kingston Warren, Oxon

**FOCUS**
The inner of the straight was dolled out 14yds at 6f and 6yds at the winning post. The top bend was dolled out 12yds from normal inner configuration, adding 47yds to race distances of 1m and further. This was no more than a fair juvenile maiden, though the winner travelled well throughout.

## 3064 DAILY UNIBET EARLY PRICES FROM 9AM CLAIMING STKS 1m 2f 7y
6:50 (6:50) (Class 5) 3-Y-O+ £2,587 (£770; £384; £192) Stalls Centre

Form RPR
3000 1 **Anaconda (FR)**[32] 2085 5-10-0 **89**............ RichardKingscote 3 80
(Tom Dascombe) *t.k.h: led after 2f: mde rest: hanging lft fr 3f out: rdn over 2f out: ended against far rail but hld on* **11/10**[1]
631 2 nk **Incendo**[16] 2547 8-9-2 **72**............(v) GeorgeDowning(5) 8 73
(Ian Williams) *pushed along first few strides: wl in tch: rdn and hanging lft fr over 2f out: wnt 2nd over 1f out: chal fnl f: nvr quite got there* **3/1**[2]
305 3 2 **Arcamante (ITY)**[28] 2221 3-8-9 **72**............(b) DanielMuscutt(5) 9 74
(Marco Botti) *t.k.h: hld up: pushed along to chse ldrs over 3f out: rdn and racd awkwardly over 2f out: prog into 3rd fnl f and styd on: unable to chal* **14/1**
-506 4 5 **Filosofo (IRE)**[28] 2222 3-9-1 **75**............ RichardHughes 4 66
(Richard Hannon) *t.k.h: trckd wnr 6f out: rdn wl over 2f out: lost 2nd and wknd over 1f out* **4/1**[3]
2-40 5 1 3/4 **Kingston Eucalypt**[14] 2628 4-9-4 **69**............ DaneO'Neill 6 53
(David Elsworth) *trckd ldrs: rdn to dispute 2nd wl over 2f out to wl over 1f out: wknd* **20/1**
-100 6 3 1/2 **Archie Rice (USA)**[39] 1899 8-9-6 **68**............ RobertTart(3) 1 52
(Tom Keddy) *t.k.h: hld up: pushed along over 3f out: no prog and wl btn 2f out* **25/1**
20/- 7 2 1/2 **Carrowbeg (IRE)**[486] 4251 6-9-4 **65**............(t) TomQueally 2 42
(Lawney Hill) *led 2f: chsd wnr to 6f out: pushed along 4f out: struggling 3f out* **66/1**
1453 8 nse **Matraash (USA)**[81] 1034 8-9-8 **72**............(be) ShaneKelly 5 46
(Daniel Mark Loughnane) *t.k.h: hld up: last after 3f: pushed along and no prog 3f out: no ch after* **20/1**

2m 8.53s (-0.17) **Going Correction** -0.125s/f (Firm)
**WFA** 3 from 4yo+ 13lb 8 Ran SP% **114.1**
Speed ratings (Par 103): **95,94,93,89,87 84,82,82**
CSF £4.23 TOTE £2.30: £1.30, £1.10, £3.70; EX 5.20 Trifecta £31.00.Arcamante was claimed by Mr K R Burke for £14,000. Incendo was claimed by Mr Conor Dore for £8,000.
**Owner** The MHS 8X8 Partnership **Bred** Haras Du Quesnay **Trained** Malpas, Cheshire
■ Stewards' Enquiry : Daniel Muscutt two-day ban: used whip above permitted level (Jun 26-27)

**FOCUS**
No great depth to this muddling claimer.

## 3065 FREEBETS.CO.UK WORLD CUP BETTING H'CAP 1m 2f 7y
7:20 (7:20) (Class 4) (0-85,83) 4-Y-O+ £4,851 (£1,443; £721; £360) Stalls Centre

Form RPR
6423 1 **Perfect Cracker**[21] 2382 6-8-6 **73**............ RyanTate(5) 8 81
(Clive Cox) *hld up in midfield: trckd ldrs 3f out: wnt 2nd wl over 1f out: edgd lft but styd on fnl f to ld last strides* **10/1**
23-1 2 nk **Red Warrior (IRE)**[48] 1636 4-9-6 **82**............ TomQueally 3 89
(Ismail Mohammed) *trckd ldr after 3f: rdn to ld jst over 2f out: hanging lft after: kpt on but hdd last strides* **5/1**[2]
0-21 3 1 1/4 **Bobbyscot (IRE)**[26] 2248 7-8-13 **75**............ KierenFallon 4 80
(Mark Hoad) *dwlt: hld up in midfield: pushed along 4f out: rdn and effrt over 2f out: edgd lft but kpt on fr over 1f out: wnt 3rd nr fin* **6/1**[3]
145- 4 shd **Headline News (IRE)**[220] 7659 5-9-7 **83**............ ChrisCatlin 6 88
(Rae Guest) *hld up in last pair: pushed along 4f out: stl last and pushed along over 1f out: r.o fnl f: gaining qckly at fin* **7/1**
40-0 5 1/2 **Monsieur Rieussec**[24] 2311 4-9-5 **81**............ RichardHughes 9 87+
(Jonathan Portman) *trckd ldng trio: cl up fr 3f out: rdn over 2f out: edgd lft u.p: cl 3rd but hld whn n.m.r against far rail nr fin and snatched up* **10/1**
3231 6 hd **Starwatch**[14] 2627 7-9-2 **78**............ WilliamCarson 1 82
(John Bridger) *chsd ldr 3f: prom after: rdn over 3f out: lost pl over 2f out: kpt on again nr fin* **12/1**
/15- 7 2 **Flashheart (IRE)**[380] 2660 4-9-0 **81**............ LouisSteward(5) 2 81
(Marcus Tregoning) *hld up towards rr: rdn and in tch over 2f out: no hdwy over 1f out: fdd* **20/1**
-000 8 2 **Persepolis (IRE)**[63] 1351 4-9-3 **82**............ OisinMurphy(3) 7 78
(Brett Johnson) *t.k.h: hld up in last pair: rdn and no prog 3f out: wl btn fnl 2f* **20/1**
-621 9 nk **Jupiter Storm**[7] 2851 5-9-7 **83** 6ex............(p) GeorgeBaker 10 78
(Gary Moore) *fast away: led and clr: breather 4f out: rdn and no rspnse over 2f out: sn hdd & wknd* **7/4**[1]

2m 5.89s (-2.81) **Going Correction** -0.125s/f (Firm) 9 Ran SP% **115.2**
Speed ratings (Par 105): **106,105,104,104,104 104,102,100,100**
CSF £59.16 CT £326.49 TOTE £11.10: £3.00, £1.60, £2.20; EX 68.40 Trifecta £288.90.
**Owner** Mildmay Racing **Bred** Mildmay Bloodstock Ltd **Trained** Lambourn, Berks
■ Stewards' Enquiry : Tom Queally two-day ban: careless riding (Jun 23-24)

**FOCUS**
A fair handicap that was run at a good gallop and, as in the previous race, the principals drifted across to the far rail in the straight, having started out near to the stands' side.

## 3066 EVERYMIND FILLIES' H'CAP 1m 67y
7:50 (7:50) (Class 4) (0-85,83) 4-Y-O+ £4,851 (£1,443; £721; £360) Stalls Low

Form RPR
1431 1 **Waveguide (IRE)**[17] 2528 5-8-4 **73**............ LewisWalsh(7) 4 78
(David Simcock) *hld up in last: clsd 1/2-way: led wl over 2f out: shkn up wl over 1f out: hrd pressed fnl f but pushed out firmly and a holding on* **5/1**[3]
6-04 2 1/2 **Oddysey (IRE)**[23] 2351 5-9-7 **83**............ RichardHughes 1 87
(Michael Dods) *trckd ldr 2f: last and pushed along jst over 3f out: hrd rdn and rallied over 1f out: tk 2nd last 100yds: styd on but hld* **7/4**[2]
54-6 3 1 **Anya**[31] 2121 5-8-13 **75**............ DaneO'Neill 2 77
(Henry Candy) *led: shkn up and hdd wl over 2f out: kpt on wl tl one pce and lost 2nd last 100yds* **14/1**
1- 4 15 **History Book (IRE)**[214] 7791 4-9-4 **80**............ WilliamBuick 3 64
(Charlie Appleby) *trckd ldr after 2f: upsides and shkn up 3f out: hd high and fnd nil: wknd 2f out* **11/10**[1]

1m 43.41s (-1.29) **Going Correction** -0.125s/f (Firm) 4 Ran SP% **107.3**
Speed ratings (Par 102): **101,100,99,84**
CSF £13.80 TOTE £4.30; EX 9.40 Trifecta £24.20.
**Owner** Tick Tock Partnership **Bred** T Darcy & Vincent McCarthy **Trained** Newmarket, Suffolk

**FOCUS**
Questionable small-field form, with the pace a steady one.

## 3067 BUGLER DEVELOPMENTS CLASSIFIED STKS 6f
8:20 (8:21) (Class 5) 3-Y-O £2,587 (£770; £384; £192) Stalls Low

Form RPR
6-02 1 **Spring Fling**$^{36}$ 1980 3-9-0 75 DaneO'Neill 2 83+
(Henry Candy) *mde all: rdn wl over 1f out: styd on steadily and nvr seriously in danger* 1/1$^{1}$
2-02 2 1 1/4 **Miss Brazil (IRE)**$^{46}$ 1669 3-9-0 74 RichardHughes 8 79
(Richard Hannon) *a chsng wnr: rdn over 2f out: kpt on but nvr able to chal* 15/2
0-1 3 3/4 **Pactolus (IRE)**$^{137}$ 291 3-9-0 75 AdamBeschizza 9 76
(Stuart Williams) *chsd ldrs on outer: rdn over 2f out: kpt on to take 3rd over 1f out: nvr able to chal* 14/1
00-0 4 1 3/4 **Chutney (IRE)**$^{36}$ 1985 3-8-7 73 CamHardie(7) 10 71
(Richard Hannon) *mostly in last trio: rdn on outer over 2f out: kpt on fr over 1f out: nrst fin but no threat* 33/1
1-02 5 3/4 **Pennine Warrior**$^{9}$ 2768 3-9-0 73 (p) LukeMorris 7 68
(Scott Dixon) *chsd ldng pair: rdn over 2f out: lost 3rd and one pce over 1f out* 12/1
6-43 6 1 **Persian Bolt (USA)**$^{13}$ 2639 3-9-0 72 JohnFahy 6 65
(Eve Johnson Houghton) *n.m.r s and dropped to last: shkn up 2f out: one pce and nvr on terms* 20/1
3143 7 1 **Searchlight**$^{21}$ 2406 3-9-0 75 (b$^{1}$) JamieSpencer 4 62
(Kevin Ryan) *n.m.r sn after s: mostly in last trio: rdn 2f out: no hdwy over 1f out* 7/1$^{3}$
-300 8 3 **Black Caesar (IRE)**$^{25}$ 2281 3-9-0 75 RichardKingscote 3 52
(Philip Hide) *chsd ldrs: rdn over 2f out: no prog wl over 1f out: wknd* 40/1
5-03 9 8 **Arranger (IRE)**$^{10}$ 2745 3-9-0 74 WilliamBuick 1 43
(Martyn Meade) *chsd ldng pair to over 2f out: wknd: eased fnl f* 5/1$^{2}$

1m 11.52s (-1.48) **Going Correction** -0.35s/f (Firm) 9 Ran SP% 115.4
Speed ratings (Par 99): **95,93,92,90,89 87,86,82,71**
CSF £8.89 TOTE £2.40: £1.10, £2.30, £5.20; EX 10.50 Trifecta £83.30.
**Owner** Six Too Many/T A Frost/ G Wilson **Bred** Mrs C R D Wilson **Trained** Kingston Warren, Oxon

**FOCUS**
Little got into this decent classified sprint.

## 3068 FREEBETS.CO.UK SUPPORTING ENGLAND IN BRAZIL H'CAP (BOBIS RACE) 5f 10y
8:50 (8:50) (Class 4) (0-85,82) 3-Y-O £4,851 (£1,443; £721; £360) Stalls Low

Form RPR
63-1 1 **High On Life**$^{14}$ 2625 3-8-12 73 RichardHughes 1 85
(Jamie Osborne) *mde all against nr side rail: wl in command over 1f out: pushed out firmly* 4/1$^{1}$
0-03 2 2 3/4 **Grecian (IRE)**$^{14}$ 2626 3-9-4 79 (t) LukeMorris 4 81
(Paul Cole) *trckd ldng trio: drvn 2f out: styd on to take 2nd jst ins fnl f: no imp on wnr* 13/2$^{3}$
2032 3 1 **Amahoro**$^{14}$ 2626 3-9-2 80 WilliamTwiston-Davies(3) 8 78
(Mick Channon) *stdd s: hld up in last: stl there 2f out: urged along and prog over 1f out: rdn and kpt on fnl f to take 3rd last strides* 13/2$^{3}$
310- 4 hd **Online Alexander (IRE)**$^{240}$ 7207 3-9-7 82 WilliamBuick 6 80
(Kevin Ryan) *pressed ldng pair: wnt 2nd 1/2-way: drvn and no imp over 1f out: one pce ins fnl f* 5/1$^{2}$
021- 5 4 1/2 **Royal Birth**$^{165}$ 8396 3-9-3 78 JamieSpencer 5 62
(Stuart Williams) *t.k.h: hld up in last pair: shkn up 2f out: wnt 5th over 1f out: no imp on ldrs: wknd and eased ins fnl f* 4/1$^{1}$
21-0 6 nk **Chorlton Manor (IRE)**$^{32}$ 2090 3-9-2 77 StevieDonohoe 7 57
(Tim Pitt) *towards rr: rdn on outer over 2f out: hanging and fnd nil: wknd over 1f out* 16/1
4-24 7 2 **Captain Whoosh (IRE)**$^{35}$ 2035 3-8-11 72 RichardKingscote 3 45
(Tom Dascombe) *chsd wnr to 1/2-way: sn lost pl and btn* 4/1$^{1}$
015- 8 12 **Autumns Blush (IRE)**$^{297}$ 5476 3-9-7 82 KierenFallon 2 25
(Jeremy Noseda) *chsd ldrs: rdn over 2f out: sn wknd: t.o* 16/1

58.3s (-2.00) **Going Correction** -0.35s/f (Firm) 8 Ran SP% 115.1
Speed ratings (Par 101): **102,97,96,95,88 88,84,65**
CSF £30.48 CT £166.34 TOTE £3.30: £1.50, £2.20, £2.90; EX 31.10 Trifecta £85.40.
**Owner** Michael Buckley **Bred** Moyns Park Estate And Stud Ltd **Trained** Upper Lambourn, Berks

**FOCUS**
A fair 3yo sprint that produced another all-the-way winner.
T/Plt: £62.90 to a £1 stake. Pool: £115,562.34 - 1,341.08 winning units T/Qpdt: £18.80 to a £1 stake. Pool: £8,978.30 - 351.85 winning units JN

3069 - 3072a (Foreign Racing) - See Raceform Interactive

# 2006 MUNICH (L-H)
Monday, June 9

**OFFICIAL GOING: Turf: good**

## 3073a RACEBETS.COM BAVARIAN CLASSIC (GROUP 3) (3YO) (TURF) 1m 2f
3:35 (12:00) 3-Y-O
£26,666 (£9,166; £4,583; £2,500; £1,666; £1,250)

RPR
1 **Magic Artist (IRE)**$^{29}$ 3-9-2 0 DavidProbert 3 108+
(W Figge, Germany) *towards rr early: sn settled in midfield on inner: pushed along to chse ldr over 2f out: led under 1 1/2f out: drvn clr fnl f: readily* 9/1
2 3 1/2 **Speedy Approach**$^{43}$ 1781 3-9-2 0 EPedroza 5 101
(A Wohler, Germany) *midfield on outer: hdwy over 1 1/2f out: rdn and chsd ldrs appr fnl f: styd on to go 2nd last 100yds: nvr on terms w wnr* 129/10
3 1/2 **Nordico (GER)**$^{22}$ 2377 3-9-2 0 (p) FrederikTylicki 6 100
(Mario Hofer, Germany) *hld up towards rr: rdn and prog 2f out: chsd ldng pair appr fnl f: kpt on u.p: nt gng pce to trble wnr* 33/10$^{2}$
4 1 1/4 **Born To Run (GER)**$^{29}$ 3-9-2 0 (b) MartinDwyer 7 98
(R Dzubasz, Germany) *dwlt and sltly hmpd leaving stalls: in rr: hdwy on outer 2f out: styd on u.p fr 1 1/2f out: run flattened out fnl 100yds* 10/1
5 3 **Oil Of England (GER)**$^{22}$ 2376 3-9-2 0 MarcLerner 2 92
(M Figge, Germany) *led: hdd under 1 1/2f out: fdd ins fnl f* 48/10$^{3}$
6 2 **Lindaro (GER)**$^{29}$ 3-9-2 0 AdriedeVries 8 88
(P Schiergen, Germany) *wnt lft s: trckd ldr early bef dropping towards rr: rdn and mod prog 2f out: sn btn* 121/10
7 3 **Lac Leman (GER)**$^{50}$ 3-9-2 0 MartinLane 1 82
(R Dzubasz, Germany) *midfield on inner early: sn trcking ldr on rail: scrubbed along and lost pl over 2f out: sn btn* 7/5$^{1}$
8 2 **Invador**$^{19}$ 3-9-2 0 FilipMinarik 4 78
(Jean-Pierre Carvalho, Germany) *pressed ldr on outer: rdn and nt qckn 2f out: sn wknd* 99/10

2m 7.83s (-1.14) 8 Ran SP% 125.3
WIN (incl. 10 euro stake): 100, PLACES: 27, 34, 23. SF: 967.
**Owner** Stall Salzburg **Bred** Darley **Trained** Germany

# 2993 LINGFIELD (L-H)
Tuesday, June 10

**OFFICIAL GOING: Turf course - good to firm (8.8); all-weather - standard**
Wind: Fresh, behind Weather: Fine, warm

## 3074 32RED FREE £10 BONUS MAIDEN STKS 7f 140y
5:25 (5:29) (Class 5) 3-Y-O+ £2,587 (£770; £384; £192) Stalls Centre

Form RPR
5 1 **Felwah**$^{17}$ 2560 3-8-5 0 NathanAlison(5) 5 77+
(William Haggas) *w ldrs: led 1/2-way: drew clr fr 2f out: easily* 7/4$^{1}$
2 4 1/2 **Flawless Pink** 3-8-10 0 SebSanders 4 66+
(Jeremy Noseda) *hld up in rr: prog wl over 2f out and pushed along: styd on encouragingly to take 2nd ins fnl f* 9/2$^{3}$
3 2 **Law Appeal** 3-9-1 0 KierenFallon 12 66
(Brian Meehan) *led against nr side rail: hdd 1/2-way: lft bhd by wnr over 2f out: kpt on same pce: lost 2nd ins fnl f* 10/1
03 4 3/4 **Border Guard**$^{43}$ 1790 3-9-1 0 LukeMorris 7 64?
(Milton Bradley) *chsd ldrs: rdn wl over 2f out: effrt to dispute 2nd over 1f out: fdd last 100yds* 100/1
50 5 3 1/2 **Miss Moppet**$^{13}$ 2681 3-8-10 0 NickyMackay 8 50+
(Hughie Morrison) *hld up wl in rr: nt clr run 4f out: swtchd to wd outside 3f out and prog: no imp wl over 1f out: fdd* 20/1
6 9 **The Reel Way (GR)** 3-8-10 0 LiamJones 9 28
(Patrick Chamings) *t.k.h early: in tch: shkn up sn after 1/2-way: sn lft bhd* 33/1
00 7 1 1/4 **Cypress Point (FR)**$^{32}$ 2109 3-8-10 0 (t) JimmyQuinn 3 25
(Ed Vaughan) *chsd ldrs: rdn 3f out: steadily wknd* 33/1
5 8 3 **Scafell Pike**$^{18}$ 2525 3-8-12 0 RobertTart(3) 1 22
(Dr Jon Scargill) *chsd ldrs but pushed along after 2f: wknd u.p wl over 2f out* 50/1
0- 9 1 1/4 **Graceful Willow**$^{299}$ 5444 4-9-4 0 SimonPearce(3) 6 17
(John E Long) *sn detached in last and pushed along: a bhd: passed a few stragglers late on* 100/1
0-0 10 1/2 **Almax**$^{7}$ 2877 3-9-1 0 TomQueally 10 18
(Michael Bell) *chsd ldrs: struggling by 1/2-way: sn btn* 16/1
11 1 **Highly Excited (USA)** 3-9-1 0 AndreaAtzeni 11 15
(Roger Varian) *w ldr 3f: lost pl qckly: wl in rr over 2f out* 11/4$^{2}$
12 1 **Dire Straits (IRE)** 3-9-1 0 JackMitchell 2 13
(Chris Wall) *nvr on terms w ldrs: rdn on wd outside over 3f out: sn btn* 7/1

1m 29.67s (-2.63) **Going Correction** -0.375s/f (Firm)
**WFA** 3 from 4yo 11lb 12 Ran SP% 123.3
Speed ratings (Par 103): **98,93,91,90,87 78,77,74,72,72 71,70**
CSF £9.94 TOTE £2.80: £1.20, £2.30, £4.60; EX 12.10 Trifecta £109.50.
**Owner** Khalil Alsayegh **Bred** Khalil Al Sayegh **Trained** Newmarket, Suffolk

**FOCUS**
Not as competitvive a maiden as the numbers would suggest.

## 3075 32RED TOMB RAIDER SLOT H'CAP 7f 140y
5:55 (5:57) (Class 6) (0-55,56) 4-Y-O+ £2,264 (£673; £336; £168) Stalls Centre

Form RPR
2445 1 **Carrera**$^{12}$ 2689 4-9-5 54 MartinHarley 11 64
(Michael Blanshard) *hld up in rr against rail: prog and swtchd lft over 2f out: clsd to ld 1f out: sn rdn clr* 9/2$^{2}$
2032 2 1 3/4 **Byrd In Hand (IRE)**$^{11}$ 2723 7-9-2 51 (v) WilliamCarson 10 57
(John Bridger) *led against rail: rdn over 2f out: hdd and outpcd 1f out: kpt on to hold 2nd pl* 10/1
P451 3 1/2 **Botanist**$^{8}$ 2844 7-9-3 52 6ex BenCurtis 12 56
(Shaun Harris) *trckd ldrs against rail: rdn 2f out: squeezed through jst over 1f out: kpt on same pce after* 6/1$^{3}$
331 4 1 1/4 **Last Minute Lisa (IRE)**$^{7}$ 2864 4-9-7 56 6ex RichardHughes 4 57
(Sylvester Kirk) *stdd s: hld up in rr: rdn jst over 2f out: prog over 1f out then swtchd to outer: kpt on one pce* 5/2$^{1}$
663 5 1 3/4 **The Happy Hammer (IRE)**$^{14}$ 2646 8-9-5 54 (b) MartinDwyer 8 51
(Eugene Stanford) *pressed ldr: rdn over 2f out: losing pl whn short of room and snatched up 1f out: fdd* 6/1$^{3}$
0-00 6 1 3/4 **Hawk Moth (IRE)**$^{36}$ 2021 6-9-5 54 (b) LukeMorris 9 47
(John Spearing) *chsd ldrs: drvn over 2f out: no imp over 1f out: wknd fnl f* 14/1
2002 7 2 3/4 **Lutine Charlie (IRE)**$^{7}$ 2864 7-9-4 53 (p) TomQueally 2 39
(Pat Eddery) *chsd ldrs: shkn up over 2f out: no prog wl over 1f out: wknd* 8/1
-006 8 6 **Lewamy (IRE)**$^{39}$ 1917 4-9-2 51 HayleyTurner 6 22
(John Best) *pressed ldng pair: shoved along after 3f: lost pl over 3f out: sn btn* 33/1
00-0 9 5 **Three Choirs (IRE)**$^{97}$ 838 4-8-9 51 (b) KieranShoemark(7) 3 9
(William Stone) *a in rr: rdn by 1/2-way: struggling after* 50/1
-120 10 1 **Bond Artist (IRE)**$^{36}$ 2019 5-9-3 55 RobertTart(3) 1 11
(Geoffrey Oldroyd) *racd wd in rr: rdn 4f out: sn struggling* 12/1

1m 29.15s (-3.15) **Going Correction** -0.375s/f (Firm) 10 Ran SP% 114.8
Speed ratings (Par 101): **100,98,97,96,94 93,90,84,79,78**
CSF £48.08 CT £226.41 TOTE £6.40: £2.70, £4.10, £3.20; EX 65.60 Trifecta £426.40.
**Owner** D Carroll **Bred** Norman Court Stud **Trained** Upper Lambourn, Berks

**FOCUS**
A moderate race on paper, won in convincing fashion.

## 3076 32RED CASINO MAIDEN FILLIES' STKS (BOBIS RACE) 6f
6:25 (6:27) (Class 5) 2-Y-O £2,587 (£770; £384; £192) Stalls Centre

Form RPR
1 **Pack Together** 2-9-0 0 RichardHughes 3 75+
(Richard Hannon) *trckd ldrs: clsd to ld jst over 1f out: hrd pressed fnl f: shkn up and styd on wl* 11/4$^{2}$

2 nk **Sulaalaat** 2-9-0 0 PaulHanagan 2 74+
(Brian Meehan) *chsd ldrs on outer: rdn over 2f out: prog to chal jst over 1f out: pressed wnr hrd and styd on: a hld* **7/1**[3]

3 1 1/4 **Commandaria (USA)** 2-9-0 0 ShaneKelly 11 70+
(Jeremy Noseda) *trckd ldrs against rail: shkn up over 2f out: clsd over 1f out: wnt 3rd fnl f: styd on same pce* **7/1**[3]

4 1/2 **Prize Exhibit** 2-8-9 0 RachealKneller(5) 10 71+
(Jamie Osborne) *trckd ldrs: gng wl but fruitless wait for gap to appear fr jst over 2f out: got through fnl f and styd on: no ch to chal* **20/1**

5 hd **Hollie Point** 2-9-0 0 AndreaAtzeni 1 68
(Charlie Appleby) *racd on outer: off the pce: shkn up over 2f out: prog over 1f out: styd on but nvr able to chal* **10/1**

6 1 1/4 **Terse** 2-9-0 0 TomQueally 5 64
(David Lanigan) *dwlt: off the pce towards rr: shkn up and clsd on ldng gp fr 2f out: one pce fnl f* **12/1**

7 3/4 **Goldcrest** 2-9-0 0 FergusSweeney 8 61
(Henry Candy) *led or disp ld: hdd jst over 1f out: fdd* **14/1**

8 2 **Superlative (IRE)** 2-9-0 0 KierenFallon 4 55+
(James Tate) *pressed ldrs: pushed along 1/2-way: lost pl over 1f out: wl btn whn short of room nr fin* **9/4**[1]

9 1 **Lady Mascot (IRE)** 2-9-0 0 JimmyQuinn 6 52
(Richard Hannon) *a towards rr and off the pce: rdn and no real prog 2f out: plugged on* **25/1**

10 1 3/4 **Old Fashion** 2-9-0 0 DaneO'Neill 9 46
(Ed Dunlop) *dwlt: rn green and a wl in rr: nvr a factor* **33/1**

11 1 3/4 **Fine Judgment** 2-9-0 0 MartinDwyer 7 41
(William Muir) *disp ld to wl over 1f out: wknd* **50/1**

12 38 **Bella Alamoto** 2-9-0 0 WilliamCarson 12
(John Bridger) *s.s: veered fr ins draw to wd outside: a bhd: t.o* **66/1**

1m 10.27s (-0.93) **Going Correction** -0.375s/f (Firm) **12 Ran SP% 120.9**
Speed ratings (Par 90): **91,90,88,88,88 86,85,82,81,79 76,26**
CSF £21.73 TOTE £3.10: £1.10, £1.80, £3.60; EX 24.30 Trifecta £99.10.
**Owner** The Queen **Bred** The Queen **Trained** East Everleigh, Wilts

**FOCUS**
Some big yards were represented and much to like from the principals.

## 3077 32RED (S) STKS 5f
**6:55** (6:55) (Class 6) 3-Y-O+ **£1,940** (£577; £288; £144) **Stalls** Centre

Form RPR

0204 1 **Sir Pedro**[8] 2838 5-9-12 77 PaddyAspell 2 78
(Robert Cowell) *wl away: mde all: drew clr wl over 1f out: rdn out* **1/2**[1]

-402 2 6 **Paradise Spectre**[6] 2887 7-9-12 62 (p) RichardHughes 5 57
(Zoe Davison) *outpcd and pushed along in 3rd: rdn 2f out: kpt on fnl f to take 2nd nr fin* **5/2**[2]

5520 3 1/2 **Island Legend (IRE)**[43] 1787 8-9-12 49 (b) LukeMorris 3 55
(Milton Bradley) *w wnr to jst over 2f out: no ch over 1f out: wknd and lost 2nd nr fin* **8/1**[3]

0300 4 4 1/2 **Brandywell Boy (IRE)**[20] 2459 11-9-7 42 (b) JoshBaudains(5) 4 39
(Dominic Ffrench Davis) *outpcd and rdn: a last* **33/1**

57.27s (-0.93) **Going Correction** -0.375s/f (Firm) **4 Ran SP% 109.3**
Speed ratings (Par 101): **92,82,81,74**
CSF £2.05 TOTE £1.70; EX 1.90 Trifecta £3.40.Winner bought in for 6,000gns.
**Owner** T W Morley **Bred** C J Mills **Trained** Six Mile Bottom, Cambs

**FOCUS**
A one-sided, small-field seller.

## 3078 32RED ON THE APP STORE H'CAP 1m 7f 169y(P)
**7:25** (7:25) (Class 5) (0-75,75) 4-Y-O+ **£2,587** (£770; £384; £192) **Stalls** Low

Form RPR

3220 1 **Sir Frank Morgan (IRE)**[11] 2739 4-9-8 74 JoeFanning 1 84
(Mark Johnston) *mde all: kicked on 4f out: drvn and styd on stoutly fr 2f out* **5/1**[2]

12-4 2 2 3/4 **Aiyana**[56] 1501 4-9-0 66 RichardHughes 3 73
(Hughie Morrison) *prog fr rr to trck wnr after 3f out: rdn over 2f out: kpt on but nvr able to chal* **7/4**[1]

-420 3 1 1/2 **First Warning**[32] 2119 4-9-9 75 StevieDonohoe 2 80
(Tim Pitt) *trckd ldng pair after 6f: rdn 3f out: no imp wl over 1f out: kpt on u.p* **6/1**[3]

6000 4 3/4 **Bramshill Lass**[13] 2683 5-8-9 67 KieranShoemark(7) 8 71
(Amanda Perrett) *hld up in last: stl only 7th and pushed along 2f out: prog on inner to chal for 3rd 1f out: no ex last 100yds* **20/1**

2010 5 4 1/2 **King Olav (UAE)**[25] 2305 9-9-6 71 LukeMorris 9 70
(Tony Carroll) *chsd wnr 3f: styd prom: rdn over 3f out: racd awkwardly and nt qckn over 2f out: wknd over 1f out* **16/1**

1555 6 4 1/2 **Poitin**[21] 2430 4-9-5 71 TomQueally 4 64
(Harry Dunlop) *hld up towards rr: rdn over 3f out: no prog over 2f out: sn wknd* **7/1**

1432 7 1 1/4 **Munsarim (IRE)**[14] 2651 7-9-8 73 (b) AmirQuinn 6 65
(Lee Carter) *dwlt: in tch in rr: rdn and no prog over 3f out: wknd jst over 2f out* **7/1**

-524 8 5 **Montjess (IRE)**[13] 2683 4-9-4 70 (p) LiamJones 5 56
(Laura Mongan) *in tch on outer: pushed along 5f out: wknd over 3f out: sn bhd* **8/1**

3m 24.92s (-0.78) **Going Correction** +0.05s/f (Slow)
**WFA** 4 from 5yo+ 1lb **8 Ran SP% 114.1**
Speed ratings (Par 103): **103,101,100,100,98 96,95,92**
CSF £14.10 CT £52.77 TOTE £6.90: £1.10, £1.20, £2.40; EX 11.50 Trifecta £84.20.
**Owner** Paul Dean **Bred** Airlie Stud **Trained** Middleham Moor, N Yorks

**FOCUS**
A modest staying handicap in which few ever got into it.

## 3079 32RED.COM FILLIES' H'CAP 1m 4f (P)
**7:55** (7:55) (Class 4) (0-80,74) 4-Y-O+ **£5,175** (£1,540; £769; £384) **Stalls** Low

Form RPR

0332 1 **Jewelled**[10] 2770 8-9-1 68 RichardHughes 4 74
(Ralph J Smith) *led: set mod pce: sed dash for home over 3f out: hrd rdn over 1f out: kpt on: jst hld on* **9/2**[3]

10-2 2 shd **Silk Train**[20] 2467 4-9-3 70 KierenFallon 3 76
(David Simcock) *trckd ldr 3f and rdn to go 2nd again 2f out: hrd drvn over 1f out: grad clsd fnl f: jst failed* **11/10**[1]

506 3 1 1/2 **Lady Lunchalot (USA)**[7] 2862 4-9-7 74 LiamJones 1 77
(Laura Mongan) *trckd wnr after 3f: rdn over 3f out: lost 2nd 2f out: kpt on same pce after* **2/1**[2]

2520 4 6 **Conserve (IRE)**[29] 2199 4-8-13 66 (b) JimmyQuinn 2 60
(Neil King) *s.s: a last: rdn over 3f out: no imp after* **8/1**

2m 33.41s (0.41) **Going Correction** +0.05s/f (Slow) **4 Ran SP% 110.2**
Speed ratings (Par 102): **100,99,98,94**
CSF £10.19 TOTE £4.80; EX 10.70 Trifecta £10.00.
**Owner** Fishdance & Cheval Court Stud **Bred** Wyck Hall Stud Ltd **Trained** Epsom, Surrey

**FOCUS**
A poorly contested, muddling event.

## 3080 32RED THUNDERSTRUCK SLOT H'CAP 1m 2f (P)
**8:25** (8:25) (Class 5) (0-70,69) 4-Y-O+ **£2,943** (£875; £437; £218) **Stalls** Low

Form RPR

3315 1 **Lily Edge**[12] 2693 5-8-8 56 (v) WilliamCarson 4 64
(John Bridger) *chsd ldng pair to 2f out: looked hld u.p: rallied wl fnl f to ld last 120yds: styd on* **25/1**

5665 2 1 1/4 **If I Were A Boy (IRE)**[34] 2084 7-8-9 57 (be) LukeMorris 10 62
(Dominic Ffrench Davis) *hld up in last pair: wdst of all bnd 2f out and drvn: r.o u.p over 1f out: tk 2nd last strides* **20/1**

-304 3 nse **Ana Shababiya (IRE)**[29] 2199 4-9-5 67 TomQueally 9 72
(Ismail Mohammed) *chsd ldng trio: rdn wl over 3f out: lost pl u.p over 2f out: rallied wl fnl f: tk 3rd last strides* **10/1**

0065 4 hd **Red Dragon (IRE)**[20] 2471 4-9-4 66 FergusSweeney 1 71
(Michael Blanshard) *chsd ldrs disputng 5th: rdn over 2f out: nt clr run briefly over 1f out: styd on fnl f: nrst fin* **8/1**[3]

000 5 nk **Spin Artist (USA)**[15] 2603 4-9-7 69 JoeFanning 5 73
(Mark Johnston) *racd wd in midfield: rdn over 2f out: prog over 1f out: hrd rdn and kpt on: nvr able to chal* **16/1**

1-30 6 nk **Posh Boy (IRE)**[43] 1798 4-9-5 67 GeorgeBaker 6 70+
(Chris Wall) *hld up in midfield: smooth prog 3f out to trck ldng pair 2f out: led over 1f out: hdd & wknd tamely last 120yds* **6/4**[1]

3215 7 nk **Tijuca (IRE)**[18] 2523 5-9-1 63 FrederikTylicki 12 66
(Ed de Giles) *stdd s: hld up in last pair: stl only 10th 2f out: prog on inner 1f out: styd on: nvr quite able to chal* **8/1**[3]

0355 8 3/4 **Diletta Tommasa (IRE)**[45] 1729 4-9-0 62 (p) ShaneKelly 7 63
(John Stimpson) *hld up towards rr: rdn over 2f out: keeping on fnl f but no ch whn n.m.r nr fin* **14/1**

0365 9 2 **Understory (USA)**[39] 1919 7-8-13 61 (b) HayleyTurner 2 58
(Tim McCarthy) *led at str pce: hdd & wknd over 1f out* **10/1**

00-0 10 5 **L'Hirondelle (IRE)**[66] 1302 10-8-10 58 KierenFox 3 45
(Michael Attwater) *pushed up to press ldr: lost 2nd and wknd qckly wl over 1f out* **66/1**

3320 11 17 **Standing Strong (IRE)**[7] 2862 6-9-0 62 (p) RichardHughes 8 15
(Zoe Davison) *stdd s: hld up in last trio: no prog 3f out: virtually p.u over 1f out* **5/1**[2]

2m 4.81s (-1.79) **Going Correction** +0.05s/f (Slow) **11 Ran SP% 119.7**
Speed ratings (Par 103): **109,108,107,107,107 107,107,106,104,100 87**
CSF £436.47 CT £5250.58 TOTE £25.70: £6.40, £4.70, £3.00; EX 307.20 Trifecta £1457.60 Part won. Pool: £1,943.56 - 0.63 winning units..
**Owner** J J Bridger **Bred** W J Wyatt **Trained** Liphook, Hants

**FOCUS**
A strongly run finale.
T/Plt: £93.40 to a £1 stake. Pool: £67,410.55 - 526.32 winning tickets. T/Qpdt: £14.70 to a £1 stake. Pool: £5,362.02 - 269.25 winning tickets. JN

# 2487 SALISBURY (R-H)
## Tuesday, June 10

**OFFICIAL GOING: Good to firm (good in places; 8.8)**
Wind: mild breeze against Weather: sunny with cloudy periods

## 3081 BATHWICK TYRES MAIDEN AUCTION STKS (DIV I) 6f
**1:55** (1:57) (Class 5) 2-Y-O **£2,911** (£866; £432; £216) **Stalls** Low

Form RPR

1 **Room Key** 2-9-0 0 DaneO'Neill 11 75+
(Eve Johnson Houghton) *rn green leaving stalls: sn cl up travelling wl: j. path over 3f out: led 2f out: rdn and kpt on wl fnl f* **12/1**

2 2 3/4 **Little Palaver**[18] 2499 2-8-6 0 RyanTate(5) 5 70
(Clive Cox) *chsd ldrs: rdn 2f out: sn chsng wnr: edgd lft jst over 1f out: kpt on same pce* **10/11**[1]

03 3 1 **Divine Law**[15] 2622 2-9-4 0 RichardHughes 8 74
(Richard Hannon) *hld up but in tch: rdn and hdwy fr 2f out: kpt on fnl f but nt pce to get on terms* **5/1**[2]

002 4 nk **Well Fleeced**[15] 2623 2-8-11 0 JohnFahy 4 66
(J S Moore) *trckd ldrs: rdn 2f out: short of room briefly jst over 1f out: kpt on fnl 120yds* **15/2**

42 5 1/2 **Buckleberry**[15] 2622 2-9-0 0 JamesDoyle 6 68
(Jonathan Portman) *trckd ldrs: rdn 2f out: kpt on tl no ex fnl 75yds* **6/1**[3]

463 6 1 3/4 **Chetan**[27] 2246 2-8-11 0 BenCurtis 1 59
(Milton Bradley) *led tl rdn 2f out: wknd ins fnl f* **25/1**

7 1 1/4 **Pivot Point (IRE)** 2-9-0 0 JimmyFortune 10 59
(Brian Meehan) *hld up: nt clr run bhd ldrs over 2f out: nt pce to get involved whn clr run over 1f out: fdd fnl 120yds* **20/1**

8 4 **Hidden Agenda** 2-8-6 0 DavidProbert 9 39
(Michael Blanshard) *hld up: rdn over 2f out: wknd over 1f out* **66/1**

0 9 4 **Mullionheir**[13] 2680 2-9-0 0 SteveDrowne 3 35
(John Best) *w ldr tl rdn 3f out: wknd wl over 1f out* **50/1**

1m 15.02s (0.22) **Going Correction** -0.10s/f (Good) **9 Ran SP% 114.9**
Speed ratings (Par 93): **94,93,91,91,90 88,86,81,75**
CSF £22.82 TOTE £16.10: £2.60, £1.10, £1.80; EX 31.30 Trifecta £189.60.
**Owner** The Picnic Partnership **Bred** R J C Wilmot-Smith **Trained** Blewbury, Oxon

**FOCUS**
A modest 2yo maiden.

## 3082 BATHWICK TYRES MAIDEN AUCTION STKS (DIV II) 6f
**2:25** (2:26) (Class 5) 2-Y-O **£2,911** (£866; £432; £216) **Stalls** Low

Form RPR

2 1 **Jaganory (IRE)**[8] 2829 2-9-0 0 AdamKirby 9 73
(David Evans) *sn led: rdn over 1f out: kpt on wl to assert fnl f: rdn out* **3/1**[1]

6 2 1 3/4 **Vegas Rebel (IRE)**[13] 2680 2-9-4 0 JimmyFortune 5 72
(Peter Chapple-Hyam) *mid-div: rdn 2f out: hdwy 1f out: r.o strly to go 2nd fnl 100yds: a being hld by wnr* **9/1**[3]

5 3 shd **Cape Cay**[15] 2623 2-8-9 0 AndreaAtzeni 3 62
(Ralph Beckett) *trckd ldrs: pushed along 3f out: rdn 2f out: short of room whn swtchd lft fnl 160yds: kpt on* **3/1**[1]

4 1½ **Fayreway (IRE)** 2-8-6 0 ........ DavidProbert 4 55+
(Martyn Meade) *hld up: hdwy 3f out: rdn 2f out: ev ch jst over 1f out: no ex fnl 120yds* **33/1**

3 5 1 **Wolfofwallstreet (IRE)**[42] 1859 2-9-0 0 ........ WilliamBuick 7 60
(Ed Walker) *in tch: swtchd lft over 2f out: sn rdn and hdwy: keeping on at same pce virtually disputing 3rd whn briefly short of room fnl 75yds* **13/2[2]**

0 6 1 **Bakht A Rawan (IRE)**[15] 2623 2-9-4 0 ........ DaneO'Neill 2 61
(Mark Usher) *slowly away: in tch: nt clrest of runs fr over 2f out but rdn: kpt on fnl f but nvr any threat* **12/1**

0 7 2¼ **Gavarnie Encore**[15] 2622 2-8-11 0 ........ SteveDrowne 6 47
(Michael Blanshard) *hld up: rdn over 2f out: nvr any imp* **100/1**

8 4½ **Runner Runner (IRE)** 2-8-13 0 ........ FergusSweeney 8 36
(George Baker) *towards rr: rdn over 2f out: no imp: wknd fnl f* **33/1**

9 18 **Grenade** 2-9-0 0 ........ RichardHughes 11 +
(Richard Hannon) *sn trcking wnr: rdn over 2f out: wknd qckly* **3/1[1]**

5 10 5 **Edmund Halley (FR)**[43] 1807 2-8-8 0 ........(b[1]) ThomasBrown(3) 10
(Harry Dunlop) *chsd ldrs for 3f: sn wknd* **100/1**

1m 14.62s (-0.18) **Going Correction** -0.10s/f (Good) **10 Ran SP% 113.9**
Speed ratings (Par 93): **97,94,94,92,91 89,86,80,56,50**
CSF £31.36 TOTE £3.60: £1.40, £1.80, £1.40; EX 24.40 Trifecta £98.90.
**Owner** Wayne Clifford **Bred** Canice Farrell Jnr **Trained** Pandy, Monmouths

**FOCUS**
The second division of the 2yo maiden was run in a time 0.4sec faster than the first.

## 3083 BATHWICK TYRES MAIDEN STKS 6f 212y
2:55 (2:56) (Class 5) 3-Y-O+ £3,234 (£962; £481; £240) Stalls Low

Form RPR

2-3 1 **Outlawed**[11] 2733 3-9-3 0 ........ GeorgeBaker 4 85+
(Ed Walker) *trckd ldrs: swtchd lft over 2f out: rdn to ld jst ins fnl f: r.o wl fnl 120yds: readily* **13/8[1]**

0- 2 1¾ **Fyrecracker (IRE)**[315] 4858 3-9-3 0 ........ RichardHughes 8 80
(Marcus Tregoning) *mid-div: hdwy 3f out: rdn to press ldr wl over 1f out: ev ch ent fnl f: nt pce of wnr fnl 120yds* **5/1[3]**

0- 3 hd **Certificate**[221] 7654 3-9-3 0 ........ AndreaAtzeni 12 79+
(Roger Varian) *mid-div: j. path over 3f out: rdn and hdwy fr 2f out: kpt on nicely ins fnl f: wnt 3rd cl home* **9/4[2]**

0 4 ½ **Marydale**[24] 2339 3-8-12 0 ........ DaneO'Neill 2 73+
(Henry Candy) *s.i.s: towards rr: swtchd lft wl over 2f out: sn rdn: hdwy over 1f out: kpt on wl fnl f* **16/1**

2 5 nse **Debit**[13] 2667 3-9-3 0 ........ AdamKirby 7 78
(Clive Cox) *prom: led over 2f out: sn rdn: hdd jst ins fnl f: no ex fnl 120yds* **10/1**

0-4 6 9 **Maymyo (IRE)**[8] 2846 3-9-3 0 ........ JamesDoyle 1 54
(Sylvester Kirk) *mid-div: rdn 2f out: nvr threatened: wknd fnl f* **33/1**

46- 7 2¾ **Roring Samson (IRE)**[239] 7251 3-9-3 0 ........ FergusSweeney 6 46
(George Baker) *trckd ldrs: rdn 2f out: wknd over 1f out* **66/1**

8 1 **Frankie** 3-8-10 0 ........ CamHardie(7) 3 44
(Jimmy Fox) *mid-div: rn green u.p over 2f out: wknd over 1f out* **100/1**

04- 9 5 **Dark Reality (IRE)**[230] 7466 3-8-12 0 ........ JamieSpencer 10 25
(Ralph Beckett) *hmpd sn after s: a towards rr: wknd over 1f out* **9/1**

10 1½ **Sea Whisper** 3-8-12 0 ........ DavidProbert 5 21
(Jo Crowley) *led tl rdn over 2f out: sn wknd* **66/1**

0 11 ½ **Franklin Nights**[22] 2381 4-9-13 0 ........ SamHitchcott 9 29
(Polly Gundry) *a towards rr* **200/1**

1m 28.54s (-0.06) **Going Correction** -0.10s/f (Good)
**WFA** 3 from 4yo 10lb **11 Ran SP% 117.9**
Speed ratings (Par 103): **96,94,93,93,93 82,79,78,72,71 70**
CSF £10.29 TOTE £2.30: £1.10, £1.90, £2.00; EX 12.50 Trifecta £45.40.
**Owner** Laurence A Bellman **Bred** Snailwell Stud Co Ltd **Trained** Newmarket, Suffolk

**FOCUS**
Not a bad maiden, but the form is a bit muddling.

## 3084 SHARP'S DOOM BAR H'CAP 5f
3:25 (3:27) (Class 5) (0-70,71) 3-Y-O £2,911 (£866; £432; £216) Stalls Low

Form RPR

4-06 1 **Mr Dandy Man (IRE)**[22] 2406 3-9-5 68 ........ RobertWinston 5 77
(Ronald Harris) *mde all: clr over 2f out: in command after: readily* **8/1**

6-12 2 2¾ **Gulland Rock**[18] 2505 3-9-4 67 ........ MartinDwyer 2 66
(William Muir) *prom tl lost pl after 2f whn looking short of room: sn drvn in 3rd: kpt on to regain 2nd jst ins fnl f: a being readily hld by wnr* **11/8[1]**

1434 3 nk **The Dandy Yank (IRE)**[6] 2889 3-9-8 71 ow1 ........ RichardHughes 4 69
(Jamie Osborne) *hld up in cl 5th: swtchd to far rails sn after s: swtchd lft 2f out: sn rdn: r.o to chal for 2nd ins fnl f: a being readily hld by wnr* **13/8[2]**

60-0 4 3 **Dark Phantom (IRE)**[37] 1980 3-8-2 51 ........(t) SilvestreDeSousa 3 38
(Peter Makin) *chsd ldrs: rdn over 2f out: chsd wnr sn after tl no ex jst ins fnl f* **14/1**

4334 5 2¾ **Jazz Bay**[18] 2505 3-8-2 51 oh1 ........ WilliamCarson 6 28
(John Bridger) *chsd ldrs: chsd wnr over 3f out tl rdn 2f out: wknd ins fnl f* **15/2[3]**

1m 0.62s (-0.38) **Going Correction** -0.10s/f (Good) **5 Ran SP% 109.7**
Speed ratings (Par 99): **99,94,94,89,84**
CSF £19.54 TOTE £5.10: £3.70, £1.10; EX 22.30 Trifecta £40.00.
**Owner** S & A Mares **Bred** Oliver Donlon **Trained** Earlswood, Monmouths

**FOCUS**
A moderate little sprint handicap.

## 3085 EBF STALLIONS BREEDING WINNERS MARGADALE FILLIES' H'CAP 1m 1f 198y
3:55 (3:55) (Class 4) (0-85,83) 3-Y-O+ £6,469 (£1,925; £962; £481) Stalls Low

Form RPR

4-03 1 **Rosehill Artist (IRE)**[26] 2277 3-9-1 83 ........ JamieSpencer 4 93
(Charles Hills) *trckd ldrs: rdn 3f out: led jst ins fnl f: styd on w enough in hand fnl 120yds: rdn out* **8/1**

01 2 nk **Seagull (IRE)**[25] 2310 3-9-0 82 ........ WilliamBuick 2 91+
(John Gosden) *hld up towards rr: rdn wl over 2f out: little imp tl hdwy jst over 1f out: styd on strly to go 2nd fnl 100yds: nvr quite getting to wnr* **11/4[1]**

1-05 3 1 **Likelihood (USA)**[13] 2685 3-8-12 80 ........ JamesDoyle 7 87
(John Gosden) *trckd ldr: led over 3f out: rdn over 2f out: hdd jst ins fnl f: kpt on but no ex fnl 120yds* **8/1**

4-31 4 3¾ **Crystal Nymph (IRE)**[26] 2277 3-8-9 77 ........ RichardHughes 5 77
(Richard Hannon) *mid-div: rdn 3f out: styd on fr over 1f out but nt pce to get on terms* **13/2[3]**

3-24 5 ½ **Cascading**[26] 2280 3-8-10 78 ........ JimmyFortune 10 77
(Hughie Morrison) *trckd ldrs: rdn 3f out: nvr threatened: one pce fnl 2f* **9/1**

1-23 6 hd **Mystery Drama**[12] 2700 4-9-8 77 ........ AdamKirby 6 77
(Alan King) *hld up bhd: rdn over 3f out: no imp tl styd on fnl f: nvr any danger* **11/1**

3-15 7 3¾ **Passing By**[21] 2431 3-8-0 75 ........ CamHardie(7) 1 66
(Richard Hannon) *mid-div: hung rt over 5f out: rdn 3f out: nvr threatened: wknd fnl f* **12/1**

1 8 hd **Hidden Gold (IRE)**[26] 2279 3-9-0 82 ........ SilvestreDeSousa 3 73
(Saeed bin Suroor) *hld up towards rr: rdn wl over 2f out: nvr any imp* **7/2[2]**

4-33 9 3½ **Play Street**[39] 1910 5-9-3 75 ........ MatthewLawson(3) 9 60
(Jonathan Portman) *led untl over 3f out: chsd ldr: sn rdn: wknd ent fnl f* **50/1**

2m 7.28s (-2.62) **Going Correction** -0.10s/f (Good)
**WFA** 3 from 4yo+ 13lb **9 Ran SP% 112.4**
Speed ratings (Par 102): **106,105,104,101,101 101,98,98,95**
CSF £29.31 CT £181.65 TOTE £9.20: £2.90, £1.10, £3.10; EX 32.60 Trifecta £258.70.
**Owner** John C Grant **Bred** Tullamaine Castle Stud **Trained** Lambourn, Berks

**FOCUS**
A fair fillies' handicap run at a good pace.

## 3086 ROA OWNERS JACKPOT H'CAP 1m 4f
4:25 (4:26) (Class 5) (0-70,70) 4-Y-O+ £2,911 (£866; £432; £216) Stalls Low

Form RPR

00-0 1 **Sunny Future (IRE)**[39] 1909 8-9-5 68 ........ GeorgeBaker 8 80
(Malcolm Saunders) *mde all: shkn up to assert ent fnl f: styd on wl: comf* **7/1[3]**

60-2 2 2¾ **Fanzine**[25] 2301 4-9-7 70 ........ JimmyFortune 1 78
(Hughie Morrison) *racd keenly: hld up: making hdwy whn nt clr run on rails 4f out: smooth prog over 2f out: trcking wnr whn swtchd lft for brief effrt jst over 1f out: nt qckn and sn hld* **7/2[1]**

0030 3 2½ **Honourable Knight (IRE)**[6] 2885 6-8-9 58 ........(v) DavidProbert 5 62
(Mark Usher) *trckd ldrs: rdn wl over 2f out: edgd lft over 1f out: styd on fnl f* **14/1**

22-1 4 hd **Men Don't Cry (IRE)**[20] 2465 5-8-12 61 ........ FrederikTylicki 2 64
(Ed de Giles) *chsd wnr: rdn whn sltly outpcd 3f out: styd on fnl f* **9/2[2]**

-356 5 hd **Nave (USA)**[15] 2627 7-9-6 69 ........ MartinLane 7 72
(David Simcock) *hld up: rdn to chse ldrs over 2f out: rdr dropped whip jst ins fnl f: styd on clsng stages* **9/2[2]**

6231 6 shd **Ivor's Princess**[12] 2693 5-9-6 69 ........(b) SeanLevey 4 72
(Rod Millman) *in tch: rdn to chse ldrs 3f out: styd on same pce fnl 2f* **7/1[3]**

45-2 7 1¾ **Shades Of Grey**[12] 2693 7-9-0 68 ........ RyanTate(5) 3 68
(Clive Cox) *chsd wnr: rdn 3f out: lost 2nd over 1f out: wknd ins fnl f* **7/2[1]**

2m 37.8s (-0.20) **Going Correction** -0.10s/f (Good) **7 Ran SP% 112.5**
Speed ratings (Par 103): **96,94,92,92,92 92,91**
CSF £30.52 CT £331.42 TOTE £8.50: £2.90, £3.10; EX 37.50 Trifecta £417.30.
**Owner** M S Saunders **Bred** Mrs G Stanga **Trained** Green Ore, Somerset

**FOCUS**
A modest handicap with an all-the-way winner.

## 3087 MOLSON COORS H'CAP 6f 212y
4:55 (4:57) (Class 6) (0-65,64) 3-Y-O £2,587 (£770; £384; £192) Stalls Low

Form RPR

3364 1 **Seven Lucky Seven**[21] 2447 3-9-1 58 ........ JamesDoyle 8 71
(Nick Littmoden) *mid-div: smooth hdwy over 2f out: led over 1f out: sn pushed clr: edgd rt: easily* **14/1**

40-6 2 3¾ **Dream Impossible (IRE)**[14] 2647 3-8-11 54 ........ MartinLane 11 57
(Peter Makin) *mid-div: rdn over 2f out: stdy prog over 1f out: styd on wl fnl f: wnt 2nd fnl 120yds: no ch w easy wnr* **16/1**

0-12 3 1¾ **Biotic**[62] 1379 3-9-5 62 ........ SeanLevey 7 60
(Rod Millman) *chsd ldrs: rdn and ev ch 2f out: sn hld chsng wnr: no ex whn lost 2nd ins fnl f* **5/1[2]**

-502 4 1½ **Tubeanie (IRE)**[7] 2860 3-9-2 59 ........ AdamKirby 4 54
(Clive Cox) *chsd ldrs: rdn over 2f out: twice short of room over 1f out: kpt on same pce* **7/2[1]**

4005 5 1½ **Nutbush**[13] 2668 3-8-1 51 ........ PaddyPilley(7) 10 42
(Mick Channon) *mid-div: rdn over 2f out: no imp tl styd on ent fnl f* **25/1**

005- 6 1 **Ventura Ice (IRE)**[250] 6974 3-8-11 61 ........ GaryMahon(7) 14 49
(Richard Hannon) *hld up towards rr: rdn and hdwy into midfield 2f out: no further imp fnl f* **8/1**

3500 7 1 **La Napoule**[26] 2274 3-9-3 60 ........ KieranO'Neill 9 45
(Richard Hannon) *s.i.s: towards rr: rdn wl over 2f out: sme late prog: nvr any danger* **25/1**

324 8 1 **Dandys Perier (IRE)**[26] 2281 3-9-2 59 ........ RobertWinston 3 42
(Ronald Harris) *w ldr: rdn wl over 2f out: hld over 1f out: wknd ent fnl f* **15/2**

-140 9 2¾ **Speed Society**[29] 2209 3-9-2 59 ........ FrederikTylicki 13 35
(Jim Boyle) *led: rdn over 2f out: hdd over 1f out: wknd* **10/1**

-000 10 1 **Stan Nineteen (IRE)**[12] 2695 3-9-1 58 ........ SteveDrowne 6 31
(Simon Hodgson) *a towards rr* **50/1**

0-06 11 8 **Borough Belle**[12] 2688 3-8-5 53 ........ AmyScott(5) 16 5
(Henry Candy) *s.i.s: sn mid-div: rdn and wknd over 2f out* **7/1[3]**

0-50 12 9 **Paradise Child**[9] 2802 3-7-11 45 ........ PhilipPrince(5) 17
(Bill Turner) *s.i.s: a towards rr* **66/1**

2340 13 4 **Blacke Forest**[20] 2470 3-9-4 61 ........ SilvestreDeSousa 1
(William Muir) *chsd ldrs tl wknd over 2f out* **20/1**

55-4 14 45 **Cueca (FR)**[42] 1832 3-8-13 56 ........ JimmyFortune 5
(Jonathan Portman) *mid-div: stmbld on path: sn bhd tl wknd over 2f out: t.o* **16/1**

1m 27.84s (-0.76) **Going Correction** -0.10s/f (Good) **14 Ran SP% 117.7**
Speed ratings (Par 97): **100,95,93,92,90 89,88,86,83,82 73,63,58,7**
CSF £203.14 CT £1282.13 TOTE £13.60: £3.80, £6.60, £2.70; EX 210.90 Trifecta £3487.40 Part won. Pool: £4,649.87 - 0.56 winning units..
**Owner** Franconson Partners **Bred** Llety Farms **Trained** Newmarket, Suffolk

**FOCUS**
A wide-open, low-grade handicap.

## 3088 CGA RACING EXCELLENCE APPRENTICE H'CAP (WHIPS SHALL BE CARRIED BUT NOT USED) 6f
5:30 (5:30) (Class 5) (0-75,75) 4-Y-O+ £2,911 (£866; £432; £216) Stalls Low

Form RPR

3640 1 **Meridius (IRE)**[6] 2887 4-9-0 63 ........(p) JordanVaughan 18 72
(Nick Littmoden) *chsd ldrs: str chal fr 2f out: kpt on wl to ld nring fin* **16/1**

0536 2 nk **Intomist (IRE)**[19] 2486 5-9-3 66 ........(p) DanielCremin 10 74
(Jim Boyle) *trckd ldrs: narrow advantage 2f out: kpt on fnl f: hdd nring fin* **6/1[1]**

0246 3 ½ **Dark Lane**[31] 2174 8-8-5 59 ........ HollieDoyle(5) 2 65
(David Evans) *chsd ldrs: r.o ins fnl f: clsng wl at fin* **14/1**

0-02 **4** 1 1/2 **Jontleman (IRE)**[32] 2124 4-9-6 **74** PaddyPilley(5) 5 76+
(Mick Channon) *mid-div: short of room on far rails most of way tl hdwy 2f out: styd on same pce fnl f: drifted lft nring fin* **7/1**[2]

4612 **5** 1/2 **Catalinas Diamond (IRE)**[27] 2250 6-8-9 **58** (t) RobJFitzpatrick 17 58
(Pat Murphy) *hld up towards rr: stdy prog fr 2f out: kpt on ins fnl f: nt rch ldrs* **8/1**[3]

1300 **6** 1/2 **Masai Moon**[25] 2300 10-9-3 **66** (b) PatMillman 13 64
(Rod Millman) *bhd: swtchd lft 2f out: r.o wl fnl f: nvr threatened ldrs* **25/1**

-066 **7** *hd* **Freddy With A Y (IRE)**[20] 2462 4-9-5 **75** (p) HectorCrouch(7) 7 73
(Gary Moore) *mid-div: styd on fnl f: nvr threatened* **6/1**[1]

-001 **8** *nse* **Night Trade (IRE)**[8] 2831 7-8-6 **58** 6ex (p) DavidParkes(3) 8 56
(Ronald Harris) *mid-div: kpt on ins fnl f: nvr threatened* **14/1**

6-60 **9** *1* **Koharu**[19] 2486 4-8-10 **64** (tp) ChrisMeehan(5) 3 58
(Peter Makin) *mid-div: chsd ldrs 2f out: one pce fnl f* **25/1**

2206 **10** 1/2 **Top Cop**[12] 2691 5-9-3 **73** (p) AbieKnowles(7) 1 66
(Ronald Harris) *disp ld tl 2f out: wknd fnl f* **14/1**

5-30 **11** *hd* **Dream Catcher (FR)**[27] 2250 6-9-2 **68** CharlotteJenner(3) 12 60
(Henry Candy) *disp ld tl 2f out: wknd fnl f* **8/1**[3]

040- **12** 1 1/4 **The Wee Chief (IRE)**[199] 8023 8-8-5 **57** CamHardie(3) 16 45
(Jimmy Fox) *a towards rr* **14/1**

-522 **13** 1/2 **George Baker (IRE)**[20] 2471 7-9-2 **72** AlfieDavies(7) 4 59
(George Baker) *a towards rr* **11/1**

000- **14** *2* **Aye Aye Skipper (IRE)**[173] 8345 4-9-4 **72** PaulBooth(5) 14 52
(Dean Ivory) *mid-div tl wknd over 1f out* **33/1**

1420 **15** *hd* **Encapsulated**[19] 2488 4-8-3 **59** (p) RhiainIngram(7) 9 39
(Roger Ingram) *mid-div tl wknd over 1f out* **14/1**

1m 14.09s (-0.71) **Going Correction** -0.10s/f (Good) **15** Ran SP% **121.5**
Speed ratings (Par 103): **100,99,98,96,96 95,95,95,93,93 93,91,90,88,87**
CSF £107.19 CT £1439.32 TOTE £22.50: £6.20, £2.20, £4.00; EX 179.10 Trifecta £1163.40 Part won. Pool: £1,551.25 - 0.54 winning units..
**Owner** Franconson Partners **Bred** Pendley Farm **Trained** Newmarket, Suffolk

**FOCUS**
A wide-open race of its type.
T/Plt: £24.50 to a £1 stake. Pool: £69,823.04 - 2,075.33 winning tickets. T/Qpdt: £8.10 to a £1 stake. Pool: £4,533.19 - 411.35 winning tickets. TM

# 2290 LE CROISE-LAROCHE
Tuesday, June 10

**OFFICIAL GOING: Turf: heavy**

## 3089a PRIX PAUL-NOEL DELAHOUTRE (CLAIMER) (5YO+) (AMATEUR RIDERS) (TURF) 1m 2f 110y
**1:05** (1:05) 5-Y-0+ **£6,250** (£2,500; £1,875; £1,250; £625)

RPR

**1** **Al Nejmaa (IRE)**[89] 7-10-11 0 DennisSchiergen 9 76
(N Sauer, Germany) **9/5**[1]

**2** 3/4 **Sirocco De Pame (FR)**[45] 8-10-7 0 ow4 MrChristopheGuimard 3 71
(R Le Gal, France) **133/10**

**3** *snk* **Garlin Blues (FR)**[63] 6-10-11 0 MrFlorentGuy 11 74
(J Phelippon, France) **9/2**[2]

**4** 1 3/4 **Nice Chief (FR)**[27] 5-10-0 0 MrDamienArtu(4) 10 64
(J-Y Artu, France) **137/10**

**5** 1 1/4 **Pedregalejo (IRE)**[18] 6-10-3 0 (b) MrJean-PhilippeBoisgontier 8 60
(P Van De Poele, France) **15/2**[3]

**6** 1 1/4 **Saute**[130] 8-10-8 0 (b) MlleDelphineGarcia-Dubois 7 63
(Mlle K Hoste, Belgium) **109/10**

**7** *1* **Valbucca (IRE)**[25] 2294 7-10-0 0 (b) MrEdouardMonfort 1 53
(Amy Weaver) *missed break: rushed up to chse ldrs on rail: rdn and outpcd over 1 1/2f out: fdd fnl f* **41/5**

**8** *snk* **Butler (IRE)**[382] 7-10-3 0 MrThomasGuineheux(5) 12 61
(Braem Horse Racing Sprl, Belgium) **35/1**

**9** 1 1/4 **Arluno (FR)**[310] 5042 5-9-13 0 MrCharles-AntoinePrunault(4) 4 53
(J-Y Artu, France) **26/1**

**10** *5* **Dark Ambition (IRE)**[598] 7266 5-10-8 0 MlleGaelleGernay 2 49
(N Minner, Belgium) **23/1**

**11** *2* **Eldarion (IRE)**[34] 6-10-4 0 ow1 (b) MrPierreJFertillet 6 41
(A Lyon, France) **28/1**

**12** *5* **Doctor Sim (IRE)**[34] 5-10-12 0 MrYannickMergirie 5 39
(D De Waele, France) **147/10**

2m 22.3s (142.30) **12** Ran SP% **119.2**
WIN (incl. 1 euro stake): 2.80. PLACES: 1.30, 3.00, 1.70. DF: 17.80. SF: 21.70.
**Owner** Stall Ori **Bred** Team Hogdala A B **Trained** Germany

# TABY (R-H)
Tuesday, June 10

**OFFICIAL GOING: Turf: good to soft**

## 3090a STOCKHOLMS STORA PRIS (GROUP 3) (4YO+) (TURF) 1m 1f 165y
**8:12** (12:00) 4-Y-0+ **£37,523** (£18,761; £9,005; £6,003; £3,752)

RPR

**1** **Bank Of Burden (USA)**[45] 7-9-2 0 Per-AndersGraberg 10 103
(Niels Petersen, Norway) *hld up towards rr: hdwy over 2 1/2f out: rdn to take a narrow ld ins fnl f: r.o gamely u.p* **107/20**[3]

**2** 1/2 **Hurricane Red (IRE)**[28] 2245 4-9-2 0 ElioneChaves 3 102
(Lennart Reuterskiold Jr, Sweden) *settled in midfield: hdwy on outer over 2 1/2f out: rdn to ld appr 1f out: hdd ins fnl f: rallied gamely u.p* **13/10**[1]

**3** *3* **Jubilance (IRE)**[12] 5-9-2 0 NikolajStott 11 96
(Bent Olsen, Denmark) *settled in rr: hdwy over 2 1/2f out: wnt 3rd ins fnl f: styd on but nvr on terms w first two* **51/1**

**4** 1 1/2 **Fearless Hunter (GER)**[207] 4-9-2 0 PatDobbs 7 93
(Rune Haugen, Norway) *midfield on inner: 6th and styng on 3f out: short of room and sltly hmpd 2 1/2f out: rdn to chse leaqders 1 1/2f out: one pce u.p fnl f* **42/1**

**5** *1* **Berling (IRE)**[28] 2245 7-9-2 0 OliverWilson 8 91
(Jessica Long, Sweden) *hld up towards rr: effrt on outer over 2 1/2f out but no real imp: styd on fr over 1f out: nrest at fin* **147/10**

**6** 1 1/2 **Without Fear (FR)**[45] 6-9-2 0 RafaelSchistl 12 88
(Niels Petersen, Norway) *hld up towards rr: outpcd and pushed along 3f out: sn in last: hrd rdn and hdwy under 2f out: swtchd off rail and kpt on wl fnl f: nvr nrr* **17/2**

**7** *nk* **Coprah**[12] 6-9-2 0 ManuelSantos 9 87
(Cathrine Erichsen, Norway) *tk a t.k.h in midfield: plld way to front bef 1/2-way: hdd appr 1f out: sn wknd* **209/10**

**8** *3* **Funinthesand (IRE)**[28] 2245 5-9-2 0 RobertHavlin 6 81
(Wido Neuroth, Norway) *chsd ldrs: rdn and nt qckn over 2f out: grad fdd fr 1 1/2f out* **269/10**

**9** 1/2 **Old Pal (FR)**[12] 5-9-2 0 ShaneKarlsson 5 80
(Niels Petersen, Norway) *trckd ldr on outer: lost pl 2f out: grad dropped away* **25/1**

**10** *2* **Energia El Gigante (BRZ)**[488] 553 5-9-2 0 RafaeldeOliveira 2 76
(Fabricio Borges, Sweden) *led: hdd 1/2-way: lost pl over 2 1/2f out: wknd fnl 1 1/2f* **7/2**[2]

**11** *hd* **Probably (IRE)**[289] 4-9-2 0 JacobJohansen 1 75
(Rune Haugen, Norway) *tk v t.k.h: restrained on heels of ldr: settled and chsd ldng pair fr 1/2-way: rdn and wknd fnl 1 1/2f* **7/1**

1m 57.6s (-1.70) **11** Ran SP% **127.1**
PARI-MUTUEL (all including 1sek stake): WIN 6.33; PLACE 2.26, 1.37, 5.23; SF 25.08.
**Owner** Stall Trick Or Treat **Bred** Bjarne Minde **Trained** Norway

# 2540 BEVERLEY (R-H)
Wednesday, June 11

**OFFICIAL GOING: Good to soft (soft in places) changing to good to soft after race 1 (2.20)**
Wind: Light against Weather: Cloudy with sunny periods

## 3091 RACE HORSE TRADER CLAIMING STKS 5f
**2:20** (2:21) (Class 6) 2-Y-O **£2,264** (£673; £336; £168) **Stalls** Low

Form RPR

450 **1** **Fairweather Trader (IRE)**[9] 2824 2-8-9 0 PaulMulrennan 3 53
(Paul Midgley) *mde all: rdn and edgd lft ent fnl f: drvn and hung lft last 50yds: hld on* **3/1**[3]

3260 **2** *nk* **Just Marion (IRE)**[24] 2359 2-8-3 0 DeclanBates(3) 6 49
(David Evans) *bmpd s: chsd ldrs on wd outside: rdn along wl over 1f out: edgd rt ent fnl f: drvn and styng on whn hmpd last 50yds* **5/2**[2]

60 **3** 1 1/2 **Astrea**[16] 2615 2-8-4 0 AndrewMullen 4 42
(Nigel Tinkler) *chsd wnr: rdn along 2f out: drvn and n.m.r ins fnl f: kpt on same pce* **7/1**

016 **4** 1/2 **Tagtale (IRE)**[24] 2360 2-8-2 0 (b) PatrickMathers 5 38
(Richard Fahey) *wnt lft s: chsd ldrs: rdn along 2f out: edgd lft over 1f out: drvn and hld whn n.m.r and snatched up last 50yds* **2/1**[1]

60 **5** *shd* **Autumn Revue**[12] 2736 2-8-6 0 (b[1]) DuranFentiman 2 42
(Tim Easterby) *in rr and sn pushed along: hdwy on inner 2f out: rdn to chse wnr whn sltly hmpd and swtchd rt ent fnl f: sn one pce* **8/1**

1m 8.36s (4.86) **Going Correction** +0.70s/f (Yiel) **5** Ran SP% **110.5**
Speed ratings (Par 91): **89,88,86,85,85**
CSF £10.89 TOTE £5.20: £1.80, £2.30; EX 9.40 Trifecta £56.40.
**Owner** The Traders **Bred** Crown Bloodstock **Trained** Westow, N Yorks
■ Stewards' Enquiry : Declan Bates four-day ban: used whip above permitted level (Jun 25-28)

**FOCUS**
A very ordinary juvenile claimer.

## 3092 FOLLOW US ON TWITTER @RACEHORSETRADER H'CAP (DIV I) 5f
**2:50** (2:51) (Class 6) (0-65,68) 3-Y-0+ **£2,264** (£673; £336; £168) **Stalls** Low

Form RPR

-000 **1** **Ichimoku**[12] 2724 4-8-9 **46** oh1 RoystonFrench 8 56
(Bryan Smart) *in tch on outer: pushed along 2f out: hdwy and rdn over 1f out: led ins fnl f: sn edgd rt and styd on* **25/1**

51-1 **2** 1 1/2 **Adiator**[22] 2421 6-9-9 **65** AdamCarter(5) 3 70+
(Neville Bycroft) *hld up: hdwy wl over 1f out: rdn to ld briefly jst ins fnl f: sn drvn and hdd: kpt on same pce* **7/4**[1]

0436 **3** 1 1/4 **Red Shadow**[15] 2653 5-8-9 **46** (p) RobertWinston 11 46
(Alan Brown) *sltly hmpd s: in rr and sn swtchd rt: pushed along and hdwy on inner 2f out: effrt and nt clr run over 1f out: rdn and kpt on fnl f: nrst fin* **25/1**

-023 **4** *nse* **Lees Anthem**[12] 2743 7-9-5 **56** DavidAllan 9 56
(Mel Brittain) *wnt lft s: towards rr: hdwy over 1f out: sn rdn and kpt on fnl f: nrst fin* **6/1**

01 **5** 2 1/4 **Sir Geoffrey (IRE)**[5] 2951 8-9-12 **68** 6ex (p) MatthewHopkins(5) 4 60
(Scott Dixon) *led: rdn along wl over 1f out: drvn and hdd ent fnl f: one pce* **11/2**[3]

0-00 **6** 1 1/4 **Arch Walker (IRE)**[19] 2514 7-9-1 **52** DuranFentiman 7 39
(John Weymes) *chsd ldr: rdn along over 2f out: wknd over 1f out* **33/1**

-340 **7** *1* **Iggy**[30] 2219 4-9-8 **59** (t) JamesSullivan 1 43
(Michael Easterby) *trckd ldrs on inner: hdwy 2f out: rdn over 1f out: wknd fnl f* **3/1**[2]

00-3 **8** 1 1/4 **Flirtinaskirt**[132] 383 4-9-8 **62** JasonHart(3) 6 41
(Ed McMahon) *prom: rdn along 1/2-way: wknd wl over 1f out* **6/1**

1m 6.64s (3.14) **Going Correction** +0.70s/f (Yiel) **8** Ran SP% **116.0**
Speed ratings (Par 101): **102,99,97,97,93 91,90,88**
CSF £69.16 CT £1178.69 TOTE £27.80: £5.90, £1.10, £3.00; EX 62.30 Trifecta £714.10.
**Owner** Crossfields Racing **Bred** Crossfields Bloodstock Ltd **Trained** Hambleton, N Yorks
■ Stewards' Enquiry : Matthew Hopkins two-day ban: careless riding (Jun 26-27)

**FOCUS**
Low-grade stuff and a real turn up.

## 3093 FOLLOW US ON TWITTER @RACEHORSETRADER H'CAP (DIV II) 5f
**3:20** (3:21) (Class 6) (0-65,66) 3-Y-0+ **£2,264** (£673; £336; £168) **Stalls** Low

Form RPR

/03 **1** **Incomparable**[14] 2675 9-8-6 **48** (p) MatthewHopkins(5) 4 58
(Scott Dixon) *hmpd at s and t.k.h on inner: trckd ldr: effrt over 1f out: swtchd lft and rdn to chal ent fnl f: led last 100yds: styd on* **9/1**

0000 **2** 1 1/2 **Decision By One**[14] 2669 5-9-2 **56** (t) DeclanBates(3) 5 61
(David Evans) *hmpd s: sn chsng ldr: rdn along wl over 1f out: drvn ent fnl f: kpt on* **10/1**

6-66 **3** 1/2 **Singing Star (IRE)**[23] 2388 3-7-13 **50** RobertDodsworth(7) 2 50
(Mel Brittain) *sltly hmpd s: hld up in rr: hdwy 2f out: effrt and nt clr run towards inner over 1f out: rdn and kpt on fnl f: nrst fin* **13/2**

0436 **4** *hd* **Pull The Pin (IRE)**[21] 2459 5-9-2 **58**....................(bt) ShirleyTeasdale(5) 8 60
(Ann Stokell) *qckly away and wnt sharply rt s: led: rdn over 1f out: hdd and drvn last 100yds: wknd towards fin* **8/1**

-020 **5** *2 1/2* **Addictive Nature (IRE)**[32] 2174 4-8-10 **52**............(v[1]) LouisSteward(5) 3 45
(John Gallagher) *hmpd s: chsd ldrs: rdn along over 2f out: wknd over 1f out* **5/1**[3]

4251 **6** *nk* **Bond Club**[9] 2838 4-9-12 **66** 6ex....................................(b) RobertTart(3) 7 58
(Geoffrey Oldroyd) *in rr and sn pushed along: swtchd lft to outer 1/2-way: drifted lft to stands' rail and rdn wl over 1f out: styd on fnl f: nrst fin* **10/3**[1]

600- **7** *4 1/2* **Mr Mo Jo**[207] 7937 6-10-0 **65**.................................................. DavidAllan 6 41+
(Les Eyre) *hmpd s: chsd ldrs: rdn along over 2f out: sn wknd* **9/1**

-050 **8** *1 3/4* **Choc'A'Moca (IRE)**[16] 2606 7-9-3 **54**........................(v) PaulMulrennan 9 24
(Paul Midgley) *in tch on outer: rdn along over 2f out: sn wknd* **9/2**[2]

0U0- **9** *1/2* **Fair Bunny**[183] 8233 7-8-9 **46** oh1.....................................(b) PaulPickard 1 14
(Alan Brown) *sltly hmpd at s and in rr: swtchd lft 1/2-way: sn rdn along and n.d* **50/1**

33-2 **10** *7* **Knockamany Bends (IRE)**[125] 502 4-8-13 **50**............ PaddyAspell 10
(John Wainwright) *wnt lft s: sn chsng ldrs: rdn along 1/2-way: sn wknd* **20/1**

1m 6.77s (3.27) **Going Correction** +0.70s/f (Yiel)
**WFA** 3 from 4yo+ 7lb **10** Ran SP% **118.2**
Speed ratings (Par 101): **101,98,97,97,93 93,85,83,82,71**
CSF £96.58 CT £631.49 TOTE £11.90: £3.30, £4.30, £2.80; EX 95.10 Trifecta £543.30.
**Owner** Paul J Dixon **Bred** Mrs Yvette Dixon **Trained** Babworth, Notts
■ Stewards' Enquiry : Shirley Teasdale eight-day ban: careless riding (Jun 25-30,Jul 1-2); one-day ban: failed to ride to draw (Jul 3)

**FOCUS**
Another run-of-the-mill sprint run in a slightly slower time than the first division..

## 3094 RACE HORSE TRADER "COMMISSION FREE" H'CAP 1m 100y
**3:50** (3:50) (Class 4) (0-80,78) 4-Y-0+ **£6,817** (£2,013; £1,007) **Stalls** Low

Form RPR

000- **1** **Eeny Mac (IRE)**[229] 7498 7-9-0 **71**.......................................... AndrewElliott 1 80
(Neville Bycroft) *mde all: rdn wl over 1f out: edgd lft and drvn ins fnl f: kpt on gamely* **10/1**

0306 **2** *1* **Al Muheer (IRE)**[16] 2603 9-9-4 **75**...............................(p) JamesSullivan 4 82
(Ruth Carr) *trckd ldrs: effrt over 2f out: rdn along on inner over 1f out: styd on to chse wnr ins fnl f: drvn and no imp towards fin* **5/1**[3]

0003 **3** *2 1/4* **Staffhoss**[4] 3005 4-8-5 **62**.................................................. JoeFanning 3 64
(Mark Johnston) *trckd wnr: effrt 2f out: sn rdn: drvn and ch ent fnl f: kpt on same pce* **7/1**

4015 **4** *2 3/4* **Ted's Brother (IRE)**[29] 2234 6-9-1 **72**........................(e) RobertWinston 2 67
(Richard Guest) *chsd ldrs: rdn along 2f out: drvn over 1f out: kpt on one pce fnl f* **3/1**[1]

003 **5** *1 1/2* **Bob**[11] 2763 4-9-3 **74**.................................................................. DavidAllan 5 66
(Les Eyre) *chsd ldrs: effrt over 2f out and sn rdn: drvn over 1f out: one pce fnl f* **7/1**

5635 **6** *4* **Ardmay (IRE)**[13] 2699 5-9-7 **78**..........................................(p) AmyRyan 8 61
(Kevin Ryan) *stdd s and hld up in rr: hdwy and in tch: 3f out: rdn wl over 2f out and sn btn* **9/2**[2]

20-0 **7** *3* **The Blue Banana (IRE)**[19] 2519 5-8-6 **63**....................(p) BarryMcHugh 7 39
(Edwin Tuer) *hld up: a in rr: rdn along 3f out and sn outpcd* **14/1**

0464 **8** *8* **No Poppy (IRE)**[16] 2604 6-9-5 **76**..........................(b) PaulMulrennan 6 33
(Tim Easterby) *in tch: pushed along and lost pl after 3f: hung bdly lft and wd bnd at 1/2-way: sn bhd* **13/2**

1m 48.3s (0.70) **Going Correction** +0.225s/f (Good) **8** Ran SP% **113.9**
Speed ratings (Par 105): **105,104,101,99,97 93,90,82**
CSF £58.62 CT £375.50 TOTE £11.90: £2.80, £1.70, £1.80; EX 58.20 Trifecta £525.30.
**Owner** Mrs J Dickinson **Bred** Kenneth Heelan **Trained** Norton, N Yorks

**FOCUS**
A race of mainly exposed/disappointing types.

## 3095 BUY RACE HORSES ONLINE AT RACEHORSETRADER.COM H'CAP 1m 1f 207y
**4:20** (4:21) (Class 5) (0-70,69) 4-Y-0+ **£3,234** (£962; £481; £240) **Stalls** Low

Form RPR

00-0 **1** **Carragold**[64] 1362 8-9-3 **65**.................................................. DavidAllan 8 74
(Mel Brittain) *in rr: pushed along over 2f out: hdwy wl over 1f out: swtchd rt and rdn ent fnl f: led last 100yds: drvn out* **8/1**

-426 **2** *1/2* **Tukitinyasok (IRE)**[46] 1718 7-8-6 **54**.................................. BarryMcHugh 2 62
(Clive Mulhall) *trckd ldrs: hdwy over 2f out: rdn over 1f out: styd on to ld briefly 100yds out: sn hdd and kpt on same pce* **12/1**

-036 **3** *1 1/4* **Tinseltown**[8] 2728 8-8-12 **65**.................................(p) ShirleyTeasdale(5) 9 71
(Brian Rothwell) *led: pushed along 3f out and sn jnd: rdn 2f out: drvn over 1f out: edgd rt ent fnl f: hdd and no ex last 100yds* **10/1**

-550 **4** *2 3/4* **Bold And Free**[12] 2738 4-8-7 **55**................................(p) RoystonFfrench 1 55
(David Thompson) *trckd ldng pair on inner: effrt wl over 2f out: rdn wl over 1f out: one pce ent fnl f* **9/1**

23-0 **5** *1* **Rex Whistler (IRE)**[22] 2423 4-9-7 **69**..........................[1] PaulMulrennan 6 68
(Julie Camacho) *trckd ldrs: effrt over 2f out: rdn wl over 1f out: wknd appr fnl f* **9/2**[2]

1-52 **6** *2* **Thankyou Very Much**[18] 2540 4-9-1 **63**.................................. JoeFanning 5 58
(James Bethell) *trckd ldr: smooth hdwy 3f out: sn cl up: rdn to chal wl over 1f out: sn ev ch tl drvn and wknd appr fnl f* **11/8**[1]

3-64 **7** *9* **Unex Michelangelo (IRE)**[149] 155 5-9-1 **63**............................ PhillipMakin 3 41
(Michael Easterby) *in rr: pushed along 3f out: rdn 2f out: sn btn* **6/1**[3]

2m 9.57s (2.57) **Going Correction** +0.225s/f (Good) **7** Ran SP% **112.5**
Speed ratings (Par 103): **98,97,96,94,93 92,84**
CSF £90.39 CT £962.01 TOTE £9.10: £4.40, £3.90; EX 85.80 Trifecta £326.70.
**Owner** Mel Brittain **Bred** Darley **Trained** Warthill, N Yorks
■ Stewards' Enquiry : Barry McHugh two-day ban: used whip above permitted level (Jun 25-26)

**FOCUS**
There was a strong gallop to this handicap thanks to Tinseltown and that set things up nicely for a late thrust from the winner.

## 3096 SELL RACE HORSES ONLINE AT RACEHORSETRADER.COM H'CAP 7f 100y
**4:50** (4:51) (Class 5) (0-70,70) 4-Y-0+ **£3,234** (£962; £481; £240) **Stalls** Low

Form RPR

0550 **1** **Zaitsev (IRE)**[25] 2341 4-9-6 **69**........................................ RobertWinston 4 80
(Ollie Pears) *mde all: rdn along over 2f out: drvn ent fnl f: styd on gamely towards fin* **11/2**[2]

3532 **2** *1* **Imaginary World (IRE)**[43] 1857 6-9-3 **69**..........................(p) JasonHart(3) 8 77
(John Balding) *trckd ldrs: hdwy over 2f out: rdn to chse wnr over 1f out: drvn ins fnl f: no imp towards fin* **8/1**

-443 **3** *4 1/2* **Violent Velocity (IRE)**[48] 1673 11-8-6 **62**............................ JoeDoyle(7) 12 59
(John Quinn) *towards rr: hdwy over 2f out: nt clr run wl over 1f out: styd on wl fnl f* **9/1**

1142 **4** *1* **Alluring Star**[16] 2605 6-9-4 **67**............................................ BarryMcHugh 9 62
(Michael Easterby) *prom: rdn along wl over 2f out: drvn over 1f out: sn one pce* **8/1**

2640 **5** *3/4* **Icy Blue**[18] 2546 6-8-13 **62**............................................(p) PhillipMakin 3 55
(Richard Whitaker) *chsd ldrs: hdwy 3f out: rdn along over 2f out: drvn and one pce fr over 1f out* **7/1**[3]

45-0 **6** *2 1/2* **Rasselas (IRE)**[20] 2477 7-9-2 **65**............................................ JoeFanning 1 51
(David Nicholls) *midfield: sme hdwy over 2f out: sn rdn along and n.d* **12/1**

5405 **7** *1 1/4* **Mysterial**[16] 2607 4-9-5 **68**................................................ JamesSullivan 13 51
(Ruth Carr) *trckd ldrs on outer: hdwy to chse wnr 1/2-way: rdn along over 2f out: drvn wl over 1f out: grad wknd* **10/1**

450- **8** *hd* **Black Rider (IRE)**[249] 7024 4-9-7 **70**................................ PaulMulrennan 7 53
(Julie Camacho) *bhd tl sme late hdwy* **20/1**

-231 **9** *nk* **Mitchell**[15] 2653 4-8-10 **59**..............................................(p) PaddyAspell 2 41
(David Thompson) *trckd ldrs on inner: hdwy wl over 2f out: sn rdn: wknd over 1f out* **5/1**[1]

-330 **10** *nk* **Steel Stockholder**[32] 2169 8-9-3 **66**.......................................... DavidAllan 6 47
(Mel Brittain) *nvr bttr than midfield* **7/1**[3]

0540 **11** *nk* **Decent Fella (IRE)**[12] 2718 8-8-13 **67**...................(tp) ShirleyTeasdale(5) 5 48
(Ann Stokell) *a towards rr* **33/1**

06-0 **12** *2 1/4* **Last Destination (IRE)**[18] 2546 6-8-2 **51** oh3.............. AndrewMullen 10 26
(Nigel Tinkler) *a in rr* **22/1**

345- **13** *11* **Sugar Town**[174] 8348 4-8-2 **51** oh1................................ DuranFentiman 11
(Peter Niven) *in tch: rdn along 3f out: sn wknd* **25/1**

1m 35.43s (1.63) **Going Correction** +0.225s/f (Good) **13** Ran SP% **122.0**
Speed ratings (Par 103): **99,97,92,91,90 87,86,86,85,85 85,82,70**
CSF £47.65 CT £411.95 TOTE £7.40: £3.00, £2.30, £5.40; EX 47.90 Trifecta £470.30.
**Owner** Mrs Z Wentworth **Bred** J F Tuthill **Trained** Norton, N Yorks

**FOCUS**
Another soundly run event and nothing got involved from off the pace. The first two came clear.

## 3097 SYNDICATE YOUR HORSE AT RACEHORSETRADER.COM MAIDEN STKS 7f 100y
**5:20** (5:23) (Class 5) 3-Y-0+ **£3,234** (£962; £481; £240) **Stalls** Low

Form RPR

3-40 **1** **Mu'Ajiza**[11] 2790 4-9-8 68.......................................... RobertWinston 6 76
(Paul Midgley) *trckd ldrs: smooth hdwy over 2f out: rdn to ld jst over 1f out: edgd rt ins fnl f and sn clr* **3/1**[3]

4 **2** *4* **Laftah (IRE)**[19] 2511 3-8-12 0........................................[1] JackMitchell 9 62
(Roger Varian) *trckd ldrs: hdwy wl over 2f out: rdn to chal wl over 1f out: ev ch tl drvn ent fnl f and kpt on same pce* **2/1**[1]

0- **3** *3/4* **Maggie's Diamond**[292] 5727 3-8-12 0.............................. TonyHamilton 2 60+
(Richard Fahey) *towards rr: hdwy wl over 2f out: rdn over 1f out: styd on fnl f: nrst fin* **5/2**[2]

**4** *1 3/4* **Cliff (IRE)** 4-9-13 0...................................................... PhillipMakin 11 65
(Nigel Tinkler) *midfield: hdwy 1/2-way: chsd ldrs over 2f out: sn rdn and kpt on same pce* **50/1**

3-03 **5** *3 1/4* **Zainda (IRE)**[153] 97 4-9-8 47............................................ JamesSullivan 4 52
(Paul Midgley) *led: rdn along wl over 2f out: drvn and hdd jst over 1f out: sn wknd* **28/1**

3-0 **6** *1/2* **Dual Mac**[22] 2425 7-9-13 74.............................................. AndrewElliott 12 55
(Neville Bycroft) *prom: sn chsng ldr: rdn along wl over 2f out: drvn wl over 1f out: sn wknd* **8/1**

4 **7** *1 1/4* **Far Ranging (USA)**[23] 2392 3-8-12 0................................ BarryMcHugh 7 43
(Julie Camacho) *towards rr: hdwy over 2f out: sn rdn and n.d* **10/1**

00-5 **8** *2* **My Boy Bob**[18] 2551 3-9-3 44............................................ DavidNolan 5 43
(Richard Fahey) *a towards rr* **25/1**

00- **9** *4 1/2* **Stream Of Light**[235] 7371 3-8-12 0...................................... PaddyAspell 8 27
(John Mackie) *a towards rr* **66/1**

4 **10** *8* **Cayjo**[48] 1662 3-9-3 0...................................................... JoeFanning 1 12
(Mark Johnston) *prom: rdn along wl over 2f out: sn wknd* **16/1**

00 **11** *20* **Cool Reception**[23] 2389 3-8-7 0................................ JacobButterfield(5) 3
(Ollie Pears) *chsd ldrs on inner: rdn along 3f out: sn lost pl and bhd* **100/1**

1m 36.44s (2.64) **Going Correction** +0.225s/f (Good)
**WFA** 3 from 4yo+ 10lb **11** Ran SP% **124.7**
Speed ratings (Par 103): **93,88,87,85,81 81,79,77,72,63 40**
CSF £9.82 TOTE £4.80: £1.60, £1.70, £1.20; EX 10.80 Trifecta £51.90.
**Owner** Ms Julie French **Bred** Darley **Trained** Westow, N Yorks

**FOCUS**
Not a strong maiden in terms of depth.

## 3098 PROMOTE YOUR HORSE PRE-AUCTION AT RACEHORSETRADER.COM H'CAP (BEVERLEY MIDDLE DISTANCE SERIES) 1m 4f 16y
**5:55** (5:57) (Class 6) (0-60,60) 3-Y-0 **£2,587** (£770; £384; £192) **Stalls** Low

Form RPR

60-2 **1** **Chivers (IRE)**[16] 2621 3-9-6 **59**........................................ TonyHamilton 9 65
(Tim Easterby) *trckd ldng pair: hdwy 2f out: rdn over 1f out: drvn to chal ent fnl f: edgd rt and led last 100yds* **9/2**[3]

5-56 **2** *nk* **Moving Waves (IRE)**[8] 2867 3-9-0 **53**......................(p) RobertWinston 6 58
(Ollie Pears) *prom: led after 1f: pushed along 3f out: rdn wl over 1f out: drvn ent fnl f: hdd and no ex last 100yds* **16/1**

3633 **3** *1/2* **Nam Ma Prow**[8] 2867 3-8-9 **51**......................................(p) JasonHart(3) 1 55
(Simon West) *hld up towards rr: stdy hdwy 3f out: chsd ldrs on inner over 1f out: rdn to chal and n.m.r ins fnl f: sn drvn and no ex towards fin* **7/2**[1]

-005 **4** *3/4* **Telegraphy (USA)**[16] 2621 3-9-7 **60**..................(b[1]) PaulMulrennan 4 63
(Ed Dunlop) *hld up in rr: hdwy 3f out: chsd ldrs 2f out: swtchd lft and rdn over 1f out: styd on fnl f: nrst fin* **12/1**

-030 **5** *1* **Kashstaree**[16] 2616 3-8-9 **48**............................................ DavidAllan 10 49
(David Barron) *in tch: hdwy over 3f out: rdn to chse ldrs 2f out: drvn appr fnl f: kpt on same pce* **12/1**

-302 **6** *nk* **Where's Tiger**[23] 2393 3-9-5 **58**........................................ PhillipMakin 8 59
(Jedd O'Keeffe) *t.k.h: sn trcking ldr: effrt 3f out: rdn 2f out: drvn and wknd appr fnl f* **4/1**[2]

0-05 **7** *1/2* **Shamouti (IRE)**[14] 2679 3-8-6 **50**.............................. JacobButterfield(5) 7 50
(Ollie Pears) *chsd ldrs: rdn along over 2f out: drvn over 1f out: hld whn n.m.r ins fnl f* **40/1**

660- **8** *3 1/4* **Little Bruv**[252] 6938 3-8-10 **49**...................................... DuranFentiman 11 44
(Tim Easterby) *hld up in rr: sme hdwy over 2f out: sn rdn along and n.d* **16/1**

3420 **9** 1 3/4 **Hello Sweetness**[23] 2393 3-8-13 **52**........................ JamesSullivan 3 44
(Jason Ward) *in tch: hdwy to chse ldrs 3f out: rdn along 2f out: sn drvn and btn* **16/1**

3050 **10** 4 **Enquiring**[30] 2198 3-9-2 **55**........................ JoeFanning 5 41
(Mark Johnston) *in tch: hdwy over 3f out: rdn along on outer 2f out: sn drvn and wknd over 1f out* **7/1**

0-44 **11** 19 **Barbara Elizabeth**[15] 2655 3-9-2 **55**........................ BarryMcHugh 2 10
(Tony Coyle) *led tl hung bdly lft and rn wd bnd after 1f: sn bhd* **7/1**

2m 47.19s (7.39) **Going Correction** +0.225s/f (Good) **11** Ran SP% **120.9**
Speed ratings (Par 97): **84,83,83,82,82 82,81,79,78,75 63**
CSF £76.48 CT £285.99 TOTE £5.60: £2.00, £3.50, £1.40; EX 90.50 Trifecta £368.50.
**Owner** C H Stevens **Bred** Epona Bloodstock Ltd **Trained** Great Habton, N Yorks

**FOCUS**
A low-grade middle-distance handicap that was run at what looked a very steady gallop. It produced a stirring finish.
T/Plt: £1807.90 to a £1 stake. Pool: £56,591.67 - 22.85 winning units. T/Qpdt: £554.60 to a £1 stake. Pool: £3672.58 - 4.90 winning units. JR

2909 **HAMILTON** (R-H)
Wednesday, June 11
**OFFICIAL GOING: Soft (good to soft in places; 6.5)**
Wind: Breezy, across Weather: Cloudy

## 3099 HAMILTON-PARK.CO.UK AMATEUR RIDERS' H'CAP 6f 5y
6:10 (6:14) (Class 6) (0-60,60) 4-Y-O+ £1,975 (£607; £303) Stalls High

Form RPR

1222 **1** **Hab Reeh**[6] 2914 6-10-13 **59**........................ MissSBrotherton 6 70
(Ruth Carr) *in tch centre: hdwy to ld 1f out: kpt on strly last 100yds* **6/4**[1]

045 **2** 2 3/4 **Amis Reunis**[20] 2479 5-9-7 **46** oh1........................(p) JasonNuttall(7) 7 48
(Alan Berry) *led centre: rdn and hdd 1f out: rallied: hld last 100yds* **25/1**

2342 **3** hd **Rock Canyon (IRE)**[6] 2909 5-10-2 **48**........................ MissCWalton 4 50
(Linda Perratt) *hld up bhd ldng gp centre: effrt and rdn over 1f out: drifted lft and kpt on ins fnl f* **8/1**[2]

403- **4** 3 1/2 **Spoken Words**[235] 7380 5-10-0 **46** oh1........................ MrJHamilton 2 36
(John David Riches) *in tch: drvn 1/2-way: hdwy over 1f out: nvr able to chal* **66/1**

00-5 **5** hd **Blue Clumber**[9] 2838 4-9-11 **48**........................ MrGrahamCarson(5) 14 38
(Shaun Harris) *towards rr and sn outpcd: hdwy over 1f out: kpt on fnl f: n.d* **20/1**

0-50 **6** 2 1/4 **Amethyst Dawn (IRE)**[109] 718 8-10-7 **58**........................ MrWEasterby(5) 12 41
(Tim Easterby) *in tch: drvn and outpcd over 2f out: rallied fnl f: no imp* **17/2**[3]

5002 **7** 3/4 **Lexi's Beauty (IRE)**[15] 2658 4-10-2 **48**........................ MrHAABannister 1 28
(Brian Baugh) *cl up centre tl rdn and wknd 1f out* **28/1**

-244 **8** nk **Iceblast**[143] 248 6-10-10 **59**........................ MissJoannaMason(3) 3 38
(Michael Easterby) *missed break: bhd centre tl hdwy over 1f out: kpt on: n.d* **17/2**[3]

5560 **9** shd **Methaaly (IRE)**[9] 2830 11-9-9 **48**........................(be) MrHFNugent(7) 11 27
(Michael Mullineaux) *s.i.s: bhd and outpcd: sme late hdwy: nvr on terms* **33/1**

420 **10** 1 3/4 **Bix (IRE)**[33] 2135 4-9-9 **46** oh1........................ MrJohnWilley(5) 9 19
(Alan Berry) *s.v.s: nvr on terms* **28/1**

0046 **11** nk **Tadalavil**[6] 2909 9-10-8 **54**........................ MrsCBartley 5 26
(Linda Perratt) *t.k.h: in tch tl rdn and wknd fr 2f out* **22/1**

0242 **11** dht **Novalist**[7] 2907 6-9-8 **47**........................(b) MrRAsquith(7) 8 19
(Robin Bastiman) *hld up in midfield: struggling over 2f out: sn btn* **12/1**

26-1 **13** 2 1/2 **Minty Jones**[14] 2667 5-10-11 **60**........................(v) MissMMullineaux(3) 10 24
(Michael Mullineaux) *prom: drvn along and outpcd over 2f out: n.d after* **16/1**

01-0 **14** 3 1/2 **Fol Hollow (IRE)**[6] 2909 9-10-11 **60**........................ MrTHamilton(3) 13 13
(Stuart Coltherd) *prom stands' side tl rdn and wknd over 2f out* **25/1**

1m 14.74s (2.54) **Going Correction** +0.375s/f (Good) **14** Ran SP% **113.9**
Speed ratings (Par 101): **98,94,94,89,89 86,85,84,84,82 81,81,78,73**
CSF £49.26 CT £233.21 TOTE £2.00: £1.10, £8.70, £3.20; EX 46.80 Trifecta £466.60.
**Owner** Grange Park Racing & Mrs B Taylor **Bred** The Anglo Irish Choral Society **Trained** Huby, N Yorks

**FOCUS**
After a warm, dry day, the going was soft, good to soft in places. A moderate amateur riders' sprint to start.

## 3100 BOOK NOW FOR SAINTS & SINNERS H'CAP 5f 4y
6:40 (6:41) (Class 6) (0-65,66) 3-Y-O £2,385 (£704; £352) Stalls Centre

Form RPR

4014 **1** **Tinsill**[10] 2802 3-9-7 **64**........................ GrahamLee 6 68
(Nigel Tinkler) *prom: drvn and outpcd over 2f out: rallied over 1f out: hung rt and rdr dropped reins ins fnl f: styd on to ld towards fin* **6/1**

00-3 **2** hd **White Flag**[29] 2230 3-8-9 **52**........................ TomEaves 5 55
(Tim Easterby) *led: rdn 2f out: kpt on fnl f: edgd lft and hdd nr fin* **22/1**

5-21 **3** hd **Raise A Billion**[14] 2675 3-8-7 **50**........................ PatrickMathers 3 53
(Alan Berry) *cl up: drvn and outpcd wl over 1f out: kpt on fnl f: hld nr fin* **11/4**[2]

31-0 **4** 2 1/2 **Dark Crystal**[52] 1601 3-9-1 **61**........................ ConnorBeasley(3) 4 55
(Linda Perratt) *cl up: rdn along over 2f out: outpcd over 1f out: no imp fnl f* **16/1**

-221 **5** shd **Scoreline**[6] 2932 3-9-6 **66** 6ex........................ JulieBurke(3) 1 59
(David O'Meara) *t.k.h: cl up: effrt and rdn over 1f out: no ex ins fnl f* **7/2**[3]

1 **U** **Lady Ranger (IRE)**[14] 2668 3-8-8 **58**........................ MeganCarberry(7) 2
(Adrian Paul Keatley, Ire) *t.k.h: prom whn hmpd: clipped heels and uns rdr over 3f out* **7/4**[1]

1m 2.56s (2.56) **Going Correction** +0.375s/f (Good) **6** Ran SP% **109.8**
Speed ratings (Par 97): **94,93,93,89,89**
CSF £98.35 TOTE £7.60: £3.60, £4.90; EX 35.60 Trifecta £341.40.
**Owner** Crawford Society 1 **Bred** L T Roberts **Trained** Langton, N Yorks
■ Stewards' Enquiry : Julie Burke nine-day ban: careless riding (Jun 25-Jul 3)
Patrick Mathers four-day ban: used whip above permitted level (Jun 25-28)

**FOCUS**
A small field for this 3yo sprint, but they bunched up the centre of the track in the early stages, which caused the favourite to clip heels and take a heavy fall. The complexion of the race changed in the closing stages.

## 3101 RACING UK FREE 1 MONTH TRIAL H'CAP 1m 3f 16y
7:10 (7:10) (Class 6) (0-65,66) 4-Y-O+ £2,385 (£704; £352) Stalls Low

Form RPR

0-01 **1** **Operateur (IRE)**[6] 2913 6-9-0 **58** 6ex........................ KevinStott(5) 7 66
(Ben Haslam) *trckd ldr: rdn over 2f out: edgd rt over 1f out: rallied to ld ins fnl f: kpt on wl towards fin* **4/1**[3]

6652 **2** 1/2 **Latin Rebel (IRE)**[6] 2915 7-9-2 **55**........................(p) GrahamLee 4 62
(Jim Goldie) *led at ordinary gallop: rdn and qcknd 3f out: hdd ins fnl f: rallied: hld nr fin* **9/2**

1101 **3** 3 1/2 **Precision Strike**[4] 2980 4-9-10 **66** 6ex........................(v) ConnorBeasley(3) 2 67
(Richard Guest) *dwlt: hld up in tch: stdy hdwy over 3f out: effrt and drvn over 2f out: one pce over 1f out* **15/8**[1]

06-2 **4** 1/2 **Tropenfeuer (FR)**[2] 3051 7-8-3 **47** ow1........................ EmmaSayer(5) 1 47
(Dianne Sayer) *t.k.h: cl up: drvn and outpcd over 2f out: rallied over 1f out: no imp fnl f* **3/1**[2]

04-6 **5** 22 **Wolf Heart (IRE)**[20] 2475 6-8-6 **48**........................ IanBrennan(3) 5 11
(Lucy Normile) *in tch: drvn over 3f out: wknd over 2f out: t.o* **7/1**

2m 27.92s (2.32) **Going Correction** +0.275s/f (Good) **5** Ran SP% **110.5**
Speed ratings (Par 101): **102,101,99,98,82**
CSF £21.26 TOTE £4.60: £1.90, £2.10; EX 15.30 Trifecta £31.20.
**Owner** Mrs Alison Royston & Mrs C Barclay **Bred** Razza Pallorsi **Trained** Middleham Moor, N Yorks

**FOCUS**
Two penalised runners topped the weights in this modest handicap and one of them defied the extra weight.

## 3102 STRATHCLYDE LOCH H'CAP 6f 5y
7:40 (7:40) (Class 4) (0-80,78) 4-Y-O+ £6,469 (£1,925; £962; £481) Stalls High

Form RPR

40-2 **1** **George Rooke (IRE)**[21] 2453 4-9-5 **76**........................(p) TomEaves 6 88
(Keith Dalgleish) *prom: hdwy to ld ins fnl f: sn rdn and edgd rt: kpt on towards fin* **10/3**[2]

2214 **2** hd **Khelman (IRE)**[18] 2549 4-9-4 **78**........................ GeorgeChaloner(3) 5 89
(Richard Fahey) *chsd ldrs: drvn and outpcd 1/2-way: rallied over 1f out: styd on wl u.p fnl f: jst hld* **3/1**[1]

-000 **3** 1/2 **Baron Run**[14] 2677 4-8-6 **68**........................ JoeyHaynes(5) 3 78
(K R Burke) *taken early to post: t.k.h: led: rdn over 2f out: hdd ins fnl f: rallied: hld towards fin* **7/1**

4131 **4** 2 1/2 **Monel**[2] 3053 6-8-5 **65** 6ex........................ IanBrennan(3) 8 67
(Jim Goldie) *dwlt: hld up in last pl: rdn over 2f out: kpt on fnl f: nvr able to chal* **11/2**

6113 **5** 3/4 **Economic Crisis (IRE)**[14] 2677 5-9-1 **72**........................ GrahamLee 2 71
(Alan Berry) *t.k.h: w ldr to over 1f out: outpcd ins fnl f* **4/1**[3]

3400 **6** 2 **Jinky**[14] 2677 6-8-7 **67**........................ ConnorBeasley(3) 1 60
(Linda Perratt) *hld up in tch: rdn and hdwy over 2f out: wknd over 1f out* **14/1**

5101 **7** 1 3/4 **Goninodaethat**[2] 3054 6-8-1 **63** 6ex........................ SammyJoBell(5) 7 50
(Jim Goldie) *hld up in tch: drvn and edgd lft over 2f out: wknd over 1f out* **17/2**

1m 13.58s (1.38) **Going Correction** +0.375s/f (Good) **7** Ran SP% **113.2**
Speed ratings (Par 105): **105,104,104,100,99 97,94**
CSF £13.47 CT £63.48 TOTE £4.90: £2.80, £2.40; EX 13.80 Trifecta £57.70.
**Owner** Mrs Janis Macpherson **Bred** Rockfield Farm **Trained** Carluke, S Lanarks

**FOCUS**
The feature race and a fair sprint, with the time 1.16secs faster than the opening contest.

## 3103 MONKLANDS MAIDEN STKS 1m 1f 36y
8:10 (8:11) (Class 5) 3-Y-O+ £3,234 (£962; £481; £240) Stalls Low

Form RPR

6-3 **1** **Some Site (IRE)**[27] 2279 3-8-9 0........................ MartinLane 4 79
(David Simcock) *hld up in tch: niggled briefly 1/2-way: smooth hdwy to chse ldr over 3f out: rdn and slt ld over 1f out: edgd rt ins fnl f: drvn out* **8/11**[1]

-224 **2** 1/2 **Maracuja**[26] 2292 3-8-9 74........................ FrannyNorton 1 78
(Mark Johnston) *t.k.h: led: qcknd over 3f out: hdd over 1f out: rallied and styd upsides: kpt on fnl f: hld nr fin* **11/4**[2]

05 **3** 9 **Archie's Advice**[5] 2952 3-8-9 0........................ KevinStott(5) 2 64
(Keith Dalgleish) *hld up in tch: effrt and pushed along 3f out: chsd clr ldling pair over 1f out: no imp* **20/1**

**4** 5 **Hatton Springs (IRE)** 3-8-9 0........................ PJMcDonald 3 49
(Stuart Coltherd) *trckd ldrs: rdn over 3f out: wknd over 1f out* **33/1**

0 **5** 2 1/2 **Drinks For Losers (IRE)**[22] 2422 3-9-0 0........................ DaleSwift 8 48
(Ian Semple) *hld up: drvn and struggling 4f out: sme late hdwy: nvr on terms* **50/1**

0/ **6** nk **Claude Carter**[14] 3901 10-9-7 0........................ GarryWhillans(5) 5 50
(Alistair Whillans) *hld up: rdn and outpcd over 4f out: sme late hdwy: n.d* **28/1**

22- **7** 2 **Pressure Point**[369] 3047 4-9-12 0........................ TomEaves 9 46
(Keith Dalgleish) *prom: shkn up and edgd lft over 2f out: wknd over 1f out* **9/2**[3]

4-0 **8** 9 **Mystical King**[38] 1969 4-9-12 0........................ LucyAlexander 6 27
(Linda Perratt) *chsd ldr to over 3f out: sn rdn and wknd* **50/1**

0 **9** 14 **Bannock Town**[26] 2292 3-8-11 0........................ IanBrennan(3) 7
(Linda Perratt) *hld up: struggling over 4f out: hung rt and wknd 3f out* **66/1**

2m 1.49s (1.79) **Going Correction** +0.275s/f (Good)
**WFA** 3 from 4yo+ 12lb **9** Ran SP% **119.3**
Speed ratings (Par 103): **103,102,94,90,87 87,85,77,65**
CSF £2.87 TOTE £1.50: £1.10, £1.40, £3.30; EX 4.10 Trifecta £17.30.
**Owner** Mrs Marcella Burns **Bred** Herbertstown House Stud **Trained** Newmarket, Suffolk

**FOCUS**
Limited experience among the runners in this maiden and a three-horse race according to the betting. In the end the two market leaders fought out the finish.

## 3104 AUCHINRAITH H'CAP 5f 4y
8:40 (8:40) (Class 6) (0-55,52) 3-Y-O+ £2,045 (£603; £302) Stalls Centre

Form RPR

0211 **1** **Classy Anne**[6] 2909 4-9-7 **52**........................ GrahamLee 5 70
(Jim Goldie) *t.k.h: trckd ldrs: smooth hdwy to ld over 1f out: pushed out fnl f: readily* **2/5**[1]

3462 **2** *2 ¾* **Captain Scooby**[9] 2830 8-9-1 **49**................................ ConnorBeasley(3) 8 57
(Richard Guest) *hld up: drvn along 1/2-way: hdwy to chse wnr ins fnl f: kpt on: no imp* **7/2**[2]

00-0 **3** *1 ¾* **Hellolini**[19] 2514 4-8-12 **46**................................ NeilFarley(3) 3 48
(Robin Bastiman) *led: rdn and hdd over 1f out: kpt on same pce fnl f* **25/1**

2034 **4** *¾* **Flow Chart (IRE)**[7] 2907 7-9-1 **46**................................ TomEaves 4 45
(Peter Grayson) *bmpd s: hld up in tch: rdn over 2f out: hdwy over 1f out: kpt on fnl f: no imp* **25/1**

0052 **5** *hd* **Ishetoo**[79] 1081 10-9-1 **46**................................ PJMcDonald 9 45
(Peter Grayson) *in tch: drvn and outpcd over 2f out: rallied fnl f: no imp* **18/1**

1554 **6** *nk* **Busy Bimbo (IRE)**[6] 2909 5-9-4 **49**................................(b) PatrickMathers 2 47
(Alan Berry) *bhd: drvn along and hdwy on outside 2f out: no imp fnl f* **9/1**[3]

00-0 **7** *8* **Wicked Wilma (IRE)**[110] 693 10-8-7 **45**................................ JordanHibberd(7) 7 14
(Alan Berry) *t.k.h: hld up bhd ldng gp: outpcd over 2f out: sn btn* **28/1**

350- **8** *shd* **Running Water**[262] 6669 6-8-9 **47**................................ AlistairRawlinson(7) 1 15
(John David Riches) *chsd ldrs: drvn along over 2f out: sn wknd* **40/1**

1m 1.61s (1.61) **Going Correction** +0.375s/f (Good) **8** Ran SP% **122.5**
Speed ratings (Par 101): **102,97,94,93,93 92,80,79**
CSF £2.28 CT £16.33 TOTE £1.20: £1.02, £1.50, £6.60; EX 2.40 Trifecta £18.20.
**Owner** The Vital Sparks **Bred** Jonayro Investments **Trained** Uplawmoor, E Renfrews

**FOCUS**
A really moderate sprint won by an in-form filly.

## 3105 FOLLOW @HAMILTONPARKRC ON TWITTER H'CAP — 1m 65y

**9:10** (9:10) (Class 6) (0-60,60) 3-Y-O+ **£2,264** (£673; £336; £168) **Stalls** Low

Form RPR

6000 **1** **Look On By**[22] 2426 4-9-6 **52**................................ RaulDaSilva 5 62
(Ruth Carr) *mde all at stdy pce: rdn over 2f out: hld on wl fnl f* **20/1**

4625 **2** *1 ¾* **Vosne Romanee**[2] 3053 3-9-0 **57**................................(b) TomEaves 6 60
(Keith Dalgleish) *hld up: stdy hdwy over 2f out: rdn over 1f out: kpt on fnl f to take 2nd cl home: nt rch wnr* **7/1**

0430 **3** *shd* **Nothing Special**[14] 2676 3-9-3 **60**................................(tp) GrahamLee 1 63
(Tom Dascombe) *pressed wnr: rdn and outpcd over 2f out: rallied to regain 2nd appr fnl f: kpt on same pce last 75yds: lost 2nd cl home* **4/1**[2]

0012 **4** *hd* **Tortoise**[2] 3053 3-8-7 **53**................................(b) ConnorBeasley(3) 3 56
(Richard Guest) *cl up: effrt and chsd wnr over 2f out: rdn and edgd lft appr fnl f: kpt on same pce* **6/4**[1]

0-34 **5** *1* **Rokeby**[12] 2729 3-8-9 **52**................................ PJMcDonald 7 52
(George Moore) *hld up: rdn and outpcd 3f out: rallied and edgd lft over 1f out: styd on wl fnl f: nrst fin* **14/1**

3-06 **6** *4* **Uncle Brit**[20] 2476 8-9-8 **57**................................ GeorgeChaloner(3) 4 51
(Malcolm Jefferson) *hld up in tch: stdy hdwy 3f out: rdn and wknd over 1f out* **6/1**[3]

-000 **7** *4 ½* **Joshua The First**[6] 2911 5-9-10 **56**................................(p[1]) DaleSwift 8 40
(Ian Semple) *hld up: hdwy on outside 3f out: rdn and wknd wl over 1f out* **20/1**

3500 **8** *½* **Torridon**[19] 2517 3-8-7 **50**................................ FrannyNorton 9 30
(Mark Johnston) *hld up: rdn and struggling over 3f out: sn btn* **25/1**

236 **9** *4 ½* **Mornin Mr Norris**[49] 1647 3-8-1 **47**................................(p) IanBrennan(3) 2 16
(John Quinn) *in tch: struggling wl over 2f out: sn btn* **9/1**

1m 51.39s (2.99) **Going Correction** +0.275s/f (Good)
**WFA** 3 from 4yo+ 11lb **9** Ran SP% **116.8**
Speed ratings (Par 101): **96,94,94,93,92 88,84,83,79**
CSF £150.64 CT £688.98 TOTE £20.20: £7.00, £2.00, £1.60; EX 155.30 Trifecta £598.80.
**Owner** J A Swinburne **Bred** S L Edwards **Trained** Huby, N Yorks

**FOCUS**
A low-grade handicap and those who raced prominently filled three of the first four places.
T/Plt: £125.30 to a £1 stake. Pool: £59,625.38 - 347.21 winning units. T/Qpdt: £6.10 to a £1 stake. Pool: £5436.91 - 657.03 winning units. RY

# 2763 HAYDOCK (L-H)

Wednesday, June 11

**OFFICIAL GOING: Soft (7.4)**
Wind: light 1/2 against Weather: overcast

## 3106 STARSPREADS.COM NOW ONLINE MAIDEN STKS — 1m 3f 200y

**2:10** (2:12) (Class 5) 3-Y-O+ **£2,587** (£770; £384; £192) **Stalls** Centre

Form RPR

-54 **1** **Allegria (IRE)**[15] 2650 3-8-8 0................................ RobertHavlin 5 83
(John Gosden) *mde all: set v stdy pce: qcknd and wnt clr over 4f out: drvn out: unchal* **5/1**[3]

0-2 **2** *3 ¾* **Button Down**[27] 2279 3-8-8 0................................ RichardHughes 8 77
(Lady Cecil) *rn wout declared tongue-tie: trckd ldrs: t.k.h: 2nd over 3f out: drvn over 2f out: no imp* **11/10**[1]

**3** *1 ¼* **Montbazon (FR)**[32] 7-10-0 0................................ FergusSweeney 6 80+
(Alan King) *s.i.s: hld up in rr: drvn over 3f out: swtchd ins and hdwy over 1f out: styd on* **9/2**[2]

**4** *¾* **Mizzou (IRE)** 3-8-13 0................................ DanielTudhope 7 79+
(Luca Cumani) *s.i.s: hld up in rr: pushed along over 3f out: kpt on fnl f* **13/2**

02 **5** *1* **Quenelle**[16] 2613 3-8-8 0................................ AndreaAtzeni 4 72
(Ed Dunlop) *chsd ldrs: drvn 4f out: one pce* **10/1**

**6** *3 ¾* **Carraig Rock**[232] 4-10-0 0................................ GrahamLee 1 71
(Hughie Morrison) *trckd ldrs: t.k.h: pushed along 4f out: wknd fnl f* **40/1**

4-0 **7** *hd* **Shining Glitter (IRE)**[27] 2271 3-8-8 0................................ FrederikTylicki 9 66
(James Fanshawe) *hld up in rr: drvn over 3f out: fdd over 1f out* **10/1**

**8** *11* **Starchaser (USA)**[37] 4-9-11 0................................(b[1]) WilliamTwiston-Davies(3) 3 53
(Philip Hobbs) *hld up in rr: sme hdwy 6f out: drvn 4f out: lost pl over 2f out* **66/1**

2m 36.32s (2.52) **Going Correction** +0.075s/f (Good)
**WFA** 3 from 4yo+ 15lb **8** Ran SP% **117.9**
Speed ratings (Par 103): **94,91,90,90,89 87,86,79**
CSF £11.28 TOTE £8.20: £1.80, £1.10, £1.60; EX 13.70 Trifecta £42.90.
**Owner** Al Asayl Bloodstock Ltd **Bred** Sheikh Sultan Bin Khalifa Al Nayhan **Trained** Newmarket, Suffolk

**FOCUS**
All races were run on the inner home straight. Overnight rain had eased the going and Rab Havlin and Richard Hughes described the ground as "slow", Havlin adding: "It's not squelchy and seems to be drying out. It will be hard work later on." Just a fair maiden and steadily run.

## 3107 CJM IRISH STALLION FARMS EBF MAIDEN FILLIES' STKS (BOBIS RACE) — 6f

**2:40** (2:42) (Class 5) 2-Y-O **£2,911** (£866; £432; £216) **Stalls** High

Form RPR

2 **1** **Tigrilla (IRE)**[16] 2612 2-9-0 0................................ RyanMoore 7 87+
(Roger Varian) *mid-div: hdwy to ld 2f out: pushed clr 1f out: v readily* **8/11**[1]

**2** *3 ¾* **Think Snow (USA)** 2-9-0 0................................ FrannyNorton 1 76
(Mark Johnston) *dwlt: hdwy over 2f out: styd on to take 2nd 1f out* **14/1**[3]

**3** *3 ¼* **You're My Cracker** 2-9-0 0................................ GrahamLee 10 72+
(Donald McCain) *hmpd s: in rr and pushed along: hdwy and 6th whn nt clr run over 1f out: nt clr run and swtchd lft ins fnl f: styd on to take 3rd nr fin* **25/1**

**4** *½* **Tohfa (IRE)** 2-9-0 0................................ RichardHughes 9 65+
(Richard Hannon) *wnt rt s: sn chsng ldrs: drvn over 2f out: one pce over 1f out* **4/1**[2]

22 **5** *2 ¾* **Persun**[15] 2641 2-8-11 0................................ WilliamTwiston-Davies(3) 6 56+
(Mick Channon) *led: hdd 2f out: fdd fnl f* **4/1**[2]

03 **6** *½* **Midnight Destiny (IRE)**[15] 2641 2-9-0 0................................ DaleSwift 4 55
(Derek Shaw) *chsd ldrs: drvn over 2f out: fdd fnl f* **50/1**

**7** *6* **Kansai** 2-9-0 0................................ AndreaAtzeni 2 37
(David Simcock) *chsd ldrs: drvn over 3f out: wknd over 1f out* **20/1**

0 **8** *5* **Supreme Belle (IRE)**[7] 2888 2-8-7 0................................ AdamMcLean(7) 8 22
(Derek Shaw) *a towards rr* **100/1**

**9** *1 ½* **Crystal Wish** 2-9-0 0................................ TomEaves 11 17+
(Kevin Ryan) *t.k.h: sn trcking ldrs: upsides over 3f out: wknd 2f out* **20/1**

**10** *9* **Hafina** 2-9-0 0................................ GrahamGibbons 5
(Michael Easterby) *in rr: bhd fnl 2f: eased clsng stages* **80/1**

1m 16.41s (2.61) **Going Correction** +0.20s/f (Good) **10** Ran SP% **122.1**
Speed ratings (Par 90): **90,85,80,80,76 75,67,61,59,47**
CSF £13.24 TOTE £2.00: £1.10, £3.30, £5.50; EX 13.80 Trifecta £286.50.
**Owner** Cheveley Park Stud **Bred** Old Carhue Stud **Trained** Newmarket, Suffolk

**FOCUS**
Ordinary maiden form, but the winner was impressive.

## 3108 STARSPREADS.COM SPORT SPREAD BETTING H'CAP (BOBIS RACE) — 1m

**3:10** (3:11) (Class 3) (0-90,87) 3-Y-O **£8,086** (£2,406; £1,202; £601) **Stalls** Low

Form RPR

51-2 **1** **Beach Bar (IRE)**[49] 1655 3-9-4 **84**................................ RyanMoore 8 91+
(William Knight) *stdd and swtchd lft s: t.k.h: drvn and hdwy over 2f out: upsides jst ins fnl f: led post* **2/1**[2]

3241 **2** *shd* **Lesha (IRE)**[30] 2203 3-8-10 **76**................................ TomEaves 3 82+
(Kevin Ryan) *sn chsng ldrs: led 1f out: hdd post* **14/1**

04 **3** *1 ¼* **Nonno Giulio (IRE)**[13] 2706 3-9-7 **87**................................ RobertHavlin 6 90
(John Gosden) *hld up towards rr: hdwy over 2f out: kpt on to take 3rd last 100yds* **25/1**

0042 **4** *3 ¾* **King Of Macedon (IRE)**[4] 3002 3-8-12 **78**................................ FrannyNorton 1 73
(Mark Johnston) *led: hdd and hmpd over 5f out: led over 2f out: hdd 1f out: wknd fnl 100yds* **9/1**[3]

21- **5** *1 ¼* **Baarez (USA)**[236] 7335 3-9-7 **87**................................ AndreaAtzeni 2 79
(Roger Varian) *blind rt eye: trckd ldr: led and edgd lft over 5f out: hdd over 2f out: wknd jst ins fnl f* **1/1**[1]

2-10 **6** *1 ¼* **Rogue Wave (IRE)**[28] 2257 3-9-0 **80**................................ GrahamLee 4 69
(Timothy Jarvis) *chsd ldrs: sn drvn along: outpcd over 4f out: one pce fnl 3f* **22/1**

3-50 **7** *½* **Riverboat Springs (IRE)**[18] 2565 3-9-3 **86**.. WilliamTwiston-Davies(3) 7 74
(Mick Channon) *in rr: drvn over 3f out: nvr a factor* **16/1**

1m 43.11s (-0.59) **Going Correction** +0.075s/f (Good) **7** Ran SP% **114.1**
Speed ratings (Par 103): **105,104,103,99,98 97,96**
CSF £28.91 CT £536.73 TOTE £2.50: £1.30, £3.70; EX 20.70 Trifecta £135.40.
**Owner** P Winkworth & Mrs Bex Seabrook **Bred** Iona Equine **Trained** Patching, W Sussex

**FOCUS**
They went a brisk early gallop in this fair handicap.

## 3109 STARSPREADS.COM ENGLAND WORLD CUP OFFERS H'CAP — 1m

**3:40** (3:40) (Class 3) (0-95,95) 4-Y-O+ **£8,086** (£2,406; £1,202; £601) **Stalls** Low

Form RPR

0002 **1** **Chosen Character (IRE)**[13] 2699 6-9-3 **91**................................(vt) HayleyTurner 3 99
(Tom Dascombe) *mde all: kpt on gamely fnl f: all out* **5/1**[3]

1-56 **2** *nse* **Multi Bene**[39] 1958 5-9-2 **90**................................ GrahamGibbons 4 98
(Ed McMahon) *trckd ldrs: 2nd 6f out: upsides over 1f out: kpt on: jst hld* **7/2**[1]

20-3 **3** *1* **Magic Of Reality (FR)**[53] 1577 4-9-4 **92** ow2................................ RichardHughes 2 98
(Lady Cecil) *stdd s: sn trcking ldrs: dropped bk over 5f out: 3rd and pushed along over 2f out: kpt on same pce fnl f* **7/2**[1]

2-34 **4** *1 ¾* **Kakatosi**[26] 2311 7-8-8 **82**................................ AndreaAtzeni 8 84
(Mike Murphy) *hld up in rr: effrt on inner over 3f out: 4th 2f out: edgd lft and one pce* **9/2**[2]

4-20 **5** *hd* **Stand My Ground (IRE)**[39] 1948 7-9-7 **95**................................ DanielTudhope 5 96
(David O'Meara) *hld up in rr: effrt over 3f out: swtchd rt over 2f out: edgd lft and kpt on last 100yds* **6/1**

0-25 **6** *2 ¾* **Ginger Jack**[16] 2618 7-8-12 **86**................................ PJMcDonald 1 81
(Geoffrey Harker) *chsd wnr 2f: drvn 3f out: wknd over 1f out* **7/1**

40-6 **7** *¾* **Mujazif (IRE)**[18] 2548 4-9-1 **89**................................ AdrianNicholls 6 82
(David Nicholls) *hld up in mid-div: hdwy to chse ldrs 4f out: drvn 3f out: wknd over 1f out* **11/1**

1m 42.55s (-1.15) **Going Correction** +0.075s/f (Good) **7** Ran SP% **114.4**
Speed ratings (Par 107): **108,107,106,105,105 102,101**
CSF £22.80 CT £68.51 TOTE £6.70: £2.20, £4.20; EX 27.40 Trifecta £117.60.
**Owner** Aykroyd And Sons Ltd **Bred** Moyglare Stud Farm Ltd **Trained** Malpas, Cheshire

**FOCUS**
Not a particularly strong race for the grade. The first two filled the same positions virtually throughout.

## 3110 CJM MAINTENANCE SOLUTIONS H'CAP (BOBIS RACE) — 1m 6f

**4:10** (4:10) (Class 4) (0-85,82) 3-Y-O **£5,175** (£1,540; £769; £384) **Stalls** Low

Form RPR

3-51 **1** **Vent De Force**[20] 2494 3-9-6 **81**................................ RyanMoore 1 92+
(Hughie Morrison) *in rr: hdwy 5f out: drvn over 3f out: sn chsng ldrs: led over 1f out: styd on strly* **7/4**[1]

-334 **2** 2 3/4 **Rite To Reign**[26] 2319 3-8-10 **76** DannyBrock(5) 3 83
(Philip McBride) *trckd ldrs: 2nd over 6f out: led 4f out: hdd over 2f out: kpt on same pce appr fnl f* **5/1**[3]
2222 **3** 2 **New Tarabela**[20] 2494 3-9-5 **80** AndreaAtzeni 6 84
(James Tate) *sn drvn along in rr: hdwy over 3f out: styd on to take 3rd last 75yds* **15/2**
010 **4** 3 **Nam Hai (IRE)**[35] 2077 3-8-10 **74** WilliamTwiston-Davies(3) 7 74
(Michael Bell) *trckd ldrs: styd far side in home st: led over 2f out: hdd over 1f out: wknd last 75yds* **25/1**
4-10 **5** *shd* **Lady Yeats**[35] 2077 3-8-11 **72** PJMcDonald 9 72
(George Moore) *mid-div: hdwy over 3f out: edgd lft and kpt on fnl f* **12/1**
-125 **6** 9 **Late Shipment**[11] 2761 3-9-1 **76** FrannyNorton 10 63
(Mark Johnston) *chsd ldrs: pushed along 7f out: sn dropped bk: lost pl 4f out* **14/1**
3-1 **7** 4 1/2 **Morning Watch (IRE)**[63] 1391 3-9-6 **81** RichardHughes 8 62
(Lady Cecil) *led: hdd over 11f out: drvn over 4f out: lost pl 3f out* **5/2**[2]
-364 **8** 13 **Love Tangle (IRE)**[12] 2719 3-8-11 **72** (p) StevieDonohoe 2 35
(Brian Meehan) *w ldrs: t.k.h: led over 11f out: hdd 4f out: lost pl over 2f out: eased fnl f* **20/1**
4150 **9** 8 **Zamra (IRE)**[26] 2319 3-8-12 **73** (v[1]) DanielTudhope 5 25
(David O'Meara) *hld up in rr: effrt 4f out: wknd and eased over 1f out* **40/1**

3m 1.38s (-0.62) **Going Correction** +0.075s/f (Good) **9** Ran SP% **118.8**
Speed ratings (Par 101): **104,102,101,99,99 94,91,84,79**
CSF £11.11 CT £53.86 TOTE £2.30: £1.10, £1.60, £1.60; EX 12.00 Trifecta £40.20.
**Owner** The Fairy Story Partnership **Bred** Deepwood Farm Stud **Trained** East Ilsley, Berks

**FOCUS**
An interesting handicap for the grade. With the exception of the fourth, they came down the centre once into the straight, before the principals drifted over to the far rail.

## 3111 STARSPREADS.COM LIVE HORSE RACING MARKETS H'CAP 1m 3f 200y
**4:40** (4:40) (Class 3) (0-95,95) 4-Y-O+ **£9,703** (£2,887; £1,443; £721) **Stalls** Centre

Form RPR
2-51 **1** **Magic Hurricane (IRE)**[21] 2461 4-9-2 **90** FrederikTylicki 1 99
(James Fanshawe) *hld up in rr: hdwy over 3f out: chal over 2f out: sn led: jnd appr fnl f: edgd rt: styd on to gain upper hand clsng stages* **3/1**[2]
-156 **2** 1 **Esteaming**[18] 2561 4-9-3 **91** GrahamGibbons 3 98
(David Barron) *trckd ldrs: effrt 4f out: swtchd rt over 1f out: sn upsides: no ex clsng stages* **3/1**[2]
6-22 **3** 5 **Jazz Master**[21] 2461 4-8-13 **87** (b) RobertHavlin 9 86
(Luca Cumani) *set stdy pce: increased gallop over 4f out: hdd 2f out: one pce fnl f* **15/2**[3]
12-2 **4** 1 1/2 **Sea Meets Sky (FR)**[25] 2331 4-9-1 **89** RichardHughes 2 86
(Lady Cecil) *trckd ldr: effrt 4f out: sn rdn: one pce over 1f out* **1/1**[1]
00-0 **5** 15 **Buckland (IRE)**[38] 1973 6-9-7 **95** NickyMackay 8 68
(Charlie Fellowes) *s.i.s: sn chsng ldrs: drvn 4f out: wknd 2f out: eased ins fnl f* **33/1**

2m 33.33s (-0.47) **Going Correction** +0.075s/f (Good) **5** Ran SP% **114.7**
Speed ratings (Par 107): **104,103,100,99,89**
CSF £12.81 TOTE £4.00: £2.20, £1.90; EX 12.00 Trifecta £40.80.
**Owner** Dragon Gate **Bred** Pat & Eoghan Grogan **Trained** Newmarket, Suffolk

**FOCUS**
Half the declared field in this fair handicap were missing because of the ground. They went a reasonable gallop and the first two came from the rear, and the time was three seconds quicker than the opening maiden, albeit on drying ground. The runners stayed on the inside in the home straight this time.
T/Plt: £34.40 to a £1 stake. Pool: £79,100.05 - 1677.39 winning units. T/Qpdt: £25.30 to a £1 stake. Pool: £3512.40 - 102.40 winning units. WG

# 2916 KEMPTON (A.W) (R-H)
Wednesday, June 11

**OFFICIAL GOING: Standard**
Wind: Moderate, half against Weather: Fine but cloudy, warm

## 3112 IRISH NIGHT ON 09.07.14 APPRENTICE H'CAP 1m (P)
**5:50** (5:50) (Class 5) (0-75,81) 4-Y-O+ **£2,587** (£770; £384; £192) **Stalls** Low

Form RPR
-661 **1** **Barnmore**[14] 2687 6-9-2 **70** RobHornby(5) 3 78
(Peter Hedger) *dwlt: hld up in last: pushed along over 3f out: prog over 2f out: chsd ldr fnl f: styd on to ld post* **6/1**
301- **2** *nse* **Stormbound (IRE)**[195] 8087 5-9-2 **68** CamHardie(3) 5 76
(Paul Cole) *chsd ldrs: rdn and prog over 2f out to ld over 1f out: kpt on but hdd post* **3/1**[1]
10-3 **3** 1 1/4 **Dana's Present**[35] 2079 5-9-8 **71** GeorgeDowning 6 76
(George Baker) *hld up in 6th: rdn over 2f out: prog to chal 1f out: nt qckn fnl f* **5/1**[2]
2212 **4** 2 **Hierarch (IRE)**[79] 1082 7-8-13 **69** (p) PaigeRanger(7) 4 69
(David Simcock) *led 100yds: trckd ldrs: pushed up to try to chal 2f out: nt qckn jst over 1f out: outpcd after* **10/1**
6321 **5** *nk* **Ocean Legend (IRE)**[12] 2721 9-9-9 **72** RyanTate 8 72
(Tony Carroll) *hld up in last trio: rdn and nt qckn over 2f out: sn last: kpt on fr over 1f out: n.d* **11/2**[3]
4126 **6** 1 1/2 **Cathedral**[13] 2702 5-9-11 **74** (p) TimClark 10 70
(Ed de Giles) *urged along to ld after 100yds: drvn over 2f out: hdd over 1f out: steadily wknd* **5/1**[2]
0 **7** 1/2 **Settle For Red (IRE)**[15] 2646 4-8-10 **64** DavidParkes(5) 2 59
(Jeremy Gask) *a in last trio: rdn over 2f out: racd against far rail and no prog over 1f out* **25/1**
40-0 **8** 2 1/2 **Speedy Writer**[37] 2012 4-9-4 **72** CharlotteJenner(5) 9 61
(Henry Candy) *trckd ldr after 1f to 2f out: steadily lost pl: no ch whn hmpd 100yds out* **16/1**
4-56 **9** 1 1/4 **Top Set (IRE)**[14] 2687 4-9-8 **71** (b) MarcMonaghan 1 57
(Marco Botti) *trckd ldr after 1f to 2f out: steadily wknd* **8/1**

1m 39.52s (-0.28) **Going Correction** -0.025s/f (Stan) **9** Ran SP% **117.9**
Speed ratings (Par 103): **100,99,98,96,96 94,94,91,90**
CSF £24.92 CT £98.44 TOTE £8.20: £2.80, £1.30, £2.70; EX 34.20 Trifecta £160.20.
**Owner** P C F Racing Ltd **Bred** J J Whelan **Trained** Dogmersfield, Hampshire

**FOCUS**
This handicap for apprentice riders looked wide open with six previous course winners in attendance. The pace steadied somewhat going into the turn, but it was still fair enough and there was a cracking finish.

## 3113 BETBRIGHT MOBILE MAIDEN STKS 6f (P)
**6:20** (6:22) (Class 5) 2-Y-O **£2,587** (£770; £384; £192) **Stalls** Low

Form RPR
**1** **Limato (IRE)** 2-9-5 0 DavidProbert 10 90+
(Henry Candy) *trckd ldng pair: led on bit over 1f out: sn pushed clr: styd on wl: comf* **8/1**
**2** 2 1/2 **Hawkesbury** 2-9-5 0 RyanMoore 2 83+
(Charlie Appleby) *v awkward s: mostly in last trio and rn green: shkn up over 2f out: gd prog over 1f out: chsd wnr jst ins fnl f: styd on but no imp* **11/8**[1]
0 **3** 3 3/4 **Frostman (FR)**[63] 1402 2-9-0 0 PhilipPrince(5) 5 70
(Jo Hughes) *t.k.h: pressed ldr: led jst over 2f out to over 1f out: sn outpcd* **33/1**
5 **4** 2 1/4 **Speed Machine (IRE)**[10] 2800 2-9-5 0 AdamKirby 8 64+
(Paul Cole) *towards rr and rn green: shkn up over 2f out and in last pair: styd on fr over 1f out: tk 4th ins fnl f* **14/1**
**5** 2 **Honcho (IRE)** 2-9-5 0 WilliamCarson 7 58
(David Elsworth) *in tch: shkn up over 2f out: no prog over 1f out: outpcd after* **6/1**[3]
0 **6** 1 1/2 **Just Because**[19] 2499 2-9-5 0 PatCosgrave 1 53
(Edward Creighton) *t.k.h: trckd ldrs: wknd steadily fr 2f out* **100/1**
**7** 2 **Father Stone** 2-9-5 0 SilvestreDeSousa 3 47
(David Elsworth) *dwlt: rn green and sn in last: shoved along bef 1/2-way: nvr a factor: passed a few late on* **16/1**
0 **8** *hd* **Next Generation (IRE)**[32] 2151 2-9-0 0 AndreaAtzeni 6 41
(Olly Stevens) *towards rr: shkn up and no prog over 2f out: sn btn* **20/1**
**9** 1/2 **Muqarred (USA)** 2-9-5 0 DaneO'Neill 9 45
(Saeed bin Suroor) *s.s: rn green in rr: sme prog and in tch 2f out: sn wknd* **3/1**[2]
0 **10** 1 **Birdie Must Fly**[11] 2771 2-9-0 0 KieranO'Neill 4 37
(Jimmy Fox) *led to jst over 2f out: wknd* **33/1**

1m 13.74s (0.64) **Going Correction** -0.025s/f (Stan) **10** Ran SP% **116.7**
Speed ratings (Par 93): **94,90,85,82,80 78,75,75,74,73**
CSF £18.92 TOTE £15.00: £3.90, £1.10, £5.00; EX 34.60 Trifecta £1497.30 Part won..
**Owner** Paul G Jacobs **Bred** Seamus Phelan **Trained** Kingston Warren, Oxon

**FOCUS**
This looked an interesting 2yo maiden and, while they were strung out at the finish, it's well worth being positive about the first two home.

## 3114 BETBRIGHT MONEYBACK OFFERS H'CAP 6f (P)
**6:50** (6:50) (Class 5) (0-75,75) 3-Y-O **£2,587** (£770; £384; £192) **Stalls** Low

Form RPR
54-1 **1** **Johara (IRE)**[19] 2525 3-9-7 **75** TedDurcan 5 87
(Chris Wall) *trckd ldr: shkn up to ld wl over 1f out and sn 2 l clr: styd on wl: readily* **7/1**[3]
12 **2** 1 3/4 **Double Up**[33] 2122 3-9-7 **75** AndreaAtzeni 9 82
(Roger Varian) *hld up in midfield: prog over 2f out: rdn to chse wnr jst over 1f out: styd on but no imp* **5/6**[1]
1444 **3** 1 1/2 **Exceeding Power**[22] 2429 3-9-5 **73** AdamKirby 3 75
(Martin Bosley) *trckd ldrs: clsd 2f out: sn rdn and nt qckn: disp 2nd briefly 1f out: one pce* **16/1**
5501 **4** 1 1/4 **Nova Princesse (GER)**[69] 1260 3-9-1 **74** (t) MarcMonaghan(5) 10 72
(Marco Botti) *hld up in rr: shkn up and outpcd over 2f out: styd on fr over 1f out to take 4th ins fnl f* **20/1**
2-32 **5** 2 1/4 **Bold Spirit**[9] 2846 3-9-5 **73** RyanMoore 4 64
(Richard Hannon) *t.k.h: trckd ldrs: shkn up over 2f out: nt qckn and outpcd wl over 1f out: no hdwy after* **5/1**[2]
42-0 **6** 1 **Red Cossack (CAN)**[46] 1725 3-9-4 **72** DaneO'Neill 2 60
(Paul Webber) *t.k.h in rr: rdn and hanging over 2f out: n.d after: plugged on* **14/1**
050- **7** 1/2 **Les Gar Gan (IRE)**[221] 7695 3-9-3 **71** PatCosgrave 6 57
(Keith Dalgleish) *chsd ldr to over 2f out: steadily wknd* **10/1**
2200 **8** 3 **Mimi Luke (USA)**[53] 1570 3-8-8 **62** (v) SilvestreDeSousa 7 38
(Alan Bailey) *led to wl over 1f out: wknd qckly fnl f* **33/1**
560 **9** 8 **Crafty Business (IRE)**[14] 2682 3-9-0 **68** SteveDrowne 1 19
(Mark Hoad) *a wl in rr: bhd fnl 2f* **50/1**
553 **10** 6 **Dove Mountain (IRE)**[123] 536 3-9-2 **70** SamHitchcott 8
(Gary Brown) *hld up in rr: rdn and lost tch over 2f out: t.o* **100/1**

1m 13.02s (-0.08) **Going Correction** -0.025s/f (Stan) **10** Ran SP% **116.0**
Speed ratings (Par 99): **99,96,94,93,90 88,88,84,73,65**
CSF £12.84 CT £95.98 TOTE £8.00: £1.90, £1.10, £5.20; EX 14.70 Trifecta £178.70.
**Owner** Mrs Claude Lilley **Bred** Tribesmen Syndicate **Trained** Newmarket, Suffolk

**FOCUS**
A fair sprint handicap for the class and the form looks solid.

## 3115 GOFFS LONDON SALE - KEMPTON-BREEZE/KENSINGTON-SALE 16.06.14 H'CAP 1m 3f (P)
**7:20** (7:20) (Class 6) (0-55,55) 4-Y-O+ **£1,940** (£577; £288; £144) **Stalls** Low

Form RPR
6612 **1** **Glennten**[30] 2212 5-9-7 **55** SilvestreDeSousa 14 63
(Sean Curran) *wl away fr wd draw: led 1f: trckd ldr: rdn to ld over 2f out: hrd pressed fr over 1f out: hld on wl last 100yds* **9/4**[1]
3563 **2** *nk* **Polydamos**[11] 2770 5-9-2 **50** AdamKirby 12 57
(Tony Carroll) *hld up in midfield: prog over 2f out gng bttr than most: chal over 1f out: w wnr fnl f: outbattled nr fin* **5/1**[2]
0400 **3** 1/2 **Entrapping**[8] 2875 4-9-5 **53** SamHitchcott 3 59
(John E Long) *t.k.h: hld up in midfield: prog on inner wl over 2f out: drvn to press ldrs over 1f out: kpt on* **25/1**
0206 **4** *shd* **Ice Tres**[40] 1919 5-9-2 **50** AndreaAtzeni 9 56
(Rod Millman) *prom: drvn to chal 2f out: cl up bhd ldng pair fnl f: kpt on but nt qckn after* **6/1**[3]
103 **5** 1 1/2 **Appyjack**[22] 2443 6-8-12 **51** RyanTate(5) 7 54+
(Tony Carroll) *stdd s: hld up in last and detahced after 4f: prog over 2f out but ldrs already gone for home: kpt on fr over 1f out: nrst fin* **8/1**
6400 **6** 3/4 **Booktheband (IRE)**[8] 2875 4-9-1 **49** (b[1]) RyanMoore 6 51
(Clive Brittain) *led after 1f to over 2f out: styd cl up tl fdd ins fnl f* **8/1**
433 **7** 2 **Poste Restante**[86] 997 4-8-6 **47** GeorgeBuckell(7) 5 46
(David Simcock) *hld up towards rr: rdn over 2f out: kpt on fr over 1f out: nvr pce to threaten* **10/1**

-060 **8** *1* **Capetown Kid**[6] 2923 4-8-13 **47**........................ DaneO'Neill 11 44
(Sylvester Kirk) *stdd s: hld up in rr: drvn 3f out: limited prog and nvr rchd ldrs: plugged on* **33/1**

0354 **9** *1* **Sixties Queen**[8] 2875 4-9-0 **53**........................ TimClark(5) 13 48
(Alan Bailey) *stdd s: hld up in last trio: drvn over 2f out: plugged on one pce after: no ch* **20/1**

045 **10** *5* **Lambert Pen (USA)**[16] 2614 4-8-12 **46**..................(p) PatCosgrave 8 33
(Peter Hiatt) *chsd ldrs: shoved along 5f out: wknd over 2f out* **20/1**

0050 **11** *11* **Mazij**[6] 2923 6-8-13 **47**........................ WilliamCarson 10 15
(Peter Hiatt) *pushed up to press ldng trio: wknd rapidly over 2f out: t.o* **16/1**

44-0 **12** *hd* **Sir Tyto (IRE)**[13] 2693 6-9-6 **54**..................[1] SteveDrowne 4 22
(Peter Makin) *pushed along in midfield after 4f: no prog: wknd 3f out: t.o* **25/1**

0/ **13** *15* **Uncle Bunge (IRE)**[1191] 330 8-8-10 **49**..............(t) PhilipPrince(5) 2
(Liam Corcoran) *a towards rr: rdn fr 1/2-way: btn over 3f out: wl t.o* **50/1**

2m 21.55s (-0.35) **Going Correction** -0.025s/f (Stan) **13** Ran SP% **121.0**
Speed ratings (Par 101): **100,99,99,99,98 97,96,95,94,91 83,83,72**
CSF £11.56 CT £229.74 TOTE £3.60: £1.20, £1.70, £10.00; EX 12.90 Trifecta £265.80.
**Owner** Bob Cooper & Val Dean **Bred** The Hon Mrs R Pease **Trained** Upper Lambourn, Berks

**FOCUS**
A very weak handicap with winning form thin on the ground. There was no hanging about early on.

## 3116 BETBRIGHT - LIVE MOMENT H'CAP (LONDON MIDDLE DISTANCE SERIES QUALIFIER) 1m 3f (P)
**7:50** (7:50) (Class 5) (0-70,70) 3-Y-O **£2,587** (£770; £384; £192) **Stalls** Low

Form RPR

-254 **1** **High Master (IRE)**[22] 2433 3-9-7 **70**........................ RyanMoore 6 75+
(Richard Hannon) *forced to r wd: towards rr: rdn and prog over 2f out: led jst over 1f out: drvn out* **11/8**[1]

2-44 **2** *1¼* **Spirit Or Soul (FR)**[41] 1904 3-9-3 **66**..................(p) MartinHarley 7 69
(Marco Botti) *trckd ldng pair: drvn over 2f out: kpt on fr over 1f out to take 2nd last stride* **11/2**[3]

-135 **3** *shd* **Opera Fan (FR)**[12] 2719 3-9-3 **66**........................ SilvestreDeSousa 1 69
(Mark Johnston) *won battle for ld early on: drvn and hrd pressed over 2f out: hdd jst over 1f out: kpt on but lost 2nd last stride* **12/1**

0-06 **4** *nk* **Malory Towers**[44] 1797 3-9-2 **65**........................ AdamKirby 8 67
(James Fanshawe) *mostly in 8th: nt clr run briefly 3f out: rdn over 2f out: styd on fr over 1f out: nrly snatched a pl nr fin* **8/1**

2540 **5** *shd* **Mary Le Bow**[16] 2621 3-9-2 **65**..................(p) DavidProbert 4 67
(Lucy Wadham) *pressed ldr: rdn to chal over 2f out: upsides over 1f out: one pce ins fnl f* **16/1**

030 **6** *2½* **Dynamic Vision (IRE)**[29] 2236 3-9-6 **69**........................ AndreaAtzeni 3 67
(Roger Varian) *w ldr early: rn in snatches in midfield after: stl in tch over 1f out: fdd fnl f* **5/1**[2]

0660 **7** *1* **Bongo Beat**[41] 1898 3-8-7 **63**........................ CamHardie(7) 2 59
(Michael Attwater) *s.i.s: towards rr: rdn over 2f out: no imp on ldrs over 1f out but stl in tch: fdd* **50/1**

000 **8** *30* **Mountain Dew**[22] 2418 3-8-11 **60**........................ SebSanders 5 5
(Ralph Beckett) *forced to r wd: chsd ldrs: wknd rapidly over 3f out: eased and wl t.o* **16/1**

006 **9** *19* **Its Not Me Its You**[14] 2682 3-9-5 **68**........................ TomQueally 9
(Brendan Powell) *sn urged along in last: lost tch 4f out: wl t.o* **25/1**

2m 20.99s (-0.91) **Going Correction** -0.025s/f (Stan) **9** Ran SP% **110.5**
Speed ratings (Par 99): **102,101,101,100,100 98,98,76,62**
CSF £8.24 CT £57.30 TOTE £2.00: £1.10, £1.20, £3.20; EX 8.30 Trifecta £43.90.
**Owner** J G Davis **Bred** Mrs M Hillman & M Roden **Trained** East Everleigh, Wilts

**FOCUS**
This ordinary 3yo handicap was run at an uneven pace and those held up were at a disadvantage.

## 3117 BETBRIGHT.COM FILLIES' H'CAP (BOBIS RACE) 7f (P)
**8:20** (8:21) (Class 4) (0-85,85) 3-Y-O **£4,690** (£1,395; £697; £348) **Stalls** Low

Form RPR

331- **1** **Maria Bella (IRE)**[217] 7763 3-9-1 **79**........................ SilvestreDeSousa 13 87
(Charlie Appleby) *mde all: drvn over 1f out: kpt on wl fnl f: hld on nr fin* **8/1**

10 **2** *nk* **Rekdhat (IRE)**[25] 2333 3-8-13 **77**..................[1] AndreaAtzeni 3 84
(Roger Varian) *towards rr: urged along fr 1/2-way: rdn and prog 2f out: sustained effrt to take 2nd ins fnl f: clsng on wnr fin* **12/1**

21- **3** *nk* **Perfect Persuasion**[162] 8451 3-9-0 **78**........................ RyanMoore 11 87+
(William Haggas) *hld up in last: shkn up over 2f out and no immediate rspnse: rapid prog on outer over 1f out: fin strly to snatch 3rd on line: too much to do* **7/4**[1]

3-20 **4** *½* **Miss Atomic Bomb**[12] 2745 3-9-4 **82**........................ MartinHarley 4 87
(Marco Botti) *hld up in last trio: prog 2f out: squeezed through fnl f and styd on: nrst fin* **20/1**

-210 **5** *½* **Tea Leaf (IRE)**[28] 2257 3-9-5 **83**........................ SebSanders 1 87
(Ralph Beckett) *trckd ldng pair: rdn to go 2nd over 1f out: a hld by wnr: one pce and lost pls ins fnl f* **12/1**

-01 **6** *1* **Zman Awal (IRE)**[33] 2126 3-8-12 **76**........................ TomQueally 7 77+
(James Fanshawe) *in tch in midfield: rdn and prog to chse ldrs over 1f out: kpt on but nt pce to threaten fnl f* **9/1**

14-2 **7** *2¼* **Bold Lass (IRE)**[23] 2383 3-8-13 **77**........................ TedDurcan 10 72+
(David Lanigan) *trckd ldng trio: rdn jst over 2f out: nt qckn over 1f out: fdd fnl f* **7/2**[2]

13-5 **8** *1¼* **Dutch S**[25] 2340 3-8-13 **77**........................ AdamKirby 6 69+
(Clive Cox) *t.k.h: trckd ldrs: rdn 2f out: nt qckn over 1f out: fdd fnl f* **6/1**[3]

165- **9** *shd* **Ligeia**[228] 7537 3-9-7 **85**........................ PatDobbs 2 77
(Richard Hannon) *hld up towards rr: swtchd to inner over 1f out and nt clr run sn after: no ch but keeping on at fin* **16/1**

5-00 **10** *¾* **Dancealot**[36] 2063 3-9-0 **78**........................ WilliamCarson 14 68
(Clive Brittain) *chsd wnr to over 1f out: wknd* **50/1**

100- **11** *1¾* **La Tinta Bay**[238] 7300 3-8-13 **84**........................ CamHardie(7) 12 69
(Richard Hannon) *tk fierce hold: hld up in rr: rdn and no prog over 2f out* **50/1**

5-40 **12** *2¾* **New Row**[16] 2624 3-8-6 **70**........................ DavidProbert 9 48
(William Jarvis) *racd wd in midfield: rdn and no prog 2f out: sn wknd* **33/1**

164- **13** *3* **Cafetiere**[232] 7568 3-8-12 **76**........................ PatCosgrave 5 63
(Paul Cole) *t.k.h early: hld up in midfield: stl there but hld whn hmpd on inner over 1f out: eased* **66/1**

1m 25.62s (-0.38) **Going Correction** -0.025s/f (Stan) **13** Ran SP% **128.4**
Speed ratings (Par 98): **101,100,100,99,99 98,95,94,93,93 91,87,84**
CSF £103.40 CT £258.03 TOTE £8.10: £2.90, £4.60, £1.10; EX 127.40 Trifecta £765.10.
**Owner** Godolphin **Bred** Darley **Trained** Newmarket, Suffolk
■ Stewards' Enquiry : Adam Kirby two-day ban: careless riding (Jun 25-26)

**FOCUS**
A competitive fillies' handicap, run at an average pace.

## 3118 BETBRIGHT.COM H'CAP 7f (P)
**8:50** (8:51) (Class 4) (0-80,78) 4-Y-O+ **£4,690** (£1,395; £697; £348) **Stalls** Low

Form RPR

-003 **1** **Gravitational (IRE)**[19] 2522 4-9-3 **77**..................[1] AshleyMorgan(3) 1 87
(Chris Wall) *trckd ldr: clsd fr 2f out: shkn up to ld 1f out: in command after: styd on wl* **4/1**[2]

5-16 **2** *1½* **Mac's Superstar (FR)**[14] 2684 4-9-6 **77**........................ ShaneKelly 5 83
(James Fanshawe) *trckd ldrs disputing 4th: rdn and prog jst over 2f out: styd on to take 2nd last 100yds: no real imp on wnr* **4/1**[2]

0-25 **3** *1* **Bayleyf (IRE)**[36] 2059 5-9-3 **74**........................ AmirQuinn 10 77
(Lee Carter) *led: drew clr 1/2-way: rdn 2f out: hdd 1f out: kpt on* **20/1**

00-6 **4** *½* **Messila Star**[42] 1873 4-9-4 **75**..................(v) SilvestreDeSousa 6 77
(Jeremy Noseda) *t.k.h: hld up towards rr: rdn and outpcd over 2f out: styd on fr over 1f out to take 4th last strides* **10/1**

0430 **5** *nk* **New Leyf (IRE)**[14] 2684 8-8-13 **70**..................(b) SeanLevey 8 71
(Jeremy Gask) *chsd ldrs: disputing 4th: rdn and nt qckn over 2f out: n.d after: plugged on fr over 1f out* **14/1**

0-06 **6** *shd* **Dominium (USA)**[26] 2312 7-9-2 **73**..................(b) MartinHarley 3 74
(Jeremy Gask) *s.i.s: hld up in last pair: prog jst over 2f out: tried to cl on ldrs over 1f out: one pce fnl f* **10/1**

3222 **7** *2¾* **Rome**[14] 2684 4-9-7 **78**........................ RyanMoore 7 72
(Gary Moore) *disp 2nd pl to over 2f out: pushed along and steadily fdd* **5/2**[1]

-446 **8** *3¾* **Top Offer**[126] 496 5-8-9 **66**........................ SteveDrowne 2 50
(Peter Crate) *in tch: pushed along fr over 2f out: steadily wknd* **7/1**[3]

0-40 **9** *22* **Hilali (IRE)**[14] 2687 5-8-13 **70**..................(p) TedDurcan 4
(Gary Brown) *mostly in last: lost tch sn after 1/2-way: t.o* **50/1**

1m 25.56s (-0.44) **Going Correction** -0.025s/f (Stan) **9** Ran SP% **112.6**
Speed ratings (Par 105): **101,99,98,97,97 97,93,89,64**
CSF £19.77 CT £279.64 TOTE £6.30: £1.80, £2.30, £2.90; EX 24.20 Trifecta £172.30.
**Owner** David Gilbert **Bred** Joseph Broderick **Trained** Newmarket, Suffolk

**FOCUS**
This modest handicap was another race where it paid to race handily.
T/Jkpt: Not won. T/Plt: £8.60 to a £1 stake. Pool: £68,795.64 - 5831.74 winning units. T/Qpdt: £3.70 to a £1 stake. Pool: £6449.74 - 1282.00 winning units. JN

# 2873 YARMOUTH (L-H)
### Wednesday, June 11

**OFFICIAL GOING: Good to firm (7.3)**
Wind: virtually nil Weather: sunny and warm

## 3119 GUIDE DOGS FOR THE BLIND MAIDEN STKS 5f 43y
**2:30** (2:31) (Class 5) 2-Y-O **£2,911** (£866; £432; £216) **Stalls** Centre

Form RPR

06 **1** **Indescribable (IRE)**[11] 2756 2-9-2 0........................ MichaelJMMurphy(3) 4 77
(Mark Johnston) *mde all: rdn over 1f out: clr and hung bdly lft ins fnl f: r.o wl* **12/1**

64 **2** *2½* **Zuzinia (IRE)**[20] 2493 2-8-11 0........................ CharlesBishop(3) 8 63
(Mick Channon) *in tch in midfield: rdn and effrt wl over 1f out: chsd clr wnr ins fnl f: kpt on but no imp* **9/1**

**3** *1* **Siren's Cove** 2-9-0 0........................ JimmyQuinn 6 59+
(James Tate) *s.i.s: rn green and pushed along in rr: hdwy ins fnl f: r.o strly fnl 100yds* **50/1**

50 **4** *nk* **Foxtrot Knight**[19] 2499 2-9-5 0........................ HarryBentley 7 63
(Olly Stevens) *in tch in midfield: rdn and outpcd wl over 1f out: rallied and styd on again ins fnl f* **66/1**

3 **5** *hd* **Burning The Clocks (IRE)**[16] 2612 2-9-5 0........................ JamieSpencer 9 63
(Peter Chapple-Hyam) *stdd s and dropped in bhd: hld up in tch in last trio: rdn and effrt over 1f out: styd on same pce ins fnl f* **11/8**[1]

6 **6** *nk* **Black Granite (IRE)**[26] 2308 2-9-5 0........................ ShaneKelly 5 62+
(Jeremy Noseda) *in tch in midfield: rdn and outpcd over 1f out: kpt on again ins fnl f* **5/1**[3]

05 **7** *¾* **Barchan (USA)**[8] 2859 2-9-5 0..................(t) AhmedAjtebi 2 59
(Charlie Appleby) *chsd ldrs: rdn and unable qck over 1f out: wknd ins fnl f* **15/2**

0 **8** *¾* **Stone Roses (IRE)**[12] 2744 2-9-0 0........................ TomQueally 1 51
(Michael Bell) *chsd wnr: rdn and unable qck over 1f out: wknd ins fnl f* **9/2**[2]

**9** *9* **Red Springer (IRE)** 2-9-5 0........................ BenCurtis 3 24
(Alan McCabe) *s.i.s: rn green in rr: rdn and hung lft over 2f out: lost tch over 1f out* **50/1**

1m 1.81s (-0.89) **Going Correction** -0.45s/f (Firm) **9** Ran SP% **111.8**
Speed ratings (Par 93): **89,85,83,82,82 82,80,79,65**
CSF £108.20 TOTE £18.00: £3.20, £2.80, £8.70; EX 117.80 Trifecta £2888.70 Part won..
**Owner** Sheikh Hamdan bin Mohammed Al Maktoum **Bred** Darley **Trained** Middleham Moor, N Yorks

**FOCUS**
A fair maiden run at a sound pace.

## 3120 EASTERN DAILY PRESS H'CAP 1m 6f 17y
**3:00** (3:01) (Class 5) (0-70,66) 3-Y-O **£2,587** (£770; £384; £192) **Stalls** High

Form RPR

3260 **1** **Frederic Chopin**[6] 2926 3-9-1 **60**..................(t) HarryBentley 6 66
(Stuart Williams) *in tch in midfield: effrt 2f out: rdn to chal over 1f out: led fnl 150yds: styd on* **17/2**

-060 **2** *¾* **Rock Of Leon**[6] 2927 3-8-3 **48**........................ JimmyQuinn 3 53
(Michael Bell) *hld up in tch: rdn and effrt to chse ldr 2f out: ev ch over 1f out: styd on same pce fnl 75yds* **12/1**

2064 **3** *½* **Drifter (IRE)**[14] 2671 3-9-4 **63**........................ GeorgeBaker 2 67
(Tom Dascombe) *stdd s: hld up in rr: swtchd rt over 3f out: rdn and effrt press ldrs over 1f out: nt qckn and one pce ins fnl f* **7/1**

5-03 **4** *2¼* **Stout Cortez**[7] 2893 3-9-4 **66**........................ MichaelJMMurphy(3) 5 67
(Mark Johnston) *led: rdn ent fnl 2f: drvn and hrd pressed over 1f out: hdd fnl 150yds: wknd towards fin* **11/8**[1]

3233 **5** *½* **Halluoella**[16] 2621 3-9-2 **61**..................(p) LukeMorris 1 61
(James Tate) *chsd ldrs: wnt 2nd and rdn 3f out: lost 2nd 2f and sn outpcd: plugged on same pce after* **6/1**[3]

0-00 **6** *13* **No Second Thoughts (IRE)**[6] 2927 3-7-11 **47** oh2(b[1]) NoelGarbutt(5) 4 29
(Michael Squance) *s.i.s: in tch towards rr: rdn over 4f out: wknd over 1f out* **100/1**

-044 7 1 ¾ **Olymnia**[16] 2616 3-8-10 **62**........................ KieranShoemark(7) 7 41
(Robert Eddery) *chsd ldr tl 3f out: lost pl and drvn 2f out: sn wknd* **4/1**[2]

3m 3.97s (-3.63) **Going Correction** -0.30s/f (Firm) **7** Ran SP% **108.1**
Speed ratings (Par 99): **98,97,97,96,95 88,87**
CSF £88.77 TOTE £7.40: £3.20, £5.30; EX 61.50 Trifecta £300.40.
**Owner** Mrs A Shone **Bred** Brook Stud **Trained** Newmarket, Suffolk

**FOCUS**
They went a steady pace in this modest handicap.

## 3121 INJURED JOCKEYS FUND APPRENTICE (S) STKS 1m 1f
3:30 (3:31) (Class 6) 3-Y-O £1,940 (£577; £288; £144) **Stalls** Low

Form RPR

4050 1 **Kisanji**[10] 2805 3-8-12 67........................ CharlesBishop 6 69
(Mick Channon) *taken down early: hld up in midfield: clsd to trck ldrs 3f out: led 2f out: drvn fnl f: hld on* **5/2**[1]

5 2 *hd* **Distant High**[22] 2442 3-8-4 0........................ NoelGarbutt(3) 8 63
(Rae Guest) *hld up in last trio: hdwy 4f out: pressed ldrs 2f out: rdn and ev ch over 1f out: kpt on u.p fnl f: a jst hld* **5/2**[1]

4-60 3 1 ½ **Lady Red Oak**[12] 2740 3-8-7 62........................ RossAtkinson 9 60
(Tom Dascombe) *stdd and wnt rt s: hld up in last trio: hdwy over 3f out: jnd ldrs 2f out: drvn over 1f out: no ex and outpcd fnl 100yds* **11/4**[2]

2045 4 9 **Previous Acclaim (IRE)**[40] 1918 3-8-4 44........................ ShelleyBirkett(3) 3 41
(Julia Feilden) *t.k.h: chsd ldrs: wnt 2nd 4f out: led and rdn over 2f out: hdd 2f out: wknd over 1f out* **16/1**

0600 5 8 **Appellez Baileys (FR)**[19] 2526 3-8-5 46........................ ThomasHemsley(7) 1 29
(Chris Dwyer) *rdn along early: in tch in midfield: rdn 4f out: wknd u.p 2f out: bhd fnl f* **80/1**

000 6 2 ¼ **Jay Gee Speedfit (IRE)**[14] 2682 3-8-7 58........................(t) JordanVaughan(5) 2 25
(George Margarson) *t.k.h: led: hung rt over 4f out: hdd over 2f out: wknd 2f out: bhd fnl f* **25/1**

400- 7 4 **Escarlata Rossa**[274] 6279 3-8-7 45........................ RosieJessop 7 11
(J S Moore) *hld up in rr: effrt on inner 4f out: rdn and btn over 2f out: sn wknd: bhd fnl f* **33/1**

50-5 8 6 **Kirkstall Abbey (IRE)**[51] 1606 3-8-2 58........................ RyanWhile(5) 5
(Simon Hodgson) *t.k.h: pressed ldr: carried rt over 4f out: lost pl and btn 3f out: bhd fnl 2f: t.o* **8/1**[3]

1m 53.91s (-1.89) **Going Correction** -0.30s/f (Firm) **8** Ran SP% **108.8**
Speed ratings (Par 97): **96,95,94,86,79 77,73,68**
CSF £8.00 TOTE £3.40: £1.10, £1.70, £1.10; EX 11.10 Trifecta £35.90.Kisanji was bought for 7400gns to Alan McCabe. Distant High was claimed by Mr R J Price for £5000.
**Owner** Box 41 **Bred** Rabbah Bloodstock Limited **Trained** West Ilsley, Berks
■ Stewards' Enquiry : Charles Bishop two-day ban: used whip above permitted level (Jun 25-26)

**FOCUS**
A weak and muddling seller, confined to apprentice riders.

## 3122 PLEASUREWOOD HILLS H'CAP 6f 3y
4:00 (4:00) (Class 3) (0-90,90) 3-Y-O+ £7,246 (£2,168; £1,084; £542; £270) **Stalls** Centre

Form RPR

-502 1 **Green Monkey**[22] 2446 4-8-13 **75**........................ ShaneKelly 6 86
(James Fanshawe) *broke wl: stdd and hld up in tch in midfield: hdwy to ld and travelling wl over 2f out: rdn ent fnl 2f: hrd drvn and hld on ins fnl f* **14/1**

523- 2 *shd* **Mission Approved**[251] 6977 4-9-5 **81**........................ LemosdeSouza 1 92
(Luca Cumani) *in tch in midfield: hdwy to press wnr over 2f out: ev ch and rdn over 1f out: sustained chal and r.o fnl f: jst hld* **8/1**[3]

010 3 ¾ **Little Shambles**[12] 2745 3-8-4 **77**........................ MichaelJMMurphy(3) 8 83
(Mark Johnston) *broke wl: sn in tch in midfield: rdn and effrt ent fnl 2f: drvn to chse ldrs over 1f out: ev ch ins fnl f: one pce fnl 100yds* **50/1**

150 4 2 **Jubilee Brig**[6] 2919 4-9-4 **83**........................(v) RossAtkinson(3) 5 85
(Sean Curran) *in tch towards rr: rdn over 2f out: hdwy u.p over 1f out: styd on to go 4th ins fnl f: nt rch ldrs* **28/1**

/1-3 5 3 **Foxy Forever (IRE)**[27] 2275 4-9-12 **88**........................ JamieSpencer 4 80
(Michael Wigham) *in tch in midfield: hdwy over 2f out: rdn to chse ldrs wl over 1f out: no ex 1f out: wknd ins fnl f* **2/1**[1]

61 6 *nk* **Role Player**[14] 2681 4-9-4 **80**........................ TomQueally 3 71
(Michael Bell) *sn led: hdd after 2f: chsd ldr tl over 2f out: rdn and unable qck 2f out: wknd fnl f* **20/1**

3-11 7 ½ **Dreese (IRE)**[44] 1818 3-8-13 **83**........................ LukeMorris 7 71
(James Tate) *dwlt: in tch in rr: drvn over 2f out: sme hdwy and edging rt over 1f out: styd on but no threat to ldrs* **8/1**[3]

5055 8 1 **Jiroft (ITY)**[23] 2390 7-9-10 **86**........................ AdamBeschizza 10 73
(Robert Cowell) *chsd ldrs: rdn ent fnl 2f: no ex u.p over 1f out: wknd fnl f* **16/1**

-060 9 1 **Dubawi Sound**[32] 2145 6-10-0 **90**........................(bt) MartinDwyer 11 73
(Hugo Palmer) *hld up in tch towards rr: rdn and effrt ent fnl 2f: no hdwy whn edgd lft and hmpd over 1f out: wl hld after* **7/2**[2]

10-0 10 *nk* **Trucanini**[58] 1492 4-9-8 **84**........................ GeorgeBaker 9 66
(Chris Wall) *hld up in tch towards rr: rdn and effrt wl over 1f out: no hdwy: wknd 1f out* **8/1**[3]

104- 11 4 **Fast Finian (IRE)**[369] 3060 5-9-12 **88**........................(b) SeanLevey 2 58
(Paul D'Arcy) *sn chsng ldr: led after 2f tl over 2f out: lost pl qckly 2f out: bhd fnl f* **10/1**

1m 11.28s (-3.12) **Going Correction** -0.45s/f (Firm)
**WFA** 3 from 4yo+ 8lb **11** Ran SP% **120.7**
Speed ratings (Par 107): **102,101,100,98,94 93,93,91,90,90 84**
CSF £122.18 CT £5471.31 TOTE £15.80: £4.70, £2.90, £7.50; EX 64.30 Trifecta £1220.50.
**Owner** Mr & Mrs P Hopper, Mr & Mrs M Morris **Bred** Jan & Peter Hopper **Trained** Newmarket, Suffolk

**FOCUS**
The pace was honest for this decent handicap. It paid to race handily.

## 3123 GREAT YARMOUTH TOURIST AUTHORITY MAIDEN H'CAP 1m 3y
4:30 (4:30) (Class 6) (0-65,65) 4-Y-O+ £2,264 (£673; £336; £168) **Stalls** Centre

Form RPR

6442 1 **Refuse Colette (IRE)**[7] 2901 5-8-2 **46** oh1........................ PaoloSirigu 3 59
(Mick Quinn) *racd in centre: led gp and chsd ldrs overall: rdn and edgd rt ent fnl 2f: chsd ldr 2f out: led over 1f out: pressed whn lft in command ins fnl f: r.o* **12/1**

-242 2 3 ¾ **Specialty (IRE)**[19] 2529 4-9-1 **62**........................ RossAtkinson(3) 4 68
(Pam Sly) *racd in centre: t.k.h early: in tch in midfield: effrt jst over 2f: out drvn and chsd wnr ent fnl f: jst over 1 l down and styng on whn rein broke jst ins fnl f: nt rcvr and eased fnl 50yds* **10/3**[1]

0660 3 ½ **Avidly**[27] 2270 4-9-2 **60**........................(b) GeorgeBaker 2 63
(Julia Feilden) *racd in centre: hld up in last trio: hdwy over 2f out: rdn and chsd ldrs over 1f out: no hdwy 1f out: styd on same pce ins fnl f* **11/2**[3]

-040 4 1 **Aomen Rock**[14] 2687 4-9-6 **64**........................ ShaneKelly 11 65
(James Fanshawe) *c to r stands' side: overall ldr tl over 5f out: chsd ldr tl led again over 2f out: hdd and hung lft over 1f out: no ex 1f out: plugged on same pce fnl f* **4/1**[2]

20/- 5 *nk* **Tin Pan Alley**[706] 3793 6-9-7 **65**........................ SeanLevey 5 65
(Sean Curran) *racd in centre: in tch in midfield: rdn over 2f out: outpcd and looked wl hld 2f out: rallied u.p 1f out: kpt on but no threat to wnr ins fnl f* **10/3**[1]

0-65 6 4 ½ **Alberto**[12] 2723 4-7-13 **46** oh1........................(p[1]) RyanPowell(3) 9 36
(Alastair Lidderdale) *carried rt after s: chsd overall ldr: swtchd lft after 1f: hdwy to ld over 1f out: hdd and rdn over 2f out: styng on same pce whn hmpd over 1f out: wknd fnl f* **40/1**

0035 7 3 ½ **Severiano (USA)**[23] 2400 4-9-1 **59**........................(be) BenCurtis 1 41
(Alan McCabe) *racd in centre: in tch in midfield: rdn over 2f out: wknd over 1f out* **11/1**

0-40 8 1 ¾ **Staines Massive**[22] 2442 4-7-12 **47**........................ NoelGarbutt(5) 6 25
(Jane Chapple-Hyam) *racd in centre: s.i.s: a towards rr: rdn 1/2-way: wknd wl over 1f out* **25/1**

-020 9 3 ¼ **Zammy**[40] 1917 5-8-5 **49**........................ LukeMorris 8 19
(Michael Wigham) *racd stands' side: in tch in midfield: rdn 1/2-way: lost pl and drvn 2f out: bhd fnl f* **14/1**

000- 10 8 **Jack Firefly**[364] 3213 5-8-2 **46** oh1........................ JimmyQuinn 7
(Michael Murphy) *racd in centre: hld up in last trio: rdn and struggling over 2f out: sn bhd* **20/1**

1m 37.75s (-2.85) **Going Correction** -0.45s/f (Firm) **10** Ran SP% **115.3**
Speed ratings (Par 101): **96,92,91,90,90 85,82,80,77,69**
CSF £50.26 CT £219.11 TOTE £14.50: £6.50, £1.70, £1.20; EX 60.20 Trifecta £412.20.
**Owner** YNWA Partnership **Bred** Patrick O'Reilly **Trained** Newmarket, Suffolk
■ Stewards' Enquiry : Shane Kelly two-day ban: careless riding (Jun 25-26)

**FOCUS**
Not much pace for this uncompetitive maiden handicap.

## 3124 BBC RADIO NORFOLK H'CAP 6f 3y
5:00 (5:13) (Class 6) (0-65,65) 3-Y-O £1,940 (£577; £288; £144) **Stalls** Centre

Form RPR

20-3 1 **Royal Brave (IRE)**[36] 2044 3-9-4 **62**........................ MartinDwyer 9 73
(William Muir) *restless in stalls: in tch in midfield: hdwy to chse ldr over 2f out: led 2f out: sn rdn: hrd drvn and kpt on ins fnl f: all out* **7/2**[1]

00-4 2 *nk* **Katawi**[33] 2125 3-9-2 **60**........................ GeorgeBaker 6 70
(Chris Wall) *hld up in tch in midfield: hdwy to trck ldrs 2f out: jnd ldr over 1f out: ev ch and rdn 1f out: drvn and nt qckn ins fnl f* **4/1**[2]

5-56 3 2 ¾ **Kiss From A Rose**[23] 2387 3-9-0 **58**........................ ChrisCatlin 3 59
(Rae Guest) *chsd ldrs: wnt 2nd 4f out tl over 2f out: 3rd and drvn over 1f out: styd on same pce ins fnl f* **9/2**[3]

500- 4 *nk* **Reaffirmed (IRE)**[214] 7817 3-9-3 **61**........................ LukeMorris 4 61
(Ed Vaughan) *t.k.h: hld up in tch in midfield: rdn and effrt 2f out: kpt on u.p ins fnl f* **9/2**[3]

6-04 5 1 ½ **Henke (IRE)**[19] 2524 3-8-13 **57**........................ J-PGuillambert 2 52
(Nigel Tinkler) *in tch in midfield: rdn and effrt 2f out: kpt on same pce ins fnl f* **16/1**

-000 6 ½ **Palace Princess (FR)**[15] 2647 3-9-1 **59**........................(b[1]) HarryBentley 7 53
(Ed Dunlop) *s.i.s: sn rcvrd and in tch in midfield: rdn over 2f out: styd on same pce and no imp fnl 2f* **20/1**

-450 7 9 **Rostrum Farewell**[23] 2388 3-8-11 **55**........................(b[1]) SeanLevey 5 20
(David Brown) *led tl over 2f out: rdn 2f out: btn over 1f out: sn eased* **20/1**

450- 8 4 **Hot Amber (USA)**[180] 8273 3-8-5 **49**........................(p) AdamBeschizza 10
(Robert Cowell) *v.s.a: bhd: sme hdwy u.p over 2f out: no hdwy 2f out: sn wknd* **16/1**

1360 9 3 ½ **Razin' Hell**[30] 2204 3-9-6 **64**........................ BenCurtis 1
(Alan McCabe) *sn outpcd in rr: nvr on terms* **12/1**

034- 10 2 ¾ **Brave Imp**[251] 6966 3-9-7 **65**........................ JamieSpencer 8
(Kevin Ryan) *chsd ldr tl over 2f out: sn rdn and struggling: lost pl 2f out: wl bhd and eased ins fnl f* **12/1**

1m 11.8s (-2.60) **Going Correction** -0.45s/f (Firm) **10** Ran SP% **115.3**
Speed ratings (Par 97): **99,98,94,94,92 91,79,74,69,66**
CSF £17.16 CT £63.24 TOTE £3.70: £1.30, £1.90, £1.90; EX 16.40 Trifecta £85.00.
**Owner** Muir Racing Partnership - Ascot **Bred** M Fahy **Trained** Lambourn, Berks

**FOCUS**
Plenty of unexposed types in this 3yo handicap, which was run at a fair pace.

## 3125 NORFOLK AND SUFFOLK ANIMAL TRUST FILLIES' H'CAP 6f 3y
5:30 (5:41) (Class 5) (0-75,75) 4-Y-O+ £2,587 (£770; £384; £192) **Stalls** Centre

Form RPR

0-43 1 **Ada Lovelace**[22] 2435 4-8-5 **59**........................ BenCurtis 8 72
(John Gallagher) *chsd ldr after 1f: shkn up to ld over 1f out: rdn clr and in command fnl f: r.o: comf* **7/2**[3]

1343 2 2 ¼ **Broughtons Charm (IRE)**[16] 2608 4-9-7 **75**........................ ChrisCatlin 4 81
(Willie Musson) *in rr of main gp: rdn over 2f out: hdwy u.p jst over 1f out: chsd wnr and edgd lft fnl 100yds: kpt on but no imp* **9/4**[1]

/U6- 3 *nk* **Ziggy's Secret**[300] 5441 4-9-5 **73**........................ DougieCostello 1 78
(Lucy Wadham) *stdd after s: hld up in tch: swtchd lft and effrt over 1f out: styd on to go 3rd fnl 100yds: kpt on: no threat to wnr* **16/1**

11-2 4 2 **Honeymoon Express (IRE)**[26] 2312 4-9-2 **75**........(p) ShelleyBirkett(5) 2 74
(Julia Feilden) *chsd ldrs: rdn and unable qck over 1f out: no ch w wnr and kpt on same pce fnl f* **5/2**[2]

3332 5 1 **Amosite**[23] 2398 8-9-4 **72**........................(v) AdamBeschizza 5 67
(J R Jenkins) *sn led: rdn and hdd over 1f out: unable qck and btn 1f out: lost 2nd and wknd fnl 100yds* **12/1**

401- 6 1 **Miakora**[321] 4691 6-8-2 **56** oh6........................ PaoloSirigu 3 48
(Mick Quinn) *led early: sn hdd: chsd ldrs tl lost pl and rdn over 2f out: btn ent fnl f: short of room and swtchd lft jst ins fnl f: wknd* **40/1**

0-53 7 *hd* **Olney Lass**[12] 2718 7-8-12 **69**........................ SimonPearce(3) 6 61
(Lydia Pearce) *sn outpcd and bustled along in rr: sme hdwy but no ch whn carried lft jst ins fnl f: n.d* **8/1**

530- 8 1 **Saskia's Dream**[162] 8456 6-8-9 **63**........................(b) LukeMorris 7 51
(Jane Chapple-Hyam) *in tch in midfield: rdn and unable qck over 1f out: hung lft and wknd ins fnl f* **14/1**

1m 11.01s (-3.39) **Going Correction** -0.45s/f (Firm) **8** Ran SP% **115.4**
Speed ratings (Par 100): **104,101,100,97,96 95,95,93**
CSF £11.94 CT £109.49 TOTE £4.40: £1.60, £1.50, £1.50; EX 16.40 Trifecta £194.40.
**Owner** D A Clark **Bred** D A Clark **Trained** Chastleton, Oxon

**FOCUS**
A fair fillies' handicap run at an honest pace.
T/Plt: £1091.00 to a £1 stake. Pool: £72,863.96 - 48.75 winning units. T/Qpdt: £12.10 to a £1 stake. Pool: £6831.38 - 416.74 winning units. SP

3126 - 3133a (Foreign Racing) - See Raceform Interactive

# 3106 HAYDOCK (L-H)

Thursday, June 12

**OFFICIAL GOING: Good to soft (good in places; 7.8)**

Wind: Light, half against Weather: Sunny

## 3134 BETDAQ HAYDOCK PARK APPRENTICE TRAINING SERIES H'CAP (RACING EXCELLENCE INITIATIVE) 1m 3f 200y

6:10 (6:11) (Class 5) (0-70,70) 4-Y-O+ £2,587 (£770; £384; £192) Stalls Centre

Form RPR

-432 1 **Nolecce**11 2801 7-8-6 **53** JackGarritty(3) 3 60
(Tony Forbes) *chsd ldr: led 4f out: hdd 2f out: abt a nk down 1f out: rallied to regain narrow ld fnl 50yds: hld on wl* 9/41

6323 2 nse **Merchant Of Medici**14 2701 7-8-13 **60** MeganCarberry(3) 2 66
(Micky Hammond) *in tch: hdwy over 3f out: led 2f out: rdn abt a nk up 1f out: hdd narrowly fnl 50yds: kpt on* 3/12

4460 3 1 1/4 **Ferdy (IRE)**27 2296 5-8-12 **56** KevinStott 7 60
(Paul Green) *stdd s: hld up: rdn and hdwy over 2f out: sn chsd ldrs: kpt on u.p ins fnl f: nt qckn towards fin* 8/1

0160 4 nse **Cavalieri (IRE)**13 2728 4-9-9 **70** EvaMoscrop(3) 1 75
(Philip Kirby) *chsd ldrs: effrt over 2f out: edgd lft over 1f out: nt clr run thrght fnl f: kpt on but nowhere to go on inner* 6/1

3132 5 2 1/2 **Call Of Duty (IRE)**7 2913 9-8-7 **51** (b) EmmaSayer 6 51
(Dianne Sayer) *hld up: hdwy on inner 3f out: rdn to chse ldrs 2f out: btn ent fnl f: no ex* 4/13

6433 6 6 **Noguchi (IRE)**8 2904 9-9-10 **68** (b) LouisSteward 5 58
(George Margarson) *chsd ldrs: effrt over 2f out: wknd 2f out* 15/2

5305 7 6 **Another Journey**17 2609 5-8-7 **51** oh6 (p) ShirleyTeasdale 8 32
(Lisa Williamson) *racd keenly: led: hdd 4f out: rdn and wknd over 2f out* 66/1

2m 32.97s (-0.83) **Going Correction** -0.325s/f (Firm) 7 Ran SP% **114.4**

Speed ratings (Par 103): **89,88,88,88,86 82,78**

CSF £9.23 CT £43.84 TOTE £4.10: £1.90, £1.70; EX 10.80 Trifecta £66.00.

**Owner** Tony Forbes **Bred** Hedsor Stud **Trained** Stramshall, Staffs

**FOCUS**

The course, which had soaked up 17mm of rain on Tuesday night, continued to dry out after a warm night and day.\n\x\x All the races were run on the inner home straight, reducing the official distances on the round course by approximately 2yds. Mainly exposed performers in a modest handicap. The gallop was on the steady side to the 3f marker and the first four finished in a heap. The winner is rated to his latest form.

## 3135 VISIT SILK MILL RIPPONDEN H'CAP 1m 2f 95y

6:40 (6:40) (Class 5) (0-70,69) 3-Y-O £3,234 (£962; £481; £240) Stalls Centre

Form RPR

4202 1 **Suni Dancer**11 2805 3-8-2 **50** oh1 RaulDaSilva 9 59
(Paul Green) *hld up: hdwy 3f out: led over 1f out: kpt on wl towards fin* 14/1

6313 2 3/4 **Jazri**16 2643 3-9-0 **62** DanielTudhope 8 69
(Milton Bradley) *midfield: hdwy over 2f out: sn led: hdd u.p over 1f out: continued to chal ins fnl f: hld towards fin* 20/1

5-32 3 3 1/4 **Interconnection**35 2095 3-9-4 **66** RichardKingscote 10 67
(Ed Vaughan) *midfield: effrt over 2f out: stdy hdwy u.p over 1f out: kpt on ins fnl f: tk 3rd cl home: no imp on ldrs* 11/22

5-05 4 shd **Kinema (IRE)**13 2735 3-9-0 **67** LouisSteward(5) 5 68
(Ed Walker) *hld up: pushed along 5f out: rdn and hdwy over 3f out: chalng 2f out: nt qckn over 1f out: kpt on same pce and no imp on ldrs ins fnl f* 9/1

0-55 5 2 1/4 **Unfinishedbusiness**34 2133 3-8-13 **61** TonyHamilton 11 58
(Richard Fahey) *hld up: nt clr run briefly over 2f out: sn rdn: kpt on ins fnl f: nvr able to trble ldrs* 20/1

-521 6 1/2 **Trinity Star (IRE)**24 2393 3-8-12 **63** (p) ConnorBeasley(3) 1 59
(Michael Dods) *pushed along early to sn trck ldrs: wnt 2nd wl over 4f out: sn rdn: chalng 2f out: nt qckn over 1f out: no ex fnl f* 11/22

4646 7 7 **Tashbeeh (IRE)**13 2729 3-8-10 **63** EmmaSayer(5) 4 45
(Dianne Sayer) *bhd: pushed along over 4f out: plugged on fnl f: nvr a threat* 33/1

3463 8 1 1/2 **Sherston**40 1947 3-9-4 **66** FrannyNorton 7 45
(Mark Johnston) *prom: pushed along over 4f out: wknd over 2f out* 8/1

624- 9 3/4 **Supa U**202 8005 3-9-0 **62** (t1) DavidAllan 3 40
(Tim Easterby) *hld up: rdn 3f out: no imp* 16/1

4252 10 1 3/4 **Aldreth**9 2867 3-8-9 **57** (b1) GrahamGibbons 12 32
(Michael Easterby) *in tch: rdn over 3f out: wknd over 2f out* 13/23

0-11 11 2 1/4 **Aurelia Cotta (IRE)**23 2417 3-9-7 **69** SeanLevey 6 39
(Charles Hills) *led: rdn over 2f out: sn hdd: wknd over 1f out: eased whn btn ins fnl f* 5/11

-601 12 3/4 **Bognor (USA)**7 2936 3-9-6 **68** 6ex AndrewMullen 2 37
(Michael Appleby) *trckd ldrs tl rdn and wknd 4f out* 8/1

2m 13.14s (-2.36) **Going Correction** -0.325s/f (Firm) 12 Ran SP% **118.0**

Speed ratings (Par 99): **96,95,92,92,90 90,84,83,83,81 79,79**

CSF £267.06 CT £1730.96 TOTE £23.70: £5.50, £3.00, £1.90; EX 289.70 Trifecta £966.80 Part won..

**Owner** Ian Furlong **Bred** Mickley Stud And G A Greaves **Trained** Lydiate, Merseyside

**FOCUS**

A few recent winners in a modest handicap but a race in which a couple of the market leaders disappointed. The gallop was reasonable and the first two pulled clear in the closing stages. Several riders reported the ground was good but the time suggested it was just on the easy side. The form is rated around the third and fourth.

## 3136 SILK MILL WELCOMES YOU MAIDEN STKS (C&G) 7f

7:10 (7:11) (Class 5) 2-Y-O £2,587 (£770; £384; £192) Stalls Low

Form RPR

1 **Archie (IRE)** 2-9-0 0 RichardKingscote 8 83+
(Tom Dascombe) *chsd ldr: led 2f out: rdn over 1f out: kpt on wl fnl f* 11/42

0 2 1 1/4 **Medrano**20 2507 2-9-0 0 GrahamLee 9 80
(David Brown) *midfield: hdwy 2f out: rdn over 1f out: chsd wnr wl ins fnl f: styd on but no real imp* 16/1

04 3 2 1/4 **Billy Slater**12 2756 2-9-0 0 TomEaves 12 74
(Richard Fahey) *chsd ldrs: rdn and ev ch 2f out: nt qckn over 1f out: kpt on u.p ins fnl f* 8/1

4 shd **Songye** 2-9-0 0 JamieSpencer 1 74+
(Kevin Ryan) *hld up: hmpd 4f out: hdwy whn swtchd rt over 1f out: gd prog to chse wnr briefly fnl 150yds: no ex towards fin* 12/1

5 3 1/2 **Ventriloquist** 2-9-0 0 PaulMulrennan 6 65
(Charlie Appleby) *swtchd lft s: towards rr: pushed along 3f out: hdwy over 2f out: rdn whn chsng ldrs over 1f out: wknd ins fnl f* 12/1

6 1 1/2 **Freight Train (IRE)** 2-9-0 0 FrannyNorton 5 62
(Mark Johnston) *led: hdd 2f out: rdn and wknd over 1f out* 9/41

00 7 hd **Alpine Affair**27 2298 2-9-0 0 SeanLevey 2 61
(Brian Meehan) *midfield: hdwy over 2f out: one pce u.p over 1f out: no imp* 33/1

3 8 1 3/4 **Tansfeeq**21 2480 2-9-0 0 GrahamGibbons 10 57
(B W Hills) *racd keenly: in tch: rdn over 2f out: wknd over 1f out* 4/13

9 2 **Chadic** 2-9-0 0 AdrianNicholls 3 52
(Mark Johnston) *chsd ldrs: rn green: rdn 4f out: wknd over 2f out* 20/1

10 1 **Stardrifter** 2-9-0 0 TonyHamilton 11 49
(Richard Fahey) *sed awkwardly: v green: a bhd: nvr on terms* 25/1

1m 29.04s (-1.66) **Going Correction** -0.325s/f (Firm) 10 Ran SP% **121.4**

Speed ratings (Par 93): **96,94,92,91,87 86,85,83,81,80**

CSF £46.77 TOTE £4.50: £2.10, £4.90, £3.20; EX 96.60 Trifecta £941.90.

**Owner** Seamus Burns,Tom Flaherty,Sabina Kelly **Bred** P Kelly **Trained** Malpas, Cheshire

**FOCUS**

A race won last year by dual Listed winner Washaar and this year's winner looks a potentially decent prospect. The gallop was no more than fair.

## 3137 FOR FRIENDLY SERVICE - SILK MILL H'CAP (BOBIS RACE) 7f

7:40 (7:41) (Class 4) (0-85,85) 3-Y-O £5,175 (£1,540; £769; £384) Stalls Low

Form RPR

-312 1 **Regiment**13 2734 3-9-4 **82** TonyHamilton 4 88
(Richard Fahey) *chsd ldrs: wnt 2nd over 1f out: sn led: drvn clr and r.o wl fnl 75yds* 3/12

1603 2 2 1/4 **Proclamationofwar**20 2517 3-8-5 **69** MartinLane 5 69
(Kevin Ryan) *chsd ldr: led over 2f out: sn rdn: hdd 1f out: no ex towards fin* 14/1

03 3 1/2 **Captain Midnight (IRE)**26 2333 3-9-4 **85** ConnorBeasley(3) 2 84
(David Brown) *hld up: pushed along and hdwy 3f out: rdn whn chsng ldrs over 2f out: kpt on ins fnl f* 6/1

6-23 4 3/4 **Mfiftythreedotcom (IRE)**38 2027 3-8-5 **69** PatrickMathers 6 66
(Richard Fahey) *s.i.s: in rr: pushed along 5f out: rdn over 2f out: impr to chse ldrs over 1f out: kpt on u.p ins fnl f: nvr able to chal* 10/1

3-11 5 11 **Despot (IRE)**37 2058 3-9-2 **80** RobertWinston 3 48
(Charles Hills) *racd keenly: in tch: rdn over 2f out: sn wknd* 9/41

1-30 6 1 1/4 **Tree Of Grace (FR)**66 1352 3-9-5 **83** SeanLevey 7 48
(Richard Hannon) *hld up: hdwy over 4f out: pushed along 3f out: wknd over 2f out* 5/13

321 7 hd **Sitting Pretty (IRE)**19 2553 3-8-13 **77** (p) RichardKingscote 1 41
(Tom Dascombe) *racd keenly: led: rdn and hdd over 2f out: sn hung lft: wknd over 1f out* 8/1

1m 27.94s (-2.76) **Going Correction** -0.325s/f (Firm) 7 Ran SP% **113.6**

Speed ratings (Par 101): **102,99,98,98,85 84,83**

CSF £41.42 CT £236.06 TOTE £3.70: £1.10, £18.30; EX 51.40 Trifecta £186.20.

**Owner** T G & Mrs M E Holdcroft **Bred** Bearstone Stud **Trained** Musley Bank, N Yorks

**FOCUS**

A useful handicap run at just an ordinary gallop. The first four finished clear of a couple who disappointed. The form is rated through the third and fourth.

## 3138 SILK MILL FOR GREAT BEER H'CAP 5f

8:10 (8:13) (Class 4) (0-80,79) 3-Y-O+ £5,175 (£1,540; £769; £384) Stalls High

Form RPR

50-0 1 **Bispham Green**16 2656 4-9-12 **77** DanielTudhope 7 89
(David O'Meara) *chsd ldrs: led over 1f out: edgd lft ins fnl 100yds: sn r.o wl to draw clr* 15/2

1203 2 2 1/2 **Bapak Bangsawan**17 2606 4-9-4 **69** JamieSpencer 17 73
(Kevin Ryan) *hld up: hdwy 2f out: sn swtchd lft: wnt 2nd 1f out: styd on: no further imp on wnr fnl 75yds* 11/21

0-05 3 1 1/4 **Bondi Beach Boy**16 2656 5-10-0 **79** GrahamLee 10 79
(James Turner) *dwlt: hld up: hdwy into midfield over 3f out: styd on ins fnl f: nt rch ldrs* 7/13

0-0 4 1 3/4 **Eland Ally**26 2332 6-9-5 **70** AndrewElliott 6 64
(Tom Tate) *hld up in rr: rdn and hdwy 1f out: kpt on ins fnl f: nt rch ldrs* 12/1

40-0 5 1/2 **Dusty Storm (IRE)**40 1961 4-9-11 **76** GrahamGibbons 13 69
(Ed McMahon) *chsd ldrs: rdn and hung lft over 1f out: kpt on same pce fnl 100yds: nt gng pce to chal* 7/13

-006 6 1 **Bosun Breese**13 2727 9-9-9 **74** PaulMulrennan 9 64
(Paul Midgley) *led: hdd over 3f out: rdn over 2f out: wknd over 1f out* 16/1

100- 7 1 **Hazelrigg (IRE)**239 7313 9-9-11 **76** (e) DavidAllan 14 62
(Tim Easterby) *hld up: rdn over 1f out: nvr able to trble ldrs* 12/1

1440 8 nk **Sleepy Blue Ocean**40 1961 8-9-12 **77** (p) RobertWinston 4 62
(John Balding) *w ldrs: rdn and ch over 1f out: wknd fnl 75yds* 11/1

02-1 9 hd **Little Eli**53 1602 4-8-10 **64** JasonHart(3) 3 49
(Eric Alston) *racd keenly: w ldrs: led over 3f out: rdn and hdd over 1f out: wknd fnl 100yds* 7/13

2456 10 1 3/4 **National Service (USA)**76 1146 3-9-0 **72** SeanLevey 5 48
(Stuart Williams) *midfield: rdn over 1f out: sn outpcd* 11/1

0304 11 1/2 **Oldjoesaid**16 2656 10-9-12 **77** PhillipMakin 15 55
(Paul Midgley) *hld up: rdn over 1f out: no imp* 6/12

0636 12 1 1/4 **Lucky Dan (IRE)**33 2167 8-8-11 **62** RaulDaSilva 2 36
(Paul Green) *reminder s: in tch early: outpcd and lost pl after 1f: struggling after* 16/1

1m 0.7s (-0.10) **Going Correction** +0.125s/f (Good)

**WFA** 3 from 4yo+ 7lb 12 Ran SP% **122.8**

Speed ratings (Par 105): **105,101,99,96,95 93,92,91,91,88 87,85**

CSF £50.27 CT £314.76 TOTE £10.70: £3.10, £1.40, £2.80; EX 58.80 Trifecta £280.70.

**Owner** David W Armstrong **Bred** Highfield Farm Llp **Trained** Nawton, N Yorks

**FOCUS**

Mainly exposed sorts in a fair handicap. The gallop was decent and this form should prove reliable, the winner rated in line with a best view of his 3yo form.

## 3139 SEE YOU AT SILK RIPPONDEN H'CAP 1m 2f 95y

8:40 (8:40) (Class 4) (0-80,80) 4-Y-O+ £5,175 (£1,540; £769; £384) Stalls Centre

Form RPR

-601 1 **Martinas Delight (USA)**31 2199 4-8-11 **70** RobertWinston 1 77
(Timothy Jarvis) *hld up: pushed along 3f out: hdwy over 2f out: led over 1f out: sn rdn: r.o fnl f: strly pressed fnl 75yds: kpt on gamely* 13/2

/003 2 nk **Engrossing**16 2654 5-8-10 **69** (e) JamesSullivan 6 75
(Ruth Carr) *hld up: nt clr run whn gng wl over 2f out: rdn over 1f out: sn wnt 2nd: str chal fnl 75yds: styd on for press: jst hld* 9/1

034/ **3** *3 ¾* **Kudu Country (IRE)**[85] 5660 8-8-11 **70**.............................. GrahamLee 3 69
(Tom Tate) *led after 1f: rdn over 2f out: hdd over 1f out: styd on same pce ins fnl f* **6/1**

6442 **4** *nk* **Hydrant**[12] 2762 8-9-3 **79**.............................. ConnorBeasley(3) 2 78
(Richard Guest) *led for 1f: remained handy: rdn 3f out: styd on same pce fnl f* **5/1[3]**

-025 **5** *4* **Save The Bees**[26] 2351 6-8-12 **78**.............................. LukeLeadbitter(7) 7 69
(Declan Carroll) *chsd ldr to 7f out: remained handy: rdn over 3f out: wknd over 1f out* **9/2[2]**

-105 **6** *1* **Patrona Ciana (FR)**[24] 2398 4-9-6 **79**.............................. DanielTudhope 9 68
(David O'Meara) *trckd ldrs early: sn lost pl: u.p over 2f out: no imp* **11/1**

-145 **7** *1* **Red Runaway**[12] 2782 4-9-7 **80**.............................. JamieSpencer 5 67
(Ed Dunlop) *sn trckd ldrs: wnt 2nd 7f out: rdn to chal over 2f out: wknd over 1f out* **15/8[1]**

2m 12.99s (-2.51) **Going Correction** -0.325s/f (Firm) 7 Ran SP% **115.6**
Speed ratings (Par 105): **97,96,93,93,90 89,88**
CSF £62.34 CT £370.14 TOTE £7.20: £3.50, £5.30; EX 90.30 Trifecta £397.20.
**Owner** T&J Partnership **Bred** Lerici Syndicate **Trained** Twyford, Bucks

**FOCUS**
A fair handicap in which the pace was on the steady side. The winner is rated back to his early best.
T/Plt: £1,394.20 to a £1 stake. Pool of £64471.80 - 33.76 winning tickets. T/Qpdt: £106.80 to a £1 stake. Pool of £6253.20 - 43.30 winning tickets. DO

## 2770 NEWBURY (L-H)
### Thursday, June 12

**OFFICIAL GOING: Good to firm (good in places)**
Wind: Almost nil Weather: Fine, very warm

## 3140 PHEASANT INN MAIDEN STKS (BOBIS RACE) 6f 110y
**1:50** (1:52) (Class 4) 2-Y-O **£3,881** (£1,155; £577; £288) **Stalls** Centre

Form RPR

2 **1** **Estidhkaar (IRE)**[21] 2480 2-9-5 0.............................. PaulHanagan 4 90+
(Richard Hannon) *pressed ldr: pushed into ld wl over 2f out: shkn up whn pressed over 1f out: edgd lft and rdn out last 100yds* **7/4[1]**

0 **2** *½* **Mustadeem (IRE)**[27] 2298 2-9-5 0.............................. WilliamBuick 7 89+
(Brian Meehan) *trckd ldrs: plld out and shkn up to go 2nd jst over 2f out: str chal fr over 1f out: styd on wl but a hld* **3/1[2]**

**3** *6* **Laidback Romeo (IRE)** 2-9-5 0.............................. AdamKirby 1 72+
(Clive Cox) *trckd ldrs: outpcd but tk 3rd wl over 1f out: no ch w ldng pair* **25/1**

4 **4** *2 ¾* **St Brelades Bay (IRE)**[33] 2146 2-9-5 0.............................. RichardHughes 9 65
(Richard Hannon) *stdd s: hld up in last trio early: prog fr 1/2-way: pushed along and kpt on one pce to take 4th fnl f: nvr involved* **5/1[3]**

22 **5** *2* **Flying Machine (IRE)**[25] 2359 2-9-5 0.............................. DavidNolan 5 59
(Richard Fahey) *led to wl over 2f out: steadily wknd u.p* **8/1**

**6** *2 ¼* **Hawkmeister (IRE)** 2-9-5 0.............................. PatDobbs 2 53
(Richard Hannon) *dwlt: rn green in last trio and pushed along early: bhd fr 1/2-way: kpt on quite wl fnl f* **40/1**

**7** *½* **Fitzwilliam** 2-9-2 0.............................. WilliamTwiston-Davies(3) 6 52
(Mick Channon) *trckd ldrs: pushed along and easily lft bhd fr over 2f out: fdd* **50/1**

3 **8** *hd* **Grigolo**[14] 2698 2-9-5 0.............................. SilvestreDeSousa 8 51
(Mark Johnston) *pressed ldr: drvn over 2f out: sn lft bhd: wknd over 1f out* **11/2**

06 **9** *2 ½* **Western Playboy (IRE)**[9] 2859 2-9-5 0.............................. TomQueally 10 44
(Sylvester Kirk) *in tch to 1/2-way: sn lft bhd and btn* **100/1**

**10** *1 ½* **Raspberry Ripple** 2-9-0 0.............................. KieranO'Neill 11 35
(Richard Hannon) *s.s: rn green but in tch in last pair after 1f: wknd sn after 1/2-way* **66/1**

**11** *7* **Noble Master** 2-9-5 0.............................. MartinHarley 3 21
(Sylvester Kirk) *a in rr: bhd fr 3f out: t.o* **100/1**

1m 18.71s (-0.59) **Going Correction** -0.225s/f (Firm) 11 Ran SP% **116.2**
Speed ratings (Par 95): **94,93,86,83,81 78,78,77,74,73 65**
CSF £6.68 TOTE £2.70: £1.40, £1.30, £5.80; EX 9.30 Trifecta £254.40.
**Owner** Hamdan Al Maktoum **Bred** BEC Bloodstock **Trained** East Everleigh, Wilts

**FOCUS**
Pat Dobbs described the ground as "good to firm", while Martin Harley felt it was riding "perfect". The rail had been moved out since the last meeting from the 5f to the 8f on the round course. Therefore all round course races were run over 8m further than advertised. The front pair, both useful prospects, drew clear in what looked a good juvenile maiden. There's better to come from the winner.

## 3141 CROSSLAND MAIDEN FILLIES' STKS (BOBIS RACE) (DIV I) 1m 2f 6y
**2:20** (2:23) (Class 4) 3-Y-O **£4,690** (£1,395; £697; £348) **Stalls** Low

Form RPR

2 **1** **Hoop Of Colour (USA)**[24] 2404 3-9-0 0.............................. RichardHughes 9 79+
(Lady Cecil) *mostly trckd ldr: led over 2f out: drvn whn pressed over 1f out: edgd lft fnl f: a holding on: eased nr fin* **6/4[1]**

2-3 **2** *½* **Oh Star (USA)**[15] 2681 3-9-0 0.............................. WilliamBuick 7 77
(John Gosden) *trckd ldrs: clsd to chal over 2f out: wandered and nt qckn fr wl over 1f out: styd on* **7/2[2]**

0 **3** *nse* **Pleasant Valley (IRE)**[34] 2129 3-9-0 0.............................. AndreaAtzeni 4 78+
(Luca Cumani) *trckd ldrs: shkn up over 2f out: swtchd ins to dispute 2nd jst over 1f out: trying to cl but looked hld whn short of room 120yds out* **7/1**

06- **4** *2 ½* **By Jupiter**[218] 7764 3-9-0 0.............................. TomQueally 3 72+
(Michael Bell) *trckd ldrs: pushed along over 2f out: tried to cl and shkn up over 1f out: one pce after* **16/1**

**5** *1* **Deuce Again** 3-9-0 0.............................. SteveDrowne 10 71+
(John Gosden) *dwlt: hld up and in last tl over 3f out: pushed along and prog over 2f out: kpt on quite encouragingly fnl f* **14/1**

5 **6** *nk* **Elshaadin**[47] 1722 3-9-0 0.............................. PaulHanagan 2 70
(Roger Varian) *led: shkn up and hdd over 2f out: steadily fdd over 1f out* **5/1[3]**

0 **7** *1 ½* **Smageta**[36] 2081 3-9-0 0.............................. MartinHarley 8 67
(Marco Botti) *hld up in midfield: rdn to chse ldrs over 2f out: no imp over 1f out: grad fdd* **50/1**

**8** *7* **Silken Waters** 3-9-0 0.............................. JohnFahy 6 54
(Eve Johnson Houghton) *dwlt: hld up in rr: sme prog on outer over 3f out: wknd over 2f out* **33/1**

6 **9** *2 ¼* **Pendley Legacy**[23] 2418 3-9-0 0.............................. AdamKirby 5 50
(Clive Cox) *t.k.h: hld up in rr: no prog 3f out: wknd 2f out* **16/1**

6 **10** *1 ½* **Lola Montez (IRE)**[16] 2649 3-9-0 0.............................. MartinLane 1 47
(David Lanigan) *a in rr: wknd over 3f out* **66/1**

2m 9.8s (1.00) **Going Correction** -0.175s/f (Firm) 10 Ran SP% **116.2**
Speed ratings (Par 98): **89,88,88,86,85 85,84,78,76,75**
CSF £6.49 TOTE £2.10: £1.10, £1.70, £2.10; EX 7.70 Trifecta £32.90.
**Owner** Niarchos Family **Bred** Flaxman Holdings Limited **Trained** Newmarket, Suffolk
■ Stewards' Enquiry : Richard Hughes two-day ban: careless riding (Jun 26-27)

**FOCUS**
This looked the stronger of the two divisions on paper, although it was run at a fairly steady gallop and they finished quite well bunched. Not as strong a race as recent runnings, the winner rated close to her debut effort.

## 3142 CROSSLAND MAIDEN FILLIES' STKS (BOBIS RACE) (DIV II) 1m 2f 6y
**2:50** (2:54) (Class 4) 3-Y-O **£4,690** (£1,395; £697; £348) **Stalls** Low

Form RPR

6-4 **1** **Carnevale**[16] 2649 3-9-0 0.............................. SilvestreDeSousa 2 78
(Ralph Beckett) *trckd ldr: led over 2f out: rdn clr over 1f out: styd on strly* **9/4[2]**

65 **2** *5* **Cape Mystery**[20] 2511 3-9-0 0.............................. MartinHarley 5 68
(Peter Chapple-Hyam) *led: drew clr w wnr 3f out: hdd over 2f out: outpcd fr over 1f out* **8/1**

**3** *1 ½* **Saint Lucy** 3-9-0 0.............................. WilliamBuick 7 65+
(John Gosden) *dwlt: sn trckd ldng pair: pushed along 4f out: outpcd 3f out: n.d after: styd on fnl f* **15/8[1]**

**4** *2 ¼* **Emily Yeats** 3-9-0 0.............................. PatDobbs 8 61
(Paul Webber) *trckd ldrs: outpcd fr 3f out: kpt on* **25/1**

**5** *¾* **Emerald Swell (IRE)** 3-9-0 0.............................. MartinLane 4 59
(Brian Meehan) *hld up in last trio: pushed along 4f out: lft bhd 3f out: nvr on terms after* **7/1[3]**

**6** *¾* **May Queen** 3-9-0 0.............................. HayleyTurner 3 58
(Chris Wall) *in tch: pushed along over 3f out: sn outpcd: reminder and flashed tail over 2f out: no prog* **14/1**

0 **7** *2 ¾* **Bowberry**[23] 2418 3-9-0 0.............................. AdamKirby 1 53
(Clive Cox) *hld up in last trio: lft bhd fr 3f out: nudged along and no real prog* **16/1**

**8** *2* **Medicean Queen (IRE)** 3-9-0 0.............................. TomQueally 6 49
(Clive Brittain) *difficult to load into stalls: dwlt: a in last trio and rn green: pushed along and no prog 4f out* **14/1**

2m 10.01s (1.21) **Going Correction** -0.175s/f (Firm) 8 Ran SP% **112.2**
Speed ratings (Par 98): **88,84,82,81,80 79,77,76**
CSF £19.82 TOTE £2.80: £1.10, £2.00, £1.10; EX 11.90 Trifecta £38.20.
**Owner** Prince A A Faisal **Bred** Nawara Stud Co Ltd **Trained** Kimpton, Hants

**FOCUS**
Less depth than the first division, but although run at a steady gallop the race produced a clear-cut winner. The form is rated cautiously and below the race's recent standard.

## 3143 LORD WEINSTOCK MEMORIAL STKS (REGISTERED AS THE BALLYMACOLL STUD STAKES) (LISTED RACE) (FILLIES) 1m 2f 6y
**3:25** (3:26) (Class 1) 3-Y-O
**£20,982** (£7,955; £3,981; £1,983; £995; £499) **Stalls** Low

Form RPR

2-22 **1** **Eastern Belle**[21] 2484 3-9-0 99.............................. WilliamBuick 4 98+
(John Gosden) *trckd ldr: pushed along over 3f out: drvn to ld over 1f out: styd on but ld fast dwindling at fin* **9/4[1]**

-016 **2** *nk* **Pelerin (IRE)**[27] 2316 3-9-0 93.............................. MartinHarley 7 97+
(Marco Botti) *hld up in last: gng easily whn no clr run over 2f out tl swtchd outside 1f out whn only 7th: str run fnl f: post c too sn* **8/1**

1-15 **3** *1 ¼* **Queen Of Ice**[29] 2255 3-9-0 93.............................. RichardHughes 8 94
(William Haggas) *led: rdn over 2f out: hdd over 1f out: kpt on same pce* **5/1[3]**

5-46 **4** *½* **Mutatis Mutandis (IRE)**[33] 2152 3-9-0 88.............................. HayleyTurner 3 93
(Ed Walker) *dwlt: hld up: prog against far rail over 2f out: clsd to chal 1f out: 2nd briefly ins fnl f: one pce last 100yds* **25/1**

-120 **5** *2 ¼* **Groovejet**[36] 2072 3-9-0 83.............................. PatDobbs 6 89
(Peter Chapple-Hyam) *prom: rdn wl over 2f out: nt qckn and no imp: kpt on* **66/1**

0-46 **6** *hd* **Uchenna (IRE)**[21] 2484 3-9-0 87.............................. AdamKirby 2 88
(David Simcock) *trckd ldrs: rdn wl over 2f out: one pce and no imp fnl 2f* **16/1**

1-20 **7** *2 ¾* **Jordan Princess**[21] 2484 3-9-0 89.............................. AndreaAtzeni 5 83
(Luca Cumani) *hld up in midfield: rdn 3f out: nt qckn over 2f out: no imp after: wknd fnl f* **5/1[3]**

15 **8** *3* **Belle De Lawers**[27] 2316 3-9-0 94.............................. PaulHanagan 10 77
(James Bethell) *hld up in last pair: shkn up on outer over 3f out: nt gng wl and wandering after: no ch and eased fnl f* **4/1[2]**

-316 **9** *¾* **Latenightrequest**[29] 2255 3-9-0 86.............................. (p) DavidNolan 1 76
(Richard Fahey) *sn prom: rdn 3f out: lost pl over 2f out: wknd over 1f out* **14/1**

2m 5.56s (-3.24) **Going Correction** -0.175s/f (Firm) 9 Ran SP% **113.1**
Speed ratings (Par 104): **105,104,103,103,101 101,99,96,96**
CSF £20.71 TOTE £2.70: £1.20, £2.90, £2.00; EX 20.80 Trifecta £104.60.
**Owner** A E Oppenheimer **Bred** Hascombe And Valiant Studs **Trained** Newmarket, Suffolk

**FOCUS**
Not a strong Listed race, any number being in with a chance inside the final 2f, and it's doubtful any of these will be capable of going on to score at a higher level. It was the best of the C&D times but the time was still ordinary. It's doubtful the winner had to match her pre-race form.

## 3144 AL BASTI EQUIWORLD H'CAP 1m (S)
**4:00** (4:01) (Class 5) (0-75,77) 3-Y-O **£2,587** (£770; £384; £192) **Stalls** Centre

Form RPR

-644 **1** **Know Your Name**[24] 2383 3-9-2 **70**.............................. (v) AdamKirby 6 79
(David Evans) *prom in main gp: rdn wl over 2f out: led 2f out and edgd lft: drvn and kpt rivals at bay fnl f* **8/1[3]**

0-44 **2** *nk* **Spirit Raiser (IRE)**[31] 2201 3-9-2 **70**.............................. HayleyTurner 8 78+
(James Fanshawe) *hld up in rr: plld out and prog over 2f out: nudged by rival sn after: clsd to chal fnl f: styd on but jst hld* **8/1[3]**

-041 **3** *½* **Craftsmanship (FR)**[11] 2805 3-9-6 **74** 6ex.............................. (p) AndreaAtzeni 4 81
(Robert Eddery) *trckd ldrs: rdn 3f out: prog to chal jst over 1f out: styd on but a hld* **10/1**

1- **4** *1 ¼* **The Third Man**[176] 8333 3-9-7 **75**.............................. WilliamBuick 9 79+
(John Gosden) *hld up in rr: plld out and prog over 2f out: drvn wl over 1f out: tried to cl on ldrs fnl f: one pce* **7/4[1]**

-500 **5** *4* **Aristocratic Duty**[12] 2775 3-8-10 **64**.............................. MartinHarley 5 59
(Sylvester Kirk) *wl in tch: shkn up and nt qckn over 2f out: no imp on ldrs after: styd on ins fnl f* **100/1**

3-64 **6** ½ **Fiftyshadesfreed (IRE)**[16] 2647 3-9-0 **68**................(p) FergusSweeney 2 62
(George Baker) *trckd rival on far side: shkn up and nt qckn over 2f out: kpt on fnl f: no ch* **25/1**

3331 **7** 3½ **After The Goldrush**[10] 2847 3-9-9 **77** 6ex.................(b) RichardHughes 1 63
(Richard Hannon) *overall ldr in far side pair to 1/2-way: shkn up 3f out: carried lft briefly and steadily wknd fr 2f out* **12/1**

2434 **8** 1 **Boogangoo (IRE)**[17] 2624 3-9-5 **73**.................................. AmirQuinn 11 58
(Grace Harris) *prom: overall ldr 1/2-way to 2f out: wknd over 1f out: eased last 150yds* **25/1**

34-4 **9** 2¼ **Marmarus**[49] 1681 3-8-6 **65**................................. RyanTate(5) 7 43
(Clive Cox) *prom: rdn 3f out: sn lost pl: rallied 2f out: wknd over 1f out* **20/1**

0-44 **10** 3¾ **Ninety Minutes (IRE)**[27] 2307 3-8-13 **67**...................... SteveDrowne 14 37
(John Best) *s.i.s: a towards rr: rdn and no prog wl over 2f out* **16/1**

2501 **11** 4 **Choice Of Destiny**[9] 2878 3-8-7 **66** 6ex....................... DannyBrock(5) 13 27
(Philip McBride) *hld up and sn wl bhd in 13th: drvn and sme prog 3f out: wknd qckly 2f out* **15/2[2]**

5-44 **12** 8 **Foxford**[40] 1946 3-9-1 **69**.......................................... SilvestreDeSousa 12 11
(Patrick Chamings) *prom 5f: wknd 2f out: heavily eased* **20/1**

500 **13** 10 **Greengage Summer**[12] 2773 3-8-9 **66**....... WilliamTwiston-Davies(3) 10
(Mick Channon) *s.i.s: in tch: rdn 3f out: sn wknd qckly: t.o* **33/1**

0-50 **14** ½ **Bowsers Bold**[16] 2647 3-8-0 **59**...................................[1] KatiaScallan(5) 3
(Marcus Tregoning) *blindfold stl on whn stalls opened and lost many l: a wl bhd: t.o* **40/1**

1m 37.71s (-1.99) **Going Correction** -0.225s/f (Firm) **14** Ran SP% **116.6**
Speed ratings (Par 99): **100,99,99,97,93 93,89,88,86,82 78,70,60,60**
CSF £62.43 CT £650.66 TOTE £10.10: £2.60, £3.10, £4.00; EX 96.40 Trifecta £844.20.
**Owner** Livvys Racing Group **Bred** Mill Farm Stud **Trained** Pandy, Monmouths

**FOCUS**
Just a fair handicap, the winner among the more exposed. He's rated back to his 2yo best. The field merged back into one at halfway, after both After The Goldrush and Fiftyshadesfreed had raced on their own near to the far rail early.

## 3145 BE WISER INSURANCE H'CAP 7f (S)
**4:30** (4:33) (Class 5) (0-75,75) 3-Y-O **£2,587** (£770; £384; £192) **Stalls** Centre

Form RPR

-052 **1** **Maraayill (IRE)**[9] 2879 3-9-7 **75**........................(tp) MartinHarley 6 81
(Marco Botti) *hld up wl in rr: prog to chse clr ldr over 1f out: drvn and styd on to ld last strides* **3/1[2]**

0-06 **2** hd **Llyrical**[31] 2224 3-8-1 **60**................................................ DannyBrock(5) 9 65
(Derek Haydn Jones) *racd v freely: led: clr after 3f: rdn wl over 1f out: kpt on wl but hdd last strides* **33/1**

2-23 **3** ¾ **Brigliadoro (IRE)**[44] 1861 3-9-4 **72**............................. RichardHughes 1 78+
(Philip McBride) *hld up wl in rr: waiting for a gap 2f out: gd prog jst over 1f out: chsd ldng pair ins fnl f: clsd on them fin: too much to do* **11/4[1]**

2-00 **4** 1 **Go For Broke**[4] 3037 3-9-1 **69**..................................... PatDobbs 12 69
(Richard Hannon) *in tch in chsng gp: rdn and prog 2f out: chsd ldng pair briefly ins fnl f: styd on same pce* **25/1**

0-02 **5** 1½ **Supersta**[40] 1940 3-9-3 **74**.......................... WilliamTwiston-Davies(3) 5 71
(Ronald Harris) *prom in chsng gp: rdn over 2f out: lost pl and btn over 1f out: kpt on again fnl f* **16/1**

-544 **6** hd **Honey Meadow**[16] 2657 3-9-0 **68**.............................. AndreaAtzeni 4 64
(Robert Eddery) *rrd bef stalls opened: prom in chsng gp: nt qckn 2f out: kpt on same pce fr over 1f out* **16/1**

642- **7** hd **Lacock**[240] 7271 3-9-4 **72**.............................................. FergusSweeney 8 68
(Henry Candy) *prom in chsng gp: rdn over 2f out: no prog over 1f out: one pce after* **8/1[3]**

4-50 **8** ½ **Headlong (IRE)**[17] 2624 3-8-13 **67**............................. TomQueally 7 61
(Brian Meehan) *hld up in rr: rdn 2f out: no threat to ldrs: plugged on* **20/1**

0246 **9** ¾ **Double Czech (IRE)**[17] 2624 3-8-13 **67**..............(v[1]) SilvestreDeSousa 3 59
(Patrick Chamings) *tk fierce hold: hld up in midfield: lost pl 2f out: reminders over 1f out: eased off whn no ch fnl f* **16/1**

62-2 **10** 1 **Suitsus**[28] 2278 3-9-3 **71**.............................................. SteveDrowne 13 61
(Peter Makin) *hld up in rr: stdy prog jst over 2f out: rdn over 1f out: wknd qckly ins fnl f* **14/1**

-204 **11** ¾ **Perfect Pursuit**[7] 2929 3-9-4 **72**.................................. AdamKirby 11 60
(Clive Cox) *chsd ldr: no imp and edgd lft fr 2f out: lost 2nd and wknd over 1f out* **25/1**

5253 **12** 3½ **Penny's Boy**[4] 3037 3-9-2 **70**...............................(t) GeorgeBaker 2 49
(Sylvester Kirk) *in tch in chsng gp: no prog 2f out: wknd jst over 1f out* **8/1[3]**

060- **13** 3¼ **Nashmi**[287] 5924 3-9-0 **68**............................................. WilliamBuick 10 38
(George Peckham) *v awkward s: a in rr: shkn up and no prog over 2f out* **25/1**

1m 25.5s (-0.20) **Going Correction** -0.225s/f (Firm) **13** Ran SP% **117.4**
Speed ratings (Par 99): **92,91,90,89,88 87,87,87,86,85 84,80,76**
CSF £109.77 CT £316.72 TOTE £3.80: £1.30, £9.30, £1.30; EX 184.40 Trifecta £1101.80.
**Owner** Sheikh Mohammed Bin Khalifa Al Maktoum **Bred** S F Bloodstock **Trained** Newmarket, Suffolk

**FOCUS**
Modest handicap form, with outsider Llyrical very nearly stealing it from the front. The level of the form is hard to pin down.

## 3146 INSURE WISER H'CAP 1m 4f 5y
**5:05** (5:06) (Class 5) (0-70,70) 3-Y-O **£2,587** (£770; £384; £192) **Stalls** Low

Form RPR

4-23 **1** **Loving Your Work**[31] 2225 3-9-3 **66**.............................. WilliamBuick 6 74
(George Baker) *hld up in midifeld: gng bttr than most 3f out: rdn and prog 2f out: clsd to ld 100yds out w hd high: kpt on* **12/1**

2435 **2** ¾ **Samtu (IRE)**[12] 2769 3-9-5 **68**.................................... MartinHarley 9 74
(Clive Brittain) *racd freely: disp ld at decent pce: def advantage 4f out: jnd and drvn 2f out: kpt on tl hdd and hung rt 100yds out* **14/1**

5-11 **3** shd **Nyanza (GER)**[36] 2080 3-9-4 **70**............... WilliamTwiston-Davies(3) 1 76
(Alan King) *prom: rdn 3f out: lost pl over 2f out and looked btn: rallied over 1f out: chal fnl f: kpt on* **12/1**

0-34 **4** ¾ **Winter Spice (IRE)**[34] 2133 3-9-0 **63**............................. AdamKirby 3 68
(Clive Cox) *wl plcd: prog to chse ldr over 3f out: chal and upsides jst over 2f out: fnd little and hld jst over 1f out: hmpd last 75yds* **14/1**

0-23 **5** 2½ **Gavlar**[21] 2492 3-9-6 **69**................................................ AndreaAtzeni 4 70
(William Knight) *prom: chsd ldr 3f out: upsides and drvn 2f out: nt qckn and btn over 1f out: fdd* **11/1**

6001 **6** 1 **Graphene**[14] 2694 3-8-5 **61**.......................................... CamHardie(7) 12 60+
(Rod Millman) *hld up in last: rdn 4f out: kpt on fr over 2f out: nvr rchd ldrs: nrst fin* **16/1**

0-34 **7** nk **Mollasses**[28] 2277 3-9-6 **69**........................................... TomQueally 7 68
(Jonathan Portman) *hld up in rr: shkn up and no prog 4f out: modest hdwy over 2f out: nvr rchd ldrs* **8/1[2]**

0-50 **8** 1½ **Hallbeck**[28] 2280 3-9-6 **69**....................................... FergusSweeney 11 66
(Henry Candy) *hld up towards rr: sme prog and swtchd ins 2f out: no hdwy over 1f out: fdd* **17/2[3]**

5066 **9** 2¾ **Assoluta (IRE)**[7] 2927 3-7-12 **52**............................... DannyBrock(5) 15 44
(Sylvester Kirk) *dropped in fr wd draw and wl in rr: rdn wl over 3f out: sme prog 2f out: no ch and wknd fnl f* **66/1**

060 **10** hd **Censorius**[31] 2221 3-9-3 **66**..................................... GeorgeBaker 14 58
(Ed Walker) *racd wd: towards rr: rdn 4f out: hanging and limited prog fr 3f out: wknd over 1f out* **14/1**

0256 **11** 7 **Brownsville (USA)**[17] 2617 3-9-5 **68**....................... SilvestreDeSousa 10 54
(Mark Johnston) *cl up bhd ldrs: rdn jst over 3f out: wknd 2f out: eased fnl f* **25/1**

520- **12** 4 **Mr Wickfield**[176] 8328 3-9-5 **68**................................. SteveDrowne 2 42
(John Best) *nvr beyond midfield: rdn and wknd over 3f out: sn bhd* **80/1**

350 **13** 2½ **Dream Big (IRE)**[16] 2650 3-9-4 **67**.............................. PatDobbs 13 37
(Jo Crowley) *a wl in rr: pushed along and no prog over 2f out: wknd qckly over 1f out* **66/1**

4630 **14** 11 **Flying Cape (IRE)**[27] 2319 3-9-6 **69**.............................. HayleyTurner 5 22
(Andrew Hollinshead) *disp ld at decent pce to 4f out: sn wknd: t.o* **14/1**

-501 **15** 6 **Storm Rider (IRE)**[7] 2927 3-8-13 **62** 6ex.................. RichardHughes 8 48
(Richard Hannon) *hld up wl in rr: drvn and no rspnse 4f out: heavily eased whn btn 2f out: t.o* **2/1[1]**

2m 33.51s (-1.99) **Going Correction** -0.175s/f (Firm) **15** Ran SP% **119.3**
Speed ratings (Par 99): **99,98,98,97,96 95,95,94,92,92 87,85,83,76,72**
CSF £164.80 CT £2065.17 TOTE £9.60: £3.40, £3.10, £2.70; EX 89.50 Trifecta £194.80.
**Owner** The Loving Your Work Syndicate **Bred** Dukes Stud & Overbury Stallions Ltd **Trained** Manton, Wilts

**FOCUS**
This was a competitive 3yo handicap for the class and it was run at a decent pace, but still few got in a serious blow. The form is a little below the expected standard for the race.

## 3147 WISER ACADEMY GENTLEMAN AMATEUR RIDERS' H'CAP 1m 2f 6y
**5:35** (5:35) (Class 5) (0-70,69) 4-Y-O+ **£2,495** (£774; £386; £193) **Stalls** Low

Form RPR

-530 **1** **Automotive**[6] 2963 6-10-13 **61**....................................... MrRBirkett 1 70
(Julia Feilden) *hld up: prog to trck ldr 2f out: led over 1f out and sn in command: rdn out* **9/2[2]**

34-3 **2** 1 **Hector's Chance**[75] 1167 5-11-5 **67**............................. MrSWalker 3 72
(Heather Main) *t.k.h: trckd ldr: led 3f out: rdn and hdd over 1f out: kpt on fnl f but readily hld* **5/4[1]**

-035 **3** hd **Royal Etiquette (IRE)**[101] 821 7-10-1 **54**..........(tp) MrAlexFerguson(5) 5 59
(Lawney Hill) *trckd ldng pair: gng easily 3f out: disp 2f out but nt qckn 2f out: swtchd to inner and n.m.r fr over 1f out: kpt on but nvr really threatened* **12/1**

-405 **4** 4½ **Petrify**[10] 2834 4-10-0 **53**.............................................(t) SeanBowen(5) 2 49
(Bernard Llewellyn) *led to 3f out: hrd rdn and steadily wknd fr 2f out* **12/1**

246- **5** 3¼ **Mandy's Boy (IRE)**[25] 6734 4-11-7 **69**.......................... MrHAABannister 7 59
(Ian Williams) *hld up in last pair: rdn wl over 2f out: no prog wl over 1f out: wknd* **5/1[3]**

6-30 **6** 1¼ **Hallingham**[15] 2672 4-10-9 **60**..................................... MrJHarding(3) 4 48
(Jonathan Portman) *dwlt: mostly in last: pushed along and no prog over 3f out: wknd over 2f out* **9/1**

35-0 **7** ½ **Whinging Willie (IRE)**[132] 405 5-10-13 **68**............... JasonNuttall(7) 6 55
(Gary Moore) *t.k.h: racd wd: in tch: rdn wl over 3f out: wknd over 2f out* **8/1**

2m 10.91s (2.11) **Going Correction** -0.175s/f (Firm) **7** Ran SP% **115.8**
Speed ratings (Par 103): **84,83,83,79,76 75,75**
CSF £10.85 TOTE £6.50: £4.10, £1.30; EX 16.00 Trifecta £127.80.
**Owner** Stowstowquickquickstow Partnership **Bred** Juddmonte Farms Ltd **Trained** Exning, Suffolk

**FOCUS**
An ordinary handicap for gentleman amateur riders. The winner seems better than ever.
T/Plt: £20.20 to a £1 stake. Pool of £69670.85 - 2514.78 winning tickets. T/Qpdt: £13.10 to a £1 stake. Pool of £4018.31 - 226.94 winning tickets. JN

# 2888 NOTTINGHAM (L-H)
### Thursday, June 12

**OFFICIAL GOING: Good (7.8)**
Wind: Light across Weather: Fine and dry

## 3148 BRITISH STALLION STUDS EBF MAIDEN STKS 6f 15y
**2:00** (2:01) (Class 5) 2-Y-O **£3,234** (£962; £481; £240) **Stalls** Centre

Form RPR

3 **1** **Ustinov**[20] 2507 2-9-5 0.................................................. JamieSpencer 6 79+
(Brian Meehan) *hld up in rr: swtchd rt and hdwy on outer 2f out: rdn to chal ent fnl f: sn led: edgd lft and kpt on* **4/7[1]**

**2** 1¾ **Sugar Lump** 2-9-5 0.......................................................... JoeFanning 5 71
(Richard Hannon) *trckd ldrs: hdwy and cl up 2f out: rdn to ld briefly ent fnl f: sn hdd and kpt on same pce* **16/1**

**3** ½ **Super Kid** 2-9-5 0............................................................ KierenFallon 9 69
(Saeed bin Suroor) *chsd ldrs: hdwy over 2f out: cl up and rdn over 1f out: kpt on same pce* **9/2[2]**

**4** nse **Shootingsta (IRE)** 2-9-5 0.............................................. PaulMulrennan 7 69
(Bryan Smart) *slt ld: rdn along 2f out: drvn and hdd ent fnl f: kpt on towards fin* **25/1**

**5** ½ **Henley** 2-9-5 0.................................................................. GrahamLee 2 68
(William Jarvis) *cl up: rdn wl over 1f out: kpt on same pce fnl f* **50/1**

23 **6** 2¼ **Rita's Boy (IRE)**[27] 2291 2-9-5 0.................................. DanielTudhope 1 61
(K R Burke) *chsd ldrs: rdn along 2f out: grad wknd appr fnl f* **10/1[3]**

**7** shd **Yorkshire Dales (IRE)** 2-9-5 0...................................... WilliamCarson 4 61
(David Elsworth) *in tch: hdwy on wd outside to chse ldrs over 2f out: sn rdn and wknd appr fnl f* **25/1**

**8** 2¼ **On The Tiles** 2-9-5 0........................................................ SeanLevey 8 54
(Ed McMahon) *trckd ldrs: hdwy 1/2-way: cl up 2f out: sn rdn and wknd appr fnl f* **33/1**

**9** 17 **Ghalib (IRE)** 2-9-5 0......................................................... LukeMorris 10 3
(Marco Botti) *racd wd: rdn along wl over 2f out: a towards rr* **12/1**

**10** 7 **La Brana** 2-9-5 0................................................................ DaleSwift 3
(Derek Shaw) *t.k.h: a towards rr* **100/1**

1m 14.37s (-0.33) **Going Correction** -0.25s/f (Firm) **10** Ran SP% **118.1**
Speed ratings (Par 93): **92,89,89,88,88 85,85,82,59,50**
CSF £11.65 TOTE £1.70: £1.10, £2.90, £1.20; EX 11.10 Trifecta £33.80.
**Owner** Mrs P Good **Bred** Mrs P Good **Trained** Manton, Wilts

**FOCUS**
The opening contest on an eight-race card was a fairly good juvenile maiden in which they went an even gallop on good ground. The winner was value for extra but it's hard to be sure about the form's overall level.

## 3149 CARLING BRILLIANTLY REFRESHING H'CAP (DIV I) 6f 15y
2:30 (2:39) (Class 6) (0-65,64) 3-Y-O+ £2,587 (£770; £384; £192) Stalls Centre

Form RPR
4634 1 **Medam**[21] 2479 5-8-13 **52**........................................ NeilFarley(3) 7 62
(Shaun Harris) *in tch: hdwy to chse ldrs over 2f out: rdn along wl over 1f out: swtchd lft and led ent fnl f: sn jnd and drvn: kpt on wl towards fin* **7/1**[1]
0601 2 *hd* **Climaxfortackle (IRE)**[23] 2435 6-9-12 **62**........................ JoeFanning 15 71
(Derek Shaw) *in rr: pushed along 1/2-way: hdwy wl over 2f out: rdn along wl over 1f out: styd on wl to chal ins fnl f: ev ch tl drvn and no ex towards fin* **8/1**[2]
-430 3 *3/4* **Lucky Lodge**[33] 2171 4-9-4 **61**.......................(b) RobertDodsworth(7) 6 68
(Mel Brittain) *prom: cl up 1/2-way: led over 2f out: rdn wl over 1f out: hdd appr fnl f: sn drvn and kpt on* **8/1**[2]
0020 4 *1 1/4* **Dancing Maite**[34] 2127 9-8-13 **54**.......................(b) PhilipPrince(5) 12 57
(Roy Bowring) *prom: led after 2f: pushed along and hdd over 2f out: cl up and sn rdn: ev ch tl drvn ent fnl f and kpt on same pce* **14/1**
0-00 5 *nse* **Nelson's Pride**[22] 2470 3-9-0 **58**.......................(b) JamieSpencer 3 59
(Kevin Ryan) *mdfield: hdwy over 2f out: rdn to chse ldrs and hung lft over 1f out: kpt on u.p fnl f* **25/1**
0-02 6 *shd* **Ishi Honest**[10] 2838 4-9-6 **56**........................................ GrahamLee 16 59
(Mark Usher) *in rr: hdwy wl over 2f out: rdn wl over 1f out: kpt on fnl f: nrst fin* **12/1**
0050 7 *1* **Divine Call**[8] 2887 7-9-10 **60**.......................(v[1]) DavidProbert 9 59
(Milton Bradley) *dwlt sltly: hdwy and in tch over 4f out: chsd ldrs over 2f out: rdn wl over 1f out and kpt on one pce* **12/1**
3065 8 *1 3/4* **Secret City (IRE)**[22] 2451 8-9-5 **58**.......................(b) JasonHart(3) 11 52
(Robin Bastiman) *towards rr: rdn along bef 1/2-way: styd on fr wl over 1f out: n.d* **12/1**
4-20 9 *2* **Bilash**[23] 2414 7-9-9 **64**........................................ JackDuern(5) 10 51
(Andrew Hollinshead) *midfield: effrt over 2f out: sn rdn and no imp* **10/1**[3]
5-10 10 *2 1/2* **Euroquip Boy (IRE)**[23] 2435 7-9-1 **56**........................ NoelGarbutt(5) 8 35
(Michael Scudamore) *t.k.h: chsd ldrs: rdn along wl over 2f out: sn wknd* **7/1**[1]
6003 11 *1 3/4* **Burnhope**[34] 2127 5-9-5 **55**.......................(p) LukeMorris 5 29
(Scott Dixon) *prom: rdn along 1/2-way: wknd over 2f out* **8/1**[2]
656- 12 *4* **Elite Freedom (IRE)**[204] 7973 3-8-12 **56**........................ DuranFentiman 17 15
(Brian Baugh) *racd wd: chsd ldrs: rdn along wl over 2f out and sn wknd* **33/1**
0-44 13 *2* **Frosted Off**[49] 1668 4-8-11 **47**........................................ WilliamCarson 4 2
(John Spearing) *slt ld 2f: cl up: rdn along wl over 2f out: sn wknd* **12/1**
-000 14 *1 3/4* **Sophie's Beau (USA)**[16] 2637 7-8-9 **52**..............(bt) BradleyBosley(7) 13 1
(Michael Chapman) *a towards rr* **100/1**
30-6 15 *4* **Hidden Talent**[139] 320 4-10-0 **64**.......................(p[1]) GrahamGibbons 2
(Steph Hollinshead) *towards rr: rdn along 1/2-way: n.d* **33/1**
04-0 16 *1* **Lucky Surprise**[20] 2505 3-9-4 **62**.......................(b[1]) SeanLevey 1
(Jeremy Gask) *a towards rr* **25/1**

1m 13.82s (-0.88) **Going Correction** -0.25s/f (Firm)
**WFA** 3 from 4yo+ 8lb **16** Ran SP% **119.4**
Speed ratings (Par 101): **95,94,93,92,92 91,90,88,85,82 79,74,71,69,64 62**
CSF £56.51 CT £484.28 TOTE £7.40: £2.00, £2.40, £2.80, £3.50; EX 49.60 Trifecta £354.70.
**Owner** Burton Agnes Bloodstock **Bred** Burton Agnes Stud Co Ltd **Trained** Carburton, Notts

**FOCUS**
The first division of a modest big-field sprint handicap in which they went a contested gallop. The form is rated around the form.

## 3150 CARLING BRILLIANTLY REFRESHING H'CAP (DIV II) 6f 15y
3:05 (3:07) (Class 6) (0-65,64) 3-Y-O+ £2,587 (£770; £384; £192) Stalls Centre

Form RPR
54 1 **Avonmore Star**[34] 2127 6-9-4 **54**........................................ GrahamLee 15 67
(Alan McCabe) *trckd ldr on stands' rail: hdwy wl over 1f out: rdn ent fnl f: sn swtchd lft and styd on strly to ld nr fin* **6/1**[2]
0234 2 *1/2* **Lees Anthem**[1] 3092 7-9-6 **56**........................................ DavidAllan 16 67
(Mel Brittain) *led and sn clr on stands' rail: rdn along over 1f out: drvn ins fnl f: hdd and no ex nr fin* **5/1**[1]
-220 3 *1 1/2* **Niceonemyson**[17] 2606 5-9-6 **61**........................................ KevinStott(5) 17 67
(Christopher Wilson) *racd towards stands' rail: chsd ldr: hdwy 2f out: rdn wl over 1f out: drvn and kpt on same pce ins fnl f* **6/1**[2]
6220 4 *1* **Indian Affair**[46] 1766 4-10-0 **64**........................................ DavidProbert 7 67
(Milton Bradley) *trckd ldrs: hdwy over 2f out: rdn over 1f out: one pce fnl f* **10/1**
-000 5 *hd* **Verus Delicia (IRE)**[29] 2250 5-9-11 **61**........................ ShaneKelly 4 63
(Daniel Mark Loughnane) *chsd ldrs: rdn along wl over 1f out: kpt on same pce fnl f* **16/1**
6414 6 *3/4* **Prigsnov Dancer (IRE)**[6] 2955 9-9-6 **63**........................ DavidParkes(7) 5 67+
(Deborah Sanderson) *in tch: effrt whn n.m.r and hmpd 2f out: swtchd rt wl over 1f out: styd on fnl f: nrst fin* **8/1**[3]
-000 7 *1/2* **Song Of Rowland (IRE)**[91] 936 3-8-13 **60**.............. SimonPearce(3) 6 56+
(John Spearing) *trckd ldrs: hdwy 2f out: n.m.r and rdn wl over 1f out: kpt on same pce fnl f* **25/1**
1-32 8 *shd* **Borough Boy (IRE)**[153] 121 4-9-6 **56**.......................(v) DaleSwift 13 54
(Derek Shaw) *towards rr: hdwy 2f out: sn rdn and kpt on fnl f: nrst fin* **9/1**
16-0 9 *1/2* **Queen Hermione (IRE)**[8] 2890 6-9-5 **62**..............(vt) AdamMcLean(7) 10 58
(Derek Shaw) *dwlt and swtchd lft s: in rr tl styd on fnl 2f: n.d* **16/1**
46-2 10 *1/2* **Divertimenti (IRE)**[160] 34 10-9-0 **55**.......................(b) PhilipPrince(5) 9 50
(Roy Bowring) *racd towards centre: prom: rdn along 2f out: drvn over 1f out and sn wknd* **20/1**
-006 11 *4 1/2* **Trending (IRE)**[16] 2648 5-9-10 **60**.......................(bt) HarryBentley 8 40
(Jeremy Gask) *in tch: rdn along and hung lft jst over 2f out: sn drvn and wknd* **25/1**
1300 12 *1/2* **Red Cape (FR)**[19] 2552 11-9-8 **58**.......................(b) JamesSullivan 3 37
(Ruth Carr) *racd towards centre: chsd ldrs: rdn along over 2f out: wknd over 1f out* **20/1**
-400 13 *2* **Errigal Lad**[54] 1584 9-8-10 **49**........................................ JasonHart(3) 11 21
(Garry Woodward) *sn outpcd and a in rr* **16/1**
5055 14 *nk* **Elle West**[31] 2204 3-8-4 **55**.......................(p) AnnaHesketh(7) 1 24
(Michael Easterby) *racd wd: chsd ldrs: rdn along over 2f out: grad wknd* **20/1**
600 15 *5* **Reginald Claude**[16] 2648 6-8-12 **55**.......................(v) CharlotteJenner(7) 14 10
(Mark Usher) *cl up centre: rdn along over 2f out: wkng whn carried rt wl over 1f out: sn in rr* **25/1**
4103 16 *nk* **Black Truffle (FR)**[16] 2648 4-9-1 **51**.......................(v) SeanLevey 2 6
(Mark Usher) *chsd ldrs on outer: rdn along wl over 2f out: sn wknd* **20/1**

1m 13.81s (-0.89) **Going Correction** -0.25s/f (Firm)
**WFA** 3 from 4yo+ 8lb **16** Ran SP% **123.7**
Speed ratings (Par 101): **95,94,92,91,90 89,89,88,88,87 81,80,78,77,71 70**
CSF £32.13 CT £160.43 TOTE £8.00: £2.30, £1.90, £1.80, £2.30; EX 44.90 Trifecta £193.40.
**Owner** Mrs M J McCabe **Bred** Miss J R Tooth **Trained** Averham Park, Notts

**FOCUS**
The second division of a modest big-field sprint handicap and the second horse home set a decent gallop up the stands' rail. The time was similar to division I. The winner is rated in line with his better runs in the past year.

## 3151 DOOM BAR ALWAYS BEST IN TAKES (H'CAP) 1m 6f 15y
3:40 (3:40) (Class 5) (0-75,75) 4-Y-O+ £2,587 (£770; £384; £192) Stalls Low

Form RPR
55-1 1 **Hallstatt (IRE)**[23] 2430 8-9-0 **68**.......................(t) PaulMulrennan 6 75
(John Mackie) *trckd ldng pair: hdwy on inner whn nt clr run and hmpd over 2f out: swtchd rt and rdn over 1f out: styd on to chal ent fnl f: led last 100yds* **3/1**[2]
3336 2 *1/2* **Lineman**[33] 2160 4-9-0 **68**........................................ RobertWinston 8 73
(Andrew Hollinshead) *hld up: hdwy on outer over 3f out: cl up over 2f out: rdn and slt ld over 1f out: drvn ins fnl f: hdd and no ex last 100yds* **10/1**
3004 3 *1* **Keep Calm**[11] 2801 4-8-9 **63**.......................(b[1]) JoeFanning 10 67
(John Mackie) *trckd ldng pair: hdwy over 3f out: sn cl up: slt ld wl over 1f out: drvn and hdd appr fnl f: kpt on same pce towards fin* **8/1**
2-56 4 *1 1/2* **Grayswood**[16] 2651 4-8-10 **64**.......................(p) MartinDwyer 9 66
(William Muir) *hld up in rr: hdwy on outer 3f out: rdn to chse ldrs wl over 1f out: edgd lft appr fnl f and sn no imp* **7/1**
3-65 5 *1/2* **Desert Recluse (IRE)**[44] 1849 7-9-7 **75**........................ StevieDonohoe 3 76
(Ian Williams) *sn led: pushed along over 3f out: rdn and edgd lft over 2f out: hdd and drvn wl over 1f out: wknd appr fnl f* **5/1**[3]
4011 6 *2* **Arashi**[8] 2885 8-9-3 **71** 6ex.......................(v) DaleSwift 4 69
(Derek Shaw) *hld up: hdwy over 3f out: rdn along wl 2f out: sn one pce* **14/1**
0241 7 *2 1/2* **Afro**[12] 2774 4-8-11 **68**.......................(p) CharlesBishop(3) 1 63
(Peter Hedger) *trckd ldr: cl up 4f out: rdn along over 3f out: wknd over 2f out* **2/1**[1]

3m 5.3s (-1.70) **Going Correction** -0.375s/f (Firm) **7** Ran SP% **114.4**
Speed ratings (Par 103): **89,88,88,87,87 85,84**
CSF £31.99 CT £217.04 TOTE £3.50: £1.90, £13.10; EX 40.70 Trifecta £124.30.
**Owner** NSU Leisure & Mrs Carolyn Seymour **Bred** Darley **Trained** Church Broughton , Derbys

**FOCUS**
A very ordinary staying handicap in which the tempo increased markedly in the home straight. Rather ordinary form.

## 3152 ABG LAW CLASSIC H'CAP 6f 15y
4:10 (4:10) (Class 3) (0-90,90) 4-Y-O+
£7,470 (£2,236; £1,118; £559; £279; £140) Stalls Centre

Form RPR
-220 1 **Joey's Destiny (IRE)**[34] 2110 4-9-6 **89**........................ MartinDwyer 1 101
(George Baker) *trckd ldrs: swtchd lft and hdwy wl over 1f out: rdn to chal ent fnl f: qcknd wl to ld last 75yds* **7/2**[3]
16 2 *1 1/2* **Run With Pride (IRE)**[19] 2562 4-8-11 **80**........................ DaleSwift 4 87
(Derek Shaw) *cl up: chal over 2f out: led wl over 1f out: sn rdn: drvn ent fnl f: hdd and no ex last 75yds* **5/2**[1]
33-5 3 *1* **Tatlisu (IRE)**[22] 2453 4-8-10 **82**........................ GeorgeChaloner(3) 3 86
(Richard Fahey) *trckd ldng pair: cl up 1/2-way: rdn to chal wl over 1f out: ev ch ins fnl f tl drvn and nt qckn last 100yds* **5/1**
0-04 4 *1 3/4* **Monsieur Chevalier (IRE)**[26] 2336 7-9-6 **89**.............. JamieSpencer 7 87
(P J O'Gorman) *dwlt and hld up: hdwy over 2f out: rdn to chse ldrs over 1f out: sn no imp* **11/4**[2]
-636 5 *3 3/4* **Noble Deed**[124] 534 4-9-7 **90**........................................ KierenFox 2 76
(Michael Attwater) *hld up: hdwy on outer 1/2-way: chsd ldrs over 2f out: sn rdn and wknd over 1f out* **10/1**
13/0 6 *9* **Just Charlie**[48] 1695 4-9-0 **83**........................................ GrahamLee 6 41
(Henry Candy) *slt ld: rdn along wl over 2f out: hdd wl over 1f out and sn wknd* **12/1**
000- 7 *15* **Captain Carey**[299] 5519 8-9-3 **86**........................................ RobertWinston 5
(Malcolm Saunders) *hld up: pushed along wl over 2f out: sn rdn along and wknd* **33/1**

1m 12.07s (-2.63) **Going Correction** -0.25s/f (Firm) **7** Ran SP% **113.9**
Speed ratings (Par 107): **107,105,103,101,96 84,64**
CSF £12.58 TOTE £3.90: £1.50, £1.50; EX 17.10 Trifecta £82.60.
**Owner** Delancey **Bred** Brian Wallace **Trained** Manton, Wilts

**FOCUS**
The feature race on the card was a decent sprint handicap in which they went a contested gallop. The winner resumed his progress and the form is rated slightly positively.

## 3153 1ST SECURITY SOLUTIONS LTD MAIDEN STKS 1m 75y
4:45 (4:48) (Class 5) 3-Y-O+ £3,234 (£962; £481; £240) Stalls High

Form RPR
-22 1 **Lacan (IRE)**[23] 2432 3-9-2 0........................................ LukeMorris 7 89+
(Clive Cox) *trckd ldrs: hdwy over 3f out: effrt and nt clr run over 2f out: swtchd rt and rdn over 1f out: sn chal: drvn to ld ins fnl f: kpt on* **11/10**[1]
22-2 2 *2 1/2* **Musaddas**[131] 443 4-9-13 85........................................ KierenFallon 10 86
(Saeed bin Suroor) *t.k.h: trckd ldrs: hdwy 4f out: cl up 3f out: rdn to ld wl over 1f out: hdd ins fnl f: kpt on same pce* **9/2**[3]
4-0 3 *nk* **Elusive Guest (FR)**[66] 1353 3-9-2 0........................ BarryMcHugh 8 82
(George Margarson) *in tch: hdwy on outer over 3f out: chsd ldng pair over 1f out: sn rdn and no imp ins fnl f* **10/1**
04-3 4 *1* **Express Himself (IRE)**[43] 1880 3-9-2 78........................ PhillipMakin 1 80
(Ed McMahon) *prom: cl up 1/2-way: led 3f out: sn rdn: hdd wl over 1f out: a sn one pce* **11/4**[2]
5 *1* **Patterned** 3-8-11 0........................................ LemosdeSouza 9 74+
(Luca Cumani) *hld up towards rr: hdwy on inner 3f out: rdn along 2f out: kpt on: nrst fin* **25/1**
0 6 *2 1/4* **Mantou (IRE)**[9] 2877 3-9-2 0........................................ JoeFanning 5 72+
(Michael Bell) *hld up towards rr: hdwy over 2f out: rdn along wl over 1f out: sn no imp* **100/1**
0 7 *7* **Varsovian**[8] 2883 4-9-13 0........................................ SebSanders 13 58
(Dean Ivory) *t.k.h: chsd ldr tl led after 1f: rdn along and hdd 3f out: grad wknd* **33/1**
0-6 8 *1 1/4* **Matravers**[9] 2877 3-9-2 0........................................ ShaneKelly 11 52+
(Sir Michael Stoute) *a towards rr* **20/1**
9 *2 1/2* **Dunnington** 5-9-13 0........................................ PatCosgrave 6 49
(Mel Brittain) *a towards rr* **50/1**

00 **10** *9* **Ballyfarsoon (IRE)**[38] 2026 3-9-2 0............................ StevieDonohoe 4 24
(Ian Williams) *s.i.s: a in rr* **100/1**
**11** *3 ½* **Wimboldsley** 3-9-2 0.......................................................[1] PJMcDonald 2 16
(Scott Dixon) *plld hrd: led 1f: chsd ldr tl wknd qckly 4f out: sn in rr* **100/1**
**12** *29* **Exton** 5-9-13 0...................................................................... DaleSwift 3
(James Given) *v.s.i.s: a wl bhd* **100/1**

1m 45.45s (-3.55) **Going Correction** -0.375s/f (Firm)
**WFA** 3 from 4yo+ 11lb **12** Ran SP% **119.0**
Speed ratings (Par 103): **102,99,99,98,97 94,87,86,84,75 71,42**
CSF £6.11 TOTE £2.40: £1.10, £1.80, £2.40; EX 7.00 Trifecta £38.00.
**Owner** Al Asayl Bloodstock Ltd **Bred** Sheikh Sultan Bin Khalifa Al Nahyan **Trained** Lambourn, Berks

**FOCUS**
A decent maiden in which they went quite steadily in the formative stage of the race. The form makes a fair bit of sense.

## 3154 DOWNLOAD THE NEW RACINGUK IPAD APP H'CAP (JOCKEY CLUB GRASSROOTS FLAT MIDDLE DISTANCE SERIES) 1m 2f 50y
**5:15** (5:15) (Class 5) (0-75,75) 3-Y-O **£3,234** (£962; £481; £240) **Stalls** Low

Form RPR
-351 **1** **Lisamour (IRE)**[21] 2492 3-9-7 **75**...................................... LukeMorris 1 82
(Paul Cole) *mde all: pushed along over 3f out and sn jnd: rdn over 2f out: drvn over 1f out: kpt on gamely ins fnl f* **7/1**
6-24 **2** *¾* **Shama's Song (IRE)**[28] 2279 3-9-3 **71**................................. ShaneKelly 9 76
(Sir Michael Stoute) *hld up: hdwy over 2f out: rdn wl over 1f out: styd on fnl f* **6/1**[3]
030 **3** *hd* **Every Time**[21] 2497 3-9-6 **74**............................................ DavidProbert 2 82+
(Andrew Balding) *hld up towards rr: hdwy on inner wl over 2f out: nt clr run and hmpd wl over 1f out: sn swtchd rt and rdn: styd on strly fnl f* **7/1**
4-23 **4** *½* **Award (IRE)**[24] 2404 3-9-0 **75**.............................. KieranShoemark(7) 5 79
(John Gosden) *trckd ldrs: lost pl and towards rr 1/2-way: swtchd rt to wd outside and rdn along 3f out: drvn 2f out: styd on to chse ldrs ins fnl f: kpt on: nrst fin* **3/1**[1]
601- **5** *½* **Ejadah (IRE)**[239] 7310 3-9-6 **74**........................................ JackMitchell 4 77
(Roger Varian) *t.k.h: prom: effrt 3f out: rdn along 2f out: drvn and one pce fnl f* **8/1**
6-54 **6** *1 ½* **Alphabetique**[27] 2310 3-8-9 **70**................................ JordanNason(7) 3 70
(Peter Chapple-Hyam) *chsd ldrs on inner: rdn along 3f out: drvn wl over 1f out: kpt on same pce appr fnl f* **10/1**
04-3 **7** *1 ¼* **Silver Mirage**[34] 2129 3-9-5 **73**...................................... JoeFanning 10 70
(Michael Bell) *hld up in rr: hdwy on outer over 3f out: sn cl up: rdn to chal wl over 1f out: sn ev ch tl drvn and wknd ins fnl f* **8/1**
**8** *7* **Koliakhova (FR)**[79] 3-9-6 **74**........................................... PatCosgrave 8 58
(George Baker) *hld up: hdwy to chse ldrs 6f out: effrt over 3f out: rdn along 2f out: sn wknd* **20/1**
2-04 **9** *7* **White Russian**[31] 2224 3-8-10 **64**..................................... KierenFallon 7 35
(Henry Candy) *trckd ldrs: hdwy to chse ldr after 3f: cl up over 4f out: rdn along over 2f out: drvn wl over 1f out and sn wknd* **4/1**[2]

2m 11.02s (-3.28) **Going Correction** -0.375s/f (Firm) **9** Ran SP% **120.4**
Speed ratings (Par 99): **98,97,97,96,96 95,94,88,83**
CSF £50.68 CT £311.73 TOTE £5.70: £1.50, £2.00, £3.90; EX 43.60 Trifecta £505.30.
**Owner** Frank Stella **Bred** Anthony Rafferty **Trained** Whatcombe, Oxon

**FOCUS**
A fair 3yo fillies' handicap in which they went a modest tempo and finished in a bunch. The winner confirmed her latest Salisbury form.

## 3155 1ST SECURITY SOLUTIONS LTD H'CAP 1m 2f 50y
**5:45** (5:45) (Class 6) (0-60,60) 4-Y-O+ **£1,940** (£577; £288; £144) **Stalls** Low

Form RPR
1121 **1** **I'm Harry**[18] 2593 5-9-7 **60**..........................................(vt) PatCosgrave 12 72
(George Baker) *trckd ldrs: hdwy whn sltly hmpd and swtchd rt 2f out: led over 1f out: rdn clr ins fnl f* **3/1**[1]
0056 **2** *2 ¼* **Sutton Sid**[11] 2806 4-9-0 **60**.......................................(b) DavidParkes(7) 8 67
(John Balding) *towards rr: hdwy 3f out and sn rdn along: drvn to chse ldrs over 1f out: kpt on u.p fnl f* **10/1**
2504 **3** *2 ½* **Elegant Ophelia**[7] 2916 5-9-6 **59**....................................(t) SebSanders 3 61
(Dean Ivory) *trckd ldng pair on inner: hdwy 3f out: rdn along 2f out: drvn ent fnl f: kpt on same pce* **10/1**
-036 **4** *½* **Loucal**[9] 2864 4-8-13 **57**..........................................(b) TobyAtkinson(5) 14 58
(Noel Quinlan) *trckd ldrs: hdwy over 4f out: rdn to chse ldrs and edgd lft 2f out: sn drvn and one pce appr fnl f* **10/1**
10-0 **5** *¾* **Kheskianto (IRE)**[143] 252 8-8-0 **46**.........................(t) BradleyBosley(7) 15 46
(Michael Chapman) *towards rr: hdwy 3f out: rdn and sltly hmpd 2f out: kpt on fnl f: nrst fin* **33/1**
044/ **6** *2 ¼* **Treasury Bond**[1794] 3958 7-8-7 **46** oh1........................ RoystonFfrench 7 41
(Oliver Sherwood) *towards rr: hdwy wl over 2f out: rdn wl over 1f out: kpt on fnl f: nrst fin* **50/1**
-040 **7** *nk* **Seldom (IRE)**[19] 2546 8-8-10 **56**............................ RobertDodsworth(7) 10 51
(Mel Brittain) *led 1f: cl up tl led again 4f out: rdn wl over 2f out: hdd over 1f out: wknd fnl f* **16/1**
0304 **8** *nse* **Amtired**[11] 2806 8-8-11 **50**.........................................(b) BarryMcHugh 5 45
(Marjorie Fife) *trckd ldrs: hdwy on inner over 3f out: rdn along over 2f out: sn no imp* **9/2**[2]
0/00 **9** *½* **Audacious**[28] 2270 6-9-5 **58**.........................................(t[1]) MichaelStainton 1 52
(Charles Pogson) *s.i.s: a in rr* **10/1**
3-34 **10** *2 ¾* **Think**[115] 639 7-8-7 **46**...................................................(t) PJMcDonald 11 34
(Clive Mulhall) *chsd ldrs: rdn along over 3f out: sn wknd* **14/1**
-415 **11** *6* **Monopoli**[9] 2863 5-9-7 **60**............................................(p) JoeFanning 13 37
(Chris Dwyer) *a towards rr* **8/1**
4224 **12** *1 ¼* **Sofias Number One (USA)**[24] 2400 6-8-7 **51**..........(b) PhilipPrince(5) 6 26
(Roy Bowring) *chsd ldr: led after 1f: hdd 4f out: rdn over 3f out and sn wknd* **7/1**[3]
43-0 **13** *42* **Priestley's Reward (IRE)**[15] 2672 5-9-5 **58**.................... LukeMorris 9
(Alan Phillips) *chsd ldrs: lost pl after 3f: bhd fnl 4f* **33/1**

2m 10.17s (-4.13) **Going Correction** -0.375s/f (Firm) **13** Ran SP% **123.5**
Speed ratings (Par 101): **101,99,97,96,96 94,94,94,93,91 86,85,52**
CSF £34.87 CT £279.22 TOTE £2.90: £2.30, £2.00, £4.30; EX 24.40 Trifecta £69.10.
**Owner** Wickfield Stud And Hartshill Stud **Bred** Wickfield Stud And Hartshill Stud **Trained** Manton, Wilts

**FOCUS**
The concluding contest was modest handicap for older horses. The winner is rated back to his early best.
T/Jkpt: £7,100.00 to a £1 stake. Pool of £10,000.00 - 1.00 winning ticket. T/Plt: £27.70 to a £1 stake. Pool of £59719.93 - 1572.40 winning tickets. T/Qpdt: £9.60 to a £1 stake. Pool of £3823.40 - 293.20 winning tickets. JR

# 3119 YARMOUTH (L-H)
Thursday, June 12

**OFFICIAL GOING: Good to firm (7.7)**
Wind: medium, behind Weather: sunny and warm

## 3156 BHEST RACING TO SCHOOL MAIDEN STKS 6f 3y
**2:10** (2:10) (Class 5) 3-Y-O+ **£3,234** (£962; £481; £240) **Stalls** Centre

Form RPR
232- **1** **Jacob's Pillow**[224] 7638 3-9-5 79..........................................[1] RyanMoore 9 88+
(William Haggas) *in tch in midfield: rdn and effrt to chse ldr 2f: led over 1f out: edging rt and drvn ins fnl f: kpt on* **5/4**[1]
2-34 **2** *1* **Intermedium**[36] 2083 3-9-5 82........................................... JimmyQuinn 2 84
(Charlie Appleby) *led: rdn and hdd over 1f out: styd pressing wnr: nt qckn u.p and hld ins fnl f* **11/4**[2]
3-33 **3** *2 ½* **Al Senad**[24] 2384 3-9-5 74............................................ FrederikTylicki 7 76
(Peter Chapple-Hyam) *t.k.h: hld up in tch in midfield: rdn and hdwy to chse ldng pair jst over 1f out: no imp fnl f* **10/3**[3]
36 **4** *4 ½* **Dancing Angel**[10] 2846 3-9-0 0........................................ PaddyAspell 8 57
(James Eustace) *chsd ldrs: wnt 2nd 4f out tl 2f out: 4th and btn jst over 1f out: wknd ins fnl f* **40/1**
**5** *nk* **Ecliptic Sunrise** 3-9-0 0.......................................... AdamBeschizza 10 56
(Des Donovan) *hld up in rr of main gp: pushed along ent fnl 2f: rdn and outpcd over 1f out: wl hld and plugged on same pce fnl f* **66/1**
44-0 **6** *2 ¼* **Stroll On (IRE)**[49] 1677 3-9-0 70..................................... ChrisCatlin 4 48
(Rae Guest) *chsd ldrs: rdn 2f out: sn struggling and btn over 1f out: wknd ins fnl f* **16/1**
**7** *4 ½* **Oasis Mirage** 3-9-0 0.................................................... NickyMackay 6 34+
(Robert Cowell) *rdr struggling to remove hood and v.s.a: a in rr: rdn over 2f out: wknd wl over 1f out* **16/1**
06 **8** *hd* **Happy Jack (IRE)**[20] 2525 3-9-5 0...................................... LiamJones 1 38
(Michael Wigham) *stdd after s: hld up in rr of main gp: rdn over 3f out: wknd 2f out: sn bhd* **150/1**
**9** *24* **Emmessess (IRE)** 3-9-2 0................................... MichaelJMMurphy(3) 5
(Christine Dunnett) *chsd ldr for 2f: lost pl and rdn over 2f out: sn bhd: t.o fnl f* **100/1**

1m 12.05s (-2.35) **Going Correction** -0.325s/f (Firm) **9** Ran SP% **111.5**
Speed ratings (Par 103): **102,100,97,91,90 87,81,81,49**
CSF £4.50 TOTE £2.00: £1.10, £1.20, £1.70; EX 5.60 Trifecta £10.10.
**Owner** Lael Stable **Bred** Lael Stables **Trained** Newmarket, Suffolk

**FOCUS**
With Makhfar a non-runner, the three at the head of the market had all had a few chances and this was probably not a maiden to be getting too carried away with. The form is rated around the second and third.

## 3157 WEDDINGS AT GREAT YARMOUTH RACECOURSE (S) STKS 7f 3y
**2:40** (2:48) (Class 6) 2-Y-O **£1,940** (£577; £288; £144) **Stalls** Centre

Form RPR
0 **1** **Cafe Cortado (IRE)**[13] 2725 2-8-1 0.................................... JoeyHaynes(5) 4 55
(K R Burke) *t.k.h: mde virtually all: rdn and rn green over 1f out: hrd pressed and drvn ins fnl f: hld on towards fin* **3/1**[2]
60 **2** *nk* **Wink Oliver**[9] 2859 2-8-4 0.......................................... DanielCremin(7) 5 59
(Mick Channon) *stdd s: hld up in tch in midfield: rdn 2f out: hdwy to chse clr wnr over 1f out: styd on and chal ins fnl f: hld towards fin* **11/4**[1]
004 **3** *3 ½* **Baileys Pursuit**[44] 1859 2-8-6 0...................................... NickyMackay 3 45
(Chris Dwyer) *t.k.h: w wnr for 1f: chsd wnr tl over 3f out: effrt u.p 2f out: 3rd and no ex ins fnl f: wknd fnl 100yds* **9/2**[3]
4 **4** *1 ¼* **Marti Ella**[36] 2064 2-8-6 0.............................................. LiamJones 8 41
(J S Moore) *t.k.h: chsd ldrs: wnt 2nd over 3f out tl over 1f out: wknd ins fnl f* **13/2**
5 **5** *6* **Please Don't Tease (IRE)**[49] 1663 2-8-6 0....................... RyanWhile(5) 1 30
(Bill Turner) *hld up in last pair: rdn and effrt over 2f out: sn struggling and wl btn over 1f out* **10/1**
**6** *24* **Marilyn Mon** 2-8-6 0....................................................... JimmyQuinn 2
(Jo Hughes) *v.s.a: sn rcvrd and in tch in rr: rdn over 2f out: wknd 2f out: t.o and eased ins fnl f* **10/1**
**7** *6* **Rosie Cheeks** 2-8-6 0....................................................... ChrisCatlin 6
(Chris Dwyer) *t.k.h: w ldr tl j. path and lost pl 5f out: rdn and struggling over 2f out: sn bhd: t.o and eased ins fnl f* **9/1**

1m 27.94s (1.34) **Going Correction** -0.325s/f (Firm) **7** Ran SP% **111.4**
Speed ratings (Par 91): **79,78,74,73,66 38,32**
CSF £11.04 TOTE £3.50: £1.40, £1.70; EX 13.30 Trifecta £53.80.There was no bid for the winner. Wink Oliver was claimed by M Fife for 5000.
**Owner** Mrs E Burke & Mrs T Burns **Bred** Rathasker Stud **Trained** Middleham Moor, N Yorks

**FOCUS**
The first 7f 2yo seller of the year. This looked a desperate affair beforehand and although the market leaders came to the fore and pulled clear of the third, it needs emphasising how weak a contest it was.

## 3158 SIS LIVE CLASSIFIED STKS 1m 3y
**3:15** (3:15) (Class 6) 3-Y-O **£1,940** (£577; £288; £144) **Stalls** Centre

Form RPR
06- **1** **Derbyshire (IRE)**[218] 7773 3-8-9 64.................................. ShaneGray(5) 3 73
(Kevin Ryan) *chsd ldr: rdn over 3f out: almost 3 l down and looked hld 1f out: kpt on u.p to ld fnl 50yds: sn in command* **7/4**[1]
5243 **2** *1 ¾* **Handwoven (IRE)**[20] 2516 3-8-11 65..........(b[1]) MichaelJMMurphy(3) 8 69
(Mark Johnston) *led: clr and stl travelling wl over 1f out: rdn and hld hd high ins fnl f: hdd fnl 50yds: immediately btn* **6/1**
0122 **3** *2 ¼* **Plucky Dip**[9] 2878 3-8-7 58............................................. JoeDoyle(7) 4 64
(John Ryan) *hld up in last pair: clsd 6f out: effrt u.p over 2f out: 3rd and kpt on same pce fr over 1f out* **5/2**[2]
0-30 **4** *¾* **Bishan Bedi (IRE)**[23] 2442 3-9-0 64.................................[1] RyanMoore 1 62
(William Jarvis) *stdd s: hld up in rr: niggled along 6f out: rdn 1/2-way: hdwy and swtchd lft over 2f out: no prog fr over 1f out* **7/2**[3]
156- **5** *3* **Born To Fly (IRE)**[269] 6474 3-8-7 61............................ JordanVaughan(7) 7 55
(Nick Littmoden) *t.k.h: chsd ldrs: rdn over 2f out: lost pl u.p 2f out: wknd over 1f out* **20/1**
005- **6** *2* **Vied (USA)**[209] 7902 3-9-0 64........................................... NickyMackay 2 51
(Robert Cowell) *chsd ldrs: rdn over 2f out: struggling and lost pl 2f out: wknd over 1f out* **25/1**

1m 38.29s (-2.31) **Going Correction** -0.325s/f (Firm) **6** Ran SP% **110.1**
Speed ratings (Par 97): **98,96,94,93,90 88**
CSF £12.22 TOTE £2.20: £1.30, £1.60; EX 10.20 Trifecta £26.50.
**Owner** Matt & Lauren Morgan **Bred** Sas Haras De La Huderie **Trained** Hambleton, N Yorks

**FOCUS**
Low-grade fare, but the well-backed winner did have some potential and came through strongly in the closing stages. The form is rated around the third.

## 3159 NORFOLK CHAMBER OF COMMERCE H'CAP (BOBIS RACE) 1m 3y
**3:50** (3:50) (Class 4) (0-80,80) 3-Y-O **£4,690** (£1,395; £697; £348) **Stalls** Centre

Form RPR
61 **1** **Etaab (USA)**[41] 1920 3-9-7 **80**................................ DaneO'Neill 7 91+
(William Haggas) *stdd after s: hld up in tch in last trio: pushed and gd hdwy to ld 2f out: edgd lft ins fnl f: kpt on and a hoding runner-up fnl 100yds* **7/4**[1]

521 **2** ½ **Halation (IRE)**[24] 2392 3-8-11 **75**.............................. MarcMonaghan(5) 6 83+
(Marco Botti) *hld up wl in tch in midfield: rdn and effrt over 2f out: hdwy over 1f out: chsd wnr ins fnl f: chal fnl 100yds: kpt on: a hld* **9/2**[2]

41-0 **3** 2½ **Sbraase**[57] 1509 3-9-4 **77**.................................. JimmyQuinn 5 79
(James Tate) *hld up in tch in rr: effrt u.p 2f out: edging lft over 1f out: kpt on ins fnl f: wnt 3rd towards fin* **8/1**

4345 **4** ½ **Gratzie**[15] 2671 3-8-1 **67**.................................. DanielCremin(7) 3 68
(Mick Channon) *t.k.h: chsd ldr: drvn and chsd wnr wl over 1f out: no ex 1f out: lost 2 pls ins fnl f* **25/1**

3-42 **5** 1 **D'Avignon (USA)**[27] 2307 3-9-3 **76**.............................(p) NickyMackay 8 75
(John Gosden) *t.k.h: wl in tch in midfield: effrt u.p ent fnl 2f: drvn and no ex 1f out: wknd ins fnl f* **7/1**

-524 **6** 4½ **Heho**[23] 2431 3-9-1 **74**.................................. RyanMoore 1 62
(Sir Michael Stoute) *chsd ldrs: rdn jst over 2f out: no ex and btn 1f out: wknd ins fnl f* **5/1**[3]

453- **7** 3 **This Is The Day**[188] 8176 3-9-0 **73**.............................[1] FrederikTylicki 2 54
(Charlie Fellowes) *stdd s: hld up in tch in last trio: rdn and effrt over 2f out: wknd over 1f out* **20/1**

05-0 **8** 16 **Street Force (USA)**[48] 1696 3-9-7 **80**.............................(b) LiamJones 4 25
(Clive Brittain) *t.k.h: led tl 2f: sn rdn and dropped out: wl bhd ins fnl f* **14/1**

1m 37.8s (-2.80) **Going Correction** -0.325s/f (Firm) **8** Ran SP% **110.1**
Speed ratings (Par 101): **101,100,98,97,96 92,89,73**
CSF £8.72 CT £43.69 TOTE £2.70: £1.20, £1.20, £3.40; EX 12.30 Trifecta £76.60.
**Owner** Hamdan Al Maktoum **Bred** Shadwell Farm LLC **Trained** Newmarket, Suffolk

**FOCUS**
An interesting 3yo handicap run at a steady pace and the well-bred, unexposed winner did it in the style of a filly with a bright future. She rates better than the bare form.

## 3160 SEALIFE CENTRE AT GREAT YARMOUTH H'CAP 7f 3y
**4:20** (4:20) (Class 6) (0-65,68) 4-Y-O+ **£1,940** (£577; £288; £144) **Stalls** Centre

Form RPR
3-54 **1** **Be Royale**[12] 2775 4-9-3 **60**.................................. DaneO'Neill 5 73
(Michael Appleby) *hld up in tch in midfield: hdwy to chse ldrs 1/2-way: led 2f out: rdn and clr 1f out: edgd lft but in command fnl f: eased cl home* **7/1**[2]

1132 **2** ½ **Global Leader (IRE)**[8] 2884 4-9-7 **64**.............................. RyanMoore 4 74
(Paul D'Arcy) *hld up in tch in midfield: rdn and effrt 2f out: swtchd lft and hdwy over 1f out: chsd clr wnr 1f out: r.o u.p and swtchd rt towards fin: nvr gng to rch wnr* **5/4**[1]

0-36 **3** 2¼ **Gift Of Silence**[23] 2448 5-9-7 **64**.............................. PaddyAspell 6 68
(John Berry) *stdd s: hld up in tch in rr: hdwy and nt clr run 2f out: rdn and effrt over 1f out: styd on to go 3rd wl ins fnl f: no threat to ldrs* **25/1**

46-0 **4** 1¼ **Fever Few**[52] 1613 5-9-4 **64**.............................. AshleyMorgan(3) 2 65
(Chris Wall) *chsd ldr: rdn and ev ch 2f out: drvn and unable qck over 1f out: wknd ins fnl f* **8/1**[3]

6-05 **5** 2¼ **Not Rigg (USA)**[104] 780 4-8-9 **59**.............................. JordanVaughan(7) 8 54
(Nick Littmoden) *t.k.h: hld up in tch in midfield: effrt u.p over 2f out: 4th and no ex 1f out: wknd ins fnl f* **7/1**[2]

4400 **6** 3¾ **Indus Valley (IRE)**[16] 2646 7-9-1 **58**.............................(b) LiamJones 9 43
(Des Donovan) *t.k.h: hld up in tch in midfield: effrt u.p over 2f out: hrd drvn and btn over 1f out: wknd fnl f* **16/1**

0-30 **7** 1½ **Orders From Rome (IRE)**[13] 2721 5-9-5 **62**.............................. FrederikTylicki 10 43
(Charlie Fellowes) *stdd s: hld up in tch towards rr: swtchd rt and effrt u.p 3f out: no imp 2f out: wknd over 1f out* **20/1**

0-11 **8** shd **Putin (IRE)**[8] 2901 6-9-6 **68** 6ex.............................(bt) RachealKneller(5) 7 49
(Phil McEntee) *led tl 2f out: sn rdn and unable qck: btn over 1f out: wknd fnl f* **12/1**

064 **9** 2¾ **Two No Bids (IRE)**[20] 2527 4-9-2 **62**.............................. RobertTart(3) 12 36
(Phil McEntee) *hld up in tch in rr: rdn and no hdwy over 2f out: sn hld up in tch towards rr: rdn over 2f out: sn wknd* **16/1**

-400 **10** 1¼ **Vermuyden**[107] 740 5-8-11 **57**.............................(t) RyanPowell(3) 11 28
(Pam Sly) *hld up in tch towards rr: effrt over 2f out: sn struggling: wknd and hung lft 2f out* **33/1**

0-05 **11** nse **Sairaam (IRE)**[51] 1639 8-7-10 **46** ow1.............................. AaronJones(7) 1 17
(Charles Smith) *chsd ldrs tl over 2f out: sn struggling: wknd over 1f out* **50/1**

4026 **12** 3¾ **Coach Montana (IRE)**[8] 2907 5-8-5 **48** ow2..........(b) AdamBeschizza 3 9
(Christine Dunnett) *wl in tch in midfield: rdn over 2f out: no ex and btn 2f out: sn wknd* **20/1**

1m 24.7s (-1.90) **Going Correction** -0.325s/f (Firm) **12** Ran SP% **118.3**
Speed ratings (Par 101): **97,96,93,92,89 85,83,83,80,79 79,74**
CSF £14.96 CT £216.91 TOTE £7.50: £2.20, £1.10, £6.30; EX 16.30 Trifecta £515.90.
**Owner** Wayne Brackstone, Steve Whitear **Bred** W Brackstone & S J Whitear **Trained** Danethorpe, Notts

**FOCUS**
Competitive enough for the grade, but the pace wasn't overly strong. The first pair were clear and the form is interesting for the grade.

## 3161 FACEBOOK AT GREAT YARMOUTH RACECOURSE H'CAP 1m 3f 101y
**4:55** (4:57) (Class 4) (0-85,84) 4-Y-O+ **£4,690** (£1,395; £697; £348) **Stalls** Low

Form RPR
13-1 **1** **Nullarbor Sky (IRE)**[23] 2445 4-9-3 **80**.............................(p) RyanMoore 1 89+
(Lucy Wadham) *sn led: rdn and qcknd 2f out: clr over 1f out: pressed and drvn ins fnl f: a holding runner-up: drvn out* **1/2**[1]

0-34 **2** ½ **Ethics Girl (IRE)**[19] 2547 8-8-2 **65**.............................(t) NickyMackay 3 73
(John Berry) *hld up in tch in rr: swtchd rt and shkn up over 2f out: hdwy to chse wnr and rdn wl over 1f out: styd on pressing wnr ins fnl f: hld towards fin* **12/1**

-454 **3** 4½ **The Ducking Stool**[23] 2445 7-8-0 **68** ow2.............. ShelleyBirkett(5) 4 68
(Julia Feilden) *pressed wnr: rdn over 2f out: outpcd u.p over 1f out: batlling for 3rd and one pce fnl f* **11/2**[3]

50-6 **4** shd **Art Scholar (IRE)**[12] 2783 7-9-0 **84**.............................. AlistairRawlinson(7) 2 84
(Michael Appleby) *trckd ldng pair: clsd and ev ch 3f out: rdn 2f out: outpcd u.p over 1f out: battling for 3rd and one pce fnl f* **9/2**[2]

2m 25.67s (-3.03) **Going Correction** -0.125s/f (Firm) **4** Ran SP% **107.9**
Speed ratings (Par 105): **106,105,102,102**
CSF £6.92 TOTE £1.20; EX 6.30 Trifecta £8.20.
**Owner** Tim Wood **Bred** Vincent Hannon **Trained** Newmarket, Suffolk

**FOCUS**
A small field and Ryan Moore was seen to good effect on the winner, making much of the running and having enough left to see off a persistent challenger. The level of the form is tricky to pin down.

## 3162 SCROBY SANDS AT GREAT YARMOUTH H'CAP 1m 1f
**5:25** (5:25) (Class 5) (0-75,77) 4-Y-O+ **£2,587** (£770; £384; £192) **Stalls** Low

Form RPR
2431 **1** **Genius Boy**[9] 2876 4-9-9 **77** 6ex.............................. RyanMoore 6 92+
(James Tate) *hld up in tch in last pair: rdn and effrt over 3f out: hdwy and racing wd of rivals 2f out: led over 1f out: stl shifting rt but in command ins fnl f: r.o: rdn out* **2/5**[1]

0002 **2** 3¼ **Ocean Applause**[23] 2444 4-8-12 **73**.............................(t) JoeDoyle(7) 2 79
(John Ryan) *chsd ldng pair: nt enough room on inner fr 3f out: rdn 2f out: swtchd rt r.o to snatch 2nd on post* **16/1**

-663 **3** nse **Enriching (USA)**[23] 2444 6-8-11 **65**.............................. J-PGuillambert 4 71
(Nick Littmoden) *led for 2f: chsd ldr after: rdn 3f out: unable qck u.p over 1f out: styd on to chse clr wnr fnl 100yds: no imp: lost 2nd on post* **12/1**

3 **4** 2¼ **Buzz Law (IRE)**[10] 2823 6-7-12 **57**.............................(v) JoeyHaynes(5) 1 58
(K R Burke) *t.k.h: chsd ldr tl led 7f out: rdn over 2f out: hdd and unable qck over 1f out: lost 2nd and wknd fnl 100yds* **15/2**[2]

0-25 **5** ½ **Rouge Nuage (IRE)**[8] 2882 4-9-4 **72**.............................. JimmyQuinn 5 72
(Conrad Allen) *in tch in midfield: rdn and effrt 3f out: no ex u.p jst ins fnl f: wknd fnl 100yds* **16/1**

-201 **6** 2¾ **Silver Alliance**[23] 2444 6-9-2 **75**.............................(p) ShelleyBirkett(5) 3 69
(Julia Feilden) *stdd s: hld up in tch in last pair: rdn and effrt 2f out: no imp and btn 1f out: eased cl home* **11/1**[3]

1m 53.96s (-1.84) **Going Correction** -0.125s/f (Firm) **6** Ran SP% **111.0**
Speed ratings (Par 103): **103,100,100,98,97 95**
CSF £8.27 TOTE £1.20: £1.10, £4.60; EX 7.90 Trifecta £33.00.
**Owner** Sheikh Juma Dalmook Al Maktoum **Bred** Meon Valley Stud **Trained** Newmarket, Suffolk

**FOCUS**
A warm order in the finale and the winner completed another treble for Ryan Moore.
T/Plt: £6.90 to a £1 stake. Pool of £55653.11 - 5834.81 winning tickets. T/Qpdt: £4.70 to a £1 stake. Pool of £2946.23 - 459.0 winning tickets. SP

3163 - 3166a (Foreign Racing) - See Raceform Interactive

# 2969 LEOPARDSTOWN (L-H)
Thursday, June 12

**OFFICIAL GOING: Good**

## 3167a BALLYOGAN STKS (GROUP 3) (F&M) 6f
**7:50** (7:52) 3-Y-O+ **£32,500** (£9,500; £4,500; £1,500)

RPR
**1** **Majestic Queen (IRE)**[33] 2144 4-9-8 95.............................. PatSmullen 5 102
(Tracey Collins, Ire) *chsd ldr: mod 2nd 1/2-way: rdn and clsd on outer to ld over 1f out: styd on wl towards fin* **8/1**[3]

**2** 2½ **Joyeuse**[19] 2564 3-9-0 109.............................. JamesDoyle 3 92
(Lady Cecil) *w.w: mod 7th 1/2-way: hdwy over 2f out into 2nd far side ins fnl f: kpt on same pce u.p towards fin wout ever troubling wnr* **8/13**[1]

**3** nk **Sparrow (IRE)**[74] 1201 3-9-0 96.............................(t) JosephO'Brien 8 91
(A P O'Brien, Ire) *hld up in tch: mod 4th 1/2-way: tk clsr order u.p 1 1/2f out: no imp on wnr in 3rd ins fnl f: kpt on same pce* **8/1**[3]

**4** 1½ **Seas Of Wells (IRE)**[10] 2857 3-9-0 .............................. DeclanMcDonogh 1 86
(John M Oxx, Ire) *dwlt sltly: sn chsd ldrs: mod 3rd 1/2-way: tk clsr order under 2f out: rdn and no ex u.p in 4th ins fnl f: kpt on one pce* **10/1**

**5** 1½ **Califante**[10] 2823 4-9-8 74.............................. RonanWhelan 2 83
(T Hogan, Ire) *dwlt sltly: hld up in tch in rr: last 1/2-way: rdn and tk clsr order in 7th ent fnl f: kpt on u.p towards fin: nvr nrr* **66/1**

**6** nk **Gathering Power (IRE)**[19] 2564 4-9-8 102.............................. FergalLynch 6 82
(Edward Lynam, Ire) *chsd ldrs: racd keenly: mod 5th 1/2-way: tk clsr order under 2f out: rdn in 6th over 1f out and no imp on ldrs: kpt on one pce* **9/2**[2]

**7** nk **Body Beautiful (IRE)**[13] 2752 3-9-0 78.............................. ColinKeane 4 79
(G M Lyons, Ire) *led and sn clr: 4 l clr 1/2-way: reduced advantage under 2f out and hdd u.p over 1f out: sn wknd* **25/1**

**8** 5½ **Morning Frost (IRE)**[20] 2532 4-9-8 95.............................. ShaneFoley 7 64
(M Halford, Ire) *hld up: mod 6th 1/2-way: rdn into st and sn no imp u.p: dropped to rr 1f out: eased* **50/1**

1m 15.81s (1.71) **Going Correction** +0.425s/f (Yiel)
**WFA** 3 from 4yo 8lb **8** Ran SP% **118.7**
Speed ratings: **105,101,101,99,97 96,96,89**
CSF £13.88 TOTE £8.10: £1.50, £1.02, £2.20; DF 21.50 Trifecta £157.80.
**Owner** Thomas J Rogers **Bred** Sunderland Holdings Ltd **Trained** The Curragh, Co Kildare

**FOCUS**
A fourth win and a career-best performance by Majestic Queen, who landed a race run at a strong pace.

3168 - 3169a (Foreign Racing) - See Raceform Interactive

# 2880 LONGCHAMP (R-H)
Thursday, June 12

**OFFICIAL GOING: Turf: very soft**

## 3170a PRIX DU CHERCHE MIDI (CONDITIONS) (2YO) (TURF) 5f (S)
**11:45** (12:00) 2-Y-O **£12,083** (£4,833; £3,625; £2,416; £1,208)

RPR
**1** **Queen Bee (FR)**[23] 2-8-10 0.............................. GregoryBenoist 5 89
(E Lellouche, France) **1/1**[1]

**2** 3½ **Pierre Precieuse (FR)**[5] 3027 2-8-10 0.............................. SebastienMaillot 2 76
(E Caroux, France) **74/10**

**3** 1½ **Something Lucky (IRE)**[8] 2-8-11 0.............................. AntoineHamelin 1 72
(Matthieu Palussiere, France) **83/10**

**4** 2½ **Archange (FR)**[35] 2-8-10 0.............................. FabriceVeron 4 62
(H-A Pantall, France) **27/10**[2]

**5** 4 **Sandy De Luz (FR)**[23] 2-8-8 0.............................. UmbertoRispoli 3 46
(L Edon, France) **214/10**

6 *hd* **Thumper (FR)**[10] 2837 2-8-11 0.................. Christophe-PatriceLemaire 6 48
(Robert Cowell) *sn led: pushed along 2f out: hdd over 1f out: rdn and wknd* **54/10**[3]

59.5s (3.20) **6** Ran SP% **119.8**
WIN (incl. 1 euro stake): 2.00. PLACES: 1.40, 2.60. SF: 8.90.
**Owner** G Augustin-Normand & Ecurie La Boetie **Bred** Earl Haras Du Logis & J Ince **Trained** Lamorlaye, France

## 3171a LA COUPE (GROUP 3) (4YO+) (TURF) 1m 2f
1:50 (12:00) 4-Y-0+ **£33,333** (£13,333; £10,000; £6,666; £3,333)

RPR

1 **Narniyn (IRE)**[226] 7613 4-8-13 0.......................... ChristopheSoumillon 1 112
(A De Royer-Dupre, France) *hld up in midfield on inner: clsd 1/2-way: gng best 2f out: shkn up to chal over 1f out and rdn to ld ent fnl f: styd on wl and a doing enough* **2/1**[2]

2 ½ **Ipswich (IRE)**[20] 2631 4-8-8 0.......................................... GeraldMosse 6 106
(A De Royer-Dupre, France) *hld up in last: rdn over 2f out: styd on and wnt 2nd ins fnl 120yds: clsng on wnr at fin but a hld* **127/10**

3 1 ¾ **Ocovango**[100] 837 4-8-11 0.......................................... MaximeGuyon 2 106
(A Fabre, France) *midfield in tch: clsd on outer 1/2-way but qckly restrained: rdn 2f out: styd on and wnt 3rd cl home: nt pce to chal* **9/5**[1]

4 *nk* **Celtic Rock**[46] 5-9-2 0.......................................... J-LMartinez 5 110
(J C Fernandez, Spain) *led: rdn 2f out: strly pressed over 1f out and hdd ent fnl f: kpt on but sn outpcd by wnr: no ex and lost 2 pl fnl 120yds* **87/10**

5 6 **Calvin Williams (FR)**[70] 1274 4-8-11 0...................... AnthonyCrastus 3 93
(E Lellouche, France) *hld up in midfield on outer: last 3f out: rdn 2f out: outpcd and btn fnl f: eased towards fin: nvr threatened* **63/10**

6 12 **Belle De Crecy (IRE)**[46] 1783 5-9-1 0.......................... FrankieDettori 4 73
(Mme C Head-Maarek, France) *t.k.h: trckd ldr: clsd 2nd 3f out: rdn over 2f out: sn no ex and btn: wknd and dropped to last: eased* **41/10**[3]

2m 10.19s (6.19) **6** Ran SP% **120.0**
WIN (incl. 1 euro stake): 3.00. PLACES: 2.20, 4.60. SF: 21.20.
**Owner** H H Aga Khan **Bred** His Highness The Aga Khan's Studs S C **Trained** Chantilly, France

## 3172a PRIX DE VILLE D'AVRAY (CLAIMER) (4YO+) (TURF) 1m 2f
2:55 (12:00) 4-Y-0+ **£9,583** (£3,833; £2,875; £1,916; £958)

RPR

1 **Esles (FR)**[12] 6-8-11 0.................................. JeremieCatineau(8) 3 89
(C Laffon-Parias, France) **7/5**[1]

2 ¾ **Tagar Bere (FR)**[18] 7-9-5 0.......................................... MaximeGuyon 2 87
(Y Barberot, France) **9/5**[2]

3 *snk* **Storm River (FR)**[301] 5-8-13 0..................................(p) MickaelBerto(5) 6 86
(C Gourdain, France) **19/2**

4 1 **Quart De Rhum (FR)**[254] 1570 5-9-1 0.............................. UmbertoRispoli 7 81
(Yannick Fouin, France) **124/10**

5 1 ¼ **Lone Ranger (FR)**[12] 6-9-1 0.......................................... StephanePasquier 1 79
(Y Gourraud, France) **77/10**[3]

6 2 ½ **Idee Libre (FR)**[63] 4-8-11 0.......................................... AnthonyCrastus 9 70
(Yannick Fouin, France) **25/1**

7 1 **Commissar**[10] 2851 5-9-1 0.............................. MllePaulineDominois(5) 5 77
(Ian Williams) *trckd ldr: cl 2nd 3f out: rdn to chal 2f out: sn outpcd by wnr: no ex and fdd fnl f: eased nring fin* **14/1**

8 2 ½ **Masiyann (FR)**[26] 4-9-1 0..........................................(p) RonanThomas 4 67
(A Bonin, France) **33/1**

2m 15.89s (11.89) **8** Ran SP% **119.3**
WIN (incl. 1 euro stake): 2.40. PLACES: 1.20, 1.10, 1.50. DF: 2.30. SF: 4.40.
**Owner** Mme Georgiana Cabrero **Bred** Janus Bloodstock Inc **Trained** Chantilly, France

# 2829 CHEPSTOW (L-H)
Friday, June 13

**OFFICIAL GOING: Good (good to firm in places; 7.4)**
Wind: slight behind Weather: sunny spells

## 3173 EBF STALLIONS NOVICE STKS (BOBIS RACE) 6f 16y
5:30 (5:33) (Class 4) 2-Y-0 **£6,469** (£1,925; £962; £481) **Stalls** Centre

Form RPR

2 1 **Smaih (GER)**[11] 2845 2-9-0 0.......................................... FrankieDettori 6 82+
(Richard Hannon) *chsd ldrs: pushed along 2f out: sn led: edgd lft and rdn clr fnl f* **2/7**[1]

2 3 **Paddys Motorbike (IRE)** 2-9-0 0.......................................... SteveDrowne 8 71+
(David Evans) *s.i.s: sn in tch: pushed along and hdwy 1/2-way: rdn and outpcd by ldng pair 2f out: styd on ins fnl f to snatch 2nd post* **9/1**[3]

0331 3 *nse* **Union Rose**[15] 2692 2-9-4 0.......................................... LiamJones 9 75+
(Ronald Harris) *led: rdn 2f out: hdd over 1f out: outpcd by wnr fnl f: wknd 100yds out: ct for 2nd post* **4/1**[2]

4 2 ½ **Vita Mina** 2-8-9 0.......................................... DavidProbert 5 58+
(David Evans) *hld up: rdn 2f out: r.o ins fnl f: nt trble ldrs* **33/1**

4 5 1 ¼ **Go White Lightning (IRE)**[30] 2246 2-8-9 0.......................... MartinLane 4 55
(David Evans) *chsd ldrs: rdn 1/2-way: sn outpcd by principals: kpt on same pce fnl 2f* **20/1**

0 6 4 **Tilly Range (IRE)**[8] 2928 2-8-9 0.......................................... ChrisCatlin 2 43
(David Evans) *cl up: rdn over 3f out and grad lost pl: no ch after* **33/1**

020 7 *shd* **Blue Burmese (IRE)**[13] 2771 2-8-2 0.......................... CharlotteJenner(7) 1 42
(Mark Usher) *chsd ldrs: rdn over 2f out: wknd fnl f* **10/1**

8 3 ¾ **Madame Ascension** 2-8-6 0.......................................... DeclanBates(3) 3 31
(David Evans) *uns rdr leaving paddock: rdn and hung lft after 2f: a towards rr* **25/1**

1m 11.97s (-0.03) **Going Correction** -0.075s/f (Good) **8** Ran SP% **131.3**
Speed ratings (Par 95): **97,93,92,89,87 82,82,77**
CSF £5.35 TOTE £1.10: £1.02, £3.00, £1.10; EX 7.00 Trifecta £16.90.
**Owner** Al Shaqab Racing **Bred** Stiftung Gestut Fahrhof **Trained** East Everleigh, Wilts

**FOCUS**
Only one previous winner lined-up in this novice event but the odds-on favourite scored with plenty in hand and the third adds substance to the form. It's possible the second and fourth are flattered a little.

## 3174 LOOKERS JEEP CARDIFF MAIDEN FILLIES' STKS 1m 4f 23y
6:05 (6:05) (Class 5) 3-Y-0+ **£3,881** (£1,155; £577; £288) **Stalls** Low

Form RPR

2-2 1 **Swan Lakes (IRE)**[28] 2310 3-8-12 0.......................................... FergusSweeney 1 79
(David Simcock) *trckd ldng pair: pushed along to chal 3f out: kpt on u.p to take def ld fnl 50yds: plld away cl home* **2/1**[2]

55 2 1 ¼ **Fiery Sunset**[48] 1738 3-8-12 0.......................................... PatCosgrave 2 77
(Michael Bell) *hld up in tch: racd keenly: wnt 3rd over 3f out: sn rdn: kpt on ins fnl f to go 2nd post* **14/1**

4-2 3 *shd* **Sea The Bloom**[60] 1491 3-8-12 0.......................................... JimmyFortune 5 77
(Sir Michael Stoute) *led: jnd and rdn 3f out: hrd drvn fnl 2f: hdd and no ex fnl 50yds: lost 2nd post* **11/8**[1]

40 4 1 ½ **Grace And Favour**[28] 2299 3-8-12 0.......................................... DavidProbert 3 74
(Andrew Balding) *t.k.h: in tch: rdn and hdwy on outside over 3f out: drvn over 2f out: styd on same pce fnl f: nvr quite able to chal* **8/1**

5 10 **May Hay**[104] 4-9-13 0.......................................... WilliamCarson 7 58
(Anthony Carson) *dwlt: bhd: in tch w main body of field after 3f: hdwy over 4f out: rdn 3f out: one pce fnl 2f* **33/1**

0 6 14 **Mikey Miss Daisy**[29] 2279 3-8-9 0.......................................... DeclanBates(3) 8 36
(Martin Hill) *chsd ldrs: rdn 4f out: sn outpcd by ldrs: wknd fnl f* **66/1**

7 25 **Italian Symphony (IRE)**[9] 4-9-13 0.......................................... HayleyTurner 6
(Brendan Powell) *chsd ldrs tl rdn and wknd 5f out: t.o* **100/1**

8 24 **Curved** 3-8-12 0.......................................... FrankieDettori 9
(Lady Cecil) *trckd ldr: swished tail repeatedly 2f: lost 2nd 4f out: sn rdn and wknd: t.o* **6/1**[3]

0 9 3 ¾ **Sunsational Girl**[16] 2667 5-9-13 0..................................(b[1]) ChrisCatlin 4
(Dai Burchell) *s.i.s and sn rdn along: a in rr: lost tch 4f out: t.o* **100/1**

2m 37.78s (-1.22) **Going Correction** +0.05s/f (Good)
**WFA** 3 from 4yo+ 15lb **9** Ran SP% **113.9**
Speed ratings (Par 100): **106,105,105,104,97 88,71,55,52**
CSF £28.39 TOTE £2.60: £1.20, £3.40, £1.10; EX 41.60 Trifecta £72.20.
**Owner** Al Asayl Bloodstock Ltd **Bred** Old Carhue Stud **Trained** Newmarket, Suffolk

**FOCUS**
The two market leaders had a sustained battle up the straight in this maiden and second and fourth stayed on well from off the pace. The first four were clear and the form makes sense. The winner is rated to form.

## 3175 COUNTRY MARQUEES H'CAP 1m 2f 36y
6:40 (6:40) (Class 5) (0-75,74) 4-Y-0+ **£2,587** (£770; £384; £192) **Stalls** Low

Form RPR

204 1 **Dandy (GER)**[9] 2882 5-9-7 **74**..................................(v) JimmyFortune 1 83
(Andrew Balding) *trckd ldr tl led 2f out: drvn and r.o wl* **9/2**

-043 2 2 **April Ciel**[7] 2947 5-8-10 **63**..................................(p) LiamJones 7 68
(Ronald Harris) *racd keenly: led at modest pce: rdn over 2f out: sn hdd: one pce fnl f but hld 2nd* **3/1**[2]

60-1 3 ½ **Belle Park**[16] 2672 7-8-1 **61** ow2.............................. KieranShoemark(7) 4 65+
(Victor Dartnall) *s.i.s: hld up in rr: clsd 3f out and sn chsng ldng pair: styd on same pce u.p fnl f* **2/1**[1]

424- 4 3 ¼ **Frozen Over**[19] 6562 6-9-7 **74**..................................(t) PatCosgrave 6 72
(Chris Down) *s.i.s: chsd ldng pair after 2f: rdn 3f out: one pce* **7/2**[3]

-555 5 ¾ **Bold Duke**[6] 2981 6-9-4 **74**.......................................... DeclanBates(3) 5 71
(Edward Bevan) *hld up in tch: relegated to last 4f out: rdn and one pce after* **8/1**

2m 12.78s (2.18) **Going Correction** +0.05s/f (Good) **5** Ran SP% **109.8**
Speed ratings (Par 103): **93,91,91,88,87**
CSF £17.90 TOTE £5.50: £3.10, £2.90; EX 16.50 Trifecta £33.70.
**Owner** Robert E Tillett **Bred** Gestut Rottgen **Trained** Kingsclere, Hants

**FOCUS**
It was quite tactical in this handicap and the favourite couldn't make an impact under a hold-up ride. A small personal best from the winner.

## 3176 "MCL LOGISTICS" FILLIES' H'CAP 1m 14y
7:15 (7:19) (Class 5) (0-75,72) 4-Y-0+ **£2,587** (£770; £384; £192) **Stalls** Centre

Form RPR

0405 1 **Tenbridge**[13] 2775 5-8-7 **58**..................................(v) DavidProbert 6 67
(Derek Haydn Jones) *led narrowly: wnt 1 l up over 2f out: rdn over 1f out: hld on u.p fnl f* **9/4**[2]

50-0 2 *nk* **Lady Bayside**[16] 2669 6-9-3 **68**.......................................... FergusSweeney 5 76
(Malcolm Saunders) *racd keenly: hld up in tch: chsd wnr over 1f out: rdn and r.o ins fnl f: jst hld* **15/2**

2005 3 5 **Oratorio's Joy (IRE)**[14] 2750 4-9-7 **72**.......................................... WilliamCarson 4 69
(Jamie Osborne) *s.i.s: cl up after 2f: rdn 3f out: outpcd by ldrs 1f out: kpt on to take 3rd nr fin* **4/1**[3]

00-0 4 *nk* **Silvas Romana (IRE)**[25] 2399 5-9-3 **68**.......................................... LiamJones 1 64
(Mark Brisbourne) *trckd ldrs: rdn 3f out: sn chsng wnr: lost 2nd over 1f out: wknd fnl f and lost 3rd nr fin* **12/1**

540/ 5 19 **Swift Act**[615] 6892 5-8-2 **53** oh3.......................................... PaoloSirigu 3 5
(Nikki Evans) *chsd ldrs: rdn 3f out: wknd 2f out: t.o* **50/1**

3-24 6 10 **Lady Guinevere**[22] 2498 4-9-2 **67**.......................................... PatCosgrave 7
(Stuart Williams) *racd keenly: angled to stands' rail after 2f: w wnr tl rdn 3f out: wknd 2f out: t.o* **11/8**[1]

1m 35.79s (-0.41) **Going Correction** +0.05s/f (Good) **6** Ran SP% **114.3**
Speed ratings (Par 100): **104,103,98,98,79 69**
CSF £19.40 CT £63.36 TOTE £4.40: £2.70, £3.40; EX 18.60 Trifecta £49.60.
**Owner** Mrs E M Haydn Jones **Bred** Mrs M L Parry **Trained** Efail Isaf, Rhondda C Taff

**FOCUS**
They went a steady pace in this handicap. The first two pulled clear and the favourite finished tailed off. Muddling form.

## 3177 HICKS LOGISTICS H'CAP 7f 16y
7:50 (7:52) (Class 5) (0-75,75) 4-Y-0+ **£2,587** (£770; £384; £192) **Stalls** Centre

Form RPR

-653 1 **Bountybeamadam**[16] 2669 4-9-2 **70**..................................(p) PatCosgrave 6 77
(George Baker) *led: rdn 2f out: jnd 1f out: hld on gamely u.p* **4/1**[2]

1134 2 *shd* **Caramack**[52] 1630 4-9-4 **75**.......................................... DeclanBates(3) 7 81
(Richard Lee) *trckd ldrs: rdn 2f out: sn chsng wnr: chal 1f out: r.o: lost out on nod* **7/2**[1]

1030 3 1 ¼ **Kakapuka**[69] 1297 7-8-13 **67**.......................................... JimmyFortune 11 69
(Anabel K Murphy) *chsd ldrs: rdn over 2f out: styd on u.p fnl f* **12/1**

-055 **4** *nk* **Peak Storm**[11] 2833 5-9-3 **71**....(p) FergusSweeney 9 73
(John O'Shea) *hld up towards rr: rdn over 2f out: r.o ins fnl f: gaining nr fin* **5/1**[3]

-050 **5** *½* **Perfect Mission**[131] 451 6-8-3 **64**....(v) KieranShoemark(7) 1 64
(Andrew Balding) *cl up: drvn over 2f out: one pce fnl f: no ex and lost 2 pls last 100yds* **6/1**

100- **6** *hd* **Just Isla**[238] 7354 4-8-5 **59**....(p) MartinLane 4 59
(Peter Makin) *t.k.h early: chsd ldrs: rdn over 2f out: one pce fnl f* **12/1**

0-0 **7** *9* **Dougal Philps**[16] 2684 5-9-0 **75**.... DavidParkes(7) 2 51
(Jeremy Gask) *dwlt: towards rr: rdn and no imp over 2f out: wknd 1f out* **22/1**

-000 **8** *8* **Federal Blue (USA)**[7] 2947 4-8-13 **67**....(v[1]) DavidProbert 5 23
(Milton Bradley) *swtchd rt to r alone on stands' rail over 4f out: a towards rr: bhd fnl 2f* **25/1**

1m 22.83s (-0.37) **Going Correction** +0.05s/f (Good) **8** Ran SP% **96.8**
Speed ratings (Par 103): **104,103,102,102,101 101,91,81**
CSF £12.90 CT £76.59 TOTE £3.00: £1.40, £1.60, £2.00; EX 12.20 Trifecta £100.20.

**Owner** Whitsbury Hopefuls **Bred** Brightwalton Stud **Trained** Manton, Wilts

■ Al's Memory and Secret Beau were withdrawn. Prices at time of withdrawal 8-1 and 7-1. Rule 4 applies to all bets - deduction 20p in the pound.

■ Stewards' Enquiry : Declan Bates four-day ban: used whip above permitted level (Jun 29-Jul 2)

**FOCUS**
The two market leaders were always prominent and had good battle in this handicap. The winner was up slightly on her C&D latest.

## 3178 SIMPLICITY 10 YEAR ANNIVERSARY MAIDEN H'CAP 6f 16y
**8:25** (8:33) (Class 5) (0-70,60) 3-Y-O+ **£2,587** (£770; £384; £192) **Stalls** Centre

Form RPR

-404 **1** **Bajan Story**[16] 2669 5-8-13 **45**.... FergusSweeney 2 54
(Michael Blanshard) *in tch: trckd ldrs fr 1/2-way: rdn over 2f out: sn chal: led 1f out: drvn out* **9/4**[1]

26-6 **2** *¾* **Logans Lad (IRE)**[22] 2488 4-10-0 **60**....(bt[1]) FrankieMcDonald 7 67
(Daniel Mark Loughnane) *a.p: rdn over 2f out: hung rt over 1f out: r.o u.p to go 2nd last strides* **10/1**

3-43 **3** *½* **Trillian Astra (IRE)**[9] 2886 3-9-6 **60**....(p) SteveDrowne 4 63
(Clive Cox) *chsd ldr: led narrowly over 2f out: rdn and hdd 1f out: kpt on: lost 2nd last strides* **3/1**[2]

0-03 **4** *1 ¼* **Trigger Park (IRE)**[16] 2668 3-9-0 **54**.... LiamJones 3 53
(Ronald Harris) *chsd ldrs: rdn 1/2-way: one pce fnl 2f: styd on u.p to go 4th post* **9/2**[3]

404- **5** *shd* **Monty Fay (IRE)**[191] 8146 5-9-0 **46**.... DavidProbert 9 47
(Derek Haydn Jones) *led to s: led tl over 2f out: sn rdn: one pce fnl f: ct for 4th post* **5/1**

0-00 **6** *3* **Beaumont Cooper**[106] 754 5-8-6 **45**.... KieranShoemark(7) 5 36
(Anabel K Murphy) *towards rr: rdn over 2f out: no imp on ldrs* **10/1**

00-5 **7** *5* **Permsiri (IRE)**[70] 1287 3-8-5 **45**.... KieranO'Neill 8 18
(Malcolm Saunders) *sn outpcd: rdn 1/2-way: no ch fnl 2f* **20/1**

5300 **8** *9* **Avondream**[55] 1573 5-9-7 **53**....(t) WilliamCarson 6
(Milton Bradley) *sn outpcd: no ch fnl 2f* **12/1**

1m 11.27s (-0.73) **Going Correction** -0.075s/f (Good)
**WFA** 3 from 4yo+ 8lb **8** Ran SP% **121.3**
Speed ratings (Par 103): **101,100,99,97,97 93,86,74**
CSF £27.92 CT £72.07 TOTE £3.10: £1.40, £2.40, £1.70; EX 22.90 Trifecta £146.30.

**Owner** A D Jones **Bred** Mr And Mrs C McKenna **Trained** Upper Lambourn, Berks

■ Stewards' Enquiry : Frankie McDonald four-day ban: used whip above permitted level (Jun 27-30)

**FOCUS**
A longstanding maiden landed a gamble in this weak handicap. He was on a good mark based on his best form.

## 3179 PAYROLLSIMPLY.CO.UK H'CAP 2m 49y
**8:55** (8:57) (Class 6) (0-65,65) 4-Y-O+ **£1,940** (£577; £288; £144) **Stalls** Low

Form RPR

0235 **1** **Annaluna (IRE)**[30] 1895 5-8-12 **56**....(v) DeclanBates(3) 4 65
(David Evans) *chsd ldrs: led 4f out: rdn over 2f out: jnd 1f out: styd on wl and asserted fnl 50yds* **7/2**[2]

-041 **2** *¾* **Taste The Wine (IRE)**[20] 2252 8-9-6 **61**....(t) MartinLane 3 69
(Bernard Llewellyn) *hld up towards rr: hdwy over 5f out: chsd wnr 3f out: ev ch 1f out tl no ex fnl 50yds* **3/1**[1]

04-3 **3** *6* **Fuzzy Logic (IRE)**[8] 1915 5-8-5 **46** oh1.... DavidProbert 6 47
(Bernard Llewellyn) *in tch: rdn and hdwy over 4f out: chsd ldng pair 2f out: kpt on same pce* **7/2**[2]

5-15 **4** *3 ¾* **Captain Sharpe**[20] 2252 6-8-12 **60**....(t) DavidParkes(7) 7 56
(Bernard Llewellyn) *s.i.s: in rr: rdn and hdwy over 4f out: one pce and no further imp fnl 2f* **6/1**[3]

-430 **5** *nk* **Descaro (USA)**[11] 2836 8-8-13 **54**....(p) FergusSweeney 10 50
(John O'Shea) *prom: wnt 2nd after 2f: rdn over 3f out: one pce fnl 2f* **10/1**

005 **6** *20* **Hazel Brook**[18] 2613 5-9-8 **63**....(p) HayleyTurner 1 35
(Mary Hambro) *racd keenly: hld up towards rr: rdn 4f out: one pce and no imp on ldrs: wknd over 1f out: t.o* **8/1**

0/3- **7** *4 ½* **Eseej (USA)**[116] 3012 9-9-7 **62**.... WilliamCarson 5 29
(Geoffrey Deacon) *t.k.h: led tl hdd 4f out: wknd qckly: t.o* **20/1**

605/ **8** *9* **Akbabend**[75] 5158 8-9-10 **65**....(p) PatCosgrave 2 21
(Chris Gordon) *chsd ldr 2f: sn sltly hmpd and rdr briefly lost iron: styd prom tl wknd over 3f out: t.o* **20/1**

3m 42.83s (3.93) **Going Correction** +0.05s/f (Good) **8** Ran SP% **113.5**
Speed ratings (Par 101): **92,91,88,86,86 76,74,69**
CSF £14.20 CT £37.55 TOTE £4.50: £1.10, £1.40, £1.70; EX 19.10 Trifecta £50.50.

**Owner** Nick Shutts **Bred** Michael Dalton **Trained** Pandy, Monmouths

**FOCUS**
The first two pulled clear in this minor staying handicap, which was run at a modest pace. Both could rate a bit higher on their Flat form.

T/Plt: £17.10 to a £1 stake. Pool: £65,260.87 - 2781.41 winning units. T/Qpdt: £20.50 to a £1 stake. Pool: £3064.10 - 110.50 winning units. RL

# 3031 GOODWOOD (R-H)
Friday, June 13

**OFFICIAL GOING: Good (good to firm in places on round course; overall 7.6, round course 7.8)**
Wind: light, across Weather: light cloud, warm

## 3180 NAUGHTY BOY APPRENTICE STKS (H'CAP) 7f
**6:15** (6:15) (Class 4) (0-85,85) 4-Y-O+ **£5,175** (£1,540; £769; £384) **Stalls** Low

Form RPR

4514 **1** **Bravo Echo**[55] 1576 8-9-1 **77**.... LouisSteward(3) 8 86
(Michael Attwater) *mde all: 5 l clr and rdn 2f out: reduced advantage fnl f but a holding on: nvr seriously chal: pushed out* **11/2**[3]

20-3 **2** *¾* **Related**[21] 2500 4-9-4 **82**.... GeorgeBuckell(5) 6 92+
(David Simcock) *chsd wnr thrght: 5 l down and rdn over 1f out: styd on u.p and steadily clsd fnl f: nvr quite getting to wnr* **4/1**[1]

-654 **3** *6* **Good Authority (IRE)**[16] 2684 7-9-11 **84**.... RobertTart 9 75+
(Karen George) *t.k.h: hld up in last pair: effrt ent fnl 2f: stl bhd and nt clr run over 1f out: swtchd lft 1f out: styd on to go 3rd nr fin: nvr nr wnr* **9/2**[2]

1-33 **4** *nk* **Scottish Glen**[39] 2012 8-8-13 **72**.... ThomasBrown 10 63
(Patrick Chamings) *t.k.h: in midfield tl dropped to last pair after 2f: rdn and effrt wl over 1f out: styd on and battling for 3rd 1f out: kpt on: nvr nr wnr* **16/1**

0211 **5** *½* **Eastern Dragon (IRE)**[16] 2669 4-9-2 **75**.... WilliamTwiston-Davies 1 64
(Michael Scudamore) *chsd ldng trio: rdn and effrt jst over 2f out: wnt 3rd but no ch w ldrs 1f out: styd on same pce: lost 2 pls nr fin* **4/1**[1]

4666 **6** *¾* **Atlantis Crossing (IRE)**[13] 2772 5-8-6 **68**.... NathanAlison(3) 7 55
(Jim Boyle) *t.k.h: hld up towards rr: rdn and hdwy over 2f out: chsd clr ldng pair over 1f out tl 1f out: plugged on same pce and lost 2 pls towards fin* **12/1**

5365 **7** *1 ¼* **Gracious George (IRE)**[16] 2684 4-8-8 **72**....(p) CamHardie(5) 2 56
(Jimmy Fox) *chsd ldrs: rdn and no hdwy over 2f out: lost 3rd over 1f out: wknd ins fnl f* **12/1**

-126 **8** *hd* **Whipper Snapper (IRE)**[8] 2922 4-9-4 **82**.... JennyPowell(5) 4 66
(William Knight) *hld up in midfield: rdn and effrt ent fnl 2f: no hdwy and lost pl over 1f out: bhd fnl f* **6/1**

6456 **9** *1 ¼* **Loud**[28] 2293 4-8-10 **69**.... MichaelJMMurphy 5 49
(Mark Johnston) *hld up in midfield: rdn over 2f out: no prog: lost pl over 1f out: wknd ins fnl f* **16/1**

1m 26.59s (-0.41) **Going Correction** -0.15s/f (Firm) **9** Ran SP% **115.0**
Speed ratings (Par 105): **96,95,88,87,87 86,85,84,83**
CSF £27.65 CT £107.16 TOTE £6.90: £2.50, £1.70, £2.10; EX 24.90 Trifecta £157.40.

**Owner** Canisbay Bloodstock **Bred** Juddmonte Farms Ltd **Trained** Epsom, Surrey

■ Stewards' Enquiry : Cam Hardie one-day ban: careless riding (Jun 27)

**FOCUS**
This was nicked from the front, the winner allowed a soft lead. The first pair finished clear.

## 3181 THREE FRIDAY NIGHTS MAIDEN AUCTION STKS (BOBIS RACE) 6f
**6:50** (6:51) (Class 4) 2-Y-O **£3,234** (£962; £481; £240) **Stalls** High

Form RPR

3 **1** **Step To The Shears**[21] 2499 2-9-3 0.... PatDobbs 1 78+
(Richard Hannon) *chsd ldng pair and travelled strly: clsd and jnd ldrs 2f out: rdn and led jst ins fnl f: r.o wl: readily* **2/1**[1]

5 **2** *1 ¼* **L'Etacq**[29] 2276 2-9-4 0.... RichardHughes 8 75
(Richard Hannon) *trckd ldrs on stands' rail: switching rt off rail fr 2f out: effrt and rdn jst over 1f out: hdwy to chse wnr fnl 100yds: r.o but no imp* **11/4**[2]

0 **3** *¾* **Twin Turbo (IRE)**[18] 2601 2-9-3 0.... FrannyNorton 6 72
(Mark Johnston) *led and crossed to r against stands' rail: rdn over 1f out: hdd jst ins fnl f: styd on same pce and lost 2nd fnl 100yds* **8/1**[3]

55 **4** *2* **Gamesters Lad**[11] 2829 2-8-10 0.... RichardKingscote 4 59
(Tom Dascombe) *pressed ldr: rdn wl over 1f out: unable qck 1f out: outpcd and btn fnl 150yds* **20/1**

**5** *¾* **Red Rebel** 2-8-12 0.... LukeMorris 3 59
(Clive Cox) *m green: in tch in last trio: rdn 3f out: hdwy over 2f out: outpcd u.p over 1f out: rallied and kpt on again ins fnl f* **16/1**

2 **6** *¾* **The Dapper Tapper (IRE)**[10] 2859 2-8-13 0.... ShaneKelly 7 57
(Eve Johnson Houghton) *hld up in tch in midfield: effrt and carried rt over 1f out: sn rdn and no hdwy: wknd ins fnl f* **11/4**[2]

**7** *2* **Dream Approval (IRE)** 2-8-6 0.... ThomasBrown(3) 5 47
(Daniel Kubler) *s.i.s: rn green: in tch in rr: hmpd over 3f out: rdn and outpcd over 1f out: styd on same pce after* **50/1**

0 **8** *1 ½* **Magic Mac**[13] 2771 2-8-6 0.... NickyMackay 2 40
(Hughie Morrison) *in tch in last pair: rdn 2f out: no imp over 1f out: bhd and one pce fnl f* **66/1**

1m 13.48s (1.28) **Going Correction** +0.175s/f (Good) **8** Ran SP% **111.9**
Speed ratings (Par 95): **98,96,95,92,91 90,88,86**
CSF £7.28 TOTE £2.70: £1.10, £1.50, £2.30; EX 7.60 Trifecta £71.20.

**Owner** Pall Mall Partners **Bred** Shinko Foods International Ltd **Trained** East Everleigh, Wilts

**FOCUS**
A one-two for Richard Hannon, with improvement from the placed horses.

## 3182 MAZDA JINBA ITTAI STKS (H'CAP) (BOBIS RACE) 1m 1f 192y
**7:25** (7:26) (Class 3) (0-90,87) 3-Y-O **£7,762** (£2,310; £1,154; £577) **Stalls** Low

Form RPR

410- **1** **Mount Logan (IRE)**[244] 7195 3-9-5 **85**.... AdamKirby 6 97+
(Luca Cumani) *hld up wl in tch in last pair: rdn and effrt 2f out: hdwy to ld jst over 1f out: sn clr and in command: r.o wl: comf* **5/2**[1]

1-25 **2** *2 ¾* **Warrior Of Light (IRE)**[22] 2496 3-9-7 **87**.... TedDurcan 2 93+
(David Lanigan) *dwlt: hld up wl in tch in last pair: clsd on ldrs but gap nvr opened over 2f out: swtchd lft and effrt bhd wnr on outer over 1f out: hdwy u.p 1f out: chsd wnr ins fnl f: r.o but no imp* **3/1**[2]

0-52 **3** *2 ½* **Bureau (IRE)**[24] 2431 3-8-12 **78**.... FrannyNorton 3 79
(Mark Johnston) *led: rdn and qcknd ent fnl 2f: hdd over 1f out and immediately outpcd: lost 3rd and wknd ins fnl f* **8/1**

01-6 **4** *3* **Strait Run (IRE)**[7] 2968 3-9-0 **80**.... RichardHughes 1 75
(Richard Hannon) *chsd ldng trio: effrt on inner ent fnl 2f: rdn and btn jst over 1f out: wknd fnl f* **7/1**

02-1 **5** *¾* **Rasameel (USA)**[32] 2211 3-9-5 **85**.... DaneO'Neill 5 79
(B W Hills) *t.k.h: chsd ldng pair: rdn and effrt 2f out: 5th and btn jst over 1f out: wknd fnl f* **8/1**

15- **6** *6* **Emirates Galloper (IRE)**[315] 4959 3-9-3 **83**.................... KierenFallon 4 65
(Saeed bin Suroor) *dwlt: sn rcvrd to chse ldr: rdn and ev ch ent fnl 2f: btn and lost pl over 1f out: wknd fnl f* **7/2**[3]

2m 8.35s (0.25) **Going Correction** -0.15s/f (Firm) **6** Ran SP% **110.5**
Speed ratings (Par 103): **93,90,88,86,85 81**
CSF £9.88 TOTE £3.60: £1.90, £2.20; EX 8.80 Trifecta £67.50.
**Owner** Sheikh Mohammed Obaid Al Maktoum **Bred** Ladyswood Stud & Canning Downs Stud Aus **Trained** Newmarket, Suffolk

**FOCUS**
A good-quality 3yo handicap, rated around the third. The winner built on his maiden win.

## 3183 CRIMBOURNE STUD STKS (H'CAP) (BOBIS RACE) 1m 4f
**8:00** (8:00) (Class 4) (0-85,82) 3-Y-O **£6,469** (£1,925; £962; £481) **Stalls** High

Form RPR

1-62 **1** **Oasis Fantasy (IRE)**[14] 2719 3-8-12 **76**.......................... OisinMurphy(3) 7 85+
(Ed Dunlop) *hld up in tch towards rr: swtchd rt and nt clr run over 2f out: swtchd lft and hdwy over 1f out: str run to ld ins fnl f: r.o strly and gng away at fin* **7/2**[2]

042 **2** *2* **Rocket Ship**[15] 2696 3-9-5 **80**.......................... JamesDoyle 5 86
(Sir Michael Stoute) *t.k.h: led for 1f: chsd ldrs: lost pl briefly 1/2-way: shkn up and hdwy to join ldr 5f out: rdn to ld 3f out: kpt on u.p tl hdd and one pce ins fnl f* **8/1**[3]

4-21 **3** *1* **Sebastian Beach (IRE)**[29] 2273 3-9-5 **80**.................... RichardHughes 4 85
(Richard Hannon) *t.k.h: hdwy to chse ldr after 2f: rdn and ev ch over 1f out: unable qck and styd on same pce ins fnl f* **5/2**[1]

2603 **4** *1* **Arantes**[13] 2761 3-9-4 **82**.......................... WilliamTwiston-Davies(3) 2 85
(Mick Channon) *hld up in tch in last trio: hdwy and nt clr run 2f out: swtchd rt and drvn to press ldrs 1f out: no ex and styd on same pce ins fnl f* **8/1**[3]

2-23 **5** *½* **Artful Rogue (IRE)**[24] 2418 3-8-13 **74**.................... RichardKingscote 6 76
(Amanda Perrett) *in tch: hdwy to chse ldrs 1/2-way: edgd rt u.p and unable qck over 1f out: styd on same pce ins fnl f* **14/1**

1044 **6** *2¾* **Maxie T**[22] 2494 3-9-2 **77**.......................... FrannyNorton 3 75
(Mark Johnston) *prom early: stdd bk and hld up in tch in midfield: rdn 4f out: drvn and chsd ldrs 3f out: no ex over 1f out: wknd ins fnl f* **10/1**

-401 **7** *2¾* **Taws**[9] 2893 3-7-9 **63** 6ex.......................... CamHardie(7) 9 56
(Rod Millman) *hld up in tch in rr: rdn 3f out: no prog and wl hld over 1f out: no ch but styd on ins fnl f* **12/1**

4-21 **8** *3¾* **Placidia (IRE)**[17] 2650 3-9-7 **82**.......................... TedDurcan 1 75
(David Lanigan) *broke wl: stdd and hld up in tch in midfield: hdwy on outer and travelling wl over 2f out: pressing ldrs and effrt over 1f out: flashed tail and hung rt over 1f out: sn btn: bhd and eased ins fnl f* **8/1**[3]

2-43 **9** *1* **Black Label**[11] 2850 3-8-13 **74**.......................... LukeMorris 8 60
(Harry Dunlop) *nt best away and bustled along leaving stalls: hdwy to ld after 1f: rdn and hdd 3f out: wknd u.p over 1f out* **16/1**

-655 **10** *46* **Poker Gold (FR)**[22] 2494 3-8-10 **71**....................(t) NickyMackay 10
(Heather Main) *t.k.h: in tch: hdwy to chse ldrs 7f out: rdn and wknd over 2f out: t.o and eased over 1f out* **16/1**

2m 35.93s (-2.47) **Going Correction** -0.15s/f (Firm) **10** Ran SP% **119.3**
Speed ratings (Par 101): **102,100,100,99,99 97,95,92,92,61**
CSF £32.67 CT £83.12 TOTE £5.00: £2.20, £2.10, £1.50; EX 23.10 Trifecta £93.80.
**Owner** Windflower Overseas & J L Dunlop OBE **Bred** Windflower Overseas **Trained** Newmarket, Suffolk

**FOCUS**
A fair 3yo handicap which looked sound run. The form makes a fair bit of sense.

## 3184 FRANKIE'S 27TH ANNIVERSARY MAIDEN STKS 1m
**8:35** (8:36) (Class 5) 3-Y-O **£3,234** (£962; £481; £240) **Stalls** Low

Form RPR

-020 **1** **Dursey Island (USA)**[13] 2773 3-9-5 81.......................... RichardHughes 5 79+
(Richard Hannon) *trckd ldng pair: clsd 2f out: jnd ldr ent fnl f: rdr delayed effrt tl pushed along and qcknd to ld ins fnl f: sn in command: pushed out* **11/4**[2]

**2** *¾* **Dreaming Beauty** 3-9-0 0.......................... JamesDoyle 6 73
(Jeremy Noseda) *s.i.s: in tch in rr: swtchd lft and effrt wl over 1f out: hdwy u.p to chse ldrs ins fnl f: r.o to snatch 2nd last stride* **4/1**[3]

3-42 **3** *shd* **Hanno (USA)**[11] 2842 3-9-5 79.......................... AdamKirby 4 77
(Ed Dunlop) *chsd ldr: rdn and effrt over 2f out: led over 1f out: drvn and hdd ins fnl f: r.o same pce: lost 2nd last stride* **1/1**[1]

0 **4** *2¾* **Artistic Muse (IRE)**[25] 2404 3-9-0 0.......................... DaneO'Neill 2 66
(B W Hills) *t.k.h: hld up wl in tch: rdn 2f out: styd on same pce ins fnl f: eased towards fin* **14/1**

00 **5** *3¼* **Triple Star**[15] 2690 3-9-0 0.......................... KierenFallon 1 58
(Hughie Morrison) *led tl rdn and hdd over 1f out: no ex u.p: wknd ins fnl f* **16/1**

1m 41.33s (1.43) **Going Correction** -0.15s/f (Firm) **5** Ran SP% **109.2**
Speed ratings (Par 99): **86,85,85,82,79**
CSF £13.48 TOTE £3.20: £2.30, £1.80; EX 10.60 Trifecta £18.00.
**Owner** Mrs J Williamson & T Hyde **Bred** Swifty Farms Inc & Darley **Trained** East Everleigh, Wilts

**FOCUS**
Not a bad little maiden and straightforward form, the winner rated close to his best.

## 3185 GOLF AT GOODWOOD STKS (H'CAP) (BOBIS RACE) 6f
**9:05** (9:06) (Class 4) (0-85,85) 3-Y-O **£5,175** (£1,540; £769; £384) **Stalls** High

Form RPR

01-2 **1** **Souville**[24] 2429 3-9-1 **79**.......................... GeorgeBaker 3 87+
(Chris Wall) *t.k.h: led for 1f: hld up wl in tch: clsd to join ldrs 2f out: rdn to ld ent fnl f: r.o wl: comf* **7/4**[1]

-060 **2** *1¼* **Flying Bear (IRE)**[28] 2317 3-8-10 **74**.......................... SeanLevey 2 76
(Jeremy Gask) *stdd s: hld up in tch in rr: rdn and effrt over 1f out: chsd wnr ins fnl f: r.o but no imp* **5/1**

-560 **3** *nk* **Meritocracy (IRE)**[27] 2344 3-9-7 **85**..........................(p) LukeMorris 1 86
(Paul Cole) *in tch in midfield: drvn over 2f out: hdwy and edgd lft u.p 1f out: battling for 2nd and r.o same pce ins fnl f* **8/1**

0-13 **4** *2¾* **Strategic Force (IRE)**[41] 1952 3-9-5 **83**.......................... AdamKirby 6 75
(Clive Cox) *chsd ldr tl led after 1f: hdd over 3f out: chsd ldr after tl rdn to ld again 2f out: drvn and hdd ent fnl f: lost 2nd and wknd fnl 150yds* **4/1**[2]

4541 **5** *8* **Royal Warrior**[14] 2717 3-8-11 **78**.......................... OisinMurphy(3) 4 45
(Alan McCabe) *restless in stalls: dwlt: in rr tl hdwy on outer to ld over 3f out: hdd and rdn 2f out: btn whn short of room 1f out: sn wknd and eased towards fin* **8/1**

14-5 **6** *3¼* **Peak Royale**[25] 2383 3-8-12 **76**..........................(b[1]) RichardHughes 5 32
(Richard Hannon) *hld up in tch: rdn over 2f out: btn over 1f out: bhd and eased ins fnl f* **9/2**[3]

1m 12.93s (0.73) **Going Correction** +0.175s/f (Good) **6** Ran SP% **113.4**
Speed ratings (Par 101): **102,100,99,96,85 81**
CSF £11.08 TOTE £2.40: £1.60, £2.20; EX 13.20 Trifecta £56.20.
**Owner** Hughes & Scott **Bred** Stowell Park Stud **Trained** Newmarket, Suffolk

**FOCUS**
A rather muddling sprint handicap and some doubts over the form, but the winner is progressing.
T/Plt: £44.60 to a £1 stake. Pool: £59,534.56 - 2781.41 winning units. T/Qpdt: £21.40 to a £1 stake. Pool: £3592.49 - 123.70 winning units. SP

# 3000 MUSSELBURGH (R-H)
### Friday, June 13

**OFFICIAL GOING: Good to soft (good in places; 7.5)**
Wind: Virtually Nil Weather: Cloudy, steady drizzle between 2nd and 4th

## 3186 EBF STALLIONS PURVIS GROUP MAIDEN STKS (BOBIS RACE) 7f 30y
**1:50** (1:50) (Class 4) 2-Y-O **£4,204** (£1,251; £625; £312) **Stalls** Low

Form RPR

**1** **Jumeirah Glory (IRE)** 2-9-5 0.......................... TonyHamilton 5 75+
(Richard Fahey) *s.i.s: sn trckd ldr on inner: n.m.r over 2f out: angled lft into clr 2f out: led over 1f out: a holding on firmly pushed out* **3/1**[2]

**2** *½* **Three Merry Lads** 2-9-5 0.......................... JoeFanning 1 74
(Mark Johnston) *led: rdn whn hdd over 1f out: edgd lft ins fnl f: kpt on but a hld* **10/11**[1]

**3** *5* **Forgiving Glance** 2-8-9 0.......................... ShirleyTeasdale(5) 3 57
(Philip Kirby) *trckd ldr: rdn to chal over 2f out: wknd fnl f* **33/1**

4 **4** *1* **Star Ascending (IRE)**[26] 2359 2-9-5 0.......................... DaleSwift 6 59
(Brian Ellison) *racd keenly in tch: rdn over 2f out: sn btn* **5/1**[3]

**5** *3½* **Battleranger (IRE)** 2-9-5 0.......................... TomEaves 4 51
(Keith Dalgleish) *racd keenly hld up: rdn over 2f out: sn wknd* **9/1**

1m 31.41s (2.41) **Going Correction** +0.075s/f (Good) **5** Ran SP% **107.0**
Speed ratings (Par 95): **89,88,82,81,77**
CSF £5.79 TOTE £2.80: £1.10, £1.10; EX 5.70 Trifecta £50.50.
**Owner** Sheikh Rashid Dalmook Al Maktoum **Bred** Robert Norton **Trained** Musley Bank, N Yorks

**FOCUS**
Home and back straight at widest position and all distances as advertised. Not much depth to this juvenile event but the first two pulled clear and both have a future.

## 3187 HBJ CLAIM SOLUTIONS SOLICITORS H'CAP (BOBIS RACE) 1m
**2:20** (2:21) (Class 4) (0-80,76) 3-Y-O **£6,469** (£1,925; £962; £481) **Stalls** Low

Form RPR

4-53 **1** **Majorities**[21] 2510 3-8-13 **71**.......................... ConnorBeasley(3) 5 81+
(Brian Meehan) *hld up: rdn and hdwy over 2f out: chal over 1f out: edgd rt: kpt on to ld 50yds out* **6/4**[1]

1111 **2** *½* **Desert Colours**[54] 1601 3-9-2 **76**..........................(b) KevinStott(5) 1 85
(Kevin Ryan) *led narrowly: rdn over 2f out: kpt on: hdd 50yds out* **8/1**

5-32 **3** *3* **Rainbow Rock (IRE)**[8] 2936 3-9-1 **70**..........................(v[1]) JoeFanning 3 72
(Mark Johnston) *dwlt: sn in tch racing keenly: rdn to chal over 2f out: one pce and hld in 3rd fr over 1f out* **2/1**[2]

26-4 **4** *3* **Porthos Du Vallon**[11] 2827 3-8-11 **66**.......................... TomEaves 4 61
(Keith Dalgleish) *pressed ldr: rdn over 2f out: wknd over 1f out* **16/1**

20-5 **5** *3¾* **In Focus (IRE)**[21] 2524 3-8-2 **62**.......................... JoeyHaynes(5) 2 48
(Alan Swinbank) *racd keenly in tch: rdn over 2f out: wknd over 1f out* **25/1**

0-01 **6** *9* **Spiceupyourlife (IRE)**[20] 2545 3-9-7 **76**.......................... TonyHamilton 6 42
(Richard Fahey) *in tch on outside: lost pl 1/2-way: wknd over 2f out* **11/2**[3]

1m 40.8s (-0.40) **Going Correction** +0.075s/f (Good) **6** Ran SP% **109.6**
Speed ratings (Par 101): **105,104,101,98,94 85**
CSF £13.33 TOTE £2.10: £1.80, £2.20; EX 14.50 Trifecta £35.40.
**Owner** T G & Mrs M E Holdcroft **Bred** Bearstone Stud **Trained** Manton, Wilts

**FOCUS**
This looked a fair race for the grade, despite the limited field size. The pace was sound and the winner rates similar to his Haydock latest.

## 3188 CALA HOMES AUCTION STKS (CONDITIONS RACE) (BOBIS RACE) 5f
**2:50** (2:50) (Class 3) 2-Y-O **£8,086** (£2,406; £1,202; £601) **Stalls** High

Form RPR

16 **1** **Diamond Creek (IRE)**[6] 3001 2-7-8 0.......................... JackGarritty(7) 2 80+
(Richard Fahey) *led: rdn whn hdd over 1f out: rallied to ld again ins fnl f: kpt on* **11/10**[1]

6 **2** *4* **Grey Zeb (IRE)**[7] 2949 2-8-8 0.......................... TomEaves 1 73
(Keith Dalgleish) *trckd ldng pair: smooth hdwy to ld over 1f out: sn rdn: hdd ins fnl f: wknd qckly* **17/2**

010 **3** *1¼* **Lazy Days In Loule (IRE)**[28] 2313 2-7-10 0 ow1.......... JoeyHaynes(5) 3 61
(Noel Wilson) *w ldr: rdn 2f out: sn outpcd by ldng pair: no threat after* **9/2**[3]

52 **4** *1½* **Alderaan (IRE)**[14] 2725 2-8-0 0.......................... DuranFentiman 4 55
(Tony Coyle) *hld up: pushed along 3f out: nvr threatened* **2/1**[2]

1m 0.78s (0.38) **Going Correction** +0.075s/f (Good) **4** Ran SP% **109.7**
Speed ratings (Par 97): **99,92,90,88**
CSF £9.96 TOTE £2.00; EX 12.00 Trifecta £21.40.
**Owner** Middleham Park Racing CVII & Partner **Bred** Oliver Donlon **Trained** Musley Bank, N Yorks

**FOCUS**
A disappointing turnout for the money. The form could feasibly be rated 5lb higher.

## 3189 INVESTEC WEALTH AND INVESTMENT H'CAP 7f 30y
**3:25** (3:26) (Class 2) (0-100,98) 4-Y-O+ **£12,938** (£3,850; £1,924; £962) **Stalls** Low

Form RPR

-023 **1** **Majestic Moon (IRE)**[14] 2747 4-8-12 **89**.......................... TonyHamilton 4 103
(Richard Fahey) *led after 1f: mde rest: rdn fnl f: kpt on wl* **11/4**[1]

5100 **2** *2¾* **Heavy Metal**[13] 2762 4-8-8 **85**.......................... JoeFanning 2 92
(Mark Johnston) *trckd ldng pair on inner: rdn over 2f out: kpt on but no ch w wnr fnl f* **25/1**

0634 **3** *2* **Silver Rime (FR)**[22] 2478 9-8-3 **83**.......................... ConnorBeasley(3) 5 85
(Linda Perratt) *dwlt: hld up: hdwy over 2f out: rdn in dispute of 2nd over 1f out: no ex and hld in 3rd fnl 110yds* **16/1**

5364 **4** *2¾* **Newstead Abbey**[13] 2758 4-9-5 **96**.......................... TomEaves 6 91
(David Barron) *trckd ldng pair: rdn over 2f out: wknd fnl f* **11/2**[3]

0310 **5** *hd* **Just Paul (IRE)**[20] 2548 4-7-13 **81**.......................... JoeyHaynes(5) 8 75
(Philip Kirby) *hld up: rdn over 2f out: nvr threatened* **11/4**[1]

-425 **6** *½* **Laffan (IRE)**[13] 2758 5-8-9 **93**.......................... RachelRichardson(7) 7 86
(Tim Easterby) *in tch on outside: rdn over 2f out: sn wknd* **11/2**[3]

0-14 **7** *5* **Best Of Order (IRE)**[13] 2784 7-9-7 **98**..........................(b) DavidNolan 1 78
(David O'Meara) *led for 1f: prom: rdn over 2f out: wknd appr fnl f* **9/2**[2]

1m 27.85s (-1.15) **Going Correction** +0.075s/f (Good) **7** Ran SP% **112.0**
Speed ratings (Par 109): **109,105,103,100,100 99,93**
CSF £66.32 CT £915.70 TOTE £3.80: £2.00, £6.60; EX 44.30 Trifecta £250.30.
**Owner** James Gaffney **Bred** Tony Cosgrave **Trained** Musley Bank, N Yorks

**FOCUS**
The winner very much had the run of the race and the form is rated a bit cautiously.

## 3190 INVESTEC WEALTH AND INVESTMENT EDINBURGH H'CAP — 1m 1f
4:00 (4:00) (Class 4) (0-80,79) 4-Y-O+ £6,469 (£1,925; £962; £481) Stalls Low

Form RPR
512 1 **Baraweez (IRE)**[31] 2234 4-9-7 79 DaleSwift 8 92+
(Brian Ellison) trckd ldng pair on inner: swtchd lft 2f out: led ins fnl f: kpt on wl: comf 2/1[1]
-533 2 2 1/4 **Never Forever**[8] 2912 5-8-12 70 TomEaves 2 76
(Jim Goldie) led narrowly: rdn whn hdd over 1f out: kpt on: regained 2nd post 9/1
10-1 3 nse **Border Bandit (USA)**[21] 2519 6-8-11 69 (p) JoeFanning 5 75
(Tracy Waggott) w ldr: rdn to ld over 1f out: hdd ins fnl f: one pce: lost 2nd post 7/2[2]
0336 4 1 1/4 **Karaka Jack**[13] 2790 7-9-4 76 AdrianNicholls 4 79
(David Nicholls) midfield: rdn over 2f out: kpt on same pce 5/1[3]
5033 5 3/4 **Dhaular Dhar (IRE)**[8] 2911 12-7-9 60 JackGarritty(7) 1 62
(Jim Goldie) s.i.s: hld up on inner: n.m.r over 2f out tl wl over 1f out: one pce and nvr threatened 22/1
-025 6 hd **Shadowtime**[18] 2603 9-9-3 75 DavidNolan 6 76
(Tracy Waggott) hld up: rdn over 2f out: nvr threatened 20/1
5102 7 1 1/2 **Cravat**[10] 2862 5-8-13 74 ConnorBeasley(3) 7 72
(Ed de Giles) midfield: rdn over 2f out: wknd fnl f 10/1
2231 8 2 1/2 **Outlaw Torn (IRE)**[21] 2518 5-8-4 67 (e) JoeyHaynes(5) 3 60
(Richard Guest) trckd ldng pair: rdn over 2f out: wknd over 1f out 7/1

1m 53.08s (-0.82) **Going Correction** +0.075s/f (Good) 8 Ran SP% **112.9**
Speed ratings (Par 105): **106,104,103,102,102 102,100,98**
CSF £20.54 CT £59.21 TOTE £3.10: £1.10, £4.00, £1.10; EX 30.20 Trifecta £169.60.
**Owner** A Barnes **Bred** Sunderland Holdings Inc **Trained** Norton, N Yorks

**FOCUS**
The pace held up again and the winner resumed his progress.

## 3191 HBJ EMPLOYMENT SOLUTIONS H'CAP (QUALIFIER FOR £15,000 BETFAIR SCOTTISH SPRINT SERIES FINAL) — 5f
4:30 (4:31) (Class 5) (0-75,75) 3-Y-O+ £5,175 (£1,540; £769; £384) Stalls High

Form RPR
2264 1 **Bunce (IRE)**[8] 2914 6-9-4 65 JoeFanning 10 74
(Linda Perratt) midfield: pushed along 1/2-way: hdwy over 1f out: r.o to ld towards fin 8/1[3]
106- 2 nk **Algar Lad**[242] 7240 4-10-0 75 DavidNolan 2 83
(David O'Meara) dwlt and swtchd lft s: hld up in tch: hdwy whn briefly n.m.r over 1f out: led 1f out: kpt on: edgd rt fnl 110yds: hdd towards fin 11/2[2]
6036 3 2 1/4 **Haajes**[26] 2364 10-9-7 73 (v) ShirleyTeasdale(5) 13 73
(Paul Midgley) chsd ldrs: rdn 1/2-way: kpt on 20/1
2111 4 3/4 **Classy Anne**[2] 3104 4-8-4 58 6ex JackGarritty(7) 11 55
(Jim Goldie) w ldr: rdn 2f out: no ex ins fnl f 11/10[1]
44-6 5 1 3/4 **Gran Canaria Queen**[28] 2297 5-9-7 68 TonyHamilton 14 59
(Tim Easterby) chsd ldrs: n.m.r and lost pl over 1f out: one pce fnl f 12/1
-053 6 3/4 **Spirit Of Alsace (IRE)**[22] 2474 3-8-3 57 RoystonFfrench 1 42
(Jim Goldie) s.i.s: hld up: rdn 1/2-way: kpt on fnl f: nvr threatened 33/1
/340 7 1 1/4 **New Lease Of Life**[16] 2675 5-8-9 56 oh1 TomEaves 9 40
(Jim Goldie) sn outpcd in rr: bhd tl kpt on fnl f 33/1
6231 8 3/4 **Roy's Legacy**[21] 2514 5-9-2 63 DuranFentiman 7 44
(Shaun Harris) led narrowly: rdn 1/2-way: hdd 1f out: wknd 12/1
0505 9 1 1/2 **Chloe's Dream (IRE)**[16] 2675 4-8-5 59 JoeDoyle(7) 12 35
(Linda Perratt) racd keenly: w ldr: wknd over 1f out 66/1
0215 10 2 **Captain Royale (IRE)**[18] 2606 9-9-10 71 (p) DaleSwift 8 39
(Tracy Waggott) chsd ldrs: rdn 1/2-way: wknd fnl f 11/2[2]
-600 11 3/4 **The Nifty Fox**[6] 3006 10-9-4 65 (v) AndrewElliott 5 31
(Tim Easterby) hld up: nvr threatened 28/1
002- 12 8 **Gottcher**[242] 7240 6-9-8 74 GarryWhillans(5) 6 11
(Ian Semple) chsd ldrs on outside: wknd over 1f out 33/1

1m 0.08s (-0.32) **Going Correction** +0.075s/f (Good)
**WFA** 3 from 4yo+ 7lb 12 Ran SP% **123.4**
Speed ratings (Par 103): **105,104,100,99,96 95,93,92,90,86 85,72**
CSF £50.14 CT £885.17 TOTE £13.60: £1.60, £2.30, £5.60; EX 40.00 Trifecta £557.10.
**Owner** Peter Tsim & Helen Perratt **Bred** John Doyle **Trained** East Kilbride, S Lanarks

**FOCUS**
This was a deal more competitive than the market suggested. The favourite was below her recent level and it's a long time since the winner was rated any higher.

## 3192 JAMES DONALDSON AND SONS LTD H'CAP (LADY AMATEURS) (QUALIFIER FOR £15000 BETFAIR SCOTTISH STAYERS) — 1m 4f 100y
5:05 (5:05) (Class 4) (0-85,82) 4-Y-O+ £4,991 (£1,548; £773; £387) Stalls Centre

Form RPR
6-22 1 **Northside Prince (IRE)**[6] 3004 8-9-1 67 MissMeganNicholls(5) 2 76
(Alan Swinbank) sn trckd ldr: led gng wl over 1f out: rdn clr fnl f 6/4[1]
60-2 2 3 1/2 **Merchant Of Dubai**[21] 2515 9-9-13 74 MrsCBartley 4 77
(Jim Goldie) sn led: rdn whn hdd over 1f out: kpt on but no ch w wnr 4/1[3]
13-6 3 1/2 **Perennial**[26] 1935 5-10-7 82 MissCWalton 1 84
(Philip Kirby) dwlt: hld up in tch: rdn 2f out: kpt on fnl f 5/2[2]
4-06 4 1 3/4 **El Bravo**[13] 2762 8-9-7 68 MissSBrotherton 3 68
(Shaun Harris) trckd ldr: rdn to chal over 2f out: wknd fnl f 5/1
06-0 5 2 **Tapis Libre**[48] 1710 6-9-9 73 (p) MissJoannaMason(3) 5 69
(Michael Easterby) hld up in tch: rdn over 2f out: sn wknd 16/1

2m 46.27s (4.27) **Going Correction** +0.075s/f (Good) 5 Ran SP% **111.1**
Speed ratings (Par 105): **88,85,85,84,82**
CSF £7.94 TOTE £1.90: £1.80, £2.30; EX 7.90 Trifecta £10.90.
**Owner** Mrs J M Penney **Bred** F Dunne **Trained** Melsonby, N Yorks
■ The first Flat winner for Megan Nicholls.

**FOCUS**
This was less competitive than in previous years and there are some doubts over the form. It has been rated through the runner-up.
T/Plt: £494.40 to a £1 stake. Pool: £43,799.45 - 64.66 winning units. T/Qpdt: £220.20 to a £1 stake. Pool: £2857.50 - 9.60 winning units. AS

# 2702 SANDOWN (R-H)
Friday, June 13

**OFFICIAL GOING: Good (good to firm in places on round course; rnd 8.1, str 7.6)**
Wind: Almost nil Weather: Fine but cloudy, very warm

## 3193 OPENWORK FOUNDATION CARES 4 KIDS EBF SPRINT MAIDEN STKS — 5f 6y
2:10 (2:11) (Class 5) 2-Y-O £3,881 (£1,155; £577; £288) Stalls Low

Form RPR
1 **Ivawood (IRE)** 2-9-5 0 RichardHughes 4 91+
(Richard Hannon) trckd ldng pair and racd against rail: squeezed through and pushed along to ld jst ins fnl f: styd on wl: taking debut 8/11[1]
06 2 2 1/4 **Magical Memory (IRE)**[37] 2071 2-9-5 0 GeorgeBaker 2 80+
(Charles Hills) s.i.s: hld up in 6th: gd prog on outer to ld jst over 1f out: edgd rt and hdd jst ins fnl f: styd on but no match for wnr 6/1[3]
02 3 2 **Kinematic**[14] 2744 2-8-11 0 OisinMurphy(3) 3 68
(Andrew Balding) led but racd jst off ins rail: shkn up and hdd jst over 1f out: impeded sn after: one pce 11/4[2]
4 3 1/2 **Squats (IRE)** 2-9-5 0 KierenFallon 1 60
(William Haggas) pushed along in 5th: no prog 2f out and outpcd: modest late hdwy 16/1
43 5 1/2 **British Embassy (IRE)**[22] 2487 2-9-5 0 JohnFahy 5 58
(Eve Johnson Houghton) chsd ldng trio: clsd 2f out: shkn up and wknd over 1f out 33/1
6 2 **Lady In White (IRE)** 2-9-0 0 JamesDoyle 6 46
(Roger Varian) chsd ldr to over 1f out: wknd 25/1
7 7 **Goldslinger (FR)** 2-9-5 0 AdamKirby 7 26
(Dean Ivory) dwlt: a detached in last 66/1

1m 1.02s (-0.58) **Going Correction** -0.075s/f (Good) 7 Ran SP% **113.0**
Speed ratings (Par 93): **101,97,94,88,87 84,73**
CSF £5.62 TOTE £2.00: £1.20, £2.70; EX 6.00 Trifecta £15.60.
**Owner** Carmichael Jennings **Bred** Ms M Davison & Ms D Kitchin **Trained** East Everleigh, Wilts

**FOCUS**
A warm day and they raced on drying ground. The rail on the round course was dolled out up to five yards from its inner position from the 1m1f point to the winning post with the bend at mid-configuration, adding eight yards to race distances. The winner looks sure to rate a good deal higher.

## 3194 ENTERPRISE FINANCE EBF MAIDEN STKS — 7f 16y
2:40 (2:44) (Class 5) 2-Y-O £3,881 (£1,155; £577; £288) Stalls Low

Form RPR
1 **Tupi (IRE)** 2-9-5 0 RichardHughes 3 81+
(Richard Hannon) off the pce in 8th: pushed along 3f out: prog on outer 2f out: r.o wl to ld last 100yds 11/4[1]
2 3/4 **Marshall Jennings (IRE)** 2-9-5 0 SeanLevey 13 79+
(Richard Hannon) chsd clr ldrs in 6th: clsd 2f out: rdn to chal 1f out: styd on but rn green: upsides 100yds out: outpcd after 8/1
3 nse **Red Rubles (IRE)** 2-9-2 0 ThomasBrown(3) 1 79+
(Andrew Balding) off the pce in 9th: clsd over 2f out: nt clr run and swtchd sharply lft wl over 1f out: styd on strly fnl f: clsng fast at fin 25/1
4 1/2 **Diaz (IRE)** 2-9-5 0 FrannyNorton 5 78
(Mark Johnston) green in preliminaries: chsd ldr: rdn to ld over 1f out: hdd and outpcd last 100yds 6/1[3]
46 5 1 1/4 **The Paco Kid**[34] 2146 2-9-5 0 PatDobbs 4 75
(Olly Stevens) trckd ldrs in 5th: gng strly 2f out: brought to chal jst over 1f out: rdn and nt qckn fnl f 4/1[2]
6 1 **Classic Villager** 2-9-5 0 AdamKirby 10 75+
(Philip Hide) off the pce in midfield: pushed along in 7th bef 1/2-way: clsd on ldrs 2f out: styng on wl and ch of winning whn nowhere to go ins fnl f: nt rcvr 33/1
0 7 hd **Groor**[25] 2386 2-9-5 0 KierenFallon 2 74
(James Tate) trckd ldng pair: cl up whn nt clr run over 1f out: stl cl up but nowhere to go ins fnl f: nt rcvr 10/1
0 8 3 1/4 **Foylesideview (IRE)**[7] 2964 2-9-5 0 ShaneKelly 7 66
(Luke Dace) led and stretched field: rdn and hdd over 1f out: hld whn tightened up against rail ins fnl furong: eased 100/1
9 hd **Moonadee (IRE)** 2-9-5 0 DaneO'Neill 8 63+
(B W Hills) dwlt: mostly in last trio and wl off the pce: pushed along and kpt on fnl 2f: nt disgracd 7/1
0 10 1 1/2 **My Mate (IRE)**[28] 2308 2-9-5 0 JamesDoyle 6 59
(Clive Brittain) t.k.h early: chsd ldng trio: wknd over 1f out 14/1
0 11 2 3/4 **Celestine Abbey**[28] 2306 2-9-0 0 AdamBeschizza 9 47
(Julia Feilden) a towards rr: no prog and btn over 2f out 80/1
0 12 15 **Playboy Bay**[28] 2298 2-9-2 0 WilliamTwiston-Davies(3) 14 15
(Mick Channon) a in rr: pushed along bef 1/2-way: no prog: t.o 50/1
13 hd **Synodic (USA)** 2-9-5 0 (t) TomQueally 12 14
(David Lanigan) s.s: a in last pair: t.o 16/1
00 14 5 **Royal Street**[18] 2623 2-9-5 0 (t) GeorgeBaker 11
(Seamus Durack) a in rr: wknd 3f out: t.o 100/1

1m 30.16s (0.66) **Going Correction** -0.075s/f (Good) 14 Ran SP% **118.2**
Speed ratings (Par 93): **93,92,92,91,90 88,88,85,84,83 79,62,62,56**
CSF £23.89 TOTE £3.70: £1.70, £3.20, £6.20; EX 29.40 Trifecta £424.80.
**Owner** Michael Kerr-Dineen & Martin Hughes **Bred** Kabansk Ltd & Rathbarry Stud **Trained** East Everleigh, Wilts
■ Stewards' Enquiry : Sean Levey two-day ban: careless riding (Jun 27-28)

**FOCUS**
They went a good gallop here. A number should progress from the bare form.

## 3195 GIFTOFRACING.CO.UK FILLIES' H'CAP (BOBIS RACE) — 1m 14y
3:15 (3:16) (Class 4) (0-85,81) 3-Y-O £6,469 (£1,925; £962; £481) Stalls Low

Form RPR
-154 1 **Cay Dancer**[27] 2340 3-8-12 79 CamHardie(7) 8 89
(Richard Hannon) trckd ldrs in 5th: prog over 2f out to ld wl over 1f out: sn hdd: styd on wl to ld again last 100yds: rdn out 10/1
6-11 2 nk **Lady Tiana**[22] 2498 3-9-5 79 LukeMorris 2 88
(Lucy Wadham) trckd ldng pair: gng strly 2f out: brought to ld over 1f out and asked to go for home: nt qckn and hdd last 100yds 6/1[2]
1-2 3 3/4 **Token Of Love**[27] 2340 3-9-6 80 RichardHughes 3 88
(William Haggas) hld up in 8th: pushed along and prog over 2f out: chsd ldng pair over 1f out: drvn and styd on but nvr able to chal 5/4[1]

0-43 **4** 3 1/2 **Swiss Kiss**[24] 2442 3-9-1 **75**............................ WilliamBuick 1 75
(John Gosden) *trckd ldrs in 6th: effrt over 2f out: kpt on to take 4th 1f out: nt pce to trble ldrs* **14/1**

1-60 **5** 1 **Laurelita (IRE)**[29] 2277 3-9-7 **81**............................ PatCosgrave 6 78
(George Baker) *dwlt: hld up in last trio: pushed along and prog on outer 2f out: one pce and no further imp fnl f* **33/1**

01-0 **6** 2 **Bright Cecily (IRE)**[44] 1868 3-9-6 **80**............................ AdamKirby 9 73
(Clive Cox) *dwlt: hld up in last trio: shkn up and prog on wd outside 2f out: edgd rt and no hdwy 1f out* **25/1**

6-44 **7** 1 **Darting**[25] 2404 3-8-9 **72**............................ OisinMurphy(3) 7 62
(Andrew Balding) *t.k.h: trckd ldng trio: rdn and lost pl 2f out: no real prog after* **8/1[3]**

21-5 **8** 1 1/4 **Dynaglow (USA)**[21] 2504 3-9-4 **78**............................ RobertHavlin 11 65
(John Gosden) *hld up in last trio: pushed along over 2f out: mod late prog: nvr involved* **12/1**

5-21 **9** 2 **Ghinia (IRE)**[29] 2274 3-9-3 **77**............................ DaneO'Neill 10 60
(Pam Sly) *sn pressed ldr: led over 2f out to wl over 1f out: wknd* **10/1**

2231 **10** 2 1/2 **Rough Courte (IRE)**[24] 2433 3-8-10 **73**............................ CharlesBishop(3) 4 50
(Mick Channon) *led to over 2f out: wknd over 1f out* **14/1**

010- **11** 4 1/2 **Light Weight (IRE)**[265] 6619 3-8-12 **72**............................ JamieSpencer 5 39
(Kevin Ryan) *racd in 7th and off the pce: rdn and no prog over 2f out: sn wknd* **33/1**

1m 41.56s (-1.74) **Going Correction** -0.075s/f (Good) **11 Ran SP% 118.8**
Speed ratings (Par 98): **105,104,103,100,99 97,96,95,93,90 86**
CSF £68.38 CT £129.22 TOTE £14.00: £2.40, £1.80, £1.30; EX 93.10 Trifecta £403.90.
**Owner** R Barnett **Bred** W And R Barnett Ltd **Trained** East Everleigh, Wilts

**FOCUS**
There was a solid gallop on here and the form should work out all right. The race is rated slightly positively.

## 3196 GEORGE LINDON-TRAVERS MEMORIAL H'CAP 1m 2f 7y

**3:50** (3:50) (Class 3) (0-90,88) 4-Y-0+
**£9,337** (£2,796; £1,398; £699; £349; £175) **Stalls** Low

Form RPR

2011 **1** **Chain Of Events**[15] 2702 7-8-13 **80**............................ WilliamBuick 4 88
(Michael Wigham) *trckd ldng pair: led on inner jst over 2f out: hrd pressed after: hld on wl fnl f* **6/1[3]**

1-50 **2** 1/2 **Vital Evidence (USA)**[51] 1651 4-9-7 **88**............................(p) JamesDoyle 9 95
(Sir Michael Stoute) *trckd ldng trio: rdn to chal 2f out: nt qckn fnl f but styd on* **9/1**

210- **3** hd **Lady Pimpernel**[243] 7223 4-9-6 **87**............................ DaneO'Neill 10 94
(Henry Candy) *trckd ldr tl pressed new ldr (and wnr) 2f out: sustained chal after: jst hld and lost 2nd nr fin* **8/1**

-100 **4** hd **Tobacco Road (IRE)**[15] 2707 4-9-0 **88**............................ CamHardie(7) 6 94
(Richard Hannon) *trckd ldrs in 6th: lost pl jst over 3f out: renewed effrt 2f out on outer: kpt on fr over 1f out: nvr quite pce to chal* **16/1**

2630 **5** 1/2 **Echo Brava**[22] 2482 4-8-9 **76**............................ LukeMorris 3 81
(Luke Dace) *hld up towards rr: swtchd outside and prog jst over 3f out: tried to chal fr wl over 1f out: nt qckn fnl f* **20/1**

5042 **6** 2 1/2 **Sheila's Buddy**[18] 2627 5-8-9 **76**............................ JohnFahy 8 77
(J S Moore) *t.k.h: hld up in last pair in r where first 3 home racd promly: prog on inner over 2f out: chsd ldrs over 1f out: no hdwy fnl f* **14/1**

1-20 **7** 1 1/4 **Gone Dutch**[28] 2309 4-9-4 **85**............................ ShaneKelly 2 83
(James Fanshawe) *trckd ldrs in 5th: shkn up over 2f out: tried to cl over 1f out: fdd ins fnl f* **9/2[2]**

3600 **8** 13 **Veeraya**[41] 1948 4-9-2 **83**............................(b) AdamBeschizza 11 56
(Julia Feilden) *a towards rr: rdn and no prog over 2f out: wknd: t.o* **33/1**

3023 **9** 3 1/2 **First Post (IRE)**[13] 2772 7-8-10 **77**............................ JamieSpencer 7 44
(Derek Haydn Jones) *hld up towards rr: rdn and no prog over 2f out: wknd and t.o* **8/1**

04- **10** 2 1/2 **Guising**[217] 7805 5-9-0 **81**............................ KierenFallon 1 55
(David Brown) *led to jst over 2f out: wknd: t.o* **12/1**

-212 **11** 7 **Kastini**[15] 2702 4-8-10 **77**............................(v) RichardHughes 5 38
(Denis Coakley) *t.k.h: hld up in last pair: sme prog over 2f out: btn whn nt clr run briefly wl over 1f out: heavily eased* **11/4[1]**

2m 8.84s (-1.66) **Going Correction** -0.075s/f (Good) **11 Ran SP% 119.3**
Speed ratings (Par 107): **103,102,102,102,101 99,98,88,85,83 78**
CSF £60.03 CT £440.85 TOTE £5.80: £2.10, £2.60, £2.90; EX 45.70 Trifecta £574.90.
**Owner** P J Edwards **Bred** Bishop Wilton Stud **Trained** Newmarket, Suffolk

**FOCUS**
They went a sensible pace and it paid to race handily. A bunch finish and it's hard to rate the form as anything other than ordinary.

## 3197 ONE MONTH FREE TRIAL AT RACINGUK.COM H'CAP (BOBIS RACE) 1m 2f 7y

**4:20** (4:21) (Class 4) (0-80,80) 3-Y-0 **£5,175** (£1,540; £769; £384) **Stalls** Low

Form RPR

-444 **1** **Rydan (IRE)**[5] 3031 3-9-7 **80**............................ TomQueally 8 87
(Robert Mills) *hld up in last trio: stdy prog on outer over 2f out: cajoled along to chal 1f out: edgd rt but drvn to ld ins fnl f: styd on* **10/1**

41 **2** 1/2 **Reesha**[48] 1730 3-9-6 **79**............................ DaneO'Neill 1 85
(Roger Varian) *pushed up to ld after 100yds: rdn 2f out: hdd and nt qckn ins fnl f* **6/1[2]**

0-64 **3** 1 1/2 **Raise Your Gaze**[22] 2481 3-9-4 **77**............................ AdamKirby 7 80
(Clive Cox) *in tch in midfield: rdn and no immediate prog over 2f out: trying to cl whn nt clr run and swtchd lft jst over 1f out: styd on wl to take 3rd nr fin* **7/1[3]**

4122 **4** nk **Cotton Club (IRE)**[21] 2506 3-8-13 **79**............................ PatMillman(7) 9 81
(Rod Millman) *hld up towards rr: rdn and prog over 2f out: cl up and ch 1f out: styd on one pce* **7/1[3]**

-555 **5** 3/4 **Best Kept**[7] 2968 3-9-5 **78**............................ PatDobbs 3 79
(Amanda Perrett) *in tch in midfield: pushed along over 2f out: no prog tl rdn and styd on fnl f: n.d* **5/1[1]**

41-4 **6** 1 1/4 **Master Dancer**[22] 2496 3-9-1 **74**............................ GeorgeBaker 11 73
(Philip Hide) *trckd ldrs: cl up 2f out and gng strly: shkn up and sing to lose pl whn squeezed out jst over 1f out* **5/1[1]**

-010 **7** nk **Gannicus**[28] 2307 3-9-0 **73**............................ KierenFallon 6 71
(Brendan Powell) *mostly in last trio: rdn 3f out: last and no ch over 1f out: hanging but styd on fnl f* **33/1**

221- **8** 1/2 **Billy Blue (IRE)**[176] 8340 3-9-3 **76**............................ WilliamBuick 10 73
(John Gosden) *trckd ldr after 2f: rdn to chal over 2f out: hd high and nt qckn: lost 2nd and wknd over 1f out* **15/2**

66-3 **9** shd **Sea Here**[83] 1069 3-9-0 **73**............................ JamesDoyle 5 70
(Ralph Beckett) *led 100yds: chsd ldr to 8f out: wl in tch tl rdn over 2f out: sn lost pl and btn* **6/1[2]**

2221 **10** 1 1/4 **Bobby Benton (IRE)**[80] 1090 3-9-2 **75**............................ LukeMorris 4 70
(Luke Dace) *rrd s and slowly away: in tch in rr: tried to make prog on inner 2f out: sn no hdwy* **33/1**

2m 9.41s (-1.09) **Going Correction** -0.075s/f (Good) **10 Ran SP% 115.5**
Speed ratings (Par 101): **101,100,99,99,98 97,97,96,96,95**
CSF £68.17 CT £451.79 TOTE £10.10: £3.70, £1.50, £2.60; EX 48.70 Trifecta £450.20.
**Owner** Jacobs Construction & Mrs B B Mills **Bred** R Coffey **Trained** Headley, Surrey

**FOCUS**
Solid form for the level, rated slightly positively with reasons for seeing possible improvement from the front six.

## 3198 BECK H'CAP 7f 16y

**4:55** (4:56) (Class 5) (0-75,75) 3-Y-0 **£3,881** (£1,155; £577; £288) **Stalls** Low

Form RPR

4-24 **1** **Twin Point**[53] 1612 3-9-7 **75**............................ WilliamBuick 7 82
(John Gosden) *trckd ldng pair: led 2f out and sent for home: drvn and a holding rivals fnl f* **13/8[1]**

6-04 **2** 1 1/4 **Cornish Path**[29] 2274 3-9-7 **75**............................ JamesDoyle 1 79
(Henry Candy) *trckd ldrs: shkn up 2f out: prog to take 3rd over 1f out: nvr able to chal but styd on to take 2nd last stride* **11/4[2]**

66-3 **3** nse **Hoon (IRE)**[24] 2447 3-9-1 **69**............................ AdamKirby 5 73
(Rae Guest) *trckd ldrs: rdn and prog to chse wnr over 1f out: edgd rt but kpt on: a hld and lost 2nd last stride* **5/1[3]**

5-06 **4** 2 **Cincuenta Pasos (IRE)**[9] 2886 3-9-2 **70**............................ TomQueally 6 69
(Joseph Tuite) *hld up in last trio: prog on outer 2f out: drvn over 1f out: no imp on ldng trio and edgd rt* **16/1**

0-44 **5** 1 3/4 **Lady Lydia (IRE)**[14] 2745 3-9-7 **75**............................ GeorgeBaker 8 69
(Conrad Allen) *stdd s: hld up in detached last: clsd gng wl enough 2f out: shkn up jst over 1f out: no prog* **8/1**

5554 **6** 1/2 **Spinning Cobblers**[38] 2049 3-8-8 **62**............................ AdamBeschizza 3 55
(Stuart Williams) *led: rdn and hdd jst over 2f out: steadily wknd* **25/1**

00-1 **7** 1 **Comanchero (IRE)**[30] 2249 3-8-8 **65**............................ OisinMurphy(3) 2 55
(Andrew Balding) *hld up in last trio: rdn on inner 2f out: no real prog* **12/1**

310- **8** 1 1/4 **Lady Crossmar (IRE)**[165] 8442 3-9-4 **72**............................ SeanLevey 4 59
(Richard Hannon) *trckd ldr: led briefly jst over 2f out: wknd over 1f out: eased* **25/1**

1m 29.05s (-0.45) **Going Correction** -0.075s/f (Good) **8 Ran SP% 113.8**
Speed ratings (Par 99): **99,97,97,95,93 92,91,90**
CSF £6.05 CT £16.53 TOTE £2.90: £1.30, £1.20, £2.00; EX 8.20 Trifecta £27.70.
**Owner** HRH Princess Haya Of Jordan **Bred** V I Araci **Trained** Newmarket, Suffolk

**FOCUS**
Just a fair handicap. The winner is rated in line with his Yarmouth run.
T/Plt: £44.00 to a £1 stake. Pool: £70,272.62 - 1164.28 winning units. T/Qpdt: £9.40 to a £1 stake. Pool: 5391.25 - 420.83 winning units. JN

# 2784 YORK (L-H)

Friday, June 13

**OFFICIAL GOING: Good (overall 6.4; home straight: far side 6.5, centre 6.5, stands' side 6.3)**
Wind: light 1/2 against Weather: overcast, light rain after race 1

## 3199 CONSTANT SECURITY IRISH STALLION FARMS EBF MAIDEN STKS (BOBIS RACE) 5f

**2:00** (2:00) (Class 3) 2-Y-0 **£6,792** (£2,021; £1,010; £505) **Stalls** Low

Form

2 **1** **Pres Rapide (IRE)**[32] 2214 2-9-5 0............................ PhillipMakin 8 81+
(John Quinn) *trckd ldrs: t.k.h: upsides over 2f out: led 1f out: drvn out* **5/6[1]**

**2** 1 1/2 **Short N Sweet** 2-9-0 0............................ DavidAllan 4 71+
(Tim Easterby) *chsd ldr: led over 3f out: hdd 1f out: styd on same pce* **20/1**

6 **3** 3/4 **Tachophobia**[20] 2541 2-9-5 0............................ RyanMoore 1 73+
(Richard Fahey) *led over 1f: chsd ldrs: styd on same pce fnl f* **9/1**

**4** 1/2 **Al Gomry** 2-9-5 0............................ PaulHanagan 2 71+
(Richard Fahey) *dwlt: sn chsng ldrs hanging lft: kpt on same pce fnl f* **7/2[2]**

06 **5** hd **Ventura Shadow**[10] 2866 2-8-11 0............................ GeorgeChaloner(3) 3 65
(Richard Fahey) *chsd ldrs: kpt on same pce appr fnl f* **33/1**

**6** 2 **Fast Lola** 2-9-0 0............................ HarryBentley 7 58
(Olly Stevens) *dwlt: hdwy to chse ldrs 3f out: kpt on same pce over 1f out* **6/1[3]**

**7** 2 **Bushtown Boy (IRE)** 2-9-5 0............................ SilvestreDeSousa 5 56
(Mark Johnston) *s.i.s: rr-div: outpcd over 2f out: nvr a factor* **16/1**

**8** 12 **Charlie Lad** 2-9-5 0............................ RobertWinston 6 13
(Ollie Pears) *wnt rt sn after s: in rr: sme hdwy over 3f out: hung rt and lost pl 2f out: eased and bhd ins fnl f* **33/1**

1m 0.65s (1.35) **Going Correction** +0.075s/f (Good) **8 Ran SP% 117.6**
Speed ratings (Par 97): **92,89,88,87,87 84,80,61**
CSF £24.27 TOTE £1.90: £1.10, £3.30, £2.20; EX 20.50 Trifecta £145.40.
**Owner** Ross Harmon **Bred** Newlands House Stud **Trained** Settrington, N Yorks

**FOCUS**
The ground had dried out slightly from that advertised and was officially described as good all over. This is usually a decent juvenile maiden. They The race average and the winner guide the initial level. They raced up the centre.

## 3200 NEPTUNE INVESTMENT MANAGEMENT STKS (H'CAP) (BOBIS RACE) 1m 2f 88y

**2:30** (2:30) (Class 3) (0-95,95) 3-Y-0 **£16,172** (£4,812; £2,405; £1,202) **Stalls** Low

Form RPR

31 **1** **Connecticut**[27] 2334 3-8-10 **84**............................ AndreaAtzeni 2 97+
(Luca Cumani) *trckd ldrs: n.m.r over 2f out: w ldr 1f out: styd on to ld nr fin* **6/4[1]**

-146 **2** hd **Donny Rover (IRE)**[22] 2481 3-8-7 **81**............................ AndrewMullen 4 93
(Michael Appleby) *hld up in rr: hdwy 7f out: chsng ldrs over 3f out: led over 1f out: hdd nr fin* **28/1**

0-11 **3** nk **Arabian Comet (IRE)**[11] 2827 3-8-8 **82** 6ex............................ HarryBentley 8 93
(William Haggas) *hld up in rr: hdwy on outside 3f out: kpt on wl towards fin* **7/1**

-012 **4** 3 1/2 **Penhill**[28] 2319 3-8-4 **78**............................ PJMcDonald 5 82
(James Bethell) *s.i.s: sn chsng ldrs: led over 2f out: hdd over 1f out: wknd last 75yds* **8/1**

33-6 **5** 2 1/2 **Snow Squall**[57] 1540 3-8-7 **81**............................ SilvestreDeSousa 9 81
(Mark Johnston) *led over 1f: chsd ldrs: wknd fnl f* **20/1**

-051 **6** *7* **Farquhar (IRE)**[13] 2769 3-9-2 **90** RyanMoore 3 79
(Peter Chapple-Hyam) *hld up in rr: effrt over 3f out: chsng ldrs over 2f out: eased whn wl hld fnl 50yds* **11/2**[2]

61 **7** *nse* **Tabreek (USA)**[29] 2271 3-9-2 **90** PaulHanagan 7 76
(Richard Hannon) *trckd ldrs: drvn over 3f out: lost pl over 1f out* **13/2**[3]

-312 **8** *3/4* **Alquimia (IRE)**[29] 2274 3-8-2 **76** oh1 PatrickMathers 10 61
(Richard Fahey) *drvn to sn chse ldrs: lost pl over 1f out* **25/1**

03-4 **9** *6* **Tiger Twenty Two**[30] 2257 3-8-9 **86** GeorgeChaloner(3) 1 59
(Richard Fahey) *trckd ldrs: led 9f out: hdd over 2f out: lost pl over 1f out* **9/1**

2m 10.45s (-2.05) **Going Correction** +0.075s/f (Good) **9** Ran SP% **114.4**
Speed ratings (Par 103): **111,110,110,107,105 100,100,99,94**
CSF £55.37 CT £233.75 TOTE £2.40: £1.10, £8.20, £2.50; EX 56.70 Trifecta £960.10.
**Owner** Sheikh Mohammed Obaid Al Maktoum **Bred** Whatton Manor Stud **Trained** Newmarket, Suffolk

**FOCUS**
A decent 3yo handicap with a thrilling finish and, although the early pace didn't look that strong, the form looks solid. The first three could be a bit better than their profiles.

## 3201 SKF ROUS (S) STKS 6f
**3:05** (3:05) (Class 3) 2-Y-O **£7,762** (£2,310; £1,154; £577) **Stalls** Low

Form RPR

04 **1** **Sudest (IRE)**[16] 2673 2-9-0 0 PaulMulrennan 14 73
(Kevin Ryan) *led tl over 1f out: styd on to ld again nr fin* **8/1**

44 **2** *1/2* **Izzthatright (IRE)**[20] 2541 2-9-0 0 SilvestreDeSousa 7 72
(Nigel Tinkler) *w ldrs: t.k.h: led narrowly over 1f out: hdd and no ex clsng stages* **5/1**[2]

63 **3** *4 1/2* **Atreus**[7] 2949 2-9-0 0 GrahamGibbons 9 58+
(Michael Easterby) *chsd ldrs: drvn and outpcd over 2f out: sn swtchd rt: kpt on fnl f: tk 3rd clsng stages* **4/1**[1]

2 **4** *1* **Strategic Order (IRE)**[43] 1901 2-9-0 0 GrahamLee 1 55
(Paul Midgley) *w ldrs: kpt on same pce over 1f out* **8/1**

60 **5** *3/4* **Fazenda's Girl**[20] 2541 2-8-9 0 (b[1]) JamesSullivan 13 48
(Michael Easterby) *mid-div: chsd ldrs and edgd lft over 2f out: one pce over 1f out* **50/1**

045 **6** *hd* **Toytown (IRE)**[27] 2328 2-8-7 0 AdamMcLean(7) 4 52
(Derek Shaw) *chsd ldrs: 3rd over 1f out: fdd last 75yds* **6/1**[3]

5 **7** *2 3/4* **Fly Grazer (IRE)**[30] 2246 2-8-4 0 PhilipPrince(5) 5 39
(J S Moore) *in rr: sme hdwy over 2f out: nvr a factor* **66/1**

404 **8** *3/4* **Binky Blue (IRE)**[43] 1900 2-8-9 0 (b[1]) BarryMcHugh 8 37
(Tony Coyle) *s.i.s: hdwy to chse ldrs over 2f out: wknd over 1f out* **8/1**

3 **9** *1 3/4* **Studio Star**[20] 2541 2-8-9 0 JacobButterfield(5) 3 36
(Ollie Pears) *t.k.h: w ldrs: lost pl over 1f out* **7/1**

**10** *6* **Secret House** 2-8-9 0 DavidAllan 15
(Michael Easterby) *s.s: a bhd* **16/1**

065 **11** *1 1/2* **Endislie (IRE)**[7] 2976 2-9-0 0 (b) AndreaAtzeni 6
(J S Moore) *chsd ldrs: lost pl 2f out: eased ins fnl f* **14/1**

025 **12** *7* **Johnny Sorrento**[48] 1741 2-9-0 0 StevieDonohoe 2
(Tim Pitt) *chsd ldrs: t.k.h: lost pl over 2f out: sn bhd* **25/1**

1m 14.22s (2.32) **Going Correction** +0.075s/f (Good) **12** Ran SP% **116.6**
Speed ratings (Par 97): **87,86,80,79,78 77,74,73,70,62 60,51**
CSF £46.41 TOTE £10.80: £3.10, £2.00, £1.80; EX 47.40 Trifecta £311.50.The winner was bought in for 11,000gns. Izzthatright was claimed by Mr Dan Gilbert for £12,000.
**Owner** Mrs J Ryan **Bred** Kenneth Heelan **Trained** Hambleton, N Yorks

**FOCUS**
A valuable 2yo seller, but the front pair dominated throughout. They improved in line with the race average.

## 3202 GEOFF PEMBERTON MEMORIAL STKS (H'CAP) 7f
**3:40** (3:42) (Class 3) (0-95,95) 4-Y-0+ **£7,439** (£2,213; £1,106; £553) **Stalls** Low

Form RPR

4-44 **1** **Alejandro (IRE)**[20] 2548 5-8-13 **87** SilvestreDeSousa 6 100
(David O'Meara) *mde all: t.k.h: fnd ex clsng stages* **7/1**[3]

-065 **2** *1 1/2* **Foxtrot Romeo (IRE)**[32] 2202 5-9-0 **88** (tp) MartinHarley 11 97
(Marco Botti) *hld up in rr: effrt and nt clr run over 1f out: styd on to take 2nd clsng stages: no imp nr fin* **9/1**

4-51 **3** *nk* **Dusky Queen (IRE)**[28] 2318 4-9-0 **88** RyanMoore 3 97
(Richard Fahey) *chsd ldrs: pushed along 3f out: nt clr run 1f out: styd on wl to take 3rd towards fin* **5/1**[1]

-461 **4** *3/4* **Dubai Hills**[13] 2763 8-9-0 **88** DanielTudhope 8 94
(David O'Meara) *chsd ldrs: kpt on same pce fnl f* **12/1**

-453 **5** *hd* **Green Howard**[20] 2548 6-8-5 **82** (p) JasonHart(3) 16 88+
(Robin Bastiman) *in rr: hdwy over 2f out: styd on wl ins fnl f* **15/2**

6-36 **6** *hd* **Kalk Bay (IRE)**[56] 1564 7-8-8 **82** (t) GrahamGibbons 7 87
(Michael Easterby) *chsd ldrs on inner: kpt on same pce fnl f* **6/1**[2]

4424 **7** *2 1/4* **Grissom (IRE)**[20] 2562 8-8-11 **85** DavidAllan 15 84
(Tim Easterby) *in rr: hdwy on wd outside over 2f out: nt rch ldrs* **16/1**

0-12 **8** *hd* **Escape To Glory (USA)**[27] 2351 6-8-10 **84** PaulMulrennan 4 83
(Michael Dods) *hld up in tch: effrt over 2f out: one pce over 1f out* **11/1**

05-0 **9** *1/2* **Smarty Socks (IRE)**[10] 2869 10-9-4 **95** SamJames(3) 1 93
(David O'Meara) *dwlt: hdwy on ins over 3f out: chsng ldrs over 1f out: wknd towards fin* **16/1**

50-2 **10** *nk* **Personal Touch**[32] 2202 5-8-6 **80** PatrickMathers 5 77
(Richard Fahey) *chsd ldrs: one pce over 1f out* **33/1**

6565 **11** *hd* **Joe Eile (IRE)**[20] 2548 6-8-12 **86** PhillipMakin 9 84
(John Quinn) *unruly in stalls: mid-div: hdwy over 2f out: one pce whn n.m.r over 1f out* **16/1**

5506 **12** *nk* **Lazarus Bell**[15] 2699 4-8-7 **81** BenCurtis 14 77
(Alan Brown) *in rr on outer: nvr on terms* **25/1**

2211 **13** *1* **True Pleasure (IRE)**[7] 2954 7-8-4 **78** 6ex PJMcDonald 2 71
(James Bethell) *chsd ldrs on inner: effrt over 2f out: wknd fnl f* **16/1**

-221 **14** *1/2* **Johnny Cavagin**[20] 2549 5-8-11 **85** (t) StevieDonohoe 10 77
(Richard Guest) *t.k.h: trckd ldrs on outer: lost pl over 1f out* **12/1**

**15** *17* **Secret Recipe**[230] 7552 4-9-7 **95** PaulHanagan 13 42
(David Nicholls) *in rr: lost pl 3f out: eased over 1f out: t.o* **33/1**

1m 24.47s (-0.83) **Going Correction** +0.075s/f (Good) **15** Ran SP% **122.2**
Speed ratings (Par 107): **107,105,104,104,103 103,101,100,100,99 99,99,98,97,78**
CSF £68.03 CT £355.75 TOTE £6.40: £2.60, £4.90, £2.00; EX 72.70 Trifecta £530.80.
**Owner** Lydonford Ltd **Bred** Yeomanstown Stud **Trained** Nawton, N Yorks

**FOCUS**
A competitive handicap, but another contest where it paid to race handily. A small personal best from the winner.

## 3203 BETBRIGHT FOR YOUR WORLD CUP BETS CHOOSE EBF NOMINATED FILLIES' STKS (H'CAP) 6f
**4:10** (4:11) (Class 2) (0-100,100) 4-Y-O+ **£16,172** (£4,812; £2,405; £1,202) **Stalls** Low

Form RPR

251 **1** **Willbeme**[20] 2542 6-8-2 **81** oh1 AndrewMullen 6 98
(Neville Bycroft) *w ldr: led over 3f out: styd on strly to forge clr last 100yds* **12/1**

1216 **2** *3 1/4* **Bondesire**[6] 2992 4-9-3 **96** DanielTudhope 2 103
(David O'Meara) *led over 2f out: hung lft and swtchd rt 1f out: styd on to take 2nd clsng stages* **7/2**[1]

-013 **3** *1 1/4* **Love Island**[13] 2757 5-9-2 **95** RyanMoore 3 98
(Richard Whitaker) *trckd ldrs: upsides over 1f out: styd on same pce* **7/2**[1]

0-05 **4** *1 1/4* **Misplaced Fortune**[28] 2318 9-8-6 **85** (v) AndreaAtzeni 4 84
(Nigel Tinkler) *mid-div: outpcd lost pl 3f out: hdwy over 1f out: edgd lft and styd on fnl 100yds* **7/1**

3-00 **5** *nk* **The Gold Cheongsam (IRE)**[134] 396 4-9-7 **100** (t) SebSanders 1 98
(Jeremy Noseda) *dwlt: hdwy over 2f out: one pce over 1f out* **10/1**

-652 **6** *2 1/2* **Royal Rascal**[13] 2757 4-9-2 **95** (b[1]) DavidAllan 7 85
(Tim Easterby) *hld up in rr: hdwy over 2f out: wknd over 1f out* **6/1**[3]

2-25 **7** *1/2* **Mar Mar (IRE)**[34] 2149 4-9-3 **96** (p) SilvestreDeSousa 5 84
(Saeed bin Suroor) *trckd ldrs: drvn over 2f out: hung lft and sn wknd* **11/2**[2]

11-0 **8** *2* **Rocksilla**[55] 1576 4-8-8 **87** HarryBentley 8 69
(Chris Wall) *in rr: drvn over 2f out: lost pl over 1f out* **16/1**

303- **9** *1/2* **Maid A Million**[230] 7538 4-9-0 **93** PaulHanagan 9 73
(David Elsworth) *hld up in rr: effrt over 2f out: lost pl over 1f out* **14/1**

1m 10.54s (-1.36) **Going Correction** +0.075s/f (Good) **9** Ran SP% **115.9**
Speed ratings (Par 96): **112,107,106,104,103 100,99,97,96**
CSF £54.07 CT £183.24 TOTE £15.00: £3.40, £1.70, £1.40; EX 65.60 Trifecta £442.40.
**Owner** P D Burrow **Bred** Mrs J M Russell **Trained** Norton, N Yorks

**FOCUS**
A decent fillies' sprint handicap, but more of the same with the winner making all. The winner rates better than ever.

## 3204 GARBUTT & ELLIOTT STKS (H'CAP) 1m 6f
**4:40** (4:43) (Class 3) (0-90,90) 4-Y-0+ **£7,439** (£2,213; £1,106; £553) **Stalls** Low

Form RPR

16-3 **1** **Totalize**[20] 2558 5-8-10 **86** MeganCarberry(7) 14 98
(Brian Ellison) *in rr: drvn 4f out: chsng ldrs whn wnt lft over 1f out: led jst ins fnl f: styd on strly* **8/1**

-023 **2** *3 1/2* **Eagle Rock (IRE)**[13] 2782 6-9-0 **83** (p) JamesSullivan 15 90
(Tom Tate) *chsd ldng pair: 2nd 10f out: led 2f out: hmpd over 1f out: hdd and no ex jst ins fnl f* **14/1**

300- **3** *2* **Kiwayu**[210] 7496 5-9-3 **86** PhillipMakin 4 90
(Philip Kirby) *mid-div: hdwy over 3f out: chsng ldrs whn hmpd over 1f out: kpt on* **50/1**

3-06 **4** *nk* **Grandorio (IRE)**[13] 2787 4-9-5 **88** DanielTudhope 9 92
(David O'Meara) *hld up in rr: stdy hdwy over 2f out: kpt on fnl f* **9/1**

2/34 **5** *2* **Local Hero (GER)**[13] 2787 7-8-12 **81** (b) PaulHanagan 16 82
(Steve Gollings) *mid-div: hdwy on outside over 3f out: kpt on same pce over 1f out* **10/1**

0-65 **6** *1* **Dr Irv**[29] 2289 5-8-7 **76** PJMcDonald 3 76
(Philip Kirby) *in rr: hdwy 4f out: chsng ldrs and rdn over 2f out: one pce over 1f out* **9/1**

3-60 **7** *3 1/2* **Party Line**[13] 2785 5-9-6 **89** (v) SilvestreDeSousa 6 84
(Mark Johnston) *chsd ldrs: drvn 4f out: upsides over 1f out: sn wknd* **9/1**

5344 **8** *1/2* **Mr Snoozy**[14] 2739 5-8-8 **80** (b[1]) JasonHart(3) 10 74
(Mark Walford) *chsd ldr: drvn 4f out: wknd over 1f out* **16/1**

161- **9** *3 1/2* **Bin Singspiel**[230] 7542 4-9-5 **88** GrahamLee 11 77
(James Tate) *awkward to load: chsd ldrs: pushed along over 5f out: wknd over 1f out* **13/2**[3]

4-02 **10** *nse* **Bohemian Rhapsody (IRE)**[34] 2160 5-9-2 **85** RobertWinston 1 74
(Seamus Durack) *mid-div: drvn on inner over 4f out: wknd 2f out* **6/1**[2]

220- **11** *3/4* **Bowdler's Magic**[244] 7210 7-8-10 **79** (t) JimmyQuinn 13 67
(David Thompson) *s.i.s and swtchd lft after s: detached in last: nvr on terms* **50/1**

052- **12** *1* **Stopped Out**[118] 7338 9-8-12 **81** (p) RussKennemore 5 68
(Philip Kirby) *led: hdd 2f out: sn wknd* **33/1**

310- **13** *23* **Phaenomena (IRE)**[225] 7650 4-9-7 **90** RyanMoore 2 44
(Lady Cecil) *mid-div: pushed along over 4f out: wknd over 2f out: heavily eased fnl f: virtually p.u: t.o* **3/1**[1]

1326 **14** *4 1/2* **Singzak**[49] 1692 6-8-6 **75** BarryMcHugh 12 23
(Michael Easterby) *chsd ldrs: lost pl over 2f out: eased and bhd fnl f: virtually p.u: t.o* **33/1**

2m 58.58s (-1.62) **Going Correction** +0.075s/f (Good) **14** Ran SP% **125.2**
Speed ratings (Par 107): **107,105,103,103,102 101,99,99,97,97 97,96,83,80**
CSF £117.01 CT £5215.66 TOTE £12.80: £3.90, £4.90, £15.60; EX 122.50 Trifecta £3361.30.
**Owner** D Gilbert, M Lawrence, A Bruce **Bred** Meon Valley Stud **Trained** Norton, N Yorks
■ Stewards' Enquiry : Megan Carberry two-day ban: careless riding (Jun 27-28)

**FOCUS**
They seemed to go a decent pace in this useful staying handicap with a trio soon skipping clear. A personal best for the winner, helped by the rider's claim.

## 3205 JIGSAW SPONSORSHIP SERVICES APPRENTICE STKS (H'CAP) 1m 4f
**5:15** (5:15) (Class 4) (0-80,82) 4-Y-0+ **£6,469** (£1,925; £962; £481) **Stalls** Centre

Form RPR

0211 **1** **Saved By The Bell (IRE)**[10] 2872 4-10-1 **82** 6ex SamJames 3 96+
(David O'Meara) *hld up in rr: stdy hdwy 3f out: r.o to ld last 50yds* **4/1**[1]

/6-0 **2** *3/4* **Only Orsenfoolsies**[13] 2790 5-9-0 **67** NeilFarley 11 74
(Micky Hammond) *chsd ldrs: upsides over 3f out: led over 1f out: hdd and no ex clsng stages* **25/1**

4332 **3** *1 1/2* **High Office**[13] 2787 8-9-11 **78** GeorgeChaloner 4 83
(Richard Fahey) *in tch: chsd ldrs over 2f out: styd on same pce last 150yds* **5/1**[2]

115- **4** *1/2* **Mister Fizz**[220] 7739 6-9-7 **79** DanielCremin(5) 14 83
(Miss Imogen Pickard) *chsd ldrs: led over 3f out: hdd over 1f out: kpt on same pce* **25/1**

04-0 **5** *4 1/2* **Eltheeb**[34] 2168 7-9-5 **77** (p) EvaMoscrop(5) 17 74
(Philip Kirby) *hld up in mid-div: effrt over 2f out: one pce* **14/1**

0-15 **6** *2* **Arthurs Secret**[21] 2520 4-9-5 **72** (b[1]) IanBrennan 6 66
(John Quinn) *in tch: effrt over 2f out: one pce* **14/1**

-004 **7** *2 1/4* **Prophesy (IRE)**[21] 2520 5-9-6 **73** (p) JasonHart 7 63
(Tim Easterby) *in rr: hdwy over 3f out: one pce fnl 2f* **8/1**

323- **8** ½ **Chant (IRE)**260 6775 4-8-11 **71** ........................ RowanScott(7) 2 60
(Ann Duffield) *in tch: effrt over 2f out: one pce* **20/1**

60-5 **9** ½ **Rock A Doodle Doo (IRE)**15 2700 7-8-13 **71** .....(p) MeganCarberry(5) 5 60
(Sally Hall) *in rr: effrt and edgd rt 3f out: nvr a factor* **7/1**3

21-0 **10** *nk* **Mallory Heights (IRE)**29 2272 4-9-4 **78** ................ GianlucaSanna(7) 15 66
(Luca Cumani) *in tch: effrt over 2f out: fdd over 1f out* **14/1**

65-0 **11** ¾ **Christmas Light**13 2790 7-9-0 **74** ........................ KevinLundie(7) 13 61
(Brian Ellison) *s.i.s: sme hdwy on wd outside 3f out: carried rt and sn lost pl* **14/1**

-206 **12** ½ **Al Furat (USA)**17 2654 6-8-4 **60** oh4 .......................... NoelGarbutt(3) 9 46
(Ron Barr) *mid-div: effrt 4f out: nvr a factor* **50/1**

-603 **13** ½ **Pertemps Networks**6 2980 10-8-10 **70** ...........(b1) DannielleMooney(7) 16 55
(Michael Easterby) *led: hdd over 3f out: lost pl over 1f out* **33/1**

22-6 **14** ½ **Aneedh**26 1659 4-9-5 **75** ........................ JacobButterfield(3) 12 60
(Jedd O'Keeffe) *in rr: drvn over 5f out: carried rt and lost pl 3f out* **25/1**

32-0 **15** 3¼ **Sioux Chieftain (IRE)**21 2520 4-9-7 **79** ............ AlistairRawlinson(5) 10 58
(Michael Appleby) *in tch: drvn 4f out: lost pl over 1f out* **8/1**

1-03 **16** 12 **A Star In My Eye (IRE)**44 1882 4-9-9 **79** ........................ ShaneGray(3) 1 39
(Kevin Ryan) *chsd ldrs: lost pl over 1f out: heavily eased ins fnl f* **14/1**

2m 32.96s (-0.24) **Going Correction** +0.075s/f (Good) **16** Ran SP% **125.9**
Speed ratings (Par 105): **103,102,101,101,98 96,95,95,94,94 93,93,93,92,90 82**
CSF £118.11 CT £530.66 TOTE £4.10: £1.60, £5.60, £1.60, £5.70; EX 211.80 Trifecta £1436.60.

**Owner** J Blackburn & A Turton **Bred** Dowager Countess Harrington **Trained** Nawton, N Yorks

**FOCUS**
Another competitive handicap, but unlike in the earlier races on the card these apprentices stuck centre-to-far side in the home straight. The pace looked ordinary and a few were inclined to take a pull. The third gives the form a bit of substance.
T/Jkpt: Not won. T/Plt: £194.60 to a £1 stake. Pool: £110,187.68 - 413.13 winning units. T/Qpdt: £92.10 to a £1 stake. Pool: £6038.22 - 48.50 winning units. WG

3206 - 3207a (Foreign Racing) - See Raceform Interactive

## 2942 BATH (L-H)
### Saturday, June 14

**OFFICIAL GOING: Firm (10.8)**
Wind: light breeze across Weather: warm

## 3208 FSB PENSION SCHEME FOR MEMBERS H'CAP — 1m 2f 46y
**2:35** (2:36) (Class 6) (0-55,54) 4-Y-O+ **£2,045** (£603; £302) **Stalls** Low

Form RPR

5244 **1** **Herbalist**15 2720 4-8-13 **53** ........................ CamHardie(7) 10 66
(Sean Curran) *trckd ldrs: rdn to ld over 1f out: strly chal fnl f: hld on: all out* **13/2**

5-41 **2** *hd* **Elizabeth Coffee (IRE)**11 2875 6-9-1 **51** .......... MichaelJMMurphy(3) 12 63
(John Weymes) *hld up towards rr: hdwy fr 3f out: rdn 2f out: str chal thrght fnl f: kpt on: lost on nod* **4/1**1

0-40 **3** 3¼ **Gabrial The Thug (FR)**24 2457 4-9-7 **54** .................... JimmyFortune 9 60
(Richard Fahey) *hld up towards rr: rdn and stdy prog fr over 2f out: wnt 3rd ent fnl f: styd on* **9/2**2

3463 **4** 1½ **Petersboden**11 2863 5-9-2 **49** ........................ SteveDrowne 11 52
(Michael Blanshard) *hld up towards rr: pushed along whn hmpd after 2f: rdn and stdy prog fr over 2f out: nvr threatened: styd on same pce fnl f* **10/1**

0060 **5** 1¼ **Kristal Hart**46 1835 5-9-0 **52** ........................ RyanWhile(5) 7 53
(Neil Mulholland) *mid-div: rdn and hdwy over 2f out: styd on same pce fnl f* **50/1**

4540 **6** 1¼ **Omotesando**23 2475 4-8-13 **46** ........................(p) LiamJones 8 44
(Mark Brisbourne) *trckd ldr: rdn to ld 2f out: hdd over 1f out: no ex fnl f* **28/1**

2-00 **7** ¾ **Elusive Band (USA)**17 2672 4-8-13 **53** ..................(tp) DavidParkes(7) 3 50
(Bernard Llewellyn) *s.i.s: sn pushed along in mid-div: rdn over 4f out: nvr threatened: wknd fnl f* **28/1**

0004 **8** 5 **Greyemkay**12 2834 6-8-7 **45** ........................ NoelGarbutt(5) 5 32
(Richard Price) *in tch tl outpcd over 2f out: n.d after* **16/1**

03 **9** *hd* **To The Sky (IRE)**6 3035 6-9-2 **49** ........................(p) WilliamCarson 6 36
(John O'Shea) *dwlt: a towards rr* **8/1**

5630 **10** *hd* **Devote Myself (IRE)**16 2689 5-9-1 **48** ..................(bt) J-PGuillambert 1 35
(John Flint) *led: rdn and hdd 2f out: wknd fnl f* **16/1**

4005 **11** 9 **Medburn Cutler**9 2923 4-9-5 **52** ........................ PatCosgrave 4 22
(George Baker) *trckd ldrs: rdn 4f out: wknd over 2f out* **6/1**3

5320 **P** **K Lightning (IRE)**12 2836 4-9-5 **52** ........................ JimmyQuinn 2
(Sarah Humphrey) *mid-div whn lost action and p.u after 2f: fatally injured* **7/1**

2m 9.16s (-1.84) **Going Correction** -0.175s/f (Firm) **12** Ran SP% **119.1**
Speed ratings (Par 101): **100,99,97,96,95 94,93,89,89,89 81,**
CSF £32.30 CT £131.85 TOTE £7.10: £3.00, £1.50, £1.20; EX 29.20 Trifecta £117.40.
**Owner** The Milk Sheiks **Bred** Girsonfield Ltd **Trained** Upper Lambourn, Berks
■ Stewards' Enquiry : Michael J M Murphy four-day ban: used whip above permitted level (Jun 28-Jul 1)

**FOCUS**
A moderate handicap in which they went a contested gallop on firm ground.

## 3209 FSB INSURANCE SERVICE H'CAP — 1m 3f 144y
**3:10** (3:10) (Class 6) (0-60,58) 4-Y-O+ **£1,940** (£577; £288; £144) **Stalls** Low

Form RPR

40-2 **1** **Captain Oats (IRE)**12 2836 11-8-12 **54** .................. RachealKneller(5) 7 63
(Pam Ford) *hld up bhd: swtchd rt and stdy prog fr over 2f out: led ins fnl f: styd on wl: pushed out* **7/1**

0-56 **2** 2¼ **Indian Scout**10 2894 6-8-9 **46** ........................(b1) JohnFahy 10 51
(Anabel K Murphy) *sn pushed along to join ldrs: rdn for str chal fr over 2f out: led jst ins fnl f: no ex whn hdd fnl 75yds* **10/1**

0500 **3** 2¼ **Shirataki (IRE)**9 2916 6-9-4 **55** ........................ ChrisCatlin 5 57
(Peter Hiatt) *led: rdn and hrd pressed fr over 2f out: hdd jst ins fnl f: no ex* **10/1**

00/5 **4** 1¾ **Just Duchess**15 2720 4-8-6 **46** ow1 ........................ ThomasBrown(3) 6 45
(Michael Blanshard) *in tch tl dropped to last pair and struggling 6f out: styd on wl ent fnl f: wnt 4th towards fin* **6/1**2

-060 **5** ½ **Roy Rocket (FR)**38 2084 4-8-3 **45** ........................ NoelGarbutt(5) 2 43
(John Berry) *hld up: hdwy on inner fr over 4f out: rdn to chse ldrs wl over 2f out: kpt on same pce fnl f* **16/1**

643- **6** 2 **Lucky Diva**287 5977 7-8-11 **53** ........................(p) RyanWhile(5) 4 48
(Bill Turner) *trckd ldrs: rdn over 2f out: styd on same pce* **7/1**

5005 **7** *hd* **Rainford Glory (IRE)**15 2738 4-9-4 **55** ..................(p) JimmyFortune 3 50
(Richard Fahey) *in tch: rdn to dispute cl 3rd over 2f out: fdd ins fnl f* **9/4**1

2-66 **8** 17 **Hendry Trigger**12 2836 5-8-6 **50** ........................(p) DavidParkes(7) 8 17
(Bernard Llewellyn) *prom tl rn wd whn losing pl on bnd 5f out: sn bhd* **8/1**

61 **9** 24 **Alhaban (IRE)**9 2937 8-9-7 **58** ........................(p) SteveDrowne 9
(Ronald Harris) *trckd ldrs tl wknd qckly u.p over 3f out: virtually p.u fnl f* **13/2**3

2m 29.24s (-1.36) **Going Correction** -0.175s/f (Firm) **9** Ran SP% **118.6**
Speed ratings (Par 101): **97,95,94,92,92 91,91,79,63**
CSF £76.20 CT £706.06 TOTE £5.80: £1.60, £3.40, £3.00; EX 88.00 Trifecta £344.00 Part won..
**Owner** Miss Tori Davies **Bred** Airlie Stud **Trained** Preston Wynne, H'fords

**FOCUS**
A moderate middle-distance handicap for older horses in which they went a contested pace. The form is rated around the runner-up.

## 3210 FSB LOBBYING FOR SMALL BUSINESSES MAIDEN AUCTION STKS — 5f 11y
**3:45** (3:49) (Class 5) 2-Y-O **£2,587** (£770; £384; £192) **Stalls** Centre

Form RPR

0 **1** **Pillar Box (IRE)**21 2541 2-9-4 0 ........................ LiamJones 7 85+
(William Haggas) *chsd ldr: rdn to ld over 1f out: r.o strly: readily* **3/1**2

62 **2** 4½ **Jimmy's Girl (IRE)**16 2692 2-8-1 0 ........................ CamHardie(7) 8 58
(Richard Hannon) *sn led: rdn whn hdd over 1f out: sn hung lft: kpt on but nt pce of wnr fnl f* **9/2**

5 **3** 1½ **Red Perdita (IRE)**47 1788 2-8-13 0 ........................ PatCosgrave 3 60
(George Baker) *chsd ldr: rdn 2f out: disputing hld 3rd whn short of room ent fnl f: kpt on same pce* **4/1**3

34 **4** ¾ **Celestial Vision (USA)**30 2269 2-8-11 0 .................. JennyPowell(7) 2 62
(Tom Dascombe) *chsd ldrs: rdn 2f out: disputing hld 3rd whn short of room ent fnl f: kpt on same pce* **9/4**1

0322 **5** 1¾ **Arlecchino's Leap**7 2993 2-9-1 0 ........................(b1) SteveDrowne 9 51
(Mark Usher) *in tch: rdn over 2f out: nvr gng pce to get involved* **5/1**

00 **6** 3 **Karluk (IRE)**40 2022 2-8-8 0 ........................ JohnFahy 6 32
(Eve Johnson Houghton) *sn pushed along in last trio: sme minor prog over 2f out but nvr gng pce to get involved* **20/1**

0 **7** 6 **Magic Round (IRE)**30 2276 2-8-8 0 ........................(p) RyanWhile(5) 5 15
(Bill Turner) *sn pushed along in last trio: nvr a threat: wknd fnl f* **25/1**

U0 **8** 3½ **Saphira Silver (IRE)**25 2413 2-8-4 0 ow1 .......... MatthewCosham(3) 11
(Nikki Evans) *outpcd in last trio: nvr any danger: wknd jst over 1f out* **100/1**

1m 1.88s (-0.62) **Going Correction** -0.175s/f (Firm) **8** Ran SP% **120.2**
Speed ratings (Par 93): **97,89,87,86,83 78,69,63**
CSF £17.61 TOTE £4.10: £1.20, £2.00, £1.70; EX 26.30 Trifecta £116.80.
**Owner** The Super Sprinters **Bred** Mrs Anne Marie Burns **Trained** Newmarket, Suffolk

**FOCUS**
A fair juvenile sprint maiden in which they went a decent gallop. Improvement from the winner.

## 3211 FSB PRINT AND MAIL/EBF STALLIONS NOVICE STKS (BOBIS RACE) — 5f 11y
**4:20** (4:21) (Class 4) 2-Y-O **£6,469** (£1,925; £962; £481) **Stalls** Centre

Form RPR

41 **1** **Beacon**30 2276 2-9-7 0 ........................ JimmyFortune 5 95+
(Richard Hannon) *trckd ldrs: led ent fnl f: qcknd clr: readily* **5/4**1

32 **2** 3 **One Moment**13 2800 2-8-9 0 ........................ LiamJones 1 70
(Robert Cowell) *led: rdn 2f out: hdd ent fnl f: kpt on but nt pce of ready wnr* **4/1**3

632 **3** 2 **Amber Crystal**15 2716 2-8-6 0 ........................ MichaelJMMurphy(3) 6 63
(John Gallagher) *kpt wd: prom: rdn 2f out: kpt on same pce fnl f* **10/1**

6251 **4** ½ **River Spirit**7 2993 2-8-10 0 ........................ WilliamTwiston-Davies(3) 2 65
(Mick Channon) *chsd ldrs: rdn 2f out: nt best of runs jst over 1f out: swtchd rt: kpt on same pce fnl f* **10/1**

001 **5** ½ **Areion (IRE)**17 2680 2-8-6 0 ........................(b) CamHardie(7) 4 63
(J S Moore) *sn pushed along in tch: rdn to chse ldrs 2f out: kpt on but nt pce to get on terms* **28/1**

120 **6** 8 **Cheerio Sweetie (IRE)**38 2071 2-8-13 0 ........................ PatCosgrave 3 33
(David Evans) *s.i.s: sn outpcd: a last* **11/4**2

1m 1.61s (-0.89) **Going Correction** -0.175s/f (Firm) **6** Ran SP% **112.7**
Speed ratings (Par 95): **100,95,92,91,90 77**
CSF £6.72 TOTE £1.80: £1.10, £2.90; EX 5.50 Trifecta £31.50.
**Owner** Highclere Thoroughbred Racing (Albany) **Bred** J M Cole **Trained** East Everleigh, Wilts

**FOCUS**
A decent juvenile novice sprint. The winner was value for a bit extra.

## 3212 FSB DATA SERVICES H'CAP — 1m 5y
**4:55** (4:55) (Class 3) (0-90,89) 4-Y-O+ **£8,409** (£2,502; £1,250; £625) **Stalls** Low

Form RPR

0-02 **1** **Ogbourne Downs**26 2382 4-8-11 **79** ........................ SteveDrowne 3 87
(Charles Hills) *s.i.s: in last pair but wl in tch: hdwy 2f out: led jst ins fnl f: r.o wl: pushed out* **4/1**

-552 **2** *nk* **Fleckerl (IRE)**38 2068 4-8-4 **75** ........................ MichaelJMMurphy(3) 2 82
(William Muir) *s.i.s: in last pair but wl in tch: hdwy over 1f out: nt clr run briefly ent fnl f: kpt on wl against far rails to go 2nd towards fin* **9/4**1

110- **3** 1¼ **Wandsworth (IRE)**166 8445 4-8-10 **78** ........................ JimmyFortune 5 82
(Roger Varian) *led: rdn wl over 1f out: hdd jst ins fnl f: kpt on but no ex whn lost 2nd towards fin* **3/1**3

5503 **4** 1¼ **Gramercy (IRE)**7 2984 7-9-7 **89** ........................ PatCosgrave 1 91
(David Simcock) *trckd ldrs: rdn 2f out: kpt on but nt pce to chal* **11/4**2

-415 **5** *nk* **Al Manaal**11 2861 4-8-11 **82** ........................ WilliamTwiston-Davies(3) 4 83
(Mick Channon) *trckd ldrs: rdn 2f out: kpt on same pce fnl f* **8/1**

1m 41.3s (0.50) **Going Correction** -0.175s/f (Firm) **5** Ran SP% **113.5**
Speed ratings (Par 107): **90,89,88,87,86**
CSF £13.81 TOTE £4.50: £2.30, £1.80; EX 15.60 Trifecta £86.60.
**Owner** S W Group Logistics Limited **Bred** Bumble Bloodstock & Mrs S Nicholls **Trained** Lambourn, Berks

**FOCUS**
The feature race of the day was a decent small-field handicap for older horses in which they went a modest gallop. The winner is rated back to his best.

## 3213 FSB TELECOM H'CAP — 5f 161y
**5:30** (5:31) (Class 4) (0-80,78) 3-Y-O+ **£5,822** (£1,732; £865; £432) **Stalls** Centre

Form RPR

1313 **1** **Spellmaker**43 1921 5-9-0 **68** ........................ MichaelJMMurphy(3) 7 76
(Tony Newcombe) *hld up: hdwy 2f out: rdn to ld over 1f out: sn hung lft: kpt on: drvn out* **7/1**

53-5 **2** *nk* **Angelito**8 2945 5-9-10 **75** ........................ LiamJones 6 82
(Ed McMahon) *chsd ldrs: rdn to chal 2f out: tight of room but ev ch thrght fnl f: kpt on* **5/1**3

5061 **3** *1* **Diamondhead (IRE)**[25] 2414 5-9-13 **78**........................ PatCosgrave 2 82
(Ed de Giles) *w ldr: led wl over 2f out: sn rdn: hdd over 1f out: tight of room but kpt on w ev ch tl no ex nring fin* **4/1**[2]

5066 **4** *½* **Vallarta (IRE)**[8] 2945 4-9-4 **72**.................. WilliamTwiston-Davies(3) 1 74+
(Mick Channon) *rrd leaving stalls: bhd: hdwy 2f out: sn rdn to chse ldrs: kpt on but nvr finding pce to chal* **5/2**[1]

340 **5** *1* **Noverre To Go (IRE)**[9] 2919 8-9-12 **77**..........................(p) SteveDrowne 4 76
(Ronald Harris) *in tch: rdn whn swtchd rt over 1f out: kpt on ins fnl f* **11/1**

113 **6** *2 ¼* **Hamoody (USA)**[9] 2933 10-9-8 **76**........................ ThomasBrown(3) 3 68
(Joseph Tuite) *led tl wl over 2f out: sn rdn: hld in cl 4th whn squeezed out ent fnl f: no ex fnl120yds* **8/1**

-136 **7** *4 ½* **Dreams Of Glory**[15] 2718 6-9-9 **74**................................ JimmyFortune 8 51
(Ron Hodges) *in tch: effrt 2f out: wknd fnl f* **7/1**

3224 **8** *4 ½* **New Decade**[11] 2865 5-8-9 **67**...................................(t) DavidParkes(7) 5 29
(Milton Bradley) *chsd ldrs tl wknd over 1f out* **20/1**

1m 10.61s (-0.59) **Going Correction** -0.175s/f (Firm) **8** Ran SP% **114.4**
Speed ratings (Par 105): **96,95,94,93,92 89,83,77**
CSF £41.76 CT £159.86 TOTE £5.90: £2.30, £2.20, £1.70; EX 38.10 Trifecta £230.60.
**Owner** Joli Racing **Bred** Dxb Bloodstock Ltd **Trained** Yarnscombe, Devon
■ Stewards' Enquiry : Michael J M Murphy (1st incident)-four-day ban: careless riding (Jul 2-4,6); (2nd)-one-day ban: careless riding (Jul 7)

**FOCUS**
A fair sprint handicap in which they went a contested gallop, but the time was relatively ordinary. The winner carried ove similar form from the AW.

## 3214 FSB CARE H'CAP 5f 161y
**6:00** (6:02) (Class 6) (0-55,55) 3-Y-O **£2,045** (£603; £302) **Stalls** Centre

Form RPR

50-0 **1** **Connaught Water (IRE)**[43] 1914 3-9-4 **55**............ MatthewLawson(3) 4 62
(Jonathan Portman) *slowly away: towards rr: hdwy whn nt clr run over 2f out: swtchd rt over 1f out: sn rdn: str run ent fnl f: led fnl 75yds* **16/1**

5431 **2** *½* **Crystalized (IRE)**[39] 2045 3-9-4 **52**................................ ChrisCatlin 11 57
(Dean Ivory) *hld up: hdwy over 2f out: chal ins fnl f: led v briefly fnl 120yds: kpt on but no ex* **2/1**[1]

2556 **3** *2* **Clear Focus (IRE)**[17] 2668 3-8-12 **46** oh1......................(v¹) LiamJones 1 45
(Brendan Powell) *chsd ldrs: sn pushed along: rdn wl over 2f out: kpt on ins fnl f: snatched 3rd fnl stride* **10/1**

000- **4** *nse* **Warm Order**[206] 7978 3-8-13 **50**.................. WilliamTwiston-Davies(3) 12 49
(Tony Carroll) *broke wl: led: rdn over 1f out: hdd fnl 120yds: sn no ex: lost 3rd fnl stride* **16/1**

065 **5** *2 ¼* **Go Charlie**[9] 2932 3-9-1 **49**........................................ SteveDrowne 8 40
(Ronald Harris) *hld up bhd: hdwy but nt best of runs fr 2f out: kpt on ins fnl f: nvr trbld ldrs* **20/1**

0606 **6** *1 ¾* **Dover The Moon (IRE)**[11] 2860 3-8-12 **46**........................ ASandesh 3 31
(Sylvester Kirk) *mid-div: rdn over 2f out: kpt on same pce* **25/1**

0055 **7** *½* **Nutbush**[4] 3087 3-8-10 **51**...................................... DanielCremin(7) 13 35
(Mick Channon) *in tch: rdn over 2f out: sn one pce* **11/2**[3]

-004 **8** *nk* **Eugenic**[17] 2668 3-9-4 **52**..........................................(v¹) JimmyFortune 15 35
(Rod Millman) *nvr bttr than mid-div* **9/2**[2]

4462 **9** *1* **Brean Splash Susie**[19] 2625 3-8-13 **52**.......................... RyanWhile(5) 9 31
(Bill Turner) *chsd ldrs: rdn wl over 2f out: wknd ent fnl f* **15/2**

04-0 **10** *2 ¾* **Spider Lily**[9] 2931 3-8-10 **47**.............................. MichaelJMMurphy(3) 5 17
(Peter Makin) *s.i.s: a towards rr* **20/1**

0-44 **11** *5* **Notnow Penny**[72] 1264 3-8-7 **48**................................ DavidParkes(7) 14 2
(Milton Bradley) *chsd ldrs: rdn over 2f out: wknd over 1f out* **20/1**

000 **12** *1* **Distant Shadow**[17] 2682 3-9-0 **48**................................ JackMitchell 6
(Chris Wall) *mid-div: rdn over 2f out: wknd over 1f out* **10/1**

1m 11.54s (0.34) **Going Correction** -0.175s/f (Firm) **12** Ran SP% **126.7**
Speed ratings (Par 97): **90,89,86,86,83 81,80,80,78,75 68,67**
CSF £48.94 CT £374.61 TOTE £25.70: £10.00, £1.40, £3.40; EX 127.00 Trifecta £758.40 Part won..
**Owner** Prof C D Green **Bred** Mrs Caroline Green **Trained** Upper Lambourn, Berks

**FOCUS**
A moderate 3yo sprint handicap.
T/Plt: £80.10 to a £1 stake. Pool of £54389.95 - 495.58 winning tickets. T/Qpdt: £13.40 to a £1 stake. Pool of £3135.34 - 172.90 winning tickets. TM

# 2756 CHESTER (L-H)
## Saturday, June 14

**OFFICIAL GOING: Good (good to firm in places; 7.4)**
Wind: light 1/2 against Weather: fine and sunny

## 3215 HALEWOOD INTERNATIONAL MAIDEN STKS (BOBIS RACE) 5f 16y
**3:05** (3:09) (Class 4) 2-Y-O **£6,469** (£1,925; £962; £481) **Stalls** Low

Form RPR

**1** **Seve** 2-9-5 0........................................................ RobertWinston 3 81+
(Tom Dascombe) *fast away: mde all: edgd rt jst ins fnl f: styd on strly* **11/2**

6 **2** *1 ½* **Crawford Avenue**[36] 2107 2-9-0 0................................ AdamKirby 4 71
(Clive Cox) *chsd ldrs: 2nd over 1f out: chalng whn edgd lft 1f out: kpt on same pce* **3/1**[2]

5 **3** *1 ½* **Anonymous John (IRE)**[14] 2756 2-9-5 0........................ FrannyNorton 5 72+
(David Evans) *mid-div: hdwy 2f out: sn swtchd rt: kpt on fnl f* **9/2**[3]

03 **4** *6* **Grazed Knees (IRE)**[13] 2800 2-9-5 0............................ SeanLevey 1 49
(David Brown) *mid-div: effrt 2f out: nvr a factor* **9/4**[1]

4 **5** *¾* **Spend A Penny (IRE)**[29] 2291 2-9-5 0.......................... PhillipMakin 9 46
(John Quinn) *hld up in rr-div: hdwy 2f out: nvr nr ldrs* **5/1**

04 **6** *¾* **Lady Zodiac (IRE)**[17] 2680 2-9-0 0.......................... StevieDonohoe 6 39
(Tim Pitt) *mid-div: sme hdwy over 1f out: nvr a factor* **50/1**

**7** *nse* **Fast Scat (USA)** 2-9-0 0........................................ AdrianNicholls 2 38
(David Evans) *dwlt: in rr: sme hdwy over 1f out: nvr on terms* **22/1**

0 **8** *1 ½* **Miss Mullberry**[19] 2601 2-9-0 0.................................. PJMcDonald 8 33
(David O'Meara) *chsd wnr: wknd over 1f out* **20/1**

06 **9** *hd* **Featsdontfailmenow**[28] 2348 2-8-9 0.......................... ShirleyTeasdale(5) 7 32
(Lisa Williamson) *chsd ldrs: lost pl over 1f out* **100/1**

4 **10** *2 ¼* **Little Belter (IRE)**[13] 2800 2-9-5 0............................ StephenCraine 11 29
(Tom Dascombe) *a in rr* **14/1**

000 **11** *4 ½* **Toni's A Star**[19] 2601 2-9-0 0.................................. RaulDaSilva 10 8
(Paul Green) *awkward to load: a in rr: bhd fnl 2f* **50/1**

1m 1.62s (0.62) **Going Correction** 0.0s/f (Good) **11** Ran SP% **126.7**
Speed ratings (Par 95): **95,92,90,80,79 78,78,75,75,71 64**
CSF £23.38 TOTE £7.90: £3.30, £1.10, £2.00; EX 28.70 Trifecta £88.90.
**Owner** Mrs P Good **Bred** Mrs P Good **Trained** Malpas, Cheshire

**FOCUS**
There was just 0.5mm of rain overnight and the ground was given as good, good to firm in places. After riding in the opener, Stephen Craine said "The ground felt on the quicker side of good" and Sean Levey said "It's good to firm." The winning time of 1min 1.62 sec was 2.02sec over Racing Post standard, suggesting the ground was between good and good to firm. One or two of these had already shown fair form, but it went to an above average newcomer. The first three were clear.

## 3216 LAMBRINI H'CAP 6f 18y
**3:40** (3:41) (Class 4) (0-85,83) 4-Y-O+ **£6,469** (£1,925; £962; £481) **Stalls** Low

Form RPR

0-00 **1** **Springinmystep (IRE)**[22] 2522 5-9-2 **78**........................ FrannyNorton 2 88
(Ed de Giles) *in rr: hdwy on inner and n.m.r 2f out: styd on wl fnl f: led nr fin* **7/1**

1120 **2** *hd* **Lexi's Hero (IRE)**[117] 644 6-9-7 **83**..............................(v) PJMcDonald 3 92
(Richard Fahey) *led over 1f: led over 1f out: no ex and hdd nr fin* **4/1**[1]

0-20 **3** *1 ¾* **Tango Sky (IRE)**[8] 2953 5-8-12 **74**............................ PatrickMathers 8 77+
(Richard Fahey) *s.i.s: hdwy over 1f out: styd on to take 3rd post* **16/1**

-040 **4** *nse* **Panther Patrol (IRE)**[25] 2414 4-8-4 **66**........................(v) AdrianNicholls 4 69
(Eve Johnson Houghton) *chsd ldrs: drvn over 2f out: kpt on same pce fnl f* **6/1**

001 **5** *½* **Monumental Man**[30] 2275 5-9-6 **82**..................................(p) AdamKirby 6 84
(James Unett) *chsd ldr: led over 4f out: hdd over 1f out: fdd fnl f* **11/2**[3]

0250 **6** *2 ¼* **Smokethatthunders (IRE)**[28] 2341 4-8-8 **70**..........(tp) StevieDonohoe 1 64
(Tim Pitt) *in rr-div: sme hdwy 2f out: nvr nr ldrs* **5/1**[2]

0023 **7** *¾* **Cruise Tothelimit (IRE)**[12] 2849 6-9-0 **81**........................ JoeyHaynes(5) 7 73
(Ian Williams) *chsd ldrs: drvn over 2f out: fdd over 1f out* **4/1**[1]

0150 **8** *8* **Lastchancelucas**[15] 2732 4-8-12 **81**.............................. LukeLeadbitter(7) 5 47
(Declan Carroll) *in rr: drvn over 2f out: sn lost pl: eased whn bhd ins fnl f* **7/1**

1m 13.78s (-0.02) **Going Correction** 0.0s/f (Good) **8** Ran SP% **117.2**
Speed ratings (Par 105): **100,99,97,97,96 93,92,82**
CSF £36.03 CT £441.08 TOTE £6.70: £1.80, £2.40, £10.40; EX 29.80 Trifecta £1205.80.
**Owner** T Gould **Bred** Dr D Harron **Trained** Ledbury, H'fords
■ Stewards' Enquiry : Franny Norton trainer said, regarding apparent improvement in form, that the gelding was better suited by the track and the good (good to firm in places) ground.

**FOCUS**
A fair handicap featuring exposed horses. It was sound run and the form is rated through the second to his winter AW form.

## 3217 CRABBIE'S ORIGINAL H'CAP 1m 2f 75y
**4:15** (4:17) (Class 2) (0-105,100) 3-Y-O+ **£32,345** (£9,625; £4,810; £2,405) **Stalls** High

Form RPR

-123 **1** **Running Deer (IRE)**[22] 2501 5-8-4 **85**........................ LouisSteward(5) 6 97
(Eve Johnson Houghton) *in rr: hdwy over 3f out: led 1f out: styd on wl* **8/1**

0 **2** *1 ¾* **Tahira (GER)**[31] 2253 4-9-7 **97**.................................. PhillipMakin 7 105
(John Quinn) *mid-div: hdwy 3f out: chsd wnr last 75yds: no imp* **5/1**[3]

0050 **3** *2 ¼* **Strictly Silver (IRE)**[19] 2618 5-8-8 **89**..........................(p) TimClark(5) 13 92
(Alan Bailey) *prom: effrt over 3f out: 2nd over 1f out: kpt on same pce* **14/1**

3356 **4** *1* **Energia Davos (BRZ)**[77] 1170 6-9-5 **100**................ MarcMonaghan(5) 9 102
(Marco Botti) *mid-div: hdwy over 3f out: styd on fnl f* **20/1**

0601 **5** *½* **Las Verglas Star (IRE)**[14] 2762 6-8-9 **85**.................... PatrickMathers 8 86
(Richard Fahey) *in rr: hdwy 3f out: styd on over 1f out: nt rch ldrs* **12/1**

1006 **6** *nk* **Life And Times (USA)**[11] 2868 6-8-3 **79**...................... FrannyNorton 12 79
(Mark Johnston) *s.i.s: hdwy on ins over 2f out: kpt on: nt rch ldrs* **16/1**

3053 **7** *1 ½* **Marcret (ITY)**[14] 2758 7-9-3 **93**.................................. PJMcDonald 2 90
(David O'Meara) *trckd ldrs on inner: effrt over 1f out: wknd last 150yds* **4/1**[2]

12-6 **8** *shd* **Croquembouche (IRE)**[66] 1399 5-8-12 **88**........................ SeanLevey 3 85
(Ed de Giles) *led: hdd 1f out: fdd* **8/1**

-220 **9** *18* **Pilgrims Rest (IRE)**[14] 2760 5-8-13 **89**...................... StevieDonohoe 5 52
(Tim Pitt) *chsd ldrs: effrt over 3f out: sn lost pl and bhd: t.o* **14/1**

4523 **10** *8* **Modernism**[14] 2779 5-9-0 **90** ow1.................................. AdamKirby 14 38
(David Simcock) *mid-div: lost pl 3f out: sn bhd: t.o* **16/1**

0-21 **11** *4 ½* **Stellar Express (IRE)**[37] 2091 5-9-2 **92**...................... RobertWinston 11 31
(Michael Appleby) *trckd ldrs: drvn over 3f out: lost pl over 2f out: bhd and eased over 1f out: t.o* **7/2**[1]

00-0 **12** *5* **Montaser (IRE)**[38] 2073 5-9-6 **96**.............................. StephenCraine 10 25
(David Simcock) *s.i.s: in rr: bhd fnl 3f: t.o* **20/1**

2m 8.74s (-2.46) **Going Correction** 0.0s/f (Good) **12** Ran SP% **123.4**
Speed ratings (Par 109): **109,107,105,105,104 104,103,103,88,82 78,74**
CSF £49.81 CT £560.97 TOTE £9.60: £2.40, £2.20, £2.60; EX 60.20 Trifecta £1506.50 Part won..
**Owner** W H Ponsonby **Bred** Mrs E Henry **Trained** Blewbury, Oxon

**FOCUS**
A decent handicap, although luck in running played a part. The form looks sound enough among the principals.

## 3218 TSINGTAO CHINESE BEER FILLIES' H'CAP 1m 4f 66y
**4:50** (4:51) (Class 4) (0-85,83) 4-Y-O+ **£6,469** (£1,925; £962; £481) **Stalls** Low

Form RPR

1220 **1** **Wilhana (IRE)**[22] 2520 4-9-2 **78**.................................. StephenCraine 5 85
(Pam Sly) *led: drvn 3f out: clr 2f out: kpt on: unchal* **14/1**

22-3 **2** *1* **Missed Call (IRE)**[28] 2331 4-9-7 **83**.............................. FrannyNorton 3 88+
(Martyn Meade) *s.i.s: sn chsng ldrs: styd on and 2nd over 1f out: kpt on: nt rch wnr* **6/4**[1]

-202 **3** *1 ½* **Vicky Valentine**[16] 2701 4-8-4 **66** ow2.............................. PJMcDonald 6 69
(Alistair Whillans) *in rr: pushed along over 5f out: hdwy 2f: kpt on to take 3rd in clsng stages* **12/1**

4142 **4** *hd* **Taro Tywod (IRE)**[8] 2947 5-8-8 **70**................................ RobertWinston 2 74+
(Mark Brisbourne) *hld up in mid-div: hdwy over 3f out: hmpd 2f out: nt clr run 1f out: kpt on: fin 5th: plcd 4th* **9/2**[3]

0-04 **5** *nse* **Magic Art (IRE)**[28] 2331 4-9-1 **82**............................ MarcMonaghan(5) 1 85+
(Marco Botti) *trckd ldrs: t.k.h: drvn and hmpd over 2f out: one pce: fin 6th: plcd 5th* **15/2**

6-31 **6** *1* **Pandorica**[12] 2834 6-8-10 **72**.......................................(p) StevieDonohoe 7 74
(Bernard Llewellyn) *chsd ldrs: drvn over 2f out: hung lft: kpt on same pce fnl f: fin 4th: disqualified and plcd 6th* **14/1**

0-01 **7** *4* **Lady Of Yue**[19] 2628 4-8-4 **71**.................................... LouisSteward(5) 4 66+
(Eugene Stanford) *hld up in rr: effrt over 3f out: wknd 2f out* **7/2**[2]

2m 40.45s (1.95) **Going Correction** 0.0s/f (Good) **7** Ran SP% **113.2**
Speed ratings (Par 102): **93,92,91,90,90 90,87**
CSF £34.93 TOTE £14.20: £5.90, £1.10; EX 42.30 Trifecta £300.40.
**Owner** David L Bayliss **Bred** Darley **Trained** Thorney, Cambs

**FOCUS**
A tactical affair in which Stephen Craine dictated a sedate gallop aboard the winner. The winner is rated to the bset view of his previous form.

## 3219 CRABBIE'S STRAWBERRY AND LIME H'CAP (BOBIS RACE) 5f 16y
**5:25** (5:26) (Class 3) (0-95,93) 3-Y-O **£9,703** (£2,887; £1,443; £721) **Stalls** Low

Form RPR
-240 1 **Peterkin (IRE)**[14] 2778 3-8-13 **85** FrannyNorton 3 96
(Mark Johnston) *mde all: drvn over 1f out: kpt on wl* 3/1[2]
1514 2 1 1/4 **Scarborough (IRE)**[29] 2317 3-8-8 **80** RobertWinston 1 86
(Michael Appleby) *mid-div: hdwy over 2f out: 3rd over 1f out: 2nd ins fnl f: kpt on* 11/4[1]
5-31 3 1 3/4 **Noble Asset**[33] 2217 3-8-2 **74** RaulDaSilva 4 74
(John Quinn) *chsd ldrs 2nd over 1f out: kpt on same pce* 14/1
4401 4 3/4 **Captain Myles (IRE)**[25] 2429 3-8-7 **79** (b) StevieDonohoe 7 76
(Tim Pitt) *dwlt: in rr: hdwy 2f out: styd on fnl f* 20/1
2101 5 3/4 **Piazon**[19] 2626 3-8-13 **90** LouisSteward(5) 5 84
(Michael Bell) *in rr: hdwy over 1f out: nvr nr to chal* 6/1
31-2 6 2 1/4 **Speed Hawk (USA)**[29] 2317 3-9-6 **92** PJMcDonald 9 78+
(Robert Cowell) *in rr: hdwy 2f out: kpt on: nvr nr ldrs* 4/1[3]
-454 7 2 1/4 **Lexington Abbey**[14] 2768 3-8-10 **82** NickyMackay 8 60
(Kevin Ryan) *in rr: sme hdwy over 1f out: nvr a factor* 20/1
45-0 8 2 1/4 **Excel's Beauty**[56] 1572 3-9-7 **93** (b) SeanLevey 2 63
(James Tate) *w wnr: wknd over 1f out* 8/1
5-56 9 1 **Fine 'n Dandy (IRE)**[36] 2116 3-9-6 **92** StephenCraine 6 58
(Tom Dascombe) *mid-div: lost pl 2f out* 20/1
2-00 10 1 1/4 **Pushkin Museum (IRE)**[37] 2090 3-8-6 **78** PatrickMathers 10 40
(Richard Fahey) *in rr: bhd fnl 2f* 40/1
1m 0.49s (-0.51) **Going Correction** 0.0s/f (Good) **10** Ran SP% **120.5**
Speed ratings (Par 103): **104,102,99,98,96 93,89,86,84,82**
CSF £11.46 CT £100.26 TOTE £3.40: £1.10, £1.80, £6.50; EX 13.70 Trifecta £128.90.
**Owner** Sheikh Hamdan bin Mohammed Al Maktoum **Bred** Darley **Trained** Middleham Moor, N Yorks

**FOCUS**
The first three were well placed. The winner recorded a small personal best.

## 3220 LAMB'S NAVY RUM FILLIES' H'CAP 7f 122y
**5:55** (5:57) (Class 4) (0-80,79) 4-Y-O+ **£6,469** (£1,925; £962; £481) **Stalls** Low

Form RPR
-552 1 **Lulu The Zulu (IRE)**[25] 2448 6-9-2 **74** RaulDaSilva 9 85
(Michael Appleby) *dwlt: swtchd lft after s: in rr: hdwy and swtchd outside over 1f out: styd on wl to ld last 100yds* 5/2[1]
1003 2 2 3/4 **Celtic Sixpence (IRE)**[8] 2954 6-9-3 **75** MichaelStainton 1 79
(Nick Kent) *led: hdd 5f out: 2nd over 1f out: styd on same pce last 150yds* 6/1[3]
5116 3 1 3/4 **Real Tigress (IRE)**[35] 2169 5-9-2 **74** RobertWinston 2 77+
(Les Eyre) *w ldrs: rt hand rein sn snapped: led 5f out: hdd last 100yds: eased* 5/2[1]
5314 4 3/4 **Kosika (USA)**[19] 2608 4-9-6 **78** FrannyNorton 5 76
(Mark Johnston) *chsd ldrs: kpt on one pce over 1f out* 9/2[2]
/055 5 6 **La Danza**[24] 2454 4-7-11 **60** oh2 ShirleyTeasdale(5) 4 43
(Lisa Williamson) *mid-div: drvn and sme hdwy over 2f out: sn wl outpcd* 25/1
100- 6 3/4 **Mandy The Nag (USA)**[264] 6700 4-9-1 **73** PatrickMathers 3 54
(Richard Fahey) *mid-div: effrt over 2f out: nvr a factor* 11/1
15-6 7 15 **Dutch Mistress**[19] 2608 5-8-9 **67** StevieDonohoe 7 10
(James Unett) *chsd ldrs: lost pl over 2f out: sn wl bhd: t.o* 16/1
1m 32.81s (-0.99) **Going Correction** 0.0s/f (Good) **7** Ran SP% **107.7**
Speed ratings (Par 102): **104,101,99,98,92 92,77**
CSF £15.70 CT £30.04 TOTE £3.80: £1.20, £3.40; EX 20.70 Trifecta £55.40.
**Owner** The Ab Kettlebys **Bred** Hong Kong Breeders Club **Trained** Danethorpe, Notts
■ Rule 4 of 10p in the pound applies to all bets; Withdrawn: Silvas Romana

**FOCUS**
The second, third and fourth held the first three positions for most of the race. A length personal best from the winner.

## 3221 CRABBIE'S SCOTTISH RASPBERRY H'CAP 7f 122y
**6:25** (6:28) (Class 4) (0-85,85) 3-Y£18,903 (£5,658; £2,829; £1,416; £705) **Stalls** Low

Form RPR
1334 1 **Dubai Dynamo**[11] 2869 9-9-9 **84** PJMcDonald 2 94
(Ruth Carr) *mid-div: drvn over 2f out: hdwy on ins over 1f out: styd on wl to ld ins fnl f* 4/1[1]
2002 2 2 **Piceno (IRE)**[10] 2905 6-9-0 **80** (p) MatthewHopkins(5) 4 85
(Scott Dixon) *led: hdd and no ex ins fnl f* 8/1
-001 3 hd **Johnno**[19] 2603 5-9-6 **81** (b) AdrianNicholls 16 86
(David Nicholls) *w ldr: kpt on same pce last 150yds* 8/1
2501 4 shd **Swift Cedar (IRE)**[26] 2381 4-9-0 **75** FrannyNorton 10 79+
(David Evans) *hld up in rr: hdwy on inner over 2f out: styd on ins fnl f* 8/1
5205 5 1 1/2 **Hadaj**[14] 2778 5-9-8 **83** (p) SeanLevey 7 84
(Ruth Carr) *chsd ldrs: kpt on one pce appr fnl f* 5/1[2]
016- 6 1 3/4 **Gatepost (IRE)**[235] 7452 5-9-7 **82** PatrickMathers 5 78
(Richard Fahey) *in rr: hdwy over 2f out: kpt on: nt rch ldrs* 14/1
3522 7 2 1/4 **Powerful Presence (IRE)**[8] 2953 8-9-5 **83** JulieBurke(3) 17 74
(David O'Meara) *hld up in rr: hdwy over 2f out: kpt on fnl f: nvr a threat* 14/1
-000 8 1 **Postscript (IRE)**[49] 1721 6-9-10 **85** RobertWinston 8 73
(David Simcock) *mid-div: hdwy over 2f out: nvr a factor* 7/1[3]
2000 9 1/2 **Brocklebank (IRE)**[8] 2959 5-9-8 **83** NickyMackay 1 70
(Simon Dow) *s.s: bhd: sme hdwy over 2f out: nvr on terms* 12/1
5235 10 3/4 **Capaill Liath (IRE)**[24] 2469 6-9-4 **79** (p) AmyRyan 6 64
(Kevin Ryan) *in rr: sme hdwy over 1f out: nvr on terms* 12/1
2-50 11 9 **Talent Scout (IRE)**[42] 1957 8-9-0 **82** (p) GemmaTutty(7) 12 44
(Karen Tutty) *chsd ldrs: lost pl over 1f out* 20/1
3306 12 nk **King Of Eden (IRE)**[14] 2763 8-8-9 **75** MarcMonaghan(5) 15 37
(Eric Alston) *s.s: a bhd* 25/1
20/0 13 4 1/2 **Gabrial's Bounty (IRE)**[36] 2117 5-9-5 **80** StephenCraine 3 30
(Richard Fahey) *chsd ldrs: wknd appr fnl f* 16/1
-600 14 38 **Best Trip (IRE)**[7] 2992 7-9-8 **83** PaulPickard 11
(Brian Ellison) *mid-div: lost pl over 3f out: sn bhd: t.o whn eased over 1f out: virtually p.u* 14/1
1m 32.29s (-1.51) **Going Correction** 0.0s/f (Good) **14** Ran SP% **132.4**
Speed ratings (Par 105): **107,105,104,104,103 101,99,98,97,96 87,87,83,45**
CSF £39.68 CT £269.46 TOTE £5.30: £1.80, £3.00, £2.70; EX 35.30 Trifecta £870.30 Part won..
**Owner** The Bottom Liners **Bred** T K & Mrs P A Knox **Trained** Huby, N Yorks

**FOCUS**
They seemed to go pretty quick here, but for all that the winner, who likes a strong pace to run at, came from midfield, the second and third were up there the whole way. The winner's best figure for a year.
T/Plt: £174.30 to a £1 stake. Pool of £55588.29 - 232.81 winning tickets. T/Qpdt: £28.50 to a £1 stake. Pool of £3493.03 - 90.50 winning tickets. WG

# 2837 LEICESTER (R-H)
Saturday, June 14

**OFFICIAL GOING: Good (good to firm in places)**
Wind: Light against Weather: Overcast

## 3222 SIX HILLS H'CAP 5f 2y
**6:15** (6:16) (Class 5) (0-70,70) 3-Y-O+ **£3,234** (£962; £481; £240) **Stalls** High

Form RPR
14-0 1 **Poyle Vinnie**[32] 2233 4-9-6 **65** RyanPowell(3) 9 76
(George Margarson) *a.p: chsd ldr 4f out: led over 1f out: rdn out* 7/1[3]
-000 2 3/4 **Noodles Blue Boy**[27] 2364 8-9-9 **70** (p) JacobButterfield(5) 7 78
(Ollie Pears) *mid-div: sn pushed along: hdwy over 1f out: r.o* 8/1
4260 3 nk **Solemn**[16] 2691 9-9-9 **65** (v) FrederikTylicki 8 72
(Milton Bradley) *mid-div: sn pushed along: hdwy u.p over 1f out: r.o* 5/1[2]
1406 4 1 1/2 **West Coast Dream**[25] 2434 7-9-6 **65** DeclanBates(3) 11 67
(Roy Brotherton) *led 4f out: rdn and hdd over 1f out: styd on same pce ins fnl f* 9/1
10-0 5 1 3/4 **Passionada**[145] 259 5-9-8 **64** MartinLane 4 59
(Ed McMahon) *led 1f: chsd ldrs: rdn over 1f out: no ex fnl f* 8/1
55-0 6 1/2 **Comptonspirit**[25] 2414 10-9-9 **65** SaleemGolam 1 58
(Brian Baugh) *chsd ldrs: lost pl over 3f out: r.o ins fnl f* 20/1
0450 7 1 1/4 **Ceelo**[10] 2887 4-8-13 **58** (b) SimonPearce(3) 2 47
(Lydia Pearce) *chsd ldrs: rdn and hung rt over 1f out: wknd fnl f* 5/1[2]
-000 8 nse **Rylee Mooch**[27] 2364 6-9-7 **70** (e) KieranShoemark(7) 12 59
(Richard Guest) *chsd ldrs: rdn and hung lft over 1f out: wknd fnl f* 11/1
200- 9 2 3/4 **Baby Queen (IRE)**[296] 5669 8-9-11 **67** JimmyQuinn 6 46
(Brian Baugh) *chsd ldrs: rdn over 1f out: sn wknd* 12/1
00-0 10 1 1/4 **Irish Boy (IRE)**[25] 2434 6-9-2 **65** (tp) JoeDoyle(7) 10 39
(Christine Dunnett) *sn pushed along in rr: bhd fr 1/2-way* 25/1
-100 11 shd **Walta (IRE)**[35] 2163 3-8-11 **65** (b) PhilipPrince(5) 3 36
(Roy Bowring) *s.i.s: nvr on terms* 20/1
0-00 12 13 **Saga Lout**[16] 2691 4-9-4 **60** (p) KieranO'Neill 5
(Ray Peacock) *sn pushed along in rr: bhd fr 1/2-way* 66/1
1m 0.87s (0.87) **Going Correction** +0.05s/f (Good)
**WFA** 3 from 4yo+ 7lb **12** Ran SP% **118.8**
Speed ratings (Par 103): **95,93,93,90,88 87,85,85,80,78 78,57**
CSF £59.15 CT £309.34 TOTE £9.10: £3.20, £3.30, £1.50; EX 80.70 Trifecta £222.60.
**Owner** Cecil And Miss Alison Wiggins **Bred** Cecil And Miss Alison Wiggins **Trained** Newmarket, Suffolk
■ Stewards' Enquiry : Philip Prince five-day ban: used whip when out of contention (Jun 28-Jul 2)

**FOCUS**
Few came into this weak handicap with a semblance of any form, but the form makes sense. They raced predominantly up the centre of the track and it was one of the lesser exposed horses who won.

## 3223 TONY GIBBONS HITS BIG SIXTY MAIDEN FILLIES' STKS (BOBIS RACE) 5f 218y
**6:45** (6:47) (Class 5) 2-Y-O **£3,234** (£962; £481; £240) **Stalls** High

Form RPR
0 1 **Calypso Beat (USA)**[24] 2460 2-8-7 0 JoeDoyle(7) 3 75
(Kevin Ryan) *mde all: shkn up over 1f out: styd on* 20/1
2 1/2 **Shahralasal (IRE)** 2-9-0 0 PaulHanagan 5 74+
(Roger Varian) *a.p: chsd wnr over 1f out: sn rdn: edgd lft and ev ch: styd on* 7/4[1]
3 1 1/4 **Taaqah (USA)** 2-9-0 0 JimmyQuinn 11 70+
(James Tate) *hld up: hdwy 1/2-way: rdn and hung rt fr over 1f out: styd on* 5/1[2]
4 2 1/2 **Finial** 2-9-0 0 AdamKirby 10 62+
(Clive Cox) *trckd wnr tl rdn over 1f out: hmpd and no ex ins fnl f* 10/1
5 1 1/4 **Pulcinella (IRE)** 2-9-0 0 MartinLane 2 59
(Charlie Appleby) *s.i.s: sn mid-div: hdwy over 2f out: rdn over 1f out: no ex fnl f* 7/1[3]
6 2 3/4 **Maybe Now Baby (IRE)** 2-9-0 0 LukeMorris 1 50
(David Simcock) *s.i.s: hld up: stmbld 4f out: rdn over 1f out: hung lft ins fnl f: n.d* 12/1
6 7 1 1/2 **Oud Malakiy (IRE)**[33] 2200 2-9-0 0 FrederikTylicki 8 46
(Richard Fahey) *rdn over 2f out: wknd fnl f* 16/1
0 8 3/4 **Larch (IRE)**[24] 2460 2-9-0 0 KieranO'Neill 9 44
(Richard Hannon) *prom: rdn over 2f out: wknd over 1f out* 12/1
0 9 2 **Whoopie Do**[49] 1726 2-8-9 0 JoeyHaynes(5) 7 38
(John Gallagher) *s.i.s: hld up: pushed along 1/2-way: wknd over 1f out* 50/1
0054 10 nk **Seamoor Secret**[25] 2436 2-9-0 0 HayleyTurner 6 37
(Alex Hales) *mid-div: rdn over 2f out: wknd over 1f out* 10/1
11 2 3/4 **Hawkin (IRE)** 2-9-0 0 OscarPereira 4 28
(Ralph Beckett) *s.i.s: sn pushed along in rr: wknd over 2f out* 20/1
1m 14.2s (1.20) **Going Correction** +0.05s/f (Good) **11** Ran SP% **116.5**
Speed ratings (Par 90): **94,93,91,88,86 83,81,80,77,76 73**
CSF £53.64 TOTE £25.30: £6.20, £1.10, £1.40; EX 88.90 Trifecta £896.90.
**Owner** Cockerill Hillen & Graham **Bred** P Cockerill, S Graham & Sh Bloodstock **Trained** Hambleton, N Yorks

**FOCUS**
Probably an ordinary maiden with the market headed by two newcomers. The centre of the track was again the place to be and it was one with previous experience who drew clear with the market leaders.

## 3224 HARBY CLAIMING STKS 1m 1f 218y
**7:15** (7:15) (Class 6) 3-4-Y-O **£1,940** (£577; £288; £144) **Stalls** Low

Form RPR
-460 1 **Gabrial The Duke (IRE)**[14] 2762 4-9-7 66 (p) AdamKirby 8 66
(David Simcock) *led after 1f: qcknd over 3f out: hdd over 2f out: sn rdn: rallied to ld and edgd lft ins fnl f: styd on* 2/1[1]
6434 2 1/2 **Ronya (IRE)**[26] 2393 3-8-0 58 JoeyHaynes(5) 6 61
(K R Burke) *a.p: jnd ldrs over 2f out: rdn to ld over 1f out: hdd and n.m.r ins fnl f: styd on* 4/1

-642 **3** ½ **Travis Bickle (IRE)**[8] 2948 3-8-7 63 LukeMorris 4 62
(Sylvester Kirk) *hld up: hdwy over 3f out: led over 2f out: rdn and hdd over 1f out: kpt on* **7/2**[3]

406 **4** 7 **Handsome Stranger (IRE)**[53] 1638 4-9-7 63 (v) FrederikTylicki 5 51
(Alan Bailey) *chsd ldrs: rdn over 2f out: wknd over 1f out* **8/1**

-432 **5** 17 **Banreenahreenkah (IRE)**[19] 2609 4-8-8 58 (tp) KieranShoemark(7) 7 12
(Paul Fitzsimons) *plld hrd and prom: trckd wnr 8f out tl rdn over 2f out: wknd wl over 1f out* **3/1**[2]

00- **6** 16 **Shock**[304] 5399 3-8-8 0 [1] KimberleyVanderVegt(7) 2
(Daniel Kubler) *s.i.s: a bhd* **66/1**

0000 **7** 4 **Tingle Tangle (USA)**[16] 2689 4-9-5 42 (t) JimmyQuinn 3
(Tony Carroll) *hld up: rdn and wknd wl over 2f out* **33/1**

00 **8** 23 **Ninny Noodle**[16] 2696 4-8-11 0 DeclanBates(3) 1
(Miss Imogen Pickard) *led 1f: chsd ldrs tl rdn and wknd over 3f out* **66/1**

2m 7.27s (-0.63) **Going Correction** +0.05s/f (Good)
**WFA** 3 from 4yo 13lb **8** Ran SP% **117.6**
Speed ratings (Par 101): **104,103,103,97,84 71,68,49**
CSF £10.77 TOTE £2.70: £1.10, £1.60, £1.60; EX 13.20 Trifecta £40.90.Travis Bickle was claimed by J L Flint for £7000.
**Owner** Dr Marwan Koukash **Bred** Old Carhue & Graeng Bloodstock **Trained** Newmarket, Suffolk

**FOCUS**
A modest claimer in which the pace was fair and there was a rousing finish with a trio drawing clear of the remainder. The form is rated around the third.

## 3225 KIRBY GATE H'CAP (BOBIS RACE) 5f 218y
**7:45** (7:45) (Class 4) (0-80,80) 3-Y-O **£6,469** (£1,925; £962; £481) **Stalls** High

Form RPR

-656 **1** **Quiet Warrior (IRE)**[28] 2333 3-9-7 **80** (b[1]) MartinHarley 3 89
(Marco Botti) *hld up: hdwy over 1f out: rdn to ld and edgd lft ins fnl f: r.o* **7/1**

2140 **2** hd **Elusive George (IRE)**[42] 1940 3-8-5 **71** JoeDoyle(7) 13 79
(John Quinn) *mid-div: hdwy over 1f out: rdn and ev ch ins fnl f: r.o* **12/1**

1-50 **3** 3¼ **Look Here's Al**[25] 2429 3-8-9 **68** JimmyQuinn 8 66
(Andrew Hollinshead) *hld up: rdn over 1f out: r.o to go 3rd nr fin: nt trble ldrs* **25/1**

3100 **4** nk **Android (IRE)**[8] 2945 3-9-3 **76** (v[1]) AdamKirby 7 73
(Clive Cox) *plld hrd and prom: led over 3f out: rdn and hdd over 1f out: ev ch whn hmpd ins fnl f: no ex* **14/1**

-623 **5** 1½ **Baars Causeway (IRE)**[17] 2686 3-8-3 **67** TimClark(5) 1 59
(Timothy Jarvis) *w ldrs: racd keenly: led over 1f out: rdn: edgd lft and hdd ins fnl f: no ex* **20/1**

110 **6** 1¼ **Desert Ranger (IRE)**[59] 1518 3-9-3 **76** LukeMorris 4 64
(James Tate) *hld up in tch: plld hrd: rdn over 2f out: styd on same pce fr over 1f out* **8/1**

4-35 **7** ¾ **Gold Club**[25] 2429 3-8-9 **68** FrederikTylicki 10 54
(Ed McMahon) *trckd ldrs: rdn over 2f out: wknd ins fnl f* **9/2**[2]

0-12 **8** shd **Iftaar (IRE)**[22] 2508 3-9-5 **78** PaulHanagan 12 63
(Charles Hills) *led: hdd over 3f out: chsd ldrs: rdn over 1f out: wknd ins fnl f* **11/4**[1]

4-03 **9** 1¼ **Wickhambrook (IRE)**[15] 2734 3-9-3 **76** MartinLane 5 57
(Ismail Mohammed) *hld up: rdn over 2f out: hdwy over 1f out: sn edgd rt and wknd* **11/2**[3]

0-66 **10** 1¼ **Smart Salute**[9] 2921 3-9-2 **75** (p) HayleyTurner 6 52
(Ed Walker) *s.i.s: sme hdwy over 2f out: rdn and wknd over 1f out* **9/1**

1m 12.64s (-0.36) **Going Correction** +0.05s/f (Good) **10** Ran SP% **116.8**
Speed ratings (Par 101): **104,103,99,99,97 95,94,94,92,90**
CSF £87.57 CT £2018.89 TOTE £7.70: £2.10, £3.30, £4.20; EX 109.80 Trifecta £954.50 Part won..
**Owner** Global First Racing & Bloodstock **Bred** John R Jeffers **Trained** Newmarket, Suffolk

**FOCUS**
The centre of the track was again the place to be for this competitive 3yo handicap. The form looks useful despite some disappointments among the market leaders. The winner belatedly built on his maiden win.

## 3226 EAST LEAKE H'CAP 1m 3f 183y
**8:15** (8:16) (Class 5) (0-75,74) 4-Y-O+ **£3,234** (£962; £481; £240) **Stalls** Low

Form RPR

3526 **1** **Flying Power**[22] 2520 6-9-0 **72** JacobButterfield(5) 10 81
(John Norton) *led 4f: chsd ldr tl led again over 4f out: rdn over 1f out: styd on gamely* **12/1**

31-0 **2** hd **Wall Street Boss (USA)**[47] 1798 4-9-1 **68** FrederikTylicki 6 77
(James Fanshawe) *a.p: chsd wnr over 2f out: rdn and ev ch ins fnl f: styd on* **7/1**[2]

43-5 **3** hd **Poetic Verse**[15] 2728 4-8-9 **69** JoeDoyle(7) 7 77+
(John Quinn) *hld up: hdwy over 2f out: rdn and hung rt over 1f out: ev ch ins fnl f: styd on* **5/1**[1]

-003 **4** 3½ **Hurry Home Poppa (IRE)**[11] 2872 4-8-9 **62** JimmyQuinn 1 65
(John Mackie) *mid-div: hdwy over 4f out: rdn over 2f out: styd on same pce fnl f* **7/1**[2]

0-33 **5** ¾ **Evervescent (IRE)**[11] 2862 5-9-3 **70** AdamKirby 4 72
(Graeme McPherson) *hld up: hdwy 4f out: rdn over 2f out: no ex fnl f* **8/1**

1356 **6** 3¼ **A Little Bit Dusty**[20] 1628 6-9-7 **74** (b) HayleyTurner 14 70
(Conor Dore) *chsd ldrs: rdn over 2f out: wknd fnl f* **8/1**

0-52 **7** 2½ **Master Of Song**[9] 2935 7-7-13 **57** ow2 (p) PhilipPrince(5) 2 49
(Roy Bowring) *trckd ldr tl led 8f out: hdd over 4f out: rdn and wknd over 1f out* **12/1**

10-0 **8** 4½ **Bold Cross (IRE)**[8] 2947 11-8-9 **67** JoeyHaynes(5) 3 52
(Edward Bevan) *hld up: hdwy over 3f out: rdn and wknd over 1f out* **25/1**

0-05 **9** 1 **Rosaceous**[22] 2501 4-9-6 **73** LukeMorris 8 57
(Daniel Kubler) *prom: rdn over 2f out: wknd over 1f out* **15/2**[3]

6565 **10** 2½ **Gabrial The Terror (IRE)**[25] 2444 4-8-12 **65** MartinHarley 5 45
(David Simcock) *s.s and then swvd lft: hdwy to go prom 10f out: rdn and wknd over 2f out* **9/1**

001/ **11** hd **Casual Mover (IRE)**[554] 8020 6-9-0 **67** RobertHavlin 9 46
(John Best) *hld up: hdwy 3f out: sn rdn: wknd 2f out* **33/1**

1-11 **12** 25 **The Ginger Berry**[135] 382 4-8-8 **64** RobertTart(3) 11 3
(Dr Jon Scargill) *hld up: racd keenly: hdwy over 7f out: wknd over 2f out* **5/1**[1]

2m 34.05s (0.15) **Going Correction** +0.05s/f (Good) **12** Ran SP% **124.5**
Speed ratings (Par 103): **101,100,100,98,97 95,94,91,90,88 88,71**
CSF £98.37 CT £489.43 TOTE £12.90: £4.20, £2.40, £2.30; EX 107.20 Trifecta £713.20.
**Owner** Jaffa Racing Syndicate **Bred** Rabbah Bloodstock Limited **Trained** High Hoyland, S Yorks
■ Stewards' Enquiry : Joe Doyle two-day ban: used whip above permitted level (Jun 28-29)

**FOCUS**
The early pace was modest for this fair handicap and they spread across the track with 2f to run. The winner is rated to his old turf best.

## 3227 CREAM GORSE H'CAP 7f 9y
**8:45** (8:45) (Class 4) (0-80,75) 3-Y-O+ **£6,301** (£1,886; £943; £472; £235) **Stalls** High

Form RPR

5304 **1** **Illustrious Prince (IRE)**[12] 2841 7-9-11 **72** FrederikTylicki 6 83
(Julie Camacho) *racd centre: a.p: rdn to chse ldr over 1f out: r.o to ld nr fin* **4/1**[1]

33-4 **2** ½ **Available (IRE)**[159] 69 5-10-0 **75** (tp) JimmyQuinn 2 84
(John Mackie) *overall ldr in centre: shake up over 1f out: hdd nr fin* **10/1**

6106 **3** 5 **Darnathean**[15] 2721 5-8-9 **63** (p) JoeDoyle(7) 5 59
(Paul D'Arcy) *racd centre: hld up: rdn over 1f out: r.o ins fnl f: wnt 3rd nr fin: nt trble ldrs* **7/1**

1240 **4** nk **Llewellyn**[19] 2602 6-9-9 **73** JasonHart(3) 8 68
(Declan Carroll) *racd centre: hld up: hdwy over 2f out: sn rdn: styd on same pce ins fnl f* **10/1**

3060 **5** 2¾ **Daring Dragon**[17] 2687 4-9-9 **70** HayleyTurner 3 58
(Ed Walker) *racd centre: hld up: rdn over 2f out: styd on ins fnl f: nvr nrr* **20/1**

32 **6** hd **Inkerman (IRE)**[10] 2902 4-10-0 **75** AdamKirby 1 63
(Jamie Osborne) *racd centre: trckd ldr tl rdn over 1f out: wknd ins fnl f* **9/2**[2]

03-0 **7** ½ **Galatian**[10] 2884 7-9-3 **67** OisinMurphy(3) 11 53
(Rod Millman) *hld up: racd stands' side tl swtchd centre over 5f out: hdwy over 1f out: sn rdn: wknd ins fnl f* **5/1**[3]

6060 **8** nk **Bogsnog (IRE)**[21] 2549 4-9-5 **71** JacobButterfield(5) 10 56
(Kristin Stubbs) *led stands' side trio tl lft to r alone over 5f out: prom: rdn 1/2-way: wknd fnl f* **12/1**

0-10 **9** 1¾ **Another Try (IRE)**[17] 2684 9-9-10 **71** LukeMorris 9 52
(Timothy Jarvis) *racd stands' side tl swtchd centre over 5f out: chsd ldrs: rdn over 2f out: wknd over 1f out* **8/1**

2215 **10** 1¾ **Clubland (IRE)**[10] 2890 5-9-7 **73** PhilipPrince(5) 4 49
(Roy Bowring) *racd centre: chsd ldrs: rdn over 2f out: wknd fnl f* **10/1**

1m 25.82s (-0.38) **Going Correction** +0.05s/f (Good)
**WFA** 3 from 4yo+ 10lb **10** Ran SP% **118.2**
Speed ratings (Par 105): **104,103,97,97,94 94,93,93,91,89**
CSF £45.10 CT £275.28 TOTE £5.40: £2.10, £4.50, £2.80; EX 54.00 Trifecta £518.10.
**Owner** Lee Bolingbroke,Graeme Howard & Partners **Bred** Rathbarry Stud **Trained** Norton, N Yorks

**FOCUS**
Very few got into this fair sprint handicap, which was run at a generous pace. The form is rated around the runner-up.

## 3228 ASFORDBY H'CAP 5f 2y
**9:15** (9:15) (Class 6) (0-60,62) 3-Y-O **£1,940** (£577; £288; £144) **Stalls** High

Form RPR

-003 **1** **Bashiba (IRE)**[26] 2387 3-8-7 **46** oh1 (t) HayleyTurner 3 56
(Nigel Tinkler) *chsd ldrs: shkn up to ld over 1f out: rdn out* **9/2**[2]

553 **2** 1½ **Champagne Charley**[19] 2625 3-9-4 **60** OisinMurphy(3) 1 64
(Des Donovan) *hld up: hdwy over 1f out: rdn to chse wnr ins fnl f: no ex towards fin* **7/2**[1]

6150 **3** 1¾ **Biscuiteer**[17] 2675 3-9-6 **59** (b) LukeMorris 7 57
(Scott Dixon) *led: rdn and hdd over 1f out: edgd rt and styd on same pce ins fnl f* **8/1**

-661 **4** 2¼ **By Rights**[13] 2802 3-9-4 **62** JoeyHaynes(5) 4 52
(Tony Carroll) *w ldrs: rdn and ev ch over 1f out: wknd ins fnl f* **7/2**[1]

5536 **5** ½ **Artemis (IRE)**[17] 2686 3-9-5 **58** JimmyQuinn 6 46
(Conrad Allen) *hld up: plld hrd: hdwy over 1f out: rdn and wknd ins fnl f* **10/1**

0-00 **6** hd **Classical Diva**[26] 2387 3-8-12 **54** JasonHart(3) 5 41
(Declan Carroll) *trckd ldrs: plld hrd: rdn over 1f out: wknd ins fnl f* **7/1**[3]

2630 **7** 1 **Chuckamental**[11] 2870 3-9-0 **53** (b[1]) RoystonFfrench 8 37
(Bryan Smart) *chsd ldrs: rdn 1/2-way: wknd fnl f* **11/1**

0061 **8** nk **Robbian**[32] 2230 3-9-0 **53** RobbieFitzpatrick 2 36
(Charles Smith) *s.i.s: sn pushed along in rr: n.d* **8/1**

00-0 **9** 3¾ **Triple O Seven (IRE)**[53] 1634 3-8-11 **50** RobertHavlin 9 19
(John Best) *hld up: rdn 1/2-way: wknd over 1f out* **33/1**

1m 1.42s (1.42) **Going Correction** +0.05s/f (Good) **9** Ran SP% **117.7**
Speed ratings (Par 97): **90,87,84,81,80 80,78,78,72**
CSF £21.11 CT £124.42 TOTE £8.00: £1.40, £2.10, £2.20; EX 25.50 Trifecta £136.60.
**Owner** Y T Szeto **Bred** John T Heffernan & Grainne Dooley **Trained** Langton, N Yorks

**FOCUS**
A very modest 3yo sprint handicap with two market leaders having it to themselves from a furlong out.
T/Plt: £402.70 to a £1 stake. Pool of £50450.27 - 91.45 winning tickets. T/Qpdt: £81.30 to a £1 stake. Pool of £5178.30 - 47.10 winning tickets. CR

# 3074 LINGFIELD (L-H)
Saturday, June 14

**OFFICIAL GOING: Turf course - good; all-weather - standard**
Wind: light, half against Weather: warm, bright spells

## 3229 TBA NEXT GENERATION CLUB MEDIAN AUCTION MAIDEN STKS 7f
**6:05** (6:06) (Class 6) 3-4-Y-O **£2,199** (£654; £327; £163) **Stalls** Centre

Form RPR

62 **1** **Doctor Sardonicus**[17] 2681 3-9-2 0 JamieSpencer 5 84
(David Simcock) *mde all and sn crossed to r against stands' rail: rdn over 1f out: battled on wl u.p fnl f: rdn out* **9/2**[3]

223 **2** ½ **Between Wickets**[28] 2339 3-9-2 82 RichardHughes 2 82+
(Marcus Tregoning) *t.k.h early: hld up wl in tch: wnt 3rd 2f out: swtchd lft and drvn over 1f out: styd on to press wnr fnl 100yds: kpt on* **7/4**[2]

54-5 **3** 2 **Whaleweigh Station**[17] 2682 3-9-2 96 RichardKingscote 7 77
(Tom Dascombe) *chsd wnr: rdn and ev ch over 1f out: no ex ins fnl f: lost 2nd and btn fnl 100yds* **6/4**[1]

00 **4** 6 **Goddess Of Gloom**[14] 2780 3-8-12 0 ow1 DaneO'Neill 6 57
(Peter Chapple-Hyam) *s.i.s: hld up in rr: rdn and effrt in centre over 1f out: no ch w ldng trio over 1f out: kpt on to go modest 4th ins fnl f* **50/1**

06 **5** ½ **Royal College**[19] 2625 4-9-12 0 GeorgeBaker 8 64
(Gary Moore) *t.k.h early: hld up wl in tch in midfield: pushed along 2f out: sn outpcd and modest 4th over 1f out: kpt on same pce* **50/1**

00- **6** nk **Clodoaldo (IRE)**[252] 7019 3-8-13 0 RyanClark(3) 4 59
(Brian Meehan) *hld up in last trio: rdn and effrt ent fnl 2f: outpcd and btn over 1f out: wl hld and one pce fnl f* **25/1**

0- **7** *3 ¼* **Abatis (USA)**[313] 5061 3-8-11 0 JamesDoyle 3 46
(Charles Hills) *t.k.h: hld up in tch in midfield: rdn and no rspnse over 2f out: wl btn over 1f out: wknd fnl f* **8/1**

4626 **8** *1 ½* **Sebs Sensei (IRE)**[87] 1008 3-9-2 68 AdamBeschizza 10 47
(Mark Hoad) *dwlt: sn bustled up and hdwy to chse ldrs after 1f: rdn and unable qck 2f out: sn wknd* **25/1**

00- **9** *3 ¾* **Amadiva (IRE)**[213] 7853 3-8-11 0 SamHitchcott 9 32
(Dean Ivory) *hld up in tch in rr: rdn over 2f out: sn struggling: bhd fnl f* **66/1**

1m 24.66s (1.36) **Going Correction** +0.275s/f (Good)
**WFA** 3 from 4yo 10lb **9** Ran SP% **118.8**
Speed ratings (Par 101): **103,102,100,93,92 92,88,86,82**
CSF £12.84 TOTE £5.80: £2.10, £1.10, £1.10; EX 14.80 Trifecta £25.00.
**Owner** Charles Wentworth **Bred** D M James **Trained** Newmarket, Suffolk

**FOCUS**
The first three look above average for maiden grade, while the others are probably waiting for handicaps. The favourite was a long way off last year's Group form. The winner has progressed with each run.

## 3230 SAMWORTH BROTHERS H'CAP 7f
**6:35** (6:36) (Class 6) (0-55,55) 3-Y-O+ **£2,587** (£770; £384; £192) **Stalls** Centre

Form RPR

505- **1** **Royal Caper**[251] 6930 4-8-11 **49** JackGilligan(7) 4 59
(Miss Joey Ellis) *hld up in midfield: hdwy to chse ldr 2f out: ev ch and rdn over 1f out: led ins fnl f: hld on wl cl home* **25/1**

0322 **2** *hd* **Byrd In Hand (IRE)**[4] 3075 7-9-6 **51** (v) WilliamCarson 9 60
(John Bridger) *chsd ldr tl led 1/2-way: drvn and hrd pressed over 1f out: hdd ins fnl f: rallied u.p fnl 50yds: hld cl home* **5/2**[1]

2032 **3** *1 ¼* **Schottische**[47] 1813 4-9-5 **50** (v) DaneO'Neill 2 56
(Derek Haydn Jones) *pushed along early: racd in midfield: hdwy u.p over 1f out: chsd ldrs and one pce u.p fnl f* **7/1**[3]

20-0 **4** *1 ¼* **Clear Loch**[141] 319 4-9-2 **47** RichardHughes 3 50
(John Spearing) *chsd ldrs: rdn and swtchd lft ent fnl 2f: no ex u.p fnl 150yds: wknd towards fin* **10/1**

/00- **5** *1* **Trust Me Boy**[34] 2534 6-9-1 **46** FrankieMcDonald 10 46
(John E Long) *chsd ldrs tl lost pl and rdn 1/2-way: bhd 2f out: rallied 1f out: styd on wl ins fnl f: eased towards fin* **50/1**

00- **6** *¾* **Natalia**[199] 8063 5-9-4 **54** JackDuern(5) 5 52
(Andrew Hollinshead) *stdd s: hld up in rr: effrt on outer 2f out: hdwy over 1f out: kpt on same pce ins fnl f* **25/1**

0554 **6** *dht* **Claude Greenwood**[6] 3035 4-8-10 **46** (b) JoshBaudains(5) 11 44
(Linda Jewell) *in tch in midfield: rdn and effrt to chse ldrs 2f out: no ex 1f out: wknd ins fnl f* **8/1**

500 **8** *2 ¼* **Patronella (IRE)**[84] 1069 3-9-0 **55** JamieSpencer 12 44
(David Simcock) *hld up in tch towards rr: swtchd lft and effrt 2f out: styng on same pce and hld whn nt clr run ins fnl f: eased wl ins fnl f* **4/1**[2]

4502 **9** *3* **Silvee**[11] 2864 7-9-4 **49** (p) SamHitchcott 1 34
(John Bridger) *slowly away and swtchd sharply rt after s: bhd: swtchd lft and drvn 2f out: no imp* **12/1**

0-00 **10** *6* **Thrasos (IRE)**[100] 858 5-9-2 **47** [1] MartinDwyer 7 16
(Jo Crowley) *v awkward leaving stalls: hld up in rr: swtchd lft and rdn wl over 2f out: wknd over 1f out: bhd and eased ins fnl f* **25/1**

1260 **11** *1 ¾* **Doctor Hilary**[10] 2907 12-9-6 **51** (v) AdamBeschizza 6 16
(Mark Hoad) *in tch in midfield: rdn and lost pl 3f out: wknd over 1f out: bhd and eased ins fnl f* **25/1**

0000 **12** *nk* **Ghostwing**[15] 2722 7-9-5 **50** RichardKingscote 8 14
(Ralph J Smith) *led tl 1/2-way: hld hd high and rdn over 2f out: wknd 2f out: bhd and eased ins fnl f* **7/1**[3]

1m 25.09s (1.79) **Going Correction** +0.275s/f (Good)
**WFA** 3 from 4yo+ 10lb **12** Ran SP% **118.8**
Speed ratings (Par 101): **100,99,98,96,95 94,94,92,88,82 80,79**
CSF £83.57 CT £516.86 TOTE £29.30: £9.50, £1.10, £2.80; EX 120.00 Trifecta £331.30.
**Owner** Mrs Angela Ellis **Bred** P And Mrs A G Venner **Trained** Newmarket, Suffolk

**FOCUS**
They went a strong pace in this selling-class event, and there was an early tendency for the runners to head for the formerly favoured stands' rail, but no draw bias was apparent and the winner was more towards the middle. The runner-up helps with the standard.

## 3231 INDUS CATERING H'CAP 6f
**7:05** (7:06) (Class 6) (0-60,58) 3-Y-O+ **£2,587** (£770; £384; £192) **Stalls** Centre

Form RPR

3406 **1** **Caminel (IRE)**[24] 2470 3-9-4 **58** TomQueally 6 65
(Jeremy Gask) *hld up in tch towards rr: rdn and hdwy ent fnl 2f: overall ldr jst ins fnl f: in command fnl 100yds: pushed out* **14/1**

1-35 **2** *1 ¼* **Assertive Agent**[113] 687 4-9-11 **57** RichardHughes 7 64+
(Tony Carroll) *hld up in tch towards rr: hdwy but nt clr run 2f out tl jst ins fnl f: r.o wl to go 2nd towards fin: no threat to wnr* **5/1**[3]

2-36 **3** *½* **Birdie Queen**[132] 448 4-9-9 **55** GeorgeBaker 8 58
(Gary Moore) *taken down early: t.k.h: hld up wl in tch in midfield: rdn and effrt over 1f out: kpt on same pce ins fnl f* **10/1**

4-62 **4** *nk* **Goadby**[21] 2553 3-9-4 **58** SebSanders 2 58
(John Holt) *racd along on far rail: overall ldr: rdn 2f out: hdd jst ins fnl f: no ex: wknd towards fin* **25/1**

4443 **5** *nk* **Picc Of Burgau**[23] 2488 4-9-10 **56** RichardKingscote 11 57
(Geoffrey Deacon) *led nr side gp and chsd overall ldr: ev ch and drvn over 1f out: no ex and one pce ins fnl f* **4/1**[2]

0104 **6** *2 ½* **Red Invader (IRE)**[25] 2435 4-9-4 **57** (b[1]) JackBudge(7) 12 50
(Charles Hills) *hld up in tch in midfield: nt clr run and shuffled bk over 2f out: swtchd lft jst over 1f out: no ch but styd on ins fnl f* **11/4**[1]

0456 **7** *hd* **El Mirage (IRE)**[7] 2994 4-9-8 **54** DaneO'Neill 3 46
(Dean Ivory) *wl in tch in midfield: rdn and effrt 2f out: unable qck over 1f out: hld and one pce fnl f* **7/1**

3200 **8** *½* **Catalyze**[41] 1986 6-9-11 **57** (t) WilliamCarson 4 48
(Paddy Butler) *rrd as stalls opened and slowly away: steadily rcvrd and in tch in midfield after 2f out: rdn and unable qck over 1f out: wknd ins fnl f* **33/1**

-406 **9** *shd* **Tiger's Home**[15] 2723 4-9-7 **53** AdamBeschizza 1 43
(Julia Feilden) *chsd ldrs: rdn and ev ch 2f out: no ex over 1f out: wknd ins fnl f* **14/1**

64-0 **10** *2 ½* **Compton Albion (IRE)**[18] 2648 4-9-7 **53** (b) DavidProbert 10 35
(Jeremy Gask) *stdd and dropped in bhd after s: hld up in rr: n.d* **20/1**

232 **11** *1 ¼* **Christopher Chua (IRE)**[12] 2831 5-8-12 **49** (p) JackDuern(5) 5 27
(Michael Scudamore) *stdd s: hld up in tch in midfield: hdwy 4f out: chsd ldrs and rdn 2f out: btn 1f out: sn wknd* **10/1**

1m 12.67s (1.47) **Going Correction** +0.275s/f (Good)
**WFA** 3 from 4yo+ 8lb **11** Ran SP% **118.9**
Speed ratings (Par 101): **101,99,98,98,97 94,94,93,93,90 88**
CSF £81.71 CT £748.67 TOTE £22.40: £7.20, £2.00, £3.60; EX 117.00 Trifecta £1103.90.
**Owner** Mark Allen **Bred** The Kathryn Stud **Trained** Sutton Veny, Wilts

**FOCUS**
This was a moderate race dominated by fillies, but the pace was decent and quite a few of these should find a suitable opening. The time wasn't bad.

## 3232 VIN DI FRANCO MEMORIAL MEDIAN AUCTION MAIDEN FILLIES' STKS 5f
**7:35** (7:39) (Class 6) 2-Y-O **£2,199** (£654; £327; £163) **Stalls** Centre

Form RPR

**1** **Sunny York (IRE)** 2-9-0 0 RichardHughes 6 71+
(James Tate) *in tch in midfield: clsd on ldrs and nt clr run over 1f out: swtchd lft and qcknd to chal ins fnl f: led fnl 75yds: rn green in front but r.o wl* **10/1**

0 **2** *¾* **Artfilly (IRE)**[58] 1528 2-9-0 0 AdamBeschizza 3 68
(Ed Walker) *chsd ldrs: rdn 2f out: chsd ldr over 1f out: ev ch fnl 100yds: kpt on* **20/1**

02 **3** *nk* **Khawaater**[18] 2644 2-9-0 0 DaneO'Neill 1 67
(Roger Varian) *nt best away sn rcvrd and led after 1f out: rdn ent f: hdd fnl 75yds: no ex* **4/5**[1]

**4** *hd* **Rosie's Premiere (IRE)** 2-9-0 0 SebSanders 4 66
(Dean Ivory) *in tch in midfield: rdn and hdwy 2f out: ev ch u.p fnl 100yds: no ex* **20/1**

**5** *3* **Showstoppa** 2-9-0 0 MartinDwyer 7 56+
(Mark Johnston) *dwlt and short of room after s: rn green towards rr: sme hdwy into midfield 1/2-way: no prog over 1f out: wknd ins fnl f* **7/1**[3]

4 **6** *1 ¼* **Icandi**[7] 2993 2-9-0 0 RichardKingscote 5 51
(Tom Dascombe) *chsd ldrs: wnt 2nd 2f out tl over 1f out: wknd ins fnl f* **10/1**

6 **7** *2 ½* **Mary Ann Bugg (IRE)**[46] 1859 2-8-9 0 RachealKneller(5) 10 42
(Phil McEntee) *chsd ldrs tl shuffled bk and nt clr run 1/2-way: rdn and wknd over 1f out* **50/1**

3 **8** *1* **Ocean Crystal**[7] 2993 2-9-0 0 DavidProbert 2 38
(John Ryan) *in tch in midfield: rdn and effrt on outer over 2f out: no prog: wknd over 1f out* **14/1**

5 **9** *3* **Euthenia**[9] 2928 2-9-0 0 SamHitchcott 9 28
(Mick Channon) *rn green: broke wl: sn lost pl and towards rr: rdn 1/2-way: no prog bhd fnl f* **6/1**[2]

**10** *2 ¼* **Tribal Diamond** 2-8-7 0 CharlotteJenner(7) 8 20
(Edward Creighton) *edgd lft and jostled sn after s: a towards rr: rdn and no hdwy 2f out: swtchd lft and wknd wl over 1f out* **66/1**

59.99s (1.79) **Going Correction** +0.275s/f (Good) **10** Ran SP% **120.2**
Speed ratings (Par 88): **96,94,94,94,89 87,83,81,76,73**
CSF £191.47 TOTE £12.50: £3.10, £6.00, £1.02; EX 143.70 Trifecta £328.30.
**Owner** Saif Ali **Bred** Ken Lynch **Trained** Newmarket, Suffolk

**FOCUS**
This was a fair maiden containing some relatively pricey juveniles, run at a good pace. Several of these look likely to win at a realistic level in the coming months. They finished in a bunch and it's hard to rate the form any higher.

## 3233 CHARLIE MARTELL "THE ADVENTURER" H'CAP 1m 1y(P)
**8:05** (8:06) (Class 6) (0-60,60) 4-Y-O+ **£2,587** (£770; £384; £192) **Stalls** High

Form RPR

3030 **1** **For Shia And Lula (IRE)**[11] 2864 5-9-5 **58** FrankieMcDonald 10 70
(Daniel Mark Loughnane) *mde virtually all: rdn 2f out: clr and in command 1f out: r.o wl: comf* **8/1**

-404 **2** *3 ¼* **Celestial Ray**[11] 2864 5-9-5 **58** SebSanders 3 63
(Linda Jewell) *t.k.h early: chsd ldrs: rdn 2f out: chsd clr wnr 1f out: kpt on but no imp* **3/1**[1]

1050 **3** *1* **Bold Ring**[18] 2646 8-8-11 **57** CharlotteJenner(7) 2 59
(Edward Creighton) *chsd ldrs: rdn and effrt wl over 1f out: kpt on ins fnl f: wnt 3rd towards fin: no threat to wnr* **16/1**

4052 **4** *½* **Cyflymder (IRE)**[33] 2219 8-8-11 **50** (v) DavidProbert 4 51
(David C Griffiths) *chsd wnr: rdn jst over 2f out: unable qck and lost 2nd 1f out: styd on same pce fnl f* **4/1**[2]

-000 **5** *1* **Pastoral Jet**[66] 1387 6-8-6 **50** DannyBrock(5) 5 49
(Richard Rowe) *dwlt: sn in tch in midfield: effrt u.p on inner wl over 1f out: 5th and styd on same pce fnl f* **20/1**

-020 **6** *1* **Jumbo Prado (USA)**[24] 2457 5-9-5 **58** (p) MartinDwyer 8 54
(John Stimpson) *hld up in tch in last trio: rdn and effrt over 1f out: styd on ins fnl f: nvr trbld ldrs* **16/1**

000- **7** *½* **My New Angel (IRE)**[242] 7283 5-8-8 **54** LouiseDay(7) 12 49
(Daniel Mark Loughnane) *hld up in last trio: stl last 2f out: pushed along and hdwy jst over 1f out: styd on fnl f: nvr trbld ldrs* **33/1**

5/06 **8** *½* **Royal Mizar (SPA)**[29] 2301 4-9-4 **57** DaneO'Neill 9 51
(Alastair Lidderdale) *s.i.s: hld up in last trio: rdn over 2f out: c wd wl over 1f out: styd on fnl f: nvr trbld ldrs* **12/1**

3015 **9** *1* **One Way Or Another (AUS)**[11] 2864 11-9-4 **57** (t) RichardHughes 11 49
(David Evans) *hld up in tch in midfield: rdn and effrt 2f out: no prog and btn over 1f out: wknd fnl f* **7/1**

6246 **10** *7* **Midnight Feast**[100] 852 6-9-7 **60** (v) TomQueally 7 36
(Lee Carter) *hld up in midfield: rdn and outpcd 2f out: wknd over 1f out: bhd fnl f* **5/1**[3]

2100 **11** *1 ¾* **Indian Violet (IRE)**[38] 2069 8-9-0 **53** (p) WilliamCarson 1 25
(Zoe Davison) *hld up in tch in midfield: rdn and lost pl over 2f out: wknd wl ovef 1f out: bhd fnl f* **12/1**

1m 38.23s (0.03) **Going Correction** +0.10s/f (Slow) **11** Ran SP% **120.1**
Speed ratings (Par 101): **103,99,98,98,97 96,95,95,94,87 85**
CSF £32.91 CT £393.90 TOTE £9.90: £2.90, £1.60, £4.90; EX 35.90 Trifecta £742.20.
**Owner** Over The Moon Racing IV **Bred** A M F Persse **Trained** Baldwin's Gate, Staffs

**FOCUS**
The pace was ordinary in this moderate event until the race began 3f out. The first four were always prominent and the winner is rated to last year's C&D best.

## 3234 HEART FM 97.5 FM H'CAP 1m 7f 169y(P)
**8:35** (8:35) (Class 5) (0-75,74) 4-Y-O+ **£3,557** (£1,058; £529; £264) **Stalls** Low

Form RPR

5164 **1** **See And Be Seen**[14] 2774 4-8-6 **57** (p) MartinDwyer 2 73+
(Sylvester Kirk) *mde all and set stdy gallop: qcknd over 4f out: rdn and wnt clr 3f out: in n.d 1f out: eased wl ins fnl f: unchal* **6/1**

46 **2** *4* **Teak (IRE)**[6] 3034 7-9-5 **74** GeorgeDowning(5) 4 80
(Ian Williams) *hld up in tch: rdn over 4f out: nt clr run on inner 2f out: swtchd rt and hdwy to chse clr wnr over 1f out: r.o but no ch w wnr* **6/4**[1]

1023 **3** *14* **Maison Brillet (IRE)**[10] 2885 7-8-13 **63** ow1 (p) SebSanders 5 52
(Clive Drew) *chsd wnr: rdn 4f out: 3rd and outpcd over 2f out: wl btn over 1f out* **9/2**[3]

2340 **4** *5* **Keep Kicking (IRE)**[6] 3034 7-9-5 **69** RichardHughes 3 52
(Simon Dow) *trckd ldrs: rdn over 3f out: chsd clr wnr over 2f out: btn and lost 2nd over 1f out: wknd and eased wl ins fnl f* **7/4**[2]

3m 25.9s (0.20) **Going Correction** +0.10s/f (Slow)
**WFA** 4 from 7yo+ 1lb **4** Ran SP% **108.8**
Speed ratings (Par 103): **103,101,94,91**
CSF £15.39 TOTE £4.90; EX 16.80 Trifecta £41.30.
**Owner** Timothy Pearson **Bred** Exors Of The Late T E Pocock **Trained** Upper Lambourn, Berks

**FOCUS**
In an uncompetitive staying event, the pace was modest until they quickened 4f out, with the front-running winner in control throughout. It's not clear where he found this form from and there are some doubts over the field. He was 8l clear when eased.

## 3235 BUTTERFLIES & BOWS VENUE DECORATION H'CAP 1m 2f (P)
**9:05** (9:05) (Class 5) (0-70,70) 4-Y-O+ **£3,557** (£1,058; £529; £264) **Stalls** Low

Form RPR

4445 **1** **Bennelong**[11] 2862 8-8-2 **58** (b) CharlotteJenner(7) 2 68
(Lee Carter) *hld up in tch towards rr: hdwy to chse ldrs and rdn 2f out: edgd rt fr over 1f out: no hdwy tl r.o to ld fnl 75yds: stormed clr towards fin* **8/1**

4313 **2** *2 ¾* **Run It Twice (IRE)**[9] 2930 4-9-7 **70** (b) RichardHughes 7 75
(David Evans) *wl in tch in midfield on outer: clsd 3f out: rdn and effrt wl over 1f out: drvn ins fnl f: edgd rt but r.o to go 2nd nr fin* **3/1**[2]

0600 **3** *shd* **Idol Deputy (FR)**[35] 2162 8-9-2 **70** (p) RachealKneller(5) 4 74
(James Bennett) *t.k.h: hld up wl in tch in midfield: nt clr run wl over 1f out tl ins fnl f: rdn and r.o fnl 150yds: snatched 3rd on post* **20/1**

4335 **4** *nse* **The Firm (IRE)**[19] 2610 5-9-4 **67** FrankieMcDonald 6 71
(Daniel Mark Loughnane) *t.k.h: led and set stdy gallop: rdn and qcknd 2f out: drvn over 1f out: hdd fnl 75yds: no ex and lost 2 pls nr fin* **11/4**[1]

05-6 **5** *¾* **Ballyshonagh**[23] 2498 4-8-13 **62** TedDurcan 3 65
(Chris Wall) *chsd ldr for 2f: styd chsng ldrs: effrt wl over 1f out: swtchd lft and drvn 1f out: styd on same pce ins fnl f* **4/1**[3]

565- **6** *¾* **Gilded Frame**[257] 6898 4-8-11 **60** DavidProbert 9 62
(J S Moore) *stdd s: hld up wl in tch in rr: rdn and effrt on outer over 1f out: kpt on but nvr threatened ldrs* **10/1**

-600 **7** *1 ¼* **Kelpie Blitz (IRE)**[77] 940 5-9-4 **67** (p[1]) AdamBeschizza 1 66
(Paul Morgan) *hld up wl in tch towards rr: nt clr run over 2f out: rdn and effrt wl over 1f out: no prog 1f out: outpcd ins fnl f* **16/1**

00 **8** *hd* **Alpine Mist**[24] 2471 4-8-13 **62** TomQueally 5 61
(Peter Makin) *chsd ldr after 2f: rdn and effrt ent fnl 2f: no ex u.p jst ins fnl f: wknd ins fnl f* **7/1**

2m 8.41s (1.81) **Going Correction** +0.10s/f (Slow) **8** Ran SP% **115.0**
Speed ratings (Par 103): **96,93,93,93,93 92,91,91**
CSF £32.49 CT £467.72 TOTE £9.60: £2.30, £1.50, £3.00; EX 36.60 Trifecta £965.50.
**Owner** John Joseph Smith **Bred** The National Stud **Trained** Epsom, Surrey

**FOCUS**
The pace was pedestrian and didn't make this much of a test. The winner seemed to find a bit on his spring form.
T/Plt: £261.80 to a £1 stake. Pool of £59388.32 - 165.57 winning tickets. T/Qpdt: £112.90 to a £1 stake. Pool of £4045.98 - 26.50 winning tickets. SP

# 3186 MUSSELBURGH (R-H)
Saturday, June 14

**OFFICIAL GOING: Soft (good to soft in places; 7.0)**
Wind: Virtually Nil Weather: Fine and Sunny

## 3236 MADELEINE CUP MAIDEN AUCTION STKS 5f
**1:00** (1:00) (Class 5) 2-Y-O **£3,234** (£962; £481; £240) **Stalls** High

Form RPR

0 **1** **Just The Tip (IRE)**[29] 2291 2-8-9 0 TomEaves 4 71+
(Keith Dalgleish) *dwlt: hld up in tch: hdwy 2f out: rdn to chal strly fnl f: kpt on: led towards fin* **9/2**[2]

05 **2** *hd* **Straightothepoint**[15] 2731 2-8-13 0 RoystonFfrench 3 74+
(Bryan Smart) *w ldr: led 2f out: sn rdn: strly pressed fnl f: kpt on: hdd towards fin* **9/2**[2]

23 **3** *5* **Lily Moreton (IRE)**[15] 2725 2-8-8 0 DuranFentiman 1 51
(Noel Wilson) *chsd ldng pair on outer: pushed along 1/2-way: rdn over 1f out: sn one pce and hld in 3rd* **4/5**[1]

0340 **4** *4 ½* **Penalty Scorer**[51] 1656 2-8-3 0 NeilFarley(3) 5 33
(Richard Guest) *led narrowly: rdn whn hdd 2f out: wknd fnl f* **9/2**[2]

**5** *7* **Come On Galey** 2-8-11 0 BenCurtis 2 13
(Kristin Stubbs) *dwlt: sn outpcd in rr: a bhd* **25/1**[3]

1m 2.04s (1.64) **Going Correction** +0.35s/f (Good) **5** Ran SP% **113.9**
Speed ratings (Par 93): **100,99,91,84,73**
CSF £24.52 TOTE £5.90: £2.90, £2.60; EX 24.70 Trifecta £46.90.
**Owner** Straightline Construction Ltd **Bred** Knocklong House Stud **Trained** Carluke, S Lanarks

**FOCUS**
Probably not a strong maiden, with leading form contender Lily Moreton proving disappointing.

## 3237 M-PACT BUILDING SERVICES LTD H'CAP 7f 30y
**1:30** (1:36) (Class 5) (0-70,70) 3-Y-O+ **£5,175** (£1,540; £769; £384) **Stalls** Low

Form RPR

2013 **1** **Mowhoob**[7] 3000 4-9-10 **66** GrahamLee 1 76
(Jim Goldie) *mde all: rdn over 2f out: drvn fnl f: diminishing advantage towards fin but a holding* **7/2**[1]

3054 **2** *nk* **Guishan**[26] 2398 4-8-8 **57** AlistairRawlinson(7) 2 66
(Michael Appleby) *trckd ldr: rdn over 2f out: kpt on: clsng at fin but a jst hld* **6/1**

0165 **3** *5* **Imperator Augustus (IRE)**[7] 3000 6-9-1 **64** JackGarritty(7) 8 60+
(Patrick Holmes) *s.i.s: hld up: hdwy on outer over 2f out: wnt 3rd over 1f out: kpt on but no threat to ldng pair* **6/1**

-500 **4** *1 ¾* **Surround Sound**[35] 2162 4-9-9 **65** DuranFentiman 3 57
(Tim Easterby) *trckd ldr: rdn 3f out: grad wknd fr over 1f out* **15/2**

2360 **5** *3 ¾* **Kyllachy Star**[12] 2841 8-9-11 **67** (v) PaulMulrennan 6 49
(Richard Fahey) *hld up: rdn over 3f out: nvr threatened* **9/1**

3421 **6** *hd* **Belle Bayardo (IRE)**[15] 2722 6-9-1 **57** RonanWhelan 7 38
(Tony Carroll) *in tch on outer: rdn 3f out: wknd over 1f out* **4/1**[2]

0-60 **7** *6* **Natures Law (IRE)**[17] 2676 4-9-4 **60** TomEaves 5 26
(Keith Dalgleish) *midfield: rdn 3f out: sn wknd* **16/1**

1333 **8** *½* **Fleurtille**[21] 2552 5-9-11 **70** ConnorBeasley(3) 10 35
(Robert Johnson) *hld up: pushed along 1/2-way: nvr threatened* **5/1**[3]

4-00 **9** *4* **Classy Lassy (IRE)**[11] 2870 3-8-3 **62** KevinLundie(7) 4 12
(Brian Ellison) *s.i.s: hld up: rdn over 3f out: nvr threatened* **25/1**

1m 31.5s (2.50) **Going Correction** +0.40s/f (Good)
**WFA** 3 from 4yo+ 10lb **9** Ran SP% **119.0**
Speed ratings (Par 103): **101,100,94,92,88 88,81,81,76**
CSF £25.65 CT £124.57 TOTE £4.30: £1.70, £2.70, £2.30; EX 27.50 Trifecta £199.70.
**Owner** Johnnie Delta Racing **Bred** Scuderia Archi Romani **Trained** Uplawmoor, E Renfrews

**FOCUS**
Not many got into this. The winner is rated back to his best.

## 3238 WILLIAM HILL H'CAP 1m 4f 100y
**2:00** (2:00) (Class 6) (0-65,71) 4-Y-O+ **£3,234** (£962; £481; £240) **Stalls** Centre

Form RPR

6/1 **1** **Lysino (GER)**[5] 3051 5-9-13 **71** 6ex TomEaves 8 83
(Keith Dalgleish) *sn in tch: moved upsides 4f out: rdn to ld 2f out: kpt on wl to assert ins fnl f* **1/2**[1]

505 **2** *2* **Ronald Gee (IRE)**[16] 2696 7-9-0 **61** GaryBartley(3) 9 69
(Jim Goldie) *led: jnd 4f out: rdn whn hdd 2f out: kpt on wl but a hld ins fnl f* **10/1**

604/ **3** *11* **Cadore (IRE)**[114] 4429 6-8-10 **61** ow1 (p) MeganCarberry(7) 5 53
(Lucy Normile) *hld up: rdn over 3f out: plugged on into modest 3rd over 1f out: no threat to ldng pair* **20/1**

100- **4** *1 ½* **Downtown Boy (IRE)**[170] 3910 6-8-10 **57** (p) ConnorBeasley(3) 6 46
(Ray Craggs) *midfield: rdn 3f out: sn btn* **13/2**[3]

6-35 **5** *7* **Geanie Mac (IRE)**[22] 2515 5-8-12 **56** (p) GrahamLee 7 35
(Linda Perratt) *trckd ldr: rdn over 5f out: wknd 2f out* **5/1**[2]

5-00 **6** *32* **Slip Of A Girl (IRE)**[15] 2738 4-7-9 **46** oh1 (p) JackGarritty(7) 3
(Patrick Holmes) *dwlt: hld up: a bhd* **22/1**

2m 49.46s (7.46) **Going Correction** +0.40s/f (Good) **6** Ran SP% **114.9**
Speed ratings (Par 101): **91,89,82,81,76 55**
CSF £7.09 CT £49.50 TOTE £1.40: £1.10, £4.90; EX 7.50 Trifecta £60.80.
**Owner** Straightline Construction Ltd **Bred** Gestut Hof Ittlingen **Trained** Carluke, S Lanarks

**FOCUS**
A weak handicap with a reduced field, and the form is a bit shaky. The winner matched his Ayr figure.

## 3239 WILLIAM HILL SCOTTISH SPRINT CUP CONSOLATION H'CAP 5f
**2:30** (2:31) (Class 3) 4-Y-O+ **£12,938** (£3,850; £1,924; £962) **Stalls** High

Form RPR

6-42 **1** **Robot Boy (IRE)**[28] 2352 4-9-5 **87** GrahamGibbons 11 98
(David Barron) *chsd ldrs: rdn 2f out: drvn to ld 110yds out: kpt on wl* **11/4**[1]

1060 **2** *1 ¼* **Red Baron (IRE)**[7] 3006 5-9-0 **85** IanBrennan(3) 6 92
(Eric Alston) *led towards centre: rdn and edgd lft over 1f out: hdd 110yds out: kpt on* **20/1**

6-43 **3** *hd* **Jack Luey**[18] 2656 7-9-3 **85** DuranFentiman 17 91
(Lawrence Mullaney) *in tch: rdn 1/2-way: angled rt ent fnl f: kpt on* **14/1**

0514 **4** *1 ¼* **Go Go Green (IRE)**[7] 3006 8-8-1 **74** 6ex SammyJoBell(5) 2 75
(Jim Goldie) *hld up: pushed along 1/2-way: hdwy on outside over 1f out: kpt on fnl f* **28/1**

-360 **5** *nk* **Jamaican Bolt (IRE)**[14] 2786 6-9-3 **92** (p) MeganCarberry(7) 8 92
(Geoffrey Oldroyd) *hld up: rdn 1/2-way: kpt on fnl f: nrst fin* **13/2**[3]

4435 **6** *1 ½* **Singeur (IRE)**[14] 2786 7-9-4 **89** NeilFarley(3) 9 84
(Robin Bastiman) *hld up: pushed along 1/2-way: hdwy whn briefly n.m.r ins fnl f: kpt on* **8/1**

40-3 **7** *shd* **Lexington Place**[7] 3006 4-8-10 **81** SamJames(3) 4 75
(David O'Meara) *s.i.s: hld up: rdn over 1f out: kpt on fnl f: nvr threatened* **10/1**

5102 **8** *½* **Silvanus (IRE)**[30] 2275 9-9-1 **83** PaulMulrennan 5 76
(Paul Midgley) *chsd ldrs: rdn 1/2-way: wknd ins fnl f* **16/1**

2441 **9** *nk* **Rothesay Chancer**[7] 3006 6-8-8 **79** 6ex GaryBartley(3) 14 71
(Jim Goldie) *hld up: rdn 1/2-way: kpt on ins fnl f: nvr threatened* **12/1**

000- **10** *¾* **Midnight Dynamo**[265] 6665 7-7-12 **73** JackGarritty(7) 3 62
(Jim Goldie) *hld up: rdn 1/2-way: nvr threatened* **25/1**

0510 **11** *nk* **Tumblewind**[14] 2786 4-9-8 **90** PaulQuinn 10 78+
(Richard Whitaker) *dwlt: hld up: hdwy whn short of room over 1f out tl jst ins fnl f: swtchd rt: no ch after* **16/1**

0200 **12** *1 ¼* **Chooseday (IRE)**[7] 2992 5-9-7 **89** (p) TomEaves 13 72
(Kevin Ryan) *prom: rdn 1/2-way: wknd over 1f out* **18/1**

4260 **13** *nse* **Bronze Beau**[15] 2727 7-8-6 **79** (t) ShaneGray(5) 1 62
(Kristin Stubbs) *w ldr on outside: rdn 1/2-way: wknd over 1f out* **40/1**

-202 **14** *1* **Rasaman (IRE)**[24] 2456 10-9-2 **84** GrahamLee 16 64
(Jim Goldie) *hld up: nvr threatened* **6/1**[2]

0-55 **15** *nse* **Perfect Blossom**[48] 1759 7-8-4 **72** RoystonFfrench 15 51
(Alan Berry) *hld up: nvr threatened* **33/1**

-215 **16** *1* **Go Nani Go**[38] 2074 8-9-2 **87** ConnorBeasley(3) 7 63
(Ed de Giles) *midfield: rdn 1/2-way: wknd over 1f out* **10/1**

604- **17** *4* **Above Standard (IRE)**[246] 7171 6-8-12 **87** DanielleMooney(7) 12 48
(Michael Easterby) *midfield: rdn 1/2-way: wknd over 1f out* **16/1**

1m 0.89s (0.49) **Going Correction** +0.35s/f (Good) **17** Ran SP% **138.3**
Speed ratings (Par 107): **110,108,107,105,105 102,102,101,101,100 99,97,97,96,95 94,87**
CSF £72.64 CT £759.93 TOTE £3.70: £1.80, £5.50, £4.70, £4.30; EX 99.00 Trifecta £1016.60 Part won..
**Owner** Laurence O'Kane & Paul Murphy **Bred** Corduff Stud Ltd **Trained** Maunby, N Yorks

**FOCUS**
A really competitive sprint handicap, and the time comes out similar to the main event. The winner is back to his 3yo best.

## 3240 STOBO CASTLE LADIES DAY CUP H'CAP 2m
**3:00** (3:01) (Class 4) (0-85,81) 4-Y-O+ **£9,703** (£2,887; £1,443; £721) **Stalls** High

Form RPR

54-0 **1** **Caledonia**[55] 1599 7-8-2 **66** ow1 JordanNason(7) 7 78+
(Jim Goldie) *hld up: rdn and gd hdwy over 2f out: led appr fnl f: edgd rt ins fnl f: kpt on wl* **12/1**

514- **2** *2 ¾* **Enchanted Garden**[27] 3627 6-8-6 **66** SamJames(3) 10 74+
(Malcolm Jefferson) *midfield: hdwy to chse ldr over 2f out: sn rdn: kpt on but no ch w wnr ins fnl f* **7/2**[1]

0-02 **3** *2 ¼* **Nashville (IRE)**[15] 2739 5-9-6 **77** GrahamGibbons 1 83
(Richard Fahey) *midfield: pushed along and lost pl 5f out: rdn and outpcd 3f out: styd on fr over 1f out: wnt 3rd towards fin* **13/2**[3]

-431 **4** *nk* **Aleksandar**[22] 2515 5-8-13 **70**........................................ GrahamLee 8 75
(Jim Goldie) *led at stdy pce: pushed along into clr ld 4f out: rdn and reduced advantage 2f out: hdd appr fnl f: wknd and lost 2 more pls ins fnl f* **13/2**[3]

0-13 **5** *2* **A Southside Boy (GER)**[17] 2678 6-8-1 **65**.................. JackGarritty(7) 5 68
(Jim Goldie) *hld up: hdwy on outer over 2f out: one pce ins fnl f* **16/1**

3233 **6** *1 1/2* **Entihaa**[21] 2561 6-9-9 **80**........................................ BenCurtis 4 81
(Alan Swinbank) *in tch: rdn over 3f out: wknd fnl f* **7/2**[1]

-300 **7** *6* **Man Of Plenty**[15] 2739 5-9-9 **80**........................(p) PaulMulrennan 6 74
(Ed Dunlop) *hld up in rr: pushed along over 3f out: swtchd lft over 2f out: briefly n.m.r over 1f out: nvr threatened* **16/1**

4144 **8** *1* **Choisan (IRE)**[10] 2900 5-9-2 **73**........................(tp) DuranFentiman 3 66
(Tim Easterby) *trckd ldr: rdn over 2f out: wknd fnl f* **20/1**

-150 **9** *nk* **Jonny Delta**[21] 2561 7-9-7 **81**........................ IanBrennan(3) 11 73
(Jim Goldie) *dwlt: hld up: rdn over 3f out: sn btn* **11/1**

42/1 **10** *3* **Pass Muster**[27] 1599 7-9-7 **78**........................ RoystonFfrench 2 67
(Philip Kirby) *hld up in midfield: rdn over 3f out: sn struggling* **6/1**[2]

400- **11** *2 1/2* **Harrison's Cave**[228] 7597 6-8-9 **66**........................ TomEaves 9 52
(Keith Dalgleish) *trckd ldr: wknd over 2f out* **14/1**

3m 37.87s (4.37) **Going Correction** +0.40s/f (Good) **11 Ran SP% 124.6**
Speed ratings (Par 105): **105,103,102,102,101 100,97,97,96,95 94**
CSF £57.08 CT £312.45 TOTE £14.60: £4.10, £1.90, £3.00; EX 61.30 Trifecta £884.80 Part won..
**Owner** Johnnie Delta Racing **Bred** E W Hyslop **Trained** Uplawmoor, E Renfrews

**FOCUS**
A competitive enough handicap, but the pace steadied markedly mid-race and that allowed long-time leader Aleksandar to kick from the front on the home turn and immediately get all of his rivals off the bridle. A personal best on the Flat from the winner.

## 3241 WILLIAM HILL SCOTTISH SPRINT CUP (HERITAGE H'CAP) 5f
3:35 (3:37) (Class 2) 4-Y-0+

**£62,250** (£18,640; £9,320; £4,660; £2,330; £1,170) **Stalls High**

Form RPR

401- **1** **Demora**[259] 6830 5-8-8 **98**........................ AlistairRawlinson(7) 3 108
(Michael Appleby) *mde all: rdn 1/2-way: kpt on wl* **10/1**

6020 **2** *1 1/4* **Masamah (IRE)**[14] 2786 8-9-5 **102**........................(p) PaddyAspell 7 108
(Marco Botti) *hld up: rdn and hdwy on outside over 1f out: kpt on* **25/1**

1406 **3** *hd* **Dinkum Diamond (IRE)**[14] 2766 6-9-10 **107**.................. BenCurtis 10 112
(Henry Candy) *hld up: rdn 1/2-way: hdwy over 1f out: kpt on* **12/1**

0302 **4** *nk* **Body And Soul (IRE)**[14] 2786 4-9-3 **100**.................. DuranFentiman 14 104+
(Tim Easterby) *trckd ldrs: rdn and ev ch ins fnl f: one pce fnl 75yds* **4/1**[1]

2000 **5** *2 1/4* **Racy**[7] 2989 7-8-10 **100**........................(p) MeganCarberry(7) 1 96
(Brian Ellison) *prom: rdn 1/2-way: edgd lft over 1f out: wknd ins fnl f* **14/1**

1321 **6** *nk* **Caspian Prince (IRE)**[7] 2989 5-9-6 **103** 6ex..............(t) RonanWhelan 17 98
(Tony Carroll) *w ldr: rdn 1/2-way: wknd ins fnl f* **6/1**[2]

4350 **7** *1/2* **Hawkeyethenoo (IRE)**[21] 2563 8-9-8 **105**.................. GrahamLee 15 98
(Jim Goldie) *hld up: rdn 1/2-way: kpt on fnl f: nvr threatened* **8/1**[3]

0000 **8** *nk* **Doc Hay (USA)**[7] 2992 7-8-11 **97**........................ IanBrennan(3) 12 89+
(Brian Ellison) *hld up: n.m.r jst ins fnl f: kpt on fnl 110yds: nvr threatened* **20/1**

3-40 **9** *1/2* **Tangerine Trees**[7] 2989 9-9-2 **99**........................(v) RoystonFfrench 16 89
(Bryan Smart) *dwlt: sn chsd ldrs: rdn 1/2-way: wknd ins fnl f* **16/1**

5-00 **10** *hd* **Magical Macey (USA)**[14] 2786 7-9-3 **100**..............(b) GrahamGibbons 8 89
(David Barron) *prom: rdn 1/2-way: wknd ins fnl f* **18/1**

-045 **11** *hd* **Confessional**[14] 2766 7-8-11 **94**........................(e) PaulMulrennan 11 83+
(Tim Easterby) *hld up: bdly hmpd over 1f out: no ch after* **10/1**

40-4 **12** *1 1/2* **Move In Time**[14] 2766 6-9-5 **105**........................ SamJames(3) 5 88
(David O'Meara) *dwlt: sn chsd ldrs: rdn 1/2-way: wknd ins fnl f* **8/1**[3]

00- **13** *1/2* **Burning Thread (IRE)**[218] 7803 7-8-3 **93**..............(b) JackGarritty(7) 9 74+
(Tim Etherington) *sn outpcd towards rr: keeping on whn short of room ins fnl f* **25/1**

4043 **14** *nk* **Addictive Dream (IRE)**[7] 2989 7-8-12 **102**.................. JordanNason(7) 2 82
(David Nicholls) *chsd ldrs: rdn 1/2-way: wknd ins fnl f* **9/1**

0-20 **15** *nk* **Borderlescott**[38] 2076 12-8-12 **98**........................ NeilFarley(3) 13 77
(Robin Bastiman) *midfield: wknd over 1f out* **16/1**

/0-6 **16** *6* **Fire Eyes**[57] 1561 4-8-10 **96**........................ ConnorBeasley(3) 6 54
(David Brown) *chsd ldrs: wknd over 1f out* **25/1**

-500 **17** *7* **Ballesteros**[7] 2989 5-9-2 **99**........................ TomEaves 4 31+
(Richard Fahey) *prom: losing pl whn bdly hmpd over 1f out: eased* **16/1**

1m 0.67s (0.27) **Going Correction** +0.35s/f (Good) **17 Ran SP% 138.3**
Speed ratings (Par 109): **111,109,108,108,104 104,103,102,102,101 101,99,98,97,97 87,76**
CSF £264.94 CT £3148.54 TOTE £13.30: £2.90, £6.70, £3.60, £1.60; EX 366.30 Trifecta £2587.30 Part won..
**Owner** A M Wragg **Bred** A M Wragg **Trained** Danethorpe, Notts

**FOCUS**
A hugely competitive sprint handicap in which the principals came down the middle of the track, avoiding trouble down the inside. The time was very similar to the consolation race. Demora continued her fine progress.

## 3242 GAYNOR WINYARD APPRENTICE H'CAP 1m
4:10 (4:14) (Class 6) (0-55,65) 4-Y-0+ **£3,234** (£962; £481; £240) **Stalls Low**

Form RPR

4/05 **1** **Mazeppa**[5] 3054 4-9-7 **65**........................ ConnorBeasley 9 77
(Keith Dalgleish) *mde all: rdn over 2f out: kpt on wl: edgd lft ins fnl f: comf* **4/1**[2]

3-52 **2** *5* **Lil Sophella (IRE)**[9] 2911 5-8-9 **58**........................ JackGarritty(5) 7 59
(Patrick Holmes) *trckd ldr: rdn over 2f out: kpt on but no ch w wnr* **5/1**[3]

4322 **3** *2 3/4* **Ewell Place (IRE)**[12] 2823 5-9-1 **64**..............(p) SammyJoBell(5) 5 58
(Richard Fahey) *trckd ldr: rdn and lost pl over 2f out: plugged on in modest 3rd fnl f* **2/1**[1]

-503 **4** *hd* **Running Reef (IRE)**[19] 2605 5-9-4 **62**........................ IanBrennan 2 56
(Tracy Waggott) *hld up in tch: rdn over 2f out: one pce nvr threatened* **8/1**

0052 **5** *9* **Admirable Art (IRE)**[17] 2669 4-9-3 **61**..............(p) RonanWhelan 1 34
(Tony Carroll) *s.i.s: hld up: rdn over 3f out: sn btn* **4/1**[2]

3-65 **6** *2* **Tony Hollis**[10] 2901 6-8-1 **48** ow1..............(vt) ShaneGray(3) 4 16
(Michael Appleby) *racd keenly: trckd ldr: rdn over 2f out: wknd over 1f out* **10/1**

336- **7** *8* **Royal Straight**[225] 7669 9-9-5 **63**........................(t) SamJames 6 13
(Linda Perratt) *hld up in tch: rdn 3f out: sn wknd* **16/1**

0004 **8** *3/4* **Daneside (IRE)**[9] 2937 7-8-2 **46** oh1..............(v) NeilFarley 3
(Simon West) *hld up on outside: rdn 1/2-way: sn wknd* **20/1**

1m 43.48s (2.28) **Going Correction** +0.40s/f (Good) **8 Ran SP% 120.8**
Speed ratings (Par 101): **104,99,96,96,87 85,77,76**
CSF £25.87 CT £52.31 TOTE £5.30: £1.80, £1.70, £1.10; EX 24.10 Trifecta £64.60.
**Owner** Gordon McDowall **Bred** Gordon McDowall **Trained** Carluke, S Lanarks

**FOCUS**
A modest handicap taken in emphatic fashion by the winner, and the form could be rated a length higher at least.
T/Plt: £314.20 to a £1 stake. Pool: £52,735.76 - 122.51 winning units. T/Qpdt: £14.80 to a £1 stake. Pool: £5,508.14 - 274.65 winning units. AS

# 3193 SANDOWN (R-H)
### Saturday, June 14

**OFFICIAL GOING: Good (good to soft in places on round course; rnd 7.8, str 7.5)**
Wind: Moderate, behind Weather: Cloudy

## 3243 BETFRED "COME ON ENGLAND" H'CAP (BOBIS RACE) 1m 1f
1:50 (1:52) (Class 3) (0-90,87) 3-Y-0

**£12,450** (£3,728; £1,864; £932; £466; £234) **Stalls Low**

Form RPR

1 **1** **Agent Murphy**[16] 2690 3-9-4 **84**........................ GeorgeBaker 1 94
(Brian Meehan) *t.k.h: trckd ldng pair: rdn to ld over 1f out: hrd pressed nr fin: hld on wl* **9/1**

0050 **2** *hd* **Torchlighter (IRE)**[8] 2962 3-9-2 **82**.................. SilvestreDeSousa 12 91
(Mark Johnston) *racd on outer: chsd ldng trio: rdn over 2f out: styd on to chse wnr ins fnl f: chal last 75yds: jst hld* **10/1**

25-1 **3** *2* **Shafrah (IRE)**[84] 1069 3-9-5 **85**........................ ShaneKelly 2 90
(Richard Hannon) *led: rdn 2f out: hdd over 1f out: kpt on same pce* **11/1**

-114 **4** *1* **Examiner (IRE)**[115] 659 3-9-6 **86**........................ SebSanders 10 89+
(William Haggas) *rousted early in last pair: drvn and stl there 3f out: prog 2f out: edgd rt fnl f but styd on: n.d* **25/1**

-210 **5** *1* **Provident Spirit**[31] 2257 3-9-7 **87**........................ WilliamBuick 5 88
(John Gosden) *trckd ldr: chal 2f out: upsides over 1f out: nt qckn and fdd fnl f* **6/1**[2]

4-11 **6** *3/4* **Reedcutter**[23] 2495 3-9-1 **84**........................ RobertTart(3) 8 83+
(James Toller) *t.k.h: hld up towards rr: prog and rdn on inner 2f out: edgd lft over 1f out: checked briefly ins fnl f: one pce* **17/2**[3]

11-4 **7** *1 3/4* **Lawyer (IRE)**[54] 1614 3-9-1 **81**........................ AndreaAtzeni 3 76
(Luca Cumani) *wl in tch: rdn and no prog over 2f out: n.d after* **10/1**

020 **8** *nk* **Triple Chief (IRE)**[17] 2681 3-8-12 **78**.................. RichardKingscote 13 73
(Rod Millman) *racd wd in midfield: rdn and no prog over 2f out: n.d after* **33/1**

1-42 **9** *2* **Gothic**[23] 2481 3-9-5 **85**........................ RyanMoore 7 76
(Sir Michael Stoute) *sn t.k.h towards rr: rdn over 2f out: no prog and wl btn over 1f out* **2/1**[1]

3034 **10** *3 1/2* **Mr Matthews (IRE)**[21] 2567 3-9-1 **81**.................. DanielTudhope 4 64
(K R Burke) *trckd ldrs: rdn and no prog over 2f out: wknd over 1f out: eased nr fin* **20/1**

3003 **11** *5* **Whitby High Light**[18] 2655 3-8-6 **72**........................ DavidProbert 11 45
(Andrew Hollinshead) *t.k.h hld up in rr: rdn and no prog over 2f out* **100/1**

4-05 **12** *8* **Malachim Mist (IRE)**[36] 2112 3-9-1 **81**..............(p) RichardHughes 6 37
(Richard Hannon) *a towards rr: wknd over 2f out: eased fnl f* **16/1**

1245 **13** *12* **Our Gabrial (IRE)**[12] 2839 3-8-12 **78**..............(b) JamieSpencer 9 9
(Richard Fahey) *v s.i.s: a last: eased over 2f out: t.o* **20/1**

1m 56.35s (0.65) **Going Correction** +0.225s/f (Good) **13 Ran SP% 117.8**
Speed ratings (Par 103): **106,105,104,103,102 101,100,99,98,94 90,83,72**
CSF £88.25 CT £1046.74 TOTE £11.70: £3.80, £3.70, £3.80; EX 78.70 Trifecta £1887.20 Part won..
**Owner** W A Harrison-Allan **Bred** Wellsummers Stud **Trained** Manton, Wilts

**FOCUS**
This was a good-quality 3yo handicap. It was run at just an average pace, though, and those in the firing line early were at a marked advantage, as they were through the card. The form is rated on the positive side.

## 3244 BETFRED "DOUBLE DELIGHT" H'CAP 1m 14y
2:20 (2:24) (Class 2) (0-100,100) 3-Y-0+

**£31,125** (£9,320; £4,660; £2,330; £1,165; £585) **Stalls Low**

Form RPR

44-1 **1** **Sea Shanty (USA)**[56] 1578 4-9-7 **93**........................ RichardHughes 6 102
(Richard Hannon) *wl in tch: u.p jst over 3f out: no prog tl squeezed through over 1f out: drvn to ld nr fin: jst hld on* **5/1**[2]

0-00 **2** *shd* **Tanseeb**[14] 2778 3-8-1 **84**........................ SilvestreDeSousa 3 90
(Mark Johnston) *prom: rdn over 2f out: angled out over 1f out: drvn to chal ins fnl f: kpt on nr fin: jst hld* **20/1**

0511 **3** *nk* **St Moritz (IRE)**[11] 2868 8-9-4 **90**..............(v) DanielTudhope 14 98
(David O'Meara) *led after 1f at gd pce: drvn and pressed 2f out: kpt on wl but hdd nr fin* **15/2**

50-0 **4** *1 1/2* **Enobled**[63] 1437 4-8-12 **84**........................ RyanMoore 2 89+
(Sir Michael Stoute) *w.w in midfield: rdn over 2f out: prog and cl up bhd ldrs against rail 1f out: one pce after* **9/2**[1]

2052 **5** *hd* **Apostle (IRE)**[14] 2758 5-9-4 **90**........................ JamieSpencer 15 94
(David Simcock) *trckd ldrs: rdn wl over 2f out: prog to dispute 2nd 1f out: one pce after* **10/1**

1532 **6** *1 3/4* **George Guru**[23] 2483 7-9-10 **96**........................ TomQueally 12 96+
(Michael Attwater) *hld up towards rr: rdn 2f out: kpt on fr jst over 1f out: too late to pose a threat* **9/1**

05-0 **7** *3/4* **Directorship**[42] 1948 8-9-7 **93**........................ DaneO'Neill 5 92
(Patrick Chamings) *wl in rr: rdn 3f out: sme prog on outer 2f out: no hdwy fnl f* **14/1**

2141 **8** *1 3/4* **Ishikawa (IRE)**[16] 2707 6-8-7 **86**.................. RobJFitzpatrick(7) 10 81
(K R Burke) *t.k.h: trckd ldrs: wnt 2nd wl over 2f out and sn chalng: stl upsides over 1f out: wknd qckly jst ins fnl f* **7/1**[3]

4000 **9** *1 1/4* **Set The Trend**[14] 2758 8-9-6 **92**........................(p) SebSanders 7 84
(David Dennis) *wl in rr: rdn on outer 3f out: sme prog u.str.p 2f out: wknd fnl f* **33/1**

-600 **10** *1 1/4* **Vainglory (USA)**[8] 2959 10-8-10 **82**........................ MartinLane 13 71
(David Simcock) *sn pushed along and detached in last pair: nvr a factor* **25/1**

0610 **11** *4* **Amulet**[8] 2956 4-9-3 **89**........................ ShaneKelly 9 69
(Eve Johnson Houghton) *led 1f: chsd ldr to wl over 2f out: wkng whn short of room jst over 1f out* **8/1**

0265 **12** *9* **Trader Jack**[21] 2562 5-8-12 **84**........................ AndreaAtzeni 16 43
(David Flood) *dwlt and dropped in fr wd draw: detached in last pair: no prog over 2f out: t.o* **8/1**

1m 43.34s (0.04) **Going Correction** +0.225s/f (Good)
**WFA** 3 from 4yo+ 11lb **12 Ran SP% 118.6**
Speed ratings (Par 109): **108,107,107,106,105 104,103,101,100,99 95,86**
CSF £103.97 CT £761.69 TOTE £3.60: £1.40, £8.60, £2.90; EX 87.70 Trifecta £651.30.



The Form Book, Raceform Ltd, Newbury, RG14 5SJ

**Owner** The Queen **Bred** Her Majesty The Queen **Trained** East Everleigh, Wilts

**FOCUS**

Competitive fare. Yet again it was another contest on the round course here where it paid to race handy and it got messy around the furlong marker. The winner built on his reappearance win.

## 3245 BETFRED 'HAT TRICK HEAVEN' SCURRY STKS (LISTED RACE) 5f 6y

2:55 (2:57) (Class 1) 3-Y-O

£20,982 (£7,955; £3,981; £1,983; £995; £499) Stalls Low

Form RPR

2-04 **1** **Wind Fire (USA)**[29] 2304 3-8-12 98 JamieSpencer 14 105
(David Brown) *quick s fr wd draw and sn crossed towards far side: pressed ldr after 1f: chal over 1f out: carried lft thrght fnl f: drvn and last strides* **17/2**[3]

0-26 **2** *nk* **Hay Chewed (IRE)**[30] 2287 3-8-9 94 MartinDwyer 8 101
(Conrad Allen) *wl away fr middle draw: led against far rail: drvn and hung bdly lft hroughout fnl f: hdd last strides* **33/1**

2-11 **3** *1* **G Force (IRE)**[29] 2317 3-9-0 103 DanielTudhope 11 102+
(David O'Meara) *w.w in midfield: swtchd to outer and prog over 1f out: chsd clr ldng pair fnl f: styd on but nvr quite rchd them* **5/4**[1]

-562 **4** *¾* **One Chance (IRE)**[30] 2287 3-8-9 93 TomQueally 5 95
(John Butler) *chsd ldrs towards far rail: rdn over 2f out: styd on fr over 1f out: nrst fin* **16/1**

313 **5** *1* **Perfect Blessings (IRE)**[21] 2564 3-8-9 95 JamesDoyle 12 91
(Clive Cox) *chsd ldrs: rdn 2f out: kpt on fr over 1f out but nvr gng pce to chal* **16/1**

30-0 **6** *3* **Simple Magic (IRE)**[29] 2304 3-8-9 92 WilliamBuick 4 80+
(John Gosden) *dwlt: wl in rr: rdn over 2f out: prog over 1f out: styd on fnl f: nrst fin* **25/1**

4-10 **7** *1* **Speedfiend**[45] 1867 3-9-0 105 DaneO'Neill 15 82
(Noel Quinlan) *hld up fr wd draw: in tch in midfield 2f out and rdn: no hdwy after* **28/1**

111- **8** *½* **Strategical (USA)**[288] 5955 3-9-0 102 RichardHughes 10 80
(Charlie Appleby) *dwlt: racd wd towards rr: rdn 2f out: sme prog over 1f out: no hdwy after* **8/1**[2]

40-5 **9** *1* **Ambiance (IRE)**[30] 2287 3-9-3 101 (b[1]) AndreaAtzeni 2 79
(Roger Varian) *racd against rail: chsd ldr 1f: rdn 3f out: wknd jst over 1f out* **10/1**

360- **10** *2* **Abbakova (IRE)**[252] 7011 3-8-9 90 DavidProbert 13 64
(Paul Cole) *racd on outer: prom 3f: wknd qckly fnl f* **66/1**

34-0 **11** *2* **Extortionist (IRE)**[42] 1949 3-9-3 102 JimCrowley 3 65
(Olly Stevens) *sltly s.i.s: impeded whn towards rr over 3f out: nvr on terms after* **9/1**

12-0 **12** *nk* **Langavat (IRE)**[29] 2304 3-9-0 99 PatDobbs 9 61
(Richard Hannon) *a in rr: outpcd fr 1/2-way* **25/1**

421- **13** *10* **Merletta**[240] 7328 3-8-9 95 ShaneKelly 7 20
(Jeremy Noseda) *a in rr: no prog 1/2-way: t.o* **33/1**

-001 **14** *7* **Sleepy Sioux**[26] 2406 3-8-9 88 (p) SilvestreDeSousa 1 +
(David Elsworth) *prom 1f: snatched up on inner over 3f out: dropped rt out and eased 2f out: t.o* **14/1**

1m 0.03s (-1.57) **Going Correction** -0.05s/f (Good) **14 Ran SP% 122.1**
Speed ratings (Par 107): **110,109,107,106,105 100,98,97,96,93 89,89,73,62**
CSF £277.18 TOTE £10.80: £2.90, £9.30, £1.10; EX 383.40 Trifecta £2809.90 Part won..
**Owner** Qatar Racing Limited **Bred** Kinsman Farm **Trained** Averham Park, Notts
■ Stewards' Enquiry : Martin Dwyer three-day ban: careless riding (Jun 28-30)

**FOCUS**

There was no hanging about and the first pair, who ended up nearer the stands' side late in the day, forced the pace from the outset. The winning time was solid. The winner is rated back to his best.

## 3246 BETFRED "YOUR WORLD CUP BOOKMAKER" H'CAP (JOCKEY CLUB GRASSROOTS FLAT SPRINT SERIES QUALIFIER) 5f 6y

3:30 (3:31) (Class 4) (0-80,80) 4-Y-0+ £5,822 (£1,732; £865; £432) Stalls Low

Form RPR

0-42 **1** **Tagula Night (IRE)**[10] 2890 8-9-3 76 (bt) RyanMoore 12 89
(Dean Ivory) *chsd clr ldng quartet: rdn and clsd fr over 1f out: drvn ahd ins fnl f: styd on wl* **5/1**[3]

1041 **2** *1* **Amenable (IRE)**[10] 2907 7-8-12 71 (p) TomQueally 8 80
(Ann Stokell) *mostly chsd ldr: rdn to ld 1f out: styd on but hdd and outpcd ins fnl f* **11/1**

3-21 **3** *3 ¾* **Pucon**[18] 2645 5-9-0 73 JamesDoyle 11 69
(Roger Teal) *fast away fr wd draw: led and crossed to far rail: hld together tl shkn up jst over 1f out: edgd lft: sn hdd and nt qckn* **10/1**

2004 **4** *nk* **Ubetterbegood (ARG)**[25] 2446 6-9-3 76 (v[1]) PatDobbs 1 71
(Robert Cowell) *racd against far rail: disp 2nd pl to 1/2-way: rdn and nt qckn over 1f out: kpt on* **15/2**

5632 **5** *2 ½* **Welease Bwian (IRE)**[11] 2865 5-8-0 66 AaronJones(7) 2 52+
(Stuart Williams) *s.s: a off the pce in rr: tried to make prog 2f out: sn no hdwy* **7/1**

214- **6** *nk* **Holley Shiftwell**[315] 4989 4-9-5 78 AndreaAtzeni 4 63
(Stuart Williams) *prom: rdn 2f out: lost pl and btn over 1f out: fdd* **9/2**[2]

6-00 **7** *hd* **Tidal's Baby**[18] 2645 5-9-0 78 GeorgeDowning(5) 7 62+
(Tony Carroll) *s.s: a off the pce in rr: rdn and no prog 2f out* **14/1**

-500 **8** *1* **Lupo D'Oro (IRE)**[19] 2629 5-9-3 76 (v[1]) JamieSpencer 3 56+
(John Best) *s.v.s: mostly in last and wl off the pce: rdn and no real prog 2f out* **7/2**[1]

-000 **9** *nk* **Red Explorer (USA)**[9] 2933 4-8-3 69 (t) NoraLooby(7) 5 48
(Ann Stokell) *taken down early: broke on terms but sn off the pce towards rr: no prog 2f out* **20/1**

6606 **10** *1* **Malaysian Boleh**[24] 2471 4-8-3 62 HayleyTurner 9 38+
(Simon Dow) *s.s: a off the pce towards rr: pushed along and no prog 2f out* **16/1**

1m 0.67s (-0.93) **Going Correction** -0.05s/f (Good) **10 Ran SP% 116.1**
Speed ratings (Par 105): **105,103,97,96,92 92,92,90,90,88**
CSF £58.47 CT £407.20 TOTE £4.30: £1.80, £2.90, £2.60; EX 56.80 Trifecta £326.00.
**Owner** Hufford & Papworth **Bred** Carpet Lady Partnership **Trained** Radlett, Herts

**FOCUS**

Just a modest sprint handicap, but it's fair form for the class. The pace was good.

## 3247 TOTEPOOL.COM H'CAP (BOBIS RACE) 7f 16y

4:05 (4:06) (Class 3) (0-95,95) 3-Y-O

£12,450 (£3,728; £1,864; £932; £466; £234) Stalls Low

Form RPR

0-12 **1** **Captain Bob (IRE)**[37] 2088 3-8-9 83 WilliamBuick 4 91
(Charles Hills) *mde all: rdn 2f out: hrd pressed fnl f: styd on wl to hold on* **5/1**[2]

110- **2** *nk* **Silent Bullet (IRE)**[261] 6765 3-9-7 95 [1] SilvestreDeSousa 6 102+
(Saeed bin Suroor) *hld up in last pair: prog on outer 2f out: drvn to chse wnr jst over 1f out: str chal last 150yds: styd on and kpt trying but jst hld* **16/1**

3-60 **3** *2* **Ticking Katie (IRE)**[57] 1563 3-8-6 87 (p) RobJFitzpatrick(7) 11 89
(K R Burke) *racd wd: trckd ldrs: chsd wnr over 2f out to jst over 1f out: nt qckn after* **22/1**

4-66 **4** *1 ¾* **Mime Dance**[8] 2962 3-8-2 76 oh1 DavidProbert 7 73
(Andrew Balding) *trckd ldrs: rdn over 2f out: no imp over 1f out: one pce* **15/2**

21-5 **5** *¾* **Erroneous (IRE)**[37] 2088 3-8-10 84 ow1 JamieSpencer 8 80
(David Simcock) *chsd wnr after 1f to over 2f out: steadily fdd over 1f out* **8/1**

3-15 **6** *2 ¾* **Destiny's Kitten (IRE)**[21] 2567 3-8-11 85 RichardKingscote 3 73
(Tom Dascombe) *towards rr: pushed along 3f out: last and no ch over 1f out: styd on fnl f* **25/1**

1-11 **7** *1* **Aertex (IRE)**[28] 2340 3-8-13 87 RichardHughes 2 73
(Richard Hannon) *t.k.h: hld up in midfield: rdn and no prog over 2f out: n.d after* **2/1**[1]

25-1 **8** *½* **Banaadeer (IRE)**[38] 2083 3-8-12 86 DaneO'Neill 5 70
(Richard Hannon) *t.k.h early: hld up towards rr: rdn and no prog over 2f out: no ch after* **7/1**[3]

130- **9** *hd* **Dutch Interior**[227] 7626 3-8-6 80 AdamBeschizza 9 64
(Gary Moore) *hld up in last: pushed along 1/2-way: rdn on outer over 2f out: sn no prog* **50/1**

1-20 **10** *3 ¼* **Secret Archive (USA)**[36] 2112 3-8-5 79 AndreaAtzeni 10 55
(Ralph Beckett) *nvr bttr than midfield: rdn and no prog over 2f out: sn wknd* **8/1**

3-21 **11** *6* **Galvanize**[36] 2138 3-8-12 86 RyanMoore 1 46
(Kevin Ryan) *chsd wnr 1f: lost pl and rdn over 2f out: sn wknd* **16/1**

1m 29.4s (-0.10) **Going Correction** +0.225s/f (Good) **11 Ran SP% 118.4**
Speed ratings (Par 103): **109,108,106,104,103 100,99,98,98,94 87**
CSF £80.26 CT £1646.76 TOTE £5.80: £1.90, £3.40, £6.20; EX 53.40 Trifecta £948.60.
**Owner** A L R Morton **Bred** Martyn J McEnery **Trained** Lambourn, Berks

**FOCUS**

Once again this 3yo handicap was suited to those racing handy and there was an all-the-way winner. Decent form, if a little shaky, rated through the third.

## 3248 BETFRED "ENGLAND EXPECTS" EBF MAIDEN STKS 1m 2f 7y

4:40 (4:43) (Class 5) 3-Y-O £3,881 (£1,155; £577; £288) Stalls Low

Form RPR

4 **1** **Kings Fete**[14] 2773 3-9-5 0 JamesDoyle 6 94+
(Sir Michael Stoute) *trckd ldng trio: clsd to ld over 1f out: shkn up and styd on wl* **4/1**[3]

5 **2** *1 ¼* **Obsidian (USA)**[28] 2334 3-9-5 0 WilliamBuick 1 93+
(John Gosden) *trckd ldng pair: waiting for gap over 2f out: rdn over 1f out: styd on to take 2nd ins fnl f: unable to chal* **11/4**[1]

3343 **3** *1 ¼* **Karraar**[15] 2746 3-9-5 84 RyanMoore 15 89
(Richard Hannon) *trckd ldr: led wl over 2f out and sent for home: hdd over 1f out: one pce* **5/1**

0 **4** *1 ½* **New Story**[28] 2334 3-9-5 0 JamieSpencer 5 86+
(Ismail Mohammed) *trckd ldng quartet: shkn up and cl up over 2f out: outpcd over 1f out: kpt on* **3/1**[2]

5- **5** *4* **Almerzem (USA)**[302] 5490 3-9-5 0 AndreaAtzeni 9 79+
(Saeed bin Suroor) *wl in tch: prog and cl up bhd ldrs over 2f out: shkn up and comf outpcd fnl 2f* **9/1**

55 **6** *4 ½* **Fastnet Red**[14] 2773 3-9-5 0 MartinDwyer 7 70+
(John Gosden) *drvn early in last pair: no prog tl styd on fnl 2f: nrst fin* **14/1**

03 **7** *2* **Mawaseel**[23] 2497 3-9-5 0 DaneO'Neill 10 66
(B W Hills) *nvr bttr than midfield: modest prog into 6th over 1f out but ldrs clr: no hdwy after* **33/1**

0-0 **8** *3 ¾* **Secure Cloud (IRE)**[30] 2271 3-9-5 0 DanielTudhope 4 59
(B W Hills) *wl in rr: outpcd fr 3f out: no ch after: passed a few late on* **100/1**

0-24 **9** *shd* **Moontown**[92] 951 3-9-5 77 SilvestreDeSousa 11 59
(Charles Hills) *towards rr: rdn on outer wl over 2f out: sn no prog and wknd* **20/1**

**10** *½* **Lu's Buddy (GR)** 3-9-5 0 PatDobbs 13 58
(Amanda Perrett) *coltish preliminaries: a towards rr: shkn up and no prog over 2f out* **50/1**

00- **11** *6* **Exceed Policy**[262] 6739 3-9-5 0 SebSanders 3 47
(David Dennis) *nvr bttr than midfield: drvn and no prog over 2f out: sn bhd* **80/1**

6-0 **12** *2* **Cinnamon Spice**[14] 2773 3-9-5 0 TomQueally 14 43
(Harry Dunlop) *chsd ldrs: shkn up wl over 2f out: sn wknd* **66/1**

0 **13** *6* **Beaver Creek**[28] 2334 3-9-5 0 RichardKingscote 8 31
(Ralph J Smith) *led to wl over 2f out: wknd rapidly* **100/1**

**14** *12* **Chuck Hatch** 3-9-5 0 GeorgeBaker 12 9
(Ed Walker) *a last: t.o fr 1/2-way* **33/1**

2m 13.14s (2.64) **Going Correction** +0.225s/f (Good) **14 Ran SP% 122.3**
Speed ratings (Par 99): **98,97,96,94,91 88,86,83,83,82 78,76,71,62**
CSF £14.95 TOTE £5.10: £2.00, £1.60, £1.90; EX 18.70 Trifecta £70.40.
**Owner** K Abdullah **Bred** Juddmonte Farms Ltd **Trained** Newmarket, Suffolk

**FOCUS**

A good 3yo maiden, rated around the third. They went a sound enough pace but once again the pace bias towards those racing prominently played out.

## 3249 BETFRED "WORLD CUP IN PLAY" H'CAP 1m 6f

5:15 (5:16) (Class 4) (0-85,84) 4-Y-0+ £5,822 (£1,732; £865; £432) Stalls Low

Form RPR

-441 **1** **Spice Fair**[9] 2920 7-9-2 79 RyanMoore 12 89
(Mark Usher) *hld up wl in rr: stdy prog fr over 3f out: clsd on ldrs 2f out: rdn to ld jst over 1f out: drvn out* **3/1**[1]

06-2 **2** *1 ¾* **English Summer**[8] 2950 7-8-6 69 (t) SilvestreDeSousa 10 76
(Richard Fahey) *trckd ldr 1f: settled into 4th: rdn and clsd over 2f out: led briefly over 1f out: one pce fnl f* **8/1**

104- **3** *2 ¾* **Hi Note**[182] 6573 6-8-11 79 HarryPoulton(5) 2 82
(Sheena West) *t.k.h: trckd ldr after 4f: rdn to ld over 2f out: hdd and no ex over 1f out* **18/1**

02-0 **4** *2 ¾* **Snowy Dawn**[42] 1935 4-9-2 79 (p) TomQueally 1 78
(Andrew Hollinshead) *in tch in midfield: rdn wl over 2f out: nt qckn and sn lft bhd: plugged on* **7/1**

0-31 **5** *1 ¾* **Happy Families**[25] 2419 4-8-5 68 AndreaAtzeni 4 65
(Heather Main) *led at gd pce: rdn and hdd over 2f out: steadily wknd* **7/2**[2]

5-30 **6** 1¾ **Softsong (FR)**[9] 2920 6-9-2 **84** (b[1]) DavidKenny(5) 7 78
(James Evans) *s.s: wl in rr: rdn and no prog wl over 2f out: no ch after* **20/1**

/0-6 **7** 1¾ **Aazif (IRE)**[35] 2142 5-9-3 **80** (t) WilliamBuick 8 72
(Ian Williams) *chsd ldr after 1f tl after 4f: drvn and wknd over 2f out* **11/2**[3]

16-0 **8** 1¾ **Azrag (USA)**[24] 2461 6-9-7 **84** (p) SebSanders 6 73
(Michael Attwater) *walked to post: in tch: urged along over 4f out: no prog and struggling wl over 2f out* **25/1**

0-65 **9** 13 **Saborido (USA)**[9] 2920 8-9-1 **78** PatDobbs 5 49
(Amanda Perrett) *dropped to rr and struggling by 1/2-way: sn btn* **15/2**

00-0 **10** dist **Ermyn Lodge**[23] 2490 8-8-4 **70** (vt) JemmaMarshall(3) 9
(Pat Phelan) *early reminder: last after 4f: t.o fr 1/2-way: virtually p.u* **28/1**

3m 4.95s (0.45) **Going Correction** +0.225s/f (Good) **10 Ran SP% 115.3**
Speed ratings (Par 105): **107,106,104,102,101 100,99,98,91,**
CSF £26.40 CT £367.42 TOTE £4.40: £1.90, £2.30, £3.90; EX 20.90 Trifecta £379.60.
**Owner** Saxon House Racing **Bred** Mrs D Hughes **Trained** Upper Lambourn, Berks

**FOCUS**
They were strung out from an early stage in this modest staying handicap and that played right into the hands of the winner, who built on his AW latest.

T/Plt: £426.00 to a £1 stake. Pool: £136,608.03 - 234.07 winning tickets. T/Qpdt: £19.40 to a £1 stake. Pool: £7958.14 - 302.40 winning tickets. JN

## [3199]YORK (L-H)

Saturday, June 14

**OFFICIAL GOING: Good changing to good (good to firm in places) after race 2 (2.40)**

Wind: Light against Weather: Cloudy with sunny periods

## 3250 QUEEN MOTHER'S CUP LADY AMATEUR RIDERS STKS (H'CAP) 1m 4f

**2:05** (2:05) (Class 3) (0-95,87) 3-Y-0+ **£12,478** (£3,870; £1,934; £968) **Stalls** Centre

Form RPR

510- **1** **Pearl Castle (IRE)**[42] 6741 4-10-13 **86** MissSBrotherton 9 94
(John Quinn) *lw: trckd ldrs: hdwy 3f out: chal wl over 1f out: rdn to ld ent fnl f: drvn out* **4/1**[1]

-656 **2** 1 **Saptapadi (IRE)**[7] 2991 8-11-0 **87** (t) MsKWalsh 7 94
(Brian Ellison) *hld up in rr: gd hdwy 3f out: trckd ldrs 2f out: rdn over 1f out: ev ch ins fnl f: no imp towards fin* **9/2**[2]

4345 **3** 1 **Mica Mika (IRE)**[14] 2790 6-9-11 **76** (p) MissEmilyBullock(6) 3 81
(Richard Fahey) *t.k.h: trckd ldr: led 3f out: rdn wl over 1f out: hdd ent fnl f: kpt on same pce* **13/2**

1 **4** 1¼ **Tiger Lilly (IRE)**[42] 1960 3-9-2 **76** MissADeniel 6 79
(Richard Fahey) *in tch: hdwy over 3f out: rdn along to chse ldrs wl over 2f out: sltly outpcd over 1f out: styd on wl fnl f: nrst fin* **6/1**[3]

0/31 **5** ¾ **Kings Bayonet**[18] 2640 7-10-6 **82** MissMeganNicholls(3) 4 84
(Alan King) *hld up in rr: tk clsr order 1/2-way: stdy hdwy on outer 3f out: cl up 2f out: rdn over 1f out and ev ch tl drvn and wknd ins fnl f* **7/1**

0201 **6** 8 **Sherman McCoy**[8] 2950 8-9-8 **70** MissNHayes(3) 2 59
(Marjorie Fife) *prom on inner: pushed along over 3f out: rdn over 2f out: grad wknd* **10/1**

000- **7** 4 **Nanton (USA)**[205] 7990 12-10-3 **76** MrsCBartley 8 59
(Jim Goldie) *hld up: a bhd* **18/1**

0-00 **8** 11 **Crackentorp**[14] 2787 9-10-3 **76** MissHayleyMoore 11 41
(Tim Easterby) *trckd ldrs on outer: cl up 5f out: rdn along over 3f out: sn wknd* **12/1**

-600 **9** ½ **Warlu Way**[14] 2787 7-10-6 **79** MissJoannaMason 5 43
(Michael Easterby) *lw: chsd ldrs on inner: rdn along over 3f out: sn wknd* **8/1**

1-00 **10** 1¾ **Ultimate**[7] 3004 8-10-2 **75** (b) MissHBethell 10 36
(Brian Ellison) *t.k.h: set stdy pce: pushed along 4f out: hdd 3f out and sn wknd* **25/1**

2m 33.31s (0.11) **Going Correction** +0.05s/f (Good)
**WFA** 3 from 4yo+ 15lb **10 Ran SP% 115.3**
Speed ratings (Par 107): **101,100,99,98,98 93,90,83,82,81**
CSF £21.52 CT £113.98 TOTE £4.50: £1.80, £1.90, £2.30; EX 23.70 Trifecta £132.10.
**Owner** Mr & Mrs Paul Gaffney **Bred** Mogeely Stud **Trained** Settrington, N Yorks
■ Stewards' Enquiry : Ms K Walsh four-day ban: used whip above permitted level (Jun 30,Jul 5,6,10)

**FOCUS**
The ground remained officially good. One of the big races for lady amateurs and the winners of the last three runnings of the race, Crackentorp (twice) and Nanton, were back again, though neither figured. They went a steady pace until things quickened up coming to the last 3f and the winning time was 5.21sec outside standard. The winner built on his 3yo form.

## 3251 JCB STKS (H'CAP) 1m 208y

**2:40** (2:40) (Class 2) (0-105,102) 3-Y-0+**£17,466** (£5,197; £2,597; £1,298) **Stalls** Low

Form RPR

-000 **1** **Spirit Of The Law (IRE)**[8] 2959 5-8-9 **83** oh1 PaulHanagan 7 92
(Richard Fahey) *led: pushed along and jnd over 2f out: sn rdn: drvn and hdd narrowly wl ins fnl f: rallied gamely to ld again nr fin* **14/1**

1100 **2** shd **Busatto (USA)**[8] 2959 4-9-1 **89** JoeFanning 10 98
(Mark Johnston) *trckd wnr: cl up over 3f out: rdn to chal wl over 1f out: drvn and slt ld wl ins fnl f: hdd and no ex nr fin* **20/1**

5-20 **3** ½ **Roserrow**[42] 1948 5-9-0 **91** OisinMurphy(3) 3 99
(Andrew Balding) *trckd ldng pair: hdwy over 3f out: cl up 2f out: sn rdn along: drvn ent fnl f and kpt on towards fin* **12/1**

2-14 **4** 1¼ **Flow (USA)**[14] 2783 4-9-4 **92** (t) MartinHarley 1 97
(Lady Cecil) *lw: in tch: hdwy on inner over 3f out: cl up 2f out: sn rdn and ev ch wh edgd lft ent fnl f and kpt on same pce* **3/1**[1]

230- **5** nse **Tarikhi (USA)**[322] 4743 4-9-7 **95** KierenFallon 4 100+
(Saeed bin Suroor) *lw: hld up: hdwy into midfield 1/2-way: effrt to chse ldrs 2f out: sn rdn and edgd lft wl over 1f out: kpt on same pce u.p fnl f* **11/2**[2]

0106 **6** 1 **Whispering Warrior (IRE)**[19] 2618 5-9-3 **91** FergusSweeney 12 94+
(David Simcock) *hld up in rr: hdwy 3f out: rdn to chse ldrs wl over 1f out: swtchd rt and drvn ent fnl f: sn no imp* **12/1**

-004 **7** 3½ **Boots And Spurs**[7] 2984 5-9-0 **88** (tp) HarryBentley 8 84
(Stuart Williams) *trckd ldrs: effrt wl over 2f out: rdn wl over 1f out: grad wknd* **10/1**

0202 **8** ½ **Spa's Dancer (IRE)**[19] 2618 7-10-0 **102** LukeMorris 2 97
(James Eustace) *swtg: hld up towards rr: hdwy over 3f out: chsd ldrs 2f out: sn rdn and grad wknd* **9/1**

0-04 **9** 1¼ **Fury**[8] 2959 6-9-4 **92** (p) FrankieDettori 11 84
(William Haggas) *hld up in rr: hdwy on wd outside over 2f out: sn rdn and n.d* **6/1**[3]

1-45 **10** 1 **Mabait**[23] 2483 8-8-13 **94** GeorgeBuckell(7) 6 84
(David Simcock) *hld up in rr: hdwy over 3f out: rdn 2f out: sn no imp* **25/1**

1002 **11** 1½ **Maven**[12] 2826 6-8-7 **88** RachelRichardson(7) 13 75
(Tim Easterby) *midfield: hdwy on outer to chse ldrs 1/2-way: rdn along over 3f out: wknd over 2f out* **20/1**

-035 **12** 1¼ **Shahdaroba (IRE)**[11] 2869 4-8-8 **85** JasonHart(3) 9 69
(Micky Hammond) *chsd ldrs: rdn along 4f out: sn wknd* **20/1**

4500 **13** 2¾ **Sweet Lightning**[30] 2286 9-9-8 **96** (p) DavidNolan 5 74
(David O'Meara) *hld up towards rr: hdwy on wd outside over 3f out: rdn along over 2f out: sn wknd* **14/1**

1m 50.2s (-1.80) **Going Correction** +0.05s/f (Good) **13 Ran SP% 122.0**
Speed ratings (Par 109): **110,109,109,108,108 107,104,103,102,101 100,99,96**
CSF £274.48 CT £3008.66 TOTE £19.10: £5.50, £5.90, £4.10; EX 334.30 Trifecta £2677.60 Part won..
**Owner** The Matthewman One Partnership **Bred** Georgestown Stud **Trained** Musley Bank, N Yorks

**FOCUS**
A decent handicap and a truly run race, but as was the case here the previous day those that raced up with the pace were at a major advantage. The first, second and third held those positions throughout. The winner matched his best figures.

## 3252 IAN AND KATE HALL MACMILLAN GANTON STKS (LISTED RACE) 1m

**3:15** (3:15) (Class 1) 3-Y-0+

**£20,982** (£7,955; £3,981; £1,983; £995; £499) **Stalls** Low

Form RPR

00-4 **1** **Guest Of Honour (IRE)**[77] 1162 5-9-7 110 (p) MartinHarley 1 114
(Marco Botti) *lw: trckd ldrs: hdwy wl over 2f out: led over 1f out and sn rdn: drvn ins fnl f: kpt on wl towards fin* **3/1**[2]

2342 **2** ½ **Fencing (USA)**[33] 2223 5-9-7 110 FrankieDettori 4 113
(John Gosden) *lw: hld up in rr: smooth hdwy on inner 3f out: cl up 2f out: sn chal: rdn and ev ch over 1f out: drvn ins fnl f: kpt on same pce towards fin* **5/2**[1]

3220 **3** ¾ **Custom Cut (IRE)**[14] 2765 5-9-7 108 DavidNolan 7 111
(David O'Meara) *trckd ldr: cl up 1/2-way: rdn 2f out and ev ch tl drvn and kpt on same pce ins fnl f* **11/1**

20-3 **4** ¾ **Lockwood**[35] 2150 5-9-7 112 KierenFallon 3 110
(Saeed bin Suroor) *trckd ldrs: hdwy over 2f out: rdn wl over 1f out: kpt on fnl f* **4/1**[3]

4-05 **5** 1¼ **Cordite (IRE)**[27] 2377 3-8-10 104 AndrewMullen 6 104
(Michael Appleby) *t.k.h: led: rdn along and jnd over 2f out: drvn wl over 1f out: sn hdd and grad wknd* **12/1**

6-01 **6** ½ **Dutch Rose (IRE)**[14] 2784 5-9-2 102 LukeMorris 2 101
(David O'Meara) *trckd ldng pair: hdwy and cl up 3f out: chal 2f out: sn rdn and ev ch tl wknd appr fnl f* **5/1**

63-0 **7** 1½ **Snowboarder (USA)**[121] 596 4-9-7 106 PaulHanagan 5 102
(Charlie Appleby) *lw: hld up: effrt over 2f out: sn rdn along and no imp* **12/1**

1m 38.45s (-0.55) **Going Correction** +0.05s/f (Good)
**WFA** 3 from 4yo+ 11lb **7 Ran SP% 114.0**
Speed ratings (Par 111): **104,103,102,102,100 100,98**
CSF £10.88 TOTE £4.30: £2.20, £1.60; EX 14.20 Trifecta £87.90.
**Owner** Giuliano Manfredini **Bred** Azienda Agricola Gennaro Stimola **Trained** Newmarket, Suffolk

**FOCUS**
An interesting Listed event and they went a solid gallop. The form makes sense overall with the winner close to his best.

## 3253 BETBRIGHT CHARITY SPRINT (H'CAP) (BOBIS RACE) 6f

**3:50** (3:52) (Class 2) (0-105,104) 3-Y-O

**£62,250** (£18,640; £9,320; £4,660; £2,330; £1,170) **Stalls** Low

Form RPR

2-24 **1** **See The Sun**[36] 2116 3-8-7 **90** DavidAllan 12 100
(Tim Easterby) *mde all: rdn over 1f out: drvn and edgd rt ins fnl f: hld on wl towards fin* **20/1**

1-32 **2** nk **Naadirr (IRE)**[29] 2304 3-9-5 **102** MartinHarley 5 111
(Marco Botti) *slightly on toes: towards rr: hdwy 2f out: effrt over 1f out: rdn and str run ins fnl f: ev ch last 50yds tl no ex nr fin* **12/1**

5231 **3** 1 **Kickboxer (IRE)**[19] 2611 3-8-6 **89** LukeMorris 6 95
(Mick Channon) *lw: in tch: hdwy 2f out: sn rdn and styd on to chse wnr ins fnl f: kpt on same pce towards fin* **14/1**

01-0 **4** ¾ **Gamesome (FR)**[28] 2343 3-9-1 **98** HarryBentley 16 102
(Olly Stevens) *lw: trckd ldrs: hdwy to chse wnr over 1f out: rdn and swtchd lft ins fnl f: sn drvn and kpt on same pce* **25/1**

-641 **5** ½ **Eastern Impact (IRE)**[28] 2344 3-8-13 **96** TonyHamilton 11 98
(Richard Fahey) *in tch: hdwy 2f out and sn rdn: styd on u.p fnl f: nrst fin* **12/1**

0-03 **6** ¾ **Ventura Mist**[36] 2116 3-8-6 **96** (p) RachelRichardson(7) 18 96
(Tim Easterby) *towards rr: hdwy on outer 2f out: sn rdn and kpt on fnl f: nrst fin* **33/1**

610- **7** 2½ **Royal Mezyan (IRE)**[252] 7011 3-8-7 **93** OisinMurphy(3) 8 85
(William Haggas) *chsd ldrs: hdwy and cl up over 2f out: rdn and edgd lft ent fnl f: one pce* **10/1**[3]

3-45 **8** shd **Charles Molson**[28] 2344 3-8-7 **90** FergusSweeney 1 81
(Henry Candy) *chsd ldrs on outer: rdn along 2f out: n.m.r and swtchd rt ins fnl f: one pce* **8/1**[2]

01-1 **9** nk **Danzeno**[59] 1518 3-9-4 **101** AndrewMullen 9 91
(Michael Appleby) *dwlt: sn cl up: rdn along and wandered wl over 1f out: drvn and hung lft ent fnl f: sn wknd* **7/2**[1]

1-02 **10** 2½ **Betimes**[14] 2767 3-9-0 **97** RobertHavlin 2 79
(John Gosden) *in rr: hdwy 2f out: rdn over 1f out: sn no imp* **11/1**

46-0 **11** 2¼ **Sleeper King (IRE)**[28] 2344 3-9-2 **99** BarryMcHugh 20 74
(Kevin Ryan) *dwlt: a in rr* **33/1**

6-06 **12** 1¾ **Supplicant**[21] 2556 3-9-4 **104** GeorgeChaloner(3) 13 74
(Richard Fahey) *towards rr: sme hdwy 2f out: sn rdn and n.d* **20/1**

-123 **13** ½ **Eccleston**[30] 2287 3-8-12 **95** DavidNolan 19 63
(David O'Meara) *a towards rr* **20/1**

4-30 **14** nk **Rufford (IRE)**[29] 2304 3-9-0 **100** JasonHart(3) 17 67
(Richard Fahey) *in tch: rdn along 2f out: sn wknd* **25/1**

210- **15** nk **Zaraee (IRE)**[275] 6328 3-8-6 **89** PaulHanagan 3 55
(William Haggas) *chsd ldrs: rdn along 2f out: sn wknd* **20/1**

-211 **16** 1 **Rural Celebration**[10] 2897 3-8-2 **88** JulieBurke(3) 14 51
(David O'Meara) *chsd ldrs: rdn along and edgd lft 2f out: sn wknd* **16/1**

4061 **17** 1½ **Almargo (IRE)**[8] 2962 3-8-6 **89** JoeFanning 4 47
(Mark Johnston) *prom: rdn along over 2f out: sn drvn and wknd over 1f out* **11/1**

0-10 **18** 7 **Ben Hall (IRE)**[14] 2767 3-8-7 **95** KevinStott(5) 7 31
(Mike Murphy) *lw: prom: rdn along 1/2-way: sn wknd* **50/1**

202- **19** 3½ **Invincible Strike (IRE)**[210] 7933 3-9-2 **99**........................ KierenFallon 15 23
(James Tate) *a towards rr* **20/1**

0-30 **20** 3¼ **Deeds Not Words (IRE)**[28] 2344 3-8-6 **92**............. CharlesBishop(3) 10 6
(Mick Channon) *chsd ldrs: rdn along 1/2-way: sn wknd: bhd whn eased over 1f out* **33/1**

1m 12.03s (0.13) **Going Correction** +0.15s/f (Good) **20** Ran SP% **129.3**
Speed ratings (Par 105): **105,104,103,102,101 100,97,97,96,93 90,88,87,87,86 85,83,73,69,64**
CSF £219.71 CT £3564.90 TOTE £17.30: £3.50, £2.90, £3.40, £8.60; EX 356.90 Trifecta £9593.30.
**Owner** C H Stevens **Bred** R C Dollar **Trained** Great Habton, N Yorks

**FOCUS**
The ground continued to dry out and was now good to firm. This traditionally hot 3yo sprint handicap looked well up to scratch this year and although it was another case of the winner making just about all, the form still has a solid look to it and plenty of winners will come out of this. A 6lb best from the winner. The main action unfolded up the centre of the track.

## 3254 ICE CO SUPPORTING MACMILLAN STKS (H'CAP) 1m 208y
4:25 (4:27) (Class 4) (0-80,80) 4-Y-0+ **£7,762** (£2,310; £1,154; £577) **Stalls** Low

Form RPR

-054 **1** **Eurystheus (IRE)**[14] 2763 5-9-4 **77**...........................(p) AndrewMullen 2 85
(Michael Appleby) *trckd ldrs: hdwy and cl up over 3f out: led 2f out and sn rdn: drvn and hdd ins fnl f: rallied gamely to ld again last 50yds* **11/1**

-004 **2** *hd* **Artful Prince**[21] 2540 4-9-0 **73**..........................................(b) DaleSwift 9 81
(James Given) *led: rdn along and jnd 3f out: hdd 2f out and sn drvn: cl up and ev ch ins fnl f: no ex towards fin* **25/1**

3405 **3** *nse* **Toga Tiger (IRE)**[22] 2519 7-9-1 **74**.......................... HarryBentley 17 81
(Kevin Frost) *dwlt and in rr: hdwy 3f out: chsd ldrs on outer 2f out: rdn over 1f out: drvn to take slt ld ins fnl f: hdd and no ex last 50yds* **16/1**

-021 **4** ½ **Barren Brook**[35] 2162 7-9-6 **79**.............................. BarryMcHugh 19 85
(Michael Easterby) *dwlt and towards rr: hdwy over 3f out: rdn wl over 1f out: styd on strly fnl f* **12/1**

-403 **5** ½ **Fazza**[22] 2519 7-9-2 **75**...................................... JamesSullivan 14 80+
(Edwin Tuer) *hld up towards rr: hdwy on outer 3f out: swtchd lft and rdn wl over 1f out: styd on strly fnl f: nrst fin* **14/1**

3-10 **6** ½ **Correggio**[32] 2234 4-9-1 **77**................................ JasonHart(3) 10 81
(Micky Hammond) *in tch: hdwy on inner to trck ldrs 4f out: rdn along 2f out: drvn over 1f out: kpt on fnl f* **16/1**

3-06 **7** ½ **Bishop's Castle (USA)**[54] 1607 5-9-1 **77**............. OisinMurphy(3) 18 80
(Brian Ellison) *dwlt and in rr: pushed along over 3f out: hdwy on inner wl over 2f out: sn rdn and styd on wl fnl f: nrst fin* **4/1**[1]

-100 **8** 1¾ **Indian Trifone (IRE)**[16] 2702 4-8-11 **70**.................... LukeMorris 20 70
(Ed Walker) *midfield: hdwy 3f out: rdn along 2f out: drvn and edgd lft over 1f out: kpt on same pce fnl f* **33/1**

0300 **9** *nk* **Steelriver (IRE)**[38] 2079 4-8-13 **72**........................... DavidAllan 7 71
(James Bethell) *towards rr: hdwy wl over 2f out: rdn over 1f out: kpt on fnl f: nrst fin* **25/1**

-235 **10** ¾ **Ingleby Symphony (IRE)**[23] 2477 4-8-9 **71**.......... GeorgeChaloner(3) 6 68
(Richard Fahey) *prom: rdn along 3f out: drvn wl over 1f out and grad wknd* **11/1**

2022 **11** ½ **Dakota Canyon (IRE)**[9] 2912 5-8-13 **72**..................(p) TonyHamilton 12 68
(Richard Fahey) *chsd ldrs on outer: hdwy 3f out: rdn along 2f out: drvn and one pce fr over 1f out* **12/1**

0-P4 **12** *nk* **Pivotman**[12] 2823 6-8-10 **69**........................................ AndrewElliott 15 65
(Michael Easterby) *hld up in rr tl styd on fnl 2f: n.d* **33/1**

-006 **13** *nk* **Kingscroft (IRE)**[32] 2234 6-9-0 **73**........................ RobertHavlin 13 69
(Michael Herrington) *towards rr: hdwy 3f out: rdn 2f out: styng on whn n.m.r and hmpd over 1f out: nt rcvr* **50/1**

-604 **14** ½ **Anderiego (IRE)**[16] 2699 6-9-7 **80**.................................(v) DavidNolan 8 74
(David O'Meara) *trckd ldrs: hdwy on outer over 3f out: rdn along over 2f out: sn drvn and wknd over 1f out* **6/1**[2]

0411 **15** 8 **Run Fat Lass Run**[12] 2823 4-8-1 **67**.......................... EvaMoscrop(7) 5 44
(Philip Kirby) *chsd ldr on inner: cl up 1/2-way: rdn along 3f out and sn wknd* **8/1**[3]

-442 **16** 2¾ **King Of The Celts (IRE)**[11] 2868 6-8-3 **69**....... RachelRichardson(7) 16 40
(Tim Easterby) *chsd ldrs: rdn along over 2f out: sn wknd* **20/1**

-501 **17** 1½ **Patriotic (IRE)**[107] 767 6-9-2 **75**..................................(p) JoeFanning 3 43
(Chris Dwyer) *a towards rr* **16/1**

1 **18** 17 **Cool Music (IRE)**[26] 2389 4-9-2 **75**.............................. KierenFallon 11 8
(Mel Brittain) *w'like: a towards rr: bhd and eased fnl 2f* **10/1**

1m 50.59s (-1.41) **Going Correction** +0.05s/f (Good) **18** Ran SP% **131.2**
Speed ratings (Par 105): **108,107,107,107,106 106,106,104,104,103 103,102,102,102,94 92,91,76**
CSF £282.65 CT £4502.64 TOTE £13.10: £3.20, £8.30, £4.40, £4.10; EX 406.90 Trifecta £3085.70 Part won..
**Owner** Midest Partnership **Bred** Calley House Uk **Trained** Danethorpe, Notts
■ Stewards' Enquiry : Andrew Elliott Fine: £140, failed to report gelding was unsuited by the ground.

**FOCUS**
A competitive handicap run at a true pace and again it paid to be handy. Sound if fairly ordinary form.

## 3255 REG GRIFFIN APPRECIATION EBF STALLIONS MAIDEN STKS (BOBIS RACE) 6f
5:00 (5:00) (Class 3) 2-Y-O **£7,439** (£2,213; £829; £829) **Stalls** Low

Form RPR

3 **1** **Pallister**[15] 2731 2-9-5 0.............................................. JoeFanning 5 80
(Mark Johnston) *lengthy: cl up: slt ld over 1f out: sn rdn and edgd rt ent fnl f: kpt on wl* **3/1**[2]

33 **2** 1¼ **Winstanley (IRE)**[31] 2258 2-9-5 0.............................. DavidNolan 1 76
(Richard Fahey) *trckd ldrs: swtchd lft and hdwy over 1f out: rdn ent fnl f: kpt on* **9/1**[3]

2 **3** *nse* **Intiwin (IRE)**[16] 2698 2-9-5 0................................ TonyHamilton 2 76
(Richard Fahey) *w'like: trckd ldng pair: hdwy 2f out: rdn to chal over 1f out: sn ev ch tl drvn and no ex wl ins fnl f* **11/4**[1]

56 **3** *dht* **Bonds Choice**[14] 2788 2-8-11 0................................ JasonHart(3) 4 71
(Richard Fahey) *trckd ldrs: effrt and nt clr run over 1f out and again ent fnl f: sn rdn and styd on wl: nrst fin* **20/1**

**5** ½ **Super Quick (IRE)** 2-8-11 0.............................. GeorgeChaloner(3) 10 70
(Richard Fahey) *athletic: trckd ldrs: hdwy and cl up 2f out: sn rdn and one pce ent fnl f* **25/1**

**6** ¾ **Pipe Bomb** 2-9-5 0............................................... HarryBentley 6 72
(Kevin Ryan) *str: sn slt ld: pushed along 2f out: rdn and hdd over 1f out: wknd ins fnl f* **3/1**[2]

4 **7** 2¾ **Speedy Move (IRE)**[14] 2777 2-9-5 0.............................. MartinHarley 7 64
(Ismail Mohammed) *w'like: trckd ldrs: hdwy 2f out: sn rdn and wknd appr fnl f* **10/1**

**8** 10 **North Bay Lady (IRE)** 2-9-0 0.................................. JamesSullivan 8 29
(John Wainwright) *leggy: s.i.s: green and a bhd* **33/1**

6 **9** 1¾ **Birkdale Boy (IRE)**[26] 2386 2-9-2 0............................ OisinMurphy(3) 9 29
(Richard Fahey) *tall: lengthy: dwlt: green and towards rr: outpcd and bhd fr 1/2-way* **14/1**

**10** 4 **What Usain** 2-9-5 0...................................................... DavidAllan 3 17
(Geoffrey Oldroyd) *w'like: bit bkwd: dwlt: green and a outpcd in rr* **20/1**

1m 13.74s (1.84) **Going Correction** +0.15s/f (Good) **10** Ran SP% **118.7**
Speed ratings (Par 97): **93,91,91,91,90 89,85,72,70,64**
WIN: 3.90 Pallister; PL: 1.70 Pallister, 2.70 Winstanley, 2.80 Bonds Choice, .60 Intiwin; EX: 27.40; CSF: 28.83; TC: ; TF: 50.90, 23160.00;.
**Owner** Sheikh Hamdan bin Mohammed Al Maktoum **Bred** Darley **Trained** Middleham Moor, N Yorks

**FOCUS**
Richard Fahey trained half the field in this maiden, but couldn't stop it from going to Mark Johnston. A compressed finish but a race that should produce winnes.

## 3256 CHARLES HENRY MEMORIAL STKS (H'CAP) 6f
5:35 (5:36) (Class 4) (0-80,80) 3-Y-O+ **£7,115** (£2,117; £1,058; £529) **Stalls** Low

Form RPR

5403 **1** **Highland Acclaim (IRE)**[36] 2138 3-8-13 **80**.............. OisinMurphy(3) 11 90+
(David O'Meara) *hld up in rr: hdwy over 2f out: rdn over 1f out: chal ins fnl f: sn drvn and kpt on wl to ld last 50yds* **16/1**

-064 **2** *nk* **Dark Castle**[15] 2732 5-9-7 **80**.................................. JasonHart(3) 1 91
(Micky Hammond) *hld up towards rr: hdwy over 2f out: swtchd lft over 1f out and rdn to ld ent fnl f: sn drvn: hdd and no ex last 50yds* **12/1**

5421 **3** 3 **Mon Brav**[8] 2953 7-9-8 **78**............................................ DaleSwift 2 79
(Brian Ellison) *dwlt and in rr: hdwy over 2f out: rdn wl over 1f out: styd on fnl f: nrst fin* **7/1**[2]

361 **4** 1¾ **Teetotal (IRE)**[22] 2522 4-9-2 **77**......................... ShelleyBirkett(5) 3 73+
(Nigel Tinkler) *chsd ldrs: rdn wl over 1f out: drvn and kpt on same pce fnl f* **10/1**

04-3 **5** *shd* **Master Bond**[35] 2167 5-9-3 **73**.................................. DavidNolan 6 68+
(David O'Meara) *trckd ldrs: smooth hdwy to dispute ld 2f out: rdn over 1f out and grad wknd* **10/1**

2602 **6** ¾ **Commanche**[28] 2332 5-9-8 **78**.................................... JoeFanning 13 71
(Chris Dwyer) *towards rr: hdwy over 2f out: rdn wl over 1f out: kpt on fnl f: nrst fin* **8/1**[3]

0052 **7** 1 **Relight My Fire**[12] 2825 4-9-2 **72**........................(b) AndrewElliott 15 62
(Tim Easterby) *racd towards stands' rail: chsd ldrs: hdwy to ld 2f: sn rdn: hdd ent fnl f and sn wknd* **16/1**

-052 **8** 6 **Line Of Reason (IRE)**[22] 2522 4-9-10 **80**................... KierenFallon 9 51+
(Paul Midgley) *trckd ldrs: effrt whn nt clr run and hmpd 2f out: sn swtchd rt and rdn: no imp* **6/1**[1]

4-00 **9** ¾ **L'Ami Louis (IRE)**[24] 2456 6-9-3 **78**....................... GarryWhillans(5) 14 46
(Ian Semple) *sn led: hdd 1/2-way and cl up tl rdn and wknd wl over 1f out* **20/1**

4403 **10** ¾ **We'll Deal Again**[57] 1566 7-9-4 **74**...........................(b) JamesSullivan 8 40
(Michael Easterby) *a towards rr* **25/1**

20-0 **11** 1 **Threes Grand**[30] 2275 4-9-7 **77**................................ TonyHamilton 12 40+
(Scott Dixon) *in tch: effrt over 2f out: rdn along whn hmpd 2f out: sn btn* **20/1**

-401 **12** *nk* **Bachotheque (IRE)**[19] 2602 4-9-6 **76**........................(p[1]) DavidAllan 4 38
(Tim Easterby) *chsd ldrs: rdn along on over 2f out: sn wknd* **12/1**

1450 **13** 1½ **Trade Secret**[28] 2332 7-9-8 **78**................................ RobertHavlin 17 35
(Mel Brittain) *blind removed late and s.i.s: a in rr* **20/1**

400- **14** *nk* **Piddie's Power**[168] 8431 7-9-5 **75**............................ HarryBentley 16 31+
(Kevin Frost) *racd nr stands' rail: chsd ldrs: rdn along whn hmpd 2f out: sn btn* **20/1**

1-20 **15** ¾ **Be Lucky**[41] 1967 4-9-4 **74**...................................... BarryMcHugh 20 28+
(Michael Easterby) *hld up towards rr: sme hdwy whn hmpd 2f out: sn wknd* **20/1**

-205 **16** ¾ **Mayfield Girl (IRE)**[27] 2361 4-8-12 **75**.............. RobertDodsworth(7) 19 26
(Mel Brittain) *racd nr stands' rail: chsd ldrs: hdwy and cl up over 2f out: sn rdn and wknd* **33/1**

0016 **17** 1 **Banovallum**[21] 2552 4-9-5 **75**................................ AndrewMullen 5 23
(Michael Easterby) *cl up: rdn along over 2f out: sn wknd* **25/1**

4-03 **P** **Time And Place**[28] 2332 4-9-5 **78**......................(b[1]) GeorgeChaloner(3) 7
(Richard Fahey) *cl up: led 1/2-way: hdd and lost pl qckly 2f out: sn p.u* **7/1**[2]

1m 12.04s (0.14) **Going Correction** +0.15s/f (Good)
**WFA** 3 from 4yo+ 8lb **18** Ran SP% **130.2**
Speed ratings (Par 105): **105,104,100,98,98 97,95,87,86,85 84,84,82,81,80 79,78,**
CSF £180.47 CT £1542.13 TOTE £21.80: £4.40, £3.80, £2.30, £3.20; EX 349.40 Trifecta £2216.00 Part won..
**Owner** Evan M Sutherland **Bred** Rathbarry Stud **Trained** Nawton, N Yorks

**FOCUS**
A good sprint handicap in which they raced centre-to-stands' side. The contest rather bucked the trend of the past two days with the first three home coming from well back, suggesting the leaders may have gone off too quick. The runner-up helps set the standard.
T/Jkpt: Not won. T/Plt: £2,892.80 to a £1 stake. Pool of £184901.60 - 46.66 winning tickets.
T/Qpdt: £88.70 to a £1 stake. Pool of £9143.26 - 76.20 winning tickets. JR

3257 - 3266a (Foreign Racing) - See Raceform Interactive

# 2979 DONCASTER (L-H)
Sunday, June 15

**OFFICIAL GOING: Good (8.0)**
Wind: Light; half behind Weather: Fine

## 3267 RAF BENEVOLENT FUND BRITISH STALLIONS EBF MAIDEN FILLIES' STKS (BOBIS RACE) 7f
2:00 (2:01) (Class 5) 2-Y-O **£3,234** (£962; £481; £240) **Stalls** Low

Form RPR

4 **1** **Caltra Colleen**[19] 2652 2-8-11 0.................. WilliamTwiston-Davies(3) 12 75
(Mick Channon) *trckd ldr: led wl over 1f out: hld on wl clsng stages* **14/1**

3 **2** *nk* **Crystal Malt (IRE)**[22] 2557 2-9-0 0................................ RyanMoore 3 74
(Richard Hannon) *trckd ldrs: upsides 1f out: no ex towards fin* **2/1**[1]

0 **3** 1½ **Astrelle (IRE)**[10] 2918 2-9-0 0...................................... LukeMorris 6 70
(Marco Botti) *trckd ldrs: 4th 1f out: kpt on to take 3rd nr line* **40/1**

5 **4** *hd* **Abbey Angel (IRE)**[17] 2697 2-9-0 0.............................. TonyHamilton 5 70
(Richard Fahey) *mid-div: effrt on outer over 2f out: chsng ldng pair 1f out: kpt on same pce* **10/1**

5 1 1/4 **Adelasia (IRE)** 2-9-0 0 WilliamBuick 7 67+
(Charlie Appleby) *s.i.s: drvn 3f out: styd on steadily fnl f* **6/1[2]**

6 shd **Nufooth (IRE)** 2-9-0 PaulHanagan 1 66+
(Richard Hannon) *s.i.s: effrt over 2f out: kpt on fnl f* **8/1[3]**

7 3 1/4 **Strong Flame** 2-9-0 0 JamieSpencer 9 58
(David Brown) *hld up in mid-div: effrt over 2f out: nvr a factor* **8/1[3]**

4 8 1 3/4 **Our Kylie (IRE)**[16] 2736 2-9-0 0 BarryMcHugh 2 53
(Tony Coyle) *s.i.s: in rr: drvn over 2f out: sme late hdwy* **12/1**

9 2 1/4 **Pixey Punk** 2-9-0 0 DuranFentiman 10 47
(Tim Easterby) *dwlt: hld up in rr: nvr on terms* **40/1**

4 10 hd **Winter Queen**[19] 2644 2-9-0 0 AdamKirby 11 47
(Charlie Appleby) *led: hdd wl over 1f out: hung lft and sn lost pl* **8/1[3]**

0 11 3 **Eileen Gray (IRE)**[31] 2276 2-9-0 0 RobertWinston 13 39
(Charles Hills) *hld up in mid-div: effrt over 2f out: edgd lft and wknd fnl f* **33/1**

12 10 **Azamaara (IRE)** 2-9-0 0 PaulMulrennan 4 13
(James Tate) *chsd ldrs: lost pl 2f out: sn bhd* **20/1**

6 13 nk **Pixie**[19] 2644 2-9-0 0 StevieDonohoe 8 12
(Ian Williams) *mid-div: lost pl 3f out: sn bhd* **100/1**

1m 27.42s (1.12) **Going Correction** -0.025s/f (Good) **13 Ran SP% 118.0**
Speed ratings (Par 90): **92,91,89,89,88 88,84,82,79,79 76,64,64**
CSF £40.09 TOTE £15.30: £4.50, £1.10, £11.30; EX 53.40 Trifecta £1029.70.
**Owner** Anne & Steve Fisher **Bred** Steven Fisher **Trained** West Ilsley, Berks

**FOCUS**
A fair juvenile fillies' maiden, but probably at the lower end of the race averages. The field were quick to track down the centre and there was an average pace on, so little surprise the first pair were always up there.

## 3268 TWEET US AT @RAFBF CLASSIFIED STKS 1m 2f 60y
**2:30** (2:31) (Class 5) 3-Y-O £3,234 (£962; £481; £240) **Stalls** Low

Form RPR

2334 1 **Truancy (IRE)**[12] 2867 3-9-0 68 (p) DanielTudhope 5 74
(K R Burke) *sn led: qcknd pce over 3f out: hld on gamely clsng stages* **9/1**

1-52 2 1 **Maiden Approach**[16] 2740 3-9-0 68 RyanMoore 1 72
(Richard Fahey) *trckd ldrs: upsides 2f out: rallied ins fnl f: kpt on same pce last 75yds* **3/1[2]**

003 3 3/4 **Semaral (IRE)**[41] 2025 3-9-0 70 TedDurcan 8 71
(Chris Wall) *hld up in mid-div: hdwy 4f out: 3rd and swtchd rt 1f out: carried hd awkwardly and ducked lft ins fnl f: styd on towards fin* **16/1**

550- 4 1 3/4 **Mishko (IRE)**[256] 6954 3-9-0 70 PaulHanagan 9 67
(Steve Gollings) *trckd ldrs: drvn 4f out: kpt on same pce over 1f out* **9/1**

20-0 5 3/4 **Heartstrings**[27] 2404 3-8-11 70 WilliamTwiston-Davies(3) 7 66
(Mick Channon) *hld up in rr: effrt over 2f out: kpt on: nvr a threat* **25/1**

-105 6 2 **The Silver Kebaya (FR)**[31] 2274 3-9-0 70 WilliamBuick 4 62
(Jeremy Noseda) *led early: chsd ldrs: chal over 2f out: fdd appr fnl f* **7/1**

0-03 7 1/2 **Ralphy Lad (IRE)**[37] 2133 3-9-0 69 DavidAllan 2 61
(Alan Swinbank) *mid-div: drvn over 3f out: fdd fnl f* **13/2[3]**

5301 8 2 **Sellingallthetime (IRE)**[10] 2934 3-9-1 71 (p) RaulDaSilva 3 58
(Michael Appleby) *hld up in rr: effrt outside over 3f out: chsng ldrs and rdn over 2f out: wknd over 1f out* **5/2[1]**

0-0 9 57 **Dream And Search (GER)**[23] 2506 3-9-0 69 (bt[1]) JamieSpencer 6
(Charles Hills) *dwlt and wnt lft s: hld up in rr: t.k.h: hdwy on outer over 5f out: chsng ldrs over 2f out: sn wknd: bhd whn eased over 1f out: virtually p.u: hopelessly t.o* **20/1**

2m 12.74s (3.34) **Going Correction** +0.075s/f (Good) **9 Ran SP% 113.9**
Speed ratings (Par 99): **89,88,87,86,85 84,83,82,36**
CSF £35.70 TOTE £8.10: £1.50, £1.70, £4.40; EX 32.30 Trifecta £334.80.
**Owner** Market Avenue Racing Club Ltd **Bred** Keogh Family **Trained** Middleham Moor, N Yorks

**FOCUS**
A very tight 3yo affair. It was run at a fair pace which lifted seriously 3f out.

## 3269 RAF WADDINGTON APPRENTICE H'CAP 1m 6f 132y
**3:05** (3:05) (Class 5) (0-70,67) 4-Y-O+ £3,234 (£962; £481; £240) **Stalls** Low

Form RPR

/0-4 1 **Eastern Magic**[57] 1574 7-8-9 53 JackDuern(3) 1 59
(Andrew Hollinshead) *trckd ldrs: drvn to chse ldrs over 3f out: led appr fnl f: hld on wl* **14/1**

-511 2 1 **Anne's Valentino**[20] 2620 4-9-1 56 GeorgeChaloner 6 61
(Malcolm Jefferson) *sn trcking ldrs: led over 2f out: hdd appr fnl f: styd on same pce last 75yds* **11/4[1]**

4104 3 nk **Dr Finley (IRE)**[23] 2531 7-8-7 55 (v) JackGilligan(7) 4 59
(Lydia Pearce) *prom: hdwy on ins to chse ldrs over 3f out: cl 3rd whn rdr mistk winning post and eased briefly 110yds out: kpt on same pce* **8/1[3]**

2-06 4 3/4 **Blue Top**[20] 2620 5-9-5 60 (p) JasonHart 8 63
(Mark Walford) *hld up in mid-div: hdwy over 3f out: swtchd lft over 1f out: kpt on fnl f* **9/2[2]**

0352 5 nk **My Destination (IRE)**[16] 2738 5-9-2 62 (b) LukeLeadbitter(5) 3 65
(Declan Carroll) *hld up in rr: hdwy on inner over 3f out: kpt on same pce fnl f* **11/1**

2035 6 1/2 **Yasir (USA)**[11] 2885 6-9-9 64 (p) MichaelJMMurphy 11 66
(Conor Dore) *in rr: effrt over 2f out: kpt on fnl f* **8/1[3]**

-021 7 nk **Kathlatino**[16] 2738 7-9-4 59 (v) NeilFarley 9 61
(Micky Hammond) *trckd ldrs: kpt on same pce fnl f* **10/1**

/0-0 8 1/2 **Phase Shift**[34] 2216 6-8-11 57 (t) MeganCarberry(5) 10 58
(Brian Ellison) *strated v slowly: in rr: hdwy over 5f out: kpt on fnl f* **11/1**

226- 9 3/4 **Chapter Five**[203] 6960 7-9-9 67 (p) GeorgeDowning(3) 7 67
(Ian Williams) *chsd ldr: upsides 8f out: led over 4f out: hdd over 2f out: wknd and eased last 75yds* **9/1**

042- 10 30 **Princeofthedesert**[29] 7951 8-8-11 52 ConnorBeasley 5 13
(Garry Woodward) *led: hdd over 4f out: lost pl over 2f out: sn bhd: t.o* **20/1**

3m 14.42s (7.02) **Going Correction** +0.075s/f (Good) **10 Ran SP% 114.3**
Speed ratings (Par 103): **84,83,83,82,82 82,82,82,81,65**
CSF £51.46 CT £337.24 TOTE £16.50: £4.40, £1.60, £3.10; EX 70.20 Trifecta £421.70.
**Owner** Mrs Christine Stevenson **Bred** Mrs C A Stevenson **Trained** Upper Longdon, Staffs
■ Stewards' Enquiry : Jack Gilligan seven-day ban: failed to ride out gelding that could have finished 2nd (Jul 11-12,14-18)
Jack Duern seven-day ban: used whip above permitted level (Jun 29-Jul 5)

**FOCUS**
This moderate staying apprentice riders' handicap was another race where it paid to race handily.

## 3270 RAFBF.ORG MAIDEN STKS 1m 4f
**3:40** (3:40) (Class 4) 3-Y-O+ £5,175 (£1,540; £769; £384) **Stalls** Low

Form RPR

0-2 1 **Forever Now**[16] 2746 3-8-12 0 WilliamBuick 3 102+
(John Gosden) *led: qcknd pce over 4f out: pushed clr 2f out: hung rt nr line* **8/13[1]**

02 2 8 **Altaayil (IRE)**[24] 2485 3-8-12 0 PaulHanagan 4 86
(Sir Michael Stoute) *trckd ldrs: shkn up over 4f out: sn drvn: wnt 2nd and edgd lft over 1f out: no ch w wnr* **3/1[2]**

00-2 3 1 1/4 **Asteroidea**[46] 1880 3-8-7 73 GrahamGibbons 5 79
(Pam Sly) *t.k.h: trckd wnr: drvn 3f out: swtchd rt over 1f out: kpt on same pce* **9/1[3]**

0 4 nk **Limousine**[64] 1438 3-8-7 0 RobertWinston 1 78
(Charles Hills) *stdd s: hld up in last: swtchd rt 4f out: sn drvn: one pce fnl 2f* **14/1**

64 5 9 **Kagami**[10] 2924 3-8-12 0 JamieSpencer 2 69
(Jeremy Noseda) *trckd ldrs: effrt 3f out: lost pl appr fnl f: eased last 100yds* **16/1**

2m 35.58s (0.68) **Going Correction** +0.075s/f (Good) **5 Ran SP% 109.5**
Speed ratings (Par 105): **100,94,93,93,87**
CSF £2.65 TOTE £1.60: £1.10, £1.90; EX 2.60 Trifecta £5.30.
**Owner** Lady Bamford **Bred** Lady Bamford **Trained** Newmarket, Suffolk

**FOCUS**
A decent little maiden.

## 3271 RAF FALCONS H'CAP 6f
**4:15** (4:17) (Class 3) (0-95,95) 3-Y-O+ £8,409 (£2,502; £1,250; £625) **Stalls** Low

Form RPR

2-12 1 **Golden Steps (FR)**[20] 2611 3-8-10 85 RyanMoore 6 96+
(Marco Botti) *t.k.h in mid-div: hdwy over 2f out: chal 1f out: styd on to ld last 50yds* **4/1[1]**

-000 2 1/2 **Out Do**[22] 2562 5-9-7 88 DanielTudhope 1 100
(David O'Meara) *trckd ldr: led over 1f out: hdd and no ex last 50yds* **11/2[2]**

0320 3 1 3/4 **Yeeoow (IRE)**[32] 2254 5-9-7 93 JoeyHaynes(5) 12 99
(K R Burke) *chsd ldng pair: upsides over 1f out: styd on same pce* **6/1[3]**

1003 4 1/2 **Ansaab**[17] 2699 6-9-5 86 (t) AdamKirby 8 90
(Alan McCabe) *led: drvn over 2f out: hdd over 1f out: styd on same pce* **14/1**

650- 5 nk **Mississippi**[323] 4780 5-9-6 87 GrahamGibbons 3 90
(David Barron) *chsd ldrs: kpt on one pce appr fnl f* **11/1**

40-6 6 1/2 **Gabbiano**[37] 2110 5-9-6 87 AndreaAtzeni 13 89
(Jeremy Gask) *dwlt: hdwy 2f out: kpt on: nvr a threat* **16/1**

02-0 7 1/2 **Secondo (FR)**[42] 1975 4-9-9 93 WilliamTwiston-Davies(3) 5 93
(Roger Charlton) *dwlt: hld up in rr: hdwy on outside over 1f out: nvr rchd ldrs* **9/1**

2-00 8 hd **Picture Dealer**[15] 2778 5-9-6 90 SimonPearce(3) 9 90
(Lydia Pearce) *hld up in rr: effrt outside 2f out: nvr trbld ldrs* **12/1**

400- 9 3/4 **Secret Look**[214] 7851 4-9-7 88 FrannyNorton 7 85
(Ed McMahon) *chsd ldrs: one pce over 1f out* **33/1**

131 10 hd **Crisis Averted (IRE)**[94] 936 3-8-4 79 PaulHanagan 10 74
(Richard Fahey) *trckd ldrs: t.k.h: drvn 2f out: fdd appr fnl f* **12/1**

5053 11 hd **Secret Witness**[15] 2786 8-10-0 95 (b) LukeMorris 4 91
(Ronald Harris) *mid-div: drvn over 2f out: nvr a threat* **12/1**

0-16 12 shd **Huntsmans Close**[13] 2849 4-9-7 88 JamesDoyle 2 84
(Roger Charlton) *hld up in rr: hdwy over 1f out: nt clr run and eased last 75yds* **14/1**

20-0 13 nk **Fairway To Heaven (IRE)**[37] 2110 5-9-11 92 RobertWinston 11 87
(Michael Wigham) *dwlt: in rr: sme hdwy over 2f out: fdd fnl f* **16/1**

1m 12.17s (-1.43) **Going Correction** -0.025s/f (Good)
**WFA** 3 from 4yo+ 8lb **13 Ran SP% 119.1**
Speed ratings (Par 107): **108,107,105,104,103 103,102,102,101,101 100,100,100**
CSF £24.47 CT £137.33 TOTE £4.40: £2.10, £2.80, £3.60; EX 26.40 Trifecta £79.30.
**Owner** M A A Al-Mannai **Bred** T Jeffroy, B Jeffroy Et Al **Trained** Newmarket, Suffolk

**FOCUS**
A decent sprint handicap and solid form.

## 3272 RAF BENEVOLENT FUND H'CAP 1m (R)
**4:50** (4:52) (Class 4) (0-80,80) 4-Y-O+ £5,175 (£1,540; £769; £384) **Stalls** Low

Form RPR

134 1 **Self Employed**[25] 2462 7-8-11 70 LukeMorris 4 79
(Garry Woodward) *dwlt: hdwy on ins over 3f out: led over 1f out: kpt on wl* **12/1**

6465 2 1 1/4 **Tatting**[15] 2762 5-9-4 77 AdamKirby 2 83
(Chris Dwyer) *rr-div: hdwy on ins over 2f out: chsng ldrs over 1f out: tk 2nd last 75yds* **18/1**

2536 3 nk **Millkwood**[22] 2549 4-9-3 76 (b) PhillipMakin 7 81
(John Davies) *mid-div: hdwy over 2f out: chsng ldrs on inner over 1f out: kpt on to take 3rd last 75yds* **14/1**

60-0 4 1 **Mazaaher**[15] 2772 4-8-12 71 PaulHanagan 8 74
(B W Hills) *trckd ldrs: effrt on outer 3f out: kpt on ins fnl f: tk 4th last strides* **6/1[2]**

31-4 5 nk **It Must Be Faith**[26] 2444 4-9-0 73 AndrewMullen 5 75
(Michael Appleby) *trckd ldrs: t.k.h: led over 3f out: hdd over 1f out: one pce* **7/1[3]**

-460 6 1/2 **No Dominion (IRE)**[15] 2762 5-9-4 77 JamesDoyle 11 78
(James Given) *dwlt: hdwy over 2f out: chsng ldrs on inner over 1f out: kpt on same pce* **12/1**

313 7 1 3/4 **Glorious Star (IRE)**[23] 2527 4-8-13 72 WilliamBuick 1 69
(Ed Walker) *mid-div: effrt on ins over 2f out: one pce* **8/1**

-233 8 shd **Simply Shining (IRE)**[20] 2604 4-9-0 73 RyanMoore 9 70
(Richard Fahey) *chsd ldrs: upsides over 2f out: fdd fnl f* **11/2[1]**

-102 9 shd **Kiwi Bay**[20] 2603 9-9-7 80 PaulMulrennan 13 77
(Michael Dods) *chsd ldrs: one pce whn nt clr run over 1f out* **8/1**

5-40 10 1/2 **Red Paladin (IRE)**[36] 2169 4-8-9 68 (p) TonyHamilton 10 64
(Kevin Ryan) *in rr-div: sme hdwy on outer over 2f out: nvr a factor* **16/1**

0-20 11 hd **Thorntoun Lady (USA)**[25] 2454 4-8-3 69 JackGarritty(7) 12 64
(Jim Goldie) *hld up in rr: sme hdwy over 2f out: swtchd rt ins fnl f: nvr on terms* **33/1**

4-40 12 7 **Goldstorm**[37] 2117 6-9-7 80 (p) PaddyAspell 6 59
(Brian Baugh) *prom: effrt on outer over 2f out: lost pl over 1f out* **33/1**

3140 13 20 **Silverware (USA)**[41] 2017 6-9-5 78 TomEaves 14 11
(Kristin Stubbs) *w ldr: t.k.h: led over 4f out: hdd over 3f out: lost pl over 2f out: sn bhd: t.o* **33/1**

11-0 **14** *nk* **Cape Samba**[37] 2131 5-9-5 **78**........................ JamieSpencer 3 10
(Ismail Mohammed) *led: hdd over 4f out: lost pl over 2f out: bhd whn eased over 1f out: t.o* **6/1**[2]

1m 39.2s (-0.50) **Going Correction** +0.075s/f (Good) **14** Ran **SP% 120.7**
Speed ratings (Par 105): **105,103,103,102,102 101,99,99,99,99 99,92,72,71**
CSF £208.48 CT £3022.61 TOTE £15.10: £4.00, £4.70, £2.00; EX 229.50 Trifecta £3102.80 Part won..
**Owner** J Pownall **Bred** R G Percival And Mrs A Lockhart **Trained** Maltby, S Yorks

**FOCUS**
This looked very competitive for the grade. There was a fair early pace on and the came down the middle once straightened for home.

## 3273 BEN ELEPHANT H'CAP (BOBIS RACE) 1m (R)
**5:20** (5:22) (Class 4) (0-85,84) 3-Y-O **£5,175** (£1,540; £769; £384) **Stalls** Low

Form RPR

1-53 **1** **Billingsgate (IRE)**[40] 2063 3-9-5 **82**........................ AdamKirby 7 90
(Charlie Appleby) *dwlt: in rr: hdwy on outer over 2f out: str run fnl f: led nr fin* **8/1**[3]

1-31 **2** *3/4* **Sahra Al Khadra**[41] 2027 3-8-11 **74**........................ PaulHanagan 4 80
(Charles Hills) *trckd ldrs on outer: led 1f out: hdd and no ex nr fin* **8/1**[3]

1-42 **3** *1* **Gilbey's Mate**[34] 2203 3-9-2 **79**........................(p) WilliamBuick 3 83
(John Gosden) *chsd ldrs: upsides 1f out: kpt on same pce* **6/1**[2]

41-5 **4** *3/4* **Idder (IRE)**[72] 1279 3-9-3 **80**........................ AndreaAtzeni 8 82
(Roger Varian) *in rr: hdwy on inner over 2f out: chsng ldrs over 1f out: kpt on same pce* **3/1**[1]

4101 **5** *hd* **Basil Berry**[29] 2333 3-9-4 **84**........................ ConnorBeasley(3) 1 86
(Chris Dwyer) *sn w ldr: led over 3f out: hung lft and hdd 1f out: kpt on same pce* **9/1**

5264 **6** *nk* **Instant Attraction (IRE)**[15] 2781 3-9-4 **81**........................ RussKennemore 5 82
(Jedd O'Keeffe) *mid-div: effrt 3f out: one pce over 1f out* **8/1**[3]

0143 **7** *1/2* **Sakhalin Star (IRE)**[14] 2805 3-8-6 **72** ow2........................ SimonPearce(3) 11 72
(Richard Guest) *hld up in rr: hdwy over 2f out: kpt on fnl f* **25/1**

1-45 **8** *shd* **Dullingham**[20] 2617 3-9-7 **84**........................ JamieSpencer 9 85+
(Charlie Appleby) *hld up in rr: swtchd lft sn after s: hdwy over 2f out: swtchd lft over 1f out: swtchd rt and nt clr run wl ins fnl f: eased towards fin* **25/1**

112- **9** *1 3/4* **Hiking (USA)**[241] 7326 3-9-6 **83**........................ JamesDoyle 6 83+
(Roger Charlton) *hld up in rr: hdwy 5f out: chsng ldrs on inner over 1f out: one pce whn hmpd and eased wl ins fnl f* **6/1**[2]

0-41 **10** *nk* **Mayfield Boy**[16] 2749 3-8-13 **76**........................ DavidAllan 13 71
(Mel Brittain) *led: hdd over 4f out: wknd fnl 100yds* **20/1**

-126 **11** *4* **Kantara Castle (IRE)**[51] 1690 3-8-9 **72**........................(t) PaulMulrennan 2 58
(John Mackie) *chsd ldrs: lost pl over 1f out* **66/1**

3661 **12** *13* **Bridie ffrench**[19] 2639 3-8-10 **76**........................ WilliamTwiston-Davies(3) 10 32
(Mick Channon) *trckd ldrs on outer: t.k.h: lost pl over 1f out: sn heavily eased* **16/1**

1m 39.59s (-0.11) **Going Correction** +0.075s/f (Good) **12** Ran **SP% 116.7**
Speed ratings (Par 101): **103,102,101,100,100 100,99,99,97,97 93,80**
CSF £66.37 CT £414.68 TOTE £8.30: £3.30, £1.60, £1.50; EX 70.50 Trifecta £278.50.
**Owner** Godolphin **Bred** Darley **Trained** Newmarket, Suffolk

**FOCUS**
A fair 3yo handicap, run at a sound pace.
T/Jkpt: Not won. T/Plt: £531.30 to a £1 stake. Pool: £125,365.97 - 172.25 winning units T/Qpdt: £110.50 to a £1 stake. Pool: £10,057.20 - 67.30 winning units WG

# 3081 SALISBURY (R-H)
Sunday, June 15

**OFFICIAL GOING: Good to firm (firm in places; 9.5)**
Wind: Mild breeze; against Weather: Overcast

## 3274 PETER SYMONDS CATERING H'CAP 1m 4f
**1:45** (1:45) (Class 4) (0-85,83) 4-Y-O+ **£4,851** (£1,443; £721; £360) **Stalls** Low

Form RPR

0-12 **1** **Xinbama (IRE)**[11] 2882 5-9-0 **76**........................ KierenFallon 2 85
(B W Hills) *trckd ldrs: pushed along 4f out: nt clrest of runs over 2f out: led over 1f out: drifted lft: styd on wl: rdn out* **10/3**[3]

5040 **2** *1* **Icebuster**[30] 2309 6-9-7 **83**........................ GeorgeBaker 3 90
(Rod Millman) *hld up bhd ldng quartet: hdwy over 2f out: sn rdn: styd on ins fnl f: wnt 2nd towards fin* **5/1**

-551 **3** *nk* **Barwick**[30] 2305 6-8-8 **77**........................ CamHardie(7) 4 84
(Lady Herries) *trckd ldrs: rdn to mount chal wl over 1f out: styd on same pce fnl f: lost 2nd towards fin* **7/4**[1]

20/0 **4** *7* **Benbecula**[38] 427 5-8-13 **75**........................(b) HayleyTurner 5 71
(Richard Mitchell) *led: pushed along 4f out: rdn wl over 2f out: edgd lft and hdd over 1f out: no ex fnl f* **16/1**

54-0 **5** *3 3/4* **Australia Day (IRE)**[41] 1493 11-9-5 **81**........................ MartinDwyer 1 71
(Paul Webber) *trckd ldr: rdn wl over 2f out: hld over 1f out: fdd fnl f* **11/4**[2]

2m 34.39s (-3.61) **Going Correction** -0.20s/f (Firm) **5** Ran **SP% 108.7**
Speed ratings (Par 105): **104,103,103,98,95**
CSF £18.69 TOTE £3.80: £1.40, £2.70; EX 17.70 Trifecta £44.60.
**Owner** Tony Waspe Partnership **Bred** P Heffernan **Trained** Upper Lambourn, Berks

**FOCUS**
With two regular front-runners (the last two to finish) in this mid-range handicap, a good pace was guaranteed, although it wasn't a crazy gallop. The winner has been rated as running a personal best.

## 3275 WESTOVER GROUP H'CAP 5f
**2:15** (2:16) (Class 4) (0-85,85) 3-Y-O+ **£4,851** (£1,443; £721; £360) **Stalls** Low

Form RPR

-600 **1** **Extrasolar**[8] 2992 4-9-8 **79**........................(t) PatDobbs 3 90
(Amanda Perrett) *trckd ldrs: pushed along 2f out: led jst ins fnl f: r.o strly* **8/1**

54-4 **2** *1 1/4* **Angel Way (IRE)**[31] 2275 5-9-2 **73**........................ ShaneKelly 10 80
(Mike Murphy) *disp ld after 1f: narrow advantage over 2f out: rdn over 1f out: hdd jst ins fnl f: kpt on but no ex* **15/2**

0643 **3** *3/4* **Ginzan**[9] 2945 6-8-8 **70**........................ RyanWhile(5) 9 74
(Malcolm Saunders) *trckd ldrs: rdn 2f out: kpt on fnl f: wnt 3rd nring fin* **9/1**

1-10 **4** *nse* **Pal Of The Cat**[43] 1944 4-9-8 **82**........................(tp) OisinMurphy(3) 2 86
(Brian Gubby) *led: jnd after 1f: narrowly hdd over 2f out: kpt on same pce fnl f* **5/1**[3]

5420 **5** *1/2* **Waseem Faris (IRE)**[23] 2503 5-9-3 **81**........................ PaddyPilley(7) 8 83
(Mick Channon) *in tch: short of room briefly whn swtchd lft 2f out: sn rdn: kpt on but nt pce to get on terms fnl f* **15/2**

3033 **6** *3/4* **Secret Missile**[19] 2645 4-9-9 **80**........................(b) MartinDwyer 4 79
(William Muir) *in tch: rdn over 2f out: kpt on but nt pce to get on terms fnl f* **10/1**

-054 **7** *1 1/2* **Rebecca Romero**[9] 2945 7-9-5 **76**........................ RichardHughes 6 70
(Denis Coakley) *fly-leapt leaving stalls: hld up: swtchd lft 2f out: sn rdn: nvr any imp* **3/1**[1]

21-2 **8** *hd* **Agerzam**[148] 234 4-9-11 **82**........................ KierenFallon 7 75
(Roger Varian) *sn pushed along in tch: swtchd lft over 2f out: sn rdn and edgd lft: nvr finding pce to get involved* **9/2**[2]

59.79s (-1.21) **Going Correction** -0.20s/f (Firm) **8** Ran **SP% 113.6**
Speed ratings (Par 105): **101,99,97,96 95,93,93**
CSF £64.84 CT £555.80 TOTE £12.80: £3.50, £2.70, £2.60; EX 71.90 Trifecta £409.70.
**Owner** Odile Griffith & John Connolly **Bred** Brook Stud Bloodstock Ltd **Trained** Pulborough, W Sussex

**FOCUS**
This was a strongly run sprint, and the first four all raced closer to the far rail than the others. The third and fourth have been rated to their recent bests.

## 3276 WATERAID MILDREN CONSTRUCTION MAIDEN FILLIES' STKS (BOBIS RACE) (DIV I) 1m
**2:45** (2:49) (Class 5) 3-Y-O **£3,234** (£962; £481; £240) **Stalls** Low

Form RPR

-2 **1** **Belle D'Or (USA)**[15] 2780 3-9-0 0........................ RobertHavlin 3 88+
(John Gosden) *cl up: edgd lft briefly whn mounting chal over 1f out: led ent fnl f: r.o strly: readily* **5/6**[1]

2-63 **2** *4 1/2* **Makruma**[28] 2365 3-9-0 77........................ DaneO'Neill 8 77
(B W Hills) *in tch: swtchd lft 2f out: sn rdn: kpt on to go 2nd fnl 110yds: nvr gng pce of ready wnr* **7/1**

55 **3** *1* **Lilly Junior**[26] 2422 3-9-0 0........................ RichardHughes 9 75
(William Haggas) *sn cl up: rdn to dispute 2nd over 1f out: kpt on same pce fnl f* **7/2**[2]

2-04 **4** *nk* **Alys Love**[27] 2384 3-9-0 79........................ GrahamLee 10 74
(William Muir) *hld up: stmbld 4f out: pushed along and hdwy 2f out: sn rdn: tight of room over 1f out: kpt on same pce fnl f* **13/2**[3]

0 **5** *1 1/2* **Dubai Hadeia**[40] 2061 3-9-0 0........................ AhmedAjtebi 5 70
(Charlie Appleby) *trckd ldr: rdn over 2f out: nt quite pce to chal: no ex fnl 110yds* **25/1**

0- **6** *3 1/4* **Cayman Cry (USA)**[318] 4921 3-9-0 0........................ KierenFallon 2 65
(Brian Meehan) *led: rdn over 1f out: hdd ent fnl f: wknd fnl 110yds* **9/1**

**7** *15* **Perfect Outcome** 3-9-0 0........................ DavidProbert 4 26
(Patrick Chamings) *s.i.s: sn in tch: rdn over 2f out: wknd over 1f out* **66/1**

**8** *2 1/2* **Shanghai Sunrise** 3-8-7 0........................[1] DavidParkes(7) 1 20
(Keiran Burke) *trckd ldrs: rdn over 2f out: sn wknd* **50/1**

1m 41.54s (-1.96) **Going Correction** -0.20s/f (Firm) **8** Ran **SP% 119.9**
Speed ratings (Par 96): **101,96,95,95,93 90,75,72**
CSF £8.14 TOTE £1.70: £1.10, £2.10, £1.70; EX 7.50 Trifecta £26.70.
**Owner** A E Oppenheimer **Bred** Hascombe Stud **Trained** Newmarket, Suffolk

**FOCUS**
The winner showed she is significantly better than the others, although several of her opponents should find suitable races. The pace was ordinary. The slower of the two divisions. The second has been rated to her best.

## 3277 WATERAID MILDREN CONSTRUCTION MAIDEN FILLIES' STKS (BOBIS RACE) (DIV II) 1m
**3:20** (3:23) (Class 5) 3-Y-O **£3,234** (£962; £481; £240) **Stalls** Low

Form RPR

03 **1** **Palerma**[22] 2560 3-8-11 0........................ CharlesBishop(3) 4 80+
(Mick Channon) *in tch: swtchd lft wl over 2f out: sn pushed along: str run ent fnl f: led fnl 120yds: r.o wl* **7/2**[2]

**2** *1 1/4* **Blue Waltz** 3-9-0 0........................ LemosdeSouza 2 77+
(Luca Cumani) *trckd ldrs: rdn 2f out: ev ch briefly fnl 120yds: kpt on but nt pce of wnr* **10/1**

45 **3** *1 1/4* **Affaire De Coeur**[39] 2082 3-9-0 0........................ JimCrowley 9 74+
(David Simcock) *hld up: swtchd lft wl over 2f out: sn rdn: stdy prog frwl over 1f out: r.o wl ins fnl f: snatched 3rd fnl stride* **14/1**

3-5 **4** *hd* **Water Queen**[15] 2780 3-9-0 0........................ RichardHughes 1 73
(William Haggas) *led: rdn over 1f out: no ex whn hdd fnl 120yds: lost 3rd fnl stride* **15/8**[1]

63 **5** *1* **Sejel (IRE)**[18] 2682 3-9-0 0........................ DaneO'Neill 3 71
(John Gosden) *trckd ldrs: rdn over 2f out: kpt on same pce* **9/2**[3]

00- **6** *3 1/2* **Good Hope**[232] 7532 3-9-0 0........................ HayleyTurner 10 63
(Michael Bell) *hld up: pushed along over 3f out: rdn over 2f out: styd on but nvr gng pce to get on terms* **16/1**

06 **7** *1 3/4* **High Drama (IRE)**[17] 2690 3-9-0 0........................ DavidProbert 6 61
(Andrew Balding) *trckd ldr tl rdn 2f out: sn squeezed out: wknd fnl f* **6/1**

06 **8** *3 1/4* **Mystic Angel (IRE)**[14] 2804 3-9-0 0........................ MartinDwyer 8 51
(William Muir) *mid-div tl rdn over 2f out: sn btn* **40/1**

0 **9** *10* **Purple Spot**[18] 2682 3-9-0 0........................ SteveDrowne 5 27
(Rod Millman) *hld up: struggling 1/2-way: sn lost tch* **100/1**

1m 40.8s (-2.70) **Going Correction** -0.20s/f (Firm) **9** Ran **SP% 114.5**
Speed ratings (Par 96): **105,103,102,102,101 97,96,92,82**
CSF £37.88 TOTE £4.30: £1.50, £3.00, £3.70; EX 34.60 Trifecta £445.20.
**Owner** Jon and Julia Aisbitt **Bred** Whatton Manor Stud **Trained** West Ilsley, Berks
■ Stewards' Enquiry : Lemos de Souza one-day ban: careless riding (Jun 29)

**FOCUS**
This was more competitive than the first division, and they went a better gallop. The faster division but the form isn't as strong.

## 3278 EBF STALLIONS CATHEDRAL STKS (LISTED RACE) 6f
**3:55** (3:55) (Class 1) 3-Y-O+
**£22,684** (£8,600; £4,304; £2,144; £1,076; £540) **Stalls** Low

Form RPR

0-0 **1** **Indignant**[29] 2336 4-9-0 96........................ PatDobbs 5 106
(Richard Hannon) *a.p: led 2f out: sn rdn: r.o: rdn out* **18/1**

3-43 **2** *nk* **Professor**[13] 2848 4-9-5 108........................ RichardHughes 1 110+
(Richard Hannon) *hmpd s: in last pair: little outpcd over 3f out: swtchd lft over 2f out: sn rdn: hdwy over 1f out: r.o wl fnl f: clsng qckly on wnr but a being jst hld* **1/1**[1]

43-0 **3** *1 1/2* **Valonia**[64] 1435 3-8-6 97........................ HarryBentley 2 98
(Henry Candy) *led tl rdn 2f out: kpt on but no ex fnl 110yds* **7/1**[3]

54-0 **4** *nk* **Minalisa**[13] 2848 5-9-0 99........................ MartinDwyer 7 99
(Rae Guest) *trckd ldrs: rdn over 2f out: kpt on same pce fnl f* **8/1**

12-6 **5** *2 1/2* **Artistic Jewel (IRE)**[36] 2161 5-9-0 105........................ GrahamLee 4 91
(Ed McMahon) *trckd ldrs: rdn over 2f out: kpt on same pce fr over 1f out* **4/1**[2]

0363 6 6 **Ballista (IRE)**[39] 2074 6-9-5 101 RichardKingscote 3 77
(Tom Dascombe) *trckd ldrs: rdn over 2f out: wknd ent fnl f* **8/1**

406- 7 1 1/2 **Fig Roll**[226] 7657 3-8-6 98 (b[1]) ChrisCatlin 6 65
(Daniel Mark Loughnane) *hld up in last pair: pushed along over 3f out: rdn over 2f out: nvr any imp: wknd over 1f out* **33/1**

1m 11.81s (-2.99) **Going Correction** -0.20s/f (Firm)
**WFA** 3 from 4yo+ 8lb 7 Ran SP% **112.9**
Speed ratings (Par 111): **111,110,108,108,104 96,94**
CSF £35.97 TOTE £10.80: £4.20, £1.20; EX 23.80 Trifecta £187.10.
**Owner** Theakston Stud Syndicate **Bred** Theakston Stud **Trained** East Everleigh, Wilts

**FOCUS**
This was a classy line-up, but the pace wasn't anything special for such a good sprint. The form and time are ordinary for the level.

## 3279 BRIDGET SWIRE MEMORIAL MAIDEN STKS (BOBIS RACE) 6f
**4:30** (4:30) (Class 2) 2-Y-O **£9,703** (£2,887; £1,443; £721) **Stalls** Low

| Form | | | | RPR |
|---|---|---|---|---|
| 2 | 1 | | **Sixty (IRE)**[9] 2964 2-9-5 0 RichardHughes 4 *(Richard Hannon) mde all: shkn up over 1f out: r.o wl: pushed out* **10/11**[1] | 84 |
| 36 | 2 | 1 | **Silver Ranger**[19] 2642 2-9-5 0 PatDobbs 5 *(Richard Hannon) trckd wnr most of way: rdn 2f out: kpt on but nvr finding pce to get on terms fnl f* **6/1**[3] | 81 |
| | 3 | nk | **Dutch Connection** 2-9-5 0 GeorgeBaker 6 *(Charles Hills) hld up: hdwy 2f out: sn rdn: chal for 2nd over 1f out: kpt on same pce fnl f* **12/1** | 80+ |
| 6 | 4 | shd | **Markaz (IRE)**[23] 2507 2-9-5 0 DaneO'Neill 2 *(B W Hills) trckd ldrs: rdn to chal for 2nd fr wl over 1f out: wnt 2nd jst ins fnl f but hld by wnr: lost 2nd whn no ex nring fin* **7/2**[2] | 80 |
| | 5 | 7 | **Ghost Cat** 2-9-5 0 SeanLevey 3 *(Brian Meehan) cl up: rdn whn outpcd wl over 1f out: nt a danger after* **25/1** | 59 |
| 5 | 6 | nk | **Arc Cara (ITY)**[15] 2776 2-9-5 0 JimCrowley 1 *(Ralph Beckett) trckd wnr tl rdn 2f out: wknd ent fnl f* **8/1** | 58 |
| | 7 | 5 | **Pixeleen** 2-8-11 0 OisinMurphy(3) 7 *(Malcolm Saunders) in tch: effrt to cl over 3f out: sn rdn: wknd over 1f out* **50/1** | 38 |

1m 13.68s (-1.12) **Going Correction** -0.20s/f (Firm) 7 Ran SP% **113.5**
Speed ratings (Par 99): **99,97,97,97,87 87,80**
CSF £6.91 TOTE £1.50: £1.10, £3.00; EX 5.40 Trifecta £29.20.
**Owner** Mrs J Wood **Bred** Kevin & Meta Cullen **Trained** East Everleigh, Wilts

**FOCUS**
This was just a fair maiden for a track that stages many good ones, and the winner dictated at a routine tempo. The runner-up has been rated to his debut form.

## 3280 SARUM ASBESTOS LTD FILLIES' H'CAP 6f 212y
**5:05** (5:06) (Class 5) (0-75,76) 3-Y-O+ **£2,911** (£866; £432; £216) **Stalls** Centre

| Form | | | | RPR |
|---|---|---|---|---|
| 020 | 1 | | **Dorraar (IRE)**[27] 2404 3-9-1 72 KierenFallon 6 *(Roger Varian) cl up: pushed along over 2f out: led wl over 1f out: sn in command: r.o wl fnl f* **10/3**[3] | 78+ |
| 6-62 | 2 | 2 1/4 | **Royal Connection**[15] 2775 3-8-13 70 RichardHughes 7 *(Richard Hannon) stdd s: pushed along wl over 2f out: no hdwy tl ent fnl f: r.o wl to go 2nd fnl 75yds: a being hld by wnr* **5/2**[1] | 69 |
| 4-66 | 3 | 3/4 | **Djinni (IRE)**[16] 2749 3-9-1 72 SeanLevey 1 *(Richard Hannon) broke wl: led for 1f: trckd ldr: rdn whn sltly outpcd 2f out: kpt on ins fnl f* **10/1** | 69 |
| 6-00 | 4 | 1/2 | **Lady Phill**[48] 1789 4-9-9 70 KierenFox 3 *(Michael Attwater) led after 1f: rdn and hdd wl over 1f out: kpt on same pce fnl f* **22/1** | 70? |
| 5-21 | 5 | 1 | **A Legacy Of Love (IRE)**[10] 2929 3-9-5 76 GeorgeBaker 2 *(Amanda Perrett) racd keenly: trckd ldr: rdn 2f out: kpt on tl no ex fnl 110yds* **3/1**[2] | 69 |
| -436 | 6 | nk | **Persian Bolt (USA)**[6] 3067 3-9-1 72 (p) JohnFahy 5 *(Eve Johnson Houghton) hld up in tch: rdn wl over 1f out: nt pce to get involved* **6/1** | 64 |
| 10-0 | 7 | 1 1/4 | **It's Taboo**[15] 2775 4-9-6 67 DavidProbert 4 *(Mark Usher) cl up: rdn 2f out: fdd ins fnl f* **9/1** | 60 |

1m 27.34s (-1.26) **Going Correction** -0.20s/f (Firm)
**WFA** 3 from 4yo 10lb 7 Ran SP% **114.4**
Speed ratings (Par 100): **99,96,95,95,93 93,92**
CSF £12.13 TOTE £4.40: £2.20, £2.10; EX 9.90 Trifecta £76.80.
**Owner** Sheikh Ahmed Al Maktoum **Bred** Darley **Trained** Newmarket, Suffolk

**FOCUS**
This was a routine fillies' handicap, run at a medium pace until the leader kicked on 3f out. The runner-up has been rated to form.

## 3281 GOLDRING SECURITY SERVICES "HANDS AND HEELS" APPRENTICE SERIES H'CAP (EXCELLENCE INITATIVE) 1m
**5:35** (5:36) (Class 6) (0-65,65) 3-Y-O **£2,587** (£770; £384; £192) **Stalls** Low

| Form | | | | RPR |
|---|---|---|---|---|
| 5430 | 1 | | **Prim And Proper**[17] 2695 3-9-2 57 JennyPowell 9 *(Brendan Powell) awkwardly away: hld up: smooth hdwy fr over 3f out: led wl over 1f out: kpt on wl fnl f: pushed out* **7/1** | 64 |
| 6240 | 2 | 3/4 | **Fruit Pastille**[20] 2624 3-9-7 65 CharlieBennett(3) 2 *(Hughie Morrison) fly-leapt leaving stalls: trckd ldrs: led wl over 2f out: hdd wl over 1f out: kpt on fnl f: a being hld by wnr* **5/1**[2] | 70 |
| 05-2 | 3 | nse | **Stybba**[39] 2078 3-9-4 62 KieranShoemark(3) 4 *(Andrew Balding) mid-div: hdwy 3f out: shkn up 2f out: kpt on fnl f but a being hld* **6/4**[1] | 67 |
| -602 | 4 | 5 | **Dylan's Centenary**[44] 1918 3-8-13 59 SophieKilloran(5) 3 *(Rod Millman) mid-div: kpt on same pce fnl 2f: nvr threatened* **10/1** | 52 |
| 0-00 | 5 | 6 | **Moneypennie**[26] 2416 3-8-9 50 CharlotteJenner 10 *(Marcus Tregoning) trckd ldrs: effrt 3f out: wknd fnl f* **25/1** | 30 |
| 0023 | 6 | 5 | **Stoneham**[12] 2878 3-9-4 62 PaddyPilley(3) 7 *(Mick Channon) disp ld tl wl over 2f out: sn hld: wknd fnl f* **11/2**[3] | 30 |
| 600 | 7 | 4 1/2 | **Tohaveandtohold**[15] 2780 3-8-7 56 (p) GeorgiaCox(8) 1 *(William Haggas) disp ld tl wl over 2f out: wknd over 1f out* **8/1** | 14 |
| 0404 | 8 | 5 | **Lord Brantwood**[9] 2948 3-9-8 63 PatrickO'Donnell 6 *(Mick Channon) a towards rr* **16/1** | 9 |
| 00-0 | 9 | 14 | **D'Arcy Indiana**[52] 1684 3-8-5 46 (p) MichaelKenneally 11 *(Amy Weaver) awkward leaving stalls: a towards rr* **33/1** | |

1m 42.07s (-1.43) **Going Correction** -0.20s/f (Firm) 9 Ran SP% **117.4**
Speed ratings (Par 97): **99,98,98,93,87 82,77,72,58**
CSF £42.62 CT £81.27 TOTE £6.40: £1.50, £2.30, £1.30; EX 42.20 Trifecta £146.30.
**Owner** Mr & Mrs A J Mutch **Bred** Mrs J L Egan **Trained** Upper Lambourn, Berks

**FOCUS**
The pace was decent and the standard wasn't bad for an apprentice race. The first three came clear and the form makes a bit of sense.
T/Plt: £213.10 to a £1 stake. Pool: £68,142.80 - 233.38 winning units T/Qpdt: £7.50 to a £1 stake. Pool: £7,147.78 - 699.56 winning units TM

3282 - 3283a (Foreign Racing) - See Raceform Interactive

# 2532 CORK (R-H)
Sunday, June 15

**OFFICIAL GOING: Round course - good to firm; sprint course - good changing to good to firm after race 1 (2.10) changing to good to firm (firm in places) after race 4 (3.50)**

## 3284a MIDSUMMER SPRINT STKS (LISTED RACE) 5f
**3:15** (3:15) 3-Y-O+ **£21,666** (£6,333; £3,000; £1,000)

| | | | RPR |
|---|---|---|---|
| 1 | | **Timeless Call (IRE)**[48] 1824 6-9-7 100 PatSmullen 7 *(Reginald Roberts, Ire) led and disp: rdn w narrow advantage over 1f out and wnt 1 l clr: kpt on wl towards fin* **8/1** | 104 |
| 2 | 1/2 | **Jamesie (IRE)**[78] 1180 6-9-9 105 FergalLynch 1 *(David Marnane, Ire) hld up on outer: pushed along in 6th under 2f out: swtchd and clsd far side into 2nd fnl 100yds where edgd lft: kpt on wl towards fin to cl on wnr: nvr on terms* **12/1** | 104+ |
| 3 | 1 1/2 | **Master Speaker (IRE)**[10] 2939 4-9-9 94 (t) SJHassett 3 *(Martin Hassett, Ire) dwlt sltly: chsd ldrs: rdn in 6th over 1f out and clsd between horses ins fnl f into 3rd ins fnl 100yds where sltly impeded: nt trble wnr* **33/1** | 99 |
| 4 | 1/2 | **Eton Rifles (IRE)**[15] 2766 9-9-12 106 JosephO'Brien 6 *(Stuart Williams) chsd ldrs: 4th 1/2-way: rdn in 3rd 1 1/2f out and no imp on wnr in 2nd briefly ins fnl f: wknd towards fin* **2/1**[1] | 100 |
| 5 | hd | **Cape Of Approval (IRE)**[239] 7364 5-9-12 105 BillyLee 8 *(T Stack, Ire) w.w: last gng wl bhd horses ent fnl f: sn tk clsr order and kpt on wl under hands and heels wout ever threatening: dismntd qckly after line* **7/1**[3] | 99 |
| 6 | 1 3/4 | **Scream Blue Murder (IRE)**[23] 2532 4-9-4 102 (p) WayneLordan 4 *(T Stack, Ire) chsd ldrs: 5th 1/2-way: stl gng wl and n.m.r bhd horses ent fnl f: sn dropped to rr and no imp: kpt on again towards fin* **5/2**[2] | 85 |
| 7 | hd | **My Good Brother (IRE)**[10] 2939 5-9-9 104 (p) ColinKeane 2 *(T G McCourt, Ire) cl up on outer: 3rd 1/2-way: rdn and wknd fr over 1f out: no imp whn sltly hmpd ins fnl f* **10/1** | 89 |
| 8 | shd | **An Saighdiur (IRE)**[22] 2570 7-9-12 106 DeclanMcDonogh 5 *(Andrew Slattery, Ire) cl up: rdn in cl 2nd fr 1/2-way and sn no ex u.p 1 1/2f out: wknd fnl f* **8/1** | 92 |

57.56s (-1.64) 8 Ran SP% **116.4**
CSF £98.20 TOTE £7.00: £1.10, £4.50, £4.90; DF 113.50 Trifecta £1622.80.
**Owner** Reginald Roberts **Bred** John Quinn **Trained** Rathangan, Co Kildare

**FOCUS**
A competitive Listed race.

## 3285a MUNSTER OAKS STKS (GROUP 3) 1m 4f
**3:50** (3:52) 3-Y-O+ **£40,625** (£11,875; £5,625; £1,875)

| | | | RPR |
|---|---|---|---|
| 1 | | **Venus De Milo (IRE)**[9] 2973 4-9-12 112 JosephO'Brien 3 *(A P O'Brien, Ire) hld up: 6th 1/2-way: impr to chse ldrs far side over 2f out: sn rdn and clsd u.p to ld over 1f out: edgd lft briefly and styd on wl to extend advantage* **5/2**[2] | 106+ |
| 2 | 1 1/4 | **Dazzling (IRE)**[9] 2960 3-8-9 100 (p) SeamieHeffernan 6 *(A P O'Brien, Ire) sn led narrowly tl jnd bef 1/2-way: 1 l clr appr st: sn rdn and strly pressed: hdd over 1f out and kpt on wl towards fin wout matching wnr* **9/2**[3] | 101 |
| 3 | 3/4 | **Circling (IRE)**[17] 2714 3-8-9 92 (p) WayneLordan 2 *(David Wachman, Ire) prom: sn settled bhd ldrs: 4th 1/2-way: tk clsr order into st: sn rdn in 2nd and no ex u.p in 3rd over 1f out: kpt on same pce* **14/1** | 100 |
| 4 | 1 3/4 | **Morga (IRE)**[32] 2263 4-9-9 96 KevinManning 1 *(Desmond McDonogh, Ire) w.w in rr: last 1/2-way: rdn into st and wnt mod 6th u.p 2f out: kpt on wl ins fnl f: nvr nrr* **16/1** | 96 |
| 5 | 1 1/2 | **Drifting Mist**[9] 2973 4-9-9 94 (t) ShaneFoley 5 *(M Halford, Ire) chsd ldrs: 3rd 1/2-way: tk clsr order bhd ldrs into st: sn rdn and dropped to 5th u.p under fr 2f out: kpt on one pce* **14/1** | 94 |
| 6 | nse | **Edelmira (IRE)**[59] 1547 3-8-9 PatSmullen 4 *(D K Weld, Ire) chsd ldrs: 5th 1/2-way: rdn over 2f out and wnt 4th u.p over 1 1/2f out: no ex u.p ins fnl f: dropped to 6th nr fin* **6/4**[1] | 95 |
| 7 | 18 | **Cristal Fashion (IRE)**[32] 2263 3-8-9 97 [1] ColinKeane 7 *(G M Lyons, Ire) trckd ldrs on outer tl got on terms bef 1/2-way: pushed along in 2nd 4f out and sn no ex u.p in 6th: wknd* **8/1** | 66 |

2m 32.75s (-15.15)
**WFA** 3 from 4yo 15lb 7 Ran SP% **117.1**
CSF £14.83 TOTE £3.30: £1.50, £2.80; DF 17.40 Trifecta £77.60.
**Owner** Mrs John Magnier & Michael Tabor & Derrick Smith **Bred** Tullpark Ltd **Trained** Cashel, Co Tipperary

**FOCUS**
A good performance from the winner.

3286 - 3288a (Foreign Racing) - See Raceform Interactive

# 3027 CHANTILLY (R-H)
Sunday, June 15

**OFFICIAL GOING: Turf: good**

## 3289a PRIX DE DIANE LONGINES (GROUP 1) (3YO FILLIES) (TURF) 1m 2f 110y
**2:45** (12:00) 3-Y-O
**£476,166** (£190,500; £95,250; £47,583; £11,916; £11,916)

| | | | RPR |
|---|---|---|---|
| 1 | | **Avenir Certain (FR)**[35] 2195 3-9-0 0 GregoryBenoist 7 *(J-C Rouget, France) wnt lft s: hld up towards rr: hdwy on wd outside fr 2f out: rdn over 1f out: styd on strly and chal 100yds out: sn led and qckly clr: readily* **9/2**[2] | 113+ |
| 2 | 1 | **Amour A Papa (FR)**[32] 2267 3-9-0 0 Pierre-CharlesBoudot 4 *(J-Y Artu, France) hld up in midfield: rdn and hdwy fr over 1f out: styd on wl fnl f and wnt 2nd cl home: nt pce of wnr* **33/1** | 111 |

**3** *snk* **Xcellence (FR)**$^{35}$ 2195 3-9-0 0.......................... GeraldMosse 2 111
(F Doumen, France) *midfield in tch on inner: swtchd off rail and pushed along 2f out: rdn to chal over 1f out: w ldr ent fnl f: styd on but hdd fnl 100yds: hld and dropped to 3rd cl home* **14/1**

**4** *shd* **Shamkala (FR)**$^{32}$ 2267 3-9-0 0.......................... ChristopheSoumillon 6 111
(A De Royer-Dupre, France) *midfield on outer: pushed along 2f out: rdn over 1f out: nt qckn: styd on fnl f but nt pce of wnr* **11/10$^{1}$**

**5** *½* **Miss France (IRE)**$^{42}$ 1976 3-9-0 0.......................... MaximeGuyon 1 110
(A Fabre, France) *trckd ldr on inner: rdn 2f out and shuffled bk whn swtchd off rail to avoid wkng pcemaker: styd on wl fnl f and forced dead-heat for 5th post but nvr able to chal* **5/1$^{3}$**

**5** *dht* **Ball Dancing (USA)**$^{14}$ 2816 3-9-0 0..........................(b) AntoineHamelin 8 110
(Mme Pia Brandt, France) *wnt lft and bmpd rival s: prom on outer: rdn 2f out: chal over 1f out and ev ch ent fnl f: styd on but nt pce of wnr and jnd for 5th post* **28/1**

**7** *nse* **Bawina (IRE)**$^{35}$ 2195 3-9-0 0.......................... OlivierPeslier 12 110
(C Laffon-Parias, France) *broke wl fr wdst draw and led early: trckd ldr on outer once hdd: pushed along to ld again 2f out and angled to rail: rdn and jnd ent fnl f: styd on but hdd fnl 100yds: no ex* **9/1**

**8** *shd* **Bocaiuva (IRE)**$^{32}$ 2267 3-9-0 0.......................... Christophe-PatriceLemaire 3 110
(F Chappet, France) *hld up in midfield on inner: pushed along and angled off rail 2f out: rdn over 1f out: styd on wl fnl f but nt quite pce to chal* **66/1**

**9** *¾* **Lavender Lane (IRE)**$^{40}$ 3-9-0 0.......................... FabienLefebvre 5 108
(J E Hammond, France) *hld up towards rr on inner: angled off rail 2f out: pushed along and hdwy ent fnl f: sn swtchd rt: styng on wl whn nt clr run fnl 100yds: nt rcvr* **14/1**

**10** *10* **Feodora (GER)**$^{21}$ 2584 3-9-0 0.......................... StephanePasquier 11 89
(Frau R Weissmeier, Germany) *bmpd s: dropped in and hld up in last pair on inner: rdn over 2f out: sn outpcd and btn: eased fnl f: nvr a factor* **66/1**

**11** *8* **Bereni Ka (FR)**$^{21}$ 2586 3-9-0 0.......................... ThierryThulliez 9 73
(Y Gourraud, France) *bmpd s: stdd and hld up: a in rr: rdn 2f out: sn outpcd and btn: nvr a factor* **50/1**

**12** *1 ¼* **Local Hero (FR)**$^{30}$ 3-9-0 0.......................... MickaelBarzalona 10 71
(Y Durepaire, France) *bmpd s: sn led and crossed to rail: pushed along into st: rdn and hdd 2f out: sn no ex and btn: wknd on rail: eased and dropped to last fnl 100yds* **50/1**

2m 5.37s (-3.43) **Going Correction** +0.025s/f (Good) **12** Ran SP% **119.1**
Speed ratings: **113,112,112,112,111 111,111,111,111,103 97,97**
WIN (incl. 1 euro stake): 4.10. PLACES: 2.10, 6.70, 5.50. DF: 57.10. SF: 84.90.
**Owner** A Caro & G Augustin-Normand **Bred** Mme E Vidal **Trained** Pau, France

**FOCUS**
The English and French Guineas winners were in the line-up, together with the strongly fancied unbeaten Aga Khan filly Shamkala, and this looked a pretty good race on paper. However, despite a solid enough gallop they finished in a bit of a heap behind the impressive winner.

## 3290a PRIX DU LYS LONGINES (GROUP 3) (3YO COLTS & GELDINGS) (TURF) 1m 4f
4:05 (12:00) 3-Y-O £33,333 (£13,333; £10,000; £6,666; £3,333)

RPR

**1** **Guardini (FR)**$^{38}$ 3-8-11 0.......................... ChristopheSoumillon 7 105
(Jean-Pierre Carvalho, Germany) *mde all: rdn over 1f out: styd on strly and asserted fnl f: easing down and diminishing advantage at fin but in control: comf* **9/2$^{3}$**

**2** *½* **Teletext (USA)**$^{30}$ 3-8-11 0.......................... Christophe-PatriceLemaire 1 104
(P Bary, France) *prom early: sn midfield in tch: pushed along over 2f out: rdn over 1f out: styd on wl fnl f and wnt 2nd cl home: clsng on wnr at fin but a hld* **5/2$^{1}$**

**3** *nk* **Norse Prize (FR)**$^{43}$ 1965 3-8-11 0.......................... AlexisBadel 2 104
(Mme M Bollack-Badel, France) *sn trcking ldr on inner: pushed along 2f out: wnt 2nd and ev ch over 1f out: outpcd by wnr fnl f: styd on but hld and dropped to 3rd cl home* **6/1**

**4** *nk* **Glaring**$^{27}$ 3-8-11 0.......................... MaximeGuyon 3 103
(A Fabre, France) *midfield: rdn and hdwy on outer fr 2f out: styd on wl fnl f but nt pce to chal* **3/1$^{2}$**

**5** *¾* **Auvray (FR)**$^{37}$ 2141 3-8-11 0.......................... GregoryBenoist 5 102
(E Lellouche, France) *prom early: sn restrained and hld up towards rr: pushed along whn nt clr run fr 2f out tl swtchd lft over 1f out: rdn and styd on wl fnl f: wnt 5th towards fin but nvr able to chal* **7/1**

**6** *½* **Swansirized (IRE)**$^{26}$ 3-8-11 0.......................... AdrienFouassier 9 101
(Alain Couetil, France) *trckd ldr on outer: pushed along and effrt to chal 2f out: outpcd by wnr over 1f out: styd on but wl hld fnl f and dropped to 6th towards fin* **25/1**

**7** *1* **Sizing Stars**$^{21}$ 2585 3-8-11 0.......................... ThierryJarnet 4 99
(J Bertran De Balanda, France) *dwlt: pushed along and reminder early: hld up in rr: stdy hdwy on outer and prom 5f out: pushed along 2f out: sn outpcd: styd on but wl hld fnl f* **12/1**

**8** *1 ¼* **Sailor (FR)**$^{37}$ 2141 3-8-11 0..........................(b) IoritzMendizabal 6 97
(J Heloury, France) *t.k.h: sn midfield on inner: rdn over 2f out: outpcd and btn fnl f: plugged on* **25/1**

**9** *1 ¾* **Blushing Bere (FR)**$^{37}$ 2141 3-8-11 0.......................... FabriceVeron 8 95
(E Leenders, France) *hld up and a in rr: rdn 2f out: outpcd and btn fnl f: nvr a factor* **14/1**

2m 30.45s (-0.55) **Going Correction** +0.025s/f (Good) **9** Ran SP% **120.6**
Speed ratings: **102,101,101,101,100 100,99,98,97**
WIN (incl. 1 euro stake): 4.30. PLACES: 1.70, 1.60, 2.30. DF: 9.90. SF: 23.00.
**Owner** Stall Ullmann **Bred** Gestut Schlenderhan **Trained** Germany

## 3291a PRIX BERTRAND DU BREUIL LONGINES (PRIX DU CHEMIN DE FER DU NORD) (GROUP 3) (4YO+) (TURF) 1m
5:15 (12:00) 4-Y-O+ £33,333 (£13,333; £10,000; £6,666; £3,333)

RPR

**1** **Pinturicchio (IRE)**$^{45}$ 1908 6-8-11 0.......................... AnthonyCrastus 6 112
(E Lellouche, France) *midfield early: hld up towards rr after 3f: nudged along and effrt on outer under 2f out: rdn to chse ldrs over 1f out: r.o to ld 100yds out: a holding runner-up to win a shade cosily* **6/1$^{3}$**

**2** *hd* **Spoil The Fun (FR)**$^{65}$ 5-8-11 0.......................... JulienAuge 4 112
(C Ferland, France) *sn racing in midfield: 6th on inner and short of room 2f out: rousted and hdwy over 1f out: r.o u.p fnl 150yds: nvr quite getting up* **22/1**

**3** *½* **Silas Marner (FR)**$^{26}$ 2449 7-8-11 0.......................... ChristopheSoumillon 11 110
(J-C Rouget, France) *hld up towards rr: pushed along and hdwy on outer 1 1/2f out: styd on u.p fnl f to press eventual wnr 100yds out: rn flattened out fnl 75yds* **5/2$^{1}$**

**4** *1 ¼* **Felician (GER)**$^{273}$ 6451 6-8-11 0.......................... ThierryThulliez 10 108
(Ferdinand J Leve, Germany) *hld up in rr: last and rdn over 1f out: styd on wl fnl f: nrest at fin* **20/1**

**5** *shd* **Market Share**$^{26}$ 2449 4-8-11 0.......................... Christophe-PatriceLemaire 1 107
(P Bary, France) *reluctant to enter stalls: trckd ldrs on rail: qcknd to ld ent fnl f: hdd 100yds out: no ex* **7/1**

**6** *nk* **Pilote (IRE)**$^{45}$ 1908 4-8-11 0.......................... OlivierPeslier 8 107
(A Fabre, France) *w.w towards rr: bhd wall of horses on inner fr 2f out: in clr and nt qckn immediately appr 1f out: kpt on wl ins fnl f: nvr on terms* **10/1**

**7** *shd* **Akemi (IRE)**$^{26}$ 2449 4-8-8 0.......................... MaximeGuyon 3 103
(X Thomas-Demeaulte, France) *midfield: rdn and no imp 1 1/2f out: styd on ins fnl f: n.d* **20/1**

**8** *snk* **Empire Storm (GER)**$^{15}$ 2765 7-8-11 0.......................... MickaelBarzalona 2 106
(Michael Attwater) *led: rdn and lened over 1 1/2f out: hdd ent fnl f: grad fdd* **16/1**

**9** *shd* **Sparkling Beam (IRE)**$^{48}$ 1827 4-8-8 0.......................... ThierryJarnet 9 103
(J E Pease, France) *midfield on outer: 6th and travelling wl 4f out: rdn to chse ldrs over 1 1/2f out: cl 3rd and ev ch ent fnl f: grad outpcd last 100yds* **9/2$^{2}$**

**10** *snk* **Fire Ship**$^{34}$ 2223 5-8-11 0.......................... GeraldMosse 7 105
(William Knight) *prom on outer: rdn to chal over 2f out: sn no imp: grad lft bhd fnl f* **8/1**

**11** *2* **Dylar (FR)**$^{14}$ 7-8-11 0.......................... VincentVion 5 101
(L Nyffels, France) *tk a t.k.h: chsd ldrs: wknd appr fnl f: eased* **20/1**

1m 35.49s (-2.51) **Going Correction** +0.025s/f (Good) **11** Ran SP% **118.3**
Speed ratings: **113,112,112,111,110 110,110,110,110,110 108**
WIN (incl. 1 euro stake): 7.70. PLACES: 2.10, 4.80, 1.40. DF: 66.70. SF: 138.70.
**Owner** Mlle Julia Rusu **Bred** Dayton Investments Ltd **Trained** Lamorlaye, France

3292 - (Foreign Racing) - See Raceform Interactive

# 2377 COLOGNE (R-H)
Sunday, June 15

**OFFICIAL GOING: Turf: good**

## 3293a OPPENHEIM-UNION-RENNEN (GROUP 2) (3YO) (TURF) 1m 3f
3:15 (12:00) 3-Y-O
£33,333 (£12,916; £5,416; £3,333; £2,083; £1,250)

RPR

**1** **Sea The Moon (GER)**$^{35}$ 3-9-2 0.......................... AHelfenbein 2 110+
(Markus Klug, Germany) *mde all: led on ins rail: pushed along over 2 1/2f out: chal on both side fr 2f out: rdn and edgd lft fr 1 1/2f out to end up on stands' rail ins fnl f: r.o wl and asserted fnl 100yds: readily* **7/10$^{1}$**

**2** *3* **Rapido (GER)**$^{28}$ 3-9-2 0.......................... FrederikTylicki 7 104
(Andreas Lowe, Germany) *settled in 5th: 4th and wl in tch 1/2-way: rdn to chal on outer 2f out: twice sltly impeded by rivals edging lft fr 1 1/2f out: styd on ent fnl f: nt pce of wnr but tk 2nd cl home* **76/10**

**3** *nk* **Swacadelic (GER)**$^{28}$ 3-9-2 0.......................... FilipMinarik 1 103
(Jean-Pierre Carvalho, Germany) *trckd ldr on inner: rdn to chal over 2f out: edgd lft fr 1 1/2f out: kpt on at one pce fnl f: lost 2nd cl home* **29/10$^{2}$**

**4** *6* **Chartbreaker (FR)**$^{28}$ 3-9-2 0.......................... EPedroza 3 92
(A Wohler, Germany) *trckd ldrs on outer: lost pl 1/2-way: rdn and no imp fr over 2f out: one pce fnl f* **122/10**

**5** *½* **Open Your Heart (GER)**$^{28}$ 3-9-2 0.......................... MartinLane 5 91
(R Dzubasz, Germany) *w.w towards rr on inner: hrd rdn 2f out: plugged on at same pce fnl f: nvr threatened ldrs* **152/10**

**6** *10* **Suracon (GER)**$^{29}$ 3-9-2 0.......................... AdrianNicholls 6 73
(A Wohler, Germany) *scrubbed along in rr: last and hrd rdn 2f out: nvr in contention* **26/1**

**7** *3 ½* **Giant's Cauldron (GER)**$^{15}$ 3-9-2 0.......................... AdriedeVries 4 67
(P Schiergen, Germany) *trckd ldr on outer: rdn and edgd lft fr 1 1/2f out: wknd qckly appr fnl f: heavily eased* **51/10$^{3}$**

2m 17.76s (-3.04) **7** Ran SP% **129.9**
WIN (incl. 10 euro stake): 17. PLACES: 13, 22. SF: 76.
**Owner** Gestut Gorlsdorf **Bred** Gestut Gorlsdorf **Trained** Germany

# 2823 CARLISLE (R-H)
Monday, June 16

**OFFICIAL GOING: Good to firm (7.7)**
Wind: Breezy, half behind Weather: Cloudy, sunny spells

## 3296 GERMANY V PORTUGAL LIVE @ FOOTBALLSCORES.COM MAIDEN AUCTION STKS (DIV I) 5f 193y
2:15 (2:16) (Class 5) 2-Y-O £2,587 (£770; £384; £192) Stalls Low

Form RPR

**1** **Fugleman (IRE)** 2-8-13 0.......................... KevinStott$^{(5)}$ 1 80+
(Ben Haslam) *hld up bhd ldng gp: hdwy over 1f out: led ins fnl f: drifted lft: kpt on wl* **20/1**

**2** *1 ¾* **Arabian Bride (IRE)** 2-8-13 0.......................... JoeFanning 5 70
(Mark Johnston) *t.k.h early: pressed ldr: rdn and ev ch over 1f out: chsd wnr ins fnl f: kpt on fin* **3/1$^{1}$**

**3** *hd* **Mrs Biggs** 2-8-5 0.......................... NeilFarley$^{(3)}$ 6 64
(Declan Carroll) *trckd ldrs on outside: hdwy to ld over 1f out: rdn and hdd ins fnl f: kpt on same pce* **18/1**

3 **4** *3* **Ocean Sheridan (IRE)**$^{21}$ 2601 2-9-1 0.......................... ConnorBeasley$^{(3)}$ 4 65
(Michael Dods) *plld hrd early: trckd ldrs: effrt and rdn 2f out: kpt on same pce fnl f* **4/1$^{2}$**

**5** *½* **Monksford Lady** 2-8-10 0.......................... GrahamLee 9 56+
(Donald McCain) *hld up on outside: effrt and pushed along 2f out: edgd rt and one pce fnl f* **16/1**

5 **6** *1 ¼* **Miss Van Gogh**$^{37}$ 2173 2-8-10 0.......................... TonyHamilton 2 53
(Richard Fahey) *trckd ldrs: rdn along 1/2-way: outpcd over 1f out: btn fnl f* **9/2$^{3}$**

4 **7** *¾* **Charles Messier**$^{24}$ 2513 2-9-4 0.......................... RoystonFfrench 3 58
(Bryan Smart) *led tl rdn and hdd over 1f out: wknd ins fnl f* **3/1$^{1}$**

**8** *5* **Magic Empress (IRE)** 2-8-8 0.......................... BarryMcHugh 8 33
(Tony Coyle) *dwlt: t.k.h and sn prom: rdn over 2f out: wknd over 1f out* **100/1**

0 **9** 1/2 **Flying Grange**[12] 2895 2-8-13 0 ........................ DavidAllan 10 36
(Tim Easterby) *bhd and sn pushed along: drvn 1/2-way: nvr on terms* **28/1**

6 **10** 3/4 **Queen Of The Scots**[35] 2206 2-8-10 0 ........................ TomEaves 7 31
(Keith Dalgleish) *t.k.h: hld up on outside: effrt whn nt clr run over 2f out: sn rdn and btn* **14/1**

1m 12.84s (-0.86) **Going Correction** -0.225s/f (Firm) **10** Ran SP% **115.2**
Speed ratings (Par 93): **96,93,93,89,88 87,86,79,78,77**
CSF £77.61 TOTE £25.50: £5.80, £2.00, £3.70; EX 131.50 Trifecta £2015.70.

**Owner** Middleham Park Racing XXVII **Bred** J Osborne **Trained** Middleham Moor, N Yorks

**FOCUS**

After a dry morning, the going was changed to good to firm all round. Those with previous experience didn't set a demanding standard for the newcomers to aim at and debutants filled the first three places. Inside rail moved out 2yds from 1m start around Old Stable bend and races on Round course increased by 4yds.

## 3297 GERMANY V PORTUGAL LIVE @ FOOTBALLSCORES.COM MAIDEN AUCTION STKS (DIV II) 5f 193y

**2:45** (2:46) (Class 5) 2-Y-O **£2,587** (£770; £384; £192) **Stalls** Low

Form RPR

0 **1** **Sakhee's Return**[29] 2358 2-8-13 0 ........................ DuranFentiman 7 75
(Tim Easterby) *in tch: effrt and rn green over 2f out: led and edgd rt over 1f out: kpt on strly to go clr fnl f* **20/1**

**2** 2 1/4 **Alans Pride (IRE)** 2-8-10 0 ........................ ConnorBeasley(3) 2 68
(Michael Dods) *hld up bhd ldng gp: effrt and pushed along over 2f out: chsd wnr last 100yds: kpt on: no imp* **4/1**[2]

053 **3** 2 1/4 **Diatomic (IRE)**[19] 2673 2-9-1 0 ........................ StephenCraine 3 63
(Tom Dascombe) *led: rdn and hdd over 1f out: kpt on same pce and lost 2nd last 100yds* **6/1**

**4** 1 1/2 **Tantric Lady** 2-8-8 0 ........................ BenCurtis 1 52
(Alan McCabe) *dwlt: bhd and pushed along over 3f out: hdwy over 1f out: kpt on fnl f: nvr able to chal* **14/1**

**5** 2 3/4 **Grand Proposal** 2-9-4 0 ........................ PaulMulrennan 5 53
(Kevin Ryan) *hld up in tch on outside: effrt and rdn over 2f out: no ex fr over 1f out* **7/1**

0 **6** 2 3/4 **Sunhill Lodge Lady**[46] 1900 2-8-6 0 ........................ PJMcDonald 6 33
(Ann Duffield) *chsd ldrs: drvn over 2f out: wknd over 1f out* **12/1**

**7** 3/4 **Ifittakesforever (IRE)** 2-9-4 0 ........................ StevieDonohoe 4 43
(Tim Pitt) *dwlt: bhd and sn pushed along: nvr on terms* **25/1**

35 **8** 8 **Howlin'For You**[35] 2206 2-8-10 0 ........................ RobertWinston 9 11
(David Brown) *t.k.h: hld up on outside: effrt and rdn over 2f out: wknd wl over 1f out* **9/2**[3]

4 **9** 10 **Elizabeth Ernest**[30] 2349 2-8-5 0 ........................ GeorgeChaloner(3) 8 +
(Richard Fahey) *plld hrd early and sddle sn slipped forward: w ldr to 2f out: struggling whn rdr rode wout irons and eased fr over 1f out* **3/1**[1]

1m 12.87s (-0.83) **Going Correction** -0.225s/f (Firm) **9** Ran SP% **112.9**
Speed ratings (Par 93): **96,93,90,88,84 80,79,69,55**
CSF £96.27 TOTE £19.80: £6.80, £1.60, £1.70; EX 108.80 Trifecta £774.90.

**Owner** Ontoawinner, M Hulin & Partner **Bred** W Brackstone & S J Whitear **Trained** Great Habton, N Yorks

**FOCUS**

This didn't look particularly strong beforehand, but the winner did it decisively and the time was only 0.03 seconds slower than the first division.

## 3298 MOLSON COORS H'CAP 5f 193y

**3:15** (3:16) (Class 5) (0-70,70) 3-Y-O+ **£2,587** (£770; £384; £192) **Stalls** Low

Form RPR

0306 **1** **Meandmyshadow**[10] 2955 6-9-7 63 ........................ DaleSwift 3 72
(Alan Brown) *mde all: rdn over 2f out: hld on gamely fnl f* **6/1**[2]

-300 **2** 1 **Salvatore Fury (IRE)**[19] 2677 4-9-9 65 ........................ (p) GrahamLee 10 71
(Keith Dalgleish) *plld hrd early: hld up: hdwy on outside over 1f out: hdwy to chse wnr ins fnl f: edgd rt: kpt on* **8/1**

0542 **3** hd **Consistant**[38] 2127 6-9-0 56 ........................ DuranFentiman 8 61
(Brian Baugh) *prom on outside: effrt and rdn over 2f out: chsd wnr briefly ins fnl f: kpt on: hld nr fin* **10/1**

140 **4** 3/4 **Shillito**[21] 2606 4-9-5 61 ........................ BarryMcHugh 2 64
(Tony Coyle) *in tch: hdwy to chse wnr over 1f out to ins fnl f: kpt on same pce* **16/1**

0342 **5** nk **Mission Impossible**[10] 2955 9-9-4 60 ........................ (p) RobertWinston 4 62
(Tracy Waggott) *trckd ldrs: n.m.r over 2f out: effrt and rdn on ins over 1f out: one pce fnl f* **10/1**

21- **6** 1 1/4 **Kirtling Belle**[297] 5710 3-9-4 67 ........................ TomEaves 6 63
(Keith Dalgleish) *midfield: rdn along over 2f out: hdwy over 1f out: kpt on: nt pce to chal* **16/1**

25-3 **7** 1/2 **Rich Again (IRE)**[14] 2825 5-9-8 64 ........................ JoeFanning 7 60+
(James Bethell) *s.i.s: hld up on ins: effrt whn n.m.r over 2f out: effrt over 1f out: no imp* **4/1**[1]

646- **8** shd **Paddy's Rock (IRE)**[294] 5826 3-8-9 58 ........................ [1] PJMcDonald 5 52
(Ann Duffield) *dwlt: bhd and pushed along: drvn over 2f out: kpt on fnl f: nvr able to chal* **20/1**

6652 **9** 1 1/4 **Thatcherite (IRE)**[21] 2606 6-10-0 70 ........................ (t) StephenCraine 9 62+
(Tony Coyle) *hld up: effrt whn nt clr run over 2f out and over 1f out: nvr able to chal* **13/2**[3]

25-6 **10** 1 1/2 **Red Cobra (IRE)**[21] 2606 4-9-2 58 ........................ DavidAllan 1 45
(Tim Easterby) *t.k.h in midfield: effrt whn n.m.r briefly over 2f out: effrt wl over 1f out: btn ins fnl f* **6/1**[2]

3400 **11** 1/2 **Iggy**[5] 3092 4-9-3 59 ........................ (t) GrahamGibbons 12 44
(Michael Easterby) *pressed wnr: drvn over 2f out: wkng whn hmpd ins fnl f* **12/1**

0040 **12** 9 **Great Demeanor (USA)**[26] 2452 4-8-10 57 ........................ EmmaSayer(5) 11 14
(Dianne Sayer) *bhd and sn pushed along: struggling fr 1/2-way: nvr on terms* **100/1**

1m 11.77s (-1.93) **Going Correction** -0.225s/f (Firm)
**WFA** 3 from 4yo+ 7lb **12** Ran SP% **116.4**
Speed ratings (Par 103): **103,101,101,100,100 98,97,97,95,93 93,81**
CSF £52.43 CT £481.03 TOTE £8.40: £2.80, £6.60, £2.40; EX 57.20 Trifecta £931.40.

**Owner** G Morrill **Bred** M J Dawson **Trained** Yedingham, N Yorks

■ Stewards' Enquiry : Dale Swift two-day ban: careless riding (Jun 30-Jul 1)

**FOCUS**

A run-of-the-mill sprint handicap with the winner showing a good attitude to make all from her good draw.

## 3299 WORLD CUP LIVE UPDATES @BOOKMAKERS.CO.UK H'CAP 7f 200y

**3:45** (3:46) (Class 5) (0-70,70) 4-Y-O+ **£2,587** (£770; £384; £192) **Stalls** Low

Form RPR

**1** **Senor George (IRE)**[43] 1992 7-8-13 62 ........................ PJMcDonald 7 73
(Tony Coyle) *hld up in midfield: pushed along over 2f out: hdwy over 1f out: disp ld last 100yds: led cl home* **8/1**

6031 **2** shd **Mercers Row**[21] 2605 7-8-12 68 ........................ GemmaTutty(7) 10 78
(Karen Tutty) *t.k.h in rr: rdn and gd hdwy on outside over 1f out: led ins fnl f: sn edgd lft and jnd: hdd cl home* **8/1**

23-2 **3** 2 1/2 **Live Dangerously**[35] 2215 4-9-6 69 ........................ (t) TomEaves 9 73
(Keith Dalgleish) *trckd ldrs: rdn over 2f out: led over 1f out to ins fnl f: kpt on same pce* **5/1**[2]

0-06 **4** 1 1/4 **Kuwait Star**[23] 2546 5-9-2 65 ........................ TonyHamilton 1 66
(Michael Herrington) *in tch on ins: drvn over 2f out: rallied over 1f out: nt qckn ins fnl f* **16/1**

0-02 **5** nk **Byron's Dream**[27] 2426 4-8-11 60 ........................ RussKennemore 4 61
(Jedd O'Keeffe) *t.k.h: hld up in tch: effrt and ch appr fnl f: outpcd last 150yds* **8/1**

14-3 **6** 1 3/4 **Pat's Legacy (USA)**[21] 2607 8-9-0 63 ........................ BarryMcHugh 3 60
(Marjorie Fife) *led tl rdn and hdd over 1f out: sn no ex* **3/1**[1]

2000 **7** 3 1/4 **Rio Cobolo (IRE)**[16] 2763 8-8-11 60 ........................ (b) PhillipMakin 8 49
(Philip Kirby) *missed break: bhd: gd hdwy against ins rail over 1f out: no imp fnl f* **22/1**

00-0 **8** 1 3/4 **Majestic Dream (IRE)**[56] 1610 6-9-7 70 ........................ GrahamGibbons 5 55
(Michael Easterby) *pressed ldr: drvn over 2f out: wknd over 1f out* **40/1**

01 **9** 6 **Poor Duke (IRE)**[65] 1450 4-9-7 70 ........................ (p) JoeFanning 11 41
(Michael Mullineaux) *hld up in midfield on outside: struggling over 2f out: btn over 1f out* **13/2**[3]

6000 **10** 3 3/4 **Jebel Tara**[7] 3054 9-8-13 62 ........................ (p[1]) RobertWinston 2 25
(Alan Brown) *hld up on ins: drvn along over 3f out: nvr on terms* **16/1**

502 **11** 3 1/4 **Alanos (IRE)**[25] 2477 5-9-7 70 ........................ PaulMulrennan 6 25
(James Ewart) *prom tl rdn and wknd fr 2f out* **14/1**

200- **12** 8 **Tanforan**[262] 6803 12-8-9 58 ........................ DavidAllan 12
(Brian Baugh) *bhd on outside: struggling 3f out: edgd rt and wknd over 2f out* **66/1**

1m 38.25s (-1.75) **Going Correction** -0.225s/f (Firm) **12** Ran SP% **115.0**
Speed ratings (Par 103): **99,98,96,95,94 93,89,88,82,78 75,67**
CSF £67.40 CT £353.77 TOTE £11.40: £5.00, £1.70, £1.90; EX 84.50 Trifecta £1323.10.

**Owner** B Dunn **Bred** T Kilduff **Trained** Norton, N Yorks

**FOCUS**

A cracking finish in a truly run contest with the winner getting up late to make a successful start for his new stable.

## 3300 EBF STALLIONS WORLD CUP FREE BETS FILLIES' H'CAP (BOBIS RACE) 6f 192y

**4:15** (4:17) (Class 4) (0-80,78) 3-Y-O **£7,762** (£2,310; £1,154; £577) **Stalls** Low

Form RPR

01-2 **1** **Jacquotte Delahaye**[11] 2929 3-9-4 78 ........................ (b) ConnorBeasley(3) 8 83
(David Brown) *midfield: rdn and hdwy to ld over 1f out: hld on wl fnl f* **7/1**[3]

-061 **2** 1 **Miaplacidus (IRE)**[17] 2729 3-7-13 61 ........................ SammyJoBell(5) 10 63
(Richard Fahey) *hld up on outside: hdwy to chse wnr over 1f out: kpt on: nt pce to chal* **8/1**

05-4 **3** 1/2 **Augusta Ada**[29] 2361 3-9-6 77 ........................ PaulMulrennan 4 78+
(Ollie Pears) *trckd ldrs: effrt whn nt clr run and swtchd lft over 2f out: rallied and hung rt appr fnl f: r.o* **8/1**

-550 **4** nk **Imshivalla (IRE)**[35] 2218 3-8-13 70 ........................ TonyHamilton 7 70
(Richard Fahey) *prom: hdwy and ev ch wl over 1f out: sn rdn: edgd rt and one pce ent fnl f* **12/1**

3032 **5** 1 1/2 **Jive**[17] 2745 3-8-13 70 ........................ JoeFanning 2 66
(Richard Hannon) *hld up bhd ldng gp: n.m.r briefly over 2f out: effrt over 1f out: no imp fnl f* **11/4**[1]

-613 **6** 1 **Bajan Rebel**[14] 2828 3-8-2 59 ........................ JamesSullivan 6 53
(Michael Easterby) *s.i.s: bhd: pushed along 3f out: hdwy over 1f out: kpt on: nvr nrr* **18/1**

51-0 **7** 1 1/2 **L'Artiste (IRE)**[17] 2740 3-8-13 70 ........................ PhillipMakin 11 60
(John Quinn) *hld up towards rr: drvn along over 2f out: no imp fr over 1f out* **25/1**

0133 **8** 3/4 **Election Night**[13] 2870 3-8-13 70 ........................ DuranFentiman 3 58
(Tim Easterby) *taken early to post: t.k.h: led tl rdn and hdd over 2f out: wknd over 1f out* **11/2**[2]

-150 **9** nk **Platinum Pearl**[32] 2274 3-9-0 71 ........................ GrahamLee 1 58
(Peter Chapple-Hyam) *t.k.h: trckd ldrs tl rdn and wknd over 1f out* **15/2**

535- **10** 1 1/4 **Scots Law (IRE)**[269] 6582 3-9-0 71 ........................ TomEaves 5 55
(Keith Dalgleish) *t.k.h: cl up: led over 2f out to over 1f out: sn wknd* **20/1**

0020 **11** 3 1/4 **Clever Miss**[17] 2929 3-8-9 69 ........................ (b[1]) JasonHart(3) 9 44
(Alan McCabe) *s.s: bhd: struggling over 3f out: nvr on terms* **18/1**

1m 26.63s (-0.47) **Going Correction** -0.225s/f (Firm) **11** Ran SP% **115.4**
Speed ratings (Par 98): **93,91,91,90,89 88,86,85,85,83 80**
CSF £60.76 CT £465.32 TOTE £6.90: £1.40, £3.30, £3.40; EX 81.90 Trifecta £877.70.

**Owner** Just For Girls Partnership **Bred** A S Denniff **Trained** Averham Park, Notts

**FOCUS**

This looked a competitive enough handicap on paper, but it produced a ready winner.

## 3301 MARTIN RUDDICK "MARRIED TO PENRITH AUCTION" H'CAP (JOCKEY CLUB GRASSROOTS MIDDLE DISTANCE SERIES) 1m 1f 61y

**4:45** (4:58) (Class 5) (0-70,70) 4-Y-O+ **£2,587** (£770; £384; £192) **Stalls** Low

Form RPR

4315 **1** **Ellaal**[11] 2912 5-9-2 65 ........................ PaulMulrennan 9 73
(Ruth Carr) *prom: shkn up to ld over 1f out: drvn and hld on wl fnl f* **7/2**[2]

-006 **2** nk **Tectonic (IRE)**[14] 2823 5-9-3 66 ........................ (p) TomEaves 1 73
(Keith Dalgleish) *hld up in tch: hdwy to chse wnr over 1f out: kpt on fnl f: hld nr fin* **5/1**[3]

2015 **3** hd **Push Me (IRE)**[9] 3005 7-9-7 70 ........................ GrahamLee 8 77
(Iain Jardine) *hld up in midfield: hdwy to chse ldrs over 1f out: drvn and hld on wl fnl f: hld towards fin* **12/1**

3-00 **4** 2 **Triple Eight (IRE)**[13] 2872 6-9-4 67 ........................ (b) RussKennemore 2 70+
(Philip Kirby) *missed break: hld up: rdn and hdwy on outside over 2f out: edgd rt and styd on fnl f: nrst fin* **17/2**

0431 **5** 2 1/4 **Cameroooney**[11] 2911 11-8-13 69 ........................ (p) MeganCarberry(7) 11 67
(Marjorie Fife) *led at ordinary gallop: rdn and hdd over 1f out: kpt on same pce fnl f* **3/1**[1]

0 **6** *hd* **Dabuki (FR)**[24] 2520 4-9-6 **69**..............(p) PJMcDonald 12 67
(Geoffrey Harker) *pressed ldr: drvn over 2f out: edgd rt and outpcd over 1f out* **33/1**

-406 **7** *2* **Gold Chain (IRE)**[13] 2872 4-8-8 **62**.............. EmmaSayer(5) 4 55
(Dianne Sayer) *hld up towards rr: drvn along over 2f out: no imp fr over 1f out* **14/1**

6-05 **8** *2 1/4* **Eastward Ho**[11] 2911 6-8-10 **59**.............. TonyHamilton 5 48
(Michael Herrington) *in tch: drvn over 2f out: wknd over 1f out* **11/1**

6-50 **9** *nse* **Time Of My Life (IRE)**[30] 2327 5-8-4 **60**..............(t) JackGarritty(7) 6 49
(Patrick Holmes) *t.k.h in midfield: drvn over 2f out: wknd over 1f out* **6/1**

55-0 **10** *7* **Yorkshireman (IRE)**[17] 2738 4-8-9 **58** ow1.............. DaleSwift 7 32
(Lynn Siddall) *s.i.s: bhd: struggling wl over 2f out: sn btn* **50/1**

-000 **11** *shd* **Roc Fort**[17] 2724 5-7-10 **52** oh6 ow1..............(b) JoeDoyle(7) 10 26
(James Moffatt) *hld up on outside: drvn and struggling 3f out: sn btn* **150/1**

1m 55.04s (-2.56) **Going Correction** -0.225s/f (Firm) **11** Ran SP% **117.0**
Speed ratings (Par 103): **102,101,101,99,97 97,95,93,93,87 87**
CSF £21.18 CT £189.65 TOTE £4.50: £2.20, £2.70, £2.90; EX 27.00 Trifecta £153.00.
**Owner** The Bottom Liners & Paul Saxton **Bred** W And R Barnett Ltd **Trained** Huby, N Yorks

**FOCUS**
Only a handful of these made much appeal going into the race, but the winner landed good support, coming out best in a three-way finish.

## 3302 WORLD CUP PRICE BOOSTS @BOOKMAKERS.CO.UK MAIDEN STKS 1m 1f 61y
**5:15** (5:26) (Class 5) 3-Y-O+ **£2,587** (£770; £384; £192) **Stalls** Low

Form RPR

56 **1** **Queens Park (FR)**[17] 2737 3-8-12 0.............. PJMcDonald 2 68
(John Davies) *in tch: effrt and rdn over 2f out: led ins fnl f: drvn out* **7/1**[3]

4 **2** *1 1/2* **Dancin Alpha**[17] 2737 3-9-3 0.............. BenCurtis 7 70
(Alan Swinbank) *led at modest gallop: jnd and rdn over 2f out: hdd ins fnl f: kpt on same pce* **15/8**[1]

**3** *3* **Vodka Wells (FR)**[51] 4-9-7 0..............(t[1]) MeganCarberry(7) 4 65
(Brian Ellison) *hld up in midfield on outside: hdwy to chal 2f out: sn pushed along: one pce fnl f* **4/1**[2]

**4** *1 1/4* **Spot The Pro (IRE)**[9] 5-10-0 0.............. BrianHughes 11 62+
(Rebecca Menzies) *dwlt: hld up: shkn up over 2f out: reminder over 1f out: pushed along and kpt on wl fnl f: nvr nrr* **16/1**

**5** *2* **Ben Bulben Pace (IRE)** 3-9-3 0.............. JoeFanning 12 57
(Mark Johnston) *dwlt: bhd: hdwy on outside and prom 1/2-way: rdn and ev ch over 2f out to over 1f out: outpcd fnl f* **4/1**[2]

3 **6** *2 3/4* **Wor Lass**[10] 2952 6-9-9 0.............. DavidAllan 6 47
(Iain Jardine) *hld up towards rr: drvn and outpcd over 2f out: sme late hdwy: nvr able to chal* **12/1**

3-0 **7** *2 1/2* **Malraaj**[17] 2733 3-9-3 0.............. TonyHamilton 8 46
(Richard Fahey) *t.k.h early: hld up in midfield: drvn and outpcd over 2f out: n.d after* **16/1**

0/6 **8** *2* **Claude Carter**[5] 3103 10-9-9 0.............. GarryWhillans(5) 1 43
(Alistair Whillans) *hld up: rdn over 3f out: no imp fr 2f out* **50/1**

5 **9** *1/2* **Blue Jacket (USA)**[23] 2553 3-8-7 0.............. EmmaSayer(5) 3 36
(Dianne Sayer) *t.k.h: chsd ldr: rdn over 2f out: wknd wl over 1f out* **100/1**

6 **10** *3 1/4* **Charedal**[11] 2910 6-9-9 0.............. PaulMulrennan 5 30
(Iain Jardine) *t.k.h: chsd ldrs tl rdn and wknd over 2f out* **150/1**

**11** *2 1/2* **Pal Ella** 3-8-12 0.............. TomEaves 10 24
(Keith Dalgleish) *s.i.s: bhd: struggling over 3f out: sn btn* **25/1**

2m 0.39s (2.79) **Going Correction** -0.225s/f (Firm)
**WFA** 3 from 4yo+ 11lb **11** Ran SP% **114.2**
Speed ratings (Par 103): **78,76,74,72,71 68,66,64,64,61 59**
CSF £19.63 TOTE £8.40: £2.80, £1.40, £1.80; EX 23.60 Trifecta £120.90.
**Owner** Mr & Mrs R Scott **Bred** Ecurie Des Monceaux **Trained** Piercebridge, Durham

**FOCUS**
A weak maiden run at a steady pace and not a great deal to get carried away with.

## 3303 DOWNLOAD THE FREE APP @BOOKMAKERS.CO.UK H'CAP 1m 3f 107y
**5:45** (5:51) (Class 5) (0-70,70) 3-Y-O **£2,587** (£770; £384; £192) **Stalls** High

Form RPR

-312 **1** **Emerahldz (IRE)**[17] 2735 3-9-2 **70**.............. SammyJoBell(5) 6 80
(Richard Fahey) *cl up: led over 2f out: rdn and edgd lft appr fnl f: hld on wl last 100yds* **10/3**[1]

0-42 **2** *nk* **Mister Uno (IRE)**[42] 2028 3-8-4 **53**.............. PJMcDonald 3 62
(Ann Duffield) *trckd ldrs: effrt and wnt 2nd over 1f out: sn carried rt: swtchd rt and styd on wl fnl f: hld nr fin* **10/1**

5216 **3** *3 1/4* **Trinity Star (IRE)**[4] 3135 3-9-0 **63**..............[1] PaulMulrennan 8 67
(Michael Dods) *hld up on outside: hdwy over 2f out: rdn and kpt on same pce fnl f* **7/2**[2]

25-5 **4** *3 1/4* **Branston De Soto**[109] 761 3-8-13 **62**.............. JoeFanning 12 60
(Mark Johnston) *hld up on outside: effrt whn n.m.r over 2f out: swtchd rt wl over 1f out: kpt on fnl f: no imp* **9/2**[3]

0-55 **5** *1 3/4* **Running Wolf (IRE)**[38] 2132 3-9-3 **69**..............(p) ConnorBeasley(3) 4 64
(Michael Dods) *led: rdn and hdd over 2f out: edgd lft: one pce over 1f out* **18/1**

2434 **6** *2 3/4* **Clear Spell (IRE)**[16] 2769 3-9-1 **67**.............. JasonHart(3) 7 58
(Alistair Whillans) *t.k.h: hld up: drvn along over 3f out: rallied over 2f out: no imp fr over 1f out* **13/2**

0305 **7** *2 1/4* **Kashstaree**[5] 3098 3-7-9 **51** oh3.............. JackGarritty(7) 9 38
(David Barron) *hld up: drvn along over 3f out: no imp fr 2f out* **8/1**

50-0 **8** *1/2* **Crakehall Lad (IRE)**[24] 2506 3-9-0 **63**.............. BenCurtis 10 49
(Alan Swinbank) *hld up: drvn along over 3f out: nvr able to chal* **20/1**

61-6 **9** *9* **Neuf Des Coeurs**[19] 2676 3-8-13 **62**.............. TomEaves 1 33
(Keith Dalgleish) *hld up in tch: effrt and edgd lft 3f out: wknd fr 2f out* **12/1**

0-00 **10** *12* **Reflection**[27] 2416 3-8-3 **52** oh6 ow1.............. PatrickMathers 5 4
(Brian Baugh) *in tch: drvn and outpcd over 3f out: sn btn: t.o* **100/1**

2m 23.71s (0.61) **Going Correction** -0.225s/f (Firm) **10** Ran SP% **115.7**
Speed ratings (Par 99): **88,87,85,83,81 79,78,77,71,62**
CSF £36.92 CT £123.94 TOTE £3.30: £1.80, £2.90, £2.10; EX 24.90 Trifecta £85.60.
**Owner** Mrs H Steel **Bred** D G Iceton **Trained** Musley Bank, N Yorks

**FOCUS**
Not as many progressive sorts as can be the case in 3yo middle-distance handicaps, but the winner came here in good form and it looks solid enough for the grade.
T/Jkpt: Not won. T/Plt: £943.40 to a £1 stake. Pool: £78406.60 - 60.67 winning tickets T/Qpdt: £68.30 to a £1 stake. Pool: £7597.14 - 82.20 winning tickets RY

# 3148 NOTTINGHAM (L-H)
Monday, June 16

**OFFICIAL GOING: Good to firm (good in places; 8.5)**
Wind: Light half-behind Weather: Overcast

## 3304 RACING UK ANYWHERE AVAILABLE NOW MEDIAN AUCTION MAIDEN STKS 5f 13y
**6:20** (6:20) (Class 5) 2-Y-O **£2,749** (£818; £408; £204) **Stalls** Centre

Form RPR

0 **1** **Kingsbridge**[10] 2964 2-9-5 0.............. SebSanders 4 76+
(Rod Millman) *chsd ldrs: led wl over 1f out: sn rdn and edgd lft: r.o* **12/1**

**2** *2 3/4* **Gleneely Girl (IRE)** 2-9-0 0.............. ChrisCatlin 5 61+
(Rae Guest) *s.s: outpcd: hdwy 2f out: r.o to go 2nd wl ins fnl f: nt trble wnr* **12/1**

05 **3** *3* **Clampdown**[23] 2541 2-9-5 0.............. KierenFallon 1 55+
(James Tate) *sn pushed along and prom: rdn over 2f out: styd on same pce fr over 1f out* **8/1**[3]

33 **4** *1 1/4* **Dominic Cork**[24] 2513 2-9-5 0.............. JamieSpencer 2 51
(Kevin Ryan) *led 2f: chsd ldr: rdn and ev ch over 1f out: wknd ins fnl f* **4/9**[1]

60 **5** *2* **Mary Ann Bugg (IRE)**[2] 3232 2-9-0 0.............. LukeMorris 3 38
(Phil McEntee) *chsd ldr tl led 4f out: rdn and hdd wl over 1f out: wknd fnl f* **33/1**

1m 0.37s (-1.13) **Going Correction** -0.275s/f (Firm) **5** Ran SP% **109.2**
Speed ratings (Par 93): **98,93,88,86,83**
CSF £45.47 TOTE £6.90: £2.50, £4.10; EX 59.30 Trifecta £227.50.
**Owner** D J Deer **Bred** D J And Mrs Deer **Trained** Kentisbeare, Devon

**FOCUS**
An ordinary 2yo maiden. Outer track used and rail moved out around whole course and distances increased by 30yds on Round course.

## 3305 EXECUTIVE NETWORK LEGAL FILLIES' H'CAP 6f 15y
**6:50** (6:50) (Class 4) (0-85,85) 3-Y-O+ **£6,469** (£1,925; £962; £481) **Stalls** Centre

Form RPR

0-00 **1** **Diamond Lady**[44] 1952 3-8-13 **77**.............. FrederikTylicki 6 84
(William Stone) *chsd ldr: rdn over 1f out: r.o to ld towards fin* **20/1**

-013 **2** *shd* **Lady Horatia**[21] 2611 3-9-2 **80**.............. MartinDwyer 7 86
(William Muir) *sn led: rdn over 1f out: hdd towards fin* **9/4**[1]

655 **3** *3/4* **Marjong**[10] 2965 4-9-5 **76**.............. SebSanders 3 82
(Simon Dow) *s.i.s: hld up: hdwy over 1f out: sn rdn: r.o* **9/2**[3]

0-31 **4** *7* **Spiraea**[25] 2488 4-8-10 **67**.............. KierenFallon 5 51
(Mark Rimell) *prom: rdn over 2f out: wknd fnl f* **10/1**

020- **5** *2 1/4* **Monakova (IRE)**[230] 7595 4-10-0 **85**.............. DanielTudhope 2 61
(David O'Meara) *prom: rdn over 2f out: wknd over 1f out* **6/1**

0103 **6** *7* **Little Shambles**[5] 3122 3-8-10 **77**.............. MichaelJMMurphy(3) 1 29
(Mark Johnston) *chsd ldrs: rdn over 2f out: hung lft and wknd over 1f out* **4/1**[2]

2232 **7** *19* **Barbs Princess**[23] 2542 4-9-0 **71**.............. WilliamBuick 4
(Charles Hills) *chsd ldrs: lost pl over 3f out: rdn and wknd wl over 1f out* **6/1**

1m 12.32s (-2.38) **Going Correction** -0.275s/f (Firm)
**WFA** 3 from 4yo 7lb **7** Ran SP% **111.4**
Speed ratings (Par 102): **104,103,102,93,90 81,55**
CSF £61.82 TOTE £8.90: £7.60, £1.10; EX 70.10 Trifecta £406.70.
**Owner** The Going Great Guns Partnership **Bred** Mickley Stud **Trained** West Wickham, Cambs

**FOCUS**
Not a bad fillies' sprint handicap.

## 3306 RACINGUK.COM H'CAP 1m 75y
**7:20** (7:20) (Class 4) (0-85,85) 4-Y-O+ **£4,851** (£1,443; £721; £360) **Stalls** Centre

Form RPR

55-4 **1** **Balducci**[26] 2453 7-9-4 **82**..............(v[1]) DanielTudhope 2 101
(David O'Meara) *mde all: rdn clr fr over 1f out: eased nr fin* **8/1**

0000 **2** *6* **Luhaif**[37] 2154 4-8-10 **79**..............(b) ShelleyBirkett(5) 1 84
(Julia Feilden) *chsd wnr: rdn over 2f out: styd on same pce fr over 1f out* **16/1**

6646 **3** *2 1/2* **Circumvent**[44] 1948 7-9-4 **82**.............. LukeMorris 5 81
(Paul Cole) *sn pushed along and prom: lost pl 6f out: rdn over 3f out: hdwy over 2f out: styd on u.p* **9/4**[1]

0030 **4** *nse* **Talented Kid**[26] 2453 5-9-4 **85**.............. MichaelJMMurphy(3) 4 84
(Mark Johnston) *chsd ldrs: rdn over 2f out: styd on same pce* **5/1**

0-10 **5** *3 3/4* **Harry Bosch**[16] 2772 4-9-4 **82**.............. JamieSpencer 6 73
(Brian Meehan) *hld up: rdn over 2f out: wknd over 1f out* **7/2**[3]

1-45 **6** *3/4* **It Must Be Faith**[1] 3272 4-8-9 **73**.............. AndrewMullen 3 62
(Michael Appleby) *s.i.s: hld up: hdwy over 2f out: sn rdn: wknd fnl f* **11/4**[2]

1m 45.48s (-3.52) **Going Correction** -0.275s/f (Firm) **6** Ran SP% **113.3**
Speed ratings (Par 105): **106,100,97,97,93 92**
CSF £109.43 TOTE £9.80: £3.20, £5.80; EX 58.90 Trifecta £147.50.
**Owner** Direct Racing **Bred** G Russell **Trained** Nawton, N Yorks

**FOCUS**
Few got involved here.

## 3307 VOUTE SALES WARWICKSHIRE OAKS (LISTED RACE) 1m 2f 50y
**7:50** (7:50) (Class 1) 4-Y-O+
**£22,684** (£8,600; £4,304; £2,144; £1,076; £540) **Stalls** Low

Form RPR

30-2 **1** **Secret Gesture**[32] 2284 4-9-0 **108**.............. JamieSpencer 3 100
(Ralph Beckett) *a.p: rdn over 1f out: r.o to ld nr fin* **4/7**[1]

1-10 **2** *1/2* **Wall Of Sound**[44] 1942 4-9-0 **95**.............. RichardKingscote 10 99
(Tom Dascombe) *led 1f: chsd ldr: rdn over 1f out: led wl ins fnl f: hdd nr fin* **10/1**

6-02 **3** *3/4* **We'll Go Walking (IRE)**[33] 2263 4-9-0 **102**.............. SeamieHeffernan 9 98
(J P Murtagh, Ire) *racd keenly: led after 1f: rdn over 1f out: hdd and unable qck wl ins fnl f* **7/1**[2]

3-22 **4** *hd* **Toast Of The Town (IRE)**[20] 2649 4-9-0 **84**..............(p) WilliamBuick 4 97
(John Gosden) *chsd ldrs: rdn over 1f out: kpt on* **20/1**

45-0 **5** *1* **Rock Choir**[44] 1948 4-9-0 **93**.............. SebSanders 5 95
(William Haggas) *sn pushed along and prom: lost pl over 5f out: hdwy over 2f out: sn rdn: rdr dropped whip over 1f out: styd on same pce ins fnl f* **12/1**

0-60 **6** *3* **Madame Defarge (IRE)**[16] 2764 4-9-0 **90**.............. FrederikTylicki 6 90
(Michael Bell) *s.i.s: hld up: rdn over 2f out: n.d* **33/1**

0-05 **7** *1 ¼* **Auction (IRE)**[23] 2554 4-9-0 94....................(p) OisinMurphy 11 87
(Ed Dunlop) *hld up: hdwy over 2f out: sn rdn: swtchd rt over 1f out: styd on same pce* **20/1**

5040 **8** *nk* **Moment In Time (IRE)**[16] 2764 5-9-0 99.................. FergusSweeney 8 87
(David Simcock) *hld up: hdwy over 3f out: rdn over 2f out: sn btn* **8/1**[3]

44-2 **9** *1* **Sinaadi (IRE)**[58] 1568 4-9-0 78.................. StevieDonohoe 2 85?
(Brian Meehan) *hld up: hdwy over 5f out: outpcd fr over 2f out* **100/1**

2m 11.24s (-3.06) **Going Correction** 0.0s/f (Good) **9** Ran SP% **121.8**
Speed ratings: **112,111,111,110,110 107,106,106,105**
CSF £8.18 TOTE £1.40: £1.10, £2.20, £2.00; EX 9.60 Trifecta £38.00.

**Owner** Qatar Racing Ltd & Newsells Park Stud **Bred** Newsells Park Stud **Trained** Kimpton, Hants

■ Stewards' Enquiry : William Buick two-day ban: used whip above permitted level (Jun 30-Jul 1)

Seamie Heffernan two-day ban: used whip above permitted level (Jun 30-Jul 1)

**FOCUS**
A fair turnout numerically, as is often the case for this event, and a decent pace cut out by the Irish raider.

## 3308 DOWNLOAD THE RACING UK IPAD APP H'CAP — 1m 2f 50y
**8:20** (8:20) (Class 6) (0-65,65) 4-Y-0+ **£1,940** (£577; £288; £144) **Stalls** Low

Form RPR

50 **1** **Ferryview Place**[73] 1288 5-7-11 46 oh1....................(p) JoeyHaynes(5) 6 56
(Ian Williams) *hld up: hdwy over 2f out: rdn over 1f out: r.o to ld wl ins fnl f* **5/1**[3]

2-31 **2** *½* **Giantstepsahead (IRE)**[27] 2443 5-9-6 64.................. SebSanders 10 73
(Denis Quinn) *sn led: hdd 8f out: chsd ldr tl led again 4f out: rdn over 1f out: hdd wl ins fnl f* **7/4**[1]

22-2 **3** *nk* **Pink Lips**[14] 2843 6-9-1 59.................. FrederikTylicki 11 67
(J R Jenkins) *hld up: hdwy over 2f out: rdn over 1f out: r.o* **4/1**[2]

62-0 **4** *3 ¼* **Youm Jamil (USA)**[10] 2942 7-8-5 49.................. FrannyNorton 7 51
(Tony Carroll) *hld up: hdwy over 3f out: rdn over 1f out: no ex ins fnl f* **25/1**

3550 **5** *1* **Diletta Tommasa (IRE)**[6] 3080 4-9-4 62....................(p) LukeMorris 5 62
(John Stimpson) *sn prom: chsd ldr over 3f out: rdn and ev ch over 2f out: no ex ins fnl f* **10/1**

200- **6** *½* **Elsie Bay**[230] 7605 5-9-7 65.................. FergusSweeney 8 64
(Gary Moore) *hld up: hdwy over 2f out: rdn over 1f out: styd on same pce fnl f* **16/1**

5416 **7** *nk* **Teide Peak (IRE)**[67] 1406 5-9-1 62.................. OisinMurphy(3) 3 61
(Paul D'Arcy) *hld up in tch: rdn and ev ch over 2f out: no ex fnl f* **4/1**[2]

530 **8** *1* **Lindsay's Dream**[11] 2923 8-8-1 48 oh1 ow2..........(p) SimonPearce(3) 4 45
(Zoe Davison) *sn pushed along in rr: hdwy 2f out: wknd ins fnl f* **33/1**

-506 **9** *6* **Chella Thriller (SPA)**[13] 2863 5-8-6 55..............(v[1]) DanielMuscutt(5) 1 41
(Alastair Lidderdale) *mid-div: rdn and wknd over 2f out* **50/1**

2000 **10** *11* **Pentameter**[32] 2270 5-9-5 63.................. MartinHarley 2 28
(John Butler) *chsd ldrs: rdn over 3f out: wknd over 2f out* **33/1**

05-5 **11** *23* **Perci French**[11] 2913 4-7-13 46 oh1.................. JulieBurke(3) 9
(David O'Meara) *led 8f out: hdd 4f out: rdn and wknd over 2f out* **25/1**

2m 13.71s (-0.59) **Going Correction** 0.0s/f (Good) **11** Ran SP% **123.5**
Speed ratings (Par 101): **102,101,101,98,97 97,97,96,91,82 64**
CSF £14.24 CT £40.73 TOTE £8.10: £1.70, £1.60, £1.60; EX 27.10 Trifecta £111.60.

**Owner** John F O'Shea **Bred** Bishopswood Bloodstock & Trickledown Stud **Trained** Portway, Worcs

■ Stewards' Enquiry : Joey Haynes four-day ban: used whip above permitted level (Jun 30-Jul 3)

Seb Sanders two-day ban: used whip above permitted level (Jun 30-Jul 1)

**FOCUS**
A moderate contest won in a time nearly 2.5 seconds slower than the preceding Listed event, and a sizeable gamble landed.

## 3309 JOIN US FOR SPORTS NIGHT TOMORROW H'CAP — 1m 6f 15y
**8:50** (8:50) (Class 6) (0-60,60) 4-Y-0+ **£1,940** (£577; £288; £144) **Stalls** Low

Form RPR

446- **1** **Maoi Chinn Tire (IRE)**[224] 7735 7-8-10 52.................. OisinMurphy(3) 4 60+
(Jennie Candlish) *trckd ldrs: racd keenly: rdn over 2f out: led ins fnl f: styd on* **3/1**[1]

366 **2** *½* **Rowlestone Lass**[10] 2942 4-8-8 47.................. ChrisCatlin 1 54
(Richard Price) *chsd ldrs: led over 2f out: rdn over 1f out: hdd ins fnl f: kpt on* **12/1**

4563 **3** *2 ¼* **Fair Comment**[11] 2923 4-9-0 53.................. MartinHarley 5 57
(Michael Blanshard) *trckd ldr: rdn over 2f out: hung lft over 1f out: no ex ins fnl f* **5/1**[2]

4U1 **4** *¾* **Graylyn Ruby (FR)**[46] 1895 9-9-2 55.................. FrederikTylicki 3 58
(Robert Eddery) *mid-div: hdwy 6f out: rdn over 2f out: styd on same pce fnl f* **6/1**[3]

-055 **5** *1 ¾* **Impeccability**[65] 1453 4-8-7 46 oh1.................. FrannyNorton 8 47
(John Mackie) *hld up: hdwy over 2f out: sn rdn: no imp fnl f* **7/1**

2006 **6** *4* **Turbulent Priest**[11] 2923 6-8-4 46 oh1..............(p) SimonPearce(3) 11 41
(Zoe Davison) *hld up: rdn over 2f out: styd on ins fnl f: nt trble ldrs* **25/1**

0046 **7** *1* **Wild Desert (FR)**[18] 2693 9-9-7 60.................. LukeMorris 2 54
(Tony Carroll) *led: rdn over 3f out: hdd over 2f out: wknd fnl f* **5/1**[2]

06-2 **8** *6* **Walter De La Mare (IRE)**[10] 2942 7-8-7 46.................. MartinDwyer 7 31
(Anabel K Murphy) *hld up: rdn over 3f out: wknd over 2f out* **7/1**

600- **9** *3 ½* **Iceman George**[268] 6632 10-8-12 56.................. TimClark(5) 9 36
(Denis Quinn) *hld up: rdn over 3f out: sn wknd* **8/1**

00-0 **10** *½* **Diamond Pro (IRE)**[15] 361 5-8-5 49....................(bt) JackDuern(5) 6 29
(Christopher Kellett) *hld up: rdn and wknd 3f out* **33/1**

3m 8.14s (1.14) **Going Correction** 0.0s/f (Good) **10** Ran SP% **123.2**
Speed ratings (Par 101): **96,95,94,94,93 90,90,86,84,84**
CSF £44.41 CT £182.58 TOTE £6.00: £1.70, £3.30, £1.80; EX 35.80 Trifecta £454.50.

**Owner** The Best Club In The World **Bred** Mrs E Thompson **Trained** Basford Green, Staffs

■ Stewards' Enquiry : Chris Catlin four-day ban: used whip above permitted level (Jun 30-Jul 3)

**FOCUS**
Not strong even for this modest grade, with half the field rated more than 10lb below the ceiling.

T/Plt: £472.70 to a £1 stake. Pool: £52422.19 - 80.95 winning tickets T/Qpdt: £19.30 to a £1 stake. Pool: £6441.72 - 246.01 winning tickets CR

# 3063 WINDSOR (R-H)
Monday, June 16

**OFFICIAL GOING: Good (7.7)**
Wind: Light, against Weather: Overcast

## 3310 MACDONALD WINDSOR HOTEL APPRENTICE H'CAP — 1m 3f 135y
**6:05** (6:06) (Class 5) (0-70,76) 4-Y-0+ **£2,587** (£770; £384; £192) **Stalls** Low

Form RPR

311 **1** **Thecornishcowboy**[7] 3052 5-9-13 **76** 6ex..........(t) JordonMcMurray(5) 9 84
(John Ryan) *hld up in 6th: prog over 3f out to ld over 2f out: sn jnd: edgd lft fr over 1f out: gd battle w runner-up and won on the nod* **5/1**[3]

5-63 **2** *nse* **Eton Rambler (USA)**[18] 2693 4-9-11 **69**.................. CamHardie 11 77
(George Baker) *hld up in 5th: trckd ldrs 3f: jnd wnr 2f out: edgd lft but gd battle after: jst pipped* **11/4**[1]

0246 **3** *1 ½* **Palus San Marco (IRE)**[31] 2305 5-9-12 **70**..............[1] JordanVaughan 10 76
(Tony Carroll) *dwlt: hld up in last pair: rdn and prog on far side fr jst over 2f out: tk 3rd fnl f: styd on but unable to chal* **5/1**[3]

4120 **4** *1 ¾* **Highlife Dancer**[10] 2942 6-9-2 **65**.................. PaddyPilley(5) 5 68
(Mick Channon) *trckd ldng pair: chal over 2f out: nt qckn wl over 1f out: hung lft fnl f* **8/1**

5066 **5** *5* **Joyful Motive**[15] 2394 5-8-2 **51** oh4.................. BradleyBosley(5) 8 46
(Michael Chapman) *led 3f: chsd ldr: urged along over 5f out: lost pl qckly over 2f out* **33/1**

441- **6** *½* **Waahej**[263] 6783 8-9-7 **65**.................. JoshBaudains 1 59
(Peter Hiatt) *hld up in last pair: in tch over 3f out: rdn and wknd over 2f out* **16/1**

0103 **7** *1 ¼* **Cabuchon (GER)**[26] 2465 7-8-12 **61**..............(t) KieranShoemark(5) 7 53
(David Evans) *hld up in 6th: cl enough 3f out: sn rdn and wknd* **10/1**

0-01 **8** *8* **Shahrazad (IRE)**[48] 1857 5-8-7 **56**..............(t) JackGilligan(5) 2 35
(Patrick Gilligan) *led after 3f to over 2f out: sn wknd rapidly* **7/2**[2]

5/P- **U** **Sacrilege**[396] 2383 9-9-9 **67**..............[1] RyanWhile 3
(Daniel O'Brien) *virtually ref to r: t.o whn swvd and uns rdr after 100yds* **40/1**

2m 31.66s (2.16) **Going Correction** +0.10s/f (Good) **9** Ran SP% **113.7**
Speed ratings (Par 103): **96,95,94,93,90 90,89,83,**
CSF £18.81 CT £71.28 TOTE £5.90: £2.20, £2.00, £2.20; EX 22.20 Trifecta £72.90.

**Owner** C Letcher & J Ryan **Bred** Hadi Al Tajir **Trained** Newmarket, Suffolk

**FOCUS**
A weak handicap, confined to apprentice riders. The pace was uneven and the field bunched up 3f out, but the first pair dominated the finish. Top bend dolled out 12yds from normal configuration adding 49yds to races of one mile and beyond. Inner of Straight dolled out 18yds at 6f and 9yds at Winning Post.

## 3311 EBF STALLIONS MAIDEN STKS — 5f 10y
**6:35** (6:35) (Class 5) 2-Y-O **£2,911** (£866; £432; £216) **Stalls** Low

Form RPR

52 **1** **Sunset Sail (IRE)**[25] 2487 2-9-5 0.................. RichardHughes 6 83+
(Richard Hannon) *mde all: pushed clr over 1f out: styd on wl* **1/2**[1]

4 **2** *4* **Latch Onto Blue**[44] 1936 2-9-5 0.................. JamesDoyle 2 71
(Charles Hills) *chsd ldrs: outpcd and shkn up 2f out: kpt on to take 2nd ins fnl f: no ch w wnr* **4/1**[2]

55 **3** *1* **Emef Rock (IRE)**[10] 2944 2-9-2 0.................. WilliamTwiston-Davies(3) 7 68
(Mick Channon) *prom: rdn to chse wnr over 1f out to ins fnl f: one pce* **20/1**

**4** *1 ¾* **Ticks The Boxes (IRE)** 2-9-5 0.................. AdamKirby 8 63+
(Clive Cox) *in tch: outpcd 1/2-way: reminder 2f out: kpt on steadily fr over 1f out* **6/1**[3]

**5** *4 ½* **Equally Fast** 2-9-5 0.................. DougieCostello 1 49
(William Muir) *fractious preliminaries: gd spd to press wnr to 2f out: lost 2nd and wknd over 1f out* **20/1**

**6** *nk* **Weardiditallgorong** 2-9-0 0.................. DavidProbert 4 43
(Des Donovan) *nvr on terms w ldrs: n.d fr 2f out* **66/1**

**7** *5* **Gangbuster** 2-9-5 0.................. SeanLevey 3 33
(Richard Hannon) *outpcd and a bhd* **12/1**

**8** *½* **Bonita Brown Eyes (IRE)** 2-9-0 0.................. LiamJones 5 27
(J S Moore) *s.i.s: rn green and a bhd* **50/1**

**9** *4 ½* **Somedaysrdiamonds** 2-9-0 0.................. JohnFahy 9 13
(J S Moore) *spd 2f: wknd qckly* **33/1**

1m 1.08s (0.78) **Going Correction** +0.10s/f (Good) **9** Ran SP% **124.6**
Speed ratings (Par 93): **97,90,89,86,79 78,70,69,62**
CSF £3.02 TOTE £1.40: £1.02, £1.70, £3.90; EX 4.30 Trifecta £17.00.

**Owner** H Robin Heffer **Bred** Patrick F Kelly **Trained** East Everleigh, Wilts

**FOCUS**
This was all about the clear-cut winner.

## 3312 MANHEIM (S) STKS — 6f
**7:05** (7:05) (Class 5) 2-Y-O **£2,587** (£770; £384; £192) **Stalls** Low

Form RPR

2602 **1** **Just Marion (IRE)**[5] 3091 2-8-6 0.................. AndreaAtzeni 11 59
(David Evans) *chsd ldrs: pushed along bef 1/2-way: struggling over 2f out: prog over 1f out: drvn to ld last 75yds* **3/1**[1]

0 **2** *½* **Shamrock Sheila (IRE)**[72] 1314 2-8-1 0..............[1] PhilipPrince(5) 3 58
(J S Moore) *chsd ldrs: rdn over 2f out: led over 1f out: wandered in front: hdd and nt qckn last 75yds* **33/1**

**3** *nse* **Robin Hill** 2-8-6 0.................. SamHitchcott 8 57
(William Muir) *s.i.s: hld up in rr: shkn up and prog jst over 2f out: drvn to chse ldrs fnl f: clsng at fin* **20/1**

**4** *nse* **Shar Shar (IRE)** 2-8-6 0.................. SilvestreDeSousa 10 57
(Chris Dwyer) *s.i.s: t.k.h in rr: rdn and prog on wd outside 2f out: chal fnl f: nt qckn nr fin* **25/1**

**5** *¾* **Summer Stroll (IRE)** 2-7-13 0.................. CamHardie(7) 5 55+
(Richard Hannon) *s.i.s: outpcd in last and rn green: pushed along and gd prog over 1f out: clsd on ldrs fnl f: one pce last 75yds* **4/1**[2]

436 **6** *1 ¼* **Diminutive (IRE)**[28] 2395 2-8-6 0.................. HarryBentley 4 51
(Jamie Osborne) *towards rr: rdn over 2f out: edgd lft over 1f out: kpt on but n.d* **10/1**

006 **7** *shd* **Ciaras Cookie (IRE)**[21] 2623 2-8-6 0.................. DavidProbert 2 51
(David Evans) *mde most to over 1f out: steadily fdd* **33/1**

300 **8** *2 ¼* **Sparbrook (IRE)**[35] 2206 2-8-6 0....................(v[1]) JimmyQuinn 1 44
(George Baker) *cl up: on terms w ldrs against nr side rail wl over 1f out: wknd qckly fnl f* **14/1**

405 **9** *1 ¾* **As A Dream (IRE)**[27] 2436 2-8-6 0.................. MartinLane 12 39
(David Evans) *prog on outer to join ldrs 1/2-way: wknd over 1f out* **8/1**[3]

3630 **10** 3 ¾ **Basil The Great**[11] 2928 2-8-11 0 HayleyTurner 6 33
(Tom Dascombe) *pressed ldr to over 2f out: wandered and wknd* **3/1**[1]

55 **11** *hd* **Please Don't Tease (IRE)**[4] 3157 2-8-6 0 (p) RyanWhile(5) 9 32
(Bill Turner) *pressed ldrs to 2f out: wknd over 1f out* **40/1**

6 **12** *16* **Artic Promise**[12] 2903 2-8-11 0 (b[1]) JimmyFortune 7
(Brian Meehan) *in tch tl wknd rapidly over 2f out: t.o* **25/1**

1m 14.63s (1.63) **Going Correction** +0.10s/f (Good) **12** Ran SP% **117.6**
Speed ratings (Par 93): **93,92,92,92,91 89,89,86,84,79 78,57**
CSF £118.86 TOTE £4.00: £1.70, £11.00, £7.00; EX 82.60 Trifecta £1753.00.There were no bid for the winner. Robin Hill was subject to a friendly claim of £8,000. Shar Shar was claimed by Mr Brian Ellison for £8,000. Summer Stroll was claimed by Mr D. O'Meara for £8,000

**Owner** Exors of the late Mrs Sally Edwards **Bred** M A Doyle **Trained** Pandy, Monmouths

**FOCUS**
This juvenile seller is always a lively betting heat. The form is rated around the winner.

## 3313 BETDAQ EXCHANGE 0% MULTIPLES DURING WORLD CUP H'CAP 6f

**7:35** (7:37) (Class 4) (0-85,85) 4-Y-0+ **£5,175** (£1,540; £769; £384) **Stalls** Low

Form RPR

50-6 **1** **Amadeus Wolfe Tone (IRE)**[14] 2833 5-9-4 **82** (b) AdamKirby 9 91
(Jamie Osborne) *s.i.s: hld up in last pair: stl there over 1f out: gd prog on outside fnl f: squeezed through and str burst to ld last strides* **16/1**

05-2 **2** *hd* **Tidentime (USA)**[9] 2995 5-9-1 **82** WilliamTwiston-Davies(3) 12 90
(Mick Channon) *hld up in rr: gd prog jst over 1f out on outside: drvn to ld last 75yds: hdd fnl strides* **7/1**[3]

6443 **3** ½ **O'Gorman**[21] 2629 5-9-2 **80** GeorgeBaker 10 87
(Gary Brown) *taken down early: hld up in rr: prog on outside over 1f out: led briefly ins fnl f: outpcd nr fin* **7/2**[2]

-030 **4** *nk* **Langley Vale**[45] 1921 5-8-9 **73** HayleyTurner 6 79+
(Roger Teal) *taken down early: trckd ldrs: rdn 2f out: clsd to chal towards outside fnl f: upsides 100yds out: one pce* **33/1**

066 **5** *shd* **Dominate**[16] 2778 4-9-2 **80** (b[1]) SeanLevey 8 85
(Richard Hannon) *t.k.h: hld up in midfield: cl up over 1f out but nt clr run: drvn and styd on ins fnl f: unable to chal* **8/1**

-556 **6** *nk* **Jungle Bay**[20] 2645 7-8-11 **75** (b) TedDurcan 11 80
(Jane Chapple-Hyam) *hld up in last pair: prog on wd outside 2f out: tried to cl 1f out: rdn and nt qckn ins fnl f* **25/1**

0 **7** *1* **Salvado (IRE)**[20] 2648 4-8-6 **70** JimmyQuinn 4 71
(Tony Carroll) *take steadily to post: hld up towards rr: drvn against nr side rail over 1f out: kpt on fnl f but n.d* **66/1**

1500 **8** 2 ½ **Time Medicean**[18] 2691 8-8-4 **68** DavidProbert 7 61
(Tony Carroll) *sn pressed ldr: rdn to ld over 1f out: hdd & wknd ins fnl f* **66/1**

5-10 **9** *nk* **Apricot Sky**[30] 2352 4-9-7 **85** DaneO'Neill 5 77
(Henry Candy) *led: styd against nr side rail fr 1/2-way: hdd over 1f out: sn wknd* **7/1**[3]

-531 **10** ½ **Italian Tom (IRE)**[12] 2887 7-8-6 **70** LiamJones 1 61
(Ronald Harris) *trckd ldrs: cl up and rdn over 1f out: n.m.r sn after and wknd* **14/1**

0-03 **11** ¾ **Generalyse**[9] 2995 5-8-13 **77** (v[1]) JimCrowley 13 65
(Ben De Haan) *in tch on outer: rdn 2f out: sn lost pl and btn* **8/1**

4-11 **12** ¾ **Breccbennach**[63] 1490 4-9-3 **81** (tp) RichardHughes 3 67
(Seamus Durack) *trckd ldrs: cl up over 1f out: nt qckn u.p: wknd* **3/1**[1]

1m 12.59s (-0.41) **Going Correction** +0.10s/f (Good) 12 Ran SP% **116.8**
Speed ratings (Par 105): **106,105,105,104,104 104,102,99,99,98 97,96**
CSF £119.37 CT £487.27 TOTE £16.50: £6.00, £2.80, £2.10; EX 145.90 Trifecta £1836.40.

**Owner** B T McDonald **Bred** Brian Williamson **Trained** Upper Lambourn, Berks

**FOCUS**
There was plenty of pace on in this fair sprint handicap and it saw plenty in with a chance half a furlong out.

## 3314 £10,000,000 RISK FREE ON BETDAQ COLUSSUS H'CAP 1m 67y

**8:05** (8:11) (Class 4) (0-80,80) 4-Y-0+ **£5,175** (£1,540; £769; £384) **Stalls** Low

Form RPR

56-0 **1** **Unison (IRE)**[10] 2947 4-8-6 **65** SilvestreDeSousa 9 75
(Peter Makin) *led after 1f: mde rest: kicked on 3f out and had rest off the bridle: drvn over 1f out: styd on* **16/1**

3-55 **2** ½ **Lord Ofthe Shadows (IRE)**[11] 2922 5-9-6 **79** RichardHughes 11 88
(Richard Hannon) *hld up in midfield: rdn over 2f out: prog to chse wnr fnl f: styd on but nvr quite getting there* **5/1**[3]

10-2 **3** 1 ½ **Magique (IRE)**[17] 2750 4-9-4 **77** JamesDoyle 1 83
(Jeremy Noseda) *dwlt: t.k.h: hld up towards rr: rdn over 2f out: prog over 1f out: tk 3rd ins fnl f: kpt on* **7/2**[1]

-640 **4** *1* **Good Luck Charm**[8] 3036 5-9-7 **80** GeorgeBaker 10 83
(Gary Moore) *hld up in last pair: rdn 2f out: kpt on fr over 1f out: nvr able to chal* **13/2**

0030 **5** *nse* **Whitby Jet (IRE)**[19] 2687 6-8-6 **72** CamHardie(7) 3 75
(Ed Vaughan) *t.k.h: hld up in midfield: rdn and lost pl over 2f out: styd out wd and styd on again fnl f* **14/1**

2123 **6** *shd* **Liberty Jack (IRE)**[75] 1234 4-9-5 **78** PatCosgrave 5 81
(Jim Boyle) *hld up towards rr: shkn up over 2f out: rdn and kpt on fr over 1f out: nvr able to threaten* **5/1**[3]

4-03 **7** *1* **Pleasure Bent**[26] 2462 4-9-6 **79** (b[1]) AndreaAtzeni 6 80
(Luca Cumani) *trckd ldrs: rdn and nt qckn over 2f out: lost pl and btn over 1f out* **4/1**[2]

0-44 **8** *1* **Siouxperhero (IRE)**[17] 2721 5-8-8 **67** (p) SteveDrowne 2 65
(William Muir) *led 1f: pressed wnr: rdn over 2f out: styd against nr side rail: lost 2nd and wknd 1f out* **10/1**

3340 **9** 1 ¾ **Rakaan (IRE)**[11] 2922 7-8-13 **79** JennyPowell(7) 8 73
(Brendan Powell) *pressed ldng pair: pushed along over 2f out: steadily wknd* **16/1**

61-4 **10** 4 ½ **Take A Note**[40] 2068 5-9-7 **80** JimCrowley 7 64
(Patrick Chamings) *hld up in last pair: pushed along over 2f out: no prog whn reminder wl over 1f out: wknd* **12/1**

1m 46.62s (1.92) **Going Correction** +0.10s/f (Good) **10** Ran SP% **124.1**
Speed ratings (Par 105): **94,93,92,91,90 90,89,88,87,82**
CSF £100.17 CT £364.96 TOTE £19.30: £5.60, £2.10, £1.50; EX 116.00 Trifecta £646.30.

**Owner** J P Carrington **Bred** Alan Dargan **Trained** Ogbourne Maisey, Wilts

**FOCUS**
A modest handicap, run at a fair pace.

## 3315 BETDAQ 0% ON WORLD CUP CORRECT SCORES MAIDEN STKS 1m 2f 7y

**8:35** (8:38) (Class 5) 3-Y-0+ **£2,587** (£770; £384; £192) **Stalls** Centre

Form RPR

42 **1** **Igider (IRE)**[16] 2773 3-9-1 0 AndreaAtzeni 8 86+
(Roger Varian) *trckd ldrs: prog to chal 3f out: rdn to ld 2f out: jnd fnl f: jst prevailed* **9/4**[1]

35 **2** *nse* **Kleo (GR)**[28] 2404 3-8-10 0 JamesDoyle 15 81+
(Luca Cumani) *trckd ldrs: prog over 2f out: rdn to chal over 1f out: w wnr fnl f: jst denied* **9/2**[3]

**3** ½ **Razor Wind (IRE)** 3-9-1 0 MartinLane 4 85
(Charlie Appleby) *wl in tch: rdn and prog over 2f out: chsd ldng pair over 1f out and n.m.r: styd on strly nr fin* **25/1**

**4** 4 ½ **Wakea (USA)** 3-9-1 0 SilvestreDeSousa 10 76+
(Jeremy Noseda) *dwlt: hld up in last pair: shkn up and prog wl over 1f out: styd on to take 4th ins fnl f: should improve* **25/1**

4 **5** 2 ½ **Savant (IRE)**[25] 2497 3-9-1 0 SeanLevey 2 71
(Sir Michael Stoute) *t.k.h: prom: drvn over 2f out: wknd jst over 1f out* **10/1**

00- **6** *shd* **Hoist The Colours (IRE)**[179] 8340 3-9-1 0 TedDurcan 5 71+
(David Lanigan) *hld up towards rr: jst pushed along fr over 2f out: one pce but shaped w sme promise* **33/1**

5 **7** *hd* **Cabin Fever**[38] 2109 3-8-10 0 JimCrowley 14 66
(Ralph Beckett) *pressed ldr: led over 3f out to 2f out: wknd* **11/4**[2]

04 **8** 1 ½ **Inspector Norse**[46] 1894 3-9-1 0 DavidProbert 6 68
(Sylvester Kirk) *towards rr: rdn over 2f out: no imp on ldrs: one pce* **25/1**

**9** *nk* **Bathrat Amal (JPN)** 4-9-8 0 RichardHughes 7 62+
(Charlie Appleby) *hld up in midfield: effrt on wd outside 3f out: no prog 2f out: wknd* **8/1**

30 **10** 3 ½ **Chantecler**[19] 2682 3-9-1 0 JimmyFortune 9 61+
(Hughie Morrison) *hld up in last: pushed along over 2f out: nvr in it but passed wkng rivals fnl 2f* **33/1**

05 **11** ¾ **Scillonian Sunset (IRE)**[38] 2118 3-8-10 0 DaneO'Neill 1 58
(Charles Hills) *chsd ldrs: rdn 3f out: steadily wknd over 2f out* **50/1**

03 **12** 3 ¼ **Fresh Kingdom (IRE)**[14] 2842 3-9-1 0 HayleyTurner 11 53
(James Fanshawe) *towards rr: pushed along firmly over 3f out and no prog* **25/1**

04 **13** *1* **Hammered Silver (IRE)**[55] 1627 4-9-10 0 SladeO'Hara(3) 13 51
(Mike Murphy) *s.i.s: a towards rr: n.d fr over 2f out* **100/1**

5 **14** 2 ½ **Sir Woodgate**[9] 2997 3-9-1 0 JimmyQuinn 16 47
(Edward Creighton) *s.i.s: sn wl plcd: rdn and cl up over 3f out: sn wknd* **100/1**

0-0 **15** *13* **Fiftyshadesdarker (IRE)**[19] 2682 3-9-1 0 PatCosgrave 12 22
(George Baker) *a wl in rr: t.o* **66/1**

50 **16** ¾ **Crazy Train**[14] 2846 5-9-1 0 DavidParkes(7) 3 15
(Keiran Burke) *awkward to post: led to over 3f out: wknd rapidly: t.o* **100/1**

2m 8.68s (-0.02) **Going Correction** +0.10s/f (Good)
**WFA** 3 from 4yo+ 12lb **16** Ran SP% **123.5**
Speed ratings (Par 103): **104,103,103,99,97 97,97,96,96,93 92,90,89,87,77 76**
CSF £11.41 TOTE £3.70: £1.40, £2.20, £7.00; EX 14.90 Trifecta £277.50.

**Owner** Saleh Al Homaizi & Imad Al Sagar **Bred** M Morrissey **Trained** Newmarket, Suffolk

**FOCUS**
A good maiden.

## 3316 ROYAL WINDSOR FESTIVAL WEEKEND H'CAP 1m 2f 7y

**9:05** (9:06) (Class 5) (0-70,68) 3-Y-0 **£2,587** (£770; £384; £192) **Stalls** Centre

Form RPR

30-4 **1** **Go Sakhee**[15] 2805 3-9-7 **68** AndreaAtzeni 9 75
(Roger Varian) *trckd ldrs: rdn over 2f out: prog to chse ldr jst over 1f out: drvn ahd last 100yds* **9/2**[2]

4-30 **2** ½ **Glebe Spirit (IRE)**[8] 3037 3-9-5 **66** SeanLevey 7 72
(Richard Hannon) *hld up in rr: swtchd to outer and rdn over 2f out: prog over 1f out: styd on to take 2nd nr fin: unable to chal* **8/1**

6-41 **3** ½ **Allergic Reaction (IRE)**[20] 2643 3-9-2 **63** RichardHughes 5 68
(William Knight) *led: kicked on 3f out: styd against nr side rail after: looked in charge over 1f out: edgd lft and hdd last 100yds* **7/1**

0-00 **4** *shd* **Beakers N Num Nums (IRE)**[14] 2850 3-9-7 **68** JamesDoyle 2 73
(William Jarvis) *hld up in midfield: rdn over 2f out: styd on u.p fr over 1f out: nt quite rch ldrs* **7/1**

3251 **5** *1* **Khee Society**[18] 2688 3-9-5 **66** GeorgeBaker 1 70+
(David Evans) *hld up in last: pushed along 2f out and looking for room: shkn up fnl f: n.m.r but styd on: nvr involved* **4/1**[1]

3330 **6** *shd* **Needless Shouting (IRE)**[9] 2998 3-9-5 **66** (v) SamHitchcott 3 69
(Mick Channon) *hld up in rr: hrd rdn over 2f out: kpt on fnl f: nvr able to chal* **12/1**

6433 **7** *nk* **Indira**[18] 2688 3-9-0 **61** JimCrowley 6 63
(John Berry) *chsd ldr: rdn over 2f out: no imp over 1f out: lost 2nd sn after and fdd* **8/1**

4-04 **8** 1 ¾ **Majestic Sun (IRE)**[48] 1847 3-9-1 **62** [1] JimmyFortune 8 61
(Peter Chapple-Hyam) *hld up in rr: rdn on outer over 2f out: no prog over 1f out* **6/1**[3]

-200 **9** *4* **My Secret Dream (FR)**[8] 3037 3-8-9 **56** DavidProbert 4 47
(Ron Hodges) *trckd ldrs: rdn 3f out: wknd 2f out* **25/1**

50 **10** ¾ **Garraun (IRE)**[38] 2126 3-9-6 **67** DaneO'Neill 10 57
(Jeremy Noseda) *dwlt: chsd ldng pair tl wknd over 2f out* **20/1**

2m 9.51s (0.81) **Going Correction** +0.10s/f (Good) **10** Ran SP% **116.0**
Speed ratings (Par 99): **100,99,99,99,98 98,98,96,93,92**
CSF £40.17 CT £249.36 TOTE £5.20: £1.20, £3.60, £1.70; EX 50.30 Trifecta £449.50.

**Owner** K Allen G Moss R & S Marchant & G Jarvis **Bred** Whitsbury Manor Stud And Mrs M E Slade **Trained** Newmarket, Suffolk

**FOCUS**
Not a bad 3yo handicap for the class, although it was run at an uneven tempo and that resulted in something of a muddling finish.

T/Plt: £32.10 to a £1 stake. Pool: £113,011.72 - 2,564.30 winning tickets T/Qpdt: £12.70 to a £1 stake. Pool: £6642.42 - 386.40 winning tickets JN

## [2142]ASCOT (R-H)

Tuesday, June 17

**OFFICIAL GOING: Good (stands' side 8.7, centre 8.9, far side 8.6, round 7.8)**

Wind: Light to medium; across Weather: Sunny

### 3317 QUEEN ANNE STKS (BRITISH CHAMPIONS SERIES) (GROUP 1) (STRAIGHT COURSE) 1m (S)

**2:30** (2:32) (Class 1) 4-Y-O+

**£229,854** (£87,142; £43,611; £21,724; £10,902; £5,471) **Stalls** Centre

Form RPR

216- **1** **Toronado (IRE)**[300] 5654 4-9-0 125 RichardHughes 8 124+
(Richard Hannon) *hld up: swtchd lft arnd the field and hdwy 2f out: str run to ld 1f out: edgd rt ins fnl f: r.o wl: in command towards fin* **4/5**[1]

04-3 **2** ¾ **Verrazano (USA)**[31] 2338 4-9-0 117 JosephO'Brien 4 122
(A P O'Brien, Ire) *swtg: midfield: pushed along over 3f out: hdwy 2f out: rdn and chalng 1f out: nt qckn ins fnl f* **6/1**[2]

0-52 **3** 1¼ **Anodin (IRE)**[23] 2587 4-9-0 117 OlivierPeslier 5 119
(F Head, France) *lengthy: lw: midfield: effrt 2f out: led over 1f out: sn hdd: kpt on and stl ch ins fnl f: no ex cl home* **9/1**

-212 **4** ½ **Tullius (IRE)**[31] 2338 6-9-0 117 JimmyFortune 2 118
(Andrew Balding) *hld up: niggled along over 4f out: big effrt over 1f out: styd on whn wanted to lug rt ins fnl f: nt quite pce to get to ldrs* **11/1**

101- **5** ¾ **Producer**[282] 6254 5-9-0 111 RyanMoore 10 116
(Richard Hannon) *stdd s: hld up in rr: pushed along over 2f out: styd on ins fnl f: nrst fin* **25/1**

0-02 **6** ¾ **Soft Falling Rain (SAF)**[80] 1176 5-9-0 120 PaulHanagan 3 115
(M F De Kock, South Africa) *chsd ldrs: effrt over 3f out: rdn and chalng over 1f out: no ex fnl 100yds* **8/1**[3]

6-0 **7** 1¼ **Glory Awaits (IRE)**[80] 1176 4-9-0 110 (b) JamesDoyle 9 112
(Kevin Ryan) *racd alone away fr main gp: chsd ldrs: pushed along over 3f out: rdn over 2f out: outpcd over 1f out: kpt on same pce but no imp ins fnl f* **50/1**

-010 **8** *nse* **Mull Of Killough (IRE)**[30] 2379 8-9-0 114 AdamKirby 6 112
(Jane Chapple-Hyam) *lw: led: hdd 5f out: remained w ldr: rdn to regain ld 2f out: hdd over 1f out: sn btn* **20/1**

-045 **9** 2 **Side Glance**[30] 2379 7-9-0 115 JamieSpencer 1 107
(Andrew Balding) *hld up: rdn over 2f out: tried to keep on ins fnl f: no imp whn eased fnl 75yds* **25/1**

420- **10** 5 **Ansgar (IRE)**[15] 2853 6-9-0 109 (t) RoryCleary 7 95
(Sabrina J Harty, Ire) *pushed along s to r w ldr: racd w zest: led 5f out: rdn and hdd 2f out: wnt sltly rt over 1f out: sn wknd* **80/1**

1m 37.73s (-3.07) **Going Correction** -0.025s/f (Good) course record **10** Ran SP% **114.9**
Speed ratings (Par 117): **114,113,112,111,110 110,108,108,106,101**
CSF £5.17 CT £25.54 TOTE £1.80: £1.20, £1.80, £2.30; EX 4.70 Trifecta £36.80.
**Owner** Al Shaqab Racing **Bred** Paul Nataf **Trained** East Everleigh, Wilts

**FOCUS**

The meeting kicked off on ground officially described as good, but it would have been drying on a warm, sunny day and the time of the opening contest strongly suggested it was on the quick side, although there may have been a wind helping them up the straight. The rail on the Round course was positioned approximately 3yds out from the 9f marker to the home straight, adding 6-12yds to races. Hardly the deepest edition of this race, but it was run at a strong gallop and the right horses came to the fore.

### 3318 COVENTRY STKS (GROUP 2) 6f

**3:05** (3:07) (Class 1) 2-Y-O

**£68,052** (£25,800; £12,912; £6,432; £3,228; £1,620) **Stalls** Centre

Form RPR

1 **1** **The Wow Signal (IRE)**[27] 2450 2-9-1 0 FrankieDettori 1 110+
(John Quinn) *athletic: travelled strly: chsd ldr: rdn and ev ch 2f out: led ent fnl f: r.o strly and asserted ins fnl f: rdn out* **5/1**[1]

1 **2** 1¾ **Cappella Sansevero**[24] 2569 2-9-1 0 JamieSpencer 13 105
(G M Lyons, Ire) *str: stdd after s: hld up in tch in last trio: rdn over 2f out: hdwy over 1f out: styd on strly u.p ins fnl f: snatched 2nd last stride* **6/1**[3]

31 **3** *shd* **Jungle Cat (IRE)**[11] 2964 2-9-1 0 JoeFanning 15 104
(Mark Johnston) *str: lw: chsd ldrs: rdn and effrt 2f out: ev ch u.p over 1f out: nt quite pce of wnr ins fnl f: kpt on to chse wnr towards fin: lost 2nd last stride* **12/1**

6111 **4** *nk* **Justice Good (IRE)**[15] 2845 2-9-1 0 RyanMoore 2 104
(David Elsworth) *t.k.h: sn led: rdn 2f out: hdd ent fnl f: nt pce of wnr and btn ins fnl f: one pce fnl 100yds and lost 2 pls towards fin* **16/1**

2 **5** *nk* **Kodi Bear (IRE)**[32] 2298 2-9-1 0 AdamKirby 8 104+
(Clive Cox) *leggy: scope: hld up in tch in midfield: shuffled bk and n.m.r wl over 1f out: plenty to do and rallied 1f out: styd on wl ins fnl f: no threat to wnr* **20/1**

1 **6** *nk* **Angelic Lord (IRE)**[14] 2866 2-9-1 0 RichardKingscote 14 102
(Tom Dascombe) *w'like: in tch in midfield: hdwy u.p and edging rt over 1f out: kpt on same pce ins fnl f* **20/1**

51 **7** *hd* **Dr No**[28] 2428 2-9-1 0 PatDobbs 16 101
(Richard Hannon) *leggy: unf: wl in tch in midfield: rdn and effrt over 1f out: unable qck 1f out: styd on same pce ins fnl f* **25/1**

11 **8** *nk* **Adaay (IRE)**[14] 2873 2-9-1 0 PaulHanagan 12 101
(William Haggas) *cmpt hld up in tch: rdn and hdwy over 1f out: no imp u.p 1f out: kpt on again fnl 100yds: nvr gng to rch ldrs and eased cl home* **5/1**[1]

3 **9** ½ **War Envoy (USA)**[15] 2855 2-9-1 0 JosephO'Brien 11 99
(A P O'Brien, Ire) *lengthy: lw: stdd s: hld up in tch in rr: effrt and wnt lft u.p over 1f out: hdwy and edging rt ins fnl f: wnt lft again u.p ins fnl f: kpt on: nvr trbld ldrs* **11/2**[2]

1 **10** ½ **Bossy Guest (IRE)**[33] 2288 2-9-1 0 WilliamTwiston-Davies 7 97
(Mick Channon) *hld up wl in tch in midfield: effrt and unable qck ent fnl f: styd on same pce u.p fnl f* **20/1**

12 **11** *shd* **Cock Of The North**[19] 2703 2-9-1 0 FrederikTylicki 9 97
(Scott Dixon) *str: taken down early: wl in tch in midfield: rdn 1/2-way: outpcd and struggling over 1f out: hld and plugged on same pce fnl f* **20/1**

111 **12** ¾ **Kool Kompany (IRE)**[15] 2855 2-9-1 0 RichardHughes 10 95
(Richard Hannon) *str: lw: stdd s: t.k.h: hld up in tch in last trio: effrt and wnt sharply rt over 1f out: drvn ent fnl f: kpt on same pce and no imp after: nvr trbld ldrs* **6/1**[3]

12 **13** 4½ **Kasb (IRE)**[25] 2521 2-9-1 0 DaneO'Neill 6 81+
(John Gosden) *lw: stdd s: t.k.h: hld up in tch towards rr: rdn and effrt 2f out: drvn and btn over 1f out: fdd fnl f* **28/1**

51 **14** 5 **Portamento (IRE)**[26] 2480 2-9-1 0 WilliamBuick 3 66
(Charlie Appleby) *t.k.h: chsd ldrs: rdn and wknd qckly over 1f out: fdd fnl f* **14/1**

**P** **Case Statement**[10] 3015 2-9-1 0 OisinMurphy 5
(M D O'Callaghan, Ire) *w'like: chsd ldrs tl lost action and dropped out rapidly over 2f out: p.u and dismntd 2f out: fatally injured* **66/1**

1m 12.99s (-1.51) **Going Correction** -0.025s/f (Good) **15** Ran SP% **125.4**
Speed ratings (Par 105): **109,106,106,106,105 105,105,104,104,103 103,102,96,89,**
CSF £32.02 CT £363.32 TOTE £5.20: £2.30, £2.40, £4.00; EX 41.90 Trifecta £516.50.
**Owner** Al Shaqab Racing **Bred** Mrs T Stack **Trained** Settrington, N Yorks

**FOCUS**

A typically warm Coventry Stakes with 11 of the 15 remaining runners last-time-out winners, six of whom came into this unbeaten. They seemed to go a decent pace up the centre of the track, without going mad, but the winning time was still just 0.53sec outside the 2yo course record set by Henrythenavigator in this race seven years ago. The prize had gone across the Irish Sea for the past three years, but this was one for the home team.

### 3319 KING'S STAND STKS (BRITISH CHAMPIONS SERIES & GLOBAL SPRINT CHALLENGE) (GROUP 1) 5f

**3:45** (3:45) (Class 1) 3-Y-O+

**£212,662** (£80,625; £40,350; £20,100; £10,087; £5,062) **Stalls** Centre

Form RPR

-401 **1** **Sole Power**[45] 1949 7-9-4 115 RichardHughes 8 120
(Edward Lynam, Ire) *hld up: swtchd rt and hdwy over 1f out: str run ins fnl f: led fnl 75yds: r.o and wl on top fin* **5/1**[3]

5434 **2** 1¼ **Stepper Point**[16] 2820 5-9-4 110 (p) MartinDwyer 4 116
(William Muir) *mainly disp ld: advantage 2f out: rdn whn strly pressed over 1f out: hdd fnl 75yds: kpt on but unable to go w wnr cl home* **50/1**

2-31 **3** *nk* **Hot Streak (IRE)**[24] 2563 3-8-12 117 JamieSpencer 11 112
(Kevin Ryan) *chsd ldrs: rdn and str chal fr 1f out: r.o u.p: hld fnl strides* **3/1**[1]

3114 **4** *nk* **Medicean Man**[80] 1179 8-9-4 112 (tp) HarryBentley 10 113
(Jeremy Gask) *lw: midfield: pushed along 2f out: rdn and hdwy over 1f out: edgd rt ins fnl f: styd on: nt quite pce of ldrs: hld fnl strides* **33/1**

0222 **5** ½ **Ahtoug**[80] 1179 6-9-4 116 WilliamBuick 13 112
(Charlie Appleby) *lw: trckd ldrs: effrt 2f out: rdn and nt qckn over 1f out: styd on ins fnl f: one pce fnl strides* **16/1**

-314 **6** *hd* **Steps (IRE)**[10] 2989 6-9-4 110 (b) KierenFallon 15 111
(Roger Varian) *squeezed out early: in rr and sn pushed along: hdwy whn swtchd lft ent fnl f: styd on: gng on at fin but nt pce to chal ldrs* **12/1**

-365 **7** *shd* **Jack Dexter**[24] 2563 5-9-4 113 GrahamLee 3 110
(Jim Goldie) *chsd ldrs: rdn over 1f out: one pce fnl 100yds* **20/1**

102- **8** *nk* **Take Cover**[213] 7928 7-9-4 103 DavidProbert 12 109
(David C Griffiths) *mainly disp ld tl rdn 2f out: sn hung rt: kpt on same pce ins fnl f: wl hld fnl 150yds* **50/1**

0-23 **9** 1¼ **Es Que Love (IRE)**[34] 2256 5-9-4 108 (p) AdamKirby 17 105
(Clive Cox) *chsd ldrs: rdn and hung rt 2f out: continued to hang after: nt qckn over 1f out: no ex fnl 150yds* **12/1**

-102 **10** 1¼ **Pearl Secret**[24] 2563 5-9-4 115 OlivierPeslier 7 100
(David Barron) *racd keenly in midfield: rdn over 1f out: outpcd ins fnl f: eased whn hld fnl 50yds* **8/1**

2-13 **11** 1¾ **Shea Shea (SAF)**[80] 1179 7-9-4 116 ChristopheSoumillon 2 94
(M F De Kock, South Africa) *hld up: effrt in tch over 1f out: no imp: eased fnl 75yds* **9/2**[2]

010- **12** ¾ **Green Door (IRE)**[248] 7191 3-8-12 107 JimCrowley 6 89
(Olly Stevens) *s.i.s: hld up: rdn and no imp whn carried rt over 1f out: nvr a threat* **66/1**

-444 **13** 1¾ **Justice Day (IRE)**[15] 2848 3-8-12 108 PaulHanagan 5 83
(David Elsworth) *lw: in tch: effrt whn chsng ldrs over 1f out: wknd ins fnl f* **66/1**

**14** *nk* **Ancil (USA)**[46] 5-9-4 103 (t) JamesDoyle 1 84
(Mrs Joan Scott, U.S.A) *in tch: rdn 2f out: wknd wl over 1f out* **66/1**

20-2 **15** *nk* **Rex Imperator**[15] 2848 5-9-4 110 (p) FrankieDettori 16 83
(William Haggas) *racd keenly: hld up: rdn over 2f out: nvr able to trble ldrs* **25/1**

1 **16** *hd* **Guerre (USA)**[50] 1824 3-8-12 110 RyanMoore 14 80
(A P O'Brien, Ire) *athletic: lw: chsd ldrs: rdn 2f out: sn lost pl: outpcd and bhd fnl f* **8/1**

58.85s (-1.65) **Going Correction** -0.025s/f (Good)
**WFA** 3 from 5yo+ 6lb **16** Ran SP% **123.3**
Speed ratings (Par 117): **111,109,108,108,107 106,106,106,104,102 99,98,95,95,94 94**
CSF £254.60 CT £888.12 TOTE £6.80: £2.30, £12.10, £1.70; EX 306.80 Trifecta £1911.40.
**Owner** Mrs S Power **Bred** G Russell **Trained** Dunshaughlin, Co Meath

**FOCUS**

A wide-open Group 1 sprint, as if often the case these days, and they were spread across the track.

### 3320 ST JAMES'S PALACE STKS (BRITISH CHAMPIONS SERIES) (GROUP 1) (ROUND COURSE) 1m (R)

**4:25** (4:28) (Class 1) 3-Y-O

**£212,662** (£80,625; £40,350; £20,100; £10,087; £5,062) **Stalls** Low

Form RPR

-121 **1** **Kingman**[24] 2571 3-9-0 125 JamesDoyle 7 128+
(John Gosden) *lw: stdd s: hld up in tch in last pair: clsd ent fnl 2f: rdn and effrt to chse ldr 1f out: shifting rt but qcknd smartly to ld fnl 100yds: sn clr: impressive* **8/11**[1]

1-21 **2** 2¼ **Night Of Thunder (IRE)**[45] 1951 3-9-0 120 RichardHughes 1 121
(Richard Hannon) *lw: led and dictated gallop: rdn and qcknd 2f out: drvn and hdd fnl 100yds: immediately outpcd by wnr and kpt on same pce after* **3/1**[2]

31-0 **3** 1 **Outstrip**[45] 1951 3-9-0 117 WilliamBuick 2 119
(Charlie Appleby) *chsd ldrs: n.m.r briefly ent fnl 2f: rdn and rdr dropped whip over 1f out: 5th and outpcd 1f out: rallied to go 3rd fnl 100yds: styd on: no threat to wnr* **33/1**

11-0 **4** ½ **War Command (USA)**[45] 1951 3-9-0 118 (p) JosephO'Brien 6 118
(A P O'Brien, Ire) *stdd s: hld up in last pair: rdn and effrt wl over 1f out: no hdwy tl styd on wl fnl 150yds: no threat to wnr* **9/1**

23-1 **5** 1 **Yuften**[31] 2346 3-9-0 93 AndreaAtzeni 4 116
(William Haggas) *chsd ldr: upsides and rdn 2f out: 3rd and outpcd 1f out: no ex and lost 2 pls fnl 100yds* **66/1**

1-10 **6** 1¼ **Toormore (IRE)**[45] 1951 3-9-0 118 RyanMoore 5 113
(Richard Hannon) *t.k.h: hld up wl in tch in midfield: rdn and effrt 2f out: drvn and outpcd 1f out: wknd ins fnl f: eased cl home* **7/1**[3]

7 shd **Prince Of All**[62] 1521 3-9-0 102 ChrisHayes 3 113
(P D Deegan, Ire) *w'like: t.k.h: hld up in tch in midfield: rdn 2f out: outpcd and lost pl over 1f out: wl hld and plugged on same pce fnl f* **66/1**

1m 39.06s (-1.64) **Going Correction** -0.025s/f (Good) **7** Ran SP% **111.3**
Speed ratings (Par 113): **107,104,103,103,102 101,100**
CSF £2.88 TOTE £1.60: £1.10, £1.60; EX 2.70 Trifecta £24.50.
**Owner** K Abdullah **Bred** Juddmonte Farms Ltd **Trained** Newmarket, Suffolk

**FOCUS**
Five of the seven runners had run in last month's 2,000 Guineas and the form of the Newmarket race could hardly be working out better, producing the first and second in the Epsom Derby, the first and second in the Irish 2,000 Guineas, plus the winners of the French Derby, Dante and a Group 3 at Chantilly. However, there was still a question mark over the first Classic due to the main protagonists taking varying routes up the Rowley Mile, so this was a chance to put the record straight and a few questions were certainly answered, as the winner put up a stunning performance. Even though the pace didn't look breakneck, it was solid enough and they again dipped under standard time in the first race run on the round course.

## 3321 ASCOT STKS (H'CAP) 2m 4f
**5:00** (5:04) (Class 2) (0-95,95) 4-Y-O+
**£37,350** (£11,184; £5,592; £2,796; £1,398; £702) **Stalls** Low

Form RPR

1/0- **1** **Domination**[37] 2189 7-9-7 92 FMBerry 17 105
(C Byrnes, Ire) *hld up bhd: hdwy on outer over 2f out: edgd rt fr wl over 1f out: led 1f out: styd on wl and in command ins fnl f* **12/1**

50-6 **2** 2 1/2 **Another Cocktail**[55] 1651 4-9-3 90 JimmyFortune 4 100
(Hughie Morrison) *in tch: hdwy 4f out: rdn to ld wl over 2f out: hdd wl over 1f out: kpt on u.p ins fnl f but wl hld by wnr* **20/1**

11-4 **3** hd **Sizzler**[52] 1735 4-9-8 95 JimCrowley 6 105
(Ralph Beckett) *midfield: hdwy 4f out: n.m.r over 3f out: nt clr run over 2f out: sn plld off inner and big effrt: led wl over 1f out: hdd 1f out: kpt on u.p after but wl hld by wnr* **16/1**

1-32 **4** 2 1/4 **Sohar**[17] 2782 6-9-4 89 GeorgeBaker 2 97
(James Toller) *hld up: hdwy over 3f out: chsd ldrs over 2f out: tried to chal over 1f out: one pce fnl 100yds* **16/1**

61-1 **5** 2 3/4 **Perfect Heart**[53] 1692 5-9-7 92 AndreaAtzeni 10 97+
(Roger Varian) *lw: trckd ldrs: lost pl and n.m.r over 3f out: sn outpcd: rallied over 1f out: styd on ins fnl f but no imp* **5/1**[1]

0-00 **6** 1 3/4 **Ray Ward (IRE)**[17] 2779 4-9-2 89 KierenFallon 5 92+
(David Simcock) *in tch: hmpd and lost pl over 3f out: sn towards rr w plenty to do: styd on and gd prog over 1f out: eased whn no ch of getting there fnl 75yds* **12/1**

323- **7** 1 **Lieutenant Miller**[67] 7193 8-9-8 93 RyanMoore 20 95
(Nicky Henderson) *hld up towards rr: hdwy over 2f out: hmpd wl over 1f out: kpt on tl no ex fnl 100yds* **8/1**[3]

00-6 **8** nk **Suraj**[33] 2289 5-9-5 90 JamieSpencer 15 92
(Nicky Henderson) *racd keenly: hld up: hdwy over 4f out: rdn and nt clr run over 3f out: chsng ldrs and cl up over 2f out: one pce over 1f out* **8/1**[3]

6-04 **9** 1 **Brockwell**[24] 2561 5-9-2 87 (p) RichardKingscote 3 88+
(Tom Dascombe) *prom: n.m.r and hmpd over 3f out: sn lost pl: styd on fr over 1f out but no ch* **10/1**

**10** 3/4 **Plinth (IRE)**[21] 7405 4-9-6 93 (tp) JosephO'Brien 7 93
(A P O'Brien, Ire) *midfield: hdwy over 3f out: rdn over 2f out: kpt on fnl f: nvr able to chal* **10/1**

12-6 **11** 1 **Ballinderry Boy**[29] 2405 4-9-4 94 OisinMurphy(3) 14 93
(Andrew Balding) *racd keenly in midfield: hdwy 3f out: rdn whn chsng ldrs over 2f out: sn no imp: wl btn ins fnl f* **13/2**[2]

1451 **12** 2 1/2 **Villa Royale**[33] 2289 5-9-8 93 AndrewMullen 13 90
(Michael Appleby) *lw: chsd ldrs: effrt to ld 4f out: hdd over 2f out: wknd ins fnl f* **14/1**

6024 **13** 6 **Gabrial's King (IRE)**[9] 3034 5-9-4 89 RichardHughes 12 80
(David Simcock) *dwlt: hld up bhd: rdn 3f out: nvr able to get on terms* **33/1**

3-04 **14** 1 1/4 **Body Language (IRE)**[32] 2294 6-9-7 92 (p) JamesDoyle 19 81
(Ian Williams) *midfield: hdwy over 4f out: rdn to chse ldrs 3f out: wknd wl over 1f out* **25/1**

**15** 6 **Agreement (IRE)**[35] 4973 4-9-4 91 PhillipMakin 18 74
(John Quinn) *midfield: pushed along and lost pl over 4f out: rdn and nt clr run over 3f out: bhd fnl 2f* **33/1**

42-0 **16** 21 **Waterclock (IRE)**[41] 2073 5-9-5 90 (p) GrahamLee 9 52+
(Jedd O'Keeffe) *chsd ldrs: rdn over 3f out: sn n.m.r and lost pl: bhd after* **25/1**

**17** 6 **Sardinia (IRE)**[37] 2189 4-9-3 90 (b) PatDobbs 8 46
(Paul Nolan, Ire) *chsd ldr after 2f tl rdn over 3f out: sn wknd* **33/1**

12-0 **18** 75 **Asbaab (USA)**[44] 1973 4-9-7 94 PaulHanagan 1
(Brian Meehan) *led: rdn and hdd 4f out: wknd over 3f out: t.o* **33/1**

0-50 **P** **Sir Graham Wade (IRE)**[59] 1581 5-9-10 95 (p) JoeFanning 16
(Mark Johnston) *hld up: u.p over 5f out: n.m.r and hmpd over 3f out: sn wnt wrong and p.u: fatally injured* **20/1**

4m 20.3s (-4.50) **Going Correction** -0.025s/f (Good)
**WFA** 4 from 5yo+ 2lb **19** Ran SP% **133.2**
Speed ratings (Par 109): **108,107,106,106,104 104,103,103,103,103 102,101,99,98,96 87,85,55,**
CSF £247.58 CT £3838.26 TOTE £17.00: £3.60, £5.00, £4.40, £4.70; EX 459.80 Trifecta £9242.60.
**Owner** Ms Carol Cleary **Bred** M Kerr-Dineen **Trained** Ballingarry, Co Limerick
■ Stewards' Enquiry : F M Berry two-day ban: used whip above permitted level (Jul 1-2)

**FOCUS**
Run at a steady tempo early, the pace increased a fair way out and only the strongest stayers could hack it.

## 3322 WINDSOR CASTLE STKS (LISTED RACE) 5f
**5:35** (5:44) (Class 1) 2-Y-O
**£34,026** (£12,900; £6,456; £3,216; £1,614; £810) **Stalls** Centre

Form RPR

**1** **Hootenanny (USA)**[32] 2-9-3 0 (b) VictorEspinoza 25 108+
(Wesley A Ward, U.S.A) *str: lengthy: lw: racd towards stands' side: mde virtually all: rdn and asserted ent fnl f: r.o strly and gng away at fin: impressive* **7/2**[1]

3313 **2** 3 1/2 **Union Rose**[4] 3173 2-9-3 0 (p) WilliamTwiston-Davies 21 94
(Ronald Harris) *racd towards stands' side: chsd ldrs: pressing wnr and drvn over 1f out: outpcd and brushed aside by wnr ins fnl f: wkng but hld on gamely for 2nd nr fin* **100/1**

21 **3** nk **Mubtaghaa (IRE)**[16] 2800 2-9-3 0 PaulHanagan 17 93
(William Haggas) *racd in centre: off the pce in midfield: rdn 1/2-way: hdwy u.p over 1f out: styd on wl to 3rd fnl 75yds: pressing for 2nd nr fin: no ch w wnr* **7/1**[3]

216 **4** 3/4 **Sarista (IRE)**[32] 2313 2-8-12 0 RobertWinston 6 86+
(David Barron) *racd towards far side: chsd ldrs overall: rdn and effrt 2f out: 3rd and hung lft u.p fr 1f out: kpt on same pce and lost 3rd fnl 75yds* **25/1**

213 **5** nse **Haxby (IRE)**[15] 2845 2-9-3 0 AndreaAtzeni 24 90
(Roger Varian) *w'like: racd towards stands' side: chsd ldrs overall: rdn and effrt wl over 1f out: no ch w wnr and styd on same pce fnl f* **20/1**

0 **6** 1 1/4 **Cotai Glory**[28] 2428 2-9-3 0 GeorgeBaker 19 86+
(Charles Hills) *unf: dismntd and led most of way to s: stdd and hmpd sn after s: racd centre and wl in rr: shifting lft and hdwy over 1f out: r.o wl ins fnl f: nvr trbld ldrs* **66/1**

123 **7** 1 **Roudee**[19] 2703 2-9-3 0 [1] RichardKingscote 11 82
(Tom Dascombe) *racd towards far side: chsd ldrs: edgd lft u.p over 1f out: wknd ins fnl f* **20/1**

31 **8** 3/4 **Fuwairt (IRE)**[15] 2829 2-9-3 0 FrankieDettori 20 80
(Richard Hannon) *unf: scope: racd in centre: wnt rt s and slowly away: off the pce in rr: hdwy u.p over 1f out: no ex 1f out: wknd ins fnl f* **14/1**

41 **9** nk **Among Angels**[22] 2623 2-9-3 0 RichardHughes 8 81+
(Richard Hannon) *w'like: str: racd towards far side: stdd s: wl off the pce in rr: rdn 2f out: hdwy u.p jst over 1f out: no imp fnl 150yds: nvr trbld ldrs* **20/1**

22 **10** 3/4 **Commander Patten (IRE)**[17] 2776 2-9-3 0 OisinMurphy 7 76+
(Alan Bailey) *lengthy: racd towards far side: chsd ldrs: rdn and effrt wl over 1f out: no ex 1f out: wknd ins fnl f* **33/1**

261 **11** 1/2 **Denzille Lane (IRE)**[13] 2903 2-9-3 0 JoeFanning 4 74+
(Mark Johnston) *racd towards far side: chsd ldrs overall: pressing ldrs and hung lft over 1f out: stl hanging and btn 1f out: fdd ins fnl f* **50/1**

211 **12** nk **Midterm Break (IRE)**[24] 2543 2-9-3 0 GrahamGibbons 15 73
(David Barron) *racd in centre: off the pce in midfield: rdn 2f out: drvn and btn ent fnl f: wknd ins fnl f* **12/1**

332 **13** 1/2 **Harry Hurricane**[27] 2458 2-9-3 0 PatCosgrave 23 71
(George Baker) *racd towards stands' side: in tch in midfield overall: rdn wl over 1f out: no imp u.p over 1f out: wknd ins fnl f* **40/1**

41 **14** hd **Majestic Hero (IRE)**[20] 2666 2-9-3 0 DavidProbert 9 70+
(Ronald Harris) *racd towards far side: off the pce in midfield: effrt u.p over 1f out: sme hdwy 1f out: kpt on but nvr trbld ldrs* **28/1**

12 **15** nk **Mind Of Madness (IRE)**[14] 2873 2-9-3 0 JamieSpencer 14 72+
(David Brown) *racd in centre: hld up off the pce in rr: hdwy and swtchd rt over 1f out: keeping on same pce and hld whn nt clr run ins fnl f: eased after* **5/1**[2]

01 **16** nk **Four Seasons (IRE)**[21] 2642 2-9-3 0 WilliamBuick 16 68+
(Charlie Appleby) *racd in centre: in tch in midfield overall: rdn 1/2-way: drvn and btn ent fnl f: wknd fnl 150yds* **12/1**

12 **17** 1 **Merdon Castle (IRE)**[29] 2403 2-9-3 0 RyanMoore 13 68
(David Elsworth) *lengthy: lw: racd in centre: wl off the pce in rr: rdn 1/2-way: sme hdwy u.p 1f out: n.d whn nt clr run ins fnl f: eased* **7/1**[3]

541 **18** 1/2 **Casterbridge**[26] 2472 2-9-3 0 JasonHart 5 65+
(Eric Alston) *racd towards far side: w wnr: rdn and ev ch over 1f out: no ex 1f out: wkng whn hmpd ins fnl f: fdd fnl 100yds* **66/1**

63 **19** 3/4 **Goring (GER)**[21] 2642 2-9-3 0 JimmyFortune 2 62+
(Eve Johnson Houghton) *w'like: racd towards far side: off the pce in midfield: rdn 2f out: no prog over 1f out: wknd ins fnl f: eased towards fin* **66/1**

**20** nk **Biting Bullets (USA)** 2-9-3 0 AdamKirby 3 59+
(Jo Hughes) *leggy: racd towards far side: s.i.s: off pce in rr: rdn 2f out: no hdwy: n.d* **100/1**

414 **21** 1 **Prince Bonnaire**[10] 3001 2-9-3 0 GrahamLee 10 56
(David Brown) *racd in centre: a off the pce towards rr: no hdwy u.p whn hmpd ent fnl f: n.d* **40/1**

314 **22** shd **Flyball**[62] 1512 2-9-3 0 PatDobbs 12 55+
(Richard Hannon) *racd towards far side: off the pce in midfield: rdn and effrt over 1f out: no hdwy: wknd ins fnl f* **50/1**

3 **23** 1 1/2 **Boann (IRE)**[20] 2666 2-8-12 0 PhilipPrince 22 45
(J S Moore) *racd in centre: s.i.s and wnt rt s: hung rt and flashed tail thrght: a bhd* **125/1**

6 **24** shd **Bwana (IRE)**[15] 2855 2-9-3 0 JamesDoyle 18 49
(P J Prendergast, Ire) *racd in centre: off the pce in midfield: rdn 2f out: no prog and wknd ent fnl f* **25/1**

59.05s (-1.45) **Going Correction** -0.025s/f (Good) **24** Ran SP% **130.4**
Speed ratings (Par 101): **110,104,103,102,102 100,99,97,97,96 95,94,94,93,93 92,91,90,89,88 87,86,84,84**
CSF £430.81 CT £2478.72 TOTE £4.50: £2.00, £27.40, £2.80; EX 531.20 Trifecta £9915.50 Part won..
**Owner** Derrick Smith & Mrs John Magnier & Michael Tabor **Bred** Barronstown **Trained** North America

**FOCUS**
A race for juveniles just below Group class at this stage of their career, the Windsor Castle has produced some surprise winners in recent years, with a 100-1 shot successful in 2008 and a 33-1 winner in 2009, but the 9-4 favourite managed to score in 2011. High-drawn horses had won the last four runnings and again those that raced nearside were at an advantage, even though the early pace came from those drawn low.
T/Jkpt: £9,498.90 to a £1 stake. Pool: £80,272.50 - 6.00 winning units T/Plt: £200.20 to a £1 stake. Pool: £583,035.93 - 2,125.10 winning units T/Qpdt: £94.20 to a £1 stake. Pool: £23,816.61 - 186.98 winning units SP

# 2859 BRIGHTON (L-H)
Tuesday, June 17

**OFFICIAL GOING: Good to firm (firm in places; 7.2)**
Wind: Moderate; half against Weather: Sunny and warm

## 3323 STARSPREADS.COM NOW ONLINE H'CAP 5f 59y
**6:00** (6:01) (Class 6) (0-60,60) 3-Y-O+ **£1,940** (£577; £288; £144) **Stalls** Low

Form RPR

653- **1** **Tychaios**[239] 7432 4-9-10 58 SeanLevey 2 69
(Stuart Williams) *chsd ldrs: wnt 2nd and drew clr w wnr 2f out: led ins fnl f: rdn out* **7/4**[1]

2634 **2** 1 1/2 **Bubbly Bailey**[15] 2830 4-9-3 51 (v) FrederikTylicki 4 57
(J R Jenkins) *led at str pce: hrd rdn wl over 1f out: hdd and one pce ins fnl f* **11/4**[2]

0000 **3** 3 1/2 **Back On Baileys**[12] 2931 3-8-3 **46** oh1 (v[1]) RyanPowell(3) 7 38
(John Ryan) *in rr: rdn over 2f out: styd on fr over 1f out* **20/1**
6406 **4** 2 **Mossgo (IRE)**[109] 777 4-9-10 **58** (t) WilliamCarson 3 45
(John Best) *chsd ldr tl rdn and btn 2f out* **12/1**
042- **5** 1 1/2 **High Tone**[314] 5128 4-9-3 **51** FergusSweeney 6 33
(Dean Ivory) *chsd ldrs tl wknd 2f out* **4/1**[3]
456- **6** 3 1/4 **Captain Ryan**[253] 7074 3-9-6 **60** SteveDrowne 9 28
(Peter Makin) *in tch and wd: wknd 2f out* **8/1**
-060 **7** 1 3/4 **Fleeting Indian (IRE)**[18] 2723 5-8-12 **46** oh1 (p) SaleemGolam 8 10
(Linda Jewell) *in tch towards outer: squeezed and lost pl 3f out: sn struggling* **50/1**
46-0 **8** 2 **Burnt Cream**[43] 2008 7-9-5 **53** (t) RobertHavlin 10 10
(Martin Bosley) *sn outpcd in rr: sddle slipped* **20/1**
1m 2.16s (-0.14) **Going Correction** -0.125s/f (Firm)
**WFA** 3 from 4yo+ 6lb **8** Ran SP% **113.3**
Speed ratings (Par 101): **96,93,88,84,82 77,74,71**
CSF £6.38 CT £65.85 TOTE £2.10: £1.10, £2.10, £4.00; EX 7.90 Trifecta £108.50.
**Owner** Panny Ellinas **Bred** L Ellinas & Old Mill Stud **Trained** Newmarket, Suffolk
**FOCUS**
Sean Levey, who rode the opening winner, said: "The ground's good to firm but there's a little bit of juice in it and it feels safe as anything." A very moderate handicap in which the first two came clear. Races on inner line and distances as advertised.

## 3324 IRISH STALLION FARMS EBF/STARSPREADS.COM MAIDEN STKS 5f 213y
**6:30** (6:30) (Class 5) 2-Y-O **£2,911** (£866; £432; £216) **Stalls** Low

Form RPR
4 **1** **Geological (IRE)**[11] 2964 2-9-5 0 SeanLevey 4 76+
(Richard Hannon) *mde virtually all: edgd lft ins fnl f: hld on wl* **7/4**[1]
6 **2** 3/4 **Steady Major (IRE)**[17] 2776 2-9-5 0 FergusSweeney 1 74
(David Simcock) *hld up in last: rdn and hdwy over 1f out: chsd wnr ins fnl f: r.o* **5/1**[2]
**3** 1 1/2 **Faraajh (IRE)** 2-9-0 0 JimmyQuinn 2 65
(James Tate) *w wnr: cl 2nd and rdn whn hmpd on rail ins fnl f: nt rcvr* **25/1**
52 **4** 2 3/4 **Town Crier (IRE)**[29] 2380 2-9-5 0 LiamJones 3 61
(William Haggas) *hld up in 4th: rdn over 2f out: sltly unbalanced on camber: drvn along and btn over 1f out* **7/4**[1]
543 **5** 1/2 **Popeswood (IRE)**[17] 2756 2-9-2 0 CharlesBishop(3) 5 60
(Mick Channon) *chsd ldng pair: rdn 2f out: btn over 1f out* **6/1**[3]
1m 10.42s (0.22) **Going Correction** -0.125s/f (Firm) **5** Ran SP% **107.5**
Speed ratings (Par 93): **93,92,90,86,85**
CSF £10.38 TOTE £2.70: £1.30, £6.80; EX 13.80 Trifecta £99.90.
**Owner** The Royal Ascot Racing Club **Bred** Mrs Helen Keaveney **Trained** East Everleigh, Wilts
**FOCUS**
An interesting little maiden for the class.

## 3325 STARSPREADS.COM SPORTS SPREAD BETTING FILLIES' H'CAP 1m 1f 209y
**7:00** (7:00) (Class 4) (0-80,74) 4-Y-O+ **£4,690** (£1,395; £697; £348) **Stalls** High

Form RPR
1425 **1** **Taro Tywod (IRE)**[3] 3218 5-8-10 **70** CamHardie(7) 3 81
(Mark Brisbourne) *trckd ldng pair: effrt on ins rail and led 2f out: drvn clr* **11/4**[2]
30-1 **2** 4 1/2 **Trulee Scrumptious**[18] 2750 5-8-7 **60** JimmyQuinn 1 62
(Peter Charalambous) *led and restrained in front: qcknd ins fnl 3f: hdd and outpcd by wnr 2f out* **5/2**[1]
4116 **3** 2 1/2 **Choral Festival**[22] 2628 8-9-1 **68** WilliamCarson 5 65
(John Bridger) *hld up in 4th: rdn 3f out: one pce fnl 2f* **9/2**
1333 **4** nk **Tilstarr (IRE)**[18] 2750 4-9-4 **74** RobertTart(3) 4 71
(Roger Teal) *chsd ldr tl hrd rdn and btn 2f out* **4/1**[3]
5220 **5** 2 **Sian Gwalia**[22] 2628 4-9-0 **67** MartinLane 2 60
(David Simcock) *a last: rdn 4f out: wknd 2f out* **5/1**
2m 2.17s (-1.43) **Going Correction** -0.125s/f (Firm) **5** Ran SP% **110.1**
Speed ratings (Par 102): **100,96,94,94,92**
CSF £9.97 TOTE £3.10: £1.80, £2.10; EX 13.70 Trifecta £60.20.
**Owner** Rasio Cymru Racing 1 **Bred** Pat Fullam **Trained** Great Ness, Shropshire
**FOCUS**
A modest fillies' handicap run at a steady initial gallop.

## 3326 STARSPREADS.COM ENGLAND WORLD CUP OFFERS H'CAP 1m 1f 209y
**7:30** (7:31) (Class 6) (0-60,59) 3-Y-O **£1,940** (£577; £288; £144) **Stalls** High

Form RPR
-000 **1** **Redlorryellowlorry (IRE)**[19] 2694 3-8-7 **45** (t) MartinLane 4 51
(George Baker) *s.i.s: rdn early: bhd: hrd rdn 3f out: rapid hdwy to ld nr fin* **66/1**
0-44 **2** 3/4 **Bishop Wulstan (IRE)**[14] 2860 3-9-0 **52** SeanLevey 12 57
(Richard Hannon) *t.k.h in midfield: gd hdwy 1f out: disp ld 75yds out: outpcd by wnr nr fin* **3/1**[1]
5-03 **3** 3/4 **Ametrine (IRE)**[12] 2927 3-9-4 **59** ThomasBrown(3) 3 62+
(William Jarvis) *t.k.h: trckd ldrs: rdn and lost pl 4f out: styd on wl fnl f* **7/1**[2]
0-43 **4** nk **King Calypso**[19] 2694 3-8-0 **45** CamHardie(7) 8 50+
(Denis Coakley) *mid-div: j. road 6f out: hdwy towards outer whn nt clr run wl over 1f out: swtchd lft: squeezed on rail ins fnl f: r.o* **7/1**[2]
0-00 **5** hd **Oracle Boy**[50] 1793 3-9-2 **54** MartinDwyer 9 56+
(William Muir) *chsd ldrs: rdn over 2f out: nt best of runs over 1f out: one pce fnl f* **8/1**[3]
0-00 **6** 1 3/4 **Mystical Maze**[35] 2237 3-8-7 **45** WilliamCarson 6 44
(Mark Brisbourne) *prom: drvn to ld ins fnl f: hng lft: hdd and no ex fnl 75yds* **66/1**
60-0 **7** 1/2 **Jersey Cream (IRE)**[28] 2416 3-9-3 **55** AdamBeschizza 10 53
(Gary Moore) *pressed ldr: led 3f out: rdn 2f out: hdd and n.m.r ins fnl f: no ex* **16/1**
4331 **8** 5 **Sandy Cove**[41] 2066 3-9-6 **58** FergusSweeney 1 57+
(James Eustace) *in tch: effrt 2f out: chsng ldrs whn bdly hmpd ins fnl f: nt rcvr* **3/1**[1]
6005 **9** 1 1/4 **Appellez Baileys (FR)**[6] 3121 3-8-8 **46** (v[1]) NickyMackay 2 32
(Chris Dwyer) *led tl 3f out: disp 5th and btn whn n.m.r ins fnl f: eased clsd home* **50/1**
050 **10** 1/2 **Pouncing Tiger**[54] 1680 3-9-1 **53** SteveDrowne 14 38
(Stuart Williams) *mid-div: rdn and hng lft 2f out: no hdwy* **16/1**
2-60 **11** 4 1/2 **Sarlat**[152] 198 3-8-2 **45** NoelGarbutt(5) 11 22
(Mark Brisbourne) *mid-div: hmpd 1/2-way: sme hdwy on rail wl over 1f out: sn wknd* **66/1**
1224 **12** 3 1/4 **Shannon Haven (IRE)**[83] 1098 3-9-6 **58** (p) ShaneKelly 13 29
(Daniel Mark Loughnane) *hld up: hdwy 4f out: n.m.r and wknd over 1f out* **12/1**
-445 **13** 3/4 **Female Strategy (IRE)**[120] 645 3-9-0 **52** LiamJones 5 21
(Mark Brisbourne) *chsd ldrs tl hrd rdn and wknd 2f out* **25/1**
2-U2 **14** 22 **Columbian Roulette (IRE)**[147] 267 3-9-4 **56** (b) PaddyAspell 7
(Charles Hills) *sn bhd: drvn along and lost tch 5f out* **10/1**
2m 3.6s **Going Correction** -0.125s/f (Firm) **14** Ran SP% **124.9**
Speed ratings (Par 97): **95,94,93,93,93 92,91,87,86,86 82,80,79,61**
CSF £265.53 CT £1646.41 TOTE £35.00: £9.90, £2.00, £3.40; EX 735.80 Trifecta £1141.60 Part won..
**Owner** PJL Racing **Bred** Tally-Ho Stud **Trained** Manton, Wilts
■ Stewards' Enquiry : Cam Hardie two-day ban: careless riding (Jul 1-2)
William Carson three-day ban: careless riding (Jul 1-3)
**FOCUS**
A weak, low-grade handicap in which the picture changed rapidly late on. It was a rough race and isn't form to take too seriously.

## 3327 STARSPREADS.COM IN PLAY TRADING H'CAP 7f 214y
**8:00** (8:03) (Class 6) (0-65,65) 4-Y-O+ **£1,940** (£577; £288; £144) **Stalls** Low

Form RPR
4-30 **1** **Elle Rebelle**[26] 2479 4-7-11 **48** CamHardie(7) 6 55
(Mark Brisbourne) *plld hrd in 6th: rdn and dropped to rr over 2f out: hung lft: str run to ld nr fin* **6/1**[3]
6123 **2** nk **Who's That Chick (IRE)**[11] 2963 5-8-12 **63** DanielCremin(7) 7 69
(Ralph J Smith) *towards rr: hdwy 2f out: hung lft and led ins fnl f: kpt on u.p: hdd nr fin* **2/1**[1]
5233 **3** 3/4 **Pick A Little**[18] 2721 6-9-7 **65** SteveDrowne 5 69
(Michael Blake) *pressed ldr: rdn to chal 2f out: unable qck ins fnl f* **12/1**
0602 **4** 1 1/2 **Fairy Mist (IRE)**[18] 2722 7-8-3 **47** (b) WilliamCarson 4 48
(John Bridger) *hld up in rr: hdwy on rail to ld 2f out: hdd and one pce ins fnl f* **10/1**
4U46 **5** shd **Interakt**[18] 2722 7-7-10 **47** (b) NoraLooby(7) 9 47
(Joseph Tuite) *mde most tl 2f out: prom whn squeezed out ins fnl f: nt rcvr* **16/1**
4-00 **6** 1 3/4 **Woolston Ferry (IRE)**[41] 2079 8-9-5 **63** FergusSweeney 1 59
(Henry Candy) *towards rr: rdn and sme hdwy over 1f out: no imp fnl f* **16/1**
5054 **7** 2 3/4 **Greensward**[12] 2930 8-9-5 **63** (v) MartinLane 3 53
(Conor Dore) *t.k.h: chsd ldrs tl outpcd fnl 2f* **8/1**
0051 **8** 1/2 **Little Indian**[48] 1876 4-9-4 **62** FrederikTylicki 8 51
(J R Jenkins) *in tch: rdn over 2f out: wknd wl over 1f out: eased whn btn fnl f* **3/1**[2]
0064 **9** 14 **Laguna Belle**[41] 2069 4-8-5 **49** oh1 ow3 AdamBeschizza 2 6
(Pat Phelan) *prom: rdn over 2f out: sn wknd* **25/1**
1m 35.27s (-0.73) **Going Correction** -0.125s/f (Firm) **9** Ran SP% **116.1**
Speed ratings (Par 101): **98,97,96,95,95 93,90,90,76**
CSF £18.50 CT £141.18 TOTE £8.10: £2.50, £1.20, £2.10; EX 27.20 Trifecta £321.70.
**Owner** The Bourne Connection **Bred** Mette Campbell-Andenaes **Trained** Great Ness, Shropshire
**FOCUS**
Moderate form.

## 3328 STARSPREADS.COM ROYAL ASCOT SPREAD BETTING H'CAP 6f 209y
**8:30** (8:30) (Class 6) (0-65,64) 4-Y-O+ **£1,940** (£577; £288; £144) **Stalls** Low

Form RPR
-022 **1** **Mrs Warren**[27] 2463 4-9-6 **63** MartinDwyer 3 75
(George Baker) *chsd ldrs: led and edgd lft ins fnl f: drvn out* **9/2**[3]
4513 **2** nk **Shifting Star (IRE)**[13] 2884 9-9-5 **62** (vt) WilliamCarson 7 73
(John Bridger) *led 2f: chsd ldr after: chalng whn brushed by wnr and carried lft ins fnl f: kpt on* **8/1**
005 **3** 3 **Mambo Spirit (IRE)**[59] 1573 10-8-12 **58** OisinMurphy(3) 6 61
(Tony Newcombe) *led after 2f and set gd pce: hrd rdn and hdd ins fnl f: wknd* **7/2**[2]
1063 **4** 3 1/2 **Darnathean**[3] 3227 5-9-6 **63** (p) SeanLevey 4 57
(Paul D'Arcy) *chsd ldrs tl wknd over 1f out* **5/2**[1]
6-04 **5** 3 **Eager To Bow (IRE)**[42] 2048 8-9-4 **64** (p) ThomasBrown(3) 2 50
(Patrick Chamings) *hld up in 6th: sme hdwy over 1f out: wknd fnl f* **8/1**
0062 **6** nk **High On The Hog (IRE)**[15] 2844 6-7-11 **45** NoelGarbutt(5) 5 31
(Mark Brisbourne) *in tch: rdn over 2f out: sn wknd* **10/1**
6551 **7** 2 **Perfect Pastime**[18] 2723 6-8-9 **59** (b) DanielCremin(7) 1 39
(Jim Boyle) *s.i.s: outpcd in rr* **6/1**
1m 21.66s (-1.44) **Going Correction** -0.125s/f (Firm) **7** Ran SP% **114.6**
Speed ratings (Par 101): **103,102,99,95,91 91,89**
CSF £39.28 TOTE £4.70: £2.10, £2.80; EX 18.90 Trifecta £81.00.
**Owner** Peter Russell **Bred** Freedom Farm Stud **Trained** Manton, Wilts
**FOCUS**
A fair race for the grade.

## 3329 STARSPREADS.COM H'CAP 5f 213y
**9:00** (9:00) (Class 5) (0-70,66) 3-Y-O+ **£2,587** (£770; £384; £192) **Stalls** Low

Form RPR
41 **1** **Avonmore Star**[5] 3150 6-9-5 **60** 6ex OisinMurphy(3) 3 72
(Alan McCabe) *mde most: drvn clr ins fnl f* **10/11**[1]
-600 **2** 3 1/4 **Koharu**[7] 3088 4-9-12 **64** (tp) SteveDrowne 2 66
(Peter Makin) *broke wl: stdd bk in tch: rdn to chse wnr 1f out: kpt on same pce* **9/2**[2]
0-00 **3** 1/2 **Orlando Star (CAN)**[15] 2847 3-8-12 **60** (v[1]) RobertTart(3) 1 58
(Roger Teal) *in tch: effrt 2f out: drvn to briefly chse wnr on ins rail over 1f out: one pce fnl f* **10/1**
-400 **4** 1/2 **Princess Cammie (IRE)**[10] 2994 4-8-9 **47** oh2 (p) WilliamCarson 5 46
(John Bridger) *dwlt: chsd wnr after 1f tl over 1f out: no ex* **14/1**
366 **5** 2 **Volito**[77] 1221 8-9-11 **63** MartinLane 6 55
(Anabel K Murphy) *hld up in rr: effrt on outer 2f out: no imp* **6/1**[3]
5540 **6** 1 3/4 **Blazing Knight (IRE)**[13] 2884 4-10-0 **66** (b) SeanLevey 4 53
(Chris Gordon) *chsd ldrs tl wknd over 1f out* **8/1**
1m 10.01s (-0.19) **Going Correction** -0.125s/f (Firm)
**WFA** 3 from 4yo+ 7lb **6** Ran SP% **111.7**
Speed ratings (Par 103): **96,91,91,90,87 85**
CSF £5.24 TOTE £1.80: £1.10, £2.20; EX 5.20 Trifecta £41.10.
**Owner** Mrs M J McCabe **Bred** Miss J R Tooth **Trained** Averham Park, Notts
**FOCUS**
Not much of a race.
T/Plt: £140.80 to a £1 stake. Pool: £49,841.72 - 258.39 winning units T/Qpdt: £36.60 to a £1 stake. Pool: £5,631.10 - 113.80 winning units LM

# [3304]NOTTINGHAM (L-H)

Tuesday, June 17

**OFFICIAL GOING: Good to firm (8.4)**
Wind: Light; half behind Weather: Cloudy

## 3330 FOR YOUR COMFORT DG TAXIS 01159500500 MEDIAN AUCTION MAIDEN STKS 6f 15y
**6:10** (6:11) (Class 5) 2-Y-O **£2,587** (£770; £384; £192) **Stalls** Centre

Form RPR

1 **Lieutenant Kaffee (USA)** 2-9-5 0 TonyHamilton 8 80+
(Richard Fahey) *racd towards stands' rail: trckd ldrs: hdwy over 2f out: rdn to chal ent fnl f: led last 100yds: kpt on strly* **7/1**

62 2 2 **Vegas Rebel (IRE)**[7] 3082 2-9-5 0 MartinHarley 9 74
(Peter Chapple-Hyam) *racd towards stands' rail: trckd ldrs: cl up 1/2-way: rdn over 1f out: led ent fnl f: sn drvn and hdd last 100yds: kpt on same pce* **9/4**[1]

3 3 **Scarlet Bounty (IRE)** 2-9-0 0 DavidNolan 4 60+
(Richard Fahey) *sltly hmpd s: in tch: trckd ldrs 1/2-way: hdwy 2f out and sn ev ch: rdn ent fnl f: sn one pce* **20/1**

5 4 ½ **Muradif (IRE)**[17] 2788 2-9-5 0 SebSanders 7 64
(William Haggas) *in tch: hdwy to chse ldrs wl over 2f out: sn pushed along: rdn over 1f out: kpt on fnl f* **5/1**[3]

05 5 2¾ **Lyfka**[36] 2220 2-8-11 0 AshleyMorgan(3) 6 50
(Paul Cole) *led: pushed along 2f out: rdn over 1f out: hdd ent fnl f: sn wknd* **25/1**

6 9 **Fast Magic (IRE)** 2-9-5 0 TomEaves 1 28
(Kevin Ryan) *cl up: rdn along wl over 2f out: sn wknd* **16/1**

5 7 6 **Alakhtal (IRE)**[17] 2777 2-9-5 0 ChrisCatlin 3 10+
(Charles Hills) *hmpd s: sn chsng ldrs on outer: hdwy and cl up 1/2-way: rdn 2f out and sn wknd* **3/1**[2]

5 8 6 **Native Charmer**[22] 2612 2-9-5 0 DaleSwift 2
(Ed McMahon) *wnt rt s: towards rr: outpcd and bhd fr 1/2-way* **10/1**

0 9 4 **Red Flute**[25] 2507 2-9-5 0 JohnFahy 5
(Alan McCabe) *wnt lft s: sn prom: rdn along wl over 2f out: sn wknd* **33/1**

1m 13.43s (-1.27) **Going Correction** -0.225s/f (Firm) **9** Ran SP% **111.5**
Speed ratings (Par 93): **99,96,92,91,88 76,68,60,54**
CSF £21.74 TOTE £6.90: £2.50, £1.20, £2.40; EX 29.70 Trifecta £268.00.
**Owner** Richard Fahey Ebor Racing Club Ltd **Bred** St George Farm LLC **Trained** Musley Bank, N Yorks

**FOCUS**
A dry run up to a meeting that had seen 17mm of water applied to the track since Friday (3mm applied to home straight overnight). A couple of interesting newcomers in a race run at a reasonable gallop throughout. The first two pulled clear. Outer track used and rail moved out around whole course and distances increased by 30yds on Round course.

## 3331 CORPORATE RELIABILITY DG TAXIS H'CAP (BOBIS RACE) 5f 13y
**6:40** (6:41) (Class 4) (0-85,83) 3-Y-O **£4,690** (£1,395; £697; £348) **Stalls** Centre

Form RPR

-300 1 **Desert Ace (IRE)**[22] 2626 3-9-2 83 (tp) RyanTate(5) 10 91
(Clive Cox) *racd nr stands' rail: hld up: hdwy wl over 1f out: rdn ent fnl f: kpt on to ld nr fin* **8/1**

-211 2 1¼ **Naivasha**[11] 2943 3-8-13 75 TedDurcan 9 79+
(Robert Cowell) *racd nr stands' rail: led: rdn along over 1f out: drvn ins fnl f: edgd lft last 100yds: sn hdd and no ex* **7/2**[1]

5415 3 hd **Royal Warrior**[4] 3185 3-9-2 78 JohnFahy 1 81
(Alan McCabe) *prom on outer: hdwy and cl up 2f out: rdn and ev ch ent fnl f tl drvn and no ex last 75yds* **25/1**

31 4 1 **Saakhen (IRE)**[40] 2093 3-9-4 80 (t) TonyHamilton 4 79
(Richard Fahey) *chsd ldrs: effrt wl over 1f out: sn rdn: kpt on same pce ins fnl f* **4/1**[2]

0040 5 1¾ **Oriental Relation (IRE)**[32] 2317 3-9-6 82 (b) DaleSwift 3 75
(James Given) *dwlt and sltly hmpd s: in rr: pushed along 1/2-way: rdn wl over 1f out: styd on fnl f: nrst fin* **20/1**

0-54 6 hd **Distant Past**[43] 2015 3-8-11 73 TomEaves 7 65
(Kevin Ryan) *chsd ldrs: rdn along 2f out: grad wknd* **6/1**[3]

21-5 7 3 **Royal Birth**[8] 3068 3-9-2 78 DavidNolan 6 60
(Stuart Williams) *in tch: pushed along 1/2-way: sn rdn and n.d* **8/1**

-240 8 1½ **Captain Whoosh (IRE)**[8] 3068 3-8-10 72 (p) ChrisCatlin 8 48
(Tom Dascombe) *a towards rr* **10/1**

2-00 9 ½ **Hatha Hooh**[32] 2317 3-9-0 79 MichaelJMMurphy(3) 5 53
(Ismail Mohammed) *chsd ldrs: rdn along over 2f out: sn wknd* **14/1**

16-6 10 2¼ **Hopefilly (IRE)**[22] 2626 3-9-2 78 MartinHarley 2 63
(Ed Walker) *racd towards centre: cl up: rdn along over 2f out: sn drvn and wknd over 1f out: lost action and virtually p.u wl ins fnl f* **8/1**

59.57s (-1.93) **Going Correction** -0.225s/f (Firm) **10** Ran SP% **114.2**
Speed ratings (Par 101): **106,104,103,102,99 98,94,91,90,87**
CSF £35.36 CT £685.78 TOTE £9.10: £3.40, £1.80, £4.70; EX 69.60 Trifecta £909.50.
**Owner** Arabian Knights **Bred** Kildaragh Stud **Trained** Lambourn, Berks

**FOCUS**
A useful handicap in which the gallop was sound throughout and this form should prove reliable.

## 3332 WILLIAM (PATRICK) BILL CORR MEMORIAL MEDIAN AUCTION MAIDEN STKS 1m 75y
**7:10** (7:12) (Class 6) 3-4-Y-O **£2,045** (£603; £302) **Stalls** Centre

Form RPR

5 1 **Betty Bere (FR)**[76] 1233 3-8-12 0 MartinHarley 3 71+
(K R Burke) *set stdy pce: qcknd over 3f out: pushed along and qcknd over 2f out: rdn wl over 1f out: drvn ins fnl f: hld on gamely towards fin* **5/2**[3]

02 2 hd **Gang Warfare**[14] 2871 3-9-3 0 HarryBentley 6 75
(Olly Stevens) *t.k.h: cl up: chal wl over 2f out: rdn and edgd lft over 1f out: drvn and n.m.r ins fnl f: ev ch tl no ex nr fin* **9/4**[2]

3 nk **Tabjeel** 3-9-3 0 DaneO'Neill 4 74+
(Saeed bin Suroor) *trckd ldng pair: hdwy 3f out: swtchd rt and cl up on outer 2f out: rdn over 1f out and sn ev ch: drvn ins fnl f and no ex towards fin* **6/4**[1]

0-5 4 4½ **Walk Like A Giant**[30] 2365 3-9-3 0 AndrewElliott 2 63
(Tom Tate) *trckd ldng pair on inner: pushed along wl over 2f out: sn rdn and one pce* **16/1**

5 5 **Norfolk Sound** 3-8-12 0 TedDurcan 5 46
(Chris Wall) *hld up in tch: hdwy on outer 3f out: chsd ldrs over 2f out: sn rdn and wknd over 1f out* **20/1**

6 7 **Forceful Beacon** 4-9-8 0 GeorgeDowning(5) 7 37
(Tony Carroll) *s.i.s: a bhd* **50/1**

00- 7 2 **Aster's Approval**[73] 5064 4-9-13 0 (bt[1]) TomEaves 1 32
(Mrs Ilka Gansera-Leveque) *t.k.h: in tch: rdn along 3f out: sn outpcd* **100/1**

1m 49.47s (0.47) **Going Correction** -0.175s/f (Firm)
**WFA** 3 from 4yo 10lb **7** Ran SP% **112.9**
Speed ratings (Par 101): **90,89,89,85,80 73,71**
CSF £8.31 TOTE £3.90: £2.20, £1.60; EX 10.30 Trifecta £23.00.
**Owner** Market Avenue Racing Club & Mrs E Burke **Bred** S N C Regnier **Trained** Middleham Moor, N Yorks

**FOCUS**
A race lacking anything in the way of strength-in-depth and a steady gallop to the 2f marker saw the three market leaders finish in a line.

## 3333 SAFE BET DG TAXIS 01159500500 H'CAP 1m 75y
**7:40** (7:45) (Class 6) (0-60,59) 3-Y-O **£2,045** (£603; £302) **Stalls** Centre

Form RPR

4444 1 **Kalahari Kingdom (IRE)**[14] 2879 3-9-5 57 (p) TonyHamilton 1 65
(Richard Fahey) *mde most: pushed along and jnd 2f out: rdn jst over 1f out: styd on strly fnl f* **5/2**[1]

0002 2 1½ **Green Zone (IRE)**[18] 2742 3-9-2 59 (p) ShelleyBirkett(5) 12 62
(Nigel Tinkler) *a.p: hdwy 3f out: cl up 2f out: sn rdn and ev ch tl drvn and kpt on same pce fnl f* **5/1**[3]

6-52 3 1 **Rockie Road (IRE)**[18] 2729 3-9-1 53 RaulDaSilva 3 54
(Paul Green) *trckd ldrs: hdwy 3f out: rdn along 2f out: drvn and edgd rt jst over 1f out: kpt on same pce fnl f* **10/1**

-060 4 1¼ **China In My Hands**[25] 2517 3-9-5 57 TedDurcan 2 55
(James Bethell) *towards rr: hdwy 3f out: chsd ldrs 2f out: sn rdn: drvn and one pce fr over 1f out: edgd lft ins fnl f* **10/1**

050- 5 ½ **Victory Danz (IRE)**[239] 7418 3-9-4 56 DavidNolan 5 54
(David O'Meara) *dwlt and towards rr: hdwy on inner 3f out: effrt to chse ldrs 2f out: sn rdn: plugging on whn n.m.r jst over 1f out: hld whn hmpd ins fnl f* **8/1**

005- 6 2¾ **Urban Sanctuary**[231] 7606 3-8-12 50 MartinHarley 9 40
(Ed Walker) *towards rr: effrt and sme hdwy over 2f out: sn rdn along and nvr nr ldrs* **3/1**[2]

0-00 7 2½ **Skinny Latte**[18] 2742 3-8-7 45 (v[1]) PatrickMathers 8 29
(Micky Hammond) *dwlt and in rr tl plugged on fnl 2f* **50/1**

5-60 8 2¼ **Vera Lou (IRE)**[12] 2926 3-8-9 47 (b) BenCurtis 10 26
(Pat Eddery) *midfield: hdwy on outer over 3f out: rdn along over 2f out: n.d* **50/1**

06-0 9 3¾ **Rehanaat (USA)**[50] 1794 3-9-5 57 DaneO'Neill 4 27
(Ed Dunlop) *chsd ldrs: rdn along 3f out: wknd over 2f out* **14/1**

640 10 18 **Navajo Dream**[28] 2432 3-8-7 45 HarryBentley 11
(Michael Appleby) *racd wd: a in rr* **10/1**

50-5 11 ¾ **Motamayezah**[49] 1852 3-8-8 46 ow1 (v[1]) JohnFahy 6
(Alan McCabe) *cl up: rdn along over 3f out: sn wknd* **50/1**

1m 48.1s (-0.90) **Going Correction** -0.175s/f (Firm) **11** Ran SP% **121.2**
Speed ratings (Par 97): **97,95,94,93,92 90,87,85,81,63 62**
CSF £15.74 CT £108.61 TOTE £3.60: £1.40, £2.10, £2.20; EX 20.20 Trifecta £84.80.
**Owner** Mrs H Steel **Bred** Churchtown House Stud **Trained** Musley Bank, N Yorks

**FOCUS**
A moderate handicap in which the gallop was an ordinary one and those held up were at a disadvantage.

## 3334 MOST RELIABLE BET DG TAXIS H'CAP 1m 1f
**8:10** (8:10) (Class 5) (0-70,69) 4-Y-O+ **£2,587** (£770; £384; £192) **Stalls** Low

Form RPR

6053 1 **Frontline Phantom (IRE)**[14] 2875 7-8-2 55 JoeyHaynes(5) 5 65
(K R Burke) *trckd ldrs on inner: hdwy over 3f out: sn cl up: slt ld 2f out and sn rdn: drvn ent fnl f: kpt on* **7/2**[2]

005 2 1½ **Spin Artist (USA)**[7] 3080 4-9-4 69 MichaelJMMurphy(3) 1 76
(Mark Johnston) *dwlt: sn pushed along inner and hdwy to ld after 1f: rdn along over 2f out and sn narrowly hdd: cl up and drvn over 1f out: ev ch tl kpt on same pce ins fnl f* **5/1**

3344 3 4 **Arlecchino (IRE)**[29] 2382 4-9-5 67 (b) DaleSwift 3 66
(Ed McMahon) *in tch on inner: rdn along and sltly outpcd 3f out: styd on appr fnl f* **5/2**[1]

300/ 4 1 **Mini's Destination**[795] 1358 6-8-12 60 StevieDonohoe 8 57
(John Holt) *hld up towards rr: hdwy on outer 3f out: rdn along 2f out: drvn and no imp fr wl over 1f out* **33/1**

2310 5 1¼ **Outlaw Torn (IRE)**[4] 3190 5-8-12 67 (e) KieranShoemark(7) 7 61
(Richard Guest) *t.k.h: trckd ldng pair on outer: effrt 3f out: rdn along 2f out: grad wknd* **5/1**

-650 6 1 **Angel Cake (IRE)**[113] 736 5-8-8 56 RaulDaSilva 4 48
(Michael Appleby) *sn detached in rr: pushed along 3f out: kpt on fnl 2f: n.d* **16/1**

1252 7 ¾ **Benandonner (USA)**[19] 2689 11-8-8 56 ow1 TomEaves 6 46
(Mike Murphy) *chsd ldrs: pushed along 3f out: rdn over 2f out: sn drvn and btn* **4/1**[3]

00/0 8 12 **Morna's Glory**[55] 1649 5-7-12 53 JackGarritty(7) 2 18
(Michael Herrington) *led 1f: cl up: rdn along 3f out: sn wknd* **50/1**

1m 55.69s (-1.91) **8** Ran SP% **114.9**
CSF £21.49 CT £50.78 TOTE £4.10: £1.10, £3.10, £1.40; EX 22.50 Trifecta £70.20.
**Owner** Ontoawinner & Mrs E Burke **Bred** Joe Rogers **Trained** Middleham Moor, N Yorks

**FOCUS**
A modest handicap run at a modest gallop until the pace lifted passing the 3f pole. The first two pulled clear in the last quarter-mile.

## 3335 ODDS ON FAVOURITE DG TAXIS 01159500500 H'CAP 1m 2f 50y
**8:40** (8:40) (Class 4) (0-80,79) 4-Y-O+ **£4,690** (£1,395; £697; £348) **Stalls** Low

Form RPR

-430 1 **Raskova (USA)**[17] 2783 4-9-4 76 TedDurcan 1 89
(William Jarvis) *trckd ldrs on inner: effrt and nt clr run over 2f out: sn swtchd rt and rdn to chal: led ent fnl f: kpt on strly* **9/4**[1]

2662 2 3 **No Win No Fee**[25] 2519 4-8-8 66 AndrewMullen 2 73
(Michael Appleby) *trckd ldr: cl up 3f out: rdn to ld 2f out: drvn and hdd ent fnl f: kpt on same pce* **3/1**[2]

4424 3 2¼ **Hydrant**[5] 3139 8-9-0 79 KieranShoemark(7) 6 82
(Richard Guest) *set stdy pce: qcknd over 3f out: rdn along over 2f out: sn hdd and one pce appr fnl f* **7/1**

4-02 4 ½ **Soul Intent (IRE)**[33] 2272 4-9-5 77 ChrisCatlin 5 79
(B W Hills) *t.k.h: trckd ldrs: effrt on outer 3f out: rdn along whn bmpd 2f out: sn drvn and one pce* **4/1**[3]

3320 **5** *1 ¼* **Syncopate**[38] 2162 5-9-5 **77**............................................ StephenCraine 4 76
(Pam Sly) *t.k.h: stmbld after 150yds: hld up in rr: hdwy on outer whn hmpd 2f out: sn rdn and btn after* **7/1**

3530 **6** *½* **Chapter And Verse (IRE)**[33] 2270 8-8-10 **68**..................... TomEaves 3 66
(Mike Murphy) *t.k.h: hld up: effrt and sme hdwy on inner 3f out: rdn along over 2f out and sn btn* **12/1**

2m 15.12s (0.82) **Going Correction** -0.175s/f (Firm) **6** Ran SP% **108.5**
Speed ratings (Par 105): **89,86,84,84,83 83**
CSF £8.50 TOTE £3.60: £1.60, £1.50; EX 8.90 Trifecta £44.20.
**Owner** Kevin Hickman **Bred** Dean Fleming **Trained** Newmarket, Suffolk
■ Stewards' Enquiry : Chris Catlin two-day ban: careless riding (Jul 1-2)

**FOCUS**
Mainly exposed sorts in a fair handicap. The gallop was on the steady side and this bare form doesn't look reliable.

## 3336 WINNING WAY WITH DG TAXIS H'CAP — 1m 6f 15y
**9:10** (9:10) (Class 6) (0-60,60) 4-Y-0+ **£1,940** (£577; £288; £144) **Stalls** Low

Form RPR

46-1 **1** **Maoi Chinn Tire (IRE)**[1] 3309 7-9-5 **58** 6ex................. StephenCraine 2 66+
(Jennie Candlish) *trckd ldrs: hdwy to ld wl over 2f out: sn clr: rdn and styd strly fnl f: readily* **11/4**[2]

604 **2** *3 ¾* **Innoko (FR)**[20] 2672 4-9-2 **60**........................................(t) JoeyHaynes(5) 8 60
(Tony Carroll) *t.k.h: hld up in rr: hdwy wl over 2f out: rdn to chse wnr wl over 1f out: sn hung lft: drvn and no imp fnl f* **14/1**

-400 **3** *shd* **Rhinestone Rebel (IRE)**[13] 2885 8-8-7 **46** oh1................. ChrisCatlin 4 46
(Peter Hiatt) *trckd ldng pair: hdwy 3f out: rdn along over 2f out: n.m.r and swtchd rt over 1f out: sn drvn and kpt on one pce* **50/1**

645 **4** *½* **Kastela Stari**[119] 649 7-9-2 **55**........................................(t) TomEaves 1 54
(Tim Fitzgerald) *hld up in rr: hdwy on outer 3f out: rdn over 2f out: kpt on fnl f: nrst fin* **14/1**

00/3 **5** *1 ½* **Cappielow Park**[15] 2836 5-8-12 **51**..................................(p) DaneO'Neill 5 48
(Ali Stronge) *trckd ldrs: effrt 3f out: rdn along over 2f out: sn no imp* **5/4**[1]

-651 **6** *2* **Father Shine (IRE)**[27] 2455 11-9-2 **55**...................... DuranFentiman 10 49
(Shaun Harris) *trckd ldr: effrt over 3f out: sn rdn along and outpcd fnl 2f* **12/1**

0140 **7** *5* **Dubara Reef (IRE)**[16] 2801 7-8-10 **49**........................... RaulDaSilva 7 36
(Paul Green) *led: rdn along and hung rt 3f out: sn hdd & wknd* **9/2**[3]

3m 13.53s (6.53) **Going Correction** -0.175s/f (Firm) **7** Ran SP% **112.3**
Speed ratings (Par 101): **74,71,71,71,70 69,66**
CSF £37.31 CT £1528.97 TOTE £4.60: £2.10, £4.00; EX 44.70 Trifecta £1180.80.
**Owner** The Best Club In The World **Bred** Mrs E Thompson **Trained** Basford Green, Staffs

**FOCUS**
A moderate handicap in which the gallop was on the steady side to the home straight.
T/Plt: £37.10 to a £1 stake. Pool: £50,063.45 - 983.30 winning units T/Qpdt: £7.00 to a £1 stake. Pool: £4,671.65 - 492.35 winning units JR

# 2348 THIRSK (L-H)
Tuesday, June 17

**OFFICIAL GOING: Good to firm (good in places; watered; 9.0)**
Wind: Light; half against Weather: Fine

## 3337 IRISH STALLION FARMS EBF NOVICE STKS (BOBIS RACE) — 5f
**2:20** (2:21) (Class 4) 2-Y-0 **£7,439** (£2,213; £1,106; £553) **Stalls** High

Form RPR

152 **1** **Don't Tell Annie**[10] 3001 2-9-2 0.......................................... DavidAllan 3 71
(Tim Easterby) *w ldr: led 2f out: edgd lft fnl f: pushed out* **2/5**[1]

**2** *¾* **Mighty Warrior** 2-9-0 0.......................................... TonyHamilton 4 66+
(Richard Fahey) *chsd ldrs: outpcd over 2f out: tk 3rd last 150yds: fin strly to take 2nd post* **5/1**[3]

15 **3** *shd* **Firgrove Bridge (IRE)**[24] 2543 2-9-7 0............................ PaulMulrennan 1 73
(Kevin Ryan) *wnt lft s: led: hdd 2f out: kpt on same pce* **4/1**[2]

00 **4** *5* **Shamkhani**[18] 2736 2-8-11 0.......................................... SladeO'Hara(3) 2 46?
(Alan Berry) *s.s: sn chsng ldrs: sn drvn along: wknd fnl f* **200/1**

1m 1.71s (2.11) **Going Correction** +0.15s/f (Good) **4** Ran SP% **108.6**
Speed ratings (Par 95): **89,87,87,79**
CSF £2.89 TOTE £1.40; EX 2.50 Trifecta £3.90.
**Owner** Dale & Ann Wilsdon & Partner **Bred** Wilsdon & Habton **Trained** Great Habton, N Yorks

**FOCUS**
Ground on the fast side of good for this eight-race card. A good prize on offer here, but just four runners, one of which, Shamkhani, had no chance on the book.

## 3338 BBC RADIO YORK GOOD NIGHT'S SLEEP APPEAL H'CAP — 5f
**2:55** (2:56) (Class 6) (0-65,65) 3-Y-0+ **£2,726** (£805; £402) **Stalls** High

Form RPR

5030 **1** **Lady Poppy**[55] 1643 4-8-13 **58**.............................. KieranSchofield(7) 3 69
(George Moore) *racd far side: chsd ldr: led that gp over 2f out: overall ldr over 1f out: drvn out* **28/1**

00-0 **2** *¾* **Mr Mo Jo**[6] 3093 6-9-13 **65**..................................................[1] DavidAllan 8 73
(Les Eyre) *swtchd lft after s: racd far side: led 3 others in gp: hdd over 2f out: kpt on same pce fnl f* **25/1**

0500 **3** *1 ½* **Choc'A'Moca (IRE)**[6] 3093 7-9-2 **54**......................(v) PaulMulrennan 14 57+
(Paul Midgley) *racd stands' side: chsd ldrs: led that gp jst ins fnl f: kpt on* **14/1**

0505 **4** *nk* **Chosen One (IRE)**[18] 2724 9-9-4 **56**............................. JamesSullivan 2 58
(Ruth Carr) *racd far side: chsd ldrs: kpt on fnl f* **20/1**

3523 **5** *¾* **Windforpower (IRE)**[11] 2951 4-9-11 **63**...................(p) PaulPickard 19 62
(Tracy Waggott) *racd stands' side: chsd ldrs: led that gp appr fnl f: hdd and no ex last 150yds* **6/1**[1]

1-12 **6** *1 ¼* **Adiator**[6] 3092 6-9-8 **65**.............................................. AdamCarter(5) 1 60
(Neville Bycroft) *chsd ldrs far side: kpt on one pce over 1f out* **13/2**[2]

-004 **7** *1* **Tuibama (IRE)**[18] 2743 5-9-3 **55**..................................(p) DaleSwift 18 46
(Tracy Waggott) *led stands' side gp: hdd that side appr fnl f: sn fdd* **15/2**

0605 **8** *1* **Mey Blossom**[57] 1604 9-9-0 **55**.........................(p) GeorgeChaloner(3) 17 42
(Richard Whitaker) *in rr stands' side: kpt on fnl 2f: nvr nr ldrs* **12/1**

0005 **9** *1 ½* **Sunrise Dance**[18] 2743 5-9-10 **65**........................ ConnorBeasley(3) 13 47
(Robert Johnson) *racd stands' side: bhd tl sme hdwy over 1f out: nvr on terms* **12/1**

4104 **10** *2* **Dodina (IRE)**[24] 2542 4-9-6 **65**.........................(p) MeganCarberry(7) 6 40
(Brian Ellison) *s.i.s: sn mid-div centre: nvr a factor* **10/1**

3-60 **11** *3 ¼* **Straits Of Malacca**[28] 2429 3-9-2 **65**............................. ShaneGray(5) 4 26
(Kevin Ryan) *swtchd rt after s: racd centre: mid-div: wknd over 1f out* **10/1**

00-3 **12** *hd* **A J Cook (IRE)**[18] 2726 4-9-1 **58**.............................. ShirleyTeasdale(5) 9 20
(Ron Barr) *racd centre: nvr nr ldrs* **50/1**

0402 **13** *nk* **I'll Be Good**[11] 2951 5-9-7 **62**.......................................(t) SladeO'Hara(3) 15 23
(Alan Berry) *in rr towards stands' side: edgd rt 2f out: nvr a factor* **12/1**

3000 **14** *2 ¾* **Electric Qatar**[12] 2933 5-9-12 **64**..................(p) StephenCraine 10 15
(Alan McCabe) *w ldr centre: edgd lft over 2f out: lost pl over 1f out* **33/1**

20-0 **15** *7* **Rat Catcher (IRE)**[28] 2435 4-9-4 **56**...................................(b) TomEaves 11
(Lisa Williamson) *racd centre: w ldrs: wknd 2f out* **66/1**

000- **16** *7* **Master Rooney (IRE)**[231] 7598 8-9-8 **60**......................(p) PJMcDonald 12
(Geoffrey Harker) *tubed: chsd ldrs: lost pl 2f out: sn bhd* **25/1**

5152 **17** *½* **Spring Bird**[25] 2514 5-9-6 **58**............................................ AdrianNicholls 16
(David Nicholls) *racd stands' side: w ldrs: heavily eased wl over 1f out: virtually p.u* **7/1**[3]

1m 0.85s (1.25) **Going Correction** +0.15s/f (Good)
**WFA** 3 from 4yo+ 6lb **17** Ran SP% **122.1**
Speed ratings (Par 101): **96,94,92,91,90 88,87,85,83,79 74,74,73,69,58 47,46**
CSF £580.70 CT £10066.45 TOTE £36.10: £7.70, £5.90, £5.10, £4.60; EX 1552.70 Trifecta £2073.20 Part won..
**Owner** Ingham Racing Syndicate **Bred** Whatton Manor Stud **Trained** Middleham Moor, N Yorks

**FOCUS**
Mainly exposed sprinters in this modest heat. They were spread right across the track, but the first two home raced on the far side.

## 3339 CARDALE ASSET MANAGEMENT H'CAP (DIV I) — 7f
**3:30** (3:31) (Class 5) (0-70,69) 3-Y-0+ **£3,234** (£962; £481; £240) **Stalls** Low

Form RPR

4-56 **1** **Orpsie Boy (IRE)**[10] 3000 11-9-7 **62**..................................... LukeMorris 3 73
(Ruth Carr) *chsd ldrs: led appr fnl f: styd on wl* **15/2**

504- **2** *3 ¾* **World Record (IRE)**[253] 7065 4-9-7 **65**........................ IanBrennan(3) 8 66
(John Quinn) *t.k.h: trckd ldrs: effrt on ins over 2f out: n.m.r: styd on to take 2nd last 50yds* **9/4**[1]

00-6 **3** *1* **No Quarter (IRE)**[57] 1606 7-9-7 **62**................................... PaulPickard 4 61
(Tracy Waggott) *t.k.h: w ldr: led over 3f out: edgd lft over 2f out: hdd appr fnl f: styd on same pce* **12/1**

5-30 **4** *nse* **Mysterious Wonder**[28] 2427 4-9-2 **57**........................ RussKennemore 1 56
(Philip Kirby) *s.i.s: sn chsng ldrs: swtchd rt 2f out: styd on same pce appr fnl f* **10/1**

4322 **5** *1 ¾* **Hellbender (IRE)**[10] 3000 8-8-9 **50**......................... DuranFentiman 6 44
(Shaun Harris) *chsd ldrs: kpt on one pce fnl 2f* **4/1**[2]

314- **6** *2* **Dream Scenario**[197] 8134 4-10-0 **69**...................................... DavidAllan 9 58
(Mel Brittain) *in rr: swtchd lft after 1f: kpt on fnl 2f: nvr a factor* **7/1**[3]

0-05 **7** *7* **Eium Mac**[21] 2658 5-8-9 **50** oh1....................................... AndrewElliott 5 21
(Neville Bycroft) *mid-div on outer: outpcd over 3f out: wknd 2f out* **15/2**

-000 **8** *1 ½* **One Kool Dude**[20] 2677 5-8-10 **51**..............................(p) PatrickMathers 7 18
(Micky Hammond) *strated slowly: nvr on terms* **22/1**

02-0 **9** *3 ½* **Wotalad**[35] 2232 4-8-10 **54**.......................................(p) GeorgeChaloner(3) 2 12
(Richard Whitaker) *led: hdd over 3f out: lost pl over 1f out* **28/1**

1m 26.39s (-0.81) **Going Correction** -0.025s/f (Good) **9** Ran SP% **111.4**
Speed ratings (Par 103): **103,98,97,97,95 93,85,83,79**
CSF £23.45 CT £196.40 TOTE £7.00: £2.00, £1.40, £3.70; EX 28.80 Trifecta £404.00.
**Owner** Miss Vanessa Church **Bred** Minch Bloodstock **Trained** Huby, N Yorks

**FOCUS**
A soundly run contest, the fastest of the three C&D times on the day, which was won in emphatic style.

## 3340 EBF STALLIONS BREEDING WINNERS FILLIES' H'CAP — 1m
**4:10** (4:10) (Class 3) (0-90,85) 3-Y-0+ **£8,086** (£2,406; £1,202; £601) **Stalls** Low

Form RPR

-142 **1** **Flycatcher (IRE)**[18] 2749 3-8-5 **75**............................ GeorgeChaloner(3) 8 84
(Richard Fahey) *w ldr: led over 3f out: styd on wl fnl f: readily* **13/8**[1]

-042 **2** *3* **Oddysey (IRE)**[8] 3066 5-9-9 **83**.................................. ConnorBeasley(3) 7 87
(Michael Dods) *trckd ldrs 3f: hdwy to chse ldrs over 3f out: 2nd and drvn over 2f out: kpt on same pce* **9/4**[2]

4640 **3** *2 ¾* **No Poppy (IRE)**[6] 3094 6-9-5 **76**.............................. SilvestreDeSousa 6 73
(Tim Easterby) *chsd ldrs: drvn 3f out: 3rd over 1f out: one pce* **4/1**[3]

0-00 **4** *8* **Just The Tonic**[22] 2602 7-9-3 **74**..................................... DanielTudhope 1 52
(Marjorie Fife) *hld up in rr: hdwy to trck ldrs over 3f out: wknd appr fnl f: eased clsng stages* **16/1**

16-3 **5** *12* **Mitchelton (FR)**[15] 2826 3-8-12 **79**..................................... FrannyNorton 5 26
(Mark Johnston) *led tl over 3f out: wknd wl over 1f out: eased clsng stages* **7/1**

1m 39.76s (-0.34) **Going Correction** -0.025s/f (Good)
**WFA** 3 from 4yo+ 10lb **5** Ran SP% **107.2**
Speed ratings (Par 104): **100,97,94,86,74**
CSF £5.20 TOTE £3.10: £1.80, £1.20; EX 5.70 Trifecta £13.40.
**Owner** Mrs P B E P Farr **Bred** Worksop Manor Stud **Trained** Musley Bank, N Yorks

**FOCUS**
Not strong form for the level given the top weight was rated just 83, 7lb below the ceiling for the grade.

## 3341 THEAKSTON BEST BITTER H'CAP — 1m 4f
**4:45** (4:45) (Class 3) (0-90,89) 4-Y-0+ **£7,439** (£2,213; £1,106; £553) **Stalls** High

Form RPR

15-0 **1** **Dolphin Village (IRE)**[45] 1934 4-8-7 **78**................. GeorgeChaloner(3) 2 87+
(Richard Fahey) *hld up in mid-div: drvn to chse ldrs 3f out: led wl over 1f out: kpt on wl* **10/1**

0302 **2** *1 ½* **Tepmokea (IRE)**[10] 2981 8-8-12 **80**..............................(p) HayleyTurner 9 86
(Conor Dore) *led after 1f: hung rt and wnt wd bnd over 8f out: reminders bnd over 4f out: hdd wl over 1f out: styd on same pce* **6/1**[3]

/052 **3** *hd* **Deepsand (IRE)**[18] 2728 5-8-9 **77**.................................(p) DavidAllan 7 82
(Tim Easterby) *hld up in rr: drvn over 4f out: hdwy over 2f out: chsng ldrs over 1f out: kpt on same pce* **12/1**

132 **4** *2 ½* **Arizona John (IRE)**[25] 2520 9-8-13 **81**.............................. FrannyNorton 5 82
(John Mackie) *t.k.h: trckd ldrs: edgd lft wl over 1f out: one pce* **7/1**

6-3 **5** *½* **Double Discount (IRE)**[32] 2309 4-9-5 **87**........................ BarryMcHugh 1 87
(Tom Dascombe) *led 1f: trckd ldrs: effoert over 2f out: one pce over 1f out* **7/2**[2]

030- **6** *1* **Almagest**[235] 7496 6-9-1 **86**.............................................. SamJames(3) 3 85
(David O'Meara) *rrd s: trckd ldrs: drvn over 3f out: one pce fnl 2f* **25/1**

-4 **7** *hd* **Semeen**[38] 2142 5-9-7 **89**........................................................ LukeMorris 10 88
(Luca Cumani) *chsd ldrs: one pce whn n.m.r wl over 1f out* **2/1**[1]

014- **8** *1 ¼* **Handsome Ransom**[284] 6165 5-8-13 **81**........................... DanielTudhope 8 78
(David O'Meara) *dwlt: hld up in rr: hdwy on outside over 2f out: nvr a threat* **12/1**

0000 9 1 3/4 **Bayan Kasirga (IRE)**[17] 2760 4-8-5 **78**....................(p) SammyJoBell(5) 6 72
(Richard Fahey) *mid-div: drvn over 4f out: chsng ldrs over 2f out: fdd over 1f out* **25/1**

2m 37.0s (0.80) **Going Correction** -0.025s/f (Good) **9** Ran SP% **114.5**
Speed ratings (Par 107): **96,95,94,93,92 92,92,91,90**
CSF £68.05 CT £725.64 TOTE £15.10: £4.40, £3.20, £4.70; EX 75.00 Trifecta £1027.80.
**Owner** Y Nasib **Bred** Gerrardstown House Stud **Trained** Musley Bank, N Yorks

**FOCUS**
A decent heat, but the market principals didn't run their races which casts a doubt over the strength of this form.

## 3342 MARKET CROSS JEWELLERS H'CAP 6f
**5:20** (5:20) (Class 4) (0-85,85) 3-Y-O+ **£4,851** (£1,443; £721; £360) **Stalls** High

Form RPR

0520 1 **Line Of Reason (IRE)**[3] 3256 4-9-9 **80**.................... PaulMulrennan 4 90+
(Paul Midgley) *t.k.h in rr: hdwy over 2f out: led 1f out: hld on towards fin* **4/1**[2]

0-06 2 *nk* **Disclosure**[17] 2768 3-8-5 **69**.................... RoystonFfrench 8 74+
(Les Eyre) *hld up in rr-div: hdwy over 2f out: nt clr run over 1f out: swtchd lft: nt clr run ins fnl f: fin strly to take 2nd nr fin* **33/1**

-022 3 *hd* **Avon Breeze**[21] 2656 5-9-11 **82**.................... RussKennemore 3 88
(Richard Whitaker) *fly-jmpd s: sn trcking ldrs: led briefly over 1f out: hung lft and kpt on last 50yds* **7/1**

0005 4 1 1/4 **Head Space (IRE)**[15] 2825 6-9-6 **77**....................(p) JamesSullivan 6 79
(Ruth Carr) *hld up in last: hdwy and swtchd lft 2f out: chsng ldrs over 1f out: kpt on same pce* **6/1**[3]

3460 5 3/4 **Mutafaakir (IRE)**[13] 2898 5-9-9 **80**....................(p) PJMcDonald 7 80
(Ruth Carr) *w ldr: led 3f out: hdd over 1f out: one pce* **4/1**[2]

-000 6 1 **Polski Max**[24] 2562 4-9-9 **85**.................... SammyJoBell(5) 2 82
(Richard Fahey) *led 3f: kpt on one pce appr fnl f* **11/1**

00-4 7 *nk* **Bop It**[31] 2352 5-10-0 **85**.................... DanielTudhope 9 81+
(David O'Meara) *trckd ldrs on inner: nt clr run over 1f out and jst ins fnl f: nt rcvr* **3/1**[1]

300 8 1/2 **Lady Frances**[24] 2556 3-9-6 **84**.................... FrannyNorton 5 76
(Mark Johnston) *chsd ldrs: hung lft over 2f out: one pce whn sltly hmpd ins fnl f* **16/1**

5005 9 8 **Burren View Lady (IRE)**[11] 2953 4-9-2 **73**.................... DavidAllan 1 42
(Tim Easterby) *chsd ldrs on outside: lost pl 3f out: bhd whn eased over 1f out* **25/1**

1m 12.77s (0.07) **Going Correction** +0.15s/f (Good)
**WFA** 3 from 4yo+ 7lb **9** Ran SP% **112.8**
Speed ratings (Par 105): **105,104,104,102,101 100,99,99,88**
CSF £115.91 CT £893.91 TOTE £7.30: £2.20, £6.70, £2.10; EX 97.60 Trifecta £1854.20.
**Owner** Taylor's Bloodstock Ltd **Bred** Corduff Stud Ltd, J Corcoran & J Judd **Trained** Westow, N Yorks

**FOCUS**
An open sprint handicap in which the action unfolded down the middle of the track in the final furlong.

## 3343 BREEDERS BACKING RACING EBF MAIDEN STKS 7f
**5:50** (5:52) (Class 5) 3-Y-O **£3,881** (£1,155; £577; £288) **Stalls** Low

Form RPR

1 **Fajry (USA)** 3-9-5 0.................... SilvestreDeSousa 8 84+
(Saeed bin Suroor) *gave problems loading: w ldrs: led over 2f out: edgd lft over 1f out: drvn clr* **11/8**[1]

06 2 4 **Incredible Fresh (IRE)**[28] 2432 3-9-5 0.................... HayleyTurner 10 74+
(James Fanshawe) *chsd ldrs: outpcd over 3f out: hdwy 2f out: styd on to take 2nd last 100yds* **14/1**

4-02 3 2 1/4 **Percy's Gal**[18] 2737 3-8-7 70.................... GemmaTutty(7) 9 63
(Karen Tutty) *t.k.h on outside: sn trcking ldrs: 2nd over 1f out: kpt on same pce* **7/4**[2]

4 4 2 1/2 **Dutch Descent (IRE)**[45] 1959 3-9-5 0.................... PaulMulrennan 1 61
(David Barron) *trckd ldrs: kpt on one pce over 1f out* **7/1**[3]

4-00 5 2 3/4 **Edward Elgar**[43] 2020 3-9-2 52....................(p) GeorgeChaloner(3) 2 54
(Richard Whitaker) *chsd ldrs: outpcd over 3f out: kpt on ins fnl f* **66/1**

0-6 6 3/4 **Humour (IRE)**[29] 2384 3-9-5 0....................[1] LukeMorris 6 52
(Roger Varian) *led: hdd over 2f out: wknd ins fnl f* **14/1**

40 7 7 **Ermine Ruby**[61] 1534 3-9-0 0.................... DanielTudhope 3 29
(Charles Hills) *s.i.s: in rr and hung rt bnd 5f out: sme hdwy on ins over 2f out: wknd over 1f out: eased ins fnl f* **12/1**

650- 8 5 **Different Scenario**[224] 7755 3-9-0 44.................... DavidAllan 5 16
(Mel Brittain) *in rr: bhd and drvn 5f out* **66/1**

0-4 9 8 **Panzi Potter Too**[28] 2420 3-8-11 0....................(b) ConnorBeasley(3) 4
(Michael Dods) *chsd ldrs: drvn over 4f out: lost pl over 3f out: sn bhd: eased ins fnl f* **33/1**

1m 27.05s (-0.15) **Going Correction** -0.025s/f (Good) **9** Ran SP% **117.9**
Speed ratings (Par 99): **99,94,91,89,85 85,77,71,62**
CSF £23.23 TOTE £1.90: £1.50, £3.20, £1.10; EX 20.00 Trifecta £49.10.
**Owner** Godolphin **Bred** Shadwell Farm LLC **Trained** Newmarket, Suffolk

**FOCUS**
The 70-rated Percy's Gal set the standard from those to have raced, but they were all blown away by the Godolphin newcomer.

## 3344 CARDALE ASSET MANAGEMENT H'CAP (DIV II) 7f
**6:20** (6:21) (Class 5) (0-70,68) 3-Y-O+ **£3,234** (£962; £481; £240) **Stalls** Low

Form RPR

-605 1 **Space War**[24] 2546 7-9-8 **62**.................... BarryMcHugh 6 74
(Michael Easterby) *hld up in mid-div: hdwy 3f out: styd on to ld last 100yds* **7/2**[2]

00-4 2 2 3/4 **Dialogue**[57] 1606 8-9-9 **63**.................... JamesSullivan 5 68
(Geoffrey Harker) *hld up in rr: hdwy 2f out: edgd lft ins fnl f: kpt on to take 2nd nr fin* **12/1**

0-03 3 *nk* **Eastlands Lad (IRE)**[36] 2219 5-8-9 **49**....................(v[1]) SilvestreDeSousa 1 53
(Micky Hammond) *t.k.h: trckd ldrs: effrt over 2f out: 2nd last 50yds: no ex* **3/1**[1]

610- 4 1 1/2 **Destination Aim**[280] 6291 7-9-11 **68**.................... NeilFarley(3) 7 68
(Frederick Watson) *swtchd lft after s: led: hdd last 100yds: fdd* **22/1**

3465 5 2 **Thrust Control (IRE)**[43] 2019 7-8-10 **50**....................(p) PaulPickard 2 45
(Tracy Waggott) *chsd ldrs: fdd fnl f: eased nr fin* **17/2**

-605 6 1/2 **Madame Mirasol (IRE)**[15] 2828 3-8-13 **67**....................(p) KevinStott(5) 3 58
(Kevin Ryan) *mid-div: drvn over 4f out: kpt on fnl 2f: nvr a threat* **8/1**

5-50 7 *nse* **Bearskin (IRE)**[47] 1906 3-8-8 **57**....................(p) PJMcDonald 9 47
(Ann Duffield) *in rr: drvn over 3f out: kpt on fnl f: no threat* **8/1**

60-0 8 *hd* **Grey Destiny**[73] 1310 4-8-13 **53**.................... DavidAllan 8 46
(Mel Brittain) *chsd ldrs in 2nd over 3f out: wknd fnl f* **33/1**

2-03 9 3/4 **Kalithea**[21] 2653 4-9-0 **54**....................[1] PaulMulrennan 4 45
(Julie Camacho) *stdd s: hld up in rr: effrt on inner and nt clr run 2f out: swtchd rt jst ins fnl f: nvr a factor* **9/2**[3]

1m 27.69s (0.49) **Going Correction** -0.025s/f (Good)
**WFA** 3 from 4yo+ 9lb **9** Ran SP% **113.1**
Speed ratings (Par 103): **96,92,92,90,88 87,87,87,86**
CSF £43.67 CT £139.29 TOTE £5.00: £1.20, £4.60, £1.30; EX 42.20 Trifecta £236.80.
**Owner** D Standring & T Langley **Bred** Shutford Stud And O F Waller **Trained** Sheriff Hutton, N Yorks

**FOCUS**
This looked to be run at a strong pace.
T/Plt: £530.10 to a £1 stake. Pool: £49,233.97 - 67.80 winning units T/Qpdt: £39.50 to a £1 stake. Pool: £3,928.41 - 73.53 winning units WG

3345 - 3351a (Foreign Racing) - See Raceform Interactive

3317
# ASCOT (R-H)
### Wednesday, June 18

**OFFICIAL GOING: Good changing to good to firm (good in places on round course) after race 1 (2:30)**
Weather: Fine

## 3352 JERSEY STKS (GROUP 3) 7f
**2:30** (2:33) (Class 1) 3-Y-O
**£42,532** (£16,125; £8,070; £4,020; £2,017; £1,012) **Stalls** Centre

Form RPR

2-13 1 **Mustajeeb**[25] 2571 3-9-4 114.................... PatSmullen 19 121+
(D K Weld, Ire) *swtg: chsd ldr tl led over 2f out: rdn 2f out: clr w 2 rivals over 1f out: r.o strly and in command 100yds: rdn out* **9/2**[1]

1-14 2 1 **Muwaary**[38] 2196 3-9-1 114.................... PaulHanagan 4 115+
(John Gosden) *t.k.h: chsd ldrs: jnd wnr ent fnl 2f: sn rdn: no ex and nt quite gng pce of wnr jst ins fnl f: r.o for clr 2nd* **9/2**[1]

2-40 3 2 1/4 **Giovanni Boldini (USA)**[16] 2853 3-9-1 110.................... JosephO'Brien 14 109
(A P O'Brien, Ire) *t.k.h: chsd ldrs: effrt to press ldng pair and wnt clr of field 2f out: 3rd and outpcd 1f out: wknd but hld on for 3rd fnl 100yds* **14/1**

1-03 4 1/2 **Windfast (IRE)**[32] 2343 3-9-1 102.................... JimmyFortune 22 108
(Brian Meehan) *lw: chsd ldrs: rdn and effrt 2f out: chsd clr ldng trio over 1f out: edgd lft u.p ent fnl f: styd on but no imp* **25/1**

4 5 *nk* **Waltzing Matilda (IRE)**[38] 2186 3-8-12 0.................... WayneLordan 21 104
(T Stack, Ire) *w'like: hld up in midfield: hdwy u.p over 1f out: edgd rt 1f out: styd on wl: no threat to ldrs* **33/1**

-031 6 1 **Brazos (IRE)**[40] 2111 3-9-1 101.................... WilliamBuick 17 104
(Clive Brittain) *in tch in midfield: nt clr run and shuffled bk towards rr 3f out: hdwy over 1f out: short of room and sltly hmpd 1f out: styd on wl ins fnl f: nvr trbld ldrs* **25/1**

20-1 7 2 **Coulsty (IRE)**[32] 2343 3-9-1 103.................... SeanLevey 16 99
(Richard Hannon) *in tch in midfield: rdn and unable qck 2f out: no threat to ldrs and styd on same pce fnl f* **33/1**

8 *nse* **Redbrook (IRE)**[41] 3-9-1 100.................... FrankieDettori 18 99
(A De Royer-Dupre, France) *stdd s: t.k.h: hld up in tch in rr: rdn and effrt ent fnl 2f: styd on past btn horses ins fnl f: nvr trbld ldrs* **6/1**[2]

111 9 *nk* **That Is The Spirit**[12] 2961 3-9-1 106.................... DanielTudhope 20 98
(David O'Meara) *led tl rdn and hdd over 2f out: sn rdn and outpcd over 1f out: btn whn sltly hmpd 1f out: wknd ins fnl f* **8/1**[3]

6-22 10 *nk* **Toofi (FR)**[32] 2343 3-9-1 102.................... AndreaAtzeni 7 98
(Roger Varian) *lw: chsd ldrs: rdn and unable qck ent fnl 2f: outpcd and btn over 1f out: plugged on* **16/1**

3-2 11 *hd* **Shining Emerald**[16] 2857 3-9-1 105....................(p) ChrisHayes 15 97
(P D Deegan, Ire) *stdd s: t.k.h: hld up in rr: rdn and effrt 2f out: hdwy jst over 1f out: edging rt and styd on ins fnl f: nvr trbld ldrs* **80/1**

14-5 12 3/4 **Anjaal**[62] 1532 3-9-6 111.................... DaneO'Neill 11 100
(Richard Hannon) *stdd s: t.k.h: hdwy into midfield after 1f: rdn and unable qck jst over 2f out: drvn and btn over 1f out: wknd fnl f* **50/1**

2-0 13 1/2 **Michaelmas (USA)**[25] 2571 3-9-1 102....................(p) ColmO'Donoghue 10 94
(A P O'Brien, Ire) *lw: swtchd lft sn after s: in tch in midfield: rdn and outpcd over 2f out: drvn over 1f out: kpt on but no threat to ldrs ins fnl f* **80/1**

1112 14 3/4 **Passing Star**[61] 1555 3-9-1 103.................... RobertWinston 23 92
(Charles Hills) *lengthy: lw: stdd and swtchd rt s: hld up in tch towards rr: rdn and effrt wl over 2f out: no imp over 1f out: nvr trbld ldrs* **33/1**

-604 15 *nk* **Miracle Of Medinah**[12] 2961 3-9-4 102.................... DavidProbert 13 94
(Mark Usher) *in tch in midfield: rdn and outpcd jst over 2f out: wl hld and styd on same pce u.p fnl f* **100/1**

1-1 16 1/2 **Glorious Empire (IRE)**[70] 1390 3-9-1 85.................... GeorgeBaker 3 90
(Ed Walker) *tall: lengthy: t.k.h: hld up in tch towards rr: hdwy over 2f out: rdn and btn over 1f out: wknd ins fnl f* **33/1**

5432 17 *nk* **Parbold (IRE)**[12] 2961 3-9-1 105.................... RyanMoore 2 89
(Richard Fahey) *dropped to rr after 1f: niggled along 5f out: pushed along and switching lft over 1f out: no ch but wnt past btn horses ins fnl f: nvr trbld ldrs* **14/1**

1-21 18 1 3/4 **Musical Comedy**[33] 2304 3-9-1 106.................... RichardHughes 8 84
(Richard Hannon) *stdd s: t.k.h early: hld up in tch towards rr: rdn and effrt 2f out: swtchd rt and hdwy over 1f out: wknd ins fnl f* **20/1**

22-5 19 3/4 **Big Time (IRE)**[25] 2571 3-9-1 113.................... ShaneFoley 12 83
(John Joseph Murphy, Ire) *stdd and swtchd lft s: t.k.h: hld up in tch towards rr: rdn and effrt 2f out: no imp and wl hld whn swtchd rt 1f out* **14/1**

125- 20 2 1/4 **Sudirman (USA)**[16] 2857 3-9-6 115....................(b) BillyLee 6 82
(David Wachman, Ire) *t.k.h: hld up in tch in midfield: hdwy to chse ldrs 4f out: rdn over 2f out: wknd over 1f out: bhd ins fnl f: eased nr fin* **20/1**

10-6 21 3/4 **Great White Eagle (USA)**[25] 2571 3-9-4 105.................... SeamieHeffernan 9 78
(A P O'Brien, Ire) *t.k.h: in tch in midfield: rdn and lost pl jst over 2f out: drvn and wknd over 1f out: bhd ins fnl f* **33/1**

3303 22 *nk* **Major Crispies**[33] 2304 3-9-1 100.................... RyanTate 5 74
(James Eustace) *in tch in midfield: rdn 1/2-way: struggling and lost pl over 2f out: n.d after: bhd ins fnl f* **100/1**

-361 23 1/2 **Aeolus**[18] 2767 3-9-1 109.................... GrahamGibbons 1 73
(Ed McMahon) *chsd ldrs tl over 2f out: sn rdn and lost pl: bhd 1f out* **20/1**

1m 24.54s (-3.06) **Going Correction** -0.075s/f (Good) **23** Ran SP% **130.7**
Speed ratings (Par 109): **114,112,110,109,109 108,105,105,105,105 104,104,103,102,102 101,101,99,98,96 95,94,94**
CSF £19.44 CT £283.42 TOTE £5.10: £2.20, £2.30, £4.80; EX 15.90 Trifecta £181.40.
**Owner** Hamdan Al Maktoum **Bred** Shadwell Estate Company Limited **Trained** Curragh, Co Kildare

**FOCUS**
After winning the first Pat Smullen described it as "beautiful, good ground, perfectly safe." Paul Hanagan, who finished second, said: "It's dried out a hell of a lot from yesterday." The time was just 0.26sec outside the track record, suggesting that the ground had indeed dried out since Tuesday. This was the biggest field for many years in this event, but although they initially split into two groups they soon merged together. The runner-up was the only one of the first nine home to have raced in the group of ten nearer the far side. It helped to be up with the pace and there was an absence of hard-luck stories. Rail on Round course positioned 3yds out from 1m1f to home straight and Old Mile increased by 6yds, 1m2f by 9yds and 1m4f+ by 12yds.

## 3353 QUEEN MARY STKS (GROUP 2) (FILLIES) 5f
3:05 (3:11) (Class 1) 2-Y-O

**£56,710** (£21,500; £10,760; £5,360; £2,690; £1,350) **Stalls** Centre

| Form | | | | RPR |
|---|---|---|---|---|
| | **1** | | **Anthem Alexander (IRE)**[13] 2938 2-9-0 0 PatSmullen 12 (Edward Lynam, Ire) *str: s.i.s: sn in tch: clsd travelling strly 2f out: led over 1f out: pressed and jnd fnl 150yds: kpt on wl and fnd ex cl home* **9/4**[1] | 106+ |
| 1121 | **2** | *nk* | **Tiggy Wiggy (IRE)**[20] 2703 2-9-0 0 RichardHughes 22 (Richard Hannon) *a.p: rdn and outpcd over 2f out: hdwy over 1f out: edgd rt ins fnl f: chal fnl 150yds: r.o but hld fnl strides* **7/2**[3] | 104 |
| 5 | **3** | ½ | **Newsletter (IRE)**[16] 2856 2-9-0 0 (t) ShaneFoley 20 (K J Condon, Ire) *w'like: str: s.i.s: hld up in rr: rdn and hdwy 2f out: str chal whn hung lft and drew level fnl 150yds: hld whn sltly short of room fnl strides* **33/1** | 102 |
| | **4** | 1¾ | **Spanish Pipedream (USA)**[55] 2-9-0 0 (bt) VictorEspinoza 13 (Wesley A Ward, U.S.A) *lengthy: prom: rdn and hung lft over 1f out: nt qckn w ldrs: hung rt ins fnl f: no ex fnl 100yds* **11/4**[2] | 96 |
| 231 | **5** | *hd* | **Littlemissblakeney**[28] 2458 2-9-0 0 WayneLordan 7 (Hugo Palmer) *leggy: prom: led 2f out: rdn and hdd over 1f out: kpt on ins fnl f but nt gng pce of ldrs* **100/1** | 95 |
| 01 | **6** | *nse* | **Arabian Queen (IRE)**[30] 2402 2-9-0 0 SilvestreDeSousa 1 (David Elsworth) *athletic: hld up in rr: hdwy over 2f out: chsd ldrs over 1f out and ch: kpt on ins fnl f but nt gng pce of ldrs clsng stages* **33/1** | 95 |
| 2 | **7** | 3 | **La Cuesta (IRE)**[12] 2944 2-9-0 0 OlivierPeslier 2 (Jamie Osborne) *w'like: hld up in rr: rdn and hdwy 2f out: chsd ldrs over 1f out: styd on same pce fnl 100yds* **66/1** | 84+ |
| 1 | **8** | ½ | **Harry's Dancer (IRE)**[32] 2348 2-9-0 0 FrankieDettori 5 (John Quinn) *athletic: hld up: hdwy over 2f out: rdn to chse ldrs over 1f out: kpt on same pce ins fnl f* **10/1** | 82 |
| 5 | **9** | *hd* | **Pastoral Girl**[32] 2348 2-9-0 0 GrahamLee 21 (James Given) *str: towards rr: pushed along and outpcd 3f out: hung rt over 1f out: styd on ins fnl f: nt pce to trble ldrs* **100/1** | 82+ |
| 1 | **10** | ½ | **Dangerous Moonlite (IRE)**[40] 2107 2-9-0 0 RyanMoore 11 (Richard Hannon) *lengthy: prom: effrt and ev ch 2f out: intimidated over 1f out and lost pl: kpt on ins fnl f but n.d* **12/1** | 80 |
| 3 | **11** | ¾ | **Adulation (IRE)**[15] 2866 2-9-0 0 JimmyFortune 9 (William Haggas) *athletic: hld up in midfield: effrt over 2f out: chsd ldrs over 1f out: kpt on same pce ins fnl f* **50/1** | 77 |
| 6101 | **12** | ½ | **Ko Cache (IRE)**[11] 3001 2-9-0 0 TomEaves 4 (Keith Dalgleish) *chsd ldrs: rdn and outpcd over 2f out: plugged on ins fnl f: no imp* **100/1** | 75 |
| 4 | **13** | 2¼ | **Coto (IRE)**[25] 2569 2-9-0 0 ColinKeane 15 (M J Tynan, Ire) *w'like: midfield: hdwy over 2f out: effrt to chse ldrs over 1f out: btn ins fnl f: hld whn bmpd 110yds out* **66/1** | 67 |
| 22 | **14** | ½ | **Al Fareej (IRE)**[15] 2866 2-9-0 0 KierenFallon 14 (James Tate) *chsd ldrs: rdn and outpcd over 2f out: plugged on ins fnl f: no imp* **50/1** | 65 |
| 211 | **15** | *hd* | **Clouds Rest**[33] 2302 2-9-0 0 PaulHanagan 6 (Richard Fahey) *neat: racd w ldr: rdn and outpcdf 2f out: wknd qckly ins fnl f* **25/1** | 65 |
| 0421 | **16** | ½ | **London Life (IRE)**[22] 2641 2-9-0 0 RichardKingscote 3 (Tom Dascombe) *in tch: rdn and outpcd over 2f out: wknd over 1f out* **66/1** | 63 |
| 21 | **17** | 2 | **Polar Vortex (IRE)**[40] 2128 2-9-0 0 AdamKirby 17 (Clive Cox) *w'like: hld up: rdn over 2f out: nvr on terms* **50/1** | 56 |
| | **18** | 1¾ | **Lady Gemini** 2-9-0 0 OisinMurphy 19 (Jo Hughes) *w'like: lengthy: midfield: rdn and lost pl 3f out: struggling after* **100/1** | 49 |
| 5 | **19** | 1¾ | **Lady Marita (IRE)**[25] 2557 2-9-0 0 PhilipPrince 18 (J S Moore) *missed break: in rr: rdn 3f out: edgd rt whn struggling over 1f out: nvr on terms* **150/1** | 43 |
| 31 | **20** | 2 | **Blue Aegean**[14] 2888 2-9-0 0 WilliamBuick 10 (Charlie Appleby) *cmpt: prom: chalng 2f out: rdn and wknd over 1f out* **20/1** | 36 |
| 22 | **21** | 3¼ | **Al Ghuwariyah (IRE)**[47] 1924 2-9-0 0 DeclanMcDonogh 8 (Kevin Ryan) *sn led: rdn and hdd 2f out: sn wknd* **100/1** | 24 |

59.15s (-1.35) **Going Correction** -0.075s/f (Good) **21** Ran SP% **126.9**
Speed ratings (Par 102): **107,106,105,102,102 102,97,96,96,95 94,93,90,89,89 88,85,82,79,76 71**
CSF £9.28 CT £223.30 TOTE £3.20: £1.50, £1.60, £8.30; EX 10.60 Trifecta £325.60.
**Owner** Noel O'Callaghan **Bred** Mountarmstrong Stud **Trained** Dunshaughlin, Co Meath

**FOCUS**
A big field of unexposed fillies, but the market didn't think this was anywhere near as competitive as the numbers suggested, with the front three being backed almost to the exclusion of the rest, and with them filling three of the first four places this is probably sound form. They initially raced in two groups before merging with 3f to run.

## 3354 PRINCE OF WALES'S STKS (BRITISH CHAMPIONS SERIES) (GROUP 1) 1m 2f
3:45 (3:47) (Class 1) 4-Y-O+

**£297,727** (£112,875; £56,490; £28,140; £14,122; £7,087) **Stalls** Low

| Form | | | | RPR |
|---|---|---|---|---|
| 22-0 | **1** | | **The Fugue**[81] 1181 5-8-11 123 WilliamBuick 7 (John Gosden) *hld up in midfield: clsd to trck ldr 2f out: rdn and qcknd to ld over 1f out: asserting and shifting rt 1f out: in command fnl and r.o wl fnl 150yds: rdn out* **11/2**[2] | 126 |
| -612 | **2** | 1¾ | **Magician (IRE)**[24] 2580 4-9-0 123 (t) JosephO'Brien 8 (A P O'Brien, Ire) *prom in main gp: 3rd and rdn to cl on ldr wl over 2f out: led over 2f out: hdd over 1f out: edgd rt 1f out: styd on same pce and hld on for 2nd ins fnl f* **6/1**[3] | 125 |
| 11-2 | **3** | 1 | **Treve (FR)**[52] 1783 4-8-11 130 FrankieDettori 2 (Mme C Head-Maarek, France) *str: racd off the pce in 6th: clsd on ldr over 2f out: rdn and effrt 2f out: edgd lft u.p over 1f out: sme hdwy and battling for 2nd fnl 150yds: r.o same pce and no threat to wnr* **8/13**[1] | 120 |
| 15-2 | **4** | 1½ | **Mukhadram**[81] 1183 5-9-0 120 PaulHanagan 1 (William Haggas) *lw: racd in 4th: rdn and clsd on ldr over 2f out: 4th and styng on same pce whn sltly hmpd and swtchd lft 1f out: no imp after* **6/1**[3] | 120 |
| 11-3 | **5** | 6 | **Dank**[81] 1181 5-8-11 117 RyanMoore 6 (Sir Michael Stoute) *stdd s: t.k.h: hld up in last pair: rdn and short-lived effrt jst over 2f out: wl btn over 1f out* **10/1** | 105 |
| 0-62 | **6** | ½ | **Parish Hall (IRE)**[44] 2040 5-9-0 113 (t) KevinManning 5 (J S Bolger, Ire) *stdd after s: chsd clr ldr: rdn and clsd to press ldrs briefly over 2f out: sn struggling and btn 2f out: sn wknd* **33/1** | 107 |
| 030 | **7** | 6 | **Zambucca (SAF)**[102] 901 6-9-0 107 PatCosgrave 3 (Gay Kelleway) *lw: stdd after s: hld up in rr: rdn over 2f out: sn outpcd and wknd wl over 1f out* **100/1** | 95 |
| 6-04 | **8** | 16 | **Elkaayed (USA)**[32] 2335 4-9-0 104 DaneO'Neill 4 (Roger Varian) *awkward leaving stalls and nt best away: sn rcvrd to ld and clr after 2f: 10 l clr 4f out: rdn and hdd over 2f out: sn btn: t.o ins fnl f* **66/1** | 63 |

2m 1.9s (-5.50) **Going Correction** -0.075s/f (Good) course record **8** Ran SP% **120.4**
Speed ratings (Par 117): **119,117,116,115,110 110,105,92**
CSF £39.77 CT £48.30 TOTE £5.80: £1.60, £1.80, £1.10; EX 38.50 Trifecta £54.40.
**Owner** Lord Lloyd-Webber **Bred** Watership Down Stud **Trained** Newmarket, Suffolk

**FOCUS**
Another terrific edition of this race, which was elevated to Group 1 status in 2001. The pacemaker did his job well and the first three home all broke the track record, set by Cirrus Des Aigles in the 2011 Champion Stakes.

## 3355 DUKE OF CAMBRIDGE STKS (GROUP 2) (F&M) (STRAIGHT COURSE) 1m (S)
4:25 (4:26) (Class 1) 4-Y-O+

**£82,881** (£31,422; £15,725; £7,833; £3,931; £1,973) **Stalls** Centre

| Form | | | | RPR |
|---|---|---|---|---|
| 12-2 | **1** | | **Integral**[45] 1974 4-9-0 115 RyanMoore 9 (Sir Michael Stoute) *lw: in tch: jst bhd ldr bef qckning up to ld over 1f out: edgd rt whn r.o wl and in command fnl 150yds* **9/4**[1] | 119 |
| -210 | **2** | 2 | **L'Amour De Ma Vie (USA)**[102] 902 5-9-3 111.. ChristopheSoumillon 7 (Mme Pia Brandt, France) *trckd ldrs: led over 2f out: rdn and hdd over 1f out: no match for wnr fnl 150yds* **20/1** | 116 |
| 55-1 | **3** | 2 | **Purr Along**[25] 2572 4-9-0 109 JamieSpencer 12 (J P Murtagh, Ire) *lw: racd keenly: hld up in last pl: hdwy 2f out: effrt to chse ldrs over 1f out: styd on ins fnl f: no imp on front two fnl 110yds* **9/1** | 109 |
| 1-62 | **4** | 1 | **Fiesolana (IRE)**[25] 2572 5-9-3 114 BillyLee 4 (W McCreery, Ire) *lw: midfield: hdwy 2f out: sn chsd ldrs and tried to chal: nt qckn 1f out: styd on same pce fnl 110yds* **14/1** | 110 |
| 510- | **5** | ½ | **Sky Lantern (IRE)**[192] 8210 4-9-5 119 RichardHughes 3 (Richard Hannon) *hld up: swtchd rt and hdwy over 2f out: rdn whn swtchd lft over 1f out: kpt on ins fnl f: nvr able to get to ldrs* **9/2**[2] | 110 |
| 360- | **6** | ¾ | **Woodland Aria**[320] 4949 4-9-0 98 WilliamBuick 11 (John Gosden) *hld up: rdn over 2f out: styd on ins fnl f: nvr able to rch ldrs* **50/1** | 104 |
| 5-20 | **7** | *hd* | **Peace Burg (FR)**[25] 2572 4-9-0 110 (t) JosephO'Brien 2 (A P O'Brien, Ire) *sn dropped into midfield: rdn and hdwy 2f out: chsd ldrs over 1f out: one pce fnl 150yds* **40/1** | 103 |
| 4-00 | **8** | 1 | **Kenhope (FR)**[26] 4-9-0 103 OlivierPeslier 1 (H-A Pantall, France) *racd keenly: hld up: pushed along 3f out: rdn over 1f out: hung rt ins fnl f: plugged on wout threatening* **28/1** | 101 |
| 0-41 | **9** | ¾ | **Esoterique (IRE)**[45] 1974 4-9-0 113 MaximeGuyon 5 (A Fabre, France) *prom: rdn whn chalng 2f out: nt qckn over 1f out: fdd fnl 110yds* **11/2**[3] | 99 |
| 14-3 | **10** | ½ | **Annecdote**[39] 2155 4-9-0 107 RichardKingscote 13 (Jonathan Portman) *hld up: impr into midfield after 1f: pushed along over 2f out: no imp u.p after* **16/1** | 98 |
| 4-23 | **11** | 2 | **Princess Loulou (IRE)**[25] 2572 4-9-0 105 AndreaAtzeni 6 (Roger Varian) *trckd ldrs: pushed along over 4f out: rdn 2f out: sn lost pl: wkng whn sltly short of room over 1f out* **33/1** | 93 |
| 1/14 | **12** | 4½ | **Certify (USA)**[118] 682 4-9-3 113 JamesDoyle 10 (Charlie Appleby) *racd keenly: hld up in midfield: rdn 2f out: no imp: wl btn whn sltly short of room 1f out* **8/1** | 86 |
| 3-44 | **13** | 4 | **Masarah (IRE)**[12] 2956 4-9-0 100 KierenFallon 8 (Clive Brittain) *led: rdn and hdd over 2f out: wknd over 1f out* **100/1** | 74 |
| 5-30 | **14** | 7 | **Gifted Girl (IRE)**[34] 2284 5-9-0 108 TomQueally 14 (Paul Cole) *edgy in stalls: missed break: impr into midfield after 1f: chsd ldrs over 3f out: wknd 2f out* **20/1** | 58 |

1m 37.09s (-3.71) **Going Correction** -0.075s/f (Good) course record **14** Ran SP% **119.3**
Speed ratings (Par 115): **115,113,111,110,109 108,108,107,106,106 104,99,95,88**
CSF £55.73 CT £355.16 TOTE £3.30: £1.30, £5.20, £2.50; EX 53.60 Trifecta £813.50.
**Owner** Cheveley Park Stud **Bred** Cheveley Park Stud Ltd **Trained** Newmarket, Suffolk

**FOCUS**
Another course record was lowered here in a race run at a sound pace. They were well strung out for much of the race, but it's hard to say the leaders went too fast early when the second was prominent throughout, the winner came from mid-division and the third from last.

## 3356 ROYAL HUNT CUP (HERITAGE H'CAP) (STRAIGHT COURSE) 1m (S)
5:00 (5:04) (Class 2) 3-Y-O+

**£108,937** (£32,620; £16,310; £8,155; £4,077; £2,047) **Stalls** Centre

| Form | | | | RPR |
|---|---|---|---|---|
| 050- | **1** | | **Field Of Dream**[263] 6838 7-9-1 **101** (b) AdamKirby 33 (Jamie Osborne) *swtg: stdd s: hld up in tch in rr: hdwy whn swtchd sharply rt over 1f out: drvn: edgd lft but qcknd to ld fnl 150yds: r.o strly and in command fnl 75yds* **20/1** | 112 |
| 0001 | **2** | 1¼ | **Chil The Kite**[32] 2336 5-9-9 **109** GeorgeBaker 14 (Hughie Morrison) *stdd s: t.k.h: hld up in rr: hdwy and swtchd rt over 1f out: nt clr run 1f out: wnt between horses and str run ins fnl f: chsd wnr fnl 50yds: r.o but wnr had flown* **14/1** | 117+ |
| /450 | **3** | 1¼ | **Steeler (IRE)**[118] 681 4-9-6 **106** SilvestreDeSousa 23 (Charlie Appleby) *racd keenly: pressed ldr tl led over 2f out: sn rdn: drvn and hdd fnl 150yds: no ex and styd on same pce after* **33/1** | 111 |
| 4-11 | **4** | *shd* | **Sea Shanty (USA)**[4] 3244 4-8-12 **98** 5ex RichardHughes 29 (Richard Hannon) *lw: pressed ldrs: rdn and ev ch 2f out: styd on same pce u.p ins fnl f* **14/1** | 103 |
| 1-34 | **5** | ½ | **Ayaar (IRE)**[39] 2145 4-8-11 **97** FrankieDettori 16 (Luca Cumani) *stdd s: t.k.h: hld up in tch in rr: hdwy whn pushed rt and hmpd over 1f out: tk time to rcvr: hdwy and r.o wl fnl 100yds* **16/1** | 104+ |
| 0054 | **6** | ½ | **Tales Of Grimm (USA)**[34] 2286 5-9-2 **102** OlivierPeslier 25 (Richard Fahey) *chsd ldrs: rdn over 2f out: drvn over 1f out: sltly hmpd and styd on same pce ins fnl f* **33/1** | 105 |

60-3 **7** ½ **Belgian Bill**[39] 2145 6-9-2 **102**........................(tp) PatCosgrave 28 104+
(George Baker) *hld up in tch in midfield: travelling wl but nt clr run fr 2f out: nvr enough room after tl nudged along and kpt on towards fin: nvr able to chal and fin full of running* **8/1**[3]

3121 **8** ¾ **Abseil (USA)**[12] 2959 4-8-11 **97** 5ex........................ JamesDoyle 22 97
(Sir Michael Stoute) *swtg: t.k.h: chsd ldrs: rdn and pressed ldrs over 1f out: no ex and n.m.r jst ins fnl f: wknd fnl 100yds* **7/2**[1]

00-1 **9** hd **Niceofyoutotellme**[46] 1948 5-8-11 **97**........................ JimCrowley 18 98+
(Ralph Beckett) *stdd s: hld up in midfield: rdn and effrt whn pushed rt and hmpd over 1f out: tk time to rcvr: kpt on same pce ins fnl f* **25/1**

0440 **10** hd **Regulation (IRE)**[87] 1078 5-9-0 **100**........................ ShaneFoley 19 99
(Neil King) *stdd s: hld up in tch towards rr: effrt and nt clr run over 1f out: hdwy 1f out: styd on wl fnl 100yds: nvr trbld ldrs* **100/1**

0-31 **11** hd **Pacific Heights (IRE)**[18] 2758 5-9-0 **100** 5ex........................ DaleSwift 12 98
(Brian Ellison) *swtchd lft sn after s: chsd ldrs: rdn 3f out: drvn and unable qck over 1f out: wknd ins fnl f* **33/1**

/302 **12** nk **Artigiano (USA)**[14] 2891 4-9-5 **105**........................ WilliamBuick 9 103
(Charlie Appleby) *swtg: swtchd lft sn after s: hld up in tch in midfield: effrt jst over 2f out: hdwy u.p and chsd ldrs over 1f out: wknd ins fnl f* **25/1**

000 **13** 1½ **Burano (IRE)**[46] 1948 5-8-13 **99**........................ JimmyFortune 24 93
(Brian Meehan) *hld up towards rr: rdn and effrt over 1f out: styd on ins fnl f: nvr trbld ldrs* **20/1**

4110 **14** ½ **Ocean Tempest**[20] 2715 5-9-8 **115**........................ JoeDoyle(7) 26 108
(John Ryan) *led tl over 2f out: outpcd u.p over 1f out: btn whn short of room jst ins fnl f: wknd fnl 150yds* **33/1**

0043 **15** ½ **Santefisio**[60] 1578 8-9-0 **100**........................(b) TomEaves 31 92
(Keith Dalgleish) *hld up in tch towards rr: plenty to do and nt clr run whn swtchd rt over 1f out: sme hdwy ins fnl f: nvr trbld ldrs* **33/1**

-000 **16** hd **Levitate**[34] 2286 6-9-0 **100**........................(v) MartinHarley 20 92
(John Quinn) *wl in tch in midfield: rdn over 2f out: unable qck u.p and lost pl 2f out: hld and plugged on same pce fr over 1f out* **100/1**

6124 **17** ¾ **Gabrial's Kaka (IRE)**[41] 2086 4-9-3 **103**........................ JamieSpencer 4 93+
(Richard Fahey) *stdd s: sn swtchd lft: hld up in rr: hdwy whn nt clr run: hmpd and swtchd lft over 1f out: swtchd rt and forced way between horses 1f out: sn drvn and no hdwy: wknd fnl 100yds* **20/1**

0-03 **18** shd **Red Avenger (USA)**[12] 2959 4-8-10 **96**........................ PaulHanagan 11 86
(Ed Dunlop) *swtchd lft sn after s: wl in tch in midfield: hdwy to chse ldrs and rdn 2f out: drvn and unable qck over 1f out: wknd ins fnl f* **20/1**

3-50 **19** 1 **Loving Spirit**[39] 2145 6-8-10 **99**........................ RobertTart(3) 27 86
(James Toller) *in tch in midfield: effrt u.p jst over 2f out: drvn and btn over 1f out: wknd 1f out* **25/1**

060- **20** nse **Queensberry Rules (IRE)**[263] 6838 4-9-0 **100**........................ RyanMoore 32 87
(William Haggas) *in toouch in midfield: clsd but nt clr run on stands' rail over 1f out: nvr able to cl: btn 1f out and eased ins fnl f* **7/1**[2]

0066 **21** nk **Starboard**[25] 2554 5-8-8 **97**........................ WilliamTwiston-Davies(3) 2 84
(David Simcock) *swtchd lft sn after s: hld up in tch in midfield: rdn and hdwy ent fnl 2f: chsd ldrs and drvn over 1f out: no ex and wknd ins fnl f* **100/1**

0124 **22** ¾ **Fort Bastion (IRE)**[14] 2891 5-8-11 **97**........................ JamesSullivan 1 82
(Ruth Carr) *swtchd lft sn after s: hld up in tch in midfield: effrt u.p ent fnl 2f: no hdwy over 1f out: wknd ins fnl f* **33/1**

1030 **23** 1¼ **Rebellious Guest**[61] 1559 5-9-0 **100**........................ KierenFallon 7 82
(George Margarson) *swtchd lft sn after s: hld up in tch in midfield: rdn and unable qck over 1f out: btn 1f out: eased ins fnl f* **50/1**

00-3 **24** 2¾ **Prince Of Johanne (IRE)**[34] 2286 8-9-1 **101**........................(p) GrahamLee 5 77
(Tom Tate) *racd solo in centre: pressed ldrs: rdn 3f out: struggling u.p 2f out: wknd over 1f out* **22/1**

0-15 **25** shd **Here Comes When (IRE)**[18] 2765 4-9-3 **106**........................ OisinMurphy(3) 3 81
(Andrew Balding) *lw: swtchd lft sn after s: wl in tch in midfield: rdn over 2f out: sn struggling and lost pl 2f out: wknd over 1f out* **20/1**

115- **26** ¾ **Short Squeeze (IRE)**[249] 7196 4-9-6 **106**........................ PatSmullen 6 80
(Hugo Palmer) *swtchd lft sn after s: t.k.h: chsd ldrs: rdn jst over 2f out: sn struggling and btn: wknd over 1f out* **11/1**

-520 **27** ½ **Ingleby Angel (IRE)**[34] 2286 5-8-11 **97**........................ DanielTudhope 10 69
(David O'Meara) *swtchd lft sn after s: in tch towards rr: rdn and effrt 2f out: no imp whn pushed rt over 1f out bhd fnl f* **33/1**

6-54 **28** shd **Trumpet Major (IRE)**[46] 1948 5-9-6 **106**........................ PatDobbs 13 78
(Richard Hannon) *rn wout declared tongue tie: swtchd lft after s: in tch in midfield: rdn and lost pl 2f out: bhd 1f out* **25/1**

1m 37.88s (-2.92) **Going Correction** -0.075s/f (Good) course record **28** Ran SP% **142.4**
Speed ratings (Par 109): **111,109,108,108,107 107,106,106,105,105 105,105,103,103,102 102,101,101,100,100 100,99,98,95,9**
CSF £239.98 CT £9023.55 TOTE £24.00: £6.30, £4.20, £9.40, £2.40; EX 528.00 Trifecta £10002.80 Part won..
**Owner** N A Jackson **Bred** Grundy Bloodstock Srl **Trained** Upper Lambourn, Berks
■ Stewards' Enquiry : Adam Kirby three-day ban: careless riding (Jul 2-4)

**FOCUS**
Another classy renewal of this long-established handicap, in which a rating of 96 was needed to get a run, compared with 87 a decade ago. They soon raced in one group, bar the 2012 winner Prince Of Johannes who continued to race solo, and it was a race dominated by those drawn high, with 12th home Artigiano the only finisher in the first 16 with a single-figure draw.

## 3357 SANDRINGHAM H'CAP (LISTED RACE) (FILLIES) (STRAIGHT COURSE) 1m (S)
5:35 (5:40) (Class 1) (0-110,103) 3-Y-O
**£39,697** (£15,050; £7,532; £3,752; £1,883; £945) **Stalls** Centre

Form RPR
1-11 **1** **Muteela**[18] 2781 3-8-13 **95**........................ PaulHanagan 22 102+
(Mark Johnston) *lw: mde virtually all: rdn 2f out: hrd pressed ins fnl f: all out: jst hld on* **9/2**[1]

3-50 **2** shd **Queen Catrine (IRE)**[38] 2195 3-9-6 **102**........................ JamieSpencer 18 108+
(Charles Hills) *hld up in last pl: swtchd rt and hdwy 3f out: c arnd whole field: r.o strly ins fnl f: jst failed: too much to do* **14/1**

2321 **3** ½ **Wee Jean**[25] 2556 3-8-11 **93**........................ WilliamTwiston-Davies 24 97
(Mick Channon) *hld up: rdn and hdwy over 2f out: hung rt over 1f out: chal ins fnl f: r.o u.p: hld towards fin* **16/1**

**4** nk **Graceful Grit (IRE)**[36] 2243 3-8-12 **94**...... Christophe-PatriceLemaire 20 98
(F-H Graffard, France) *w'like: chsd ldrs: ch 2f out: nt qckn over 1f out: styd on ins fnl f: nt quite pce of ldrs* **25/1**

-403 **5** nk **Lady Lara (IRE)**[33] 2316 3-9-2 **98**........................ KierenFallon 8 101
(Timothy Jarvis) *in tch: effrt to chal wl over 2f out: stl ev ch ins fnl f: hld towards fin* **25/1**

1-32 **6** ½ **Feedyah (USA)**[111] 771 3-9-0 **96**........................ RichardHughes 19 98
(Charlie Appleby) *midfield: hdwy 3f out: r.o and chalng ins fnl f: no ex nr fin* **20/1**

-405 **7** 1¼ **Lamar (IRE)**[33] 2299 3-8-11 **93**........................ LukeMorris 23 92
(James Tate) *midfield: pushed along over 3f out: styd on ins fnl f: edgd rt fnl 150yds: nt pce to chal ldrs* **16/1**

1-43 **8** 1 **Psychometry (FR)**[27] 2484 3-8-8 **89** oh1 ow1........................ RyanMoore 1 91+
(Sir Michael Stoute) *hld up in rr: hdwy 2f out: nt clr run over 1f out: nt clr run again and hmpd ins fnl f: styd on: gng on at fin* **9/1**

**9** ½ **Odisseia (IRE)**[31] 2372 3-8-9 **91**........................ WayneLordan 6 87
(Edward Lynam, Ire) *w'like: hld up in midfield: rdn 3f out: sme hdwy over 2f out: kpt on ins fnl f: nt trble ldrs* **15/2**[3]

1-64 **10** ½ **Dutch Courage**[33] 2316 3-9-0 **96**........................ GrahamLee 10 90
(Richard Fahey) *midfield: rdn 3f out: no imp: one pce fnl f* **14/1**

-211 **11** 1 **Crowley's Law**[16] 2840 3-9-2 **98**........................ RichardKingscote 2 90
(Tom Dascombe) *lw: racd keenly: chsd ldrs: rdn over 2f out: no ex fnl 100yds* **13/2**[2]

1445 **12** ¾ **Nakuti (IRE)**[12] 2962 3-8-7 **89** oh6........................ MartinDwyer 12 79
(Sylvester Kirk) *lw: prom: ev ch 3f out: rdn and one pce over 1f out: fdd ins fnl f* **50/1**

50 **13** nk **Queen Of Power (IRE)**[24] 2581 3-9-1 **97**........................ DeclanMcDonogh 17 87
(M D O'Callaghan, Ire) *str: s.i.s: hld up: pushed along over 3f out: kpt on ins fnl f: nvr able to chal* **25/1**

6-20 **14** 1¼ **Midnite Angel (IRE)**[33] 2316 3-8-8 **90**........................(b) AndreaAtzeni 15 77
(Richard Hannon) *racd keenly: chsd ldrs: rdn over 2f out: sn wknd* **33/1**

1111 **15** 1½ **Alumina (IRE)**[78] 1225 3-8-8 **90**........................ DavidProbert 7 73
(Andrew Balding) *hld up: rdn in midfield 4f out: wknd over 2f out* **50/1**

4-34 **16** ¾ **Hot Coffee (IRE)**[25] 2565 3-8-8 **90**........................ HayleyTurner 9 72
(Tom Dascombe) *midfield: rdn 4f out: wknd over 2f out* **25/1**

1-36 **17** 1¾ **Majeyda (USA)**[45] 1976 3-9-7 **103**........................ WilliamBuick 3 81
(Charlie Appleby) *midfield: rdn 3f out: no imp over 1f out: nvr a threat* **14/1**

2-10 **18** ½ **Adhwaa**[33] 2316 3-8-10 **92**........................ DaneO'Neill 5 68
(B W Hills) *hld up towards rr: rdn 3f out: nvr on terms* **25/1**

150- **19** ¾ **Stealth Missile (IRE)**[228] 7695 3-8-7 **89** oh2........................ LiamJones 11 64
(Clive Brittain) *prom: pushed along 3f out: rdn and wknd over 2f out* **66/1**

2231 **20** nk **Polar Eyes**[19] 2740 3-8-7 **89** oh8........................ JimmyQuinn 16 63
(Peter Chapple-Hyam) *midfield tl rdn and wknd 3f out* **66/1**

060 **21** ½ **Alutiq (IRE)**[32] 2343 3-8-9 **91**........................ HarryBentley 14 64
(Eve Johnson Houghton) *prom: rdn 3f out: wknd 2f out: eased whn wl btn fnl 100yds* **25/1**

2-06 **22** nk **Oxsana**[132] 506 3-8-11 **93**........................(p) TomQueally 13 65
(William Haggas) *racd keenly: hld up: pushed along over 3f out: bhd fnl 2f* **20/1**

1125 **23** 2¾ **Secret Pursuit (IRE)**[27] 2484 3-9-0 **96**........................ OisinMurphy 4 62
(Marcus Tregoning) *chsd ldrs: pushed along over 3f out: wknd over 2f out* **33/1**

11-0 **24** 11 **Coral Mist**[67] 1435 3-9-3 **99**........................ FrankieDettori 25 40
(Charles Hills) *hld up: struggling 2f out: nvr on terms* **20/1**

1m 37.93s (-2.87) **Going Correction** -0.075s/f (Good) course record **24** Ran SP% **135.2**
Speed ratings (Par 104): **111,110,110,110,109 109,108,107,106,106 105,104,104,102,101 100,98,98,97,97 96,96,93,82**
CSF £56.91 CT £981.59 TOTE £5.20: £1.90, £3.90, £4.50, £7.50; EX 76.60 Trifecta £1749.80.
**Owner** Hamdan Al Maktoum **Bred** Shadwell Estate Company Limited **Trained** Middleham Moor, N Yorks
■ Stewards' Enquiry : Jamie Spencer three-day ban: used whip without giving filly time to respond (Jul 2-4)
William Twiston-Davies two-day ban: used whip above permitted level (Jul 2-3)

**FOCUS**
As in the Hunt Cup, they all edged over to race stands' side, and the pace, while sound enough, wasn't overly strong.
T/Jkpt: Not won. T/Plt: £86.70 to a £1 stake. Pool: £596,187.90 - 5017.38 winning tickets T/Qpdt: £32.60 to a £1 stake. Pool: £24,549.54 - 555.78 winning tickets SP

# 3099 HAMILTON (R-H)
Wednesday, June 18

**OFFICIAL GOING: Good (good to firm in places on straight; watered; 8.5)**
Wind: Breezy, half behind Weather: Sunny, hot

## 3358 BRITISH STALLION STUDS EBF MAIDEN STKS 6f 5y
1:50 (1:51) (Class 5) 2-Y-O
**£3,234** (£962; £481; £240) **Stalls** High

Form RPR
4 **1** **Lady Desire (IRE)**[23] 2601 2-8-11 0........................ JasonHart(3) 7 76+
(Keith Dalgleish) *dwlt: hung rt thrght: sn pushed along in rr: hdwy over 2f out: led over 1f out: rdn clr fnl f* **7/1**

**2** 2¾ **My Dream Boat (IRE)** 2-9-2 0........................ PJMcDonald 1 70
(Donald McCain) *restless in stalls: wnt rt s: sn outpcd: hdwy over 1f out: chsd (clr) wnr ins fnl f: no imp* **33/1**

33 **3** ¾ **Miami Carousel (IRE)**[16] 2824 2-9-5 0........................ PhillipMakin 2 71
(John Quinn) *trckd ldrs: effrt and wnt 2nd over 1f out to ins fnl f: kpt on same pce* **7/2**[2]

2 **4** nse **Split The Atom (IRE)**[19] 2736 2-9-5 0........................ RonanWhelan 3 70
(John Patrick Shanahan, Ire) *trckd ldrs: rdn over 2f out: kpt on same pce ins fnl f* **5/1**[3]

**5** 1 **Disavow** 2-8-11 0........................ FrannyNorton 8 59
(Mark Johnston) *w ldr: ev ch over 1f out: outpcd ins fnl f: bttr for r* **8/1**

**6** ½ **Charlotte's Secret** 2-9-2 0........................ TonyHamilton 4 63
(Richard Fahey) *in tch: pushed along and outpcd wl over 1f out: no imp fnl f* **12/1**

4 **7** 1¾ **Seeking Approval (IRE)**[30] 2386 2-9-0 0........................ PaulMulrennan 5 56
(Kevin Ryan) *slt ld to over 1f out: sn rdn and wknd* **13/8**[1]

**8** 33 **Warapito** 2-8-9 0........................ PaulMcGiff(7) 6
(Richard Guest) *missed break: bhd and outpcd: no ch fr 1/2-way* **100/1**

1m 12.21s (0.01) **Going Correction** -0.075s/f (Good) **8** Ran SP% **112.2**
Speed ratings (Par 93): **96,92,91,91,89 89,86,42**
CSF £182.08 TOTE £6.40: £1.80, £8.20, £1.10; EX 288.10 Trifecta £665.70.
**Owner** G Brogan **Bred** Rockhart Trading Ltd **Trained** Carluke, S Lanarks

**FOCUS**
The going was good, good to firm in places (watered). They went a decent pace for this maiden. Rail realignment around the loop increased in distance by about 50yds on Round course.

## 3359 SAM COLLINGWOOD-CAMERON H'CAP 6f 5y
2:20 (2:22) (Class 5) (0-75,75) 3-Y-O+
**£2,911** (£866; £432; £216) **Stalls** High

Form RPR
0412 **1** **Amenable (IRE)**[4] 3246 7-9-5 **71**........................(p) ShirleyTeasdale(5) 8 80
(Ann Stokell) *taken early to post: mde all: rdn over 1f out: hld on wl fnl f* **7/2**[1]

3060 **2** *nk* **King Of Eden (IRE)**[4] 3221 8-9-11 **75**.......... JasonHart(3) 10 83
(Eric Alston) *prom towards stands' rail: rdn and persistently hung rt fr over 2f out: chsd wnr over 1f out: kpt on fnl f: hld towards fin* **4/1**[2]

2000 **3** *3/4* **Gold Beau (FR)**[23] 2602 4-9-10 **71**..........(b[1]) AmyRyan 5 77
(Kristin Stubbs) *taken early to post: cl up: drvn along over 2f out: kpt on same pce ins fnl f* **20/1**

2221 **4** *1* **Hab Reeh**[7] 3099 6-8-12 **66** 6ex.......... GemmaTutty(7) 4 69
(Ruth Carr) *t.k.h early: prom: pushed along over 2f out: effrt over 1f out: edgd rt and one pce fnl f* **4/1**[2]

1135 **5** *nk* **Economic Crisis (IRE)**[7] 3102 5-9-11 **72**.......... PaulMulrennan 3 74
(Alan Berry) *taken early to post: hld up bhd ldng gp: hdwy over 1f out: kpt on fnl f: nvr able to chal* **12/1**

4000 **6** *1/2* **Baltic Spirit (IRE)**[12] 2951 3-8-2 **59**.......... ConnorBeasley(3) 6 57
(Keith Dalgleish) *taken early to post: chsd ldrs: drvn along 2f out: kpt on same pce fnl f* **12/1**

50-0 **7** *1 1/4* **Les Gar Gan (IRE)**[7] 3114 3-9-3 **71**..........(b[1]) PhillipMakin 2 65
(Keith Dalgleish) *dwlt: bhd: pushed along over 2f out: no imp fnl f* **17/2**

0561 **8** *1/2* **Alexandrakollontai (IRE)**[21] 2677 4-9-5 **69**..........(b) JulieBurke(3) 7 64
(Alistair Whillans) *trckd ldrs: rdn 2f out: wknd fnl f* **8/1**[3]

-500 **9** *1 1/4* **Oak Bluffs (IRE)**[12] 2955 3-8-6 **60**.......... PJMcDonald 11 49
(Richard Fahey) *hld up: swtchd to bk of centre gp after 1f: rdn over 2f out: sn n.d* **28/1**

4004 **10** *4 1/2* **Bapak Muda (USA)**[23] 2605 4-8-9 **61**..........(b) KevinStott(5) 1 37
(Kevin Ryan) *prom: rdn over 2f out: hung rt over 1f out: sn btn* **9/1**

1m 11.16s (-1.04) **Going Correction** -0.075s/f (Good)
**WFA** 3 from 4yo+ 7lb 10 Ran SP% **117.5**
Speed ratings (Par 103): **103,102,101,100,99 99,97,96,95,89**
CSF £17.55 CT £245.17 TOTE £4.20: £1.80, £1.60, £5.10; EX 25.70 Trifecta £501.80.
**Owner** Stephen Arnold **Bred** Michael Downey & Roalso Ltd **Trained** Lincoln, Lincolnshire

**FOCUS**
The pace was honest for this competitive handicap.

## 3360 D M HALL H'CAP 1m 65y
**2:55** (2:56) (Class 5) (0-70,69) 3-Y-O £2,911 (£866; £432; £216) Stalls Low

Form RPR

6-44 **1** **Porthos Du Vallon**[5] 3187 3-9-0 **65**..........(p) JasonHart(3) 4 74
(Keith Dalgleish) *plld hrd: sn midfield: effrt and swtchd lft wl over 1f out: edgd rt and led ins fnl f: kpt on strly* **7/2**[1]

-642 **2** *1 3/4* **Light Of Asia (IRE)**[16] 2847 3-9-7 **69**.......... PaddyAspell 9 74
(Ed Dunlop) *hld up: stdy hdwy on outside 4f out: rdn and outpcd over 2f out: rallied over 1f out: styd on to take 2nd nr fin: nt rch wnr* **10/1**

2432 **3** *3/4* **Handwoven (IRE)**[6] 3158 3-9-3 **65**..........(b) FrannyNorton 7 68
(Mark Johnston) *t.k.h: led: rdn over 2f out: hdd ins fnl f: kpt on same pce: lost 2nd nr fin* **5/1**[3]

0320 **4** *nk* **Aran Sky (IRE)**[17] 2805 3-9-7 **69**.......... PhillipMakin 5 72
(K R Burke) *hld up: rdn and outpcd over 2f out: rallied over 1f out: kpt on wl fnl f: nrst fin* **11/2**

0-60 **5** *hd* **Bahamian C**[44] 2020 3-9-0 **62**.......... TonyHamilton 8 64
(Richard Fahey) *t.k.h early: hld up: rdn over 2f out: no imp tl styd on fnl f: nvr able to chal* **25/1**

0040 **6** *1* **Eddiemaurice (IRE)**[17] 2805 3-9-0 **62**.......... PatrickMathers 1 62
(Richard Guest) *dwlt: hld up on ins: effrt and pushed along 3f out: no imp fnl f* **12/1**

\- **7** *1/2* **Helen's Armada (IRE)**[20] 2712 3-9-3 **65**.......... RonanWhelan 6 64
(John Patrick Shanahan, Ire) *prom: effrt and drvn along over 2f out: wknd fnl f* **7/1**

-044 **8** *shd* **Lomond Lassie**[9] 3054 3-8-9 **57**.......... PJMcDonald 2 55
(Keith Dalgleish) *prom: rdn and ev ch over 1f out: wknd ins fnl f* **9/1**

0-55 **9** *1 3/4* **Smart Alec (IRE)**[22] 2657 3-8-7 **58**.......... SamJames(3) 3 52
(Alan Swinbank) *pressed ldr: effrt and rdn over 2f out: wknd appr fnl f* **9/2**[2]

1m 48.44s (0.04) **Going Correction** -0.075s/f (Good) 9 Ran SP% **115.6**
Speed ratings (Par 99): **96,94,93,93,93 92,91,91,89**
CSF £39.36 CT £176.09 TOTE £5.10: £1.60, £3.10, £1.70; EX 35.10 Trifecta £172.90.
**Owner** Lamont Racing **Bred** Aiden Murphy **Trained** Carluke, S Lanarks

**FOCUS**
An open handicap, run at a steady pace.

## 3361 BOTHWELL CASTLE H'CAP 1m 65y
**3:30** (3:31) (Class 4) (0-80,80) 3-Y-O+ £6,469 (£1,925; £962; £481) Stalls Low

Form RPR

2612 **1** **Sir Guy Porteous (IRE)**[16] 2827 3-9-2 **78**.......... FrannyNorton 11 86
(Mark Johnston) *mde all: rdn over 2f out: kpt on strly fnl f* **4/1**[1]

0-00 **2** *1/2* **Argaki (IRE)**[23] 2603 4-9-7 **76**.......... JasonHart(3) 9 85
(Keith Dalgleish) *hld up in midfield: stdy hdwy to chse wnr 4f out: drvn 2f out: edgd rt fnl f: r.o* **10/1**

-010 **3** *1 1/2* **Ralphy Boy (IRE)**[23] 2603 5-9-6 **72**.......... PJMcDonald 3 78
(Alistair Whillans) *chsd wnr to 4f out: sn rdn: rallied: kpt on same pce fnl f* **10/1**

0154 **4** *1/2* **Ted's Brother (IRE)**[7] 3094 6-8-13 **72**..........(e) ARawlinson(7) 4 76
(Richard Guest) *hld up: swtchd lft and effrt on outside over 2f out: hung rt and one pce over 1f out* **11/2**[3]

221- **5** *1* **Hanalei Bay (IRE)**[194] 8185 4-9-2 **68**.......... PhillipMakin 5 70
(Keith Dalgleish) *hld up: effrt and rdn over 2f out: hdwy over 1f out: no imp fnl f* **8/1**

0335 **6** *1/2* **Dhaular Dhar (IRE)**[5] 3190 12-8-6 **61** oh2.......... IanBrennan(3) 7 62
(Jim Goldie) *hld up: effrt and rdn whn n.m.r briefly over 2f out: no imp fr over 1f out* **25/1**

1-24 **7** *1/2* **Dancing Cosmos (IRE)**[40] 2117 4-10-0 **80**.......... RonanWhelan 1 80
(John Patrick Shanahan, Ire) *prom: drvn along over 3f out: outpcd over 2f out: no imp fr over 1f out* **9/2**[2]

3142 **8** *1/2* **I'm Super Too (IRE)**[18] 2790 7-9-5 **74**.......... SamJames(3) 2 73
(Alan Swinbank) *s.i.s: hld up on ins: drvn and outpcd over 2f out: n.d after* **4/1**[1]

500 **9** *8* **Haames (IRE)**[19] 2733 7-8-3 **62**.......... CamHardie(7) 6 42
(Kevin Morgan) *hld up: drvn along over 2f out: struggling wl over 1f out* **66/1**

-100 **10** *2* **Swehan (IRE)**[29] 2423 4-9-1 **72**.......... KevinStott(5) 8 48
(Kevin Ryan) *cl up: rdn along wl over 2f out: wknd over 1f out* **14/1**

1m 46.72s (-1.68) **Going Correction** -0.075s/f (Good)
**WFA** 3 from 4yo+ 10lb 10 Ran SP% **114.9**
Speed ratings (Par 105): **105,104,103,102,101 101,100,100,92,90**
CSF £43.86 CT £379.84 TOTE £3.60: £1.90, £8.40, £4.10; EX 40.80 Trifecta £503.80.
**Owner** Paul Dean **Bred** Rabbah Bloodstock Limited **Trained** Middleham Moor, N Yorks

**FOCUS**
An open handicap, run at a fair pace.

## 3362 RACINGUK.COM/FREETRIAL MAIDEN AUCTION STKS 1m 65y
**4:10** (4:11) (Class 5) 3-Y-O £2,726 (£805; £402) Stalls Low

Form RPR

20- **1** **Jacob Black**[311] 5307 3-9-2 0.......... JasonHart(3) 4 78
(Keith Dalgleish) *mde all at stdy gallop: rdn and qcknd clr over 2f out: eased ins fnl f: easily* **5/2**[1]

0-03 **2** *3 1/4* **Solid Justice (IRE)**[14] 2902 3-9-5 0.......... PJMcDonald 8 69
(Jason Ward) *s.i.s: hld up: hdwy on outside 2f out: chsd (clr) wnr ins fnl f: r.o: flattered by proximity to eased-down wnr* **18/1**

40-3 **3** *7* **Ice Mayden**[14] 2896 3-9-0 **54**.......... RoystonFfrench 5 47
(Bryan Smart) *trckd ldrs: effrt and chsd (clr) wnr over 1f out to ins fnl f: sn btn* **11/1**

3630 **4** *1* **Lynngale**[32] 2355 3-8-9 **57**..........[1] ShaneGray(5) 3 45
(Kristin Stubbs) *prom: drvn wl over 2f out: no imp fr over 1f out* **10/1**[3]

0-00 **5** *1/2* **Miguela McGuire**[16] 2828 3-8-11 **47**.......... NeilFarley(3) 2 44
(Eric Alston) *s.i.s: hld up: drvn and outpcd over 3f out: rallied over 1f out: n.d* **40/1**

5332 **6** *1/2* **Petergate**[16] 2828 3-9-5 **59**..........(p) BarryMcHugh 6 48
(Brian Rothwell) *prom: rdn over 2f out: sn outpcd* **4/1**[2]

5 **7** *1* **Tom Mann (IRE)**[118] 675 3-9-5 0.......... AndrewMullen 1 46
(David Barron) *hld up in midfield: drvn and outpcd 3f out: no imp fr 2f out* **5/2**[1]

606- **8** *1/2* **Darling Boyz**[245] 7309 3-9-5 **57**.......... PhillipMakin 7 44
(John Quinn) *hld up: rdn along 3f out: no imp fr 2f out* **10/1**[3]

50 **9** *13* **Blue Jacket (USA)**[2] 3302 3-8-9 0.......... EmmaSayer(5) 9 9
(Dianne Sayer) *chsd wnr tl rdn and wknd qckly over 1f out* **80/1**

1m 47.72s (-0.68) **Going Correction** -0.075s/f (Good) 9 Ran SP% **112.6**
Speed ratings (Par 99): **100,96,89,88,88 87,86,86,73**
CSF £50.32 TOTE £5.50: £1.50, £4.50, £2.10; EX 44.90 Trifecta £293.80.
**Owner** Redgate Bloodstock **Bred** Miss Emma Foley **Trained** Carluke, S Lanarks
■ Stewards' Enquiry : Emma Sayer two-day ban: careless riding (Jul 2-3)

**FOCUS**
A steady pace for this modest maiden.

## 3363 SAINTS & SINNERS NEXT WEEK H'CAP (DIV I) 1m 1f 36y
**4:45** (4:45) (Class 6) (0-60,61) 3-Y-O+ £1,940 (£577; £288; £144) Stalls Low

Form RPR

0042 **1** **Raamz (IRE)**[21] 2674 7-9-7 **57**.......... CamHardie(7) 1 65
(Kevin Morgan) *trckd ldrs: effrt and rdn over 2f out: led over 1f out: drvn out fnl f* **3/1**[2]

0531 **2** *1/2* **Frontline Phantom (IRE)**[1] 3334 7-9-11 **61** 6ex.......... PeterSword(7) 8 68
(K R Burke) *t.k.h: pressed ldr: led over 4f out to over 1f out: styd upsides tl one pce last 75yds* **15/8**[1]

0-64 **3** *1 3/4* **Diddy Eric**[21] 2674 4-9-6 **49**..........(b) PJMcDonald 3 52
(Micky Hammond) *hld up in tch: rdn and hdwy to chse ldng pair over 1f out: kpt on fnl f: nt pce to chal* **14/1**

3062 **4** *nk* **Ebony Clarets**[9] 3056 5-8-13 **45**..........(p) ConnorBeasley(3) 2 48
(Linda Perratt) *hld up in tch: effrt and rdn over 2f out: kpt on same pce fnl f* **14/1**

1 **5** *1/2* **Carraroe Flyer (IRE)**[9] 3056 4-9-2 **45**..........(p) PaddyAspell 9 47
(Adrian Paul Keatley, Ire) *in tch: rdn over 3f out: edgd rt and kpt on same pce fr 2f out* **7/2**[3]

60-0 **6** *2* **Benidorm**[103] 869 6-9-2 **45**..........(e[1]) PhillipMakin 7 42
(Richard Guest) *hld up: rdn over 3f out: hdwy over 1f out: nvr rchd ldrs* **66/1**

0050 **7** *6* **Cheeky Wee Red**[21] 2676 6-9-2 **45**..........(t) BarryMcHugh 6 30
(Alistair Whillans) *hld up: drvn and outpcd over 2f out: sn btn* **25/1**

3006 **8** *1 1/4* **Primary Route (IRE)**[9] 3052 4-9-4 **50**.......... JasonHart(3) 4 32
(Keith Dalgleish) *led to over 4f out: rdn 3f out: wknd wl over 1f out* **15/2**

1m 59.94s (0.24) **Going Correction** -0.075s/f (Good) 8 Ran SP% **112.4**
Speed ratings (Par 101): **95,94,93,92,92 90,85,84**
CSF £8.69 CT £62.81 TOTE £4.60: £2.40, £1.30, £1.20; EX 10.80 Trifecta £50.80.
**Owner** Roemex Ltd **Bred** Shadwell Estate Company Limited **Trained** Gazeley, Suffolk

**FOCUS**
A moderate handicap run at a steady pace. It paid to race handy.

## 3364 SAINTS & SINNERS NEXT WEEK H'CAP (DIV II) 1m 1f 36y
**5:20** (5:21) (Class 6) (0-60,57) 3-Y-O+ £1,940 (£577; £288; £144) Stalls Low

Form RPR

6252 **1** **Vosne Romanee**[7] 3105 3-9-3 **57**..........(b) PhillipMakin 5 66
(Keith Dalgleish) *s.s: hld up: nudged along and stdy hdwy to chse ldrs 2f out: shkn up to ld wl ins fnl f: drvn out* **7/2**[3]

0204 **2** *1 3/4* **Gadobout Dancer**[9] 3056 7-8-13 **45**.......... JasonHart(3) 9 51
(Keith Dalgleish) *t.k.h: led: rdn and qcknd over 2f out: hung lft and hdd wl ins fnl f: one pce* **7/1**

3-11 **3** *1 1/2* **Remember Rocky**[21] 2674 5-9-5 **55**..........(p) MeganCarberry(7) 8 58
(Lucy Normile) *prom: drvn along over 2f out: edgd rt wl over 1f out: kpt on ins fnl f* **5/2**[1]

00-5 **4** *1/2* **Spokesperson (USA)**[29] 2426 6-8-13 **45**..........(p) NeilFarley(3) 1 47
(Frederick Watson) *midfield: drvn and outpcd 3f out: rallied appr fnl f: kpt on: nrst fin* **25/1**

0040 **5** *4* **Taxiformissbyron**[29] 2427 4-9-3 **49**..........(b) SamJames(3) 2 43
(Iain Jardine) *trckd ldr: effrt and rdn over 2f out: wknd over 1f out* **11/1**

-445 **6** *2 1/4* **Kolonel Kirkup**[13] 2915 4-9-10 **56**..........(bt) ConnorBeasley(3) 4 45
(Michael Dods) *hld up in tch: drvn and outpcd over 2f out: n.d after* **3/1**[2]

23-0 **7** *3/4* **Maillot Jaune (IRE)**[19] 2729 4-8-13 **49**.......... JackGarritty(7) 3 36
(Patrick Holmes) *trckd ldrs: drvn over 3f out: wknd over 2f out* **33/1**

0-50 **8** *1/2* **Mount Cheiron (USA)**[16] 2828 3-8-10 **55**.......... EmmaSayer(5) 7 40
(Dianne Sayer) *hld up: drvn along wl over 2f out: sn btn* **12/1**

504 **9** *14* **Samoan (IRE)**[12] 2950 5-9-2 **45**..........(b) PatrickMathers 6
(Alan Berry) *towards rr: hdwy on outside 1/2-way: rdn and wknd fr 3f out* **66/1**

1m 58.76s (-0.94) **Going Correction** -0.075s/f (Good)
**WFA** 3 from 4yo+ 11lb 9 Ran SP% **112.6**
Speed ratings (Par 101): **101,99,98,97,94 92,91,91,78**
CSF £26.84 CT £69.93 TOTE £3.80: £1.30, £2.80, £1.20; EX 21.40 Trifecta £105.00.
**Owner** Straightline Construction Ltd **Bred** Mrs L M G Walsh **Trained** Carluke, S Lanarks

**FOCUS**
The pace was sound for this modest handicap.

## 3365 SODEXO APPRENTICE H'CAP (ROUND TWO OF THE HAMILTON PARK APPRENTICE RIDER SERIES) 1m 4f 17y
5:55 (5:55) (Class 6) (0-60,61) 4-Y-0+ £2,045 (£603; £302) Stalls Low

Form RPR
-011 1 **Operateur (IRE)**[7] 3101 6-9-5 **61** 6ex................ KevinStott(3) 5 72+
(Ben Haslam) *trckd ldrs: rdn to ld over 1f out: styd on strly to go clr fnl f* **3/1**[2]
0365 2 3¾ **Isdaal**[21] 2678 7-8-11 **55**................ CamHardie(5) 3 60
(Kevin Morgan) *hld up in tch: hdwy on outside and ev ch over 2f out: chsd wnr ins fnl f: kpt on* **11/2**
0400 3 ½ **Sergeant Pink (IRE)**[23] 2424 8-8-9 **51**................ EmmaSayer(3) 2 55
(Dianne Sayer) *prom: dropped in rr and pushed along after 4f: rallied over 2f out: kpt on fnl f: nrst fin* **16/1**
000/ 4 1 **Strobe**[34] 6315 10-8-4 **46**................(p) ShaneGray(3) 6 49
(Lucy Normile) *mde most tl rdn and hdd over 1f out: no ex and lost two pls ins fnl f* **33/1**
553- 5 2½ **Yourholidayisover (IRE)**[24] 6722 7-8-3 **47**................ JackGarritty(5) 4 46
(Patrick Holmes) *trckd ldrs: stdy hdwy on ins over 3f out: rdn over 2f out: no ex over 1f out* **8/1**
0-00 6 6 **Travis County (IRE)**[18] 2790 5-9-0 **58**................ MeganCarberry(5) 7 47
(Brian Ellison) *dwlt: hld up: rdn over 4f out: no imp fr 2f out* **4/1**[3]
6522 7 4½ **Latin Rebel (IRE)**[7] 3101 7-9-2 **55**................(v[1]) ConnorBeasley 8 37
(Jim Goldie) *t.k.h: w ldr to over 2f out: sn wknd* **9/4**[1]

2m 37.03s (-1.57) **Going Correction** -0.075s/f (Good) **7** Ran SP% **111.1**
Speed ratings (Par 101): **102,99,99,98,96 92,89**
CSF £18.53 CT £212.58 TOTE £3.60: £1.90, £2.50; EX 17.70 Trifecta £71.60.
**Owner** Mrs A Royston,Mrs C Barclay,M T Buckley **Bred** Razza Pallorsi **Trained** Middleham Moor, N Yorks
■ Stewards' Enquiry : Shane Gray three-day ban: careless riding (Jul 2-4)

**FOCUS**
A weak apprentice handicap run at a fair pace.
T/Plt: £203.00 to a £1 stake. Pool: £49343.04 - 177.36 winning tickets T/Qpdt: £30.30 to a £1 stake. Pool: £4203.08 - 102.56 winning tickets RY

# 2895 RIPON (R-H)
Wednesday, June 18

**OFFICIAL GOING: Good (8.2)**
Wind: Virtually nil Weather: Fine and sunny

## 3366 MIDDLEHAM RACING BREAKS APPRENTICE H'CAP 6f
6:50 (6:50) (Class 6) (0-65,60) 3-Y-0+ £3,234 (£962; £481; £240) Stalls High

Form RPR
1311 1 **Fathom Five (IRE)**[16] 2830 10-9-9 **55**................ GeorgiaCox 8 66
(Shaun Harris) *mde all: rdn over 1f out: kpt on* **7/2**[2]
0021 2 1½ **Cadeaux Pearl**[12] 2955 6-9-13 **59**................ SophieKilloran 2 66
(Scott Dixon) *chsd ldr: rdn 2f out: kpt on: edgd lft ins fnl f: wnt 2nd post* **10/3**[1]
4622 3 hd **Captain Scooby**[7] 3104 8-9-5 **51**................(v) MelissaThompson 3 57
(Richard Guest) *midfield: pushed along 1/2-way: hdwy to chse wnr over 1f out: one pce fnl f: lost 2nd post* **4/1**[3]
6646 4 2½ **Cape Of Hope (IRE)**[19] 2726 4-10-0 **60**................ JamesMerrett 5 58
(David Nicholls) *chsd ldr: rdn 1/2-way: plugged on* **4/1**[3]
0-00 5 5 **Lazy Sioux**[16] 2828 3-8-10 **49**................ PaulaMuir 1 29
(Philip Kirby) *slowly away: hld up: hdwy over 2f out: wknd fnl f* **17/2**
-405 6 2½ **Lady Montenegro**[50] 1855 3-8-9 **48**................ TomasHarrigan 7 20
(Ann Duffield) *hld up: nvr threatened* **14/1**
0635 7 5 **Upper Lambourn (IRE)**[14] 2907 6-8-13 **45**...(t) KimberleyVanderVegt 11 3
(Christopher Kellett) *slowly away: hld up in rr: a bhd* **25/1**
56-0 8 ½ **Harpers Ruby**[76] 1270 4-8-13 **45**................ JackBudge 6 1
(Neville Bycroft) *in tch: rdn over 2f out: sn wknd* **25/1**
40 9 ½ **Exkaliber**[97] 937 5-8-13 **45**................(t) NicolaGrundy 4
(Richard Ford) *hld up: edgd rt over 2f out: nvr threatened* **33/1**
5045 10 8 **Lady Dancer (IRE)**[19] 2726 3-8-6 **45**................(b) KieranSchofield 9
(George Moore) *chsd ldr: wknd over 2f out* **40/1**

1m 12.84s (-0.16) **Going Correction** -0.125s/f (Firm)
**WFA** 3 from 4yo+ 7lb **10** Ran SP% **115.6**
Speed ratings (Par 101): **96,94,93,90,83 80,73,73,72,61**
CSF £14.80 CT £48.98 TOTE £4.00: £1.30, £2.10, £3.00; EX 16.50 Trifecta £31.10.
**Owner** Nottinghamshire Racing **Bred** Eamonn Connolly **Trained** Carburton, Notts

**FOCUS**
Having been dry since the weekend, 2mm of irrigation had been applied to the whole track overnight and the ground was officially given as good. After winning the second race, jockey Paul Mulrennan called it "quick". All rails were placed at their innermost positions. A handicap for apprentices who had yet to ride a winner and it looks to be weak form.

## 3367 BONDGATE MAIDEN AUCTION STKS 5f
7:20 (7:21) (Class 5) 2-Y-0 £3,234 (£962; £481; £240) Stalls High

Form RPR
4 1 **Olivia Fallow (IRE)**[43] 2051 2-9-0 0................ PaulMulrennan 1 67+
(Paul Midgley) *wnt rt s: sn swtchd lft: trckd ldng pair: rdn over 1f out: led ins fnl f: edgd rt: kpt on* **13/8**[1]
526 2 1 **Stanghow**[32] 2328 2-9-5 0................ DavidAllan 5 68
(Mel Brittain) *led narrowly: rdn and edgd rt over 1f out: hdd ins fnl f: one pce* **7/2**[2]
3 nk **Arthur MartinLeake (IRE)** 2-9-5 0................ BenCurtis 4 67+
(K R Burke) *s.i.s: hld up: sn pushed along: rdn and hdwy appr fnl f: kpt on* **13/8**[1]
004 4 7 **On Appro**[30] 2395 2-8-7 0................ RachelRichardson(7) 2 37
(Tim Easterby) *chsd ldng pair: wknd over 1f out* **20/1**
5 1¼ **Jebediah Shine** 2-8-11 0................ JulieBurke(3) 3 32
(David O'Meara) *w ldr: wknd over 1f out* **14/1**[3]

1m 0.24s (0.24) **Going Correction** -0.125s/f (Firm) **5** Ran SP% **109.8**
Speed ratings (Par 93): **93,91,90,79,77**
CSF £7.69 TOTE £2.70: £2.00, £1.90; EX 9.50 Trifecta £12.90.
**Owner** A Bell **Bred** Mark Salmon **Trained** Westow, N Yorks

**FOCUS**
The three that had experience did not look to set an insurmountable standard in this juvenile maiden, but the newcomers were unable to capitalise and it looks only modest form.

## 3368 RIPON-RACES.CO.UK H'CAP 1m 1f 170y
7:50 (7:50) (Class 4) (0-85,80) 4-Y-0+ £5,175 (£1,540; £769; £384) Stalls Low

Form RPR
-513 1 **Maybeme**[15] 2868 8-8-12 **71**................(p) AndrewElliott 5 80
(Neville Bycroft) *dwlt: hld up in rr: rdn 3f out: no imp initially and stl last over 1f out: r.o: led towards fin* **3/1**[3]
-000 2 nk **Muffin McLeay (IRE)**[11] 2981 6-9-7 **80**................ GrahamGibbons 2 88
(David Barron) *trckd ldng pair: hdwy and upsides fr over 2f out: drvn to ld over appr fnl f: one pce fnl 110yds: hdd towards fin* **13/2**
36 3 1½ **Shouranour (IRE)**[13] 2912 4-9-4 **77**................(p) DavidNolan 3 82
(David O'Meara) *led narrowly: rdn and jnd over 2f out: wandered and hdd appr fnl f: no ex fnl 110yds* **11/4**[2]
6356 4 1½ **Ardmay (IRE)**[7] 3094 5-9-5 **78**................(b) AmyRyan 1 80
(Kevin Ryan) *racd keenly: trckd ldng pair: rdn over 2f out: sn one pce* **9/2**
0-04 5 10 **Dolphin Rock**[18] 2762 7-9-2 **75**................ RobertWinston 4 56
(Brian Ellison) *w ldr: rdn 4f out: outpcd and dropped to 4th over 2f out: btn over 1f out: eased ins fnl f* **5/2**[1]

2m 1.98s (-3.42) **Going Correction** -0.125s/f (Firm) **5** Ran SP% **111.8**
Speed ratings (Par 105): **108,107,106,105,97**
CSF £21.29 TOTE £3.60: £2.00, £1.50; EX 27.10 Trifecta £53.70.
**Owner** Mrs J Dickinson **Bred** Harts Farm And Stud **Trained** Norton, N Yorks

**FOCUS**
A fair race and all five could be given a chance. A good pace contributed to an exciting finish, with the winner coming from last to first.

## 3369 WELLS MEMORIAL CHALLENGE TROPHY H'CAP (BOBIS RACE) 6f
8:20 (8:21) (Class 3) (0-95,95) 3-Y-0 £7,561 (£2,263; £1,131; £566; £282) Stalls High

Form RPR
2313 1 **Kickboxer (IRE)**[4] 3253 3-8-12 **89**................ CharlesBishop(3) 3 98
(Mick Channon) *prom on outer: led 2f out: sn rdn clr: edgd rt: kpt on* **1/1**[1]
-055 2 2¼ **No Leaf Clover (IRE)**[18] 2767 3-9-7 **95**................ RobertWinston 5 97
(Ollie Pears) *trckd ldrs: pushed along over 2f out: briefly n.m.r over 1f out: rdn to go 2nd jst ins fnl f: one pce and no imp on wnr* **5/1**[3]
20-0 3 nk **Makin The Rules (IRE)**[35] 2257 3-8-1 **78** oh1 ow2................ IanBrennan(3) 1 79
(John Quinn) *led narrowly: hdd 2f out: sn no ch w wnr: lost 2nd jst ins fnl f: one pce* **12/1**
-461 4 2¼ **The Hooded Claw (IRE)**[41] 2090 3-8-13 **87**................ DavidAllan 2 81
(Tim Easterby) *w ldr: rdn over 2f out: wknd fnl f* **10/3**[2]
1-06 5 1 **Roachdale House (IRE)**[46] 1937 3-8-12 **89**................ GeorgeChaloner(3) 4 79
(Richard Fahey) *trckd ldrs: rdn over 2f out: wknd fnl f* **7/1**

1m 11.43s (-1.57) **Going Correction** -0.125s/f (Firm) **5** Ran SP% **109.9**
Speed ratings (Par 103): **105,102,101,98,97**
CSF £6.38 TOTE £1.80: £1.90, £1.10; EX 7.30 Trifecta £25.40.
**Owner** Living Legend Racing Partnership 1 **Bred** Rathasker Stud **Trained** West Ilsley, Berks

**FOCUS**
Despite the small field, this had the look of a decent sprint handicap.

## 3370 SIS LIVE MAIDEN STKS 6f
8:50 (8:50) (Class 5) 3-Y-0 £3,234 (£962; £481; £240) Stalls High

Form RPR
-262 1 **Dutch Breeze**[18] 2789 3-9-5 78................ DavidAllan 5 84
(Tim Easterby) *mde all: pushed clr fr over 1f out: edgd rt ins fnl f* **8/15**[1]
43 2 3¼ **Piccadilly Jim (IRE)**[18] 2789 3-9-2 0................ GeorgeChaloner(3) 3 73
(Richard Fahey) *chsd ldng pair: rdn 2f out: kpt on to go 2nd ins fnl f: no ch w wnr* **18/1**
23 3 4 **Eternitys Gate**[16] 2846 3-9-5 0................ RobertHavlin 2 60
(Peter Chapple-Hyam) *wnt rt s: sn w ldr: rdn 2f out: wknd ins fnl f* **11/4**[2]
- 4 4½ **Bon Chance** 3-9-5 0................ BarryMcHugh 6 45
(Michael Easterby) *s.i.s: hld up: pushed along 1/2-way: nvr threatened* **40/1**
5 1¾ **It's A Yes From Me** 3-9-5 0................ ShaneKelly 4 40
(James Fanshawe) *sn outpcd towards rr: a bhd* **8/1**[3]

1m 11.51s (-1.49) **Going Correction** -0.125s/f (Firm) **5** Ran SP% **110.7**
Speed ratings (Par 99): **104,99,94,88,86**
CSF £11.98 TOTE £1.40: £1.10, £6.60; EX 10.70 Trifecta £11.70.
**Owner** Mr And Mrs J D Cotton **Bred** Wilsdon & Habton **Trained** Great Habton, N Yorks

**FOCUS**
An uncompetitive maiden, but the time compared favourably to the preceding Class 3 handicap.

## 3371 IT'S LADIES DAY TOMORROW H'CAP 1m 4f 10y
9:20 (9:21) (Class 5) (0-75,75) 4-Y-0+ £3,234 (£962; £481; £240) Stalls Low

Form RPR
1462 1 **Pertuis (IRE)**[15] 2872 8-8-11 **70**................(p) JoeyHaynes(5) 8 75+
(Micky Hammond) *t.k.h in midfield: hdwy 3f out: rdn to ld wl over 1f out: kpt on* **3/1**[1]
406- 2 ½ **Bright Applause**[57] 6631 6-9-1 **69**................ BarryMcHugh 1 73
(Tracy Waggott) *trckd ldr on inner: pushed along and n.m.r 2f out: swtchd lft over 1f out: sn rdn: kpt on: wnt 2nd towards fin* **15/2**
-003 3 shd **Cloud Monkey (IRE)**[19] 2728 4-9-2 **70**................ PhillipMakin 7 74
(Martin Todhunter) *hld up: hdwy over 2f out: rdn over 1f out: kpt on* **7/1**[3]
4005 4 ¾ **Aryal**[11] 3004 4-9-7 **75**................(b) AdrianNicholls 6 78
(Mark Johnston) *led at stdy pce: rdn and edgd lft 2f out: sn hdd: remained 2nd tl no ex and lost 2 pls towards fin* **9/1**
366- 5 7 **Bossa Nova Baby (IRE)**[280] 6313 4-9-0 **68**................ RobertHavlin 4 59
(Peter Chapple-Hyam) *midfield on inner: rdn over 2f out: wknd over 1f out* **16/1**
-155 6 16 **Emulating (IRE)**[29] 2445 4-9-4 **72**................ ShaneKelly 5 38+
(James Fanshawe) *trckd ldr: pushed along whn bdly hmpd and stmbld 2f out: eased* **7/2**[2]

2m 43.35s (6.65) **Going Correction** -0.125s/f (Firm) **6** Ran SP% **87.4**
Speed ratings (Par 103): **72,71,71,71,66 55**
CSF £14.49 CT £53.62 TOTE £3.30: £1.90, £2.40; EX 10.50 Trifecta £110.50.
**Owner** M H O G **Bred** Killeen Castle Stud **Trained** Middleham Moor, N Yorks
■ Rule 4 of 25p in the pound applies to all bets; Withdrawn: Good Speech

**FOCUS**
A modest handicap which was further weakened by a late withdrawal of the gambled-on Good Speech. They went no pace before it lifted for the final 3f.
T/Plt: £17.80 to a £1 stake. Pool: £58968.38 - 2412.55 winning tickets T/Qpdt: £4.60 to a £1 stake. Pool: £5991.90 - 961.35 winning tickets AS

## 2976 COMPIEGNE (L-H)

Wednesday, June 18

**OFFICIAL GOING: Turf: good to soft**

### 3372a PRIX DE BLERANCOURT (CLAIMER) (3YO) (TURF) 1m

1:35 (12:00) 3-Y-O £9,583 (£3,833; £2,875; £1,916; £958)

RPR

1 **Reding (FR)**[15] 3-8-10 0.......................................... JeremieCatineau(8) 8 89
(C Laffon-Parias, France) **33/10**[1]

2 ½ **Zashka (FR)**[12] 2978 3-8-8 0.......................................... GregoryBenoist 6 78
(J-P Gallorini, France) **123/10**

3 nk **Winitall**[55] 3-8-11 0..........................................(p) TheoBachelot 9 80
(S Cerulis, France) **49/10**[2]

4 2½ **Star Dolois (FR)**[15] 3-8-11 0..........................................(b[1]) RonanThomas 5 74
(A Bonin, France) **101/10**

5 hd **Victordina (FR)**[51] 3-9-1 0.......................................... UmbertoRispoli 4 78
(R Rohne, Germany) **161/10**

6 2 **Pink Chalice**[38] 3-8-11 0..........................................(p) CristianDemuro 14 69
(F Doumen, France) **225/10**

7 1½ **Isyalia (FR)**[21] 3-8-3 0.......................................... MlleAmelieFoulon(5) 10 63
(A Fabre, France) **91/10**

8 2½ **Suhali (FR)**[239] 3-8-8 0.......................................... EddyHardouin 15 57
(J Heloury, France) **78/1**

9 snk **Parfum De Roi (FR)**[58] 1620 3-9-1 0.......................................... MickaelBarzalona 17 64
(Y-M Porzier, France) **224/10**

10 nk **Visioner (FR)**[43] 3-9-6 0.......................................... JohanVictoire 7 68
(C Boutin, France) **113/10**

11 3 **Live Grace (IRE)**[13] 3-8-11 0.......................................... StephaneLaurent 11 52
(Mlle B Renk, France) **94/1**

12 ¾ **Conquete (FR)**[215] 3-8-3 0.......................................... SoufyaneMoulin(5) 12 47
(P Bary, France) **102/10**

13 5 **Twombly (SPA)**[154] 193 3-9-2 0.......................................... AnthonyCrastus 16 44
(C Boutin, France) **159/10**

14 5 **Lizalia (FR)**[47] 1920 3-8-8 0..........................................(b) AurelienLemaitre 13 24
(Jo Hughes) *chsd ldng gp on outer: pushed along and lost pl over 2f out: bhd whn eased fnl f* **115/1**

15 10 **Crepusculedesdieux (FR)**[55] 3-9-4 0..........................................(b) StephanePasquier 2 11
(M Delcher Sanchez, France) **71/10**[3]

1m 44.0s (104.00) **15** Ran SP% **119.5**
WIN (incl. 1 euro stake): 4.30. PLACES: 1.80, 2.80, 1.90. DF: 35.30. SF: 47.50.
**Owner** Sarl Darpat France **Bred** Sarl Darpat France **Trained** Chantilly, France

### 3373a PRIX DE RESSONS (CLAIMER) (4YO+) (TURF) 1m

2:05 (12:00) 4-Y-0+ £7,916 (£3,166; £2,375; £1,583; £791)

RPR

1 **Cabidochop (FR)**[360] 5-9-1 0.......................................... AntoineHamelin 1 82
(A De Watrigant, France) **8/1**

2 nse **Smooth Operator (GER)**[38] 8-8-11 0..........................................(p) UmbertoRispoli 7 78
(Mario Hofer, Germany) **77/10**[3]

3 ¾ **Pont Marie (FR)**[36] 4-9-4 0..........................................(p) GregoryBenoist 2 83
(F Chappet, France) **79/10**

4 1¼ **Montalban (FR)**[41] 7-9-4 0..........................................(b) ThomasMessina 8 80
(D De Waele, France) **30/1**

5 hd **Lower East Side**[302] 4-9-1 0.......................................... TheoBachelot 11 77
(S Wattel, France) **119/10**

6 ½ **Nova Valorem (IRE)**[63] 6-9-5 0.......................................... StephanePasquier 15 80
(C Boutin, France) **33/10**[1]

7 ¾ **Polarix**[90] 8-9-1 0.......................................... FabriceVeron 17 74
(H-A Pantall, France) **6/1**[2]

8 1½ **Mirandola (FR)**[36] 5-8-3 0.......................................... MllePaulineDominois(5) 18 64
(Yves de Nicolay, France) **33/1**

9 shd **Very Bad Trip (FR)**[18] 5-9-3 0.......................................... ThibaultSpeicher(5) 10 77
(T Castanheira, France) **102/10**

10 ¾ **Cool Star (FR)**[18] 9-8-11 0..........................................(b) RonanThomas 13 65
(A Bonin, France) **146/10**

11 2 **Esprit Des Temps (GER)**[182] 7-8-11 0.......................................... EddyHardouin 12 60
(W Mongil, Germany) **269/10**

12 snk **Forester (IRE)**[333] 4548 4-9-4 0..........................................(p) AurelienLemaitre 9 67
(Mlle P Peelman, Belgium) **68/1**

13 2 **Unfuwan (IRE)**[696] 4-9-1 0.......................................... PierantonioConvertino 5 59
(A De Mieulle, France) **139/1**

14 hd **Akton City (FR)**[18] 7-9-8 0.......................................... ThierryThulliez 16 66
(J-P Delaporte, France) **47/1**

15 snk **Le Falgoux (FR)**[349] 7-8-8 0.......................................... SoufyaneMoulin(3) 4 54
(C Boutin, France) **42/1**

16 nk **Hecton Lad (USA)**[865] 423 7-9-1 0..........................................(b) MarcSwinnens 3 58
(Mme L De Blende, Belgium) **118/1**

17 1¼ **Royal Talisman**[1062] 6-9-4 0.......................................... MickaelBarzalona 14 58
(Jo Hughes) *w ldrs on outer: disputing 2nd 1/2-way: rdn appr 2f out and nt qckn: grad lft bhd by ldrs: wknd fnl f* **14/1**

18 1¼ **Taweel (FR)** 4-8-11 0.......................................... StephaneLaurent 6 48
(Mlle B Renk, France) **124/1**

1m 36.23s (96.23) **18** Ran SP% **119.1**
WIN (incl. 1 euro stake): 9.00. PLACES: 2.70, 3.00, 2.70. DF: 32.80. SF: 96.40.
**Owner** Alain Chopard **Bred** A Chopard **Trained** France

## 3352 ASCOT (R-H)

Thursday, June 19

**OFFICIAL GOING: Good to firm (good in places on round course)**

Wind: Light, across Weather: Fine

### 3374 NORFOLK STKS (GROUP 2) 5f

2:30 (2:31) (Class 1) 2-Y-O

£45,368 (£17,200; £8,608; £4,288; £2,152; £1,080) **Stalls** Centre

Form RPR

211 1 **Baitha Alga (IRE)**[12] 2987 2-9-1 0.......................................... FrankieDettori 7 106
(Richard Hannon) *lw: in tch: qcknd to ld over 1f out: sn rdn and asserted: r.o wl: pushed out whn wl in command towards fin* **8/1**[3]

120 2 1½ **Mind Of Madness (IRE)**[2] 3322 2-9-1 0.......................................... RyanMoore 9 101
(David Brown) *hld up: pushed along 2f out: swtchd lft and hdwy over 1f out: r.o to take 2nd fnl 110yds: nt rch wnr* **14/1**

1 3 2¼ **Ahlan Emarati (IRE)**[61] 1571 2-9-1 0.......................................... JamieSpencer 4 95
(Peter Chapple-Hyam) *str: in rr: pushed along over 2f out: hdwy for press over 1f out: proging whn checked ins fnl f: rn to take 3rd ins fnl 50yds: gng on at fin but nt pce to trble front two* **25/1**

1 4 ¾ **Snap Shots (IRE)**[20] 2731 2-9-1 0.......................................... RichardKingscote 5 90
(Tom Dascombe) *leggy: displayed plenty of spd and prom: rdn 2f out: stl ev ch 1f out: no ex fnl 100yds* **16/1**

5 2 **The Great War (USA)**[45] 2036 2-9-1 0..........................................(t) JosephO'Brien 1 83
(A P O'Brien, Ire) *str: in tch: shkn up 2f out: effrt to chal over 1f out: wandered after and nt qckn: wknd fnl 100yds* **5/6**[1]

11 6 1¼ **Mukhmal (IRE)**[43] 2071 2-9-1 0.......................................... PaulHanagan 8 78+
(Mark Johnston) *str: lw: racd w plenty of zest: led: rdn and hdd over 1f out: wknd ins fnl f* **4/1**[2]

220 7 ½ **Fine Prince (IRE)**[12] 2987 2-9-1 0.......................................... TomQueally 2 76
(Robert Mills) *hld up towards rr: pushed along over 2f out: rdn whn hung rt over 1f out: no imp* **50/1**

515 8 1¼ **Mignolino (IRE)**[12] 3001 2-9-1 0..........................................(b[1]) GrahamGibbons 6 72+
(David Barron) *displayed plenty of spd and prom: rdn whn chalng 2f out: wknd over 1f out* **50/1**

9 6 **To Be Determined (USA)**[41] 2-8-12 0..........................................(bt) VictorEspinoza 3 47+
(Wesley A Ward, U.S.A) *lengthy: upset at s: dwlt: in rr: pushed along and outpcd over 2f out: eased whn bhd and wl btn fnl f* **10/1**

59.81s (-0.69) **Going Correction** -0.15s/f (Firm) **9** Ran SP% **115.1**
Speed ratings (Par 105): **99,96,93,91,88 86,85,83,74**
CSF £107.99 CT £2643.45 TOTE £7.20: £1.80, £2.40, £3.50; EX 92.20 Trifecta £694.00.
**Owner** Al Shaqab Racing **Bred** Ms Theresa Killen **Trained** East Everleigh, Wilts

**FOCUS**

After 4mm of water had been applied overnight, the ground remained good to firm, good in places on the Round course. The consensus amongst the jockeys was that it was good to firm, though Jamie Spencer said "It's lovely ground, but you can tell it's been watered as it's a bit loose on top." Rail on Round course positioned 3yds out from 1m1f to home straight and Old Mile increased by 6yds, 1m2f by 9yds and 1m4f+ by 12yds. Six of the last eight winners of this Group 2 contest had won their only previous starts, but this year those with more experience came to the fore, with the front pair both having their fourth outings.

### 3375 TERCENTENARY STKS (GROUP 3) 1m 2f

3:05 (3:05) (Class 1) 3-Y-O

£42,532 (£16,125; £8,070; £4,020; £2,017; £1,012) **Stalls** Low

Form RPR

2-11 1 **Cannock Chase (USA)**[33] 2337 3-9-0 97.......................................... RyanMoore 7 111+
(Sir Michael Stoute) *athletic: lw: hld up in tch in last trio: rdn and hdwy on outer to ld over 1f out: edgd rt to inner rail ins fnl f: r.o wl: rdn out* **7/4**[1]

-221 2 1½ **Mutakayyef**[28] 2497 3-9-0 107.......................................... PaulHanagan 1 108
(William Haggas) *lw: t.k.h: chsd ldrs: rdn ent fnl 2f out: 3rd and drvn over 1f out: kpt on: lft 2nd wl ins fnl f: no imp* **7/1**

2-34 3 nk **Postponed (IRE)**[47] 1953 3-9-0 104.......................................... AndreaAtzeni 3 107+
(Luca Cumani) *lw: hld up in tch in last pair: hdwy on inner to trck ldrs and nt clr run 1f out: swtchd lft ins fnl f: styd on wl towards fin: wnt 3rd cl home* **8/1**

-152 4 nk **Cloudscape (IRE)**[20] 2748 3-9-0 100..........................................(t) WilliamBuick 5 109+
(John Gosden) *lw: t.k.h: hld up wl in tch in midfield: nt clr run over 2f out: swtchd rt over 1f out: stl nt clr run and sn swtchd lft sharply: styd on wl fnl 100yds: wnt 4th last stride* **8/1**

2414 5 shd **Barley Mow (IRE)**[27] 2502 3-9-0 108.......................................... RichardHughes 4 108+
(Richard Hannon) *chsd ldr tl led over 8f out: rdn ent fnl 2f: drvn and hdd over 1f out: keeping on but hld by wnr whn hmpd and snatched up wl ins fnl f: nt rcvr and lost 3 pls after* **13/2**[3]

1-1 6 1½ **Spark Plug (IRE)**[33] 2330 3-9-0 91.......................................... JimmyFortune 9 104
(Brian Meehan) *w'like: stdd and dropped in bhd after s: hld up in rr: rdn and effrt 2f out: kpt on u.p fnl f: nvr able to chal* **20/1**

0-53 7 nse **Somewhat (USA)**[41] 2114 3-9-0 102.......................................... JoeFanning 8 104
(Mark Johnston) *led tl over 8f out: chsd ldr after: rdn and ev ch 2f out: 5th and outpcd 1f out: plugged on same pce after* **12/1**

20 8 30 **Obliterator (IRE)**[26] 2571 3-9-0 109..........................................(t) JamieSpencer 6 44
(G M Lyons, Ire) *bustled along leaving stalls: chsd ldng trio: pushed along over 4f out: rdn 3f out: struggling whn hmpd over 1f out: sn wl btn and virtually p.u ins fnl f: t.o* **9/2**[2]

2m 5.31s (-2.09) **Going Correction** -0.025s/f (Good) **8** Ran SP% **115.1**
Speed ratings (Par 109): **107,105,105,105,105 104,104,80**
CSF £14.72 CT £77.89 TOTE £2.60: £1.10, £2.20, £2.10; EX 12.90 Trifecta £85.90.
**Owner** Saeed Suhail **Bred** Hascombe Stud **Trained** Newmarket, Suffolk

■ Stewards' Enquiry : William Buick one-day ban: careless riding (Jul 3)
Ryan Moore two-day ban: careless riding (Jul 3-4)

**FOCUS**

Perhaps not the deepest edition of the race and it was run at just an ordinary gallop, with there being a couple who looked a little unfortunate, at least not to push the winner harder anyway. Most of these had form that tied in with one another.

### 3376 RIBBLESDALE STKS (GROUP 2) (FILLIES) 1m 4f

3:45 (3:46) (Class 1) 3-Y-O

£98,335 (£37,281; £18,657; £9,294; £4,664; £2,340) **Stalls** Low

Form RPR

0-10 1 **Bracelet (IRE)**[46] 1976 3-9-0 105..........................................[1] JosephO'Brien 3 107
(A P O'Brien, Ire) *midfield: rdn over 2f out: hdwy under 2f out: led jst over 1f out: drvn out ins fnl f: styd on gamley: a in control towards fin* **10/1**

0-51 2 ½ **Lustrous**[34] 2316 3-9-0 100.......................................... RichardHughes 8 106
(Richard Hannon) *hld up in rr: rdn over 2f out: swtchd lft and hdwy wl over 1f out: styd on ins fnl f: tk 2nd nr fin: nvr gng to get there* **16/1**

-312 3 hd **Criteria (IRE)**[40] 2152 3-9-0 93.......................................... JamesDoyle 7 105
(John Gosden) *swtg: in tch: effrt on outer to chse ldrs over 3f out: chalng over 1f out: styd on and stl ev ch ins fnl f: hld fnl 50yds* **20/1**

12 4 1 **Vazira (FR)**[25] 2586 3-9-0 109.......................................... ChristopheSoumillon 10 104+
(A De Royer-Dupre, France) *athletic: hld up in rr: rdn and nt pick-up over 2f out: hdwy u.p over 1f out: styd on ins fnl f: nvr able to rch ldrs* **9/4**[1]

1 5 nk **Final Score (IRE)**[25] 2590 3-9-3 103.......................................... FabioBranca 9 106
(Stefano Botti, Italy) *lengthy: tall: midfield: rdn over 2f out: sn nt qckn and hung rt: styd on fnl f: nvr able to get to ldrs* **16/1**

31 6 1¼ **Wonderstruck (IRE)**[20] 2746 3-9-0 87.......................................... FrankieDettori 4 101
(William Haggas) *str: lw: trckd ldrs: rdn 3f out: tried to chal over 1f out: nt qckn: kpt on same pce fnl 100yds* **7/1**



The Form Book, Raceform Ltd, Newbury, RG14 5SJ

-313 **7** *1 ½* **Talmada (USA)**[33] 2347 3-9-0 92 ........ AndreaAtzeni 2 99
(Roger Varian) *lw: trckd ldr: chal 3f out: rdn to ld 2f out: hdd jst over 1f out: no ex fnl 100yds* **16/1**

424 **8** *1 ½* **Nancy From Nairobi**[36] 2255 3-9-0 90 ........ WilliamTwiston-Davies 12 97
(Mick Channon) *lw: hld up: rdn over 2f out: edgd rt ins fnl f: kpt on: nvr able to trble ldrs* **33/1**

-144 **9** *1 ½* **Emaratiya Ana (IRE)**[28] 2484 3-9-0 90 ........ TomQueally 6 94
(Roger Varian) *hld up in midfield: rdn over 2f out: nvr able to rch ldrs: no imp over 1f out: one pce after* **66/1**

5 **10** *4* **Terrific (IRE)**[43] 2072 3-9-0 97 ........ (b) RyanMoore 5 88
(A P O'Brien, Ire) *lw: bustled along to ld: rdn over 2f out: sn hdd: wknd fnl f* **20/1**

13 **11** *6* **Bright Approach (IRE)**[43] 2072 3-9-0 97 ........ WilliamBuick 1 78
(John Gosden) *lw: racd keenly: trckd ldrs: pushed along over 3f out: outpcd over 2f out: wknd over 1f out* **5/1**[3]

-144 **P** **Inchila**[13] 2960 3-9-0 109 ........ JamieSpencer 11
(Peter Chapple-Hyam) *hld up: effrt into midfield whn wnt wrong over 2f out: sn p.u* **7/2**[2]

2m 30.92s (-1.58) **Going Correction** -0.025s/f (Good) **12** Ran SP% **122.9**
Speed ratings (Par 108): **104,103,103,102,102 101,100,99,98,96 92,**
CSF £156.75 CT £3141.49 TOTE £10.30: £2.60, £6.10, £7.30; EX 215.80 Trifecta £2335.70.
**Owner** Michael Tabor & Derrick Smith & Mrs John Magnier **Bred** Roncon & Chelston **Trained** Cashel, Co Tipperary

**FOCUS**
An interesting Ribblesdale in which they seemed to go an even gallop thanks to the pacemaker Terrific, who held on to the advantage until passing the 2f pole. However, the winning time suggested that they didn't go mad. The race was marred by the injury sustained by the Oaks fourth Inchila.

## 3377 GOLD CUP (BRITISH CHAMPIONS SERIES) (GROUP 1) 2m 4f
**4:25** (4:29) (Class 1) 4-Y-0+
**£212,662** (£80,625; £40,350; £20,100; £10,087; £5,062) **Stalls** Low

Form RPR

10-1 **1** **Leading Light (IRE)**[32] 2370 4-9-0 118 ........ (p) JosephO'Brien 14 118+
(A P O'Brien, Ire) *lw: chsd ldrs: drvn and effrt 3f out: chal and edgd rt u.p over 1f out: led 1f out: sn wnt lft and then bk rt u.p ins fnl f: pushed along and a holding rivals fnl 100yds* **10/11**[1]

23-4 **2** *shd* **Missunited (IRE)**[13] 2973 7-8-13 107 ........ JimCrowley 10 115
(Michael Winters, Ire) *led: rdn and fnd ex 3f out: hrd pressed and drvn over 1f out: hdd 1f out: 3rd and ev ch ins fnl f: kpt on gamely but a jst hld* **40/1**

0-11 **3** *4 ½* **Brown Panther**[21] 2704 6-9-2 115 ........ RichardKingscote 4 113
(Tom Dascombe) *lw: t.k.h early: chsd ldr tl 14f out: wnt 2nd again over 3f out: rdn over 2f out: ev ch whn bmpd jst over 1f out: 4th and btn jst ins fnl f: wknd fnl 100yds* **5/1**[2]

-506 **4** *nk* **Simenon (IRE)**[50] 1869 7-9-2 111 ........ FrankieDettori 15 113
(W P Mullins, Ire) *stdd and dropped in bhd after s: hld up in rr: hdwy on outer 6f out: effrt u.p over 2f out: styd on past btn horses over 1f out: kpt on but no threat to ldrs fnl f* **14/1**

6-30 **5** *3 ¾* **Oriental Fox (GER)**[21] 2704 6-9-2 105 ........ JoeFanning 5 108
(Mark Johnston) *hld up in tch in midfield: travelling wl and nt clr run 4f out: rdn and hdwy over 2f out: 6th and no prog over 1f out: wknd fnl f* **50/1**

10-1 **6** *3 ¼* **Altano (GER)**[39] 2229 8-9-2 117 ........ (t) EPedroza 1 105
(A Wohler, Germany) *dwlt: sn rcvrd to chse ldng trio: rdn over 5f out: nt clr run and shuffled bk 3f out: tried to rally u.p 2f out: no prog and plugged on same pce after* **7/1**[3]

0-65 **7** *nk* **Havana Beat (IRE)**[19] 2779 4-9-0 102 ........ DavidProbert 11 105
(Andrew Balding) *stdd s: hld up in last quartet: swtchd lft and effrt 3f out: drvn and no hdwy whn edgd rt 2f out: plugged on same pce and wl hld after* **66/1**

-363 **8** *shd* **Shwaiman (IRE)**[19] 2785 4-9-0 104 ........ TomQueally 3 104
(James Fanshawe) *swtg: hld up in last quartet: rdn and effrt over 2f out: stl plenty to do whn nt clr run and hmpd wl over 1f out: plugged on same pce after* **50/1**

20-6 **9** *3 ¼* **Ahzeemah (IRE)**[34] 2315 5-9-2 111 ........ (p) KierenFallon 7 105
(Saeed bin Suroor) *hld up in tch in midfield: rdn and hdwy over 2f out: 5th and no hdwy u.p over 1f out: sn btn: wl hld and heavily eased ins fnl furlonfg* **25/1**

-006 **10** *13* **Saddler's Rock (IRE)**[32] 2370 6-9-2 108 ........ (b[1]) WilliamBuick 9 87
(John M Oxx, Ire) *lw: t.k.h early: chsd ldrs early: steadily dropped bk and in midfield: 12f out: rdn over 2f out: sn btn: bhd and eased ins fnl f* **33/1**

51-2 **11** *18* **Royal Diamond (IRE)**[32] 2370 8-9-2 114 ........ RichardHughes 13 67
(J P Murtagh, Ire) *stdd s: t.k.h: hld up but nt settle towards rr: hdwy to chse ldr 14f out tl over 3f out: sn rdn and wknd 3f out: wl bhd and eased fnl f: t.o* **12/1**

4051 **12** *12* **Ralston Road (IRE)**[19] 2785 4-9-0 107 ........ RonanWhelan 2 54
(John Patrick Shanahan, Ire) *hld up in tch in midfield: rdn 5f out: lost pl over 3f out: lost tch 2f out: eased fnl f: t.o: fin lame* **66/1**

110- **D** *nk* **Estimate (IRE)**[243] 7363 5-8-13 112 ........ RyanMoore 6 115
(Sir Michael Stoute) *hld up wl in tch in midfield: effrt to chse ldrs and swtchd rt over 2f out: drvn and ev ch over 1f out: battled on gamely u.p: a jst hld fnl 100yds* **8/1**

4m 21.09s (-3.71) **Going Correction** -0.025s/f (Good)
**WFA** 4 from 5yo+ 2lb **13** Ran SP% **123.2**
Speed ratings (Par 117): **106,105,104,103,102 101,101,100,99,94 87,82,105**
CSF £8.84 CT £191.69 TOTE £2.10: £1.50, £1.80, £7.80; EX 12.20 Trifecta £271.80.
**Owner** Derrick Smith & Mrs John Magnier & Michael Tabor **Bred** Lynch-Bages Ltd **Trained** Cashel, Co Tipperary
■ Stewards' Enquiry : Jim Crowley four-day ban: used whip above permitted level (Jul 3,4,6,7)
Joseph O'Brien seven-day ban: used whip above permitted level (Jul 3-9)

**FOCUS**
The premier staying event of the season. They went a steady pace early, but got racing from a fair way out and it resulted in a pulsating three-way finish. Rock-solid staying form.

## 3378 BRITANNIA STKS (HERITAGE H'CAP) (BOBIS RACE) (STRAIGHT COURSE) 1m (S)
**5:00** (5:09) (Class 2) (0-105,104) 3-Y-O
**£74,700** (£22,368; £11,184; £5,592; £2,796; £1,404) **Stalls** Centre

Form RPR

312 **1** **Born In Bombay**[47] 1954 3-8-4 87 ........ DavidProbert 26 95
(Andrew Balding) *lw: racd stands' side: chsd ldrs: overall ldr over 2f out: rdn over 1f out: pressed ins fnl f: styd on gamely towards fin: 1st of 20 in gp* **14/1**

0152 **2** *½* **Bow Creek (IRE)**[41] 2114 3-9-7 104 ........ RyanMoore 20 111
(Mark Johnston) *racd stands' side: in tch: rdn and hdwy over 1f out: chal fnl 110yds: r.o u.p: edgd lft towards fin: 2nd of 20 in gp* **25/1**

2-51 **3** *½* **Hors De Combat**[47] 1954 3-8-13 96 ........ FrederikTylicki 12 102
(James Fanshawe) *lw: racd stands' side: midfield: rdn and hdwy 2f out: chalng ins fnl f: styd on: hld towards fin: 3rd of 20 in gp* **8/1**[2]

1-16 **4** *½* **Bilimbi (IRE)**[26] 2565 3-8-7 90 ........ (p) AndreaAtzeni 30 95
(William Haggas) *lw: racd stands' side: hld up: rdn and hdwy over 2f out: chsd ldrs over 1f out: styd on: one pce towards fin: 4th of 20 in gp* **7/1**[1]

1-22 **5** *½* **Zarwaan**[26] 2565 3-9-4 101 ........ PaulHanagan 24 105+
(Ed Dunlop) *lw: racd stands' side: midfield: effrt over 2f out: chsd ldrs over 1f out: styd on towards fin: 5th of 20 in gp* **8/1**[2]

2234 **6** *½* **American Hope (USA)**[62] 1555 3-9-2 99 ........ ShaneKelly 8 101+
(Mike Murphy) *racd far side: hld up racing keenly: hdwy 3f out: led gp over 1f out: edgd rt ins fnl f: styd on but hld by ldrs in other gp: 1st of 10 in gp* **50/1**

21-6 **7** *½* **Madeed**[64] 1516 3-8-6 89 ........ (t) MartinDwyer 5 90+
(Brian Meehan) *lw: racd far side: prom: led gp 2f out: hdd over 1f out: continued to chal: swtchd lft fnl 120yds: styd on: hld towards fin: 2nd of 10 in gp* **33/1**

5-51 **8** *hd* **Legend Rising (IRE)**[42] 2088 3-8-9 92 ........ JimCrowley 25 93
(Martyn Meade) *racd stands' side: hld up: rdn and hdwy over 2f out: styd on ins fnl f: nrst fin 6th of 20 in gp* **33/1**

6-33 **9** *hd* **First Flight (IRE)**[26] 2565 3-8-9 92 ........ KierenFallon 1 92+
(Saeed bin Suroor) *racd far side: hld up: rdn and hdwy over 2f out: chsd ldrs over 1f out: styd on: hld towards fin: 3rd of 10 in gp* **14/1**

0610 **10** *2* **Almargo (IRE)**[5] 3253 3-8-6 89 ........ SilvestreDeSousa 15 85
(Mark Johnston) *racd stands' side: chsd ldrs: chal fr 2f out: nt qckn ins fnl f: no ex fnl 75yds: 7th of 20 in gp* **50/1**

5-62 **11** *1* **Free Code (IRE)**[33] 2330 3-8-10 93 ow1 ........ MartinHarley 32 86
(James Tate) *racd stands' side: hld up in rr: rdn over 2f out: hdwy over 1f out: styd on ins fnl f: gng on at fin: 8th of 20 in gp* **50/1**

-121 **12** *½* **Chatez (IRE)**[26] 2565 3-9-1 98 ........ FergusSweeney 13 90
(Alan King) *lw: racd stands' side: in midfield: rdn and hdwy over 1f out: in midfield ins fnl f: no imp on ldrs: 9th of 20 in gp* **14/1**

**13** *½* **Third Dimension**[54] 1746 3-8-9 95 ........ ColinKeane(3) 31 86
(G M Lyons, Ire) *racd stands' side: hld up: rdn over 2f out: nt clr run and snatched up wl over 1f out: prog after: styd on ins fnl f: nt rch ldrs: 10th of 20 in gp* **14/1**

**14** *nk* **Table Rock (IRE)**[17] 2858 3-9-2 99 ........ (b) JosephO'Brien 6 89
(A P O'Brien, Ire) *str: racd far side: in tch: rdn and ev ch 2f out: nt qckn over 1f out: styd on same pce fnl 120yds: 4th of 10 in gp* **12/1**

5305 **15** *½* **Lyn Valley**[12] 2986 3-8-12 95 ........ FrankieDettori 27 84
(Mark Johnston) *racd stands' side: hld up: hdwy 3f out: ev ch 2f out: nt qckn over 1f out: fdd and eased fnl 110yds: 11th of 20 in gp* **18/1**

1-01 **16** *¾* **Idea (USA)**[14] 2921 3-8-7 90 ow1 ........ JamesDoyle 18 78
(Sir Michael Stoute) *racd stands' side: hld up: rdn over 2f out: kpt on ins fnl f: nvr trbld ldrs: 12th of 20 in gp* **10/1**[3]

01-1 **17** *nk* **Magnus Maximus**[64] 1513 3-9-4 101 ........ RichardHughes 16 88
(Richard Hannon) *racd stands' side: hld up: rdn 2f out: kpt on ins fnl f: nvr trbld ldrs: 13th of 20 in gp* **16/1**

36-6 **18** *nk* **Pupil (IRE)**[47] 1953 3-8-9 92 ........ PatDobbs 11 78
(Richard Hannon) *racd far side: prom tl rdn and outpcd over 2f out: n.d after: 5th of 10 in gp* **66/1**

0-31 **19** *nk* **Abbey Village (IRE)**[20] 2733 3-8-2 85 ........ PatrickMathers 2 70
(Richard Fahey) *w'like: racd far side: trckd ldrs: rdn 3f out: outpcd over 2f out: rallied ins fnl f: styd on: nt pce of ldrs: 6th of 10 in gp* **40/1**

00-3 **20** *1* **Suzi's Connoisseur**[13] 2962 3-8-7 95 ........ NoelGarbutt(5) 9 78
(Hugo Palmer) *racd far side: hld up: hdwy 4f out: rdn and ev ch 2f out: wknd ins fnl f: 7th of 10 in gp* **50/1**

1-05 **21** *1* **Complicit (IRE)**[33] 2343 3-9-2 99 ........ LukeMorris 14 80
(Paul Cole) *racd stands' side: in tch: rdn over 2f out: sn outpcd: no imp after: 14th of 20 in gp* **33/1**

-323 **22** *nse* **Beau Nash (IRE)**[26] 2556 3-8-9 92 ........ KieranO'Neill 33 73
(Richard Hannon) *lw: racd stands' side: chsd ldrs: effrt 3f out: wknd over 2f out: 15th of 20 in gp* **50/1**

151 **23** *½* **Mindurownbusiness (IRE)**[51] 1861 3-8-2 85 ........ HayleyTurner 4 65
(David Simcock) *w'like: racd far side: prom and racd keenly: effrt over 2f out: wknd over 1f out: 8th of 10 in gp* **16/1**

0-00 **24** *nk* **Nezar (IRE)**[126] 594 3-8-12 95 ........ TomQueally 21 74
(George Margarson) *swtg: racd stands' side: hld up: rdn over 2f out: no imp: one pce fnl f: 16th of 20 in gp* **50/1**

2150 **25** *5* **Zampa Manos (USA)**[12] 2986 3-8-8 94 ........ (v[1]) OisinMurphy(3) 3 61
(Andrew Balding) *racd far side: led gp tl rdn and hdd 2f out: wknd over 1f out: 9th of 10 in gp* **50/1**

-601 **26** *¾* **Ifwecan**[12] 3002 3-8-8 91 ........ FrannyNorton 19 57
(Mark Johnston) *racd stands' side: prom: rdn and wkng whn hmpd over 1f out: bhd after: 17th of 20 in gp* **28/1**

0-60 **27** *3 ¼* **Mawfoor (IRE)**[26] 2565 3-8-10 93 ........ JimmyFortune 23 51
(Brian Meehan) *racd stands' side: prom: rdn 3f out: wknd over 2f out: 18th of 20 in gp* **50/1**

4-04 **28** *¾* **Hunters Creek (IRE)**[33] 2345 3-9-0 97 ........ WilliamBuick 17 54
(John Gosden) *racd stands' side: in midfield: rdn 3f out: wknd over 2f out: bhd after: 19th of 20 in gp* **16/1**

0241 **29** *8* **Crowdmania**[26] 2544 3-8-5 88 ........ JoeFanning 28 26
(Mark Johnston) *racd stands' side: led overall: rdn and hdd over 2f out: wknd over 1f out: 20th of 20 in gp* **33/1**

-005 **30** *6* **Dubawi Fun**[112] 770 3-8-6 92 ow2 ........ WilliamTwiston-Davies(3) 10 16
(Ismail Mohammed) *racd far side: hld up: struggling 3f out: bhd after: 10th of 10 in gp* **100/1**

1m 38.4s (-2.40) **Going Correction** -0.15s/f (Firm) **30** Ran SP% **140.7**
Speed ratings (Par 105): **106,105,105,104,104 103,103,102,102,100 99,99,98,98,97 97,96,96,96,95 94,94,93,93,88 87,84,83**
CSF £354.57 CT £3053.86 TOTE £16.10: £3.20, £8.80, £2.60, £3.00; EX 395.90 Trifecta £6029.40.
**Owner** George Strawbridge **Bred** George Strawbridge **Trained** Kingsclere, Hants
■ Stewards' Enquiry : Andrea Atzeni two-day ban: used whip above permitted level (Jul 4,6)

**FOCUS**
The annual cavalry charge for the Britannia and, unlike in the previous day's Royal Hunt Cup, those drawn lowest (ten of them) stayed far side, headed by the first-time visored Zampa Manos, while the rest, headed by a couple of Mark Johnston inmates in Crowdmania and Ifwecan, came towards the nearside. Despite the first five home coming up the nearside, there wasn't much between the two groups at the line and this looks very strong form.

## 3379 KING GEORGE V STKS (H'CAP) (BOBIS RACE) 1m 4f
5:35 (5:40) (Class 2) (0-105,100) 3-Y-O
£46,687 (£13,980; £6,990; £3,495; £1,747; £877) Stalls Low

Form RPR
1-31 **1** **Elite Army**[28] 2496 3-9-1 **94** KierenFallon 14 109+
(Saeed bin Suroor) *t.k.h: hld up wl in tch: chsng ldrs and nt clr run ent fnl 2f: gap opened and qcknd between horses 1f out: drvn to ld fnl 75yds: r.o strly: eased nr fin* **4/1**[1]

-212 **2** ¾ **Windshear**[33] 2337 3-9-2 **95** RichardHughes 21 107
(Richard Hannon) *lw: chsd ldrs: clsd to chal 2f out: rdn to ld over 1f out: forged clr jst ins fnl f: hdd and outpcd fnl 75yds: kpt on for clr 2nd* **4/1**[1]

-121 **3** 3¼ **Captain Morley**[19] 2761 3-8-11 **90** JamieSpencer 22 97
(David Simcock) *hld up in tch in midfield: rdn and effrt ent fnl 2f: drvn and hdwy over 1f out: styd on wl u.p to go 3rd nr fin: no threat to ldng pair* **10/1**[3]

3-22 **4** ½ **Venezia (IRE)**[35] 2271 3-8-10 **89** RyanMoore 2 95
(Martyn Meade) *hld up off the pce towards rr: swtchd lft and effrt over 2f out: hdwy u.p over 1f out: styd on wl u.p fnl f: wnt 4th cl home: nvr trbld ldrs* **20/1**

-111 **5** ½ **Arab Dawn**[22] 2685 3-8-11 **90** JimmyFortune 15 95
(Hughie Morrison) *chsd ldrs: rdn and effrt jst over 2f out: pressing ldrs u.p over 1f out: no ex jst ins fnl f: wknd fnl 100yds: lost 2 pls nr fin* **10/1**[3]

2-00 **6** *hd* **Trip To Paris (IRE)**[12] 3003 3-8-6 **85** (b) LukeMorris 3 90
(Ed Dunlop) *hld up off the pce in midfield: effrt u.p over 2f out: hrd drvn and hdwy whn swtchd rt 1f out: styd on wl towards fin: no threat to ldrs* **33/1**

40 **7** *hd* **Carlo Bugatti (IRE)**[42] 2087 3-9-7 **100** (p) JosephO'Brien 8 105
(A P O'Brien, Ire) *lw: hld up in midfield: rdn and effrt on outer 3f out: hdwy u.p over 1f out: styd on ins fnl f: no threat to ldrs* **16/1**

-120 **8** 1 **Alex My Boy (IRE)**[12] 3003 3-8-8 **87** FrannyNorton 19 90
(Mark Johnston) *v.s.a and reminders sn after s: wl off the pce in rr: hdwy u.p over 1f out: swtchd rt and styd on strly ins fnl f: nvr trbld ldrs* **10/1**[3]

2-23 **9** *nse* **Gold Trail (IRE)**[12] 2982 3-8-11 **90** AndreaAtzeni 18 93
(Charlie Appleby) *led and grad crossed to inner: rdn over 2f out: drvn and hdd over 1f out: stl pressing ldrs but no ex 1f out: wknd fnl 150yds* **25/1**

1-12 **10** ½ **Personal Opinion**[34] 2303 3-8-12 **91** WilliamBuick 6 93
(Charlie Appleby) *hld up in midfield: rdn and effrt jst over 2f out: hdwy and swtchd lft ent fnl f: styd on: nvr trbld ldrs* **7/1**[2]

-363 **11** 3 **Truth Or Dare**[33] 2345 3-8-13 **99** CamHardie(7) 13 96
(Richard Hannon) *hld up in midfield: effrt u.p over 2f out: no imp whn sltly hmpd over 1f out: wl hld and one pce fnl f* **25/1**

4113 **12** *hd* **Black Schnapps (IRE)**[26] 2566 3-9-1 **94** MartinDwyer 10 91
(William Muir) *lw: w ldr on inner: rdn and ev ch over 2f out: no ex and btn over 1f out: wknd ins fnl f* **16/1**

-356 **13** 1½ **Stars Over The Sea (USA)**[12] 2986 3-9-6 **99** JoeFanning 20 94
(Mark Johnston) *lw: t.k.h: chsd ldrs and styd wd early: rdn over 2f out: struggling to qckn and losing pl whn short of room over 1f out: wknd fnl f* **14/1**

1030 **14** 2 **Swivel**[12] 3003 3-8-8 **90** MichaelJMMurphy(3) 11 81
(Mark Johnston) *off the pce towards rr: rdn an bhd over 2f out: n.d but plugged on ins fnl f* **66/1**

2-61 **15** 1¾ **Zee Zeely**[46] 1979 3-8-8 **87** (p) PaulHanagan 4 76
(William Haggas) *racd off the pce towards rr: rdn and effrt 2f out: drvn and no real imp over 1f out: nvr trbld ldrs* **14/1**

1-05 **16** 8 **Bremner**[20] 2748 3-8-13 **92** (tp) JamesDoyle 1 68
(Hugo Palmer) *wl in tch in midfield: rdn and no hdwy ent fnl 2f: btn over 1f out: wknd qckly fnl f* **50/1**

3-44 **17** 8 **Fire Fighting (IRE)**[12] 2982 3-8-9 **88** SilvestreDeSousa 7 51
(Mark Johnston) *chsd ldrs: hmpd and lost pl after 2f: dropped to rr and pushed along briefly 8f out: rdn over 2f out: sn wl btn* **20/1**

2-31 **18** 2¼ **Art Of War (IRE)**[32] 2365 3-8-9 **88** RichardKingscote 9 47
(Tom Dascombe) *stdd s: hld up in rr: effrt on inner 2f out: racd awkwardky and no prog: sn wl btn: bhd fnl f: t.o* **20/1**

2m 30.59s (-1.91) **Going Correction** -0.025s/f (Good) **18 Ran SP% 133.2**
Speed ratings (Par 105): **105,104,102,102,101 101,101,100,100,100 98,98,97,95,94 89,84,82**
CSF £17.10 CT £163.45 TOTE £5.20: £1.80, £1.90, £2.90, £4.90; EX 22.30 Trifecta £252.70.
**Owner** Godolphin **Bred** Darley **Trained** Newmarket, Suffolk
■ Stewards' Enquiry : Joseph O'Brien two-day ban: used whip above permitted level (Jul 10,14)

**FOCUS**
A quality 3yo handicap that was run at a good gallop, with two bang in-form progressive types, evidently ahead of the handicapper, coming clear. The form looks strong.
T/Jkpt: £35,500.00 to a £1 stake. Pool of £133854.36- 4 winning units. T/Plt: £1376.60 to a £1 stake. Pool of £605950.31 - 321.31 winning units. T/Qpdt: £137.80 to a £1 stake. Pool of £45,112.89 - 242.11 winning units. SP

# 3222 LEICESTER (R-H)
Thursday, June 19

**OFFICIAL GOING: Good to firm (8.3)**
Wind: Light against Weather: Overcast

## 3380 HARRINGTON H'CAP 7f 9y
6:00 (6:00) (Class 6) (0-65,65) 3-Y-O
£1,940 (£577; £288; £144) Stalls High

Form RPR
-302 **1** **The Dukkerer (IRE)**[45] 2020 3-9-2 **60** AdamKirby 10 67
(Garry Moss) *led: hdd over 4f out: chsd ldr: rdn over 1f out: led ins fnl f: styd on* **9/2**[2]

-530 **2** 1½ **McCarthy Mor (IRE)**[16] 2878 3-9-0 **58** (v[1]) TonyHamilton 7 61
(Richard Fahey) *hld up: racd keenly: hdwy 3f out: rdn over 1f out: r.o to go 2nd nr fin* **12/1**

5022 **3** *shd* **Bonjour Steve**[22] 2668 3-9-4 **62** (p) DaneO'Neill 5 65
(Richard Price) *w ldr tl led over 4f out: rdn over 1f out: hdd and unable qck ins fnl f* **6/1**[3]

2404 **4** 7 **Molly Ahoy**[15] 2902 3-9-1 **62** BillyCray(3) 11 47
(Alan McCabe) *s.i.s: in rr: rdn over 2f out: styd on ins fnl f: nvr nrr* **25/1**

-045 **5** ¾ **Henke (IRE)**[8] 3124 3-8-13 **57** J-PGuillambert 4 40
(Nigel Tinkler) *chsd ldrs: rdn 1/2-way: wknd fnl f* **10/1**

3641 **6** ½ **Seven Lucky Seven**[9] 3087 3-8-13 **64** 6ex JordanVaughan(7) 13 45
(Nick Littmoden) *prom: rdn over 2f out: wknd fnl f* **7/4**[1]

3035 **7** ½ **Sexy Secret**[16] 2878 3-9-1 **59** RobertHavlin 3 39
(Lydia Pearce) *prom: rdn 1/2-way: sn lost pl: n.d after* **10/1**

0260 **8** 1¼ **Keep To The Beat**[27] 2526 3-8-9 **58** KevinStott(5) 12 35
(Kevin Ryan) *chsd ldrs: rdn 1/2-way: wknd over 1f out* **25/1**

250 **9** 5 **Va Benny**[16] 2877 3-9-0 **58** (v[1]) HarryBentley 6 22
(J R Jenkins) *chsd ldrs: rdn over 2f out: wknd wl over 1f out* **20/1**

3600 **10** 3 **Razin' Hell**[8] 3124 3-8-13 **64** AnnaHesketh(7) 8 20
(Alan McCabe) *mid-div: pushed along 1/2-way: wknd over 2f out* **33/1**

2-4 **11** 3 **Jaeger Connoisseur (IRE)**[51] 1855 3-8-0 **51** RobJFitzpatrick(7) 1
(K R Burke) *chsd ldrs: rdn over 2f out: sn wknd* **12/1**

005 **P** **Adaptability**[18] 2804 3-9-7 **65** SeanLevey 9
(Brian Meehan) *hld up: wknd 1/2-way: sn eased and p.u* **8/1**

1m 25.36s (-0.84) **Going Correction** -0.125s/f (Firm) **12 Ran SP% 128.9**
Speed ratings (Par 97): **99,97,97,89,88 87,87,85,80,76 73,**
CSF £59.99 CT £346.41 TOTE £5.40: £1.60, £4.30, £1.90; EX 112.80 Trifecta £548.20.
**Owner** Willam G Pett & Ron Hull **Bred** Mrs Sarah Maccann **Trained** Tickhill, S Yorks

**FOCUS**
This modest opener was taken in convincing style by the winner.

## 3381 DINGLEY MAIDEN STKS (BOBIS RACE) 7f 9y
6:30 (6:31) (Class 4) 2-Y-O
£3,881 (£1,155; £577; £288) Stalls High

Form RPR
**1** **Muqaawel (USA)** 2-9-5 0 DaneO'Neill 4 80+
(Mark Johnston) *s.i.s: hdwy over 5f out: led 2f out: hung lft ins fnl f: r.o: readily* **7/1**[3]

3 **2** 1¼ **Critical Risk (IRE)**[17] 2837 2-9-5 0 SeanLevey 9 77
(Brian Meehan) *s.i.s: hdwy over 5f out: rdn and ev ch 2f out: nt clr run ins fnl f: styd on same pce* **4/6**[1]

4 **3** *nk* **Azraff (IRE)**[23] 2642 2-9-5 0 HarryBentley 3 76+
(Marco Botti) *trckd ldrs: rdn over 1f out: hung lft ins fnl f: styd on* **4/1**[2]

0 **4** 5 **Goolagong Girl (IRE)**[14] 2918 2-8-7 0 LewisWalsh(7) 8 58
(Jane Chapple-Hyam) *s.i.s: hld up: hdwy u.p over 1f out: no ex ins fnl f* **50/1**

**5** *hd* **Toofeeg (IRE)** 2-9-5 0 LiamJones 5 63
(William Haggas) *s.i.s: pushed along and hdwy 1/2-way: rdn and hung rt over 1f out: no ex ins fnl f* **12/1**

**6** 5 **Duc De Seville (IRE)** 2-9-5 0 AdamKirby 7 50
(Clive Cox) *chsd ldrs: rdn over 2f out: sn ev ch: wknd fnl f* **7/1**[3]

**7** 9 **Keen Move** 2-9-5 0 RobertHavlin 6 26
(Ismail Mohammed) *w ldr: plld hrd: led over 5f out: rdn and hdd 2f out: wknd over 1f out* **20/1**

**8** 2¾ **Virtualise** 2-9-0 0 LouisSteward(5) 1 19
(John Gallagher) *led: hdd over 5f out: chsd ldrs: rdn and wknd wl over 1f out* **50/1**

1m 28.23s (2.03) **Going Correction** -0.125s/f (Firm) **8 Ran SP% 121.4**
Speed ratings (Par 95): **83,81,81,75,75 69,59,56**
CSF £12.81 TOTE £16.80: £3.00, £1.10, £1.10; EX 23.50 Trifecta £94.80.
**Owner** Hamdan Al Maktoum **Bred** Shadwell Farm LLC **Trained** Middleham Moor, N Yorks

**FOCUS**
Mark Johnston is no stranger to success in this maiden and he made it three wins in the last four years.

## 3382 TOWN HALL CLAIMING STKS 1m 60y
7:05 (7:06) (Class 6) 3-Y-O+
£1,940 (£577; £288; £144) Stalls Low

Form RPR
0520 **1** **Kimbali (IRE)**[29] 2469 5-9-2 67 [1] AdamKirby 5 76
(David Evans) *s.i.s: hld up: plld hrd: hdwy over 3f out: led 2f out: rdn and hung rt ins fnl f: r.o* **8/1**[3]

4151 **2** 1½ **Licence To Till (USA)**[11] 3035 7-8-13 81 JennyPowell(7) 6 77
(Tom Dascombe) *sn led: rdn and hdd 2f out: styd on same pce ins fnl f* **4/6**[1]

0454 **3** 4½ **Prime Exhibit**[31] 2381 9-8-13 67 (t) LouisSteward(5) 1 64
(Daniel Mark Loughnane) *hld up: hdwy over 2f out: rdn over 1f out: nt clr run over 1f out: no ex ins fnl f* **8/1**[3]

1656 **4** 2¼ **Justonefortheroad**[11] 3035 8-9-2 74 TonyHamilton 4 57
(Richard Fahey) *hld up: hdwy over 2f out: sn rdn: styd on same pce* **4/1**[2]

1405 **5** 1 **Slinky McVelvet**[14] 2936 3-8-4 66 BillyCray(3) 3 54
(Garry Moss) *chsd ldrs: rdn over 3f out: wknd fnl f* **20/1**

50 **6** 8 **Lindart (ITY)**[33] 2339 3-9-0 0 SeanLevey 2 42
(Richard Hannon) *chsd ldr: reminder 5f out: rdn over 3f out: wknd 2f out* **25/1**

1m 44.39s (-0.71) **Going Correction** -0.125s/f (Firm)
**WFA** 3 from 5yo+ 10lb **6 Ran SP% 110.8**
Speed ratings (Par 101): **98,96,92,89,88 80**
CSF £13.60 TOTE £6.40: £2.60, £1.10; EX 21.50 Trifecta £40.00.Kimbali was claimed by S Bryan for £6000. Licence To Till was claimed by A Berry for £8000.
**Owner** J A Wilcox **Bred** P Kelly **Trained** Pandy, Monmouths

**FOCUS**
Betting at this lowly level comes with a health warning attached and those that took the plunge on recent runaway Goodwood winner Licence To Till were left licking their wounds.

## 3383 FOSTON H'CAP 1m 60y
7:35 (7:35) (Class 4) (0-85,85) 3-Y-O+
£4,690 (£1,395; £697; £348) Stalls Low

Form RPR
6463 **1** **Circumvent**[3] 3306 7-9-11 **82** (b) RaulDaSilva 4 92
(Paul Cole) *sn pushed along to join ldr: led 6f out: rdn clr 2f out: hld on* **7/2**[2]

6040 **2** ½ **Anderiego (IRE)**[5] 3254 6-9-9 **80** DanielTudhope 1 89
(David O'Meara) *hld up: hdwy over 2f out: rdn to go 2nd over 1f out: r.o: nt rch wnr* **5/2**[1]

2-53 **3** 4 **Meteoroid (USA)**[38] 2222 3-8-12 **79** (b[1]) SeanLevey 3 77
(Lady Cecil) *prom: rdn over 2f out: hung rt over 1f out: no ex fnl f* **7/2**[2]

631- **4** 6 **My Target (IRE)**[231] 7646 3-9-1 **82** AhmedAjtebi 5 66
(Saeed bin Suroor) *s.i.s: hld up: hdwy over 2f out: rdn and edgd lft sn after: wknd over 1f out* **7/2**[2]

231- **5** 1 **Ocean Storm (IRE)**[282] 6275 3-9-4 **85** AdamKirby 6 67
(James Tate) *led over 2f: chsd wnr: rdn over 2f out: sn hung rt: wknd over 1f out* **10/1**

0-00 **6** 7 **Henry The Aviator (USA)**[13] 2959 4-10-0 **85** DaneO'Neill 2 53
(Mark Johnston) *trckd ldrs: rdn over 3f out: wknd over 1f out* **8/1**[3]

1m 42.82s (-2.28) **Going Correction** -0.125s/f (Firm)
**WFA** 3 from 4yo+ 10lb **6 Ran SP% 115.4**
Speed ratings (Par 105): **106,105,101,95,94 87**
CSF £13.18 TOTE £5.40: £2.80, £1.10; EX 17.50 Trifecta £78.60.
**Owner** The Fairy Story Partnership **Bred** Deepwood Farm Stud **Trained** Whatcombe, Oxon

**FOCUS**
Doubts surrounded most of these beforehand and it's difficult to know what was required.

## 3384 WALTHAM-ON-THE-WOLDS FILLIES' H'CAP 5f 218y
8:10 (8:11) (Class 5) (0-75,75) 3-Y-O+ £2,587 (£770; £384; £192) Stalls High

Form RPR
2243 1 **Serenity Spa**30 2448 4-9-12 **73**.................... AdamKirby 4 85
(Tony Carroll) *hld up: hdwy 2f out: rdn to ld ins fnl f: r.o* 5/1[3]
-020 2 1 **Diamond Blue**24 2602 6-9-2 **63**....................(p) TonyHamilton 6 71
(Richard Fahey) *hld up: hdwy over 1f out: sn rdn: r.o* 16/1
-003 3 2 1/2 **Red Lady (IRE)**19 2768 3-9-6 **74**....................(p) SeanLevey 2 72
(Brian Meehan) *w ldr tl led 2f out: rdn over 1f out: hdd and unable qck ins fnl f* 7/1
00-0 4 nk **Jamesbo's Girl**40 2167 4-9-8 **69**.................... GrahamGibbons 7 68
(David Barron) *chsd ldrs: rdn over 1f out: nt clr run ins fnl f: styd on* 9/2[2]
00-0 5 2 1/4 **Piddie's Power**5 3256 7-10-0 **75**....................(p) BenCurtis 9 67
(Kevin Frost) *s.i.s: rdn over 2f out: sn edgd rt: styd on ins fnl f: nt trble ldrs* 9/1
3061 6 hd **Meandmyshadow**3 3298 6-9-8 **69** 6ex.................... DaleSwift 10 60
(Alan Brown) *prom: rdn over 2f out: styd on same pce fnl f* 5/2[1]
-050 7 1 1/4 **Sairaam (IRE)**7 3160 8-8-6 **56** oh11....................(p) BillyCray(3) 5 43
(Charles Smith) *led: rdn and hdd 2f out: wknd ins fnl f* 66/1
0/53 8 2 3/4 **Koala Bear**12 2985 4-9-3 **64**.................... ShaneKelly 1 42
(James Fanshawe) *s.i.s: hdwy over 3f out: rdn over 1f out: wknd fnl f* 5/1[3]
3514 9 6 **Clock Opera (IRE)**34 2312 4-8-13 **65**.................... LouisSteward(5) 8 24
(William Stone) *hld up in tch: racd keenly: rdn over 2f out: wknd over 1f out* 10/1
1254 10 1 1/4 **Mill I Am (USA)**78 1230 4-8-12 **59**.................... HarryBentley 3 14
(Stuart Williams) *prom: rdn over 2f out: wknd over 1f out* 25/1

1m 11.53s (-1.47) **Going Correction** -0.125s/f (Firm)
**WFA** 3 from 4yo+ 7lb 10 Ran SP% **122.9**
Speed ratings (Par 100): **104,102,99,98,95 95,94,90,82,80**
CSF £85.93 CT £574.47 TOTE £4.80: £1.40, £3.00, £3.20; EX 70.40 Trifecta £717.20.
**Owner** Seasons Holidays **Bred** Barry Hurley **Trained** Cropthorne, Worcs

**FOCUS**
A competitive handicap on paper.

## 3385 GLEBE MAIDEN STKS 1m 3f 183y
8:40 (8:41) (Class 5) 3-Y-O+ £2,587 (£770; £384; £192) Stalls Low

Form RPR
3-44 1 **Bajan Beauty (IRE)**31 2385 3-8-7 67.................... RobertHavlin 4 75
(Charles Hills) *led after 1f: rdn over 1f out: styd on* 12/1
5-4 2 1 3/4 **Mustadaam (IRE)**64 1517 3-8-12 0.................... DaneO'Neill 5 77
(Brian Meehan) *a.p: chsd wnr 7f out: rdn over 2f out: styd on same pce ins fnl f* 4/6[1]
40 3 1 **Chatham House Rule**30 2422 3-8-12 0.................... BenCurtis 2 76
(Michael Bell) *led 1f: chsd ldr tl 7f out: remained handy: rdn over 3f out: styd on same pce fnl f* 20/1
4 1 3/4 **Social Riser (IRE)** 3-8-7 0.................... FrannyNorton 7 68+
(Charles Hills) *prom: rdn over 4f out: outpcd 3f out: rallied over 1f out: kpt on* 25/1
2223 5 1 1/4 **Mbhali (IRE)**117 717 3-8-12 75.................... AdrianNicholls 10 71
(Mark Johnston) *chsd ldrs: rdn over 3f out: styd on same pce fr over 1f out* 4/1[2]
6 2 1/4 **Di's Gift**41 5-9-12 0.................... TonyHamilton 1 67
(Richard Guest) *s.s: hld up: hdwy over 4f out: outpcd 3f out: rallied over 1f out: wknd ins fnl f* 25/1
50 7 15 **Double Dealites**35 2280 4-9-2 0.................... HarryPoulton(5) 8 38
(Jamie Poulton) *hld up: a in rr: bhd fnl 4f* 50/1
8 2 1/4 **Dizzy River (IRE)**390 9-9-12 0.................... DaleSwift 12 40
(Brian Ellison) *s.s: hld up: a in rr: bhd fnl 5f* 33/1
0 9 2 1/2 **Uncle Muf (USA)**14 2917 4-9-12 0.................... AdamKirby 9 36
(Ali Stronge) *hld up: a in rr: bhd fnl 5f* 25/1
10 nk **Upper Street (IRE)** 3-8-8 0 ow1.................... ShaneKelly 6 31
(Sir Michael Stoute) *s.s: a in rr: bhd fnl 5f* 8/1[3]
0 11 7 **Nancy**14 2924 3-8-7 0.................... HarryBentley 11 19
(Mark H Tompkins) *s.s: sn pushed along into mid-div: rdn over 5f out: sn wknd* 66/1
6-00 12 18 **Lara Lipton (IRE)**14 2917 3-8-0 49....................(v[1]) LewisWalsh(7) 3
(Jane Chapple-Hyam) *prom: pushed along 7f out: wknd 4f out* 100/1

2m 32.62s (-1.28) **Going Correction** -0.125s/f (Firm)
**WFA** 3 from 4yo+ 14lb 12 Ran SP% **122.5**
Speed ratings (Par 103): **99,97,97,96,95 93,83,82,80,80 75,63**
CSF £19.92 TOTE £17.00: £4.60, £1.10, £4.00; EX 33.20 Trifecta £668.70.
**Owner** Decadent Racing II **Bred** Miss Sarah Thompson **Trained** Lambourn, Berks
■ Stewards' Enquiry : Harry Bentley caution: failed to take all reasonable and permissable measures to obtain best possible placing.

**FOCUS**
A modest maiden.

## 3386 IBSTOCK H'CAP 5f 2y
9:10 (9:10) (Class 4) (0-85,85) 3-Y-O+ £4,690 (£1,395; £697; £348) Stalls High

Form RPR
06-2 1 **Algar Lad**6 3191 4-9-2 **75**.................... DanielTudhope 4 93+
(David O'Meara) *hld up in tch: led on bit over 1f out: clr ins fnl f: easily* 4/5[1]
6-60 2 3 **Corncockle**31 2390 3-8-13 **78**.................... DavidNolan 2 79
(David O'Meara) *s.i.s: sn pushed along in rr: swtchd rt and hdwy over 1f out: styd on to go 2nd nr fin: no ch w wnr* 12/1
1110 3 nse **Taurus Twins**19 2786 8-9-8 **81**....................(b) DaneO'Neill 5 84
(Richard Price) *led: pushed along 1/2-way: rdn and hdd over 1f out: no ex ins fnl f* 12/1
6111 4 3/4 **Ladweb**21 2691 4-9-7 **85**.................... LouisSteward(5) 7 85
(John Gallagher) *chsd ldr: rdn and ev ch over 1f out: no ex ins fnl f* 3/1[2]
-223 5 6 **Arctic Lynx (IRE)**30 2446 7-9-9 **82**....................[1] AdamKirby 1 61
(Robert Cowell) *chsd ldrs: rdn over 1f out: wknd ins fnl f* 11/2[3]

59.83s (-0.17) **Going Correction** -0.125s/f (Firm)
**WFA** 3 from 4yo+ 6lb 5 Ran SP% **111.3**
Speed ratings (Par 105): **96,91,91,89,80**
CSF £11.53 TOTE £1.50: £1.10, £6.00; EX 13.00 Trifecta £99.30.
**Owner** Great Northern Partnership **Bred** Highclere Stud **Trained** Nawton, N Yorks

**FOCUS**
Some in-form sprinters locked horns in this finale and it saw a hugely impressive performance from the winner.
T/Plt: £52.30 to a £1 stake. Pool of £37427.32 - 522.25 winning tickets. T/Qpdt: £24.00 to a £1 stake. Pool of £3648.59 - 112.40 winning tickets. CR

# 3229 LINGFIELD (L-H)
Thursday, June 19

**OFFICIAL GOING: Standard**
Wind: Light, half against Weather: Cloudy, warm

## 3387 NECK REFUNDS AT 888SPORT.COM MAIDEN STKS 6f 1y(P)
5:50 (5:52) (Class 5) 2-Y-O £2,846 (£847; £423; £211) Stalls Low

Form RPR
52 1 **Power Play (IRE)**40 2172 2-9-5 0.................... ChrisCatlin 2 77+
(Richard Hannon) *mde all: hrd rdn and hld on gamely fnl f* 11/4[2]
2 shd **Midlander (IRE)** 2-9-5 0.................... RoystonFrench 8 77+
(Mark Johnston) *towards rr and wd: rdn 3f out: styd on wl fr 2f out: str chal fnl 100yds: jst denied* 6/1[3]
32 3 1 **Colour Catcher**44 2057 2-9-5 0.................... MartinLane 4 74
(Charlie Appleby) *chsd ldrs: rdn to press ldrs in centre over 1f out: r.o* 5/6[1]
4 1 **Drumkilbo** 2-9-5 0.................... GeorgeBaker 1 71+
(Lady Cecil) *chsd ldrs: rdn to press ldrs on inner over 1f out: one pce* 7/1
06 5 4 **Just Because**8 3113 2-9-5 0.................... PatCosgrave 3 59
(Edward Creighton) *pressed wnr tl hrd rdn and wknd 1f out* 50/1
6 3 1/2 **Stamp Of Approval (IRE)** 2-8-11 0.................... AshleyMorgan(3) 7 43
(Chris Wall) *sn wl bhd: rdn into mod 6th 2f out: no further prog* 16/1
7 1/2 **Prima Pagina** 2-8-11 0.................... RobertTart(3) 6 42+
(Dr Jon Scargill) *s.i.s: towards rr: lost tch 3f out: styng on at fin* 33/1
0 8 27 **Bella Alamoto**9 3076 2-9-0 0.................... WilliamCarson 5
(John Bridger) *s.i.s: t.k.h: sn in midfield: rdn 3f out: sn wknd and bhd* 100/1

1m 13.7s (1.80) **Going Correction** -0.025s/f (Stan) 8 Ran SP% **119.8**
Speed ratings (Par 93): **87,86,85,84,78 74,73,37**
CSF £20.51 TOTE £3.80: £1.20, £2.60, £1.02; EX 22.30 Trifecta £62.90.
**Owner** Mohamed Saeed Al Shahi **Bred** Barnane Stud **Trained** East Everleigh, Wilts

**FOCUS**
A fair maiden in which the gallop was an ordinary one and a race in which a couple of the newcomers shaped with promise. The winner raced just off the inside rail throughout.

## 3388 "CASH IN EARLY" AT 888SPORT.COM (S) STKS 6f 1y(P)
6:20 (6:20) (Class 6) 3-Y-O £2,199 (£654; £327; £163) Stalls Low

Form RPR
022 1 **Black Vale (IRE)**15 2906 3-8-12 67....................(t) DannyBrock(5) 4 72
(Phil McEntee) *sluggish s: rushed up to ld after 1f: rdn clr over 1f out: sn in command* 9/2[3]
3640 2 2 3/4 **Kodafine (IRE)**15 2886 3-8-7 65.................... ChrisCatlin 6 53
(David Evans) *led 1f: pressed wnr after tl hrd rdn and btn over 1f out: jst hld on for 2nd* 7/2[1]
4156 3 hd **Coiste Bodhar (IRE)**35 2281 3-9-3 66....................(p) GeorgeBaker 8 63
(Joseph Tuite) *t.k.h in rr: rdn and hdwy over 1f out: styd on* 6/1
2504 4 1 1/2 **El Duque**37 2230 3-8-12 64.................... RyanWhile(5) 5 58
(Bill Turner) *in tch: outpcd over 2f out: rallied on inner over 1f out: styd on same pce* 20/1
3110 5 nse **Intense Feeling (IRE)**23 2647 3-8-7 62.................... NathanAlison(5) 7 53
(Lee Carter) *s.i.s: sn in tch: rdn to chse ldrs 2f out: one pce appr fnl f* 4/1[2]
64-0 6 2 **Cafetiere**8 3117 3-8-7 76.................... MartinLane 1 41
(Paul Cole) *outpcd and rdn along: sn bhd: styng on at fin* 5/1
1115 7 3/4 **Emerald Breeze (IRE)**84 1130 3-8-12 70....................(b) StevieDonohoe 2 44
(Tim Pitt) *prom: rdn over 2f out: wknd 1f out* 5/1

1m 12.28s (0.38) **Going Correction** -0.025s/f (Stan) 7 Ran SP% **112.8**
Speed ratings (Par 97): **96,92,92,90,90 87,86**
CSF £19.98 TOTE £5.50: £3.20, £1.30; EX 28.40 Trifecta £213.50.Cafetiere was claimed by P O'Callaghan for £6000.
**Owner** Mrs Rebecca McEntee **Bred** Michael Downey & Roalso Ltd **Trained** Newmarket, Suffolk

**FOCUS**
A competitive seller on paper, but the gallop was an ordinary one and not many figured. The winner raced down the centre in the straight.

## 3389 ISG H'CAP 1m 1y(P)
6:55 (6:58) (Class 6) (0-60,60) 3-Y-O £2,587 (£770; £384; £192) Stalls High

Form RPR
60-3 1 **Crafted (IRE)**52 1805 3-9-3 **56**.................... RoystonFrench 9 70
(Mark Johnston) *disp ld after 1f: led over 2f out: rdn 5 l clr over 1f out: comf* 6/1
-236 2 3 1/2 **Choral Clan (IRE)**30 2417 3-9-6 **59**....................(t) JackMitchell 12 63+
(Philip Mitchell) *sn bhd: nt clr run over 2f out: rdn and hdwy over 1f out: styd on wl to take 2nd nr fin* 4/1[1]
3256 3 nk **Happydoingnothing**16 2879 3-9-6 **59**.................... AdamBeschizza 4 62
(Christine Dunnett) *in tch: hrd rdn over 2f out: chsd wnr 1f out: a wl hld: lost 2nd nr fin* 33/1
1221 4 2 1/2 **Clapperboard**16 2860 3-9-7 **60**....................(b) WilliamCarson 6 57
(Paul Fitzsimons) *led 1f: prom: rdn over 2f out: wknd 1f out* 9/2[2]
1500 5 3/4 **Plough Boy (IRE)**38 2224 3-9-7 **60**.................... ChrisCatlin 8 55
(Willie Musson) *in tch on outer: rdn 2f out: styd on same pce* 6/1
0600 6 nk **Buckland Beau**23 2647 3-9-6 **59**.................... MartinLane 5 53
(Charlie Fellowes) *sn chsng ldrs: outpcd fnl 2f* 16/1
0-00 7 3 **Excedo Praecedo**14 2927 3-9-3 **56**.................... GeorgeBaker 11 42
(Amanda Perrett) *disp ld after 1f tl over 2f out: hrd rdn and wknd over 1f out* 8/1
0-00 8 nse **Venus Marina**22 2681 3-8-11 **53**.................... AshleyMorgan(3) 10 39
(Chris Wall) *s.i.s: on and off the bridle: bhd: hdwy on outer 3f out: rdn and lost pl 2f out: styd on fnl f* 20/1
-604 9 shd **Lifejacket (IRE)**14 2927 3-9-5 **58**.................... SebSanders 1 44
(Ed Dunlop) *in tch on rail: drvn along over 2f out: sn btn* 5/1[3]
600 10 2 1/2 **Purana**45 2025 3-9-4 **57**.................... SteveDrowne 3 36
(Tony Carroll) *plld hrd early: sn stdd towards rr: rdn wl over 1f out: n.d* 33/1
0000 11 3 3/4 **Scariff Hornet (IRE)**21 2688 3-9-1 **59**.................... JoshBaudains(5) 2 28
(Sylvester Kirk) *towards rr: rdn over 4f out: sn struggling* 50/1
-404 12 1 **Starlite Jewel**27 2526 3-8-10 **52**.................... RyanPowell(3) 7 19
(George Margarson) *s.i.s: towards rr: rdn 4f out: sn struggling* 25/1

1m 37.62s (-0.58) **Going Correction** -0.025s/f (Stan) 12 Ran SP% **116.9**
Speed ratings (Par 97): **101,97,97,94,93 93,90,90,90,88 84,83**
CSF £27.96 CT £746.47 TOTE £7.00: £1.80, £1.90, £11.70; EX 33.70 Trifecta £709.00.
**Owner** Sheikh Hamdan bin Mohammed Al Maktoum **Bred** Joe Osborne **Trained** Middleham Moor, N Yorks

**FOCUS**
There were a couple of unexposed sorts in this moderate handicap. The gallop was an ordinary one to the home turn and the ready winner edged into the centre in the closing stages.

## 3390 ADVANCED ROOFING STEPS & LADDERS FILLIES' H'CAP 1m 1y(P)
**7:25** (7:25) (Class 5) (0-70,62) 4-Y-0+ **£3,234** (£962; £481; £240) **Stalls High**

Form RPR
1-52 **1** **Sonnetation (IRE)**[14] 2930 4-9-7 **62**.......... PatCosgrave 3 68
(Jim Boyle) *trckd ldr: led over 2f out: jnd by runner-up ins fnl f: jst prevailed* **5/4**[1]
3420 **2** *shd* **Two In The Pink (IRE)**[19] 2775 4-9-5 **60**.......... MartinHarley 2 65
(Ralph J Smith) *hld up in 6th: rdn and hdwy ent st: drvn to dispute ld ins fnl f: jst denied* **5/1**[2]
-066 **3** *½* **Ashkalara**[21] 2689 7-8-8 **49**.......... MartinLane 1 53
(Stuart Howe) *chsd ldrs: hrd rdn over 1f out: r.o* **16/1**
0-00 **4** *nk* **Anginola (IRE)**[38] 2212 5-8-4 **52**..........(p) CharlotteJenner(7) 6 55
(Laura Mongan) *s.i.s: bhd: rdn over 3f out: styd on wl fnl 2f* **33/1**
5002 **5** *1 ½* **Princess Spirit**[23] 2646 5-9-3 **61**..........(p) AshleyMorgan(3) 8 61
(Edward Creighton) *stdd s: plld hrd: in tch on outer: effrt and wd on bnd into st: styd on same pce* **5/1**[2]
2116 **6** *¾* **Welsh Inlet (IRE)**[19] 2775 6-9-2 **57**.......... WilliamCarson 4 55
(John Bridger) *t.k.h: chsd ldrs: rdn 3f out: btn 2f out* **10/1**
0503 **7** *¾* **Bold Ring**[5] 3233 8-8-9 **57**.......... MeganCarberry(7) 7 53
(Edward Creighton) *towards rr: no room on rail after 2f: rdn wl over 1f out: unable to chal* **10/1**
2631 **8** *4 ½* **Meddling**[48] 1917 4-9-0 **60**.......... ShelleyBirkett(5) 5 45
(Julia Feilden) *led tl over 2f out: wknd over 1f out* **7/1**[3]
1m 37.55s (-0.65) **Going Correction** -0.025s/f (Stan) **8 Ran SP% 117.3**
Speed ratings (Par 100): **102,101,101,101,99 98,98,93**
CSF £8.05 CT £68.25 TOTE £2.10: £1.30, £1.60, £3.80; EX 11.00 Trifecta £210.90.
**Owner** The 'In Recovery' Partnership **Bred** Dr Dean Harron **Trained** Epsom, Surrey
**FOCUS**
A modest fillies' handicap run at a modest gallop. The winner came down the centre in the straight.

## 3391 AIREY MILLER NEWBIES H'CAP 1m 4f (P)
**8:00** (8:00) (Class 5) (0-70,69) 3-Y-0 **£3,234** (£962; £481; £240) **Stalls Low**

Form RPR
-006 **1** **Daydreamer**[20] 2735 3-9-4 **66**.......... SebSanders 3 72+
(William Haggas) *prom: drvn to ld 1f out: wnt rt and collided w rival 50yds out: all out* **11/4**[1]
4306 **2** *hd* **Masterpaver**[12] 2998 3-9-4 **69**..........(v) RobertTart(3) 1 74
(Alan Bailey) *in rr: effrt over 2f out and wd into st: r.o wl fnl f: edgd lft and bmpd rival: jst hld* **7/2**[2]
1310 **3** *1* **Jarlath**[15] 2893 3-9-6 **68**.......... SteveDrowne 5 72
(Seamus Mullins) *dwlt: sn in tch: jnd ldr 2f out: chalng between rivals whn bdly squeezed and bmpd on both sides fnl 50yds: nt rcvr* **7/1**
0-06 **4** *½* **Rochambeau (IRE)**[17] 2850 3-9-5 **67**..........(b[1]) GeorgeBaker 6 70
(Roger Charlton) *sn stdd towards rr: effrt on inner over 1f out: styd on fnl f* **7/2**[2]
1353 **5** *1 ¼* **Opera Fan (FR)**[8] 3116 3-9-4 **66**.......... JoeFanning 2 68
(Mark Johnston) *led: hrd rdn and hdd 1f out: disputing 4th and btn whn hmpd and snatched up 50yds out* **5/1**[3]
0-61 **6** *1* **Chesil Beach**[12] 2997 3-8-5 **60**.......... RobHornby(7) 7 59
(Andrew Balding) *dwlt: hdwy to press ldr after 1f tl over 5f out: rdn and outpcd fnl 3f* **14/1**
3420 **7** *8* **Flying Author (IRE)**[21] 2694 3-7-12 **51** oh2 ow1......(tp) DannyBrock(5) 4 37
(Phil McEntee) *s.s: bhd: gd hdwy on outer to press ldr over 5f out: wknd 2f out* **33/1**
2m 31.51s (-1.49) **Going Correction** -0.025s/f (Stan) **7 Ran SP% 109.9**
Speed ratings (Par 99): **103,102,102,101,101 100,95**
CSF £11.51 TOTE £4.60: £1.20, £4.30; EX 17.10 Trifecta £113.20.
**Owner** Mr & Mrs R Scott **Bred** Mr & Mrs R & P Scott **Trained** Newmarket, Suffolk
**FOCUS**
A modest handicap, but one featuring a couple of unexposed sorts. The pace was on the steady side to the home turn and the winner raced centre-to-far side in the straight.

## 3392 DOWNLOAD 888SPORT.COM MOBILE APP H'CAP 5f 6y(P)
**8:30** (8:32) (Class 6) (0-65,71) 4-Y-0+ **£2,587** (£770; £384; £192) **Stalls High**

Form RPR
1300 **1** **Seamster**[24] 2606 7-9-5 **63**..........(bt) GeorgeBaker 8 77
(Richard Ford) *mde all at str pce: in control over 1f out: rdn out* **3/1**[2]
002 **2** *1 ¼* **Decision By One**[8] 3093 5-8-9 **56**..........(t) DeclanBates(3) 2 66
(David Evans) *chsd wnr: hrd rdn and hld over 1f out: kpt on fnl f* **11/4**[1]
4150 **3** *1 ¼* **Dishy Guru**[40] 2174 5-9-7 **65**..........(b) MartinHarley 3 70+
(Michael Blanshard) *dwlt: towards rr: rdn and hdwy over 1f out: styd on* **11/4**[1]
0440 **4** *3 ¼* **Volcanic Dust (IRE)**[45] 2008 6-8-9 **53**..........(t) SteveDrowne 5 46
(Milton Bradley) *in tch: rdn over 2f out: one pce* **25/1**
0344 **5** *½* **Danzoe (IRE)**[43] 2070 7-9-0 **58**.......... SebSanders 4 50
(Christine Dunnett) *in tch on outer: hrd rdn 3f out: sn btn* **8/1**
4455 **6** *1 ¾* **Pharoh Jake**[16] 2865 6-9-1 **59**..........(v[1]) WilliamCarson 6 44
(John Bridger) *pushed along to chse ldrs: rdn over 2f out: wknd over 1f out* **8/1**
00-3 **7** *nse* **Hit The Lights (IRE)**[43] 2070 4-9-2 **63**.......... ThomasBrown(3) 7 48
(Patrick Chamings) *dwlt: outpcd: a bhd* **5/1**[3]
306 **8** *3 ¼* **Give Us A Belle (IRE)**[20] 2724 5-9-4 **62**..........(vt) AdamBeschizza 1 35
(Christine Dunnett) *pushed along: prom on rail: drvn and lost pl 3f out* **12/1**
58.63s (-0.17) **Going Correction** -0.025s/f (Stan) **8 Ran SP% 128.8**
Speed ratings (Par 101): **100,98,96,90,90 87,87,81**
CSF £13.54 CT £27.18 TOTE £3.80: £1.50, £1.90, £1.10; EX 34.90 Trifecta £205.90.
**Owner** P Bamford **Bred** D G Hardisty Bloodstock **Trained** Garstang, Lancs
**FOCUS**
Exposed sprinters in a modest handicap. Although the gallop was sound, very few figured and the winner raced centre-to-far side in the straight.

## 3393 £88 IN FREE BETS AT 888SPORT.COM H'CAP 6f 1y(P)
**9:00** (9:02) (Class 6) (0-65,65) 3-Y-0+ **£2,587** (£770; £384; £192) **Stalls Low**

Form RPR
0500 **1** **Billy Red**[16] 2865 10-9-2 **61**..........(b) DannyBrock(5) 5 70
(J R Jenkins) *mde virtually all: hld on wl fnl f* **25/1**
2303 **2** *½* **Victorian Number (FR)**[15] 2901 6-9-9 **63**.......... GeorgeBaker 7 70
(Geoffrey Deacon) *prom: hrd rdn wl over 1f out: chsd wnr fnl f: r.o: jst hld* **9/4**[1]
5305 **3** *¾* **Sewn Up**[30] 2435 4-9-4 **58**..........(p) RoystonFfrench 2 63+
(Andrew Hollinshead) *rn wout declared tongue-tie: mid-div on rail: hdwy over 1f out: r.o wl fnl f* **12/1**
2212 **4** *½* **Ghost Train (IRE)**[79] 1221 5-9-11 **65**..........(p) HayleyTurner 4 68
(Tim McCarthy) *mid-div: hdwy to dispute 2nd 1f out: no ex fnl 100yds* **5/2**[2]
300 **5** *½* **Compton Prince**[15] 2887 5-9-8 **62**..........(b) SteveDrowne 8 63
(Milton Bradley) *towards rr: hdwy over 1f out: one pce fnl f* **16/1**
2000 **6** *nk* **Catalyze**[5] 3231 6-8-12 **57**..........(t) RyanWhile(5) 6 57
(Paddy Butler) *bhd: rdn and r.o fr over 1f out: nrest at fin* **20/1**
3023 **7** *¾* **Major Muscari (IRE)**[14] 2909 6-8-13 **56**..........(p) NeilFarley(3) 11 54
(Shaun Harris) *in rr: rdn and sme hdwy over 1f out: nt rch ldrs* **8/1**
000 **8** *nk* **Reginald Claude**[7] 3150 6-8-10 **57**..........(v) CharlotteJenner(7) 12 54
(Mark Usher) *towards rr: rdn and kpt on fnl 2f: unable to chal* **25/1**
0-65 **9** *1* **All Or Nothin (IRE)**[23] 2648 5-9-3 **62**.......... DavidKenny(5) 10 56
(Paddy Butler) *in tch on outer: rdn 3f out: no hdwy fnl 2f* **25/1**
2530 **10** *hd* **Commandingpresence (USA)**[12] 2994 8-9-3 **57**........ WilliamCarson 3 50
(John Bridger) *chsd wnr tl wknd 1f out* **25/1**
50-0 **11** *2 ½* **Going French (IRE)**[15] 2890 7-9-9 **63**.......... PaddyAspell 9 48
(Grace Harris) *chsd ldrs tl hrd rdn and wknd 1f out* **25/1**
1322 **12** *2 ¾* **Johnny Splash (IRE)**[23] 2648 5-9-1 **58**..........(v) RobertTart(3) 1 34
(Roger Teal) *prom tl lost pl 3f out* **7/1**[3]
1m 12.13s (0.23) **Going Correction** -0.025s/f (Stan) **12 Ran SP% 120.5**
Speed ratings (Par 101): **97,96,95,94,94 93,92,92,90,90 87,83**
CSF £76.70 CT £741.46 TOTE £18.90: £4.80, £1.80, £4.00; EX 112.30 Trifecta £583.60.
**Owner** Mrs Irene Hampson **Bred** D R Tucker **Trained** Royston, Herts
**FOCUS**
Another very ordinary handicap and the fourth sprint winner on the card to make all or most of the running. The gallop was reasonable and the winner raced centre-to-far side in the straight.
T/Plt: £19.10 to a £1 stake. Pool of £40664.48 - 1553.58 winning tickets. T/Qpdt: £13.50 to a £1 stake. Pool of £4004.20 - 219.20 winning tickets. LM

# 3366 RIPON (R-H)
Thursday, June 19
**OFFICIAL GOING: Good (good to firm in places)**
Wind: virtually nil Weather: Fine and sunny

## 3394 BRITISH STALLION STUDS EBF MAIDEN STKS 6f
**2:10** (2:13) (Class 5) 2-Y-0 **£3,881** (£1,155; £577; £288) **Stalls High**

Form RPR
62 **1** **Roossey (IRE)**[32] 2358 2-9-5 0.......... GrahamLee 7 82
(William Haggas) *racd keenly: prom: led 4f out: rdn 2f out: strly pressed fr over 1f out: kpt on* **10/11**[1]
**2** *nk* **Grand Beauty (IRE)** 2-9-0 0.......... TonyHamilton 4 76+
(Richard Fahey) *chsd ldrs: rdn to chal strly fr over 1f out: kpt on: hld nr fin* **14/1**
4 **3** *2* **Gaudy (IRE)**[35] 2288 2-9-5 0.......... HarryBentley 6 75+
(Kevin Ryan) *s.i.s: sn in tch: rdn 2f out: one pce and hld by ldng pair fr over 1f out* **15/8**[2]
00 **4** *1 ¾* **Penny Royale**[19] 2788 2-9-0 0.......... AndrewElliott 2 65+
(Tim Easterby) *hld up: nudged along and hdwy 2f out: kpt on fnl f* **100/1**
06 **5** *7* **Dragline**[47] 1955 2-9-5 0.......... DavidAllan 3 49
(Tim Easterby) *hld up: pushed along 1/2-way: nvr threatened* **50/1**
**6** *5* **Prince Of Clowns (IRE)** 2-9-5 0.......... PhillipMakin 5 34
(John Quinn) *midfield: pushed along 1/2-way: nvr threatened* **14/1**
**7** *4 ½* **Mutafarrej** 2-9-5 0.......... AdrianNicholls 8 21
(Mark Johnston) *w ldrs: rdn over 2f out: wknd over 1f out* **12/1**[3]
4 **8** *2 ½* **Godric**[14] 2928 2-9-5 0.......... StephenCraine 9
(Tom Dascombe) *led narrowly: hdd 4f out: sn btn* **14/1**
0 **9** *nk* **Hafina**[8] 3107 2-9-0 0.......... JamesSullivan 1
(Michael Easterby) *hld up: a towards rr* **100/1**
1m 14.18s (1.18) **Going Correction** +0.05s/f (Good) **9 Ran SP% 118.8**
Speed ratings (Par 93): **94,93,90,88,79 72,66,63,62**
CSF £17.45 TOTE £1.80: £1.10, £4.00, £1.10; EX 17.50 Trifecta £52.70.
**Owner** Sheikh Ahmed Al Maktoum **Bred** Ballyreddin Stud **Trained** Newmarket, Suffolk
**FOCUS**
The going was riding just on the fast side despite overnight watering. Course at innermost configuration and distances as advertised. An interesting maiden with several speedily bred debutants taking on more experienced rivals, but a pair with experience dominated the betting and one of those came out best.

## 3395 SIS LIVE CLAIMING STKS 6f
**2:45** (2:45) (Class 5) 3-Y-0+ **£3,234** (£962; £481; £240) **Stalls High**

Form RPR
0056 **1** **Emily Davison (IRE)**[15] 2906 3-8-5 45..........(p) GemmaTutty(7) 3 62
(Karen Tutty) *led: hdd over 4f out: briefly outpcd 1/2-way: hdwy over 1f out: led again ins fnl f: kpt on* **66/1**
3000 **2** *2 ¾* **Inxile (IRE)**[19] 2786 9-9-10 91..........(p) AdrianNicholls 2 60
(David Nicholls) *s.i.s: racd keenly and led over 4f out: rdn whn hdd jst ins fnl f: no ex* **4/5**[1]
0066 **3** *1* **Bosun Breese**[7] 3138 9-8-12 74.......... PaulMulrennan 1 45
(Paul Midgley) *prom: rdn over 2f out: no ex fnl f* **5/2**[2]
0-00 **4** *shd* **Swendab (IRE)**[11] 3033 6-9-10 85..........(b) GrahamLee 6 57
(John O'Shea) *chsd ldrs: rdn and outpcd 1/2-way: plugged on fnl f* **5/1**[3]
-316 **5** *2 ½* **Foreign Rhythm (IRE)**[26] 2542 9-8-6 63.......... ShirleyTeasdale(5) 4 36
(Ron Barr) *hld up: pushed along 1/2-way: nvr threatened* **14/1**
1m 13.5s (0.50) **Going Correction** +0.05s/f (Good)
**WFA** 3 from 6yo+ 7lb **5 Ran SP% 109.0**
Speed ratings (Par 103): **98,94,93,92,89**
CSF £120.43 TOTE £13.70: £7.00, £1.10; EX 87.40 Trifecta £188.50.
**Owner** Thoroughbred Homes Ltd **Bred** Rathbarry Stud **Trained** Osmotherley, N Yorks
**FOCUS**
Not a bad claimer.

## 3396 CURVY BRIDAL BOROUGHBRIDGE H'CAP (BOBIS RACE) 1m 4f 10y
**3:20** (3:20) (Class 4) (0-80,76) 3-Y-0 **£5,175** (£1,540; £769; £384) **Stalls Low**

Form RPR
-051 **1** **Maid In Rio (IRE)**[20] 2735 3-9-3 **72**.......... PaulMulrennan 3 89+
(Mark Johnston) *in tch: led gng wl 2f out: sn rdn clr: eased towards fin* **7/2**[2]
0014 **2** *7* **Full Day**[12] 3003 3-9-2 **71**.......... PaulPickard 5 75
(Brian Ellison) *pressed ldr: led 3f out: rdn whn hdd 2f out: sn no ch w wnr: plugged on* **9/2**[3]

-632 **3** 3/4 **Loch Ma Naire (IRE)**[22] 2671 3-9-4 **73**..........(b) GrahamLee 2 76
(Ed Dunlop) *hld up: pushed along over 4f out: plugged on into modest 3rd ins fnl f* **6/1**

2-34 **4** 4 **Grand Meister**[22] 2685 3-9-7 **76**.......... PJMcDonald 1 72
(Michael Bell) *s.i.s: sn trckd ldrs: rdn over 2f out: sn one pce: wknd fnl f* **5/4**[1]

054 **5** 2 1/2 **Mendelita**[32] 2365 3-8-7 **62**.......... JamesSullivan 4 54
(Richard Fahey) *hld up: pushed along over 5f out: nvr threatened* **16/1**

36-4 **6** 19 **Fine Vintage (FR)**[21] 2696 3-9-5 **74**.......... AdrianNicholls 6 54
(Mark Johnston) *led: rdn whn hdd 3f out: sn wknd* **12/1**

2m 33.67s (-3.03) **Going Correction** -0.10s/f (Good) **6** Ran SP% **112.7**
Speed ratings (Par 101): **106,101,100,98,96 83**
CSF £19.43 TOTE £5.20: £2.60, £2.40; EX 20.50 Trifecta £56.90.
**Owner** The New Fairyhouse Partnership **Bred** Miss Susan Bates And Suzannah Dwyer **Trained** Middleham Moor, N Yorks

**FOCUS**
A tight 3yo handicap on paper, but a clear-cut winner.

## 3397 LADIES DAY H'CAP 1m 1f
**4:00** (4:00) (Class 3) (0-90,90) 4-Y-0+ **£7,561** (£2,263; £1,131; £566; £282) **Stalls** Low

Form RPR

-113 **1** **Hit The Jackpot (IRE)**[16] 2869 5-9-4 **87**.......... DanielTudhope 1 102
(David O'Meara) *in tch: pushed along over 2f out: rdn to ld over 1f out: sn clr: eased fnl 110yds* **7/4**[1]

1322 **2** 5 **Bold Prediction (IRE)**[16] 2869 4-9-2 **90**.......... JoeyHaynes(5) 2 94
(K R Burke) *trckd ldr: led 3f out: sn rdn: hdd over 1f out: sn no ex and no ch w wnr* **3/1**[3]

0431 **3** 2 1/4 **Bartack (IRE)**[12] 3005 4-9-0 **86**..........(v) SamJames(3) 4 85
(David O'Meara) *trckd ldrs: rdn over 2f out: sn outpcd: wnt modest 3rd 110yds out* **13/2**

1002 **4** 2 **Busatto (USA)**[5] 3251 4-9-6 **89**.......... AdrianNicholls 5 84
(Mark Johnston) *s.i.s: hld up: rdn and hdwy on outer over 2f out: sn chsd ldr: wknd fnl f: lost 3rd 100yds out* **11/4**[2]

05-6 **5** 38 **Suits Me**[16] 2869 11-9-4 **87**.......... PhillipMakin 3
(David Barron) *sn led: rdn whn hdd 3f out: sn wknd: eased* **11/1**

1m 52.21s (-2.49) **Going Correction** -0.10s/f (Good) **5** Ran SP% **109.7**
Speed ratings (Par 107): **107,102,100,98,65**
CSF £7.20 TOTE £3.10: £1.30, £1.90; EX 5.80 Trifecta £15.20.
**Owner** Hambleton Racing Ltd XXX **Bred** Moyglare Stud Farm Ltd **Trained** Nawton, N Yorks

**FOCUS**
A decent prize produced a good handicap, despite the smallish field, but the winner scored with plenty in hand.

## 3398 BEAUMONT ROBINSON LADIES' DERBY H'CAP (LADY AMATEUR RIDERS) 1m 4f 10y
**4:35** (4:36) (Class 6) (0-65,65) 4-Y-0+ **£3,119** (£967; £483; £242) **Stalls** Low

Form RPR

00-5 **1** **Tropical Bachelor (IRE)**[16] 2872 8-9-5 **49**.......... MissSBrotherton 4 63
(Brian Baugh) *trckd ldr: rdn to ld 2f out: kpt on wl to go clr* **9/2**[2]

-400 **2** 5 **Patavium (IRE)**[24] 2620 11-8-12 **47**..........(p) MissNHayes(5) 1 53
(Edwin Tuer) *midfield on inner: angled towards outer over 2f out: sn rdn: wnt 2nd 1f out: edgd rt: kpt on: no threat wnr* **16/1**

0363 **3** 1 1/2 **Tinseltown**[8] 3095 8-10-7 **65**.......... MissADeniel 6 69
(Brian Rothwell) *led: rdn whn hdd over 3f out: plugged on* **6/1**

-303 **4** 1 3/4 **Politbureau**[20] 2738 7-9-1 **48**..........(b) MissJoannaMason(3) 2 49
(Michael Easterby) *hld up: sme hdwy over 3f out: kpt on one pce: wnt 4th towards fin* **6/1**

55-5 **5** 1/2 **Amir Pasha (UAE)**[24] 2620 9-9-0 **47**..........(b) MissJRRichards(3) 9 47
(Micky Hammond) *racd keenly: trckd ldr: rdn to ld 3f out: hdd 2f out: wkng whn sltly short of room ins fnl f* **11/1**

2360 **6** 7 **Mcbirney (USA)**[13] 2963 7-10-0 **63**.......... MrsRWilson(5) 3 52
(Paul D'Arcy) *v.s.a: hld up wl in rr: nvr threatened* **11/2**[3]

3232 **7** 3/4 **Merchant Of Medici**[7] 3134 7-10-2 **60**.......... MissAliceMills 10 48
(Micky Hammond) *in tch: wknd over 2f out* **7/2**[1]

1-00 **8** 1 3/4 **Royal Trooper (IRE)**[125] 609 8-9-13 **60**..........(t) BeckyBrisbourne(3) 11 45
(Mark Brisbourne) *hld up in rr: a bhd* **25/1**

-640 **9** 11 **Cabal**[53] 1761 7-9-1 **50**..........(b) MissKMargarson(5) 12 17
(Andrew Crook) *in tch on outer: wknd over 3f out* **20/1**

0000 **U** **Flag Of Glory**[21] 2701 7-9-5 **54**.......... MissMEdden(5) 8
(Peter Hiatt) *stmbld and uns rdr leaving stall* **12/1**

2m 36.47s (-0.23) **Going Correction** -0.10s/f (Good) **10** Ran SP% **114.9**
Speed ratings (Par 101): **96,95,91,90,90 85,85,83,76,**
CSF £72.39 CT £434.78 TOTE £5.10: £2.90, £4.50, £1.90; EX 104.30 Trifecta £783.50 Part won. Pool of £1044.76 - 0.60 winning units..
**Owner** Pippa Bickerton **Bred** George Ward **Trained** Audley, Staffs
■ Stewards' Enquiry : Mrs R Wilson 14-day ban: failed to take all reasonable and permissable measures to obtain best possible placing (tbn)

**FOCUS**
A grand title, but a modest contest that was weakened by the absence of the likely favourite.

## 3399 NORTH ORMESBY WMC TONY BENNETT MEMORIAL H'CAP 5f
**5:10** (5:12) (Class 5) (0-75,75) 3-Y-0+ **£3,234** (£962; £481; £240) **Stalls** High

Form RPR

5333 **1** **Adam's Ale**[32] 2364 5-9-11 **72**.......... GrahamLee 1 83
(Paul Midgley) *sn prom: led over 1f out: pushed out fnl f* **5/4**[1]

2150 **2** 1 1/4 **Captain Royale (IRE)**[6] 3191 9-9-10 **71**..........(p) JamesSullivan 2 78
(Tracy Waggott) *sn led: rdn whn hdd over 1f out: kpt on but a hld by wnr* **16/1**

5120 **3** 1/2 **Boxing Shadows**[32] 2364 4-9-5 **66**.......... RobertWinston 4 71
(Les Eyre) *midfield: hdwy to chse ldr 2f out: sn rdn: kpt on* **6/1**[2]

364- **4** hd **Innocently (IRE)**[296] 5859 3-9-5 **75**.......... JulieBurke(3) 8 77
(David O'Meara) *trckd ldrs: rdn 2f out: n.m.r over 1f out: angled rt jst ins fnl f: kpt on* **14/1**

0030 **5** 1/2 **Ambitious Icarus**[18] 2803 5-10-0 **75**..........(e) RobbieFitzpatrick 13 77+
(Richard Guest) *s.i.s: hld up: swtchd rt to wd outside 2f out: kpt on fnl f* **16/1**

005 **6** nk **Medici Time**[14] 2914 9-9-4 **65**..........(v) PhillipMakin 10 66
(Tim Easterby) *dwlt: hld up: rdn 2f out: kpt on fnl f* **14/1**

-006 **7** 1 1/4 **Ypres**[24] 2602 5-9-10 **71**.......... AndrewElliott 7 68+
(Jason Ward) *hld up: nvr threatened* **9/1**[3]

0004 **8** nse **Holy Angel (IRE)**[13] 2953 5-9-9 **70**..........(e) DavidAllan 9 66
(Tim Easterby) *t.k.h in midfield: rdn over 1f out: n.m.r ins fnl f: nvr threatened* **11/1**

3040 **9** hd **Lady Mai (IRE)**[18] 2802 3-7-12 **56** oh2.......... SammyJoBell(5) 6 50
(Richard Fahey) *chsd ldrs: rdn 2f out: wknd ins fnl f* **22/1**

3100 **10** nk **Lorimer's Lot (IRE)**[20] 2727 3-9-5 **72**.......... PJMcDonald 11 65
(Mark Walford) *midfield on inner: pushed along 1/2-way: nvr threatened* **10/1**

0000 **11** 1 3/4 **Mister Manannan (IRE)**[44] 2056 7-9-11 **72**.......... AdrianNicholls 12 60+
(David Nicholls) *dwlt and bmpd s: hld up: stl gng wl whn n.m.r over 1f out tl ins fnl f: no ch after* **25/1**

0000 **12** 1 3/4 **The Strig**[24] 2606 7-9-5 **66**..........(p) PaulMulrennan 5 48
(Nigel Tinkler) *slowly into stirde: sn in tch towards outer: wknd fnl f* **33/1**

59.75s (-0.25) **Going Correction** +0.05s/f (Good)
**WFA** 3 from 4yo+ 6lb **12** Ran SP% **122.4**
Speed ratings (Par 103): **104,102,101,100,100 99,97,97,97,96 93,91**
CSF £24.98 CT £100.37 TOTE £2.00: £1.10, £2.80, £3.10; EX 19.70 Trifecta £89.20.
**Owner** Mrs M Hills **Bred** Mrs M J Hills **Trained** Westow, N Yorks

**FOCUS**
A fair sprint handicap in which the first two held those positions throughout.

## 3400 RACING AGAIN ON MONDAY 7TH JULY H'CAP 1m
**5:45** (5:46) (Class 5) (0-75,75) 4-Y-0+ **£3,234** (£962; £481; £240) **Stalls** Low

Form RPR

0-13 **1** **Border Bandit (USA)**[6] 3190 6-9-1 **69**..........(p) RobertWinston 4 77
(Tracy Waggott) *hld up in tch: hdwy over 3f out: swtchd lft 2f out: sn chal: led 110yds out: kpt on* **6/4**[1]

3062 **2** 1/2 **Al Muheer (IRE)**[8] 3094 9-9-7 **75**..........(p) JamesSullivan 5 82
(Ruth Carr) *trckd ldrs on inner: rdn over 2f out: kpt on fnl f: wnt 2nd post* **3/1**[2]

5000 **3** hd **Al Mukhdam**[13] 2953 4-9-7 **75**.......... PhillipMakin 6 81
(Ed de Giles) *prom: led 6f out: hdd over 2f out: sn rdn: led again 1f out: hdd 110yds out: no ex: lost 2nd post* **10/1**

6300 **4** 3 **Shamaheart (IRE)**[27] 2519 4-9-5 **73**..........(p) PJMcDonald 2 72
(Geoffrey Harker) *led: hdd 6f out: trckd ldr: led again over 2f out: sn rdn: hdd 1f out: wknd* **10/1**

4-05 **5** nk **Janaab (IRE)**[24] 2605 4-8-7 **61**..........(t) DavidAllan 7 60
(Tim Easterby) *trckd ldrs: rdn 3f out: wknd fnl f* **12/1**

-010 **6** 3 **Charles De Mille**[27] 2519 6-8-8 **62**.......... AndrewElliott 8 54
(George Moore) *s.i.s: hld up in rr: pushed along over 3f out: nvr threatened* **12/1**

-400 **7** 2 1/2 **Woody Bay**[23] 2654 4-9-5 **73**..........(b[1]) GrahamLee 3 59
(James Given) *dwlt: racd keenly hld up: rdn over 3f out: nvr threatened* **6/1**[3]

1m 39.38s (-2.02) **Going Correction** -0.10s/f (Good) **7** Ran SP% **112.9**
Speed ratings (Par 103): **106,105,105,102,102 99,96**
CSF £5.87 CT £30.11 TOTE £2.60: £1.80, £1.20; EX 5.20 Trifecta £32.90.
**Owner** Elsa Crankshaw Gordon Allan **Bred** Darley **Trained** Spennymoor, Co Durham

**FOCUS**
An ordinary handicap, but a close finish.
T/Plt: £33.20 to a £1 stake. Pool of £50884.85 - 1115.56 winning tickets. T/Qpdt: £18.40 to a £1 stake. Pool of £2696.40 - 108.35 winning tickets. AS

# 2931 SOUTHWELL (L-H)
### Thursday, June 19

**OFFICIAL GOING: Standard**
Wind: Light across Weather: Cloudy

## 3401 32RED MEDIAN AUCTION MAIDEN STKS 1m 3f (F)
**2:20** (2:20) (Class 5) 3-4-Y-0 **£2,587** (£770; £384; £192) **Stalls** Low

Form RPR

632 **1** **Holberg Suite**[14] 2924 3-8-10 71.......... NickyMackay 3 76
(John Gosden) *cl up: rdn along and lost pl 5f out: drvn to chse clr ldr over 2f out: styd on u.p fnl f: led last 40yds* **10/11**[1]

22 **2** 3/4 **Lamorak (FR)**[23] 2655 3-9-1 0.......... SeanLevey 4 80+
(Hugo Palmer) *prom: trckd ldr after 4f: cl up 4f out: led over 3f out: pushed clr wl over 2f out: rdn and edgd lft over 1f out: drvn and hung rt ent fnl f: sn wknd: hdd last 40yds* **9/4**[2]

3 **3** 23 **Vodka Wells (FR)**[3] 3302 4-10-0 0..........(t) DaleSwift 2 41
(Brian Ellison) *s.i.s: sn detached and pushed along: sme hdwy on outer over 4f out: rdn along and plugged on fnl 3f: tk remote 3rd ins fnl f* **5/1**[3]

6 **4** nk **Carraig Rock**[8] 3106 4-10-0 0.......... RobertHavlin 1 40
(Hughie Morrison) *prom on inner whn n.m.r and lost pl bnd after 1 1/2f: chsd ldrs: rdn along over 4f out: bhd and wd st: n.d* **9/1**

00-0 **5** nk **Key To Your Heart**[15] 2883 3-8-10 0.......... TomEaves 5 35+
(Hughie Morrison) *sn led on outer: rdn along and jnd 4f out: hdd over 3f out: sn drvn and wknd wl over 2f out* **25/1**

2m 31.59s (3.59) **Going Correction** +0.075s/f (Slow)
**WFA** 3 from 4yo 13lb **5** Ran SP% **113.7**
Speed ratings (Par 103): **89,88,71,71,71**
CSF £3.37 TOTE £2.10: £1.70, £1.10; EX 3.60 Trifecta £4.60.
**Owner** Cheveley Park Stud **Bred** Cheveley Park Stud Ltd **Trained** Newmarket, Suffolk
■ Stewards' Enquiry : Nicky Mackay sev en-day ban: used whip above permitted level (Jul 3-9)
Sean Levey one-day ban: careless riding (Jul 3)

**FOCUS**
Probably a fair maiden for round here and the pace was generous.

## 3402 32RED CASINO H'CAP 7f (F)
**2:55** (2:55) (Class 4) (0-80,80) 4-Y-0+ **£4,690** (£1,395; £697; £348) **Stalls** High

Form RPR

6000 **1** **The Great Gabrial**[14] 2922 5-9-6 **79**..........(p) BenCurtis 3 93
(Alan McCabe) *towards rr: gd hdwy over 2f out: rdn to ld appr fnl f: kpt on strly* **11/1**

030 **2** 2 **Al Khan (IRE)**[22] 2677 5-8-7 **71**.......... JacobButterfield(5) 7 80
(Ollie Pears) *chsd ldng pair: pushed along 3f out: rdn and sltly outpcd over 1f out: edgd rt and kpt on u.p fnl f* **10/1**

5322 **3** 3/4 **Imaginary World (IRE)**[8] 3096 6-8-7 **69**..........(t) JasonHart(3) 5 76
(John Balding) *hld up: wd st: hdwy over 2f out: rdn to chse ldrs over 1f out: edgd lft and kpt on same pce fnl f* **7/2**[2]

-100 **4** 3/4 **Exzachary**[17] 2833 4-8-13 **79**..........(t) HarryBurns(7) 6 84
(Jo Hughes) *dwlt and bhd: rdn and hdwy wl over 1f out: kpt on fnl f: nrst fin* **25/1**

2101 **5** 1 1/4 **Two Moons**[15] 2905 4-9-5 **78**.......... BarryMcHugh 2 80
(Tony Coyle) *in tch on inner: swtchd rt and hdwy over 2f out: rdn to chal over 1f out: sn ev ch: drvn ent fnl f and sn one pce* **2/1**[1]

5024 **6** nk **Subtle Knife**[16] 2861 5-9-7 **80**.......... PatrickDonaghy 4 81
(Giles Bravery) *swtchd rt to outer sn after s: sn in rr and wd st: rdn over 2f out: styd on fnl f: nrst fin* **8/1**

1125 **7** *1 ¾* **Khajaaly (IRE)**[17] 2844 7-9-1 **74**..............(vt) AndrewMullen 10 71
(Michael Appleby) *trckd ldrs: hdwy to chse clr ldr 3f out: rdn along 2f out: sn wknd* **13/2[3]**

0-01 **8** *3 ¾* **Welliesinthewater (IRE)**[84] 1125 4-7-13 **65** ow1...(v) AdamMcLean[(7)] 1 52
(Derek Shaw) *a towards rr* **16/1**

5606 **9** *shd* **Pabusar**[15] 2905 6-7-10 **62**.............. NoraLooby[(7)] 9 49
(Ann Stokell) *led: pushed clr 1/2-way: rdn along 2f out: hdd & wknd appr fnl f* **66/1**

0604 **10** *5* **Foie Gras**[15] 2901 4-8-2 **61**.............. RaulDaSilva 8 35
(Chris Dwyer) *cl up: rdn along 3f out: sn wknd* **16/1**

1m 29.53s (-0.77) **Going Correction** +0.075s/f (Slow) **10** Ran SP% **114.5**
Speed ratings (Par 105): **107,104,103,103,101 101,99,94,94,89**
CSF £113.58 CT £466.17 TOTE £16.90: £4.80, £3.50, £2.00; EX 116.50 Trifecta £580.40.
**Owner** Tariq Al Nisf **Bred** Juddmonte Farms Ltd **Trained** Averham Park, Notts
**FOCUS**
A fair handicap for thr track.

## 3403 ALL NEW 32REDSPORT.COM MAIDEN AUCTION STKS 6f (F)
**3:30** (3:31) (Class 5) 2-Y-O **£2,587** (£770; £384; £192) **Stalls** Low

Form RPR

422 **1** **Make On Madam (IRE)**[26] 2541 2-8-0 0.............. JackGarritty[(7)] 3 66
(Brian Ellison) *trckd ldrs: hdwy to chse ldng pair 1/2-way: rdn wl over 1f out: styd on to chal ent fnl f: drvn to ld and hung lft last 100yds: kpt on* **11/4[2]**

32 **2** *1* **Grosmont**[15] 2903 2-9-1 0.............. TomEaves 2 71
(James Given) *led: rdn over 1f out: drvn ent fnl f: hdd and no ex last 100yds* **15/2**

2 **3** *hd* **Spindle (IRE)**[72] 1363 2-8-6 0.............. AndrewMullen 6 61
(Mark Usher) *prom: chsd ldng pair after 2f: rdn along and sltly outpcd wl over 1f out: kpt on and ch ins fnl f: hld whn hmpd nr fin* **5/1[3]**

22 **4** *3 ¾* **Denton Dawn (IRE)**[28] 2472 2-8-5 0.............. ConnorBeasley[(3)] 5 52
(Michael Dods) *prom: chsd ldr after 2f: effrt over 2f out: rdn wl over 1f out: drvn and wknd appr fnl f* **11/10[1]**

**5** *8* **Regal Accolade** 2-9-0 0.............. DavidNolan 7 34
(David O'Meara) *dwlt and sn rdn along: outpcd and wd st: n.d* **20/1**

**6** *8* **Theydon Thunder** 2-8-8 0.............. RosieJessop[(3)] 1 7
(Peter Charalambous) *s.i.s: green and a bhd* **50/1**

1m 17.84s (1.34) **Going Correction** +0.075s/f (Slow) **6** Ran SP% **109.4**
Speed ratings (Par 93): **94,92,92,87,76 66**
CSF £21.47 TOTE £2.30: £1.80, £3.20; EX 14.80 Trifecta £47.50.
**Owner** Keith Brown **Bred** Mrs T Brudenell **Trained** Norton, N Yorks
■ Stewards' Enquiry : Jack Garritty four-day ban: careless riding (Jul 3-4,6-7)
**FOCUS**
A fair 2yo maiden auction race.

## 3404 BET NOW AT 32REDSPORT.COM H'CAP 2m (F)
**4:10** (4:10) (Class 6) (0-60,59) 4-Y-O+ **£1,940** (£577; £288; £144) **Stalls** Low

Form RPR

221- **1** **Katie Gale**[273] 6558 4-9-3 **55**.............. AndrewMullen 7 68+
(Michael Appleby) *midfield: pushed along and jnd ldng gp after 6f: prom on outer over 4f out: sn cl up: rdn and slt ld over 2f out: drvn over 1f out: hung rt to stands' rail ins fnl f: styd on* **7/4[1]**

-603 **2** *6* **Mister Bob (GER)**[14] 2935 5-9-3 **55**..............(p) TedDurcan 12 63
(James Bethell) *trckd ldng pair: cl up 1/2-way: led 4f out: rdn along 3f out: hdd over 2f out and sn rdn: drvn and one pce fnl f* **5/1[2]**

0055 **3** *6* **Layla's Boy**[14] 2935 7-8-5 **46**..............(t[1]) JasonHart[(3)] 10 45
(Simon West) *hld up and bhd: hdwy 5f out: rdn along 3f out: plugged on fnl 2f: no imp* **33/1**

0665 **4** *1 ¼* **Joyful Motive**[3] 3310 5-8-2 **47**.............. BradleyBosley[(7)] 9 44
(Michael Chapman) *prom: rdn along and lost pl 6f out: plugged on u.p fnl 3f* **6/1[3]**

2005 **5** *7* **Our Golden Girl**[14] 2916 4-8-12 **50**..............(b) RaulDaSilva 11 39
(Shaun Lycett) *trckd ldrs: hdwy to ld 1/2-way: rdn along and hdd 4f out: drvn over 3f out and sn outpcd* **10/1**

00/3 **6** *3 ½* **Freedom Flying**[93] 1004 11-8-7 **45**..............(p) DuranFentiman 6 30
(Lee James) *in rr: bhd 1/2-way: plugged on u.p fnl 3f: nvr a factor* **33/1**

-353 **7** *¾* **Lacey**[77] 1265 5-9-1 **58**..............(e) JackDuern[(5)] 4 42
(Andrew Hollinshead) *a in rr* **7/1**

1-36 **8** *40* **Rock Of Ages**[15] 2904 5-9-7 **59**..............(b) LiamJones 5
(Michael Murphy) *tardy s: hdwy on outer to join ldrs after1f: led after 6f: hdd 1/2-way: rdn along over 5f out: sn drvn and wknd wl over 3f out* **5/1[2]**

5010 **9** *16* **Kingaroo (IRE)**[18] 2801 8-8-8 **49**.............. ConnorBeasley[(3)] 8
(Garry Woodward) *midfield: rdn along 6f out: sn bhd* **20/1**

/0-0 **10** *1 ¼* **All That Remains (IRE)**[61] 1359 9-8-13 **51**..............(t) DaleSwift 3
(Brian Ellison) *a in rr: bhd fnl 4f* **14/1**

5-00 **11** *23* **Bullseye Babe**[15] 2885 4-8-9 **47**..............(e[1]) RobertHavlin 2
(Mark Usher) *led 6f: rdn along and lost pl over 7f out: sn bhd: t.o fnl 4f* **50/1**

3364 **12** *50* **Uncle Bernie (IRE)**[15] 2885 4-9-3 **55**..............(p) JimmyQuinn 1
(Andrew Hollinshead) *a in rr: lost pl after 6f: sn bhd and t.o fnl 6f* **12/1**

3m 46.08s (0.58) **Going Correction** +0.075s/f (Slow) **12** Ran SP% **132.5**
Speed ratings (Par 101): **101,98,95,94,90 89,88,68,60,60 48,23**
CSF £11.58 CT £243.97 TOTE £2.20: £1.30, £2.20, £9.60; EX 14.90 Trifecta £352.20.
**Owner** Ferrybank Properties Limited **Bred** Netherfield House Stud **Trained** Danethorpe, Notts
**FOCUS**
A low-grade stayers' handicap. Plenty of Southwell regulars, but surprisingly no C&D winner in the line-up.

## 3405 RACING SPECIALS AT 32REDSPORT.COM H'CAP 7f (F)
**4:45** (4:45) (Class 5) (0-75,72) 3-Y-O **£2,587** (£770; £384; £192) **Stalls** High

Form RPR

110 **1** **Red Primo (IRE)**[30] 2429 3-9-7 **72**.............. BenCurtis 8 82+
(Alan McCabe) *trckd ldrs: hdwy 3f out: cl up on outer over 2f: rdn to ld wl over 1f out: drvn and edgd lft ins fnl f: kpt on wl towards fin* **9/4[1]**

0000 **2** *1 ¼* **Outbacker (IRE)**[14] 2929 3-9-7 **72**.............. LiamJones 6 79
(Mark Johnston) *cl up: led over 4f out: rdn along wl over 2f out: hdd wl over 1f out: drvn and rallied ins fnl f: no ex last 100yds* **7/1**

-166 **3** *3 ¼* **Two Shades Of Grey (IRE)**[30] 2429 3-8-13 **67**.... GeorgeChaloner[(3)] 3 66
(Richard Fahey) *prom whn hmpd after 1f: chsd ldrs: rdn along 3f out: styd on u.p fr wl over 1f out: no imp fnl f* **6/1**

-424 **4** *¾* **Injaz**[16] 2870 3-8-4 **60**.............. ShaneGray[(5)] 7 57
(Kevin Ryan) *cl up on outer: rdn along wl over 2f out: wknd over 1f out: edgd rt ins fnl f* **13/2**

6-50 **5** *¾* **Buy Out Boy**[84] 1124 3-8-11 **62**.............. AndrewMullen 4 57
(Michael Appleby) *towards rr: rdn along 1/2-way: styd on fnl 2f: n.m.r ins fnl f: nrst fin* **7/2[2]**

2103 **6** *shd* **Wildcat Lass (USA)**[14] 2936 3-9-4 **69**.............. DavidNolan 2 63
(David O'Meara) *cl up: rdn along 1/2-way: wknd over 2f out* **5/1[3]**

-346 **7** *7* **Miss Acclaimed (IRE)**[27] 2517 3-8-0 **58**..............(p) JackGarritty[(7)] 5 34
(Brian Ellison) *prom whn hmpd and lost pl after 1f: sn towards rr* **14/1**

-000 **8** *3 ¾* **Hickster (IRE)**[15] 2889 3-8-13 **69**..............(v) PhilipPrince[(5)] 1 35
(Roy Bowring) *slt ld on inner: hdd over 4f out: rdn along over 3f out: sn wknd* **25/1**

1m 30.3s **Going Correction** +0.075s/f (Slow) **8** Ran SP% **120.3**
Speed ratings (Par 99): **103,101,97,97,96 96,88,83**
CSF £20.03 CT £87.23 TOTE £3.60: £1.70, £3.10, £1.50; EX 21.40 Trifecta £126.40.
**Owner** Craig and Maureen Buckingham **Bred** E O'Gorman **Trained** Averham Park, Notts
**FOCUS**
A fair 3yo handicap.

## 3406 32RED.COM H'CAP 6f (F)
**5:20** (5:22) (Class 6) (0-65,65) 3-Y-O **£1,940** (£577; £288; £144) **Stalls** Low

Form RPR

140- **1** **Musical Molly (IRE)**[241] 7418 3-9-1 **59**.............. DaleSwift 1 68
(Brian Ellison) *slt ld: hdd over 4f out: cl up on inner: chal over 2f out: rdn to ld wl over 1f out: drvn out* **9/1**

4302 **2** *¾* **Meebo (IRE)**[14] 2931 3-9-0 **58**..............(vt) NickyMackay 6 64
(J R Jenkins) *cl up: led 3f out: rdn over 2f out: hdd wl over 1f out: ev ch tl drvn and no ex ins fnl f* **5/1[3]**

5-00 **3** *3 ½* **Street Boss (IRE)**[38] 2204 3-8-11 **55**.............. DuranFentiman 2 50
(Tim Easterby) *chsd ldrs on inner: pushed along and outpcd 1/2-way: rdn 2f out: styd on to take 3rd ins fnl f* **20/1**

0511 **4** *½* **Shades Of Silk**[14] 2931 3-8-11 **58**.............. ConnorBeasley[(3)] 5 51
(James Given) *in tch: wd st: hdwy over 2f out: rdn along wl over 1f out: sn no imp* **1/1[1]**

54-4 **5** *¾* **Tahchee**[15] 2886 3-9-1 **59**.............. TomEaves 4 50
(James Fanshawe) *trckd ldrs: effrt wl over 2f out: sn rdn and no imp fr over 1f out* **4/1[2]**

1000 **6** *1 ¾* **Walta (IRE)**[5] 3222 3-9-2 **65**..............(b) PhilipPrince[(5)] 7 50
(Roy Bowring) *s.i.s and bhd: rdn along and rapid hdwy on outer to ld over 4f out: hdd 3f out: drvn 2f out and grad wknd* **5/1[3]**

50-0 **7** *99* **Hot Amber (USA)**[8] 3124 3-8-5 **49**..............(e[1]) AndrewMullen 3
(Robert Cowell) *dwlt: a in rr: detached 1/2-way and vritually p.u over 2f out* **20/1**

1m 17.78s (1.28) **Going Correction** +0.075s/f (Slow) **7** Ran SP% **122.9**
Speed ratings (Par 97): **94,93,88,87,86 84,**
CSF £57.38 TOTE £9.80: £4.40, £2.70; EX 43.30 Trifecta £320.10.
**Owner** Mrs J A Martin **Bred** W Maxwell Ervine **Trained** Norton, N Yorks
**FOCUS**
The first two home had this to themselves from the halfway mark.

## 3407 32RED ON THE APP STORE H'CAP 1m (F)
**5:55** (5:55) (Class 6) (0-55,55) 3-Y-O **£1,940** (£577; £288; £144) **Stalls** Low

Form RPR

-050 **1** **Gold Class**[31] 2393 3-9-7 **55**..............(b) DaleSwift 5 62
(Ed McMahon) *tardy and reminders s: sn swtchd rt to outer: rdn along and gd hdwy on outer over 3f out: wd st: hdwy to chse ldng pair wl over 1f out: drvn to chal jst ins fnl f: edgd lft: led last 75yds* **14/1**

6-50 **2** *1 ¼* **Irene Hull (IRE)**[16] 2878 3-9-4 **55**.............. JasonHart[(3)] 8 59
(Garry Moss) *cl up: led after 3f: rdn and jnd over 2f out: drvn over 1f out: edgd rt ins fnl f: hdd and no ex last 75yds* **7/1**

2344 **3** *2 ¾* **Sleet (IRE)**[15] 2906 3-9-2 **50**..............(b[1]) AndrewMullen 12 53
(Michael Appleby) *in tch on outer: hdwy 1/2-way: chsd ldr 3f out: rdn to chal over 2f out: drvn over 1f out: ev ch tl hld whn n.m.r and sltly hmpd last 100yds* **9/2[1]**

0-45 **4** *6* **Notts So Blue**[20] 2742 3-8-12 **46** oh1..............(be[1]) DuranFentiman 1 30
(Shaun Harris) *bhd and rdn along 1/2-way: hdwy over 2f out: kpt on u.p fr over 1f out: nrst fin* **14/1**

360 **5** *½* **Mornin Mr Norris**[8] 3105 3-8-13 **47**.............. RaulDaSilva 6 30
(John Quinn) *led 3f: chsd ldr: rdn along over 3f out: drvn over 2f out and plugged on same pce* **11/2[3]**

4-30 **6** *3 ¾* **Jayeff Herring (IRE)**[16] 2878 3-9-0 **55**.............. MichaelKenneally[(7)] 3 29
(Michael Bell) *chsd ldrs on inner: rdn along wl over 2f out: sn wknd* **16/1**

-034 **7** *1 ½* **Sweet Cherry (IRE)**[21] 2688 3-8-9 **50** ow1..............[1] ChrisMeehan[(7)] 2 21
(Peter Makin) *a towards rr* **5/1[2]**

3120 **8** *1* **Cascadia (IRE)**[18] 2805 3-9-6 **54**.............. TomEaves 9 22
(Alison Hutchinson) *chsd ldrs: rdn along over 3f out: sn wknd* **9/2[1]**

4600 **9** *1 ¼* **Harlequin Jinks**[22] 2667 3-8-7 **46** oh1.............. RachealKneller[(5)] 11 12
(Mark Usher) *dwlt: a bhd* **33/1**

6033 **10** *1* **Casper Lee (IRE)**[14] 2931 3-8-12 **51**..............(b) JacobButterfield[(5)] 4 14
(Michael Herrington) *t.k.h: chsd ldrs: rdn along 3f out: sn wknd* **8/1**

44-0 **11** *1 ¾* **Modify**[20] 2742 3-9-4 **52**.............. DavidNolan 7 11
(David O'Meara) *a towards rr* **15/2**

06-6 **12** *nk* **Hoof's So Lucky**[14] 2931 3-8-12 **46** oh1.............. BarryMcHugh 10 5
(Michael Easterby) *a towards rr* **25/1**

1m 45.27s (1.57) **Going Correction** +0.075s/f (Slow) **12** Ran SP% **129.8**
Speed ratings (Par 97): **95,93,91,85,84 80,79,78,77,76 74,73**
CSF £119.08 CT £539.17 TOTE £23.30: £5.60, £4.40, £1.20; EX 186.00 Trifecta £1062.20 Part won. Pool of £1416.36 - 0.36 winning units..
**Owner** The C H F Partnership **Bred** The C H F Partnership **Trained** Lichfield, Staffs
**FOCUS**
A wide-open low-grade handicap and not many got into it in the home straight.
T/Plt: £206.70 to a £1 stake. Pool of £40919.74 - 144.45 winning tickets. T/Qpdt: £30.90 to a £1 stake. Pool of £2910.26 - 69.60 winning tickets. JR

3408 - 3411a (Foreign Racing) - See Raceform Interactive

# 3163 LEOPARDSTOWN (L-H)
Thursday, June 19

**OFFICIAL GOING: Good to firm**

## 3412a BALLYCORUS STKS (GROUP 3) 7f
**8:05** (8:05) 3-Y-O+ **£32,500** (£9,500; £4,500; £1,500)

RPR

**1** **Wannabe Better (IRE)**[26] 2572 4-9-6 **102**.............. WayneLordan 1 107+
(T Stack, Ire) *settled bhd ldrs: dropped to 6th 1/2-way: rdn into 4th over 1f out and kpt on wl u.p on outer towards fin to ld cl home* **10/1**

**2** *½* **Eastern Rules (IRE)**[82] 1176 6-9-9 **108**.............. ShaneFoley 4 109
(M Halford, Ire) *hld up in tch: clsr in 5th 1/2-way: tk clsr order in 4th over 2f out and wnt 2nd over 1f out: clsd u.p to dispute fnl 100yds tl hdd cl home* **7/1[3]**

3 hd **Brendan Brackan (IRE)**[39] 2185 5-9-12 112.................... GaryCarroll 5 111
(G M Lyons, Ire) *led: 1 l clr 1/2-way: extended advantage 2f out: strly pressed ent fnl f and jnd fnl 100yds: sn hdd and dropped to 3rd cl home* **6/4**[1]

4 1 1/2 **Big Break**[26] 2572 4-9-6 106.................................(b[1]) PatSmullen 2 101
(D K Weld, Ire) *sn chsd ldrs: clsd into 2nd over 2f out: rdn and no imp on ldr in 3rd 1 1/2f out: kpt on one pce in 4th ins fnl f* **5/2**[2]

5 1/2 **Leitir Mor (IRE)**[7] 3166 4-9-12 106...............(tp) KevinManning 3 106+
(J S Bolger, Ire) *s.i.s and racd in rr: no imp into st: sme hdwy fr 2f out to chse ldrs in 5th ent fnl f: kpt on towards fin wout troubling principals* **10/1**

6 6 **One Spirit (IRE)**[7] 3166 6-9-6 99.................................. NGMcCullagh 6 84
(F Dunne, Ire) *chsd ldrs: 3rd 1/2-way: rdn into st and sn no ex u.p: wknd* **16/1**

7 14 **Fountain Of Youth (IRE)**[26] 2571 3-9-0 98..........(p) SeamieHeffernan 8 46
(A P O'Brien, Ire) *sn chsd ldr in 2nd: rdn fr 3f out and wknd into st: eased fnl f* **12/1**

1m 25.43s (-3.27) **Going Correction** -0.125s/f (Firm)
**WFA** 3 from 4yo+ 9lb 7 Ran SP% 112.8
Speed ratings: **113,112,112,110,109 103,87**
CSF £73.83 TOTE £8.40: £3.70, £2.90; DF 108.90 Trifecta £112.40.
**Owner** Mrs T Gaffney **Bred** Churchtown House Stud **Trained** Golden, Co Tipperary

**FOCUS**
Another race that would have produced a very different result if it had been run in a contrasting manner. Favourite Brendan Bracken was pestered by Fountain Of Youth over a trip short of his best and had another challenge in the straight, getting tired close home and setting it up for a closer.

3413 - 3414a (Foreign Racing) - See Raceform Interactive

## 3374 ASCOT (R-H)
### Friday, June 20

**OFFICIAL GOING: Good to firm (good in places on round course; stands' side 9.1, centre 8.9, far side 8.9, round 7.7)**

## 3415 ALBANY STKS (GROUP 3) (FILLIES) 6f
2:30 (2:32) (Class 1) 2-Y-O

**£39,697** (£15,050; £7,532; £3,752; £1,883; £945) **Stalls** Centre

Form RPR

1 1 **Cursory Glance (USA)**[30] 2460 2-9-0 0.................. AndreaAtzeni 17 105+
(Roger Varian) *dwlt: sn rcvrd and in tch in midfield: rdn and gd hdwy to chse ldrs over 1f out: led fnl 75yds: r.o strly and gng away at fin* **14/1**

2 2 **Sunset Glow (USA)**[14] 2-9-0 0..............................(b) VictorEspinoza 11 99
(Wesley A Ward, U.S.A) *led: stl travelling strly 2f out: jnd and rdn over 1f out: kpt on wl u.p: rdr dropped whip fnl 100yds: sn hdd and brushed aside by wnr: battled on to hold 2nd* **7/1**[3]

11 3 nk **Patience Alexander (IRE)**[35] 2313 2-9-0 0.................... AdamKirby 10 98
(David Evans) *chsd ldrs: wnt 2nd over 2f out: drvn and ev ch over 1f out: kpt on wl but outpcd by wnr fnl 75yds* **9/2**[1]

2 4 hd **Malabar**[22] 2697 2-9-0 0.......................... WilliamTwiston-Davies 14 98+
(Mick Channon) *hld up towards rr: effrt and swtchd lft over 1f out: gd hdwy u.p and edging rt 1f out: styd on strly fnl 100yds* **25/1**

2 5 4 **Osaila (IRE)**[16] 2888 2-9-0 0.................................. FrankieDettori 4 86
(Richard Hannon) *in tch in midfield: rdn and effrt 2f out: chsd ldrs and drvn over 1f out: 4th and btn 1f out: wknd ins fnl f* **16/1**

1 6 1 **Peace And War (USA)**[24] 2644 2-9-0 0......................... JamieSpencer 5 83
(Olly Stevens) *hld up in tch in midfield: rdn and effrt 2f out: hdwy u.p over 1f out: kpt on but no threat to ldrs fnl f* **25/1**

1 7 3/4 **Bitter Lake (USA)**[21] 2744 2-9-0 0.............................. WilliamBuick 19 80
(Charlie Appleby) *in tch in midfield: rdn and effrt ent fnl 2f: drvn and no hdwy over 1f out tl styd on ins fnl f: no threat to ldrs* **9/1**

1 8 shd **Effusive**[18] 2824 2-9-0 0.................................. SilvestreDeSousa 1 80
(William Haggas) *in tch in midfield: effrt 2f out: sme hdwy u.p over 1f out: no imp 1f out: wknd ins fnl f* **16/1**

9 hd **Sexy Legs**[27] 2568 2-9-0 0...................................... WayneLordan 13 79
(David Wachman, Ire) *wl in tch in midfield: rdn ent fnl 2f: drvn and unable qck over 1f out: 6th and btn 1f out: wknd ins fnl f* **9/2**[1]

614 10 1/2 **Appleberry (IRE)**[35] 2313 2-9-0 0............................ AndrewMullen 3 78
(Michael Appleby) *chsd ldrs: rdn 1/2-way: drvn and btn over 1f out: wknd ins fnl f* **33/1**

11 11 1 1/4 **Bond's Girl**[28] 2521 2-9-0 0.................................. RichardHughes 23 77+
(Richard Fahey) *hld up in rr: effrt but stl plenty to do whn swtchd rt and hdwy over 1f out: pushed along and kpt on fnl f: nvr trbld ldrs* **14/1**

1 12 1 3/4 **Secret Liaison (IRE)**[34] 2349 2-9-0 0.......................... JamesDoyle 15 69
(James Tate) *chsd ldr tl over 2f out: sn rdn: drvn and btn over 1f out: wknd fnl f* **66/1**

31 13 nse **Bazzana**[25] 2622 2-9-0 0.......................................... RyanMoore 24 70+
(Martyn Meade) *wnt lft and stdd s: t.k.h: hld up towards rr: stl plenty to do whn nt clr run and swtchd lft and rt wl over 1f out: no imp after* **8/1**

4 14 1/2 **Gilded Lace**[20] 2771 2-9-0 0........................................ LiamJones 22 67
(J S Moore) *s.i.s: sn pushed along and outpcd in rr: sme hdwy and pushed rt over 1f out: nvr trbld ldrs* **100/1**

2 15 1 1/4 **Secret Lightning (FR)**[15] 2928 2-9-0 0....................... MartinHarley 8 63
(Sylvester Kirk) *in tch in midfield: rdn and unable qck ent fnl 2f: lost pl and btn over 1f out: wknd fnl f* **100/1**

03 16 2 1/2 **York Express**[22] 2697 2-9-0 0.................................... TomQueally 7 56
(Ismail Mohammed) *in tch towards rr: rdn and effrt 2f out: no prog over 1f out: wl hld fnl f* **100/1**

51 17 3 3/4 **Showcard**[27] 2557 2-9-0 0........................................ JimmyFortune 9 45
(Gary Moore) *hld up towards rr: effrt but stl plenty to do and swtchd rt over 1f out: no imp fnl f: n.d* **50/1**

1 18 3/4 **Elite Gardens (USA)**[47] 1977 2-9-0 0.......................... KierenFallon 21 42
(Saeed bin Suroor) *hld up in tch midfield: rdn 2f out: sn hung lft and btn: no ch and eased ins fnl f* **6/1**[2]

41 19 6 **Expensive Date**[21] 2716 2-9-0 0.................................. LukeMorris 6 24
(Paul Cole) *in tch in midfield: rdn and struggling ent fnl 2f: sn lost pl: bhd fnl f* **40/1**

01 20 3/4 **Gold Waltz**[31] 2436 2-9-0 0........................................ JimCrowley 16 22
(Ralph Beckett) *t.k.h: wl in tch in midfield: rdn and lost pl over 2f out: bhd fnl f* **80/1**

464 21 nk **Fujiano**[16] 2888 2-9-0 0.......................................... DavidProbert 2 21
(Derek Haydn Jones) *in tch in midfield: rdn over 2f out: sn struggling and lost pl: bhd fnl f* **100/1**

1m 13.85s (-0.65) **Going Correction** +0.05s/f (Good) 21 Ran SP% 131.1
Speed ratings (Par 100): **106,103,102,102,97 96,95,94,94,93 92,89,89,89,87 84,79,78,70,69 68**
CSF £108.37 CT £530.77 TOTE £20.00: £5.30, £3.30, £2.30; EX 184.60 Trifecta £867.40.
**Owner** Merry Fox Stud Limited **Bred** Merry Fox Stud Limited **Trained** Newmarket, Suffolk

**FOCUS**
False rail removed to provide fresh ground and distances as advertised. A total of 4mm of water was put on the straight track after racing the previous day, but the Round course was not watered. The going remained good to firm, good in places on the Round course. On the face of it, this is pretty strong form as the placed horses were well fancied (the third had the standout form coming into the race), while Mick Channon, who has a good record in this race, holds the fourth in high regard and there was a nice gap back to the fifth, so there's every chance the winner is a really good filly in the making.

## 3416 WOLFERTON H'CAP (LISTED RACE) 1m 2f
3:05 (3:06) (Class 1) (0-110,108) 4-Y-O+

**£39,697** (£15,050; £7,532; £3,752; £1,883; £945) **Stalls** Low

Form RPR

4-13 1 **Contributer (IRE)**[56] 1697 4-9-5 **106**.......................... GeorgeBaker 15 115
(Ed Dunlop) *hld up in rr: nt clr run whn hdwy and swtchd lft under 2f out: r.o to ld on outer ins fnl f: sn edgd rt: kpt on wl towards fin* **9/1**

10-3 2 1/2 **Bold Sniper**[48] 1948 4-9-1 **102**................................ RyanMoore 1 110
(Sir Michael Stoute) *trckd ldrs: rdn and outpcd over 2f out: styd on to chse ldrs over 1f out: chalng ins fnl f: nt quite gng pce of wnr: hld towards fin* **2/1**[1]

2-61 3 1 3/4 **Cafe Society (FR)**[32] 2405 4-8-11 **98**........................ JimCrowley 9 103
(Gai Waterhouse, Australia) *hld up: nt clr run over 2f out: rdn and wanted to lug rt whn swtchd rt to make hdwy over 1f out: r.o ins fnl f: gng on at fin: nt rch front two* **6/1**[3]

1200 4 nk **Sennockian Star**[14] 2957 4-9-1 **102**..........................(v) JoeFanning 3 106
(Mark Johnston) *led: hdd over 6f out: remained w ldr: rdn to regain ld 2f out: hrd pressed after: hdd ins fnl f: kpt on same pce fnl 100yds* **25/1**

35 5 1 1/2 **Hall Of Mirrors (IRE)**[26] 2580 4-9-5 **106**..............(p) JosephO'Brien 4 107
(A P O'Brien, Ire) *trckd ldrs: effrt over 2f out: sn chalng: edgd rt and nt qckning ent fnl f: no ex fnl 150yds* **14/1**

6/65 6 nk **Energizer (GER)**[111] 810 5-9-2 **103**........................ AdamKirby 14 104
(Charlie Appleby) *racd keenly: hld up: effrt and hdwy 2f out: rdn over 1f out: prog ins fnl f: styd on fnl 100yds: nt pce to rch ldrs* **16/1**

1-42 7 1 1/2 **Dick Doughtywylie**[63] 1559 6-9-1 **102**....................(t) WilliamBuick 7 100
(John Gosden) *racd keenly: w ldrs: led over 6f out: rdn and hdd 2f out: no ex ent fnl f: fdd fnl 150yds* **12/1**

42-5 8 hd **Boomshackerlacker (IRE)**[51] 1870 4-9-4 **105**..........(p) PatCosgrave 16 103
(George Baker) *racd keenly in midfield: rdn over 2f out: no imp over 1f out: one pce ins fnl f* **16/1**

0300 9 1 1/2 **Rebellious Guest**[2] 3356 5-9-0 **100** ow1...................... OlivierPeslier 11 96
(George Margarson) *hld up: pushed along over 2f out: plugged on fnl f: nvr able to trble ldrs* **33/1**

02-6 10 1 1/4 **Wigmore Hall (IRE)**[43] 2085 7-9-4 **105**........................ TomQueally 5 97
(Michael Bell) *bustled along whn s.i.s: sn in midfield: rdn and nt qckn over 2f out: no imp over 1f out: plugged on whn n.d ins fnl f* **14/1**

4666 11 2 1/2 **Edu Querido (BRZ)**[14] 2958 5-9-5 **106**..................(p) MartinHarley 6 94
(Marco Botti) *midfield: rdn and struggling to hold pl whn n.m.r and hmpd over 2f out: struggling in rr after* **50/1**

-030 12 17 **First Mohican**[20] 2785 6-9-4 **105**..........................(b[1]) RichardHughes 8 60
(Alan King) *trckd ldrs: clsd on outer and w ldr over 5f out: pushed along 3f out: hung rt and nt qckn over 2f out: wkng whn continuing hang over 1f out: eased whn btn fnl f* **16/1**

-613 13 12 **Saxo Jack (FR)**[111] 812 4-9-4 **105**..........................(p) KierenFallon 2 37
(Saeed bin Suroor) *racd keenly: proiminent: pushed along 4f out: wknd over 2f out: eased whn wl btn fnl f* **5/1**[2]

2m 4.98s (-2.42) **Going Correction** +0.05s/f (Good) 13 Ran SP% 121.7
Speed ratings (Par 111): **111,110,109,108,107 107,106,106,104,103 101,88,78**
CSF £27.28 CT £124.07 TOTE £10.10: £3.00, £1.50, £2.60; EX 38.00 Trifecta £218.80.
**Owner** George Bolton **Bred** Petra Bloodstock Agency Ltd **Trained** Newmarket, Suffolk

**FOCUS**
It's a shame that classy Just the Judge got scratched, but this was still a decent edition of the Listed Wolferton Handicap. There was something of a muddling pace on, although the winner did come from last to first, and the form looks solid.

## 3417 KING EDWARD VII STKS (GROUP 2) (C&G) 1m 4f
3:45 (3:45) (Class 1) 3-Y-O

**£113,788** (£43,139; £21,589; £10,754; £5,397; £2,708) **Stalls** Low

Form RPR

14 1 **Eagle Top**[55] 1727 3-9-0 92.......................................... WilliamBuick 5 118+
(John Gosden) *dwlt: hld up in rr: rdn over 2f out: clsd qckly to join ldrs and rdr stdd wl over 1f out: rdn and qcknd to ld ent fnl f: shifting rt but sn in command: r.o wl: readily* **12/1**

21 2 3 1/4 **Adelaide (IRE)**[26] 2579 3-9-0 111.............................. JosephO'Brien 4 112
(A P O'Brien, Ire) *dwlt: sn in tch in midfield: rdn and effrt on outer 3f out: drvn to ld 2f out: hdd ent fnl f: no ch w wnr but styd on for clr 2nd fnl f* **6/5**[1]

1-43 3 2 1/4 **Scotland (GER)**[43] 2087 3-9-0 95.................................. JimCrowley 6 109
(Andrew Balding) *hld up in tch in last trio: rdn and effrt ent fnl 2f: no real imp: styd on steadily ins fnl f to go 3rd nr fin: no ch w wnr* **25/1**

0-21 4 1/2 **Snow Sky**[41] 2153 3-9-0 108........................................ JamesDoyle 3 108+
(Sir Michael Stoute) *chsd ldr: wnt 2nd over 3f out: rdn and effrt over 2f out: ev ch 2f out tl ent fnl f: sn outpcd and btn: wknd and lost 3rd nr fin* **6/1**[2]

21-5 5 3 3/4 **Bunker (IRE)**[36] 2285 3-9-0 107.............................. FrankieDettori 10 102
(Richard Hannon) *chsd ldrs early: settled in midfield after 2f: rdn and hdwy to chal between horses 2f out: 4th and outpcd jst over 1f out: wknd ins fnl f* **8/1**

1-21 6 1 **Miner's Lamp (IRE)**[34] 2347 3-9-0 105.............................. RyanMoore 7 100
(Charlie Appleby) *dwlt: hld up in tch in last pair: clsd and nt clr run briefly ent fnl f: sn drvn and no hdwy over 1f out: wknd fnl f* **7/1**[3]

5-14 7 4 1/2 **Odeon**[36] 2285 3-9-0 105.............................................. GrahamLee 2 93
(James Given) *led: pushed along 4f out: rdn and hdd 2f out: sn btn: wknd over 1f out* **16/1**

1 8 5 **Dylan Mouth (IRE)**[33] 2376 3-9-3 111.......................... FabioBranca 8 88
(Stefano Botti, Italy) *t.k.h: chsd ldr tl over 3f out: sn struggling u.p: wknd wl over 1f out: bhd 1f out* **9/1**

1-34 9 8 **Seagull Star**[43] 2087 3-9-0 97.................................. AndreaAtzeni 1 72
(William Haggas) *chsd ldng trio after 2f: rdn 4f out: lost pl and bhd over 2f out: wknd 2f out: wl bhd fnl f* **25/1**

2m 27.98s (-4.52) **Going Correction** +0.05s/f (Good) 9 Ran SP% 114.6
Speed ratings (Par 111): **117,114,113,113,110 109,106,103,98**
CSF £26.65 CT £363.54 TOTE £15.10: £3.80, £1.10, £4.90; EX 35.80 Trifecta £542.40.
**Owner** Lady Bamford **Bred** Lady Bamford **Trained** Newmarket, Suffolk
■ Stewards' Enquiry : William Buick caution: careless riding.

**FOCUS**
With Western Hymn a non-runner, there was no representative from the Derby this year, but the well-fancied Gallinule Stakes winner Adelaide, together with the Lingfield Derby Trial winner Snow Sky, who had been quietly fancied by some for the Derby before a setback ruled him out of Epsom, set a decent standard.

## 3418 CORONATION STKS (BRITISH CHAMPIONS SERIES) (GROUP 1) (FILLIES) (ROUND COURSE) 1m (R)

**4:25** (4:26) (Class 1) 3-Y-O

**£212,662** (£80,625; £40,350; £20,100; £10,087; £5,062) **Stalls** Low

Form RPR

12-0 **1** **Rizeena (IRE)**[47] 1976 3-9-0 111 ........................................ RyanMoore 7 113
(Clive Brittain) *racd keenly: a.p: led over 1f out: edgd rt ins fnl f: r.o wl: a in command towards fin* **11/2**[3]

2-10 **2** *3/4* **Lesstalk In Paris (IRE)**[40] 2195 3-9-0 110.......... ChristopheSoumillon 8 111+
(J-C Rouget, France) *hld up in midfield: hdwy on outer over 1f out: r.o ins fnl f: clsd to take 2nd cl home: nt quite able to chal wnr* **15/2**

-125 **3** *hd* **Euro Charline**[47] 1976 3-9-0 106 ........................................ AndreaAtzeni 1 111
(Marco Botti) *in tch: effrt wl over 1f out: sn swtchd rt: running on against inner rail and c through narrow wl ins fnl f: plld off rail fnl 50yds: hld fnl strides* **16/1**

1- **4** *1 1/4* **My Titania (IRE)**[264] 6881 3-9-0 106 ......................... DeclanMcDonogh 4 108
(John M Oxx, Ire) *racd keenly: led for 2f: trckd ldr after: rdn and ev ch 2f out: nt qckn over 1f out: styd on towards fin but lacked pce of ldrs* **7/2**[2]

0-10 **5** *hd* **Sandiva (IRE)**[47] 1976 3-9-0 107 ........................................ FrankieDettori 5 107
(Richard Fahey) *midfield: pushed along and outpcd over 2f out: styd on fnl 100yds: nt pce to get to ldrs* **25/1**

13-0 **6** *3/4* **Tapestry (IRE)**[47] 1976 3-9-0 111 ........................................ JosephO'Brien 2 105
(A P O'Brien, Ire) *midfield: effrt 2f out: rdn and nt qckn over 1f out: styd on ins fnl f: nt clr run fnl 75yds: allowed to coast home whn no ch* **14/1**

0-10 **7** *shd* **J Wonder (USA)**[40] 2195 3-9-0 104 ........................................ JimmyFortune 11 105
(Brian Meehan) *racd keenly: prom: led after 2f: rdn and hdd over 1f out: no ex fnl 75yds* **20/1**

14-2 **8** *nk* **Radiator**[35] 2316 3-9-0 99 ........................................ JamesDoyle 10 104
(Sir Michael Stoute) *hld up: plld out over 2f out: kpt on ins fnl f: nvr able to chal* **16/1**

4-22 **9** *nk* **Lightning Thunder**[26] 2581 3-9-0 111 ........................................ OlivierPeslier 9 104
(Olly Stevens) *in tch: effrt over 2f out: no imp u.p over 1f out: no ex fnl 100yds* **5/2**[1]

123- **10** *shd* **Kiyoshi**[265] 6836 3-9-0 111 ........................................ JamieSpencer 3 104
(Charles Hills) *hld up: pushed along 2f out: kpt on ins fnl f: nt pce to trble ldrs* **16/1**

11-0 **11** *5* **Lucky Kristale**[47] 1976 3-9-0 108 ........................................ RichardHughes 6 92
(George Margarson) *hld up in rr: pushed along over 2f out: outpcd after: nvr able to get on terms* **20/1**

3- **U** **Rosalind (USA)**[49] 1933 3-9-0 110 ........................................ KierenFallon 12
(Kenneth McPeek, U.S.A) *stmbld and uns rdr coming out of stalls* **20/1**

1m 40.73s (0.03) **Going Correction** +0.05s/f (Good) **12** Ran SP% **120.4**
Speed ratings (Par 110): **101,100,100,98,98 97,97,97,97,97 92,**
CSF £44.25 CT £640.73 TOTE £7.20: £2.40, £3.00, £4.20; EX 48.60 Trifecta £572.20.
**Owner** Sheikh Rashid Dalmook Al Maktoum **Bred** Roundhill Stud **Trained** Newmarket, Suffolk

**FOCUS**
With no Guineas winner in attendance this wasn't the strongest Coronation Stakes. The anticipated lack of early pace was borne out, with J Wonder pulling her way into the lead after 2f or so, and those held up proved at a definite disadvantage. There was also drama from the stalls as US raider Rosalind got rid of Kieren Fallon when badly diving as they flew open.

## 3419 QUEEN'S VASE (LISTED RACE) 2m

**5:00** (5:01) (Class 1) 3-Y-O

**£48,203** (£18,275; £9,146; £4,556; £2,286; £1,147) **Stalls** Low

Form RPR

3-52 **1** **Hartnell**[41] 2153 3-9-3 103 ........................................ JoeFanning 2 105
(Mark Johnston) *chsd ldrs: clsd and nt clr run 3f out: rdn to ld on inner 2f out: clr 1f out: hung bdly lft fnl 100yds: hld on cl home* **7/2**[2]

0-4 **2** *nk* **Century (IRE)**[42] 2114 3-9-3 97 ........................................ JosephO'Brien 10 104
(A P O'Brien, Ire) *stdd s: hld up in tch in rr: hdwy on outer 5f out: rdn to chse ldng trio over 2f out: drvn over 1f out: styd on to chse wnr fnl 100yds: clsd and chalng hanging wnr whn bmpd nr fin: hld after* **5/1**[3]

1-22 **3** *1 3/4* **Marzocco (USA)**[28] 2502 3-9-3 100 ........................................ WilliamBuick 7 103
(John Gosden) *chsd ldng trio: clsd over 3f out: rdn and effrt over 2f out: drvn and chsd clr wnr 1f out: keeping on and pressing hanging wnr in cl 3rd whn bmpd and hmpd fnl 75yds: nt rcvr and eased towards fin* **11/8**[1]

6-21 **4** *1 1/4* **Big Orange**[52] 1830 3-9-3 83 ........................................ TomQueally 6 100
(Michael Bell) *awkward leaving stalls: sn rcvrd to chse ldr: clsd over 3f out: rdn to ld wl over 2f out: hdd 2f out: lost 2nd 1f out: styd on same pce after* **33/1**

-122 **5** *6* **Montaly**[27] 2566 3-9-3 88 ........................................ DavidProbert 3 93
(Andrew Balding) *s.i.s: hld up in tch towards rr: rdn and effrt to go 5th over 2f out: sn no imp: wl hld over 1f out: plugged on* **9/1**

34 **6** *5* **Hatsaway (IRE)**[21] 2746 3-9-3 0 ........................................ LiamJones 4 87
(Clive Brittain) *hld up in tch in last quartet: rdn and effrt on outer over 3f out: sn struggling: past btn horses to go modest 6th 2f out: plugged on* **33/1**

4-31 **7** *25* **Gold Approach**[30] 2466 3-8-12 89 ........................................ SilvestreDeSousa 9 52
(William Haggas) *t.k.h: led tl hdd and rdn wl over 2f out: sn btn: t.o and eased fnl f* **16/1**

-231 **8** *15* **Loving Your Work**[8] 3146 3-9-3 66 ........................................ PatCosgrave 12 39
(George Baker) *stdd after s: hld up in tch in rr: rdn 4f out: wknd over 2f out: t.o over 1f out: eased ins fnl f* **33/1**

2110 **9** *39* **Anglo Irish**[44] 2077 3-9-3 81 ........................................ FrankieDettori 5
(John Gosden) *t.k.h early: hld up in tch in midfield: rdn wl over 2f out: sn btn and bhd: t.o wl over 1f out: eased* **12/1**

1353 **10** *10* **God's Speed (IRE)**[51] 1883 3-9-3 82 ........................................ ChrisCatlin 11
(Rae Guest) *hld up in tch in midfield: rdn and dropped to last 4f out: sn struggling and lost tch: t.o and eased over 1f out* **20/1**

3m 24.73s (-4.27) **Going Correction** +0.05s/f (Good) **10** Ran SP% **118.2**
Speed ratings (Par 107): **112,111,110,110,107 104,92,84,65,60**
CSF £20.78 CT £33.62 TOTE £4.60: £1.90, £2.20, £1.10; EX 17.70 Trifecta £39.00.
**Owner** Sheikh Hamdan bin Mohammed Al Maktoum **Bred** Darley **Trained** Middleham Moor, N Yorks

**FOCUS**
The last two winners of this race have gone on to take the following year's Gold Cup. The pace was fair and the time was good.

## 3420 BUCKINGHAM PALACE STKS (H'CAP) 7f

**5:35** (5:38) (Class 2) (0-105,105) 3-Y-O+

**£62,250** (£18,640; £9,320; £4,660; £2,330; £1,170) **Stalls** Centre

Form RPR

-020 **1** **Louis The Pious**[41] 2145 6-9-4 99 ........................................ SilvestreDeSousa 29 109
(David O'Meara) *racd stands' side: midfield: rdn and hdwy over 2f out: led overall wl over 1f out: r.o ins fnl f: a doing enough towards fin: 1st of 22 in gp* **33/1**

13-1 **2** *3/4* **Horsted Keynes (FR)**[52] 1862 4-9-5 100 ........................................ JamieSpencer 21 108
(Roger Varian) *racd stands' side: hld up in rr: rdn over 2f out: swtchd lft and hdwy over 1f out: r.o ins fnl f: nt quite get to wnr: 2nd of 22 in gp* **8/1**[2]

-134 **3** *3/4* **Watchable**[16] 2898 4-9-0 95 ........................................ DanielTudhope 25 101
(David O'Meara) *racd stands' side: hld up: hdwy 3f out: rdn 2f out: chalng ins fnl f: r.o for press: hld towards fin: 3rd of 22 in gp* **14/1**

0-05 **4** *shd* **Bronze Angel (IRE)**[34] 2336 5-8-13 94 ........................................(b) MartinDwyer 30 100
(Marcus Tregoning) *racd stands' side: midfield: swtchd rt and hdwy 3f out: rdn to chal 2f out: stl ev ch ins fnl f: no ex fnl strides: 4th of 22 in gp* **10/1**

0-02 **5** *nse* **Jack's Revenge (IRE)**[48] 1943 6-9-0 95 ........................................(bt) PatCosgrave 17 101
(George Baker) *racd stands' side: midfield: hdwy over 2f out: chalng ins fnl f: styd on: hld towards fin: 5th of 22 in gp* **20/1**

0430 **6** *nse* **Santefisio**[2] 3356 8-9-5 100 ........................................(b) JimmyFortune 18 105
(Keith Dalgleish) *s.i.s: racd stands' side: in rr: rdn and hdwy 2f out: r.o ins fnl f: gng on at fin: 6th of 22 in gp* **20/1**

0063 **7** *1 1/4* **Intransigent**[83] 1174 5-9-4 102 ........................................ OisinMurphy[(3)] 23 107+
(Andrew Balding) *racd stands' side: in tch: rdn and outpcd over 2f out: rallied ins fnl f: styd on: nt trble ldrs: 7th of 22 in gp* **33/1**

0410 **8** *1/2* **Georgian Bay (IRE)**[41] 2145 4-9-4 99 ........................................(v) GrahamLee 28 103+
(K R Burke) *racd stands' side: midfield: effrt whn n.m.r and hmpd wl over 1f out: styd on fnl 100yds: hld towards fin: 8th of 22 in gp* **20/1**

00-6 **9** *1/2* **Pastoral Player**[41] 2145 7-9-4 99 ........................................ HayleyTurner 3 94
(Hughie Morrison) *racd far side: hld up: rdn and hdwy 2f out: r.o to ld gp towards fin: unable to go pce of other gp: 1st of 6 in gp* **16/1**

0-60 **10** *1/2* **Deauville Prince (FR)**[20] 2758 4-9-0 95 ..............(t) RichardKingscote 14 89
(Tom Dascombe) *racd stands' side: prom: rdn whn chalng 2f out: nt qckn over 1f out: styd on same pce fnl 100yds: 10th of 22 in gp* **100/1**

-016 **11** *1/2* **Secret Art (IRE)**[22] 2707 4-8-13 94 ........................................ JimCrowley 26 86
(William Knight) *racd stands' side: hld up in midfield and t.k.h: lost pl over 4f out: outpcd over 2f out: styd on fnl 150yds: nvr able to rch ldrs: 11th of 22 in gp* **25/1**

1321 **12** *hd* **Hillbilly Boy (IRE)**[21] 2747 4-9-2 97 ........................................ AndreaAtzeni 12 89+
(Martin Smith) *swtchd to r far side after 1f: led gp over 5f out: rdn over 2f out: hdd and no ex towards fin: 2nd of 6 in gp* **9/1**[3]

0-00 **13** *1/2* **Zanetto**[20] 2778 4-8-13 97 ........................................ ThomasBrown[(3)] 19 88
(Andrew Balding) *racd stands' side: towards rr: rdn over 2f out: styd on ins fnl f: nvr able to trble ldrs: 12th of 22 in gp* **66/1**

0-00 **14** *3/4* **Tamayuz Star (IRE)**[21] 2747 4-8-11 92 ........................................ LiamJones 32 81
(George Margarson) *racd stands' side: led overall: rdn 3f out: hdd wl over 1f out: no ex fnl 100yds: 13th of 22 in gp* **50/1**

-351 **15** *1/2* **Blessington (IRE)**[42] 2110 4-9-2 97 ........................................(t) WilliamBuick 27 84+
(John Gosden) *missed break: racd stands' side: hld up: rdn over 2f out: kpt on ins fnl f: no imp under hand ride fnl 100yds: 14th of 22 in gp* **8/1**[2]

4002 **16** *nk* **Sir Reginald**[13] 2984 6-8-12 93 ........................................ TonyHamilton 8 80
(Richard Fahey) *racd far side: prom: rdn over 2f out: hung rt and nt qckn over 1f out: kpt on same pce: 3rd of 6 in gp* **33/1**

0-53 **17** *shd* **Blaine**[37] 2254 4-9-1 96 ........................................ JamesDoyle 1 82
(Kevin Ryan) *racd farside: hld up: rdn over 2f out: kpt on same pce ins fnl f: no imp: 4th of 6 in gp* **20/1**

-450 **18** *nk* **Mabait**[6] 3251 8-8-6 94 ........................................(b[1]) GeorgeBuckell[(7)] 22 80
(David Simcock) *racd stands' side: hld up: n.m.r and hmpd over 4f out: bhd after: 15th of 22 in gp* **50/1**

20-0 **19** *nk* **One Word More (IRE)**[69] 1437 4-9-0 95 ........................................ FrankieDettori 16 80
(Charles Hills) *racd stands' side: midfield: rdn over 2f out: no imp over 1f out: eased whn btn ins fnl f: 16th of 22 in gp* **33/1**

6-66 **20** *3/4* **Bubbly Bellini (IRE)**[9] 3127 7-8-9 97 ........................................(p) SeanCorby[(7)] 20 80
(Adrian McGuinness, Ire) *racd stands' side: chsd ldrs: rdn to chal 2f out: wknd over 1f out: 17th of 22 in gp* **50/1**

-103 **21** *nk* **Brae Hill (IRE)**[20] 2784 8-8-11 97 ........................................ SammyJoBell[(5)] 24 79
(Richard Fahey) *racd stands' side: prom: rdn and wknd over 2f out: btn whn n.m.r and hmpd ins fnl f: 18th of 22 in gp* **50/1**

-660 **22** *nk* **Heaven's Guest (IRE)**[41] 2145 4-9-3 101 ............. GeorgeChaloner[(3)] 15 82
(Richard Fahey) *racd stands' side: prom: rdn to chal 2f out: no ex over 1f out: fdd fnl 150yds: 19th of 22 in gp* **33/1**

22-1 **23** *4* **Rene Mathis (GER)**[20] 2778 4-8-13 94 ........................................ DavidNolan 7 65
(Richard Fahey) *racd farside: led gp: hdd over 2f out: rdn and wknd ins fnl f: 5th of 6 in gp* **20/1**

00-0 **24** *2 3/4* **Excellent Guest**[41] 2145 7-8-10 94 ............. WilliamTwiston-Davies[(3)] 11 58
(George Margarson) *racd stands' side: midfield: rdn and outpcd over 2f out: eased whn btn ins fnl f: 20th of 22 in gp* **25/1**

2-00 **25** *6* **Mezzotint (IRE)**[37] 2254 5-9-2 97 ........................................ JosephO'Brien 31 45
(Stuart Williams) *racd stands' side: trckd ldrs: rdn over 2f out: wknd over 1f out: eased whn wl btn ins fnl f: 21st of 22 in gp* **25/1**

300- **26** *24* **Jammy Guest (IRE)**[342] 4295 4-8-12 93 ........................................ JoeFanning 5
(George Margarson) *racd far side: prom tl rdn and wknd over 2f out: eased whn btn fnl f: 6th of 6 in gp* **66/1**

63-2 **27** *2* **Fort Knox**[34] 2336 4-9-10 105 ........................................ RichardHughes 4
(Charlie Appleby) *swtchd to r in stands' gp early: hld up: rdn and no imp over 2f out: eased whn btn over 1f out: 22nd of 22 in gp* **12/1**

2-21 **D** *1 3/4* **Russian Realm**[29] 2483 4-9-1 96 ........................................ RyanMoore 13 92+
(Sir Michael Stoute) *racd stands' side: midfield: rdn over 2f out: one pce ins fnl f: nvr able to trble ldrs: 9th of 22 in gp* **5/1**[1]

1m 26.85s (-0.75) **Going Correction** +0.05s/f (Good) **28** Ran SP% **140.1**
Speed ratings (Par 109): **106,105,104,104,104 104,102,102,99,98 98,98,97,96,96 95,95,95,94,94 93,93,88,85,78 51,49,100**
CSF £247.62 CT £3973.20 TOTE £35.20: £8.40, £2.40, £3.50, £3.60; EX 310.50 Trifecta £3822.80.
**Owner** F Gillespie **Bred** Ashbrittle Stud **Trained** Nawton, N Yorks
■ Stewards' Enquiry : Martin Dwyer three-day ban: careless riding (Jul 4,6,7); four-day ban: used whip above permitted level (Jul 8-9,14)

**FOCUS**
As ever this season's Buckingham Palace was fiendishly competitive on paper. The bias towards those drawn high played out, however, and few managed to get in a serious blow at the business end.

T/Jkpt: Not won. T/Plt: £84.20 to a £1 stake. Pool: £622105.20 - 5393.14 winning tickets T/Qpdt: £24.00 to a £1 stake. Pool: £32936.59 - 1012.42 winning tickets SP

# 3180 GOODWOOD (R-H)

Friday, June 20

**OFFICIAL GOING: Good (good to firm in places on round course; 7.4)**

Wind: Light, across away from stands Weather: Fine and warm

## 3421 ZANE LOWE APPRENTICE STKS (H'CAP) 1m 1f 192y

6:15 (6:15) (Class 5) (0-75,74) 3-Y-O £3,234 (£962; £481; £240) Stalls Low

Form RPR

06-0 1 **Golden Journey (IRE)**58 1655 3-9-4 71 RyanTate 7 78
(Clive Cox) chsd ldrs: led over 2f out: drvn out 7/1[3]

5553 2 3/4 **Hedge End (IRE)**14 2968 3-9-4 74 CamHardie(3) 5 80
(Richard Hannon) hld up in rr: rdn and hdwy over 2f out: chal fnl f: r.o 3/1[1]

510 3 1 **Barye**21 2748 3-9-2 72 LewisWalsh(3) 2 76
(David Simcock) plld hrd: chsd ldrs: outpcd over 2f out: styd on fnl f 12/1

4-25 4 3/4 **Castle Combe (IRE)**55 1727 3-9-3 73 CharlotteJenner(3) 6 76
(Marcus Tregoning) w ldr: led after 3f tl over 2f out: one pce fnl f 5/1[2]

06-4 5 2 **Scoppio Del Carro**18 2850 3-8-12 68 (t) JackGarritty(3) 8 67
(Andrew Balding) towards rr: effrt 3f out: styd on same pce fnl 2f 5/1[2]

60-5 6 1 1/4 **Cape Summit**13 2998 3-9-0 70 AlistairRawlinson(3) 1 66
(Ed Dunlop) hld up in rr: hdwy over 2f out: wknd over 1f out 3/1[1]

30-5 7 nk **Chess Valley**17 2879 3-9-5 72 [1] NoelGarbutt 4 68
(Rae Guest) t.k.h in 5th: outpcd 3f out: sme hdwy over 1f out: no ex fnl f 10/1

-220 8 11 **Template (IRE)**29 2494 3-9-0 72 KieranShoemark(5) 3 47
(Amanda Perrett) led 3f: chsd ldr tl 3f out: sn wknd 16/1

2m 9.02s (0.92) **Going Correction** +0.125s/f (Good) 8 Ran SP% 118.5
Speed ratings (Par 99): **101,100,99,99,97 96,96,87**
CSF £29.44 CT £254.12 TOTE £10.60: £2.90, £1.10, £3.00; EX 35.30 Trifecta £330.00.
**Owner** Peter Ridgers **Bred** Cbs Bloodstock **Trained** Lambourn, Berks

**FOCUS**
Several unexposed types lined-up in this handicap and a gamble was landed. First 2f of 1m course dolled out 5yds. Lower bend dolled out 5yds and races incorporating that bend increased by about 10yds.

## 3422 TFN STKS (H'CAP) 6f

6:45 (6:46) (Class 5) (0-70,70) 4-Y-0+ £3,234 (£962; £481; £240) Stalls High

Form RPR

5350 1 **Chevise (IRE)**29 2486 6-7-11 53 (b) CamHardie(7) 2 63
(Steve Woodman) mid-div: hdwy to chse ldr over 1f out: led ins fnl f: rdn out: jst hld on 10/1

0315 2 nse **Pettochside**21 2718 5-9-2 70 RyanTate(5) 1 80
(Chris Gordon) towards rr: gd hdwy over 1f out: r.o wl fnl f: clsng on wnr nr fin: jst failed 3/1[2]

0-60 3 4 **Lucky Di**16 2884 4-9-1 67 CharlesBishop(3) 11 64
(Peter Hedger) chsd ldrs: led wl over 1f out tl wknd ins fnl f 6/1[3]

-431 4 3 **Ada Lovelace**9 3125 4-8-13 65 6ex MichaelJMMurphy(3) 9 53
(John Gallagher) chsd ldr: led 3f out tl wl over 1f out: sn wknd 9/4[1]

0003 5 1/2 **Gung Ho Jack**16 2887 5-8-12 61 SteveDrowne 10 47
(John Best) mid-div: rdn and no hdwy fnl 3f 16/1

4203 6 3 3/4 **Rigolleto (IRE)**16 2890 6-9-7 70 JohnFahy 6 44
(Anabel K Murphy) bhd: rdn 3f out: n.d 8/1

-253 7 4 **Bayleyf (IRE)**9 3118 5-9-5 68 AmirQuinn 5 29
(Lee Carter) prom tl wknd 2f out 6/1[3]

2514 8 2 3/4 **Seek The Fair Land**13 2995 8-9-5 68 (b) StevieDonohoe 12 20
(Lee Carter) led and set str pce for 3f: wknd 2f out 16/1

40-0 9 nk **The Name Is Frank**23 2669 9-8-3 52 oh4 ow1 (tp) FrankieMcDonald 7 3
(Mark Gillard) s.s: outpcd: drvn along 3f out: a bhd 33/1

2006 10 2 1/4 **Pastoral Dancer**106 858 5-7-13 51 oh6 RyanPowell(3) 8
(Richard Rowe) outpcd: a bhd 66/1

1m 11.08s (-1.12) **Going Correction** -0.10s/f (Good) 10 Ran SP% 120.7
Speed ratings (Par 103): **103,102,97,93,92 87,82,78,78,75**
CSF £41.63 CT £207.26 TOTE £15.40: £3.30, £1.50, £2.90; EX 46.60 Trifecta £1097.60 Not won..
**Owner** The Chevise Partnership **Bred** Paul And Mrs Jenny Green **Trained** East Lavant, W Sussex

**FOCUS**
The leaders went off hard in this sprint handicap. The first came from off the pace and finished clear.

## 3423 GLORIOUS GOODWOOD MAIDEN FILLIES' STKS 1m 1f

7:20 (7:21) (Class 5) 3-Y-0+ £3,234 (£962; £481; £240) Stalls Low

Form RPR

1 **Tearless** 4-9-11 MartinLane 9 91
(Charlie Appleby) s.i.s: t.k.h in rr: hdwy 3f out: led over 1f out: rdn out 12/1

5-62 2 1 1/4 **Almashooqa (USA)**33 2365 3-9-0 82 DaneO'Neill 4 88
(Roger Varian) led: jnd over 2f out: rdn and ev ch over 1f out: unable qck ins fnl f 6/4[2]

32-0 3 nk **Casual Smile**41 2152 3-9-0 89 DavidProbert 7 87
(Andrew Balding) pressed ldr: disp ld over 2f out tl over 1f out: no ex ins fnl f 5/4[1]

3-0 4 11 **Dianora**34 2339 3-9-0 RichardHughes 5 64
(Sir Michael Stoute) chsd ldrs: outpcd 2f out: sn btn 5/1[3]

45 5 1 **Sixties Love**30 2466 3-9-0 SteveDrowne 6 62
(Simon Dow) s.i.s: bhd: rdn over 2f out: n.d 33/1

00- 6 2 1/2 **Highland Stardust**288 6140 3-8-9 RyanTate(5) 2 57
(Clive Cox) hld up in 5th: wknd over 2f out 40/1

05 7 5 **Pink Diamond**18 2850 3-9-0 JohnFahy 3 46
(Eve Johnson Houghton) prom: rdn 3f out: sn wknd 20/1

1m 56.56s (0.26) **Going Correction** +0.125s/f (Good) 7 Ran SP% 118.9
**WFA** 3 from 4yo 11lb
Speed ratings (Par 100): **103,101,101,91,90 88,84**
CSF £31.91 TOTE £8.10: £2.90, £2.10; EX 28.90 Trifecta £67.00.
**Owner** Godolphin **Bred** Darley **Trained** Newmarket, Suffolk

**FOCUS**
A 12-1 Godolphin debutante overhauled the two market leaders in this maiden and the first three finished a long way clear.

## 3424 MAZDA JINBA ITTAI STKS (H'CAP) 1m 6f

7:50 (7:50) (Class 3) (0-95,91) 4-Y-0+
£7,470 (£2,236; £1,118; £559; £279; £140) Stalls Low

Form RPR

-236 1 **Lion Beacon**20 2782 4-8-13 83 SebSanders 7 91
(Amanda Perrett) mde all: qcknd 4f out: sn rdn: hld on wl fnl 2f 5/1[2]

5650 2 1 3/4 **Swing Alone (IRE)**30 2461 5-9-6 90 RichardHughes 1 96
(Gay Kelleway) stdd s: plld hrd in 6th: rdn 3f out: no imp tl styd on wl fr over 1f out: snatched 2nd on line 14/1

61-0 3 shd **Great Fighter**20 2787 4-9-1 85 AndreaAtzeni 2 90
(Saeed bin Suroor) chsd ldrs: pushed along 4f out: drvn to chse wnr fnl 100yds: lost 2nd on line 5/1[2]

1320 4 3/4 **Arty Campbell (IRE)**29 2482 4-8-6 76 MartinLane 4 80
(Bernard Llewellyn) t.k.h in 5th: hdwy in centre over 2f out: drvn to chal over 1f out: one pce ins fnl f 14/1

5-12 5 nse **Debdebdeb**27 2558 4-9-7 91 DavidProbert 5 95
(Andrew Balding) t.k.h: chsd wnr tl over 1f out: one pce 1/1[1]

-600 6 4 1/2 **Party Line**7 3204 5-9-2 89 (v) MichaelJMMurphy(3) 6 87
(Mark Johnston) chsd ldrs: rdn along and outpcd in 5th whn hmpd over 2f out: n.d after 7/1[3]

0-60 7 7 **Aazif (IRE)**6 3249 5-8-10 80 StevieDonohoe 3 68
(Ian Williams) a bhd 20/1

3m 2.69s (-0.91) **Going Correction** +0.125s/f (Good) 7 Ran SP% 113.9
Speed ratings (Par 107): **107,106,105,105,105 102,98**
CSF £67.02 TOTE £7.00: £2.80, £3.30; EX 72.90 Trifecta £117.70.
**Owner** Mrs Alexandra J Chandris **Bred** The Late A M Jenkins & J Chandris **Trained** Pulborough, W Sussex

**FOCUS**
The winner showed a good attitude to make all in this decent handicap.

## 3425 THREE FRIDAY NIGHTS FILLIES' (H'CAP) 7f

8:25 (8:25) (Class 4) (0-85,83) 3-Y-0+ £5,175 (£1,540; £769; £384) Stalls Low

Form RPR

3133 1 **Alice's Dancer (IRE)**17 2861 5-9-8 80 MichaelJMMurphy(3) 6 89
(William Muir) t.k.h: chsd ldr: led 2f out: drvn out 9/2

01 2 1 1/2 **Temptress (IRE)**48 1946 3-9-2 80 DavidProbert 1 82
(Roger Charlton) hld up in 5th: rdn and hdwy over 1f out: chsd wnr fnl f: kpt on 4/1[3]

3221 3 nse **Saucy Minx (IRE)**17 2861 4-9-7 83 (b) KieranShoemark(7) 2 88
(Amanda Perrett) chsd clr ldrs: rdn 2f out: styd on fnl f 6/1

12 4 nk **Khatiba (IRE)**93 1013 3-8-12 76 AndreaAtzeni 4 77
(Roger Varian) chsd clr ldrs: clsd 2f out: hrd rdn over 1f out: kpt on 5/2[1]

-001 5 nk **Baby Bush (IRE)**21 2745 3-9-4 82 RichardHughes 3 82
(Richard Hannon) stdd s: hld up in rr: rdn and hdwy over 1f out: one pce fnl 100yds 11/4[2]

56-0 6 3 1/4 **Plover**30 2462 4-9-6 82 CamHardie(7) 5 77
(Michael Attwater) led tl outpcd and lost pl 2f out 16/1

1m 27.24s (0.24) **Going Correction** +0.125s/f (Good)
**WFA** 3 from 4yo+ 9lb 6 Ran SP% 113.6
Speed ratings (Par 102): **103,101,101,100,100 96**
CSF £22.91 TOTE £6.80: £2.90, £2.60; EX 28.20 Trifecta £201.30.
**Owner** Perspicacious Punters Racing Club **Bred** Rathasker Stud **Trained** Lambourn, Berks

**FOCUS**
Three last-time-out winners lined-up in this handicap, but they went a steady pace and there was a bunch finish.

## 3426 GOODWOOD FARM SHOP STKS (H'CAP) 6f

8:55 (8:56) (Class 5) (0-70,69) 3-Y-0 £3,408 (£1,006; £503) Stalls High

Form RPR

1362 1 **Dont Have It Then**16 2886 3-9-6 68 ChrisCatlin 1 83
(Willie Musson) outpcd towards rr: gd hdwy 2f out: led 1f out: rdn clr: comf 7/2[2]

4-04 2 4 **Faure Island**12 3037 3-9-7 69 DaneO'Neill 7 71
(Henry Candy) sn prom: led briefly wl over 1f out: sn outpcd by wnr 9/4[1]

0-31 3 3/4 **Royal Brave (IRE)**9 3124 3-9-3 68 6ex MichaelJMMurphy(3) 2 68
(William Muir) rrd s and missed break: chsd ldrs after 2f: rdn to chal 2f out: one pce 9/4[1]

-300 4 3 1/2 **Why Not Now**31 2429 3-8-11 59 ow1 (b[1]) RichardHughes 5 48
(Roger Charlton) chsd ldr tl outpcd over 2f out 6/1[3]

56-6 5 3 1/4 **Captain Ryan**3 3323 3-8-12 60 SteveDrowne 9 38
(Peter Makin) led tl wl over 1f out: sn wknd 10/1

65-4 6 hd **Pelagian (USA)**23 2686 3-7-13 54 CamHardie(7) 4 32
(Michael Attwater) in tch tl outpcd 1/2-way 16/1

000- 7 9 **Ignight**205 8061 3-8-2 50 DavidProbert 3
(Mark Usher) a towards rr: bhd and struggling over 2f out 20/1

0-06 8 2 **Spirited Silver**28 2505 3-7-13 50 oh5 [1] RyanPowell(3) 8
(John Bridger) outpcd after 2f: sn bhd 33/1

1m 11.67s (-0.53) **Going Correction** -0.10s/f (Good) 8 Ran SP% 120.7
Speed ratings (Par 99): **99,93,92,88,83 83,71,68**
CSF £12.61 CT £21.85 TOTE £5.50: £1.90, £1.30, £1.40; EX 15.60 Trifecta £29.70.
**Owner** Laurence Mann **Bred** Charley Knoll Partnership **Trained** Newmarket, Suffolk

**FOCUS**
The winner forged clear from the two market leaders in this sprint handicap.
T/Plt: £675.50 to a £1 stake. Pool: £62694.67 - 67.75 winning tickets T/Qpdt: £45.30 to a £1 stake. Pool: £5332.35 - 87.10 winning tickets LM

# 2776 NEWMARKET (R-H)

Friday, June 20

**OFFICIAL GOING: Good to firm (7.5)**

Wind: Light half-behind Weather: Cloudy with sunny spells

## 3427 ADNAMS NEWMARKET NIGHTS APPRENTICE H'CAP 1m

5:55 (5:56) (Class 5) (0-70,69) 4-Y-0+ £3,234 (£962; £481; £240) Stalls High

Form RPR

0B00 1 **Roxy Lane**108 833 5-8-7 50 oh5 JoshBaudains 8 60
(Peter Hiatt) chsd ldrs: rdn over 2f out: r.o to ld wl ins fnl f 66/1

6556 2 1/2 **Lady Sylvia**14 2963 5-9-4 64 JennyPowell(3) 9 73
(Joseph Tuite) hld up: swtchd rt and hdwy over 2f out: rdn over 1f out: r.o 12/1

0204 **3** *nk* **Living Leader**[14] 2963 5-9-0 **62**....................(p) RobHornby(5) 6 70
(Grace Harris) *mid-div: hdwy over 3f out: led over 2f out: rdn over 1f out: hdd wl ins fnl f* **7/1**[2]

-660 **4** *5* **Jonnie Skull (IRE)**[17] 2876 8-9-5 **67**....................(vt) JackGilligan(5) 11 64
(Lydia Pearce) *led: rdn and hdd over 2f out: wknd ins fnl f* **14/1**

34 **5** *nk* **Buzz Law (IRE)**[8] 3162 6-8-10 **56**.................... RobJFitzpatrick(3) 5 52
(K R Burke) *prom: rdn over 2f out: styd on same pce fr over 1f out* **8/1**[3]

6603 **6** *2½* **Avidly**[9] 3123 4-9-3 **60**....................(b) ShelleyBirkett 10 50
(Julia Feilden) *s.i.s: racd keenly and sn prom: rdn and edgd rt over 1f out: wknd ins fnl f* **14/1**

-000 **7** *2¼* **Duke Of Destiny (IRE)**[15] 2930 5-9-3 **67**....................(p) CliffordLee(7) 15 52
(Ed Walker) *mid-div: hdwy 3f out: rdn and hung rt over 1f out: wknd fnl f* **12/1**

-440 **8** *½* **Siouxperhero (IRE)**[4] 3314 5-9-10 **67**....................(tp) JoeyHaynes 3 51
(William Muir) *hld up: rdn over 3f out: n.d* **9/2**[1]

2124 **9** *½* **Hierarch (IRE)**[9] 3112 7-9-5 **69**.................... SophieKilloran(7) 4 52
(David Simcock) *hld up: nvr trbld ldrs* **16/1**

3114 **10** *nk* **Kasbhom**[28] 2529 4-9-8 **68**....................(t) MeganCarberry(3) 1 50
(Anthony Carson) *hld up: racd keenly: rdn over 2f out: hung rt over 1f out: n.d* **8/1**[3]

3041 **11** *2½* **Secret Success**[15] 2930 4-9-12 **69**.................... NathanAlison 12 45
(Paul Cole) *chsd ldrs: rdn over 2f out: wknd over 1f out* **8/1**[3]

64-0 **12** *2½* **Norwegian Reward (IRE)**[49] 1917 6-8-7 **50**....................(p) LouisSteward 2 20
(Conrad Allen) *hld up: rdn and wknd over 1f out: b.b.v* **14/1**

6633 **13** *1½* **Enriching (USA)**[8] 3162 6-9-5 **65**.................... JordanVaughan(3) 7 32
(Nick Littmoden) *chsd ldrs: rdn whn hmpd over 3f out: wknd over 2f out* **8/1**[3]

640 **14** *hd* **Two No Bids (IRE)**[8] 3160 4-9-5 **62**.................... DannyBrock 13 28
(Phil McEntee) *s.s: hdwy 1/2-way: rdn and wknd wl over 2f out* **25/1**

1m 39.98s (-0.02) **Going Correction** +0.20s/f (Good) **14** Ran SP% **121.7**
Speed ratings (Par 103): **108,107,107,102,101 99,97,96,96,95 93,90,89,89**
CSF £743.77 CT £6166.96 TOTE £67.40: £15.00, £4.00, £2.90; EX 1953.40 Trifecta £628.90 Not won..
**Owner** R G Robinson & R D Robinson **Bred** R G Percival And Miss S M Rhodes **Trained** Hook Norton, Oxon
■ Stewards' Enquiry : Shelley Birkett caution: careless riding.

**FOCUS**
A warm and dry run up to the meeting saw 6mm of water applied to the track on Thursday and the relocation of the bend into the home straight increased the distance of the 1m2f and 1m5f races by 22m. Not many in-form sorts in a modest handicap. The gallop was a reasonable one.

## 3428 NEWMARKETRACECOURSES.CO.UK H'CAP (BOBIS RACE) 1m 2f
**6:30** (6:31) (Class 4) (0-80,80) 3-Y-O **£6,469** (£1,925; £962; £481) **Stalls** Centre

Form RPR

15 **1** **Lungarno Palace (USA)**[47] 1979 3-9-5 **78**....................(bt) MartinHarley 3 86+
(Marco Botti) *hld up: hdwy u.p over 1f out: led ins fnl f: styd on* **10/1**

0-02 **2** *nk* **Swanwick Shore (IRE)**[31] 2418 3-9-1 **74**.................... SeanLevey 4 81
(Richard Hannon) *chsd ldr: rdn over 2f out: styd on* **16/1**

-604 **3** *shd* **Grandest**[15] 2936 3-9-4 **77**.................... RobertHavlin 1 84
(John Gosden) *led: plld hrd: rdn and edgd rt over 1f out: hdd ins fnl f: styd on* **12/1**

5-53 **4** *2¼* **Ganges (IRE)**[47] 1979 3-9-1 **77**.................... RobertTart(3) 2 80
(James Toller) *chsd ldrs: pushed along 3f out: rdn and nt clr run over 1f out: styd on towards fin* **11/4**[1]

6-46 **5** *nk* **Mairise**[35] 2319 3-8-12 **71**.................... ShaneKelly 8 73
(Sir Michael Stoute) *trckd ldrs: plld hrd: rdn and hung rt over 1f out: styd on same pce ins fnl f* **7/2**[2]

-510 **6** *2¼* **Ice Slice (IRE)**[20] 2781 3-9-7 **80**.................... LukeMorris 9 78
(James Eustace) *hld up: hdwy over 3f out: sn rdn: no ex ins fnl f* **8/1**

2-33 **7** *2½* **Invasor Luck (USA)**[52] 1830 3-9-2 **75**.................... TomQueally 6 68
(James Fanshawe) *prom: pushed along over 3f out: rdn over 1f out: sn wknd* **10/1**

4-00 **8** *12* **Miss Buckshot (IRE)**[14] 2968 3-9-5 **78**.................... AdamKirby 5 48
(Rae Guest) *hld up: hdwy u.p over 1f out: wknd fnl f* **6/1**[3]

-056 **9** *8* **Xanthos**[21] 2734 3-9-5 **78**.................... PaulHanagan 7 33
(Ed Walker) *stdd s: hld up: pushed along over 3f out: rdn and wknd over 1f out* **14/1**

45-5 **10** *2¾* **L Ge R**[60] 1616 3-8-2 **61** oh1.................... JimmyQuinn 10 11
(Peter Charalambous) *prom: rdn over 2f out: wknd over 1f out* **25/1**

2m 7.55s (2.05) **Going Correction** +0.25s/f (Good) **10** Ran SP% **116.6**
Speed ratings (Par 101): **101,100,100,98,98 96,94,85,78,76**
CSF £156.94 CT £1935.70 TOTE £12.10: £3.40, £3.20, £3.30; EX 157.40 Trifecta £844.50.
**Owner** Giuliano Manfredini **Bred** Galleria Bloodstock & Samac **Trained** Newmarket, Suffolk
■ Stewards' Enquiry : Martin Harley two-day ban: used whip above permitted level (Jul 4,6)

**FOCUS**
A fair handicap featuring a couple of unexposed types. The gallop was no more than fair.

## 3429 NEWMARKETEXPERIENCE.CO.UK MAIDEN STKS (BOBIS RACE) 6f
**7:05** (7:06) (Class 4) 2-Y-O **£3,881** (£1,155; £577; £288) **Stalls** High

Form RPR

3 **1** **Epithet (IRE)**[20] 2776 2-9-5 0.................... AdamKirby 6 86
(Charlie Appleby) *mde all: shkn up and qcknd clr over 1f out: easily* **5/6**[1]

0 **2** *4* **British Art**[51] 1879 2-9-5 0.................... LukeMorris 10 74+
(Paul Cole) *trckd ldrs: rdn and edgd rt over 1f out: r.o: no ch w wnr* **33/1**

**3** *½* **Fanciful Angel (IRE)** 2-9-5 0.................... MartinHarley 11 73+
(Marco Botti) *hld up: hdwy 1/2-way: rdn over 1f out: sn chsng wnr: styd on same pce wl ins fnl f* **8/1**[3]

**4** *2¾* **Maftoon (IRE)** 2-9-5 0.................... PaulHanagan 14 64+
(Richard Hannon) *s.s: pushed along and nt clr run over 2f out: hdwy over 1f out: r.o ins fnl f: nt trble ldrs* **3/1**[2]

63 **5** *1½* **Big McIntosh (IRE)**[11] 3049 2-9-5 0....................(t) TomQueally 13 60
(John Ryan) *chsd wnr tl rdn over 1f out: wknd ins fnl f* **14/1**

**6** *½* **Indelible Ink (IRE)** 2-9-2 0.................... RobertTart(3) 9 58+
(Sir Michael Stoute) *hld up: shkn up over 2f out: nvr trbld ldrs* **16/1**

**7** *½* **Guiding Light (IRE)** 2-9-5 0.................... RobertHavlin 7 57
(Andrew Balding) *trckd ldrs: rdn: edgd rt and wknd over 1f out* **16/1**

**8** *¾* **Duke Of North (IRE)** 2-9-5 0.................... ShaneKelly 4 55
(James Fanshawe) *s.i.s: hld up: pushed along over 2f out: n.d* **33/1**

56 **9** *½* **Mr Shekells**[33] 2359 2-9-0 0.................... DannyBrock(5) 8 53
(Philip McBride) *chsd ldrs: rdn and edgd rt over 1f out: sn wknd* **40/1**

**10** *4½* **Gea And Tea** 2-9-5 0.................... JimmyQuinn 2 40
(Robert Eddery) *hld up: nvr on terms* **33/1**

0 **11** *12* **Sky Steps (IRE)**[47] 1977 2-9-5 0....................(t) JackMitchell 5 4
(Philip McBride) *hld up: a in rr* **66/1**

**12** *37* **Emperors Warrior (IRE)** 2-9-5 0.................... SeanLevey 12
(Richard Hannon) *nvr travelling: sn bhd: eased fnl 2f* **25/1**

1m 13.48s (0.98) **Going Correction** +0.20s/f (Good) **12** Ran SP% **125.7**
Speed ratings (Par 95): **101,95,95,91,89 88,88,87,86,80 64,15**
CSF £51.76 TOTE £2.30: £1.10, £7.20, £2.90; EX 40.90 Trifecta £357.90.
**Owner** Godolphin **Bred** Darley **Trained** Newmarket, Suffolk

**FOCUS**
Several top stables were represented in a race that has been won for the last two years by a smart sort, but the betting suggested this wasn't a competitive event and the winner won unchallenged. The gallop was fair.

## 3430 32RED CASINO H'CAP 1m
**7:35** (7:37) (Class 5) (0-75,75) 3-Y-O **£3,881** (£1,155; £577; £288) **Stalls** High

Form RPR

4-36 **1** **Baynunah (USA)**[31] 2433 3-9-0 **68**.................... TomQueally 5 78
(James Fanshawe) *trckd ldr in centre: rdn over 2f out: led over 1f out: styd on wl* **8/1**

0501 **2** *½* **Kisanji**[9] 3121 3-8-9 **63**.................... MartinHarley 6 72
(Alan McCabe) *s.i.s: racd centre: hld up: hdwy over 1f out: sn rdn and ev ch: styd on* **16/1**

1-35 **3** *8* **Argot**[21] 2749 3-9-4 **72**.................... WilliamCarson 8 63
(Anthony Carson) *led far side trio: rdn and edgd rt over 2f out: wknd ins fnl f* **7/2**[2]

3262 **4** *hd* **Baltic Fire (IRE)**[41] 2165 3-8-3 **62**.................... JoeyHaynes(5) 9 52
(K R Burke) *chsd ldr far side: rdn and edgd rt over 2f out: wknd ins fnl f* **4/1**[3]

0460 **5** *2¼* **Saalib (USA)**[13] 2998 3-9-0 **68**....................(tp) PaulHanagan 1 53
(Brian Meehan) *overall ldr in centre: clr 5f out: rdn and hdd over 1f out: hung lft and wknd ins fnl f* **12/1**

-233 **6** *½* **Brigliadoro (IRE)**[8] 3145 3-9-4 **72**.................... ShaneKelly 7 56
(Philip McBride) *s.i.s: hld up and racd far side: swtchd rt: hdwy and jnd centre over 3f out: shkn up over 1f out: wknd fnl f* **11/8**[1]

60-0 **7** *28* **Nashmi**[8] 3145 3-9-0 **68**.................... LukeMorris 4
(George Peckham) *racd centre: chsd ldrs: rdn over 2f out: wknd over 1f out* **25/1**

1m 40.62s (0.62) **Going Correction** +0.20s/f (Good) **7** Ran SP% **112.9**
Speed ratings (Par 99): **104,103,95,95,93 92,64**
CSF £113.63 CT £526.23 TOTE £9.00: £3.70, £4.40; EX 112.90 Trifecta £645.30.
**Owner** Mohamed Obaida **Bred** Rabbah Bloodstock Llc **Trained** Newmarket, Suffolk

**FOCUS**
A fair handicap in which the field raced in two groups to halfway. Although the gallop seemed reasonable, the first two did well to pull clear in the closing stages.

## 3431 ALL NEW 32REDSPORT.COM H'CAP 7f
**8:05** (8:05) (Class 3) (0-95,93) 3-Y-O+ **£9,056** (£2,695; £1,346; £673) **Stalls** High

Form RPR

3-13 **1** **Dark Emerald (IRE)**[12] 3036 4-9-6 **87**.................... AdamKirby 6 98
(Brendan Powell) *led: hdd over 5f out: edgd lft sn after: led again 1/2-way: rdn over 1f out: styd on wl* **6/1**[3]

/002 **2** *1½* **Englishman**[25] 2629 4-9-6 **87**.................... JamieSpencer 2 94
(Charles Hills) *hld up in tch: rdn and hung lft fr over 1f out: chsd wnr ins fnl f: styd on same pce* **10/1**

0-32 **3** *1½* **Life Partner (IRE)**[21] 2747 4-9-12 **93**.................... WilliamBuick 3 96+
(Charlie Appleby) *hld up: rdn and hung rt over 1f out: hung lft and r.o ins fnl f: nt rch ldrs* **3/1**[1]

3-15 **4** *¾* **Sir Mike**[35] 2311 5-9-9 **90**.................... FrankieDettori 5 91
(Luca Cumani) *hld up: hdwy over 2f out: rdn over 1f out: styd on* **4/1**[2]

3500 **5** *2¼* **Showboating (IRE)**[27] 2548 6-9-7 **88**....................(tp) MartinHarley 7 83
(Alan McCabe) *hld up: rdn over 2f out: sn outpcd: styd on ins fnl f* **11/1**

03-0 **6** *nse* **Maid A Million**[7] 3203 4-9-7 **93**.................... JoeyHaynes(5) 4 88
(David Elsworth) *chsd ldrs: rdn over 1f out: no ex ins fnl f* **20/1**

-013 **7** *hd* **So Beloved**[29] 2483 4-9-12 **93**....................(b[1]) JamesDoyle 8 88
(Roger Charlton) *s.i.s: sn rcvrd to r alone on far side: led over 5f out to 1/2-way: rdn over 1f out: wknd ins fnl f* **6/1**[3]

-042 **8** *3* **Zacynthus (IRE)**[31] 2425 6-8-11 **83**.................... LouisSteward(5) 9 70
(Michael Bell) *chsd ldrs: rdn over 1f out: sn wknd* **7/1**

24-0 **9** *6* **Equity Risk (USA)**[29] 2483 4-9-8 **89**.................... PaulHanagan 1 60
(Kevin Ryan) *w ldrs: rdn over 1f out: sn wknd* **12/1**

1m 25.69s (-0.01) **Going Correction** +0.20s/f (Good) **9** Ran SP% **115.9**
Speed ratings (Par 107): **108,106,104,103,101 101,100,97,90**
CSF £64.23 CT £216.71 TOTE £8.20: £2.30, £2.30, £1.50; EX 83.10 Trifecta £240.60.
**Owner** K Rhatigan **Bred** Olive O'Connor **Trained** Upper Lambourn, Berks

**FOCUS**
Mainly exposed sorts in a very useful handicap. The gallop was no more than fair.

## 3432 BREEDERS BACKING RACING EBF MAIDEN STKS (BOBIS RACE) 1m 2f
**8:40** (8:42) (Class 4) 3-Y-O **£5,498** (£1,636; £817; £408) **Stalls** Centre

Form RPR

4 **1** **Winter Thunder**[42] 2126 3-9-5 0.................... SilvestreDeSousa 1 94+
(Saeed bin Suroor) *hld up in tch: rdn over 3f out: led and hung lft ins fnl f: r.o wl* **3/1**[2]

-333 **2** *4* **Loving Home**[29] 2481 3-9-5 80.................... WilliamBuick 8 86
(John Gosden) *chsd ldr tl led over 3f out: rdn over 1f out: edgd rt and hdd ins fnl f: styd on same pce* **7/4**[1]

**3** *2* **Tryster (IRE)** 3-9-5 0.................... AdamKirby 9 83
(Charlie Appleby) *hld up: hdwy 4f out: rdn over 2f out: ev ch over 1f out: hung lft and no ex ins fnl f* **9/1**

54-5 **4** *nk* **Courageous Rock (USA)**[72] 1394 3-9-5 78.................... LukeMorris 3 82
(Ed Vaughan) *chsd ldrs: rdn over 2f out: ev ch over 1f out: no ex ins fnl f* **12/1**

**5** *2¾* **Orkney Island** 3-9-5 0.................... JamieSpencer 2 77+
(Charlie Appleby) *s.i.s: hld up: effrt and nt clr run over 2f out: outpcd over 1f out: kpt on nr fin* **14/1**

**6** *¾* **Gold Struck** 3-9-5 0.................... JamesDoyle 7 75
(John Gosden) *s.i.s: plld hrd and hld up in tch: rdn over 1f out: wknd ins fnl f* **5/1**[3]

0-0 **7** *3¾* **Mutaraadif (USA)**[16] 2881 3-9-5 0.................... PaulHanagan 4 68
(Roger Varian) *led: hdd over 3f out: rdn and wknd over 1f out* **12/1**

**8** *5* **Tasaaboq** 3-9-5 0....................(t) SeanLevey 5 59
(Brian Meehan) *prom: rdn over 2f out: wknd over 1f out* **25/1**

60 **9** *2½* **Pindora (GER)**[18] 2850 3-8-9 0....................(t) TobyAtkinson(5) 6 49
(Noel Quinlan) *hld up: pushed along over 3f out: wknd wl over 1f out* **50/1**

2m 10.02s (4.52) **Going Correction** +0.25s/f (Good) **9** Ran SP% **115.9**
Speed ratings (Par 101): **91,87,86,85,83 83,80,76,74**
CSF £8.66 TOTE £4.40: £1.60, £1.30, £2.80; EX 9.60 Trifecta £71.90.
**Owner** Godolphin **Bred** Darley **Trained** Newmarket, Suffolk

**FOCUS**
A useful maiden in which the gallop was an ordinary one.

## 3433 TURFTV H'CAP 5f
**9:10** (9:11) (Class 5) (0-75,75) 3-Y-O £3,881 (£1,155; £577; £288) **Stalls** High

Form RPR
-431 1 **War Spirit**[13] 2985 3-9-3 71 SeanLevey 9 82
(Richard Hannon) *hld up: hdwy 1/2-way: shkn up to ld over 1f out: rdn out* **7/2**[1]
4321 2 1 3/4 **Groundworker (IRE)**[28] 2505 3-9-6 74 JamesDoyle 6 79
(Sylvester Kirk) *hld up: hdwy over 1f out: rdn to chse wnr ins fnl f: r.o* **7/2**[1]
0602 3 1 1/4 **Touch The Clouds**[16] 2889 3-8-13 74 MeganCarberry(7) 2 75
(William Stone) *chsd ldrs: rdn over 1f out: edgd lft and styd on same pce ins fnl f* **16/1**
4560 4 nk **National Service (USA)**[8] 3138 3-9-4 72 MartinHarley 8 71
(Stuart Williams) *hld up: swtched rt and r.o ins fnl f: nt rch ldrs* **25/1**
2240 5 1 1/4 **Argent Touch**[19] 2802 3-8-0 61 AdamMcLean(7) 5 56
(Derek Shaw) *s.i.s: hld up: racd keenly: rdn over 1f out: hung rt and r.o ins fnl f: nvr nrr* **33/1**
-445 6 1/2 **Lady Lydia (IRE)**[7] 3198 3-9-7 75 (p) AdamKirby 12 68
(Conrad Allen) *mid-div: hdwy 1/2-way: rdn over 1f out: no ex ins fnl f* **5/1**[2]
5646 7 3/4 **Anfield**[52] 1860 3-8-2 56 oh8 (t) PaoloSirigu 4 46
(Mick Quinn) *led: rdn and hdd over 1f out: no ex ins fnl f* **40/1**
2114 8 shd **Saffire Song**[99] 936 3-9-0 73 NatashaEaton(5) 3 63
(Alan Bailey) *chsd ldrs: rdn over 1f out: no ex ins fnl f* **25/1**
-460 9 1/2 **Kalon Brama (IRE)**[36] 2274 3-7-11 58 BradleyBosley(7) 1 46
(Peter Charalambous) *hld up: plld hrd: rdn over 1f out: n.d* **25/1**
6-50 10 1/2 **Inheritance**[23] 2681 3-8-6 60 PaulHanagan 11 48
(Sir Michael Stoute) *hld up: pushed along 1/2-way: nt trble ldrs* **7/2**[1]
2122 11 1/2 **Hustle Bustle (IRE)**[30] 2470 3-8-9 68 MarcMonaghan(5) 10 53
(David Brown) *chsd ldrs: rdn over 1f out: wknd ins fnl f* **14/1**
0-05 12 2 **He's My Boy (IRE)**[23] 2686 3-8-11 65 FrederikTylicki 7 42
(James Fanshawe) *prom: rdn over 1f out: wknd fnl f* **10/1**[3]

1m 0.05s (0.95) **Going Correction** +0.20s/f (Good) **12 Ran SP% 121.9**
Speed ratings (Par 99): **100,97,95,94,92 91,90,90,89,88 88,84**
CSF £14.79 CT £181.04 TOTE £5.20: £1.90, £1.50, £3.60; EX 14.90 Trifecta £148.80.
**Owner** Mohamed Saeed Al Shahi **Bred** Biddestone Stud Ltd **Trained** East Everleigh, Wilts

**FOCUS**
A fair handicap run at a decent gallop and this form should prove reliable.
T/Plt: £405.80 to a £1 stake. Pool: £63039.12 - 113.40 winning tickets T/Qpdt: £44.50 to a £1 stake. Pool: £7114.34 - 118.08 winning tickets CR

# 2652 REDCAR (L-H)
## Friday, June 20

**OFFICIAL GOING: Good to firm (8.7)**
Wind: Light across Weather: Fine & dry

## 3434 WIN A VIP DAY OUT @ REDCARRACING.CO.UK MAIDEN STKS 1m 2f
**2:20** (2:20) (Class 5) 3-Y-O+ £2,587 (£770; £384; £192) **Stalls** Low

Form RPR
65 1 **Perfect Light (IRE)**[35] 2310 3-8-9 0 FrannyNorton 2 84
(William Haggas) *trckd ldr: swtchd rt and hdwy over 2f out: sn cl up: rdn to ld wl over 1f out: kpt on wl u.p fnl f* **7/2**[3]
2 3/4 **Mythical Madness** 3-9-0 0 AhmedAjtebi 4 87
(Charlie Appleby) *trckd ldrs: effrt over 2f out: sn swtchd rt to outer: rdn wl over 1f out: styd on wl fnl f* **8/1**
35 3 2 1/4 **Potent Embrace (USA)**[24] 2650 3-8-9 0 AdrianNicholls 7 78
(Mark Johnston) *led: pushed along over 3f out: rdn over 2f out: hdd wl over 1f out: sn drvn and one pce fnl f* **4/1**
4 3/4 **Absolute Sway** 3-9-0 0 PaulMulrennan 1 82+
(Charlie Appleby) *dwlt: green and bhd: hdwy 3f out: rdn along over 2f out: styd on appr fnl f: nrst fin* **3/1**[2]
063 5 4 1/2 **Randwick (IRE)**[29] 2485 3-9-0 90 RobertWinston 6 75
(Charles Hills) *trckd ldng pair: hdwy to chse ldr over 4f out: pushed along wl over 2f out: sn rdn and edgd lft: drvn wl over 1f out and sn wknd* **11/4**[1]
6 12 **Giovanni Jack**[13] 4-9-12 0 BenCurtis 5 50
(Alan Swinbank) *towards rr: pushed along and sme hdwy 4f out: sn rdn and outpcd fnl 3f* **33/1**
6 7 13 **Yawail**[33] 2365 3-8-9 0 BarryMcHugh 8 21
(Brian Rothwell) *in tch: rdn along 4f out: sn outpcd and bhd* **66/1**
0 8 10 **King Couture (IRE)**[16] 2899 3-9-0 0 GrahamGibbons 3 7
(Michael Easterby) *a in rr: outpcd and wl bhd fnl 3f* **66/1**

2m 6.07s (-1.03) **Going Correction** -0.05s/f (Good)
**WFA** 3 from 4yo 12lb **8 Ran SP% 110.9**
Speed ratings (Par 103): **102,101,99,99,95 85,75,67**
CSF £28.85 TOTE £4.60: £1.70, £1.80, £1.70; EX 32.50 Trifecta £106.10.
**Owner** Liam Sheridan **Bred** Beauty Bright Syndicate **Trained** Newmarket, Suffolk

**FOCUS**
After the opening race Robert Winston said: "It's beautiful ground, good to firm with no jar." This looked a decent maiden on paper, but there are one or two doubts over the form.

## 3435 DOWNLOAD THE NEW RACINGUK IPAD APP (S) STKS 7f
**2:55** (2:56) (Class 6) 2-Y-O £1,940 (£577; £288; £144) **Stalls** Centre

Form RPR
4040 1 **Binky Blue (IRE)**[7] 3201 2-8-6 0 BarryMcHugh 7 59
(Tony Coyle) *trckd ldrs: cl up 1/2-way: rdn to ld wl over 1f out and sn edgd lft: drvn ins fnl f: kpt on wl towards fin* **2/1**[1]
50 2 2 **Fly Grazer (IRE)**[7] 3201 2-8-6 0 BenCurtis 2 54
(J S Moore) *hld up in tch: smooth hdwy on outer 1/2-way: slt ld over 2f out: rdn and hung lft wl over 1f out: sn hdd: rallied to chal ent fnl f and ev ch tl drvn and no ex last 100yds* **20/1**
605 3 1 3/4 **Fazenda's Girl**[7] 3201 2-8-6 0 JamesSullivan 8 49
(Michael Easterby) *wnt rt s: hld up in rr: hdwy over 2f out: rdn along wl over 1f out: styd on fnl f: nrst fin* **6/1**[3]
504 4 1 3/4 **Reet Petite (IRE)**[33] 2360 2-8-3 0[1] ConnorBeasley(3) 3 44
(Michael Dods) *hld up in rr: hdwy over 2f out: rdn along to chse ldrs over 1f out: sn one pce* **9/2**[2]
605 5 1 **Autumn Revue**[9] 3091 2-8-6 0 (b) DuranFentiman 6 41
(Tim Easterby) *trckd ldrs: rdn along 3f out and sn outpcd: rallied u.p and plugged on fr over 1f out* **16/1**
4501 6 11 **Fairweather Trader (IRE)**[9] 3091 2-9-3 0 PaulMulrennan 5 23
(Paul Midgley) *led: rdn along 3f out: sn hdd & wknd wl over 1f out* **9/2**[2]
44 7 5 **Marti Ella**[8] 3157 2-8-6 0 AdrianNicholls 4
(J S Moore) *prom: rdn to ld briefly wl over 2f out: sn hdd & wknd* **10/1**

8 3 3/4 **Cheeco**[16] 2903 2-8-11 0 PJMcDonald 1
(Ruth Carr) *wnt lft s: in rr and t.k.h: hdwy and cl up after 2f: rdn along 3f out: sn wknd* **10/1**

1m 27.1s (2.60) **Going Correction** +0.25s/f (Good) **8 Ran SP% 112.8**
Speed ratings (Par 91): **95,92,90,88,87 75,69,65**
CSF £44.93 TOTE £2.70: £1.30, £3.50, £2.20; EX 38.00 Trifecta £196.00.The winner was bought in for 5,500gns.
**Owner** B Dunn **Bred** Gerard & Anne Corry **Trained** Norton, N Yorks

**FOCUS**
The first three in this poor race all contested the relatively valuable Rous seller over 6f at York last week, won by Sudest, and finished in the reverse order this time.

## 3436 WATCH ON 3 DEVICES RACINGUK.COM/ANYWHERE H'CAP 1m 2f
**3:30** (3:30) (Class 5) (0-70,70) 4-Y-O+ £2,587 (£770; £384; £192) **Stalls** Low

Form RPR
2450 1 **Gabrial's Hope (FR)**[25] 2607 5-8-3 52 FrannyNorton 3 63
(Tracy Waggott) *hld up: hdwy to trck ldrs over 3f out: swtchd rt and effrt to ld 2f out: rdn clr over 1f out: drvn out* **8/1**
3500 2 2 1/2 **Magnolia Ridge (IRE)**[17] 2872 4-9-4 67 (p) AmyRyan 7 73
(Kristin Stubbs) *hld up in rr: swtchd rt to wd outside 3f out: gd hdwy 2f out: rdn over 1f out: chsd wnr ins fnl f: no imp towards fin* **10/1**
0-00 3 4 **Printmaker (IRE)**[25] 2607 6-8-7 56 (p) PJMcDonald 6 55
(Tim Easterby) *trckd ldrs: hdwy 3f out: rdn along 2f out: drvn and one pce ent fnl f* **9/1**
00-6 4 1 1/2 **Gala Casino Star (IRE)**[28] 2519 9-8-12 68 (v) JordanNason(7) 5 64
(Deborah Sanderson) *trckd ldng pair: hdwy on inner 4f out: disp ld 3f out and sn rdn: drvn wl over 1f out and sn wknd* **2/1**[1]
4040 5 6 **Gioia Di Vita**[55] 1724 4-9-6 69 RaulDaSilva 9 53
(David Thompson) *trckd ldr: cl up over 4f out: slt ld 3f out: sn rdn: hdd 2f out: sn drvn and wknd* **3/1**[2]
0033 6 3 **Staffhoss**[9] 3094 4-8-11 60 (b[1]) AdrianNicholls 8 39
(Mark Johnston) *trckd ldrs: pushed along 4f out: rdn over 3f out: sn drvn and wknd* **11/2**[3]
0-00 7 7 **Mcmonagle (USA)**[57] 1673 6-8-11 60 (tp) RobertWinston 4 40
(Alan Brown) *led: jnd and pushed along over 4f out: rdn and hdd 3f out: sn wknd* **10/1**

2m 5.74s (-1.36) **Going Correction** -0.05s/f (Good) **7 Ran SP% 113.0**
Speed ratings (Par 103): **103,101,97,96,91 89,83**
CSF £79.07 CT £730.87 TOTE £7.10: £3.90, £4.70; EX 100.40 Trifecta £512.50.
**Owner** David Tate **Bred** Mrs G Forien & G Forien **Trained** Spennymoor, Co Durham

**FOCUS**
Decidely moderate handicap form, none of these looking progressive. They went a good, contested gallop and the first two came from the rear. The time was slightly quicker than the opening Class 5 maiden.

## 3437 ANDERSON BARROWCLIFF H'CAP (QUALIFIER FOR THE REDCAR STRAIGHT-MILE CHAMPIONSHIP) 1m
**4:10** (4:10) (Class 3) (0-90,88) 3-Y-O+ £7,439 (£2,213; £1,106; £553) **Stalls** Centre

Form RPR
4311 1 **Genius Boy**[8] 3162 4-9-7 84 6ex PaulMulrennan 4 96+
(James Tate) *hld up in rr: stdy hdwy on outer wl over 2f out: rdn to chal jst over 1f out: drvn ins fnl f: styd wl on to ld nr fin* **11/8**[1]
2006 2 1/2 **Sound Advice**[29] 2478 5-9-8 85 TomEaves 3 96
(Keith Dalgleish) *cl up: led after 2f: rdn along wl over 1f out: drvn ins fnl f: hdd and no ex towards fin* **6/1**[3]
-014 3 2 **Hakuna Matata**[25] 2603 7-8-13 79 (b) ConnorBeasley(3) 2 85
(Michael Dods) *hld up: hdwy to trck ldrs on outer 3f out: rdn to chal wl over 1f out: ev ch tl drvn ins fnl f and kpt on same pce* **7/1**
1020 4 2 **Kiwi Bay**[5] 3272 9-9-3 80 PJMcDonald 6 82
(Michael Dods) *trckd ldrs: pushed along wl over 2f out: sn rdn and sltly outpcd: kpt on u.p fnl f* **8/1**
5060 5 1/2 **Lazarus Bell**[7] 3202 4-8-13 81 (p) JacobButterfield(5) 1 82
(Alan Brown) *cl up: rdn 2f out and ev ch tl drvn appr the fnl f and grad wknd* **12/1**
0400 6 1 1/4 **Osteopathic Remedy (IRE)**[17] 2869 10-9-11 88 PhillipMakin 5 86
(Michael Dods) *led 2f: cl up: rdn along over 2f out: wknd wl over 1f out* **20/1**
-316 7 27 **Yourartisonfire**[41] 2156 4-9-10 87 (v) BenCurtis 7 23
(K R Burke) *trckd ldrs: effrt 3f out: sn rdn along: wknd 2f out and sn bhd* **4/1**[2]

1m 37.08s (0.48) **Going Correction** +0.25s/f (Good) **7 Ran SP% 112.5**
Speed ratings (Par 107): **107,106,104,102,102 100,73**
CSF £9.73 CT £41.48 TOTE £2.00: £1.10, £3.70; EX 12.60 Trifecta £54.60.
**Owner** Sheikh Juma Dalmook Al Maktoum **Bred** Meon Valley Stud **Trained** Newmarket, Suffolk
■ Stewards' Enquiry : Tom Eaves three-day ban: used whip without giving gelding time to respond (Jul 4,6,7)

**FOCUS**
Not a strong handicap for the class. They quickly split into two small groups before converging by halfway.

## 3438 REDCAR RACECOURSE SHOWGROUND & OUTDOOR EVENTS CLASSIFIED CLAIMING STKS 1m 2f
**4:45** (4:45) (Class 6) 3-Y-O+ £2,045 (£603; £302) **Stalls** Low

Form RPR
6312 1 **Incendo**[11] 3064 8-9-12 72 (v) PaulMulrennan 1 78
(Conor Dore) *hld up: stdy hdwy 3f out: swtchd rt and chal on bit over 1f out: shkn up ins fnl f: kpt on to ld last 75yds* **7/4**[1]
4530 2 nk **Matraash (USA)**[11] 3064 8-9-4 72 (p) StephenCraine 3 69
(Daniel Mark Loughnane) *trckd ldng pair: smooth hdwy over 3f out: led on bit 2f out: jnd and rdn ent fnl f: sn drvn: hdd and no ex last 75yds* **14/1**
3230 3 3 **Aqua Ardens (GER)**[20] 2772 6-10-0 74 (t) TomEaves 4 74
(George Baker) *hld up in tch: hdwy over 2f out: rdn to chse ldng pair appr fnl f: sn no imp* **2/1**[2]
00-4 4 3 **Yorksters Prince (IRE)**[24] 2654 7-8-11 57 (b) ShirleyTeasdale(5) 2 56
(Marjorie Fife) *led: pushed along over 3f out: rdn and hdd 2f out: sn wknd* **7/2**[3]
140- 5 10 **Carthaginian (IRE)**[12] 4810 5-9-2 72 (p) PhillipMakin 5 37
(Martin Todhunter) *a bhd* **8/1**
666 6 1 1/4 **Some Boy Lukey**[14] 2952 3-8-4 45 RaulDaSilva 7 35
(David Thompson) *chsd ldr: rdn along wl over 3f out: sn wknd* **33/1**

2m 7.45s (0.35) **Going Correction** -0.05s/f (Good)
**WFA** 3 from 5yo+ 12lb **6 Ran SP% 112.6**
Speed ratings (Par 101): **96,95,93,90,82 81**
CSF £25.68 TOTE £2.90: £1.20, £5.70; EX 21.40 Trifecta £61.40.
**Owner** Mrs Louise Marsh **Bred** London Thoroughbred Services Ltd **Trained** Hubbert's Bridge, Lincs

**FOCUS**
A very modest claimer run at an ordinary pace. It was the slowest of the three C&D times.

## 3439 RACING UK ANYWHERE AVAILABLE NOW H'CAP 1m
**5:20** (5:21) (Class 5) (0-70,70) 3-Y-O+ **£2,587** (£770; £384; £192) **Stalls** Centre

Form RPR
5-60 **1** **Tanawar (IRE)**[39] 2215 4-9-4 **60** ........ JamesSullivan 13 69
(Ruth Carr) *hld up towards rr: stdy hdwy 3f out: chsd ldrs over 1f out: rdn to ld ins fnl f: kpt on wl* **6/1**[1]
0153 **2** *nk* **Push Me (IRE)**[4] 3301 7-9-9 **70** ........ ShaneGray(5) 10 78
(Iain Jardine) *hld up in rr: hdwy over 2f out: effrt and nt clr run over 1f out: sn swtchd rt and rdn: nt clr run and swtchd lft ins fnl f: styd on wl towards fin* **9/1**
6004 **3** *½* **Hard Core Debt**[13] 3005 4-9-7 **63** ........ RobertWinston 16 70
(Brian Ellison) *hld up in rr: gd hdwy over 2f out: rdn to chal ent fnl f: sn drvn and ev ch tl no ex towards fin* **16/1**
55-5 **4** *½* **Broctune Papa Gio**[60] 1609 7-9-11 **67** ........ TomEaves 11 73
(Keith Reveley) *a.p: effrt 2f out: rdn over 1f out: ev ch ent fnl f: sn drvn and no ex last 100yds* **16/1**
-602 **5** *nk* **Shearian**[31] 2427 4-9-1 **60** ........ ConnorBeasley(3) 15 65
(Tracy Waggott) *sn led: rdn along 2f out: drvn over 1f out: hdd & wknd ins fnl f* **14/1**
0-42 **6** *1 ¼* **Nelson's Bay**[28] 2518 5-9-1 **62** ........ KevinStott(5) 4 64
(Wilf Storey) *trckd ldrs: hdwy and cl up 1/2-way: rdn along wl over 1f out: drvn ent fnl f: sn wknd* **6/1**[1]
40-0 **7** *shd* **Prostate Awareness (IRE)**[34] 2355 3-8-7 **59** ........ AndrewElliott 8 59
(Patrick Holmes) *prom: rdn along wl over 2f out: drvn over 1f out: grad wknd* **22/1**
-121 **8** *shd* **Reggie Bond**[55] 1718 4-9-11 **67** ........(b) DavidAllan 9 69
(Geoffrey Oldroyd) *trckd ldrs: hdwy over 2f out: rdn wl over 1f out: kpt on same pce fnl f* **13/2**[2]
23-5 **9** *3 ¾* **King Pin**[60] 1607 9-9-11 **67** ........(p) DaleSwift 12 60
(Tracy Waggott) *hld up: hdwy on outer to chse ldrs over 3f out: rdn along 2f out: grad wknd* **7/1**[3]
50-0 **10** *6* **Black Rider (IRE)**[9] 3096 4-10-0 **70** ........ PaulMulrennan 6 49
(Julie Camacho) *hld up: hdwy on outer 3f out: chsd ldrs 2f out: sn rdn and wknd* **20/1**
50-0 **11** *nk* **Clock On Tom**[41] 2171 4-9-2 **58** ........ GrahamGibbons 14 37
(Michael Easterby) *nvr bttr than midfield* **20/1**
-604 **12** *nk* **Midnight Warrior**[24] 2658 4-8-5 **52** oh3........ ShirleyTeasdale(5) 1 30
(Ron Barr) *prom: chsd ldr 1/2-way: rdn along wl over 2f out: sn wknd* **25/1**
2460 **13** *1* **Silly Billy (IRE)**[46] 2019 6-8-13 **58** ........(p) JasonHart(3) 2 34
(John Balding) *t.k.h early: trckd ldrs: rdn along 2f out: sn wknd* **7/1**[3]
060- **14** *10* **Miss Matiz**[298] 5830 7-8-10 **52** oh7........ RoystonFfrench 3 5
(Tracy Waggott) *chsd ldrs: rdn along 3f out: sn wknd* **100/1**
00-0 **15** *9* **Finn Mac**[24] 2658 4-8-10 **52** oh4........ PaddyAspell 5
(John Norton) *midfield: rdn along 1/2-way: sn lost pl and bhd* **66/1**

1m 37.68s (1.08) **Going Correction** +0.25s/f (Good)
**WFA** 3 from 4yo+ 10lb **15** Ran SP% **115.5**
Speed ratings (Par 103): **104,103,103,102,102 101,101,100,97,91 90,90,89,79,70**
CSF £51.03 CT £838.29 TOTE £8.10: £2.60, £2.30, £8.00; EX 74.80 Trifecta £1537.00 Part won..
**Owner** JB & MD **Bred** J Hanly, Castlemartin Sky & Skymarc Far **Trained** Huby, N Yorks

**FOCUS**
Quite a competitive handicap and the form makes sense. The principals came from the rear.

## 3440 COME RACING TOMORROW ON LADIES' DAY MAIDEN H'CAP 5f
**5:50** (5:51) (Class 5) (0-70,62) 3-Y-O+ **£2,587** (£770; £384; £192) **Stalls** Centre

Form RPR
-242 **1** **Red Forever**[13] 2985 3-9-2 **60** ........ SladeO'Hara(3) 2 66
(Alan Berry) *prom: hdwy 2f out: led over 1f out: rdn ins fnl f: kpt on* **5/1**[2]
3-20 **2** *½* **Knockamany Bends (IRE)**[9] 3093 4-9-1 **50**........ PaddyAspell 9 56
(John Wainwright) *in rr: hdwy on outer wl over 1f out: sn rdn: styd on strly fnl f* **25/1**
-306 **3** *1 ¼* **Another Royal**[18] 2828 3-9-0 **55** ........(b) DavidAllan 3 55
(Tim Easterby) *hld up towards rr: hdwy 2f out: rdn to chse ldrs on outer over 1f out: drvn and kpt on fnl f* **15/8**[1]
0-20 **4** *1* **Tell Me When**[24] 2657 3-9-0 **55** ........ BarryMcHugh 5 51
(Brian Rothwell) *towards rr: hdwy 2f out: rdn over 1f out: kpt on fnl f: nrst fin* **8/1**
20-3 **5** *nk* **See Vermont**[28] 2514 6-8-10 **48** ........ NeilFarley(3) 6 45
(Robin Bastiman) *prom: cl up over 2f out: rdn and ev ch over 1f out: drvn ent fnl f: sn wknd* **13/2**
5-30 **6** *1 ¾* **Cheeky Peta'S**[145] 346 3-8-9 **53**........(v) ConnorBeasley(3) 1 42
(James Given) *led: rdn along 2f out: sn drvn: hdd & wknd over 1f out* **20/1**
06-4 **7** *¾* **Pavers Bounty**[29] 2474 3-9-7 **62** ........ DuranFentiman 4 48
(Noel Wilson) *t.k.h early: chsd ldrs: rdn along 2f out: wknd appr fnl f* **10/1**
-504 **8** *2 ½* **Spinner Lane**[25] 2619 3-8-5 **46** ........ FrannyNorton 7 23
(Richard Whitaker) *in rr: rdn along 1/2-way: sn outpcd and bhd* **16/1**
44-5 **9** *3* **Princess Myla (IRE)**[58] 1642 3-9-1 **56**........(p) PaulMulrennan 8 22
(Paul Midgley) *prom: cl up 1/2-way: rdn along 2f out: sn wknd* **6/1**[3]

59.86s (1.26) **Going Correction** +0.25s/f (Good)
**WFA** 3 from 4yo+ 6lb **9** Ran SP% **113.8**
Speed ratings (Par 103): **99,98,96,94,94 91,90,86,81**
CSF £114.66 CT £315.17 TOTE £5.90: £1.90, £7.40, £1.30; EX 67.50 Trifecta £225.30.
**Owner** Sporting Kings **Bred** Bearstone Stud **Trained** Cockerham, Lancs

**FOCUS**
The topweight ran off 8lb below the permitted rating ceiling in this maiden handicap, and this isn't form to get excited about.
T/Plt: £794.70 to a £1 stake. Pool: £46781.93 - 42.97 winning tickets T/Qpdt: £37.10 to a £1 stake. Pool: £3050.02 - 60.70 winning tickets JR

3441 - 3447a (Foreign Racing) - See Raceform Interactive

# [3415]ASCOT (R-H)
Saturday, June 21

**OFFICIAL GOING: Good to firm (good in places on round course; stands' side 9.4, centre 9.5, far side 9.1, round 8.4)**

## 3448 CHESHAM STKS (LISTED RACE) 7f
**2:30** (2:35) (Class 1) 2-Y-O
**£34,026** (£12,900; £6,456; £3,216; £1,614; £810) **Stalls** Centre

Form RPR
4 **1** **Richard Pankhurst**[21] 2776 2-9-3 0........[1] WilliamBuick 7 111+
(John Gosden) *athletic: hld up: swtchd lft and hdwy 2f out: r.o to ld ins fnl f: sn edgd rt and dashed clr: comf* **10/1**
2 **2** *3 ¾* **Toscanini (IRE)**[19] 2855 2-9-3 0........ ShaneFoley 15 101
(M Halford, Ire) *athletic: lw: hld up: hdwy travelling strly over 2f out: led wl over 1f out: sn rdn: hdd ins fnl f: kpt on but outpcd and no ch w wnr after* **4/1**[2]
**3** *hd* **Dick Whittington (IRE)**[7] 3257 2-9-3 0........ JosephO'Brien 4 100
(A P O'Brien, Ire) *str: in tch: clsd to go prom 4f out: rdn whn chalng over 1f out: nt qckn ins fnl f: kpt on after but nt gng pce of wnr* **15/8**[1]
**4** *¾* **Nafaqa (IRE)** 2-9-3 0........ PaulHanagan 14 98+
(B W Hills) *w'like: completely missed break: in rr: rdn and hdwy under 2f out: swtchd rt over 1f out: r.o ins fnl f: nrst fin* **40/1**
1 **5** *3* **Justice Well**[21] 2777 2-9-3 0........ WilliamCarson 6 90
(David Elsworth) *athletic: hld up in midfield: hdwy 3f out: chalng under 2f out: edgd lft over 1f out: nt qckn: kpt on same pce ins fnl f* **12/1**
**6** *1 ¼* **Cordero (IRE)** 2-9-3 0........(bt[1]) RyanMoore 10 87
(Wesley A Ward, U.S.A) *chsd ldrs: pushed along over 2f out: keeping on for press but struggling to qckn whn n.m.r and hmpd over 1f out: kpt on same pce whn n.d ins fnl f* **6/1**[3]
**7** *½* **Franklin D (USA)** 2-9-3 0........ TomQueally 2 86
(Michael Bell) *tall: lw: hld up: pushed along and hdwy 3f out: rdn whn hung lft and no real imp over 1f out: one pce ins fnl f* **50/1**
2 **8** *1* **Caprior Bere (FR)**[33] 2386 2-9-3 0........ MartinHarley 3 83
(K R Burke) *str: in tch: effrt to ld over 2f out: rdn and hdd wl over 1f out: wknd ins fnl f* **66/1**
41 **9** *1* **Juventas**[36] 2306 2-8-12 0........ WilliamTwiston-Davies 12 76
(Mick Channon) *leggy: racd keenly: hld up in midfield: outpcd and losing pl whn n.m.r and hmpd over 2f out: sn wl btn* **20/1**
**10** *¾* **Crown The Kitten (USA)**[15] 2-9-3 0........(bt) VictorEspinoza 11 78+
(Wesley A Ward, U.S.A) *w'like: led: rdn and hdd over 2f out: u.p and hld whn n.m.r and hmpd over 1f out: sn dropped away* **12/1**
15 **11** *¾* **Via Via (IRE)**[23] 2703 2-9-3 0........ RichardHughes 8 78
(Clive Brittain) *prom: rdn 2f out: wknd over 1f out: eased whn btn fnl 100yds* **14/1**
00 **12** *2 ½* **Groor**[8] 3194 2-9-3 0........ KierenFallon 1 70
(James Tate) *str: in tch: rdn 3f out: outpcd 2f out: btn ins fnl f: eased whn wl hld clsng stages* **33/1**
21 **13** *4 ½* **Jaganory (IRE)**[11] 3082 2-9-3 0........ AdamKirby 9 57
(David Evans) *str: w'like: racd keenly: chsd ldrs: rdn over 2f out: sn wknd* **25/1**
1 **14** *3 ½* **Loretta Martin**[52] 1872 2-8-12 0........ CharlesBishop 5 43
(Mick Channon) *leggy: midfield: pushed along and wknd 3f out: wl bhd fnl 2f* **50/1**

1m 27.58s (-0.02) **Going Correction** -0.125s/f (Firm) **14** Ran SP% **119.6**
Speed ratings (Par 101): **95,90,90,89,86 84,84,83,81,81 80,77,72,68**
CSF £46.71 CT £113.19 TOTE £12.10: £3.40, £1.80, £1.30; EX 59.60 Trifecta £164.70.
**Owner** Ms Rachel D S Hood **Bred** J H M Gosden **Trained** Newmarket, Suffolk

**FOCUS**
False rail removed to provide fresh ground and distances as advertised. The final day of what had been a truly memorable meeting saw the going remain unchanged from the previous two days, despite no watering of the track taking place overnight. Some decent types have won this in the past, but it's still to produce a winner in recent times that has gone on to be a truly Group-class performer as a 3yo. On the positive side, the first four home last year (Berkshire, Bunker, Ihtimal and Somewhat) went on to land two Group 2s, a Group 3 and a couple of Listed events before the end of their juvenile campaigns.

## 3449 DUKE OF EDINBURGH STKS (H'CAP) 1m 4f
**3:05** (3:07) (Class 2) (0-105,104) 3-Y-O+
**£46,687** (£13,980; £6,990; £3,495; £1,747; £877) **Stalls** Low

Form RPR
-111 **1** **Arab Spring (IRE)**[36] 2314 4-9-10 **104**........ RyanMoore 12 115+
(Sir Michael Stoute) *chsd ldng pair: rdn and effrt to chse ldr 2f out: led over 1f out: asserting and edging rt 1f out: styd on strly: rdn out* **11/4**[1]
1040 **2** *2* **Salutation (IRE)**[15] 2957 4-8-12 **95**........ MichaelJMMurphy(3) 11 103
(Mark Johnston) *lw: racd keenly: led: rdn over 2f out: hdd over 1f out: keeping on same pce and btn whn hmpd and swtchd lft jst ins fnl f: kpt on for clr 2nd* **25/1**
133- **3** *1 ¼* **Havana Cooler (IRE)**[301] 5764 4-9-3 **97**........ AdamKirby 9 103+
(Luca Cumani) *hld up in tch in midfield on inner: hdwy but nt clr run over 1f out: gap opened: hdwy u.p and battling for 3rd fnl f: styd on* **12/1**
3-13 **4** *nk* **Elidor**[42] 2143 4-9-2 **99**........ WilliamTwiston-Davies(3) 16 105
(Mick Channon) *t.k.h: hld up in tch in midfield: rdn and effrt over 2f out: hdwy u.p and battling for 3rd 1f out: styd on* **8/1**[3]
62-4 **5** *1* **Dashing Star**[21] 2779 4-9-6 **100**........ JamieSpencer 5 104
(David Elsworth) *t.k.h: chsd ldr: rdn and lost 2nd 2f out: unable qck u.p over 1f out: styd on same pce and lost 2 pls fnl f* **20/1**
20-0 **6** *¾* **Elhaame (IRE)**[48] 1973 4-9-0 **94**........ AndreaAtzeni 7 97
(Luca Cumani) *t.k.h: hld up wl in tch in midfield: rdn and unable qck ent fnl 2f: drvn and styd on same pce fr over 1f out* **12/1**
00-1 **7** *½* **Wadi Al Hattawi (IRE)**[21] 2787 4-9-5 **99**........(p) KierenFallon 14 105+
(Saeed bin Suroor) *t.k.h: hld up in midfield: n.m.r and hmpd 5f out: effrt but stl lots to do whn nt clr run and swtchd lft over 1f out: styd on wl ins fnl f: nvr trbld ldrs* **12/1**
5365 **8** *nk* **Aussie Reigns (IRE)**[15] 2957 4-9-8 **102**........ GeorgeBaker 13 103
(William Knight) *stdd s: hld up towards rr: hdwy on inner 2f out: nt clr run and swtchd lft over 1f out: kpt on ins fnl f: nvr trbld ldrs* **33/1**
6-44 **9** *½* **Continuum**[42] 2143 5-9-1 **98**........ CharlesBishop(3) 15 99
(Peter Hedger) *short of room and stmbld sn after s: hld up towards rr: swtchd lft and hdwy on outer 5f out: midfield and unable qck u.p whn edgd rt over 1f out: kpt on same pce after* **25/1**

0-00 **9** *dht* **Lahaag**[21] 2779 5-9-3 **97** .......... PaulHanagan 18 98
(John Gosden) *t.k.h: hld up towards rr: rdn and effrt over 2f out: pushed rt and squeezed for room wl over 1f out: hdwy u.p over 1f out: kpt on but no threat to ldrs* **25/1**

50-1 **11** *2 ¾* **Groundbreaking**[36] 2309 4-9-9 **103** .......... WilliamBuick 4 99
(Charlie Appleby) *swtg: stdd after s: hld up towards rr: swtchd lft and effrt on outer over 2f out: kpt on u.p but no imp: nvr threatened ldrs* **12/1**

30-5 **12** *1 ¼* **Eshtiaal (USA)**[28] 2558 4-8-13 **93** .......... (bt) JimmyFortune 2 87
(Brian Meehan) *chsd ldrs: rdn and struggling wl over 2f out: wkng whn squeezed for room wl over 1f out: wl hld 1f out* **33/1**

11-2 **13** *nse* **Hamelin (IRE)**[42] 2142 4-9-2 **96** .......... JamesDoyle 6 90
(Lady Cecil) *lw: t.k.h: hld up in tch in midfield: rdn and effrt to chse ldrs 3f out: drvn and unable qck 2f out: wknd 1f out* **4/1**[2]

00-0 **14** *½* **Macbeth (IRE)**[21] 2779 5-9-1 **95** .......... AndrewMullen 17 88
(Michael Appleby) *in tch in midfield: rdn and hdwy over 2f out: no imp whn carried rt and hmpd wl over 1f out: wknd over 1f out* **33/1**

0-16 **15** *1 ½* **Beacon Lady**[14] 2988 5-8-11 **96** .......... JackDuern(5) 19 87
(William Knight) *stdd s: hld up in rr: rdn 3f out: no real prog: n.d* **33/1**

5210 **16** *2 ¼* **Viewpoint (IRE)**[48] 1973 5-9-5 **99** .......... RichardHughes 22 86
(Richard Hannon) *styd wd early: hld up towards rr: rdn and effrt whn pushed lft 2f out: no prog: n.d* **40/1**

1413 **17** *3* **One Pursuit (IRE)**[14] 2981 6-8-6 **93** .......... JennyPowell(7) 3 76
(Brendan Powell) *chsd ldrs: rdn and lost pl 3f out: bhd and sltly hmpd wl over 1f out* **50/1**

-134 **18** *38* **Squire Osbaldeston (IRE)**[44] 2085 4-9-4 **98** .......... FrankieDettori 8 20
(Martyn Meade) *t.k.h: hld up wl in tch in midfield: rdn and hdwy to chse ldrs over 2f out: wkng whn bdly hmpd over 1f out: sn bhd and heavily eased ins fnl f: t.o* **14/1**

2m 28.85s (-3.65) **Going Correction** -0.05s/f (Good) **18** Ran SP% **127.7**
Speed ratings (Par 109): **110,108,107,107,106 106,106,105,105,105 103,102,102,102,101 100,98,72**
CSF £83.86 CT £760.53 TOTE £4.10: £1.70, £5.30, £3.10, £2.20; EX 93.10 Trifecta £1124.80.
**Owner** Ballymacoll Stud **Bred** Ballymacoll Stud Farm Ltd **Trained** Newmarket, Suffolk

**FOCUS**
A typically strong and competitive renewal of this middle-distance handicap, run at a sound pace, with the whole field covered by 11lb on official ratings. Eight of the previous ten winners had been drawn in double figures and the trend continued.

## 3450 HARDWICKE STKS (GROUP 2) 1m 4f
**3:45** (3:46) (Class 1) 4-Y-0+

**£120,962** (£45,859; £22,951; £11,432; £5,737; £2,879) **Stalls** Low

Form RPR

1-22 **1** **Telescope (IRE)**[44] 2086 4-9-1 114 .......... RyanMoore 8 125
(Sir Michael Stoute) *swtg: trckd ldrs: led over 2f out: qcknd clr over 1f out: r.o wl and in command after: impressive* **7/4**[1]

6-02 **2** *7* **Hillstar**[43] 2115 4-9-1 115 .......... FrankieDettori 2 114+
(Sir Michael Stoute) *hld up: nt clr run over 2f out: rdn and hdwy over 1f out: styd on ins fnl f: tk 2nd nr fin: no ch w wnr* **7/1**[3]

1-22 **3** *hd* **Pether's Moon (IRE)**[42] 2143 4-9-1 110 .......... RichardHughes 5 113
(Richard Hannon) *prom: trcking ldrs waitong for run over 2f out: rdn to take 2nd over 1f out: no imp on wnr: no ch fnl f: lost 2nd nr fin* **8/1**

54-2 **4** *2 ¾* **Forgotten Voice (IRE)**[35] 2335 9-9-1 110 .......... KierenFallon 6 109
(Nicky Henderson) *racd keenly: hld up: pushed along over 3f out: rdn over 2f out: hdwy u.p over 1f out: kpt on ins fnl f but nvr able to trble ldrs* **10/1**

01-1 **5** *½* **Sharestan (IRE)**[23] 2705 6-9-1 111 .......... AndreaAtzeni 10 108
(Saeed bin Suroor) *midfield: hdwy over 2f out: sn wnt 2nd: no imp on wnr and lost 2nd over 1f out: fdd fnl 100yds* **12/1**

125- **6** *3 ¼* **Dandino**[228] 7761 7-9-1 115 .......... MartinHarley 9 103
(Marco Botti) *midfield: pushed along 3f out: no imp u.p over 1f out: one pce after: wl btn ins fnl f* **5/1**[2]

6050 **7** *nk* **Joshua Tree (IRE)**[14] 2988 7-9-1 110 .......... AdamKirby 7 103
(Ed Dunlop) *hld up: rdn over 2f out: no imp: one pce under hand ride ins fnl f: nvr trbld ldrs* **33/1**

1-00 **8** *14* **Camborne**[23] 2704 6-9-1 112 .......... (p) WilliamBuick 3 80
(John Gosden) *missed break: hld up in rr: swtchd lft u.p over 2f out: nvr on terms: eased whn wl btn ins fnl f* **16/1**

/23- **9** *6* **Eye Of The Storm (IRE)**[15] 2973 4-9-1 111 .......... JosephO'Brien 4 71
(A P O'Brien, Ire) *swtg: sn chsd ldr: led 3f out: rdn and hdd over 2f out: sn wknd: eased whn wl btn over 1f out* **8/1**

S0-5 **10** *20* **Ektihaam (IRE)**[44] 2086 5-9-1 112 .......... [1] PaulHanagan 1 39
(Roger Varian) *led: hdd 3f out: rdn and wknd 2f out: eased whn wl btn over 1f out: t.o* **20/1**

2m 27.45s (-5.05) **Going Correction** -0.05s/f (Good) **10** Ran SP% **118.1**
Speed ratings (Par 115): **114,109,109,107,107 104,104,95,91,78**
CSF £14.52 CT £80.33 TOTE £2.50: £1.10, £2.30, £2.80; EX 8.60 Trifecta £68.30.
**Owner** Highclere Thoroughbred Racing -Wavertree **Bred** Barronstown Stud **Trained** Newmarket, Suffolk

**FOCUS**
An interesting renewal of this always quality contest, which featured five previous winners at this meeting. It was run at a decent gallop, in a time 1.4 seconds quicker than the handicap that preceded it, and one colt proved far superior to his rivals. Sir Michael Stoute had a strong record in this race, having won four of the last eight renewals, and he added to that total.

## 3451 DIAMOND JUBILEE STKS (BRITISH CHAMPIONS SERIES & GLOBAL SPRINT CHALLENGE) (GROUP 1) 6f
**4:25** (4:26) (Class 1) 3-Y-0+

**£297,727** (£112,875; £56,490; £28,140; £14,122; £7,087) **Stalls** Centre

Form RPR

10-1 **1** **Slade Power (IRE)**[28] 2570 5-9-4 119 .......... WayneLordan 4 123
(Edward Lynam, Ire) *swtg: racd far side: chsd ldng pair: clsd and upsides ldrs 2f out: rdn to ld over 1f out: r.o wl: in command whn edgd lft towards fin: 1st of 9 in gp* **7/2**[1]

**2** *1 ½* **Due Diligence (USA)**[19] 2857 3-8-11 113 .......... (t) RyanMoore 12 116
(A P O'Brien, Ire) *lw: racd nr side: led gp but midfield overall: rdn and effrt over 2f out: carried rt but hdwy over 1f out: chsd clr wnr ins fnl f: keeping on but hld whn hmpd and snatched up cl home: 1st of 3 in gp* **5/1**[3]

10-3 **3** *hd* **Aljamaaheer (IRE)**[65] 1531 5-9-4 115 .......... (b[1]) PaulHanagan 6 117
(Roger Varian) *racd far side: taken down early: bhd: rdn and effrt 2f out: hdwy jst over 1f out: styd on wl ins fnl f: wnt 3rd nr fin: nvr gng to rch wnr: 2nd of 9 in gp* **4/1**[2]

2-16 **4** *1* **Music Master**[19] 2848 4-9-4 108 .......... FergusSweeney 14 113+
(Henry Candy) *racd nr side: stdd s: hld up in rr: hdwy over 2f out: rdn to ld gp 2f out: hanging lft after but hdwy to chse wnr 1f out tl ins fnl f: kpt on one pce after: 2nd of 3 in gp* **16/1**

05-1 **5** *2 ¼* **American Devil (FR)**[21] 2799 5-9-4 110 .......... Pierre-CharlesBoudot 15 106
(E Libaud, France) *str: racd nr side: stdd s: hld up and midfield overall: rdn and effrt 2f out: hdwy 1f out: edgd rt and kpt on ins fnl f: nvr trbld ldrs: 3rd of 3 in gp* **8/1**

1-52 **6** *1 ¼* **Astaire (IRE)**[38] 2256 3-8-11 114 .......... JamieSpencer 3 100
(Kevin Ryan) *racd far side: overall ldr: rdn and hdd over 1f out: lost 2nd 1f out: wknd fnl 100yds: 3rd of 9 in gp* **8/1**

3650 **7** *½* **Jack Dexter**[4] 3319 5-9-4 113 .......... GrahamLee 10 101
(Jim Goldie) *racd in centre: s.i.s: bhd: rdn 2f out: hdwy and styd on past btn horses ins fnl f: nvr trbld ldrs: 1st of 2 in gp* **20/1**

-160 **8** *½* **Gordon Lord Byron (IRE)**[48] 2004 6-9-4 118 .......... WilliamBuick 1 99
(T Hogan, Ire) *racd far side: chsd ldr: rdn and ev ch over 1f out: unable qck and btn 1f out: wknd ins fnl f: 4th of 9 in gp* **10/1**

-050 **9** *hd* **Tropics (USA)**[38] 2256 6-9-4 112 .......... RobertWinston 11 98
(Dean Ivory) *racd nr side: hld up in midfield overall: swtchd to centre after 2f: rdn and hdwy 1/2-way: edgd rt and no imp over 1f out: wknd ins fnl f: 2nd of 2 in gp* **25/1**

13-6 **10** *½* **Darwin (USA)**[28] 2570 4-9-4 114 .......... (t) JosephO'Brien 5 97
(A P O'Brien, Ire) *lw: racd far side: in tch in midfield: effrt and rdn 2f out: no rspnse whn hung lft and flashed tail u.p over 1f out: wknd ins fnl f: 5th of 9 in gp* **16/1**

-230 **11** *nk* **Es Que Love (IRE)**[4] 3319 5-9-4 108 .......... (p) AdamKirby 8 96
(Clive Cox) *racd far side: hld up in midfield: effrt u.p over 1f out: no prog 1f out: wknd ins fnl f: 6th of 9 in gp* **20/1**

-200 **12** *1 ½* **Montiridge (IRE)**[19] 2848 4-9-4 113 .......... RichardHughes 2 91
(Richard Hannon) *racd far side: wnt rt s and s.i.s: sn rcvrd and in midfield: rdn and effrt 2f out: unable qck and btn whn n.m.r over 1f out: wknd fnl f: 7th of 9 in gp* **25/1**

1144 **13** *nk* **Medicean Man**[4] 3319 8-9-4 112 .......... (tp) HarryBentley 9 90
(Jeremy Gask) *lw: racd far side: towards rr: rdn and sme hdwy over 2f out: drvn and no hdwy over 1f out: wknd ins fnl f: 8th of 9 in gp* **25/1**

3500 **14** *7* **Hawkeyethenoo (IRE)**[7] 3241 8-9-4 103 .......... AndreaAtzeni 7 68
(Jim Goldie) *racd far side: a in rr: rdn and effrt jst over 2f out: no prog and wknd over 1f out: 9th of 9 in gp* **40/1**

1m 12.4s (-2.10) **Going Correction** -0.125s/f (Firm)
**WFA** 3 from 4yo+ 7lb **14** Ran SP% **125.5**
Speed ratings (Par 117): **109,107,106,105,102 100,100,99,99,98 98,96,95,86**
CSF £19.49 CT £78.44 TOTE £4.20: £1.50, £2.00, £2.00; EX 22.00 Trifecta £128.20.
**Owner** Mrs S Power **Bred** Mrs S Power **Trained** Dunshaughlin, Co Meath
■ Stewards' Enquiry : Wayne Lordan one-day ban: careless riding (Jul 6)

**FOCUS**
Perhaps not the strongest or most international renewal of this top sprint in recent years, with no challengers from Australia or Hong Kong. The field split into two groups before converging somewhat up the centre of the track in the last furlong. It proved the pinnacle of a week to remember for trainer Edward Lynam, who recorded his third win and second Group 1 of the week, following Sole Power in the King's Stand and Anthem Alexander in the Queen Mary.

## 3452 WOKINGHAM STKS (HERITAGE H'CAP) 6f
**5:00** (5:01) (Class 2) (0-110,110) 3-Y-0+

**£108,937** (£32,620; £16,310; £8,155; £4,077; £2,047) **Stalls** Centre

Form RPR

0-22 **1** **Baccarat (IRE)**[38] 2254 5-9-2 **105** .......... GeorgeChaloner(3) 27 116
(Richard Fahey) *racd stands' side: hld up: hdwy over 2f out: led overall 1f out: r.o ins fnl f: wl on top at fin: 1st of 10 in gp* **9/1**

-432 **2** *1 ½* **Professor**[6] 3278 4-9-8 **108** .......... RyanMoore 18 114
(Richard Hannon) *racd in centre gp: midfield: pushed along over 2f out: swtchd lft and hdwy over 1f out: edgd rt ins fnl f: r.o: nt rch wnr: 1st of 9 in gp* **10/1**

2123 **3** *¾* **Rivellino**[64] 1557 4-9-4 **104** .......... WilliamBuick 12 108
(K R Burke) *racd in centre gp: hld up: hdwy 2f out: rdn over 1f out: r.o ins fnl f: nt quite pce of front two: 2nd of 9 in gp* **25/1**

5140 **4** *nk* **Alben Star (IRE)**[21] 2786 6-9-4 **104** .......... PaulHanagan 25 107
(Richard Fahey) *racd stands' side: a prominent: rdn to ld overall over 2f out: hdd over 1f out: r.o u.p: styd on same pce fnl 100yds: 2nd of 10 in gp* **16/1**

1-00 **5** *¾* **Boomerang Bob (IRE)**[19] 2848 5-9-0 **100** .......... SebSanders 20 100
(B W Hills) *racd in centre gp: trckd ldrs: big effrt to ld gp over 1f out: r.o ins fnl f: hld towards fin: 3rd of 9 in gp* **33/1**

1-01 **6** *hd* **Rocky Ground (IRE)**[19] 2848 4-9-8 **108** 5ex .......... FrankieDettori 29 108
(Roger Varian) *racd stands' side: hld up: hdwy and swtchd rt over 2f out: styd on ins fnl f: one pce and no imp fnl 100yds: 3rd of 10 in gp* **6/1**[2]

-403 **7** *nse* **Dont Bother Me (IRE)**[21] 2778 4-8-12 **98** .......... (p) MartinHarley 31 98
(Marco Botti) *racd stands' side: hld up in midfield: rdn and hdwy over 1f out: r.o ins fnl f: gng on at fin: 4th of 10 in gp* **14/1**

-062 **8** *¾* **Sirius Prospect (USA)**[21] 2784 6-9-5 **105** .......... RobertWinston 14 102
(Dean Ivory) *racd in centre gp: in tch: effrt 2f out: tried to chal over 1f out: kpt on ins fnl f: nt quite pce of ldrs: 4th of 9 in gp* **33/1**

-212 **9** *¾* **Glen Moss (IRE)**[42] 2145 5-9-4 **104** .......... SeanLevey 2 99
(David Brown) *lw: racd far side: chsd ldrs: rdn 2f out: r.o to ld gp fnl 75yds: hld by ldrs in other gps: 1st of 9 in gp* **16/1**

0005 **10** *hd* **Racy**[7] 3241 7-9-0 **100** .......... (p) JosephO'Brien 23 94
(Brian Ellison) *racd stands' side: trckd ldrs: rdn and ev ch over 1f out: styd on same pce fnl 100yds: 5th of 10 in gp* **33/1**

2-02 **11** *½* **Seeking Magic**[14] 2989 6-8-10 **99** .......... (t) RyanTate(3) 30 92
(Clive Cox) *racd stands' side: trckd ldrs: rdn over 2f out: nt qckn over 1f out: styd on same pce fnl 110yds: 6th of 10 in gp* **12/1**

5000 **12** *½* **Lancelot Du Lac (ITY)**[19] 2848 4-9-2 **102** .......... TomQueally 5 93
(Dean Ivory) *swtg: racd far side: trckd ldrs: led gp 2f out: styng on whn edgd lft fr over 1f out: hld by ldrs in other gps and hdd fnl 75yds: no ex: 2nd of 9 in gp* **33/1**

00-3 **13** *½* **Ninjago**[48] 1975 4-9-3 **103** .......... RichardHughes 17 92
(Richard Hannon) *racd in centre gp: hld up: rdn over 2f out: hdwy and edgd lft over 1f out: kpt on ins fnl f: no ex fnl 75yds: 5th of 9 in gp* **8/1**[3]

-610 **14** *¾* **Hamza (IRE)**[41] 2197 5-9-10 **110** .......... (b) JamesDoyle 7 97
(Kevin Ryan) *racd far side: led gp: rdn and hdd 2f out: kpt on u.p: no ex fnl 100yds: 3rd of 9 in gp* **25/1**

3021 **15** *2 ¾* **Absolutely So (IRE)**[49] 1943 4-8-11 **100** .......... OisinMurphy(3) 24 78
(Andrew Balding) *racd stands' side: midfield: rdn and wknd over 2f out: 7th of 10 in gp* **4/1**[1]

0 **16** *nk* **Secret Asset (IRE)**[21] 2778 9-8-12 **98** .......... (p) RobertHavlin 21 75
(Jane Chapple-Hyam) *racd in centre gp: trckd ldrs: effrt over 2f out: outpcd over 1f out: plugged on ins fnl f: 6th of 9 in gp* **66/1**

5-33 **17** *1* **Hoof It**[84] 1172 7-9-5 **105** .......... KierenFallon 10 79
(Michael Easterby) *swtchd to r far side early: hld up: rdn and hdwy 2f out: styd on ins fnl f: eased whn no imp fnl 100yds: 4th of 9 in gp* **16/1**

0114 **18** *nk* **Fast Shot**[38] 2254 6-8-4 **97**........................ RachelRichardson(7) 3 70
(Tim Easterby) *lw: racd far side: chsd ldrs: outpcd 2f out: kpt on ins fnl f but n.d: 5th of 9 in gp* **50/1**

0-00 **19** *nk* **Arnold Lane (IRE)**[149] 304 5-9-2 **102**........................ SamHitchcott 13 74
(Mick Channon) *racd in centre gp: trckd ldrs: rdn over 2f out: wknd ins fnl f: 7th of 9 in gp* **50/1**

20-1 **20** *1 1/4* **Barracuda Boy (IRE)**[77] 1313 4-8-12 **98**........................ RichardKingscote 4 66
(Tom Dascombe) *racd far side: prom: rdn 2f out: nt qckn over 1f out: fdd fnl 100yds: 6th of 9 in gp* **33/1**

1-00 **21** *1 1/2* **Dungannon**[121] 680 7-8-10 **99**........................ ThomasBrown(3) 15 62
(Andrew Balding) *lw: dwlt: swtchd rt to r far side over 4f out: in rr: pushed along over 3f out: no imp fnl f: 8th of 10 in gp* **33/1**

404- **22** *nse* **Dandy Boy (ITY)**[19] 2853 8-9-1 **101**........................(t) PatDobbs 9 64
(David Marnane, Ire) *swtchd rt to r far side over 4f out: in rr: outpcd over 2f out: nvr on terms: 7th of 9 in gp* **25/1**

-422 **23** *1 3/4* **Annunciation**[42] 2149 4-9-5 **105**........................ JimmyFortune 6 63
(Richard Hannon) *racd far side: hld up: rdn 2f out: no imp: eased whn n.d fnl 100yds: 8th of 9 in gp* **40/1**

2123 **24** *2* **Trinityelitedotcom (IRE)**[45] 2076 4-9-1 **101**........................ GeorgeBaker 26 52
(Tom Dascombe) *racd stands' side: led overall: rdn and hdd over 2f out: wknd over 1f out: 9th of 10 in gp: lame* **25/1**

-420 **25** *nk* **Jimmy Styles**[48] 1975 10-9-3 **103**........................(p) AdamKirby 8 53
(Clive Cox) *racd far side: in tch: rdn and wknd over 1f out: 9th of 9 in gp* **50/1**

10-0 **26** *1 1/4* **Zero Money (IRE)**[48] 1975 8-8-6 **97**........................(b) NoelGarbutt(5) 19 43
(Hugo Palmer) *racd in centre gp: led gp: rdn over 3f out: hdd wl over 1f out: sn wknd: 8th of 9 in gp* **66/1**

00-3 **27** *1 3/4* **Nocturnal Affair (SAF)**[29] 2532 8-9-3 **103**........................ WayneLordan 22 44
(David Marnane, Ire) *racd stands' side: in rr: struggling over 2f out: nvr on terms: 10th of 10 in gp* **50/1**

22-0 **28** *10* **York Glory (USA)**[21] 2766 6-9-9 **109**........................(b) JamieSpencer 11 18
(Kevin Ryan) *racd in centre gp: hld up bhd: rdn over 2f out: no imp: eased whn wl btn fnl f: 9th of 9 in gp* **14/1**

1m 12.09s (-2.41) **Going Correction** -0.125s/f (Firm)
**WFA** 3 from 4yo+ 7lb **28** Ran SP% **149.5**
Speed ratings (Par 109): **111,109,108,107,106 106,106,105,104,104 103,102,102,101,97 96,95,95,94,93 91,91,88,86,85 84,8**
CSF £95.59 CT £2303.64 TOTE £9.10: £1.80, £3.70, £8.20, £7.90; EX 157.70 Trifecta £8660.30.

**Owner** Sir Robert Ogden **Bred** Twelve Oaks Stud **Trained** Musley Bank, N Yorks
■ Stewards' Enquiry : Thomas Brown three-day ban: careless riding (Jul 6-8)
William Buick two-day ban: careless riding (Jul 6-7)

**FOCUS**
This was a classy event, illustrated by the fact that leading ante-post fancy Intrinsic missed that cut by some margin. It goes without saying that the pace was quick from the outset (the winning time was quicker than the Diamond Jubilee Stakes), and the field split into three groups, which turned into two about 2f from home. There didn't look a great deal of trouble in-running, although a couple of jockeys got bans for careless riding (one after half a furlong, the other at the 5f pole), which should make this result pretty reliable, but those drawn high or who raced down the middle appeared to have an advantage.

## 3453 QUEEN ALEXANDRA STKS (CONDITIONS RACE) 2m 5f 159y
5:35 (5:36) (Class 2) 4-Y-0+
**£37,350** (£11,184; £5,592; £2,796; £1,398; £702) **Stalls** Low

Form RPR

**1** **Pique Sous (FR)**[27] 2582 7-9-2 96........................(t) RyanMoore 15 101+
(W P Mullins, Ire) *t.k.h: hld up towards rr: hdwy to chse ldrs 3f out: rdn to ld 2f out: clr and in command 1f out: styd on: drvn out* **11/4[2]**

4-20 **2** *1 1/2* **El Salvador (IRE)**[13] 3041 5-9-2 105........................ JosephO'Brien 3 99+
(A P O'Brien, Ire) *chsd ldr for 8f: sn shuffled bk into midfield: nt clr run on inner 3f out: rdn and effrt jst over 2f out: styng on whn swtchd rt ent fnl f: kpt on to go 2nd fnl 50yd: nvr gng to rch wnr* **10/1**

-155 **3** *nk* **Brass Ring**[35] 2335 4-9-0 103........................[1] JamesDoyle 17 99+
(John Gosden) *lw: t.k.h: hld up in last pair but nt settle: hdwy to chse ldr 14f out: led 11f out: rdn and hdd 2f out: edgd lft u.p over 1f out: kpt on but lost 2nd fnl 50yds* **6/1**

0-35 **4** *6* **Tiger Cliff (IRE)**[23] 2704 5-9-2 112........................ TomQueally 6 93+
(Alan King) *t.k.h: hld up in tch in midfield: wnt 2nd and pressing ldr over 3f out: rdn and ev ch over 2f out: 3rd and outpcd over 1f out: wknd ins fnl f: lost action after fin: fatally injured* **5/2[1]**

-660 **5** *nk* **Argent Knight**[28] 2561 4-9-0 86........................(v) FrankieDettori 2 93
(William Jarvis) *lw: chsd ldrs: nt clr run and swtchd lft ent fnl 2f: sn outpcd u.p: 5th and wl hld 1f out: plugged on* **50/1**

-341 **6** *3 1/4* **Number One London (IRE)**[13] 3034 4-9-0 80........................(p) WilliamBuick 8 91
(Brian Meehan) *t.k.h: chsd ldrs: wnt 2nd 5f out tl over 3f out: short of room and lost pl 3f out: rdn and btn over 2f out: plugged on* **25/1**

0-56 **7** *nk* **First Avenue**[14] 1770 9-9-2 77........................ AmirQuinn 16 90
(Laura Mongan) *stdd and dropped in bhd after s: hld up in rr: clsd 5f out: rdn and outpcd over 2f out: 7th and wl hld whn swtchd rt over 1f out* **33/1**

5-00 **8** *10* **Romeo Montague**[21] 2779 6-9-2 83........................ GeorgeBaker 11 81
(Ed Dunlop) *stdd s: hld up in tch in midfield: clsd on ldrs 4f out: rdn and effrt whn pushed lft 2f out: no prog and sn btn: eased ins fnl f* **33/1**

-005 **9** *10* **Statutory (IRE)**[21] 2785 4-9-3 100........................ KierenFallon 5 75
(Saeed bin Suroor) *t.k.h: hld up wl in tch in midfield: clsd 5f out: rdn and effrt whn pushed lft 2f out: sn drvn and btn: eased ins fnl f: t.o* **5/1[3]**

**10** *5* **Royal Irish Hussar (IRE)**[49] 4741 4-9-0 98........................(p) JamieSpencer 9 67
(Nicky Henderson) *t.k.h: hld up wl in tch in midfield: hmpd and lost pl 3f out: sn rdn: wknd jst over 2f out: eased fnl f: t.o* **11/1**

30/0 **11** *39* **Dollar Bill**[11] 1941 5-9-2 65........................(v[1]) SamHitchcott 1 32
(Nick Gifford) *led tl 11f out: chsd ldr tl 5f out: sn rdn and los pl: lost tch over 2f out: t.o* **66/1**

006/ **P** **Petara Bay (IRE)**[585] 4800 10-9-2 95........................ SaleemGolam 13
(Sophie Leech) *iwnt rt s: in tch in midfield: rdn and dropped to rr 4f out: sn lost tch: t.o 3f out tl p.u ins fnl f: lame* **66/1**

-256 **P** **Dark Ranger**[16] 2920 8-9-2 82........................ OisinMurphy 12
(Tim Pitt) *pushed rt and stdd s: t.k.h: hld up in tch in rr: sddle slipped and hdwy on outer 12f out: lost pl qckly 5f out: sn t.o: p.u and dismntd 2f out* **50/1**

4m 49.82s (0.42) **Going Correction** -0.05s/f (Good)
**WFA** 4 from 5yo+ 2lb **13** Ran SP% **120.2**
Speed ratings (Par 109): **97,96,96,94,94 92,92,89,85,83 69, ,**
CSF £29.16 CT £156.41 TOTE £3.30: £1.50, £2.80, £2.20; EX 31.50 Trifecta £209.70.
**Owner** Supreme Horse Racing Club **Bred** Elevage Avicole Lozac'H-Leyan Et Al **Trained** Muine Beag, Co Carlow
■ Stewards' Enquiry : Saleem Golam ten-day ban: failed to dismount on gelding which was lame (Jul 5-12,14-15)

**FOCUS**
The final race of the meeting is the longest Flat race in the calendar. The last eight winners were all drawn high, and that was the case again. The two Irish trainers with runners had both been successful in this race in the previous six runnings, and they supplied the first two home.
T/Jkpt: £47,333.30 to a £1 stake. Pool: £200,000.00 - 3.00 winning tickets. T/Plt: £38.40 to a £1 stake. Pool: £678,500.61 - 12,873.35 winning tickets. T/Qpdt: £15.90 to a £1 stake. Pool: £29,301.36 - 1,355.33 winning tickets.

# 3049 AYR (L-H)
Saturday, June 21

**OFFICIAL GOING: Good to firm (9.3)**
Wind: Breezy, half against Weather: Overcast

## 3454 SUNSPORT/BRITISH STALLION STUDS EBF MAIDEN STKS (BOBIS RACE) 6f
**1:50** (1:51) (Class 4) 2-Y-O **£4,528** (£1,347; £673; £336) **Stalls** Low

Form RPR

4 **1** **Squats (IRE)**[8] 3193 2-9-5 0........................ LiamJones 7 82+
(William Haggas) *trckd ldrs: rdn to ld over 1f out: jnd last 100yds: kpt on gamely towards fin* **8/1**

**2** *hd* **Surewecan** 2-9-5 0........................ FrannyNorton 6 81+
(Mark Johnston) *trckd ldrs: effrt and pushed along over 1f out: disp ld last 100yds: kpt on: jst hld* **11/2**

**3** *3 1/4* **Salateen** 2-9-5 0........................ DavidProbert 2 72
(Kevin Ryan) *w ldr: pushed along over 1f out: kpt on same pce fnl f* **5/1[3]**

642 **4** *2* **Zuzinia (IRE)**[10] 3119 2-9-0 0........................ MartinDwyer 4 61
(Mick Channon) *led tl rdn and hdd over 1f out: wknd ins fnl f* **9/2[2]**

6 **5** *2 3/4* **Sandgate**[22] 2736 2-9-5 0........................ PJMcDonald 9 57
(Richard Fahey) *stdd s: sn rn green in rr: pushed along and hdwy over 2f out: kpt on fnl f: nvr able to chal* **10/1**

**6** *nk* **Spirit Of The Sea (IRE)** 2-8-11 0........................ GaryBartley(3) 1 52
(Jim Goldie) *missed break: bhd: stdy hdwy 1/2-way: pushed along 2f out: kpt on fnl f: n.d* **25/1**

**7** *2 1/2* **Classic Flyer** 2-9-5 0........................ DanielTudhope 3 49
(David O'Meara) *green in paddock: chsd ldrs: pushed along over 2f out: wknd over 1f out* **7/1**

**8** *3 1/2* **Tecumseh (IRE)** 2-9-0 0........................ JoeyHaynes(5) 5 39
(K R Burke) *t.k.h early: in tch: lost pl over 2f out: sn struggling* **10/3[1]**

**9** *nk* **Sir Acclam (IRE)** 2-9-5 0........................ TomEaves 8 38
(Keith Dalgleish) *hld up bhd ldng gp: pushed along and outpcd over 2f out: wknd over 1f out* **8/1**

1m 12.63s (0.23) **Going Correction** +0.125s/f (Good) **9** Ran SP% **121.0**
Speed ratings (Par 95): **103,102,98,95,92 91,88,83,83**
CSF £54.03 TOTE £5.50: £2.00, £2.70, £2.60; EX 47.20 Trifecta £305.60.
**Owner** Sheikh Rashid Dalmook Al Maktoum **Bred** Paul McEnery **Trained** Newmarket, Suffolk

**FOCUS**
A fair juvenile maiden that was won by subsequent Group 1 winner Wootton Bassett on his debut in 2010 and Sandringham runner-up Queen Catrine on her second start last year. They went a contested gallop on good to firm ground. Track at full width and distances as advertised.

## 3455 SCOTTISH SUN ON SUNDAY H'CAP (BOBIS RACE) 1m
**2:20** (2:20) (Class 2) (0-100,95) 3-Y-O
**£15,562** (£4,660; £2,330; £1,165; £582; £292) **Stalls** Low

Form RPR

1-2 **1** **Pretzel (IRE)**[21] 2781 3-9-2 **90**........................ FrederikTylicki 4 104+
(Roger Varian) *sn trcking ldr: shkn up to ld wl over 1f out: edgd lft and pushed clr fnl f: readily* **10/11[1]**

6-02 **2** *4 1/2* **Braidley (IRE)**[14] 2983 3-9-0 **88**........................ PJMcDonald 5 92
(James Bethell) *t.k.h early: prom: effrt and rdn 2f out: chsd (clr) wnr last 100yds: readily* **12/1**

6121 **3** *1/2* **Sir Guy Porteous (IRE)**[3] 3361 3-8-10 **84** 6ex........................ FrannyNorton 7 87
(Mark Johnston) *led: rdn and hdd wl over 1f out: one pce and lost 2nd last 100yds* **9/2[2]**

-664 **4** *1/2* **Mime Dance**[7] 3247 3-8-2 **76** oh1........................ DavidProbert 2 78
(Andrew Balding) *prom: checked after 1f: effrt whn n.m.r briefly over 2f out: rdn and hung lft over 1f out: kpt on ins fnl f* **8/1**

-632 **5** *3/4* **Homestretch**[15] 2968 3-8-7 **81**........................ MartinDwyer 6 81
(Mick Channon) *hld up in tch: hdwy on outside and hung lft 2f out: sn no imp* **11/2[3]**

0103 **6** *4 1/2* **Azagal (IRE)**[14] 2983 3-9-7 **95**........................ DuranFentiman 3 85
(Tim Easterby) *t.k.h early: chsd ldrs: rdn over 2f out: wknd over 1f out* **25/1**

0340 **7** *1 1/4* **Mr Matthews (IRE)**[7] 3243 3-8-0 **79**........................ JoeyHaynes(5) 1 66
(K R Burke) *hld up: rdn over 3f out: struggling over 2f out: sn btn* **22/1**

1m 39.83s (-3.97) **Going Correction** -0.375s/f (Firm) **7** Ran SP% **112.9**
Speed ratings (Par 105): **104,99,99,98,97 93,92**
CSF £13.21 TOTE £1.60: £1.20, £4.20; EX 13.20 Trifecta £41.80.
**Owner** Normandie Stud Ltd **Bred** Normandie Stud Ltd **Trained** Newmarket, Suffolk

**FOCUS**
A decent 3yo handicap in which they went a respectable gallop.

## 3456 SLATERS H'CAP 1m
**2:55** (2:56) (Class 2) (0-105,97) 4-Y-O+
**£15,562** (£4,660; £2,330; £1,165; £582; £292) **Stalls** Low

Form RPR

-043 **1** **Two For Two (IRE)**[17] 2891 6-9-6 **96**........................ DanielTudhope 8 106+
(David O'Meara) *stdd in last pl: angled to outside 2f out: qcknd to ld over 1f out: edgd lft: rdn out fnl f* **5/2[1]**

3341 **2** *2* **Dubai Dynamo**[7] 3221 9-8-12 **88**........................ PJMcDonald 4 92
(Ruth Carr) *hld up in tch: effrt and chsd wnr over 1f out: kpt on ins fnl f: nt pce to chal* **9/2[3]**

1000 **3** *1 3/4* **Trail Blaze (IRE)**[15] 2959 5-8-10 **91**........................(b) ShaneGray(5) 3 91
(Kevin Ryan) *pressed ldr: led over 2f out to over 1f out: kpt on same pce fnl f* **14/1**

0000 **4** *nk* **Norse Blues**[21] 2758 6-8-9 **88**........................ JasonHart(3) 7 87
(David Barron) *hld up: effrt whn n.m.r over 2f out: rdn whn n.m.r appr fnl f: kpt on: nrst fin* **13/2**

5001 **5** *1* **Balty Boys (IRE)**[17] 2891 5-9-7 **97**........................(b) PaulPickard 1 94
(Brian Ellison) *dwlt: sn rdn to chse ldrs: drvn along fr 3f out: rallied: kpt on same pce fnl f* **11/1**

1 **6** *3 1/4* **Capo Rosso (IRE)**[34] 2362 4-9-5 **95**........................ StephenCraine 2 85
(Tom Dascombe) *led: rdn and hdd over 2f out: wknd over 1f out* **4/1[2]**

5111 **7** 3 **Lawmans Thunder**[31] 2462 4-9-5 **95**....... MartinDwyer 9 78
(Ismail Mohammed) *hld up in tch: effrt and pushed along over 2f out: wknd fnl f* **5/1**

603 **8** 2 3/4 **Stonefield Flyer**[50] 1928 5-8-9 **85**....... TomEaves 6 61
(Keith Dalgleish) *t.k.h early: prom: gng wl over 2f out: rdn and wknd over 1f out* **16/1**

1m 38.95s (-4.85) **Going Correction** -0.375s/f (Firm) **8** Ran SP% **117.6**
Speed ratings (Par 109): **109,107,105,104,103 100,97,94**
CSF £14.40 CT £132.42 TOTE £3.50: £1.40, £1.90, £4.50; EX 15.80 Trifecta £124.30.
**Owner** High Hopes Partnership & Partner **Bred** Patrick Fahey **Trained** Nawton, N Yorks

**FOCUS**
Another good 1m handicap, but this time for older horses and they went a strong gallop.

## 3457 ARNOLD CLARK H'CAP 1m 2f
**3:35** (3:36) (Class 3) (0-95,93) 4-Y-0+ **£9,703** (£2,887; £1,443; £721) **Stalls** Low

Form RPR

0503 **1** **Strictly Silver (IRE)**[7] 3217 5-9-2 **88**....... (p) LiamJones 3 97
(Alan Bailey) *trckd ldrs: led over 2f out: edgd lft over 1f out: hld on wl fnl f* **4/1**[3]

0-52 **2** 3/4 **One Pekan (IRE)**[18] 2876 4-8-8 **80**....... FrederikTylicki 4 88
(Roger Varian) *in tch: effrt and rdn over 2f out: hdwy to chse wnr ins fnl f: kpt on* **11/4**[2]

-002 **3** 1 **Argaki (IRE)**[3] 3361 4-7-11 **76**....... JackGarritty(7) 6 82
(Keith Dalgleish) *prom on outside: hdwy to chse wnr over 2f out: sn rdn: lost 2nd ins fnl f: one pce* **12/5**[1]

00-1 **4** hd **Muharrer**[32] 2423 5-9-1 **87**....... TomEaves 2 92
(Michael Dods) *t.k.h: hld up in tch: effrt whn n.m.r briefly over 2f out: hdwy over 1f out: kpt on same pce ins fnl f* **7/1**

-505 **5** 3/4 **Cosmic Halo**[19] 2826 5-7-12 **75**....... SammyJoBell(5) 8 80
(Richard Fahey) *hld up: hdwy over 2f out: styng on whn no room last 150yds: nt rcvr* **25/1**

-516 **6** nse **Love Marmalade (IRE)**[14] 3004 4-8-7 **79**....... PJMcDonald 7 83
(Alistair Whillans) *hld up: rdn over 3f out: hdwy over 1f out: kpt on ins fnl f: nrst fin* **16/1**

23-5 **7** 5 **Beaumont's Party (IRE)**[17] 2891 7-9-7 **93**....... DaleSwift 5 87
(Brian Ellison) *trckd ldr to over 2f out: sn rdn: wknd over 1f out* **20/1**

2611 **8** 1 3/4 **San Cassiano (IRE)**[12] 3055 7-8-13 **85**....... JamesSullivan 1 76
(Ruth Carr) *led tl rdn and hdd over 2f out: sn btn* **8/1**

2m 6.59s (-5.41) **Going Correction** -0.375s/f (Firm) **8** Ran SP% **114.2**
Speed ratings (Par 107): **106,105,104,104,103 103,99,98**
CSF £15.39 CT £31.09 TOTE £5.20: £1.80, £1.30, £1.10; EX 14.40 Trifecta £46.40.
**Owner** Allan McNamee & Alan Bailey **Bred** Langton Stud **Trained** Newmarket, Suffolk

**FOCUS**
A decent handicap for older horses in which they went a good, even gallop.

## 3458 SCOTTISH SUN MISS SCOTLAND H'CAP 5f
**4:15** (4:16) (Class 3) (0-95,93) 3-Y-0+ **£9,703** (£2,887; £1,443; £721) **Stalls** Low

Form RPR

00-0 **1** **Burning Thread (IRE)**[7] 3241 7-9-9 **90**....... (b) JamesSullivan 4 99
(Tim Etherington) *hld up: rdn over 1f out: gd hdwy on outside fnl f: led cl home* **12/1**

0112 **2** nse **Bear Behind (IRE)**[17] 2898 5-9-12 **93**....... StephenCraine 3 102
(Tom Dascombe) *led at decent gallop to over 1f out: drvn and rallied to regain ld last 100yds: ct cl home* **11/2**

2-60 **3** shd **Alaskan Bullet (IRE)**[19] 2825 5-8-7 **74**....... PaulPickard 8 82
(Brian Ellison) *missed break: hld up: gd hdwy over 1f out: disp ld last 100yds: jst hld* **20/1**

5001 **4** 1 1/4 **Doctor Parkes**[13] 3033 8-8-13 **85**....... JoeyHaynes(5) 9 89
(Stuart Williams) *prom on outside: effrt and ev ch over 1f out to ins fnl f: kpt on same pce last 75yds* **13/2**

2020 **5** 1/2 **Rasaman (IRE)**[7] 3239 10-9-0 **84**....... GaryBartley(3) 10 86
(Jim Goldie) *hld up: rdn and effrt over 1f out: kpt on fnl f: nvr able to chal* **10/1**

10-0 **6** nk **New Fforest**[14] 2989 4-9-11 **92**....... DavidProbert 5 93
(Andrew Balding) *t.k.h: pressed ldr: led over 1f out to last 100yds: sn no ex* **10/3**[1]

-000 **7** 2 **L'Ami Louis (IRE)**[7] 3256 6-8-9 **75** ow1....... TomEaves 2 70
(Ian Semple) *trckd ldrs: pushed along whn n.m.r briefly over 1f out: sn outpcd* **20/1**

4-05 **8** 1/2 **Exceptionelle**[43] 2123 4-9-5 **86**....... (b[1]) FrederikTylicki 6 78
(Roger Varian) *t.k.h: in tch: effrt and pushed along over 1f out: sn no imp* **5/1**[3]

0-01 **9** 2 1/2 **Bispham Green**[9] 3138 4-9-4 **85**....... DanielTudhope 7 68
(David O'Meara) *hld up bhd ldng gp: rdn over 2f out: wknd wl over 1f out* **7/2**[2]

58.93s (-0.47) **Going Correction** +0.125s/f (Good) **9** Ran SP% **117.0**
Speed ratings (Par 107): **108,107,107,105,104 104,101,100,96**
CSF £77.47 CT £1317.26 TOTE £15.00: £3.80, £2.00, £7.10; EX 114.40 Trifecta £2023.20 Part won. Pool: £2,697.66 - 0.19 winning units..
**Owner** Tim Etherington **Bred** James Lombard **Trained** Norton, N Yorks

**FOCUS**
A useful sprint handicap.

## 3459 SCOTTISH SUN/EBF STALLIONS LAND O'BURNS FILLIES' STKS (LISTED RACE) 5f
**4:50** (4:54) (Class 1) 3-Y-0+
**£22,684** (£8,600; £4,304; £2,144; £1,076; £540) **Stalls** Low

Form RPR

-262 **1** **Hay Chewed (IRE)**[7] 3245 3-8-12 **99**....... TomEaves 10 102
(Conrad Allen) *sn trcking ldrs: led wl over 1f out: drvn and edgd lft ins fnl f: kpt on wl* **17/2**[3]

2-13 **2** 1 **Inyordreams**[38] 2257 3-8-12 **80**....... DaleSwift 4 98
(James Given) *chsd ldrs: effrt and rdn 2f out: chsng wnr whn checked sltly ins fnl f: r.o* **12/1**

0-2 **3** 1 1/2 **Reroute (IRE)**[63] 1572 3-8-12 **98**....... HayleyTurner 7 93
(Ed Walker) *t.k.h: hld up in midfield: hdwy to chse wnr over 1f out: rdn: edgd rt and lost 2nd ins fnl f: one pce* **4/1**[1]

643- **4** 1/2 **Survived**[337] 4486 3-8-12 **92**....... LiamJones 5 91
(William Haggas) *hld up in midfield: drvn and outpcd over 2f out: rallied over 1f out: kpt on ins fnl f* **16/1**

3-03 **5** 1/2 **Valonia**[6] 3278 3-8-12 **97**....... FrederikTylicki 3 89
(Henry Candy) *w ldr: drvn wl over 1f out: kpt on same pce fnl f* **4/1**[1]

4-00 **6** 1/2 **Riskit Fora Biskit (IRE)**[41] 2197 4-9-4 **98**....... PJMcDonald 1 90
(Michael Bell) *led at decent gallop: rdn and hdd wl over 1f out: outpcd fnl f* **12/1**

1312 **7** 1 1/4 **Divine (IRE)**[15] 2965 3-8-12 **90**....... MartinDwyer 13 83
(Mick Channon) *hld up: rdn and hdwy over 1f out: no imp fnl f* **6/1**[2]

01/5 **8** 3 **Kune Kune**[63] 1572 5-9-4 **95**....... (t) JoeyHaynes 8 74
(Rae Guest) *bhd and sn outpcd: sme hdwy over 1f out: nvr able to chal* **25/1**

-210 **9** 1 **Blithe Spirit**[28] 2564 3-8-12 **97**....... JasonHart 6 69
(Eric Alston) *prom: drvn over 2f out: wknd wl over 1f out* **12/1**

00-0 **10** 1/2 **Midnight Dynamo**[7] 3239 7-9-4 **71**....... GaryBartley 12 69
(Jim Goldie) *bhd and sn struggling: no ch fr 1/2-way* **33/1**

0-06 **11** 6 **Cincinnati Kit**[37] 2275 5-9-4 **79**....... (t) JamesSullivan 11 47
(Stuart Williams) *bhd and outpcd: nvr on terms* **40/1**

59.01s (-0.39) **Going Correction** +0.125s/f (Good)
**WFA** 3 from 4yo+ 6lb **11** Ran SP% **101.2**
Speed ratings (Par 108): **108,106,104,103,102 101,99,94,93,92 82**
CSF £86.22 TOTE £7.00: £2.00, £3.90, £1.70; EX 105.80 Trifecta £318.40.
**Owner** John C Davies **Bred** Newlands House Stud **Trained** Newmarket, Suffolk
■ Rule 4 of 25p in the pound applies to all bets; Withdrawn: Swan Song

**FOCUS**
A good Listed fillies' sprint won in 2011 by Margot Did a couple months prior to her Group 1 Nunthorpe success under Hayley Turner. The time was slightly slower than the previous handicap, though, raising some doubts over the form.

## 3460 LEITH H'CAP (BOBIS RACE) 6f
**5:25** (5:26) (Class 4) (0-80,80) 3-Y-0 **£5,175** (£1,540; £769; £384) **Stalls** Low

Form RPR

0536 **1** **Spirit Of Alsace (IRE)**[8] 3191 3-7-9 **61** oh6....... JackGarritty(7) 4 68
(Jim Goldie) *t.k.h: in tch: hdwy to chse clr ldr over 2f out: sn hung lft: coaxed along to ld ins fnl f: kpt on* **7/1**

-140 **2** 1/2 **Signore Piccolo**[36] 2317 3-9-4 **80**....... JasonHart(3) 1 85+
(Eric Alston) *led and sn clr: rdn 2f out: hdd ins fnl f: rallied: hld towards fin* **11/4**[1]

2-62 **3** 3 **Heroique (IRE)**[17] 2897 3-9-2 **75**....... (e) DuranFentiman 2 69
(Tim Easterby) *chsd clr ldr tl outpcd over 2f out: rallied over 1f out: kpt on ins fnl f* **4/1**[3]

-641 **4** 1/2 **Sleeper Class**[30] 2474 3-8-6 **65**....... HayleyTurner 3 57+
(Jim Goldie) *dwlt: bhd: hdwy and hung lft fr 1/2-way: effrt and drvn over 1f out: no ex ins fnl f* **7/2**[2]

1-54 **5** 7 **Sandra's Diamond (IRE)**[36] 2295 3-9-4 **77**....... TomEaves 7 44
(Keith Dalgleish) *wnt rt s: hld up: rdn over 2f out: sn btn* **11/4**[1]

0000 **6** 12 **Aspirant**[16] 2936 3-8-10 **69**....... (b[1]) PaulPickard 5
(Brian Ellison) *chsd ldrs tl rdn and wknd over 2f out* **12/1**

1m 13.48s (1.08) **Going Correction** +0.125s/f (Good) **6** Ran SP% **115.7**
Speed ratings (Par 101): **97,96,92,91,82 66**
CSF £27.48 TOTE £9.70: £3.20, £1.70; EX 47.10 Trifecta £167.50.
**Owner** The Reluctant Suitor's **Bred** Ecurie Des Monceaux **Trained** Uplawmoor, E Renfrews

**FOCUS**
This was a fair 3yo sprint handicap.
T/Plt: £89.90 to a £1 stake. Pool: £74464.98 - 604.54 winning tickets T/Qpdt: £14.70 to a £1 stake. Pool: £5334.5 - 266.95 winning tickets RY

# 3134 HAYDOCK (L-H)
### Saturday, June 21

**OFFICIAL GOING: Good to firm (8.2)**
Wind: light 1/2 against Weather: fine

## 3461 LJF ENGINEERING MAIDEN STKS 5f
**6:50** (6:51) (Class 5) 2-Y-O **£3,234** (£962; £481; £240) **Stalls** Centre

Form RPR

**1** **Steve Prescott** 2-9-5 0....... DavidNolan 6 86+
(Richard Fahey) *wnt rt s: w ldrs: led over 1f out: wnt clr ins fnl f: v readily* **2/1**[2]

4 **2** 3 1/2 **Mumford**[19] 2837 2-9-5 0....... FrannyNorton 5 74+
(Richard Hannon) *chsd ldrs: drvn over 2f out: sn outpcd: styd on wl fnl f: tk 2nd last 75yds* **6/4**[1]

50 **3** 1/2 **Belle Fille**[43] 2107 2-9-0 0....... PhillipMakin 3 67
(David Brown) *trckd ldrs: swtchd lft over 1f out: chsd wnr jst ins fnl f: kpt on same pce* **5/1**[3]

405 **4** 6 **Soie D'Leau**[19] 2824 2-9-5 0....... AmyRyan 2 50
(Kristin Stubbs) *w ldrs: hung lft over 1f out: wknd fnl f* **25/1**

5 **5** hd **Poolstock**[31] 2450 2-9-2 0....... SamJames(3) 4 50
(David O'Meara) *led: hdd over 1f out: wknd fnl f* **6/1**

**6** 4 **Frank The Barber (IRE)** 2-9-5 0....... RussKennemore 7 35
(Steph Hollinshead) *carried rt s: sn chsng ldrs: wknd over 1f out* **25/1**

**7** 10 **Blue Eyed Boy** 2-9-2 0....... DeclanBates(3) 8
(Roy Brotherton) *hmpd s: in rr: reminders after 1f: bhd fnl 2f* **25/1**

1m 1.64s (0.84) **Going Correction** +0.025s/f (Good) **7** Ran SP% **115.8**
Speed ratings (Par 93): **94,88,87,78,77 71,55**
CSF £5.42 TOTE £3.10: £2.20, £2.00; EX 6.90 Trifecta £18.10.
**Owner** Dr Marwan Koukash **Bred** J A And M A Knox **Trained** Musley Bank, N Yorks

**FOCUS**
All races on Inner home straight and distances on Round course increased by 3yds. An interesting juvenile maiden that was won in good style.

## 3462 WATCH ON 3 DEVICES RACINGUK.COM/ANYWHERE FILLIES' H'CAP (JC GRASSROOTS SPRINT SERIES QUALIFIER) 5f
**7:20** (7:20) (Class 5) (0-75,75) 3-Y-0+ **£3,234** (£962; £481; £240) **Stalls** Centre

Form RPR

0054 **1** **Hannahs Turn**[21] 2757 4-9-7 **75**....... MarcMonaghan(5) 7 84
(Chris Dwyer) *wnt rt s: sn trcking ldrs: effrt 2f out: r.o to ld last 150yds* **8/1**

6-00 **2** 2 1/4 **Jamboree Girl**[36] 2317 3-9-2 **71**....... PhillipMakin 1 70
(Tim Easterby) *led over 1f: led over 1f out: hdd jst ins fnl f: styd on same pce* **9/2**[3]

4-42 **3** 1 1/2 **Angel Way (IRE)**[6] 3275 5-9-7 **73**....... SladeO'Hara(3) 5 69
(Mike Murphy) *stdd s: t.k.h: hdwy to ld over 3f out: hdd over 1f out: kpt on same pce* **2/1**[1]

-550 **4** 1 1/4 **Perfect Blossom**[7] 3239 7-9-7 **70**....... PaulMulrennan 2 61
(Alan Berry) *chsd ldrs: drvn over 2f out: one pce over 1f out* **12/1**

6-20 **5** nse **Flighty Clarets (IRE)**[16] 2914 4-8-13 **67**....... SammyJoBell(5) 6 58
(Richard Fahey) *stdd s: hld up towards rr: effrt over 2f out: kpt on fnl f* **8/1**

5-14 **6** 1/2 **Where The Boys Are (IRE)**[15] 2943 3-8-10 **65**....... FrannyNorton 4 52
(Ed McMahon) *chsd ldrs: rdn over 1f out: one pce* **7/2**[2]

-535 **7** 2 3/4 **Value (IRE)**[21] 2768 3-8-5 **65** ........ JackDuern(5) 3 42
(Gay Kelleway) *chsd ldrs: drvn over 3f out: outpcd and edgd lft over 1f out: sn wknd* **12/1**

1m 0.72s (-0.08) **Going Correction** +0.025s/f (Good)
**WFA** 3 from 4yo+ 6lb **7 Ran SP% 114.8**
Speed ratings (Par 100): **101,97,95,93,92 92,87**
CSF £43.70 TOTE £11.30: £3.90, £1.80; EX 34.70 Trifecta £258.60.
**Owner** Mrs K W Sneath **Bred** Wayland Stud **Trained** Newmarket, Suffolk

**FOCUS**
Probably just an ordinary fillies' handicap.

## 3463 SOCKSHOP H'CAP 1m
**7:50** (7:50) (Class 4) (0-85,83) 4-Y-O+ **£5,498** (£1,636; £817; £408) **Stalls** Low

Form RPR
0060 **1** **Kingscroft (IRE)**[7] 3254 6-8-5 **72** ........(b) JacobButterfield(5) 6 81
(Michael Herrington) *t.k.h in rr: effrt and edgd rt over 1f out: led and edgd lft last 100yds: kpt on towards fin* **4/1**[2]

0000 **2** 1/2 **Postscript (IRE)**[7] 3221 6-9-7 **83** ........ DavidNolan 3 91
(David Simcock) *trckd ldr: led over 1f out: hdd last 100yds: crowded: no ex* **5/2**[1]

5000 **3** 3 1/2 **Party Royal**[34] 2362 4-9-5 **81** ........ PhillipMakin 5 81
(Mark Johnston) *led: hdd over 1f out: kpt on same pce* **4/1**[2]

**4** hd **Zeftan (IRE)**[29] 2535 5-8-13 **75** ........(p) PaulMulrennan 1 74
(Adrian Paul Keatley, Ire) *hld up in rr: hdwy on ins over 4f out: nt clr run and swtchd ins over 1f out: kpt on ins fnl f* **4/1**[2]

0530 **5** 1 3/4 **Skytrain**[12] 3050 4-9-7 **83** ........ FrannyNorton 2 78
(Mark Johnston) *chsd ldrs: drvn over 3f out: one pce fnl 2f* **8/1**[3]

1-06 **6** 3 3/4 **Berlusca (IRE)**[131] 560 5-9-2 **81** ........ SamJames(3) 7 68
(David O'Meara) *trckd ldrs: t.k.h: effrt over 2f out: wknd fnl 100yds* **12/1**

1-00 **7** 5 **Cape Samba**[6] 3272 5-8-11 **78** ........ MarcMonaghan(5) 4 53
(Ismail Mohammed) *trckd ldrs: t.k.h: effrt over 2f out: wknd over 1f out* **14/1**

1m 40.92s (-2.78) **Going Correction** -0.175s/f (Firm) **7 Ran SP% 114.0**
Speed ratings (Par 105): **106,105,102,101,100 96,91**
CSF £14.36 TOTE £5.50: £2.70, £2.40; EX 16.30 Trifecta £105.60.
**Owner** Darren & Annaley Yates **Bred** J Beckett **Trained** Cold Kirby, N Yorks

**FOCUS**
A muddling race as they crawled early on and the form is unlikely to be reliable.

## 3464 RACING UK ANYWHERE AVAILABLE NOW H'CAP (BOBIS RACE) 1m
**8:20** (8:22) (Class 4) (0-80,80) 3-Y-O **£5,498** (£1,636; £817; £408) **Stalls** Low

Form RPR
2412 **1** **Lesha (IRE)**[10] 3108 3-9-7 **80** ........ BrianHughes 1 88+
(Kevin Ryan) *trckd ldrs: nt clr run fr over 2f out tl ins fnl f: led last 75yds: hld on towards fin* **5/1**[2]

422 **2** 1/2 **Voyageofdiscovery (USA)**[58] 1680 3-9-3 **76** ........ JohnFahy 2 85+
(Clive Cox) *hld up in mid-div: t.k.h: nt clr run fr over 2f out tl burst through last 50yds: r.o: nt quite rch wnr* **10/1**

221- **3** 1 1/4 **El Beau (IRE)**[254] 7146 3-9-3 **76** ........ PhillipMakin 10 79
(John Quinn) *hld up in rr: hdwy on outside over 3f out: chal and edgd lft 1f out: styd on same pce last 100yds* **7/1**

0424 **4** 3/4 **King Of Macedon (IRE)**[10] 3108 3-9-5 **78** ........ FrannyNorton 4 79
(Mark Johnston) *led: hdd and no ex last 75yds* **9/2**[1]

1-03 **5** 1 **Sbraase**[9] 3159 3-9-4 **77** ........(p) GrahamLee 5 76+
(James Tate) *s.i.s: hld up in rr: hdwy on ins over 3f out: nt clr run fr over 2f out: nt rcvr* **13/2**

1230 **6** nk **Jaahiez (USA)**[51] 1897 3-9-2 **75** ........(p) PaulMulrennan 8 73+
(Roger Varian) *hld up in rr: nt clr run on inner over 2f out: swtchd rt over 1f out: edgd lft ins fnl f: kpt on same pce* **13/2**

2-30 **7** 2 1/4 **Emef Diamond**[30] 2481 3-9-3 **79** ........ CharlesBishop(3) 3 72
(Mick Channon) *mid-div: t.k.h: hmpd bnd over 4f out: nt clr run over 2f out: nvr a threat* **11/2**[3]

210- **8** 3/4 **Desert Society (IRE)**[239] 7492 3-9-6 **79** ........ KieranO'Neill 9 72
(Richard Hannon) *trckd ldrs on outer: keeping on same pce whn hmpd and eased last 100yds* **16/1**

2-00 **9** 5 **Syros (IRE)**[17] 2897 3-8-7 **73** ........ DanielleMooney(7) 6 53
(Michael Easterby) *chsd ldrs: lost pl over 2f out* **33/1**

2105 **10** shd **Mariners Moon (IRE)**[19] 2827 3-9-2 **75** ........ DanielTudhope 7 66
(David O'Meara) *chsd ldr: hmpd and dropped bk 1f out: bmpd and heavily eased 100yds out* **10/1**

1m 41.76s (-1.94) **Going Correction** -0.175s/f (Firm) **10 Ran SP% 116.4**
Speed ratings (Par 101): **102,101,100,99,98 98,95,95,90,90**
CSF £54.02 CT £358.92 TOTE £6.20: £2.10, £2.60, £2.30; EX 57.60 Trifecta £203.40.
**Owner** Mubarak Al Naemi **Bred** Michael Conlon **Trained** Hambleton, N Yorks
■ Stewards' Enquiry : John Fahy two-day ban: careless riding (Jul 6-7)

**FOCUS**
An ordinary gallop and with plenty or the runners meeting trouble in running this was a thoroughly unsatisfactory race from a form point of view.

## 3465 MUSIC NIGHT HERE 19TH JULY MAIDEN STKS 1m
**8:50** (8:50) (Class 5) 3-Y-O+ **£3,234** (£962; £481; £240) **Stalls** Low

Form RPR
6-4 **1** **Alketios (GR)**[32] 2432 3-9-2 0 ........ DanielTudhope 5 82+
(Luca Cumani) *trckd ldrs: effrt over 2f out: edgd rt over 1f out: styd on u.p to ld last 100yds* **7/4**[2]

42 **2** 1 **Taqneen (IRE)**[18] 2877 3-9-2 0 ........ PaulMulrennan 6 79
(Ed Dunlop) *trckd ldr: effrt over 3f out: led 1f out: hdd and no ex ins fnl f* **11/8**[1]

0-2 **3** 1 1/2 **Protected**[29] 2516 3-9-2 0 ........ GrahamLee 1 75
(James Tate) *led: qcknd pce over 4f out: hdd 1f out: kpt on same pce* **5/1**[3]

0- **4** 11 **Pantoloni**[232] 7655 3-9-2 0 ........ AhmedAjtebi 4 49
(Charlie Appleby) *led to s: stdd sn after s: t.k.h: effrt over 3f out: hung lft 2f out: sn wknd* **7/1**

560- **5** 1 3/4 **Vale Mentor (IRE)**[204] 8091 3-9-2 50 ........ PhillipMakin 2 45
(Tim Easterby) *trckd ldrs: wknd over 1f out* **16/1**

6-00 **6** 49 **Echologic**[121] 673 4-9-12 36 ........[1] JohnFahy 3
(Brian Baugh) *s.s: bhd and reminders after 2f: t.o 3f out* **50/1**

1m 41.89s (-1.81) **Going Correction** -0.175s/f (Firm)
**WFA** 3 from 4yo 10lb **6 Ran SP% 115.5**
Speed ratings (Par 103): **102,101,99,88,86 37**
CSF £4.74 TOTE £3.60: £1.80, £1.40; EX 4.40 Trifecta £8.80.
**Owner** Leonidas Marinopoulos **Bred** Figaia Stud **Trained** Newmarket, Suffolk

**FOCUS**
Hard to know what to make of this maiden. The pace wasn't strong, the first three were clear but the two main contenders both raced as though they were feeling the ground.

## 3466 HAYDOCK-PARK.CO.UK H'CAP 1m 2f 95y
**9:20** (9:20) (Class 4) (0-80,80) 3-Y-O+ **£5,498** (£1,636; £817; £408) **Stalls** Centre

Form RPR
-523 **1** **New Street (IRE)**[26] 2617 3-9-1 **79** ........ DavidNolan 1 88
(Richard Fahey) *trckd ldrs: effrt over 1f out: led jst ins fnl f: r.o wl: readily* **11/4**[1]

0-03 **2** 1 1/2 **Emaad (USA)**[14] 2998 3-8-4 **68** ........ FrannyNorton 8 74
(Mark Johnston) *led: t.k.h: qcknd pce over 3f out: hdd jst ins fnl f: styd on same pce* **11/4**[1]

2220 **3** 1 **Watersmeet**[18] 2867 3-8-6 **70** ........ AdrianNicholls 2 74
(Mark Johnston) *trckd ldrs on inner: nt clr run and swtchd rt over 1f out: styd on to take 3rd nr fin* **20/1**

10-0 **4** nk **Shankly**[71] 1419 3-8-13 **77** ........[1] HarryBentley 4 81
(Clive Cox) *sn trcking wnr: kpt on same pce fnl f* **3/1**[2]

0-33 **5** 4 **Discovery Bay**[29] 2515 6-9-6 **72** ........ PaulMulrennan 5 68
(Brian Ellison) *hld up towards rr: hdwy on ins over 3f out: nt clr run over 2f out: one pce over 1f out* **7/1**

24-0 **6** 1 1/2 **Mustamir (IRE)**[66] 1517 3-8-10 **74** ........ GrahamLee 3 67
(James Tate) *mid-div: pushed along over 4f out: one pce fnl 2f* **6/1**[3]

0-60 **7** 3 **Rising Breeze (FR)**[42] 2148 3-9-2 **80** ........ PhillipMakin 7 67
(K R Burke) *hld up in rr: effrt on outside over 2f out: wknd over 1f out* **16/1**

2m 12.17s (-3.33) **Going Correction** -0.175s/f (Firm)
**WFA** 3 from 5yo+ 12lb **7 Ran SP% 115.8**
Speed ratings (Par 105): **106,104,104,103,100 99,96**
CSF £10.91 CT £122.53 TOTE £4.10: £2.10, £2.40; EX 11.00 Trifecta £152.10.
**Owner** David W Armstrong **Bred** New Deal Partnership **Trained** Musley Bank, N Yorks

**FOCUS**
Something of a tactical race with a moderate early pace. The first four finished clear.
T/Plt: £114.80 to a £1 stake. Pool: £63,087.00 - 401.10 winning tickets. T/Qpdt: £7.90 to a £1 stake. Pool: £4,697.00 - 435.50 winning tickets. WG

# 3387 LINGFIELD (L-H)
## Saturday, June 21

**OFFICIAL GOING: Turf course - good to firm (8.6); all-weather - standard**
Wind: none Weather: Light cloud

## 3467 32RED MAIDEN AUCTION STKS 7f
**6:05** (6:06) (Class 6) 2-Y-O **£2,264** (£673; £336; £168) **Stalls** Centre

Form RPR
425 **1** **Buckleberry**[11] 3081 2-8-11 ........ MatthewLawson(3) 10 72
(Jonathan Portman) *trckd ldrs: pushed along 2f out: led 1f out: hrd rdn and strly pressed fnl 50yds, jst hld on* **3/1**[1]

**2** nse **Taper Tantrum (IRE)** 2-9-2 ........ MartinLane 4 74+
(Michael Bell) *prom: disp ld 2f out: hdd 1f out: rallied wl: strly pressed wnr fnl 50yds: jst hld* **5/1**

0 **3** 2 3/4 **Azure Amour (IRE)**[21] 2771 2-8-12 ........ StevieDonohoe 5 62
(Ralph Beckett) *led after 1f: disp ld 2f out: sn rdn: kpt on fnl f: nt gng pce of wnr* **9/2**[3]

**4** 1/2 **Saumur** 2-8-7 ........ JimmyQuinn 7 56+
(Denis Coakley) *s.s: towards rr: n.m.r after 1f: pushed along 3f out: r.o wl fnl f: nrst fin* **4/1**[2]

0 **5** 1 1/2 **Paco's Dream**[21] 2771 2-8-10 ........ PatCosgrave 2 55
(Harry Dunlop) *trckd ldrs after 1f: wd: disp ld 2f out: rdn and wknd fnl f* **10/1**

**6** 3 1/4 **Pyrocumulus (IRE)** 2-8-10 ........ PhilipPrince(5) 3 51
(Jo Hughes) *trckd ldrs after 1f: disp ld 3f out: rdn 2f out: wknd fnl f* **20/1**

0 **7** 2 1/2 **Hidden Agenda**[11] 3081 2-8-8 ........ SteveDrowne 1 38
(Michael Blanshard) *hld up in mid-div: wd: pushed along 4f out: rdn 3f out: styd on same pce fnl f* **25/1**

00 **8** 2 **Sarah Catherine**[54] 1788 2-8-0 ........ CharlotteJenner(7) 6 31
(Mark Usher) *trckd ldrs after 1f: pushed along 3f out: stl prom tl wknd fnl f* **25/1**

**9** 1 **Epsom Poems** 2-8-12 ........ TedDurcan 8 33
(Pat Phelan) *s.s: towards rr: rdn 3f out: sn wl btn* **14/1**

00 **10** 5 **Overstone Lass (IRE)**[26] 2622 2-8-7 ........ WilliamCarson 9 15
(John Spearing) *hld up in mid-div: stl prom tl rdn 3f out: grad wknd fnl 2f* **33/1**

0 **11** 2 **St Paul's Square (IRE)**[16] 2928 2-8-11 ........ RachealKneller(5) 11 19
(Jamie Osborne) *prom after 1f: lost pl 4f out: wknd qckly 3f out* **12/1**

1m 25.24s (1.94) **Going Correction** -0.15s/f (Firm) **11 Ran SP% 118.7**
Speed ratings (Par 91): **82,81,78,78,76 72,69,67,66,60 58**
CSF £17.20 TOTE £3.20: £1.50, £2.80, £1.30; EX 17.80 Trifecta £35.90.
**Owner** Berkeley Racing **Bred** Whitsbury Manor Stud & Pigeon House Stud **Trained** Upper Lambourn, Berks

**FOCUS**
A modest auction maiden for 2yo's that were sold for less than £21,000 at 2013 yearling sales or 2014 breeze-up sales. Despite the stalls being spread across the track, the runners made a beeline for the near rail.

## 3468 SYLVIE & TIM BROWN MEMORIAL H'CAP 7f 140y
**6:35** (6:36) (Class 5) (0-75,76) 4-Y-O+ **£3,234** (£962; £481; £240) **Stalls** Centre

Form RPR
3-43 **1** **Jaladee**[46] 2048 4-9-7 **75** ........ AndreaAtzeni 4 82
(Roger Varian) *s.s: chsd ldrs after 1f: pushed along 3f out: rdn over 1f out: r.o wl fnl f to ld fnl 50yds* **9/4**[1]

5522 **2** nk **Fleckerl (IRE)**[7] 3212 4-9-5 **76** ........ MichaelJMMurphy(3) 6 82
(William Muir) *hld up towards rr: pushed along and gd prog 2f out: r.o wl fnl f to dispute ld: hdd fnl 50yds* **9/4**[1]

0660 **3** shd **Freddy With A Y (IRE)**[11] 3088 4-9-5 **73** ........(p) RichardHughes 5 79
(Gary Moore) *led after 1f: hdd and pushed along 2f out: rallied ins fnl f to press ldrs: jst hld* **7/1**[3]

0453 **4** 2 3/4 **Jack Of Diamonds (IRE)**[16] 2922 5-9-5 **73** ........ RobertWinston 8 72
(Roger Teal) *s.s: towards rr: rdn 2f out: r.o fnl f* **3/1**[2]

5220 **5** 1 **George Baker (IRE)**[11] 3088 7-8-9 **70** ........ ChrisMeehan(7) 7 67
(George Baker) *trckd ldrs: prom and rdn ent fnl f: wknd fnl 100yds* **16/1**

3-64 **6** 1 1/2 **Sarangoo**[28] 2559 6-9-7 **75** ........ SebSanders 2 68
(Malcolm Saunders) *disp ld after 1f: led 3f out: pushed along 2f out: wknd fnl f* **16/1**

00-0 7 6 **Tommy's Secret**[16] 2919 4-9-7 75 AdamKirby 1 53
(Jane Chapple-Hyam) *hld up towards rr: rdn 3f out: wl btn fnl 2f* 16/1
1m 30.06s (-2.24) **Going Correction** -0.15s/f (Firm) 7 Ran SP% 116.7
Speed ratings (Par 103): **105,104,104,101,100 99,93**
CSF £7.79 CT £29.40 TOTE £3.30: £2.30, £2.60; EX 9.10 Trifecta £70.00.
**Owner** Sheikh Ahmed Al Maktoum **Bred** Darley **Trained** Newmarket, Suffolk
■ Stewards' Enquiry : Andrea Atzeni two-day ban: used whip above permitted level (Jul 7-8)
**FOCUS**
Competitive stuff, despite just the seven runners for this extended 7f handicap.

## 3469 IMTECH MAIDEN STKS 6f
7:05 (7:07) (Class 5) 3-Y-O+ £2,587 (£770; £384; £192) Stalls Centre

Form RPR
4-2 1 **Amber Isle (USA)**[24] 2682 3-9-0 (be[1]) RichardHughes 9 78
(Roger Charlton) *broke wl: led after 1f: pushed along ent fnl f: r.o strly* 6/4[1]
23- 2 1 ¾ **Makhfar (IRE)**[309] 5494 3-9-5 RobertHavlin 7 77
(John Gosden) *trckd ldrs after 1f: cl up ent fnl 2f: sn rdn: kpt on: nt gng pce of wnr* 2/1[2]
0- 3 shd **Lady Sparkler (IRE)**[330] 4702 3-9-0 AndreaAtzeni 5 72
(Roger Varian) *s.s: towards rr: gd prog 3f out to trck ldrs: rdn ent fnl f: nt gng pce of wnr: lost 2nd cl home* 9/4[3]
60- 4 1 ¼ **Foxtrot Pearl (IRE)**[244] 7393 3-9-0 StevieDonohoe 11 68
(John Holt) *trckd ldrs after 1f: rdn 2f out: styd on same pce fnl f* 33/1
3 5 ½ **Vecheka (IRE)**[29] 2525 3-8-12 RobHornby(7) 6 71
(Andrew Balding) *s.s: in rr: detached by 3 l: sme prog 3f out to mid-div: rdn fnl f: one pce* 16/1
0-5 6 7 **Loot**[19] 2846 3-9-0 RyanWhile(5) 2 49
(Bill Turner) *s.s: towards rr: wd: gd prog 3f out: rdn ent fnl 2f: sn btn* 25/1
0 7 ½ **Sterling Kate**[30] 2489 3-8-7 RhiainIngram(7) 8 42
(Roger Ingram) *broke wl: disp ld after 1f: rdn 2f out: sn wknd* 50/1
0 8 10 **Phantom Spirit**[30] 2489 3-9-0 PatCosgrave 1 10
(George Baker) *s.s: towards rr: rdn and short of room 2f out: a bhd* 50/1
1m 11.16s (-0.04) **Going Correction** -0.15s/f (Firm)
**WFA** 3 from 4yo+ 7lb 8 Ran SP% 120.7
Speed ratings (Par 103): **94,91,91,89,89 79,79,65**
CSF £5.04 TOTE £2.50: £1.10, £1.10, £1.20; EX 6.10 Trifecta £8.60.
**Owner** K Abdullah **Bred** Juddmonte Farms Inc **Trained** Beckhampton, Wilts
**FOCUS**
An average sprint maiden for 3yos and up.

## 3470 32RED CASINO H'CAP 5f
7:35 (7:36) (Class 5) (0-75,81) 3-Y-O+ £3,234 (£962; £481; £240) Stalls Centre

Form RPR
3-11 1 **High On Life**[12] 3068 3-9-12 81 RichardHughes 2 92
(Jamie Osborne) *broke wl on outside to dispute ld after 1f: led and rdn ent fnl f: r.o wl: won gng away* 11/10[1]
21-0 2 2 **Silverrica (IRE)**[47] 2030 4-9-7 70 RobertWinston 5 76
(Malcolm Saunders) *hld up in mid-div: rdn ent fnl 2f: r.o wl fnl f: nt gng pce of wnr* 10/1
6325 3 ½ **Welease Bwian (IRE)**[7] 3246 5-8-9 65 AaronJones(7) 8 69
(Stuart Williams) *hld up towards rr: rdn whn nt clr run 2f out: swtchd lft and r.o wl fnl f to take 3rd* 7/1[3]
2041 4 1 **Sir Pedro**[11] 3077 5-9-12 75 PaddyAspell 4 76
(Robert Cowell) *trckd ldrs after 1f: disp ld out wd 3f out: rdn fnl 2f: one pce fnl f* 6/1[2]
4561 5 1 ¼ **Whitecrest**[14] 2994 6-9-6 72 WilliamTwiston-Davies(3) 7 68
(John Spearing) *s.s: towards rr: pushed along 3f out: rdn along fnl f: r.o: nvr nrr* 7/1[3]
6-00 6 1 ¾ **Howyadoingnotsobad (IRE)**[25] 2645 6-9-1 69 (tp) RyanWhile(5) 6 59
(Bill Turner) *trckd ldrs after 1f: pushed along 2f out: wknd ent fnl f* 16/1
-020 7 2 **Royal Acquisition**[25] 2645 4-9-9 72 SteveDrowne 3 55
(Robert Cowell) *disputed ld after 1f: hdd 2f out: sn wknd* 33/1
50 8 1 ¼ **Triple Dream**[68] 1490 9-9-11 74 (tp) RichardKingscote 1 52
(Milton Bradley) *hld up in mid-div: rdn 3f out: wknd fnl f* 16/1
4200 9 1 ½ **Encapsulated**[11] 3088 4-8-9 58 (p) RobertHavlin 9 31
(Roger Ingram) *s.s and pushed along after 1f: detached in rr 3f out: a bhd* 16/1
57.26s (-0.94) **Going Correction** -0.15s/f (Firm)
**WFA** 3 from 4yo+ 6lb 9 Ran SP% 116.6
Speed ratings (Par 103): **101,97,97,95,93 90,87,85,83**
CSF £13.58 CT £56.38 TOTE £1.90: £1.10, £2.00, £2.30; EX 11.30 Trifecta £39.60.
**Owner** Michael Buckley **Bred** Moyns Park Estate And Stud Ltd **Trained** Upper Lambourn, Berks
**FOCUS**
The strong favourite prevailed in this handicap over the minimum trip.

## 3471 ALL NEW 32REDSPORT.COM (S) STKS 1m 4f (P)
8:05 (8:05) (Class 6) 3-Y-O £2,264 (£673; £336; £168) Stalls Low

Form RPR
2002 1 **Passionate Affair (IRE)**[14] 2997 3-8-12 65 (tp) RichardKingscote 6 65
(Tom Dascombe) *trckd ldrs after 1f: cl up bhd ldr 2f out: rdn to chse ldr fnl f: hrd rdn fnl 50yds to ld on post* 1/2[1]
0-00 2 nse **Archduchess**[16] 2924 3-8-10 30 ow3 (b[1]) MartinLane 5 63
(Rae Guest) *pushed along to ld after 1f: strly pressed fnl f: r.o wl: hdd fnl strides* 33/1
5000 3 11 **Monsieur Chabal**[16] 2927 3-8-12 54 RichardHughes 8 47
(Jamie Osborne) *hld up towards rr: rdn 3f out: r.o: passed btn horses fnl f to take 3rd* 4/1[2]
5466 4 hd **Witch From Rome**[54] 1812 3-8-12 55 StevieDonohoe 2 47
(John Holt) *hld up towards rr: prog to mid-div 4f out: pushed along 2f out: one pce* 12/1
0003 5 1 ¾ **Beauchamp Melba**[14] 2997 3-8-7 50 (p) WilliamCarson 4 39
(Paul Fitzsimons) *trckd ldr after 1f: pushed along 2f out and sn rdn: wknd ent fnl f* 8/1[3]
0-00 6 3 ¾ **Burmese Breeze**[45] 2081 3-8-12 51 TedDurcan 1 38
(Chris Wall) *trckd ldrs after 1f: prom tl 3f out where pushed along: sn lost pl and wknd qckly* 12/1
006- 7 4 ½ **Black Tie Dancer (IRE)**[219] 7883 3-8-12 40 PatCosgrave 7 31
(Gay Kelleway) *hld up in mid-div: rdn 3f out: wknd 2f out: sn wl btn* 16/1
0- 8 3 ½ **Blazing Chilli**[443] 1344 3-8-7 RyanWhile(5) 3 25
(Bill Turner) *v.s.a: pushed along: a in rr* 20/1
2m 33.48s (0.48) **Going Correction** -0.125s/f (Stan) 8 Ran SP% 126.7
Speed ratings (Par 97): **93,92,85,85,84 81,78,76**
CSF £29.57 TOTE £1.50: £1.10, £6.50, £1.90; EX 33.00 Trifecta £93.50.The winner was sold to Jamie Osborne for 6,000gns.
**Owner** The Passionate Partnership **Bred** Ballyreddin Stud **Trained** Malpas, Cheshire
■ Stewards' Enquiry : Martin Lane three-day ban: weighed in heavy (Jul 6-8)
**FOCUS**
A weak seller for 3yos.

## 3472 BET NOW AT 32REDSPORT.COM H'CAP 1m 4f (P)
8:35 (8:35) (Class 5) (0-75,75) 4-Y-O+ £3,234 (£962; £481; £240) Stalls Low

Form RPR
6-64 1 **The Holyman (IRE)**[87] 1108 6-9-2 70 AdamKirby 7 79
(Jo Crowley) *trckd ldr after 1f: rdn to dispute ld 2f out: hdd ent fnl f: rallied ent fnl 100yds: won gng away* 8/1
0-23 2 ½ **Warrigal (IRE)**[25] 2640 4-9-2 70 ChrisCatlin 6 78
(Jeremy Noseda) *hld up in mid-div: smooth prog 2f out to dispute ld: rdn to ld ent fnl f: sn hrd drvn and hdd fnl 50yds* 7/2[2]
26-3 3 2 ½ **Dalgig**[16] 2924 4-9-3 71 RichardHughes 8 75
(Jamie Osborne) *led after 1f: set gd pce: rdn ent 3f out: sn hdd and styd on same pce fnl f* 11/4[1]
5-31 4 ½ **Atalanta Bay (IRE)**[50] 1919 4-8-13 67 ShaneKelly 3 70
(Marcus Tregoning) *mid-div: rdn ent fnl 3f: styd on same pl fnl f* 7/2[2]
02-0 5 1 **Little Buxted (USA)**[17] 2882 4-9-4 75[1] WilliamTwiston-Davies(3) 4 77
(Robert Mills) *hld up in mid-div: pushed along 4f out: one pce fnl f* 9/2[3]
6003 6 3 ¾ **Idol Deputy (FR)**[7] 3235 8-8-10 69 (p) RachealKneller(5) 5 65
(James Bennett) *hld up towards rr: prog 4f out to mid-div: rdn ent fnl 2f one pce* 20/1
06-0 7 5 **Couloir Extreme (IRE)**[26] 2627 4-9-7 75 AdamBeschizza 1 63
(Gary Moore) *mid-div: pushed along 4f out: sn wknd* 25/1
4320 8 4 **Munsarim (IRE)**[11] 3078 7-9-4 72 (b) AmirQuinn 9 53
(Lee Carter) *s.s and veered lft: a towards rr* 14/1
220- 9 19 **Passion Play**[364] 3587 6-8-11 70 RyanWhile(5) 2 21
(Bill Turner) *trckd ldrs after 1f: pushed along 5f out: lost pl and wknd qckly after* 33/1
2m 29.64s (-3.36) **Going Correction** -0.125s/f (Stan) 9 Ran SP% 118.6
Speed ratings (Par 103): **106,105,104,103,103 100,97,94,81**
CSF £36.36 CT £98.94 TOTE £10.50: £2.90, £2.00, £1.60; EX 44.90 Trifecta £215.80.
**Owner** Kilstone Limited **Bred** Old Carhue Stud **Trained** Whitcombe, Dorset
**FOCUS**
A fair middle-distance handicap for older horses.

## 3473 32RED.COM H'CAP 1m 2f (P)
9:05 (9:05) (Class 6) (0-65,63) 4-Y-O+ £2,458 (£731; £365; £182) Stalls Low

Form RPR
04 1 **With Hindsight (IRE)**[33] 2396 6-8-1 50 CamHardie(7) 2 59
(John Spearing) *hld up: sn trckd ldr: rdn ent fnl 2f: hrd rdn to press ldr 1f out: styd on strly towards fin to ld fnl 50yds* 7/2[1]
0/-5 2 nk **Tin Pan Alley**[10] 3123 6-9-6 62 AdamKirby 8 70
(Sean Curran) *broke wl to ld after 1f: rdn into ld ent fnl 2f where strly pressed: hdd ent fnl f: rallied to chse ldr fnl 50yds* 9/2[2]
5-65 3 ¾ **Ballyshonagh**[7] 3235 4-9-5 61 TedDurcan 7 67
(Chris Wall) *trckd ldrs after 1f: rdn to chse ldrs 2f out: styd on wl: nt gng pce of wnr* 10/1
3151 4 ½ **Lily Edge**[11] 3080 5-9-4 60 (v) WilliamCarson 6 65
(John Bridger) *trckd ldr after 1f: pushed along 2f out: r.o fnl f* 8/1
4451 5 ½ **Bennelong**[7] 3235 8-8-13 62 (b) CharlotteJenner(7) 1 66
(Lee Carter) *s.s: in rr: pushed along 3f out: r.o wl fnl f: passed btn horses: nvr nrr* 6/1
6 1 ½ **City Of Angkor Wat (IRE)**[332] 4646 4-8-10 57 PhilipPrince(5) 9 58
(Jo Hughes) *hld up in mid-div: pushed along 4f out: rdn ent fnl 2f: one pce fnl f* 25/1
-003 7 1 **Rezwaan**[58] 1664 7-9-7 63 (be) ShaneKelly 3 62
(Murty McGrath) *hld up in mid-div: pushed along ent fnl 2f: sn wknd* 5/1[3]
3540 8 2 **Highly Likely (IRE)**[18] 2863 5-8-10 55 (b[1]) WilliamTwiston-Davies(3) 5 50
(Steve Woodman) *hld up towards rr: pushed along 3f out: wknd ent fnl f* 33/1
220 9 hd **Salient**[22] 2720 10-8-6 48 KierenFox 10 43
(Michael Attwater) *prom: trckd ldrs out wd after 2f: pushed along 3f out: fdd 2f out* 16/1
2455 10 1 ¾ **Thane Of Cawdor (IRE)**[24] 2672 5-9-4 60 RichardHughes 11 51+
(Joseph Tuite) *s.s: in rr: a bhd* 5/1[3]
2m 5.14s (-1.46) **Going Correction** -0.125s/f (Stan) 10 Ran SP% 120.9
Speed ratings (Par 101): **100,99,99,98,98 97,96,94,94,93**
CSF £19.93 CT £147.87 TOTE £4.90: £1.50, £2.40, £3.50; EX 24.60 Trifecta £349.10.
**Owner** G N Barot **Bred** Thomas Doherty **Trained** Kinnersley, Worcs
**FOCUS**
A modest 1m2f handicap.
T/Plt: £3.50 to a £1 stake. Pool: £55,788.38 - 1,1367.28 winning tickets. T/Qpdt: £2.30 to a £1 stake. Pool: £4,900.96 - 1,513.55 winning tickets. NF

# 3427 NEWMARKET (R-H)
Saturday, June 21
**OFFICIAL GOING: Good to firm changing to good to firm (firm in places) after race 3 (3:25)**
Wind: Light across Weather: Cloudy with sunny spells

## 3474 HOUSE COLLECTION EBF STALLIONS MAIDEN STKS (BOBIS RACE) 7f
2:15 (2:15) (Class 4) 2-Y-O £4,528 (£1,347; £673; £336) Stalls High

Form RPR
4 1 **Diaz (IRE)**[8] 3194 2-9-5 0 JoeFanning 4 83
(Mark Johnston) *led: hdd over 5f out: chsd ldrs: shkn up to ld over 1f out: rdn out* 7/2[2]
2 1 ¼ **Azmaam (IRE)** 2-9-5 0 DaneO'Neill 8 80+
(Richard Hannon) *a.p: pushed along over 2f out: swtchd rt over 1f out: r.o* 5/2[1]
3 3 hd **Red Rubles (IRE)**[8] 3194 2-9-2 0 ThomasBrown(3) 9 79
(Andrew Balding) *plld hrd: led over 5f out: rdn and hdd over 1f out: styd on same pce ins fnl f* 4/1[3]
0 4 4 **Faithful Creek (IRE)**[21] 2776 2-9-5 0 StevieDonohoe 3 68
(Brian Meehan) *prom: rdn over 2f out: styd on same pce fr over 1f out* 16/1
5 2 ¾ **Sharp Sailor (USA)** 2-9-5 0 LukeMorris 1 61+
(Marco Botti) *wnt rt s: hld up: rdn over 2f out: kpt on ins fnl f: nvr nrr* 7/1
6 4 ½ **Digital Rebellion (IRE)** 2-9-5 0 SilvestreDeSousa 7 52+
(Charlie Appleby) *hld up: plld hrd: hdwy over 2f out: rdn and wknd over 1f out* 5/1

7 1 ¼ **Crack Shot (IRE)** 2-9-0 0 ............ DannyBrock(5) 2 45
(Clive Brittain) *hld up: pushed along 1/2-way: wknd over 1f out* **33/1**

0 8 hd **Father Stone**[10] 3113 2-9-5 0 ............ PaoloSirigu 6 45
(David Elsworth) *w ldr tl over 5f out: remained handy tl rdn and wknd over 1f out* **66/1**

9 15 **Andretti** 2-9-5 0 ............ ShaneKelly 5
(Sir Michael Stoute) *prom: pushed along 1/2-way: wknd 2f out* **20/1**

1m 26.8s (1.10) **Going Correction** -0.125s/f (Firm) **9** Ran SP% **115.0**
Speed ratings (Par 95): **92,90,90,85,82 77,76,75,58**
CSF £12.40 TOTE £4.40: £1.50, £1.20, £1.60; EX 14.30 Trifecta £44.10.

**Owner** Jonathan S Dean **Bred** Kilfrush Stud **Trained** Middleham Moor, N Yorks

**FOCUS**
A couple of the newcomers were well backed in this decent maiden, while the pair with the best form were relatively weak, but it went to one of those with previous experience. Far side course used. Stalls Far Side except 1m5f: Centre.

## 3475 PADDOCKS HOUSE H'CAP 1m 5f
**2:50** (2:52) (Class 5) (0-75,75) 4-Y-0+ **£3,881** (£1,155; £577; £288) **Stalls** Centre

Form RPR

-413 1 **Meetings Man (IRE)**[19] 2835 7-9-0 **75** ............(p) CamHardie(7) 6 83+
(Ali Stronge) *a.p: led over 4f out: pushed along and swtchd rt over 2f out: clr over 1f out: styd on* **5/1**

221 2 1 ½ **Northside Prince (IRE)**[8] 3192 8-9-7 **75** ............ BenCurtis 4 79
(Alan Swinbank) *a.p: rdn over 3f out: chsd wnr over 1f out: styd on* **4/1**[3]

0-00 3 3 ¼ **Ex Oriente (IRE)**[38] 2259 5-9-4 **72** ............(t) AdamBeschizza 5 71
(Stuart Williams) *s.s: hld up: rdn over 3f out: hdwy 2f out: styd on to go 3rd towards fin: nt trble ldrs* **8/1**

6113 4 ¾ **Camelopardalis**[17] 2894 5-8-3 **62** ............ DannyBrock(5) 2 60
(Philip McBride) *chsd ldrs: rdn over 3f out: no ex ins fnl f* **2/1**[1]

0500 5 12 **St Ignatius**[16] 2920 7-8-8 **67** ............(v) TimClark(5) 7 47
(Alan Bailey) *plld hrd: trckd ldr tl led 7f out: rdn and hdd over 4f out: wknd over 1f out* **14/1**

1006 6 34 **Archie Rice (USA)**[12] 3064 8-8-9 **66** ow1 ............ RyanClark(3) 3
(Tom Keddy) *led 6f: chsd ldr: rdn over 3f out: wknd over 2f out* **28/1**

-331 7 8 **Corn Maiden**[18] 2874 5-8-8 **62** ............ LukeMorris 1
(Lydia Pearce) *hld up: rdn over 5f out: wknd over 2f out* **7/2**[2]

2m 48.14s (4.14) **Going Correction** +0.425s/f (Yiel) **7** Ran SP% **113.4**
Speed ratings (Par 103): **104,103,101,100,93 72,67**
CSF £24.74 TOTE £5.00: £2.60, £2.30; EX 18.50 Trifecta £107.10.

**Owner** Mrs Bettine Evans **Bred** Hakan Keles **Trained** Eastbury, Berks

**FOCUS**
This was an ordinary staying handicap and even though the early pace didn't look anything special, it provided a slow-motion finish and they finished very tired.

## 3476 EASTERN COUNTIES FINANCE EBF STALLIONS FILLIES' H'CAP 1m
**3:25** (3:25) (Class 4) (0-85,82) 3-Y-0+ **£6,469** (£1,925; £962; £481) **Stalls** High

Form RPR

1-23 1 **Token Of Love**[8] 3195 3-9-4 **82** ............ JoeFanning 1 91+
(William Haggas) *hld up: hdwy over 2f out: shkn up to ld ins fnl f: r.o: comf* **7/4**[1]

4311 2 1 ½ **Waveguide (IRE)**[12] 3066 5-9-0 **75** ............ LewisWalsh(7) 4 82
(David Simcock) *a.p: led over 1f out: rdn and hdd ins fnl f: styd on same pce* **12/1**

31-1 3 5 **Sequined (USA)**[80] 1240 3-9-4 **82** ............ SilvestreDeSousa 2 76
(Charlie Appleby) *hld up: racd keenly: hdwy 2f out: sn rdn and hung lft: no ex ins fnl f* **7/2**[2]

0440 4 ¾ **Coincidently**[36] 2318 4-9-1 **72** ............ RobertTart(3) 6 66
(Alan Bailey) *led: rdn and hdd over 1f out: no ex ins fnl f* **20/1**

130- 5 4 ½ **Lunette (IRE)**[226] 7785 4-9-5 **73** ............ JimCrowley 8 57
(Ralph Beckett) *w ldr: rdn over 1f out: wknd fnl f* **5/1**[3]

1-23 6 nk **Tullia (IRE)**[29] 2504 3-8-13 **77** ............ ShaneKelly 5 58
(William Knight) *prom: rdn over 2f out: wknd over 1f out* **6/1**

01 7 1 **Sensible Way (USA)**[15] 2967 3-9-1 **79** ............ DaneO'Neill 9 58
(Richard Hannon) *chsd ldrs: rdn over 2f out: wknd fnl f* **8/1**

15-5 8 10 **Boadicee**[17] 2892 3-8-11 **75** ............[1] ChrisCatlin 3 31
(Rae Guest) *s.s: hld up: pushed along over 3f out: wknd over 2f out* **40/1**

1m 37.65s (-2.35) **Going Correction** -0.125s/f (Firm)
**WFA** 3 from 4yo+ 10lb **8** Ran SP% **115.5**
Speed ratings (Par 102): **106,104,99,98,94 93,92,82**
CSF £25.30 CT £68.20 TOTE £2.30: £1.20, £2.00, £1.70; EX 19.40 Trifecta £33.10.

**Owner** A E Oppenheimer **Bred** Hascombe And Valiant Studs **Trained** Newmarket, Suffolk

**FOCUS**
A nice fillies' handicap run at a fair pace. The last four runnings of this had gone to a 3yo, none of whom had run more than three times previously, and that trend was extended.

## 3477 POETS HOUSE EBF STALLIONS MAIDEN STKS (BOBIS RACE) 1m
**4:05** (4:07) (Class 4) 3-Y-0 **£5,498** (£1,636; £817; £408) **Stalls** High

Form RPR

1 **Dream Spirit (IRE)** 3-9-5 0 ............ JimCrowley 1 90
(William Haggas) *wnt rt s: hld up: hdwy to chse ldr over 2f out: shkn up over 1f out: led and hung lft ins fnl f: r.o* **4/1**[2]

2 2 ¾ **Made With Love**[65] 1529 3-9-5 0 ............ DaneO'Neill 4 88
(Roger Varian) *led: rdn and hung lft over 1f out: hdd ins fnl f: unable qck towards fin* **2/11**[1]

00- 3 14 **Tuddenham (USA)**[233] 7646 3-9-5 0 ............ LukeMorris 6 56
(Anthony Carson) *prom: chsd ldr over 5f out tl rdn over 2f out: wknd over 1f out* **25/1**

4 2 ¼ **Four Cheers (IRE)** 3-9-0 0 ............ DannyBrock(5) 5 51
(Clive Brittain) *chsd ldrs: rdn over 2f out: wknd over 1f out* **12/1**[3]

05- 5 1 **Bushy Glade (IRE)**[326] 4861 3-9-0 0 ............ AdamBeschizza 2 43
(Julia Feilden) *chsd ldr over 2f: remained handy: rdn over 2f out: wknd over 1f out* **40/1**

0 6 36 **Remy**[21] 2780 3-9-0 0 ............ J-PGuillambert 3
(Nick Littmoden) *prom: rdn over 3f out: wknd over 2f out* **28/1**

1m 38.92s (-1.08) **Going Correction** -0.125s/f (Firm) **6** Ran SP% **122.0**
Speed ratings (Par 101): **100,99,85,83,82 46**
CSF £5.66 TOTE £7.00: £2.30, £1.10; EX 9.00 Trifecta £38.30.

**Owner** Roberts Green Whittall-Williams Savidge **Bred** Tom & Paul Monaghan **Trained** Newmarket, Suffolk

**FOCUS**
The ground was changed to good to firm, firm in places before this race. An uncompetitive maiden, which looked at the mercy of the long odds-on favourite, but those who took the skinny prices about him had their fingers burnt.

## 3478 BRIGADIER GERARD H'CAP (BOBIS RACE) 5f
**4:40** (4:41) (Class 2) (0-105,100) 3-Y-0 **£12,450** (£3,728; £1,864; £932; £466; £234) **Stalls** High

Form RPR

4-00 1 **Extortionist (IRE)**[7] 3245 3-9-7 **100** ............ JimCrowley 10 113
(Olly Stevens) *trckd ldrs: swtchd rt over 1f out: rdn to ld wl ins fnl f: r.o: readily* **8/1**

1-26 2 1 ½ **Speed Hawk (USA)**[7] 3219 3-8-13 **92** ............ SilvestreDeSousa 4 100
(Robert Cowell) *chsd ldrs: rdn and ev ch over 1f out: styd on* **11/4**[1]

1-20 3 nk **Stars Above Me**[35] 2344 3-8-4 **90** ............ CamHardie(7) 7 97
(Roger Charlton) *led 4f out: rdn over 1f out: hdd and unable qck wl ins fnl f* **6/1**[3]

110- 4 shd **Fast Track**[274] 6584 3-8-6 **85** ............ RoystonFfrench 1 92+
(David Barron) *hld up: hmpd over 1f out: rdn and r.o wl ins fnl f: nt rch ldrs* **16/1**

2401 5 ¾ **Peterkin (IRE)**[7] 3219 3-8-12 **91** ............ JoeFanning 8 95
(Mark Johnston) *led 1f: w ldr: rdn and ev ch ins fnl f: styd on same pce* **7/1**

401 6 nk **Royal Seal**[32] 2442 3-8-7 **86** ow1 ............ ShaneKelly 2 89
(Sir Michael Stoute) *s.i.s: effrt and nt clr run over 1f out: rdn and hung lft ins fnl f: nt rch ldrs* **16/1**

-300 7 nk **Deeds Not Words (IRE)**[7] 3253 3-8-11 **90** ............ LukeMorris 3 92
(Mick Channon) *sn pushed along in rr: rdn over 1f out: styd on ins fnl f: nvr nrr* **25/1**

1015 8 ½ **Piazon**[7] 3219 3-8-6 **90** ............ LouisSteward(5) 5 90
(Michael Bell) *hld up: hung lft fnl 2f: n.d* **12/1**

0-50 9 1 ½ **Ambiance (IRE)**[7] 3245 3-9-5 **98** ............(b) DaneO'Neill 6 93
(Roger Varian) *chsd ldrs: rdn 2f out: no ex ins fnl f* **20/1**

2221 10 8 **Soul Brother (IRE)**[32] 2420 3-8-7 **86** ............ BenCurtis 9 52
(Tim Easterby) *prom: lost pl 4f out: rdn over 1f out: wknd fnl f* **3/1**[2]

57.78s (-1.32) **Going Correction** -0.125s/f (Firm) **10** Ran SP% **117.6**
Speed ratings (Par 105): **105,102,102,101,100 100,99,99,96,83**
CSF £30.55 CT £147.84 TOTE £12.20: £2.50, £1.60, £2.70; EX 40.60 Trifecta £306.60.

**Owner** Sheikh Suhaim Al Thani **Bred** Mrs Louise Lyons **Trained** Chiddingfold, Surrey

**FOCUS**
This was a decent 3yo sprint handicap and the form looks rock-solid.

## 3479 ECF H'CAP 6f
**5:15** (5:16) (Class 4) (0-85,85) 3-Y-0+ **£6,469** (£1,925; £962; £481) **Stalls** High

Form RPR

1165 1 **Ex Ex**[16] 2919 4-9-7 **78** ............(v[1]) J-PGuillambert 6 89
(Nick Littmoden) *hld up in tch: rdn over 1f out: r.o to ld wl ins fnl f* **12/1**

210- 2 hd **Tanzeel (IRE)**[282] 6328 3-9-7 **85** ............ DaneO'Neill 1 93+
(Charles Hills) *s.i.s: plld hrd and sn prom: rdn over 1f out: led ins fnl f: sn hdd: r.o* **9/4**[1]

3-02 3 ¾ **Shore Step (IRE)**[28] 2562 4-9-13 **84** ............ LukeMorris 5 92
(Mick Channon) *led 5f out: hrd rdn fr over 1f out: hdd ins fnl f: kpt on* **5/2**[2]

0003 4 nk **Go Far**[16] 2919 4-9-2 **78** ............(b) TimClark(5) 4 85
(Alan Bailey) *racd alone: prom: pushed along 1/2-way: rdn and hung rt over 1f out: r.o* **10/1**

0040 5 1 ½ **Joe Packet**[14] 2992 7-10-0 **85** ............ JimCrowley 8 87
(Jonathan Portman) *chsd ldrs: rdn over 1f out: no ex ins fnl f* **3/1**[3]

4-00 6 1 **Footstepsintherain (IRE)**[13] 3036 4-9-9 **80** ............ SilvestreDeSousa 2 79
(David Dennis) *slowly into strde: hld up: rdn and hung lft over 2f out: styd on ins fnl f: nvr trbld ldrs* **7/1**

000- 7 1 ½ **Someone's Darling**[250] 7240 4-8-12 **72** ............ SimonPearce(3) 7 66
(Lydia Pearce) *led 1f: chsd ldr: rdn over 1f out: wknd ins fnl f* **25/1**

1m 12.24s (-0.26) **Going Correction** -0.125s/f (Firm)
**WFA** 3 from 4yo+ 7lb **7** Ran SP% **117.5**
Speed ratings (Par 105): **96,95,94,94,92 91,89**
CSF £40.98 CT £92.92 TOTE £9.60: £3.10, £2.10; EX 49.90 Trifecta £154.10.

**Owner** Nick Littmoden **Bred** Mr & Mrs A E Pakenham **Trained** Newmarket, Suffolk

**FOCUS**
A fair sprint handicap.

## 3480 HOUSE COLLECTION H'CAP (BOBIS RACE) 7f
**5:50** (5:54) (Class 4) (0-85,86) 3-Y-0 **£6,469** (£1,925; £962; £481) **Stalls** High

Form RPR

11-2 1 **Outback Traveller (IRE)**[73] 1390 3-9-6 **84** ............ ShaneKelly 12 93
(Jeremy Noseda) *led: hdd over 5f out: led again over 2f out: rdn out* **8/1**

4221 2 ¾ **Baltic Brave (IRE)**[18] 2879 3-8-6 **77** ............(t) CharlieBennett(7) 4 84
(Hughie Morrison) *hld up: swtchd rt and hdwy over 1f out: rdn and r.o ins fnl f: nt rch wnr* **12/1**

-121 3 shd **Red Pike (IRE)**[29] 2508 3-9-4 **82** ............ RoystonFfrench 10 89
(Bryan Smart) *chsd ldrs: rdn and ev ch whn hung rt ins fnl f: r.o* **8/1**

-424 4 1 **Showpiece**[42] 2148 3-9-4 **82** ............ JoeFanning 2 86
(Richard Hannon) *hld up: rdn and edgd lft over 1f out: r.o: nt rch ldrs* **7/2**[1]

313- 5 2 ¾ **Dutch Art Dealer**[226] 7782 3-9-0 **78** ............ JimCrowley 1 75
(Paul Cole) *hld up: hdwy over 2f out: rdn over 1f out: edgd lft and no ex ins fnl f* **4/1**[2]

16-5 6 nk **Almuheet**[56] 1714 3-9-7 **85** ............ DaneO'Neill 11 81
(Sir Michael Stoute) *s.i.s: sn prom: rdn over 1f out: no ex ins fnl f* **10/1**

40-3 7 shd **Biography**[45] 2083 3-8-10 **81** ............ CamHardie(7) 7 77
(Richard Hannon) *chsd ldrs: rdn over 2f out: no ex fnl f* **20/1**

4031 8 3 ¼ **Highland Acclaim (IRE)**[7] 3256 3-9-8 **86** ............ SilvestreDeSousa 8 72+
(David O'Meara) *t.k.h: led over 5f out tl over 2f out: wknd ins fnl f* **7/1**[3]

-344 9 3 **Finn Class (IRE)**[14] 3002 3-8-13 **82** ............ LouisSteward(5) 9 61
(Michael Bell) *prom: rdn over 2f out: wknd fnl f* **7/1**[3]

-310 10 1 **Skaters Waltz (IRE)**[16] 2921 3-9-6 **84** ............ LukeMorris 5 60
(Paul Cole) *chsd ldrs: rdn over 2f out: hmpd and wknd over 1f out* **20/1**

4033 11 hd **Spreadable (IRE)**[22] 2717 3-8-6 **70** ............(b) ChrisCatlin 6 46
(Nick Littmoden) *hld up: rdn and wknd over 1f out* **33/1**

424- 12 nk **Applejack Lad**[172] 8452 3-8-5 **76** ............(t) JordonMcMurray(7) 3 51
(John Ryan) *hld up: rdn over 2f out: wknd over 1f out* **40/1**

1m 25.07s (-0.63) **Going Correction** -0.125s/f (Firm) **12** Ran SP% **121.1**
Speed ratings (Par 101): **98,97,97,95,92 92,92,88,84,83 83,82**
CSF £97.21 CT £813.61 TOTE £4.60: £2.30, £3.20, £3.90; EX 64.80 Trifecta £403.00.

**Owner** Saeed Suhail **Bred** Tally-Ho Stud **Trained** Newmarket, Suffolk

**FOCUS**
A competitive handicap in which they split into two groups early, with the larger group coming up the centre while three stayed against the far rail, including the winner and third.

T/Plt: £15.30 to a £1 stake. Pool: £65,965.10 - 3,146.34 winning tickets. T/Qpdt: £5.70 to a £1 stake. Pool: £3,696.25 - 475.15 winning tickets. CR

## 3434 REDCAR (L-H)

Saturday, June 21

**OFFICIAL GOING: Good to firm (8.7)**

Wind: Light across Weather: Cloudy with sunny periods

### 3481 BRITISH STALLION STUDS EBF MARKET CROSS JEWELLERS MAIDEN STKS 7f

2:05 (2:05) (Class 5) 2-Y-O £3,234 (£962; £481; £240) Stalls Centre

Form RPR

2 **1** **Home Cummins (IRE)**[21] 2788 2-9-0 0 TonyHamilton 10 77+
(Richard Fahey) *trckd ldr: effrt over 2f out: shkn up ent fnl f: sn rdn and kpt on to ld last 75yds* 1/2[1]

53 **2** *1* **Ythan Waters**[33] 2386 2-9-5 0 PaulMulrennan 13 79
(Bryan Smart) *led: pushed along over 2f out: rdn over 1f out: drvn ins fnl f: hdd and no ex last 75yds* 5/1[3]

**3** *8* **Sekuras Girl (IRE)** 2-8-11 0 ConnorBeasley(3) 6 52+
(Michael Dods) *trckd ldrs: hdwy over 2f out: rdn along wl over 1f out: kpt on same pce u.p fnl f* 33/1

**4** *nse* **Sweet Talker** 2-9-0 0 AndrewElliott 11 52+
(Tim Easterby) *hld up towards rr: swtchd rt to outer and gd hdwy 2f out: rdn to chse ldrs over 1f out: edgd lft and one pce ins fnl f* 66/1

**5** *3* **Stormin Tom (IRE)** 2-9-5 0 DavidNolan 9 49
(Tim Easterby) *in tch: hdwy to chse ldrs 1/2-way: rdn along over 2f out: sn one pce* 50/1

0 **6** *1/2* **Chilworth Bells**[15] 2964 2-9-5 0 GrahamGibbons 12 48
(Mick Channon) *hld up: hdwy on wd outside 3f out: pushed along to chse ldrs 2f out: cl up and rdn over 1f out: wknd ins fnl f* 16/1

**7** *2* **Lord Of Words (IRE)** 2-8-12 0 MeganCarberry(7) 7 42
(Brian Ellison) *towards rr: hdwy wl over 2f out: rdn wl over 1f out: sn no imp* 33/1

0 **8** *1* **Chollima**[34] 2358 2-9-5 0 DavidAllan 8 40
(Tim Easterby) *chsd ldrs to 1/2-way: sn wknd* 50/1

**9** *1/2* **Youonlyliveonce (IRE)** 2-9-2 0 IanBrennan(3) 2 38
(John Quinn) *nvr bttr than midfield* 33/1

**10** *8* **Heading Home (FR)** 2-9-5 0 PhillipMakin 4 17
(John Quinn) *midfield: pushed along 1/2-way: sn outpcd* 9/2[2]

0 **11** *nk* **Pencaitland**[33] 2386 2-8-11 0 NeilFarley(3) 5
(Noel Wilson) *a towards rr* 100/1

**12** *22* **Brightside** 2-8-12 0 KevinLundie(7) 1
(Tracy Waggott) *s.i.s: a in rr* 80/1

1m 26.46s (1.96) **Going Correction** -0.025s/f (Good) **12** Ran SP% **123.9**
Speed ratings (Par 93): **87,85,76,76,73 72,70,69,68,59 59,34**
CSF £3.50 TOTE £1.70: £1.10, £1.50, £4.50; EX 4.50 Trifecta £36.70.
**Owner** Mrs H Steel **Bred** Yeguada De Milagro Sa **Trained** Musley Bank, N Yorks

**FOCUS**
A modest 2yo maiden.

### 3482 TEESSIDE HOSPICE FASHION SHOW H'CAP 1m 6f 19y

2:40 (2:40) (Class 6) (0-65,65) 4-Y-0+ £2,587 (£770; £384; £192) Stalls Low

Form RPR

00-4 **1** **Hot Spice**[59] 1644 6-9-4 62 GrahamGibbons 12 75
(Michael Easterby) *cl up: led after 2f: pushed along and qcknd 3f out: jnd and rdn 2f out: drvn ent fnl f: styd on strly* 4/1[2]

6-11 **2** *3 3/4* **Maoi Chinn Tire (IRE)**[4] 3336 7-8-13 64 12ex JoeDoyle(7) 2 72
(Jennie Candlish) *hld up in midfield: stdy hdwy on inner 4f out: trckd wnr wl over 2f out: effrt to chal 2f out: sn rdn and ev ch tl drvn and oner pce ent fnl f* 5/2[1]

224- **3** *1 1/2* **Danceintothelight**[175] 7098 7-8-9 56 NeilFarley(3) 6 62
(Micky Hammond) *trckd ldrs on inner: pushed along and sltly outpcd 3f out: rdn 2f out: styd on appr fnl f* 20/1

-005 **4** *2* **Madrasa (IRE)**[28] 2550 6-9-2 65 (b) JacobButterfield(5) 4 68
(Keith Reveley) *hld up in rr: hdwy over 3f out: rdn along 2f out: styd on appr fnl f: nrst fin* 9/2[3]

36-5 **5** *2* **Spiekeroog**[17] 2900 8-9-1 59 DavidNolan 10 59
(Alan Brown) *prom: chsd wnr 1/2-way: rdn along 3f out: drvn wl over 1f out: sn one pce* 14/1

4/63 **6** *1 1/2* **Rockabilly Riot (IRE)**[16] 2915 4-9-4 62 PhillipMakin 5 60
(Martin Todhunter) *trckd ldrs: hdwy over 3f out: rdn along 2f out: sn drvn and no imp* 5/1

054 **7** *4 1/2* **Saddlers Mot**[17] 2904 10-8-9 60 GemmaTutty(7) 3 52
(Karen Tutty) *hld up: a in rr: bled fr nose* 28/1

000- **8** *shd* **Speedy Star (IRE)**[28] 7376 5-8-2 46 oh1 PaulQuinn 1 38
(Tina Jackson) *t.k.h early: hld up: a in rr* 100/1

0-06 **9** *1/2* **Golden Future**[29] 2512 11-8-9 53 PaulMulrennan 11 44
(Peter Niven) *midfield: rdn along wl over 3f out: n.d* 20/1

-000 **10** *10* **Musikhani**[20] 2801 4-9-5 63 RussKennemore 8 40
(Philip Kirby) *sn trcking ldrs on outer: pushed along 4f out: rdn 3f out and sn wknd* 10/1

004 **11** *14* **Lacocodanza**[15] 2952 5-7-9 46 oh1 KieranSchofield(7) 7 3
(George Moore) *towards rr: hdwy on outer to chse ldrs 1/2-way: rdn along 4f out: sn wknd* 20/1

50-0 **12** *8* **Turjuman (USA)**[32] 2424 9-8-2 46 oh1 RaulDaSilva 9
(Simon West) *led 2f: cl up: rdn along 4f out: sn wknd* 66/1

3m 2.84s (-1.86) **Going Correction** -0.075s/f (Good) **12** Ran SP% **119.4**
Speed ratings (Par 101): **102,99,99,97,96 95,93,93,92,87 79,74**
CSF £13.29 CT £181.37 TOTE £5.50: £2.10, £1.10, £3.40; EX 15.30 Trifecta £159.00.
**Owner** S Hull, D Swales, A Turton & J Blackburn **Bred** J L Dunlop **Trained** Sheriff Hutton, N Yorks

**FOCUS**
A low-grade staying handicap run at a decent pace.

### 3483 H JARVIS 136TH ANNIVERSARY H'CAP 7f

3:15 (3:16) (Class 3) (0-90,89) 4-Y-0+ £7,762 (£2,310; £1,154; £577) Stalls Centre

Form RPR

1002 **1** **Heavy Metal**[8] 3189 4-9-3 85 AdrianNicholls 8 95
(Mark Johnston) *in tch: pushed along 1/2-way: gd hdwy 2f out: rdn to ld over 1f out: edgd lft ins fnl f: drvn out* 10/1

0002 **2** *2 3/4* **Out Do**[6] 3271 5-9-6 88 DavidNolan 6 91
(David O'Meara) *trckd ldrs: hdwy and cl up over 2f out: effrt wl over 1f out and ev ch tl rdn and kpt on same pce fnl f* 2/1[1]

3060 **3** *1* **Chilworth Icon**[53] 1862 4-9-7 89 PhillipMakin 7 89
(Mick Channon) *trckd ldrs: hdwy over 2f out: rdn over 1f out: swtchd rt ins fnl f: kpt on same pce* 12/1

3-42 **4** *1/2* **Available (IRE)**[7] 3227 5-8-11 79 (tp) PaulMulrennan 1 78
(John Mackie) *prom: led 4f out: rdn along over 2f out: hdd over 1f out and grad wknd* 8/1[3]

0126 **5** *2 1/4* **Corporal Maddox**[40] 2202 7-9-7 89 (p) BarryMcHugh 2 82
(Ronald Harris) *hld up in tch: swtchd lft to outer and hdwy 2f out: sn rdn and no imp fnl f* 20/1

-000 **6** *2 1/2* **Evanescent (IRE)**[28] 2548 5-8-6 77 IanBrennan(3) 9 64
(John Quinn) *prom: cl up 1/2-way: rdn along over 2f out: sn drvn and wknd* 18/1

2200 **7** *6* **Orbit The Moon (IRE)**[26] 2602 6-8-2 73 (bt) ConnorBeasley(3) 5 44
(Michael Dods) *hld up towards rr: sme hdwy on outer wl over 2f out: sn rdn along and wknd* 10/1

-366 **8** *1/2* **Kalk Bay (IRE)**[8] 3202 7-9-0 82 (t) GrahamGibbons 4 52
(Michael Easterby) *towards rr: pushed along 3f out: rdn over 2f out: sn btn* 10/3[2]

-300 **9** *7* **Wannabe King**[28] 2548 8-8-13 86 (v) KevinStott(5) 3 38
(Geoffrey Harker) *led 3f: cl up tl rdn along over 2f out and sn wknd* 17/2

1m 24.09s (-0.41) **Going Correction** -0.025s/f (Good) **9** Ran SP% **113.9**
Speed ratings (Par 107): **101,97,96,96,93 90,83,83,75**
CSF £29.95 CT £247.60 TOTE £8.50: £4.10, £1.70, £3.90; EX 21.60 Trifecta £189.60.
**Owner** Sheikh Hamdan bin Mohammed Al Maktoum **Bred** Darley **Trained** Middleham Moor, N Yorks

**FOCUS**
A fair handicap.

### 3484 TEC4M BUILDING THE FUTURE H'CAP (BOBIS RACE) 5f

3:55 (3:56) (Class 4) (0-85,82) 3-Y-O £6,469 (£1,925; £962; £481) Stalls Centre

Form RPR

65-1 **1** **Money Team (IRE)**[47] 2015 3-9-5 80 GrahamGibbons 6 95
(David Barron) *led 1f: cl up: effrt whn hmpd and carried lft over 1f out: rdn to chal ins fnl f: kpt on wl to ld last 75yds* 7/2[1]

10-4 **2** *1* **Online Alexander (IRE)**[12] 3068 3-9-7 82 AmyRyan 9 93
(Kevin Ryan) *wnt rt s: towards rr: hdwy and cl up bef 1/2-way: rdn to chal wl over 1f out: sn led: drvn and edgd lft ins fnl f: hdd and no ex last 75yds* 5/1[2]

3305 **3** *4* **Meadway**[17] 2897 3-9-5 80 PaulMulrennan 1 75
(Bryan Smart) *in tch on outer: hdwy over 2f out: sn rdn: kpt on fnl f* 6/1[3]

514- **4** *3/4* **Go Glamorous (IRE)**[279] 6432 3-9-1 76 BarryMcHugh 10 68
(Ronald Harris) *prom: led after 1f: rdn and hung lft wl over 1f out: sn hdd and one pce* 28/1

1310 **5** *shd* **Crisis Averted (IRE)**[6] 3271 3-9-4 79 (v[1]) TonyHamilton 8 71
(Richard Fahey) *towards rr: pushed along over 2f out: sn rdn and styd on fnl f: nrst fin* 13/2

3106 **6** *5* **One Boy (IRE)**[17] 2897 3-9-4 82 ConnorBeasley(3) 4 54
(Michael Dods) *chsd ldrs: rdn wl over 1f out: sn wknd* 15/2

-001 **7** *1/2* **Baytown Kestrel**[16] 2933 3-8-11 79 (p) MeganCarberry(7) 2 49
(Brian Ellison) *prom: rdn along 1/2-way: sn wknd* 9/1

11-0 **8** *3/4* **Pull The Plug (IRE)**[22] 2745 3-9-4 82 NeilFarley(3) 7 49
(Declan Carroll) *chsd ldrs: rdn along bef 1/2-way: sn outpcd* 6/1[3]

234- **9** *11* **Gilmer (IRE)**[246] 7349 3-9-5 80 [1] AhmedAjtebi 5 3
(Charlie Appleby) *trckd ldrs: pushed along after 2f: rdn 1/2-way: sn lost pl and bhd* 10/1

58.21s (-0.39) **Going Correction** -0.025s/f (Good) **9** Ran SP% **115.1**
Speed ratings (Par 101): **102,100,94,92,92 84,83,82,65**
CSF £20.71 CT £101.64 TOTE £3.50: £1.30, £2.10, £2.50; EX 18.70 Trifecta £140.20.
**Owner** Hardisty Rolls II **Bred** Mrs Claire Doyle **Trained** Maunby, N Yorks

**FOCUS**
An interesting 3yo sprint handicap with some progressive, unexposed types on show.

### 3485 ALLEN TURNER MEMORIAL CLAIMING STKS 7f

4:30 (4:30) (Class 5) 3-Y-O+ £3,234 (£962; £481; £240) Stalls Centre

Form RPR

0-00 **1** **Native Falls (IRE)**[42] 2166 3-8-8 58 DavidAllan 13 72
(Alan Swinbank) *led to 1/2-way: cl up: led again wl over 2f out: rdn appr fnl f: kpt on* 20/1

3041 **2** *2* **Illustrious Prince (IRE)**[7] 3227 7-9-1 78 IanBrennan(3) 8 71
(Julie Camacho) *prom: rdn along over 2f out: drvn to chse wnr ent fnl f: sn edgd lft and no imp towards fin* 1/1[1]

-400 **3** *2 1/2* **Red Paladin (IRE)**[6] 3272 4-9-5 68 [1] TonyHamilton 3 65
(Kevin Ryan) *bhd: rdn along and hdwy over 2f out: drvn and kpt on fnl f: nrst fin* 7/2[2]

60-3 **4** *1 1/2* **Whispered Times (USA)**[61] 1606 7-8-9 59 (p) JacobButterfield(5) 1 56
(Tracy Waggott) *cl up on outer: led 1/2-way: rdn along and hdd over 2f out: drvn and hung rt over 1f out: sn wknd* 11/1

0510 **5** *4 1/2* **Ad Vitam (IRE)**[40] 2215 6-9-1 56 (vt) GrahamGibbons 6 46
(David C Griffiths) *chsd ldrs: rdn along over 2f out: sn drvn and wknd* 16/1

5-06 **6** *hd* **Rasselas (IRE)**[10] 3096 7-8-7 63 (v) AnnaHesketh(7) 11 44
(David Nicholls) *chsd ldrs: rdn along wl over 2f out: sn outpcd* 11/1

4-10 **7** *4 1/2* **Medecis Mountain**[140] 428 5-8-10 48 KevinStott(5) 4 33
(John Wainwright) *chsd ldrs: rdn along 3f out: sn outpcd* 50/1

00 **8** *9* **Beaulie**[25] 2653 4-8-6 0 NataliaGemelova(3) 7 4
(Keith Reveley) *a in rr: bhd fnl 2f* 100/1

00-0 **9** *3/4* **San Remo Rose (IRE)**[61] 1611 3-8-0 43 PatrickMathers 12
(Tony Coyle) *dwlt: a towards rr: rdn along 1/2-way: bhd fnl 2f* 50/1

2310 **U** **Mitchell**[10] 3096 4-9-0 59 (p) ConnorBeasley(3) 5
(David Thompson) *wnt lft and uns rdr s* 7/1[3]

1m 24.6s (0.10) **Going Correction** -0.025s/f (Good)
**WFA** 3 from 4yo+ 9lb **10** Ran SP% **116.9**
Speed ratings (Par 103): **98,95,92,91,86 85,80,70,69,**
CSF £40.23 TOTE £22.70: £4.40, £1.10, £1.50; EX 80.50 Trifecta £1021.00.Mitchell was claimed by Mr Tim Dykes for £8,000.
**Owner** Anthea Findlay & The Twopin Partnership **Bred** John Foley **Trained** Melsonby, N Yorks

**FOCUS**
A strong pace for this claimer where few got involved.

### 3486 WATCH ON 3 DEVICES RACINGUK.COM/ANYWHERE MEDIAN AUCTION MAIDEN STKS 6f

5:05 (5:19) (Class 5) 3-5-Y-O £3,234 (£962; £481; £240) Stalls Centre

Form RPR

53 **1** **Sleeping Apache (IRE)**[33] 2392 4-9-9 0 ConnorBeasley(3) 8 72
(Philip Kirby) *chsd ldrs: hdwy over 2f out: rdn to ld over 1f out: kpt on wl* 3/1[2]

553 **2** 2 ½ **Hoy Hoy (IRE)**[24] 2667 3-9-5 72 GrahamGibbons 10 62
(Mick Channon) *led: rdn along 2f out: hdd over 1f out: drvn and kpt on same pce fnl f* **11/4**[1]

3-44 **3** ½ **Alpine Flower (IRE)**[14] 2985 3-9-0 70 DavidAllan 9 55
(Tim Easterby) *towards rr: hdwy 1/2-way: chsd ldrs 2f out: sn rdn: drvn and kpt on same pce fnl f* **9/2**[3]

5 **4** ¾ **Linda's Sister**[14] 2985 4-9-4 0 IanBrennan(3) 5 55
(John Quinn) *prom: rdn along 2f out: sn drvn and kpt on one pce* **8/1**

3 **5** ½ **Highland Rebel (IRE)**[53] 1853 3-9-5 0 TonyHamilton 6 56
(Richard Fahey) *cl up: rdn along over 2f out: drvn over 1f out: sn wknd* **6/1**

4-0 **6** *nse* **Saranta**[22] 2737 3-9-0 0 PatrickMathers 3 51
(Richard Fahey) *dwlt and in rr: hdwy on outer 2f out: sn rdn and styd on fnl f: nrst fin* **8/1**

**7** *nse* **Clabare** 3-9-0 0 GarryWhillans(5) 7 56?
(Ian Semple) *dwlt and in rr: hdwy wl over 1f out: sn rdn and kpt on fnl f: nrst fin* **33/1**

0 **8** *nk* **Kaytom**[33] 2389 3-9-0 0 BarryMcHugh 1 50?
(John Wainwright) *in tch: hdwy over 2f out: rdn over 1f out: kpt on fnl f: nrst fin* **66/1**

0-44 **9** *14* **Lunesdale Buddy**[28] 2551 3-9-0 45 KevinStott(5) 4 10
(Alan Berry) *prom: rdn along 1/2-way: wknd over 2f out* **66/1**

1m 12.58s (0.78) **Going Correction** -0.025s/f (Good)
**WFA** 3 from 4yo 7lb **9** Ran SP% **112.3**
Speed ratings (Par 103): **93,89,89,88,87 87,87,86,68**
CSF £11.20 TOTE £4.00: £1.20, £1.10, £2.00; EX 13.60 Trifecta £67.80.
**Owner** Geoff & Sandra Turnbull **Bred** Airlie Stud **Trained** Middleham, N Yorks

**FOCUS**
A moderate sprint maiden.

## 3487 LADIES AND GENTS EVENING, 23RD AUGUST H'CAP 5f
**5:40** (5:44) (Class 6) (0-65,65) 3-Y-O £2,726 (£805; £402) **Stalls** Centre

Form RPR

04 **1** **Dancing Juice**[80] 1246 3-8-2 **53** ow1 (v[1]) RobJFitzpatrick(7) 8 59
(K R Burke) *mde most: jnd 2f out and sn rdn: drvn ent fnl f: kpt on gamely towards fin* **16/1**

0031 **2** *nk* **Bashiba (IRE)**[7] 3228 3-8-3 **52** (t) ShelleyBirkett(5) 7 57
(Nigel Tinkler) *trckd ldrs: pushed along and sltly outpcd over 1f out: sn rdn and styd on strly ins fnl f: jst hld* **8/1**[3]

0-00 **3** *nse* **Tweety Pie (IRE)**[25] 2657 3-9-3 **64** NeilFarley(3) 5 69
(Declan Carroll) *cl up: rdn along wl over 1f out: drvn and kpt on wl fnl f: jst hld* **9/1**

-341 **4** ½ **Storyline (IRE)**[33] 2387 3-9-7 **65** DavidAllan 10 68
(Tim Easterby) *cl up: effrt 2f out: sn rdn and ev ch tl drvn and no ex wl ins fnl f* **5/4**[1]

20-0 **5** ¾ **Secret Applause**[61] 1611 3-9-0 **61** ConnorBeasley(3) 6 62
(Michael Dods) *towards rr: rdn along 1/2-way: hdwy over 1f out: kpt on u.p fnl f: nrst fin* **33/1**

4426 **6** *shd* **Fredricka**[20] 2802 3-9-4 **62** (p) GrahamGibbons 2 62
(Garry Moss) *trckd ldrs: hdwy and cl up 2f out: rdn over 1f out: ev ch tl drvn and one pce wl ins fnl f* **7/1**[2]

-622 **7** 1 ½ **Vodka Chaser (IRE)**[15] 2943 3-8-9 **60** AlistairRawlinson(7) 4 55
(Alison Hutchinson) *chsd ldrs: rdn along and n.m.r over 1f out: swtchd lft ent fnl f: kpt on same pce* **7/1**[2]

-213 **8** *hd* **Raise A Billion**[10] 3100 3-8-8 **52** PatrickMathers 3 46
(Alan Berry) *chsd ldrs: rdn along 2f out: sn drvn and grad wknd* **9/1**

-000 **9** 1 ½ **Classy Lassy (IRE)**[7] 3237 3-8-7 **58** KevinLundie(7) 9 47
(Brian Ellison) *dwlt: a in rr* **33/1**

4003 **10** *4* **Sandsman's Girl (IRE)**[19] 2838 3-9-2 **60** BarryMcHugh 1 34
(James Given) *chsd ldrs on outer: rdn along 2f out: sn wknd* **16/1**

58.74s (0.14) **Going Correction** -0.025s/f (Good) **10** Ran SP% **118.2**
Speed ratings (Par 97): **97,96,96,95,94 94,91,91,89,82**
CSF £139.72 CT £1231.13 TOTE £16.60: £3.80, £2.90, £3.80; EX 169.70 Trifecta £837.30 Part won. Pool: £1,116.46 - 0.32 winning units..
**Owner** Market Avenue Racing Club Ltd **Bred** P Scholes **Trained** Middleham Moor, N Yorks

**FOCUS**
An ordinary handicap, rated around the runner-up.
T/Plt: £4.60 to a £1 stake. Pool: £58,451.36 - 9,271.36 winning tickets. T/Qpdt: £3.40 to a £1 stake. Pool: £3,337.02 - 712.12 winning tickets. JR

# 2751 DOWN ROYAL (R-H)
Saturday, June 21

**OFFICIAL GOING: Good to firm**

## 3491a MAGNERS ULSTER DERBY (PREMIER H'CAP) 1m 3f
**4:10** (4:10) 3-Y-O
**£50,000** (£15,833; £7,500; £2,500; £1,666; £833)

RPR

**1** **Wexford Town (IRE)**[38] 2264 3-8-13 **83** (t) KevinManning 5 87+
(J S Bolger, Ire) *slowly away and niggled along in detached rr: 2 l detached in rr 1/2-way: rdn to cl on outer fr 4f out: hdwy u.p to go cl 5th ent fnl f: kpt on strly to dispute ld 100yds out: led 50yds out* **7/1**

**2** *hd* **Magnolia Beach (IRE)**[47] 2038 3-9-9 **96** ColinKeane(3) 9 100
(G M Lyons, Ire) *hld up towards rr: 7th 1/2-way: prog fr over 2f out: rdn to go 3rd ent fnl f: kpt on strly u.p to dispute ld 100yds out: hdd 50yds out* **6/1**[3]

**3** ½ **Azurite (IRE)**[47] 2041 3-9-5 **89** GaryCarroll 2 92
(G M Lyons, Ire) *chsd ldrs: 3rd 1/2-way: rdn to chal under 3f out: led under 2f out: kpt on wl u.p whn chal ins fnl f: hdd 100yds out and no ex* **9/2**[1]

**4** 1 ¼ **Abushamah (IRE)**[12] 3069 3-8-13 **83** ChrisHayes 4 84?
(Kevin Prendergast, Ire) *hld up towards rr: bit clsr in 6th 1/2-way: gd prog fr 3f out to go 2nd under 2f out: kpt on wl u.p but no ex cl home and dropped to 4th 100yds out* **16/1**

**5** 2 ¾ **Zafayan (IRE)**[19] 2858 3-9-9 **93** (p) PatSmullen 6 89
(D K Weld, Ire) *hld up in rr: 8th 1/2-way: rdn fr 3f out and hdwy on outer to go 4th ent fnl f: sltly short of room jst ins fnl f and swtchd ins: kpt on same pce* **11/2**[2]

**6** 3 ¼ **Urban Moon (IRE)**[13] 3044 3-9-11 **95** NGMcCullagh 7 85
(J P Murtagh, Ire) *sn led: set brisk pce: rdn whn pressed for ld 3f out: hdd under 2f out: no ex and wknd ent fnl f* **9/2**[1]

**7** 6 ½ **Blue Atlantic (USA)**[14] 3003 3-8-4 **77** ConorHoban(3) 3 55
(Mark Johnston) *restless in stalls and hld by handler: sn chsd ldrs: 4th 1/2-way: rdn over 3f out and wnt 3rd briefly u.p: sn no ex and wknd fr 2f out* **12/1**

**8** *15* **Notarised**[14] 3003 3-8-12 **82** FMBerry 1 33
(Mark Johnston) *cl up: sn trckd ldr in 2nd: rdn over 3f out and sn no ex: wknd and eased ins fnl f* **9/2**[1]

**9** 8 ½ **Abby Cadabby (IRE)**[13] 3043 3-8-10 **83** ConnorKing(3) 8 19
(A Oliver, Ire) *settled in mid-div: 5th 1/2-way: pushed along fr 4f out: sn dropped to rr: no imp* **14/1**

2m 19.95s (139.95) **9** Ran SP% **117.0**
CSF £49.16 CT £211.92 TOTE £6.50: £1.80, £2.70, £1.90; DF 68.20 Trifecta £245.50.
**Owner** Mrs J S Bolger **Bred** J S Bolger **Trained** Coolcullen, Co Carlow

**FOCUS**
A relatively big field in the context of a fixture with only 44 runners in total, but still only a single-figure turn-out for the most important event in Northern Ireland's Flat-racing calendar. Confined to members of the Classic generation this year having previously been open to older horses.

# 3048 LES LANDES
Friday, June 20

**OFFICIAL GOING: Good to firm**

## 3495a EPISODE FUND H'CAP 1m 4f
**7:05** (7:05) 3-Y-O+ **£1,460** (£525; £315)

RPR

**1** **Sweet Liberta (IRE)**[13] 5-8-13 MatthewCosham 3 65
(T Le Brocq, Jersey) **5/2**[2]

**2** *5* **Rossetti**[13] 2991 6-10-2 (p) MattieBatchelor 2 74
(Mrs A Malzard, Jersey) **1/2**[1]

**3** *7* **King Kenny**[13] 9-8-5 oh17 (p) NoraLooby 1 38
(Mrs A Corson, Jersey) **5/2**[2]

2m 47.0s (-3.00) **3** Ran SP% **123.8**

**Owner** G Amy & T Le Brocq **Bred** W Maxwell Ervine **Trained** Jersey

## 3496a QUILTER CHEVIOT H'CAP 5f 110y
**7:40** (7:40) 3-Y-O+ **£1,905** (£685; £410)

RPR

**1** **Kersivay**[13] 8-8-12 (p) JemmaMarshall 6 37
(Mrs A Malzard, Jersey) **2/1**[2]

**2** *1* **Country Blue (FR)**[13] 5-9-10 (p) CraigWalker 1 46
(Mrs A Malzard, Jersey) **5/2**[3]

**3** ½ **Purley Queen (IRE)**[13] 5-10-8 MrFTett 4 56
(Mrs C Gilbert, Jersey) **2/1**[2]

**4** *5* **Novabridge**[46] 2598 6-10-12 (b) MattieBatchelor 2 44
(Neil Mulholland) **11/8**[1]

**5** *1* **Chester'slittlegem (IRE)**[13] 5-9-12 HarryPoulton 3 26
(Mrs A Corson, Jersey) **6/1**

**6** *3* **Lively Little Lady**[13] 4-8-5 oh2 NoraLooby 5
(Mrs A Corson, Jersey) **14/1**

1m 7.0s (67.00) **6** Ran SP% **158.3**

**Owner** Fast And Furious Racing **Bred** Brook Stud Bloodstock Ltd **Trained** St Ouen, Jersey

# 2519 PONTEFRACT (L-H)
Sunday, June 22

**OFFICIAL GOING: Good (good to firm in places; 7.8)**
Wind: light 1/2 against Weather: fine

## 3497 TOTEJACKPOT/BRITISH STALLION STUDS EBF MAIDEN FILLIES' STKS (BOBIS RACE) 6f
**2:10** (2:12) (Class 5) 2-Y-O £4,528 (£1,347; £673; £336) **Stalls** Low

Form RPR

**1** **Bimbo** 2-8-11 0 [1] GeorgeChaloner(3) 9 78+
(Richard Fahey) *chsd ldrs on outside: drvn over 2f out: styd on to ld towards fin* **33/1**

2 **2** ¾ **Lady Moscou (IRE)**[13] 3063 2-9-0 0 KierenFallon 1 76
(James Tate) *sn trcking ldrs: led on ins over 3f out: hdd and no ex clsng stages* **10/3**[2]

0 **3** 1 ¼ **Lacing**[66] 1528 2-9-0 0 RyanMoore 5 72
(Richard Fahey) *led tl over 3f out: upsides over 1f out: drvn and kpt on same pce last 100yds* **5/6**[1]

**4** 2 ¼ **Caius College Girl (IRE)** 2-9-0 0 GrahamGibbons 6 66
(David Barron) *trckd ldrs: one pce appr fnl f* **14/1**

**5** ½ **Multi Grain** 2-9-0 0 RobertWinston 8 64
(Brian Ellison) *chsd ldrs: one pce over 1f out* **66/1**

0 **6** *8* **Mistress Makfi (IRE)**[66] 1536 2-9-0 0 SilvestreDeSousa 4 40
(Mark Johnston) *s.i.s: drvn along in rr: bhd over 1f out: eased ins fnl f* **25/1**

0433 **7** *7* **Rose Of Kiev (IRE)**[37] 2306 2-9-0 0 FrannyNorton 2 19
(Mark Johnston) *in rr and drvn along: bhd over 1f out: eased ins fnl f* **7/1**[3]

6 **8** 2 ¼ **Terse**[12] 3076 2-9-0 0 TedDurcan 7 12+
(David Lanigan) *dwlt: hdwy over 3f out: sn chsng ldrs: lost pl wl over 1f out: sn bhd: eased ins fnl f* **10/1**

1m 17.37s (0.47) **Going Correction** -0.275s/f (Firm) **8** Ran SP% **114.2**
Speed ratings (Par 90): **85,84,82,79,78 68,58,55**
CSF £138.76 TOTE £17.60: £4.50, £1.20, £1.10; EX 144.60 Trifecta £280.90.
**Owner** Lady Halifax **Bred** Lady Halifax **Trained** Musley Bank, N Yorks
■ Elevator Action (33-1) was withdrawn. Rule 4 does not apply.

**FOCUS**
False rail in place about 5yds from permanent inside rail which increased distances by about 12yds. Despite the surprise result, this wasn't a bad maiden and the second and third are capable of winning a similar event.

## 3498 TOTEPLACEPOT RACING'S FAVOURITE BET MAIDEN AUCTION STKS 1m 4f 8y
**2:40** (2:40) (Class 5) 3-Y-O **£4,528** (£1,347; £673; £336) **Stalls** Low

Form RPR
6 **1** **Westerly**[26] 2650 3-8-6 0 LiamJones 4 71+
(William Haggas) *dwlt: in rr: hdwy over 7f out: chsng ldrs over 5f out: led and edgd lft over 1f out: drvn out* **16/1**

32 **2** *1 1/2* **Smiling Stranger (IRE)**[36] 2334 3-8-12 0 OisinMurphy(3) 7 77
(Andrew Balding) *trckd ldrs: drvn over 2f out: upsides whn hmpd over 1f out: styd on same pce* **4/11**[1]

5633 **3** *nk* **Mambo Rhythm**[27] 2616 3-8-8 65 FrannyNorton 5 69
(Mark Johnston) *trckd ldrs: rdn 2f out: kpt on to take 3rd last 100yds* **10/1**[3]

03 **4** *3/4* **Strawberry Martini**[27] 2613 3-8-8 0 AndreaAtzeni 3 68
(William Muir) *dwlt: in rr: drvn 5f out: sn chsng ldrs: outpcd over 2f out: styd on fnl f: tk 4th last 50yds* **11/1**

-034 **5** *6* **Stout Cortez**[11] 3120 3-8-12 65 SilvestreDeSousa 1 62
(Mark Johnston) *led: hdd and hmpd over 1f out: wknd fnl f* **8/1**[2]

-440 **6** *27* **Barbara Elizabeth**[11] 3098 3-8-6 55 BarryMcHugh 6 13
(Tony Coyle) *chsd ldrs: lost pl over 2f out: sn bhd: t.o* **50/1**

0-4 **7** *24* **Petite Madame (IRE)**[63] 1600 3-8-7 0 JimmyQuinn 2
(David Thompson) *mid-div: drvn and lost pl over 5f out: sn bhd: t.o over 2f out* **50/1**

2m 38.42s (-2.38) **Going Correction** -0.275s/f (Firm) **7** Ran SP% **111.7**
Speed ratings (Par 99): **96,95,94,94,90 72,56**
CSF £21.55 TOTE £11.20: £5.20, £1.10; EX 22.00 Trifecta £218.90.
**Owner** Mrs Charles Cyzer **Bred** C A Cyzer **Trained** Newmarket, Suffolk

**FOCUS**
The field lacked experience, but the first five should be fine in handicaps, with the winner having some potential. The leader was restrained in front, but still set a good pace.

## 3499 TOTEQUADPOT FOUR PLACES IN FOUR RACES H'CAP 1m 2f 6y
**3:10** (3:12) (Class 3) (0-90,93) 3-Y-O+
**£12,450** (£3,728; £1,864; £932; £466; £234) **Stalls** Low

Form RPR
3-20 **1** **Epic Battle (IRE)**[109] 840 4-9-7 83 KierenFallon 1 89
(George Margarson) *trckd ldrs: pushed along over 5f out: chsd ldr over 1f out: styd on to ld last 50yds* **20/1**

32-5 **2** *nk* **Legal Waves (IRE)**[62] 1608 4-9-3 79 BenCurtis 2 84
(Alan Swinbank) *t.k.h: hld up: hdwy to trck ldrs over 3f out: effrt over 2f out: rdr lost whip appr fnl f: styd on to take 2nd clsng stages* **20/1**

41-0 **3** *shd* **Cactus Valley (IRE)**[60] 1653 5-10-0 90 JamesDoyle 3 95
(Roger Charlton) *s.i.s: hld up in rr: hdwy on outside over 1f out: styd on ins fnl f: tk cl 3rd fnl strides* **7/1**[3]

1131 **4** *1/2* **Hit The Jackpot (IRE)**[3] 3397 5-10-3 93 6ex DanielTudhope 4 97
(David O'Meara) *led: qcknd pce over 2f out: hdd and no ex last 50yds* **15/8**[2]

-106 **5** *3/4* **Correggio**[8] 3254 4-9-1 77 PJMcDonald 5 80
(Micky Hammond) *hld up: hdwy on ins 6f out: sn trcking ldrs: effrt over 2f out: kpt on same pce fnl f* **10/1**

01 **6** *10* **Comedy King (IRE)**[33] 2422 3-8-10 84 AndreaAtzeni 7 68
(Luca Cumani) *trckd ldrs: effrt over 2f out: wknd appr fnl f: eased clsng stages* **13/8**[1]

0066 **7** *2 1/2* **Life And Times (USA)**[8] 3217 6-9-2 78 SilvestreDeSousa 6 57
(Mark Johnston) *w ldr: drvn over 3f out: wknd fnl f: eased towards fin* **12/1**

2m 11.46s (-2.24) **Going Correction** -0.275s/f (Firm)
**WFA** 3 from 4yo+ 12lb **7** Ran SP% **111.7**
Speed ratings (Par 107): **97,96,96,96,95 87,85**
CSF £309.54 TOTE £14.60: £5.70, £3.90; EX 120.50 Trifecta £490.60.
**Owner** Saleh Al Homaizi & Imad Al Sagar **Bred** Castlemartin Sky & Skymarc Farm **Trained** Newmarket, Suffolk

**FOCUS**
In a valuable and well-contested handicap, several of the runners returned to form in a blanket finish. The pace was solid without being excessive.

## 3500 TOTEPOOL PONTEFRACT CASTLE STKS (LISTED RACE) 1m 4f 8y
**3:40** (3:41) (Class 1) 4-Y-O+ **£22,684** (£8,600; £4,304; £2,144; £1,076) **Stalls** Low

Form RPR
-232 **1** **Freedom's Light**[22] 2764 4-8-10 100 WilliamBuick 3 107
(John Gosden) *trckd ldrs: effrt over 2f out: led over 1f out: hld on towards fin* **7/4**[2]

10-4 **2** *1/2* **Waila**[50] 1942 4-8-10 104 RyanMoore 5 106
(Sir Michael Stoute) *hld up in last: effrt over 2f out: swtchd wd over 1f out: sn chsng wnr: styd on: jst hld* **11/8**[1]

61-3 **3** *12* **Familliarity**[47] 2047 4-8-10 80 AndreaAtzeni 2 87
(Roger Varian) *trckd ldrs: effrt over 2f out: swtchd rt ins fnl f: tk modest 3rd nr fin* **25/1**

020 **4** *1/2* **Mirsaale**[15] 2991 4-9-1 98 (p) KierenFallon 1 91
(James Tate) *set sound pce: pushed along over 5f out: hdd over 1f out: sn fdd* **20/1**

2-00 **5** *nk* **Harris Tweed**[43] 2143 7-9-1 109 (p) GeorgeBaker 6 91
(William Haggas) *w ldr: chal over 1f out: fdd fnl f* **7/2**[3]

2m 34.1s (-6.70) **Going Correction** -0.275s/f (Firm) **5** Ran SP% **109.3**
Speed ratings (Par 111): **111,110,102,102,102**
CSF £4.46 TOTE £2.50: £1.30, £1.20; EX 4.90 Trifecta £25.80.
**Owner** George Strawbridge **Bred** George Strawbridge **Trained** Newmarket, Suffolk

**FOCUS**
The first two proved a class above the rest, two of whom have been out of form. With the tempo being set by a pair of horses who have often done well out in front, the race was set up for the more patiently ridden runners.

## 3501 TOTEPOOL.COM PONTEFRACT CUP (H'CAP) 2m 1f 216y
**4:10** (4:10) (Class 4) (0-85,80) 4-Y-O+ **£6,469** (£1,925; £962; £481) **Stalls** Low

Form RPR
62 **1** **Teak (IRE)**[8] 3234 7-9-2 72 (p) StevieDonohoe 8 78
(Ian Williams) *chsd ldrs: effrt on ins over 2f out: chsng ldr over 1f out: sn led: drvn out* **10/1**

-613 **2** *1 1/2* **Rosairlie (IRE)**[23] 2739 6-9-10 80 PJMcDonald 7 85
(Micky Hammond) *hld up in rr: hdwy 4f out: nt clr run on ins over 2f out: styd on to take 2nd last 150yds* **9/1**

14-3 **3** *1 1/4* **Embsay Crag**[30] 2520 8-9-5 75 RussKennemore 9 78
(Philip Kirby) *dwlt: hld up in rr: hdwy 4f out: led over 2f out: hdd over 1f out: kpt on same pce* **7/1**[3]

20-0 **4** *shd* **Bowdler's Magic**[9] 3204 7-9-5 75 (t) JimmyQuinn 10 78
(David Thompson) *s.i.s: hld up in rr: hdwy 3f out: chsng ldrs over 1f out: kpt on same pce* **33/1**

00/0 **5** *2 1/4* **Nafaath (IRE)**[23] 2739 8-9-5 75 GrahamLee 5 75
(Donald McCain) *mid-div: pushed along 7f out: chsng ldrs over 3f out: one pce over 1f out* **20/1**

-000 **6** *5* **Herostatus**[38] 2289 7-9-10 80 KierenFallon 11 77
(Jason Ward) *mid-div: hdwy on outside over 2f out: no imp whn eased ins fnl f* **7/2**[1]

4-60 **7** *1/2* **Riptide**[31] 2482 8-9-7 77 PaulMulrennan 1 71
(Michael Scudamore) *chsd ldrs: drvn to ld 4f out: hdd over 2f out: wknd last 100yds* **9/1**

550- **8** *4 1/2* **Cloudy Spirit**[137] 4873 9-9-8 78 WilliamBuick 3 67
(Andrew Hollinshead) *hld up in rr: drvn and sme hdwy over 4f out: wknd over 1f out* **9/1**

-100 **9** *1 3/4* **New Youmzain (FR)**[31] 2482 5-9-8 78 (p) AndrewMullen 4 65
(Michael Appleby) *t.k.h: led: clr after 5f tl over 5f out: hdd 4f out: lost pl over 2f out* **8/1**

2201 **10** *1 1/4* **Sir Frank Morgan (IRE)**[12] 3078 4-9-7 78 SilvestreDeSousa 2 64
(Mark Johnston) *chsd ldrs: upsides over 2f out: lost pl over 1f out* **5/1**[2]

-060 **11** *30* **Palazzo Bianco**[14] 3034 6-9-8 78 (p) RobertWinston 6 31
(Brian Ellison) *sn chsng ldr: drvn 6f out: lost pl 4f out: sn bhd: t.o whn eased over 1f out* **10/1**

3m 58.67s (2.47) **Going Correction** -0.275s/f (Firm)
**WFA** 4 from 5yo+ 1lb **11** Ran SP% **118.4**
Speed ratings (Par 105): **83,82,81,81,80 78,78,76,75,74 61**
CSF £97.50 CT £679.40 TOTE £13.70: £3.30, £2.10, £2.50; EX 90.70 Trifecta £562.00.
**Owner** Farranamanagh **Bred** Michael Morrissey **Trained** Portway, Worcs

**FOCUS**
Although the other runners ignored the tearaway leader, this was still a good test.

## 3502 TOTEEXACTA PICK THE 1, 2 FILLIES' H'CAP 1m 2f 6y
**4:40** (4:40) (Class 4) (0-85,84) 3-Y-O+ **£6,469** (£1,925; £962; £481) **Stalls** Low

Form RPR
-523 **1** **Bureau (IRE)**[9] 3182 3-8-9 77 SilvestreDeSousa 2 86
(Mark Johnston) *trckd ldrs: drvn to ld appr fnl f: styd on wl* **4/1**[2]

2350 **2** *1 1/4* **Ingleby Symphony (IRE)**[8] 3254 4-9-0 70 RyanMoore 1 76
(Richard Fahey) *hld up towards rr: pushed along 4 f out: hdwy on ins over 1f out: styd on to take 2nd ins fnl f* **7/1**

1411 **3** *1 1/4* **Thurayaat**[33] 2431 3-9-2 84 PaulHanagan 5 88
(Roger Varian) *led: drvn over 2f out: hdd appr fnl f: kpt on same pce* **5/1**

1-35 **4** *1 3/4* **Annawi**[22] 2772 4-9-11 81 DaneO'Neill 6 81
(Henry Candy) *dwlt: hld up in rr: hdwy on outside over 2f out: 4th 1f out: kpt on one pce* **9/2**[3]

06-4 **5** *1 1/4* **By Jupiter**[10] 3141 3-8-4 72 AndreaAtzeni 4 70
(Michael Bell) *hld up towards rr: hdwy to trck ldrs over 3f out: drvn over 2f out: hung lft over 1f out: one pce* **7/1**

-053 **6** *4* **Likelihood (USA)**[12] 3085 3-9-0 82 JamesDoyle 3 77
(John Gosden) *trckd ldrs: pushed along over 2f out: wknd over 1f out: eased clsng stages* **2/1**[1]

2m 12.48s (-1.22) **Going Correction** -0.275s/f (Firm)
**WFA** 3 from 4yo 12lb **6** Ran SP% **113.2**
Speed ratings (Par 102): **93,92,91,89,88 85**
CSF £31.04 TOTE £6.20: £2.90, £3.40; EX 34.30 Trifecta £144.50.
**Owner** Sheikh Hamdan bin Mohammed Al Maktoum **Bred** Darley **Trained** Middleham Moor, N Yorks

**FOCUS**
A decent mid-class fillies' race, run at a medium gallop.

## 3503 TOTETRIFECTA AVAILABLE ON ALL RACES H'CAP 6f
**5:10** (5:11) (Class 5) (0-75,75) 3-Y-O **£3,881** (£1,155; £577; £288) **Stalls** Low

Form RPR
-052 **1** **Foxy Clarets (IRE)**[31] 2474 3-9-7 75 (b) RyanMoore 5 87
(Richard Fahey) *racd wd: mde all: drvn clr over 1f out: styd on wl* **11/4**[2]

0-03 **2** *5* **Makin The Rules (IRE)**[4] 3369 3-9-4 75 IanBrennan(3) 2 71
(John Quinn) *chsd ldrs: 2nd over 1f out: no imp* **11/8**[1]

-343 **3** *3 1/4* **Lendal Bridge**[26] 2657 3-8-4 58 BarryMcHugh 4 44
(Tony Coyle) *chsd ldrs: drvn over 2f out: one pce over 1f out* **8/1**

2-06 **4** *2* **Red Cossack (CAN)**[11] 3114 3-9-2 70 DaneO'Neill 1 49
(Paul Webber) *dwlt: in rr and hung rt: effrt over 2f out: sddle slipped and fdd over 1f out* **8/1**

4-32 **5** *1/2* **My Inspiration (IRE)**[22] 2759 3-9-7 75 DavidAllan 3 53
(Tim Easterby) *chsd ldrs: effrt over 2f out: wknd fnl f* **9/2**[3]

1m 17.05s (0.15) **Going Correction** -0.275s/f (Firm) **5** Ran SP% **109.2**
Speed ratings (Par 99): **88,81,77,74,73**
CSF £6.85 TOTE £3.00: £1.70, £1.70; EX 8.60 Trifecta £33.80.
**Owner** Hazel Tattersall & G Hyde **Bred** Simon Holt David Thorpe & R J Beggan **Trained** Musley Bank, N Yorks

**FOCUS**
This was won with remarkable ease for a race of this type, but the bare result looks a bit deceptive.
T/Plt: £335.40 to a £1 stake. Pool: £67,980.92 - 147.95 winning tickets. T/Qpdt: £109.90 to a £1 stake. Pool: £3,594.68 - 24.20 winning tickets. WG

3504 - 3510a (Foreign Racing) - See Raceform Interactive

# DORTMUND (R-H)
Sunday, June 22

**OFFICIAL GOING: Turf: good**

## 3511a GROSSER PREIS DER WIRTSCHAFT (GROUP 3) (3YO+) (TURF) 1m 165y
**4:10** (12:00) 3-Y-O+
**£26,666** (£9,166; £4,583; £2,500; £1,666; £1,250)

RPR
**1** **Amaron**[52] 1908 5-9-5 0 FabienLefebvre 6 110
(Andreas Lowe, Germany) *trckd ldr: chal gng strly into st: rdn to ld 2f out: strly pressed fnl f: kpt on wl and asserted towards fin* **6/4**[1]

2 *1* **Simba**[231] 7726 3-8-7 0 ow1........................ EPedroza 7 106
(A Wohler, Germany) *t.k.h: midfield in tch: rdn 2f out: r.o and wnt 2nd towards fin: nt quite pce of wnr* **32/5**

3 *nk* **Red Dubawi (IRE)**[24] 2715 6-9-5 0........................ EddyHardouin 3 107
(Frau Erika Mader, Germany) *stdd and hld up in last: pushed along and hdwy on wd outside fr 2f out: wnt 2nd jst over 1f out: edgd rt and chal fnl f: kpt on but hld towards fin and dropped to 3rd* **43/5**

4 *nk* **Peace At Last (IRE)**[24] 2715 4-9-1 0........................ FabriceVeron 4 102
(H-A Pantall, France) *t.k.h: hld up in tch on inner: rdn and angled out over 2f out: sltly outpcd whn squeezed for room jst over 1f out: kpt on wl fnl f and wnt 4th post: nvr able to chal* **9/2**[3]

5 *nk* **Szoff (GER)**[32] 4-9-1 0........................ FilipMinarik 1 102
(Jean-Pierre Carvalho, Germany) *led: strly pressed into st and sn rdn: hdd 2f out: styd on same pce and sn hld: dropped to 5th post* **139/10**

6 *1/2* **Neatico (GER)**[28] 2587 7-9-10 0........................ AdriedeVries 8 110
(P Schiergen, Germany) *midfield in tch on outer: rdn into st: effrt to chal 2f out: outpcd by wnr fnl f: kpt on but wl hld* **12/5**[2]

7 *5* **King's Hall**[24] 2715 6-9-1 0........................(b) SHellyn 5 90
(M Figge, Germany) *hld up in tch on outer: in rr and rdn whn squeezed out by rivals and snatched up 2f out: nt rcvr and sn btn: wknd* **39/1**

8 *hd* **Nadelwald**[35] 2377 3-8-6 0........................ MrVinzenzSchiergen 2 90
(P Schiergen, Germany) *t.k.h: prom on inner: rdn over 2f out: no ex and btn over 1f out: wknd fnl f* **8/1**

1m 49.23s (109.23)
**WFA** 3 from 4yo+ 11lb **8** Ran SP% **131.8**
WIN (incl. 10 euro stake): 25. PLACES: 14, 16, 21. SF: 205.
**Owner** Gestut Winterhauch **Bred** Genesis Green Stud Ltd **Trained** Germany

# FRAUENFELD (R-H)
Sunday, June 22

**OFFICIAL GOING: Turf: good**

## 3512a SWISS DERBY (CONDITIONS) (3YO COLTS & FILLIES) (TURF) 1m 4f
**3:15** (12:00) 3-Y-O **£32,432** (£12,972; £9,729; £6,486; £3,243)

RPR

1 **Oak Harbour**[28] 2585 3-9-2 0........................ MaximeGuyon 10 95
(A De Royer-Dupre, France) **9/10**[1]

2 *hd* **Firestorm (GER)**[225] 3-9-2 0........................ DanielePorcu 2 95
(P Schiergen, Germany) **16/1**

3 *nk* **Master Of Finance (IRE)**[15] 3003 3-9-2 0........................ IoritzMendizabal 7 94
(Mark Johnston) *t.k.h: trckd ldr on outer in share of 2nd: rdn to press ldr fr 1 1/2f out: kpt on u.p fnl f: no ex fnl 50yds* **19/5**[2]

4 *2 1/2* **Filou (SWI)**[252] 7235 3-9-2 0........................(b) OlivierPeslier 1 90
(P Schaerer, Switzerland) **49/10**[3]

5 *1/2* **Cazador (IRE)** 3-9-2 0........................ MSuerland 8 89
(A Wohler, Germany) **107/10**

6 *nk* **Semilla (FR)**[22] 3-8-13 0........................ FredericSpanu 6 86
(A Schaerer, Switzerland) **118/10**

7 *nk* **Ajasam** 3-9-2 0........................ OlivierPlacais 3 88
(M Weiss, Switzerland) **134/10**

8 *1 3/4* **Archandel Michael (CZE)** 3-9-2 0........................ ThomasMessina 4 86
(Christina Bucher, Switzerland) **239/10**

9 *1/2* **Hard Man (FR)** 3-9-2 0........................ Christophe-PatriceLemaire 5 85
(P Schaerer, Switzerland) **11/2**

10 *7* **Jim (GER)**[70] 3-9-2 0........................ AurelienLemaitre 9 74
(Christina Bucher, Switzerland) **103/10**

2m 31.33s (151.33) **10** Ran SP% **147.9**
PARI-MUTUEL (all including 1 chf stakes): WIN 1.90; PLACE 1.70, 2.60, 1.60; SF 28.30.
**Owner** P Baumgartner **Bred** All Along Llc **Trained** Chantilly, France

# 3047 SAN SIRO (R-H)
Sunday, June 22

**OFFICIAL GOING: Turf: good to soft**

## 3513a PREMIO MARIO INCISA DELLA ROCCHETTA (GROUP 3) (3YO FILLIES) (TURF) 1m 2f
**4:20** (12:00) 3-Y-O **£29,166** (£12,833; £7,000; £3,500)

RPR

1 **So Many Shots (IRE)**[28] 2590 3-8-11 0........................ CristianDemuro 1 95
(Stefano Botti, Italy) *w.w in tch: shkn up to ld 2 1/2f out: drvn and sn clr ent fnl f: comf* **51/50**[1]

2 *4* **Oryetta (USA)**[46] 3-8-11 0........................ MircoDemuro 7 87
(G Botti, France) *in rr: hdwy to chse ldr over 2f out: kpt on at one pce fnl f: no ch w wnr* **101/20**

3 *5 1/2* **Francine (IRE)**[56] 1780 3-8-11 0........................ DPerovic 5 76
(Stefano Botti, Italy) *w.w towards rr: rdn and effrt 2f out: kpt on u.p to go 3rd ins fnl f: nvr on terms* **29/1**

4 *1 1/2* **Donna Prassede (ITY)**[28] 2590 3-8-11 0........................ CFiocchi 3 73
(Stefano Botti, Italy) *settled in 5th on outer: rdn and nt qckn over 2f out: plugged on ins fnl f: nvr threatened ldrs* **127/10**

5 *1 3/4* **Finidaprest (IRE)**[28] 2590 3-8-11 0........................ DarioVargiu 4 70
(B Grizzetti, Italy) *tk a v t.k.h: led: hdd 2 1/2f out: grad lft bhd by ldrs* **51/20**[2]

6 *1/2* **Albadorata (IRE)**[84] 3-8-11 0........................ LManiezzi 2 69
(Gianluca Bietolini, Italy) *chsd ldng pair: 5th between horses 1/2-way: rdn along to hold pl fr 2 1/2f out: wknd fnl f* **222/10**

7 *2 1/2* **Legal Trip (IRE)** 3-8-11 0........................ FabioBranca 6
(Stefano Botti, Italy) *pressed ldr: lost pl 2f out: sn btn* **19/5**[3]

2m 3.5s (-3.20) **7** Ran SP% **130.0**
WIN (incl. 1 euro stake): 2.02. PLACES: 1.38, 2.20. DF: 5.56.
**Owner** Dioscuri Srl **Bred** Sandro Garavelli **Trained** Italy

# 3173 CHEPSTOW (L-H)
Monday, June 23

**OFFICIAL GOING: Good to firm (8.8)**
Wind: slight behind Weather: cloudy but warm

## 3514 32RED CASINO MEDIAN AUCTION MAIDEN STKS 1m 4f 23y
**2:00** (2:02) (Class 5) 3-5-Y-O **£2,587** (£770; £384; £192) **Stalls** Low

Form RPR

-034 1 **Mabdhool (IRE)**[16] 2998 3-8-13 67........................ DaneO'Neill 4 73
(Marcus Tregoning) *led 1f: trckd ldr: pushed along to ld narrowly 3f out: rdn and a jst holding persistent chalr after* **3/1**[2]

6-03 2 *1/2* **Norse Light**[23] 2773 3-8-13 79........................ JimCrowley 5 72
(Ralph Beckett) *led after 1f tl narrowly hdd 3f out: kpt on wl u.p after but a jst being hld* **4/6**[1]

3 *2* **Cape Victoria** 3-8-5 0........................ OisinMurphy(3) 1 64
(Andrew Balding) *green in preliminaries: dwlt: sn in tch in last: gained a pl after 4f: rdn and slty outpcd by ldng pair 3f out: kpt on same pce and no real imp* **5/1**[3]

4 *25* **Magic Magnolia (IRE)**[50] 2000 3-8-8 0........................ JohnFahy 2 24
(Mark Gillard) *racd in 3rd tl relegated to last after 4f: rdn and outpcd over 4f out: lost tch 2f out: t.o* **50/1**

2m 40.86s (1.86) **Going Correction** -0.225s/f (Firm) **4** Ran SP% **103.6**
Speed ratings (Par 103): **84,83,82,65**
CSF £5.04 TOTE £3.70; EX 4.40 Trifecta £6.70.
**Owner** Hamdan Al Maktoum **Bred** Woodcote Stud Ltd **Trained** Whitsbury, Hants
■ Rule 4 of 5p in the pound applies to all bets; Withdrawn: En Reve

**FOCUS**
Not much pace for this uncompetitive maiden. Muddling, weak form.

## 3515 32RED ON THE APP STORE H'CAP 1m 2f 36y
**2:30** (2:31) (Class 5) (0-75,75) 4-Y-0+ **£2,587** (£770; £384; £192) **Stalls** Low

Form RPR

0560 1 **Jacob Cats**[17] 2959 5-9-7 75........................(v) JimCrowley 6 85
(William Knight) *trckd ldrs: wnt 2nd over 3f out: shkn up to ld over 2f out: sn rdn clr and in command* **2/1**[1]

5-41 2 *5* **Jebril (FR)**[23] 2770 4-9-4 75........................ MatthewLawson(3) 5 75
(Jonathan Portman) *racd keenly: w ldr: led 4f out tl rdn and hdd over 2f out: sn outpcd by wnr but kpt on to hold 2nd* **2/1**[1]

5433 3 *2* **St Paul De Vence (IRE)**[19] 2882 4-9-3 71........................(b) LukeMorris 3 67
(Paul Cole) *broke wl: hld up in 4th: niggled along 5f out: wnt 3rd over 2f out: sn drvn: nt qckn u.p and a being hld* **11/4**[2]

0-00 4 *3 3/4* **Bold Cross (IRE)**[9] 3226 11-8-8 65........................ OisinMurphy(3) 2 54
(Edward Bevan) *hld up in last: rdn 3f out: one pce and no real imp* **12/1**[3]

1000 5 *24* **Hill Fort**[85] 1196 4-9-2 70........................ BenCurtis 1 13
(Ronald Harris) *sn tk narrow ld: rdn and hdd 4f out: wknd over 2f out: eased over 1f out: t.o* **12/1**[3]

2m 7.22s (-3.38) **Going Correction** -0.225s/f (Firm) **5** Ran SP% **108.7**
Speed ratings (Par 103): **104,100,98,95,76**
CSF £6.09 TOTE £2.70: £1.10, £1.50; EX 5.80 Trifecta £11.10.
**Owner** Canisbay Bloodstock **Bred** Highclere Stud **Trained** Patching, W Sussex

**FOCUS**
A fair handicap for the grade run at a steady pace, in a relatively quick time. The winner is rated back to last season's form.

## 3516 32RED CLASSIFIED STKS 1m 14y
**3:05** (3:05) (Class 5) 3-Y-O **£2,587** (£770; £384; £192) **Stalls** Centre

Form RPR

-004 1 *nk* **Go For Broke**[11] 3145 3-9-0 68........................ PatDobbs 4 73
(Richard Hannon) *chsd ldrs: rdn to ld narrowly 2f out: hdd 100yds out: jst hld* **11/4**[2]

54-4 2 *nse* **Serena Grae**[82] 1237 3-9-0 68........................ MartinDwyer 3 73
(Marcus Tregoning) *t.k.h: racd keenly: trckd ldrs: rdn and ev ch over 2f out: sn hung lft: kpt on u.p but jst hld* **12/1**

5-06 3 *1 1/4* **Canova (IRE)**[52] 1913 3-9-0 69........................ DaneO'Neill 6 70
(Roger Charlton) *hld up in 4th: clsd 3f out: drvn and ev ch over 2f out tl no ex fnl 100yds* **5/1**

2515 4 *1 3/4* **Khee Society**[7] 3316 3-9-0 66........................ JimCrowley 5 66
(David Evans) *hld up: rdn over 2f out: one pce and nvr able to chal* **2/1**[1]

-010 5 *1 1/4* **Zambeasy**[17] 2968 3-8-11 67........................ OisinMurphy(3) 1 63
(Philip Hide) *wnt to s early: led: isolated towards far side fr 1/2-way: rdn and hdd 2f out: wknd 1f out* **4/1**[3]

6-66 D **Charlie Wells (IRE)**[21] 2847 3-9-0 63........................ JohnFahy 7 74
(Eve Johnson Houghton) *hld up: hdwy 3f out: sn drvn: r.o to ld 100yds out: hld on* **16/1**

1m 32.8s (-3.40) **Going Correction** -0.225s/f (Firm) **6** Ran SP% **110.2**
Speed ratings (Par 99): **107,107,106,104,103 108**
CSF £57.36 TOTE £21.10: £6.40, £1.70; EX 98.30 Trifecta £455.00.
**Owner** Lady Whent **Bred** Raffin Bloodstock **Trained** East Everleigh, Wilts

**FOCUS**
The pace was steady for this tight contest. The field raced up the centre and the winner is rated back to his debut form.

## 3517 32RED.COM MAIDEN STKS 1m 14y
**3:40** (3:41) (Class 5) 3-Y-O+ **£2,587** (£770; £384; £192) **Stalls** Centre

Form RPR

2-3 1 **Potentate (IRE)**[60] 1681 3-9-3 77........................ PatDobbs 3 81
(Richard Hannon) *mde all: drvn over 1f out: a holding runner-up fnl f* **2/1**[2]

24-4 2 *1 1/4* **Hesbaan (IRE)**[16] 2996 3-9-3 75........................ DaneO'Neill 4 78
(Marcus Tregoning) *trckd ldrs: wnt 2nd over 3f out to 2f out: chsd wnr again early ins fnl f: r.o u.p* **3/1**[3]

3 3 *5* **New Identity (IRE)**[25] 2690 3-9-3 0........................ PatCosgrave 6 70
(Denis Coakley) *t.k.h: trckd ldrs: rdn and wnt 2nd 2f out: wknd early ins fnl f* **1/1**[1]

4 *12* **Ronnie Rockcake**[11] 4-9-13 0........................ JohnFahy 7 41
(Ben Pauling) *s.i.s: towards rr: clsd 1/2-way: drvn over 2f out: one pce and no ch w principals after* **33/1**

6 5 *7* **Forceful Beacon**[6] 3332 4-9-13 0........................ SteveDrowne 2 25
(Tony Carroll) *t.k.h: cl up: rdn and outpcd by ldrs over 3f out: sn no ch: wknd over 1f out* **50/1**

0 6 *23* **Planet Rock**[18] 2917 3-8-10 0........................ DavidParkes(7) 5
(Keiran Burke) *hld up in rr: rdn and outpcd over 4f out: qckly lost tch: t.o* **66/1**

7 4 1/2 **Zand Man** 4-9-10 0..............(t) OisinMurphy(3) 1
(Milton Bradley) *t.k.h in rr: rdn along after 3f: qckly lost tch: t.o* **50/1**

1m 33.91s (-2.29) **Going Correction** -0.225s/f (Firm)
**WFA** 3 from 4yo 10lb **7 Ran SP% 116.7**
Speed ratings (Par 103): **102,100,95,83,76 53,49**
CSF £8.61 TOTE £2.20: £1.10, £2.90; EX 8.60 Trifecta £12.20.
**Owner** Saleh Al Homaizi & Imad Al Sagar **Bred** Mrs Celine Collins **Trained** East Everleigh, Wilts
■ Stewards' Enquiry : Dane O'Neill two-day ban: use of whip (7-8 July)

**FOCUS**
Not much pace for this maiden which was dominated by the 3yos. The winner is rated to form.

## 3518 32RED.COM H'CAP 7f 16y
4:10 (4:12) (Class 5) (0-70,70) 3-Y-O **£2,587** (£770; £384; £192) **Stalls** Centre

Form RPR
0-15 1 **Frangipanni (IRE)**[33] 2470 3-9-3 **66**.............. GeorgeBaker 2 78+
(Roger Charlton) *hld up towards rr: rdn over 2f out: stmbld and lurchd lft 1f out: r.o to ld fnl 50yds: cosily* **3/1**[1]
02-5 2 *nk* **Half Way**[48] 2058 3-8-12 **66**.............. AmyScott(5) 10 74
(Henry Candy) *s.i.s: hdwy to join ldr after 2f: def ld 4f out: rdn over 2f out: edgd rt ins fnl f: hdd fnl 50yds* **8/1**
0-10 3 *2* **Comanchero (IRE)**[10] 3198 3-8-11 **63**.............. OisinMurphy(3) 9 66
(Andrew Balding) *chsd ldrs: rdn and sltly outpcd 3f out: renewed effrt to chse ldr briefly ent fnl f: one pce after* **8/1**
6-40 4 *2* **Concrete Mac**[39] 2278 3-9-7 **70**.............. PatDobbs 5 68
(Hughie Morrison) *led 3f: styd cl up: lost 2nd ent fnl f: one pce* **7/1**
4-00 5 *5* **Cameley Dawn**[56] 1792 3-8-8 **57**.............. MartinLane 4 42
(Malcolm Saunders) *prom: rdn over 3f out: sn outpcd by ldrs: kpt on but no threat after* **25/1**
5024 6 *1 3/4* **Tubeanie (IRE)**[13] 3087 3-8-13 **62**.............. LukeMorris 3 42
(Clive Cox) *mid-div: pushed along over 4f out: kpt on one pce u.p fnl 2f* **10/1**
30-6 7 *1/2* **Big Boned (USA)**[79] 1315 3-9-3 **66**.............. JamieSpencer 8 45
(Ed Dunlop) *wnt lft and bmpd rival s: hld up in rr: rdn and clsng whn hmpd 1f out: nt rcvr and wknd rapidly* **10/1**
0-22 8 *2 1/4* **Fantasy Justifier (IRE)**[20] 2870 3-9-5 **68**.............. SteveDrowne 6 41
(Ronald Harris) *t.k.h in mid-div: pushed along 2f out: unable qck: wknd fnl f* **5/1**[3]
-062 9 *2 1/2* **Llyrical**[11] 3145 3-9-0 **63**.............. DaneO'Neill 1 30
(Derek Haydn Jones) *chsd ldrs: rdn over 2f out: wknd over 1f out* **9/2**[2]
034 10 *4* **Border Guard**[13] 3074 3-9-1 **64**.............. BenCurtis 7 20
(Milton Bradley) *wnt to post early: bmpd s: rdn over 3f out: a towards rr* **33/1**

1m 21.67s (-1.53) **Going Correction** -0.225s/f (Firm) **10 Ran SP% 119.5**
Speed ratings (Par 99): **99,98,96,94,88 86,85,83,80,75**
CSF £28.54 CT £182.92 TOTE £5.10: £1.90, £1.50, £4.20; EX 34.80 Trifecta £189.90.
**Owner** Lady Rothschild **Bred** Kincorth Investments Inc **Trained** Beckhampton, Wilts

**FOCUS**
A decent pace for this open handicap. The winner is rated a bit better than the bare form.

## 3519 32RED FREE £10 BONUS H'CAP 6f 16y
4:45 (4:46) (Class 5) (0-75,75) 3-Y-O+ **£2,587** (£770; £384; £192) **Stalls** Centre

Form RPR
0504 1 **See The Storm**[70] 1487 6-9-1 **65**.............. CharlesBishop(3) 2 73
(Ian Williams) *hld up: hdwy over 3f out: shkn up to ld early ins fnl f: r.o wl* **7/2**[3]
2060 2 *1/2* **Top Cop**[13] 3088 5-9-11 **72**..............(be) SteveDrowne 1 78
(Ronald Harris) *trckd ldr: let down to ld 1f out but qckly hdd: r.o u.p* **10/1**
006- 3 *1 3/4* **Fair Ranger**[221] 7879 3-9-7 **75**.............. PatDobbs 4 74
(Richard Hannon) *led early: chsd ldrs: rdn over 2f out: kpt on fnl f* **3/1**[2]
3523 4 *1/2* **Broadway Ranger (IRE)**[23] 2759 3-9-4 **72**.............. DaneO'Neill 7 69
(Charles Hills) *sn led: pushed along 2f out: hdd 1f out: one pce and edgd rt ins fnl f* **6/1**
2204 5 *3/4* **Indian Affair**[11] 3150 4-8-13 **63**.............. OisinMurphy(3) 5 60
(Milton Bradley) *chsd ldrs: rdn and outpcd 3f out: kpt on same pce and no threat after* **11/4**[1]
6-10 6 *1 1/4* **For Ayman**[19] 2886 3-9-2 **70**..............(t) GeorgeBaker 3 61
(Seamus Durack) *s.i.s: a last: detached after 2f: rdn 2f out: sme hdwy fnl f* **9/2**

1m 10.84s (-1.16) **Going Correction** -0.225s/f (Firm)
**WFA** 3 from 4yo+ 7lb **6 Ran SP% 115.4**
Speed ratings (Par 103): **98,97,95,94,93 91**
CSF £36.69 TOTE £5.70: £2.70, £4.10; EX 34.30 Trifecta £159.00.
**Owner** Keating Bradley Fold Ltd **Bred** D R Botterill **Trained** Portway, Worcs

**FOCUS**
A fair handicap run at a strong pace. The runner-up helps the standard.

## 3520 32REDPOKER.COM H'CAP 5f 16y
5:15 (5:15) (Class 6) (0-60,57) 3-Y-O+ **£1,940** (£577; £288; £144) **Stalls** Centre

Form RPR
4435 1 **Picc Of Burgau**[9] 3231 4-9-8 **55**.............. GeorgeBaker 6 70+
(Geoffrey Deacon) *hld up in mid-div: nudged along to cl gng wl over 1f out: qcknd to ld 75yds out: comf* **7/4**[1]
4404 2 *1 1/4* **Volcanic Dust (IRE)**[4] 3392 6-9-3 **53**..............(t) MichaelJMMurphy(3) 8 61
(Milton Bradley) *w ldr: def advantage over 1f out: r.o u.p: hdd 75yds out: no ch w wnr* **12/1**
600 3 *2 1/4* **Spray Tan**[34] 2435 4-9-7 **54**.............. PatDobbs 5 54
(Tony Carroll) *trckd ldrs: rdn and ev ch over 1f out: unable qck ins fnl f* **5/1**[2]
0-60 4 *2* **Ryan Style (IRE)**[148] 351 8-8-11 **49**.............. ShirleyTeasdale(5) 2 42
(Lisa Williamson) *in tch towards rr: pushed along over 2f out: styd on fnl f: nvr able to chal* **10/1**
04-5 5 *1/2* **Monty Fay (IRE)**[10] 3178 5-8-12 **45**.............. PatCosgrave 10 36
(Derek Haydn Jones) *chsd ldrs: rdn over 2f out: kpt on one pce* **6/1**[3]
-050 6 *1 1/4* **Lady Rain**[26] 2667 5-8-12 **45**.............. BenCurtis 7 31
(Ronald Harris) *s.i.s: sn rdn along and outpcd in rr: styng on whn n.m.r ent fnl f: nvr nr to chal* **33/1**
0403 7 *1* **Spic 'n Span**[21] 2830 9-8-13 **46**..............(p) SteveDrowne 3 29+
(Ronald Harris) *taken to post early: fly-leapt s: rdn over 2f out: a towards rr* **5/1**[2]
1110 8 *nk* **Louis Vee (IRE)**[44] 2174 6-9-7 **57**..............(t) DeclanBates(3) 12 39
(Roy Brotherton) *chsd ldrs: rdn over 2f out: wknd over 1f out* **12/1**
5203 9 *20* **Island Legend (IRE)**[13] 3077 8-8-13 **49**..............(b) OisinMurphy(3) 4
(Milton Bradley) *narrow ldr: rdn over 2f out: hdd and hung lft over 1f out: wknd qckly: virtually p.u ins fnl f: t.o* **9/1**

58.86s (-0.44) **Going Correction** -0.225s/f (Firm) **9 Ran SP% 121.4**
Speed ratings (Par 101): **94,92,88,85,84 82,80,80,48**
CSF £27.15 CT £95.70 TOTE £3.30: £1.40, £2.00, £2.10; EX 26.50 Trifecta £178.10.
**Owner** The Outta Lunch Partnership **Bred** Mrs G S Rees **Trained** Compton, Berks

**FOCUS**
A modest handicap run at a decent pace. The winner was the least exposed and the runner-up sets the standard.
T/Plt: £436.80 to a £1 stake. Pool: £52,883.37 - 88.37 winning units. T/Qpdt: £51.60 to a £1 stake. Pool: £5239.67 - 75.00 winning units. RL

# 3467 LINGFIELD (L-H)
Monday, June 23

**OFFICIAL GOING: Standard**
Wind: Nil Weather: Fine

## 3521 32RED AMATEUR RIDERS' (S) STKS 1m 4f (P)
2:15 (2:15) (Class 6) 4-Y-O+ **£1,871** (£580; £290; £145) **Stalls** Low

Form RPR
000- 1 **Investissement**[17] 4233 8-10-12 **84**..............(p) MrSWalker 8 71
(Charlie Longsdon) *a.p: chsd ldr over 4f out: led over 2f out: pushed clr fr over 1f out* **1/1**[1]
/06- 2 *4 1/2* **Edgeworth (IRE)**[295] 4195 8-10-7 **59**..............(p) MissMeganNicholls(5) 3 64
(David Bridgwater) *a.p: chsd ldr over 6f out tl over 5f out: hdd over 2f out: styd on same pce fr over 1f out* **14/1**
0/00 3 *10* **Osgood**[18] 2916 7-10-9 **59**..............(v) MissHayleyMoore(3) 7 48
(Gary Moore) *hld up: hdwy 4f out: rdn over 2f out: wknd over 1f out* **10/1**
0-03 4 *2 3/4* **Evergreen Forest (IRE)**[18] 2916 6-10-7 **61**..............(b) MrLKilgarriff(5) 9 44
(Natalie Lloyd-Beavis) *chsd ldrs: rdn over 3f out: wknd over 1f out* **9/2**[2]
1030 5 *2 1/4* **Cabuchon (GER)**[7] 3310 7-10-10 **61**..............(t) MissKFBegley(7) 1 45
(David Evans) *hld up: hdwy 4f out: wknd 2f out* **5/1**[3]
6 *8* **Lion On The Prowl (IRE)**[35] 10-10-12 **0**..............(tp) MrsAlexDunn 10 27
(Alexandra Dunn) *dwlt: plld hrd and hdwy to join ldr after 1f: pushed along and lost pl over 6f out: wknd 4f out* **20/1**
0000 7 *2 1/2* **Ghostwing**[9] 3230 7-10-7 **48**.............. MissEllaSmith(5) 5 23
(Ralph J Smith) *sn led: hdd over 5f out: wknd over 3f out* **25/1**
3050 8 *13* **Another Journey**[11] 3134 5-10-5 **40**..............(e[1]) MrCEllingham(7) 2
(Lisa Williamson) *trckd ldrs: racd keenly: lost pl after 2f: wknd over 5f out* **66/1**
6-00 9 *3/4* **Heading To First**[27] 570 7-10-7 **40**.............. MissMBryant(5) 4
(Paddy Butler) *hld up: wknd over 4f out* **50/1**
/060 10 *44* **Royal Mizar (SPA)**[9] 3233 4-10-12 **54**.............. MissZoeLilly 6
(Alastair Lidderdale) *dwlt: sn outpcd* **16/1**

2m 32.89s (-0.11) **Going Correction** +0.075s/f (Slow) **10 Ran SP% 118.5**
Speed ratings (Par 101): **103,100,93,91,90 84,83,74,73,44**
CSF £17.45 TOTE £2.00: £1.80, £3.60, £1.60; EX 12.90 Trifecta £108.00.Investissement was bought by Lee Carter for 4000gns.
**Owner** Countrywide Vehicle Rentals Taxi Hire **Bred** Wertheimer Et Frere **Trained** Over Norton, Oxon

**FOCUS**
Not much to dwell on in this uncompetitive event. The gallop was an ordinary one and the winner raced close to the far rail in the straight. He was a class above and didn't need to be near even last year's form.

## 3522 32RED CASINO H'CAP 5f 6y(P)
2:45 (2:47) (Class 5) (0-75,75) 3-Y-O **£3,234** (£962; £481; £240) **Stalls** Low

Form RPR
6254 1 **Minley**[24] 2717 3-9-5 **73**..............(v[1]) FrederikTylicki 1 75
(Charlie Fellowes) *trckd ldrs: rdn over 1f out: r.o to ld wl ins fnl f* **5/4**[2]
5365 2 *3/4* **Artemis (IRE)**[9] 3228 3-8-2 **56**.............. JimmyQuinn 4 55
(Conrad Allen) *trckd ldrs: racd keenly: rdn over 1f out: ev ch ins fnl f: r.o* **8/1**[3]
1650 3 *nk* **Thataboy (IRE)**[17] 2945 3-9-7 **75**..............(t) RichardKingscote 2 73
(Tom Dascombe) *led: shkn up over 1f out: rdn and hdd wl ins fnl f* **1/1**[1]
050 4 *1* **Khelfan**[31] 2525 3-8-2 **56** oh11.............. NickyMackay 5 51
(Martin Smith) *sn pushed along in rr: rdn over 1f out: r.o ins fnl f: nt rch ldrs* **33/1**
0-00 5 *4 1/2* **Ellingham (IRE)**[35] 2397 3-8-2 **56** oh1.............. DavidProbert 3 34
(Christine Dunnett) *chsd ldr tl rdn wl over 1f out: wknd ins fnl f* **33/1**
5530 6 *10* **Dove Mountain (IRE)**[12] 3114 3-8-11 **65**.............. TedDurcan 6 7
(Gary Brown) *sn outpcd* **25/1**

59.8s (1.00) **Going Correction** +0.075s/f (Slow) **6 Ran SP% 115.3**
Speed ratings (Par 99): **95,93,93,91,84 68**
CSF £11.44 TOTE £2.30: £1.10, £3.40; EX 10.60 Trifecta £15.70.
**Owner** J H Richmond-Watson **Bred** C J Mills **Trained** Newmarket, Suffolk

**FOCUS**
A fair handicap in which none of the runners came here in top form. The gallop was sound and the winner raced against the far rail in the straight. The time was slow and this is unconvincing form.

## 3523 ALL NEW 32REDSPORT.COM CLAIMING STKS 6f 1y(P)
3:20 (3:21) (Class 5) 3-Y-O **£3,234** (£962; £481; £240) **Stalls** Low

Form RPR
6402 1 **Kodafine (IRE)**[4] 3388 3-8-2 **65**.............. DavidProbert 2 64
(David Evans) *chsd ldr: shkn up over 1f out: r.o to ld wl ins fnl f* **4/1**[2]
0221 2 *nk* **Black Vale (IRE)**[4] 3388 3-8-4 **67**..............(t) CamHardie(7) 1 72
(Phil McEntee) *led: shkn up over 1f out: edgd rt: hdd and unable qck wl ins fnl f* **5/6**[1]
34 3 *1 3/4* **Skinny Love**[16] 2994 3-8-10 **68**..............(p) AdamBeschizza 8 65
(Zoe Davison) *chsd ldrs: rdn over 2f out: styd on same pce ins fnl f* **8/1**[3]
1563 4 *3 1/4* **Coiste Bodhar (IRE)**[4] 3388 3-8-8 **66**..............(p) ThomasBrown(3) 5 56
(Joseph Tuite) *prom: hmpd over 5f out: rdn over 2f out: styd on same pce fr over 1f out* **10/1**
1105 5 *1 1/4* **Intense Feeling (IRE)**[4] 3388 3-7-13 **62**.............. NoelGarbutt(5) 6 45
(Lee Carter) *hld up: rdn over 1f out: nvr on terms* **10/1**
00 6 *1* **Calamity Jane**[30] 2560 3-8-4 **0**..............[1] SilvestreDeSousa 7 42
(Ralph Beckett) *s.i.s: hld up: rdn over 1f out: n.d: eased nr fin* **10/1**
5044 7 *1 1/4* **El Duque**[4] 3388 3-8-2 **64**..............(p) RyanWhile(5) 3 41
(Bill Turner) *prom: nt clr run over 5f out: rdn whn hmpd over 2f out: sn wknd* **25/1**
00 8 *62* **Jamie Lee's Girl**[34] 2418 3-7-12 **0** ow1.............. PhilipPrince(5) 4
(David Flood) *s.s: outpcd* **66/1**

1m 11.85s (-0.05) **Going Correction** +0.075s/f (Slow) **8 Ran SP% 118.3**
Speed ratings (Par 99): **103,102,100,95,94 92,91,8**
.Black Vale was claimed by Mr R Smith for £7,000.\n\x\x Skinny Love was claimed Mr K Burke for £9,000.
**Owner** Mrs E Evans **Bred** Tally-Ho Stud **Trained** Pandy, Monmouths
■ Stewards' Enquiry : Adam Beschizza two-day ban: careless riding (7-8 July)
Thomas Brown three-day ban: careless riding (9, 10, 14 July)

**FOCUS**
A modest claimer and, although the gallop was sound throughout, it proved difficult to make ground from behind. The winner came down the centre and the first three finished clear. Five of these, including the 1-2, ran in a C&D seller last week.

## 3524 32RED.COM/BRITISH STALLION STUDS EBF MAIDEN STKS 6f 1y(P)
3:55 (3:55) (Class 5) 2-Y-O £3,234 (£962; £481; £240) Stalls Low

Form RPR
52 1 **L'Etacq**[10] 3181 2-9-5 0 SeanLevey 5 72
(Richard Hannon) *chsd ldrs: rdn over 1f out: r.o to ld nr fin* **5/4**[1]
53 2 *hd* **Anonymous John (IRE)**[9] 3215 2-9-5 0 MartinHarley 7 71
(David Evans) *chsd ldr 5f out: rdn to ld over 1f out: edgd lft: hdd nr fin* **11/4**[2]
6 3 *1* **Big Chill (IRE)**[51] 1936 2-9-5 0 JamesDoyle 6 69
(Charles Hills) *hld up: hdwy u.p and hung lft fr over 1f out: r.o* **8/1**
30 4 *1* **Sportlobster (IRE)**[68] 1504 2-9-5 0 RichardKingscote 4 65
(Tom Dascombe) *led early: lost pl 5f out: r.o ins fnl f* **20/1**
5 *shd* **Blame Love (USA)** 2-9-5 0 SilvestreDeSousa 1 65
(Mark Johnston) *sn pushed along in rr: hdwy over 4f out: rdn over 1f out: styd on* **7/1**[3]
00 6 *2* **Foylesideview (IRE)**[10] 3194 2-9-5 0 ShaneKelly 2 59
(Luke Dace) *sn led: rdn and hdd over 1f out: no ex ins fnl f* **16/1**
7 *1* **Rashash (IRE)** 2-9-5 0 JackMitchell 3 56
(Roger Varian) *sn pushed along and rn green in rr: no ch whn hung lft fnl f* **8/1**

1m 13.93s (2.03) **Going Correction** +0.075s/f (Slow) **7** Ran SP% **116.5**
Speed ratings (Par 93): **89,88,87,86,85 83,81**
CSF £5.00 TOTE £1.90: £1.10, £1.80; EX 5.40 Trifecta £20.30.
**Owner** Coriolan Partnership **Bred** Mrs S M Mitchell **Trained** East Everleigh, Wilts

**FOCUS**
A fair maiden in which the gallop was soon reasonable and the winner raced centre-to-far side in the straight. The form is rated around the first two.

## 3525 BET NOW AT 32REDSPORT.COM MEDIAN AUCTION MAIDEN STKS 1m 1y(P)
4:25 (4:26) (Class 5) 3-Y-O £3,234 (£962; £481; £240) Stalls Low

Form RPR
22 1 **Telefono**[19] 2883 3-9-5 0 JamesDoyle 7 83
(Amanda Perrett) *trckd ldr tl led over 5f out: rdn and edgd rt over 1f out: styd on u.p* **4/5**[1]
2 2 *½* **Wrood (USA)**[42] 2211 3-9-0 0 ShaneKelly 4 76
(James Fanshawe) *a.p: chsd wnr over 4f out: rdn over 2f out: styd on* **7/4**[2]
3 *6* **Kicking The Can (IRE)** 3-9-5 0 RobertHavlin 1 67
(Peter Chapple-Hyam) *chsd ldrs: rdn over 2f out: no ex ins fnl f* **10/1**[3]
0-0 4 *3* **Danglydontask**[26] 2682 3-9-5 0 (b) PaddyAspell 9 59
(David Arbuthnot) *hld up: rdn over 3f out: styd on fnl 2f: nvr trbld ldrs* **66/1**
5- 5 *6* **Tolly McGuiness**[328] 4862 3-9-0 0 ShelleyBirkett(5) 10 45
(Julia Feilden) *prom: racd keenly: rdn and wknd over 2f out* **50/1**
6 *1 ¼* **Too Bend** 3-9-2 0 ThomasBrown(3) 6 42
(Patrick Chamings) *s.s: sn pushed along in rr: nvr on terms* **50/1**
7 *1* **Auf Wiedersehen** 3-9-5 0 FrederikTylicki 3 40
(James Fanshawe) *prom: lost pl over 4f out: wknd 3f out* **10/1**[3]
8 *9* **Hannington** 3-9-5 0 (t) DavidProbert 8 18
(Andrew Balding) *s.s: sn pushed along and a in rr* **16/1**
6 9 *10* **Fleetwood Bella**[79] 1296 3-9-0 0 JimmyQuinn 2
(Michael Attwater) *racd keenly: led: hdd over 5f out: wknd over 3f out* **66/1**

1m 37.26s (-0.94) **Going Correction** +0.075s/f (Slow) **9** Ran SP% **122.9**
Speed ratings (Par 99): **107,106,100,97,91 90,89,80,70**
CSF £2.59 TOTE £2.20: £1.02, £1.30, £2.10; EX 2.60 Trifecta £9.10.
**Owner** K Abdullah **Bred** Juddmonte Farms Ltd **Trained** Pulborough, W Sussex

**FOCUS**
The betting suggested this was between the two market leaders and that's how it turned out. The winner came down the centre in the straight. There was little depth to this.

## 3526 RACING SPECIALS AT 32REDSPORT.COM H'CAP 1m 1y(P)
5:00 (5:00) (Class 6) (0-65,65) 4-Y-O+ £2,264 (£673; £336; £168) Stalls Low

Form RPR
2430 1 **Prince Of Burma (IRE)**[17] 2947 6-9-7 65 (b) SilvestreDeSousa 5 77
(David Evans) *s.i.s: sn prom: shkn up to ld over 1f out: r.o wl: eased nr fin* **2/1**[1]
0301 2 *4 ½* **For Shia And Lula (IRE)**[9] 3233 5-9-2 65 EoinWalsh(5) 2 68
(Daniel Mark Loughnane) *sn led: rdn and hdd over 1f out: no ex ins fnl f* **11/4**[2]
4-00 3 *4* **Sweet Marwell (IRE)**[131] 582 4-9-3 61 FergusSweeney 6 53
(Jo Crowley) *mid-div: hdwy over 3f out: sn rdn: styd on same pce fr over 1f out* **8/1**
2-60 4 *½* **Fiducia**[109] 853 4-9-6 64 JamesDoyle 3 55
(Simon Dow) *mid-div: hdwy over 3f out: chsd ldr over 2f out: sn rdn: no ex fnl f* **14/1**
0640 5 *1 ¼* **Nifty Kier**[18] 2923 5-8-2 46 DavidProbert 4 34
(Phil McEntee) *hld up: hdwy over 2f out: styd on same pce fr over 1f out* **10/1**
2465 6 *1 ¾* **Tax Reform (IRE)**[27] 2646 4-9-6 64 (b) RobertHavlin 1 48
(Mark Hoad) *sn chsng ldr: rdn and lost 2nd over 2f out: wknd over 1f out* **9/2**[3]
0640 7 *2 ¼* **Laguna Belle**[6] 3327 4-7-9 46 oh1 CamHardie(7) 8 25
(Pat Phelan) *hld up: rdn over 3f out: n.d* **20/1**
66-0 8 *9* **Two Sugars**[54] 1874 6-8-3 47 JimmyQuinn 9 6
(Edward Creighton) *sn pushed along to chse ldrs: rdn over 4f out: wknd over 2f out* **25/1**
-400 9 *21* **Hilali (IRE)**[12] 3118 5-9-6 64 TedDurcan 7
(Gary Brown) *sn pushed along in rr: bhd fnl 5f* **20/1**

1m 37.77s (-0.43) **Going Correction** +0.075s/f (Slow) **9** Ran SP% **118.4**
Speed ratings (Par 101): **105,100,96,96,94 93,90,81,60**
CSF £7.51 CT £36.15 TOTE £2.90: £1.10, £1.40, £2.30; EX 9.20 Trifecta £73.00.
**Owner** E R Griffiths **Bred** P Burns **Trained** Pandy, Monmouths

**FOCUS**
Exposed performers in a modest handicap. The gallop was reasonable and the winner raced close to the far rail in the straight. A step up on the winner's winter form.

## 3527 32RED ON THE APP STORE H'CAP (DIV I) 7f 1y(P)
5:30 (5:30) (Class 6) (0-60,60) 3-Y-O+ £2,264 (£673; £336; £168) Stalls High

Form RPR
4006 1 **Indus Valley (IRE)**[11] 3160 7-9-8 56 (b) DavidProbert 1 68
(Des Donovan) *hld up: hdwy over 2f out: rdn to ld wl ins fnl f: sn clr* **3/1**[1]
1160 2 *2 ¾* **Exceedexpectations (IRE)**[19] 2887 5-9-12 60 (p) StevieDonohoe 4 65
(Lee Carter) *chsd ldrs: rdn over 1f out: led ins fnl f: sn hdd and outpcd* **7/2**[2]
/2-0 3 *hd* **Silvala Dance**[35] 2399 4-9-2 50 TedDurcan 10 54
(Chris Wall) *a.p: rdn over 1f out: ev ch ins fnl f: styd on same pce* **8/1**[3]
0260 4 *1 ¼* **Coach Montana (IRE)**[11] 3160 5-8-12 46 (b) RichardKingscote 8 47
(Christine Dunnett) *sn led: rdn over 1f out: hdd and no ex ins fnl f* **12/1**
-060 5 *¾* **Borough Belle**[13] 3087 3-8-8 51 FergusSweeney 2 47
(Henry Candy) *hld up: rdn over 1f out: r.o ins fnl f: nt trble ldrs* **12/1**
5666 6 *¾* **Hinton Admiral**[34] 2435 10-9-0 48 (p) JimmyQuinn 9 45
(Pat Eddery) *sn pushed along and prom: rdn over 2f out: no ex ins fnl f* **20/1**
6043 7 *6* **Dividend Dan (IRE)**[33] 2469 4-9-9 57 ShaneKelly 6 39
(Mike Murphy) *sn w ldr tl rdn over 2f out: wknd fnl f* **3/1**[1]
-656 8 *3 ¾* **Alberto**[12] 3123 4-8-12 46 oh1 (p) WilliamCarson 7 18
(Alastair Lidderdale) *hld up: wknd 2f out* **16/1**
0150 9 *4* **One Way Or Another (AUS)**[9] 3233 11-9-7 55 (t) SilvestreDeSousa 11 17
(David Evans) *sn pushed along to chse ldrs: rdn over 2f out: sn wknd* **8/1**[3]
00-0 10 *7* **Divine Bay**[25] 2694 3-7-10 46 oh1 (v[1]) HectorCrouch(7) 5
(Gary Moore) *s.i.s: outpcd* **25/1**

1m 25.5s (0.70) **Going Correction** +0.075s/f (Slow)
**WFA** 3 from 4yo+ 9lb **10** Ran SP% **124.3**
Speed ratings (Par 101): **99,95,95,94,93 92,85,81,76,68**
CSF £14.62 CT £82.04 TOTE £5.50: £2.50, £2.40, £2.50; EX 20.80 Trifecta £107.50.
**Owner** W P Flynn **Bred** P Morris & B McKenna **Trained** Exning, Suffolk

**FOCUS**
A moderate handicap run at a fair gallop. The cosy winner came down the centre in the straight. The winner is rated up a little on his spring form.

## 3528 32RED ON THE APP STORE H'CAP (DIV II) 7f 1y(P)
6:00 (6:00) (Class 6) (0-60,59) 3-Y-O+ £2,264 (£673; £336; £168) Stalls High

Form RPR
-026 1 **Ishi Honest**[11] 3149 4-9-8 55 SilvestreDeSousa 6 62
(Mark Usher) *a.p: chsd ldr over 4f out: led over 2f out: rdn out* **7/1**[3]
0-45 2 *¾* **Golly Miss Molly**[18] 2931 3-8-6 48 HayleyTurner 3 50
(Jeremy Gask) *led: hdd over 5f out: sn edgd lft: remained handy: chsd wnr 2f out: sn rdn and ev ch: styd on* **33/1**
0524 3 *hd* **Cyflymder (IRE)**[9] 3233 8-9-0 50 ThomasBrown(3) 1 55
(David C Griffiths) *a.p: hmpd 5f out: rdn over 1f out: styd on* **3/1**[2]
6230 4 *1* **Greek Islands (IRE)**[24] 2722 6-9-7 54 JimmyQuinn 2 54
(Edward Creighton) *s.i.s: hld up: rdn and r.o ins fnl f: nvr nrr: fin 5th: plcd 4th* **8/1**
5020 5 *½* **Silvee**[9] 3230 7-9-2 49 (p) WilliamCarson 10 48
(John Bridger) *led over 5f out: rdn and hdd over 2f out: no ex ins fnl f: fin 6th: plcd 5th* **20/1**
14-0 6 *1* **Squirrel Wood (IRE)**[25] 2689 6-9-9 56 FergusSweeney 8 52
(Mary Hambro) *hld up: r.o ins fnl f: nvr on terms: fin 7th: plcd 6th* **14/1**
00- 7 *1* **Genax (IRE)**[188] 8317 3-8-8 53 IanBrennan(3) 4 43
(John Wainwright) *chsd ldrs: rdn and hung rt over 1f out: no ex: fin 8th: plcd 7th* **6/4**[1]
00-0 8 *½* **Exceed Policy**[9] 3248 3-8-3 45 FrankieMcDonald 9 33
(David Dennis) *hld up: rdn over 1f out: n.d: fin 9th: plcd 8th* **20/1**
0000 9 *3 ¼* **Mists Of Time (IRE)**[60] 1664 4-9-0 47 (p) StevieDonohoe 5 30
(Pat Eddery) *prom: rdn over 2f out: hmpd and wknd over 1f out: fin 10th: plcd 9th* **50/1**
5510 D *¾* **Perfect Pastime**[6] 3328 6-9-12 59 (b) ShaneKelly 7 62
(Jim Boyle) *hld up: rdn over 1f out: r.o ins fnl f: nt rch ldrs: finshed 4th: disq & plcd last* **7/1**[3]

1m 25.98s (1.18) **Going Correction** +0.075s/f (Slow)
**WFA** 3 from 4yo+ 9lb **10** Ran SP% **122.2**
Speed ratings (Par 101): **96,95,94,92,92 91,90,89,85,94**
CSF £222.87 CT £867.63 TOTE £7.50: £2.90, £5.90, £1.30; EX 128.50 Trifecta £652.60.
**Owner** Saxon House Racing **Bred** Miss A V Hill **Trained** Upper Lambourn, Berks
■ Stewards' Enquiry : Shane Kelly three-day ban: failed to weigh in (7, 8, 9 Jul)
Ian Brennan two-day ban: careless riding (7-8 July)

**FOCUS**
The second division of a moderate handicap. The gallop was an ordinary one to the home turn and the winner came down the centre. He's rated to last year's form.
T/Plt: £3.80 to a £1 stake. Pool: £61,431.48 - 11,752.40 winning units. T/Qpdt: £1.20 to a £1 stake. Pool: £3176.59 - 3176.08 winning units. CR

# 3337 THIRSK (L-H)
## Monday, June 23

**OFFICIAL GOING: Good to firm (9.3)**
Wind: light 1/2 against Weather: fine and sunny

## 3529 RACING UK ANYWHERE AVAILABLE NOW MAIDEN AUCTION STKS 6f
6:20 (6:24) (Class 6) 2-Y-O £2,726 (£805; £402) Stalls High

Form RPR
3 1 **Mrs Biggs**[7] 3296 2-8-11 0 NeilFarley(3) 14 65
(Declan Carroll) *mde all: styd on towards fin* **7/2**[1]
54 2 *¾* **Ingleby Spring (IRE)**[28] 2615 2-9-0 0 TonyHamilton 2 63
(Richard Fahey) *chsd wnr: ev ch fnl f: no ex fnl 50yds* **11/1**
633 3 *1 ½* **Atreus**[10] 3201 2-8-12 0 DanielleMooney(7) 1 63
(Michael Easterby) *chsd ldrs: ev ch 1f out: kpt on same pce last 75yds* **20/1**
5 4 *1* **Lucilla Aurelius (IRE)**[36] 2359 2-9-0 0 PJMcDonald 15 55
(Tony Coyle) *chsd ldrs: kpt on same pce appr fnl f* **9/2**[3]
64 5 *4 ½* **Upward Trend (IRE)**[23] 2788 2-9-5 0 DavidAllan 9 51+
(Tim Easterby) *in rr: hdwy whn nt clr run over 1f out: swtchd ins fnl f: styd on* **4/1**[2]
44 5 *dht* **Star Ascending (IRE)**[10] 3186 2-8-12 0 MeganCarberry(7) 13 51+
(Brian Ellison) *in rr-div: effrt on ins whn nt clr run 2f out: kpt on fnl f: nvr on terms: dead-heated for 5th* **6/1**
7 *1 ¾* **Oricano** 2-8-7 0 GemmaTutty(7) 10 37
(Karen Tutty) *dwlt: in rr: sme hdwy over 2f out: nvr nr ldrs* **20/1**
0 8 *½* **Just No Rules**[27] 2652 2-9-0 0 JamesSullivan 4 35
(Tony Coyle) *wnt lft s: t.k.h: swtchd rt after 1f: chsd ldrs: hung lft and wknd over 1f out* **66/1**
9 *1 ½* **Equiaire** 2-9-0 0 PhillipMakin 8 31
(John Weymes) *chsd ldrs: wknd over 1f out* **50/1**

10 *10* **Caeser The Gaeser (IRE)** 2-9-0 0 ........ DuilioDaSilva[(5)] 5 6
(Richard Guest) *dwlt: sn bhd* **50/1**
0 **11** *½* **Secret House**[10] 3201 2-9-0 0 ........ GrahamGibbons 3
(Michael Easterby) *hmpd s: in rr: sme hdwy over 2f out: sn lost pl: bhd whn eased ins fnl f* **66/1**

1m 14.72s (2.02) **Going Correction** +0.175s/f (Good) **11** Ran SP% **99.5**
Speed ratings (Par 91): **93,92,90,88,82 82,80,79,77,64 63**
CSF £27.37 TOTE £4.00: £1.30, £2.40, £2.50; EX 29.40 Trifecta £108.10.
**Owner** Kenneth Mackay & Martin Percival **Bred** Martin Percival **Trained** Sledmere, E Yorks
■ Cumbrianna was withdrawn. Price at time of withdrawal 5-1. Rule 4 applies to all bets - deduction 15p in the pound.

**FOCUS**
The ground was officially good to firm but the time was 4.12secs slower than standard. This didn't look a strong maiden but the form has been given a small chance. The first four were always prominent.

## 3530 RACING UK IPAD APP RACINGUK.COM/MOBILE H'CAP 6f
**6:50** (6:53) (Class 6) (0-60,60) 3-Y-0+ **£2,726** (£805; £402) **Stalls** High

Form RPR
0452 **1** **Amis Reunis**[12] 3099 5-8-12 **46** ........ (p) PatrickMathers 16 57
(Alan Berry) *racd stands' side: chsd ldrs: hmpd: swtchd lft and 2nd over 2f out: styd on to ld ins fnl f: drvn out* **16/1**
2342 **2** *1* **Lees Anthem**[11] 3150 7-9-11 **59** ........ DavidAllan 10 67
(Mel Brittain) *swtchd rt after s: racd stands' side: led that gp after 2f: edgd lft over 2f out: hdd and no ex ins fnl f* **12/1**
06-0 **3** *1½* **Abraham Monro**[17] 2955 4-9-5 **53** ........ JamesSullivan 20 56
(Ruth Carr) *racd stands' side: in rr: hdwy over 2f out: styd on fnl f* **8/1[2]**
-005 **4** *shd* **Nelson's Pride**[11] 3149 3-9-2 **57** ........ (b) GrahamLee 12 58
(Kevin Ryan) *hld up in rr stands' side: hdwy over 2f out: kpt on wl fnl f* **12/1**
6050 **5** *1¼* **Mey Blossom**[6] 3338 9-9-4 **55** ........ (v) GeorgeChaloner[(3)] 18 54
(Richard Whitaker) *racd stands' side: mid-div: effrt over 2f out: kpt on same pce fnl f* **16/1**
040- **6** *¾* **Redalani (IRE)**[254] 7203 4-9-6 **54** ........ RobertWinston 13 50
(Alan Brown) *racd stands' side: chsd ldrs: carried lft and sddle slipped over 2f out: one pce over 1f out* **25/1**
10-5 **7** *3¾* **Monsieur Royale**[163] 141 4-9-7 **58** ........ (b) RobertTart[(3)] 17 42
(Geoffrey Oldroyd) *racd stands' side: mid-div: hdwy over 2f out: edgd lft and wknd over 1f out* **8/1[2]**
40-0 **8** *1¼* **Charlemagne Diva**[30] 2542 4-9-4 **57** ........ DuilioDaSilva[(5)] 19 37
(Richard Guest) *racd stands' side: led that gp 2f: hmpd over 2f out: kpt on one pce* **20/1**
300- **9** *1* **Gambino (IRE)**[248] 7345 4-8-6 **47** ow1 ........ AlistairRawlinson[(7)] 7 23
(John David Riches) *racd far side: w ldr: led that gp over 1f out: no ch w stands' side* **25/1**
6200 **10** *1½* **See Clearly**[17] 2955 5-9-9 **57** ........ (p) TonyHamilton 11 29
(Tim Easterby) *racd stands' side: mid-div: drvn over 2f out: nvr a factor* **10/1[3]**
6223 **11** *1¼* **Captain Scooby**[5] 3366 8-9-0 **51** ........ (v) BillyCray[(3)] 8 19
(Richard Guest) *racd far side: in rr: sme hdwy over 1f out: nvr a factor* **14/1**
5510 **12** *½* **Absolute Bearing (IRE)**[16] 3000 5-9-1 **49** ........ TomEaves 15 16
(Tim Etherington) *dwlt in rr stands' side: kpt on fnl 2f: nvr a factor* **25/1**
0650 **13** *shd* **Secret City (IRE)**[11] 3149 8-9-8 **56** ........ (b) DanielTudhope 9 22
(Robin Bastiman) *racd far side: sn drvn along: nvr a factor* **16/1**
-060 **14** *nk* **Pavers Star**[32] 2473 5-8-13 **47** ........ PaulMulrennan 3 12
(Noel Wilson) *led far side gp tl hdd & wknd over 1f out* **66/1**
-000 **15** *¾* **Dream Ally (IRE)**[44] 2171 4-9-12 **60** ........ PJMcDonald 2 23
(Micky Hammond) *restless in stalls: hood removed late: racd far side: a in rr* **22/1**
0-00 **16** *hd* **Locky Taylor (IRE)**[20] 2870 3-9-0 **60** ........ ShaneGray[(5)] 1 20
(Kevin Ryan) *racd far side: chsd ldrs: drvn 3f out: lost pl 2f out: eased clsng stages* **50/1**
-006 **17** *¾* **Here Now And Why (IRE)**[31] 2514 7-9-6 **54** ........ (b) PhillipMakin 5 14
(Philip Kirby) *racd far side: mid-div: effrt over 2f out: lost pl over 1f out* **22/1**
3000 **18** *7* **Red Cape (FR)**[11] 3150 11-9-7 **55** ........ (b) DaleSwift 14
(Ruth Carr) *racd stands' side: chsd ldrs: lost pl over 1f out: sn eased* **28/1**
3111 **19** *2* **Fathom Five (IRE)**[5] 3366 10-9-0 **55** ........ GeorgiaCox[(7)] 4
(Shaun Harris) *racd far side: chsd ldrs: lost pl over 1f out: eased whn bhd* **5/1[1]**
2440 **U** **Iceblast**[12] 3099 6-9-3 **58** ........ DanielleMooney[(7)] 6
(Michael Easterby) *racd far side: in rr whn fly-jmpd and uns rdr sn after s* **20/1**

1m 13.41s (0.71) **Going Correction** +0.175s/f (Good)
**WFA** 3 from 4yo+ 7lb **20** Ran SP% **124.3**
Speed ratings (Par 101): **102,100,98,98,96 95,90,89,87,85 84,83,83,83,82 81,80,71,68,**
CSF £169.89 CT £1705.89 TOTE £22.10: £4.70, £2.90, £2.20, £3.10; EX 139.60 Trifecta £1408.90 Part won..
**Owner** A B Parr **Bred** Paddock Space **Trained** Cockerham, Lancs

**FOCUS**
This was a low-grade sprint handicap featuring plenty of sorts that are hard to win with. The field split into two groups initially, with those drawn 1-9 racing middle to far side, though the two groups merged in the last 2f. Unlike the big-field sprint here last week, the stands' side seemed the place to be. The winner's best form for this yard.

## 3531 RACINGUK.COM/ANYWHERE: 3DEVICES, 1PRICE MAIDEN STKS 5f
**7:20** (7:21) (Class 5) 3-4-Y-0 **£3,234** (£962; £481; £240) **Stalls** High

Form RPR
042- **1** **Zac Brown (IRE)**[255] 7173 3-9-3 86 ........ GrahamGibbons 4 70+
(David Barron) *mde all: shkn up over 1f out: sn clr: v easily* **1/7[1]**
06 **2** *3¾* **Escaping Midge (IRE)**[20] 2871 3-8-12 0 ........ DuranFentiman 3 51
(Tim Easterby) *chsd ldrs: drvn over 2f out: kpt on to take 2nd last 50yds* **12/1**
**3** *1¼* **Blaze It** 3-8-12 0 ........ PaulPickard 5 47
(Brian Ellison) *mid-div: swtchd lft over 2f out: sn chsng ldrs: 2nd over 1f out: one pce* **7/1[2]**
0- **4** *3¼* **Parisian Melody**[422] 1839 3-8-12 0 ........ DavidAllan 2 35
(Mel Brittain) *rrd and wnt lft s: in last: drvn over 2f out: tk n.d 4th nr fin* **11/1[3]**
560 **5** *1¼* **Jiminy**[27] 2658 4-9-9 44 ........ (b) PatrickMathers 1 37
(Alan Berry) *chsd wnr: drvn over 2f out: wknd over 1f out* **33/1**

1m 0.66s (1.06) **Going Correction** +0.175s/f (Good)
**WFA** 3 from 4yo 6lb **5** Ran SP% **119.0**
Speed ratings (Par 103): **98,92,90,84,82**
CSF £4.19 TOTE £1.10: £1.02, £3.80; EX 3.40 Trifecta £16.70.
**Owner** R G Toes **Bred** Tally-Ho Stud **Trained** Maunby, N Yorks

**FOCUS**
This was a weak and uncompetitive maiden. The winner's bare form was 2st+ off his 2yo best, with the time slow.

## 3532 YORKSHIRE OUTDOORS ADVENTURE EXPERIENCES H'CAP 2m
**7:50** (7:50) (Class 5) (0-70,70) 4-Y-0+ **£2,587** (£770; £384; £192) **Stalls** Low

Form RPR
0023 **1** **Longshadow**[63] 1605 4-8-13 **62** ........ (v[1]) AndrewElliott 6 76
(Jason Ward) *t.k.h: sn trcking ldrs: drvn over 3f out: led over 2f out: hdd appr fnl f: rallied to regain ld clsng stages* **4/1[2]**
5-53 **2** *½* **Beat The Tide**[34] 2424 4-9-4 **70** ........ (p) ConnorBeasley[(3)] 8 83
(Michael Dods) *hld up in rr: hdwy 8f out: led appr fnl f: hdd and no ex clsng stages* **3/1[1]**
3525 **3** *7* **My Destination (IRE)**[8] 3269 5-8-7 **63** ow1 ........ (b) LukeLeadbitter[(7)] 2 68
(Declan Carroll) *hld up in rr: hdwy over 2f out: kpt on to take modest 3rd last 30yds* **16/1**
2-54 **4** *1¾* **Beat The Shower**[28] 2620 8-8-8 **57** ........ RobertWinston 7 60
(Peter Niven) *trckd ldrs: effrt over 3f out: one pce fnl 2f* **7/1**
-024 **5** *3¼* **Medieval Bishop (IRE)**[31] 2515 5-9-2 **65** ........ (p) JasonHart 5 64
(Mark Walford) *trckd ldrs: drvn over 3f out: wknd fnl f* **9/2[3]**
0201 **6** *4½* **Jan Smuts (IRE)**[34] 2424 6-9-3 **66** ........ (tp) GrahamLee 3 60
(Wilf Storey) *hld up in mid-div: drvn over 3f out: wknd over 1f out* **17/2**
5-55 **7** *hd* **Amir Pasha (UAE)**[4] 3398 9-8-2 **51** oh4 ........ (v) DuranFentiman 1 44
(Micky Hammond) *chsd ldrs: drvn over 4f out: wknd over 1f out* **25/1**
0020 **8** *4½* **Hunting Ground (USA)**[23] 2760 4-9-7 **70** ........ FrannyNorton 4 58
(Mark Johnston) *led: drvn over 3f out: hdd over 2f out: lost pl over 1f out* **11/2**

3m 33.91s (5.61) **Going Correction** +0.175s/f (Good) **8** Ran SP% **111.3**
Speed ratings (Par 103): **92,91,88,87,85 83,83,81**
CSF £15.50 CT £163.08 TOTE £4.00: £1.10, £1.20, £3.50; EX 17.70 Trifecta £131.70.
**Owner** David Robertson & J Ward **Bred** Miss K Rausing **Trained** Middleham, N Yorks

**FOCUS**
Quite a competitive handicap for the grade but the pace was no more than ordinary, though the tempo increased soon after the turn into the straight. The first two came clear and the winner is rated back to his Irish best.

## 3533 JONATHAN TROWELL MEMORIAL STKS (H'CAP) 7f
**8:20** (8:21) (Class 4) (0-80,78) 4-Y-0+ **£4,851** (£1,443; £721; £360) **Stalls** Low

Form RPR
1413 **1** **Repetition**[19] 2905 4-9-4 **75** ........ TomEaves 9 86
(Kristin Stubbs) *led: swtchd lft after 1f: hdd narrowly appr fnl f: styd on to regain ld last 100yds* **4/1[2]**
0000 **2** *1¼* **Snow Bay**[30] 2549 8-9-1 **72** ........ GrahamLee 5 80
(Paul Midgley) *trckd ldrs: t.k.h: handy 2nd over 3f out: led narrowly appr fnl f: hdd and no ex last 100yds* **8/1**
6405 **3** *nk* **Icy Blue**[12] 3096 6-8-4 **61** ........ (p) FrannyNorton 6 68
(Richard Whitaker) *sn chsng ldrs: drvn 3f out: edgd rt and styd on ins fnl f* **10/1**
1-21 **4** *1½* **Cara's Request (AUS)**[16] 3000 9-8-13 **73** ........ ConnorBeasley[(3)] 10 76
(Michael Dods) *in rr-div: effrt over 3f out: styd on fnl f* **3/1[1]**
1163 **5** *hd* **Real Tigress (IRE)**[9] 3220 5-9-3 **74** ........ DavidAllan 6 77
(Les Eyre) *in rr-div: effrt over 3f out: one pce over 1f out* **5/1[3]**
0520 **6** *¾* **Relight My Fire**[9] 3256 4-9-1 **72** ........ (b) PJMcDonald 7 73
(Tim Easterby) *chsd ldrs: drvn 3f out: one pce over 1f out* **12/1**
3-10 **7** *7* **Flexible Flyer**[44] 2169 5-9-4 **75** ........ (t[1]) DougieCostello 3 57
(Mark Walford) *in rr: drvn 3f out: lost pl over 1f out: eased towards fin* **9/1**
-021 **8** *2¾* **Smalljohn**[147] 359 8-8-11 **68** ........ (v) RoystonFfrench 8 43
(Bryan Smart) *chsd ldrs: drvn over 3f out: wknd over 1f out* **20/1**
0613 **9** *3¾* **Diamondhead (IRE)**[9] 3213 5-9-7 **78** ........ PhillipMakin 2 44
(Ed de Giles) *in rr: drvn over 2f out: nvr on terms: eased fnl f* **9/1**
030- **10** *19* **Slim Chance (IRE)**[268] 6855 5-8-9 **66** ........ AndrewElliott 4
(Simon West) *s.i.s: in rr: wd and lost pl over 2f out: sn bhd and eased* **40/1**

1m 27.63s (0.43) **Going Correction** +0.175s/f (Good) **10** Ran SP% **116.8**
Speed ratings (Par 105): **104,102,102,100,100 99,91,88,84,62**
CSF £36.16 CT £307.77 TOTE £5.60: £2.00, £4.70, £3.80; EX 44.70 Trifecta £166.90.
**Owner** The B P J Partnership **Bred** G Reed **Trained** Norton, N Yorks

**FOCUS**
They looked to go a decent gallop here but the first two were in the first two throughout. This was quite a competitive contest. The winner had improved again on the AW since his last turf start.

## 3534 BET ON THE MOVE WITH RACING UK'S ANDROID APP H'CAP 1m
**8:50** (8:51) (Class 6) (0-65,65) 3-Y-0 **£2,726** (£805; £402) **Stalls** Low

Form RPR
0406 **1** **Eddiemaurice (IRE)**[5] 3360 3-9-4 **62** ........ (v[1]) RobertWinston 3 74
(Richard Guest) *in rr: hdwy over 2f out: styd on to ld last 100yds* **3/1[2]**
0022 **2** *1¾* **Green Zone (IRE)**[6] 3333 3-9-1 **59** ........ (p) PhillipMakin 7 67
(Nigel Tinkler) *trckd ldrs: drvn 3f out: led over 1f out: hdd and no ex ins fnl f* **5/2[1]**
0-26 **3** *3* **Coin Broker (IRE)**[24] 2740 3-9-7 **65** ........ DanielTudhope 11 66
(David O'Meara) *mid-div: drvn over 4f out: styd on to take 3rd ins fnl f* **9/2[3]**
-500 **4** *1¾* **Bearskin (IRE)**[6] 3344 3-8-13 **57** ........ (b[1]) PJMcDonald 9 54
(Ann Duffield) *wnt lft s: sn led: hdd over 1f out: one pce* **12/1**
5200 **5** *2¼* **Belle Peinture (FR)**[28] 2616 3-8-2 **46** oh1 ........ JamesSullivan 5 38
(Alan Lockwood) *led early: chsd ldrs: one pce fnl 2f* **40/1**
0-01 **6** *hd* **Oly'Roccs (IRE)**[55] 1852 3-8-9 **53** ........ PaulMulrennan 4 44
(Philip Kirby) *chsd ldrs: nt clr run on inner over 1f out: one pce* **12/1**
56-3 **7** *nk* **Jimmy Crackle (IRE)**[79] 1304 3-8-9 **60** ........ MeganCarberry[(7)] 12 51
(Brian Ellison) *awkward to load: mid-div: outpcd over 3f out: kpt on fnl f* **6/1**
5-60 **8** *2* **Ofelia (IRE)**[24] 2741 3-8-4 **48** ........ PaulPickard 1 34
(Brian Ellison) *hld up in rr: sme hdwy on outside over 2f out: nvr on terms* **25/1**
-006 **9** *4* **Classical Diva**[9] 3228 3-8-4 **51** ........ NeilFarley[(3)] 6 28
(Declan Carroll) *t.k.h in rr: lost pl over 2f out: sn bhd* **25/1**
06-0 **10** *40* **Paparima (IRE)**[22] 2802 3-7-9 **46** oh1 ........ JackGarritty[(7)] 8
(Paul Green) *t.k.h on outside in rr: bhd fnl 3f: t.o over 1f out: virtually p.u* **100/1**
00-0 **11** *dist* **Evie Jay (IRE)**[28] 2606 3-9-2 **60** ........ RaulDaSilva 2
(Paul Green) *mid-div: t.k.h: lost pl over 2f out: sddle slipped: sn eased and virtually p.u: eventually completed* **40/1**

1m 42.36s (2.26) **Going Correction** +0.175s/f (Good) **11** Ran SP% **115.0**
Speed ratings (Par 97): **95,93,90,88,86 86,85,83,79,39**
CSF £10.11 CT £32.78 TOTE £3.90: £1.10, £1.10, £2.90; EX 10.80 Trifecta £46.50.
**Owner** Advance Group UK Ltd **Bred** Declan Murphy **Trained** Wetherby, W Yorks

**FOCUS**
A low-grade and ordinary handicap but the pace was strong. The winner is rated back to his 2yo best, which came over C&D.

## 3535 DOWNLOAD NEW RACINGUK IPAD APP H'CAP 1m 4f
**9:20** (9:21) (Class 6) (0-60,60) 4-Y-O+ **£2,587** (£770; £384; £192) **Stalls High**

Form RPR
0444 **1** **Amazing Blue Sky**[14] 3052 8-8-10 **49**.................... JamesSullivan 8 57
(Ruth Carr) *hld up in midfield: hdwy to chse ldrs over 3f out: 2nd over 2f out: led over 1f out: kpt on wl* **10/3**[1]
4603 **2** *1 ½* **Ferdy (IRE)**[11] 3134 5-9-3 **56**.................... RaulDaSilva 6 62
(Paul Green) *mid-div: hdwy over 3f out: kpt on to take 2nd ins fnl f: no real imp* **7/1**[3]
6-00 **3** *3 ½* **Noosa Sound**[26] 2674 4-8-7 **46** oh1....................(t) RoystonFfrench 7 46
(John Davies) *chsd ldrs: led over 4f out: hdd over 1f out: one pce* **20/1**
-064 **4** *1 ½* **Blue Top**[8] 3269 5-9-7 **60**....................(p) JasonHart 10 58
(Mark Walford) *t.k.h in mid-div: hdwy over 3f out: kpt on one pce fnl 2f* **4/1**[2]
40-6 **5** *½* **District Attorney (IRE)**[11] 2738 5-8-7 **46**....................(v[1]) MichaelStainton 3 43+
(Chris Fairhurst) *mid-div: lost pl over 3f out: styd on fnl 2f* **11/1**
5504 **6** *½* **Bold And Free**[12] 3095 4-9-0 **53**....................(p) GrahamLee 11 49
(David Thompson) *t.k.h in mid-div on outside: hdwy to chse ldrs over 4f out: wknd fnl 75yds* **8/1**
0-00 **7** *3* **Euston Square**[32] 2476 8-9-0 **58**....................[1] GarryWhillans(5) 9 49
(Alistair Whillans) *dwlt: in rr: kpt on fnl 2f: nvr a factor* **25/1**
00-4 **8** *6* **Downtown Boy (IRE)**[9] 3238 6-9-1 **54**....................(p) TomEaves 2 36
(Ray Craggs) *led 2f: chsd ldrs: 2nd over 4f out: wknd over 1f out* **16/1**
500- **9** *1 ½* **Needwood Park**[164] 4052 6-8-4 **46** oh1....................(p) ConnorBeasley(3) 13 25
(Ray Craggs) *chsd ldrs: led after 2f: hdd over 4f out: lost pl 3f out* **50/1**
0530 **10** *1 ¼* **Stamp Duty (IRE)**[28] 2614 6-8-0 **46** oh1.................... JoeDoyle(7) 5 23
(Suzzanne France) *in rr: bhd fnl 3f* **25/1**
044- **11** *4* **Rust (IRE)**[230] 7741 4-9-6 **59**.................... PJMcDonald 1 30
(Ann Duffield) *chsd ldrs: wknd 2f out: eased nr fin* **7/1**[3]
0066 **12** *2 ¼* **Chaparella (IRE)**[18] 2915 4-8-7 **46**.................... FrannyNorton 4 13
(Mark Johnston) *chsd ldrs: lost pl over 3f out* **16/1**
0040 **13** *4* **Daneside (IRE)**[9] 3242 7-8-7 **46** oh1....................(e) AndrewElliott 12 7
(Simon West) *in rr: bhd fnl 3f* **40/1**

2m 40.59s (4.39) **Going Correction** +0.175s/f (Good) **13 Ran SP% 116.1**
Speed ratings (Par 101): **92,91,88,87,87 87,85,81,80,79 76,75,72**
CSF £23.95 CT £404.03 TOTE £3.80: £1.70, £2.50, £6.80; EX 19.50 Trifecta £864.80 Part won..
**Owner** G Scruton, D Williamson & R Carr **Bred** Hong Kong Breeders Club **Trained** Huby, N Yorks

**FOCUS**
Mainly exposed and ordinary sorts in this 40-60 handicap which was run at a rather a stop-start gallop with the pace slowing markedly down the far side. The form looks sound.
T/Jkpt: Not won. T/Plt: £31.80 to a £1 stake. Pool: £70,398.02 - 1611.35 winning units. T/Qpdt: £9.10 to a £1 stake. pool: £3857.75 - 313.20 winning units. WG

# [3310]WINDSOR (R-H)
### Monday, June 23

**OFFICIAL GOING: Good to firm (good in places; 8.6)**
Top bend out 15yds adding 59yds to races of 1m+. Inner of Straight out 18yds at 6f and 9yds at WP.
Wind: Almost nil Weather: Cloudy becoming bright, sultry

## 3536 3M UNITED KINGDOM PLC MEDIAN AUCTION MAIDEN STKS 6f
**6:40** (6:40) (Class 5) 2-Y-O **£2,587** (£770; £384; £192) **Stalls Low**

Form RPR
**1** **Louie De Palma** 2-9-2 0.................... RyanTate(3) 6 81+
(Clive Cox) *outpcd in 7th and pushed along: clsd over 2f out: swtchd outside over 1f out: shkn up to ld ins fnl f: pushed out* **3/1**[2]
3 **2** *1 ¼* **Arthur MartinLeake (IRE)**[5] 3367 2-9-5 0.................... MartinHarley 7 74
(K R Burke) *sn trckd ldrs on outer: shkn up to ld over 1f out: rdn and hdd ins fnl f: outpcd but kpt on* **6/4**[1]
6 **3** *nk* **Guilty (IRE)**[17] 2944 2-9-5 0.................... SeanLevey 4 73
(Richard Hannon) *disp ld to over 1f out: drvn and upsides ins fnl f: outpcd last 100yds: kpt on* **5/1**[3]
**4** *5* **Field Game** 2-9-5 0.................... JimmyFortune 2 58
(Hughie Morrison) *racd against rail: w ldrs to wl over 1f out: wknd* **10/1**
**5** *¾* **Jargon (FR)** 2-9-5 0.................... JamieSpencer 3 56
(Michael Bell) *disp ld to 2f out: hanging and wknd over 1f out* **5/1**[3]
**6** *14* **Akavit (IRE)** 2-9-5 0.................... FrederikTylicki 1 14
(Ed de Giles) *dwlt: wl outpcd in last and a t.o: passed two stragglers nr fin* **33/1**
**7** *½* **Blackasyourhat (IRE)** 2-9-5 0.................... SebSanders 5 12
(Roger Ingram) *s.i.s: outpcd in 6th and pushed along: wknd 2f out: t.o* **66/1**
0 **8** *2 ½* **Goldslinger (FR)**[10] 3193 2-9-5 0.................... ChrisCatlin 8 5
(Dean Ivory) *spd on outer to 1/2-way: sn wknd qckly: t.o* **33/1**

1m 13.04s (0.04) **Going Correction** -0.175s/f (Firm) **8 Ran SP% 114.8**
Speed ratings (Par 93): **92,90,89,83,82 63,62,59**
CSF £7.86 TOTE £4.80: £1.50, £1.20, £1.20; EX 9.90 Trifecta £31.80.
**Owner** Peter Ridgers **Bred** Pantile Stud **Trained** Lambourn, Berks

**FOCUS**
Not a bad 2yo maiden, run at a brisk pace. The race average suggests that the form should be pitched higher.

## 3537 WSM COMMUNICATIONS IN AID OF CLIC SARGENT MAIDEN STKS 1m 67y
**7:10** (7:10) (Class 5) 3-Y-O **£2,911** (£866; £432; £216) **Stalls Low**

Form RPR
0-3 **1** **Certificate**[13] 3083 3-9-5 0.................... FrederikTylicki 5 87
(Roger Varian) *trckd ldr: shkn up to ld wl over 1f out: crossed to rail sn after: pushed out firmly fnl f* **9/4**[2]
3 **2** *½* **Old Guard**[60] 1680 3-9-5 0.................... JamesDoyle 12 85
(Roger Charlton) *led: jinked briefly at intersection over 3f out: hdd wl over 1f out: checked and swtchd lft sn after: styd on fnl f: a hld* **2/1**[1]
0- **3** *4* **Weekendatbernies (IRE)**[286] 6277 3-9-5 0.................... JamieSpencer 3 76
(Ed de Giles) *trckd ldng pair: shkn up and nt qckn jst over 2f out: kpt on to take 3rd fnl f: no ch w ldng pair* **6/1**[3]
0-4 **4** *1 ½* **Lil Rockerfeller (USA)**[143] 403 3-9-5 0.................... KieranO'Neill 6 72
(Richard Hannon) *chsd ldng pair: shkn up and outpcd over 2f out: lost 3rd and one pce fnl f* **14/1**
00 **5** *¾* **Capmonde (IRE)**[23] 2780 3-9-0 0.................... MartinDwyer 1 66
(William Knight) *hld up in midfield: shkn up over 2f out: reminder wl over 1f out: hanging but kpt on fnl f* **25/1**
5- **6** *1* **Mountain Kingdom (IRE)**[258] 7089 3-9-5 0.................... LukeMorris 9 68
(Sir Mark Prescott Bt) *t.k.h: hld up towards rr: awkward on bnd over 5f out: pushed along on wd outside over 2f out: n.d but kpt on* **14/1**
04 **7** *1* **Artistic Muse (IRE)**[10] 3184 3-9-0 0.................... DaneO'Neill 4 61
(B W Hills) *hld up towards rr: pushed along and kpt on one pce fr over 2f out: n.d* **16/1**
0 **8** *½* **Dire Straits (IRE)**[13] 3074 3-9-5 0.................... TedDurcan 14 65
(Chris Wall) *wl in tch: shkn up over 2f out: sn outpcd: plugged on* **40/1**
**9** *9* **House Captain** 3-9-5 0.................... SeanLevey 7 44
(Richard Hannon) *s.i.s: t.k.h in rr: shkn up over 3f out: no prog* **16/1**
50 **10** *shd* **Mr Soprano**[34] 2432 3-9-5 0.................... SaleemGolam 2 44
(Stuart Williams) *s.i.s: t.k.h in rr: sme prog into midfield 3f out: wknd 2f out* **66/1**
**11** *1 ½* **Il Gran Capo (IRE)** 3-9-5 0.................... RobertHavlin 11 40
(Roger Ingram) *s.s: hld up in last: no prog 3f out* **66/1**
00 **12** *hd* **Femme De Menage**[26] 2681 3-9-0 0.................... DavidProbert 13 35
(Andrew Balding) *chsd ldrs tl wknd over 2f out* **66/1**
0 **13** *5* **Fly A Kite**[50] 1984 3-9-5 0.................... SamHitchcott 10 29
(Jonathan Portman) *s.i.s: a in rr: wknd over 2f out: wl bhd* **66/1**

1m 44.87s (0.17) **Going Correction** -0.025s/f (Good) **13 Ran SP% 115.7**
Speed ratings (Par 99): **98,97,93,92,91 90,89,88,79,79 78,77,72**
CSF £6.54 TOTE £2.90: £1.20, £1.20, £2.80; EX 7.30 Trifecta £27.70.
**Owner** Cheveley Park Stud **Bred** Cheveley Park Stud Ltd **Trained** Newmarket, Suffolk
■ Stewards' Enquiry : Frederik Tylicki one-day ban: careless riding (7 July)

**FOCUS**
A 3yo maiden markedly weakened by the non-runner. It was run at a fair early pace but yet again at this course it paid to race handily. Fair form, the first two improving.

## 3538 UNIBET-BY PLAYERS FOR PLAYERS H'CAP (BOBIS RACE) 1m 67y
**7:40** (7:40) (Class 4) (0-85,84) 3-Y-O **£4,851** (£1,443; £721; £360) **Stalls Low**

Form RPR
4222 **1** **Voyageofdiscovery (USA)**[2] 3464 3-8-10 **76**.................... RyanTate(3) 6 86
(Clive Cox) *trckd ldng pair: wnt 2nd over 2f out: shkn up to ld wl over 1f out: in command fnl f: pushed out* **13/8**[1]
3-51 **2** *1 ¾* **Ravenous**[61] 1654 3-9-1 **78**.................... JimCrowley 1 83
(Ralph Beckett) *led: rdn and hdd wl over 1f out: no ch w wnr fnl f but kpt on* **6/1**[3]
-005 **3** *1 ¼* **Cool Bahamian (IRE)**[18] 2921 3-9-1 **83**.................... LouisSteward(5) 3 85
(Eve Johnson Houghton) *hld up disputing 5th: eased to outer and rdn 2f out: chsd ldng pair over 1f out: nt qckn fnl f* **6/1**[3]
3054 **4** *1 ¼* **Grevillea (IRE)**[19] 2892 3-9-2 **82**.................... WilliamTwiston-Davies(3) 2 81
(Mick Channon) *hld up in last: plenty to do whn swtchd to wd outside and rdn over 2f out: kpt on but no ch* **10/1**
01-0 **5** *½* **Constantine**[18] 2921 3-9-2 **79**.................... SeanLevey 4 77
(Richard Hannon) *t.k.h: trckd ldng pair: rdn and nt qckn over 2f out: fdd fnl f* **20/1**
-450 **6** *3 ¼* **Dullingham**[8] 3273 3-9-7 **84**.................... JamieSpencer 5 77
(Charlie Appleby) *hld up disputing 5th: pushed along and no prog 3f out: wl hld over 1f out: eased ins fnl f* **5/2**[2]
0-03 **7** *2 ¼* **Capers Royal Star (FR)**[17] 2948 3-8-2 **65** oh2.................... LukeMorris 7 50
(Alastair Lidderdale) *t.k.h: chsd ldr to over 2f out: wknd qckly* **40/1**

1m 43.91s (-0.79) **Going Correction** -0.025s/f (Good) **7 Ran SP% 111.5**
Speed ratings (Par 101): **102,100,99,97,97 94,91**
CSF £11.37 TOTE £3.10: £1.60, £2.20; EX 11.70 Trifecta £47.10.
**Owner** The Navigators **Bred** Look Out Lorie Partnership **Trained** Lambourn, Berks

**FOCUS**
A modest 3yo handicap. They went a routine sort of pace and kicked at the top of the home straight. Sound, if ordinary form.

## 3539 UNIBET.CO.UK DAILY ENHANCED PLACE TERMS H'CAP (BOBIS RACE) 6f
**8:10** (8:11) (Class 4) (0-85,85) 3-Y-O **£4,851** (£1,443; £721; £360) **Stalls Low**

Form RPR
2100 **1** **Nova Champ (IRE)**[17] 2962 3-8-13 **77**....................(p) JamieSpencer 9 83
(Stuart Williams) *racd alone in centre: led 1f: prom: rdn over 2f out and looked in trble: rallied 1f out: drvn ahd last strides* **17/2**
4114 **2** *hd* **Iseemist (IRE)**[17] 2965 3-8-9 **78**.................... LouisSteward(5) 7 83
(John Gallagher) *pressed ldr after 1f: drvn to take narrow ld fnl f: kpt on but hdd last strides* **10/1**
2220 **3** *shd* **Lincoln (IRE)**[17] 2962 3-9-3 **84**.................... WilliamTwiston-Davies(3) 1 89
(Mick Channon) *taken down early: led after 1f and racd against nr side rail: drvn 2f out: narrowly hdd fnl f: kpt on but lost 2nd nr fin* **7/2**[2]
1-00 **4** *1 ¼* **Miss Lillie**[27] 2639 3-9-2 **80**....................(p) JamesDoyle 6 81
(Roger Teal) *free to post: hld up in rr: taken to wd outside and rdn over 2f out: kpt on fr over 1f out: nvr able to chal* **25/1**
51 **5** *nk* **Polybius**[21] 2846 3-9-6 **84**.................... TedDurcan 2 85
(David Lanigan) *t.k.h: hld up: trckd ldrs 1/2-way: shkn up 2f out: nt qckn between rivals over 1f out: no imp fnl f* **7/4**[1]
5603 **6** *½* **Meritocracy (IRE)**[10] 3185 3-9-7 **85**.................... LukeMorris 3 83
(Paul Cole) *chsd ldrs: urged along 1/2-way: lost pl and struggling 2f out: tried to rally fnl f: one pce* **12/1**
-134 **7** *1 ¼* **Strategic Force (IRE)**[10] 3185 3-9-1 **82**....................(b[1]) RyanTate(3) 8 76
(Clive Cox) *t.k.h and sn prom: rdn over 2f out: sn lost pl and btn* **16/1**
-446 **8** *hd* **Fiftyshadesofgrey (IRE)**[46] 2090 3-9-2 **80**....................(bt[1]) PatCosgrave 5 74
(George Baker) *hld up in rr: drvn and no prog over 2f out: no imp after* **14/1**
1-44 **9** *1 ¾* **Exceeder**[46] 2090 3-9-1 **79**.................... MartinHarley 4 67
(Marco Botti) *a towards rr: rdn and no prog over 2f out* **8/1**[3]

1m 11.65s (-1.35) **Going Correction** -0.175s/f (Firm) **9 Ran SP% 113.4**
Speed ratings (Par 101): **102,101,101,99,99 98,97,96,94**
CSF £87.78 CT £354.00 TOTE £5.20: £2.00, £3.20, £1.60; EX 78.60 Trifecta £796.70.
**Owner** Qatar Racing Limited **Bred** Hyde Park Stud & Paddy Conney **Trained** Newmarket, Suffolk

**FOCUS**
A fair 3yo sprint handicap that threw up a very tight three-way finish. A personal best from the winner.

## 3540 DOWNLOAD THE UNIBET PRO APP FILLIES' H'CAP 1m 2f 7y
**8:40** (8:40) (Class 5) (0-70,69) 4-Y-O+ **£2,911** (£866; £432; £216) **Stalls Centre**

Form RPR
400- **1** **Panettone (IRE)**[237] 7611 5-9-1 **63**.................... PaddyAspell 2 71
(Roger Varian) *a in ldng trio: trckd ldr 6f out: rdn to chal whn bmpd 2f out: styd w ldrs: kpt on to ld last 100yds* **6/1**[2]

6652 **2** ½ **If I Were A Boy (IRE)**[13] 3080 7-8-10 **58**..........................(b) LukeMorris 1 65
(Dominic Ffrench Davis) *led: rdn and jnd whn nudged by rival 2f out: hdd briefly 1f out: drvn and hdd last 100yds: kpt on* **8/1**[3]

-131 **3** *nk* **Stockhill Diva**[17] 2947 4-9-7 **69**.......................................... KierenFallon 7 75+
(Brendan Powell) *hld up in last and wl off the pce: pushed along and prog 4f out: squeezed between rivals to chal 2f out: led briefly 1f out: nt qckn last 150yds* **5/6**[1]

0-54 **4** 3 **Beep**[15] 3032 4-8-8 **63** ow3.......................................... NedCurtis(7) 5 64
(Lydia Richards) *t.k.h: hld up off the pce in last trio: clsd on ldrs 3f out: shkn up and nt qckn 2f out: fdd ins fnl f* **14/1**

-340 **5** *nk* **Zinnobar**[21] 2836 4-8-2 **50** oh2..........................(p) NickyMackay 8 50
(Jonathan Portman) *chsd ldr to 6f out: rdn over 3f out: steadily fdd fr wl over 1f out* **14/1**

2150 **6** 2 **Tijuca (IRE)**[13] 3080 5-8-8 **56**.......................................... ChrisCatlin 3 52
(Ed de Giles) *hld up in last trio and off the pce: pushed along and no prog over 3f out: n.d after* **11/1**

66 **7** 16 **Remix (IRE)**[28] 2609 5-8-9 **57**..........................(p) StevieDonohoe 6 23
(Ian Williams) *hld up in 4th: shkn up and lost pl over 3f out: wknd 2f out: t.o* **9/1**

2m 9.97s (1.27) **Going Correction** -0.025s/f (Good) **7** Ran SP% **111.6**
Speed ratings (Par 100): **93,92,92,89,89 88,75**
CSF £49.02 CT £76.98 TOTE £8.70: £3.20, £2.50; EX 26.60 Trifecta £74.20.
**Owner** Duncan Jones & Dr Sosie Kassab **Bred** Bjorn Nielsen **Trained** Newmarket, Suffolk

**FOCUS**
A moderate fillies' handicap, run at an ordinary pace and with no depth. The winner is rated to form.

## 3541 CITI PRIVATE BANK SUPPORTING CLIC SARGENT H'CAP 1m 3f 135y
**9:10** (9:10) (Class 5) (0-75,73) 3-Y-O **£2,911** (£866; £432; £216) **Stalls** Centre

Form RPR
2-03 **1** **Classical Art (IRE)**[23] 2769 3-9-6 **72**.......................................... KierenFallon 5 77
(Roger Varian) *hld up in 4th: pushed along and prog over 3f out: rdn to ld over 1f out: kpt on fnl f: jst hld on* **2/1**[1]

-344 **2** *shd* **Winter Spice (IRE)**[11] 3146 3-8-10 **65**..........................(b[1]) RyanTate(3) 6 69
(Clive Cox) *hld up in last: hld together tl prog wl over 1f out: cajoled along to cl on wnr last 75yds: jst failed* **5/1**[3]

4-20 **3** 1 **Armourer (IRE)**[24] 2735 3-9-0 **66**.......................................... MartinDwyer 1 68
(William Muir) *led at mod pce: veered bdly lft over 4f out: str reminders and flashed tail: drvn and hdd over 1f out: nt qckn* **14/1**

0023 **4** 1½ **New Colours**[26] 2671 3-9-1 **67**..........................(v[1]) BenCurtis 2 67
(Marcus Tregoning) *t.k.h: trckd ldng pair: wnt 2nd 4f out: rdn and nt qckn whn cl up wl over 1f out: one pce after* **8/1**

4-13 **5** 4 **Cosette (IRE)**[39] 2273 3-9-7 **73**.......................................... DaneO'Neill 3 66
(Henry Candy) *trckd ldr to 4f out: drvn over 2f out: wknd over 1f out* **9/4**[2]

0-33 **6** 4½ **Epsom Hill (SWE)**[19] 2899 3-9-6 **72**..........................(v[1]) FrederikTylicki 4 57
(Charlie Fellowes) *dwlt: hld up in last pair: shkn up and cl enough bhd ldrs over 2f out: wknd qckly over 1f out* **6/1**

2m 35.97s (6.47) **Going Correction** -0.025s/f (Good) **6** Ran SP% **112.8**
Speed ratings (Par 99): **77,76,76,75,72 69**
CSF £12.52 TOTE £2.50: £1.40, £1.90; EX 13.60 Trifecta £151.00.
**Owner** Mrs Susan Roy **Bred** J Dorrian **Trained** Newmarket, Suffolk

**FOCUS**
Due to a tactical pace this 3yo handicap was a muddling affair, although the first three came from the back.
T/Plt: £56.10 to a £1 stake. Pool: £82,979.07 - 1078.56 winning units. T/Qpdt: £36.40 to a £1 stake. Pool: £4616.03 - 93.80 winning units. JN

# 3091 BEVERLEY (R-H)
Tuesday, June 24

**OFFICIAL GOING: Good to firm changing to good to firm (good in places) after race 3 (2.45)**
Inside rail around bottom bend moved in and races on Round course increased by 19yds.
Wind: fresh across Weather: Overcast, couple of heavy showers before 1st

## 3542 WATCH ON THREE DEVICES RACINGUK.COM/ANYWHERE MAIDEN AUCTION STKS 7f 100y
**1:45** (1:45) (Class 6) 2-Y-O **£2,264** (£673; £336; £168) **Stalls** Low

Form RPR
64 **1** **Special Venture (IRE)**[20] 2895 2-9-1 0.......................................... DavidAllan 5 73+
(Tim Easterby) *mde all: pressed fr over 2f out tl 1f out: kpt on wl and firmly in command ins fnl f* **5/2**[2]

40 **2** 2½ **Our Kylie (IRE)**[9] 3267 2-8-10 0.......................................... BarryMcHugh 6 62
(Tony Coyle) *trckd ldr: pressed wnr fr over 2f out tl 1f out: no ex ins fnl f* **6/1**[3]

3 **3** ½ **Flatcapper (IRE)**[28] 2652 2-8-10 0.......................................... TonyHamilton 1 61
(Richard Fahey) *trckd ldr: rdn over 2f out: one pce* **11/10**[1]

0 **4** ¾ **Mistral**[24] 2771 2-8-1 0.......................................... JackDuern(5) 3 55
(Steph Hollinshead) *dwlt: sn in tch: rdn over 2f out: kpt on fnl f* **66/1**

00 **5** 3¾ **Sparkle Girl**[36] 2386 2-8-6 0.......................................... DuranFentiman 4 46
(Tim Easterby) *midfield: pushed along 1/2-way: one pce and nvr threatened* **66/1**

**6** 2 **Electric (IRE)** 2-8-6 0.......................................... PhilipPrince(5) 2 47
(Jo Hughes) *s.i.s: hld up: nvr threatened* **25/1**

**7** *nse* **Yukos Flyer (IRE)** 2-8-6 0.......................................... PatrickMathers 7 41
(Richard Fahey) *hld up: nvr threatened* **16/1**

4 **8** 2¾ **Tantric Lady**[8] 3297 2-8-6 0.......................................... BenCurtis 8 35
(Alan McCabe) *wnt sltly lft s: racd keenly hld up: rdn over 2f out: sn btn* **8/1**

1m 35.67s (1.87) **Going Correction** -0.075s/f (Good) **8** Ran SP% **114.3**
Speed ratings (Par 91): **86,83,82,81,77 75,75,71**
CSF £17.64 TOTE £3.60: £1.20, £2.00, £1.10; EX 17.70 Trifecta £33.70.
**Owner** David Scott & Co Ltd & E A Brook **Bred** Eimear Mulhern & Abbeville Stud **Trained** Great Habton, N Yorks

**FOCUS**
The inside rail round the bottom bend was moved out, extending the distance of all races on the round course by 19 yards. They went an average pace for this 2yo maiden, which suited those prominent. The time was slow but the form has been given a chance.

## 3543 RACING UK PROFITS ALL RETURNED TO RACING MEDIAN AUCTION MAIDEN STKS 1m 100y
**2:15** (2:17) (Class 5) 3-Y-O **£3,408** (£1,006; £503) **Stalls** Low

Form RPR
3-3 **1** **Mange All**[38] 2334 3-9-5 0.......................................... LiamJones 1 85+
(William Haggas) *mde all: c clr on bit fnl 3f* **1/10**[1]

40 **2** 10 **Far Ranging (USA)**[13] 3097 3-9-0 0.......................................... BarryMcHugh 2 57
(Julie Camacho) *in tch: rdn over 3f out: wnt 2nd over 2f out: one pce and no threat wnr* **4/1**[2]

0000 **3** 4½ **Tawan**[21] 2867 3-9-2 37..........................(b[1]) ConnorBeasley(3) 4 52
(Brian Rothwell) *in tch: hdwy to chse ldr 4f out: lost 2nd over 2f out: no ex* **50/1**

**4** 2¼ **Fillydelphia (IRE)** 3-9-0 0..........................[1] AndrewMullen 5 41
(Patrick Holmes) *sn pushed along in rr: nvr threatened* **12/1**[3]

0 **5** 3¼ **Pepperello**[21] 2871 3-9-5 0.......................................... JamesSullivan 3 39
(Tim Etherington) *prom: lost pl 4f out: sn btn* **33/1**

1m 46.96s (-0.64) **Going Correction** -0.075s/f (Good) **5** Ran SP% **123.5**
Speed ratings (Par 99): **100,90,85,83,80**
CSF £1.53 TOTE £1.10: £1.10, £1.60; EX 1.60 Trifecta £9.10.
**Owner** B Haggas **Bred** J B Haggas **Trained** Newmarket, Suffolk

**FOCUS**
This was weak and little more than an exercise gallop for the heavily odds-on winner. He's likely to better this.

## 3544 RACING UK ANYWHERE AVAILABLE NOW H'CAP 1m 1f 207y
**2:45** (2:45) (Class 4) (0-80,78) 4-Y-O+ **£6,469** (£1,925; £962; £481) **Stalls** Low

Form RPR
0054 **1** **Aryal**[6] 3371 4-9-4 **75**..........................(b) FrannyNorton 6 85
(Mark Johnston) *stmbld sltly leaving stall: sn trckd ldr: rdn over 2f out: led wl over 1f out: kpt on wl* **9/2**[2]

0022 **2** 1¾ **Ocean Applause**[12] 3162 4-8-9 **73**..........................(t) JoeDoyle(7) 5 79
(John Ryan) *hld up: rdn and hdwy over 2f out: wnt 2nd 110yds out: kpt on* **13/2**

/0-0 **3** 2¼ **Quite Sparky**[31] 2540 7-7-9 **59**..........................(p) JackGarritty(7) 4 60
(Mike Sowersby) *midfield: rdn and hdwy over 2f out: one pce fnl f* **66/1**

00-1 **4** *nse* **Eeny Mac (IRE)**[13] 3094 7-9-4 **75**.......................................... AndrewElliott 8 76
(Neville Bycroft) *led: rdn whn hdd wl over 1f out: no ex ins fnl f* **11/2**

-640 **5** *hd* **Unex Michelangelo (IRE)**[13] 3095 5-8-5 **62**.......................................... BarryMcHugh 3 63
(Michael Easterby) *hld up: rdn 2f out: kpt on fnl f: nrst fin* **33/1**

4420 **6** *hd* **King Of The Celts (IRE)**[10] 3254 6-8-5 **69**.......................................... RachelRichardson(7) 2 70
(Tim Easterby) *trckd ldr: rdn over 2f out: no ex ins fnl f* **8/1**

4120 **7** ½ **Red Shuttle**[63] 1636 7-9-4 **78**.......................................... RobertTart(3) 10 78
(Andi Brown) *hld up: rdn over 2f out: kpt on fnl f* **8/1**

5-00 **8** 19 **Christmas Light**[11] 3205 7-9-1 **72**.......................................... TomEaves 1 35
(Brian Ellison) *in tch: rdn over 2f out: sn wknd* **5/1**[3]

-623 **9** ½ **Tafawuk (USA)**[18] 2966 5-9-1 **72**.......................................... FrederikTylicki 7 35
(Roger Varian) *in tch: pushed along over 3f out: rdn over 2f out: sn wknd* **7/2**[1]

104- **10** 9 **Enzaal (USA)**[279] 6514 4-9-7 **78**.......................................... PhillipMakin 9 23
(Philip Kirby) *midfield: rdn over 3f out: sn btn* **20/1**

2m 4.95s (-2.05) **Going Correction** -0.075s/f (Good) **10** Ran SP% **117.2**
Speed ratings (Par 105): **105,103,101,101,101 101,101,85,85,78**
CSF £33.42 CT £1694.98 TOTE £5.30: £2.10, £2.10, £7.20; EX 40.60 Trifecta £1119.70.
**Owner** Sheikh Hamdan bin Mohammed Al Maktoum **Bred** Newsells Park Stud **Trained** Middleham Moor, N Yorks

**FOCUS**
The pace was honest for this fair handicap. A turf best from the winner.

## 3545 RACING UK ON SKY 432 H'CAP 1m 1f 207y
**3:15** (3:16) (Class 6) (0-65,65) 3-Y-O **£2,726** (£805; £402) **Stalls** Low

Form RPR
3-24 **1** **Miss Lucy Jane**[32] 2523 3-9-3 **64**.......................................... GeorgeChaloner(3) 6 72
(Richard Fahey) *dwlt: sn midfield towards outer: rdn and hdwy over 2f out: r.o wl fr over 1f out: led 110yds out* **9/2**[3]

50-5 **2** ½ **Victory Danz (IRE)**[7] 3333 3-8-12 **56**.......................................... DanielTudhope 4 64
(David O'Meara) *hld up in midfield: pushed along 3f out: briefly n.m.r over 2f out: swtchd to wd outside over 1f out: r.o wl: wnt 2nd 100yds out* **4/1**[2]

-050 **3** 4½ **Shamouti (IRE)**[13] 3098 3-8-2 **49**..........................(p) IanBrennan(3) 7 48
(Ollie Pears) *led narrowly: rdn over 2f out: hdd 110yds out: no ex* **28/1**

00-4 **4** *nk* **Sequester**[43] 2210 3-9-7 **65**.......................................... TedDurcan 8 63
(David Lanigan) *trckd ldng pair: rdn over 2f out: no ex fnl f* **3/1**[1]

004 **5** ½ **Fickle Feelings (IRE)**[20] 2899 3-8-9 **53**.......................................... GrahamGibbons 3 50
(David Barron) *trckd ldng pair: rdn over 2f out: no ex fnl f* **7/1**

-346 **6** ¾ **Speedbird One**[28] 2643 3-9-1 **62**.......................................... ConnorBeasley(3) 1 58
(James Given) *midfield: rdn over 2f out: one pce and nvr threatened* **20/1**

5430 **7** ¾ **Kraka Gym (IRE)**[45] 2165 3-9-2 **60**.......................................... BarryMcHugh 5 54
(Michael Easterby) *hld up: rdn over 2f out: nvr threatened* **11/1**

0-35 **8** *shd* **Frosty The Snowman (IRE)**[47] 2098 3-9-4 **62**.......................................... JamesSullivan 2 56
(Ruth Carr) *hld up: rdn over 2f out: nvr threatened* **16/1**

3360 **9** 6 **Power Up**[17] 2998 3-9-7 **65**.......................................... FrannyNorton 10 48
(Mark Johnston) *w ldr: rdn over 2f out: already wkng whn sltly short of room jst ins fnl f* **8/1**

0124 **10** 11 **Tortoise**[13] 3105 3-8-11 **55**..........................(b) RobertWinston 11 17
(Richard Guest) *trckd ldng pair towards outier: rdn over 2f out: wknd over 1f out* **14/1**

2m 6.9s (-0.10) **Going Correction** -0.075s/f (Good) **10** Ran SP% **115.9**
Speed ratings (Par 97): **97,96,93,92,92 91,91,91,86,77**
CSF £22.72 CT £450.09 TOTE £4.80: £2.30, £2.10, £7.10; EX 27.50 Trifecta £541.50.
**Owner** R J Bown **Bred** Miss J Chaplin **Trained** Musley Bank, N Yorks

**FOCUS**
Plenty of unexposed types in this handicap which was run at a sound pace. The front two pulled clear and the form is taken literally.

## 3546 RACING UK ANDROID APP RACINGUK.COM/MOBILE H'CAP 1m 4f 16y
**3:45** (3:45) (Class 5) (0-70,70) 4-Y-O+ **£3,234** (£962; £481; £240) **Stalls** Low

Form RPR
111 **1** **Thecornishcowboy**[8] 3310 5-9-0 **70**..........................(t) JoeDoyle(7) 3 81
(John Ryan) *in tch: pushed along and hdwy over 1f out: rdn to ld ins fnl f: jst hld on* **5/4**[1]

51 **2** *hd* **Spanish Plume**[57] 1815 6-9-1 **69**.................................(p) JackDuern(5) 4 79
(Andrew Hollinshead) *hld up: pushed along and hdwy 2f out: briefly nt much appr fnl f: angled lft into clr jst ins fnl f: r.o: jst hld* **8/1**

2-00 **3** *2 ½* **Gambol (FR)**[50] 2025 4-9-7 **70**........................................... DaneO'Neill 8 76
(B W Hills) *wnt sltly lft s: hld up and t.k.h: rdn over 2f out: hdwy on outer over 1f out: one pce in 3rd fnl 110yds* **11/2**[3]

6030 **4** *2 ¾* **Pertemps Networks**[11] 3205 10-9-2 **65**..................... GrahamGibbons 2 67
(Michael Easterby) *trckd ldr: rdn over 2f out: no ex ins fnl f* **16/1**

4-01 **5** *½* **Valantino Oyster (IRE)**[29] 2607 7-8-13 **62**......................(p) DaleSwift 7 63
(Tracy Waggott) *led: rdn over 2f out: hdd ins fnl f: wknd* **9/2**[2]

0-05 **6** *1* **Kheskianto (IRE)**[12] 3155 8-7-9 **51** oh5..................(t) BradleyBosley(7) 1 50
(Michael Chapman) *dwlt: sn trckd ldrs: rdn over 2f out: wknd ins fnl f* **33/1**

/63- **7** *1* **Sheila's Castle**[367] 3589 10-8-0 **54**......................... ShirleyTeasdale(5) 6 52
(Sean Regan) *in tch on outer: rdn over 2f out: wknd over 1f out* **10/1**

-600 **8** *¾* **Valentine's Gift**[21] 2872 6-8-8 **60**...................................... JulieBurke(3) 5 56
(Neville Bycroft) *hld up in tch: rdn over 2f out: wknd fnl f* **12/1**

2m 40.23s (0.43) **Going Correction** -0.075s/f (Good) **8** Ran SP% **114.7**
Speed ratings (Par 103): **95,94,93,91,91 90,89,89**
CSF £12.24 CT £41.59 TOTE £2.80: £1.50, £1.80, £2.50; EX 10.70 Trifecta £41.00.
**Owner** C Letcher & J Ryan **Bred** Hadi Al Tajir **Trained** Newmarket, Suffolk

**FOCUS**
A fair handicap for the grade, run at a steady pace. The winner did not have to match his Windsor win.

## 3547 WATCH LIVE RACING AND BET WITH RACING UK H'CAP 7f 100y
**4:15** (4:16) (Class 5) (0-70,70) 3-Y-O+ **£3,234** (£962; £481; £240) **Stalls** Low

Form RPR

05-1 **1** **Jacbequick**[42] 2236 3-9-0 **70**.................................... JacobButterfield(5) 13 74+
(Ollie Pears) *prom: rdn over 2f out: led narrowly 110yds out: edgd lft: rdr dropped rein nr fin: jst hld on* **12/1**

6-00 **2** *hd* **Last Destination (IRE)**[13] 3096 6-8-9 **51** oh3............... AndrewMullen 5 58
(Nigel Tinkler) *midfield: rdn over 2f out: hdwy over 1f out: ev ch ins fnl f: kpt on: jst hld* **10/1**

4655 **3** *nk* **Thrust Control (IRE)**[7] 3344 7-8-9 **51** oh1................(p) FrannyNorton 14 57
(Tracy Waggott) *led: rdn over 2f out: strly pressed fr over 1f out: hdd 110yds out: kpt on* **20/1**

4050 **4** *nk* **Mysterial**[13] 3096 4-9-10 **66**............................................ JamesSullivan 9 71
(Ruth Carr) *hld up in midfield on inner: rdn and hdwy over 1f out: kpt on fnl f* **6/1**[3]

-541 **5** *½* **Be Royale**[12] 3160 4-9-10 **66**............................................. DaneO'Neill 10 70+
(Michael Appleby) *hld up: rdn and hdwy on outer over 1f out: kpt on fnl f* **4/1**[1]

6051 **6** *nk* **Space War**[7] 3344 7-9-12 **68** 6ex................................ GrahamGibbons 11 71
(Michael Easterby) *prom towards outer: rdn and ev ch over 1f out: no ex fnl 100yds* **13/2**

5004 **7** *nk* **Surround Sound**[10] 3237 4-9-7 **63**...................................... DavidAllan 4 66
(Tim Easterby) *hld up: rdn over 2f out: hdwy whn n.m.r ins fnl f: swtchd rt: kpt on* **4/1**[1]

0312 **8** *1* **Mercers Row**[8] 3299 7-9-5 **68**.................................... GemmaTutty(7) 12 68+
(Karen Tutty) *racd keenly: hld up in midfield on outer: rdn and hdwy 2f out: no ex fnl 110yds* **11/2**[2]

502/ **9** *3* **Rocky's Pride (IRE)**[309] 5600 8-8-9 **51** oh4.......................... PaulQuinn 2 44
(Richard Whitaker) *chsd ldrs: rdn over 2f out: wknd fnl f* **25/1**

0000 **10** *hd* **Rio Cobolo (IRE)**[8] 3299 8-9-4 **60**...............................(b) PhillipMakin 8 52
(Philip Kirby) *trckd ldrs: rdn over 2f out: wknd ins fnl f* **25/1**

0460 **11** *2 ¾* **Blazeofenchantment (USA)**[20] 2901 4-8-10 **52**............. PaulPickard 1 37
(John Wainwright) *dwlt: hld up: rdn 3f out: nvr threatened* **20/1**

6-04 **12** *2 ¾* **Wolfwood**[20] 2896 3-7-7 **51** oh6.................................... JackGarritty(7) 6 26
(John Davies) *midfield: rdn over 2f out: wknd over 1f out* **50/1**

1m 33.12s (-0.68) **Going Correction** -0.075s/f (Good)
**WFA** 3 from 4yo+ 9lb **12** Ran SP% **119.0**
Speed ratings (Par 103): **100,99,99,99,98 98,97,96,93,93 89,86**
CSF £117.01 CT £2417.01 TOTE £13.00: £2.80, £3.80, £4.70; EX 180.40 Trifecta £1547.70.
**Owner** Cherry Garth Racing **Bred** Russ Wake **Trained** Norton, N Yorks
■ Stewards' Enquiry : Jacob Butterfield one-day ban: careless riding (Jul 8)

**FOCUS**
They went a strong pace for this open-looking contest, in the best time on the card. A bunch finish and the form is ordinary.

## 3548 GO RACING IN YORKSHIRE FUTURE STARS APPRENTICE H'CAP (ROUND 4) 5f
**4:45** (4:46) (Class 6) (0-60,60) 3-Y-O+ **£2,264** (£673; £336; £168) **Stalls** Low

Form RPR

5003 **1** **Choc'A'Moca (IRE)**[7] 3338 7-8-13 **51**..........................(v) JoshDoyle(5) 11 61
(Paul Midgley) *in tch: rdn 1/2-way: kpt on: led towards fin* **5/1**[2]

03-4 **2** *hd* **Spoken Words**[13] 3099 5-8-10 **46** oh1......................... GaryMahon(3) 13 55
(John David Riches) *hld up in rr: rdn and hdwy over 1f out: kpt on wl: jst failed* **50/1**

4500 **3** *¾* **Rostrum Farewell**[13] 3124 3-8-8 **52**...........................(b) ClaireMurray(5) 5 56
(David Brown) *led: sn clr: rdn and reduced advantage ins fnl f: hdd towards fin* **33/1**

446 **4** *1 ¾* **Bondi Beach Babe**[17] 2985 4-9-5 **57**............................ PeterSword(5) 12 57
(James Turner) *hld up: rdn 1/2-way: kpt on fnl f* **18/1**

031 **5** *nk* **Incomparable**[13] 3093 9-9-2 **54**..............................(p) PatrickO'Donnell(5) 7 53
(Scott Dixon) *chsd ldr: rdn 1/2-way: no ex ins fnl f* **7/1**

0-32 **6** *¾* **White Flag**[13] 3100 3-9-1 **54**.................................... RachelRichardson 9 48
(Tim Easterby) *chsd ldr: rdn 1/2-way: no ex fnl f* **11/1**

0230 **7** *1* **Major Muscari (IRE)**[5] 3393 6-9-4 **56**...........(p) MrAidenBlakemore(5) 10 49
(Shaun Harris) *dwlt: hld up: nvr threatened* **11/1**

0505 **8** *1 ½* **Mey Blossom**[1] 3530 9-9-5 **55**.....................................(v) AaronJones(3) 1 42+
(Richard Whitaker) *awkward s: hld up: rdn 1/2-way: nvr threatened* **5/1**[2]

4056 **9** *nse* **Lady Montenegro**[6] 3366 3-8-4 **48**.............................(p) RowanScott(5) 8 33
(Ann Duffield) *midfield: rdn 1/2-way: nvr threatened* **14/1**

0001 **10** *hd* **Ichimoku**[13] 3092 4-9-0 **52**...................................... MichaelKenneally(5) 3 38
(Bryan Smart) *midfield: rdn 1/2-way: wknd fnl f* **6/1**[3]

0000 **11** *1 ½* **Sophie's Beau (USA)**[12] 3149 7-8-12 **50**.................(t) BradleyBosley(5) 6 31
(Michael Chapman) *midfield: sn pushed along: wknd 2f out* **20/1**

2505 **U** **Manatee Bay**[18] 2955 4-9-10 **60**.................................... AnnaHesketh(3) 4
(David Nicholls) *awkward leaving stall and uns rdr* **4/1**[1]

1m 2.9s (-0.60) **Going Correction** -0.075s/f (Good)
**WFA** 3 from 4yo+ 6lb **12** Ran SP% **118.4**
Speed ratings (Par 101): **101,100,99,96,96 95,93,91,90,90 88,**
CSF £240.78 CT £7357.74 TOTE £5.30: £1.80, £9.20, £10.90; EX 212.80 Trifecta £2977.70 Part won. Pool: £3,970.31 - 0.40 winning units..
**Owner** John Milburn - Andrew Stephenson **Bred** Yeomanstown Stud **Trained** Westow, N Yorks

**FOCUS**
Plenty of pace for the modest apprentice handicap. The winner built on his latest form.

T/Plt: £111.10 to a £1 stake. Pool: £61,137.81 - 401.49 winning tickets. T/Qpdt: £71.00 to a £1 stake. Pool: £5,123.82 - 53.39 winning tickets. AS

# 3323 BRIGHTON (L-H)
### Tuesday, June 24

**OFFICIAL GOING: Good to firm (fim in places)**
Races on inner line and distances as advertised.
Wind: Moderate, against Weather: Fine and warm

## 3549 JIM DARVILL MEMORIAL H'CAP 5f 213y
**1:30** (1:30) (Class 6) (0-60,65) 3-Y-O+ **£1,940** (£577; £288; £144) **Stalls** Low

Form RPR

0005 **1** **Verus Delicia (IRE)**[12] 3150 5-9-12 **60**.................................. ShaneKelly 6 73
(Daniel Mark Loughnane) *in tch: effrt and hung lft fr over 1f out: led ins fnl f: rdn out* **7/1**

0060 **2** *1 ¾* **Homeboy (IRE)**[22] 2830 6-8-7 **46** oh1.........................(b) NoelGarbutt(5) 1 53
(David Evans) *led tl ins fnl f: one pce* **50/1**

411 **3** *¾* **Avonmore Star**[7] 3329 6-10-0 **65** 6ex.............................. OisinMurphy(3) 4 70
(Alan McCabe) *chsd ldr: rdn to chal over 1f out: one pce fnl f* **6/4**[1]

6606 **4** *¾* **Little Choosey**[50] 2008 4-9-0 **48**........................................ MartinHarley 2 51
(Anabel K Murphy) *towards rr: hdwy on rail 2f out: styd on same pce fnl f* **14/1**

4216 **5** *hd* **Belle Bayardo (IRE)**[10] 3237 6-9-9 **57**............................. LukeMorris 10 59
(Tony Carroll) *mid-div on outer: rdn over 2f out: styd on fnl f* **5/1**[2]

6205 **6** *2 ½* **Haadeeth**[20] 2887 7-9-8 **56**.................................................(t) AdamKirby 7 50
(David Evans) *towards rr: sme hdwy over 1f out: no imp fnl f* **8/1**

0000 **7** *nse* **Song Of Rowland (IRE)**[12] 3150 3-9-1 **59**...................... SimonPearce(3) 5 51
(John Spearing) *broke wl: prom tl wknd wl over 1f out* **6/1**[3]

5105 **8** *1 ¼* **Ad Vitam (IRE)**[3] 3485 6-9-8 **56**.................................(bt) MartinDwyer 3 46
(David C Griffiths) *outpcd and bhd: nvr nr ldrs* **12/1**

4004 **9** *8* **Princess Cammie (IRE)**[7] 3329 4-8-12 **46** oh1.........(p) WilliamCarson 8 10
(John Bridger) *s.s: sn in midfield on outer: wknd over 2f out* **33/1**

0003 **10** *9* **Back On Baileys**[7] 3323 3-8-2 **46** oh1..........................(v) RyanPowell(3) 9
(John Ryan) *prom for 2f: bhd and struggling fr 1/2-way* **40/1**

1m 9.73s (-0.47) **Going Correction** +0.025s/f (Good)
**WFA** 3 from 4yo+ 7lb **10** Ran SP% **116.3**
Speed ratings (Par 101): **104,101,100,99,99 96,96,94,83,71**
CSF £303.99 CT £814.08 TOTE £10.70: £2.80, £6.10, £1.10; EX 376.90 Trifecta £1820.00 Part won. Pool: £2,426.71 - 0.81 winning units..
**Owner** R M Brilley **Bred** R Fagan **Trained** Baldwin's Gate, Staffs

**FOCUS**
A moderate sprint handicap in which few got involved. The form is rated slightly positively.

## 3550 STARSPREADS.COM NOW ONLINE MAIDEN AUCTION STKS 5f 213y
**2:00** (2:02) (Class 5) 2-Y-O **£2,587** (£770; £384; £192) **Stalls** Low

Form RPR

0 **1** **Dream Approval (IRE)**[11] 3181 2-8-7 ...................... ThomasBrown(3) 6 69+
(Daniel Kubler) *t.k.h: sn prom: led 2f out: rdn clr fnl f: readily* **5/1**[3]

00 **2** *2 ¾* **Sculptured (FR)**[35] 2413 2-8-10 ....................................... PatCosgrave 3 60
(Jo Hughes) *in tch: chsd wnr over 1f out: kpt on same pce* **8/1**

0 **3** *1 ½* **Fast Scat (USA)**[10] 3215 2-8-10 ...................................... MartinHarley 2 56
(David Evans) *in tch: outpcd 3f out: rallied over 1f out: kpt on fnl f* **3/1**[2]

664 **4** *2* **Itsindebag**[25] 2716 2-7-13 ............................................. CamHardie(7) 7 46
(J S Moore) *s.s: hdwy over 2f out: wknd 1f out* **7/1**

006 **5** *1 ¾* **Karluk (IRE)**[10] 3210 2-8-8 ................................................(b[1]) JohnFahy 4 42
(Eve Johnson Houghton) *led tl 2f out: wknd over 1f out* **12/1**

**6** *4* **Jimmy's Hall** 2-8-10 ....................................................... OisinMurphy(3) 5 35
(J S Moore) *towards rr: mod effrt in centre 2f out: unbalanced on trck: sn wknd* **11/4**[1]

0 **7** *3 ½* **Powerfulstorm**[87] 1169 2-8-6 ............................................. LukeMorris 1 18
(Ronald Harris) *prom tl wknd over 2f out* **5/1**[3]

1m 10.56s (0.36) **Going Correction** +0.025s/f (Good) **7** Ran SP% **116.3**
Speed ratings (Par 93): **98,94,92,89,87 82,77**
CSF £44.60 TOTE £4.60: £2.30, £3.90; EX 46.00 Trifecta £172.20.
**Owner** Denarius Consulting Ltd **Bred** Myles Sunderland **Trained** Whitsbury, Hants

**FOCUS**
Very modest form amongst those with previous experience in this maiden. The second to fifth are the key. The time was 0.83secs slower than the opening contest over the same trip.

## 3551 STARSPREADS.COM COSTA RICA V ENG TRADE IN PLAY H'CAP 5f 59y
**2:30** (2:30) (Class 4) (0-80,80) 3-Y-O+ **£4,690** (£1,395; £697; £348) **Stalls** Low

Form RPR

4000 **1** **Powerful Wind (IRE)**[110] 863 5-9-9 **77**........................... DavidProbert 6 86
(Ronald Harris) *mde virtually all: hrd rdn fnl f: hld on by diminishing margin nr fin* **16/1**

623 **2** *¾* **Secret Millionaire (IRE)**[16] 3033 7-9-5 **73**...................... LukeMorris 3 79
(Tony Carroll) *hld up in 5th: hdwy and edgd lft over 1f out: chsd wnr fnl f: clsng qckly at fin: jst hld* **7/4**[1]

0336 **3** *5* **Secret Missile**[9] 3275 4-9-12 **80**.................................(b) MartinDwyer 4 69
(William Muir) *prom: rdn over 2f out: edgd rt over 1f out: one pce* **7/2**[3]

6410 **4** *hd* **Clear Praise (USA)**[25] 2718 7-9-8 **76**.............................. HayleyTurner 7 64
(Simon Dow) *chsd wnr tl 2f out: rdn and lost pl: kpt on again ins fnl f* **8/1**

665 **5** *¾* **Volito**[7] 3329 8-8-2 **63**........................................ KieranShoemark(7) 1 49
(Anabel K Murphy) *s.s: outpcd and wl bhd tl r.o fnl f* **12/1**

3304 **6** *1 ¾* **Fair Value (IRE)**[16] 3033 6-9-12 **80**................................... SebSanders 5 59
(Simon Dow) *chsd ldrs: rdn into 2nd 2f out: wknd 1f out: 3rd and btn whn eased: sddle slipped* **9/4**[2]

1m 1.8s (-0.50) **Going Correction** +0.025s/f (Good) **6** Ran SP% **114.0**
Speed ratings (Par 105): **105,103,95,95,94 91**
CSF £45.63 TOTE £13.70: £4.80, £1.30; EX 50.60 Trifecta £91.20.
**Owner** Anthony Cooke **Bred** Miss Ciara Doyle **Trained** Earlswood, Monmouths

**FOCUS**
The feature race and quite a competitive sprint, despite the small field, but something of an upset. The winner is rated close to his best.

## 3552 PIPECENTER.CO.UK H'CAP 1m 3f 196y
**3:00** (3:00) (Class 6) (0-65,61) 4-Y-O+ **£1,940** (£577; £288; £144) **Stalls** High

Form RPR

2-14 **1** **Men Don't Cry (IRE)**[14] 3086 5-9-4 **61**.......................... OisinMurphy(3) 6 70
(Ed de Giles) *chsd ldrs: disp ld 4f out: sustained battle w runner-up: hung lft fnl f: forged ahd fnl 100yds* **3/1**[2]

2622 **2** *½* **Litmus (USA)**[21] 2863 5-8-9 **49**.................................(b) HayleyTurner 4 57
(Simon Dow) *led: disp ld fr 4f out and kpt on gamely: worn down fnl 100yds* **5/1**[3]

4634 **3** *9* **Petersboden**[10] 3208 5-8-8 **48** ........ FergusSweeney 2 42
(Michael Blanshard) *hld up in 4th: rdn into 3rd 3f out: one pce: nvr trbld ldng pair* **12/1**

33-0 **4** *8* **Thundering Home**[18] 2942 7-8-11 **54** ........ WilliamTwiston-Davies(3) 1 35
(Richard Mitchell) *stdd s: a bhd: passed btn horses fnl 2f* **5/1**[3]

0066 **5** *2 1/2* **Turbulent Priest**[8] 3309 6-8-5 **45** ........ (b) LukeMorris 5 22
(Zoe Davison) *chsd ldr tl 1/2-way: hrd rdn and wknd 3f out* **25/1**

1311 **6** *1/2* **Novel Dancer**[19] 2916 6-8-8 **55** ........ JennyPowell(7) 3 31
(Lydia Richards) *bhd: modest hdwy 2f out: nvr nr ldrs: sn wknd* **8/1**

0-21 **7** *3* **Hamble**[19] 2923 5-9-4 **58** ........ PatrickDonaghy 7 29
(Giles Bravery) *stdd s: bhd: hdwy 6f out: hrd rdn and wknd 3f out* **15/8**[1]

2m 32.14s (-0.56) **Going Correction** +0.025s/f (Good) 7 Ran SP% **115.8**
Speed ratings (Par 101): **102,101,95,90,88 88,86**
CSF £18.82 TOTE £3.40: £2.10, £2.80; EX 18.30 Trifecta £67.30.

**Owner** Clarke, King & Lewis **Bred** Ecurie Des Monceaux **Trained** Ledbury, H'fords

**FOCUS**
Another moderate contest and the first two had it between them throughout, finishing clear. The form is rated around the runner-up.

## 3553 CLIMATECENTER.CO.UK H'CAP — 1m 1f 209y
**3:30** (3:32) (Class 6) (0-65,65) 4-Y-O+ £1,940 (£577; £288; £144) **Stalls** High

Form RPR

5650 **1** **Gabrial The Terror (IRE)**[10] 3226 4-9-4 **62** ........ MartinHarley 1 72
(David Simcock) *chsd ldng pair: wnt 2nd 3f out: chal and n.m.r on rail over 1f out: led ins fnl f: wl on top nr fin* **9/2**[3]

0-30 **2** *1 3/4* **Cherry Princess**[19] 2923 4-8-6 **53** ........ OisinMurphy(3) 2 60
(Stuart Williams) *led: rdn and hld on wl fnl 2f tl hdd and no ex ins fnl f* **6/1**

-562 **3** *2 1/2* **Indian Scout**[10] 3209 6-7-11 **48** ........ (b) CamHardie(7) 6 50
(Anabel K Murphy) *chsd ldr tl 3f out: hrd rdn wl over 1f out: hung lft: wknd fnl f* **7/2**[2]

0221 **4** *1 3/4* **Auden (USA)**[25] 2720 6-9-7 **65** ........ (v) PatDobbs 3 64
(J R Jenkins) *plld hrd in 4th: plld outside 3f out: sn rdn: one pce* **6/4**[1]

1410 **5** *1 1/4* **Anjuna Beach (USA)**[23] 2084 4-9-7 **65** ........ ShaneKelly 5 62
(Gary Moore) *s.s: bhd: rdn 3f out: n.d* **10/1**

33-0 **6** *3/4* **Green Earth (IRE)**[19] 2916 7-8-12 **59** ........ JemmaMarshall(3) 4 54
(Pat Phelan) *in tch: rdn 3f out: sn outpcd* **10/1**

2m 3.88s (0.28) **Going Correction** +0.025s/f (Good) 6 Ran SP% **112.9**
Speed ratings (Par 101): **99,97,95,94,93 92**
CSF £30.73 TOTE £6.20: £2.20, £2.20; EX 34.60 Trifecta £125.90.

**Owner** Dr Marwan Koukash **Bred** Mrs Joan Murphy **Trained** Newmarket, Suffolk

**FOCUS**
An ordinary handicap. The winner rates a 4lb personal best.

## 3554 STARSPREADS.COM IN-PLAY TRADING H'CAP — 7f 214y
**4:00** (4:01) (Class 6) (0-55,55) 3-Y-O+ £1,940 (£577; £288; £144) **Stalls** Low

Form RPR

6024 **1** **Fairy Mist (IRE)**[7] 3327 7-9-2 **47** ........ (b) WilliamCarson 4 56
(John Bridger) *hld up: hdwy 3f out: nt clr run and swtchd rt over 1f out: hrd rdn fnl f: led fnl strides* **6/1**[3]

2640 **2** *hd* **Abigails Angel**[19] 2923 7-8-12 **46** oh1 ........ WilliamTwiston-Davies(3) 9 54
(Brett Johnson) *sn led: kpt on u.p fnl 2f: hdd fnl strides* **10/1**

-006 **3** *nk* **Hawk Moth (IRE)**[14] 3075 6-9-7 **52** ........ (b) LukeMorris 1 59
(John Spearing) *chsd ldrs: wnt 2nd 2f out: drvn to chal fnl f: r.o* **6/1**[3]

-301 **4** *1 1/2* **Elle Rebelle**[7] 3327 4-9-2 **54** 6ex ........ CamHardie(7) 3 58
(Mark Brisbourne) *dwlt: bhd: rdn and sme hdwy 2f out: styd on: nvr able to chal* **9/4**[1]

5406 **5** *4 1/2* **Omotesando**[10] 3208 4-9-1 **46** oh1 ........ (p) ShaneKelly 7 39
(Mark Brisbourne) *prom: chsd ldr over 4f out tl over 2f out: sn btn* **5/1**[2]

0-00 **6** *1/2* **Jersey Cream (IRE)**[7] 3326 3-9-0 **55** ........ AdamBeschizza 5 45
(Gary Moore) *s.s: plld hrd in rr: rdn 3f out: n.d* **5/1**[2]

0660 **7** *1/2* **Autopilot**[26] 2688 3-9-0 **55** ........ (p) MartinHarley 8 44
(Anabel K Murphy) *in tch tl outpcd fnl 3f* **5/1**[2]

0/00 **8** *34* **Make A Fuss**[44] 1232 5-8-12 **46** oh1 ........ (b[1]) RyanPowell(3) 2
(Gerry Enright) *pressed ldr tl 1/2-way: wknd 3f out* **50/1**

1m 36.54s (0.54) **Going Correction** +0.025s/f (Good)
**WFA** 3 from 4yo+ 10lb 8 Ran SP% **120.4**
Speed ratings (Par 101): **98,97,97,96,91 91,90,56**
CSF £66.54 CT £384.71 TOTE £4.90: £2.10, £2.10, £1.90; EX 24.30 Trifecta £150.80.

**Owner** J J Bridger **Bred** Sandro Garavelli **Trained** Liphook, Hants

■ Stewards' Enquiry : William Twiston-Davies four-day ban: used whip above permitted level (Jul 8-10,14)

**FOCUS**
Another low-grade handicap but the best finish of the day. The winner was close to his old best.

## 3555 STARSPREADS.COM ENGLAND WORLD CUP OFFERS H'CAP — 6f 209y
**4:30** (4:31) (Class 5) (0-70,68) 3-Y-O+ £2,587 (£770; £384; £192) **Stalls** Low

Form RPR

0303 **1** *nk* **Kakapuka**[11] 3177 7-9-13 **67** ........ MartinHarley 6 74
(Anabel K Murphy) *led: kpt on wl u.p fnl f: hdd fnl 75yds* **9/2**

-604 **2** *nk* **Alcando (IRE)**[20] 2884 4-9-11 **65** ........ ShaneKelly 5 71
(Denis Coakley) *chsd ldr tl ins fnl f: kpt on* **7/2**[3]

00-6 **3** *1* **Just Isla**[11] 3177 4-9-4 **58** ........ (p) SebSanders 4 61
(Peter Makin) *hld up in 5th: hdwy and hung lft over 1f out: r.o fnl f* **3/1**[2]

2536 **4** *nk* **Sleipnir**[31] 2545 3-9-5 **68** ........ (be) PatDobbs 1 68
(Philip Hide) *dwlt: t.k.h: sn in 4th: hrd rdn 2f out: kpt on fnl f* **8/1**

000- **5** *38* **Stonecrabstomorrow (IRE)**[230] 7772 11-8-12 **55** ........ AshleyMorgan(3) 2
(Michael Attwater) *s.i.s: a in rr: no ch fnl 2f* **12/1**

215 **D** **Ocean Legend (IRE)**[13] 3112 9-9-13 **67** ........ AdamKirby 3 75
(Tony Carroll) *prom: rdn over 2f out: r.o to ld fnl 75yds* **9/4**[1]

1m 22.79s (-0.31) **Going Correction** +0.025s/f (Good)
**WFA** 3 from 4yo+ 9lb 6 Ran SP% **115.0**
Speed ratings (Par 103): **101,101,100,99,56 102**
CSF £13.19 TOTE £2.90: £1.70, £2.40; EX 8.00 Trifecta £22.50.

**Owner** Aiden Murphy & All The Kings Horses **Bred** Paradime Ltd **Trained** Wilmcote, Warwicks

**FOCUS**
A tight little race and a finish to match. The winner is rated back to his 2012 level.

T/Plt: £751.40 to a £1 stake. Pool: £58,955.84 - 57.27 winning tickets. T/Qpdt: £100.80 to a £1 stake. Pool: £5,260.59 - 38.60 winning tickets. LM

# 3140 NEWBURY (L-H)
Tuesday, June 24

**OFFICIAL GOING: Good (7.0)**
Rail moved back in and all distances as advertised.
Wind: Light, across Weather: Fine, warm

## 3556 PUMP TECHNOLOGY APPRENTICE H'CAP — 1m 3f 5y
**6:20** (6:20) (Class 5) (0-70,70) 4-Y-O+ £3,234 (£962; £481; £240) **Stalls** Low

Form RPR

5-00 **1** **Whinging Willie (IRE)**[12] 3147 5-9-1 **66** ........ (p) HectorCrouch(7) 8 76
(Gary Moore) *dwlt: t.k.h: hld up in last pair: swtchd rt and gd prog over 2f out: rdn to chal jst over 1f out: led last 100yds: styd on* **25/1**

2562 **2** *1 1/4* **Emman Bee (IRE)**[16] 3032 5-8-12 **61** ........ KieranShoemark(5) 5 68
(Luke Dace) *hld up in midfield: smooth prog to trck ldr over 2f out: n.m.r over 1f out and shkn up: fnd nil and btn ins fnl f* **10/1**

4543 **3** *3 1/4* **The Ducking Stool**[12] 3161 7-9-7 **65** ........ ShelleyBirkett 6 66
(Julia Feilden) *hld up in tch: pushed along over 3f out: nvr quite pce to threaten ldrs but kpt on* **8/1**

0143 **4** *2* **Rockweiller**[15] 3052 7-8-9 **58** ........ GeorgiaCox(5) 2 56
(Shaun Harris) *mde most to over 1f out: steadily fdd* **12/1**

3566 **5** *1 1/4* **A Little Bit Dusty**[10] 3226 6-9-12 **70** ........ (p) JoeyHaynes 3 66
(Conor Dore) *trckd ldrs on inner: pushed along over 3f out: wl there but rdn 2f out: fdd over 1f out* **14/1**

40-5 **6** *7* **Guilded Spirit**[78] 1355 4-9-11 **69** ........ LouisSteward 4 53
(Stuart Kittow) *mostly chsd ldr to over 2f out: wknd qckly over 1f out* **4/1**[2]

0-16 **7** *10* **Conquestadim**[27] 2670 4-9-7 **70** ........ CharlieBennett(5) 11 37
(Hughie Morrison) *prom: rdn over 3f out: wknd wl over 2f out* **7/1**

4-32 **8** *6* **Hector's Chance**[12] 3147 5-9-7 **68** ........ GeorgeBuckell(3) 10 25
(Heather Main) *chsd ldrs: rdn 4f out: sn btn* **6/1**[3]

50-0 **9** *9* **Bridge That Gap**[19] 2916 6-8-12 **63** ........ RhiainIngram(7) 7 4
(Roger Ingram) *dwlt: prog on outer after 3f to chse ldrs: wl there 3f out: sn wknd rapidly* **40/1**

54-0 **10** *10* **Pahente**[24] 2770 6-9-4 **62** ........ (p) NathanAlison 9
(Tony Carroll) *in tch 7f: wknd: t.o* **50/1**

-632 **D** *1/2* **Eton Rambler (USA)**[8] 3310 4-9-11 **69** ........ RyanTate 1 78
(George Baker) *hld up in last pair: prog and squeezed through over 2f out: rdn to ld over 1f out and edgd rt: hdd and nt qckn last 100yds* **9/4**[1]

2m 23.15s (1.95) **Going Correction** +0.20s/f (Good) 11 Ran SP% **120.4**
Speed ratings (Par 103): **100,98,96,94,94 88,81,77,70,63 99**
CSF £82.19 CT £639.45 TOTE £15.80: £4.80, £1.60, £3.70; EX 117.10 Trifecta £370.60.

**Owner** P B Moorhead **Bred** Joe Rogers **Trained** Lower Beeding, W Sussex

■ Hector Crouch's first winner under rules.

**FOCUS**
The ground was good all round after overnight rain. Race times suggested the ground was perhaps on the easy side of good. An ordinary event. They went what looked a fairly modest gallop, but the first two both came from the back of the field. The winner's best form since he was a 2yo.

## 3557 WIN RACES WITH JONATHAN PORTMAN MAIDEN AUCTION FILLIES' STKS (BOBIS RACE) — 6f 8y
**6:55** (6:56) (Class 4) 2-Y-O £3,881 (£1,155; £577; £288) **Stalls** Centre

Form RPR

0 **1** **Feeling Easy (IRE)**[19] 2928 2-8-6 0 ........ AndreaAtzeni 4 72
(Robert Eddery) *trckd ldrs: prog to go 2nd over 2f out: rdn over 1f out: styd on to ld last 100yds* **12/1**

3 **2** *3/4* **Secret Spirit**[24] 2771 2-8-9 0 ........ RyanTate(3) 13 76
(Clive Cox) *led: pushed along and hung lft over 2f out: rdn over 1f out: hdd and nt qckn last 100yds* **15/8**[1]

6 **3** *shd* **Dubai Breeze (IRE)**[39] 2306 2-8-12 0 ........ RyanMoore 2 76
(Clive Brittain) *hld up towards rr: prog towards far side over 2f out: rdn wl over 1f out: styd on fnl f to press for 2nd nr fin* **11/4**[2]

**4** *2* **Loumarin (IRE)** 2-8-6 0 ........ DavidProbert 1 64
(Martyn Meade) *trckd ldrs: prog over 2f out: rdn to dispute 2nd over 1f out: fdd ins fnl f* **66/1**

**5** *3* **Rosie Royale (IRE)** 2-8-10 0 ........ JamesDoyle 8 59+
(Roger Teal) *in tch in midfield: shkn up wl over 2f out: sn outpcd: kpt on quite encouragingly fr over 1f out to take 5th fnl f* **33/1**

00 **6** *3 1/2* **Magic Mac**[11] 3181 2-8-6 0 ........ NickyMackay 12 44
(Hughie Morrison) *mostly chsd ldr to over 2f out: steadily wknd* **66/1**

5 **7** *3* **June's Moon**[71] 1488 2-8-7 0 ........ MatthewLawson(3) 9 39
(Jonathan Portman) *disp 2nd pl to over 2f out: steadily fdd* **25/1**

0 **8** *hd* **Lady Mascot (IRE)**[14] 3076 2-8-12 0 ........ SeanLevey 7 41
(Richard Hannon) *hld up wl in rr: sme prog over 2f out: no ch w ldrs* **16/1**

**9** *1/2* **Ragtime Dancer** 2-8-8 0 ........ RichardKingscote 3 35
(Jonathan Portman) *s.s: wl in rr: pushed along over 2f out: sme prog wl over 1f out: nvr in it but plugged on* **16/1**

5 **10** *3/4* **Diracan (IRE)**[28] 2652 2-8-12 0 ........ J-PGuillambert 5 37
(Nick Littmoden) *wl in rr and sn pushed along: sme prog 2f out but nowhere nr ldrs: no hdwy fnl f* **33/1**

**11** *1* **Berkshire Beauty** 2-8-9 0 ........ OisinMurphy(3) 6 34
(Andrew Balding) *a in rr and rn green: shkn up and struggling 1/2-way: nvr a factor* **25/1**

**12** *14* **Flashy Diva** 2-8-8 0 ........ FergusSweeney 14
(Henry Candy) *s.s: rcvrd and sn in tch: wknd 1/2-way: t.o* **12/1**

6 **13** *13* **Baronessa (IRE)**[24] 2771 2-8-12 0 ........ RichardHughes 10
(Richard Hannon) *chsd ldrs but nvr gng wl and sn pushed along: wknd 1/2-way: t.o* **7/1**[3]

**14** *7* **Spirit In Time (IRE)** 2-8-3 0 ........ RyanWhile(5) 11
(Malcolm Saunders) *s.s: a in rr: t.o fnl 2f* **66/1**

**15** *11* **Chefchaouen (IRE)** 2-8-6 0 ........ JohnFahy 15
(J S Moore) *dwlt: a bhd: t.o sn after 1/2-way* **66/1**

1m 14.36s (1.36) **Going Correction** +0.10s/f (Good) 15 Ran SP% **120.6**
Speed ratings (Par 92): **94,93,92,90,86 81,77,77,76,75 74,55,38,28,14**
CSF £32.72 TOTE £20.10: £4.40, £1.10, £1.80; EX 59.40 Trifecta £181.00.

**Owner** Edwin Phillips & Mrs Pamela Aitken **Bred** Hyde Park Stud & Lisglen **Trained** Newmarket, Suffolk

**FOCUS**
The first two home in this event in 2012, Maureen and Annecdote, both went on to win in Group 3 company, as did the 2008 winner Pyrrha. These principals are unlikely to reach the same heights, but this was still a fair auction maiden, if ordinary for the track.

## 3558 PUMPMATIC PUMP STATIONS BY PUMP TECHNOLOGY MAIDEN FILLIES' STKS (BOBIS RACE) 7f (S)
7:25 (7:27) (Class 4) 2-Y-O £3,881 (£1,155; £577; £288) Stalls Centre

| Form | | | | RPR |
|---|---|---|---|---|
| | 1 | | **Alonsoa (IRE)** 2-9-0 0 FergusSweeney 2 (Henry Candy) *dwlt hld up towards rr: prog 1/2-way: shkn up to ld wl over 1f out: styd on wl and in command fnl f* 8/1 | 80+ |
| | 2 | 2 ¼ | **Abaq** 2-9-0 0 PaulHanagan 7 (Richard Hannon) *t.k.h: trckd ldr: led over 2f out to wl over 1f out: one pce fnl f* 3/1[1] | 74+ |
| | 3 | hd | **All Rounder (USA)** 2-9-0 0 JamesDoyle 13 (John Gosden) *led: set mod pce early: shkn up and hdd over 2f out: nt qckn but styd on fnl f* 7/1[3] | 73+ |
| | 4 | hd | **Ya Latif (IRE)** 2-9-0 0 AndreaAtzeni 8 (Roger Varian) *trckd ldrs: shkn up and outpcd 2f out: styd on again fnl f* 6/1[2] | 73+ |
| | 5 | 1 ½ | **Star Of Spring (IRE)** 2-9-0 0 GeorgeBaker 5 (Charles Hills) *hld up in last pair: pushed along and prog fr over 2f out: styd on fnl f: nrst fin* 3/1[1] | 69+ |
| | 6 | nk | **Zubaidah** 2-9-0 0 PatCosgrave 3 (George Baker) *s.s: sn wl in tch: rdn over 2f out: nvr gng pce to chal but kpt on* 33/1 | 68+ |
| 4 | 7 | 1 ¼ | **Hound Music**[25] 2744 2-9-0 0 ShaneKelly 1 (Jonathan Portman) *hld up in last pair early: sme prog 3f out: shkn up and one pce fnl 2f: nvr involved* 6/1[2] | 65 |
| 6 | 8 | nk | **All My Love (IRE)**[19] 2918 2-9-0 0 RichardHughes 4 (Richard Hannon) *pressed ldrs: rdn and cl up 2f out: wknd jst over 1f out* 12/1 | 64 |
| | 9 | 1 ¾ | **Starlight June** 2-9-0 0 RichardKingscote 10 (Jonathan Portman) *dwlt: a in rr: lost tch w main gp 2f out: pushed along and kpt on steadily fnl f* 50/1 | 59 |
| 45 | 10 | 4 | **Go White Lightning (IRE)**[11] 3173 2-9-0 0 SilvestreDeSousa 9 (David Evans) *t.k.h: trckd ldrs: drvn over 2f out: wknd over 1f out: eased last 100yds* 25/1 | 48 |
| | 11 | 10 | **Rave Dancer** 2-8-9 0 ShelleyBirkett(5) 11 (Stuart Kittow) *a towards rr: wknd over 2f out: t.o* 50/1 | 21 |
| | 12 | 2 ¾ | **Mikandy (IRE)** 2-9-0 0 AdamKirby 12 (Clive Cox) *dwlt: sn chsd ldrs: wknd over 2f out: t.o* 22/1 | 14 |

1m 28.02s (2.32) **Going Correction** +0.10s/f (Good) 12 Ran SP% 124.9
Speed ratings (Par 92): **90,87,87,86,85 84,83,83,81,76 65,62**
CSF £32.60 TOTE £12.10: £3.10, £1.60, £2.70; EX 52.70 Trifecta £349.50.
**Owner** Mrs Patricia J Burns **Bred** Lodge Park Stud **Trained** Kingston Warren, Oxon

**FOCUS**
Five of the last ten winners of this maiden have gone on to Group/Grade success, most notably 2012 winner Just The Judge, who took the Irish 1,000 Guineas, and 2011 scorer Questing who won twice at the top level when trained in the USA. However they went a steady pace and finished compressed behind the winner, so the form is rated at the bottom end of the race averages.

## 3559 JUNG PUMPEN & PUMP TECHNOLOGY H'CAP 1m 7y(R)
8:00 (8:01) (Class 5) (0-70,68) 3-Y-O £3,234 (£962; £481; £240) Stalls Centre

| Form | | | | RPR |
|---|---|---|---|---|
| 302 | 1 | | **Glebe Spirit (IRE)**[8] 3316 3-9-4 65 RichardHughes 3 (Richard Hannon) *trckd ldrs: prog on outer over 2f out: rdn to ld over 1f out: styd on wl fnl f: readily* 9/4[1] | 78+ |
| -552 | 2 | 2 ½ | **Mister Mayday (IRE)**[26] 2688 3-9-1 62 (b[1]) PatCosgrave 6 (George Baker) *taken down early: stdd s: t.k.h and hld up in last pair: prog over 2f out: rdn to chse wnr ins fnl f: styd on but no imp* 12/1 | 67 |
| 3-30 | 3 | 4 | **What A Dandy (IRE)**[29] 2624 3-9-4 65 AdamKirby 8 (Jim Boyle) *t.k.h: w ldr: led 3f out: drvn and hdd over 1f out: sn lft bhd* 12/1 | 61 |
| 6650 | 4 | 1 | **Mendacious Harpy (IRE)**[16] 3037 3-9-0 68 (b[1]) CamHardie(7) 2 (George Baker) *t.k.h: trckd ldrs: rdn to try to cl on ldrs wl over 1f out: sn outpcd* 7/1[3] | 62 |
| 5-00 | 5 | ½ | **Classic Mission**[35] 2417 3-9-3 64 RichardKingscote 4 (Jonathan Portman) *s.i.s: towards rr: rdn over 2f out: plugged on but nvr gng pce to threaten* 20/1 | 56 |
| 4636 | 6 | 1 ¼ | **Honiton Lace**[26] 2695 3-8-8 55 SilvestreDeSousa 7 (B W Hills) *taken down early: hld up in rr: rdn over 2f out: sn outpcd and btn* 22/1 | 44 |
| -030 | 7 | 1 ¼ | **Peacemaker (IRE)**[19] 2936 3-9-7 68 JohnFahy 10 (Eve Johnson Houghton) *trckd ldrs: rdn over 2f out: wknd over 1f out* 20/1 | 55 |
| 4301 | 8 | 1 | **Prim And Proper**[9] 3281 3-8-3 57 JennyPowell(7) 9 (Brendan Powell) *hld up in last pair: lft bhd 2f out: brief effrt over 1f out: sn no prog* 15/2 | 41 |
| 3500 | 9 | 5 | **Dream Big (IRE)**[12] 3146 3-9-4 65 PatDobbs 1 (Jo Crowley) *trckd ldrs on inner: cl enough over 2f out: sn wknd* 33/1 | 38 |
| 4051 | 10 | 22 | **Woodbridge**[16] 3037 3-9-6 67 RyanMoore 5 (Richard Fahey) *led: rdn and hdd 3f out: wknd 2f out: eased over 1f out: t.o* 5/2[2] | |

1m 40.51s (1.81) **Going Correction** +0.20s/f (Good) 10 Ran SP% 115.8
Speed ratings (Par 99): **98,95,91,90,90 88,87,86,81,59**
CSF £27.84 CT £276.42 TOTE £3.00: £1.10, £3.00, £3.50; EX 35.10 Trifecta £404.50.
**Owner** Glebe Farm Stud **Bred** Knockainey Stud **Trained** East Everleigh, Wilts

**FOCUS**
This modest handicap was run at a decent gallop. With the second favourite failing to run his race it may not have taken much winning, but the winner is accorded another perdonal best.

## 3560 PEGASUS PUMPS LTD FILLIES' H'CAP (BOBIS RACE) 1m 2f 6y
8:35 (8:35) (Class 4) (0-85,85) 3-Y-O £4,690 (£1,395; £697; £348) Stalls Low

| Form | | | | RPR |
|---|---|---|---|---|
| 11 | 1 | | **My Spirit (IRE)**[22] 2826 3-9-7 85 RyanMoore 1 (William Haggas) *hld up in 5th: prog to chse ldr over 2f out: sn rdn: no imp 1f out: drvn and styd on wl to ld last stride* 7/4[1] | 99+ |
| 41- | 2 | hd | **Asyad (IRE)**[245] 7450 3-8-12 76 FrankieDettori 3 (Sir Michael Stoute) *trckd ldng pair: led over 3f out gng strly: rdn 2f out: over a l up 1f out: kpt on but hdd last stride* 5/1[3] | 90+ |
| 5-51 | 3 | 5 | **Wahgah (USA)**[28] 2649 3-9-2 80 PaulHanagan 4 (Saeed bin Suroor) *trckd ldng trio: rdn to dispute 2nd over 2f out to jst over 1f out: fdd but hld on for 3rd* 16/1 | 85 |
| 0-14 | 4 | hd | **Cameo Tiara (IRE)**[32] 2504 3-9-2 80 RichardHughes 5 (Richard Hannon) *hld up in last: prog and squeezed through jst over 2f out: drvn over 1f out: no ch w ldng pair but pressed for 3rd nr fin* 16/1 | 84 |
| 21-2 | 5 | 4 | **Gay Marriage (IRE)**[33] 2498 3-8-12 76 WilliamBuick 8 (John Gosden) *t.k.h: trckd ldr: lost pl wl over 2f out: steadily fdd* 8/1 | 73 |
| 0-22 | 6 | 1 | **Joys Of Spring (IRE)**[18] 2967 3-9-0 78 AndreaAtzeni 7 (Luca Cumani) *hld up in 7th: effrt 3f out: no imp on ldrs wl over 1f out: fdd* 4/1[2] | 73 |
| -312 | 7 | 10 | **Stereo Love (FR)**[32] 2504 3-9-2 80 AdamKirby 6 (Clive Cox) *taken down early: t.k.h: hld up in 6th: effrt on outer 3f out: no prog 2f out: sn wknd* 10/1 | 56 |
| 1-03 | 8 | 26 | **Kind Invitation**[35] 2431 3-9-4 82 SilvestreDeSousa 2 (Charlie Appleby) *led to over 3f out: sn dropped away t.o* 11/1 | |

2m 9.12s (0.32) **Going Correction** +0.20s/f (Good) 8 Ran SP% 113.3
Speed ratings (Par 98): **106,105,101,101,98 97,89,68**
CSF £10.40 CT £101.33 TOTE £2.50: £1.20, £1.70, £2.70; EX 12.00 Trifecta £57.20.
**Owner** Miss Pat O'Kelly **Bred** Kilcarn Stud **Trained** Newmarket, Suffolk

**FOCUS**
An interesting fillies' handicap in which the first two contested a fine finish, clear of the remainder. The first two can make their marks outside handicaps.

## 3561 LEE SAN MARINE SANITATION H'CAP 5f 34y
9:05 (9:05) (Class 5) (0-70,70) 3-Y-O+ £3,234 (£962; £481; £120; £120) Stalls Centre

| Form | | | | RPR |
|---|---|---|---|---|
| 2-22 | 1 | | **Perfect Muse**[17] 2994 4-9-9 67 AdamKirby 9 (Clive Cox) *hld up in tch: smooth prog wl over 1f out: produced to ld last 100yds: drvn and styd on wl* 9/4[1] | 79+ |
| 2310 | 2 | 1 | **Roy's Legacy**[11] 3191 5-9-5 63 SilvestreDeSousa 4 (Shaun Harris) *prom: rdn over 2f out: led jst over 1f out: hdd and outpcd last 100yds* 6/1[3] | 71 |
| 4064 | 3 | ½ | **West Coast Dream**[10] 3222 7-9-3 64 DeclanBates(3) 7 (Roy Brotherton) *mde most to jst over 1f out: kpt on same pce fnl f* 33/1 | 70 |
| 6433 | 4 | 1 | **Ginzan**[9] 3275 6-9-7 70 RyanWhile(5) 2 (Malcolm Saunders) *hld up in tch: prog 2f out gng wl: poised to chal over 1f out: rdn and fnd nil* 11/2[2] | 73 |
| 2463 | 4 | dht | **Dark Lane**[14] 3088 8-9-2 60 AndreaAtzeni 5 (David Evans) *wl in tch: rdn 2f out: n.m.r over 1f out: kpt on fnl f: nrst fin* 12/1 | 63 |
| 2220 | 6 | ½ | **Katja**[32] 2505 3-8-12 62 PaulHanagan 6 (B W Hills) *n.m.r s: wl in rr: rdn over 2f out: prog over 1f out: kpt on but nt pce to threaten* 25/1 | 61 |
| 50-3 | 7 | 1 ¼ | **Monarch Maid**[17] 2994 3-9-1 65 ChrisCatlin 12 (Peter Hiatt) *chsd ldrs towards nr side: rdn and nt qckn 2f out: one pce fnl f* 14/1 | 59 |
| 2603 | 8 | ½ | **Solemn**[10] 3222 9-9-7 65 (v) DavidProbert 8 (Milton Bradley) *chsd ldrs 3f: sn lost pl and btn: one pce after* 9/1 | 60 |
| 3-56 | 9 | ¾ | **Edged Out**[35] 2414 4-9-9 70 OisinMurphy(3) 11 (Christopher Mason) *in tch in rr: rdn and no prog 2f out: n.d after* 17/2 | 62 |
| 4343 | 10 | 1 ¾ | **The Dandy Yank (IRE)**[14] 3084 3-9-6 70 RichardHughes 3 (Jamie Osborne) *hld up: shkn up whn n.m.r over 1f out: wknd fnl f* 7/1 | 54 |
| 0-05 | 11 | 4 | **First Rebellion**[22] 2830 5-8-7 54 (b) JoeyHaynes(3) 10 (Tony Carroll) *mostly chsd ldr to 2f: wknd qckly* 40/1 | 25 |
| 1002 | 12 | nk | **Only Ten Per Cent (IRE)**[19] 2933 6-9-9 67 (v) PatDobbs 1 (J R Jenkins) *hld up in tch: rdn and no prog 2f out: wknd over 1f out* 16/1 | 37 |

1m 1.41s (0.01) **Going Correction** +0.10s/f (Good)
**WFA** 3 from 4yo+ 6lb 12 Ran SP% 122.9
Speed ratings (Par 103): **103,101,100,99,99 98,96,95,94,91 85,84**
CSF £15.66 CT £370.65 TOTE £3.00: £1.70, £2.90, £7.20; EX 17.30 Trifecta £1759.00.
**Owner** R J Vines **Bred** R J Vines **Trained** Lambourn, Berks

**FOCUS**
Ordinary sprint handicap form. The winner is likely to do better.
T/Jkpt: Not won. T/Plt: £15.70 to a £1 stake. Pool: £73,782.90 - 471.31 winning tickets. T/Qpdt: £52.60 to a £1 stake. Pool: £5,842.94 - 82.05 winning tickets. JN

# 3208 BATH (L-H)
## Wednesday, June 25

**OFFICIAL GOING: Firm (12.3)**
Races incorporating bottom bend increased in distance by about 10yds.
Wind: virtually nil Weather: sunny

## 3562 PREMIER CONSERVATORY ROOFS GUARDIAN WARM ROOF H'CAP 1m 5y
6:10 (6:10) (Class 5) (0-70,70) 4-Y-O+ £2,587 (£770; £384; £192) Stalls Low

| Form | | | | RPR |
|---|---|---|---|---|
| 01-2 | 1 | | **Stormbound (IRE)**[14] 3112 5-8-13 62 LukeMorris 2 (Paul Cole) *trckd ldrs: rdn over 3f out: styd on ins fnl f: led fnl 30yds: drvn out* 11/4[2] | 71 |
| -055 | 2 | hd | **Not Rigg (USA)**[13] 3160 4-8-8 57 JackMitchell 4 (Nick Littmoden) *sn w ldr: led after 2f: rdn over 2f out: kpt on but no ex whn hdd fnl 30yds* 8/1[3] | 66 |
| 1564 | 3 | 1 ½ | **Wilfred Pickles (IRE)**[28] 2687 8-9-7 70 (p) FergusSweeney 1 (Jo Crowley) *mid-div: rdn wl over 2f out: hdwy over 1f out: sn swtchd rt: kpt on ins fnl f* 12/1 | 75 |
| 0-00 | 4 | shd | **Speedy Writer**[14] 3112 4-9-5 68 [1] DaneO'Neill 7 (Henry Candy) *hld up: hdwy whn rdn over 2f out: sn chsng ldrs: kpt on ins fnl f* 10/1 | 73 |
| 4451 | 5 | ¾ | **Carrera**[15] 3075 4-8-11 60 DavidProbert 3 (Michael Blanshard) *hld up: hdwy whn nt clr run over 1f out: sn rdn: kpt on same pce fnl f* 5/2[1] | 63 |
| 2333 | 6 | 2 ¾ | **Pick A Little**[8] 3327 6-9-2 65 SteveDrowne 8 (Michael Blake) *led for 2f: trckd ldr: rdn 3f out: wknd ins fnl f* 8/1[3] | 62 |
| 553 | 7 | 6 | **Rutterkin (USA)**[85] 1228 6-8-2 51 oh6 AndrewMullen 6 (James Moffatt) *in tch: rdn 3f out: wknd over 1f out* 25/1 | 34 |
| 0020 | 8 | 2 ¼ | **Lutine Charlie (IRE)**[15] 3075 7-8-4 53 MartinDwyer 9 (Pat Eddery) *trckd ldrs: rdn over 2f out: wknd ent fnl f* 8/1[3] | 31 |
| 2100 | 9 | 12 | **Spirit Of Gondree (IRE)**[21] 2884 6-8-13 65 (b) MatthewLawson(3) 5 (Milton Bradley) *s.i.s: struggling 4f out: a in rr* 33/1 | 15 |

1m 38.36s (-2.44) **Going Correction** -0.225s/f (Firm) 9 Ran SP% 112.1
Speed ratings (Par 103): **103,102,101,101,100 97,91,89,77**
CSF £24.09 CT £221.60 TOTE £3.00: £1.20, £4.40, £3.30; EX 24.90 Trifecta £185.40.
**Owner** P F I Cole Ltd **Bred** A Footstep Away Syndicate **Trained** Whatcombe, Oxon



The Form Book, Raceform Ltd, Newbury, RG14 5SJ

**FOCUS**
No rain locally for a fortnight, so predictably fast ground at a track unable to water. All races using the bottom bend were run over 10 yards further than advertised owing to rail movements. A fast-run opener secured in the final strides by the winner.

## 3563 FUND FORCE/EBF STALLIONS MAIDEN FILLIES' STKS (BOBIS RACE) 5f 161y
6:40 (6:42) (Class 5) 2-Y-O £2,911 (£866; £432; £216) Stalls Centre

Form RPR

0 **1** **Rathaath (IRE)**[20] 2918 2-9-0 0 DaneO'Neill 10 76+
(Brian Meehan) *sn pressing ldr: led over 2f out: kpt on wl: pushed out* **7/4**[1]

**2** *1 1/4* **Ajaadat** 2-9-0 0 JackMitchell 3 72
(Roger Varian) *chsd ldrs: rdn 3f out: chsd wnr ent fnl f: kpt on nicely fnl 120yds but a being hld* **10/3**[3]

0 **3** *3 1/4* **Lady Gemini**[7] 3353 2-9-0 0 MartinDwyer 1 61
(Jo Hughes) *led: hdd over 2f out: sn rdn: kpt chsng wnr tl no ex ent fnl f* **8/1**

5 **4** *4* **Anastazia**[20] 2918 2-9-0 0 SeanLevey 6 48
(Paul D'Arcy) *trckd ldrs: rdn over 2f out: fdd fnl 120yds* **20/1**

**5** *nk* **The Wispe** 2-9-0 0 SteveDrowne 8 47+
(Robert Cowell) *sn outpcd in rr: hdwy over 1f out: styd on fnl f: nvr trbld ldrs* **40/1**

**6** *1/2* **Gumhrear (IRE)** 2-9-0 0 LukeMorris 4 45
(James Tate) *sn pushed along in tch: rdn wl over 2f out: nvr any imp* **10/1**

0 **7** *2 1/2* **Heavenlyfriendship**[21] 2888 2-8-7 0 JennyPowell(7) 5 37
(Brendan Powell) *sn outpcd in rr: nvr any threat* **66/1**

2020 **8** *5* **Exentricity**[18] 2987 2-8-11 0 CharlesBishop(3) 7 21
(Mick Channon) *in tch: rdn whn outpcd wl over 2f out: nvr any imp: eased whn btn ins fnl f* **3/1**[2]

U00 **9** *7* **Saphira Silver (IRE)**[11] 3210 2-8-9 0 PhilipPrince(5) 2
(Nikki Evans) *in tch tl outpcd 3f out: sn bhd* **100/1**

1m 9.7s (-1.50) **Going Correction** -0.30s/f (Firm) **9** Ran SP% **114.3**
Speed ratings (Par 90): **98,96,92,86,86 85,82,75,66**
CSF £7.46 TOTE £2.80: £1.20, £1.40, £2.30; EX 8.10 Trifecta £72.10.
**Owner** Hamdan Al Maktoum **Bred** Shadwell Estate Company Limited **Trained** Manton, Wilts

**FOCUS**
This maiden proved fairly straightforward for the favourite. The time and race average offer guidance.

## 3564 GUARDIAN WARM ROOF PREMIER CONSERVATORY ROOFS H'CAP 5f 161y
7:10 (7:12) (Class 6) (0-60,60) 3-Y-O £1,940 (£577; £288; £144) Stalls Centre

Form RPR

5563 **1** **Clear Focus (IRE)**[11] 3214 3-8-7 **46** oh1 (v) AndreaAtzeni 12 51
(Brendan Powell) *trckd ldrs: rdn to chal 2f out: led ent fnl f: hld on: all out* **8/1**

0655 **2** *nk* **Go Charlie**[11] 3214 3-8-8 **47** SteveDrowne 10 51
(Ronald Harris) *hld up bhd: hdwy fr wl over 2f out: cl up whn rdn over 1f out: sn edgd lft: ev ch fnl 120yds: jinked lft nring fin* **16/1**

56-0 **3** *1/2* **Elite Freedom (IRE)**[13] 3149 3-9-1 **54** (p) AndrewMullen 11 56
(Brian Baugh) *mid-div: rdn and hdwy over 2f out: chsd ldrs over 1f out: bmpd jst ins fnl f: ev ch fnl 120yds: bdly hmpd nring fin* **25/1**

0-01 **4** *1 1/4* **Connaught Water (IRE)**[11] 3214 3-9-4 **60** MatthewLawson(3) 2 58+
(Jonathan Portman) *rrd leaving stalls: bhd: swtchd rt to centre over 2f out: sn rdn and hdwy: kpt on wl fnl f* **4/1**[2]

050- **5** *1/2* **Prize**[223] 7874 3-9-3 **56** SeanLevey 8 55+
(Sylvester Kirk) *mid-div: swtchd rt whn nt clr run 2f out: bmpd jst ins fnl f: kpt on but nt clrest of runs fnl 120yds* **12/1**

-360 **6** *shd* **Princess Rose**[22] 2870 3-9-3 **59** (b) WilliamTwiston-Davies(3) 5 55
(John Weymes) *chsd ldrs: rdn whn nt best of runs fr over 1f out: kpt on but hld fnl f* **12/1**

4312 **7** *shd* **Crystalized (IRE)**[11] 3214 3-9-2 **55** FergusSweeney 6 51+
(Dean Ivory) *hld up towards rr: hdwy whn nt clr run and lost pl 2f out: r.o wl whn clr run ent fnl f: nt rch ldrs* **3/1**[1]

-533 **8** *1 1/4* **Wedgewood Estates**[19] 2943 3-9-3 **56** LukeMorris 1 48+
(Tony Carroll) *s.i.s: towards rr: hdwy over 2f out: sn rdn: one pce fnl f* **6/1**[3]

0550 **9** *4 1/2* **Nutbush**[11] 3214 3-8-7 **49** CharlesBishop(3) 3 26
(Mick Channon) *mid-div: rdn 3f out: wknd ent fnl f* **9/1**

00-4 **10** *hd* **Warm Order**[11] 3214 3-8-11 **50** ow1 JimCrowley 7 26
(Tony Carroll) *trckd lde: rdn to ld 2f out: hdd ent fnl f: wknd* **10/1**

-440 **11** *4 1/2* **Notnow Penny**[11] 3214 3-8-7 **46** DavidProbert 4 7
(Milton Bradley) *led tl 2f out: sn wknd* **50/1**

-500 **12** *3/4* **Paradise Child**[15] 3087 3-8-7 **46** oh1 MartinDwyer 9 5
(Bill Turner) *chsd ldrs: nt clr run 2f out: lost action and eased ent fnl f* **80/1**

1m 10.45s (-0.75) **Going Correction** -0.30s/f (Firm) **12** Ran SP% **117.8**
Speed ratings (Par 97): **93,92,91,90,89 89,89,87,81,81 75,74**
CSF £126.15 CT £1919.46 TOTE £7.50: £3.60, £4.20, £7.80; EX 140.70 Trifecta £1346.50 Part won..
**Owner** K Rhatigan **Bred** Yvonne&gerard Kennedy&intense Focus Syn **Trained** Upper Lambourn, Berks

**FOCUS**
Seven of the line-up were reopposing just 11 days after clashing in a C&D 0-55. Those on the inner largely got in each other's way in the final quarter mile.

## 3565 GUARDIAN WARM ROOF H'CAP (BOBIS RACE) 5f 11y
7:40 (7:40) (Class 4) (0-85,89) 3-Y-O £4,690 (£1,395; £697) Stalls Centre

Form RPR

3001 **1** **Desert Ace (IRE)**[8] 3331 3-9-10 **89** 6ex (tp) RyanTate(3) 3 94
(Clive Cox) *disp ld tl clr ldr 2f out: rdn ent fnl f: sn strly chal: hld on gamely: all out* **6/4**[1]

0323 **2** *shd* **Amahoro**[16] 3068 3-9-1 **80** WilliamTwiston-Davies(3) 4 84
(Mick Channon) *trckd ldrs: trckd wnr jst over 1f out: rdn for str chal fnl 120yds: kpt on: jst hld* **5/2**[3]

314 **3** *6* **Saakhen (IRE)**[8] 3331 3-9-4 **80** (t) DaneO'Neill 1 62
(Richard Fahey) *disp ld tl rdn 2f out: sn dropped to 3rd and hld* **13/8**[2]

1m 0.61s (-1.89) **Going Correction** -0.30s/f (Firm) **3** Ran SP% **106.7**
Speed ratings (Par 101): **103,102,93**
CSF £5.04 TOTE £1.90; EX 4.70 Trifecta £2.90.
**Owner** Arabian Knights **Bred** Kildaragh Stud **Trained** Lambourn, Berks
■ Stewards' Enquiry : Ryan Tate two-day ban: used whip above permitted level (Jul 9-10)

**FOCUS**
Already a disappointing numerical turnout for this feature event before Groundworker was taken out, and not quite as frantic an early gallop as in the preceding contests.

## 3566 PREMIER CONSERVATORY ROOFS GUARDIAN WARM ROOF CLASSIFIED STKS 5f 161y
8:10 (8:10) (Class 5) 3-Y-O £2,587 (£770; £384; £192) Stalls Centre

Form RPR

10-4 **1** **Picks Pinta**[81] 1315 3-8-9 62 PhilipPrince(5) 4 74
(Jo Hughes) *disp ld tl clr ldr over 2f out: drifted rt fr over 1f out: kpt on wl: pushed out* **3/1**[2]

4-06 **2** *2 3/4* **Stroll On (IRE)**[13] 3156 3-9-0 68 [1] ChrisCatlin 1 65
(Rae Guest) *sn pushed along to chse ldrs: chsd wnr over 1f out: kpt on but a being hld* **5/1**[3]

10-0 **3** *2 1/4* **Lady Crossmar (IRE)**[12] 3198 3-8-7 70 CamHardie(7) 3 58
(Richard Hannon) *sn pushed along chsng ldrs: wnt 3rd ent fnl f: kpt on but nvr gng pce to get involved* **3/1**[2]

0-40 **4** *3* **Tolmias (GR)**[18] 2996 3-9-0 67 AndreaAtzeni 2 48
(Luca Cumani) *disp ld tl rdn over 2f out: sn sltly outpcd by wnr: lost 2nd over 1f out: wknd fnl 120yds* **6/5**[1]

1m 9.92s (-1.28) **Going Correction** -0.30s/f (Firm) **4** Ran SP% **112.1**
Speed ratings (Par 99): **96,92,89,85**
CSF £16.38 TOTE £3.10; EX 16.80 Trifecta £42.00.
**Owner** Chester Racing Club Ltd **Bred** Heatherwold Stud **Trained** Lambourn, Berks

**FOCUS**
All four runners here were on retrieval missions, having disappointed to varying degrees last time out.

## 3567 PREMIER CONSERVATORY ROOFS H'CAP 1m 3f 144y
8:40 (8:41) (Class 6) (0-60,60) 3-Y-O £1,940 (£577; £288; £144) Stalls Low

Form RPR

0500 **1** **Enquiring**[14] 3098 3-8-8 **50** MichaelJMMurphy(3) 5 61
(Mark Johnston) *trckd ldr: rdn 3f out: led over 1f out: edgd lft: styd on strly* **10/1**

-442 **2** *3* **Bishop Wulstan (IRE)**[8] 3326 3-8-6 **52** CamHardie(7) 12 57
(Richard Hannon) *mid-div: hdwy over 3f out: wnt 3rd over 2f out: styd on to snatch 2nd nring fin: n.d to wnr* **6/4**[1]

0660 **3** *shd* **Assoluta (IRE)**[13] 3146 3-8-11 **50** MartinDwyer 4 54
(Sylvester Kirk) *led: kicked clr 3f out: sn rdn: hdd over 1f out: hld whn sltly hmpd and swtchd rt sn after: styd on: lost 2nd fnl strides* **20/1**

0-02 **4** *3 1/2* **Maid Of Tuscany (IRE)**[20] 2926 3-8-12 **58** CharlotteJenner(7) 7 57
(Mark Usher) *hld up towards rr: rdn and hdwy 3f out: styd on fnl 2f: nvr threatening to trble ldrs* **8/1**[3]

-616 **5** *hd* **Chesil Beach**[6] 3391 3-9-7 **60** DavidProbert 9 58
(Andrew Balding) *hld up towards rr of midfield: rdn 3f out: styd on steadily but nvr gng pce to get on terms* **10/1**

0005 **6** *1 3/4* **Dark Days**[20] 2926 3-9-3 **56** (t) LukeMorris 10 51
(Paul Cole) *trckd ldrs: rdn wl over 2f out: sn one pce* **3/1**[2]

0-30 **7** *nse* **Tete Orange**[17] 3037 3-8-9 **51** (b[1]) WilliamTwiston-Davies(3) 11 46
(Stuart Williams) *s.i.s: bhd: hdwy into midfield u.p over 2f out: no further imp fr over 1f out* **25/1**

005- **8** *hd* **Bright Society (IRE)**[336] 4630 3-8-2 **46** oh1 (b) PhilipPrince(5) 1 41
(Sean Curran) *chsd ldrs tl outpcd over 2f out: hld whn short of room ins fnl f* **33/1**

00-6 **9** *1 1/2* **Kelamita (IRE)**[58] 1792 3-8-11 **50** AndreaAtzeni 2 43
(Hughie Morrison) *a towards rr* **14/1**

00 **10** *8* **Lizalia (FR)**[7] 3372 3-8-13 **59** HarryBurns(7) 8 38
(Jo Hughes) *mid-div: rdn over 3f out: wknd 2f out* **66/1**

0000 **11** *10* **Mountain Dew**[14] 3116 3-9-4 **57** JimCrowley 6 20
(Ralph Beckett) *hld up towards rr: midfield after 4f: sn rdn: wknd over 2f out* **20/1**

2m 29.57s (-1.03) **Going Correction** -0.225s/f (Firm) **11** Ran SP% **118.8**
Speed ratings (Par 97): **94,92,91,89,89 88,88,88,87,81 75**
CSF £24.21 CT £312.54 TOTE £9.00: £3.20, £1.20, £5.90; EX 30.50 Trifecta £1051.50.
**Owner** Sheikh Hamdan bin Mohammed Al Maktoum **Bred** D J Bloodstock, G Roddick & Wrottesley Ltd **Trained** Middleham Moor, N Yorks

**FOCUS**
A modest handicap.

## 3568 PREMIER CONSERVATORY ROOFS GUARDIAN WARM ROOF MAIDEN STKS 1m 3f 144y
9:10 (9:10) (Class 5) 3-Y-O+ £2,587 (£770; £384; £192) Stalls Low

Form RPR

0 **1** *hd* **Mymatechris (IRE)**[152] 316 3-8-13 0 DavidProbert 5 75+
(Andrew Balding) *trckd ldrs: gng wl whn chalng wnr 2f out: sn carried bdly rt: kpt on wl w ev ch fnl f: jst hld: fin 2nd, hd: awardd r* **2/1**[2]

00 **2** **Special Fighter (IRE)**[38] 2365 3-8-10 0 MichaelJMMurphy(3) 6 76+
(Mark Johnston) *mde all: edgd rt whn jnd 2f out: sn rdn: veered rt over 1f out: kpt on gamely fnl f: all out: fin first: disqualified and plcd 2nd* **5/1**[3]

00 **3** *1 1/4* **Statsminister**[21] 2881 3-8-8 0 JackMitchell 2 68
(Luke Dace) *in tch: rdn 3f out: hdwy 2f out: styd on wl fnl f* **50/1**

04 **4** *3 1/4* **Approaching Star (FR)**[49] 2082 3-8-8 0 AndreaAtzeni 3 63
(William Haggas) *trckd ldrs: rdn 3f out: styd on same pce fnl 2f* **6/5**[1]

50 **5** *5* **Chindeni**[19] 2967 3-8-8 0 LukeMorris 4 54
(Ed Vaughan) *hld up in tch: rdn over 3f out: nvr a threat: one pce fnl 2f* **33/1**

56 **6** *3/4* **Cape Karli (IRE)**[53] 1959 3-8-8 0 SteveDrowne 7 53
(Charles Hills) *trckd wnr tl rdn 2f out: wknd ent fnl f* **10/1**

**7** *59* **Koben Sky**[689] 6-9-3 0 PhilipPrince(5) 1
(Bernard Llewellyn) *rn v green: s.i.s: sn detached and drvn: in tch 6f out: wknd wl over 2f out: t.o* **50/1**

2m 30.8s (0.20) **Going Correction** -0.225s/f (Firm)
**WFA** 3 from 6yo 14lb **7** Ran SP% **111.4**
Speed ratings (Par 103): **89,90,89,86,83 83,43**
CSF £11.60 TOTE £4.10: £2.10, £2.40; EX 6.80 Trifecta £65.80.
**Owner** David Brownlow **Bred** Derrick Fisher **Trained** Kingsclere, Hants

**FOCUS**
The most dramatic event of the evening.
T/Plt: £2,090.60 to a £1 stake. Pool: £64,152.75 - 22.40 winning tickets T/Qpdt: £398.60 to a £1 stake. Pool: £5494.42 - 10.20 winning tickets TM

# [3296]CARLISLE (R-H)

Wednesday, June 25

**OFFICIAL GOING: Good to firm (good in places; 7.2)**

Old Stable bend inside rail moved out 4yds and races on Round course increased by 7yds.

Wind: Light, half against Weather: Overcast

## 3569 OUR LOCAL HERO'S FOUNDATION IRISH STALLION FARMS EBF MAIDEN STKS — 5f 193y

**2:00** (2:01) (Class 5) 2-Y-O **£2,911** (£866; £432; £216) **Stalls** Low

Form | | | | RPR
1 **George Bowen (IRE)** 2-9-5 0 TonyHamilton 2 84+
(Richard Fahey) *noisy and green in preliminaries: dwlt: sn led: pushed along whn hrd pressed over 1f out: drvn and edgd lft wl ins fnl f: kpt on wl: improve* **15/8[2]**

4 **2** ½ **Songye**[13] 3136 2-9-5 0 JamieSpencer 4 82
(Kevin Ryan) *sn pressing ldr: pushed along and hung rt over 2f out: disp ld over 1f out to wl ins fnl f: hld cl home* **5/4[1]**

03 **3** 5 **Twin Turbo (IRE)**[12] 3181 2-9-5 0 FrannyNorton 9 67
(Mark Johnston) *t.k.h: prom on outside: hdwy to chse clr ldng pair over 1f out: edgd rt: no imp fnl f* **11/2[3]**

**4** 4 **Black Pudding (IRE)** 2-9-5 0 PJMcDonald 6 55+
(Ann Duffield) *in tch: effrt and pushed along over 2f out: wknd over 1f out* **33/1**

05 **5** 9 **Triggers Broom (IRE)**[21] 2895 2-8-11 0 GeorgeChaloner(3) 1 22
(Richard Fahey) *early ldr: chsd ldrs tl rdn and wknd over 1f out* **20/1**

50 **6** 5 **Bobby's Flyer (IRE)**[38] 2359 2-9-5 0 DavidAllan 3 12
(Tim Easterby) *prom tl rdn and wknd over 2f out* **33/1**

**7** 11 **Sovereign Bounty** 2-9-5 0 [1] GrahamLee 7
(Jedd O'Keeffe) *bhd and sn struggling: lost tch fr 1/2-way: t.o* **33/1**

1m 14.43s (0.73) **Going Correction** +0.075s/f (Good) **7 Ran SP% 108.2**
Speed ratings (Par 93): **98,97,90,85,73 66,52**
CSF £3.96 TOTE £3.00: £1.30, £1.10; EX 4.00 Trifecta £13.80.
**Owner** M A Scaife **Bred** Kevin Blake **Trained** Musley Bank, N Yorks

**FOCUS**
Old stable bend moved out 4yds adding 7yds to races at 7f and further. The ground was officially good to firm, good in places. Little depth to this maiden and the two market leaders pulled clear. The form looks better than the race average.

## 3570 EDMUNDSON ELECTRICAL CARLISLE MAIDEN AUCTION STKS — 5f

**2:30** (2:32) (Class 5) 2-Y-O **£2,587** (£770; £384; £192) **Stalls** Low

Form | | | | RPR
5 **1** **Fast Act (IRE)**[82] 1276 2-9-4 0 JamieSpencer 10 84+
(Kevin Ryan) *trckd ldrs on outside: hdwy to ld over 1f out: drifted rt ins fnl f: rdn out* **9/4[2]**

02 **2** 1¼ **Bahamian Sunrise**[39] 2328 2-8-8 0 GeorgeChaloner(3) 2 70+
(Richard Fahey) *in tch: pushed along over 2f out: effrt over 1f out: hung lft ins fnl f: chsd wnr last 50yds: r.o* **6/4[1]**

052 **3** ¾ **Straightothepoint**[11] 3236 2-8-13 0 RoystonFfrench 9 69
(Bryan Smart) *pressed ldr: led briefly wl over 1f out: kpt on fnl f: no ex and lost 2nd last 50yds* **3/1[3]**

6 **4** ¾ **Danot (IRE)**[44] 2214 2-8-13 0 TomEaves 8 67+
(Keith Dalgleish) *led: hung lft thrght: hdd wl over 1f out: rallied: kpt on same pce fnl f* **20/1**

**5** 2¾ **Perfect Girl (IRE)** 2-8-10 0 [1] DavidAllan 3 54+
(Tim Easterby) *hld up bhd ldng gp: pushed along 1/2-way: hdwy over 1f out: kpt on fnl f: nrst fin* **16/1**

0 **6** 1¼ **Cupulation**[29] 2642 2-8-11 0 GrahamLee 5 50
(Amy Weaver) *t.k.h in midfield: drvn and outpcd wl over 1f out: sn btn* **50/1**

**7** 3 **Invincible Wish (IRE)** 2-8-11 0 PaulPickard 1 39+
(Brian Ellison) *bhd: pushed along and outpcd 1/2-way: sme hdwy over 1f out: nvr nrr* **33/1**

**8** 5 **Maid In Rome (IRE)** 2-8-8 0 DuranFentiman 6 18
(Tim Easterby) *t.k.h: hld up: hdwy on outside 1/2-way: wknd wl over 1f out* **28/1**

0 **9** 5 **Ubedizzy (IRE)**[30] 2615 2-8-11 0 JasonHart 7 3
(Noel Wilson) *plld hrd: chsd ldrs tl rdn and wknd wl over 1f out* **50/1**

1m 2.01s (1.21) **Going Correction** +0.075s/f (Good) **9 Ran SP% 116.7**
Speed ratings (Par 93): **93,91,89,88,84 82,77,69,61**
CSF £5.77 TOTE £3.00: £1.20, £1.10, £1.20; EX 6.90 Trifecta £15.10.
**Owner** Hambleton Racing Ltd XXXII **Bred** Newlands House Stud **Trained** Hambleton, N Yorks

**FOCUS**
A fair maiden. The winner was value for a bit extra and there's more to come.

## 3571 BET ON UK RACING WITH TOTEPOOL H'CAP — 5f

**3:00** (3:00) (Class 4) (0-85,83) 3-Y-O+ **£5,175** (£1,540; £769; £384) **Stalls** Low

Form | | | | RPR
4410 **1** **Rothesay Chancer**[11] 3239 6-9-7 76 GrahamLee 9 86
(Jim Goldie) *bhd and sn outpcd: plenty to do 1/2-way: gd hdwy over 1f out: led wl ins fnl f: kpt on wl* **16/1**

1203 **2** 1¼ **Boxing Shadows**[6] 3399 4-8-11 66 DavidAllan 6 71
(Les Eyre) *hld up bhd ldng gp: effrt and rdn 2f out: hdwy and ev ch wl ins fnl f: kpt on same pce towards fin* **11/2**

2055 **3** ¾ **Hadaj**[11] 3221 5-9-8 82 (b) KevinStott(5) 11 84
(Ruth Carr) *in tch: lost pl after 2f: rdn and gd hdwy fnl f: kpt on: nrst fin* **11/4[1]**

-053 **4** nk **Bondi Beach Boy**[13] 3138 5-9-9 78 SilvestreDeSousa 3 79
(James Turner) *led at decent gallop: rdn 2f out: hung lft and hdd wl ins fnl f: sn no ex* **7/2[3]**

0223 **5** 3½ **Avon Breeze**[8] 3342 5-9-10 82 GeorgeChaloner(3) 1 71
(Richard Whitaker) *prom: effrt and rdn 2f out: outpcd fnl f* **3/1[2]**

1040 **6** 1¼ **Dodina (IRE)**[8] 3338 4-8-10 65 (b[1]) TomEaves 4 49
(Brian Ellison) *hld up: stdy hdwy over 2f out: drvn and rival's whip ct in reins over 1f out: edgd rt and sn btn* **40/1**

0010 **7** nse **Baytown Kestrel**[4] 3484 3-9-4 79 RobertWinston 5 61
(Brian Ellison) *awkward s: chsd ldr: drvn over 2f out: wknd ent fnl f* **16/1**

1020 **8** nk **Silvanus (IRE)**[11] 3239 9-10-0 83 PaulMulrennan 2 66
(Paul Midgley) *taken early to post: t.k.h: prom: effrt whn whip ct in rival's reins and plld out of rdr's hand over 1f out: wknd fnl f* **12/1**

2400 **9** 2½ **Tax Free (IRE)**[19] 2953 12-9-11 80 AdrianNicholls 10 54
(David Nicholls) *trckd ldrs: rdn over 2f out: wknd over 1f out* **18/1**

1m 0.37s (-0.43) **Going Correction** +0.075s/f (Good)
**WFA** 3 from 4yo+ 6lb **9 Ran SP% 116.4**
Speed ratings (Par 105): **106,104,102,102,96 94,94,94,90**
CSF £102.11 CT £321.22 TOTE £13.60: £4.20, £2.20, £1.30; EX 172.70 Trifecta £708.90.
**Owner** The McMaster Springford Partnership **Bred** Mrs S R Kennedy **Trained** Uplawmoor, E Renfrews

**FOCUS**
A useful sprint handicap and the pace was strong, which favoured the closers. The winner is rated back to his best.

## 3572 DOWNLOAD THE FREE APP @BOOKMAKERS.CO.UK CARLISLE BELL CONSOLATION RACE (H'CAP) — 7f 200y

**3:35** (3:35) (Class 4) (0-85,85) 3-Y-O+ **£6,469** (£1,925; £962; £481) **Stalls** Low

Form | | | | RPR
2103 **1** **Another For Joe**[16] 3050 6-9-6 75 GrahamLee 17 85
(Jim Goldie) *cl up: effrt and rdn over 1f out: led ins fnl f: kpt on strly* **14/1**

0062 **2** 1½ **Tectonic (IRE)**[9] 3301 5-8-11 66 (p) TomEaves 9 73
(Keith Dalgleish) *t.k.h in midfield: stdy hdwy over 2f out: led over 1f out: rdn: edgd lft and hdd ins fnl f: one pce* **14/1**

0-21 **3** shd **George Rooke (IRE)**[14] 3102 4-9-10 79 (p) SilvestreDeSousa 3 90+
(Keith Dalgleish) *hld up: plenty to do ent st: hdwy on wd outside 2f out: kpt on strly fnl f: nrst fin* **11/2[1]**

052 **4** 1¼ **Spin Artist (USA)**[8] 3334 4-9-0 69 FrannyNorton 14 73
(Mark Johnston) *trckd ldrs: effrt and chal wl over 1f out: one pce whn checked ins fnl f* **10/1**

1-62 **5** nk **Ventura Quest (USA)**[54] 1927 3-9-6 85 TonyHamilton 10 86
(Richard Fahey) *hld up towards rr: hdwy on outside over 1f out: sn drvn: kpt on ins fnl f: nrst fin* **15/2[3]**

-131 **6** ¾ **Border Bandit (USA)**[6] 3400 6-9-7 76 6ex (p) RobertWinston 4 77
(Tracy Waggott) *prom: effrt and rdn 2f out: kpt on same pce fnl f* **8/1**

4315 **7** ¾ **Cameroonéy**[9] 3301 11-8-9 69 (p) NathanAlison(5) 7 69
(Marjorie Fife) *led: rdn and hdd over 1f out: outpcd fnl f* **25/1**

0622 **8** 1 **Al Muheer (IRE)**[6] 3400 9-9-8 77 (p) JamesSullivan 15 74
(Ruth Carr) *towards rr: rdn over 2f out: kpt on fnl f: nvr able to chal* **11/1**

-000 **9** nk **Act Your Shoe Size**[40] 2293 5-9-0 69 JasonHart 12 66
(Keith Dalgleish) *in tch: drvn over 2f out: no ex over 1f out* **25/1**

0256 **10** hd **Shadowtime**[12] 3190 9-9-5 74 PaulMulrennan 13 70
(Tracy Waggott) *plld hrd: trckd ldrs tl rdn and wknd over 1f out* **25/1**

4035 **11** hd **Fazza**[11] 3254 7-9-1 75 KevinStott(5) 16 71
(Edwin Tuer) *hld up: shortlived effrt on outside over 2f out: sn no imp* **8/1**

1653 **12** ½ **Imperator Augustus (IRE)**[11] 3237 6-8-4 64 JackGarritty(5) 5 59
(Patrick Holmes) *hld up on ins: drvn over 2f out: sn no imp* **14/1**

5363 **13** 1¼ **Millkwood**[10] 3272 4-9-7 76 (b) PhillipMakin 8 68
(John Davies) *s.i.s: hld up: rdn 3f out: nvr on terms* **11/1**

2242 **14** 8 **Who's Shirl**[30] 2604 8-9-7 76 MichaelStainton 2 49
(Chris Fairhurst) *bhd: struggling 3f out: sn btn* **25/1**

1102 **P** **Eutropius (IRE)**[18] 3005 5-9-10 79 BenCurtis 1
(Alan Swinbank) *dwlt: bhd and hmpd after 1f: nvr gng wl after: struggling and eased 2f out: p.u towards fin: b.b.v* **7/1[2]**

1m 39.46s (-0.54) **Going Correction** +0.025s/f (Good)
**WFA** 3 from 4yo+ 10lb **15 Ran SP% 123.0**
Speed ratings (Par 105): **103,101,101,100,99 99,98,97,97,96 96,96,94,86,**
CSF £190.87 CT £1228.99 TOTE £13.10: £3.80, £4.80, £2.40; EX 252.50 Trifecta £1310.10.
**Owner** Mr & Mrs Gordon Grant & J S Goldie **Bred** G Merkel **Trained** Uplawmoor, E Renfrews

**FOCUS**
A fair handicap for those declared to run in the Carlisle Bell, but were eliminated at the 48-hour declaration stage. The early pace fractions were steady until the pace picked up on the turn into the straight. The form is rated around the runner-up.

## 3573 BOOKMAKERS.CO.UK CARLISLE BELL (H'CAP) — 7f 200y

**4:10** (4:11) (Class 4) (0-85,88) 3-Y-O+

**£18,675** (£5,592; £2,796; £1,398; £699; £351) **Stalls** Low

Form | | | | RPR
0013 **1** **Johnno**[11] 3221 5-9-3 81 AdrianNicholls 12 95
(David Nicholls) *pressed ldr: led and rdn over 1f out: edgd rt and kpt on wl fnl f* **7/1[3]**

0062 **2** 1 **Sound Advice**[5] 3437 5-9-7 85 TomEaves 16 97
(Keith Dalgleish) *prom: effrt and chsd wnr over 1f out: kpt on u.p fnl f: hld nr fin* **13/2[2]**

5-41 **3** 2¾ **Balducci**[9] 3306 7-9-10 88 6ex (v) DanielTudhope 13 93
(David O'Meara) *in tch: effrt and rdn 2f out: kpt on same pce fnl f* **9/2[1]**

0003 **4** 1½ **Party Royal**[4] 3463 4-9-3 81 SilvestreDeSousa 10 83
(Mark Johnston) *prom: effrt and drvn along over 2f out: kpt on same pce appr fnl f* **11/1**

0214 **5** nk **Barren Brook**[11] 3254 7-9-2 80 GrahamGibbons 9 81
(Michael Easterby) *t.k.h: hld up towards rr: rdn and edgd rt 2f out: swtchd lft and styd on wl fnl f: nrst fin* **8/1**

-256 **6** ¾ **Ginger Jack**[14] 3109 7-9-7 85 (p) PJMcDonald 3 85
(Geoffrey Harker) *in tch on ins: drvn along over 2f out: no imp over 1f out* **12/1**

3105 **7** ½ **Just Paul (IRE)**[12] 3189 4-8-11 80 JackGarritty(5) 6 78
(Philip Kirby) *midfield on ins: drvn along over 2f out: effrt over 1f out: nvr able to chal* **12/1**

-500 **8** 1¾ **Talent Scout (IRE)**[11] 3221 8-8-9 80 (p) GemmaTutty(7) 5 74
(Karen Tutty) *led: rdn and hdd over 1f out: wknd fnl f* **25/1**

20-0 **9** 2 **Shesastar**[87] 1191 6-9-3 81 FrannyNorton 8 71
(David Barron) *hld up: rdn along over 2f out: edgd rt and sme hdwy over 1f out: nvr rchd ldrs* **28/1**

1122 **10** 2½ **High Time Too (IRE)**[50] 2062 4-9-6 84 JamieSpencer 7 68
(Hugo Palmer) *midfield: drvn along on outside over 2f out: btn fnl f* **16/1**

-120 **11** hd **Escape To Glory (USA)**[12] 3202 6-9-6 84 PaulMulrennan 11 68
(Michael Dods) *hld up: rdn along over 2f out: nvr on terms* **22/1**

6343 **12** 1¾ **Silver Rime (FR)**[12] 3189 9-9-4 82 PhillipMakin 2 62
(Linda Perratt) *midfield: drvn and outpcd over 2f out: sn btn* **16/1**

0350 **13** shd **Shahdaroba (IRE)**[11] 3251 4-9-5 83 GrahamLee 17 62
(Micky Hammond) *hld up towards rr: struggling over 2f out: sn wknd* **14/1**

-000 **14** ¾ **Lord Of The Dance (IRE)**[27] 2699 8-8-13 80 RyanClark(3) 4 58
(Michael Mullineaux) *dwlt: bhd: drvn along wl over 2f out: nvr on terms* **12/1**

-364 **15** 2½ **Toto Skyllachy**[43] 2234 9-9-3 84 SamJames(3) 1 56
(David O'Meara) *s.i.s: bhd: drvn along wl over 2f out: sn btn* **20/1**

1-20 **16** 1 3/4 **Circuitous**[23] 2825 6-9-4 **82**................................ JasonHart 15 50
(Keith Dalgleish) *towards rr: drvn along 3f out: btn fnl 2f* **20/1**
1m 38.69s (-1.31) **Going Correction** +0.025s/f (Good) **16** Ran SP% **126.1**
Speed ratings (Par 105): **107,106,103,101,101 100,100,98,96,93 93,92,91,91,88 86**
CSF £49.46 CT £197.67 TOTE £6.60: £2.50, £2.30, £1.70, £3.00; EX 58.50 Trifecta £266.60.
**Owner** Alan Zheng **Bred** Gestut Sohrenhof **Trained** Sessay, N Yorks
**FOCUS**
Another big field and a strongly contested renewal of this celebrated handicap, first run in 1599, but those that raced prominently were favoured and not many got competitive from off the pace. The winning time was 0.77 seconds faster than the consolation race. The winner is rated back to his old best.

## 3574 TOTEPOOL CUMBERLAND PLATE (H'CAP) 1m 3f 107y
**4:45** (4:45) (Class 4) (0-85,85) 3-Y-0+
**£18,675** (£5,592; £2,796; £1,398; £699; £351) **Stalls** High

Form RPR
3-54 **1** **Noble Alan (GER)**[25] 2760 11-9-1 **79**........................ IanBrennan(3) 16 88
(Nicky Richards) *hld up gng wl: smooth hdwy and swtchd to wd outside 2f out: qcknd to ld ins fnl f: drifted rt: kpt on strly* **13/2**[1]
0510 **2** 1 1/4 **Streets Of Newyork**[25] 2787 7-9-4 **79**.................... RobertWinston 6 86+
(Brian Ellison) *hld up: effrt whn hmpd 2f out: rcvrd and hdwy whn hmpd again 1f out: styd on wl to take 2nd nr fin: nt rch wnr* **15/2**[3]
4-05 **3** *hd* **Eltheeb**[12] 3205 7-9-1 **76**...................................(p[1]) PaulMulrennan 11 83
(Philip Kirby) *hld up: stdy hdwy on ins 2f out: carried rt and chsd wnr ins fnl f: no ex and lost 2nd nr fin* **10/1**
1142 **4** 1/2 **Memory Cloth**[36] 2423 7-9-2 **82**........................ JackGarritty(5) 14 89
(Brian Ellison) *hld up: effrt whn nt clr run and swtchd rt wl over 1f out: n.m.r 1f out: kpt on ins fnl f: no imp* **20/1**
4-11 **5** 1/2 **Aramist (IRE)**[33] 2520 4-9-6 **81**.................................... BenCurtis 17 86+
(Alan Swinbank) *hld up: reminders over 4f out: hdwy over 2f out: chsng ldrs whn carried rt 1f out: one pce* **7/1**[2]
051 **6** *nk* **Laughing Jack**[19] 2966 6-8-12 **78**...................... GeorgeDowning(5) 12 83
(George Baker) *t.k.h: prom on outside: rdn and hung rt over 2f out: rallied: carried rt ins fnl f: one pce* **14/1**
13-0 **7** 3 **Endless Credit (IRE)**[25] 2787 4-9-9 **84**.................. GrahamGibbons 2 84
(Luca Cumani) *t.k.h early: trckd ldrs: led over 1f out: carried rt and hdd ins fnl f: sn no ex* **7/1**[2]
41-6 **8** 4 **Satanic Beat (IRE)**[40] 1377 5-9-5 **80**.......................... GrahamLee 8 73
(Jedd O'Keeffe) *prom: effrt and rdn over 2f out: wknd appr fnl f* **25/1**
0-01 **9** 2 3/4 **Dance King**[18] 3004 4-9-2 **77**.......................................... DavidAllan 13 65
(Tim Easterby) *cl up: led over 2f out to over 1f out: wknd fnl f* **8/1**
-250 **10** 1 1/2 **Burnham**[20] 2920 5-9-1 **76**...........................................(p) DanielTudhope 9 62
(Hughie Morrison) *trckd ldrs: effrt and rdn over 2f out: cl up whn hmpd ent fnl f: sn btn* **10/1**
/0-0 **11** 7 **Rosslyn Castle**[35] 2461 5-9-5 **83**........................ GeorgeChaloner(3) 3 57
(Philip McBride) *hld up in midfield: drvn along over 2f out: sn btn* **40/1**
2-60 **12** 1 1/2 **Croquembouche (IRE)**[11] 3217 5-9-10 **85**.................. PhillipMakin 5 57
(Ed de Giles) *led to over 2f out: rdn and wknd over 1f out* **15/2**[3]
000- **13** 8 **Cousin Khee**[228] 7823 7-9-7 **82**.................................. JamieSpencer 4 41
(Hughie Morrison) *hld up: effrt and rdn over 2f out: wknd over 1f out: eased* **16/1**
3323 **14** 3 **High Office**[12] 3205 8-9-5 **80**........................................ DavidNolan 10 34
(Richard Fahey) *midfield: drvn and outpcd over 2f out: sn btn* **14/1**
2m 23.74s (0.64) **Going Correction** +0.025s/f (Good) **14** Ran SP% **121.4**
Speed ratings (Par 105): **98,97,96,96,96 96,93,90,88,87 82,81,75,73**
CSF £53.17 CT £494.14 TOTE £6.90: £2.70, £3.20, £5.40; EX 61.20 Trifecta £1998.30.
**Owner** Craig Bennett **Bred** Gestut Kussaburg **Trained** Greystoke, Cumbria
■ Stewards' Enquiry : Ian Brennan one-day ban: careless riding (Jul 9)
**FOCUS**
A useful handicap but a messy race, with the winner edging right approaching the final furlong and causing a concertina effect. The first four raced in rear and the winner built on a better latest run.

## 3575 EBF WORLD CUP FREE BETS @BOOKMAKERS.CO.UK FILLIES H'CAP 6f 192y
**5:15** (5:17) (Class 4) (0-80,76) 3-Y-0+ **£6,469** (£1,925; £962; £481) **Stalls** Low

Form RPR
3144 **1** **Kosika (USA)**[11] 3220 4-10-0 **76**.................................... FrannyNorton 7 88
(Mark Johnston) *t.k.h: mde virtually all: rdn over 1f out: kpt on wl fnl f* **6/1**
5361 **2** 1 1/4 **Spirit Of Alsace (IRE)**[4] 3460 3-7-13 **61** 6ex................ JackGarritty(5) 2 66
(Jim Goldie) *dwlt: hld up: rdn and hdwy over 1f out: chsd wnr ins fnl f: r.o* **6/1**
1424 **3** 1 1/2 **Alluring Star**[14] 3096 6-9-5 **67**................................ GrahamGibbons 5 71
(Michael Easterby) *w wnr to over 2f out: rdn and kpt on same pce fnl f* **9/1**
0612 **4** 1 1/4 **Miaplacidus (IRE)**[9] 3300 3-7-13 **61**........................ SammyJoBell(5) 3 59
(Richard Fahey) *prom: drvn and outpcd over 2f out: rallied fnl f: no imp* **9/2**[2]
5610 **5** 3/4 **Alexandrakollontai (IRE)**[7] 3359 4-9-7 **69**..................(b) PJMcDonald 10 68
(Alistair Whillans) *hld up: rdn over 2f out: kpt on fnl f: nvr able to chal* **16/1**
221- **6** 1 1/4 **Angel Flores (IRE)**[208] 8091 3-9-0 **71**........................ TonyHamilton 4 64
(Richard Fahey) *t.k.h early: prom: effrt and swtchd rt over 1f out: wknd ins fnl f* **3/1**[1]
6341 **7** *shd* **Medam**[13] 3149 5-8-6 **60** oh3.......................................... NeilFarley(3) 1 52
(Shaun Harris) *hld up: rdn 3f out: no imp fr 2f out* **12/1**
0-02 **8** 1 **Gladsome**[19] 2954 6-8-6 **60** oh3.............................. ConnorBeasley(3) 9 50
(Michael Herrington) *hld up: effrt and rdn over 2f out: nvr able to chal* **28/1**
0-52 **9** 4 **Penina (IRE)**[32] 2545 3-8-8 **65**.......................................... PaulPickard 6 44
(Brian Ellison) *t.k.h: cl up: rdn over 2f out: wknd fnl f* **11/2**[3]
1m 26.95s (-0.15) **Going Correction** +0.025s/f (Good)
**WFA** 3 from 4yo+ 9lb **9** Ran SP% **114.2**
Speed ratings (Par 105): **101,99,97,96,95 94,94,92,88**
CSF £41.25 CT £323.45 TOTE £8.40: £2.50, £2.50, £3.00; EX 40.80 Trifecta £414.60.
**Owner** Sheikh Hamdan bin Mohammed Al Maktoum **Bred** Betz Thoroughbred Et Al **Trained** Middleham Moor, N Yorks
**FOCUS**
Not the strongest handicap for the grade, but it was run at a good pace. The form is worth a bit more at face value.
T/Jkpt: Not won. T/Plt: £49.20 to a £1 stake. Pool: £75659.30 - 1120.57 winning tickets T/Qpdt: £33.70 to a £1 stake. Pool: £4261.66 - 93.40 winning tickets RY

# 3112 KEMPTON (A.W) (R-H)
Wednesday, June 25

**OFFICIAL GOING: Standard**
Wind: Almost nil Weather: Fine, warm

## 3576 IRISH NIGHT ON 09.07.14 APPRENTICE H'CAP 1m (P)
**5:50** (5:51) (Class 6) (0-60,60) 4-Y-0+ **£1,940** (£577; £288; £144) **Stalls** Low

Form RPR
2361 **1** **Zed Candy Girl**[27] 2689 4-9-0 **53**................................(p) TimClark 1 63
(Dai Burchell) *trckd ldng pair: wnt 2nd 2f out: rdn and clsd to ld 1f out: hung lft but kpt on* **8/1**[3]
1035 **2** 1 3/4 **Appyjack**[14] 3115 6-8-12 **51**.......................................... JoeyHaynes 4 57
(Tony Carroll) *settled in mdifeld: urged along over 3f out: prog on inner over 2f out: kpt on fr over 1f out to take 2nd last stride* **6/1**[1]
2305 **3** *nse* **Greek Islands (IRE)**[2] 3528 6-8-8 **54**................ RhiainIngram(7) 10 60
(Edward Creighton) *sn w ldr: led 3f out: edgd lft and hdd 1f out: one pce and lost 2nd last stride* **14/1**
2010 **4** 1 1/4 **Katmai River (IRE)**[26] 2720 7-8-13 **55**................ CharlotteJenner(3) 2 58
(Mark Usher) *trckd ldrs: disp 3rd wl over 1f out but no imp on ldng pair: one pce after* **10/1**
4435 **5** 3/4 **Warbond**[20] 2930 6-9-0 **56**...........................................(b[1]) RyanWhile(3) 14 57+
(Michael Madgwick) *dropped in fr wd draw and hld up in last trio: brought wd in st and shkn up: no prog tl styd on wl fr over 1f out: nrst fin* **7/1**[2]
-500 **6** 1 **Diamonds A Dancing**[21] 2884 4-8-12 **51**.................. MarcMonaghan 8 50
(Brian Gubby) *wl in rr: urged along over 3f out: kpt on fnl 2f: nrst fin* **10/1**
5632 **7** *nse* **Polydamos**[14] 3115 5-9-0 **53**....................................(v) LouisSteward 12 52
(Tony Carroll) *racd wd: chsd ldrs: effrt over 2f out: no imp over 1f out: one pce after* **6/1**[1]
003 **8** 1/2 **Delightful Sleep**[23] 2844 6-9-1 **57**...................... AlistairRawlinson(3) 6 55
(David Evans) *hld up towards rr: rdn over 2f out: sme prog over 1f out: one pce fnl f* **6/1**[1]
0562 **9** 1 1/2 **Sutton Sid**[13] 3155 4-9-2 **60**........................................(b) DavidParkes(5) 9 54
(Ann Stokell) *hld up in last trio: pushed along over 3f out: no prog tl rdn and styd on fr over 1f out: nrst fin* **12/1**
6600 **10** 4 1/2 **Divine Rule (IRE)**[22] 2864 6-9-1 **59**....................(p) SophieRalston(5) 11 43
(Laura Mongan) *racd wd: hld up towards rr: pushed along and no prog over 2f out* **20/1**
066- **11** 1 1/2 **Know No Fear**[189] 7429 9-9-2 **60**................................(p) PaulBooth(5) 13 40
(Alastair Lidderdale) *dropped in fr wd draw and hld up in last trio: shkn up and no prog over 2f out* **25/1**
0-00 **12** 1 1/2 **L'Hirondelle (IRE)**[15] 3080 10-9-2 **55**............................ NoelGarbutt 5 32
(Michael Attwater) *nvr bttr than midfield: rdn and no prog over 2f out: sn wknd* **16/1**
0-60 **13** 8 **Hidden Talent**[13] 3149 4-9-7 **60**................................(b[1]) JackDuern 7 19
(Steph Hollinshead) *led to 3f out: sn wknd: t.o* **33/1**
50-0 **14** 18 **Douglas Pasha (IRE)**[23] 2843 4-8-8 **52**........................ GaryMahon(5) 3
(Martin Smith) *prom: rdn 1/2-way: wknd 3f out: wl t.o* **33/1**
1m 39.77s (-0.03) **Going Correction** 0.0s/f (Stan) **14** Ran SP% **119.4**
Speed ratings (Par 101): **100,98,98,96,96 95,95,94,93,88 87,85,77,59**
CSF £52.48 CT £683.52 TOTE £8.60: £3.20, £1.90, £6.60; EX 61.80 Trifecta £964.40.
**Owner** Robert Emmanuel **Bred** H H L Bloodstock **Trained** Briery Hill, Blaenau Gwent
**FOCUS**
The pace was decent and fair for all.

## 3577 BETDAQ £25 NO LOSE FREE BET H'CAP (LONDON MILE SERIES QUALIFIER) 1m (P)
**6:20** (6:20) (Class 4) (0-85,84) 3-Y-0+ **£4,690** (£1,395; £697; £348) **Stalls** Low

Form RPR
3-02 **1** **Buckstay (IRE)**[25] 2772 4-9-12 **82**.................................. ShaneKelly 11 94+
(Peter Chapple-Hyam) *hld up in last trio: stdy prog fr 3f out: clsd on ldrs over 1f out: pushed into ld ins fnl f: quite comf* **6/1**
2-22 **2** 1/2 **Musaddas**[13] 3153 4-9-13 **83**..........................................[1] KierenFallon 1 93
(Saeed bin Suroor) *trckd ldr after 1f: shkn up to ld 2f out: drvn over 1f out: hdd and nt qckn ins fnl f* **7/2**[2]
0-64 **3** 3/4 **Messila Star**[14] 3118 4-9-3 **73**..................................(v) WilliamBuick 2 82
(Jeremy Noseda) *trckd ldrs: cl up 2f out: hrd rdn to chal over 1f out: nt qckn fnl f* **14/1**
2316 **4** 3/4 **Tenor (IRE)**[16] 3050 4-9-11 **81**..................................(t) GeorgeBaker 4 88
(John Ryan) *led 1f: trckd ldng pair after: rdn to chal wl over 1f out: nt qckn fnl f* **7/1**
10-1 **5** 6 **Suehail**[20] 2922 5-9-13 **83**.............................................. PatDobbs 12 76
(Robert Cowell) *hld up in last trio: rdn and struggling in 7th over 2f out: plugged on fr over 1f out* **8/1**
-010 **6** 1 1/2 **Shahrazad (IRE)**[9] 3310 5-8-3 **66** oh4..................(t) JackGilligan(7) 13 56
(Patrick Gilligan) *led after 1f to 2f out: wknd qckly over 1f out* **33/1**
1350 **7** 2 **Hagree (IRE)**[20] 2921 3-9-4 **84**..................................(t) MartinHarley 9 67
(Marco Botti) *hld up in last trio: rdn over 2f out: no prog on inner wl over 1f out: sn wknd* **5/1**[3]
1- **8** 1 **Furas (IRE)**[224] 7852 3-9-4 **84**.................................. PaulHanagan 6 65
(Saeed bin Suroor) *racd wd: struggling fr 1/2-way: last and wl btn over 2f out* **9/4**[1]
3-03 **9** 11 **Soaring Spirits (IRE)**[23] 2833 4-9-9 **79**....................(b) JimmyQuinn 5 37
(Dean Ivory) *sltly awkward s: t.k.h in midfield: wknd qckly 2f out: t.o* **25/1**
1m 38.59s (-1.21) **Going Correction** 0.0s/f (Stan)
**WFA** 3 from 4yo+ 10lb **9** Ran SP% **121.0**
Speed ratings (Par 105): **106,105,104,104,98 96,94,93,82**
CSF £28.74 CT £292.65 TOTE £9.00: £2.50, £1.70, £5.00; EX 29.60 Trifecta £457.50.
**Owner** Mrs Fitri Hay **Bred** M Phelan & Lawman Syndicate **Trained** Newmarket, Suffolk
**FOCUS**
The pace increased after the first furlong but was still no better than medium.

## 3578 BETDAQ NO PREMIUM CHARGE MAIDEN STKS 7f (P)
**6:50** (6:56) (Class 5) 2-Y-0 **£2,587** (£770; £384; £192) **Stalls** Low

Form RPR
3 **1** **Disegno (IRE)**[25] 2777 2-9-5 0.......................................... RyanMoore 11 88+
(Sir Michael Stoute) *pressed ldr: drew wl clr w runner-up fr 3f out: rdn to chal 2f out: led 1f out: styd on* **4/5**[1]
5 **2** 1 1/2 **Ventriloquist**[13] 3136 2-9-5 0.................................... WilliamBuick 12 84+
(Charlie Appleby) *led: drew wl clr w wnr fr 3f out: rdn 2f out: kpt on wl but hdd 1f out: hld after* **7/2**[2]
**3** 6 **Indianaughty (USA)** 2-9-5 0.......................................... MartinHarley 1 70+
(Marco Botti) *s.s: hld up in last pair: prog over 2f out: pushed along and styd on steadily to take 3rd ins fnl f: shaped wl* **10/1**[3]

4 ½ **Tom Hark (FR)** 2-9-5 0 PatDobbs 6 66
(Richard Hannon) *chsd ldng pair: lft wl bhd by them fr 3f out: kpt on steadily fr 2f out but lost 3rd ins fnl f* **10/1**3

5 4 ½ **Mountainside** 2-9-5 0 MartinLane 10 54+
(Charlie Appleby) *s.v.s: rousted along to get in tch: v awkward bnd 5f out and reminders: no ch fr 3f out: modest late hdwy* **14/1**

6 2 ¼ **Prince Of Paris** 2-9-5 0 RobertHavlin 8 48
(Roger Ingram) *chsd ldrs: lft bhd w the rest fr 3f out: wknd 2f out* **33/1**

7 shd **Eben Dubai (IRE)** 2-9-5 0 PaulHanagan 9 48
(Sir Michael Stoute) *green in preliminaries: nvr bttr than midfield: lft bhd w the rest whn ldng pair drew clr 3f out: no prog after* **10/1**3

8 8 **Wolf Of Windlesham (IRE)** 2-9-5 0 JamesDoyle 2 26
(B W Hills) *s.i.s: a wl in rr: no ch fnl 3f* **25/1**

50 9 4 **Edmund Halley (FR)**15 3082 2-9-5 0 (b) PatCosgrave 3 16
(Harry Dunlop) *chsd ldrs: lft bhd fr 3f out: sn wknd* **50/1**

40 10 nk **Storming Harry**46 2172 2-9-5 0 (t) WilliamCarson 4 15
(Robin Dickin) *s.s: in tch in midfield: lost grnd qckly over 3f out and then snatched up: bhd after* **50/1**

11 ½ **Olympic Charm** 2-9-5 0 DaleSwift 7 13
(Derek Shaw) *chsd ldrs to 1/2-way: wknd qckly over 2f out* **50/1**

1m 27.19s (1.19) **Going Correction** 0.0s/f (Stan) **11 Ran SP% 124.4**
Speed ratings (Par 93): **93,91,84,83,78 76,76,66,62,61 61**
CSF £3.78 TOTE £1.50: £1.10, £2.00, £2.60; EX 4.70 Trifecta £23.30.
**Owner** Niarchos Family **Bred** Niarchos Family **Trained** Newmarket, Suffolk

**FOCUS**
The pace was adequate and the first two created a positive impression in drawing well clear, but several of the others are also interesting.

## 3579 DIZZEE RASCAL LIVE AT KEMPTON 06.09.14 H'CAP 2m (P)
**7:20** (7:21) (Class 6) (0-65,65) 4-Y-0+ **£1,940** (£577; £288; £144) **Stalls** Low

Form RPR

1641 1 **See And Be Seen**11 3234 4-9-4 62 (p) JamesDoyle 1 75+
(Sylvester Kirk) *mde all: rdn and firmly in control fr 2f out: styd on wl* **5/2**1

5/45 2 3 ½ **Soundbyte**24 2801 9-8-3 50 (v) JoeyHaynes(3) 4 59
(John Gallagher) *trckd ldrs: rdn to chse wnr jst over 2f out: styd on but nvr any imp* **5/1**2

54-5 3 8 **Bold Adventure**29 380 10-9-0 58 StevieDonohoe 5 57
(Willie Musson) *hld up in last trio: prog on inner 3f out: outpcd fr 2f out: tk modest 3rd ins fnl f* **14/1**

-060 4 1 ¼ **The Absent Mare**7 2885 6-8-11 55 WilliamCarson 10 53
(Robin Dickin) *s.s: hld up in last trio: rdn and prog over 2f out: sn lft bhd by ldng pair: plugged on fnl f* **16/1**

30-3 5 ½ **Money Talks**28 2683 4-9-7 65 GeorgeBaker 11 62+
(Michael Madgwick) *hld up in last trio and racd wd: quick prog on wd outside bnd 5f out to 4f out to press wnr over 3f out: rdn over 2f out: sn lost 2nd and btn: wknd fnl f* **5/2**1

300- 6 2 ¼ **Sure Fire (GER)**275 6696 9-7-11 46 NoelGarbutt(5) 6 41
(David Evans) *in tch: rdn 5f out: outpcd fr over 2f out: no ch after* **20/1**

0056 7 shd **Hazel Brook**12 3179 5-9-2 60 PatDobbs 2 54
(Mary Hambro) *chsd wnr to over 3f out: sn wknd* **20/1**

5325 8 28 **Rocky Rebel**33 872 6-9-3 61 DaleSwift 9 22
(Michael Blake) *chsd ldrs: rdn 6f out: wkng whn v wd bnd 3f out: wl t.o* **6/1**3

1206 9 1 ¼ **Royal Defence (IRE)**16 3051 8-8-9 53 (bt1) FrederikTylicki 8 12
(Richard Ford) *racd wd: prom: rdn and lost pl over 3f out: wd bnd sn after and wknd: wl t.o* **10/1**

3m 31.98s (1.88) **Going Correction** 0.0s/f (Stan) **9 Ran SP% 119.3**
Speed ratings (Par 101): **95,93,89,88,88 87,87,73,72**
CSF £15.85 CT £142.93 TOTE £3.10: £1.20, £3.10, £4.10; EX 27.80 Trifecta £237.00.
**Owner** Timothy Pearson **Bred** Exors Of The Late T E Pocock **Trained** Upper Lambourn, Berks

**FOCUS**
The front-running winner was allowed to set a modest pace, and that was just what he wanted.

## 3580 IRISH STALLION FARMS EBF NOVICE STKS (BOBIS RACE) 6f (P)
**7:50** (7:50) (Class 3) 2-Y-0
**£6,225** (£1,864; £932; £466; £233; £117) **Stalls** Low

Form RPR

1 1 **Limato (IRE)**14 3113 2-9-7 0 JamesDoyle 4 97+
(Henry Candy) *trckd ldr after 2f: led jst over 1f out: sn drew clr: easily* **4/6**1

13 2 2 ¼ **Natural Order (USA)**22 2873 2-9-7 0 WilliamBuick 7 86
(K R Burke) *hld up in 4th: clsd 2f out: rdn to chal over 1f out: chsd wnr fnl f and styd on but no ch* **4/1**2

143 3 2 **Bronze Maquette (IRE)**37 2403 2-9-2 0 RyanMoore 1 75
(Gary Moore) *hld up in 5th: rdn 2f out: cl up bhd ldrs over 1f out: kpt on one pce to take 3rd ins fnl f* **8/1**

01 4 1 ¼ **Assault On Rome (IRE)**18 2979 2-9-2 0 KierenFallon 3 72
(Mark Johnston) *led: kicked on over 2f out: hdd jst over 1f out: wknd* **10/1**

015 5 ½ **Lightning Stride**18 2987 2-9-7 0 HarryBentley 2 75
(Brian Meehan) *trckd ldr 2f: styd cl up: rdn to chal over 1f out: wknd fnl f* **7/1**3

6 15 **Junior Ben** 2-9-0 0 DaleSwift 5 23
(Derek Shaw) *slowly away: a in last: wknd over 2f out: t.o* **66/1**

1m 13.38s (0.28) **Going Correction** 0.0s/f (Stan) **6 Ran SP% 114.2**
Speed ratings (Par 97): **98,95,92,90,90 70**
CSF £3.83 TOTE £1.70: £1.10, £2.20; EX 3.70 Trifecta £16.70.
**Owner** Paul G Jacobs **Bred** Seamus Phelan **Trained** Kingston Warren, Oxon

**FOCUS**
The pace was just medium and the winner smothered the opposition for finishing speed. The smart winner looks likely to rate a good few lengths higher.

## 3581 CASH OUT ON THE BETDAQ + APP FILLIES' H'CAP 6f (P)
**8:20** (8:20) (Class 4) (0-80,80) 3-Y-0+ **£4,690** (£1,395; £697; £348) **Stalls** Low

Form RPR

11-2 1 **Oh So Sassy**29 2645 4-10-0 80 GeorgeBaker 9 97
(Chris Wall) *trckd ldr: led 2f out gng easily: pushed clr over 1f out: readily* **3/1**2

0002 2 3 ¼ **Outbacker (IRE)**6 3405 3-8-13 72 RyanMoore 2 75
(Mark Johnston) *hld up in last: rdn and prog jst over 2f out: tk 2nd ins fnl f: no ch w wnr* **11/4**1

6111 3 shd **Moonspring (IRE)**21 2886 3-8-13 75 (e) OisinMurphy(3) 4 78
(Robert Cowell) *chsd ldng pair: rdn over 2f out: disp 2nd u.p fnl f: kpt on* **7/1**

214 4 ½ **Joie De Reve (IRE)**67 1579 3-9-1 74 WilliamBuick 8 75
(David Simcock) *hld up in 5th: shkn up 2f out: nt qckn and lost pl: styd on again ins fnl f* **7/2**3

100 5 ½ **Glastonberry**36 2435 6-9-12 78 HayleyTurner 6 80
(Geoffrey Deacon) *sltly awkward s: settled in last pair: urged along over 2f out: sme prog over 1f out: one pce fnl f* **16/1**

4-10 6 ¾ **Clearing**19 2965 4-9-5 71 PatCosgrave 5 70
(Jim Boyle) *led to 2f out: no ch w wnr sn after: wknd fnl f* **16/1**

-405 7 1 ¾ **Light Rose (IRE)**21 2884 4-8-10 69 (p) DavidParkes(7) 1 63
(Jeremy Gask) *in tch in 6th: rdn and no prog 2f out: wl btn over 1f out* **16/1**

421 8 3 ¼ **Backstage Gossip**34 2489 3-8-10 69 RobertHavlin 10 50
(Hughie Morrison) *chsd ldng trio on outer: wknd over 2f out* **7/1**

1m 12.33s (-0.77) **Going Correction** 0.0s/f (Stan)
**WFA** 3 from 4yo+ 7lb **8 Ran SP% 116.5**
Speed ratings (Par 102): **105,100,100,99,99 98,95,91**
CSF £11.99 CT £52.63 TOTE £3.60: £1.10, £1.50, £2.10; EX 13.30 Trifecta £47.10.
**Owner** The Eight Of Diamonds **Bred** Mrs C J Walker **Trained** Newmarket, Suffolk

**FOCUS**
The pace was ordinary for these mid-range fillies, but the winner quickened impressively.

## 3582 BETDAQ SUPPORTING THE INJURED JOCKEYS FUND H'CAP (LONDON MIDDLE DISTANCE SERIES QUALIFIER) 1m 3f (P)
**8:50** (8:50) (Class 4) (0-85,83) 4-Y-0+ **£4,690** (£1,395; £697; £348) **Stalls** Low

Form RPR

-200 1 **Gone Dutch**12 3196 4-9-7 83 FrederikTylicki 2 93+
(James Fanshawe) *trckd ldrs: rdn and prog over 2f out: led over 1f out: drvn out* **7/4**1

6-01 2 ½ **Qanan**21 2882 5-9-3 79 TedDurcan 7 88+
(Chris Wall) *trckd ldrs: rdn over 2f out: clsd to chse wnr jst over 1f out: styd on but a hld* **9/4**2

2316 3 1 ¾ **Starwatch**16 3065 7-9-1 77 WilliamCarson 4 83
(John Bridger) *led: stdd pce after 3f and sn hdd: chsd ldr after: tried to cl 2f out but sn lost 2nd: plugged on* **16/1**

0-44 4 1 **Lyric Ballad**30 2628 4-8-11 73 RobertHavlin 5 77
(Hughie Morrison) *wl in tch: reminder 4f out: drvn and gradual prog over 2f out: chsd ldrs 1f out: one pce after* **12/1**

-650 5 nk **Storm (IRE)**30 2628 4-8-5 67 HayleyTurner 8 71
(Charles Hills) *hld up in last trio: rdn over 2f out: gradual prog to cl on ldrs 1f out: one pce after* **20/1**

3050 6 6 **Thatchmaster (USA)**32 2540 4-9-4 80 RyanMoore 1 74
(Mark Johnston) *hld up: t.k.h whn pce dropped after 3f: sn dropped to last: shkn up and no prog over 3f out: bhd after* **5/1**3

3133 7 hd **Back Burner (IRE)**28 2670 6-9-3 79 SamHitchcott 3 72
(Dai Burchell) *trckd ldrs: quick move to ld over 7f out: clr over 2f out: hdd & wknd qckly over 1f out* **16/1**

1266 8 3 **Cathedral**14 3112 5-8-7 72 OisinMurphy(3) 6 60
(Ed de Giles) *s.v.s: a in last pair: struggling 3f out: no ch after* **8/1**

2m 20.71s (-1.19) **Going Correction** 0.0s/f (Stan) **8 Ran SP% 119.1**
Speed ratings (Par 105): **104,103,102,101,101 97,96,94**
CSF £6.16 CT £46.07 TOTE £3.00: £1.40, £1.10, £3.30; EX 6.40 Trifecta £162.40.
**Owner** The Ice Syndicate **Bred** Cheveley Park Stud Ltd **Trained** Newmarket, Suffolk

**FOCUS**
The pace was modest for the first 4f, and significantly stronger thereafter.
T/Plt: £23.80 to a £1 stake. Pool: £57241.11 - 1754.23 winning tickets T/Qpdt: £3.30 to a £1 stake. Pool: £6571.55 - 1458.02 winning tickets JN

# 3274 SALISBURY (R-H)
Wednesday, June 25

**OFFICIAL GOING: Good to firm (firm in places; firm, good to firm in places between 7f & 4f; 9.4)**
Wind: virtually nil Weather: dry and bright

## 3583 ASHBRITTLE STUD BRITISH STALLION STUDS EBF MAIDEN FILLIES' STKS (BOBIS RACE) 5f
**2:10** (2:16) (Class 4) 2-Y-0 **£4,204** (£1,251; £625; £312) **Stalls** Low

Form RPR

4 1 **Indaria**27 2692 2-8-11 0 OisinMurphy(3) 8 80
(Rod Millman) *racd keenly: chsd ldr tl led over 3f out: rdn over 1f out: styd on wl: rdn out* **14/1**

4 2 1 ¼ **Prize Exhibit**15 3076 2-9-0 0 RyanMoore 1 75
(Jamie Osborne) *uns and galloped loose to s: hld up in rr: swtchd lft and hdwy over 2f out: drvn to chse ldng pair over 1f out: wnt 2nd fnl 75yds: kpt on but a hld* **5/4**1

6 3 1 ¼ **Zifena**21 2888 2-9-0 0 JimmyFortune 2 71
(Eve Johnson Houghton) *chsd ldng pair: rdn and chsd wnr wl over 1f out: no imp and lost 2nd fnl 75yds* **20/1**

4 6 **Piping Dream (IRE)** 2-9-0 0 PatDobbs 4 49
(Richard Hannon) *hld up in midfield: rdn and effrt ent fnl 2f: outpcd and wl btn 1f out: wnt modest 4th ins fnl f* **12/1**

6 5 hd **Lady In White (IRE)**12 3193 2-9-0 0 1 AndreaAtzeni 3 48
(Roger Varian) *awkward leaving stalls: a towards rr of main gp: rdn and no hdwy 2f out: wl hld whn swtchd lft ins fnl f* **7/1**

00 6 nk **True Course**18 2979 2-9-0 0 WilliamBuick 6 47
(Charlie Appleby) *chsd ldng trio: rdn and no hdwy ent fnl 2f: drifted rt and wl btn ent fnl f* **7/2**3

322 7 2 ½ **One Moment**11 3211 2-9-0 0 RichardHughes 5 52
(Robert Cowell) *led and crossed to r against far rail: hdd over 3f out: rdn and btn over 1f out: 4th and wl hld whn slt stumble and heavily eased ins fnl f* **5/2**2

8 44 **Red Renee** 2-9-0 0 JohnFahy 7
(Mark Gillard) *awkward leaving stalls: rn green and immediately outpcd: t.o fnl 3f* **100/1**

1m 0.7s (-0.30) **Going Correction** -0.175s/f (Firm) **8 Ran SP% 127.8**
Speed ratings (Par 92): **95,93,91,81,81 80,76,6**
CSF £36.02 TOTE £16.60: £3.90, £1.10, £4.30; EX 61.80 Trifecta £1179.90.
**Owner** K L Dare **Bred** Poulton Farm Stud **Trained** Kentisbeare, Devon

**FOCUS**
Not a bad 2yo fillies' maiden with the principals coming clear. The form is taken at face value.

## 3584 NEW F-TYPE COUPE AT WESTOVER JAGUAR MAIDEN STKS 6f
**2:40** (2:42) (Class 5) 2-Y-0 **£3,234** (£962; £481; £240) **Stalls** Low

Form RPR

2 1 **Sugar Lump**13 3148 2-9-5 0 RichardHughes 5 76+
(Richard Hannon) *led early: sn hdd and chsd ldr: led and effrt to chal 2f out: drvn 1f out: rdn hands and heels fnl 100yds: led fnl 50yds: r.o* **10/11**1

644 **2** *nk* **Brazen Spirit**[34] 2487 2-9-2 0 RyanTate(3) 7 75
(Clive Cox) *stdd s: t.k.h: sn led: rdn 2f out: hung lft over 1f out but sustained duel w wnr after: hdd and no ex fnl 50yds* **5/1**[3]

3 **3** *2 1/4* **Three Robins**[21] 2888 2-9-0 0 RyanMoore 1 63
(Richard Hannon) *t.k.h: hld up in tch: switching lft and hdwy to chse ldrs over 1f out: pushed along and styd on same pce ins fnl f* **7/2**[2]

**4** *1* **Essaka (IRE)** 2-9-2 0 WilliamTwiston-Davies(3) 2 65
(Mick Channon) *t.k.h: chsd ldrs: rdn and effrt 2f out: swtchd rt and no ex ins fnl f: wknd fnl 100yds* **12/1**

54 **5** *3 1/4* **Offshore**[22] 2859 2-9-5 0 RichardKingscote 8 56
(James Tate) *wnt lft s: sn rcvrd and chsd ldrs: rdn 3f out: no ex and btn over 1f out: wknd ins fnl f* **11/1**

**6** *3/4* **Francis Scott Key (IRE)** 2-9-5 0 JimmyFortune 6 53
(Brian Meehan) *hld up in tch towards rr: effrt whn pushed lft over 1f out: sn btn and wknd fnl f* **16/1**

**7** *hd* **Cartmell Cleave** 2-9-5 0 TomQueally 4 53
(Stuart Kittow) *hld up in tch: rdn and hdwy over 2f out: no hdwy over 1f out: wknd ins fnl f* **50/1**

**8** *8* **Cape Point** 2-9-5 0 DavidProbert 3 29
(Michael Blanshard) *t.k.h: hld up in tch: rdn and effrt 2f out: btn and ducked lft over 1f out: wknd and eased ins fnl f* **66/1**

**9** *3/4* **Henrietta Dancer** 2-8-9 0 RyanWhile(5) 9 21
(Malcolm Saunders) *wnt lft s: rn green in rr: rdn 1/2-way: bhd fnl 2f* **66/1**

1m 14.71s (-0.09) **Going Correction** -0.175s/f (Firm) **9** Ran SP% **118.1**
Speed ratings (Par 93): **93,92,89,88,83 82,82,72,71**
CSF £6.09 TOTE £1.60: £1.10, £2.20, £1.70; EX 8.20 Trifecta £21.60.
**Owner** M Hughes & M Kerr-Dineen **Bred** T J Cooper **Trained** East Everleigh, Wilts

**FOCUS**
A modest 2yo maiden and straightforward enough form.

## 3585 BATHWICK TYRES H'CAP 1m 1f 198y
**3:10** (3:19) (Class 5) (0-70,70) 4-Y-0+ **£2,911** (£866; £432; £216) **Stalls** Low

Form RPR

4601 **1** **Gabrial The Duke (IRE)**[11] 3224 4-9-3 **66** (p) JimCrowley 4 76
(David Simcock) *chsd ldr: rdn to ld 2f out: sn hdd but drew clr w runner-up: drvn to ld again 1f out: drew clr fnl 100yds: eased towards fin* **2/1**[1]

060- **2** *3 3/4* **Miss Blakeney**[189] 8336 5-9-7 **70** MartinDwyer 3 73
(Marcus Tregoning) *hld up in tch in midfield: rdn and gd hdwy to join wnr 2f out: drvn to ld over 1f out: hdd 1f out: sn btn: wknd fnl 100yds* **10/1**

260- **3** *1 1/2* **Russian Royale**[254] 7256 4-9-7 **70** TomQueally 2 70
(Stuart Kittow) *s.i.s: sn rcvrd and in tch in midfield: hdwy and switching lft over 1f out: wnt 3rd 1f out: styd on: no threat to wnr* **14/1**

2064 **4** *3* **Ice Tres**[14] 3115 5-8-3 **52** (v[1]) AndreaAtzeni 7 46
(Rod Millman) *t.k.h: chsd ldrs: rdn over 2f out: wnt 3rd but no threat to ldng pair over 1f out: lost 3rd and wknd ins fnl f* **7/1**[3]

-400 **5** *1 1/4* **Freddy Q (IRE)**[19] 2947 5-8-5 **57** MichaelJMMurphy(3) 5 49
(Tony Newcombe) *stdd s: hld up in tch in last trio: pushed along and stl plenty to do whn nt clr run over 1f out: kpt on ins fnl f: nvr trbld ldrs* **7/2**[2]

0654 **6** *nse* **Red Dragon (IRE)**[15] 3080 4-9-4 **67** FergusSweeney 8 59
(Michael Blanshard) *stdd s: t.k.h: hld up in tch in last trio: shkn up 2f out: kpt on fnl f: nvr trbld ldrs* **14/1**

2263 **7** *nse* **Nubar Boy**[35] 2471 7-9-3 **69** (p) OisinMurphy(3) 1 61
(Ian Williams) *chsd ldrs: rdn and unable qck over 2f out: losing pl whn short of room over 1f out: wknd fnl f* **8/1**

0432 **8** *1/2* **April Ciel**[12] 3175 5-8-13 **65** (p) WilliamTwiston-Davies(3) 6 56
(Ronald Harris) *led and set stdy gallop: rdn and qcknd over 3f out: hdd 2f out: outpcd and lost 3rd over 1f out: wknd fnl f* **8/1**

0-40 **9** *21* **Precision Five**[19] 2947 5-9-2 **65** (p) SeanLevey 10 16
(Jeremy Gask) *hld up in tch in last trio: rdn and short-lived effrt over 2f out: wl btn and drifted rt 1f out: eased ins fnl f: t.o* **14/1**

2m 7.37s (-2.53) **Going Correction** -0.175s/f (Firm) **9** Ran SP% **119.4**
Speed ratings (Par 103): **103,100,98,96,95 95,95,94,78**
CSF £24.48 CT £229.79 TOTE £2.90: £1.60, £2.50, £4.20; EX 35.30 Trifecta £268.60.
**Owner** Dr Marwan Koukash **Bred** Old Carhue & Graeng Bloodstock **Trained** Newmarket, Suffolk

**FOCUS**
There was a near ten-minute delay to this moderate handicap due to Medal Of Valour bursting the stalls and running loose. It paid to race handy as the pace steadied around halfway and then turned into a dash from 2f out. The winner is rated back to his best.

## 3586 ALAN & THOMAS INSURANCE GROUP MAIDEN FILLIES' STKS (BOBIS RACE) 6f 212y
**3:45** (3:46) (Class 5) 3-Y-0 **£3,234** (£962; £481; £240) **Stalls** Low

Form RPR

42 **1** **Laftah (IRE)**[14] 3097 3-9-0 0 PaulHanagan 2 81
(Roger Varian) *mde all: rdn and qcknd ent fnl 2f: pressed and drvn 1f out: r.o wl and in command ins fnl f: rdn out* **5/1**

2 **2** *3/4* **Elizona**[36] 2442 3-9-0 0 FrederikTylicki 5 79
(James Fanshawe) *hld up in tch in last pair: rdn and hdwy whn barging match w rival over 1f out: chal 1f out: r.ofor clr 2nd but hld by wnr fnl 100yds* **2/1**[1]

-022 **3** *5* **Miss Brazil (IRE)**[16] 3067 3-9-0 76 RichardHughes 6 66+
(Richard Hannon) *chsd ldrs: effrt 2f out: edging lft and barging match w rival over 1f out: 3rd and btn 1f out: wknd ins fnl f* **11/4**[3]

52 **4** *3/4* **Lead A Merry Dance**[19] 2946 3-9-0 0 RyanMoore 3 64
(Sylvester Kirk) *t.k.h: chsd wnr: rdn ent fnl 2f: 4th and btn whn swtchd rt 1f out: wknd ins fnl f* **14/1**

-036 **5** *2 1/2* **Venus Grace**[20] 2929 3-9-0 75 JimCrowley 4 58
(Ralph Beckett) *stdd s: hld up in last pair: rdn and short-lived effrt wl over 1f out: sn btn: wknd fnl f* **5/2**[2]

1m 28.67s (0.07) **Going Correction** -0.175s/f (Firm) **5** Ran SP% **111.9**
Speed ratings (Par 96): **92,91,85,84,81**
CSF £15.67 TOTE £5.80: £3.00, £1.10; EX 16.60 Trifecta £44.90.
**Owner** Hamdan Al Maktoum **Bred** Bernard Cooke **Trained** Newmarket, Suffolk

**FOCUS**
An ordinary 3yo fillies' maiden in which the winner made all in a slow time. A big step up on her first two runs.

## 3587 ASHBRITTLE STUD BIBURY CUP (H'CAP) (BOBIS RACE) 1m 4f
**4:20** (4:20) (Class 3) (0-95,88) 3-Y-0
**£12,450** (£3,728; £1,864; £699; £699; £234) **Stalls** Low

Form RPR

441 **1** **Kinshasa**[21] 2881 3-9-3 **84** AndreaAtzeni 4 90+
(Luca Cumani) *hld up wl in tch in midfield: nt clr run over 2f out: swtchd lft and rdn to chal ent fnl f: led wl ins fnl f: r.o wl* **9/4**[1]

2-21 **2** *3/4* **Pack Leader (IRE)**[17] 3031 3-9-7 **88** RichardKingscote 5 92
(Amanda Perrett) *led: rdn over 2f out: edgd lft u.p and hdd wl ins fnl f: kpt on* **14/1**

2241 **3** *1 1/2* **Cape Caster (IRE)**[23] 2850 3-9-0 **81** JimCrowley 2 83+
(Ralph Beckett) *hld up wl in tch in midfield: shuffled bk to last pair 4f out: nt clr run 2f out: swtchd lft 1f out: styd on to go 3rd towards fin: no threat to ldng pair* **5/1**[2]

1224 **4** *1/2* **Cotton Club (IRE)**[12] 3197 3-8-5 **79** CamHardie(7) 1 80
(Rod Millman) *hld up in tch in last pair: swtchd lft and effrt 2f out: no imp u.p over 1f out: styd on same pce ins fnl f* **7/1**[3]

2210 **4** *dht* **Norse Star (IRE)**[34] 2494 3-8-13 **80** RyanMoore 8 81?
(Sylvester Kirk) *chsd ldr: ev ch and wandered u.p over 1f out: no ex and btn ins fnl f: lost 3rd towards fin* **14/1**

3-65 **6** *1/2* **Snow Squall**[12] 3200 3-8-7 **77** MichaelJMMurphy(3) 3 77
(Mark Johnston) *chsd ldrs: nt clr run on inner over 2f out: swtchd lft over 1f out: stl chsng ldrs whn short of room and hmpd 1f out: one pce and hld after* **8/1**

-153 **7** *11* **Hymenaios (IRE)**[18] 2986 3-9-6 **87** RichardHughes 7 75
(Richard Hannon) *hld up in last pair: clsd and chsd ldrs 4f out: drvn and unable qck 2f out: pushed lft and btn over 1f out: wknd* **9/4**[1]

2m 37.76s (-0.24) **Going Correction** -0.175s/f (Firm) **7** Ran SP% **115.1**
Speed ratings (Par 103): **93,92,91,91,91 90,83**
CSF £36.76 CT £144.59 TOTE £2.90: £1.70, £3.90; EX 37.50 Trifecta £147.50.
**Owner** Fittocks Stud **Bred** Fittocks Stud Ltd **Trained** Newmarket, Suffolk

**FOCUS**
This well-established handicap was a tactical affair and threw up something of a messy finish. The bare form is likely only ordinary.

## 3588 NEW FOREST FARM MACHINERY/JOHN DEERE FILLIES' H'CAP 6f
**4:55** (4:55) (Class 5) (0-70,69) 3-Y-0 **£2,911** (£866; £432; £216) **Stalls** Low

Form RPR

4640 **1** **Poetic Choice**[35] 2470 3-9-4 **66** J-PGuillambert 4 79
(Nick Littmoden) *pressed ldr tl led 1/2-way: rdn and qcknd clr over 1f out: sddle slipped bk but in command 1f out: r.o wl: comf* **12/1**

3406 **2** *3 3/4* **Invoke (IRE)**[19] 2943 3-9-7 **69** TomQueally 3 70
(Michael Bell) *t.k.h: led tl 1/2-way: rdn and unable qck over 1f out: no ch w wnr but kpt on to hold 2nd fnl f* **11/2**

0-00 **3** *1 1/4* **Popping Candy**[59] 1767 3-8-12 **60** [1] AndreaAtzeni 8 57
(Roger Varian) *hld up in last pair: swtchd lft and effrt 2f out: styd on ins fnl f: no threat to wnr* **3/1**[2]

000 **4** *1 3/4* **Swiss Lait**[25] 2780 3-9-0 **62** LiamKeniry 6 53
(David Elsworth) *wnt sharply rt s and slowly away: rdn along in rr: swtchd lft over 1f out: styd on past btn horses fnl f: nvr trbld ldrs* **12/1**

-433 **5** *2 1/2* **Trillian Astra (IRE)**[12] 3178 3-8-10 **61** (p) RyanTate(3) 7 44
(Clive Cox) *bmpd s: in tch in midfield: chsd ldrs over 3f out: rdn: unable qck and edgd rt over 1f out: wknd fnl f* **11/4**[1]

6235 **6** *3* **Baars Causeway (IRE)**[11] 3225 3-9-3 **65** (v[1]) JimCrowley 5 39
(Timothy Jarvis) *bmpd s: chsd ldrs: rdn and unable qck 2f out: wknd ent fnl f* **4/1**[3]

10-5 **7** *3/4* **Gower Princess**[19] 2943 3-8-13 **64** WilliamTwiston-Davies(3) 1 35
(Ronald Harris) *chsd ldrs tl 1/2-way: sn u.p and lost pl: wknd over 1f out* **9/1**

5-40 **8** *8* **Cueca (FR)**[15] 3087 3-8-0 **55** CamHardie(7) 2
(Jonathan Portman) *in tch in last trio: rdn and no hdwy ent fnl 2f: wknd over 1f out* **20/1**

1m 13.54s (-1.26) **Going Correction** -0.175s/f (Firm) **8** Ran SP% **117.2**
Speed ratings (Par 96): **101,96,94,92,88 84,83,73**
CSF £77.95 CT £255.07 TOTE £17.60: £3.00, £1.90, £1.40; EX 92.20 Trifecta £462.50.
**Owner** A A Goodman, L Stratton, N Littmoden **Bred** Larry Stratton **Trained** Newmarket, Suffolk

**FOCUS**
A weak 3yo fillies' sprint handicap, run at a fair pace. The winner is rated back to her standout AW win.

## 3589 IJF 50TH ANNIVERSARY H'CAP (FOR GENTLEMAN AMATEUR RIDERS) 6f 212y
**5:25** (5:26) (Class 6) (0-65,65) 4-Y-0+ **£2,495** (£774; £386; £193) **Stalls** Centre

Form RPR

0505 **1** **Perfect Mission**[12] 3177 6-10-12 **63** (v) MrHHunt(7) 1 72
(Andrew Balding) *mde all: rdn ent fnl f: kpt on wl: rdn out* **4/1**[1]

2110 **2** *1/2* **Hail Promenader (IRE)**[25] 2770 8-11-2 **65** (tp) MrGrahamCarson(5) 7 72
(Anthony Carson) *in tch in midfield: rdn and hdwy 2f out: pressed ldng pair over 1f out: chsd wnr wl ins fnl f: kpt on* **12/1**

40-2 **3** *3/4* **Harwoods Star (IRE)**[42] 2251 4-10-11 **62** MrRyanDuthie(7) 3 67
(Amanda Perrett) *chsd ldrs: rdn and ev ch over 1f out: no ex and styd on same pce ins fnl f* **5/1**[3]

-203 **4** *2 1/4* **Substantivo (IRE)**[35] 2463 4-11-0 **61** MrORJSangster(3) 4 61
(Timothy Jarvis) *chsd ldr: rdn ent fnl 2f: ev ch tl 4th and outpcd 1f out: styd on same pce after* **4/1**[1]

4460 **5** *2 1/2* **Top Offer**[14] 3118 5-11-1 **64** MrGeorgeCrate(5) 9 58
(Peter Crate) *stdd and dropped in bhd after s: t.k.h: hld up in tch in rr: hdwy into midfield and switching lft over 2f out: rdn over 1f out: wknd 1f out* **14/1**

0-00 **6** *1 1/4* **The Name Is Frank**[5] 3422 9-9-12 **47** MrAlexFerguson(5) 6 38
(Mark Gillard) *in tch in last trio: drvn and unable qck wl over 1f out: wl hld and plugged on same pce fnl f* **25/1**

635 **7** *1/2* **The Happy Hammer (IRE)**[15] 3075 8-10-9 **53** MrPCollington 8 43
(Eugene Stanford) *hld up in tch in last trio: swtchd lft and effrt 2f out: no hdwy u.p over 1f out: wknd fnl f* **5/1**[3]

U465 **8** *2 1/4* **Interakt**[8] 3327 7-10-0 **47** (b) MrChrisMartin(3) 2 32
(Joseph Tuite) *chsd ldrs: rdn and unable qck over 2f out: edgd lft and wknd over 1f out* **14/1**

533- **9** *54* **Takitwo**[299] 5948 11-10-8 **55** MrJHarding(3) 10
(Geoffrey Deacon) *in tch in midfield on outer: rdn and lost pl over 2f out: bhd and eased over 1f out: t.o* **9/2**[2]

1m 27.71s (-0.89) **Going Correction** -0.175s/f (Firm) **9** Ran SP% **116.4**
Speed ratings (Par 101): **98,97,96,94,91 89,89,86,24**
CSF £52.83 CT £247.09 TOTE £4.90: £1.60, £2.70, £1.50; EX 22.80 Trifecta £183.00.
**Owner** Mildmay Racing & D H Caslon **Bred** Mildmay Bloodstock Ltd **Trained** Kingsclere, Hants

**FOCUS**
This moderate handicap for gentleman amateur riders looked wide open. There was a sound early pace on but few got seriously involved. The winner didn't have to match last year's C&D form.
T/Plt: £68.60 to a £1 stake. Pool: £48935.27 - 520.49 winning tickets T/Qpdt: £42.30 to a £1 stake. Pool: £3015.52 - 52.70 winning tickets SP

3590 - 3598a (Foreign Racing) - See Raceform Interactive

# 3569 CARLISLE (R-H)

Thursday, June 26

**OFFICIAL GOING: Good to firm (firm in places; 7.5)**

Course at normal configuration and distances as advertised.

Wind: light 1/2 against Weather: fine

## 3599 DOWNLOAD THE FREE APP @BOOKMAKERS.CO.UK H'CAP (GRASSROOTS FLAT SPRINT SERIES QUALIFIER) 5f 193y

2:10 (2:13) (Class 4) (0-80,79) 3-Y-O+ £6,469 (£1,925; £962; £481) Stalls Low

| Form | | | | RPR |
|---|---|---|---|---|
| 302 | 1 | | **Al Khan (IRE)**[7] 3402 5-9-3 71 ....(p) JasonHart 1 *(Ollie Pears) chsd ldrs: 2nd over 2f out: led over 1f out: hld on towards fin* **7/2**[3] | 81+ |
| 0040 | 2 | nk | **Holy Angel (IRE)**[7] 3399 5-9-2 70 ....(e) AndrewElliott 3 *(Tim Easterby) mid-div: hdwy on ins over 1f out: chsd wnr jst ins fnl f: styng on at fin* **20/1** | 79 |
| 4031 | 3 | 3 ¾ | **Sunraider (IRE)**[24] 2825 7-9-11 79 .... GrahamLee 5 *(Paul Midgley) in rr: drvn 3f out: styd on fnl f: tk modest 3rd in clsng stages* **11/4**[1] | 76 |
| 0530 | 4 | 1 ½ | **Arctic Feeling (IRE)**[19] 2992 6-9-7 78 ....(v) GeorgeChaloner(3) 7 *(Richard Fahey) mde most tl over 1f out: fdd in clsng stages* **13/2** | 70 |
| 0003 | 5 | 1 ¾ | **Gold Beau (FR)**[8] 3359 4-9-3 71 ....(b) AmyRyan 4 *(Kristin Stubbs) chsd ldrs: rdn 2f out: one pce* **7/1** | 58 |
| 614 | 6 | 2 ¾ | **Teetotal (IRE)**[12] 3256 4-9-9 77 .... SilvestreDeSousa 2 *(Nigel Tinkler) t.k.h early: sn trcking ldrs: drvn over 2f out: one pce* **3/1**[2] | 55 |
| 40-1 | 7 | 4 ½ | **Mandalay King (IRE)**[21] 2914 9-8-13 70 ....(p) IanBrennan(3) 6 *(Marjorie Fife) rrd s: hld up in rr: swtchd lft over 2f out: sn wknd* **12/1** | 33 |
| 4030 | 8 | 1 | **We'll Deal Again**[12] 3256 7-9-4 72 ....(b) BarryMcHugh 8 *(Michael Easterby) w ldr 3f: lost pl 2f out* **25/1** | 32 |

1m 13.38s (-0.32) **Going Correction** +0.075s/f (Good) **8 Ran SP% 116.0**

Speed ratings (Par 105): **105,104,99,97,95 91,85,84**

CSF £68.41 CT £221.75 TOTE £4.10: £1.40, £4.20, £1.10; EX 73.00 Trifecta £342.00.

**Owner** Richard Walker **Bred** Galadari Sons Stud Company Limited **Trained** Norton, N Yorks

**FOCUS**

A competitive opener, run on ever-quickening ground.

## 3600 WORLD CUP PRICE BOOSTS @BOOKMAKERS.CO.UK H'CAP 5f

2:40 (2:41) (Class 5) (0-70,70) 3-Y-O £2,587 (£770; £384; £192) Stalls Low

| Form | | | | RPR |
|---|---|---|---|---|
| 35-0 | 1 | | **Lexington Rose**[68] 1585 3-9-7 70 .... RoystonFfrench 8 *(Bryan Smart) hld up in rr: t.k.h: gd hdwy on outside over 1f out: styd on to ld in clsng stages* **10/1** | 76 |
| 21-6 | 2 | ½ | **Kirtling Belle**[10] 3298 3-9-4 67 .... JasonHart 7 *(Keith Dalgleish) chsd ldrs: kpt on ins fnl f: tk 2nd nr fin* **5/1**[2] | 71 |
| 63-1 | 3 | hd | **Thornaby Princess**[23] 2870 3-9-3 66 .... SilvestreDeSousa 9 *(Marjorie Fife) wnt lft s: t.k.h in rr: hdwy over 2f out: led 1f out: hdd and no ex in clsng stages* **9/4**[1] | 69+ |
| 05-3 | 4 | 1 ½ | **Ty Cobb (IRE)**[31] 2619 3-8-5 57 .... IanBrennan(3) 1 *(John Quinn) w ldrs: kpt on same pce ins fnl f* **10/1** | 55 |
| 2421 | 5 | shd | **Red Forever**[6] 3440 3-9-0 66 6ex .... SladeO'Hara(3) 3 *(Alan Berry) w ldr: led over 3f out: hdd 1f out: kpt on same pce* **11/2**[3] | 64 |
| -554 | 6 | hd | **Madagascar Moll (IRE)**[20] 2951 3-8-10 66 .... JoshDoyle(7) 2 *(David O'Meara) chsd ldrs: upsides over 1f out: one pce* **11/1** | 63 |
| 4-50 | 7 | 1 | **Princess Myla (IRE)**[6] 3440 3-8-7 56 .... BarryMcHugh 5 *(Paul Midgley) mid-div: n.m.r 2f out: upsides over 1f out: one pce* **33/1** | 49 |
| 0141 | 8 | 1 | **Tinsill**[15] 3100 3-9-4 67 .... GrahamLee 6 *(Nigel Tinkler) in rr: hdwy 2f out: n.m.r jst ins fnl f: fdd towards fin* **5/1**[2] | 57 |
| 4050 | 9 | 6 | **Danfazi (IRE)**[52] 2015 3-9-4 67 .... AmyRyan 4 *(Kristin Stubbs) led over 1f out: lost pl over 1f out: sn bhd* **11/1** | 35 |

1m 1.62s (0.82) **Going Correction** +0.075s/f (Good) **9 Ran SP% 117.3**

Speed ratings (Par 99): **96,95,94,92,92 90,88,79**

CSF £60.25 CT £149.62 TOTE £13.50: £3.50, £2.30, £1.10; EX 50.30 Trifecta £178.60.

**Owner** Middleham Park Racing VIII & Partners **Bred** Mickley Stud & Richard Kent **Trained** Hambleton, N Yorks

**FOCUS**

The winner was on a good mark compared to her early 2yo form.

## 3601 WORLD CUP LIVE UPDATES @BOOKMAKERS.CO.UK MAIDEN STKS 6f 192y

3:10 (3:12) (Class 5) 3-Y-O+ £2,587 (£770; £384; £192) Stalls Low

| Form | | | | RPR |
|---|---|---|---|---|
| - | 1 | | **Zain Empire** 3-9-3 0 .... GrahamLee 6 *(Robert Cowell) mid-div: shkn up over 4f out: hdwy over 2f out: chsd ldr 1f out: styd on to ld nr fin* **7/2**[2] | 71+ |
| 0 | 2 | hd | **Enliven**[76] 1422 3-8-12 0 .... JamesDoyle 7 *(Andrew Balding) trckd ldrs: led over 2f out: hdd and no ex nr fin* **1/1**[1] | 65 |
| 00-0 | 3 | 4 ½ | **Gambino (IRE)**[3] 3530 4-9-5 46 .... AlistairRawlinson(7) 2 *(John David Riches) in rr: hdwy over 2f out: chsng ldr over 1f out: kpt on same pce* **20/1** | 62 |
| 44 | 4 | 1 ¼ | **Dutch Descent (IRE)**[9] 3343 3-9-3 0 .... JasonHart 4 *(David Barron) led: hdd over 2f out: one pce* **4/1**[3] | 56 |
| 5 | 5 | nk | **Showtime Star**[47] 2170 4-9-12 0 .... BenCurtis 3 *(Alan Swinbank) sn trcking ldrs: drvn over 3f out: one pce fnl 2f* **20/1** | 58 |
| 4 | 6 | 2 ½ | **Cliff (IRE)**[15] 3097 4-9-12 0 .... SilvestreDeSousa 8 *(Nigel Tinkler) mid-div: effrt over 2f out: sn chsng ldrs: fdd clsng stages* **6/1** | 51 |
| 000 | 7 | 30 | **Cool Reception**[15] 3097 3-8-9 0 .... IanBrennan(3) 5 *(Ollie Pears) t.k.h: chsd ldrs: lost pl over 2f out: sn bhd: eased ins fnl f: t.o* **100/1** | |
| | 8 | 5 | **Perfect Print (IRE)**[18] 5-9-12 0 ....(t) RoystonFfrench 1 *(Maurice Barnes) dwlt: in rr: drvn over 3f out: sn outpcd and hung lft: t.o fnl 2f* **80/1** | |

1m 26.37s (-0.73) **Going Correction** -0.075s/f (Good)

**WFA** 3 from 4yo+ 9lb **8 Ran SP% 118.3**

Speed ratings (Par 103): **101,100,95,94,93 91,56,51**

CSF £7.51 TOTE £5.30: £1.70, £1.10, £3.00; EX 12.10 Trifecta £75.30.

**Owner** Asaad Al Banwan **Bred** Mascalls Stud **Trained** Six Mile Bottom, Cambs

**FOCUS**

A weak maiden.

## 3602 WORLD CUP FREE BETS @BOOKMAKERS.CO.UK MAIDEN STKS 1m 1f 61y

3:40 (3:40) (Class 5) 3-Y-O+ £2,587 (£770; £384; £192) Stalls Low

| Form | | | | RPR |
|---|---|---|---|---|
| 2 | 1 | | **Scallop**[30] 2650 3-8-9 0 .... JamesDoyle 1 *(Sir Michael Stoute) mde all: pushed along 2f out: wnt clr fnl f: easily* **30/100**[1] | 82+ |
| | 2 | 4 ½ | **Law Keeper (IRE)** 3-8-9 0 .... SilvestreDeSousa 6 *(James Tate) trckd ldrs: t.k.h: effrt over 2f out: styd on same pce appr fnl f* **7/1**[3] | 69+ |
| | 3 | 6 | **Mediate** 3-9-0 0 .... FrannyNorton 5 *(Mark Johnston) in rr-div: sn pushed along and green: hdwy over 2f out: swtchd lft over 1f out: styd on to go modest 3rd in clsng stages* **9/2**[2] | 62+ |
| 36 | 4 | ¾ | **Wor Lass**[10] 3302 6-9-6 0 .... JasonHart 2 *(Iain Jardine) chsd ldrs: edgd lft over 1f out: one pce* **50/1** | 56 |
| | 5 | 6 | **Legal Advisor** 3-9-0 0 .... RoystonFfrench 7 *(Philip Kirby) dwlt: in rr: drvn over 4f out: sn chsng ldrs: lost pl 2f out* **25/1** | 47 |
| | 6 | 12 | **Sorcier (FR)**[103] 8-9-11 0 .... GrahamLee 3 *(Iain Jardine) dwlt: in rr: sme hdwy over 4f out: lost pl 2f out: sn bhd* **66/1** | 23 |

1m 57.73s (0.13) **Going Correction** -0.075s/f (Good)

**WFA** 3 from 5yo+ 11lb **6 Ran SP% 114.9**

Speed ratings (Par 103): **96,92,86,86,80 70**

CSF £3.33 TOTE £1.30: £1.10, £2.70; EX 3.60 Trifecta £6.90.

**Owner** K Abdullah **Bred** Juddmonte Farms Ltd **Trained** Newmarket, Suffolk

**FOCUS**

A weak maiden run in a slow time and the bare form is limited initially around the fourth. The winner did not need to improve.

## 3603 FOLLOW TONIGHT'S WORLD CUP @FOOTBALLSCORES.COM H'CAP (GRASSROOTS FLAT MIDDLE DISTANCE QUALIFIER) 1m 1f 61y

4:10 (4:10) (Class 5) (0-70,67) 3-Y-O £2,587 (£770; £384; £192) Stalls Low

| Form | | | | RPR |
|---|---|---|---|---|
| 2466 | 1 | | **Incurs Four Faults**[17] 3053 3-8-8 54 .... JasonHart 1 *(Keith Dalgleish) mde all: styd on wl fnl f: drvn out* **7/1** | 65 |
| 2521 | 2 | 2 ¼ | **Vosne Romanee**[8] 3364 3-9-3 63 6ex ....(b) JamesDoyle 2 *(Keith Dalgleish) dwlt: sn mid-div: effrt and chsd ldrs over 2f out: edgd lft ins fnl f: tk 2nd nr fin* **7/2**[2] | 69 |
| 4630 | 3 | ½ | **Sherston**[14] 3135 3-9-5 65 .... FrannyNorton 4 *(Mark Johnston) chsd wnr: drvn 4f out: kpt on same pce fnl f* **7/2**[2] | 70 |
| 240- | 4 | ¾ | **Nakeeta**[252] 7320 3-9-7 67 .... [1] GrahamLee 8 *(Iain Jardine) hld up in rr-div: hdwy over 3f out: swtchd rt ins fnl f: styd on to go 4th nr fin* **16/1** | 70 |
| 0-05 | 5 | ½ | **Mitcd (IRE)**[23] 2867 3-8-5 54 .... GeorgeChaloner(3) 6 *(Richard Fahey) chsd ldrs: drvn over 3f out: n.m.r on inner over 1f out: one pce* **12/1** | 56 |
| 5-23 | 6 | 8 | **Stybba**[11] 3281 3-9-2 62 ....(p) JamieSpencer 7 *(Andrew Balding) hld up in mid-div: trcking ldrs over 3f out: effrt over 2f out: wknd and eased last 150yds* **5/2**[1] | 48 |
| 2021 | 7 | 9 | **Suni Dancer**[14] 3135 3-8-9 55 .... SilvestreDeSousa 3 *(Paul Green) hld up in rr: t.k.h: sme hdwy over 2f out: sn rdn: wknd and eased appr fnl f* **9/2**[3] | 22 |
| 0-00 | 8 | 7 | **D'Arcy Indiana**[11] 3281 3-7-9 48 oh2 ....(b[1]) JoeDoyle(7) 5 *(Amy Weaver) s.s: t.k.h in rr: drvn and wandered over 3f out: sn lost pl and bhd* **100/1** | |

1m 57.39s (-0.21) **Going Correction** -0.075s/f (Good) **8 Ran SP% 118.3**

Speed ratings (Par 99): **97,95,94,93,93 86,78,72**

CSF £32.89 CT £102.31 TOTE £8.60: £3.80, £1.50, £1.30; EX 46.10 Trifecta £248.30.

**Owner** J S Morrison **Bred** Baldernock Bloodstock Ltd **Trained** Carluke, S Lanarks

**FOCUS**

The winner enjoyed an easy lead.

## 3604 DOWNLOAD THE BOOKMAKERS.CO.UK APP "HANDS AND HEELS" APPRENTICE SERIES H'CAP (EXCELLENCE INITATIVE) 7f 200y

4:40 (4:41) (Class 5) (0-70,63) 4-Y-O+ £2,587 (£770; £384; £192) Stalls Low

| Form | | | | RPR |
|---|---|---|---|---|
| -066 | 1 | | **Rasselas (IRE)**[5] 3485 7-9-9 63 ....(b[1]) AnnaHesketh(3) 1 *(David Nicholls) mde all: sn clr: pushed along over 1f out: kpt on: unchal* **10/1** | 73 |
| 0065 | 2 | 4 ½ | **Cono Zur (FR)**[17] 3056 7-9-4 58 .... DanielleMooney(3) 5 *(Ruth Carr) chsd wnr: drvn 3f out: 2nd 1f out: kpt on same pce* **11/2**[3] | 58 |
| 60-0 | 3 | nk | **Indian Giver**[17] 3052 6-8-10 50 .... GaryMahon(3) 8 *(John David Riches) in rr: hdwy over 3f out: chsng ldrs over 1f out: kpt on same pce to take 3rd post* **14/1** | 49 |
| 2146 | 4 | nse | **Echo Of Lightning**[45] 2215 4-9-4 58 .... KevinLundie(3) 4 *(Brian Ellison) trckd wnr: drvn 3f out: kpt on same pce appr fnl f* **7/4**[1] | 57 |
| 3344 | 5 | 4 ½ | **Dansili Dutch (IRE)**[21] 2911 5-9-7 61 .... JoshDoyle(3) 6 *(David O'Meara) trckd ldrs: effrt over 3f out: wknd over 1f out* **7/2**[2] | 50 |
| 3050 | 6 | 2 ½ | **Baltic Prince (IRE)**[21] 2914 4-9-6 57 .... LewisWalsh 7 *(Paul Green) hld up towards rr: hdwy 4f out: chsng ldrs and drvn over 2f out: wknd fnl f* **7/1** | 40 |
| 0336 | 7 | 1 | **Staffhoss**[6] 3436 4-9-4 60 .... PaulaMuir(5) 3 *(Mark Johnston) s.i.s: bhd and drvn over 4f out: nvr on terms* **7/1** | 41 |
| -500 | 8 | 9 | **Card High (IRE)**[27] 2724 4-8-8 45 ....(t) RachelRichardson 9 *(Wilf Storey) t.k.h toward rr on outer: lost pl over 2f out: sn bhd* **50/1** | 5 |

1m 39.18s (-0.82) **Going Correction** -0.075s/f (Good) **8 Ran SP% 116.7**

Speed ratings (Par 103): **101,96,96,96,91 89,88,79**

CSF £64.99 CT £785.76 TOTE £10.10: £2.50, £2.80, £3.30; EX 61.30 Trifecta £759.40.

**Owner** J P Honeyman **Bred** Lynch Bages Ltd **Trained** Sessay, N Yorks

**FOCUS**

First-time blinkers revived the winner and this rates his best form since he was a 3yo.

T/Plt: £102.00 to a £1 stake. Pool of £51474.15 - 368.30 winning tickets. T/Qpdt: £19.60 to a £1 stake. Pool of £3228.50 - 121.83 winning tickets. WG

3358 **HAMILTON** (R-H)
Thursday, June 26

**OFFICIAL GOING: Good (good to firm in places; 7.9)**
Rail realignment around the loop increased in distance by about 50yds on Round course.
Wind: Light against Weather: Cloudy

## 3605 SAINTS & SINNERS LADY AMATEUR RIDERS' H'CAP (FOR SAINTS & SINNERS CHALLENGE CUP) 1m 5f 9y
6:20 (6:20) (Class 6) (0-65,64) 4-Y-O+ £2,305 (£709; £354) Stalls Low

Form RPR
0111 1 **Operateur (IRE)**[8] 3365 6-9-13 61 MissMeganNicholls(5) 2 74+
(Ben Haslam) *midfield: smooth hdwy 4f out: led 2f out: sn rdn clr: eased fnl 50yds* 4/5[1]
00-0 2 3 1/2 **Harrison's Cave**[12] 3240 6-10-5 62 MrsCBartley 1 66
(Keith Dalgleish) *led: hdd 9f out: trckd ldr: rdn and outpcd over 2f out: kpt on fnl f: wnt 2nd towards fin* 3/1[2]
04-0 3 1 **Silver Tigress**[69] 1567 6-8-12 48 MissKMabon(7) 6 50
(Iain Jardine) *trckd ldr: led 9f out: rdn whn hdd 2f out: no ex fnl f: lost 2nd towards fin* 22/1
4/6- 4 3/4 **Hunting Tower**[219] 5933 10-10-2 64 (t) MissJWalton(5) 4 65
(J J Lambe, Ire) *hld up: rdn and hdwy 3f out: plugged on* 10/1[3]
0-05 5 22 **Edas**[28] 2701 12-9-5 51 MissHCuthbert(3) 5 19
(Thomas Cuthbert) *hld up: nvr threatened* 16/1
4-00 6 5 **Jebulani**[125] 695 4-9-0 46 MissJRRichards(3) 3 7
(Barry Murtagh) *racd keenly: prom: rdn 4f out: sn wknd* 12/1
06-6 7 22 **Grethel (IRE)**[31] 2213 10-9-2 45 MissADeniel 7
(Alan Berry) *s.i.s: hld up in rr: a bhd* 40/1
2m 52.61s (-1.29) **Going Correction** -0.05s/f (Good) 7 Ran SP% 110.0
Speed ratings (Par 101): **101,98,98,97,84 81,67**
CSF £2.98 TOTE £1.50: £1.10, £2.80; EX 3.40 Trifecta £29.80.
**Owner** Mrs A Royston,Mrs C Barclay,M T Buckley **Bred** Razza Pallorsi **Trained** Middleham Moor, N Yorks
**FOCUS**
A weak handicap.

## 3606 JORDAN ELECTRICS MAIDEN AUCTION STKS 6f 5y
6:50 (6:51) (Class 5) 2-Y-O £3,234 (£962; £481; £240) Stalls High

Form RPR
2 1 **Arabian Bride (IRE)**[10] 3296 2-8-12 0 JoeFanning 6 81+
(Mark Johnston) *mde all: pushed clr fnl f* 4/6[1]
0 2 6 **Lady Charlie**[20] 2944 2-8-6 0 BenCurtis 1 54
(Jo Hughes) *in tch on outer: rdn and hdwy 2f out: wnt 2nd appr fnl f: kpt on but no ch w wnr* 33/1
40 3 1 **Elizabeth Ernest**[10] 3297 2-8-5 0 GeorgeChaloner(3) 7 53
(Richard Fahey) *dwlt: sn trckd ldr on inner racing keenly: rdn 2f out: kpt on same pce* 7/1
5 4 3/4 **Grand Proposal**[10] 3297 2-8-12 0 KevinStott(5) 4 60
(Kevin Ryan) *dwlt: sn trckd ldrs: rdn over 2f out: one pce* 5/1[2]
5 2 1/2 **Why No Rein (IRE)** 2-9-5 0 GrahamLee 5 54+
(Richard Fahey) *s.i.s: hld up: pushed along 1/2-way: nvr threatened* 11/2[3]
0 6 4 1/2 **Blencathra**[20] 2944 2-8-6 0 PhilipPrince(5) 2 33
(Jo Hughes) *w ldr: lost pl over 3f out: wknd 2f out* 50/1
1m 12.99s (0.79) **Going Correction** -0.05s/f (Good) 6 Ran SP% 109.4
Speed ratings (Par 93): **92,84,82,81,78 72**
CSF £24.29 TOTE £1.50: £1.10, £9.50; EX 19.60 Trifecta £120.00.
**Owner** Jaber Abdullah **Bred** Kabansk Ltd & Rathbarry Stud **Trained** Middleham Moor, N Yorks
**FOCUS**
Not much depth here.

## 3607 IRN BRU OPEN MAIDEN STKS 1m 1f 36y
7:20 (7:21) (Class 5) 3-4-Y-O £3,234 (£962; £481; £240) Stalls Low

Form RPR
32 1 **Maid Of The Glens (IRE)**[25] 2804 3-8-11 0 RonanWhelan 3 82
(John Patrick Shanahan, Ire) *mde all: rdn clr fnl 2f* 13/8[2]
40-0 2 6 **Ehtifaal (IRE)**[45] 2201 3-9-2 74 GrahamLee 4 74
(William Haggas) *trckd ldng pair: rdn over 2f out: one pce: wnt 2nd 50yds out: no threat wnr* 1/1[1]
30 3 1 1/2 **First Move**[54] 1960 4-9-13 0 JoeFanning 6 72
(Mark Johnston) *w ldr: rdn over 2f out: one pce and no ch w wnr fr over 1f out: lost 2nd 50yds out* 11/2[3]
6- 4 7 **Blue Sonic**[301] 5919 4-9-5 0 GaryBartley(3) 5 52
(Jim Goldie) *in tch: rdn over 2f out: wknd fnl f* 50/1
05 5 11 **Drinks For Losers (IRE)**[15] 3103 3-9-2 0 JasonHart 2 33
(Ian Semple) *hld up: rdn over 4f out: sn struggling* 33/1
1m 58.25s (-1.45) **Going Correction** -0.05s/f (Good)
**WFA** 3 from 4yo 11lb 5 Ran SP% 108.4
Speed ratings (Par 103): **104,98,97,91,81**
CSF £3.46 TOTE £2.40: £1.40, £1.20; EX 3.30 Trifecta £5.20.
**Owner** Thistle Bloodstock Limited **Bred** Thistle Bloodstock Ltd **Trained** Kells, Co Kilkenny
**FOCUS**
Another modest maiden and another easy winner.

## 3608 EBF STALLIONS CAPTAIN J.C. STEWART FILLIES' H'CAP 1m 65y
7:50 (7:50) (Class 4) (0-80,81) 3-Y-O+ £6,469 (£1,925; £962; £481) Stalls Low

Form RPR
-401 1 **Mu'Ajiza**[15] 3097 4-9-10 74 RobertWinston 8 88
(Paul Midgley) *hld up: hdwy 3f out: rdn to ld appr fnl f: kpt on wl to go clr* 9/2[2]
1421 2 2 3/4 **Flycatcher (IRE)**[9] 3340 3-9-4 81 6ex GeorgeChaloner(3) 6 86
(Richard Fahey) *pressed ldr: rdn to ld narrowly over 2f out: hdd appr fnl f: kpt on but sn no ch w wnr* 1/1[1]
3-03 3 2 **Pigeon Pie**[29] 2676 3-8-7 67 JoeFanning 4 68
(Mark Johnston) *led narrowly: rdn whn hdd over 2f out: plugged on* 8/1
1056 4 6 **Patrona Ciana (FR)**[14] 3139 4-10-0 78 DavidNolan 5 67
(David O'Meara) *hld up in tch: rdn over 2f out: nvr threatened* 18/1
2546 5 1 **Spavento (IRE)**[19] 3005 8-9-1 65 JasonHart 1 52
(Eric Alston) *trckd ldng pair: rdn over 3f out: wknd fnl 2f* 16/1
0000 6 3 **Act Your Shoe Size**[1] 3572 5-9-5 69 TomEaves 3 49
(Keith Dalgleish) *dwlt: sn trckd ldng pair: rdn 3f out: sn wknd* 6/1[3]
0-63 7 1 1/4 **Hala Hala (IRE)**[22] 2892 3-9-2 76 GrahamLee 7 51
(Michael Bell) *in tch on outside early: dropped in and hld up 6f out: rdn over 2f out: sn wknd* 12/1
1m 46.89s (-1.51) **Going Correction** -0.05s/f (Good)
**WFA** 3 from 4yo+ 10lb 7 Ran SP% 112.4
Speed ratings (Par 102): **105,102,100,94,93 90,89**
CSF £9.07 CT £32.65 TOTE £7.20: £2.80, £1.20; EX 11.20 Trifecta £37.60.
**Owner** Ms Julie French **Bred** Darley **Trained** Westow, N Yorks
**FOCUS**
This looked to be run at quite a brisk tempo and the winner is better than ever.

## 3609 SUPER TINA WEBSTER SUPERSEAL (S) H'CAP 5f 4y
8:20 (8:22) (Class 6) (0-60,60) 3-Y-O+ £2,385 (£704; £352) Stalls Centre

Form RPR
0561 1 **Emily Davison (IRE)**[7] 3395 3-8-2 51 6ex (p) GemmaTutty(7) 5 58
(Karen Tutty) *hld up: rdn 1/2-way: r.o wl fnl f: led towards fin* 7/1[3]
6464 2 nk **Cape Of Hope (IRE)**[8] 3366 4-9-10 60 (v) AdrianNicholls 1 68
(David Nicholls) *outpcd in rr tl r.o fr over 1f out: wnt 2nd nr fin* 13/2[2]
-254 3 1/2 **Straight Gin**[21] 2910 3-8-5 47 (b[1]) JamesSullivan 11 51
(Alan Berry) *racd isolated towards stands' rail: w ldr: rdn to ld over 1f out: no ex fnl 110yds and hdd towards fin* 14/1
6535 4 hd **Greenhead High**[21] 2909 6-8-10 53 (v) AnnaHesketh(7) 2 58
(David Nicholls) *trckd ldrs: smooth hdwy 2f out: rdn and ev ch ins fnl f: no ex towards fin* 7/1[3]
3423 5 1 1/4 **Rock Canyon (IRE)**[15] 3099 5-8-11 50 GeorgeChaloner(3) 6 51
(Linda Perratt) *chsd ldrs: rdn 2f out: no ex fnl 110yds* 7/1[3]
4364 6 1/2 **Pull The Pin (IRE)**[15] 3093 5-9-8 58 (b) PaulMulrennan 4 57
(Ann Stokell) *rn wout declared tongue tie: led narrowly: rdn whn hdd over 1f out: wknd fnl 110yds* 11/2[1]
0006 7 hd **Baltic Spirit (IRE)**[8] 3359 3-9-3 59 TomEaves 3 55
(Keith Dalgleish) *hld up: rdn 1/2-way: one pce and nvr threatened* 8/1
0525 8 4 **Ishetoo**[15] 3104 10-8-10 46 JoeFanning 10 30
(Peter Grayson) *hld up: rdn 1/2-way: sn btn* 25/1
2605 9 1/2 **Commandable (AUS)**[35] 2473 10-9-1 51 (b) JasonHart 9 33
(Ian Semple) *prom: rdn 1/2-way: wknd over 1f out* 7/1[3]
5050 10 2 3/4 **Chloe's Dream (IRE)**[13] 3191 4-9-6 56 GrahamLee 8 28
(Linda Perratt) *w ldr: wknd fnl f* 10/1
064- 11 5 **Myjestic Melody (IRE)**[212] 8051 6-8-10 46 oh1 (v[1]) BenCurtis 7
(Shaun Harris) *prom: rdn 1/2-way: wknd over 1f out* 16/1
59.48s (-0.52) **Going Correction** -0.05s/f (Good)
**WFA** 3 from 4yo+ 6lb 11 Ran SP% 115.3
Speed ratings (Par 101): **102,101,100,100,98 97,97,90,90,85 77**
CSF £50.96 CT £631.96 TOTE £8.20: £2.50, £2.30, £4.10; EX 60.40 Trifecta £379.10.The winner was bought in 6,200gns.
**Owner** Thoroughbred Homes Ltd **Bred** Rathbarry Stud **Trained** Osmotherley, N Yorks
**FOCUS**
Quite a competitive heat for the grade and the pace must have been strong as the picture changed dramatically in the final half-furlong.

## 3610 PATERSONS OF GREENOAKHILL H'CAP 6f 5y
8:50 (8:50) (Class 4) (0-80,80) 3-Y-O+ £6,469 (£1,925; £962; £481) Stalls High

Form RPR
2142 1 **Khelman (IRE)**[15] 3102 4-9-11 80 GeorgeChaloner(3) 5 89
(Richard Fahey) *prom: rdn to ld over 1f out: kpt on wl* 13/8[1]
454 2 nk **Funding Deficit (IRE)**[34] 2518 4-8-9 61 GrahamLee 2 69
(Jim Goldie) *led: rdn whn hdd over 1f out: kpt on but a jst hld* 5/1[3]
0602 3 2 1/2 **King Of Eden (IRE)**[8] 3359 8-9-7 73 JasonHart 1 73
(Eric Alston) *prom: rdn and outpcd by ldng pair over 2f out: plugged on but no threat after* 5/2[2]
6606 4 2 1/4 **Bonnie Charlie**[20] 2951 8-9-0 66 PaulQuinn 4 59
(David Nicholls) *hld up in tch: rdn over 2f out: wknd ins fnl f* 12/1
2641 5 4 1/2 **Bunce (IRE)**[13] 3191 6-9-5 71 JoeFanning 6 49
(Linda Perratt) *hld up in tch: rdn over 2f out: wknd fnl f* 5/1[3]
1m 11.19s (-1.01) **Going Correction** -0.05s/f (Good)
**WFA** 3 from 4yo+ 7lb 5 Ran SP% 107.7
Speed ratings (Par 105): **104,103,100,97,91**
CSF £9.49 TOTE £2.70: £1.70, £2.30; EX 10.00 Trifecta £23.10.
**Owner** S & G Clayton **Bred** Oghill House Stud & Jimmy Hyland **Trained** Musley Bank, N Yorks
**FOCUS**
Only a small field but okay form.

## 3611 STUART ANDERSON 21ST BIRTHDAY CELEBRATION H'CAP 5f 4y
9:20 (9:21) (Class 5) (0-75,75) 3-Y-O+ £3,408 (£1,006; £503) Stalls Centre

Form RPR
0-02 1 **Mr Mo Jo**[9] 3338 6-9-0 63 (b) DavidAllan 7 72
(Les Eyre) *chsd ldr: rdn to ld 1f out: kpt on* 6/1[2]
0060 2 nk **Ypres**[7] 3399 5-9-5 71 (p) JoeyHaynes(3) 4 79
(Jason Ward) *midfield: hdwy to chse ldr over 1f out: ev ch fnl f: kpt on: jst hld* 11/1
3002 3 1 3/4 **Salvatore Fury (IRE)**[10] 3298 4-9-2 65 (p) JoeFanning 2 67
(Keith Dalgleish) *racd keenly: hld up: hdwy 2f out: n.m.r hust bhd ldrs appr fnl f: swtchd rt ins fnl f: rdn and one pce* 3/1[1]
0363 4 1/2 **Haajes**[13] 3191 10-9-10 73 (v) GrahamLee 10 73
(Paul Midgley) *midfield: rdn 2f out: kpt on ins fnl f* 3/1[1]
-000 5 1 1/4 **Sunny Side Up (IRE)**[33] 2552 5-8-9 65 (t) GemmaTutty(7) 6 60
(Karen Tutty) *s.i.s: hld up: rdn 2f out: kpt on ins fnl f: nvr threatened* 14/1
6660 6 nk **Majestic Manannan (IRE)**[47] 2167 5-9-3 66 AdrianNicholls 8 60
(David Nicholls) *led: rdn whn hdd 1f out: wknd* 12/1
0000 7 1 **Red Explorer (USA)**[12] 3246 4-9-3 66 (p) BenCurtis 5 57
(Ann Stokell) *midfield on outer: rdn 1/2-way: nvr threatened* 25/1
1355 8 1/2 **Economic Crisis (IRE)**[8] 3359 5-9-9 72 PaulMulrennan 1 61
(Alan Berry) *s.i.s: hld up: nvr threatened* 8/1[3]
2600 9 6 **Bronze Beau**[12] 3239 7-9-12 75 (t) JamesSullivan 9 42
(Kristin Stubbs) *racd keenly hld up: nvr threatened* 17/2
02-0 10 13 **Gottcher**[13] 3191 6-9-10 73 JasonHart 3
(Ian Semple) *prom: wknd over 1f out: eased* 25/1
59.36s (-0.64) **Going Correction** -0.05s/f (Good) 10 Ran SP% 116.3
Speed ratings (Par 103): **103,102,99,98,96 96,94,94,84,63**
CSF £69.78 CT £238.43 TOTE £5.80: £2.80, £2.30, £1.50; EX 63.90 Trifecta £604.40.
**Owner** Sunpak Potatoes **Bred** D A Flavell **Trained** Catton, North Yorkshire
**FOCUS**
The pace looked sound and the hold-up horses ended up dominating. The winner has been rated close to his best and the runner-up to his best.
T/Plt: £12.40 to a £1 stake. Pool of £48334.26 - 2845.10 winning tickets. T/Qpdt: £11.30 to a £1 stake. Pool of £4089.66 - 266.04 winning tickets. AS

# 3380 LEICESTER (R-H)

Thursday, June 26

**OFFICIAL GOING: Good to firm (8.5)**

Wind: Light against Weather: Cloudy

## 3612 LANGHAM LADIES' H'CAP (LADY AMATEUR RIDERS) 5f 2y

5:40 (5:40) (Class 5) (0-75,74) 3-Y-0+ £2,495 (£774; £386; £193) Stalls High

Form RPR

0233 1 **Tyfos**37 2434 9-10-3 70 MissSBrotherton 2 84
(Brian Baugh) *mde all: clr 4f out: shkn up over 1f out: styd on: unchal* 11/41

0002 2 2 3/4 **Noodles Blue Boy**12 3222 8-9-13 71 (p) MissHDukes(5) 5 75
(Ollie Pears) *chsd wnr who was clr 4f out: rdn 1/2-way: tk clsr order over 1f out: styd on same pce ins fnl f* 7/22

024 3 3 1/2 **Jontleman (IRE)**16 3088 4-10-7 74 MissEJJones 6 66
(Mick Channon) *chsd ldrs: rdn 1/2-way: styd on to go 3rd wl ins fnl f: nt trble front pair* 6/13

0400 4 1/2 **Two Turtle Doves (IRE)**24 2831 8-8-13 55 oh2.. MissMMullineaux(3) 3 45
(Michael Mullineaux) *chsd clr ldrs: rdn 1/2-way: rdr dropped whip over 1f out: styd on same pce* 50/1

3301 5 2 **Storm Lightning**23 2865 5-10-2 72 BeckyBrisbourne(3) 1 55
(Mark Brisbourne) *chsd clr ldrs: rdn 1/2-way: no ex fnl f* 11/41

-200 6 3 3/4 **Be Lucky**12 3256 4-10-2 72 (t) MissJoannaMason(3) 7 41
(Michael Easterby) *sn outpcd* 6/13

0-00 6 dht **Irish Boy (IRE)**12 3222 6-9-4 62 (tp) MissLWilson(5) 8 31
(Christine Dunnett) *in rr: pushed along 1/2-way: nvr on terms* 33/1

00-6 8 3 1/2 **Magical Speedfit (IRE)**50 2070 9-9-7 65 MissKMargarson(5) 4 21
(George Margarson) *sn outpcd* 33/1

**Going Correction** -0.175s/f (Firm) 8 Ran SP% 112.0

Speed ratings (Par 103): **93,88,83,82,79 73,73,67**

CSF £11.99 CT £51.01 TOTE £2.90: £1.10, £1.50, £2.40; EX 11.20 Trifecta £70.30.

**Owner** Magnate Racing **Bred** J Tomlinson And G Williams **Trained** Audley, Staffs

**FOCUS**

A warm, dry evening and they raced on watered ground. A fair sprint handicap for lady amateur riders, which very few got into. The winner is rated to his early 2013 form.

## 3613 INJURED JOCKEYS FUND 50TH ANNIVERSARY MAIDEN AUCTION STKS 5f 218y

6:10 (6:11) (Class 5) 2-Y-O £2,587 (£770; £384; £192) Stalls High

Form RPR

062 1 **Magical Memory (IRE)**13 3193 2-9-2 0 GeorgeBaker 5 84
(Charles Hills) *trckd ldrs: rdn to wl ld ins fnl f: r.o* 5/41

2 nk **Publilia** 2-8-11 0 WilliamBuick 3 78+
(Mark Johnston) *disp ld tl led over 1f out: sn rdn: hdd wl ins fnl f: r.o* 25/1

3 3/4 **Fingal's Cave (IRE)** 2-8-8 0 WilliamTwiston-Davies(3) 8 76+
(Mick Channon) *trckd ldrs: racd keenly: shkn up over 1f out: r.o* 9/1

00 4 1 1/4 **Johnny B Goode (IRE)**61 1726 2-8-6 0 SammyJoBell(5) 4 72
(Richard Fahey) *trckd ldrs: shkn up over 1f out: edgd lft ins fnl f: styd on same pce* 50/1

4 5 1 1/2 **Heaven's Secret (IRE)**24 2824 2-8-13 0 RyanMoore 7 70
(Richard Fahey) *disp ld tl rdn over 1f out: styd on same pce ins fnl f* 7/23

6 nk **Thecornishassassin** 2-8-8 0 OisinMurphy(3) 10 67
(Robert Eddery) *mid-div: outpcd over 2f out: r.o ins fnl f* 50/1

3 7 2 1/4 **Laidback Romeo (IRE)**14 3140 2-8-13 0 RyanTate(3) 11 65
(Clive Cox) *disp ld tl rdn over 2f out: edgd rt and no ex fnl f* 3/12

8 9 **Right Madam (IRE)** 2-8-6 0 MartinDwyer 6 28
(Andrew Hollinshead) *s.i.s: a in rr* 66/1

9 1/2 **Stec (IRE)** 2-8-9 0 JennyPowell(7) 9 36
(Tom Dascombe) *sn pushed along and a in rr* 66/1

3 10 13 **Maesmor Magic (IRE)**28 2692 2-8-4 0 DavidProbert 2
(Martyn Meade) *w ldrs tl rdn over 3f out: wknd over 1f out* 20/1

00 U **St Paul's Square (IRE)**5 3467 2-8-6 0 RachealKneller(5) 1
(Jamie Osborne) *uns rdr leaving stalls* 200/1

1m 12.46s (-0.54) **Going Correction** -0.175s/f (Firm) 11 Ran SP% 117.7

Speed ratings (Par 93): **96,95,94,92,90 90,87,75,74,57**

CSF £42.66 TOTE £2.90: £1.30, £5.50, £2.10; EX 27.70 Trifecta £191.30.

**Owner** Kennet Valley Thoroughbreds I **Bred** Wardstown Stud Ltd **Trained** Lambourn, Berks

**FOCUS**

An interesting maiden and although the pace was ordinary, the form looks solid, rated around pre-race form and the race average.

## 3614 SIS LIVE FILLIES' H'CAP 1m 60y

6:40 (6:40) (Class 5) (0-70,69) 3-Y-0+ £2,587 (£770; £384; £192) Stalls Low

Form RPR

3-06 1 **Adore**34 2504 3-8-13 64 RyanMoore 7 71
(Sir Michael Stoute) *trckd ldr: rdn to ld over 1f out: r.o* 9/41

-034 2 1 1/2 **Thatchereen (IRE)**27 2740 3-9-3 68 TomQueally 2 71
(Michael Bell) *hld up: racd keenly: hdwy over 2f out: rdn over 1f out: r.o to go 2nd post: nt rch wnr* 3/12

2402 3 shd **Fruit Pastille**11 3281 3-8-7 65 CharlieBennett(7) 4 68
(Hughie Morrison) *sn led: rdn and hdd over 1f out: edgd lft ins fnl f: styd on same pce* 9/41

0 4 6 **Trikala (IRE)**21 2929 3-8-13 69 MarcMonaghan(5) 5 58
(Marco Botti) *hld up: rdn over 2f out: nt trble ldrs* 7/13

00/4 5 7 **Mini's Destination**9 3334 6-9-5 60 StevieDonohoe 1 35
(John Holt) *prom: rdn over 2f out: wknd over 1f out* 16/1

203 6 3 1/2 **Chanceuse**31 2609 3-8-3 54 DavidProbert 6 19
(Gay Kelleway) *chsd ldrs: rdn over 2f out: wknd over 1f out* 20/1

1m 44.81s (-0.29) **Going Correction** -0.075s/f (Good)

**WFA** 3 from 5yo+ 10lb 6 Ran SP% 109.7

Speed ratings (Par 100): **98,96,96,90,83 79**

CSF £8.82 TOTE £2.50: £1.60, £1.80; EX 8.20 Trifecta £14.80.

**Owner** Cheveley Park Stud **Bred** Cheveley Park Stud Ltd **Trained** Newmarket, Suffolk

■ Acton Gold was withdrawn. Price at time of withdrawal 28/1. Rule 4 does not apply.

**FOCUS**

A modest fillies' handicap with all bar one of them a 3yo and the market proved correct with the front three in the betting filling the first three places. The winner is among the stable's lesser lights.

## 3615 INJURED JOCKEYS FUND 50TH ANNIVERSARY FILLIES' H'CAP (BOBIS RACE) 7f 9y

7:10 (7:10) (Class 4) (0-85,85) 3-Y-O £4,690 (£1,395; £697; £348) Stalls High

Form RPR

51 1 **Felwah**16 3074 3-8-13 77 PaulHanagan 5 86+
(William Haggas) *trckd ldrs: wnt 2nd over 4f out: rdn to ld over 1f out: edgd rt ins fnl f: r.o* 11/41

31-1 2 2 1/4 **Maria Bella (IRE)**15 3117 3-9-5 83 RyanMoore 3 87
(Charlie Appleby) *racd keenly: led: rdn and hdd over 1f out: styd on same pce ins fnl f* 10/32

1-50 3 hd **Dynaglow (USA)**13 3195 3-8-11 75 WilliamBuick 4 78
(John Gosden) *plld hrd: trckd ldr tl over 4f out: remained handy: rdn over 1f out: styd on* 9/2

-204 4 3 **Miss Atomic Bomb**15 3117 3-9-5 83 MartinHarley 6 78
(Marco Botti) *trckd ldrs: shkn up over 1f out: no ex ins fnl f* 15/2

3-50 5 3/4 **Dutch S**15 3117 3-8-8 75 1 RyanTate(3) 1 68
(Clive Cox) *s.i.s: sn pushed along in rr: styd on ins fnl f: nvr nrr* 7/23

352- 6 1 **Threetimesalady**278 6628 3-9-7 85 LukeMorris 2 76
(Sir Mark Prescott Bt) *hld up: rdn over 1f out: wknd ins fnl f* 12/1

1m 24.57s (-1.63) **Going Correction** -0.175s/f (Firm) 6 Ran SP% 109.6

Speed ratings (Par 98): **102,99,99,95,94 93**

CSF £11.50 TOTE £3.70: £1.90, £1.10; EX 10.30 Trifecta £45.60.

**Owner** Khalil Alsayegh **Bred** Khalil Al Sayegh **Trained** Newmarket, Suffolk

**FOCUS**

They went an end-to-end gallop and the form of this competitive 3yo fillies' handicap looks useful. the first two can do better.

## 3616 HYDROVANE COMPRESSORS MANUFACTURED IN U.K. H'CAP 1m 1f 218y

7:40 (7:40) (Class 5) (0-70,70) 4-Y-O+ £2,587 (£770; £384; £192) Stalls Low

Form RPR

0053 1 **Oratorio's Joy (IRE)**13 3176 4-9-7 70 WilliamCarson 2 76
(Jamie Osborne) *hld up in tch: chsd ldr over 2f out: rdn over 1f out: r.o to ld post* 5/13

2630 2 hd **Nubar Boy**1 3585 7-9-1 69 (p) GeorgeDowning(5) 6 74
(Ian Williams) *led: shkn up over 1f out: rdn ins fnl f: hdd post* 7/1

5301 3 1 3/4 **Automotive**14 3147 6-9-2 65 RyanMoore 5 67
(Julia Feilden) *hld up: pushed along and hdwy over 2f out: styd on: nt rch ldrs* 9/42

10 4 5 **Poor Duke (IRE)**10 3299 4-9-2 70 (v1) TimClark(5) 3 62
(Michael Mullineaux) *hld up: rdn over 3f out: sn outpcd* 20/1

4-06 5 1 **Saint Thomas (IRE)**13 2540 7-9-2 65 TomQueally 4 55
(John Mackie) *chsd ldr tl rdn over 2f out: wknd over 1f out* 2/11

000- P **Kazak**244 7505 4-9-4 67 GeorgeBaker 1
(Robert Stephens) *chsd ldrs: rdn over 2f out: wknd over 1f out: p.u and dismntd ins fnl f* 8/1

2m 6.2s (-1.70) **Going Correction** -0.075s/f (Good) 6 Ran SP% 109.1

Speed ratings (Par 103): **103,102,101,97,96**

CSF £35.68 TOTE £5.50: £3.00, £2.60; EX 25.10 Trifecta £53.40.

**Owner** A F Tait **Bred** R Mahon & J Reilly **Trained** Upper Lambourn, Berks

**FOCUS**

A modest handicap and the pace was indifferent. The form is rated around the runner-up to his old turf best.

## 3617 BRUNTINGTHORPE H'CAP 1m 3f 183y

8:10 (8:10) (Class 6) (0-65,65) 4-Y-O+ £1,940 (£577; £288; £144) Stalls Low

Form RPR

3150 1 **Royal Marskell**25 2801 5-9-4 65 OisinMurphy(3) 4 74
(Alison Hutchinson) *pushed along to chse ldr after 1f: led over 3f out: rdn over 1f out: styd on wl* 2/11

3460 2 3 **Golden Jubilee (USA)**41 2300 5-9-3 64 (v) WilliamTwiston-Davies(3) 3 68
(Nigel Twiston-Davies) *a.p: chsd wnr over 2f out: rdn and ev ch ins fnl f: no ex* 3/13

3150 3 4 1/2 **Well Owd Mon**20 2942 4-8-7 56 JackDuern(5) 2 53
(Andrew Hollinshead) *hld up: racd keenly: hdwy over 7f out: shkn up 2f out: wknd ins fnl f* 4/1

1204 4 15 **Highlife Dancer**10 3310 6-9-0 65 DanielCremin(7) 5 38
(Mick Channon) *led over 8f: rdn and wknd over 1f out* 9/42

2m 32.23s (-1.67) **Going Correction** -0.075s/f (Good) 4 Ran SP% 109.1

Speed ratings (Par 101): **102,100,97,87**

CSF £8.11 TOTE £2.30; EX 9.30 Trifecta £17.60.

**Owner** Miss Chantal Wootten **Bred** Miss V Woodward **Trained** Exning, Suffolk

**FOCUS**

A paucity of runners for this modest and uncompetitive handicap, in which the quartet of riders all claimed. Although the pace was not even, it was far from a tactical affair. The winner is rated to his AW form.

## 3618 SKEFFINGTON H'CAP 1m 60y

8:40 (8:40) (Class 5) (0-70,70) 3-Y-O £2,587 (£770; £384; £192) Stalls Low

Form RPR

3454 1 **Gratzie**14 3159 3-9-0 66 WilliamTwiston-Davies(3) 5 71
(Mick Channon) *sn trcking ldr: led over 2f out: rdn and edgd lft ins fnl f: r.o* 5/22

04-0 2 1 1/2 **Slingsby**40 2355 3-8-5 54 LukeMorris 3 55
(Michael Easterby) *set stdy pce tl qcknd over 3f out: rdn and hdd over 2f out: r.o* 14/1

4013 3 1/2 **Caledonia Laird**28 2695 3-8-10 59 MartinDwyer 4 61
(Jo Hughes) *trckd ldrs: plld hrd: wnt 2nd over 2f out: rdn over 1f out: edgd rt and styd on same pce ins fnl f* 9/41

1430 4 1/2 **Sakhalin Star (IRE)**11 3273 3-9-4 70 BillyCray(3) 7 69
(Richard Guest) *hld up: rdn over 1f out: styd on ins fnl f: nt rch ldrs* 3/13

-300 5 2 1/4 **Steele Ranger**57 1884 3-8-12 68 JordanNason(7) 2 62
(Peter Chapple-Hyam) *hld up: racd keenly: rdn over 2f out: styd on same pce fnl f* 9/2

1m 50.08s (4.98) **Going Correction** -0.075s/f (Good) 5 Ran SP% 109.2

Speed ratings (Par 99): **72,70,70,69,67**

CSF £29.74 TOTE £3.90: £1.60, £3.80; EX 20.20 Trifecta £93.20.

**Owner** C Corbett, David Hudd, Chris Wright **Bred** John Troy & Robert Levitt **Trained** West Ilsley, Berks

**FOCUS**

This modest 3yo handicap turned into something of a sprint after a sluggish early pace, making the worth of form open to question. The winner is rated to this year's form.

T/Plt: £53.60 to a £1 stake. Pool of £49445.26 - 673.30 winning tickets. T/Qpdt: £19.00 to a £1 stake. Pool of £4358.90 - 169.0 winning tickets. CR

# 2736 NEWCASTLE (L-H)

Thursday, June 26

**OFFICIAL GOING: Good to firm (good in places) changing to good to firm after race 2 (3.00)**
All Round course on fresh ground.
Wind: Light, half behind Weather: Overcast

## 3619 BETFRED RACING FOLLOW US ON TWITTER NOVICE STKS (BOBIS RACE) 6f
2:30 (2:31) (Class 4) 2-Y-O £6,469 (£1,925; £962; £481) Stalls Centre

Form RPR
22 1 **Aktabantay**[37] 2428 2-9-0 0 DanielTudhope 4 90+
(Hugo Palmer) *t.k.h early: trckd ldrs: shkn up to ld ins fnl f: edgd lft: pushed out: comf* **6/5**[1]
1 2 1 1/4 **Geordie George (IRE)**[22] 2895 2-9-7 0 PhillipMakin 6 91
(John Quinn) *dwlt: sn rcvrd and led: rdn over 1f out: hdd ins fnl f: kpt on: nt rch wnr* **9/4**[2]
13 3 1/2 **Sea Wolf (IRE)**[33] 2543 2-9-7 0 PaulMulrennan 2 89
(Michael Dods) *trckd ldrs: effrt and rdn over 1f out: kpt on same pce ins fnl f* **8/1**
5123 4 3/4 **Vimy Ridge**[19] 3001 2-9-4 0 TonyHamilton 1 84
(Richard Fahey) *early ldr: trckd ldr: effrt and rdn over 1f out: hung lft and one pce ins fnl f* **9/2**[3]
5 3 1/4 **Dominada (IRE)** 2-9-0 0 PJMcDonald 3 70+
(Brian Ellison) *dwlt: hld up in tch: hdwy over 2f out: hung lft and wknd over 1f out: bttr for r* **66/1**
01 6 shd **Just The Tip (IRE)**[12] 3236 2-8-13 0 TomEaves 5 69
(Keith Dalgleish) *hld up in tch: rdn along wl over 1f out: sn btn* **28/1**
1m 15.65s (1.05) **Going Correction** -0.25s/f (Firm) 6 Ran SP% **110.5**
Speed ratings (Par 95): **83,81,80,79,75 75**
CSF £3.95 TOTE £2.70: £1.30, £1.50; EX 4.90 Trifecta £16.80.
**Owner** V I Araci **Bred** Fittocks Stud Ltd **Trained** Newmarket, Suffolk
**FOCUS**
After the opener, Tony Hamilton reported the going as 'quick ground' and Paul Mulrennan said it was 'good to firm'. Probably just a fair maiden, and the early pace wasn't that strong. It pretty much developed into a 2f sprint. The winner has been rated more or less to the level of his taking debut.

## 3620 BETFRED WORLD CUP GOALS GALORE EXTRA MEDIAN AUCTION MAIDEN STKS 6f
3:00 (3:00) (Class 6) 2-Y-O £1,940 (£577; £288; £144) Stalls Centre

Form RPR
1 **Great Park (IRE)** 2-9-5 0 PhillipMakin 1 73
(Martyn Meade) *cl up: rdn over 1f out: led last 100yds: pushed out* **17/2**
432 2 nk **Indian Keys**[29] 2673 2-8-9 0 ShaneGray(5) 3 67
(Kevin Ryan) *led: rdn over 1f out: edgd lft and hdd ins fnl f: rallied: hld cl home* **8/1**
3 1 1/2 **Third Time Lucky (IRE)** 2-9-5 0 TonyHamilton 2 68
(Richard Fahey) *t.k.h early: trckd ldrs: effrt over 1f out: checked ins fnl f: kpt on same pce* **11/4**[1]
0533 4 2 1/2 **Diatomic (IRE)**[10] 3297 2-9-5 0 RichardKingscote 7 60
(Tom Dascombe) *trckd ldrs: drvn along over 2f out: kpt on same pce fnl f* **9/1**
3 5 nse **Danny O'Ruairc (IRE)**[27] 2736 2-9-5 0 TomEaves 4 60+
(James Moffatt) *hld up: shkn up and hdwy over 1f out: kpt on fnl f: nvr nr ldrs* **8/1**
6 1 1/2 **Aprovado (IRE)** 2-9-5 0 PaulMulrennan 5 55
(Michael Dods) *dwlt: hld up: effrt on outside over 2f out: outpcd fnl f* **7/2**[2]
06 7 nk **Secret Of Dubai**[22] 2895 2-9-0 0 PaulPickard 6 49
(Brian Ellison) *hld up: drvn along over 2f out: no imp fr over 1f out* **80/1**
02 8 3/4 **The Card Players (IRE)**[56] 1900 2-9-5 0 DaleSwift 10 53
(Brian Ellison) *cl up: drvn and edgd rt over 1f out: sn outpcd* **9/2**[3]
9 nk **Fast Charlie (IRE)** 2-9-5 0 PJMcDonald 9 51
(Ann Duffield) *hld up bhd ldng gp: effrt and pushed along over 2f out: wknd over 1f out* **16/1**
0 10 15 **Tobouggan Run**[61] 1726 2-9-5 0 RaulDaSilva 8 6
(Michael Appleby) *hld up: struggling over 2f out: sn btn: t.o* **40/1**
1m 14.92s (0.32) **Going Correction** -0.25s/f (Firm) 10 Ran SP% **119.4**
Speed ratings (Par 91): **87,86,84,81,81 79,78,77,77,57**
CSF £76.48 TOTE £11.50: £3.90, £1.60, £2.10; EX 72.00 Trifecta £626.50.
**Owner** David Caddy **Bred** Brinkley Stud, Ficomontanino, Bego Blu **Trained** Newmarket, Suffolk
**FOCUS**
Not much early pace on and this is probably ordinary form. The runner-up seemed to post a minor personal best.

## 3621 BETFRED.COM FREE BET OFFERS SEATON DELAVAL H'CAP 1m 3y(S)
3:30 (3:30) (Class 2) (0-105,97) 4-Y-O+
£12,450 (£3,728; £1,864; £932; £466; £234) Stalls Centre

Form RPR
3026 1 shd **Dance And Dance (IRE)**[20] 2959 8-9-1 91 RichardKingscote 3 100
(Ed Vaughan) *in tch: effrt over 1f out: ev ch and rdn whn bmpd last 100yds: kpt on: hld nr fin: fin 2nd: awrdd the r* **9/2**[2]
5121 2 **Baraweez (IRE)**[13] 3190 4-8-10 86 DaleSwift 5 95
(Brian Ellison) *trckd ldr: rdn to ld over 1f out: edgd rt and bmpd rival last 100yds: hld on wl towards fin: fin first: plcd 2nd* **3/1**[1]
3412 3 1 **Dubai Dynamo**[5] 3456 9-8-12 88 PJMcDonald 8 94
(Ruth Carr) *hld up bhd ldng gp: rdn and hdwy over 1f out: kpt on ins fnl f* **15/2**
0530 4 1 1/4 **Marcret (ITY)**[12] 3217 7-9-2 92 DanielTudhope 7 95
(David O'Meara) *hld up: rdn and hdwy over 1f out: kpt on wl fnl f: nvr able to chal* **12/1**
3222 5 2 **Bold Prediction (IRE)**[7] 3397 4-8-11 90 JoeyHaynes(3) 2 88
(K R Burke) *led at ordinary gallop: rdn and hdd over 1f out: sn outpcd* **8/1**
1240 6 hd **Fort Bastion (IRE)**[8] 3356 5-9-7 97 JamesSullivan 4 95
(Ruth Carr) *hld up in tch: drvn and effrt 2f out: sn no imp* **6/1**[3]
0004 7 2 3/4 **Norse Blues**[5] 3456 6-8-12 88 GrahamGibbons 9 79
(David Barron) *t.k.h: hld up in tch: effrt and rdn over 2f out: no imp over 1f out* **6/1**[3]
0021 8 6 **Heavy Metal**[5] 3483 4-9-1 91 6ex JoeFanning 1 68
(Mark Johnston) *pressed ldrs: drvn along over 2f out: wknd over 1f out* **15/2**
1m 39.44s (-3.96) **Going Correction** -0.25s/f (Firm) 8 Ran SP% **114.1**
Speed ratings (Par 109): **108,109,107,106,104 104,101,95**
CSF £18.33 CT £98.62 TOTE £4.90: £1.70, £1.70, £2.20; EX 23.00 Trifecta £98.70.
**Owner** Mohammed Rashid **Bred** Darley **Trained** Newmarket, Suffolk
**FOCUS**
The going was changed to good to firm prior to this race. A useful contest. Once again the early gallop appeared far from strong. The third sets the level with the runner-up close last summer's form.

## 3622 BETFRED RACING LIKE US ON FACEBOOK H'CAP 2m 19y
4:00 (4:00) (Class 4) (0-80,80) 4-Y-O+ £4,690 (£1,395; £697; £348) Stalls Low

Form RPR
0-30 1 **Knightly Escapade**[62] 1692 6-8-10 69 PJMcDonald 3 79
(Brian Ellison) *hld up: smooth hdwy to trck ldrs over 2f out: shkn up to ld ins fnl f: pushed out: comf* **9/2**[3]
2336 2 2 1/4 **Entihaa**[12] 3240 6-9-7 80 DavidAllan 4 87
(Alan Swinbank) *chsd ldrs: smooth hdwy to ld over 2f out: sn rdn: hdd ins fnl f: no ch w wnr* **6/5**[1]
/2-2 3 4 1/2 **Rumble Of Thunder (IRE)**[22] 2900 8-8-12 71 RussKennemore 2 73
(Philip Kirby) *chsd clr ldr: smooth hdwy and ev ch over 2f out: sn drvn: outpcd appr fnl f* **11/4**[2]
-000 4 25 **Crackentorp**[12] 3250 9-8-13 72 GrahamGibbons 6 44
(Tim Easterby) *t.k.h: hld up: drvn and outpcd over 3f out: sn btn: t.o* **15/2**
-000 5 10 **Ultimate**[12] 3250 8-8-12 71 PaulPickard 7 31
(Brian Ellison) *led at decent gallop and clr to over 3f out: hdd over 2f out: sn wknd: t.o* **16/1**
3m 31.1s (-8.30) **Going Correction** -0.375s/f (Firm) 5 Ran SP% **108.0**
Speed ratings (Par 105): **105,103,101,89,84**
CSF £10.02 TOTE £5.70: £2.60, £1.40; EX 13.30 Trifecta £22.40.
**Owner** Mrs J A Martin **Bred** M Meacock & The Late I Stewart-Brown **Trained** Norton, N Yorks
**FOCUS**
The winner was off a career-low mark and not far off his best, with the runner-up in line with solid recent form.

## 3623 BETFRED WORLD CUP GOALS GALORE H'CAP 1m 2f 32y
4:30 (4:32) (Class 6) (0-60,61) 4-Y-O+ £1,940 (£577; £288; £144) Stalls Centre

Form RPR
403 1 **Gabrial The Thug (FR)**[12] 3208 4-9-2 53 (t) DavidNolan 4 65
(Richard Fahey) *prom: smooth hdwy to ld wl over 1f out: drvn and hrd pressed fnl f: hld on gamely nr fin* **11/2**[3]
4501 2 shd **Gabrial's Hope (FR)**[6] 3436 5-9-7 58 6ex RobertWinston 5 70
(Tracy Waggott) *t.k.h early: hld up: stdy hdwy on ins 3f out: effrt and chal appr fnl f: hung lft ins fnl f: kpt on: hld nr fin* **11/4**[1]
0-06 3 6 **Monthly Medal**[37] 2426 11-8-4 46 (t) ShaneGray(5) 3 47
(Wilf Storey) *hld up: stdy hdwy over 2f out: chsd clr ldng pair 1f out: kpt on: no imp* **22/1**
-603 4 2 1/4 **Captain Rhyric**[21] 2913 5-8-4 46 JackGarritty(5) 2 42
(James Moffatt) *led: rdn and hdd wl over 1f out: sn outpcd* **22/1**
2060 5 1/2 **Al Furat (USA)**[13] 3205 6-9-5 56 PaulPickard 1 51
(Ron Barr) *hld up in midfield: stdy hdwy whn n.m.r briefly over 2f out: sn rdn: no imp over 1f out* **16/1**
5312 6 1 1/2 **Frontline Phantom (IRE)**[8] 3363 7-9-7 61 6ex JoeyHaynes(3) 9 54
(K R Burke) *hld up in midfield: effrt and rdn over 2f out: no imp over 1f out* **3/1**[2]
-003 7 1 3/4 **Printmaker (IRE)**[6] 3436 6-9-5 56 (p) GrahamGibbons 15 45
(Tim Easterby) *prom on outside: drvn and outpcd over 3f out: rallied 2f out: btn fnl f* **12/1**
0-44 8 16 **Yorksters Prince (IRE)**[6] 3438 7-9-6 57 (b) DanielTudhope 11 16
(Marjorie Fife) *cl up: rdn over 3f out: sn wknd* **9/1**
4/54 9 2 **Snooker (GER)**[35] 2476 8-9-1 52 JamesSullivan 8 7
(Rose Dobbin) *dwlt: hld up: rdn along over 2f out: nvr on terms* **10/1**
050 10 1 1/4 **Tight Knit (USA)**[36] 2455 4-8-11 48 (b) DuranFentiman 13
(John Weymes) *hld up in midfield: pushed along over 2f out: wknd over 1f out* **100/1**
0500 11 shd **Cheeky Wee Red**[8] 3363 6-8-5 45 (bt[1]) ConnorBeasley(3) 10
(Alistair Whillans) *dwlt: hld up: drvn along over 2f out: sn btn* **28/1**
-006 12 5 **Travis County (IRE)**[8] 3365 5-9-7 58 (b[1]) DaleSwift 14
(Brian Ellison) *slowly away and early reminders: t.k.h and sn prom: rdn over 3f out: wknd over 2f out* **25/1**
2m 9.69s (-2.21) **Going Correction** -0.375s/f (Firm) 12 Ran SP% **116.7**
Speed ratings (Par 101): **93,92,88,86,85 84,83,70,68,67 67,63**
CSF £19.29 CT £310.99 TOTE £6.60: £2.40, £1.40, £7.30; EX 20.30 Trifecta £718.10.
**Owner** Dr Marwan Koukash **Bred** Alain Plainfosse **Trained** Musley Bank, N Yorks
■ Stewards' Enquiry : David Nolan four-day ban: used whip above permitted level down the shoulder in the forehand (Jul, 10,14-16)
**FOCUS**
This moderate contest was run at a decent gallop. The winner posted his best figure since last summer and the runner-up was back to his best.

## 3624 BETFRED SUPPORTS JACK BERRY HOUSE H'CAP 1m 2f 32y
5:00 (5:02) (Class 5) (0-75,75) 4-Y-O+ £2,587 (£770; £384; £192) Stalls Centre

Form RPR
-033 1 **Corton Lad**[19] 3004 4-9-5 73 (tp) TomEaves 1 82
(Keith Dalgleish) *t.k.h: mde all: qcknd clr over 3f out: pushed along and kpt on wl fr 2f out: unchal* **7/4**[1]
6202 2 3 3/4 **Bling King**[30] 2654 5-9-7 75 PJMcDonald 2 76
(Geoffrey Harker) *chsd wnr: rdn along 3f out: kpt on same pce fr 2f out* **11/4**[2]
3105 3 1 1/4 **Outlaw Torn (IRE)**[9] 3334 5-8-8 67 (e) DuilioDaSilva(5) 3 66
(Richard Guest) *taken early to post: t.k.h: hld up in tch: effrt and rdn over 2f out: kpt on fnl f: no imp* **11/2**
003- 4 1 **Painted Tail (IRE)**[182] 2974 7-8-11 65 DavidAllan 6 62
(Alan Swinbank) *hld up: drvn along over 2f out: sme hdwy fnl f: nvr on terms* **16/1**
310- 5 1 **Woodstock (IRE)**[31] 6552 4-8-9 68 GarryWhillans(5) 5 63
(Alistair Whillans) *chsd ldrs: drvn along 3f out: wknd over 1f out* **28/1**
1641 6 3 3/4 **Jacobs Son**[21] 2935 6-9-1 69 RaulDaSilva 4 57
(Michael Appleby) *hld up in tch: drvn and hung lft over 2f out: sn wknd* **7/2**[3]
2m 10.64s (-1.26) **Going Correction** -0.375s/f (Firm) 6 Ran SP% **110.0**
Speed ratings (Par 103): **90,87,86,85,84 81**
CSF £6.47 TOTE £2.70: £1.50, £1.70; EX 7.10 Trifecta £21.50.
**Owner** J Hutton **Bred** Frank Brady And Brian Scanlon **Trained** Carluke, S Lanarks

**FOCUS**
The winner is rated back to his 3yo form.

## 3625 BETFRED HALF TIME IN-PLAY BOOSTS H'CAP 7f
5:30 (5:30) (Class 5) (0-75,73) 3-Y-O £2,587 (£770; £384; £192) Stalls Centre

Form RPR
5213 1 **Twin Appeal (IRE)**19 3002 3-9-7 73.....................(b1) GrahamGibbons 2 87+
(David Barron) *trckd ldrs: pushed along 1/2-way: hdwy to ld 1f out: rdn out* 7/4[1]
-001 2 1 3/4 **Native Falls (IRE)**5 3485 3-8-12 64 6ex............................. DavidAllan 3 75+
(Alan Swinbank) *led: rdn over 2f out: hdd 1f out: rallied: one pce last 100yds* 7/2[2]
-003 3 1 3/4 **Street Boss (IRE)**7 3406 3-8-3 55.............................. DuranFentiman 5 60
(Tim Easterby) *hld up: rdn and hdwy over 2f out: chsd ldrs over 1f out: kpt on same pce ins fnl f* 33/1
6032 4 1 3/4 **Proclamationofwar**14 3137 3-8-12 69........................ ShaneGray(5) 6 69
(Kevin Ryan) *cl up: rdn over 2f out: edgd rt over 1f out: sn no ex* 9/2[3]
2310 5 hd **Rough Courte (IRE)**13 3195 3-9-7 73......................... SamHitchcott 4 73
(Mick Channon) *taken early to post: in tch: drvn and outpcd over 2f out: no imp fr over 1f out* 10/1
0440 6 3 **Lomond Lassie**8 3360 3-8-4 56.............................. JamesSullivan 8 48
(Keith Dalgleish) *hld up: pushed along over 2f out: nvr able to chal* 16/1
1663 7 hd **Two Shades Of Grey (IRE)**7 3405 3-9-1 67.............. TonyHamilton 9 59
(Richard Fahey) *hld up bhd ldng gp: drvn and outpcd over 2f out: n.d after* 13/2
01-0 8 2 **Giant Samurai (USA)**19 3002 3-9-6 72.........................(b) PhillipMakin 7 58
(John Quinn) *in tch: drvn and outpcd over 2f out: btn over 1f out* 28/1

1m 25.24s (-2.56) **Going Correction** -0.25s/f (Firm) 8 Ran SP% 111.5
Speed ratings (Par 99): **104,102,100,98,97 94,94,91**
CSF £7.40 CT £132.52 TOTE £2.60: £1.20, £1.30, £4.00; EX 10.50 Trifecta £234.30.
**Owner** Twinacre Nurseries Ltd **Bred** Glashare House Stud **Trained** Maunby, N Yorks

**FOCUS**
A fair handicap run at a strong gallop. The winner posted a clear personal best and this looks form to be positive about.
T/Jkpt: £29435.50 to a £1 stake. Pool of £41458.59 - 0.50 winning units. T/Plt: £10.60 to a £1 stake. Pool of £79361.59 - 5445.37 winning tickets. T/Qpdt: £4.20 to a £1 stake. Pool of £5350.39 - 924.23 winning tickets. RY

# 3156 YARMOUTH (L-H)
Thursday, June 26

**OFFICIAL GOING: Good to firm (7.4)**
Bottom bend dolled out 1.5m and races on Round course increased by 7m.
Wind: light, across Weather: dry and sunny

## 3626 HAVEN SEASHORE AT GREAT YARMOUTH MAIDEN STKS 6f 3y
2:20 (2:23) (Class 5) 2-Y-O £3,234 (£962; £481; £240) Stalls Centre

Form RPR
1 **Belardo (IRE)** 2-9-5 0.................................... AndreaAtzeni 2 89+
(Roger Varian) *hld up wl in tch in midfield: shkn up and clsd to join ldr over 1f out: nudged along to ld ins fnl f: qcknd clr fnl 100yds: readily* 8/13[1]
0 2 2 1/4 **Heartbreak Hero**26 2777 2-9-5 0.............................. SebSanders 3 78
(William Haggas) *led for 2f: chsd ldr tl led again ent fnl 2f: rdn wl over 1f out: hdd ins fnl f: sn brushed aside by wnr but kpt on for clr 2nd* 5/1[3]
3 3 3 1/4 **Siren's Cove**15 3119 2-9-0 0.................................. KierenFallon 8 63
(James Tate) *wl in tch in midfield: rdn and effrt 2f out: 4th and unable qck 1f out: no ch w ldrs but plugged on to go 3rd fnl 100yds* 7/2[2]
0 4 nk **Pivot Point (IRE)**16 3081 2-9-5 0........................... RobertHavlin 4 67
(Brian Meehan) *slowly in to stride: in tch in rr of main gp: rdn and effrt 2f out: 5th and wl hld 1f out: styd on and battling for 3rd fnl 100yds* 14/1
0 5 2 1/4 **Bushtown Boy (IRE)**13 3199 2-9-2 0.................. MichaelJMMurphy(3) 7 60
(Mark Johnston) *chsd ldrs: wnt 2nd ent fnl 2f: sn rdn: 3rd and outpcd 1f out: wknd and lost 2 pls fnl 100yds* 16/1
6 9 **Ya Halla (IRE)** 2-9-0 0.................................. FrederikTylicki 6 28
(Robert Cowell) *chsd ldr after 1f tl led 4f out: hdd ent fnl 2f: sn lost pl: wknd jst over 1f out* 33/1
7 nk **Presto Boy** 2-9-5 0........................................ HayleyTurner 1 32
(James Fanshawe) *chsd ldr for 1f out: steadily lost pl and in rr of main gp 1/2-way: rdn over 1f out: sn wknd* 16/1
8 43 **Hold Firm** 2-9-5 0.......................................... TedDurcan 5
(Mark H Tompkins) *v.s.a: sn detached in last: t.o 4f out* 66/1

1m 11.77s (-2.63) **Going Correction** -0.325s/f (Firm) 8 Ran SP% 123.7
Speed ratings (Par 93): **104,101,96,96,93 81,80,23**
CSF £4.94 TOTE £1.40: £1.10, £1.80, £1.20; EX 5.30 Trifecta £11.60.
**Owner** Prince A A Faisal **Bred** Ballylinch Stud **Trained** Newmarket, Suffolk

**FOCUS**
The going was fast despite watering and the jockeys described it as "quick but safe". Quite an interesting maiden that has thrown up Gimcrack winner Showcasing, plus several Listed winners, in recent seasons, and this looked another strong edition.

## 3627 CONFERENCES AT GREAT YARMOUTH H'CAP 7f 3y
2:50 (2:54) (Class 6) (0-65,65) 3-Y-O £1,940 (£577; £288; £144) Stalls Centre

Form RPR
-426 1 **Tyrsal (IRE)**47 2163 3-9-7 65.............................. AndreaAtzeni 6 71
(Robert Eddery) *in tch: rdn and hdwy to ld 1f out: r.o wl and drew clr fnl 100yds: readily* 11/4[2]
0-00 2 2 3/4 **Hot Amber (USA)**7 3406 3-7-10 47.............................[1] CamHardie(7) 7 46
(Robert Cowell) *chsd ldrs: rdn and effrt to chal 2f out: led over 1f out: hdd 1f out: outpcd by wnr fnl 100yds: plugged on to hold 2nd* 33/1
4323 3 hd **Handwoven (IRE)**8 3360 3-9-4 65...................(b) MichaelJMMurphy(3) 1 63
(Mark Johnston) *chsd ldr tl led 2f out: sn rdn and nt qckn: hdd over 1f out: outpcd by wnr fnl 100yds* 9/4[1]
0006 4 1/2 **Palace Princess (FR)**15 3124 3-9-0 58 ow2................(b) SebSanders 3 55
(Ed Dunlop) *stdd and bmpd s: hld up in tch in last pair: effrt u.p over 1f out: no ch w wnr but kpt on ins fnl f* 14/1
44-5 5 nk **Libra Romana (IRE)**155 280 3-8-8 52............................ LukeMorris 8 48
(Sir Mark Prescott Bt) *in tch in midfield: rdn over 2f out: unable qck ent fnl f: no ch w wnr and edgd lft ins fnl f* 12/1
00-4 6 2 1/2 **Reaffirmed (IRE)**15 3124 3-9-2 60.............................. PatCosgrave 5 50
(Ed Vaughan) *stdd s: t.k.h: hld up wl in tch in midfield: rdn and effrt over 1f out: wknd 1f out* 3/1[3]
460 7 1/2 **Marweena (IRE)**48 2126 3-9-2 65.......................... LouisSteward(5) 4 53
(Michael Bell) *hld up in tch in last pair: rdn and effrt 2f out: chsd ldrs and drvn over 1f out: no ex: wknd fnl f* 12/1
0454 8 1/2 **Previous Acclaim (IRE)**15 3121 3-8-2 46 oh1................ JimmyQuinn 2 33
(Julia Feilden) *led tl 2f: sn btn: bhd 1f out* 20/1

1m 24.77s (-1.83) **Going Correction** -0.325s/f (Firm) 8 Ran SP% 112.2
Speed ratings (Par 97): **97,93,93,92 89,89,88**
CSF £77.86 CT £234.40 TOTE £4.60: £1.50, £7.30, £1.10; EX 83.20 Trifecta £253.80.
**Owner** Phillips, Fullerton & Riesebieter **Bred** Daniel Furini **Trained** Newmarket, Suffolk
■ Stewards' Enquiry : Seb Sanders three-day ban: weighed in 2lb heavy (Jul 16-18)

**FOCUS**
This probably didn't take much winning and the winner is rated in line with better view of AW form.

## 3628 BURLINGTON PALM HOTEL H'CAP 7f 3y
3:20 (3:20) (Class 5) (0-75,74) 4-Y-O+ £2,587 (£770; £384; £192) Stalls Centre

Form RPR
3550 1 **Pearl Nation (USA)**51 2054 5-9-6 74............................ AndrewMullen 5 84+
(Michael Appleby) *chsd ldng pair: shkn up 3f out: rdn and hdwy to ld over 1f out: hdd and bmpd fnl 100yds: fought bk to ld again fnl 50yds: pushed out* 11/8[1]
0664 2 nk **Vallarta (IRE)**12 3213 4-9-4 72............................... TedDurcan 1 81
(Mick Channon) *stdd s: hld up in tch in rr: rdn and effrt over 1f out: drvn to ld: edgd lft and bmpd wnr fnl 100yds: hdd and no ex fnl 50yds* 11/4[2]
3/ 3 3 1/2 **Don't Be**195 4-9-4 72............................................ LukeMorris 3 72
(Sir Mark Prescott Bt) *chsd ldr: rdn over 2f out: drvn and ev ch over 1f out: outpcd 1f out: wknd ins fnl f* 10/1
3122 4 3 3/4 **Sakash**38 2400 4-9-4 72.......................................... FrederikTylicki 4 62
(J R Jenkins) *racd keenly: led tl rdn and hdd over 1f out: 4th and btn 1f out: wknd ins fnl f* 9/2[3]
4063 5 1/2 **Fantasy Gladiator**126 677 8-9-2 70.............................. PatCosgrave 2 59
(John Quinn) *stdd s: hld up in tch: effrt u.p 2f out: no imp over 1f out: wknd ins fnl f* 7/1

1m 23.54s (-3.06) **Going Correction** -0.325s/f (Firm) 5 Ran SP% 108.5
Speed ratings (Par 103): **104,103,99,95,94**
CSF £5.18 TOTE £3.20: £1.30, £1.50; EX 6.20 Trifecta £41.30.
**Owner** Iddon, M&C Dixon, Taylor, Finn, O'Brien **Bred** William A Carl Estate **Trained** Danethorpe, Notts

**FOCUS**
A tight little handicap on paper, despite the small field, and run 1.23secs faster than the preceding 3yo contest. The winner looked at least as good as ever.

## 3629 GREENE KING FESTIVAL AT YARMOUTH H'CAP 1m 3y
3:50 (3:50) (Class 4) (0-80,79) 4-Y-O+ £4,787 (£1,424; £711; £355) Stalls Centre

Form RPR
0002 1 **Luhaif**10 3306 4-9-2 79........................................(b) ShelleyBirkett(5) 2 84
(Julia Feilden) *mde all: 4 l clr 1/2-way: rdn 2f out: pressed ins fnl f: fnd ex and holding rivals towards fin* 2/1[2]
-510 2 1/2 **Hot Mustard**17 3056 4-7-9 60.............................. CamHardie(7) 1 64
(Michael Bell) *t.k.h: sn chsng wnr: rdn ent fnl 2f: drvn over 1f out: styd on and pressing wnr fnl 100yds: styd on same pce and hld towards fin* 15/8[1]
2631 3 1/2 **Mishrif (USA)**57 1886 8-9-4 76.................................(v) FrederikTylicki 4 79
(J R Jenkins) *hld up in rr: rdn 2f out: styd on wl ins fnl f: wnt 3rd towards fin: nvr gng to rch wnr* 9/2
-255 4 1/2 **Rouge Nuage (IRE)**14 3162 4-8-12 70.........................(b) JimmyQuinn 3 72
(Conrad Allen) *t.k.h: chsd ldng pair: rdn 2f out: styd on u.p and pressing wnr fnl 100yds: styd on same pce and lost 3rd towards fin* 7/2[3]

1m 37.66s (-2.94) **Going Correction** -0.325s/f (Firm) 4 Ran SP% 108.5
Speed ratings (Par 105): **101,100,100,99**
CSF £6.10 TOTE £3.30; EX 9.00 Trifecta £16.30.
**Owner** R J Creese **Bred** T R G Vestey **Trained** Exning, Suffolk

**FOCUS**
The feature race and an all-the-way success for the top weight.

## 3630 LADIES NIGHT AT GREAT YARMOUTH H'CAP 6f 3y
4:20 (4:21) (Class 6) (0-65,65) 4-Y-O+ £1,940 (£577; £288; £144) Stalls Centre

Form RPR
34-0 1 **Uprise**36 2463 5-9-1 62..........................................(t) RyanPowell(3) 3 73
(George Margarson) *stdd and bmpd s: hld up in tch in rr: gd hdwy over 1f out: led 1f out: in command whn edgd lft u.p ins fnl f: r.o: comf* 8/1
6-00 2 2 1/4 **Copper To Gold**35 2479 5-7-9 46 oh1............................ CamHardie(7) 5 50+
(Robin Bastiman) *taken down early: awkward as stalls opened and slowly away: reminder after s: sn rcvrd and in tch in midfield: rdn and unable qck over 1f out: styd on ins fnl f: wnt 2nd towards fin* 6/1[3]
-000 3 1 1/4 **Jack Barker**30 2658 5-8-2 46 oh1.................................... JimmyQuinn 7 46
(Robin Bastiman) *led: rdn ent fnl 2f: hdd 1f out: sn outpcd and wnr and styd on same pce after* 33/1
4210 4 hd **Sweet Talking Guy (IRE)**47 2147 4-9-4 65............(t) SimonPearce(3) 1 64
(Lydia Pearce) *hld up in tch towards rr: hdwy over 2f out: drvn and chsng ldrs over 1f out: chsd wnr but outpcd ins fnl f: lost 2 pls towards fin* 7/4[1]
052- 5 1 **Aaranyow (IRE)**301 5930 6-8-3 52............................... NathanAlison(5) 8 48
(Clifford Lines) *chsd ldrs: chsd ldr 4f out: drvn and unable qck over 1f out: lost 2nd jst ins fnl f: sn outpcd* 8/1
5-06 6 3/4 **Emerald Sea**22 2887 4-9-7 65.........................................(b1) TedDurcan 6 59
(Chris Wall) *in tch in midfield: hdwy over 2f out: drvn and chsd ldrs over 1f out: no ex 1f out: wknd ins fnl f* 4/1[2]
01-6 7 4 **Miakora**15 3125 6-8-6 50........................................ PaoloSirigu 2 31
(Mick Quinn) *chsd ldr for 2f: rdn over 3f out: struggling and btn over 1f out: wknd fnl f* 14/1
6033 8 6 **Senora Lobo (IRE)**24 2831 4-7-11 46 oh1..............(p) NatashaEaton(5) 4 8
(Lisa Williamson) *t.k.h: chsd ldrs tl 2f: sn lost pl u.p: bhd fnl f* 14/1

1m 12.56s (-1.84) **Going Correction** -0.325s/f (Firm) 8 Ran SP% 109.1
Speed ratings (Par 101): **99,96,94,94,92 91,86,78**
CSF £49.93 CT £1367.86 TOTE £8.20: £2.20, £2.30, £6.60; EX 62.80 Trifecta £2152.30.
**Owner** Pitfield Partnership **Bred** Cheveley Park Stud Ltd **Trained** Newmarket, Suffolk

**FOCUS**
A modest sprint handicap run 0.79secs slower than the opening juvenile contest. The winner is rated in line with last year's form off a career-low mark.

## 3631 GREAT YARMOUTH SCOOTER RALLY MEDIAN AUCTION MAIDEN STKS 1m 2f 21y
4:50 (4:50) (Class 6) 3-Y-O £2,587 (£770; £384; £192) Stalls Low

Form RPR
1 **Redkirk** 3-9-5 0............................................... SebSanders 5 89+
(William Haggas) *t.k.h: hld up in tch in last pair: clsd to join ldrs over 2f out: led wl over 1f out: shkn up and readily wnt clr 1f out: in n.d after: easily* 6/1[3]
2 2 5 **Perspicace**50 2081 3-8-12 0........................................ CamHardie(7) 6 77
(Roger Charlton) *t.k.h: chsd ldr: rdn and ev ch over 2f out: brushed aside by wnr over 1f out: kpt on and wnt 2nd fnl 100yds* 1/1[1]



The Form Book, Raceform Ltd, Newbury, RG14 5SJ

362 **3** 2 1/4 **Cincinnati Girl (IRE)**[24] 2850 3-9-0 69 PatCosgrave 1 68
(Denis Coakley) *led and set stdy gallop: rdn over 2f out: hdd and brushed aside by wnr over 1f out: lost 2nd and wknd fnl 100yds* **5/2**[2]

50-4 **4** 2 **Mishko (IRE)**[11] 3268 3-9-5 70 FrederikTylicki 7 69
(Steve Gollings) *t.k.h: wl in tch in midfield: rdn over 2f out: 4th and btn whn edgd lft u.p 1f out: wknd ins fnl f* **16/1**

**5** 1 1/2 **Roxy Hart** 3-9-0 0 JimmyQuinn 4 61
(Ed Vaughan) *hld up in tch: rdn over 2f out: outpcd 2f out: wknd over 1f out* **50/1**

2-45 **6** 1/2 **Swilken**[22] 2883 3-9-5 69 TedDurcan 3 65
(Mark H Tompkins) *t.k.h: chsd ldng pair: n.m.r 3f out: rdn ent fnl 2f: unable qck and btn over 1f out: wknd fnl f* **12/1**

**7** 23 **Focail Mear** 3-8-11 0 RyanPowell(3) 2 16
(John Ryan) *s.i.s: a in rr: rdn and lost tch over 2f out: t.o fnl f* **66/1**

2m 9.95s (-0.55) **Going Correction** +0.125s/f (Good) **7 Ran SP% 109.9**
Speed ratings (Par 97): **107,103,101,99,98 98,79**
CSF £11.46 TOTE £6.10: £3.60, £1.50; EX 14.60 Trifecta £33.00.
**Owner** Scotney/Symonds/Fisher Partnership **Bred** Mrs R D Peacock **Trained** Newmarket, Suffolk

**FOCUS**
Those with form set a modest standard in this 3yo maiden and they were brushed aside by one of the newcomers.

## 3632 FOLLOW US ON TWITTER YARMOUTH RACECOURSE H'CAP 1m 6f 17y
5:20 (5:20) (Class 5) (0-70,70) 4-Y-0+ **£2,587** (£770; £384; £192) **Stalls High**

Form RPR

33-2 **1** 2 **Dumbfounded (FR)**[21] 2916 6-8-10 66 CamHardie(7) 6 71
(Lady Herries) *hld up in tch in last pair: hdwy 3f out: rdn and ev ch 2f out: edgd lft and styd on same pce ins fnl f* **15/8**[1]

1043 **2** 1/2 **Dr Finley (IRE)**[11] 3269 7-8-3 55 (v) SimonPearce(3) 1 59
(Lydia Pearce) *sn led: rdn over 2f out: hrd pressed 2f out: hdd 1f out: styd on same pce after* **10/1**

6326 **3** 1 1/2 **No Such Number**[23] 1501 6-9-4 67 KierenFallon 2 69
(Julia Feilden) *chsd ldr tl over 3f out: nt clr run on inner and swtchd rt over 1f out: nt clr run and swtchd rt again jst ins fnl f: kpt on u.p: no threat to wnr* **10/3**[2]

-U00 **4** nk **Baan (USA)**[88] 1197 11-8-1 53 RosieJessop(3) 5 55
(James Eustace) *hld up in tch in last pair: rdn and effrt ent fnl 2f: kpt on same pce u.p fnl f* **7/1**

463- **5** 2 1/2 **Hell Hath No Fury**[322] 5196 5-8-2 51 oh5 AndrewMullen 4 49
(Michael Appleby) *chsd ldrs: wnt 2nd over 3f out: rdn and ev ch 2f out: no ex and btn whn short of room ins fnl f: sn wknd: eased towards fin* **9/2**[3]

0506 **6** 34 **Berkeley Street (USA)**[24] 2843 4-7-11 51 oh1 (p) NoelGarbutt(5) 7 2
(Jane Chapple-Hyam) *in tch in midfield: rdn and effrt over 3f out: wknd 2f out: t.o fnl f* **25/1**

4300 **D** **Royal Alcor (IRE)**[28] 2701 7-9-2 70 (t) ShelleyBirkett(5) 3 78
(Gay Kelleway) *hld up in tch: clsd over 2f out: nt clr run 2f out: swtchd rt over 1f out: rdn and str run to ld 1f out: r.o wl* **12/1**

3m 11.11s (3.51) **Going Correction** +0.125s/f (Good) **7 Ran SP% 109.2**
Speed ratings (Par 103): **92,92,91,91,90 70,94**
CSF £31.86 TOTE £10.00: £4.80, £1.30; EX 35.80 Trifecta £186.50.
**Owner** Lady Sarah Clutton **Bred** Haras Du Taillis **Trained** Patching, W Sussex

**FOCUS**
An ordinary staying handicap, run at a moderate early gallop. The winner bounced back from two poor runs for a personal best on turf, mirroring AW progress.
T/Plt: £68.40 to a £1 stake. Pool of £56565.12 - 603.60 winning tickets. T/Qpdt: £55.50 to a £1 stake. Pool of £2399.82 - 31.99 winning tickets. SP

3633 - 3639a (Foreign Racing) - See Raceform Interactive

# 805 DEAUVILLE (R-H)
Thursday, June 26

**OFFICIAL GOING: Turf: good; polytrack: standard**

## 3640a PRIX DE L'HOTELLERIE (MAIDEN) (2YO) (POLYTRACK) 6f 110y
3:40 (12:00) 2-Y-0 **£10,416** (£4,166; £3,125; £2,083; £1,041)

RPR

**1** **Speed Machine (IRE)**[15] 3113 2-9-2 0 IoritzMendizabal 8 82
(Paul Cole) *worked across fr wdst draw and sn led on rail: mde rest: rdn and qcknd 2f out: edgd lft u.p fnl f but kpt on wl and in control: readily* **47/10**[2]

**2** 1 **First Company (FR)**[28] 2-9-2 0 ChristopheSoumillon 4 79
(J-C Rouget, France) **7/10**[1]

**3** snk **Raison D'Etre (FR)** 2-8-9 0 AnthonyCrastus 7 72
(F Vermeulen, France) **112/10**

**4** 3 **Vianella (FR)**[6] 2-8-13 0 TheoBachelot 1 67
(S Wattel, France) **11/2**[3]

**5** 1 1/4 **Maply (FR)** 2-9-2 0 MorganDelalande 2 67
(Y Barberot, France) **68/1**

**6** 5 **Maisie's Minion** 2-9-2 0 MaximeGuyon 6 53
(F-H Graffard, France) **79/10**

**7** 2 **Stocksandshares (IRE)** 2-9-2 0 AntoineHamelin 3 47
(Matthieu Palussiere, France) **29/1**

**8** 6 **Danish Design (FR)** 2-8-9 0 Christophe-PatriceLemaire 5 23
(J E Pease, France) **269/10**

1m 20.77s (80.77) **8 Ran SP% 119.6**
WIN (incl. 1 euro stake): 5.70. PLACES: 1.50, 1.10, 1.90. DF: 4.10. SF: 11.50.
**Owner** Lane Racing Ltd **Bred** R Jeffcock **Trained** Whatcombe, Oxon

3641 - (Foreign Racing) - See Raceform Interactive

# 3215 CHESTER (L-H)
Friday, June 27

**OFFICIAL GOING: Good (7.2) changing to good to soft after race 3 (7.20)**
Rail between 6f and 1f moved out 3yd with drop in at that point and races increased in distance by 13yds.
Wind: almost nil Weather: overcast, light rain 1st 2 races

## 3642 STELLA ARTOIS MAIDEN FILLIES' STKS (BOBIS RACE) 7f 2y
6:20 (6:20) (Class 4) 2-Y-0 **£6,469** (£1,925; £962; £481) **Stalls Low**

Form RPR

5 **1** **Disavow**[9] 3358 2-9-0 0 FrannyNorton 2 69
(Mark Johnston) *mde all: drvn over 2 l clr over 1f out: lasted home* **13/8**[1]

50 **2** 1/2 **Euthenia**[13] 3232 2-8-11 0 WilliamTwiston-Davies(3) 3 68
(Mick Channon) *hld up in last: hdwy on outside over 2f out: styd on to take 2nd nr fin* **25/1**

3 **3** 3/4 **You're My Cracker**[16] 3107 2-9-0 0 RobertHavlin 6 66+
(Donald McCain) *chsd ldrs: effrt over 3f out: styd on to take 2nd last 50yds* **5/1**[3]

**4** 1/2 **Elle Dorado** 2-9-0 0 RichardKingscote 4 65+
(Tom Dascombe) *chsd ldrs: effrt 3f out: nt clr run over 2f out: swtchd lft over 1f out: kpt on* **11/1**

5 **5** 1 **Super Quick (IRE)**[13] 3255 2-9-0 0 DavidNolan 5 62
(Richard Fahey) *chsd ldr: hung rt and reminder over 3f out: one pce over 1f out* **7/4**[2]

4 **6** 1 **Vita Mina**[14] 3173 2-9-0 0 StephenCraine 1 60
(David Evans) *half-rrd s: sn chsng ldrs: drvn 3f out: hit rail over 1f out: wknd last 100yds* **16/1**

1m 31.3s (4.80) **Going Correction** +0.525s/f (Yiel) **6 Ran SP% 109.2**
Speed ratings (Par 92): **93,92,91,91,89 88**
CSF £34.86 TOTE £3.10: £1.20, £10.40; EX 23.50 Trifecta £91.80.
**Owner** Sheikh Hamdan bin Mohammed Al Maktoum **Bred** Darley **Trained** Middleham Moor, N Yorks

**FOCUS**
Some afternoon/evening rain meant the ground was changed to good from good to firm before racing. However, the opening two times were both slow, suggesting the ground may have been slower than that, possibly good to soft. The race average is modest and this looks ordinary again.

## 3643 LINDOP TOYOTA GT86 H'CAP (BOBIS RACE) 1m 2f 75y
6:50 (6:51) (Class 4) (0-80,75) 3-Y-0 **£6,469** (£1,925; £962; £481) **Stalls High**

Form RPR

2450 **1** **Our Gabrial (IRE)**[13] 3243 3-9-7 75 DavidNolan 1 89
(Richard Fahey) *led 1f: trckd ldrs: t.k.h: 2nd over 2f out: hung lft and led last 100yds: kpt on* **5/1**[3]

2-01 **2** 3/4 **Empress Ali (IRE)**[23] 2899 3-9-2 73 WilliamTwiston-Davies(3) 9 86
(Tom Tate) *swtchd lft after s: led after 1f: drvn over 2f out: hdd and crowded ins fnl f: no ex* **4/1**[1]

42-6 **3** 8 **Alpine Storm (IRE)**[77] 1427 3-9-4 72 FrannyNorton 2 69
(Mark Johnston) *trckd ldrs: t.k.h: effrt over 2f out: 3rd over 1f out: one pce* **15/2**

3132 **4** 5 **Jazri**[15] 3135 3-8-11 65 RichardKingscote 4 53
(Milton Bradley) *trckd ldrs: drvn over 3f out: wknd appr fnl f* **9/2**[2]

-525 **5** 1/2 **Pershing**[43] 2273 3-9-5 73 PaoloSirigu 7 60
(Marco Botti) *dwlt: hld up in rr: j. path over 7f out: kpt on fnl 2f: nvr a factor* **15/2**

3062 **6** 3/4 **Masterpaver**[8] 3391 3-8-10 67 (v) RobertTart(3) 8 53
(Alan Bailey) *mid-div: drvn over 4f out: sn chsng ldrs: one pce* **6/1**

1516 **7** 2 1/2 **Solo Hunter**[27] 2761 3-9-6 74 StephenCraine 5 55
(David Evans) *mid-div: drvn over 3f out: nvr a factor* **10/1**

050- **8** 18 **Enfys Hud**[256] 7252 3-8-6 63 ThomasBrown(3) 3 10
(David Evans) *in rr: drvn 5f out: sn bhd: t.o* **20/1**

-600 **9** 13 **Berrahri (IRE)**[21] 2962 3-9-5 73 RobertHavlin 6
(John Best) *dwlt: hld up in rr: effrt 3f out: eased and lost pl over 2f out: virtually p.u: t.o* **25/1**

2m 14.98s (3.78) **Going Correction** +0.525s/f (Yiel) **9 Ran SP% 110.4**
Speed ratings (Par 101): **105,104,98,94,93 93,91,76,66**
CSF £23.50 CT £138.26 TOTE £5.80: £2.60, £1.60, £2.50; EX 21.80 Trifecta £144.70.
**Owner** Dr Marwan Koukash **Bred** Michael Woodlock & Seamus Kennedy **Trained** Musley Bank, N Yorks

**FOCUS**
Not strong form for the level with the topweight and winner rated 5lb below the ceiling for the grade, but the front two pulled clear in what appeared a soundly run contest.

## 3644 GROSVENOR SHOPPING CENTRE/EBF STALLIONS FILLIES' H'CAP 1m 2f 75y
7:20 (7:21) (Class 3) (0-90,88) 3-Y-0+ **£9,703** (£2,887; £1,443; £721) **Stalls High**

Form RPR

-212 **1** **Cosseted**[27] 2783 4-9-13 87 RobertHavlin 3 97+
(James Fanshawe) *rr-div: pushed along over 7f out: hdwy over 3f out: styd on to ld last 150yds: drvn out* **6/4**[1]

4404 **2** 1 1/2 **Coincidently**[6] 3476 4-8-10 73 ow1 RobertTart(3) 8 80
(Alan Bailey) *hld up in rr: hdwy over 3f out: styd on fnl f: tk 2nd post* **10/1**

2242 **3** nse **Maracuja**[16] 3103 3-8-2 74 FrannyNorton 4 81
(Mark Johnston) *chsd ldrs: chal over 2f out: edgd lft and kpt on same pce last 100yds* **4/1**[3]

0020 **4** 1 1/2 **Maven**[13] 3251 6-9-7 88 RachelRichardson(7) 1 92
(Tim Easterby) *led: hdd and no ex jst ins fnl f* **8/1**

21-1 **5** 1 1/2 **Tears Of The Sun**[28] 2719 3-8-8 80 HarryBentley 2 86
(Roger Varian) *trckd ldrs: swtchd ins over 1f out: sn nt clr run and eased: nt rcvr* **7/2**[2]

-314 **6** 3 3/4 **Pandorica**[13] 3218 6-8-12 72 oh1 (p) StevieDonohoe 6 66
(Bernard Llewellyn) *rr-div: drvn to chse ldrs 3f out: fdd ins fnl f* **33/1**

4251 **7** 39 **Taro Tywod (IRE)**[10] 3325 5-8-13 76 6ex WilliamTwiston-Davies(3) 7
(Mark Brisbourne) *in rr: drvn over 4f out: bhd fnl 3f: t.o* **16/1**

445 **8** 39 **Arianrhod (IRE)**[20] 1817 3-8-0 72 oh4 (b) PaoloSirigu 5
(Donald McCain) *hld up in rr: t.k.h: trckd ldrs after 2f: drvn over 4f out: sn lost pl: t.o 2f out: virtually p.u* **40/1**

2m 14.5s (3.30) **Going Correction** +0.525s/f (Yiel)
**WFA** 3 from 4yo+ 12lb **8 Ran SP% 113.7**
Speed ratings (Par 104): **107,105,105,104,103 100,69,37**
CSF £18.05 CT £50.63 TOTE £3.30: £1.40, £3.10, £1.10; EX 15.70 Trifecta £80.20.
**Owner** Cheveley Park Stud **Bred** Cheveley Park Stud Ltd **Trained** Newmarket, Suffolk

**FOCUS**
A strongly run handicap. The winner continues to progress and the runner-up ran as well as ever.

## 3645 MOET & CHANDON CLAIMING STKS 7f 122y
7:55 (7:55) (Class 4) 4-Y-0+ **£6,469** (£1,925; £962; £481) **Stalls Low**

Form RPR

0-00 **1** **Big Johnny D (IRE)**[49] 2113 5-9-0 96 FrannyNorton 4 83
(David Barron) *trckd ldrs: effrt and edgd rt over 1f out: r.o to ld fnl strides* **9/2**[2]

0001 **2** nk **Anaconda (FR)**[18] 3064 5-9-0 89 RichardKingscote 7 83
(Tom Dascombe) *led: drvn over 1 l ahd over 1f out: hdd and no ex nr fin: fatally injured* **5/2**[1]

1030 **3** 1 3/4 **Brae Hill (IRE)**[7] 3420 8-9-3 97 DavidNolan 2 81
(Richard Fahey) *chsd ldr: drvn over 2f out: kpt on same pce appr fnl f* **5/2**[1]

2350 **4** 3/4 **Capaill Liath (IRE)**[13] 3221 6-8-7 77 (p) ShaneGray(5) 3 74
(Kevin Ryan) *dwlt: in rr: effrt over 2f out: styd on fnl f* **14/1**

3011 **5** *½* **Conry (IRE)**[34] 2548 8-8-13 85 ........ StevieDonohoe 6 74
(Ian Williams) *hld up in rr: effrt over 2f out: kpt on fnl f* **8/1**[3]

5243 **6** *4* **Cyflymder (IRE)**[4] 3528 8-8-9 50 ........ HarryBentley 1 60
(David C Griffiths) *dwlt: sn chsng ldrs: drvn over 2f out: wknd fnl f* **50/1**

5000 **7** *2* **Sweet Lightning**[13] 3251 9-8-10 93 ........ SamJames(3) 5 59
(David O'Meara) *in rr: effrt over 2f out: wknd fnl f: eased nr fin* **9/2**[2]

1m 36.73s (2.93) **Going Correction** +0.525s/f (Yiel) **7** Ran SP% **113.2**
Speed ratings (Par 105): **106,105,103,103,102 98,96**
CSF £15.86 TOTE £9.50: £7.00, £1.50; EX 20.80 Trifecta £74.20.Capaill Liath was claimed by Mr Claes Bjorling for £12,000.
**Owner** Clive Washbourn **Bred** David McGuinness **Trained** Maunby, N Yorks

**FOCUS**
A good-quality claimer, but an ordinary pace and the sixth limits the form.

## 3646 CHESTER STANDARD H'CAP — 7f 2y

**8:30** (8:31) (Class 4) (0-85,83) 3-Y-O+ **£6,469** (£1,925; £962; £481) **Stalls** Low

Form RPR

0103 **1** **Ralphy Boy (IRE)**[9] 3361 5-9-3 **72** ........ RichardKingscote 1 81
(Alistair Whillans) *mde all: kpt on fnl f: jst hld on* **9/2**[2]

5014 **2** *hd* **Swift Cedar (IRE)**[13] 3221 4-9-6 **75** ........ FrannyNorton 5 83+
(David Evans) *mid-div: effrt on ins over 2f out: hdwy over 1f out: 2nd last 100yds: styd on: jst hld* **15/8**[1]

16-6 **3** *1½* **Gatepost (IRE)**[13] 3221 5-9-13 **82** ........ DavidNolan 10 87
(Richard Fahey) *trckd wnr: t.k.h: rdn and hung lft fr over 1f out: kpt on same pce* **9/1**

1342 **4** *3¾* **Caramack**[14] 3177 4-9-3 **77** ........ EoinWalsh(5) 2 72
(Richard Lee) *s.i.s: in rr: sme hdwy over 1f out: nvr a factor* **5/1**[3]

5462 **5** *1½* **Pashan Garh**[25] 2833 5-9-0 **69** ........ StevieDonohoe 4 60
(Pat Eddery) *chsd ldrs: wknd over 1f out* **12/1**

5-22 **6** *1¾* **Tidentime (USA)**[11] 3313 5-9-10 **82** ........ WilliamTwiston-Davies(3) 8 68
(Mick Channon) *hld up in rr: effrt on outer over 1f out: nvr on terms* **13/2**

5220 **7** *1¼* **Powerful Presence (IRE)**[13] 3221 8-9-11 **83** ........ SamJames(3) 9 66
(David O'Meara) *chsd ldrs: effrt over 2f out: wknd over 1f out* **12/1**

0331 **8** *1* **Sheikh The Reins (IRE)**[23] 2884 5-9-1 **70** ........(v) RobertHavlin 6 51
(John Best) *mid-div: effrt over 2f out: wknd over 1f out* **20/1**

1m 29.84s (3.34) **Going Correction** +0.525s/f (Yiel) **8** Ran SP% **113.1**
Speed ratings (Par 105): **101,100,99,94,93 91,89,88**
CSF £13.05 CT £71.26 TOTE £6.70: £1.60, £1.10, £2.40; EX 14.90 Trifecta £81.10.
**Owner** Frank Lowe **Bred** Frank Lowe **Trained** Newmill-On-Slitrig, Borders

**FOCUS**
An ordinary enough handicap in which the front three finished clear. This was the winner's best performance since he was a 2yo, and the runner-up is rated to last year's best.

## 3647 CRUISE NIGHTCLUB H'CAP (BOBIS RACE) — 7f 122y

**9:00** (9:03) (Class 4) (0-80,77) 3-Y-O **£6,469** (£1,925; £962; £481) **Stalls** Low

Form RPR

1 **1** **Buredyma**[34] 2560 3-9-7 **77** ........ RichardKingscote 3 85+
(William Haggas) *in rr: sn drvn along: hdwy on outer over 1f out: hmpd wl ins fnl f: led post* **2/1**[2]

-234 **2** *hd* **Mfiftythreedotcom (IRE)**[15] 3137 3-8-12 **68** ........ TonyHamilton 4 74
(Richard Fahey) *chsd ldng pair: drvn over 2f out: hmpd and swtchd lft wl ins fnl f: led clsng stages: hdd post* **4/1**[3]

0-31 **3** *¾* **Crafted (IRE)**[8] 3389 3-8-6 **62** 6ex ........ FrannyNorton 1 66+
(Mark Johnston) *w ldr: led after 1f: drvn over 1f out: hung bdly rt ins fnl f: hdd clsng stages* **7/4**[1]

2-04 **4** *1½* **Rangi Chase (IRE)**[24] 2871 3-9-4 **74** ........ DavidNolan 5 74
(Richard Fahey) *wnt rt s: hld up in rr: hdwy over 2f out: n.m.r over 1f out: kpt on same pce fnl f* **10/1**

-145 **5** *2¼* **Cahal (IRE)**[35] 2517 3-8-2 **58** oh1 ........ RaulDaSilva 2 53+
(David Nicholls) *led 1f: w ldr: drvn 3f out: wknd fnl 100yds* **8/1**

1m 38.31s (4.51) **Going Correction** +0.525s/f (Yiel) **5** Ran SP% **109.9**
Speed ratings (Par 101): **98,97,97,95,93**
CSF £10.16 TOTE £2.50: £1.10, £2.40; EX 9.50 Trifecta £16.70.
**Owner** Saleh Al Homaizi & Imad Al Sagar **Bred** Pantile Stud **Trained** Newmarket, Suffolk
■ Stewards' Enquiry : Franny Norton two-day ban: careless riding (Jul 14-15)

**FOCUS**
A soundly run affair as Crafted and Cahal took each other on at the head of affairs and that rather set things up for the winner. The runner-up has been rated as posting a small personal best, and possibly even better if the fourth confirms this level.
T/Plt: £75.70 to a £1 stake. Pool: £52,579.30 - 506.84 winning tickets. T/Qpdt: £11.90 to a £1 stake. Pool: £5,131.37 - 317.40 winning tickets. WG

# 3267 DONCASTER (L-H)

Friday, June 27

**OFFICIAL GOING: Good to firm (firm in places; 9.8) changing to good to firm after race 1 (2.00)**
Round course railed out from 10f to where it joins the straight and races of 10f and over increased by 15yds.
Wind: Light half behind Weather: Overcast and showers

## 3648 BETDAQ THE SPORTS BETTING EXCHANGE EBF STALLIONS MAIDEN FILLIES' STKS (BOBIS RACE) — 6f

**2:00** (2:00) (Class 5) 2-Y-O **£2,911** (£866; £432; £216) **Stalls** High

Form RPR

4 **1** **Fruity (IRE)**[29] 2697 2-9-0 0 ........ JamieSpencer 11 79+
(Clive Cox) *trckd ldrs: hdwy 1/2-way: sn cl up: rdn to ld wl over 1f out: clr ent fnl f: kpt on strly* **7/1**[3]

**2** *1¼* **Shahah** 2-9-0 0 ........ FrankieDettori 7 75+
(Richard Hannon) *hld up in tch: hdwy over 2f out: rdn to chse wnr ins fnl f: no imp towards fin* **8/1**

**3** *2¼* **Encore L'Amour** 2-9-0 0 ........ MartinHarley 9 69+
(David Simcock) *in rr: gd hdwy wl over 1f out: styd on strly fnl f: nrst fin* **50/1**

2 **4** *½* **Shahralasal (IRE)**[13] 3223 2-9-0 0 ........ PaulHanagan 3 67
(Roger Varian) *cl up: slt ld 1/2-way: rdn along and hdd wl over 1f out: drvn and wknd ent fnl f* **6/4**[1]

**5** *¾* **Simple Elegance (USA)** 2-9-0 0 ........ MartinLane 8 65
(Charlie Appleby) *dwlt and green in rr: hdwy and pushed along wl over 2f out: sn rdn: kpt on fnl f: nrst fin* **28/1**

5 **6** *½* **Hollie Point**[17] 3076 2-9-0 0 ........ WilliamBuick 5 63
(Charlie Appleby) *trckd ldrs: hdwy wl over 2f out: rdn along wl over 1f out: sn one pce* **10/3**[2]

**7** *1½* **Angels Wings (IRE)** 2-9-0 0 ........ JamesDoyle 2 59
(Charles Hills) *dwlt and towards rr: gd hdwy on wd outside over 2f out: rdn to chse ldrs wl over 1f out: sn one pce* **9/1**

5 **8** *1¼* **Summer Stroll (IRE)**[11] 3312 2-9-0 0 ........ DanielTudhope 4 55
(David O'Meara) *chsd ldrs: rdn along wl over 2f out: grad wknd* **20/1**

524 **9** *1¼* **Alderaan (IRE)**[14] 3188 2-9-0 0 ........[1] BarryMcHugh 1 51
(Tony Coyle) *t.k.h: cl up: rdn along wl over 2f out: wknd appr fnl f* **20/1**

0 **10** *7* **North Bay Lady (IRE)**[13] 3255 2-9-0 0 ........ GrahamLee 6 30
(John Wainwright) *in tch: rdn along 1/2-way: sn wknd* **100/1**

**11** *4½* **Ryedale Mist** 2-9-0 0 ........ DuranFentiman 10 17
(Tim Easterby) *slt ld: hdd 1/2-way: sn rdn along and wknd* **66/1**

1m 12.33s (-1.27) **Going Correction** -0.275s/f (Firm) **11** Ran SP% **114.1**
Speed ratings (Par 90): **97,95,92,91,90 90,88,86,84,75 69**
CSF £54.62 TOTE £8.30: £2.40, £2.20, £9.70; EX 65.20 Trifecta £2239.40 Part won. Pool: £2,985.91 - 0.36 winning tickets..
**Owner** Qatar Racing Limited **Bred** Rossenarra Bloodstock Limited **Trained** Lambourn, Berks

**FOCUS**
Overcast and cooler than of late. The ground was described as loose in places by a couple of jockeys. They came up the centre of the track in this decent 2yo fillies' maiden and the gallop was solid.

## 3649 BETDAQ 0% ON WORLD CUP CORRECT SCORES NOVICE STKS (BOBIS RACE) — 7f

**2:30** (2:30) (Class 4) 2-Y-O **£6,469** (£1,925; £962; £481) **Stalls** High

Form RPR

2 **1** **Hawkesbury**[16] 3113 2-9-0 0 ........ WilliamBuick 3 100+
(Charlie Appleby) *hld up in rr: smooth hdwy 3f out and sn cl up: led on bit appr fnl f: sn clr: easily* **4/5**[1]

1 **2** *7* **Russian Punch**[31] 2652 2-8-13 0 ........ GrahamLee 4 75
(James Given) *prom: led 3f out: rdn along 2f out: hdd and drvn appr fnl f: kpt on same pce* **11/1**

215 **3** *1* **Doomah (IRE)**[25] 2845 2-8-13 0 ........ FrankieDettori 1 72
(Richard Hannon) *t.k.h early: led: hdd 3f out: sn pushed along: rdn 2f out and sn one pce* **4/1**[3]

1 **4** *4½* **Jumeirah Glory (IRE)**[14] 3186 2-9-7 0 ........ PaulHanagan 2 68
(Richard Fahey) *trckd ldr: rdn along wl over 2f out: sn outpcd* **3/1**[2]

1m 24.9s (-1.40) **Going Correction** -0.275s/f (Firm) **4** Ran SP% **108.9**
Speed ratings (Par 95): **97,89,87,82**
CSF £9.42 TOTE £1.90; EX 8.10 Trifecta £15.30.
**Owner** Godolphin **Bred** Darley **Trained** Newmarket, Suffolk

**FOCUS**
The pace was fair despite the paucity of runners, with two travelling up the centre of the track and two against the stands' rail. The winner really impressed and the runner-up has been rated close to her debut win.

## 3650 BETDAQ £25 NO LOSE FREE BET H'CAP — 6f

**3:00** (3:01) (Class 5) (0-70,70) 3-Y-O **£3,234** (£962; £481; £240) **Stalls** High

Form RPR

0-42 **1** **Katawi**[16] 3124 3-9-2 **65** ........ GeorgeBaker 3 79+
(Chris Wall) *cl up: led 1/2-way: rdn clr ent fnl f: kpt on strly* **10/3**[1]

-455 **2** *2* **Traditionelle**[26] 2802 3-8-6 **55** ........ AndrewElliott 9 61+
(Tim Easterby) *in rr: rdn along and hdwy 2f out: str run ins fnl f: nt rch wnr* **12/1**

5302 **3** *2¼* **McCarthy Mor (IRE)**[8] 3380 3-8-9 **58** ........(v) PaulHanagan 7 57
(Richard Fahey) *t.k.h: trckd ldrs: hdwy 2f out: sn rdn: kpt on u.p fnl f* **6/1**[3]

0-00 **4** *¾* **Les Gar Gan (IRE)**[9] 3359 3-9-6 **69** ........(b) GrahamLee 5 66
(Keith Dalgleish) *trckd ldrs: hdwy over 2f out: rdn along wl over 1f out: drvn and kpt on fnl f* **6/1**[3]

-062 **5** *nk* **Disclosure**[10] 3342 3-9-6 **69** ........ RoystonFfrench 12 65
(Les Eyre) *t.k.h early: in tch: hdwy 2f out: sn rdn: styd on fnl f: nrst fin* **9/2**[2]

-204 **6** *nse* **Tell Me When**[7] 3440 3-8-6 **55** ........ BarryMcHugh 1 50
(Brian Rothwell) *cl up: effrt over 2f out: sn rdn and ev ch tl drvn appr fnl f: one pce* **25/1**

2405 **7** *1¾* **Argent Touch**[7] 3433 3-8-12 **61** ........ DaleSwift 10 51
(Derek Shaw) *s.i.s and in rr: hdwy 2f out: sn rdn and no imp* **22/1**

0325 **8** *½* **Jive**[11] 3300 3-9-7 **70** ........ JimmyFortune 2 58
(Richard Hannon) *trckd ldrs: hdwy 2f out: rdn over 1f out: wknd ent fnl f* **7/1**

64-0 **9** *2* **Winter Picnic (IRE)**[28] 2741 3-8-2 **51** oh2 ........ DuranFentiman 6 33
(Tim Easterby) *slt ld: pushed along and hdd 1/2-way: rdn over 2f out and sn wknd* **50/1**

0006 **10** *½* **Walta (IRE)**[8] 3406 3-8-8 **60** ........(b) BillyCray(3) 4 40
(Roy Bowring) *s.i.s and bhd: gd hdwy on wd outside over 2f out: sn cl up and rdn: wknd appr fnl f* **40/1**

-503 **11** *1* **Look Here's Al**[13] 3225 3-8-13 **67** ........ JackDuern(5) 8 44
(Andrew Hollinshead) *a towards rr* **8/1**

00-0 **12** *1¼* **Stream Of Light**[16] 3097 3-7-9 **51** oh6 ........ JoeDoyle(7) 13 24
(John Mackie) *cl up: rdn along 1/2-way: sn wknd* **100/1**

-206 **13** *1¼* **False Witness (IRE)**[36] 2474 3-8-9 **65** ........ AnnaHesketh(7) 11 34
(David Nicholls) *in tch on wd outside: rdn along bef 1/2-way: sn lost pl and bhd* **50/1**

1m 12.09s (-1.51) **Going Correction** -0.275s/f (Firm) **13** Ran SP% **116.7**
Speed ratings (Par 99): **99,96,93,92,91 91,89,88,86,85 84,82,80**
CSF £41.33 CT £240.29 TOTE £3.40: £1.70, £4.80, £2.00; EX 52.80 Trifecta £377.80.
**Owner** Moyns Park Stud **Bred** Moyns Park Estate And Stud Ltd **Trained** Newmarket, Suffolk

**FOCUS**
A modest, if reasonably competitive 3yo handicap. It paid to be up with the pace, which was not strong early. There was another impressive winner.

## 3651 BETDAQ 3% COMMISSION H'CAP (BOBIS RACE) — 1m (R)

**3:35** (3:36) (Class 3) (0-95,90) 3-Y-O **£7,762** (£2,310; £1,154; £577) **Stalls** Low

Form RPR

361 **1** **Moohaarib (IRE)**[24] 2871 3-9-2 **85** ........ MartinHarley 5 99+
(Marco Botti) *hld up: smooth hdwy 3f out: chal over 1f out: shkn up to ld jst ins fnl f: rdn and edgd lft last 100yds: kpt on wl towards fin* **3/1**[2]

6-63 **2** *¾* **Championship (IRE)**[22] 2921 3-9-6 **89** ........ JimmyFortune 1 101
(Richard Hannon) *dwlt and hld up in rr: hdwy to trck ldrs 5f out: chal over 2f out: led wl over 1f out and sn rdn: hdd jst ins fnl f and sn drvn: edgd lft and rt: no ex last 75yds* **7/1**

1 **3** *5* **Knavery (USA)**[30] 2682 3-9-7 **90** ........ JamieSpencer 6 91
(Roger Varian) *trckd ldrs: hdwy over 2f out: rdn along wl over 1f out: sn one pce* **2/1**[1]

043 **4** *3½* **Nonno Giulio (IRE)**[16] 3108 3-9-4 **87** ........ WilliamBuick 3 79
(John Gosden) *dwlt: plld hrd and sn led: rdn along and jnd over 2f out: hdd wl over 1f out: sn wknd* **4/1**[3]

3121 **5** *4 1/2* **Regiment**[15] 3137 3-9-4 **87** TonyHamilton 2 69
(Richard Fahey) *t.k.h: trckd ldng pair: hdwy to chse ldr 1/2-way: rdn along wl over 2f out: sn outpcd* **9/2**

1-00 **6** *11* **Scrutiny**[55] 1937 3-9-2 **85** LiamJones 4 42
(William Haggas) *hld up in rr: pushed along 3f out: rdn along over 2f out: sn outpcd and bhd* **33/1**

1m 38.43s (-1.27) **Going Correction** -0.075s/f (Good) **6** Ran SP% **112.0**
Speed ratings (Par 103): **103,102,97,93,89 78**
CSF £23.19 TOTE £3.50: £2.30, £3.20; EX 19.20 Trifecta £50.00.
**Owner** Sheikh Mohammed Bin Khalifa Al Maktoum **Bred** Watership Down Stud **Trained** Newmarket, Suffolk

**FOCUS**
A decent 3yo handicap and useful form. They turned in to race up the centre of the course off a sedate early pace and the trio who pulled hard in the early stages filled the last three places.

## 3652 BETDAQ £200 FREE BET GAMES BONUS MAIDEN FILLIES' STKS (DIV I) 1m 2f 60y
**4:10** (4:11) (Class 5) 3-Y-O+ **£2,911** (£866; £432; £216) **Stalls** Low

Form RPR

-234 **1** **Award (IRE)**[15] 3154 3-9-0 76 WilliamBuick 3 82
(John Gosden) *mde most: pushed along 3f out: jnd and rdn 2f out: drvn ent fnl f: hdd narrowly last 100yds: rallied to ld again last 50yds* **5/4**[1]

6-4 **2** *nk* **Muhawalah (IRE)**[21] 2967 3-9-0 0 [1] PaulHanagan 4 81
(Roger Varian) *prom: effrt over 2f out and sn rdn along: carried hd high: drvn to chal ins fnl f: slt ld last 100yds: sn edgd lft and hdd last 50yds* **9/4**[2]

3 **3** *3 3/4* **Dream Child (IRE)**[31] 2650 3-9-0 0 MartinLane 6 74
(Charlie Appleby) *dwlt: sn trcking ldrs: hdwy 3f out: cl up 2f out: rdn wl over 1f out and ev ch tl drvn and one pce ent fnl f* **4/1**[3]

0 **4** *2 1/4* **Petticoat Lane**[63] 1701 3-9-0 0 LemosdeSouza 2 70
(Luca Cumani) *in tch: hdwy on inner over 3f out: cl up 2f out: sn rdn and ev ch tl wknd appr fnl f* **33/1**

**5** *3* **Gale Force** 3-9-0 0 ShaneKelly 10 64
(James Fanshawe) *midfield: hdwy over 4f out: chsd ldrs 3f out: rdn along over 2f out: sn no imp* **14/1**

0-0 **6** *4* **Sheer Poetry (IRE)**[25] 2850 3-9-0 0 (e) GrahamLee 1 56
(Mike Murphy) *chsd ldrs: rdn along wl over 3f out: grad wknd* **100/1**

6 **7** *3/4* **May Queen**[15] 3142 3-8-11 0 AshleyMorgan(3) 11 55
(Chris Wall) *nvr bttr than midfield* **25/1**

60 **8** *2 3/4* **Pendley Legacy**[15] 3141 3-9-0 0 JohnFahy 7 50
(Clive Cox) *a towards rr* **40/1**

0 **9** *5* **Wilful Minx (FR)**[26] 2804 3-9-0 0 JimmyFortune 8 40
(James Given) *a towards rr* **66/1**

00 **10** *1/2* **Smageta**[15] 3141 3-9-0 0 AntonioFresu 9 39
(Marco Botti) *in tch: effrt over 3f out: sn rdn along and n.d* **40/1**

**11** *39* **Red Legacy**[66] 6-9-12 0 MichaelStainton 5
(Sean Regan) *s.i.s: a bhd* **150/1**

2m 12.71s (3.31) **Going Correction** -0.075s/f (Good)
**WFA** 3 from 6yo 12lb **11** Ran SP% **116.7**
Speed ratings (Par 100): **83,82,79,77,75 72,71,69,65,65 33**
CSF £3.91 TOTE £2.80: £1.10, £1.10, £1.90; EX 5.40 Trifecta £13.20.
**Owner** Al Asayl Bloodstock Ltd **Bred** Flor Ryan **Trained** Newmarket, Suffolk

**FOCUS**
They dawdled early and this first division of an uncompetitive fillies' maiden turned into something of a sprint turning in, with the first three in the market, backed to exclusion, filling the first three places. The winner and runner-up posted personal-best performances, but the third was a bit off her AW debut figure.

## 3653 BETDAQ £200 FREE BET GAMES BONUS MAIDEN FILLIES' STKS (DIV II) 1m 2f 60y
**4:45** (4:46) (Class 5) 3-Y-O+ **£2,911** (£866; £432; £216) **Stalls** Low

Form RPR

-6 **1** **Galactic Heroine**[38] 2422 3-9-0 0 GrahamLee 3 86
(James Given) *led and sn clr: wd st: pushed along over 3f out: hdd and rdn over 2f out: styd on wl u.p fr over 1f out: led last 75yds* **11/1**

2-32 **2** *1 1/4* **Oh Star (USA)**[15] 3141 3-9-0 76 WilliamBuick 7 83
(John Gosden) *sn trcking clr ldr: styd nr inner rail st: hdwy and cl up over 3f out: led wl over 2f out: rdn clr over 1f out: edgd rt and drvn ent fnl f: wknd and hdd last 75yds* **2/1**[2]

42 **3** *8* **Colourful**[31] 2649 3-9-0 0 JamesDoyle 9 68
(Lady Cecil) *trckd ldrs: hdwy to chse ldng pair 4f out: rdn along 3f out: drvn and no imp fnl 2f* **7/4**[1]

00- **4** *1/2* **Bella Varenna (IRE)**[272] 6828 3-8-9 0 MarcMonaghan(5) 1 67
(Marco Botti) *in tch: pushed along 4f out: rdn 3f out: kpt on u.p fnl f* **33/1**

65- **5** *2 1/4* **Super Moment (IRE)**[244] 7533 3-9-0 0 KierenFallon 8 63
(Saeed bin Suroor) *in tch: effrt and hdwy over 3f out: rdn along wl over 2f out: sn no imp* **5/1**[3]

0- **6** *nk* **Sealed With A Kiss**[212] 8067 3-9-0 0 LiamKeniry 2 62
(James Fanshawe) *dwlt and in rr tl styd on fnl 2f: n.d* **50/1**

**7** *1* **Undress (IRE)** 3-9-0 0 LiamJones 6 60
(William Haggas) *towards rr: stdy hdwy over 4f out: chsd ldng pair over 2f out: sn rdn and wknd appr fnl f* **12/1**

0 **8** *2 1/4* **Queen's Dream (IRE)**[26] 2804 3-9-0 0 [1] JimmyFortune 5 56
(Roger Varian) *t.k.h early: nvr bttr than midfield* **20/1**

0 **9** *28* **Bathrat Amal (JPN)**[11] 3315 4-9-12 0 MartinLane 10 3
(Charlie Appleby) *a towards rr* **22/1**

00-0 **10** *8* **Connexion Francais**[35] 2517 3-8-7 44 JoeDoyle(7) 4
(Tim Etherington) *chsd ldng pair: rdn along 4f out: sn wknd* **200/1**

2m 10.14s (0.74) **Going Correction** -0.075s/f (Good)
**WFA** 3 from 4yo 12lb **10** Ran SP% **116.9**
Speed ratings (Par 100): **94,93,86,86,84 84,83,81,59,52**
CSF £32.27 TOTE £12.90: £2.70, £1.50, £1.10; EX 39.70 Trifecta £129.20.
**Owner** Biddestone Racing Partnership V 1 **Bred** Tareq Al Mazeedi **Trained** Willoughton, Lincs

**FOCUS**
Division two of the fillies' maiden was run at a muddling pace and very few got into it, with the front two, wide apart across the track, having it to themselves in the final half-mile. The level is fluid, but the second has been rated up on her previous runs.

## 3654 BETDAQ NO PREMIUM CHARGE H'CAP 1m 6f 132y
**5:20** (5:20) (Class 4) (0-85,85) 4-Y-O+ **£5,175** (£1,540; £769; £384) **Stalls** Low

Form RPR

0232 **1** **Eagle Rock (IRE)**[14] 3204 6-9-7 **85** (p) AndrewElliott 1 93
(Tom Tate) *led: pushed along over 3f out: rdn and hdd over 2f out: drvn and rallied to ld again narrowly ent fnl f: kpt on gamely towards fin* **13/8**[2]

5-11 **2** *hd* **Hallstatt (IRE)**[15] 3151 8-8-1 **72** (t) JoeDoyle(7) 3 79
(John Mackie) *trckd ldng pair on inner: hdwy and cl up over 3f out: rdn to ld over 2f out: drvn and hdd ent fnl f: kpt on gamely and ev ch tl no ex nr fin* **6/1**[3]

14-0 **3** *2 1/2* **Handsome Ransom**[10] 3341 5-9-3 **81** [1] JamieSpencer 4 85
(David O'Meara) *hld up in tch: hdwy over 2f out: rdn wl over 1f out: kpt on same pce fnl f* **7/1**

1-34 **4** *nk* **Innsbruck**[20] 2981 4-9-3 **81** JamesDoyle 2 85
(John Quinn) *trckd wnr: cl up over 3f out: chal 2f out: sn rdn and ev ch tl drvn and one pce ins fnl f* **11/8**[1]

3m 14.67s (7.27) **Going Correction** -0.075s/f (Good) **4** Ran SP% **107.0**
Speed ratings (Par 105): **77,76,75,75**
CSF £10.21 TOTE £2.30; EX 9.20 Trifecta £18.90.
**Owner** The Ivy Syndicate **Bred** Silk Fan Syndicate **Trained** Tadcaster, N Yorks

**FOCUS**
Not a strong handicap for the class with just four runners, but a fair pace and a tight finish. The winner is better than ever.

## 3655 CASH OUT ON THE BETDAQ+ APP H'CAP 1m 4f
**5:50** (5:51) (Class 5) (0-75,74) 3-Y-O **£3,234** (£962; £481; £240) **Stalls** Low

Form RPR

4153 **1** **Innocent Touch (IRE)**[20] 3003 3-9-3 **70** TonyHamilton 6 78+
(Richard Fahey) *prom: cl up 4f out: chal over 2f out: rdn to ld 1 1/2f out: drvn ent fnl f: jst hld on* **15/8**[1]

000 **2** *shd* **Injun Sands**[28] 2746 3-8-13 **66** JamieSpencer 2 73+
(Jane Chapple-Hyam) *hld up in rr: hdwy wl over 2f out: rdn to chse ldrs over 1f out: swtchd lft to inner jst ins fnl f: fin strly: jst failed* **12/1**

5-54 **3** *1* **Micras**[37] 2466 3-9-6 **73** DavidProbert 9 78
(Andrew Balding) *slt ld: pushed along 3f out: rdn over 2f out: hdd 1 1/2f out: sn drvn and ev ch tl no ex last 100yds* **12/1**

0100 **4** *1 1/4* **Gannicus**[14] 3197 3-9-4 **71** JimmyFortune 7 74
(Brendan Powell) *prom on outer: hdwy and cl up 3f out: rdn 2f out and ev ch tl drvn ent fnl f: wknd last 100yds* **11/1**

0-21 **5** *2 3/4* **Chivers (IRE)**[16] 3098 3-8-9 **62** AndrewElliott 4 61
(Tim Easterby) *t.k.h: cl up: pushed along 3f out: rdn 2f out and ev ch tl drvn and wknd appr fnl f* **12/1**

6-30 **6** *1* **Sea Here**[14] 3197 3-9-5 **72** MartinLane 5 69
(Ralph Beckett) *trckd ldrs: hdwy over 3f out: rdn over 2f out: no imp fr over 1f out* **6/1**[2]

2-56 **7** *7* **Dorset Cream**[49] 2133 3-9-6 **73** JamesDoyle 1 59
(Lady Cecil) *hld up in rr: hdwy on inner 3f out: effrt to chse ldrs 2f out: sn rdn and wknd* **8/1**[3]

-423 **8** *nk* **Alzammaar (USA)**[36] 2494 3-9-7 **74** (b[1]) PaulHanagan 10 59
(Charles Hills) *trckd ldrs on outer: pushed along wl over 3f out: sn rdn and wknd wl over 2f out* **9/1**

-064 **9** *3 3/4* **Malory Towers**[16] 3116 3-9-0 **67** LiamKeniry 3 46
(James Fanshawe) *trckd ldrs: rdn along 3f out: wknd over 2f out* **12/1**

0-31 **10** *3 1/4* **That Be Grand**[32] 2621 3-8-3 **61** LouisSteward(5) 8 35
(Shaun Harris) *a in rr* **14/1**

2m 36.68s (1.78) **Going Correction** -0.075s/f (Good) **10** Ran SP% **115.9**
Speed ratings (Par 99): **91,90,90,89,87 86,82,82,79,77**
CSF £26.01 CT £215.37 TOTE £3.30: £1.90, £5.60, £1.90; EX 27.60 Trifecta £391.80.
**Owner** Nicholas Wrigley & Kevin Hart **Bred** B Kennedy **Trained** Musley Bank, N Yorks

**FOCUS**
They went no great pace early and came up the centre of the track turning for home in this fair handicap. This was a bit muddling, but the winner made a slight step up, in line with his profile, while the third also stepped up and the fourth ran to form.
T/Plt: £131.80 to a £1 stake. Pool: £89,717.74 - 496.71 winning tickets. T/Qpdt: £9.20 to a £1 stake. Pool: £9,204.60 - 739.20 winning tickets. JR

# 3236 MUSSELBURGH (R-H)
### Friday, June 27

**OFFICIAL GOING: Good to firm (7.7)**
Wind: fresh half behind Weather: Cloudy

## 3656 BRITISH STALLION STUDS EBF MAIDEN STKS (BOBIS RACE) 5f
**2:10** (2:10) (Class 4) 2-Y-O **£4,204** (£1,251; £625; £312) **Stalls** High

Form RPR

5 **1** **Showstoppa**[13] 3232 2-9-0 0 JoeFanning 7 69
(Mark Johnston) *mde all: rdn over 1f out: strly pressed fnl 110yds: kpt on* **4/1**[3]

00 **2** *hd* **Miss Mullberry**[13] 3215 2-9-0 0 TomEaves 4 68
(David O'Meara) *racd keenly: trckd ldrs: rdn and hdwy appr fnl f: ev ch fnl 110yds: kpt on but a jst hld* **12/1**

**3** *1 1/2* **She's A Worldie (IRE)** 2-9-0 0 PaulMulrennan 5 66+
(Bryan Smart) *dwlt: sn trckd ldr on inner: pushed along whn hmpd over 1f out: remained short of room tl fnl 75yds: kpt on* **5/1**

**4** *1 1/4* **Dark Reckoning** 2-9-0 0 PJMcDonald 1 58
(Ann Duffield) *chsd ldrs: rdn 2f out: hung rt ins fnl f: wknd fnl 110yds* **5/2**[2]

4330 **5** *1* **Hell Of A Lord**[35] 2507 2-9-0 0 RyanWhile(5) 6 60
(Bill Turner) *pressed ldr: rdn 2f out: wknd ins fnl f* **7/4**[1]

59.57s (-0.83) **Going Correction** -0.45s/f (Firm) **5** Ran SP% **109.3**
Speed ratings (Par 95): **88,87,85,83,81**
CSF £40.93 TOTE £3.90: £1.60, £4.70; EX 31.50 Trifecta £80.40.
**Owner** Hot To Trot & Whitsbury Manor Stud **Bred** Whitsbury Manor Stud **Trained** Middleham Moor, N Yorks

**FOCUS**
The opener was won in a time of 59.57sec, which was 1.57sec slower than standard, but the jockeys in the first confirmed that the ground was riding quick. Fair maiden form. The winner and second have been rated as improving, but the level is fluid.

## 3657 ROTECH M & P LTD H'CAP 1m 4f 100y
**2:40** (2:40) (Class 6) (0-65,67) 4-Y-O+ **£3,234** (£962; £481; £240) **Stalls** Centre

Form RPR

-233 **1** **Eilean Mor**[18] 3056 6-8-1 **48** ow1 ConnorBeasley(3) 2 55
(R Mike Smith) *trckd ldr: dropped to 3rd 6f out: rdn and hdwy to ld 2f out: kpt on* **9/2**[3]

-414 **2** *3/4* **Rocky Two (IRE)**[22] 2915 4-8-11 **55** PaulMulrennan 7 61
(Philip Kirby) *midfield: hdwy to trck ldr 6f out: led narrowly over 2f out: hdd 2f out: carried hd bit awkwardly u.p and a jst hld* **5/2**[2]

1111 **3** *3/4* **Operateur (IRE)**[1] 3605 6-9-4 **67** 6ex KevinStott(5) 6 72
(Ben Haslam) *led at stdy pce: rdn whn hdd over 2f out: outpcd over 1f out: kpt on ins fnl f* **6/5**[1]

6043 **4** 2 ¾ **Grand Diamond (IRE)**[18] 3051 10-8-4 **55**.................. JordanNason(7) 1 56
(Jim Goldie) *hld up: rdn over 2f out: one pce and nvr threatened* **15/2**

0405 **5** 1 ¼ **Taxiformissbyron**[9] 3364 4-8-0 **49**..............................(p) JackGarritty(5) 5 48
(Iain Jardine) *hld up: rdn over 2f out: nvr threatened* **12/1**

2m 50.55s (8.55) **Going Correction** -0.35s/f (Firm) **5** Ran SP% **111.7**
Speed ratings (Par 101): **57,56,56,54,53**
CSF £16.22 TOTE £5.30: £3.00, £1.60; EX 16.80 Trifecta £31.30.
**Owner** R Michael Smith **Bred** Triple H Stud Ltd **Trained** Galston, E Ayrshire

**FOCUS**
A low-grade handicap which was run at a slow pace, and in a time over 10sec outside standard. The form is of very limited value. They raced a few horse widths off the rail in the home straight. The winner is rated to last year's best in an unsatisfactory race.

## 3658 SHAWBROOK BANK (S) STKS 5f
**3:10** (3:13) (Class 4) 2-Y-O **£6,469** (£1,925; £962; £481) **Stalls** High

Form RPR

61 **1** **Honest Bob'S**[40] 2360 2-8-12 0.................................. JackGarritty(5) 6 73
(Brian Ellison) *trckd ldr: led over 1f out: rdn clr* **11/4**[2]

065 **2** 4 **Ventura Shadow**[14] 3199 2-8-2 0.............................. SammyJoBell(5) 1 49
(Richard Fahey) *wnt rt s: chsd ldrs towards outer: rdn 2f out: wnt 2nd jst ins fnl f: kpt on but no ch w wnr* **9/4**[1]

55 **3** 2 ¼ **Decisive Rebel**[30] 2673 2-8-12 0.................................... JoeFanning 5 46
(Jo Hughes) *led: hdd 4f out: rdn to ld again 2f out: hdd over 1f out: no ex ins fnl f* **11/4**[2]

60 **4** 1 ¾ **Queen Of The Scots**[11] 3296 2-8-7 0..............................(p) TomEaves 3 34
(Keith Dalgleish) *hld up in tch: rdn 1/2-way: flashed tail u.p over 1f out: nvr threatened* **8/1**[3]

06 **5** 8 **Cupulation**[2] 3570 2-8-12 0.......................................... PaulMulrennan 7 10
(Amy Weaver) *prom: led 4f out: hdd 2f out: wknd* **18/1**

630 **6** 3 ½ **Hell For Leather**[21] 2944 2-8-7 0..................................(b[1]) RyanWhile(5) 2
(Bill Turner) *wnt rt s: a outpcd in rr* **12/1**

59.23s (-1.17) **Going Correction** -0.45s/f (Firm) **6** Ran SP% **108.2**
Speed ratings (Par 95): **91,84,81,78,65 59**
CSF £8.62 TOTE £2.20: £1.10, £2.30; EX 6.70 Trifecta £15.80.There was no bid for the winner.
**Owner** Ms Y Lowe **Bred** Norman Court Stud & Mike Channon B/S Ltd **Trained** Norton, N Yorks

**FOCUS**
A valuable seller, the richest race on the card, and it was run in a time 0.34sec quicker than the earlier maiden. This has been rated cautiously and arguably deserves to be a bit higher.

## 3659 ROSS ELECTRICAL H'CAP 5f
**3:45** (3:45) (Class 4) (0-80,76) 3-Y-O+ **£5,175** (£1,540; £769; £384) **Stalls** High

Form RPR

504 **1** **Perfect Blossom**[6] 3462 7-9-2 **70**................................. SladeO'Hara(3) 1 80
(Alan Berry) *trckd ldrs: led 2f out: sn rdn: kpt on* **20/1**

4-65 **2** nk **Gran Canaria Queen**[14] 3191 5-9-2 **67**............................... DavidAllan 7 76
(Tim Easterby) *in tch: rdn 1/2-way: hdwy to chse wnr appr fnl f: kpt on* **4/1**[2]

-603 **3** 1 ¼ **Alaskan Bullet (IRE)**[6] 3458 5-9-9 **74**................................ PaulPickard 3 79
(Brian Ellison) *s.i.s: hld up: hdwy on outer 1/2-way: sn rdn: kpt on* **7/2**[1]

0-00 **4** nk **Midnight Dynamo**[6] 3459 7-9-3 **71**.............................. GaryBartley(3) 4 74
(Jim Goldie) *midfield: rdn 1/2-way: kpt on fnl f* **7/1**

6415 **5** 1 **Bunce (IRE)**[1] 3610 6-9-6 **71**........................................... JoeFanning 8 71
(Linda Perratt) *hld up: rdn 2f out: kpt on fnl f: nvr threatened* **6/1**

6-55 **6** ½ **Jofranka**[20] 3006 4-9-11 **76**.............................................. PhillipMakin 2 74
(David Barron) *w ldr: rdn 2f out: wknd ins fnl f* **11/2**[3]

0000 **7** hd **Mister Manannan (IRE)**[8] 3399 7-9-7 **72**......................... AdrianNicholls 9 69
(David Nicholls) *slowly away: hld up: swtchd rt to outside 1/2-way: sme hdwy over 1f out: wknd and eased fnl 110yds* **6/1**

1502 **8** 4 ½ **Captain Royale (IRE)**[8] 3399 9-9-5 **70**.....................(p) RobertWinston 6 51
(Tracy Waggott) *led narrowly: rdn whn hdd 2f out: wknd* **9/1**

57.54s (-2.86) **Going Correction** -0.45s/f (Firm) **8** Ran SP% **113.4**
Speed ratings (Par 105): **104,103,101,101,99 98,98,91**
CSF £96.60 CT £355.65 TOTE £27.50: £5.70, £1.80, £1.50; EX 138.40 Trifecta £1140.20.
**Owner** Alan Berry **Bred** Mrs A Morris **Trained** Cockerham, Lancs

**FOCUS**
A fair handicap run in time 0.46sec inside the standard. They finished in a heap. The winner is rated back to last year's form and the runner-up back to her best.

## 3660 VIRIDOR TRANSFORMING WASTE RACING FORWARD H'CAP 7f 30y
**4:20** (4:20) (Class 5) (0-70,70) 4-Y-O+ **£3,234** (£962; £481; £240) **Stalls** Low

Form RPR

665 **1** **Order Of Service**[18] 3050 4-8-13 **65**.............................. GaryBartley(3) 1 75
(Jim Goldie) *mde all: rdn over 2f out: pressed fnl 110yds: hld on wl* **7/1**[3]

4560 **2** nk **Loud**[14] 3180 4-9-2 **65**....................................................... JoeFanning 5 74+
(Mark Johnston) *hld up: rdn and gd hdwy on outside fr over 2f out: chal fnl 110yds: kpt on: jst hld* **9/1**

40-3 **3** 3 **Joyful Sound (IRE)**[34] 2546 6-8-9 **58**...........................(p) PaulPickard 6 59
(Brian Ellison) *midfield: rdn over 2f out: kpt on: wnt 3rd post* **15/2**

0-34 **4** shd **Whispered Times (USA)**[6] 3485 7-8-10 **59**...........(p) RobertWinston 10 60
(Tracy Waggott) *trckd ldrs: rdn to chse wnr 2f out: lost 2nd ins fnl f: wknd and lost 3rd post* **14/1**

3-23 **5** 2 ¼ **Live Dangerously**[11] 3299 4-9-6 **69**..................................(t) TomEaves 4 64
(Keith Dalgleish) *trckd ldrs: drvn and outpcd over 1f out: no threat after* **11/4**[1]

5-00 **6** 1 **Fabled City (USA)**[20] 3000 5-8-11 **60**................................(t) JasonHart 9 53
(Keith Dalgleish) *hld up: rdn over 2f out: nvr threatened* **8/1**

4433 **7** 1 **Beckermet (IRE)**[18] 3053 12-9-0 **63**................................ JamesSullivan 7 53
(Ruth Carr) *in tch: rdn and outpcd 2f out: wknd ins fnl f* **12/1**

1-42 **8** 11 **Next Door (IRE)**[28] 2726 4-9-2 **65**..................................... PhillipMakin 3 27
(David Barron) *prom: rdn over 2f out: wknd over 1f out* **14/1**

-004 **9** ¾ **Mishaal (IRE)**[25] 2825 4-9-2 **70**.............................(b) JacobButterfield(5) 2 30
(Michael Herrington) *v.s.a: hld up in rr: a bhd* **3/1**[2]

1m 26.57s (-2.43) **Going Correction** -0.35s/f (Firm) **9** Ran SP% **118.1**
Speed ratings (Par 103): **99,98,95,95,92 91,90,77,76**
CSF £69.46 CT £494.48 TOTE £10.20: £2.30, £3.00, £1.70; EX 56.90 Trifecta £905.90.
**Owner** Whitestonecliffe Racing Partnership **Bred** Cheveley Park Stud Ltd **Trained** Uplawmoor, E Renfrews

**FOCUS**
A modest handicap. The winner is rated to his turf best and the runner-up, much the best of those from off the pace, ran to his best since AW in the spring.

## 3661 BOOGIE IN THE MORNING H'CAP (QUALIFIER FOR THE £15,000 BETFAIR SCOTTISH STAYERS SERIES FINAL) 2m
**4:55** (4:55) (Class 6) (0-65,68) 4-Y-O+ **£3,234** (£962; £481; £240) **Stalls** Centre

Form RPR

0231 **1** **Longshadow**[4] 3532 4-9-7 **68** 6ex..................................(v) JoeyHaynes(3) 1 77
(Jason Ward) *hld up: smooth hdwy 4f out: rdn to chal over 2f out: led over 1f out: hung rt ins fnl f: styd on wl* **5/6**[1]

0-34 **2** 3 ¾ **Mason Hindmarsh**[38] 2424 7-9-4 **65**......................... ConnorBeasley(3) 4 69
(Karen McLintock) *midfield: chsd ldr 4f out: rdn to ld over 2f out: hdd over 1f out: plugged on* **5/1**[2]

000- **3** nk **Underwritten**[182] 8417 5-8-6 **50**............................................ JasonHart 8 54
(Shaun Harris) *trckd ldr: rdn and outpcd over 3f out: styd on fnl f: wnt 3rd post* **10/1**

00/4 **4** nk **Strobe**[9] 3365 10-7-13 **46**............................................(p) IanBrennan(3) 5 49
(Lucy Normile) *trckd ldr: led 5f out: rdn whn hdd over 2f out: plugged on: lost 3rd post* **20/1**

6601 **5** 1 ½ **Voice From Above (IRE)**[22] 2915 5-8-3 **52**..............(p) JackGarritty(5) 3 53
(Patrick Holmes) *in tch: rdn over 3f out: one pce and nvr rchd ldrs* **17/2**

063- **6** 22 **Indepub**[19] 5087 5-9-1 **64**..............................................(v) KevinStott(5) 2 39
(Martin Todhunter) *hld up: rdn over 5f out: sn btn* **22/1**

22-0 **7** ¾ **Hero's Story**[20] 3004 4-8-11 **58**.................................. GaryBartley(3) 7 32
(Jim Goldie) *hld up: nvr threatened* **16/1**

2/00 **8** 21 **Spruzzo**[74] 1485 8-8-11 **55**.................................................. JoeFanning 9 4
(Chris Fairhurst) *led: rdn whn hdd 5f out: wknd* **8/1**[3]

00-0 **9** 29 **Hayley**[36] 2476 4-7-11 **46** oh1.......................................... SammyJoBell(5) 6
(Jim Goldie) *slowly away: sn midfield on outside: wknd over 4f out* **50/1**

3m 26.66s (-6.84) **Going Correction** -0.35s/f (Firm) **9** Ran SP% **118.9**
Speed ratings (Par 101): **103,101,100,100,100 89,88,78,63**
CSF £5.29 CT £26.26 TOTE £1.80: £1.10, £1.80, £5.50; EX 6.10 Trifecta £57.40.
**Owner** David Robertson & J Ward **Bred** Miss K Rausing **Trained** Middleham, N Yorks

**FOCUS**
A moderate staying handicap in which the pace steadied down the back. The winner is better than ever and the runner-up is rated close to this year's form, and the fourth to latest.

## 3662 WILLIAM HILL-BET ON THE MOVE H'CAP (QUALIFIER FOR THE £15,000 BETFAIR SCOTTISH MILE SERIES FINAL) 1m
**5:30** (5:30) (Class 6) (0-65,69) 3-Y-O **£3,234** (£962; £481; £240) **Stalls** Low

Form RPR

-605 **1** **Bahamian C**[9] 3360 3-9-1 **62**.......................................... SammyJoBell(5) 5 71
(Richard Fahey) *hld up: rdn 3f out: gd hdwy on outside over 1f out: kpt on: led last 75yds* **6/1**

0-41 **2** ½ **Picks Pinta**[2] 3566 3-9-7 **68** 6ex....................................... PhilipPrince(5) 4 76
(Jo Hughes) *in tch towards outer: rdn and hdwy over 2f out: led appr fnl f: kpt on: hdd fnl 75yds* **4/1**[2]

0-00 **3** 3 **Prostate Awareness (IRE)**[7] 3439 3-8-12 **59**...........(p) JackGarritty(5) 7 60
(Patrick Holmes) *w ldr: rdn over 3f out: led 2f out: hdd appr fnl f: edgd rt: wknd fnl 110yds* **8/1**

-441 **4** 4 **Porthos Du Vallon**[9] 3360 3-9-13 **69** 6ex.............................(p) JasonHart 6 61+
(Keith Dalgleish) *led narrowly: rdn over 2f out: hdd 2f out: wknd fnl f* **15/8**[1]

3513 **5** 1 **It's All A Game**[18] 3054 3-9-7 **63**.................................(b) RobertWinston 2 53
(Richard Guest) *trckd ldng pair: rdn over 3f out: wknd over 1f out* **5/1**[3]

3460 **6** ¾ **Miss Acclaimed (IRE)**[8] 3405 3-9-2 **58**..........................(b[1]) PaulPickard 3 46
(Brian Ellison) *dwlt: hld up: rdn 3f out: nvr threatened* **20/1**

1-60 **7** 26 **Neuf Des Coeurs**[11] 3303 3-9-6 **62**...............................(b[1]) JoeFanning 1
(Keith Dalgleish) *racd keenly: trckd ldng pair: rdn over 3f out: sn wknd: eased* **15/2**

1m 38.45s (-2.75) **Going Correction** -0.35s/f (Firm) **7** Ran SP% **113.4**
Speed ratings (Par 97): **99,98,95,91,90 89,63**
CSF £29.48 TOTE £6.30: £2.20, £2.70; EX 44.60 Trifecta £278.00.
**Owner** S & G Clayton **Bred** Giles Wates **Trained** Musley Bank, N Yorks

**FOCUS**
A very modest event, but the time dipped inside standard. The winner produced his best figure since his debut, while the third possibly paid for chasing the pace but has been rated to latest.
T/Plt: £256.40 to a £1 stake. Pool: £48,289.55 - 137.47 winning tickets. T/Qpdt: £24.30 to a £1 stake. Pool: £4,453.15 - 135.10 winning tickets. AS

# 3619 NEWCASTLE (L-H)
Friday, June 27

**OFFICIAL GOING: Good to firm (watered; 8.0)**
All Round course on fresh ground.
Wind: Slight, half against Weather: Overcast

## 3663 BETFRED WIN TICKETS ON FACEBOOK CLASSIFIED STKS 7f
**6:10** (6:10) (Class 5) 3-Y-O **£2,587** (£770; £384; £192) **Stalls** Centre

Form RPR

6-00 **1** **Top Of The Glas (IRE)**[36] 2481 3-9-0 75.............................. DaleSwift 2 82
(Brian Ellison) *prom: rdn 2f out: hdwy to ld last 75yds: kpt on wl* **7/2**[3]

01 **2** 1 **Mr McLaren**[22] 2910 3-9-0 75........................................ DanielTudhope 5 79
(David O'Meara) *chsd ldrs: drvn and outpcd over 2f out: rallied appr fnl f: wnt 2nd last 50yds: r.o* **5/2**[2]

3120 **3** ½ **Alquimia (IRE)**[14] 3200 3-8-11 75.............................. GeorgeChaloner(3) 3 78
(Richard Fahey) *pressed ldr: drvn and led over 1f out: edgd lft: hdd and no ex last 75yds* **13/8**[1]

3-06 **4** 6 **Centre Haafhd**[42] 2295 3-9-0 75.................................... GrahamGibbons 1 63
(David Barron) *led at modest gallop: rdn over 2f out: hdd over 1f out: wknd fnl f* **5/1**

1425 **5** 20 **Secret Suspect**[72] 1507 3-9-0 73...................................... PaulMulrennan 4 11
(James Tate) *hld up in tch: rdn and struggling over 2f out: lost tch over 1f out* **10/1**

1m 27.17s (-0.63) **Going Correction** -0.225s/f (Firm) **5** Ran SP% **114.6**
Speed ratings (Par 99): **94,92,92,85,62**
CSF £13.14 TOTE £4.90: £2.40, £1.20; EX 12.10 Trifecta £43.20.
**Owner** Market Avenue Racing Club Ltd **Bred** Seamus McConnon **Trained** Norton, N Yorks

**FOCUS**
All races on the round course were run on fresh ground. This was a fair little contest. They raced up the middle and the winner and runner-up took a while to get going, but the third didn't really go through with her challenge. The winner has been rated to his standout 2yo run.

## 3664 BETFRED ANYTIME GOAL SCORER MAIDEN FILLIES' STKS 7f
**6:40** (6:42) (Class 5) 3-Y-O+ **£2,587** (£770; £384; £192) **Stalls** Centre

Form RPR
4 **1** **Free Rein**[27] 2780 3-8-12 0 ........ JimCrowley 2 79
(Ralph Beckett) *in tch gng wl: smooth hdwy 2f out: rdn to ld over 1f out: hld on wl towards fin* **13/8**[1]
**2** *hd* **Cloud Line** 3-8-12 0 ........ MartinHarley 4 78
(William Haggas) *dwlt: hld up: smooth hdwy over 2f out: effrt and chsd wnr over 1f out: kpt on wl fnl f: jst hld: improve* **3/1**[2]
-45 **3** *11* **Haidees Reflection**[52] 2053 4-9-7 0 ........ BarryMcHugh 7 53?
(Lucy Normile) *led tl rdn and hdd over 1f out: sn dropped by first two* **100/1**
**4** *¾* **French Flirt** 3-8-12 0 ........ DanielTudhope 6 48
(Timothy Jarvis) *slowly away: t.k.h: hld up: rdn over 2f out: hung bdly lft to far rail over 1f out: no imp* **11/1**
0- **5** *¾* **Bay Street Belle**[282] 6512 3-8-12 0 ........ GrahamGibbons 5 46
(David Barron) *t.k.h: hld up in tch: shkn up and outpcd over 2f out: sn btn* **14/1**
54- **6** *¾* **La Havrese (FR)**[282] 6512 3-8-12 0 ........ PJMcDonald 1 44
(Ann Duffield) *trckd ldrs: pushed along over 2f out: wknd over 1f out* **10/1**[3]
2 **7** *3* **Gotcha**[39] 2389 3-8-12 0 ........ DaleSwift 3 36
(James Bethell) *t.k.h: trckd ldrs: rdn over 2f out: sn btn* **3/1**[2]
60 **8** *3* **Charedal**[11] 3302 6-9-7 0 ........ PaulMulrennan 8 31
(Iain Jardine) *cl up tl rdn and wknd over 2f out* **100/1**

1m 27.06s (-0.74) **Going Correction** -0.225s/f (Firm)
**WFA** 3 from 4yo+ 9lb **8 Ran SP% 114.2**
Speed ratings (Par 100): **95,94,82,81,80 79,76,72**
CSF £6.63 TOTE £2.20: £1.10, £1.10, £20.30; EX 5.20 Trifecta £181.40.
**Owner** The Eclipse Partnership **Bred** Car Colston Hall Stud **Trained** Kimpton, Hants

**FOCUS**
The front two, both likely types on paper, pulled a long way clear off what looked a modest early pace, in the process clocking a time slightly quicker time than the preceding classified event, and the pair of them look decent prospects. Again, the action was up the middle.

## 3665 BETFRED TV/EBF STALLIONS HOPPINGS STKS (LISTED RACE) (FILLIES' & MARES) 1m 2f 32y
**7:10** (7:10) (Class 1) 3-Y-O+
**£22,684** (£8,600; £4,304; £2,144; £1,076; £540) **Stalls** Low

Form RPR
1-30 **1** **Regardez**[21] 2960 3-8-7 92 ........ GrahamGibbons 3 104
(Ralph Beckett) *early ldr: sn chsd ldr: led and qcknd over 2f out: clr over 1f out: kpt on strly fnl f* **7/1**[3]
164- **2** *6* **Regal Hawk**[274] 6764 4-9-5 88 ........ GrahamLee 1 93
(James Tate) *chsd ldng pair: effrt and wnt 2nd over 2f out: one pce fr over 1f out* **11/1**
0-33 **3** *1 ¼* **Magic Of Reality (FR)**[16] 3109 4-9-5 92 ........ PhillipMakin 2 91
(Lady Cecil) *in tch: effrt and rdn over 2f out: kpt on same pce fr over 1f out* **9/1**
-050 **4** *2 ¼* **Auction (IRE)**[11] 3307 4-9-5 94 ........(b[1]) JimCrowley 4 86
(Ed Dunlop) *hld up: stdy hdwy over 2f out: rdn over 1f out: kpt on fnl f: nvr rchd ldrs* **22/1**
0162 **5** *2 ¼* **Pelerin (IRE)**[15] 3143 3-8-7 97 ........ MartinHarley 6 82
(Marco Botti) *s.i.s: hld up in last pl: smooth hdwy 3f out: rdn wl over 1f out: no imp fnl f* **5/4**[1]
-620 **6** *2* **Lily Rules (IRE)**[21] 2960 3-8-7 96 ........ BarryMcHugh 5 78
(Tony Coyle) *hld up in tch: rdn wl over 2f out: btn over 1f out* **9/4**[2]
55-0 **7** *1* **Hollowina**[27] 2764 4-9-5 76 ........(b[1]) PJMcDonald 7 76
(David Brown) *led: rdn and hdd over 2f out: wknd over 1f out* **66/1**

2m 9.16s (-2.74) **Going Correction** -0.10s/f (Good)
**WFA** 3 from 4yo 12lb **7 Ran SP% 111.9**
Speed ratings (Par 108): **106,101,100,98,96 95,94**
CSF £73.57 TOTE £9.10: £3.80, £3.40; EX 92.10 Trifecta £279.80.
**Owner** J H Richmond-Watson **Bred** Lawn Stud **Trained** Kimpton, Hants

**FOCUS**
A weak fillies' Listed race, and the first three sat second, third and fourth (behind the rag) for most of the way. The winner has improved with the runner-up to form.

## 3666 BETFRED MOBILE GOSFORTH PARK CUP (H'CAP) 5f
**7:45** (7:45) (Class 2) (0-105,97) 3-Y-O+
**£12,450** (£3,728; £1,864; £932; £466; £234) **Stalls** Centre

Form RPR
-421 **1** **Robot Boy (IRE)**[13] 3239 4-9-7 **92** ........ GrahamGibbons 15 110
(David Barron) *dwlt: sn cl up and angled to centre: led after 2f: rdn clr over 1f out: kpt on strly fnl f* **10/3**[1]
0031 **2** *3* **Another Wise Kid (IRE)**[39] 2390 6-9-5 **90** ........ GrahamLee 14 97
(Paul Midgley) *hld up in tch: effrt and rdn over 1f out: chsd (clr) wnr ins fnl f: no imp* **9/1**
0-00 **3** *¾* **Fitz Flyer (IRE)**[51] 2074 8-8-13 **84** ........(v) RoystonFfrench 9 88
(David Nicholls) *t.k.h early: hld up in midfield: effrt and rdn 1/2-way: kpt on fnl f: nrst fin* **33/1**
0450 **4** *1 ¾* **Confessional**[13] 3241 7-9-8 **93** ........(e) DavidAllan 10 91
(Tim Easterby) *prom: chsd wnr over 2f out to ins fnl f: sn outpcd* **8/1**
6-21 **5** *½* **Algar Lad**[8] 3386 4-9-1 **86** 6ex ........ DanielTudhope 13 82
(David O'Meara) *hld up nr side of gp: effrt and rdn wl over 1f out: kpt on fnl f: nt pce to chal* **5/1**[2]
046 **6** *¾* **Barnet Fair**[20] 2989 6-9-6 **91** ........ AdrianNicholls 12 85+
(David Nicholls) *s.i.s: hld up: effrt and hdwy over 1f out: nt clr run ins fnl f: sn no imp* **13/2**[3]
4356 **7** *½* **Singeur (IRE)**[13] 3239 7-9-2 **87** ........ PaulMulrennan 11 79
(Robin Bastiman) *hld up: drvn along over 2f out: kpt on fnl f: nvr able to chal* **12/1**
3-01 **8** *1 ½* **Asian Trader**[26] 2803 5-8-9 **87** ........ GeorgiaCox[(7)] 7 73
(William Haggas) *in tch: effrt and rdn 2f out: wknd ins fnl f* **11/1**
0133 **9** *4 ½* **Love Island**[14] 3203 5-9-7 **95** ........ GeorgeChaloner[(3)] 6 65
(Richard Whitaker) *prom: drvn over 2f out: wknd over 1f out* **14/1**
0-01 **10** *1* **Burning Thread (IRE)**[6] 3458 7-9-11 **96** 6ex ........(b) JamesSullivan 4 63
(Tim Etherington) *hld up in midfield: struggling over 2f out: btn over 1f out* **33/1**
0000 **11** *2 ¾* **Doc Hay (USA)**[13] 3241 7-9-6 **94** ........ IanBrennan[(3)] 2 51
(Brian Ellison) *bhd and sn struggling: plenty to do 1/2-way: nvr on terms* **12/1**
0602 **12** *16* **Red Baron (IRE)**[13] 3239 5-8-12 **86** ........ NeilFarley[(3)] 3
(Eric Alston) *led towards far side 2f: hung lft and wknd 2f out: t.o* **14/1**
10-0 **13** *½* **Lover Man (IRE)**[41] 2353 5-9-12 **97** ........(t) TomEaves 1
(Keith Dalgleish) *disp ld far side 2f: rdn and wknd fr 2f out: t.o* **40/1**

58.94s (-2.16) **Going Correction** -0.225s/f (Firm) **13 Ran SP% 119.6**
Speed ratings (Par 109): **108,103,102,99,98 97,96,94,86,85 80,55,54**
CSF £33.04 CT £882.85 TOTE £4.60: £1.70, £3.30, £5.10; EX 34.90 Trifecta £1735.20 Part won. Pool: £2,313.67 - 0.60 winning tickets..
**Owner** Laurence O'Kane & Paul Murphy **Bred** Corduff Stud Ltd **Trained** Maunby, N Yorks

**FOCUS**
This was all about the potentially Group-class winner, who is an improved horse, with the runner-up rated to form. They raced up the middle.

## 3667 BETFRED SUPPORTS JACK BERRY HOUSE H'CAP 1m 3y(S)
**8:20** (8:20) (Class 4) (0-85,85) 3-Y-O+ **£4,690** (£1,395; £697; £348) **Stalls** Centre

Form RPR
21-4 **1** **Big Storm Coming**[20] 3000 4-8-12 **69** ........ BenCurtis 3 76
(Brian Ellison) *trckd ldrs: rdn and sltly outpcd over 2f out: rallied over 1f out: led ins fnl f: edgd rt nr fin: kpt on wl* **11/2**[3]
-106 **2** *nk* **Rogue Wave (IRE)**[16] 3108 3-8-11 **78** ........ JimCrowley 4 82
(Timothy Jarvis) *pressed ldr: led over 2f out: rdn over 1f out: hdd ins fnl f: kpt on: hld nr fin* **13/2**
0402 **3** *nk* **Anderiego (IRE)**[8] 3383 6-9-7 **78** ........ DanielTudhope 7 83
(David O'Meara) *hld up in tch: hdwy over 2f out: rdn and ev ch over 1f out to ins fnl f: hld towards fin* **6/4**[1]
-200 **4** *1 ½* **Thorntoun Lady (USA)**[12] 3272 4-8-12 **69** ........ GrahamLee 1 71
(Jim Goldie) *in tch: rdn along over 2f out: kpt on ins fnl f: nt rch first three* **9/1**
-035 **5** *½* **Sbraase**[6] 3464 3-8-10 **77** ........(p) PaulMulrennan 2 76
(James Tate) *in tch: drvn along over 2f out: kpt on same pce fnl f* **5/2**[2]
50/0 **P** **Vito Volterra (IRE)**[38] 2423 7-9-6 **77** ........ AndrewMullen 5
(Michael Smith) *led at stdy pce: rdn and hdd over 2f out: wknd over 1f out: no ch whn broke down bdly and dismntd ins fnl f* **33/1**

1m 41.65s (-1.75) **Going Correction** -0.225s/f (Firm)
**WFA** 3 from 4yo+ 10lb **6 Ran SP% 110.2**
Speed ratings (Par 105): **99,98,98,96,96**
CSF £37.70 CT £73.92 TOTE £6.00: £2.00, £3.20; EX 35.50 Trifecta £77.70.
**Owner** Fishlake Commercial Motors Ltd **Bred** Bearstone Stud **Trained** Norton, N Yorks

**FOCUS**
A fair handicap and again the action was up the middle.

## 3668 BETFRED EXCLUSIVE COMPETITIONS ON TWITTER H'CAP 6f
**8:50** (8:50) (Class 5) (0-70,70) 3-Y-O+ **£2,587** (£770; £384; £192) **Stalls** Centre

Form RPR
0450 **1** **Exotic Guest**[36] 2473 4-9-3 **61** ........ JamesSullivan 15 71
(Ruth Carr) *hld up: gd hdwy 2f out: led ins fnl f: drvn out* **12/1**
0202 **2** *¾* **Diamond Blue**[8] 3384 6-9-2 **63** ........(p) GeorgeChaloner[(3)] 7 70
(Richard Fahey) *midfield: rdn and hdwy over 2f out: chsd wnr ins fnl f: r.o* **7/2**[1]
-520 **3** *shd* **Penina (IRE)**[2] 3575 3-9-0 **65** ........ BenCurtis 10 70
(Brian Ellison) *hld up: rdn and hdwy over 1f out: kpt on fnl f: hld nr fin* **9/1**
6520 **4** *shd* **Thatcherite (IRE)**[11] 3298 6-9-12 **70** ........(t) BarryMcHugh 16 77
(Tony Coyle) *hld up and bhd: rdn and hdwy over 1f out: kpt on ins fnl f* **11/2**[2]
4350 **5** *½* **Bajan Bear**[121] 746 6-9-10 **68** ........ AdrianNicholls 3 73
(David Nicholls) *hld up in midfield: smooth hdwy to ld over 1f out: sn rdn and edgd rt: hdd ins fnl f: kpt on same pce* **9/1**
6064 **6** *¾* **Bonnie Charlie**[1] 3610 8-9-8 **66** ........ PaulQuinn 14 70
(David Nicholls) *hld up: stdy hdwy over 2f out: edgd rt over 1f out: n.m.r ins fnl f: one pce* **10/1**
-306 **7** *shd* **Jumbo Steps (IRE)**[20] 3006 7-9-11 **69** ........ GrahamLee 4 71
(Jim Goldie) *cl up: led main centre gp after 2f: rdn and hdd over 1f out: rallied: one pce ins fnl f* **8/1**
25-4 **8** *2 ¾* **Sakhee's Rose**[102] 993 4-9-6 **64** ........(b) DaleSwift 13 58
(Ed McMahon) *hld up: pushed along and hdwy over 1f out: nvr able to chal* **25/1**
10-4 **9** *6* **Destination Aim**[10] 3344 7-9-10 **68** ........ JasonHart 12 42
(Frederick Watson) *chsd ldrs: drvn over 2f out: wknd over 1f out* **20/1**
-600 **10** *7* **Natures Law (IRE)**[13] 3237 4-8-13 **57** ........[1] TomEaves 5 9
(Keith Dalgleish) *prom: drvn over 2f out: wkng whn hmpd over 1f out* **20/1**
0212 **11** *1 ¾* **Cadeaux Pearl**[9] 3366 6-9-1 **59** ........ MartinHarley 8 5
(Scott Dixon) *midfield: rdn over 2f out: wknd over 1f out* **6/1**[3]
0600 **12** *23* **Bogsnog (IRE)**[13] 3227 4-9-11 **69** ........ GrahamGibbons 2
(Kristin Stubbs) *racd far side: led 2f: hung lft and wknd over 2f out: t.o* **16/1**
0050 **13** *6* **Sunrise Dance**[10] 3338 5-9-7 **65** ........ AndrewMullen 1
(Robert Johnson) *w ldr far side: rdn and wknd over 2f out: t.o* **25/1**

1m 13.46s (-1.14) **Going Correction** -0.225s/f (Firm)
**WFA** 3 from 4yo+ 7lb **13 Ran SP% 122.9**
Speed ratings (Par 103): **98,97,96,96,96 95,94,91,83,73 71,40,32**
CSF £52.44 CT £423.88 TOTE £12.30: £2.80, £2.10, £3.40; EX 58.00 Trifecta £1160.10 Part won. Pool: £1,546.80 - 0.42 winning tickets..
**Owner** 21st Century Racing,A Swinburne,R Carr **Bred** D Cantillon And E Cantillon **Trained** Huby, N Yorks
■ Stewards' Enquiry : Paul Quinn two-day ban: careless riding (Jul 14-15)

**FOCUS**
They raced up the middle and this was a bit messy. The winner is rated to his best since last year's 5f win here, with a small personal best from the third, and the fourth running as well as ever.

## 3669 BETFRED WORLD CUP ENHANCED MATCH PRICES H'CAP 5f
**9:20** (9:20) (Class 5) (0-75,75) 3-Y-O **£2,587** (£770; £384; £192) **Stalls** Centre

Form RPR
-000 **1** **Pushkin Museum (IRE)**[13] 3219 3-9-6 **74** ........ PJMcDonald 6 83
(Richard Fahey) *t.k.h early: mde all: rdn whn hung lft ins fnl f: kpt on wl* **25/1**
1-62 **2** *1 ¼* **Kirtling Belle**[1] 3600 3-8-13 **67** ........ TomEaves 3 71
(Keith Dalgleish) *chsd wnr: rdn over 2f out: carried lft ins fnl f: kpt on towards fin* **13/2**
-313 **3** *hd* **Noble Asset**[13] 3219 3-9-6 **74** ........ PhillipMakin 2 77
(John Quinn) *in tch: effrt on outside over 1f out: kpt on ins fnl f* **6/1**[3]
0-26 **4** *hd* **Rozene (IRE)**[23] 2889 3-9-2 **70** ........ GrahamGibbons 7 73
(David Barron) *chsd ldrs: drvn and outpcd over 2f out: rallied over 1f out: kpt on fnl f* **5/1**[2]

4150 **5** 1/2 **Skye's The Limit**27 2768 3-9-4 75 1 GeorgeChaloner(3) 5 76
(Richard Fahey) *t.k.h: chsd ldrs: effrt and drvn 2f out: kpt on same pce ins fnl f* **7/4**1

0-05 **6** 1 1/4 **Secret Applause**6 3487 3-8-4 61 ConnorBeasley(3) 1 57
(Michael Dods) *wnt lft s: bhd and outpcd: hdwy fnl f: nvr able to chal* **10/1**

5340 **7** 3/4 **Inciting Incident (IRE)**23 2886 3-8-13 67 (b) GrahamLee 4 61
(Ed McMahon) *t.k.h: hld up: stdy hdwy over 2f out: rdn wl over 1f out: sn no imp* **13/2**

40-1 **8** 4 1/2 **Musical Molly (IRE)**8 3406 3-8-11 65 6ex DaleSwift 8 42
(Brian Ellison) *hld up in tch: drvn along over 2f out: wknd over 1f out* **7/1**

1m 0.17s (-0.93) **Going Correction** -0.225s/f (Firm) **8** Ran SP% **119.4**
Speed ratings (Par 99): **98,96,95,95,94 92,91,84**
CSF £184.29 CT £1137.56 TOTE £23.20: £4.40, £1.70, £2.00; EX 163.10 Trifecta £755.30.
**Owner** Dr Marwan Koukash **Bred** Miss Nicola Cullen **Trained** Musley Bank, N Yorks
■ Stewards' Enquiry : P J McDonald caution: careless riding.

**FOCUS**
Ordinary form with the winner rated a length off his AW best, and the third posting a personal best.
T/Jkpt: Not won. T/Plt: £1079.00 to a £1 stake. Pool: £77,305.41 - 52.30 winning tickets. T/Qpdt: £168.40 to a £1 stake. Pool: £5,828.79 - 25.60 winning tickets. RY

# 3474 NEWMARKET (R-H)

Friday, June 27

**OFFICIAL GOING: Good to firm (7.9)**
Realignment of bend into home straight increased distances of 10f, 12f, and 13f races by 22m.
Wind: virtually nil Weather: dry, showers races 1 and 2

## 3670 NEWMARKETRACECOURSES.CO.UK H'CAP 1m
5:55 (5:55) (Class 5) (0-75,75) 3-Y-O+ £3,881 (£1,155; £577; £288) Stalls High

Form RPR

-442 **1** **Spirit Raiser (IRE)**15 3144 3-9-3 74 HayleyTurner 3 83+
(James Fanshawe) *sn chsng ldr: rdn to ld wl over 1f out: drifting rt but r.o wl fnl f: rdn out* **9/4**1

-312 **2** 1 1/2 **Sahra Al Khadra**12 3273 3-9-3 74 DaneO'Neill 5 79
(Charles Hills) *hld up in tch in last trio: clsd to chse ldrs and rdn 2f out: chsd wnr over 1f out: kpt on but drifting rt and no imp after* **9/4**1

-500 **3** 3/4 **Headlong (IRE)**15 3145 3-8-8 65 SilvestreDeSousa 6 68
(Brian Meehan) *stdd s: hld up in tch in rr: swtchd rt and hdwy 2f out: chsd ldrs 1f out: kpt on but no imp ins fnl f* **11/1**

1223 **4** 1 3/4 **Plucky Dip**15 3158 3-7-13 61 DannyBrock(5) 4 60
(John Ryan) *in tch in midfield: rdn over 2f out: drvn and unable qck over 1f out: styd on same pce fnl f* **10/1**

1-56 **5** 1 1/4 **Tea In Transvaal (IRE)**23 2892 3-9-4 75 RyanMoore 8 71
(Richard Hannon) *chsd ldrs: rdn and effrt over 2f out: carried rt and unable qck ent fnl f: styd on same pce after* **11/2**2

3-20 **6** 1 1/2 **Pure Amber (IRE)**35 2510 3-9-3 74 AdamKirby 7 67
(Ismail Mohammed) *led: rdn over 2f out: hdd wl over 1f out: edgd rt u.p and outpcd ent fnl f: wknd fnl 100yds* **8/1**3

2200 **7** 14 **Appease**37 2462 5-10-0 75 (p) TomQueally 2 38
(John Butler) *hld up in tch in last trio: rdn ent fnl 2f: sn btn: bhd fnl f* **20/1**

1m 39.58s (-0.42) **Going Correction** +0.05s/f (Good)
**WFA** 3 from 5yo 10lb **7** Ran SP% **110.2**
Speed ratings (Par 103): **104,102,101,100,98 97,83**
CSF £6.47 CT £38.46 TOTE £2.60: £2.10, £2.30; EX 5.20 Trifecta £82.00.
**Owner** Lord Vestey **Bred** Stowell Park Stud **Trained** Newmarket, Suffolk

**FOCUS**
The pace was not very strong in this handicap, but progressive 3yos filled the first two places and the form looks sound.

## 3671 BRITISH STALLION STUDS EBF MAIDEN FILLIES' STKS (BOBIS RACE) 6f
6:30 (6:39) (Class 4) 2-Y-O £4,528 (£1,347; £673; £336) Stalls High

Form RPR

**1** **Muraaqaba** 2-9-0 0 DaneO'Neill 14 85+
(Mark Johnston) *wnt rt s: mde all and set stdy gallop: rdn over 1f out: r.o wl and drew clr ins fnl f: gng away at fin: readily* **2/1**1

**2** 3 1/4 **Exceedingly** 2-9-0 0 NickyMackay 5 75+
(John Gosden) *chsd wnr early: stdd and chsd ldng trio: rdn and effrt over 1f out: styd on ins fnl f: wnt 2nd on post: no threat to wnr* **12/1**

**3** hd **East Coast Lady (IRE)** 2-9-0 0 FrederikTylicki 2 75
(William Stone) *sn chsng wnr: rdn 2f out: outpcd by wnr fnl f but kpt on wl: lost 2nd on post* **25/1**

**4** 3/4 **Disprove (IRE)** 2-8-9 0 NoelGarbutt(5) 16 72
(Hugo Palmer) *t.k.h: chsd ldrs: rdn ent fnl 2f: outpcd by wnr jst ins fnl f: styd on same pce after* **25/1**

**5** 1/2 **Black Cherry** 2-8-7 0 CamHardie(7) 1 71+
(Richard Hannon) *s.i.s: sn rcvrd and in tch in midfield after 1f: rdn and effrt over 2f out: edgd lft and no imp fnl f* **9/1**

**6** 1 1/4 **On High** 2-9-0 0 KieranO'Neill 13 67
(Richard Hannon) *sltly hmpd s: in tch in midfield: rdn and effrt 2f out: no imp ent fnl f: no ch w wnr and kpt on same pce after* **25/1**

**7** 1 3/4 **Tamarin** 2-9-0 0 RyanMoore 7 62
(Sir Michael Stoute) *in tch in midfield: rdn over 2f out: unable qck over 1f out: no ch w wnr and one-pce fnl f* **10/1**

**8** hd **Hundi (IRE)** 2-9-0 0 FrankieDettori 12 61+
(Charles Hills) *v.s.a: rcvrd and in tch after 1f: chsd ldrs and rdn ent fnl 2f: no ex over 1f out: btn and eased ins fnl f* **10/3**2

**9** hd **Coolcalmcollected (IRE)** 2-9-0 0 TedDurcan 4 61
(Chris Wall) *stdd after s: hld up in tch towards rr: rdn over 1f out: no real imp: plugged on same pce after* **20/1**

**10** 5 **Stocking** 2-9-0 0 AndreaAtzeni 11 46
(Roger Varian) *dwlt: flashed tail regularly: in tch in midfield: rdn and nt qckn 2f out: wknd 1f out* **11/2**3

**11** 1 **Recover (USA)** 2-9-0 0 TomQueally 3 43
(Brian Meehan) *stdd s: in tch towards rr: rdn and effrt over 2f out: no prog: wknd over 1f out* **25/1**

**12** 3 3/4 **Decibelle** 2-9-0 0 HayleyTurner 10 31
(Jane Chapple-Hyam) *t.k.h: hld up in tch towards rr: rdn 1/2-way: wknd over 1f out* **50/1**

6 **13** 1 1/4 **Weardiditallgorong**11 3311 2-9-0 0 SamHitchcott 8 28
(Des Donovan) *in tch in rr: rdn 1/2-way: wknd wl over 1f out: bhd fnl f* **66/1**

1m 14.53s (2.03) **Going Correction** +0.05s/f (Good) **13** Ran SP% **122.2**
Speed ratings (Par 92): **88,83,83,82,81 80,77,77,77,70 69,64,62**
CSF £26.46 TOTE £3.70: £1.60, £2.80, £6.80; EX 33.20 Trifecta £608.70.
**Owner** Hamdan Al Maktoum **Bred** Shadwell Estate Company Limited **Trained** Middleham Moor, N Yorks
■ Stewards' Enquiry : Nicky Mackay caution: careless riding.

**FOCUS**
A majority of newcomers lined-up in this interesting maiden and the favourite scored in good style. This Is Too was withdrawn after getting loose out of the front of the stalls. The race average is decent and there were some nice types on show. The opening level is fluid but likely this good or better.

## 3672 32RED CASINO H'CAP (BOBIS RACE) 7f
7:05 (7:08) (Class 4) (0-80,80) 3-Y-O £5,175 (£1,540; £769; £384) Stalls High

Form RPR

2-31 **1** **Outlawed**17 3083 3-9-7 80 GeorgeBaker 1 87+
(Ed Walker) *hld up in tch in last trio: clsd 2f out: rdn and chal 1f out: led fnl 100yds: r.o wl and asserted towards fin* **11/4**1

10-0 **2** 1/2 **Desert Society (IRE)**6 3464 3-9-6 79 RyanMoore 5 85
(Richard Hannon) *sn led: rdn ent fnl 2f: hrd pressed and drvn 1f out: hdd fnl 100yds: battled on wl but no ex towards fin* **6/1**2

0-10 **3** hd **Battle Command (USA)**35 2510 3-9-5 78 FrankieDettori 9 83
(Peter Chapple-Hyam) *hld up in tch in last trio: rdn and hdwy 2f out: chal 1f out: kpt on wl u.p: no ex towards fin* **7/1**3

-241 **4** 1/2 **Twin Point**14 3198 3-9-6 79 NickyMackay 8 83
(John Gosden) *chsd ldrs: rdn and effrt wl over 1f out: ev ch and drvn 1f out: kpt on tl no ex and eased towards fin* **11/4**1

0-13 **5** 2 1/4 **Pactolus (IRE)**18 3067 3-9-2 75 AdamBeschizza 3 73
(Stuart Williams) *chsd ldrs: n.m.r 2f out: swtchd rt and effrt over 1f out: styd on same pce and no imp fnl f* **8/1**

-104 **6** 1/2 **Nirva (IRE)**31 2639 3-9-5 78 TomQueally 4 75
(Ralph Beckett) *hld up in tch in rr: rdn and effrt 2f out: kpt on but no threat to ldrs fnl f* **12/1**

0365 **7** 1 1/2 **Tarrafal (IRE)**34 2545 3-8-3 71 oh9 SilvestreDeSousa 6 55
(Mark Johnston) *chsd ldr: rdn over 2f out: drvn and lost pl over 1f out: wknd ins fnl f* **20/1**

-120 **8** 5 **Iftaar (IRE)**13 3225 3-9-5 78 DaneO'Neill 7 58
(Charles Hills) *stdd after s: t.k.h: hld up in tch in midfield: rdn and effrt 2f out: wknd 1f out* **10/1**

1m 25.51s (-0.19) **Going Correction** +0.05s/f (Good) **8** Ran SP% **112.8**
Speed ratings (Par 101): **103,102,102,101,99 98,96,91**
CSF £19.07 CT £102.66 TOTE £3.80: £1.40, £1.90, £2.00; EX 19.30 Trifecta £92.20.
**Owner** Laurence A Bellman **Bred** Snailwell Stud Co Ltd **Trained** Newmarket, Suffolk

**FOCUS**
There was a tight four-way finish in this steadily run handicap. The winner looks a nice type, and the runner-up and third stepped up on their maiden wins.

## 3673 INVESCO PERPETUAL H'CAP (BOBIS RACE) 1m 5f
7:35 (7:37) (Class 4) (0-80,78) 3-Y-O £5,175 (£1,540; £769; £384) Stalls Centre

Form RPR

0511 **1** **Maid In Rio (IRE)**8 3396 3-9-7 78 6ex SilvestreDeSousa 8 93
(Mark Johnston) *t.k.h: chsd ldrs: jnd ldr 3f out: led 2f out: rdn and edgd rt over 1f out: hrd pressed wl ins fnl f: hld on* **10/3**2

03-5 **2** nk **Battersea**69 1587 3-9-5 76 FrederikTylicki 6 90
(Roger Varian) *in tch in midfield: rdn and effrt over 2f out: chsd wnr jst ins fnl f: r.o wl and clsng on wnr towards fin* **7/1**

5-32 **3** 5 **Curbyourenthusiasm (IRE)**36 2492 3-9-3 74 FergusSweeney 3 80
(David Simcock) *stdd after s: hld up in tch towards rr: hdwy 5f out: rdn and effrt over 2f out: 4th and no imp 1f out: kpt on to go 3rd ins fnl f* **9/2**3

3342 **4** 2 3/4 **Rite To Reign**16 3110 3-9-7 78 RyanMoore 7 80
(Philip McBride) *chsd ldr tl led 3f out: hdd 2f out: no ex u.p over 1f out: wknd ins fnl f* **9/4**1

-053 **5** 5 **Cinnilla**28 2735 3-8-11 68 TomQueally 2 62
(Ralph Beckett) *chsd ldrs: rdn over 3f out: struggling u.p over 2f out: wl btn but plugged on ins fnl f* **16/1**

2221 **6** 1/2 **Bold Runner**36 2491 3-9-0 71 FrankieDettori 4 65
(Jose Santos) *stdd s: t.k.h: hld up in tch in rr: effrt on outer but racing awkwardly over 2f out: wknd over 1f out* **7/1**

022- **7** 3 1/2 **Rawoof (IRE)**276 6716 3-9-1 72 DaneO'Neill 1 60
(Ed Dunlop) *stdd s: hld up in tch towards rr: swtchd lft off of rail 3f out: rdn and btn over 2f out: wknd over 1f out* **12/1**

0050 **8** 36 **Appellez Baileys (FR)**10 3326 3-8-2 59 oh14 NickyMackay 5
(Chris Dwyer) *led tl rdn and hdd over 3f out: dropped to rr 2f out: sn lost tch: t.o* **100/1**

2m 46.99s (2.99) **Going Correction** +0.05s/f (Good) **8** Ran SP% **111.6**
Speed ratings (Par 101): **92,91,88,87,83 83,81,59**
CSF £25.40 CT £101.87 TOTE £3.30: £1.40, £1.80, £1.80; EX 19.70 Trifecta £138.90.
**Owner** The New Fairyhouse Partnership **Bred** Miss Susan Bates And Suzannah Dwyer **Trained** Middleham Moor, N Yorks

**FOCUS**
This looked a good race for the grade with the front four all interesting. The winner more than confirmed her Ripon win, while the runner-up posted a big personal best.

## 3674 EBF STALLIONS HYPHEN BLOODSTOCK FILLIES' CONDITIONS STKS 6f
8:10 (8:10) (Class 3) 3-Y-O+ £9,056 (£2,695; £1,346; £673) Stalls High

Form RPR

40-0 **1** **Remember**27 2781 3-8-6 88 KieranO'Neill 5 95
(Richard Hannon) *chsd ldr tl rdn and qcknd to ld over 1f out: 2 l clr 1f out: r.o wl* **9/1**

00-2 **2** 1 1/2 **Hoodna (IRE)**27 2778 4-8-13 100 KierenFallon 7 92
(Saeed bin Suroor) *stdd s: hld up in tch in midfield: clsd to chse ldrs 2f out: sn rdn: battling for 2nd but no imp on wnr fnl f* **5/6**1

14-3 **3** shd **Our Queenie (IRE)**21 2965 3-7-13 87 CamHardie(7) 8 90
(Richard Hannon) *in tch in midfield: rdn and effrt ent fnl 2f: battling for 2nd but no imp on wnr fnl f* **8/1**

-010 **4** 1 3/4 **Front Page News**19 3036 4-8-6 78 KieranShoemark(7) 9 86?
(Robert Eddery) *in tch in midfield: rdn and hdwy 2f out: styd on same pce and no imp fnl f* **33/1**

3-06 **5** 3/4 **Maid A Million**7 3431 4-8-13 90 RyanMoore 3 84
(David Elsworth) *led: rdn ent fnl 2f: drvn and hdd over 1f out: outpcd and btn 1f out: kpt on* **6/1**2

31-0 **6** *hd* **Artistic Charm**[72] 1515 3-8-9 85 LukeMorris 1 84
(David Simcock) *wnt rt s: hld up in tch in rr: clsd and n.m.r 2f: drvn and effrt over 1f out: one-pced fnl f* **16/1**

60 **7** *1 3/4* **March**[25] 2848 4-8-13 99 [1] FrankieDettori 2 77
(Robert Cowell) *s.i.s: sn rcvrd and hld up in tch in rr: hdwy 2f out: rdn and no imp over 1f out: wknd ins fnl f* **7/1**[3]

0-60 **8** *2 3/4* **Melody Of Love**[21] 2956 4-8-13 92 TomQueally 4 69
(Brian Meehan) *chsd ldrs: rdn 2f out: unable qck and lost pl ent fnl f: wknd fnl 150yds* **14/1**

1m 12.07s (-0.43) **Going Correction** +0.05s/f (Good)
**WFA** 3 from 4yo 7lb 8 Ran SP% **117.9**
Speed ratings (Par 104): **104,102,101,99,98 98,95,92**
CSF £17.55 TOTE £11.70: £2.60, £1.10, £2.20; EX 25.40 Trifecta £101.00.
**Owner** Saeed Manana **Bred** Fittocks Stud **Trained** East Everleigh, Wilts

**FOCUS**
A bit muddling, the fourth key to the level. The runner-up was keen early and is rated a stone below solid handicap latest.

## 3675 ANN LEWITT HALF CENTURY H'CAP 1m 2f
8:40 (8:40) (Class 4) (0-80,80) 3-Y-O+ £4,998 (£1,509; £764; £391; £205) Stalls Centre

Form RPR

2115 **1** **Insaany**[18] 3055 3-9-2 80 DaneO'Neill 2 89
(Mark Johnston) *chsd clr ldr: clsd and travelling best over 2f out: rdn to ld over 1f out: clr and drvn ins fnl f: edgd rt towards fin: a holding on* **4/1**[2]

623- **2** *1 1/4* **Itsnowcato**[200] 8221 3-8-10 74 LukeMorris 6 79
(Ed Walker) *hld up off the pce in last pair: rdn 3f out: drvn and wnt 3rd ent fnl f: chsd wnr wl ins fnl f: kpt on* **9/1**

-410 **3** *shd* **Sayed Youmzain**[36] 2496 3-9-1 79 (b[1]) SilvestreDeSousa 3 84
(Marco Botti) *t.k.h: hld up in midfield: rdn and effrt over 2f out: chsd clr wnr jst over 1f out: lost 2nd wl ins fnl f: kpt on: nt clr run and eased last strides* **11/2**[3]

0-12 **4** *5* **Trulee Scrumptious**[10] 3325 5-8-9 61 oh1 (v) JimmyQuinn 4 56
(Peter Charalambous) *led: racd away fr rivals nr inner rail fr 8f out: rdn over 2f out: drvn and hdd over 1f out: wknd 1f out* **8/1**

123 **5** *6* **Luck Of The Game (USA)**[35] 2506 3-9-1 79 RyanMoore 5 63
(David Simcock) *hld up off the pce in last pair: rdn 3f out: drvn and hung lft over 1f out: wl hld 1f out: eased towards fin* **11/8**[1]

-320 **P** **Classic Devotion (USA)**[30] 2685 3-9-2 80 WilliamBuick 1
(Charlie Appleby) *hld up in midfield: rdn 3f out: dropped to last and btn over 1f out: sn eased: p.u ins fnl f* **7/1**

2m 6.6s (1.10) **Going Correction** +0.05s/f (Good)
**WFA** 3 from 5yo 12lb 6 Ran SP% **111.1**
Speed ratings (Par 105): **97,96,95,91,87**
CSF £36.24 TOTE £4.30: £2.10, £3.00; EX 28.20 Trifecta £181.10.
**Owner** Hamdan Al Maktoum **Bred** Qatar Bloodstock Ltd **Trained** Middleham Moor, N Yorks

**FOCUS**
Trulee Scrumptious set a strong pace before weakening in this handicap and the first three pulled clear. The winner has been progressing and this was another step up, while the runner-up improved in line with maiden form.

## 3676 ALL NEW 32RED SPORT H'CAP 5f
9:10 (9:10) (Class 4) (0-85,85) 3-Y-O+ £5,175 (£1,540; £769; £384) Stalls High

Form RPR

0151 **1** **Sandfrankskipsgo**[56] 1922 5-9-12 85 GeorgeBaker 5 94
(Peter Crate) *hld up in midfield: clsd over 1f out: rdn to ld ins fnl f: hld on wl towards fin* **7/1**

14-6 **2** *nk* **Holley Shiftwell**[13] 3246 4-9-4 77 JamesDoyle 8 85
(Stuart Williams) *racd off the pce in rr: rdn 2f out: clsd u.p over 1f out: chsd wnr ins fnl f: r.o wl: hld towards fin* **4/1**[1]

015 **3** *2 1/2* **Monumental Man**[13] 3216 5-9-9 82 (p) AdamKirby 2 81
(James Unett) *chsd ldr: rdn and ev ch 2f out: led over 1f out: hdd ins fnl f: outpcd fnl 100yds* **9/2**[2]

0414 **4** *1 3/4* **Sir Pedro**[6] 3470 5-8-11 75 MarcMonaghan(5) 4 68
(Robert Cowell) *chsd ldrs: clsd and upsides ldrs 2f out: rdn over 1f out: no ex ins fnl f: wknd fnl 100yds* **6/1**

0-14 **5** *1/2* **Ruby's Day**[52] 2050 5-8-11 77 ClaireMurray(7) 7 68
(David Brown) *s.i.s: pushed along and outpcd in rr: hung lft wl over 1f out: kpt on fnl f: nvr trbld ldrs* **11/2**[3]

110 **6** *1 1/4* **Breccbennach**[11] 3313 4-9-8 81 (tp) DaneO'Neill 6 67
(Seamus Durack) *chsd ldrs: rdn and pressing ldrs 2f out: no ex jst over 1f out: sn wknd* **9/2**[2]

0550 **7** *4 1/2* **Jiroft (ITY)**[16] 3122 7-9-12 85 PatCosgrave 3 55
(Robert Cowell) *led tl rdn and hdd over 1f out: sn lost pl: fdd ins fnl f* **6/1**

59.23s (0.13) **Going Correction** +0.05s/f (Good) 7 Ran SP% **112.8**
Speed ratings (Par 105): **100,99,95,92,91 89,82**
CSF £33.91 CT £139.21 TOTE £7.70: £3.30, £2.10; EX 21.60 Trifecta £61.50.
**Owner** Peter Crate **Bred** Peter Crate **Trained** Newdigate, Surrey

**FOCUS**
The leaders got involved in a pace duel and the first two came from some way back. The level is fluid given the pace collapsed, but the runner-up is unexposed and this rates a small personal best.
T/Plt: £20.90 to a £1 stake. Pool: £55,955.53 - 1946.41 winning tickets. T/Qpdt: £10.10 to a £1 stake. Pool: £4,459.44 - 325.37 winning tickets. SP

# 3626 YARMOUTH (L-H)
### Friday, June 27

**OFFICIAL GOING: Good to firm (firm in places; 7.5) changing to good after race 4 (3.55)**
Bottom bend dolled out 1.5m and races on Round course increased by 7m.
Wind: light breeze Weather: sunny; 18 degrees, heavy rain race 3

## 3677 GEORGE DAVIES 21ST BIRTHDAY MAIDEN STKS 6f 3y
2:20 (2:25) (Class 5) 3-Y-O+ £3,234 (£962; £481; £240) Stalls Centre

Form RPR

-342 **1** **Intermedium**[15] 3156 3-9-5 81 AdamKirby 2 84
(Charlie Appleby) *mde all: rdn clr over 1f out: untrbld after* **1/4**[1]

0 **2** *6* **Oasis Mirage**[15] 3156 3-9-0 0 FrederikTylicki 4 60
(Robert Cowell) *cl up: rdn and sltly outpcd 2f out: wnt 2nd over 1f out: no ch w wnr* **20/1**

5 **3** *1 1/4* **Ecliptic Sunrise**[15] 3156 3-8-11 0 OisinMurphy(3) 6 56
(Des Donovan) *t.k.h: pressed ldrs: rdn 1/2-way: disp 2nd over 2f out tl btn over 1f out* **8/1**[2]

00- **4** *1 1/4* **Shaft Of Light**[224] 7893 3-9-5 0 LukeMorris 5 57
(Sir Mark Prescott Bt) *cl up: drvn and outpcd 1/2-way: racd awkwardly fnl 2f: no ch after: plugged on* **16/1**[3]

00-0 **5** *1/2* **Aster's Approval**[10] 3332 4-9-12 0 (vt[1]) PaddyAspell 1 57?
(Mrs Ilka Gansera-Leveque) *sweating: taken down early: lost 6 l s: a bhd: rdn and plugged on ins fnl f* **100/1**

55 **6** *shd* **Dubawi Coast**[32] 2625 3-9-0 0 (p) JimmyQuinn 7 50
(James Tate) *sn shkn up and rn green: chsd ldrs: effrt and disp 2nd over 2f out tl btn over 1f out: fdd ins fnl f* **16/1**[3]

**7** *16* **Belle Star** 3-9-0 0 PatCosgrave 3
(Noel Quinlan) *cl up tl rdn 1/2-way: fdd bdly over 2f out: t.o* **25/1**

1m 12.88s (-1.52) **Going Correction** -0.225s/f (Firm)
**WFA** 3 from 4yo 7lb 7 Ran SP% **112.5**
Speed ratings (Par 103): **101,93,91,89,89 88,67**
CSF £8.88 TOTE £1.10: £1.10, £6.50; EX 7.40 Trifecta £31.50.
**Owner** Godolphin **Bred** Darley **Trained** Newmarket, Suffolk

**FOCUS**
An uncompetitive opener, run on drying ground. The winner gave the third a similar beating to their C&D meeting last time, and the runner-up, from the same race, improved.

## 3678 WATERAID CHARITY H'CAP 1m 3y
2:50 (2:51) (Class 6) (0-65,64) 4-Y-O+ £1,940 (£577; £288; £144) Stalls Centre

Form RPR

2422 **1** **Specialty (IRE)**[16] 3123 4-9-5 62 AdamKirby 2 76
(Pam Sly) *led: drvn over 2f out: hdd over 1f out: battled on and level again 100yds out: jst prevailed* **3/1**[1]

4421 **2** *nse* **Refuse Colette (IRE)**[16] 3123 5-8-7 50 oh5 AndreaAtzeni 4 64
(Mick Quinn) *racd keenly in 2nd: drvn to ld over 1f out: remained hrd pressed but r.o gamely: jst pipped* **6/1**[3]

-363 **3** *6* **Gift Of Silence**[15] 3160 5-9-7 64 PaddyAspell 7 64
(John Berry) *last away and hld up: rdn and prog 2f out: wnt mod 3rd ins fnl f* **10/1**

00-5 **4** *1/2* **My Guardian Angel**[68] 852 5-9-7 64 TedDurcan 5 63
(Mark H Tompkins) *chsd ldrs: effrt 1/2-way: rdn 3f out: outpcd by ldng pair 2f out: plugged on* **14/1**

0364 **5** *nk* **Loucal**[15] 3155 4-8-7 55 TobyAtkinson(5) 8 53
(Noel Quinlan) *chsd ldrs: hrd rdn 3f out: struggling 2f out* **10/1**

B001 **6** *1 1/2* **Roxy Lane**[7] 3427 5-8-2 45 oh10 LukeMorris 3 40
(Peter Hiatt) *prom: pushed along 1/2-way: outpcd by ldng pair 2f out: lost mod 3rd ins fnl f* **4/1**[2]

5562 **7** *1 1/4* **Lady Sylvia**[7] 3427 5-9-4 64 OisinMurphy(3) 1 56
(Joseph Tuite) *towards rr: rdn over 2f out: sn btn* **3/1**[1]

5005 **8** *3/4* **Mr Chocolate Drop (IRE)**[26] 2806 10-8-2 45 oh10 (t) JimmyQuinn 6 35
(Mandy Rowland) *bhd: pushed along 1/2-way: struggling fnl 3f* **25/1**

1m 38.24s (-2.36) **Going Correction** -0.225s/f (Firm) 8 Ran SP% **113.0**
Speed ratings (Par 101): **102,101,95,95,95 93,92,91**
CSF £20.87 CT £157.64 TOTE £3.10: £1.10, £2.10, £3.00; EX 15.50 Trifecta £61.80.
**Owner** Michael H Sly Dr T Davies Mrs Pam Sly **Bred** M H Sly, Dr T Davies & Mrs P Sly **Trained** Thorney, Cambs

**FOCUS**
The one-two have been rated as running a bit better than when finishing two-one over C&D last time, the level fluid with the pair clear.

## 3679 COLMANS OF NORWICH 200TH ANNIVERSARY H'CAP 5f 43y
3:20 (3:20) (Class 6) (0-60,60) 3-Y-O £1,940 (£577; £288; £144) Stalls Centre

Form RPR

6220 **1** **Vodka Chaser (IRE)**[6] 3487 3-9-2 60 TimClark(5) 3 69
(Alison Hutchinson) *chsd ldrs gng wl: rdn and wnt 2nd 2f out: led ins fnl f: sn in command: readily* **3/1**[1]

2000 **2** *3 1/2* **Mimi Luke (USA)**[16] 3114 3-9-6 59 (v) AdamKirby 7 55
(Alan Bailey) *sn led: drvn 2f out: hdd ins fnl f: sn outbattled* **4/1**[3]

6-40 **3** *2* **Astral Rose**[35] 2505 3-8-12 54 (b) OisinMurphy(3) 6 43
(Jonathan Portman) *mounted on crse: immediately drvn: effrt 1/2-way: no imp fnl 2f: plugged on into mod 3rd ins fnl f* **8/1**

3652 **4** *1/2* **Artemis (IRE)**[4] 3522 3-9-3 56 JimmyQuinn 8 43
(Conrad Allen) *plld hrd: sn prom: rdn and outpcd wl over 1f out: lost 3rd ins fnl f* **7/2**[2]

0610 **5** *3 3/4* **Robbian**[13] 3228 3-8-13 52 RobbieFitzpatrick 1 26
(Charles Smith) *a abt same pl: rdn 1/2-way: fdd 2f out* **8/1**

0030 **6** *1 1/4* **Back On Baileys**[3] 3549 3-8-7 46 oh1 (v) ChrisCatlin 2 15
(John Ryan) *taken down early: dwlt: sn pushed along in rr: wl btn 2f out* **16/1**

3530 **7** *1* **Rosie Prospects**[79] 1389 3-8-5 51 (p) RhiainIngram(7) 5 17
(Roger Ingram) *a bhd: wl btn 2f out* **20/1**

6460 **8** *1 1/2* **Anfield**[7] 3433 3-8-9 48 (p) PatCosgrave 4 8
(Mick Quinn) *w ldr for over 1f: sn rdn: wknd 1/2-way: wl btn fnl 2f* **5/1**

1m 2.45s (-0.25) **Going Correction** -0.225s/f (Firm) 8 Ran SP% **116.8**
Speed ratings (Par 97): **93,87,84,83,77 75,73,71**
CSF £15.61 CT £87.38 TOTE £2.80: £1.10, £1.60, £3.00; EX 13.90 Trifecta £128.30.
**Owner** L P Keane **Bred** Tally-Ho Stud **Trained** Exning, Suffolk

**FOCUS**
This was desperately weak with no recent winners amongst the eight who took part. However, they appeared to go plenty quick enough up front. The winner is rated to her 2yo best but with little confidence.

## 3680 ESSEX AND SUFFOLK WATER H'CAP 2m
3:55 (3:55) (Class 5) (0-75,81) 4-Y-O+ £2,587 (£770; £384; £192) Stalls High

Form RPR

211/ **1** **Solar View (IRE)**[665] 5798 5-9-7 75 LukeMorris 4 85
(Sir Mark Prescott Bt) *settled in 3rd: drvn over 4f out: wnt 2nd over 2f out: led u.p over 1f out: sn edgd clr* **4/1**[2]

-412 **2** *2 3/4* **Wannabe Your Man**[27] 2774 4-9-7 75 AndreaAtzeni 1 82
(Roger Varian) *led at v slow pce tl reined bk 11f out: shkn up over 4f out: led over 2f out: rdn and hdd over 1f out: fnd little and wl hld fnl f* **4/11**[1]

-564 **3** *12* **Grayswood**[15] 3151 4-8-9 63 (p) MartinDwyer 2 56
(William Muir) *hld up last: drvn and outpcd over 4f out: edgd lft 3f out: tk remote 3rd ins fnl f and styd on* **10/1**[3]

0-06 **4** *6* **Bouggatti**[30] 2683 6-8-12 66 (v[1]) TedDurcan 3 51
(Lady Herries) *2nd tl led 11f out: rdn and hdd over 2f out: dropped out v tamely* **20/1**

3m 33.42s (1.02) **Going Correction** -0.10s/f (Good) 4 Ran SP% **107.2**
Speed ratings (Par 103): **93,91,85,82**
CSF £6.00 TOTE £2.50; EX 7.60 Trifecta £8.20.
**Owner** Neil Greig - Osborne House **Bred** Lady Richard Wellesley **Trained** Newmarket, Suffolk

**FOCUS**
A torrential downpour before the start of this race and a suspicion that the ground rode slower than described. The absence of Meetings Man meant that this was not as competitive as was advertised and it remains to be seen what was achieved by the winner.

## 3681 GREENE KING FESTIVAL AT YARMOUTH H'CAP 1m 3f 101y
**4:30** (4:30) (Class 4) (0-80,78) 4-Y-O+ **£5,498** (£1,636; £817; £408) **Stalls** Low

Form RPR
-003 **1** **Ex Oriente (IRE)**[6] 3475 5-9-1 **72**................................. AdamBeschizza 6 83
(Stuart Williams) *hld up last tl effrt on outer fr 4f out: sn rdn: wnt 2nd 2f out: drvn to ld 100yds out: styd on stoutly* **7/1**

211 **2** ½ **Ifan (IRE)**[24] 2862 6-9-0 **74**.................................. OisinMurphy(3) 1 84
(Tim Vaughan) *taken down early: chsd clr ldr: clsd 3f out: rdn to ld 2f out: hdd fnl 100yds: kpt on same pce* **3/1**[1]

1253 **3** 8 **Sagesse**[111] 891 4-9-7 **78**........................................ LukeMorris 4 75
(Sir Mark Prescott Bt) *chsd ldng pair: pushed along 4f out: racd awkwardly: unbalanced and outpcd over 2f out: last jst over 1f out: rallied and styd on nicely to take modest 3rd* **10/3**[2]

6-02 **4** 2 ¼ **Colinca's Lad (IRE)**[20] 2980 12-8-10 **70**.................... RosieJessop(3) 2 63
(Peter Charalambous) *rdn to ld at str pce: sent 8 l clr 1/2-way: rdn over 2f out: sn hdd: kpt trying but btn 1f out: lost 3rd fnl 75yds* **5/1**[3]

0-22 **5** 1 ¾ **Silk Train**[17] 3079 4-8-13 **70**.................................... PatCosgrave 3 60
(David Simcock) *nvr bttr than 4th: rdn over 2f out: plugged on same pce after* **3/1**[1]

1406 **6** ½ **Secular Society**[24] 2876 4-9-3 **74**........................ FergusSweeney 5 64
(George Baker) *in last pair: pushed along 4f out: rdn and effrt 3f out: fdd over 1f out* **12/1**

2m 25.97s (-2.73) **Going Correction** -0.10s/f (Good) **6** Ran SP% **109.9**
Speed ratings (Par 105): **105,104,98,97,95 95**
CSF £26.90 TOTE £9.40: £3.50, £1.80; EX 30.20 Trifecta £179.10.

**Owner** Mrs J Morley & GJSS **Bred** Mrs Vanessa Hutch **Trained** Newmarket, Suffolk

**FOCUS**
A disappointing turnout for this feature but it was run at a good pace. The runner-up earned a personal-best rating.

## 3682 BOOK THE TRAFALGAR RESTAURANT AT YARMOUTH H'CAP 1m 3f 101y
**5:05** (5:05) (Class 6) (0-60,59) 4-Y-O+ **£1,940** (£577; £288; £144) **Stalls** Low

Form RPR
330 **1** **Poste Restante**[16] 3115 4-8-2 **47**........................... LewisWalsh(7) 7 57
(David Simcock) *hld up in last pair: rdn and str run to go 2nd 3f out: sn w ldr: urged clr fnl 120yds* **12/1**

5003 **2** 2 **Shirataki (IRE)**[13] 3209 6-9-2 **54**................................. ChrisCatlin 1 61
(Peter Hiatt) *led: rdn and hrd pressed wl over 2f out: hdd and outpcd fnl 120yds* **8/1**

3253 **3** 1 ¾ **Bethan**[24] 2874 5-9-0 **57**..............................(p) ShelleyBirkett(5) 2 61
(Julia Feilden) *prom: rdn 3f out: one pce and wl hld by ldng pair fnl 2f but kpt trying* **9/2**[2]

2-23 **4** 2 **Pink Lips**[11] 3308 6-9-4 **59**..................................... OisinMurphy(3) 3 60
(J R Jenkins) *towards rr: slipped on home turn: sn drvn: making no imp fr over 2f out and wl btn after* **11/8**[1]

350- **5** 13 **Helamis**[251] 7382 4-8-12 **50**....................................... JackMitchell 4 29
(Denis Quinn) *midfield: shkn up 1/2-way: struggling over 2f out* **5/1**[3]

4006 **6** 4 ½ **Booktheband (IRE)**[16] 3115 4-8-10 **48**......................(b) LukeMorris 5 20
(Clive Brittain) *midfield: effrt to go 2nd home turn: lost pl 3f out: nt look keen: drvn and fdd bdly: t.o* **16/1**

6654 **7** 6 **Joyful Motive**[8] 3404 5-8-2 **47**............................ BradleyBosley(7) 8 9
(Michael Chapman) *drvn to go prom but nvr travelling: racd wd: stopped v qckly over 4f out: t.o after* **16/1**

046/ **8** 9 **Black Iceman**[792] 1631 6-9-0 **55**.......................... SimonPearce(3) 6 2
(Lydia Pearce) *lost 6 l s: pushed along and lost tch over 4f out: sn hopelessly t.o* **20/1**

2m 27.46s (-1.24) **Going Correction** -0.10s/f (Good) **8** Ran SP% **112.3**
Speed ratings (Par 101): **100,98,97,95,86 83,78,72**
CSF £98.95 CT £498.10 TOTE £16.20: £4.00, £2.80, £2.30; EX 86.60 Trifecta £528.10.

**Owner** Tick Tock Partnership **Bred** Dunchurch Lodge Stud Company **Trained** Newmarket, Suffolk

**FOCUS**
A weak race, but the winner was having only her second turf start and stepped up on her AW form from earlier in the year.

## 3683 ARENARACINGCOMPANY.CO.UK H'CAP 1m 2f 21y
**5:40** (5:40) (Class 5) (0-70,70) 3-Y-O **£2,587** (£770; £384; £192) **Stalls** Low

Form RPR
0306 **1** **Dynamic Vision (IRE)**[16] 3116 3-9-3 **66**....................(b[1]) JackMitchell 1 71
(Roger Varian) *mde all: shkn up 3f out: rdn 2 l clr over 1f out: all out cl home* **10/1**

-551 **2** ½ **Avocadeau (IRE)**[21] 2948 3-9-5 **68**........................(p) MartinDwyer 3 72
(William Muir) *pressed wnr: drvn 3f out: outpcd wl over 1f out: rallied fnl 75yds: gaining cl home* **5/1**[3]

3310 **3** 2 ½ **Sandy Cove**[10] 3326 3-8-6 **58**.................................... RyanTate(3) 4 57
(James Eustace) *racd keenly in 3rd: pushed along over 3f out: outpcd 2f out: kpt on steadily ins fnl f: no ch w ldrs* **7/2**[2]

0-04 **4** 6 **Anjin (IRE)**[160] 230 3-9-2 **65**........................................ LukeMorris 5 53
(Sir Mark Prescott Bt) *a same pl: rdn 4f out: sn edgd lft: btn 2f out* **11/10**[1]

2230 **5** 4 **Speechday (IRE)**[36] 2492 3-9-0 **66**....................... OisinMurphy(3) 6 46
(Marco Botti) *sn last pair: rdn 4f out: sn btn* **16/1**

-556 **6** 5 **Lucky Visione**[28] 2719 3-9-2 **70**........................ ShelleyBirkett(5) 2 41
(Gay Kelleway) *s.i.s: a last: pushed along and struggling over 4f out: eased ins fnl f* **8/1**

2m 8.66s (-1.84) **Going Correction** -0.10s/f (Good) **6** Ran SP% **112.6**
Speed ratings (Par 99): **103,102,100,95,92 88**
CSF £57.59 TOTE £8.70: £3.90, £2.00; EX 38.70 Trifecta £107.60.

**Owner** Saif Ali **Bred** Rabbah Bloodstock Limited **Trained** Newmarket, Suffolk

**FOCUS**
The field finished in the order they raced, the winner stepping up a little on shaky maiden best. The second stepped up on his weak Bath win, with the third close to recent form.

T/Plt: £171.40 to a £1 stake. Pool: £60,594.41 - 258.07 winning tickets. T/Qpdt: £64.50 to a £1 stake. Pool: £3,565.90 - 40.90 winning tickets. IM

# [3038] CURRAGH (R-H)
Friday, June 27

**OFFICIAL GOING: Good to firm**

## 3686a TODAY FM H'CAP 5f
**6:25** (6:27) (60-90,89) 3-Y-O+ **£8,912** (£2,066; £904; £516)

RPR
**1** **Kernoff (IRE)**[29] 2709 3-9-12 **89**...............................(p) ShaneFoley 8 100+
(M Halford, Ire) *hld up: niggled along in 7th bef 1/2-way: impr on outer into 4th ent fnl f: kpt on wl u.p to ld ins fnl 100yds: drvn clr* **5/1**[3]

**2** 2 **Lady Mega (IRE)**[44] 2262 3-9-0 **84**....................... RobbieDowney(7) 3 88
(Edward Lynam, Ire) *chsd ldrs: 4th 1/2-way: impr into 2nd 1 1/2f out: disp ent fnl f and sn led narrowly briefly tl hdd ins fnl 100yds: no ex* **5/2**[1]

**3** nk **Tylery Wonder (IRE)**[33] 2578 4-10-0 **85**........................(b) BillyLee 9 90
(W McCreery, Ire) *disp early tl led narrowly after 1f: over 1 l clr 1/2-way: rdn 2f out and jnd ent fnl f: sn hdd narrowly and no ex in 3rd ins fnl 100yds* **9/2**[2]

**4** nk **Pencil Hill (IRE)**[19] 3040 9-9-7 **78**................................. PatSmullen 10 82
(Tracey Collins, Ire) *chsd ldrs: 3rd 1/2-way: rdn over 1f out and sn swtchd rt: n.m.r bhd horses and sn no imp on wnr in 4th: kpt on same pce* **7/1**

**5** ½ **Speed Dream (IRE)**[285] 6439 10-9-0 **78**............... DylanRobinson(7) 12 80
(James M Barrett, Ire) *s.i.s and racd towards rr: 9th 1/2-way: tk clsr order in 6th ent fnl f: nt clr run ins fnl f: kpt on towards fin: nvr nrr* **20/1**

**6** ¾ **Kiss The Stars (IRE)**[13] 3260 4-9-3 **77**......................(p) ColinKeane(3) 6 76
(T G McCourt, Ire) *chsd ldrs: 5th 1/2-way: gng wl 2f out: rdn over 1f out and n.m.r between horses ins fnl f: swtchd rt and kpt on towards fin* **9/2**[2]

**7** 1 **Big Bad Lily (IRE)**[13] 3260 6-8-6 **63**............................(vt) WayneLordan 11 59
(K J Condon, Ire) *missed kick and racd towards rr: 8th 1/2-way: rdn in rr ent fnl f and sn swtchd rt into 7th: kpt on same pce* **12/1**

**8** 4 ¾ **Persian Caliph (IRE)**[69] 1591 3-9-3 **80**...................... NGMcCullagh 2 57
(Mrs John Harrington, Ire) *chsd ldrs: 6th 1/2-way: rdn on outer under 2f out and no imp on ldrs over 1f out: wknd* **16/1**

**9** 1 ¼ **Lager Time (IRE)**[37] 2459 4-9-0 **71**.................................. JFEgan 1 45
(David Evans) *disp early tl racd in cl 2nd after 1f: rdn and no ex fr 2f out: wknd ins fnl f whn n.m.r between horses: eased* **14/1**

1m 0.02s (-2.88) **Going Correction** -0.40s/f (Firm)
**WFA** 3 from 4yo+ 6lb **9** Ran SP% **119.1**
Speed ratings: **107,103,103,102,102 100,99,91,89**
CSF £18.54 CT £61.60 TOTE £6.60: £1.80, £1.50, £2.00; DF 22.50 Trifecta £111.60.
**Owner** J D Clague **Bred** Newberry Stud Company **Trained** Doneany, Co Kildare
**FOCUS**
The second and sixth help set the level with the winner posting a personal best.

3687 - 3690a (Foreign Racing) - See Raceform Interactive

# CLAIREFONTAINE (R-H)
Friday, June 27

**OFFICIAL GOING: Turf: very soft**

## 3691a PRIX DES COSMOS (CLAIMER) (2YO) (TURF) 7f
**12:50** (12:50) 2-Y-O **£11,250** (£4,500; £3,375; £2,250; £1,125)

RPR
**1** **Portenio (FR)**[66] 2-9-1 0........................................ MarcLerner 5 74
(C Lerner, France) **41/1**

**2** hd **Safzebos (FR)**[23] 2-9-1 0........................................ JulienAuge 8 73
(C Ferland, France) **41/10**[3]

**3** 1 ½ **Well Fleeced**[17] 3081 2-8-11 0.......................... IoritzMendizabal 3 65
(J S Moore) *dwlt sltly and pushed along early: midfield on inner: rdn over 2f out: kpt on wl u.p and chal ins fnl f: ev ch tl outpcd by front pair and hld towards fin: jst prevailed in battle for 3rd* **23/5**

**4** shd **Cornwallville (IRE)**[14] 2-9-6 0................................. FlavienPrat 4 74
(D Windrif, France) **19/5**[2]

**5** 2 ½ **Baiafa (ITY)** 2-9-1 0.............................................. CristianDemuro 7 63
(G Botti, France) **60/1**

**6** hd **Grand Argentier (FR)**[12] 2-9-4 0......................... AntoineHamelin 9 65
(Matthieu Palussiere, France) **54/10**

**7** ½ **Freaky Girl (FR)**[20] 2-9-1 0................... Christophe-PatriceLemaire 10 61
(Robert Collet, France) **39/1**

**8** 12 **Voila Baileys (FR)**[21] 2976 2-8-8 0.............................. TheoBachelot 11 24
(F-H Graffard, France) **74/10**

**9** 2 **Eliminator (FR)** 2-9-1 0................................ ChristopheSoumillon 6 26
(J-C Rouget, France) **37/10**[1]

**10** 2 ½ **Gentledor (FR)**[21] 2976 2-9-1 0...................................... FabriceVeron 1 20
(Y Barberot, France) **158/10**

1m 18.6s (78.60) **10** Ran SP% **119.6**
WIN (incl. 1 euro stake): 42.40. PLACES: 6.80, 2.30, 2.10. DF: 92.10. SF: 250.00.
**Owner** Michel Tocze **Bred** Haras De Ulia Sl **Trained** France

# [3642] CHESTER (L-H)
Saturday, June 28

**OFFICIAL GOING: Good to soft (soft in places; 6.7)**
Rail between 6f & 1f out another 3yds, 6 in total with a drop in at that point. Races 1,2&6 increased by 20yds, 3&4 by 24yds, 5 by 38yds and 7 by 46yds.
Wind: almost nil Weather: steady rain 1st 2, light rain race 6

## 3692 INJURED JOCKEYS FUND 50TH ANNIVERSARY NOVICE STKS (BOBIS RACE) 5f 16y
**2:10** (2:11) (Class 4) 2-Y-O **£6,469** (£1,925; £962; £481) **Stalls** Low

Form RPR
**1** **Showing Character** 2-9-0 0................................ RichardKingscote 1 93+
(Tom Dascombe) *mde all: shkn up appr fnl f: sn rdn clr: v readily* **3/1**[2]

1 **2** 4 ½ **Steve Prescott**[7] 3461 2-9-7 0....................................... DavidNolan 2 84
(Richard Fahey) *chsd wnr: drvn over 2f out: kpt on same pce fnl f: no imp* **4/5**[1]

061 **3** 3 ¾ **Indescribable (IRE)**[17] 3119 2-9-7 0........................... FrannyNorton 5 71
(Mark Johnston) *dwlt: sn drvn along and outpcd: hdwy over 2f out: chsng ldrs on inner over 1f out: wknd last 100yds* **10/3**[3]

060 **4** *15* **Featsdontfailmenow**[14] 3215 2-8-9 0.................................. BenCurtis 3 5
(Lisa Williamson) *sn w ldrs on outside: lost pl over 2f out: sn wl bhd* **40/1**

1m 5.63s (4.63) **Going Correction** +0.775s/f (Yiel) **4** Ran SP% **106.1**
Speed ratings (Par 95): **93,85,79,55**
CSF £5.71 TOTE £5.00; EX 7.50 Trifecta £8.40.
**Owner** The Mad March Hares **Bred** Jeremy Green And Sons **Trained** Malpas, Cheshire

**FOCUS**
There had been 4mm of rain over the previous 24 hours and there was more rain prior to racing, leaving the ground officially good to soft, soft in places. The winning time of the opener confirmed that conditions were quite testing. Only the four runners, but there were a couple of well-regarded colts in the line-up and the winner showed serious ability.

## 3693 CHALICE H'CAP 5f 16y
**2:45** (2:46) (Class 3) (0-90,88) 3-Y-0+ **£9,703** (£2,887; £1,443; £721) **Stalls** Low

Form RPR
0-02 **1** **B Fifty Two (IRE)**[26] 2849 5-9-12 **88**.....................(bt) RichardKingscote 3 101
(B W Hills) *mde all: drvn 3 l clr 1f out: styd on* **7/4**[1]

0306 **2** *3* **Jillnextdoor (IRE)**[28] 2757 4-9-9 **88**............. WilliamTwiston-Davies(3) 1 90
(Mick Channon) *wnt rt s: chsd ldrs: effrt 2f out: chsd wnr over 1f out: no imp* **9/2**

16-3 **3** *2* **Withernsea (IRE)**[24] 2897 3-9-0 **82**..................................... DavidNolan 5 78+
(Richard Fahey) *chsd ldrs: nt clr run over 2f out tl lost pl and swtchd rt over 1f out: styd on wl to take 3rd last 75yds* **7/2**[2]

0000 **4** *3* **Forest Edge (IRE)**[28] 2758 5-9-12 **88**.................................(b) BenCurtis 6 72
(David Evans) *wnt rt s: sn chsng ldrs: drvn over 2f out: wknd fnl f* **8/1**

1100 **5** *2 1/2* **Come On Dave (IRE)**[23] 2933 5-8-10 **72**......................... PaddyAspell 8 47
(David Nicholls) *hood removed late: s.i.s: hdwy on outside over 3f out: sn chsng ldrs: wknd fnl f* **12/1**

0014 **6** *3 1/4* **Doctor Parkes**[7] 3458 8-9-9 **85**............................................. LiamJones 4 48
(Stuart Williams) *w ldrs: drvn over 2f out: lost pl over 1f out* **4/1**[3]

1m 4.61s (3.61) **Going Correction** +0.775s/f (Yiel)
**WFA** 3 from 4yo+ 6lb **6** Ran SP% **115.6**
Speed ratings (Par 107): **102,97,94,89,85 80**
CSF £10.47 CT £24.63 TOTE £2.30: £1.30, £2.70; EX 9.50 Trifecta £43.00.
**Owner** Gary And Linnet Woodward **Bred** Mull Enterprises Ltd **Trained** Upper Lambourn, Berks

**FOCUS**
Once again early speed paid off. The winner is getting close to his old form and the runner-up was a length off this year's form.

## 3694 £25 FREE MOBILE BET AT CORBETTSPORTS.COM H'CAP (BOBIS RACE) 7f 2y
**3:20** (3:20) (Class 2) (0-100,95) 3-Y-**£12,602** (£3,772; £1,886; £944; £470) **Stalls** Low

Form RPR
-065 **1** **Roachdale House (IRE)**[10] 3369 3-8-11 **85**..................... TedDurcan 1 95
(Richard Fahey) *trckd ldrs: effrt over 2f out: led 1f out: styd on wl* **7/2**[2]

1015 **2** *2 1/4* **Basil Berry**[13] 3273 3-8-10 **84**............................................... BenCurtis 3 88
(Chris Dwyer) *drvn to ld: hdd 1f out: kpt on same pce* **5/1**[3]

3-40 **3** *3* **Tiger Twenty Two**[15] 3200 3-8-11 **85**............................. PhillipMakin 5 81+
(Richard Fahey) *in rr: pushed along and outpcd 4f out: hdwy over 2f out: styd on wl fnl f: tk 3rd towards fin* **13/2**

3131 **4** *1 1/4* **Kickboxer (IRE)**[10] 3369 3-9-4 **95**................. WilliamTwiston-Davies(3) 4 88
(Mick Channon) *trckd ldrs: rdn over 1f out: wknd last 150yds* **15/8**[1]

000 **5** *6* **Lady Frances**[11] 3342 3-8-8 **82**....................................... FrannyNorton 8 60
(Mark Johnston) *in rr: sn chsng ldrs: wknd 2f out* **14/1**

1634 **6** *5* **Pool House**[35] 2544 3-9-7 **95**........................................ RobertHavlin 7 60
(Andrew Balding) *in rr: sn drvn along: nvr on terms* **10/1**

-301 **7** *12* **Yagheer (IRE)**[24] 2902 3-8-4 **78**.......................................... LiamJones 6 11
(Roger Varian) *chsd ldr: drvn over 4f out: lost pl over 2f out: sn bhd* **8/1**

1m 30.48s (3.98) **Going Correction** +0.775s/f (Yiel) **7** Ran SP% **113.9**
Speed ratings (Par 105): **108,105,102,100,93 88,74**
CSF £21.02 CT £107.29 TOTE £6.70: £4.40, £2.40; EX 30.10 Trifecta £169.00.
**Owner** G Devlin **Bred** G Devlin **Trained** Musley Bank, N Yorks

**FOCUS**
Very few got into this. The winner is getting back to his 2yo best and looked like rating higher then, so may do so.

## 3695 BUDWEISER MAIDEN STKS 7f 122y
**3:55** (4:00) (Class 4) 3-Y-0+ **£6,469** (£1,925; £962; £481) **Stalls** Low

Form RPR
2232 **1** **Between Wickets**[14] 3229 3-9-3 82.............................. BenCurtis 8 71+
(Marcus Tregoning) *carried rt s: sn w ldr: led over 1f out: rdn and styd on wl last 100yds* **7/4**[1]

52 **2** *1 1/4* **Distant High**[17] 3121 3-8-12 0......................... RichardKingscote 2 62
(Richard Price) *chsd ldrs: upsides on inner 1f out: kpt on same pce ins fnl f* **4/1**[3]

0- **3** *4* **Essanar**[253] 7335 3-8-12 0.............................................. JackDuern(5) 1 57
(Andrew Hollinshead) *in rr: drvn 3f out: sn outpcd: hdwy over 1f out: one pce* **16/1**

0- **4** *3/4* **Nabeel (IRE)**[269] 6939 3-9-3 0..........................................[1] TedDurcan 3 55
(Saeed bin Suroor) *stmbld sn after s: sn trcking ldrs: drvn over 2f out: stmbld and swtchd lft over 1f out: kpt on to take modest 4th nr fin* **15/8**[2]

24-4 **5** *3/4* **Market Storm (FR)**[63] 1720 3-9-3 67..............................(b) PhillipMakin 5 53
(Michael Mullineaux) *led: edgd rt and hdd over 1f out: one pce* **10/1**

**6** *22* **Gifted Spirit** 4-9-8 0.................................................... WilliamCarson 6
(Mark Brisbourne) *in rr: hdwy over 3f out: lost pl over 2f out: sn bhd t.o* **16/1**

00- **7** *12* **Hares Grove (IRE)**[453] 1291 5-9-13 0............................ SaleemGolam 7
(Richard Price) *wnt rt s: t.k.h in rr: swtchd ins after 1f: lost pl over 2f out: sn bhd: t.o* **50/1**

1m 41.63s (7.83) **Going Correction** +0.925s/f (Soft)
**WFA** 3 from 4yo+ 10lb **7** Ran SP% **114.0**
Speed ratings (Par 105): **97,95,91,91,90 68,56**
CSF £9.21 TOTE £2.30: £1.20, £2.10; EX 6.00 Trifecta £50.50.
**Owner** R C C Villers **Bred** Miss K J Keir **Trained** Whitsbury, Hants

**FOCUS**
A modest maiden. The winner didn't need to match his best with the unexposed fourth not improving as much as the market expected. The level has been set around the runner-up.

## 3696 SMILES AND MORE H'CAP 1m 4f 66y
**4:30** (4:33) (Class 4) (0-80,80) 3-Y-0+ **£6,469** (£1,925; £962; £481) **Stalls** Low

Form RPR
6-22 **1** **English Summer**[14] 3249 7-9-7 **73**.................................(t) DavidNolan 2 82
(Richard Fahey) *trckd ldrs: cl 2nd over 3f out: rdn to ld over 1f out: hung lft: drvn out* **2/1**[1]

3150 **2** *1 1/4* **Right Of Appeal**[29] 2728 3-8-3 **69**.............................. LiamJones 5 76
(Mark Johnston) *led: qcknd pce over 5f out: hdd over 1f out: kpt on wl ins fnl f* **11/4**[2]

1450 **3** *7* **Red Runaway**[16] 3139 4-9-12 **78**.................................... TedDurcan 3 75
(Ed Dunlop) *dwlt: in rr: hdwy to chse ldrs after 3f: drvn and outpcd over 5f out: rallied and handy 3rd over 2f out: one pce over 1f out: eased whn wl hld clsng stages* **3/1**[3]

3022 **4** *16* **Tepmokea (IRE)**[11] 3341 8-10-0 **80**...............................(b[1]) PhillipMakin 6 58
(Conor Dore) *trckd ldrs: drvn 4f out: wknd over 2f out: bhd whn eased over 1f out* **4/1**

04 **5** *38* **Poor Duke (IRE)**[2] 3616 4-8-13 **70**...............................(b) TimClark(5) 4
(Michael Mullineaux) *sn chsng ldrs: drvn 4f out: lost pl over 2f out: sn wl bhd: t.o* **9/1**

2m 47.84s (9.34) **Going Correction** +0.925s/f (Soft)
**WFA** 3 from 4yo+ 14lb **5** Ran SP% **115.0**
Speed ratings (Par 105): **105,104,99,88,63**
CSF £8.23 TOTE £2.40: £1.70, £2.00; EX 7.00 Trifecta £30.40.
**Owner** Dr Marwan Koukash **Bred** Juddmonte Farms Ltd **Trained** Musley Bank, N Yorks

**FOCUS**
The runner-up is rated back in line with his spring AW form, and the winner built on his recent debut for Richard Fahey. There was little depth to this.

## 3697 STELLA CIDRE H'CAP 5f 16y
**5:05** (5:05) (Class 4) (0-85,84) 4-Y-0+ **£6,469** (£1,925; £962; £481) **Stalls** Low

Form RPR
05-6 **1** **Cheworee**[60] 1850 5-9-2 **79**...................................(tp[1]) RichardKingscote 4 88
(Tom Dascombe) *mde all: jst hld on* **7/2**[1]

3040 **2** *shd* **Oldjoesaid**[16] 3138 10-8-13 **76**.................................. PhillipMakin 2 84
(Paul Midgley) *chsd ldrs: n.m.r over 1f out: styd on to take 2nd last 50yds: jst failed* **5/1**[2]

-203 **3** *3/4* **Tango Sky (IRE)**[14] 3216 5-8-6 **74**............................ ShaneGray(5) 8 79+
(Richard Fahey) *dwlt: in rr: hdwy on outside over 1f out: styd on to take cl 3rd nr line* **7/1**

0100 **4** *1 1/4* **Pandar**[21] 2992 5-9-7 **84**............................................... BenCurtis 9 85+
(Milton Bradley) *w wnr: kpt on same pce fnl f* **14/1**

3015 **5** *1 1/4* **Storm Lightning**[2] 3612 5-8-9 **72**........................... WilliamCarson 6 71+
(Mark Brisbourne) *mid-div: drvn over 2f out: hmpd over 1f out: styd on down outside fnl f* **7/1**

0060 **6** *shd* **Royal Bajan (USA)**[56] 1961 6-8-6 **74**.............................(v) JackDuern(5) 1 70
(James Given) *chsd wnr: drvn 2f out: upsides 1f out: fdd last 50yds* **11/2**[3]

2650 **7** *1/2* **Trader Jack**[14] 3244 5-9-6 **83**.....................................(tp) StephenCraine 3 77
(David Flood) *mid-div: nt clr run on ins over 1f out: kpt on same pce ins fnl f* **6/1**

2-10 **8** *1 1/2* **Little Eli**[16] 3138 4-8-2 **65** oh1.......................................... PaulQuinn 5 54
(Eric Alston) *dwlt: in rr: nvr a factor* **14/1**

4205 **9** *3 1/4* **Waseem Faris (IRE)**[13] 3275 5-9-0 **80**....... WilliamTwiston-Davies(3) 11 57
(Mick Channon) *trckd ldrs: rdn over 1f out: sn wknd* **9/1**

1m 5.01s (4.01) **Going Correction** +0.925s/f (Soft) **9** Ran SP% **116.9**
Speed ratings (Par 105): **104,103,102,100,98 98,97,95,90**
CSF £21.10 CT £117.40 TOTE £5.00: £2.70, £2.40, £3.40; EX 19.90 Trifecta £101.60.
**Owner** S Stoneham,E Van Cutsem,A Hoctor-Duncan **Bred** Sarah Stoneham **Trained** Malpas, Cheshire

**FOCUS**
An open race but once again it paid to be up there. The winner was close to her best, and the runner-up ran to his best since last spring.

## 3698 BECKS H'CAP 1m 7f 195y
**5:40** (5:42) (Class 4) (0-85,80) 4-Y-0+ **£6,469** (£1,925; £962; £481) **Stalls** Low

Form RPR
0222 **1** **Kashgar**[20] 3034 5-9-4 **80**.................................. WilliamTwiston-Davies(3) 2 90
(Bernard Llewellyn) *trckd ldr: led over 1f out: edgd lft: drvn out* **15/8**[1]

023 **2** *1 3/4* **Nashville (IRE)**[14] 3240 5-9-4 **77**.............................. DavidNolan 1 84
(Richard Fahey) *wnt rt s: led: qcknd pce over 4f out: hdd over 1f out: swtchd rt: kpt on same pce* **15/8**[1]

-411 **3** *13* **Miss Macnamara (IRE)**[35] 2550 5-9-0 **73**...................... PhillipMakin 7 64
(Martin Todhunter) *hld up in last: hdwy over 3f out: modest 3rd 2f out: eased nr fin* **11/4**[2]

0412 **4** *6* **Taste The Wine (IRE)**[15] 3179 8-8-6 **65**............................(t) LiamJones 3 49
(Bernard Llewellyn) *chsd ldrs: pushed along over 6f out: one pce over 2f out* **16/1**

2023 **5** *54* **Vicky Valentine**[14] 3218 4-8-7 **66**.............................. WilliamCarson 5
(Alistair Whillans) *chsd ldrs: drvn 4f out: lost pl over 2f out: bhd whn eased fnl f: t.o* **12/1**[3]

3m 40.41s (12.41) **Going Correction** +0.925s/f (Soft) **5** Ran SP% **109.8**
Speed ratings (Par 105): **105,104,97,94,67**
CSF £5.62 TOTE £2.20: £2.10, £1.30; EX 5.10 Trifecta £11.30.
**Owner** Alex James **Bred** J L C Pearce **Trained** Fochriw, Caerphilly

**FOCUS**
The winner ran a personal best when taking this last year and this rates an even better effort.
T/Plt: £159.90 to a £1 stake. Pool: £57,692.29 - 263.25 winning tickets. T/Qpdt: £12.90 to a £1 stake. Pool: £4,188.25 - 238.85 winning tickets. WG

# 3648 DONCASTER (L-H)
Saturday, June 28

**OFFICIAL GOING: Good to firm (9.3)**
Round course railed out from 10f to where it joins the straight and races of 10f and over increased by 15yds.
Wind: Light half behind Weather: Overcast

## 3699 BEAVER 84 H'CAP 1m 4f
**5:25** (5:25) (Class 5) (0-75,75) 4-Y-0+ **£2,911** (£866; £432; £216) **Stalls** Low

Form RPR
3-53 **1** **Poetic Verse**[14] 3226 4-9-0 **71**.................................. ConnorBeasley(3) 13 79
(John Quinn) *hld up towards rr: hdwy over 3f out: trckd ldrs over 2f out: chal wl over 1f out: rdn to ld appr fnl f: sn drvn and hld on wl towards fin* **4/1**[2]

4203 **2** *nk* **Sporting Gold (IRE)**[26] 2851 5-9-7 **75**..........................(b) PaddyAspell 11 82
(Roger Varian) *in tch: hdwy 4f out: led wl over 2f out and sn rdn: drvn and hdd appr fnl f: kpt on gamely: jst hld* **8/1**

332- **3** *nse* **Highway Code (USA)**[43] 7539 8-8-12 **71**........................(t) EoinWalsh(5) 5 78
(Richard Lee) *dwlt: hld up in rr: stdy hdwy 3f out: chsd ldrs 2f out: sn rdn to chal and ev ch tl drvn and no ex last 50yds* **14/1**

1-02 **4** *hd* **Wall Street Boss (USA)**[14] 3226 4-9-2 **70**................. FrederikTylicki 10 77
(James Fanshawe) *trckd ldrs: hdwy 4f out: cl up 3f out: rdn wl over 1f out and ev ch tl drvn ins fnl f: no ex towards fin* **7/2**[1]

1604 **5** *1½* **Cavalieri (IRE)**[16] 3134 4-9-2 **70**................. AmyRyan 9 75
(Philip Kirby) *hld up in rr: hdwy 3f out: rdn 2f out: styd on appr fnl f: nrst fin* **8/1**

1013 **6** *4* **Precision Strike**[17] 3101 4-8-7 **66**.............................(v) DuilioDaSilva(5) 4 64
(Richard Guest) *trckd ldrs: wd st: rdn along 3f out: ch 2f out: sn drvn and grad wknd* **20/1**

06-2 **7** *1¾* **Bright Applause**[10] 3371 6-9-2 **70**................................ BarryMcHugh 3 65
(Tracy Waggott) *trckd ldrs: hdwy on inner 4f out: cl up 3f out: sn rdn and wknd 2f out* **14/1**

54-0 **8** *hd* **Good Speech (IRE)**[45] 2259 4-9-3 **71**.......................... AndrewElliott 8 66
(Tom Tate) *cl up: wd st: rdn along 3f out: grad wknd* **9/1**

5261 **9** *nk* **Flying Power**[14] 3226 6-9-2 **75**........................ JacobButterfield(5) 2 70
(John Norton) *prom: cl up over 4f out: rdn along 3f out: sn wknd* **7/1**[3]

3040 **10** *¾* **Reflect (IRE)**[27] 2806 6-8-9 **63** ow1...................................(v) DaleSwift 1 56
(Derek Shaw) *a towards rr* **22/1**

3260 **11** *9* **Singzak**[15] 3204 6-9-0 **73**........................................ JackGarritty(5) 7 52
(Michael Easterby) *led: rdn along over 4f out: hdd wl over 2f out and sn wknd* **20/1**

2110 **12** *5* **Dubai Celebration**[10] 2540 6-9-5 **73**........................ PatrickDonaghy 6 44
(Julie Camacho) *hld up: a towards rr* **25/1**

1435 **13** *2¾* **Rockweiller**[4] 3556 7-8-4 **58**................................ DuranFentiman 12 25
(Shaun Harris) *chsd ldrs: pushed along on outer and wd st: rdn wl over 3f out and sn wknd* **12/1**

2m 33.58s (-1.32) **Going Correction** 0.0s/f (Good) **13** Ran SP% **125.7**
Speed ratings (Par 103): **104,103,103,103,102 99,98,98,98,97 91,88,86**
CSF £36.02 CT £426.30 TOTE £3.90: £2.00, £2.80, £3.70; EX 33.80 Trifecta £314.60.
**Owner** J N Blackburn **Bred** The Links Partnership **Trained** Settrington, N Yorks

**FOCUS**
The ground was just on the fast side, Paddy Aspell describing it as 'good to firm, but good in places.' They went a fair gallop to this handicap, which comprised mainly exposed sorts and half a length separated the first four home, while the first five were clear of the rest, but the form looks sound.

## 3700 M & G SERVICES "ASBESTOS ABATEMENT & SURVEYING" MAIDEN STKS 6f
**5:55** (5:58) (Class 5) 3-Y-O+ **£3,234** (£962; £481; £240) **Stalls** High

Form RPR

23-2 **1** **Makhfar (IRE)**[7] 3469 3-9-5 80........................ RobertHavlin 3 81
(John Gosden) *chsd ldrs: hdwy 1/2-way: rdn to ld over 1f out: hung lft and hdd jst ins fnl f: drvn and rallied to ld again last 75yds: kpt on* **1/2**[1]

-226 **2** *½* **Royal Connoisseur (IRE)**[42] 2329 3-9-0 74.............. JackGarritty(5) 1 79
(Richard Fahey) *in tch: hdwy wl over 2f out: rdn to chal over 1f out: led jst ins fnl f: sn drvn: fnd little and hdd last 50yds* **7/2**[2]

0 **3** *12* **Wimboldsley**[16] 3153 3-9-5 0........................................ DaleSwift 4 41
(Scott Dixon) *prom: rdn along over 2f out: sn drvn and one pce: tk remote 3rd ins fnl f* **33/1**

6-0 **4** *2* **Jenny Twigg**[21] 2985 4-9-7 0.............................. MichaelStainton 5 31
(Chris Fairhurst) *cl up: rdn along 1/2-way: outpcd fnl 2f* **50/1**

**5** *½* **Smart Dj** 3-9-5 0........................................................ PaddyAspell 8 33
(Andrew Hollinshead) *qckly away and led: rdn along and hung lft over 2f out: hdd over 1f out and sn wknd* **11/1**

3-0 **6** *3¾* **Celestial Knight**[26] 2846 3-9-5 0........................ FrederikTylicki 2 21
(James Fanshawe) *a towards rr* **6/1**[3]

- **7** *½* **Bond's Gift** 4-9-7 0.................................................. BarryMcHugh 6 16
(Geoffrey Oldroyd) *s.i.s: a bhd* **14/1**

**8** *3¼* **Bond Empire** 4-9-12 0.................................................. RaulDaSilva 7 11
(Geoffrey Oldroyd) *s.i.s: a bhd* **16/1**

1m 13.18s (-0.42) **Going Correction** -0.125s/f (Firm)
**WFA** 3 from 4yo 7lb **8** Ran SP% **129.0**
Speed ratings (Par 103): **97,96,80,77,77 72,71,67**
CSF £3.29 TOTE £1.50: £1.02, £1.40, £7.00; EX 2.70 Trifecta £43.40.
**Owner** Hamdan Al Maktoum **Bred** Centaur Bloodstock Agency **Trained** Newmarket, Suffolk

**FOCUS**
An uncompetitive sprint maiden in which the first two had the best form and ran close to thier marks.

## 3701 JORDAN ROAD SURFACING IRISH STALLION FARMS EBF MAIDEN STKS 7f
**6:30** (6:31) (Class 5) 2-Y-O **£2,911** (£866; £432; £216) **Stalls** High

Form RPR

6 **1** **Freight Train (IRE)**[16] 3136 2-9-5 0........................ FrannyNorton 11 82
(Mark Johnston) *mde all: rdn wl over 1f out: styd on strly fnl f* **1/1**[1]

**2** *3¼* **Pensax Boy** 2-9-5 0................................................ RobertWinston 4 73+
(Ian Williams) *trckd ldrs: hdwy 3f out: rdn wl over 1f out: kpt on same pce fnl f* **25/1**

**3** *½* **Sands Chorus** 2-9-2 0.............................. ConnorBeasley(3) 10 72+
(James Given) *towards rr: hdwy 1/2-way: rdn to chse ldrs 2f out: kpt on same pce fnl f* **20/1**

**4** *½* **Loom Of Life (IRE)** 2-9-5 0........................................ TonyHamilton 5 71+
(Richard Fahey) *dwlt and in rr: pushed along over 3f out: rdn over 2f out: styd on wl fnl f: nrst fin* **9/2**[3]

**5** *2¼* **River Of Dreams (IRE)** 2-9-5 0.................................. BarryMcHugh 8 64+
(Kevin Ryan) *prom: cl up 1/2-way: rdn along 2f out: grad wknd* **12/1**

**6** *2½* **Rocky Desert (IRE)** 2-9-5 0........................................ LukeMorris 3 58
(Marco Botti) *in tch: hdwy on outer wl over 2f out: rdn wl over 1f out: sn one pce* **4/1**[2]

5 **7** *1¾* **Roman De Brut (IRE)**[30] 2698 2-9-5 0........................ RobertHavlin 7 53
(Ian Williams) *a towards rr* **33/1**

05 **8** *4½* **Forcible**[44] 2269 2-9-5 0........................................ HarryBentley 9 41
(David Brown) *t.k.h: chsd ldrs: rdn along wl over 2f out: sn wknd* **10/1**

6 **9** *1½* **Hangon Harriet**[21] 2979 2-9-0 0.................................. PJMcDonald 1 32
(Pam Sly) *prom: rdn along 1/2-way: sn wknd* **25/1**

1m 27.08s (0.78) **Going Correction** -0.125s/f (Firm) **9** Ran SP% **120.4**
Speed ratings (Par 93): **90,86,85,85,82 79,77,72,70**
CSF £38.90 TOTE £2.50: £1.10, £6.40, £3.80; EX 37.60 Trifecta £544.80.
**Owner** A D Spence **Bred** Rozelle Bloodstock **Trained** Middleham Moor, N Yorks

**FOCUS**
Probably no more than an average juvenile maiden.

## 3702 BEAVER 84 HIRE PLETTAC H'CAP 6f
**7:05** (7:05) (Class 4) (0-85,86) 3-Y-O+ **£5,175** (£1,540; £769; £384) **Stalls** High

Form RPR

1-35 **1** **Greeb**[33] 2611 3-9-4 **82**................................................ TedDurcan 1 92+
(Charles Hills) *dwlt: hdwy to trck ldrs after 2f: effrt on outer 2f out: chal over 1f out: sn rdn and kpt on wl to ld last 100yds* **9/2**[1]

0-04 **2** *¾* **Eland Ally**[16] 3138 6-8-11 **68**........................................ AndrewElliott 4 78
(Tom Tate) *led and sn clr: rdn along and jnd wl over 1f out: drvn ent fnl f: hdd and no ex last 100yds* **25/1**

23-2 **3** *1¾* **Mission Approved**[17] 3122 4-10-0 **85**........................ LukeMorris 10 89
(Luca Cumani) *hld up towards rr: hdwy 2f out: swtchd rt and rdn over 1f out: styd on fnl f: nrst fin* **5/1**[2]

0642 **4** *1¼* **Dark Castle**[14] 3256 5-10-0 **85**.................................... PJMcDonald 7 85
(Micky Hammond) *t.k.h: trckd ldrs: pushed along and lost pl over 2f out: sn rdn: styd on fnl f: nrst fin* **13/2**

0054 **5** *½* **Head Space (IRE)**[11] 3342 6-9-5 **76**........................(p) JamesSullivan 11 75
(Ruth Carr) *prom: chsd ldr over 2f out: rdn and ev ch over 1f out: drvn and one pce fnl f* **7/1**

2150 **6** *½* **Clubland (IRE)**[14] 3227 5-8-10 **72**................................ TimClark(5) 16 69
(Roy Bowring) *prom: hdwy to chse ldr wl over 1f out: ev ch tl drvn ent fnl f and grad wknd* **25/1**

4213 **7** *¾* **Mon Brav**[14] 3256 7-9-7 **78**........................................ RobertWinston 5 73
(Brian Ellison) *in tch on outer: rdn along and outpcd 1/2-way: kpt on u.p fnl f: n.d* **17/2**

0425 **8** *hd* **Naabegha**[21] 2995 7-9-9 **80**........................................(p) HarryBentley 17 74
(Alan McCabe) *hld up: hdwy over 2f out: rdn wl over 1f out: no imp fnl f* **22/1**

0-61 **9** *½* **Amadeus Wolfe Tone (IRE)**[12] 3313 5-10-1 **86**..........(b) GrahamLee 12 79
(Jamie Osborne) *in rr: effrt 2f out: sn rdn along and sme late hdwy* **9/1**

0-40 **10** *2¾* **Bop It**[11] 3342 5-10-0 **85**........................................ DanielTudhope 13 69
(David O'Meara) *chsd clr ldr: rdn along over 2f out: sn wknd* **15/2**

056 **11** *2¾* **Medici Time**[9] 3399 9-8-9 **66** oh2..................................(v) TonyHamilton 14 41
(Tim Easterby) *in tch: pushed along 1/2-way: sn lost pl and bhd* **25/1**

5021 **12** *10* **Green Monkey**[17] 3122 4-9-9 **80**.................................. FrederikTylicki 15 23
(James Fanshawe) *in rr: rdn along over 2f out: sn bhd and eased* **11/2**[3]

1m 11.93s (-1.67) **Going Correction** -0.125s/f (Firm)
**WFA** 3 from 4yo+ 7lb **12** Ran SP% **124.2**
Speed ratings (Par 105): **106,105,102,101,100 99,98,98,97,94 90,77**
CSF £127.10 CT £585.95 TOTE £8.80: £2.80, £8.70, £2.10; EX 164.10 Trifecta £1066.60.
**Owner** Hamdan Al Maktoum **Bred** Shadwell Estate Company Limited **Trained** Lambourn, Berks

**FOCUS**
Mainly exposed sorts in this sprint in which they raced towards the centre of the track and it seemed an advantage to race close to the pace as few featured. The well-backed winner continues on the up, and the second is rated to last year's form.

## 3703 AFI GROUP H'CAP 1m (R)
**7:40** (7:41) (Class 3) (0-90,88) 4-Y-O+ **£7,762** (£2,310; £1,154; £577) **Stalls** Low

Form RPR

22-2 **1** **Extraterrestrial**[28] 2763 10-8-8 **75**........................(p) TonyHamilton 1 83
(Richard Fahey) *trckd ldrs on inner: hdwy over 2f out: squeezed through to chal jst over 1f out: rdn to ld last 100yds: styd on* **11/1**

-060 **2** *1¼* **Bishop's Castle (USA)**[14] 3254 5-8-7 **77**.................... OisinMurphy(3) 9 82
(Brian Ellison) *prom: trckd ldr 1/2-way: cl up 3f out: rdn to chal wl over 1f out: sn ev ch: drvn ins fnl f: kpt on same pce towards fin* **7/4**[1]

3500 **3** *½* **Shahdaroba (IRE)**[3] 3573 4-9-2 **83**..............................(p) GrahamLee 2 87
(Micky Hammond) *a.p: rdn along over 2f out: drvn over 1f out: kpt on towards fin* **8/1**

-162 **4** *nse* **Mac's Superstar (FR)**[17] 3118 4-8-10 **77**.................. FrederikTylicki 8 81
(James Fanshawe) *trckd ldrs: effrt 3f out: rdn along 2f out: drvn and kpt on same pce fnl f* **14/1**

4614 **5** *¾* **Dubai Hills**[15] 3202 8-9-7 **88**.................................... DanielTudhope 3 90
(David O'Meara) *led: rdn along and jnd 2f out: drvn over 1f out: hdd ins fnl f: wknd towards fin* **6/1**[3]

0601 **6** *nk* **Kingscroft (IRE)**[7] 3463 6-8-5 **77** ow1.................... JacobButterfield(5) 7 78
(Michael Herrington) *in tch: pushed along wl over 2f out: rdn wl over 1f out: kpt on u.p fnl f: nrst fin* **9/2**[2]

5005 **7** *hd* **Showboating (IRE)**[8] 3431 6-9-6 **87**............................(tp) SeanLevey 6 88
(Alan McCabe) *hld up towards rr: hdwy 3f out: rdn 2f out: sn drvn and kpt on same pce fnl f* **12/1**

341 **8** *nk* **Self Employed**[13] 3272 7-8-8 **75**.................................... LukeMorris 4 75
(Garry Woodward) *dwlt and in rr: hdwy wl over 2f out: sn rdn: kpt on u.p fnl f: nrst fin* **13/2**

4652 **9** *4½* **Tatting**[13] 3272 5-8-7 **79**........................................ MarcMonaghan(5) 5 69
(Chris Dwyer) *a in rr* **14/1**

1m 39.64s (-0.06) **Going Correction** 0.0s/f (Good) **9** Ran SP% **122.6**
Speed ratings (Par 107): **100,98,98,98,97 97,96,96,92**
CSF £32.64 CT £176.45 TOTE £10.80: £2.60, £1.20, £2.30; EX 38.20 Trifecta £761.50.
**Owner** G J Paver **Bred** Lostford Manor Stud **Trained** Musley Bank, N Yorks

**FOCUS**
Quite a competitive handicap run at a fair gallop. The winner is rated to last year's form, with the runner-up to this season's form.

## 3704 PANELCRAFT QUALITY ACCESS PANELS H'CAP (BOBIS RACE) 5f 140y
**8:15** (8:16) (Class 4) (0-85,88) 3-Y-O **£5,175** (£1,540; £769; £384) **Stalls** High

Form RPR

-111 **1** **High On Life**[7] 3470 3-9-10 **88**.................................... DanielTudhope 7 100
(Jamie Osborne) *qckly away: mde all: rdn over 1f out: kpt on strly* **2/1**[1]

4-11 **2** *1¾* **Johara (IRE)**[17] 3114 3-9-5 **83**........................................ TedDurcan 2 88
(Chris Wall) *in tch: hdwy on outer to chse ldrs over 2f out: rdn wl over 1f out: chsd wnr appr fnl f: sn drvn and no imp* **5/1**

3030 **3** *½* **Munfallet (IRE)**[36] 2510 3-8-13 **77**.................................. SeanLevey 8 80
(David Brown) *chsd ldrs on inner: hdwy 2f out: rdn over 1f out: swtchd lft and drvn ins fnl f: kpt on: nrst fin* **14/1**

0534 **4** *1* **Jazz (IRE)**[33] 2626 3-9-5 **83**........................................ RobertWinston 10 86+
(Charles Hills) *towards rr: hdwy over 2f out: rdn wl over 1f out: styd on fnl f: nrst fin* **7/2**[2]

4153 **5** *½* **Royal Warrior**[11] 3331 3-8-13 **80**.............................. OisinMurphy(3) 3 78
(Alan McCabe) *chsd wnr: rdn along over 2f out: drvn wl over 1f out: wknd ent fnl f* **12/1**

1-05 **6** *2* **Kenny The Captain (IRE)**[56] 1937 3-9-5 **83**.............. DuranFentiman 6 75
(Tim Easterby) *chsd ldrs: rdn along 1/2-way: grad wknd* **12/1**

0-40 **7** *½* **Canyari (IRE)**[43] 2317 3-9-4 **85**............................ GeorgeChaloner(3) 1 75
(Richard Fahey) *chsd ldng pair: rdn along over 2f out: sn wknd* **9/2**[3]



The Form Book, Raceform Ltd, Newbury, RG14 5SJ

01-0 **8** *1* **Kaab (IRE)**[73] 1518 3-9-7 **85**.............................. RobertHavlin 5 72
(Ed Dunlop) *in tch: effrt over 2f out: sn rdn and wknd* **20/1**

-006 **9** *2 3/4* **Khalice**[41] 2361 3-8-10 **74**.............................. GrahamLee 9 52
(James Given) *dwlt: a in rr* **25/1**

1m 7.47s (-1.33) **Going Correction** -0.125s/f (Firm) **9** Ran SP% **121.1**
Speed ratings (Par 101): **103,100,100,98,98 95,94,93,89**
CSF £13.08 CT £115.50 TOTE £3.10: £1.80, £1.60, £4.20; EX 8.50 Trifecta £170.70.
**Owner** Michael Buckley **Bred** Moyns Park Estate And Stud Ltd **Trained** Upper Lambourn, Berks

**FOCUS**
This was a decent sprint for three-year-olds. The winner continues to progress, the runner-up confirmed her AW form and, while the third is less obvious, his penultimate run here had been franked.

## 3705 STABILISED PAVEMENTS FILLIES' H'CAP — 1m 2f 60y
**8:45** (8:45) (Class 5) (0-70,67) 4-Y-O+ **£2,911** (£866; £432; £216) **Stalls** Low

Form RPR

-412 **1** **Elizabeth Coffee (IRE)**[14] 3208 6-8-9 **55**.............................. LukeMorris 4 66
(John Weymes) *chsd clr ldr: swtchd wd 3f out: clsd up over 2f out: rdn to ld wl over 1f out: drvn and clr whn edgd rt ent fnl f: kpt on strly* **2/1**[1]

20 **2** *7* **Ela Goog La Mou**[39] 2444 5-8-11 **60**.............................. RosieJessop(3) 5 58
(Peter Charalambous) *t.k.h: led and sn clr: pushed along and jnd over 2f out: sn rdn: drvn and kpt on one pce fr over 1f out* **3/1**[2]

40/0 **3** *1* **Snow Dancer (IRE)**[30] 2701 10-8-10 **63**.............................. AlistairRawlinson(7) 1 59
(John David Riches) *hld up: hdwy 4f out: rdn along over 2f out: drvn and kpt on one pce appr fnl f* **8/1**

2205 **4** *1 3/4* **Sian Gwalia**[11] 3325 4-8-10 **63**.............................. GeorgeBuckell(7) 2 56
(David Simcock) *trckd ldrs: hdwy to take clsr order wl over 2f out: sn rdn: drvn wl over 1f out and sn one pce* **10/3**[3]

2430 **5** *1* **Coillte Cailin (IRE)**[27] 2806 4-9-2 **67**.............................. EoinWalsh(5) 3 58
(Daniel Mark Loughnane) *hld up in tch: hdwy 4f out: rdn along wl over 2f out: sn edgd lft and wknd* **7/2**

2m 12.15s (2.75) **Going Correction** 0.0s/f (Good) **5** Ran SP% **114.7**
Speed ratings (Par 100): **89,83,82,81,80**
CSF £8.71 TOTE £2.10: £1.60, £2.00; EX 5.20 Trifecta £19.10.
**Owner** Highmoor Racing 4 & Tag Racing **Bred** David Carey **Trained** Middleham Moor, N Yorks

**FOCUS**
An ordinary fillies' handicap with most of the five rather out of form. The gallop was a modest one.
T/Plt: £29.60 to a £1 stake. Pool of £101551.36 - 2501.51 winning tickets. T/Qpdt: £9.60 to a £1 stake. Pool of £7583.56 - 581.60 winning tickets. JR

# 3521 LINGFIELD (L-H)
### Saturday, June 28

**OFFICIAL GOING: Turf - good; all-weather - standard**
Wind: virtually nil Weather: dry after showers before racing

## 3706 ARMED FORCES DAY/BRITISH STALLION STUDS EBF MAIDEN STKS — 5f
**5:50** (5:51) (Class 5) 2-Y-O **£2,911** (£866; £432; £216) **Stalls** Centre

Form RPR

**1** **New Providence** 2-8-9 0.............................. NoelGarbutt(5) 1 68+
(Hugo Palmer) *s.i.s: rn green and pushed along in rr: hdwy 1/2-way: chsng ldrs and nt clr run over 1f out: swtchd lft and effrt in centre 1f out: chal fnl 100yds: r.o wl to ld nr fin* **12/1**

6424 **2** *nk* **Zuzinia (IRE)**[7] 3454 2-8-11 0.............................. CharlesBishop(3) 5 67
(Mick Channon) *hld up in tch: sltly hmpd after 1f: clsd to chse ldrs and nt clr run over 1f out: swtchd lft and drvn to chal 1f out: led fnl 100yds: hdd and no ex nr fin* **7/2**[2]

43 **3** *1* **Golden Zephyr (IRE)**[23] 2918 2-9-0 0.............................. ChrisCatlin 2 63
(B W Hills) *led and crossed to r against stands' rail: shkn up over 1f out: hrd pressed and drvn 1f out: hung lft and hdd fnl 100yds: wknd towards fin* **4/5**[1]

03 **4** *4 1/2* **Surrey Pink (FR)**[32] 2644 2-9-0 0.............................. HayleyTurner 3 47
(William Muir) *chsd ldr: swtchd lft over 3f out: rdn 2f out: no ex and btn 1f out: wknd ins fnl f* **14/1**

**5** *10* **Creative Genius** 2-9-5 0.............................. GeorgeBaker 4 16
(Ed Walker) *chsd ldng pair tl lost pl over 1f out: sn btn and nt given a hrd time: bhd fnl f* **4/1**[3]

58.93s (0.73) **Going Correction** +0.075s/f (Good) **5** Ran SP% **112.1**
Speed ratings (Par 93): **97,96,94,87,71**
CSF £52.37 TOTE £13.20: £6.90, £2.80; EX 67.50 Trifecta £150.10.
**Owner** Chris Humber **Bred** James Ortega Bloodstock **Trained** Newmarket, Suffolk

**FOCUS**
Probably just ordinary maiden form rated around the runner-up.

## 3707 CLARK - 3 GENERATIONS OF BIRTHDAYS H'CAP — 5f
**6:20** (6:22) (Class 5) (0-70,70) 3-Y-O+ **£3,234** (£962; £481; £240) **Stalls** Centre

Form RPR

3145 **1** **Dawn Catcher**[21] 2994 4-9-9 **67**.............................. GeorgeBaker 1 77
(Geoffrey Deacon) *racd far side thrght: chsd ldrs: rdn and effrt to ld ent fnl f: r.o wl* **7/1**

110 **2** *1 1/4* **Putin (IRE)**[16] 3160 6-9-3 **68**..............................(bt) JennyPowell(7) 8 73
(Phil McEntee) *led: swtchd lft and racd in centre fr 1/2-way: rdn and hdd ent fnl f: stydon on same pce after* **8/1**

0000 **3** *1* **Rylee Mooch**[14] 3222 6-9-10 **68**..............................(e) AdamKirby 5 69
(Richard Guest) *dwlt: racd in centre: rdn and hdwy 2f out: chsd ldrs and drifting lft 1f out: styd on same pce ins fnl f* **6/1**[3]

-342 **4** *3/4* **Indian Tinker**[41] 2364 5-9-9 **67**.............................. RichardHughes 7 66
(Robert Cowell) *racd in centre: in tch in midfield: effrt u.p over 1f out: styd on same pce ins fnl f* **9/4**[1]

3430 **5** *1* **The Dandy Yank (IRE)**[4] 3561 3-9-1 **70**..............................(b[1]) RachealKneller(5) 4 63+
(Jamie Osborne) *racd in centre: v.s.a: wl bhd: styd on past btn horses fnl f: nvr trbld ldrs* **10/1**

3220 **6** *1/2* **Johnny Splash (IRE)**[9] 3393 5-8-7 **51**..............................(v) ChrisCatlin 6 44
(Roger Teal) *racd in centre: chsd ldrs: drvn and unable qck over 1f out: drifting lft and wknd ins fnl f* **25/1**

1503 **7** *1/2* **Dishy Guru**[9] 3392 5-9-4 **62**..............................(b) LiamKeniry 3 54
(Michael Blanshard) *racd in centre: s.i.s: bhd: rdn and effrt ent fnl f: styd on: nvr trbld ldrs* **16/1**

3123 **8** *1 1/4* **Picansort**[25] 2865 7-9-6 **64**..............................(v) SebSanders 2 51
(Peter Crate) *chsd ldr: grad switching rt: racing along on stands' rail fr over 3f out: drvn and btn over 1f out: wknd fnl f* **9/2**[2]

5532 **9** *2 1/2* **Champagne Charley**[14] 3228 3-8-12 **62**.............................. DavidProbert 9 38
(Des Donovan) *racd nr stands' rail: in midfield: rdn: hung lft and racing in centre fr 1/2-way: wknd over 1f out* **7/1**

58.79s (0.59) **Going Correction** +0.075s/f (Good)
**WFA** 3 from 4yo+ 6lb **9** Ran SP% **118.2**
Speed ratings (Par 103): **98,96,94,93,91 90,90,88,84**
CSF £63.00 CT £361.53 TOTE £8.70: £2.30, £2.80, £2.10; EX 79.90 Trifecta £753.10.
**Owner** Mayden Stud & Associates **Bred** Mayden Stud, J A And D S Dewhurst **Trained** Compton, Berks

**FOCUS**
An open sprint handicap in which most of the field eventually ended up on the far side. The winner is rated a length up on April's Nottingham win, with the runner-up close to his penultimate figure at Southwell.

## 3708 ERIC GAGER 80TH BIRTHDAY FILLIES' H'CAP — 7f
**6:55** (6:56) (Class 5) (0-75,80) 3-Y-O+ **£3,234** (£962; £481; £240) **Stalls** Centre

Form RPR

6-04 **1** **Fever Few**[16] 3160 5-8-12 **62**.............................. AshleyMorgan(3) 5 73
(Chris Wall) *taken down early: stdd s: travelled wl: chsd ldrs tl jnd ldrs 1/2-way: led and gng best over 2f out: pushed clr over 1f out: r.o wl: comf* **4/1**[2]

0-04 **2** *2 1/2* **Chutney (IRE)**[19] 3067 3-8-9 **72**.............................. CamHardie(7) 1 74
(Richard Hannon) *in tch: rdn and 1/2-way: styd on u.p to chse clr wnr 1f out: kpt on but no imp* **5/1**[3]

0201 **3** *5* **Dorraar (IRE)**[13] 3280 3-9-10 **80**.............................. KierenFallon 4 69
(Roger Varian) *stdd s: t.k.h: hld up in last pair: hdwy to ld 1/2-way: hdd over 2f out: btn over 1f out: 3rd and wknd 1f out* **4/5**[1]

5/30 **4** *6* **Sandaura (IRE)**[40] 2404 4-9-9 **70**.............................. AdamKirby 2 46
(Clive Cox) *chsd ldr tl led after 1f: hdd 1/2-way: sn rdn: wknd over 1f out* **14/1**

1-24 **5** *6* **Honeymoon Express (IRE)**[17] 3125 4-9-9 **75**........(p) ShelleyBirkett(5) 6 35
(Julia Feilden) *led for 1f: dropped to rr and rdn 1/2-way: wknd 2f out* **6/1**

1m 24.23s (0.93) **Going Correction** +0.075s/f (Good)
**WFA** 3 from 4yo+ 9lb **5** Ran SP% **113.2**
Speed ratings (Par 100): **97,94,88,81,74**
CSF £23.44 TOTE £6.70: £2.90, £2.40; EX 20.10 Trifecta £46.70.
**Owner** Mrs C A Wall & R Wayman **Bred** Redgate Bloodstock Ltd & Mrs Z Wise **Trained** Newmarket, Suffolk

**FOCUS**
A modest handicap in which the odds-on favourite proved disappointing. The winner is rated to her best, with the runner-up to her 2yo best.

## 3709 CGG H'CAP — 7f
**7:25** (7:26) (Class 5) (0-75,75) 3-Y-O **£3,234** (£962; £481; £240) **Stalls** Centre

Form RPR

6-36 **1** **Mr Win (IRE)**[20] 3037 3-8-8 **65**.............................. AshleyMorgan(3) 2 87
(Chris Wall) *chsd ldr after 1f: clr wl over 1f out: rdn and qcknd to ld over 1f out: r.o strly and drew wl clr fnl f* **5/2**[2]

-223 **2** *9* **Newton's Law (IRE)**[21] 2996 3-9-7 **75**..............................(t) RichardHughes 5 78
(Brian Meehan) *stdd s: t.k.h: sn led: wnt clr w wnr and rdn wl over 1f out: hdd ent fnl f: sn brushed aside by wnr and wl btn fnl f: eased towards fin* **6/4**[1]

-646 **3** *1/2* **Fiftyshadesfreed (IRE)**[16] 3144 3-8-13 **67**..................(p) PatCosgrave 1 64
(George Baker) *dwlt: hld up wl in tch in last trio: rdn: swtchd lft and effrt over 2f out: modest 4th over 1f out: wnt 3rd ins fnl f: plugged on but no ch w wnr* **7/1**[3]

2-20 **4** *7* **Suitsus**[16] 3145 3-9-2 **70**.............................. SteveDrowne 4 49
(Peter Makin) *stdd s: t.k.h: hld up wl in tch in midfield: rdn and hdwy to chse clr ldng pair wl over 1f out: no imp: lost 3rd and wknd ins fnl f* **14/1**

4-40 **5** *2 1/2* **Marmarus**[16] 3144 3-8-6 **63**.............................. RyanTate(3) 8 36
(Clive Cox) *in tch in last trio: rdn and effrt over 2f out: sn btn: wknd wl over 1f out* **7/1**[3]

4061 **6** *4 1/2* **Caminel (IRE)**[14] 3231 3-8-9 **63**.............................. LiamKeniry 7 24
(Jeremy Gask) *led early: chsd ldrs: rdn and btn over 2f out: wknd wl over 1f out* **12/1**

420- **7** *1* **Monte Viso**[259] 7202 3-8-11 **65** ow1.............................. TomQueally 6 23
(Stuart Kittow) *chsd ldrs: rdn over 2f out: sn struggling: wknd wl over 1f out* **33/1**

00-0 **8** *2 3/4* **Stapleford Lad**[31] 2681 3-8-12 **66**.............................. AdamBeschizza 3 17
(Stuart Williams) *t.k.h: hld up wl in tch in midfield: rdn over 2f out: sn btn: wl bhd fnl f* **25/1**

1m 22.59s (-0.71) **Going Correction** +0.075s/f (Good) **8** Ran SP% **114.7**
Speed ratings (Par 99): **107,96,96,88,85 80,79,75**
CSF £6.65 CT £21.38 TOTE £3.40: £1.50, £1.10, £2.00; EX 7.90 Trifecta £37.70.
**Owner** Des Thurlby **Bred** Kevin Blake **Trained** Newmarket, Suffolk

**FOCUS**
They finished strung out like three-mile chasers in this modest handicap. A clear personal best from the winner, with the third close to latest.

## 3710 TANDRIDGE TRIUMPH (S) STKS — 1m 4f (P)
**8:00** (8:00) (Class 6) 3-Y-O+ **£2,134** (£635; £317; £158) **Stalls** Low

Form RPR

/00- **1** **Ninfea (IRE)**[27] 7622 6-9-3 57.............................. AdamKirby 1 51
(Neil King) *stdd s: chsd ldrs: rdn and chal between rivals over 2f out: led 2f out: asserted ins fnl f: styd on wl* **7/1**[2]

0060 **2** *2 1/2* **Illegale (IRE)**[26] 2836 8-9-3 42..............................(bt) DavidProbert 6 47
(Nikki Evans) *hld up in tch in last: rdn and effrt over 2f out: 3rd and drvn over 1f out: styd on ins fnl f: wnt 2nd towards fin: no threat to wnr* **20/1**[3]

0-04 **3** *3/4* **Red Willow**[57] 1923 8-9-3 42..............................(p) SamHitchcott 2 46
(John E Long) *led and set stdy gallop: rdn and qcknd wl when pressed over 2f out: hdd 2f out: ev ch tl btn ins fnl f: wknd and lost 2nd towards fin* **7/1**[2]

1125 **4** *17* **Stand Guard**[24] 2904 10-9-13 80.............................. TomQueally 5 47
(John Butler) *mostly chsd ldr: rdn and unable qck over 2f out: dropped to last and btn whn wd bnd 2f out: wl hld and eased ins fnl f* **1/4**[1]

2m 35.01s (2.01) **Going Correction** -0.125s/f (Stan) **4** Ran SP% **109.8**
Speed ratings (Par 101): **88,86,85,74**
CSF £67.95 TOTE £4.60; EX 22.00 Trifecta £55.40.
**Owner** The St Gatien Racing For Fun Partnership **Bred** Kilco Builders **Trained** Newmarket, Suffolk

**FOCUS**
With the favourite flopping, this looks very weak form with the 57-rated winner accounting for two rivals rated in the 40s. The runner-up and third are rated to this year's form.

## 3711 THIEPVAL MEMORIAL DAY H'CAP — 1m 4f (P)
**8:30** (8:30) (Class 6) (0-65,65) 3-Y-O — **£2,587** (£770; £384; £192) **Stalls** Low

Form — RPR

000- **1** **Red Passiflora**[226] 7875 3-9-4 **62** ... ChrisCatlin 14 — 77+
(Sir Mark Prescott Bt) *t.k.h: in tch: hdwy to ld 9f out: mde rest: rdn clr w rival 3f out: 3 l clr ins fnl f: kpt on: a jst holding on* **8/1**

-450 **2** *nk* **Sweetheart Abbey**[23] 2927 3-9-0 **58** ... TomQueally 6 — 72
(William Knight) *taken down early: in tch in midfield: 5th and outpcd u.p 5th: rallied 2f out: chsd clr wnr ins fnl f: styd on wl: nvr quite getting to wnr* **10/1**

0600 **3** *5* **Censorius**[16] 3146 3-9-7 **65** ... (v[1]) PatCosgrave 7 — 69
(Ed Walker) *dwet and rdn leaving stalls: chsd ldrs after 2f: chsd wnr 8f out: rdn and drew clr w wnr 3f out: hung rt and btn over 1f out: plugged on to hold 3rd ins fnl f* **16/1**

-040 **4** *1* **Majestic Sun (IRE)**[12] 3316 3-8-11 **60** ... NoelGarbutt(5) 10 — 62
(Peter Chapple-Hyam) *stdd s: hld up in rr: rdn and plenty to do 3f out: hdwy 2f out: styd on wl ins fnl f: nvr threatened ldrs* **16/1**

0-40 **5** *1* **Musalaha (IRE)**[61] 1793 3-8-12 **56** ... DaneO'Neill 4 — 56
(Ed Dunlop) *chsd ldrs: 4th and outpcd 3f out: rallied u.p over 1f out: no ex and plugged on same pce fnl f* **16/1**

-354 **6** *3 ½* **Nissaki Kasta**[30] 2695 3-8-13 **57** ... HayleyTurner 13 — 51
(Hughie Morrison) *led tl 9f out: chsd ldrs after: 3rd and outpcd u.p 3f out: no imp: wknd 1f out* **20/1**

0-50 **7** *¾* **Third Strike**[161] 230 3-9-6 **64** ... LiamKeniry 16 — 56
(Gary Moore) *t.k.h: hld up in tch in midfield: rdn and outpcd 3f out: n.d after: plugged on* **20/1**

0021 **8** *½* **Passionate Affair (IRE)**[7] 3471 3-9-7 **65** ... (bt[1]) RichardHughes 9 — 56
(Jamie Osborne) *stdd after s: t.k.h: hld up in rr: outpcd and rdn over 3f out: no real imp and wl hld after* **6/1**[3]

060 **9** *¾* **Ophir**[30] 2690 3-9-7 **65** ... DougieCostello 1 — 55
(William Muir) *hld up in tch towards rr: rdn and outpcd over 3f out: plugged on but n.d after* **10/1**

-460 **10** *17* **Last Echo (IRE)**[88] 1220 3-8-8 **59** ... JaneElliott(7) 15 — 16
(Ralph Beckett) *s.i.s and hmpd sn after s: in tch in midfield: rdn over 4f out: lost tch 3f out: t.o* **25/1**

-055 **11** *5* **Improvized**[32] 2643 3-8-13 **57** ... (t) SteveDrowne 8
(William Muir) *hld up towards rr: rdn over 3f out: sn wl btn: t.o over 1f out* **25/1**

046 **12** *1* **Catadupa**[44] 2279 3-9-5 **63** ... GeorgeBaker 5 — 9
(Roger Charlton) *taken down early: t.k.h: chsd ldrs tl rdn and btn over 3f out: wl bhd and eased over 1f out: t.o* **3/1**[1]

0060 **13** *47* **Its Not Me Its You**[17] 3116 3-9-0 **65** ... JennyPowell(7) 2
(Brendan Powell) *in tch in midfield: rdn over 4f out: sn dropped out: t.o fnl 2f* **33/1**

-033 **14** *1 ½* **Lochalsh (IRE)**[23] 2926 3-9-2 **60** ... AdamKirby 3
(William Knight) *t.k.h: chsd ldrs for 2f: midfield after: rdn and btn over 3f out: eased wl over 1f out: t.o* **9/2**[2]

2m 30.8s (-2.20) **Going Correction** -0.125s/f (Stan) — **14** Ran — SP% **124.6**
Speed ratings (Par 97): **102,101,98,97,97 94,94,93,93,82 78,78,46,45**
CSF £82.02 CT £1276.20 TOTE £7.50: £3.10, £3.80, £7.40; EX 115.30 Trifecta £1727.40 Part won..
**Owner** Cheveley Park Stud **Bred** Cheveley Park Stud Ltd **Trained** Newmarket, Suffolk

**FOCUS**
The front two finished nicely clear in this weak handicap. Improved form from the winner, with the third earning a small personal best and the fourth to his last two turf marks.

## 3712 ROYAL BRITISH LEGION SURREY MAIDEN AUCTION STKS — 1m 2f (P)
**9:00** (9:02) (Class 6) 3-Y-O — **£2,264** (£673; £336; £168) **Stalls** Low

Form — RPR

4 **1** **Crown Of Aragon**[24] 2883 3-9-1 0 ... (v[1]) PatCosgrave 11 — 74+
(Denis Coakley) *t.k.h early: hld up wl in tch: rdn and effrt on inner to chse ldrs 2f out: led 1f out: kpt on u.p: drvn out* **11/4**[1]

-430 **2** *¾* **Black Label**[15] 3183 3-9-1 73 ... DaneO'Neill 9 — 72
(Harry Dunlop) *nt best away: hdwy to chse ldr after 2f: rdn and ev ch 2f: unable qck 1f out: one pce and hld fnl 100yds* **7/2**[2]

0-40 **3** *1 ¼* **Tiptree Lace**[22] 2967 3-8-13 72 ... TomQueally 7 — 68
(William Knight) *chsd ldrs: rdn and effrt ent fnl 2f: 3rd and kpt on same pce ins fnl f* **5/1**[3]

0 **4** *½* **Soundtrack (IRE)**[30] 2690 3-9-1 0 ... AdamKirby 10 — 69+
(William Knight) *hld up towards rr: pushed along 3f out: hdwy and swtchd rt over 1f out: kpt on wl ins fnl f: nt rch ldrs* **8/1**

066- **5** *1* **Tipsy Star**[212] 8085 3-8-10 58 ... (v[1]) DavidProbert 1 — 62
(Jonathan Geake) *broke wl: t.k.h: stdd and chsd ldrs: rdn and effrt ent fnl 2f: nt clr run and swtchd rt over 1f out: kpt on same pce fnl f* **14/1**

06 **6** *2 ¼* **Nelson Of The Nile**[20] 3031 3-8-8 0 ... MatthewLawson(3) 2 — 59
(Jonathan Portman) *hld up towards rr: rdn along over 4f out: stl plenty to do and wd bnd 2f out: hdwy and swtchd rt 1f out: styd on wl ins fnl f: nvr trbld ldrs* **20/1**

0-6 **7** *hd* **Footsieonehundred (IRE)**[24] 2883 3-8-3 0 ... (t) SimonPearce(3) 6 — 53
(Patrick Gilligan) *led: rdn ent fnl 2f: hdd 1f out: wknd ins fnl f* **33/1**

0 **8** *½* **Exclusive Contract (IRE)**[38] 2466 3-8-8 0 ... RachealKneller(5) 8 — 59
(Jamie Osborne) *t.k.h: chsd ldrs: rdn and unable qck ent fnl 2f: btn whn pushed rt over 1f out: wknd fnl f* **20/1**

**9** *1* **Jack Bear** 3-8-11 0 ... RichardHughes 12 — 55
(Jonathan Portman) *hld up in midfield: rdn and hdwy on outer 3f out: no imp over 1f out: btn whn hmpd ins fnl f: wknd* **5/1**[3]

**10** *¾* **Saturation Point** 3-8-6 0 ow1 ... RobertTart(3) 13 — 52
(James Toller) *wnt rt s and s.i.s: rdn 3f out: plugged on but nvr trbld ldrs* **16/1**

00 **11** *10* **Oakbank (USA)**[61] 1797 3-8-8 0 ... DanielMuscutt(5) 4 — 37
(Brett Johnson) *hld up in tch in midfield: rdn and lost pl over 3f out: bhd fnl 2f* **50/1**

**12** *1 ¾* **Mountain River (IRE)** 3-8-13 0 ... LiamKeniry 3 — 34
(J S Moore) *s.i.s: hld up in rr: rdn 4f out: bhd fnl 2f* **16/1**

2m 5.88s (-0.72) **Going Correction** -0.125s/f (Stan) — **12** Ran — SP% **126.2**
Speed ratings (Par 97): **97,96,95,95,94 92,92,91,91,90 82,81**
CSF £12.51 TOTE £4.00: £1.50, £1.60, £2.10; EX 14.50 Trifecta £55.00.
**Owner** Fairmount Partnership **Bred** Executive Bloodlines **Trained** West Ilsley, Berks

**FOCUS**
Probably just ordinary maiden form which can be rated around the reliable runner-up.
T/Plt: £3,620.50 to a £1 stake. Pool of £55398.90 - 11.17 winning tickets. T/Qpdt: £145.20 to a £1 stake. Pool of £6242.05 - 31.80 winning tickets. SP

# [3663] NEWCASTLE (L-H)
Saturday, June 28

**OFFICIAL GOING: Good to firm (8.1)**
Wind: Light, half behind Weather: Overcast

## 3713 BETFRED/IRISH STALLION FARMS EBF MAIDEN STKS (BOBIS RACE) — 5f
**1:35** (1:36) (Class 4) 2-Y-O — **£4,075** (£1,212; £606; £303) **Stalls** Centre

Form — RPR

4 **1** **Al Gomry**[15] 3199 2-9-5 0 ... PaulHanagan 6 — 83+
(Richard Fahey) *colty in paddock: cl up: led and edgd lft 2f out: pushed out fnl f* **5/4**[1]

**2** *¾* **Gerry The Glover (IRE)** 2-9-5 0 ... PaulPickard 5 — 80+
(Brian Ellison) *dwlt: hld up: rdn and hdwy over 2f out: pressed wnr over 1f out: kpt on: hld last 50yds* **25/1**

**3** *4 ½* **Eastern Racer (IRE)** 2-9-5 0 ... TomEaves 4 — 65
(Brian Ellison) *t.k.h: prom: effrt and ev ch whn blkd 2f out: outpcd by first two fnl f* **12/1**

0 **4** *4 ½* **Classic Flyer**[7] 3454 2-9-2 0 ... SamJames(3) 3 — 48
(David O'Meara) *t.k.h: led tl hdd 2f out: wknd fnl f* **8/1**[3]

40 **5** *nse* **Bowson Fred**[46] 2231 2-9-5 0 ... JamesSullivan 2 — 48
(Michael Easterby) *t.k.h: chsd ldrs: rdn and outpcd wl over 1f out: n.d after* **8/1**[3]

2 **6** *5* **Short N Sweet**[15] 3199 2-9-0 0 ... DavidAllan 1 — 25
(Tim Easterby) *disp ld to 2f out: rdn and wknd appr fnl f* **15/8**[2]

004 **7** *10* **Shamkhani**[11] 3337 2-9-5 0 ... SilvestreDeSousa 8
(Alan Berry) *hld up bhd ldng gp: struggling 1/2-way: sn btn* **66/1**

1m 0.54s (-0.56) **Going Correction** -0.20s/f (Firm) — **7** Ran — SP% **114.5**
Speed ratings (Par 95): **96,94,87,80,80 72,56**
CSF £34.58 TOTE £2.10: £1.30, £4.20; EX 46.00 Trifecta £195.50.
**Owner** Al Shaqab Racing **Bred** Horizon Bloodstock Limited **Trained** Musley Bank, N Yorks

**FOCUS**
Paul Hanagan said that the ground was "quick, but with no jar", while Paul Pickard described it as "fast, maybe quicker than good to firm". The opener was 1.54sec outside standard. A fairly ordinary maiden. The first two raced on what looked the quickest part of the track and finished clear.

## 3714 BETFRED HALF TIME IN-PLAY BOOSTS H'CAP — 6f
**2:05** (2:05) (Class 2) (0-100,99) 3-Y-O+
**£12,450** (£3,728; £1,864; £932; £466; £234) **Stalls** Centre

Form — RPR

3-53 **1** **Tatlisu (IRE)**[16] 3152 4-8-11 **82** ... GrahamLee 8 — 97
(Richard Fahey) *in tch: effrt and rdn over 1f out: led ins fnl f: kpt on strly* **10/1**

5- **2** *nk* **Muthmir (IRE)**[308] 5748 4-9-2 **87** ... PaulHanagan 9 — 101+
(William Haggas) *dwlt: plld hrd in rr: hdwy 2f out: effrt and pressed wnr last 100yds: kpt on: hld nr fin* **9/4**[1]

0106 **3** *2 ¼* **Kimberella**[42] 2353 4-9-4 **89** ... AdrianNicholls 3 — 96
(David Nicholls) *t.k.h: led: rdn 2f out: hdd ins fnl f: kpt on same pce* **7/1**[2]

50-5 **4** *1 ½* **Mississippi**[13] 3271 5-9-2 **87** ... SilvestreDeSousa 6 — 89
(David Barron) *midfield: drvn and hdwy over 2f out: kpt on fnl f: nrst fin* **15/2**[3]

4240 **5** *nk* **Grissom (IRE)**[15] 3202 8-8-13 **84** ... DavidAllan 10 — 85
(Tim Easterby) *hld up in tch: rdn over 2f out: wknd over 1f out* **16/1**

-433 **6** *2* **Jack Luey**[14] 3239 7-9-1 **86** ... DuranFentiman 4 — 81
(Lawrence Mullaney) *chsd ldrs: drvn over 2f out: wknd appr fnl f* **12/1**

-105 **7** *nk* **Tarooq (USA)**[24] 2898 8-9-0 **85** ... GrahamGibbons 12 — 79
(David Barron) *hld up: rdn along over 2f out: no imp* **8/1**

211- **8** *½* **Pipers Note**[355] 4117 4-9-4 **92** ... GeorgeChaloner(3) 2 — 84
(Richard Whitaker) *prom: rdn along over 2f out: wknd fnl f* **20/1**

0-30 **9** *½* **Lewisham**[21] 2992 4-8-11 **82** ... JoeFanning 5 — 73
(David Nicholls) *dwlt: t.k.h in rr: pushed along over 2f out: nvr able to chal* **14/1**

-401 **10** *3* **Clear Spring (IRE)**[26] 2849 6-10-0 **99** ... TomEaves 14 — 80
(John Spearing) *hld up in tch: drvn over 2f out: wknd over 1f out* **9/1**

00-0 **11** *1 ¼* **Nameitwhatyoulike**[91] 1164 5-9-2 **87** ... BarryMcHugh 13 — 64
(Michael Easterby) *hld up: rdn over 2f out: nvr able to chal* **28/1**

04-0 **12** *35* **Above Standard (IRE)**[14] 3239 6-8-8 **86** ... DanielleMooney(7) 7
(Michael Easterby) *chsd ldrs to 1/2-way: sn lost pl: lost tch over 1f out* **33/1**

1m 11.89s (-2.71) **Going Correction** -0.20s/f (Firm) — **12** Ran — SP% **116.6**
Speed ratings (Par 109): **110,109,106,104,104 101,101,100,99,95 94,47**
CSF £31.39 CT £176.34 TOTE £13.90: £3.10, £1.30, £2.70; EX 35.20 Trifecta £551.40.
**Owner** Middleham Park Racing LIV **Bred** J C And Rocal Bloodstock **Trained** Musley Bank, N Yorks

**FOCUS**
A decent handicap, but not many were able to get involved. The time was just inside the standard. The winner posted a personal best and there's a case for rating this even higher.

## 3715 BETFRED TV CHIPCHASE STKS (GROUP 3) — 6f
**2:40** (2:41) (Class 1) 3-Y-O+
**£34,026** (£12,900; £6,456; £3,216; £1,614; £810) **Stalls** Centre

Form — RPR

1-10 **1** **Danzeno**[14] 3253 3-8-10 101 ... AndrewMullen 6 — 108
(Michael Appleby) *dwlt: t.k.h and sn trcking ldrs: led and hung lft over 1f out: kpt on wl fnl f* **9/4**[2]

0102 **2** *¾* **Ruwaiyan (USA)**[20] 3036 5-9-3 95 ... (p) DavidAllan 2 — 108
(James Tate) *prom: drvn and outpcd over 2f out: rallied over 1f out: styd on to chse wnr towards fin* **7/1**

16-4 **3** *1* **Saayerr**[73] 1514 3-8-10 108 ... GrahamLee 5 — 103
(William Haggas) *t.k.h: cl up: led after 2f: rdn and hdd over 1f out: carried lft: kpt on same pce ins fnl f: lost 2nd nr fin* **2/1**[1]

3024 **4** *1 ½* **Body And Soul (IRE)**[14] 3241 4-9-0 102 ... DuranFentiman 3 — 97
(Tim Easterby) *t.k.h: led 2f: cl up: drvn over 2f out: kpt on same pce fnl f* **4/1**[3]

0300 **5** *shd* **Hitchens (IRE)**[26] 2848 9-9-3 100 ... GrahamGibbons 1 — 100
(David Barron) *hld up in last pl: rdn and outpcd 2f out: kpt on ins fnl f: nvr rchd ldrs* **20/1**

03-1 **6** *shd* **Sir Maximilian (IRE)**52 2074 5-9-3 96 StevieDonohoe 7 99
(Tim Pitt) *hld up in tch: drvn and outpcd over 2f out: rallied fnl f: nvr able to chal* **11/1**

1m 12.53s (-2.07) **Going Correction** -0.20s/f (Firm)
**WFA** 3 from 4yo+ 7lb **6** Ran SP% **109.7**
Speed ratings (Par 113): **105,104,102,100,100 100**
CSF £16.96 TOTE £3.50: £2.00, £4.00; EX 18.80 Trifecta £57.20.
**Owner** A M Wragg **Bred** A M Wragg **Trained** Danethorpe, Notts

**FOCUS**
Not a strong race for the grade, and unlikely to produce any winners of the Abbaye (Maarek) or July Cup (Mayson) as the 2012 race did. The winner is rated back to his Newmarket success, with the second improving on this year's handicap form and looking key to the level.

## 3716 BETFRED WORLD CUP DOUBLE DELIGHT H'CAP 7f
3:15 (3:15) (Class 2) (0-105,104) 3-Y-O+
£12,450 (£3,728; £1,864; £932; £466; £234) **Stalls** Centre

Form RPR

6100 **1** **Almargo (IRE)**9 3378 3-8-4 89 JoeFanning 6 98+
(Mark Johnston) *mde virtually all: qcknd clr over 1f out: edgd lft ins fnl f: pushed out* **11/2**2

6526 **2** *1 ¾* **Royal Rascal**15 3203 4-9-4 94 DavidAllan 10 100
(Tim Easterby) *hld up: rdn and hdwy over 2f out: kpt on fnl f to take 2nd last stride* **14/1**

0652 **3** *nse* **Foxtrot Romeo (IRE)**15 3202 5-9-1 91 (tp) MartinHarley 3 97+
(Marco Botti) *hld up: stdy hdwy over 2f out: effrt and chsd (clr) wnr over 1f out: kpt on same pce ins fnl f: lost 2nd last stride* **15/2**

1035 **4** *hd* **Farlow (IRE)**22 2959 6-9-0 90 PaulHanagan 8 95
(Richard Fahey) *hld up: rdn along over 2f out: hdwy over 1f out: kpt on u.p fnl f* **6/1**3

0525 **5** *3 ¾* **Apostle (IRE)**14 3244 5-9-0 90 LukeMorris 1 86
(David Simcock) *chsd ldrs: effrt and rdn over 2f out: outpcd fnl f* **11/1**

5-00 **6** *4* **Smarty Socks (IRE)**15 3202 10-8-12 91 SamJames(3) 7 76
(David O'Meara) *slowly away: hld up: rdn over 2f out: sme late hdwy: nvr on terms* **16/1**

-632 **7** *½* **My Freedom (IRE)**121 768 6-10-0 104 SilvestreDeSousa 5 88
(Saeed bin Suroor) *t.k.h: prom: rdn and outpcd 2f out: n.d after* **5/1**1

-003 **8** *½* **Cosmic Chatter**24 2898 4-9-3 93 GrahamGibbons 12 76
(David Barron) *prom: rdn over 2f out: hung lft and wknd wl over 1f out* **12/1**

2532 **9** *1 ½* **Dream Walker (FR)**30 2707 5-8-12 91 OisinMurphy(3) 9 70
(Brian Ellison) *midfield: drvn and outpcd wl over 2f out: n.d after* **5/1**1

1114 **10** *2 ½* **Victoire De Lyphar (IRE)**29 2747 7-9-6 96 (e) JamesSullivan 11 68
(Ruth Carr) *taken early to post: t.k.h: cl up tl hung lft and wknd 2f out* **17/2**

4001 **11** *5* **Clockmaker (IRE)**20 3036 8-9-4 94 PaulMulrennan 2 53
(Conor Dore) *disp ld to 3f out: drvn and outpcd whn hmpd wl over 1f out: sn btn* **14/1**

1m 24.57s (-3.23) **Going Correction** -0.20s/f (Firm)
**WFA** 3 from 4yo+ 9lb **11** Ran SP% **120.5**
Speed ratings (Par 109): **110,108,107,107,103 98,98,97,96,93 87**
CSF £81.98 CT £599.45 TOTE £5.90: £3.00, £5.00, £2.80; EX 135.90 Trifecta £1197.80.
**Owner** Sheikh Hamdan bin Mohammed Al Maktoum **Bred** Mountarmstrong Stud **Trained** Middleham Moor, N Yorks

**FOCUS**
This looked a warm handicap, and it was run inside the standard. The winner and runner-up are better than ever, and the fourth helps set the standard.

## 3717 JOHN SMITH'S NORTHUMBERLAND PLATE (HERITAGE H'CAP) 2m 19y
3:50 (3:54) (Class 2) 3-Y-O+
£86,226 (£25,956; £12,978; £6,468; £3,248; £1,638) **Stalls** Low

Form RPR

4412 **1** **Angel Gabrial (IRE)**52 2073 5-8-12 96 GeorgeChaloner(3) 1 107
(Richard Fahey) *in tch: pushed along over 2f out: swtchd rt and hdwy to ld over 1f out: hung rt: kpt on wl fnl f* **4/1**1

2-31 **2** *3 ½* **Suegioo (FR)**52 2073 5-9-4 99 (p) MartinHarley 10 106
(Marco Botti) *hld up in tch: effrt over 2f out: chsd wnr ins fnl f: kpt on: nt pce to chal* **12/1**

-506 **3** *2 ½* **Repeater**28 2785 5-9-4 102 SamJames(3) 8 106+
(David O'Meara) *hld up and wl bhd: gd hdwy against far rail fr over 2f out: kpt on to take 3rd last stride* **28/1**

241 **4** *shd* **Noble Silk**35 2561 5-9-0 95 (p) PaulMulrennan 15 100+
(Lucy Wadham) *s.i.s: hld up on ins: effrt on ins over 2f out: styng on whn checked ins fnl f: r.o* **14/1**

0-00 **5** *nse* **Ardlui (IRE)**43 2314 6-8-10 91 (b) DavidAllan 6 95
(Tim Easterby) *t.k.h: led at ordinary gallop: hdd 1/2-way: regained ld over 4f out: qcknd over 3f out: hdd over 1f out: one pce ins fnl f* **20/1**

-306 **6** *½* **Oriental Fox (GER)**9 3377 6-9-10 105 JoeFanning 3 108
(Mark Johnston) *t.k.h: hld up in midfield: effrt over 2f out: edgd lft over 1f out: kpt on ins fnl f* **8/1**2

6-31 **7** *½* **Totalize**15 3204 5-8-10 91 5ex RobertWinston 12 94
(Brian Ellison) *t.k.h in midfield: effrt and rdn 3f out: kpt on fr 2f out: nt pce to chal* **9/1**3

-650 **8** *1 ¼* **Glenard**35 2561 4-8-10 91 GrahamGibbons 5 92
(Charles Hills) *chsd ldrs: wnt 2nd over 3f out: effrt and drvn over 2f out: wknd ins fnl f* **18/1**

-151 **9** *3 ¾* **Lord Van Percy**42 2342 4-8-11 95 OisinMurphy(3) 22 92
(Andrew Balding) *stdd and swtchd lft s: hld up and wl bhd: rdn and styd on fr over 2f out: nvr able to chal* **9/1**3

16- **10** *2 ¼* **Dark Crusader (IRE)**36 2537 4-9-0 95 FergusSweeney 9 89
(A J Martin, Ire) *hld up: effrt and pushed along 3f out: no imp fr 2f out* **9/1**3

1-44 **11** *4* **Sir Ector (USA)**22 2973 7-9-6 101 GrahamLee 18 90
(J J Lambe, Ire) *t.k.h: hld up: rdn along over 3f out: nvr on terms* **22/1**

0/ **12** *¾* **Lucky Bridle (IRE)**36 2537 5-9-2 97 PaulHanagan 11 85
(W P Mullins, Ire) *midfield: effrt and drvn on outside over 3f out: edgd lft and wknd wl over 1f out* **8/1**2

030- **13** *1* **Boite (IRE)**352 4211 4-8-9 97 JordanNason(7) 19 84
(Peter Chapple-Hyam) *hld up and wl bhd: drvn over 3f out: nvr on terms* **40/1**

45-3 **14** *1 ¾* **Tropical Beat**42 2342 6-9-2 97 SilvestreDeSousa 17 82
(David O'Meara) *hld up on outside: shortlived effrt 4f out: rdn and wknd fr 3f out* **14/1**

650/ **15** *6* **Buthelezi (USA)**78 2278 6-9-0 95 (t) TomEaves 13 73
(Brian Ellison) *chsd ldrs: rdn over 4f out: wkng whn hmpd over 2f out* **33/1**

0 **16** *6* **Agreement (IRE)**11 3321 4-8-7 91 (p) IanBrennan(3) 20 62
(John Quinn) *in tch tl rdn and wknd fr over 3f out* **66/1**

151- **17** *9* **Big Thunder**274 6793 4-9-3 98 LukeMorris 16 58
(Sir Mark Prescott Bt) *prom on outside: rdn over 3f out: hung lft and wknd fr 2f out* **14/1**

20-0 **18** *4 ½* **Mawaqeet (USA)**15 2073 5-8-10 91 (p) PJMcDonald 14 45
(Donald McCain) *towards rr: drvn along 4f out: btn over 2f out* **33/1**

2-00 **19** *18* **Waterclock (IRE)**11 3321 5-8-9 90 (p) RussKennemore 21 23
(Jedd O'Keeffe) *w ldr: led 1/2-way to over 4f out: sn drvn and lost pl: t.o* **66/1**

3m 28.96s (-10.44) **Going Correction** -0.40s/f (Firm) **19** Ran SP% **129.0**
Speed ratings (Par 109): **110,108,107,106,106 106,106,105,103,102 100,100,99,99,96 93,88,86,77**
CSF £49.78 CT £1236.93 TOTE £4.70: £1.80, £3.30, £6.00, £4.00; EX 41.60 Trifecta £2435.10.
**Owner** Dr Marwan Koukash **Bred** K And Mrs Cullen **Trained** Musley Bank, N Yorks

**FOCUS**
Ante-post favourite Pique Sous was an absentee, as was the fellow Wille Mullins-trained Simenon, the latter's absence meaning the weights were raised 5lb. Another leading contender missing was Duke Of Clarence, representing the winning connections. They went a fairly ordinary gallop in a typically competitive renewal of this famous race, which is likely to be run on the hurdles track from 2015. It was a triumph for owner Dr Marwan Koukash and a reversal of the Chester Cup 1-2 from May, neither of the protagonists having been out since. Both upped their level a bit with the fourth rated to form.

## 3718 BETFRED WORLD CUP BET IN-PLAY H'CAP 1m 2f 32y
4:25 (4:30) (Class 4) (0-85,85) 4-Y-O+ £4,690 (£1,395; £697; £348) **Stalls** Low

Form RPR

6110 **1** **San Cassiano (IRE)**7 3457 7-9-7 85 JamesSullivan 3 95
(Ruth Carr) *mde all at modest gallop: qcknd clr wl over 2f out: drvn and styd on wl fnl f* **8/1**

4642 **2** *2 ¾* **Amaze**19 3055 6-8-8 75 (p) OisinMurphy(3) 1 80
(Brian Ellison) *in tch: effrt and pushed along over 2f out: chsd wnr over 2f out: clsd ent fnl f: one pce last 100yds* **7/4**1

1000 **3** *3 ¾* **Sky Khan**33 2618 5-9-0 81 (p) IanBrennan(3) 8 79
(John Wainwright) *t.k.h: hld up: rdn and effrt over 2f out: kpt on fnl f: nt rch first two* **15/2**

0220 **4** *9* **Dakota Canyon (IRE)**14 3254 5-8-8 72 (p) PaulHanagan 7 53
(Richard Fahey) *prom: drvn and outpcd over 3f out: rallied over 1f out: nvr able to chal* **6/1**3

1512 **5** *7* **Licence To Till (USA)**9 3382 7-9-2 80 SilvestreDeSousa 12 63
(Alan Berry) *in tch: hdwy to join wnr 1/2-way: rdn and outpcd over 2f out: 4th and hld whn looked to break down appr fnl f* **16/1**

600- **6** *8* **It's A Mans World**56 5580 8-8-8 72 TomEaves 2 24
(Brian Ellison) *hld up: drvn along over 3f out: nvr on terms* **16/1**

-350 **7** *3 ½* **Well Painted (IRE)**138 559 5-9-6 84 GrahamLee 5 29
(William Haggas) *hld up: rdn along over 3f out: btn fnl 2f* **5/1**2

5305 **8** *1 ½* **Skytrain**7 3463 4-9-3 81 JoeFanning 4 24
(Mark Johnston) *chsd ldrs tl rdn and wknd over 2f out* **8/1**

1053 **9** *9* **Outlaw Torn (IRE)**2 3624 5-8-4 68 oh1 ow2 (e) AdrianNicholls 11
(Richard Guest) *t.k.h: hld up: rdn along over 3f out: sn n.d* **14/1**

2m 10.01s (-1.89) **Going Correction** -0.40s/f (Firm) **9** Ran SP% **119.7**
Speed ratings (Par 105): **91,88,85,78,73 66,63,62,55**
CSF £23.28 CT £115.14 TOTE £10.40: £3.00, £1.20, £2.60; EX 32.40 Trifecta £214.90.
**Owner** S Jackson, L Shaw, Mrs R Carr **Bred** Peter Savill **Trained** Huby, N Yorks

**FOCUS**
Not a strong race for the grade, and few got into it as they finished strung out behind the winer, who set a steady gallop. The winner is rated as good as ever.

## 3719 BETFRED.COM FREE BETS OFFERS H'CAP (BOBIS RACE) 1m (R)
5:00 (5:00) (Class 4) (0-85,85) 3-Y-O £4,690 (£1,395; £697; £348) **Stalls** Low

Form RPR

5212 **1** **Halation (IRE)**16 3159 3-9-2 80 MartinHarley 7 89+
(Marco Botti) *hld up in tch: smooth hdwy over 2f out: swtchd lft and led 1f out: pushed along and hld on wl* **9/4**1

1-55 **2** *nk* **Erroneous (IRE)**14 3247 3-9-1 82 OisinMurphy(3) 4 90
(David Simcock) *prom: hdwy to ld over 2f out: sn rdn: edgd lft and hdd 1f out: rallied: hld nr fin* **5/2**2

-300 **3** *3* **Act Of Charity (IRE)**55 1979 3-9-7 85 (b) TomEaves 1 86
(Gay Kelleway) *trckd ldrs: no room fr 3f out tl swtchd rt over 1f out: kpt on fnl f: no ch w first two* **25/1**

60-1 **4** *2 ¾* **Amood (IRE)**24 2883 3-9-1 79 PaulHanagan 5 74
(Charles Hills) *t.k.h: hld up in tch: hdwy on outside and cl up over 2f out: edgd rt and wknd over 1f out* **9/2**3

61- **5** *nk* **Ryeolliean**256 7276 3-9-0 78 SilvestreDeSousa 8 72
(David O'Meara) *t.k.h early: pressed ldr: drvn over 2f out: wknd over 1f out* **5/1**

1112 **6** *37* **Desert Colours**15 3187 3-8-11 80 (b) KevinStott(5) 3
(Kevin Ryan) *led to over 2f out: rdn and wknd wl over 1f out: eased whn no ch fnl f* **5/1**

1m 41.94s (-3.36) **Going Correction** -0.40s/f (Firm) **6** Ran SP% **114.7**
Speed ratings (Par 101): **100,99,96,93,93 56**
CSF £8.49 CT £104.42 TOTE £3.10: £1.80, £1.90; EX 8.60 Trifecta £70.70.
**Owner** Al Asayl Bloodstock Ltd **Bred** Sheikh Sultan Bin Khalifa Al Nayhan **Trained** Newmarket, Suffolk

**FOCUS**
A fair handicap for three-year-olds in which they quite a steady gallop. The winner is progressing and this could be rated a length higher.
T/Jkpt: Part won. T/Plt: £66.60 to a £1 stake. Pool: £178,010.38 - 1949.75 winning tickets.
T/Qpdt: £29.80 to a £1 stake. Pool: £12,842.70 - 318.4 winning tickets. RY

# 3670 NEWMARKET (R-H)

Saturday, June 28

**OFFICIAL GOING: Good to firm (8.3) changing to good to soft after race 2 (2.20) changing to soft after race 3 (2.55)**

Realignment of bend into home straight increased distances of 10f & 12f. races by 22m.

Wind: almost nil Weather: sunny early, heavy rain with thunder and lightning races 2 and 3; becoming chilly

## 3720 BET365 MAIDEN STKS (BOBIS RACE) 7f

**1:45** (1:45) (Class 4) 2-Y-O **£3,881** (£1,155; £577; £288) **Stalls** High

Form RPR

1 **Zephuros (IRE)** 2-9-5 0 WilliamBuick 7 87+
(Charlie Appleby) *t.k.h: prom: led wl over 1f out: edgd rt 1f out: drvn and hld on wl cl home* **9/4**[2]

2 ½ **Lexington Times (IRE)** 2-9-5 0 PatDobbs 4 86+
(Richard Hannon) *trckd ldrs: shkn up 1/2-way: outpcd briefly: rallied and wnt 2nd ins fnl f: kpt on stoutly cl home: promising* **9/2**[3]

3 3 ¼ **Holland Park** 2-9-5 0 RyanMoore 3 77+
(Richard Hannon) *pressed ldr: rdn over 2f out: ev ch over 1f out: sn lost tch w ldng pair ins fnl f* **2/1**[1]

4 4 **Landwade Lad** 2-9-5 0 HayleyTurner 1 66
(James Fanshawe) *t.k.h early: rdn 1/2-way: sn outpcd and n.d after* **14/1**

5 2 ¾ **Giantouch (USA)** 2-9-5 0 AntonioFresu 2 59
(Marco Botti) *a in last trio: swtchd lft and rdn: outpcd on outer 2f out* **12/1**

000 6 1 ¼ **Framley Garth (IRE)**[28] 2776 2-9-5 0 LiamKeniry 5 55
(David Elsworth) *led tl hdd wl over 1f out: rdn and sn lost pl* **40/1**

7 ¾ **Austin Friars** 2-9-5 0 MartinLane 6 53
(Charlie Appleby) *dwlt: rn green in rr: rdn and outpcd on outer 2f out* **6/1**

1m 26.49s (0.79) **Going Correction** +0.075s/f (Good) **7 Ran SP% 113.4**
Speed ratings (Par 95): **98,97,93,89,86 84,83**
CSF £12.62 TOTE £3.00: £1.80, £3.00; EX 16.50 Trifecta £31.60.
**Owner** Godolphin **Bred** Darley **Trained** Newmarket, Suffolk

**FOCUS**
Far side course used. Stalls Far Side except 10 &12f: Centre. Realignment of bend into home straight increased distances of 10f & 12f. races by 22m. The predicted rain began to fall just before the first race. A maiden that has been won by some decent types, most noticeably 2013 champion 2yo Kingman. Some choicely bred sorts lined up for this contest which was run at an honest pace. It's a race with a strong average rating and this looked a race to be positive about.

## 3721 BET365 EMPRESS STKS (FILLIES) (LISTED RACE) 6f

**2:20** (2:33) (Class 1) 2-Y-O

**£14,744** (£5,590; £2,797; £1,393; £699; £351) **Stalls** High

Form RPR

01 1 **Calypso Beat (USA)**[14] 3223 2-9-0 0 WilliamBuick 5 92
(Kevin Ryan) *led: pushed along 2f out: drvn 1f out: drifted rt: kpt on strly: readily* **25/1**

21 2 ½ **Parsley (IRE)**[36] 2499 2-9-0 0 PatDobbs 3 91
(Richard Hannon) *hld up: rdn and hdwy 2f out: ev ch 1f out: no imp fnl 100yds* **9/1**

21 3 1 ¼ **Tigrilla (IRE)**[17] 3107 2-9-0 0 RyanMoore 1 87
(Roger Varian) *cl up: rdn 1/2-way: drvn to chal 1f out: nt qckn fnl 100yds* **5/2**[1]

51 4 ½ **Zeb Un Nisa**[22] 2944 2-9-0 0 JamesDoyle 8 85
(Roger Charlton) *hld up: effrt 2f out: drvn to chal 1f out: nt qckn fnl 100yds* **3/1**[2]

1 5 ½ **Accipiter**[23] 2918 2-9-0 0 AshleyMorgan 4 84
(Chris Wall) *wnt down early: pressed wnr: drvn and ev ch 1f out: btn whn squeezed for room 100yds out* **11/2**

14 6 1 ½ **Bonnie Grey**[30] 2703 2-9-0 0 MartinLane 7 79
(Rod Millman) *bhd early: rdn 3f out: nvr trbld ldrs* **12/1**

2315 7 ¾ **Littlemissblakeney**[10] 3353 2-9-0 0 FrankieDettori 2 77
(Hugo Palmer) *prom: rdn over 1f out: wknd steadily* **5/1**[3]

410 8 nse **Juventas**[7] 3448 2-9-0 0 DanielTudhope 6 77
(Mick Channon) *dwlt: a bhd* **16/1**

010 9 ¾ **Cajoling (IRE)**[30] 2703 2-9-0 0 HarryBentley 9 75
(Jonathan Portman) *toward rr: drvn and btn over 2f out* **80/1**

1m 12.79s (0.29) **Going Correction** +0.075s/f (Good) **9 Ran SP% 114.3**
Speed ratings (Par 98): **101,100,98,98,97 95,94,94,93**
CSF £229.28 TOTE £17.60: £4.10, £2.30, £1.20; EX 103.20 Trifecta £705.20.
**Owner** Cockerill Hillen & Graham **Bred** P Cockerill, S Graham & Sh Bloodstock **Trained** Hambleton, N Yorks

**FOCUS**
The race was delayed due to a heavy storm. A decent renewal with all the field having won on either of their last two starts. It was run at a fair pace with the runners coming up the centre. The average rating for this is modest given the grade.

## 3722 BET365 FRED ARCHER STKS (LISTED RACE) 1m 4f

**2:55** (3:03) (Class 1) 4-Y-O+

**£20,982** (£7,955; £3,981; £1,983; £995; £499) **Stalls** Centre

Form RPR

3602 1 **Sheikhzayedroad**[30] 2705 5-9-0 109 MartinLane 7 105
(David Simcock) *settled towards rr: hrd rdn wl over 3f out: effrt over 2f out: sustained chal u.p fnl f: led 75yds out: all out* **11/2**[2]

-211 2 ½ **Gatewood**[35] 2555 6-9-3 105 WilliamBuick 4 107
(John Gosden) *trckd ldrs: wnt 2nd 3f out: led over 2f out: sn rdn: hdd and no ex wl ins fnl f* **9/4**[1]

-320 3 ¾ **Chancery (USA)**[43] 2314 6-9-0 97 DanielTudhope 1 103
(David O'Meara) *settled in rr: effrt 4f out: drvn 2f out: styd on steadily ins fnl f but nvr gng to get there* **16/1**

3524 4 1 ½ **Rawaki (IRE)**[28] 2785 6-9-0 108 DavidProbert 5 101
(Andrew Balding) *prom: rdn 3f out: plugged on same pce fnl f* **13/2**[3]

3-10 5 18 **Battalion (IRE)**[42] 2335 4-9-0 110 RyanMoore 6 88
(William Haggas) *prom: rdn 5f out: hung lft and tired qckly: virtually p.u ins fnl f: t.o* **9/4**[1]

116- 6 2 ¾ **Cameron Highland (IRE)**[287] 6385 5-9-0 105 FrankieDettori 8 67
(Roger Varian) *led at stdy pce: rdn and hdd over 2f out: fdd over 1f out* **8/1**

0300 7 44 **Zambucca (SAF)**[10] 3354 6-9-0 100 PatCosgrave 3
(Gay Kelleway) *last pair: drvn and struggling 1/2-way: eased over 2f out: sn t.o* **33/1**

00 8 14 **Energia Eros (BRZ)**[149] 398 5-9-0 105 (b[1]) AntonioFresu 2
(Marco Botti) *bhd: struggling u.p 3f out: t.o and heavily eased over 2f out* **40/1**

2m 36.75s (3.85) **Going Correction** +0.475s/f (Yiel) **8 Ran SP% 112.6**
Speed ratings (Par 111): **106,105,105,104,92 90,61,51**
CSF £17.72 TOTE £6.00: £1.80, £1.20, £3.90; EX 15.90 Trifecta £191.40.
**Owner** Mohammed Jaber **Bred** Rabbah Bloodstock Limited **Trained** Newmarket, Suffolk

**FOCUS**
A strong contest for the grade run at a sound pace in the conditions which suited those coming from off the pace. It was run in torrential rain with the front four finishing clear. The winner was the pick of the weights and is rated close to form. The third is key to the level and earned a small personal best.

## 3723 BET365 CRITERION STKS (GROUP 3) 7f

**3:30** (3:34) (Class 1) 3-Y-O+

**£36,861** (£13,975; £6,994; £3,484; £1,748; £877) **Stalls** High

Form RPR

06-5 1 **Gregorian (IRE)**[22] 2958 5-9-3 113 WilliamBuick 5 117
(John Gosden) *cl up: rdn to ld over 1f out: drvn and fnd plenty fnl 100yds* **9/2**[2]

3-54 2 1 **Garswood**[28] 2765 4-9-3 114 (b[1]) RyanMoore 9 114
(Richard Fahey) *led after 1f: drvn and hdd 2f out: pressed wnr hrd fnl f: hld fnl 100yds* **5/1**[3]

5-13 3 2 ½ **Eton Forever (IRE)**[28] 2765 7-9-3 110 FrankieDettori 1 108
(Roger Varian) *settled towards rr: rdn 1/2-way: drvn and clsd over 1f out: no further imp last 100yds* **13/2**

2-45 4 2 ½ **Highland Colori (IRE)**[26] 2848 6-9-3 109 DavidProbert 2 101
(Andrew Balding) *led 1f: pressed ldr tl led again 2f out: drvn and hdd over 1f out: sn outpcd* **8/1**

41-0 5 1 ¼ **Tawhid**[28] 2765 4-9-3 111 (p) HarryBentley 6 98
(Saeed bin Suroor) *hld up towards rr: drvn over 1f out: hung fire fnl f: wl hld after* **10/1**

-463 6 3 ¼ **Top Notch Tonto (IRE)**[30] 2705 4-9-8 110 JamesDoyle 8 95
(Brian Ellison) *a abt same pl: rdn and tried to get on terms 2f out: no further hdwy: btn over 1f out* **8/1**

-051 7 nk **Gabriel's Lad (IRE)**[49] 2145 5-9-3 110 GeorgeBaker 3 89
(Denis Coakley) *stdd in last pair: rdn 1/2-way: sn struggling* **5/2**[1]

3610 8 ½ **Penitent**[22] 2958 8-9-8 113 DanielTudhope 7 93
(David O'Meara) *prom: rdn wl over 1f out: sn lost pl* **20/1**

1m 26.78s (1.08) **Going Correction** +0.475s/f (Yiel) **8 Ran SP% 112.8**
Speed ratings (Par 113): **112,110,108,105,103 100,99,99**
CSF £26.42 TOTE £4.60: £1.80, £1.70, £1.90; EX 21.80.
**Owner** HRH Princess Haya Of Jordan **Bred** Rathasker Stud **Trained** Newmarket, Suffolk

**FOCUS**
The ground was changed to soft from good to soft. A typically high-class field for this Group 3 contest which was run at a fair pace. The winner is rated to his best.

## 3724 EBF STALLIONS BET365 ETERNAL STKS (LISTED RACE) 7f

**4:05** (4:09) (Class 1) 3-Y-O

**£22,684** (£8,600; £4,304; £2,144; £1,076; £540) **Stalls** High

Form RPR

124 1 **Evita Peron**[34] 2584 3-9-0 103 JimCrowley 2 105
(Ralph Beckett) *trckd ldrs: only one on bridle whn qcknd to ld wl over 1f out: sn rdn and in command after: edgd sltly lft fnl 100yds* **3/1**[1]

2123 2 2 ¾ **Penny Drops**[22] 2961 3-9-0 93 FrankieDettori 1 98
(William Haggas) *plld hrd: hld up: rdn and effrt 2f out: chsd wnr fnl f: no imp* **9/2**[2]

1 3 1 ¼ **Swift Campaign (IRE)**[28] 2780 3-9-0 84 WilliamBuick 8 95
(John Gosden) *hld up last tl past 1/2-way: drvn and effrt over 1f out: kpt on same pce ins fnl f: n.d* **13/2**[3]

-146 4 2 ¾ **Wedding Ring (IRE)**[73] 1513 3-9-0 96 MartinLane 6 87
(Charlie Appleby) *towards rr: rdn and effrt over 2f out: nt qckn over 1f out: passed two rivals fnl strides* **14/1**

0-22 5 nse **Musicora**[26] 2840 3-9-0 92 SeanLevey 9 87
(Richard Hannon) *t.k.h: chsd ldrs: rdn and effrt 2f out: no imp and btn over 1f out* **20/1**

-640 6 nk **Dutch Courage**[10] 3357 3-9-0 96 TonyHamilton 10 87
(Richard Fahey) *chsd ldrs: rdn over 2f out: btn over 1f out* **8/1**

-541 7 2 ¼ **Manderley (IRE)**[27] 2804 3-9-0 109 PatDobbs 5 81
(Richard Hannon) *fly leapt fr stalls: sn led: drvn 2f out: hdd wl over 1f out: sn hung lft and lost pl* **3/1**[1]

13-0 8 15 **Along Again (IRE)**[73] 1515 3-9-0 99 RyanMoore 3 42+
(Sir Michael Stoute) *t.k.h: chsd ldrs: drvn 2f out: sn btn: heavily eased and t.o ins fnl f* **17/2**

1110 9 1 ¾ **Alumina (IRE)**[10] 3357 3-9-0 90 DavidProbert 4 37
(Andrew Balding) *prom tl rdn and wknd over 2f out: heavily eased and t.o ins fnl f* **25/1**

-521 10 4 **Relation Alexander (IRE)**[39] 2447 3-9-0 74 LiamKeniry 7 27
(Paul D'Arcy) *prom: rdn 2f out: sn btn: heavily eased and t.o ins fnl f* **66/1**

1m 27.81s (2.11) **Going Correction** +0.475s/f (Yiel) **10 Ran SP% 119.9**
Speed ratings (Par 107): **106,102,101,98,98 97,95,78,76,71**
CSF £16.72 TOTE £4.20: £2.00, £1.80, £2.60; EX 16.20 Trifecta £176.80.
**Owner** Newsells Park Stud **Bred** Newsells Park Stud **Trained** Kimpton, Hants

**FOCUS**
The first time this Listed contest had been run at Newmarket, having been switched from Warwick. The pace was honest. The winner (rated to top race standard from the past decade) and runner-up are progressive.

## 3725 BET365.COM FILLIES' H'CAP 1m 4f

**4:40** (4:40) (Class 3) (0-95,91) 3-Y-O+ **£9,056** (£2,695; £1,346; £673) **Stalls** Centre

Form RPR

3-12 1 **Melrose Abbey (IRE)**[44] 2277 3-8-5 **82** MartinLane 1 95
(Ralph Beckett) *hld up trcking ldrs: drvn over 3f out: led 2f out: styd on strly after and wl in command 1f out* **9/4**[2]

012 2 3 ½ **Seagull (IRE)**[18] 3085 3-8-9 **86** WilliamBuick 6 93+
(John Gosden) *disp 2nd: rdn over 2f out: nt qckn after: wnt 2nd but no imp ins fnl f* **11/8**[1]

5231 3 3 ¼ **Bureau (IRE)**[6] 3502 3-8-6 **83** 6ex RoystonFfrench 7 85
(Mark Johnston) *led: rdn and hdd 2f out: chsd wnr vainly tl lost 2nd and wknd ins fnl f* **14/1**

-031 4 ¾ **Rosehill Artist (IRE)**[18] 3085 3-8-11 **88** FrankieDettori 3 89
(Charles Hills) *chsd ldrs: rdn 4f out: btn 2f out: plugged on* **8/1**[3]

556- 5 hd **Kikonga**[240] 7650 4-10-0 **91** JamesDoyle 4 91
(Luca Cumani) *t.k.h: disp 2nd tl rdn 3f out: btn 2f out* **10/1**

13-0 **6** *61* **Empress Adelaide**[28] 2762 4-9-8 **85** RyanMoore 5
(William Haggas) *last pair: drvn and floundering over 4f out: sn t.o: hacked home* **8/1**3

2m 39.73s (6.83) **Going Correction** +0.475s/f (Yiel)
**WFA** 3 from 4yo 14lb **6** Ran SP% **110.9**
Speed ratings (Par 104): **96,93,91,91,90 50**
CSF £5.57 CT £27.79 TOTE £3.40: £2.00, £1.20; EX 6.50 Trifecta £50.60.
**Owner** J H Richmond-Watson **Bred** Lawn Stud **Trained** Kimpton, Hants

**FOCUS**
Improved form from the well-bred winner, with the front-running third close to her Pontefract win.

## 3726 BET365.COM H'CAP 1m 2f
**5:15** (5:16) (Class 2) (0-100,99) 3-Y-O+ **£12,938** (£3,850; £1,924; £962) **Stalls** Centre

Form RPR
-012 **1** **Llanarmon Lad (IRE)**[22] 2959 5-9-4 **89** RyanMoore 3 99
(Brian Ellison) *stdd to r in 3rd: pushed along 3f out: hrd drvn to ld 2f out: kpt on gamely and holding rivals fnl f* **5/4**1

0024 **2** *2 1/4* **Busatto (USA)**[9] 3397 4-9-7 **92** JimCrowley 8 98
(Mark Johnston) *set slow pce: rdn 3f out: hdd 2f out: nt qckn ins fnl f: jst hld 2nd* **4/1**3

06-0 **3** *nk* **Proud Chieftain**[56] 1948 6-9-10 **95** JimmyQuinn 7 100
(Clifford Lines) *pressed ldr in slowly run r: rdn and outpcd over 2f out: last briefly 1f out: rallied gamely ins fnl f: nrly ct 2nd but no ch w wnr* **14/1**

26-0 **4** *3/4* **Urban Dance (IRE)**[55] 1973 4-9-13 **98** WilliamBuick 1 102
(Charlie Appleby) *stdd to r in 4th: effrt over 2f out: sn rdn: chal 1f out: nt qckn after and lost 3rd fnl 50yds* **9/4**2

4400 **5** *3* **Regulation (IRE)**[10] 3356 5-10-0 **99** MartinLane 9 97
(Neil King) *stdd to r in last: effrt over 2f out: flattered briefly: rdn and btn 1f out: eased cl home* **17/2**

2m 12.63s (7.13) **Going Correction** +0.475s/f (Yiel)
**WFA** 3 from 4yo+ 12lb **5** Ran SP% **112.4**
Speed ratings (Par 109): **90,88,87,87,84**
CSF £6.85 TOTE £1.90: £1.50, £1.90; EX 5.40 Trifecta £27.00.
**Owner** Middleham Park Racing XLIII & Partner **Bred** Miss Sarah Thompson **Trained** Norton, N Yorks

**FOCUS**
A steady pace but the form makes sense.

## 3727 BET365 EBF STALLIONS FILLIES' H'CAP 1m
**5:45** (5:47) (Class 3) (0-95,93) 3-Y-O+ **£9,056** (£2,695; £1,346; £673) **Stalls** High

Form RPR
-200 **1** **Midnite Angel (IRE)**[10] 3357 3-8-13 **88** (b) FrankieDettori 2 101
(Richard Hannon) *settled in rr: t.k.h: effrt gng wl 2f out: drvn to ld 1f out: sn surged clr* **9/2**3

3112 **2** *4* **Waveguide (IRE)**[7] 3476 5-8-4 **76** LewisWalsh(7) 9 82
(David Simcock) *trckd ldrs: led gng wl 2f out: hdd 1f out: sn rdn: nt match strides w wnr after* **3/1**2

2213 **3** *2 3/4* **Saucy Minx (IRE)**[8] 3425 4-9-4 **83** (b) JimCrowley 6 82
(Amanda Perrett) *midfield: effrt 2f out: drvn and ch over 1f out: edgd lft and nt keen whn making no imp after* **10/1**

-421 **4** *2 1/4* **Starlight Serenade**[36] 2504 3-8-0 **75** oh3 JimmyQuinn 1 67
(Ralph Beckett) *plld hrd: prom: rdn 2f out: wknd over 1f out* **9/4**1

0-23 **5** *1 1/4* **Magique (IRE)**[12] 3314 4-8-12 **77** JamesDoyle 8 68
(Jeremy Noseda) *towards rr: rdn over 2f out: sn btn* **8/1**

65-0 **6** *2* **Ligeia**[17] 3117 3-8-8 **83** MartinLane 7 68
(Richard Hannon) *disp ld tl rdn and lost pl qckly over 2f out* **25/1**

1-00 **7** *4* **Folk Melody (IRE)**[43] 2316 3-9-4 **93** WilliamBuick 5 69
(Charlie Appleby) *midfield: rdn 2f out: sn btn: eased ins fnl f* **6/1**

155 **8** *5* **Al Manaal**[14] 3212 4-9-2 **81** RyanMoore 4 47
(Mick Channon) *disp ld tl hrd rdn and lost pl over 2f out: eased ins fnl f* **20/1**

1m 42.39s (2.39) **Going Correction** +0.475s/f (Yiel)
**WFA** 3 from 4yo+ 10lb **8** Ran SP% **117.0**
Speed ratings (Par 104): **107,103,100,98,96 94,90,85**
CSF £18.92 CT £129.67 TOTE £5.20: £1.90, £1.70, £2.10; EX 22.90 Trifecta £163.10.
**Owner** Al Shaqab Racing **Bred** O Bourke **Trained** East Everleigh, Wilts

**FOCUS**
A personal best from the winner and the runner-up is rated close to her latest.
T/Plt: £33.40 to a £1 stake. Pool: £112,814.76 - 2460.67 winning tickets. T/Qpdt: £7.00 to a £1 stake. Pool: £9,281.10 - 973.3 winning tickets. IM

# 3536 WINDSOR (R-H)
## Saturday, June 28

**OFFICIAL GOING: Good (watered; 9.0) changing to good to soft after race 3 (3.05)**
Top bend dolled out 5yds from normal inner configuration adding 16yds to races of one mile and beyond. Inner of Straight on normal racing line.
Wind: Almost nil Weather: Changeable - heavy shower before race 3.

## 3728 NEW HORSE RACING ODDS AT UNIBET.CO.UK MAIDEN STKS 6f
**1:55** (1:58) (Class 5) 2-Y-O **£2,587** (£770; £384; £192) **Stalls** Low

Form RPR
44 **1** **St Brelades Bay (IRE)**[16] 3140 2-9-5 0 RichardHughes 9 82+
(Richard Hannon) *hld up in midfield: swtchd fr inner to outer over 2f out: prog after: clsd to ld last 120yds: comf* **5/6**1

**2** *1 1/2* **Home Of The Brave (IRE)** 2-9-5 0 JimmyFortune 8 76+
(Hugo Palmer) *stdd s: t.k.h: hld up in rr: hmpd over 2f out: prog over 1f out: pushed along and styd on to take 2nd last stride: encouraging debut* **9/2**2

6 **3** *shd* **Quintus Cerialis (IRE)**[37] 2480 2-9-5 0 AdamKirby 7 73
(Clive Cox) *mde most: rdn over 1f out: hdd and outpcd last 120yds: lost 2nd post* **20/1**

0 **4** *2 1/2* **Hawkin (IRE)**[14] 3223 2-9-0 0 SebSanders 10 61
(Ralph Beckett) *cl up: rdn to dispute 3rd 2f out to over 1f out: one pce after* **66/1**

**5** *hd* **Inniscastle Lad** 2-9-5 0 DougieCostello 11 65
(William Muir) *in tch on outer: shkn up wl over 1f out: kpt on but nvr gng pce to threaten* **50/1**

**6** *3/4* **First Class Mail** 2-9-2 0 CharlesBishop(3) 2 63
(Mick Channon) *chsd ldrs: rdn to dispute 3rd 2f out to over 1f out: fdd* **33/1**

0 **7** *1/2* **Pixeleen**[13] 3279 2-9-0 0 TomQueally 5 56
(Malcolm Saunders) *towards rr: pushed along 2f out: kpt on steadily fnl f: nvr nrr* **50/1**

**8** *6* **Total Demolition (IRE)** 2-9-5 0 JamieSpencer 1 43
(Olly Stevens) *dwlt but sn rcvrd to join ldr: wknd over 1f out: eased* **16/1**

06 **9** *1 3/4* **Bakht A Rawan (IRE)**[18] 3082 2-9-5 0 JohnFahy 3 38
(Mark Usher) *disp ld 1f: chsd ldrs to 1/2-way: sn wknd* **33/1**

**10** *1* **Soldier Sam (IRE)** 2-9-5 0 DaneO'Neill 12 35
(Richard Hannon) *slowly away: rn green in rr: nvr a factor* **14/1**

**11** *2 3/4* **Dutch Falcon** 2-9-5 0 SteveDrowne 6 27
(William Muir) *chsd ldrs to 1/2-way: sn wknd* **25/1**

**12** *2 1/4* **Blue Amazon (IRE)** 2-8-11 0 ThomasBrown(3) 4 15
(Lee Carter) *w ldrs 2f: wknd over 2f out* **100/1**

4 **13** *7* **Doctor Kehoe**[29] 2731 2-9-5 0 KierenFallon 13
(Richard Fahey) *wnt lft s: a in last pair: t.o* **8/1**3

1m 13.06s (0.06) **Going Correction** +0.10s/f (Good) **13** Ran SP% **117.3**
Speed ratings (Par 93): **103,101,100,97,97 96,95,87,85,83 80,77,67**
CSF £3.80 TOTE £1.80: £1.10, £2.00, £4.00; EX 6.40 Trifecta £48.90.
**Owner** Carmichael Jennings **Bred** J C Bloodstock **Trained** East Everleigh, Wilts
■ Stewards' Enquiry : Richard Hughes 1st incident; caution: careless riding. (2nd) three-day ban: careless riding (Jul 14-16)

**FOCUS**
Probably not a maiden with a great deal of depth to it, but the winner has quickly got his career back on track, while there was plenty to like about the runner-up's performance on debut.

## 3729 UNIBET - BY PLAYERS FOR PLAYERS MAIDEN STKS 6f
**2:30** (2:31) (Class 5) 3-Y-O **£2,587** (£770; £384; £192) **Stalls** Low

Form RPR
-025 **1** **Supersta**[16] 3145 3-9-5 **73** SteveDrowne 6 76
(Ronald Harris) *disp ld 2f: chsd ldr: rdn 2f out: led 1f out: hung lft fnl f: drvn out* **3/1**3

4- **2** *1/2* **Anna's Vision (IRE)**[255] 7294 3-9-0 0 RichardHughes 2 69+
(Jeremy Noseda) *hld up in tch: prog on outer 2f out: rdn to chal 1f out: carried lft ins fnl f: hld whn hmpd last strides* **5/2**2

2 **3** *2* **Inis Airc (IRE)**[37] 2489 3-9-0 0 JimmyFortune 3 63
(Sylvester Kirk) *disp ld to over 4f out: lost pl: effrt and hrd rdn over 1f out: hung lft but kpt on to take 3rd nr fin* **9/4**1

60 **4** *3/4* **Silken Poppy**[22] 2946 3-8-11 0 ThomasBrown(3) 7 61
(Patrick Chamings) *led after 2f: shkn up and hdd 1f out: nt qckn* **20/1**

**5** *1/2* **Unbridled Joy (IRE)** 3-9-0 0 AdamKirby 4 59
(Clive Cox) *chsd ldrs: pushed along 1/2-way: rdn to chal over 1f out: one pce fnl f* **5/1**

- **6** *2 1/2* **Simma (IRE)** 3-9-0 0 DaneO'Neill 5 51
(Sylvester Kirk) *v.s.a: ct up in rr over 3f out: rdn over 1f out: fdd* **16/1**

1m 13.55s (0.55) **Going Correction** +0.10s/f (Good) **6** Ran SP% **111.7**
Speed ratings (Par 99): **100,99,96,95,95 91**
CSF £10.80 TOTE £4.70: £2.20, £1.80; EX 11.60 Trifecta £15.10.
**Owner** Mrs Ruth Serrell & Ridge House Stables **Bred** Cheveley Park Stud Ltd **Trained** Earlswood, Monmouths
■ Stewards' Enquiry : Richard Hughes three-day ban: careless riding (Jul 14-16)

**FOCUS**
Fair form at best in this sprint maiden. The winner set the standard and has been rated to his best.

## 3730 DAILY UNIBET EARLY PRICES FROM 9AM H'CAP 1m 3f 135y
**3:05** (3:05) (Class 2) (0-100,97) 4-Y-O+ **£12,938** (£3,850; £1,924; £962) **Stalls** Centre

Form RPR
54-1 **1** **Al Saham**[49] 2142 5-9-7 **97** KierenFallon 4 106
(Saeed bin Suroor) *prog to trck ldr over 6f out: rdn over 2f out: persistent chal fnl 2f: styd on to ld nr fin* **3/1**1

0-00 **2** *hd* **Nicholascopernicus (IRE)**[28] 2787 5-8-12 **88** JamieSpencer 11 96
(Ed Walker) *cl up: led 7f out: hrd rdn wl over 1f out: kpt on but hdd nr fin* **7/1**3

3453 **3** *3/4* **Mica Mika (IRE)**[14] 3250 6-7-11 **78** oh1 (p) SammyJoBell(5) 1 87+
(Richard Fahey) *wl in tch: shkn up to trck ldng pair on inner wl over 1f out: gng strly whn insufficient gap fnl f: nvr able to chal* **12/1**

0-33 **4** *1/2* **Border Legend**[28] 2783 5-9-2 **92** JimmyFortune 8 98+
(Roger Charlton) *hld up in lat trio: pushed along over 3f out: swtchd to outer and prog 2f out: tried to cl on ldrs fnl f: nvr quite rchd them* **7/2**2

-630 **5** *nse* **Kelinni (IRE)**[21] 2991 6-9-2 **97** DanielMuscutt(5) 10 103+
(Marco Botti) *hld up in rr: pushed along over 3f out: prog on outer 2f out: tried to cl on ldrs fnl f: nvr quite rchd them* **8/1**

2100 **6** *1* **Viewpoint (IRE)**[7] 3449 5-9-4 **94** RichardHughes 2 98
(Richard Hannon) *led to 7f out: chsd ldng pair: rdn over 3f out: no imp 2f out: kpt on same pce* **7/1**3

5230 **7** *1* **Modernism**[14] 3217 5-8-13 **89** SebSanders 7 92
(David Simcock) *prom: rdn to dispute 3rd over 3f out: no imp 2f out: one pce after* **20/1**

23-6 **8** *3/4* **Ajman Bridge**[49] 2154 4-9-1 **91** (b1) AdamKirby 3 92
(Luca Cumani) *in tch: shkn up over 2f out: sme prog over 1f out: nt qckn and lost pl fnl f* **9/1**

-044 **9** *11* **Pasaka Boy**[21] 2991 4-8-10 **86** JohnFahy 9 69
(Jonathan Portman) *chsd ldrs: rdn wl over 3f out: wknd over 2f out: sn bhd* **10/1**

0-00 **10** *6* **Resurge (IRE)**[22] 2957 9-8-12 **88** (bt) TomQueally 6 61
(Stuart Kittow) *s.i.s: a in last trio: no hdwy over 2f out: wknd wl over 1f out* **25/1**

2m 28.94s (-0.56) **Going Correction** -0.025s/f (Good) **10** Ran SP% **118.7**
Speed ratings (Par 109): **100,99,99,99,99 98,97,97,89,85**
CSF £24.95 CT £224.49 TOTE £3.20: £1.80, £2.10, £2.60; EX 27.50 Trifecta £330.80.
**Owner** Godolphin **Bred** Darley **Trained** Newmarket, Suffolk

**FOCUS**
A useful handicap. The pace steadied around halfway, not quickening again until over 2f out, and not that many threatened to land a serious blow. The third looked unlucky. The winner posted a small personal best and the runner-up was close to last year's best.

## 3731 UNIBET "ROAD TO RIO CHALLENGE" MIDSUMMER STKS (LISTED RACE) 1m 67y
**3:40** (3:42) (Class 1) 3-Y-O+
**£20,982** (£7,955; £3,981; £1,983; £995; £499) **Stalls** Low

Form RPR
2203 **1** **Custom Cut (IRE)**[14] 3252 5-9-4 **108** JamieSpencer 11 112
(David O'Meara) *pressed ldr after 1f: pressed new ldr over 3f out: led over 1f out: hrd rdn fnl f: hld on wl* **8/1**

-044 **2** *nk* **Baltic Knight (IRE)**35 2554 4-9-4 104 RichardHughes 8 111
(Richard Hannon) *hld up in rr: last of main gp over 3f out: prog over 2f out: rdn to take 2nd fnl f: chal last 100yds: nt qckn* **7/1**3

5560 **3** *2* **Empire Storm (GER)**13 3291 7-9-4 105 (t) CamHardie 3 107
(Michael Attwater) *cl up: led over 3f out: drvn and hdd over 1f out: one pce* **25/1**

-630 **4** *¾* **Fire Ship**13 3291 5-9-4 105 TomQueally 6 107+
(William Knight) *towards rr: shkn up over 3f out: prog on inner over 2f out: chsd ldng pair briefly over 1f out but nt clr run sn after: nt rcvr* **10/1**

15-0 **5** *½* **Short Squeeze (IRE)**10 3356 4-9-4 106 JimmyFortune 4 104
(Hugo Palmer) *hld up towards rr: clsd on ldrs over 2f out and gng bttr than most: rdn and fnd nil over 1f out: wl hld after* **9/2**2

-203 **6** *1½* **Roserrow**14 3251 5-9-4 93 SteveDrowne 10 100
(Andrew Balding) *wl in tch: rdn over 3f out: nt qckn over 2f out: no prog after* **20/1**

2-56 **7** *1* **Emell**91 1162 4-9-4 100 KieranO'Neill 2 98
(Richard Hannon) *trckd ldrs: shkn up over 3f out: no imp 2f out: fdd* **33/1**

6261 **8** *18* **Free Wheeling (AUS)**119 808 6-9-4 110 (t) KierenFallon 7 57
(Saeed bin Suroor) *hld up in rr: shkn up and no prog over 3f out: wl btn over 2f out: eased and t.o* **7/1**3

0161 **9** *6* **Fanoos**33 2608 5-8-13 83 (e1) RobertTart 9 38
(Dr Jon Scargill) *s.i.s: hld up in last: unsteerable bnd over to 5f out and nrly rn off the crse: continued t.o* **33/1**

1100 **10** *1* **Ocean Tempest**10 3356 5-9-7 115 AdamKirby 1 44
(John Ryan) *pushed up to ld: rdn and hdd over 3f out: sn dropped out: t.o and eased fnl f* **6/4**1

1m 42.2s (-2.50) **Going Correction** -0.025s/f (Good) **10 Ran SP% 117.9**
Speed ratings (Par 111): **111,110,108,107,107 105,104,86,80,79**
CSF £60.36 TOTE £8.10: £2.50, £1.80, £6.80; EX 66.20 Trifecta £1558.50 Part won..
**Owner** Gary Douglas & Pat Breslin **Bred** Moyglare Stud Farm Ltd **Trained** Nawton, N Yorks

**FOCUS**
Not a particularly strong Listed race, particularly with the favourite underperforming. The gallop didn't look overly strong, the runner-up possibly deserving of a little extra credit after coming from the back of the field. The winner has been rated to his best, and the sixth helps set the level.

## 3732 ROHLIG LOGISTICS UK 30TH ANNIVERSARY H'CAP 6f
4:10 (4:13) (Class 2) (0-105,105) 3-Y-O+

**£18,675** (£5,592; £2,796; £1,398; £699; £351) **Stalls** Low

Form RPR

0-00 **1** **Fairway To Heaven (IRE)**13 3271 5-8-12 89 JackMitchell 9 102
(Michael Wigham) *hld up in detached last: stl there 2f out: rapid prog against nr side rail over 1f out: hrd rdn and r.o wl to ld last strides* **22/1**

1-04 **2** *1* **Gamesome (FR)**14 3253 3-9-0 98 JamieSpencer 6 106+
(Olly Stevens) *trckd ldrs: gng easily 2f out: prog to ld jst over 1f out: drvn ins fnl f: ct last strides* **3/1**2

-000 **3** *1¾* **Arnold Lane (IRE)**7 3452 5-9-9 100 SamHitchcott 2 104
(Mick Channon) *chsd ldrs: rdn wl over 2f out: nvr gng pce to chal but kpt on fnl f to take 3rd last strides* **16/1**

-340 **4** *nk* **Desert Law (IRE)**44 2283 6-9-7 98 1 KierenFallon 4 101
(Saeed bin Suroor) *chsd ldr: led over 3f out: dashed for home over 2f out: drvn and hdd jst over 1f out: fdd* **25/1**

4006 **5** *1¼* **El Viento (FR)**28 2786 6-9-0 91 (v) DaneO'Neill 11 90
(Richard Fahey) *in tch: pushed along 1/2-way: nvr gng pce to threaten ldrs: one pce over 1f out* **8/1**

00-0 **6** *½* **Humidor (IRE)**36 2503 7-9-5 96 AdamKirby 10 93
(George Baker) *prom: chsd ldr 1/2-way to wl over 1f out: steadily wknd* **12/1**

-000 **7** *2* **Valbchek (IRE)**26 2848 5-9-7 98 (b) TomQueally 1 89
(Jeremy Noseda) *hld up in rr: shkn up 1/2-way: no imp on ldrs 2f out: wl btn after* **14/1**

0421 **8** *7* **Ashpan Sam**21 2992 5-10-0 105 RichardHughes 13 92
(John Spearing) *led to over 3f out: wknd 2f out: heavily eased fnl f* **15/8**1

0-40 **9** *4* **Morache Music**26 2848 6-10-0 105 SebSanders 8 61
(Peter Makin) *a wl in rr: rdn and no prog over 2f out* **7/1**3

0530 **10** *10* **Secret Witness**13 3271 8-9-3 94 (b) SteveDrowne 5 18
(Ronald Harris) *a towards rr: wknd over 2f out: eased over 1f out: t.o* **16/1**

1m 12.1s (-0.90) **Going Correction** +0.10s/f (Good)
**WFA** 3 from 5yo+ 7lb **10 Ran SP% 117.7**
Speed ratings (Par 109): **110,108,106,105,104 103,100,91,86,72**
CSF £88.28 CT £1155.76 TOTE £20.90: £4.60, £1.60, £4.50; EX 140.50 Trifecta £815.20.
**Owner** Palatinate Thoroughbred Racing Limited **Bred** J Cullinan **Trained** Newmarket, Suffolk

**FOCUS**
A useful sprint, the first two both progressive and the third and fourth, who may also be well treated, helping to set the level.

## 3733 UNIBET INJURY TIME INSURANCE IN BRAZIL FILLIES' H'CAP 1m 67y
4:45 (4:45) (Class 5) (0-75,70) 3-Y-O+ **£2,587** (£770; £384; £192) **Stalls** Low

Form RPR

-516 **1** **Sweet Martoni**23 2930 4-10-0 70 TomQueally 2 78
(William Knight) *mde all: sent for home 3f out: rdn and edgd lft fr jst over 1f out: styd on wl* **11/2**3

6305 **2** *1* **Rocksee (IRE)**27 2805 3-9-0 66 (p) SteveDrowne 5 70
(Tom Dascombe) *pressed wnr: rdn wl over 2f out: nt qckn and hld wl over 1f out: kpt on to maintain 2nd nr fin* **14/1**

31-0 **3** *hd* **Tides Reach (IRE)**42 2340 3-9-1 70 RobertTart(3) 7 74+
(Roger Charlton) *t.k.h: hld up in last pair: rdn and prog on outer fr over 2f out: kpt on to press for 2nd ins fnl f* **7/1**

-622 **4** *2½* **Royal Connection**13 3280 3-9-4 70 RichardHughes 1 68
(Richard Hannon) *t.k.h early: trckd ldng pair: rdn and nt qckn over 2f out: no imp after* **11/8**1

0-00 **5** *½* **It's Taboo**13 3280 4-9-8 64 AdamKirby 9 63
(Mark Usher) *s.i.s: hld up then bustled along early: in tch: shkn up and nt qckn over 2f out: n.d after* **14/1**

-200 **6** *½* **Flamborough Breeze**115 843 5-9-6 69 (t) CamHardie(7) 4 66
(Ed Vaughan) *hld up in 6th: rdn over 2f out: no imp on ldrs: one pce after* **12/1**

0-02 **7** *1¼* **Lady Bayside**15 3176 6-10-0 70 KierenFallon 3 65
(Malcolm Saunders) *chsd ldrs: pushed along 4f out: rdn and no imp over 2f out: wl hld after* **9/2**2

610- **8** *5* **Alderley**179 8452 3-9-4 70 JohnFahy 8 51
(Martyn Meade) *t.k.h: hld up in last: prog on inner over 2f out: wknd qckly jst over 1f out* **20/1**

1m 46.45s (1.75) **Going Correction** -0.025s/f (Good)
**WFA** 3 from 4yo+ 10lb **8 Ran SP% 114.0**
Speed ratings (Par 100): **90,89,88,86,85 85,84,79**
CSF £76.14 CT £547.18 TOTE £8.50: £2.20, £2.70, £2.20; EX 74.30 Trifecta £1189.70 Part won..
**Owner** Lavell Willis **Bred** Mrs M Lavell **Trained** Patching, W Sussex

**FOCUS**
Another race on the card in which a handy position proved vital, the first two home occupying those positions almost throughout. The runner-up posted a small personal best with the third running to her maiden form.

## 3734 DOWNLOAD THE UNIBET PRO APP APPRENTICE H'CAP 6f
5:20 (5:20) (Class 5) (0-70,70) 4-Y-O+ **£2,726** (£805; £402) **Stalls** Low

Form RPR

5362 **1** **Intomist (IRE)**18 3088 5-9-5 68 (p) DanielCremin(5) 11 77
(Jim Boyle) *mde all: rdn over 1f out: kpt on fnl f: hld on* **7/2**1

6666 **2** *nk* **Atlantis Crossing (IRE)**15 3180 5-9-4 65 NathanAlison(3) 4 73+
(Jim Boyle) *s.i.s: sn in tch then t.k.h: prog 2f out: tk 2nd u.p jst ins fnl f: clsd on wnr at fin* **7/2**1

352 **3** *1* **Assertive Agent**14 3231 4-9-1 59 RyanTate 12 64
(Tony Carroll) *chsd ldrs: rdn 2f out: wnt 2nd briefly 1f out: styd on same pce* **4/1**2

6125 **4** *1½* **Catalinas Diamond (IRE)**18 3088 6-8-13 57 (t) RyanClark 13 57
(Pat Murphy) *hld up in last pair: prog on outer 2f out: drvn and kpt on same pce fnl f: n.d* **5/1**3

6060 **5** *nk* **Malaysian Boleh**14 3246 4-8-9 60 (b1) KieranShoemark(7) 8 59
(Simon Dow) *slowly away: t.k.h in last: prog 2f out: kpt on fnl f: nvr able to threaten* **12/1**

31-0 **6** *1¾* **Tregereth (IRE)**28 2775 4-9-2 60 MatthewLawson 7 53
(Jonathan Portman) *prom: chsd wnr after 2f to 1f out: steadily wknd* **20/1**

055 **7** *3* **Fossa**31 2687 4-9-2 67 PaulBooth(7) 9 51
(Dean Ivory) *in tch in rr: shkn up 1/2-way: no prog on outer over 2f out: wknd over 1f out* **8/1**

-004 **8** *2¾* **Lady Phill**13 3280 4-9-4 67 JordanVaughan(5) 10 42
(Michael Attwater) *chsd wnr 2f: sn pushed along: wknd over 2f out* **8/1**

1m 13.6s (0.60) **Going Correction** +0.10s/f (Good) **8 Ran SP% 115.8**
Speed ratings (Par 103): **100,99,98,96,95 93,89,85**
CSF £16.09 CT £50.69 TOTE £3.80: £1.50, £1.50, £1.70; EX 23.60 Trifecta £53.70.
**Owner** The Clueless Syndicate **Bred** P M Guerin **Trained** Epsom, Surrey

**FOCUS**
An ordinary sprint handicap. The winner came back to his best with the third helping to set the level.
T/Plt: £525.60 to a £1 stake. Pool: £86,973.73 - 120.79 winning tickets. T/Qpdt: £322.80 to a £1 stake. Pool: £4,973.24 - 11.40 winning tickets. JN

3735 - (Foreign Racing) - See Raceform Interactive

# 3684 CURRAGH (R-H)
Saturday, June 28

**OFFICIAL GOING: Good to firm**

## 3736a DUBAI DUTY FREE FINEST SURPRISE SAPPHIRE STKS (GROUP 3) 5f
3:45 (3:45) 3-Y-O+

**£32,500** (£10,291; £4,875; £1,625; £1,083; £541)

RPR

**1** **Fountain Of Youth (IRE)**9 3412 3-9-3 94 (b1) SeamieHeffernan 5 108
(A P O'Brien, Ire) *chsd ldrs: pushed along into 3rd early: rdn 2f out and clsd u.p to chal in 2nd ins fnl f: kpt on best to ld cl home* **14/1**

**2** *hd* **Extortionist (IRE)**7 3478 3-9-3 100 ColinKeane 4 107
(Olly Stevens) *trckd ldr tl disp bef 1/2-way: rdn w narrow advantage over 1 1/2f out: strly pressed u.p ins fnl f and hdd cl home* **2/1**1

**3** *¾* **Monsieur Joe (IRE)**21 2989 7-9-9 104 JosephO'Brien 3 106
(Paul Midgley) *chsd ldrs: pushed along in 4th 1/2-way and clsd u.p into 3rd wl ins fnl f: kpt on same pce: a hld* **5/1**3

**4** *½* **Jamesie (IRE)**13 3284 6-9-9 105 FergalLynch 2 105+
(David Marnane, Ire) *w.w: 5th 1/2-way: rdn 2f out and clsd u.p bhd horses ins fnl f: kpt on towards fin wout ever threatening principals* **7/2**2

**5** *1¾* **Timeless Call (IRE)**13 3284 6-9-6 101 PatSmullen 6 95
(Reginald Roberts, Ire) *broke wl to ld narrowly tl jnd bef 1/2-way: hdd u.p over 1 1/2f out and sn no ex u.p: wknd wl ins fnl f* **7/2**2

**6** *5* **Scream Blue Murder (IRE)**13 3284 4-9-6 101 WayneLordan 1 77
(T Stack, Ire) *stmbld sltly leaving gate and racd in rr: in tch 1/2-way: rdn on outer 2f out and no imp: wknd* **8/1**

59.01s (-3.89) **Going Correction** -0.40s/f (Firm)
**WFA** 3 from 4yo+ 6lb **6 Ran SP% 112.2**
Speed ratings: **115,114,113,112,109 101**
CSF £42.39 TOTE £7.10: £3.50, £1.80; DF 34.10 Trifecta £172.50.
**Owner** Mrs John Magnier & Michael Tabor & Derrick Smith **Bred** Floors Farming **Trained** Cashel, Co Tipperary

**FOCUS**
The second and fourth help set the standard on their recent best.

## 3737a PADDY POWER SCURRY (PREMIER H'CAP) 6f 63y
4:15 (4:17) 3-Y-O+

**£50,000** (£15,833; £7,500; £2,500; £1,666; £833)

RPR

**1** **Line Of Reason (IRE)**11 3342 4-8-3 85 5ex LeighRoche(3) 18 96
(Paul Midgley) *chsd ldrs nr side: hdwy travelling wl fr 2f out to ld ent fnl f: rdn and kpt on wl u.p towards fin* **18/1**

**2** *½* **Zalty (FR)**26 2854 4-8-5 87 (b1) ConorHoban(3) 7 96+
(David Marnane, Ire) *chsd ldrs far side: hdwy 2f out to chal over 1f out: kpt on wl towards fin: hld* **20/1**

**3** *nk* **Discussiontofollow (IRE)**75 1492 4-8-10 89 ShaneKelly 21 97
(Mike Murphy) *chsd ldrs nr side: rdn to chal in 3rd ins fnl f and sn no imp on wnr: kpt on same pce* **8/1**2

**4** *¾* **Alben Star (IRE)**7 3452 6-9-11 104 JosephO'Brien 25 110
(Richard Fahey) *chsd ldrs nr side: 5th 1/2-way: nt clr run 2f out and sn lost several pls: sn swtchd rt and r.o wl ins fnl f: nrst fin* **4/1**1

**5** *1½* **Dashwood**23 2939 7-8-7 86 (t) ShaneFoley 1 87
(J F Levins, Ire) *towards rr far side: rdn 2f out and prog u.p to chse ldrs ins fnl f: kpt on same pce* **25/1**

**6** *nk* **Intensical (IRE)**17 3127 3-8-13 99 KevinManning 6 97
(J S Bolger, Ire) *chsd ldrs far side: rdn 2f out and sme hdwy u.p over 1f out: no imp on ldrs ins fnl f* **25/1**

**7** *½* **Yeeoow (IRE)**13 3271 5-8-11 93 JoeyHaynes(3) 3 91
(K R Burke) *disp early far side: rdn almost on terms 2f out and no ex u.p ins fnl f: wknd towards fin* **16/1**

**8** *hd* **Harry Trotter (IRE)**[23] 2939 5-9-1 **94**.................................. FMBerry 10 92
(David Marnane, Ire) *hld up towards rr nr side: tk clsr order on outer 1 1/2f out: kpt on* **33/1**

**9** *nk* **Earth Drummer (IRE)**[6] 3507 4-8-9 **88**.......................... RonanWhelan 9 85
(J S Bolger, Ire) *chsd ldrs far side: rdn and no ex 1f out: one pce towards fin* **25/1**

**10** *1* **Shipyard (USA)**[14] 3258 5-8-10 **89**............................... GaryCarroll 22 82
(A Oliver, Ire) *chsd ldrs nr side: 3rd 1/2-way: rdn and no ex 1 1/2f out: wknd* **14/1**

**11** *3/4* **Yulong Baoju (IRE)**[23] 2939 4-9-3 **96**...................(t) ColmO'Donoghue 16 87
(Edward Lynam, Ire) *hld up in rr of mid-div nr side: sme hdwy over 1f out where n.m.r between horses and edgd rt: kpt on one pce* **25/1**

**12** *hd* **Fly To The Moon (IRE)**[45] 2262 3-8-8 **94**................(p) WayneLordan 12 82
(David Wachman, Ire) *hld up in mid-div in centre gp early: pushed along over 2f out and no imp ent fnl f: kpt on one pce* **16/1**

**13** *nk* **Antiquus (IRE)**[14] 3258 5-8-4 **83** oh2..........................(p[1]) RoryCleary 20 72
(Ms Joanna Morgan, Ire) *chsd ldrs nr side: 4th 1/2-way: rdn and wknd fr under 2f out* **33/1**

**14** *hd* **Srucahan (IRE)**[34] 2578 5-8-12 **91**..............................(v) ChrisHayes 15 80
(P D Deegan, Ire) *in rr of mid-div: rdn 2f out and nt clr run over 1f out: squeezed between horses ins fnl f: kpt on one pce* **20/1**

**15** *1 1/4* **Twenty One Choice (IRE)**[20] 3036 5-8-5 **84**................ AndreaAtzeni 8 69
(Ed de Giles) *chsd ldrs nr side: rdn and wknd over 1f out* **25/1**

**16** *1/2* **Alkasser (IRE)**[54] 2038 3-9-6 **106**.................................. PatSmullen 5 87
(D K Weld, Ire) *chsd ldrs far side: rdn and no imp over 1f out: wknd and eased* **4/1**[1]

**17** *hd* **Arbitrageur (IRE)**[14] 3258 5-8-5 **84** oh3 ow1.......................... JFEgan 24 67
(Donal Kinsella, Ire) *rrd and uns rdr bef s: led to post and loaded wout rdr: s.i.s: tk clsr order in mid-div nr side 1/2-way: rdn and no ex over 1f out: wknd* **33/1**

**18** *1 1/2* **Barkston Ash**[35] 2562 6-9-4 **97**..................................(p) JasonHart 23 75
(Eric Alston) *chsd ldrs nr side: 2nd 1/2-way: rdn over 2f out and sn no ex u.p: wknd* **12/1**

**19** *1* **Burn The Boats (IRE)**[49] 2145 5-8-12 **94**...............(p) ColinKeane[(3)] 13 69
(G M Lyons, Ire) *prom in centre gp: rdn 2f out and wknd over 1f out* **9/1**[3]

**20** *1/2* **Seanie (IRE)**[41] 2369 5-8-10 **92**...................................... ConnorKing[(3)] 14 65
(David Marnane, Ire) *prom in centre grouP: 10th 1/2-way: rdn under 2f out and hmpd between horses ent fnl f: no imp after: wknd* **12/1**

**21** *1 1/4* **Grey Danube (IRE)**[92] 1157 5-8-4 **83** oh11..............(bt) NGMcCullagh 19 52
(D J Bunyan, Ire) *led nr side: rdn and hdd under 2f out: wknd* **50/1**

**22** *2* **Greek Canyon (IRE)**[14] 3258 5-8-13 **92**.................. EmmetMcNamara 17 55
(G M Lyons, Ire) *hld up in tch: rdn in 9th nr side 1/2-way and sn no ex: wknd* **16/1**

**23** *1 1/4* **Arctic (IRE)**[34] 2578 7-9-2 **95**................................... MichaelHussey 2 54
(Tracey Collins, Ire) *chsd ldrs far side: rdn and no imp 2f out: wknd and eased fnl f* **33/1**

1m 15.18s (-3.92) **Going Correction** -0.40s/f (Firm)
**WFA** 3 from 4yo+ 7lb **23** Ran SP% **148.6**
Speed ratings: **110,109,108,107,105 105,104,104,104,102 101,101,101,100,99 98,98,96,95,94 92,90,88**
CSF £367.91 CT £3197.94 TOTE £24.20: £4.80, £7.80, £2.60, £2.10; DF 1162.30.
**Owner** Taylor's Bloodstock Ltd **Bred** Corduff Stud Ltd, J Corcoran & J Judd **Trained** Westow, N Yorks

**FOCUS**
A typical Scurry, ultra competitive and with its share of hard-luck stories.

## 3738a GAIN RAILWAY STKS (GROUP 2) 6f
4:50 (4:51) 2-Y-O

**£50,000** (£15,833; £7,500; £2,500; £1,666; £833)

RPR

**1** **Kool Kompany (IRE)**[11] 3318 2-9-3 ....................................... FMBerry 1 112
(Richard Hannon) *hooded to load: sn led and tacked over to nr side: 1 l clr 1/2-way: rdn over 1f out and pressed: kpt on wl u.p to assert ins fnl f* **6/1**[3]

**2** *2* **Ahlan Emarati (IRE)**[9] 3374 2-9-3 ............................... PatSmullen 3 106
(Peter Chapple-Hyam) *broke wl: sn settled bhd ldrs: 4th 1/2-way: tk clsr order in 3rd over 2f out: rdn into 2nd over 1f out and kpt on wl towards fin wout matching wnr* **6/1**[3]

**3** *1 3/4* **War Envoy (USA)**[11] 3318 2-9-3 .............................(bt[1]) JosephO'Brien 4 101
(A P O'Brien, Ire) *hld up in tch: 5th 1/2-way: swtchd rt to outer 2f out: rdn in 4th ent fnl f and sn no imp on wnr in 3rd: kpt on same pce* **5/2**[2]

**4** *hd* **Rapid Applause**[70] 1589 2-9-3 ..................................... FergalLynch 8 100
(M D O'Callaghan, Ire) *on toes befhand: w.w in rr: swtchd rt to outer 2f out and rdn into 3rd ent fnl f: sn no imp on wnr and dropped to 4th: kpt on same pce* **14/1**

**5** *1* **Cappella Sansevero**[11] 3318 2-9-3 ................................ ColinKeane 5 97
(G M Lyons, Ire) *reluctant to load: trckd ldrs: cl 2nd 1/2-way: rdn 1 1/2f out and sn no imp on wnr: dropped to 5th ins fnl f and kpt on one pce* **6/4**[1]

**6** *hd* **Battle Of Marathon (USA)**[9] 3408 2-9-3 ............... SeamieHeffernan 6 97
(A P O'Brien, Ire) *hld up in tch: 6th 1/2-way: rdn 2f out and no imp on ldrs in rr ent fnl f: kpt on one pce* **9/1**

**7** *nse* **I Will Excel (IRE)**[9] 3408 2-9-3 ........................... DeclanMcDonogh 2 96
(M D O'Callaghan, Ire) *chsd ldrs: sltly hmpd early: 3rd 1/2-way: rdn in 4th 1 1/2f out and sn no ex: one pce and dropped to rr cl home* **33/1**

1m 12.6s (-2.90) **Going Correction** -0.40s/f (Firm) **7** Ran SP% **116.8**
Speed ratings: **103,100,98,97,96 96,96**
CSF £42.46 TOTE £6.30: £2.10, £3.20; DF 23.80 Trifecta £129.40.
**Owner** Middleham Park Racing LXXXVI **Bred** Miss Imelda O'Shaughnessy **Trained** East Everleigh, Wilts

**FOCUS**
Different tactics and a very different result for the winner. The opening level is fluid, the winner progressing well and the runner-up building on his Norfolk run.

## 3739a DUBAI DUTY FREE IRISH DERBY (GROUP 1) (ENTIRE COLTS & FILLIES) 1m 4f
5:30 (5:30) 3-Y-O **£604,166** (£197,916; £93,750; £31,250; £20,833)

RPR

**1** **Australia**[21] 2990 3-9-0 123............................................ JosephO'Brien 5 121+
(A P O'Brien, Ire) *settled bhd ldrs in 3rd: travelling wl into st and smooth hdwy on outer fr 2f out to ld on bit ent fnl f: eased clr: easily* **1/8**[1]

**2** *2 1/2* **Kingfisher (IRE)**[21] 2990 3-9-0 105...................... ColmO'Donoghue 7 113
(A P O'Brien, Ire) *sn led: 2 l clr 1/2-way: reduced advantage appr st: rdn 2f out and strly pressed: hdd over 1f out and no ch w easy wnr in 3rd briefly: kpt on same pce in 2nd ins fnl f* **25/1**

**3** *2 1/2* **Orchestra (IRE)**[21] 2990 3-9-0 110........................ SeamieHeffernan 2 109
(A P O'Brien, Ire) *chsd ldr in 2nd: tk clsr order bhd ldr appr st where lost action briefly: rdn to ld briefly over 1f out where hung: sn hdd and no ch w easy wnr in 3rd ins fnl f: kpt on same pce* **12/1**[3]

**4** *3* **Ponfeigh (IRE)**[14] 3261 3-9-0 102........................... DeclanMcDonogh 1 104+
(John M Oxx, Ire) *w.w: 4th 1/2-way: rdn over 2f out and no imp on ldrs: kpt on one pce* **12/1**[3]

**5** *1/2* **Fascinating Rock (IRE)**[21] 2990 3-9-0 112........................ PatSmullen 3 103+
(D K Weld, Ire) *w.w: last 1/2-way: rdn into st and no imp on ldrs 2f out: kpt on one pce* **8/1**[2]

2m 33.19s (-5.31) **Going Correction** -0.375s/f (Firm) **5** Ran SP% **119.2**
Speed ratings: **102,100,98,96,96**
CSF £8.15 TOTE £1.10: £1.02, £4.40; DF 11.70 Trifecta £22.40.
**Owner** D Smith/Mrs J Magnier/M Tabor/T Ah Khing **Bred** Stanley Estate And Stud Co **Trained** Cashel, Co Tipperary

**FOCUS**
The withdrawal of Kingston Hill in particular meant this was likely to be a stroll for Australia - and so it proved. It was a weak renewal, but the runner-up's Chester win is working out and this has been rated in line with the best view of that form.

3740 - 3743a (Foreign Racing) - See Raceform Interactive

# [3640] DEAUVILLE (R-H)
Saturday, June 28

**OFFICIAL GOING: Turf: very soft; fibresand: standard**

## 3744a PRIX DE LA CHAUSSEY (CLAIMER) (2YO) (TURF) 5f
11:45 (12:00) 2-Y-O **£11,250** (£4,500; £3,375; £2,250; £1,125)

RPR

**1** **Loose Cannon (FR)**[22] 2976 2-8-8 0.........................(b) GregoryBenoist 9 79
(D Windrif, France) **227/10**

**2** *3/4* **Join Up (FR)**[19] 2-9-2 0.......................................(p) ChristopheSoumillon 4 84
(J-C Rouget, France) **13/10**[1]

**3** *1/2* **Hesat (FR)**[21] 3027 2-8-8 0........................................ MickaelBarzalona 3 74
(M Boutin, France) **129/10**

**4** *1* **Something Lucky (IRE)**[16] 3170 2-9-1 0.................. AntoineHamelin 5 77
(Matthieu Palussiere, France) **158/10**

**5** *1/2* **Pearlred (FR)**[8] 2-8-8 0............................. Christophe-PatriceLemaire 6 69
(M Boutin, France) **17/5**[2]

**6** *nk* **Little Mask (FR)**[8] 2-8-5 0.......................................... ValentinGambart[(8)] 7 73
(M Boutin, France) **37/1**

**7** *3* **Baie Fleurie (FR)** 2-9-1 0............................................. AnthonyCrastus 10 64
(J Rossi, France) **42/10**[3]

**8** *3/4* **Shamrock Sheila (IRE)**[12] 3312 2-8-5 0................. SoufyaneMoulin[(3)] 2 54
(J S Moore) *t.k.h: w ldrs: pushed along 2f out: rdn and lost pl over 1f out: no ex and btn fnl f: wknd* **141/10**

**9** *nk* **Dayaday (FR)** 2-8-11 0............................................ StephanePasquier 8 56
(M Delcher Sanchez, France) **238/10**

**10** *1 1/4* **Sulphur (FR)**[39] 2-8-8 0..............................................(p) TheoBachelot 1 48
(Mario Hofer, Germany) **206/10**

59.79s (2.29) **10** Ran SP% **120.7**
WIN (incl. 1 euro stake): 23.70. PLACES: 4.30, 1.40, 2.80. DF: 26.20. SF: 84.90.
**Owner** Passion Racing Club **Bred** Haras Du Logis Saint Germain **Trained** France

## 3745a PRIX DE BRETONCELLES (CLAIMER) (3YO) (POLYTRACK) 1m 4f 110y
1:15 (12:00) 3-Y-O **£9,583** (£3,833; £2,875; £1,916; £958)

RPR

**1** **Art Of Zapping (FR)**[27] 3-9-6 0.................................(b) MaximeGuyon 3 75
(C Escuder, France) **9/5**[1]

**2** *nk* **Adam's Peak (IRE)**[35] 3-9-1 0...................................... AnthonyCrastus 1 70
(D Sepulchre, France) **76/10**

**3** *nk* **Amative (FR)** 3-8-11 0..............................................(b) TheoBachelot 9 66
(S Wattel, France) **76/10**

**4** *snk* **Jed Water (FR)**[4] 3-9-1 0......................... Christophe-PatriceLemaire 6 69
(C Boutin, France) *fin 5th: plcd 4th* **93/10**

**5** *shd* **In For A Pound (FR)** 3-9-1 0...................................... MathieuAndrouin 8 69
(P Monfort, France) *fin 4th: disqualified and plcd 5th* **99/10**

**6** *snk* **Hualapai (IRE)**[25] 3-8-8 0..........................................(p) CristianDemuro 2 62
(G Botti, France) **71/10**[3]

**7** *1* **Kais (FR)** 3-9-1 0............................................................(p) FabriceVeron 7 67
(F Monnier, France) **37/1**

**8** *2* **Gaelic Way (FR)**[27] 3-9-4 0........................................... AntoineHamelin 5 67
(J Merienne, France) **58/10**[2]

**9** *4 1/2* **Starlight Princess (IRE)**[129] 659 3-9-3 0..........(b) SoufyaneMoulin[(3)] 4 63
(J S Moore) *dwlt and hld up in last: clsd on outer bef st: rdn over 2f out: sn outpcd: dropped to last again and btn over 1f out: wknd and eased fnl f* **15/2**

2m 45.28s (165.28) **9** Ran SP% **119.3**
WIN (incl.1 euro stake): 2.80. PLACES: 1.40, 2.00, 2.50. DF: 11.20. SF: 16.10.
**Owner** Ecurie Ze **Bred** Mme B Moser **Trained** France

## 3746a PRIX DE RIS-ORANGIS (GROUP 3) (3YO+) (TURF) 6f
2:25 (12:00) 3-Y-O+ **£33,333** (£13,333; £10,000; £6,666; £3,333)

RPR

**1** **Thawaany (IRE)**[28] 2799 4-8-10 0..................................... OlivierPeslier 9 113
(F Head, France) *travelled strly: trckd ldr: rdn to chal over 1f out and sn led: r.o strly and asserted fnl f: readily* **6/1**[3]

**2** *1 1/2* **Zejel**[34] 4-8-10 0.............................................................. JulienAuge 5 108
(C Ferland, France) *midfield: rdn and hdwy fr over 1f out: r.o and wnt 2nd ins fnl f: nt pce of wnr* **204/10**

**3** *nse* **Signs Of Blessing (IRE)**[48] 2197 3-8-7 0............... StephanePasquier 8 110
(F Rohaut, France) *hld up in rr: last 1/2-way: pushed along 2f out: rdn and r.o fnl f: wnt 3rd towards fin and almost snatched 2nd post but nvr able to chal* **12/5**[1]

**4** *1 1/4* **Daraybi (FR)**[15] 3206 3-8-7 0........................................ ThierryJarnet 7 106
(A De Royer-Dupre, France) *chsd ldr: rdn to chal over 1f out: ev ch ent fnl f: sn outpcd by wnr: no ex and fdd fnl 75yds* **37/10**[2]

**5** *snk* **Abu Sidra (FR)**[21] 3030 5-9-0 0........................ ChristopheSoumillon 6 107
(J-F Bernard, France) *in tch: rdn 2f out: outpcd and shuffled bk over 1f out: rallied u.p fnl f: r.o and wnt 5th post* **91/10**

6 *shd* **Gammarth (FR)**[27] 2814 6-9-0 0 ........ FabriceVeron 1 107
(H-A Pantall, France) *chsd ldr: rdn 2f out: effrt to chal over 1f out and ev ch ent fnl f: sn outpcd by wnr: kpt on but wl hld and dropped to 6th post* **97/10**

7 *nse* **Dibajj (FR)**[27] 2820 4-9-1 0 ........ GeraldMosse 3 108
(A De Royer-Dupre, France) *sn midfield: pushed along 1/2-way: rdn 2f out: outpcd in rr ent fnl f: rallied and kpt on wl towards fin but nvr able to chal* **67/10**

8 *½* **Ice Love (FR)**[48] 2195 3-8-4 0 ........ RaphaelMarchelli 4 100
(T Castanheira, France) *hld up towards rr: pushed along 2f out: rdn over 1f out: kpt on same pce and wl hld fnl f* **33/1**

9 *2* **Aksil (FR)**[5] 4-8-10 0 ........ ValentinGambart 10 95
(M Boutin, France) *t.k.h: midfield: rdn and effrt to chal over 1f out: ev ch ent fnl f: no ex and btn fnl 120yds: wknd* **45/1**

10 *½* **Myasun (FR)**[67] 1641 7-9-4 0 ........ GregoryBenoist 11 101
(C Baillet, France) *hld up towards rr: rdn 2f out: outpcd and btn fnl f: eased towards fin* **94/10**

11 *2* **Omaticaya (IRE)**[41] 2375 3-8-8 0 ........ GFois 2 90
(Manila Illuminati, Italy) *led: rdn and strly pressed over 1f out: sn hdd: no ex and wknd: dropped to last ins fnl f and eased nring fin* **32/1**

1m 9.65s (-1.35)
**WFA** 3 from 4yo+ 7lb **11** Ran SP% **119.6**
WIN (incl.1 euro stake): 7.00. PLACES: 2.30, 3.80, 1.60. DF: 75.00. SF: 109.10.
**Owner** Hamdan Al Maktoum **Bred** Mrs A J Donnelly **Trained** France

3747 - (Foreign Racing) - See Raceform Interactive

# 3583 SALISBURY (R-H)

Sunday, June 29

**OFFICIAL GOING: Straight course - good to firm (firm in places); loop section - good (good to firm in places) (9.1)**
Wind: virtually nil Weather: sunny

## 3748 BATHWICK TYRES EBF STALLIONS BLAGRAVE MAIDEN STKS (BOBIS RACE) 6f 212y

**2:10** (2:12) (Class 4) 2-Y-O **£4,851** (£1,443; £721; £360) **Stalls** Centre

Form RPR

3 **1** **Marcano (IRE)**[44] 2298 2-9-5 0 ........ RobertHavlin 3 82+
(Rod Millman) *mde all: shkn up to draw ahd 2f out: kpt on wl and in command fnl f: rdn out* **9/5**[1]

5 **2** *2¼* **Harlequin Striker (IRE)**[23] 2964 2-9-5 0 ........ SilvestreDeSousa 9 76
(Mick Channon) *disp ld tl rdn 2f out: kpt on but nt pce of wnr fnl f* **7/1**

**3** *nk* **Misterioso (IRE)** 2-9-5 0 ........ RichardHughes 8 76+
(Richard Hannon) *hld up: swtchd lft and hdwy over 2f out: rdn over 1f out: kpt on wl to go 3rd ins fnl f wout ever threatening* **11/4**[2]

6 **4** *1* **Hawkmeister (IRE)**[17] 3140 2-9-5 0 ........ PatDobbs 6 72
(Richard Hannon) *sn trcking ldrs: rdn over 2f out: kpt on same pce fnl f* **9/1**

6 **5** *4* **Classic Villager**[16] 3194 2-9-5 0 ........ LiamKeniry 10 62
(Philip Hide) *sn trcking ldrs: rdn over 2f out: one pce fnl f* **5/1**[3]

**6** *shd* **Tumut (IRE)** 2-9-2 0 ........ CharlesBishop(3) 11 61
(Mick Channon) *trckd ldrs: rdn over 2f out: sn one pce* **50/1**

**7** *7* **Percy Veer** 2-9-0 0 ........ JoshBaudains(5) 2 42
(Sylvester Kirk) *s.i.s: towards rr: struggling over 3f out: nvr gng pce to get on terms* **50/1**

**8** *4½* **Mutamid** 2-9-5 0 ........ TomQueally 7 30
(Ismail Mohammed) *in tch: rdn over 2f out: wknd fnl f* **25/1**

0 **9** *5* **Noble Master**[17] 3140 2-9-5 0 ........ LukeMorris 5 17
(Sylvester Kirk) *trckd ldrs tl wknd 2f out* **66/1**

**10** *19* **Quae Supra** 2-9-5 0 ........ TedDurcan 1
(Richard Hannon) *sn outpcd towards rr: lost tch over 3f out: t.o* **18/1**

1m 29.03s (0.43) **Going Correction** -0.05s/f (Good) **10** Ran SP% **116.1**
Speed ratings (Par 95): **95,92,92,90,86 86,78,73,67,45**
CSF £14.84 TOTE £2.90: £1.20, £3.10, £1.20; EX 12.90 Trifecta £40.00.
**Owner** The Links Partnership **Bred** David Barry **Trained** Kentisbeare, Devon

**FOCUS**
An interesting maiden. The pace was steady but the favourite delivered and his main market rival shaped with promise in third.

## 3749 DEREK BURRIDGE GOLF & RACING TROPHIES H'CAP (A SENIORS' SPRINT) 5f

**2:40** (2:41) (Class 4) (0-80,80) 6-Y-O+ **£5,175** (£1,540; £769; £384) **Stalls** Low

Form RPR

232 **1** **Secret Millionaire (IRE)**[5] 3551 7-9-0 **73** ........ LukeMorris 5 83
(Luke Dace) *in tch: rdn and hdwy 2f out: nt clr run whn swtchd lft jst over 1f out: r.o strly to ld fnl 75yds* **3/1**[1]

405 **2** *1* **Noverre To Go (IRE)**[15] 3213 8-9-3 **76** ........ (p) SteveDrowne 9 82
(Ronald Harris) *hld up: rdn and hdwy over 1f out: r.o strly ins fnl f: wnt 2nd towards fin* **11/1**

230 **3** *¾* **Cruise Tothelimit (IRE)**[15] 3216 6-9-7 **80** ........ SilvestreDeSousa 7 84
(Ian Williams) *disp ld tl clr ldr over 3f out: rdn over 2f out: kpt on tl hdd fnl 75yds: lost 2nd whn no ex towards fin* **3/1**[1]

4334 **4** *1¾* **Ginzan**[5] 3561 6-8-11 **70** ........ TomQueally 8 67
(Malcolm Saunders) *chsd ldrs: sn pushed along to hold pl: rdn wl over 2f out: bmpd jst over 1f out: kpt on to go 4th towards fin: nt pce to get involved* **9/2**[2]

0-15 **5** *¾* **Aye Aye Digby (IRE)**[36] 2559 9-9-4 **77** ........ RichardHughes 6 72
(Patrick Chamings) *disp ld tl over 3f out: rdn to chse ldr over 2f out: drifted lft over 1f out: no ex fnl 120yds* **8/1**

000/ **6** *2¼* **Living It Large (FR)**[729] 3608 7-9-4 **80** ........ OisinMurphy(3) 1 67
(Ed de Giles) *chsd ldrs: effrt over 2f out: wknd ins fnl f* **11/2**[3]

0044 **7** *1* **Ubetterbegood (ARG)**[15] 3246 6-9-1 **74** ........ (v) PatDobbs 2 57
(Robert Cowell) *t.k.h: trckd ldrs: rdn 2f out: bmpd jst over 1f out: wknd ins fnl f* **10/1**

0/0- **8** *hd* **My Meteor**[300] 6040 7-7-11 **61** oh1 ........ NoelGarbutt(5) 3 43
(Tony Newcombe) *towards rr: effrt over 2f out: wknd ins fnl f* **66/1**

1m 0.11s (-0.89) **Going Correction** -0.05s/f (Good) **8** Ran SP% **113.6**
Speed ratings: **105,103,102,99,98 94,93,92**
CSF £36.97 CT £106.74 TOTE £3.60: £1.30, £3.30, £1.20; EX 37.40 Trifecta £160.30.
**Owner** Robert E Lee Syndicate **Bred** James Delaney **Trained** Okehurst Lane, W Sussex

**FOCUS**
A competitive sprint handicap. The early pace was not strong but the first two finished well from out the back.

## 3750 BATHWICK TYRES MAIDEN STKS 1m 1f 198y

**3:10** (3:11) (Class 5) 3-Y-O+ **£4,204** (£1,251; £625; £312) **Stalls** Low

Form RPR

04 **1** **New Story**[15] 3248 3-9-0 0 ........ TomQueally 10 93
(Ismail Mohammed) *trckd ldr: led 2f out: sn pushed clr: comf* **5/2**[1]

0-2 **2** *4* **Dalmatia (IRE)**[25] 2881 3-8-9 0 ........ ShaneKelly 13 79
(Sir Michael Stoute) *wnt lft s: sn led: rdn and hdd 2f out: kpt on but sn hld by wnr* **7/1**

04 **3** *½* **High Church (IRE)**[48] 2221 3-8-11 0 ........ OisinMurphy(3) 3 83
(Roger Charlton) *hld up: pushed along over 3f out: stdy prog fr over 2f out: wnt 3rd ent fnl f: styd on wl towards fin* **9/2**[3]

0-25 **4** *1½* **Green Light**[21] 3031 3-9-0 0 ........ JimCrowley 12 80
(Ralph Beckett) *mid-div: pushed along for stdy prog fr 2f out: wnt 4th ent fnl f: styd on but nt pce to get involved* **14/1**

-363 **5** *3¼* **Carthage (IRE)**[21] 3030 3-9-0 80 ........ RichardHughes 2 74
(Richard Hannon) *mid-div: rdn and hdwy 3f out: wnt 3rd 2f out: wknd ent fnl f* **11/4**[2]

02- **6** *6* **Arabian Beauty (IRE)**[247] 7493 3-8-9 0 ........ KierenFallon 5 57
(Saeed bin Suroor) *trckd ldrs: rdn 3f out: wknd ent fnl f* **11/2**

0 **7** *3* **Silken Waters**[17] 3141 3-8-9 0 ........ JohnFahy 7 51
(Eve Johnson Houghton) *a towards rr* **80/1**

**8** *3¼* **Bikini Island (USA)** 3-8-9 0 ........ [1] LiamKeniry 11 44
(Andrew Balding) *trckd ldrs: rdn 3f out: sn wknd* **18/1**

0- **9** *15* **Hopeigetlucky**[257] 7270 3-9-0 0 ........ LukeMorris 9 19
(Stuart Kittow) *struggling 5f out: a towards rr* **66/1**

60 **10** *11* **Lola Montez (IRE)**[17] 3141 3-8-9 0 ........ TedDurcan 8
(David Lanigan) *mid-div: rdn 4f out: wknd 2f out* **100/1**

2m 8.83s (-1.07) **Going Correction** -0.05s/f (Good) **10** Ran SP% **117.0**
Speed ratings (Par 103): **102,98,98,97,94 89,87,84,72,64**
CSF £20.86 TOTE £4.00: £1.40, £2.20, £2.00; EX 20.60 Trifecta £92.70.
**Owner** Sultan Ali **Bred** Chancery Bourse Investments Ltd **Trained** Newmarket, Suffolk

**FOCUS**
A decent maiden but the first two were always prominent and nothing got involved from off the steady pace.

## 3751 BATHWICK TYRES AUCTION STKS (CONDITIONS RACE) (BOBIS RACE) 6f

**3:40** (3:41) (Class 3) 2-Y-O **£7,762** (£2,310; £1,154; £577) **Stalls** Low

Form RPR

31 **1** **Step To The Shears**[16] 3181 2-8-11 0 ........ PatDobbs 5 91
(Richard Hannon) *broke wl: mde all: kpt on gamely whn strly chal fnl f: rdn out* **10/1**

1 **2** *nk* **Room Key**[19] 3081 2-8-5 0 ........ JohnFahy 3 84
(Eve Johnson Houghton) *travelled wl: trckd ldrs: str chal ent fnl f: sn rdn: kpt on wl w ev ch: hld nring fin* **8/1**[3]

14 **3** *6* **Percy Alleline**[27] 2845 2-8-12 0 ........ JimCrowley 7 73
(Ralph Beckett) *trckd wnr: rdn over 2f out: lost 2nd over 1f out: outpcd by front pair fnl f* **5/4**[1]

2 **4** *3¼* **Paddys Motorbike (IRE)**[16] 3173 2-8-10 0 ........ SilvestreDeSousa 2 61
(David Evans) *s.i.s: last but in tch: hdwy over 3f out to chse ldrs: outpcd 2f out: kpt on to regain 4th fnl f* **14/1**

410 **5** *6* **Among Angels**[12] 3322 2-8-8 0 ........ RichardHughes 1 53
(Richard Hannon) *trckd ldrs: rdn to dispute 2nd 2f out: eased whn appeared to lose action over 1f out* **7/4**[2]

221 **6** *9* **Brown Velvet**[40] 2413 2-7-13 0 ........ (v) NoelGarbutt(5) 6 10
(Hugo Palmer) *plld hrd: trckd ldrs: rdn over 2f out: sn wknd* **33/1**

1m 14.41s (-0.39) **Going Correction** -0.05s/f (Good) **6** Ran SP% **110.6**
Speed ratings (Par 97): **100,99,91,87,79 67**
CSF £78.80 TOTE £8.30: £3.00, £2.70; EX 51.00 Trifecta £209.80.
**Owner** Pall Mall Partners **Bred** Shinko Foods International Ltd **Trained** East Everleigh, Wilts

**FOCUS**
The favourite was well held in this conditions event and the first two pulled clear.

## 3752 H S LESTER MEMORIAL H'CAP 1m 6f 21y

**4:15** (4:15) (Class 4) (0-85,83) 4-Y-O+ **£5,175** (£1,540; £769; £384)

Form RPR

0-01 **1** **Sunny Future (IRE)**[19] 3086 8-8-11 **73** ........ RichardHughes 3 84
(Malcolm Saunders) *trckd ldng pair: sneaked up inner to ld jst over 3f out: styd on wl to draw clr fnl 120yds: comf* **7/4**[1]

0402 **2** *4½* **Icebuster**[14] 3274 6-9-7 **83** ........ RobertHavlin 9 88
(Rod Millman) *trckd ldng trio: rdn to chse wnr 2f out: styd on but a being comf hld fnl 120yds* **10/3**[3]

621 **3** *3¼* **Teak (IRE)**[7] 3501 7-9-2 **78** 6ex ........ (p) StevieDonohoe 8 78
(Ian Williams) *trckd ldr: pressed ldr over 3f out: rdn wl over 2f out: styd on same pce* **2/1**[2]

-315 **4** *9* **Happy Families**[15] 3249 4-8-6 **68** ........ LukeMorris 6 56
(Heather Main) *led tl hdd jst over 3f out: sn rdn: wknd ent fnl f* **5/1**

3m 4.02s (-3.38) **Going Correction** -0.05s/f (Good) **4** Ran SP% **109.4**
Speed ratings (Par 105): **107,104,102,97**
CSF £7.72 TOTE £2.30; EX 6.10 Trifecta £12.00.
**Owner** M S Saunders **Bred** Mrs G Stanga **Trained** Green Ore, Somerset

**FOCUS**
There were stacks of non-runners in this staying handicap. They went a stop-start gallop and the winner forged clear.

## 3753 MOLSON COORS H'CAP 1m

**4:45** (4:47) (Class 2) (0-100,100) 3-Y-O+
**£12,450** (£3,728; £1,864; £932; £466; £234) **Stalls** Low

Form RPR

**1** **The Rectifier (USA)**[64] 1721 7-10-0 **100** ........ (t) FergusSweeney 6 111
(Seamus Durack) *mde all: kpt on gamely fnl f: rdn out* **6/1**

-004 **2** *1* **Magic City (IRE)**[38] 2483 5-9-7 **93** ........ RichardHughes 11 102+
(Richard Hannon) *awkwardly away: hld up: stdy hdwy fr over 2f out: swtchd rt over 1f out: sn chsng wnr: kpt on but a being hld* **7/2**[2]

4416 **3** *4½* **Verse Of Love**[38] 2483 5-9-1 **87** ........ SilvestreDeSousa 7 85
(David Evans) *trckd wnr: rdn wl over 2f out: nt quite pce to chal: lost 2nd over 1f out: kpt on same pce* **11/1**

6543 **4** *nk* **Good Authority (IRE)**[16] 3180 7-8-9 **84** ........ OisinMurphy(3) 10 82
(Karen George) *little awkward leaving stall: hld up: rdn over 2f out: hdwy over 1f out: styd on fnl f* **9/2**[3]

10-2 **5** 2 3/4 **Silent Bullet (IRE)**[15] 3247 3-9-4 **100** KierenFallon 2 89
(Saeed bin Suroor) *trckd ldrs: swtchd lft for effrt 2f out: nt pce to get on terms: fdd ins fnl f* **9/4**[1]

5-00 **6** 1/2 **Directorship**[15] 3244 8-9-5 **91** JimCrowley 5 81
(Patrick Chamings) *cl up: rdn over 2f out: sn outpcd* **11/1**

40-0 **7** 1/2 **Valais Girl**[50] 2155 4-9-4 **90** (p) HarryBentley 4 79
(Marcus Tregoning) *hld up in tch: rdn over 2f out: nvr threatened: one pce fnl f* **25/1**

00 **8** 9 **Tellovoi (IRE)**[29] 2758 6-9-6 **92** (v) LukeMorris 8 60
(Ann Stokell) *trckd ldrs: rdn over 2f out: wknd over 1f out* **14/1**

0000 **9** 2 3/4 **Brocklebank (IRE)**[15] 3221 5-8-2 **81** KieranShoemark(7) 3 43
(Simon Dow) *struggling over 3f out: a towards rr* **20/1**

1m 41.13s (-2.37) **Going Correction** -0.05s/f (Good)
**WFA** 3 from 4yo+ 10lb **9 Ran SP% 117.4**
Speed ratings (Par 109): **109,108,103,103,100 99,99,90,87**
CSF £27.80 CT £229.61 TOTE £7.40: £2.30, £2.00, £1.80; EX 32.60 Trifecta £286.50.
**Owner** Mrs Anne Cowley **Bred** Ceka Ireland Ltd **Trained** Upper Lambourn, Berkshire

**FOCUS**
The winner made all in this useful handicap.

## 3754 CGA RACING EXCELLENCE APPRENTICE H'CAP (WHIPS SHALL BE CARRIED BUT NOT USED) 1m
**5:15** (5:16) (Class 6) (0-60,58) 3-Y-O **£2,587** (£770; £384; £192) **Stalls Low**

Form RPR

0040 **1** **Eugenic**[15] 3214 3-8-13 **50** JordanVaughan 10 56
(Rod Millman) *mid-div: hdwy to dispute ld over 3f out: led over 2f out: strly pressed fr over 1f out: drifted rt fnl f: hld on wl* **13/2**

6044 **2** 3/4 **Mercury Magic**[33] 2643 3-9-2 **58** PatrickO'Donnell(5) 8 62
(Ralph Beckett) *towards rr: pushed along fr over 4f out: hdwy 3f out: drifted rt over 2f out: chal over 1f out: kpt on tl no ex nring fin* **9/2**[3]

0-04 **3** 6 **Dark Phantom (IRE)**[19] 3084 3-8-8 **50** (t) ChrisMeehan(5) 11 40
(Peter Makin) *hld up: hdd over 3f out: disp hld 3rd fr over 1f out: kpt on same pce fnl f* **14/1**

-500 **4** shd **Dancing Sal (IRE)**[26] 2860 3-9-1 **57** HectorCrouch(5) 7 47
(Gary Moore) *mid-div: hdwy to dispute ld over 3f out: hdd wl over 2f out: kpt on same pce fr over 1f out* **9/1**

5000 **5** 5 **La Napoule**[19] 3087 3-9-1 **57** GaryMahon(5) 4 35
(Richard Hannon) *trckd ldrs tl lost pl over 4f out: nt a threat after* **17/2**

00-0 **6** 3 1/4 **Pacific Trip**[25] 2883 3-8-10 **52** KieranShoemark(5) 5 23
(Andrew Balding) *sn pushed along: nvr bttr than mid-div* **4/1**[2]

0-00 **7** 4 **Macnamara**[24] 2927 3-8-1 **45** [1] Leah-AnneAvery(7) 1 7
(Harry Dunlop) *led tl over 3f out: sn btn* **25/1**

-060 **8** 7 **Spirited Silver**[9] 3426 3-8-8 **45** CharlotteJenner 9
(John Bridger) *s.i.s: sn trcking ldrs: disp ld briefly over 3f out: wknd over 2f out* **25/1**

4600 **9** 1 3/4 **Lady Knight (IRE)**[23] 2978 3-9-1 **57** (b) JosephineGordon(5) 6
(J S Moore) *trckd ldrs: disp ld briefly over 3f out: wknd over 2f out* **20/1**

6024 **U** **Dylan's Centenary**[14] 3281 3-8-13 **57** SophieKilloran(7) 3
(Rod Millman) *trckd ldrs: disputing ld whn sddle slipped over 3f out: nt rcvr and uns rdr sn after* **11/4**[1]

0-50 **B** **Permsiri (IRE)**[16] 3178 3-8-8 **45** AdamMcLean 2
(Malcolm Saunders) *trckd ldrs for 4f: towards rr: b.d whn clipping heels over 2f out* **50/1**

1m 46.07s (2.57) **Going Correction** -0.05s/f (Good) **11 Ran SP% 119.8**
Speed ratings (Par 97): **85,84,78,78,73 69,65,58,57,**
CSF £34.99 CT £323.34 TOTE £8.30: £3.10, £2.10, £2.70; EX 45.30 Trifecta £424.90.
**Owner** Chris Scott **Bred** M S Saunders And Chris Scott **Trained** Kentisbeare, Devon
■ Stewards' Enquiry : Patrick O'Donnell seven-day ban: used whip contrary to race conditions (tbn)

**FOCUS**
The first two pulled clear in this minor handicap and there was plenty of drama.
T/Plt: £54.10 to a £1 stake. Pool: £91,058.78 - 1228.46 winning units. T/Qpdt: £24.60 to a £1 stake. Pool: 4981.78 - 149.33 winning units. TM

# 3728 WINDSOR (R-H)
Sunday, June 29

**OFFICIAL GOING: Good (8.1)**
Top bend dolled out 5yds from normal inner configuration adding 16yds to races of one mile and beyond. Inner of Straight on normal racing line.
Wind: Light, half behind Weather: Fine but cloudy

## 3755 UNIBET.CO.UK MAIDEN FILLIES' STKS 1m 67y
**2:00** (2:00) (Class 5) 3-5-Y-O **£2,587** (£770; £384; £192) **Stalls Low**

Form RPR

22 **1** **Principle Equation (IRE)**[31] 2690 3-9-0 0 RyanMoore 3 81+
(Ralph Beckett) *pressed ldr: led over 2f out: rdn whn pressed 1f out: styd on and in command last 100yds* **8/13**[1]

-044 **2** 1 3/4 **Alys Love**[14] 3276 3-9-0 74 DaneO'Neill 1 77
(William Muir) *trckd ldng trio: rdn to chse wnr jst over 1f out: styd on but hld last 100yds: eased nr fin* **10/1**

6 **3** 2 1/2 **Venturous Spirit (IRE)**[29] 2780 3-9-0 0 WilliamBuick 11 71
(John Gosden) *trckd ldng pair: rdn to take 2nd briefly over 1f out: one pce fnl f* **4/1**[2]

**4** 1 1/2 **Past Forgetting (IRE)** 3-9-0 0 MartinHarley 4 67+
(Luca Cumani) *s.i.s: hld up in last trio and off the pce: pushed along over 2f out: kpt on steadily fr over 1f out: nrst fin* **14/1**

05 **5** 1/2 **Dubai Hadeia**[14] 3276 3-9-0 0 MartinLane 7 66
(Charlie Appleby) *hld up in last trio and off the pce: jst pushed along fr over 2f out: kpt on steadily fr over 1f out: nrst fin* **25/1**

**6** nse **Elusive Ellen (IRE)**[343] 4570 4-9-3 0 JennyPowell(7) 8 68?
(Brendan Powell) *s.i.s: hld up in 7th and off the pce: pushed along 3f out: prog over 2f out: hung lft fr over 1f out: n.d but kpt on* **100/1**

00- **7** 3 **Luna Sunrise**[289] 6355 3-9-0 0 SamHitchcott 10 59?
(Timothy Jarvis) *led to over 2f out: shkn up and wknd over 1f out* **66/1**

00- **8** 4 **Savanna Spring (IRE)**[261] 7175 3-9-0 0 DanielTudhope 2 49
(Timothy Jarvis) *s.i.s: in tch in midfield: shkn up and wknd 2f out* **66/1**

54- **9** 1/2 **Redinha**[330] 5003 3-9-0 0 AdamKirby 6 48+
(Clive Cox) *hld up in last trio and off the pce: brief effrt over 2f out: wknd over 1f out* **8/1**[3]

0-6 **10** 20 **Cayman Cry (USA)**[14] 3276 3-9-0 0 JoeFanning 9
(Brian Meehan) *plld hrd: chsd ldrs tl wknd 3f out: t.o* **33/1**

1m 42.6s (-2.10) **Going Correction** -0.225s/f (Firm)
**WFA** 3 from 4yo 10lb **10 Ran SP% 119.6**
Speed ratings (Par 100): **101,99,96,95,94 94,91,87,87,67**
CSF £8.25 TOTE £1.50: £1.10, £3.70, £1.60; EX 6.70 Trifecta £20.90.
**Owner** Clipper Logistics **Bred** Kilcarn Stud **Trained** Kimpton, Hants

**FOCUS**
Top bend dolled out 5yds from normal inner configuration adding 16yds to races of one mile and beyond. Inner of Straight on normal racing line. Fair form in this maiden. The gallop was not overly strong.

## 3756 UNIBET - BY PLAYERS FOR PLAYERS H'CAP 5f 10y
**2:30** (2:30) (Class 5) (0-75,75) 3-Y-O **£2,587** (£770; £384; £192) **Stalls Low**

Form RPR

3212 **1** **Groundworker (IRE)**[9] 3433 3-9-7 **75** RyanMoore 1 82
(Sylvester Kirk) *chsd ldng pair: shoved along fr 1/2-way: plld out and drvn over 1f out: styd on to ld ins fnl f* **10/11**[1]

-122 **2** 1 **Gulland Rock**[19] 3084 3-8-13 **67** DaneO'Neill 4 70
(William Muir) *led: jnd 2f out: kpt on but hdd and outpcd ins fnl f* **9/2**[3]

64-4 **3** nk **Innocently (IRE)**[10] 3399 3-9-7 **75** DanielTudhope 2 77
(David O'Meara) *pressed ldr: upsides fr 2f out but could nvr overtake: wnr wnt past ins fnl f* **2/1**[2]

2500 **4** 15 **Va Benny**[10] 3380 3-7-9 **56** oh1 (v) CamHardie(7) 3
(J R Jenkins) *dwlt: outpcd and a last: t.o* **20/1**

1m 0.1s (-0.20) **Going Correction** -0.025s/f (Good) **4 Ran SP% 108.7**
Speed ratings (Par 99): **100,98,97,73**
CSF £5.35 TOTE £1.80; EX 4.10 Trifecta £3.10.
**Owner** Deauville Daze Partnership **Bred** Knockainey Stud **Trained** Upper Lambourn, Berks

**FOCUS**
A small field but it did at least feature a couple of in-form sprinters and the winner looks progressive.

## 3757 BRITISH STALLION STUDS EBF FILLIES' CONDITIONS STKS (BOBIS RACE) 5f 10y
**3:00** (3:00) (Class 2) 2-Y-O **£10,271** (£3,075; £1,537) **Stalls Low**

Form RPR

10 **1** **Dangerous Moonlite (IRE)**[11] 3353 2-9-1 0 RyanMoore 3 89+
(Richard Hannon) *mde virtually all: pushed along quite firmly to draw clr over 1f out* **1/10**[1]

**2** 3 3/4 **Tongue Twista** 2-8-10 0 J-PGuillambert 2 71+
(Nick Littmoden) *sn pushed along: chsd wnr 1/2-way: no ch fr over 1f out but kpt on* **16/1**[3]

50 **3** 6 **Lady Marita (IRE)**[11] 3353 2-8-12 0 LiamJones 1 51
(J S Moore) *chsd wnr to 1/2-way: kpt in tch tl wknd over 1f out* **12/1**[2]

59.9s (-0.40) **Going Correction** -0.025s/f (Good) **3 Ran SP% 104.5**
Speed ratings (Par 96): **102,96,86**
CSF £2.29 TOTE £1.10; EX 2.10 Trifecta £2.80.
**Owner** Mrs J Wood **Bred** J K Thoroughbreds **Trained** East Everleigh, Wilts

**FOCUS**
An extremely weak race for the money on offer and no surprise if the winner proves a lot better than the bare form.

## 3758 DAILY UNIBET EARLY PRICES FROM 9AM H'CAP (BOBIS RACE) 1m 2f 7y
**3:30** (3:30) (Class 3) (0-90,89) 3-Y-O **£7,439** (£2,213; £1,106; £553) **Stalls Low**

Form RPR

0502 **1** **Torchlighter (IRE)**[15] 3243 3-9-4 **86** JoeFanning 3 100
(Mark Johnston) *led 1f: sn hld up in 4th: pushed along over 3f out: clsd fr 2f out: rdn to ld 1f out: styd on wl* **11/4**[2]

-144 **2** 1 **Yenhaab (IRE)**[22] 2986 3-9-3 **85** RyanMoore 6 97
(William Haggas) *trckd ldr after 1f: chal over 2f out: upsides but nt qckn over 1f out: chsd new ldr (and wnr) fnl f: a hld* **7/4**[1]

1541 **3** nk **Cay Dancer**[16] 3195 3-8-9 **84** CamHardie(7) 1 96
(Richard Hannon) *trckd ldng pair after 3f: nt clr run 2f out: swtchd ins and tried to chal 1f out: kpt on same pce* **6/1**

4-31 **4** 1 1/4 **Anglophile**[27] 2839 3-9-7 **89** WilliamBuick 5 98
(Charlie Appleby) *led after 1f: hrd pressed over 2f out: hdd 1f out: lost pl qckly* **4/1**[3]

06-4 **5** 1 1/2 **Tall Ship (IRE)**[89] 1216 3-8-6 **74** JimmyQuinn 2 80
(Sir Michael Stoute) *hld up in last: rdn and no imp on ldrs jst over 2f out: one pce after* **8/1**

2m 4.8s (-3.90) **Going Correction** -0.225s/f (Firm) **5 Ran SP% 108.4**
Speed ratings (Par 103): **106,105,104,103,102**
CSF £7.73 TOTE £4.40: £1.80, £1.70; EX 8.10 Trifecta £29.50.
**Owner** Sheikh Hamdan bin Mohammed Al Maktoum **Bred** Darley **Trained** Middleham Moor, N Yorks

**FOCUS**
A fairly useful handicap run in a fair time.

## 3759 NEW HORSE RACING ODDS AT UNIBET.CO.UK H'CAP 1m 67y
**4:05** (4:05) (Class 3) (0-90,88) 3-Y-O+ **£7,439** (£2,213; £1,106; £553) **Stalls Low**

Form RPR

00- **1** **Homage (IRE)**[291] 6308 4-9-13 **88** RyanMoore 4 104+
(William Haggas) *hld up in 5th prog on inner over 2f out: led over 1f out: pushed out fnl f: readily* **7/4**[1]

-552 **2** 2 1/2 **Lord Ofthe Shadows (IRE)**[13] 3314 5-9-7 **82** SeanLevey 5 89
(Richard Hannon) *trckd ldng trio: rdn wl over 2f out: prog to take 2nd 1f out: styd on but no ch w wnr* **6/1**

0304 **3** 1 **Talented Kid**[13] 3306 5-9-8 **83** JoeFanning 7 88
(Mark Johnston) *t.k.h: hld up in last: shkn up over 2f out: prog wl over 1f out: styd on to take 3rd ins fnl f: n.d* **9/2**[3]

2110 **4** 4 1/2 **Uncle Dermot (IRE)**[29] 2772 6-9-13 **88** AdamKirby 2 82
(Brendan Powell) *led: kicked on 3f out: hdd & wknd over 1f out* **3/1**[2]

3060 **5** 4 1/2 **Spiritual Star (IRE)**[21] 3036 5-9-10 **85** WilliamCarson 3 69
(Anthony Carson) *pushed along early and reminder: then t.k.h: trckd ldng pair: chsd ldr 3f out: chal 2f out: wknd qckly over 1f out* **12/1**

360- **6** 16 **Tobougg Happy**[290] 6328 3-9-2 **87** MartinHarley 8 32
(James Tate) *chsd ldr to 3f out: wknd qckly over 2f out: t.o* **8/1**

0- **7** 9 **Game Mascot**[167] 4-9-11 **86** ChrisCatlin 6 13
(Peter Hiatt) *t.k.h: hld up in last pair: wknd 3f out: t.o* **33/1**

1m 41.5s (-3.20) **Going Correction** -0.225s/f (Firm)
**WFA** 3 from 4yo+ 10lb **7 Ran SP% 115.6**
Speed ratings (Par 107): **107,104,103,99,94 78,69**
CSF £13.26 CT £40.76 TOTE £2.50: £1.30, £2.90; EX 13.00 Trifecta £60.60.
**Owner** Highclere Thoroughbred Racing - Dalmeny **Bred** J Hanly **Trained** Newmarket, Suffolk

**FOCUS**
Not a particularly strong race overall but a taking performance from the winner on his first start for a new stable. The winning time was the best of the three run over the C&D.

## 3760 UNIBET.CO.UK DAILY ENHANCED ODDS H'CAP 1m 67y
4:35 (4:36) (Class 5) (0-75,77) 3-Y-O £2,587 (£770; £384; £192) Stalls Low

Form RPR
31-6 1 **Rayoumti (IRE)**[64] 1711 3-9-3 71 ........ MartinHarley 5 78
(George Margarson) *trckd ldr: shkn up to ld over 1f out: rdn to assert ins fnl f* **14/1**
5064 2 1 1/4 **Filosofo (IRE)**[20] 3064 3-9-3 71 ........ SeanLevey 3 75
(Richard Hannon) *led: set mod pce tl kicked on 3f out: drvn and hdd over 1f out: kpt on but readily hld last 100yds* **14/1**
1-4 3 1 1/2 **The Third Man**[17] 3144 3-9-7 75 ........ WilliamBuick 6 77+
(John Gosden) *hld up in 5th: pushed along 3f out: swtchd to outer and drvn 2f out: tk 3rd 1f out but nt pce to threaten ldng pair* **4/11**[1]
2-35 4 1 **Final Countdown**[153] 357 3-8-12 66 ........ WilliamCarson 4 64
(Anthony Carson) *hld up in last: shoved along over 3f out: stl last and reminder over 1f out: kpt on to take 4th nr fin: nvr involved* **25/1**
42-0 5 1/2 **Lacock**[17] 3145 3-9-2 70 ........ DaneO'Neill 7 67
(Henry Candy) *hld up in 4th: rdn and no prog over 2f out: one pce after* **6/1**[2]
0301 6 nk **Sweet Alibi (IRE)**[31] 2695 3-8-4 65 ........ CamHardie(7) 1 61
(J S Moore) *trckd ldng pair: cl enough and rdn 2f out: nt qckn and wl hld after* **8/1**[3]
1m 43.45s (-1.25) **Going Correction** -0.225s/f (Firm) 6 Ran SP% **115.9**
Speed ratings (Par 99): **97,95,94,93,92 92**
CSF £171.93 CT £255.81 TOTE £13.70: £3.10, £4.90; EX 90.50 Trifecta £117.20.
**Owner** Saleh Al Homaizi & Imad Al Sagar **Bred** Denis & David McDonnell **Trained** Newmarket, Suffolk

**FOCUS**
A fair handicap. It was steadily run, the first two home sharing those positions throughout, and the form could be a bit muddling. The favourite disappointed having not been well placed.

## 3761 DOWNLOAD THE UNIBET PRO APP H'CAP 1m 3f 135y
5:05 (5:06) (Class 5) (0-70,85) 4-Y-O+ £2,726 (£805; £402) Stalls Centre

Form RPR
1111 1 **Thecornishcowboy**[5] 3546 5-10-1 85 6ex........(t) JordonMcMurray(7) 2 92
(John Ryan) *hld up in tch: pushed along over 2f out: steadily clsd on outer over 1f out: rdn to ld last 75yds* **5/1**[3]
-306 2 1/2 **Posh Boy (IRE)**[19] 3080 4-9-4 67 ........ SebSanders 5 73
(Chris Wall) *hld up in last pair: prog 3f out: rdn to chse ldr wl over 1f out: led ins fnl f: hdd and one pce last 75yds* **8/1**
-232 3 3/4 **Warrigal (IRE)**[8] 3472 4-9-7 70 ........(p) RyanMoore 6 75
(Jeremy Noseda) *trckd ldrs: prog to ld 7f out: kicked on 3f out: drvn over 1f out: hdd and nt qckn ins fnl f* **6/4**[1]
0303 4 1/2 **Honourable Knight (IRE)**[19] 3086 6-8-9 58 ........(v) MartinHarley 3 62
(Mark Usher) *led to 7f out: chsd ldr: rdn 3f out: lost 2nd wl over 1f out: kpt on same pce after* **16/1**
0-20 5 1 3/4 **Urban Space**[23] 2947 8-8-5 54 ........(t) WilliamCarson 7 55
(John Flint) *trckd ldrs: rdn 3f out: disp 2nd briefly wl over 1f out: nt qckn after: hld whn short of room nr fin* **8/1**
2463 6 shd **Palus San Marco (IRE)**[13] 3310 5-9-7 70 ........ JoeFanning 4 71
(Tony Carroll) *s.s: hld up in last: urged along 3f out: nvr on terms but kpt on steadily fr over 1f out* **9/2**[2]
0-35 7 3 1/2 **Tingo In The Tale (IRE)**[39] 2464 5-8-13 66 WilliamTwiston-Davies(3) 1 60
(David Arbuthnot) *trckd ldr 4f: styd cl up: rdn 3f out: one pce after tl wknd fnl f* **8/1**
41-6 8 28 **Waahej**[13] 3310 8-9-0 63 ........ ChrisCatlin 8 12
(Peter Hiatt) *in tch: rdn and wknd 3f out: t.o* **33/1**
2m 29.7s (0.20) **Going Correction** -0.225s/f (Firm) 8 Ran SP% **117.0**
Speed ratings (Par 103): **90,89,89,88,87 87,85,66**
CSF £45.18 CT £88.27 TOTE £4.30: £1.60, £2.60, £1.30; EX 32.50 Trifecta £108.40.
**Owner** C Letcher & J Ryan **Bred** Hadi Al Tajir **Trained** Newmarket, Suffolk

**FOCUS**
A fair handicap that saw the winner produce another personal best. The pace was on the steady side for a long way.
T/Plt: £110.00 to a £1 stake. Pool: £69,686.64 - 462.35 winning units. T/Qpdt: £88.60 to a £1 stake. Pool: £3489.84 - 29.12 winning units. JN

# 3735 CURRAGH (R-H)
Sunday, June 29

**OFFICIAL GOING: Good to firm**

## 3763a GRANGECON STUD STKS (GROUP 3) 6f
2:45 (2:46) 2-Y-O £35,208 (£10,291; £4,875; £1,625)

RPR
1 **I Am Beautiful (IRE)**[17] 3163 2-9-0 ........ SeamieHeffernan 11 98
(A P O'Brien, Ire) *sn led: 1 l clr 1/2-way: rdn and extended advantage under 2f out: strly pressed wl ins fnl f: all out towards fin to jst hold on* **12/1**
2 shd **Jeanne Girl (IRE)**[36] 2568 2-9-0 ........ NGMcCullagh 7 98
(Mrs John Harrington, Ire) *disp early tl sn settled bhd ldr: 2nd 1/2-way: rdn under 2f out and clsd u.p to strly press wnr wl ins fnl f: jst hld* **9/2**[3]
3 nse **Quinta Verde (IRE)**[23] 2969 2-9-0 ........ JamieSpencer 4 98
(Edward Lynam, Ire) *w.w towards rr: 10th 1/2-way: impr fr 2f out to chse ldrs in 4th ent fnl f: clsd u.p on ldng pair towards fin: jst failed* **7/1**
4 2 3/4 **Pleascach (IRE)** 2-9-0 ........ KevinManning 10 89+
(J S Bolger, Ire) *on toes befhand: s.i.s and racd in rr: last 1/2-way: hdwy on outer fr 2f out into 6th fnl 100yds: kpt on wl into nvr nrr 4th fnl stride: nt trble principals* **16/1**
5 hd **Back To Base (IRE)**[22] 3014 2-9-0 ........ FMBerry 2 88
(David Wachman, Ire) *w.w on outer: racd keenly: 8th 1/2-way: rdn into 3rd ent fnl f and sn no imp on ldrs in 4th: kpt on one pce and dropped to 5th fnl stride* **10/3**[2]
6 nk **Avenue Montaigne (IRE)**[14] 3283 2-9-0 ........ ShaneFoley 5 87
(John Joseph Murphy, Ire) *hld up in tch: 6th 1/2-way: rdn in 5th and no imp on ldrs ent fnl f: kpt on one pce* **33/1**
7 2 **Leading Actress (IRE)**[14] 3283 2-9-0 ........ BillyLee 3 81
(W McCreery, Ire) *hld up in tch: 7th 1/2-way: rdn between horses 1f out and sn no ex: kpt on one pce* **12/1**
8 1 1/4 **As Good As Gold (IRE)**[18] 3126 2-9-0 ........ JosephO'Brien 9 77
(A P O'Brien, Ire) *chsd ldrs: 5th 1/2-way: niggled along 2f out and sn no imp: kpt on one pce in 8th towards fin* **10/1**
9 1/2 **Perfect Fit (IRE)**[18] 3126 2-9-0 ........ WayneLordan 8 76
(David Wachman, Ire) *hld up in tch: 9th 1/2-way: rdn and no imp fr 2f out* **33/1**
10 1/2 **Stormfly (IRE)**[27] 2856 2-9-0 ........ PatSmullen 6 74
(D K Weld, Ire) *disp early tl sn settled bhd ldrs: 3rd 1/2-way: rdn and wknd fr under 2f out: eased fnl f* **3/1**[1]
11 nk **Belle Et Bete (IRE)**[18] 3126 2-9-0 ........ ColinKeane 1 73
(G M Lyons, Ire) *chsd ldrs: 4th 1/2-way: rdn and no ex 1 1/2f out: wknd and eased ins fnl f* **20/1**
1m 12.56s (-2.94) **Going Correction** -0.40s/f (Firm) 11 Ran SP% **119.8**
Speed ratings: **103,102,102,99,98 98,95,94,93,92 92**
CSF £65.28 TOTE £14.30: £3.60, £1.90, £3.10; DF 87.50 Trifecta £1725.10.
**Owner** Mrs John Magnier & Michael Tabor & Flaxman Stables **Bred** Quay Bloodstock And The Niarchos Family **Trained** Cashel, Co Tipperary

**FOCUS**
A fair compliment was paid to the Leopardstown victory of Queen Nefertiti here as the winner and the third home almost ran to the pound from that contest.

## 3764a AT THE RACES CURRAGH CUP (GROUP 3) 1m 6f
3:15 (3:16) 3-Y-O+

£32,500 (£10,291; £4,875; £1,625; £1,083; £541)

RPR
1 **Ernest Hemingway (IRE)**[92] 1177 5-10-0 116........(t) JosephO'Brien 5 114+
(A P O'Brien, Ire) *w.w: 6th 1/2-way: hdwy on outer fr over 2f out into 2nd 1 1/2f out: sn led gng best and rdn clr: styd on wl* **6/4**[1]
2 2 **Certerach (IRE)**[92] 1177 6-10-0 113 ........ JamieSpencer 9 111
(M Halford, Ire) *hld up in rr: last 1/2-way: hdwy in rr fr under 2f out to chse ldrs in 4th ent fnl f: styd on wl into 2nd ins fnl 100yds: nt trble wnr* **11/2**[3]
3 1/2 **Tarana (IRE)**[23] 2973 4-9-8 101 ........ DeclanMcDonogh 3 104
(John M Oxx, Ire) *led: narrow advantage 1/2-way: rdn and strly pressed into st: hdd u.p over 1f out and sn no ch w wnr: dropped to 3rd ins fnl 100yds* **4/1**[2]
4 1 1/2 **Dabadiyan (IRE)**[92] 1177 4-9-11 107 ........ ShaneFoley 4 105
(M Halford, Ire) *chsd ldrs: t.k.h early: 4th 1/2-way: clsr in 3rd appr st: rdn 2f out and no imp on wnr in 4th ins fnl f: kpt on same pce* **6/1**
5 1 1/4 **Shu Lewis (IRE)**[23] 2973 8-9-8 100 ........ SeamieHeffernan 8 100
(Ms M Dowdall Blake, Ire) *trckd ldr in 2nd: almost on terms into st: sn rdn and no ex u.p in 4th fr under 2f out: one pce fnl f* **8/1**
6 1/2 **Chicago (IRE)**[23] 2973 5-9-11 99 ........ RonanWhelan 2 102
(John Patrick Shanahan, Ire) *hld up bhd ldrs: 5th 1/2-way: rdn 2f out and sn no imp on ldrs: one pce fnl f* **25/1**
7 1 1/2 **El Salvador (IRE)**[8] 3453 5-9-11 105 ........ AnaO'Brien 1 100
(A P O'Brien, Ire) *sweated up befhand: chsd ldrs in 3rd tl dropped to 4th into st: rdn and no ex over 2f out: wknd to rr 1f out* **10/1**
3m 4.68s (-4.72) **Going Correction** 0.0s/f (Good) 7 Ran SP% **113.7**
Speed ratings: **113,111,111,110,110 109,108**
CSF £10.06 TOTE £2.10: £1.50, £2.30; DF 9.60 Trifecta £31.00.
**Owner** Mrs John Magnier & Michael Tabor & Derrick Smith **Bred** Barronstown Stud **Trained** Cashel, Co Tipperary

**FOCUS**
Ernest Hemingway, a five-length winner of this event a year ago, had less to spare on this occasion but still won quite comfortably. The pace was moderate and it developed into a sprint.

## 3765a FRIARSTOWN STUD INTERNATIONAL STKS (GROUP 3) 1m 2f
3:45 (3:47) 3-Y-O+ £33,854 (£9,895; £4,687; £1,562)

RPR
1 **Mekong River (IRE)**[35] 2579 3-8-12 107........(p) SeamieHeffernan 4 110
(A P O'Brien, Ire) *sweated up befhand: led: 1 l clr 1/2-way: rdn into st and hdd u.p fr 2f out: rallied far side ent fnl f to regain advantage fnl 100yds: kpt on wl* **5/1**[3]
2 nk **Parish Hall (IRE)**[11] 3354 5-9-12 112........(t) KevinManning 3 111
(J S Bolger, Ire) *chsd ldr: t.k.h early: 2nd 1/2-way almost on terms gng wl into st and led fr 2f out: sn rdn and strly pressed ent fnl f: hdd fnl 100yds and kpt on wl towards fin wout matching wnr* **9/4**[2]
3 2 3/4 **Ebanoran (IRE)**[22] 2990 3-8-12 112 ........ DeclanMcDonogh 5 104+
(John M Oxx, Ire) *dwlt and w.w: 4th 1/2-way: tk clsr order appr st: rdn in 3rd fr 2f out and sn no imp on ldrs: kpt on one pce ins fnl f* **5/4**[1]
4 1/2 **Elleval (IRE)**[92] 1176 4-9-9 109 ........ FergalLynch 2 102+
(David Marnane, Ire) *w.w: racd keenly: last 1/2-way: tk clsr order bhd ldrs 2f out: sn rdn in 4th and no imp on ldrs ent fnl f: kpt on one pce* **10/1**
5 5 **Agena (IRE)**[15] 3261 3-8-12 ........ ColmO'Donoghue 1 95
(A P O'Brien, Ire) *chsd ldrs: 3rd 1/2-way: rdn in 4th over 2f out and sn no ex: wknd to rr 1 1/2f out* **7/1**
2m 6.3s (-3.00) **Going Correction** 0.0s/f (Good)
**WFA** 3 from 4yo+ 12lb 5 Ran SP% **113.5**
Speed ratings: **112,111,109,109,105**
CSF £17.09 TOTE £3.90: £1.90, £1.50; DF 10.20 Trifecta £25.60.
**Owner** Mrs John Magnier & Michael Tabor & Derrick Smith **Bred** Roncon, Wynatt & Chelston **Trained** Cashel, Co Tipperary

**FOCUS**
Despite getting into a muck sweat beforehand, Mekong River was tough in victory and looks one to try in one of the traditional St Leger trials. This has been rated around the runner-up.

## 3766a NEWBRIDGE SILVERWARE PRETTY POLLY STKS (F&M) (GROUP 1) 1m 2f
4:20 (4:23) 3-Y-O+

£100,000 (£31,666; £15,000; £5,000; £3,333; £1,666)

RPR
1 **Thistle Bird**[23] 2956 6-9-10 113 ........ GeorgeBaker 5 115+
(Roger Charlton) *chsd ldrs: 4th 1/2-way: tk clsr order bhd ldrs in 3rd into st: hdwy on outer 2f out to chal gng best: rdn to ld over 1f out and styd on wl towards fin* **4/1**[3]
2 2 3/4 **Venus De Milo (IRE)**[14] 3285 4-9-10 112 ........ JosephO'Brien 7 110
(A P O'Brien, Ire) *trckd ldr in 2nd: clsd on outer to ld fr 3f out: strly pressed fr under 2f out and hdd over 1f out: sn no ch w wnr: kpt on same pce* **7/2**[2]
3 3/4 **Just The Judge (IRE)**[23] 2956 4-9-10 108 ........ JamieSpencer 10 108+
(Charles Hills) *hld up in tch: 5th 1/2-way: rdn over 2f out and clsd u.p into 4th ent fnl f: wnt 3rd ins fnl 150yds and kpt on wl: nt trble wnr* **11/2**

4 ¾ **My Ambivalent (IRE)**[22] 2988 5-9-10 112 ........................ AndreaAtzeni 9 107
(Roger Varian) *reluctant to load: led: pushed along appr st and hdd fr 3f out: no imp on ldrs in 3rd 1 1/2f out: kpt on one pce and dropped to 3rd ins fnl 150yds* **15/8**[1]

5 1 ¾ **Peace Burg (FR)**[11] 3355 4-9-10 108 ........................(t) SeamieHeffernan 1 103
(A P O'Brien, Ire) *w.w: 6th 1/2-way: rdn into 4th briefly fr 2f out: sn no ex u.p in 5th: kpt on one pce ins fnl f* **28/1**

6 hd **Pearl Of Africa (IRE)**[17] 3166 4-9-10 107 ........................ ColinKeane 2 103
(Edward Lynam, Ire) *hld up towards rr: 7th 1/2-way: rdn into st and sme hdwy on outer fr 2f out to chse ldrs in 6th over 1f out: kpt on one pce* **10/1**

7 2 **Avenue Gabriel**[35] 2581 3-8-12 103 ........................ ChrisHayes 3 99
(P D Deegan, Ire) *w.w in rr: last 1/2-way: rdn and no imp into st: kpt on one pce fnl 2f* **12/1**

8 9 **Harasiya (IRE)**[21] 3041 4-9-10 104 ........................ DeclanMcDonogh 8 81
(John M Oxx, Ire) *chsd ldrs: 3rd 1/2-way: rdn in 4th fr 3f out and sn no imp on ldrs: wknd under 2f out: eased fnl f* **25/1**

2m 5.58s (-3.72) **Going Correction** 0.0s/f (Good)
**WFA** 3 from 4yo+ 12lb **8** Ran SP% **116.5**
Speed ratings: **114,111,111,110,109 109,107,100**
CSF £18.82 TOTE £3.90: £1.70, £1.70, £2.10; DF 15.90 Trifecta £108.90.
**Owner** Lady Rothschild **Bred** The Rt Hon Lord Rothschild **Trained** Beckhampton, Wilts

**FOCUS**
Having gone close on a couple of occasions at this level, Thistle Bird finally broke her Group 1 duck and deservedly so. The winner is rated back to her best with the runner-up and third close to last year's form.

3767 - 3769a (Foreign Racing) - See Raceform Interactive

## HAMBURG (R-H)
Sunday, June 29
**OFFICIAL GOING: Turf: good to soft**

### 3770a LUCKY SPEED HANSA-PREIS (GROUP 2) (3YO+) (TURF) 1m 4f
**4:10** (12:00) 3-Y-0+
**£33,333** (£12,916; £5,416; £3,333; £2,083; £1,250)

RPR

1 **Protectionist (GER)**[28] 2815 4-9-6 0 ........................ EPedroza 4 112+
(A Wohler, Germany) *hld up in last pair on inner: swtchd to outer and hdwy into midfield 5f out: rdn and prom into st: chal ent fnl f: edgd rt u.p: styd on strly and led towards fin: pushed out and asserted* **29/10**[2]

2 1 **Singing (FR)**[52] 2106 4-9-6 0 ........................ JBojko 1 110
(A Wohler, Germany) *prom on inner: pushed along to chal into st and led 2f out: edgd rt to rail jst over 1f out: strly pressed ent fnl f: styd on wl but hdd towards fin and hld* **109/10**

3 1 **Sirius (GER)**[29] 3-8-6 0 ........................(b) SHellyn 2 109
(Andreas Lowe, Germany) *midfield on inner: rdn and angled out into st: wnt 3rd ent fnl f: short of room and swtchd lft sn after: styd on wl fnl 150yds but nt pce of front pair* **48/10**[3]

4 1 ¼ **Lucky Speed (IRE)**[28] 2815 4-9-6 0 ........................ AdriedeVries 6 107
(P Schiergen, Germany) *hld up towards rr: last 4f out: pushed along into st: swtchd to outer and rdn over 1f out: edgd rt u.p but styd on and wnt 4th wl ins fnl f: nvr able to chal* **6/4**[1]

5 1 ¼ **Nymphea (IRE)**[37] 2631 5-9-3 0 ........................ DanielePorcu 9 102
(P Schiergen, Germany) *led and sn crossed to rail: rdn and strly pressed into st: hdd 2f out: hmpd on rail jst over 1f out and lost 2nd: hld fnl f: fdd and dropped to 5th* **125/10**

6 1 **Vif Monsieur (GER)**[28] 2815 4-9-6 0 ........................ KClijmans 5 103
(S Smrczek, Germany) *midfield: pushed along and fanned wd into st: rdn 2f out: hung rt and outpcd by ldrs over 1f out: styd on wout threatening fnl f* **133/10**

7 1 **Berlin Berlin**[32] 5-9-3 0 ........................ MartinSeidl 3 99
(Markus Klug, Germany) *hld up in midfield: towards rr 5f out: rdn over 2f out: styd on same pce on rail fr over 1f out and nvr threatened* **222/10**

8 4 ½ **Schulz (GER)**[98] 4-9-6 0 ........................ APietsch 7 94
(Markus Klug, Germany) *midfield in tch: pushed along 3f out: rdn and outpcd in st: fdd: eased whn btn fnl 100yds* **168/10**

9 10 **Elis Gury**[27] 4-9-6 0 ........................ FilipMinarik 10 78
(M G Mintchev, Germany) *wnt lft s and racd alone early: sn worked across to join remainder and trckd ldr on outer: rdn into st: sn lost pl and btn: wknd: eased fnl f* **118/10**

10 2 ½ **Hey Little Gorl (GER)**[294] 6248 4-9-3 0 ........................ AHelfenbein 8 71
(Markus Klug, Germany) *t.k.h: hld up in rr: hdwy into midfield on outer bef 1/2-way: pushed along and shuffled bk to rr again 3f out: rdn in last and btn 2f out: bhd and eased fnl f* **133/10**

2m 31.8s (-2.75)
**WFA** 3 from 4yo+ 14lb **10** Ran SP% **130.4**
WIN (incl. 10 euro stake): 39. PLACES: 18, 34, 21. SF: 439.
**Owner** Dr Christoph Berglar **Bred** Dr Christoph Berglar **Trained** Germany

3771 - (Foreign Racing) - See Raceform Interactive

## KLAMPENBORG
Sunday, June 29
**OFFICIAL GOING: Turf: good**

### 3772a HARKILA SCANDINAVIAN OPEN CHAMPIONSHIP (GROUP 3) (3YO+) (TURF) 1m 4f
**2:50** (12:00) 3-Y-0+ **£33,370** (£11,123; £5,561; £3,337; £2,224)

RPR

1 **Without Fear (FR)**[19] 3090 6-9-6 0 ........................ RafaelSchistl 8 105
(Niels Petersen, Norway) *mde virtually all: set stdy gallop: qcknd tempo fr 1/2-way: hrd pressed and rdn 2f out: r.o appr 1f out: drvn out fnl f: readily* **758/100**[3]

2 2 **Bank Of Burden (USA)**[19] 3090 7-9-6 0 ........................ Per-AndersGraberg 2 102
(Niels Petersen, Norway) *tk v t.k.h and prom early: restrained bhd ldrs: chsd ldr over 2f out: rdn and nt qckn over 1f out: one pce fnl f* **13/10**[1]

3 2 **Hurricane Red (IRE)**[19] 3090 4-9-4 0 ........................ ElioneChaves 9 97
(Lennart Reuterskiold Jr, Sweden) *towards rr: hdwy to chse ldng gp 2 1/2f out: cl 3rd and rdn 1 1/2f out: one pce fnl f* **6/4**[2]

4 2 **Free House**[428] 5-9-4 0 ........................(b) CarlosLopez 4 93
(Jessica Long, Sweden) *hld up towards rr: rdn and no imp 2f out: styd on u.p fnl f: wnt 4th cl home: nt pce to trble ldrs* **42/1**

5 ½ **Stubbs (IRE)**[246] 7525 3-8-4 0 ........................ ShaneKarlsson 6 93
(Bettina Andersen, Denmark) *in rr: gd hdwy on outer to press ldrs over 2f out: sn rdn and nt qckn 1 1/2f out: kpt on at same pce: lost 4th cl home* **112/10**

6 1 ½ **Lindenthaler (GER)**[245] 6-9-4 0 ........................ ValmirDeAzeredo 7 90
(Fredrik Reuterskiold, Sweden) *midfield: rdn and chsd ldrs over 2f out: sn no further imp: one pce fnl f* **53/1**

7 ½ **Jubilance (IRE)**[19] 3090 5-9-4 0 ........................ JacobJohansen 5 89
(Bent Olsen, Denmark) *midfield early: sn restrained towards rr: creeping clsr whn nt clr run and snatched up over 1 1/2f out: swtchd ins and rdn but no imp fnl f* **123/10**

8 dist **Berling (IRE)**[19] 3090 7-9-6 0 ........................ OliverWilson 10
(Jessica Long, Sweden) *midfield on outer early: pressed ldr after 2f: 4th and rdn over 2f out: sn wknd* **119/10**

9 dist **Funinthesand (IRE)**[19] 3090 5-9-4 0 ........................ Jan-ErikNeuroth 3
(Wido Neuroth, Norway) *t.k.h: towards rr: rdn and wl btn fnl 3f* **46/1**

10 1 ½ **Fearless Hunter (GER)**[19] 3090 4-9-4 0 ........................ NikolajStott 1
(Rune Haugen, Norway) *t.k.h: trckd ldrs: rdn and wknd over 1 1/2f out* **33/1**

2m 30.8s (150.80)
**WFA** 3 from 4yo+ 14lb **10** Ran SP% **127.8**
PARI-MUTUEL (all including 1krone stakes): WIN 8.54; PLACE 1.86, 1.24, 1.31; SF 40.67.
**Owner** Stall Bonne Nuit **Bred** Zamim Ralphy Meahjohn **Trained** Norway

## 2630 SAINT-CLOUD (L-H)
Sunday, June 29
**OFFICIAL GOING: Turf: good to soft**

### 3773a ABU DHABI PRIX DE MALLERET (GROUP 2) (3YO FILLIES) (TURF) 1m 4f
**1:30** (12:00) 3-Y-0 **£71,250** (£27,500; £13,125; £8,750; £4,375)

RPR

1 **Dolniya (FR)**[23] 2977 3-8-11 0 ........................ ChristopheSoumillon 1 109+
(A De Royer-Dupre, France) *hld up in tch: hdwy on outer and pushed along to chal 2f out: rdn to ld over 1f out: edgd lft u.p fnl f but styd on wl and asserted: readily* **7/4**[1]

2 ¾ **Savanne (IRE)**[28] 2816 3-8-11 0 ........................ MaximeGuyon 5 108
(A Fabre, France) *led early: sn hdd and trckd ldr: pushed along to chal 2f out and sn led: rdn and hdd over 1f out: styd on wl but nt pce of wnr fnl f and hld* **10/3**[3]

3 snk **Lavender Lane (IRE)**[14] 3289 3-8-11 0 ........................ GeraldMosse 3 108
(J E Hammond, France) *t.k.h: hld up in last: pushed along to cl fr 2f out: rdn over 1f out: styd on and wnt 3rd wl ins fnl f but nvr able to chal* **5/2**[2]

4 ½ **Indonesienne (IRE)**[49] 2195 3-8-11 0 ........................ OlivierPeslier 4 107
(C Ferland, France) *t.k.h: midfield in tch on outer: pushed along to chal 2f out: styd on but nt pce of wnr: dropped to 4th wl ins fnl f and hld* **6/1**

5 5 **Hug And A Kiss (USA)**[46] 2267 3-8-11 0 ........................ Pierre-CharlesBoudot 2 100
(A Fabre, France) *midfield in tch on inner: pushed along and shuffled bk 2f out: sn outpcd in rr: wl btn and n.d fnl f* **10/1**

6 7 **Mintaka (FR)**[23] 2977 3-8-11 0 ........................ FreddyDiFede 6 89
(A De Royer-Dupre, France) *sn led: 3 l clr into st: strly pressed fr 2f out and sn hdd: pushed along and qckly btn: wknd on rail and dropped to last over 1f out: eased fnl 120yds* **100/1**

2m 34.8s (-5.60) **6** Ran SP% **112.4**
WIN (incl. 1 euro stake): 2.70 (Dolniya coupled with Mintaka). PLACES: 1.40, 1.70. SF: 6.40.
**Owner** H H Aga Khan **Bred** S A Aga Khan **Trained** Chantilly, France

### 3774a GRAND PRIX DE SAINT-CLOUD (GROUP 1) (4YO+) (TURF) 1m 4f
**2:40** (12:00) 4-Y-0+ **£190,466** (£76,200; £38,100; £19,033; £9,533)

RPR

1 hd **Noble Mission**[35] 2580 5-9-2 0 ........................ JamesDoyle 4 119
(Lady Cecil) *led: kicked and 3 l clr into st: pushed along over 2f out: rdn over 1f out: stl 3 l in front and looked in control 100yds out: tired and rapidly diminishing advantage towards fin: hdd fnl stride* **2/1**[2]

2 snk **Siljan's Saga (FR)**[37] 2631 4-8-13 0 ........................ Pierre-CharlesBoudot 2 115+
(J-P Gauvin, France) *midfield in tch on outer: pushed along 2f out: rdn in 3rd ent fnl f: styd on strly towards fin as ldr tired and almost snatched 2nd post: nt quite pce of wnr* **14/1**

3 1 ¾ **Narniyn (IRE)**[17] 3171 4-8-13 0 ........................ ChristopheSoumillon 6 113
(A De Royer-Dupre, France) *t.k.h: hld up in tch on outer: pushed along over 2f out: hung lft and appeared to be toiling whn rdn over 1f out: flashed tailed u.p fnl f: styd on for wl-hld 4th* **6/1**[3]

4 1 ½ **Flintshire**[22] 2988 4-9-2 0 ........................ MaximeGuyon 1 113
(A Fabre, France) *midfield in tch on inner: pushed along 3f out: rdn and outpcd by ldr 2f out: styd on same pce u.p fr over 1f out and nvr able to chal* **13/8**[1]

5 1 ¼ **Meleagros (IRE)**[52] 2106 5-9-2 0 ........................ AdrienFouassier 3 111
(Alain Couetil, France) *hld up in tch on inner: rdn over 2f out: styd on same pce fr over 1f out and nvr able to chal* **25/1**

6 15 **Empoli (GER)**[22] 2988 4-9-2 0 ........................ UmbertoRispoli 7 87
(P Schiergen, Germany) *restrained and hld up in last: rdn 3f out: toiling in rr and no imp in st: wl btn whn eased over 1f out* **16/1**

D **Spiritjim (FR)**[28] 2819 4-9-2 0 ........................ Christophe-PatriceLemaire 5 119
(P Bary, France) *trckd ldr: pushed along over 2f out: rdn and no imp on ldr over 1f out: 3 l down in 2nd and looked hld 100yds out: styd on strly as ldr tired towards fin and jst got up to ld fnl stride* **8/1**

2m 34.83s (-5.57) **7** Ran SP% **113.2**
WIN (incl. 1 euro stake): 6.60. PLACES: 2.70, 1.70. SF: 27.60.
**Owner** K Abdullah **Bred** Juddmonte Farms Ltd **Trained** Newmarket, Suffolk

**FOCUS**
This was perhaps an ordinary renewal of this Group 1 prize. There was a thunderstorm prior to the off but the ground didn't appear to be riding too soft. For most of the journey it looked as if Noble Mission would win unchallenged, but it all changed in the final 100m.

# 3513 SAN SIRO (R-H)

Sunday, June 29

**OFFICIAL GOING: Turf: soft**

## 3775a PREMIO PRIMI PASSI (GROUP 3) (2YO) (TURF) 6f

2:55 (12:00) 2-Y-O £21,000 (£21,000; £7,000; £3,500)

RPR

1 **Ginwar (ITY)**27 2-8-11 0 CFiocchi 4 99
(Stefano Botti, Italy) *broke wl and led: edgd rt fr 2f out: rdn and responded 1 1/2f out: r.o gamely u.p fnl f: jnd on line* 6/4[2]

1 dht **Fontanelice (IRE)**14 2-8-8 0 MircoDemuro 2 96
(Stefano Botti, Italy) *pressed ldr on outer: swtchd ins over 2f out: rdn to chal fnl f: r.o u.str.p: got up to dead-heat on line* 6/4[2]

3 1 ½ **Arte Volante**14 2-8-8 0 FabioBranca 3 92
(B Grizzetti, Italy) *chsd ldng pair on inner: pushed along and outpcd over 2f out: styd on u.p fnl f: nt pce to trble ldrs* 174/10[3]

4 5 **Pensierieparole** 2-8-11 0 DarioVargiu 5 80+
(B Grizzetti, Italy) *missed break: sn trcking ldrs on outer: rdn and effrt 2f out: sn outpcd: wknd and eased ins fnl f* 6/5[1]

1m 11.0s (-0.80) 4 Ran SP% 130.9
WIN (incl. 1 euro stake): 1.25 (Fontanelice), 1.26 (Ginwar), PLACES: 1.40 (Fontanelice), 1.51 (Ginwar). DF: 2.70.
**Owner** Intra Srl **Bred** Intra Srl **Trained** Italy
**Owner** Stefano Botti **Bred** John Martin McLoughney **Trained** Italy

## 3776a PREMIO DEL GIUBILEO (GROUP 3) (3YO+) (TURF) 1m 1f

4:45 (12:00) 3-Y-O+ £23,333 (£10,266; £5,600; £2,800)

RPR

1 **Steaming Kitten (USA)**21 3047 3-8-7 0 FabioBranca 6 104
(Gianluca Bietolini, Italy) *led early: sn hdd and trckd ldr on inner: smooth hdwy to chal and led again 3f out: rdn clr 2f out: in control and pushed out fnl f: easing down at fin: comf* 7/5[1]

2 2 **Pattaya (ITY)**42 2374 6-9-3 0 MEsposito 5 100
(Stefano Botti, Italy) *dwlt and hld up in rr: last into st: pushed along 3f out: stl in rr 2f out: rdn and r.o fnl f: wnt 2nd cl home: nrst fin but no ch w wnr* 42/10[3]

3 snk **Kramulkie (IRE)**56 4-9-3 0 FBossa 10 99
(A Marcialis, Italy) *hld up in rr: rdn over 2f out: r.o fnl f and wnt 3rd fnl strides but nvr able to chal: nrst fin* 101/10

4 hd **Verdetto Finale**35 2589 4-9-3 0 MircoDemuro 8 99
(R Biondi, Italy) *trckd ldr on outer: swtchd ins and pushed along to chal 3f out: rdn and outpcd by wnr fnl 2f: hung rt ent fnl f: kpt on but lost 2 pls cl home* 2/1[2]

5 snk **Porsenna (IRE)**35 2589 4-9-3 0 PBorrelli 2 99
(Stefano Botti, Italy) *dwlt sltly and hld up towards rr on inner: rdn 3f out: swtchd lft and styd on wl fnl 120yds but nvr able to chal* 109/10

6 snk **Prato Mariante (ITY)**56 5-9-3 0 DPerovic 3 98
(M Corradini, Italy) *prom early but qckly restrained into midfield: rdn 2f out: nt qckn in 3rd whn carried rt ent fnl f: kpt on but lost 3 pls cl home* 187/10

7 7 **Demeteor (ITY)**21 3047 4-9-3 0 LManiezzi 4 84
(R Menichetti, Italy) *sweated up: dwlt sltly but qckly rcvrd and sn led: rdn and hdd 3f out: no ex and btn 2f out: steadily fdd and eased fnl f* 148/10

8 2 ½ **Teixidor (ITY)**63 5-9-3 0 SSulas 7 78
(Ottavio Di Paolo, Italy) *prom: rdn 3f out: sn outpcd and btn: wknd and eased ent fnl f* 202/10

9 1 **Peng (ITY)**49 4-9-3 0 CFiocchi 1 76
(Stefano Botti, Italy) *t.k.h: midfield in tch: rdn 3f out: outpcd and btn ent fnl f: sn eased and wknd* 232/10

10 dist **Vola E Va**35 2589 5-9-3 0 DarioVargiu 9
(B Grizzetti, Italy) *broke wl but stdd and settled in midfield: pushed along 3f out: no imp whn eased qckly as if smething amiss jst ins fnl 2f: dropped to last and t.o* 96/10

1m 50.9s (-7.00)
**WFA** 3 from 4yo+ 11lb 10 Ran SP% 141.3
WIN (incl. 1 euro stake): 2.42. PLACES: 1.39, 1.69, 2.24. DF: 11.55.
**Owner** Kenneth L & Sarah K Ramsey **Bred** Kenneth L & Sarah K Ramsey **Trained** Italy

# FFOS LAS (L-H)

Monday, June 30

**OFFICIAL GOING: Good (good to firm in places; 8.1)**
Wind: moderate behind Weather: sunny spells

## 3778 RACING EXCELLENCE APPRENTICE TRAINING SERIES H'CAP 1m 4f (R)

6:15 (6:16) (Class 6) (0-65,67) 4-Y-O+ £1,940 (£577; £288; £144) Stalls Low

Form RPR

-141 1 **Men Don't Cry (IRE)**6 3552 5-9-12 67 6ex DavidParkes(3) 5 76
(Ed de Giles) *hld up in last pair: hdwy over 3f out: led over 1f out: rdn out* 6/5[1]

6000 2 1 ¼ **Kelpie Blitz (IRE)**16 3235 5-9-12 64 (p) CamHardie 1 71
(Paul Morgan) *trckd ldrs: chal and nt qckn 2f out: kpt on ins fnl f* 7/1

40/1 3 2 **Lady Percy (IRE)**28 2836 5-9-3 55 CharlotteJenner 3 59
(Mark Usher) *led 3f: trckd ldr tl rdn to ld again 3f out: hdd over 1f out: one pce* 7/2[2]

500- 4 1 ½ **Jawinski (IRE)**350 4352 4-8-5 48 KieranShoemark(5) 7 49
(David Evans) *hld up in last pair: rdn over 3f out: styd on fnl 2f: nt trble ldrs* 16/1

4054 5 2 **Petrify**18 3147 4-8-4 47 (tp) MichaelKenneally(5) 2 45
(Bernard Llewellyn) *trckd ldr tl led after 3f: hdd 3f out: one pce* 5/1[3]

-000 6 18 **Elusive Band (USA)**16 3208 4-8-12 50 (tp) JordanVaughan 4 19
(Bernard Llewellyn) *chsd ldrs: rdn over 2f out: sn wknd: t.o* 10/1

40/5 7 2 ¾ **Swift Act**17 3176 5-8-7 50 [1] ChrisMeehan(5) 6 15
(Nikki Evans) *chsd ldrs: rdn over 3f out: sn wknd: t.o* 33/1

2m 36.8s (-0.60) **Going Correction** -0.125s/f (Firm) 7 Ran SP% 114.8
Speed ratings (Par 101): **97,96,94,93,92 80,78**
CSF £10.61 TOTE £2.00: £2.30, £2.40; EX 10.60 Trifecta £25.90.
**Owner** Clarke, King & Lewis **Bred** Ecurie Des Monceaux **Trained** Ledbury, H'fords

**FOCUS**
Cam Hardie, rider of the runner-up, described the ground as being "a little bit dead". A lowly handicap won readily by a penalised recent scorer. The form is rated around the third.

## 3779 IRISH STALLION FARMS EBF MAIDEN STKS 5f

6:45 (6:46) (Class 5) 2-Y-O £2,911 (£866; £432; £216) Stalls High

Form RPR

024 1 **Kibaar**41 2413 2-9-5 0 PaulHanagan 1 75
(B W Hills) *racd keenly: mde all: rdn 1f out: r.o and a holding rival* 4/11[1]

2 ½ **Aussie Ruler (IRE)** 2-9-5 0 SteveDrowne 4 73+
(Ronald Harris) *chsd wnr after 1f: rdn over 1f out: kpt on ins fnl f but a being hld* 8/1[3]

553 3 7 **Emef Rock (IRE)**14 3311 2-9-5 0 WilliamTwiston-Davies 3 48
(Mick Channon) *in tch: rdn 2f out: sn outpcd by ldng pair* 4/1[2]

4 1 ½ **Bannister Bell (IRE)** 2-9-5 0 LiamKeniry 5 43
(David Evans) *chsd ldrs: rdn 1/2-way: sn outpcd by principals* 12/1

0 5 10 **Steel Blaze**41 2436 2-8-11 0 OisinMurphy(3) 2 2
(Nikki Evans) *a in last: swtchd rt 1/2-way: qckly outpcd and lost tch* 50/1

57.71s (-0.59) **Going Correction** -0.125s/f (Firm) 5 Ran SP% 114.1
Speed ratings (Par 93): **99,98,87,84,68**
CSF £4.52 TOTE £1.10: £1.10, £4.20; EX 3.70 Trifecta £8.80.
**Owner** Hamdan Al Maktoum **Bred** Laundry Cottage Stud Farm **Trained** Upper Lambourn, Berks

**FOCUS**
The front pair drew clear in what looked an ordinary maiden. The winner was 10lb below his Ascot form, but this run might be underestimated.

## 3780 IWEC ELECTRICAL H'CAP 2m (R)

7:15 (7:17) (Class 6) (0-60,59) 4-Y-O+ £1,940 (£577; £288; £144) Stalls Low

Form RPR

43-6 1 **Lucky Diva**16 3209 7-8-12 50 (v) PaulHanagan 3 58
(Bill Turner) *trckd ldrs: rdn to ld 2f out: styd on wl* 7/1[3]

3456 2 2 **Willow Island (IRE)**11 2885 5-8-2 45 (t) NoelGarbutt(5) 5 49
(David Evans) *mid-div: rdn over 3f out: styd on u.p fnl 2f: wnt 2nd last strides* 20/1

-154 3 nk **Captain Sharpe**17 3179 6-9-7 59 (t) WilliamTwiston-Davies 8 63
(Bernard Llewellyn) *trckd ldrs: rdn 2f out: kpt on same pce to dispute 2nd fnl f* 10/1

65-2 4 ½ **Halling's Wish**25 2923 4-9-2 54 GeorgeBaker 1 57
(Gary Moore) *trckd ldr tl over 2f out: rdn and kpt on same pce: disp 2nd fnl f* 1/1[1]

4-33 5 shd **Fuzzy Logic (IRE)**17 3179 5-8-7 45 LukeMorris 2 48
(Bernard Llewellyn) *led: shied at path and reminders after 4f: rdn along 4f out: hdd 2f out: kpt on same pce* 6/1[2]

33-4 6 2 ¼ **Wasabi (IRE)**62 1865 5-8-9 50 OisinMurphy(3) 7 51
(John Berry) *hld up in rr: pushed along and hdwy 3f out: nt clr run over 2f out: swtchd rt over 1f out: unable qck* 7/1[3]

035/ 7 3 ¼ **Maggie Aron**350 4004 8-8-7 50 (t) DanielMuscutt(5) 4 47
(Tim Vaughan) *racd keenly: hld up: hdwy 5f out: rdn 3f out: sltly hmpd over 2f out: fdd over 1f out* 8/1

440/ 8 1 ¾ **Bogey Hole (IRE)**945 7569 5-8-4 49 CamHardie(7) 9 44
(Nikki Evans) *hld up in rr: rdn over 3f out: no real imp* 50/1

0500 9 20 **Another Journey**7 3521 5-8-2 45 [1] EoinWalsh(5) 6 16
(Lisa Williamson) *t.k.h towards rr: rdn over 3f out: wknd over 2f out: t.o* 100/1

3m 39.97s (9.97) **Going Correction** -0.125s/f (Firm) 9 Ran SP% 117.2
Speed ratings (Par 101): **70,69,68,68,68 67,65,64,54**
CSF £128.29 CT £1398.80 TOTE £9.90: £1.80, £3.10, £2.70; EX 176.00 Trifecta £983.90.
**Owner** Darren Coombes **Bred** Gracelands Stud **Trained** Sigwells, Somerset
■ Stewards' Enquiry : Paul Hanagan one-day ban: careless riding (14 Jul)

**FOCUS**
This was run at a steady gallop, with several of them racing keenly. The winner is rated to last year's form.

## 3781 THREE RIVERS H'CAP 1m (R)

7:45 (7:51) (Class 6) (0-60,58) 3-Y-O+ £1,940 (£577; £288; £144) Stalls Low

Form RPR

0-62 1 **Dream Impossible (IRE)**20 3087 3-8-12 54 SteveDrowne 9 64
(Peter Makin) *mid-div: hdwy over 2f out: rdn over 1f out: r.o wl to ld fnl 100yds* 9/2[2]

0040 2 1 ¾ **Greyemkay**16 3208 6-8-10 45 OisinMurphy(3) 5 53
(Richard Price) *a.p: rdn to ld over 1f out: hdd fnl 100yds* 7/2[1]

030 3 nk **Delightful Sleep**5 3576 6-9-11 57 LiamKeniry 10 64
(David Evans) *hld up: hdwy over 2f out: rdn over 1f out: r.o ins fnl f* 8/1[3]

0340 4 1 ½ **Sweet Cherry (IRE)**11 3407 3-8-7 49 PaulHanagan 7 51
(Peter Makin) *hld up: rdn and clsd 2f out: r.o ins fnl f* 8/1[3]

660- 5 ¾ **Flipping**217 8038 7-9-3 49 WilliamTwiston-Davies 8 51
(Stuart Kittow) *trckd ldrs: rdn wl over 1f out: sn edgd rt: one pce* 16/1

00-0 6 3 ½ **My New Angel (IRE)**16 3233 5-9-5 56 EoinWalsh(5) 6 50
(Daniel Mark Loughnane) *mid-div: rdn and sme hdwy over 3f out: one pce fnl f* 20/1

600- 7 1 ¼ **Alba Verde**193 8342 3-8-3 45 LukeMorris 3 34
(Sir Mark Prescott Bt) *w ldr: led over 3f out: drvn and hdd over 1f out: wknd fnl f* 7/2[1]

0104 8 ¾ **Katmai River (IRE)**5 3576 7-9-2 55 CharlotteJenner(7) 11 44
(Mark Usher) *in rr: rdn and sme hdwy over 3f out: kpt on fnl f* 8/1[3]

6300 9 3 ¼ **Devote Myself (IRE)**16 3208 5-8-11 46 (bt) RyanClark(3) 4 28
(John Flint) *wnt to post early: dwlt: mid-div: nt clr run over 2f out: sn rdn: wknd over 1f out* 20/1

200/ 10 1 **Rockinit (IRE)**1946 741 8-9-2 55 CamHardie(7) 12 35
(Peter Bowen) *reluctant to enter stalls: wnt rt s: towards rr: rdn and hdwy over 3f out: wknd over 1f out* 33/1

60-0 11 19 **Foiled**66 1691 4-8-10 45 MatthewCosham(3) 2
(Nikki Evans) *led: drvn and hdd over 3f out: wknd 2f out: t.o* 100/1

-500 12 12 **Dutchartcollector**32 2695 3-9-2 58 (b[1]) GeorgeBaker 1
(Gary Moore) *s.i.s: sn chsng ldrs: rdn over 3f out: wknd over 2f out: virtually p.u ins fnl f: t.o* 14/1

1m 39.08s (-1.92) **Going Correction** -0.125s/f (Firm)
**WFA** 3 from 4yo+ 10lb 12 Ran SP% 122.0
Speed ratings (Par 101): **104,102,101,100,99 96,94,94,90,89 70,58**
CSF £20.44 CT £128.44 TOTE £5.40: £2.00, £1.70, £3.40; EX 26.00 Trifecta £140.60.
**Owner** Mrs J N Humphreys **Bred** Glending Bloodstock **Trained** Ogbourne Maisey, Wilts

**FOCUS**
Plenty of exposed sorts here and no surprise to see one of the more lightly raced 3yos triumph. The form is rated around the third and fourth.

## 3782 LONETREE LTD MCDONALDS H'CAP 1m (R)
**8:15** (8:18) (Class 4) (0-80,80) 3-Y-0+ **£4,690** (£1,395; £697) **Stalls** Low

Form RPR
1-42 **1** **Kafeel (USA)**[24] 2962 3-9-4 **80**........................ PaulHanagan 2 91+
(Roger Varian) *mde all: nudged along 2f out: sn drew clr: easily* **1/2**[1]
3424 **2** *3* **Caramack**[3] 3646 4-9-11 **77**........................ GeorgeBaker 4 78
(Richard Lee) *hld up in last: rdn over 2f out: r.o u.p ins fnl f to go 2nd nr fin: nvr threatened wnr* **4/1**[3]
6441 **3** *hd* **Know Your Name**[18] 3144 3-8-13 **75**........................(v) LiamKeniry 3 74
(David Evans) *pressed wnr: rdn over 2f out: sn one pce: ct for 2nd nr fin* **7/2**[2]
1m 38.95s (-2.05) **Going Correction** -0.125s/f (Firm)
**WFA** 3 from 4yo 10lb **3** Ran SP% **108.9**
Speed ratings (Par 105): **105,102,101**
CSF £2.84 TOTE £1.40; EX 2.60 Trifecta £2.90.
**Owner** Hamdan Al Maktoum **Bred** Shadwell Farm LLC **Trained** Newmarket, Suffolk
**FOCUS**
A straightforward opportunity for the hot favourite, who was value for 5l.

## 3783 BARRY WALTERS CATERING H'CAP 6f
**8:45** (8:47) (Class 4) (0-80,79) 3-Y-0+ **£4,690** (£1,395; £697; £348) **Stalls** High

Form RPR
0022 **1** **Decision By One**[11] 3392 5-8-2 **60** oh2........................(t) NoelGarbutt(5) 7 68
(David Evans) *hld up bhd ldrs: rdn 2f out: r.o to ld last strides* **7/1**
006 **2** *nse* **Light From Mars**[25] 2919 9-9-5 **79**........................(p) MikeyEnnis(7) 6 86
(Ronald Harris) *cl up: led over 1f out: sn rdn: hdd last strides* **10/1**
30-0 **3** *hd* **Dutch Interior**[16] 3247 3-9-4 **78**........................ GeorgeBaker 3 82
(Gary Moore) *hld up: rdn over 1f out: r.o u.p ins fnl f: jst hld* **9/2**[3]
6642 **4** *3/4* **Vallarta (IRE)**[4] 3628 4-9-5 **72**........................ WilliamTwiston-Davies 2 76
(Mick Channon) *hld up: rdn 2f out: one pce fnl f* **6/4**[1]
6130 **5** *3 3/4* **Diamondhead (IRE)**[7] 3533 5-9-8 **78**........................ OisinMurphy(3) 8 70
(Ed de Giles) *prom: rdn over 2f out: wknd over 1f out* **3/1**[2]
-004 **6** *2 1/2* **Swendab (IRE)**[11] 3395 6-9-5 **79**........................(v) CamHardie(7) 1 63
(John O'Shea) *led narrowly: rdn over 2f out: edgd lft and hdd over 1f out: wknd fnl f* **14/1**
1m 8.66s (-1.34) **Going Correction** -0.125s/f (Firm)
**WFA** 3 from 4yo+ 7lb **6** Ran SP% **111.4**
Speed ratings (Par 105): **103,102,102,101,96 93**
CSF £67.00 CT £340.86 TOTE £6.70: £2.10, £4.70; EX 64.50 Trifecta £314.30.
**Owner** Mrs I M Folkes **Bred** G E Amey **Trained** Pandy, Monmouths
**FOCUS**
A fair sprint in which there was little to separate the first three at the line.

## 3784 STRADEY PARK H'CAP 5f
**9:15** (9:16) (Class 6) (0-65,62) 3-Y-0+ **£1,940** (£577; £288; £144) **Stalls** High

Form RPR
3006 **1** **Outbid**[28] 2831 4-8-4 **47**........................ CamHardie(7) 7 56
(Tony Carroll) *hld up bhd ldrs: qcknd to ld 1f out: edgd rt: drvn out* **5/1**[2]
-604 **2** *1/2* **Ryan Style (IRE)**[7] 3520 8-8-10 **49**........................ RyanClark(3) 3 56
(Lisa Williamson) *hld up in last: rdn over 1f out: r.o ins fnl f: jst hld* **10/1**[3]
4030 **3** *3/4* **Spic 'n Span**[7] 3520 9-8-10 **46**........................(p) LukeMorris 5 51
(Ronald Harris) *wnt to s early: cl up: rdn 2f out: r.o same pce fnl f* **5/1**[2]
4634 **4** *hd* **Dark Lane**[6] 3561 8-9-10 **60**........................ LiamKeniry 2 64
(David Evans) *chsd ldrs: rdn 1/2-way: kpt on ins fnl f* **7/4**[1]
6-65 **5** *2* **Captain Ryan**[10] 3426 3-9-1 **57**........................ SteveDrowne 4 52
(Peter Makin) *led: rdn over 1f out: sn hdd: fdd ins fnl f* **5/1**[2]
0602 **6** *1/2* **Homeboy (IRE)**[6] 3549 6-8-4 **45**........................(b) NoelGarbutt(5) 1 40
(David Evans) *racd alone in centre: in tch: rdn 2f out: sn edgd rt and nt go pce of ldrs* **5/1**[2]
57.34s (-0.96) **Going Correction** -0.125s/f (Firm)
**WFA** 3 from 4yo+ 6lb **6** Ran SP% **112.1**
Speed ratings (Par 101): **102,101,100,99,96 95**
CSF £49.30 TOTE £8.00: £1.70, £4.20; EX 52.40 Trifecta £169.80.
**Owner** Richard Ward **Bred** Llety Stud **Trained** Cropthorne, Worcs
**FOCUS**
Moderate sprinting form. The winner is rated to her spring AW form.
T/Plt: £119.20 to a £1 stake. Pool of £58918.06 - 360.66 winning tickets. T/Qpdt: £76.10 to a £1 stake. Pool of £5330.69 - 51.80 winning tickets. RL

# 3497 PONTEFRACT (L-H)
Monday, June 30

**OFFICIAL GOING: Good (7.1)**
Wind: Virtually nil Weather: Fine and dry

## 3785 PATRICIA GEORGE MEMORIAL LADIES' H'CAP (LADY AMATEUR RIDERS) 1m 2f 6y
**2:30** (2:36) (Class 5) (0-75,75) 3-Y-0+ **£3,119** (£967; £483; £242) **Stalls** Low

Form RPR
-064 **1** **El Bravo**[17] 3192 8-9-12 **66**........................ MrsCBartley 3 74
(Shaun Harris) *chsd clr ldr: tk cl order 4f out: sn led: rdn and jnd wl over 1f out: hdd narrowly ent fnl f: drvn and rallied to ld again last 100yds: kpt on* **9/2**[3]
000U **2** *1/2* **Flag Of Glory**[11] 3398 7-8-11 **56** oh2........................ MissMEdden(5) 1 63
(Peter Hiatt) *trckd ldrs: hdwy 3f out: chsd wnr wl over 1f out: slt ld ent fnl f: hdd and no ex last 100yds* **5/1**
0-30 **3** *1 1/2* **Hernando Torres**[30] 2770 6-9-1 **60**........................(p) MrsRWilson(5) 5 64
(Michael Easterby) *hld up in rr: hdwy over 4f out: chsd ldng pair wl over 1f out: sn rdn and no imp* **7/1**
1420 **4** *5* **I'm Super Too (IRE)**[12] 3361 7-10-1 **74**........................ MissMeganNicholls(5) 6 69
(Alan Swinbank) *hld up in tch: hdwy on outer over 4f out: chsd ldng pair 2f out: sn rdn and no imp* **3/1**[2]
4621 **5** *16* **Pertuis (IRE)**[12] 3371 8-10-4 **72**........................(p) MissSBrotherton 8 36
(Micky Hammond) *trckd ldrs: hdwy and cl up 3f out: rdn along wl over 1f out: sn btn* **2/1**[1]
0/0- **6** *6* **Pindar (GER)**[12] 4604 10-9-3 **57**........................(p) MissADeniel 7 10
(Joanne Foster) *led and sn clr: rdn along 4f out: sn wknd and hdd 3f out: sn bhd* **50/1**
234- **7** *19* **Volcanic Jack (IRE)**[194] 5420 6-9-6 **60**........................ MissAliceMills 2
(Michael Chapman) *a in rr: bhd fnl 3f* **14/1**
2m 17.5s (3.80) **Going Correction** +0.35s/f (Good) **7** Ran SP% **114.3**
Speed ratings (Par 103): **98,97,96,92,79 74,59**
CSF £26.95 CT £154.25 TOTE £5.00: £3.10, £3.60; EX 32.10 Trifecta £249.70.
**Owner** www.nottinghamshireracing.co.uk (2) **Bred** D J And Mrs Deer **Trained** Carburton, Notts
■ Stewards' Enquiry : Miss A Deniel five-day ban: use of whip (15-17 23 & 26 July)
**FOCUS**
False rail in place, distances increased by about 12yds. The going was good, although the clerk of the course felt the last 2f was probably just on the slower side. A fair handicap, confined to lady amateur riders, run at a sound pace. The well-backed Aldwick Bay bolted to post and was withdrawn. The winner is rated to his best in the last two years.

## 3786 SPINDRIFTER CONDITIONS STKS (BOBIS RACE) 6f
**3:00** (3:01) (Class 2) 2-Y-0
**£9,337** (£2,796; £1,398; £699; £349; £175) **Stalls** Low

Form RPR
31 **1** **Pallister**[16] 3255 2-9-0 0........................ FrannyNorton 2 82+
(Mark Johnston) *chsd ldrs: rdn along and edgd lft 1/2-way: drvn wl over 1f out: edgd rt and swtchd to outer ent fnl f: styd on strly to ld last 40yds* **5/2**[2]
332 **2** *1 1/4* **Winstanley (IRE)**[16] 3255 2-8-12 0........................ GrahamLee 1 76
(Richard Fahey) *cl up on inner: disp ld 2f out: rdn over 1f out: led jst ins fnl f: sn drvn: hdd and no ex last 40yds* **10/1**
413 **3** *1 1/4* **Red Icon (IRE)**[23] 2987 2-9-0 0........................ RichardKingscote 6 75
(Tom Dascombe) *sn led: rdn along 2f out: drvn and edgd rt ent fnl f: sn hdd and kpt on same pce* **11/8**[1]
24 **4** *2 1/4* **Strategic Order (IRE)**[17] 3201 2-8-12 0........................ PaulMulrennan 5 66
(Paul Midgley) *hld up in rr: pushed along 2f out: kpt on fnl f: nrst fin* **100/1**
41 **5** *3* **Olivia Fallow (IRE)**[12] 3367 2-8-7 0........................ PJMcDonald 3 53
(Paul Midgley) *trckd ldrs: n.m.r on inner whn hit rail and almost uns rdr 2f out: no ch after* **25/1**
1 **6** *1* **Son Of Africa**[21] 3063 2-9-0 0........................ DaneO'Neill 4 56
(Henry Candy) *dwlt: sn trcking ldrs on outer: cl up 1/2-way: chal 2f out and ev ch: rdn and edgd lft appr fnl f: sn wknd* **3/1**[3]
1m 20.36s (3.46) **Going Correction** +0.35s/f (Good) **6** Ran SP% **109.6**
Speed ratings (Par 99): **90,88,86,83,79 78**
CSF £24.68 TOTE £3.60: £2.10, £2.60; EX 12.80 Trifecta £56.00.
**Owner** Sheikh Hamdan bin Mohammed Al Maktoum **Bred** Darley **Trained** Middleham Moor, N Yorks
**FOCUS**
A typically small but select field for this conditions race, which was run at a sound pace. The winner repeated his York form with the runner-up.

## 3787 JACK SMITH - A LIFETIME IN RACING H'CAP 1m 4f 8y
**3:30** (3:32) (Class 4) (0-80,80) 3-Y-0+ **£5,175** (£1,540; £769) **Stalls** Low

Form RPR
6-02 **1** **Only Orsenfoolsies**[17] 3205 5-9-5 **71**........................ PJMcDonald 4 82+
(Micky Hammond) *mde all: rdn 3f out: clr wl over 1f out: kpt on strly* **7/2**[2]
0000 **2** *8* **Bayan Kasirga (IRE)**[13] 3341 4-9-3 **74**........................ SammyJoBell(5) 1 72
(Richard Fahey) *trckd ldng pair: pushed along and outpcd 3f out: rdn 2f out: plugged on one pce to take modest 2nd ins fnl f: no ch w wnr* **7/1**[3]
4-21 **3** *10* **Ruwasi**[24] 2952 3-9-0 **80**........................ PaulMulrennan 3 71
(James Tate) *trckd wnr: effrt and cl up 3f out: rdn along 2f out: sn drvn and wknd over 1f out* **2/5**[1]
2m 43.55s (2.75) **Going Correction** +0.35s/f (Good)
**WFA** 3 from 4yo+ 14lb **3** Ran SP% **106.2**
Speed ratings (Par 105): **104,98,92**
CSF £15.49 TOTE £2.40; EX 10.40 Trifecta £9.40.
**Owner** Foolsies **Bred** Redmyre Bloodstock & Newhall Farm Estate **Trained** Middleham, N Yorks
**FOCUS**
A disappointing turnout for this handicap, which was run at a fair pace. It took no winning.

## 3788 EBF STALLIONS BREEDING WINNERS PARK SUITE FILLIES' H'CAP 6f
**4:00** (4:00) (Class 3) (0-90,89) 3-Y-0+
**£9,337** (£2,796; £1,398; £699; £349; £175) **Stalls** Low

Form RPR
1-01 **1** **Stepping Out (IRE)**[24] 2965 3-9-4 **86**........................ RichardKingscote 5 96+
(Tom Dascombe) *t.k.h: trckd ldng pair: hdwy and cl up 2f out: led wl over 1f out: sn rdn and edgd lft ins fnl f: kpt on* **3/1**[1]
0132 **2** *1 1/4* **Lady Horatia**[14] 3305 3-9-0 **82**........................ StevieDonohoe 4 88+
(William Muir) *dwlt and in rr: hdwy wl over 1f out and sn n.m.r: swtchd rt and rdn appr fnl f: styd on strly towards fin* **11/2**[3]
-054 **3** *3/4* **Misplaced Fortune**[17] 3203 9-9-9 **84**........................(v) SilvestreDeSousa 8 92+
(Nigel Tinkler) *midfield: n.m.r and lost pl over 2f out: hdwy whn bdly hmpd over 1f out: swtchd rt and rdn ent fnl f: styd on strly: nrst fin* **8/1**
5100 **4** *3/4* **Tumblewind**[16] 3239 4-9-10 **88**........................ GeorgeChaloner(3) 3 91
(Richard Whitaker) *trckd ldrs on inner: hdwy wl over 1f out: swtchd rt and rdn appr fnl f: kpt on fnl f* **14/1**
-623 **5** *1 3/4* **Heroique (IRE)**[9] 3460 3-8-7 **75**........................(e) DuranFentiman 2 70
(Tim Easterby) *slt ld: rdn along 2f out: drvn and hdd wl over 1f out: grad wknd fnl f* **25/1**
0-20 **6** *nk* **Tight Fit**[45] 2318 4-9-13 **88**........................ DaneO'Neill 10 84
(Henry Candy) *hld up in rr: hdwy on outer over 2f out: rdn and hung lft over 1f out: sn drvn and no imp fnl f* **16/1**
5-43 **7** *nk* **Augusta Ada**[14] 3300 3-8-10 **78**........................ PaulMulrennan 1 71
(Ollie Pears) *t.k.h: trckd ldng pair on inner: effrt and nt clr run wl over 1f out: sn swtchd rt and shkn up: wknd appr fnl f* **8/1**
600 **8** *7* **Alutiq (IRE)**[12] 3357 3-9-7 **89**........................ JamieSpencer 6 60
(Eve Johnson Houghton) *in tch: pushed along over 2f out: rdn wl over 1f out: sn hmpd and wknd* **9/2**[2]
1111 **9** *23* **Ishiamber**[24] 2945 4-9-10 **85**........................ PatCosgrave 7
(George Baker) *in tch: hdwy on outer 2f out: rdn whn bdly hmpd over 1f out: no ch after* **6/1**
0116 **10** *23* **Links Drive Lady**[24] 2965 6-9-13 **88**........................ RobertWinston 9
(Dean Ivory) *cl up: rdn along 2f out: sn wknd* **20/1**
1m 18.38s (1.48) **Going Correction** +0.35s/f (Good)
**WFA** 3 from 4yo+ 7lb **10** Ran SP% **116.2**
Speed ratings (Par 104): **104,102,101,100,98 97,97,87,57,26**
CSF £19.28 TOTE £4.20: £1.20, £2.40, £3.00; EX 20.90 Trifecta £108.90.
**Owner** Attenborough Bellman Ingram Lowe **Bred** Glending Bloodstock **Trained** Malpas, Cheshire
■ Stewards' Enquiry : George Chaloner two-day ban: careless riding (14-15 July)

**FOCUS**
This competitive handicap was run at a steady pace. Another step up from the winner.

## 3789 WAYNE CONWAY MEMORIAL H'CAP — 1m 4f 8y
4:30 (4:31) (Class 5) (0-70,69) 3-Y-O — £3,234 (£962; £481; £240) Stalls Low

Form — RPR
0-00 1 **Craggaknock**[31] 2735 3-9-1 63 JasonHart 13 76+
(Mark Walford) *mde all: rdn along and green over 2f out: sn clr: styd on strly* **8/1**
44-0 2 2 **Inevitable**[55] 2060 3-9-6 68 FrannyNorton 6 78+
(Mark Johnston) *a.p: hdwy to chse wnr 2f out: drvn appr fnl f: no imp* **8/1**
-323 3 9 **Interconnection**[18] 3135 3-9-4 66 RichardKingscote 5 62
(Ed Vaughan) *chsd ldrs: hdwy 3f out: rdn along 2f out: drvn wl over 1f out and sn one pce* **9/2**[2]
-500 4 1 3/4 **Hallbeck**[18] 3146 3-9-5 67 DaneO'Neill 2 60
(Henry Candy) *hld up and bhd: hdwy over 2f out: rdn wl over 1f out: kpt on: n.d* **4/1**[1]
3026 5 6 **Where's Tiger**[19] 3098 3-8-10 58 RussKennemore 11 41
(Jedd O'Keeffe) *hld up towards rr: stdy hdwy 3f out: rdn 2f out: plugged on: nvr nr ldrs* **16/1**
-235 6 7 **Gavlar**[18] 3146 3-9-6 68 JimCrowley 7 40
(William Knight) *towards rr: hdwy over 3f out: rdn along over 2f out: n.d* **6/1**[3]
-030 7 2 1/4 **Ralphy Lad (IRE)**[15] 3268 3-9-7 69 BenCurtis 1 37
(Alan Swinbank) *hld up and bhd: sme hdwy on inner 2f out: sn rdn and n.d* **20/1**
-555 8 3 **Unfinishedbusiness**[18] 3135 3-8-8 59 GeorgeChaloner(3) 10 23
(Richard Fahey) *in tch: hdwy on outer over 3f out: rdn to chse ldng pair 2f out: sn drvn and wknd* **7/1**
0-35 9 10 **Master Clockmaker (IRE)**[61] 1880 3-9-7 69 PJMcDonald 4 17
(Ann Duffield) *hld up: hdwy and in tch over 4f out: rdn along 3f out: sn wknd* **20/1**
0004 10 7 **To Begin**[35] 2621 3-8-2 50 oh3 SilvestreDeSousa 14
(Tim Easterby) *chsd wnr: rdn along wl over 2f out: sn drvn and wknd wl over 1f out* **28/1**
-555 11 39 **Running Wolf (IRE)**[14] 3303 3-9-5 67 (p) PaulMulrennan 9
(Michael Dods) *chsd ldrs: rdn along over 3f out: sn wknd* **25/1**
2520 12 7 **Aldreth**[18] 3135 3-8-11 59 (p) GrahamGibbons 8
(Michael Easterby) *in tch: rdn along over 3f out: sn wknd* **20/1**
0-50 13 31 **Oscuro**[26] 2899 3-8-6 54 (b[1]) DuranFentiman 15
(Tim Easterby) *midfield: rdn along over 5f out: sn bhd* **40/1**

2m 40.04s (-0.76) **Going Correction** +0.35s/f (Good) **13 Ran SP% 117.1**
Speed ratings (Par 99): **116,114,108,107,103 98,97,95,88,84 58,53,32**
CSF £61.43 CT £326.29 TOTE £9.10: £3.30, £3.30, £1.70; EX 62.40 Trifecta £531.90.
**Owner** Mrs Mary & David Longstaff **Bred** Lady Davis **Trained** Sherriff Hutton, N Yorks

**FOCUS**
The pace was sound for this open handicap and it was the standout time on the card. It paid to race handy. Improvement from the winner.

## 3790 WILFRED UNDERWOOD MEMORIAL CLASSIFIED STKS — 6f
5:00 (5:00) (Class 5) 3-Y-O — £3,234 (£962; £481; £240) Stalls Low

Form — RPR
-214 1 **Boy In The Bar**[26] 2897 3-9-0 75 (b) RobertWinston 7 87
(David Barron) *chsd ldrs: hdwy on outer and cl up over 2f out: rdn to ld wl over 1f out: sn clr and kpt on strly* **5/1**[2]
U221 2 5 **Naggers (IRE)**[35] 2619 3-9-0 75 GrahamLee 1 77+
(Paul Midgley) *dwlt sltly: t.k.h and sn trcking ldrs: nt clr run and sltly hmpd over 2f out: effrt and n.m.r wl over 1f out: sn rdn and kpt on fnl f: no ch w wnr* **10/11**[1]
3 3 3 1/4 **Jaeger Train (IRE)**[58] 1940 3-9-0 73 BenCurtis 5 61
(K R Burke) *led: rdn along over 2f out: hdd and drvn wl over 1f out: grad wknd* **5/1**[2]
-345 4 5 **Got To Dance**[31] 2717 3-9-0 73 JimCrowley 4 45
(Ralph Beckett) *towards rr: hdwy 2f out: sn rdn and plugged on: nvr nr ldrs* **9/1**
1430 5 2 1/2 **Searchlight**[21] 3067 3-9-0 75 JamieSpencer 2 37
(Kevin Ryan) *prom: rdn along over 2f out: wknd wl over 1f out* **8/1**[3]
1-06 6 2 1/4 **Chorlton Manor (IRE)**[21] 3068 3-9-0 75 (p) StevieDonohoe 3 29
(Tim Pitt) *chsd ldrs: rdn along over 2f out: sn wknd* **25/1**
1004 7 11 **Android (IRE)**[16] 3225 3-9-0 75 (v) DaneO'Neill 6
(Clive Cox) *hld up: a in rr: bhd and eased fr wl over 1f out* **20/1**

1m 18.21s (1.31) **Going Correction** +0.35s/f (Good) **7 Ran SP% 115.4**
Speed ratings (Par 99): **105,98,94,87,84 81,66**
CSF £10.17 TOTE £5.40: £2.10, £1.50; EX 14.40 Trifecta £33.40.
**Owner** S Rudolf **Bred** Brinkley Stud S R L **Trained** Maunby, N Yorks

**FOCUS**
Only 2lb covered the seven runners for this classified stakes, which was run at an honest pace. The winner is rated in line with his maiden win.

## 3791 ANN & GEORGE DUFFIELD - SUNHILL-LODGES.CO.UK H'CAP — 1m 4y
5:30 (5:30) (Class 5) (0-75,76) 3-Y-O+ — £3,234 (£962; £481; £240) Stalls Low

Form — RPR
2560 1 **Shadowtime**[5] 3572 9-9-13 74 RobertWinston 8 83
(Tracy Waggott) *in tch on inner: effrt over 2f out: rdn along wl over 1f out: swtchd rt to outer and hdwy ent fnl f: styd on strly to ld nr fin* **9/1**
0-00 2 hd **Checkpoint**[49] 2215 5-9-2 63 BarryMcHugh 4 71
(Tony Coyle) *hld up in tch: hdwy wl over 1f out: rdn ent fnl f: led last 100yds: drvn and hdd nr fin* **10/1**
-055 3 1/2 **Janaab (IRE)**[11] 3400 4-8-12 59 (t) DavidAllan 3 66
(Tim Easterby) *led: rdn along over 2f out: hrd pressed and drvn over 1f out: hdd and no ex last 100yds* **10/1**
-200 4 3 **Sword Of The Lord**[35] 2603 4-10-0 75 (t) JamieSpencer 5 75
(George Margarson) *dwlt and in rr: hdwy on outer over 2f out: rdn to chal over 1f out: ev ch tl drvn: edgd lft and one pce ins fnl f* **4/1**[2]
6025 5 1 3/4 **Shearian**[10] 3439 4-8-13 60 FrannyNorton 1 56
(Tracy Waggott) *trckd ldr on inner: rdn along over 2f out: drvn wl over 1f out: grad wknd fnl f* **4/1**[2]
4513 6 nk **Botanist**[20] 3075 7-8-9 56 oh4 BenCurtis 7 51
(Shaun Harris) *in tch: hdwy on outer 1/2-way and sn cl up: rdn to chal 2f out: sn ev ch tl drvn and wknd ins fnl f* **16/1**
3151 7 14 **Ellaal**[14] 3301 5-9-7 68 PaulMulrennan 6 31
(Ruth Carr) *chsd ldrs: rdn along wl over 2f out: sn wknd* **7/2**[1]
0000 8 34 **Rocket Ronnie (IRE)**[44] 2351 4-9-13 74 AdrianNicholls 9
(David Nicholls) *prom: cl up 1/2-way: rdn along over 2f out: wknd qckly: sn bhd and eased* **9/2**[3]

1m 48.26s (2.36) **Going Correction** +0.35s/f (Good) **8 Ran SP% 114.5**
Speed ratings (Par 103): **102,101,101,98,96 96,82,48**
CSF £93.25 CT £925.89 TOTE £11.30: £3.10, £2.50, £1.70; EX 138.40 Trifecta £878.80.
**Owner** H Conlon **Bred** Darley **Trained** Spennymoor, Co Durham
■ Stewards' Enquiry : Robert Winston two-day ban: use of whip (14-15 July)

**FOCUS**
They went a sound pace for this fair handicap. The winner's best form in the past year.
T/Plt: £345.20 to a £1 stake. Pool of £83196.43 - 175.90 winning tickets. T/Qpdt: £13.50 to a £1 stake. Pool of £6613.52 - 360.21 winning tickets. JR

# 3401 SOUTHWELL (L-H)
Monday, June 30

**OFFICIAL GOING: Standard**
Wind: Almost nil Weather: Cloudy with sunny spells

## 3792 32RED H'CAP — 6f (F)
2:15 (2:16) (Class 6) (0-65,65) 3-Y-O — £2,264 (£673; £336; £168) Stalls Low

Form — RPR
-230 1 **Misstemper (IRE)**[29] 2802 3-9-6 64 RaulDaSilva 10 69
(Jose Santos) *chsd ldrs: rdn 1/2-way: swtchd rt over 1f out: r.o to ld post* **7/2**[2]
3022 2 hd **Meebo (IRE)**[11] 3406 3-9-2 60 (vt) NickyMackay 6 64
(J R Jenkins) *led: hdd over 3f out: rdn over 1f out: led ins fnl f: hdd post* **5/2**[1]
0060 3 2 1/4 **Classical Diva**[7] 3534 3-8-4 51 (b) NeilFarley(3) 9 48
(Declan Carroll) *s.i.s: hdwy on outer over 4f out: led over 3f out: rdn and edgd lft over 1f out: hdd and unable qck ins fnl f* **14/1**
2030 4 2 3/4 **Roomie**[42] 2388 3-8-7 51 (be) AndrewElliott 12 39
(Tim Easterby) *chsd ldrs: pushed along over 3f out: sn outpcd: styd on appr fnl f* **5/1**
2025 5 1/2 **Under Approval**[48] 2230 3-8-13 62 GemmaTutty(5) 5 48
(Karen Tutty) *sn outpcd: r.o wl ins fnl f: nt rch ldrs* **16/1**
0-34 6 shd **Templar Boy**[25] 2932 3-8-8 55 ConnorBeasley(3) 11 41
(J R Jenkins) *s.i.s: hdwy over 3f out: sn outpcd: hung lft and styd on ins fnl f* **4/1**[3]
0-00 7 11 **Stream Of Light**[3] 3650 3-8-3 47 oh1 ow1 JoeFanning 7
(John Mackie) *prom: lost pl over 4f out: wknd over 3f out* **12/1**
34-0 8 2 3/4 **Brave Imp**[19] 3124 3-9-4 62 [1] TomEaves 2 4
(Kevin Ryan) *sn pushed along to chse ldrs: rdn over 3f out: sn wknd* **10/1**
0-00 9 2 1/4 **Weisse Girl**[44] 2355 3-8-5 49 (p) JamesSullivan 8
(Nick Kent) *hmpd sn after s: in rr: wknd over 3f out* **33/1**
000- 10 9 **Sherry For Nanny (IRE)**[279] 6725 3-8-5 49 (b[1]) RoystonFfrench 4
(Marjorie Fife) *prom tl rdn and wknd over 3f out* **33/1**

1m 18.34s (1.84) **Going Correction** +0.175s/f (Slow) **10 Ran SP% 122.7**
Speed ratings (Par 97): **94,93,90,87,86 86,71,67,64,52**
CSF £13.45 CT £110.74 TOTE £6.40: £2.00, £1.30, £4.60; EX 13.20 Trifecta £178.80.
**Owner** Bob Cooper & Val Dean **Bred** Orbit Performance & John Cullinan **Trained** Upper Lambourn, Berks
■ The first winner for Brazilian trainer Jose Santos.

**FOCUS**
A couple of unexposed sorts in a modest handicap. Although the gallop was sound, the time suggested the surface was on the slow side and the action unfolded in the centre. The winner is rated to her maiden best.

## 3793 ALL NEW 32REDSPORT.COM (S) STKS — 5f (F)
2:45 (2:45) (Class 6) 3-Y-O+ — £2,102 (£625; £312; £156) Stalls Low

Form — RPR
5215 1 **Abi Scarlet (IRE)**[26] 2905 5-8-12 80 CharlieBennett(7) 4 79
(Hughie Morrison) *chsd ldrs: outpcd 1/2-way: rallied and swtchd rt over 1f out: led ins fnl f: sn clr* **4/6**[1]
400 2 2 1/2 **First In Command (IRE)**[25] 2933 9-9-5 72 (t) ShaneKelly 6 70
(Daniel Mark Loughnane) *chsd ldrs: wnt 2nd 2f out: led on bit 1f out: shkn up and hdd ins fnl f: styd on same pce* **7/1**[3]
0066 3 3 **Foxy Music**[25] 2933 10-9-10 80 (b) TonyHamilton 5 64
(Tony Coyle) *chsd ldrs: outpcd wl over 3f out: styd on ins fnl f: wnt 3rd nr fin* **4/1**[2]
5261 4 hd **Dissent (IRE)**[88] 1270 5-9-7 58 (b) ConnorBeasley(3) 1 63
(James Given) *chsd ldrs: led 2f out: rdn and hdd 1f out: no ex* **8/1**
0330 5 3 1/2 **Casper Lee (IRE)**[11] 3407 3-8-8 51 (b) JacobButterfield(5) 3 44
(Michael Herrington) *s.s: outpcd* **25/1**
2063 6 2 3/4 **Pearl Noir**[26] 2907 4-9-5 58 (b) TomEaves 7 36
(Scott Dixon) *led 3f: sn rdn: wknd fnl f* **16/1**

1m 0.52s (0.82) **Going Correction** +0.20s/f (Slow)
**WFA** 3 from 4yo+ 6lb **6 Ran SP% 113.3**
Speed ratings (Par 101): **101,97,92,91,86 81**
CSF £6.26 TOTE £1.40: £1.10, £3.20; EX 5.90 Trifecta £17.60.The winner was bought by S Dixon for 10,250gns.
**Owner** H Morrison **Bred** Henry O'Callaghan **Trained** East Ilsley, Berks

**FOCUS**
A range of ability on show. The gallop was sound and the useful winner raced towards the stands' side from halfway. The form is rated on the cautious side.

## 3794 32RED CASINO BRITISH STALLION STUDS EBF MAIDEN STKS — 7f (F)
3:15 (3:17) (Class 5) 2-Y-O — £3,396 (£1,010; £505; £252) Stalls High

Form — RPR
23 1 **Spindle (IRE)**[11] 3403 2-9-0 0 AndrewMullen 3 69
(Mark Usher) *mde all: shkn up 2f out: styd on wl* **6/4**[2]
2 3 1/2 **Polarisation** 2-9-5 0 JoeFanning 4 65+
(Mark Johnston) *chsd wnr: shkn up over 2f out: edgd lft over 1f out: styd on same pce fnl f* **5/6**[1]
6 3 10 **Theydon Thunder**[11] 3403 2-9-2 0 RosieJessop(3) 2 38
(Peter Charalambous) *chsd ldrs: rdn over 2f out: edgd lft and wknd wl over 1f out* **50/1**
3 4 3 **Forgiving Glance**[17] 3186 2-9-0 0 TomEaves 1 24
(Philip Kirby) *w wnr tl over 4f out: rdn and wknd over 2f out* **10/1**[3]
5 69 **Capitaine** 2-8-12 0 GaryMahon(7) 6
(Seamus Mullins) *s.s: outpcd* **33/1**

1m 31.88s (1.58) **Going Correction** +0.175s/f (Slow) **5 Ran SP% 108.5**
Speed ratings (Par 93): **97,93,81,78,**
CSF £2.96 TOTE £2.30: £1.10, £1.10; EX 3.50 Trifecta £23.90.
**Owner** Saxon House Racing **Bred** M Vsetecka **Trained** Upper Lambourn, Berks


The Form Book, Raceform Ltd, Newbury, RG14 5SJ

**FOCUS**
A most uncompetitive maiden in which the gallop was no more than fair. The winner came down the centre and the bare form is ordinary.

## 3795 BET NOW AT 32REDSPORT.COM APPRENTICE CLAIMING STKS 7f (F)
3:45 (3:46) (Class 6) 4-Y-0+ £2,296 (£683; £341; £170) Stalls High

Form RPR
0-00 1 **Gaelic Wizard (IRE)**56 2029 6-8-11 57 GemmaTutty(3) 9 64
(Karen Tutty) *a.p: rdn 1/2-way: led over 1f out: hdd wl ins fnl f: styd on to ld nr fin* **50/1**
0053 2 nk **Warfare**42 2399 5-9-12 63 (b) KevinStott 6 75
(Kevin Ryan) *chsd ldr tl led 1/2-way: rdn and hdd over 1f out: rallied to ld wl ins fnl f: hdd nr fin* **12/1**
0543 3 1 1/4 **My Son Max**28 2841 6-9-3 79 JackGarritty(3) 2 66
(Michael Blake) *s.i.s: hld up: drvn along 1/2-way: hdwy 2f out: styd on* **9/2**3
3006 4 hd **Masai Moon**20 3088 10-9-0 68 (b) PatMillman(3) 3 62
(Rod Millman) *sn pushed along in rr: r.o ins fnl f: nrst fin* **16/1**
4504 5 3/4 **Intrepid (IRE)**26 2905 4-9-4 71 GeorgeDowning 4 61
(Ian Williams) *hld up in tch: rdn over 1f out: styd on same pce ins fnl f* **2/1**1
-220 6 1/2 **Midaz**33 2669 4-9-7 66 CharlieBennett(5) 7 68
(Hughie Morrison) *chsd ldrs: rdn 1/2-way: outpcd over 2f out: rallied over 1f out: styd on same pce ins fnl f* **6/1**
04-0 7 2 1/4 **Fast Finian (IRE)**19 3122 5-9-1 85 (b) JoeDoyle(3) 5 54
(Paul D'Arcy) *led to 1/2-way: rdn over 1f out: no ex fnl f* **9/4**2
0000 8 6 **Red Explorer (USA)**4 3611 4-8-11 60 (b1) GaryMahon(5) 10 37
(Ann Stokell) *chsd ldrs: rdn 1/2-way: wknd fnl f* **20/1**
2006 9 3 **Officer In Command (USA)**26 2901 8-9-3 62 (p) GeorgiaCox(5) 8 35
(John Butler) *s.i.s: sn pushed along and a in rr* **50/1**

1m 31.59s (1.29) **Going Correction** +0.175s/f (Slow) 9 Ran SP% **118.8**
Speed ratings (Par 101): **99,98,97,97,96 95,93,86,82**
CSF £560.04 TOTE £48.60: £12.20, £3.30, £1.30; EX 677.50 Trifecta £4968.60 Part won..
**Owner** Grange Park Racing **Bred** Mrs Mary Gallagher **Trained** Osmotherley, N Yorks

**FOCUS**
A reasonable claimer on paper, but a race that took less winning than seemed likely with a couple of the market leaders disappointing. The winner came down the in the straight and the form is rated a bit cautiously.

## 3796 RACING SPECIALS AT 32REDSPORT.COM MEDIAN AUCTION MAIDEN STKS 1m 4f (F)
4:15 (4:16) (Class 6) 3-4-Y-0 £2,264 (£673; £336; £168) Stalls Low

Form RPR
0 1 **Dino Mite**66 1701 3-8-9 0 ShaneKelly 3 83+
(Peter Chapple-Hyam) *s.i.s: rcvrd to ld after 1f: clr over 4f out: canter* **3/1**2
0-62 2 18 **Kirkman (IRE)**35 2616 3-9-0 58 TedDurcan 6 55
(James Bethell) *led 1f: chsd wnr: rdn over 4f out: styd on same pce fnl 3f* **3/1**2
2335 3 10 **Hallouella**19 3120 3-8-9 59 (p) JimmyQuinn 1 41
(James Tate) *sn pushed along to chse ldrs: rdn over 5f out: wknd 3f out: eased fnl f* **4/1**3
4 10 **Air Squadron**234 4-9-7 0 PatrickO'Donnell(7) 7 36
(Ralph Beckett) *chsd ldrs: rdn over 5f out: wknd over 3f out: eased over 1f out* **6/4**1
0 5 shd **Arryzona**27 2877 3-9-0 0 AdamBeschizza 4 23
(Christine Dunnett) *prom: racd keenly: hung rt and lost pl after 2f: bhd fnl 8f* **50/1**
6 61 **Big Fortune** 4-10-0 0 (t) DavidProbert 2
(David C Griffiths) *s.i.s: hld up: rdn over 6f out: sn wknd* **25/1**

2m 42.66s (1.66) **Going Correction** +0.175s/f (Slow)
**WFA** 3 from 4yo 14lb 6 Ran SP% **115.8**
Speed ratings (Par 101): **101,89,82,75,75 34**
CSF £12.95 TOTE £5.40: £2.30, £2.20; EX 14.60 Trifecta £36.80.
**Owner** P Cunningham **Bred** P Cunningham **Trained** Newmarket, Suffolk

**FOCUS**
A very one-sided maiden in which the gallop was reasonable. The winner came down the centre in the straight. The time was 30lb slower than the following handicapand it's hard to know what the winner chieved.

## 3797 32RED.COM H'CAP (BOBIS RACE) 1m 4f (F)
4:45 (4:45) (Class 4) (0-80,80) 3-Y-0 £5,175 (£1,540; £769; £384) Stalls Low

Form RPR
1 1 **From Frost**97 1088 3-9-7 80 (t) DavidProbert 5 96
(Andrew Balding) *prom: pushed along and lost pl over 7f out: hdwy over 3f out: led over 2f out: rdn clr fr over 1f out: eased nr fin* **9/2**3
0061 2 9 **Daydreamer**11 3391 3-8-10 71 oh2 MartinHarley 4 71+
(William Haggas) *trckd ldrs: wnt 2nd over 2f out: sn rdn: styd on same pce fr over 1f out* **3/1**2
-202 3 2 1/2 **Ultimate Act**25 2925 3-9-2 75 ShaneKelly 2 73
(Seamus Mullins) *led: rdn and hdd over 4f out: led again over 3f out: hdd over 2f out: styd on same pce* **8/1**
3010 4 7 **Sellingallthetime (IRE)**15 3268 3-8-5 72 oh1 ow1(p) AlistairRawlinson(7) 1 58
(Michael Appleby) *s.i.s: hdwy over 7f out: led over 4f out tl over 3f out: rdn and wknd over 1f out* **6/4**1
0026 5 28 **Master Dan**35 2621 3-8-4 71 oh5 (b1) ConnorBeasley(3) 6 8
(James Given) *chsd ldr after 1f tl 1/2-way: rdn over 4f out: wknd 3f out* **20/1**
-150 6 13 **Blue Atlantic (USA)**9 3491 3-9-3 76 JoeFanning 3
(Mark Johnston) *chsd ldrs tl rdn and wknd over 3f out* **7/1**

2m 40.57s (-0.43) **Going Correction** +0.175s/f (Slow) 6 Ran SP% **111.6**
Speed ratings (Par 101): **108,102,100,95,77 68**
CSF £18.04 TOTE £4.40: £2.50, £2.10; EX 15.90 Trifecta £59.40.
**Owner** George Strawbridge **Bred** George Strawbridge **Trained** Kingsclere, Hants

**FOCUS**
A couple of previous winners came to the fore in a fair handicap. The pace was fair and the ready winner came down the centre, in a time 301lb faster than the previous maiden. The form could be rated a bit higher.

## 3798 32RED ON THE APP STORE H'CAP 1m (F)
5:15 (5:16) (Class 6) (0-60,57) 3-Y-0+ £2,264 (£673; £336; £168) Stalls Low

Form RPR
-405 1 **Hayek**41 2427 7-9-3 46 (b) AndrewElliott 4 56
(Tim Easterby) *hld up: hdwy over 1f out: r.o to ld nr fin* **20/1**
U20 2 1/2 **Columbian Roulette (IRE)**13 3326 3-9-2 55 PaddyAspell 9 62+
(Charles Hills) *a.p: chsd ldr over 6f out: rdn over 1f out: styd on to ld wl ins fnl f: hdd nr fin* **7/2**1
0-06 3 nk **Benidorm**12 3363 6-8-11 45 (e) DuilioDaSilva(5) 8 53
(Richard Guest) *hld up: hdwy over 4f out: rdn over 3f out: ev ch wl ins fnl f: unable qck nr fin* **33/1**
2-00 4 4 1/2 **Wotalad**13 3339 4-9-9 52 TonyHamilton 6 50
(Richard Whitaker) *led 1f: chsd ldrs: rdn over 1f out: styd same pce fr over 1f out* **16/1**
0355 5 1 **Puppet Theatre (IRE)**25 2937 4-8-13 45 SamJames(3) 10 41+
(David O'Meara) *led 7f out: clr 3f out: rdn over 1f out: wknd and hdd wl ins fnl f* **9/2**3
2222 6 2 1/2 **General Tufto**25 2937 9-9-10 56 (b) BillyCray(3) 2 46
(Charles Smith) *sn outpcd: sme hdwy u.p over 1f out: nvr on terms* **4/1**2
0-30 7 hd **Pim Street (USA)**25 2937 4-10-0 57 (v) DanielTudhope 3 46
(David O'Meara) *prom: rdn over 2f out: wknd over 1f out* **6/1**
2103 8 4 1/2 **Just Five (IRE)**65 1745 8-9-2 48 (v) ConnorBeasley(3) 7 27
(John Weymes) *s.i.s: sn outpcd* **5/1**
0400 9 4 **Daneside (IRE)**7 3535 7-9-2 45 (vt) PaulPickard 11 15
(Simon West) *s.i.s: hdwy over 6f out: rdn and wknd over 3f out* **33/1**
4325 10 3 1/2 **Banreenahreenkah (IRE)**16 3224 4-9-13 56 (b1) DavidProbert 1 18
(Paul Fitzsimons) *mid-div: lost pl over 5f out: wknd over 3f out* **20/1**
0040 11 2 1/4 **Habeshia**32 2689 4-9-6 49 (vt) JohnFahy 5 6
(John Best) *chsd ldrs tl rdn and wknd over 3f out* **7/1**

1m 47.65s (3.95) **Going Correction** +0.175s/f (Slow)
**WFA** 3 from 4yo+ 10lb 11 Ran SP% **125.1**
Speed ratings (Par 101): **87,86,86,81,80 78,78,73,69,66 63**
CSF £91.30 CT £2418.14 TOTE £21.90: £6.10, £2.20, £10.10; EX 158.50 Trifecta £3604.50.
**Owner** Habton Farms **Bred** Cranford Stud **Trained** Great Habton, N Yorks

**FOCUS**
Not many unexposed types in a moderate handicap. The gallop was strong and the winner raced centre-to-far side in the straight. He arrested a slide over the last couple of years.
T/Plt: £24.80 to a £1 stake. Pool of £73768.46 - 2169.44 winning tickets. T/Qpdt: £9.50 to a £1 stake. Pool of £5379.97 - 417.80 winning tickets. CR

# 3755 WINDSOR (R-H)
Monday, June 30

**OFFICIAL GOING: Good (8.6)**
Wind: Almost nil Weather: Cloudy, becoming fine after race 4

## 3799 EBF STALLIONS MEDIAN AUCTION MAIDEN FILLIES' STKS (BOBIS RACE) 5f 10y
6:00 (6:01) (Class 5) 2-Y-0 £2,911 (£866; £432; £216) Stalls Low

Form RPR
4 1 **Rosie's Premiere (IRE)**16 3232 2-8-11 0 RyanTate(3) 8 78+
(Dean Ivory) *chsd ldrs in 6th and racd on outer: gd prog fr 2f out to ld 1f out: stl green but cajoled along and sn clr* **15/2**3
3 2 2 **Robin Hill**14 3312 2-9-0 0 SamHitchcott 4 71
(William Muir) *chsd ldng pair: urged along over 2f out: styd on fr over 1f out to take 2nd nr fin* **25/1**
62 3 1/2 **Crawford Avenue**16 3215 2-9-0 0 AdamKirby 7 69
(Clive Cox) *w ldr: led 2f out: sn rdn: hdd 1f out: one pce and lost 2nd nr fin* **4/6**1
0 4 4 **Kansai**19 3107 2-9-0 0 AndreaAtzeni 1 55
(David Simcock) *sltly awkward s: chsd ldrs in 5th: shkn up 2f out and no imp 2f out: fdd fnl f* **12/1**
5 1 1/2 **Mazoula (IRE)** 2-9-0 0 RichardHughes 3 49+
(Hugo Palmer) *dwlt: off the pce in last trio: taken to outer over 1f out: nudged along and kpt on steadily* **8/1**
0 6 3/4 **Fine Judgment**20 3076 2-9-0 0 HayleyTurner 6 47
(William Muir) *led to 2f out: wknd over 1f out* **33/1**
7 2 1/4 **Vinamar (IRE)** 2-9-0 0 SeanLevey 2 38+
(Roger Teal) *dwlt: off the pce in last trio: nvr a factor* **50/1**
8 3 3/4 **Noble Cause** 2-9-0 0 FergusSweeney 5 25+
(Luke Dace) *s.v.s: detached in last most of way* **33/1**
5 9 1/2 **Strategise (IRE)**26 2888 2-9-0 0 StephenCraine 9 23
(Tom Dascombe) *dwlt: rcvrd to chse ldrs: wknd qckly 2f out* **7/1**2

1m 0.05s (-0.25) **Going Correction** -0.275s/f (Firm) 9 Ran SP% **114.7**
Speed ratings (Par 90): **91,87,87,80,78 77,73,67,66**
CSF £167.78 TOTE £8.50: £2.00, £2.90, £1.10; EX 58.20 Trifecta £116.30.
**Owner** Mrs Heather Yarrow **Bred** Yeomanstown Stud **Trained** Radlett, Herts

**FOCUS**
Top bend dolled out 5yds from normal inner configuration adding 16yds to races of one mile and beyond. Inner of Straight on normal racing line. Probably just an ordinary fillies' maiden. The form fits in with the race average.

## 3800 UNIBET ROAD TO RIO CHALLENGE (S) STKS 6f
6:30 (6:30) (Class 6) 3-Y-0+ £1,940 (£577; £288; £144) Stalls Low

Form RPR
2151 1 **Ocean Legend (IRE)**6 3555 9-9-8 67 AdamKirby 5 66
(Tony Carroll) *trckd ldr: shkn up to ld wl over 1f out: v hrd pressed fnl f: jst hld on* **6/5**2
33-3 2 nse **Hipz (IRE)**87 1277 3-8-5 70 MartinLane 4 54
(George Baker) *hld up bhd ldrs: prog on outer to go 2nd over 1f out: hrd rdn and sustained chal fnl f: jst failed* **10/11**1
0600 3 3 3/4 **Fleeting Indian (IRE)**13 3323 5-8-10 41 (v1) DanielCremin(7) 2 49
(Linda Jewell) *led: rdn over 2f out: hdd wl over 1f out: one pce after* **50/1**
-400 4 4 **Staines Massive**19 3123 4-9-3 45 (v1) RobertHavlin 3 36
(Jane Chapple-Hyam) *trckd ldng pair: shkn up and no rspnse over 2f out: wl btn over 1f out* **20/1**3
65 5 1/2 **Forceful Beacon**7 3517 4-9-3 0 WilliamCarson 6 35
(Tony Carroll) *stdd s: hld up in last: nvr on terms: no ch whn rdn fnl f* **20/1**3

1m 12.7s (-0.30) **Going Correction** -0.275s/f (Firm)
**WFA** 3 from 4yo+ 7lb 5 Ran SP% **109.3**
Speed ratings (Par 101): **91,90,85,80,79**
CSF £2.51 TOTE £2.00: £1.10, £1.10; EX 2.60 Trifecta £15.40.There was no bid for the winner. Hipz was claimed by L J Mongan for £5000.
**Owner** W McLuskey **Bred** Mark Commins **Trained** Cropthorne, Worcs

**FOCUS**
An uncompetitive affair, effectively a match. The poor third limits the form.

## 3801 UNIBET INJURY TIME INSURANCE IN BRAZIL MAIDEN FILLIES' STKS 6f

**7:00** (7:01) (Class 5) 3-4-Y-0 **£2,587** (£770; £384; £192) **Stalls** Low

Form RPR

23-2 **1** **Mia San Triple**[52] 2126 3-9-0 76 RichardHughes 13 82
(Jeremy Noseda) *taken down early: mde all: shkn up and looked wl in command over 1f out: rdn out last 150yds* **6/4**[1]

43 **2** 3/4 **Belletriste (FR)**[24] 2946 3-8-9 0 JoshBaudains(5) 6 79
(Sylvester Kirk) *dwlt: wl off the pce early: gd prog on outer over 2f out: tk 2nd ins fnl f: styd on but unable to chal* **16/1**

0-3 **3** 3 **Lady Sparkler (IRE)**[9] 3469 3-9-0 0 AndreaAtzeni 11 70
(Roger Varian) *sn chsd wnr: rdn and no imp wl over 1f out: one pce and lost 2nd ins fnl f* **5/2**[2]

04 **4** 1 3/4 **Marydale**[20] 3083 3-9-0 0 FergusSweeney 4 64
(Henry Candy) *hld up in midfield: lft bhd by ldrs over 2f out: shkn up and kpt on fr 2f out: n.d* **3/1**[3]

0- **5** 4 **Plauseabella**[260] 7218 3-9-0 0 TomQueally 5 51
(Stuart Kittow) *t.k.h: chsd ldrs: outpcd over 2f out: no imp after* **33/1**

0-0 **6** hd **Diamond Solitaire (IRE)**[52] 2125 3-9-0 0 SamHitchcott 1 51
(Timothy Jarvis) *chsd ldng pair: rdn over 2f out: wknd fnl f* **50/1**

30 **7** 1/2 **Lunarian**[24] 2946 3-8-11 0 CharlesBishop(3) 2 49
(Mick Channon) *a in midfield: outpcd over 2f out: shkn up and no prog after* **25/1**

**8** 1 1/4 **Hardy Pink (IRE)** 3-9-0 0 AdamKirby 14 45
(Jamie Osborne) *slowly away: wl off the pce in last pair: nvr a factor: passed a few late on* **12/1**

5 **9** 1/2 **Nora Batty**[24] 2946 3-8-9 0 RyanWhile(5) 10 43
(Bill Turner) *spped to 1/2-way: sn wknd* **40/1**

00 **10** shd **Sterling Kate**[9] 3469 3-9-0 0 RobertHavlin 8 43
(Roger Ingram) *a towards rr: lft bhd fr over 2f out: pushed along and nvr on terms after* **80/1**

**11** 13 **Tobago Cays** 3-8-9 0 MarcMonaghan(5) 12
(Bill Turner) *s.s: a detached in last: t.o* **100/1**

1m 11.3s (-1.70) **Going Correction** -0.275s/f (Firm) **11** Ran SP% **120.6**
Speed ratings (Par 100): **100,99,95,92,87 87,86,84,84,83 66**
CSF £28.46 TOTE £2.60: £1.50, £3.60, £1.10; EX 25.40 Trifecta £33.40.
**Owner** Gute Freunde Partnership **Bred** Aiden Murphy **Trained** Newmarket, Suffolk

**FOCUS**
Not many got into this ordinary fillies' maiden but those with the best form on the board came to the fore and the winner has an official rating of 76. The form could be rated a few pounds higher.

## 3802 NEW HORSE RACING ODDS AT UNIBET.CO.UK H'CAP 1m 2f 7y

**7:30** (7:30) (Class 4) (0-85,84) 4-Y-0+ **£5,175** (£1,540; £769; £384) **Stalls** Low

Form RPR

231 **1** **Perfect Cracker**[21] 3065 6-8-10 76 RyanTate(3) 1 85
(Clive Cox) *hld up in 7th: stdy prog towards outer over 2f out gng strly: clsd on ldrs over 1f out: led jst ins fnl f: drvn out* **4/1**[3]

3-12 **2** 1 **Red Warrior (IRE)**[21] 3065 4-9-7 84 TomQueally 2 91
(Ismail Mohammed) *t.k.h early: hld up in 5th: drvn and prog on outer 2f out: styd on to take 2nd wl ins fnl f: unable to chal* **9/4**[1]

0400 **3** 1 1/4 **Tinshu (IRE)**[35] 2627 8-9-0 77 (p) HayleyTurner 5 82
(Derek Haydn Jones) *trckd ldng trio: clsd on outer over 2f out: led over 1f out: drvn and hdd jst ins fnl f: one pce* **16/1**

2-06 **4** 2 1/4 **Silver Dixie (USA)**[26] 2882 4-8-12 78 CharlesBishop(3) 8 79
(Peter Hedger) *led: rdn 2f out: hdd over 1f out: fdd fnl f* **9/1**

0640 **5** 2 **Karam Albaari (IRE)**[93] 1175 6-9-4 81 FrederikTylicki 4 78
(J R Jenkins) *hld up in 6th: jst pushed along over 2f out: no ch whn shkn up over 1f out: kpt on fnl f: nvr involved* **16/1**

540 **6** 1 1/2 **Commissar**[18] 3172 5-8-13 76 RichardHughes 3 70
(Ian Williams) *dwlt: hld up in last: shkn up over 2f out: modest prog over 1f out: no ch and eased nr fin* **7/1**

35-0 **7** 7 **Al Jamal**[25] 2922 4-9-5 82 SeanLevey 7 63
(Jeremy Gask) *sn chsd ldng pair: rdn over 2f out: sn wknd* **25/1**

006- **8** 1 1/4 **Greeleys Love (USA)**[345] 4537 4-9-4 81 AdamKirby 6 59
(Mark Johnston) *sn pressed ldr: rdn over 2f out: lost 2nd and wknd qckly wl over 1f out* **3/1**[2]

2m 3.9s (-4.80) **Going Correction** -0.325s/f (Firm) **8** Ran SP% **113.9**
Speed ratings (Par 105): **106,105,104,102,100 99,94,93**
CSF £13.31 CT £126.16 TOTE £4.60: £1.60, £1.60, £3.40; EX 7.50 Trifecta £91.90.
**Owner** Mildmay Racing **Bred** Mildmay Bloodstock Ltd **Trained** Lambourn, Berks

**FOCUS**
A straightforward handicap to assess, with the winner confirming C&D latest with the runner-up.

## 3803 UNIBET - BY PLAYERS FOR PLAYERS FILLIES' H'CAP 1m 3f 135y

**8:00** (8:00) (Class 5) (0-70,69) 3-Y-0+ **£2,911** (£866; £432; £216) **Stalls** Centre

Form RPR

3325 **1** **Yeah Baby (IRE)**[49] 2225 3-9-0 69 TomQueally 8 76
(Charles Hills) *hld up in rr: progres fr jst over 3f out: drvn to cl on ldrs over 1f out: edgd rt but led 150yds: kpt on* **10/1**

-034 **2** nk **Dark Amber**[31] 2750 4-9-10 65 KierenFallon 12 72
(Brendan Powell) *hld up in rr: prog fr 3f out: swtchd outside 2f out: drvn and styd on to take 2nd nr fin: jst hld* **8/1**[3]

0-40 **3** 1/2 **Special Miss**[27] 2867 3-8-7 62 AndreaAtzeni 2 68
(Marco Botti) *trckd ldng pair after 3f: led on inner over 2f out and sent for home: drvn over 1f out: edgd rt and hdd last 150yds: nt qckn and jst hld after: lost 2nd nr fin* **4/1**[1]

060 **4** 2 3/4 **High Love (IRE)**[45] 2310 3-8-8 63 HayleyTurner 1 64
(Tom Dascombe) *plld hrd: prog to join ldr after 2f: disp tl hdd over 2f out: hrd rdn and nt qckn w hd at awkward angle: stl on terms over 1f out: fdd* **14/1**

2316 **5** 4 1/2 **Ivor's Princess**[20] 3086 5-9-13 68 (b) SeanLevey 6 62
(Rod Millman) *hld up in midfield: rdn and tried to cl on ldrs over 2f out: no imp over 1f out: wknd* **12/1**

1163 **6** 3 **Choral Festival**[13] 3325 8-9-12 67 WilliamCarson 7 56
(John Bridger) *hld up in midfield: prog on outer 3f out: rdn and on terms 2f out: wknd over 1f out* **8/1**[3]

66-5 **7** 2 1/2 **Bossa Nova Baby (IRE)**[12] 3371 4-9-9 64 RobertHavlin 10 49
(Peter Chapple-Hyam) *dwlt: hld up in midfield: pushed along and dropped to rr 3f out: nvr on terms after* **25/1**

243 **8** nk **Tracks Of My Tears**[35] 2628 4-9-3 61 RyanPowell(3) 11 45
(Giles Bravery) *t.k.h: hld up in last: rdn and wl off the pce 4f out: taken to outer and sme prog over 2f out: nvr a threat* **8/1**[3]

5405 **9** 1 1/2 **Mary Le Bow**[19] 3116 3-8-6 61 (p) MartinLane 3 43
(Lucy Wadham) *led after 1f: mde most to over 2f out: wknd* **14/1**

1-35 **10** 1 1/4 **Uganda Glory (USA)**[35] 2628 4-9-9 64 (v) AdamKirby 13 44
(George Baker) *trckd ldrs: rdn over 3f out: wknd qckly fr 2f out* **5/1**[2]

4-00 **11** 6 **Pink And Black (IRE)**[41] 2418 3-8-13 68 FrederikTylicki 4 38
(William Muir) *t.k.h: hld up towards rr: rdn and struggling wl over 3f out* **14/1**

00-6 **12** 85 **Elsie Bay**[14] 3308 5-9-7 62 (p) RichardHughes 9
(Gary Moore) *led 1f: steadily lost pl: rdn 4f out: wknd rapidly and t.o over 2f out: virtually p.u* **10/1**

2m 25.1s (-4.40) **Going Correction** -0.325s/f (Firm)
**WFA** 3 from 4yo+ 14lb **12** Ran SP% **119.7**
Speed ratings (Par 100): **101,100,100,98,95 93,91,91,90,89 85,29**
CSF £88.64 CT £379.65 TOTE £9.90: £3.50, £3.70, £2.50; EX 56.70 Trifecta £1113.20.
**Owner** Tony Elliott & Jeff King **Bred** Lynch Bages, Camas Park & Summerhill B/S **Trained** Lambourn, Berks

■ Stewards' Enquiry : Hayley Turner two-day ban: use of whip (14-15 Jul)

**FOCUS**
A weak fillies' handicap in which the first three finished clear. The winner was not an obvious improver.

## 3804 UNIBET BEST FOR BETS IN BRAZIL MAIDEN STKS 1m 67y

**8:30** (8:31) (Class 5) 3-Y-0 **£2,726** (£805; £402) **Stalls** Low

Form RPR

4-03 **1** **Elusive Guest (FR)**[18] 3153 3-9-5 80 KierenFallon 11 85
(George Margarson) *led over 6f out: mde rest: rdn over 2f out: jnd over 1f out: edgd lft sn after: drvn into narrow ld nr fin* **5/2**[2]

5 **2** nk **Above The Rest (IRE)**[31] 2733 3-9-5 0 AdamKirby 10 84
(Timothy Jarvis) *trckd wnr after 2f: rdn over 2f out: str chal and upsides fr over 1f out: jst hld last strides* **14/1**

0-3 **3** 3 1/2 **Weekendatbernies (IRE)**[7] 3537 3-9-5 0 FrederikTylicki 7 76
(Ed de Giles) *in tch: chsd ldng trio over 4f out: drvn to take 3rd wl over 1f out: no imp on ldng pair* **8/1**

**4** hd **Baha** 3-9-5 0 RobertHavlin 8 75+
(John Gosden) *dwlt: wl in rr: long way adrift of ldrs whn shkn up over 2f out: picked up over 1f out: fin strly* **7/1**[3]

**5** 4 **Dalasi (IRE)** 3-9-0 0 FergusSweeney 1 61
(Henry Candy) *dwlt: towards rr: shkn up and tk 5th over 3f out: no imp on ldrs after* **16/1**

4 **6** 1 1/4 **Four Cheers (IRE)**[9] 3477 3-9-5 0 TomQueally 9 63
(Clive Brittain) *chsd ldng pair 6f out: rdn 3f out: lost 3rd and wknd wl over 1f out* **50/1**

05 **7** 2 1/4 **Sir Rosco**[25] 2917 3-9-5 0 ShaneKelly 5 57
(Sir Michael Stoute) *chsd ldrs: carried lft 4f out: sn rdn: no prog fr over 2f out* **16/1**

05 **8** hd **I Am Not Here (IRE)**[49] 2201 3-9-5 0 SamHitchcott 6 57
(Timothy Jarvis) *slowest out of the stalls: hld up wl in rr: shkn up 3f out: nvr a factor* **66/1**

0 **9** 16 **Il Gran Capo (IRE)**[7] 3537 3-8-12 0 RhiainIngram(7) 4 19
(Roger Ingram) *a in rr: wknd over 2f out: t.o* **100/1**

00 **10** 2 **Dire Straits (IRE)**[7] 3537 3-9-5 0 TedDurcan 3 14
(Chris Wall) *a in rr: rdn 3f out: wknd and t.o* **33/1**

0245 **11** 99 **Bon Voyage**[32] 2690 3-9-5 82 (p) RichardHughes 2
(Richard Hannon) *pushed up to ld: tk str hold after 1f: sn stdd and hdd: hung lft 4f out and sn dropped away completely: virtually p.u over 2f out: eventually fin* **13/8**[1]

1m 42.8s (-1.90) **Going Correction** -0.325s/f (Firm) **11** Ran SP% **116.1**
Speed ratings (Par 99): **96,95,92,92,88 86,84,84,68,66**
CSF £36.22 TOTE £3.70: £1.70, £3.20, £2.50; EX 30.80 Trifecta £212.30.
**Owner** John Guest Racing **Bred** Ecurie Haras Du Cadran & J C Seroul **Trained** Newmarket, Suffolk

**FOCUS**
Not a bad 3yo maiden. The winner matched his Nottingham latest.

## 3805 ROYAL WINDSOR RACECOURSE MONDAY NIGHT CLUB H'CAP 1m 67y

**9:00** (9:01) (Class 5) (0-70,66) 3-Y-0+ **£2,911** (£866; £432; £216) **Stalls** Low

Form RPR

5132 **1** **Shifting Star (IRE)**[13] 3328 9-9-12 64 (vt) WilliamCarson 6 74
(John Bridger) *mde all gng best over 2f out: pressed and drvn 1f out: styd on wl fnl f* **5/1**[2]

4042 **2** 1 1/4 **Celestial Ray**[16] 3233 5-9-6 58 RobertHavlin 7 65
(Linda Jewell) *trckd ldng trio: rdn over 2f out: prog to take 2nd jst over 1f out and sn chalng: nt qckn ins fnl f* **6/1**[3]

4400 **3** 2 3/4 **Siouxperhero (IRE)**[10] 3427 5-9-12 64 (bt) DougieCostello 3 65
(William Muir) *trckd wnr: rdn over 2f out: wl hld sn after: lost 2nd jst over 1f out: fdd but hld on for 3rd* **9/1**

0016 **4** nse **My Manekineko**[38] 2529 5-9-11 63 KierenFallon 4 64
(J R Jenkins) *hld up in last trio: rdn 2f out: sme prog over 1f out: kpt on fnl f: nvr rchd ldrs* **14/1**

-030 **5** 2 3/4 **Capers Royal Star (FR)**[7] 3538 3-9-1 63 AdamKirby 2 55
(Alastair Lidderdale) *trckd ldrs in 5th: rdn over 2f out: no prog and wl hld over 1f out* **7/1**

610- **6** 3/4 **Bertie Moon**[251] 7437 4-10-0 66 HayleyTurner 1 59
(Geoffrey Deacon) *t.k.h: chsd ldng pair: shkn up wl over 2f out: wknd over 1f out* **16/1**

323- **7** 1 3/4 **Star Anise (FR)**[210] 8132 3-9-0 62 SamHitchcott 5 48
(Harry Dunlop) *walked to post early: hld up in last trio: rdn and no prog over 2f out* **25/1**

0-23 **8** 3 **Harwoods Star (IRE)**[5] 3589 4-9-10 62 RichardHughes 8 44
(Amanda Perrett) *dwlt: hld up in last trio: effrt on outer 3f out: no prog 2f out: wl btn after: wknd* **5/4**[1]

1m 43.0s (-1.70) **Going Correction** -0.325s/f (Firm)
**WFA** 3 from 4yo+ 10lb **8** Ran SP% **114.3**
Speed ratings (Par 103): **95,93,91,90,88 87,85,82**
CSF £34.79 CT £263.12 TOTE £5.50: £1.40, £2.30, £2.90; EX 19.90 Trifecta £235.20.
**Owner** Night Shadow Syndicate **Bred** Hardys Of Kilkeel Ltd **Trained** Liphook, Hants

**FOCUS**
A moderate handicap. The winner is rated close to the level of last year's turf form.
T/Jkpt: £2366.60 to a £1 stake. Pool: £7294.50 - 3.00 winning units. T/Plt: £5.80 to a £1 stake. Pool of £95736.03 - 11913.71 winning tickets T/Qpdt: £5.70 to a £1 stake. Pool of £7671.39 - 989.52 winning tickets. JN

## [3289] CHANTILLY (R-H)
Monday, June 30

**OFFICIAL GOING: Turf: good to soft**

### 3806a PRIX DU BOIS (GROUP 3) (2YO) (TURF) 5f
1:50 (12:00) 2-Y-O £33,333 (£13,333; £10,000; £6,666; £3,333)

RPR

1 **Goken (FR)**[45] 2-8-11 0 FabriceVeron 8 107+
(H-A Pantall, France) *sn led and mde rest: pushed along and qcknd clr fr 2f out: rdn and r.o strly fnl f: comf* **7/4**[1]

2 2 **Jane's Memory (IRE)**[23] 3027 2-8-8 0 AndreaAtzeni 3 97+
(Rae Guest) *in tch: pushed along 2f out: rdn and wnt 2nd over 1f out: r.o and chsd wnr fnl f but no imp and wl hld* **13/2**

3 2 **Lehaim (FR)**[23] 2-8-11 0 (p) TheoBachelot 1 93+
(M Nigge, France) *midfield on inner: pushed along 2f out: rdn and wnt 3rd jst ins fnl f: kpt on but nt pce to chal* **20/1**

4 3 **Cheik Bere (FR)**[40] 2-8-11 0 FlavienPrat 6 82
(M Figge, Germany) *pressed ldr: cl 2nd 2f out: rdn and outpcd by wnr over 1f out: fdd and dropped to 4th fnl f* **12/1**

5 nk **Preciously (FR)**[23] 3027 2-8-8 0 IoritzMendizabal 5 78
(D Guillemin, France) *midfield: shuffled bk to rr 3f out: rdn over 1f out: r.o fnl f and wnt 5th towards fin: nvr able to chal* **16/1**

6 nk **Spirit Of Xian (IRE)**[28] 2856 2-8-8 0 MickaelBarzalona 7 77
(Richard Hannon) *in tch: pushed along and outpcd 2f out: kpt on u.p fnl f but wl hld* **9/1**

7 snk **Lostinparadise**[6] 2-8-8 0 AntoineHamelin 4 76
(Matthieu Palussiere, France) *in tch: clsd and pushed along to chal 2f out: rdn and outpcd by wnr over 1f out: fdd fnl f* **33/1**

8 1 3/4 **Super Ale (FR)**[53] 2-8-11 0 FrankieDettori 2 75
(G Botti, France) *hld up in rr: pushed along and effrt to cl 2f out: outpcd and btn fnl f: eased towards fin* **5/2**[2]

9 3/4 **Queen Bee (FR)**[18] 3170 2-8-8 0 GregoryBenoist 9 69
(E Lellouche, France) *midfield: pushed along 2f out: outpcd in rr whn short of room ins fnl f: btn after and eased* **6/1**[3]

10 1 1/2 **Wolcharo (IRE)**[45] 2-8-11 0 EddyHardouin 10 66
(Matthieu Palussiere, France) *prom: pushed along and lost pl qckly over 2f out: rdn and in last and btn ent fnl f: eased towards fin* **40/1**

58.52s (0.22) **10 Ran SP% 126.3**
WIN (incl. 1 euro stake): 2.40. PLACES: 1.50, 2.50, 5.40. DF: 7.30. SF: 12.00.
**Owner** Guy Pariente **Bred** Guy Pariente Holding **Trained** France

### 3807a PRIX DAPHNIS (GROUP 3) (3YO COLTS & GELDINGS) (TURF) 1m 1f
2:50 (12:00) 3-Y-O £33,333 (£13,333; £10,000; £6,666; £3,333)

RPR

1 **Master Carpenter (IRE)**[32] 2706 3-8-11 0 ChristopheSoumillon 5 106
(Rod Millman) *midfield in tch on outer: rdn over 1f out: chal ent fnl f: r.o wl and led 100yds out: pushed out and asserted: shade cosily* **9/2**[2]

2 1/2 **Calling Out (FR)**[48] 2242 3-8-11 0 AntoineHamelin 2 105
(J-P Gauvin, France) *trckd ldr on inner: pushed along and looking for clr run over 1f out: rdn and squeezed between rivals jst ins fnl f: r.o and wnt 2nd fnl strides: nt quite pce of wnr* **16/1**

3 shd **Mr Pommeroy (FR)**[29] 2818 3-8-11 0 FabriceVeron 3 105
(H-A Pantall, France) *led: pushed along into st: rdn and strly pressed fr 2f out: kpt on gamely u.p but hdd 100yds out and hld after: dropped to 3rd fnl strides* **5/1**[3]

4 1 1/2 **Zuri Chop (FR)**[5] 3597 3-8-11 0 JulienAuge 8 102
(A De Watrigant, France) *stdd and hld up in last: rdn over 1f out: r.o and tk nvr nrr 4th wl ins fnl f* **14/1**

5 hd **Army Bulletin (IRE)**[23] 3028 3-8-11 0 MaximeGuyon 4 101
(A Fabre, France) *awkward s and dwlt: hld up in last trio on inner: pushed along and angled out over 1f out: kpt on fnl f but nvr able to chal* **9/2**[2]

6 3/4 **Bodhi (FR)**[48] 2242 3-9-1 0 Jean-BernardEyquem 1 104
(J-F Bernard, France) *midfield in tch on inner: pushed along 2f out: angled out for clr run over 1f out: kpt on same pce fnl f and nvr able to chal* **11/8**[1]

7 nse **High Duty**[30] 2799 3-8-11 0 AdriedeVries 6 100
(P Schiergen, Germany) *trckd ldr on outer: chal gng strly 2f out: rdn over 1f out: nt qckn u.p and fdd fnl f: eased whn hld nring fin and lost 6th post* **20/1**

8 1 1/2 **Guiliani (IRE)**[26] 2908 3-8-11 0 CristianDemuro 7 96
(Jean-Pierre Carvalho, Germany) *hld up in last trio on outer: pushed along 2f out: rdn and outpcd over 1f out: dropped to last and wl hld fnl f: plugged on: eased nring fin* **10/1**

1m 54.37s (3.27) **8 Ran SP% 121.5**
WIN (incl. 1 euro stake): 5.70. PLACES: 2.20, 3.50, 2.40. DF: 36.90. SF: 83.90.
**Owner** Links Partnership/Cheveley Park Stud **Bred** Naiff Sa & Newtown Stud **Trained** Kentisbeare, Devon

### 3808a PRIX CHLOE (GROUP 3) (3YO FILLIES) (TURF) 1m 1f
3:20 (12:00) 3-Y-O £33,333 (£13,333; £10,000; £6,666; £3,333)

RPR

1 **Wunder (GER)**[30] 3-8-11 0 AdriedeVries 1 107
(Markus Klug, Germany) *trckd ldr on inner: angled off rail and rdn over 1f out: chal ins fnl f and sn led: r.o strly and asserted: readily* **12/1**

2 1 1/2 **Delivery**[29] 2816 3-8-11 0 MaximeGuyon 6 104
(A Fabre, France) *sn led: pushed along and qcknd 2f out: rdn over 1f out: strly pressed and hdd fnl f: readily outpcd by wnr but kpt on wl for 2nd* **13/2**

3 nk **Be My Gal**[58] 1945 3-8-11 0 JamesDoyle 2 103
(Roger Charlton) *midfield on inner: hdwy on rail fr 2f out: pushed along and wnt 3rd over 1f out: rdn and swtchd lft for clr run fnl f: kpt on wl but nt quite pce to chal* **7/1**

4 shd **Felcine (IRE)**[24] 2977 3-8-11 0 CristianDemuro 3 103
(G Botti, France) *hld up in midfield: gng strly whn nt clr run 2f out: rdn and angled lft over 1f out: r.o and wnt 4th ins fnl f: fin wl but nvr able to chal* **33/1**

5 2 **Defrost My Heart (IRE)**[27] 3-8-11 0 GeraldMosse 9 99
(A De Royer-Dupre, France) *hld up in rr: rdn over 1f out: kpt on down wd outside and tk n.d 5th fnl 100yds* **10/1**

6 1/2 **Anahita (FR)**[48] 2243 3-8-11 0 ChristopheSoumillon 5 98
(J-C Rouget, France) *hld up towards rr: angled out and rdn over 1f out: kpt on same pce and hld fnl f* **7/2**[2]

7 2 **Royalmania**[85] 1339 3-8-11 0 OlivierPeslier 10 94
(F Head, France) *hld up towards rr on outer: pushed along and clsd 2f out: rdn and edgd rt over 1f out: no ex and fdd fnl f* **2/1**[1]

8 1 1/4 **Ming Zhi Cosmos (FR)**[29] 3-8-11 0 ThierryThulliez 7 91
(N Clement, France) *t.k.h: midfield in tch: rdn over 1f out: no ex and btn fnl f: fdd* **20/1**

9 6 **Delhi**[27] 2880 3-8-11 0 Christophe-PatriceLemaire 4 78
(P Bary, France) *trckd ldr on outer: pushed along 2f out: lost pl qckly over 1f out: btn and dropped to rr fnl f: eased* **25/1**

10 snk **Cladocera (GER)**[27] 2880 3-8-11 0 AntoineHamelin 8 78
(A De Royer-Dupre, France) *midfield on outer: clsd 4f out: pushed along and lost pl steadily fr 2f out: last and btn ent fnl f: eased fnl 100yds* **9/2**[3]

1m 51.96s (0.86) **10 Ran SP% 127.9**
WIN (incl. 1 euro stake): 15.90. PLACES: 4.70, 2.50, 2.90. DF: 86.80. SF: 168.30.
**Owner** Gestut Gorlsdorf **Bred** Gestut Gorlsdorf **Trained** Germany

**FOCUS**
This was 30lb quicker than the colts in the Prix Daphnis.

### 3809a PRIX DU FOUR A TUILE (CLAIMER) (3YO) (TURF) 6f
3:50 (12:00) 3-Y-O £7,916 (£3,166; £2,375; £1,583; £791)

RPR

1 **Molesne Chop (FR)**[10] 3-8-6 0 (b) MllePaulineDominois(5) 13 68
(Mlle C Cardenne, France) **159/10**

2 3/4 **Yosra (FR)**[31] 3-9-5 0 EddyHardouin 4 74
(J Heloury, France) **117/10**

3 hd **La Goutte D'Or (FR)**[10] 3-8-8 0 JohanVictoire 7 62
(M Seror, France) **45/1**

4 3/4 **Meritocracy (IRE)**[7] 3539 3-9-4 0 (p) ChristopheSoumillon 9 70
(Paul Cole) *trckd ldrs: sltly short of room and dropped to last 1/2-way: swtchd outside and hdwy 1 1/2f out: styd on u.p fnl f: nt pce to get on terms w ldrs* **7/5**[1]

5 nse **Color Code (FR)**[10] 3-8-11 0 KorentinNaimi(8) 2 70
(M Boutin, France) **125/10**

6 2 1/2 **Larra Chope (FR)**[10] 3-8-7 0 (p) MickaelBerto(6) 1 56
(C Boutin, France) **45/1**

7 1 1/2 **Yuki (IRE)**[262] 7185 3-8-8 0 UmbertoRispoli 8 47
(B Goudot, France) **44/1**

8 3 **Nabulio (FR)**[45] 3-8-11 0 (p) CristianDemuro 3 40
(F Chappet, France) **224/10**

9 hd **Faith In You**[31] 3-8-8 0 GregoryBenoist 12 36
(R Chotard, France) **13/2**[3]

10 1 1/2 **Spanish Whipper (IRE)**[77] 3-8-11 0 StephanePasquier 11 35
(M Delcher Sanchez, France) **69/10**

11 hd **Orangefield (FR)**[31] 3-9-4 0 (b) FabriceVeron 10 41
(H-A Pantall, France) **39/10**[2]

12 7 **Realyfrajj (FR)**[198] 3-8-11 0 FranckBlondel 6 12
(Mlle S-V Tarrou, France) **85/1**

1m 12.22s (0.82) **12 Ran SP% 121.3**
WIN (incl. 1 euro stake): 16.90. PLACES: 4.30, 3.70, 10.10. DF: 81.60. SF: 209.80.
**Owner** Mlle Chrystelle Cardenne **Bred** A Chopard & M Perret **Trained** France

## NANTES (R-H)
Monday, June 30

**OFFICIAL GOING: Turf: soft**

### 3810a PRIX DE HAUTE FORET (CONDITIONS) (3YO) (TURF) 1m
4:05 (12:00) 3-Y-O £11,250 (£4,500; £3,375; £2,250; £1,125)

RPR

1 **Kenbest (FR)**[17] 3-9-0 0 ThierryJarnet 7 96
(H-A Pantall, France) **8/5**[1]

2 2 1/2 **Silver Treasure (FR)**[24] 2961 3-9-0 0 AlexandreRoussel 6 90
(Amy Weaver) *broke wl and led: set decent gallop: rdn and kicked clr over 1 1/2f out: c wd fnl bnd into st and racd alone in centre: hdd 150yds out: jst hld on for 2nd* **26/5**[3]

3 snk **Malka (FR)**[293] 6292 3-8-10 0 TonyPiccone 3 86
(Matthieu Palussiere, France) **26/5**[3]

4 hd **Vacationer**[30] 3-8-5 0 SebastienMartino(5) 2 85
(H-A Pantall, France) **7/1**

5 nse **Nomad Arrow (IRE)**[183] 3-8-8 0 (p) ValentinSeguy(6) 4 89
(X Thomas-Demeaulte, France) **122/10**

6 3/4 **Createur (IRE)**[45] 3-9-0 0 AdrienFouassier 8 87
(Alain Couetil, France) **43/10**[2]

7 8 **Super City (FR)**[144] 3-8-10 0 JeromeClaudic 5 65
(J-L Mace, France) **97/10**

8 2 1/2 **Quiaa Nominoor (FR)**[23] 3-9-0 0 (p) MathieuTavaresDaSilva 1 63
(Remy Nerbonne, France) **60/1**

1m 41.74s (101.74) **8 Ran SP% 120.6**
WIN (incl. 1 euro stake): 2.60. PLACES: 1.30, 1.50, 1.80. DF: 7.60. SF: 12.70.
**Owner** Guy Pariente **Bred** G Pariente **Trained** France

3811 - 3812a (Foreign Racing) - See Raceform Interactive

## [3562] BATH (L-H)
Tuesday, July 1

**OFFICIAL GOING: Firm (11.4)**
Wind: virtually nil Weather: sunny periods

### 3813 BATHWICK CAR AND VAN HIRE MAIDEN AUCTION STKS 5f 11y
6:10 (6:12) (Class 6) 2-Y-O £1,940 (£577; £288; £144) Stalls Centre

Form RPR

600 1 **Multi Quest**[53] 2128 2-8-6 0 FrannyNorton 6 55
(Jo Hughes) *a.p: rdn 2f out: led fnl 120yds: kpt on* **5/1**[1]

6 2 1 **Frank The Barber (IRE)**[10] 3461 2-9-1 0 RussKennemore 4 60
(Steph Hollinshead) *led: rdn over 2f out: hung lft whn hdd fnl 120yds: no ex* **20/1**

3 1/2 **Scent Of Power** 2-8-1 0 NoelGarbutt(5) 8 50+
(Anthony Carson) *trckd ldrs: rdn to chal over 1f out: ev ch tl squeezed up whn looking hld fnl 120yds* **5/1**[1]

0 4 4 **Spirit In Time (IRE)**[7] 3557 2-8-10 0 .......... FergusSweeney 2 38
(Malcolm Saunders) *trckd ldrs: rdn 2f out: wknd ins fnl f* **25/1**

5 6 **King's Bond** 2-9-1 0 .......... SteveDrowne 1 20
(Ronald Harris) *s.i.s: sn outpcd and detached: nvr threatened* **14/1**[2]

00 6 3 ¾ **Powerfulstorm**[7] 3550 2-8-6 0 ..........(b[1]) LiamJones 5
(Ronald Harris) *sn pushed along to chse ldrs: rdn over 2f out: wknd over 1f out* **16/1**[3]

1m 1.84s (-0.66) **Going Correction** -0.20s/f (Firm) **6** Ran SP% **54.5**
Speed ratings (Par 92): **97,95,94,88,78 72**
CSF £20.31 TOTE £3.20: £1.60, £3.80; EX 26.10 Trifecta £65.10.
**Owner** H Downs **Bred** Mrs C Lloyd **Trained** Lambourn, Berks
■ Rule 4 of 55p in the pound applies to all bets; Withdrawn: Jimmy's Girl

**FOCUS**
Races incorporating bottom bend increased in distance by about 10yds. The withdrawal of the odds-on Jimmy's Girl turned a weak race into an even weaker one and it's hard to get too excited about the form. The winner is rated as a small improver.

## 3814 PETER AND CARA'S HONEYMOON H'CAP 1m 2f 46y
**6:40** (6:40) (Class 5) (0-75,75) 3-Y-O **£2,587** (£770; £384; £192) **Stalls** Low

Form RPR

-110 1 **Aurelia Cotta (IRE)**[19] 3135 3-9-1 **69** .......... SteveDrowne 7 77
(Charles Hills) *a.p: rdn over 2f out: led wl over 1f out: styd on and in command fnl f* **11/2**[3]

6303 2 1 **Sherston**[5] 3603 3-8-11 **65** ..........(b[1]) FrannyNorton 4 71
(Mark Johnston) *chsd ldrs: rdn whn sltly outpcd 3f out: nt best of runs 2f out: styd on ent fnl f wnt 2nd fnl 120yds: a being hld* **4/1**[2]

-254 3 1 ¾ **Castle Combe (IRE)**[11] 3421 3-9-6 **74** ..........(p) DaneO'Neill 3 77
(Marcus Tregoning) *led after 1f: rdn wl over 2f out: hdd wl over 1f out: hld ent fnl f: no ex whn lost 2nd fnl 120yds* **6/1**

15-0 4 ½ **Jelly Fish**[32] 2719 3-9-7 **75** ..........(t[1]) JamesDoyle 8 77
(Amanda Perrett) *helld up mid-div: pushed along over 4f out: rdn 3f out: no imp tl styd on ent fnl f: wnt 4th towards fin* **13/2**

2665 5 1 ½ **Tunnel Tiger (IRE)**[23] 3037 3-8-4 **58** .......... KieranO'Neill 6 57
(William Knight) *trckd ldrs: rdn wl over 2f out: nt pce to chal: fdd fnl 100yds* **8/1**

0-23 6 3 ¾ **Protected**[10] 3465 3-9-7 **75** .......... RichardHughes 5 67
(James Tate) *mid-div: rdn wl over 2f out: nvr finding pce to get involved: wknd fnl 120yds* **8/1**

003- 7 6 **Sharp Lookout**[216] 8067 3-9-7 **75** .......... GeorgeBaker 1 55
(Roger Charlton) *hld up towards rr: pushed along over 4f out: rdn 3f out: nvr any imp: wknd ent fnl f* **7/2**[1]

5-50 8 nk **Haleo**[29] 2850 3-9-2 **70** .......... MartinDwyer 2 50
(William Muir) *sn struggling in last: nvr any danger: wknd ent fnl f* **25/1**

2m 7.95s (-3.05) **Going Correction** -0.20s/f (Firm) **8** Ran SP% **111.3**
Speed ratings (Par 100): **104,103,101,101,100 97,92,92**
CSF £26.20 CT £131.15 TOTE £5.50: £2.50, £1.60, £1.80; EX 26.90 Trifecta £244.50.
**Owner** Decadent Racing II **Bred** W J Kennedy **Trained** Lambourn, Berks

**FOCUS**
Modest form. The pace held up. Another step up from the winner.

## 3815 CREST NICHOLSON BATH RIVERSIDE H'CAP 1m 2f 46y
**7:10** (7:10) (Class 5) (0-75,81) 4-Y-0+ **£2,587** (£770; £384; £192) **Stalls** Low

Form RPR

0426 1 **Sheila's Buddy**[18] 3196 5-9-7 **75** ..........[1] RichardHughes 1 84
(J S Moore) *mde all: 6 l clr 7f out: kpt on wl fnl 2f: unchal* **4/1**[3]

5601 2 4 ½ **Jacob Cats**[8] 3515 5-9-13 **81** 6ex ..........(v) JimCrowley 4 81
(William Knight) *s.i.s: racd in 4th and pushed along early: rdn wl over 2f out: styd on to go 2nd ent fnl f: nvr threatened wnr* **11/8**[1]

0541 3 1 ½ **Aryal**[7] 3544 4-9-13 **81** 6ex ..........(b) FrannyNorton 2 79
(Mark Johnston) *trckd wnr: rdn 2f out: nt pce to get on terms w wnr: lost 2nd whn no ex ent fnl f* **15/8**[2]

10-1 4 5 **Heezararity**[85] 1354 6-9-2 **70** .......... JimmyFortune 3 58
(Jonathan Geake) *trckd ldng pair: rdn wl over 2f out: kpt on same pce tl no ex ins fnl f* **8/1**

2m 7.57s (-3.43) **Going Correction** -0.20s/f (Firm) **4** Ran SP% **108.0**
Speed ratings (Par 103): **105,101,100,96**
CSF £9.90 TOTE £5.20; EX 7.30 Trifecta £11.90.
**Owner** Ray Styles **Bred** Mrs Anita R Dodd **Trained** Upper Lambourn, Berks

**FOCUS**
Three of the four had won last time. This was all about the winner, who dominated.

## 3816 BATHWICK CAR AND VAN HIRE MAIDEN STKS 5f 161y
**7:40** (7:40) (Class 5) 3-Y-O **£2,587** (£770; £384) **Stalls** Centre

Form RPR

0-2 1 **Fyrecracker (IRE)**[21] 3083 3-9-5 0 .......... RichardHughes 3 74+
(Marcus Tregoning) *mde all: pushed clr fnl f: easily* **1/10**[1]

6552 2 6 **Go Charlie**[6] 3564 3-9-5 47 .......... SteveDrowne 2 54
(Ronald Harris) *taken to s early: t.k.h early: trckd ldrs: rdn to chal for 2nd fr 2f out but nvr gng pce to threaten wnr: wnt 2nd fnl 40yds* **9/1**[2]

0-56 3 nk **Loot**[10] 3469 3-9-0 59 .......... RyanWhile[(5)] 4 53
(Bill Turner) *trckd wnr: rdn whn chal for 2nd fr 2f out: kpt on but nvr gng pce to threaten wnr: lost 2nd fnl 40yds* **20/1**[3]

1m 11.41s (0.21) **Going Correction** -0.20s/f (Firm) **3** Ran SP% **105.7**
Speed ratings (Par 100): **90,82,81**
CSF £1.48 TOTE £1.10; EX 1.40 Trifecta £1.30.
**Owner** Mrs Lynn Turner & Guy Brook **Bred** Miss Nicola Cullen **Trained** Whitsbury, Hants

**FOCUS**
As uncompetitive a maiden as you'll see, this proved nothing more than an exercise canter for the long odds-on favourite. The form is rated around the runner-up.

## 3817 BATHWICK CAR AND VAN HIRE FILLIES' H'CAP 5f 161y
**8:10** (8:11) (Class 5) (0-75,75) 3-Y-0+ **£2,587** (£770; £384; £192) **Stalls** Centre

Form RPR

0033 1 **Red Lady (IRE)**[12] 3384 3-9-4 **73** ..........[1] JimmyFortune 2 81
(Brian Meehan) *w ldr: led wl over 1f out: sn rdn: hld on gamely fnl f: drvn out* **11/2**

0540 2 ½ **Rebecca Romero**[16] 3275 7-9-12 **75** .......... JamesDoyle 5 82
(Denis Coakley) *broke wl: sn stdd into last pair: hdwy over 1f out: chal jst ins fnl f: kpt on but hld enaring fin* **9/2**[3]

1-02 3 ¾ **Silverrica (IRE)**[10] 3470 4-9-7 **70** .......... RichardHughes 3 75
(Malcolm Saunders) *trckd ldrs: rdn over 1f out: flattered briefly: hld ins fnl f* **5/2**[2]

10-3 4 7 **Shilla (IRE)**[73] 1585 3-9-1 **70** .......... DaneO'Neill 6 51
(Henry Candy) *trckd ldrs: rdn over 2f out: nt pce to get on terms: fdd fnl f* **7/4**[1]

5-06 5 2 ¼ **Comptonspirit**[17] 3222 10-8-11 **63** .......... MatthewLawson[(3)] 4 37
(Brian Baugh) *sn pushed along in last pair: rdn over 2f out: nvr threatened: wknd fnl f* **16/1**

14-4 6 9 **Go Glamorous (IRE)**[10] 3484 3-9-5 **74** .......... SteveDrowne 1 18
(Ronald Harris) *sn led: rdn and hdd wl over 1f out: sn wknd* **14/1**

1m 9.82s (-1.38) **Going Correction** -0.20s/f (Firm)
**WFA** 3 from 4yo+ 6lb **6** Ran SP% **111.1**
Speed ratings (Par 100): **101,100,99,90,87 75**
CSF £29.06 TOTE £5.00: £3.30, £3.00; EX 24.50 Trifecta £119.20.
**Owner** D J Burke **Bred** Brook Stud Bloodstock Ltd **Trained** Manton, Wilts

**FOCUS**
It can be difficult to make up ground from off the pace on a surface such as this and the winner was always on the speed. Modest fillies' form.

## 3818 UNIBET BY PLAYERS FOR PLAYERS MAIDEN H'CAP 1m 5f 22y
**8:40** (8:40) (Class 5) (0-70,70) 3-Y-0+ **£2,587** (£770; £384; £192) **Stalls** High

Form RPR

5022 1 **The Kid**[27] 2893 3-9-0 **70** ..........(tp) RichardKingscote 10 81+
(Tom Dascombe) *mid-div: hdwy in centre 2f out: swtchd lft over 1f out: rdn for str run ins fnl f: led nring fin* **6/4**[1]

40-0 2 nk **Sound Of Summer (IRE)**[35] 2655 3-8-13 **69** .......... SteveDrowne 7 76
(Charles Hills) *led: qcknd clr wl over 2f out: sn rdn: kpt on: hdd nring fin* **25/1**

50-4 3 nse **Deauville Dancer (IRE)**[55] 2080 3-8-7 **63** .......... LukeMorris 5 70+
(Sir Mark Prescott Bt) *mid-div: rdn and hdwy over 2f out: chsd ldrs ent fnl f: styd on wl towards fin* **8/1**[3]

5633 4 ½ **Fair Comment**[15] 3309 4-9-0 **56** oh3 .......... RobertHavlin 9 62
(Michael Blanshard) *trckd ldr: rdn over 2f out: styd on ins fnl f* **22/1**

5 5 1 ¾ **Quadriller (FR)**[25] 2942 7-9-4 **60** ..........(t) RichardHughes 8 64
(Philip Hobbs) *hld up towards rr: pushed along and hdwy 3f out: sn rdn: chsd ldrs over 1f out: no ex fnl 100yds* **8/1**[3]

3306 6 ¾ **Needless Shouting (IRE)**[15] 3316 3-8-10 **66** .......... SamHitchcott 3 68
(Mick Channon) *mid-div: hdwy over 2f out: sn rdn to chse ldrs: no ex fnl 120yds* **12/1**

400 7 9 **Bergan (GER)**[26] 2917 3-8-8 **64** .......... LiamJones 6 53
(Mick Channon) *a towards rr* **33/1**

65-6 8 1 ¼ **Gilded Frame**[17] 3235 4-9-3 **59** .......... JohnFahy 1 46
(J S Moore) *a towards rr* **33/1**

6463 9 9 **Angus Glens**[23] 3032 4-9-10 **66** ..........(p) JimCrowley 4 40
(David Dennis) *trckd ldrs: rdn 3f out: sn wknd* **12/1**

5-54 10 10 **Branston De Soto**[15] 3303 3-8-6 **62** .......... FrannyNorton 11 21
(Mark Johnston) *trckd ldrs: effrt over 2f out: lost action over 1f out: immediately eased: fatally injured* **11/4**[2]

2m 51.97s (-0.03) **Going Correction** -0.20s/f (Firm)
**WFA** 3 from 4yo+ 14lb **10** Ran SP% **118.3**
Speed ratings (Par 103): **92,91,91,91,90 89,84,83,78,71**
CSF £50.76 CT £236.85 TOTE £2.60: £1.10, £3.10, £2.80; EX 43.00 Trifecta £461.90.
**Owner** D Ward **Bred** D Boocock **Trained** Malpas, Cheshire

**FOCUS**
Modest and rather muddling form, limited by the fourth. The winner is perhaps a bit better than the bare form.

## 3819 BATHWICK CAR AND VAN HIRE H'CAP 1m 3f 144y
**9:10** (9:10) (Class 6) (0-60,56) 3-Y-O **£2,587** (£770; £384; £192) **Stalls** Low

Form RPR

4422 1 **Bishop Wulstan (IRE)**[6] 3567 3-9-4 **53** .......... RichardHughes 1 63
(Richard Hannon) *trckd ldrs tl lost pl sltly over 5f out: hdwy over 2f out: sn rdn: led jst over 1f out: styd on wl* **3/1**[2]

5001 2 ¾ **Enquiring**[6] 3567 3-9-7 **56** 6ex .......... FrannyNorton 8 64
(Mark Johnston) *trckd ldr: rdn wl over 2f out: sltly hmpd over 1f out: styd on to go 2nd ins fnl f* **9/4**[1]

6603 3 1 ½ **Assoluta (IRE)**[6] 3567 3-9-1 **50** .......... JamesDoyle 6 55
(Sylvester Kirk) *led: travelling best over 2f out: rdn and edgd rt over 1f out: sn hdd: lost 2nd and no ex ins fnl f* **8/1**

000 4 ¾ **Little Flo**[31] 2773 3-9-3 **52** .......... FergusSweeney 7 56
(Brendan Powell) *hld up: hdwy fr 3f out: rdn to chse ldrs over 2f out: styd on same pce fnl f* **16/1**

4-00 5 1 ¾ **Windshield**[148] 456 3-9-7 **56** .......... LukeMorris 2 57
(Sir Mark Prescott Bt) *trckd ldrs: pushed along over 4f out: rdn 3f out: styd on same pce fnl 2f* **4/1**[3]

0001 6 2 ¼ **Redlorryyellowlorry (IRE)**[14] 3326 3-8-12 **47** ..........(t) MartinLane 4 44
(George Baker) *hld up: rdn over 3f out: sme prog over 2f out: styd on but nvr gng pce to get involved* **10/1**

-005 7 24 **Oracle Boy**[14] 3326 3-9-5 **54** .......... MartinDwyer 3 12
(William Muir) *a towards rr: eased whn btn fnl f* **7/1**

6000 8 7 **Dark Tsarina (IRE)**[36] 2621 3-9-0 **52** .......... OisinMurphy[(3)] 5
(Michael Madgwick) *trckd ldrs: rdn 3f out: wknd 2f out: eased fnl f* **50/1**

2m 28.81s (-1.79) **Going Correction** -0.20s/f (Firm) **8** Ran SP% **116.3**
Speed ratings (Par 98): **97,96,95,95,93 92,76,71**
CSF £10.41 CT £47.81 TOTE £3.00: £1.20, £1.80, £1.50; EX 11.10 Trifecta £45.80.
**Owner** Middleham Park Racing XIV & James Pak **Bred** Scuderia Pieffegi Sas **Trained** East Everleigh, Wilts

**FOCUS**
This was trappy. The first two stepped up on the form of their C&D meeting last week.
T/Plt: £90.40 to a £1 stake. Pool: £47,383.95 - 382.62 winning tickets. T/Qpdt: £30.50 to a £1 stake. Pool: £3,753.85 - 91.02 winning tickets. TM

# 3549 BRIGHTON (L-H)
### Tuesday, July 1

**OFFICIAL GOING: Firm (good to firm in places; 7.4)**
Wind: Fresh, across towards stand Weather: Fine and warm

## 3820 BRIGHTONCARBOOTSALE.CO.UK H'CAP 5f 213y
**2:30** (2:30) (Class 6) (0-55,55) 3-Y-0+ **£1,940** (£577; £288; £144) **Stalls** Low

Form RPR

363 1 **Birdie Queen**[17] 3231 4-9-7 **55** .......... GeorgeBaker 8 69
(Gary Moore) *trckd ldr: led over 1f out: rdn out* **7/2**[2]

2206 2 3 **Johnny Splash (IRE)**[3] 3707 5-9-3 **51** ..........(v) AdamKirby 6 55
(Roger Teal) *led tl over 1f out: sn outpcd* **4/1**[3]

05-1 3 3 ¼ **Royal Caper**[17] 3230 4-8-12 **53** .......... JackGilligan[(7)] 2 47
(Miss Joey Ellis) *outpcd and bhd: styd on fr over 1f out: nt rch ldrs* **7/2**[2]

40-0 4 ½ **The Wee Chief (IRE)**[21] 3088 8-9-7 **55** .......... PatDobbs 4 47
(Jimmy Fox) *towards rr: hdwy 2f out: one pce appr fnl f* **8/1**



The Form Book, Raceform Ltd, Newbury, RG14 5SJ

6560 **5** *3* **Alberto**[8] 3527 4-8-12 **46** oh1..........................(b[1]) PatCosgrave 7 28
(Alastair Lidderdale) *s.i.s: racd wd: sn outpcd* **33/1**
3345 **6** *½* **Jazz Bay**[21] 3084 3-8-9 **49**..........................(p) SeanLevey 5 29
(John Bridger) *mainly 4th tl wknd 2f out* **12/1**
42-5 **7** *1¾* **High Tone**[14] 3323 4-9-3 **51**.......................... KierenFallon 3 26
(Dean Ivory) *chsd ldrs: rdn over 2f out: wknd wl over 1f out: eased whn wl btn ins fnl f* **11/4**[1]
1m 8.98s (-1.22) **Going Correction** -0.275s/f (Firm)
**WFA** 3 from 4yo+ 6lb **7** Ran SP% **112.9**
Speed ratings (Par 101): **97,93,88,88,84 83,81**
CSF £17.36 CT £50.89 TOTE £3.00: £1.80, £2.60; EX 15.20 Trifecta £72.20.
**Owner** The Golf Partnership **Bred** D R Tucker **Trained** Lower Beeding, W Sussex

**FOCUS**
Rail out 3yds from 6f to 2.5f and distances increased about 8yds. A very weak handicap in which the first two were always to the fore. This rates a personal best from the winner.

## 3821 MR & MRS FOAT 25TH ANNIVERSARY H'CAP 6f 209y
**3:00** (3:01) (Class 5) (0-70,70) 3-Y-O **£2,587** (£770; £384; £192) **Stalls** Low

Form RPR
2040 **1** **Perfect Pursuit**[19] 3145 3-9-1 **67**.......................... RyanTate(3) 6 73
(Clive Cox) *in tch: drvn along over 2f out: styd on wl fr over 1f out: led fnl strides* **6/1**
4-32 **2** *nk* **Bereka**[102] 1045 3-8-12 **61**.......................... KierenFallon 4 66
(James Tate) *t.k.h: trckd ldrs: rdn to ld ins fnl f: jst ct* **5/1**[3]
2530 **3** *3¼* **Penny's Boy**[19] 3145 3-9-7 **70**.......................... PatDobbs 1 67
(Sylvester Kirk) *chsd ldr: led over 1f out tl ins fnl f: wknd fnl 100yds* **3/1**[2]
3-16 **4** *2½* **Castorienta**[110] 936 3-9-4 **67**.......................... PatCosgrave 2 57
(George Baker) *chsd ldrs tl wknd fnl f* **10/1**
-003 **5** *nk* **Orlando Star (CAN)**[14] 3329 3-8-9 **58**..........................(v) LukeMorris 5 47
(Roger Teal) *led tl wknd over 1f out* **20/1**
0236 **6** *3* **Stoneham**[16] 3281 3-8-8 **60**.......................... CharlesBishop(3) 3 42
(Mick Channon) *towards rr: effrt over 2f out: hung lft and wknd over 1f out* **16/1**
3233 **7** *2½* **Handwoven (IRE)**[5] 3627 3-9-2 **65**..........................(b) SilvestreDeSousa 7 40
(Mark Johnston) *s.v.s and wl bhd: mod effrt 3f out: nvr able to chal* **7/4**[1]
1m 21.93s (-1.17) **Going Correction** -0.275s/f (Firm) **7** Ran SP% **112.1**
Speed ratings (Par 100): **95,94,90,88,87 84,81**
CSF £34.12 TOTE £12.20: £4.30, £2.10; EX 35.00 Trifecta £132.10.
**Owner** John Drew **Bred** Mildmay Bloodstock Ltd **Trained** Lambourn, Berks

**FOCUS**
A slightly better handicap than the opener, this time for 3yos. The winner is rated around last year's debut.

## 3822 WINNER RENTAL SERVICES MAIDEN STKS 1m 1f 209y
**3:30** (3:35) (Class 5) 3-Y-O **£3,234** (£962; £481; £240) **Stalls** High

Form RPR
3 **1** **Tryster (IRE)**[11] 3432 3-9-5 0.......................... AdamKirby 3 89+
(Charlie Appleby) *trckd ldr: led on bit over 1f out: edgd lft: canter* **5/6**[1]
2235 **2** *5* **Mbhali (IRE)**[12] 3385 3-9-5 74.......................... SilvestreDeSousa 2 74
(Mark Johnston) *led tl over 1f out: no ch w wnr* **9/4**[2]
0 **3** *5* **Executrix**[75] 1534 3-9-0 0.......................... ShaneKelly 1 60
(Sir Michael Stoute) *t.k.h: trckd ldrs: chal 2f out: wknd over 1f out* **8/1**
0- **4** *6* **Dream And Hope**[334] 4921 3-9-0 0..........................[1] KierenFallon 5 48
(Clive Brittain) *s.s: in rr: pushed along 6f out: n.d fnl 3f* **6/1**[3]
0 **5** *19* **Red Inferno (IRE)**[26] 2925 3-8-12 0.......................... JackGilligan(7) 4 17
(Miss Joey Ellis) *hld up in 4th: rdn 5f out: wknd 3f out* **100/1**
2m 1.05s (-2.55) **Going Correction** -0.275s/f (Firm) **5** Ran SP% **111.7**
Speed ratings (Par 100): **99,95,91,86,71**
CSF £3.03 TOTE £2.10: £1.10, £1.70; EX 3.00 Trifecta £6.20.
**Owner** Godolphin **Bred** Herbertstown House Stud **Trained** Newmarket, Suffolk

**FOCUS**
Not a bad little 3yo maiden and a promising winner, but it lacked depth. The form is rated around the runner-up.

## 3823 STREAMLINE TAXIS SUPPORTS THE MARTLETTS HOSPICE H'CAP 1m 3f 196y
**4:00** (4:02) (Class 5) (0-70,70) 3-Y-O+ **£2,587** (£770; £384; £192) **Stalls** High

Form RPR
2253 **1** **Libeccio (FR)**[26] 2934 3-9-0 **69**.......................... LiamKeniry 2 79
(Andrew Balding) *hld up in 5th: hdwy 2f out: led ins fnl f: pushed out* **8/1**
00-1 **2** *1¾* **Red Passiflora**[3] 3711 3-8-13 **68** 6ex.......................... LukeMorris 1 75
(Sir Mark Prescott Bt) *dwlt: sn in cl 3rd: pushed along 4f out: unbalanced on trck: drvn into ld and edgd lft 1f out: hdd and one pce ins fnl f* **11/8**[1]
1502 **3** *5* **Right Of Appeal**[3] 3696 3-9-0 **69**.......................... SilvestreDeSousa 3 75
(Mark Johnston) *led: hdd and bdly squeezed on rail 1f out: snatched up: nt rcvr* **6/4**[2]
00-3 **4** *5* **Nordic Quest (IRE)**[13] 2702 5-10-0 **70**.......................... TomQueally 5 61
(Nicky Henderson) *dwlt: sn trcking ldr: rdn over 2f out: sn wknd* **7/1**[3]
2601 **5** *4* **Frederic Chopin**[20] 3120 3-8-6 **61**..........................(t) HarryBentley 4 46
(Stuart Williams) *hld up in 4th: rdn and wknd 2f out* **16/1**
2m 28.26s (-4.44) **Going Correction** -0.275s/f (Firm)
**WFA** 3 from 5yo 13lb **5** Ran SP% **111.6**
Speed ratings (Par 103): **103,101,98,95,92**
CSF £19.95 TOTE £8.10: £3.00, £1.30; EX 24.30 Trifecta £65.90.
**Owner** Mick and Janice Mariscotti **Bred** Capricorn Stud Sa **Trained** Kingsclere, Hants
■ Stewards' Enquiry : Luke Morris three-day ban: careless riding (Jul 15-17)

**FOCUS**
Fair enough form for the class, with a personal best from the winner.

## 3824 MAYO WYNNE BAXTER SOLICITORS H'CAP 1m 1f 209y
**4:30** (4:31) (Class 6) (0-55,55) 4-Y-O+ **£1,940** (£577; £288; £144) **Stalls** High

Form RPR
3314 **1** **Last Minute Lisa (IRE)**[21] 3075 4-9-5 **53**.......................... PatDobbs 9 63
(Sylvester Kirk) *hld up in rr: stdy hdwy 3f out: led ins fnl f: rdn clr* **7/2**[2]
-302 **2** *2½* **Cherry Princess**[7] 3553 4-9-5 **53**.......................... HarryBentley 4 58
(Stuart Williams) *prom: led 1f out: hdd and outpcd ins fnl f* **7/2**[2]
154 **3** *hd* **Stanlow**[28] 2863 4-9-7 **55**..........................(b[1]) ShaneKelly 1 60
(Daniel Mark Loughnane) *in tch: led 2f out tl 1f out: one pce* **6/1**[3]
6222 **4** *1½* **Litmus (USA)**[7] 3552 5-9-1 **49**..........................(b) HayleyTurner 12 51
(Simon Dow) *sn prom: rdn 4f out: outpcd over 2f out: styd on fnl f* **11/4**[1]
4-00 **5** *6* **Sir Tyto (IRE)**[20] 3115 6-8-9 **50**..........................(p) ChrisMeehan(7) 6 41
(Peter Makin) *towards rr: hdwy over 2f out: wknd over 1f out* **33/1**
00-0 **6** *½* **Bridge Builder**[33] 2689 4-9-4 **55**.......................... CharlesBishop(3) 10 48
(Peter Hedger) *led after 1f tl 2f out: wknd over 1f out* **50/1**

0050 **7** *6* **Medburn Cutler**[17] 3208 4-9-2 **50**..........................(v[1]) PatCosgrave 5 28
(George Baker) *s.i.s: sn in midfield: rdn 3f out: no ch whn hung lft 2f out* **12/1**
0000 **8** *¾* **Ghostwing**[8] 3521 7-8-11 **48**.......................... RyanTate(3) 3 25
(Ralph J Smith) *led 1f: prom tl wknd wl over 1f out* **20/1**
0206 **9** *12* **Silvee**[8] 3528 7-9-1 **49**..........................(p) SeanLevey 11 3
(John Bridger) *bhd: mod effrt over 2f out: sn wknd* **25/1**
0066 **10** *53* **Booktheband (IRE)**[4] 3682 4-9-0 **48**..........................(bt) KierenFallon 7
(Clive Brittain) *mid-div: struggling 6f out: wl bhd fnl 4f* **16/1**
2m 1.1s (-2.50) **Going Correction** -0.275s/f (Firm) **10** Ran SP% **112.5**
Speed ratings (Par 101): **99,97,96,95,90 90,85,85,75,33**
CSF £14.79 CT £68.79 TOTE £3.90: £1.90, £1.50, £2.00; EX 15.70 Trifecta £78.30.
**Owner** Gerry Dolan **Bred** Geoffrey Croke **Trained** Upper Lambourn, Berks

**FOCUS**
They went a fair pace in this moderate handicap, thanks to a disputed lead, and that played into the hands of the winner. The first four came clear. The winner matched her winter AW form.

## 3825 MARTLETS.ORG.UK H'CAP 7f 214y
**5:00** (5:00) (Class 5) (0-70,70) 4-Y-O+ **£2,587** (£770; £384; £192) **Stalls** Low

Form RPR
1232 **1** **Who's That Chick (IRE)**[14] 3327 5-9-2 **65**.......................... AdamKirby 4 77
(Ralph J Smith) *cl up in 3rd: trckd ldr over 4f out: rdn over 2f out: led and hung lft over 1f out: drvn out* **11/8**[1]
3222 **2** *1½* **Byrd In Hand (IRE)**[17] 3230 7-8-5 **54**..........................(b) HayleyTurner 2 62
(John Bridger) *led tl over 1f out: one pce* **7/2**[2]
0305 **3** *2¼* **Whitby Jet (IRE)**[15] 3314 6-9-7 **70**.......................... LiamKeniry 3 73
(Ed Vaughan) *hld up in 4th: effrt and hrd rdn 2f out: styd on same pce appr fnl f* **4/1**[3]
5406 **4** *7* **Annes Rocket (IRE)**[126] 740 9-9-4 **67**..........................(p) PatDobbs 6 54
(Jimmy Fox) *hld up in rr: rdn over 2f out: n.d* **20/1**
0200 **5** *4* **Lutine Charlie (IRE)**[6] 3562 7-8-4 **53**..........................(p) SilvestreDeSousa 1 31
(Pat Eddery) *chsd ldr tl over 3f out: hrd rdn and wknd wl over 1f out* **4/1**[3]
1m 33.4s (-2.60) **Going Correction** -0.275s/f (Firm) **5** Ran SP% **109.1**
Speed ratings (Par 103): **102,100,98,91,87**
CSF £6.31 TOTE £1.90: £1.10, £2.10; EX 5.90 Trifecta £7.50.
**Owner** Piper, Churchill, Hirschfeld **Bred** T Hirschfeld **Trained** Epsom, Surrey

**FOCUS**
An ordinary handicap, but they went a decent pace and the first three pulled clear. The runner-up sets the level with the winner continuing her recent progress.

## 3826 HARRINGTONS LETTINGS H'CAP 5f 59y
**5:30** (5:31) (Class 5) (0-70,67) 3-Y-O+ **£2,587** (£770; £384) **Stalls** Low

Form RPR
3253 **1** **Welease Bwian (IRE)**[10] 3470 5-8-12 **65**..........................(t) AaronJones(7) 4 74
(Stuart Williams) *chsd ldng pair: shkn up and led jst ins fnl f: rdn clr* **6/4**[1]
64-6 **2** *2¼* **Excellent Aim**[132] 663 7-8-9 **62**..........................(t) JordanVaughan(7) 2 63
(George Margarson) *w ldr: hung lft and led briefly 1f out: sn hdd and no ex* **13/8**[2]
5001 **3** *6* **Billy Red**[12] 3393 10-9-5 **65**..........................(b) KierenFallon 1 52
(J R Jenkins) *dwlt: sn in narrow ld and restrained in front: rdn and carried hd awkwardly fr 2f out: hdd & wknd 1f out* **11/4**[3]
1m 1.99s (-0.31) **Going Correction** -0.275s/f (Firm)
**WFA** 3 from 5yo+ 5lb **3** Ran SP% **104.8**
Speed ratings (Par 103): **91,87,77**
CSF £4.02 TOTE £1.70; EX 3.40 Trifecta £3.80.
**Owner** W E Enticknap **Bred** Nils Koop **Trained** Newmarket, Suffolk

**FOCUS**
With only three horses remaining this modest sprint was always going to be tactical. The winner is rated to his turf best.
T/Plt: £38.50 to a £1 stake. Pool: £60,785.94 - 347.41 winning tickets. T/Qpdt: £6.20 to a £1 stake. Pool: £5,495.45 - 649.09 winning tickets. LM

# 3605 HAMILTON (R-H)
### Tuesday, July 1

**OFFICIAL GOING: Good (good to firm in places; 7.9)**
Wind: Almost nil Weather: Sunny, hot

## 3827 AVON GORGE MAIDEN STKS 6f 5y
**2:15** (2:16) (Class 5) 2-Y-O **£3,408** (£1,006; £503) **Stalls** High

Form RPR
2 **1** **Surewecan**[10] 3454 2-9-5 0.......................... JoeFanning 4 84+
(Mark Johnston) *trckd ldr: led over 2f out: pushed along and edgd lft over 1f out: kpt on strly to go clr fnl f* **8/13**[1]
5 **2** *3¾* **Battleranger (IRE)**[18] 3186 2-9-5 0.......................... TomEaves 6 72
(Keith Dalgleish) *led: rdn and hdd over 2f out: rallied: kpt on ins fnl f: nt rch wnr* **50/1**
**3** *1¼* **Spring Offensive (IRE)** 2-9-5 0.......................... TonyHamilton 2 68+
(Richard Fahey) *s.i.s: plld hrd bhd ldng gp: drvn and rn green 1/2-way: rallied over 1f out: edgd rt: kpt on same pce fnl f: improve* **20/1**[3]
**4** *1½* **Golden Spun (USA)** 2-9-5 0.......................... PaulMulrennan 5 64+
(Bryan Smart) *s.i.s: t.k.h and sn in tch: effrt and rdn 2f out: kpt on same pce whn n.m.r briefly ins fnl f* **28/1**
6 **5** *7* **Pipe Bomb**[17] 3255 2-9-5 0.......................... JamieSpencer 3 43+
(Kevin Ryan) *colty in paddock: trckd ldrs: effrt and rdn over 2f out: wknd over 1f out: eased whn no ch ins fnl f* **15/8**[2]
06 **6** *5* **Sunhill Lodge Lady**[15] 3297 2-9-0 0.......................... PJMcDonald 1 23
(Ann Duffield) *t.k.h: hld up bhd ldng gp: drvn and struggling over 2f out: sn btn* **150/1**
1m 12.56s (0.36) **Going Correction** +0.05s/f (Good) **6** Ran SP% **107.5**
Speed ratings (Par 94): **99,94,92,90,81 74**
CSF £35.94 TOTE £1.20: £1.10, £11.10; EX 21.10 Trifecta £87.40.
**Owner** Douglas Livingston **Bred** Christopher & Annabelle Mason **Trained** Middleham Moor, N Yorks

**FOCUS**
Rail alignment in the loop meant races of 1m and beyond measured 50yds more than the advertised distances. A false rail was in place around the bend into the straight. Not many runners but a decent bunch on looks and a useful performance by the winner. The form is taken at face value.

## 3828 SUNDAY MAIL SUMMER RACENIGHT NEXT WEEK H'CAP 1m 65y
**2:45** (2:45) (Class 6) (0-60,60) 3-Y-O+ **£2,045** (£603; £302) **Stalls** Low

Form RPR
0-03 **1** **Indian Giver**[5] 3604 6-8-9 **50**.................................. AlistairRawlinson(7) 3 61
(John David Riches) *hld up in midfield: effrt and drvn over 2f out: hdwy to ld over 1f out: hung lft: pushed out fnl f* **9/2**[3]
3500 **2** *2* **Her Red Devil (IRE)**[52] 2165 3-8-6 **52**.................... GeorgeChaloner(3) 8 56
(Richard Fahey) *hld up: rdn over 3f out: hdwy 2f out: chsd (clr) wnr ins fnl f: r.o* **9/1**
3356 **3** *1 3/4* **Dhaular Dhar (IRE)**[13] 3361 12-9-10 **58**.......................... GrahamLee 12 60
(Jim Goldie) *hld up: drvn along over 2f out: hdwy over 1f out: kpt on ins fnl f: nrst fin* **5/1**
0-55 **4** *hd* **Blue Clumber**[20] 3099 4-8-13 **47**.......................................... BenCurtis 9 49
(Shaun Harris) *pressed ldr: rdn over 2f out: led briefly wl over 1f out: one pce and lost two pls ins fnl f* **20/1**
0604 **5** *5* **China In My Hands**[14] 3333 3-8-12 **55**........................[1] JamieSpencer 2 43
(James Bethell) *s.i.s: hld up: rdn over 2f out: hdwy over 1f out: kpt on fnl f: no imp* **7/2**[1]
0001 **6** *nk* **Look On By**[20] 3105 4-9-8 **56**............................................. RaulDaSilva 5 45
(Ruth Carr) *led: rdn and hung lft over 2f out: hdd over 1f out: wknd ins fnl f* **4/1**[2]
-513 **7** *2 1/2* **Dutch Lady**[32] 2741 3-9-2 **59**.......................................... PatrickMathers 11 41
(John Holt) *hld up in midfield on outside: effrt and rdn over 2f out: no imp over 1f out* **13/2**
0000 **8** *14* **Jebel Tara**[15] 3299 9-9-12 **60**..........................................(bt) RobertWinston 7 11
(Alan Brown) *t.k.h in midfield: effrt over 3f out: hung rt and wknd 2f out: t.o* **25/1**
-000 **9** *nk* **Skinny Latte**[14] 3333 3-8-3 **46** oh1..................................(b[1]) DuranFentiman 10
(Micky Hammond) *s.i.s: t.k.h: hld up on outside: struggling over 2f out: hung rt and sn btn: t.o* **50/1**
06-0 **10** *3/4* **Arabian Sunset (IRE)**[45] 2355 3-8-7 **50**.................... RoystonFfrench 1
(Simon Waugh) *t.k.h: trckd ldrs tl lost pl qckly over 3f out: sn struggling: t.o* **66/1**

1m 48.22s (-0.18) **Going Correction** +0.05s/f (Good)
**WFA** 3 from 4yo+ 9lb **10** Ran SP% **112.5**
Speed ratings (Par 101): **102,100,98,98,93 92,90,76,75,75**
CSF £40.75 CT £211.48 TOTE £5.40: £1.60, £4.50, £2.70; EX 49.90 Trifecta £269.30.
**Owner** J D Riches **Bred** M C Denning **Trained** Pilling, Lancashire
■ A first training success for John Riches.

**FOCUS**
This was a low-grade handicap featuring mainly hard-to-win-with sorts and it was run at a bit of a stop-start gallop. The winner's best form since her 2012 form.

## 3829 FERNIGAIR H'CAP 1m 4f 17y
**3:15** (3:16) (Class 5) (0-75,79) 3-Y-O+ **£3,881** (£1,155; £577; £288) **Stalls** Low

Form RPR
4314 **1** **Aleksandar**[17] 3240 5-9-11 **70**.......................................... GrahamLee 6 78
(Jim Goldie) *trckd ldrs: effrt and ev ch over 2f out: edgd rt and led over 1f out: hld on gamely towards fin* **11/2**[3]
-355 **2** *1/2* **Geanie Mac (IRE)**[17] 3238 5-8-9 **54** oh1......................(p) PJMcDonald 3 61
(Linda Perratt) *in tch: smooth hdwy over 2f out: effrt and ev ch over 1f out: flashed tail ins fnl f: kpt on: hld nr fin* **28/1**
36-0 **3** *nk* **Royal Straight**[17] 3242 9-8-12 **62**..............................(t) SammyJoBell(5) 1 69
(Linda Perratt) *hld up: stdy hdwy over 2f out: swtchd lft and effrt over 1f out: kpt on ins fnl f: hld nr fin* **50/1**
0331 **4** *3 1/2* **Corton Lad**[5] 3624 4-10-1 79 6ex....................................(tp) KevinStott(5) 2 80
(Keith Dalgleish) *in tch on ins: faltered bnd 5f out: effrt and hung lft over 2f out: one pce fnl f* **2/1**[1]
6333 **5** *2 1/4* **Mambo Rhythm**[9] 3498 3-8-7 **65**.......................................... JoeFanning 5 63
(Mark Johnston) *in tch: hdwy to ld over 2f out: hdd over 1f out: outpcd fnl f* **9/4**[2]
35-5 **6** *6* **La Bacouetteuse (FR)**[60] 1929 9-9-7 **66**..........................(b) DavidAllan 8 54
(Iain Jardine) *wnt lft s: hld up: outpcd over 3f out: sme late hdwy: nvr on terms* **22/1**
3020 **7** *6* **Rookery (IRE)**[46] 2319 3-8-12 **70**................................... PaulMulrennan 7 48
(Mark Johnston) *led at ordinary gallop: rdn and hdd over 2f out: sn btn* **9/1**
0454 **8** *3 3/4* **King Of Paradise (IRE)**[28] 2868 5-10-0 **73**........................ JasonHart 4 45
(Eric Alston) *cl up tl rdn and wknd over 2f out* **8/1**

2m 37.43s (-1.17) **Going Correction** +0.05s/f (Good)
**WFA** 3 from 4yo+ 13lb **8** Ran SP% **110.4**
Speed ratings (Par 103): **105,104,104,102,100 96,92,90**
CSF £130.28 CT £6373.39 TOTE £6.20: £1.90, £4.60, £5.90; EX 80.80 Trifecta £680.80.
**Owner** Mrs M Craig **Bred** Fittocks Stud Ltd **Trained** Uplawmoor, E Renfrews

**FOCUS**
A fair handicap in which a couple of the market leaders disappointed. The gallop was no more than fair. Sound form, the winner back to his best.

## 3830 EBF STALLIONS SOBA CONDITIONS STKS 5f 4y
**3:45** (3:45) (Class 3) 3-Y-O+ **£9,337** (£2,796; £1,398; £699; £349) **Stalls** Centre

Form RPR
-050 **1** **Hopes N Dreams (IRE)**[24] 2989 6-8-12 94.......................... PaulMulrennan 3 95
(Kevin Ryan) *mde all against stands' rail: rdn over 1f out: kpt on wl fnl f* **7/2**[3]
-400 **2** *nk* **Tangerine Trees**[17] 3241 9-9-3 95..........................................(v) TomEaves 1 99
(Bryan Smart) *racd wd: cl up: rdn 2f out: hung rt 1f out: kpt on fnl f: hld cl home* **9/4**[2]
3-16 **3** *1/2* **Sir Maximilian (IRE)**[3] 3715 5-9-3 96............................. StevieDonohoe 2 97
(Tim Pitt) *hung rt thrght: in tch: effrt and hdwy 2f out: drifted rt: kpt on fnl f: hld towards fin* **11/8**[1]
10-0 **4** *3/4* **Victory Laurel (IRE)**[24] 3030 4-9-3 103...........................(v[1]) JamieSpencer 4 94
(Robert Cowell) *trckd ldrs: effrt and drvn over 1f out: kpt on same pce ins fnl f* **13/2**
200 **5** *12* **Bix (IRE)**[20] 3099 4-8-10 44.......................................... JordanHibberd(7) 5 51?
(Alan Berry) *bhd: struggling after 2f: sn lost tch* **300/1**

59.01s (-0.99) **Going Correction** +0.05s/f (Good) **5** Ran SP% **108.8**
Speed ratings (Par 107): **109,108,107,106,87**
CSF £11.44 TOTE £4.70: £1.30, £1.70; EX 11.40 Trifecta £19.70.
**Owner** JCG Chua & CK Ong **Bred** J & Mrs Brennan & Edward & Mrs O'Regan **Trained** Hambleton, N Yorks

**FOCUS**
Quite an interesting 5f conditions race. The winner is rated close to her best.

## 3831 CHATELHERAULT PALACE H'CAP 5f 4y
**4:15** (4:15) (Class 4) (0-80,75) 3-Y-O+ **£5,175** (£1,540; £769; £384) **Stalls** Centre

Form RPR
4-35 **1** **Master Bond**[17] 3256 5-9-10 **73**.......................................... DanielTudhope 7 82
(David O'Meara) *in tch: effrt and drvn over 1f out: led ins fnl f: kpt on strly* **11/8**[1]
51-0 **2** *nk* **Tom Sawyer**[35] 2656 6-9-6 **72**...............................(b) ConnorBeasley(3) 1 80
(Julie Camacho) *cl up on outside: effrt and rdn 2f out: pressed wnr ins fnl f: r.o: hld nr fin* **16/1**
3550 **3** *1 1/2* **Economic Crisis (IRE)**[5] 3611 5-9-8 **71**........................ PaulMulrennan 3 74
(Alan Berry) *taken early to post: led and sn tacked over to stands' rail: rdn 2f out: edgd rt and hdd ins fnl f: one pce* **8/1**
0560 **4** *hd* **Medici Time**[3] 3702 9-9-1 **64**..........................................(v) TonyHamilton 5 66
(Tim Easterby) *hld up: rdn and hdwy over 1f out: kpt on fnl f: no imp* **10/1**
4155 **5** *shd* **Bunce (IRE)**[4] 3659 6-9-5 **71**.......................................... GeorgeChaloner(3) 6 72
(Linda Perratt) *chsd ldrs: drvn and outpcd 1/2-way: kpt on fnl f: nvr able to chal* **7/1**[3]
5-65 **6** *1* **Ingenti**[38] 2542 6-8-11 **65**.......................................... KevinStott(5) 4 63
(Christopher Wilson) *chsd ldr: drvn and chal over 1f out to ins fnl f: kpt on same pce* **7/1**[3]
0305 **7** *1 3/4* **Ambitious Icarus**[12] 3399 5-9-12 **75**..............................(e) RobertWinston 8 73
(Richard Guest) *sn drvn bhd ldng gp: hdwy over 1f out: keeping on whn nt clr run ins fnl f: sn no imp* **6/1**[2]
6000 **8** *2 1/2* **Findog**[34] 2675 4-8-10 **59**..........................................[1] PJMcDonald 2 42
(Linda Perratt) *taken early to post: dwlt: bhd and outpcd: nvr on terms* **28/1**

59.77s (-0.23) **Going Correction** +0.05s/f (Good) **8** Ran SP% **110.9**
Speed ratings (Par 105): **103,102,100,99,99 98,95,91**
CSF £24.42 CT £125.28 TOTE £2.00: £1.20, £2.00, £2.00; EX 21.20 Trifecta £112.70.
**Owner** Bonded Twentyten Partnership **Bred** Bond Thoroughbred Corporation **Trained** Nawton, N Yorks

**FOCUS**
Most of these were quite exposed. The form is rated around the runner-up.

## 3832 FOLLOW @HAMILTONPARKRC ON TWITTER MAIDEN STKS 6f 5y
**4:45** (4:47) (Class 5) 3-Y-O+ **£3,234** (£962; £481; £240) **Stalls** High

Form RPR
24-2 **1** **Epic Voyage (USA)**[26] 2932 3-9-5 80.............................. PJMcDonald 6 69+
(Brian Ellison) *t.k.h: chsd ldrs: drvn over 2f out: rallied over 1f out: led ins fnl f: drvn out* **4/9**[1]
3- **2** *2* **Bifocal**[301] 6082 3-9-0 0.......................................... GarryWhillans(5) 3 62
(Ian Semple) *led: rdn 2f out: hdd ins fnl f: kpt on u.p* **10/1**[3]
40-6 **3** *shd* **Redalani (IRE)**[8] 3530 4-9-6 54..............................(p) RobertWinston 1 58
(Alan Brown) *cl up on outside: rdn and hung rt over 1f out: kpt on same pce ins fnl f* **10/3**[2]
**4** *4 1/2* **Flaming Star** 3-9-0 0.......................................... StevieDonohoe 5 43
(John Holt) *dwlt: bhd and outpcd: nvr able to chal* **20/1**

1m 13.11s (0.91) **Going Correction** +0.05s/f (Good)
**WFA** 3 from 4yo 6lb **4** Ran SP% **106.2**
Speed ratings (Par 103): **95,92,92,86**
CSF £5.23 TOTE £1.40; EX 3.30 Trifecta £4.70.
**Owner** Koo's Racing Club **Bred** Juddmonte Farms Inc **Trained** Norton, N Yorks

**FOCUS**
A most uncompetitive maiden in which the market leader didn't have to reproduce his best to win in workmanlike fashion. The second and third set a modest standard. The gallop was reasonable.

## 3833 100% RACING UK PROFITS RETURNED TO RACING H'CAP 6f 5y
**5:15** (5:17) (Class 6) (0-65,61) 3-Y-O+ **£2,045** (£603; £302) **Stalls** High

Form RPR
4235 **1** **Rock Canyon (IRE)**[5] 3609 5-9-0 **50**.......................... ConnorBeasley(3) 12 56
(Linda Perratt) *towards rr and sn drvn along: hdwy towards stands' rail to ld appr fnl f: hld on wl u.p cl home* **7/1**[3]
4521 **2** *hd* **Amis Reunis**[8] 3530 5-9-5 **52** 6ex..................................(p) PatrickMathers 5 57
(Alan Berry) *hld up in tch: effrt and drvn towards stands' side over 1f out: ev ch wl ins fnl f: jst hld* **7/1**[3]
-000 **3** *1/2* **Locky Taylor (IRE)**[8] 3530 3-9-7 **60**..............................(p) TomEaves 6 63
(Kevin Ryan) *spd towards stands' side: outpcd and hung rt 1/2-way: rallied over 1f out: kpt on ins fnl f* **33/1**
0500 **4** *2 1/4* **Chloe's Dream (IRE)**[5] 3609 4-9-4 **56**.......................... KevinStott(5) 1 53
(Linda Perratt) *led centre tl edgd lft and hdd appr fnl f: kpt on same pce last 100yds* **22/1**
3-42 **5** *nk* **Spoken Words**[7] 3548 5-8-5 **45**.......................... AlistairRawlinson(7) 8 41
(John David Riches) *chsd ldrs: drvn and hung rt wl over 1f out: kpt on same pce fnl f* **7/2**[2]
542 **6** *1 1/2* **Funding Deficit (IRE)**[5] 3610 4-10-0 **61**.......................... GrahamLee 14 52
(Jim Goldie) *hung rt thrght: prom towards stands' side: rdn over 2f out: one pce over 1f out* **5/4**[1]
4363 **7** *1/2* **Red Shadow**[20] 3092 5-8-13 **46**..........................................(p) RobertWinston 7 35
(Alan Brown) *missed break: bhd towards stands' side: hdwy and hung rt over 1f out: nvr able to chal* **16/1**
0-30 **8** *3 1/4* **Monte Cassino (IRE)**[106] 996 9-9-5 **55**.......................... GeorgeChaloner(3) 10 34
(Bryan Smart) *dwlt: sn prom centre: drvn 1/2-way: wknd over 1f out* **33/1**
0460 **9** *1 1/4* **Tadalavil**[20] 3099 9-9-0 **52**.......................................... SammyJoBell(5) 13 27
(Linda Perratt) *hld up towards stands' side: rdn along 1/2-way: sn no imp* **25/1**
4-03 **10** *3/4* **Greenbury (IRE)**[69] 1647 3-8-12 **51**..............................(p) PJMcDonald 2 22
(Ann Duffield) *in tch centre: effrt and rdn over 2f out: wknd over 1f out* **16/1**
00-0 **11** *2 3/4* **Secret Kode (IRE)**[75] 1543 3-9-6 **59**.............................. RoystonFfrench 4 22
(Simon Waugh) *dwlt: a outpcd in centre* **33/1**

1m 12.48s (0.28) **Going Correction** +0.05s/f (Good)
**WFA** 3 from 4yo+ 6lb **11** Ran SP% **120.4**
Speed ratings (Par 101): **100,99,99,96,95 93,93,88,87,86 82**
CSF £52.91 CT £1530.42 TOTE £7.60: £1.90, £2.20, £6.10; EX 36.60 Trifecta £2399.10.
**Owner** Mrs Helen Perratt **Bred** Patrick J Connolly **Trained** East Kilbride, S Lanarks

**FOCUS**
This was a low-grade sprint handicap in which the runners were spread out from the centre to the nearside rails. It's doubtful the winner suddenly improved.
T/Plt: £127.70 to a £1 stake. Pool: £60,785.94 - 347.41 winning tickets. T/Qpdt: £24.00 to a £1 stake. Pool: £4,438.21 - 136.54 winning tickets. RY

## 2949 CATTERICK (L-H)

Wednesday, July 2

**OFFICIAL GOING: Good to firm (firm in places; 9.5)**

Wind: Moderate across Weather: Cloudy

### 3841 BRITISH STALLION STUDS EBF MAIDEN FILLIES' STKS (BOBIS RACE) 5f

2:30 (2:31) (Class 5) 2-Y-O £2,911 (£866; £432; £216) Stalls Low

| Form | | | | RPR |
|---|---|---|---|---|
| 30 | 1 | | **Adulation (IRE)**[14] 3353 2-9-0 0 GrahamGibbons 5 (William Haggas) *qckly away: mde all: clr over 2f out: readily* 4/9[1] | 81+ |
| 430 | 2 | 3 ¼ | **Magic Florence (IRE)**[47] 2313 2-9-0 0 GrahamLee 3 (James Given) *chsd wnr: rdn along 2f out: drvn over 1f out and sn no imp* 9/2[2] | 63 |
| 0 | 3 | 1 ¼ | **Crystal Wish**[21] 3107 2-8-9 0 KevinStott(5) 4 (Kevin Ryan) *trckd ldrs: hdwy to chse ldng pair 1/2-way: rdn along wl over 1f out: kpt on same pce* 16/1 | 59 |
| 0 | 4 | ½ | **Little Sista**[79] 1482 2-9-0 0 PaulMulrennan 1 (Bryan Smart) *chsd ldrs on inner: hdwy 2f out: sn rdn and kpt on appr fnl f* 14/1 | 57 |
| 56 | 5 | 3 ¼ | **Miss Van Gogh**[16] 3296 2-9-0 0 TonyHamilton 11 (Richard Fahey) *towards rr: hdwy wl over 1f out: sn rdn and kpt on fnl f: nvr nr ldrs* 9/1[3] | 45+ |
| 5 | 6 | 1 | **Jebediah Shine**[14] 3367 2-9-0 0 DanielTudhope 8 (David O'Meara) *chsd ldrs: rdn along over 2f out: sn one pce* 18/1 | 41 |
| 6 | 7 | 2 ¾ | **Savannah Beau**[33] 2731 2-9-0 0 RussKennemore 7 (Marjorie Fife) *prom: rdn along 1/2-way: sn wknd* 14/1 | 32 |
| | 8 | 13 | **Threatorapromise (IRE)** 2-9-0 0 BarryMcHugh 10 (Tony Coyle) *a in rr: outpcd and bhd fr 1/2-way* 33/1 | |
| | 9 | 5 | **Poppy In The Wind** 2-9-0 0 RobertWinston 6 (Alan Brown) *s.i.s: a bhd* 50/1 | |

59.44s (-0.36) **Going Correction** -0.175s/f (Firm) **9 Ran SP% 126.8**
Speed ratings (Par 91): **95,89,87,87,81 80,75,55,47**
CSF £3.44 TOTE £1.70: £1.10, £1.40, £5.30; EX 3.00 Trifecta £44.30.
**Owner** Cheveley Park Stud **Bred** E Mulryan **Trained** Newmarket, Suffolk

**FOCUS**
The winner apart, this looked a weak maiden. The winner is value for extra.

### 3842 EBFSTALLIONS.COM MEDIAN AUCTION MAIDEN STKS 5f 212y

3:00 (3:01) (Class 5) 2-Y-O £2,911 (£866; £432; £216) Stalls Low

| Form | | | | RPR |
|---|---|---|---|---|
| 63 | 1 | | **Tachophobia**[19] 3199 2-9-5 0 TonyHamilton 6 (Richard Fahey) *prom: effrt to chal 2f out: led over 1f out: sn rdn: drvn ins fnl f: kpt on* 7/4[2] | 77 |
| | 2 | hd | **Summer Times** 2-9-5 0 JoeFanning 3 (Mark Johnston) *trckd ldrs: green and pushed along 1/2-way: gd hdwy to trck ldrs 2f out: nt clr run over 1f out: swtchd rt and rdn to chse wnr ins fnl f: styd on strly: jst failed* 14/1[3] | 78+ |
| 0 | 3 | 4 ½ | **Captain Marmalade (IRE)**[47] 2298 2-9-5 0 GrahamLee 2 (Roger Charlton) *trckd ldrs: cl up 1/2-way: led over 2f out: rdn and hdd over 1f out: sn one pce* 4/6[1] | 63 |
| 4 | 4 | 5 | **Snoway**[45] 2358 2-9-0 0 BarryMcHugh 5 (Tony Coyle) *t.k.h: in tch: pushed along and outpcd 1/2-way: sn rdn and kpt on appr fnl f* 22/1 | 43 |
| 06 | 5 | 5 | **Cerise Firth**[36] 2652 2-9-0 0 GrahamGibbons 1 (Steph Hollinshead) *slt ld: jnd wl over 2f out: sn hdd & wknd* 50/1 | 28+ |
| 0 | 6 | 1 ¼ | **Jubilee Spirit**[39] 2541 2-9-5 0 TomEaves 7 (Geoffrey Oldroyd) *dwlt and sltly hmpd s: a in rr: bhd fr 1/2-way* 66/1 | 29 |
| 00 | 7 | 1 ¼ | **Just No Rules**[9] 3529 2-8-7 0 LauraBarry(7) 4 (Tony Coyle) *sn outpcd in rr: bhd fr 1/2-way* 80/1 | 21 |

1m 13.63s (0.03) **Going Correction** -0.175s/f (Firm) **7 Ran SP% 112.1**
Speed ratings (Par 94): **92,91,85,79,72 70,69**
CSF £21.34 TOTE £4.70: £2.00, £3.90; EX 9.20 Trifecta £20.90.
**Owner** A Rhodes Haulage And P Timmins **Bred** Springcombe Park Stud **Trained** Musley Bank, N Yorks

**FOCUS**
Three of these dominated the final stages. There's probably better to come from the winner.

### 3843 WEAR A YELLOW JERSEY H'CAP (A QUALIFIER FOR THE 2014 CATTERICK TWELVE FURLONG SERIES FINAL) 1m 3f 214y

3:30 (3:30) (Class 6) (0-65,65) 4-Y-O+ £3,408 (£1,006; £503) Stalls Low

| Form | | | | RPR |
|---|---|---|---|---|
| 06 | 1 | | **Dabuki (FR)**[16] 3301 4-9-7 65 (p) PJMcDonald 7 (Geoffrey Harker) *mde all: rdn clr over 1f out: drvn ins fnl f: kpt on* 4/1[2] | 71 |
| 4666 | 2 | nk | **Monzino (USA)**[87] 1117 6-7-9 46 oh1 BradleyBosley(7) 1 (Michael Chapman) *t.k.h: trckd ldng pair: hdwy over 2f out: sn rdn: chsd wnr ent fnl f: kpt on wl towards fin: jst hld* 12/1 | 51 |
| /636 | 3 | 5 | **Rockabilly Riot (IRE)**[11] 3482 4-9-3 61 PhillipMakin 2 (Martin Todhunter) *hld up in tch: hdwy 3f out: rdn along 2f out: drvn and kpt on same pce appr fnl f* 11/4[1] | 58 |
| 4002 | 4 | ½ | **Patavium (IRE)**[13] 3398 11-7-10 47 (p) RachelRichardson(7) 8 (Edwin Tuer) *t.k.h: trckd ldrs: hdwy to chse wnr after 3f: rdn along over 2f out: drvn over 1f out: sn one pce* 4/1[2] | 43 |
| 3-00 | 5 | 1 | **Maillot Jaune (IRE)**[14] 3364 4-7-11 46 JackGarritty(5) 3 (Patrick Holmes) *hld up in tch: hdwy on inner over 3f out: rdn to chse ldrs 2f out: drvn and one pce fr over 1f out* 9/1 | 40 |
| 530- | 6 | 2 ¼ | **Weybridge Light**[10] 6216 9-8-8 52 (b) RaulDaSilva 5 (David Thompson) *hld up towards rr: hdwy 3f out: rdn along over 2f out: plugged on appr fnl f: n.d* 12/1 | 43 |
| 5-00 | 7 | 5 | **Yorkshireman (IRE)**[16] 3301 4-8-10 54 ow2 DaleSwift 6 (Lynn Siddall) *a in rr* 25/1 | 37 |
| 0-65 | 8 | 2 ½ | **District Attorney (IRE)**[9] 3535 5-8-2 46 (v) DuranFentiman 9 (Chris Fairhurst) *a towards rr* 13/2[3] | 25 |
| 0-00 | 9 | ½ | **Turjuman (USA)**[11] 3482 9-7-13 46 oh1 (v) NeilFarley(3) 4 (Simon West) *chsd ldrs: rdn along over 3f out: wknd 2f out* 40/1 | 24 |

2m 37.23s (-1.67) **Going Correction** -0.175s/f (Firm) **9 Ran SP% 111.7**
Speed ratings (Par 101): **98,97,94,94,93 91,88,86,86**
CSF £48.30 CT £149.08 TOTE £5.90: £1.70, £5.40, £1.80; EX 70.90 Trifecta £495.20.
**Owner** J Blackburn & A Turton **Bred** Catherine Niederhauser **Trained** Thirkleby, N Yorks

**FOCUS**
Modest form and it paid to be handy. The ex-French winner's fisrt real turf form.

### 3844 YORKSHIRE WELCOMES LE GRAND DEPART H'CAP 7f

4:00 (4:00) (Class 4) (0-80,79) 3-Y-O+ £6,469 (£1,925; £962; £481) Stalls Low

| Form | | | | RPR |
|---|---|---|---|---|
| 1036 | 1 | | **Little Shambles**[16] 3305 3-9-6 79 JoeFanning 4 (Mark Johnston) *mde all: jnd and rdn 2f out: drvn clr over 1f out: styd on strly* 5/1[3] | 88 |
| 3453 | 2 | 2 ¾ | **Solar Spirit (IRE)**[26] 2953 9-9-10 75 RobertWinston 1 (Tracy Waggott) *t.k.h: hld up: gd hdwy 2f out: chsd wnr over 1f out and sn rdn: drvn and no imp ins fnl f* 5/1[3] | 81 |
| 0043 | 3 | 1 ¼ | **Hard Core Debt**[12] 3439 4-8-13 64 DaleSwift 7 (Brian Ellison) *towards rr: hdwy wl over 2f out: rdn to chse ldrs over 1f out: kpt on same pce fnl f* 5/1[3] | 66 |
| -006 | 4 | 1 ¾ | **Lightnin Hopkins (IRE)**[26] 2953 4-9-12 77 (p) DanielTudhope 2 (David O'Meara) *trckd ldrs on inner: effrt over 2f out: sn rdn: drvn and wknd over 1f out* 7/2[2] | 74 |
| 0-63 | 5 | 1 ¼ | **No Quarter (IRE)**[15] 3339 7-8-11 62 RoystonFfrench 3 (Tracy Waggott) *t.k.h: trckd ldng pair: hdwy and cl up 2f out: sn rdn and ev ch tl wknd appr fnl f* 12/1 | 56 |
| -004 | 6 | hd | **Just The Tonic**[15] 3340 7-9-7 72 BarryMcHugh 5 (Marjorie Fife) *in rr: effrt and hdwy over 2f out: rdn wl over 1f out: no imp* 16/1 | 65 |
| 3512 | 7 | 1 ¼ | **Kung Hei Fat Choy (USA)**[65] 1803 5-9-12 77 (b) GrahamLee 6 (James Given) *hld up in tch: smooth hdwy on outer 1/2-way: chsd ldrs 2f out: rdn over 1f out: wknd ent fnl f* 3/1[1] | 67 |
| 30-0 | 8 | 9 | **Slim Chance (IRE)**[9] 3533 5-9-1 66 AndrewElliott 8 (Simon West) *t.k.h: cl up: rdn along 2f out: sn wknd* 33/1 | 33 |

1m 25.3s (-1.70) **Going Correction** -0.175s/f (Firm)
**WFA** 3 from 4yo+ 8lb **8 Ran SP% 113.7**
Speed ratings (Par 105): **102,98,97,95,94 93,92,82**
CSF £29.76 CT £131.07 TOTE £5.40: £1.60, £2.80, £1.80; EX 30.60 Trifecta £111.10.
**Owner** Sheikh Hamdan bin Mohammed Al Maktoum **Bred** Darley **Trained** Middleham Moor, N Yorks

**FOCUS**
A fair handicap. The winner was another to make all and rates a length personal best.

### 3845 RACINGUK.COM/ANYWHERE 3DEVICES 1PRICE H'CAP 1m 7f 177y

4:30 (4:30) (Class 5) (0-75,74) 4-Y-O+ £2,911 (£866; £432; £216) Stalls Low

| Form | | | | RPR |
|---|---|---|---|---|
| 0-41 | 1 | | **Hot Spice**[11] 3482 6-9-2 69 GrahamGibbons 3 (Michael Easterby) *mde all: stdd gallop after 7f: qckng over 3f out: rdn and qckd 2f out: drvn ins fnl f and kpt on strly* 3/1[2] | 79 |
| -656 | 2 | 2 ½ | **Dr Irv**[19] 3204 5-9-7 74 PJMcDonald 1 (Philip Kirby) *trckd ldng pair: hdwy on inner over 3f out: chsd wnr over 2f out: rdn wl over 1f out: drvn ins fnl f: sn no imp* 5/4[1] | 81 |
| 6032 | 3 | 14 | **Ferdy (IRE)**[9] 3535 5-8-3 56 RaulDaSilva 6 (Paul Green) *hld up in rr: hdwy over 2f out: rdn to take 3rd over 1f out: n.d* 8/1 | 46 |
| 24-3 | 4 | ¾ | **Danceintothelight**[11] 3482 7-7-13 55 NeilFarley(3) 4 (Micky Hammond) *trckd ldng pair: pushed along 4f out: rdn over 3f out: sn outpcd* 9/1 | 44 |
| 5112 | 5 | 1 ¼ | **Anne's Valentino**[17] 3269 4-8-4 57 JamesSullivan 2 (Malcolm Jefferson) *trckd ldr: rdn along 3f out: wknd 2f out* 9/2[3] | 45 |
| 0-60 | 6 | ½ | **Sohcahtoa (IRE)**[10] 1763 8-7-11 55 oh2 (e) JackGarritty(5) 5 (Andrew Crook) *hld up: a towards rr* 25/1 | 42 |

3m 27.25s (-4.75) **Going Correction** -0.175s/f (Firm) **6 Ran SP% 112.6**
Speed ratings (Par 103): **104,102,95,95,94 94**
CSF £7.22 TOTE £4.20: £2.20, £1.80; EX 13.00 Trifecta £45.50.
**Owner** S Hull, D Swales, A Turton & J Blackburn **Bred** J L Dunlop **Trained** Sheriff Hutton, N Yorks

**FOCUS**
A fair staying event. The winner's best form since he was a 3yo.

### 3846 RACING AGAIN NEXT WEDNESDAY CLASSIFIED STKS 7f

5:00 (5:00) (Class 6) 3-Y-O+ £2,385 (£704; £352) Stalls Low

| Form | | | | RPR |
|---|---|---|---|---|
| -313 | 1 | | **Crafted (IRE)**[5] 3647 3-8-12 64 JoeFanning 5 (Mark Johnston) *mde all: qcknd 2f out: rdn clr over 1f out: styd on strly* 5/4[1] | 78+ |
| 3021 | 2 | 3 ¾ | **The Dukkerer (IRE)**[13] 3380 3-8-12 64 JasonHart 6 (Garry Moss) *trckd wnr: cl up 1/2-way: rdn along 2f out: drvn and edgd lft over 1f out: kpt on same pce* 11/4[2] | 65 |
| 5004 | 3 | 2 ½ | **Bearskin (IRE)**[9] 3534 3-8-12 54 (v[1]) PJMcDonald 1 (Ann Duffield) *t.k.h: trckd ldrs on inner: hdwy to chse ldng pair wl over 2f out: swtchd rt and rdn over 1f out: sn drvn and no imp* 12/1 | 59 |
| 404 | 4 | 3 ¼ | **Shillito**[16] 3298 4-8-13 60 LauraBarry(7) 8 (Tony Coyle) *dwlt and towards rr: hdwy wl over 2f out: swtchd rt and rdn 1 1/2f out: kpt on: nrst fin* 13/2[3] | 53 |
| 46-0 | 5 | 1 | **Paddy's Rock (IRE)**[16] 3298 3-8-5 56 RowanScott(7) 4 (Ann Duffield) *dwlt and towards rr: hdwy on inner over 2f out: sn rdn along and plugged on: nrst fin* 14/1 | 47 |
| 5034 | 6 | 4 | **Graceful Act**[26] 2954 6-9-6 56 TomEaves 12 (Ron Barr) *prom on outer: pushed along 3f out: rdn over 2f out: grad wknd* 50/1 | 40 |
| 5313 | 7 | 1 ¾ | **Betty Boo (IRE)**[26] 2955 4-9-6 60 DuranFentiman 3 (Shaun Harris) *dwlt and in rr tl sme late hdwy* 10/1 | 36 |
| 6666 | 8 | 1 ¼ | **Some Boy Lukey**[12] 3438 3-8-12 45 RaulDaSilva 9 (David Thompson) *chsd ldrs: rdn along wl over 2f out: sn wknd* 100/1 | 29 |
| 00-0 | 9 | nk | **Koolgreycat (IRE)**[33] 2724 5-8-13 51 PeterSword(7) 7 (Noel Wilson) *t.k.h: a towards rr* 100/1 | 31 |
| 6040 | 10 | 3 ¾ | **Midnight Warrior**[12] 3439 4-9-6 49 PaulPickard 11 (Ron Barr) *a towards rr* 66/1 | 22 |
| -050 | 11 | 5 | **St Paul'S (IRE)**[36] 2657 3-8-12 54 (tp) AdrianNicholls 2 (David C Griffiths) *chsd ldrs: rdn wl over 2f out: sn wknd* 25/1 | 6 |
| 60-0 | 12 | nk | **Miss Matiz**[12] 3439 7-9-6 44 RoystonFfrench 10 (Tracy Waggott) *midfield: effrt and sme hdwy wl over 2f out: sn rdn and wknd* 100/1 | 8 |

1m 25.49s (-1.51) **Going Correction** -0.175s/f (Firm)
**WFA** 3 from 4yo+ 8lb **12 Ran SP% 118.2**
Speed ratings (Par 101): **101,96,93,90,89 84,82,81,80,76 70,70**
CSF £4.41 TOTE £2.60: £1.50, £1.10, £3.20; EX 6.70 Trifecta £55.50.
**Owner** Sheikh Hamdan bin Mohammed Al Maktoum **Bred** Joe Osborne **Trained** Middleham Moor, N Yorks

**FOCUS**
It had become obvious during the meeting that front-runners were favoured, so Joe Fanning was quick to get his mount to the front. Improved form from the winner.

T/Plt: £11.30 to a £1 stake. Pool: £57191.00 - 3683.58 winning tickets T/Qpdt: £4.70 to a £1 stake. Pool: £3627.83 - 569.85 winning tickets JR

# 3514 CHEPSTOW (L-H)

Wednesday, July 2

**OFFICIAL GOING: Good to firm**

Wind: slight behind Weather: sunny spells

## 3847 EBF STALLIONS BET365 MAIDEN STKS — 6f 16y

**6:10** (6:10) (Class 5) 2-Y-O — **£2,911** (£866; £432; £216) **Stalls** Centre

Form — RPR

0 **1** **Guiding Light (IRE)**[12] 3429 2-9-5 0 ... JimmyFortune 7 76+
(Andrew Balding) *w ldr: led 2f out: jnd ent fnl f: sn edgd rt u.p: asserted fnl 50yds* **7/2**[2]

**2** 3/4 **La Estatua** 2-9-0 0 ... JimmyQuinn 9 69+
(James Tate) *hld up towards rr: pushed along and hdwy over 1f out: chal ent fnl f: sn carried rt: hld fnl 50yds* **12/1**

**3** 3 **Wonder Of Qatar (IRE)** 2-9-5 0 ... RichardHughes 4 65+
(Richard Hannon) *hld up in tch: rdn over 2f out: chsd ldng pair fnl f: kpt on same pce: improve* **4/5**[1]

00 **4** 4 1/2 **Air Of York (IRE)**[58] 2007 2-9-5 0 ... DavidProbert 6 51
(Ronald Harris) *chsd ldrs: pushed along whn n.m.r and swtchd rt over 2f out: styd on u.p ins fnl f* **66/1**

46 **5** 1 1/2 **Arizona Snow**[58] 2007 2-9-5 0 ... SteveDrowne 5 47
(Ronald Harris) *t.k.h: led narrowly tl rdn and hdd 2f out: wknd ins fnl f* **20/1**

056 **6** 1/2 **Smugglers Lane (IRE)**[30] 2837 2-9-5 0 ... LiamKeniry 8 45
(David Evans) *chsd ldrs: rdn over 2f out: grad outpcd fr over 1f out* **33/1**

524 **7** 1 3/4 **Town Crier (IRE)**[15] 3324 2-9-5 0 ... LiamJones 3 40
(William Haggas) *s.i.s: towards rr: rdn and hdwy to press ldrs over 2f out: wknd over 1f out* **5/1**[3]

40 **8** 3 1/4 **Godric**[13] 3394 2-9-5 0 ... RichardKingscote 2 30
(Tom Dascombe) *prom: pushed along fr 1/2-way: wknd over 1f out* **16/1**

50 **9** 4 **Abba Zabba (IRE)**[26] 2944 2-9-5 0 ... BenCurtis 1 18
(David Evans) *a in rr: lost tch 1/2-way* **66/1**

1m 12.73s (0.73) **Going Correction** -0.025s/f (Good) **9** Ran SP% **118.7**

Speed ratings (Par 94): **94,93,89,83,81 80,78,73,68**

CSF £43.10 TOTE £4.40: £1.10, £3.70, £1.10; EX 42.90 Trifecta £176.20.

**Owner** Thurloe Thoroughbreds XXXIV **Bred** Providence Stud **Trained** Kingsclere, Hants

**FOCUS**

The front pair drew clear in what was an ordinary juvenile maiden. The time and the sixth limit the form.

## 3848 BINGO AT BET365 H'CAP — 6f 16y

**6:40** (6:40) (Class 6) (0-65,71) 3-Y-O+ — **£1,940** (£577; £216; £216) **Stalls** Centre

Form — RPR

-100 **1** **Euroquip Boy (IRE)**[20] 3149 7-8-13 **55** ... NoelGarbutt(5) 17 65
(Michael Scudamore) *sed awkwardly: sn chsng ldrs stands' side: led gp 2f out: overall ldr appr fnl f: r.o u.p* **8/1**

0500 **2** 3/4 **Divine Call**[20] 3149 7-9-4 **58** ... (v) OisinMurphy(3) 15 66
(Milton Bradley) *hld up in rr stands' side: rdn over 2f out: hdwy over 1f out: chsd wnr ins fnl f: kpt on* **16/1**

5423 **3** 2 1/4 **Consistant**[16] 3298 6-9-5 **56** ... AndrewMullen 10 57
(Brian Baugh) *s.i.s: chsd ldrs on stands' side: rdn over 2f out: edgd lft over 1f out: wnt rt ins fnl f: kpt on* **6/1**[2]

0051 **3** dht **Verus Delicia (IRE)**[8] 3549 5-10-1 **66** 6ex ... ShaneKelly 16 70
(Daniel Mark Loughnane) *chsd ldrs stands' side: pushed along 1/2-way: keeping on against rail whn hmpd early ins fnl f: r.o* **7/1**[3]

0654 **5** nk **Diamond Vine (IRE)**[30] 2831 6-8-9 **46** ... (p) LukeMorris 11 46
(Ronald Harris) *led stands' side 2f: styd prom: rdn 1/2-way: kpt on* **20/1**

5041 **6** 1 **See The Storm**[9] 3519 6-10-3 **71** 6ex ... CharlesBishop(3) 7 68
(Ian Williams) *towards rr far side: rdn and hdwy over 2f out: r.o fnl f* **10/1**

5000 **7** nk **New Rich**[28] 2887 4-9-5 **61** ... (p) GeorgeDowning(5) 8 57
(Eve Johnson Houghton) *s.i.s: towards rr far side: rdn over 2f out: n.m.r wl over 1f out: r.o ins fnl f* **25/1**

0221 **8** 2 1/2 **Decision By One**[2] 3783 5-9-6 **64** 6ex ... (t) HollieDoyle(7) 14 52
(David Evans) *cl up stands' side: led gp after 2f to 2f out: sn rdn: wknd fnl f* **7/1**[3]

0010 **9** shd **Night Trade (IRE)**[22] 3088 7-9-5 **56** ... (p) SteveDrowne 3 43
(Ronald Harris) *towards rr far side: hdwy over 2f out: kpt on: nvr rchd ldrs* **25/1**

6205 **10** nk **Hamis Al Bin (IRE)**[43] 2414 5-9-7 **58** ... (t) RichardKingscote 6 44
(Milton Bradley) *chsd ldr far side: rdn over 2f out: one pce* **14/1**

1344 **11** 1/2 **Colourbearer (IRE)**[88] 1311 7-8-11 **48** ... (t) BenCurtis 5 33
(Milton Bradley) *led far side and overall ldr: drvn over 2f out: hdd appr fnl f: sn wknd* **20/1**

4351 **12** 3/4 **Picc Of Burgau**[9] 3520 4-9-10 **61** 6ex ... GeorgeBaker 1 43
(Geoffrey Deacon) *wnt to post early: chsd ldr far side: rdn and wknd over 1f out* **4/1**[1]

6-62 **13** 2 **Logans Lad (IRE)**[19] 3178 4-9-11 **62** ... (bt) FrankieMcDonald 4 38
(Daniel Mark Loughnane) *racd keenly: hld up bhd ldrs far side: drvn over 2f out: wknd over 1f out* **16/1**

0-50 **14** 3 **Assembly**[33] 2718 4-9-13 **64** ... RichardHughes 13 30
(Mark Rimell) *chsd ldrs stands' side: lost pl 1/2-way: no ch fnl 2f* **20/1**

00-0 **15** 1 1/2 **Basle**[110] 963 7-8-6 **48** ... (tp) JoshBaudains(5) 9 10
(Roy Brotherton) *wnt to post early: towards rr far side: pushed along 1/2-way: wknd over 1f out* **33/1**

0-06 **16** 2 **Fortrose Academy (IRE)**[81] 1448 5-9-3 **54** ... (p) LiamKeniry 2 9
(Chris Gordon) *towards rr far side: rdn and wknd over 1f out* **25/1**

1m 12.07s (0.07) **Going Correction** -0.025s/f (Good) **16** Ran SP% **126.7**

Speed ratings (Par 101): **98,97,94,94,93 92,91,88,88,88 87,86,83,79,77 75**

WIN: 16.30 Euroquip Boy; PL: 2.30 Verus Delicia, 3.10 Euroquip Boy, 1.40 Consistant, 4.30 Divine Call; EX: 238.60; CSF: 120.65; TC: 331.45, 421.30; TF: 973.00, TRIFECTA Part won..

**Owner** Ted Bennett **Bred** Gerard And Yvonne Kennedy **Trained** Bromsash, H'fords

■ Stewards' Enquiry : Oisin Murphy two-day ban: careless riding (Jul 16-17)

**FOCUS**

Spread across the track, it was those nearest the stands' rail who came out on top. The winner's best form for the past two years.

## 3849 BET365.COM MEDIAN AUCTION MAIDEN STKS — 7f 16y

**7:10** (7:10) (Class 6) 3-4-Y-O — **£2,045** (£603; £302) **Stalls** Centre

Form — RPR

5532 **1** **Hoy Hoy (IRE)**[11] 3486 3-9-3 70 ... GeorgeBaker 4 69
(Mick Channon) *hld up in tch: rdn 3f out: hdwy to chse ldr appr fnl f: r.o to ld fnl 50yds* **2/1**[1]

-440 **2** 1/2 **Foxford**[20] 3144 3-8-12 67 ... LiamKeniry 8 63
(Patrick Chamings) *led narrowly: pushed along over 2f out: 2 l up ent fnl f: sn drvn and hung lft: hdd and no ex fnl 50yds* **7/2**[3]

0 **3** 2 1/2 **Mad Endeavour**[65] 1808 3-9-3 0 ... MartinLane 2 62
(Stuart Kittow) *racd keenly: a.p: rdn over 2f out: kpt on same pce* **12/1**

-034 **4** 1 1/2 **Trigger Park (IRE)**[19] 3178 3-9-3 53 ... SteveDrowne 9 58
(Ronald Harris) *mid-div: rdn 3f out: styd on fnl 2f: nt rch ldrs* **10/1**

6 **5** 2 1/4 **Avon Scent**[35] 2667 4-9-6 0 ... DavidProbert 5 50
(Christopher Mason) *w ldr to 1/2-way: styd prom tl rdn and lost pl 2f out: styd on again fnl f* **25/1**

**6** 1/2 **Adimendis (IRE)** 3-9-3 0 ... [1] JohnFahy 6 50+
(J S Moore) *s.i.s: towards rr: rdn 1/2-way and rn green: sn no ch w ldrs: pushed along and kpt on fnl f* **20/1**

-000 **7** hd **Reflection**[16] 3303 3-8-12 42 ... AndrewMullen 7 45
(Brian Baugh) *mid-div: rdn and hdwy 3f out: one pce fnl 2f* **100/1**

04 **8** 1 1/4 **Field Force**[35] 2681 3-9-3 0 ... RichardHughes 1 47
(Amanda Perrett) *chsd ldrs: rdn 3f out: wknd 1f out* **9/4**[2]

00- **9** 4 **With A Twist**[268] 7069 3-8-9 0 ... OisinMurphy(3) 3 31
(Andrew Balding) *s.s: in rr: pushed along and sme hdwy 3f out: wknd over 1f out* **16/1**

4500 **10** 14 **Luv U Honey**[58] 2023 3-8-12 35 ... JimmyQuinn 10
(Brian Baugh) *in rr: rdn over 3f out: lost tch 2f out* **50/1**

1m 24.62s (1.42) **Going Correction** -0.025s/f (Good)

**WFA** 3 from 4yo 8lb **10** Ran SP% **120.5**

Speed ratings (Par 101): **90,89,86,84,82 81,81,80,75,59**

CSF £9.45 TOTE £2.90: £1.10, £2.00, £6.20; EX 10.00 Trifecta £111.00.

**Owner** Sheikh Mohammed Bin Khalifa Al Maktoum **Bred** J K Thoroughbreds **Trained** West Ilsley, Berks

**FOCUS**

Quite a modest maiden. The winner was probably a bit better than the bare form.

## 3850 BET365 H'CAP — 1m 14y

**7:40** (7:41) (Class 5) (0-75,74) 3-Y-O+ — **£2,587** (£770; £384; £192) **Stalls** Centre

Form — RPR

6531 **1** **Bountybeamadam**[19] 3177 4-9-13 **73** ... (p) PatCosgrave 9 83
(George Baker) *led stands' side: led overall 1/2-way: pushed along over 2f out: idled u.p ins fnl f: styd on wl* **7/1**

-661 **2** 1 3/4 **Charlie Wells (IRE)**[9] 3516 3-9-0 **69** 6ex ... JohnFahy 1 73+
(Eve Johnson Houghton) *chsd other pair in centre: in tch overall: rdn over 3f out: pressed ldrs 2f out: r.o fnl f to go 2nd last strides* **5/1**[2]

4051 **3** nk **Tenbridge**[19] 3176 5-9-1 **61** ... (v) DavidProbert 7 66
(Derek Haydn Jones) *wnt to post early: trckd wnr stands' side: rdn over 2f out: r.o: no ex fnl 100yds: ct for 2nd last strides* **6/1**[3]

-020 **4** 1/2 **Lady Bayside**[4] 3733 6-9-10 **70** ... GeorgeBaker 6 74
(Malcolm Saunders) *trckd ldrs stands' side: nt clr run briefly over 2f out: rdn whn hit on hd by rival's whip over 1f out: kpt on same pce fnl f* **5/1**[2]

0554 **5** 2 **Peak Storm**[19] 3177 5-9-10 **70** ... (p) LukeMorris 5 69
(John O'Shea) *s.i.s: towards rr stands' side: pushed along 1/2-way: sme hdwy u.p over 2f out: kpt on fnl f* **8/1**

326 **6** 1 1/4 **Inkerman (IRE)**[18] 3227 4-10-0 **74** ... (t) RichardHughes 8 70
(Jamie Osborne) *in rr stands' side: pushed along fnl 2f: kpt on ins fnl f: nvr trbld ldrs* **8/1**

5-02 **7** 2 1/2 **Imperial Glance**[33] 2721 4-9-5 **68** ... OisinMurphy(3) 4 59
(Andrew Balding) *trckd ldr in centre trio: rdn to chse overall ldr over 2f out: wknd fnl f* **11/4**[1]

4340 **8** 17 **Boogangoo (IRE)**[20] 3144 3-9-2 **71** ... StevieDonohoe 2 21
(Grace Harris) *c stands' side after 1f: a in rr: rdn over 2f out: wknd over 1f out: t.o* **10/1**

-255 **9** 2 1/4 **Citizen Kaine (IRE)**[58] 2596 3-8-12 **67** ... LiamJones 3 11
(Jo Hughes) *led trio in centre and overall: hdd 1/2-way: drvn and wknd over 2f out: t.o* **25/1**

1m 35.06s (-1.14) **Going Correction** -0.025s/f (Good)

**WFA** 3 from 4yo+ 9lb **9** Ran SP% **121.9**

Speed ratings (Par 103): **104,102,101,101,99 98,95,78,76**

CSF £44.36 CT £230.85 TOTE £7.00: £2.10, £2.30, £2.60; EX 68.20 Trifecta £328.70.

**Owner** Whitsbury Hopefuls **Bred** Brightwalton Stud **Trained** Manton, Wilts

**FOCUS**

As in the earlier handicap on the card, it proved an advantage to race near to the stands' rail. Improvement from the winner.

## 3851 CASINO AT BET365 H'CAP — 2m 49y

**8:10** (8:10) (Class 5) (0-75,81) 4-Y-O+ — **£2,587** (£770; £384; £192) **Stalls** Low

Form — RPR

2351 **1** **Annaluna (IRE)**[19] 3179 5-8-7 **61** ... (v) DavidProbert 6 69
(David Evans) *chsd ldng pair after 1f: chal 3f out: sn led: rdn ent fnl f: styd on wl* **10/1**

4-25 **2** 1 1/2 **Our Folly**[41] 2482 6-9-5 **73** ... (t) PatCosgrave 2 79
(Stuart Kittow) *hld up in 5th: hdwy u.p 3f out: chsd wnr appr fnl f: no ex fnl 50yds* **6/1**[2]

0-02 **3** 2 **Jezza**[35] 2683 8-8-12 **66** ... (bt) RichardHughes 1 70
(Karen George) *dwlt: hld up in last: rdn over 2f out: styd on ins fnl f to go 3rd cl home* **14/1**

11/1 **4** hd **Solar View (IRE)**[5] 3680 5-9-13 **81** 6ex ... LukeMorris 8 84
(Sir Mark Prescott Bt) *wnt to post early: hld up in 6th: niggled along over 5f out: n.m.r over 2f out: sn chsng ldng pair: one pce u.p fnl f: lost 3rd cl home* **4/7**[1]

655 **5** 2 1/4 **Desert Recluse (IRE)**[20] 3151 7-9-6 **74** ... StevieDonohoe 9 75
(Ian Williams) *chsd ldr: rdn and ev ch 3f out: fdd appr fnl f* **16/1**

-200 **6** 2 1/4 **Ashdown Lad**[24] 3034 5-9-4 **75** ... (p) OisinMurphy(3) 3 73
(Tom Symonds) *led: drvn 3f out: sn hdd: wknd over 1f out* **8/1**[3]

0-00 **7** 1 **Significant Move**[65] 1811 7-9-0 **68** ... MartinLane 4 65
(Stuart Kittow) *racd mainly in 4th tl drvn 3f out: wknd over 1f out* **20/1**

3m 40.14s (1.24) **Going Correction** +0.225s/f (Good) **7** Ran SP% **115.5**

Speed ratings (Par 103): **105,104,103,103,102 100,100**

CSF £68.48 CT £845.50 TOTE £8.50: £2.80, £3.00; EX 52.10 Trifecta £150.80.

**Owner** Nick Shutts **Bred** Michael Daiton **Trained** Pandy, Monmouths

**FOCUS**
A modest handicap. Another step up from the winner but the favourite disappointed.

**3852** **POKER AT BET365 H'CAP** **1m 4f 23y**
8:40 (8:40) (Class 6) (0-60,60) 4-Y-O+ £1,940 (£577; £288; £144) Stalls Low

Form RPR
645 1 **Crouching Harry (IRE)**[30] 2836 5-8-11 50....(p) JohnFahy 3 58
(Anabel K Murphy) *mid-div: rdn and hdwy over 2f out: swtchd rt over 1f out: led 100yds out: r.o* 10/1
662 2 ½ **Rowlestone Lass**[16] 3309 4-8-11 50.... ShaneKelly 9 57
(Richard Price) *racd keenly: chsd ldrs: wnt 2nd 4f out: led on bit 2f out: shkn up ent fnl f: hdd 100yds out: no ex* 3/1[1]
05-0 3 *nk* **On Stage**[74] 1574 5-9-3 56.... MartinLane 10 62
(Stuart Kittow) *s.s: in rr: rdn and hdwy 3f out: styd on wl ins fnl f* 5/1[2]
0-21 4 2 ¼ **Captain Oats (IRE)**[18] 3209 11-9-2 60.... RachealKneller(5) 2 62
(Pam Ford) *s.i.s: in rr: stdy hdwy 3f out: rdn 2f out: one pce and no further imp fnl f* 10/1
040/ 5 1 **Surprise Us**[60] 7018 7-8-6 46 ow2.... OisinMurphy(3) 4 48
(Mark Gillard) *led: drvn over 3f out: hdd 2f out: one pce after* 33/1
665- 6 3 **Hollywood All Star (IRE)**[7] 2237 5-8-7 46.... DavidProbert 5 42
(Graeme McPherson) *mid-div: rdn 3f out: one pce and no real imp* 20/1
-041 7 6 **Glens Wobbly**[26] 2942 6-8-12 54.... RyanTate(3) 6 40
(Jonathan Geake) *trckd ldr to 4f out: sn drvn: one pce and hld whn hmpd over 1f out* 3/1[1]
6-04 8 *hd* **Ninepointsixthree**[30] 2836 4-8-10 49....(p) LukeMorris 1 35
(John O'Shea) *trckd ldrs: rdn over 4f out: grad wknd fnl 2f* 8/1[3]
042 9 22 **Innoko (FR)**[15] 3336 4-9-7 60....(t) RichardHughes 8 42
(Tony Carroll) *hld up: hdwy 6f out: drvn 3f out: wknd 2f out: eased ent fnl f: t.o* 5/1[2]
2m 42.43s (3.43) **Going Correction** +0.225s/f (Good) 9 Ran SP% 120.3
Speed ratings (Par 101): **97,96,96,94,94 92,88,88,73**
CSF £41.93 CT £174.80 TOTE £9.50: £3.00, £2.00, £2.00; EX 55.50 Trifecta £369.20.
**Owner** Touchwood Racing **Bred** Moyglare Stud Farm Ltd **Trained** Wilmcote, Warwicks
**FOCUS**
Lowly but straightforward form and the pace was fairly steady.

**3853** **BET365.COM H'CAP** **1m 2f 36y**
9:10 (9:10) (Class 6) (0-65,68) 4-Y-O+ £1,940 (£577; £288; £144) Stalls Low

Form RPR
4320 1 **April Ciel**[7] 3585 5-9-7 65....(p) LukeMorris 9 74
(Ronald Harris) *mde all: rdn over 2f out: edgd rt over 1f out: hld on wl u.p* 9/2[3]
0663 2 1 ¼ **Ashkalara**[13] 3390 7-8-5 49.... MartinLane 4 56
(Stuart Howe) *taken steadily to post: t.k.h in rr: hdwy 3f out: styd on u.p to go 2nd fnl 100yds: nt rch wnr* 12/1
6501 3 *hd* **Gabrial The Terror (IRE)**[8] 3553 4-9-7 68 6ex.... OisinMurphy(3) 8 74
(David Simcock) *mid-div: hdwy 3f out: r.o u.p fnl f* 7/4[1]
-306 4 1 ½ **Hallingham**[20] 3147 4-9-0 58....(b[1]) RichardKingscote 2 61
(Jonathan Portman) *prom: trckd wnr after 2f: rdn 3f out: no ex and lost two pls fnl 100yds* 12/1
0-13 5 2 ½ **Belle Park**[19] 3175 7-8-8 59.... KieranShoemark(7) 7 58
(Victor Dartnall) *hld up in rr: rdn over 2f out: styd on ins fnl f: nt trble ldrs* 3/1[2]
10-3 6 1 ¼ **Acapulco Bay**[30] 2834 10-8-5 49....(p) DavidProbert 3 45
(Dai Burchell) *hld up towards rr: rdn 3f out: styd on same pce fnl 2f* 16/1
2-04 7 7 **Youm Jamil (USA)**[16] 3308 7-8-4 48.... JimmyQuinn 10 31
(Tony Carroll) *chsd ldrs: rdn 2f out: wknd qckly fnl f* 14/1
0-00 8 9 **Bondi Mist (IRE)**[26] 2942 5-8-8 55....(v) RyanTate(3) 1 21
(Jonathan Geake) *chsd wnr 2f: styd prom: rdn 4f out: wknd 2f out* 12/1
2m 12.4s (1.80) **Going Correction** +0.225s/f (Good) 8 Ran SP% 115.2
Speed ratings (Par 101): **101,100,99,98,96 95,90,82**
CSF £56.25 CT £128.34 TOTE £6.20: £2.00, £3.00, £1.50; EX 45.00 Trifecta £167.20.
**Owner** Paul & Ann de Weck **Bred** Paul And Ann De Weck **Trained** Earlswood, Monmouths
**FOCUS**
This was run at just a steady gallop. The winner is rated back to his best.
T/Jkpt: Not won. T/Plt: £228.30 to a £1 stake. Pool: £92462.18 - 295.58 winning tickets T/Qpdt: £33.10 to a £1 stake. Pool: £8331.97 - 186.10 winning tickets RL

## [3576]KEMPTON (A.W) (R-H)
### Wednesday, July 2

**OFFICIAL GOING: Standard**
Wind: Moderate, across Weather: Fine, very warm

**3854** **IRISH NIGHT 09.07.14 APPRENTICE H'CAP** **6f (P)**
5:50 (5:54) (Class 5) (0-75,75) 4-Y-O+ £2,587 (£770; £384; £192) Stalls Low

Form RPR
-000 1 **Almanack**[26] 2955 4-9-2 67.... NathanAlison 7 76
(Ian Williams) *settled in 7th: urged along and hd high 2f out: stl only 5th 1f out: str run fnl f to ld post* 16/1
-603 2 *shd* **Lucky Di**[12] 3422 4-8-10 66.... RobHornby(5) 10 75
(Peter Hedger) *trckd ldr: rdn to ld over 1f out: styd on fnl f but hdd post* 4/1[1]
5140 3 2 ¼ **Seek The Fair Land**[12] 3422 8-9-7 75....(b) CharlotteJenner(3) 1 77
(Lee Carter) *t.k.h: led: rdn and hdd over 1f out: one pce and lost 2nd ins fnl f* 7/1[3]
3222 4 *nk* **Ray Of Joy**[55] 2096 8-9-7 72....(v) DannyBrock 4 73
(J R Jenkins) *chsd ldng trio: rdn and nt qckn 2f out: kpt on fnl f to press for 3rd nr fin* 8/1
5566 5 ¾ **Jungle Bay**[16] 3313 7-9-10 75....(p) DavidKenny 2 73
(Jane Chapple-Hyam) *chsd ldng pair: rdn to chal on inner over 1f out: nt qckn and lost pl fnl f* 4/1[1]
-320 6 1 ¼ **Borough Boy (IRE)**[20] 3150 4-8-9 60....(v) JacobButterfield 5 54
(Derek Shaw) *stdd s: hld up in last trio: pushed along and no prog over 2f out: no ch whn rdn over 1f out: kpt on: nvr involved* 12/1
000- 7 1 ¼ **Rocket Rob (IRE)**[186] 8431 8-9-5 75.... JordonMcMurray(5) 6 65
(Willie Musson) *racd wd: hld up in last trio: pushed along 1/2-way: nt on terms after: nvr involved* 12/1
4022 8 3 **Paradise Spectre**[22] 3077 7-8-13 64....(p) ShelleyBirkett 11 45
(Zoe Davison) *s.s: a in last trio: rdn and no prog over 2f out* 25/1
540 9 *hd* **Kuanyao (IRE)**[24] 3033 8-9-7 72....(b) LouisSteward 3 52
(Conor Dore) *sn pushed along in 6th: no prog 2f out: wknd over 1f out* 11/2[2]
-005 10 *nse* **Rafaaf (IRE)**[97] 1125 6-8-3 59.... KieranShoemark(5) 12 39
(Richard Phillips) *chsd ldrs on outer tl wknd over 2f out* 16/1
1m 13.39s (0.29) **Going Correction** +0.075s/f (Slow) 10 Ran SP% 110.0
Speed ratings (Par 103): **101,100,97,97,96 94,93,89,88,88**
CSF £71.30 CT £438.85 TOTE £23.30: £5.90, £1.90, £2.80; EX 111.30 Trifecta £756.10.
**Owner** Phil Slater **Bred** Ed's Stud Ltd **Trained** Portway, Worcs
■ Rule 4 of 5p in the pound applies to all bets; Withdrawn: Aeolian Blue
**FOCUS**
The track had been watered ahead of a decent eight-race card. An okay race of its type, weakened with the defection of Aeolian Blue who sat down in the stalls and had to be withdrawn, and there was a bit of a turn-up.

**3855** **JOCKEY CLUB H'CAP (JOCKEY CLUB GRASSROOTS FLAT SPRINT SERIES QUALIFIER)** **6f (P)**
6:20 (6:23) (Class 5) (0-70,70) 3-Y-O £2,587 (£770; £384; £192) Stalls Low

Form RPR
0055 1 **Classic Pursuit**[28] 2886 3-9-3 66....(p) TomQueally 7 73
(Ronald Harris) *t.k.h: hld up in last: gd prog fr 2f out: rdn to ld last 120yds: edgd lft nr fin but styd on* 7/2[3]
-123 2 ¾ **Biotic**[22] 3087 3-8-12 61.... JamesDoyle 8 66
(Rod Millman) *chsd ldng trio: rdn over 2f out: clsd over 1f out: chal and upsides ins fnl f: nt qckn last 100yds* 11/4[2]
-135 3 ½ **Dynamo Walt (IRE)**[28] 2889 3-8-13 67.... JacobButterfield(5) 4 70
(Derek Shaw) *chsd ldrs in 5th: urged along and clsd on inner fr 2f out: chal ins fnl f: nt qckn last 100yds* 16/1
5446 4 1 ½ **Honey Meadow**[20] 3145 3-9-4 67.... DaneO'Neill 6 66
(Robert Eddery) *hld up in last trio: shkn up and no prog over 2f out: kpt on fr over 1f out to take 4th last strides: nvr in it* 10/1
50-5 5 *nk* **Prize**[7] 3564 3-8-7 56.... KieranO'Neill 5 54
(Sylvester Kirk) *chsd ldng pair: rdn and clsd to ld jst over 1f out: hdd & wknd quite qckly last 120yds* 20/1
1220 6 2 **Hustle Bustle (IRE)**[12] 3433 3-9-5 68.... SeanLevey 2 59
(David Brown) *t.k.h: disp ld at str pce: clr w one rival 1/2-way: hdd & wknd jst over 1f out* 20/1
2522 7 1 **Serata Di Gala (FR)**[35] 2686 3-9-2 70....[1] MarcMonaghan(5) 1 58
(Marco Botti) *disp ld at str pce: clr w one rival 1/2-way: hdd & wknd jst over 1f out* 10/1
6461 8 4 **More Beau (USA)**[36] 2657 3-9-7 70.... PaddyAspell 9 45
(Ed Dunlop) *racd wd in last trio: urged along and no prog over 2f out: wknd over 1f out: lame* 9/4[1]
1m 12.84s (-0.26) **Going Correction** +0.075s/f (Slow) 8 Ran SP% 113.2
Speed ratings (Par 100): **104,103,102,100,99 97,95,90**
CSF £13.29 CT £130.65 TOTE £4.30: £1.50, £1.80, £4.00; EX 15.40 Trifecta £201.20.
**Owner** David & Gwyn Joseph **Bred** B & B Equine Limited **Trained** Earlswood, Monmouths
**FOCUS**
Just modest fare but it was competitive enough. A strong pace set it up for the closers. The winner was close to his best.

**3856** **BETBRIGHT.COM MAIDEN STKS (DIV I)** **1m 4f (P)**
6:50 (6:50) (Class 5) 3-Y-O+ £2,587 (£770; £384; £192) Stalls Low

Form RPR
4 1 **Wakea (USA)**[16] 3315 3-8-13 0.... SilvestreDeSousa 8 88+
(Jeremy Noseda) *trckd ldr after 4f: led 3f out: rdn 2f out: drew clr over 1f out: pushed out firmly* 1/1[1]
04 2 6 **Fort Berkeley (IRE)**[27] 2917 3-8-10 0.... AshleyMorgan(3) 7 78
(Paul Cole) *led: hung lft bnd after 3f and hdd: sn dropped to 3rd: effrt to chse wnr 2f out: outpcd over 1f out: kpt on* 10/1
3 ¾ **Elbereth** 3-8-5 0.... ThomasBrown(3) 2 72+
(Andrew Balding) *chsd ldrs in 5th: pushed along over 3f out: kpt on to take 3rd 2f out: no ch w wnr* 33/1
3 4 ¾ **Saint Lucy**[20] 3142 3-8-8 0.... RobertHavlin 3 71+
(John Gosden) *hld up towards rr: pushed along and sme prog over 2f out: rdn over 1f out: kpt on but no threat* 8/1[3]
5-5 5 9 **Almerzem (USA)**[18] 3248 3-8-13 0.... KierenFallon 9 61
(Saeed bin Suroor) *dwlt: t.k.h and sn trckd ldr: impeded but led after 3f: shkn up and hdd 3f out: lost 2nd 2f out: wknd* 15/8[2]
64 6 1 ¾ **Carraig Rock**[13] 3401 4-9-12 0.... HayleyTurner 5 58+
(Hughie Morrison) *t.k.h: chsd ldng trio tl wknd qckly 2f out* 50/1
00 7 2 ¼ **Prince Of Islay (IRE)**[27] 2924 3-8-6 0....(p) GeorgeBuckell(7) 11 55
(Robert Mills) *nvr bttr than midfield: rdn 4f out: wknd over 2f out* 100/1
00 8 3 ¼ **Uncle Muf (USA)**[13] 3385 4-9-12 0.... JimCrowley 6 50
(Ali Stronge) *a towards rr: rdn 4f out: wknd over 2f out* 33/1
6 9 1 **New Reaction**[27] 2917 3-8-13 0.... PatDobbs 4 48
(Amanda Perrett) *a in rr: urged along 4f out: wknd over 2f out* 12/1
10 29 **Izzy Piccolina (IRE)**[100] 6-9-7 0.... SebSanders 10
(Geoffrey Deacon) *a towards rr: wknd qckly 3f out: t.o* 66/1
0 11 1 ¾ **Canadian Diamond (IRE)**[8] 2917 7-9-12 0.... DaneO'Neill 1
(Brendan Powell) *s.s: a last: lost tch over 3f out: t.o* 50/1
2m 33.69s (-0.81) **Going Correction** +0.075s/f (Slow)
**WFA** 3 from 4yo+ 13lb 11 Ran SP% 125.0
Speed ratings (Par 103): **105,101,100,100,94 92,91,89,88,69 68**
CSF £13.74 TOTE £2.80: £1.10, £4.20, £10.70; EX 15.80 Trifecta £244.20.
**Owner** Sanford R Robertson **Bred** Sanford R Robertson **Trained** Newmarket, Suffolk
**FOCUS**
The first division of a maiden that was taken by subsequent Listed-winning filly Astonishing last year. This was tactical and uncompetitive but the winner could prove up to a similar standard. It was the fastest of the three C&D times.

**3857** **BETBRIGHT.COM MAIDEN STKS (DIV II)** **1m 4f (P)**
7:20 (7:20) (Class 5) 3-Y-O+ £2,587 (£770; £384; £192) Stalls Low

Form RPR
22 1 **Desert Snow**[27] 2917 3-8-8 0.... KierenFallon 10 89
(Saeed bin Suroor) *trckd ldr: led over 2f out: urged along over 1f out: rdn clr fnl f* 3/1[3]
0422 2 4 ½ **Rocket Ship**[19] 3183 3-8-13 82.... JamesDoyle 1 86
(Sir Michael Stoute) *led at mod pce: tried to kick on 4f out: hdd over 2f out: nt qckn and hld over 1f out: outpcd fnl f* 5/2[2]
3 3 4 **Montbazon (FR)**[21] 3106 7-9-12 0.... FergusSweeney 2 80
(Alan King) *trckd ldng pair: pushed along firmly and outpcd fr over 2f out: kpt on* 8/1
6 4 3 ¼ **Fighting Back**[28] 2881 3-8-13 0.... TomQueally 11 75
(Amanda Perrett) *trckd ldng trio: rdn over 3f out: sn outpcd and btn: kpt on fnl f* 9/4[1]
6- 5 *hd* **Robertson (IRE)**[291] 6402 4-9-12 0.... JimCrowley 9 74
(James Fanshawe) *hld up in last trio: rdn and wl adrift 3f out: stl looked green but plugged on fr over 1f out* 25/1

663 **6** ½ **Race To Glory (FR)**34 2696 3-8-13 78 RyanMoore 4 74
(Roger Charlton) *chsd ldrs in 5th: shkn up to take 4th over 2f out but already outpcd: no hdwy after: lost 2 pls nr fin* **7/1**

0- **7** 1¼ **Sarpech (IRE)**266 7128 3-8-13 0 HarryBentley 5 72
(Sir Mark Prescott Bt) *hld up in midfield: outpcd and reminder over 2f out: nvr on terms after* **20/1**

0 **8** 17 **Tribulina**48 2279 3-8-8 0 PaoloSirigu 3 39
(Marco Botti) *a towards rr: wknd over 2f out: fin slowly and t.o* **66/1**

**9** 22 **Sirrah Star (IRE)**22 6-9-7 0 PaddyAspell 6 4
(Neil Mulholland) *s.s: a in last: wknd 3f out: wl t.o* **100/1**

2m 34.4s (-0.10) **Going Correction** +0.075s/f (Slow)
**WFA** 3 from 4yo+ 13lb **9** Ran SP% **119.0**
Speed ratings (Par 103): **103,100,97,95,95 94,93,82,67**
CSF £11.04 TOTE £4.80: £1.90, £1.50, £2.10; EX 12.40 Trifecta £51.70.
**Owner** Godolphin **Bred** Darley **Trained** Newmarket, Suffolk

**FOCUS**
This looked more competitive than the first division, although it ended up being nearly a second slower. Steps up from the first two.

## 3858 LEONARD CURTIS/BRITISH STALLION STUDS EBF MAIDEN FILLIES' STKS (BOBIS RACE) 7f (P)

**7:50** (7:51) (Class 5) 2-Y-0 **£2,911** (£866; £432; £216) **Stalls** Low

Form RPR

2 **1** **Panda Spirit (USA)**27 2918 2-9-0 0 RyanMoore 3 80+
(Sir Michael Stoute) *trckd ldr: led 2f out: pushed clr over 1f out: comf* **2/5**1

**2** 4 **Arethusa** 2-9-0 0 JamesDoyle 5 66+
(Ed Dunlop) *settled towards rr: prog over 2f out: pushed along and kpt on to take 2nd last 75yds: no ch w wnr* **33/1**

53 **3** ¾ **Red Perdita (IRE)**18 3210 2-9-0 0 MartinDwyer 9 64
(George Baker) *led at mod pce: rdn and hdd 2f out: sn outpcd: lost 2nd last 75yds* **10/1**3

**4** 1¾ **Romance Story (IRE)** 2-9-0 0 KierenFallon 10 59+
(Saeed bin Suroor) *unsettled as stalls opened and slowly away: hld up in last: reminder over 2f out and rn green: pushed along and prog on outer over 1f out: kpt on fnl f* **3/1**2

0 **5** 1¼ **Old Fashion**22 3076 2-9-0 0 DaneO'Neill 2 56
(Ed Dunlop) *chsd ldrs: tried to cl jst over 2f out: sn outpcd and btn* **25/1**

**6** nse **Nelsons Trick** 2-9-0 0 RobertHavlin 11 56+
(Rod Millman) *racd wd: trckd ldng pair: lost pl and outpcd over 2f out: kpt on again fnl f* **20/1**

00 **7** 1½ **Heavenlyfriendship**7 3563 2-9-0 0 FergusSweeney 8 52
(Brendan Powell) *hld up in last trio: shkn up and brief prog 2f out: sn no hdwy* **50/1**

0 **8** ½ **Papier**44 2402 2-9-0 0 SeanLevey 6 50
(Richard Hannon) *in tch in midfield: shkn up and outpcd fr 2f out: fdd* **16/1**

**9** 4 **Quiet Beauty** 2-9-0 0 JimCrowley 1 40
(Robert Cowell) *trckd ldng pair: rdn over 2f out: wknd over 1f out* **20/1**

00 **10** 6 **Birdie Must Fly**21 3113 2-9-0 0 KieranO'Neill 4 23
(Jimmy Fox) *t.k.h: hld up in last pair: wknd over 2f out: sddle slipped* **50/1**

1m 29.33s (3.33) **Going Correction** +0.075s/f (Slow) **10** Ran SP% **131.6**
Speed ratings (Par 91): **83,78,77,75,74 74,72,71,67,60**
CSF £35.72 TOTE £1.60: £1.02, £8.30, £2.10; EX 24.80 Trifecta £136.00.
**Owner** Robert Ng **Bred** SF Bloodstock LLC **Trained** Newmarket, Suffolk

**FOCUS**
An ordinary fillies' maiden lacking depth. The winner was value for a little extra.

## 3859 BETBRIGHT.COM H'CAP 2m (P)

**8:20** (8:21) (Class 3) (0-90,90) 4-Y-0+ **£7,439** (£2,213; £1,106; £553) **Stalls** Low

Form RPR

-145 **1** **Presto Volante (IRE)**24 3034 6-9-3 86 (p) JamesDoyle 1 95
(Amanda Perrett) *trckd clr ldng pair: clsd over 2f out: hrd rdn to ld over 1f out: pressed after: jnd nr fin: jst hld on* **4/1**2

00-1 **2** shd **Poyle Thomas**32 2782 5-9-7 90 JimCrowley 2 99+
(Ralph Beckett) *hld up off the pce: drvn over 2f out: chsd clr ldng trio wl over 1f out: clsd u.p fnl f: tk 2nd nr fin and jnd wnr: jst pipped* **6/5**1

5210 **3** ½ **Story Writer**24 3034 5-8-8 77 KierenFallon 5 85
(William Knight) *hld up off the pce: prog over 4f out: clsd on ldrs over 2f out: drvn to chal over 1f out: pressed wnr but nt qckn fnl f: lost 2nd nr fin* **7/1**3

-233 **4** 3¼ **Rosie Rebel**41 2490 4-8-7 76 SilvestreDeSousa 3 80
(Rae Guest) *t.k.h: led and abt 3 l clr: drvn and hdd over 1f out: fdd fnl f* **12/1**

4411 **5** 1¾ **Spice Fair**18 3249 7-9-2 85 RyanMoore 9 87
(Mark Usher) *slowly away: hld up in last pair: drvn over 2f out: mod prog over 1f out: nvr on terms* **7/1**3

16-2 **6** ½ **Clerk's Choice (IRE)**67 591 8-8-10 79 HayleyTurner 8 81
(William Jarvis) *hld up in last trio: urged along over 3f out: modest prog 2f out: no hdwy fnl f* **10/1**

0-06 **7** 2¼ **Ascendant**58 2034 8-8-3 77 DannyBrock(5) 4 76
(Andrew Reid) *hld up off the pce: hrd rdn over 2f out: no real prog on inner and wl btn over 1f out* **66/1**

6-00 **8** 17 **Azrag (USA)**18 3249 6-8-12 81 (p) SebSanders 7 60
(Michael Attwater) *trckd ldr and clr of rest: wknd qckly and lost 2nd over 2f out: t.o* **33/1**

030 **9** 38 **Storm Hawk (IRE)**27 2920 7-8-3 72 (b) NickyMackay 6 5
(Pat Eddery) *s.s and had to be urged to leave stalls: rapid prog fr rr to chse ldrs 10f out: wknd rapidly 5f out: sn wl t.o and eased* **66/1**

3m 27.89s (-2.21) **Going Correction** +0.075s/f (Slow) **9** Ran SP% **113.2**
Speed ratings (Par 107): **108,107,107,106,105 104,103,95,76**
CSF £8.89 CT £30.04 TOTE £5.20: £1.20, £1.10, £2.70; EX 12.30 Trifecta £51.60.
**Owner** Mrs S Conway Mr & Mrs M Swayne Mr A Brooke Mrs R D **Bred** R A Major **Trained** Pulborough, W Sussex

**FOCUS**
A good staying handicap. They went a fair gallop and there was a pulsating finish. The third is rated to form.

## 3860 BETBRIGHT MOBILE H'CAP 1m 4f (P)

**8:50** (8:52) (Class 3) (0-95,93) 4-Y-0+ **£7,439** (£2,213; £1,106; £553) **Stalls** Low

Form RPR

32-0 **1** **Expert Fighter (USA)**46 2342 5-9-7 93 KierenFallon 8 102
(Saeed bin Suroor) *mde all: set stdy pce tl wound up fr 4f out: kicked for home over 2f out and sn over 2 l clr: ld dwindled nr fin but a holding on* **3/1**2

-230 **2** nk **Ridgeway Storm (IRE)**59 1981 4-8-5 77 HarryBentley 6 86+
(Alan King) *hld up in 4th: rdn and outpcd over 2f out: prog over 1f out: tk 2nd 150yds out: clsd on wnr but nvr gng to get there* **7/2**3

0-05 **3** 2¾ **Buckland (IRE)**21 3111 6-9-4 90 FrederikTylicki 3 94
(Charlie Fellowes) *trckd ldng pair: rdn to chse wnr over 2f out but outpcd: no imp after: lost 2nd last 150yds* **8/1**

3121 **4** 1¾ **Incendo**12 3438 8-8-5 77 (v) HayleyTurner 7 78
(Conor Dore) *hld up in 6th in slowly run event: rdn and outpcd over 2f out: kpt on fr over 1f out: no ch* **16/1**

2014 **5** ¾ **Shavansky**95 1171 10-9-0 91 ShelleyBirkett(5) 1 91
(Rod Millman) *t.k.h: hld up in 5th: shkn up to dispute 2nd wl over 1f out but no imp: hanging and fdd sn after* **8/1**

0-64 **6** 4½ **Art Scholar (IRE)**20 3161 7-8-9 81 JamesDoyle 4 74
(Michael Appleby) *hld up in 7th in slowly run event: no ch once pce lifted over 2f out: no prog* **10/1**

4/0- **7** 3¾ **War Singer (USA)**347 3345 7-8-13 85 (t) JimCrowley 2 72
(Johnny Farrelly) *stdd s: hld up in last in slowly run event: no ch once pce lifted over 2f out: no prog* **33/1**

-561 **8** ½ **Aldborough (IRE)**35 2670 4-8-4 76 (p) SilvestreDeSousa 5 62
(Ralph Beckett) *trckd wnr: pushed along over 3f out: hung lft and wknd over 2f out* **5/2**1

2m 35.9s (1.40) **Going Correction** +0.075s/f (Slow) **8** Ran SP% **115.9**
Speed ratings (Par 107): **98,97,95,94,94 91,88,88**
CSF £14.22 CT £75.29 TOTE £4.50: £1.40, £2.20, £2.40; EX 25.50 Trifecta £173.50.
**Owner** Godolphin **Bred** Darley **Trained** Newmarket, Suffolk

**FOCUS**
A race taken last year by Seal Of Approval before she went on to record a Group One victory. Unsurprisingly, with this being contested by mainly exposed older horses, there looks to be nothing of that standard in this year's renewal. The slowest of the three races over this trip on the evening, and not form to be confident about.

## 3861 BETBRIGHT - LIVE THE MOMENT H'CAP (LONDON MILE SERIES QUALIFIER) 1m (P)

**9:20** (9:20) (Class 4) (0-85,83) 3-Y-0+ **£4,690** (£1,395; £697; £348) **Stalls** Low

Form RPR

3164 **1** **Tenor (IRE)**7 3577 4-9-5 81 (t) JoeDoyle(7) 2 100
(John Ryan) *mde all: drew clr fr 2f out: drvn over 1f out: in n.d after* **7/1**

-643 **2** 4½ **Messila Star**7 3577 4-9-4 73 (v) JamesDoyle 10 82
(Jeremy Noseda) *w wnr: rdn and outpcd 2f out: no imp after but kpt on for clr 2nd* **13/2**3

31-4 **3** 2½ **My Target (IRE)**13 3383 3-9-4 82 KierenFallon 3 83
(Saeed bin Suroor) *chsd ldrs: rdn over 2f out: kpt on to take 3rd fnl f: no ch w ldng pair* **6/1**2

-334 **4** ¾ **Scottish Glen**19 3180 8-9-13 82 JimCrowley 9 83
(Patrick Chamings) *t.k.h: hld up in rr: pushed along over 2f out: prog over 1f out: kpt on to take 4th last strides: no ch* **20/1**

6611 **5** nse **Barnmore**21 3112 6-9-2 74 CharlesBishop(3) 4 75
(Peter Hedger) *mounted on crse: hld up in rr: dropped to last 1/2-way: rdn 3f out: prog on inner 2f out: kpt on to press for 4th nr fin: no ch* **16/1**

0031 **6** 1½ **Gravitational (IRE)**21 3118 4-9-10 82 AshleyMorgan(3) 7 80
(Chris Wall) *prom: chsd ldng pair 3f out: outpcd and drvn 2f out: no imp after: wknd fnl f* **11/4**1

0-00 **7** 1½ **Tommy's Secret**11 3468 4-9-10 79 PatDobbs 12 73
(Jane Chapple-Hyam) *hld up in midfield: rdn over 2f out: sn outpcd and no ch* **50/1**

0-33 **8** 1¾ **Dana's Present**21 3112 5-9-2 71 FergusSweeney 11 61
(George Baker) *mounted on crse: racd wd: hld up wl in rr: cajoled along and no real prog over 2f out: nvr in it* **25/1**

**9** ¾ **Zarliman (IRE)**229 4-9-8 77 TomQueally 6 65
(Martyn Meade) *hld up in rr: sme prog into midfield 2f out: no hdwy after: fdd fnl f* **8/1**

606- **10** ¾ **Chelwood Gate (IRE)**274 6925 4-9-11 83 ThomasBrown(3) 5 70
(Patrick Chamings) *hld up in midfield: shkn up and no prog over 2f out: sn wl btn* **33/1**

4053 **11** ½ **Toga Tiger (IRE)**18 3254 7-9-8 77 SeanLevey 1 63
(Kevin Frost) *dwlt: rushed up on inner to chse ldrs: rdn to dispute 3rd 3f out: wknd over 2f out* **7/1**

321 **12** 12 **Space Walker (IRE)**37 2624 3-8-12 76 DaneO'Neill 8 32
(Harry Dunlop) *dwlt: rapid prog on outer fr rr 1/2-way: disp 3rd over 3f out: sn wknd rapidly: t.o* **8/1**

1m 38.61s (-1.19) **Going Correction** +0.075s/f (Slow)
**WFA** 3 from 4yo+ 9lb **12** Ran SP% **120.9**
Speed ratings (Par 105): **108,103,101,100,100 98,97,95,94,93 93,81**
CSF £51.02 CT £300.27 TOTE £9.80: £3.20, £2.60, £2.40; EX 68.30 Trifecta £1366.00.
**Owner** Kilco (International) Ltd **Bred** Epona Bloodstock Ltd And P A Byrne **Trained** Newmarket, Suffolk

■ Stewards' Enquiry : Joe Doyle 21-day ban (of which seven days will be deferred): Jul 25 - Aug 7 used whip above permitted level, 5th offence in 6mths.

**FOCUS**
This had the look of a good, competitive event, but little got into it and once again being on the pace was the place to be. The form is rated around the runner-up.
T/Plt: £22.80 to a £1 stake. Pool: £67916.45 - 2170.28 winning tickets T/Qpdt: £3.40 to a £1 stake. Pool: £7123.35 - 1519.30 winning tickets JN

# 3126 FAIRYHOUSE (R-H)

Wednesday, July 2

**OFFICIAL GOING: Good to firm**

## 3864a IRISH STALLION FARMS EUROPEAN BREEDERS FUND BROWNSTOWN STKS (GROUP 3) (F&M) 7f

**7:00** (7:01) 3-Y-0+ **£40,625** (£11,875; £5,625; £1,875)

RPR

**1** **Tobann (IRE)**4 3742 4-9-8 101 (t) KevinManning 7 104+
(J S Bolger, Ire) *ponied to s: chsd ldrs: 5th 1/2-way: tk clsr order bhd ldrs 2f out: rdn into 2nd under 2f out and led ent fnl f: kpt on wl u.p and extended advantage towards fin* **3/1**1

**2** 1½ **Majestic Queen (IRE)**20 3167 4-9-11 103 PatSmullen 1 103
(Tracey Collins, Ire) *dwlt and towards rr early tl prog to chse ldr in 2nd after 1f: got on terms into st and led narrowly under 2f out: hdd u.p ent fnl f and sn no ex: kpt on same pce* **3/1**1

**3** ¾ **Califante**4 3742 4-9-8 75 RonanWhelan 3 98?
(T Hogan, Ire) *w.w: last 1/2-way: impr on outer fr over 2f out into 4th ent fnl f: no imp on ldrs u.p in 3rd wl ins fnl f: kpt on same pce* **66/1**

4 shd **Wannabe Better (IRE)**13 3412 4-9-11 106 WayneLordan 4 101
(T Stack, Ire) *hld up: 6th 1/2-way: prog far side bhd ldrs 2f out where n.m.r: rdn ent fnl f and sn no imp on ldrs in 4th: kpt on same pce* **7/2**2
5 2 **Sparrow (IRE)**20 3167 3-9-2 96 ow2 (t) JosephO'Brien 2 89
(A P O'Brien, Ire) *chsd ldrs: 4th 1/2-way: tk clsr order bhd ldrs 2f out: sn rdn and no ex ins fnl f: kpt on one pce* **4/1**3
6 1 1/4 **Whimsical (IRE)**4 3742 5-9-8 89 (p1) ChrisHayes 8 89
(P D Deegan, Ire) *sn led: over 1 l clr 1/2-way: jnd into st and hdd under 2f out: sn no ex and dropped to 6th ins fnl f: kpt on one pce* **20/1**
7 3 **Seas Of Wells (IRE)**20 3167 3-9-0 93 DeclanMcDonogh 5 78
(John M Oxx, Ire) *hld up towards rr: 7th 1/2-way: tk clsr order bhd ldrs over 2f out: n.m.r and sn rdn in rr: no imp over 1f out: kpt on one pce* **10/1**
8 nk **Exactement (IRE)**20 3166 4-9-8 96 GaryCarroll 6 80
(Sabrina J Harty, Ire) *chsd ldr in 2nd tl dropped to 3rd after 1f: rdn over 2f out and sn wknd* **14/1**

1m 28.44s (-2.06)
**WFA** 3 from 4yo+ 8lb **8** Ran SP% **114.2**
CSF £12.15 TOTE £3.70: £1.02, £1.20, £7.70; DF 12.20 Trifecta £494.50.
**Owner** Mrs J S Bolger **Bred** J S Bolger **Trained** Coolcullen, Co Carlow

**FOCUS**
There was no obvious up-and-coming potential star in this. What we had was a genuine Group 3 that was both open and competitive. The gallop seemed fair and the first two help with the standard.

## 3744 DEAUVILLE (R-H)
### Wednesday, July 2

**OFFICIAL GOING: Turf: good to soft; polytrack: standard**

### 3869a PRIX DU COCHET (MAIDEN) (3YO COLTS & GELDINGS) (POLYTRACK) 1m 1f 110y
12:00 (12:00) 3-Y-O £10,416 (£4,166; £3,125; £2,083; £1,041)

RPR
1 **Dominandros (FR)**40 2630 3-9-2 0 Pierre-CharlesBoudot 9 78
(Gay Kelleway) *broke wl and t.k.h: hld up in tch: 7th and travelling wl 2 1/2f out: hdwy in centre of trck 1 1/2f out: shkn up and r.o wl fnl f: led cl home to win a shade cosily* **42/1**
2 1/2 **Labaik (FR)**46 3-9-2 0 FabienLefebvre 5 77
(J E Hammond, France) **97/10**
3 1 3/4 **Diyoudar (FR)**59 2003 3-9-2 0 IoritzMendizabal 1 73
(J-C Rouget, France) **83/10**3
4 1 1/4 **Hellain (FR)**90 3-9-2 0 GregoryBenoist 8 71
(E Lellouche, France) **97/10**
5 3/4 **Amirli (IRE)**15 3-9-2 0 ChristopheSoumillon 2 69
(A De Royer-Dupre, France) **11/10**1
6 1 **Maninthemirror (FR)** 3-8-13 0 AntoineHamelin 4 64
(Mme Pia Brandt, France) **35/1**
7 1 1/2 **Dark Noir (FR)**27 3-9-2 0 TonyPiccone 11 64
(B Dutruel, France) **17/2**
8 1/2 **Main De Fer**27 3-9-2 0 MaximeGuyon 6 63
(A Fabre, France) **13/2**2
9 2 **Rochefort (FR)** 3-8-13 0 CesarPasserat(3) 3 59
(Mme C Head-Maarek, France) **211/10**
10 2 1/2 **Medaillon (FR)**27 3-9-2 0 TheoBachelot 10 54
(Mario Hofer, Germany) **124/10**
11 9 **Just Soldier (FR)**23 3-9-2 0 AntoineCoutier 7 35
(F Chappet, France) **70/1**

2m 3.53s (123.53) **11** Ran SP% **119.4**
WIN (incl. 1 euro stake): 42.60. PLACES: 9.60, 2.80, 2.20. DF: 257.70. SF: 622.60.
**Owner** Winterbeck Manor Stud & Partners **Bred** S C E A Haras De La Perelle **Trained** Exning, Suffolk

### 3871a PRIX DU FEUILLARD (CLAIMER) (2YO COLTS & GELDINGS) (POLYTRACK) 6f 110y
1:05 (12:00) 2-Y-O £7,916 (£3,166; £2,375; £1,583; £791)

RPR
1 **Well Fleeced**5 3691 2-9-2 0 (p) IoritzMendizabal 8 68
(J S Moore) *mde virtually all: swtchd ins to rail after 1f: rdn and lened 1 1/2f out: drvn clr fnl f: comf* **21/10**1
2 3 **Persevere (FR)** 2-8-9 0 JohanVictoire 1 53
(Y Durepaire, France) **128/10**
3 1 1/4 **Atilla (FR)**17 2-9-2 0 Christophe-PatriceLemaire 4 56
(M Boutin, France) **15/2**
4 shd **Monsieur Royal (FR)**9 2-9-2 0 (p) JulienGuillochon 3 56
(C Plisson, France) **12/5**2
5 1 1/2 **Mr Bright Eyes (FR)** 2-9-2 0 (b1) AntoineHamelin 2 52
(Matthieu Palussiere, France) **131/10**
6 1/2 **Jimmy's Hall**8 3550 2-9-2 0 MickaelBarzalona 10 50
(J S Moore) *sn trcking ldr on outer: rdn but nt qckn 2f out: wknd appr fnl f* **42/10**3
7 1 1/4 **Last Honours (FR)**28 2-9-2 0 (p) AlexisBadel 7 47
(C Boutin, France) **132/10**
8 5 **Mister Papy (FR)**46 2-9-2 0 (p) StephaneLaurent 5 33
(C Plisson, France) **57/1**
9 1/2 **Camden Market (FR)** 2-8-13 0 CristianDemuro 9 28
(F Vermeulen, France) **26/1**

1m 21.56s (81.56) **9** Ran SP% **119.5**
WIN (incl. 1 euro stake): 3.10. PLACES: 1.70, 2.90, 2.20. DF: 10.90. SF: 19.00.
**Owner** The Well Fleeced Partnership **Bred** Theakston Stud **Trained** Upper Lambourn, Berks

### 3872a PRIX DES MARAIS (CLAIMER) (2YO FILLIES) (POLYTRACK) 6f 110y
1:35 (12:00) 2-Y-O £7,916 (£3,166; £2,375; £1,583; £791)

RPR
1 **La Mezcla (FR)** 2-9-2 0 JohanVictoire 4 69
(Y Durepaire, France) **39/10**2
2 3/4 **Whole Lotta Love (FR)** 2-8-13 0 TheoBachelot 10 64
(Mario Hofer, Germany) **141/10**
3 hd **Who Knows (IRE)** 2-8-9 0 MarcLerner 3 59
(C Lerner, France) **118/10**
4 snk **Qoosine (FR)**12 2-9-2 0 StephanePasquier 5 66
(Rod Collet, France) **63/10**
5 3/4 **Nimble (IRE)**63 1872 2-8-9 0 ThierryJarnet 11 57
(J S Moore) *dwlt: in rr: pushed along fr 2f out: styd on fnl f: nrest at fin* **59/10**3
6 1 **Meshavita (FR)**26 2976 2-8-13 0 FranckBlondel 12 58
(M Pimbonnet, France) **142/10**
7 1 **All Blues (FR)**33 2-8-10 0 ow1 Pierre-CharlesBoudot 8 52
(M Boutin, France) **89/10**
8 3/4 **Marlinda (FR)**26 2976 2-8-9 0 (b1) AlexisBadel 7 49
(C Boutin, France) **34/1**
9 1/2 **Sister Love (FR)** 2-8-9 0 TristanNormand 2 48
(L Baudron, France) **48/1**
10 1/2 **Mylenachope (FR)**28 2-8-9 0 AnthonyCrastus 9 46
(C Boutin, France) **227/10**
11 3/4 **Boann (IRE)**15 3322 2-9-2 0 IoritzMendizabal 6 51
(J S Moore) *chsd ldrs: 5th and gng wl 2 1/2f out: nt clr run 2f out and 1 1/2f out: rdn and nt qckn immediately whn hmpd 1f out: nt rcvr and nt given a hrd time* **13/5**1
12 9 **Poursuite (FR)** 2-8-13 0 GregoryBenoist 1 23
(R Martens, France) **41/1**

1m 22.29s (82.29) **12** Ran SP% **119.0**
WIN (incl. 1 euro stake): 4.90. PLACES: 2.10, 5.30, 3.40. DF: 47.10. SF: 45.00.
**Owner** Kubla Racing **Bred** J-P Larrieu & S Hillou-Lespes **Trained** France

## 3770 HAMBURG (R-H)
### Wednesday, July 2

**OFFICIAL GOING: Turf: good**

### 3873a FRANZ-GUNTHER VON GAERTNER-GEDACHTNISRENNEN (GROUP 3) (3YO+ FILLIES & MARES) (TURF) 1m
6:25 (12:00) 3-Y-O+ £26,666 (£9,166; £4,583; £2,500; £1,666; £1,250)

RPR
1 **Calyxa**34 2715 4-9-2 0 AdriedeVries 7 107+
(Ferdinand J Leve, Germany) *w.w towards rr: hdwy on outer over 1 1/2f out: r.o wl to ld fnl 100yds: drvn out* **19/5**3
2 1 1/2 **Diamond Dove (GER)**38 2584 3-8-9 0 AndreBest 1 104
(Andreas Lowe, Germany) *tk v t.k.h: trckd ldr on inner: rdn to chse ldr over 1 1/2f out: led 1f out: hdd fnl 100yds: no ex* **33/10**2
3 1 1/4 **Artwork Genie (IRE)**38 2584 3-8-7 0 FilipMinarik 3 99
(Jean-Pierre Carvalho, Germany) *trckd ldr on outer: hrd rdn over 1 1/2f out: kpt on u.p fnl f: jst hld on for 3rd* **83/10**
4 hd **Forever Beauty (GER)**23 4-9-0 0 FXWeissmeier 4 99
(Frau R Weissmeier, Germany) *midfield on inner: n.m.r 2f out and swtchd: nt clr run and switch bk ins 1 1/2f out: styd on u.p fnl f: jst missed 3rd* **159/10**
5 3/4 **Indian Rainbow (IRE)**38 2584 3-8-7 0 JBojko 6 97+
(Andreas Lowe, Germany) *w.w in rr: c wd into st: styd on u.p fnl f: nrest at fin* **26/5**
6 nk **Daksha (FR)**40 2631 4-9-4 0 APietsch 8 100
(Waldemar Hickst, Germany) *w.w in midfield on outer: pushed along to hold pl 2f out: sn rdn and nt qckn 1 1/2f out: kpt on at same pce fnl f* **5/1**
7 1 1/2 **Quaduna**59 1974 4-9-4 0 EPedroza 2 97
(A Wohler, Germany) *led: rdn over 1 1/2f out: hdd 1f out: sn wknd* **5/2**1
8 2 1/2 **Money Time (IRE)**23 4-9-0 0 (p) AHelfenbein 5 87
(A Wohler, Germany) *hld up towards rr: sme prog into midfield 1/2-way: rdn and outpcd over 2f out: wknd fnl f* **10/1**

1m 38.45s (98.45)
**WFA** 3 from 4yo 9lb **8** Ran SP% **131.2**
WIN (incl. 10 euro stake): 48. PLACES: 16, 14, 24 SF: 207.
**Owner** Gestut Haus Ittlingen **Bred** Gestut Haus Ittlingen **Trained** Germany

## 2986 EPSOM (L-H)
### Thursday, July 3

**OFFICIAL GOING: Good to firm (8.5)**
Wind: Moderate, across (towards stands) Weather: Sunny, very warm

### 3874 CHALK LANE H'CAP 1m 4f 10y
6:05 (6:08) (Class 5) (0-75,75) 4-Y-O+ £3,234 (£962; £481; £240) Stalls Centre

Form RPR
0324 1 1/2 **Granell (IRE)**27 2966 4-8-11 68 (b) RyanClark(3) 8 75
(Brian Meehan) *dwlt: hld up: 7th st: rdn and prog over 2f out: chsd wnr fnl f and sn chalng: nt qckn last 100yds* **10/1**
3565 2 nk **Nave (USA)**23 3086 7-9-1 69 MartinLane 5 76
(David Simcock) *dwlt: hld up: last st: prog on outer fr 3f out but a wanting to hang lft: drvn and clsd on ldng pair ins fnl f: nvr quite able to chal* **3/1**2
3334 3 3 1/2 **Tilstarr (IRE)**16 3325 4-9-1 72 OisinMurphy(3) 4 73
(Roger Teal) *hld up: 6th st: clsd over 2f out: sn drvn and nt qckn: one pce after* **12/1**
-024 4 3 1/4 **Colinca's Lad (IRE)**6 3681 12-8-13 70 RosieJessop(3) 6 66
(Peter Charalambous) *led and sn clr: c bk to field over 2f out: hdd & wknd jst over 1f out* **6/1**3
3321 5 6 **Jewelled**23 3079 8-9-1 69 PatDobbs 7 55
(Ralph J Smith) *chsd clr ldrs in 4th: clsd 3f out: wnt 2nd jst over 2f out to over 1f out: wknd qckly* **8/1**
6-00 6 3 1/4 **Couloir Extreme (IRE)**12 3472 4-9-4 72 (b1) LiamKeniry 3 53
(Gary Moore) *chsd clr ldng pair: wnt 2nd over 3f out to jst over 2f out: wknd* **25/1**
6-65 7 1/2 **Dellbuoy**35 2702 5-8-10 64 TedDurcan 1 44
(Pat Phelan) *dwlt: hld up: 8th st: rdn and no prog wl over 2f out* **20/1**
5240 8 4 1/2 **Montjess (IRE)**23 3078 4-9-1 69 (p) LiamJones 2 42
(Laura Mongan) *chsd clr ldr and clr of rest: wknd over 3f out* **33/1**
-024 D **Soul Intent (IRE)**16 3335 4-9-7 75 GeorgeBaker 9 83+
(B W Hills) *hld up: 5th st: prog 3f out: clsd to ld jst over 1f out: hrd pressed fnl f: drvn and kpt on wl* **7/4**1

2m 36.29s (-2.61) **Going Correction** -0.175s/f (Firm) **9** Ran SP% **115.1**
Speed ratings (Par 103): **100,100,98,95,91 89,89,86,101**
CSF £19.98 CT £50.08 TOTE £3.10: £1.70, £2.60, £1.70; EX 22.10 Trifecta £84.60.
**Owner** Native Colony Partnership **Bred** Gigginstown House Stud **Trained** Manton, Wilts

**FOCUS**
Rail dolled out 3yds from 1m to Winning Post increasing 1m races by 12yds, 7f by 6yds and 6f by 5yds. A modest contest featuring only one horse with a win in its last three starts. Sound form.

## 3875 BRITISH STALLION STUDS EBF MEDIAN AUCTION MAIDEN STKS 7f
6:35 (6:36) (Class 5) 2-Y-O £3,881 (£1,155; £577; £288) Stalls Low

Form RPR
0 **1** **Scutum (IRE)**[33] 2777 2-9-5 0 GeorgeBaker 1 74+
(Brian Meehan) *trckd ldng pair: swtchd rt 3f out: pushed along and prog 2f out: led jst ins fnl f: rdn out to hold on* **7/1**[3]

0 **2** *nk* **Chadic**[21] 3136 2-9-5 0 SilvestreDeSousa 6 73
(Mark Johnston) *wl away: led: shkn up 3f out: hdd jst ins fnl f: kpt on wl nr fin but jst hld* **4/1**[2]

0 **3** *2 ½* **Lwah (IRE)**[24] 3063 2-9-5 0 FrankieDettori 3 67+
(Richard Hannon) *hld up: 5th st: swtchd rt 2f out: rdn and nt qckn sn after: kpt on fnl f to take 3rd last strides* **10/11**[1]

03 **4** *hd* **Azure Amour (IRE)**[12] 3467 2-9-0 0 MartinLane 2 61
(Ralph Beckett) *hld up: last but in tch st: prog on inner and cl up 2f out: chsd ldng pair over 1f out but nt qckn: no imp after: lost 3rd last strides* **10/1**

06 **5** *6* **Chilworth Bells**[12] 3481 2-9-5 0 SamHitchcott 7 50
(Mick Channon) *in tch: 6th and losing pl st: sn rdn and struggling* **33/1**

564 **6** *1* **Invincible Zeb (IRE)**[31] 2829 2-9-5 0 SteveDrowne 4 47
(Ronald Harris) *pressed ldr: rdn over 2f out: wknd qckly over 1f out: eased ins fnl f* **7/1**[3]

0 **7** *5* **Hold Firm**[7] 3626 2-9-5 0 TedDurcan 5 34
(Mark H Tompkins) *chsd ldrs: 4th st: wknd 3f out* **66/1**

1m 24.12s (0.82) **Going Correction** -0.175s/f (Firm) **7 Ran SP% 110.9**
Speed ratings (Par 94): **88,87,84,84,77 76,70**
CSF £32.74 TOTE £8.90: £2.70, £1.90; EX 38.40 Trifecta £117.00.
**Owner** The Pony Club **Bred** Tally-Ho Stud **Trained** Manton, Wilts

**FOCUS**
No more than a fair maiden normally, and this looked no different.

## 3876 TOTEPOOL SUPPORTING THE SPORT YOU LOVE H'CAP 6f
7:10 (7:10) (Class 3) (0-95,90) 3-Y-O+ £7,439 (£2,213; £1,106; £553) Stalls High

Form RPR
0502 **1** **Swiss Cross**[26] 2992 7-9-9 86 (bt) SilvestreDeSousa 7 94
(Phil McEntee) *nt that wl away but sn pressed ldr: pushed along 1/2-way: rdn to ld 2f out: hrd pressed last 100yds: jst hld on* **11/4**[1]

0603 **2** *shd* **Chilworth Icon**[12] 3483 4-9-12 89 SamHitchcott 6 97
(Mick Channon) *chsd clr ldng trio: rdn and prog 2f out: tk 2nd 1f out: str chal last 100yds: jst failed* **12/1**

-160 **3** *1 ¼* **Huntsmans Close**[18] 3271 4-9-10 87 GeorgeBaker 5 91
(Roger Charlton) *hld up in 5th: pushed along over 2f out: prog over 1f out but hanging lft: kpt on to take 3rd ins fnl f* **6/1**

0-40 **4** *hd* **Muir Lodge**[78] 1513 3-9-7 90 [1] DavidProbert 2 92
(Andrew Balding) *trckd ldng pair: rdn and nt qckn wl over 1f out: kpt on fnl f but nvr able to chal* **5/1**[3]

4104 **5** *1* **Clear Praise (USA)**[9] 3551 7-8-13 76 LiamKeniry 8 76
(Simon Dow) *led: rdn and hdd 2f out: fdd fnl f* **33/1**

665 **6** *¾* **Dominate**[17] 3313 4-9-3 80 (b) PatDobbs 3 77
(Richard Hannon) *mostly in 6th: nt on terms st: rdn and no prog over 2f out: kpt on ins fnl f* **4/1**[2]

53 **7** *½* **Marjong**[17] 3305 4-8-10 76 OisinMurphy(3) 1 72
(Simon Dow) *hld up in last pair: pushed along and no prog over 2f out: no ch whn rdn fnl f: kpt on* **4/1**[2]

1265 **8** *¾* **Corporal Maddox**[12] 3483 7-9-11 88 (p) SteveDrowne 4 81
(Ronald Harris) *hld up in last pair: nvr on terms: shkn up and no prog over 2f out: kpt on nr fin* **16/1**

1m 7.8s (-1.60) **Going Correction** -0.175s/f (Firm)
**WFA** 3 from 4yo+ 6lb **8 Ran SP% 114.1**
Speed ratings (Par 107): **103,102,101,100,99 98,97,96**
CSF £37.07 CT £182.68 TOTE £2.90: £1.20, £3.60, £2.50; EX 23.70 Trifecta £117.30.
**Owner** Steve Jakes **Bred** Lordship Stud **Trained** Newmarket, Suffolk
■ Stewards' Enquiry : Silvestre De Sousa two-day ban: used whip above permitted level (Jul 17-18)

**FOCUS**
A steadily run sprint handicap. The winner was close to last year's turf form.

## 3877 EBF STALLIONS ARTHUR BUDGETT MEMORIAL MAIDEN FILLIES' STKS 1m 4f 10y
7:45 (7:45) (Class 4) 3-4-Y-O £5,175 (£1,540; £769; £384) Stalls Centre

Form RPR
-245 **1** **Cascading**[23] 3085 3-8-12 76 PatDobbs 2 82
(Hughie Morrison) *led: kicked on 3f out: drvn and hdd over 1f out: rallied to ld ins fnl f: styd on* **9/2**[2]

-224 **2** *1* **Toast Of The Town (IRE)**[17] 3307 4-9-11 95 (p) FrankieDettori 6 80
(John Gosden) *hld up in 4th: prog to trck wnr over 2f out: pushed into ld over 1f out: fnd little in front: hdd and drvn ins fnl f: outbattled* **1/3**[1]

54 **3** *5* **Shadows Ofthenight (IRE)**[38] 2613 3-8-12 0 SilvestreDeSousa 7 72
(Mick Channon) *hld up in rr: 5th and rdn st: hanging lft but drvn into 3rd over 1f out: no ch w ldng pair* **14/1**[3]

4 **4** *3* **Social Riser (IRE)**[14] 3385 3-8-12 0 SteveDrowne 5 68
(Charles Hills) *chsd ldr to over 2f out: steadily wknd* **14/1**[3]

25 **5** *4 ½* **Elpida (USA)**[37] 2649 3-8-12 0 ShaneKelly 1 60
(David Simcock) *awkward s: hld up in 5th: brief effrt 3f out: pushed along and lft bhd 2f out: reminder and no hdwy over 1f out* **20/1**

505 **6** *7* **Chindeni**[8] 3568 3-8-12 0 LiamKeniry 4 49
(Ed Vaughan) *chsd ldng pair tl wknd 3f out* **50/1**

2m 36.86s (-2.04) **Going Correction** -0.175s/f (Firm)
**WFA** 3 from 4yo 13lb **6 Ran SP% 113.3**
Speed ratings (Par 102): **99,98,95,93,90 85**
CSF £6.51 TOTE £9.60: £2.40, £1.02; EX 7.20 Trifecta £18.00.
**Owner** Thurloe Thoroughbreds XXXI **Bred** Ecurie Des Monceaux & Partners **Trained** East Ilsley, Berks

**FOCUS**
Suspect maiden form.

## 3878 PETER ANDRE 10 JULY H'CAP (JOCKEY CLUB GRASSROOTS FLAT MIDDLE DISTANCE SERIES QUALIFIER) 1m 2f 18y
8:20 (8:20) (Class 4) (0-80,79) 3-Y-O+ £4,690 (£1,395; £697; £348) Stalls Low

Form RPR
-154 **1** **Jakey (IRE)**[45] 2405 4-10-0 79 TedDurcan 1 88
(Pat Phelan) *dwlt: hld up in last: rdn and prog over 2f out: clsd on ldrs over 1f out: squeezed through fnl f to ld last 100yds* **3/1**[2]

6-16 **2** *nk* **Lilac Tree**[138] 623 4-9-12 77 SilvestreDeSousa 6 85
(Mark Johnston) *chsd ldr: rdn wl over 2f out: led over 1f out: kpt on u.p but hdd and outpcd last 100yds* **11/4**[1]

0222 **3** *½* **Ocean Applause**[9] 3544 4-9-1 73 (t) JoeDoyle(7) 4 80
(John Ryan) *in tch: 5th st: rdn to chse ldng pair over 2f out: clsd 1f out: styd on but outpcd last 100yds* **4/1**[3]

1020 **4** *2 ½* **Cravat**[20] 3190 5-9-6 74 OisinMurphy(3) 10 76
(Ed de Giles) *in tch: dropped to 6th and shoved along st: tried to make prog on outer fr 2f out but hanging lft: kpt on to take 4th last strides* **6/1**

-124 **5** *nk* **Trulee Scrumptious**[6] 3675 5-8-9 60 (v) JimmyQuinn 3 64
(Peter Charalambous) *led: stretched field fr 5f out: drvn and hdd over 1f out: cl up but hld whn hmpd ins fnl f* **7/1**

4515 **6** *5* **Bennelong**[12] 3473 8-8-11 62 (b) StevieDonohoe 2 54
(Lee Carter) *trckd ldng pair to over 2f out: wknd wl over 1f out* **20/1**

3200 **7** *7* **Munsarim (IRE)**[12] 3472 7-9-6 71 (v) AmirQuinn 5 50
(Lee Carter) *dwlt: pushed up to go prom: 4th st: rdn over 3f out: wknd 2f out* **33/1**

0000 **8** *10* **Persepolis (IRE)**[24] 3065 4-10-0 79 (b[1]) GeorgeBaker 9 39
(Brett Johnson) *t.k.h: hld up: 7th st: hanging and wknd wl over 2f out: t.o* **10/1**

2m 6.58s (-3.12) **Going Correction** -0.175s/f (Firm) **8 Ran SP% 115.2**
Speed ratings (Par 105): **105,104,104,102,102 98,92,84**
CSF £11.83 CT £32.40 TOTE £3.80: £1.10, £2.00, £1.80; EX 13.80 Trifecta £49.30.
**Owner** Allen B Pope **Bred** Cliveden Stud Ltd **Trained** Epsom, Surrey

**FOCUS**
A modest handicap, run at a fair pace. Ordinary but sound form.

## 3879 BANSTEAD H'CAP 7f
8:50 (8:51) (Class 4) (0-85,85) 3-Y-O+ £4,690 (£1,395; £697; £348) Stalls Low

Form RPR
1441 **1** **Kosika (USA)**[8] 3575 4-9-11 82 6ex SilvestreDeSousa 11 92
(Mark Johnston) *led: drvn 2f out: hdd over 1f out: battled bk wl to ld again last 100yds* **7/2**[1]

3621 **2** *½* **Intomist (IRE)**[5] 3734 5-8-4 68 (p) DanielCremin(7) 12 77
(Jim Boyle) *sn trckd ldr: rdn to ld over 1f out: hdd and nt qckn last 100yds* **5/1**[2]

2530 **3** *1 ¾* **Bayleyf (IRE)**[13] 3422 5-8-9 66 oh1 (p) StevieDonohoe 7 70
(Lee Carter) *t.k.h: trckd ldng trio: rdn to go 3rd 2f out: nt qckn and no imp after* **33/1**

1600 **4** *1 ¾* **Forceful Appeal (USA)**[25] 3036 6-9-9 83 OisinMurphy(3) 4 82
(Simon Dow) *hld up: 6th st: drvn and no prog over 2f out: kpt on fr over 1f out: n.d* **5/1**[2]

6404 **5** *¾* **Good Luck Charm**[17] 3314 5-9-7 78 GeorgeBaker 3 76
(Gary Moore) *hld up: 7th st: hld together tl rdn over 1f out: mod late prog: no ch* **7/2**[1]

0304 **6** *1* **Langley Vale**[17] 3313 5-9-2 73 SebSanders 1 68
(Roger Teal) *chsd ldrs: 5th st: sn rdn: outpcd fr 2f out: n.d after* **10/1**[3]

2210 **7** *nk* **Firmdecisions (IRE)**[55] 2110 4-10-0 85 PatDobbs 5 79
(Brett Johnson) *chsd ldng pair to 2f out: sn wl outpcd: plugged on* **12/1**

-211 **8** *nk* **Meet Me Halfway**[44] 2448 4-9-8 82 AshleyMorgan(3) 10 75
(Chris Wall) *hld up in rr: 8th st: shkn up on outer and no prog over 2f out: no ch after* **5/1**[2]

6560 **9** *1* **Lionheart**[54] 2147 4-9-2 73 (b[1]) ShaneKelly 2 64
(Peter Crate) *hld up in last: gng bttr than most 2f out but stl wl in rr: rdn and no rspnse jst over 1f out* **20/1**

1m 21.26s (-2.04) **Going Correction** -0.175s/f (Firm) **9 Ran SP% 118.9**
Speed ratings (Par 105): **104,103,101,99,98 97,97,96,95**
CSF £21.84 CT £501.41 TOTE £3.80: £1.60, £2.10, £6.00; EX 22.70 Trifecta £738.50.
**Owner** Sheikh Hamdan bin Mohammed Al Maktoum **Bred** Betz Thoroughbred Et Al **Trained** Middleham Moor, N Yorks

**FOCUS**
A good, competitive handicap.
T/Plt: £30.10 to a £1 stake. Pool: £74,168.12 - 1795.25 winning units. T/Qpdt: £4.00 to a £1 stake. Pool: £6,982.62 - 1286.06 winning units. JN

# 3461 HAYDOCK (L-H)
### Thursday, July 3

**OFFICIAL GOING: Good changing to good to soft after race 1 (2.20)**
Wind: light 1/2 against Weather: overcast, light showers becoming dry and sunny

## 3880 GLASS TIMES H'CAP 1m 2f 95y
2:20 (2:20) (Class 5) (0-70,70) 3-Y-O+ £2,587 (£770; £384; £192) Stalls Centre

Form RPR
2203 **1** **Watersmeet**[12] 3466 3-9-3 70 JoeFanning 8 80+
(Mark Johnston) *mde all: qcknd pce over 3f out: drvn over 1f out: kpt on: unchal* **15/8**[1]

501 **2** *3 ½* **Ferryview Place**[17] 3308 5-8-9 51 oh1 (p) RobertWinston 3 54
(Ian Williams) *mid-div: t.k.h: effrt over 3f out: chsd wnr appr fnl f: kpt on same pce* **8/1**

3000 **3** *hd* **Steelriver (IRE)**[19] 3254 4-10-0 70 DavidAllan 5 73
(James Bethell) *hld up in rr: effrt over 3f out: 3rd 1f out: kpt on same pce* **8/1**

-335 **4** *4* **Evervescent (IRE)**[19] 3226 5-10-0 70 PaulHanagan 6 65
(Graeme McPherson) *mid-div: t.k.h: effrt over 3f out: one pce* **9/2**[3]

045 **5** *¾* **Poor Duke (IRE)**[5] 3696 4-10-0 70 TomEaves 4 64
(Michael Mullineaux) *sn chsng ldrs: drvn over 3f out: one pce* **33/1**

2450 **6** *½* **All Reddy**[26] 2998 3-9-2 69 RichardKingscote 1 62
(Tom Dascombe) *chsd ldrs: pushed along over 5f out: one pce fnl 2f* **4/1**[2]

-523 **7** *¾* **Rockie Road (IRE)**[16] 3333 3-8-0 53 RaulDaSilva 7 45
(Paul Green) *trckd ldrs: t.k.h: chsd wnr over 3f out: wknd appr fnl f* **8/1**

350- **8** *13* **Tenhoo**[314] 5706 8-10-0 70 JasonHart 2 37
(Eric Alston) *stdd s: hld up in rr: sme hdwy on inner 4f out: sn wknd: bhd fnl 2f* **20/1**

000- **9** *1* **Idarose (IRE)**[281] 6759 5-8-4 51 oh6 GemmaTutty(5) 9 16
(John David Riches) *mid-div: drvn over 3f out: sn lost pl: bhd fnl 2f* **100/1**

2m 14.25s (-1.25) **Going Correction** -0.125s/f (Firm)
**WFA** 3 from 4yo+ 11lb **9 Ran SP% 115.0**
Speed ratings (Par 103): **100,97,97,93,93 92,92,81,81**
CSF £17.56 CT £97.58 TOTE £2.20: £1.10, £2.30, £2.40; EX 16.80 Trifecta £130.70.
**Owner** J Barson **Bred** Stetchworth & Middle Park Studs **Trained** Middleham Moor, N Yorks



The Form Book, Raceform Ltd, Newbury, RG14 5SJ

**FOCUS**
All races on Inner Home straight and distances reduced by 5yds on Round course. This looked a race devoid of pace on paper, but the winner dominated. The form is rated around the second.

## 3881 DISTINCTION DOORS EBF STALLIONS MAIDEN STKS 6f
2:50 (2:51) (Class 5) 2-Y-O £2,911 (£866; £432; £216) Stalls Centre

Form RPR
1 **Faydhan (USA)** 2-9-5 0 PaulHanagan 10 100+
(John Gosden) *wnt rt s: rr-div: hdwy over 3f out: led 1f out: wnt clr* **10/11**[1]
3 2 6 **Dutch Connection**[18] 3279 2-9-5 0 WilliamBuick 5 80
(Charles Hills) *w ldrs: led over 2f out: hdd 1f out: no ch w wnr* **7/4**[2]
40 3 1 1/4 **Speedy Move (IRE)**[19] 3255 2-9-5 0 JoeFanning 8 76
(Ismail Mohammed) *led: hdd over 3f out: kpt on same pce fnl f* **16/1**
40 4 2 1/4 **Little Belter (IRE)**[19] 3215 2-9-5 0 RichardKingscote 6 70
(Tom Dascombe) *mid-div: pushed along 3f out: one pce* **25/1**
4 5 2 1/2 **Shootingsta (IRE)**[21] 3148 2-9-5 0 PaulMulrennan 7 62
(Bryan Smart) *w ldrs: led over 3f out: hdd over 2f out: wknd fnl f* **7/1**[3]
6 3/4 **Dark Wonder (IRE)** 2-9-5 0 GrahamLee 2 60
(James Given) *in rr-div: kpt on fnl 2f: nvr a factor* **25/1**
0 7 hd **On The Tiles**[21] 3148 2-9-5 0 SeanLevey 11 59
(Ed McMahon) *dwlt: hld up in rr: effrt over 2f out: kpt on fnl f: nvr a factor* **40/1**
8 3 3/4 **Horsetracker** 2-8-9 0[1] GeorgeDowning(5) 4 43
(Ian Williams) *s.s: sn drvn along: sme hdwy 3f out: lost pl over 1f out* **66/1**
9 6 **Retro Valley (IRE)** 2-9-5 0 DanielTudhope 3 30
(David Dennis) *dwlt: in rr: bhd whn eased clsng stages* **66/1**
6 10 11 **Millgate**[48] 2291 2-9-2 0 GeorgeChaloner(3) 9
(Richard Fahey) *wnt rt s: chsd ldrs: lost pl over 2f out: bhd whn eased ins fnl f* **20/1**

1m 14.23s (0.43) **Going Correction** +0.275s/f (Good) **10** Ran SP% **125.0**
Speed ratings (Par 94): **108,100,98,95,92 91,90,85,77,63**
CSF £2.72 TOTE £2.40: £1.10, £1.10, £3.30; EX 3.50 Trifecta £23.30.
**Owner** Hamdan Al Maktoum **Bred** Keithshire Farm **Trained** Newmarket, Suffolk

**FOCUS**
The ground was changed from good to good to soft immediately after the running of the first. The next four home all had previous experience which makes the winner's performance all the more impressive.

## 3882 BOHLE GROUP H'CAP (JOCKEY CLUB GRASSROOTS FLAT SPRINT SERIES QUALIFIER) 6f
3:20 (3:22) (Class 4) (0-80,81) 3-Y-O+ £5,175 (£1,540; £769; £384) Stalls Centre

Form RPR
0521 1 **Foxy Clarets (IRE)**[11] 3503 3-9-4 81 6ex (b) GeorgeChaloner(3) 4 89
(Richard Fahey) *chsd ldrs: led over 3f out: drvn rt out: hld on towards fin* **9/2**[2]
1-05 2 1/2 **Constantine**[10] 3538 3-9-5 79 SeanLevey 5 85
(Richard Hannon) *in rr-div: hdwy over 2f out: styd on fnl f: tk 2nd last 50yds* **12/1**
0616 3 nk **Meandmyshadow**[14] 3384 6-8-13 67 DaleSwift 2 73
(Alan Brown) *drvn to ld: hdd over 3f out: kpt on same pce fnl f* **16/1**
5-30 4 3/4 **Rich Again (IRE)**[17] 3298 5-8-9 63 JoeFanning 6 67
(James Bethell) *s.i.s: hdwy 3f out: sn chsng ldrs: kpt on same pce ins fnl f* **8/1**[3]
211 5 3 **Dreams Of Reality**[43] 2470 3-9-1 75 RichardKingscote 11 68+
(Tom Dascombe) *mid-div: stmbld over 4f out: clipped heels: stmbld bdly and lost pl over 3f out: kpt on fnl f* **9/2**[2]
0402 6 hd **Holy Angel (IRE)**[7] 3599 5-9-0 68 (e) DavidAllan 12 61
(Tim Easterby) *dwlt and wnt rt s: bhd: hdwy over 2f out: kpt on: nvr a factor* **4/1**[1]
042 7 1 3/4 **Eland Ally**[5] 3702 6-9-0 68 AndrewElliott 10 56
(Tom Tate) *sn chsng ldrs: dropped bk over 2f out: kpt on fnl f* **4/1**[1]
6-10 8 5 **Minty Jones**[22] 3099 5-8-7 61 oh6 (v) RaulDaSilva 8 33
(Michael Mullineaux) *w ldrs: reminders over 3f out: wknd 2f out* **50/1**
101- 9 1/2 **Brother Tiger**[230] 7896 5-9-5 73 RobertHavlin 7 43
(David C Griffiths) *trckd ldrs: lost pl over 1f out* **8/1**[3]
-030 10 11 **Generalyse**[17] 3313 5-9-9 77 (bt) PaulHanagan 1 12
(Ben De Haan) *prom: lost pl over 4f out: bhd fnl 2f: eased clsng stages* **20/1**

1m 15.05s (1.25) **Going Correction** +0.275s/f (Good)
**WFA** 3 from 4yo+ 6lb **10** Ran SP% **118.9**
Speed ratings (Par 105): **102,101,100,99,95 95,93,86,86,71**
CSF £58.54 CT £598.66 TOTE £4.70: £1.50, £3.50, £4.20; EX 60.10 Trifecta £647.30.
**Owner** Hazel Tattersall & G Hyde **Bred** Simon Holt David Thorpe & R J Beggan **Trained** Musley Bank, N Yorks

**FOCUS**
This was competitive but it's dubious as to how many of these would have appreciated the morning rain. The winner confirmed his Pontrefact form.

## 3883 TUFFX GLASS EBF STALLIONS NOVICE STKS (BOBIS RACE) 7f
3:50 (3:51) (Class 4) 2-Y-O £6,469 (£1,925; £962; £481) Stalls Low

Form RPR
1 1 **Lieutenant Kaffee (USA)**[16] 3330 2-9-2 0 PaulHanagan 3 90+
(Richard Fahey) *hld up in last: t.k.h: hdwy 3f out: styd on to ld last 75yds: kpt on wl* **4/1**[2]
41 2 3/4 **Diaz (IRE)**[12] 3474 2-9-5 0 JoeFanning 5 90
(Mark Johnston) *led: edgd rt over 1f out: hdd and no ex last 75yds* **4/1**[2]
3 1 1/2 **Henrytheaeroplane (USA)** 2-8-12 0 TonyHamilton 1 79+
(Richard Fahey) *dwlt: sn trcking ldrs: hdwy over 3f out: swtchd lft and chsd ldrs 1f out: kpt on same pce* **28/1**[3]
31 4 4 1/2 **Epithet (IRE)**[13] 3429 2-9-5 0 WilliamBuick 6 74
(Charlie Appleby) *trckd ldrs: 2nd 4f out: drvn to chal over 1f out: wknd fnl 150yds* **4/7**[1]
5 9 **Joshua Potman (IRE)** 2-8-12 0 RichardKingscote 2 46
(Tom Dascombe) *sn chsng ldrs: drvn over 3f out: lost pl 2f out: bhd whn eased towards fin* **33/1**

1m 29.23s (-1.47) **Going Correction** -0.125s/f (Firm) **5** Ran SP% **110.0**
Speed ratings (Par 96): **103,102,100,95,85**
CSF £19.50 TOTE £5.20: £2.90, £1.70; EX 17.80 Trifecta £57.30.
**Owner** Richard Fahey Ebor Racing Club Ltd **Bred** St George Farm LLC **Trained** Musley Bank, N Yorks

**FOCUS**
This was run at a strong pace.

## 3884 RITEC CLEARSHIELD ECO-SYSTEMS H'CAP (BOBIS RACE) 1m 6f
4:20 (4:20) (Class 2) (0-100,87) 3-Y-O £16,172 (£4,812; £2,405; £1,202) Stalls Low

Form RPR
1200 1 **Alex My Boy (IRE)**[14] 3379 3-9-7 87 JoeFanning 4 101+
(Mark Johnston) *sn chsng ldrs: led 3f out: drvn over 1f out: styd on wl* **4/6**[1]
022 2 3 3/4 **Altaayil (IRE)**[18] 3270 3-9-7 87 PaulHanagan 2 95+
(Sir Michael Stoute) *dwlt: hld up in last: shkn up 6f out: hdwy to chal 3f out: sn rdn and wandered: kpt on same pce appr fnl f* **4/1**[3]
5135 3 8 **Ujagar (IRE)**[57] 2077 3-8-11 77 (b) RichardKingscote 1 74
(Tom Dascombe) *sed awkwardly: led: qcknd pce 4f out: hdd 3f out: wknd over 1f out* **10/1**
14 4 3 3/4 **Tiger Lilly (IRE)**[19] 3250 3-8-10 76 TonyHamilton 3 68
(Richard Fahey) *trckd ldrs: drvn and outpcd 4f out: lost pl over 1f out* **7/2**[2]

3m 3.92s (1.92) **Going Correction** -0.125s/f (Firm) **4** Ran SP% **111.3**
Speed ratings (Par 106): **89,86,82,80**
CSF £3.87 TOTE £2.00; EX 3.70 Trifecta £12.20.
**Owner** Jaber Abdullah **Bred** Orpendale, Chelston & Wynatt **Trained** Middleham Moor, N Yorks

**FOCUS**
A desperately disappointing turnout for such a valuable prize and hard to get overly excited by the form, but the first two are likely to be better than their marks.

## 3885 FGI TANGERINE FILLIES' H'CAP 1m
4:50 (4:53) (Class 5) (0-75,74) 3-Y-O+ £2,587 (£770; £384; £192) Stalls Low

Form RPR
01-5 1 **Ejadah (IRE)**[21] 3154 3-9-5 74 PaulHanagan 4 87
(Roger Varian) *wore net muzzle: w ldr: led over 6f out: drvn and styd on wl appr fnl f* **9/2**[2]
5504 2 4 1/2 **Imshivalla (IRE)**[17] 3300 3-8-12 70[1] GeorgeChaloner(3) 5 73
(Richard Fahey) *mid-div: effrt and chsng ldrs over 3f out: 3rd appr fnl f: styd on to take 2nd clsng stages: no ch w wnr* **8/1**
2165 3 1/2 **Dalmarella Dancer (IRE)**[34] 2740 3-9-4 73 DanielTudhope 9 75
(K R Burke) *hld up in rr: hdwy on ins over 3f out: chsng wnr over 1f out: kpt on same pce* **9/1**
1056 4 3 1/2 **The Silver Kebaya (FR)**[18] 3268 3-9-0 69 (p) WilliamBuick 6 63
(Jeremy Noseda) *chsd ldrs: drvn over 3f out: one pce fnl 2f* **6/1**[3]
1303 5 nk **Burnt Fingers (IRE)**[33] 2775 4-9-6 66 GrahamLee 10 61
(Rod Millman) *hld up in rr: effrt over 3f out: hdwy on outside over 1f out: nvr a factor* **11/4**[1]
-506 6 2 1/2 **Amethyst Dawn (IRE)**[22] 3099 8-8-10 56 DavidAllan 7 45
(Tim Easterby) *t.k.h in rr: effrt 3f out: wknd fnl f* **16/1**
5465 7 1 3/4 **Spavento (IRE)**[7] 3608 8-9-5 65 JasonHart 2 50
(Eric Alston) *sn led: hdd over 6f out: wknd appr fnl f* **28/1**
0210 8 10 **Suni Dancer**[7] 3603 3-8-0 55 RaulDaSilva 3 15
(Paul Green) *led early: chsd ldrs: drvn over 3f out: lost pl over 1f out: bhd whn eased clsng stages* **10/1**

1m 41.42s (-2.28) **Going Correction** -0.125s/f (Firm)
**WFA** 3 from 4yo+ 9lb **8** Ran SP% **98.7**
Speed ratings (Par 100): **106,101,101,97,97 94,92,82**
CSF £29.00 CT £188.12 TOTE £3.80: £1.50, £2.00, £2.90; EX 26.20 Trifecta £192.10.
**Owner** Hamdan Al Maktoum **Bred** Herbertstown House Stud **Trained** Newmarket, Suffolk
■ Rule 4 of 15p in the pound applies to all bets; Withdrawn: Announcement

**FOCUS**
The winer set a reasonable pace and posted a clear personal best.

## 3886 SUPALITE TILED ROOF SYSTEM H'CAP 1m
5:20 (5:20) (Class 3) (0-95,95) 3-Y-O+ £8,086 (£2,406; £1,202; £601) Stalls Low

Form RPR
-413 1 **Balducci**[8] 3573 7-9-12 93 (v) DanielTudhope 2 103
(David O'Meara) *mde all: drvn over 2f out: kpt on wl ins fnl f* **13/2**
-562 2 1 1/4 **Multi Bene**[22] 3109 5-9-11 92 GrahamGibbons 8 99
(Ed McMahon) *trckd ldrs: chsd wnr over 1f out: kpt on same pce ins fnl f* **3/1**[1]
0021 3 3/4 **Chosen Character (IRE)**[22] 3109 6-9-13 94 (vt) RichardKingscote 6 99
(Tom Dascombe) *chsd ldrs: drvn over 2f out: kpt on same pce over 1f out* **9/2**[3]
-040 4 1 **Hunters Creek (IRE)**[14] 3378 3-9-5 95 RobertHavlin 3 96
(John Gosden) *s.i.s: sn chsng ldrs: drvn and outpcd over 3f out: swtchd outside and chsng ldrs over 2f out: kpt on same pce fnl f* **7/2**[2]
0-30 5 2 3/4 **Storm King**[50] 2253 5-9-10 91 SeanLevey 9 88
(David C Griffiths) *trckd ldrs: 2nd over 3f out: wknd last 100yds* **12/1**
-323 6 10 **Life Partner (IRE)**[13] 3431 4-9-12 93 PaulHanagan 4 67
(Charlie Appleby) *sn detached in last: drvn over 5f out: nvr on terms: eased ins fnl f* **3/1**[1]
/5-0 7 1 **Mezmaar**[26] 2984 5-9-12 93 GrahamLee 5 64
(Kevin Morgan) *in rr-div: drvn over 5f out: lost pl over 3f out: sn bhd: eased nr fin* **50/1**

1m 41.03s (-2.67) **Going Correction** -0.125s/f (Firm)
**WFA** 3 from 4yo+ 9lb **7** Ran SP% **113.4**
Speed ratings (Par 107): **108,106,106,105,102 92,91**
CSF £25.83 CT £96.35 TOTE £6.90: £3.20, £2.40; EX 29.40 Trifecta £123.90.
**Owner** Direct Racing **Bred** G Russell **Trained** Nawton, N Yorks

**FOCUS**
A competitive finale, run at a stern pace. The form looks solid.
T/Plt: £204.10 to a £1 stake. Pool: £69,716.73 - 249.30 winning units. T/Qpdt: £74.70 to a £1 stake. Pool: £3948.26 - 39.10 winning units. WG

# 3556 NEWBURY (L-H)
Thursday, July 3

**OFFICIAL GOING: Good (good to firm in places; 7.1)**
Wind: mild breeze across Weather: sunny

## 3887 ANDREW LLOYD WEBBER FOUNDATION APPRENTICE H'CAP 5f 34y
6:25 (6:25) (Class 5) (0-70,76) 4-Y-O+ £2,911 (£866; £432; £216) Stalls High

Form RPR
1451 1 **Dawn Catcher**[5] 3707 4-9-6 73 6ex PaddyPilley(5) 7 82
(Geoffrey Deacon) *trckd ldr tl disp ld after 2f: clr ldr 2f out: edgd lft fnl 100yds: hld on nr fin* **8/1**
2331 2 nk **Tyfos**[7] 3612 9-10-0 76 6ex TimClark 1 84
(Brian Baugh) *trckd ldrs: rdn 2f out: kpt on wl: hld nring fin* **4/1**[3]

4-01 **3** *hd* **Poyle Vinnie**[19] 3222 4-9-4 **69** JordanVaughan(3) 4 76
(George Margarson) *trckd ldrs: swtchd rt 2f out: sn rdn: kpt on ins fnl f: nvr quite getting there* **4/1**[3]

0404 **4** *1½* **Panther Patrol (IRE)**[19] 3216 4-8-12 **65** (v) KieranShoemark(5) 5 67
(Eve Johnson Houghton) *disp ld tl rdn 2f out: kpt pressing ldr: keeping on at same pce but hld in cl 4th whn short of room nring fin* **11/4**[1]

0003 **5** *2* **Rylee Mooch**[5] 3707 6-9-6 **68** (e) PhilipPrince 8 62
(Richard Guest) *broke wl: led for 2f: sn rdn to chse ldrs: one pce whn edgd lft fnl f* **14/1**

000- **6** *1* **Celestial Bay**[206] 8220 5-9-8 **70** JoshBaudains 2 61
(Sylvester Kirk) *awkward leaving stalls: sn outpcd in last pair: nvr on terms* **20/1**

53-1 **7** *½* **Tychaios**[16] 3323 4-8-12 **65** AaronJones(5) 3 54
(Stuart Williams) *sn outpcd in last pair: nvr on terms* **7/2**[2]

1m 1.99s (0.59) **Going Correction** -0.025s/f (Good) **7 Ran SP% 111.4**
Speed ratings (Par 103): **94,93,93,90,87 86,85**
CSF £37.66 CT £143.72 TOTE £9.50: £3.40, £1.80; EX 48.60 Trifecta £163.20.
**Owner** Mayden Stud & Associates **Bred** Mayden Stud, J A And D S Dewhurst **Trained** Compton, Berks

■ Stewards' Enquiry : Tim Clark four-day ban: used whip above permitted level (Jul 17-20)
Paddy Pilley one-day ban: careless riding (Jul 17)

**FOCUS**
Rail realignment increased distances on Round course by 13m. Four last-time-out winners in this modest apprentice handicap, and three of them contested the finish, so the form has a sound look to it. The winner improved again on her Leciester win. The first two are both by Bertolini.

## 3888 DENFORD STUD IRISH CHAMPIONS WEEKEND EBF MAIDEN FILLIES' STKS (BOBIS RACE) 6f 8y
**7:00** (7:01) (Class 4) 2-Y-O **£4,851** (£1,443; £721; £360) **Stalls** High

Form RPR

0 **1** **Goldcrest**[23] 3076 2-9-0 0 DaneO'Neill 4 80+
(Henry Candy) *mde all in centre: edgd rt after 1f: qcknd clr over 1f out: readily* **9/2**[2]

32 **2** *2* **Crystal Malt (IRE)**[18] 3267 2-9-0 0 RichardHughes 1 74
(Richard Hannon) *trckd wnr in centre thrght: rdn 2f out: kpt on but nt pce of wnr fr over 1f out* **2/1**[1]

**3** *1½* **Dolorous** 2-9-0 0 WilliamBuick 7 70+
(John Gosden) *mid-div in centre: hdwy over 2f out: wnt 3rd over 1f out: kpt on nicely but nt pce to threaten* **8/1**[3]

**4** *6* **Teosroyal (IRE)** 2-9-0 0 RoystonFfrench 2 52+
(Clive Brittain) *racd centre: s.i.s: towards rr: stdy prog fr over 2f out: styd on nicely fnl f but nvr any threat* **50/1**

**5** *2¼* **Moon River (IRE)** 2-9-0 0 JimmyFortune 3 45+
(Brian Meehan) *racd centre: towards rr: hanging lft whn hdwy over 2f out: kpt on but nt pce to rch ldrs fnl f* **16/1**

20 **6** *1¼* **Secret Lightning (FR)**[13] 3415 2-8-9 0 JoshBaudains(5) 6 41
(Sylvester Kirk) *edgy in stalls: trckd ldrs in centre: swtchd rt whn lost pl over 2f out: kpt on but nt pce to threaten ldrs fnl f* **12/1**

**7** *¾* **Dusty Blue** 2-9-0 0 PatCosgrave 14 44+
(Paul Cole) *racd stands' side: mid-div: rdn 2f out: sn swtchd lft: one pce fnl f* **66/1**

**8** *½* **Beauty Of The Sea** 2-9-0 0 FrederikTylicki 16 42+
(Roger Varian) *racd stands' side: trckd ldrs: rdn 2f out: fdd fnl f* **11/1**

**9** *hd* **Bellajeu** 2-9-0 0 HarryBentley 8 37
(Olly Stevens) *nvr bttr than mid-div in centre gp* **8/1**[3]

**10** *nse* **Fast Romance (USA)** 2-9-0 0 LukeMorris 15 42+
(Paul Cole) *racd stands' side: trckd ldr: rdn over 2f out: wknd over 1f out* **33/1**

**11** *nk* **Gen I Am** 2-9-0 0 KieranO'Neill 9 36
(Richard Hannon) *mid-div in centre tl wknd over 1f out* **40/1**

**12** *3* **Epic Find (USA)** 2-8-11 0 RobertTart(3) 5 27
(Charles Hills) *racd centre: s.i.s: sn outpcd: a towards rr* **20/1**

**13** *hd* **Victorina** 2-8-11 0 RyanTate(3) 11 26
(Stuart Kittow) *racd centre: mid-div tl wknd 2f out* **100/1**

**14** *1½* **Its Lady Mary** 2-9-0 0 FergusSweeney 10 22
(Paul Cole) *prom in centre gp: rdn 2f out: sn wknd* **66/1**

6 **15** *2¼* **Maybe Now Baby (IRE)**[19] 3223 2-9-0 0 WilliamTwiston-Davies 12 20+
(David Simcock) *racd stands' side: trckd ldr tl wknd 2f out* **28/1**

**16** *6* **Sister Of Mercy (IRE)** 2-9-0 0 JamesDoyle 13 +
(Roger Charlton) *racd stands' side: trckd ldrs tl wknd 2f out* **16/1**

1m 13.2s (0.20) **Going Correction** -0.025s/f (Good) **16 Ran SP% 121.1**
Speed ratings (Par 93): **97,94,92,84,81 79,78,78,77,77 77,73,73,71,68 60**
CSF £12.77 TOTE £5.30: £2.00, £1.60, £3.10; EX 19.50 Trifecta £128.10.
**Owner** Lady Whent **Bred** Lady Whent **Trained** Kingston Warren, Oxon

**FOCUS**
Probably not a particularly strong maiden. Just four of this large field had previous racecourse experience, including the first two. Not many got into the race and a low draw proved highly advantageous.

## 3889 JLT MAIDEN STKS (BOBIS RACE) 5f 34y
**7:35** (7:37) (Class 4) 2-Y-O
**£4,980** (£1,491; £745; £372; £186; £93) **Stalls** High

Form RPR

**1** *3* **Judicial (IRE)** 2-9-5 0 [1] JamesDoyle 9 83+
(Roger Charlton) *racd centre for 2f: in tch: rdn 2f out: chsd wnr ent fnl f: kpt on but no ch w ready wnr* **16/1**

**2** *5* **Profitable (IRE)** 2-9-2 0 RyanTate(3) 5 65+
(Clive Cox) *racd centre for 2f: in tch: rdn 2f out: sn sed to drift lft: hung bdly lft ent fnl f: sn wnt 3rd: fin on far side rails: kpt on but no ch* **2/1**[2]

4 **3** *1¼* **Essaka (IRE)**[8] 3584 2-9-5 0 WilliamTwiston-Davies 6 61
(Mick Channon) *racd centre for 2f: trckd ldrs: rdn 2f out: kpt on same pce fnl f* **7/1**[3]

5 **4** *2¾* **Shackled N Drawn (USA)**[60] 1977 2-9-5 0 (t) KierenFallon 11 51+
(Olly Stevens) *racd alone on stands' side rails for 2f: led: edging lft whn rdn and hdd over 1f out: sn hld: fdd fnl 120yds* **13/8**[1]

**5** *½* **Rotherwick (IRE)** 2-9-5 0 LukeMorris 1 49
(Paul Cole) *racd centre for 2f: in tch: rdn 2f out: sn outpcd* **14/1**

**6** *1¼* **Galago (IRE)** 2-9-5 0 JimmyFortune 7 45
(Sylvester Kirk) *racd centre for 2f: slowly away and wnt lft s: in last pair: nvr gng pce to get on terms* **50/1**

**7** *9* **Arthur's Way (IRE)** 2-9-5 0 PatCosgrave 8 12
(Paul Cole) *racd centre for 2f: s.i.s: sn rdn along in last pair: nvr any danger* **40/1**

0 **8** *2* **Tribal Diamond**[19] 3232 2-9-0 0 AdamBeschizza 2
(Edward Creighton) *racd centre for 2f: chsd ldrs tl wknd 2f out* **250/1**

**D** **Strath Burn** 2-9-5 0 WilliamBuick 3 94+
(Charles Hills) *led chsng gp in centre tl swtchd to stands' side after 2f: led over 1f out: sn in command: readily* **7/1**[3]

1m 1.24s (-0.16) **Going Correction** -0.025s/f (Good) **9 Ran SP% 113.8**
Speed ratings (Par 96): **95,87,85,80,80 78,63,60,100**
CSF £105.75 TOTE £7.40: £1.80, £3.20, £1.10; EX 61.40 Trifecta £155.50.
**Owner** Elite Racing Club **Bred** Elite Racing Club **Trained** Beckhampton, Wilts

■ John Joiner was withdrawn. Price at time of withdrawal 66-1. Rule 4 does not apply.

**FOCUS**
A reasonable maiden that should produce winners. In contrast to the earlier fillies' race, where a low draw was required, the field all raced on the stands' side after two furlongs. They finished strung out behind the winner.

## 3890 BETFAIR FILLIES' H'CAP 7f (S)
**8:10** (8:11) (Class 4) (0-80,80) 3-Y-O+ **£4,690** (£1,395; £697; £348) **Stalls** High

Form RPR

1- **1** **Alzanti (USA)**[217] 8084 3-9-4 **78** JamesDoyle 1 87
(Amanda Perrett) *trckd ldrs: chal ent fnl f: shkn up to ld fnl 120yds: cosily* **4/1**[2]

400- **2** *¾* **Gown (IRE)**[250] 7537 3-9-2 **76** WilliamBuick 2 83
(Charles Hills) *prom: led over 2f out: rdn over 1f out: hdd fnl 120yds: kpt on but no ex* **14/1**

00-0 **3** *2¾* **Annina (IRE)**[54] 2157 4-10-0 **80** DaneO'Neill 8 83
(Henry Candy) *led tl over 2f out: sn rdn: drifted lft ent fnl f: kpt on same pce* **14/1**

5131 **4** *1½* **Pretty Bubbles**[33] 2775 5-9-6 **72** FrederikTylicki 7 71
(J R Jenkins) *in tch: swtchd rt over 2f out: sn rdn to chse ldrs: kpt on same pce fnl f* **8/1**

1243 **5** *2½* **Nimble Kimble**[28] 2929 3-8-11 **74** RyanTate(3) 3 64
(James Eustace) *hld up: hdwy fr 3f out: rdn to chse ldrs 2f out: no ex ins fnl f* **7/1**[3]

663 **6** *6* **Djinni (IRE)**[18] 3280 3-8-3 **70** CamHardie(7) 5 44
(Richard Hannon) *trckd ldr: rdn 2f out: sn wknd* **9/1**

-151 **7** *9* **Frangipanni (IRE)**[10] 3518 3-8-12 **72** 6ex RichardHughes 6 23
(Roger Charlton) *racd keenly trcking ldrs: short-lived effrt over 2f out: qckly btn* **6/4**[1]

005 **8** *1½* **Triple Star**[20] 3184 3-8-3 **63** LukeMorris 11 10
(Hughie Morrison) *in tch: rdn over 2f out: sn wknd* **22/1**

0025 **9** *dist* **Princess Spirit**[14] 3390 5-8-9 **61** oh1 (p) AdamBeschizza 9
(Edward Creighton) *hld up: stirrup leather broke 2f out: sn eased: p.u to a walk fnl f* **40/1**

1m 25.01s (-0.69) **Going Correction** -0.025s/f (Good)
**WFA** 3 from 4yo+ 8lb **9 Ran SP% 113.7**
Speed ratings (Par 102): **102,101,98,96,93 86,76,74,**
CSF £56.93 CT £714.21 TOTE £4.70: £1.60, £4.00, £3.20; EX 64.70 Trifecta £499.00.
**Owner** K Abdullah **Bred** Juddmonte Farms Inc **Trained** Pulborough, W Sussex

**FOCUS**
The first two were among three who raced in the centre slightly apart from the others, stall one beating stall two. With the favourite flopping, the form doesn't look especially solid.

## 3891 CHEVELEY PARK STUD MAIDEN STKS 1m 4f 5y
**8:40** (8:40) (Class 5) 3-Y-O+ **£3,234** (£962; £481; £240) **Stalls** Low

Form RPR

**1** **Stella Bellissima (IRE)** 3-8-10 0 WilliamBuick 10 88+
(John Gosden) *dwlt: bhd: racd wdst home bnd: smooth hdwy fr 4f out: pushed along 2f out: led fnl 175yds: styd on wl* **4/1**[2]

5 **2** *1½* **Gwafa (IRE)**[49] 2271 3-9-1 0 MartinHarley 5 82
(Marco Botti) *trckd ldrs: rdn over 2f out: styd on fnl f: wnt 2nd towards fin* **12/1**[3]

03 **3** *nk* **Pleasant Valley (IRE)**[21] 3141 3-8-10 0 AndreaAtzeni 8 77
(Luca Cumani) *trckd ldr: led 4f out: rdn wl over 2f out: hdd fnl 175yds: no ex whn lost 2nd towards fin* **4/1**[2]

5 **4** *2¾* **Pennine Panther**[42] 2485 3-9-1 0 DaneO'Neill 4 78
(Henry Candy) *hld up: hdwy over 3f out: rdn over 2f out: kpt on fnl f but nt pce to get on terms* **50/1**

2424 **5** *hd* **Three Peaks**[34] 2733 3-9-1 79 (p) JamesDoyle 9 77
(Charles Hills) *s.i.s: sn in tch: hdwy over 2f out: sn rdn: kpt on same pce tl no ex fnl 120yds* **12/1**[3]

-224 **6** *4½* **Venezia (IRE)**[14] 3379 3-9-1 89 RichardHughes 7 70
(Martyn Meade) *led tl 4f out: rdn wl over 2f out: sn hld: wknd ent fnl f* **4/7**[1]

**7** *shd* **Guard of Honour (IRE)** 3-9-1 0 PatCosgrave 2 70
(Rebecca Curtis) *mid-div: rdn over 2f out: no imp: wknd fnl f* **33/1**

50 **8** *29* **Sir Woodgate**[17] 3315 3-9-1 0 AdamBeschizza 1 24
(Edward Creighton) *a towards rr: wknd over 2f out: t.o* **100/1**

0 **9** *13* **Italian Symphony (IRE)**[20] 3174 4-9-9 0 (p) BrendanPowell 6
(Brendan Powell) *mid-div: pushed along after 2f: last and struggling 4f out: wknd over 2f out: t.o* **100/1**

2m 33.51s (-1.99) **Going Correction** -0.025s/f (Good)
**WFA** 3 from 4yo+ 13lb **9 Ran SP% 125.9**
Speed ratings (Par 103): **105,104,103,101,101 98,98,79,70**
CSF £52.90 TOTE £4.40: £1.60, £2.80, £1.20; EX 54.80 Trifecta £160.70.
**Owner** Normandie Stud Ltd **Bred** Normandie Stud Ltd **Trained** Newmarket, Suffolk

**FOCUS**
This was run a second quicker than the concluding handicap. With the favourite bombing out the form is not what it might have been, but this was still a bright start from the winner, and the form makes a fair bit of sense, rated around the third and fifth.

## 3892 ABN AMRO H'CAP (BOBIS RACE) 1m 4f 5y
**9:10** (9:11) (Class 4) (0-85,85) 3-Y-O **£4,690** (£1,395; £697; £348) **Stalls** Low

Form RPR

2-1 **1** **Second Step (IRE)**[33] 2773 3-9-7 **85** AndreaAtzeni 8 97+
(Luca Cumani) *in tch: hdwy over 4f out: led wl over 2f out: sn rdn: styd on wl to assert fnl f* **7/1**

1 **2** *2* **Arabian Revolution**[28] 2924 3-9-6 **84** KierenFallon 6 93
(Saeed bin Suroor) *s.i.s: mid-div after 2f: hdwy over 3f out: rdn over 2f out: sn pressing wnr: styd on same pce fnl f* **7/4**[1]

556 **3** *1½* **Fastnet Red**[19] 3248 3-8-12 **76** WilliamBuick 7 82
(John Gosden) *hld up: pushed along over 4f out: hdwy over 2f out: wnt 3rd over 1f out: styd on wout rching ldrs* **9/2**[2]

2413 **4** *2* **Cape Caster (IRE)**[8] 3587 3-9-3 **81** JamesDoyle 10 84
(Ralph Beckett) *hld up: rdn for stdy prog in centre fr over 2f out: styd on to go 4th fnl 120yds* **5/1**[3]

-213 **5** *1* **Sebastian Beach (IRE)**[20] 3183 3-9-2 **80** RichardHughes 9 81
(Richard Hannon) *trckd ldr: led briefly 3f out: sn rdn: kpt chsng ldrs tl no ex fnl 120yds* **6/1**



The Form Book, Raceform Ltd, Newbury, RG14 5SJ

3-10 **6** *1 3/4* **Purple Spectrum**[33] 2761 3-9-1 **79**....................(p) LiamJones 5 78
(William Haggas) *sn pushed into ld: rdn and hdd 3f out: wknd jst over 1f out* **16/1**

0-36 **7** *5* **What A Scorcher**[49] 2280 3-8-12 **76**.................... LukeMorris 1 67
(Clive Cox) *in tch: rdn 4f out: nvr threatened: wknd over 1f out* **50/1**

1-15 **8** *4 1/2* **Fun Mac (GER)**[40] 2566 3-9-5 **83**.................... JimmyFortune 4 71
(Hughie Morrison) *broke wl: trckd ldr: rdn wl over 2f out: wknd over 1f out* **10/1**

2m 34.56s (-0.94) **Going Correction** -0.025s/f (Good) **8** Ran SP% **114.9**
Speed ratings (Par 102): **102,100,99,98,97 96,93,90**
CSF £19.82 CT £61.98 TOTE £7.00: £1.60, £1.50, £1.90; EX 20.40 Trifecta £86.40.
**Owner** Merry Fox Stud Limited **Bred** Merry Fox Stud Limited **Trained** Newmarket, Suffolk

**FOCUS**
This fair handicap was run at a reasonable gallop, but the time was around a second slower than the previous maiden. The form is rated around the fourth, with improvement from the first three.
T/Jkpt: Not won. T/Plt: £391.00 to a £1 stake. Pool: £81,593.34 - 152.30 winning units. T/Qpdt: £46.40 to a £1 stake. Pool: £8129.48 - 129.40 winning units. TM

# 3677 YARMOUTH (L-H)

Thursday, July 3

**OFFICIAL GOING: Good to firm (firm in places) changing to firm after race 1 (2.10)**
Wind: light, half against Weather: sunny and warm

## 3893 BRITISH STALLION STUDS EBF MAIDEN STKS 6f 3y
**2:10** (2:10) (Class 5) 2-Y-O **£3,234** (£962; £481; £240) **Stalls** Centre

Form RPR

3 **1** **Fanciful Angel (IRE)**[13] 3429 2-9-5 0.................... MartinHarley 5 86+
(Marco Botti) *in tch in midfield: pushed along to chse wnr and wandered over 1f out: led ins fnl f: sn clr: comf* **11/10[1]**

2 **2** *2 3/4* **Midlander (IRE)**[14] 3387 2-9-5 0.................... RoystonFfrench 3 77
(Mark Johnston) *led: rdn over 1f out: wnt lft u.p and hdd ins fnl f: sn btn and one pce after* **15/8[2]**

4 **3** *3 1/2* **Drumkilbo**[14] 3387 2-8-12 0.................... CamHardie(7) 1 67
(Lady Cecil) *chsd ldr: rdn ent fnl 2f: 3rd and outpcd over 1f out: kpt on same pce after* **8/1**

2 **4** *9* **Mighty Warrior**[16] 3337 2-9-5 0.................... DavidNolan 7 40
(Richard Fahey) *chsd ldng pair: rdn ent fnl 2f: 4th and btn over 1f out: wknd fnl f* **7/1[3]**

**5** *14* **What A Party (IRE)** 2-8-9 0.................... ShelleyBirkett(5) 4
(Gay Kelleway) *s.i.s: bhd: pushed along 4f out: lost tch over 1f out: t.o* **66/1**

**6** *7* **Duke Of Romance** 2-9-5 0.................... JackMitchell 2
(John Ryan) *s.i.s: a bhd: lost tch over 1f out: t.o* **50/1**

1m 12.52s (-1.88) **Going Correction** -0.25s/f (Firm) **6** Ran SP% **109.5**
Speed ratings (Par 94): **101,97,92,80,62 52**
CSF £3.16 TOTE £2.10: £1.10, £1.70; EX 3.50 Trifecta £10.90.
**Owner** Scuderia Blueberry **Bred** Berjis Desai **Trained** Newmarket, Suffolk

**FOCUS**
Bottom bend dolled out 1.5m and races on Round course increased by 7m. The most interesting race on the card, with four of these already showing plenty of ability on their respective debuts. The quartet duly dominated with the two newcomers proving green from the start. They raced up the centre.

## 3894 LADIES NIGHT AT GREAT YARMOUTH RACECOURSE (S) STKS 6f 3y
**2:40** (2:40) (Class 6) 2-Y-O **£1,940** (£577; £288; £144) **Stalls** Centre

Form RPR

0043 **1** **Baileys Pursuit**[21] 3157 2-8-6 0.................... AndreaAtzeni 2 60
(Chris Dwyer) *chsd ldrs: wnt 2nd 2f out: rdn to ld over 1f out: clr ins fnl f: styd on wl: rdn out* **7/2[2]**

64 **2** *2 1/4* **Ho Yam Lay**[38] 2622 2-8-6 0.................... HayleyTurner 4 53
(Michael Bell) *chsd ldr: 3rd and unable qck whn swtchd lft ins fnl f: wnt 2nd ins fnl f: no imp* **1/1[1]**

350 **3** *2 1/4* **Howlin'For You**[17] 3297 2-7-13 0....................(v[1]) CamHardie(7) 5 46
(David Brown) *led: drvn and hdd over 1f out: 3rd and wknd ins fnl f* **4/1[3]**

0164 **4** *7* **Tagtale (IRE)**[22] 3091 2-8-11 0.................... PatrickMathers 1 30
(Richard Fahey) *s.i.s: bhd: detached last and rdn over 3f out: n.d after: wnt modest 4th ins fnl f* **13/2**

00 **5** *4* **May One**[63] 1901 2-8-1 0.................... KatiaScallan(5) 3 13
(Mick Channon) *t.k.h: hld up wl in tch: rdn and effrt 2f out: wknd over 1f out: fdd fnl f* **25/1**

1m 13.6s (-0.80) **Going Correction** -0.25s/f (Firm) **5** Ran SP% **109.4**
Speed ratings (Par 92): **95,92,89,79,74**
.Baileys Pursuit was bought in for £5,000.\n\x\x Ho Yam Lay was claimed by Mr Nick Littmoden for £5,000.
**Owner** G R Bailey Ltd (Baileys Horse Feeds) **Bred** P And Mrs A G Venner **Trained** Newmarket, Suffolk

**FOCUS**
Although open to colts and gelding, five fillies went to post for this moderate seller and again they raced up the middle. The winning time was over a second slower than the opening maiden.

## 3895 GREENE KING FESTIVAL AT YARMOUTH RACECOURSE H'CAP 7f 3y
**3:10** (3:10) (Class 5) (0-75,74) 3-Y-0+ **£2,846** (£847; £423; £211) **Stalls** Centre

Form RPR

1106 **1** **Desert Ranger (IRE)**[19] 3225 3-9-6 **74**.................... KierenFallon 3 80
(James Tate) *awkward leaving stalls and s.i.s: t.k.h: hld up in tch: effrt and rdn to chse ldr 2f out: edging lft but drvn to ld ins fnl f: sn clr: readily* **15/8[1]**

30-0 **2** *3 1/2* **Saskia's Dream**[22] 3125 6-8-8 **61**....................(v) CamHardie(7) 1 61
(Jane Chapple-Hyam) *led: rdn 2f out: edgd lft u.p and hdd ins fnl f: sn outpcd: plugged on* **11/2[3]**

-025 **3** *3* **Shasta Daisy**[28] 2929 3-9-5 **73**....................[1] MartinHarley 4 62
(Lady Cecil) *chsd ldrs: rdn and unable qck over 2f out: 3rd and wl btn 1f out* **5/2[2]**

6604 **4** *3* **Jonnie Skull (IRE)**[13] 3427 8-9-6 **66**....................(vt) JimmyQuinn 2 50
(Lydia Pearce) *led for 2f: chsd ldr tl over 2f out: sn struggling u.p: bhd over 1f out* **5/2[2]**

1m 27.4s (0.80) **Going Correction** -0.25s/f (Firm) **4** Ran SP% **107.3**
**WFA** 3 from 6yo+ 8lb
Speed ratings (Par 103): **85,81,77,74**
CSF £11.19 TOTE £1.90; EX 10.80 Trifecta £25.30.
**Owner** Sheikh Juma Dalmook Al Maktoum **Bred** Tally-Ho Stud **Trained** Newmarket, Suffolk

**FOCUS**
The four runners in this modest handicap started off racing closer to the nearside rail than they had in the first couple of races, but the front pair edged away to the centre of the track late on. Weakish form, the winner building on his AW wins.

## 3896 SCOOTER RALLY AT GREAT YARMOUTH RACECOURSE H'CAP 5f 43y
**3:40** (3:41) (Class 6) (0-60,55) 3-Y-O+ **£1,940** (£577; £288; £144) **Stalls** Centre

Form RPR

6-00 **1** **Burnt Cream**[16] 3323 7-9-7 **52**....................(t) MartinHarley 7 63+
(Martin Bosley) *stdd s: hld up in rr: clsd and travelling strly 2f out: led and stl on bit ent fnl f: rdn and r.o fnl 150yds: comf* **9/1**

5003 **2** *1 1/2* **Rostrum Farewell**[9] 3548 3-8-9 **52**....................(b) CamHardie(7) 1 56
(David Brown) *led: rdn 2f out: edgd lft u.p and hdd ent fnl f: styd on same pce fnl 150yds* **5/1[3]**

6342 **3** *hd* **Bubbly Bailey**[16] 3323 4-9-8 **53**....................(v) AndreaAtzeni 6 58
(J R Jenkins) *chsd ldr: rdn ent fnl 2f: stl cl 3rd 1f out: styd on same pce after* **2/1[1]**

0400 **4** *1 1/2* **Lady Mai (IRE)**[14] 3399 3-9-3 **53**.................... DavidNolan 4 51
(Richard Fahey) *chsd ldrs: drvn 2f out: unable qck over 1f out: kpt on same pce fnl f* **4/1[2]**

060 **5** *1* **Give Us A Belle (IRE)**[14] 3392 5-9-4 **54**....................(vt) EoinWalsh(5) 5 50
(Christine Dunnett) *in tch in last trio: pushed along ent fnl 2f: hld hd high and no imp fnl f* **12/1**

0205 **6** *shd* **Addictive Nature (IRE)**[22] 3093 4-9-1 **51**....................(v) LouisSteward(5) 3 47
(John Gallagher) *wl in toouch in midfield: rdn and effrt jst over 2f out: unable qck over 1f out: wknd ins fnl f* **5/1[3]**

0421 **7** *3/4* **College Doll**[79] 1500 5-9-10 **55**....................(t) JimmyQuinn 2 48
(Christine Dunnett) *in tch in midfield: effrt over 2f out: no ex over 1f out: wknd ins fnl f* **20/1**

-005 **8** *8* **Ellingham (IRE)**[10] 3522 3-9-5 **55**.................... SebSanders 8 17
(Christine Dunnett) *in tch in last trio: rdn and no hdwy ent fnl 2f: wknd 1f out: bhd and eased towards fin* **33/1**

1m 3.61s (0.91) **Going Correction** -0.25s/f (Firm)
**WFA** 3 from 4yo+ 5lb **8** Ran SP% **112.1**
Speed ratings (Par 101): **82,79,79,76,75 75,73,61**
CSF £51.14 CT £125.84 TOTE £9.70: £2.70, £2.50, £1.10; EX 75.70 Trifecta £253.40.
**Owner** Mrs Patricia Brown **Bred** C Eddington And Partners **Trained** Chalfont St Giles, Bucks

**FOCUS**
A moderate sprint handicap with the top weight officially rated 55. The field split into two with a group of five racing up the middle, while three raced centre-to-far side. The winner improved and has possibly improved.

## 3897 FAMILY FUNDAY AT GREAT YARMOUTH RACECOURSE H'CAP (BOBIS RACE) 1m 1f
**4:10** (4:10) (Class 4) (0-80,80) 3-Y-O **£5,013** (£1,491; £745; £372) **Stalls** Low

Form RPR

-644 **1** **Damascene**[41] 2506 3-9-2 **75**....................(p) MartinHarley 3 83
(Marco Botti) *chsd ldng pair: effrt to ld 2f out: sn rdn: forged clr ins fnl f: styd on wl: rdn out* **5/2[2]**

6-1 **2** *2 3/4* **Derbyshire (IRE)**[21] 3158 3-8-5 **69**.................... KevinStott(5) 6 71
(Kevin Ryan) *chsd ldr: rdn over 2f out: ev ch 2f out tl unable qck 1f out: kpt on same pce after: wnt 2nd last stride* **11/10[1]**

4321 **3** *shd* **Starlit Cantata**[26] 2998 3-8-12 **71**.................... JohnFahy 1 73
(Eve Johnson Houghton) *hld up in tch in last pair: hdwy 3f out: rdn and ev ch 2f out: unable qck w wnr ins fnl f: kpt on same pce: lost 2nd last stride* **10/1**

**4** *1/2* **Gangster Squad (FR)**[238] 3-8-12 **78**.................... CamHardie(7) 4 79
(Martyn Meade) *hld up in rr: clsd to press ldrs and rdn ent fnl 2f: styd on same pce ins fnl f* **16/1**

-300 **5** *6* **Emef Diamond**[12] 3464 3-9-1 **77**.................... CharlesBishop(3) 2 65
(Mick Channon) *racd keenly: led: clr 6f out: rdn over 2f out: hdd 2f out: btn over 1f out: wknd fnl f* **4/1[3]**

1m 53.1s (-2.70) **Going Correction** -0.25s/f (Firm) **5** Ran SP% **111.2**
Speed ratings (Par 102): **102,99,99,99,93**
CSF £5.74 TOTE £4.60: £1.80, £1.30; EX 6.00 Trifecta £15.40.
**Owner** Prince A A Faisal **Bred** Nawara Stud Co Ltd **Trained** Newmarket, Suffolk

**FOCUS**
They seemed to go a decent pace in this fair handicap, but all five runners were in a line across the track passing the 2f pole. The winner continues to progress.

## 3898 INJURED JOCKEYS FUND H'CAP 1m 2f 21y
**4:40** (4:40) (Class 5) (0-70,72) 3-Y-O+ **£2,846** (£847; £423; £211) **Stalls** Low

Form RPR

-004 **1** **Beakers N Num Nums (IRE)**[17] 3316 3-9-3 **68**.......... MartinDwyer 1 78
(William Jarvis) *hld up in tch: clsd and pushed along 3f out: led over 1f out: edgd lft u.p whn asserting 1f out: r.o wl* **7/4[2]**

6330 **2** *3* **Enriching (USA)**[13] 3427 6-9-10 **64**.................... J-PGuillambert 2 68
(Nick Littmoden) *chsd ldr for 2f: chsd ldrs after: rdn to ld over 2f out: hdd over 1f out: styd on same pce fnl f* **6/1[3]**

6011 **3** *3/4* **Gabrial The Duke (IRE)**[8] 3585 4-9-11 **72** 6ex.......... GeorgeBuckell(7) 6 75
(David Simcock) *chsd ldrs tl wnt 2nd after 2f: led 7f out: rdn and hdd over 2f out: styd on same pce u.p fr over 1f out* **11/10[1]**

2600 **4** *7* **Sparkling Ice (IRE)**[35] 2688 3-8-10 **61**....................(b[1]) JohnFahy 7 50
(Eve Johnson Houghton) *led tl 7f out: chsd ldr tl 4f out: lost pl u.p 3f out: bhd fnl f* **12/1**

2m 7.25s (-3.25) **Going Correction** -0.25s/f (Firm)
**WFA** 3 from 4yo+ 11lb **4** Ran SP% **106.0**
Speed ratings (Par 103): **103,100,100,94**
CSF £10.66 TOTE £2.50; EX 8.80 Trifecta £17.20.
**Owner** The Willie Robertson Partnership **Bred** Deerfield Farm **Trained** Newmarket, Suffolk

**FOCUS**
An ordinary handicap hit by three non-runners. The form is not entirely solid.

## 3899 TRAFALGAR RESTAURANT "HANDS AND HEELS" APPRENTICE SERIES H'CAP RACING EXCELLENCE INITIATIVE) 1m 3f 101y
**5:10** (5:10) (Class 6) (0-65,65) 4-Y-O+ **£1,940** (£577; £288; £144) **Stalls** Low

Form RPR

3525 **1** **Layline (IRE)**[37] 2651 7-9-5 **65**.................... TomasHarrigan(5) 2 72
(Gay Kelleway) *sn chsd ldr: rdn and ev ch 2f out: led ins fnl f: styd on wl* **9/4[2]**

3310 **2** *1 1/4* **Corn Maiden**[12] 3475 5-9-7 **62**.................... LewisWalsh 4 67
(Lydia Pearce) *led: rdn over 1f out: hdd and no ex ins fnl f* **11/10[1]**

506 **3** *6* **Sawwala**[38] 2613 4-9-2 **60**.................... CharlieBennett(3) 1 55
(J R Jenkins) *chsd ldrs: rdn over 3f out: 3rd and no imp over 1f out: plugged on* **7/2[3]**

4300 4 24 **Candesta (USA)**[62] 1919 4-9-7 **62**................................(b[1]) DavidParkes 3 18
(Julia Feilden) *hld up in tch: rdn over 3f out: wknd 2f out: wl bhd fnl f* **12/1**
2m 27.86s (-0.84) **Going Correction** -0.25s/f (Firm) **4** Ran SP% **108.3**
Speed ratings (Par 101): **93,92,87,70**
CSF £5.16 TOTE £2.50; EX 6.00 Trifecta £9.80.
**Owner** Kelleway, Smith & Scandrett **Bred** Mrs M E Slade **Trained** Exning, Suffolk
■ Tomas Harrigan's first winner.

**FOCUS**
A moderate hands and heels apprentice handicap. The runner-up is rated to his penultimate C&D win.
T/Plt: £26.80 to a £1 stake. Pool: £54,045.66 - 1469.95 winning units. T/Qpdt: £21.60 to a £1 stake. Pool: 3360.50 - 115.00 winning units. SP

3900 - 3906a (Foreign Racing) - See Raceform Interactive

## 3869 DEAUVILLE (R-H)
Thursday, July 3

**OFFICIAL GOING: Turf: good; polytrack: standard**

### 3907a PRIX DE CARROUGES (CLAIMER) (5YO+) (POLYTRACK) 1m 1f 110y
**2:05** (12:00) 5-Y-O+ **£7,916** (£3,166; £2,375; £1,583; £791)

RPR
1 **Cashpoint**[26] 2991 9-9-5 0................................................ MaximeGuyon 7 80
(Ian Williams) *in tch: pushed along into st: chal over 1f out and led ent fnl f: rdn and r.o strly: diminishing advantage towards fin but in control* **15/2**
2 nk **Touch Of Honour (GER)**[397] 5-8-9 0 ow1...................... GeraldMosse 4 70
(W Mongil, Germany) **49/1**
3 nk **Russian Khan (GER)**[67] 6-9-4 0...................................... EddyHardouin 3 78
(W Mongil, Germany) **165/10**
4 1 ½ **Blazon (FR)**[192] 7-9-4 0......................................... AnthonyCrastus 5 75
(Mlle C Gryson, France) **122/10**
5 hd **Caroz (FR)**[57] 7-9-2 0......................................(p) Pierre-CharlesBoudot 10 73
(J-P Gauvin, France) **13/2**[3]
6 2 **Nova Valorem (IRE)**[15] 3373 6-9-5 0....................... StephanePasquier 1 71
(C Boutin, France) **84/10**
7 shd **Gaily Game**[404] 6-9-1 0.......................................... ChristopheSoumillon 9 67
(J-C Rouget, France) **19/10**[1]
8 ¾ **Stormy Ocean (FR)**[219] 6-9-4 0...................................... TonyPiccone 8 69
(C Lotoux, France) **154/10**
9 ½ **Circumvent**[14] 3383 7-9-8 0......................................(b) IoritzMendizabal 6 72
(Paul Cole) *pushed along to go forward early and sn led: rdn and strly pressed 2f out: hdd over 1f out: no ex and btn fnl f: wknd* **29/10**[2]
10 1 ¾ **Risquillo (FR)**[18] 8-9-2 0..........................(p) Christophe-PatriceLemaire 2 62
(M Boutin, France) **35/1**
2m 0.99s (120.99) **10** Ran SP% **120.0**
WIN (incl. 1 euro stake): 8.50. PLACES: 3.10, 11.10, 5.10. DF: 242.30. SF: 470.10.
**Owner** Macable Partnership **Bred** Stowell Park Stud **Trained** Portway, Worcs

## 3542 BEVERLEY (R-H)
Friday, July 4

**OFFICIAL GOING: Good to firm (8.3)**
Wind: light 1/2 against Weather: overcast, rain after race 2

### 3908 RACING AGAIN TOMORROW (S) STKS 7f 100y
**6:30** (6:31) (Class 6) 3-Y-O+ **£2,264** (£673; £336; £168) **Stalls** Low

Form RPR
5201 1 **Kimbali (IRE)**[15] 3382 5-9-1 70.......................... LukeLeadbitter(7) 12 73
(Declan Carroll) *swtchd rt after s: hld up in rr-div: t.k.h: hdwy on outer over 2f out: styd on to ld towards fin* **6/1**[3]
-344 2 ½ **Whispered Times (USA)**[7] 3660 7-9-3 57................(p) RobertWinston 2 67
(Tracy Waggott) *chsd ldrs: led over 1f out: hdd and no ex towards fin* **7/1**
4543 3 4 **Prime Exhibit**[15] 3382 9-9-3 67.................................(t) EoinWalsh(5) 6 62
(Daniel Mark Loughnane) *in rr and sn drvn along: hdwy on ins over 2f out: swtchd lft over 1f out: styd on to take 3rd nr fin* **14/1**
0-42 4 nk **Dialogue**[17] 3344 8-9-3 63.................................. JamesSullivan 11 56
(Geoffrey Harker) *rr-div: hdwy over 2f out: kpt on* **12/1**
-235 5 1 ¾ **Live Dangerously**[7] 3660 4-9-3 69..........................(tp) JasonHart 10 52
(Keith Dalgleish) *led 1f: chsd ldr: led over 3f out: hdd over 1f out: wknd last 75yds* **15/8**[1]
0661 6 1 ¾ **Rasselas (IRE)**[8] 3604 7-8-10 61...............................(v) AnnaHesketh(7) 8 48+
(David Nicholls) *sn bhd: hdwy on outer over 1f out: kpt on towards fin* **4/1**[2]
6553 7 2 ¾ **Thrust Control (IRE)**[10] 3547 7-9-3 49.....................(p) FrannyNorton 15 41
(Tracy Waggott) *trckd ldrs: t.k.h: wknd fnl f* **14/1**
02/0 8 2 **Rocky's Pride (IRE)**[10] 3547 8-9-0 47................ GeorgeChaloner(3) 16 36
(Richard Whitaker) *in rr: rn wd bnd over 5f out: kpt on fnl 2f* **66/1**
6 9 1 ¼ **Lady Jamesway (IRE)**[65] 1888 3-7-11 0....................... RowanScott(7) 4 25
(Ann Duffield) *chsd ldrs: fdd fnl 2f* **50/1**
-100 10 nse **Medecis Mountain**[13] 3485 5-9-3 47.....................(p) JacobButterfield(5) 3 37
(John Wainwright) *dwlt: sn mid-div: one pce fnl 2f* **50/1**
560- 11 2 ½ **Let's Go Live**[290] 6497 4-9-3 64......................................[1] BarryMcHugh 13 26
(Tony Coyle) *s.i.s: a in rr* **25/1**
3400 12 1 ¼ **Plunder**[25] 3056 4-9-0 55................................................(b) SladeO'Hara(3) 1 23
(Alan Berry) *a in rr* **33/1**
-000 13 1 ½ **Mcmonagle (USA)**[14] 3436 6-9-3 58.............................(tp) DavidNolan 5 19
(Alan Brown) *led after 1f: hdd over 3f out: sn wknd* **33/1**
0006 14 3 **Aspirant**[13] 3460 3-8-9 65............................................. AndrewElliott 9 9
(Brian Ellison) *chsd ldrs: hung rt and lost pl over 1f out* **20/1**
0-06 15 1 ¼ **Magical Mischief**[46] 2389 4-8-13 44 ow1..................... MichaelStainton 7 5
(Chris Fairhurst) *mid-div: wd bnd 4f out: wknd 2f out* **66/1**
000- 16 ½ **Shatin Secret**[286] 6655 4-8-10 51.................................. PeterSword(7) 14 7
(Noel Wilson) *in rr: bhd fnl 3f* **100/1**
1m 31.15s (-2.65) **Going Correction** -0.275s/f (Firm)
**WFA** 3 from 4yo+ 8lb **16** Ran SP% **125.0**
Speed ratings (Par 101): **104,103,98,98,96 94,91,89,87,87 84,83,81,78,76 76**
CSF £45.33 TOTE £4.90: £2.60, £2.10, £4.20; EX 47.50 Trifecta £556.70.There was no bid for the winner.
**Owner** Mrs Sarah Bryan **Bred** P Kelly **Trained** Sledmere, E Yorks

**FOCUS**
They went a strong pace in this seller and were strung out an early stage. The runner-up is the key to the form.

### 3909 EBF AUNT BESSIE'S YORKSHIRE PUDDING NOVICE STKS 5f
**7:00** (7:01) (Class 5) 2-Y-O **£6,469** (£1,925; £962; £481) **Stalls** Low

Form RPR
3 1 **She's A Worldie (IRE)**[7] 3656 2-8-9 0.......................... PaulMulrennan 4 79
(Bryan Smart) *mde all: edgd lft ins fnl f: kpt on wl* **5/2**[2]
2 2 1 **Grand Beauty (IRE)**[15] 3394 2-8-9 0.............................. TonyHamilton 6 75
(Richard Fahey) *rdn rnd paddock by lad: t.k.h: trckd ldrs: drvn to chal 1f out: styd on same pce* **5/6**[1]
51 3 3 ¾ **Showstoppa**[7] 3656 2-9-2 0............................................ FrannyNorton 3 69
(Mark Johnston) *chsd wnr: drvn over 2f out: one pce fnl f* **5/1**[3]
0103 4 3 ½ **Lazy Days In Loule (IRE)**[21] 3188 2-8-13 0.................. DuranFentiman 2 53
(Noel Wilson) *chsd ldrs: drvn over 2f out: wknd fnl 150yds* **12/1**
5 1 **Belle Nellie (IRE)** 2-8-9 0.................................................. JasonHart 7 45
(Nigel Tinkler) *dwlt and wnt rt s: hdwy over 2f out: edgd rt and wknd last 150yds* **20/1**
00 6 5 **Sparkling Sapphire**[30] 2895 2-8-9 0.............................. PaulQuinn 5 27+
(Richard Whitaker) *half-rrd s: sn chsng ldrs: wknd over 1f out* **50/1**
1m 3.51s (0.01) **Going Correction** -0.05s/f (Good) **6** Ran SP% **114.2**
Speed ratings (Par 94): **97,95,89,83,82 74**
CSF £5.08 TOTE £3.20: £1.50, £1.10; EX 5.80 Trifecta £14.10.
**Owner** Fiddes, Chappell & Salthouse **Bred** Tally-Ho Stud **Trained** Hambleton, N Yorks

**FOCUS**
The odds-on favourite was turned over by her main market rival in this novice event. Straightforward form which fits in with the race averages.

### 3910 JACKSON'S YORKSHIRE CHAMPION BREAD H'CAP 7f 100y
**7:30** (7:30) (Class 4) (0-80,80) 3-Y-O+ **£6,469** (£1,925; £962; £481) **Stalls** Low

Form RPR
5206 1 **Relight My Fire**[11] 3533 4-9-6 **72**...............................(b) DavidAllan 8 78
(Tim Easterby) *trckd ldng pair: styd on fnl f: led towards fin* **7/1**[3]
-066 2 ½ **Berlusca (IRE)**[13] 3463 5-10-0 **80**................................ DanielTudhope 3 86+
(David O'Meara) *hld up in rr: hdwy 3f out: nt clr run 2f out: sn swtchd lft: styd on wl fnl f: tk 2nd post* **25/1**
5501 3 nse **Zaitsev (IRE)**[23] 3096 4-9-9 **75**.................................... RobertWinston 1 80+
(Ollie Pears) *t.k.h: led: kpt on wl fnl 2f: hdd nr fin* **9/4**[1]
4244 4 2 ¼ **King Of Macedon (IRE)**[13] 3464 3-9-3 **77**..............(b[1]) RoystonFfrench 2 73
(Mark Johnston) *chsd ldr: drvn over 2f out: wknd fnl 50yds* **3/1**[2]
0-14 5 ¾ **Eeny Mac (IRE)**[10] 3544 7-9-9 **75**................................. AndrewElliott 6 72
(Neville Bycroft) *sn bhd and pushed along: sme hdwy over 1f out: styng on at fin* **7/1**[3]
5602 6 4 **Loud**[7] 3660 4-8-13 **65**................................................ FrannyNorton 5 52
(Mark Johnston) *sn in rr and pushed along: hdwy over 4f out: chsng ldrs over 1f out: sn wknd* **3/1**[2]
0-04 7 3 **Desert Creek (IRE)**[69] 1710 8-9-7 **73**............................ AdrianNicholls 4 53
(David Nicholls) *hld up in mid-div: effrt over 2f out: hmpd over 1f out: swtchd rt and wknd 1f out* **14/1**
1m 30.87s (-2.93) **Going Correction** -0.275s/f (Firm)
**WFA** 3 from 4yo+ 8lb **7** Ran SP% **116.3**
Speed ratings (Par 105): **105,104,104,101,100 96,92**
CSF £146.63 CT £517.59 TOTE £7.50: £3.60, £9.10; EX 91.70 Trifecta £345.10.
**Owner** Jonathan Gill **Bred** J Gill **Trained** Great Habton, N Yorks
■ Stewards' Enquiry : Franny Norton one-day ban: careless riding (Jul 18)

**FOCUS**
There was a tight finish in this handicap and the third can be marked for going close after setting a strong pace. Sound form, the winner back to his best.

### 3911 SWAN INDUSTRIAL DRIVES H'CAP 1m 100y
**8:00** (8:00) (Class 5) (0-75,74) 3-Y-O **£3,408** (£1,006; £503) **Stalls** Low

Form RPR
4061 1 **Eddiemaurice (IRE)**[11] 3534 3-9-0 **67** 6ex...............(v) RobertWinston 9 78
(Richard Guest) *hld up in rr: hdwy over 4f out: sn chsng ldrs: led over 1f out: drvn clr ins fnl f* **5/1**[3]
0033 2 5 **Street Boss (IRE)**[8] 3625 3-8-2 **55** oh2.....................(p) DuranFentiman 5 58
(Tim Easterby) *chsd ldrs: nt clr run over 1f out: swtchd lft and nt clr run 1f out: c to outside: carried lft ins fnl f: styd on to take 2nd last strides* **10/1**
6-35 3 nk **Mitchelton (FR)**[17] 3340 3-9-7 **74**................................ FrannyNorton 3 73
(Mark Johnston) *led tl 7f out: chsd ldrs: kpt on same pce appr fnl f* **8/1**
1050 4 ¾ **Mariners Moon (IRE)**[13] 3464 3-9-7 **74**........................ DanielTudhope 6 71
(David O'Meara) *t.k.h in rr: hdwy 3f out: edgd lft and kpt on same pce fnl f* **5/1**[3]
4441 5 nk **Kalahari Kingdom (IRE)**[17] 3333 3-8-10 **63**................(p) TonyHamilton 2 59
(Richard Fahey) *drvn to chse ldrs: led 7f out: hdd over 1f out: one pce* **11/4**[1]
-000 6 ½ **Syros (IRE)**[13] 3464 3-9-3 **70**.......................................(v) GrahamGibbons 1 65
(Michael Easterby) *stdd s: t.k.h in rr: outpcd and lost pl 3f out: hdwy on ins over 1f out: kpt on ins fnl f* **16/1**
4414 7 hd **Porthos Du Vallon**[7] 3662 3-9-3 **70**..............................(p) JasonHart 7 65
(Keith Dalgleish) *t.k.h in rr: outpcd and lost pl 3f out: kpt on fr 1f out* **4/1**[2]
4300 8 2 ¼ **Kraka Gym (IRE)**[10] 3545 3-8-7 **60**..............................(b) BarryMcHugh 8 50
(Michael Easterby) *half-rrd s: sn trcking ldrs: chal over 2f out: wknd last 75yds* **12/1**
1m 47.48s (-0.12) **Going Correction** -0.275s/f (Firm) **8** Ran SP% **113.8**
Speed ratings (Par 100): **89,84,83,82,82 82,81,79**
CSF £52.45 CT £394.31 TOTE £5.40: £2.10, £2.90, £2.80; EX 45.60 Trifecta £462.60.
**Owner** Advance Group UK Ltd **Bred** Declan Murphy **Trained** ingmanthorpe, W Yorks

**FOCUS**
It was raining. This looked a competitive handicap but the winner powered clear from off the steady pace. He built on his Thirsk win.

### 3912 BERYL AND JOE TURNER MEMORIAL H'CAP 1m 4f 16y
**8:30** (8:32) (Class 6) (0-60,60) 3-Y-O+ **£2,587** (£770; £384; £192) **Stalls** Low

Form RPR
0050 1 **Rainford Glory (IRE)**[20] 3209 4-9-4 **53**................... GeorgeChaloner(3) 9 63
(Richard Fahey) *chsd ldrs: hung rt over 2f out: led over 1f out: drvn out* **12/1**
0404 2 1 **Majestic Sun (IRE)**[6] 3711 3-9-1 **60**............................ PaulMulrennan 3 68+
(Peter Chapple-Hyam) *hld up in mid-div on ins: hdwy over 4f out: nt clr run and swtchd lft over 1f out: chsd wnr ins fnl f: styng on at fin* **4/1**[2]
-562 3 3 ¼ **Moving Waves (IRE)**[23] 3098 3-8-10 **55**.....................(p) RobertWinston 1 58
(Ollie Pears) *led 1f: chsd ldrs: swtchd lft over 2f out: kpt on same pce appr fnl f* **7/1**[3]

4441 **4** *2* **Amazing Blue Sky**[11] 3535 8-9-9 **55** 6ex.................... JamesSullivan 10 55
(Ruth Carr) *hld up in rr: hdwy on ins over 2f out: kpt on fnl f* **11/1**

0-03 **5** *1/2* **Quite Sparky**[10] 3544 7-9-13 **59**....................................(p) BrianHughes 2 58
(Mike Sowersby) *hld up in rr: hdwy over 4f out: n.m.r over 1f out: one pce* **16/1**

0012 **6** *1 1/4* **Enquiring**[3] 3819 3-8-11 **56** 6ex...................................... FrannyNorton 11 53
(Mark Johnston) *drvn to chse ldrs: nt clr run 2f out: one pce over 1f out* **5/2**[1]

6000 **7** *1/2* **Valentine's Gift**[10] 3546 6-10-0 **60**.................................(p) AndrewElliott 7 56
(Neville Bycroft) *hld up in rr: t.k.h: sme hdwy over 2f out: nvr a factor* **33/1**

3034 **8** *1 1/4* **Politbureau**[15] 3398 7-9-1 **47**......................................(b) GrahamGibbons 4 41
(Michael Easterby) *dwlt: in rr: hdwy over 3f out: nvr a factor* **14/1**

6-55 **9** *3/4* **Spiekeroog**[13] 3482 8-9-12 **58**.........................................(b) DavidNolan 6 51
(Alan Brown) *t.k.h: sn mid-div: effrt over 2f out: nvr a factor* **33/1**

4-03 **10** *hd* **Silver Tigress**[8] 3605 6-9-2 **48**........................................ DavidAllan 12 41
(Iain Jardine) *led after 1f: t.k.h: hdd over 1f out: wknd last 150yds* **16/1**

0-52 **11** *6* **Victory Danz (IRE)**[10] 3545 3-8-7 **55**................................ SamJames(3) 8 38
(David O'Meara) *hld up in rr: hdwy on outer over 5f out: drvn over 3f out: sn lost pl: eased whn bhd clsng stages* **4/1**[2]

2m 36.92s (-2.88) **Going Correction** -0.275s/f (Firm)
**WFA** 3 from 4yo+ 13lb **11** Ran SP% **121.4**
Speed ratings (Par 101): **98,97,95,93,93 92,92,91,91,90 86**
CSF £61.55 CT £372.04 TOTE £18.00: £3.80, £1.70, £2.40; EX 107.20 Trifecta £515.00.
**Owner** Dr Marwan Koukash **Bred** Her Diamond Necklace **Trained** Musley Bank, N Yorks

**FOCUS**
The prominent runners faded after setting a good pace and first two pulled clear. The winner is rated back to his best.

## 3913 FERGUSON FAWSITT ARMS H'CAP 5f
**9:00** (9:04) (Class 6) (0-60,60) 3-Y-O+ **£2,264** (£673; £336; £168) **Stalls** Low

Form RPR

2120 **1** **Cadeaux Pearl**[7] 3668 6-9-9 **59**.................................... FrederikTylicki 12 69
(Scott Dixon) *rr-div: hdwy over 1f out: edgd rt ins fnl f: styd on wl to ld nr fin* **10/1**

0031 **2** *nk* **Choc'A'Moca (IRE)**[10] 3548 7-9-3 **53**.........................(v) PaulMulrennan 6 62
(Paul Midgley) *chsd ldrs: kpt on wl fnl f: tk 2nd post* **7/2**[2]

505U **3** *hd* **Manatee Bay**[10] 3548 4-9-10 **60**......................................... FrannyNorton 7 68
(David Nicholls) *mid-div: hdwy 2f out: edgd lft ins fnl f: led last 50yds: hdd clsng stages* **3/1**[1]

5440 **4** *hd* **Hazard Warning (IRE)**[56] 2127 4-9-2 **52**..................(b) JamesSullivan 4 59
(James Given) *s.i.s: hdwy on ins over 1f out: swtchd lft jst ins fnl f: styng on wl whn nt clr run wl towards fin* **14/1**

2230 **5** *2 1/4* **Captain Scooby**[11] 3530 8-8-10 **51**.......................(v) DuilioDaSilva(5) 14 50
(Richard Guest) *in rr: hdwy over 1f out: nt rch ldrs* **10/1**

0-35 **6** *hd* **See Vermont**[14] 3440 6-8-9 **48**..................................(p) NeilFarley(3) 16 46
(Robin Bastiman) *chsd ldrs on outer: one pce fnl f* **33/1**

0636 **7** *1/2* **Pearl Noir**[4] 3793 4-9-4 **54**.............................................(b) DavidNolan 1 51
(Scott Dixon) *led: hdd last 50yds: fdd* **17/2**

0-50 **8** *3 3/4* **Monsieur Royale**[11] 3530 4-9-8 **58**............................(b) BarryMcHugh 15 41
(Geoffrey Oldroyd) *dwlt: swtchd rt after s: hdwy over 1f out: styng on at fin* **16/1**

5546 **9** *hd* **Busy Bimbo (IRE)**[23] 3104 5-8-12 **48**............................(b) PaddyAspell 8 30
(Alan Berry) *mid-div: drvn over 2f out: nvr a factor* **16/1**

1520 **10** *hd* **Spring Bird**[17] 3338 5-9-8 **58**....................................... GrahamGibbons 9 40
(David Nicholls) *chsd ldrs: rdn over 2f out: fdd fnl f: eased towards fin* **14/1**

-500 **11** *3/4* **Princess Myla (IRE)**[8] 3600 3-9-0 **55**............................ TonyHamilton 5 32
(Paul Midgley) *chsd ldrs: wknd appr fnl f* **20/1**

0600 **12** *8* **Pavers Star**[11] 3530 5-8-11 **47**............................................. JasonHart 3
(Noel Wilson) *chsd ldrs: wknd jst ins fnl f: heavily eased* **7/1**[3]

0040 **13** *1 3/4* **Tuibama (IRE)**[17] 3338 5-9-3 **53**..............................(p) RobertWinston 13
(Tracy Waggott) *chsd ldrs: rdr briefly lost iron 2f out: sn lost plm bhd whn heavily eased ins fnl f* **9/1**

0000 **14** *2* **Classy Lassy (IRE)**[13] 3487 3-8-7 **55**............................ KevinLundie(7) 11
(Brian Ellison) *bhd: hdwy on ins 2f out: hung lft and wknd ins fnl f: sn eased* **25/1**

1m 3.1s (-0.40) **Going Correction** -0.05s/f (Good)
**WFA** 3 from 4yo+ 5lb **14** Ran SP% **135.1**
Speed ratings (Par 101): **101,100,100,99,96 95,95,89,88,88 87,74,71,68**
CSF £49.49 CT £141.78 TOTE £12.60: £3.60, £1.10, £3.40; EX 72.90 Trifecta £243.40.
**Owner** P J Dixon & Partners **Bred** Catridge Farm Stud Ltd **Trained** Babworth, Notts
■ Lees Anthem was withdrawn. Price at time of withdrawal 5-1. Rule 4 applies to bets placed prior to withdrawal but not to SP bets - deduction 10p in the pound. New market formed.

**FOCUS**
There was an exciting finish to this low-grade handicap. Lees Anthem was reluctant to go to the start and was withdrawn. The winner is rated up a length on his recent form.
T/Plt: £843.70 to a £1 stake. Pool: £69,116 - 59.80 winning tickets T/Qpdt: £202.60 to a £1 stake. Pool: £5,560 - 20.30 winning tickets WG

# 3699 DONCASTER (L-H)
Friday, July 4

**OFFICIAL GOING: Good to firm (9.1)**
Wind: Moderate half against Weather: Cloudy with sunny periods

## 3914 RICKY BOND WORLDPAY MAIDEN STKS 7f
**2:20** (2:28) (Class 5) 3-Y-O **£3,234** (£962; £481; £240) **Stalls** High

Form RPR

02 **1** **Jailawi (IRE)**[27] 2996 3-9-5 0........................................ MartinHarley 5 85+
(Ismail Mohammed) *mulish at s: a.p: cl up 1/2-way: led wl over 2f out: rdn over 1f out: kpt on strly fnl f* **11/4**[3]

2450 **2** *2* **Bon Voyage**[4] 3804 3-9-5 82.................................. SilvestreDeSousa 6 79
(Richard Hannon) *trckd ldrs: pushed along 3f out: cl up 2f out: sn rdn to chal and ev ch tl drvn and one pce ins fnl f* **5/2**[2]

06 **3** *1 3/4* **Mantou (IRE)**[22] 3153 3-9-5 0............................................ BenCurtis 9 74
(Michael Bell) *in rr and pushed along 1/2-way: rdn over 2f out: styd on wl on outer over 1f out: kpt on ins fnl f: nrst fin* **20/1**

00 **4** *nk* **Captain George (IRE)**[45] 2442 3-9-5 0............................ ShaneKelly 12 73
(James Fanshawe) *towards rr: pushed along 3f out: rdn over 2f out: styd on wl appr fnl f: nrst fin* **20/1**

5 **5** *2 1/2* **Duelling Dragon (USA)**[140] 605 3-9-5 0.................... GrahamGibbons 4 67
(David Barron) *hld up in rr: pushed along and n.m.r wl over 1f out: swtchd rt and hdwy 1f out: rdn whn green and edgd lft ins fnl f: kpt on: nrst fin* **12/1**

00- **6** *shd* **Presidente**[295] 6334 3-9-5 0................................................. GeorgeBaker 8 66
(Ed Walker) *t.k.h: trckd ldrs: effrt over 2f out: rdn along wl over 1f out: sn one pce* **33/1**

6 **7** *3/4* **Tap Your Toes (IRE)**[32] 2842 3-9-5 0......................... LemosdeSouza 1 65
(Luca Cumani) *trckd ldrs: hdwy 3f out: cl up 2f out: sn rdn to chal and ev ch tl drvn and wknd appr fnl f* **20/1**

32- **8** *nse* **Nathr (USA)**[407] 2591 3-9-5 0.............................................. DaneO'Neill 7 64
(Charles Hills) *prom: cl up 1/2-way: rdn along 2f out and ev ch tl drvn and wknd over 1f out* **7/4**[1]

-4 **9** *6* **Bon Chance**[16] 3370 3-9-5 0............................................ BarryMcHugh 2 49
(Michael Easterby) *hld up a towards rr* **66/1**

**10** *3/4* **Up Pompeii** 3-9-5 0............................................................ FrederikTylicki 10 47
(George Peckham) *nvr bttr than midfield* **50/1**

03 **11** *7* **Wimboldsley**[6] 3700 3-9-5 0.......................................... JamesSullivan 13 29
(Scott Dixon) *led: rdn along 3f out: sn hdd & wknd* **33/1**

6660 **12** *7* **Some Boy Lukey**[2] 3846 3-9-5 45...................................... RaulDaSilva 11 10
(David Thompson) *cl up: rdn along 1/2-way: sn wknd* **100/1**

0 **13** *43* **Emmessess (IRE)**[22] 3156 3-9-0 0.................................... EoinWalsh(5) 3
(Christine Dunnett) *s.i.s: a outpcd and bhd: t.o fnl 3f* **100/1**

1m 27.75s (1.45) **Going Correction** -0.025s/f (Good) **13** Ran SP% **124.9**
Speed ratings (Par 100): **90,87,85,85,82 82,81,81,74,73 65,57,8**
CSF £9.59 TOTE £3.90: £1.30, £1.90, £5.20; EX 11.40 Trifecta £134.10.
**Owner** Saeed H Al Tayer **Bred** Stock Vale Ltd **Trained** Newmarket, Suffolk

**FOCUS**
Round course railed out from 10f to where it joins the straight and races of 10f and over increased by 10yds. After riding in the opener George Baker said: "It is good to firm ground" and Frederik Tylicki said: "It is a little bit on the quick side, but there is a nice cover of grass." Not much depth to this maiden, and they went a steady early pace. The time was slow, 4.45sec outside the standard, but the form makes sense, rated around the second.

## 3915 CHRISTA PRICE WORLDPAY CLAIMING STKS 1m (S)
**2:50** (2:51) (Class 5) 4-Y-O+ **£2,911** (£866; £432; £216) **Stalls** High

Form RPR

260- **1** **Classic Colori (IRE)**[280] 6801 7-8-8 80..................(p) CamHardie(5) 5 84
(Ali Stronge) *hld up in rr: smooth hdwy on outer 3f out: chal 1 1/2f out and sn rdn: drvn to ld last 150yds: kpt on wl towards fin* **5/4**[2]

3000 **2** *3/4* **Wannabe King**[13] 3483 8-9-3 84...........................(p) SilvestreDeSousa 1 86
(Geoffrey Harker) *sn led and set stdy pce: pushed along and qcknd wl over 2f out: jnd and rdn 1 1/2f out: drvn ent fnl f: hdd and no ex last 150yds* **1/1**[1]

351- **3** *9* **Kingswinford (IRE)**[448] 1514 8-8-13 68............................ PaddyAspell 3 62
(John Norton) *t.k.h: trckd ldr: effrt and n.m.r on inner over 2f out: sn rdn: drvn and one pce fr over 1f out* **10/1**[3]

1050 **4** *hd* **Ad Vitam (IRE)**[10] 3549 6-8-11 55...............................(t[1]) AdrianNicholls 4 59
(David C Griffiths) *t.k.h: trckd ldr: rdn along over 2f out: sn drvn and one pce* **22/1**

1m 41.29s (1.99) **Going Correction** -0.025s/f (Good) **4** Ran SP% **107.9**
Speed ratings (Par 103): **89,88,79,79**
CSF £2.82 TOTE £2.30; EX 2.80 Trifecta £6.30.Classic Colori was claimed by Mr M. Keighley for £8,000.
**Owner** Miss Ali Brewer **Bred** Frank Dunne **Trained** Eastbury, Berks

**FOCUS**
They didn't go much of a gallop until the runner-up stepped it up a notch going to the two pole, and from there the race predictably developed into a match. Shaky form.

## 3916 NICK STEVENS WORLDPAY MAIDEN FILLIES' STKS 7f
**3:25** (3:28) (Class 5) 3-Y-O+ **£3,234** (£962; £481; £240) **Stalls** High

Form RPR

54- **1** **Pageant Belle**[287] 6607 3-8-9 0...................................... CamHardie(5) 12 80+
(Roger Charlton) *trckd ldrs: smooth hdwy 3f out: led over 2f out: rdn appr fnl f: kpt on strly* **8/1**

**2** *1* **Better Chance (IRE)** 3-9-0 0......................................... AhmedAjtebi 8 75+
(Saeed bin Suroor) *prom: effrt and cl up 2f out: sn rdn and ev ch tl drvn and no imp ins fnl f* **11/2**[3]

635 **3** *2 1/2* **Sejel (IRE)**[19] 3277 3-9-0 71.............................................. DaneO'Neill 11 68
(John Gosden) *led: rdn along and hdd over 2f out: drvn over 1f out: kpt on same pce* **5/2**[2]

2 **4** *2 1/2* **Flawless Pink**[24] 3074 3-9-0 0........................................... SebSanders 13 62
(Jeremy Noseda) *trckd ldrs: pushed along 1/2-way: rdn and sltly outpcd over 1f out: kpt on ins fnl f* **11/10**[1]

003- **5** *nk* **Cordial**[284] 6691 3-9-0 75.................................................. MartinHarley 4 61
(Stuart Williams) *in tch: hdwy to chse ldrs over 2f out: rdn wl over 1f: wknd appr fnl f* **14/1**

-0 **6** *nk* **Bond's Gift**[6] 3700 4-9-8 0............................................. BarryMcHugh 9 63
(Geoffrey Oldroyd) *towards rr: pushed along wl over 2f out: swtchd rt to stands' rail over 1f out: styd on fnl f: nrsest fin* **100/1**

0-5 **7** *3/4* **Bay Street Belle**[7] 3664 3-9-0 0.................................... GrahamGibbons 1 58
(David Barron) *towards rr: hdwy over 2f out: sn rdn along: kpt on u.p fnl f: nrst fin* **33/1**

60 **8** *2* **Yawail**[14] 3434 3-9-0 0.................................................... JamesSullivan 7 52
(Brian Rothwell) *a towards rr* **100/1**

**9** *2* **Mygameanyours (IRE)** 6-9-8 0............................................. LiamKeniry 2 50
(Tony Carroll) *towards rr: gd hdwy on wd outside over 2f out: rdn to chse ldrs wl over 1f out: wknd ent fnl f* **100/1**

535- **10** *1 1/2* **Noble Reach**[296] 6295 3-8-7 53....................................... JordanNason(7) 6 43
(Deborah Sanderson) *chsd ldrs: pushed along 4f out: sn wknd* **66/1**

006- **11** *7* **Dr Victoria**[322] 5487 5-9-8 42........................................... PaddyAspell 14 27
(John Norton) *a towards rr* **100/1**

00 **12** *8* **Phantom Spirit**[13] 3469 3-9-0 0........................................ MartinLane 5 3
(George Baker) *s.i.s: a in rr* **100/1**

**13** *35* **Give It A Whirl** 3-8-9 0..........................................(p) EoinWalsh(5) 10
(Christine Dunnett) *dwlt: sn in midfield: rdn along 1/2-way and sn wknd* **100/1**

1m 27.82s (1.52) **Going Correction** -0.025s/f (Good)
**WFA** 3 from 4yo+ 8lb **13** Ran SP% **119.7**
Speed ratings (Par 100): **90,88,86,83,82 82,81,79,77,75 67,58,18**
CSF £51.40 TOTE £8.50: £2.30, £2.10, £1.10; EX 61.00 Trifecta £200.30.
**Owner** Axom XLV **Bred** Redgate Bloodstock Ltd **Trained** Beckhampton, Wilts

**FOCUS**
A fairly ordinary fillies' maiden, and another steadily run race. The form has been taken at face value, but there are doubts.

## 3917 KATHLEEN SNELL WORLDPAY H'CAP — 7f
**4:00** (4:01) (Class 3) (0-90,89) 3-Y-0+ **£7,762** (£2,310; £1,154; £577) **Stalls** High

Form RPR
1 **1** **Invincible Fresh (IRE)**[27] 2996 3-9-2 **85**... FrederikTylicki 2 95+
(James Fanshawe) *hld up in tch: smooth hdwy wl over 2f out: led over 1f out: sn rdn and kpt on strly* **7/2**[2]
3410 **2** *2* **Self Employed**[6] 3703 7-8-11 **75**... ConnorBeasley(3) 8 82
(Garry Woodward) *hld up towards rr: hdwy over 2f out: rdn to chse ldrs over 1f out: drvn and kpt on ins fnl f* **12/1**
0034 **3** *nk* **Ansaab**[19] 3271 6-9-11 **86**...(t) MartinHarley 5 92
(Alan McCabe) *led 1 1/2f: cl up tl led again over 3f out: rdn over 2f out: hdd over 1f out: sn drvn and kpt on same pce fnl f* **6/1**[3]
0-60 **4** *3/4* **Mujazif (IRE)**[23] 3109 4-9-12 **87**...(t) AdrianNicholls 3 91
(David Nicholls) *hld up towards rr: hdwy on wd outside over 2f out: rdn wl over 1f out: kpt on fnl f: nrst fin* **20/1**
1-21 **5** *3* **Outback Traveller (IRE)**[13] 3480 3-9-6 **89**... ShaneKelly 4 82
(Jeremy Noseda) *prom: cl up 3f out: rdn along over 2f out: drvn and wknd over 1f out* **3/1**[1]
31-0 **6** *3 1/4* **Bouclier (IRE)**[29] 2922 4-9-4 **79**... GrahamGibbons 6 67
(Luca Cumani) *chsd ldrs: rdn along over 2f out: sn drvn and one pce* **7/1**
4535 **7** *1 1/4* **Green Howard**[21] 3202 6-9-7 **82**...(p) JasonHart 7 67
(Robin Bastiman) *trckd ldrs: hdwy 3f out: rdn 2f out: sn btn* **8/1**
-050 **8** *3* **Malachim Mist (IRE)**[20] 3243 3-8-4 **78**... CamHardie(5) 1 52
(Richard Hannon) *chsd ldrs on outer: rdn along wl over 2f out: sn wknd* **10/1**
0-00 **9** *11* **Shesastar**[9] 3573 6-9-6 **81**... SilvestreDeSousa 9 29
(David Barron) *s.i.s: a bhd* **7/1**
115/ **10** *2 1/4* **Schoolmaster**[589] 7823 6-9-7 **82**... PatCosgrave 10 25
(Giles Bravery) *racd wd towards stands' rail: prom: led after 1 1/2f: rdn along and hdd over 3f out: sn wknd* **50/1**

1m 25.26s (-1.04) **Going Correction** -0.025s/f (Good)
**WFA** 3 from 4yo+ 8lb **10** Ran SP% **121.1**
Speed ratings (Par 107): **104,101,101,100,97 93,91,88,75,73**
CSF £47.18 CT £257.12 TOTE £5.50: £2.20, £4.80, £3.80; EX 47.50 Trifecta £393.80.
**Owner** Cheng Wai Tao **Bred** Roundhill Stud **Trained** Newmarket, Suffolk

**FOCUS**
They went a respectable clip in this fair handicap and the time was just 1.96sec over Racing Post standard, which suggests the ground was pretty close to the official verdict. Sound form, with a step up from the winner.

## 3918 HARRIET PYKE WORLDPAY FILLIES' H'CAP — 1m 4f
**4:35** (4:35) (Class 4) (0-85,84) 3-Y-0+ **£5,175** (£1,540; £769; £384) **Stalls** Low

Form RPR
10 **1** **Hidden Gold (IRE)**[24] 3085 3-8-13 **82**... SilvestreDeSousa 5 89
(Saeed bin Suroor) *t.k.h early: trckd ldng pair: pushed along and sltly outpcd over 3f out: smooth hdwy and cl up over 2f out: sn chal and rdn: led jst ins fnl f: sn drvn and hld on wl towards fin* **4/1**[3]
412 **2** *shd* **Reesha**[21] 3197 3-8-13 **82**... FrederikTylicki 2 88
(Roger Varian) *trckd ldr: cl up 3f out: rdn 2f out and sn ev ch: drvn ins fnl f: kpt on: jst hld* **1/1**[1]
-541 **3** *1* **Allegria (IRE)**[23] 3106 3-9-1 **84**... RobertHavlin 1 88
(John Gosden) *set stdy pce: qcknd over 4f out: jnd and rdn 3f out: drvn over 1f out: hdd jst ins fnl f: kpt on* **3/1**[2]
552 **4** *1/2* **Fiery Sunset**[21] 3174 3-8-8 **77**... BenCurtis 3 80
(Michael Bell) *t.k.h: trckd ldng pair on inner: effrt whn n.m.r on inner over 2f out: swtchd rt and sltly outpcd 1 1/2f out: rdn and styd on wl fnl f: nrst fin* **7/1**
634- **5** *7* **Rainbow Beauty**[52] 7895 4-9-6 **76**...(tp) PaddyAspell 6 68
(Tom George) *hld up: hdwy to chse ldrs 3f out: rdn over 2f out: sn one pce* **25/1**
1/0- **6** *19* **Mafeteng**[438] 1728 6-9-1 **71**... RaulDaSilva 4 33
(David Thompson) *hld up: a in rr: rdn along 3f out: sn outpcd* **50/1**

2m 33.59s (-1.31) **Going Correction** -0.025s/f (Good)
**WFA** 3 from 4yo+ 13lb **6** Ran SP% **113.3**
Speed ratings (Par 102): **103,102,102,101,97 84**
CSF £8.60 TOTE £4.80: £2.90, £1.30; EX 12.00 Trifecta £24.60.
**Owner** Godolphin **Bred** Darley **Trained** Newmarket, Suffolk

**FOCUS**
This race was over about ten yards longer than advertised as the round course was railed out. This wasn't strong for the grade, with the top weight 9lb below the race ceiling. The pace was fairly steady and there was a bunch finish. The form is rated through the runner-up.

## 3919 RICHARD BLAND WORLDPAY H'CAP — 1m 4f
**5:05** (5:05) (Class 5) (0-70,70) 4-Y-0+ **£3,234** (£962; £481; £240) **Stalls** Low

Form RPR
-003 **1** **Gambol (FR)**[10] 3546 4-9-7 **70**... GeorgeBaker 2 81
(B W Hills) *hld up in rr: hdwy 3f out: effrt to chse ldr over 1f out: sn rdn and edged lft: drvn and edgd lft ins fnl f: styd on to ld on line* **15/8**[1]
1211 **2** *nse* **I'm Harry**[22] 3155 5-9-3 **66**...(vt) PatCosgrave 8 76
(George Baker) *trckd ldrs: hdwy over 3f out: cl up 2f out: sn led: rdn ent fnl f: sn drvn and kpt on: hdd on line* **7/2**[2]
3443 **3** *8* **Arlecchino (IRE)**[17] 3334 4-9-3 **66**...(b) RoystonFfrench 7 63
(Ed McMahon) *chsd ldng pair: pushed along over 3f out: rdn and outpcd over 2f out: styd on u.p fnl f: tk modest 3rd nr fin* **5/1**[3]
5002 **4** *shd* **Magnolia Ridge (IRE)**[14] 3436 4-9-5 **68**...(p) AmyRyan 1 65
(Kristin Stubbs) *hld up in rr: hdwy over 3f out: rdn to chse ldrs 2f out: sn drvn and one pce: lost modest 3rd nr fin* **7/1**
3-05 **5** *2 3/4* **Rex Whistler (IRE)**[23] 3095 4-9-4 **67**... PaulMulrennan 4 60
(Julie Camacho) *t.k.h: chsd ldr: cl up 3f out: sn rdn: led briefly 2f out: sn hdd & wknd* **7/1**
0405 **6** *nk* **Gioia Di Vita**[14] 3436 4-9-4 **67**...(p) RaulDaSilva 6 59
(David Thompson) *set gd pce: rdn along and jnd 3f out: drvn and hdd 2f out: sn wknd* **12/1**
0106 **7** *2 1/4* **Charles De Mille**[15] 3400 6-8-13 **62**... PJMcDonald 5 51
(George Moore) *chsd ldng pair: tk clsr order over 4f out: rdn along over 3f out: sn drvn and wknd* **14/1**

2m 33.51s (-1.39) **Going Correction** -0.025s/f (Good) **7** Ran SP% **113.0**
Speed ratings (Par 103): **103,102,97,97,95 95,94**
CSF £8.30 CT £26.63 TOTE £2.30: £1.50, £1.50; EX 8.70 Trifecta £27.20.
**Owner** Hamdan Al Maktoum **Bred** Baron Georg Von Ullmann **Trained** Upper Lambourn, Berks

**FOCUS**
This race was over about ten yards longer than advertised as the round course was railed out. It was just a modest handicap, run at an ordinary gallop, but the first two finished clear. The winner built on his latest form.

## 3920 WALLY OLUSOA WORLDPAY FILLIES' H'CAP — 5f
**5:35** (5:35) (Class 4) (0-80,78) 4-Y-0+ **£5,175** (£1,540; £769; £384) **Stalls** High

Form RPR
1413 **1** **Iffranesia (FR)**[47] 2361 4-9-6 **77**...[1] AdamBeschizza 7 90
(Robert Cowell) *trckd ldrs: hdwy 2f out: sn chal: rdn to ld jst ins fnl f: drvn out* **5/1**[3]
-112 **2** *1 3/4* **Random Success (IRE)**[132] 714 4-9-1 **72**... GeorgeBaker 3 79
(Roger Charlton) *dwlt: hld up: swtchd lft to outer and hdwy 2f out: rdn to chse ldrs ent fnl f: sn drvn: no imp towards fin* **4/1**[1]
0050 **3** *nse* **Burren View Lady (IRE)**[17] 3342 4-8-12 **69**...(e) DavidAllan 6 76
(Tim Easterby) *cl up: slt ld 2f out: sn rdn: drvn and hdd jst ins fnl f: kpt on same pce* **9/1**
5615 **4** *1 3/4* **Whitecrest**[13] 3470 6-9-1 **72**... PJMcDonald 5 72
(John Spearing) *chsd ldrs: rdn along and sltly outpcd wl over 1f out: kpt on under pressure fnl f* **14/1**
-556 **5** *2* **Jofranka**[7] 3659 4-9-5 **76**... GrahamGibbons 9 69
(David Barron) *cl up: effrt to dispute ld 2f out: sn rdn and ev ch tl drvn ent fnl f and sn wknd* **5/1**[3]
2431 **6** *1 1/2* **Serenity Spa**[15] 3384 4-9-7 **78**... LiamKeniry 1 66
(Tony Carroll) *in tch on outer: hdwy to chse ldrs 2f out: sn rdn and btn* **9/2**[2]
0-00 **7** *2 3/4* **Threes Grand**[20] 3256 4-9-4 **75**... FrederikTylicki 2 53
(Scott Dixon) *chsd ldrs: rdn along 2f out: sn wknd* **6/1**
1036 **8** *3 3/4* **Six Wives**[26] 3033 7-8-10 **67**...(p) ShaneKelly 4 31
(Scott Dixon) *slt ld: rdn along and hdd 2f out: sn wknd* **10/1**
0301 **9** *4* **Lady Poppy**[17] 3338 4-8-0 **64**... KieranSchofield(7) 8 14
(George Moore) *anticipated s and stmbld as gates opened: a bhd* **10/1**

59.71s (-0.79) **Going Correction** -0.025s/f (Good) **9** Ran SP% **120.6**
Speed ratings (Par 102): **105,102,102,99,96 93,89,83,76**
CSF £26.60 CT £180.47 TOTE £5.60: £2.50, £1.20, £3.10; EX 18.90 Trifecta £214.70.
**Owner** Cyril Humphris **Bred** Cyril Humphris **Trained** Six Mile Bottom, Cambs

**FOCUS**
An ordinary handicap in which the winner resumed her progress.
T/Plt: £105.70 to a £1 stake. Pool: £82918.79 - 572.57 winning tickets T/Qpdt: £18.00 to a £1 stake. Pool: £5837.33 - 239.20 winning tickets JR

# 3880 HAYDOCK (L-H)
### Friday, July 4

**OFFICIAL GOING: Soft (8.7)**
Wind: Moderate, half against Weather: Rain

## 3921 BETDAQ HAYDOCK PARK APPRENTICE TRAINING SERIES H'CAP (PART OF THE RACING EXCELLENCE INITIATIVE) — 5f
**6:45** (6:47) (Class 5) (0-75,74) 3-Y-0+ **£2,587** (£770; £384; £192) **Stalls** Centre

Form RPR
-000 **1** **Captain Dunne (IRE)**[27] 3006 9-9-7 **69**... RachelRichardson(4) 9 82
(Tim Easterby) *mde all: rdn over 1f out: kpt on wl fnl f* **13/2**
002 **2** *3* **First In Command (IRE)**[4] 3793 9-9-10 **72**...(t) LouiseDay(4) 4 74
(Daniel Mark Loughnane) *racd keenly: chsd ldrs: wnt 2nd 1f out: kpt on ins fnl f: nt trble wnr* **4/1**[1]
0-05 **3** *2* **Passionada**[20] 3222 5-9-5 **63**... KevinStott 8 58
(Ed McMahon) *racd keenly: chsd ldrs: rdn over 2f out: nt qckn: kpt on same pce ins fnl f* **4/1**[1]
4045 **4** *1* **Beau Mistral (IRE)**[39] 2602 5-9-8 **70**... JamesKendrick(4) 6 61
(Paul Green) *hld up: pushed along over 3f out: styd on ins fnl f: nt trble ldrs* **4/1**[1]
041 **5** *nk* **Perfect Blossom**[7] 3659 7-9-12 **74** 6ex... JordanHibberd(4) 7 64
(Alan Berry) *missed break: hld up: effrt 2f out: one pce ins fnl f* **9/2**[2]
-050 **6** *nk* **De Repente (IRE)**[49] 2295 3-9-0 **65**... DanielCremin(2) 2 52
(Paul Green) *prom: rdn over 1f out: one pce ins fnl f* **6/1**[3]
224- **7** *15* **Jawking**[442] 1650 5-8-13 **59**... JennyPowell(2) 5
(James Unett) *in tch: pushed along and lost pl 3f out: bhd over 2f out* **16/1**

1m 2.38s (1.58) **Going Correction** +0.425s/f (Yiel)
**WFA** 3 from 4yo+ 5lb **7** Ran SP% **111.7**
Speed ratings (Par 103): **104,99,96,94,93 93,69**
CSF £30.90 CT £114.82 TOTE £6.50: £3.00, £2.70; EX 35.30 Trifecta £197.20.
**Owner** Middleham Park Racing XV & Partners **Bred** Ballybrennan Stud Ltd **Trained** Great Habton, N Yorks

**FOCUS**
All races on Inner Home straight and distances reduced by 5yds on Round course. A modest apprentices' handicap but a return to winning form for a veteran, who cashed in on a reduced mark. Not form to be too literal about.

## 3922 ADAPT (UK) TRAINING SERVICES CELEBRATION NURSERY H'CAP (BOBIS RACE) — 6f
**7:15** (7:17) (Class 4) 2-Y-O **£5,175** (£1,540; £769; £384) **Stalls** Centre

Form RPR
344 **1** **No One Knows**[46] 2402 2-8-13 **72**... MartinLane 10 75
(B W Hills) *hld up in tch: rdn over 1f out: r.o to ld wl ins fnl f: in command cl home* **11/4**[1]
423 **2** *1* **Ar Colleen Aine**[58] 2064 2-8-9 **68**... JoeFanning 4 68
(Mick Channon) *hld up: hdwy 2f out: chal fr over 1f out: nt qckn and hld towards fin* **6/1**
331 **3** *1 1/4* **Perardua**[35] 2725 2-8-13 **72**... PatrickMathers 6 68
(Richard Fahey) *racd keenly: w ldr: led over 1f out: sn rdn: hdd wl ins fnl f: no ex towards fin* **7/2**[2]
344 **4** *2 1/4* **Celestial Vision (USA)**[20] 3210 2-9-5 **78**... StephenCraine 3 67
(Tom Dascombe) *led: rdn and hdd over 1f out: hld whn n.m.r briefly wl ins fnl f: sn wknd* **5/1**[3]
145 **5** *nk* **Magical Roundabout (IRE)**[51] 2258 2-9-7 **80**... SeanLevey 2 68
(Richard Hannon) *prom tl rdn and btn over 1f out: sn hung lft: edgd rt clsng stages* **6/1**
21 **6** *2 1/2* **Mecca's Mirage (IRE)**[46] 2395 2-9-5 **78**... AndrewMullen 8 59
(Michael Dods) *hld up: effrt 2f out: sn cl up: wknd ins fnl f* **5/1**[3]

1m 17.02s (3.22) **Going Correction** +0.425s/f (Yiel) **6** Ran SP% **110.8**
Speed ratings (Par 96): **95,93,92,89,88 85**
CSF £18.74 CT £54.73 TOTE £3.60: £2.00, £2.80; EX 16.40 Trifecta £103.20.
**Owner** Gary And Linnet Woodward **Bred** Gary Woodward **Trained** Upper Lambourn, Berks

**FOCUS**
The field for this nursery was almost cut in half by withdrawals, but produced a good finish. The third looks the best guide.

## 3923 BETFRED SAYS FAREWELL TO WILLIAM SIMUKULWA H'CAP (BOBIS RACE) 1m 2f 95y
7:45 (7:45) (Class 4) (0-85,83) 3-Y-O £5,175 (£1,540; £769; £384) Stalls Centre

Form RPR
1 **1** **Wee Frankie (IRE)**[49] 2292 3-9-3 **79** SeanLevey 3 91
(Keith Dalgleish) *racd keenly: prom: rdn to take 2nd over 2f out: sn hung rt: str chal ins fnl f: led fnl 75yds: styd on dourly* **6/4**[1]

2124 **2** ½ **Solidarity**[32] 2839 3-9-6 **82** AndrewMullen 1 93
(Charlie Appleby) *hld up: hdwy 5f out: led over 3f out: rdn 2f out: hrd pressed ins fnl f: hdd fnl 75yds: no ex* **2/1**[2]

5-42 **3** 9 **Mustadaam (IRE)**[15] 3385 3-9-7 **83** DaneO'Neill 5 77
(Brian Meehan) *s.i.s: in tch: chsd ldr over 6f out: rdn and outpcd over 2f out: no ch w front pair fr over 1f out: eased whn wl btn wl ins fnl f* **3/1**[3]

2-63 **4** 12 **Alpine Storm (IRE)**[7] 3643 3-8-10 **72** JoeFanning 2 43
(Mark Johnston) *racd keenly: led: rdn and hdd over 3f out: wknd over 2f out* **12/1**

0-34 **5** 2 ¼ **Guaracha**[105] 1044 3-8-13 **75** MartinLane 7 42
(Clive Brittain) *prom: lost pl 5f out: rdn over 4f out: sn wknd* **25/1**

2m 15.86s (0.36) **Going Correction** +0.125s/f (Good) 5 Ran SP% **109.9**
Speed ratings (Par 102): **103,102,95,85,84**
CSF £4.77 TOTE £2.40: £1.70, £1.50; EX 5.80 Trifecta £8.70.
**Owner** Lamont Racing **Bred** Oak Lodge Bloodstock **Trained** Carluke, S Lanarks
■ Stewards' Enquiry : Sean Levey two-day ban: used whip above permitted level (Jul 18-19)

**FOCUS**
This 3yo handicap was a three-horse race judged on the betting. That was how it turned out, but it looked hard work in the conditions and only two mattered in the closing stages. The winner looked on a good mark.

## 3924 IRISH CHAMPIONS WEEKEND EBF MAIDEN STKS 7f
8:15 (8:15) (Class 5) 2-Y-O £2,911 (£866; £432; £216) Stalls Low

Form RPR
0 **1** **Stec (IRE)**[8] 3613 2-8-12 0 JennyPowell(7) 1 80
(Tom Dascombe) *led: rdn and hdd narrowly over 1f out: regained ld wl ins fnl f: styd on and fnd ex* **33/1**

43 **2** 1 **Azraff (IRE)**[15] 3381 2-9-5 0 MartinHarley 7 78
(Marco Botti) *prom over 5f out: travelled wl: rdn to chal over 1f out: kpt on but hld cl home* **5/4**[1]

**3** hd **Here Now** 2-9-5 0 SilvestreDeSousa 8 77+
(Charlie Appleby) *hld up: hdwy over 2f out: rdn to ld narrowly over 1f out: hdd wl ins fnl f: no ex cl home* **9/2**[3]

0 **4** 1 ¼ **Maraakib (IRE)**[28] 2964 2-9-5 0 DaneO'Neill 2 74
(Brian Meehan) *trckd ldrs: effrt 2f out: rdn whn chalng over 1f out: nt qckn ins fnl f: kpt on same pce fnl 150yds* **4/1**[2]

**5** nk **Kifaaya** 2-9-5 0 JoeFanning 4 73+
(Mark Johnston) *prom: pushed along and outpcd over 2f out: prog ins fnl f: styd on towards fin: nt pce to chal* **7/1**

0 **6** 7 **Stardrifter**[22] 3136 2-9-5 0 PatrickMathers 5 56
(Richard Fahey) *rrd s: hld up: pushed along briefly 4f out: rdn over 2f out: no imp* **16/1**

55 **7** 7 **Robben**[39] 2601 2-9-0 0 KevinStott(5) 6 38
(Kevin Ryan) *in tch: pushed along briefly 5f out: rdn 2f out: wknd over 1f out* **11/1**

1m 30.94s (0.24) **Going Correction** +0.125s/f (Good) 7 Ran SP% **112.3**
Speed ratings (Par 94): **103,101,101,100,99 91,83**
CSF £72.79 TOTE £36.90: £9.70, £1.50; EX 119.70 Trifecta £744.50 Part won..
**Owner** D Ward **Bred** D G Iceton **Trained** Malpas, Cheshire

**FOCUS**
A complete surprise in this juvenile maiden, although the time compared reasonably with the preceding handicap. The winner left his debut well behind.

## 3925 MILLIE ROSE MEMORIAL MAIDEN STKS 1m
8:45 (8:45) (Class 5) 3-Y-O+ £2,587 (£770; £384; £192) Stalls Low

Form RPR
4-34 **1** **Express Himself (IRE)**[22] 3153 3-9-3 78 SteveDrowne 7 83+
(Ed McMahon) *hld up: rdn over 2f out: hdwy over 1f out: styd on to ld narrowly wl ins fnl f: a doing enough nr fin* **7/2**[1]

353 **2** hd **Potent Embrace (USA)**[14] 3434 3-8-12 77 JoeFanning 5 75
(Mark Johnston) *led: rdn whn pressed over 1f out: hdd narrowly wl ins fnl f: kpt on: hld nr fin* **11/2**[3]

-5 **3** ¾ **The Character (IRE)**[58] 2075 3-9-3 0 StephenCraine 10 78
(Tom Dascombe) *chsd ldr: rdn 2f out: chal fr over 1f out: no ex fnl strides* **9/2**[2]

**4** 3 **Esteban** 3-9-3 0 MartinHarley 8 71
(Marco Botti) *midfield: hdwy over 3f out: rdn and chsd ldrs over 1f out: no ex fnl 100yds* **17/2**

56- **5** 1 ¾ **Racing's Dream**[207] 8213 3-9-3 0 SeanLevey 4 67
(Brian Meehan) *chsd ldrs: rdn 2f out: kpt on same pce fnl f* **14/1**

04 **6** ¾ **Quasqazah**[34] 2789 3-9-3 0 (b[1]) DaneO'Neill 3 65
(Roger Varian) *chsd ldrs: rdn over 2f out: one pce fr over 1f out* **12/1**

**7** nk **Crowded** 3-9-3 0 MartinLane 6 64
(Charlie Appleby) *in tch: rdn over 2f out: sn wknd* **7/2**[1]

**8** 5 **Trimoulet** 5-9-9 0 ConnorBeasley(3) 12 55
(Daniel Kubler) *hld up: hdwy 4f out: chsd ldrs 3f out: rdn and wknd over 1f out* **25/1**

**9** 8 **Divine Warrior (IRE)** 3-9-3 0 BenCurtis 9 35
(Timothy Jarvis) *bhd: pushed along 5f out: rdn and hung lft over 2f out: nvr on terms* **25/1**

**10** shd **Endless Seas** 3-8-12 0 AndrewMullen 11 29
(Michael Appleby) *hld up: niggled along over 3f out: rdn and hung lft over 2f out: nvr on terms* **20/1**

4 **11** 3 ¾ **Dutch Lady Roseane**[112] 962 3-8-12 0 (e[1]) AdamBeschizza 1 21
(James Unett) *s.s: towards rr: struggling over 3f out: bhd over 2f out: nvr on terms* **66/1**

1m 45.77s (2.07) **Going Correction** +0.125s/f (Good)
**WFA** 3 from 5yo 9lb 11 Ran SP% **116.8**
Speed ratings (Par 103): **94,93,93,90,88 87,87,82,74,74 70**
CSF £21.59 TOTE £5.10: £1.70, £2.00, £1.50; EX 20.20 Trifecta £152.10.
**Owner** Milton Express Limited **Bred** Barouche Stud Ireland Ltd **Trained** Lichfield, Staffs

**FOCUS**
Subsequent Group 3 winner Green Destiny was the best recent winner of this 3yo maiden. Ordinary form, the form horses dominating.

## 3926 MUSIC HERE ON 8TH AUGUST H'CAP 1m 3f 200y
9:15 (9:15) (Class 4) (0-85,83) 4-Y-O+ £5,175 (£1,540; £769) Stalls Centre

Form RPR
15-4 **1** **Mister Fizz**[21] 3205 6-8-11 **80** DanielCremin(7) 1 91+
(Miss Imogen Pickard) *mde all: rdn over 3f out: drew clr over 2f out: styd on wl: unchal* **2/1**[3]

0134 **2** 10 **Brigadoon**[55] 2160 7-9-7 **83** AndrewMullen 4 78
(Michael Appleby) *hld up in rr: rdn whn c over to stands' side over 3f out: no imp u.p over 2f out: kpt on to take 2nd fnl 150yds: no ch w wnr* **15/8**[2]

6011 **3** 2 ¾ **Martinas Delight (USA)**[22] 3139 4-8-12 **74** DaneO'Neill 6 67
(Timothy Jarvis) *chsd wnr: rdn and c over to stands' side over 3f out: no imp on wnr over 2f out: lost 2nd fnl 150yds: sn eased* **7/4**[1]

2m 38.1s (4.30) **Going Correction** +0.125s/f (Good) 3 Ran SP% **104.5**
Speed ratings (Par 105): **90,83,81**
CSF £5.51 TOTE £2.30; EX 7.80 Trifecta £3.90.
**Owner** Mrs Margaret J Wilson **Bred** Mrs Margaret J Wilson **Trained** Kingsland, Herefordshire

**FOCUS**
Half the field were taken out of this handicap, but there was not much between the trio in the betting. However, there was a difference of opinion in the straight and the one that stayed towards the far side came home alone. The winner was the only one to show his best.
T/Plt: £108.90 to a £1 stake. Pool: £69,523 - 465.75 winning tickets T/Qpdt: £9.80 to a £1 stake. Pool: £6,396 - 481.90 winning tickets DO

# 3243 SANDOWN (R-H)
Friday, July 4

**OFFICIAL GOING: Round course - good to firm; sprint course - good (good to firm in places; round course 8.6; sprint course 8.4)**
Wind: Moderate, against Weather: Fine, hot

## 3927 PALACEGATE TOUCH H'CAP 5f 6y
2:00 (2:01) (Class 3) (0-95,95) 3-Y-O+ £9,337 (£2,796; £1,398; £699; £349; £175) Stalls Low

Form RPR
5-40 **1** **Milly's Gift**[34] 2757 4-9-2 **88** RyanTate(3) 5 97
(Clive Cox) *trckd ldrs: clsd gng strly over 1f out: rdn to ld jst ins fnl f: drvn out* **8/1**

0-60 **2** ½ **Ajjaadd (USA)**[42] 2503 8-9-8 **91** WilliamTwiston-Davies 16 98
(Ted Powell) *dwlt: hld up in last quartet and grad mde way fr wdst draw towards far rail: prog 2f out: r.o wl fnl f: tk 2nd last strides* **33/1**

0-14 **3** nk **Goldream**[34] 2778 5-9-12 **95** (p) AndreaAtzeni 14 101
(Robert Cowell) *chsd ldrs on outer: clsd over 1f out: rdn to chal and upsides jst ins fnl f: styd on same pce* **11/2**[2]

6500 **4** ½ **Trader Jack**[6] 3697 5-8-9 **83** PhilipPrince(5) 7 89+
(David Flood) *s.i.s: mostly in last quartet tl prog against far rail over 1f out: r.o wl fnl f: fin best of all* **25/1**

6001 **5** nk **Extrasolar**[19] 3275 4-9-2 **85** (t) PatDobbs 15 88
(Amanda Perrett) *racd on outer in last quartet: rdn and prog 2f out: chsd ldrs 1f out: styd on same pce* **25/1**

0146 **6** hd **Doctor Parkes**[6] 3693 8-9-2 **85** JamesDoyle 12 88
(Stuart Williams) *towards rr and racd on outer: rdn over 2f out: no prog tl styd on fr 1f out: nrst fin* **16/1**

-100 **7** hd **Apricot Sky**[18] 3313 4-9-0 **83** WilliamBuick 10 85
(Henry Candy) *pressed ldr: rdn to ld jst over 1f out to jst ins fnl f: wknd* **10/1**

-421 **8** nk **Tagula Night (IRE)**[20] 3246 8-8-13 **82** (bt) RyanMoore 3 89+
(Dean Ivory) *hld up in last quartet: trying to make prog against far rail whn hmpd wl over 1f out: swtchd arnd rivals fnl f: r.o towards fin but no ch to rcvr* **5/1**[1]

0020 **9** ¾ **Judge 'n Jury**[27] 2989 10-9-3 **93** (t) KieranShoemark(7) 8 91
(Ronald Harris) *led but racd sme way off far rail: hdd & wknd jst over 1f out* **25/1**

1044 **10** 1 ½ **Normal Equilibrium**[27] 2992 4-9-2 **90** (p) MarcMonaghan(5) 11 83
(Robert Cowell) *chsd ldrs: rdn and no imp over 1f out: wknd ins fnl f* **12/1**

0-06 **11** 3 ¼ **New Fforest**[13] 3458 4-9-5 **91** OisinMurphy(3) 4 84
(Andrew Balding) *chsd ldrs and racd towards far rail: rdn and wknd jst over 1f out* **7/1**[3]

1000 **12** ¾ **Taajub (IRE)**[27] 2989 7-9-6 **89** JimmyFortune 6 67
(Peter Crate) *trckd ldrs: shkn up and lost pl 2f out: struggling over 1f out* **8/1**

0-60 **13** shd **Lady Gibraltar**[27] 2989 5-9-3 **86** KierenFallon 2 67
(Timothy Jarvis) *disp 2nd pl to wl over 1f out: wknd* **8/1**

150- **14** 6 **Storm Trooper (IRE)**[266] 7170 3-8-9 **83** RichardHughes 13 37
(Richard Hannon) *trckd ldrs on outer to 1/2-way: wknd and eased over 1f out: t.o* **20/1**

-560 **15** nk **Fine 'n Dandy (IRE)**[20] 3219 3-9-0 **88** (t) RichardKingscote 9 41
(Tom Dascombe) *chsd ldrs: lost pl 1/2-way: sn btn: t.o* **50/1**

1m 0.87s (-0.73) **Going Correction** +0.075s/f (Good)
**WFA** 3 from 4yo+ 5lb 15 Ran SP% **121.8**
Speed ratings (Par 107): **108,107,106,105,105 105,104,104,103,100 95,94,94,84,84**
CSF £263.51 CT £1616.05 TOTE £8.70: £3.70, £9.50, £2.60; EX 327.00 Trifecta £2887.90 Part won..
**Owner** Ken Lock Racing **Bred** Ken Lock Racing **Trained** Lambourn, Berks
■ Stewards' Enquiry : Philip Prince two-day ban: careless riding (Jul 18-19)

**FOCUS**
Rail dolled out 4yds from 1m to Winning Post and distances on Round course increased by 8yds. Sprint track at full width. Despite 15 runners in this fair sprint handicap, it wasn't a messy affair and the main action was away from the often favoured stands' rail until the final furlong. A length best from the winner.

## 3928 DRAGON STKS (LISTED RACE) 5f 6y
2:30 (2:32) (Class 1) 2-Y-O £14,744 (£5,590; £2,797; £1,393) Stalls Low

Form RPR
411 **1** **Beacon**[20] 3211 2-9-2 0 RichardHughes 1 105+
(Richard Hannon) *t.k.h early: hld up: trckd ldr over 2f out: pushed into ld 1f out: readily drew clr* **2/1**[2]

116 **2** 4 **Mukhmal (IRE)**[15] 3374 2-9-2 0 PaulHanagan 4 91
(Mark Johnston) *t.k.h: pressed ldr: led over 3f out: shkn up and hdd 1f out: outpcd and wandered but hld on for 2nd* **15/8**[1]

14 **3** *hd* **Snap Shots (IRE)**[15] 3374 2-9-2 0 RichardKingscote 2 90
(Tom Dascombe) *led to over 3f out: dropped to 3rd over 2f out: rdn and no imp over 1f out: kpt on to press for 2nd nr fin* **3/1**[3]

3132 **4** *6* **Union Rose**[17] 3322 2-9-2 0 (p) WilliamTwiston-Davies 3 68
(Ronald Harris) *dwlt: in tch in last pair tl rdn and struggling jst over 2f out: sn btn* **6/1**

1m 2.49s (0.89) **Going Correction** +0.075s/f (Good) **4** Ran SP% **107.4**
Speed ratings (Par 102): **95,88,88,78**
CSF £6.02 TOTE £2.70; EX 5.60 Trifecta £7.20.
**Owner** Highclere Thoroughbred Racing (Albany) **Bred** J M Cole **Trained** East Everleigh, Wilts

**FOCUS**
Often an average juvenile Listed sprint, but Beacon rates the best winner for a long time. He's open to more improvement too. There wasn't that much pace on early.

## 3929 IRISH CHAMPIONS WEEKEND EBF MAIDEN STKS 7f 16y
**3:00** (3:02) (Class 5) 2-Y-O **£3,881** (£1,155; £577; £288) **Stalls** Low

Form RPR

02 **1** **Mustadeem (IRE)**[22] 3140 2-9-5 0 PaulHanagan 10 87+
(Brian Meehan) *trckd ldng pair: pushed into ld over 1f out: wl in command fnl f: pushed out* **2/5**[1]

**2** *1 3/4* **Darshini** 2-9-5 0 RyanMoore 2 80+
(Sir Michael Stoute) *trckd ldng trio: pushed along over 2f out: tk 3rd jst over 1f out: styd on fnl f to take 2nd last strides: no threat to wnr* **14/1**

4 **3** *nk* **Tom Hark (FR)**[9] 3578 2-9-5 0 RichardHughes 6 79
(Richard Hannon) *led: rdn and hdd over 1f out: one pce after: lost 2nd last strides* **10/1**[3]

0 **4** *5* **Silver Quay (IRE)**[49] 2298 2-9-5 0 PatDobbs 9 66
(Richard Hannon) *chsd ldrs in 5th: pushed along over 2f out: lost pl wl over 1f out: kpt on again fnl f to take 4th last strides* **33/1**

**5** *nk* **New Brunswick (GER)** 2-9-5 0 WilliamBuick 1 65+
(John Gosden) *settled in 8th: prog 2f out: nudged along to chse clr ldng trio wl ins fnl f: lost 4th last strides* **6/1**[2]

4 **6** *3/4* **Mistamel (IRE)**[25] 3063 2-9-5 0 JimmyFortune 11 63
(Eve Johnson Houghton) *chsd ldr to 2f out: wknd 1f out* **10/1**[3]

**7** *1* **Cahill (IRE)** 2-9-5 0 WilliamTwiston-Davies 3 60
(Alan King) *chsd ldrs in 6th: rdn over 2f out: one pce and no prog* **16/1**

**8** *2 1/4* **Althon (IRE)** 2-9-5 0 FrankieDettori 8 54
(John Gosden) *rn green in last pair: pushed along and no progrtess 3f out: no real hdwy after* **20/1**

**9** *2 1/4* **The Way You Dance (IRE)** 2-9-5 0 TomQueally 5 48+
(Ismail Mohammed) *dwlt and s.i.s: mostly detached in last: nvr a factor* **50/1**

**10** *5* **Thewaythewindblows (IRE)** 2-9-2 0 ThomasBrown(3) 4 35
(Daniel Kubler) *in tch in 7th: shkn up and rn green over 2f out: wknd wl over 1f out* **66/1**

1m 30.22s (0.72) **Going Correction** -0.20s/f (Firm) **10** Ran SP% **127.6**
Speed ratings (Par 94): **87,85,84,78,78 77,76,74,71,65**
CSF £9.49 TOTE £1.50: £1.10, £2.80, £2.70; EX 9.40 Trifecta £62.10.
**Owner** Hamdan Al Maktoum **Bred** Shadwell Estate Company Limited **Trained** Manton, Wilts

**FOCUS**
This 2yo maiden looked a cracking opportunity for the favourite and he won well. The form makes sense and is rated at the top end of the race averages.

## 3930 AMBANT GALA STKS (LISTED RACE) 1m 2f 7y
**3:35** (3:36) (Class 1) 3-Y-O+
**£20,982** (£7,955; £3,981; £1,983; £995; £499) **Stalls** Low

Form RPR

1223 **1** **Windhoek**[28] 2958 4-9-5 108 KierenFallon 2 113+
(Saeed bin Suroor) *trckd ldng pair: clsd smoothly to ld 2f out: pushed clr over 1f out: reminder fnl f: comf* **5/4**[1]

0-36 **2** *2 1/2* **Amralah (IRE)**[49] 2314 4-9-5 91 RyanMoore 1 108
(Mick Channon) *led after 1f: rdn and hdd 2f out: styd on but no match for wnr* **7/1**

-451 **3** *1 1/2* **Tha'ir (IRE)**[127] 773 4-9-5 106 AndreaAtzeni 4 105
(Saeed bin Suroor) *hld up in 4th: shkn up over 2f out: tk 3rd over 1f out: no imp on ldng pair* **4/1**[2]

-650 **4** *1/2* **Educate**[97] 1181 5-9-5 112 TomQueally 3 104
(Ismail Mohammed) *hld up in 5th: pushed along and tried to make prog fr 2f out but hanging: kpt on same pce fnl f* **9/2**[3]

3630 **5** *6* **Truth Or Dare**[15] 3379 3-8-9 97 ow1 RichardHughes 7 94
(Richard Hannon) *led 1f: trckd ldr: rdn to chal and upsides jst over 2f out: wknd qckly over 1f out* **8/1**

4160 **6** *13* **Flemish School**[34] 2779 4-9-0 90 (p) WilliamBuick 5 63
(David Elsworth) *hld up in last: shkn up and wknd 3f out: eased and t.o* **20/1**

2m 5.86s (-4.64) **Going Correction** -0.20s/f (Firm)
**WFA** 3 from 4yo+ 11lb **6** Ran SP% **111.0**
Speed ratings (Par 111): **110,108,106,106,101 91**
CSF £10.42 TOTE £2.00: £1.20, £3.30; EX 8.50 Trifecta £34.70.
**Owner** Godolphin **Bred** Horizon Bloodstock Limited **Trained** Newmarket, Suffolk

**FOCUS**
This wasn't a strong Listed race and it proved easy pickings for the heavily backed favourite, who probably didn't need to improve.

## 3931 NOELLE RENO H'CAP 1m 2f 7y
**4:10** (4:11) (Class 3) (0-95,91) 3-Y-O+
**£12,450** (£3,728; £1,864; £932; £466; £234) **Stalls** Low

Form RPR

0015 **1** **Presburg (IRE)**[39] 2627 5-9-5 85 OisinMurphy(3) 2 95
(Joseph Tuite) *hld up and last after 2f: drvn and prog on outer wl over 1f out: swept into the ld last 150yds: sn clr* **14/1**

-502 **2** *2 1/4* **Vital Evidence (USA)**[21] 3196 4-9-12 89 (p) JamesDoyle 6 95
(Sir Michael Stoute) *led: drvn and hdd 2f out: kpt on wl and upsides jst ins fnl f: outpcd after* **9/2**[3]

4441 **3** *shd* **Rydan (IRE)**[21] 3197 3-8-12 86 FrankieDettori 7 92
(Robert Mills) *hld up towards rr: prog on outer jst over 2f out sn drvn: nt qckn but styd on fnl f to press for 2nd last strides* **4/1**[2]

5-04 **4** *1/2* **Jodies Jem**[36] 2707 4-9-6 83 JoeFanning 11 88
(William Jarvis) *trckd ldng pair after 2f: moved up smoothly to ld 2f out: rdn over 1f out: hdd and no ex last 150yds* **17/2**

0111 **5** *1 1/4* **Chain Of Events**[21] 3196 7-9-6 83 WilliamBuick 12 85
(Michael Wigham) *trckd ldr: rdn to chal jst over 2f out: styd pressing tl wknd ins fnl f* **9/2**[3]

3433 **6** *nse* **Karraar**[20] 3248 3-8-11 85 PaulHanagan 1 87
(Richard Hannon) *trckd ldng pair 2f: styd cl up: rdn 2f out: nt qckn and no imp fr over 1f out* **7/2**[1]

1-03 **7** *6* **Cactus Valley (IRE)**[12] 3499 5-9-13 90 (b[1]) RyanMoore 5 81
(Roger Charlton) *s.i.s and pushed along early: sn wl in tch towards rr: rdn over 2f out: no prog and btn wl over 1f out: wknd* **11/2**

0-00 **8** *7* **Snow King (USA)**[55] 2157 4-8-11 79 MarcMonaghan(5) 10 57
(Ted Powell) *in tch: rdn wl over 2f out: wknd wl over 1f out* **66/1**

2m 6.7s (-3.80) **Going Correction** -0.20s/f (Firm)
**WFA** 3 from 4yo+ 11lb **8** Ran SP% **112.7**
Speed ratings (Par 107): **107,105,105,104,103 103,98,93**
CSF £73.41 CT £302.18 TOTE £12.70: £3.10, £1.90, £1.80; EX 86.10 Trifecta £504.60.
**Owner** www.isehove.com **Bred** Limestone And Tara Studs **Trained** Great Shefford, Berks

**FOCUS**
Despite the non-runners, this was still a fair handicap and they went a sound enough pace. The form is rated around the second.

## 3932 RACING UK PROFITS RETURNED TO RACING H'CAP 1m 6f
**4:45** (4:45) (Class 4) (0-85,85) 3-Y-O+ **£6,469** (£1,925; £962; £481) **Stalls** Low

Form RPR

300- **1** **Alwilda**[246] 7650 4-10-0 85 LukeMorris 10 92
(Sir Mark Prescott Bt) *hld up in 5th: urged along over 2f out: hrd rdn and clsd on outer fr over 1f out: sustained effrt to ld last 50yds* **10/1**

2-13 **2** *1/2* **Economy**[44] 2461 4-9-12 83 JamesDoyle 4 89
(Sir Michael Stoute) *hld up in 4th: clsd over 2f out and stl gng strly: led wl over 1f out: sn drvn and tending to hang rt: kpt on but hdd last 50yds* **11/10**[1]

0031 **3** *nk* **Ex Oriente (IRE)**[7] 3681 5-9-6 77 6ex AndreaAtzeni 2 83
(Stuart Williams) *dwlt and propped s: last tl 10f out: rdn over 2f out: grad clsd on outer fr over 1f out: nrst fin but nvr quite able to chal* **9/2**[2]

6411 **4** *hd* **See And Be Seen**[9] 3579 4-8-11 68 6ex (p) RyanMoore 6 73
(Sylvester Kirk) *trckd ldng pair: clsd to chal 2f out: drvn and pressed ldr over 1f out tl no ex and lost 2 pls last 75yds* **13/2**[3]

04-3 **5** *2 1/2* **Hi Note**[12] 3249 6-9-4 80 HarryPoulton(5) 1 82
(Sheena West) *won battle for ld and set decent pce: hrd pressed over 2f out: hdd wl over 1f out: one pce after* **20/1**

1256 **6** *nk* **Late Shipment**[23] 3110 3-8-3 75 (p) JoeFanning 3 76
(Mark Johnston) *trckd ldr and clr of rest early: rdn to chal over 2f out: lost pl and one pce over 1f out* **9/2**[2]

60 **7** *9* **Vedani (IRE)**[24] 758 5-9-2 73 (t) TomQueally 8 62
(Tony Carroll) *last after 4f: rdn and no prog wl over 2f out: sn wknd* **40/1**

3m 3.97s (-0.53) **Going Correction** -0.20s/f (Firm)
**WFA** 3 from 4yo+ 15lb **7** Ran SP% **113.6**
Speed ratings (Par 105): **93,92,92,92,91 90,85**
CSF £21.32 CT £58.53 TOTE £11.10: £4.40, £1.40; EX 23.60 Trifecta £121.00.
**Owner** Miss K Rausing **Bred** Miss K Rausing **Trained** Newmarket, Suffolk

**FOCUS**
There was no hanging around in this staying handicap and it saw a cracking finish. Solid form for the class, with the first two and the fourth progressive.
T/Jkpt: Not won. T/Plt: £94.70 to a £1 stake. Pool: £99396.19 - 765.73 winning tickets T/Qpdt: £6.50 to a £1 stake. Pool: £7456.77 - 838.34 winning tickets JN

# 2435 WARWICK (L-H)
Friday, July 4

**OFFICIAL GOING: Good (7.1)**
Wind: Light behind Weather: Cloudy with sunny spells

## 3933 BRITISH STALLION STUDS EBF MAIDEN FILLIES' STKS (BOBIS RACE) 6f
**2:10** (2:13) (Class 5) 2-Y-O **£2,911** (£866; £432; £216) **Stalls** Low

Form RPR

02 **1** **Mary McPhee**[45] 2436 2-9-0 0 HarryBentley 5 77+
(Charles Hills) *chsd ldrs: rdn to ld ins fnl f: r.o* **3/1**[2]

50 **2** *1/2* **Pastoral Girl**[16] 3353 2-9-0 0 GrahamLee 3 75
(James Given) *led: hdd over 3f out: w ldr: rdn and ev ch ins fnl f: unable qck towards fin* **5/6**[1]

**3** *3* **Caigemdar (IRE)** 2-9-0 0 PhillipMakin 11 66+
(David Barron) *w ldr tl led over 3f out: rdn over 1f out: hdd and no ex ins fnl f* **12/1**[3]

**4** *nk* **Dear Bruin (IRE)** 2-9-0 0 LiamJones 8 66+
(John Spearing) *sn pushed along and prom: rdn over 2f out: hung lft and styd on same pce fnl f* **50/1**

26 **5** *1 1/2* **Aevalon**[43] 2493 2-9-0 0 JohnFahy 1 61
(Eve Johnson Houghton) *mid-div: hdwy 1/2-way: rdn over 2f out: no ex fnl f* **12/1**[3]

50 **6** *5* **Diracan (IRE)**[10] 3557 2-9-0 0 JackMitchell 15 46
(Nick Littmoden) *s.i.s and wnt rt s: hdwy over 2f out: rdn and wknd over 1f out* **33/1**

40 **7** *3/4* **Tantric Lady**[10] 3542 2-9-0 0 [1] DavidProbert 12 44
(Alan McCabe) *s.i.s: hld up: pushed along over 2f out: nvr trbld ldrs* **33/1**

**8** *1 1/4* **Auld Fyffee (IRE)** 2-8-11 0 RyanPowell(3) 13 40+
(John Ryan) *s.i.s: outpcd: styd on ins fnl f: nvr nrr* **66/1**

**9** *2 1/2* **Josefa** 2-9-0 0 StevieDonohoe 10 33
(Noel Quinlan) *prom: rdn over 2f out: wknd over 1f out* **20/1**

00 **10** *nk* **Whoopie Do**[20] 3223 2-8-9 0 LouisSteward(5) 9 32
(John Gallagher) *mid-div: rdn and wknd over 2f out* **100/1**

**11** *hd* **Seebeedee** 2-9-0 0 SamHitchcott 2 31
(Harry Dunlop) *s.i.s: a in rr: wknd 1/2-way: b.b.v* **50/1**

0 **12** *7* **Recover (USA)**[7] 3671 2-9-0 0 SeanLevey 14 10
(Brian Meehan) *hld up in tch: rdn and wknd over 2f out* **16/1**

0 **13** *2* **Trixy**[28] 2944 2-9-0 0 JimmyQuinn 4 4
(Jo Hughes) *mid-div: wknd 1/2-way* **66/1**

6 **14** *2 1/4* **Emilys Girl (IRE)**[36] 2692 2-9-0 0 SteveDrowne 6
(Ronald Harris) *a in rr: wknd 1/2-way* **100/1**

1m 13.86s (2.06) **Going Correction** +0.20s/f (Good) **14** Ran SP% **120.4**
Speed ratings (Par 91): **94,93,89,88,86 80,79,77,74,73 73,64,61,58**
CSF £5.42 TOTE £3.80: £1.40, £1.10, £3.10; EX 7.00 Trifecta £39.50.
**Owner** J Gompertz, Sir Peter Vela, Qatar Racing **Bred** Qatar Bloodstock Ltd **Trained** Lambourn, Berks

**FOCUS**
Realignment of bend added 2.5yds to all distances. The first meeting staged here since the furore surrounding the track's last fixture in May. Up to 14mm of water had been applied to the track since Wednesday and the re-aligned sprint course rail added 2.5yards to official distances on a card made up solely of races over 5f and 6f. The market suggested this fair fillies maiden was between the two market leaders and that's how it turned out in a race where the prominent-racers dominated. The gallop was an ordinary one. The form dpends on his much the runner-up was below her Queen Mary run.

## 3934 ARDENCOTE MANOR HOTEL, COUNTRY CLUB & SPA MAIDEN AUCTION STKS 6f
**2:40** (2:43) (Class 5) 2-Y-O **£2,587** (£770; £384; £192) **Stalls** Low

Form RPR
2200 **1** **Fine Prince (IRE)**[15] 3374 2-9-4 0 GrahamLee 3 82
(Robert Mills) *led to 1/2-way: rdn to ld and hung rt over 1f out: r.o* **8/11**[1]
0 **2** ¾ **Royal Razalma (IRE)**[34] 2771 2-8-10 0 MatthewLawson(3) 2 75
(Jonathan Portman) *chsd ldrs: led 1/2-way: rdn and hdd over 1f out: edgd rt ins fnl f: styd on* **25/1**
**3** 7 **Little Miss Mighty** 2-8-8 0 JackMitchell 8 49+
(Nick Littmoden) *mid-div: pushed along over 2f out: styd on to go 3rd nr fin: nt trble ldrs* **28/1**
26 **4** ¾ **The Dapper Tapper (IRE)**[21] 3181 2-9-1 0 JohnFahy 1 54
(Eve Johnson Houghton) *prom: rdn and edgd rt over 1f out: sn wknd* **7/2**[2]
0 **5** 1 ½ **Ifittakesforever (IRE)**[18] 3297 2-9-4 0 StevieDonohoe 4 52
(Tim Pitt) *chsd ldrs: rdn over 2f out: edgd rt and wknd over 1f out* **25/1**
0 **6** nk **Somedaysrdiamonds**[18] 3311 2-8-8 0[1] LiamJones 11 41
(J S Moore) *chsd ldrs: rdn over 2f out: wknd over 1f out* **50/1**
4636 **7** 5 **Chetan**[24] 3081 2-8-11 0 FergusSweeney 5 29
(Milton Bradley) *prom: rdn 1/2-way: wknd wl over 1f out* **14/1**
6 **8** 5 **Pyrocumulus (IRE)**[13] 3467 2-9-1 0 JimmyQuinn 10 18
(Jo Hughes) *s.i.s: sn pushed along and a in rr* **20/1**
05 **9** 2 ½ **Paco's Dream**[13] 3467 2-8-10 0 HarryBentley 7 6
(Harry Dunlop) *s.i.s: outpcd* **11/1**[3]
0 **10** 5 **Henrietta Dancer**[9] 3584 2-8-6 0 DavidProbert 9
(Malcolm Saunders) *chsd ldr to 1/2-way: sn rdn: wknd 2f out* **50/1**
0 **11** 9 **Warapito**[16] 3358 2-8-4 0 PaulMcGiff(7) 12
(Richard Guest) *s.i.s: sn pushed along into mid-div: rdn: hung lft and wknd over 2f out: eased* **100/1**
**12** 6 **Amadeus Dream (IRE)** 2-8-11 0 SteveDrowne 6
(Milton Bradley) *dwlt and hmpd s: outpcd* **50/1**

1m 13.44s (1.64) **Going Correction** +0.20s/f (Good) **12** Ran SP% **117.9**
Speed ratings (Par 94): **97,96,86,85,83 83,76,69,66,59 47,39**
CSF £30.40 TOTE £1.60: £1.10, £9.40, £5.90; EX 38.30 Trifecta £678.80.
**Owner** R A Mills **Bred** Grange Stud **Trained** Headley, Surrey

**FOCUS**
Little strength in depth in an ordinary maiden where the first two home showed fair form. The gallop was only fair and the first two pulled clear in the closing stages.

## 3935 MIDSHIRE BUSINESS SYSTEMS - OFFICE TECHNOLOGY H'CAP 6f
**3:10** (3:11) (Class 5) (0-70,71) 3-Y-O+ **£2,587** (£770; £384; £192) **Stalls** Low

Form RPR
-314 **1** **Spiraea**[18] 3305 4-9-9 **67** GrahamLee 5 75
(Mark Rimell) *trckd ldrs: shkn up over 1f out: r.o to ld nr fin* **5/1**[3]
2036 **2** hd **Rigolleto (IRE)**[14] 3422 6-9-7 **70** LouisSteward(5) 2 77
(Anabel K Murphy) *w ldr tl led 1/2-way: rdn over 1f out: hdd nr fin* **5/1**[3]
3206 **3** ¾ **Borough Boy (IRE)**[2] 3854 4-8-11 **55** (v) DaleSwift 4 60
(Derek Shaw) *plld hrd: led to 1/2-way: rdn and ev ch ins fnl f: styd on* **6/1**
60-0 **4** ¾ **Orient Sky**[96] 1192 3-8-7 **57** (p) JohnFahy 7 58
(Paul Midgley) *hld up: hdwy over 2f out: rdn and hung lft ins fnl f: no ex towards fin* **10/1**
-563 **5** 1 ¼ **Kiss From A Rose**[23] 3124 3-8-7 **57** ChrisCatlin 8 54
(Rae Guest) *chsd ldrs: shkn up and hung lft over 1f out: styd on same pce ins fnl f* **3/1**[1]
-300 **6** 6 **Dream Catcher (FR)**[24] 3088 6-9-9 **67** FergusSweeney 11 46
(Henry Candy) *w ldrs tl rdn over 2f out: wknd over 1f out* **9/2**[2]
0626 **7** nk **High On The Hog (IRE)**[17] 3328 6-8-2 **51** oh6 NoelGarbutt(5) 10 29
(Mark Brisbourne) *s.i.s: hld up: racd keenly: rdn over 2f out: n.d* **25/1**
00-5 **8** 1 **Gracie's Games**[32] 2831 8-8-7 **51** oh6 (b) LiamJones 9 26
(John Spearing) *sn pushed along in rr: rdn over 1f out: wknd fnl f* **33/1**
2240 **9** ½ **New Decade**[20] 3213 5-9-4 **65** (t) MatthewLawson(3) 3 38
(Milton Bradley) *s.i.s: hdwy over 2f out: rdn and wknd over 1f out* **16/1**
040- **10** ¾ **Chellalla**[233] 7861 5-9-6 **64** StevieDonohoe 6 35
(Ian Williams) *hld up: rdn over 2f out: wknd over 1f out* **16/1**

1m 13.43s (1.63) **Going Correction** +0.20s/f (Good)
**WFA** 3 from 4yo+ 6lb **10** Ran SP% **118.4**
Speed ratings (Par 103): **97,96,95,94,93 85,84,83,82,81**
CSF £30.79 CT £138.19 TOTE £6.90: £2.00, £1.70, £2.10; EX 31.60 Trifecta £147.10.
**Owner** Mark Rimell **Bred** Coln Valley Stud **Trained** Leafield, Oxon

**FOCUS**
A modest handicap in which the gallop was an ordinary one for a sprint and those up with the pace were favoured. The first five finished clear and the winner is accorded a small personal best.

## 3936 WIGLEY GROUP H'CAP (BOBIS RACE) (JOCKEY CLUB GRASSROOTS FLAT SPRINT SERIES QUALIFIER) 6f
**3:45** (3:45) (Class 4) (0-80,80) 3-Y-O **£6,469** (£1,925; £962; £481) **Stalls** Low

Form RPR
-000 **1** **Dancealot**[23] 3117 3-8-10 **74** DannyBrock(5) 2 83
(Clive Brittain) *chsd ldr tl led over 2f out: rdn and hung rt over 1f out: r.o wl* **12/1**
3143 **2** 2 ½ **Saakhen (IRE)**[9] 3565 3-9-7 **80** (t) GrahamLee 11 81
(Richard Fahey) *a.p: rdn to chse wnr over 1f out: styd on same pce ins fnl f* **17/2**
3621 **3** 2 ¼ **Dont Have It Then**[14] 3426 3-9-2 **75** ChrisCatlin 9 69+
(Willie Musson) *hld up: hdwy 2f out: rdn over 1f out: styd on same pce ins fnl f* **5/1**[3]
-042 **4** 6 **Faure Island**[14] 3426 3-8-10 **69** FergusSweeney 1 44
(Henry Candy) *led over 3f: sn rdn: wknd fnl f* **4/1**[1]
0223 **5** 1 ¼ **Bonjour Steve**[15] 3380 3-8-3 **62** (p) DavidProbert 7 33
(Richard Price) *hld up: hdwy over 2f out: wknd over 1f out* **9/2**[2]
1315 **6** 2 **First Experience**[78] 1543 3-8-13 **72** SaleemGolam 10 36
(Rae Guest) *s.i.s: hld up: effrt over 1f out: sn wknd* **28/1**
-232 **7** 1 ¼ **Three Cliffs**[35] 2717 3-8-13 **75** RossAtkinson(3) 4 35
(Roger Varian) *s.i.s: hld up: rdn and hung rt over 1f out: n.d* **6/1**
-215 **8** 4 **A Legacy Of Love (IRE)**[19] 3280 3-9-3 **76** TedDurcan 3 23
(Amanda Perrett) *chsd ldrs: rdn over 2f out: wknd over 1f out* **12/1**
0-30 **9** ½ **Biography**[13] 3480 3-9-7 **80** KieranO'Neill 8 26
(Richard Hannon) *prom: rdn over 2f out: wknd over 1f out* **7/1**
-106 **10** 3 **Ashkari (IRE)**[39] 2611 3-9-5 **78** (p) SteveDrowne 5 14
(Clive Cox) *chsd ldrs: rdn over 2f out: wknd over 1f out: eased* **12/1**

1m 12.56s (0.76) **Going Correction** +0.20s/f (Good) **10** Ran SP% **118.7**
Speed ratings (Par 102): **102,98,95,87,86 83,81,76,75,71**
CSF £111.67 CT £598.43 TOTE £16.90: £5.50, £3.30, £1.80; EX 120.20 Trifecta £492.80.
**Owner** Saeed Manana **Bred** Mr & Mrs G Middlebrook **Trained** Newmarket, Suffolk

**FOCUS**
A fair handicap in which the gallop was no more than ordinary and another race where it paid to race up with the pace. The first three finished clear and it was the fastest of the C&D times. The winner is rated back to her 2yo level.

## 3937 RICOH - IMAGINE CHANGE - USE MIDSHIRE NURSERY H'CAP 5f
**4:20** (4:22) (Class 6) 2-Y-O **£1,940** (£577; £288; £144) **Stalls** Low

Form RPR
040 **1** **Zebs Lad (IRE)**[28] 2944 2-8-12 **66** SteveDrowne 3 75
(Ronald Harris) *chsd ldr: rdn and edgd rt over 1f out: r.o to ld wl ins fnl f* **16/1**
524 **2** ¾ **Don Sigfredo (IRE)**[28] 2944 2-9-1 **69** (p) HayleyTurner 6 75
(Tom Dascombe) *led: rdn and hung rt over 1f out: hdd wl ins fnl f* **3/1**[1]
2514 **3** 7 **River Spirit**[20] 3211 2-9-1 **69** SamHitchcott 1 50
(Mick Channon) *hld up in tch: rdn 2f out: edgd rt over 1f out: wknd ins fnl f* **7/1**[3]
046 **4** 1 ¼ **Lady Zodiac (IRE)**[20] 3215 2-8-0 **54** oh1 JimmyQuinn 10 30
(Tim Pitt) *chsd ldrs: rdn 1/2-way: wknd fnl f* **10/1**
236 **5** 2 **Rita's Boy (IRE)**[22] 3148 2-9-5 **76** JoeyHaynes(3) 8 45
(K R Burke) *sn pushed along in rr: rdn and edgd rt over 1f out: nvr trbld ldrs* **3/1**[1]
504 **6** 1 ¼ **Foxtrot Knight**[23] 3119 2-9-0 **68** HarryBentley 2 33
(Olly Stevens) *hld up: rdn 1/2-way: wknd over 1f out* **7/2**[2]
0456 **7** 1 ¾ **Toytown (IRE)**[21] 3201 2-8-5 **62** ow2 CharlesBishop(3) 4 20
(Derek Shaw) *s.i.s: in rr: rdn and wknd over 1f out* **7/1**[3]
3404 **8** 3 **Penalty Scorer**[20] 3236 2-7-12 **57** (v[1]) NoelGarbutt(5) 7 5
(Richard Guest) *hld up: hdwy over 2f out: rdn and wknd over 1f out* **25/1**

1m 0.28s (0.68) **Going Correction** +0.20s/f (Good) **8** Ran SP% **116.0**
Speed ratings (Par 92): **102,100,89,87,84 82,79,74**
CSF £64.80 CT £381.84 TOTE £19.30: £5.40, £1.30, £2.60; EX 81.70 Trifecta £778.00.
**Owner** Mrs Ruth M Serrell **Bred** Tally-Ho Stud **Trained** Earlswood, Monmouths

**FOCUS**
The first nursery of the season in which the handicap marks are estimated and for information purposes only. The gallop was an ordinary one and the first two, who pulled clear, showed fair form. Those held up were again at a disadvantage.

## 3938 RACINGUK.COM MEDIAN AUCTION MAIDEN STKS 5f
**4:55** (4:56) (Class 6) 3-5-Y-O **£1,940** (£577; £288; £144) **Stalls** Low

Form RPR
-360 **1** **Camanche Grey (IRE)**[60] 2015 3-9-5 59 GrahamLee 1 65
(Ben Haslam) *w ldr tl led 1/2-way: rdn out* **5/2**[2]
3 **2** ¾ **Eleusis**[73] 1634 3-9-0 0[1] TedDurcan 4 57
(Chris Wall) *hld up in tch: rdn to chse wnr over 1f out: ev ch ins fnl f: no ex towards fin* **10/11**[1]
604 **3** 3 ¼ **Lucky Clover**[37] 2667 3-9-0 48 DavidProbert 7 46
(Malcolm Saunders) *s.i.s and wnt rt s: sn chsng ldrs: rdn over 1f out: styd on same pce ins fnl f* **8/1**[3]
0020 **4** nk **Lexi's Beauty (IRE)**[23] 3099 4-9-5 48 LiamJones 5 47
(Brian Baugh) *w ldrs: rdn and ev ch over 1f out: no ex ins fnl f* **16/1**
0 **5** ¾ **Smile For Me (IRE)**[43] 2489 3-9-0 0 SamHitchcott 2 42
(Harry Dunlop) *s.i.s: sn pushed along in rr: hdwy over 1f out: no ex ins fnl f* **10/1**
4-00 **6** 7 **Brave Imp**[4] 3792 3-9-5 62 (b[1]) PhillipMakin 6 22
(Kevin Ryan) *unruly in stalls: sn led: hdd 1/2-way: sn rdn: wknd fnl f* **12/1**
00-0 **7** 3 ½ **Hares Grove (IRE)**[6] 3695 5-9-10 0 SaleemGolam 3 11
(Richard Price) *sn pushed along towards rr: rdn and wknd over 1f out* **50/1**

1m 0.86s (1.26) **Going Correction** +0.20s/f (Good)
**WFA** 3 from 4yo+ 5lb **7** Ran SP% **116.7**
Speed ratings (Par 101): **97,95,92,91,90 79,73**
CSF £5.31 TOTE £4.80: £1.40, £1.50; EX 7.50 Trifecta £34.70.
**Owner** L Ashmore **Bred** Peter & Elizabeth Jones **Trained** Middleham Moor, N Yorks

**FOCUS**
A weak and most uncompetitive maiden in which the two market leaders pulled clear. The gallop was reasonable. The winner is rated to his AW best.

## 3939 NASMYTH 10TH ANNIVERSARY H'CAP 5f
**5:25** (5:26) (Class 5) (0-70,70) 3-Y-O+ **£2,587** (£770; £384; £192) **Stalls** Low

Form RPR
6-10 **1** **Beach Rhythm (USA)**[26] 3033 7-8-13 **64** (v) PatMillman(7) 6 75
(Jim Allen) *w ldr: led 4f out: clr 3f out: rdn over 1f out: jst hld on* **11/2**[2]
-055 **2** hd **Alpha Delta Whisky**[26] 3033 6-9-3 **66** (v) LouisSteward(5) 10 76
(John Gallagher) *a.p: chsd wnr 2f out: rdn and ev ch ins fnl f: r.o* **6/1**[3]
1242 **3** 2 ¼ **Whipphound**[28] 2945 6-9-12 **70** DaleSwift 7 72+
(Mark Brisbourne) *s.s: hdwy over 1f out: r.o: nt trble ldrs* **11/4**[1]
600 **4** ¾ **Studfarmer**[26] 3035 4-8-2 **51** oh6 (p) NoelGarbutt(5) 1 50
(John Panvert) *sn pushed along in rr: r.o ins fnl f: nvr nrr* **33/1**
3-00 **5** 1 ½ **Little Briar Rose**[33] 2802 3-8-5 **54** LiamJones 8 46
(John Spearing) *sn pushed along towards rr: rdn over 1f out: r.o ins fnl f* **50/1**
1100 **6** ¾ **Louis Vee (IRE)**[11] 3520 6-8-10 **57** (t) DeclanBates(3) 4 48
(Roy Brotherton) *led 1f: chsd wnr tl rdn 2f out: no ex fnl f* **25/1**
6030 **7** 1 ¼ **Solemn**[10] 3561 9-9-7 **65** (v) DavidProbert 2 52
(Milton Bradley) *prom: rdn 1/2-way: hung lft and no ex fnl f* **8/1**
2506 **8** 10 **Smokethatthunders (IRE)**[20] 3216 4-9-10 **68** StevieDonohoe 5 19
(Tim Pitt) *sn pushed along in rr: wknd 1/2-way* **8/1**

1m 0.75s (1.15) **Going Correction** +0.20s/f (Good)
**WFA** 3 from 4yo+ 5lb **8** Ran SP% **87.3**
Speed ratings (Par 103): **98,97,94,92,90 89,87,71**
CSF £20.24 CT £39.99 TOTE £4.60: £1.40, £1.80, £1.20; EX 16.50 Trifecta £42.20.
**Owner** J P Allen **Bred** Christoph Amerian **Trained** Stoodleigh, Devon
■ Orient Class was withdrawn. Price at time of withdrawal 9-4f. Rule 4 applies to all bets - deduction 30p in the pound.

**FOCUS**
A modest handicap in which the market leader Orient Class was withdrawn after unseating his rider and bolting before the start. The gallop was soon sound. The winner backed up his Bath run.
T/Plt: £23.40 to a £1 stake. Pool: £56312.12 - 1751.21 winning tickets T/Qpdt: £11.00 to a £1 stake. Pool: £2700.74 - 181.20 winning tickets CR

3940 - 3944a (Foreign Racing) - See Raceform Interactive

# 3908 BEVERLEY (R-H)

Saturday, July 5

**OFFICIAL GOING: Good**

Wind: Moderate; against Weather: Cloudy with sunny periods

## 3945 AWARD-WINNING COACHMAN CARAVANS MAIDEN AUCTION STKS — 7f 100y

1:55 (1:56) (Class 6) 2-Y-O — £3,408 (£1,006; £503) Stalls Low

Form — RPR

2 **1** **Alans Pride (IRE)**[19] 3297 2-8-9 0 ConnorBeasley(3) 10 — 68
(Michael Dods) *towards rr: gd hdwy wl over 2f out: chsd ldrs over 1f out and sn rdn: drvn to chal ins fnl f: n.m.r and kpt on wl to ld nr fin* **3/1**[1]

00 **2** *hd* **Playboy Bay**[22] 3194 2-8-12 0 SamHitchcott 12 — 68
(Mick Channon) *bhd: green and pushed along 3f out: swtchd lft to outer and hdwy whn j. path and unbalanced over 1f out: sn rdn and str run to chal ins fnl f: ev ch whn edgd rt and no ex nr line* **14/1**

54 **3** *shd* **Grand Proposal**[9] 3606 2-8-10 0 ShaneGray(5) 6 — 70
(Kevin Ryan) *trckd ldrs: hdwy 2f out: rdn to chal over 1f out: drvn to ld ins fnl f: hdd and no ex nr fin* **7/1**[2]

0 **4** *3 ¾* **Lord Of Words (IRE)**[14] 3481 2-8-12 0 DaleSwift 4 — 58
(Brian Ellison) *chsd ldrs: hdwy 3f out: rdn along 2f out: drvn and kpt on same pce appr fnl f* **20/1**

33 **5** *1 ½* **Flatcapper (IRE)**[11] 3542 2-8-10 0 TonyHamilton 2 — 53+
(Richard Fahey) *led: rdn along wl over 1f out: drvn ent fnl f: hdd & wknd last 150yds* **3/1**[1]

0 **6** *2 ¾* **Yukos Flyer (IRE)**[11] 3542 2-8-4 0 GeorgeChaloner(3) 7 — 43
(Richard Fahey) *bhd: swtchd to outer 2f out: sn rdn and styd on appr fnl f: nvr nr ldrs* **16/1**

05 **7** *1 ¼* **Rutland Panther**[48] 2360 2-8-8 0 ow3 LukeLeadbitter(7) 3 — 49
(Declan Carroll) *chsd ldng pair: rdn along over 2f out: hld whn n.m.r wl over 1f out and kpt on one pce* **25/1**

**8** *2 ¼* **Brokopondo (IRE)**[27] 3038 2-8-5 0 JoeDoyle(7) 1 — 40
(Miss Evanna McCutcheon, Ire) *dwlt: sn in tch on inner: pushed along wl over 2f out: sn rdn and nvr nr ldrs* **3/1**[1]

00 **9** *hd* **Pencaitland**[14] 3481 2-8-4 0 NeilFarley(3) 5 — 35
(Noel Wilson) *a in rr* **100/1**

54 **10** *8* **Lucilla Aurelius (IRE)**[12] 3529 2-8-9 0 BarryMcHugh 11 — 18
(Tony Coyle) *cl up: rn wd bnd 4f out: rdn along wl over 2f out: sn wknd* **10/1**[3]

**11** *½* **Harps Of Bretagne** 2-8-1 0 NatashaEaton(5) 8 — 14
(Lisa Williamson) *a in rr: outpcd and bhd fr 1/2-way* **100/1**

5 **12** *2 ¼* **Regal Accolade**[16] 3403 2-8-10 0 JulieBurke(3) 9 — 16
(David O'Meara) *midfield: rdn along wl over 2f out: sn wknd* **20/1**

1m 36.14s (2.34) **Going Correction** +0.125s/f (Good) — 12 Ran SP% 124.5

Speed ratings (Par 92): **91,90,90,86,84 81,80,77,77,68 67,65**

CSF £52.87 TOTE £3.90: £1.70, £4.40, £2.50; EX 75.60 Trifecta £443.70.

**Owner** Alan Henderson & Alan Bolton **Bred** Roundhill Stud **Trained** Denton, Co Durham

**FOCUS**

Probably just a modest maiden, but the early pace was decent, so the result should be reliable.

## 3946 ELTHERINGTON STKS (H'CAP) — 7f 100y

2:30 (2:30) (Class 5) (0-70,73) 3-Y-O — £3,881 (£1,155; £577; £288) Stalls Low

Form — RPR

0-55 **1** **In Focus (IRE)**[22] 3187 3-8-9 58 DavidAllan 13 — 68
(Alan Swinbank) *sltly hmpd s: sn led and mde most: rdn along wl over 1f out: edgd lft ent fnl f: sn drvn and kpt on strly* **16/1**

5-11 **2** *2* **Jacbequick**[11] 3547 3-9-5 73 JacobButterfield(5) 11 — 78
(Ollie Pears) *trckd ldng pair: swtchd rt 2f out: rdn over 1f out: drvn to chse wnr ins fnl f: no imp towards fin* **9/2**[2]

0-33 **3** *1* **Ice Mayden**[17] 3362 3-8-3 55 ow1 ConnorBeasley(3) 3 — 57+
(Bryan Smart) *midfield on inner: swtchd lft and hdwy 2f out: sn rdn: styd on wl fnl f: nrst fin* **7/1**

6416 **4** *¾* **Seven Lucky Seven**[16] 3380 3-9-3 66 JackMitchell 6 — 66
(Nick Littmoden) *chsd wnr: rdn along and edgd lft over 2f out: drvn and hung lft to stands' rail ent fnl f: kpt on same pce* **7/1**

4541 **5** *2 ½* **Gratzie**[9] 3618 3-9-6 69 SamHitchcott 1 — 63
(Mick Channon) *t.k.h: chsd ldrs on inner: hdwy over 2f out: rdn and ev ch over 1f out: drvn and wknd ent fnl f* **8/1**

030- **6** *1 ½* **Strictly Glitz (IRE)**[277] 6914 3-7-13 55 JoeDoyle(7) 5 — 45
(John Quinn) *in tch: hdwy over 2f out: rdn along wl over 1f out: sn no imp* **28/1**

-413 **7** *½* **Sooqaan**[42] 2545 3-8-12 61 PJMcDonald 9 — 50+
(Mel Brittain) *towards rr tl styd on fnl 2f: nvr nr ldrs* **12/1**

-061 **8** *1 ½* **Adore**[9] 3614 3-9-5 68 PaulMulrennan 12 — 53
(Sir Michael Stoute) *trckd ldrs: hdwy over 2f out: rdn wl over 1f out: wknd appr fnl f* **4/1**[1]

5012 **9** *hd* **Kisanji**[15] 3430 3-9-3 69 CharlesBishop(3) 4 — 54
(Alan McCabe) *towards rr: sme hdwy into midfield 3f out: effrt on outer over 2f out: sn rdn and hung rt over 1f out: sn wknd* **11/2**[3]

3044 **10** *1 ½* **Marlismamma (FR)**[36] 2741 3-8-0 52 oh1 ow1 JulieBurke(3) 7 — 33
(David O'Meara) *towards rr: swtchd rt to inner and hdwy 2f out: sn rdn and n.d* **25/1**

1-00 **11** *shd* **L'Artiste (IRE)**[19] 3300 3-9-1 67 IanBrennan(3) 10 — 48
(John Quinn) *midfield: effrt and sme hdwy over 2f out: rdn wl over 1f out and sn btn* **16/1**

0550 **12** *2 ¼* **Elle West**[23] 3150 3-8-3 52 PaulQuinn 2 — 27
(Michael Easterby) *a in rr* **40/1**

3326 **13** *1 ¾* **Petergate**[17] 3362 3-8-10 59 (p) BarryMcHugh 14 — 30
(Brian Rothwell) *hld up: n.m.r on inner 3f out: hdwy on inner over 2f out: sn rdn and btn* **18/1**

1m 34.07s (0.27) **Going Correction** +0.125s/f (Good) — 13 Ran SP% 124.1

Speed ratings (Par 100): **103,100,99,98,95 94,93,91,91,89 89,87,85**

CSF £88.58 CT £589.80 TOTE £17.50: £3.80, £2.20, £3.20; EX 139.40 Trifecta £1179.10 Not won..

**Owner** G H Bell **Bred** Century Farms **Trained** Melsonby, N Yorks

**FOCUS**

A modest handicap in which those racing prominently did best. A 3lb best from the winner.

## 3947 BRITISH STALLION STUDS EBF LEISURE FURNISHINGS MAIDEN STKS — 5f

3:05 (3:07) (Class 5) 2-Y-O — £3,881 (£1,155; £577; £288) Stalls Low

Form — RPR

**1** **Fendale** 2-9-1 0 PaulMulrennan 2 — 83+
(Bryan Smart) *dwlt and towards rr: smooth hdwy on inner over 2f out: effrt and nt clr run over 1f out: squeezed through and qcknd to ld ins fnl f: sn hung lft and rdn clr* **7/2**[1]

34 **2** *5* **Ocean Sheridan (IRE)**[19] 3296 2-9-2 0 ConnorBeasley(3) 1 — 66
(Michael Dods) *trckd ldrs on inner: effrt wl over 1f out: rdn to ld briefly ent fnl f: sn hdd and kpt on same pce* **7/1**

3 **3** *nk* **Faraajh (IRE)**[18] 3324 2-9-0 0 DavidAllan 13 — 60
(James Tate) *chsd ldrs: effrt on outer 2f out: sn rdn and ev ch tl edgd rt ent fnl f and kpt on same pce* **4/1**[2]

4 **4** *2* **Black Pudding (IRE)**[10] 3569 2-9-5 0 PJMcDonald 3 — 58
(Ann Duffield) *in tch: effrt and n.m.r wl over 1f out: sn rdn and n.m.r again appr fnl f: kpt on* **5/1**[3]

04 **5** *hd* **Classic Flyer**[7] 3713 2-9-2 0 SamJames(3) 12 — 57
(David O'Meara) *prom: rdn along 2f out: drvn and one pce appr fnl f* **16/1**

0 **6** *2* **Cheeky Chapman**[32] 2866 2-9-2 0 GeorgeChaloner(3) 8 — 50
(Clive Mulhall) *in rr: rdn along 1/2-way: styd on on outer fr over 1f out: nrst fin* **33/1**

0 **7** *nk* **Maid In Rome (IRE)**[10] 3570 2-9-0 0 AndrewElliott 11 — 44
(Tim Easterby) *bhd: sme hdwy 2f out: sn swtchd rt to inner and rdn over 1f out: no imp* **33/1**

5240 **8** *¾* **Alderaan (IRE)**[8] 3648 2-9-0 0 BarryMcHugh 9 — 41
(Tony Coyle) *chsd ldrs: rdn along 2f out: sn wknd* **14/1**

**9** *3* **Wiseton (IRE)** 2-9-1 0 GrahamGibbons 4 — 31
(David Barron) *led: rdn along wl over 1f out: hdd & wknd ent fnl f* **16/1**

**10** *nse* **Edie White** 2-8-3 0 JoeDoyle(7) 6 — 26
(Lawrence Mullaney) *dwlt: sn outpcd and bhd* **66/1**

**11** *hd* **Lady Jade** 2-8-5 0 ShelleyBirkett(5) 7 — 25
(Nigel Tinkler) *a towards rr* **33/1**

322 **12** *1 ½* **Grosmont**[16] 3403 2-9-5 0 DaleSwift 5 — 29
(James Given) *prom: rdn along 1/2-way: sn wknd* **7/2**[1]

0 **13** *1* **Alfie Bond**[61] 2014 2-9-2 0 IanBrennan(3) 10 — 25
(Brian Rothwell) *uns rdr en route to post: a in rr* **33/1**

1m 5.11s (1.61) **Going Correction** +0.125s/f (Good) — 13 Ran SP% 125.3

Speed ratings (Par 94): **92,84,83,80,80 76,76,75,70,70 69,67,65**

CSF £28.93 TOTE £6.60: £2.30, £2.30, £1.20; EX 31.70 Trifecta £192.00.

**Owner** Ritchie Fiddes **Bred** Cheveley Park Stud Ltd **Trained** Hambleton, N Yorks

**FOCUS**

This didn't look a strong contest but the winner was impressive, and value for a bit extra.

## 3948 COACHMAN CARAVANS QUALITY H'CAP — 5f

3:40 (3:41) (Class 4) (0-85,83) 3-Y-O+ — £7,762 (£2,310; £1,154; £577) Stalls Low

Form — RPR

5204 **1** **Thatcherite (IRE)**[8] 3668 6-8-13 70 (t) BarryMcHugh 5 — 79+
(Tony Coyle) *hld up in rr: hdwy on inner whn nt clr run and hmpd over 1f out: swtchd lft and rdn ent fnl f: squeezed through last 100yds and fin strly to ld on line* **8/1**

1066 **2** *shd* **One Boy (IRE)**[14] 3484 3-9-0 79 ConnorBeasley(3) 4 — 86
(Michael Dods) *hld up: hdwy and nt clr run 1 1/2f out: rdn and squeezed through to chal ent fnl f: drvn to ld last 100yds: ct on line* **20/1**

0553 **3** *nk* **Hadaj**[10] 3571 5-9-4 82 (b) JoeDoyle(7) 8 — 90
(Ruth Carr) *trckd ldrs: hdwy 2f out: rdn to chal over 1f out: drvn and ev ch ins fnl f: no ex towards fin* **4/1**[2]

3-52 **4** *1* **Angelito**[21] 3213 5-9-6 77 DaleSwift 3 — 81
(Ed McMahon) *trckd ldrs: cl up 1/2-way: rdn over 1f out: disp ld and ev ch ent fnl f: sn drvn and one pce towards fin* **7/1**[3]

400 **5** *½* **Sleepy Blue Ocean**[23] 3138 8-9-4 75 (p) AndrewElliott 1 — 78
(John Balding) *slt ld: rdn along wl over 1f out: drvn ent fnl f: hdd & wknd last 100yds* **22/1**

0534 **6** *1* **Bondi Beach Boy**[10] 3571 5-9-3 77 GeorgeChaloner(3) 2 — 76+
(James Turner) *trckd ldrs on inner: effrt and nt clr run 1 1/2f out: rdn and kpt on ins fnl f* **11/4**[1]

0022 **7** *½* **Noodles Blue Boy**[9] 3612 8-8-9 71 (b[1]) JacobButterfield(5) 17 — 68
(Ollie Pears) *chsd ldrs: rdn along 1/2-way: chal on outer over 1f out: ev ch tl drvn ins fnl f and wknd fnl 100yds* **20/1**

1500 **8** *nse* **Lastchancelucas**[21] 3216 4-9-9 80 (b) TonyHamilton 7 — 77
(Declan Carroll) *towards rr: hdwy over 1f out: rdn to chse ldrs whn n.m.r and swtchd lft ins fnl f: kpt on: nrst fin* **25/1**

05-5 **9** *¾* **Bosham**[56] 2167 4-8-11 68 [1] GrahamGibbons 12 — 62
(Michael Easterby) *stmbld and almost uns rdr s: sn swtchd rt to inner: bhd: hdwy wl over 1f out: kpt on fnl f: nrst fin* **20/1**

3331 **10** *2 ¼* **Adam's Ale**[16] 3399 5-9-8 79 PaulMulrennan 13 — 65
(Paul Midgley) *wnt bdly lft s: a towards rr* **7/1**[3]

4000 **11** *¾* **Lost In Paris (IRE)**[60] 2056 8-8-5 69 LauraBarry(7) 9 — 52
(Tony Coyle) *a towards rr* **50/1**

-021 **12** *nk* **Mr Mo Jo**[9] 3611 6-8-6 68 (b) ShaneGray(5) 6 — 50
(Les Eyre) *cl up: rdn along wl over 1f out: drvn and wknd appr fnl f* **14/1**

2400 **12** *dht* **Rusty Rocket (IRE)**[36] 2732 5-9-11 82 RaulDaSilva 16 — 64
(Paul Green) *carried bdly lft s: racd wd: a in rr* **25/1**

2032 **14** *3 ¾* **Boxing Shadows**[10] 3571 4-8-10 67 DavidAllan 10 — 36
(Les Eyre) *chsd ldrs: rdn along 2f out: sn wknd* **11/1**

1m 4.83s (1.33) **Going Correction** +0.125s/f (Good)

**WFA** 3 from 4yo+ 5lb — 14 Ran SP% 126.1

Speed ratings (Par 105): **94,93,93,91,90 89,88,88,87,83 82,82,82,76**

CSF £164.59 CT £750.66 TOTE £11.00: £3.10, £8.70, £1.80; EX 206.40 Trifecta £1607.80.

**Owner** Brian Kerr **Bred** Taroka Equine Investments **Trained** Norton, N Yorks

**FOCUS**

A hotly contested handicap, which produced a stirring finish. The pace was strong but the overall time was slow compared with the maiden. A small personal best from the winner.

## 3949 C.G.I. H'CAP — 1m 100y

4:15 (4:16) (Class 5) (0-70,68) 3-Y-O+ — £3,881 (£1,155; £577; £288) Stalls Low

Form — RPR

04-2 **1** **World Record (IRE)**[18] 3339 4-9-8 65 IanBrennan(3) 5 — 74
(John Quinn) *trckd ldng pair: hdwy to chse ldr over 2f out: rdn to chal over 1f out: drvn ent fnl f: styd on to ld last 150yds* **4/1**[2]

4262 **2** *1* **Tukitinyasok (IRE)**[24] 3095 7-9-2 56 BarryMcHugh 1 — 63
(Clive Mulhall) *led: rdn along and jnd wl over 1f out: drvn ent fnl f: hdd and no ex last 150yds* **8/1**

0040 **3** 2¼ **Surround Sound**[11] 3547 4-9-8 **62**.............................. DavidAllan 10 64
(Tim Easterby) *hld up towards rr: hdwy on inner 2f out: swtchd lft over 1f out: rdn to chse ldng pair whn edgd lft ent fnl f: sn no imp* **3/1**[1]

-522 **4** 1 **Lil Sophella (IRE)**[21] 3242 5-9-4 **58**.............................. AndrewElliott 6 58
(Patrick Holmes) *hld up towards rr: hdwy over 2f out: rdn to chse ldrs over 1f out: drvn and sltly hmpd jst ins fnl f: sn no imp* **7/1**

0-00 **5** 2¼ **The Blue Banana (IRE)**[24] 3094 5-9-4 **61**..........(b) ConnorBeasley(3) 3 55
(Edwin Tuer) *hld up in rr: hdwy over 2f out: sn rdn and kpt on one pce appr fnl f* **12/1**

-030 **6** 2 **Day Of The Eagle (IRE)**[42] 2549 8-10-0 **68**.............. GrahamGibbons 8 58
(Michael Easterby) *trckd ldrs: rdn along 2f out: hld whn sltly hmpd ent fnl f: sn one pce* **12/1**

-002 **7** 1 **Last Destination (IRE)**[11] 3547 6-8-12 **52**.............. PaulMulrennan 4 39
(Nigel Tinkler) *in tch: hdwy to chse ldrs 2f out and sn rdn: wknd over 1f out* **8/1**

0400 **8** 6 **Seldom (IRE)**[23] 3155 8-9-0 **54**.............................. PJMcDonald 9 28
(Mel Brittain) *chsd ldrs: rdn along over 2f out: sn wknd* **16/1**

0504 **9** 12 **Mysterial**[11] 3547 4-9-5 **66**.............................. JoeDoyle(7) 2 12
(Ruth Carr) *t.k.h: chsd ldr: hung lft and rn wd bnd 4f out: rdn along over 2f out: wknd wl over 1f out: sn bhd and eased* **5/1**[3]

1m 47.16s (-0.44) **Going Correction** +0.125s/f (Good) **9** Ran SP% **117.7**
Speed ratings (Par 103): **107,106,103,102,100 98,97,91,79**
CSF £36.69 CT £110.54 TOTE £4.30: £2.10, £3.00, £1.30; EX 45.30 Trifecta £155.70.
**Owner** Carl Hinchy **Bred** Roy W Tector **Trained** Settrington, N Yorks

**FOCUS**
The early gallop didn't seem particularly strong and it paid to be prominent. A step up from the winner.

## 3950 POWERPART FILLIES' H'CAP — 1m 1f 207y
**4:50** (4:51) (Class 5) (0-70,70) 3-Y-O — **£3,234** (£962; £481; £240) **Stalls** Low

Form — RPR

-241 **1** **Miss Lucy Jane**[11] 3545 3-9-4 **70**.............................. GeorgeChaloner(3) 6 77+
(Richard Fahey) *hld up towards rr: swtchd lft to outer and hdwy 2f out: rdn over 1f out: styd on strly fnl f to ld nr fin* **6/4**[1]

561 **2** ½ **Queens Park (FR)**[19] 3302 3-9-4 **67**.............................. PJMcDonald 2 73
(John Davies) *trckd ldrs: hdwy over 2f out: chsd ldr over 1f out: drvn to chal ent fnl f: sn led: hdd and no ex towards fin* **5/1**[2]

2600 **3** 1 **Keep To The Beat**[16] 3380 3-8-2 **56**..........(p) ShaneGray(5) 1 60
(Kevin Ryan) *sn led: rdn along over 2f out: jnd and drvn over 1f out: hdd ins fnl f: kpt on same pce towards fin* **12/1**

4-00 **4** 1¾ **Acquaint (IRE)**[40] 2616 3-7-13 **55**.............................. JoeDoyle(7) 5 55
(John Wainwright) *midfield: hdwy over 2f out: rdn to chse ldrs over 1f out: swtchd rt and drvn ent fnl f: no imp* **18/1**

-263 **5** 1 **Coin Broker (IRE)**[12] 3534 3-8-12 **64**.............................. SamJames(3) 13 62
(David O'Meara) *trckd ldrs: hdwy wl over 2f out: rdn wl over 1f out: drvn and no imp appr fnl f* **8/1**

-600 **6** hd **Ofelia (IRE)**[12] 3534 3-8-2 **51** oh5.............................. RaulDaSilva 4 49
(Brian Ellison) *hld up in rr: hdwy over 2f out: swtchd lft to wd outside wl over 1f out: sn rdn and styd on fnl f: nrst fin* **25/1**

03-0 **7** 1 **Bertha Burnett (IRE)**[49] 2355 3-8-2 **54** ow2.............. IanBrennan(3) 3 50
(Brian Rothwell) *hld up towards rr: hdwy over 2f out: sn rdn along: kpt on fnl f: nrst fin* **20/1**

0-05 **8** hd **Heartstrings**[20] 3268 3-9-5 **68**.............................. SamHitchcott 12 64
(Mick Channon) *hld up in tch: hdwy over 2f out: rdn to chse ldrs wl over 1f out: sn edgd rt and btn* **14/1**

6136 **9** 1¾ **Bajan Rebel**[19] 3300 3-8-10 **59**.............................. GrahamGibbons 11 51
(Michael Easterby) *a towards rr* **7/1**[3]

-006 **10** 3 **Mystical Maze**[18] 3326 3-8-2 **51** oh6.............................. PaulQuinn 8 38
(Mark Brisbourne) *a towards rr* **25/1**

-600 **11** 1½ **Sarlat**[18] 3326 3-8-0 **54** oh6 ow3.............................. NatashaEaton(5) 10 38
(Mark Brisbourne) *chsd ldng pair: pushed along 3f out: rdn over 2f out: sn wknd* **50/1**

4406 **12** 4 **Barbara Elizabeth**[13] 3498 3-8-6 **55**.............................. BarryMcHugh 7 31
(Tony Coyle) *cl up: rdn along over 2f out: drvn wl over 1f out: sn wknd* **33/1**

3466 **13** 5 **Speedbird One**[11] 3545 3-8-11 **60**.............................. PaulMulrennan 9 27
(James Given) *t.k.h: midfield: hdwy on outer 1/2-way: chsd ldrs over 3f out: rdn along over 2f out: sn wknd* **16/1**

4200 **14** 7 **Hello Sweetness**[24] 3098 3-7-13 **51** oh5.............................. JulieBurke(3) 14 4
(Jason Ward) *a towards rr: rdn along 3f out: sn outpcd and bhd* **25/1**

2m 7.8s (0.80) **Going Correction** +0.125s/f (Good) **14** Ran SP% **121.7**
Speed ratings (Par 97): **101,100,99,98,97 97,96,96,95,92 91,88,84,78**
CSF £7.56 CT £220.55 TOTE £2.30: £1.60, £1.80, £10.80; EX 9.70 Trifecta £626.90.
**Owner** R J Bown **Bred** Miss J Chaplin **Trained** Musley Bank, N Yorks
■ Stewards' Enquiry : George Chaloner two-day ban: used whip above permitted level (Jul 19-20)

**FOCUS**
A modest contest for fillies run at just a fair gallop. The winner shaped a bit better than the bare form.

## 3951 THETFORD MAIDEN STKS — 5f
**5:25** (5:27) (Class 5) 3-Y-O+ — **£3,234** (£962; £481; £240) **Stalls** Low

Form — RPR

333 **1** **Al Senad**[23] 3156 3-9-5 74.............................. PaulMulrennan 6 82
(Peter Chapple-Hyam) *qckly away: mde most: rdn clr over 1f out: styd on strly* **13/8**[1]

54 **2** 8 **Linda's Sister**[14] 3486 4-9-2 0.............................. IanBrennan(3) 7 50
(John Quinn) *hld up: hdwy 1/2-way: swtchd lft and rdn wl over 1f out: styd on fnl f: no ch w wnr* **7/1**

262 **3** 1¼ **Royal Connoisseur (IRE)**[7] 3700 3-9-5 74.............................. TonyHamilton 5 49
(Richard Fahey) *trckd ldrs: hdwy 2f out: sn chsng wnr: rdn over 1f out and kpt on same pce* **7/4**[2]

50 **4** 4½ **Patron Of Explores (USA)**[36] 2737 3-9-5 0.............................. AndrewElliott 8 33
(Patrick Holmes) *midfield: pushed along and sltly outpcd 1/2-way: rdn 2f out: plugged on appr fnl f: nvr a factor* **50/1**

3 **5** 2¼ **Blaze It**[12] 3531 3-9-0 0.............................. PJMcDonald 2 19
(Brian Ellison) *sltly hmpd s: towards rr tl sme late hdwy* **10/1**

0-00 **6** 2¾ **Kalani's Diamond**[47] 2389 4-9-2 32..........(t) GeorgeChaloner(3) 4 12
(Bryan Smart) *chsd ldrs: rdn along wl over 1f out: wknd appr fnl f* **50/1**

3 **7** 1 **Sorry Saeed**[131] 731 3-9-0 0.............................. DavidAllan 11 6
(James Tate) *qckly away and cl up: rdn along over 2f out: wknd wl over 1f out* **9/2**[3]

00 **8** shd **Kaytom**[14] 3486 3-9-0 0.............................. BarryMcHugh 3 6
(John Wainwright) *wnt rt s: a in rr* **25/1**

0-4 **9** 6 **Parisian Melody**[12] 3531 3-8-7 0.............................. RobertDodsworth(7) 10
(Mel Brittain) *dwlt: a in rr* **40/1**

0-05 **10** 7 **Poco Piccolo**[68] 1801 3-9-5 40..........(b[1]) SamHitchcott 1
(Deborah Sanderson) *a in rr* **33/1**

1m 3.76s (0.26) **Going Correction** +0.125s/f (Good)
**WFA** 3 from 4yo 5lb **10** Ran SP% **127.4**
Speed ratings (Par 103): **102,89,87,80,76 72,70,70,60,59**
CSF £14.96 TOTE £3.30: £1.10, £2.50, £1.10; EX 19.20 Trifecta £38.20.
**Owner** Ziad A Galadari **Bred** Galadari Sons Stud Company Limited **Trained** Newmarket, Suffolk

**FOCUS**
Only one horse mattered from some way out. The winner was quite impressive in a relatively fast time but the form of the beaten horses is poor.
T/Plt: £149.40 to a £1 stake. Pool: £79,003.24 - 386.01 winning units T/Qpdt: £11.70 to a £1 stake. Pool: £5,590.41 - 353.10 winning units JR

# 3599 CARLISLE (R-H)
### Saturday, July 5

**OFFICIAL GOING: Good to firm (7.7)**
Wind: Fresh; half against Weather: Sunny; hot

## 3952 ATKINS WHITEHAVEN REWARDING ITS OUTSTANDING PERFORMERS APPRENTICE H'CAP — 5f 193y
**5:40** (5:40) (Class 5) (0-75,76) 4-Y-O+ — **£2,587** (£770; £384; £192) **Stalls** Low

Form — RPR

-652 **1** **Gran Canaria Queen**[8] 3659 5-9-3 **71**.............. RachelRichardson(5) 7 86
(Tim Easterby) *chsd clr ldr: shkn up and hdwy 2f out: led ins fnl f: pushed clr* **11/2**[3]

0-04 **2** 4½ **Jamesbo's Girl**[16] 3384 4-8-13 **67**.............................. PaulMcGiff(5) 4 68
(David Barron) *bhd and sn pushed along: hdwy on wd outside 1/2-way: chsd (clr) wnr ins fnl f: kpt on: no imp* **5/1**[2]

5034 **3** ½ **Running Reef (IRE)**[21] 3242 5-8-8 **60**.............................. JordanNason(3) 5 59
(Tracy Waggott) *bhd and sn pushed along: hdwy over 1f out: kpt on ins fnl f: no imp* **9/1**

021 **4** ¾ **Al Khan (IRE)**[9] 3599 5-9-13 **76**..........(p) KevinStott 3 73
(Ollie Pears) *prom: effrt and drvn over 2f out: kpt on same pce fnl f* **7/4**[1]

6606 **5** 1 **Majestic Manannan (IRE)**[9] 3611 5-8-10 **64**.............. AnnaHesketh(5) 2 57
(David Nicholls) *led and sn wl clr: shkn up and hdd ins fnl f: sn btn* **8/1**

5144 **6** 1¼ **Go Go Green (IRE)**[21] 3239 8-8-7 **73**.............................. SammyJoBell(3) 9 62
(Jim Goldie) *in tch: rdn over 2f out: one pce fr over 1f out* **6/1**

3400 **7** nk **New Lease Of Life**[22] 3191 5-8-4 **56** oh2.............................. JackGarritty(3) 8 44
(Jim Goldie) *in tch: outpcd and edgd rt 2f out: n.d after* **14/1**

440U **8** hd **Iceblast**[12] 3530 6-8-4 **58**.............................. DanielleMooney(5) 1 46
(Michael Easterby) *slowly away: bhd and outpcd: nvr rchd ldrs* **20/1**

1m 13.4s (-0.30) **Going Correction** +0.05s/f (Good) **8** Ran SP% **115.2**
Speed ratings (Par 103): **104,98,97,96,95 93,92,92**
CSF £33.30 CT £243.73 TOTE £5.30: £1.60, £1.70, £3.30; EX 26.60 Trifecta £160.60.
**Owner** M Gillies **Bred** H Moszkowicz And Whitsbury Manor Stud **Trained** Great Habton, N Yorks

**FOCUS**
5mm of rain overnight and sustained watering ensured good to firm ground on a sunny and breezy evening. The early pace set by Majestic Manannan was largely ignored by his rivals,

## 3953 ANDERSONS (DENTON HOLME) SAWMILLS CARLISLE MAIDEN STKS — 1m 1f 61y
**6:10** (6:11) (Class 5) 3-Y-O+ — **£2,587** (£770; £384; £192) **Stalls** Low

Form — RPR

4-23 **1** **Sea The Bloom**[22] 3174 3-8-13 75.............................. GrahamLee 3 71+
(Sir Michael Stoute) *mde all at ordinary gallop: rdn over 2f out: drew clr fnl f: comf* **4/9**[1]

5-6 **2** 4½ **Mountain Kingdom (IRE)**[12] 3537 3-9-4 0.............................. LukeMorris 6 63
(Sir Mark Prescott Bt) *hld up in tch: pushed along over 3f out: hdwy 2f out: chsd (clr) wnr last 100yds: no imp* **8/1**

00 **3** 1¼ **King's Prospect**[46] 2422 3-9-1 0.............................. ConnorBeasley(3) 1 60?
(Tracy Waggott) *prom: effrt and hdwy over 2f out: chsd wnr over 1f out to last 100yds: one pce* **80/1**

24/2 **4** 4 **Nasijah**[162] 323 4-9-9 75.............................. JamesSullivan 2 48
(James Tate) *t.k.h: trckd wnr: effrt and rdn over 2f out: lost 2nd over 1f out: sn wknd* **4/1**[2]

**5** 2¼ **Chilly Miss** 5-9-9 0.............................. TomEaves 5 43
(Malcolm Jefferson) *dwlt: hld up: rdn and outpcd over 3f out: n.d after* **15/2**[3]

4 **6** 1¾ **Hatton Springs (IRE)**[24] 3103 3-8-8 0.............................. GarryWhillans(5) 7 38
(Stuart Coltherd) *chsd ldrs: rdn and hung lft over 2f out: wknd over 1f out* **40/1**

1m 58.25s (0.65) **Going Correction** +0.05s/f (Good)
**WFA** 3 from 4yo+ 10lb **6** Ran SP% **115.8**
Speed ratings (Par 103): **99,95,93,90,88 86**
CSF £5.43 TOTE £1.20: £1.10, £3.30; EX 4.50 Trifecta £62.10.
**Owner** Cheveley Park Stud **Bred** Cheveley Park Stud Ltd **Trained** Newmarket, Suffolk

## 3954 CLEANEVENT GROUP H'CAP — 5f
**6:40** (6:41) (Class 5) (0-70,68) 3-Y-O+ — **£2,587** (£770; £384; £192) **Stalls** Low

Form — RPR

0023 **1** **Salvatore Fury (IRE)**[9] 3611 4-9-10 **66**..........(p) GrahamLee 7 75
(Keith Dalgleish) *in tch: shkn up over 1f out: coaxed along to ld ins fnl f: sn rdn and edgd rt: kpt on* **85/40**[1]

3060 **2** 1½ **Jumbo Steps (IRE)**[8] 3668 7-9-9 **68**.............................. GaryBartley(3) 12 72
(Jim Goldie) *hld up in tch: effrt and drvn wl over 1f out: kpt on fnl f to take 2nd cl home: nt rch wnr* **7/2**[2]

0005 **3** hd **Sunny Side Up (IRE)**[9] 3611 5-9-2 **63**..........(t) GemmaTutty(5) 6 66
(Karen Tutty) *dwlt: bhd: hdwy on outside 2f out: rdn and kpt on ins fnl f: nrst fin* **7/1**

0663 **4** ¾ **Bosun Breese**[16] 3395 9-9-12 **68**.............................. PhillipMakin 8 68
(Paul Midgley) *led: rdn and edgd lft over 1f out: kpt on ins fnl f* **12/1**

-656 **5** shd **Ingenti**[4] 3831 6-9-4 **65**.............................. KevinStott(5) 4 65
(Christopher Wilson) *pressed ldr: rdn to ld over 1f out: hdd ins fnl f: no ex and lost three pls nr fin* **5/1**[3]

00-0 **6** ¾ **Baby Queen (IRE)**[21] 3222 8-9-5 **64**.............................. NeilFarley(3) 11 61
(Brian Baugh) *led tl rdn and hdd over 1f out: kpt on same pce ins fnl f* **25/1**

5235 **7** nk **Windforpower (IRE)**[18] 3338 4-9-6 **62**..........(p) PaulPickard 1 58
(Tracy Waggott) *hld up bhd ldng gp: rdn over 1f out: no imp whn short of room cl home* **11/2**

1-00 **8** 2 **Fol Hollow (IRE)**24 3099 9-8-10 **57**........................ GarryWhillans(5) 2 46
(Stuart Coltherd) *t.k.h: prom tl rdn and wknd over 1f out* **33/1**

1m 1.45s (0.65) **Going Correction** +0.05s/f (Good) **8** Ran SP% **113.3**
Speed ratings (Par 103): **96,93,93,92,91 90,90,87**
CSF £9.37 CT £42.53 TOTE £2.60: £1.70, £1.10, £2.30; EX 8.40 Trifecta £62.00.
**Owner** Prestige Thoroughbred Racing **Bred** Ken Harris & Dr Brid Corkery **Trained** Carluke, S Lanarks

**FOCUS**
Still a tight-looking race for the grade despite the four absentees, and reasonably straightforward form.

## 3955 CARLISLE RACECOURSE H'CAP 7f 200y

**7:10** (7:11) (Class 4) (0-85,82) 3-Y-0+ **£5,822** (£1,732; £865; £432) **Stalls** Low

Form RPR

5000 **1** **Talent Scout (IRE)**10 3573 8-9-3 **77**........................(p) GemmaTutty(5) 2 88
(Karen Tutty) *mde all: rdn wl over 1f out: kpt on gamely fnl f: all out* **15/2**

6016 **2** *nse* **Kingscroft (IRE)**7 3703 6-9-2 **76**........................(b) JacobButterfield(5) 3 86
(Michael Herrington) *t.k.h: pressed wnr: drvn along wl over 1f out: kpt on wl last 100yds: jst hld* **7/1**

-213 **3** 2 1/4 **George Rooke (IRE)**10 3572 4-9-12 **81**........................(p) TomEaves 8 86
(Keith Dalgleish) *hld up in tch: stdy hdwy over 2f out: effrt and disputing 2nd whn edgd lft appr fnl f: edgd rt and no ex last 100yds* **5/2**1

3640 **4** 1/2 **Toto Skyllachy**10 3573 9-9-13 **82**........................ DanielTudhope 4 86
(David O'Meara) *hld up: effrt and swtchd lft wl over 1f out: kpt on ins fnl f: nvr able to chal* **11/1**

1031 **5** 3/4 **Another For Joe**10 3572 6-9-11 **80**........................ GrahamLee 5 82
(Jim Goldie) *dwlt: sn prom: rdn along over 2f out: kpt on ins fnl f: no imp* **3/1**2

6220 **6** 3/4 **Al Muheer (IRE)**10 3572 9-9-8 **77**........................(e1) JamesSullivan 9 77
(Ruth Carr) *hld up: hdwy over 2f out: rdn and hung rt over 1f out: sn outpcd* **8/1**

0034 **7** 7 **Party Royal**10 3573 4-9-10 **79**........................ PhillipMakin 1 63
(Mark Johnston) *chsd ldrs: drvn and outpcd over 2f out: btn over 1f out* **13/2**3

2404 **8** 14 **Llewellyn**21 3227 6-8-13 **71**........................ NeilFarley(3) 10 23
(Declan Carroll) *bhd: struggling over 2f out: sn btn: t.o* **18/1**

1m 38.84s (-1.16) **Going Correction** +0.05s/f (Good)
**WFA** 3 from 4yo+ 9lb **8** Ran SP% **115.9**
Speed ratings (Par 105): **107,106,104,104,103 102,95,81**
CSF £59.21 CT £170.33 TOTE £11.90: £3.00, £2.50, £1.80; EX 54.70 Trifecta £340.30.
**Owner** Thoroughbred Homes Ltd **Bred** Johnston King **Trained** Osmotherley, N Yorks

**FOCUS**
No fewer than six of the eight to stand their ground had last run at the Carlisle Bell fixture ten days previously, three in the Bell itself and three in its consolation race (both C&D).

## 3956 INTERACTIVE FILLIES' H'CAP 6f 192y

**7:40** (7:40) (Class 5) (0-75,74) 3-Y-0+ **£2,587** (£770; £384; £192) **Stalls** Low

Form RPR

-545 **1** **Sandra's Diamond (IRE)**14 3460 3-9-6 74........................ GrahamLee 4 79
(Keith Dalgleish) *t.k.h: led: rdn and hdd over 1f out: rallied to ld ins fnl f: kpt on wl u.p* **7/2**2

-004 **2** 3/4 **Les Gar Gan (IRE)**8 3650 3-9-0 68........................(b) TomEaves 6 71
(Keith Dalgleish) *t.k.h: in tch: hdwy to chal over 1f out to ins fnl f: kpt on: no ex nr fin* **4/1**3

-020 **3** 1 **Gladsome**10 3575 6-8-6 55........................ ConnorBeasley(3) 8 58
(Michael Herrington) *t.k.h: cl up: rdn to ld over 1f out: hdd ins fnl f: kpt on same pce towards fin* **8/1**

3-15 **4** 1 1/4 **Ixelles Diamond (IRE)**46 2433 3-9-1 69........................ DavidNolan 1 66
(Richard Fahey) *trckd ldrs: drvn and ev ch over 1f out: kpt on same pce ins fnl f* **3/1**1

0022 **5** 1 3/4 **Outbacker (IRE)**10 3581 3-9-1 69........................(b1) JoeFanning 5 62
(Mark Johnston) *awkward s: t.k.h in rr: stdy hdwy whn n.m.r and swtchd lft 2f out: sn rdn: outpcd fnl f* **4/1**3

2000 **6** *hd* **See Clearly**12 3530 5-8-9 55........................(p) JamesSullivan 2 50
(Tim Easterby) *hld up in tch: effrt and rdn over 2f out: no ex fr over 1f out* **6/1**

1m 27.22s (0.12) **Going Correction** +0.05s/f (Good)
**WFA** 3 from 5yo+ 8lb **6** Ran SP% **112.6**
Speed ratings (Par 100): **101,100,99,97,95 95**
CSF £17.78 CT £101.57 TOTE £4.30: £2.30, £2.40; EX 14.50 Trifecta £101.90.
**Owner** Prestige Thoroughbred Racing **Bred** Robert Norton **Trained** Carluke, S Lanarks

**FOCUS**
This fillies" handicap proved as tight as the market had suggested it might, with all six competitors still holding chances a furlong out.

## 3957 JESSIE J HERE LIVE 27TH JULY H'CAP (BOBIS RACE) 6f 192y

**8:10** (8:11) (Class 4) (0-85,84) 3-Y-0 **£5,175** (£1,540; £769; £384) **Stalls** Low

Form RPR

1213 **1** **Sir Guy Porteous (IRE)**14 3455 3-9-7 **84**........................ JoeFanning 4 95
(Mark Johnston) *mde all: rdn clr over 1f out: kpt on strly: unchal* **3/1**1

-632 **2** 3 **Zain Zone (IRE)**54 2218 3-9-0 **77**........................ JamesSullivan 3 80
(Ruth Carr) *t.k.h: chsd ldrs: wnt 2nd over 2f out: rdn and edgd lft over 1f out: kpt on same pce ins fnl f* **4/1**2

0324 **3** 6 **Proclamationofwar**9 3625 3-8-5 **68**........................ DuranFentiman 6 55
(Kevin Ryan) *t.k.h: chsd ldrs: effrt and rdn over 2f out: outpcd by first two over 1f out* **12/1**

1-00 **4** 3/4 **Pull The Plug (IRE)**14 3484 3-9-0 **80**........................ NeilFarley(3) 9 65
(Declan Carroll) *unruly bef s: t.k.h: chsd wnr to over 2f out: sn rdn: no ex over 1f out* **16/1**

52-6 **5** 4 1/2 **Threetimesalady**9 3615 3-9-6 **83**........................ LukeMorris 7 57
(Sir Mark Prescott Bt) *hld up in tch: effrt and drvn over 2f out: no imp over 1f out* **11/2**

6325 **6** 2 1/4 **Homestretch**14 3455 3-9-3 **80**........................ GrahamLee 8 48
(Mick Channon) *hld up in tch on outside: drvn over 3f out: no imp fr 2f out* **3/1**1

1-21 **7** 2 1/4 **Jacquotte Delahaye**19 3300 3-9-3 **83**........................(b) ConnorBeasley(3) 1 45
(David Brown) *s.s: bhd: effrt and drvn on outside over 2f out: sn btn* **5/1**3

1m 26.0s (-1.10) **Going Correction** +0.05s/f (Good) **7** Ran SP% **115.6**
Speed ratings (Par 102): **108,104,97,96,91 89,86**
CSF £15.61 CT £124.43 TOTE £3.80: £2.30, £2.50; EX 21.00 Trifecta £90.10.
**Owner** Paul Dean **Bred** Rabbah Bloodstock Limited **Trained** Middleham Moor, N Yorks

**FOCUS**
A winning time 1.22 seconds quicker than the preceding fillies' handicap.

## 3958 KAISER CHIEFS LIVE AFTER RACING H'CAP 1m 1f 61y

**8:40** (8:41) (Class 5) (0-70,69) 4-Y-0+ **£2,587** (£770; £384; £192) **Stalls** Low

Form RPR

-064 **1** **Kuwait Star**19 3299 5-8-11 **64**........................ JacobButterfield(5) 10 73
(Michael Herrington) *t.k.h early: mde all: rdn and hrd pressed fr 2f out: kpt on gamely towards fin* **8/1**

0622 **2** 1/2 **Tectonic (IRE)**10 3572 5-9-6 **68**........................(p) TomEaves 4 76
(Keith Dalgleish) *t.k.h: prom: swtchd lft and effrt over 1f out: coaxed along to chal ins fnl f: rdn and no ex nr fin* **11/4**1

6405 **3** 3 1/2 **Unex Michelangelo (IRE)**11 3544 5-9-0 **62**........................ JamesSullivan 3 63
(Michael Easterby) *hld up: rdn and effrt over 2f out: edgd rt and kpt on fnl f: nrst fin* **8/1**

5046 **4** *shd* **Bold And Free**12 3535 4-8-3 **51**........................(p) RaulDaSilva 2 51
(David Thompson) *t.k.h: pressed wnr and sn clr of rest: rdn and ev ch fr 2f out: wknd ins fnl f* **9/1**

-004 **5** 1 3/4 **Triple Eight (IRE)**19 3301 6-9-5 **67**........................(b) PhillipMakin 9 64
(Philip Kirby) *dwlt: hld up: rdn and hdwy wl over 1f out: kpt on fnl f: nvr able to chal* **8/1**

4060 **6** 5 **Gold Chain (IRE)**19 3301 4-8-8 **61** ow2........................ EmmaSayer(5) 6 47
(Dianne Sayer) *hld up: rdn along and hdwy over 2f out: no imp fr over 1f out* **20/1**

-426 **7** 1 **Nelson's Bay**15 3439 5-8-13 **61**........................(t) GrahamLee 5 45
(Wilf Storey) *chsd clr ldng pair: rdn over 2f out: edgd rt and wknd over 1f out* **4/1**2

00-5 **8** 11 **Rex Romanorum (IRE)**39 2654 6-9-0 **62**........................ DuranFentiman 12 23
(Patrick Holmes) *hld up in midfield: drvn and outpcd over 3f out: n.d after* **16/1**

303 **9** 4 1/2 **First Move**9 3607 4-9-7 **69**........................ JoeFanning 7 21
(Mark Johnston) *dwlt: hld up on outside: struggling 4f out: btn and eased over 1f out* **9/2**3

1m 57.19s (-0.41) **Going Correction** +0.05s/f (Good) **9** Ran SP% **118.8**
Speed ratings (Par 103): **103,102,99,99,97 93,92,82,78**
CSF £31.24 CT £187.68 TOTE £11.00: £2.60, £1.70, £2.30; EX 46.00 Trifecta £614.00.
**Owner** Miss Vivian Pratt **Bred** H & V Pratt **Trained** Cold Kirby, N Yorks

**FOCUS**
The time was 1.06 seconds quicker than that of the earlier maiden.
T/Plt: £35.10 to a £1 stake. Pool: £53,635.78 - 1,113.53 winning units T/Qpdt: £8.70 to a £1 stake. Pool: £5,726.64 - 482.78 winning units RY

3921

# HAYDOCK (L-H)

### Saturday, July 5

**OFFICIAL GOING: Soft (6.5) changing to good to soft after race 1 (1.45)**
Wind: Light; half against Weather: Fine and sunny

## 3959 CASINO AT BET365.COM H'CAP (BOBIS RACE) 5f

**1:45** (1:46) (Class 4) (0-85,82) 3-Y-0 **£6,469** (£1,925; £962; £481) **Stalls** Centre

Form RPR

4311 **1** **War Spirit**15 3433 3-9-2 **77**........................ SeanLevey 3 89+
(Richard Hannon) *hld up in rr: hdwy over 2f out: led appr fnl f: styd on wl: readily* **5/2**1

-546 **2** 1 1/4 **Distant Past**18 3331 3-8-10 **71**........................ TomEaves 4 77
(Kevin Ryan) *chsd ldrs: wnt 2nd jst ins fnl f: kpt on same pce* **14/1**

014 **3** 3/4 **Captain Myles (IRE)**21 3219 3-9-4 **79**........................(b) StevieDonohoe 9 82
(Tim Pitt) *mid-div: effrt over 2f out: styd on fnl f: tk 3rd nr fin* **9/1**

1402 **4** 1/2 **Signore Piccolo**14 3460 3-9-7 **82**........................ JasonHart 8 84
(Eric Alston) *led: hdd appr fnl f: kpt on same pce* **4/1**2

4215 **5** 4 1/2 **Red Forever**9 3600 3-8-4 **65**........................ PatrickMathers 7 50
(Alan Berry) *chsd ldrs: wknd appr fnl f* **14/1**

-002 **6** 1 **Jamboree Girl**14 3462 3-8-10 **71**........................ DuranFentiman 10 53
(Tim Easterby) *s.i.s: hdwy 3f out: wknd over 1f out* **8/1**

3101 **7** 4 **Flashy Queen (IRE)**31 2889 3-9-4 **79**........................ SteveDrowne 13 46
(Joseph Tuite) *chsd ldrs: wknd over 1f out* **9/2**3

643 **8** 1 **Fuel Injection**31 2889 3-8-4 **65**........................(v1) JamesSullivan 6 29
(Paul Midgley) *prom: lost pl over 1f out* **7/1**

1140 **9** 1 1/4 **Saffire Song**15 3433 3-8-9 **70**........................ JoeFanning 2 29
(Alan Bailey) *chsd ldrs: lost pl 3f out* **25/1**

1m 1.14s (0.34) **Going Correction** +0.10s/f (Good) **9** Ran SP% **117.5**
Speed ratings (Par 102): **101,99,97,97,89 88,81,80,78**
CSF £40.95 CT £279.54 TOTE £2.80: £1.60, £4.00, £3.20; EX 29.60 Trifecta £271.10.
**Owner** Mohamed Saeed Al Shahi **Bred** Biddestone Stud Ltd **Trained** East Everleigh, Wilts

**FOCUS**
All races on Stands side Home straight and distances on Round course increased by 57yds. After riding in the opener Sean Levey said: "It's a fresh course today and it's good to soft at worst", Joe Fanning said: "They are not getting in as much as I thought, it isn't as soft as last night" and Duran Fentiman said: "It's just on the easy side, it's lovely considering all the rain they had." The winner built on his Newmarket win.

## 3960 BET365.COM CONDITIONS STKS 6f

**2:20** (2:20) (Class 2) 3-Y-0+

**£14,940** (£4,473; £2,236; £1,118; £559; £280) **Stalls** Centre

Form RPR

4440 **1** **Justice Day (IRE)**18 3319 3-8-10 107........................ GrahamLee 3 111
(David Elsworth) *trckd ldrs: led over 2f out: styd on strly fnl f* **5/1**2

-400 **2** 1 3/4 **Morache Music**7 3732 6-8-11 104........................ TomQueally 2 101+
(Peter Makin) *s.i.s: hld up: hdwy over 2f out: nt clr run and swtchd lft appr fnl f: 3rd 150yds out: styd on to take 2nd nr fin* **7/1**

2130 **3** 1/2 **Barkston Ash**7 3737 6-8-11 97........................(p) JasonHart 7 100
(Eric Alston) *dwlt: sn drvn along: hdwy and swtchd lft 2f out: 2nd jst ins fnl f: styd on same pce* **12/1**

0330 **4** 1 3/4 **Complicate (AUS)**98 1180 5-9-2 109........................ SilvestreDeSousa 5 99
(Saeed bin Suroor) *chsd ldrs: drvn over 2f out: kpt on same pce appr fnl f* **7/1**

556- **5** 1 3/4 **Soul (AUS)**273 7013 7-8-11 107........................ AhmedAjtebi 9 89
(Saeed bin Suroor) *racd towards stands' side: chsd ldrs: drvn over 2f out: one pce over 1f out* **11/2**3

2450 **6** 1 1/2 **Captain Ramius (IRE)**56 2145 8-8-11 103........................ PhillipMakin 8 84
(Kevin Ryan) *racd towards stands' side: sn chsng ldrs: one pce over 1f out* **7/1**

1122 **7** *hd* **Bear Behind (IRE)**14 3458 5-8-11 95........................ HayleyTurner 4 83
(Tom Dascombe) *led tl over 2f out: fdd last 150yds* **11/2**3

4220 **8** 3/4 **Annunciation**[14] 3452 4-8-11 104 ........ PatDobbs 10 81
(Richard Hannon) *s.i.s: in rr: drvn over 2f out: wknd appr fnl f* **4/1**[1]

2-00 **9** 1 1/4 **Langavat (IRE)**[21] 3245 3-8-5 95 ........ KieranO'Neill 1 76
(Richard Hannon) *chsd ldrs: wknd fnl f* **33/1**

1m 12.99s (-0.81) **Going Correction** +0.10s/f (Good)
**WFA** 3 from 4yo+ 6lb **9** Ran SP% **115.6**
Speed ratings (Par 109): **109,106,106,103,101 99,99,98,96**
CSF £39.81 TOTE £6.20: £2.10, £2.60, £3.90; EX 40.30 Trifecta £526.20.

**Owner** D R C Elsworth **Bred** Gerry Kenny **Trained** Newmarket, Suffolk

**FOCUS**
The official ground description was changed to good to soft before this race, a decent conditions sprint. The winner is worth more at face value but there are doubts.

## 3961 BET365 LANCASHIRE OAKS (GROUP 2) (F&M) 1m 3f 200y
**2:55** (2:56) (Class 1) 3-Y-O+
**£52,740** (£19,995; £10,006; £4,984; £2,501; £1,255) **Stalls** Centre

Form RPR

111- **1** **Pomology (USA)**[328] 5315 4-9-5 110 ........ GrahamLee 12 113
(John Gosden) *trckd ldrs: led appr fnl f: styd on* **8/1**

11 **2** 2 1/4 **Sultanina**[35] 2764 4-9-5 101 ........ RobertHavlin 3 109
(John Gosden) *trckd ldrs: effrt 3f out: 2nd 1f out: no imp* **9/2**[2]

23-5 **3** 2 1/2 **Talent**[28] 2988 4-9-5 112 ........ JimCrowley 10 105
(Ralph Beckett) *stdd s: hld up in rr: hdwy over 2f out: styd on to take 3rd last 75yds* **7/1**

-023 **4** 1 1/4 **We'll Go Walking (IRE)**[19] 3307 4-9-5 102 ........ ShaneKelly 5 103
(J P Murtagh, Ire) *led: clr after 3f: drvn over 3f out: hdd appr fnl f: wknd last 100yds* **20/1**

3-13 **5** nk **Silk Sari**[35] 2764 4-9-5 99 ........ AndreaAtzeni 6 103
(Luca Cumani) *sn chsng ldrs: drvn 3f out: edgd lft: kpt on one pce* **5/1**[3]

0400 **6** 3/4 **Moment In Time (IRE)**[19] 3307 5-9-5 94 ........ TomQueally 4 101
(David Simcock) *hld up in rr: effrt over 3f out: one pce fnl 2f* **25/1**

1-46 **7** 1 3/4 **Astonishing (IRE)**[35] 2764 4-9-5 103 ........ PatDobbs 8 99
(Sir Michael Stoute) *mid-div: hdwy over 3f out: wknd jst ins fnl f* **14/1**

F1-4 **8** nse **Seal Of Approval**[50] 2315 5-9-5 115 ........ HayleyTurner 1 98
(James Fanshawe) *stdd s: racd in last: drvn 6f out: kpt on clsng stages: nvr a factor* **15/8**[1]

11- **9** 1 1/2 **Charity Line (IRE)**[251] 7558 4-9-5 111 ........(t) MartinHarley 7 96
(Marco Botti) *hld up in mid-div: effrt over 3f out: wknd fnl f* **14/1**

2m 31.6s (-2.20) **Going Correction** +0.10s/f (Good)
**WFA** 3 from 4yo+ 13lb **9** Ran SP% **115.2**
Speed ratings (Par 115): **111,109,107,107,106 106,105,105,104**
CSF £43.76 TOTE £8.00: £2.50, £2.40, £2.40; EX 24.80 Trifecta £215.50.

**Owner** HRH Princess Haya Of Jordan **Bred** Dr John A Chandler **Trained** Newmarket, Suffolk

**FOCUS**
Actual race distance 1m4f37yds. A strong edition of this Group 2, but the withdrawal of Lustrous meant that 3yos went unrepresented. They went a strong gallop and the form looks solid. John Gosden has won this race six times now, including three of the last four runnings, and for good measure he had the second too. Both progressed. The time was slightly quicker than the Old Newton Cup.

## 3962 BET365 OLD NEWTON CUP (HERITAGE H'CAP) 1m 3f 200y
**3:30** (3:31) (Class 2) 4-Y-O+
**£62,250** (£18,640; £9,320; £4,660; £2,330; £1,170) **Stalls** Centre

Form RPR

-001 **1** **De Rigueur**[35] 2779 6-9-4 97 ........(tp) AndreaAtzeni 19 106
(Marco Botti) *s.s: in rr: hdwy and edgd rt over 2f out: edgd lft and led last 100yds: hld on* **9/1**

/35- **2** nk **Pallasator**[266] 7193 5-9-8 101 ........ LukeMorris 16 110
(Sir Mark Prescott Bt) *mid-div: drvn and hdwy 4f out: led over 1f out: edgd lft and hdd last 100yds: no ex* **7/1**[3]

-511 **3** 3/4 **Magic Hurricane (IRE)**[24] 3111 4-9-2 95 ........ FrederikTylicki 15 103
(James Fanshawe) *hld up in mid-div: smooth hdwy to chal over 2f out: kpt on same pce last 50yds* **5/1**[2]

2-45 **4** 1/2 **Dashing Star**[14] 3449 4-9-6 99 ........ LiamKeniry 6 106
(David Elsworth) *led: hdd over 1f out: hld whn hmpd ins fnl f nr fin* **8/1**

-004 **5** shd **Quiz Mistress**[35] 2764 6-9-6 99 ........ SilvestreDeSousa 12 106
(Hughie Morrison) *rr-div: hdwy on outer over 3f out: chsng ldrs 2f out: kpt on same pce last 150yds* **7/1**[3]

33-3 **6** 1/2 **Havana Cooler (IRE)**[14] 3449 4-9-5 98 ........ AdamKirby 1 104
(Luca Cumani) *mid-div: drvn and hdwy on inner over 3f out: chsng ldrs over 1f out: edgd rt and kpt on same pce fnl f* **10/3**[1]

610- **7** 5 **Forgotten Hero (IRE)**[238] 7823 5-8-13 92 ........ MartinHarley 9 90
(Charles Hills) *hld up in rr: hdwy to trck ldrs over 2f out: wknd over 1f out* **25/1**

50/0 **8** nk **Buthelezi (USA)**[7] 3717 6-8-13 92 ........ TomEaves 14 90
(Brian Ellison) *hld up in rr: drvn over 4f out: styd on over 1f out: nvr a factor* **50/1**

-243 **9** 1 **Blue Surf**[28] 2991 5-9-6 99 ........ PatDobbs 11 95
(Amanda Perrett) *trckd ldrs: effrt over 2f out: wknd over 1f out* **14/1**

2004 **10** hd **Sennockian Star**[15] 3416 4-9-9 102 ........(v) JoeFanning 17 98
(Mark Johnston) *chsd ldrs: drvn over 3f out: wknd over 1f out* **20/1**

0015 **11** 1 1/2 **Balty Boys (IRE)**[14] 3456 5-9-4 97 ........ PaulPickard 13 90
(Brian Ellison) *chsd ldrs: lost pl after 3f: nvr a factor after* **50/1**

630- **12** hd **Fattsota**[220] 8062 6-9-10 103 ........ DanielTudhope 18 96
(David O'Meara) *trckd ldrs: drvn over 3f out: lost pl over 1f out* **16/1**

2-60 **13** 2 1/2 **Wigmore Hall (IRE)**[15] 3416 7-9-8 101 ........ TomQueally 8 90
(Michael Bell) *s.i.s: hdwy on ins over 3f out: rdn and wknd 2f out* **25/1**

5031 **14** 2 1/2 **Strictly Silver (IRE)**[14] 3457 5-8-11 93 ........(p) RobertTart(3) 10 78
(Alan Bailey) *prom: chsng ldrs over 2f out: wknd over 1f out* **20/1**

0-00 **15** 3 3/4 **Open Eagle (IRE)**[28] 2991 5-8-12 91 ........ JimCrowley 5 70
(David O'Meara) *trckd ldrs: drvn over 3f out: lost pl 2f out: eased whn bhd clsng stages* **16/1**

2m 32.35s (-1.45) **Going Correction** +0.10s/f (Good) **15** Ran SP% **125.4**
Speed ratings (Par 109): **108,107,107,106,106 106,103,103,102,102 101,101,99,97,95**
CSF £67.36 CT £360.18 TOTE £9.70: £2.80, £2.30, £2.30; EX 111.80 Trifecta £717.00.

**Owner** N A Jackson **Bred** Cheveley Park Stud Ltd **Trained** Newmarket, Suffolk

**FOCUS**
Actual race distance 1m4f37yds. A competitive heritage handicap run in a time slightly quicker than than the Lancashire Oaks. Unlike that race, the runners came down the centre in the home straight. The first six finished in a bunch, clear of the remainder, and a high draw proved no hindrance the way the race panned out. Solid enough form, with improvement from the first two.

## 3963 BET365.COM NURSERY H'CAP (BOBIS RACE) 7f
**4:05** (4:05) (Class 3) 2-Y-O **£6,469** (£1,925; £962; £481) **Stalls** Low

Form RPR

033 **1** **Divine Law**[25] 3081 2-9-4 75 ........ SeanLevey 3 76
(Richard Hannon) *trckd ldrs: drvn over 2f out: edgd lft: styd on to ld towards fin* **7/2**[2]

065 **2** nk **Dragline**[16] 3394 2-8-0 57 oh2 ........ DuranFentiman 1 57
(Tim Easterby) *trckd ldrs: t.k.h: 2nd over 5f out: led over 2f out: hrd drvn and edgd lft: hdd and no ex clsng stages* **20/1**

1 **3** 2 1/2 **Muqaawel (USA)**[16] 3381 2-9-7 78 ........ DaneO'Neill 2 72
(Mark Johnston) *dwlt: racd in last: chsng ldrs over 3f out: rdn over 2f out: kpt on same pce: unable to chal: eased nr fin* **2/5**[1]

3310 **4** 6 **Jersey Bull (IRE)**[42] 2543 2-9-4 75 ........ WilliamTwiston-Davies 4 54
(Mick Channon) *led: hdd over 2f out: wknd over 1f out: eased clsng stages* **13/2**[3]

1m 33.71s (3.01) **Going Correction** +0.10s/f (Good) **4** Ran SP% **111.7**
Speed ratings (Par 98): **86,85,82,75**
CSF £37.73 TOTE £4.70; EX 35.80 Trifecta £92.70.
**Owner** Mrs Amanda Turner **Bred** Bearstone Stud **Trained** East Everleigh, Wilts

**FOCUS**
Actual race distance 7f 57yds. Not a strong nursery, particularly with the favourite seemingly below par. There was no hanging about, and after the field had come down the middle in the home straight the first two fought out the finish on the inside rail. The runner-up is the key, and the race is rated cautiously.

## 3964 BET365 H'CAP 7f
**4:40** (4:40) (Class 2) (0-105,95) 3-Y-O+ **£16,172** (£4,812; £2,405; £1,202) **Stalls** Low

Form RPR

0210 **1** **Heavy Metal**[9] 3621 4-9-5 92 ........ JoeFanning 4 104
(Mark Johnston) *dwlt: in rr: hdwy to trck ldrs 4f out: nt clr run on ins over 2f out: swtchd rt appr fnl f: styd on to ld nr fin* **7/1**

-131 **2** 1/2 **Dark Emerald (IRE)**[15] 3431 4-9-6 93 ........ AdamKirby 5 104
(Brendan Powell) *trckd ldrs: led narrowly over 2f out: edgd lft and jnd ins fnl f: hdd and no ex clsng stages* **5/2**[1]

-441 **3** nk **Alejandro (IRE)**[22] 3202 5-9-7 94 ........ DanielTudhope 8 104
(David O'Meara) *led: qcknd pce over 3f out: hdd over 2f out: rallied and upsides whn crowded last 75yds: no ex* **3/1**[2]

6032 **4** 1 1/2 **Chilworth Icon**[2] 3876 4-9-2 89 ........ WilliamTwiston-Davies 2 95
(Mick Channon) *trckd ldrs: t.k.h: n.m.r on ins over 1f out: kpt on same pce* **3/1**[2]

4256 **5** nk **Laffan (IRE)**[22] 3189 5-9-4 91 ........ DuranFentiman 6 97
(Tim Easterby) *hld up in rr: hdwy to trck ldrs 4f out: kpt on same pce over 1f out* **9/2**[3]

1m 29.27s (-1.43) **Going Correction** +0.10s/f (Good) **5** Ran SP% **109.3**
Speed ratings (Par 109): **112,111,111,109,109**
CSF £24.13 TOTE £5.60: £2.70, £1.70; EX 21.40 Trifecta £37.30.
**Owner** Sheikh Hamdan bin Mohammed Al Maktoum **Bred** Darley **Trained** Middleham Moor, N Yorks

**FOCUS**
Actual race distance 7f 57yds. A disappointing turnout for the money, but they went a reasonable gallop and it produced a good finish. It was something of a messy race despite the small field. The winner stepped up on his penultimate form.

## 3965 BET365.COM H'CAP (BOBIS RACE) 1m 2f 95y
**5:15** (5:15) (Class 2) (0-100,94) 3-Y-O **£16,172** (£4,812; £2,405; £1,202) **Stalls** Centre

Form RPR

-311 **1** **Roseburg (IRE)**[28] 2982 3-9-7 94 ........ AndreaAtzeni 2 103+
(Luca Cumani) *hld up in rr: trcking ldrs 4f out: effrt over 2f out: led 1f out: pushed clr: readily* **5/6**[1]

-110 **2** 2 **Al Busayyir (IRE)**[28] 2986 3-9-1 88 ........ MartinHarley 3 93+
(Marco Botti) *trckd ldrs: nt clr run over 2f out: swtchd rt over 1f out: styd on to take 2nd last 75yds: no imp* **4/1**[2]

1-00 **3** 1 3/4 **Master The World (IRE)**[63] 1951 3-9-5 92 ........ LiamKeniry 7 92
(David Elsworth) *t.k.h: trckd ldr: upsides over 3f out: led over 2f out: hdd 1f out: kpt on same pce* **7/1**

1120 **4** 3/4 **Libran (IRE)**[28] 3003 3-8-12 85 ........ TomQueally 5 84
(Alan Swinbank) *hld up in rr: trcking ldrs 4f out: drvn over 2f out: kpt on one pce* **5/1**[3]

-440 **5** 15 **Fire Fighting (IRE)**[16] 3379 3-8-13 86 ........ JoeFanning 6 63
(Mark Johnston) *led: qcknd pce over 3f out: hdd over 2f out: lost pl 1f out: eased towards fin* **10/1**

2m 14.27s (-1.23) **Going Correction** +0.10s/f (Good) **5** Ran SP% **112.8**
Speed ratings (Par 106): **108,106,105,104,92**
CSF £4.69 TOTE £1.60: £1.10, £2.30; EX 4.60 Trifecta £12.60.
**Owner** Sheikh Mohammed Obaid Al Maktoum **Bred** Mrs Brid Cosgrove **Trained** Newmarket, Suffolk

**FOCUS**
Actual race distance 1m2f152yds. A decent handicap in which they stayed on the inside rail. It was sound run and the first two look potentially better than the bare form allows.
T/Plt: £485.90 to a £1 stake. Pool: £140,327.95 - 210.82 winning units T/Qpdt: £56.40 to a £1 stake. Pool: £7,635.79 - 100.10 winning units WG

# 3612 LEICESTER (R-H)
Saturday, July 5

**OFFICIAL GOING: Good to firm (good in places)**
Wind: Light; across Weather: Cloudy with sunny spells

## 3966 FENWICK OF LEICESTER FILLIES' H'CAP 5f 218y
**2:15** (2:15) (Class 5) (0-70,73) 3-Y-O+ **£3,881** (£1,155; £577; £288) **Stalls** High

Form RPR

-411 **1** **Syrian Pearl**[39] 2647 3-9-2 68 ........ AshleyMorgan(3) 11 83+
(Chris Wall) *chsd ldrs: led over 1f out: rdn out* **4/1**[1]

-624 **2** 3 **Goadby**[21] 3231 3-8-9 58 ........ WilliamCarson 6 62
(John Holt) *led: rdn and hdd over 1f out: styd on same pce ins fnl f* **8/1**

4062 **3** 1/2 **Invoke (IRE)**[10] 3588 3-9-1 69 ........ LouisSteward(5) 10 72
(Michael Bell) *chsd ldrs: rdn over 2f out: styd on same pce ins fnl f* **5/1**[2]

5140 **4** 1/2 **Clock Opera (IRE)**[16] 3384 4-8-12 62 ........ KieranShoemark(7) 1 64
(William Stone) *w ldrs: rdn over 1f out: no ex ins fnl f* **10/1**

021 **5** *nk* **Kodafine (IRE)**[12] 3523 3-8-6 **58**.................................... DeclanBates(3) 4 58
(David Evans) *sn pushed along to chse ldr: rdn over 2f out: ev ch over 1f out: no ex ins fnl f* **8/1**

1-06 **6** *½* **Tregereth (IRE)**[7] 3734 4-8-12 **58**.......................... MatthewLawson(3) 12 58
(Jonathan Portman) *hld up: rdn 1/2-way: hdwy over 2f out: styd on same pce fnl f* **15/2**[3]

0-40 **7** *nk* **See No Ships**[29] 2946 3-8-1 **50** oh2.................................... JimmyQuinn 8 48
(Mark Usher) *hld up: rdn over 2f out: r.o ins fnl f: nvr nrr* **20/1**

6-03 **8** *5* **Elite Freedom (IRE)**[10] 3564 3-8-6 **55**.................(p) AndrewMullen 7 37
(Brian Baugh) *prom: rdn over 2f out: wknd wl over 1f out* **9/1**

0-60 **9** *¾* **Big Boned (USA)**[12] 3518 3-9-2 **65**..................................[1] HarryBentley 2 44
(Ed Dunlop) *hld up: hdwy over 2f out: sn rdn: wknd fnl f* **5/1**[2]

030- **10** *5* **Seraphima**[204] 8278 4-8-6 **54**.................................... ShirleyTeasdale(5) 5 18
(Lisa Williamson) *prom: pushed along whn hmpd and lost pl 1/2-way: n.d after* **66/1**

1-60 **11** *5* **Miakora**[9] 3630 6-8-7 **50** oh1..........................................(v) PaoloSirigu 3
(Mick Quinn) *s.i.s: hdwy over 4f out: rdn and wknd over 2f out* **33/1**

1m 11.97s (-1.03) **Going Correction** -0.075s/f (Good)
**WFA** 3 from 4yo+ 6lb 11 Ran SP% **115.6**
Speed ratings (Par 100): **103,99,98,97,97 96,96,89,88,81 75**
CSF £34.89 CT £163.11 TOTE £3.90: £2.40, £3.10, £2.10; EX 23.90 Trifecta £155.00.
**Owner** The Clodhoppers **Bred** Jeremy Green And Sons **Trained** Newmarket, Suffolk

**FOCUS**
A moderate fillies' sprint handicap.

## 3967 AVAILABLE CAR (S) STKS — 5f 218y

**2:50** (2:50) (Class 5) 2-Y-O **£2,587** (£770; £384; £192) **Stalls** High

Form RPR

4366 **1** **Diminutive (IRE)**[19] 3312 2-8-6 0.................................... WilliamCarson 3 61
(Jamie Osborne) *trckd ldrs: rdn to ld over 1f out: sn hung rt: styd on* **5/2**[1]

0060 **2** *2¾* **Ciaras Cookie (IRE)**[19] 3312 2-8-6 0.................................... BenCurtis 5 53
(David Evans) *plld hrd: led: hdd over 3f out: rdn and outpcd over 1f out: styd on to go 2nd wl ins fnl f* **4/1**[2]

3425 **3** *1¾* **Kidmeforever**[35] 2771 2-8-6 0.................................... LiamJones 2 48
(J S Moore) *sn pushed along and prom: led over 2f out: rdn and hdd over 1f out: hmpd and no ex ins fnl f* **5/2**[1]

603 **4** *1¾* **Astrea**[24] 3091 2-8-6 0.................................... AndrewMullen 4 42
(Nigel Tinkler) *chsd ldrs: rdn over 2f out: styd on same pce fr over 1f out* **9/1**

0 **5** *2¼* **Madame Ascension**[22] 3173 2-8-1 0.................................... NoelGarbutt(5) 9 36+
(David Evans) *sn pushed along in rr: hdwy 1/2-way: sn outpcd: r.o ins fnl f* **25/1**

440 **6** *3¾* **Marti Ella**[15] 3435 2-7-13 0..............................(p) JosephineGordon(7) 6 24
(J S Moore) *prom: rdn and hung rt over 2f out: sn wknd* **20/1**

605 **7** *½* **Mary Ann Bugg (IRE)**[19] 3304 2-8-1 0..............................(vt[1]) DannyBrock(5) 8 23
(Phil McEntee) *chsd ldrs: led over 3f out: rdn and hdd over 2f out: wknd over 1f out* **14/1**

000 **8** *4½* **Sarah Catherine**[14] 3467 2-8-6 0.................................... HarryBentley 10 9
(Mark Usher) *hld up: rdn 1/2-way: wknd over 2f out* **8/1**[3]

1m 14.47s (1.47) **Going Correction** -0.075s/f (Good) 8 Ran SP% **113.5**
Speed ratings (Par 94): **87,83,81,78,75 70,70,64**
CSF £12.45 TOTE £3.70: £1.30, £1.50, £1.50; EX 14.70 Trifecta £36.80.
**Owner** J A Osborne **Bred** Messrs D & J Fitzgerald **Trained** Upper Lambourn, Berks
■ Stewards' Enquiry : William Carson caution: careless riding.

**FOCUS**
A typically weak race of its type.

## 3968 EBF STALLIONS BREEDING WINNERS FILLIES' H'CAP — 1m 1f 218y

**3:25** (3:25) (Class 4) (0-80,84) 3-Y-O **£7,561** (£2,263; £1,131; £566; £282) **Stalls** Low

Form RPR

41-2 **1** **Asyad (IRE)**[11] 3560 3-9-7 **84**.................................... TedDurcan 5 92+
(Sir Michael Stoute) *trckd ldrs: wnt 2nd 6f out: rdn over 1f out: styd on to ld wl ins fnl f* **4/5**[1]

2313 **2** *1½* **Bureau (IRE)**[7] 3725 3-9-5 **82**.................................... RoystonFfrench 7 87
(Mark Johnston) *led at stdy pce after 1f: qcknd over 3f out: rdn over 1f out: hdd and no ex wl ins fnl f* **9/2**[2]

6-41 **3** *hd* **Carnevale**[23] 3142 3-9-0 **77**.................................... PatCosgrave 3 82
(Ralph Beckett) *led 1f: chsd ldr tl 6f out: remained handy: rdn over 2f out: edgd lft ins fnl f: styd on* **5/1**[3]

-116 **4** *¾* **Compton Bird**[77] 1577 5-9-6 **72**.................................... LiamJones 6 75
(Paul Fitzsimons) *hld up: rdn over 2f out: r.o ins fnl f: nt rch ldrs* **14/1**

1-06 **5** *2½* **Bright Cecily (IRE)**[22] 3195 3-9-0 **77**.................................... HarryBentley 4 75
(Clive Cox) *s.i.s: plld hrd and sn prom: rdn over 2f out: nt clr run and no ex wl ins fnl f* **16/1**

-210 **6** *2¼* **Ghinia (IRE)**[22] 3195 3-9-0 **77**.................................... BenCurtis 2 71
(Pam Sly) *hld up: rdn over 2f out: nvr trbld ldrs* **9/1**

3-35 **7** *1¼* **Division Belle**[37] 2695 3-8-0 **63**.................................... PaoloSirigu 1 54
(William Muir) *hld up: racd keenly: rdn over 2f out: nvr on terms* **33/1**

2m 9.52s (1.62) **Going Correction** -0.075s/f (Good)
**WFA** 3 from 4yo+ 11lb 7 Ran SP% **115.9**
Speed ratings (Par 102): **90,88,88,88,86 84,83**
CSF £4.95 CT £11.25 TOTE £1.80: £1.20, £2.40; EX 4.70 Trifecta £13.00.
**Owner** Al Shaqab Racing **Bred** Gestut Wittekindshof **Trained** Newmarket, Suffolk

**FOCUS**
A modest fillies' handicap.

## 3969 LEXUS LEICESTER H'CAP — 7f 9y

**4:00** (4:00) (Class 3) (0-90,90) 3-Y-O **£9,451** (£2,829; £1,414; £708; £352) **Stalls** High

Form RPR

0004 **1** **Forest Edge (IRE)**[7] 3693 5-9-3 **86**..............................(b) DeclanBates(3) 3 94
(David Evans) *sn chsng ldr: led wl over 1f out: rdn and edgd lft ins fnl f: styd on* **22/1**

-130 **2** *¾* **Compton**[97] 1190 5-9-3 **83**..............................(t) HarryBentley 1 89
(Stuart Williams) *hld up: hdwy 1/2-way: rdn and ev ch over 1f out: styd on* **12/1**

0-32 **3** *nk* **Related**[22] 3180 4-9-3 **83**.................................... PatCosgrave 2 88
(David Simcock) *a.p: rdn over 1f out: styd on* **5/4**[1]

0050 **4** *1¾* **Showboating (IRE)**[7] 3703 6-9-5 **85**..............................(tp) BenCurtis 5 86
(Alan McCabe) *s.i.s: hld up: rdn over 2f out: r.o ins fnl f: nt rch ldrs* **11/2**[3]

-100 **5** *2¼* **Ben Hall (IRE)**[21] 3253 3-8-9 **90**.................................... RobJFitzpatrick(7) 8 82
(Mike Murphy) *trckd ldrs: racd keenly: hung rt fr 1/2-way: rdn over 2f out: styd on same pce fnl f* **20/1**

-000 **6** *nse* **Tamayuz Star (IRE)**[15] 3420 4-9-9 **89**.................................... LiamJones 7 84
(George Margarson) *led: rdn and hdd wl over 1f out: no ex ins fnl f* **4/1**[2]

0000 **7** *¾* **Set The Trend**[21] 3244 8-9-8 **88**..............................(v) SteveDrowne 4 81
(David Dennis) *s.i.s: hld up: rdn over 1f out: nt trble ldrs* **20/1**

0600 **8** *32* **Dubawi Sound**[24] 3122 6-9-2 **87**..............................(t) NoelGarbutt(5) 6
(Hugo Palmer) *sn drvn along and prom: wknd 1/2-way* **11/2**[3]

1m 23.62s (-2.58) **Going Correction** -0.075s/f (Good)
**WFA** 3 from 4yo+ 8lb 8 Ran SP% **116.8**
Speed ratings (Par 107): **111,110,109,107,105 105,104,67**
CSF £251.49 CT £562.37 TOTE £19.90: £4.50, £2.20, £1.30; EX 184.80 Trifecta £1889.20 Not won..
**Owner** P & K Swinnerton **Bred** Alberto Panetta **Trained** Pandy, Monmouths

**FOCUS**
A good handicap in which they went a proper gallop.

## 3970 ARCHIE MOSS VAUXHALL/BREEDERS BACKING RACING EBF RATING RELATED MAIDEN STKS — 7f 9y

**4:35** (4:35) (Class 5) 3-Y-O **£3,881** (£1,155; £577; £288) **Stalls** High

Form RPR

0-60 **1** **Matravers**[23] 3153 3-9-0 **70**.................................... TedDurcan 6 73
(Sir Michael Stoute) *s.i.s: hld up: rdn and hung rt fr over 2f out: hdwy over 1f out: styd on u.p to ld wl ins fnl f* **2/1**[1]

4366 **2** *¾* **Persian Bolt (USA)**[20] 3280 3-8-9 **70**..............................(b[1]) GeorgeDowning(5) 3 71
(Eve Johnson Houghton) *led: rdn over 1f out: hdd and unable qck wl ins fnl f* **3/1**[2]

5365 **3** *½* **Sleipnir**[11] 3555 3-9-0 **66**.................................... RobertWinston 4 70
(Philip Hide) *trckd ldr: rdn over 1f out: ev ch ins fnl f: unable qck wl ins fnl f* **6/1**

423- **4** *1¾* **Heska (IRE)**[224] 8016 3-9-0 **65**..............................(tp) AndrewMullen 2 65
(Michael Appleby) *chsd ldrs: sn pushed along: rdn over 2f out: styd on same pce ins fnl f* **4/1**[3]

3-00 **5** *6* **Charmy Dukesse (IRE)**[67] 1846 3-8-9 **67**.................................... DanielMuscutt(5) 5 50
(Marco Botti) *prom: pushed along and lost pl 4f out: n.d after* **12/1**

-062 **6** *¾* **Stroll On (IRE)**[10] 3566 3-9-0 **66**.................................... ChrisCatlin 1 48
(Rae Guest) *chsd ldrs: rdn over 2f out: wknd over 1f out* **7/1**

1m 24.57s (-1.63) **Going Correction** -0.075s/f (Good) 6 Ran SP% **112.8**
Speed ratings (Par 100): **106,105,104,102,95 94**
CSF £8.31 TOTE £3.20: £2.10, £3.00; EX 10.30 Trifecta £53.50.
**Owner** Mr & Mrs James Wigan **Bred** Mrs James Wigan & London TB Services Ltd **Trained** Newmarket, Suffolk

**FOCUS**
An ordinary 3yo maiden in which they went an honest gallop.

## 3971 EAST MIDLANDS CERAMICS H'CAP — 1m 60y

**5:05** (5:05) (Class 6) (0-65,72) 3-Y-O+ **£3,234** (£962; £481; £240) **Stalls** Low

Form RPR

5136 **1** **Botanist**[5] 3791 7-9-1 **52**.................................... BenCurtis 4 65
(Shaun Harris) *hld up: hdwy over 2f out: rdn to ld 1f out: r.o wl* **15/2**[3]

521 **2** *3¼* **Sonnetation (IRE)**[16] 3390 4-10-0 **65**.................................... PatCosgrave 6 71
(Jim Boyle) *led: hdd over 6f out: chsd ldrs: led again over 2f out: rdn and hdd 1f out: styd on same pce* **11/2**[2]

4301 **3** *¾* **Prince Of Burma (IRE)**[12] 3526 6-10-4 **72**..............................(b) RichardEvans(3) 5 78+
(David Evans) *hld up: hdwy and nt clr run over 1f out: r.o to go 3rd post: nt rch ldrs* **8/1**

5003 **4** *nk* **Headlong (IRE)**[8] 3670 3-9-2 **65**..................................[1] RyanClark(3) 11 67
(Brian Meehan) *hld up: wnt centre to r alone over 4f out: rdn and hung rt fr over 2f out: hdwy over 1f out: r.o: nt rch ldrs* **9/2**[1]

043 **5** *nse* **Living Leader**[15] 3427 5-9-5 **63**..............................(p) RobHornby(7) 10 66
(Grace Harris) *hld up: hdwy over 2f out: sn rdn: kpt on* **9/2**[1]

6405 **6** *½* **Nifty Kier**[12] 3526 5-8-4 **46** oh1.................................... DannyBrock(5) 2 48
(Phil McEntee) *hld up: hdwy over 3f out: rdn over 1f out: kpt on: n.m.r towards fin* **25/1**

0350 **7** *3½* **Sexy Secret**[16] 3380 3-8-9 **58**.................................... SimonPearce(3) 3 50
(Lydia Pearce) *hld up: rdn over 2f out: styd on ins fnl f: nvr trbld ldrs* **20/1**

4160 **8** *½* **Teide Peak (IRE)**[19] 3308 5-9-10 **61**.................................... RobertWinston 12 54
(Paul D'Arcy) *hld up: shkn up over 2f out: nvr on terms* **10/1**

3134 **9** *2¼* **Solarmaite**[30] 2935 5-9-2 **58**..............................(b) TimClark(5) 9 46
(Roy Bowring) *racd keenly: w ldrs: rdn and ev ch over 2f out: wknd over 1f out* **16/1**

1400 **10** *3¼* **Barbary (IRE)**[28] 2998 3-9-0 **60**.................................... TedDurcan 1 38
(Charlie Fellowes) *prom: rdn over 2f out: hmpd over 1f out: sn wknd* **10/1**

-520 **11** *1* **Master Of Song**[21] 3226 7-9-2 **53**..............................(p) JimmyQuinn 7 31
(Roy Bowring) *led over 6f out: rdn and hdd over 2f out: wknd over 1f out* **12/1**

6506 **12** *6* **Angel Cake (IRE)**[18] 3334 5-9-3 **54**.................................... AndrewMullen 13 18
(Michael Appleby) *chsd ldrs: rdn over 2f out: hmpd: wknd and eased over 1f out* **20/1**

0555 **13** *8* **La Danza**[21] 3220 4-8-13 **55**.................................... ShirleyTeasdale(5) 8
(Lisa Williamson) *stmbld s: sn mid-div: rdn and wknd over 2f out* **33/1**

1m 43.94s (-1.16) **Going Correction** -0.075s/f (Good)
**WFA** 3 from 4yo+ 9lb 13 Ran SP% **122.7**
Speed ratings (Par 101): **102,98,98,97,97 97,93,93,90,87 86,80,72**
CSF £47.30 CT £349.57 TOTE £10.80: £2.80, £2.40, £2.30; EX 71.60 Trifecta £162.60.
**Owner** N Blencowe, R Booth, D Cooper, M Lenton **Bred** Cheveley Park Stud Ltd **Trained** Carburton, Notts

**FOCUS**
A fair handicap in which they went a decent gallop.

## 3972 "THE RANGE" H'CAP — 5f 2y

**5:35** (5:37) (Class 5) (0-70,69) 3-Y-O **£3,881** (£1,155; £577; £288) **Stalls** Low

Form RPR

4305 **1** **The Dandy Yank (IRE)**[7] 3707 3-9-7 **69**..............................(p) WilliamCarson 5 76
(Jamie Osborne) *led: hdd over 3f out: led again 1/2-way: rdn over 1f out: edgd lft: r.o* **9/1**

2201 **2** *¾* **Vodka Chaser (IRE)**[8] 3679 3-9-0 **67**.................................... TimClark(5) 9 71
(Alison Hutchinson) *a.p: rdn over 1f out: chsd wnr wl ins fnl f: r.o* **6/1**

2206 **3** *2* **Katja**[11] 3561 3-8-13 **61**.................................... TedDurcan 6 58
(B W Hills) *a.p: rdn over 1f out: styd on same pce ins fnl f* **9/2**[3]

4-06 **4** *nk* **Pensax Lad (IRE)**[36] 2717 3-9-7 **69**.................................... SteveDrowne 11 65
(Ronald Harris) *hld up: pushed along 3f out: rdn and r.o ins fnl f: nt rch ldrs* **16/1**

41 **5** *hd* **Dancing Juice**[14] 3487 3-8-1 **56**..............................(v) RobJFitzpatrick(7) 12 51
(K R Burke) *plld hrd: trckd ldr tl led over 3f out: hdd 1/2-way: rdn over 1f out: styd on* **7/1**

0235 **6** *¾* **Diamondsinthesky (IRE)**[77] 1585 3-8-8 **56**..............................(v) HarryBentley 3 49
(Derek Shaw) *mid-div: hdwy 1/2-way: rdn over 1f out: styd on same pce fnl f* **20/1**

-050 **7** *¾* **He's My Boy (IRE)**[15] 3433 3-9-0 **62**.................................... FergusSweeney 4 52
(James Fanshawe) *hld up: hdwy over 1f out: sn rdn: no ex ins fnl f* **14/1**

2215 **8** *6* **Scoreline**[24] 3100 3-9-3 **65**.................................... BenCurtis 13 33
(David O'Meara) *chsd ldrs: rdn 1/2-way: wknd fnl f* **4/1**[2]
606- **9** *½* **Dont Tell Nan**[232] 7900 3-7-11 **50** oh2............................ NoelGarbutt(5) 8 17
(Derek Shaw) *hld up: outpcd 3f out: bhd whn hung rt fnl f* **33/1**
0312 **10** *5* **Bashiba (IRE)**[14] 3487 3-8-6 **54**...............................(t) HayleyTurner 7
(Nigel Tinkler) *prom: rdn 3f out: sn lost pl* **3/1**[1]
0030 **11** *4* **Sandsman's Girl (IRE)**[14] 3487 3-8-8 **56**...............(b) RoystonFfrench 10
(James Given) *sn pushed along in rr: wknd 3f out* **25/1**

59.33s (-0.67) **Going Correction** -0.075s/f (Good) **11** Ran SP% **124.1**
Speed ratings (Par 100): **102,100,97,97,96 95,94,84,84,76 69**
CSF £64.27 CT £284.35 TOTE £13.70: £3.50, £2.20, £2.30; EX 79.00 Trifecta £350.50.
**Owner** Chris Watkins And David N Reynolds **Bred** Martyn J McEnery **Trained** Upper Lambourn, Berks

**FOCUS**
A modest 3yo sprint handicap.
T/Plt: £9.40 to a £1 stake. Pool: £73,960.15 - 5,724.77 winning units T/Qpdt: £5.40 to a £1 stake. Pool: £4,390.38 - 591.85 winning units CR

# 3330 NOTTINGHAM (L-H)
## Saturday, July 5

**OFFICIAL GOING: Good to firm (good in places; 8.3)**
Wind: Virtually nil Weather: Light cloud, bright spells, dry

## 3973 AJA LADIES' H'CAP (FOR LADY AMATEUR RIDERS) 1m 2f 50y
6:00 (6:05) (Class 6) (0-60,65) 3-Y-O+ **£1,871** (£580; £290; £145) **Stalls** Low

Form RPR
0304 **1** **Edgware Road**[67] 1835 6-9-2 **48**................................ MissBHampson(7) 7 60
(Sean Curran) *chsd ldr: rdn to ld 1f out: drew clr ins fnl f: styd on wl: readily* **10/1**
2005 **2** *4* **Belle Peinture (FR)**[12] 3534 3-8-10 **46** oh1.......................... MissADeniel 3 50
(Alan Lockwood) *led: rdn 2f out: hdd 1f out: kpt on same pceand no ch w wnr after* **25/1**
5012 **3** *1¾* **Ferryview Place**[2] 3880 5-9-11 **50**...........................(p) MissSBrotherton 2 51
(Ian Williams) *t.k.h: chsd ldrs: rdn and effrt over 2f out: styd on same pce u.p fr over 1f out* **6/4**[1]
5623 **4** *nk* **Indian Scout**[11] 3553 6-9-9 **48**...........................(b) MrsCBartley 5 48
(Anabel K Murphy) *hld up towards rr: hdwy 4f out: drvn and kpt on same pce fr over 1f out* **12/1**
00U2 **5** *½* **Flag Of Glory**[5] 3785 7-9-10 **54**.............................. MissMEdden(5) 9 53
(Peter Hiatt) *stdd after s: hld up in rr: hdwy over 3f out: rdn and styd on same pce fnl 2f* **5/1**[2]
4121 **6** *11* **Elizabeth Coffee (IRE)**[7] 3705 6-10-7 **65**......... MissMeganNicholls(5) 1 43
(John Weymes) *taken down early: stdd after s: hld up in tch: hdwy 1/2-way: drvn and btn 2f out: wknd over 1f out* **6/1**[3]
1503 **7** *2* **Well Owd Mon**[9] 3617 4-9-13 **52**.............................. MissAliceMills 10 26
(Andrew Hollinshead) *s.i.s: hld up in rr: sme hdwy and drvn 3f out: no hdwy and wl hld fnl 2f* **14/1**
406/ **8** *7* **Dropzone (USA)**[43] 4440 5-10-4 **60**...........................(b) MissLBrooke(3) 4 21
(Richard Lee) *dwlt: sn in rcvrd and in tch in midfield: drvn and struggling 4f out: bhd fnl 2f* **33/1**
350- **9** *4½* **Having A Ball**[215] 8121 10-9-4 **50**.............................. MissLWest(7) 6 3
(Geoffrey Deacon) *chsd ldrs tl lost pl 1/2-way: bhd fnl 2f* **33/1**

2m 13.16s (-1.14) **Going Correction** -0.15s/f (Firm)
**WFA** 3 from 4yo+ 11lb **9** Ran SP% **104.1**
Speed ratings (Par 101): **98,94,93,93,92 83,82,76,73**
CSF £190.52 CT £454.80 TOTE £12.30: £3.30, £6.10, £1.10; EX 211.60 Trifecta £1518.60 Part won..
**Owner** Power Bloodstock Ltd **Bred** Juddmonte Farms Ltd **Trained** Upper Lambourn, Berks
■ Herbalist was withdrawn. Price at time of withdrawal 10-1. Rule 4 applies to all bets - deduction 5p in the pound.

**FOCUS**
Outer track used and distances as advertised. Leaden skies but warm and little wind. Despite 8.38mm of rain overnight, the ground rode as advertised. A moderate handicap confined to lady amateur riders, run at a modest early pace and up front was the place to be.

## 3974 DOWNLOAD NEW RACINGUK IPAD APP CLASSIFIED STKS 1m 2f 50y
6:30 (6:31) (Class 5) 3-Y-O **£2,726** (£805; £402) **Stalls** Low

Form RPR
-600 **1** **Rising Breeze (FR)**[14] 3466 3-8-11 74..........................1 JoeyHaynes(3) 3 81
(K R Burke) *stdd s: hld up in rr: gd hdwy to chse ldrs over 2f out: swtchd lft and chal over 1f out: rdn to ld 1f out: styd on wl* **16/1**
-425 **2** *1½* **D'Avignon (USA)**[23] 3159 3-9-0 75...........................(b) RobertHavlin 6 78
(John Gosden) *sn led: rdn 2f out: edgd rt and hdd 1f out: styd on same pce ins fnl f* **11/2**[3]
1-46 **3** *1* **Master Dancer**[22] 3197 3-9-0 73................................ RobertWinston 2 76
(Philip Hide) *t.k.h: hld up in tch: hdwy to chse ldrs 3f out: rdn and carried rt ent fnl f: styd on same pce after* **7/2**[1]
45-0 **4** *½* **Yaakooum (IRE)**[35] 2773 3-9-0 73................................ PatDobbs 7 75
(Richard Hannon) *dwlt: in tch in last pair: rdn 4f out: sme hdwy over 1f out: kpt on ins fnl f* **9/2**[2]
-522 **5** *3½* **Maiden Approach**[20] 3268 3-9-0 70...................(v[1]) PatrickMathers 1 69
(Richard Fahey) *chsd ldrs: rdn over 2f out: 4th and btn ent fnl f: wknd fnl 150yds* **12/1**
-043 **6** *½* **She's Gorgeous (IRE)**[36] 2749 3-9-0 73.................. FrederikTylicki 4 68
(James Fanshawe) *hld up in tch: rdn and effrt 2f out: unable qck and btn over 1f out: wknd fnl f* **7/2**[1]
-406 **7** *4½* **Elysian Prince**[30] 2936 3-9-0 74................................ PatCosgrave 8 59
(Paul Cole) *chsd ldrs: wnt 2nd 1/2-way tl wl over 1f out: sn lost pl: wknd fnl f* **20/1**
2352 **8** *3* **Mbhali (IRE)**[4] 3822 3-8-11 74.......................... MichaelJMMurphy(3) 5 53
(Mark Johnston) *chsd ldr tl 1/2-way: rdn and lost pl over 4f out: bhd over 1f out* **9/2**[2]

2m 11.39s (-2.91) **Going Correction** -0.15s/f (Firm) **8** Ran SP% **114.5**
Speed ratings (Par 100): **105,103,103,102,99 99,95,93**
CSF £100.88 TOTE £29.80: £5.40, £1.90, £1.70; EX 167.30 Trifecta £1100.80 Part won..
**Owner** Market Avenue Racing Club Ltd **Bred** Gerard Belloir **Trained** Middleham Moor, N Yorks

**FOCUS**
A tight 3yo affair. The pace was muddling, with the leaders slowing it up approaching the turn for home and the time was 5.39 seconds slower than standard.

## 3975 LADIES DAY ON FRIDAY 15TH AUGUST MAIDEN AUCTION FILLIES' STKS (BOBIS RACE) 5f 13y
7:00 (7:01) (Class 5) 2-Y-O **£2,587** (£770; £384; £192) **Stalls** High

Form RPR
**1** **Explosive Lady (IRE)** 2-8-10 0.......................................... BenCurtis 7 79+
(K R Burke) *niggled along early: in tch in midfield: swtchd off of rail and pushed along to chal 2f out: led over 1f out: r.o strly and drew clr fnl f: easily* **7/2**[1]
50 **2** *4½* **June's Moon**[11] 3557 2-8-10 0.......................................... PatDobbs 8 61
(Jonathan Portman) *led: rdn 2f out: hdd over 1f out: no ch w wnr but kpt on to hold 2nd ins fnl f* **5/1**[2]
**3** *¾* **Percy's Lass** 2-8-10 0.......................................... RobertWinston 3 58+
(Brian Ellison) *wnt rt s: in tch in rr: rdn and swtchd lft 2f out: hdwy to go 3rd ins fnl f: styd on: no ch w wnr* **5/1**[2]
0 **4** *3* **Freeze The Secret (IRE)**[49] 2328 2-8-6 0 ow3.......... OisinMurphy(3) 6 47
(David C Griffiths) *chsd ldrs: 3rd and unable qck over 1f out: btn 1f out: wknd ins fnl f* **14/1**
**5** *½* **Closing** 2-8-7 0 ow1.......................................... JackMitchell 1 43
(Nick Littmoden) *chsd ldrs: rdn and unable qck 2f out: btn over 1f out: wknd fnl f* **11/1**[3]
5 **6** *2¼* **Perfect Girl (IRE)**[10] 3570 2-9-0 0.......................................... TedDurcan 2 42
(Tim Easterby) *in touch in midfield: rdn ent fnl 2f: no prog: wl hld 1f out: wknd* **7/2**[1]
6 **7** *½* **Lady Of Illusion**[28] 2993 2-8-6 0.......................................... HarryBentley 5 32
(Mark Usher) *t.k.h: chsd ldrs: rdn and outpcd 2f out: wknd ent fnl f* **25/1**
**8** *¾* **Piccadillo** 2-8-7 0.......................................... ThomasBrown(3) 4 33
(Daniel Kubler) *bmpd s: sn pushed along in last pair: n.d* **5/1**[2]

1m 1.73s (0.23) **Going Correction** -0.15s/f (Firm) **8** Ran SP% **113.3**
Speed ratings (Par 91): **92,84,83,78,78 74,73,72**
CSF £20.71 TOTE £3.40: £1.10, £1.80, £2.40; EX 19.30 Trifecta £101.30.
**Owner** Market Avenue Racing Club & Mrs E Burke **Bred** Georgestown Stud **Trained** Middleham Moor, N Yorks

**FOCUS**
Not a lot of strength in this modest maiden sprint for fillies, but the winner looked a cut above.

## 3976 UISGE BEATHA MEMORIAL H'CAP 1m 6f 15y
7:30 (7:30) (Class 5) (0-70,77) 4-Y-O+ **£2,587** (£770; £384; £192) **Stalls** Low

Form RPR
0034 **1** **Hurry Home Poppa (IRE)**[21] 3226 4-8-12 **61**................ JimmyQuinn 2 68+
(John Mackie) *chsd ldrs: wnt 2nd 5f out: led 3f out: sustained duel w runner-up: forged ahd and edgd rt fnl 50yds* **11/4**[1]
26-0 **2** *1¼* **Chapter Five**[20] 3269 7-9-2 **65**...............................(p) StevieDonohoe 1 71
(Ian Williams) *chsd ldr tl led 10f out: hdd 3f out but styd upsides wnr: sustained duel after tl no ex and btn fnl 50yds: n.m.r nr fin* **7/2**[2]
3362 **3** *shd* **Lineman**[23] 3151 4-9-7 **70**.......................................... RobertWinston 6 75
(Andrew Hollinshead) *hld up in tch in last pair: effrt to chse ldng pair over 2f out: kpt on but nvr quite enough pce to chal* **7/2**[2]
4321 **4** *14* **Nolecce**[23] 3134 7-8-1 **55**.......................................... NoelGarbutt(5) 7 41
(Tony Forbes) *in tch in midfield: effrt in 3rd 4f out: 4th and btn 2f out: wknd over 1f out* **9/2**[3]
3001 **5** *7* **Royal Alcor (IRE)**[9] 3632 7-9-9 **77**...........................(t) ShelleyBirkett(5) 4 53
(Gay Kelleway) *hld up in tch in last pair: effrt 3f out: sn struggling and btn: wl bhd over 1f out* **11/2**
4003 **6** *12* **Rhinestone Rebel (IRE)**[18] 3336 8-8-2 **51** oh5.......... PatrickMathers 3 10
(Peter Hiatt) *led tl 10f out: chsd ldr tl 4f out: sn rdn and struggling: bhd 2f out: t.o* **20/1**

3m 5.75s (-1.25) **Going Correction** -0.15s/f (Firm) **6** Ran SP% **109.4**
Speed ratings (Par 103): **97,96,96,88,84 77**
CSF £11.90 TOTE £3.60: £1.90, £2.90; EX 13.30 Trifecta £78.30.
**Owner** D Ward **Bred** Kilcarn Stud **Trained** Church Broughton , Derbys

**FOCUS**
A fair staying handicap and the pace was indifferent. Very few got into it and a trio drew clear of the remainder.

## 3977 PENTAGON VAUXHALL NOTTINGHAM AND MANSFIELD H'CAP (A JOCKEY CLUB MIDDLE DISTANCE SERIES QUALIFIER) 1m 2f 50y
8:00 (8:02) (Class 4) (0-80,85) 3-Y-O+ **£6,469** (£1,925; £962; £481) **Stalls** Low

Form RPR
6622 **1** **No Win No Fee**[18] 3335 4-9-0 **66**.......................................... AndrewMullen 2 83
(Michael Appleby) *in tch in midfield: rdn and effrt 2f out: led over 1f out: gng clr and edgd lft 1f out: r.o strly: readily* **7/1**[3]
1111 **2** *6* **Thecornishcowboy**[6] 3761 5-9-12 **85** 6ex..........(t) JordonMcMurray(7) 3 91
(John Ryan) *hld up in tch in midfield: hdwy to chse ldrs over 2f out: swtchd rt wl over 1f out: no ch w wnr fnl f: kpt on to snatch 2nd on post* **9/1**
0042 **3** *nse* **Artful Prince**[21] 3254 4-9-9 **75**...........................(b) DaleSwift 7 81
(James Given) *chsd ldr: drvn to ld over 2f out: hdd over 1f out: sn outpcd and btn: kpt on but lost 2nd on post* **12/1**
0303 **4** *1¼* **Every Time**[23] 3154 3-8-10 **76**.......................................... OisinMurphy(3) 9 80
(Andrew Balding) *hld up in last pair: rdn and hdwy on outer over 2f out: no ch w wnr but battling for placings 1f out: kpt on same pce* **7/2**[2]
4243 **5** *6* **Hydrant**[18] 3335 8-9-6 **77**.......................................... DuilioDaSilva(5) 8 69
(Richard Guest) *led: rdn and hdd over 2f out: 5th and btn over 1f out: wknd fnl f* **25/1**
15-0 **6** *6* **Flashheart (IRE)**[26] 3065 4-9-12 **78**.......................................... BenCurtis 1 59
(Marcus Tregoning) *chsd ldrs: rdn and struggling 3f out: 6th and btn 2f out: sn wknd* **12/1**
1-2 **7** *18* **Tanqeya (IRE)**[43] 2510 3-9-3 **80**.......................................... DaneO'Neill 10 27
(Richard Hannon) *chsd ldrs: rdn and no rspnse over 2f out: sn btn: t.o fnl f* **5/4**[1]
1111 **8** *7* **Kindlelight Storm (USA)**[106] 1051 4-9-6 **72**.............(b) J-PGuillambert 5 5
(Nick Littmoden) *hld up in last pair: rdn 3f out: sn btn: t.o over 1f out* **40/1**
00-5 **9** *½* **Attenzione (IRE)**[31] 2881 3-8-13 **76**...........................(t) MartinHarley 4 8
(Marco Botti) *in tch in midfield: rdn and btn over 2f out: lost tch 2f out: t.o 1f out* **16/1**

2m 10.99s (-3.31) **Going Correction** -0.15s/f (Firm)
**WFA** 3 from 4yo+ 11lb **9** Ran SP% **116.7**
Speed ratings (Par 105): **107,102,102,101,96 91,77,71,71**
CSF £68.64 CT £747.19 TOTE £11.10: £2.20, £2.90, £5.00; EX 60.50 Trifecta £1051.60.
**Owner** Stephen Almond **Bred** Bearstone Stud **Trained** Danethorpe, Notts

**FOCUS**
A few improving and unexposed 3yos in this useful handicap, in which they went a solid pace, but the older generation filled the first three places.

## 3978 RACING UK ANYWHERE AVAILABLE NOW H'CAP 1m 2f 50y
**8:30** (8:31) (Class 5) (0-70,70) 3-Y-O £2,587 (£770; £384; £192) **Stalls** Low

Form RPR
4-02 1 **Inevitable**[5] 3789 3-9-2 **68** MichaelJMMurphy(3) 1 75+
(Mark Johnston) *chsd ldrs tl led over 8f out: mde rest: rdn 3f out: forged ahd over 1f out: clr ins fnl f: kpt on* **5/4**[1]

350 2 1 1/2 **Frosty The Snowman (IRE)**[11] 3545 3-8-11 **60** PaulMulrennan 7 64
(Ruth Carr) *stdd after s: hld up in rr: hdwy towards inner over 1f out: chsd wnr ins fnl f: kpt on but nvr able to chal* **33/1**

0-02 3 3/4 **Oyster (IRE)**[28] 2998 3-9-0 **63** (b[1]) J-PGuillambert 12 66
(Nick Littmoden) *s.i.s: rdn 3f out: hdwy u.p over 1f out: styd on to go 3rd ins fnl f: kpt on* **16/1**

-440 4 2 1/4 **Darting**[22] 3195 3-9-4 **70** OisinMurphy(3) 10 68
(Andrew Balding) *t.k.h: led tl over 8f out: chsd wnr after: rdn and ev ch 3f out: no ex and btn ent fnl f: wknd and lost 2 pls ins fnl f* **10/1**

0300 5 2 1/4 **Peacemaker (IRE)**[11] 3559 3-9-2 **65** (p) JohnFahy 8 59
(Eve Johnson Houghton) *s.i.s: in tch in rr: effrt u.p on outer over 2f out: styd on past btn horses fnl f: nvr threatened ldrs* **28/1**

00-6 6 1/2 **Clodoaldo (IRE)**[21] 3229 3-8-13 **65** RyanClark(3) 2 58
(Brian Meehan) *dwlt: rcvrd and hdwy to chse ldrs after 1f out: drvn and unable qck over 2f out: wknd ent fnl f* **25/1**

51 7 hd **Betty Bere (FR)**[18] 3332 3-9-7 **70** MartinHarley 3 63
(K R Burke) *hld up in tch in midfield: clsd to chse ldrs and gng wl over 2f out: wnt 3rd and rdn wl over 1f out: sn btn: wknd fnl f* **5/1**[2]

-353 8 3/4 **Argot**[15] 3430 3-9-7 **70** WilliamCarson 5 61
(Anthony Carson) *t.k.h: hld up in tch towards rr: rdn 3f out: no imp whn short of room and hmpd 2f out: n.d after* **8/1**

6010 9 1 1/4 **Bognor (USA)**[23] 3135 3-9-7 **70** AndrewMullen 4 59
(Michael Appleby) *chsd ldrs: rdn and effrt over 2f out: struggling and outpcd over 1f out: wknd fnl f* **18/1**

64-5 10 1 1/2 **Wealth (IRE)**[177] 99 3-8-11 **63** GeorgeChaloner(3) 9 49
(Richard Fahey) *in tch in midfield: hdwy u.p on outer to chse ldrs 3f out: no ex and btn over 1f out: wknd fnl f* **6/1**[3]

10-0 11 14 **Light Weight (IRE)**[22] 3195 3-9-6 **69** (p) HarryBentley 11 29
(Kevin Ryan) *chsd ldrs: rdn and struggling over 2f out: lost pl and bhd whn hmpd 2f out: bhd fnl f* **25/1**

2m 13.37s (-0.93) **Going Correction** -0.15s/f (Firm) 11 Ran SP% **120.8**
Speed ratings (Par 100): **97,95,95,93,91 91,91,90,89,88 77**
CSF £64.16 CT £498.86 TOTE £3.30: £1.90, £3.40, £4.70; EX 55.10 Trifecta £1330.20 Part won..
**Owner** Sheikh Hamdan bin Mohammed Al Maktoum **Bred** Brook Stud Bloodstock Ltd **Trained** Middleham Moor, N Yorks

■ Stewards' Enquiry : J-P Guillambert two-day ban: used whip above permitted level (Jul 19-20)

**FOCUS**
The pace was ordinary for this modest 3yo handicap but the form looks solid enough.

## 3979 WATCH RACING UK ON CHANNEL 432 H'CAP 1m 75y
**9:00** (9:01) (Class 5) (0-75,75) 3-Y-O+ £2,587 (£770; £384; £192) **Stalls** Centre

Form RPR
1544 1 **Ted's Brother (IRE)**[17] 3361 6-9-6 **72** (e) DuilioDaSilva(5) 8 81
(Richard Guest) *hld up in tch: rdn and effrt on outer over 2f out: gd hdwy 1f out: chal ins fnl f: r.o to ld cl home* **14/1**

2330 2 nk **Simply Shining (IRE)**[20] 3272 4-9-8 **72** GeorgeChaloner(3) 4 80
(Richard Fahey) *in tch in midfield: hdwy to chse ldrs 4f out: rdn to chse ldr over 2f out: sn ev ch: led jst over 1f out: kpt on tl hdd and no ex cl home* **6/1**[2]

4606 3 hd **No Dominion (IRE)**[20] 3272 5-10-0 **75** DaleSwift 1 83
(James Given) *s.i.s: t.k.h: hld uip in tch towards rr: hdwy on inner 3f out: swtchd rt and chal between horse 2f out: ev ch after: no ex cl home* **8/1**

0-00 4 3 **Majestic Dream (IRE)**[19] 3299 6-9-7 **68** (b) GrahamGibbons 6 69
(Michael Easterby) *led: rdn ent fnl 2f: hdd jst over 1f out: no ex ins fnl f: wknd fnl 100yds* **33/1**

3032 5 4 **Sherston**[4] 3814 3-8-6 **65** (b) MichaelJMMurphy(3) 3 55
(Mark Johnston) *chsd ldr for 1f: chsd ldrs after: drvn and unable qck over 2f out: outpcd over 1f out: wknd fnl f* **9/2**[1]

-565 6 2 **Tea In Transvaal (IRE)**[8] 3670 3-9-2 **72** (b[1]) PatDobbs 9 57
(Richard Hannon) *t.k.h: hdwy to chse ldr after 1f: drvn and lost 2nd over 2f out: wknd over 1f out* **8/1**

4000 7 1 **Woody Bay**[16] 3400 4-9-10 **71** PaulMulrennan 2 56
(James Given) *in tch in midfield: rdn and effrt 3f out: outpcd and btn 2f out: wknd over 1f out* **12/1**

0552 8 2 1/4 **Not Rigg (USA)**[10] 3562 4-8-13 **60** JackMitchell 7 40
(Nick Littmoden) *chsd ldrs: rdn and effrt 2f out: drvn and btn over 1f out: sn wknd* **9/2**[1]

-030 9 1 1/2 **Wickhambrook (IRE)**[21] 3225 3-9-5 **75** LiamJones 5 49
(Ismail Mohammed) *in tch in midfield: sme hdwy u.p over 2f out: no imp and btn 2f out: sn wknd* **14/1**

2-16 10 4 1/2 **Ivy Port**[156] 388 4-8-11 **58** AndrewMullen 11 24
(Michael Appleby) *sn bhd and nvr travelling in rr: nvr on terms* **12/1**

4-30 11 hd **Silver Mirage**[23] 3154 3-9-3 **73** TomQueally 10 36
(Michael Bell) *s.i.s: in tch in last trio: rdn and effrt over 2f out: sn btn: bhd over 1f out* **15/2**[3]

1m 46.51s (-2.49) **Going Correction** -0.15s/f (Firm)
**WFA** 3 from 4yo+ 9lb 11 Ran SP% **116.3**
Speed ratings (Par 103): **106,105,105,102,98 96,95,93,91,87 87**
CSF £94.71 CT £740.17 TOTE £13.00: £4.10, £2.10, £2.40; EX 98.20 Trifecta £1074.20.
**Owner** Ontoawinner & Guest **Bred** T Counihan **Trained** ingmanthorpe, W Yorks

**FOCUS**
They went hard up front and there was a tight finish to this fair handicap. The form looks viable.
T/Plt: £168.40 to a £1 stake. Pool: £51,198.92 - 221.83 winning units T/Qpdt: £35.20 to a £1 stake. Pool: £4,275.84 - 89.80 winning units SP

# 3927 SANDOWN (R-H)
Saturday, July 5

**OFFICIAL GOING: Good to firm (firm in places on the round course; round course 8.7; sprint course 8.4)**
Wind: Moderate, against Weather: Cloudy becoming overcast; rain race 4

## 3980 GARY TUCK MEMORIAL H'CAP (BOBIS RACE) 7f 16y
**1:30** (1:31) (Class 3) (0-95,90) 3-Y-O
**£9,337** (£2,796; £1,398; £699; £349; £175) **Stalls** Low

Form RPR
4016 1 **Royal Seal**[14] 3478 3-9-2 **85** [1] RyanMoore 7 96
(Sir Michael Stoute) *hld up in 5th: shkn up and prog on outer fr over 2f out: led over 1f out: drvn clr* **13/2**

64-1 2 2 **Mutawathea**[91] 1298 3-8-13 **82** PaulHanagan 4 88
(Richard Hannon) *hld up in 4th: rdn and nt qckn on outer over 2f out: styd on fr over 1f out to take 2nd last strides* **6/1**

-012 3 nk **Extremity (IRE)**[30] 2921 3-9-1 **84** JamesDoyle 1 89
(Hugo Palmer) *trckd ldng pair: rdn to cl over 1f out as wnr wnt by: chsd after and no imp: lost 2nd last strides* **5/2**[1]

-121 4 1 1/2 **Captain Bob (IRE)**[21] 3247 3-9-6 **89** WilliamBuick 2 90
(Charles Hills) *led: rdn and pressed 2f out: hdd and one pce over 1f out* **11/4**[2]

-116 5 1 1/4 **Reedcutter**[21] 3243 3-9-1 **84** RichardHughes 3 82
(James Toller) *pressed ldr: chal 2f out: edgd lft and fnd nil over 1f out: wknd* **5/1**[3]

4-53 6 2 1/4 **Whaleweigh Station**[21] 3229 3-9-7 **90** RichardKingscote 6 82
(Tom Dascombe) *hld up in last pair: shkn up 2f out: no prog over 1f out: wknd fnl f* **25/1**

-600 7 2 1/4 **Mawfoor (IRE)**[16] 3378 3-9-7 **90** [1] JimmyFortune 5 76
(Brian Meehan) *stdd s: hld up in last pair: shkn up and no prog 2f out: wl btn after* **16/1**

1m 27.67s (-1.83) **Going Correction** -0.125s/f (Firm) 7 Ran SP% **109.3**
Speed ratings (Par 104): **105,102,102,100,99 96,94**
CSF £40.37 CT £111.85 TOTE £5.40: £2.60, £3.00; EX 36.00 Trifecta £147.40.
**Owner** Cheveley Park Stud **Bred** Cheveley Park Stud Ltd **Trained** Newmarket, Suffolk

**FOCUS**
Rail at innermost position and all distances as advertised. Just 3mm of overnight rain, and a little prior to racing, left the ground riding fast, with it being slightly quicker on the round course. Paul Hanagan felt it was riding very similar to the previous day. The rail was at its innermost configuration. The closers came to the fore off a fair gallop. The winner built on his Yarmouth win and is bred to be smart.

## 3981 CORAL CHARGE (REGISTERED AS THE SPRINT STKS) (GROUP 3) 5f 6y
**2:05** (2:06) (Class 1) 3-Y-O+
**£35,443** (£13,437; £6,725; £3,350; £1,681; £843) **Stalls** Low

Form RPR
0012 1 **Extortionist (IRE)**[7] 3736 3-8-12 106 RyanMoore 4 115
(Olly Stevens) *in tch in midfield on inner: rdn and prog fr 2f out: sustained effrt fnl f to ld last 100yds: drvn out* **13/2**

0-23 2 1 1/4 **Kingsgate Native (IRE)**[42] 2563 9-9-3 112 JamesDoyle 8 113
(Robert Cowell) *trckd ldng pair: rdn to chal over 1f out: led jst ins fnl f: hdd last 100yds: styd on* **5/1**[2]

4063 3 1 1/4 **Dinkum Diamond (IRE)**[21] 3241 6-9-3 107 DavidProbert 10 108
(Henry Candy) *chsd ldrs: rdn and nt qckn 2f out: styd on fnl f to take 3rd nr fin* **9/1**

-041 4 nse **Wind Fire (USA)**[21] 3245 3-8-9 103 OisinMurphy 12 103
(David Brown) *towards rr: rdn on outer 2f out: styd on fnl f: nrly snatched 3rd fin* **15/2**

3146 5 nk **Steps (IRE)**[18] 3319 6-9-3 110 (b) KierenFallon 1 107+
(Roger Varian) *s.s: pushed along in last pair: prog whn nt clr run over 1f out: styd on ins fnl f: n.d* **4/1**[1]

4342 6 3/4 **Stepper Point**[18] 3319 5-9-3 113 (p) MartinDwyer 9 104
(William Muir) *pressed ldr: led over 2f out: rdn and hdd jst ins fnl f: fdd* **11/2**[3]

2225 7 1/2 **Ahtoug**[18] 3319 6-9-3 115 WilliamBuick 6 102
(Charlie Appleby) *chsd ldng pair: rdn over 1f out: sn lost pl: swtchd lft ins fnl f: no prog* **6/1**

10-0 8 1/2 **Green Door (IRE)**[18] 3319 3-8-12 105 JimmyFortune 11 98
(Olly Stevens) *s.i.s: t.k.h and hld up in last pair: taken to outer 2f out and gng bttr than sme: pushed along and no hdwy over 1f out: nvr in it* **25/1**

2621 9 2 **Hay Chewed (IRE)**[14] 3459 3-8-9 99 PaulHanagan 7 88
(Conrad Allen) *led against far rail: rdn and hdd over 2f out: wknd over 1f out* **14/1**

5004 10 8 **Trader Jack**[1] 3927 5-9-3 82 (b) SeamieHeffernan 5 64
(David Flood) *pushed along in midfield bef 1/2-way: lost pl and btn wl over 1f out* **66/1**

59.86s (-1.74) **Going Correction** -0.125s/f (Firm)
**WFA** 3 from 5yo+ 5lb 10 Ran SP% **113.4**
Speed ratings (Par 113): **108,106,104,103,103 102,101,100,97,84**
CSF £37.87 TOTE £8.20: £2.70, £1.80, £3.10; EX 40.10 Trifecta £476.90.
**Owner** Sheikh Suhaim Al Thani **Bred** Mrs Louise Lyons **Trained** Chiddingfold, Surrey

**FOCUS**
The leaders went off hard in this sprint and Ryan Moore was again seen to excellent effect aboard the winner. Hard form to pin down, but the winner is worth a length best.

## 3982 CORAL CHALLENGE (H'CAP) 1m 14y
**2:40** (2:41) (Class 2) 3-Y-O+
**£46,687** (£13,980; £6,990; £3,495; £1,747; £877) **Stalls** Low

Form RPR
4-40 1 **Velox**[29] 2959 4-8-0 **88** CamHardie(5) 4 102
(Luca Cumani) *chsd clr ldrs in 6th: prog over 2f out: rdn to chse ldr over 1f out: clsd to ld last 140yds: qckly drew clr* **11/2**[2]

6010 2 3 **Ifwecan**[16] 3378 3-8-0 **92** oh1 FrannyNorton 2 97+
(Mark Johnston) *led at str pce but pressed: rdn 2f out: kpt on wl and looked like holding on 1f out: hdd and outpcd last 140yds* **14/1**

1240 3 1 1/4 **Gabrial's Kaka (IRE)**[17] 3356 4-9-6 **103** FrankieDettori 9 107
(Richard Fahey) *wl bhd in last and shoved along fr 1/2-way: sed to make grnd jst over 2f out: styd on wl fr over 1f out to take 3rd last stride* **7/1**[3]

-210 4 nse **Russian Realm**[15] 3420 4-8-13 **96** RyanMoore 8 100
(Sir Michael Stoute) *hld up wl in rr: rdn and prog on outer fr over 2f out: chsd ldng pair jst over 1f out: no imp fnl f: lost 3rd fnl stride* **7/2**[1]

0-30 **5** 1/2 **Prince Of Johanne (IRE)**[17] 3356 8-9-3 **100**............(p) PaulHanagan 14 103
(Tom Tate) *wl bhd in 12th and pushed along by 1/2-way: sed to make grnd 2f out: styd on fnl f: nrst fin* **10/1**

0160 **6** 3/4 **Secret Art (IRE)**[15] 3420 4-8-10 **93**............ RichardKingscote 6 94
(William Knight) *racd in 7th and off the pce: rdn over 2f out: sn lost pl and in rr: kpt on again fnl f* **16/1**

5113 **7** 1/2 **St Moritz (IRE)**[21] 3244 8-8-6 **92**............(v) OisinMurphy(3) 11 92
(David O'Meara) *s.i.s: pushed up and rapid prog to press ldr after 2f: lost 2nd and fdd over 1f out* **10/1**

3050 **8** 1 3/4 **Lyn Valley**[16] 3378 3-8-2 **94**............ DavidProbert 10 88
(Mark Johnston) *chsd clr ldrs in 5th: rdn over 2f out: no prog after: steadily fdd* **10/1**

000 **9** 3/4 **Burano (IRE)**[17] 3356 5-9-0 **97**............ JimmyFortune 5 91
(Brian Meehan) *hld up wl in rr: pushed along over 2f out: nt clr run over 1f out and dropped to last: styd on fnl f but no ch* **12/1**

0242 **10** 1 3/4 **Busatto (USA)**[7] 3726 4-8-9 **92**............ KierenFallon 12 82
(Mark Johnston) *t.k.h: pressed ldr 2f: clr of rest in 3rd tl wknd over 1f out* **14/1**

3-00 **11** hd **Snowboarder (USA)**[21] 3252 4-9-6 **103**............ WilliamBuick 3 93
(Charlie Appleby) *chsd clr ldng trio: tried to cl over 2f out: lost pl and wknd over 1f out* **28/1**

-150 **12** 2 3/4 **Birdman (IRE)**[140] 625 4-8-9 **92**............(be) MartinLane 1 75
(David Simcock) *hld up off the pce in 8th: tried to make prog on inner over 2f out: wknd over 1f out* **50/1**

0316 **13** 3/4 **Brazos (IRE)**[17] 3352 3-8-13 **105**............ JamesDoyle 7 90
(Clive Brittain) *racd wd and wl in rr: shkn up over 2f out: no prog and wl btn over 1f out: eased* **9/1**

1m 39.35s (-3.95) **Going Correction** -0.125s/f (Firm)
**WFA** 3 from 4yo+ 9lb **13** Ran SP% **119.7**
Speed ratings (Par 109): **114,111,109,109,109 108,107,106,105,103 103,100,100**
CSF £80.59 CT £572.46 TOTE £6.00: £2.60, £4.40, £2.60; EX 83.10 Trifecta £670.50.
**Owner** S Stuckey **Bred** Stuart Stuckey **Trained** Newmarket, Suffolk

**FOCUS**
Run at 6f pace, the race set up for the closers. The winner built on his Epsom run.

## 3983 CORAL DISTAFF (LISTED RACE) (FILLIES) 1m 14y
**3:15** (3:15) (Class 1) 3-Y-O
**£20,982** (£7,955; £3,981; £1,983; £995; £499) **Stalls** Low

Form RPR

-21 **1** **Belle D'Or (USA)**[20] 3276 3-9-0 83............ WilliamBuick 6 102
(John Gosden) *chsd ldr: shkn up over 2f out: looked hld tl picked up fnl f: r.o wl to ld post* **11/2**[3]

3213 **2** nse **Wee Jean**[17] 3357 3-9-0 95............ RichardHughes 1 101
(Mick Channon) *led: sent for home over 2f out: shkn up and looked in command 1f out: styd on but hdd post* **10/1**

2110 **3** 2 1/2 **Crowley's Law**[17] 3357 3-9-0 98............ RichardKingscote 2 95
(Tom Dascombe) *trckd ldng pair: shkn up over 2f out: disp 2nd briefly over 1f out: one pce fnl f* **6/1**

66-2 **4** 2 1/2 **Veiled Intrigue**[56] 2155 3-9-0 101............ DavidProbert 4 89
(Henry Candy) *hld up in last: rdn and no prog jst over 2f out: kpt on to take mod 4th ins fnl f* **25/1**

-502 **5** 1 3/4 **Queen Catrine (IRE)**[17] 3357 3-9-0 105............ RyanMoore 3 85
(Charles Hills) *t.k.h: hld up in 4th: shkn up and no prog jst over 2f out: wl btn over 1f out* **5/4**[1]

4-20 **6** 2 **Radiator**[15] 3418 3-9-0 103............ JamesDoyle 5 80
(Sir Michael Stoute) *racd on outer: hld up in 5th: shkn up over 2f out: no prog and wl btn over 1f out* **3/1**[2]

1m 41.6s (-1.70) **Going Correction** -0.125s/f (Firm) **6** Ran SP% **112.1**
Speed ratings (Par 105): **103,102,100,97,96 94**
CSF £53.87 TOTE £5.30: £3.30, £3.50; EX 40.50 Trifecta £117.70.
**Owner** A E Oppenheimer **Bred** Hascombe Stud **Trained** Newmarket, Suffolk

**FOCUS**
It started raining again prior to this contest, a decent fillies' event that was run at a dawdling gallop and in a time a stone slower than the preceding handicap. The first two home were in the front pair throughout and the form rates at the lower end of the race averages.

## 3984 CORAL-ECLIPSE (BRITISH CHAMPIONS SERIES) (GROUP 1) 1m 2f 7y
**3:50** (3:52) (Class 1) 3-Y-O+
**£255,195** (£96,750; £48,420; £24,120; £12,105; £6,075) **Stalls** Low

Form RPR

5-24 **1** **Mukhadram**[17] 3354 5-9-7 119............ PaulHanagan 10 120
(William Haggas) *trckd ldr and clr in ldng trio: led 3f out: sent for home and clr 2f out: drvn but nvr in any danger fr over 1f out* **14/1**

23-3 **2** 2 **Trading Leather (IRE)**[63] 1950 4-9-7 119............ KevinManning 5 116
(J S Bolger, Ire) *trckd ldng pair and clr of rest: drvn over 2f out: chsd wnr wl over 1f out: kpt on but no real imp* **12/1**

-530 **3** 3/4 **Somewhat (USA)**[16] 3375 3-8-10 102............ FrannyNorton 11 114
(Mark Johnston) *led: set gd pce and stretched field: rdn and hdd 3f out: lost 2nd wl over 1f out but stl clr of rest: hld on wl for 3rd* **100/1**

1-02 **4** 1 1/4 **Kingston Hill**[28] 2990 3-8-10 120............ FrankieDettori 8 112+
(Roger Varian) *hld up in 6th and off the pce: rdn wl over 2f out: kpt on fr over 1f out: nrst fin: too much to do* **4/1**[3]

-130 **5** shd **True Story**[28] 2990 3-8-10 114............(v1) KierenFallon 4 111
(Saeed bin Suroor) *t.k.h: hld up: trckd clr ldng trio 1/2-way: rdn and nt qckn wl over 2f out: kpt on fr over 1f out: no ch* **16/1**

2-01 **6** 2 **The Fugue**[17] 3354 5-9-4 124............ WilliamBuick 1 104+
(John Gosden) *stdd s: hld up in last: trying to make prog whn nt clr run over 2f out: rdn wl over 1f out but task already hopeless: plugged on* **5/2**[1]

1-04 **7** nk **War Command (USA)**[18] 3320 3-8-10 117............(p) SeamieHeffernan 7 107
(A P O'Brien, Ire) *hld up in 8th and off the pce: rdn wl over 2f out: no prog and sn btn: plugged on fnl f* **8/1**

-212 **8** 1 3/4 **Night Of Thunder (IRE)**[18] 3320 3-8-10 120............ RichardHughes 3 103
(Richard Hannon) *hld up in 7th and off the pce: prog into 4th 2f out but nowhere nr ldng trio: rdn and no prog after: wknd fnl f* **7/2**[2]

4-32 **9** 5 **Verrazano (USA)**[18] 3317 4-9-7 120............ RyanMoore 6 93
(A P O'Brien, Ire) *chsd clr ldng trio to 1/2-way: rdn and struggling wl over 2f out: sn wknd* **7/1**

2m 4.47s (-6.03) **Going Correction** -0.125s/f (Firm)
**WFA** 3 from 4yo+ 11lb **9** Ran SP% **115.6**
Speed ratings (Par 117): **119,117,116,115,115 114,113,112,108**
CSF £168.16 CT £15029.88 TOTE £14.60: £3.00, £2.50, £14.20; EX 64.90 Trifecta £1373.90.
**Owner** Hamdan Al Maktoum **Bred** Wardall Bloodstock **Trained** Newmarket, Suffolk

**FOCUS**
What had promised to be a vintage edition of the race, featuring the 2,000 Guineas winner and Derby runner-up amongst the Classic generation, taking on several top older performers, never really materialised, with the first three racing in the front trio throughout, a little way on from the remainder, and never coming back to them. Complete outsider Somewhat was driven to lead and went fast early, taking the eventual first and second with him, but the pace then slowed a little and by the time they began racing in the home straight, the principals found themselves with too much ground to make up, resulting in something of an unsatisfactory result. Somewhat is the key to the form but there's a chance Mukhadram ran to his best. Trading Leather got close to his 3yo form.

## 3985 CORAL MARATHON (REGISTERED AS THE ESHER STKS) (LISTED RACE) 2m 78y
**4:25** (4:26) (Class 1) 4-Y-O+
**£20,982** (£7,955; £3,981; £1,983) **Stalls** Centre

Form RPR

-650 **1** **Havana Beat (IRE)**[16] 3377 4-9-0 103............ DavidProbert 4 106
(Andrew Balding) *trckd ldr: rdn to chal 2f out: nt qckn over 1f out and looked hld: rallied last 150yds: led fnl strides* **11/4**[3]

5063 **2** hd **Repeater**[7] 3717 5-9-0 102............ RyanMoore 2 106
(David O'Meara) *rel to r and lft 12 l: sn ct up as pce mod: trckd ldng pair over 6f out: cl up 2f out: swtchd ins and drvn to ld jst ins fnl f: idled and hdd last strides* **5/2**[2]

/0-1 **3** nk **Domination**[18] 3321 7-9-0 100............ FMBerry 7 105
(C Byrnes, Ire) *led at mod pce: kicked on 4f out: drvn and pressed 2f out: hdd and one pce jst ins fnl f* **11/8**[1]

040 **4** 4 1/2 **Body Language (IRE)**[18] 3321 6-8-9 90............(p) JamesDoyle 3 95
(Ian Williams) *trckd ldng pair to over 6f out: in trble once pce lifted 4f out: wl btn over 2f out* **8/1**

3m 48.57s (9.87) **Going Correction** -0.125s/f (Firm) **4** Ran SP% **108.5**
Speed ratings (Par 111): **70,69,69,67**
CSF £9.67 TOTE £3.30; EX 8.90 Trifecta £14.30.
**Owner** Mick and Janice Mariscotti **Bred** Ms Natalie Cleary **Trained** Kingsclere, Hants

**FOCUS**
With three non-runners and no obvious front-runner, this was always likely to be messy, but it did produce a gripping three-way finish. The form is rated through the winner and third.

## 3986 DOWNLOAD THE CORAL APP H'CAP (BOBIS RACE) 1m 2f 7y
**5:00** (5:00) (Class 4) (0-85,85) 3-Y-O
**£6,469** (£1,925; £962; £481) **Stalls** Low

Form RPR

-643 **1** **Raise Your Gaze**[22] 3197 3-8-10 **77**............ RyanTate(3) 11 91
(Clive Cox) *hld up in last: prog on outer over 2f out: shkn up to ld wl over 1f out and sn clr: rdn out* **5/2**[1]

4352 **2** 6 **Samtu (IRE)**[23] 3146 3-8-7 **71**............ KierenFallon 9 74
(Clive Brittain) *hld up in 5th: pushed along 3f out: no ch w wnr fr over 1f out but styd on u.p to take 2nd last 100yds* **7/2**[2]

5555 **3** 1 1/2 **Best Kept**[22] 3197 3-8-13 **77**............ JamesDoyle 4 77
(Amanda Perrett) *led 1f: sn in 4th: prog to chal and drvn 2f out: wnr sn swept past: kpt on same pce after* **9/2**[3]

-420 **4** nk **Gothic**[21] 3243 3-9-7 **85**............(b1) RyanMoore 6 85
(Sir Michael Stoute) *trckd ldr after 2f: rdn to ld over 2f out: hdd wl over 1f out and no ch w wnr after: one pce fnl f* **5/2**[1]

14-4 **5** 7 **Aristocracy**[155] 404 3-7-11 **68**............ PaddyPilley(7) 3 54
(Mick Channon) *pushed up to ld after 1f: mde most to over 2f out: wknd wl over 1f out* **16/1**

0200 **6** 15 **Rookery (IRE)**[4] 3829 3-8-6 **70**............(b1) FrannyNorton 2 28
(Mark Johnston) *mostly trckd ldng pair to 3f out: rdn and wknd over 2f out: t.o* **12/1**

2m 6.88s (-3.62) **Going Correction** -0.125s/f (Firm) **6** Ran SP% **111.1**
Speed ratings (Par 102): **109,104,103,102,97 85**
CSF £11.26 CT £34.12 TOTE £3.10: £1.50, £2.00; EX 11.50 Trifecta £40.20.
**Owner** Miss J Deadman & S Barrow **Bred** James Ortega Bloodstock **Trained** Lambourn, Berks

**FOCUS**
Another race hit by non-runners and it produced a clear-cut winner. A personal best from him, but possibly not all it looks.
T/Jkpt: Not won. T/Plt: £20,601.40 to a £1 stake. Pool: £222,946.88 - 7.90 winning tickets.
T/Qpdt: £872.40 to a £1 stake. Pool: £14,619.50 - 12.40 winning tickets. JN

3987 - 3993a (Foreign Racing) - See Raceform Interactive

# 3743 BELMONT PARK (L-H)
Saturday, July 5

**OFFICIAL GOING: Dirt: fast, turf: good**

## 3994a BELMONT DERBY INVITATIONAL STKS (GRADE 1) (3YO) (TURF) 1m 2f (T)
**9:34** (12:00) 3-Y-O
**£403,614** (£138,554; £75,301; £51,204; £30,120; £21,084)

RPR

**1** **Mr Speaker (USA)**[40] 3-8-10 0............ JLezcano 8 112+
(Claude McGaughey III, U.S.A) *hld up in rr: tk clsr order on inner 3f out: 7th and styng on 2f out: rdn and r.o fnl f: led 120yds out: drvn out to hold off rally of runner-up* **235/10**

**2** nk **Adelaide (IRE)**[15] 3417 3-8-10 0............ ColmO'Donoghue 4 111+
(A P O'Brien, Ire) *midfield: cl up in 4th after 5f: qcknd between horses to ld over 1f out: r.o: hdd 120yds out: rallied and pressed wnr to line* **9/4**[1]

**3** 3 1/2 **Flamboyant (FR)**[40] 3-8-10 0............ JRosario 5 104
(Patrick Gallagher, U.S.A) *w.w towards rr: tk clsr order 1/2-way: 6th and pushed along 3f out: swtchd outside and nowhere to go 1 1/2f out: snatched up and swtchd outside again: r.o and swtchd ins to go 3rd ins fnl f: kpt on wl but nt* **196/10**

**4** 1/2 **Gailo Chop (FR)**[75] 1621 3-8-10 0............ JulienAuge 6 103
(A De Watrigant, France) **23/5**

**5** nk **Sheldon (USA)**[23] 3-8-10 0............(b) JAlvarado 2 103
(James J Toner, U.S.A) **35/1**

**6** 3/4 **Toast Of New York (USA)**[98] 1178 3-8-10 0............ JamieSpencer 1 101
(Jamie Osborne) **9/2**[3]

**7** 1/2 **Global View (USA)**[34] 3-8-10 0............ GaryStevens 9 100
(Thomas F Proctor, U.S.A) **84/10**

**8** 8 3/4 **Bobby's Kitten (USA)**[34] 3-8-10 0............ JJCastellano 3 83
(Chad C Brown, U.S.A) **4/1**[2]

**9** 4 1/4 **Pornichet (FR)**[55] 2196 3-8-10 0............(b1) JLOrtiz 7 74
(Gai Waterhouse, Australia) **196/10**

**10** 3 3/4 **Gala Award (USA)**[40] 3-8-10 0............ JRVelazquez 10 67
(Todd Pletcher, U.S.A) **152/10**

2m 1.18s (-0.11) **10** Ran SP% **120.2**
PARI-MUTUEL (all including 2 usd stake): WIN 49.00; PLACE (1-2) 18.20, 4.40; SHOW (1-2-3) 10.80, 3.20, 7.40; SF 288.50.

**Owner** Phipps Stable **Bred** Phipps Stable **Trained** USA

## 3995a BELMONT OAKS INVITATIONAL (GRADE 1) (3YO FILLIES) (TURF) 1m 2f (T)
**10:45** (12:00) 3-Y-0
**£322,289** (£111,445; £60,240; £39,156; £24,096; £18,072)

RPR
1 **Minorette (USA)**41 3-8-9 0 JRosario 8 108
(Chad C Brown, U.S.A) **63/10**
2 2 **Sea Queen (USA)**41 3-8-9 0 IOrtizJr 10 104
(Christophe Clement, U.S.A) **91/10**
3 1 1/4 **Summer Solo (USA)**24 3-8-9 0 CHVelasquez 3 102+
(Christophe Clement, U.S.A) **34/1**
4 3/4 **Xcellence (FR)**20 3289 3-8-9 0 GeraldMosse 6 100+
(F Doumen, France) **3/1**2
5 3/4 **Wonderfully (IRE)**41 2581 3-8-9 0 ColmO'Donoghue 7 99
(A P O'Brien, Ire) **199/10**
6 3/4 **Goldy Espony (FR)**41 2586 3-8-9 0 JLezcano 1 97+
(Chad C Brown, U.S.A) **112/10**
7 1 3/4 **Room Service (USA)**34 2822 3-8-9 0 SXBridgmohan 2 94+
(Wayne Catalano, U.S.A) **13/5**1
8 3 **Flying Jib**61 2042 3-8-9 0 PatSmullen 4 88
(D K Weld, Ire) **54/10**3
9 1/2 **Rosalind (USA)**15 3418 3-8-9 0 JRLeparoux 5 87+
(Kenneth McPeek, U.S.A) **116/10**
10 2 3/4 **Recepta (USA)**41 3-8-9 0 JAlvarado 9 81
(James J Toner, U.S.A) **25/1**

2m 1.64s (0.35) **10** Ran SP% **119.6**
PARI-MUTUEL (all including 2 usd stake): WIN 14.60; PLACE (1-2) 6.30, 9.60; SHOW (1-2-3) 5.50, 6.80, 11.60; SF 106.00.
**Owner** Michael Tabor & Derrick Smith & Mrs John Magnier **Bred** Silk And Scarlet Syndicate **Trained** USA

# 2244 JAGERSRO (R-H)
Saturday, July 5

**OFFICIAL GOING: Dirt: standard**

## 3996a ZAWAWI CUP (GROUP 3) (3YO+) (DIRT) 6f (D)
**5:35** (12:00) 3-Y-0+ **£28,142** (£14,071; £6,754; £4,502; £2,814)

RPR
1 **Let'sgoforit (IRE)**53 2244 6-9-6 0 OliverWilson 6 103
(Bodil Hallencreutz, Sweden) *midfield on outer: pushed along and outpcd 2 1/2f out: styng on fr 1 1/2f out: r.o wl u.p fnl f to ld fnl strides* **758/100**
2 nk **Over The Ocean (USA)**9 4-9-6 0 Per-AndersGraberg 10 102
(Niels Petersen, Norway) *led: hrd rdn over 1f out: r.o u.p fnl f: hdd fnl strides* **36/5**
3 3/4 **Ragazzo (NOR)**9 5-9-6 0 JacobJohansen 4 100
(Annike Bye Hansen, Norway) *chsd ldrs thrght: r.o u.p fnl f: no ex last 50yds* **7/5**1
4 3 **Proud Possibility (USA)**25 4-9-6 0 RafaelSchistl 1 90
(Niels Petersen, Norway) *pressed ldr on inner: rdn and nt qckn 1 1/2f out: fdd ins fnl f* **32/5**3
5 1/2 **Energia Dust (BRZ)**53 2245 6-9-6 0 RafaeldeOliveira 5 88
(Fabricio Borges, Sweden) *towards rr: rdn and outpcd in last over 2f out: styd on u.p fnl 1 1/2f: nrest at fin* **42/10**2
6 3/4 **Alcohuaz (CHI)**20 9-9-6 0 ElioneChaves 3 86
(Lennart Reuterskiold Jr, Sweden) *chsd ldng gp: outpcd over 2f out: kpt on at same pce fnl f* **91/10**
7 2 **Ikc Dragon Heart (USA)**20 4-9-6 0 ShaneKarlsson 7 80
(Johan Reuterskiold, Sweden) *a towards rr: sme late prog: nvr in contention* **38/1**
8 1/2 **Sir Freddie (USA)**25 5-9-6 0 ValmirDeAzeredo 8 78
(Fredrik Reuterskiold, Sweden) *towards rr: rdn and no imp fr 2f out* **31/1**
9 shd **Mr David (USA)**25 7-9-6 0 (b) RebeccaColldin 2 78
(Claes Bjorling, Sweden) *midfield on inner: outpcd and dropped towards rr over 2f out: sn btn* **44/5**
10 2 1/2 **Govinda (USA)**25 7-9-6 0 ManuelSantos 9 70
(Hans-Inge Larsen, Sweden) *chsd ldrs on outer: rdn and lost pl 2f out: wknd fnl f* **33/1**

1m 10.1s (70.10) **10** Ran SP% **127.0**
PARI-MUTUEL (all including 1sek stake): WIN 8.56; PLACE 2.37, 2.05, 1.53; SF 85.52.
**Owner** Bodil Hallencreutz & Barbro L Wehtje **Bred** Castlemartin Sky & Skymarc Farm **Trained** Sweden

# 3170 LONGCHAMP (R-H)
Saturday, July 5

**OFFICIAL GOING: Turf: good to soft**

## 3997a PRIX DE LA PORTE MAILLOT (GROUP 3) (3YO+) (TURF) 7f
**4:50** (12:00) 3-Y-0+ **£33,333** (£13,333; £10,000; £6,666; £3,333)

RPR
1 **Sommerabend**35 2799 7-9-6 0 TheoBachelot 2 115
(M Rulec, Germany) *trckd ldr: shkn up and qcknd to ld 1 1/2f out: r.o fnl f: drvn out* **47/10**3
2 1/2 **American Devil (FR)**14 3451 5-9-4 0 Pierre-CharlesBoudot 1 112
(E Libaud, France) *w.w in share of 5th on inner: hdwy 1 1/2f out: rdn to chse ldr ins fnl f: r.o wl but a hld by wnr* **7/5**1
3 nk **So Long Malpic (FR)**26 3030 7-8-11 0 OlivierPeslier 5 104
(T Lemer, France) *w.w in rr of main gp: hdwy on outer over 1 1/2f out: r.o ins fnl f: nvr quite on terms w ldrs* **221/10**
4 1/2 **Vorda (FR)**62 1976 3-8-4 0 Christophe-PatriceLemaire 7 101
(P Sogorb, France) *lost hind legs as stalls opened and bdly missed break: wl adrift in rr: crept clsr to be in tch w main gp 1 1/2f out: r.o wl on outer fnl f: nrest at fin* **13/5**2
5 1 **Desert Blanc**35 2799 6-9-1 0 GregoryBenoist 8 104
(C Baillet, France) *t.k.h: hld up in share of 5th on outer: rdn and chsd ldrs appr 1f out: kpt on ins fnl f: nt pce to chal* **227/10**
6 nk **Bamiyan (FR)**35 2799 4-9-1 0 ThierryJarnet 6 103
(T Lemer, France) *chsd ldng trio: rdn 1 1/2f out: styd on ins fnl f: nvr able to get on terms* **13/2**
7 8 **Complimentor (IRE)**35 2799 4-9-1 0 MaximeGuyon 4 82
(X Thomas-Demeaulte, France) *pressed ldng pair on outer: led over 2 1/2f out: hdd 1 1/2f out: wknd fnl f* **106/10**
8 3 1/2 **Little Big Shot (IRE)**22 3206 3-8-7 0 (b) AurelienLemaitre 3 69
(F-H Graffard, France) *broke wl and led: hdd over 2 1/2f out: wknd fr 1 1/2f out: eased ins fnl f* **50/1**

1m 20.56s (-0.14)
**WFA** 3 from 4yo+ 8lb **8** Ran SP% **119.5**
WIN (incl. 1 euro stake): 5.70. PLACES: 1.70, 1.30, 3.00. DF: 4.40. SF: 12.60.
**Owner** Stall Am Alten Flies **Bred** Gestut Schlenderhan **Trained** Germany

# 3454 AYR (L-H)
Sunday, July 6

**OFFICIAL GOING: Good to firm (9.4)**
Wind: Breezy, half against Weather: Cloudy, sunny spells

## 3998 FSB BUSINESS BANKING MAIDEN STKS 1m 2f
**1:30** (1:31) (Class 5) 3-Y-O+ **£3,557** (£1,058; £529; £264) **Stalls** Low

Form RPR
3- 1 **Earl Of Menteith (IRE)**375 3695 3-9-3 0 JoeFanning 4 81+
(Mark Johnston) *noisy in paddock: t.k.h: mde all at ordinary gallop: rdn and qcknd over 1f out: kpt on strly fnl f* **7/2**3
2-52 2 1 1/2 **Legal Waves (IRE)**14 3499 4-10-0 80 BenCurtis 5 76
(Alan Swinbank) *trckd ldr to 1/2-way: effrt and rdn 2f out: regained 2nd appr fnl f: kpt on: nt pce to chal* **11/8**1
-000 3 nk **Dolce N Karama (IRE)**30 2971 3-9-3 93 RonanWhelan 2 75
(John Patrick Shanahan, Ire) *t.k.h: trckd ldrs: wnt 2nd 1/2-way: rdn and ev ch over 2f out: lost 2nd appr fnl f: kpt on same pce* **7/4**2
4 4 1/2 **Braes Of Lochalsh** 3-9-3 0 GrahamLee 6 67?
(Jim Goldie) *in tch: rdn and outpcd over 2f out: plugged on fnl f: no imp* **18/1**
5 39 **Joyful Star** 4-10-0 0 DavidAllan 1
(Frederick Watson) *s.s: hdwy to join gp after 2f: rdn and struggling 3f out: sn lost tch: t.o* **100/1**

2m 10.68s (-1.32) **Going Correction** -0.425s/f (Firm)
**WFA** 3 from 4yo 11lb **5** Ran SP% **106.9**
Speed ratings (Par 103): **88,86,86,82,51**
CSF £8.26 TOTE £4.30: £2.10, £1.10; EX 9.40 Trifecta £12.40.
**Owner** Sheikh Hamdan bin Mohammed Al Maktoum **Bred** Tullpark Ltd **Trained** Middleham Moor, N Yorks

**FOCUS**
Not a bad little maiden, but it was tactical.

## 3999 FSB HEALTH & WELLBEING H'CAP 1m 2f
**2:00** (2:00) (Class 4) (0-85,85) 3-Y-O+ **£5,498** (£1,636; £817; £408) **Stalls** Low

Form RPR
55-0 1 **Hold The Line (IRE)**9 3689 4-10-0 **85** RonanWhelan 8 93
(John Patrick Shanahan, Ire) *t.k.h early: hld up in tch: hdwy over 2f out: led over 1f out: drvn and hld on wl fnl f* **10/1**
5332 2 1/2 **Never Forever**23 3190 5-9-0 **71** GrahamLee 5 78
(Jim Goldie) *led at modest gallop: rdn and hdd over 1f out: rallied: hld towards fin* **7/1**
0524 3 1 1/4 **Spin Artist (USA)**11 3572 4-9-0 **71** PJMcDonald 4 76
(Mark Johnston) *prom: drvn and outpcd over 3f out: rallied over 1f out: kpt on fin* **14/1**
-162 4 nse **Lilac Tree**3 3878 4-9-6 **77** JoeFanning 2 83
(Mark Johnston) *trckd ldrs on ins: nt clr run over 2f out and over 1f out: sn edgd lft: rdn and kpt on steadily whn in clr fnl f* **15/8**1
5055 5 nk **Cosmic Halo**15 3457 5-9-1 **75** GeorgeChaloner(3) 3 79
(Richard Fahey) *hld up: hdwy on outside over 3f out: rdn and hung lft fr wl over 1f out: kpt on ins fnl f* **4/1**2
0023 6 3/4 **Argaki (IRE)**15 3457 4-9-8 **79** JasonHart 6 82
(Keith Dalgleish) *pressed ldr: rdn and ev ch over 2f out to over 1f out: no ex ins fnl f* **11/2**3
0032 7 14 **Engrossing**24 3139 5-9-1 **72** (e) JamesSullivan 1 48
(Ruth Carr) *t.k.h: stdd in rr on ins: drvn and struggling over 2f out: sn btn* **7/1**

2m 6.65s (-5.35) **Going Correction** -0.425s/f (Firm) **7** Ran SP% **110.9**
Speed ratings (Par 105): **104,103,102,102,102 101,90**
CSF £71.40 CT £944.37 TOTE £12.10: £5.00, £2.90; EX 46.80 Trifecta £753.00.
**Owner** Thistle Bloodstock Limited **Bred** Thistle Bloodstock Ltd **Trained** Kells, Co Kilkenny

**FOCUS**
Not a bad handicap in which they went a routine pace.

## 4000 FSB 24/7 LEGAL ADVICE LINE H'CAP 1m 2f
**2:30** (2:31) (Class 6) (0-60,58) 3-Y-O+ **£2,587** (£770; £384; £192) **Stalls** Low

Form RPR
3-46 1 **Testa Rossa (IRE)**27 3056 4-9-9 **55** GrahamLee 10 65
(Jim Goldie) *hld up in midfield: hdwy on ins to ld over 1f out: drvn out fnl f* **5/1**2
1325 2 1 1/4 **Call Of Duty (IRE)**24 3134 9-9-0 **51** (b) EmmaSayer(5) 9 57+
(Dianne Sayer) *s.i.s: bhd and sn pushed along: hdwy on wd outside over 2f out: edgd lft and chsd wnr ins fnl f: r.o* **7/1**3
5625 3 1/2 **Troy Boy**33 2875 4-8-11 **46** NeilFarley(3) 14 51
(Robin Bastiman) *led: rdn and hdd over 1f out: lost 2nd ins fnl f: kpt on same pce* **11/1**
0-54 4 2 1/4 **Spokesperson (USA)**18 3364 6-8-13 **45** (p) DavidAllan 7 45
(Frederick Watson) *bhd: pushed along over 4f out: hdwy over 2f out: kpt on ins fnl f: no imp* **12/1**
2331 5 hd **Eilean Mor**9 3657 6-8-13 **50** DuilioDaSilva(5) 12 50
(R Mike Smith) *pressed ldr: rdn and ev ch over 2f out to over 1f out: outpcd fnl f* **9/2**1
5000 6 1/2 **Wyldfire (IRE)**27 3052 4-9-9 **55** JamesSullivan 13 54
(Ruth Carr) *t.k.h: hld up: rdn along over 2f out: hdwy and edgd lft over 1f out: nvr rchd ldrs* **10/1**
0624 7 2 1/2 **Ebony Clarets**18 3363 5-8-10 **45** (p) ConnorBeasley(3) 5 39
(Linda Perratt) *midfield: effrt and rdn over 2f out: btn fnl f* **11/1**
4055 8 3 3/4 **Taxiformissbyron**9 3657 4-8-8 **45** (p) KevinStott(5) 6 32
(Iain Jardine) *trckd ldrs: rdn over 2f out: wknd over 1f out* **14/1**

0605 **9** *1 3/4* **Al Furat (USA)**[10] 3623 6-9-8 **54**..........................(p[1]) PaulPickard 1 38
(Ron Barr) *chsd ldrs: drvn along over 2f out: wknd wl over 1f out* **12/1**
-500 **10** *12* **Time Of My Life (IRE)**[20] 3301 5-9-11 **57**..................(t) DanielTudhope 3 18
(Patrick Holmes) *cl up tl rdn and wknd over 2f out* **5/1**[2]
-000 **11** *15* **Euston Square**[13] 3535 8-9-5 **56**..........................(b[1]) GarryWhillans(5) 4
(Alistair Whillans) *s.v.s: a t.o* **20/1**

2m 7.69s (-4.31) **Going Correction** -0.425s/f (Firm)
**WFA** 3 from 4yo+ 11lb **11** Ran SP% **116.6**
Speed ratings (Par 101): **100,99,98,96,96 96,94,91,89,80 68**
CSF £39.61 CT £369.62 TOTE £5.20: £1.90, £2.30, £3.90; EX 28.40 Trifecta £308.70.
**Owner** J S Morrison **Bred** Hugo Merry And Khalid Al-Mudhaf **Trained** Uplawmoor, E Renfrews
■ Stewards' Enquiry : Garry Whillans three-day ban: used whip without giving gelding time to respond (Jul 20-22)

**FOCUS**
A moderate handicap, rated around the runner-up.

## 4001 FSB CARD PAYMENT PROCESSING H'CAP 1m
**3:00** (3:00) (Class 5) (0-75,74) 3-Y-0+ **£3,234** (£962; £481; £240) **Stalls** Low

Form RPR
21-5 **1** **Hanalei Bay (IRE)**[18] 3361 4-9-7 **68**.............................. PhillipMakin 3 75
(Keith Dalgleish) *trckd ldrs: n.m.r over 2f out to wl over 1f out: sn rdn: kpt on wl fnl f to ld nr fin* **5/1**
651 **2** *nk* **Order Of Service**[9] 3660 4-9-7 **71**.............................. GaryBartley(3) 6 77
(Jim Goldie) *pressed ldr: led and rdn 2f out: edgd lft: kpt on wl fnl f: hdd nr fin* **7/1**
6222 **3** *1/2* **Tectonic (IRE)**[1] 3958 5-9-7 **68**..........................(p) JasonHart 7 73
(Keith Dalgleish) *t.k.h: stdd in rr: shkn up and hdwy over 1f out: rdn and kpt on fnl f: nrst fin* **2/1**[1]
2022 **4** *1* **Bling King**[10] 3624 5-9-13 **74**.............................. PJMcDonald 1 77
(Geoffrey Harker) *in tch: effrt and drvn over 2f out: kpt on same pce fnl f* **9/2**[3]
-601 **5** *1 1/4* **Tanawar (IRE)**[16] 3439 4-9-3 **64**.............................. JamesSullivan 2 64
(Ruth Carr) *t.k.h: hld up: rdn and hdwy over 1f out: no imp ins fnl f* **7/2**[2]
4-40 **6** *2* **Tiffany Bay (IRE)**[37] 2740 3-9-2 **72**..........................(b[1]) RonanWhelan 4 65
(John Patrick Shanahan, Ire) *led: rdn and hdd 2f out: wknd ins fnl f* **20/1**
06-0 **7** *10* **Declamation (IRE)**[27] 3050 4-9-4 **70**.............................. GarryWhillans(5) 5 42
(Alistair Whillans) *hld up in tch: rdn and struggling 2f out: sn btn* **18/1**

1m 39.84s (-3.96) **Going Correction** -0.425s/f (Firm)
**WFA** 3 from 4yo+ 9lb **7** Ran SP% **112.9**
Speed ratings (Par 103): **102,101,101,100,98 96,86**
CSF £37.89 TOTE £6.30: £3.40, £4.10; EX 41.20 Trifecta £125.00.
**Owner** Mrs Francesca Mitchell **Bred** Holborn Trust Co **Trained** Carluke, S Lanarks

**FOCUS**
A run-of-the-mill handicap, run at an average pace.

## 4002 FSB MOBILE CARD PAYMENT TERMINALS H'CAP 1m
**3:30** (3:31) (Class 3) (0-95,99) 3-Y-0+ **£9,703** (£2,887; £1,443; £721) **Stalls** Low

Form RPR
622 **1** **Sound Advice**[11] 3573 5-9-10 **90**.............................. JasonHart 5 98
(Keith Dalgleish) *t.k.h: mde all: rdn and hrd pressed over 2f out: drvn out fnl f* **13/8**[1]
0204 **2** *1* **Kiwi Bay**[16] 3437 9-8-13 **79**.............................. PaulMulrennan 7 84
(Michael Dods) *t.k.h: pressed wnr: rdn to chal over 2f out: kpt on same pce ins fnl f* **5/1**[3]
4123 **3** *4* **Dubai Dynamo**[10] 3621 9-9-9 **89**.............................. PJMcDonald 4 85
(Ruth Carr) *in tch: effrt and rdn over 2f out: no imp fr over 1f out* **85/40**[2]
3430 **4** *6* **Silver Rime (FR)**[11] 3573 9-8-11 **80**.............................. ConnorBeasley(3) 1 62
(Linda Perratt) *blinfold v slow to remove and s.s: hdwy 1/2-way: drvn and wknd fr 2f out* **11/2**
4-00 **5** *8* **Unsinkable (IRE)**[62] 1165 4-9-5 **90**.............................. GarryWhillans(5) 6 54
(Ian Semple) *blindfold sltly slow to remove and dwlt: sn trcking ldrs: drvn and wknd over 2f out* **14/1**

1m 39.23s (-4.57) **Going Correction** -0.425s/f (Firm) **5** Ran SP% **108.8**
Speed ratings (Par 107): **105,104,100,94,86**
CSF £9.73 TOTE £2.00: £1.20, £1.90; EX 7.70 Trifecta £16.90.
**Owner** G L S Partnership **Bred** G L S Partnership **Trained** Carluke, S Lanarks

**FOCUS**
What had promised to be a strong handicap was hit badly by non-runners.

## 4003 FSB FINANCE FOR BUSINESS H'CAP (DIV I) 6f
**4:00** (4:01) (Class 5) (0-75,73) 3-Y-0+ **£3,234** (£962; £481; £240) **Stalls** Low

Form RPR
4006 **1** **Jinky**[25] 3102 6-9-4 **65**.............................. JoeFanning 3 76
(Linda Perratt) *trckd ldrs: shkn up and hdwy over 1f out: led 1f out: rdn out towards fin* **9/1**
0012 **2** *1 1/2* **Native Falls (IRE)**[10] 3625 3-9-1 **68**.............................. DavidAllan 2 73
(Alan Swinbank) *led: rdn and hdd 1f out: rallied: hld towards fin* **9/4**[1]
4501 **3** *6* **Exotic Guest**[9] 3668 4-9-4 **65**.............................. JamesSullivan 8 52
(Ruth Carr) *stdd s: hld up: hdwy to chse clr ldng pair over 1f out: sn rdn and edgd lft: no imp* **11/4**[2]
0602 **4** *1 1/4* **Jumbo Steps (IRE)**[1] 3954 7-9-4 **68**.............................. GaryBartley(3) 4 51
(Jim Goldie) *chsd ldrs: drvn and outpcd over 1f out: btn fnl f* **4/1**[3]
-004 **5** *1 3/4* **Midnight Dynamo**[9] 3659 7-9-10 **71**.............................. DanielTudhope 9 48
(Jim Goldie) *hld up: rdn and outpcd 2f out: sn btn* **5/1**
1010 **6** *13* **Goninodaethat**[25] 3102 6-9-2 **63**.............................. GrahamLee 7 8
(Jim Goldie) *chsd ldr: rdn and wknd fr 2f out* **8/1**

1m 11.11s (-1.29) **Going Correction** -0.20s/f (Firm)
**WFA** 3 from 4yo+ 6lb **6** Ran SP% **115.2**
Speed ratings (Par 103): **100,98,90,88,86 68**
CSF £30.60 CT £71.90 TOTE £10.20: £4.70, £1.50; EX 33.30 Trifecta £131.60.
**Owner** John Murphy **Bred** J Breslin **Trained** East Kilbride, S Lanarks

**FOCUS**
This was a moderate sprint handicap and the first two had the final furlong all to themselves.

## 4004 FSB FINANCE FOR BUSINESS H'CAP (DIV II) 6f
**4:30** (4:32) (Class 5) (0-75,73) 3-Y-0+ **£3,234** (£962; £481; £240) **Stalls** Low

Form RPR
6000 **1** **Opt Out**[44] 2514 4-8-13 **60**..........................(b[1]) PJMcDonald 3 67
(Alistair Whillans) *hld up: hdwy and swtchd lft wl over 1f out: led 1f out: hld on wl fnl f* **18/1**
2004 **2** *nk* **Thorntoun Lady (USA)**[9] 3667 4-9-6 **67**.............................. DanielTudhope 5 73
(Jim Goldie) *in tch: smooth hdwy over 2f out: disp ld over 1f out to ins fnl f: kpt on: hld nr fin* **4/1**[3]
1314 **3** *nk* **Monel**[25] 3102 6-9-3 **64**.............................. GrahamLee 8 71+
(Jim Goldie) *in tch: effrt whn nt clr run briefly over 1f out: rdn and kpt on fnl f* **5/2**[1]
0000 **4** *1 3/4* **L'Ami Louis (IRE)**[15] 3458 6-9-7 **73**.............................. GarryWhillans(5) 6 72
(Ian Semple) *tk hold early: w ldrs: led over 2f out: edgd rt and hdd 1f out: one pce whn edgd lft ins fnl f* **5/1**
426 **5** *2 3/4* **Funding Deficit (IRE)**[5] 3833 4-9-0 **64**.............................. GaryBartley(3) 4 55
(Jim Goldie) *led to over 2f out: sn rdn: outpcd fnl f* **7/2**[2]
1555 **6** *1/2* **Bunce (IRE)**[5] 3831 6-9-6 **70**.............................. GeorgeChaloner(3) 9 59
(Linda Perratt) *w ldrs tl rdn and no ex fnl f* **9/2**
0500 **7** *6* **Fife Jo**[31] 2909 4-8-7 **54** oh9.............................. JoeFanning 7 24
(Jim Goldie) *prom: drvn and outpcd over 2f out: sn btn* **28/1**

1m 12.81s (0.41) **Going Correction** -0.20s/f (Firm) **7** Ran SP% **114.4**
Speed ratings (Par 103): **89,88,88,85,82 81,73**
CSF £87.74 CT £246.94 TOTE £22.30: £5.60, £2.70; EX 132.40 Trifecta £441.80.
**Owner** Akela Construction Ltd **Bred** Darley **Trained** Newmill-On-Slitrig, Borders

**FOCUS**
The second division of the moderate 6f handicap. The time was 1.7secs slower than the first.

## 4005 FSB FUEL CARD AMATEUR RIDERS' H'CAP 5f
**5:00** (5:01) (Class 6) (0-65,62) 4-Y-0+ **£2,495** (£774; £386; £193) **Stalls** Low

Form RPR
5054 **1** **Chosen One (IRE)**[19] 3338 9-10-7 **55**.............................. MissSBrotherton 3 67
(Ruth Carr) *mde all: rdn over 1f out: kpt on strly fnl f* **7/2**[2]
0000 **2** *2* **Black Douglas**[31] 2909 5-10-5 **53**.............................. MrsCBartley 6 58+
(Jim Goldie) *racd alone far side: bhd tl hdwy 2f out: kpt on wl fnl f: tk 2nd last stride* **6/1**[3]
-006 **3** *nse* **Saxonette**[46] 2452 6-9-9 **48**.............................. MrHStock(5) 4 53
(Linda Perratt) *prom: hdwy to chse wnr over 1f out: kpt on fnl f: lost 2nd last stride* **12/1**
4004 **4** *3/4* **Two Turtle Doves (IRE)**[10] 3612 8-10-1 **52**.......... MissMMullineaux(3) 8 54
(Michael Mullineaux) *bhd: hdwy and hung lft 2f out: kpt on fnl f: nvr able to chal* **20/1**
0-30 **5** *3/4* **A J Cook (IRE)**[19] 3338 4-10-2 **55**.............................. PhillipDennis(5) 10 54
(Ron Barr) *prom: drvn along and hung lft over 1f out: sn one pce* **20/1**
5212 **6** *nk* **Amis Reunis**[5] 3833 5-10-2 **54**..........................(p) MissADeniel 11 48
(Alan Berry) *in tch: rdn 2f out: kpt on same pce fnl f* **12/5**[1]
5004 **7** *1 1/4* **Chloe's Dream (IRE)**[5] 3833 4-10-0 **53**.......... MissMeganNicholls(5) 9 47
(Linda Perratt) *hld up bhd ldng gp: pushed along over 2f out: nvr able to chal* **13/2**
0-03 **8** *1* **Hellolini**[25] 3104 4-9-5 **46**.............................. DylanMcDonagh(7) 5 36
(Robin Bastiman) *dwlt: sn chsng ldrs: wknd 1f out* **20/1**
6000 **9** *hd* **The Nifty Fox**[23] 3191 10-10-9 **62**..........................(p) MrWEasterby(5) 1 51
(Tim Easterby) *in tch: smooth hdwy 1/2-way: rdn and wknd fnl f* **8/1**
1-00 **10** *1 1/2* **My Time**[78] 1584 5-9-12 **53**.............................. MrHFNugent(7) 7 37
(Michael Mullineaux) *dwlt: bhd and sn struggling: sme late hdwy: nvr on terms* **66/1**
0-00 **11** *2 3/4* **Wicked Wilma (IRE)**[25] 3104 10-9-6 **45**.............................. MrJohnWilley(5) 2 19
(Alan Berry) *chsd wnr tl rdn and wknd 2f out* **33/1**

59.91s (0.51) **Going Correction** -0.20s/f (Firm) **11** Ran SP% **116.8**
Speed ratings (Par 101): **87,83,83,82,81 80,78,77,76,74 70**
CSF £22.62 CT £227.72 TOTE £4.40: £1.20, £1.40, £3.90; EX 28.80 Trifecta £196.50.
**Owner** Bridget Houlston, Chris Jeffery & Co **Bred** Carl Holt **Trained** Huby, N Yorks

**FOCUS**
A weak sprint handicap, confined to amateur riders. The main action came down the middle late on.
T/Jkpt: £156,514.50 to a £1 stake. Pool: £661,329.00 - 3.00 winning tickets. T/Plt: £499.90 to a £1 stake. Pool: £97,027.62 - 141.67 winning tickets. T/Qpdt: £68.80 to a £1 stake. Pool: £6,638.61 - 71.40 winning tickets. RY

# 3873 HAMBURG (R-H)
Sunday, July 6

**OFFICIAL GOING: Turf: good**

## 4006a ALMASED CUP (HAMBURG TROPHY) (GROUP 3) (3YO+) (TURF) 1m 2f
**2:40** (12:00) 3-Y-0+

**£26,666** (£9,166; £4,583; £2,500; £1,666; £1,250)

RPR
**1** **Bermuda Reef (IRE)**[22] 4-9-2 0.............................. AdriedeVries 10 110
(P Schiergen, Germany) *trckd ldr: rdn to chal over 1 1/2f out: led appr fnl f: drvn out: readily* **17/10**[1]
**2** *1 1/4* **Vanishing Cupid (SWI)**[43] 2576 4-9-2 0..................(b) IoritzMendizabal 3 107
(H-A Pantall, France) *midfield in tch: bmpd w rival over 4f out: 3rd and swtchd outside over 2f out: styd on u.p to go 2nd 100yds out: nvr quite on terms w wnr* **7/1**
**3** *1 1/2* **Nausica Time (GER)**[39] 4-8-13 0.............................. AHelfenbein 2 101
(S Smrczek, Germany) *led: rallied whn chal over 1 1/2f out: hdd appr 1f out: one pce u.p fnl f* **11/1**
**4** *2 1/2* **Neatico (GER)**[14] 3511 7-9-8 0.............................. DanielePorcu 7 105
(P Schiergen, Germany) *hld up towards rr: hdwy on outer over 2f out: plugged on u.p to go 4th cl home: nvr nrr* **4/1**[2]
**5** *nse* **Majestic Jasmine (IRE)**[27] 4-8-13 0.............................. EPedroza 6 96
(A Wohler, Germany) *w.w towards rr: rdn to chse ldng trio over 2f out: plugged on at one pce fnl f: lost 4th cl home* **4/1**[2]
**6** *15* **Quinzieme Monarque (USA)**[35] 2815 4-9-2 0.......... DennisSchiergen 5 69
(P Schiergen, Germany) *towards rr: last and rdn 2 1/2f out: no imp and sn btn: eased fnl f* **15/2**
**7** *11* **Petit Chevalier (FR)**[22] 6-9-4 0.............................. SHellyn 4 49
(W Mongil, Germany) *midfield in tch: bmpd w rival over 4f out: lost pl 3f out: sn btn* **6/1**[3]
**8** *10* **See The Rock (IRE)**[31] 4-9-2 0.............................. FilipMinarik 9 27
(Mario Hofer, Germany) *dwlt: prog to press ldr on outer after 3f: rdn and lost pl 4f out: sn wl bhd* **8/1**

2m 8.27s (128.27) **8** Ran SP% **135.0**
WIN (incl. 10 euro stake): 27. PLACES: 16, 23, 26. SF: 211.
**Owner** Gestut Ammerland **Bred** Gestut Ammerland **Trained** Germany

## 4007a IDEE 145 DEUTSCHES DERBY (GROUP 1) (3YO COLTS & FILLIES) (TURF) 1m 4f

**4:05** (12:00) 3-Y-0 **£325,000** (£108,333; £65,000; £32,500; £10,833)

RPR

1 **Sea The Moon (GER)**[21] 3293 3-9-2 0 ............ ChristopheSoumillon 15 122+
(Markus Klug, Germany) *worked across fr wd draw and sn led: mde rest: rdn and crossed to r alone against nr side' rail in st: styd on strly and sn in full control: eased fnl f but sauntered further clr: v impressive* **9/5**[1]

2 *11* **Lucky Lion**[49] 2377 3-9-2 0 .................................... IoritzMendizabal 3 102
(Andreas Lowe, Germany) *t.k.h: a.p: ct on heels first turn: rdn into st: wnt 2nd over 1f out: styd on fnl f but absolutely no ch w wnr* **7/1**[3]

3 *2 ½* **Open Your Heart (GER)**[21] 3293 3-9-2 0 .................. MircoDemuro 20 98
(R Dzubasz, Germany) *dwlt sltly and hld up in last: stl in rr whn rdn into st: styd on wl fnl 2f and tk nvr nrr 3rd cl home* **66/1**

4 *nk* **Eric (GER)**[36] 3-9-2 0 ................................................ SHellyn 8 98
(C Von Der Recke, Germany) *hld up towards rr on inner: rdn into st: styd on fnl 2f and snatched 4th post: fin wl: nvr nrr* **65/1**

5 *shd* **Wild Chief (GER)**[35] 2818 3-9-2 0 .......................... FabienLefebvre 14 98
(J Hirschberger, Germany) *sn trcking ldr on outer: rdn into st: readily outpcd by wnr and sn wl hld: styd on: no ex and lost 2 pls cl home* **77/10**

6 *nk* **Speedy Approach**[27] 3073 3-9-2 0 .................................. EPedroza 5 97
(A Wohler, Germany) *midfield in tch on inner: rdn into st: sn outpcd by wnr: hld in 4th ent fnl f: styd on but lost 2 pls towards fin* **139/10**

7 *1 ¼* **Madurai (GER)**[56] 3-9-2 0 ........................................ APietsch 6 95
(Waldemar Hickst, Germany) *midfield on inner: swtchd off rail and rdn into st: styd on same pce fnl 2f and nvr threatened* **269/10**

8 *2* **Amorous Adventure (GER)**[14] 3-9-2 0 ...................... MaximPecheur 2 92
(K Demme, Germany) *dwlt sltly and pushed along early: hld up in rr: rdn and fanned wd into st: styd on for n.d 8th* **76/1**

9 *2* **Magic Artist (IRE)**[27] 3073 3-9-2 0 .............................. DavidProbert 13 89
(W Figge, Germany) *dwlt sltly and hld up in midfield: rdn into st: styd on same pce fnl 2f and sn wl hld: n.d* **141/10**

10 *1 ¼* **Swacadelic (GER)**[21] 3293 3-9-2 0 ................................ FilipMinarik 19 87
(Jean-Pierre Carvalho, Germany) *dwlt sltly: hld up in midfield on outer: swtchd ins and rdn into st: outpcd and wl hld fnl 2f: plugged on but nvr threatened* **101/10**

11 *½* **Karltheodor (GER)**[56] 3-9-2 0 ........................................ MartinLane 7 86
(R Dzubasz, Germany) *pushed along to go forward and led early: trckd ldr on inner once hdd: rdn 3f out: lost pl 2f out: sn no ex and btn: wknd fnl f* **79/1**

12 *1 ¼* **Weltmacht**[28] 3046 3-8-13 0 ........................................ TomQueally 9 81
(Markus Klug, Germany) *dwlt sltly but qckly rcvrd: hld up in midfield: rdn and fanned wd into st: outpcd and btn fnl 2f: hung rt u.p: nvr threatened* **168/10**

13 *4* **Russian Bolero (GER)**[14] 3-9-2 0 ...................................(b) JBojko 1 78
(A Wohler, Germany) *dwlt and pushed along to rcvr: hld up in midfield: rdn and fanned wd into st: sn outpcd and btn: eased fnl f: nvr a factor* **37/1**

14 *2* **Baltic Storm (IRE)**[14] 3-9-2 0 ................................ FrederikTylicki 4 75
(J D Hillis, Germany) *midfield: pushed along and shuffled bk 3f out: rdn and btn st: eased fnl f* **51/1**

15 *5* **Pinzolo**[29] 2990 3-9-2 0 ........................................ WilliamBuick 11 67
(Charlie Appleby) *midfield: pushed along to hold position over 3f out: rdn and outpcd into st: no ex and btn ent fnl f: sn eased* **157/10**

16 *3* **Giant's Cauldron (GER)**[21] 3293 3-9-2 0 .......................... AdriedeVries 18 62
(P Schiergen, Germany) *midfield on outer: in tch 1/2-way: rdn 3f out: outpcd and btn fnl 2f: eased ent fnl f* **175/10**

17 *28* **Geoffrey Chaucer (USA)**[29] 2990 3-9-2 0 ............................ RyanMoore 16 17
(A P O'Brien, Ire) *midfield in tch on outer: prom 1/2-way: rdn and lost pl fr 3f out: no ex and btn whn eased over 1f out: t.o* **68/10**[2]

18 *5* **Amazonit (GER)**[14] 3-9-2 0 ........................................ HarryBentley 12 9
(J Hirschberger, Germany) *midfield in tch: rdn and lost pl qckly over 3f out: dropped to last and btn into st: eased fnl 2f: t.o* **197/10**

2m 29.86s (-4.69) **18 Ran SP% 130.4**
WIN (inc 10euro stake): 28; PLACES: 19, 32, 107; SF: 188.
**Owner** Gestut Gorlsdorf **Bred** Gestut Gorlsdorf **Trained** Germany

# 3206 MAISONS-LAFFITTE (R-H)

Sunday, July 6

**OFFICIAL GOING: Turf: good**

## 4008a PRIX MESSIDOR (GROUP 3) (3YO+) (STRAIGHT) (TURF) 1m (S)

**2:40** (12:00) 3-Y-0+ **£33,333** (£13,333; £10,000; £6,666; £3,333)

RPR

1 **Graphic (IRE)**[30] 2958 5-9-1 0 ....................................(p) FrankieDettori 4 112
(William Haggas) *mde all: pushed along and qcknd fr 2f out: rdn over 1f out: r.o strly and in control fnl f: readily* **4/5**[1]

2 *1 ½* **Pilote (IRE)**[21] 3291 4-9-1 0 ........................................ OlivierPeslier 3 109
(A Fabre, France) *midfield in tch: swtchd out and pushed along 2f out: rdn and wnt 2nd over 1f out: r.o and chsd wnr fnl f but no real imp and wl hld* **4/1**[2]

3 *1 ¼* **Line Drummer (FR)**[46] 4-9-1 0 .................................... UmbertoRispoli 2 106
(J Reynier, France) *t.k.h: hld up in tch: pushed along in last 2f out: rdn and kpt on into 3rd fnl f but nvr able to chal* **22/1**

4 *1 ¼* **Matorio (FR)**[42] 2587 4-8-11 0 ........................................ FabriceVeron 1 99
(H-A Pantall, France) *hld up in last: clsd on outer 3f out: pushed along 2f out: rdn and outpcd fnl f: nvr able to chal* **4/1**[2]

5 *2 ½* **Market Share**[21] 3291 4-9-1 0 ............................ Christophe-PatriceLemaire 5 97
(P Bary, France) *trckd ldr: rdn and outpcd by wnr over 1f out: no ex and btn fnl f: fdd and dropped to last* **7/1**[3]

1m 38.1s (-4.20) **5 Ran SP% 112.4**
WIN (incl. 1 euro stake): 2.00. PLACES: 1.20, 1.50. SF: 7.20.
**Owner** The Royal Ascot Racing Club **Bred** Kevin & Meta Cullen **Trained** Newmarket, Suffolk

## 4009a PRIX AMANDINE (LISTED RACE) (3YO FILLIES) (TURF) 7f (S)

**3:10** (12:00) 3-Y-0 **£22,916** (£9,166; £6,875; £4,583; £2,291)

RPR

1 **Amy Eria (IRE)**[54] 2243 3-8-11 0 ...................................... ThierryThulliez 1 107
(F Rohaut, France) **30/1**

2 *2* **This Time (FR)**[56] 2195 3-8-11 0 ........................................ FabriceVeron 3 102+
(H-A Pantall, France) **14/5**[1]

3 *½* **Fresles (IRE)**[23] 3206 3-8-11 0 ...................................... GregoryBenoist 10 100+
(Mme Pia Brandt, France) **191/10**

4 *1 ¾* **Stormyra (FR)**[35] 2817 3-9-2 0 ...................................(p) UmbertoRispoli 4 101+
(J-P Gallorini, France) **17/5**[2]

5 *hd* **Eyeful**[23] 3206 3-8-11 0 ................................................ OlivierPeslier 8 95+
(A Fabre, France) **22/5**[3]

6 *nk* **Sea Front (FR)**[33] 3-8-11 0 ............................................ MaximeGuyon 7 94+
(E Libaud, France) **78/10**

7 *nse* **Midnite Angel (IRE)**[8] 3727 3-8-11 0 ...............................(b) FrankieDettori 2 94+
(Richard Hannon) *dwlt sltly: hld up and a towards rr: rdn 2f out: kpt on same pce and wl hld fnl f: nvr threatened* **7/1**

8 *hd* **Dancing Sands (IRE)**[94] 1273 3-8-11 0 .......................... MickaelBarzalona 6 94+
(H-A Pantall, France) *prom: rdn and outpcd fr 2f out: sn lost pl: kpt on but wl hld fnl f* **9/2**

9 *11* **Fetan Joa (FR)**[33] 2880 3-8-11 0 ........................................ ThierryJarnet 9 64+
(J Heloury, France) **45/1**

1m 25.8s (-2.20) **9 Ran SP% 120.0**
WIN (incl. 1 euro stake): 6.30 (Amy Eria coupled with Midnite Angel). PLACES: 7.20, 1.80, 4.30. DF: 43.60. SF: 130.40.
**Owner** Al Shaqab Racing **Bred** D Chassagneux **Trained** Sauvagnon, France

# MONMOUTH PARK (L-H)

Sunday, July 6

**OFFICIAL GOING: Turf: firm; dirt: fast**

## 4010a UNITED NATIONS STKS (GRADE 1) (3YO+) (TURF) 1m 3f

**11:13** (12:00) 3-Y-0+

**£180,722** (£60,240; £30,120; £18,072; £9,036; £6,024)

RPR

1 **Main Sequence (USA)**[260] 7367 5-8-6 0 ................................ RMaragh 5 113
(H Graham Motion, U.S.A) **8/1**

2 *nk* **Twilight Eclipse (USA)**[30] 5-8-8 0 ...................................... JLezcano 3 114
(Thomas Albertrani, U.S.A) **18/5**[2]

3 *1* **Side Glance**[19] 3317 7-8-6 0 ...................................... JamieSpencer 10 111
(Andrew Balding) **56/10**

4 *nse* **Winning Cause (USA)**[28] 4-8-6 0 ...................................... CDeCarlo 8 111
(Todd Pletcher, U.S.A) **174/10**

5 *nk* **Kaigun (CAN)**[29] 3025 4-8-6 0 ............................................ AGarcia 7 110
(Mark Casse, Canada) **3/1**[1]

6 *1 ¼* **Ghurair (USA)**[28] 4-8-6 0 ............................................ GaryStevens 2 108
(Chad C Brown, U.S.A) **43/10**[3]

7 *nse* **Charming Kitten (USA)**[30] 4-8-6 0 ...................................... JBravo 1 108
(Todd Pletcher, U.S.A) **47/10**

8 *2* **Exclusive Strike (USA)**[43] 7-8-6 0 ...................................(b) PLopez 6 104
(Jason Servis, U.S.A) **172/10**

9 *hd* **Manchurian High (USA)**[37] 6-8-6 0 ...................................... FBoyce 4 104
(Lilli Kurtinecz, U.S.A) **85/1**

2m 14.23s (134.23) **9 Ran SP% 121.5**
PARI-MUTUEL (all including 2 usd stake): WIN 18.00; PLACE (1-2) 8.60, 5.00; SHOW (1-2-3) 5.60, 3.80, 4.40; SF 98.40.
**Owner** Flaxman Holdings Ltd **Bred** Flaxman Holdings Ltd **Trained** USA

# 3998 AYR (L-H)

Monday, July 7

**OFFICIAL GOING: Good to firm (9.5)**

Wind: Breezy, half against Weather: Sunny

## 4011 BRITISH STALLION STUDS EBF MAIDEN STKS 5f

**2:30** (2:31) (Class 5) 2-Y-O **£3,234** (£962; £481; £240) **Stalls** Low

Form RPR

42 1 **Latch Onto Blue**[21] 3311 2-9-5 0 .............................. RobertWinston 1 74+
(Charles Hills) *mde all: rdn over 1f out: edgd rt ins fnl f: hld on wl* **5/6**[1]

26 2 *nk* **Short N Sweet**[9] 3713 2-9-0 0 ........................................ DavidAllan 3 67+
(Tim Easterby) *chsd ldrs: rdn and hdwy to chse wnr ent fnl f: kpt on towards fin* **11/4**[2]

0034 3 *2 ¼* **Bahango (IRE)**[28] 3049 2-9-5 0 ..................................[1] JamesSullivan 4 62
(Kristin Stubbs) *in tch: hdwy on outside over 1f out: edgd rt: kpt on ins fnl f: nt rch first two* **20/1**

55 4 *2 ½* **Poolstock**[16] 3461 2-9-5 0 ........................................ DanielTudhope 5 53
(David O'Meara) *stdd in tch: shkn up over 1f out: no imp fnl f* **9/1**

5 5 *nse* **Monksford Lady**[21] 3296 2-9-0 0 ........................................ GrahamLee 2 48
(Donald McCain) *w wnr tl rdn and wknd fr 1f out* **7/1**[3]

59.1s (-0.30) **Going Correction** -0.35s/f (Firm) **5 Ran SP% 108.5**
Speed ratings (Par 94): **88,87,83,79,79**
CSF £3.19 TOTE £1.60: £1.10, £1.50; EX 3.60 Trifecta £12.00.
**Owner** Jim & Susan Hill **Bred** Manor Farm Stud (rutland) **Trained** Lambourn, Berks

**FOCUS**

Home bend out 2m and distance son Round course increased by about 6yds. A dry night and with the forecast rain failing to arrive and the course applied around 5mm of water. The home turn was moved out two metres meaning an extra six yards to cover in races over 7f and beyond. An uncompetitive maiden to open proceedings, with the pair with the best form coming clear.

## 4012 INJURED JOCKEYS FUND 50TH ANNIVERSARY NURSERY H'CAP 7f 50y

**3:00** (3:00) (Class 5) 2-Y-O **£3,234** (£962; £481; £240) **Stalls** High

Form RPR

51 1 **Disavow**[10] 3642 2-9-7 77 ........................................ JoeFanning 2 77
(Mark Johnston) *t.k.h: mde all: hrd pressed fr over 2f out: asserted fnl f: hld on wl nr fin* **9/4**[2]

602 2 *½* **Wink Oliver**[25] 3157 2-8-1 60 ow2 ................................ ConnorBeasley(3) 4 59
(Marjorie Fife) *pressed wnr: rdn and ev ch over 2f out to 1f out: kpt on ins fnl f* **11/2**

542 3 *¾* **Ingleby Spring (IRE)**[14] 3529 2-8-6 65 .......................... GeorgeChaloner(3) 1 62
(Richard Fahey) *trckd ldrs: effrt and rdn 2f out: kpt on ins fnl f* **85/40**[1]

351 4 *2 ¾* **Multiplier**[40] 2673 2-9-7 77 ........................................ JamesSullivan 3 67
(Kristin Stubbs) *in tch: rdn over 2f out: hung lft over 1f out: nvr able to chal* **10/1**

554 **5** 1/2 **Gamesters Lad**[24] 3181 2-8-6 **62**........................ KieranO'Neill 5 50
(Tom Dascombe) *hld up last: rdn and outpcd 3f out: no imp fr 2f out* **7/2**[3]
1m 32.0s (-1.40) **Going Correction** -0.35s/f (Firm) **5** Ran SP% **109.5**
Speed ratings (Par 94): **94,93,92,89,88**
CSF £14.10 TOTE £2.40: £1.30, £3.10; EX 13.10 Trifecta £30.10.
**Owner** Sheikh Hamdan bin Mohammed Al Maktoum **Bred** Darley **Trained** Middleham Moor, N Yorks

**FOCUS**
Another small field and a race in which the order rarely changed, the winner given a good front-running ride.

## 4013 PENALTY SHOOTOUT MONEY BACK WITH BETVICTOR H'CAP 7f 50y
**3:30** (3:30) (Class 4) (0-85,83) 3-Y-O+ **£5,498** (£1,636; £817; £408) **Stalls** High

Form RPR
4304 **1** **Silver Rime (FR)**[1] 4002 9-9-8 **80**........................ ConnorBeasley(3) 8 89
(Linda Perratt) *dwlt: hld up in tch: hdwy over 1f out: rdn to ld ins fnl f: kpt on wl* **6/1**
5344 **2** 1/2 **Jazz (IRE)**[9] 3704 3-9-6 **83**........................ RobertWinston 3 88
(Charles Hills) *bhd and detached: gd hdwy on outside over 2f out: led and edgd lft over 1f out: hdd ins fnl f: kpt on: hld nr fin* **3/1**[1]
2200 **3** 3 **Powerful Presence (IRE)**[10] 3646 8-9-13 **82**........................ DanielTudhope 1 82
(David O'Meara) *t.k.h: led tl rdn and hdd over 1f out: kpt on same pce fnl f* **3/1**[1]
0131 **4** 2 1/4 **Mowhoob**[23] 3237 4-9-3 **72**........................ GrahamLee 2 66
(Jim Goldie) *cl up: rdn and ev ch over 2f out: outpcd over 1f out* **11/2**[3]
-016 **5** hd **Spiceupyourlife (IRE)**[24] 3187 3-8-10 **76**........................ GeorgeChaloner(3) 4 67
(Richard Fahey) *prom: rdn over 2f out: edgd lft and no ex over 1f out* **4/1**[2]
3046 **6** 5 **Klynch**[35] 2825 8-9-7 **76**........................(v[1]) JamesSullivan 9 57
(Ruth Carr) *t.k.h: cl up: rdn and ev ch over 2f out: wknd over 1f out* **10/1**
1m 29.16s (-4.24) **Going Correction** -0.35s/f (Firm)
**WFA** 3 from 4yo+ 8lb **6** Ran SP% **108.8**
Speed ratings (Par 105): **110,109,106,103,103 97**
CSF £22.63 CT £56.90 TOTE £5.50: £4.30, £1.60; EX 20.10 Trifecta £77.50.
**Owner** Ken McGarrity **Bred** Jean-Philippe Dubois **Trained** East Kilbride, S Lanarks

**FOCUS**
A competitive handicap despite the small field and run at a sound pace, the two protagonists coming from the back to fight out the finish. It's been rated around the runner-up.

## 4014 BEST ODDS IN FOOTBALL AT BETVICTOR.COM H'CAP 1m
**4:00** (4:00) (Class 6) (0-60,59) 3-Y-O+ **£2,264** (£673; £336; £168) **Stalls** Low

Form RPR
0652 **1** **Cono Zur (FR)**[11] 3604 7-9-10 **57**........................ JamesSullivan 4 69+
(Ruth Carr) *mde all: rdn over 2f out: kpt on strly fnl f* **4/1**[1]
5-00 **2** 1 3/4 **Galilee Chapel (IRE)**[28] 3054 5-8-12 **45**........................(b) JasonHart 10 52
(Alistair Whillans) *hld up: rdn over 2f out: hdwy whn n.m.r briefly over 1f out: kpt on fnl f: tk 2nd towards fin* **25/1**
3360 **3** 3/4 **Staffhoss**[11] 3604 4-9-12 **59**........................ JoeFanning 8 64
(Mark Johnston) *in tch: rdn along over 2f out: hdwy to chse wnr over 1f out: one pce and lost 2nd towards fin* **5/1**[2]
3315 **4** 3/4 **Eilean Mor**[1] 4000 6-9-3 **50**........................ RobertWinston 7 53
(R Mike Smith) *hld up towards rr: nt clr run and swtchd rt over 2f out: swtchd lft and hdwy over 1f out: kpt on fnl f* **4/1**[1]
3563 **5** 1 1/2 **Dhaular Dhar (IRE)**[6] 3828 12-9-11 **58**........................(p) GrahamLee 5 58
(Jim Goldie) *hld up: effrt whn n.m.r briefly over 2f out: n.m.r appr fnl f: kpt on: no imp* **5/1**[2]
-300 **6** hd **Pim Street (USA)**[7] 3798 4-9-10 **57**........................(v) DanielTudhope 6 56
(David O'Meara) *hld up: rdn and hdwy on outside over 2f out: kpt on fnl f: nvr able to chal* **10/1**
-500 **7** 3/4 **Mount Cheiron (USA)**[19] 3364 3-8-5 **52**........................(p) EmmaSayer(5) 3 48
(Dianne Sayer) *t.k.h: in tch: effrt and rdn over 2f out: wknd ins fnl f* **16/1**
-050 **8** 2 **Eastward Ho**[21] 3301 6-9-9 **56**........................(b[1]) BrianHughes 9 49
(Michael Herrington) *pressed wnr: rdn over 2f out: wknd over 1f out* **12/1**
0503 **9** 2 1/4 **Shamouti (IRE)**[13] 3545 3-8-4 **49**........................(p) ConnorBeasley(3) 11 35
(Ollie Pears) *t.k.h early: chsd ldrs: effrt and rdn over 2f out: wknd fnl f* **7/1**[3]
600 **10** 3 1/2 **Charedal**[10] 3664 6-8-7 **45**........................ ShaneGray(5) 1 25
(Iain Jardine) *dwlt: hld up on ins: struggling over 3f out: nvr on terms* **100/1**
1m 39.52s (-4.28) **Going Correction** -0.35s/f (Firm)
**WFA** 3 from 4yo+ 9lb **10** Ran SP% **113.3**
Speed ratings (Par 101): **107,105,104,103,102 102,101,99,97,93**
CSF £103.44 CT £519.21 TOTE £4.80: £1.70, £5.00, £2.50; EX 97.10 Trifecta £1554.20.
**Owner** Ruth Carr Racing **Bred** J P Dubois **Trained** Huby, N Yorks

**FOCUS**
A run-of-the-mill handicap in which the winner was another to make the vast majority of the running. The third and fourth have been rated close to their recent form.

## 4015 DOWNLOAD THE BETVICTOR SPINCAST APP H'CAP 1m 5f 13y
**4:30** (4:30) (Class 5) (0-75,70) 4-Y-O+ **£3,234** (£962; £481; £240) **Stalls** Low

Form RPR
0606 **1** **Gold Chain (IRE)**[2] 3958 4-8-6 **59** ow1........................ EmmaSayer(5) 6 68
(Dianne Sayer) *s.i.s: bhd and detached: gd hdwy 3f out: squeezed through to ld wl over 1f out: pushed along and edgd rt ins fnl f: styd on* **8/1**
3552 **2** 1 3/4 **Geanie Mac (IRE)**[6] 3829 5-8-4 **53**........................(p) JamesSullivan 8 58
(Linda Perratt) *hld up bhd ldng gp: effrt over 2f out: chsd wnr over 1f out: kpt on same pce ins fnl f* **11/2**
0434 **3** 3 1/4 **Grand Diamond (IRE)**[10] 3657 10-7-13 **53**........................ SammyJoBell(5) 5 54
(Jim Goldie) *hld up: stdy hdwy 3f out: effrt and ev ch 2f out: one pce appr fnl f* **8/1**
10-5 **4** 5 **Woodstock (IRE)**[11] 3624 4-9-2 **65**........................ GrahamLee 2 58
(Alistair Whillans) *t.k.h early: cl up: effrt and led over 2f out to wl over 1f out: sn outpcd* **7/1**
5052 **5** 14 **Ronald Gee (IRE)**[23] 3238 7-8-13 **65**........................ GaryBartley(3) 7 37
(Jim Goldie) *trckd ldrs: effrt and rdn over 3f out: wknd fr 2f out* **3/1**[1]
2016 **6** 1 3/4 **Sherman McCoy**[23] 3250 8-9-7 **70**........................ RobertWinston 4 39
(Marjorie Fife) *cl up: rdn over 3f out: wknd 2f out* **4/1**[2]
0200 **7** 8 **Hunting Ground (USA)**[14] 3532 4-9-3 **66**........................(b[1]) JoeFanning 3 23
(Mark Johnston) *t.k.h: led tl rdn and hdd over 2f out: wknd over 1f out* **5/1**[3]
2m 49.26s (-4.74) **Going Correction** -0.35s/f (Firm) **7** Ran SP% **111.8**
Speed ratings (Par 103): **100,98,96,93,85 84,79**
CSF £48.34 CT £359.09 TOTE £10.10: £3.70, £3.00; EX 73.80 Trifecta £399.50.
**Owner** Andrew Sayer **Bred** Sheikh Sultan Bin Khalifa Al Nahyan **Trained** Hackthorpe, Cumbria

**FOCUS**
A low-grade handicap short on progressive types and the strong pace took its toll in the closing stages. Not solid form.

## 4016 BETVICTOR WORLD CUP SPINCAST FREE BETS H'CAP 5f
**5:00** (5:01) (Class 3) (0-95,86) 3-Y-O+ **£7,762** (£2,310; £1,154; £577) **Stalls** Low

Form RPR
4605 **1** **Mutafaakir (IRE)**[20] 3342 5-9-5 **79**........................(p) JamesSullivan 7 88
(Ruth Carr) *t.k.h: mde all: rdn and edgd rt 2f out: hung lft and hld on wl ins fnl f* **9/2**[3]
0061 **2** 3/4 **Jinky**[1] 4003 6-8-8 **71**........................ GeorgeChaloner(3) 5 77
(Linda Perratt) *awkward s: sn prom: effrt and chsd wnr ins fnl f: kpt on: hld nr fin* **2/1**[2]
-215 **3** nk **Algar Lad**[10] 3666 4-9-12 **86**........................ DanielTudhope 4 91
(David O'Meara) *t.k.h: chsd ldrs: effrt and rdn over 1f out: carried lft wl ins fnl f: kpt on* **13/8**[1]
4101 **4** 1 3/4 **Rothesay Chancer**[12] 3571 6-9-7 **81**........................ GrahamLee 6 80
(Jim Goldie) *hld up in tch: effrt and pushed along over 1f out: kpt on ins fnl f: no imp* **8/1**
415 **5** nse **Perfect Blossom**[3] 3921 7-8-12 **75**........................ SladeO'Hara(3) 1 74
(Alan Berry) *cl up: rdn wl over 1f out: no ex whn carried lft ins fnl f: eased and lost one pl nr line* **10/1**
58.53s (-0.87) **Going Correction** -0.35s/f (Firm) **5** Ran SP% **109.8**
Speed ratings (Par 107): **92,90,90,87,87**
CSF £13.83 TOTE £6.10: £1.90, £2.10; EX 13.30 Trifecta £34.10.
**Owner** Ms Helen Barbour & Dario Neri **Bred** Shadwell Estate Company Limited **Trained** Huby, N Yorks
■ Stewards' Enquiry : Slade O'Hara four-day ban: failed to ride out for 4th (Jul 21-24)
James Sullivan two-day ban: careless riding (Jul 21-22)

**FOCUS**
A small field and something of a messy race although the winner, who was providing Ruth Carr and James Sullivan with a double on the card, was full value for his win having hung all over the track. The runner-up confirmed his back-to-form effort the previous day.

## 4017 ENHANCED PRICES ON BETVICTOR INSTABET APP APPRENTICE H'CAP 7f 50y
**5:30** (5:30) (Class 6) (0-65,70) 3-Y-O **£2,264** (£673; £336; £168) **Stalls** High

Form RPR
1-04 **1** **Dark Crystal**[26] 3100 3-9-1 **59**........................ MeganCarberry(5) 3 68
(Linda Perratt) *cl up: rdn and hdwy to ld over 1f out: kpt on strly fnl f* **20/1**
3131 **2** 2 1/2 **Crafted (IRE)**[5] 3846 3-9-10 **70** 6ex........................ AhmadAlSubousi(7) 9 73
(Mark Johnston) *w ldr on outside: led over 3f out: hung lft and hdd over 1f out: kpt on same pce ins fnl f* **8/15**[1]
60-5 **3** 1 1/2 **Vale Mentor (IRE)**[16] 3465 3-8-6 **50**........................ RachelRichardson(5) 8 48
(Tim Easterby) *led tl hdd over 3f out: rallied: kpt on same pce over 1f out* **16/1**
505 **4** 1 3/4 **Moonwood**[34] 2871 3-8-10 **52**........................(v[1]) JacobButterfield(5) 4 45
(Ollie Pears) *dwlt: hld up in tch: rdn along 2f out: kpt on fnl f: no imp* **33/1**
3612 **5** 8 **Spirit Of Alsace (IRE)**[12] 3575 3-9-12 **65**........................ ConnorBeasley 6 37
(Jim Goldie) *plld hrd: in tch tl hung lft and wknd fr 2f out* **7/2**[2]
000- **6** 3/4 **Queen Of Arts**[240] 7818 3-8-2 **46** oh1........................ SammyJoBell(5) 7 16
(Richard Fahey) *hld up in tch: struggling 1/2-way: sn btn* **11/1**[3]
1m 30.83s (-2.57) **Going Correction** -0.35s/f (Firm) **6** Ran SP% **109.4**
Speed ratings (Par 98): **100,97,95,93,84 83**
CSF £30.33 CT £175.45 TOTE £9.30: £4.20, £1.10; EX 31.30 Trifecta £113.00.
**Owner** Mrs Helen Perratt **Bred** R Biggs **Trained** East Kilbride, S Lanarks

**FOCUS**
A modest event further weakened by three non-runners and a surprise winner in a race in which little got into it. The winner has been rated as running a personal best, but the form is unconvincing.
T/Plt: £222.80 to a £1 stake. Pool: £56174.13 - 184.01 winning tickets T/Qpdt: £94.10 to a £1 stake. Pool: £4018.60 - 31.60 winning tickets RY

# 3394 RIPON (R-H)
Monday, July 7

**OFFICIAL GOING: Good (good to firm in places; 8.1)**
Wind: almost nil Weather: fine, light rain race 6

## 4018 HAPPY 80TH BIRTHDAY JOHN OGLANBY MAIDEN AUCTION FILLIES' STKS (BOBIS RACE) 6f
**6:40** (6:42) (Class 5) 2-Y-O **£3,234** (£962; £481; £240) **Stalls** High

Form RPR
**1** **Rosalie Bonheur** 2-8-3 0........................ RyanTate(3) 11 70+
(Clive Cox) *hmpd s: in rr: hdwy and swtchd rt 2f out: led ins fnl f: kpt on* **9/4**[1]
2 **2** hd **Gleneely Girl (IRE)**[21] 3304 2-8-12 0........................ ChrisCatlin 2 75+
(Rae Guest) *trckd ldrs: led 2f out: hdd ins fnl f: kpt on wl* **3/1**[2]
006 **3** 7 **Blazing Rose (IRE)**[40] 2673 2-8-12 0........................ GrahamGibbons 3 54
(David O'Meara) *chsd ldrs: outpcd over 2f out: kpt on to chse ldrs 1f out: wknd last 75yds* **33/1**
030 **4** 3/4 **Pickle Lilly Pearl**[52] 2313 2-8-12 0........................ RobertHavlin 7 52
(David C Griffiths) *wnt lft s: led: hdd 2f out: kpt on one pce appr fnl f* **20/1**
4330 **5** 2 **Rose Of Kiev (IRE)**[15] 3497 2-8-9 0........................ FrannyNorton 4 43
(Mark Johnston) *chsd ldrs: drvn 3f out: one pce* **3/1**[2]
46 **6** 3 1/4 **Icandi**[23] 3232 2-8-9 0........................ RichardKingscote 5 33
(Tom Dascombe) *stmbld bdly sn after s: mid-div: outpcd over 2f out: no threat* **10/1**
**7** 3 1/4 **Ellerina** 2-8-9 0........................ MichaelStainton 1 23+
(Chris Fairhurst) *wnt rt s: detached in last and racd wd: bhd tl sme late hdwy* **50/1**
**8** 1 1/2 **Riverlynx (IRE)** 2-8-9 0........................ AndrewElliott 9 19
(Ben Haslam) *in rr-div: sme hdwy over 2f out: sn wknd* **28/1**
0 **9** 2 **Pixey Punk**[22] 3267 2-9-1 0........................ DuranFentiman 6 19
(Tim Easterby) *chsd ldrs: lost pl over 1f out* **9/1**[3]
1m 13.45s (0.45) **Going Correction** -0.15s/f (Firm) **9** Ran SP% **113.0**
Speed ratings (Par 91): **91,90,81,80,77 73,69,67,64**
CSF £8.47 TOTE £4.00: £1.10, £1.40, £7.30; EX 9.20 Trifecta £239.20.
**Owner** Mrs Hugh Maitland-Jones **Bred** Mrs Hugh Maitland-Jones **Trained** Lambourn, Berks

**FOCUS**
A moderate 2yo fillies' maiden. Rail on bend from back straight to home straight moved out 3m adding about 7yds to races on Round course.

## 4019 OUR LOCAL HEROES FOUNDATION H'CAP 6f
7:10 (7:11) (Class 5) (0-70,70) 3-Y-O £3,234 (£962; £481; £240) Stalls High

Form RPR
2-06 1 **Sartori**[56] 2205 3-9-1 **64**.......... RussKennemore 14 70
(Marjorie Fife) *mde all: edgd rt ins fnl f: hld on nr fin* **20/1**
4552 2 *nk* **Traditionelle**[10] 3650 3-8-9 **58**.......... AndrewElliott 13 63+
(Tim Easterby) *hld up in rr: swtchd lft to stands' side rail 2f out: styd on wl fnl f: jst hld* **4/1[1]**
023 3 *nk* **Percy's Gal**[20] 3343 3-9-2 **70**.......... GemmaTutty(5) 3 74
(Karen Tutty) *chsd ldrs: upsides fnl f: no ex nr fin* **4/1[1]**
1455 4 *1* **Cahal (IRE)**[10] 3647 3-8-7 **56**.......... AdrianNicholls 4 57
(David Nicholls) *chsd ldrs: drvn over 2f out: kpt on same pce fnl f* **16/1**
4244 5 *¾* **Injaz**[18] 3405 3-8-12 **61**..........(p) JamesDoyle 1 59+
(Kevin Ryan) *in rr: swtchd lft after s: hdwy over 1f out: hmpd and swtchd lft ins fnl f: styd on* **8/1[3]**
-056 6 *shd* **Secret Applause**[10] 3669 3-8-10 **59**.......... PaulMulrennan 11 57
(Michael Dods) *hld up in mid-div: hdwy over 2f out: chsng ldrs 1f out: kpt on same pce* **14/1**
0-06 7 *½* **Shikari**[34] 2870 3-8-2 **51** oh2.......... AndrewMullen 8 47
(Robin Bastiman) *t.k.h: chsd ldrs: hmpd after 1f: outpcd over 2f out: kpt on ins fnl f* **25/1**
0455 8 *nk* **Henke (IRE)**[18] 3380 3-8-1 **55**..........(p) ShelleyBirkett(5) 5 51
(Nigel Tinkler) *mid-div: hdwy over 2f out: sn chsng ldrs: one pce appr fnl f* **28/1**
-003 9 *¾* **Tweety Pie (IRE)**[16] 3487 3-9-0 **66**.......... NeilFarley(3) 6 59
(Declan Carroll) *chsd ldrs: one pce over 1f out* **11/1**
5-34 10 *shd* **Ty Cobb (IRE)**[11] 3600 3-8-4 **56**.......... IanBrennan(3) 9 49
(John Quinn) *chsd ldrs: hmpd and lost pl after 1f: kpt on fnl f* **16/1**
0-04 11 *2* **Orient Sky**[3] 3935 3-8-8 **57**..........(p) PJMcDonald 7 43
(Paul Midgley) *chsd ldrs: hung rt and wknd last 100yds* **7/1[2]**
0625 12 *5* **Disclosure**[10] 3650 3-9-7 **70**.......... DavidAllan 12 40
(Les Eyre) *chsd ldrs: lost pl over 1f out* **7/1[2]**
5323 13 *2¾* **Lucky Times**[36] 2802 3-8-10 **59**.......... DuranFentiman 10 21
(Mel Brittain) *s.i.s: hdwy on outside over 2f out: wknd over 1f out* **16/1**
1m 12.17s (-0.83) **Going Correction** -0.15s/f (Firm) 13 Ran SP% **120.8**
Speed ratings (Par 100): **99,98,98,96,95 95,95,94,93,93 90,84,80**
CSF £97.51 CT £412.27 TOTE £22.60: £7.90, £1.50, £1.50; EX 92.40 Trifecta £1520.70.
**Owner** Chris Tremewan, Mike Saini, Tom Fife **Bred** D R Tucker **Trained** Stillington, N Yorks
■ Stewards' Enquiry : Russ Kennemore two-day ban: used whip above permitted level (Jul 21-22)
Gemma Tutty seven-day ban: used whip above permitted level (Jul 21-27)

**FOCUS**
An ordinary sprint handicap. The winner has been rated as running his best race for his current yard.

## 4020 FOLLOW @ATTHERACES ON TWITTER H'CAP (BOBIS RACE) 1m 4f 10y
7:40 (7:40) (Class 4) (0-80,80) 3-Y-O £5,175 (£1,540; £769; £384) Stalls Low

Form RPR
0-23 1 **Asteroidea**[22] 3270 3-9-1 **74**.......... GrahamGibbons 6 83
(Pam Sly) *led after 1f: styd on wl fnl 2f* **6/1**
0-22 2 *1½* **Button Down**[26] 3106 3-9-6 **79**.......... JamesDoyle 5 86
(Lady Cecil) *hld up in mid-div: drvn over 3f out: swtchd outside 2f out: chsd wnr and hung rt ins fnl f: no imp* **9/2[3]**
2560 3 *2¼* **Brownsville (USA)**[25] 3146 3-8-6 **65**.......... FrannyNorton 2 68
(Mark Johnston) *led 1f: chsd ldrs: drvn over 3f out: 2nd over 1f out: styd on same pce* **14/1**
332 4 *1¼* **Miss Tree**[31] 2952 3-8-10 **72**.......... IanBrennan(3) 4 73
(John Quinn) *hld up in mid-div: hdwy to trck ldrs 7f out: kpt on same pce over 1f out* **7/2[3]**
-441 5 *shd* **Bajan Beauty (IRE)**[18] 3385 3-9-2 **75**.......... RobertHavlin 3 76
(Charles Hills) *dwlt: in rr: drvn over 6f out: hdwy over 3f out: sn chsng ldrs: one pce over 1f out* **11/1**
0341 6 *3¼* **Mabdhool (IRE)**[14] 3514 3-9-7 **80**.......... PaulHanagan 1 76
(Marcus Tregoning) *chsd wnr: chal over 3f out: wknd appr fnl f* **8/1**
61 7 *1¼* **Westerly**[15] 3498 3-8-12 **71**.......... LiamJones 7 65
(William Haggas) *in rr: pushed along over 6f out: sme hdwy and edgd lft over 2f out: wknd fnl f* **10/3[2]**
2m 34.53s (-2.17) **Going Correction** -0.15s/f (Firm) 7 Ran SP% **110.7**
Speed ratings (Par 102): **101,100,98,97,97 95,94**
CSF £22.72 TOTE £7.20: £2.80, £1.30; EX 16.90 Trifecta £183.20.
**Owner** Michael H Sly Dr T Davies Mrs Pam Sly **Bred** M H Sly, Dr T Davies & Mrs P Sly **Trained** Thorney, Cambs

**FOCUS**
Not a bad handicap. The fifth and sixth have been rated close to their marks after stiff rises for maiden wins.

## 4021 ARMSTRONG MEMORIAL H'CAP (BOBIS RACE) 6f
8:10 (8:10) (Class 3) (0-90,88) 3-Y-O £7,561 (£2,263; £1,131; £566; £282) Stalls High

Form RPR
61 1 **Telmeyd**[37] 2759 3-9-7 **88**.......... SebSanders 1 101+
(William Haggas) *trckd ldrs: led over 1f out: rdn and styd on wl* **6/4[1]**
2203 2 *2* **Lincoln (IRE)**[14] 3539 3-9-1 **85**.......... CharlesBishop(3) 6 92
(Mick Channon) *trckd ldrs on stands' side rail: nt clr run over 2f out: swtchd rt over 1f out: chsd wnr jst ins fnl f: no imp* **3/1[3]**
2621 3 *2* **Dutch Breeze**[19] 3370 3-8-12 **79**.......... DavidAllan 5 80
(Tim Easterby) *chsd ldrs: drvn 2f out: kpt on same pce* **7/4[2]**
0-30 4 *½* **Alisios (GR)**[31] 2968 3-8-10 **77**.......... JamesDoyle 3 76
(Luca Cumani) *in rr: outpcd over 3f out: hdwy over 2f out: one pce* **13/2**
-210 5 *½* **Galvanize**[23] 3247 3-9-4 **85**.......... PaulMulrennan 2 82
(Kevin Ryan) *led: hdd over 1f out: one pce* **18/1**
1m 11.02s (-1.98) **Going Correction** -0.15s/f (Firm) 5 Ran SP% **113.1**
Speed ratings (Par 104): **107,104,101,101,100**
CSF £8.93 TOTE £2.20: £1.10, £1.90; EX 7.40 Trifecta £12.60.
**Owner** Sheikh Ahmed Al Maktoum **Bred** Cheveley Park Stud Ltd **Trained** Newmarket, Suffolk

**FOCUS**
A fair little sprint handicap. The runner-up sets the standard.

## 4022 SIS LIVE MAIDEN STKS 1m
8:40 (8:41) (Class 5) 3-Y-O+ £3,234 (£962; £481; £240) Stalls Low

Form RPR
262- 1 **Bold Captain (IRE)**[262] 7339 3-9-3 **72**.......... PhillipMakin 4 74+
(John Quinn) *mde all: drvn over 2f out: hld on towards fin* **7/2[3]**
4-42 2 *½* **Hesbaan (IRE)**[14] 3517 3-9-3 **74**.......... PaulHanagan 13 73
(Marcus Tregoning) *mid-div: hdwy over 3f out: styd on fnl f: tk 2nd post* **6/4[1]**
0-0 3 *shd* **Interject (USA)**[87] 1423 3-8-12 **0**.......... JamesDoyle 5 68
(Charles Hills) *chsd wnr: effrt over 2f out: kpt on same pce ins fnl f* **7/1**
4 *2¾* **Lockhart (IRE)** 3-9-3 **0**.......... FrannyNorton 1 66
(Mark Johnston) *chsd ldrs: one pce over 1f out* **11/4[2]**
46 5 *hd* **Cliff (IRE)**[11] 3601 4-9-7 **0**.......... ShelleyBirkett(5) 7 68
(Nigel Tinkler) *chsd ldrs: kpt on one pce fnl 2f* **33/1**
4 6 *3½* **Fillydelphia (IRE)**[13] 3543 3-8-12 **0**.......... AndrewMullen 2 53
(Patrick Holmes) *s.i.s: hdwy over 4f out: sn drvn: one pce fnl 2f* **100/1**
0- 7 *4* **Sr Swing**[262] 7339 3-8-12 **0**.......... RussKennemore 3 44
(Philip Kirby) *dwlt: in rr-div: hdwy over 3f out: hung lft: nvr trbld ldrs* **66/1**
0 8 *3¼* **Lacerta**[50] 2365 3-9-3 **0**.......... PJMcDonald 9 41
(Micky Hammond) *mid-div: nvr a factor* **100/1**
60- 9 *1½* **Saythatagain (IRE)**[255] 7493 3-8-12 **0**.......... DavidAllan 8 33
(Tim Easterby) *in rr: sme hdwy over 3f out: nvr on terms* **28/1**
10 *3¼* **Asha** 3-8-12 **0**.......... RobertHavlin 6 25
(David C Griffiths) *s.s: in rr: kpt on fnl 2f: nvr on terms* **66/1**
6 11 *hd* **Giovanni Jack**[17] 3434 4-9-12 **0**.......... BenCurtis 11 32
(Alan Swinbank) *s.i.s: in rr: sme hdwy over 2f out: sn lost pl* **50/1**
06 12 *10* **Shadow Of The Day**[33] 2902 7-9-12 **0**.......... DuranFentiman 12 9
(Lee James) *s.i.s: in rr: bhd fnl 3f* **100/1**
0 13 *8* **Clabare**[16] 3486 3-8-12 **0**.......... GarryWhillans(5) 10
(Ian Semple) *chsd ldrs: lost pl over 3f out: bhd whn eased ins fnl f* **25/1**
1m 39.61s (-1.79) **Going Correction** -0.15s/f (Firm)
**WFA** 3 from 4yo+ 9lb 13 Ran SP% **119.5**
Speed ratings (Par 103): **102,101,101,98,98 94,90,87,86,82 82,72,64**
CSF £8.73 TOTE £4.30: £1.90, £1.10, £2.30; EX 10.70 Trifecta £46.40.
**Owner** Highfield Racing **Bred** Danny Coogan **Trained** Settrington, N Yorks

**FOCUS**
Just fair form in this maiden. As is often the case here it paid to race handily. The runner-up shaped like the best from a poor draw and race position, while the third has been rated as improving.

## 4023 CHILDRENS FESTIVAL CIRCUS HERE 4TH AUGUST H'CAP 1m
9:10 (9:10) (Class 5) (0-70,70) 3-Y-O+ £3,234 (£962; £481; £240) Stalls Low

Form RPR
526 1 **Thankyou Very Much**[26] 3095 4-9-7 **63**..........(p) PJMcDonald 2 72
(James Bethell) *trckd ldrs on inner: led over 1f out: kpt on wl* **7/2[1]**
3650 2 *1½* **Tarrafal (IRE)**[10] 3672 3-8-7 **58**.......... FrannyNorton 5 62+
(Mark Johnston) *in rr: hdwy over 2f out: styd on strly to take 2nd last 50yds: gng on at fin* **7/1[3]**
-623 3 *¾* **Irondale Express**[38] 2740 3-9-4 **69**.......... BarryMcHugh 9 71
(Tony Coyle) *chsd ldrs: chal over 3f out: kpt on same pce ins fnl f* **14/1**
3004 4 *1½* **Shamaheart (IRE)**[18] 3400 4-9-9 **70**..........(p) KevinStott(5) 4 70
(Geoffrey Harker) *trckd ldr: led over 2f out: hdd over 1f out: kpt on one pce* **8/1**
5224 5 *nse* **Lil Sophella (IRE)**[2] 3949 5-9-2 **58**.......... AndrewElliott 8 58
(Patrick Holmes) *mid-div: hdwy on outer over 2f out: kpt on fnl f* **9/2[2]**
4053 6 *nse* **Icy Blue**[14] 3533 6-9-6 **62**..........(p) PhillipMakin 11 62
(Richard Whitaker) *in rr: hdwy over 1f out: styng on at fin* **7/1[3]**
4433 7 *hd* **Violent Velocity (IRE)**[26] 3096 11-9-3 **62**.......... IanBrennan(3) 7 62
(John Quinn) *mid-div: hdwy over 2f out: kpt on one pce: nvr a threat* **9/1**
3350 8 *2¼* **Royal Holiday (IRE)**[33] 2905 7-9-11 **67**..........(p) RussKennemore 3 62
(Marjorie Fife) *led: drvn over 4f out: hdd over 2f out: wknd over 1f out* **12/1**
-033 9 *4* **Eastlands Lad (IRE)**[20] 3344 5-8-6 **51** oh2.......... NeilFarley(3) 1 36
(Micky Hammond) *trckd ldrs on inner: t.k.h: effrt over 2f out: wknd over 1f out: eased towards fin* **16/1**
3300 10 *4½* **Steel Stockholder**[26] 3096 8-9-8 **64**.......... DavidAllan 6 39
(Mel Brittain) *mid-div: effrt over 3f out: lost pl over 2f out* **18/1**
4260 11 *6* **Nelson's Bay**[2] 3958 5-9-5 **61**..........(t) AmyRyan 10 22
(Wilf Storey) *trckd ldrs on outer: lost pl after 2f: bhd fnl 2f: eased clsng stages* **8/1**
1m 40.17s (-1.23) **Going Correction** -0.15s/f (Firm)
**WFA** 3 from 4yo+ 9lb 11 Ran SP% **123.1**
Speed ratings (Par 103): **100,98,97,96,96 96,95,93,89,85 79**
CSF £29.59 CT £322.09 TOTE £4.10: £2.20, £2.40, £4.90; EX 41.40 Trifecta £703.60.
**Owner** Robert Gibbons **Bred** Robert Gibbons **Trained** Middleham Moor, N Yorks

**FOCUS**
A moderate handicap. The third helps set the standard, with the fourth close to his recent form.
T/Plt: £18.40 to a £1 stake. Pool: £84,561.58 - 3,352.93 winning tickets T/Qpdt: £6.00 to a £1 stake. Pool: £6,851.55 - 833.70 winning tickets WG

# 3799 WINDSOR (R-H)
Monday, July 7

**OFFICIAL GOING: Good to soft**
Wind: Almost nil Weather: Heavy rain before racing, dry rest of evening

## 4024 BETDAQ 0% WORLD CUP NIL-NIL RESULTS APPRENTICE H'CAP 6f
5:50 (5:51) (Class 5) (0-75,75) 4-Y-O+ £2,587 (£770; £384; £192) Stalls Low

Form RPR
-646 1 **Sarangoo**[16] 3468 6-9-11 **74**.......... OisinMurphy 11 83
(Malcolm Saunders) *trckd ldr: rdn to ld over 1f out: hrd pressed and drvn fnl f: jst hld on* **15/2[3]**
2224 2 *shd* **Ray Of Joy**[5] 3854 8-9-2 **68**..........(v) DannyBrock(3) 10 76
(J R Jenkins) *trckd ldrs gng wl: rdn to chse wnr 1f out: str chal fnl f: jst failed* **11/1**
1102 3 *4½* **Putin (IRE)**[9] 3707 6-9-1 **69**..........(bt) JennyPowell(5) 7 62
(Phil McEntee) *led: tk field down centre of crse: rdn and hdd over 1f out: fdd but hld on for 3rd* **12/1**
5406 4 *½* **Blazing Knight (IRE)**[20] 3329 4-8-12 **64**..........(b) TimClark(3) 2 56
(Chris Gordon) *towards rr: rdn and struggling over 2f out: kpt on fnl f: n.d* **25/1**
-066 5 *shd* **Dominium (USA)**[26] 3118 7-9-8 **71**..........(p) RobertTart 9 62
(Jeremy Gask) *hld up in rr: prog on wd outside 2f out: no hdwy over 1f out: wknd fnl f* **8/1**
6662 6 *½* **Atlantis Crossing (IRE)**[9] 3734 5-9-2 **68**.......... NathanAlison(3) 4 58
(Jim Boyle) *awkward s: t.k.h and hld up in rr: prog and cl up 1/2-way: rdn over 1f out: sn wknd* **3/1[1]**
243 7 *1¼* **Jontleman (IRE)**[11] 3612 4-9-10 **73**.......... WilliamTwiston-Davies 5 59
(Mick Channon) *in tch: rdn over 2f out: wknd over 1f out* **8/1**

6423 **8** *1* **Jay Bee Blue**[39] 2691 5-9-7 **75**....................(bt) CamHardie(5) 1 58
(Sean Curran) *trckd ldrs: rdn over 2f out: wknd over 1f out* **7/2**[2]

0100 **9** *shd* **Night Trade (IRE)**[5] 3848 7-8-0 **56**....................(p) AbieKnowles(7) 3 38
(Ronald Harris) *towards rr: effrt on outer 2f out: wknd over 1f out* **20/1**

00-0 **10** *2 3/4* **Someone's Darling**[16] 3479 4-9-7 **70**.................... JoeyHaynes 8 43
(Lydia Pearce) *chsd ldng pair to over 2f out: wknd* **25/1**

1005 **11** *6* **Presumido (IRE)**[39] 2691 4-9-3 **69**.................... JackDuern(3) 6 23
(Simon Dow) *tk fierce hold: hld up and sn last: racd alone against nr side rail fr 1/2-way: nvr on terms* **25/1**

1m 12.89s (-0.11) **Going Correction** +0.125s/f (Good) **11** Ran SP% **113.5**
Speed ratings (Par 103): **105,104,98,98,98 97,95,94,94,90 82**
CSF £78.49 CT £969.79 TOTE £8.10: £3.00, £2.70, £3.50; EX 83.80 Trifecta £757.60.
**Owner** Lockstone Business Services Ltd **Bred** M S Saunders And Chris Scott **Trained** Green Ore, Somerset

**FOCUS**
A moderate handicap, confined to apprentice riders. The winner has been rated back to her form over this C&D in October. Top bend dolled out 8yds from normal inner configuration adding 29yds to races of one mile and beyond. Inner of Straight dolled out 5yds at 6f and 2yds at Winning Post.

## 4025 BRITISH STALLION STUDS EBF MAIDEN STKS 6f
**6:20** (6:21) (Class 5) 2-Y-O **£2,911** (£866; £432; £216) **Stalls** Low

Form RPR

4 **1** **Ticks The Boxes (IRE)**[21] 3311 2-9-5 0.................... AdamKirby 7 84+
(Clive Cox) *mde all: steered towards far side fr 1/2-way: rdn over 1f out: clr fnl f: styd on wl* **7/1**

**2** *2* **Atletico (IRE)** 2-9-5 0.................... TomQueally 13 78+
(Roger Varian) *s.i.s: towards rr: rdn and gd prog fr 2f out: tk 2nd ins fnl f: styd on but unable to chal* **6/1**[3]

2 **3** *1 3/4* **Aussie Ruler (IRE)**[7] 3779 2-9-5 0.................... SteveDrowne 11 73
(Ronald Harris) *prom: chsd wnr 2f out to ins fnl f: one pce* **6/1**[3]

**4** *1* **Stolen Story (IRE)** 2-9-5 0.................... KierenFallon 15 70
(George Margarson) *s.i.s: towards rr: rdn over 2f out: kpt on fr over 1f out towards far rail: tk 4th ins fnl f* **12/1**

**5** *1/2* **Rio Ronaldo (IRE)** 2-9-5 0.................... PatDobbs 12 69
(Mike Murphy) *s.i.s: t.k.h: trckd ldrs fr 1/2-way: shkn up over 1f out: one pce after* **33/1**

42 **6** *1 1/2* **Mumford**[16] 3461 2-9-5 0.................... RichardHughes 1 64
(Richard Hannon) *chsd wnr to 2f out: wkng whn hmpd jst ins fnl f* **7/2**[1]

**7** *nk* **Oriental Splendour (IRE)** 2-9-0 0.................... CamHardie(5) 10 63
(Roger Charlton) *prom: rdn 2f out: no imp on ldrs 1f out: one pce* **40/1**

0 **8** *nk* **Ghalib (IRE)**[25] 3148 2-9-5 0.................... MartinHarley 3 62
(Marco Botti) *mostly in midfield: shkn up and no prog 2f out: kpt on* **9/2**[2]

**9** *5* **Zipedeedodah (IRE)** 2-9-2 0.................... OisinMurphy(3) 4 47
(Joseph Tuite) *spd to chse ldrs: styd in centre and wknd 2f out* **25/1**

**10** *2 1/4* **Toast Of Newbury (IRE)** 2-9-5 0.................... WilliamTwiston-Davies 9 40
(Jamie Osborne) *s.s: a in rr: no ch fnl 2f* **40/1**

**11** *1 3/4* **Classic Seniority** 2-9-5 0.................... SeanLevey 2 35
(Richard Hannon) *chsd ldrs: styd in centre fr 1/2-way: wknd 2f out* **12/1**

0 **12** *1* **Total Demolition (IRE)**[9] 3728 2-9-5 0.................... JamieSpencer 14 32
(Olly Stevens) *stdd s: hld up and sn last: no prog fr 1/2-way* **25/1**

**13** *nk* **Activation** 2-9-5 0....................(p) HayleyTurner 5 31
(Hughie Morrison) *midfield early: dropped to rr and rdn 1/2-way: sn struggling* **50/1**

6 **14** *1* **Akavit (IRE)**[14] 3536 2-9-5 0.................... FrederikTylicki 8 28
(Ed de Giles) *sn in last pair: nvr a factor* **100/1**

**15** *4 1/2* **Speculator** 2-9-5 0.................... LukeMorris 6 15
(David Menuisier) *s.s: a towards rr: styd in centre fr 1/2-way and wknd* **50/1**

1m 14.13s (1.13) **Going Correction** +0.125s/f (Good) **15** Ran SP% **117.3**
Speed ratings (Par 94): **97,94,92,90,90 88,87,87,80,77 75,73,73,72,66**
CSF £43.76 TOTE £7.60: £2.40, £2.60, £2.50; EX 46.70 Trifecta £277.30.
**Owner** Miss J Deadman & S Barrow **Bred** John B Hughes **Trained** Lambourn, Berks

**FOCUS**
Probably a fair 2yo maiden.

## 4026 BETDAQ 0% WORLD CUP CORRECT SCORES CLAIMING STKS 1m 2f 7y
**6:50** (6:51) (Class 6) 3-Y-O **£2,587** (£770; £384; £192) **Stalls** Centre

Form RPR

0 **1** **Koliakhova (FR)**[25] 3154 3-8-8 72....................[1] KierenFallon 2 71
(George Baker) *mde all: wound it up fr 3f out: drvn and in command over 1f out: styd on* **3/1**[2]

5255 **2** *2 3/4* **Pershing**[10] 3643 3-9-1 72.................... MartinHarley 3 72
(Marco Botti) *trckd ldng pair: rdn to chse wnr jst over 2f out: no imp 1f out: one pce* **5/4**[1]

00 **3** *1 1/2* **Exclusive Contract (IRE)**[9] 3712 3-8-8 0.................... JamieSpencer 1 62
(Jamie Osborne) *stdd s: hld up in last: plenty to do whn asked for effrt over 2f out: drvn and hanging over 1f out: tk 3rd fnl f: no ch* **6/1**

6366 **4** *2 1/2* **Honiton Lace**[13] 3559 3-8-0 53.................... SilvestreDeSousa 5 49
(B W Hills) *t.k.h: sn pressed wnr: tried to chal 3f out: fdd 2f out* **7/2**[3]

6000 **5** *16* **Lady Knight (IRE)**[8] 3754 3-8-1 57.................... LukeMorris 4 20
(J S Moore) *racd in 4th: nt gng wl bef 1/2-way: dropped to last and wknd over 2f out: t.o* **25/1**

2m 9.21s (0.51) **Going Correction** +0.125s/f (Good) **5** Ran SP% **109.8**
Speed ratings (Par 98): **102,99,98,96,83**
CSF £7.17 TOTE £3.20: £1.70, £1.20; EX 6.80 Trifecta £21.70.Honiton Lace was claimed Mr P. S. McEntee £4,000. Koliakhova was claimed Mr J. L. Flint £12,000.
**Owner** Mrs C E S Baker **Bred** E A R L Ecurie De La Vallee Martigny **Trained** Manton, Wilts

**FOCUS**
A moderate claimer. It has been rated cautiously with the runner-up and fourth below their recent form.

## 4027 BETDAQ EXCHANGE 0% MULTIPLES DURING WORLD CUP H'CAP 5f 10y
**7:20** (7:20) (Class 4) (0-85,85) 3-Y-O+ **£4,851** (£1,443; £721; £360) **Stalls** Low

Form RPR

0400 **1** **Gladiatrix**[31] 2965 5-9-12 **85**....................(b) SilvestreDeSousa 13 95
(Rod Millman) *prom: taken towards far side fr 1/2-way: overall ldr wl over 1f out: clr fnl f: drvn out* **7/1**

-030 **2** *2 1/4* **Ziggy Lee**[29] 3033 8-9-4 **84**.................... JordanNason(7) 6 86
(Peter Hedger) *in tch: pushed along after 2f: styd towards nr side fr 1/2-way: rdn to ld gp over 1f out: kpt on but no threat to wnr* **10/1**

4-30 **3** *nse* **Port Alfred**[53] 2275 4-9-11 **84**.................... AdamKirby 7 86
(Charlie Appleby) *hld up in tch: taken towards far side fr 1/2-way: drvn to chse wnr over 1f out: kpt on but no imp fnl f* **9/2**[2]

1103 **4** *1 3/4* **Taurus Twins**[18] 3386 8-9-8 **81**....................(b) TomQueally 14 76
(Richard Price) *prom: taken towards far side fr 1/2-way and chsd wnr: fdd jst over 1f out* **8/1**

0541 **5** *1 1/4* **Hannahs Turn**[16] 3462 4-9-4 **82**.................... MarcMonaghan(5) 2 73
(Chris Dwyer) *early spd but nt pce to hold position after 2f: styd towards nr side fr 1/2-way: rdn and one pce fnl 2f* **8/1**

2050 **6** *1 3/4* **Waseem Faris (IRE)**[9] 3697 5-8-12 **78**.................... PaddyPilley(7) 11 63
(Mick Channon) *hld up in tch: taken towards far side fr 1/2-way: pushed along and no prog 2f out* **8/1**

-023 **7** *1 3/4* **Silverrica (IRE)**[6] 3817 4-8-11 **70**.................... RichardHughes 5 48
(Malcolm Saunders) *prom: styd cl to nr side fr 1/2-way: tried to chal gp ldr over 1f out: sn wknd and eased* **4/1**[1]

-000 **8** *1 1/4* **Burning Blaze**[99] 1190 4-9-9 **82**.................... JamieSpencer 12 56
(Olly Stevens) *stdd s: hld up and detached in last early: styd towards nr side fr 1/2-way: nvr remotely involved* **5/1**[3]

5500 **9** *1 1/4* **Jiroft (ITY)**[10] 3676 7-9-10 **83**....................(t) PatCosgrave 3 52
(Robert Cowell) *led: styd against nr side rail fr 1/2-way: hdd & wknd wl over 1f out* **20/1**

1m 0.45s (0.15) **Going Correction** +0.125s/f (Good)
**WFA** 3 from 4yo+ 5lb **9** Ran SP% **114.5**
Speed ratings (Par 105): **103,99,99,96,94 91,88,86,84**
CSF £73.54 CT £351.51 TOTE £7.30: £2.30, £4.60, £1.60; EX 66.10 Trifecta £526.00.
**Owner** Harry Dutfield & Partners **Bred** H G And J R Dutfield **Trained** Kentisbeare, Devon

**FOCUS**
A competitive sprint handicap. The winner has been rated back to form off a fair mark.

## 4028 WARHORSE FIREWORKS AT ROYAL WINDSOR RACECOURSE H'CAP 1m 67y
**7:50** (7:50) (Class 4) (0-85,86) 3-Y-O+ **£4,851** (£1,443; £721; £360) **Stalls** Low

Form RPR

1-40 **1** **Lawyer (IRE)**[23] 3243 3-9-4 **80**.................... AdamKirby 4 88+
(Luca Cumani) *hld up in 5th: rdn over 2f out: chsd ldr over 1f out: drvn to ld ins fnl f: sn clr* **2/1**[1]

4333 **2** *1 3/4* **St Paul De Vence (IRE)**[14] 3515 4-9-1 **68**.................... LukeMorris 8 74
(Paul Cole) *trckd ldr 2f: styd prom: rdn to chal 3f out: lost pl over 2f out: struggling over 1f out: rallied fnl f to take 2nd last strides* **5/1**[3]

6520 **3** *nk* **Tatting**[9] 3703 5-9-6 **78**.................... MarcMonaghan(5) 9 83
(Chris Dwyer) *chsd ldng trio: rdn over 2f out: nt qckn over 1f out: kpt on ins fnl f to take 3rd last stride* **16/1**

3310 **4** *hd* **After The Goldrush**[25] 3144 3-9-0 **76**....................(b) RichardHughes 2 79
(Richard Hannon) *led: hdd 3f out but nt asked for effrt: shkn up to ld again 2f out: drvn over 1f out: hdd ins fnl f: lost 2 pls last strides* **9/2**[2]

-021 **5** *nk* **Ogbourne Downs**[23] 3212 4-10-0 **81**.................... SteveDrowne 6 85
(Charles Hills) *hld up in 6th: clsd on ldrs 2f out: shkn up and nt qckn over 1f out: kpt on one pce after* **9/2**[2]

-030 **6** *1 1/4* **Soaring Spirits (IRE)**[12] 3577 4-9-10 **77**....................(b) KierenFallon 1 78
(Dean Ivory) *t.k.h early: trckd ldr after 2f: rdn to ld 3f out to 2f out: lost pl over 1f out: wl hld whn short of room nr fin* **5/1**[3]

3400 **7** *5* **Rakaan (IRE)**[21] 3314 7-9-4 **78**.................... JennyPowell(7) 3 68
(Brendan Powell) *s.s: a in last: pushed along and jst in tch 2f out: wknd over 1f out* **25/1**

1m 44.65s (-0.05) **Going Correction** +0.125s/f (Good)
**WFA** 3 from 4yo+ 9lb **7** Ran SP% **112.8**
Speed ratings (Par 105): **105,103,102,102,102 101,96**
CSF £11.97 CT £119.92 TOTE £2.70: £1.90, £2.90; EX 11.40 Trifecta £110.80.
**Owner** Sheikh Mohammed Obaid Al Maktoum **Bred** Drumlin Bloodstock **Trained** Newmarket, Suffolk

**FOCUS**
A modest handicap. The runner-up and third have been rated close to their marks.

## 4029 HAPPY BIRTHDAY MISS KATRINA THOMAS MAIDEN FILLIES' STKS 1m 67y
**8:20** (8:21) (Class 5) 3-4-Y-O **£2,587** (£770; £384; £192) **Stalls** Low

Form RPR

5 **1** **Patterned**[25] 3153 3-9-0 0.................... AdamKirby 10 76+
(Luca Cumani) *sn pressed ldr: disp ld fr 1/2-way: rdn over 2f out: gained upper hand jst over 1f out: drvn out* **11/8**[1]

-434 **2** *1 1/2* **Swiss Kiss**[24] 3195 3-9-0 73.................... RichardHughes 5 73
(John Gosden) *led: jnd 1/2-way: disp after and clr of rest wl over 2f out: rdn over 1f out: sn nt qckn and hld* **6/4**[2]

**3** *3 1/2* **Scarlet Sash** 3-9-0 0.................... FergusSweeney 11 65+
(Henry Candy) *s.i.s: sn in midfield: outpcd fr 3f out: shkn up and kpt on fr over 1f out to take 3rd last strides* **10/1**[3]

-360 **4** *hd* **Habdab**[164] 311 3-9-0 68.................... PatDobbs 9 64
(Richard Hannon) *trckd ldng trio: disp 3rd fr 3f out: outpcd over 2f out: shkn up and kpt on same pce after* **14/1**

00 **5** *2* **Purple Spot**[22] 3277 3-9-0 0.................... SteveDrowne 6 60
(Rod Millman) *trckd ldng pair: outpcd fr 3f out: pushed along after: fdd fnl f: nt disgracd* **80/1**

6 **6** *nk* **Daisy's Secret**[40] 2681 3-9-0 0.................... PatCosgrave 3 59
(George Baker) *wl in tch: outpcd and shkn up wl over 2f out: one pce after* **10/1**[3]

-6 **7** *1* **Simma (IRE)**[9] 3729 3-8-9 0.................... JoshBaudains(5) 4 57
(Sylvester Kirk) *towards rr: pushed along over 3f out: sn outpcd and rdn n.d after: kpt on fnl f* **33/1**

06 **8** *nk* **Sleeper**[63] 2031 3-9-0 0.................... OscarPereira 8 56
(Ralph Beckett) *hld up in last pair: pushed along over 3f out: sn outpcd and urged: no ch after: kpt on fnl f* **16/1**

6 **9** *2 3/4* **The Reel Way (GR)**[27] 3074 3-9-0 0.................... DavidProbert 2 50
(Patrick Chamings) *hld up in last trio: pushed along sn after 1/2-way: no prog over 2f out* **33/1**

**10** *13* **Praise N Glory** 3-9-0 0.................... LiamKeniry 1 20
(Linda Jewell) *s.s: a in last: pushed along over 3f out: wknd over 2f out: t.o* **100/1**

1m 46.64s (1.94) **Going Correction** +0.125s/f (Good) **10** Ran SP% **120.9**
Speed ratings (Par 100): **95,93,90,89,87 87,86,86,83,70**
CSF £3.78 TOTE £2.90: £1.10, £1.10, £2.30; EX 3.80 Trifecta £27.20.
**Owner** Fittocks Stud **Bred** Fittocks Stud **Trained** Newmarket, Suffolk

**FOCUS**
Not that much stength in depth here. Muddling form.

## 4030 ROYAL WINDSOR RACECOURSE MONDAY NIGHT CLUB H'CAP — 1m 2f 7y
8:50 (8:50) (Class 5) (0-75,75) 3-Y-0+ — £2,587 (£770; £384; £192) Stalls Centre

Form — RPR

10-6 **1** **Bertie Moon**[7] 3805 4-9-5 **66** ........ GeorgeBaker 8 — 78
(Geoffrey Deacon) *mde all: rdn over 1f out and sn pressed: styd on wl and in command last 150yds* — **16/1**

2112 **2** *1 ½* **I'm Harry**[3] 3919 5-9-5 **66** ........ (vt) PatCosgrave 5 — 75
(George Baker) *hld up in 4th: prog to trck wnr wl over 2f out: drvn to chal over 1f out: styd on but nt qckn and hld ins fnl f* — **11/10**[1]

0531 **3** *3 ¼* **Oratorio's Joy (IRE)**[11] 3616 4-9-11 **72** ........ WilliamCarson 1 — 75
(Jamie Osborne) *dwlt: hld up in last pair: pushed along over 3f out: prog to chse ldng pair over 2f out: drvn and lft bhd fr over 1f out* — **3/1**[2]

400- **4** *nse* **Robin Hood (IRE)**[316] 5793 6-9-7 **68** ........ JackMitchell 2 — 71
(Philip Mitchell) *trckd ldr 4f: rdn 3f out: sn lft bhd and struggling: kpt on again ins fnl f* — **12/1**

6546 **5** *2 ¾* **Red Dragon (IRE)**[12] 3585 4-9-5 **66** ........ MartinHarley 10 — 64
(Michael Blanshard) *cl up: trckd wnr after 4f to wl over 2f out: steadily wknd* — **11/1**

-004 **6** *15* **Speedy Writer**[12] 3562 4-9-7 **68** ........ FergusSweeney 11 — 37
(Henry Candy) *hld up in last pair: pushed along 4f out: wknd over 2f out: t.o* — **5/1**[3]

2m 10.18s (1.48) **Going Correction** +0.125s/f (Good)
**WFA** 3 from 4yo+ 11lb — 6 Ran SP% **111.2**
Speed ratings (Par 103): **99,97,95,95,92 80**
CSF £33.94 CT £68.66 TOTE £12.00: £4.50, £1.20; EX 21.20 Trifecta £68.40.
**Owner** Jim Kelly **Bred** M E Wates **Trained** Compton, Berks

**FOCUS**
An ordinary handicap. Muddling form with the runner-up a bit flat off the same mark as when a close second at Doncaster the previous week.
T/Jkpt: Not won. T/Plt: £88.30 to a £1 stake. Pool: £97,229.21 - 803.72 winning tickets T/Qpdt: £5.10 to a £1 stake. Pool: £8211.75 - 1185.90 winning tickets JN

# 3495 LES LANDES
Sunday, July 6
**OFFICIAL GOING: Good to soft (soft in places)**

## 4038a GEORGE AND LEONORA PERPETUAL H'CAP (TURF) — 5f 110y
3:05 (3:07) 3-Y-0+ — £1,460 (£525; £315)

RPR

**1** **Novabridge**[16] 3496 6-10-12 ........ (b) MichaelByrne 2 — 69
(Neil Mulholland) — **5/2**[2]

**2** *3* **Purley Queen (IRE)**[16] 3496 5-10-11 ........ MrFTett 3 — 58
(Mrs C Gilbert, Jersey) — **5/1**

**3** *6* **Chester'slittlegem (IRE)**[16] 3496 5-9-11 ........ (p) ShelleyBirkett 5 — 24
(Mrs A Corson, Jersey) — **9/1**

**4** *hd* **Under Review (IRE)**[135] 699 8-10-8 ........ (t) MissHHeal 6 — 35
(Liam Corcoran) — **5/1**

**5** *hd* **Pantella (IRE)**[1100] 3616 6-10-4 ........ PhilipPrince 9 — 30
(R Storp, Germany) — **7/4**[1]

**6** *1* **Kersivay**[16] 3496 8-9-4 ........ (p) JemmaMarshall 4 — 13
(Mrs A Malzard, Jersey) — **4/1**

**7** *4* **Country Blue (FR)**[16] 3496 5-10-0 ........ (p) CraigWalker 7 — 9
(Mrs A Malzard, Jersey) — **3/1**[3]

**8** *¾* **Fast Freddie**[16] 10-10-0 ........ (p) NoraLooby 1 — 7
(Mrs A Corson, Jersey) — **6/1**

**9** *dist* **Copper Falls**[76] 1623 5-9-13 ........ MattieBatchelor 8
(Mrs A Malzard, Jersey) — **7/1**

1m 8.0s (68.00) — 9 Ran SP% **180.1**

**Owner** Dajam Ltd **Bred** Bishopswood Bloodstock & Trickledown Stud **Trained** Limpley Stoke, Wilts

## 4039a HATSTONE LAWYERS H'CAP (TURF) — 7f
3:40 (3:40) 3-Y-0+ — £1,460 (£525; £315)

RPR

**1** **Wicked Tara**[410] 2581 4-8-10 ........ PhilipPrince 1 — 25
(Natalie Lloyd-Beavis) — **6/1**

**2** *2* **Lucifers Shadow (IRE)**[16] 5-10-12 ........ MrFTett 2 — 50
(Mrs C Gilbert, Jersey) — **4/6**[1]

**3** *8* **Jackpot**[29] 4-10-4 ........ JemmaMarshall 4 — 20
(Mrs A Malzard, Jersey) — **9/4**[2]

**4** *3* **Frankkie M (JER)**[29] 4-9-4 ........ ShelleyBirkett 3
(Mrs A Corson, Jersey) — **14/1**

**5** *6* **Lively Little Lady**[16] 3496 4-9-7 ........ (p) NoraLooby 6
(Mrs A Corson, Jersey) — **7/1**

**6** *11* **Buaiteoir (FR)**[42] 2592 8-10-10 ........ MatthewCosham 5
(Nikki Evans) — **5/1**[3]

1m 35.0s (5.00) — 6 Ran SP% **140.9**

**Owner** K Walters **Bred** Steve Starkey **Trained** East Garston, Berks

## 4040a "BUILDING A BETTER WORKING WORLD" H'CAP (TURF) — 1m 1f
4:15 (4:17) 3-Y-0+ — £1,460 (£525; £315)

RPR

**1** **Grey Panel (FR)**[16] 6-8-5 ........ TimClark 2 — 30
(T Le Brocq, Jersey) — **13/8**[1]

**2** *3* **Athania (IRE)**[16] 8-8-5 ........ (p) PhilipPrince 1 — 24
(Mrs A Corson, Jersey) — **9/1**

**3** *1 ½* **Rebel Woman**[16] 8-8-5 ........ ShelleyBirkett 6 — 21
(Mrs A Corson, Jersey) — **15/2**

**4** *2 ½* **Special Report (IRE)**[20] 6457 4-9-0 ........ (b) JemmaMarshall 3 — 25
(Neil Mulholland) — **9/4**[3]

**5** *7* **Rossetti**[16] 3495 6-10-12 ........ (p) CraigWalker 4 — 36
(Mrs A Malzard, Jersey) — **3/1**

**6** *1* **Beck's Bolero (IRE)**[16] 8-9-2 ........ (p) NoraLooby 5 — 10
(Mrs A Corson, Jersey) — **7/4**[2]

2m 5.0s (125.00) — 6 Ran SP% **152.0**

**Owner** The Le Brocq Boys **Bred** John Berry **Trained** Jersey

## 4041a GREAT UNCLE BULGARIA H'CAP (TURF) — 1m 4f
4:50 (4:52) 3-Y-0+ — £1,270 (£455; £275)

RPR

**1** **King Kenny**[16] 3495 9-8-12 ........ (p) ShelleyBirkett 8 — 38
(Mrs A Corson, Jersey) — **5/1**[3]

**2** *10* **Evergreen Forest (IRE)**[13] 3521 6-10-11 ........ (b) MrLKilgarriff 6 — 49
(Natalie Lloyd-Beavis) — **5/1**[3]

**3** *2* **River Du Nord (FR)**[29] 3048 7-9-4 ........ JemmaMarshall 5 — 25
(Sue Gardner) — **5/1**[3]

**4** *1* **Up In Flames (IRE)**[29] 5-9-11 ........ (p) MattieBatchelor 7 — 30
(Mrs A Malzard, Jersey) — **7/1**

**5** *2* **Sworn Mammy (GER)**[29] 3048 7-9-9 ........ PhilipPrince 4 — 25
(R Storp, Germany) — **1/2**[1]

**6** *5* **Ballyheigue (IRE)**[44] 2512 5-10-10 ........ (p) MissHHeal 1 — 32
(Liam Corcoran) — **9/4**[2]

**7** *3 ½* **Sweet Liberta (IRE)**[16] 3495 5-10-12 ........ MrRHodson 2 — 28
(T Le Brocq, Jersey) — **5/1**[3]

**8** *dist* **Premier Jack's**[115] 941 3-8-10 ........ MatthewCosham 3
(Nikki Evans) — **11/1**

2m 50.0s
**WFA** 3 from 5yo+ 13lb — 8 Ran SP% **184.9**

**Owner** The Crawford Family **Bred** D P Martin **Trained** Jersey

# 3820 BRIGHTON (L-H)
Tuesday, July 8
**OFFICIAL GOING: Good to firm (firm in places; 7.4)**
Wind: Light, half behind Weather: Showery

## 4042 BRIGHTWELLS, THE BLOODSTOCK AUCTIONEERS (S) H'CAP — 5f 213y
5:40 (5:40) (Class 6) (0-60,60) 3-Y-0+ — £2,045 (£603; £302) Stalls Low

Form — RPR

0241 **1** **Fairy Mist (IRE)**[14] 3554 7-9-0 **49** ........ (b) WilliamCarson 9 — 58
(John Bridger) *in tch: effrt 2f out: led ins fnl f: edgd lft: drvn out* — **7/2**[1]

4060 **2** *1 ¾* **Tiger's Home**[24] 3231 4-8-11 **51** ........ ShelleyBirkett(5) 10 — 56
(Julia Feilden) *chsd ldrs: led 2f out tl ins fnl f: hld whn n.m.r and eased fnl 50yds* — **9/2**[3]

6064 **3** *2 ¼* **Little Choosey**[14] 3549 4-8-12 **47** ........ JohnFahy 4 — 43
(Anabel K Murphy) *towards rr: rdn and hdwy over 1f out: r.o* — **4/1**[2]

0440 **4** *1 ¼* **El Duque**[15] 3523 3-8-13 **59** ........ (tp) RyanWhile(5) 5 — 50
(Bill Turner) *chsd ldr: led briefly over 2f out: hrd rdn and wknd over 1f out* — **20/1**

4500 **5** *1 ¾* **Ceelo**[24] 3222 4-9-5 **57** ........ (b) SimonPearce(3) 6 — 44
(Lydia Pearce) *dwlt: sn in midfield on outer: effrt in centre 2f out: no imp* — **5/1**

6260 **6** *2 ¾* **High On The Hog (IRE)**[4] 3935 6-8-6 **46** oh1 ........ NoelGarbutt(5) 7 — 24
(Mark Brisbourne) *s.s: bhd tl passed btn horses fr over 1f out* — **8/1**

6200 **7** *nk* **Where's Reiley (USA)**[39] 2723 8-9-3 **52** ........ (v) LukeMorris 1 — 29
(Michael Attwater) *prom tl wknd wl over 1f out* — **8/1**

6066 **8** *nk* **Dover The Moon (IRE)**[24] 3214 3-8-0 **48** oh1 ow2 ........ GaryMahon(7) 3 — 23
(Sylvester Kirk) *towards rr: drvn along and hdwy on rail over 2f out: wknd over 1f out* — **16/1**

64-0 **9** *6* **Myjestic Melody (IRE)**[12] 3609 6-8-11 **46** oh1 ........ JimmyQuinn 2 — 3
(Shaun Harris) *led tl over 2f out: hrd rdn and wknd wl over 1f out* — **33/1**

1m 9.79s (-0.41) **Going Correction** -0.075s/f (Good)
**WFA** 3 from 4yo+ 6lb — 9 Ran SP% **112.9**
Speed ratings (Par 101): **99,96,93,92,89 86,85,85,77**
CSF £18.80 CT £64.22 TOTE £3.70: £1.50, £3.10, £1.90; EX 25.00 Trifecta £71.80.No bid for the winner.
**Owner** J J Bridger **Bred** Sandro Garavelli **Trained** Liphook, Hants
■ Stewards' Enquiry : William Carson one-day ban: careless riding (Jul 22)

**FOCUS**
The rail was dolled out from 6f to 2.5f increasing distances by about 12yds. Despite 0.5mm of overnight rain the ground had officially changed to firm, good to firm in places (from good to firm). Weak form, nothing solid.

## 4043 RDFGROUP.COM CELEBRATES 20 SUCCESSFUL YEARS H'CAP — 5f 213y
6:10 (6:10) (Class 5) (0-75,74) 3-Y-0 — £2,726 (£805; £402) Stalls Low

Form — RPR

2330 **1** **Handwoven (IRE)**[7] 3821 3-8-12 **65** ........ (b) JoeFanning 4 — 72
(Mark Johnston) *mde all: set str pce tl stdd after 2f: rdn and r.o wl fnl 2f: readily* — **8/1**

-313 **2** *1 ¾* **Royal Brave (IRE)**[18] 3426 3-9-1 **68** ........ DaneO'Neill 2 — 69
(William Muir) *chsd ldrs: hrd rdn over 1f out: r.o to take 2nd nr fin* — **7/2**[2]

2232 **3** *nk* **Newton's Law (IRE)**[10] 3709 3-9-3 **73** ........ (t) RyanClark(3) 5 — 73
(Brian Meehan) *rring in stalls: fly-leapt s: hld up in 4th: drvn to chse wnr 2f out: one pce: lost 2nd nr fin* — **7/4**[1]

0330 **4** *1* **Spreadable (IRE)**[17] 3480 3-9-2 **69** ........ (b) LukeMorris 6 — 66
(Nick Littmoden) *in rr: effrt and hung lft over 1f out: styd on fnl f* — **10/1**

06-3 **5** *6* **Fair Ranger**[15] 3519 3-9-7 **74** ........ RichardHughes 3 — 52
(Richard Hannon) *chsd wnr tl 2f out: sn wknd* — **9/2**[3]

6-13 **6** *5* **Costa Filey**[60] 2122 3-9-7 **74** ........ JimmyQuinn 1 — 36
(Ed Vaughan) *mainly 5th tl wknd 2f out* — **8/1**

1m 9.45s (-0.75) **Going Correction** -0.075s/f (Good) — 6 Ran SP% **108.1**
Speed ratings (Par 100): **102,99,99,97,89 83**
CSF £32.76 TOTE £5.80: £2.90, £1.50; EX 17.50 Trifecta £80.10.
**Owner** Sheikh Hamdan bin Mohammed Al Maktoum **Bred** N Ormiston **Trained** Middleham Moor, N Yorks
■ Spinning Cobbler (10-1) was withdrawn. Rule 4 applies to all bets. Deduction - 5p in the pound.

**FOCUS**
A fair 3yo handicap. The runner-up and third have been rated a length or so off their bests.

## 4044 FOLLOW US ON TWITTER @RDFGROUP @RDF_RECRUITMENT MAIDEN STKS — 6f 209y
6:40 (6:40) (Class 5) 2-Y-0 — £2,587 (£770; £384; £192) Stalls Low

Form — RPR

0 **1** **Shaakis (IRE)**[38] 2776 2-9-5 ........ DaneO'Neill 5 — 69
(Marcus Tregoning) *dwlt: rdn up to chse ldr after 2f: led and qcknd over 2f out: hdd over 1f out: drvn to get bk up fnl 75yds* — **7/1**[3]

4 **2** *nk* **Oregon Gift**[57] 2214 2-9-5 .................................... JoeFanning 6 68
(Mark Johnston) *led tl over 2f out: drvn to ld again over 1f out: kpt on u.p: hdd fnal 75yds* **11/4**[1]

63 **3** *nk* **Guilty (IRE)**[15] 3536 2-9-5 .................................... RichardHughes 3 67
(Richard Hannon) *chsd ldrs: rdn to chal in centre over 2f out: sn outpcd and drvn along: r.o fnl f* **11/4**[1]

54 **4** *3/4* **Muradif (IRE)**[21] 3330 2-9-5 .................................... SebSanders 7 66
(William Haggas) *hld up in rr: hdwy to chse ldrs over 1f out: n.m.r and kpt on same pce ins fnl f* **7/2**[2]

00 **5** *3/4* **Pinter**[35] 2859 2-9-5 .................................... AhmedAjtebi 1 63
(Charlie Appleby) *dwlt: sn in tch: hrd rdn and outpcd wl over 1f out: styd on fnl f* **16/1**

6 **6** *3/4* **Tumut (IRE)**[9] 3748 2-9-2 .................................... CharlesBishop(3) 4 61
(Mick Channon) *in tch: outpcd and btn wl over 1f out: styd on same pce fnl f* **14/1**

**7** *1* **Pasticcio** 2-9-5 .................................... AdamKirby 2 66+
(Charlie Appleby) *trckd ldr: hrd rdn and sltly outpcd 2f out: cl 4th and styng on whn boxed in on rail 1f out: nt rcvr* **7/1**[3]

1m 23.74s (0.64) **Going Correction** -0.075s/f (Good) **7** Ran SP% **113.1**
Speed ratings (Par 94): **93,92,92,91,90 89,88**
CSF £25.98 TOTE £9.00: £4.70, £1.40; EX 32.50 Trifecta £132.20.
**Owner** Hamdan Al Maktoum **Bred** Sinead Bishop **Trained** Whitsbury, Hants

**FOCUS**
A fair but competitive maiden.

## 4045 DAILY RACING MARKETS AT STARSPREADS.COM FILLIES' H'CAP 1m 3f 196y
**7:10** (7:10) (Class 4) (0-80,80) 4-Y-O+ **£4,690** (£1,395; £697; £348) **Stalls** Centre

Form RPR

3216 **1** **Jewelled**[5] 3874 8-8-10 **69** .................................... RichardHughes 5 77
(Ralph J Smith) *patiently rdn in detached last: hdwy and hung lft fr 2f out: led ent fnl f: rdn out* **6/1**

2533 **2** *1/2* **Sagesse**[11] 3681 4-9-2 **75** .................................... (b[1]) LukeMorris 4 82
(Sir Mark Prescott Bt) *t.k.h: trckd ldr: chal 2f out: unable qck ins fnl f* **11/4**[2]

4-35 **3** *2 1/4* **Hi Note**[4] 3932 6-9-4 **80** .................................... CharlesBishop(3) 1 84
(Sheena West) *led: rdn over 2f out: hdd ent fnl f: no ex* **5/1**[3]

00-1 **4** *1 1/2* **Panettone (IRE)**[15] 3540 5-8-9 **68** .................................... PaddyAspell 2 69
(Roger Varian) *s.i.s: sn rcvrd into 3rd: rdn 3f out: one pce appr fnl f* **5/2**[1]

2510 **5** *2 3/4* **Taro Tywod (IRE)**[11] 3644 5-8-12 **76** .................................... CamHardie(5) 3 73
(Mark Brisbourne) *hld up in 4th: rdn over 2f out: wknd 1f out* **8/1**

5623 **6** *3/4* **Emman Bee (IRE)**[14] 3556 5-8-2 **61** .................................... (p) HayleyTurner 6 57
(Luke Dace) *hld up in 5th: rdn over 2f out: wknd over 1f out* **6/1**

2m 32.9s (0.20) **Going Correction** -0.075s/f (Good) **6** Ran SP% **111.6**
Speed ratings (Par 102): **96,95,94,93,91 90**
CSF £22.48 TOTE £6.60: £3.80, £1.80; EX 18.50 Trifecta £111.70.
**Owner** Fishdance & Cheval Court Stud **Bred** Wyck Hall Stud Ltd **Trained** Epsom, Surrey

**FOCUS**
Only a fair handicap for the grade. The winner has been rated to last year's 1m2f win here.

## 4046 ENGLAND'S TEST V INDIA WITH STARSPREADS.COM H'CAP 7f 214y
**7:40** (7:42) (Class 6) (0-55,55) 3-Y-O+ **£2,045** (£603; £302) **Stalls** Low

Form RPR

2222 **1** **Byrd In Hand (IRE)**[7] 3825 7-9-6 **54** .................................... WilliamCarson 2 64
(John Bridger) *led 1f: disp 2nd tl led again 2f out: drvn out* **5/2**[1]

0063 **2** *1 3/4* **Hawk Moth (IRE)**[14] 3554 6-9-4 **52** .................................... (b) LukeMorris 1 58
(John Spearing) *s.i.s: sn in tch: rdn to chse wnr wl over 1f out: kpt on* **3/1**[2]

6402 **3** *3/4* **Abigails Angel**[14] 3554 7-8-13 **47** .................................... RichardHughes 3 51
(Brett Johnson) *chsd ldrs: rdn and kpt on fnl 2f* **9/2**[3]

-000 **4** *hd* **Excedo Praecedo**[19] 3389 3-8-9 **52** .................................... (t[1]) PatCosgrave 7 54
(Amanda Perrett) *towards rr: pushed along over 3f out: effrt in centre 2f out: styd on fnl f* **10/1**

-006 **5** *1* **The Name Is Frank**[13] 3589 9-8-12 **46** oh1 .................................... (b[1]) LiamKeniry 10 47
(Mark Gillard) *hdwy to ld after 1f: hdd 2f out: one pce* **20/1**

6045 **6** *2 1/4* **China In My Hands**[7] 3828 3-8-12 **55** .................................... (p[1]) JoeFanning 4 49
(James Bethell) *hld up in tch: effrt whn nt clr run over 2f out: hung lft after: wknd over 1f out* **9/2**[3]

-554 **7** *1 1/4* **Blue Clumber**[7] 3828 4-8-13 **47** .................................... (b) BenCurtis 6 40
(Shaun Harris) *disp 2nd tl outpcd 2f out: btn whn n.m.r wl over 1f out: edgd lft and sn wknd* **12/1**

0-50 **8** *47* **Kirkstall Abbey (IRE)**[27] 3121 3-8-10 **53** .................................... JimmyQuinn 11
(Simon Hodgson) *a bhd: struggling 1/2-way: eased over 2f out* **33/1**

1m 34.95s (-1.05) **Going Correction** -0.075s/f (Good)
**WFA** 3 from 4yo+ 9lb **8** Ran SP% **114.4**
Speed ratings (Par 101): **102,100,99,99,98 96,94,47**
CSF £10.17 CT £30.72 TOTE £2.80: £1.10, £2.30, £1.50; EX 13.30 Trifecta £41.60.
**Owner** Marshall Bridger **Bred** Bricklow Ltd **Trained** Liphook, Hants

**FOCUS**
A low-grade handicap. Sound form, with the second and third's form franked in the opening race.

## 4047 WORLD CUP IN-PLAY AT STARSPREADS.COM FILLIES' H'CAP 6f 209y
**8:10** (8:10) (Class 5) (0-70,70) 3-Y-O+ **£2,726** (£805; £402) **Stalls** Low

Form RPR

6224 **1** **Royal Connection**[10] 3733 3-9-6 **70** .................................... RichardHughes 4 74
(Richard Hannon) *chsd ldr: drvn to dispute ld fnl f: edgd rt nr fin: jst prevailed* **6/4**[1]

5005 **2** *shd* **Aristocratic Duty**[26] 3144 3-8-12 **62** .................................... LiamKeniry 5 65
(Sylvester Kirk) *chsd ldrs: drvn to dispute ld fnl f: brushed by wnr nr fin: jst denied* **6/1**

1166 **3** *shd* **Welsh Inlet (IRE)**[19] 3390 6-9-5 **61** .................................... WilliamCarson 6 67
(John Bridger) *dwlt: in tch: rdn and swtchd wd to centre over 2f out: r.o wl fr over 1f out: clsng at fin* **6/1**

-530 **4** *2 1/4* **Olney Lass**[27] 3125 7-9-9 **68** .................................... SimonPearce(3) 1 68
(Lydia Pearce) *chsd ldrs: rdn and one pce appr fnl f* **5/1**[2]

0200 **5** *1 3/4* **Clever Miss**[22] 3300 3-9-4 **68** .................................... (v) BenCurtis 7 60
(Alan McCabe) *led at gd pce: hrd rdn and hdd 1f out: wknd fnl f* **11/2**[3]

004 **6** *10* **Goddess Of Gloom**[24] 3229 3-8-7 **62** .................................... ShelleyBirkett(5) 8 28
(Peter Chapple-Hyam) *dwlt: towards rr: hmpd over 2f out: n.d after* **10/1**

1m 22.14s (-0.96) **Going Correction** -0.075s/f (Good)
**WFA** 3 from 4yo+ 8lb **6** Ran SP% **109.7**
Speed ratings (Par 100): **102,101,101,99,97 85**
CSF £10.33 CT £36.96 TOTE £2.40: £1.50, £3.80; EX 12.30 Trifecta £45.80.
**Owner** W H Ponsonby **Bred** Wood Hall Stud Ltd & Neil Gilchrist **Trained** East Everleigh, Wilts

**FOCUS**
A fair handicap in which the pace was honest. The winner has been rated as running a small personal best.

## 4048 STARSPREADS.COM £500 REFER A FRIEND H'CAP 6f 209y
**8:45** (8:45) (Class 6) (0-60,60) 3-Y-O **£2,045** (£603; £302) **Stalls** Low

Form RPR

56-5 **1** **Born To Fly (IRE)**[26] 3158 3-9-6 **59** .................................... (b[1]) SebSanders 7 66
(Nick Littmoden) *bhd: rdn and hdwy on rail over 2f out: waited for gap over 1f out: burst through to ld narrowly ins fnl f: all out* **8/1**

-005 **2** *hd* **Moneypennie**[23] 3281 3-8-1 **47** .................................... (tp) CharlotteJenner(7) 3 53
(Marcus Tregoning) *towards rr: hdwy 3f out: jnd wnr in centre ins fnl f: sustained str chal: jst hld* **10/1**

46-0 **3** *1 1/2* **Roring Samson (IRE)**[28] 3083 3-9-7 **60** .................................... PatCosgrave 1 62
(George Baker) *fly-leapt s: sn in midfield: n.m.r and swtchd outside over 2f out: hung lft and pressed ldrs 1f out: kpt on* **3/1**[1]

5004 **4** *1 1/4* **Dancing Sal (IRE)**[9] 3754 3-9-4 **57** .................................... (b[1]) GeorgeBaker 2 56
(Gary Moore) *chsd ldrs: led 1f out tl ins fnl f: no ex* **5/1**

4-55 **5** *2 1/4* **Libra Romana (IRE)**[12] 3627 3-8-12 **51** .................................... LukeMorris 10 44
(Sir Mark Prescott Bt) *chsd ldr at str pce tl wknd 1f out* **4/1**[3]

3004 **6** *1 1/4* **Why Not Now**[18] 3426 3-8-11 **55** .................................... (b) CamHardie(5) 9 45
(Roger Charlton) *plld hrd: led at str pce tl wknd 1f out: eased* **7/2**[2]

4540 **7** *6* **Previous Acclaim (IRE)**[12] 3627 3-8-2 **46** oh1 .................................... (p) ShelleyBirkett(5) 8 20
(Julia Feilden) *chsd ldrs tl wknd 2f out* **25/1**

5500 **8** *4 1/2* **Nutbush**[13] 3564 3-8-1 **47** .................................... PaddyPilley(7) 5 10
(Mick Channon) *dwlt: bhd: rdn 3f out: nvr nr ldrs* **12/1**

040- **9** *17* **Society Diva (IRE)**[278] 6979 3-9-4 **57** .................................... FergusSweeney 6
(George Baker) *in tch early: stdd towards rr after 2f: rdn 3f out: sn no ch* **25/1**

1m 22.61s (-0.49) **Going Correction** -0.075s/f (Good) **9** Ran SP% **119.5**
Speed ratings (Par 98): **99,98,97,95,93 91,84,79,60**
CSF £87.28 CT £296.03 TOTE £10.10: £2.70, £3.90, £1.30; EX 80.20 Trifecta £647.90.
**Owner** Franconson Partners **Bred** Tally-Ho Stud **Trained** Newmarket, Suffolk

**FOCUS**
At best a moderate 3yo handicap. The winner has been rated as improving a length, and the runner-up to a small personal best.
T/Plt: £36.50 to a £1 stake. Pool: £58,933.26 - 1,177.72 winning tickets. T/Qpdt: £11.40 to a £1 stake. Pool: £5,753.76 - 371.46 winning tickets. LM

# 3706 LINGFIELD (L-H)
Tuesday, July 8

**OFFICIAL GOING: Standard**
Wind: virtually nil Weather: showers

## 4049 32RED H'CAP 6f 1y(P)
**2:15** (2:15) (Class 6) (0-60,60) 3-Y-O+ **£2,264** (£673; £336; £168) **Stalls** Low

Form RPR

2614 **1** **Dissent (IRE)**[8] 3793 5-9-5 **58** .................................... (b) ConnorBeasley(3) 6 81
(James Given) *taken down early: mde all: 5 l clr 2f out: drvn and styd on strly fr over 1f out: unchal* **5/1**[2]

0-00 **2** *10* **Proper Charlie**[139] 662 6-9-2 **52** .................................... (v) StevieDonohoe 2 43
(Lee Carter) *chsd ldrs and clr in ldng quartet: rdn and wnt 5 l 2nd ent fnl 2f: no imp: no ch w wnr but hld on for 2nd cl home* **16/1**

3053 **3** *nk* **Sewn Up**[19] 3393 4-9-8 **58** .................................... (p) JimCrowley 7 48
(Andrew Hollinshead) *stdd s: hld up off the pce in last quartet: hdwy over 1f out: styd on fnl f and pressing for 2nd nr fin: no ch w wnr* **5/1**[2]

364 **4** *shd* **Dancing Angel**[26] 3156 3-9-2 **58** .................................... PaddyAspell 4 47
(James Eustace) *racd off the pce in midfield: rdn over 2f out: hdwy to go modest 3rd 1f out: kpt on: no ch w wnr* **7/1**[3]

1254 **5** *nk* **Catalinas Diamond (IRE)**[10] 3734 6-9-6 **56** .................................... (t) AdamKirby 1 45
(Pat Murphy) *rdr struggling to remove hood and slowly away: wl bhd in last quartet: rdn over 2f out: hdwy over 1f out: kpt on fnl f: no ch w wnr* **5/1**[2]

0000 **6** *2 1/2* **Reginald Claude**[19] 3393 6-8-12 **55** .................................... CharlotteJenner(7) 9 36
(Mark Usher) *stdd s: hld up off the pce in rr: hdwy jst over 1f out: kpt on: nvr trbld ldrs* **16/1**

0035 **7** *nk* **Gung Ho Jack**[18] 3422 5-9-10 **60** .................................... GeorgeBaker 8 40
(John Best) *hld up in 5th but nvr on terms w ldrs: rdn and no hdwy wl over 1f out* **11/4**[1]

4044 **8** *3 1/4* **Molly Ahoy**[19] 3380 3-9-4 **60** .................................... TomQueally 5 28
(Alan McCabe) *sn outpcd and wl bhd: nvr a factor* **20/1**

0006 **9** *2* **Catalyze**[19] 3393 6-9-5 **55** .................................... (t) JoeFanning 10 18
(Paddy Butler) *taken down early: awkward as stalls opened and s.i.s: a bhd* **16/1**

5300 **10** *2 3/4* **Commandingpresence (USA)**[19] 3393 8-9-5 **55** .................................... WilliamCarson 12 9
(John Bridger) *taken down early: chsd ldng pair tl 1/2-way: sn struggling: losing pl and wd bnd 2f out: wknd* **25/1**

3445 **11** *1/2* **Danzoe (IRE)**[19] 3392 7-9-6 **56** .................................... SebSanders 11 9
(Christine Dunnett) *racd off the pce in midfield: drvn 1/2-way: no hdwy: wknd wl over 1f out* **25/1**

-000 **12** *1/2* **Saga Lout**[24] 3222 4-9-7 **57** .................................... (b[1]) FergusSweeney 3 8
(Ray Peacock) *chsd ldr tl over 2f out: 3rd and struggling whn sltly hmpd ent fnl 2f: lost modest 3rd 1f out: wknd* **50/1**

1m 10.04s (-1.86) **Going Correction** -0.15s/f (Stan)
**WFA** 3 from 4yo+ 6lb **12** Ran SP% **121.2**
Speed ratings (Par 101): **106,92,92,92,91 88,88,83,81,77 76,76**
CSF £79.65 CT £436.38 TOTE £6.90: £2.10, £6.40, £1.90; EX 95.30 Trifecta £960.20.
**Owner** The Cool Silk Partnership **Bred** Corduff Stud Ltd & J Corcoran **Trained** Willoughton, Lincs
■ Stewards' Enquiry : Connor Beasley four-day ban: used whip when clearly winning (Jul 22-25)

**FOCUS**
A low-grade affair in which all bar one or two looked to be fully exposed. The winner's clear-cut win was out of line with his recent form but he was a lot better 2yo and he's been rated close to that form.

## 4050 BET NOW AT 32REDSPORT.COM CLASSIFIED CLAIMING STKS 6f 1y(P)
**2:45** (2:45) (Class 5) 3-Y-O+ **£2,587** (£770; £384; £192) **Stalls** Low

Form RPR

3001 **1** **Seamster**[19] 3392 7-8-13 69 .................................... (bt) CamHardie(5) 4 82
(Richard Ford) *mde all: rdn over 1f out: in command and kpt on fnl f: unchal* **5/2**[1]

6043 **2** *2 1/4* **Alcando (IRE)**[14] 3555 4-9-0 65 .................................... RichardHughes 6 71
(Denis Coakley) *chsd wnr thrght: wl of clr of field fr 4f out: rdn and no imp over 1f out: plugged on same pce after* **3/1**[2]

4121 **3** 2 1/2 **Amenable (IRE)**[20] 3359 7-9-2 69 ................(p) HayleyTurner 5 65
(Conor Dore) *chsd ldng pair over 4f out but nvr on terms: kpt on u.p fnl f* **6/1**[3]

6040 **4** 3/4 **Foie Gras**[19] 3402 4-8-5 59 ................ ConnorBeasley(3) 2 55
(Chris Dwyer) *midfield whn short of room and lost pl 5f out: wl off the pce in last trio after: hdwy and swtchd lft 1f out: kpt on: n.d* **16/1**

2312 **5** 2 1/4 **Spitfire**[69] 1892 9-8-7 70 ................(t) VictorSantos(7) 3 53
(J R Jenkins) *hmpd and dropped to last pair 5f out: sn rdn and nvr gng wl after: no threat to ldrs* **12/1**

5652 **5** *dht* **Parisian Pyramid (IRE)**[127] 826 8-8-5 61 ..........(b) CharlotteJenner(7) 8 51
(Lee Carter) *chsd ldrs tl bmpd and lost pl 5f out: off the pce in midfield after: rdn over 2f out: no hdwy and wl btn after* **16/1**

3032 **7** *shd* **Victorian Number (FR)**[19] 3393 6-9-4 65 ................ GeorgeBaker 1 57
(Geoffrey Deacon) *midfield: 4th and outpcd 4f out: no ch w ldrs after: rdn wl over 1f out: no hdwy: wknd ins fnl f* **3/1**[2]

0220 **8** 1 3/4 **Paradise Spectre**[6] 3854 7-9-0 64 ................(p) LiamKeniry 7 47
(Zoe Davison) *v.s.a: a off the pce in rr* **50/1**

1m 11.05s (-0.85) **Going Correction** -0.15s/f (Stan) **8 Ran SP% 114.3**
Speed ratings (Par 103): **99,96,92,91,88 88,88,86**
CSF £10.18 TOTE £3.90: £1.50, £1.40, £2.40; EX 12.30 Trifecta £54.00.
**Owner** P Bamford **Bred** D G Hardisty Bloodstock **Trained** Garstang, Lancs
■ Stewards' Enquiry : Richard Hughes one-day ban: careless riding (Jul 22)

**FOCUS**
This claimer looked quite open with several having a decent chance at the weights. The winner is better than ever and the runner-up has been rated to his recent form.

## 4051 32RED CASINO H'CAP — 1m 4f (P)
**3:15** (3:15) (Class 5) (0-75,75) 3-Y-0+ — **£2,587** (£770; £384; £192) **Stalls Low**

Form — RPR

1250 **1** **Filament Of Gold (USA)**[41] 2685 3-8-12 72 ................ JoeFanning 4 82
(Mark Johnston) *in tch in midfield: rdn to chal over 1f out: led and edgd rt 1f out: r.o wl* **12/1**

-330 **2** 1 **Invasor Luck (USA)**[18] 3428 3-9-1 75 ................ TomQueally 5 83
(James Fanshawe) *in tch in midfield: clsd to trck ldrs 2f out: rdn and ev ch over 1f out: kpt on but hld by wnr ins fnl f* **8/1**

-641 **3** 3 3/4 **The Holyman (IRE)**[17] 3472 6-9-13 74 ................ AdamKirby 1 76
(Jo Crowley) *sn bustled up to ld: rdn over 2f out: hdd and carried rt 1f out: outpcd by ldng pair but hld on for 3rd ins fnl f* **7/1**[3]

1-04 **4** 1 3/4 **Crystal Pearl**[54] 2273 3-8-12 72 ................ TedDurcan 3 71
(Mark H Tompkins) *chsd ldrs: rdn and effrt ent fnl 2f: unable qck over 1f out: hld and one pce fnl f* **14/1**

404 **5** 1 3/4 **Grace And Favour**[25] 3174 3-9-0 74 ................ RyanMoore 2 70
(Andrew Balding) *mostly chsd ldr: rdn and pressed ldr 2f out: unable qck over 1f out: wknd ins fnl f* **3/1**[2]

2-00 **6** 3 1/4 **Red Pilgrim (IRE)**[38] 2774 4-9-11 72 ................(t) LiamKeniry 7 63
(James Toller) *s.i.s: hld up in tch in last pair: rdn and effrt over 2f out: sn outpcd: wknd over 1f out* **50/1**

20-0 **7** 20 **Passion Play**[17] 3472 6-9-1 67 ................(v[1]) RyanWhile(5) 6 26
(Bill Turner) *t.k.h: chsd ldrs: rdn over 4f out: lost pl 3f out: t.o fnl f* **66/1**

00/1 **8** 4 1/2 **Black Minstrel (IRE)**[70] 1835 5-9-2 63 ................ JimCrowley 8 15
(Amanda Perrett) *hld up in tch in rr: clsd 4f out: rdn and no rspnse over 2f out: sn wl btn: t.o fnl f* **5/4**[1]

2m 29.39s (-3.61) **Going Correction** -0.15s/f (Stan)
**WFA** 3 from 4yo+ 13lb **8 Ran SP% 110.9**
Speed ratings (Par 103): **106,105,102,101,100 98,85,82**
CSF £96.52 CT £699.64 TOTE £14.60: £3.40, £2.50, £1.20; EX 101.40 Trifecta £400.40.
**Owner** Sheikh Hamdan bin Mohammed Al Maktoum **Bred** Darley **Trained** Middleham Moor, N Yorks

**FOCUS**
With warm favourite Black Minstrel bombing out completely this took a little less winning than looked likely. The third has been rated a couple of lengths off his C&D latest.

## 4052 32RED MAIDEN FILLIES' STKS — 1m 2f (P)
**3:45** (3:51) (Class 5) 3-4-Y-0 — **£2,587** (£770; £384; £192) **Stalls Low**

Form — RPR

352 **1** **Kleo (GR)**[22] 3315 3-9-0 79 ................ RichardHughes 2 90+
(Luca Cumani) *chsd ldr: rdn to ld 2f out: asserted u.p 1f out: styd on and in command fnl f* **5/4**[1]

6-42 **2** 3 1/4 **Muhawalah (IRE)**[11] 3652 3-9-0 76 ................(b[1]) DaneO'Neill 1 83
(Roger Varian) *led and set gd gallop: rdn and hdd 2f out: no ex and btn 1f out: plugged on for clr 2nd* **4/1**[3]

33 **3** 2 3/4 **Dream Child (IRE)**[11] 3652 3-9-0 0 ................ AdamKirby 5 78
(Charlie Appleby) *chsd ldrs: wnt 3rd 4f out: sn wl clr of field: rdn and nt qckn wl over 1f out: styd on same pce after* **6/1**

03 **4** 4 **Jammy Moment**[137] 684 3-9-0 0 ................ HayleyTurner 7 70
(William Muir) *in toouch in midfield: wnt 4th over 3f out: sn outpcd by ldrs: n.d but kpt on ins fnl f* **50/1**

0 **5** 12 **Eloquence**[37] 2804 3-9-0 0 ................ JimCrowley 8 47
(Tom Dascombe) *wnt rt s: hld up in midfield: rdn and outpcd over 3f out: 6th and n.d over 2f out: plugged on* **33/1**

24- **6** 1 1/2 **Hadya (IRE)**[243] 7779 3-9-0 0 ................ JoeFanning 6 45
(James Tate) *in tch in midfield: rdn and outpcd over 3f out: 5th and wl btn whn hung lft over 2f out* **16/1**

5 **7** 3 3/4 **Emerald Swell (IRE)**[26] 3142 3-9-0 0 ................ StevieDonohoe 14 37
(Brian Meehan) *s.i.s: racd off the pce in last quartet: rdn over 4f out: sn wl btn* **25/1**

**8** 9 **Noble Descent** 3-9-0 0 ................ RyanMoore 3 20
(Sir Michael Stoute) *dwlt: rdn along thrght and nvr bttr than midfield: struggling over 4f out: lost tch over 3f out: t.o* **7/2**[2]

0- **9** 1 1/2 **Across The Cape**[259] 7449 3-9-0 0 ................ TomQueally 11 17
(Michael Bell) *led rdrless to s: bmpd s and slowly away: a off the pce in last quartet: rdn over 4f out: sn lost tch: t.o* **66/1**

00 **10** 4 1/2 **Nancy**[19] 3385 3-9-0 0 ................(b[1]) BenCurtis 10 9
(Mark H Tompkins) *barging match w rival sn after s and slowly away: a off the pce in rr: rdn over 4f out: sn lost tch: t.o over 1f out* **100/1**

0 **11** 21 **En Reve**[88] 1423 3-9-0 0 ................ FergusSweeney 12
(Seamus Durack) *restless in stalls: stdd after s: a off the pce towards rr: rdn and lost tch over 4f out: t.o fnl 2f* **66/1**

60 **12** 45 **May Queen**[11] 3652 3-9-0 0 ................ TedDurcan 4
(Chris Wall) *chsd ldng pair tl 4f out: sn dropped out: t.o and virtually p.u fr over 1f out* **66/1**

2m 2.9s (-3.70) **Going Correction** -0.15s/f (Stan)
**WFA** 3 from 4yo 11lb **12 Ran SP% 121.1**
Speed ratings (Par 100): **108,105,103,100,90 89,86,79,77,74 57,21**
CSF £6.34 TOTE £2.20: £1.10, £2.00, £1.70; EX 7.60 Trifecta £19.10.
**Owner** Mrs M Marinopoulos **Bred** Figaia Stud **Trained** Newmarket, Suffolk
■ Peace Palace (100-1) and Graceful Willow (100-1) were withdrawn. Rule 4 does not apply.

**FOCUS**
The fillies with the best form dominated this maiden and they were well strung out in behind. The form makes sense with the second and third close to their Doncaster latest.

## 4053 32RED.COM FILLIES' H'CAP — 7f 1y(P)
**4:15** (4:19) (Class 4) (0-85,85) 3-Y-0+ — **£5,175** (£1,540; £769; £384) **Stalls High**

Form — RPR

50-0 **1** **Stealth Missile (IRE)**[20] 3357 3-9-1 85 ................(t) DannyBrock(5) 3 93
(Clive Brittain) *chsd ldrs: styd on inner and rdn to chal over 1f out: led 1f out: r.o wl: rdn out* **10/1**

10-2 **2** 1/2 **Meeting Waters**[42] 2639 3-9-2 81 ................ RyanMoore 5 88
(William Haggas) *in tch in midfield: rdn and effrt to chse ldrs 1f out: chsd wnr fnl 100yds: r.o but a hld* **9/4**[1]

005 **3** 1 1/4 **Lady Frances**[10] 3694 3-9-6 85 ................ JoeFanning 1 88
(Mark Johnston) *led: rdn and edgd rt wl over 1f out: hdd 1f out: styd on same pce ins fnl f* **7/1**

5014 **4** 1/2 **Nova Princesse (GER)**[27] 3114 3-8-9 74 ................(t) MartinHarley 6 76
(Marco Botti) *hld up in tch towards rr: nt clr run ent fnl 2f: hdwy towards inner over 1f out: kpt on but nt enough pce to chal ins fnl f* **4/1**[2]

0-00 **5** 1 3/4 **Trucanini**[27] 3122 4-10-0 85 ................ GeorgeBaker 8 86
(Chris Wall) *t.k.h: chsd ldr: rdn and unable qck over 1f out: btn 1f out: wknd ins fnl f* **9/2**[3]

-004 **6** *hd* **Miss Lillie**[15] 3539 3-9-0 79 ................(p) RichardHughes 4 76+
(Roger Teal) *taken down early: short of room and dropped to rr sn after s: effrt on outer wl over 1f out: kpt on but nvr a threat* **7/1**

0104 **7** 1/2 **Front Page News**[11] 3674 4-9-7 78 ................ AdamKirby 7 77
(Robert Eddery) *hld up in tch in last trio: rdn over 2f out: styd on but no real imp over 1f out* **16/1**

00-0 **8** 2 **La Tinta Bay**[27] 3117 3-8-12 82 ................ CamHardie(5) 2 73
(Richard Hannon) *t.k.h: hld up wl in tch in midfield: effrt u.p towards inner over 1f out: wknd ins fnl f* **33/1**

6-06 **9** 5 **Plover**[18] 3425 4-9-8 79 ................(p[1]) RobertHavlin 9 60
(Michael Attwater) *dwlt: sn rcvrd and chsd ldrs: rdn and outpcd wl over 1f out: wknd 1f out* **50/1**

1m 23.49s (-1.31) **Going Correction** -0.15s/f (Stan)
**WFA** 3 from 4yo 8lb **9 Ran SP% 113.8**
Speed ratings (Par 102): **101,100,99,98,96 96,95,93,87**
CSF £32.34 CT £172.52 TOTE £12.30: £2.80, £1.40, £1.80; EX 42.10 Trifecta £261.50.
**Owner** Saeed Manana **Bred** Sommerville Bloodstock **Trained** Newmarket, Suffolk

**FOCUS**
An open fillies' handicap run at what looked a reasonable gallop and but not many could get in a blow from off the pace. The winner has been rated as running a personal best, the runner-up is progressive and the third is down to a good mark.

## 4054 32RED ON THE APP STORE MAIDEN AUCTION STKS — 7f 1y(P)
**4:45** (4:48) (Class 5) 2-Y-0 — **£2,587** (£770; £384; £192) **Stalls High**

Form — RPR

6 **1** **Thecornishassassin**[12] 3613 2-9-0 0 ................ AdamKirby 7 80
(Robert Eddery) *mde all: rdn and wnt clr ent fnl 2f: in command over 1f out: kpt on: rdn out* **3/1**[2]

0 **2** 1 1/2 **Runner Runner (IRE)**[28] 3082 2-8-10 0 ................ PatCosgrave 1 72
(George Baker) *chsd ldrs: rdn to chse clr wnr 2f out: styd on and grad clsng ins fnl f: nvr gng to rch wnr* **7/1**

64 **3** 3 3/4 **Hawkmeister (IRE)**[9] 3748 2-9-1 0 ................ RichardHughes 9 67
(Richard Hannon) *in tch in midfield: effrt whn v wd bnd 2f out: hdwy 1f out to go 3rd fnl 100yds: styd on but no threat to ldrs* **6/4**[1]

002 **4** 3 3/4 **Sculptured (FR)**[14] 3550 2-8-9 0 ................ StevieDonohoe 3 51
(Jo Hughes) *chsd ldrs: wnt 2nd over 2f out tl 2f out: btn and edgd rt over 1f out: wknd fnl f* **20/1**

**5** *shd* **Entente** 2-9-1 0 ................ SteveDrowne 5 56
(Peter Makin) *hld up in tch in midfield: rn green and short of room bnd 2f out: effrt on inner in 3rd over 1f out: no ex 1f out and wknd ins fnl f* **25/1**

**6** 1 1/2 **Cahar Fad (IRE)** 2-8-7 0 ................ JackDuern(5) 4 49
(Steph Hollinshead) *outpcd and pushed along in rr of main gp: effrt but stl plenty to do whn squeezed between rivals over 2f out: kpt on same pce fnl 2f: nvr danmgerous* **66/1**

40 **7** *hd* **Gilded Lace**[18] 3415 2-7-13 0 ................ JosephineGordon(7) 8 43
(J S Moore) *chsd wnr tl over 2f out: wkng whn hmpd over 1f out: fdd ins fnl f* **6/1**[3]

**8** 2 1/2 **Anna Dolce (FR)** 2-8-10 0 ................ OisinMurphy 10 40
(Harry Dunlop) *s.i.s: outpcd in rr of main gp: nvr trbld ldrs* **25/1**

00 **9** 1 3/4 **Hidden Agenda**[17] 3467 2-8-7 0 ................ RobertHavlin 11 32
(Michael Blanshard) *racd in midfield: rdn and struggling 1/2-way: wknd over 2f out* **100/1**

**10** 11 **Artesana** 2-8-3 0 ................ CamHardie(5) 6
(William Knight) *racd in midfield: rdn and struggling 1/2-way: wl bhd fnl f* **12/1**

00U **11** 12 **St Paul's Square (IRE)**[12] 3613 2-9-1 0 ................ FergusSweeney 2
(Jamie Osborne) *s.i.s: outpcd in rr of main gp: lost tch 3f out: t.o* **100/1**

**12** 12 **Picket Line** 2-8-13 0 ................ HayleyTurner 12
(Geoffrey Deacon) *v.s.a: v green and bucking early: immediately t.o* **33/1**

1m 24.22s (-0.58) **Going Correction** -0.15s/f (Stan) **12 Ran SP% 118.3**
Speed ratings (Par 94): **97,95,91,86,86 84,84,81,79,67 53,39**
CSF £22.68 TOTE £4.70: £1.50, £2.10, £1.30; EX 31.20 Trifecta £96.60.
**Owner** Horseheath Lodge Racing **Bred** Cranford Bloodstock-Houghton Bloodstock **Trained** Newmarket, Suffolk

**FOCUS**
This looked quite a decent little heat.

## 4055 RACING SPECIALS AT 32REDSPORT.COM H'CAP (DIV I) — 7f 1y(P)
**5:15** (5:19) (Class 6) (0-60,60) 3-Y-0+ — **£2,264** (£673; £336; £168) **Stalls High**

Form — RPR

1602 **1** **Exceedexpectations (IRE)**[15] 3527 5-9-12 60 ..........(v) StevieDonohoe 3 77
(Lee Carter) *wnt rt s: sn w ldr: led wl over 3f out: shkn up and qcknd wl clr wl over 1f out: in n.d after: rdn out* **7/2**[1]

2436 **2** 6 **Cyflymder (IRE)**[11] 3645 8-9-2 50 ................ OisinMurphy 11 51
(David C Griffiths) *sn chsng ldrs: rdn to chse wnr 2f out: sn outpcd: no ch w wnr but kpt on for 2nd fnl f* **6/1**[3]

2300 **3** 1 1/4 **Major Muscari (IRE)**[14] 3548 6-9-6 54 ................ BenCurtis 9 52+
(Shaun Harris) *hld up in tch in rr: rdn and effrt whn wd bnd 2f out: hdwy and edging lft 1f out: styd on but no ch w wnr* **10/1**

5030 **4** 1/2 **Bold Ring**[19] 3390 8-9-8 56 ................ AdamBeschizza 7 53
(Edward Creighton) *hld up in midfield: rdn over 2f out: hdwy u.p 1f out: kpt on but no ch w wnr* **16/1**

6666 **5** 3/4 **Hinton Admiral**[15] 3527 10-8-7 **46**... DannyBrock(5) 4 41+
(Pat Eddery) *pushed rt s: hld up in rr: nt clr run and hmpd 2f out: hdwy 1f out: styd on: no ch w wnr* **14/1**

3120 **6** 3/4 **Crystalized (IRE)**[13] 3564 3-8-13 **55**... FergusSweeney 5 45+
(Dean Ivory) *hld up in tch towards rr: nt clr run and hmpd over 2f out: nt clr run 2f out: hdwy ent fnl f: kpt on but no ch w wnr* **5/1**[2]

4625 **7** nse **Very First Blade**[77] 1631 5-9-1 **49**...(be) JimCrowley 1 42
(Michael Mullineaux) *wl in tch in midfield on inner: rdn and effrt ent fnl 2f: no ch w wnr and styd on same pce fr over 1f out* **8/1**

5-00 **8** 2 **Cadmium**[54] 2278 3-9-3 **59**... TomQueally 6 44
(Harry Dunlop) *dwlt and bmpd sn after s: detached in last and pushed along over 4f out: sme hdwy and swtchd lft 1f out: kpt on: nvr trbld ldrs* **14/1**

2604 **9** 2 1/2 **Coach Montana (IRE)**[15] 3527 5-8-12 **46** oh1...(b) RobertHavlin 2 27
(Christine Dunnett) *taken down early: led tl wl over 3f out: 3rd and btn wl over 1f out: fdd fnl f* **16/1**

1400 **10** 5 **Speed Society**[28] 3087 3-9-3 **59**... PatCosgrave 10 24
(Jim Boyle) *hld up in tch towards rr: rdn and effrt ent fnl 2f: no hdwy: wknd over 1f out* **6/1**[3]

-005 **11** 3 1/4 **Sutton Sioux**[70] 1833 3-8-4 **46** oh1...(b[1]) HayleyTurner 8
(Jeremy Gask) *chsd ldrs: rdn and lost pl ent fnl 2f: sn wknd: bhd fnl f* **66/1**

1m 23.93s (-0.87) **Going Correction** -0.15s/f (Stan)
**WFA** 3 from 5yo+ 8lb **11 Ran SP% 114.3**
Speed ratings (Par 101): **98,91,89,89,88 87,87,85,82,76 72**
CSF £23.26 CT £193.10 TOTE £4.70: £1.40, £2.30, £2.90; EX 25.10 Trifecta £334.50.
**Owner** Clear Racing **Bred** R S Cockerill (farms) Ltd & Peter Dodd **Trained** Epsom, Surrey

**FOCUS**
Mostly exposed handicappers here and, after a heavy shower that tightened up the surface even more, it proved impossible for anything to come from off the pace. There's an obvious doubt over how literally to take the form.

## 4056 RACING SPECIALS AT 32REDSPORT.COM H'CAP (DIV II) 7f 1y(P)
**5:45** (5:46) (Class 6) (0-60,59) 3-Y-0+ **£2,264** (£673; £336; £168) **Stalls High**

Form RPR

400 **1** **Ermine Ruby**[21] 3343 3-8-13 **54**... MartinHarley 7 61+
(Charles Hills) *hld up in tch in midfield: rdn and effrt ent fnl f: swtchd rt and qcknd to ld wl ins fnl f: r.o and sn in command* **11/4**[1]

00 **2** 1 1/4 **Big City Boy (IRE)**[50] 2394 6-8-7 **45**... DannyBrock(5) 5 52
(Phil McEntee) *led: rdn and fnd ex 2f out: drvn 1f out: hdd and styd on same pce wl ins fnl f* **50/1**

6203 **3** 3/4 **Alfresco**[36] 2843 10-9-6 **53**...(b) GeorgeBaker 3 58
(Martin Bosley) *t.k.h: chsd ldrs: rdn and effrt to chse ldr over 1f out: lost 2nd and styd on same pce ins fnl f* **9/2**[2]

3053 **4** nk **Greek Islands (IRE)**[13] 3576 6-9-8 **55**... AdamBeschizza 10 59
(Edward Creighton) *w ldr: rdn and ev ch 2f out tl unable qck jst over 1f out: r.o same pce fnl f* **8/1**

0261 **5** 1/2 **Ishi Honest**[15] 3528 4-9-10 **57**... JimCrowley 6 60
(Mark Usher) *chsd ldrs: rdn and effrt 2f out: unable qck ent fnl f: kpt on same pce after* **5/1**[3]

2-03 **6** 3/4 **Silvala Dance**[15] 3527 4-9-3 **50**... TedDurcan 9 51
(Chris Wall) *hld up in tch in midfield: rdn and effrt 2f out: kpt on same pce and no imp ins fnl f* **9/2**[2]

050- **7** 1/2 **Sweet Lily Pea (USA)**[258] 7461 3-8-11 **57**... TimClark(5) 4 54
(Mrs Ilka Gansera-Leveque) *dwlt: t.k.h: hld up in tch in rr: nt clr run 2f out: rdn and hdwy ent fnl f: styd on: nvr trbld ldrs* **8/1**

0060 **8** 1/2 **Lewamy (IRE)**[28] 3075 4-9-2 **49**...(v) FergusSweeney 1 47
(John Best) *shuffled bk to rr after 1f: hld up in tch: effrt on outer wl over 1f out: styd on ins fnl f: nvr trbld ldrs* **12/1**

4-60 **9** 1/2 **The Boss Of Me**[132] 745 3-8-11 **52**...(t) OisinMurphy 8 46
(Sean Curran) *t.k.h: hld up in tch: rdn wl overt 1f out: styd on same pce after: nvr trbld ldrs* **14/1**

4-00 **10** 3 1/4 **Lucky Surprise**[26] 3149 3-9-4 **59**... SteveDrowne 2 45
(Jeremy Gask) *in tch in midfield: rdn 3f out: struggling and lost pl 2f out: wknd over 1f out* **33/1**

1m 24.85s (0.05) **Going Correction** -0.15s/f (Stan)
**WFA** 3 from 4yo+ 8lb **10 Ran SP% 121.2**
Speed ratings (Par 101): **93,91,90,90,89 88,88,87,87,83**
CSF £157.90 CT £625.13 TOTE £4.30: £1.30, £4.80, £2.00; EX 147.50 Trifecta £2627.20 Part won. Pool: £3,503.03 - 0.71 winning units..
**Owner** Sir Peter Vela & The Hon Mrs P Stanley **Bred** New England Stud & P J & P M Vela **Trained** Lambourn, Berks

**FOCUS**
A weak handicap. Dubious form with the front-running runner-up 8lb out of the handicap.
T/Plt: £36.00 to a £1 stake. Pool: £86,072.32 - 1,741.32 winning tickets. T/Qpdt: £9.60 to a £1 stake. Pool: £6,768.47 - 518.88 winning tickets. SP

# 3785 PONTEFRACT (L-H)
Tuesday, July 8

**OFFICIAL GOING: Good (good to firm in places; 7.4) changing to soft after race 2 (3.00)**
Wind: Light across Weather: Cludy with sunny periods, torrential ran after 1st race

## 4057 DIANNE NURSERY H'CAP (BOBIS RACE) 6f
**2:30** (2:31) (Class 4) 2-Y-0 **£4,528** (£1,347; £673; £336) **Stalls Low**

Form RPR

333 **1** **Miami Carousel (IRE)**[20] 3358 2-8-5 **71**... JoeDoyle(7) 9 80+
(John Quinn) *t.k.h early: trckd ldrs: swtchd rt and gd hdwy wl over 1f out: rdn to ld and hung lft jst ins fnl f: rdr dropped whip: sn clr: kpt on strly* **11/1**

435 **2** 3 1/2 **British Embassy (IRE)**[25] 3193 2-8-9 **68**... SilvestreDeSousa 6 66
(Eve Johnson Houghton) *hld up in rr: hdwy on outer and wd st: rdn over 1f out: styd on fnl f: no ch w wnr* **7/2**[1]

1 **3** nk **Bimbo**[16] 3497 2-9-2 **78**... GeorgeChaloner(3) 3 75
(Richard Fahey) *hld up in rr: hdwy on inner 2f out: nt clr run and swtchd rt jst over 1f out: rdn and n.m.r ins fnl f: kpt on same pce* **4/1**[2]

01 **4** 1 **Sakhee's Return**[22] 3297 2-9-7 **80**... DuranFentiman 2 74
(Tim Easterby) *in tch on inner: hdwy 1/2-way: swtchd rt and rdn to chse ldr over 1f out: drvn and one pce fnl f* **9/2**[3]

523 **5** nse **Horsforth**[66] 1955 2-8-9 **68**... BarryMcHugh 1 62
(Tony Coyle) *led: rdn and qcknd clr wl over 1f out: hdd & wknd ins fnl f* **7/1**

304 **6** hd **Sportlobster (IRE)**[15] 3524 2-8-10 **69**... RichardKingscote 8 62
(Tom Dascombe) *chsd ldrs: rdn along 1 1/2f out: hld whn n.m.r appr fnl f: one pce after* **16/1**

056 **7** 12 **Mountain Man**[56] 2231 2-8-9 **68**... GrahamGibbons 4 25
(Michael Easterby) *chsd ldng pair: rdn along wl over 2f out: sn wknd* **16/1**

4232 **8** 14 **Ar Colleen Aine**[4] 3922 2-8-9 **68**... JamesDoyle 5
(Mick Channon) *chsd ldrs: rdn along wl over 2f out: sn wknd* **7/1**

4156 **9** 1 3/4 **Elizabeth Flynn (IRE)**[53] 2302 2-9-3 **76**... DanielTudhope 7
(K R Burke) *prom: chsd ldr after 2f: rdn along over 2f out: sn wknd* **20/1**

1m 18.88s (1.98) **Going Correction** +0.40s/f (Good) **9 Ran SP% 110.3**
Speed ratings (Par 96): **102,97,96,95,95 95,79,60,58**
CSF £45.99 CT £173.25 TOTE £12.50: £3.40, £1.30, £1.30; EX 64.40 Trifecta £212.50.
**Owner** Highfield Racing 5 **Bred** Lynn Lodge Stud **Trained** Settrington, N Yorks

**FOCUS**
False rail in place, distances increased by about 12yds. This ended up being a one-sided nursery. The gallop looked no more than a fair one until past halfway.

## 4058 HILCO APPRAISAL H'CAP 1m 2f 6y
**3:00** (3:01) (Class 5) (0-75,75) 3-Y-0+ **£3,234** (£962; £481; £240) **Stalls Low**

Form RPR

60-4 **1** **Woodacre**[64] 2016 7-8-12 **62**... GeorgeChaloner(3) 3 86
(Richard Whitaker) *trckd ldng pair on inner: hdwy 2f out: led wl over 1f out: sn rdn clr: kpt on wl towards fin* **9/2**[2]

-336 **2** nk **Epsom Hill (SWE)**[15] 3541 3-8-13 **71**...(p) FrederikTylicki 1 94
(Charlie Fellowes) *towards rr: hdwy on inner 3f out: swtchd rt and rdn over 1f out: drvn to chse wnr whn edgd lft ins fnl f: clsd up and ch whn edgd lft again last 50yds: kpt on* **8/1**

6-46 **3** 13 **Fine Vintage (FR)**[19] 3396 3-9-0 **72**... FrannyNorton 2 71
(Mark Johnston) *led: rdn along over 2f out: hdd wl over 1f out: sn drvn and plugged on one pce* **8/1**

4124 **4** 2 **Lord Franklin**[33] 2912 5-9-11 **72**... JasonHart 8 67
(Eric Alston) *trckd ldrs: hdwy 4f out: rdn to chse wnr wl over 1f out: drvn and wknd ent fnl f* **14/1**

5-14 **5** 1 3/4 **Obboorr**[158] 405 5-9-4 **65**... TomEaves 5 57
(John Wainwright) *in tch on inner: hdwy to chse ldrs over 2f out: sn rdn along and one pce fr wl over 1f out* **7/1**[3]

4-36 **6** 3 **Pat's Legacy (USA)**[22] 3299 8-9-1 **62**... DanielTudhope 4 48
(Marjorie Fife) *s.i.s and bhd tl sme late hdwy* **12/1**

5666 **7** 8 **A Little Bit Dusty**[14] 3556 6-9-7 **68**...(p) PaulHanagan 10 39
(Conor Dore) *hld up in midfield: sme hdwy on outer over 3f out: rdn along 2f out: n.d* **16/1**

345 **8** 3 1/4 **Rokeby**[27] 3105 3-7-7 **58** oh8... KieranSchofield(7) 12 23
(George Moore) *a towards rr* **50/1**

0424 **9** nk **The Osteopath (IRE)**[47] 2477 11-9-13 **74**... PJMcDonald 14 38
(John Davies) *a towards rr: bhd fnl 3f* **28/1**

3633 **10** 3 3/4 **Tinseltown**[19] 3398 8-8-13 **65**... JackGarritty(5) 7 22
(Brian Rothwell) *cl up: rdn along over 2f out: sn wknd* **18/1**

2220 **11** 47 **Missy Wells**[35] 2872 4-9-1 **62**...(p) DuranFentiman 11
(Mark Walford) *in tch: rdn along over 4f out: sn wknd and bhd* **20/1**

210- **12** 9 **Jan De Heem**[281] 6898 4-9-7 **68**... PaulMulrennan 9
(Tina Jackson) *a towards rr: wl bhd fnl 3f* **50/1**

031 **13** 3 1/4 **Gabrial The Thug (FR)**[12] 3623 4-9-0 **61**...(t) DavidNolan 6
(Richard Fahey) *a towards rr: bhd fnl 3f* **9/1**

-321 **14** 31 **Tower Power**[35] 2867 3-9-3 **75**... JamesDoyle 13
(Ismail Mohammed) *trckd ldrs on outer: rdn along over 3f out: wknd qckly: sn wl bhd and eased* **7/2**[1]

2m 18.26s (4.56) **Going Correction** +0.40s/f (Good)
**WFA** 3 from 4yo+ 11lb **14 Ran SP% 122.8**
Speed ratings (Par 103): **97,96,86,84,83 80,74,71,71,68 31,23,21,**
CSF £39.98 CT £286.35 TOTE £7.90: £3.40, £3.70, £3.80; EX 39.20 Trifecta £267.80.
**Owner** Mrs R M Whitaker **Bred** Hellwood Stud Farm **Trained** Scarcroft, W Yorks
■ Stewards' Enquiry : Kieran Schofield two-day ban: careless riding (Jul 22-23)

**FOCUS**
This was run in the middle of a torrential downpour and quite a few patently failed to give their running, the leading pair well clear.

## 4059 COLLIERS INTERNATIONAL ASSET ADVISORY H'CAP 5f
**3:30** (3:31) (Class 5) (0-75,74) 3-Y-0 **£3,234** (£962; £481; £240) **Stalls Low**

Form RPR

-600 **1** **Straits Of Malacca**[21] 3338 3-8-9 **62**... TomEaves 9 70
(Kevin Ryan) *trckd ldr on outer: cl up 2f out: led over 1f out: rdn ins fnl f: kpt on strly* **16/1**

4050 **2** 1 1/4 **Argent Touch**[11] 3650 3-8-5 **58**... FrannyNorton 8 61
(Derek Shaw) *towards rr: hdwy 2f out: rdn over 1f out: chsd wnr ins fnl f: no imp towards fin* **16/1**

1410 **3** nk **Tinsill**[12] 3600 3-9-0 **67**...(p) SilvestreDeSousa 6 69
(Nigel Tinkler) *in rr and sn rdn along: hdwy on outer 2f out: styd on u.p fnl f: nrst fin* **8/1**

-350 **4** 2 **Gold Club**[24] 3225 3-8-13 **66**... PaulHanagan 2 61
(Ed McMahon) *chsd ldrs: rdn along and outpcd wl over 1f out: kpt on fnl f* **5/2**[2]

5000 **5** 2 **Princess Myla (IRE)**[4] 3913 3-8-2 **55** oh2...[1] JamesSullivan 7 43
(Paul Midgley) *in rr: sme hdwy 2f out: sn rdn along and n.d* **33/1**

121 **6** 1 1/2 **Orient Class**[67] 1925 3-9-3 **70**...(v) GrahamLee 3 52
(Paul Midgley) *trckd ldng pair: hdwy to chse wnr 1f out: sn rdn: drvn and wknd last 100yds* **7/4**[1]

3414 **7** 9 **Storyline (IRE)**[17] 3487 3-8-12 **65**... DavidAllan 5 15
(Tim Easterby) *led: rdn along wl 2f out: hdd over 1f out and wknd qckly* **7/2**[3]

1m 8.78s (5.48) **Going Correction** +0.925s/f (Soft) **7 Ran SP% 113.0**
Speed ratings (Par 100): **93,91,90,87,84 81,67**
CSF £218.79 CT £2187.05 TOTE £14.70: £5.40, £3.90; EX 88.40 Trifecta £448.70.
**Owner** JCG Chua & CK Ong **Bred** Whitsbury Manor Stud **Trained** Hambleton, N Yorks

**FOCUS**
The ground was changed to soft prior to this race. A fair sprint. A few proved disappointing on the rain-softened ground. The winner recorded his best effort since his 2yo maiden win, while the runner-up has been rated to his best turf form.

## 4060 WEATHERBYS VAT SERVICES PIPALONG STKS (LISTED RACE) (F&M) 1m 4y
**4:00** (4:02) (Class 1) 4-Y-0+
**£22,684** (£8,600; £4,304; £2,144; £1,076; £540) **Stalls Low**

Form RPR

0-60 **1** **Audacia (IRE)**[32] 2956 4-9-0 **85**... GrahamLee 3 102
(Hugo Palmer) *trckd ldrs: hdwy 2f out: chsd ldr over 1f out: sn rdn to chal: styd on wl u.p to ld last 100yds* **12/1**

-016 **2** *1* **Dutch Rose (IRE)**[24] 3252 5-9-0 102 DanielTudhope 10 100
(David O'Meara) *trckd ldng pair on outer: hdwy and cl up 2f out: led wl over 1f out: rdn and jnd ent fnl f: sn drvn: hdd and no ex last 100yds* **13/2**

21-5 **3** *½* **Vanity Rules**[66] 1945 4-9-0 83 FrederikTylicki 5 99
(Ed Vaughan) *hld up in rr: gd hdwy over 2f out: effrt to chse ldng pair jst over 1f out: sn rdn and styd on wl fnl f: nrst fin* **14/1**

6100 **4** *11* **Amulet**[24] 3244 4-9-0 89 PaulHanagan 2 73
(Eve Johnson Houghton) *slt ld: rdn along over 2f out: hdd wl over 1f out and grad wknd* **6/1**[3]

0-15 **5** *½* **Boonga Roogeta**[52] 2331 5-9-0 91 RobertTart 9 72
(Peter Charalambous) *in tch on wd outside: rdn along over 3f out: wknd over 2f out* **40/1**

0-04 **6** *6* **Pavlosk (USA)**[59] 2155 4-9-0 100 JamesDoyle 4 58
(Sir Michael Stoute) *hld up: sme hdwy on inner 3f out: rdn along over 2f out: n.d* **7/2**[1]

0-06 **7** *17* **Butterfly McQueen (USA)**[32] 2956 4-9-0 97 DavidProbert 7 19
(Andrew Balding) *chsd ldrs: rdn along 3f out: sn outpacd* **7/1**

4011 **8** *nk* **Mu'Ajiza**[12] 3608 4-9-0 82 RobertWinston 6 19
(Paul Midgley) *hld up: hdwy 3f out: chsd ldrs wl over 1f out: sn rdn and wknd qckly* **12/1**

-210 **9** *5* **Stellar Express (IRE)**[24] 3217 5-9-0 92 AndrewMullen 8
(Michael Appleby) *cl up: rdn along 3f out: sn wknd and bhd* **8/1**

-440 **10** *15* **Masarah (IRE)**[20] 3355 4-9-0 100 SilvestreDeSousa 1
(Clive Brittain) *chsd ldrs on inner: rdn along 3f out sn wknd and bhd* **11/2**[2]

1m 52.09s (6.19) **Going Correction** +0.925s/f (Soft) **10** Ran SP% **113.3**
Speed ratings (Par 111): **106,105,104,93,93 87,70,69,64,49**
CSF £85.36 TOTE £16.50: £3.30, £2.30, £3.90; EX 122.90 Trifecta £1452.70.
**Owner** Carmichael Simmons Humber **Bred** Rathasker Stud **Trained** Newmarket, Suffolk

**FOCUS**
Clearly not a strong Listed race, the field well strung out with plenty failing to handle the ground. The pace looked sound enough under the conditions. The level is fluid, with the ground very different from that forecast.

## 4061 KING RICHARD III STKS (H'CAP) 6f
4:30 (4:30) (Class 3) (0-90,87) 3-Y-O+ **£7,762** (£2,310; £1,154; £577) **Stalls** Low

Form RPR

-110 **1** **My Name Is Rio (IRE)**[52] 2352 4-9-6 81 PaulMulrennan 13 90
(Michael Dods) *sn slt ld: pushed along over 1f out: sn jnd and rdn: drvn ins fnl f and kpt on wl towards fin* **9/1**[3]

00-0 **2** *nk* **Secret Look**[23] 3271 4-9-12 87 GrahamGibbons 7 95
(Ed McMahon) *trckd ldrs: hdwy 2f out: chsd wnr over 1f out: sn rdn to chal and ev ch tl drvn ins fnl f and no ex towards fin* **10/1**

0543 **3** *1* **Misplaced Fortune**[8] 3788 9-9-9 84 (v) SilvestreDeSousa 6 89
(Nigel Tinkler) *in tch: hdwy to trck ldrs 2f out: effrt to chal on inner ent fnl f: sn rdn and ev ch tl drvn and kpt on same pce towards fin* **3/1**[1]

0313 **4** *1 ½* **Sunraider (IRE)**[12] 3599 7-9-4 79 GrahamLee 1 79
(Paul Midgley) *hld up in rr: hdwy wl over 1f out: sn swtchd rt and rdn: styd on strly fnl f: nrst fin* **6/1**[2]

6023 **5** *2 ¾* **King Of Eden (IRE)**[12] 3610 8-9-2 77 JasonHart 11 68
(Eric Alston) *in tch on outer: wd st: hdwy to chse ldrs over 1f out: sn rdn: edgd lft and one pce ins fnl f* **20/1**

4250 **6** *4* **Naabegha**[10] 3702 7-9-4 79 (p) JamesDoyle 3 57
(Alan McCabe) *a towards rr* **12/1**

1-00 **7** *¾* **Rocksilla**[25] 3203 4-9-10 85 PaulHanagan 4 61
(Chris Wall) *cl up: rdn along 2f out: sn drvn and wknd over 1f out* **9/1**[3]

5533 **8** *½* **Hadaj**[3] 3948 5-9-7 82 (b) JamesSullivan 2 56
(Ruth Carr) *prom: pushed along 1/2-way: rdn over 2f out and sn wknd* **3/1**[1]

2000 **9** *¾* **Chooseday (IRE)**[24] 3239 5-9-12 87 [1] BrianHughes 12 59
(Kevin Ryan) *dwlt: sn chsng ldrs: cl up 1/2-way: rdn along wl over 1f out: sn drvn and wknd* **20/1**

-456 **10** *5* **It Must Be Faith**[22] 3306 4-8-11 72 AndrewMullen 10 28
(Michael Appleby) *chsd ldrs: rdn along wl over 2f out: sn wknd* **14/1**

1m 22.46s (5.56) **Going Correction** +0.925s/f (Soft)
**WFA** 3 from 4yo+ 6lb **10** Ran SP% **117.3**
Speed ratings (Par 107): **99,98,97,95,91 86,85,84,83,76**
CSF £95.81 CT £341.10 TOTE £10.10: £2.60, £4.20, £1.80; EX 112.30 Trifecta £611.30.
**Owner** K Kirkup & Mrs T Galletley **Bred** Anthony J Keane **Trained** Denton, Co Durham
■ Stewards' Enquiry : Paul Mulrennan two-day ban: used whip above permitted level (Jul 22-23)

**FOCUS**
They went steady by sprint standards here, the winner always well placed. The runner-up has been rated close to his 3yo form.

## 4062 MARVELLOUS TEA DANCE COMPANY MAIDEN STKS 1m 4f 8y
5:00 (5:00) (Class 5) 3-Y-O+ **£3,234** (£962; £481; £240) **Stalls** Low

Form RPR

4 **1** **Mizzou (IRE)**[27] 3106 3-9-0 0 DanielTudhope 2 84+
(Luca Cumani) *trckd ldrs: hdwy 4f out: swtchd rt to outer 3f out: hdwy to ld wl over 1f out: sn rdn clr: styd on strly* **1/1**[1]

6 **2** *7* **Di's Gift**[19] 3385 5-9-13 0 RobertWinston 3 71
(Richard Guest) *hld up: hdwy on inner over 5f out: cl up 4f out: led 3f out: rdn along and jnd 2f out: sn hdd and drvn: kpt on u.p fnl f: no ch w wnr* **10/1**

0 **3** *1* **Pas De Cheval (IRE)**[54] 2271 3-9-0 0 (v[1]) GrahamLee 5 69
(Sir Michael Stoute) *hld up: hdwy over 4f out: chsd ldrs 3f out: rdn wl over 1f out: kpt on one pce* **5/2**[2]

4 **4** *7* **Spot The Pro (IRE)**[22] 3302 5-9-13 0 BrianHughes 8 58
(Rebecca Menzies) *trckd ldrs: effrt 3f out: rdn along 2f out: swtchd lft and drvn appr fnl f: sn one pce* **7/1**[3]

**5** *14* **Chebsey Beau**[50] 4-9-13 0 PhillipMakin 6 36
(John Quinn) *in rr: hdwy on outer over 5f out: in tch and rdn along 3f out: sn outpcd* **8/1**

4- **6** *3* **Hope For Glory**[109] 8046 5-9-10 0 [1] JoeyHaynes[(3)] 1 31
(Jason Ward) *a in rr: bhd fnl 3f* **50/1**

42-0 **7** *74* **Princeofthedesert**[23] 3269 8-9-13 50 (p) JasonHart 4
(Garry Woodward) *led: rdn along 4f out: hdd 3f out: wknd 2f out: sn bhd and eased* **50/1**

00 **8** *8* **King Couture (IRE)**[18] 3434 3-9-0 0 JamesSullivan 7
(Michael Easterby) *chsd ldr: rdn along 5f out: sn wknd and bhd fnl 3f* **66/1**

2m 54.57s (13.77) **Going Correction** +0.925s/f (Soft)
**WFA** 3 from 4yo+ 13lb **8** Ran SP% **116.7**
Speed ratings (Par 103): **91,86,85,81,71 69,20,15**
CSF £13.13 TOTE £2.80: £1.10, £1.90, £1.40; EX 12.60 Trifecta £34.10.
**Owner** Jon S Kelly **Bred** Matrix Bloodstock **Trained** Newmarket, Suffolk

**FOCUS**
A weak maiden after the non-runners and it was plain sailing for the favourite. Doubts over the form with the runner-up no great shakes.

## 4063 PONTEFRACT SPORTS & EDUCATION FOUNDATION H'CAP 1m 4y
5:30 (5:30) (Class 5) (0-70,72) 3-Y-O **£3,234** (£962; £481; £240) **Stalls** Low

Form RPR

222 **1** **Green Zone (IRE)**[15] 3534 3-8-11 59 (p) SilvestreDeSousa 12 75
(Nigel Tinkler) *trckd ldrs: hdwy over 3f out: led over 2f out and wd st: rdn clr ent fnl f: styd on strly* **5/2**[1]

4403 **2** *5* **Sicilian Bay (IRE)**[39] 2742 3-7-12 51 ShirleyTeasdale[(5)] 5 55
(Paul Midgley) *trckd ldng pair on inner: hdwy and cl up 3f out: rdn 2f out: drvn to chse wnr ins fnl f: sn no imp* **7/2**[2]

5010 **3** *3 ½* **Choice Of Destiny**[26] 3144 3-9-4 66 GrahamGibbons 3 62
(Philip McBride) *hld up: hdwy over 3f out: chsd wnr 2f out: wd st and sn rdn: drvn and one pce ent fnl f* **13/2**

0611 **4** *1* **Eddiemaurice (IRE)**[4] 3911 3-9-10 72 6ex (v) RobertWinston 9 66
(Richard Guest) *dwlt and in rr: hdwy 3f out: rdn to chse ldrs wl over 1f out: sn drvn and no imp* **4/1**[3]

-005 **5** *6* **Edward Elgar**[21] 3343 3-8-7 55 (p) PJMcDonald 11 35
(Richard Whitaker) *cl up: rdn along 3f out: drvn 2f out and sn outpcd* **16/1**

4-02 **6** *7* **Slingsby**[12] 3618 3-8-6 54 BarryMcHugh 6 18
(Michael Easterby) *led: rdn along 3f out: sn hdd & wknd* **20/1**

6603 **7** *4* **Lady Liz**[39] 2729 3-7-9 50 (b) KieranSchofield[(7)] 10 5
(George Moore) *t.k.h: towards rr: hdwy on outer 1/2-way: cl up 3f out: pushed along whn n.m.r and sltly hmpd 3f out: sn bhd* **16/1**

-505 **8** *3 ¾* **Buy Out Boy**[19] 3405 3-9-0 62 AndrewMullen 1 8
(Michael Appleby) *chsd ldrs: rdn along 3f out: sn wknd and bhd* **9/1**

505 **9** *27* **Miss Moppet**[28] 3074 3-9-5 67 DanielTudhope 7
(Hughie Morrison) *chsd ldrs: rdn along 3f out: sn wknd and bhd* **14/1**

1m 52.92s (7.02) **Going Correction** +0.925s/f (Soft) **9** Ran SP% **117.3**
Speed ratings (Par 100): **101,96,92,91,85 78,74,70,43**
CSF £11.41 CT £50.90 TOTE £2.80: £1.20, £1.80, £2.20; EX 9.30 Trifecta £58.00.
**Owner** Sunrise **Bred** Incense Partnership **Trained** Langton, N Yorks

**FOCUS**
A modest handicap. Once again they were well strung out. The winner has been rated back to his 2yo best, and the runner-up close to form.
T/Jkpt: Not won. T/Plt: £1,772.00 to a £1 stake. Pool: £102,199.08 - 42.10 winning tickets.
T/Qpdt: £112.10 to a £1 stake. Pool: £6,766.46 - 44.66 winning tickets. JR

# 4006 HAMBURG (R-H)
Tuesday, July 8

**OFFICIAL GOING: Turf: good to soft**

## 4064a GROSSER PREIS VON LOTTO HAMBURG (HAMBURGER STUTEN-PREIS) (GROUP 3) (3YO FILLIES) (TURF) 1m 3f
5:40 (12:00) 3-Y-O

**£26,666** (£9,166; £4,583; £2,500; £1,666; £1,250)

RPR

**1** **Papagena Star (IRE)**[30] 3046 3-9-2 0 AHelfenbein 7 102
(Markus Klug, Germany) *trckd ldr on outer: pushed along into st: rdn to chal on rail over 1f out and led ent fnl f: styd on strly and drew clr: comf* **27/10**[2]

**2** *3 ½* **Lacy (GER)**[17] 3-9-2 0 APietsch 4 96
(Waldemar Hickst, Germany) *dwlt: hld up in last: hdwy and chal into st: pushed along to ld 2f out and angled towards nr side rail: rdn and strly pressed fr over 1f out: hdd ent fnl f: styd on for wl hld 2nd* **8/5**[1]

**3** *1 ½* **Oriental Magic (GER)**[44] 2584 3-9-2 0 FilipMinarik 2 93
(J Hirschberger, Germany) *hld up in tch: rdn in last 2f out: styd on and wnt 3rd ins fnl f: nt pce to chal* **108/10**

**4** *hd* **Kaldera (GER)**[19] 3-9-2 0 EPedroza 6 93
(W Mongil, Germany) *midfield in tch: rdn over 2f out: outpcd by front pair st: styd on but wl hld* **37/10**[3]

**5** *3 ½* **Lutindi (GER)** 3-9-2 0 AdriedeVries 3 87
(P Schiergen, Germany) *trckd ldr on inner: rdn over 2f out: sn outpcd and btn: fdd* **54/10**

**6** *1 ¾* **Turmalina (GER)**[30] 3046 3-9-2 0 SHellyn 5 83
(J Hirschberger, Germany) *led: rdn and strly pressed into st: hdd 2f out: sn outpcd and btn: fdd* **89/10**

**7** *6* **Amadea (GER)** 3-9-2 0 DanielePorcu 1 73
(P Schiergen, Germany) *midfield on inner: rdn over 2f out: dropped to last and btn over 1f out: wknd fnl f* **9/1**

2m 24.3s (-0.40) **7** Ran SP% **131.0**
WIN (incl. 10 euro stake): 37. Plces: 23, 19. SF: 111.
**Owner** Dr Alexandra Margarete Renz **Bred** Richard Ahern **Trained** Germany

# 3841 CATTERICK (L-H)
Wednesday, July 9

**OFFICIAL GOING: Good to firm (9.1)**
Wind: fresh against Weather: Sunny

## 4065 YORKSHIRE-OUTDOORS.CO.UK CLAIMING STKS 5f
2:30 (2:30) (Class 6) 2-Y-O **£2,385** (£704; £352) **Stalls** Low

Form RPR

536 **1** **Millar Rose (IRE)**[40] 2725 2-9-2 0 BenCurtis 3 67+
(K R Burke) *chsd ldrs: rdn to ld narrowly jst ins fnl f: kpt on* **5/2**[2]

64 **2** *hd* **Danot (IRE)**[14] 3570 2-9-7 0 TomEaves 1 71+
(Keith Dalgleish) *trckd ldr: rdn and ev ch over 1f out: kpt on but a jst hld* **2/1**[1]

0044 **3** *4 ½* **On Appro**[21] 3367 2-8-8 0 GrahamGibbons 4 42
(Tim Easterby) *led: rdn 2f out: hdd jst ins fnl f: wknd* **20/1**

5016 **4** *shd* **Fairweather Trader (IRE)**[19] 3435 2-8-13 0 PaulMulrennan 5 47+
(Paul Midgley) *hld up: rdn 1/2-way: kpt on fnl f* **11/1**

066 **5** *4 ½* **Sunhill Lodge Lady**[8] 3827 2-8-9 0 PJMcDonald 2 27
(Ann Duffield) *chsd ldrs: rdn 1/2-way: wknd over 1f out* **25/1**

553 **6** *1 ½* **Decisive Rebel**[12] 3658 2-8-7 0 (p) HarryBurns[(7)] 6 26
(Jo Hughes) *hld up: nvr threatened* **6/1**



The Form Book, Raceform Ltd, Newbury, RG14 5SJ

604 **7** ½ **Queen Of The Scots**[12] 3658 2-8-6 0................................(p) JasonHart 7 16
(Keith Dalgleish) *hld up: a towards rr* **5/1**[3]
1m 0.8s (1.00) **Going Correction** -0.125s/f (Firm) **7** Ran SP% **109.8**
Speed ratings (Par 92): **87,86,79,79,72 69,68**
CSF £7.23 TOTE £3.80: £1.30, £1.30; EX 7.70 Trifecta £80.80.
**Owner** Ontoawinner 7, M Hulin, E Burke **Bred** Patrick F Kelly And M J Foley **Trained** Middleham Moor, N Yorks

**FOCUS**
A dry run up to a meeting that was staged on good to firm ground. A modest claimer in which the pace was sound and the two with the best form were well on top at the finish. The third and fourth have been rated 5lb below their best.

## 4066 ST TERESA'S HOSPICE MEDIAN AUCTION MAIDEN STKS 1m 3f 214y
**3:00** (3:02) (Class 5) 3-4-Y-O **£2,911** (£866; £432; £216) **Stalls** Low

Form RPR
4222 **1** **Rocket Ship**[7] 3857 3-9-0 82................................ JamesDoyle 4 86+
(Sir Michael Stoute) *mde all: pushed clr fnl 2f: easily* **1/7**[1]
33 **2** 11 **Vodka Wells (FR)**[20] 3401 4-9-13 0................................ DaleSwift 1 68+
(Brian Ellison) *hld up: stl plenty to do over 3f out: pushed along and hdwy over 2f out: wnt 2nd over 1f out: no ch w wnr* **5/1**[3]
60 **3** 9 **Giovanni Jack**[2] 4022 4-9-13 0................................ BenCurtis 5 45
(Alan Swinbank) *hld up: hdwy over 3f out: briefly chsd wnr over 2f out: lost 2nd over 1f out: wknd* **20/1**
00-0 **4** 1½ **Major Rowan**[57] 2236 3-9-0 41................................(b) RoystonFfrench 2 43
(Bryan Smart) *trckd ldr: rdn over 4f out: wknd over 2f out* **50/1**
**5** ¾ **Bigindie (IRE)**[21] 4-9-13 0................................ PhillipMakin 3 42
(John Weymes) *in tch: rdn over 2f out: sn wknd* **9/2**[2]
0-00 **6** 8 **Secret Kode (IRE)**[8] 3833 3-8-9 59................................(p) DavidAllan 8 24
(Simon Waugh) *trckd ldr: rdn over 4f out: wknd over 2f out* **33/1**
**7** 23 **Kaylan's Rose**[25] 4-9-8 0................................ PaulMulrennan 9
(Barry Murtagh) *dwlt: hld up: a bhd* **20/1**
-006 **8** 1¾ **Slip Of A Girl (IRE)**[25] 3238 4-9-3 43................................[1] JackGarritty(5) 7
(Patrick Holmes) *hld up: a bhd* **66/1**
2m 35.99s (-2.91) **Going Correction** -0.125s/f (Firm)
**WFA** 3 from 4yo 13lb **8** Ran SP% **138.3**
Speed ratings (Par 103): **104,96,90,89,89 83,68,67**
CSF £2.49 TOTE £1.20: £1.02, £1.60, £4.40; EX 2.30 Trifecta £17.10.
**Owner** K Abdullah **Bred** Juddmonte Farms Ltd **Trained** Newmarket, Suffolk

**FOCUS**
A most uncompetitive maiden in which the market leader didn't have to improve to win with plenty in hand. The gallop was reasonable.

## 4067 GO RACING IN YORKSHIRE SUMMER FESTIVAL H'CAP 7f
**3:30** (3:31) (Class 5) (0-75,80) 3-Y-O **£2,911** (£866; £432; £216) **Stalls** Low

Form RPR
-551 **1** **In Focus (IRE)**[4] 3946 3-8-11 64 6ex................................ DavidAllan 3 76+
(Alan Swinbank) *mde all: pressed by 2nd tl pushed clr fr 2f out: rdn ent fnl f: kpt on wl* **15/8**[1]
5451 **2** 3½ **Sandra's Diamond (IRE)**[4] 3956 3-9-13 80 6ex................................ GrahamLee 1 83
(Keith Dalgleish) *w ldr: rdn and outpcd by wnr 2f out: kpt on ins fnl f but a comf hld* **2/1**[2]
6124 **3** 3¼ **Miaplacidus (IRE)**[14] 3575 3-8-10 63................................ TonyHamilton 2 57
(Richard Fahey) *s.i.s: sn pushed along in rr: kpt on fr over 1f out: wnt 3rd ins fnl f: nvr threatened* **7/2**[3]
-443 **4** 1¼ **Alpine Flower (IRE)**[18] 3486 3-8-12 65................................ AndrewElliott 5 56
(Tim Easterby) *chsd ldng pair: rdn over 2f out: one pce* **14/1**
2221 **5** 3¼ **Romantic Bliss (IRE)**[71] 1854 3-8-1 57................................(b) JoeyHaynes(3) 4 39
(K R Burke) *chsd ldng pair: rdn 3f out: wknd fnl f* **9/1**
4606 **6** 5 **Miss Acclaimed (IRE)**[12] 3662 3-8-4 57 ow2................................(b) BenCurtis 6 26
(Brian Ellison) *hld up: rdn and hdwy over 2f out: wknd over 1f out* **22/1**
1m 26.07s (-0.93) **Going Correction** -0.125s/f (Firm) **6** Ran SP% **111.4**
Speed ratings (Par 100): **100,96,92,90,87 81**
CSF £5.84 TOTE £2.80: £2.20, £1.30; EX 7.50 Trifecta £17.30.
**Owner** G H Bell **Bred** Century Farms **Trained** Melsonby, N Yorks

**FOCUS**
This fair handicap contained a couple of in-form types. The gallop was reasonable throughout. The balance of the second and third suggest this is a sensible level for now.

## 4068 5TH REGIMENT ROYAL ARTILLERY HEIMDALL H'CAP (FOR THE TURMERIC CHALLENGE TROPHY) 1m 7f 177y
**4:00** (4:00) (Class 4) (0-85,85) 3-Y-O+ **£6,469** (£1,925; £962; £481) **Stalls** Low

Form RPR
2010 **1** **Sir Frank Morgan (IRE)**[17] 3501 4-9-7 78................................ JoeFanning 5 88
(Mark Johnston) *mde all: rdn over 2f out: styd on wl: drew clr fr over 1f out* **5/1**[3]
6562 **2** 4½ **Dr Irv**[7] 3845 5-9-3 74................................ PJMcDonald 4 79
(Philip Kirby) *in tch: rdn to chse wnr over 1f out: sn drvn: one pce and no imp* **15/8**[1]
4113 **3** ¾ **Miss Macnamara (IRE)**[11] 3698 5-9-1 72................................ PhillipMakin 1 76
(Martin Todhunter) *trckd ldr: rdn over 2f out: one pce* **13/2**
-112 **4** nk **Hallstatt (IRE)**[12] 3654 8-9-2 73................................(t) PaulMulrennan 6 76
(John Mackie) *in tch: trckd ldr 4f out: rdn over 2f out: one pce* **8/1**
30-6 **5** ½ **Almagest**[22] 3341 6-10-0 85................................ DanielTudhope 3 88
(David O'Meara) *hld up: pushed along over 2f out: kpt on ins fnl f: nvr threatened* **3/1**[2]
0-04 **6** 1½ **Bowdler's Magic**[17] 3501 7-9-4 75................................(t) JimmyQuinn 2 76
(David Thompson) *hld up: rdn over 2f out: nvr threatened* **11/1**
3m 29.84s (-2.16) **Going Correction** -0.125s/f (Firm) **6** Ran SP% **109.2**
Speed ratings (Par 105): **100,97,97,97,96 96**
CSF £14.02 CT £53.78 TOTE £5.40: £2.90, £1.20; EX 20.70 Trifecta £67.00.
**Owner** Paul Dean **Bred** Airlie Stud **Trained** Middleham Moor, N Yorks

**FOCUS**
Mainly exposed performers in a useful handicap but a race in which the winner was allowed to dictate a modest gallop, so the form may not be reliable. The winner is progressive, while the runner-up is not the heartiest of battlers but the form is rated around him and the third.

## 4069 RACINGUK.COM H'CAP (DIV I) 7f
**4:30** (4:30) (Class 6) (0-65,62) 3-Y-O+ **£2,385** (£704; £352) **Stalls** Low

Form RPR
6530 **1** **Imperator Augustus (IRE)**[14] 3572 6-10-0 62........... DanielTudhope 7 71+
(Patrick Holmes) *dwlt: hld up in midfield: rdn and gd hdwy 2f out: chsd ldr over 1f out: kpt on to ld 75yds out* **4/1**[1]
044 **2** 2 **Shillito**[7] 3846 4-9-12 60................................ BarryMcHugh 10 64
(Tony Coyle) *led after 1f: rdn over 2f out: hdd 75yds out: no ex* **8/1**
-001 **3** 2¼ **Gaelic Wizard (IRE)**[9] 3795 6-9-4 57................................ GemmaTutty(5) 2 55
(Karen Tutty) *chsd ldrs: rdn over 2f out: one pce* **11/2**[2]
5530 **4** hd **Thrust Control (IRE)**[5] 3908 7-9-3 51................................(p) DaleSwift 11 48
(Tracy Waggott) *prom: rdn over 2f out: one pce* **7/1**[3]
050 **5** 1¾ **Mey Blossom**[15] 3548 9-9-1 52................................(p) GeorgeChaloner(3) 4 44
(Richard Whitaker) *midfield: rdn over 2f out: one pce* **14/1**
-304 **6** ¾ **Mysterious Wonder**[22] 3339 4-9-5 57................................ PhillipMakin 8 47
(Philip Kirby) *hld up: rdn over 2f out: one pce* **8/1**
4014 **7** hd **Ellies Image**[30] 3053 7-9-0 51................................ ConnorBeasley(3) 12 41
(Richard Ford) *hld up in midfield on outer: rdn over 2f out: one pce and nvr threatened* **10/1**
6-03 **8** ½ **Abraham Monro**[16] 3530 4-9-5 53................................ JamesSullivan 1 41
(Ruth Carr) *in tch: rdn over 2f out: wknd fnl f* **4/1**[1]
0000 **9** 1¼ **Skinny Latte**[8] 3828 3-8-3 45................................(b) PatrickMathers 5 27
(Micky Hammond) *s.i.s: hld up: nvr threatened* **100/1**
0400 **10** 2½ **Midnight Warrior**[7] 3846 4-8-10 49................................ ShirleyTeasdale(5) 9 27
(Ron Barr) *sn pushed along in rr: a bhd* **40/1**
5500 **11** ¾ **Elle West**[4] 3946 3-8-3 52................................ AnnaHesketh(7) 3 25
(Michael Easterby) *midfield: rdn over 2f out: sn wknd* **33/1**
0-60 **12** 1½ **Spithead**[65] 2019 4-9-2 55................................(p) JackGarritty(5) 6 27
(Mike Sowersby) *led for 1f: trckd ldr: rdn over 2f out: sn wknd* **33/1**
1m 25.43s (-1.57) **Going Correction** -0.125s/f (Firm)
**WFA** 3 from 4yo+ 8lb **12** Ran SP% **115.2**
Speed ratings (Par 101): **103,100,98,97,95 95,94,94,92,89 89,87**
CSF £34.41 CT £178.68 TOTE £4.90: £2.10, £2.30, £2.30; EX 32.30 Trifecta £160.80.
**Owner** Foulrice Park Racing Limited **Bred** Western Bloodstock **Trained** Middleham, N Yorks

**FOCUS**
A modest handicap in which the gallop was sound throughout. The first two pulled clear. The runner-up was another front-runner to run well on the card.

## 4070 RACINGUK.COM H'CAP (DIV II) 7f
**5:00** (5:01) (Class 6) (0-65,62) 3-Y-O+ **£2,385** (£704; £352) **Stalls** Low

Form RPR
40U0 **1** **Iceblast**[4] 3952 6-9-10 58................................(b) GrahamGibbons 5 69
(Michael Easterby) *trckd ldng pair: rdn to ld over 1f out: kpt on wl* **11/2**
0343 **2** 1½ **Running Reef (IRE)**[4] 3952 5-9-12 60................................ RobertWinston 8 67
(Tracy Waggott) *trckd ldng pair: rdn and ev ch over 1f out: kpt on but a hld fnl f* **9/4**[1]
6500 **3** 3 **Secret City (IRE)**[16] 3530 8-9-6 54................................(p) DanielTudhope 3 53
(Robin Bastiman) *led narrowly: rdn whn hdd over 1f out: no ex* **9/1**
635 **4** 1¼ **No Quarter (IRE)**[7] 3844 7-10-0 62................................ RoystonFfrench 10 58
(Tracy Waggott) *midfield: rdn over 2f out: kpt on fnl f* **10/1**
0452 **5** 4 **Viking Warrior (IRE)**[30] 3054 7-9-3 51................................(b) BenCurtis 6 36
(Shaun Harris) *w ldr: rdn over 2f out: wknd fnl f* **9/2**[2]
3-51 **6** 4 **Heidi's Delight (IRE)**[183] 77 5-9-5 53................................(p) PJMcDonald 2 27
(Ann Duffield) *midfield: rdn 1/2-way: wknd over 1f out* **16/1**
0-00 **7** 2 **Koolgreycat (IRE)**[7] 3846 5-8-10 51................................ PeterSword(7) 1 20
(Noel Wilson) *dwlt: hld up: rdn over 2f out: nvr threatened* **33/1**
0000 **8** hd **One Kool Dude**[22] 3339 5-9-1 49................................(p) PatrickMathers 7 17
(Micky Hammond) *midfield: rdn over 2f out: wknd over 1f out* **25/1**
4464 **9** 6 **Bondi Beach Babe**[15] 3548 4-9-9 57................................ GrahamLee 4 9
(James Turner) *hld up: nvr threatened* **5/1**[3]
-000 **10** 2 **Weisse Girl**[9] 3792 3-8-8 50 ow1................................(b) MichaelStainton 11
(Nick Kent) *hld up: nvr threatened* **66/1**
1m 25.12s (-1.88) **Going Correction** -0.125s/f (Firm)
**WFA** 3 from 4yo+ 8lb **10** Ran SP% **114.3**
Speed ratings (Par 101): **105,103,99,98,93 89,87,86,79,77**
CSF £17.59 CT £111.84 TOTE £7.20: £1.40, £2.00, £4.90; EX 24.70 Trifecta £220.60.
**Owner** Mrs Susan E Mason **Bred** A C M Spalding **Trained** Sheriff Hutton, N Yorks

**FOCUS**
Division two of a very ordinary handicap. The gallop was reasonable (first two clear) but those held up were at a disadvantage. Sound form for the grade, with the runner-up a good benchmark.

## 4071 RACING AGAIN NEXT WEDNESDAY 16TH JULY H'CAP 5f 212y
**5:30** (5:30) (Class 5) (0-75,74) 3-Y-O **£2,911** (£866; £432; £216) **Stalls** Low

Form RPR
-032 **1** **Makin The Rules (IRE)**[17] 3503 3-9-7 74................................ PhillipMakin 2 79
(John Quinn) *mde all: rdn over 1f out: kpt on wl* **10/11**[1]
3063 **2** 3 **Another Royal**[19] 3440 3-8-2 55................................(b) DuranFentiman 6 51
(Tim Easterby) *midfield: rdn and hdwy to chse wnr over 1f out: kpt on but a comf hld* **5/1**[2]
2130 **3** 3¼ **Raise A Billion**[18] 3487 3-8-2 55 oh3................................ PatrickMathers 3 41
(Alan Berry) *hld up: rdn and sme hdwy 2f out: kpt on fnl f: nvr threatened* **9/1**
3606 **4** nk **Princess Rose**[14] 3564 3-8-2 58................................(b) JoeyHaynes(3) 4 46+
(John Weymes) *dwlt: hld up: rdn over 2f out: kpt on ins fnl f: nvr threatened* **10/1**
0060 **5** ½ **Khalice**[11] 3704 3-9-3 70................................ GrahamLee 5 54
(James Given) *chsd ldrs: rdn over 2f out: wknd fnl f* **6/1**[3]
0603 **6** 2¼ **Classical Diva**[9] 3792 3-8-2 55 oh7................................(b) AndrewMullen 1 32
(Declan Carroll) *chsd ldrs: rdn over 2f out: wknd fnl f* **16/1**
2-40 **7** 7 **Jaeger Connoisseur (IRE)**[20] 3380 3-8-2 55 oh6......(b[1]) RaulDaSilva 7 11
(K R Burke) *chsd ldr: rdn over 2f out: wknd over 1f out* **25/1**
1m 12.9s (-0.70) **Going Correction** -0.125s/f (Firm) **7** Ran SP% **112.2**
Speed ratings (Par 100): **99,95,90,90,89 86,77**
CSF £5.49 TOTE £1.90: £1.10, £2.90; EX 6.00 Trifecta £15.30.
**Owner** C W Makin **Bred** Godfrey Moylan **Trained** Settrington, N Yorks

**FOCUS**
A fair handicap in which the market leader won with a bit in hand. The gallop seemed sound. The winner and fifth had a notable class edge and the winner had the run of things out in front.
T/Plt: £14.70 to a £1 stake. Pool: £56,646.06 - 2796.67 winning units. T/Qpdt: £11.20 to a £1 stake. Pool: £2952.99 - 193.70 winning units. AS

# 3854 KEMPTON (A.W) (R-H)
Wednesday, July 9

**OFFICIAL GOING: Standard**
Wind: Strong, half against Weather: Fine but cloudy, warm

## 4072 BETDAQ NO PREMIUM CHARGE APPRENTICE H'CAP 7f (P)
**6:20** (6:20) (Class 5) (0-70,69) 4-Y-O+ **£2,587** (£770; £384; £192) **Stalls** Low

Form RPR
0410 **1** **Secret Success**[19] 3427 4-9-12 69................................(t) LouisSteward 2 79
(Paul Cole) *mde all: set mod pce tl drew away fr 2f out: clr fnl f: rdn out* **6/4**[1]

1240 **2** 1 ¾ **Hierarch (IRE)**[19] 3427 7-9-5 **69**................(p) SophieKilloran(7) 4 74
(David Simcock) *mostly chsd wnr: shkn up and outpcd fr 2f out: kpt on fnl f: n.d* **14/1**

4202 **3** 1 **Two In The Pink (IRE)**[20] 3390 4-8-12 **62**.................. RhiainIngram(7) 5 65
(Ralph J Smith) *hld up in last trio: shkn up and prog fr 2f out: tk 3rd 1f out: styd on but unable to chal* **12/1**

0064 **4** ¾ **Masai Moon**[9] 3795 10-9-8 **68**......................(v) PatMillman(3) 11 69
(Rod Millman) *dwlt: hld up in last trio: prog and rdn over 1f out: tk 4th jst ins fnl f: kpt on but n.d* **25/1**

0061 **5** 3 **Indus Valley (IRE)**[16] 3527 7-9-0 **62**..................(b) DavidParkes(5) 6 54
(Des Donovan) *stdd s: hld up towards rr: sme prog on inner 2f out: no hdwy 1f out: fdd* **5/1[2]**

2205 **6** ¾ **George Baker (IRE)**[18] 3468 7-9-6 **68**.................. ChrisMeehan(5) 1 58
(George Baker) *trckd ldrs: shkn up over 2f out: no prog over 1f out: wknd* **7/1[3]**

0050 **7** nk **Keene's Pointe**[43] 2646 4-8-11 **61**.................. TylerSaunders(7) 10 51
(B W Hills) *chsd ldrs: urged along furiously over 2f out: wknd over 1f out* **12/1**

225 **8** ½ **Hellbender (IRE)**[22] 3339 8-9-4 **66**.................. MrAidenBlakemore(5) 9 54
(Shaun Harris) *chsd ldrs: rdn over 2f out: wknd over 1f out* **14/1**

0605 **9** 4 **Malaysian Boleh**[11] 3734 4-9-10 **67**..................(b) JackDuern 3 44
(Simon Dow) *s.s: hld up in last: brought wd bnd 3f out: no prog* **8/1**

-600 **10** 2 **Hidden Talent**[14] 3576 4-8-7 **55**.................. PaddyPilley(5) 7 27
(Steph Hollinshead) *chsd ldng pair tl wknd qckly over 2f out* **100/1**

1m 27.3s (1.30) **Going Correction** +0.125s/f (Slow) **10** Ran SP% **113.8**
Speed ratings (Par 103): **97,95,93,93,89 88,88,87,83,80**
CSF £24.61 CT £186.46 TOTE £3.00: £2.00, £2.40, £2.30; EX 24.20 Trifecta £169.40.
**Owner** P F I Cole Ltd **Bred** Ray Bailey **Trained** Whatcombe, Oxon

**FOCUS**
A modest handicap for apprentice riders, run at an even tempo and they came predominantly up the centre of the track, with the first four drawing a little way clear. Very few got into it. The runner-up, who is consistent but hard to win with, helps set the level, along wth the third and fourth.

## 4073 BYRNE GROUP SUPPORTING IRISH NIGHT H'CAP 1m (P)
**6:50** (6:52) (Class 6) (0-65,65) 3-Y-0+ **£1,940** (£577; £288; £144) **Stalls** Low

Form RPR

0404 **1** **Aomen Rock**[28] 3123 4-9-7 **65**..................(v[1]) DaneO'Neill 13 78+
(James Fanshawe) *hld up in midfield: shkn up and prog on outer 2f out: led jst over 1f out: pushed clr: comf* **6/1[2]**

3-00 **2** 2 ½ **Galatian**[25] 3227 7-9-0 **65**.................. PatMillman(7) 1 72
(Rod Millman) *dwlt: sn rcvrd into midfield: rdn 2f out: prog on outer to take 2nd last 100yds: styd on but no ch w wnr* **15/2**

0164 **3** 2 **My Manekineko**[9] 3805 5-9-5 **63**.................. DavidProbert 6 65
(J R Jenkins) *t.k.h: trckd ldr after 2f: led 2f out: hdd jst over 1f out: sn btn but hld on for 3rd* **16/1**

-006 **4** nk **Woolston Ferry (IRE)**[22] 3327 8-9-2 **60**.................. FergusSweeney 8 61
(Henry Candy) *trckd ldrs: rdn and tried to chal over 1f out: one pce after* **12/1**

0106 **5** ½ **Shahrazad (IRE)**[14] 3577 5-8-11 **62**..................(t) JackGilligan(7) 3 62
(Patrick Gilligan) *stdd after s: hld up towards rr: shoved along vigorously 2f out: styd on fnl f: nvr really involved* **12/1**

3336 **6** shd **Pick A Little**[14] 3562 6-9-3 **64**.................. RyanClark(3) 4 64
(Michael Blake) *led 1f: styd prom: rdn over 2f out: tried to chal over 1f out: fdd fnl f* **14/1**

0250 **7** shd **Princess Spirit**[6] 3890 5-9-2 **60**..................(p) AdamBeschizza 12 59
(Edward Creighton) *trckd ldrs on outer: rdn over 2f out: stl cl up jst over 1f out: fdd* **20/1**

4400 **8** 1 **Dimitar (USA)**[42] 2669 5-9-7 **65**.................. LiamKeniry 11 62
(Johnny Farrelly) *hld up in midfield: plenty to do whn rdn on outer 2f out: no great prog over 1f out* **7/2[1]**

065 **9** hd **Royal College**[25] 3229 4-9-7 **65**.................. GeorgeBaker 5 62
(Gary Moore) *led after 1f to 2f out: wknd jst over 1f out* **10/1**

4515 **10** ¾ **Carrera**[14] 3562 4-9-2 **60**.................. MartinHarley 9 55
(Michael Blanshard) *pushed along at various times towards rr: no prog fnl 2f* **13/2[3]**

1000 **11** ½ **Spirit Of Gondree (IRE)**[14] 3562 6-9-6 **64**..................(b) AdamKirby 7 58
(Milton Bradley) *stdd s: hld up in last quartet: jst pushed along fr 2f out: no prog and nvr remotely involved* **16/1**

10 **12** ½ **Alhaban (IRE)**[25] 3209 8-9-2 **60**..................(p) LukeMorris 2 53
(Ronald Harris) *trckd ldrs: rdn 2f out: steadily wknd on inner* **25/1**

1506 **13** 1 ¼ **Tijuca (IRE)**[16] 3540 5-9-5 **63**.................. OisinMurphy 10 53
(Ed de Giles) *s.s: hld up in last pair: shkn up over 2f out: no prog* **14/1**

2116 **14** 7 **Pipers Piping (IRE)**[111] 1036 8-9-1 **62**.................. RossAtkinson(3) 14 36
(Mandy Rowland) *broke w ldrs but heavily restrained and sn in last: rdn and no prog over 2f out: wknd* **33/1**

1m 40.04s (0.24) **Going Correction** +0.125s/f (Slow) **14** Ran SP% **122.7**
Speed ratings (Par 101): **103,100,98,98,97 97,97,96,96,95 95,94,93,86**
CSF £50.42 CT £719.01 TOTE £7.20: £3.10, £2.40, £6.50; EX 57.70 Trifecta £1441.70 Part won..
**Owner** Dragon Gate **Bred** Meon Valley Stud **Trained** Newmarket, Suffolk
■ Stewards' Enquiry : Ryan Clark two-day ban: used whip above permitted level (Jul 23-24)

**FOCUS**
A modest handicap, the pace was solid and again the main protagonists came up the centre. The third has been rated close to the balance of his recent best.

## 4074 BETDAQ £25 NO LOSE FREE BET H'CAP (LONDON MILE SERIES QUALIFIER) (BOBIS RACE) 1m (P)
**7:20** (7:20) (Class 4) (0-80,80) 3-Y-0 **£4,690** (£1,395; £697; £348) **Stalls** Low

Form RPR

1-16 **1** **Brown Eyed Honey**[55] 2277 3-8-13 **77**.................. NathanAlison(5) 9 87
(William Haggas) *trckd ldrs: prog over 2f out: led wl over 1f out: rdn and styd on wl after* **12/1**

2234 **2** 2 ¼ **Plucky Dip**[12] 3670 3-7-9 **61**.................. JoeDoyle(7) 10 66
(John Ryan) *chsd ldrs on outer: rdn over 2f out: prog to chse ldr over 1f out: styd on but nvr gng pce to chal* **25/1**

5532 **3** 1 ¼ **Hedge End (IRE)**[19] 3421 3-9-2 **80**.................. CamHardie(5) 1 82
(Richard Hannon) *wl in rr early: prog on inner fr 3f out: drvn to go 3rd jst over 1f out: kpt on but nvr able to chal* **10/1**

5106 **4** ¾ **Ice Slice (IRE)**[19] 3428 3-9-6 **79**.................. LukeMorris 5 79
(James Eustace) *settled in midfield: rdn over 2f out: prog over 1f out: tk 4th fnl f and styd on: nt pce to threaten* **20/1**

-423 **5** ½ **Gilbey's Mate**[24] 3273 3-9-7 **80**..................(p) WilliamBuick 7 79+
(John Gosden) *sn in last trio: swtchd lft over 2f out and drvn: prog over 1f out: styd on but no ch of threatening* **7/2[1]**

-210 **6** 4 **Bowie Boy (IRE)**[34] 2921 3-9-7 **80**.................. JimCrowley 13 70
(Ralph Beckett) *racd on outer: sme prog fr rr 1/2-way: rdn over 2f out: tried to cl over 1f out but n.d: wknd ins fnl f* **9/1**

0-60 **7** ½ **Footsieonehundred (IRE)**[11] 3712 3-8-2 **64** oh3 ow3(t) SimonPearce(3) 14 53
(Patrick Gilligan) *gd spd fr wdst draw to dispute ld: led briefly 2f out: wknd fnl f* **66/1**

-042 **8** ¾ **Cornish Path**[26] 3198 3-9-2 **75**.................. DaneO'Neill 8 62
(Henry Candy) *towards rr: nt clr run briefly over 2f out: tried to make prog over 1f out but sn no hdwy* **7/1[3]**

-016 **9** ¾ **Zman Awal (IRE)**[28] 3117 3-9-2 **75**.................. TomQueally 3 60
(James Fanshawe) *trckd ldrs on inner: rdn over 2f out: wknd over 1f out* **6/1[2]**

0-50 **10** nk **Crafty Exit**[32] 2996 3-8-11 **70**.................. MartinHarley 12 55
(William Knight) *hld up in last quartet: pushed along over 2f out: one reminder wl over 1f out: kpt on steadily fnl f: nvr involved* **20/1**

2646 **11** 3 **Instant Attraction (IRE)**[24] 3273 3-9-7 **80**.................. RussKennemore 4 58
(Jedd O'Keeffe) *disp ld to 2f out: wknd qckly over 1f out* **14/1**

0106 **12** 1 ¼ **Zambeasy**[16] 3516 3-8-11 **70**.................. LiamKeniry 2 45
(Philip Hide) *tk fierce hold: trckd ldrs: wknd 2f out: eased fnl f* **14/1**

24-4 **13** hd **Be Seeing You**[58] 2222 3-9-0 **73**.................. PatDobbs 6 48
(Roger Charlton) *mostly in last pair: rdn fr 1/2-way: no prog* **15/2**

24-0 **14** 15 **Applejack Lad**[18] 3480 3-8-8 **74**..................(t) JordonMcMurray(7) 11 14
(John Ryan) *prom to 1/2-way: rn v wd bnd 3f out and sn bhd: t.o* **25/1**

1m 38.58s (-1.22) **Going Correction** +0.125s/f (Slow) **14** Ran SP% **119.6**
Speed ratings (Par 102): **111,108,107,106,106 102,101,101,100,99 96,95,95,80**
CSF £290.20 CT £3187.87 TOTE £11.10: £4.10, £5.00, £2.70; EX 350.00 Trifecta £1654.80 Part won..
**Owner** M S Bloodstock Ltd **Bred** Mike Smith **Trained** Newmarket, Suffolk

**FOCUS**
They again came up the centre of the track for this fair 3yo handicap, just as they had done in the two previous events. The pace was reasonable. The runner-up has been rated a minor improver.

## 4075 IRISH CHAMPIONS WEEKEND EBF MAIDEN FILLIES' STKS (BOBIS RACE) 6f (P)
**7:50** (7:51) (Class 5) 2-Y-0 **£2,911** (£866; £432; £216) **Stalls** Low

Form RPR

2 **1** **Abaq**[15] 3558 2-9-0 0.................. PaulHanagan 5 78+
(Richard Hannon) *trckd ldng trio: clsd 2f out: shkn up to ld jst over 1f out: rdn clr fnl f* **4/6[1]**

5 **2** 2 ¼ **Simple Elegance (USA)**[12] 3648 2-9-0 0.................. WilliamBuick 7 71
(Charlie Appleby) *trckd ldr: led jst over 2f out: shkn up and hdd jst over 1f out: styd on same pce* **4/1[2]**

**3** nk **Impressive Victory (USA)** 2-9-0 0.................. DaneO'Neill 2 70
(Saeed bin Suroor) *trckd ldng pair: rdn to chal over 1f out: hanging rt and kpt on same pce* **9/2[3]**

5 **4** 1 **Rosie Royale (IRE)**[15] 3557 2-9-0 0.................. JamesDoyle 3 67
(Roger Teal) *led: shkn up and hdd jst over 2f out: styd wl in tch: one pce fnl f* **14/1**

**5** 3 ½ **Honey Required** 2-9-0 0.................. LiamJones 6 57+
(William Haggas) *rn green in rr and pushed along: kpt on to take 5th over 1f out: n.d* **20/1**

**6** ¾ **Natural Charm (IRE)** 2-9-0 0.................. TomQueally 9 55+
(Roger Varian) *s.i.s: rn green and urged along in last pair early: pushed along and kpt on steadily fnl 2f* **16/1**

**7** 1 ½ **Camdora (IRE)** 2-9-0 0.................. AdamKirby 1 50
(Jamie Osborne) *a towards rr: lft bhd over 2f out: no prog after* **33/1**

60 **8** 1 ½ **Weardiditallgorong**[12] 3671 2-9-0 0.................. DavidProbert 4 46
(Des Donovan) *chsd ldng quartet: outpcd wl over 2f out: wknd over 1f out* **100/1**

**9** nk **Freedom Rose (IRE)** 2-9-0 0.................. FrannyNorton 8 45
(Derek Shaw) *wnt lft s: rn green in last pair: pushed along and struggling sn after 1/2-way* **100/1**

1m 15.15s (2.05) **Going Correction** +0.125s/f (Slow) **9** Ran SP% **120.4**
Speed ratings (Par 91): **91,88,87,86,81 80,78,76,76**
CSF £3.81 TOTE £1.70: £1.10, £1.20, £1.70; EX 4.50 Trifecta £7.60.
**Owner** Hamdan Al Maktoum **Bred** Shadwell Estate Company Limited **Trained** East Everleigh, Wilts

**FOCUS**
Some well-bred 2yo fillies on show but they went no great pace early and, although the form should stack up, there did not appear to be a lot of strength in depth. The level is fluid but the fourth may anchor the form longer term.

## 4076 BYRNE GROUP H'CAP 2m (P)
**8:20** (8:20) (Class 5) (0-75,73) 4-Y-0+ **£2,587** (£770; £384; £192) **Stalls** Low

Form RPR

5466 **1** **Albonny (IRE)**[40] 2739 5-9-1 **67**.................. LukeMorris 6 76
(Timothy Jarvis) *trckd ldr: led wl over 2f out: drvn for home wl over 1f out and sn clr: unchal after* **7/2[2]**

3-22 **2** 2 ¼ **Dumbfounded (FR)**[13] 3632 6-8-10 **67**.................. CamHardie(5) 9 74
(Lady Herries) *trckd ldrs: impeded by rival pulling up 1/2-way and dropped to last pair: shkn up and prog 2f out but wnr already gone: r.o to take 2nd ins fnl f: no ch to chal* **11/4[1]**

5556 **3** 2 ½ **Poitin**[29] 3078 4-9-4 **70**.................. RichardKingscote 5 73
(Harry Dunlop) *trckd ldrs: chsd wnr over 2f out: sn rdn and outpcd: one pce after and lost 2nd ins fnl f* **8/1**

/05- **4** ½ **Reggie Perrin**[45] 4754 6-8-2 **61**..................(vt) SophieRalston(7) 1 64
(Pat Phelan) *pushed along early in last pair: urged along over 3f out: kpt on fnl 2f: nrst fin* **25/1**

0116 **5** ½ **Arashi**[27] 3151 8-9-5 **71**..................(v) TomQueally 2 73
(Derek Shaw) *hld up in tch: prog 3f out: disp 2nd briefly over 2f out: sn rdn and no rspnse* **5/1[3]**

-023 **6** 2 **Jezza**[7] 3851 8-9-0 **66**..................(bt) JamieSpencer 4 66
(Karen George) *squeezed out s: in tch in rr: drvn and tried to make prog over 2f out: one pce after* **5/1[3]**

421- **7** 27 **Goldan Jess (IRE)**[317] 5267 10-9-1 **67**.................. RussKennemore 3 34
(Philip Kirby) *led to wl over 2f out: wknd rapidly: t.o* **12/1**

6-10 **8** 5 **Markami (FR)**[34] 2920 4-9-5 **71**..................(t) LiamKeniry 8 32
(Johnny Farrelly) *hld up in tch: prog 6f out: rdn in 3rd 3f out: wknd rapidly: t.o* **10/1**

200- **P** **Kent Ragstone (USA)**[240] 7840 5-9-7 **73**.................. AdamKirby 7
(Murty McGrath) *prom tl p.u 1/2-way* **28/1**

3m 30.29s (0.19) **Going Correction** +0.125s/f (Slow) **9** Ran SP% **117.4**
Speed ratings (Par 103): **104,102,101,101,101 100,86,84,**
CSF £13.84 CT £71.84 TOTE £4.20: £1.90, £1.30, £2.60; EX 15.70 Trifecta £112.70.
**Owner** Mohamed Alhameli & Partners **Bred** J Costello **Trained** Twyford, Bucks


The Form Book, Raceform Ltd, Newbury, RG14 5SJ

**FOCUS**
A fair staying handicap and the pace was genuine enough. The winner has been rated close to his best.

## 4077 CASH OUT ON THE BETDAQ APP H'CAP (LONDON MIDDLE DISTANCE SERIES QUALIFIER) 1m 3f (P)
8:50 (8:51) (Class 4) (0-80,85) 3-Y-0+ £4,690 (£1,395; £697; £348) Stalls Low

Form RPR

1556 **1** **Emulating (IRE)**[21] 3371 4-9-7 **72**........ FrederikTylicki 4 83
(James Fanshawe) *trckd ldng trio: rdn over 2f out: clsd over 1f out to ld jst ins fnl f: cajoled along and hld on wl* **8/1**

-235 **2** ¾ **Artful Rogue (IRE)**[26] 3183 3-8-10 **73**........ JimCrowley 3 83
(Amanda Perrett) *trckd ldng pair: wnt 2nd over 2f out: drvn to chal over 1f out: chsd wnr ins fnl f and styd on: a hld* **9/2**[1]

3-50 **3** ¾ **Tacticus (USA)**[53] 2334 3-8-9 **72**........(v[1]) MartinHarley 10 81
(Lady Cecil) *led: didn't a r smoothly: stepped up the pce over 3f out: hrd pressed fr 2f out: hdd jst ins fnl f: styd on* **9/2**[1]

2-05 **4** 6 **Little Buxted (USA)**[18] 3472 4-9-8 **73**........ TomQueally 11 72
(Robert Mills) *hld up in midfield: rdn and outpcd over 3f out: n.d after: kpt on to take modest 4th ins fnl f* **10/1**

2210 **5** ¾ **Bobby Benton (IRE)**[26] 3197 3-8-10 **73**........[1] LukeMorris 7 71
(Luke Dace) *t.k.h: trckd ldng trio: pushed along over 3f out: steadily wknd fnl 2f* **8/1**

022 **6** ½ **Gang Warfare**[22] 3332 3-8-11 **74**........ JamieSpencer 9 73+
(Olly Stevens) *hld up in last trio: in trble once kick for home sed over 3f out: drvn and prog over 2f out but nowhere nr ldrs: no hdwy after* **5/1**[2]

00-0 **7** 2 **Cousin Khee**[14] 3574 7-10-0 **79**........ WilliamBuick 12 73
(Hughie Morrison) *sn trckd ldr: rdn to chal 3f out: wknd qckly jst over 2f out* **13/2**[3]

1112 **8** 1¼ **Thecornishcowboy**[4] 3977 5-9-13 **85** 6ex........(t) JoeDoyle(7) 1 77
(John Ryan) *hld up in midfield: in trble once kick for home sed over 3f out: no imp on ldrs 2f out: wknd* **5/1**[2]

/006 **9** 1 **Aviator (GER)**[32] 2981 6-9-13 **78**........(b) PaddyAspell 2 68
(James Eustace) *dwlt: hld up in last: no ch once sprint sed over 3f out: pushed along and no prog* **33/1**

-530 **10** *shd* **Hurricane Harry**[31] 3031 3-8-0 **68**........ CamHardie(5) 8 58
(William Knight) *hld up in rr: outpcd and rdn over 3f out: no prog after* **25/1**

4553 **11** 32 **Wildomar**[95] 1317 5-9-1 **66**........ ChrisCatlin 5
(Peter Hiatt) *a towards rr: wknd qckly over 2f out: t.o* **33/1**

2m 21.87s (-0.03) **Going Correction** +0.125s/f (Slow)
**WFA** 3 from 4yo+ 12lb **11 Ran SP% 124.1**
Speed ratings (Par 105): **105,104,103,99,99 98,97,96,95,95 72**
CSF £45.70 CT £187.35 TOTE £8.10: £2.60, £2.40, £2.40; EX 49.60 Trifecta £346.00.

**Owner** Ben CM Wong **Bred** Mrs E J O'Grady **Trained** Newmarket, Suffolk

**FOCUS**
It paid to be up with the pace and the front three drew clear in this useful handicap in which few got involved. The second and third have been rated as minor improvers.

## 4078 BETDAQ - THE SPORTS BETTING EXCHANGE H'CAP 6f (P)
9:20 (9:20) (Class 4) (0-80,80) 3-Y-0+ £4,690 (£1,395; £697; £348) Stalls Low

Form RPR

616 **1** **Role Player**[28] 3122 4-9-12 **80**........ TomQueally 11 90
(Michael Bell) *trckd ldrs on outer: rdn and clsd fr 2f out: led 1f out: drvn and r.o wl* **14/1**

260 **2** 1¾ **Vincentti (IRE)**[33] 2945 4-9-10 **78**........[1] AdamKirby 7 83
(Ronald Harris) *pressed ldr: rdn to ld 2f out: hdd 1f out: kpt on wl to hold on for 2nd but no ch w wnr* **12/1**

0-03 **3** *shd* **Dutch Interior**[9] 3783 3-9-4 **78**........ WilliamBuick 2 82
(Gary Moore) *trckd ldng pair: rdn to chal and upsides over 1f out: kpt on fnl f but no threat to wnr* **9/2**[2]

3213 **4** *hd* **Athletic**[64] 2059 5-9-5 **73**........(v) JimCrowley 9 77
(Andrew Reid) *hld up but sn in midfield on inner: effrt and swtchd lft wl over 1f out: drvn and styd on fnl f: clsd on plcd horses nr fin* **17/2**

3363 **5** 1¼ **Secret Missile**[15] 3551 4-9-11 **79**........(b) GeorgeBaker 8 79
(William Muir) *stdd s: hld up in last pair: stl there 2f out: pushed along and prog over 1f out: rdn and styd on fnl f: no ch* **16/1**

3131 **6** ½ **Spellmaker**[25] 3213 5-9-3 **74**........ MichaelJMMurphy(3) 4 73
(Tony Newcombe) *chsd ldrs: one of first to be rdn over 2f out: nvr able to threaten but kpt on fr over 1f out* **7/1**[3]

2104 **7** ½ **Sweet Talking Guy (IRE)**[13] 3630 4-8-12 **69**........(t) SimonPearce(3) 6 66
(Lydia Pearce) *hld up towards rr: pushed along and stl wl in rr 2f out: rdn and one pce fnl f: no ch* **9/1**

0001 **8** 1¾ **Almanack**[7] 3854 4-8-8 **67**........ NathanAlison(5) 1 59
(Ian Williams) *hld up in last pair: tried to make prog on inner fr 2f out: nvr gng pce to pose a threat* **4/1**[1]

4-21 **9** ½ **Amber Isle (USA)**[18] 3469 3-9-4 **78**........(be) JamesDoyle 3 68
(Roger Charlton) *led: rdn and hdd 2f out: wknd jst over 1f out* **9/2**[2]

6004 **10** *hd* **Novellen Lad (IRE)**[34] 2919 9-9-11 **79**........ ChrisCatlin 10 69
(Willie Musson) *settled in rr: c wd in st: pushed along and nvr any prog* **20/1**

423 **11** 1 **Angel Way (IRE)**[18] 3462 5-9-6 **74**........ PatDobbs 5 61
(Mike Murphy) *trckd ldrs: pushed along over 2f out: steadily lost pl* **14/1**

1m 12.96s (-0.14) **Going Correction** +0.125s/f (Slow)
**WFA** 3 from 4yo+ 6lb **11 Ran SP% 121.1**
Speed ratings (Par 105): **105,102,102,102,100 99,99,96,96,96 94**
CSF £175.88 CT £902.78 TOTE £16.90: £3.90, £3.50, £2.20; EX 189.30 Trifecta £1244.00 Part won..

**Owner** Sheikh Marwan Al Maktoum **Bred** Darley **Trained** Newmarket, Suffolk

**FOCUS**
A competitive sprint handicap and fair form. The runner-up and third help set the level.

T/Jkpt: Not won. T/Plt: £175.70 to a £1 stake. Pool: £79,033.45 - 328.20 winning units. T/Qpdt: £32.80 to a £1 stake. Pool: £6743.64 - 152.05 winning units. JN

# 4049 LINGFIELD (L-H)
Wednesday, July 9

**OFFICIAL GOING: Standard**
Wind: light, half against Weather: dry, bright spells

## 4079 OILFIELD OFFSHORE UNDERWRITING LTD MAIDEN AUCTION STKS 6f 1y(P)
2:20 (2:21) (Class 5) 2-Y-0 £2,587 (£770; £384; £192) Stalls Low

Form RPR

220 **1** **Commander Patten (IRE)**[22] 3322 2-9-3 0........ AdamKirby 7 83+
(Alan Bailey) *mde all: rdn and qcknd clr ent fnl 2f: in command after: rdn out mainly hands and heels* **30/100**[1]

030 **2** 2¼ **York Express**[19] 3415 2-8-12 0........ TomQueally 3 71+
(Ismail Mohammed) *hld up in tch in midfield: effrt and rdn to chse wnr 2f out: kpt on for clr 2nd: no imp on wnr* **4/1**[2]

03 **3** 5 **Fast Scat (USA)**[15] 3550 2-8-9 0........ JimCrowley 6 50+
(David Evans) *awkward leaving stalls and s.i.s: rcvrd to chse wnr after 1f: 3rd and outpcd u.p 2f out: wknd over 1f out* **7/1**[3]

00 **4** ¾ **Gavarnie Encore**[29] 3082 2-8-11 0........ MartinHarley 5 50
(Michael Blanshard) *chsd ldrs: 4th and outpcd u.p over 2f out: n.d fnl 2f* **16/1**

**5** *nk* **Mywayalways (IRE)** 2-9-0 0........ DavidProbert 8 52
(David Evans) *s.i.s: hld up in last trio: rdn and effrt over 2f out: 5th and wl hld over 1f out* **12/1**

00 **6** 1½ **El Campeon**[44] 2622 2-8-12 0........ JackDuern(5) 2 51
(Simon Dow) *hld up in last trio: n.d* **50/1**

0 **7** 7 **Bonita Brown Eyes (IRE)**[23] 3311 2-8-9 0........ SteveDrowne 4 22
(J S Moore) *chsd ldrs: rdn and lost pl over 2f out: bhd over 1f out* **25/1**

**8** 8 **Misu Pete** 2-8-11 0........ LiamKeniry 1
(Mark Usher) *s.i.s: pushed along thrght and a detached in last* **20/1**

1m 12.28s (0.38) **Going Correction** -0.05s/f (Stan) **8 Ran SP% 133.6**
Speed ratings (Par 94): **95,92,85,84,83 81,72,61**
CSF £2.76 TOTE £1.20: £1.02, £1.30, £1.60; EX 2.90 Trifecta £8.20.

**Owner** John Stocker **Bred** Forenaghts Stud & Dermot Cantillon **Trained** Newmarket, Suffolk

**FOCUS**
The winner set a decent enough standard in what looks straightforward form to rate.

## 4080 32RED (S) STKS 1m 2f (P)
2:50 (2:50) (Class 6) 3-Y-0+ £1,940 (£577; £288; £144) Stalls Low

Form RPR

3500 **1** **Well Painted (IRE)**[11] 3718 5-9-6 **81**........(bt[1]) AdamKirby 7 82
(William Haggas) *chsd clr ldr but stl wl clr of field: rdn and clsd qckly to ld over 2f out: sn clr and rdn: in n.d after: eased towards fin* **6/4**[1]

00-1 **2** 4½ **Investissement**[16] 3521 8-9-12 **82**........(p) StevieDonohoe 1 78
(Lee Carter) *racd off the pce in 3rd: rdn but stl plenty to do over 2f out: chsd clr wnr over 1f out: kpt on but nvr a threat* **4/1**[2]

3013 **3** *nk* **Prince Of Burma (IRE)**[4] 3971 6-9-9 **72**........(b) RichardEvans(3) 9 77
(David Evans) *hld up wl off the pce in rr of main gp: sme hdwy and nt clr run over 2f out: swtchd rt wl over 1f out: styd on fnl f and pressing for 2nd cl home: no threat to wnr* **5/1**[3]

064 **4** 12 **Handsome Stranger (IRE)**[25] 3224 4-9-9 **60**........(p) RobertTart(3) 2 54
(Alan Bailey) *racd off the pce in midfield: rdn over 2f out: no prog: n.d: fin 5th plcd 4th* **16/1**

-004 **5** 2¾ **Anginola (IRE)**[20] 3390 5-8-8 **51**........ CharlotteJenner(7) 10 38
(Laura Mongan) *racd off the pce in midfield: rdn and wl btn 6th over 2f out: nvr on terms: fin 6th plcd 5th* **33/1**

3260 **6** 9 **Menelik (IRE)**[43] 2646 5-9-12 **64**........(b) AmirQuinn 6 32
(Lee Carter) *led and sn wl clr: hdd over 2f out: sn btn: lost 2nd and fdd over 1f out: fin 7th plcd 6th* **40/1**

06/P **7** 14 **Petara Bay (IRE)**[18] 3453 10-9-6 **95**........ TomQueally 4
(Sophie Leech) *racd in midfield but nvr on terms w ldrs: rdn and lost pl over 3f out: t.o fnl 2f: eased ins fnl f: fin 8th plcd 7th* **7/1**

**8** 80 **Rose Of Marron (IRE)**[32] 7-9-6 0........ PaddyAspell 5
(John Upson) *v.s.a: a wl t.o: fin 9th plcd 8th* **100/1**

5302 **D** 1½ **Matraash (USA)**[19] 3438 8-9-12 **69**........(p) RichardHughes 3 72
(Daniel Mark Loughnane) *stdd s: hld up off the pce in midfield: hdwy but stl plenty to do over 2f out: kpt on fr over 1f out: no threat to wnr: fin 4th: disqualified and plcd last: rdr weighed in 1 1/2lbs light* **6/1**

2m 4.04s (-2.56) **Going Correction** -0.05s/f (Stan)
**WFA** 3 from 4yo+ 11lb **9 Ran SP% 115.7**
Speed ratings (Par 101): **108,104,104,93,91 83,72,8,102**
.The winner was bought by Lee Power Bloodstock for 9600gns. \n\x\x Prince Of Burma was claimed by Mr Claes Bjorling for £6,000.

**Owner** Options O Syndicate **Bred** Round Hill Stud **Trained** Newmarket, Suffolk

**FOCUS**
A decent seller that appears to make some sense, a fast pace set by the seventh helping in that regard.

## 4081 OILFIELD INSURANCE AGENCIES LTD FILLIES' H'CAP 1m 4f (P)
3:20 (3:20) (Class 5) (0-70,70) 3-Y-0+ £3,752 (£1,116; £557; £278) Stalls Low

Form RPR

00-4 **1** **Bella Varenna (IRE)**[12] 3653 3-8-10 **65**........ MartinHarley 1 71+
(Marco Botti) *chsd ldrs early: hld up wl in tch in midfield after: swtchd lft and effrt over 1f out: hdwy to ld ins fnl f: r.o wl* **9/2**[3]

6-45 **2** ¾ **By Jupiter**[17] 3502 3-9-1 **70**........ TomQueally 7 75+
(Michael Bell) *t.k.h early: hld up in tch in last trio: effrt u.p on outer wl over 1f out: hdwy 1f out: chsd wnr wl ins fnl f: kpt on* **3/1**[2]

0-00 **3** ¾ **Give Us A Reason**[34] 2924 4-8-13 **55**........ LukeMorris 3 59
(James Toller) *hld up in tch towards rr: rdn over 2f out: hdwy u.p to chal 1f out: no ex fnl 100yds* **25/1**

3652 **4** 1 **Isdaal**[21] 3365 7-8-8 **55**........(p) CamHardie(5) 4 57
(Kevin Morgan) *t.k.h: hld up wl in tch in midfield: effrt u.p and ev ch over 1f out: no ex and one pce fnl 150yds* **7/1**

1514 **5** 2¼ **Lily Edge**[18] 3473 5-9-5 **61**........(v) WilliamCarson 8 59
(John Bridger) *t.k.h: chsd ldrs: wnt 2nd over 2f out: rdn and ev ch over 2f out: no ex 1f out: wknd ins fnl f* **6/1**

6505 **6** ½ **Storm (IRE)**[14] 3582 4-9-9 **65**........ GeorgeBaker 2 63
(Charles Hills) *t.k.h: led for 2f: chsd ldrs after: effrt to chal on inner over 1f out: led 1f out: sn hdd & wknd ins fnl f* **9/4**[1]

6-04 **7** 1 **Grand Liaison**[44] 2610 5-9-7 **63**........ JimCrowley 9 59
(James Given) *in tch in midfield: hdwy to ld 10f out: rdn and hrd pressed over 2f out: hdd 1f out: sn wknd* **8/1**

0-00 **8** *41* **Three Choirs (IRE)**[29] 3075 4-8-3 **52** oh3.............. KieranShoemark(7) 6
(William Stone) *a in rr: rdn over 4f out: lost tch 3f out: t.o* **40/1**
2m 32.87s (-0.13) **Going Correction** -0.05s/f (Stan)
**WFA** 3 from 4yo+ 13lb **8** Ran SP% **118.1**
Speed ratings (Par 100): **98,97,97,96,94 94,93,66**
CSF £19.13 CT £306.72 TOTE £5.80: £1.70, £1.40, £6.00; EX 20.00 Trifecta £311.10.
**Owner** Promenade Bloodstock Limited **Bred** Laurence Kennedy **Trained** Newmarket, Suffolk
**FOCUS**
A messy affair. The winner travelled quite well and was less exposed than most.

## 4082 32RED CASINO H'CAP — 1m 7f 169y(P)
**3:50** (3:51) (Class 6) (0-60,59) 4-Y-0+ **£2,587** (£770; £384; £192) **Stalls** Low

Form RPR
00-3 **1** **Underwritten**[12] 3661 5-8-12 **50**..................... MartinHarley 11 64+
(Shaun Harris) *mde all: rdn and clr w runner-up ent fnl 2f: forged ahd over 1f out: in command and styd on wl fnl f* **4/1**[1]
5-00 **2** *3 3/4* **Epsom Salts**[160] 382 9-9-4 **59**..........................(p) JemmaMarshall(3) 13 66
(Pat Phelan) *hld up in tch but stuck on outer: hdwy 7f out: chsd wnr wl over 3f out: rdn and clr w wnr ent fnl 2f: no ex and btn 1f out: one pce after* **10/1**
/452 **3** *3 1/4* **Soundbyte**[14] 3579 9-9-0 **52**..........................(v) TomQueally 5 55
(John Gallagher) *s.i.s: hld up towards rr: clsd and wl in tch 5f out: hdwy over 2f out: wnt 3rd wl over 1f out: kpt on but no imp after* **7/1**
500 **4** *6* **Double Dealites**[20] 3385 4-9-7 **59**.......................... NeilCallan 8 59+
(Jamie Poulton) *hld up towards rr: clsd and wl in tch 5f out: nt clr run ent fnl 2f: bdly hmpd wl over 1f out: swtchd rt 1f out: styd on wl ins fnl f: no threat to ldrs* **7/1**
0-41 **5** *3/4* **Eastern Magic**[24] 3269 7-8-13 **56**..................... JackDuern(5) 12 51
(Andrew Hollinshead) *in tch in midfield: hdwy to press ldrs 4f out: 3rd and outpcd u.p jst over 2f out: 4th and wl hld over 1f out: plugged on* **6/1**[3]
3024 **6** *1 1/2* **Ice Apple**[33] 2942 6-8-10 **48**.......................... SamHitchcott 10 41
(John E Long) *s.i.s: in rr and niggled along: hdwy into midfield on outer 4f out: no imp and outpcd 2f out: wl hld after* **14/1**
0433 **7** *3/4* **Dr Finley (IRE)**[13] 3632 7-9-1 **56**..........................(v) SimonPearce(3) 7 53
(Lydia Pearce) *hld up towards rr: clsd and wl in tch 5f out: nt clr run on inner over 2f out: fnlly swtchd lft ins fnl f: all ch had gone: plugged on* **6/1**[3]
3001 **8** *2 3/4* **Omega Omega**[65] 2595 5-8-7 **45**..........................(bt) LukeMorris 3 34
(Liam Corcoran) *chsd ldr tl 12f out: styd chsng ldrs tl struggling u.p 3f out: wknd and wandered u.p over 1f out* **20/1**
0/0 **9** *8* **Uncle Bunge (IRE)**[28] 3115 8-8-4 **47**..........................(t) PhilipPrince(5) 2 26
(Liam Corcoran) *t.k.h: wl in tch in midfield: drvn and unable qck 2f out: bhd and eased wl ins fnl f* **50/1**
004 **10** *25* **Sycophantic (IRE)**[111] 1035 4-9-0 **52**.......................... AdamKirby 4
(Jamie Osborne) *chsd ldrs: wnt 2nd 12f out tl wl over 3f out: sn dropped out u.p and bhd 2f out: t.o and eased ins fnl f* **9/2**[2]
22-0 **P** **Mr Plod**[38] 2801 9-9-6 **58**.......................... JimCrowley 6
(Andrew Reid) *hld up in tch in midfield: rdn and unable qck ent fnl 2f: wknd over 1f out: bhd whn lost action ins fnl f: eased and p.u cl home: dismntd* **14/1**
3m 25.2s (-0.50) **Going Correction** -0.05s/f (Stan) **11** Ran SP% **120.9**
Speed ratings (Par 101): **99,97,95,92,92 91,91,89,85,73**
CSF £46.02 CT £278.55 TOTE £5.00: £1.70, £5.70, £2.60; EX 48.00 Trifecta £622.90.
**Owner** W A Robinson **Bred** W And R Barnett Ltd **Trained** Carburton, Notts
**FOCUS**
This was turned into procession by the winner, who had the run of things. He still has the ability to run to a higher mark, though.

## 4083 RACING SPECIALS AT 32REDSPORT.COM NURSERY H'CAP — 5f 6y(P)
**4:20** (4:24) (Class 5) 2-Y-0 **£3,234** (£962; £481; £240) **Stalls** High

Form RPR
410 **1** **Expensive Date**[19] 3415 2-9-7 **77**.......................... LukeMorris 5 80
(Paul Cole) *dwlt and bustled along in last pair: hdwy on outer and travelling bttr 1/2-way: rdn and effrt over 1f out: drvn to chal strly ins fnl f: r.o to ld towards fin* **6/1**[2]
10 **2** *1/2* **Secret Liaison (IRE)**[19] 3415 2-9-7 **77**.......................... NeilCallan 2 78+
(James Tate) *t.k.h: pressed ldr tl led wl over 1f out: rdn and edgd lft 1f out: drvn and hrd pressed fnl 100yds: hdd and no ex towards fin* **6/4**[1]
036 **3** *3 1/2* **Midnight Destiny (IRE)**[28] 3107 2-8-4 **60**.......................... FrannyNorton 4 48
(Derek Shaw) *chsd ldrs: racd awkwardly bnd 4f out: effrt on inner to chse ldr over 1f out: unable qck whn hmpd and lost 2nd ins fnl f: outpcd after* **20/1**
034 **4** *2 1/2* **Surrey Pink (FR)**[11] 3706 2-7-12 **59**.......................... CamHardie(5) 3 38
(William Muir) *dwlt: outpcd and bustled along in last pair: rdn and struggling ent fnl 2f: n.d after* **8/1**[3]
454 **5** *1/2* **Come Uppence**[47] 2499 2-9-5 **75**.......................... AdamKirby 1 53
(David Evans) *sn led: drifted rt bnd and hdd wl over 1f out: sn btn: wknd fnl f* **6/4**[1]
59.61s (0.81) **Going Correction** -0.05s/f (Stan) **5** Ran SP% **110.2**
Speed ratings (Par 94): **91,90,84,80,79**
CSF £15.58 TOTE £5.00: £2.20, £1.30; EX 12.50 Trifecta £64.80.
**Owner** Chris Wright,Holly Wright,Chloe Forsyth **Bred** Stratford Place Stud **Trained** Whatcombe, Oxon
■ Stewards' Enquiry : Neil Callan one-day ban: careless riding (Jul 23)
**FOCUS**
BHA ratings are estimated. They went off quickly in this nursery. The winner has been rated as running a small personal best.

## 4084 BET NOW AT 32REDSPORT.COM H'CAP (DIV I) — 1m 2f (P)
**4:50** (4:54) (Class 6) (0-60,60) 3-Y-0 **£2,587** (£770; £384; £192) **Stalls** Low

Form RPR
-406 **1** **Benoordenhout (IRE)**[41] 2694 3-8-8 **47**..........................(p) OisinMurphy 2 58
(Jonathan Portman) *sn pushed up to chse ldr: upsides ldr and clr over 2f out: rdn over 1f out: led u.p ins fnl f: styd on* **6/1**
066- **2** *1* **Leaderene**[329] 5379 3-8-11 **50**.......................... FrannyNorton 1 59
(Mark Johnston) *sn pushed up to ld: rdn and clr w wnr over 1f out: drvn and hdd ins fnl f: no ex* **7/2**[1]
6040 **3** *5* **Lifejacket (IRE)**[20] 3389 3-9-4 **57**.......................... GeorgeBaker 5 57
(Ed Dunlop) *broke wl: sn stdd and hld up in tch in midfield: rdn and effrt to chse clr ldng pair jst over 2f out: no imp: plugged on* **9/2**[3]
00-0 **4** *1* **Lingfield Lupus (IRE)**[34] 2926 3-8-7 **46** oh1.......................... LukeMorris 4 44
(John Best) *chsd ldrs: rdn over 5f out: 4th and outpcd u.p 2f out: plugged on same pce after* **33/1**
44-0 **5** *1/2* **Sleeping Venus (IRE)**[58] 2210 3-9-7 **60**..........................(p) PatCosgrave 9 57
(George Baker) *hld up in tch in last quartet: rdn and effrt on outer over 3f out: 5th and wl hld 2f out: plugged on ins fnl f* **25/1**
060 **6** *9* **Mystic Angel (IRE)**[24] 3277 3-9-1 **54**.......................... StevieDonohoe 8 34
(William Muir) *in tch in midfield: shuffled bk towards rr and drvn over 3f out: sn struggling: wl btn fnl 2f* **20/1**
000- **7** *9* **Sir Percy Blakeney**[296] 6460 3-9-0 **53**.......................... RichardHughes 7 16
(Marcus Tregoning) *hld up in tch in midfield: effrt over 2f out: sn btn: wl bhd and eased ins fnl f* **7/2**[1]
0600 **8** *3 1/4* **Spirited Silver**[10] 3754 3-8-7 **46** oh1.......................... WilliamCarson 10 3
(John Bridger) *hld up in tch in last pair: rdn 3f out: sn lost tch* **50/1**
5600 **9** *1* **Confiture**[41] 2688 3-8-13 **52**.......................... MartinHarley 11 7
(Michael Blanshard) *stuck wd and dropped to rr on bnd after 1f: rdn and hung rt 3f out: sn lost tch* **10/1**
2240 **10** *12* **Shannon Haven (IRE)**[22] 3326 3-9-3 **56**..........................(p[1]) AdamKirby 3
(Daniel Mark Loughnane) *chsd ldrs: rdn and btn wl over 2f out: no ch and hung lft over 1f out: sn eased: t.o* **4/1**[2]
2m 4.39s (-2.21) **Going Correction** -0.05s/f (Stan) **10** Ran SP% **119.5**
Speed ratings (Par 98): **106,105,101,100,100 92,85,83,82,72**
CSF £26.99 CT £105.91 TOTE £6.20: £2.10, £2.20, £2.00; EX 30.80 Trifecta £174.50.
**Owner** Prof C D Green **Bred** Prof C Green **Trained** Upper Lambourn, Berks
**FOCUS**
The pace held up quite well and the front three were the only ones to travel. The fourth has been rated to his mark.

## 4085 BET NOW AT 32REDSPORT.COM H'CAP (DIV II) — 1m 2f (P)
**5:20** (5:22) (Class 6) (0-60,60) 3-Y-0 **£2,587** (£770; £384; £192) **Stalls** Low

Form RPR
-434 **1** **King Calypso**[22] 3326 3-8-2 **46** oh1.......................... CamHardie(5) 6 50+
(Denis Coakley) *hld up in tch towards rr: nt clr run ent fnl 2f: hdwy to chse ldrs 1f out: swtchd lft ins fnl f: qcknd u.p to ld nr fin* **3/1**[2]
3103 **2** *nk* **Sandy Cove**[12] 3683 3-9-4 **57**.......................... RichardHughes 8 60
(James Eustace) *hld up in tch in last trio: n.m.r ent fnl 2f: hdwy over 1f out: r.o wl fnl f: pressing ldrs nr fin: snatched 2nd last strides* **11/4**[1]
5-00 **3** *hd* **Ede's The Business**[34] 2926 3-8-10 **52**..........................(v[1]) JemmaMarshall(3) 4 55
(Pat Phelan) *chsd ldr: upsides ldr and travelling bttr over 3f out: rdn to ld over 2f out: kpt on wl u.p tl hdd and lost 2 pls nr fin* **33/1**
0236 **4** *3/4* **Bourbon Prince**[40] 2742 3-8-13 **52**.......................... TomQueally 2 54
(Michael Bell) *t.k.h: chsd ldrs: rdn and effrt to press ldr 2f out: edgd rt and styd on same pce ins fnl f* **7/1**
655- **5** *2 1/4* **Palace Dragon (IRE)**[252] 7631 3-9-7 **60**.......................... LukeMorris 1 57
(Sir Mark Prescott Bt) *dwlt: sn in tch in midfield: hdwy to press ldrs over 2f out: 2nd and drvn 2f out: unable qck and lost 2nd jst ins fnl f: wknd fnl 100yds* **9/2**[3]
0401 **6** *1 1/2* **Eugenic**[10] 3754 3-8-11 **50**.......................... RobertHavlin 5 45
(Rod Millman) *in tch in midfield: nt clr run and shuffled bk over 2f out: rdn and sme hdwy over 1f out: no imp ins fnl f* **8/1**
600 **7** *5* **Topaling**[43] 2649 3-9-0 **53**.......................... TedDurcan 10 38
(Mark H Tompkins) *chsd ldrs: rdn and unable qck ent fnl 2f: wknd fnl f* **16/1**
600 **8** *nk* **Pindora (GER)**[19] 3432 3-8-10 **54**..........................(t) TobyAtkinson(5) 7 38
(Noel Quinlan) *dwlt: a in rr: rdn 4f out: nvr trbld ldrs* **25/1**
0500 **9** *7* **St Paul'S (IRE)**[7] 3846 3-9-1 **54**..........................(p) OisinMurphy 3 25
(David C Griffiths) *led: rdn over 3f out: hdd and lost pl over 2f out: bhd fnl f* **20/1**
0016 **10** *1 1/2* **Redlorryyellowlorry (IRE)**[8] 3819 3-8-8 **47**..........................(t) PatCosgrave 9 15
(George Baker) *in tch in last pair: rdn and hdwy u.p on outer 3f out: lost pl and wd bnd 2f out: sn wknd* **16/1**
2m 6.65s (0.05) **Going Correction** -0.05s/f (Stan) **10** Ran SP% **116.8**
Speed ratings (Par 98): **97,96,96,96,94 93,89,88,83,81**
CSF £11.40 CT £223.32 TOTE £4.30: £1.70, £1.40, £4.50; EX 10.90 Trifecta £273.30.
**Owner** Count Calypso Racing **Bred** Miss K Rausing **Trained** West Ilsley, Berks
**FOCUS**
This appeared to be steadily run. The third had a soft lead and limits the form.

## 4086 32RED ON THE APP STORE MEDIAN AUCTION MAIDEN STKS — 6f 1y(P)
**5:50** (5:52) (Class 6) 3-4-Y-0 **£2,587** (£770; £384; £192) **Stalls** Low

Form RPR
05-2 **1** **Major Jack**[51] 2384 3-9-5 75.......................... RichardHughes 5 78+
(Roger Charlton) *mde all: nudged along and readily asserted ent fnl f: v easily* **1/4**[1]
05 **2** *3 1/4* **Roly Tricks**[32] 2996 3-9-0 0.......................... HarryBentley 3 59
(Olly Stevens) *chsd ldr after 1f: rdn and pressing wnr ent fnl 2f: brushed aside by wnr ent fnl f: kpt on* **7/2**[2]
0/ **3** *6* **Lady Cooper**[600] 7738 4-9-6 0.......................... ChrisCatlin 1 42
(Willie Musson) *sn pushed along in rr: sme hdwy and battling for modest 3rd fnl 2f: no threat to ldrs but kpt on to go 3rd wl ins fnl f* **25/1**[3]
\- **4** *hd* **Black Widow** 3-9-0 0.......................... PatCosgrave 2 40
(Pat Eddery) *chsd wnr for 1f: 3rd and rdn over 3f out: no ch but battling for 3rd fnl 2f: kpt on but lost 3rd wl ins fnl f* **33/1**
1m 12.54s (0.64) **Going Correction** -0.05s/f (Stan)
**WFA** 3 from 4yo 6lb **4** Ran SP% **109.0**
Speed ratings (Par 101): **93,88,80,80**
CSF £1.47 TOTE £1.10; EX 1.30 Trifecta £3.10.
**Owner** D J Deer **Bred** D J And Mrs Deer **Trained** Beckhampton, Wilts
**FOCUS**
An uncompetitive maiden. The winner enjoyed a soft lead but is arguably value for further.
T/Plt: £20.40 to a £1 stake. Pool: £77,316.98 - 2760.48 winning units. T/Qpdt: £18.10 to a £1 stake. Pool: £3910.75 - 159.65 winning units. SP

# 3893 YARMOUTH (L-H)
Wednesday, July 9

**OFFICIAL GOING: Good to firm (7.3)**
Wind: Strong behind Weather: Overcast

## 4087 LADIES NIGHT AT GREAT YARMOUTH RACECOURSE MAIDEN AUCTION STKS — 5f 43y
**2:10** (2:12) (Class 6) 2-Y-0 **£2,328** (£693; £346; £173) **Stalls** Centre

Form RPR
4 **1** **Loumarin (IRE)**[15] 3557 2-8-8 0.......................... AndreaAtzeni 4 65+
(Martyn Meade) *mde all: racd keenly: shkn up over 1f out: r.o: comf* **10/11**[1]
06 **2** *2 1/2* **Somedaysrdiamonds**[5] 3934 2-8-8 0.......................... LiamJones 2 52
(J S Moore) *sn chsng wnr: rdn over 1f out: styd on same pce fnl f* **33/1**
5 **3** *nse* **Rockaroundtheclock (IRE)**[47] 2499 2-9-1 0.......... AshleyMorgan(3) 3 62
(Paul Cole) *pushed along early to chse ldrs: rdn over 1f out: styd on* **9/4**[2]

4 2 1/4 **Spring Loaded (IRE)** 2-9-4 0 RyanMoore 1 54+
(Paul D'Arcy) *prom: pushed along over 3f out: sn outpcd: kpt on ins fnl f*
**7/2**[3]

1m 0.9s (-1.80) **Going Correction** -0.625s/f (Hard) **4** Ran SP% **108.3**
Speed ratings (Par 92): **91,87,86,83**
CSF £19.40 TOTE £1.80; EX 14.00 Trifecta £37.10.
**Owner** Barry O'Connor **Bred** Oliver Donlon **Trained** Newmarket, Suffolk

**FOCUS**
Bottom bend dolled out 1.5m and races on Round course increased by 7m. A strong wind behind the runners in this low-grade maiden, and the jockeys reported the ground as "quick". The winner had the best pre-race form and enjoyed a soft lead.

## 4088 GUIDE DOGS FOR THE BLIND (S) STKS 1m 3f 101y
**2:40** (2:40) (Class 6) 3-4-Y-O **£1,940** (£577; £288; £144) **Stalls** Low

Form RPR
4630 **1** **Angus Glens**[8] 3818 4-9-12 66 (p) KierenFallon 5 62
(David Dennis) *s.i.s and hmpd s: sn rcvrd to ld and nudged along thrght: clr 7f out: eased towards fin* **7/4**[1]

3611 **2** 4 **Big Kenny**[19] 1257 3-9-5 66 (b) SebSanders 3 59
(Neil King) *hld up: pushed along over 4f out: hdwy u.p over 1f out: styd on to go 2nd wl ins fnl f: no ch w wnr* **10/3**[3]

-500 **3** 1 1/2 **Haleo**[8] 3814 3-8-11 68 MichaelJMMurphy(3) 1 51
(William Muir) *chsd ldrs: pushed along over 4f out: rdn to go 2nd over 2f out: styd on same pce fnl f* **2/1**[2]

036 **4** 6 **Chanceuse**[13] 3614 3-8-7 51 TomasHarrigan(7) 4 42
(Gay Kelleway) *edgd rt s: chsd wnr tl rdn over 2f out: wknd fnl f* **8/1**

00-0 **5** 1 3/4 **Escarlata Rossa**[28] 3121 3-8-2 43 JosephineGordon(7) 2 34
(J S Moore) *s.i.s: hld up: pushed along over 4f out: n.m.r ins fnl f: nvr on terms* **25/1**

2m 31.91s (3.21) **Going Correction** -0.625s/f (Hard)
**WFA** 3 from 4yo 12lb **5** Ran SP% **107.7**
Speed ratings (Par 101): **80,77,76,71,70**
CSF £7.52 TOTE £2.60: £1.20, £2.30; EX 7.80 Trifecta £17.80.The winner was bought in for 8000gns.
**Owner** Corbett Stud **Bred** Lady Bamford **Trained** Hanley Swan, Worcestershire

**FOCUS**
Three stood out on the ratings in this seller and they filled the places. Nothing solid and dubious form.

## 4089 HOLIDAYS ON THE NORFOLK BROADS MEDIAN AUCTION MAIDEN STKS 1m 3y
**3:10** (3:10) (Class 5) 3-Y-O **£2,846** (£847; £423; £211) **Stalls** Centre

Form RPR
-322 **1** **Oh Star (USA)**[12] 3653 3-9-0 77 WilliamBuick 5 88+
(John Gosden) *mde all: clr fr over 2f out: shkn up over 1f out: comf* **4/6**[1]

04 **2** 8 **Petticoat Lane**[12] 3652 3-9-0 0 LemosdeSouza 1 70
(Luca Cumani) *s.i.s: hld up: hdwy over 3f out: chsd wnr and edgd rt over 2f out: sn outpcd* **12/1**[3]

63- **3** 2 1/2 **Authorized Too**[236] 7902 3-9-5 0 RyanMoore 4 71+
(William Haggas) *trckd ldrs: wnt 2nd 1/2-way tl rdn and bmpd over 2f out: sn hung lft and no ex* **9/4**[2]

0 **4** 9 **Auf Wiedersehen**[16] 3525 3-9-5 0 FrederikTylicki 2 48
(James Fanshawe) *prom: pushed along over 3f out: wknd over 2f out* **25/1**

**5** 8 **Lady Lovelace** 3-8-11 0 MichaelJMMurphy(3) 3 25
(Ed Vaughan) *clipped heels nt long after s: sn pushed along in rr: wknd 3f out* **33/1**

5-5 **6** 20 **Tolly McGuiness**[16] 3525 3-9-0 0 ShelleyBirkett(5) 6
(Julia Feilden) *chsd wnr to 1/2-way: wknd wl over 2f out* **66/1**

1m 35.3s (-5.30) **Going Correction** -0.625s/f (Hard) **6** Ran SP% **106.7**
Speed ratings (Par 100): **101,93,90,81,73 53**
CSF £8.61 TOTE £1.20: £1.10, £3.90; EX 5.70 Trifecta £9.40.
**Owner** Al Asayl Bloodstock Ltd **Bred** Tenth Street Stables Llc **Trained** Newmarket, Suffolk

**FOCUS**
The favourite set a fair standard in this 3yo maiden and routed her rivals. The balance of the second, third and fourth, coupled with the winner's pre-race form, set the initial level.

## 4090 CONFERENCES AT GREAT YARMOUTH RACECOURSE H'CAP 1m 3y
**3:40** (3:40) (Class 5) (0-75,73) 3-Y-O+ **£2,587** (£770; £384; £192) **Stalls** Centre

Form RPR
1322 **1** **Global Leader (IRE)**[27] 3160 4-9-8 67 RyanMoore 5 76
(Paul D'Arcy) *mde all: rdn over 1f out: styd on* **11/8**[1]

5102 **2** 1 1/2 **Hot Mustard**[13] 3629 4-9-1 60 AndreaAtzeni 3 66
(Michael Bell) *racd keenly: trckd wnr tl stdd and lost pl over 6f out: hdwy over 1f out: sn rdn: styd on to go 2nd wl ins fnl f* **6/1**[3]

553 **3** 1/2 **Lilly Junior**[24] 3276 3-9-4 72 SebSanders 6 74
(William Haggas) *a.p: shkn up over 3f out: chsd wnr over 2f out: sn rdn: styd on same pce ins fnl f* **15/8**[2]

5010 **4** 11 **Patriotic (IRE)**[25] 3254 6-9-7 73 (p) JoshCrane(7) 1 52
(Chris Dwyer) *hld up: rdn and wknd over 2f out* **8/1**

00-4 **5** 13 **Boboli Gardens**[36] 2877 4-10-0 73 FrederikTylicki 4 22
(Mrs Ilka Gansera-Leveque) *chsd wnr over 6f out tl rdn over 2f out: wknd over 1f out* **16/1**

1m 35.26s (-5.34) **Going Correction** -0.625s/f (Hard)
**WFA** 3 from 4yo+ 9lb **5** Ran SP% **108.2**
Speed ratings (Par 103): **101,99,99,88,75**
CSF £9.52 TOTE £1.90: £1.20, £3.70; EX 6.80 Trifecta £12.50.
**Owner** Dr J S Kinnear **Bred** Thomas J Murphy **Trained** Newmarket, Suffolk

**FOCUS**
A tight little handicap on paper but the favourite became the fourth winner to make all. The race was run marginally faster than the preceding maiden. The second and third help set the level.

## 4091 GREENE KING FESTIVAL AT YARMOUTH RACECOURSE H'CAP 1m 1f
**4:10** (4:10) (Class 3) (0-90,90) 3-Y-O+ **£7,246** (£2,168; £1,084; £542) **Stalls** Low

Form RPR
3111 **1** **Genius Boy**[19] 3437 4-10-0 90 RyanMoore 5 98
(James Tate) *trckd ldr: rdn over 2f out: led over 1f out: styd on u.p* **2/1**[1]

-522 **2** 1 **One Pekan (IRE)**[18] 3457 4-9-6 82 (p[1]) AndreaAtzeni 2 88
(Roger Varian) *led: rdn and hdd over 1f out: styd on same pce ins fnl f* **2/1**[1]

1-34 **3** 3 3/4 **Don't Stare**[34] 2922 4-9-8 84 FrederikTylicki 6 83
(James Fanshawe) *hld up: hdwy over 2f out: sn rdn: styd on same pce fr over 1f out* **11/4**[2]

0660 **4** 9 **Life And Times (USA)**[17] 3499 6-8-9 74 MichaelJMMurphy(3) 4 55
(Mark Johnston) *s.i.s: sn chsng ldrs: rdn over 4f out: wknd over 2f out* **6/1**[3]

1m 55.62s (-0.18) **Going Correction** -0.625s/f (Hard)
**WFA** 3 from 4yo+ 10lb **4** Ran SP% **107.6**
Speed ratings (Par 107): **84,83,79,71**
CSF £6.19 TOTE £2.00; EX 4.20 Trifecta £4.40.
**Owner** Sheikh Juma Dalmook Al Maktoum **Bred** Meon Valley Stud **Trained** Newmarket, Suffolk

**FOCUS**
The feature contest and a good quality handicap despite the small field. The winner had won his previous three while the runner-up had lost his previous seven, and there was only ever going to be one winner once they hooked up. Straightforward form to rate.

## 4092 TRAFALGAR RESTAURANT AT GREAT YARMOUTH RACECOURSE FILLIES' H'CAP 1m 2f 21y
**4:40** (4:41) (Class 5) (0-70,68) 3-Y-O+ **£2,587** (£770; £384; £192) **Stalls** Low

Form RPR
00-6 **1** **Good Hope**[24] 3277 3-8-13 64 RyanMoore 4 78
(Michael Bell) *chsd ldr: pushed along over 4f out: rdn to ld over 2f out: styd on u.p* **3/1**[1]

-300 **2** 1 **Tete Orange**[14] 3567 3-7-11 51 oh2 RyanPowell(3) 1 63
(Stuart Williams) *trckd ldrs: rdn over 4f out: chsd wnr over 2f out: sn ev ch tl no ex nr fin* **25/1**

2533 **3** 5 **Bethan**[12] 3682 5-8-11 56 (p) ShelleyBirkett(5) 2 59
(Julia Feilden) *prom: rdn over 3f out: styd on same pce fr over 1f out* **15/2**

-546 **4** 1/2 **Alphabetique**[27] 3154 3-8-10 68 JordanNason(7) 7 70
(Peter Chapple-Hyam) *hld up: hdwy over 4f out: rdn over 2f out: styd on same pce fr over 1f out* **9/2**[3]

3043 **5** 4 **Ana Shababiya (IRE)**[29] 3080 4-9-9 68 TimClark(5) 5 62
(Ismail Mohammed) *led: clr 6f out tl rdn and hdd over 2f out: wknd fnl f* **7/1**

-033 **6** 6 **Ametrine (IRE)**[22] 3326 3-8-3 59 NoelGarbutt(5) 3 42
(William Jarvis) *s.i.s: rdn over 3f out: wknd over 2f out* **4/1**[2]

04 **7** 6 **Trikala (IRE)**[13] 3614 3-9-1 66 (p) AndreaAtzeni 6 37
(Marco Botti) *hld up: rdn over 3f out: hung lft and wknd over 2f out* **5/1**

4-00 **8** 24 **Ellen May**[32] 2994 4-8-13 53 ow1 SebSanders 8
(Nick Littmoden) *hld up: plld hrd: rdn over 4f out: wknd wl over 2f out* **16/1**

2m 7.31s (-3.19) **Going Correction** -0.625s/f (Hard)
**WFA** 3 from 4yo+ 11lb **8** Ran SP% **113.8**
Speed ratings (Par 100): **98,97,93,92,89 84,80,60**
CSF £76.29 CT £514.10 TOTE £3.60: £1.20, £7.50, £2.40; EX 78.10 Trifecta £577.70.
**Owner** The Queen **Bred** The Queen **Trained** Newmarket, Suffolk

**FOCUS**
An ordinary fillies' handicap but a good battle. The winner is well bred and improving, the runner-up has been rated as improving as well, and the third and fourth support the level.

## 4093 ARENARACING.CO.UK H'CAP 1m 6f 17y
**5:10** (5:10) (Class 5) (0-70,70) 4-Y-O+ **£2,587** (£770; £384; £192) **Stalls** High

Form RPR
5434 **1** **The Ducking Stool**[15] 3556 7-8-9 63 ShelleyBirkett(5) 3 72
(Julia Feilden) *chsd ldrs: wnt 2nd over 3f out: rdn to ld ins fnl f: styd on wl* **4/1**[3]

00-1 **2** 4 **Ninfea (IRE)**[11] 3710 6-8-3 57 NoelGarbutt(5) 5 61
(Neil King) *hld up: pushed along over 5f out: hdwy over 2f out: styd on to go 2nd post* **16/1**

1501 **3** nk **Royal Marskell**[13] 3617 5-9-7 70 RyanMoore 2 73
(Alison Hutchinson) *sn led: rdn over 1f out: hdd and no ex ins fnl f: lost 2nd nr fin* **13/8**[1]

5643 **4** 8 **Grayswood**[12] 3680 4-8-10 62 (p) MichaelJMMurphy(3) 1 55
(William Muir) *chsd ldrs: rdn over 4f out: wknd over 2f out* **5/1**

5251 **5** 21 **Layline (IRE)**[6] 3899 7-9-2 65 AndreaAtzeni 4 31
(Gay Kelleway) *s.i.s: hdwy to chse ldr over 12f out tl rdn over 3f out: wknd over 2f out: eased* **9/4**[2]

3m 4.49s (-3.11) **Going Correction** -0.625s/f (Hard) **5** Ran SP% **111.4**
Speed ratings (Par 103): **94,91,91,86,74**
CSF £50.18 TOTE £4.10: £2.40, £4.40; EX 35.90 Trifecta £148.50.
**Owner** Newmarket Equine Tours Racing Club **Bred** Cheveley Park Stud Ltd **Trained** Exning, Suffolk

**FOCUS**
This modest staying contest was run at an ordinary gallop until the straight. Modest form, weakened by the poor performance of the fifth.
T/Plt: £13.20 to a £1 stake. Pool: £50,629.38 - 2797.67 winning units. T/Qpdt: £6.30 to a £1 stake. Pool: £3268.82 - 379.34 winning units. CR

4094 - 4100a (Foreign Racing) - See Raceform Interactive

3813
# BATH (L-H)
Thursday, July 10

**OFFICIAL GOING: Firm (11.5)**
Wind: Quite strong across Weather: Sunny

## 4101 UNIBET H'CAP 5f 161y
**6:00** (6:02) (Class 6) (0-55,61) 3-Y-O+ **£1,940** (£577; £288; £144) **Stalls** Centre

Form RPR
0626 **1** **Molly Jones**[38] 2830 5-8-12 46 oh1 JohnFahy 4 58
(Derek Haydn Jones) *hld up towards rr: hdwy over 2f out: rdn to ld over 1f out: hung lft: kpt on wl* **5/1**[3]

3631 **2** 2 **Birdie Queen**[9] 3820 4-9-6 61 6ex HectorCrouch(7) 14 66
(Gary Moore) *in tch: nt clr run bhd ldrs fr jst over 2f out tl pushed through to chal over 1f out: kpt on but nt pce of wnr* **3/1**[1]

0533 **3** 1 3/4 **Sewn Up**[2] 4049 4-9-2 50 (p) RoystonFfrench 2 50+
(Andrew Hollinshead) *chsd ldrs: rdn whn sddle slipped over 2f out: nvr rcvrd w jockey unable to ride out ins fnl f but kpt on* **4/1**[2]

5522 **4** 2 **Go Charlie**[9] 3816 3-8-10 50 SteveDrowne 9 42
(Ronald Harris) *taken to s early: mid-div: hdwy 2f out: rdn whn nt best of runs over 1f out: kpt on but hld fnl 120yds* **10/1**

0061 **5** 1 1/2 **Outbid**[10] 3784 4-8-12 53 6ex KieranShoemark(7) 10 41
(Tony Carroll) *trckd ldrs: rdn and ev ch fr 2f out tl ent fnl f: no ex* **14/1**

0506 **6** 1 3/4 **Lady Rain**[17] 3520 5-8-7 46 oh1 JackDuern(5) 5 28
(Ronald Harris) *towards rr: hdwy over 2f out: styd on fnl f: nvr trbld ldrs* **33/1**

030 **7** 1/2 **Elite Freedom (IRE)**[5] 3966 3-8-12 55 (p) SimonPearce(3) 7 35
(Brian Baugh) *mid-div: effrt over 2f out: no ex ins fnl f* **8/1**

0306 **8** 1/2 **Back On Baileys**[13] 3679 3-8-3 46 oh1 (v) RyanPowell(3) 11 24
(John Ryan) *taken to s early: mid-div: rdn whn swtchd rt over 1f out: nvr any imp* **50/1**

-006 **9** *1 1/4* **Arch Walker (IRE)**[29] 3092 7-9-2 **50**..........(b) KieranO'Neill 6 25
(John Weymes) *taken to s early: prom: rdn w ev ch fr 2f out tl hmpd over 1f out: fdd ins fnl f* **7/1**

6026 **10** *1 1/2* **Homeboy (IRE)**[10] 3784 6-8-10 **47**..........(b) DeclanBates(3) 13 17
(David Evans) *trckd ldrs: rdn over 2f out: bmpd over 1f out: sn wknd* **18/1**

0003 **11** *6* **Jack Barker**[14] 3630 5-8-12 **46** oh1.......... SeanLevey 3
(Robin Bastiman) *led: rdn 2f out: hdd whn bdly squeezed up over 1f out: no ch after* **20/1**

000 **12** *34* **Jamie Lee's Girl**[17] 3523 3-7-13 **46** oh1..........(b1) RobHornby(7) 12
(David Flood) *s.i.s: a struggling in last: eased whn btn fnl 2f* **66/1**

1m 11.13s (-0.07) **Going Correction** -0.30s/f (Firm)
**WFA** 3 from 4yo+ 6lb **12** Ran SP% **117.5**
Speed ratings (Par 101): **95,92,90,87,85 83,82,81,80,78 70,24**
CSF £19.51 CT £67.34 TOTE £6.10: £1.90, £1.50, £1.80; EX 31.30 Trifecta £134.50.
**Owner** Mrs E M Haydn Jones **Bred** Mrs M L Parry & P M Steele-Mortimer **Trained** Efail Isaf, Rhondda C Taff

**FOCUS**
Races incorporating bottom bend increased in distance by about 25yds. Very quick conditions again on a hot, dry evening. A modest opener, but the in-form horses largely came to the fore. The winner is rated to last year's best.

## 4102 DOWNLOAD THE UNIBET PRO APP H'CAP 5f 161y
6:30 (6:30) (Class 5) (0-70,70) 3-Y-O+ £2,587 (£770; £384; £192) Stalls Centre

Form RPR

304 **1** **Ask The Guru**[44] 2645 4-9-7 **70**..........(v) LouisSteward(5) 8 77
(Michael Attwater) *mde all: sn clr w one other: rdn wl over 2f out: kpt on wl fnl f* **9/2**[2]

5631 **2** *3/4* **Clear Focus (IRE)**[15] 3564 3-8-1 **51** oh1..........(v) KieranO'Neill 9 55
(Brendan Powell) *chsd clr ldrs: rdn wl over 2f out: hdwy wl over 1f out: jockey sn dropped whip: ch ins fnl f: no ex nr fin* **11/2**[3]

-200 **3** *nk* **Bilash**[28] 3149 7-8-12 **61**..........(p) JackDuern(5) 3 65
(Andrew Hollinshead) *chsd clr ldrs: rdn wl over 2f out: kpt on to chse wnr fnl 120yds: no ex nr fin* **15/8**[1]

-065 **4** *nk* **Comptonspirit**[9] 3817 10-9-0 **63**..........(p) EoinWalsh(5) 4 66
(Brian Baugh) *squeezed up s: last and sn struggling: no imp tl r.o ent fnl f: clsng wl in 4th nr fin* **10/1**

003 **5** *2 1/4* **Spray Tan**[17] 3520 4-8-2 **53**.......... KieranShoemark(7) 2 49
(Tony Carroll) *in last trio: rdn wl over 2f out: kpt on ins fnl f but nvr threatened* **9/2**[2]

6530 **6** *1/2* **Zafraaj**[43] 2668 3-8-10 **60**..........(b) SteveDrowne 7 53
(Ronald Harris) *w wnr clr of remainder: rdn wl over 2f out: hld over 1f out: fdd fnl 120yds* **20/1**

/0-0 **7** *1 3/4* **My Meteor**[11] 3749 7-8-13 **60**.......... DeclanBates(3) 5 48
(Tony Newcombe) *in last pair: rdn wl over 2f out: nvr threatened* **7/1**

1m 11.65s (0.45) **Going Correction** -0.30s/f (Firm)
**WFA** 3 from 4yo+ 6lb **7** Ran SP% **112.9**
Speed ratings (Par 103): **92,91,90,90,87 86,84**
CSF £28.27 CT £60.58 TOTE £7.30: £3.30, £2.30; EX 20.70 Trifecta £49.40.
**Owner** Canisbay Bloodstock **Bred** Redmyre Bloodstock & Tweenhills Stud **Trained** Epsom, Surrey
■ Stewards' Enquiry : Jack Duern two-day ban: used whip above permitted level (Jul 24-25)

**FOCUS**
The two front-runners looked to set strong early fractions, but the winner ultimately clocked a time half a second slower than the 46-rated scorer in the opener. The winner is rated to his AW winter form.

## 4103 BATHWICK CAR AND VAN HIRE MAIDEN STKS 5f 11y
7:00 (7:01) (Class 5) 2-Y-O £2,587 (£770; £384; £192) Stalls Centre

Form RPR

06 **1** **Cotai Glory**[23] 3322 2-9-5 0.......... GeorgeBaker 4 93+
(Charles Hills) *wnt sltly rt leaving stalls: mde all: nudged clr over 1f out: easily* **4/11**[1]

0 **2** *3 3/4* **Biting Bullets (USA)**[23] 3322 2-9-5 0.......... SteveDrowne 3 74
(Jo Hughes) *in tch: hdwy to chse wnr wl over 1f out: sn rdn: kpt on but nt pce of easy wnr* **9/2**[2]

5 **3** *12* **Perfect Concord**[44] 2644 2-9-0 0.......... LukeMorris 6 21
(Michael Blanshard) *chsd wnr tl rdn wl over 1f out: sn one pce* **25/1**

**4** *9* **Bouncing Czech** 2-9-5 0.......... SeanLevey 5
(Amanda Perrett) *trckd ldrs: rdn 2f out: wknd ent fnl f* **5/1**[3]

0 **5** *5* **Blue Eyed Boy**[19] 3461 2-9-2 0.......... DeclanBates(3) 2
(Roy Brotherton) *chsd ldrs tl wknd 2f out* **66/1**

**6** *4* **What A Squirtle** 2-8-12 0..........[1] JordanVaughan(7) 1
(Dave Roberts) *wnt lft s: a outpcd and bhd* **33/1**

1m 1.47s (-1.03) **Going Correction** -0.30s/f (Firm) **6** Ran SP% **116.4**
Speed ratings (Par 94): **96,90,70,56,48 42**
CSF £2.67 TOTE £1.10: £1.10, £2.30; EX 3.00 Trifecta £15.20.
**Owner** Ms A A Yap & F Ma **Bred** Glebe Stud, J F Dean & Lady Trenchard **Trained** Lambourn, Berks

**FOCUS**
All very straightforward for the favourite. The first two finished miles clear.

## 4104 INJURED JOCKEYS FUND 50TH ANNIVERSARY H'CAP 1m 2f 46y
7:35 (7:35) (Class 4) (0-85,83) 3-Y-O+ £4,690 (£1,395; £697; £348) Stalls Low

Form RPR

2041 **1** **Dandy (GER)**[27] 3175 5-9-0 **77**..........(v) RobHornby(7) 4 83
(Andrew Balding) *mde virtually all: rdn over 2f out: kpt on fnl f: hld on whn strly pressed fnl 120yds* **9/2**[3]

6305 **2** *hd* **Echo Brava**[27] 3196 4-9-6 **76**.......... LukeMorris 3 81
(Luke Dace) *s.i.s: chsd ldrs: rdn wl over 2f out to dispute 2nd: str chal fnl 120yds: jst hld* **5/1**

-436 **3** *1* **Cricklewood Green (USA)**[49] 2496 3-9-2 **83**.......... SeanLevey 2 86
(Richard Hannon) *trckd ldrs: dropped to 4th and pushed along over 4f out: rdn to dispute 2nd over 2f out: edgd lft over 1f out: chal ent fnl f: no ex towards fin* **6/4**[1]

-600 **4** *1* **Croquembouche (IRE)**[15] 3574 5-9-12 **82**.......... GeorgeBaker 1 83
(Ed de Giles) *pressed wnr: pushed into ld briefly over 6f out: rdn wl over 2f out: disputing 2nd whn squeezed up over 1f out: hld fnl f* **7/4**[2]

2m 7.22s (-3.78) **Going Correction** -0.30s/f (Firm)
**WFA** 3 from 4yo+ 11lb **4** Ran SP% **111.2**
Speed ratings (Par 105): **103,102,102,101**
CSF £23.49 TOTE £4.10; EX 17.00 Trifecta £24.30.
**Owner** Robert E Tillett **Bred** Gestut Rottgen **Trained** Kingsclere, Hants

**FOCUS**
A disappointing numerical turnout for the feature, but a tightish contest on adjusted ratings. A decent pace, and the winner is better than ever.

## 4105 BATHWICK CAR AND VAN HIRE H'CAP 1m 2f 46y
8:10 (8:10) (Class 5) (0-60,60) 3-Y-O+ £1,940 (£577; £288; £144) Stalls Low

Form RPR

1103 **1** **Cataria Girl (USA)**[41] 2720 5-9-6 **59**..........(t) JordanVaughan(7) 8 69
(Marcus Tregoning) *hld up in tch: rdn and hdwy over 2f out: str chal ent fnl f: led fnl strides* **9/2**[2]

6522 **2** *shd* **If I Were A Boy (IRE)**[17] 3540 7-9-7 **60**..........(p) AlistairRawlinson(7) 5 69
(Dominic Ffrench Davis) *trckd ldrs: led wl over 2f out: sn rdn: strly chal fnl f: hdd fnl strides* **5/1**[3]

0402 **3** *2 1/4* **Greyemkay**[10] 3781 6-8-9 **46** oh1.......... LouisSteward(5) 7 51
(Richard Price) *trckd ldrs: rdn wl over 2f out: kpt on same pce fnl f* **7/1**

0303 **4** *1/2* **Delightful Sleep**[10] 3781 6-9-7 **56**.......... DeclanBates(3) 4 60
(David Evans) *hld up in tch: rdn to chse ldrs 2f out: kpt on same pce fnl f* **8/1**

6343 **5** *1* **Petersboden**[16] 3552 5-9-1 **47**.......... SteveDrowne 9 49
(Michael Blanshard) *hld up: hdwy whn nt clr run over 1f out: sn rdn: kpt on ins fnl f: nvr threatened* **10/1**

0605 **6** *2 1/2* **Kristal Hart**[26] 3208 5-9-3 **49**.......... WilliamCarson 1 46
(Neil Mulholland) *w ldr tl rdn wl over 2f out: sn hld: fdd fnl 120yds* **18/1**

-004 **7** *3/4* **Bold Cross (IRE)**[17] 3515 11-9-9 **60**.......... EoinWalsh(5) 3 56
(Edward Bevan) *hld up in tch: effrt over 2f out: nvr quite threatened: fdd fnl 120yds* **14/1**

000- **8** *7* **Soiree D'Ete**[337] 5131 3-8-12 **55**.......... LukeMorris 10 37
(Sir Mark Prescott Bt) *led: hdd wl over 2f out: sn rdn: wknd over 1f out* **15/8**[1]

2m 10.87s (-0.13) **Going Correction** -0.30s/f (Firm)
**WFA** 3 from 4yo+ 11lb **8** Ran SP% **114.3**
Speed ratings (Par 103): **98,97,96,95,94 92,92,86**
CSF £27.14 CT £154.21 TOTE £5.00: £2.00, £2.80, £1.60; EX 24.20 Trifecta £68.80.
**Owner** Mr And Mrs A E Pakenham **Bred** Shadwell Farm LLC **Trained** Whitsbury, Hants

**FOCUS**
Moderate form, with the favourite disappointing. The winner picked up on her spring progress.

## 4106 BATHWICK TYRES H'CAP 1m 3f 144y
8:40 (8:40) (Class 6) (0-65,65) 3-Y-O £1,940 (£577; £288; £144) Stalls Low

Form RPR

003 **1** **Statsminister**[15] 3568 3-9-5 **63**.......... FergusSweeney 2 68
(Luke Dace) *disp ld: rdn wl over 2f out: narrowly hdd ent fnl f: kpt on gamely to ld fnl stride* **9/1**

0-00 **2** *nse* **Secure Cloud (IRE)**[26] 3248 3-9-3 **61**.......... SteveDrowne 7 66
(B W Hills) *disp ld: rdn wl over 2f out: narrow advantage ent fnl f: kpt on: hdd fnl stride* **10/1**

4221 **3** *1 3/4* **Bishop Wulstan (IRE)**[9] 3819 3-9-2 **60** 6ex.......... SeanLevey 1 62
(Richard Hannon) *trckd ldng pair: rdn over 2f out: kpt on fnl f but nt pce to chal* **11/4**[1]

0210 **4** *1* **Passionate Affair (IRE)**[12] 3711 3-9-7 **65**..........(tp) WilliamCarson 8 65
(Jamie Osborne) *t.k.h early: in tch: rdn to chse ldrs fr over 2f out: kpt on but nt pce to get on terms* **16/1**

000- **5** *hd* **Moscato**[260] 7460 3-9-3 **61**.......... LukeMorris 3 61
(Sir Mark Prescott Bt) *trckd ldrs: rdn over 3f out: kpt on fnl f but nt pce to get on terms* **10/3**[2]

0016 **6** *3* **Graphene**[28] 3146 3-8-10 **61**.......... JordanVaughan(7) 5 56
(Rod Millman) *trckd ldrs: rdn into clly disp 3rd 2f out: fdd fnl f* **7/2**[3]

6361 **7** *6* **Roman Riches**[35] 2926 3-9-4 **62**..........(v) GeorgeBaker 4 47
(Gary Moore) *hld up bhd: rdn wl over 2f out: nvr any imp* **7/1**

2m 32.12s (1.52) **Going Correction** -0.30s/f (Firm) **7** Ran SP% **109.4**
Speed ratings (Par 98): **92,91,90,90,90 88,84**
CSF £83.19 CT £288.41 TOTE £16.70: £6.90, £5.70; EX 104.40 Trifecta £426.60.
**Owner** Mrs Charles Cyzer **Bred** C A Cyzer **Trained** Okehurst Lane, W Sussex

**FOCUS**
Just 5lb separated these on both official ratings and RPRs, but few got into it.

## 4107 BATHWICK TYRES IN BATH H'CAP 1m 5f 22y
9:10 (9:10) (Class 6) (0-60,60) 4-Y-O+ £1,940 (£577; £288; £144) Stalls High

Form RPR

2503 **1** **Scribe (IRE)**[21] 2595 6-9-3 **59**..........(bt) DeclanBates(3) 2 68
(David Evans) *trckd ldrs: rdn to ld wl over 1f out: edgd lft: styd on strly fnl f* **20/1**

3-61 **2** *2 1/2* **Lucky Diva**[10] 3780 7-8-12 **56** 6ex..........(v) RyanWhile(5) 10 61
(Bill Turner) *trckd ldrs: rdn over 2f out: chsd wnr jst over 1f out: kpt on but a being hld* **8/1**

06-2 **3** *3/4* **Edgeworth (IRE)**[17] 3521 8-8-13 **59**..........(p) JennyPowell(7) 8 63
(David Bridgwater) *led after 2f: rdn wl over 2f out: hdd wl over 1f out: styd on same pce fnl f* **7/1**[3]

0305 **4** *2 3/4* **Cabuchon (GER)**[17] 3521 7-9-7 **60**..........(t) GeorgeBaker 6 60
(David Evans) *hld up bhd: rdn and hdwy over 2f out: styd on fnl f wout ever threatening to rch ldrs* **7/2**[2]

0410 **5** *hd* **Glens Wobbly**[8] 3852 6-8-12 **54**.......... RyanTate(3) 1 54
(Jonathan Geake) *led for 1f: trckd ldrs: rdn wl over 2f out: styd on tl no ex ins fnl f* **3/1**[1]

/-00 **6** *1/2* **Agapanthus (GER)**[4] 2942 9-8-7 **46** oh1..........(b) WilliamCarson 9 45
(Neil Mulholland) *led after 1f: hdd after 2f: trckd ldr: rdn wl over 2f out: sn one pce* **33/1**

0/54 **7** *5* **Just Duchess**[26] 3209 4-8-7 **46** oh1.......... LukeMorris 5 37
(Michael Blanshard) *nvr really travelling in mid-div: drvn over 4f out: nvr threatened* **7/1**[3]

0055 **8** *1/2* **Our Golden Girl**[21] 3404 4-8-7 **46** oh1..........(b) JohnFahy 7 37
(Shaun Lycett) *trckd ldrs: rdn whn losing pl 4f out: nt a danger after* **12/1**

-560 **9** *1 1/4* **Peachez**[127] 848 6-9-0 **60**..........(p) PaulNO'Brien(7) 3 49
(Seamus Durack) *a towards rr* **15/2**

44/6 **10** *nk* **Treasury Bond**[28] 3155 7-8-7 **46** oh1.......... RoystonFfrench 4 34
(Oliver Sherwood) *mid-div: rdn 3f out: sn btn* **14/1**

2m 51.71s (-0.29) **Going Correction** -0.30s/f (Firm) **10** Ran SP% **117.2**
Speed ratings (Par 101): **98,96,96,94,94 93,90,90,89,89**
CSF £171.91 CT £1247.08 TOTE £21.80: £7.90, £3.00, £2.80; EX 140.30 Trifecta £401.90.
**Owner** Shropshire Wolves 3 **Bred** Lynch Bages Ltd & Samac Ltd **Trained** Pandy, Monmouths

**FOCUS**
A moderate finale. The winner was on a good mark on his Turf best.
T/Plt: £440.60 to a £1 stake. Pool: £72,587.61 - 120.25 winning units. T/Qpdt: £67.80 to a £1 stake. Pool: £4,722.53 - 51.50 winning units. TM

## 3914 DONCASTER (L-H)

Thursday, July 10

**OFFICIAL GOING: Good (8.8)**

Wind: Light half behind Weather: Fine and dry

### 4108 LES "BUDDY" CLARKE MEMORIAL H'CAP 7f

2:00 (2:02) (Class 5) (0-75,75) 3-Y-O+ £3,234 (£962; £481; £240) Stalls High

Form RPR

4003 1 **Red Paladin (IRE)**[19] 3485 4-9-4 **65** NeilCallan 4 76
(Kevin Ryan) *hld up towards rr: hdwy 1/2-way: chsd ldrs whn n.m.r and sltly hmpd wl over 1f out: rdn and hdwy to ld ent fnl f: drvn and kpt on wl towards fin* **11/2[1]**

4304 2 ½ **Sakhalin Star (IRE)**[14] 3618 3-9-1 **70** RobertWinston 2 77
(Richard Guest) *hld up towards rr: hdwy 3f out: effrt wl over 1f out: rdn to chal ent fnl f: sn drvn and ev ch tl no ex last 50yds* **7/1[2]**

0-05 3 3¼ **Piddie's Power**[21] 3384 7-9-11 **72** BrianHughes 6 73
(Kevin Frost) *trckd ldrs: hdwy wl over 2f out: rdn to chal over 1f out and ev ch: drvn and edgd rt jst ins fnl f: kpt on same pce* **16/1**

3-50 4 ½ **King Pin**[20] 3439 9-9-4 **65** (p) DaleSwift 5 65
(Tracy Waggott) *dwlt and in rr: hdwy wl over 2f out: sn rdn: styd on wl fnl f: nrst fin* **14/1**

-041 5 ¾ **Fever Few**[12] 3708 5-9-4 **68** AshleyMorgan(3) 12 66
(Chris Wall) *cl up: led wl over 2f out: sn rdn: drvn and hdd ent fnl f: grad wknd* **9/1[3]**

5415 6 ½ **Be Royale**[16] 3547 4-9-5 **66** AndrewMullen 15 63
(Michael Appleby) *swtchd lft s and hld up towards rr: hdwy 3f out: rdn along 2f out: swtchd rt to stands' rail and drvn ent fnl f: kpt on: nrst fin* **7/1[2]**

100 7 hd **Flexible Flyer**[17] 3533 5-10-0 **75** (t) DougieCostello 8 71
(Mark Walford) *prom: cl up 3f out: rdn along over 2f out: grad wknd appr fnl f* **18/1**

531 8 1¾ **Sleeping Apache (IRE)**[19] 3486 4-10-0 **75** DanielTudhope 1 67
(Philip Kirby) *hld up towards rr: hdwy on wd outside 3f out: chsd ldrs over 2f out: sn rdn and no imp appr fnl f* **10/1**

-326 9 nk **Clumber Place**[59] 2219 8-8-4 **58** AlexHopkinson(7) 10 49
(Shaun Harris) *led: rdn along and hdd wl over 2f out: cl up tl drvn and edgd lft wl over 1f out: sn wknd* **20/1**

14-6 10 ¾ **Dream Scenario**[23] 3339 4-9-7 **68** (v) DavidAllan 14 57
(Mel Brittain) *hld up in tch: hdwy to chse ldrs over 2f out: rdn along wl over 1f out: drvn appr fnl f: sn wknd* **16/1**

000 11 ¾ **Oak Bluffs (IRE)**[22] 3359 3-8-2 **57** (p) PatrickMathers 7 41
(Richard Fahey) *prom: rdn along 3f out: sn wknd* **9/1[3]**

2000 12 3½ **Orbit The Moon (IRE)**[19] 3483 6-9-7 **71** (tp) ConnorBeasley(3) 9 49
(Michael Dods) *cl up: rdn along 3f out: sn wknd* **9/1[3]**

4243 13 1 **Alluring Star**[15] 3575 6-8-13 **67** DanielleMooney(7) 13 42
(Michael Easterby) *chsd ldrs: rdn along 1/2-way: sn wknd* **20/1**

5-54 14 2½ **Broctune Papa Gio**[20] 3439 7-9-6 **67** TomEaves 11 36
(Keith Reveley) *chsd ldrs: rdn along 3f out: sn wknd* **16/1**

1m 25.29s (-1.01) **Going Correction** -0.175s/f (Firm)
**WFA** 3 from 4yo+ 8lb **14** Ran SP% **118.6**
Speed ratings (Par 103): **98,97,93,93,92 91,91,89,89,88 87,83,82,79**
CSF £41.19 CT £427.82 TOTE £5.60: £2.30, £3.20, £7.40; EX 39.90 Trifecta £1472.20.
**Owner** Hambleton Racing Ltd XXII **Bred** Noel O'Callaghan **Trained** Hambleton, N Yorks

**FOCUS**
Round course railed out from 10f to where it joins the straight and races of 10f and over increased by 10yds. On a bright and breezy day the ground had dried out and was officially good but reckoned a bit loose on top. The winner has been rated as running a small personal best.

### 4109 188BET BRITISH STALLION STUDS EBF MAIDEN STKS (DIV I) 6f

2:30 (2:33) (Class 5) 2-Y-O £3,234 (£962; £481; £240) Stalls High

Form RPR

1 **Punk Rocker (IRE)** 2-9-0 0 PaulMulrennan 7 70+
(Michael Dods) *dwlt: sn trcking ldrs: hdwy over 2f out: effrt to chal over 1f out: rdn ent fnl f: led last 100yds: kpt on strly* **9/1**

04 2 ½ **Pivot Point (IRE)**[14] 3626 2-9-5 0 SamanthaSpratt 12 73
(Brian Meehan) *led: pushed along over 2f out: rdn over 1f out: drvn and hdd last 100yds: kpt on wl u.p towards fin* **11/1**

3 nse **Cool Strutter (IRE)** 2-9-5 0 PatDobbs 5 73+
(Richard Hannon) *trckd ldrs: pushed along over 2f out: rdn: n.m.r and sltly outpcd wl over 1f out: sn swtchd rt and kpt on strly fnl f* **11/2[3]**

0 4 1 **Duke Of North (IRE)**[20] 3429 2-9-5 0 ShaneKelly 3 70
(James Fanshawe) *hld up in tch: hdwy on outer wl over 2f out: rdn to chse ldrs over 1f out: kpt on u.p fnl f: nrst fin* **12/1**

0 5 2½ **Olympic Charm**[15] 3578 2-9-5 0 DaleSwift 1 62
(Derek Shaw) *in tch: hdwy on outer 4f out: cl up over 2f out: rdn wl over 1f out: wknd ent fnl f* **100/1**

5 6 ¾ **Honcho (IRE)**[29] 3113 2-9-5 0 RobertHavlin 8 60
(David Elsworth) *prom: chsd ldr 4f out: rdn along over 2f out: sn drvn and wknd over 1f out* **9/2[1]**

6 7 1 **Francis Scott Key (IRE)**[15] 3584 2-9-5 0 MartinLane 11 57
(Brian Meehan) *chsd ldrs: rdn along wl over 2f out: grad wknd* **9/1**

8 ½ **Big Bear (FR)** 2-9-5 0 GrahamGibbons 2 56
(George Peckham) *dwlt and in rr: hdwy 1/2-way: rdn along and kpt on fnl 2f: n.d* **50/1**

9 ½ **Explain** 2-9-5 0 DavidProbert 4 54
(Martyn Meade) *prom: rdn along over 2f out: wknd wl over 1f out* **5/1[2]**

10 4½ **Bickershaw** 2-9-5 0 TomEaves 6 41
(Richard Fahey) *in tch: pushed along 1/2-way: sn rdn along and wknd 2f out* **9/1**

11 16 **Seraffimo** 2-9-5 0 [1] PaddyAspell 10
(Sharon Watt) *towards rr: rdn along bef 1/2-way: sn outpcd and bhd* **66/1**

1m 14.1s (0.50) **Going Correction** -0.175s/f (Firm) **11** Ran SP% **100.7**
Speed ratings (Par 94): **89,88,88,86,83 82,81,80,79,73 52**
CSF £75.43 TOTE £12.60: £3.90, £2.30, £1.50; EX 103.80 Trifecta £789.10.
**Owner** Mr & Mrs Paul Gaffney **Bred** Pat O'Donovan **Trained** Denton, Co Durham
■ Rule 4 of 15p in the pound applies to all bets; Withdrawn: Rise To Power

**FOCUS**
Previous form was thin on the ground. Ordinary in terms of bare form, with the field compressed in a slow time, but the winner did it well and can do better.

### 4110 188BET BRITISH STALLION STUDS EBF MAIDEN STKS (DIV II) 6f

3:05 (3:06) (Class 5) 2-Y-O £3,234 (£962; £481; £240) Stalls High

Form RPR

1 **Fox Trotter (IRE)** 2-9-5 0 MartinLane 6 88+
(Brian Meehan) *dwlt and swtchd lft s: sn trcking ldrs: hdwy 1/2-way: cl up 2f out: sn chal: rdn to ld ent fnl f: sn clr and styd on strly* **10/1**

2 2 2¾ **Burnt Sugar (IRE)**[40] 2777 2-9-5 0 PatDobbs 2 80
(Richard Hannon) *cl up: slt ld 2f out: sn jnd and rdn: drvn and hdd ent fnl f: kpt on: no ch w wnr* **8/13[1]**

03 3 5 **Kassbaan**[51] 2413 2-9-5 0 PaddyAspell 7 65
(Marco Botti) *chsd ldng pair: effrt and cl up 2f out: sn rdn and kpt on one pce appr fnl f* **5/1[2]**

4 2½ **Saltarello (IRE)** 2-9-5 0 PhillipMakin 11 57+
(John Quinn) *towards rr: rdn along wl over 2f out: hdwy over 1f out: swtchd rt and kpt on fnl f* **16/1**

0 5 nse **Yorkshire Dales (IRE)**[28] 3148 2-9-5 0 DavidProbert 5 57
(David Elsworth) *chsd ldrs: rdn along over 2f out: sn one pce* **6/1[3]**

0 6 ¾ **Rosie Crowe (IRE)**[59] 2200 2-9-0 0 RobertHavlin 4 50
(David C Griffiths) *in tch: rdn along and outpcd wl over 2f out: plugged on* **100/1**

06 7 1¾ **Jubilee Spirit**[8] 3842 2-9-5 0 BarryMcHugh 9 50
(Geoffrey Oldroyd) *s.i.s: a in rr* **100/1**

3 8 ¾ **Westhoughton**[49] 2472 2-9-5 0 DanielTudhope 3 47
(David O'Meara) *led: rdn along 1/2-way: hdd 2f out and sn wknd* **25/1**

9 5 **Smart Stepper (IRE)** 2-9-2 0 [1] ConnorBeasley(3) 8 32
(Michael Dods) *a towards rr: outpcd and bhd fnl 2f* **25/1**

5 10 3½ **Why No Rein (IRE)**[14] 3606 2-9-5 0 TomEaves 10 22
(Richard Fahey) *midfield: rdn along bef 1/2-way: sn outpcd and bhd* **50/1**

1m 13.23s (-0.37) **Going Correction** -0.175s/f (Firm) **10** Ran SP% **119.5**
Speed ratings (Par 94): **95,91,84,81,81 80,77,76,70,65**
CSF £16.79 TOTE £10.10: £2.60, £1.10, £1.70; EX 24.30 Trifecta £121.10.
**Owner** Mrs Sheila Tucker **Bred** Edmond Kent **Trained** Manton, Wilts

**FOCUS**
Less strength in depth in part two but a potentially very useful winner. The runner-up has been rated a bit below his debut form.

### 4111 188BET MAIDEN STKS 6f

3:40 (3:41) (Class 4) 3-Y-O+ £5,175 (£1,540; £769; £384) Stalls High

Form RPR

3- 1 **Secret Hint**[273] 7155 3-9-0 0 DavidProbert 5 85+
(Andrew Balding) *trckd ldrs: hdwy 2f out: rdn to ld ent fnl f: styd on wl* **11/2[3]**

4-3 2 1¾ **Marmoom**[102] 1192 3-9-5 0 GrahamGibbons 7 84
(Charles Hills) *sn trcking ldng pair: hdwy to chse ldr 1/2-way: rdn wl over 1f out: led briefly jst over 1f out: hdd ent fnl f: sn drvn and one pce* **10/11[1]**

22-3 3 4½ **Kommander Kirkup**[68] 1939 3-9-5 85 (b[1]) PaulMulrennan 2 70
(Michael Dods) *sn led: rdn along over 2f out: drvn and hdd appr fnl f: sn wknd* **3/1[2]**

42- 4 1¾ **Tiger Jim**[259] 7484 4-9-11 0 DanielTudhope 6 65+
(Jim Goldie) *towards rr: hdwy over 2f out: sn rdn: kpt on to take modest 4th fnl f* **20/1**

5 5 2½ **It's A Yes From Me**[22] 3370 3-9-5 0 ShaneKelly 1 56
(James Fanshawe) *chsd ldrs: rdn over 2f out: sn drvn and one pce* **40/1**

6 ½ **John Caesar (IRE)** 3-9-5 0 (t) PatDobbs 11 54+
(Jeremy Noseda) *towards rr tl sme late hdwy* **10/1**

30/ 7 hd **Two Pancakes**[753] 3182 4-9-8 0 NeilFarley(3) 3 55
(Declan Carroll) *in tch: rdn along 1/2-way: sn outpcd* **66/1**

53 8 1 **Ecliptic Sunrise**[13] 3677 3-9-0 0 StevieDonohoe 8 46
(Des Donovan) *a towards rr* **100/1**

9 16 **Tiger Heights** 3-9-5 0 TomEaves 4
(Jim Goldie) *dwlt: a in rr* **100/1**

5 10 3 **Smart Dj**[12] 3700 3-9-0 0 PaddyAspell(5) 9
(Andrew Hollinshead) *cl up: rdn along 1/2-way: sn wknd* **66/1**

11 4½ **Oriental Heights** 3-8-11 0 GaryBartley(3) 10
(Jim Goldie) *in tch: rdn along 1/2-way: sn outpcd* **66/1**

1m 11.54s (-2.06) **Going Correction** -0.175s/f (Firm)
**WFA** 3 from 4yo 6lb **11** Ran SP% **115.5**
Speed ratings (Par 105): **106,103,97,95,92 91,91,89,68,64 58**
CSF £10.45 TOTE £6.30: £1.80, £1.30, £1.10; EX 14.30 Trifecta £48.40.
**Owner** George Strawbridge **Bred** George Strawbridge **Trained** Kingsclere, Hants

**FOCUS**
A decent older horse sprint maiden. The form makes sense with the first two clear. It's been rated around the runner-up.

### 4112 188BET CASINO FILLIES' H'CAP 1m (R)

4:15 (4:16) (Class 4) (0-85,84) 3-Y-O+ £5,175 (£1,540; £769; £384) Stalls Low

Form RPR

21- 1 **Water Hole (IRE)**[216] 8176 3-9-1 **80** RobertHavlin 1 92+
(John Gosden) *trckd ldrs: hdwy 3f out: cl up 2f out: led wl over 1f out: sn rdn and styd on wl fnl f* **4/1[2]**

1-4 2 2 **History Book (IRE)**[31] 3066 4-9-10 **80** MartinLane 6 89+
(Charlie Appleby) *trckd ldng pair: effrt and n.m.r 2f out: sn swtchd rt and rdn: styd on to chse wnr ins fnl f: sn drvn and no imp* **33/1**

4214 3 nk **Starlight Serenade**[12] 3727 3-8-7 **72** DavidProbert 4 78+
(Ralph Beckett) *hld up in rr: hdwy on outer wl over 2f out: rdn wl over 1f out: styd on to chse ldng pair ins fnl f: nrst fin* **9/2[3]**

0422 4 3½ **Oddysey (IRE)**[23] 3340 5-9-10 **83** ConnorBeasley(3) 10 83
(Michael Dods) *hld up in rr: gd hdwy on outer 3f out: rdn to chse wnr over 1f out: sn drvn and wknd fnl f* **9/1**

-354 5 nk **Annawi**[18] 3502 4-9-10 **80** PatDobbs 9 80
(Henry Candy) *cl up: chal wl over 2f out: sn rdn and one pce fr over 1f out* **7/2[1]**

11 6 2¾ **Buredyma**[13] 3647 3-9-0 **79** GrahamGibbons 11 70
(William Haggas) *trckd ldrs: hdwy over 3f out: rdn along over 2f out: sn drvn and btn wl over 1f out* **7/2[1]**

20-5 7 1¾ **Monakova (IRE)**[24] 3305 4-10-0 **84** DanielTudhope 3 73
(David O'Meara) *trckd ldrs: effrt over 2f out: sn rdn and hld whn n.m.r wl over 1f out* **16/1**

3223 8 hd **Imaginary World (IRE)**[21] 3402 6-9-3 **73** (p) JasonHart 2 62
(John Balding) *hld up towards rr: hdwy on inner and in tch over 4f out: rdn along over 3f out: sn wknd* **16/1**

4-20 **9** 1 1/4 **Sinaadi (IRE)**[24] 3307 4-9-8 78 PaulMulrennan 8 64
(Brian Meehan) *led: pushed along wl over 2f out: rdn and hdd wl over 1f out: sn drvn and wknd* **16/1**

6403 **10** 4 1/2 **No Poppy (IRE)**[23] 3340 6-9-5 75 TomEaves 5 51
(Tim Easterby) *hld up towards rr: sme hdwy over 3f out: sn rdn and wknd* **25/1**

1m 37.71s (-1.99) **Going Correction** -0.10s/f (Good)
**WFA** 3 from 4yo+ 9lb **10** Ran SP% **117.1**
Speed ratings (Par 102): **105,103,102,99,98 96,94,94,92,88**
CSF £123.16 CT £632.29 TOTE £4.50: £1.90, £4.30, £1.70; EX 109.60 Trifecta £572.30.
**Owner** W S Farish **Bred** Barronstown Stud **Trained** Newmarket, Suffolk

**FOCUS**
After taking this competitive fillies' handicap Robert Havlin reckoned the ground had dried out further during the afternoon and by now was "on the quick side of good". The runner-up was back to form and the third is still improving.

## 4113 188BET GREAT IN PLAY PRICES H'CAP 1m 4f
**4:50** (4:50) (Class 4) (0-85,86) 3-Y-0+ **£5,175** (£1,540; £769; £384) **Stalls** Low

Form RPR

33-3 **1** **Quest For More (IRE)**[87] 1493 4-9-10 80 PatDobbs 5 86+
(Roger Charlton) *trckd ldrs: hdwy to trck ldr after 4f: cl up over 2f out: rdn to ld wl over 1f out: edgd lft ins fnl f: drvn out* **4/1**[3]

-226 **2** 3/4 **Mr Gallivanter (IRE)**[33] 3003 3-8-13 82 PhillipMakin 8 87
(John Quinn) *trckd ldrs: hdwy 3f out: rdn and ev ch wl over 1f out: drvn and kpt on fnl f* **7/2**[2]

0255 **3** hd **Save The Bees**[28] 3139 6-9-0 77 LukeLeadbitter(7) 2 82
(Declan Carroll) *set stdy pce: qcknd 4f out: rdn and qcknd again over 2f out: hdd wl over 1f out: drvn whn n.m.r on inner ins fnl f: kpt on same pce towards fin* **25/1**

00-0 **4** shd **Nanton (USA)**[26] 3250 12-9-2 72 DanielTudhope 7 77
(Jim Goldie) *hld up in rr: hdwy wl over 2f out: chsd ldrs whn n.m.r on inner over 1f out: swtchd rt and rdn ent fnl f: fin strly* **28/1**

0523 **5** nk **Deepsand (IRE)**[23] 3341 5-9-7 77 (p) DavidAllan 4 81
(Tim Easterby) *trckd ldrs: hdwy over 2f out: rdn and n.m.r over 1f out: drvn and kpt on fnl f: nrst fin* **14/1**

-235 **6** 5 **Astra Hall**[40] 2760 5-10-0 84 GrahamGibbons 1 80
(Ralph Beckett) *trckd ldr on inner: hdwy 2f out: sn rdn: drvn and wknd ent fnl f* **9/1**

11 **7** 14 **From Frost**[10] 3797 3-9-3 86 6ex (t) DavidProbert 9 60
(Andrew Balding) *hld up in rr: pushed along 4f out: rdn over 3f out: sn btn and bhd whn eased wl over 1f out* **5/4**[1]

2m 37.37s (2.47) **Going Correction** -0.10s/f (Good)
**WFA** 3 from 4yo+ 13lb **7** Ran SP% **110.6**
Speed ratings (Par 105): **87,86,86,86,86 82,73**
CSF £17.10 CT £285.31 TOTE £5.40: £2.20, £2.30; EX 18.40 Trifecta £185.50.
**Owner** H R H Sultan Ahmad Shah **Bred** Epona Bloodstock Ltd **Trained** Beckhampton, Wilts

**FOCUS**
A very steady gallop until the final 4f and there was little between the first five at the line. Muddling form with the big-priced third setting a steady pace.

## 4114 188BET H'CAP 5f
**5:25** (5:26) (Class 5) (0-75,75) 3-Y-0+ **£3,234** (£962; £481; £240) **Stalls** High

Form RPR

0545 **1** **Head Space (IRE)**[12] 3702 6-9-11 74 (v[1]) JamesSullivan 14 87
(Ruth Carr) *towards rr: hdwy over 2f out: rdn over 1f out: str run ent fnl f: sn led: drvn and hung lft last 100yds: kpt on* **3/1**[1]

-400 **2** 3/4 **Flash City (ITY)**[105] 1127 6-9-2 65 PJMcDonald 4 75
(Ruth Carr) *in tch: hdwy wl over 1f out: n.m.r and swtchd lft over 1f out: sn rdn and styd on to chal ins fnl f: drvn and no ex towards fin* **16/1**

0000 **3** 3/4 **Mister Manannan (IRE)**[13] 3659 7-9-7 70 AdrianNicholls 11 77
(David Nicholls) *dwlt and in rr: hdwy wl over 1f out: sn rdn and styd on strly fnl f: nrst fin* **12/1**

10-5 **4** 1/2 **Emjayem**[51] 2434 4-9-9 72 GrahamGibbons 9 81+
(Ed McMahon) *dwlt and sltly hmpd s: towards rr: hdwy 2f out: chsd ldrs appr fnl f: sn rdn: styng on wl and ev ch whn bdly hmpd last 100yds: nt rcvr and lost 3rd nr line* **8/1**[3]

6000 **5** 1 3/4 **Bronze Beau**[14] 3611 7-9-7 73 (t) NataliaGemelova(3) 1 72
(Kristin Stubbs) *cl up on outer: led 1/2-way: rdn over 1f out: drvn ent fnl f: sn hdd and one pce* **25/1**

3634 **6** 1 1/2 **Haajes**[14] 3611 10-9-4 72 (v) ShirleyTeasdale(5) 8 66
(Paul Midgley) *wnt rt s: towards rr: swtchd lft and hdwy on outer wl over 1f out: sn rdn and kpt on fnl f: n.d* **11/1**

5020 **7** 1 1/4 **Moorhouse Lad**[32] 3033 11-9-12 75 PaulMulrennan 5 64
(Garry Moss) *prom: rdn along 2f out: sn drvn and wknd appr fnl f* **16/1**

0001 **8** nk **Captain Dunne (IRE)**[6] 3921 9-8-13 69 RachelRichardson(7) 12 57
(Tim Easterby) *chsd ldrs: hdwy 2f out: rdn and ev ch over 1f out: wknd ent fnl f* **6/1**[2]

5020 **9** nk **Captain Royale (IRE)**[13] 3659 9-9-10 73 (p) BarryMcHugh 6 60
(Tracy Waggott) *midfield: hdwy over 2f out: rdn wl over 1f out and sn no imp* **22/1**

0606 **10** nk **Royal Bajan (USA)**[12] 3697 6-9-9 72 (v) DaleSwift 13 58
(James Given) *prom: cl up 2f out: sn rdn and ev ch: drvn and edgd lft appr fnl f: sn n.m.r and wknd* **11/1**

102 **11** 1 1/4 **Roy's Legacy**[16] 3561 5-9-2 65 JasonHart 15 46
(Shaun Harris) *racd towards stands' rail: a towards rr* **6/1**[2]

0000 **12** shd **The Strig**[21] 3399 7-8-11 63 (p) ConnorBeasley(3) 2 44
(Nigel Tinkler) *a in rr* **33/1**

6634 **13** 2 1/4 **Bosun Breese**[5] 3954 9-9-5 68 PhillipMakin 7 41
(Paul Midgley) *slt ld: hdd 1/2-way: cl up: rdn along wl over 1f out and sn wknd* **25/1**

1000 **14** 6 **Lorimer's Lot (IRE)**[21] 3399 3-9-2 70 (p) TomEaves 10 19
(Mark Walford) *in tch: rdn along 2f out: sn wknd* **16/1**

58.45s (-2.05) **Going Correction** -0.175s/f (Firm)
**WFA** 3 from 4yo+ 5lb **14** Ran SP% **121.7**
Speed ratings (Par 103): **109,107,106,105,103 100,98,98,97,97 95,95,91,81**
CSF £53.44 CT £535.47 TOTE £3.50: £2.10, £6.10, £3.80; EX 62.50 Trifecta £2707.50 Part won..
**Owner** The Bottom Liners & Mrs R Carr **Bred** Castlemartin Stud And Skymarc Farm **Trained** Huby, N Yorks

■ Stewards' Enquiry : James Sullivan three-day ban: careless riding (Jul 24,25,27)

**FOCUS**
With no less than five runners determined to make it there was plenty of pace on. The winner drifted left in the final furlong and caused plenty of interference on his inside. This is potentially better form than average for the grade.

## 4115 188BET AMATEUR JOCKEYS' ASSOCIATION H'CAP (FOR AMATEUR RIDERS) 2m 110y
**5:55** (5:55) (Class 5) (0-70,66) 4-Y-0+ **£2,495** (£774; £386; £193) **Stalls** Low

Form RPR

5253 **1** **My Destination (IRE)**[17] 3532 5-10-5 62 (b) MrWEasterby(5) 3 75
(Declan Carroll) *in tch: hdwy 5f out: cl up on outer 3f out: shkn up to ld wl over 1f out: sn rdn clr: styd on wl* **7/1**[3]

3264 **2** 11 **No Such Number**[14] 3632 6-11-0 66 MrRBirkett 2 66
(Julia Feilden) *hld up in tch: hdwy 5f out: sn trcking ldrs: effrt over 2f out and sn ev ch: rdn wl over 1f out and kpt on: no ch w wnr* **9/2**[1]

1125 **3** 3/4 **Anne's Valentino**[8] 3845 4-9-12 57 MrJTeal(7) 11 56
(Malcolm Jefferson) *trckd ldrs: hdwy over 3f out: rdn to ld over 2f out: hdd wl over 1f out: sn drvn and kpt on one pce* **5/1**[2]

-233 **4** 2 3/4 **Jawaab (IRE)**[18] 1485 10-9-11 54 (v) PhillipDennis(5) 8 50
(Philip Kirby) *led: hdd 1/2-way: sn pushed along and lost pl: rallied u.p and plugged on fnl 2f* **5/1**[2]

6516 **5** 4 **Father Shine (IRE)**[23] 3336 11-10-3 55 MrsCBartley 6 46
(Shaun Harris) *chsd ldrs: rdn along and outpcd over 6f out: in rr after* **10/1**

6662 **6** 1 **Monzino (USA)**[8] 3843 6-9-9 47 oh2 MissAliceMills 7 37
(Michael Chapman) *a in rr* **15/2**

0304 **7** 1 3/4 **Pertemps Networks**[16] 3546 10-10-9 64 MissJoannaMason(3) 5 52
(Michael Easterby) *trckd ldr: hdwy to ld 1/2-way: rdn along 4f out: hdd over 3f out and sn wknd* **14/1**

3-44 **8** nse **Candelita**[40] 2770 7-10-2 61 MrStanSheppard(7) 1 48
(Matt Sheppard) *in tch: hdwy to trck ldng pair over 5f out: sn cl up: led over 3f out: rdn and hdd over 2f out: rdr dropped whip and sn wknd* **7/1**[3]

0/36 **9** 8 **Freedom Flying**[21] 3404 11-9-4 47 oh2 (p) MrAaronJames(5) 9 25
(Lee James) *a bhd* **50/1**

4422 **10** 16 **Blazing Desert**[42] 915 10-10-1 60 MrHFNugent(7) 10 19
(William Kinsey) *racd wd: cl up: rdn along 4f out: sn wknd* **16/1**

3m 39.4s (-1.00) **Going Correction** -0.10s/f (Good) **10** Ran SP% **111.9**
Speed ratings (Par 103): **98,92,92,91,89 88,88,87,84,76**
CSF £36.87 CT £169.56 TOTE £7.40: £2.50, £1.40, £2.00; EX 46.90 Trifecta £189.30.
**Owner** Mrs Sarah Bryan **Bred** Darley **Trained** Sledmere, E Yorks

**FOCUS**
A low-grade amateur riders' handicap and the first two home came from off the pace. Dubious form, but the winner has been rated up a bit on his form from last year.
T/Plt: £57.10 to a £1 stake. Pool: £73,509.98 - 938.97 winning units. T/Qpdt: £6.10 to a £1 stake. Pool: £6,062.67 - 726.05 winning units. JR

# 3874 EPSOM (L-H)
Thursday, July 10

**OFFICIAL GOING: Good to firm (good in places; 8.4 (home straight 7.9))**
Wind: Almost nil Weather: Cloudy becoming fine

## 4116 STEVE DONOGHUE APPRENTICE H'CAP 1m 2f 18y
**6:10** (6:10) (Class 5) (0-75,75) 4-Y-0+ **£3,881** (£1,155; £577; £288) **Stalls** Low

Form RPR

3141 **1** **Last Minute Lisa (IRE)**[9] 3824 4-8-7 59 6ex JoshBaudains(3) 6 68+
(Sylvester Kirk) *stdd s: hld up: last tl prog over 1f out whn plenty to do: r.o wl fnl f to ld last 50yds* **3/1**[2]

6-33 **2** 1 1/4 **Dalgig**[19] 3472 4-9-7 75 CamHardie(5) 3 81
(Jamie Osborne) *led at decent pce: rdn over 1f out: styd on but hdd and outpcd last 50yds* **5/2**[1]

2016 **3** 3 3/4 **Silver Alliance**[28] 3162 6-9-9 75 (p) ShelleyBirkett(3) 5 74
(Julia Feilden) *trckd ldng pair 3f: 4th st: shkn up to go 3rd again over 2f out: no imp over 1f out: kpt on* **8/1**

-330 **4** 1 1/4 **Play Street**[30] 3085 5-9-9 72 MatthewLawson 2 69
(Jonathan Portman) *chsd ldr: shkn up over 2f out: no imp over 1f out: wknd fnl f* **4/1**[3]

345 **5** 1 1/4 **Buzz Law (IRE)**[20] 3427 6-8-7 56 JoeyHaynes 1 50
(K R Burke) *mostly in same pl: rdn and no prog over 2f out: wknd over 1f out* **8/1**

2214 **6** 1/2 **Auden (USA)**[16] 3553 6-8-13 65 (v) DannyBrock(3) 4 58
(J R Jenkins) *t.k.h: trckd ldng pair after 3f tl wknd over 2f out* **5/1**

2m 8.29s (-1.41) **Going Correction** -0.025s/f (Good) **6** Ran SP% **112.5**
Speed ratings (Par 103): **104,103,100,99,98 97**
CSF £10.97 TOTE £3.60: £1.70, £1.50; EX 9.50 Trifecta £25.00.
**Owner** Gerry Dolan **Bred** Geoffrey Croke **Trained** Upper Lambourn, Berks

**FOCUS**
Rail dolled out up to 6yds from 1m to Wining Post increasing races of 1m and beyond by 20yds and 6f race by 6yds. An ordinary handicap run at what looked as reasonable gallop, although Dalgig was allowed to do his own thing out in front. The runner-up has been rated to form.

## 4117 BRITISH STALLION STUDS EBF MAIDEN STKS 6f
**6:40** (6:40) (Class 5) 2-Y-0 **£3,881** (£1,155; £577; £288) **Stalls** High

Form RPR

3 **1** **Super Kid**[28] 3148 2-9-2 0 MatthewLawson(3) 6 77+
(Saeed bin Suroor) *cl up bhd ldng pair: led 2f out: pushed clr over 1f out: readily* **5/4**[1]

**2** 1 3/4 **Maftool (USA)** 2-9-2 0 JoeyHaynes(3) 4 72+
(Saeed bin Suroor) *slowly away: rn green and bdly outpcd in last: prog over 2f out: stl green but r.o to take 2nd ins fnl f* **6/1**[2]

2 **3** 2 1/4 **Publilia**[14] 3613 2-9-0 0 BenCurtis 3 60
(Mark Johnston) *led but pressed: rdn and hdd 2f out: one pce after: lost 2nd ins fnl f* **5/4**[1]

5 **4** hd **Ghost Cat**[25] 3279 2-9-0 0 CamHardie(5) 5 64
(Brian Meehan) *pressed ldr: upsides 3f out: pushed along whn wnr wnt past 2f out: one pce after* **14/1**[3]

0 **5** 5 **Vinamar (IRE)**[10] 3799 2-9-0 0 OisinMurphy 1 44
(Roger Teal) *hld up in 4th and wl in tch: pushed along 1/2-way: steadily wknd fnl 2f* **50/1**

0 **6** 19 **Lady Ballantrae (IRE)**[37] 2859 2-8-9 0 DannyBrock(5) 2
(Simon Dow) *outpcd in 5th: rdn over 2f out: wknd wl over 1f out: eased fnl f: t.o* **50/1**

1m 9.86s (0.46) **Going Correction** -0.025s/f (Good) **6** Ran SP% **113.8**
Speed ratings (Par 94): **95,92,89,89,82 57**
CSF £10.29 TOTE £2.20: £1.40, £2.70; EX 8.90 Trifecta £16.90.
**Owner** Godolphin **Bred** Darley **Trained** Newmarket, Suffolk



The Form Book, Raceform Ltd, Newbury, RG14 5SJ

**FOCUS**
This looked quite an informative little heat featuring some nice types capable of progressing. The time was ordinary and the suspicion is that the third was below form.

## 4118 TOTEPOOL HOME OF POOL BETTING H'CAP — 1m 114y
7:15 (7:15) (Class 4) (0-85,90) 3-Y-O+ £6,469 (£1,925; £962; £481) Stalls Low

Form — RPR

1510 **1** **Mindurownbusiness (IRE)**[21] 3378 3-8-13 **85**.............. CamHardie(5) 7 95
(David Simcock) *trckd ldng pair: chsd ldr 2f out: rdn and styd on wl fnl f to ld last strides* **5/2**[2]

2131 **2** *nk* **Sir Guy Porteous (IRE)**[5] 3957 3-9-9 **90** 6ex........... SilvestreDeSousa 1 99
(Mark Johnston) *trckd ldr: led over 2f out and sent for home: drvn and styd on fnl f but hdd last strides* **7/4**[1]

-130 **3** *3 1/4* **Angelic Upstart (IRE)**[34] 2959 6-9-10 **81**.................... OisinMurphy 4 86
(Andrew Balding) *trckd ldng pair: rdn wl over 2f out: hanging lft and outpcd wl over 1f out: kpt on nr fin* **3/1**[3]

1236 **4** *hd* **Liberty Jack (IRE)**[24] 3314 4-9-6 **77**............................ PatCosgrave 6 79
(Jim Boyle) *hld up in last pair: stdy prog to chse ldng pair over 1f out: rdn and nt qckn after: lost 3rd last strides* **10/1**

06-5 **5** *2 3/4* **Young Dottie**[40] 2770 8-8-7 **67**.............................. JemmaMarshall(3) 2 63
(Pat Phelan) *hld up in last pair: nt clr run on inner 2f out and swtchd out wd: shkn up and no prog after* **25/1**

105 **6** *25* **Harry Bosch**[24] 3306 4-9-9 **80**..........................(b) KierenFallon 3 18
(Brian Meehan) *sn pushed up to ld: rdn and hdd over 2f out: wkng whn short of room on inner wl over 1f out: eased and t.o* **10/1**

1m 43.57s (-2.53) **Going Correction** -0.025s/f (Good)
**WFA** 3 from 4yo+ 10lb — **6** Ran SP% **112.0**
Speed ratings (Par 105): **110,109,106,106,104 82**
CSF £7.26 TOTE £3.00: £1.90, £1.60; EX 7.20 Trifecta £20.20.
**Owner** St Albans Bloodstock I **Bred** Laundry Cottage Stud Farm **Trained** Newmarket, Suffolk

**FOCUS**
This was dominated by the two progressive 3yos in the line-up. The third has been rated to last year's C&D run.

## 4119 BEACH BOYS 17 JULY H'CAP — 1m 4f 10y
7:50 (7:51) (Class 4) (0-80,86) 4-Y-O+ £5,175 (£1,540; £769; £384) Stalls Centre

Form — RPR

-342 **1** **Ethics Girl (IRE)**[28] 3161 8-8-8 **67**............................(bt[1]) OisinMurphy 4 74
(John Berry) *hld up in 5th: prog over 2f out: rdn to chse ldr ins fnl f: r.o to ld last stride* **8/1**

5513 **2** *shd* **Barwick**[25] 3274 6-9-4 **77**.............................................. TedDurcan 3 84
(Lady Herries) *trckd ldr: pushed along over 5f out: shkn up to ld 2f out: drvn fnl f: kpt on but hdd last stride* **9/2**[3]

5653 **3** *nk* **Nave (USA)**[7] 3874 7-8-10 **69**...................................... KierenFallon 7 75
(David Simcock) *hld up and sn in rr: last st: shoved along 3f out: hanging whn rdn 2f out: urged along and r.o fnl f: gaining at fin* **9/4**[2]

-010 **4** *1 1/2* **Lady Of Yue**[26] 3218 4-8-7 **71**................................ JoshBaudains(5) 5 75
(Eugene Stanford) *hld up in rr: 6th st: rdn to cl on ldrs 2f out: stl wl in tch 1f out: one pce* **14/1**

5-41 **5** *hd* **Mister Fizz**[6] 3926 6-9-6 **86** 6ex.......................... DanielCremin(7) 6 90
(Miss Imogen Pickard) *led: set mod pce tl 4f out: rdn and hdd 2f out: styd pressing ldr tl one pce ins fnl f* **2/1**[1]

-001 **6** *1 1/2* **Whinging Willie (IRE)**[16] 3556 5-8-6 **70**....................(p) CamHardie(5) 1 71
(Gary Moore) *t.k.h: trckd ldng trio: rdn and nt qckn 2f out: one pce after* **9/1**

5005 **7** *16* **St Ignatius**[19] 3475 7-7-13 **65**.............................(v) CallumShepherd(7) 2 41
(Alan Bailey) *chsd ldr to 5f out: 3rd st: sn wknd: t.o* **33/1**

2m 39.73s (0.83) **Going Correction** -0.025s/f (Good) — **7** Ran SP% **113.0**
Speed ratings (Par 105): **96,95,95,94,94 93,82**
CSF £42.35 TOTE £9.20: £3.10, £2.80; EX 47.10 Trifecta £191.20.
**Owner** The 1997 Partnership **Bred** Newsells Park Stud **Trained** Newmarket, Suffolk

**FOCUS**
A steady pace to this handicap and they finished in a bit of a heap with most of the runners appearing to hang down the camber towards the far rail. Muddling form with a bunched finish. The runner-up has been rated to form.

## 4120 DEADMAN CONFIDENTIAL H'CAP — 1m 2f 18y
8:20 (8:22) (Class 5) (0-75,75) 3-Y-O £3,881 (£1,155; £577; £288) Stalls Low

Form — RPR

3341 **1** **Truancy (IRE)**[25] 3268 3-9-1 **72**...........................(p) JoeyHaynes(3) 3 79
(K R Burke) *mde all: rdn 2f out: kpt on wl enough and a holding rivals fr over 1f out* **6/1**

6-45 **2** *1 1/4* **Tall Ship (IRE)**[11] 3758 3-9-6 **74**...............................(v[1]) TedDurcan 6 78
(Sir Michael Stoute) *trckd ldrs: disp 3rd st: rdn and nt qckn over 2f out: keeping on whn n.m.r ins fnl f: forced way through to take 2nd last strides* **4/1**[2]

0234 **3** *hd* **New Colours**[17] 3541 3-8-13 **67**..........................................(v) BenCurtis 4 70
(Marcus Tregoning) *chsd wnr: rdn over 2f out: nt qckn and hld fr over 1f out: edgd lft ins fnl f: lost 2nd last strides* **8/1**

-413 **4** *2* **Allergic Reaction (IRE)**[24] 3316 3-8-9 **63**..................... OisinMurphy 1 62
(William Knight) *taken down early and steadily to post: hld up: pushed along in 7th st and nt on terms: drvn and kpt on fnl 2f to take 4th ins fnl f: n.d* **7/1**

0-41 **5** *1 1/2* **Go Sakhee**[24] 3316 3-9-2 **70**...................................... AndreaAtzeni 7 67
(Roger Varian) *trckd ldrs: disp 3rd st: shkn up and nt qckn over 2f out: hanging sltly over 1f out: fdd* **9/4**[1]

001 **6** *4 1/2* **Special Fighter (IRE)**[15] 3568 3-9-5 **73**................ SilvestreDeSousa 2 64
(Mark Johnston) *trckd ldng pair: urged along wl over 2f out: losing pl whn n.m.r over 1f out: wknd* **5/1**[3]

000 **7** *25* **Isabella Beeton**[49] 2498 3-8-10 **67**......................... JemmaMarshall(3) 8 8
(Pat Phelan) *stdd s: hld up: 6th st: reminders 3f out: no prog and btn 2f out: eased and t.o* **33/1**

-206 **8** *34* **Pure Amber (IRE)**[13] 3670 3-9-4 **72**............................ KierenFallon 9
(Ismail Mohammed) *mistimed s bef stalls opened: hld up: dropped to last and pushed along 5f out: eased and wl t.o* **10/1**

2m 8.46s (-1.24) **Going Correction** -0.025s/f (Good) — **8** Ran SP% **117.4**
Speed ratings (Par 100): **103,102,101,100,99 95,75,48**
CSF £31.06 CT £195.70 TOTE £6.00: £2.00, £1.30, £2.30; EX 33.40 Trifecta £266.80.
**Owner** Market Avenue Racing Club Ltd **Bred** Keogh Family **Trained** Middleham Moor, N Yorks

**FOCUS**
This looked a wide-open 3yo handicap but the pace wasn't strong and nothing could get into it from off the pace. The third has been rated close to his standout Windsor run.

## 4121 TONI-JANE HELDT & OMNI SECURITY SERVICE H'CAP (JOCKEY CLUB GRASSROOTS SPRINT SERIES QUALIFIER) — 6f
8:50 (8:50) (Class 4) (0-85,85) 3-Y-O+ £5,822 (£1,732; £865; £432) Stalls High

Form — RPR

1142 **1** **Iseemist (IRE)**[17] 3539 3-8-11 **79**.............................. JoeyHaynes(3) 5 87+
(John Gallagher) *sn trckd ldr: led 2f out gng easily: shkn up over 1f out: styd on and a in command* **5/1**[2]

-145 **2** *1* **Desert Command**[33] 2992 4-9-10 **83**............................ LiamKeniry 3 88
(Andrew Balding) *trckd ldng quartet: prog over 2f out to chse wnr wl over 1f out: styd on but nvr able to chal* **5/2**[1]

2115 **3** *1/2* **Eastern Dragon (IRE)**[27] 3180 4-8-11 **75**.................... NoelGarbutt(5) 2 78
(Michael Scudamore) *w.w: 6th st: shkn up and prog over 2f out: chsd ldng pair over 1f out: kpt on same pce after* **10/1**

150- **4** *1/2* **School Fees**[335] 5247 5-9-4 **82**.................................... CamHardie(5) 6 84
(Olly Stevens) *pushed along towards rr: 7th st: prog over 2f out: kpt on to press for 3rd fr over 1f out* **8/1**

-610 **5** *1* **Amadeus Wolfe Tone (IRE)**[12] 3702 5-9-12 **85**.........(b) AndreaAtzeni 8 84+
(Jamie Osborne) *stdd s: hld up and sn wl adrift in last: stl there 2f out: rdn over 1f out: r.o strly fnl f: far too much to do* **8/1**

0602 **6** *2* **Flying Bear (IRE)**[27] 3185 3-8-10 **75**................................ KierenFallon 9 66+
(Jeremy Gask) *awkward s: wl off the pce in 8th: drvn 3f out: nvr gng pce to make any prog* **6/1**[3]

0-00 **7** *3 1/2* **Sacrosanctus**[68] 1938 6-9-7 **80**...............................(p) SilvestreDeSousa 4 61
(Scott Dixon) *chsd ldr early: 4th st: sn rdn and lost pl: struggling in rr 2f out* **7/1**

-213 **8** *6* **Pucon**[26] 3246 5-9-0 **73**.......................................................... OisinMurphy 1 35
(Roger Teal) *led to 2f out: wknd rapidly over 1f out* **10/1**

1045 **9** *25* **Clear Praise (USA)**[7] 3876 7-9-2 **75**................................ HarryBentley 7
(Simon Dow) *walked to post early: prom: 3rd st: wknd rapidly jst over 2f out: virtually p.u* **25/1**

1m 9.34s (-0.06) **Going Correction** -0.025s/f (Good)
**WFA** 3 from 4yo+ 6lb — **9** Ran SP% **116.3**
Speed ratings (Par 105): **99,97,97,96,95 92,87,79,46**
CSF £18.04 CT £120.85 TOTE £4.80: £2.10, £1.40, £3.20; EX 19.80 Trifecta £103.30.
**Owner** K Marsden **Bred** J P Lim,K Marsden & South Hatch Racing **Trained** Chastleton, Oxon

**FOCUS**
It once again proved hard for anything to get into the race from behind. The runner-up and third have been rated close to form.
T/Plt: £76.50 to a £1 stake. Pool: £69,688.02 - 664.25 winning units. T/Qpdt: £23.90 to a £1 stake. Pool: £5,964.50 - 184.50 winning units. JN

# 3720 NEWMARKET (R-H)
Thursday, July 10

**OFFICIAL GOING: Good to firm (good in places) changing to good after race 3 (2.40) changing to good to soft after race 4 (3.15)**
Wind: light, half behind Weather: rain

## 4122 BAHRAIN TROPHY (GROUP 3) — 1m 5f
1:40 (1:44) (Class 1) 3-Y-O
£45,368 (£17,200; £8,608; £4,288; £2,152; £1,080) Stalls Centre

Form — RPR

-521 **1** **Hartnell**[20] 3419 3-9-1 103........................................... JoeFanning 4 111+
(Mark Johnston) *mde all: rdn along hands and heels and asserted jst over 1f out: awkward hd carriage but styd on strly: readily* **9/4**[2]

2122 **2** *2 3/4* **Windshear**[21] 3379 3-9-1 101........................................ RichardHughes 5 107
(Richard Hannon) *stdd s: hld up in tch in last pair: rdn 3f out: hdwy u.p to chse ldrs over 1f out: chsd wnr ins fnl f: r.o for clr 2nd but no threat to wnr* **2/1**[1]

0-21 **3** *3* **Forever Now**[25] 3270 3-9-1 96........................................ WilliamBuick 2 102
(John Gosden) *swtg: chsd wnr: upsides wnr 4f out: rdn wl over 2f out: no ex jst over 1f out: lost 2nd and wknd ins fnl f* **2/1**[1]

-110 **4** *1 3/4* **Honor Bound**[34] 2960 3-8-12 94.................................... JimCrowley 1 97
(Ralph Beckett) *dwlt: sn rcvrd and chsd ldrs: rdn over 2f out: drvn and no ex over 1f out: wknd ins fnl f* **25/1**

31 **5** *8* **The Corsican (IRE)**[35] 2917 3-9-1 82............................ MartinHarley 6 88
(David Simcock) *swtg: t.k.h: hld up wl in tch in midfield: rdn over 2f out: drvn and btn over 1f out: sn wknd* **20/1**

-511 **6** *14* **Vent De Force**[29] 3110 3-9-1 86..................................... RyanMoore 7 76
(Hughie Morrison) *lw: in tch in last pair: clsd 4f out: rdn and effrt over 2f out: sn btn: wknd over 1f out: eased ins fnl f* **12/1**[3]

2m 46.29s (2.29) **Going Correction** +0.125s/f (Good) — **6** Ran SP% **113.7**
Speed ratings (Par 110): **97,95,93,92,87 78**
CSF £7.36 TOTE £2.80: £1.70, £1.90; EX 6.90 Trifecta £16.10.
**Owner** Sheikh Hamdan bin Mohammed Al Maktoum **Bred** Darley **Trained** Middleham Moor, N Yorks

**FOCUS**
The track was using the stands' side course, which had not been raced on since August 2013. Stalls Far side except 10f, 12f, 13f: Centre. Steady light rain fell on the July course for quite a while before racing and clerk of the course Michael Prosser reported that there had been 5mm up to the opening race. It continued to fall during the afternoon. This is regarded as Newmarket's St Leger trial and Masked Marvel completed the double back in 2011, albeit he was the last winner of this race to go on to contest the final Classic. Prior to that Corsica (2010) went on to finish third at Doncaster, while Kite Wood (2009) was narrowly denied by stablemate Mastery. Plenty went right for the winner in making all at a steady pace, but he's still improving and was well on top at the finish. It's possible the form could rate higher.

## 4123 PORTLAND PLACE PROPERTIES JULY STKS (GROUP 2) (C&G) — 6f
2:10 (2:16) (Class 1) 2-Y-O
£45,368 (£17,200; £8,608; £4,288; £2,152; £1,080) Stalls High

Form — RPR

1 **1** **Ivawood (IRE)**[27] 3193 2-9-0 0.................................... RichardHughes 1 115+
(Richard Hannon) *str: lengthy: gd sort: lw: nt best away but sn pressing ldrs: led after 1f: rdn and edgd lft over 1f out: r.o strly and gng away fnl 100yds: readily* **3/1**[1]

313 **2** *2 3/4* **Jungle Cat (IRE)**[23] 3318 2-9-0 0..................................... JoeFanning 11 107
(Mark Johnston) *chsd ldrs: pressing wnr 1/2-way: rdn 2f out: outpcd by wnr ins fnl f: kpt on to hold 2nd towards fin* **13/2**[3]

1 **3** ½ **Muhaarar**[59] 2200 2-9-0 0 DaneO'Neill 8 106
(Charles Hills) *t.k.h: hld up wl in tch in midfield: effrt u.p to chse ldrs over 1f out: kpt on same pce ins fnl f* **12/1**

1 **4** *nk* **Belardo (IRE)**[14] 3626 2-9-0 0 AndreaAtzeni 7 105
(Roger Varian) *athletic: hld up in tch towards rr: hdwy 2f out: rdn and chsd ldrs ent fnl f: kpt on same pce ins fnl f* **5/1**[2]

16 **5** *nse* **Angelic Lord (IRE)**[23] 3318 2-9-0 0 RichardKingscote 4 104
(Tom Dascombe) *stdd after s: t.k.h: hld up in tch towards rr: rdn and hdwy over 1f out: kpt on wl u.p ins fnl f* **14/1**

5 **6** *1* **The Great War (USA)**[21] 3374 2-9-0 0 RyanMoore 5 101
(A P O'Brien, Ire) *hld up in tch in midfield: hdwy 2f out: edging lft u.p and no imp 1f out: kpt on same pce after* **7/1**

1202 **7** *3* **Mind Of Madness (IRE)**[21] 3374 2-9-0 0 JamieSpencer 6 92
(David Brown) *stdd after s: hld up in tch towards rr: effrt and edging lft over 1f out: no imp and btn 1f out: wknd ins fnl f* **9/1**

213 **8** *shd* **Mubtaghaa (IRE)**[23] 3322 2-9-0 0 PaulHanagan 2 92
(William Haggas) *str: hld up wl in tch in midfield: rdn and effrt 2f out: struggling and btn ent fnl f: wknd ins fnl f* **13/2**[3]

211 **9** *1 ½* **Dougal (IRE)**[55] 2308 2-9-0 0 JimCrowley 12 88
(Richard Hannon) *in tch in midfield: rdn and effrt ent fnl 2f: struggling u.p over 1f out: wknd 1f out* **25/1**

1 **10** *2* **George Bowen (IRE)**[15] 3569 2-9-0 0 TonyHamilton 9 82
(Richard Fahey) *w'like: wl in tch in midfield: lost pl and rdn over 2f out: wknd u.p over 1f out* **25/1**

0155 **11** *1 ¼* **Lightning Stride**[15] 3580 2-9-0 0 HarryBentley 3 78
(Brian Meehan) *led for 1f: chsd wnr tl 1/2-way: sn rdn and lost pl 2f out: wknd over 1f out* **100/1**

31 **12** *3 ¾* **Ustinov**[28] 3148 2-9-0 0 JimmyFortune 10 67
(Brian Meehan) *s.i.s: a bhd* **22/1**

1m 11.02s (-1.48) **Going Correction** +0.125s/f (Good) **12** Ran SP% **118.2**
Speed ratings (Par 106): **114,110,109,109,109 107,103,103,101,99 97,92**
CSF £21.28 TOTE £4.10: £1.70, £2.20, £4.10; EX 24.60 Trifecta £918.20.
**Owner** Carmichael Jennings **Bred** Ms M Davison & Ms D Kitchin **Trained** East Everleigh, Wilts

**FOCUS**
The winning time suggested the rain had yet to get into the ground. The winner was impressive and lengthened away in the style of a serious horse. The runner-up and fifth have been rated as running similar races to Royal Ascot, with the third and fourth putting up improved efforts.

## 4124 PRINCESS OF WALES'S BOYLESPORTS.COM STKS (GROUP 2) 1m 4f
2:40 (2:47) (Class 1) 3-Y-O+
**£56,710** (£21,500; £10,760; £5,360; £2,690; £1,350) **Stalls** Centre

Form RPR

6-12 **1** **Cavalryman**[103] 1177 8-9-2 115 SilvestreDeSousa 4 117
(Saeed bin Suroor) *lw: t.k.h: mde all and set v stdy gallop: rdn and qcknd wl over 2f out: sustained duel w runner-up after: r.o wl: rdn out* **9/1**

-022 **2** *nk* **Hillstar**[19] 3450 4-9-2 113 FrankieDettori 2 116
(Sir Michael Stoute) *stdd s: t.k.h: hld up in tch in last pair: swtchd lft and hdwy to join wnr over 3f out: rdn wl over 2f out: sustained duel w wnr after: r.o but hld towards fin* **7/2**[2]

223 **3** ½ **Pether's Moon (IRE)**[19] 3450 4-9-2 112 RichardHughes 1 115
(Richard Hannon) *t.k.h: hld up in tch: rdn wl over 2f out: hdwy to go 3rd and swtchd lft 1f out: pressed ldrs ins fnl f: r.o but hld towards fin* **5/1**[3]

1111 **4** *5* **Arab Spring (IRE)**[19] 3449 4-9-2 112 RyanMoore 8 107
(Sir Michael Stoute) *t.k.h: chsd wnr tl over 3f out: rdn wl over 2f out: outpcd and dropped to 4th 1f out: wknd ins fnl f* **1/1**[1]

4110 **5** *7* **Excellent Result (IRE)**[103] 1182 4-9-5 113 KierenFallon 7 99
(Saeed bin Suroor) *stdd s: hld up in tch in last pair: switching lft 4f out: rdn wl over 2f out: outpcd and btn over 1f out: sn wknd* **20/1**

25-6 **6** *3 ¼* **Dandino**[19] 3450 7-9-2 114 MartinHarley 5 90
(Marco Botti) *t.k.h: chsd ldrs: rdn and dropped to rr over 3f out: wknd over 1f out* **12/1**

2m 37.04s (4.14) **Going Correction** +0.05s/f (Good) **6** Ran SP% **111.3**
Speed ratings (Par 115): **88,87,87,84,79 77**
CSF £39.30 TOTE £11.10: £3.90, £2.00; EX 48.80 Trifecta £111.20.
**Owner** Godolphin **Bred** Darley **Trained** Newmarket, Suffolk

**FOCUS**
The early pace wasn't that strong, and quite a few took a reasonable hold, with the sprint seeming to start just over 4f from home. As had been the case in the opener, it looked an advantage to lead and stay towards the stands' rail. The runner-up and third have been rated close to their Royal Ascot figures.

## 4125 BOYLESPORTS.COM DOWNLOAD OUR APP H'CAP (BOBIS RACE) 1m 2f
3:15 (3:17) (Class 2) (0-105,101) 3-Y-O
**£43,575** (£13,048; £6,524; £3,262; £1,631; £819) **Stalls** Centre

Form RPR

5021 **1** **Torchlighter (IRE)**[11] 3758 3-8-12 **92** 6ex JoeFanning 6 105
(Mark Johnston) *chsd clr ldr: clsd qckly to ld ent fnl 2f: drvn clr ent fnl f: styd on strly: readily* **13/2**

-625 **2** *5* **Ventura Quest (USA)**[15] 3572 3-8-5 **85** JimmyQuinn 3 88
(Richard Fahey) *in tch in midfield: effrt u.p ent fnl 2f: chsd wnr over 1f out: no imp but kpt on u.p fnl f* **16/1**

10-1 **3** *1 ¼* **Mount Logan (IRE)**[27] 3182 3-9-1 **95** AndreaAtzeni 10 96
(Luca Cumani) *lw: stdd s: hld up in last pair: rdn over 2f out: 5th and swtchd lft over 1f out: no ch w wnr but kpt on u.p ins fnl f: wnt 3rd nr fin* **2/1**[1]

-101 **4** *nk* **What About Carlo (FR)**[33] 2986 3-9-7 **101** JimmyFortune 2 101
(Eve Johnson Houghton) *in tch in midfield: effrt u.p 2f out: 3rd and unable qck 1f out: kpt on same pce and no ch w wnr after: lost 3rd nr fin* **4/1**[3]

3-31 **5** *3 ½* **Mange All**[16] 3543 3-8-6 **86** LiamJones 11 79
(William Haggas) *lw: led and sn clr: rdn and hdd ent fnl 2f: btn ent fnl f: sn wknd* **7/2**[2]

033 **6** *24* **Stormardal (IRE)**[41] 2748 3-8-11 **91** TomQueally 9 39
(Ismail Mohammed) *chsd ldrs: rdn 4f out: sn struggling: bhd fnl 2f: t.o* **8/1**

-620 **7** *6* **Free Code (IRE)**[21] 3378 3-8-12 **92** SilvestreDeSousa 1 28
(James Tate) *hld up in last pair: rdn 4f out: lost tch 3f out: t.o fnl f* **9/1**

2m 4.04s (-1.46) **Going Correction** +0.05s/f (Good) **7** Ran SP% **115.9**
Speed ratings (Par 106): **107,103,102,101,98 79,74**
CSF £98.24 CT £282.11 TOTE £6.10: £2.50, £6.20; EX 97.20 Trifecta £356.90.
**Owner** Sheikh Hamdan bin Mohammed Al Maktoum **Bred** Darley **Trained** Middleham Moor, N Yorks

**FOCUS**
The ground was easing all the time. The fifth set a strong pace and the winner was well placed, but he pulled clear in good style. The third has not been rated as improving from his Goodwood win.

## 4126 PETER SILVESTER MEMORIAL EBF STALLIONS MAIDEN FILLIES' STKS (BOBIS RACE) 6f
3:50 (3:52) (Class 4) 2-Y-O
**£6,469** (£1,925; £962; £481) **Stalls** High

Form RPR

3 **1** **East Coast Lady (IRE)**[13] 3671 2-9-0 0 FrederikTylicki 14 82+
(William Stone) *tall: lengthy: racd alone against far rail: probably mde all: rdn and qcknd over 1f out: clr ins fnl f: r.o strly: readily* **12/1**

03 **2** *3 ½* **Lacing**[18] 3497 2-9-0 0 RyanMoore 3 72
(Richard Fahey) *chsd ldrs: swtchd rt and racd against stands' rail fr 1/2-way: chsd wnr and drvn 2f out: wl hld by wnr and kpt on same pce ins fnl f* **11/2**[3]

**3** *1 ½* **Jillanar (IRE)** 2-9-0 0 TomQueally 2 67+
(George Margarson) *leggy: s.i.s: in tch in rr: swtchd rt to r towards stands' side 1/2-way: rdn and hdwy 2f out: styd on to go 3rd ins fnl f: kpt on but no threat to wnr* **50/1**

**4** ½ **Umniyah (IRE)** 2-9-0 0 HarryBentley 10 66+
(Saeed bin Suroor) *str: in tch in midfield: rdn and effrt 2f out: chsd ldrs but unable qck ent fnl f: styd on same pce fnl f* **8/1**

54 **5** ½ **Anastazia**[15] 3563 2-9-0 0 MartinHarley 12 64
(Paul D'Arcy) *leggy: hld up in tch in rr: hdwy 2f out: edgd lft and no hdwy 1f out: kpt on same pce after* **66/1**

2 **6** *shd* **Exceedingly**[13] 3671 2-9-0 0 WilliamBuick 9 64
(John Gosden) *str: chsd ldrs: rdn and unable qck over 1f out: kpt on same pce ins fnl f* **9/4**[1]

**7** ¾ **Lady Of Dubai** 2-9-0 0 AndreaAtzeni 16 61+
(Luca Cumani) *cmpt: in tch in midfield: rdn and effrt 2f out: no imp and kpt on same pce fr over 1f out* **7/2**[2]

63 **8** *1* **Dubai Breeze (IRE)**[16] 3557 2-9-0 0 RichardHughes 1 58
(Clive Brittain) *lengthy: in tch in midfield: swtchd rt to r towards stands' rail over 3f out: rdn to chse ldrs over 1f out: no ex and btn 1f out: wknd ins fnl f* **11/2**[3]

**9** *nk* **Taqneyya (IRE)** 2-9-0 0 PaulHanagan 6 58
(Charles Hills) *unf: scope: dwlt: sn rcvrd and in tch in midfield: rdn and lost pl over 1f out: wknd ins fnl f* **16/1**

0 **10** *hd* **Bombay Mix**[35] 2928 2-9-0 0 JimmyFortune 5 57
(Charlie Fellowes) *w'like: led main gp and chsd wnr tl 2f out: lost pl u.p over 1f out: wknd ins fnl f* **50/1**

**11** *9* **Gipsy Doll** 2-9-0 0 PatCosgrave 11 30
(Paul Cole) *leggy: chsd ldrs: rdn 2f out: sn struggling and lost pl: wknd and bhd ins fnl f* **33/1**

**12** *nk* **La Favorita (IRE)** 2-9-0 0 JimCrowley 13 29
(Charles Hills) *w'like: s.i.s: in tch tl rdn and wknd over 1f out: bhd ins fnl f* **40/1**

1m 13.37s (0.87) **Going Correction** +0.05s/f (Good) **12** Ran SP% **119.2**
Speed ratings (Par 93): **96,91,89,88,88 87,86,85,85,84 72,72**
CSF £75.28 TOTE £16.70: £3.30, £2.20, £13.20; EX 84.90 Trifecta £2204.60.
**Owner** Horseheath Lodge Racing **Bred** Mountarmstrong Stud **Trained** West Wickham, Cambs

**FOCUS**
The ground was changed to good to soft prior to this maiden. The field was spread out all over the place. The runner-up has been rated to her Pontefract mark.

## 4127 HASTINGS DIRECT SIR HENRY CECIL STKS (LISTED RACE) 1m
4:25 (4:25) (Class 1) 3-Y-O
**£22,684** (£8,600; £4,304; £2,144; £1,076; £540) **Stalls** High

Form RPR

0 **1** **Table Rock (IRE)**[13] 3687 3-9-3 107 (b) RyanMoore 4 109
(A P O'Brien, Ire) *hld up in tch in rr: effrt in 5th wl over 1f out: hdwy u.p to chal jst ins fnl f: led on post* **4/1**[3]

1-21 **2** *nse* **Pretzel (IRE)**[19] 3455 3-9-3 111 WilliamBuick 2 108
(John Gosden) *lw: chsd ldr tl led over 2f out: rdn over 1f out: hrd pressed jst ins fnl f: kpt on wl: hdd on post* **2/1**[1]

4320 **3** *1 ¾* **Parbold (IRE)**[22] 3352 3-9-3 105 MartinHarley 7 104
(Richard Fahey) *dwlt: t.k.h: in tch in midfield: rdn and effrt to chse ldrs over 1f out: nt clrest of runs 1f out: styd on same pce fnl 100yds* **8/1**

-225 **4** *1 ¾* **Zarwaan**[21] 3378 3-9-3 102 PaulHanagan 1 100
(Ed Dunlop) *chsd ldrs: rdn and effrt wl over 1f out: no ex and btn jst ins fnl f: wknd fnl 100yds* **9/4**[2]

54-4 **5** *3 ¼* **God Willing**[82] 1580 3-9-3 105 JamieSpencer 8 92
(Ed Dunlop) *in tch in last pair: effrt 2f out: rdn and no hdwy over 1f out: wknd fnl f* **20/1**

3-00 **6** *3 ¼* **Sir Jack Layden**[68] 1953 3-9-3 105 FrankieDettori 9 85
(David Brown) *in tch in midfield: rdn and dropped to rr ent fnl 2f: wknd over 1f out* **33/1**

0-10 **7** *5* **Coulsty (IRE)**[22] 3352 3-9-6 103 RichardHughes 6 76
(Richard Hannon) *led tl over 2f out: sn rdn: 5th and btn ent fnl f: sn wknd* **11/1**

1m 38.79s (-1.21) **Going Correction** +0.05s/f (Good) **7** Ran SP% **111.3**
Speed ratings (Par 108): **108,107,106,104,101 97,92**
CSF £11.73 TOTE £4.00: £2.00, £1.60; EX 11.40 Trifecta £50.70.
**Owner** Michael Tabor & Derrick Smith & Mrs John Magnier **Bred** Whisperview Trading Ltd **Trained** Cashel, Co Tipperary

**FOCUS**
Following the success of East Coast Lady, who made all on the far side in the previous maiden, the whole field in this Listed contest tacked over to race next to the far-side rail. The winner has been a big improver since being blinkered and this was another step up. The third has yet to repeat his Free Handicap form but this rates his best run since.

## 4128 FRONTLINE BATHROOMS H'CAP 5f
5:30 (5:31) (Class 3) (0-90,90) 3-Y-O+ **£9,703** (£2,887; £1,443; £721) **Stalls** High

Form RPR

-465 **1** **Pearl Blue (IRE)**[39] 2803 6-9-8 **89** AshleyMorgan(3) 13 100
(Chris Wall) *chsd ldrs: rdn and effrt in 3rd over 1f out: str run ins fnl f to ld nr fin* **11/2**[2]

1460 **2** ½ **Megaleka**[39] 2803 4-8-13 **82** TimClark(5) 11 91
(Alan Bailey) *chsd ldr: swtchd lft and clsd u.p 1f out: led fnl 100yds: r.o: hdd and no ex nr fin* **20/1**

1005 **3** *1 ½* **Come On Dave (IRE)**[12] 3693 5-8-2 **71** oh2 DanielMuscutt(5) 14 75
(John Butler) *racd keenly: led: 3 l clr and rdn over 1f out: hdd fnl 100yds: no ex: wkng cl home* **16/1**

0034 **4** *nk* **Go Far**[19] 3479 4-9-0 **78**...(v) MartinHarley 1 81+
(Alan Bailey) *in tch in midfield: effrt u.p and edgd lft over 1f out: styd on wl fnl 100yds* **11/2**[2]
6026 **5** *1/2* **Commanche**[26] 3256 5-8-9 **78**... MarcMonaghan(5) 5 79
(Chris Dwyer) *taken down early: in tch towards rr: rdn over 1f out: styd on wl ins fnl f: nvr trbld ldrs* **6/1**[3]
5304 **6** *hd* **Arctic Feeling (IRE)**[14] 3599 6-8-13 **77**...(v) PaulHanagan 6 77
(Richard Fahey) *in tch in midfield: rdn over 1f out: hdwy ins fnl f: styd on wl towards fin* **5/1**[1]
1-21 **7** *3/4* **Oh So Sassy**[15] 3581 4-9-12 **90**... JackMitchell 10 87+
(Chris Wall) *dwlt: in tch in midfield: effrt u.p over 1f out: no imp: styd on same pce ins fnl f* **11/2**[2]
5000 **8** *1 1/4* **Lupo D'Oro (IRE)**[26] 3246 5-8-11 **75**... JamieSpencer 12 68
(John Best) *s.i.s: hld up in rr: effrt and hdwy u.p over 1f out: wknd ins fnl f* **12/1**
2150 **9** *1* **Go Nani Go**[26] 3239 8-9-8 **86**... FrederikTylicki 15 75
(Ed de Giles) *stdd s: hld up in tch towards rr: hdwy into midfield and rdn over 1f out: wknd ins fnl f* **10/1**
1400 **10** *hd* **Saffire Song**[5] 3959 3-7-13 **73** oh1 ow2... NatashaEaton(5) 3 59
(Alan Bailey) *chsd ldrs: rdn and lost pl over 1f out: wknd ins fnl f* **50/1**
3311 **11** *hd* **Harrogate Fair**[41] 2743 4-8-7 **71** oh1...(p) JoeFanning 2 59
(Michael Squance) *hld up in tch towards rr: effrt and sltly hmpd over 1f out: no imp after* **8/1**

58.64s (-0.46) **Going Correction** +0.05s/f (Good)
**WFA** 3 from 4yo+ 5lb **11** Ran SP% **117.6**
Speed ratings (Par 107): **105,104,101,101,100 100,99,97,95,95 94**
CSF £109.11 CT £1658.73 TOTE £7.50: £2.40, £8.50, £2.80; EX 138.30 Trifecta £1020.60.
**Owner** Archangels 2 **Bred** L Queally **Trained** Newmarket, Suffolk

**FOCUS**
Four came out of this, including likely favourite Doctor Parkes, but that didn't make it easier to pinpoint the winner in ground none of these were probably expecting. The whole field stayed towards the far side, although some raced nearer the middle. The winner has been rated to his old best and the runner-up to a small personal best.
T/Jkpt: Not won. T/Plt: £2,867.90 to a £1 stake. Pool: £197,416.20 - 50.25 winning units. T/Qpdt: £677.10 to a £1 stake. Pool: £10,249.38 - 11.20 winning units. SP

## 3973 NOTTINGHAM (L-H)
Thursday, July 10

**OFFICIAL GOING: Good to firm (good in places; 7.8)**
Wind: Light half-behind Weather: Fine

### 4129 EBF ANIXTER IP ASSURED MEDIAN AUCTION MAIDEN STKS 6f 15y
**2:20** (2:22) (Class 5) 2-Y-O **£2,911** (£866; £432; £216) **Stalls** Centre

Form RPR
22 **1** **Lady Moscou (IRE)**[18] 3497 2-9-0 0... JamesDoyle 8 74
(James Tate) *prom: outpcd over 2f out: rallied over 1f out: led ins fnl f: edgd lft: r.o* **9/4**[1]
6 **2** *3/4* **Spirit Of Zeb (IRE)**[84] 1536 2-9-0 0... SammyJoBell(5) 7 77
(Richard Fahey) *chsd ldrs: led 1f out: sn hdd and edgd lft: styd on* **20/1**
**3** *2 3/4* **Al Bandar (IRE)** 2-9-5 0... GeorgeBaker 9 69+
(Richard Hannon) *s.s: hdwy over 1f out: styd on to go 3rd nr fin* **5/1**
3 **4** *1/2* **Scarlet Bounty (IRE)**[23] 3330 2-8-11 0... GeorgeChaloner(3) 6 62
(Richard Fahey) *chsd ldrs: led over 1f out: sn rdn and hdd: no ex ins fnl f* **3/1**[2]
03 **5** *1* **Outback Ruler (IRE)**[45] 2623 2-9-5 0... AdamKirby 2 64
(Clive Cox) *w ldr tl led over 4f out: shkn up and rdr dropped rein over 2f out: hdd and edgd lft over 1f out: no ex ins fnl f* **7/2**[3]
0 **6** *1/2* **Right Madam (IRE)**[14] 3613 2-9-0 0... RoystonFfrench 3 58
(Andrew Hollinshead) *prom: rdn over 1f out: no ex fnl f* **50/1**
**7** *1* **Grand Spirit (IRE)** 2-9-5 0... LemosdeSouza 11 60
(Luca Cumani) *prom: outpcd over 3f out: kpt on ins fnl f* **20/1**
0 **8** *3 1/2* **Epic Find (USA)**[7] 3888 2-8-11 0... RobertTart(3) 4 44
(Charles Hills) *s.i.s: hld up: pushed along and wknd over 1f out* **25/1**
5 **9** *6* **River Of Dreams (IRE)**[12] 3701 2-9-5 0... FrannyNorton 10 31
(Kevin Ryan) *led: hdd over 4f out: rdn over 2f out: sn wknd* **10/1**
**10** *5* **Call Me Crockett (IRE)** 2-9-0 0... DuilioDaSilva(5) 5 16
(Richard Guest) *s.s: outpcd* **50/1**

1m 13.95s (-0.75) **Going Correction** -0.35s/f (Firm) **10** Ran SP% **121.0**
Speed ratings (Par 94): **91,90,86,85,84 83,82,77,69,63**
CSF £54.92 TOTE £2.90: £1.30, £2.20, £2.50; EX 52.20 Trifecta £585.10.
**Owner** Saeed Manana **Bred** Michael Downey & Roalso Ltd **Trained** Newmarket, Suffolk

**FOCUS**
Races on Outer track and distances as advertised. A fair maiden run at an honest pace. The field raced up the centre. The winner showed a good attitude and looks the type to rate higher.

### 4130 BSCL AND TECH-OLOGY SOLUTION PARTNER MAIDEN STKS 1m 75y
**2:55** (2:56) (Class 5) 3-4-Y-O **£2,587** (£770; £384; £192) **Stalls** Centre

Form RPR
0-3 **1** **Bombardment (USA)**[36] 2881 3-9-4 0... AdamKirby 2 81
(Charlie Appleby) *mde all: rdn and edgd rt over 1f out: r.o* **5/2**[1]
0-4 **2** *1 1/4* **Nabeel (IRE)**[12] 3695 3-8-11 0... AhmadAlSubousi(7) 10 78
(Saeed bin Suroor) *hld up: hdwy over 2f out: chsd wnr ins fnl f: r.o* **14/1**
0-0 **3** *hd* **Eye Contact**[85] 1517 3-9-4 0... JamesDoyle 5 78
(Sir Michael Stoute) *hld up: hdwy over 2f out: r.o* **8/1**
60 **4** *2 1/2* **Elite Force (IRE)**[73] 1795 3-9-4 0...(t) GeorgeBaker 1 72
(Roger Charlton) *chsd ldrs: rdn over 2f out: styd on same pce ins fnl f* **7/2**[2]
0 **5** *1 1/2* **Blue Army**[33] 2996 3-9-4 0... HayleyTurner 14 68
(Saeed bin Suroor) *chsd wnr after 1f: ev ch over 2f out: rdn and edgd rt over 1f out: wknd ins fnl f* **12/1**
6-3 **6** *3 1/2* **Swordbearer**[36] 2883 3-9-4 0... LiamKeniry 4 60
(James Fanshawe) *prom: rdn over 2f out: wknd over 1f out* **8/1**
00 **7** *2 3/4* **Varsovian**[28] 3153 4-9-8 0... DuilioDaSilva(5) 11 56
(Dean Ivory) *hld up: pushed along over 3f out: edgd lft over 1f out: nvr trbld ldrs* **100/1**
0-0 **8** *1* **Orion's Bow**[73] 1795 3-9-4 0...(t) NickyMackay 7 52
(John Gosden) *chsd ldrs: rdn over 2f out: wknd fnl f* **11/2**[3]
**9** *5* **Holiday Magic (IRE)** 3-9-4 0... AhmedAjtebi 8 40
(Charlie Appleby) *prom: rdn over 3f out: wknd over 2f out* **14/1**
**10** *nse* **Shaf (IRE)** 3-9-1 0... RyanTate(3) 13 40
(Ed Dunlop) *s.s: a in rr* **25/1**
**11** *1/2* **William Of Orange** 3-9-4 0... ChrisCatlin 6 39
(Sir Mark Prescott Bt) *s.i.s: hld up: rdn over 3f out: sn wknd* **20/1**
**12** *nk* **Gleese The Devil (IRE)** 3-9-1 0... GeorgeChaloner(3) 9 38
(Richard Fahey) *mid-div: rdn over 3f out: sn wknd* **20/1**
0-3 **13** *1 1/2* **Essanar**[12] 3695 3-9-4 0... PaulQuinn 12 35
(Andrew Hollinshead) *s.i.s: a in rr: wknd over 3f out* **50/1**
5 **14** *1 1/4* **Wild Hill Boy**[52] 2392 4-9-13 0... RaulDaSilva 3 34
(David C Griffiths) *hld up: rdn 1/2-way: wknd 3f out* **100/1**

1m 46.03s (-2.97) **Going Correction** -0.35s/f (Firm)
**WFA** 3 from 4yo 9lb **14** Ran SP% **126.7**
Speed ratings (Par 103): **100,98,98,95,94 90,87,86,81,81 81,80,79,78**
CSF £40.25 TOTE £2.80: £1.40, £2.20, £4.10; EX 43.60 Trifecta £458.70.
**Owner** Godolphin **Bred** Pontchartrain Stud **Trained** Newmarket, Suffolk

**FOCUS**
Some powerful stables lined up for this maiden which was run at a steady pace. The winner was the form pick on his reappearance run. The level is a bit fluid.

### 4131 DATA TECHNIQUES INSTALLING CONFIDENCE H'CAP 6f 15y
**3:30** (3:30) (Class 5) (0-75,75) 3-Y-O+ **£2,587** (£770; £384; £192) **Stalls** Centre

Form RPR
3505 **1** **Bajan Bear**[13] 3668 6-9-5 **68**... AdrianNicholls 1 80
(David Nicholls) *hld up: hdwy over 2f out: led over 1f out: r.o* **6/1**[3]
-100 **2** *1 3/4* **Le Laitier (FR)**[51] 2429 3-8-8 **68**... MatthewHopkins(5) 8 73
(Scott Dixon) *chsd ldrs: rdn over 2f out: r.o* **16/1**
0204 **3** *3/4* **Dancing Maite**[28] 3149 9-8-2 **56** oh3...(b) GemmaTutty(5) 9 60
(Roy Bowring) *led: rdn and hdd over 1f out: styd on same pce ins fnl f* **16/1**
0602 **4** *3/4* **Ypres**[14] 3611 5-9-12 **75**...(v[1]) AndrewElliott 13 76
(Jason Ward) *hld up: hdwy over 2f out: styd on: nt rch ldrs* **10/1**
1506 **5** *2 1/4* **Clubland (IRE)**[12] 3702 5-9-7 **70**... AdamKirby 11 64
(Roy Bowring) *prom: rdn over 1f out: no ex fnl f* **9/2**[2]
0646 **6** *1* **Bonnie Charlie**[13] 3668 8-9-2 **65**... PaulQuinn 5 56
(David Nicholls) *hld up: hdwy over 2f out: rdn over 1f out: styd on same pce fnl f* **7/1**
-421 **7** *1/2* **Katawi**[13] 3650 3-9-6 **75**... GeorgeBaker 7 63
(Chris Wall) *chsd ldr: rdn and ev ch wl over 1f out: wknd ins fnl f* **5/4**[1]
0-00 **8** *4 1/2* **Charlemagne Diva**[17] 3530 4-8-7 **56** oh1... RaulDaSilva 10 31
(Richard Guest) *racd alone: prom: rdn over 2f out: wknd over 1f out* **33/1**
00-0 **9** *1/2* **Aye Aye Skipper (IRE)**[30] 3088 4-9-7 **70**...(b[1]) ChrisCatlin 3 43
(Dean Ivory) *s.i.s: sn pushed along in rr: wknd 2f out* **33/1**
6-20 **10** *1 3/4* **Divertimenti (IRE)**[28] 3150 10-8-2 **56** oh3...(b) PhilipPrince(5) 2 24
(Roy Bowring) *prom tl rdn and wknd wl over 1f out* **33/1**

1m 12.7s (-2.00) **Going Correction** -0.35s/f (Firm)
**WFA** 3 from 4yo+ 6lb **10** Ran SP% **119.1**
Speed ratings (Par 103): **99,96,95,94,91 90,89,83,83,80**
CSF £95.92 CT £1488.11 TOTE £8.60: £1.70, £2.90, £4.70; EX 76.20 Trifecta £1676.50.
**Owner** C McKenna **Bred** Mr And Mrs C McKenna **Trained** Sessay, N Yorks

**FOCUS**
A decent pace for this uncompetitive sprint handicap. The winner has been rated back to his best.

### 4132 EBF COMMSCOPE SOLUTIONS FILLIES' H'CAP 6f 15y
**4:05** (4:06) (Class 4) (0-80,78) 3-Y-O+ **£6,469** (£1,925; £962; £481) **Stalls** Centre

Form RPR
0542 **1** **Guishan**[26] 3237 4-8-10 **62**... AndrewMullen 7 71+
(Michael Appleby) *w ldrs: led over 3f out: edgd lft ins fnl f: drvn out* **6/1**
124 **2** *1/2* **Khatiba (IRE)**[20] 3425 3-9-4 **76**...[1] JamesDoyle 2 82
(Roger Varian) *sn pushed along in rr: hdwy over 1f out: r.o* **7/2**[2]
424 **3** *1* **Available (IRE)**[19] 3483 5-9-12 **78**...(tp) FrannyNorton 4 82
(John Mackie) *w ldrs: rdn and ev ch over 1f out: styd on same pce ins fnl f* **11/4**[1]
-145 **4** *nk* **Ruby's Day**[13] 3676 5-9-10 **76**... AdamKirby 6 79
(David Brown) *prom: hung lft fr 1/2-way: rdn over 1f out: styd on* **8/1**
6163 **5** *8* **Meandmyshadow**[7] 3882 6-9-1 **67**... RobertWinston 3 44
(Alan Brown) *led: hdd over 3f out: rdn over 2f out: wknd fnl f* **9/2**[3]
-506 **6** *1 1/2* **Penny Garcia**[36] 2890 4-9-6 **72**... DuranFentiman 1 44
(Tim Easterby) *chsd ldrs: rdn 1/2-way: wknd over 1f out* **16/1**
1113 **7** *2 1/4* **Moonspring (IRE)**[15] 3581 3-9-3 **75**...(e) GrahamLee 5 39
(Robert Cowell) *s.i.s: outpcd* **6/1**

1m 12.62s (-2.08) **Going Correction** -0.35s/f (Firm)
**WFA** 3 from 4yo+ 6lb **7** Ran SP% **112.6**
Speed ratings (Par 102): **99,98,97,96,85 83,80**
CSF £26.34 TOTE £6.00: £2.80, £2.60; EX 22.60 Trifecta £69.90.
**Owner** Brian D Cantle **Bred** B D Cantle **Trained** Danethorpe, Notts

**FOCUS**
An open fillies' handicap run at a sound pace. Sound but ordinary form, with the runner-up back to form in the hood.

### 4133 PTC SYSTEMS H'CAP (BOBIS RACE) 5f 13y
**4:35** (4:36) (Class 4) (0-85,85) 3-Y-O **£5,175** (£1,540; £769; £384) **Stalls** Centre

Form RPR
4540 **1** **Lexington Abbey**[26] 3219 3-9-1 **79**... JamesDoyle 5 86
(Kevin Ryan) *chsd ldr: led 1f out: rdn out* **8/1**
3232 **2** *3/4* **Amahoro**[15] 3565 3-8-13 **80**... CharlesBishop(3) 7 84
(Mick Channon) *hld up: hdwy over 1f out: sn rdn: r.o* **5/1**[3]
32-1 **3** *1 1/4* **Sunrise Star**[34] 2946 3-9-7 **85**... AdamKirby 6 85
(Lady Cecil) *prom: outpcd 3f out: rdn and r.o ins fnl f* **6/4**[1]
0405 **4** *1 1/2* **Oriental Relation (IRE)**[23] 3331 3-9-2 **80**...(b) GrahamLee 8 74
(James Given) *chsd ldrs: rdn over 1f out: styd on same pce ins fnl f* **8/1**
1505 **5** *1* **Skye's The Limit**[13] 3669 3-8-8 **75**... GeorgeChaloner(3) 3 66
(Richard Fahey) *chsd ldrs: rdn 1/2-way: no ex fnl f* **4/1**[2]
-061 **6** *nk* **Mr Dandy Man (IRE)**[30] 3084 3-8-12 **76**... RobertWinston 2 66+
(Ronald Harris) *led: swvd lft 1/2-way: sn rdn: hdd 1f out: sn eased* **16/1**
01-0 **7** *1/2* **Heavens Edge**[54] 2340 3-9-1 **79**... RaulDaSilva 4 67
(Christopher Mason) *hld up: hdwy 2f out: sn rdn and btn* **33/1**
1225 **8** *3/4* **Taquka (IRE)**[45] 2626 3-9-3 **81**... DougieCostello 1 66
(Ralph Beckett) *chsd ldrs: rdn 1/2-way: wknd over 1f out* **16/1**

59.38s (-2.12) **Going Correction** -0.35s/f (Firm) **8** Ran SP% **113.6**
Speed ratings (Par 102): **102,100,98,96,94 94,93,92**
CSF £46.86 CT £91.99 TOTE £10.10: £3.20, £1.40, £1.10; EX 42.90 Trifecta £120.60.
**Owner** Middleham Park Racing Xix **Bred** D R Tucker **Trained** Hambleton, N Yorks

**FOCUS**
A fair sprint handicap run at a sound pace. The winner has been rated back to his reappearance form off a reduced mark, while the runner-up, who has had a few chances, helps set the standard.

## 4134 NG BAILEY - IT'S NOT SYSTIMAX H'CAP — 1m 6f 15y
5:10 (5:11) (Class 5) (0-70,68) 3-Y-O — £2,587 (£770; £384; £192) Stalls Low

Form — RPR

0-43 **1** **Deauville Dancer (IRE)**[9] 3818 3-9-2 **63**.......................... ChrisCatlin 2 81+
(Sir Mark Prescott Bt) *trckd ldr: led over 2f out: rdn and hung rt ins fnl f: styd on wl: readily* **4/1**[2]

4010 **2** *6* **Taws**[27] 3183 3-8-8 **62**...................................................... JennyPowell(7) 3 71
(Rod Millman) *hld up: pushed along 6f out: hdwy over 3f out: chsd wnr over 2f out: styd on same pce ins fnl f* **7/2**[1]

3442 **3** *1 ¼* **Winter Spice (IRE)**[17] 3541 3-9-4 **68**.............................(b) RyanTate(3) 5 75
(Clive Cox) *hld up: hdwy over 2f out: styd on same pce ins fnl f* **4/1**[2]

0460 **4** *3 ½* **Catadupa**[12] 3711 3-9-1 **62**................................................ JamesDoyle 1 64
(Roger Charlton) *chsd ldrs: rdn over 2f out: no ex fr over 1f out* **10/1**

0535 **5** *shd* **Cinnilla**[13] 3673 3-9-7 **68**..............................(b) DougieCostello 10 70
(Ralph Beckett) *hld up: rdn over 2f out: styd on ins fnl f: nvr nrr* **7/1**[3]

60-0 **6** *2 ¾* **Little Bruv**[29] 3098 3-7-11 **49** oh4.............................. JackGarritty(5) 11 49
(Tim Easterby) *hld up in tch: lost pl and nt clr run over 2f out: sn rdn: kpt on ins fnl f* **33/1**

0056 **7** *nk* **Dark Days**[15] 3567 3-8-8 **55**............................................(t) RaulDaSilva 7 53
(Paul Cole) *s.i.s: hld up: hdwy over 2f out: edgd lft and wknd over 1f out* **20/1**

6360 **8** *¾* **Izbushka (IRE)**[20] 2735 3-8-8 **58** ow1..................(vt) GeorgeChaloner(3) 6 55
(Ian Williams) *hld up: rdn over 4f out: wknd over 1f out* **25/1**

3135 **9** *hd* **Cape Arrow**[35] 2934 3-9-2 **63**............................................ GrahamLee 9 60
(Paul Cole) *s.i.s: sn prom: rdn over 4f out: wknd over 1f out* **10/1**

300 **10** *15* **Chantecler**[24] 3315 3-9-4 **65**........................................... HayleyTurner 4 41
(Hughie Morrison) *led: rdn and hdd over 3f out: wknd over 2f out* **8/1**

5514 **11** *3* **Blue Talisman (IRE)**[36] 2893 3-9-1 **62**.....................(b) DuranFentiman 8 33
(Tim Easterby) *chsd ldr tl led over 3f out: rdn and hdd over 2f out: wknd over 1f out* **20/1**

3m 1.11s (-5.89) **Going Correction** -0.35s/f (Firm) **11** Ran SP% **120.3**
Speed ratings (Par 100): **102,98,97,95,95 94,94,93,93,84 83**
CSF £17.87 CT £60.88 TOTE £4.50: £1.60, £1.80, £2.10; EX 21.70 Trifecta £73.20.
**Owner** Suffolk Bloodstock **Bred** Ruskerne Ltd **Trained** Newmarket, Suffolk

**FOCUS**
An open looking handicap run at a fair pace. Sound form, with the winner potentially better than the bare result, and the second and third clear of the unexposed fourth and fifth.
T/Plt: £116.40 to a £1 stake. Pool: £46,942.22 - 294.16 winning units. T/Qpdt: £30.60 to a £1 stake. Pool: £3,322.68 - 80.12 winning units. CR

4135 - 4141a (Foreign Racing) - See Raceform Interactive

# 3448 ASCOT (R-H)
### Friday, July 11

**OFFICIAL GOING: Straight course - good to firm (good in places; 8.6); round course - good (good to firm in places; 7.8)**
Wind: Light; across Weather: Cloudy

## 4142 HELICAL BAR EBF STALLIONS MAIDEN STKS (BOBIS RACE) — 6f
2:30 (2:31) (Class 3) 2-Y-O — £9,056 (£2,695; £1,346; £673) Stalls High

Form — RPR

64 **1** **Markaz (IRE)**[26] 3279 2-9-5 0................................................ DaneO'Neill 8 83
(B W Hills) *slowly away: sn wl in tch: swtchd rt wl over 1f out and sn pushed into ld: shkn up fnl f: readily* **7/2**[2]

3 **2** *1 ¼* **Fingal's Cave (IRE)**[15] 3613 2-9-5 0............... WilliamTwiston-Davies 9 79
(Mick Channon) *trckd ldrs: rdn to chal over 1f out: hanging and nt qckn fnl f* **7/1**

6 **3** *shd* **Rotherwick (IRE)**[8] 3889 2-9-5 0........................................ LukeMorris 3 79
(Paul Cole) *chsd ldrs: pushed along fr 1/2-way: rdn to chal over 1f out: styd on but no match for wnr* **14/1**

**4** *7* **Emirates Airline** 2-9-5 0.................................................... AdamKirby 5 58+
(Saeed bin Suroor) *slowly away: mostly in last pair and nvr a factor: shkn up over 1f out: styd on quite wl fnl f to take 4th post* **9/4**[1]

0 **5** *nse* **Mutafarrej**[22] 3394 2-9-5 0.................................................. KierenFallon 4 58
(Mark Johnston) *pressed ldrs: led jst over 2f out to over 1f out: wknd qckly* **20/1**

**6** *¾* **Chevallier** 2-9-5 0.............................................................. SeanLevey 6 56
(Richard Hannon) *t.k.h: w ldr: led briefly over 2f out: wknd over 1f out* **16/1**

**7** *2 ½* **Lysander The Greek** 2-9-5 0............................................ JimCrowley 1 51+
(Ralph Beckett) *slowly away: rcvrd to trck ldrs: waiting for a gap over 2f out: sing to lose pl whn impeded wl over 1f out: wknd* **4/1**[3]

0 **8** *5* **Soldier Sam (IRE)**[13] 3728 2-9-5 0.................................. JimmyFortune 7 33
(Richard Hannon) *mde most to over 2f out: sn wknd* **33/1**

**9** *nk* **Delusional** 2-9-5 0............................................................. GeorgeBaker 2 32
(Roger Charlton) *s.i.s: a in last pair: pushed along and no prog 2f out: bttr for r* **8/1**

1m 14.05s (-0.45) **Going Correction** +0.025s/f (Good) **9** Ran SP% **116.9**
Speed ratings (Par 98): **104,102,102,92,92 91,88,81,81**
CSF £28.66 TOTE £4.90: £1.40, £1.90, £4.40; EX 19.80 Trifecta £199.20.
**Owner** Hamdan Al Maktoum **Bred** Yeomanstown Stud & Doc Bloodstock **Trained** Upper Lambourn, Berks

**FOCUS**
Rail realignment added 10yds to Old Mile, 13yds to 10f, 14yds to 12f and 16yds to 14f. The forecast rain didn't arrive and the ground was good to firm, good in places. The pace was not strong in this maiden but the leading form contender scored with something in hand and the first three pulled clear. The time was 1.65 seconds outside standard. The winner ran to his recent level.

## 4143 COMMERCIAL PROPERTY LAW BY DARBYS SOLICITORS NURSERY H'CAP (BOBIS RACE) — 6f
3:05 (3:05) (Class 4) 2-Y-O — £7,762 (£2,310; £1,154; £577) Stalls High

Form — RPR

1 **1** **Louie De Palma**[18] 3536 2-8-10 **79**...................................... RyanTate(3) 5 87+
(Clive Cox) *hld up in tch: nudged by rival 2f out: prog after: rdn to ld 1f out: hrd pressed fnl f: styd on wl* **9/4**[1]

1433 **2** *½* **Bronze Maquette (IRE)**[16] 3580 2-8-11 **77**..................... JimmyFortune 7 84+
(Gary Moore) *hld up in last: swtchd rt 2f out and nudged wnr: prog to chal 1f out: hrd rdn and styd on: jst hld nr fin* **12/1**

41 **3** *2 ¼* **Squats (IRE)**[20] 3454 2-9-3 **83**........................................... LiamJones 3 83
(William Haggas) *t.k.h: w ldr: led wl over 2f out: hdd and one pce 1f out* **3/1**[2]

441 **4** *1* **St Brelades Bay (IRE)**[13] 3728 2-9-7 **87**........................... DaneO'Neill 1 84
(Richard Hannon) *hld up in tch: rdn and cl up jst over 1f out: outpcd fnl f* **5/1**[3]

3225 **5** *4* **Arlecchino's Leap**[27] 3210 2-8-8 **74**...............................(v) DavidProbert 6 59
(Mark Usher) *mde most to wl over 2f out: wknd over 1f out* **25/1**

41 **6** *1 ¼* **Geological (IRE)**[24] 3324 2-9-4 **84**..................................... SeanLevey 2 65
(Richard Hannon) *t.k.h: hld up in tch: pushed along over 2f out: nt qckn over 1f out: wknd fnl f* **8/1**

01 **7** *nk* **Kingsbridge**[25] 3304 2-8-12 **78**.......................................... JimCrowley 8 58
(Rod Millman) *pressed ldrs: shkn up and steadily lost pl fr 2f out* **5/1**[3]

0015 **8** *1* **Areion (IRE)**[27] 3211 2-7-9 **66** oh2..................................(b) CamHardie(5) 4 43
(J S Moore) *prom 4f: sn wknd* **40/1**

1m 13.79s (-0.71) **Going Correction** +0.025s/f (Good) **8** Ran SP% **114.2**
Speed ratings (Par 96): **105,104,101,100,94 93,92,91**
CSF £30.56 CT £82.55 TOTE £2.80: £1.10, £3.70, £1.70; EX 33.00 Trifecta £236.30.
**Owner** Peter Ridgers **Bred** Pantile Stud **Trained** Lambourn, Berks

**FOCUS**
Five last-time-out winners lined up in this nursery. The pace was fair and the favourite battled well to score. The form is rated slightly positively.

## 4144 CLOSE BROTHERS PROPERTY FINANCE H'CAP — 1m 6f
3:40 (3:40) (Class 3) (0-95,94) 3-Y-O+
£9,337 (£2,796; £1,398; £699; £349; £175) Stalls Low

Form — RPR

-116 **1** **Hassle (IRE)**[41] 2760 5-9-9 **89**............................................(p) AdamKirby 3 98+
(Clive Cox) *hld up in last trio: prog 2f out: rdn to chal whn hung rt and bmpd runner-up 100yds out: sn led: jst hld on* **10/3**[2]

101- **2** *hd* **Alcaeus**[285] 6876 4-10-0 **94**.............................................. LukeMorris 2 103+
(Sir Mark Prescott Bt) *dwlt: hld up in last: rdn and prog wl over 2f out: chsd ldr over 1f out: str chal u.p whn bmpd 100yds out: kpt on wl: jst failed: unlucky* **11/4**[1]

6500 **3** *nk* **Glenard**[13] 3717 4-9-10 **90**................................................[1] GeorgeBaker 8 98
(Charles Hills) *trckd ldr 5f: styd prom: led over 2f out gng strly: rdn over 1f out: bmpd and hdd 100yds: kpt on but jst hld* **10/3**[2]

2-04 **4** *5* **Snowy Dawn**[27] 3249 4-8-7 **78**....................................(p) CamHardie(5) 9 79
(Andrew Hollinshead) *t.k.h: plld way through to trck ldr after 5f: rdn to chal over 2f out: chsd ldr to over 1f out: wknd* **12/1**

-010 **5** *¾* **Dance King**[16] 3574 4-8-11 **77**........................................... TedDurcan 5 77
(Tim Easterby) *trckd ldrs: shkn up and nt qckn 2f out: steadily wknd over 1f out* **16/1**

00-2 **6** *8* **Rockfella**[68] 1981 8-8-12 **78**........................................... MartinDwyer 7 67
(Denis Coakley) *led at mod pce: kicked on 5f out: hdd & wknd over 2f out* **5/1**[3]

01-2 **7** *2 ½* **Ronaldinho (IRE)**[39] 2851 4-9-0 **80**............................. JimmyFortune 4 65
(Alan King) *sn settled bhd ldrs: cl up over 2f out: rdn and wknd wl over 1f out* **14/1**

-000 **8** *4 ½* **Azrag (USA)**[9] 3859 6-9-1 **81**........................................(p) SebSanders 1 60
(Michael Attwater) *plld hrd: hld up: rdn and wknd 3f out* **50/1**

3m 4.29s (3.29)
**WFA** 3 from 4yo+ 15lb **8** Ran SP% **111.7**
CSF £12.29 CT £30.73 TOTE £4.70: £1.60, £1.50, £1.30; EX 13.00 Trifecta £28.30.
**Owner** A D Spence **Bred** Cheval Court Stud **Trained** Lambourn, Berks

**FOCUS**
They went a steady pace in this decent handicap and there was a tight finish but the three market leaders pulled clear. The winner's style makes it hard to pin him down, but he is rated as resuming his progress here.

## 4145 CUSHMAN & WAKEFIELD FILLIES' H'CAP (FOR THE JOHN TRAVERS MEMORIAL TROPHY) — 1m 4f
4:15 (4:18) (Class 3) (0-95,91) 3-Y-O+ — £9,703 (£2,887; £1,443; £721) Stalls Low

Form — RPR

-113 **1** **Arabian Comet (IRE)**[28] 3200 3-8-10 **86**.......................... JimmyFortune 10 95
(William Haggas) *hld up in last pair: rdn and prog over 2f out: led over 1f out but pressed: drifted lft fnl f: styd on wl* **9/4**[1]

56-5 **2** *1* **Kikonga**[13] 3725 4-9-13 **90**................................................. AdamKirby 4 97
(Luca Cumani) *trckd ldng trio: rdn and prog to go 2nd over 2f out: chal over 1f out: pressed wnr fr over 1f out: nt qckn ins fnl f* **7/2**[3]

2-21 **3** *hd* **Swan Lakes (IRE)**[28] 3174 3-8-1 **77**................................... MartinLane 9 84
(David Simcock) *sn led: kicked for home over 3f out: hdd over 1f out: hld after but styd on nr fin* **11/4**[2]

-144 **4** *1* **Cameo Tiara (IRE)**[17] 3560 3-7-13 **80**................................. CamHardie(5) 2 85
(Richard Hannon) *plld hrd: trckd ldng pair: disp 2nd over 2f out: nt qckn sn after: edgd lft 1f out: styd on nr fin* **10/1**

10-3 **5** *4 ½* **Lady Pimpernel**[28] 3196 4-9-11 **88**..................................... DaneO'Neill 3 86
(Henry Candy) *mostly chsd ldr to wl over 2f out: sn lost pl and btn* **8/1**

-311 **6** *3 ¼* **Tioga Pass**[49] 2501 3-9-1 **91**............................................. LukeMorris 6 84
(Paul Cole) *t.k.h early: hld up in last pair: rdn and no rspnse wl over 2f out* **12/1**

2m 31.16s (-1.34) **Going Correction** +0.025s/f (Good)
**WFA** 3 from 4yo 13lb **6** Ran SP% **107.6**
Speed ratings (Par 104): **105,104,104,103,100 98**
CSF £9.49 CT £17.77 TOTE £3.10: £1.50, £1.80; EX 8.80 Trifecta £18.00.
**Owner** Abdulla Al Mansoori **Bred** Darley **Trained** Newmarket, Suffolk
■ Rule 4 of 5p in the pound applies to all bets; Withdrawn: Nullarbor Sky
■ Stewards' Enquiry : Jimmy Fortune caution; careless riding

**FOCUS**
The pace was not very strong in this decent handicap but the market leaders filled the first three places and the form looks solid. The runner-up is rated similar to her win in this last year.

## 4146 LONG HARBOUR H'CAP — 6f
4:50 (4:55) (Class 3) (0-90,89) 3-Y-O+ — £9,703 (£2,887; £1,443; £721) Stalls High

Form — RPR

-023 **1** **Shore Step (IRE)**[20] 3479 4-9-9 **84**................ WilliamTwiston-Davies 10 95
(Mick Channon) *mde all: drew 2 l clr 2f out: drvn and styd on wl after* **14/1**

0040 **2** *1 ½* **Trader Jack**[6] 3981 5-9-2 **82**......................................... PhilipPrince(5) 13 88
(David Flood) *in tch in midfield: rdn 2f out: prog over 1f out: styd on to take 2nd nr fin* **12/1**

0310 **3** *hd* **Highland Acclaim (IRE)**[20] 3480 3-9-2 **86**.......................... SamJames(3) 16 93+
(David O'Meara) *s.s: hld up wl in rr: rdn and prog whn nt clr run briefly 1f out: r.o wl nr fin: nrly snatched 2nd* **14/1**

3152 **4** *nk* **Pettochside**[21] 3422 5-9-0 **75**......................................... DaneO'Neill 14 80
(Chris Gordon) *prom: rdn to chse wnr over 1f out: one pce and no imp: lost 2 pls nr fin* **20/1**

0-66 **5** ¾ **Gabbiano**[26] 3271 5-9-11 **86** ........ MartinLane 4 88+
(Jeremy Gask) *hld up in rr: last 2f out: rdn over 1f out: r.o wl fnl f: nrst fin but no ch* **9/1**[3]

2211 **6** *nse* **Red Refraction (IRE)**[34] 2984 4-9-9 **89** ........ CamHardie(5) 6 91
(Richard Hannon) *trckd ldrs: rdn 2f out: nt qckn over 1f out: kpt on same pce after* **4/1**[1]

5402 **7** ½ **Rebecca Romero**[10] 3817 7-9-0 **75** ........ PatCosgrave 17 75
(Denis Coakley) *hld up in rr: rdn and nt qckn 2f out: styd on fnl f: nrst fin* **25/1**

024 **8** 2 **Azrur (IRE)**[52] 2425 4-9-7 **85** ........(t[1]) RyanTate(3) 9 79
(David Brown) *prom: rdn 2f out: wknd over 1f out* **14/1**

-000 **9** *nk* **Picture Dealer**[26] 3271 5-9-10 **88** ........ SimonPearce(3) 12 81
(Lydia Pearce) *trckd ldrs: rdn 2f out: lost pl and struggling over 1f out: n.d after* **16/1**

0512 **10** ¾ **Slip Sliding Away (IRE)**[33] 3033 7-9-10 **85** ........ AdamKirby 5 76
(Peter Hedger) *trckd ldrs: prog to dispute 2nd wl over 1f out: shkn up and wknd fnl f* **13/2**[2]

0324 **11** 1 **Chilworth Icon**[6] 3964 4-10-0 **89** ........ SamHitchcott 15 76
(Mick Channon) *prom: rdn over 2f out: wknd wl over 1f out* **10/1**

-300 **12** ¾ **Lewisham**[13] 3714 4-9-5 **80** ........(p) JimmyFortune 1 65
(David Nicholls) *in tch towards rr: rdn 2f out: no prog and wl btn over 1f out* **10/1**

1321 **13** ½ **Shaolin (IRE)**[36] 2919 4-9-9 **84** ........(t) GeorgeBaker 18 67
(Seamus Durack) *hld up in last pair: shkn up and no prog wl over 1f out* **10/1**

-050 **14** 1 **Outer Space**[56] 2317 3-9-6 **87** ........ JimCrowley 2 66
(Jamie Osborne) *t.k.h: chsd wnr to over 1f out: wknd qckly* **14/1**

-035 **15** 7 **Midnight Rider (IRE)**[46] 2629 6-9-6 **81** ........ TedDurcan 7 39
(Chris Wall) *dwlt: in tch towards rr: rdn and no prog 2f out: wknd qckly fnl f: virtually p.u nr fin* **25/1**

1m 14.47s (-0.03) **Going Correction** +0.025s/f (Good)
**WFA** 3 from 4yo+ 6lb **15** Ran SP% **123.3**
Speed ratings (Par 107): **101,99,98,98,97 97,96,93,93,92 91,90,89,88,78**
CSF £162.94 CT £2083.08 TOTE £15.10: £4.80, £3.70, £5.60; EX 210.10 Trifecta £4052.60 Part won..
**Owner** Jon and Julia Aisbitt **Bred** Lynn Lodge Stud **Trained** West Ilsley, Berks
■ Rule 4 of 5p in the pound applies to all bets; Withdrawn: Noble Deed

**FOCUS**
The pace was not strongat all in this good sprint handicap and the winner made all. The time was over 2 seconds outside standard. The winner is rated up a length on his best form of last year.

## 4147 JLL H'CAP (BOBIS RACE) 1m (R)
**5:20** (5:26) (Class 3) (0-90,90) 3-Y-O **£9,703** (£2,887; £1,443; £721) **Stalls** Low

Form RPR

51-3 **1** **Sea Defence (USA)**[62] 2176 3-8-13 **82** ........ JimmyFortune 2 97+
(Roger Charlton) *awkward s but sn trckd clr ldrs: prog to chal 2f out: led over 1f out: forged clr fnl f* **3/1**[1]

6-60 **2** 2 ¾ **Pupil (IRE)**[22] 3378 3-9-7 **90** ........ AdamKirby 10 96
(Richard Hannon) *hld up in last pair: pushed along over 3f out: prog over 2f out: styd on u.p fr over 1f out: tk 2nd last strides* **9/1**

13-5 **3** *nk* **Dutch Art Dealer**[20] 3480 3-8-8 **77** ........ KierenFallon 1 82
(Paul Cole) *t.k.h: prom: trckd ldng pair over 5f out: clsd to ld 2f out: sn jnd: hdd over 1f out: no ex fnl f: lost 2nd nr fin* **12/1**

1462 **4** *nk* **Donny Rover (IRE)**[28] 3200 3-8-9 **85** ........ AlistairRawlinson(7) 6 90
(Michael Appleby) *hld up towards rr: prog over 2f out: chsd ldrs over 1f out but no imp: styd on fnl f: nrly snatched 3rd* **10/1**

2221 **5** 1 ½ **Voyageofdiscovery (USA)**[18] 3538 3-8-10 **82** ........ RyanTate(3) 8 83
(Clive Cox) *led over 6f out to over 5f out: chsd ldr: led again briefly over 2f out: sn outpcd by ldng pair: one pce after* **7/2**[2]

0053 **6** ½ **Cool Bahamian (IRE)**[18] 3538 3-8-7 **81** ........ LouisSteward(5) 11 81
(Eve Johnson Houghton) *hld up in rr: jst abt last 3f out: prog 2f out: nt qckn over 1f out: styd on* **16/1**

2110 **7** 12 **Zerfaal**[41] 2781 3-9-2 **85** ........(p) DaneO'Neill 9 57
(John Gosden) *hld up in midfield: rdn and no prog over 2f out: sn wknd: bhd fnl f* **4/1**[3]

1-64 **8** 1 ¼ **Strait Run (IRE)**[28] 3182 3-8-2 **76** ........ CamHardie(5) 5 46
(Richard Hannon) *led to over 6f out: settled bhd clr ldrs after: wknd over 2f out: bhd fnl f* **25/1**

21-5 **9** 3 ½ **Baarez (USA)**[30] 3108 3-9-4 **87** ........ JackMitchell 4 48
(Roger Varian) *plld hrd: allowed to stride on and led over 5f out: sn stretched field: hdd & wknd jst over 2f out* **12/1**

-100 **10** ¾ **Adhwaa**[23] 3357 3-9-7 **90** ........ GeorgeBaker 7 50
(B W Hills) *s.s: hld up in last pair: rdn and no prog 2f out: bhd over 1f out* **8/1**

1m 39.94s (-0.76) **Going Correction** +0.025s/f (Good) **10** Ran SP% **122.5**
Speed ratings (Par 104): **104,101,100,100,99 98,86,85,81,81**
CSF £32.77 CT £301.09 TOTE £3.80: £1.30, £3.00, £2.90; EX 44.20 Trifecta £601.20.
**Owner** K Abdullah **Bred** Juddmonte Farms Inc **Trained** Beckhampton, Wilts

**FOCUS**
They went a stop-start gallop in this handicap and the unexposed favourite scored with quite a bit in hand. The winner was well on top.

## 4148 SIGNATURE CAPITAL APPRENTICE H'CAP 1m (S)
**5:50** (5:55) (Class 4) (0-85,84) 4-Y-O+ **£6,469** (£1,925; £962; £481) **Stalls** High

Form RPR

6434 **1** **George Cinq**[32] 3050 4-9-9 **84** ........ LouisSteward(3) 1 95+
(Michael Bell) *dwlt: hld up in last pair: smooth prog over 3f out: led jst over 2f out and only one stl gng wl: drvn over 1f out: pressed fnl f: hld on* **13/2**

01 **2** ¾ **Unison (IRE)**[25] 3314 4-8-12 **70** ........ RyanTate 6 79
(Peter Makin) *cl up: rdn wl over 2f out: prog over 1f out: chsd wnr fnl f and sn chal: no ex nr fin* **16/1**

6221 **3** 1 ½ **No Win No Fee**[6] 3977 4-8-9 **72** 6ex ........ AlistairRawlinson(5) 10 78+
(Michael Appleby) *prom: pushed along fr 1/2-way: u.p over 2f out: kpt on but nvr able to chal* **13/8**[1]

-064 **4** 1 ½ **Silver Dixie (USA)**[11] 3802 4-9-1 **78** ........ JordanNason(5) 11 80
(Peter Hedger) *dwlt: hld up: prog over 3f out: sn rdn: nt qckn 2f out: kpt on fnl f to take 4th last strides* **10/1**

1224 **5** *shd* **Sakash**[15] 3628 4-8-9 **70** ........ DannyBrock(3) 4 72
(J R Jenkins) *hld up in rr: prog and rdn over 2f out: chsd wnr wl over 1f out to fnl f: fdd* **25/1**

0021 **6** 2 **Luhaif**[15] 3629 4-9-5 **80** ........(b) ShelleyBirkett(3) 9 78
(Julia Feilden) *led at str pce: drvn and hdd jst over 2f out: steadily fdd* **16/1**

5522 **7** 1 ½ **Lord Ofthe Shadows (IRE)**[12] 3759 5-9-5 **82** ........ CamHardie(5) 7 76
(Richard Hannon) *in tch: rdn 3f out: no imp on ldrs wl over 1f out: wknd fnl f* **9/2**[2]

1260 **8** 2 **Whipper Snapper (IRE)**[28] 3180 4-9-2 **81** ........ CallumShepherd(7) 3 70
(William Knight) *in tch: rdn 3f out: wknd wl over 1f out* **20/1**

3043 **9** *nk* **Talented Kid**[12] 3759 5-9-11 **83** ........ MichaelJMMurphy 12 72
(Mark Johnston) *prom: rdn 3f out: wknd fr over 2f out* **5/1**[3]

1m 40.69s (-0.11) **Going Correction** +0.025s/f (Good) **9** Ran SP% **115.7**
Speed ratings (Par 105): **101,100,98,97,97 95,93,91,91**
CSF £102.90 CT £248.06 TOTE £9.50: £2.60, £3.60, £1.10; EX 109.20 Trifecta £470.80.
**Owner** Tamdown Group Limited **Bred** Oakhill Stud **Trained** Newmarket, Suffolk
■ Stewards' Enquiry : Ryan Tate 13-day ban; excessive use of whip (25th Jul - 6th Aug)

**FOCUS**
This was weakened by a few non-runners but they went a fair pace and the winner scored in smooth style. The form is rated around the runner-up.
T/Plt: £56.90 to a £1 stake. Pool: £89,187.70 - 1,142.85 winning units T/Qpdt: £26.10 to a £1 stake. Pool: £7,099.57 - 200.92 winning units JN

# 3847 CHEPSTOW (L-H)
Friday, July 11

**OFFICIAL GOING: Good to firm (8.2)**
Wind: Slight against Weather: Fine and warm

## 4149 GOCOMPARE.COM APPRENTICE TRAINING SERIES H'CAP (RACING EXCELLENCE INITIATIVE) 1m 4f 23y
**6:00** (6:02) (Class 5) (0-70,65) 4-Y-O+ **£2,587** (£770; £384; £192) **Stalls** Low

Form RPR

34-0 **1** **Now What**[46] 2614 7-9-2 **55** ........ NedCurtis 4 64
(Jonathan Portman) *trckd ldr 3f: racd in 3rd after: 15 l off ldng pair ent st over 4f out: rdn and hdwy 3f out: led over 2f out: sn drvn clr: comf* **4/1**[2]

40/5 **2** 4 ½ **Surprise Us**[9] 3852 7-8-2 **46** ........(p) KieranShoemark(5) 1 48
(Mark Gillard) *led: jnd after 5f: 15 l clr of remainder ent st over 4f out: rdn 3f out: sn outpcd by wnr but plugged on to hold 2nd* **10/1**[3]

0/00 **3** ¾ **Dollar Bill**[20] 3453 5-9-12 **65** ........(v) JordanVaughan 7 66
(Nick Gifford) *mainly racd in 4th: 20 l off ldng pair and rdn 4f out: styd on fnl 2f: wnt 3rd cl home* **11/4**[1]

0545 **4** ½ **Petrify**[11] 3778 4-8-3 **47** ........(tp) MichaelKenneally(5) 6 47
(Bernard Llewellyn) *s.i.s: racd keenly: in rr tl hdwy after 3f: led narrowly after 5f: 15 l clr w one other ent st over 4f out: rdn 3f out: sn hdd and one pce: lost 3rd cl home* **4/1**[2]

0/0- **5** 26 **Stafford Charlie**[19] 3953 8-8-2 **46** oh1 ........(p) AaronJones(5) 5 4
(John O'Shea) *wnt to post early: a towards rr: no ch fnl 5f: t.o* **33/1**

0006 **6** 2 ½ **Elusive Band (USA)**[11] 3778 4-8-8 **50** ........(tp) DavidParkes(3) 2 4
(Bernard Llewellyn) *wnt to post early: towards rr: rdn and disputing poor 4th ent st over 4f out: no imp: wknd 2f out: t.o* **10/1**[3]

3034 **7** *nk* **Honourable Knight (IRE)**[12] 3761 6-9-5 **58** ........(v) CharlotteJenner 3 12
(Mark Usher) *in rr: lost tch and bdly detached 1/2-way: no ch after: t.o* **11/4**[1]

2m 38.1s (-0.90) **Going Correction** -0.05s/f (Good) **7** Ran SP% **114.5**
Speed ratings (Par 103): **101,98,97,97,79 78,77**
CSF £41.94 TOTE £5.30: £2.90, £5.30; EX 43.20 Trifecta £125.80.
**Owner** Mrs S J Portman **Bred** Mrs D O Joly **Trained** Upper Lambourn, Berks

**FOCUS**
The going was good to firm after a dry night. A moderate apprentices' handicap, but a strange race with few getting involved. The winner is rated to last year's form.

## 4150 AND THEY'RE OFF WITH LEISURETIME EBF STALLIONS NOVICE STKS (BOBIS RACE) 5f 16y
**6:30** (6:32) (Class 4) 2-Y-O **£6,469** (£1,925; £962; £481) **Stalls** Centre

Form RPR

15 **1** **Accipiter**[13] 3721 2-8-13 0 ........ AshleyMorgan(3) 2 85+
(Chris Wall) *broke wl: led 1f: styd cl up: rdn to ld ent fnl f: r.o wl* **11/8**[1]

310 **2** 1 ¼ **Fuwairt (IRE)**[24] 3322 2-9-4 0 ........ SteveDrowne 5 83
(Richard Hannon) *hld up in tch: hdwy 2f out: sn rdn and r.o: ev ch 1f out tl no ex fnl 100yds* **7/4**[2]

4210 **3** ½ **London Life (IRE)**[23] 3353 2-8-9 0 ........ JennyPowell(7) 4 79
(Tom Dascombe) *cl up: led after 1f: rdn over 1f out: hdd ent fnl f: kpt on same pce* **9/1**

1 **4** 2 **Sunny York (IRE)**[27] 3232 2-8-13 0 ........ SeanLevey 1 69
(James Tate) *flashed tail early: racd keenly: trckd ldrs: rdn over 1f out and sn outpcd by principals* **8/1**[3]

2213 **5** 1 **Charlie's Star**[65] 2071 2-8-10 0 ........ DeclanBates(3) 6 65
(David Evans) *chsd ldrs: rdn over 2f out: sn outpcd by principals* **8/1**[3]

**6** 47 **Indian Tim** 2-9-0 0 ........ DavidProbert 3
(Milton Bradley) *steaded s: immediately outpcd: lost tch after 2f: t.o* **50/1**

59.59s (0.29) **Going Correction** -0.075s/f (Good) **6** Ran SP% **112.7**
Speed ratings (Par 96): **94,92,91,88,86 11**
CSF £4.06 TOTE £2.70: £1.30, £1.70; EX 4.80 Trifecta £25.60.
**Owner** Follow The Flag Partnership **Bred** The Lavington Stud **Trained** Newmarket, Suffolk

**FOCUS**
The feature contest and a fair-looking novice stakes in which the runners ended up on the far side. Straightforward form.

## 4151 NOAH'S ARK CHILDREN'S HOSPITAL CHARITY H'CAP 5f 16y
**7:05** (7:05) (Class 5) (0-70,70) 3-Y-O+ **£2,587** (£770; £384; £192) **Stalls** Centre

Form RPR

-560 **1** **Edged Out**[17] 3561 4-9-10 **68** ........ DavidProbert 9 77
(Christopher Mason) *chsd ldrs: rdn 2f out: r.o to dispute ld 1f out: sn edgd lft: led last strides* **3/1**[1]

6344 **2** *shd* **Dark Lane**[11] 3784 8-8-9 **60** ........ HollieDoyle(7) 6 69
(David Evans) *chsd ldrs: rdn 2f out: led over 1f out: sn jnd: carried lft ins fnl f: hdd last strides* **4/1**[2]

310 **3** 3 ¾ **Italian Tom (IRE)**[25] 3313 7-9-12 **70** ........ LukeMorris 7 65
(Ronald Harris) *chsd ldrs: rdn and lost pl after 2f: r.o u.p fnl f: nt trble ldng pair* **4/1**[2]

2056 **4** *nk* **Haadeeth**[17] 3549 7-8-7 **54** ........(t) DeclanBates(3) 5 48
(David Evans) *led early: chsd ldr tl led again 2f out: sn hdd: one pce* **9/1**

4-55 **5** 1 ¼ **Monty Fay (IRE)**[18] 3520 5-8-2 **51** oh6 ........ TimClark(5) 10 41
(Derek Haydn Jones) *wnt to s early: in rr: rdn 2f out: stl last 1f out: r.o: nt trble ldrs* **16/1**

0060 **6** 2 **Trending (IRE)**[29] 3150 5-8-13 **57** ........(bt) SeanLevey 1 39
(Jeremy Gask) *in tch: rdn 2f out: no imp on ldrs: wknd ins fnl f* **8/1**

4042 **7** 1 ¼ **Volcanic Dust (IRE)**[18] 3520 6-8-9 **53** ........(t) WilliamCarson 4 31
(Milton Bradley) *wnt to s early: sn led: rdn and hdd 2f out: wknd fnl f* **8/1**

2005 **8** *2 ¼* **Rambo Will**[45] 2637 6-9-5 **66**.............................. NataliaGemelova(3) 3 36
(J R Jenkins) *s.i.s: sn chsng ldrs: rdn 1/2-way: wknd appr fnl f* **5/1**[3]
59.0s (-0.30) **Going Correction** -0.075s/f (Good) **8** Ran SP% **119.8**
Speed ratings (Par 103): **99,98,92,92,90 87,85,81**
CSF £15.97 CT £49.39 TOTE £4.50: £1.50, £1.70, £1.80; EX 18.20 Trifecta £68.30.
**Owner** Christopher & Annabelle Mason **Bred** Christopher & Annabelle Mason **Trained** Caewent, Monmouthshire

**FOCUS**
A modest but quite competitive sprint handicap in which they were spread across the track and it produced a very close finish. The time was 0.59sec faster than the preceding 2yo novice stakes. The winner is rated back to her best.

## 4152 HICKS LOGISTICS FILLIES' H'CAP — 1m 14y

**7:35** (7:35) (Class 5) (0-70,70) 3-Y-O — **£2,587** (£770; £384; £192) **Stalls** Centre

Form — RPR
4-43 **1** **Serena Grae**[18] 3516 3-9-5 **68**.............................. MartinDwyer 5 75
(Marcus Tregoning) *mde all: rdn over 2f out: sn jnd: styd on wl to assert fnl f* **11/4**[1]
454- **2** *2 ½* **Real Jazz (IRE)**[204] 8346 3-8-11 **60**..............................(b[1]) LukeMorris 2 61
(Sir Mark Prescott Bt) *s.i.s: sn chsng ldng trio: drvn 3f out: r.o to go 2nd ins fnl f: no threat to wnr* **11/2**[3]
0-50 **3** *2 ¾* **Chess Valley**[21] 3421 3-9-7 **70**.............................. DavidProbert 4 65
(Rae Guest) *cl up: rdn and ev ch over 2f out tl wknd ent fnl f* **3/1**[2]
5000 **4** *1 ½* **Patronella (IRE)**[27] 3230 3-8-5 **54**.............................. ChrisCatlin 7 45
(David Simcock) *in rr: struggling in last after 3f: styd on wl fnl f: nt trble ldrs* **10/1**
0052 **5** *2 ¼* **Aristocratic Duty**[3] 4047 3-8-13 **62**.............................. LiamKeniry 3 48
(Sylvester Kirk) *prom: rdn over 2f out: wknd over 1f out* **3/1**[2]
41-0 **6** *2 ¼* **Reimpose (USA)**[73] 1846 3-9-2 **65**..............................[1] StevieDonohoe 6 46
(Pat Eddery) *chsd ldng trio tl rdn and outpcd 1/2-way: wknd over 1f out* **20/1**
3016 **7** *1 ½* **Sweet Alibi (IRE)**[12] 3760 3-8-11 **65**.............................. PhilipPrince(5) 8 43
(J S Moore) *towards rr: rdn and sme hdwy 3f out: wknd fnl f* **8/1**
1m 35.14s (-1.06) **Going Correction** -0.075s/f (Good) **7** Ran SP% **117.0**
Speed ratings (Par 97): **102,99,96,95,93 90,89**
CSF £19.04 CT £48.22 TOTE £4.40: £2.00, £2.50; EX 10.60 Trifecta £52.90.
**Owner** Mrs Heather Raw **Bred** Heather Raw **Trained** Whitsbury, Hants

**FOCUS**
An ordinary fillies' handicap that appeared to be run at a sound gallop. The winner built on her C&D run.

## 4153 JENNIFER MELLY LAW H'CAP — 1m 14y

**8:10** (8:11) (Class 5) (0-70,70) 3-Y-O+ — **£2,587** (£770; £384; £192) **Stalls** Centre

Form — RPR
5-06 **1** **Mister Musicmaster**[147] 602 5-9-5 **68**.............................. JennyPowell(7) 4 82
(Ron Hodges) *led narrowly tl pushed into 2 l ld over 3f out: rdn 2f out: r.o strly and sn drew clr* **14/1**
0435 **2** *4 ½* **Living Leader**[6] 3971 5-9-7 **63**..............................(p) StevieDonohoe 3 67
(Grace Harris) *s.i.s: sn chsng ldng pair: rdn over 2f out: r.o to go 2nd fnl 50yds: no ch w wnr* **6/1**
0513 **3** *nk* **Tenbridge**[9] 3850 5-9-5 **61**..............................(v) DavidProbert 2 64
(Derek Haydn Jones) *disp ld over 3f: rdn over 2f out: sn outpcd by wnr but kpt on: lost 2nd fnl 50yds* **7/2**[1]
0204 **4** *nse* **Lady Bayside**[9] 3850 6-9-13 **69**.............................. LiamKeniry 1 72
(Malcolm Saunders) *hld up bhd ldrs: rdn over 2f out: r.o ins fnl f* **5/1**[3]
5545 **5** *2* **Peak Storm**[9] 3850 5-10-0 **70**..............................(v) LukeMorris 7 68
(John O'Shea) *in tch: rdn over 3f out: kpt on same pce fnl 2f* **10/1**
430 **6** *2* **Emperatriz**[143] 647 4-9-5 **68**.............................. KieranShoemark(7) 5 62
(John Holt) *chsd ldrs: rdn over 3f out: one pce and no ch after* **20/1**
3034 **7** *4 ½* **Delightful Sleep**[1] 4105 6-8-11 **56**.............................. DeclanBates(3) 12 39
(David Evans) *towards rr: rdn and hdwy over 2f out: wknd fnl f* **5/1**[3]
3611 **8** *3 ¼* **Zed Candy Girl**[16] 3576 4-8-11 **58**..............................(p) TimClark(5) 9 34
(Dai Burchell) *in tch: rdn 3f out: wkng whn sltly hmpd over 1f out* **4/1**[2]
5666 **9** *½* **Thewestwalian (USA)**[42] 2720 6-8-9 **51** oh6.............................. ChrisCatlin 8 26
(Peter Hiatt) *in tch: drvn 3f out: sn outpcd by ldrs: wknd fnl f* **25/1**
3550 **10** *nk* **Xclusive**[44] 2672 4-9-1 **57**.............................. SteveDrowne 6 31
(Ronald Harris) *sn towards rr: rdn over 3f out: wknd over 2f out* **20/1**
1m 33.99s (-2.21) **Going Correction** -0.075s/f (Good) **10** Ran SP% **119.0**
Speed ratings (Par 103): **108,103,103,103,101 99,94,91,90,90**
CSF £94.73 CT £311.39 TOTE £12.50: £3.30, £2.40, £1.70; EX 112.10 Trifecta £432.00.
**Owner** Mrs L Sharpe & Mrs S G Clapp **Bred** Mrs J Fuller And S Dutfield **Trained** Charlton Mackrell, Somerset

**FOCUS**
Several C&D winners in this handicap which was run 1.15sec faster than the preceding fillies' contest. The winner's best form since last spring.

## 4154 MCL LOGISTICS H'CAP — 7f 16y

**8:40** (8:42) (Class 4) (0-85,85) 3-Y-O+ — **£4,690** (£1,395; £697; £348) **Stalls** Centre

Form — RPR
1-40 **1** **Take A Note**[25] 3314 5-9-7 **78**..............................(v) DavidProbert 7 86
(Patrick Chamings) *bustled along leaving stalls: sn trcking ldrs: rdn to chal 3f out: led wl over 1f out: edgd lft ins fnl f: hld on wl u.p* **10/1**
3-6 **2** *½* **Black Dave (IRE)**[37] 2884 4-8-6 **66**.............................. DeclanBates(3) 1 73
(David Evans) *hld up in tch: rdn 3f out: hdwy 2f out: ev ch 1f out tl cl home* **8/1**
062 **3** *½* **Light From Mars**[11] 3783 9-9-1 **79**..............................(p) MikeyEnnis(7) 5 85
(Ronald Harris) *hld up in tch: nt clr run over 1f out: sn rdn: swtchd rt ins fnl f: r.o* **6/1**
0002 **4** *1* **Postscript (IRE)**[20] 3463 6-10-0 **85**.............................. SeanLevey 3 88
(David Simcock) *cl up: led narrowly 3f out: sn rdn: hdd wl over 1f out: no ex fnl 100yds* **2/1**[1]
5051 **5** *½* **Perfect Mission**[16] 3589 6-8-2 **66**..............................(v) KieranShoemark(7) 6 68
(Andrew Balding) *racd keenly: prom tl led over 5f out: hdd 3f out: sn drvn and one pce: keeping on cl home* **9/2**[3]
6461 **6** *3 ¼* **Sarangoo**[4] 4024 6-9-3 **74**.............................. LukeMorris 2 67
(Malcolm Saunders) *led over 1f: styd prom: rdn 1/2-way: wknd appr fnl f* **3/1**[2]
00-P **7** *11* **Kazak**[15] 3616 4-8-5 **67**..............................(t) DanielMuscutt(5) 4 32
(Robert Stephens) *hld up in rr: rdn 3f out: sn outpcd: bhd fnl 2f* **25/1**
1m 22.14s (-1.06) **Going Correction** -0.075s/f (Good) **7** Ran SP% **114.8**
Speed ratings (Par 105): **103,102,101,100,100 96,83**
CSF £84.85 CT £524.79 TOTE £9.10: £3.40, £2.40; EX 97.80 Trifecta £513.90.
**Owner** The Foxford House Partnership **Bred** P J L Wright **Trained** Baughurst, Hants
■ Stewards' Enquiry : Declan Bates four-day ban; excessive use of whip (25th, 27th-29th July)

**FOCUS**
A fair contest and a good finish.

## 4155 BARTHOLOMEW HAWKINS CHARTERED FINANCIAL PLANNERS H'CAP — 6f 16y

**9:10** (9:10) (Class 5) (0-70,68) 3-Y-O — **£2,587** (£770; £384; £192) **Stalls** Centre

Form — RPR
2460 **1** **Double Czech (IRE)**[29] 3145 3-9-4 **65**..............................(v) DavidProbert 4 75
(Patrick Chamings) *chsd ldrs: rdn 2f out: led over 1f out: r.o wl u.p* **7/2**[2]
0-03 **2** *3 ½* **Lady Crossmar (IRE)**[16] 3566 3-9-4 **65**.............................. SeanLevey 3 64
(Richard Hannon) *disp ld 3f: chsd ldrs after: rdn 3f out: r.o u.p fnl f* **5/1**[3]
5634 **3** *¾* **Coiste Bodhar (IRE)**[18] 3523 3-8-10 **64**..............................(p) NoraLooby(7) 2 60
(Joseph Tuite) *racd keenly: led: rdn 3f out: hdd 2f out: one pce and hld whn rdr dropped whip ins fnl f* **6/1**
-220 **4** *½* **Fantasy Justifier (IRE)**[18] 3518 3-9-7 **68**.............................. LukeMorris 1 63+
(Ronald Harris) *s.i.s: racd keenly and sn chsng ldrs: rdn to ld 2f out: hdd over 1f out: no ex ins fnl f* **11/4**[1]
5330 **5** *1 ¼* **Wedgewood Estates**[16] 3564 3-8-8 **55**.............................. WilliamCarson 5 46
(Tony Carroll) *towards rr: rdn and sme hdwy 3f out: one pce fnl f* **7/1**
55 **6** *7* **Prize**[9] 3855 3-8-9 **56**.............................. MartinDwyer 6 24
(Sylvester Kirk) *hld up in rr: rdn over 3f out: no imp: wknd wl over 1f out* **7/2**[2]
1m 11.42s (-0.58) **Going Correction** -0.075s/f (Good) **6** Ran SP% **114.6**
Speed ratings (Par 100): **100,95,94,93,92 82**
CSF £21.48 TOTE £5.20: £2.40, £2.20; EX 24.00 Trifecta £115.70.
**Owner** K W Tyrrell **Bred** Henry O'Callaghan **Trained** Baughurst, Hants

**FOCUS**
A modest 3yo sprint but a double on the night for the trainer and a treble for the jockey. The form is rated a bit cautiously.
T/Plt: £381.40 to a £1 stake. Pool: £65,928.90 - 126.17 winning units T/Qpdt: £100.60 to a £1 stake. Pool: £7,847.78 - 57.70 winning units RL

# 3692 CHESTER (L-H)

### Friday, July 11

**OFFICIAL GOING: Good to firm (good in places; 7.6)**
Wind: Light, half against Weather: Hot and sunny

## 4156 ABODE HOTEL H'CAP (FOR LADY AMATEUR RIDERS) — 7f 122y

**6:15** (6:16) (Class 4) (0-80,80) 4-Y-O+ — **£6,586** (£2,026; £1,013) **Stalls** Low

Form — RPR
2320 **1** **My Single Malt (IRE)**[62] 2169 6-9-8 **72**..............................(p) MissLWilson(5) 4 81
(Julie Camacho) *trckd ldrs: wnt 2nd 1f out: r.o to ld fnl 100yds: a doing enough after* **9/2**[2]
-214 **2** *nk* **Cara's Request (AUS)**[18] 3533 9-9-9 **73**.............................. MissMeganNicholls(5) 3 81
(Michael Dods) *w ldr: led 5f out: hdd wl over 3f out: stl cl 2nd tl regained ld 2f out: rdn 1f out: hdd fnl 100yds: r.o for press but hld* **9/2**[2]
5433 **3** *1 ¼* **Prime Exhibit**[7] 3908 9-9-8 **67**..............................(t) MissAliceMills 6 72
(Daniel Mark Loughnane) *hld up in rr: hdwy 2f out: rdn to chse ldrs 1f out: r.o and gng on at fin: nt quite get to front pair* **20/1**
3032 **4** *1* **Kakapuka**[17] 3555 7-9-9 **68**.............................. MissJoannaMason 11 70
(Anabel K Murphy) *showed gd spd: led: hdd 5f out: remained prom: rdn over 2f out: kpt on same pce ins fnl f* **20/1**
-561 **5** *1 ¾* **Orpsie Boy (IRE)**[24] 3339 11-9-9 **68**.............................. MissSBrotherton 5 66
(Ruth Carr) *dwlt: midfield: rdn 2f out: kpt on ins fnl f: nvr able to chal* **9/2**[2]
02 **6** *1* **Checkpoint**[11] 3791 5-8-13 **63**.............................. MissHDukes(5) 2 59+
(Tony Coyle) *hld up: hdwy 2f out: kpt on fnl f: nvr able to trble ldrs* **4/1**[1]
-100 **7** *hd* **Another Try (IRE)**[27] 3227 9-9-6 **70**.............................. MissTSutherland(5) 15 65
(Timothy Jarvis) *racd on wd outer: ev ch over 3f out: one pce under hand ride fnl f* **50/1**
0455 **8** *¾* **Poor Duke (IRE)**[8] 3880 4-9-7 **66**..............................(p) MissMMullineaux 10 59
(Michael Mullineaux) *midfield: lost pl 4f out: outpcd over 2f out: kpt on u.p over 1f out: no imp* **50/1**
6603 **9** *1 ¼* **Freddy With A Y (IRE)**[20] 3468 4-10-1 **74**..........(v[1]) MissHayleyMoore 8 64
(Gary Moore) *trckd ldrs: led wl over 3f out: rdn and hdd 2f out: wknd ins fnl f* **10/1**
4-40 **10** *2 ½* **Clary (IRE)**[67] 2021 4-8-11 **61** oh13.............................. MissPFuller(5) 7 45
(James Unett) *in rr: u.p over 2f out: nvr a threat* **66/1**
620P **11** *1* **Our Boy Jack (IRE)**[48] 2548 5-10-2 **80**.............................. MissJMcLernon(5) 1 61
(Richard Fahey) *midfield: pushed along and lost pl 4f out: outpcd after and n.d* **6/1**[3]
1004 **12** *1 ¾* **Exzachary**[22] 3402 4-10-0 **73**.............................. MissEJJones 9 50
(Jo Hughes) *dwlt: sltly hmpd st after s: in rr: hdwy into midfield over 3f out: rdn over 2f out: sn wknd* **28/1**
5125 **13** *2 ½* **Licence To Till (USA)**[13] 3718 7-10-7 **80**.............................. MissJRRichards 14 51
(Alan Berry) *midfield tl wknd over 2f out* **33/1**
1m 32.1s (-1.70) **Going Correction** -0.175s/f (Firm) **13** Ran SP% **119.2**
Speed ratings (Par 105): **101,100,99,98,96 95,95,94,93,91 90,88,85**
CSF £23.17 CT £373.67 TOTE £6.50: £1.90, £2.10, £5.80; EX 33.70 Trifecta £601.70.
**Owner** Nigel Gravett **Bred** Ballylinch Stud **Trained** Norton, N Yorks
■ Stewards' Enquiry : Miss L Wilson two-day ban; used whip in the incorrect place (29th July, 1st Aug)
Miss J McLernon five-day ban; used whip when out of contention (26th, 29th, 30th July - 1st, 4th Aug)

**FOCUS**
A dry run up to a meeting run on good, good to firm ground. The running rail was at its innermost position meaning all races were run over the advertised distances. Mainly exposed performers in a fair handicap. The gallop was reasonable but those held up were at a disadvantage. The winner was close to the form which saw him finish second in the last two runnings.

## 4157 MBNA NURSERY H'CAP (BOBIS RACE) — 7f 2y

**6:45** (6:47) (Class 4) 2-Y-O — **£6,469** (£1,925; £962; £481) **Stalls** Low

Form — RPR
225 **1** **Flying Machine (IRE)**[29] 3140 2-8-11 **75** ow1.............................. FrederikTylicki 1 81+
(Richard Fahey) *led early: sn hdd: trckd ldrs after: wnt 2nd over 2f out: led jst over 1f out: r.o wl to draw clr fnl 100yds* **5/2**[2]
13 **2** *3 ½* **Buccaneers Vault (IRE)**[49] 2521 2-9-4 **85**.............................. ConnorBeasley(3) 2 82
(Michael Dods) *sn led: hdd over 5f out: chsd ldr tl rdn and lost 2nd over 2f out: nt qckn over 1f out: kpt on u.p to regain 2nd ins fnl f: no ch w wnr* **9/4**[1]
5435 **3** *nk* **Popeswood (IRE)**[24] 3324 2-8-11 **75**.............................. BenCurtis 4 71
(Mick Channon) *hld up in tch: effrt to chse ldrs over 2f out: styd on same pce fnl 100yds* **9/1**



The Form Book, Raceform Ltd, Newbury, RG14 5SJ

3046 **4** *2 ½* **Sportlobster (IRE)**[3] 4057 2-8-5 **69**...............(v[1]) HayleyTurner 6 58
(Tom Dascombe) *bustled along early to go prom: led over 5f out: rdn over 2f out: hdd jst over 1f out: wknd fnl 100yds* **10/1**

21 **5** *½* **Arabian Bride (IRE)**[15] 3606 2-9-3 **81**............... RichardKingscote 8 69
(Mark Johnston) *in tch: lost pl and outpcd over 3f out: n.d after* **3/1**[3]

01 **6** *6* **Dream Approval (IRE)**[17] 3550 2-8-2 **66**........................ PaoloSirigu 5 37
(Daniel Kubler) *hld up: hdwy on outer over 3f out: lost pl wl over 2f out: n.d after* **10/1**

6021 **P** **Just Marion (IRE)**[25] 3312 2-8-0 **64** oh2........................ RaulDaSilva 3
(David Evans) *got upset in stalls: prom: rdn thrght: wknd wl over 2f out: eased whn wl bhd over 1f out: t.o whn p.u nr fin* **33/1**

1m 26.54s (0.04) **Going Correction** -0.175s/f (Firm) 7 Ran SP% **115.5**
Speed ratings (Par 96): **92,88,87,84,84 77,**
CSF £8.77 CT £41.60 TOTE £3.00: £1.70, £1.60; EX 11.40 Trifecta £61.90.
**Owner** G Devlin **Bred** Derek Veitch And Saleh Ali Hammadi **Trained** Musley Bank, N Yorks

**FOCUS**
A useful nursery in which the gallop was fair. The winner posted a minor best and the third helps with the level.

## 4158 LDF H'CAP (BOBIS RACE) 5f 16y
7:15 (7:15) (Class 2) (0-105,105) 3-Y-O **£12,602** (£3,772; £1,886; £944) **Stalls** Low

Form RPR

4015 **1** **Peterkin (IRE)**[20] 3478 3-8-7 **91**........................ FrannyNorton 1 96
(Mark Johnston) *mde all: rdn over 1f out: pressed ins fnl f: kpt finding for press: hld on wl* **5/6**[1]

0-00 **2** *nk* **Green Door (IRE)**[6] 3981 3-9-7 **105**...............(b) JamieSpencer 2 109
(Olly Stevens) *racd keenly: chsd ldrs: wnt 2nd 2f out: str chal ins fnl f: r.o for press: hld nr fin* **11/4**[2]

0150 **3** *1 ¾* **Piazon**[20] 3478 3-8-5 **89**........................ HayleyTurner 4 87
(Michael Bell) *in rr: rdn to take 3rd over 1f out: kpt on ins fnl f: nvr able to chal front two* **7/1**

2100 **4** *9* **Blithe Spirit**[20] 3459 3-8-12 **96**........................ JasonHart 3 61
(Eric Alston) *stmbld s: chsd wnr: rdn and hung rt fr 3f out: lost 2nd 2f out: sn wknd* **13/2**[3]

58.88s (-2.12) **Going Correction** -0.175s/f (Firm) course record 4 Ran SP% **107.1**
Speed ratings (Par 106): **109,108,105,91**
CSF £3.28 TOTE £1.60; EX 4.20 Trifecta £8.20.
**Owner** Sheikh Hamdan bin Mohammed Al Maktoum **Bred** Darley **Trained** Middleham Moor, N Yorks

**FOCUS**
A disappointing turnout but nevertheless a decent handicap in which the pace was sound and a race that broke the 50-year track record. The form makes sense.

## 4159 FORTRESS MANAGEMENT SERVICES 20TH ANNIVERSARY/ EBF STALLIONS CONDITIONS STKS (BOBIS RACE) 5f 16y
7:45 (7:47) (Class 2) 2-Y-O **£12,938** (£3,850; £1,924; £962) **Stalls** Low

Form RPR

1 **1** **Showing Character**[13] 3692 2-9-1 0........................ RichardKingscote 1 97+
(Tom Dascombe) *mde all: qcknd clr ins fnl f: r.o wl and in command after* **4/7**[1]

41 **2** *2 ¾* **Rosie's Premiere (IRE)**[11] 3799 2-8-7 0........................ FrannyNorton 5 79
(Dean Ivory) *in rr: effrt on outer over 2f out: wnt 2nd 1f out: styd on ins fnl f: nt pce of wnr and no ch* **8/1**

12 **3** *1* **Steve Prescott**[13] 3692 2-9-1 0........................ DavidNolan 2 83
(Richard Fahey) *in tch: effrt 2f out: edgd rt ins fnl f: unable to go w wnr: styd on same pce fnl 100yds* **3/1**[2]

2110 **4** *5* **Clouds Rest**[23] 3353 2-8-12 0........................ TomEaves 4 62
(Richard Fahey) *prom: w wnr over 3f out: rdn and nt qckn over 1f out: sn lost 2nd: btn whn sltly short of room ins fnl f: dropped away* **7/1**[3]

5410 **5** *8* **Casterbridge**[24] 3322 2-9-1 0........................ JasonHart 3 36
(Eric Alston) *unruly bef r: racd w ldrs: dropped in bhd pce setters over 3f out: wknd 2f out: lft bhd over 1f out* **20/1**

(-1.00) **Going Correction** -0.175s/f (Firm) 5 Ran SP% **117.0**
Speed ratings (Par 100): **101,96,95,87,74**
CSF £6.80 TOTE £1.30: £1.10, £5.70; EX 3.60 Trifecta £12.60.
**Owner** The Mad March Hares **Bred** Jeremy Green And Sons **Trained** Malpas, Cheshire

**FOCUS**
A very useful conditions event in which all the runners were winners. The gallop was sound and the winner remains a smart prospect. The runner-up seems the key to the form.

## 4160 MOSS BROS H'CAP 1m 4f 66y
8:20 (8:20) (Class 3) (0-90,88) 3-Y-O+ **£8,086** (£2,406; £1,202; £601) **Stalls** Low

Form RPR

/315 **1** **Kings Bayonet**[27] 3250 7-9-8 **82**........................ HayleyTurner 6 94
(Alan King) *hld up in rr: swtchd rt and hdwy over 1f out: r.o to ld wl ins fnl f: in command cl home* **14/1**

121 **2** *1* **Xinbama (IRE)**[26] 3274 5-9-5 **79**........................ RichardKingscote 3 89
(B W Hills) *hld up: hdwy over 2f out: chsd ldrs over 1f out: chalng ins fnl f: nt pce of wnr and hld towards fin* **7/2**[1]

221 **3** *2 ¼* **English Summer**[13] 3696 7-9-5 **79**...............(t) DavidNolan 5 85
(Richard Fahey) *in tch: clsd 3f out: rdn to ld jst over 1f out: hdd wl ins fnl f: styd on same pce after* **6/1**

-656 **4** *1* **Snow Squall**[16] 3587 3-8-3 **76**........................ FrannyNorton 8 81
(Mark Johnston) *prom: rdn to ld 2f out: hdd jst over 1f out: no ex fnl 100yds* **4/1**[2]

1-33 **5** *1 ¾* **Familliarity**[19] 3500 4-9-6 **80**........................ FrederikTylicki 1 82
(Roger Varian) *trckd ldrs: swtchd lft to chal briefly over 1f out: nt qckn: wknd fnl 100yds* **9/2**[3]

2300 **6** *2 ¾* **Modernism**[13] 3730 5-10-0 **88**........................ JamieSpencer 2 86
(David Simcock) *midfield: rdn over 1f out: one pce and no imp fnl f* **9/1**

2201 **7** *nk* **Wilhana (IRE)**[27] 3218 4-9-8 **82**........................ StephenCraine 4 79
(Pam Sly) *led: rdn and hdd 2f out: stl there but u.p over 1f out: wknd ins fnl f* **10/1**

166 **8** *7* **Love Marmalade (IRE)**[20] 3457 4-9-5 **79**........................ PJMcDonald 7 65
(Alistair Whillans) *hld up: rdn and outpcd 3f out: nvr a threat* **20/1**

-115 **9** *9* **Aramist (IRE)**[16] 3574 4-9-7 **81**........................ BenCurtis 9 53
(Alan Swinbank) *prom: rdn over 3f out: wknd wl over 2f out* **7/1**

2m 34.88s (-3.62) **Going Correction** -0.175s/f (Firm)
**WFA** 3 from 4yo+ 13lb 9 Ran SP% **117.7**
Speed ratings (Par 107): **105,104,102,102,101 99,98,94,88**
CSF £63.89 CT £335.92 TOTE £10.00: £4.30, £1.30, £1.60; EX 72.70 Trifecta £287.60.
**Owner** W H Ponsonby **Bred** Mickley Stud & C J Whiston **Trained** Barbury Castle, Wilts

**FOCUS**
A useful handicap featuring mainly exposed types. The gallop seemed an ordinary one to the 3f pole but those held up filled the first two placings. The winner resumed his progress.

## 4161 HOBBS H'CAP 7f 2y
8:50 (8:51) (Class 4) (0-80,80) 3-Y-O+ **£6,469** (£1,925; £962; £481) **Stalls** Low

Form RPR

4131 **1** **Repetition**[18] 3533 4-10-0 **80**........................ TomEaves 8 91
(Kristin Stubbs) *mde all: rdn over 1f out: pressed wl ins fnl f: gamely kpt finding: hld on wl* **3/1**[1]

-412 **2** *½* **Picks Pinta**[14] 3662 3-8-12 **72**........................ FrannyNorton 7 78
(Jo Hughes) *trckd ldrs: wnt 2nd over 2f out: rdn over 1f out: chal wl ins fnl f: a hld* **5/1**[3]

0032 **3** *4* **Celtic Sixpence (IRE)**[27] 3220 6-9-9 **75**........................ MichaelStainton 6 74
(Nick Kent) *midfield: hdwy on inner over 2f out: chsd ldrs over 1f out: no ex fnl 100yds* **17/2**

-044 **4** *nk* **Rangi Chase (IRE)**[14] 3647 3-8-12 **72**........................ JamieSpencer 3 67
(Richard Fahey) *in rr: rdn and hdwy on outer over 1f out: styd on ins fnl f: no imp on front pair* **7/2**[2]

210 **5** *4 ½* **Sitting Pritty (IRE)**[29] 3137 3-9-0 **74**........................ RichardKingscote 10 58
(Tom Dascombe) *chsd wnr tl over 2f out: rdn and wknd over 1f out* **16/1**

1031 **6** *hd* **Ralphy Boy (IRE)**[14] 3646 5-9-11 **77**........................ PJMcDonald 9 63
(Alistair Whillans) *in tch: rdn 2f out: no imp on ldrs: wknd fnl f* **7/1**

0/00 **7** *7* **Gabrial's Bounty (IRE)**[27] 3221 5-9-9 **75**........................ DavidNolan 11 43
(Richard Fahey) *midfield: wknd over 1f out* **14/1**

0235 **8** *¾* **King Of Eden (IRE)**[3] 4061 8-9-11 **77**........................ JasonHart 13 43
(Eric Alston) *in rr and rdn: nvr on terms* **10/1**

4413 **9** *6* **Know Your Name**[11] 3782 3-9-1 **75**...............(v) BenCurtis 12 22
(David Evans) *chsd ldrs tl rdn and wknd over 2f out* **11/1**

1m 24.24s (-2.26) **Going Correction** -0.175s/f (Firm)
**WFA** 3 from 4yo+ 8lb 9 Ran SP% **116.9**
Speed ratings (Par 105): **105,104,99,99,94 94,86,85,78**
CSF £18.46 CT £115.30 TOTE £6.40: £1.90, £2.40, £1.90; EX 14.90 Trifecta £271.00.
**Owner** The B P J Partnership **Bred** G Reed **Trained** Norton, N Yorks

**FOCUS**
Mainly exposed sorts in a fair handicap. The gallop was an ordinary one and, as is often the case around here, not many figured. The first four all raced on the rail, and the winner continued his great run.

## 4162 TRINITY MIRROR H'CAP (BOBIS RACE) 1m 2f 75y
9:20 (9:20) (Class 4) (0-85,85) 3-Y-O **£6,469** (£1,925; £962; £481) **Stalls** High

Form RPR

1442 **1** **Yenhaab (IRE)**[12] 3758 3-9-7 **85**........................ JamieSpencer 5 99+
(William Haggas) *led after 1f: mde rest: rdn and qcknd over 1f out: drew clr ins fnl f: r.o wl: eased down towards fin* **10/11**[1]

4501 **2** *2* **Our Gabrial (IRE)**[14] 3643 3-9-5 **83**........................ DavidNolan 3 91
(Richard Fahey) *led for 1f: chsd wnr tl over 7f out: pushed along 3f out: regained 2nd 2f out: no imp on wnr fnl f and wl hld* **9/2**[3]

3132 **3** *7* **Bureau (IRE)**[6] 3968 3-9-4 **82**........................ FrannyNorton 4 77
(Mark Johnston) *chsd ldrs: dropped to rr 7f out: pushed along 5f out: outpcd 2f out: wnt poor 3rd 1f out: no ch* **5/2**[2]

0544 **4** *5* **Grevillea (IRE)**[18] 3538 3-9-2 **80**........................ GrahamGibbons 6 65
(Mick Channon) *racd keenly: hld up in rr: hdwy to chse wnr over 7f out: rdn and lost 2nd 2f out: wknd over 1f out* **11/1**

2m 8.65s (-2.55) **Going Correction** -0.175s/f (Firm) 4 Ran SP% **107.5**
Speed ratings (Par 102): **103,101,95,91**
CSF £5.22 TOTE £1.80; EX 3.70 Trifecta £5.00.
**Owner** Essafinaat & Qatar Racing **Bred** Albert Conneally **Trained** Newmarket, Suffolk

**FOCUS**
A depleted field but nevertheless a useful performance from the winner, who was allowed to do his own thing in front. The first two pulled clear in the straight.
T/Plt: £53.00 to a £1 stake. Pool: £66,988.42 - 922.13 winning units T/Qpdt: £6.70 to a £1 stake. Pool: £4,380.56 - 480.20 winning units DO

# 4122 NEWMARKET (R-H)
### Friday, July 11

**OFFICIAL GOING: Soft (5.8)**
Wind: Medium; half behind Weather: Dry and slowly brightening up after wet morning

## 4163 PRICE BAILEY EBF STALLIONS FILLIES' H'CAP (BOBIS RACE) 7f
1:40 (1:41) (Class 2) (0-100,94) 3-Y-O
**£15,562** (£4,660; £2,330; £1,165; £582; £292) **Stalls** Low

Form RPR

4450 **1** **Nakuti (IRE)**[23] 3357 3-8-10 **83**........................ RyanMoore 6 91
(Sylvester Kirk) *hld up in tch in last pair: clsd to chse ldrs and nt clr run over 1f out: rdn and hdwy between rivals to ld fnl 100yds: r.o wl u.p* **7/2**[2]

00-2 **2** *¾* **Gown (IRE)**[8] 3890 3-8-3 **76**........................ JimmyQuinn 2 82
(Charles Hills) *wl in tch in midfield: nt clr run 2f out: swtchd lft and hdwy over 1f out: edging bk rt and chsd ldrs 1f out: r.o wl to snatch 2nd nr fin* **8/1**

1464 **3** *nk* **Wedding Ring (IRE)**[13] 3724 3-9-7 **94**........................ WilliamBuick 7 99
(Charlie Appleby) *chsd ldng pair: rdn and effrt to ld ent fnl f: drvn and hdd fnl 100yds: styd on same pce after: lost 2nd towards fin* **6/1**

4-33 **4** *2 ½* **Our Queenie (IRE)**[14] 3674 3-9-0 **87**........................ KieranO'Neill 10 86
(Richard Hannon) *w ldr tl led 3f out: drvn and hdd over 1f out: sn no ex: wknd ins fnl f* **11/1**

-340 **5** *1 ¼* **Hot Coffee (IRE)**[23] 3357 3-9-2 **89**........................ RichardKingscote 9 84
(Tom Dascombe) *t.k.h early: hld up wl in tch in midfield: rdn and effrt over 1f out: unable qck and btn 1f out: wknd ins fnl f* **3/1**[1]

0361 **6** *4* **Little Shambles**[9] 3844 3-8-12 **85** 6ex........................ JoeFanning 4 70
(Mark Johnston) *led: hdd 3f out: rdn wl over 1f out: sn struggling and btn: wknd 1f out* **10/1**

41 **7** *3 ¾* **Free Rein**[14] 3664 3-8-2 **75**........................ SilvestreDeSousa 8 50
(Ralph Beckett) *stdd s: t.k.h: hld up in tch in rr: rdn and effrt over 1f out: sn btn and edgd rt 1f out: wknd* **4/1**[3]

1m 29.18s (3.48) **Going Correction** +0.525s/f (Yiel) 7 Ran SP% **110.0**
Speed ratings (Par 103): **101,100,99,96,95 90,86**
CSF £28.41 CT £149.52 TOTE £4.20: £2.50, £3.50; EX 31.20 Trifecta £226.40.
**Owner** Nelius Hayes **Bred** Eamonn McEvoy **Trained** Upper Lambourn, Berks

**FOCUS**
Stands side track used with Stalls on Stands side except 10f: Centre. The gallop was a fairly steady one for this fillies' handicap, which, following the non-runners, ended up being an average race for the grade. They raced under the stands' rail. The winner is accorded a personal best.

## 4164 DUCHESS OF CAMBRIDGE STKS (SPONSORED BY QIPCO) (GROUP 2) 6f
2:10 (2:10) (Class 1) 2-Y-O £45,368 (£17,200; £8,608; £4,288; £2,152) Stalls Low

Form RPR
016 1 **Arabian Queen (IRE)**[23] 3353 2-9-0 0 RyanMoore 6 100
(David Elsworth) *led and dictated gallop: rdn and qcknd wl over 1f out: pressed ins fnl f: fnd ex and asserted fnl 100yds: r.o wl* 4/1[2]

2 1 1/4 **High Celebrity (FR)**[21] 2-9-0 0 MaximeGuyon 1 99+
(A Fabre, France) *stdd and bmpd sn after s: swtchd lft and t.k.h in rr: clsd 2f out: rdn to chse wnr ent fnl f: drvn and pressing wnr fnl 150yds: no ex and btn fnl 100yds: eased towards fin* 4/9[1]

2 3 3 **Tongue Twista**[12] 3757 2-9-0 0 J-PGuillambert 5 87
(Nick Littmoden) *chsd ldng pair: rdn wl over 1f out: 4th: drvn and unable qck 1f out: no threat to ldng pair but kpt on to go 3rd last strides* 50/1

212 4 hd **Parsley (IRE)**[13] 3721 2-9-0 0 RichardHughes 2 87
(Richard Hannon) *chsd wnr: rdn wl over 1f out: 3rd and unable qck 1f out: styd on same pce after: lost 3rd last strides* 13/2[3]

161 5 1 1/4 **Diamond Creek (IRE)**[28] 3188 2-9-0 0 TonyHamilton 3 83
(Richard Fahey) *restless in stalls: stdd and wnt rt sn after s: t.k.h: hld up in tch in last pair: rdn wl over 1f out: no imp: wknd ins fnl f* 25/1

1m 15.14s (2.64) **Going Correction** +0.525s/f (Yiel) 5 Ran SP% 108.4
Speed ratings (Par 106): **103,101,97,97,95**
CSF £6.05 TOTE £4.60: £2.00, £1.10; EX 6.90 Trifecta £60.70.
**Owner** J C Smith **Bred** Littleton Stud **Trained** Newmarket, Suffolk

**FOCUS**
The run of the race saw Arabian Queen edge out the less-experienced High Celebrity in an interesting edition of a Group 2 formerly known as the Cherry Hinton. It looked a very weak renewal in terms of form though. The runner-up may well prove the best of these in time.

## 4165 QIPCO FALMOUTH STKS (BRITISH CHAMPIONS SERIES) (GROUP 1) (F&M) 1m
2:40 (2:41) (Class 1) 3-Y-O+
£113,420 (£43,000; £21,520; £10,720; £5,380; £2,700) Stalls Low

Form RPR
2-21 1 **Integral**[23] 3355 4-9-7 117 RyanMoore 5 119
(Sir Michael Stoute) *t.k.h: chsd ldr for 3f: styd chsng ldrs: rdn to ld wl over 1f out: 2 l clr and in command 1f out: r.o wl: drvn out* 15/8[1]

2-01 2 2 **Rizeena (IRE)**[21] 3418 3-8-12 111 OlivierPeslier 6 112
(Clive Brittain) *hld up in tch: hdwy to join ldr 5f out: led over 3f out: rdn and hdd wl over 1f out: kpt on to hold 2nd but a hld by wnr fnl f* 4/1[2]

2005 3 3/4 **Peace Burg (FR)**[12] 3766 4-9-7 108 (t) JosephO'Brien 3 113
(A P O'Brien, Ire) *hld up wl in tch in midfield: nt clr run ent fnl 2f: drvn and hdwy to chse ldng pair 1f out: edgd lft and kpt on ins fnl f: no imp on wnr* 25/1

5-13 4 3 1/2 **Purr Along**[23] 3355 4-9-7 109 JamieSpencer 7 105
(J P Murtagh, Ire) *stdd and dropped in bhd after s: hld up in tch in last pair: hdwy over 2f out: drvn and chsd ldrs over 1f out: no ex 1f out: wknd ins fnl f* 9/2[3]

10-5 5 3 1/4 **Sky Lantern (IRE)**[23] 3355 4-9-7 119 RichardHughes 1 97
(Richard Hannon) *led tl over 3f out: dropped to 3rd and nt clr run over 2f out: rdn wl over 1f out: sn outpcd and wknd ent fnl f* 4/1[2]

23-0 6 2 1/4 **Kiyoshi**[21] 3418 3-8-12 109 HarryBentley 4 90
(Charles Hills) *wl in tch in midfield: rdn and lost pl over 3f out: swtchd lft and rallied briefly 2f out: sn btn and wknd over 1f out* 11/1

/140 7 9 **Certify (USA)**[23] 3355 4-9-7 113 WilliamBuick 2 71
(Charlie Appleby) *t.k.h: hld up in tch in last pair: swtchd lft and hdwy 3f out: rdn 2f out: sn struggling and wknd over 1f out: bhd and eased ins fnl f* 14/1

1m 41.96s (1.96) **Going Correction** +0.525s/f (Yiel)
**WFA** 3 from 4yo 9lb 7 Ran SP% 111.8
Speed ratings (Par 117): **111,109,108,104,101 99,90**
CSF £9.07 TOTE £2.60: £1.30, £2.10; EX 8.40 Trifecta £79.80.
**Owner** Cheveley Park Stud **Bred** Cheveley Park Stud Ltd **Trained** Newmarket, Suffolk

**FOCUS**
The soft ground was an unknown for many of these top fillies and that, combined with the fact it was run at a dawdle through the early stages, as they grouped against the stands' rail, casts a doubt over the strength of the form. However, it makes sense amongst the front three, with Integral backing up her Ascot figure. Little got involved from off the pace.

## 4166 BETFRED MOBILE HERITAGE H'CAP (BOBIS RACE) 6f
3:15 (3:16) (Class 2) (0-105,102) 3-Y-O
£62,250 (£18,640; £9,320; £4,660; £2,330; £1,170) Stalls Low

Form RPR
3000 1 **Deeds Not Words (IRE)**[20] 3478 3-8-5 88 ow1 CharlesBishop(3) 16 98
(Mick Channon) *racd down centre thrght: chsd ldrs: drvn to ld over 1f out: styd on wl: ins fnl f: rdn out* 33/1

0-01 2 1 1/4 **Remember**[14] 3674 3-8-11 92 KieranO'Neill 2 97+
(Richard Hannon) *racd stands' side: hld up towards rr: nt clr run 2f out: swtchd lft and hdwy over 1f out: chsd wnr ins fnl f: kpt on* 11/1

-121 3 1 1/4 **Golden Steps (FR)**[26] 3271 3-8-10 91 MartinHarley 17 92+
(Marco Botti) *swtchd lft to r far side after s: hld up in midfield overall: hdwy u.p and edging rt over 1f out: 3rd and styd on same pce ins fnl f* 13/2[1]

4614 4 1 1/4 **The Hooded Claw (IRE)**[23] 3369 3-8-6 87 JasonHart 20 84
(Tim Easterby) *racd on far side: overall ldr tl hung bdly rt and hdd over 1f out: wknd ins fnl f* 8/1[2]

0-30 5 nk **Suzi's Connoisseur**[22] 3378 3-8-9 95 NoelGarbutt(5) 3 91+
(Hugo Palmer) *racd stands' side: v.s.a: clsd on to rr of gp after 2f: shifting lft and hdwy over 1f out: styd on ins fnl f: nvr trbld ldrs* 25/1

-241 6 shd **See The Sun**[27] 3253 3-9-2 97 DavidAllan 10 93
(Tim Easterby) *racd stands' side: chsd ldrs overall: rdn over 1f out: styd on same pce and no imp fnl f* 10/1

-060 7 3/4 **Supplicant**[27] 3253 3-9-2 102 JackGarritty(5) 4 95
(Richard Fahey) *racd stands' side: hld up towards rr overall: nt clr run and switching lft 2f out: hdwy u.p jst over 1f out: kpt on fnl f: nvr trbld ldrs* 16/1

0552 8 3/4 **No Leaf Clover (IRE)**[23] 3369 3-8-13 94 RobertWinston 18 85
(Ollie Pears) *racd far side: chsd ldrs overall tl edgd rt and no ex u.p jst over 1f out: wknd ins fnl f* 16/1

0161 9 1 **Royal Seal**[6] 3980 3-8-10 91 6ex RyanMoore 19 79
(Sir Michael Stoute) *racd far side: hld up towards rr overall: hdwy u.p over 1f out: no ex 1f out: wknd ins fnl f* 8/1[2]

1111 10 1 3/4 **High On Life**[13] 3704 3-9-0 95 RichardHughes 11 77
(Jamie Osborne) *racd stands' side: led gp and chsd overall ldr tl 2f out: no ex u.p over 1f out: wknd ins fnl f* 10/1

3030 11 1 1/2 **Major Crispies**[23] 3352 3-9-5 100 PaddyAspell 7 77
(James Eustace) *racd stands' side: hld up towards rr overall: rdn and effrt 2f out: no prog: wl hld but plugged on past btn horses ins fnl f* 50/1

1314 12 nk **Kickboxer (IRE)**[13] 3694 3-9-0 95 AndreaAtzeni 9 71
(Mick Channon) *racd stands' side: in tch in midfield overall: rdn 2f out: lost pl and btn over 1f out: wknd ins fnl f* 9/1[3]

1001 13 1 3/4 **Almargo (IRE)**[13] 3716 3-8-13 94 JoeFanning 6 65
(Mark Johnston) *racd stands' side: in tch in midfield overall: rdn 2f out: sn lost pl and btn over 1f out: bhd ins fnl f* 12/1

3120 14 1 1/2 **Divine (IRE)**[20] 3459 3-8-9 90 WilliamBuick 15 56
(Mick Channon) *racd stands' side: in tch overall: rdn 2f out: lost pl u.p and btn over 1f out: wknd fnl f* 12/1

-450 15 22 **Charles Molson**[27] 3253 3-8-8 89 FergusSweeney 13
(Henry Candy) *racd nr side: towards rr overall: shifting lft and rdn 2f out: no hdwy and wknd over 1f out: wl bhd and heavily eased ins fnl f: t.o* 13/2[1]

1m 13.12s (0.62) **Going Correction** +0.525s/f (Yiel) 15 Ran SP% 121.3
Speed ratings (Par 106): **116,114,112,111,110 110,109,108,107,104 102,102,100,98,68**
CSF £360.16 CT £2732.75 TOTE £46.70: £12.90, £4.10, £2.90; EX 921.70 Trifecta £3626.40 Part won..
**Owner** George Materna **Bred** B Holland, S Hillen & J Cullinan **Trained** West Ilsley, Berks

**FOCUS**
A messy race with four horses going far side, the winner alone up the middle and the others near side (early on), and they were all over the place in the closing stages. The winner showed surprise improvement.

## 4167 WEATHERBYS EBF STALLIONS MAIDEN STKS (BOBIS RACE) 7f
3:50 (3:52) (Class 4) 2-Y-O £6,469 (£1,925; £962; £481) Stalls Low

Form RPR
2 1 **Lexington Times (IRE)**[13] 3720 2-9-0 0 RichardHughes 1 87+
(Richard Hannon) *mde all and racd nrest stands' rail: rdn over 1f out: kpt on wl fnl f: rdn out* 15/8[1]

2 3/4 **Good Contact (USA)** 2-9-0 0 HarryBentley 2 85+
(Saeed bin Suroor) *chsd ldrs: rdn and effrt over 1f out: hdwy to chse wnr ins fnl f: kpt on* 7/1[3]

3 2 **Basateen (IRE)** 2-9-0 0 PaulHanagan 10 80+
(Richard Hannon) *stdd s: hld up in rr: swtchd rt and effrt over 1f out: rn green but hdwy and drifting lft fnl f: styd on wl fnl 100yds* 11/1

4 nk **Latharnach (USA)** 2-9-0 0 JamieSpencer 4 79+
(Charlie Appleby) *s.i.s: in tch in midfield: rdn and effrt over 1f out: styd on wl ins fnl f* 25/1

5 1 1/4 **Typhoon Season** 2-9-0 0 KieranO'Neill 5 76
(Richard Hannon) *t.k.h: chsd ldrs: chsd wnr 2f out: rdn over 1f out: no ex and lost 2nd ins fnl f: wknd towards fin* 33/1

6 1 **Best Of Times** 2-9-0 0 AndreaAtzeni 7 74+
(Saeed bin Suroor) *in tch: drvn and effrt jst over 1f out: swtchd rt ins fnl f: no hdwy: wknd wl ins fnl f* 3/1[2]

7 nk **Snoano** 2-9-0 0 WilliamBuick 14 73
(John Gosden) *stdd s: t.k.h: hld up in tch: hdwy and rdn to chse ldrs over 1f out: wknd ins fnl f* 12/1

8 1/2 **Space Age (IRE)** 2-9-0 0 SilvestreDeSousa 13 72
(Charlie Appleby) *in tch in midfield: rdn sme hdwy jst over 1f out: no ex and wknd ins fnl f* 14/1

9 7 **Kopassus (IRE)** 2-9-0 0 FergusSweeney 12 54
(Peter Chapple-Hyam) *stdd s: hld up in toouch towards rr: rdn 2f out: sn struggling and btn: bhd fnl f* 33/1

30 10 shd **Grigolo**[29] 3140 2-9-0 0 JoeFanning 3 54
(Mark Johnston) *chsd wnr tl 2f out: sn rdn and lost pl: wknd over 1f out* 8/1

11 13 **Dark Side Dream** 2-9-0 0 JimmyQuinn 9 22
(Chris Dwyer) *in tch towards rr: rdn 2f out: sn lost tch and bhd fnl f* 100/1

1m 29.64s (3.94) **Going Correction** +0.525s/f (Yiel) 11 Ran SP% 116.8
Speed ratings (Par 96): **98,97,94,94,93 91,91,91,83,82 68**
CSF £14.99 TOTE £2.70: £1.30, £2.40, £3.20; EX 14.50 Trifecta £136.50.
**Owner** Middleham Park Racing C **Bred** Ruskerne Ltd **Trained** East Everleigh, Wilts

**FOCUS**
This maiden has produced plenty of smart types over the years, and the race should prove a rich source of winners. The majority of these eventually decided to race up the middle of the track, the exception being Lexington Times, whose rider was content to race near side throughout. The winner is rated to his debut form.

## 4168 WOODHURST CONSTRUCTION MAIDEN STKS (BOBIS RACE) 1m 2f
4:25 (4:27) (Class 4) 3-Y-O £6,469 (£1,925; £962; £481) Stalls Centre

Form RPR
02 1 **Astronereus (IRE)**[33] 3031 3-9-5 0 RichardHughes 5 95+
(Amanda Perrett) *hld up in tch in midfield: clsd and trcking ldrs whn nt clr run 2f out: swtchd lft and effrt u.p over 1f out: led ins fnl f: sn in command: r.o wl: readily* 15/2[3]

3 2 2 **Razor Wind (IRE)**[25] 3315 3-9-5 0 RyanMoore 6 88
(Charlie Appleby) *dwlt: hld up in tch in last trio: rdn and effrt 2f out: hdwy to chal over 1f out: led jst ins fnl f: hdd fnl 100yds: sn btn and plugged on same pce after* 5/4[1]

3 3 1/4 **Ghany (IRE)** 3-9-0 0 PaulHanagan 2 77
(William Haggas) *hld up in tch in last trio: swtchd lft and pushed along ent fnl 2f: swtchd rt jst ins fnl f: kpt on steadily to go 3rd towards fin: no threat to ldrs* 22/1

00 4 1 1/2 **Goldenrod**[41] 2773 3-9-5 0 SilvestreDeSousa 8 79
(Ralph Beckett) *t.k.h: chsd ldrs tl hdwy to ld 8f out: hrd pressed and rdn 2f out: hdd jst ins fnl f: wknd fnl 100yds* 33/1

52 5 11 **Obsidian (USA)**[27] 3248 3-9-5 0 WilliamBuick 4 58
(John Gosden) *t.k.h early: chsd ldrs: wnt 2nd over 2f out and sn upsides ldr: rdn and fnd little over 1f out: btn 1f out: fdd ins fnl f* 6/4[2]

64 6 1 **Fighting Back**[9] 3857 3-9-5 0 JoeFanning 9 56
(Amanda Perrett) *s.i.s: in tch in last trio: rdn 3f out: struggling 2f out: sn wknd* 20/1

-634 7 14 **Glasgow Central**[52] 2418 3-9-5 74 RobertWinston 7 30
(Charles Hills) *led for 2f: chsd ldr tl over 2f out: sn lost pl and short of room 2f out: wknd over 1f out: wl bhd ins fnl f: t.o* 33/1

2m 8.59s (3.09) **Going Correction** +0.525s/f (Yiel) 7 Ran SP% 111.2
Speed ratings (Par 102): **108,106,103,102,93 93,81**
CSF £16.52 TOTE £8.00: £3.40, £1.30; EX 18.70 Trifecta £141.40.

**Owner** John Connolly & Odile Griffith **Bred** Team Hogdala Ab **Trained** Pulborough, W Sussex
**FOCUS**
A good maiden in recent years and the fourth looks the key. The winner showed form verging on smart.

## 4169 WOODHURST CONSTRUCTION H'CAP — 1m
**5:00** (5:00) (Class 3) (0-90,90) 3-Y-0+ **£9,703** (£2,887; £1,443; £721) **Stalls** Low

| Form | | | | RPR |
|---|---|---|---|---|
| 1-10 | **1** | | **Glorious Empire (IRE)**[23] 3352 3-9-5 **90** ... AndreaAtzeni 1 | 99+ |
| | | | (Ed Walker) *t.k.h: chsd ldr tl 1/2-way: styd trcking ldrs: shkn up to chal 1f out: rdn to ld ins fnl f: edging lft but r.o wl after* **5/2**[1] | |
| 0131 | **2** | ½ | **Johnno**[16] 3573 5-9-12 **88** ... AdrianNicholls 7 | 98 |
| | | | (David Nicholls) *led: rdn and qcknd over 2f out: drvn over 1f out: hdd ins fnl f: kpt on but a hld after* **5/2**[1] | |
| 5255 | **3** | 2¼ | **Apostle (IRE)**[13] 3716 5-9-13 **89** ... FergusSweeney 9 | 94 |
| | | | (David Simcock) *t.k.h: chsd ldrs: wnt 2nd 1/2-way: rdn ent fnl 2f: 3rd and no ex ins fnl f: outpcd fnl 150yds* **11/2**[3] | |
| 560- | **4** | 2½ | **Albaqaa**[287] 6801 9-9-4 **83** ... RobertTart[(3)] 8 | 82 |
| | | | (P J O'Gorman) *hld up in tch in last pair: rdn and effrt wl over 1f out: no ex u.p 1f out: sltly hmpd and wknd ins fnl f* **16/1** | |
| -31 | **5** | ¾ | **Potentate (IRE)**[18] 3517 3-8-6 **77** ... JoeFanning 3 | 72 |
| | | | (Richard Hannon) *t.k.h: hld up wl in tch in midfield: rdn and effrt 2f out: unable qck and btn 1f out: sn wknd* **10/3**[2] | |
| 310- | **6** | 1¾ | **Zeshov (IRE)**[306] 6233 3-8-8 **79** ... SilvestreDeSousa 2 | 70 |
| | | | (Jeremy Noseda) *stdd s: t.k.h: hld up in tch in last pair: rdn and effrt 2f out: no ex ent fnl f: sn wknd* **10/1** | |

1m 43.0s (3.00) **Going Correction** +0.525s/f (Yiel)
**WFA** 3 from 5yo+ 9lb **6** Ran SP% **110.6**
Speed ratings (Par 107): **106,105,103,100,100 98**
CSF £8.65 CT £27.46 TOTE £3.30: £2.00, £1.70; EX 10.40 Trifecta £37.60.
**Owner** Ms Judy Yap & Ms Salina Yang **Bred** Patrick Grogan **Trained** Newmarket, Suffolk
**FOCUS**
A few non-runners, but the field were quickening from the 5f point to 1f out, and two improvers came a little way clear. They gradually edged towards the far side. Improved form from the winner.
T/Plt: £57.80 to a £1 stake. Pool: £128,771.11 - 1,623.82 winning units T/Qpdt: £11.90 to a £1 stake. Pool: £10,225.68 - 635.22 winning units SP

# 3250 YORK (L-H)
### Friday, July 11
**OFFICIAL GOING: Good to firm (7.5)**
Wind: Light; half against Weather: Fine and sunny; very warm

## 4170 CAKEMARK EBF STALLIONS MAIDEN STKS (BOBIS RACE) — 5f 89y
**1:50** (1:50) (Class 3) 2-Y-0 **£7,115** (£2,117; £1,058; £529) **Stalls** Centre

| Form | | | | RPR |
|---|---|---|---|---|
| 2 | **1** | | **Maljaa**[42] 2731 2-9-5 0 ... FrederikTylicki 8 | 84+ |
| | | | (Roger Varian) *w ldr: led over 1f out: drvn out* **8/11**[1] | |
| | **2** | ½ | **Teruntum Star (FR)** 2-9-5 0 ... PaulMulrennan 7 | 80+ |
| | | | (Kevin Ryan) *chsd ldrs: effrt 2f out: styd on to take 2nd last 75yds* **11/2**[2] | |
| 5 | **3** | 1¼ | **Henley**[29] 3148 2-9-5 0 ... GrahamLee 1 | 76 |
| | | | (William Jarvis) *hld up: effrt over 2f out: styd on to take 3rd last 50yds* **13/2**[3] | |
| 4 | **4** | ½ | **Tohfa (IRE)**[30] 3107 2-9-0 0 ... PatDobbs 3 | 69 |
| | | | (Richard Hannon) *w ldrs: drvn over 2f out: kpt on same pce fnl f* **8/1** | |
| 45 | **5** | 3 | **Spend A Penny (IRE)**[27] 3215 2-9-5 0 ... PhillipMakin 6 | 64 |
| | | | (John Quinn) *led: hdd over 1f out: wknd last 150yds* **14/1** | |
| | **6** | 4½ | **Muhaarib Al Emarat (IRE)** 2-9-2 0 ... GeorgeChaloner[(3)] 5 | 48 |
| | | | (Richard Fahey) *dwlt: in rr: hdwy 3f out: wknd over 1f out* **28/1** | |
| | **7** | 4½ | **Farang Jai Dee (IRE)** 2-8-12 0 ... LukeLeadbitter[(7)] 4 | 32 |
| | | | (Declan Carroll) *s.i.s: sme hdwy over 2f out: sn wknd* **50/1** | |

1m 4.42s (0.32) **Going Correction** -0.075s/f (Good) **7** Ran SP% **109.8**
Speed ratings (Par 98): **94,93,91,90,85 78,71**
CSF £4.59 TOTE £1.80: £1.20, £3.40; EX 5.90 Trifecta £21.90.
**Owner** Hamdan Al Maktoum **Bred** Bumble Bloodstock & C Liesack **Trained** Newmarket, Suffolk
**FOCUS**
All distances as advertised. A fair juvenile contest and the first two should both do better from here.

## 4171 TOTEPOOL SUMMER STKS (GROUP 3) — 6f
**2:20** (2:22) (Class 1) 3-Y-O+
**£34,026** (£12,900; £6,456; £3,216; £1,614; £810) **Stalls** Centre

| Form | | | | RPR |
|---|---|---|---|---|
| 6510 | **1** | | **Ladies Are Forever**[58] 2256 6-9-4 106 ... (b) DanielTudhope 7 | 111 |
| | | | (Geoffrey Oldroyd) *hld up in mid-div: hdwy over 2f out: led 1f out: hld on nr fin* **7/2**[1] | |
| 3012 | **2** | hd | **Joyeuse**[29] 3167 3-8-12 108 ... JamesDoyle 14 | 109 |
| | | | (Lady Cecil) *hld up towards rr: hdwy over 2f out: struck on hd by rival rdrs whip 1f out: styd on wl ins fnl f: jst hld* **7/2**[1] | |
| 01 | **3** | 1¾ | **Indignant**[26] 3278 4-9-4 102 ... PatDobbs 12 | 105 |
| | | | (Richard Hannon) *chsd ldrs: drvn over 2f out: kpt on same pce fnl f* **10/1** | |
| 511 | **4** | 1¾ | **Willbeme**[28] 3203 6-9-4 90 ... AndrewMullen 13 | 99 |
| | | | (Neville Bycroft) *led: hdd 1f out: kpt on same pce* **12/1** | |
| 6000 | **5** | 1½ | **Ice Love (FR)**[13] 3746 3-8-12 101 ... RaphaelMarchelli 1 | 93+ |
| | | | (T Castanheira, France) *in rr: hdwy over 1f out: styng on at fin* **22/1** | |
| 43-4 | **6** | nk | **Survived**[20] 3459 3-8-12 92 ... FrannyNorton 2 | 92 |
| | | | (William Haggas) *chsd ldrs: one pce over 1f out* **12/1** | |
| 2-65 | **7** | nk | **Artistic Jewel (IRE)**[26] 3278 5-9-4 102 ... GrahamGibbons 10 | 92 |
| | | | (Ed McMahon) *chsd ldrs: drvn 2f out: one pce* **14/1** | |
| 3135 | **8** | 1 | **Perfect Blessings (IRE)**[27] 3245 3-8-12 94 ... GrahamLee 5 | 88 |
| | | | (Clive Cox) *mid-div: drvn over 2f out: nvr a factor* **15/2**[3] | |
| -132 | **9** | 4 | **Inyordreams**[20] 3459 3-8-12 96 ... DaleSwift 9 | 75 |
| | | | (James Given) *chsd ldrs: wknd over 1f out* **14/1** | |
| -036 | **10** | 2¼ | **Ventura Mist**[27] 3253 3-8-12 95 ... (p) DuranFentiman 15 | 68 |
| | | | (Tim Easterby) *wnt rt s: in rr: sme hdwy over 2f out: sn wknd* **20/1** | |
| 31 | **11** | 6 | **Emerald Star**[62] 2155 3-9-0 105 ... DanielePorcu 11 | 51 |
| | | | (P Schiergen, Germany) *in rr: eased whn bhd ins fnl f* **7/1**[2] | |

1m 9.3s (-2.60) **Going Correction** -0.20s/f (Firm)
**WFA** 3 from 4yo+ 6lb **11** Ran SP% **115.6**
Speed ratings (Par 113): **109,108,106,104,102 101,101,99,94,91 83**
CSF £13.86 TOTE £4.00: £1.70, £2.00, £2.60; EX 11.00 Trifecta £67.00.
**Owner** R C Bond **Bred** Bond Thoroughbred Corporation **Trained** Brawby, N Yorks

**FOCUS**
This was a competitive renewal and it was hard not to be impressed by the effort of the winner. The fourth looks the best guide.

## 4172 HAYLIN STKS (NURSERY H'CAP) (BOBIS RACE) — 5f
**2:55** (2:55) (Class 3) 2-Y-O **£7,439** (£2,213; £1,106; £553) **Stalls** Centre

| Form | | | | RPR |
|---|---|---|---|---|
| 0652 | **1** | | **Ventura Shadow**[14] 3658 2-8-5 **67** ... PatrickMathers 5 | 71 |
| | | | (Richard Fahey) *in rr: hdwy and edgd lft 2f out: chsng ldrs 1f out: led ins fnl f: hld on nr fin* **16/1** | |
| 21 | **2** | nk | **Pres Rapide (IRE)**[28] 3199 2-9-7 **83** ... PhillipMakin 4 | 86 |
| | | | (John Quinn) *w ldrs: led over 1f out: hdd ins fnl f: kpt on wl towards fin* **6/5**[1] | |
| 5262 | **3** | 1¼ | **Stanghow**[23] 3367 2-8-8 **70** ... PJMcDonald 7 | 68 |
| | | | (Mel Brittain) *wnt rt s: outpcd in rr: hdwy over 1f out: keeping on wl at fin* **14/1** | |
| 0613 | **4** | 2½ | **Indescribable (IRE)**[13] 3692 2-9-2 **78** ... FrannyNorton 1 | 67 |
| | | | (Mark Johnston) *led tl over 2f out: kpt on same pce appr fnl f* **9/4**[2] | |
| 405 | **5** | ½ | **Bowson Fred**[13] 3713 2-8-4 **66** ... JamesSullivan 3 | 54 |
| | | | (Michael Easterby) *chsd ldrs: kpt on same pce appr fnl f* **8/1**[3] | |
| 334 | **6** | 2½ | **Dominic Cork**[25] 3304 2-8-9 **71** ... (b[1]) TomEaves 6 | 50 |
| | | | (Kevin Ryan) *sn trcking ldrs: led over 2f out: hdd over 1f out: hung lft and sn wknd* **14/1** | |
| 2400 | **7** | 6 | **Alderaan (IRE)**[6] 3947 2-8-6 **68** ... (b[1]) BarryMcHugh 2 | 25 |
| | | | (Tony Coyle) *trckd ldr: swtchd lft sn after s: outpcd and drvn over 3f out: lost pl over 1f out* **25/1** | |

58.99s (-0.31) **Going Correction** -0.20s/f (Firm) **7** Ran SP% **110.4**
Speed ratings (Par 98): **94,93,91,87,86 82,73**
CSF £33.52 TOTE £15.20: £5.00, £1.20; EX 35.60 Trifecta £179.40.
**Owner** Middleham Park Racing LXXXVIII **Bred** Northmore Stud **Trained** Musley Bank, N Yorks
**FOCUS**
They seemed to go plenty hard enough in the early stages here and that played to the strengths of the lightly weighted winner. Straightforward form.

## 4173 GROCERYAID CHAIRMAN'S CHARITY CUP (HANDICAP STKS) — 1m 4f
**3:30** (3:30) (Class 2) (0-100,98) 3-Y-O+ **£12,291** (£3,657; £1,827; £913) **Stalls** Centre

| Form | | | | RPR |
|---|---|---|---|---|
| 41 | **1** | | **Kings Fete**[27] 3248 3-8-8 **91** ow1 ... JamesDoyle 14 | 103+ |
| | | | (Sir Michael Stoute) *v free to post: trckd ldrs: t.k.h: led over 1f out: pushed out* **5/2**[1] | |
| -010 | **2** | ½ | **Mighty Yar (IRE)**[41] 2779 4-9-10 **94** ... GrahamLee 8 | 105+ |
| | | | (Lady Cecil) *stmbld bdly s: sn chsng ldrs: drvn 3f out: sn outpcd: rallied and styd on wl fnl f* **5/2**[1] | |
| 1066 | **3** | 2¼ | **Whispering Warrior (IRE)**[27] 3251 5-9-7 **91** ... OisinMurphy 9 | 98+ |
| | | | (David Simcock) *hld up in rr: hdwy on wd outside over 2f out: edgd lft and styd on ins fnl f* **14/1** | |
| 10-1 | **4** | hd | **Pearl Castle (IRE)**[27] 3250 4-9-8 **92** ... PhillipMakin 10 | 99 |
| | | | (John Quinn) *chsd ldrs: kpt on same pce appr fnl f* **7/1**[2] | |
| 6130 | **5** | ½ | **Itlaaq**[41] 2787 8-9-0 **84** ... GrahamGibbons 5 | 90 |
| | | | (Michael Easterby) *mid-div: hdwy over 2f out: kpt on one pce over 1f out* **25/1** | |
| -002 | **6** | ½ | **Nicholascopernicus (IRE)**[13] 3730 5-9-6 **90** ... PatDobbs 11 | 95 |
| | | | (Ed Walker) *chsd ldrs: one pce fnl 2f* **14/1** | |
| 2111 | **7** | nse | **Saved By The Bell (IRE)**[28] 3205 4-9-4 **88** ... DanielTudhope 12 | 93 |
| | | | (David O'Meara) *hld up in rr-div: hdwy 7f out: drvn over 3f out: one pce whn nt clr run nr fin* **15/2**[3] | |
| -064 | **8** | nk | **Grandorio (IRE)**[28] 3204 4-9-4 **88** ... DavidNolan 3 | 93 |
| | | | (David O'Meara) *hld up in rr: t.k.h: hdwy on ins over 3f out: one pce fnl 2f* **14/1** | |
| 00-3 | **9** | ¾ | **Kiwayu**[28] 3204 5-9-2 **86** ... PJMcDonald 4 | 90 |
| | | | (Philip Kirby) *mid-div: hdwy 5f out: effrt 3f out: nvr a factor* **20/1** | |
| -061 | **10** | 1¾ | **Linguine (FR)**[34] 2981 4-9-6 **90** ... PaulMulrennan 16 | 91 |
| | | | (Paul Midgley) *swtchd lft after s: led: hdd & wknd over 1f out* **22/1** | |

2m 32.58s (-0.62) **Going Correction** -0.075s/f (Good)
**WFA** 3 from 4yo+ 13lb **10** Ran SP% **114.4**
Speed ratings (Par 109): **99,98,97,97,96 96,96,96,95,94**
CSF £7.43 CT £68.96 TOTE £3.50: £1.40, £1.50, £3.40; EX 9.40 Trifecta £93.10.
**Owner** K Abdullah **Bred** Juddmonte Farms Ltd **Trained** Newmarket, Suffolk
**FOCUS**
A two-horse race according to the betting and the pair dominated the finish. The winner is highly likely to do better.

## 4174 ACTURIS STKS (H'CAP) — 5f
**4:05** (4:05) (Class 3) (0-95,95) 3-Y-O+ **£12,291** (£3,657; £1,827; £913) **Stalls** Centre

| Form | | | | RPR |
|---|---|---|---|---|
| 2011 | **1** | | **Line Of Reason (IRE)**[13] 3737 4-9-9 **92** ... PaulMulrennan 8 | 105 |
| | | | (Paul Midgley) *hld up in mid-div: hdwy 2f out: r.o fnl f: led nr fin* **4/1**[2] | |
| 0200 | **2** | ¾ | **Silvanus (IRE)**[16] 3571 9-8-13 **82** ... PJMcDonald 11 | 92 |
| | | | (Paul Midgley) *chsd ldrs: led ins fnl f: hdd and no ex towards fin* **25/1** | |
| 2153 | **3** | 1¼ | **Algar Lad**[4] 4016 4-9-3 **86** ... DanielTudhope 2 | 92 |
| | | | (David O'Meara) *dwlt: swtchd rt after s: in rr: hdwy 2f out: kpt on wl fnl f: tk 3rd nr fin* **7/2**[1] | |
| -630 | **4** | nk | **Imperial Legend (IRE)**[51] 2456 5-9-1 **84** ... (p) AndrewMullen 13 | 88 |
| | | | (David Nicholls) *w ldr over 3f out: led over 1f out: hdd ins fnl f: fdd nr fin* **16/1** | |
| -200 | **5** | hd | **Borderlescott**[27] 3241 12-9-9 **95** ... NeilFarley[(3)] 6 | 99 |
| | | | (Robin Bastiman) *led over 1f: chsd ldrs: kpt on same pce over 1f out* **14/1** | |
| -003 | **6** | 1 | **Fitz Flyer (IRE)**[14] 3666 8-9-0 **83** ... (v) RoystonFfrench 3 | 83 |
| | | | (David Nicholls) *chsd ldrs: outpcd over 2f out: kpt on fnl f* **9/2**[3] | |
| 0 | **7** | 1¾ | **Stone Of Folca**[53] 2390 6-9-2 **85** ... RobertHavlin 1 | 79 |
| | | | (John Best) *chsd ldrs: fdd fnl f* **16/1** | |
| 5346 | **8** | ½ | **Bondi Beach Boy**[6] 3948 5-8-5 **77** ... GeorgeChaloner[(3)] 12 | 69 |
| | | | (James Turner) *hdwy to ld over 3f out: hdd over 1f out: carried hd high: wknd last 150yds* **15/2** | |
| 0312 | **9** | nk | **Another Wise Kid (IRE)**[14] 3666 6-9-7 **90** ... GrahamLee 16 | 81 |
| | | | (Paul Midgley) *prom: drvn over 2f out: wknd over 1f out* **5/1** | |
| 5000 | **10** | 6 | **Lastchancelucas**[6] 3948 4-8-11 **80** ... (b) DuranFentiman 10 | 49 |
| | | | (Declan Carroll) *chsd ldrs: lost pl over 2f out: bhd fnl f* **16/1** | |

57.35s (-1.95) **Going Correction** -0.20s/f (Firm)
**WFA** 3 from 4yo+ 5lb **10** Ran SP% **117.0**
Speed ratings (Par 107): **107,105,103,103,103 101,98,97,97,87**
CSF £97.27 CT £394.58 TOTE £4.60: £1.50, £6.50, £1.80; EX 111.70 Trifecta £427.10.
**Owner** Taylor's Bloodstock Ltd **Bred** Corduff Stud Ltd, J Corcoran & J Judd **Trained** Westow, N Yorks

**FOCUS**
This was decimated by non-runners on account of the rattling fast ground but it was still competitive and served up a good finish. The winner rates better than ever.

## 4175 CRANSWICK PLC FOOD GROUP STKS (H'CAP) 1m 2f 88y
**4:40** (4:40) (Class 4) (0-85,85) 3-Y-0+ **£7,439** (£2,213; £1,106; £553) **Stalls** Low

Form RPR
0602 **1** **Bishop's Castle (USA)**[13] 3703 5-9-7 **78** DaleSwift 3 87
(Brian Ellison) *t.k.h towards rr: hdwy on ins over 3f out: upsides over 1f out: styd on u.p to ld nr fin* **7/2**[1]
-344 **2** *hd* **Innsbruck**[14] 3654 4-9-8 **79** (b[1]) PhillipMakin 1 87
(John Quinn) *trckd ldr: t.k.h: narrow ld over 1f out: hdd and no ex clsng stages* **10/1**
2320 **3** *2 1/4* **Merchant Of Medici**[22] 3398 7-8-2 **66** oh6 (p) JoeDoyle(7) 8 70
(Micky Hammond) *hld up towards rr: hdwy over 3f out: chsng ldrs over 1f out: kpt on same pce* **25/1**
6000 **4** *2 1/2* **Warlu Way**[27] 3250 7-9-4 **75** JamesSullivan 11 74
(Michael Easterby) *trckd ldrs: dropped bk to rr after 2f: hdwy over 2f out: edgd lft and styd on wl fnl f* **16/1**
363 **5** *2 1/2* **Shouranour (IRE)**[23] 3368 4-9-6 **77** DanielTudhope 2 72
(David O'Meara) *led: hdd over 1f out: grad wknd* **11/2**[2]
6015 **6** *2* **Las Verglas Star (IRE)**[27] 3217 6-9-11 **85** GeorgeChaloner(3) 13 76
(Richard Fahey) *mid-div: hdwy over 3f out: one pce fnl 2f* **8/1**[3]
2145 **7** *nk* **Barren Brook**[16] 3573 7-9-9 **80** BarryMcHugh 16 70
(Michael Easterby) *trckd ldrs: t.k.h: fdd over 1f out* **8/1**[3]
-000 **8** *1* **Resurge (IRE)**[13] 3730 9-9-13 **84** (t) OisinMurphy 7 72
(Stuart Kittow) *s.i.s: hdwy 7f out: sn chsng ldrs: wknd over 1f out* **16/1**
-122 **9** *6* **Red Warrior (IRE)**[11] 3802 4-9-13 **84** (p) TomQueally 12 61
(Ismail Mohammed) *mid-div: hdwy on outside over 3f out: rdn over 2f out: wknd over 1f out: eased ins fnl f* **7/2**[1]
04-0 **10** *1 3/4* **Enzaal (USA)**[17] 3544 4-9-5 **76** GrahamLee 6 50
(Philip Kirby) *trckd ldrs: drvn over 3f out: wknd 2f out* **33/1**
3605 **11** *4 1/2* **Moccasin (FR)**[38] 2868 5-8-7 **71** KevinLundie(7) 10 36
(Geoffrey Harker) *s.i.s: in rr: rdn over 3f out: sn bhd* **16/1**

2m 10.26s (-2.24) **Going Correction** -0.075s/f (Good) **11 Ran SP% 115.6**
Speed ratings (Par 105): **105,104,103,101,99 97,97,96,91,90 86**
CSF £39.04 CT £755.60 TOTE £4.80: £2.00, £3.00, £5.60; EX 34.60 Trifecta £977.10.
**Owner** Koo's Racing Club & Brian Ellison **Bred** Darley **Trained** Norton, N Yorks
**FOCUS**
A strong race for the grade and plenty like about a few of these.

## 4176 ELECTROLUX APPLIANCES STKS (APPRENTICE H'CAP) (BOBIS RACE) 7f
**5:10** (5:10) (Class 3) (0-95,92) 3-Y-0 **£7,439** (£2,213; £1,106; £553) **Stalls** Low

Form RPR
-603 **1** **Ticking Katie (IRE)**[27] 3247 3-9-2 **87** (p) RobJFitzpatrick(5) 3 93
(K R Burke) *mid-div: hdwy over 3f out: rdn over 2f out: chsng ldrs over 1f out: styd on to ld nr fin* **4/1**[2]
0152 **2** *hd* **Basil Berry**[13] 3694 3-9-4 **84** JoeyHaynes 4 89+
(Chris Dwyer) *awkward s: hdwy on ins 4f out: led over 2f out: edgd lft fnl f: hdd nr fin* **15/2**[3]
1036 **3** *3/4* **Azagal (IRE)**[20] 3455 3-9-7 **92** RachelRichardson(5) 1 96
(Tim Easterby) *hld up in rr: hdwy on inner over 3f out: chsng ldrs over 1f out: kpt on same pce clsng stages* **12/1**
10-0 **4** *2 1/2* **Zaraee (IRE)**[27] 3253 3-9-4 **87** NathanAlison(3) 2 84
(William Haggas) *t.k.h: led 1f: chsd ldrs: one pce over 1f out* **9/1**
6610 **5** *6* **Bridie ffrench**[26] 3273 3-8-5 **76** DanielCremin(5) 5 57
(Mick Channon) *hld up in rr: effrt over 2f out: nvr on terms* **16/1**
2204 **6** *3 3/4* **Shot In The Sun (IRE)**[35] 2962 3-9-4 **84** GeorgeChaloner 7 56
(Richard Fahey) *chsd ldrs: drvn 3f out: lost pl wl over 1f out* **2/1**[1]
2212 **7** *shd* **Naggers (IRE)**[11] 3790 3-8-9 **75** IanBrennan 6 46
(Paul Midgley) *t.k.h: led after 1f: hdd over 2f out: wknd wl over 1f out* **4/1**[2]
033 **8** *3 3/4* **Captain Midnight (IRE)**[29] 3137 3-8-11 **84** ClaireMurray(7) 10 46
(David Brown) *sn w ldrs: wknd 2f out* **20/1**

1m 24.01s (-1.29) **Going Correction** -0.075s/f (Good) **8 Ran SP% 113.4**
Speed ratings (Par 104): **104,103,102,100,93 88,88,84**
CSF £33.17 CT £327.25 TOTE £4.60: £1.80, £2.00, £2.40; EX 34.60 Trifecta £218.20.
**Owner** Ontoawinner 6, M Hulin, E Burke **Bred** Tally-Ho Stud **Trained** Middleham Moor, N Yorks
**FOCUS**
A competitive finale which more than lived up to its billing.
T/Jkpt: £18,396.50 to a £1 stake. Pool: £64,776.57 - 2.50 winning units T/Plt: £16.60 to a £1 stake. Pool: £101,830.39 - 4,462.48 winning units T/Qpdt: £13.50 to a £1 stake. Pool: £5,617.04 - 305.90 winning units WG

# 4142 ASCOT (R-H)
Saturday, July 12
**OFFICIAL GOING: Good to firm (firm in places; straight 8.8, round 8.0)**
Wind: Almost nil Weather: Fine, very warm

## 4178 KELLY GROUP FILLIES' NURSERY H'CAP (BOBIS RACE) 7f
**1:25** (1:25) (Class 4) 2-Y-0 **£6,469** (£1,925; £962; £481) **Stalls** High

Form RPR
51 **1** **Savoy Showgirl (IRE)**[44] 2697 2-8-11 **78** LouisSteward(5) 2 87+
(Michael Bell) *hld up in 5th: prog on outer over 2f out: rdn to ld jst over 1f out: styd on wl* **6/1**
014 **2** *2 1/2* **Assault On Rome (IRE)**[17] 3580 2-9-2 **78** FrannyNorton 4 80
(Mark Johnston) *disp ld tl rdn to gain def advantage wl over 1f out: hdd jst over 1f out: styd on same pce* **4/1**[3]
502 **3** *2 1/2* **Euthenia**[15] 3642 2-8-7 **73** CharlesBishop(3) 5 68
(Mick Channon) *trckd ldrs: rdn over 2f out: nt qckn wl over 1f out: kpt on to take 3rd ins fnl f* **6/1**
0024 **4** *3/4* **Sculptured (FR)**[4] 4054 2-7-9 **62** oh4 CamHardie(5) 7 55
(Jo Hughes) *disp ld to wl over 1f out: steadily outpcd* **8/1**
41 **5** *3 1/4* **Caltra Colleen**[27] 3267 2-9-0 **76** WilliamTwiston-Davies 1 60
(Mick Channon) *trckd ldng pair: rdn wl over 2f out: stl in tch over 1f out: wknd* **3/1**[1]
050 **6** *4* **Paco's Dream**[8] 3934 2-8-0 **62** oh6 LukeMorris 3 36
(Harry Dunlop) *s.i.s: a in last pair: rdn and lost tch 1/2-way: no ch after* **25/1**
4100 **7** *17* **Juventas**[14] 3721 2-9-7 **83** GeorgeBaker 6 11
(Mick Channon) *stdd s: t.k.h: hld up in last: lost tch 1/2-way: pushed along and no rspnse over 2f out: eased and t.o* **7/2**[2]

1m 27.81s (0.21) **Going Correction** 0.0s/f (Good) **7 Ran SP% 110.8**
Speed ratings (Par 93): **98,95,92,91,87 83,63**
CSF £28.09 TOTE £4.50: £1.90, £2.50; EX 38.60 Trifecta £113.50.
**Owner** Miss Emily Asprey & Christopher Wright **Bred** Hyde Park Stud & Lisglen **Trained** Newmarket, Suffolk
**FOCUS**
Rail on Round course was out 2y at 12f and increased to 9y at bend into home straight. Old Mile increased by 10yds, 10f by 13yds, 12f by 14y and 14f by 16yds. The ground was changed to good to firm, firm in places prior to racing and the time of this opening contest very much suggested it was quick. A fair nursery, run at a reasonable pace. The winner has a good bit more to offer.

## 4179 TOTEPOOL HERITAGE H'CAP 5f
**1:55** (1:55) (Class 2) 3-Y-0+
**£62,250** (£18,640; £9,320; £4,660; £2,330; £1,170) **Stalls** High

Form RPR
33 **1** **Discussiontofollow (IRE)**[14] 3737 4-8-10 **92** ShaneKelly 1 103+
(Mike Murphy) *hld up in last pair and grad crossed fr wdst draw towards nr side gp: prog gng strly 2f out: rdn to chal 1f out: led last 120yds: kpt on* **10/1**
-401 **2** *hd* **Milly's Gift**[8] 3927 4-8-7 **92** RyanTate(3) 7 102+
(Clive Cox) *taken down early: hld up wl in rr in centre: gd prog jst over 2f out to ld gp jst over 1f out: clr of rest of that side and upsides wnr ins fnl f: jst pipped* **12/1**
4211 **3** *1/2* **Robot Boy (IRE)**[15] 3666 4-9-5 **101** GrahamGibbons 13 109
(David Barron) *chsd ldrs nr side: rdn to ld overall jst over 1f out: hdd last 120yds: styd on* **5/1**[1]
01-1 **4** *nk* **Demora**[28] 3241 5-8-13 **102** AlistairRawlinson(7) 19 109
(Michael Appleby) *sn overall ldr on nr side: hdd jst over 1f out: kpt on wl fnl f* **9/1**
0202 **5** *2* **Masamah (IRE)**[28] 3241 8-9-6 **102** (p) MartinHarley 20 102
(Marco Botti) *v fast away but sn hdd: racd against nr side rail: chsd ldrs: rdn over 1f out: kpt on same pce fnl f* **10/1**
466 **6** *nse* **Barnet Fair**[15] 3666 6-8-3 **90** CamHardie(5) 16 90
(David Nicholls) *taken down early: hld up nr side: rdn 2f out: kpt on fr over 1f out: nvr able to chal* **6/1**[2]
-262 **7** *shd* **Speed Hawk (USA)**[21] 3478 3-8-6 **93** AdamBeschizza 11 90+
(Robert Cowell) *trckd ldrs in centre: gng bttr than many 2f out: sme prog over 1f out: 2nd of gp ins fnl f: nt pce to threaten* **10/1**
0050 **8** *1 1/2* **Racy**[21] 3452 7-9-0 **96** (p) PatCosgrave 18 90
(Brian Ellison) *taken down early: chsd rival against nr side rail: plenty to do whn swtchd rt 2f out: drvn and kpt on: no ch* **14/1**
0000 **9** *3/4* **Lancelot Du Lac (ITY)**[21] 3452 4-9-5 **101** AdamKirby 8 92
(Dean Ivory) *disp ld in centre to 2f out: nt qckn u.p: steadily fdd* **7/1**[3]
-006 **10** *1/2* **Riskit Fora Biskit (IRE)**[21] 3459 4-8-8 **95** LouisSteward(5) 2 84
(Michael Bell) *taken down early: led centre gp to jst over 1f out: wknd* **25/1**
2431 **11** *3/4* **Top Boy**[42] 2786 4-8-9 **91** (v) AndrewMullen 6 78
(Derek Shaw) *racd in centre: rdn towards rr bef 1/2-way: kpt on fnl f: no ch* **20/1**
-010 **12** *3/4* **Burning Thread (IRE)**[15] 3666 7-8-11 **93** (b) WilliamTwiston-Davies 14 77
(Tim Etherington) *racd nr side: a in rr: rdn bef 1/2-way: struggling after* **50/1**
00-0 **13** *1* **Bogart**[58] 2283 5-9-2 **98** AmyRyan 12 78
(Kevin Ryan) *disp ld in centre to 2f out: wknd over 1f out* **25/1**
13-0 **14** *1/2* **Morawij**[85] 1561 4-9-10 **106** DaneO'Neill 5 84
(Roger Varian) *s.i.s: racd in centre: a in rr: rdn and no real prog 2f out* **25/1**
-000 **15** *1/2* **Dungannon**[21] 3452 7-9-1 **97** (v) JimmyFortune 10 74
(Andrew Balding) *chsd ldrs in centre: rdn and no imp 2f out: wknd over 1f out* **20/1**
1511 **16** *1 1/4* **Sandfrankskipsgo**[15] 3676 5-8-3 **90** NathanAlison(5) 15 62
(Peter Crate) *prom nr side tl wknd qckly over 1f out* **33/1**
-021 **17** *5* **B Fifty Two (IRE)**[14] 3693 5-8-12 **94** (bt) FrannyNorton 9 48
(B W Hills) *disp ld in centre to 2f out: wknd qckly* **25/1**
0-00 **18** *1 1/2* **Zero Money (IRE)**[21] 3452 8-8-8 **95** (b) NoelGarbutt(5) 3 44
(Hugo Palmer) *nvr gng wl: racd in centre: a bhd* **33/1**

58.89s (-1.61) **Going Correction** 0.0s/f (Good)
**WFA** 3 from 4yo+ 5lb **18 Ran SP% 127.8**
Speed ratings (Par 109): **112,111,110,110,107 107,106,104,103,102 101,100,98,97,96 94,86,84**
CSF £112.44 CT £709.44 TOTE £11.80: £2.70, £3.40, £1.60, £2.20; EX 154.50 Trifecta £1113.50.
**Owner** David Spratt **Bred** Jerry O'Sullivan **Trained** Westoning, Beds
**FOCUS**
A good-quality sprint that was dominated by in-form runners. The bare form almost certainly underestimates the winner.

## 4180 FRED COWLEY MBE MEMORIAL SUMMER MILE STKS (GROUP 2) 1m (R)
**2:30** (2:30) (Class 1) 4-Y-0+
**£56,710** (£21,500; £10,760; £5,360; £2,690; £1,350) **Stalls** Low

Form RPR
0-41 **1** **Guest Of Honour (IRE)**[28] 3252 5-9-1 111 (p) MartinHarley 3 117
(Marco Botti) *hld up disputing 5th: prog over 2f out: rdn to ld over 1f out: pressed after: styd on wl* **11/4**[1]
0100 **2** *1/2* **Mull Of Killough (IRE)**[25] 3317 8-9-1 114 GeorgeBaker 8 116
(Jane Chapple-Hyam) *trckd ldng pair: clsd 2f out: drvn to chal over 1f out: pressed wnr after: styd on but a hld* **9/2**[3]
0-16 **3** *1 1/2* **Long John (AUS)**[105] 1178 4-9-1 115 (b) AdamKirby 9 112
(Charlie Appleby) *hld up disputing 7th: rdn and no prog over 2f out: hdwy over 1f out: tk 3rd fnl f: styd on but nvr able to chal* **5/1**
01-5 **4** *3* **Producer**[25] 3317 5-9-1 114 DaneO'Neill 6 106
(Richard Hannon) *s.v.s: sn disputing 7th: drvn over 2f out: kpt on fr over 1f out to take modest 4th last strides* **4/1**[2]
3000 **5** *hd* **Zambucca (SAF)**[14] 3722 6-9-1 98 LukeMorris 5 105
(Gay Kelleway) *hld up and sn in last: rdn over 2f out: stl last 1f out: styd on ins fnl f: n.d* **50/1**
0624 **6** *nk* **Highland Knight (IRE)**[36] 2958 7-9-1 109 (t) DavidProbert 7 104
(Andrew Balding) *trckd ldng pair: shkn up wl over 2f out: sn lost pl: steadily wknd* **8/1**
1 **7** *hd* **The Rectifier (USA)**[13] 3753 7-9-1 106 (t) FergusSweeney 2 104
(Seamus Durack) *led: drvn over 2f out: hdd over 1f out: wknd fnl f* **8/1**
-540 **8** *1/2* **Trumpet Major (IRE)**[24] 3356 5-9-1 105 PatDobbs 4 103
(Richard Hannon) *chsd ldrs disputing 5th: rdn wl over 2f out: sn struggling and btn* **14/1**

5603 **9** 3/4 **Empire Storm (GER)**[14] 3731 7-9-1 105 (t) RobertHavlin 11 101
(Michael Attwater) *trckd ldr: rdn to chal over 2f out: lost 2nd and wknd over 1f out* 25/1

1m 39.34s (-1.36) **Going Correction** 0.0s/f (Good) **9 Ran SP% 116.2**
Speed ratings (Par 115): **106,105,104,101,100 100,100,99,99**
CSF £15.30 TOTE £4.20: £1.40, £1.80, £1.80; EX 14.90 Trifecta £109.00.
**Owner** Giuliano Manfredini **Bred** Azienda Agricola Gennaro Stimola **Trained** Newmarket, Suffolk

**FOCUS**
They went an even gallop and the form looks sound, with the placed runners from a year ago finishing first and second, albeit in a different order. The fifth limits the form a little.

## 4181 WINKWORTH H'CAP 7f
**3:05** (3:05) (Class 4) (0-85,84) 3-Y-O+ **£8,409** (£2,502; £1,250; £625) **Stalls High**

Form RPR
3344 **1** **Scottish Glen**[10] 3861 8-9-1 71 DavidProbert 7 84
(Patrick Chamings) *hld up in last quartet: prog jst over 2f out: rdn to ld jst ins fnl f: styd on wl* 10/1

5521 **2** 1 **Lulu The Zulu (IRE)**[28] 3220 6-9-9 79 AndrewMullen 5 89
(Michael Appleby) *stdd s: t.k.h: trckd ldrs: drvn over 2f out: clsd to chal 1f out u.str.p: chsd wnr sn after: kpt on but a hld* 7/2[1]

-344 **3** 1 **Kakatosi**[31] 3109 7-9-11 81 PatDobbs 4 88
(Mike Murphy) *led: drvn and pressed wl over 1f out: hdd and one pce jst ins fnl f* 8/1

-000 **4** 1 1/4 **Tommy's Secret**[10] 3861 4-8-12 68 JimmyQuinn 6 72
(Jane Chapple-Hyam) *sn in last: pushed along 3f out: sme prog 2f out: styd on u.p fnl f to take 4th last strides* 40/1

-115 **5** hd **Despot (IRE)**[30] 3137 3-9-2 80 GeorgeBaker 1 81
(Charles Hills) *trckd ldrs: rdn and nt qckn 2f out: one pce after: nvr able to chal* 8/1

5434 **6** nse **Good Authority (IRE)**[13] 3753 7-9-13 83 LukeMorris 2 87
(Karen George) *towards rr: shkn up and sme prog 3f out: nt qckn 2f out: kpt on u.p fnl f: nt pce to threaten* 8/1

0504 **7** 3/4 **Showboating (IRE)**[7] 3969 6-10-0 84 (tp) MartinHarley 14 86
(Alan McCabe) *slowly away: hld up in last pair: pushed along 3f out: stl last 2f out: styd on fr jst over 1f out: n.d* 13/2[2]

2554 **8** 1 3/4 **Rouge Nuage (IRE)**[16] 3629 4-8-8 69 (b) CamHardie(5) 13 66
(Conrad Allen) *t.k.h: wl in tch and racd sltly away fr rest: rdn over 2f out: steadily fdd* 18/1

/1-6 **9** 2 1/4 **Obliterieght (IRE)**[34] 3036 5-10-0 84 AdamKirby 10 75
(William Knight) *prom: rdn to chal wl over 1f out: wknd rapidly jst over 1f out* 7/1[3]

5141 **10** shd **Bravo Echo**[29] 3180 8-9-10 80 RobertHavlin 3 71
(Michael Attwater) *trckd ldr: rdn over 2f out: wknd wl over 1f out* 8/1

4050 **11** nk **Light Rose (IRE)**[17] 3581 4-8-12 68 ChrisCatlin 12 58
(Jeremy Gask) *nvr bttr than midfield: shkn up and struggling in rr 2f out* 25/1

3-15 **12** 1/2 **Realize**[75] 1803 4-9-8 78 JimmyFortune 11 67
(Hughie Morrison) *prom: shkn up wl over 2f out: sn lost pl and btn* 12/1

1m 26.54s (-1.06) **Going Correction** 0.0s/f (Good)
**WFA** 3 from 4yo+ 8lb **12 Ran SP% 120.8**
Speed ratings (Par 105): **106,104,103,102,102 102,101,99,96,96 96,95**
CSF £45.77 CT £304.85 TOTE £10.50: £3.90, £1.70, £2.90; EX 70.90 Trifecta £491.10.
**Owner** The Foxford House Partnership **Bred** Mrs Ann Jenkins **Trained** Baughurst, Hants
■ Stewards' Enquiry : Luke Morris £580.00 fine; used mobile phone outside designated area

**FOCUS**
A competitive handicap in which everything fell right for the winner, who posted a turf best.

## 4182 NORMAN COURT STUD FILLIES' H'CAP 1m (S)
**3:40** (3:40) (Class 3) (0-90,84) 3-Y-O+ **£9,703** (£2,887; £1,443; £721) **Stalls High**

Form RPR
012 **1** **Temptress (IRE)**[22] 3425 3-9-1 80 PatDobbs 3 94
(Roger Charlton) *hld up in last: smooth prog jst over 2f out: led over 1f out: rdn and readily drew clr* 8/1

511 **2** 4 1/2 **Felwah**[16] 3615 3-9-5 84 DaneO'Neill 1 88
(William Haggas) *hld up in tch: prog over 2f out: drvn to chal and upsides over 1f out: sn outpcd by wnr* 7/4[1]

-120 **3** nk **Saltwater Creek (IRE)**[42] 2769 3-8-7 77 CamHardie(5) 2 80
(Michael Bell) *led: drvn and hdd over 1f out: outpcd but kpt on ins fnl f* 7/1

-112 **4** 1 1/2 **Lady Tiana**[29] 3195 3-9-4 83 LukeMorris 6 83
(Lucy Wadham) *hld up in tch: prog and cl up 2f out: rdn to try to chal over 1f out: outpcd sn after* 3/1[2]

1122 **5** 1 1/4 **Waveguide (IRE)**[14] 3727 5-8-13 76 LewisWalsh(7) 7 75
(David Simcock) *trckd ldr: shkn up 2f out: cl enough over 1f out: sn nt qckn: lft bhd after* 7/2[3]

1602 **6** 23 **Bowstar**[108] 1102 5-9-7 77 (b) RobertHavlin 4 23
(Michael Attwater) *trckd ldr tl wknd rapidly jst over 2f out: eased and t.o* 33/1

1m 39.35s (-1.45) **Going Correction** 0.0s/f (Good)
**WFA** 3 from 4yo+ 9lb **6 Ran SP% 110.1**
Speed ratings (Par 104): **107,102,102,100,99 76**
CSF £21.68 TOTE £6.40: £2.40, £1.40; EX 17.40 Trifecta £192.30.
**Owner** The Pyoneers **Bred** J Hanly, A Stroud And T Stewart **Trained** Beckhampton, Wilts

**FOCUS**
A fair fillies' handicap that was won in taking style by the winner, who posted a clear personal best.

## 4183 NEPTUNE INVESTMENT MANAGEMENT H'CAP (BOBIS RACE) 1m 4f
**4:15** (4:15) (Class 2) (0-105,105) 3-Y-O
**£31,125** (£9,320; £4,660; £2,330; £1,165; £585) **Stalls Low**

Form RPR
3-52 **1** **Battersea**[15] 3673 3-8-0 84 oh2 NickyMackay 7 95+
(Roger Varian) *trckd ldr: rdn to chal jst over 1f out: led over 1f out but pressed: styd on wl to assert ins fnl f* 10/1

-621 **2** 1 3/4 **Oasis Fantasy (IRE)**[29] 3183 3-8-0 84 oh3 JimmyQuinn 2 92
(Ed Dunlop) *hld up in midfield: rdn and prog to chse ldng trio wl over 1f out: styd on fnl f to take 2nd last stride* 7/1[3]

5111 **3** nk **Maid In Rio (IRE)**[15] 3673 3-8-1 85 FrannyNorton 3 93
(Mark Johnston) *trckd ldng trio: clsd to chal 2f out: drvn and w wnr over 1f out tl jst ins fnl f: one pce and lost 2nd last stride* 8/1

0300 **4** 2 1/4 **Swivel**[23] 3379 3-8-5 89 JohnFahy 4 93
(Mark Johnston) *trckd ldng trio: rdn over 2f out: no imp over 1f out: styd on same pce after* 25/1

0-21 **5** nse **Nabatean (IRE)**[37] 2925 3-8-1 85 oh1 ow1 DavidProbert 9 89+
(Andrew Balding) *hld up and last tl 4f out: rdn over 2f out: kpt on fr over 1f out: n.d* 9/2[1]

0122 **6** 1/2 **Good Value**[45] 2685 3-7-9 84 CamHardie(5) 12 87
(Sir Michael Stoute) *led at gd pce: rdn and pressed over 2f out: hdd & wknd over 1f out* 7/1[3]

4411 **7** 2 3/4 **Kinshasa**[17] 3587 3-8-5 89 LukeMorris 1 88
(Luca Cumani) *s.i.s: hld up in last trio: rdn and sme prog over 3f out: no hdwy u.p 2f out: wknd* 9/2[1]

-120 **8** nk **Galizzi (USA)**[35] 2986 3-7-9 84 JackGarritty(5) 6 82
(Michael Bell) *fractious in preliminaries: t.k.h: hld up in last trio: rdn and no prog 3f out: wl btn 2f out* 10/1

-216 **9** 17 **Miner's Lamp (IRE)**[22] 3417 3-9-7 105 AdamKirby 5 76
(Charlie Appleby) *pushed along early then tk fierce hold towards rr: rapid prog to chse ldrs over 3f out: wknd as rapidly over 2f out: t.o* 5/1[2]

6321 **10** 28 **Hesketh Bank**[35] 3003 3-8-0 84 oh1 AndrewMullen 11 10
(Richard Fahey) *wl in tch: hung lft 4f out and sn dropped to last: wl t.o* 14/1

2m 29.12s (-3.38) **Going Correction** 0.0s/f (Good) **10 Ran SP% 117.8**
Speed ratings (Par 106): **111,109,109,108,108 107,105,105,94,75**
CSF £79.04 CT £595.46 TOTE £10.40: £3.00, £2.60, £2.60; EX 87.90 Trifecta £799.00.
**Owner** H R H Sultan Ahmad Shah **Bred** Newsells Park Stud **Trained** Newmarket, Suffolk

**FOCUS**
A good middle-distance 3yo handicap, run at a decent gallop and it should produce winners. The winner and third were tightly matched on Newmarket form.

## 4184 PLAYBOY CLUB LONDON H'CAP 1m 2f
**4:50** (4:50) (Class 3) (0-90,89) 3-Y-O+ **£9,703** (£2,887; £1,443; £721) **Stalls Low**

Form RPR
-600 **1** **Charles Camoin (IRE)**[36] 2957 6-9-11 86 JimmyFortune 10 94+
(Sylvester Kirk) *sweating profusely: stdd s: hld up in last: prog jst over 2f out: clsd on ldrs over 1f out: drvn to ld jst ins fnl f: styd on wl* 4/1[1]

4301 **2** 3/4 **Raskova (USA)**[25] 3335 4-9-10 85 TedDurcan 11 91
(William Jarvis) *trckd ldr 3f: styd handy: rdn on inner 2f out: clsd and upsides 1f out: styd on but hld ins fnl f* 5/1[2]

35 **3** nk **Double Discount (IRE)**[25] 3341 4-9-11 86 FergusSweeney 7 91
(Tom Dascombe) *t.k.h: prom: chsd ldr over 3f out: drvn 2f out: tried to chal over 1f out: nt qckn but styd on fnl f* 8/1

5406 **4** 1/2 **Commissar**[12] 3802 5-8-12 73 FrannyNorton 2 77+
(Ian Williams) *hld up in last trio: pushed along and no prog over 2f out: shkn up over 1f out: styd on fnl f: too much to do* 14/1

0-00 **5** hd **Weapon Of Choice (IRE)**[80] 1653 6-9-11 86 PatCosgrave 1 90
(Stuart Kittow) *hld up in midfield: rdn over 2f out: steadily clsd on ldrs 1f out: kpt on but nt quite pce to rch ldrs* 25/1

0541 **6** hd **Eurystheus (IRE)**[28] 3254 5-9-5 80 (p) AndrewMullen 3 84
(Michael Appleby) *t.k.h: trckd ldrs: rdn over 2f out: clsd and tried to chal jst over 1f out: nt qckn* 7/1[3]

252- **7** 3/4 **Saoi (USA)**[276] 7121 7-9-11 86 AdamKirby 9 88
(William Knight) *hld up in last trio: shkn up over 2f out: no prog over 1f out: kpt on fnl f: nvr threatened ldrs* 14/1

-201 **8** shd **Epic Battle (IRE)**[20] 3499 4-9-11 86 MartinHarley 12 88
(George Margarson) *led 3f: chsd ldr to over 3f out: stl cl up and drvn to ld over 1f out: hdd and fdd jst ins fnl f* 8/1

1004 **9** 3/4 **Tobacco Road (IRE)**[29] 3196 4-9-9 89 CamHardie(5) 4 90
(Richard Hannon) *trckd ldrs: prog to ld 6f out: drvn over 2f out: hdd over 1f out: no ex and lost pls fnl f* 7/1[3]

4003 **10** nk **Tinshu (IRE)**[12] 3802 8-8-11 77 (p) DannyBrock(5) 8 77
(Derek Haydn Jones) *prom early: sn in midfield: dropped to rr and rdn 2f out: one pce and no imp on ldrs after* 12/1

45-4 **11** 2 1/4 **Headline News (IRE)**[33] 3065 5-9-8 83 ChrisCatlin 6 79
(Rae Guest) *hld up in midfield: rdn and no prog over 2f out: eased whn btn fnl f* 8/1

2m 9.64s (2.24) **Going Correction** 0.0s/f (Good)
**WFA** 3 from 4yo+ 11lb **11 Ran SP% 119.9**
Speed ratings (Par 107): **91,90,90,89,89 89,88,88,88,87 86**
CSF £23.93 CT £156.06 TOTE £5.20: £2.00, £2.30, £3.40; EX 25.90 Trifecta £186.40.
**Owner** Chris Wright & The Hon Mrs J M Corbett **Bred** Pat Grogan **Trained** Upper Lambourn, Berks

**FOCUS**
A wide-open handicap, run at rather a muddling gallop, and any number held a chance over 1f out. The winner was entitled to take this on her best form.
T/Plt: £121.30 to a £1 stake. Pool: £126,458.11 - 760.68 winning units. T/Qpdt: £17.50 to a £1 stake. Pool: £7432.68 - 313.22 winning units. JN

# 4156 CHESTER (L-H)
Saturday, July 12

**OFFICIAL GOING: Good to firm (good in places; 7.7)**
Wind: Light to medium, across Weather: Cloudy

## 4185 £10 FREE BET AT CORBETTSPORTS.COM/ EBF STALLIONS MAIDEN STKS (BOBIS RACE) 5f 16y
**2:15** (2:16) (Class 4) 2-Y-O **£6,469** (£1,925; £962; £481) **Stalls Low**

Form RPR
220 **1** **Al Ghuwariyah (IRE)**[24] 3353 2-8-9 0 KevinStott(5) 4 73
(Kevin Ryan) *mde all: rdn over 1f out: kpt on gamely whn pressed ins fnl f* 8/1

5242 **2** nk **Don Sigfredo (IRE)**[8] 3937 2-9-5 0 (p) RichardKingscote 6 77
(Tom Dascombe) *chsd ldrs: rdn over 1f out: chalng wnr ins fnl f: nt qckn* 9/2[2]

3 **3** 1/2 **Eastern Racer (IRE)**[14] 3713 2-8-12 0 MeganCarberry(7) 7 75
(Brian Ellison) *towards rr: got unbalanced wl over 2f out: rdn 2f out: hdwy whn nt clr run over 1f out: styd on ins fnl f: nt pce to chal wnr* 25/1

532 **4** 1 **Anonymous John (IRE)**[19] 3524 2-9-2 0 (v[1]) DeclanBates(3) 2 72
(David Evans) *unruly bef s: rdn along to r w wnr: rdn whn chalng over 1f out: lost 2nd jst ins fnl f: stl wl there tl no ex fnl 75yds* 6/1[3]

4242 **5** nk **Zuzinia (IRE)**[14] 3706 2-9-0 0 SamHitchcott 1 65
(Mick Channon) *in tch: effrt whn nt clr run 1f out: sn snatched up: kpt on under hand ride after* 8/1

22 **6** 1/2 **Midlander (IRE)**[9] 3893 2-9-5 0 RoystonFfrench 3 69
(Mark Johnston) *s.i.s: in tch: rdn and outpcd 2f out: kpt on same pce ins fnl f* 10/11[1]

**7** 5 **Captain Revelation** 2-9-5 0 StephenCraine 5 51
(Tom Dascombe) *s.i.s: outpcd and bhd: nvr on terms* 25/1

1m 2.66s (1.66) **Going Correction** +0.30s/f (Good) **7 Ran SP% 114.8**
Speed ratings (Par 96): **98,97,96,95,94 93,85**
CSF £43.70 TOTE £6.90: £2.10, £2.70; EX 25.20 Trifecta £313.10.
**Owner** Mubarak Al Naemi **Bred** Sean Gorman **Trained** Hambleton, N Yorks
■ Stewards' Enquiry : Richard Kingscote three-day ban; used whip without giving gelding time to respond (27th-29th July)

**FOCUS**
The rail between the 6f and 1 1/2f point was moved out by 9m, adding 30yds to race 1, 37yds to race 2, 3,4 and 7, 70yds to race 5 and 39yds to race 6. After riding in the opener both Richard Kingscote, who switched to this meeting from Newmarket, and Royston Ffrench described the ground as "quick". No more than a fair maiden but the form could rate a few pounds higher.

## 4186 RAYMOND & KATHLEEN CORBETT MEMORIAL H'CAP (BOBIS RACE) 6f 18y
**2:50** (2:50) (Class 4) (0-80,80) 3-Y-O **£6,469** (£1,925; £962; £481) **Stalls** Low

Form RPR
215 **1** *shd* **Kodafine (IRE)**[7] 3966 3-8-3 **62** oh4 ow1 ........ AdrianNicholls 9 67
(David Evans) *chsd ldrs: pushed along 3f out: wnt 2nd 2f out: rdn to ld ins fnl f: sn edgd rt: hdd narrowly towards fin* **14/1**
0001 **2** *1 1/2* **Pushkin Museum (IRE)**[15] 3669 3-9-5 **78** ........ DavidNolan 1 78
(Richard Fahey) *led: rdn over 1f out: hdd ins fnl f: kpt on u.p: hld towards fin* **2/1**[1]
1535 **3** *nk* **Royal Warrior**[14] 3704 3-9-7 **80** ........ OisinMurphy 7 79
(Alan McCabe) *in tch: rdn over 2f out: outpcd sn after: styd on u.p ins fnl f: nt rch ldrs* **4/1**[2]
5-55 **4** *2* **Finflash (IRE)**[54] 2406 3-9-1 **74** ........ SamHitchcott 6 65
(Mick Channon) *towards rr: rdn and hdwy jst over 1f out: kpt on ins fnl f: nvr trbld ldrs* **9/1**
60-4 **5** *nk* **Foxtrot Pearl (IRE)**[21] 3469 3-8-8 **67** ........ StevieDonohoe 10 57
(John Holt) *hld up: rdn over 1f out: kpt on ins fnl f: nvr trbld ldrs* **25/1**
2115 **6** *3/4* **Dreams Of Reality**[9] 3882 3-9-2 **75** ........ RichardKingscote 4 63+
(Tom Dascombe) *awkward s: sn in midfield: effrt to chse ldrs over 1f out: one pce ins fnl f* **4/1**[2]
3-56 **7** *8* **Quantum Dot (IRE)**[61] 2208 3-8-4 **68** ........ ShirleyTeasdale(5) 2 27
(Lisa Williamson) *chsd ldr: ev ch 3f out: rdn and lost 2nd 2f out: wknd over 1f out* **14/1**
2155 **8** *nk* **Red Forever**[7] 3959 3-7-13 **65** ........ JoeDoyle(7) 11 23
(Alan Berry) *ref to settle: hld up: shkn up on wd outer over 2f out: sn outpcd and wl btn* **16/1**
2105 **D** **Jolly Red Jeanz (IRE)**[61] 2208 3-8-3 **62** ........(b) RoystonFfrench 3 68
(B W Hills) *chsd ldrs: rdn over 1f out: r.o ins fnl f: led narrowly towards fin* **8/1**[3]

1m 15.84s (2.04) **Going Correction** +0.30s/f (Good) **9** Ran SP% **117.5**
Speed ratings (Par 102): **97,95,95,92,92 91,80,80,98**
CSF £113.76 CT £313.11 TOTE £11.30: £4.60, £3.30, £1.20; EX 115.60 Trifecta £547.70.
**Owner** Mrs E Evans **Bred** Tally-Ho Stud **Trained** Pandy, Monmouths

**FOCUS**
This was run at a good pace but thr form looks ordinary at best.

## 4187 BET WITH CORBETT SPORTS CITY PLATE (LISTED RACE) 7f 2y
**3:25** (3:25) (Class 1) 3-Y-O+
**£20,982** (£7,955; £3,981; £1,983; £995; £499) **Stalls** Low

Form RPR
6-00 **1** **Glory Awaits (IRE)**[25] 3317 4-9-2 110 ........(b) IanBrennan 3 109
(Kevin Ryan) *trckd ldrs: checked after 1f and sn rdn along: n.m.r and lost pl sn after: dropped towards rr: rdn and hdwy over 1f out: r.o to ld wl ins fnl f: in control nr fin* **4/1**[3]
6040 **2** *1/2* **Miracle Of Medinah**[24] 3352 3-8-8 102 ........ StevieDonohoe 1 105
(Mark Usher) *bhd: rdn and hdwy over 1f out: r.o and str chal wl ins fnl f: hld nr fin* **9/1**
1-26 **3** *nk* **Mushir**[57] 2304 3-8-8 101 ........ SteveDrowne 2 104
(Roger Varian) *trckd ldrs: wnt 2nd over 1f out: r.o to chal ins fnl f: styd on same pce and hld fnl strides* **2/1**[1]
0630 **4** *nk* **Intransigent**[22] 3420 5-9-2 102 ........ OisinMurphy 4 106
(Andrew Balding) *chsd ldrs: effrt over 1f out: r.o to ld ins fnl f: sn hdd: no ex fnl strides* **7/2**[2]
6100 **5** *1/2* **Penitent**[14] 3723 8-9-7 112 ........ DavidNolan 6 110
(David O'Meara) *led: rdn over 1f out: hdd ins fnl f: kpt on u.p: one pce nr fin* **14/1**
5-0 **6** *nk* **Boom And Bust (IRE)**[86] 1533 7-9-2 105 ........ RoystonFfrench 5 104
(Marcus Tregoning) *towards rr: rdn over 1f out: styd on ins fnl f: nvr able to chal* **11/2**
0213 **7** *6* **Chosen Character (IRE)**[9] 3886 6-9-2 94 ........(vt) RichardKingscote 7 88
(Tom Dascombe) *w ldr tl rdn over 2f out: wknd jst over 1f out* **16/1**

1m 26.69s (0.19) **Going Correction** +0.30s/f (Good)
**WFA** 3 from 4yo+ 8lb **7** Ran SP% **113.5**
Speed ratings (Par 111): **110,109,109,108,108 107,100**
CSF £37.86 TOTE £6.10: £3.10, £3.60; EX 40.60 Trifecta £137.60.
**Owner** Ahmad Abdulla Al Shaikh & Co **Bred** J Fisher **Trained** Hambleton, N Yorks
■ Stewards' Enquiry : Stevie Donohoe two-day ban; used whip above permitted level (27th-28th July)

**FOCUS**
An open Listed event in which the pace was not overly strong and they finished in a heap. Ordinary form for the grade.

## 4188 BET ON YOUR MOBILE AT CORBETTSPORTS.COM H'CAP 6f 18y
**4:00** (4:01) (Class 2) (0-105,100) 3-Y-O+ **£12,938** (£3,850; £1,924; £962) **Stalls** Low

Form RPR
1063 **1** **Kimberella**[14] 3714 4-9-1 **89** ........ AdrianNicholls 7 102
(David Nicholls) *trckd ldrs: led jst over 1f out: sn rdn: r.o wl: in command fnl 100yds* **7/1**[3]
4504 **2** *2 1/4* **Confessional**[15] 3666 7-9-4 **92** ........(e) DavidNolan 3 98
(Tim Easterby) *broke wl: in tch: rdn over 1f out: kpt on to take 2nd ins fnl f: no imp on wnr* **8/1**
-005 **3** *1 1/4* **Boomerang Bob (IRE)**[21] 3452 5-9-10 **98** ........ SteveDrowne 6 100+
(B W Hills) *midfield: rdn and hdwy over 1f out: swtchd lft jst ins fnl f: rdr sn dropped rein: r.o: nt rch front two* **11/4**[1]
1202 **4** *3/4* **Lexi's Hero (IRE)**[28] 3216 6-8-6 **85** ........(v) SammyJoBell(5) 13 85
(Richard Fahey) *trckd ldrs: rdn over 1f out: nt qckn: styd on same pce ins fnl f* **14/1**
0003 **5** *1/2* **Arnold Lane (IRE)**[14] 3732 5-9-12 **100** ........ SamHitchcott 5 98
(Mick Channon) *midfield: effrt 2f out: kpt on u.p ins fnl f: no imp on ldrs* **10/1**
5-61 **6** *hd* **Cheworee**[14] 3697 5-8-8 **82** ........(tp) RichardKingscote 8 79
(Tom Dascombe) *led: rdn and hdd jst over 1f out: no ex and fdd fnl 100yds* **25/1**
0010 **7** *3/4* **Clockmaker (IRE)**[14] 3716 8-9-6 **94** ........ IanBrennan 4 89
(Conor Dore) *racd keenly in midfield: rdn 2f out: no hdwy: one pce ins fnl f* **20/1**
00-6 **8** *1/2* **Secretinthepark**[69] 1975 4-9-6 **94** ........ StevieDonohoe 12 87
(Ed McMahon) *towards rr: rdn over 1f out: kpt on ins fnl f: no imp* **10/1**
3005 **9** *nk* **Hitchens (IRE)**[14] 3715 9-9-10 **98** ........ RoystonFfrench 1 90+
(David Barron) *in rr: rdn over 1f out: nvr on terms* **6/1**[2]
3636 **10** *1 1/4* **Ballista (IRE)**[27] 3278 6-9-5 **100** ........(p) JennyPowell(7) 10 88
(Tom Dascombe) *chsd ldr tl rdn and nt qckn over 1f out: wknd fnl 150yds* **28/1**
4163 **11** *2 1/4* **Verse Of Love**[13] 3753 5-8-9 **86** ........ DeclanBates(3) 2 67
(David Evans) *n.m.r wl over 4f out: in rr: outpcd fnl 2f: nvr a threat* **8/1**
-530 **U** **Blaine**[22] 3420 4-9-3 **96** ........(b[1]) KevinStott(5) 11
(Kevin Ryan) *stmbld and uns rdr s* **12/1**

1m 14.39s (0.59) **Going Correction** +0.30s/f (Good) **12** Ran SP% **120.3**
Speed ratings (Par 109): **108,105,103,102,101 101,100,99,99,97 94,**
CSF £61.37 CT £194.31 TOTE £7.20: £3.00, £3.50, £1.10; EX 51.80 Trifecta £131.70.
**Owner** C Titcomb **Bred** P And Mrs A G Venner **Trained** Sessay, N Yorks

**FOCUS**
Not the strongest handicap for the grade but it was competitive and the pace was strong throughout. The winner has looked capable of reaching this sort of level.

## 4189 CSP AUDIO VISUAL H'CAP (BOBIS RACE) 1m 6f 91y
**4:35** (4:46) (Class 4) (0-80,78) 3-Y-O **£7,762** (£2,310; £1,154; £577) **Stalls** Low

Form RPR
3413 **1** **Spectator**[40] 2839 3-9-0 **71** ........(p) OisinMurphy 2 79
(Andrew Balding) *hld up: rdn 3f out: hdwy on inner 2f out: led ins fnl f: r.o gamely* **4/1**[3]
1531 **2** *3/4* **Innocent Touch (IRE)**[15] 3655 3-9-5 **76** ........ DavidNolan 3 83
(Richard Fahey) *chsd ldrs: checked sltly 2f out: rdn and chalng upsides whn edgd lft ins fnl f: hld nr fin* **11/4**[1]
0142 **3** *nk* **Full Day**[23] 3396 3-8-9 **73** ........ MeganCarberry(7) 1 79
(Brian Ellison) *in tch: hdwy on inner over 2f out: rdn and led wl over 1f out: hdd ins fnl f: continued to chal: no ex fnl strides* **7/2**[2]
-032 **4** *9* **Norse Light**[19] 3514 3-9-7 **78** ........(b[1]) RichardKingscote 5 72
(Ralph Beckett) *chsd ldr: led 2f out: rdn and hdd over 1f out: wknd ins fnl f* **16/1**
3335 **5** *6* **Mambo Rhythm**[11] 3829 3-8-10 **67** ........ RoystonFfrench 7 52
(Mark Johnston) *in tch: pushed along over 3f out: wknd 2f out* **11/1**
6-04 **6** *11* **Layla's Red Devil (IRE)**[87] 1508 3-8-4 **66** ........ SammyJoBell(5) 4 36
(Richard Fahey) *hld up: niggled along 6f out: bhd fnl 2f* **5/1**
5023 **7** *16* **Right Of Appeal**[11] 3823 3-9-0 **71** ........ AdrianNicholls 6 19
(Mark Johnston) *racd keenly: led: rdn over 2f out: sn hdd and hmpd: wknd after* **11/2**

3m 10.43s (3.43) **Going Correction** +0.30s/f (Good) **7** Ran SP% **115.2**
Speed ratings (Par 102): **102,101,101,96,92 86,77**
CSF £15.67 TOTE £5.00: £2.40, £2.10; EX 18.60 Trifecta £73.80.
**Owner** Kingsclere Racing Club **Bred** Kingsclere Stud **Trained** Kingsclere, Hants
■ Stewards' Enquiry : David Nolan caution; careless riding.

**FOCUS**
A tight 3yo handicap in which all seven runners were trying this longer trip for the first time, with the first three pulling clear of the remainder.

## 4190 IRISH CHAMPIONS WEEKEND H'CAP 1m 2f 75y
**5:10** (5:13) (Class 4) (0-80,80) 4-Y-O+ **£6,469** (£1,925; £962; £481) **Stalls** High

Form RPR
2 **1** **Spanish Plume**[18] 3546 6-8-8 **72** ........(p) KevinStott(5) 6 81+
(Andrew Hollinshead) *racd keenly: hld up: impr wl over 7f out: prom 4f out: led over 1f out: r.o wl: clr fnl 100yds: comf* **8/1**
0003 **2** *2* **Al Mukhdam**[23] 3400 4-9-3 **76** ........ OisinMurphy 4 80
(Ed de Giles) *led: rdn and hdd over 1f out: sn outpcd by wnr: no ex nr fin and jst hld on for 2nd* **7/1**
3354 **3** *shd* **The Firm (IRE)**[28] 3235 5-8-7 **66** ........ FrankieMcDonald 2 70+
(Daniel Mark Loughnane) *hld up: nt clr run over 2f out: sn swtchd to wd outside: prog ins fnl f: r.o and edgd lft: gng on at fin* **8/1**
2223 **4** *3/4* **Ocean Applause**[9] 3878 4-8-9 **75** ........(t) JoeDoyle(7) 1 77
(John Ryan) *trckd ldrs: nt clr run over 2f out: rdn over 1f out: kpt on u.p ins fnl f: no imp* **11/4**[1]
3050 **5** *1/2* **Skytrain**[14] 3718 4-9-7 **80** ........ RoystonFfrench 7 81
(Mark Johnston) *prom: lost pl 5f out: sn rdn: outpcd over 2f out: kpt on u.p ins fnl f but nt trble ldrs* **12/1**
310 **6** *hd* **Gabrial The Thug (FR)**[4] 4058 4-7-11 **61** ........(t) SammyJoBell(5) 9 62
(Richard Fahey) *prom: rdn 2f out: sn outpcd by ldrs: edgd lft u.p ins fnl f: no ex fnl 100yds* **8/1**
5013 **7** *1* **Gabrial The Terror (IRE)**[10] 3853 4-8-9 **68** ........ StevieDonohoe 3 67
(David Simcock) *in tch: hmpd on bnd under 8f out: sn lost pl: u.p towards rr over 2f out: nvr able to get on terms after* **11/2**[3]
0142 **8** *3/4* **Swift Cedar (IRE)**[15] 3646 4-9-2 **78** ........ DeclanBates(3) 5 76
(David Evans) *hld up: rdn over 2f out: no imp: wl hld ins fnl f* **4/1**[2]

2m 13.57s (2.37) **Going Correction** +0.30s/f (Good) **8** Ran SP% **115.6**
Speed ratings (Par 105): **102,100,100,99,99 99,98,97**
CSF £62.86 CT £465.17 TOTE £9.40: £3.00, £2.80, £2.30; EX 64.80 Trifecta £542.80.
**Owner** The Three R'S **Bred** Mrs J A Prescott **Trained** Upper Longdon, Staffs

**FOCUS**
A fair handicap run at a steady pace.

## 4191 CRUISE NIGHTCLUB APPRENTICE H'CAP (BOBIS RACE) 7f 122y
**5:45** (5:46) (Class 4) (0-80,78) 3-Y-O **£6,469** (£1,925; £962; £481) **Stalls** Low

Form RPR
-103 **1** **Comanchero (IRE)**[19] 3518 3-8-11 **63** ........ OisinMurphy 8 72
(Andrew Balding) *hld up: hdwy over 2f out: qcknd to ld fnl 120yds: r.o wl: pushed out and in command towards fin* **6/1**[3]
0-21 **2** *2* **Wilde Inspiration (IRE)**[43] 2737 3-9-12 **78** ........ IanBrennan 7 82
(Julie Camacho) *hld up: rdn and hdwy over 1f out: r.o ins fnl f: tk 2nd towards fin: nt trble wnr* **11/4**[1]
3105 **3** *3/4* **Rough Courte (IRE)**[16] 3625 3-9-0 **71** ........ DanielCremin(5) 9 73
(Mick Channon) *chsd ldr: rdn to chal 2f out: led 1f out: hdd fnl 120yds: kpt on same pce towards fin* **8/1**
0-40 **4** *2 1/2* **Comino (IRE)**[59] 2257 3-9-8 **77** ........ KevinStott(3) 3 73
(Kevin Ryan) *racd keenly: led: rdn over 1f out: hdd 1f out: no ex and fdd fnl 100yds: eased whn btn towards fin* **13/2**
2342 **5** *1 1/4* **Mfiftythreedotcom (IRE)**[15] 3647 3-9-0 **69** ........ SammyJoBell(3) 6 62+
(Richard Fahey) *hld up: nt clr run wl over 1f out: kpt on ins fnl f: nvr able to chal* **4/1**[2]
522 **6** *3/4* **Distant High**[14] 3695 3-8-9 **64** ........ JoeDoyle(3) 1 55
(Richard Price) *midfield: nt clr run and outpcd over 2f out: nvr able to get on terms after* **7/1**
13- **7** *nk* **Flora Medici**[289] 6770 3-9-10 **76** ........ RosieJessop 4 66
(Sir Mark Prescott Bt) *in tch: rdn whn chsng ldrs over 2f out: wknd ins fnl f* **7/1**

4-45 **8** *3 1/4* **Market Storm (FR)**[14] 3695 3-8-8 **63**........................(v) JordanNason(3) 2 45
(Michael Mullineaux) *trckd ldrs: pushed along 3f out: wknd over 2f out* **16/1**

1m 35.47s (1.67) **Going Correction** +0.30s/f (Good) **8** Ran SP% **116.3**
Speed ratings (Par 102): **103,101,100,97,96 95,95,92**
CSF £23.33 CT £125.03 TOTE £10.40: £2.40, £1.70, £2.90; EX 31.10 Trifecta £148.70.
**Owner** Kennet Valley Thoroughbreds VII **Bred** Yeomanstown Stud **Trained** Kingsclere, Hants

**FOCUS**
Only a fair 3yo handicap.
T/Plt: £402.90 to a £1 stake. Pool: £60,643.51 - 109.86 winning units. T/Qpdt: £55.80 to a £1 stake. Pool: £4465.70 - 59.20 winning units. DO

## 3827 HAMILTON (R-H)
Saturday, July 12

**OFFICIAL GOING: Good to firm (8.2)**
Wind: Light, half behind Weather: Overcast, light rain

## 4192 RACING UK ANYWHERE AVAILABLE NOW MAIDEN AUCTION STKS 5f 4y
**6:40** (6:40) (Class 5) 2-Y-O **£3,408** (£1,006; £503) **Stalls** Centre

Form RPR
**1** **Edgar Balthazar** 2-9-0 0.................................................... TomEaves 3 73+
(Keith Dalgleish) *wnt rt s: mde all: drvn along 2f out: hrd pressed fnl f: hld on gamely* **9/4**[1]

**2** *nk* **Felix Leiter** 2-9-1 0.................................................... BenCurtis 2 73
(K R Burke) *green in preliminaries: cl up: pushed along after 2f: effrt and ev ch fnl f: kpt on: hld nr fin* **11/4**[3]

0 **3** *2 1/4* **Indian Champ**[54] 2395 2-8-9 0.....................................(b) ShaneGray(5) 6 64
(Kevin Ryan) *prom: rdn: outpcd and edgd lft over 1f out: kpt on fnl f to take 3rd cl home: nt rch first two* **20/1**

**4** *1/2* **Intruder** 2-8-12 0.................................................... PJMcDonald 1 60
(Richard Fahey) *in tch: hdwy on outside over 2f out: rdn and outpcd fnl f* **7/2**

**5** *6* **George Bailey (IRE)** 2-8-13 0........................................ BarryMcHugh 4 40
(Bryan Smart) *t.k.h: cl up tl rdn and wknd wl over 1f out* **5/2**[2]

0 **6** *2 1/4* **Equiaire**[19] 3529 2-8-7 0.............................................. JoeyHaynes(3) 5 29
(John Weymes) *bhd and outpcd: no ch fr 2f out* **40/1**

59.34s (-0.66) **Going Correction** -0.275s/f (Firm) **6** Ran SP% **115.4**
Speed ratings (Par 94): **94,93,89,89,79 75**
CSF £9.21 TOTE £4.00: £1.90, £1.60; EX 8.50 Trifecta £67.50.
**Owner** Middleham Park racing XXII **Bred** Natton House Thoroughbreds **Trained** Carluke, S Lanarks

**FOCUS**
Fresh ground around the loop and all distances as advertised. Light rain started about an hour before the first race of a meeting staged on watered ground. The riders reported the ground to be as the official description. Not much to go on by way of form but just an ordinary bunch on looks and this represents modest form from the principals. The gallop was reasonable and the first two pulled clear.

## 4193 FAIR FRIDAY RACENIGHT NEXT WEEK H'CAP 5f 4y
**7:10** (7:11) (Class 6) (0-65,68) 3-Y-O **£2,587** (£770; £384; £192) **Stalls** Centre

Form RPR
6001 **1** **Straits Of Malacca**[4] 4059 3-9-5 **68** 6ex.............................. ShaneGray(5) 3 78
(Kevin Ryan) *trckd ldrs: led over 1f out: drvn clr fnl f* **15/8**[1]

0060 **2** *2 1/4* **Baltic Spirit (IRE)**[16] 3609 3-8-13 **57**..............................(b[1]) JasonHart 8 59
(Keith Dalgleish) *s.i.s: bhd and drvn along: hdwy 1/2-way: effrt and chsd (clr) wnr fnl f: no imp* **5/1**[3]

15 **3** *2 1/4* **Dancing Juice**[7] 3972 3-8-12 **56**...........................................(v) TomEaves 9 50
(K R Burke) *led tl rdn and hdd over 1f out: edgd rt and no ex ins fnl f* **13/2**

003 **4** *2 3/4* **Mossy Marie (IRE)**[37] 2910 3-8-1 **48**.................................. NeilFarley(3) 1 32
(Eric Alston) *in tch on outside: effrt 2f out: edgd rt and wknd appr fnl f* **22/1**

654- **5** *2 1/2* **Aya's Gift**[343] 5000 3-9-5 **63**.............................................. JackMitchell 4 38
(Ed Walker) *in tch: effrt and hdwy over 2f out: edgd rt and wknd over 1f out* **3/1**[2]

2543 **6** *2* **Straight Gin**[16] 3609 3-8-6 **50** ow2...................................(b) BarryMcHugh 6 18
(Alan Berry) *w ldrs: drvn along over 2f out: wknd wl over 1f out* **11/1**

6300 **7** *3/4* **Chuckamental**[28] 3228 3-8-6 **50**........................................... PJMcDonald 5 15
(Bryan Smart) *dwlt: bhd and outpcd: no ch fr 1/2-way* **9/1**

58.86s (-1.14) **Going Correction** -0.275s/f (Firm) **7** Ran SP% **112.5**
Speed ratings (Par 98): **98,94,90,86,82 79,78**
CSF £11.23 CT £48.48 TOTE £2.90: £1.60, £2.80; EX 11.00 Trifecta £51.30.
**Owner** JCG Chua & CK Ong **Bred** Whitsbury Manor Stud **Trained** Hambleton, N Yorks

**FOCUS**
Not a strong sprint handicap but it was run at a fair gallop.

## 4194 DAILY RECORD H'CAP (A QUALIFIER FOR THE £15000 BETFAIR SCOTTISH SPRINT SERIES FINAL) 6f 5y
**7:45** (7:45) (Class 5) (0-70,71) 3-Y-O+ **£3,234** (£962; £481; £240) **Stalls** High

Form RPR
0035 **1** **Gold Beau (FR)**[16] 3599 4-9-7 **70**.............................(p) JacobButterfield(5) 5 80
(Kristin Stubbs) *t.k.h early: pressed ldr: led over 2f out: drvn clr fnl f* **5/1**[3]

0231 **2** *2* **Salvatore Fury (IRE)**[7] 3954 4-9-13 **71**..............................(p) JasonHart 3 74
(Keith Dalgleish) *t.k.h: prom: effrt and rdn over 1f out: chsd wnr ins fnl f: r.o* **4/1**[1]

3165 **3** *3/4* **Lothair (IRE)**[45] 2677 5-9-12 **70**......................................... BenCurtis 6 70
(Alan Swinbank) *prom: rdn and ev ch over 1f out: edgd rt: one pce ins fnl f* **5/1**[3]

-041 **4** *1/2* **Dark Crystal**[5] 4017 3-8-9 **59**............................................. PJMcDonald 7 57
(Linda Perratt) *hld up bhd ldng gp: rdn over 2f out: kpt on fnl f: nvr able to chal* **9/2**[2]

2214 **5** *hd* **Hab Reeh**[24] 3359 6-9-3 **66**............................................. GemmaTutty(5) 8 64
(Ruth Carr) *hld up: drvn after 2f: hdwy over 1f out: kpt on: nvr able to chal* **9/2**[2]

6105 **6** *nk* **Alexandrakollontai (IRE)**[17] 3575 4-9-7 **68**.................(b) JulieBurke(3) 4 65
(Alistair Whillans) *dwlt: bhd and outpcd: kpt on fnl f: nrst fin* **15/2**

2126 **7** *2 1/2* **Amis Reunis**[6] 4005 5-8-9 **53**.......................................(p) PaddyAspell 2 42
(Alan Berry) *led to over 2f out: rdn and wknd over 1f out* **9/1**

1-00 **8** *8* **Feel The Heat**[50] 2522 7-9-7 **70**.......................................(v) AdamCarter(5) 1 33
(Bryan Smart) *in tch: hung rt thrght: rdn and wknd over 2f out* **12/1**

1m 9.93s (-2.27) **Going Correction** -0.275s/f (Firm)
**WFA** 3 from 4yo+ 6lb **8** Ran SP% **119.2**
Speed ratings (Par 103): **104,101,100,99,99 99,95,85**
CSF £26.49 CT £107.14 TOTE £7.20: £1.90, £2.00, £1.80; EX 33.90 Trifecta £215.50.
**Owner** D Arundale **Bred** Haras Du Quesnay **Trained** Norton, N Yorks

**FOCUS**
Mainly exposed sorts in a fair handicap. The gallop was sound and this form looks reliable.

## 4195 HAMILTON ADVERTISER H'CAP 6f 5y
**8:15** (8:16) (Class 6) (0-60,60) 3-Y-O+ **£2,385** (£704; £352) **Stalls** High

Form RPR
0000 **1** **Dream Ally (IRE)**[19] 3530 4-9-9 **59**.................................... PJMcDonald 8 67
(Micky Hammond) *in tch: effrt and rdn 2f out: gd hdwy to ld ins fnl f: kpt on strly* **15/2**

-500 **2** *3* **Monsieur Royale**[8] 3913 4-9-5 **55**..................................(b) BarryMcHugh 5 53
(Geoffrey Oldroyd) *hld up: rdn and hdwy over 1f out: kpt on to take 2nd nr fin: nt rch wnr* **7/1**

0-03 **3** *nk* **Gambino (IRE)**[16] 3601 4-8-12 **55**...................................... GaryMahon(7) 7 52
(John David Riches) *in tch: drvn over 2f out: chsd wnr ins fnl f tl lost 2nd cl home* **15/2**

6000 **4** *1 1/2* **Natures Law (IRE)**[15] 3668 4-9-4 **54**..............................(b[1]) JasonHart 10 46
(Keith Dalgleish) *dwlt: sn rdn and led after 2f: clr and drvn over 2f out: hdd and no ex ins fnl f* **15/2**

2351 **5** *1/2* **Rock Canyon (IRE)**[11] 3833 5-9-2 **52**.................................. AndrewElliott 6 43
(Linda Perratt) *in tch: drvn along over 2f out: edgd rt and no imp over 1f out* **9/2**[1]

005 **6** *1* **Bix (IRE)**[11] 3830 4-8-10 **46**.................................................. BenCurtis 4 33
(Alan Berry) *dwlt: bhd and outpcd: hdwy over 1f out: nvr able to chal* **18/1**

0040 **7** *1 1/4* **Chloe's Dream (IRE)**[6] 4005 4-8-12 **53**................... JacobButterfield(5) 9 36
(Linda Perratt) *t.k.h: led 2f: cl up tl wknd fnl f* **15/2**

4406 **8** *3 3/4* **Lomond Lassie**[16] 3625 3-8-11 **53**.......................................(p) TomEaves 1 23
(Keith Dalgleish) *prom: drvn over 2f out: wknd over 1f out* **11/2**[2]

0040 **9** *2 1/2* **Bapak Muda (USA)**[24] 3359 4-9-5 **60**................................ ShaneGray(5) 3 23
(Kevin Ryan) *sn bhd and outpcd: nvr on terms* **6/1**[3]

45-0 **10** *14* **Throwing Roses**[37] 2937 4-8-12 **48**.................................... PaddyAspell 2
(John Weymes) *bhd and sn struggling: no ch fr 1/2-way* **25/1**

1m 11.31s (-0.89) **Going Correction** -0.275s/f (Firm)
**WFA** 3 from 4yo+ 6lb **10** Ran SP% **116.5**
Speed ratings (Par 101): **94,90,89,87,86 85,83,78,75,56**
CSF £59.08 CT £410.75 TOTE £11.00: £4.00, £2.10, £2.00; EX 77.70 Trifecta £587.80.
**Owner** T C H **Bred** Noel & Roger O'Callaghan **Trained** Middleham, N Yorks
■ Stewards' Enquiry : Gary Mahon two-day ban; used whip above permitted level (27th-28th July)

**FOCUS**
A low-grade sprint featuring plenty of hard-to-win with sorts, but the pace was sound.

## 4196 SUNDAY MAIL H'CAP 1m 3f 16y
**8:45** (8:45) (Class 5) (0-75,75) 3-Y-O+ **£4,851** (£1,443; £721; £360) **Stalls** Low

Form RPR
3322 **1** **Never Forever**[6] 3999 5-9-10 **71**........................................... TomEaves 4 83
(Jim Goldie) *chsd ldrs: drvn over 3f out: rallied to ld over 1f out: drvn clr fnl f* **9/2**[3]

23-2 **2** *3 3/4* **Itsnowcato**[15] 3675 3-9-1 **74**................................................ JackMitchell 5 79
(Ed Walker) *hld up: hdwy over 3f out: effrt and keeping on whn lft 2nd over 1f out: kpt on same pce fnl f* **7/4**[1]

2212 **3** *9* **Northside Prince (IRE)**[21] 3475 8-10-0 **75**............................. BenCurtis 1 64
(Alan Swinbank) *chsd ldrs: drvn and outpcd over 2f out: no imp fr over 1f out* **9/1**

0312 **4** *nk* **Zanouska (USA)**[37] 2934 3-8-10 **69**.................................. AdrianNicholls 6 58
(Mark Johnston) *t.k.h: cl up tl drvn and outpcd over 2f out: sn n.d* **8/1**

1113 **5** *7* **Operateur (IRE)**[15] 3657 6-9-8 **69**.................................... AndrewElliott 3 45
(Ben Haslam) *hld up: drvn and struggling 3f out: nvr on terms* **10/1**

5441 **6** *25* **Ted's Brother (IRE)**[7] 3979 6-9-9 **75**..........................(e) DuilioDaSilva(5) 8 6
(Richard Guest) *stmbld leaving stalls: hld up: struggling over 3f out: sn btn: b.b.v* **11/1**

4661 **P** **Incurs Four Faults**[16] 3603 3-8-1 **60**..................................... RaulDaSilva 2 64
(Keith Dalgleish) *t.k.h: led: rdn 3f out: chsng wnr and keeping on same pce whn p.u over 1f out* **4/1**[2]

2m 21.27s (-4.33) **Going Correction** -0.275s/f (Firm)
**WFA** 3 from 4yo+ 12lb **7** Ran SP% **113.1**
Speed ratings (Par 103): **104,101,94,94,89 71,**
CSF £12.53 CT £65.69 TOTE £6.90: £3.20, £2.20; EX 14.50 Trifecta £135.80.
**Owner** Barry MacDonald **Bred** Millsec Limited **Trained** Uplawmoor, E Renfrews

**FOCUS**
Several in-form types in a fair handicap but, although the gallop was no more than fair, the first two finished clear.

## 4197 RACING UK ON SKY 432 H'CAP (A QUALIFIER FOR THE £15000 BETFAIR SCOTTISH MILE SERIES FINAL) 1m 65y
**9:15** (9:15) (Class 5) (0-70,70) 3-Y-O+ **£3,234** (£962; £481; £240) **Stalls** Low

Form RPR
0433 **1** **Hard Core Debt**[10] 3844 4-9-8 **64**........................................... BenCurtis 2 74
(Brian Ellison) *t.k.h: in tch: smooth hdwy to ld over 2f out: rdn and edgd rt over 1f out: kpt on strly* **9/2**[3]

0530 **2** *1 3/4* **Outlaw Torn (IRE)**[14] 3718 5-9-4 **65**.......................(e) DuilioDaSilva(5) 4 71
(Richard Guest) *t.k.h: chsd ldrs: effrt and wnt 2nd over 1f out: drifted lft and kpt on fnl f: nt rch wnr* **17/2**

2223 **3** *nk* **Tectonic (IRE)**[6] 4001 5-10-0 **70**.......................................(p) TomEaves 6 75
(Keith Dalgleish) *t.k.h: hld up in tch: stdy hdwy over 2f out: rdn over 1f out: kpt on same pce ins fnl f* **4/1**[2]

-031 **4** *2 1/4* **Indian Giver**[11] 3828 6-8-8 **57**............................................. GaryMahon(7) 1 57
(John David Riches) *s.i.s: hld up: rdn over 2f out: kpt on fnl f: nvr able to chal* **8/1**

4-21 **5** *2 1/2* **World Record (IRE)**[7] 3949 4-9-13 **69**................................ PJMcDonald 7 63
(John Quinn) *t.k.h: trckd ldr tl rdn and wknd 2f out* **5/4**[1]

0016 **6** *7* **Look On By**[11] 3828 4-9-0 **56**................................................ RaulDaSilva 5 41
(Ruth Carr) *t.k.h: led tl edgd lft and hdd over 2f out: wknd over 1f out* **14/1**

1m 46.52s (-1.88) **Going Correction** -0.275s/f (Firm) **6** Ran SP% **110.9**
Speed ratings (Par 103): **98,96,95,93,91 84**
CSF £38.65 TOTE £4.90: £2.20, £3.20; EX 43.90 Trifecta £35.50.
**Owner** Koo's Racing Club **Bred** Shadwell Estate Company Limited **Trained** Norton, N Yorks

**FOCUS**
A moderate gallop to this extended mile handicap.
T/Plt: £386.30 to a £1 stake. Pool: £65,753.41 - 124.25 winning units. T/Qpdt: £93.00 to a £1 stake. Pool: £5664.41 - 45.04 winning units. RY

4163

# NEWMARKET (R-H)

Saturday, July 12

**OFFICIAL GOING: Soft (6.3; far side 6.1, centre 6.3, stands' side 6.5) changing to good to soft after race 1 (2.05)**

Wind: Almost nil Weather: Cloudy with sunny spells

## 4198 SPA AT BEDFORD LODGE HOTEL MILE (H'CAP) (BOBIS RACE) 1m

**2:05** (2:06) (Class 2) (0-100,99) 3-Y-O

**£24,900** (£7,456; £3,728; £1,864; £932; £468) **Stalls** Low

Form RPR

1-65 **1** **Golden Town (IRE)**[70] 1954 3-9-4 **96**..................(v[1]) SilvestreDeSousa 11 107
(Saeed bin Suroor) *a.p: chsd ldr over 2f out: led over 1f out: rdn out* **8/1**

1-31 **2** *½* **You're Fired (IRE)**[43] 2734 3-8-6 **84**............................ WayneLordan 4 94
(K R Burke) *hld up: hdwy u.p over 1f out: r.o* **6/1**[1]

1144 **3** *2 ¼* **Examiner (IRE)**[28] 3243 3-8-8 **86**............................ LiamJones 16 91
(William Haggas) *hld up: hdwy over 2f out: rdn and edgd rt over 1f out: styd on same pce ins fnl f* **12/1**

4121 **4** *¾* **Lesha (IRE)**[21] 3464 3-8-7 **85**............................ HarryBentley 1 88
(Kevin Ryan) *hld up: hdwy over 2f out: rdn over 1f out: styd on same pce ins fnl f* **16/1**

1113 **5** *½* **Crystal Lake (IRE)**[42] 2781 3-8-7 **85**............................ KierenFox 14 87
(Ralph Beckett) *hld up: pushed along over 3f out: hdwy over 2f out: sn rdn: no ex ins fnl f* **7/1**[3]

-003 **6** *2 ½* **Master The World (IRE)**[7] 3965 3-8-11 **89**.................. JamieSpencer 6 85
(David Elsworth) *led 2f: chsd ldrs: rdn over 1f out: wknd ins fnl f* **8/1**

-510 **7** *2 ½* **Legend Rising (IRE)**[23] 3378 3-9-0 **92**..................... FrederikTylicki 12 85
(Martyn Meade) *hld up: hdwy over 2f out: rdn and nt clr run over 1f out: wknd ins fnl f* **13/2**[2]

0404 **8** *2 ½* **Hunters Creek (IRE)**[9] 3886 3-9-1 **93**............................ WilliamBuick 8 78
(John Gosden) *prom: rdn over 2f out: wknd over 1f out* **11/1**

4-12 **9** *shd* **Mutawathea**[7] 3980 3-8-5 **83**............................ PaulHanagan 2 67
(Richard Hannon) *chsd ldrs: rdn over 3f out: wknd over 1f out* **11/1**

-240 **10** *2 ¼* **Safety Check (IRE)**[105] 1178 3-9-7 **99**............................ MartinLane 7 78
(Charlie Appleby) *w ldr tl led 6f out: rdn and hdd over 1f out: sn wknd* **25/1**

-010 **11** *1* **Idea (USA)**[23] 3378 3-8-11 **89**............................ JamesDoyle 3 66
(Sir Michael Stoute) *hld up: pushed along over 3f out: wknd over 1f out* **6/1**[1]

0651 **12** *7* **Roachdale House (IRE)**[14] 3694 3-8-12 **90**............... TonyHamilton 13 51
(Richard Fahey) *prom: rdn over 3f out: wknd over 2f out* **16/1**

1m 39.82s (-0.18) **Going Correction** +0.325s/f (Good) 12 Ran SP% **116.6**

Speed ratings (Par 106): **113,112,110,109,109 106,104,101,101,99 98,91**

CSF £54.47 CT £585.71 TOTE £10.60: £4.00, £2.30, £4.50; EX 69.10 Trifecta £1469.90 Part won..

**Owner** Godolphin **Bred** Darley **Trained** Newmarket, Suffolk

**FOCUS**

Stands side track used with Stalls on Stands side except 12f: Centre. It had been dry since 9.00am the previous day and the ground had dried out somewhat, changed to good to soft from soft following this opening contest. They raced middle to stands' side, and it was a decent contest despite a few non-runners. The fourth and fifth help with the standard.

## 4199 666BET SUPERLATIVE STKS (GROUP 2) 7f

**2:40** (2:40) (Class 1) 2-Y-O

**£45,368** (£17,200; £8,608; £4,288; £2,152; £1,080) **Stalls** Low

Form RPR

21 **1** **Estidhkaar (IRE)**[30] 3140 2-9-1 0............................ PaulHanagan 7 114+
(Richard Hannon) *w ldr: led 3f out: rdn and edgd rt over 1f out: r.o wl* **15/8**[1]

221 **2** *4 ½* **Aktabantay**[16] 3619 2-9-1 0............................ WilliamBuick 4 103
(Hugo Palmer) *a.p: rdn to chse wnr over 1f out: styd on same pce ins fnl f* **7/1**

120 **3** *2 ¼* **Cock Of The North**[25] 3318 2-9-1 0............................ FrederikTylicki 2 97
(Scott Dixon) *w ldrs: led 4f out tl 3f out: sn rdn: no ex fnl f* **9/1**

132 **4** *1 ¾* **Natural Order (USA)**[17] 3580 2-9-1 0............................ JimCrowley 6 93
(K R Burke) *hld up: rdn over 2f out: styd on same pce fr over 1f out* **25/1**

21 **5** *½* **Mister Universe**[42] 2788 2-9-1 0............................ GrahamLee 3 92
(Mark Johnston) *led 3f: w ldrs: rdn over 2f out: wknd fnl f* **6/1**[3]

11 **6** *nk* **Lieutenant Kaffee (USA)**[9] 3883 2-9-1 0.................. TonyHamilton 9 91
(Richard Fahey) *hld up: rdn 1/2-way: wknd fnl f* **5/1**[2]

10 **7** *4* **Bossy Guest (IRE)**[25] 3318 2-9-1 0............................ JamesDoyle 10 85
(Mick Channon) *hld up in tch: racd keenly: rdn over 2f out: wknd over 1f out* **9/1**

21 **8** *10* **Smaih (GER)**[29] 3173 2-9-1 0............................ FrankieDettori 5 64
(Richard Hannon) *chsd ldrs tl wknd and eased over 1f out* **8/1**

1m 26.73s (1.03) **Going Correction** +0.325s/f (Good) 8 Ran SP% **113.2**

Speed ratings (Par 106): **107,101,99,97,96 96,91,80**

CSF £15.16 TOTE £2.60: £1.30, £1.70, £2.30; EX 17.00 Trifecta £171.80.

**Owner** Hamdan Al Maktoum **Bred** BEC Bloodstock **Trained** East Everleigh, Wilts

**FOCUS**

The action was again middle to stands' side. This can be a strong contest, winners in the past decade including Dubawi (2004), Horatio Nelson (2005) and Olympic Glory (2012), who were all subsequently successful at the top level. This year's race was weakened by the withdrawal of paper favourite Gleneagles, and also Archie, and it's questionable how many of these really wanted to go as far as 7f at this stage of their careers, especially on a soft surface. Indeed, only Lieutenant Kaffee had previously tried this trip. However, Estidhkaar is really progressing and rates a good winner of this race.

## 4200 666BET BUNBURY CUP (HERITAGE H'CAP) 7f

**3:15** (3:16) (Class 2) 3-Y-O+

**£74,700** (£22,368; £11,184; £5,592; £2,796; £1,404) **Stalls** Low

Form RPR

6600 **1** **Heaven's Guest (IRE)**[22] 3420 4-9-3 **101**..................... TonyHamilton 9 111
(Richard Fahey) *hld up: hdwy u.p over 1f out: hung lft ins fnl f: sn carried rt: r.o to ld towards fin* **12/1**

0210 **2** *½* **Absolutely So (IRE)**[21] 3452 4-9-2 **100**..................... WilliamBuick 14 109
(Andrew Balding) *chsd ldrs: wnt 2nd over 2f out: rdn to ld over 1f out: hung rt ins fnl f: hdd towards fin* **5/1**[2]

0-22 **3** *½* **Hoodna (IRE)**[15] 3674 4-9-2 **100**..................... SilvestreDeSousa 20 107
(Saeed bin Suroor) *dwlt: sn in tch: rdn over 2f out: ev ch fr over 1f out: edgd lft ins fnl f: styd on* **12/1**

2406 **4** *1 ¼* **Fort Bastion (IRE)**[16] 3621 5-8-13 **97**..................... JamesSullivan 12 101
(Ruth Carr) *mid-div: hdwy over 2f out: rdn over 1f out: unable qck towards fin* **22/1**

-110 **5** *2 ½* **Ertijaal (IRE)**[70] 1951 3-8-13 **105**.....................(b[1]) PaulHanagan 17 100
(William Haggas) *led: racd keenly: rdn and hdd over 1f out: styd on same pce* **8/1**

4100 **6** *hd* **Georgian Bay (IRE)**[22] 3420 4-9-1 **99**.....................(v) GrahamLee 18 96
(K R Burke) *racd alone far side: up w the pce: rdn over 1f out: no ex ins fnl f* **12/1**

0201 **7** *3 ¾* **Louis The Pious**[22] 3420 6-9-7 **105** 6ex..................... NeilCallan 11 92
(David O'Meara) *hld up: plld hrd: rdn over 2f out: hung lft over 1f out: nvr trbld ldrs* **14/1**

2120 **8** *2 ¾* **Glen Moss (IRE)**[21] 3452 5-9-6 **104**..................... SeanLevey 1 84
(David Brown) *hld up in tch: rdn over 1f out: wknd fnl f* **7/1**[3]

-000 **9** *½* **Mezzotint (IRE)**[22] 3420 5-8-13 **97**..................... PaulMulrennan 7 76
(Stuart Williams) *hld up: rdn over 2f out: wknd fnl f* **66/1**

-500 **10** *1 ½* **Loving Spirit**[24] 3356 6-8-12 **99**..................... RobertTart[(3)] 5 74
(James Toller) *hld up: rdn and hung lft over 1f out: nvr on terms* **10/1**

-140 **11** *2 ¾* **Best Of Order (IRE)**[29] 3189 7-8-13 **97**.....................(p) JamieSpencer 3 65
(David O'Meara) *sn pushed along in rr: rdn and wknd over 1f out* **20/1**

4322 **12** *2 ¾* **Professor**[21] 3452 4-9-10 **108**..................... RichardHughes 6 69
(Richard Hannon) *hld up in tch: rdn over 2f out: wknd over 1f out* **7/1**[3]

1210 **13** *½* **Abseil (USA)**[24] 3356 4-8-13 **97**.....................[1] JamesDoyle 15 56
(Sir Michael Stoute) *racd keenly: trckd ldr tl rdn over 2f out: wknd over 1f out* **4/1**[1]

1m 25.61s (-0.09) **Going Correction** +0.325s/f (Good)

**WFA** 3 from 4yo+ 8lb 13 Ran SP% **122.2**

Speed ratings (Par 109): **113,112,111,110,107 107,103,99,99,97 94,91,90**

CSF £71.25 CT £779.69 TOTE £18.40: £5.20, £2.30, £4.40; EX 112.10 Trifecta £1219.40.

**Owner** J K Shannon & M A Scaife **Bred** Yeomanstown Stud **Trained** Musley Bank, N Yorks

**FOCUS**

Softish ground, seven non-runners and each-way betting the first three made for an unusual Bunbury Cup, but thanks to Ertijaal being lit up by the application of blinkers for the first time they went a strong gallop and this looks solid handicap form. A small personal best from Heaven's Guest.

## 4201 DARLEY JULY CUP (BRITISH CHAMPIONS SERIES AND GLOBAL SPRINT CHALLENGE) (GROUP 1) 6f

**3:50** (3:50) (Class 1) 3-Y-O+

**£289,221** (£109,650; £54,876; £27,336; £13,719; £6,885) **Stalls** Low

Form RPR

0-11 **1** **Slade Power (IRE)**[21] 3451 5-9-6 120..................... WayneLordan 13 122
(Edward Lynam, Ire) *racd far side: trckd ldrs: rdn to ld overall over 1f out: drvn out: 1st of 7 in gp* **7/4**[1]

0500 **2** *1 ½* **Tropics (USA)**[21] 3451 6-9-6 109..................... RobertWinston 16 117
(Dean Ivory) *racd far side: a.p: rdn and ev ch over 1f out: styd on same pce wl ins fnl f: 2nd of 7 in gp* **66/1**

6-51 **3** *shd* **Gregorian (IRE)**[14] 3723 5-9-6 116..................... WilliamBuick 2 117
(John Gosden) *racd stands' side: hld up in tch: nt clr run over 1f out: sn swtchd lft: rdn to ld that side wl ins fnl f: r.o: 1st of 6 in gp* **12/1**

**4** *nk* **Undrafted (USA)**[35] 4-9-6 109..................... FrankieDettori 1 116
(Wesley A Ward, U.S.A) *racd stands' side: hld up: hdwy wl over 1f out: rdn to ld that side 1f out tl wl ins fnl f: styd on: 2nd of 6 in gp* **25/1**

**5** *1* **Cougar Mountain (IRE)**[17] 3591 3-9-0 0..................... JosephO'Brien 7 112
(A P O'Brien, Ire) *racd stands' side: trckd ldrs: rdn and ev ch fr over 2f out tl styd on same pce ins fnl f: 3rd of 6 in gp* **16/1**

12-6 **6** *1 ¼* **Noozhoh Canarias (SPA)**[70] 1951 3-9-0 116.. ChristopheSoumillon 11 108
(Enrique Leon Penate, Spain) *racd far side: led that gp tl rdn and hdd over 1f out: no ex ins fnl f: 3rd of 7 in gp* **9/2**[2]

-313 **7** *hd* **Hot Streak (IRE)**[25] 3319 3-9-0 115..................... JamieSpencer 12 107
(Kevin Ryan) *racd far side: hld up: hdwy over 1f out: sn rdn: no ex ins fnl f: 4th of 5 in gp* **15/2**[3]

0-50 **8** *2 ¾* **Moviesta (USA)**[59] 2256 4-9-6 113..................... PaulMulrennan 10 99
(Bryan Smart) *racd far side: hld up: hdwy 1/2-way: rdn over 1f out: wknd ins fnl f: 5th of 7 in gp* **40/1**

0-33 **9** *½* **Aljamaaheer (IRE)**[21] 3451 5-9-6 115.....................(b) PaulHanagan 15 98
(Roger Varian) *racd far side: trckd ldr tl rdn over 2f out: wknd fnl f: 6th of 7 in gp* **8/1**

6500 **10** *nse* **Jack Dexter**[21] 3451 5-9-6 111..................... GrahamLee 14 98
(Jim Goldie) *racd far side: prom: lost pl 1/2-way: sn pushed along: wknd fnl f: last of 7 in gp* **25/1**

-526 **11** *4* **Astaire (IRE)**[21] 3451 3-9-0 113..................... RichardHughes 5 84
(Kevin Ryan) *racd stands' side: led overall tl rdn and hdd over 1f out: wknd ins fnl f: 4th of 6 in gp* **10/1**

4401 **12** *1 ¾* **Justice Day (IRE)**[7] 3960 3-9-0 108..................... SilvestreDeSousa 9 78
(David Elsworth) *racd stands' side: chsd ldr: rdn and ev ch wl over 1f out: hmpd sn after: wknd fnl f: 5th of 6 in gp* **25/1**

0-20 **13** *19* **Rex Imperator**[25] 3319 5-9-6 108.....................(p) JimCrowley 3 18
(William Haggas) *racd stands' side: chsd ldrs: rdn over 1f out: wknd and eased fnl f: last of 6 in gp* **40/1**

1m 12.4s (-0.10) **Going Correction** +0.325s/f (Good)

**WFA** 3 from 4yo+ 6lb 13 Ran SP% **118.0**

Speed ratings (Par 117): **113,111,110,110,109 107,107,103,102,102 97,95,69**

CSF £187.50 CT £1155.95 TOTE £2.50: £1.20, £12.40, £3.90; EX 114.40 Trifecta £850.20.

**Owner** Mrs S Power **Bred** Mrs S Power **Trained** Dunshaughlin, Co Meath

**FOCUS**

The easy ground was partly responsible for only two previous Group 1 winners lining up, and it's hard to consider this anything more than ordinary form for the level. Slade Power rates the leading European sprinter and could do a bit better yet.

## 4202 ROSSDALES EBF STALLIONS MAIDEN FILLIES' STKS (BOBIS RACE) 7f

**4:25** (4:25) (Class 4) 2-Y-O **£6,469** (£1,925; £962; £481) **Stalls** Low

Form RPR

**1** **Winters Moon (IRE)** 2-9-0 0............................ HarryBentley 16 78+
(Saeed bin Suroor) *edgd lft s: sn prom: rdn to ld over 1f out: r.o* **5/2**[2]

4 **2** *1* **Shagah (IRE)**[37] 2918 2-9-0 0............................ FrankieDettori 5 75
(Richard Hannon) *trckd ldrs: rdn and ev ch over 1f out: styd on* **9/4**[1]

**3** *½* **Stroll Patrol** 2-9-0 0............................ RichardHughes 1 74+
(Philip McBride) *hld up: hdwy over 2f out: rdn and ev ch over 1f out: styd on* **14/1**

6 **4** *2* **Nufooth (IRE)**[27] 3267 2-9-0 0............................ PaulHanagan 15 69
(Richard Hannon) *trckd ldr: wnt 2nd 1/2-way: led wl over 2f out: rdn and hdd over 1f out: no ex ins fnl f* **7/2**[3]

| | | | | |
|---|---|---|---|---|
| | **5** | *nse* | **Pamushana (IRE)** 2-9-0 0 .......... TonyHamilton 2 | 69+ |
| | | | (Richard Fahey) *hld up: pushed along over 2f out: r.o ins fnl f: nvr nrr* **11/1** | |
| | **6** | *2 1/2* | **Minestrone (IRE)** 2-9-0 0 .......... GrahamLee 10 | 63 |
| | | | (Tom Dascombe) *mid-div: rdn over 1f out: no ex fnl f* **11/1** | |
| 0 | **7** | *nse* | **Auld Fyffee (IRE)**[8] 3933 2-8-11 0 .......... RyanPowell(3) 9 | 63 |
| | | | (John Ryan) *chsd ldr to 1/2-way: sn rdn: wknd ins fnl f* **50/1** | |
| 30 | **8** | *3/4* | **Ocean Crystal**[28] 3232 2-8-7 0 .......... JordonMcMurray(7) 7 | 61 |
| | | | (John Ryan) *led over 4f: sn rdn: wknd ins fnl f* **66/1** | |
| 00 | **9** | *12* | **Supreme Belle (IRE)**[31] 3107 2-9-0 0 .......... PaulMulrennan 14 | 31 |
| | | | (Derek Shaw) *hld up in tch: rdn over 2f out: wknd over 1f out* **66/1** | |
| | **10** | *13* | **Laura B** 2-9-0 0 .......... FrederikTylicki 17 | |
| | | | (Chris Wall) *wnt lft s: sn pushed along in rr: wknd 2f out* **12/1** | |

1m 28.61s (2.91) **Going Correction** +0.325s/f (Good) **10** Ran SP% **117.5**
Speed ratings (Par 93): **96,94,94,92,91 89,89,88,74,59**
CSF £8.60 TOTE £3.20: £1.40, £1.50, £5.00; EX 9.40 Trifecta £122.60.
**Owner** Godolphin **Bred** Darley **Trained** Newmarket, Suffolk

**FOCUS**
They raced middle to stands' side. Seven non-runners and the feeling this was just a fair fillies' maiden, and a little below recent renewals. The winner could prove a lot better than the bare form.

## 4203 SPA AT BEDFORD LODGE HOTEL NURSERY H'CAP (BOBIS RACE) 7f
**5:00** (5:00) (Class 2) 2-Y-O **£16,172** (£4,812; £2,405; £1,202) **Stalls** Low

| Form | | | | RPR |
|---|---|---|---|---|
| 31 | **1** | | **When Will It End (IRE)**[39] 2859 2-8-10 **74** .......... RichardHughes 5 | 79+ |
| | | | (Richard Hannon) *hld up: hdwy over 2f out: shkn up to ld over 1f out: rdn and hung lft ins fnl f: r.o* **2/1**[1] | |
| 622 | **2** | *2* | **Vegas Rebel (IRE)**[25] 3330 2-8-10 **74** .......... FrankieDettori 3 | 74 |
| | | | (Peter Chapple-Hyam) *s.i.s: hld up: hdwy over 1f out: rdn to chse wnr ins fnl f: no ex towards fin* **3/1**[2] | |
| 521 | **3** | *1/2* | **Power Play (IRE)**[23] 3387 2-9-4 **82** .......... SeanLevey 2 | 81 |
| | | | (Richard Hannon) *chsd ldr: rdn and ev ch over 1f out: hung lft ins fnl f: styd on same pce* **8/1** | |
| 635 | **4** | *1 1/4* | **Big McIntosh (IRE)**[22] 3429 2-7-13 **66** .......... (t) RyanPowell(3) 4 | 62 |
| | | | (John Ryan) *led: rdn and hdd over 1f out: hung lft and no ex ins fnl f* **12/1** | |
| 2144 | **5** | *4* | **Burtonwood**[35] 2987 2-9-7 **85** .......... PaulHanagan 1 | 71 |
| | | | (Richard Fahey) *prom: rdn over 1f out: wkng whn hung lft ins fnl f* **5/1** | |
| 511 | **6** | *1 1/4* | **Disavow**[5] 4012 2-9-3 **81** 6ex .......... SilvestreDeSousa 6 | 64 |
| | | | (Mark Johnston) *chsd ldrs: rdn over 2f out: ev ch over 1f out: hmpd and wknd ins fnl f* **4/1**[3] | |

1m 29.63s (3.93) **Going Correction** +0.325s/f (Good) **6** Ran SP% **113.8**
Speed ratings (Par 100): **90,87,87,85,81 79**
CSF £8.43 TOTE £2.60: £1.30, £1.90; EX 10.20 Trifecta £39.80.
**Owner** Michael Buckley **Bred** Mountarmstrong Stud **Trained** East Everleigh, Wilts
■ Stewards' Enquiry : Ryan Powell two-day ban; careless riding (27th-28th July)

**FOCUS**
There were just seven runners in the 2012 running of this nursery, and only five last year, and despite increased prize money there was another very disappointing turnout. They went steady and the time was much the slowest of four races at the trip. It looked a weak event for the level. The runner-up helps the standard.

## 4204 EGERTON HOUSE STABLES H'CAP 1m 4f
**5:35** (5:36) (Class 3) (0-90,89) 3-Y-O+ **£9,703** (£2,887; £1,443; £721) **Stalls** Centre

| Form | | | | RPR |
|---|---|---|---|---|
| 2-30 | **1** | | **Glorious Protector (IRE)**[63] 2142 4-10-0 **89** .......... WilliamBuick 3 | 103 |
| | | | (Ed Walker) *hld up: hdwy and nt clr run over 2f out: shkn up to ld over 1f out: r.o strly* **11/4**[1] | |
| 0-00 | **2** | *7* | **Rosslyn Castle**[17] 3574 5-9-2 **77** .......... MartinLane 10 | 80 |
| | | | (Philip McBride) *hld up: hdwy and swtchd lft over 2f out: rdn and ev ch over 1f out: sn outpcd* **16/1** | |
| 0-22 | **3** | *1* | **Merchant Of Dubai**[29] 3192 9-8-13 **74** .......... GrahamLee 6 | 75 |
| | | | (Jim Goldie) *chsd ldr over 4f: remained handy: led over 2f out: rdn and hdd over 1f out: no ex ins fnl f* **10/1** | |
| 10-0 | **4** | *6* | **Phaenomena (IRE)**[29] 3204 4-10-0 **89** .......... SeanLevey 2 | 80 |
| | | | (Lady Cecil) *chsd ldrs: rdn and ev ch over 1f out: wknd ins fnl f* **9/2**[3] | |
| -035 | **5** | *2 1/4* | **Noble Gift**[52] 2461 4-9-8 **83** .......... JimCrowley 7 | 71 |
| | | | (William Knight) *hld up: plld hrd: hdwy over 8f out: trckd ldr over 7f out: rdn and ev ch fr over 2f out tl over 1f out: wknd fnl f* **13/2** | |
| 4533 | **6** | *1 1/2* | **Mica Mika (IRE)**[14] 3730 6-9-5 **80** .......... (p) PaulHanagan 5 | 65 |
| | | | (Richard Fahey) *plld hrd and prom: lost pl over 5f out: rallied over 2f out: rdn and wknd over 1f out* **7/2**[2] | |
| 1120 | **7** | *hd* | **Thecornishcowboy**[3] 4077 5-9-5 **87** .......... (t) JordonMcMurray(7) 11 | 72 |
| | | | (John Ryan) *hld up: hdwy over 3f out: rdn and wknd over 1f out* **14/1** | |
| 06-0 | **8** | *37* | **Greeleys Love (USA)**[12] 3802 4-9-4 **79** .......... (v) SilvestreDeSousa 1 | 5 |
| | | | (Mark Johnston) *led: rdn and hdd over 2f out: sn wknd and eased* **13/2** | |

2m 34.82s (1.92) **Going Correction** +0.325s/f (Good)
**WFA** 3 from 4yo+ 13lb **8** Ran SP% **115.4**
Speed ratings (Par 107): **106,101,100,96,95 94,94,69**
CSF £48.02 CT £386.52 TOTE £3.80: £1.30, £5.10, £2.70; EX 56.90 Trifecta £876.90.
**Owner** Ms A A Yap **Bred** T Boylan **Trained** Newmarket, Suffolk

**FOCUS**
This might not be the strongest of form around, but it was hard not to be impressed with the winner.
T/Plt: £71.20 to a £1 stake. Pool: £174,495.61 - 1786.91 winning tickets. T/Qpdt: £15.30 to a £1 stake. Pool: £10,989.61 - 528.95 winning tickets. CR

# 3748 SALISBURY (R-H)
Saturday, July 12

**OFFICIAL GOING: Good to firm (8.8)**
Wind: light, half against Weather: showers

## 4205 EDWARD MILLS 40TH BIRTHDAY NOVICE AUCTION STKS 6f
**5:55** (5:55) (Class 5) 2-Y-O **£3,234** (£962; £481; £240) **Stalls** Low

| Form | | | | RPR |
|---|---|---|---|---|
| 01 | **1** | | **Feeling Easy (IRE)**[18] 3557 2-8-6 0 .......... RossAtkinson(3) 4 | 82 |
| | | | (Robert Eddery) *dropped in bhd after s: hld up in last: rdn and edgd lft 2f out: hdwy to chal ent fnl f: led fnl 150yds: r.o wl: comf* **5/1** | |
| 521 | **2** | *1 1/2* | **Be Bold**[59] 2246 2-9-0 0 .......... PatDobbs 3 | 82 |
| | | | (Richard Hannon) *chsd ldng pair: rdn and effrt over 2f out: hdwy and drvn to ld ent fnl f: hdd fnl 150yds: styd on same pce after* **5/4**[1] | |
| 210 | **3** | *3 3/4* | **Jaganory (IRE)**[21] 3448 2-8-13 0 .......... DaneO'Neill 1 | 70 |
| | | | (David Evans) *led: rdn ent fnl 2f: hdd ent fnl f: edgd lft and wknd fnl 150yds* **4/1**[3] | |
| 2153 | **4** | *1 3/4* | **Doomah (IRE)**[15] 3649 2-8-9 0 .......... RobertHavlin 2 | 61 |
| | | | (Richard Hannon) *pressed ldr: rdn and ev ch over 2f out tl no ex ent fnl f: wknd fnl 150yds* **5/2**[2] | |

1m 15.89s (1.09) **Going Correction** 0.0s/f (Good) **4** Ran SP% **109.7**
Speed ratings (Par 94): **92,90,85,82**
CSF £11.90 TOTE £5.20; EX 11.80 Trifecta £22.50.
**Owner** Edwin Phillips & Mrs Pamela Aitken **Bred** Hyde Park Stud & Lisglen **Trained** Newmarket, Suffolk

**FOCUS**
This has been a Richard Hannon benefit in recent years but, despite saddling half the field, he couldn't continue his winning run. The time was slow and this is ordinary form for a novice race.

## 4206 MANOR FARM BUTCHERS H'CAP 6f
**6:25** (6:26) (Class 5) (0-75,74) 3-Y-O+ **£2,911** (£866; £432; £216) **Stalls** Low

| Form | | | | RPR |
|---|---|---|---|---|
| 6424 | **1** | | **Vallarta (IRE)**[12] 3783 4-9-12 **74** .......... (v) WilliamTwiston-Davies 3 | 81 |
| | | | (Mick Channon) *hld up in tch in midfield: swtchd rt and effrt towards far rail 2f out: hdwy to chal 1f out: styd on wl u.p to ld towards fin* **10/3**[2] | |
| -660 | **2** | *nk* | **Smart Salute**[28] 3225 3-9-4 **72** .......... (p) GeorgeBaker 4 | 77 |
| | | | (Ed Walker) *chsd ldng pair: wnt 2nd and switching lft 2f out: drvn and effrt ent fnl f: ev ch ins fnl f: styd on: snatched 2nd last stride* **11/4**[1] | |
| 0040 | **3** | *shd* | **Lady Phill**[14] 3734 4-9-3 **65** .......... KierenFox 8 | 71 |
| | | | (Michael Attwater) *led: rdn and qcknd wl over 1f out: hrd pressed and drvn 1f out: hdd and no ex towards fin: lost 2nd last stride* **20/1** | |
| 4064 | **4** | *1* | **Annes Rocket (IRE)**[11] 3825 9-9-3 **65** .......... (p) PatDobbs 1 | 68 |
| | | | (Jimmy Fox) *hld up in tch in last pair: hdwy on far rail over 1f out: rdn and ev ch ins fnl f: no ex and outpcd fnl 75yds* **20/1** | |
| 103 | **5** | *2* | **Italian Tom (IRE)**[1] 4151 7-9-8 **70** .......... LukeMorris 6 | 66 |
| | | | (Ronald Harris) *in tch in midfield: rdn over 2f out: drvn and unable qck over 1f out: plugged on same pce fnl f* **8/1** | |
| 4443 | **6** | *3/4* | **Exceeding Power**[31] 3114 3-8-11 **72** .......... AlistairRawlinson(7) 7 | 65 |
| | | | (Martin Bosley) *chsd ldr tl 2f out: rdn and lost pl over 1f out: plugged on same pce fnl f* **4/1**[3] | |
| 655 | **7** | *hd* | **Volito**[18] 3551 8-8-11 **59** .......... JohnFahy 2 | 52 |
| | | | (Anabel K Murphy) *stdd s: t.k.h: hld up in tch in last pair: hdwy 2f out: drvn and no hdwy ent fnl f: plugged on same pce after* **16/1** | |
| 303- | **8** | *16* | **Maria Montez**[277] 7106 5-9-5 **67** .......... DaneO'Neill 5 | 31 |
| | | | (B W Hills) *dwlt: t.k.h: sn rcvrd and in tch in midfield: rdn over 2f out: sn lost pl: wl bhd and eased ins fnl f* **9/2** | |

1m 14.9s (0.10) **Going Correction** 0.0s/f (Good)
**WFA** 3 from 4yo+ 6lb **8** Ran SP% **114.4**
Speed ratings (Par 103): **99,98,98,97,94 93,93,71**
CSF £12.97 CT £152.17 TOTE £4.90: £1.70, £1.10, £4.00; EX 13.10 Trifecta £364.70.
**Owner** Tails & Bargate **Bred** Frank O'Meara **Trained** West Ilsley, Berks
■ Stewards' Enquiry : Kieren Fox four-day ban; used whip above permitted level (27th-31th July)
William Twiston-Davies two-day ban; used whip abover permitted level (27th-28th July)

**FOCUS**
It started raining just before this race but it wouldn't have had enough time to make any difference to ground conditions. A modest handicap featuring mostly exposed horses and plenty were in with a chance entering the final furlong. The form doesn't have a very strong feel to it.

## 4207 BATHWICK TYRES BRITISH STALLION STUDS EBF MAIDEN STKS (BOBIS RACE) 6f 212y
**6:55** (6:57) (Class 4) 2-Y-O **£4,204** (£1,251; £625; £216) **Stalls** Centre

| Form | | | | RPR |
|---|---|---|---|---|
| 3 | **1** | | **Misterioso (IRE)**[13] 3748 2-9-5 0 .......... RichardHughes 8 | 85+ |
| | | | (Richard Hannon) *chsd ldr: rdn to ld over 1f out: sn asserted and in command fnl f: r.o: comf* **4/9**[1] | |
| 63 | **2** | *2 1/2* | **Big Chill (IRE)**[19] 3524 2-9-5 0 .......... GeorgeBaker 6 | 77 |
| | | | (Charles Hills) *t.k.h: in tch in midfield: wnt 4th 1/2-way: rdn and effrt to chse ldng pair over 1f out: wnt 2nd ins fnl f: kpt on but no threat to wnr* **10/1**[3] | |
| 52 | **3** | *1 1/2* | **Harlequin Striker (IRE)**[13] 3748 2-9-5 0 .......... JamesDoyle 10 | 73 |
| | | | (Mick Channon) *led: jnd and rdn 2f out: drvn and hdd over 1f out: wknd and lost 2nd ins fnl f* **4/1**[2] | |
| 0 | **4** | *5* | **Gea And Tea**[22] 3429 2-9-0 0 .......... NoelGarbutt(5) 3 | 59+ |
| | | | (Robert Eddery) *hld up in midfield: rdn: rn green and veered lft over 2f out: hdwy and edging rt over 1f out: kpt on steadily but no threat to ldrs* **50/1** | |
| 3 | **5** | *shd* | **Golden Wedding (IRE)**[37] 2928 2-9-5 0 .......... JohnFahy 14 | 59 |
| | | | (Eve Johnson Houghton) *chsd ldng pair: rdn 2f out: 4th and btn ent fnl f: wknd* **14/1** | |
| | **6** | *1 1/4* | **Servery** 2-9-5 0 .......... PatDobbs 9 | 56 |
| | | | (Richard Hannon) *hld up in midfield: rdn and effrt jst over 2f out: no ch w ldrs and wnt 5th jst over 1f out: plugged on same pce after* **20/1** | |
| 00 | **7** | *2 1/2* | **Pink Ribbon (IRE)**[36] 2964 2-9-5 0 .......... LiamKeniry 4 | 49 |
| | | | (Sylvester Kirk) *t.k.h: in tch in midfield: rdn and outpcd in 5th over 2f out: wknd over 1f out* **50/1** | |
| 46 | **8** | *3/4* | **Vita Mina**[15] 3642 2-9-0 0 .......... WilliamTwiston-Davies 2 | 42 |
| | | | (David Evans) *chsd ldng trio tl 1/2-way: sn rdn: wkng and swtchd lft over 2f out: no ch fr 1f out* **40/1** | |
| 0 | **9** | *1 1/4* | **Wolf Of Windlesham (IRE)**[17] 3578 2-9-5 0 .......... RobertHavlin 11 | 44 |
| | | | (B W Hills) *hld up in midfield: rdn and effrt whn bdly hmpd over 2f out: no hdwy after* **66/1** | |
| 0 | **10** | *shd* | **Moonadee (IRE)**[29] 3194 2-9-5 0 .......... DaneO'Neill 5 | 43 |
| | | | (B W Hills) *stdd s: t.k.h: hld up in rr: pushed along: hld hd high and btn over 2f out: no ch fnl 2f* **16/1** | |
| | **11** | *8* | **That Man Of Mine (IRE)** 2-9-5 0 .......... JimmyFortune 1 | 22 |
| | | | (Jamie Osborne) *s.i.s: a in rr: lost tch 2f out* **33/1** | |
| | **12** | *1/2* | **Who'Sthedaddy** 2-9-2 0 .......... ThomasBrown(3) 13 | 20 |
| | | | (Daniel Kubler) *s.i.s: pushed along in rr: lost tch 2f out* **66/1** | |
| | **13** | *9* | **Hier Encore (FR)** 2-9-5 0 .......... LukeMorris 7 | |
| | | | (David Menuisier) *racd in last quartet: lost pl and rdn 3f out: t.o fnl f* **66/1** | |

1m 29.03s (0.43) **Going Correction** 0.0s/f (Good) **13** Ran SP% **129.4**
Speed ratings (Par 96): **97,94,92,86,86 85,82,81,80,79 70,70,59**
CSF £6.86 TOTE £1.60: £1.10, £2.60, £1.60; EX 11.80 Trifecta £22.90.
**Owner** Michael Pescod **Bred** Eyrefield Lodge Stud **Trained** East Everleigh, Wilts

**FOCUS**
Probably not a strong maiden and the market proved spot on. The pace was decent and the winner was well on top in the end.

## 4208 FERNDENE FARM H'CAP (BOBIS RACE) 1m
7:30 (7:30) (Class 4) (0-85,84) 3-Y-O £4,851 (£1,443; £721; £360) Stalls Low

Form RPR

12-0 **1** **Hiking (USA)**[27] 3273 3-9-5 **82** JamesDoyle 7 87+
(Roger Charlton) *hld up in tch in last pair: rdn and effrt 2f out: hdwy u.p 1f out: chal fnl 100yds: edgd rt but styd on wl to ld towards fin* **9/4**[2]

5160 **2** *nk* **Solo Hunter**[15] 3643 3-8-8 **74** (v) ThomasBrown(3) 4 78
(David Evans) *led: rdn and hrd pressed 2f out: kpt on and outbattled 3rd ins fnl f: hdd and no ex towards fin* **20/1**

1 **3** *½* **Fajry (USA)**[25] 3343 3-9-7 **84** DaneO'Neill 2 87
(Saeed bin Suroor) *t.k.h: chsd ldr: upsides 2f out: rdn over 1f out: hld hd high and nt qckning whn stmbld sltly ins fnl f: btn and n.m.r fnl 50yds* **6/4**[1]

5155 **4** *½* **Khee Society**[19] 3516 3-7-12 **66** NoelGarbutt(5) 5 68
(David Evans) *stdd s: hld up in tch in rr: rdn and effrt over 2f out: hdwy u.p to chse ldrs ins fnl f: kpt on: n.m.r towards fin* **16/1**

0200 **5** *nse* **Triple Chief (IRE)**[28] 3243 3-8-13 **76** RobertHavlin 6 78
(Rod Millman) *in tch in midfield: rdn and effrt 2f out: nt clrest of runs over 1f out: kpt on wl u.p fnl 100yds* **8/1**[3]

0500 **6** *nk* **Malachim Mist (IRE)**[8] 3917 3-8-12 **75** (p) RichardHughes 1 76
(Richard Hannon) *chsd ldrs: swtchd rt and rdn 2f out: stl pressing ldrs and drvn 1f out: kpt on same pce ins fnl f* **9/1**

16 **7** *6* **Tigers In Red (USA)**[107] 1122 3-9-6 **83** (b[1]) FergusSweeney 3 71
(David Simcock) *restless in stalls: in tch in midfield: rdn and effrt 2f out: btn over 1f out: wknd fnl f* **8/1**[3]

1m 42.71s (-0.79) **Going Correction** 0.0s/f (Good) 7 Ran SP% **113.6**
Speed ratings (Par 102): **103,102,102,101,101 101,95**
CSF £42.51 CT £85.51 TOTE £3.80: £2.00, £5.70; EX 31.40 Trifecta £120.80.

**Owner** K Abdullah **Bred** Juddmonte Farms Inc **Trained** Beckhampton, Wilts

**FOCUS**
Two unexposed ones in this otherwise modest handicap and the field finished in a heap after a steady early gallop, suggesting the form is probably only ordinary.

## 4209 BATHWICK TYRES H'CAP 1m 4f
8:00 (8:00) (Class 5) (0-75,78) 3-Y-O+ £2,911 (£866; £432; £216) Stalls Low

Form RPR

5-04 **1** **Jelly Fish**[11] 3814 3-9-0 **74** (t) JamesDoyle 9 88
(Amanda Perrett) *in tch in midfield: clsd to join ldrs 3f out: led over 2f out: sn rdn: hrd pressed fnl f: r.o and jst prevailed* **3/1**[1]

-135 **2** *shd* **Cosette (IRE)**[19] 3541 3-8-12 **72** DaneO'Neill 5 85
(Henry Candy) *chsd ldrs: nt clr run over 1f out: swtchd rt jst over 1f out: rdn and str chal fnl f: r.o: jst hld* **11/2**

6322 **3** *6* **Eton Rambler (USA)**[18] 3556 4-9-10 **71** PatCosgrave 2 74
(George Baker) *stdd s: hld up in rr: hdwy 3f out: rdn and effrt 2f out: keeping on whn nt clr run and hmpd 1f out: no ch w ldrs but kpt on to go 3rd wl ins fnl f* **5/1**[3]

-011 **4** *½* **Sunny Future (IRE)**[13] 3752 8-10-3 **78** RichardHughes 6 81
(Malcolm Saunders) *chsd ldr tl led 3f out: hdd and rdn over 2f out: struggling whn sltly hmpd jst over 1f out: wknd ins fnl f* **3/1**[1]

1-00 **5** *1* **Mallory Heights (IRE)**[29] 3205 4-10-0 **75** AdamKirby 10 76
(Luca Cumani) *hld up in last pair: pushed along and hdwy on outer over 3f out: drvn and ev ch 2f out: no ex and btn ent fnl f: wknd* **4/1**[2]

1324 **6** *7* **Jazri**[15] 3643 3-7-13 **64** CamHardie(5) 3 54
(Milton Bradley) *hld up in tch in midfield: rdn and effrt 2f out: no imp: wknd over 1f out* **14/1**

3201 **7** *73* **April Ciel**[10] 3853 5-9-6 **67** (p) LukeMorris 4
(Ronald Harris) *t.k.h: led tl 3f out: sn lost pl: t.o and virtually p.u fnl f* **16/1**

2m 35.87s (-2.13) **Going Correction** 0.0s/f (Good)
**WFA** 3 from 4yo+ 13lb 7 Ran SP% **114.6**
Speed ratings (Par 103): **107,106,102,102,101 97,48**
CSF £19.97 CT £78.97 TOTE £4.20: £2.50, £4.30; EX 22.50 Trifecta £151.00.

**Owner** K Abdullah **Bred** Millsec Limited **Trained** Pulborough, W Sussex

**FOCUS**
This looked an ordinary heat on paper but two broke clear in the final furlong to fight out a tight finish and look handicappers with more to offer.

## 4210 PARTY CONTINUES AT THE CHAPEL NIGHTCLUB H'CAP 1m 1f 198y
8:30 (8:32) (Class 6) (0-60,58) 3-Y-O £2,587 (£770; £384; £192) Stalls Low

Form RPR

050 **1** **Pink Diamond**[22] 3423 3-9-6 **57** JimmyFortune 2 65
(Eve Johnson Houghton) *hld up in tch in midfield: rdn and effrt to chal over 2f out: led wl over 1f out: edgd rt ins fnl f: styd on and asserted fnl 75yds* **4/1**[3]

4016 **2** *¾* **Eugenic**[3] 4085 3-9-3 **54** RobertHavlin 5 61
(Rod Millman) *chsd ldrs: clsd to join ldrs 3f out: rdn to ld over 2f out: hdd 2f out: ev ch after tl no ex and btn fnl 75yds* **10/3**[2]

6033 **3** *2* **Assoluta (IRE)**[11] 3819 3-9-1 **52** RichardHughes 4 55
(Sylvester Kirk) *chsd ldrs: rdn and effrt ent fnl 2f: chsd ldng pair 1f out: no imp and one pce after* **9/4**[1]

2366 **4** *5* **Stoneham**[11] 3821 3-9-4 **58** CharlesBishop(3) 6 52
(Mick Channon) *led: rdn and hdd over 2f out: outpcd and btn over 1f out: wknd fnl f* **10/1**

-240 **5** *1 ¼* **Snow Conditions**[37] 2926 3-9-7 **58** LiamKeniry 7 49
(Philip Hide) *chsd ldr: rdn and ev ch wl over 2f out tl outpcd and btn over 1f out: wknd fnl f* **9/1**

6600 **6** *1* **Autopilot**[18] 3554 3-9-1 **52** [1] JohnFahy 3 41
(Anabel K Murphy) *hld up in detached last: clsd to bk of field 4f out: rdn and effrt on inner 2f out: sn btn: wknd over 1f out* **11/1**

00-6 **7** *14* **Highland Stardust**[22] 3423 3-9-7 **58** AdamKirby 1 21
(Clive Cox) *in tch in rr of main gp: rdn over 3f out: btn 2f out: sn wknd and lost tch 1f out* **7/1**

2m 10.54s (0.64) **Going Correction** 0.0s/f (Good) 7 Ran SP% **113.8**
Speed ratings (Par 98): **97,96,94,90,89 89,77**
CSF £17.53 TOTE £5.20: £2.80, £2.10; EX 23.00 Trifecta £86.30.

**Owner** Dr Anne J F Gillespie **Bred** Dr A Gillespie **Trained** Blewbury, Oxon

**FOCUS**
A weak contest.

## 4211 EBF STALLIONS BREEDING WINNERS LADIES' EVENING FILLIES' H'CAP 1m 1f 198y
9:00 (9:01) (Class 3) (0-95,91) 3-Y-O+ £9,056 (£2,695; £1,346; £673) Stalls Low

Form RPR

1 **1** **Tearless**[22] 3423 4-9-13 **90** AdamKirby 1 100+
(Charlie Appleby) *chsd ldrs: rdn and effrt 2f out: led over 1f out: in command and r.o wl fnl f: comf* **9/4**[1]

-622 **2** *2* **Almashooqa (USA)**[22] 3423 3-8-12 **86** DaneO'Neill 6 92
(Roger Varian) *hld up in tch in midfield: rdn and hdwy on outer wl over 1f out: chsd wnr 1f out: styd on but no imp* **5/1**[3]

0314 **3** *1 ¼* **Rosehill Artist (IRE)**[14] 3725 3-9-0 **88** JimmyFortune 5 92
(Charles Hills) *hld up in tch in last pair: rdn and effrt on inner 2f out: chsd wnr over 1f out tl 1f out: 3rd and styd on same pce fnl f* **6/1**

3120 **4** *5* **Stereo Love (FR)**[18] 3560 3-8-3 **80** RyanTate(3) 4 74
(Clive Cox) *taken down early: in tch in midfield: rdn and effrt whn short of room and bdly hmpd wl over 1f out: rallied and kpt on fnl f: no threat to ldrs* **8/1**

1231 **5** *½* **Running Deer (IRE)**[28] 3217 5-9-9 **91** LouisSteward(5) 3 84
(Eve Johnson Houghton) *led: rdn ent fnl 2f: hdd over 1f out: sn outpcd: 4th and btn 1f out: wknd fnl f* **7/2**[2]

453 **6** *4 ½* **Affaire De Coeur**[27] 3277 3-8-0 **74** oh1 LukeMorris 9 59
(David Simcock) *stdd and flashed tail leaving stalls: hld up in last pair: rdn and effrt over 2f out: no prog: wknd over 1f out* **8/1**

15 **7** *½* **Zaeemah (IRE)**[35] 2982 3-9-2 **90** [1] HarryBentley 7 74
(Saeed bin Suroor) *chsd ldng trio: rdn and effrt over 2f out: lost pl wl over 1f out: sn wknd* **12/1**

-150 **8** *1 ½* **Passing By**[32] 3085 3-7-9 **74** oh2 CamHardie(5) 2 55
(Richard Hannon) *chsd ldr: ev ch and unable qck over 2f out: sn lost pl and edgd lft: wknd over 1f out* **20/1**

2m 8.65s (-1.25) **Going Correction** 0.0s/f (Good)
**WFA** 3 from 4yo+ 11lb 8 Ran SP% **118.6**
Speed ratings (Par 104): **105,103,102,98,98 94,94,92**
CSF £14.48 CT £60.66 TOTE £3.10: £1.10, £2.10, £3.00; EX 10.50 Trifecta £55.40.

**Owner** Godolphin **Bred** Darley **Trained** Newmarket, Suffolk

**FOCUS**
A competitive fillies' handicap but the top weight was rated 4lb below the ceiling rating for the grade.
T/Plt: £360.70 to a £1 stake. Pool: £53,932.01 - 109.14 winning units. T/Qpdt: £23.40 to a £1 stake. Pool: £5152.70 - 162.90 winning units. SP

# 4170 YORK (L-H)
Saturday, July 12

**OFFICIAL GOING: Good to firm (7.6)**
Wind: Light half behind Weather: Fine and dry

## 4212 JOHN SMITH'S RACING STKS (H'CAP) 1m
1:40 (1:40) (Class 2) (0-105,100) 3-Y-O+ £16,172 (£4,812; £2,405; £1,202) Stalls Low

Form RPR

054 **1** **Bronze Angel (IRE)**[22] 3420 5-9-8 **94** (b) MartinDwyer 11 106
(Marcus Tregoning) *hld up towards rr: gd hdwy 3f out: trckd ldrs over 2f out: swtchd rt to outer and effrt to ld wl over 1f out: sn rdn: edgd lft ins fnl f: kpt on strly* **6/1**[1]

4313 **2** *2 ¼* **Bartack (IRE)**[23] 3397 4-8-7 **86** (v) JoshDoyle(7) 12 93
(David O'Meara) *swtg: a cl up: led 3f out: rdn 2f out: sn hdd: drvn and kpt on fnl f* **25/1**

-604 **3** *½* **Mujazif (IRE)**[8] 3917 4-8-13 **85** (t) BarryMcHugh 10 91
(David Nicholls) *in tch: hdwy 3f out: cl up 2f out: sn rdn and ev ch over 1f out: drvn whn n.m.r and hld ins fnl f* **16/1**

5355 **4** *1 ¾* **Alfred Hutchinson**[42] 2784 6-9-4 **90** TomEaves 5 92
(Geoffrey Oldroyd) *trckd ldrs: smooth hdwy 3f out: cl up 2f out: ev ch tl rdn over 1f out and kpt on same pce* **10/1**[2]

1314 **5** *nk* **Hit The Jackpot (IRE)**[20] 3499 5-9-10 **96** DanielTudhope 7 97
(David O'Meara) *trckd ldrs: hdwy 3f out: rdn along 2f out: sn drvn and one pce* **10/1**[2]

022 **6** *1 ¾* **Braidley (IRE)**[21] 3455 3-8-7 **88** PJMcDonald 15 83
(James Bethell) *lw: in tch: pushed along and sltly outpcd wl over 2f out: rdn wl over 1f out: kpt on fnl f* **10/1**[2]

4200 **7** *1* **Don't Call Me (IRE)**[63] 2145 7-9-8 **94** (t) PhillipMakin 17 89
(David Nicholls) *towards rr: hdwy wl over 2f out: sn rdn along and kpt on appr fnl f: nrst fin* **20/1**

0435 **8** *nse* **Awake My Soul (IRE)**[34] 3047 5-9-5 **94** SamJames(3) 13 89
(David O'Meara) *swtg: midfield: rdn in tch over 3f out: sn rdn along and sltly outpcd: kpt on u.p fr wl over 1f out* **14/1**

4306 **9** *2* **Santefisio**[22] 3420 8-10-0 **100** (b) JoeFanning 1 90
(Keith Dalgleish) *dwlt and in rr tl styd on fnl 2f: n.d* **12/1**

4006 **10** *¾* **Osteopathic Remedy (IRE)**[22] 3437 10-8-11 **86**(t) ConnorBeasley(3) 16 75
(Michael Dods) *in rr tl sme late hdwy* **33/1**

5304 **11** *1 ¾* **Marcret (ITY)**[16] 3621 7-9-6 **92** AndrewElliott 14 76
(David O'Meara) *dwlt and bhd tl sme late hdwy* **25/1**

4500 **12** *nk* **Mabait**[22] 3420 8-8-13 **92** GeorgeBuckell(7) 3 76
(David Simcock) *midfield: hdwy on inner 3f out: chsd ldrs over 2f out: sn rdn and wknd over 1f out* **33/1**

5034 **13** *1 ¼* **Gramercy (IRE)**[28] 3212 7-9-3 **89** (p) HayleyTurner 6 70
(David Simcock) *lw: chsd ldrs: rdn along 3f out: sn wknd* **33/1**

0003 **14** *nk* **Trail Blaze (IRE)**[21] 3456 5-9-0 **91** (p) ShaneGray(5) 4 71
(Kevin Ryan) *cl up: rdn along wl over 3f out: sn wknd* **25/1**

16 **15** *1 ¼* **Capo Rosso (IRE)**[21] 3456 4-9-9 **95** AndreaAtzeni 2 72
(Tom Dascombe) *led: rdn along 4f out: hdd 3f out and sn wknd* **12/1**

-513 **16** *¾* **Dusky Queen (IRE)**[29] 3202 4-9-4 **90** RyanMoore 8 66
(Richard Fahey) *towards rr: rdn along over 3f out: nvr a factor* **6/1**[1]

5262 **17** *7* **Royal Rascal**[14] 3716 4-9-8 **94** DavidAllan 9 54
(Tim Easterby) *a in rr* **12/1**

60-1 **18** *15* **Navajo Chief**[58] 2286 7-10-0 **100** KierenFallon 18 25
(Timothy Jarvis) *midfield: rdn along 3f out: sn wknd and bhd whn eased over 1f out* **11/1**[3]

1m 35.61s (-3.39) **Going Correction** -0.225s/f (Firm)
**WFA** 3 from 4yo+ 9lb 18 Ran SP% **124.9**
Speed ratings (Par 109): **107,104,104,102,102 100,99,99,97,96 94,94,93,93,91 91,84,69**
CSF £166.56 CT £2282.98 TOTE £7.00: £2.20, £7.10, £4.60, £3.30; EX 177.60 Trifecta £1811.40 Part won..

**Owner** Lady Tennant **Bred** Rihana Partnership **Trained** Whitsbury, Hants

**FOCUS**
All distances as advertised. A decent handicap to open proceedings. The gallop appeared sound enough but the winner was actually the only one to get involved from off the pace, so his performance is probably worth marking up as a result. The third has been rated to his recent form.

## 4213 JOHN SMITH'S SILVER CUP STKS (H'CAP) (LISTED RACE) 1m 6f
**2:20** (2:24) (Class 1) (0-110,104) 3-Y-O+
**£22,684** (£8,600; £4,304; £2,144; £1,076; £540) **Stalls** Low

Form RPR
-440 **1** **Continuum**[21] 3449 5-9-6 **96**........(p[1]) JoeFanning 10 102
(Peter Hedger) *swtg: hld up in rr: hdwy 6f out: drvn 3f out: styd on to ld towards fin* **11/1**
0-42 **2** *3/4* **Waila**[20] 3500 4-9-9 **99**........ RyanMoore 1 104
(Sir Michael Stoute) *trckd ldng pair: t.k.h: effrt over 3f out: narrow ld 1f out: hdd and no ex clsng stages* **6/4[1]**
5-05 **3** *nk* **Great Hall**[156] 507 4-9-9 **99**........ PhillipMakin 4 104
(John Quinn) *mid-div: effrt over 3f out: swtchd rt and upsides fnl f: struck over hd by rivals whip ins fnl f: no ex clsng stages* **11/1**
4006 **4** *1/2* **Moment In Time (IRE)**[7] 3961 5-9-8 **98**........ HayleyTurner 9 102
(David Simcock) *hld up in rr: hdwy 3f out: hmpd 2f out: styd on wl down wd outside fnl f: gng on at fin* **14/1**
-125 **5** *1 3/4* **Debdebdeb**[22] 3424 4-9-1 **91**........ MartinDwyer 5 92
(Andrew Balding) *lw: reluctant to go bhd stalls: led after 1f: hdd 9f out: one pce fnl 2f* **13/2[3]**
0050 **6** *nk* **Statutory (IRE)**[21] 3453 4-9-8 **98**........ AndreaAtzeni 6 99
(Saeed bin Suroor) *swtg: led 1f: led 9f out: qcknd pce over 4f out: hdd 1f out: sn fdd* **10/1**
3630 **7** *3/4* **Shwaiman (IRE)**[23] 3377 4-10-0 **104**........ TomQueally 2 104
(James Fanshawe) *dwlt: hld up in rr: effrt over 3f out: kpt on ins fnl f: nvr a factor* **8/1**
4-11 **8** *1 1/4* **Al Saham**[14] 3730 5-9-11 **101**........ KierenFallon 8 99
(Saeed bin Suroor) *trckd ldrs: effrt over 3f out: edgd rt: fdd fnl f* **5/1[2]**
2m 59.52s (-0.68) **Going Correction** -0.225s/f (Firm)
**WFA** 3 from 4yo+ 15lb 8 Ran SP% 113.5
Speed ratings (Par 111): **92,91,91,91,90 89,89,88**
CSF £27.62 CT £191.46 TOTE £16.30: £3.20, £1.10, £3.20; EX 38.20 Trifecta £433.10.
**Owner** P C F Racing Ltd **Bred** Juddmonte Farms Ltd **Trained** Dogmersfield, Hampshire

**FOCUS**
This Listed staying handicap was run at a steady pace and the form probably is a bit muddling, as plenty were still in with every chance approaching the final furlong. Most have been rated close to their marks.

## 4214 55TH JOHN SMITH'S CUP (HERITAGE H'CAP) 1m 2f 88y
**2:55** (2:56) (Class 2) 3-Y-O+
**£93,375** (£27,960; £13,980; £6,990; £3,495; £1,755) **Stalls** Low

Form RPR
-551 **1** **Farraaj (IRE)**[36] 2957 5-9-11 **111**........ AndreaAtzeni 22 120
(Roger Varian) *lw: chsd ldr: effrt 2f out: rdn to chal ent fnl f: led last 100yds: kpt on strly* **6/1[3]**
02-4 **2** *1 1/2* **Zain Eagle**[52] 2461 4-8-9 **95**........ TomEaves 18 101
(Robert Cowell) *swtg: set stdy pce: qcknd over 3f out: rdn clr over 2f out: rdn and edgd lft over 1f out: drvn and hung lft ins fnl f: hdd and no ex last 100yds* **20/1**
0-32 **3** *1 3/4* **Bold Sniper**[22] 3416 4-9-2 **102**........ RyanMoore 7 105
(Sir Michael Stoute) *t.k.h early: trckd ldrs: hdwy to chse ldng pair over 3f out: rdn along 2f out: sn drvn and no imp fnl f* **4/1[1]**
6504 **4** *3/4* **Educate**[8] 3930 5-9-12 **112**........ TomQueally 6 113
(Ismail Mohammed) *hld up towards rr: hdwy towards inner over 2f out: rdn wl over 1f out: kpt on fnl f: nrst fin* **20/1**
3203 **5** *1/2* **Chancery (USA)**[14] 3722 6-8-11 **97**........ DanielTudhope 21 97+
(David O'Meara) *lw: hld up towards rr: hdwy 3f out: rdn 2f out: kpt on u.p fr over 1f out: nrst fin* **9/1**
0040 **6** *nk* **Sennockian Star**[7] 3962 4-9-2 **102**........(v) JoeFanning 3 102
(Mark Johnston) *prom: pushed along 3f out: rdn 2f out: sn drvn and kpt on one pce* **20/1**
60-0 **7** *1 1/4* **Queensberry Rules (IRE)**[24] 3356 4-9-0 **100**........(t) SebSanders 10 98
(William Haggas) *towards rr: hdwy 3f out: rdn along 2f out: sn kpt on fnl f: nrst fin* **14/1**
-310 **8** *1/2* **Pacific Heights (IRE)**[24] 3356 5-8-11 **100**........ GeorgeChaloner(3) 8 97
(Brian Ellison) *in tch: rdn along over 4f out: sltly outpcd 3f out: kpt on u.p fnl 2f* **25/1**
111 **9** *1/2* **Clever Cookie**[42] 2785 6-9-7 **107**........ PJMcDonald 12 103+
(Peter Niven) *in rr: pushed along over 3f out: hdwy 2f out: sn rdn and kpt on fnl f: nrst fin* **11/2[2]**
6130 **10** *4* **Saxo Jack (FR)**[22] 3416 4-9-5 **105**........ WilliamCarson 14 93
(Saeed bin Suroor) *lw: hld up: hdwy on inner 3f out: rdn along to chse ldrs over 2f out: sn drvn and wknd* **25/1**
-030 **11** *3/4* **Red Avenger (USA)**[24] 3356 4-8-7 **96**........ ConnorBeasley(3) 17 83
(Ed Dunlop) *lw: in tch: hdwy on outer over 3f out: rdn along to chse ldrs over 2f out: drvn and edgd lft over 1f out: sn wknd* **12/1**
02 **12** *1* **Tahira (GER)**[28] 3217 4-8-13 **99**........ PhillipMakin 5 84
(John Quinn) *swtg: in tch: hdwy to chse ldrs 3f out: rdn along over 2f out: drvn and hld whn n.m.r and wknd over 1f out* **9/1**
5200 **13** *3/4* **Ingleby Angel (IRE)**[24] 3356 5-8-11 **97**........ MartinDwyer 19 80
(David O'Meara) *t.k.h early: hld up: a in rr* **50/1**
0660 **14** *3 3/4* **Starboard**[24] 3356 5-8-11 **97**........ HayleyTurner 16 73
(David Simcock) *swtg: a in rr* **33/1**
30-5 **15** *3 1/2* **Tarikhi (USA)**[28] 3251 4-8-9 **95**........ KierenFallon 11 64
(Saeed bin Suroor) *trckd ldrs: hdwy over 3f out: rdn along over 2f out: sn drvn and wknd: collapsed after line: fatally injured* **10/1**
0431 **16** *1 1/4* **Two For Two (IRE)**[21] 3456 6-8-12 **101** 5ex........ SamJames(3) 13 68
(David O'Meara) *midfield: rdn along over 3f out: sn wknd* **20/1**
2m 7.96s (-4.54) **Going Correction** -0.225s/f (Firm) 16 Ran SP% 124.8
Speed ratings (Par 109): **109,107,106,105,105 105,104,103,103,100 99,98,98,95,92 91**
CSF £127.04 CT £550.17 TOTE £7.10: £2.00, £5.20, £1.60, £4.30; EX 192.40 Trifecta £1223.30.
**Owner** Sheikh Ahmed Al Maktoum **Bred** Darley **Trained** Newmarket, Suffolk

**FOCUS**
Tactics played a huge part in the 55th running of this highly valuable handicap, with the pace steady and very few ever threatening to land a serious blow. The first two home shared those positions throughout. Those recording top handicap figures do not always translate their form to Pattern races, but the winner would seem well placed to do so.

## 4215 JOHN SMITH'S CITY WALLS STKS (LISTED RACE) 5f
**3:30** (3:30) (Class 1) 3-Y-O+
**£22,684** (£8,600; £4,304; £2,144; £1,076; £540) **Stalls** Centre

Form RPR
02-0 **1** **Take Cover**[25] 3319 7-9-1 109........ AndreaAtzeni 14 114
(David C Griffiths) *mde all: edgd rt fnl f: styd on wl* **9/1**
-113 **2** *1 1/4* **G Force (IRE)**[28] 3245 3-8-10 103........ DanielTudhope 10 108+
(David O'Meara) *lw: dwlt: in rr: hdwy over 2f out: chsd wnr 1f out: struck over hd by rivals whip ins fnl f: kpt on same pce* **7/4[1]**
1003 **3** *1 1/4* **Monsieur Joe (IRE)**[14] 3736 7-9-1 104........ TomQueally 6 105
(Paul Midgley) *hld up towards rr: effrt 2f out: styd on fnl f* **9/1**
-232 **4** *3/4* **Kingsgate Native (IRE)**[7] 3981 9-9-1 112........ RyanMoore 5 102
(Robert Cowell) *mid-div: effrt and edgd lft over 1f out: kpt on same pce* **9/4[2]**
-23 **5** *1/2* **Reroute (IRE)**[21] 3459 3-8-5 98........(t) HayleyTurner 1 94
(Ed Walker) *w ldrs: kpt on same pce fnl f* **16/1**
0-40 **6** *1 1/4* **Move In Time**[28] 3241 6-9-1 102........ SamJames 11 96
(David O'Meara) *chsd ldrs: fdd over 1f out* **20/1**
00-0 **7** *2* **Whozthecat (IRE)**[59] 2254 7-9-1 97........ DavidAllan 12 89
(Declan Carroll) *chsd ldrs: fdd appr fnl f: edgd lft ins fnl f* **33/1**
-155 **8** *1* **Lucky Beggar (IRE)**[41] 2820 4-9-1 106........ WilliamCarson 7 85
(Charles Hills) *chsd ldrs: drvn over 2f out: lost pl over 1f out* **14/1**
2-00 **9** *4* **York Glory (USA)**[21] 3452 6-9-1 107........(b) PhillipMakin 3 71
(Kevin Ryan) *hld up in rr: effrt 2f out: no imp: hmpd and eased clsng stages* **8/1[3]**
56.5s (-2.80) **Going Correction** -0.225s/f (Firm)
**WFA** 3 from 4yo+ 5lb 9 Ran SP% 118.5
Speed ratings (Par 111): **113,111,109,107,107 105,101,100,93**
CSF £25.84 TOTE £10.40: £2.30, £1.30, £2.70; EX 30.30 Trifecta £171.50.
**Owner** Norcroft Park Stud **Bred** Norcroft Park Stud **Trained** Bawtry, S Yorks

**FOCUS**
Smart form from the principals in this Listed event. The winner made all at a good pace. The runner-up has been rated to form.

## 4216 JOHN SMITH'S MEDIAN AUCTION MAIDEN STKS (BOBIS RACE) 6f
**4:05** (4:07) (Class 3) 2-Y-O **£7,439** (£2,213; £1,106; £553) **Stalls** Centre

Form RPR
**1** **Flaming Spear (IRE)** 2-9-5 0........ RyanMoore 8 94+
(Kevin Ryan) *athletic: lw: in tch: hdwy to trck ldrs over 3f out: effrt 2f out: sn chsng ldr: rdn to chal jst ins fnl f: sn led and kpt on strly* **11/10[1]**
03 **2** *2 3/4* **Lady Gemini**[17] 3563 2-9-0 0........ DavidAllan 9 78
(Jo Hughes) *led: rdn along and clr wl over 1f out: jnd and drvn jst ins fnl f: sn hdd and kpt on same pce* **14/1**
2 **3** *4 1/2* **Polarisation**[12] 3794 2-9-5 0........ JoeFanning 6 69
(Mark Johnston) *unf: scope: chsd ldrs: hdwy 2f out: sn rdn: kpt on fnl f* **7/1[3]**
**4** *1/2* **Best Example (USA)** 2-9-5 0........ AndreaAtzeni 11 68
(Saeed bin Suroor) *str: lengthy: bit bkwd: dwlt and towards rr: hdwy and in tch 1/2-way: pushed along and outpcd over 2f out: sn rdn: kpt on appr fnl f* **9/2[2]**
**5** *1/2* **Moonlightnavigator (USA)** 2-9-5 0........ PhillipMakin 4 66
(John Quinn) *str: trckd ldrs: hdwy over 2f out: rdn over 1f out: kpt on same pce* **17/2**
**6** *2* **Arcano Gold (IRE)** 2-9-5 0........ DanielTudhope 2 60
(Richard Fahey) *str: towards rr: pushed along 1/2-way: hdwy on outer 2f out: kpt on fnl f* **25/1**
6 **7** *hd* **Charlotte's Secret**[24] 3358 2-9-5 0........ PatrickMathers 13 59
(Richard Fahey) *w'like: swtg: towards rr: pushed along 1/2-way: hdwy 2f out: rdn and edgd lft over 1f out: kpt on* **20/1**
44 **8** *2* **Essaka (IRE)**[9] 3889 2-9-5 0........ MartinDwyer 7 53
(Mick Channon) *leggy: chsd ldr: rdn along 2f out: wknd appr fnl f* **14/1**
**9** *1 1/2* **Milady Eileen (IRE)** 2-8-11 0........ GeorgeChaloner(3) 10 44
(Richard Fahey) *w'like: dwlt and sltly hmpd s: towards rr: swtchd lft and hdwy 2f out: sn rdn and wknd appr fnl f* **16/1**
44 **10** *4 1/2* **Snoway**[10] 3842 2-9-0 0........ TomQueally 12 30
(Tony Coyle) *w'like: chsd ldrs: rdn along 1/2-way: sn wknd* **66/1**
00 **11** *nse* **Chollima**[21] 3481 2-9-5 0........ DuranFentiman 5 35
(Tim Easterby) *w'like: midfield: rdn along wl over 2f out: sn outpcd* **66/1**
60 **12** *28* **Birkdale Boy (IRE)**[28] 3255 2-9-5 0........ WilliamCarson 3
(Richard Fahey) *swtg: dwlt: sn outpcd and a bhd* **40/1**
1m 10.28s (-1.62) **Going Correction** -0.225s/f (Firm) 12 Ran SP% 122.1
Speed ratings (Par 98): **101,97,91,90,90 87,87,84,82,76 76,39**
CSF £19.13 TOTE £2.10: £1.10, £3.40, £2.40; EX 19.50 Trifecta £104.50.
**Owner** Qatar Racing & Essafinaat **Bred** Gerry Flannery Developments **Trained** Hambleton, N Yorks

**FOCUS**
Not a strong race overall but the leading pair deserve credit for pulling clear. The winner is clearly highly regarded.

## 4217 JOHN SMITH'S STAYERS' STKS (H'CAP) 2m 88y
**4:40** (4:40) (Class 3) (0-95,90) 4-Y-O+ **£9,703** (£2,887; £1,443; £721) **Stalls** Low

Form RPR
0240 **1** **Gabrial's King (IRE)**[25] 3321 5-9-5 **88**........ DanielTudhope 7 98
(David Simcock) *dwlt: hld up in rr: hdwy over 3f out: chsd ldrs 2f out: styd on to ld nr fin* **14/1**
-301 **2** *nk* **Knightly Escapade**[16] 3622 6-8-3 **75**........ ConnorBeasley(3) 9 84
(Brian Ellison) *hld up in rr: hdwy over 4f out: chsng ldrs over 2f out: led over 1f out: edgd rt ins fnl f: hdd and no ex clsng stages* **11/1**
-040 **3** *3* **Brockwell**[25] 3321 5-9-2 **85**........ HayleyTurner 3 90
(Tom Dascombe) *chsd ldrs: led over 2f out: hdd over 1f out: kpt on one pce* **4/1[1]**
0-33 **4** *2 1/2* **Rhombus (IRE)**[34] 3034 4-9-7 **90**........ TomQueally 6 92
(Ismail Mohammed) *hld up in rr: hdwy to chse ldrs over 2f out: one pce whn edgd lft ins fnl f* **7/1[3]**
0232 **5** *1/2* **Nashville (IRE)**[14] 3698 5-8-5 **77**........ GeorgeChaloner(3) 10 78
(Richard Fahey) *chsd ldrs: drvn upsides over 2f out: one pce* **8/1**
2321 **6** *1 3/4* **Eagle Rock (IRE)**[15] 3654 6-9-4 **87**........(p) AndrewElliott 12 86
(Tom Tate) *lw: jnd ldr after 1f: led after 4f: hdd over 3f out: one pce fnl 2f* **9/2[2]**

-411 **7** *4 ½* **Hot Spice**[10] 3845 6-8-4 **73** ............ DuranFentiman 8 67
(Michael Easterby) *led 4f: chsd ldrs: led over 3f out: hdd over 2f out: wknd over 1f out* **7/1**[3]

50-0 **8** *8* **Cloudy Spirit**[20] 3501 9-8-6 **75** ............ PaulQuinn 5 59
(Andrew Hollinshead) *hld up in rr: drvn over 4f out: sme late hdwy: nvr on terms* **33/1**

6213 **9** *1* **Teak (IRE)**[13] 3752 7-8-6 **75** ............(v[1]) MartinDwyer 11 58
(Ian Williams) *chsd ldrs: upsides 10f out: wknd over 1f out: eased ins fnl f* **16/1**

0-06 **10** *¾* **Tappanappa (IRE)**[106] 1140 7-8-6 **75** ............[1] RaulDaSilva 13 57
(Michael Appleby) *mid-div: pushed along after 4f: drvn 7f out: lost pl 5f out* **12/1**

1-03 **11** *1 ¼* **Great Fighter**[22] 3424 4-9-2 **85** ............(p) AndreaAtzeni 1 66
(Saeed bin Suroor) *lw: mid-div: hdwy to chse ldrs over 2f out: wknd over 1f out: eased clsng stages* **8/1**

00 **12** *1 ¼* **Agreement (IRE)**[14] 3717 4-9-4 **87** ............ PhillipMakin 4 66
(John Quinn) *mid-div: drvn 4f out: lost pl over 2f out: eased whn bhd ins fnl f* **28/1**

3m 28.97s (-5.53) **Going Correction** -0.225s/f (Firm) course record **12** Ran SP% **120.4**
Speed ratings (Par 107): **104,103,102,101,100 99,97,93,93,92 92,91**
CSF £161.84 CT £741.85 TOTE £16.30: £4.60, £3.90, £1.80; EX 168.00 Trifecta £1854.10.
**Owner** Dr Marwan Koukash **Bred** Danella Partnership **Trained** Newmarket, Suffolk
■ Stewards' Enquiry : Daniel Tudhope trainers representative could offer no explanation for geldings improved form

**FOCUS**
A fairly useful staying event. The gallop looked no more than a fair one for a long way, and the race did not really begin in earnest until they approached the straight. The runner-up has been rated to his old best, while the third is consistent but hard to win with.

## 4218 JOHN SMITH'S STKS (NURSERY H'CAP) (BOBIS RACE) 6f
5:15 (5:17) (Class 2) 2-Y-O £9,703 (£2,887; £1,443; £721) Stalls Centre

Form RPR

0241 **1** **Kibaar**[12] 3779 2-8-13 **85** ............ TomQueally 5 85
(B W Hills) *hld up towards rr: smooth hdwy over 2f out: chsd ldrs over 1f out: rdn ent fnl f: styd on wl to ld on line* **6/1**[3]

2610 **2** *nse* **Denzille Lane (IRE)**[25] 3322 2-8-13 **85** ............ JoeFanning 2 85
(Mark Johnston) *mde most tl hdd 2f out and sn rdn: drvn ent fnl f: kpt on wl towards fin: jst failed* **10/1**

022 **3** *nse* **Bahamian Sunrise**[17] 3570 2-8-2 **74** ............ PatrickMathers 1 74
(Richard Fahey) *leggy: trckd ldrs on outer: hdwy and cl up 2f out: rdn to take slt ld jst ins fnl f: sn drvn: hdd and no ex on line* **10/1**

133 **4** *3 ¼* **Sea Wolf (IRE)**[16] 3619 2-9-2 **91** ............ ConnorBeasley(3) 8 81
(Michael Dods) *w'like: trckd ldrs on outer: hdwy and cl up 2f out: sn rdn and sltly outpcd: kpt on fnl f* **15/2**

314 **5** *1* **Epithet (IRE)**[9] 3883 2-9-7 **93** ............ RyanMoore 3 80
(Charlie Appleby) *trckd ldrs: hdwy 1/2-way: led 2f out: rdn over 1f out: hdd jst ins fnl f: sn wknd* **7/4**[1]

611 **6** *1 ¾* **Honest Bob'S**[15] 3658 2-8-8 **83** ............ GeorgeChaloner(3) 6 65
(Brian Ellison) *w'like: in rr: pushed along over 2f out: sn rdn and n.d* **11/2**[2]

153 **7** *4 ½* **Firgrove Bridge (IRE)**[25] 3337 2-8-8 **80** ............ MartinDwyer 4 48
(Kevin Ryan) *cmpt: cl up: disp ld 1/2-way: rdn over 2f out: sn wknd* **16/1**

61 **8** *4* **Billyoakes (IRE)**[57] 2291 2-8-9 **81** ............ AndreaAtzeni 7 37
(Mick Channon) *leggy: chsd ldrs: rdn along over 2f out: sn wknd* **7/1**

1m 10.63s (-1.27) **Going Correction** -0.225s/f (Firm) **8** Ran SP% **114.4**
Speed ratings (Par 100): **99,98,98,94,93 90,84,79**
CSF £63.10 CT £591.53 TOTE £6.90: £2.20, £3.10, £2.50; EX 53.80 Trifecta £1043.60.
**Owner** Hamdan Al Maktoum **Bred** Laundry Cottage Stud Farm **Trained** Upper Lambourn, Berks
■ Stewards' Enquiry : Patrick Mathers thwo-day ban; used whip above permitted level (27th-28th July)

**FOCUS**
Fairly decent form in this nursery, where the first three flashed across the line together. This race could rated a little higher, with the runner-up improving on his previous turf form, and the third also posting a minor personal best.
T/Jkpt: Not won. T/Plt: £37.30 to a £1 stake. Pool: £22,0077.81 - 4301.57 winning tickets.
T/Qpdt: £10.80 to a £1 stake. Pool: £12,209.84 - 835.55 winning tickets. JR

4219 - 4229a (Foreign Racing) - See Raceform Interactive

# ARLINGTON PARK (L-H)
Saturday, July 12

**OFFICIAL GOING: Turf: firm**

## 4230a AMERICAN DERBY (GRADE 3) (3YO) (TURF) 1m 1f 110y
10:55 (12:00) 3-Y-O
£68,674 (£22,891; £12,590; £6,867; £3,433; £1,204)

RPR

**1** **Divine Oath (USA)**[41] 3-8-7 0 ............ FGeroux 2 98
(Todd Pletcher, U.S.A) **18/5**[2]

**2** *½* **Our Channel (USA)**[35] 2990 3-8-9 0 ............ JamesGraham 7 99
(William Haggas) **32/5**

**3** *¾* **Highball (USA)**[27] 3-8-7 0 ............ AGarcia 3 95
(Wayne Catalano, U.S.A) **44/5**

**4** *½* **Schoolofhardrocks (USA)**[98] 1330 3-8-7 0 ............(b) VictorEspinoza 4 94
(David Hofmans, U.S.A) **13/10**[1]

**5** *¾* **Afortable (USA)**[49] 3-8-7 0 ............ JRLeparoux 10 93
(Chris Block, U.S.A) **47/10**[3]

**6** *¾* **Big Tom Prado (USA)** 3-8-7 0 ............ CHMarquezJr 1 91
(Christine K Janks, U.S.A) **68/1**

**7** *2* **Giacallure (USA)** 3-8-7 0 ............ JBravo 5 87
(Richard Scherer, U.S.A) **37/1**

**8** *¾* **Hesinfront (USA)**[99] 3-8-7 0 ............ CHill 9 86
(Dale Romans, U.S.A) **157/10**

**9** *7 ¼* **Ghostly Wonder (USA)** 3-8-7 0 ............ JEFelix 6 71
(Andrew Hansen, U.S.A) **87/1**

**P** **Chief Barker (IRE)**[49] 3-8-7 0 ............ QHamilton 8
(Larry Rivelli, U.S.A) **209/10**

1m 56.5s (1.03) **10** Ran SP% **122.3**
PARI-MUTUEL (all including 2 usd stake): WIN 9.20; PLACE (1-2) 4.60, 6.40; SHOW (1-2-3) 3.40, 4.60, 6.00; SF 67.60.
**Owner** Let's Go Stable **Bred** Sanford R Robertson **Trained** USA

# 3994 BELMONT PARK (L-H)
Saturday, July 12

**OFFICIAL GOING: Turf: firm**

## 4231a BOWLING GREEN H'CAP (GRADE 2) (4YO+) (TURF) 1m 4f
10:28 (12:00) 4-Y-O+
£72,289 (£24,096; £12,048; £6,024; £3,614; £2,409)

RPR

**1** **Hangover Kid (USA)**[34] 6-8-3 0 ............(b) JLezcano 1 108
(Jason Servis, U.S.A) **47/10**[3]

**2** *hd* **Grandeur (IRE)**[35] 3025 5-8-10 0 ............ JRosario 4 115
(Jeremy Noseda) **13/20**[1]

**3** *¾* **Sky Blazer (USA)**[36] 6-8-4 0 ow2 ............(b) RMaragh 5 107
(Barclay Tagg, U.S.A) **155/10**

**4** *½* **Boisterous (USA)**[35] 3025 7-8-8 0 ............ JRVelazquez 3 111
(Todd Pletcher, U.S.A) **42/10**[2]

**5** *¾* **Reflecting (USA)**[36] 5-8-3 0 ............(b) IOrtizJr 6 104
(Claude McGaughey III, U.S.A) **76/10**

**6** *4 ¾* **Horvat Clan (USA)**[24] 5-8-1 0 ow2 ............ JAlvarado 2 95
(David Cannizzo, U.S.A) **185/10**

2m 28.18s (-0.40) **6** Ran SP% **120.2**
PARI-MUTUEL (all including 2 usd stake): WIN 11.40; PLACE (1-2) 3.90, 2.50; SHOW (1-2-3) 3.00, 2.10, 4.40; SF 26.00.
**Owner** Four Tags Stable **Bred** Steve Taglienti **Trained** USA

4232 - 4246a (Foreign Racing) - See Raceform Interactive

# HANOVER (L-H)
Sunday, July 13

**OFFICIAL GOING: Turf: good**

## 4247a GROSSER PREIS DER VGH VERSICHERUNGEN (GROUP 2) (TURF) 1m
3:45 (12:00) 3-Y-O+
£33,333 (£12,916; £5,416; £3,333; £2,083; £1,250)

RPR

**1** **Red Dubawi (IRE)**[21] 3511 6-9-2 0 ............ EddyHardouin 7 113+
(Frau Erika Mader, Germany) *missed break: hld up in rr: c stands' side st: hdwy over 1 1/2f out: nt clr run and swtchd ins to find a gap 1f out: qcknd to ld fnl 50yds: won gng away* **152/10**

**2** *¾* **Ajaxana (GER)**[49] 2584 3-8-7 0 ............ AnthonyCrastus 6 109
(Waldemar Hickst, Germany) *midfield: tk clsr order 2f out: rdn to chse ldrs 1 1/2f out: led ent fnl f: r.o u.p: hdd 50yds out: no ex* **33/10**[2]

**3** *2* **Amaron**[21] 3511 5-9-2 0 ............ FabienLefebvre 4 107
(Andreas Lowe, Germany) *sn led: hdd after 2f and chsd ldr on inner: rdn to chal fr 2f out: led 1 1/2f out: hdd ent fnl f: readily outpcd by first two* **21/10**[1]

**4** *¾* **Avon Pearl**[45] 5-9-2 0 ............(b) PatDobbs 3 105
(Rune Haugen, Norway) *hld up towards rr: rdn and hdwy to chse ldrs 2f out: pressed ldr 1 1/2f out: grad outpcd by ldrs ins fnl f* **42/10**[3]

**5** *nk* **Gereon (GER)**[45] 2715 6-9-5 0 ............ LiamJones 2 107
(C Zschache, Germany) *midfield: rdn to chse ldrs fr 2f out: one pce u.p fnl f* **182/10**

**6** *hd* **Peace At Last (IRE)**[21] 3511 4-9-2 0 ............ DanielePorcu 8 104
(H-A Pantall, France) *w.w towards rr: rdn and prog 1 1/2f out: kpt on ins fnl f: nvr on terms w ldrs* **131/10**

**7** *nk* **Felician (GER)**[28] 3291 6-9-2 0 ............ RobertHavlin 5 103
(Ferdinand J Leve, Germany) *hld up towards rr: sme hdwy 2f out: nvr in contention* **89/10**

**8** *1 ½* **Quixote (GER)**[18] 4-9-2 0 ............ AdriedeVries 11 102
(P Schiergen, Germany) *led after 2f: rdn over 2f out: hdd 1 1/2f out and sn btn* **227/10**

**9** *1 ½* **Nordico (GER)**[34] 3073 3-8-7 0 ............ FrederikTylicki 9 97
(Mario Hofer, Germany) *pressed ldrs: 2nd and rdn over 2f out: lost pl 1 1/2f out: sn btn* **43/5**

**10** *7* **Abendwind (GER)**[36] 3028 3-8-7 0 ............ JohanVictoire 1 80
(Waldemar Hickst, Germany) *midfield on inner: rdn and no imp over 2f out: sn btn* **71/10**

**11** *13* **Konig Concorde (GER)**[42] 2814 9-9-2 0 ............ WPanov 10 53
(Christian Sprengel, Germany) *trckd ldrs: rdn to chse ldrs 2 1/2f out: wknd over 1 1/2f out* **37/1**

1m 39.69s (99.69)
**WFA** 3 from 4yo+ 9lb **11** Ran SP% **132.9**
WIN (incl. 10 euro stake): 162. PLACES: 28. 15. 14. SF: 460.
**Owner** Zalim Bifov **Bred** Haras Des Sablonnets **Trained** Germany

4248 - (Foreign Racing) - See Raceform Interactive

# 3997 LONGCHAMP (R-H)
Sunday, July 13

**OFFICIAL GOING: Turf: very soft**

## 4249a PRIX DE THIBERVILLE (LISTED RACE) (3YO FILLIES) (TURF) 1m 4f
4:45 (12:00) 3-Y-O £22,916 (£9,166; £6,875; £2,291; £416)

RPR

**1** **Zarshana (IRE)**[42] 2816 3-8-11 0 ............(p) ChristopheSoumillon 6 102+
(A De Royer-Dupre, France) **6/5**[1]

**2** *¾* **Saraaba (IRE)**[24] 3-8-11 0 ............ ThierryJarnet 2 101+
(F Head, France) **6/4**[2]

**3** *3 ½* **Elektrum (IRE)**[49] 2590 3-8-11 0 ............ CristianDemuro 5 95
(G Botti, France) **153/10**

**4** *nk* **Discrete (FR)**[57] 3-8-11 0 ............ Pierre-CharlesBoudot 4 95
(H-F Devin, France) **128/10**

**5** *3* **Emaratiya Ana (IRE)**[24] 3376 3-8-11 0 ............ WilliamBuick 7 90
(Roger Varian) *sn trcking ldr on outer: pushed along to chal 3f out: led briefly early in st: rdn and hdd 2f out: no ex and btn over 1f out: fdd* **33/1**

6 nk **Allegrezza**[20] 3-8-11 0 GregoryBenoist 1 89
(D Smaga, France) 26/5[3]

7 dist **Full Moon Fever (IRE)**[46] 2685 3-8-11 0 (p) StephanePasquier 3
(Ed Walker) *dwlt sltly but pushed along to go forward and sn led: rdn and hdd early in st: no ex and wknd qckly 2f out: dropped to last and eased: t.o* 31/1

2m 39.63s (9.23) 7 Ran SP% 121.0
WIN (incl. 1 euro stake): 2.20. PLACES: 1.40, 1.30. SF: 5.00.
**Owner** H H Aga Khan **Bred** His Highness The Aga Khan's Studs S C **Trained** Chantilly, France

## 4250a PRIX MAURICE DE NIEUIL (GROUP 2) (4YO+) (TURF) 1m 6f
5:45 (12:00) 4-Y-0+ £61,750 (£23,833; £11,375; £7,583; £3,791)

RPR

1 **Terrubi (IRE)**[49] 2588 4-8-13 0 ChristopheSoumillon 2 116+
(P Bary, France) *hld up towards rr: tk clsr order 3f out: hdwy towards outer over 2f out: led 1 1/2f out: drvn clr ins fnl f and sn in command* 5/1[2]

2 1 1/2 **Brown Panther**[24] 3377 6-8-13 0 RichardKingscote 4 114+
(Tom Dascombe) *w.w towards rr: shkn up and effrt on outer 3f out: rdn and chsd ldr fr over 1 1/2f out: kpt on under driving fnl f: nt pce to trble wnr* 5/4[1]

3 nk **Going Somewhere (BRZ)**[42] 2819 5-8-13 0 GregoryBenoist 3 113+
(D Smaga, France) *hld up in rr: hdwy on outer 2f out: styd on wl fnl f: nvr on terms w wnr* 28/1

4 4 **Seismos (IRE)**[45] 2704 6-8-13 0 MartinHarley 9 108
(Marco Botti) *trckd ldr on outer: rdn to chal 2f out: led sn after but hdd 1 1/2f out: one pce u.p appr fnl f: fdd last 100yds* 14/1

5 1 1/4 **Fly With Me (FR)**[49] 2588 4-9-2 0 (p) MaximeGuyon 6 109
(E Libaud, France) *trckd ldrs: rdn and nt qckn 2f out: one pce tl wknd ins fnl f* 5/1[2]

6 1 1/4 **Goldtara (FR)**[49] 2588 6-8-9 0 Christophe-PatriceLemaire 7 100
(A Lyon, France) *midfield: cl 5th 2 1/2f out: sn rdn and outpcd: plugged on u.p fr over 1f out: nvr trbld ldrs* 7/1[3]

7 6 **Kicky Blue (GER)**[20] 4-8-9 0 ThierryJarnet 8 92
(T Clout, France) *trckd ldrs on outer: 3rd and ev ch 2 1/2f out: rdn and no imp 2f out: sn btn and wknd fnl f* 11/1

8 dist **Remus De La Tour (FR)**[46] 5-8-13 0 NicolasPerret 5
(K Borgel, France) *led: rdn and pressed fr 2f out: hdd sn after: wknd qckly* 33/1

9 dist **Montclair (IRE)**[49] 2588 4-8-13 0 Pierre-CharlesBoudot 1
(A Fabre, France) *midfield on inner: scrubbed along and lost pl over 5f out: t.o fr 3 1/2f out* 9/1

3m 8.82s (188.82) 9 Ran SP% 121.7
WIN (incl. 1 euro stake): 5.50. PLACES: 1.70, 1.70, 3.00. DF: 9.80. SF: 24.00.
**Owner** Ecurie Jean-Louis Bouchard **Bred** Petra Bloodstock & Ecurie De Meautry **Trained** Chantilly, France

## 4251a JUDDMONTE GRAND PRIX DE PARIS (GROUP 1) (3YO COLTS & FILLIES) (TURF) 1m 4f
6:20 (12:00) 3-Y-0 £285,700 (£114,300; £57,150; £28,550; £14,300)

RPR

1 **Gallante (IRE)**[31] 3-9-2 0 Pierre-CharlesBoudot 5 118
(A Fabre, France) *led early: prom on inner once hdd: angled off rail and chal gng strly 2f out: rdn to ld over 1f out: styd on strly fnl f: diminishing advantage at fin but a doing enough* 33/1

2 snk **Prince Gibraltar (FR)**[42] 2818 3-9-2 0 ChristopheSoumillon 3 119+
(J-C Rouget, France) *restrained and hld up in midfield: in tch on outer: clsd 3f out: rdn 2f out: styd on and wnt 2nd ins fnl f: edgd rt: clsng on wnr at fin but nvr quite getting there* 10/11[1]

3 2 1/2 **Teletext (USA)**[28] 3290 3-9-2 0 Christophe-PatriceLemaire 7 114
(P Bary, France) *midfield on outer: clsd 5f out: chal gng strly 3f out: pushed along and disputing ld 2f out: rdn and hdd over 1f out: styd on but outpcd by wnr and dropped to 3rd fnl f* 16/1

4 2 **Free Port Lux**[42] 2818 3-9-2 0 (b[1]) ThierryJarnet 9 111+
(F Head, France) *hld up towards rr: pushed along and hdwy 2f out: rdn over 1f out: plugged on for 4th fnl f but nt pce to chal* 16/1

5 3/4 **Marzocco (USA)**[23] 3419 3-9-2 0 (p) WilliamBuick 10 110
(John Gosden) *worked across fr wd draw and sn led on rail: pushed along and strly pressed fr 3f out: rdn and jnd 2f out: hdd over 1f out and sn outpcd: plugged on for wl hld 5th fnl f* 20/1

6 5 **The Grey Gatsby (IRE)**[42] 2818 3-9-2 0 RyanMoore 1 102+
(Kevin Ryan) *hld up towards rr on inner: pushed along over 3f out: rdn and toiling 2f out: sn no imp on ldrs and wl hld: plugged on and tk mod 6th towards fin: n.d* 4/1[2]

7 1 **Golden Guepard (IRE)**[49] 2585 3-9-2 0 MaximeGuyon 2 100
(A Fabre, France) *midfield on inner: angled off rail and rdn over 2f out: outpcd by ldrs and hld in 6th ent fnl f: no ex and dropped to 7th towards fin* 8/1[3]

8 1 **Prince Nomad (FR)**[37] 3-9-2 0 (p) MickaelBarzalona 11 98
(X Thomas-Demeaulte, France) *dropped in fr wdst draw and hld up in last: rdn 3f out: hung rt and no imp u.p in st: plugged on past btn horses fnl f but nvr a factor* 100/1

9 2 **Machucambo (FR)**[30] 3207 3-9-2 0 GeraldMosse 6 95
(C Ferland, France) *t.k.h: w ldrs early: sn midfield in tch: rdn over 2f out: outpcd and btn over 1f out: fdd* 16/1

10 1 1/4 **Guardini (FR)**[28] 3290 3-9-2 0 OlivierPeslier 8 93
(Jean-Pierre Carvalho, Germany) *w ldrs early: sn trcking ldr on outer: cl 2nd 3f out: rdn and effrt over 2f out: fnd little and qckly lost pl: edgd rt to rail over 1f out and sn btn: wknd* 10/1

11 dist **Auvray (FR)**[28] 3290 3-9-2 0 GregoryBenoist 4
(E Lellouche, France) *hld up in midfield: pushed along 3f out: rdn and dropped to rr 2f out: sn btn: eased and t.o* 40/1

2m 41.76s (11.36) 11 Ran SP% 121.4
WIN (incl. 1 euro stake): 62.70. PLACES: 6.00, 1.10, 3.50. DF: 44.70. SF: 139.90.
**Owner** Derrick Smith & Mrs John Magnier & Michael Tabor **Bred** Lynch Bages Ltd & Camas Park Stud **Trained** Chantilly, France

**FOCUS**
Not a terribly strong race, they went a steady gallop early and even after Marzocco took over it was just an ordinary pace.

# SAINT-MALO (L-H)
Sunday, July 13

**OFFICIAL GOING: Turf: soft**

## 4252a PRIX DE COMBOURG (CONDITIONS) (3YO) (TURF) 1m 1f
1:55 (12:00) 3-Y-0 £8,333 (£3,333; £2,500; £1,666; £833)

RPR

1 **Kaskarau (FR)** 3-8-10 0 (b) ValentinSeguy[(6)] 6 85
(X Thomas-Demeaulte, France) 53/10[3]

2 3 **Blue Bere (FR)**[206] 3-8-8 0 ChristopherGrosbois 3 71
(J Boisnard, France) 179/10

3 1 **Laguna Boy (FR)**[14] 3-8-11 0 MorganDelalande 4 72
(Y Barberot, France) 81/10

4 hd **Victordina (FR)**[25] 3372 3-8-8 0 WilliamsSaraiva 9 68
(R Rohne, Germany) 32/1

5 1 1/2 **Hurricancrys (FR)**[73] 3-9-2 0 AlexandreRoussel 5 73
(J Boisnard, France) 5/1[2]

6 1/2 **Tempo Royale (FR)**[17] 3-8-13 0 JeromeCabre 7 69
(S Wattel, France) 63/10

7 1/2 **Vesly (FR)** 3-8-5 0 LukasDelozier[(8)] 8 68
(Y Barberot, France) 121/10

8 1 **Silver Treasure (FR)**[13] 3810 3-9-2 0 VincentVion 1 69
(Amy Weaver) *t.k.h early: midfield on inner in main body of field bhd clr ldr: rdn 2f out: no imp and btn fnl f: fdd and eased towards fin* 6/4[1]

9 1 1/2 **Diamond River (FR)** 3-8-8 0 YoannRousset 2 58
(P Monfort, France) 142/10

1m 51.17s (111.17) 9 Ran SP% 119.8
WIN (incl. 1 euro stake): 6.30. PLACES: 2.30, 4.90, 2.80. DF: 51.50. SF: 108.20.
**Owner** Din-Mukhammed Matkenov **Bred** De La Fuente Stud **Trained** France

# 4011 AYR (L-H)
Monday, July 14

**OFFICIAL GOING: Good changing to good to soft after race 1 (2.30)**
Wind: Breezy, half against Weather: Overcast, showers

## 4253 EBF STALLIONS MAIDEN STKS (BOBIS RACE) 7f 50y
2:30 (2:34) (Class 4) 2-Y-0 £4,204 (£1,251; £625; £312) Stalls High

Form RPR

02 1 **Chadic**[11] 3875 2-9-5 0 JoeFanning 5 85+
(Mark Johnston) *mde all: shkn up and qcknd 2f out: kpt on strly fnl f: unchal* 7/2

532 2 2 3/4 **Ythan Waters**[23] 3481 2-9-5 0 PaulMulrennan 3 78
(Bryan Smart) *trckd ldrs: effrt and rdn 2f out: wnt 2nd ins fnl f: kpt on: nt rch wnr* 5/2[1]

23 3 hd **Intiwin (IRE)**[30] 3255 2-9-5 0 TonyHamilton 8 78
(Richard Fahey) *pressed wnr: rdn over 2f out: lost 2nd ins fnl f: kpt on same pce* 10/3[3]

43 4 2 **Gaudy (IRE)**[25] 3394 2-9-5 0 DanielTudhope 1 73
(Kevin Ryan) *wnt lft s: in tch: rdn over 2f out: kpt on fnl f: no imp* 11/4[2]

35 5 hd **Danny O'Ruairc (IRE)**[18] 3620 2-9-5 0 PJMcDonald 2 72
(James Moffatt) *in tch: effrt and rdn over 2f out: edgd rt appr fnl f: no imp* 25/1

6 1 3/4 **Sir Chauvelin** 2-9-5 0 GrahamLee 7 68
(Jim Goldie) *unruly and uns rdr in paddock: dwlt: hld up: shkn up over 2f out: no imp fr over 1f out* 25/1

5 7 12 **Go On Chas**[35] 3049 2-9-0 0 GarryWhillans[(5)] 4 39
(Ian Semple) *t.k.h: hld up in tch: struggling over 2f out: sn btn* 80/1

8 11 **Sabbra Cadabra** 2-9-5 0 DuranFentiman 9 12
(Philip Kirby) *t.k.h: hld up: rdn over 2f out: sn btn* 100/1

1m 32.77s (-0.63) **Going Correction** -0.10s/f (Good) 8 Ran SP% 110.5
Speed ratings (Par 96): **99,95,95,93,93 91,77,64**
CSF £11.67 TOTE £4.90: £1.40, £1.20, £1.20; EX 12.20 Trifecta £33.50.
**Owner** Sheikh Hamdan bin Mohammed Al Maktoum **Bred** Darley **Trained** Middleham Moor, N Yorks

**FOCUS**
Rail alignment increased distances, adding 18yds to race one, two, three and six, and 24yds to race seven. After 5mm of rain prior to racing the ground had eased to good, from good to firm, firm in places to good. After riding in the opener both Joe Fanning and Tony Hamilton said the ground was "on the easy side of good". An open maiden, in which it paid to race prominently. It was slowly run and may flatter one or two.

## 4254 DOWNLOAD THE BETVICTOR APP NOW H'CAP 1m
3:00 (3:00) (Class 5) (0-75,67) 3-Y-0+ £2,911 (£866; £432; £216) Stalls Low

Form RPR

0414 1 **Dark Crystal**[2] 4194 3-8-11 59 JoeFanning 1 66
(Linda Perratt) *trckd ldrs: smooth hdwy to ld over 2f out: led and edgd lft over 1f out: drvn out* 11/4[2]

5635 2 nk **Dhaular Dhar (IRE)**[7] 4014 12-9-1 57 (p) GaryBartley[(3)] 2 64
(Jim Goldie) *hld up in tch: rdn over 2f out: hdwy over 1f out: chsd wnr ins fnl f: kpt on fin* 8/1

3223 3 1 1/4 **Ewell Place (IRE)**[30] 3242 5-9-11 64 (p) PJMcDonald 3 68
(Richard Fahey) *t.k.h: led tl rdn and hdd over 2f out: rallied: kpt on same pce wl ins fnl f* 5/2[1]

2355 4 2 1/2 **Live Dangerously**[10] 3908 4-10-0 67 (tp) TomEaves 6 65
(Keith Dalgleish) *prom: rdn and hdwy over 2f out: hung lft over 1f out: no imp fnl f* 9/2[3]

4110 5 3 **Run Fat Lass Run**[30] 3254 4-10-0 67 PhillipMakin 5 58
(Philip Kirby) *hld up: rdn over 2f out: no imp fr over 1f out* 9/1

444- 6 3 1/4 **Berbice (IRE)**[336] 5331 9-8-4 48 oh3 SammyJoBell[(5)] 7 32
(Linda Perratt) *missed break: plld hrd in rr: stdy hdwy over 2f out: rdn and wknd over 1f out* 50/1

666 7 3/4 **Rioja Day (IRE)**[35] 3054 4-9-9 62 GrahamLee 4 44
(Jim Goldie) *w ldr: rdn over 2f out: wknd wl over 1f out* 13/2

1m 41.77s (-2.03) **Going Correction** -0.10s/f (Good)
**WFA** 3 from 4yo+ 9lb 7 Ran SP% 109.8
Speed ratings (Par 103): **106,105,104,101,98 95,94**
CSF £22.50 TOTE £3.00: £2.10, £5.00; EX 29.10 Trifecta £80.70.
**Owner** Mrs Helen Perratt **Bred** R Biggs **Trained** East Kilbride, S Lanarks

**FOCUS**
The going changed to good to soft before this race. Not a strong handicap for the grade, with the two at the top rated 8lb below the ceiling.

## 4255 FOLLOW @BETVICTORRACING ON TWITTER H'CAP 1m 2f
**3:30** (3:30) (Class 5) (0-75,74) 3-Y-O+ £2,911 (£866; £432; £216) Stalls Low

Form RPR
2423 1 **Maracuja**[17] 3644 3-9-3 **74** JoeFanning 3 83+
(Mark Johnston) *mde all at modest gallop: shkn up and qcknd clr wl over 1f out: kpt on strly fnl f* **11/10**[1]
52-4 2 2 **Thorntoun Care**[52] 2516 3-8-9 **66** GrahamLee 4 70+
(Jim Goldie) *chsd wnr thrght: effrt and rdn over 2f out: kpt on fnl f: nt pce to chal* **4/1**[2]
0-54 3 1 ½ **Woodstock (IRE)**[7] 4015 4-9-0 **65** GarryWhillans(5) 2 66
(Alistair Whillans) *t.k.h early: hld up in tch: drvn along and hdwy 2f out: kpt on same pce ins fnl f* **14/1**
6-03 4 nk **Royal Straight**[13] 3829 9-8-13 **64** (t) SammyJoBell(5) 6 65
(Linda Perratt) *s.i.s: sn prom: effrt and hung lft over 1f out: no imp fnl f* **6/1**[3]
4650 5 7 **Spavento (IRE)**[11] 3885 8-9-2 **62** (b) JasonHart 1 49
(Eric Alston) *hld up on ins: struggling over 2f out: btn fnl f* **16/1**
00-6 6 1 ½ **Mandy The Nag (USA)**[30] 3220 4-9-10 **70** TomEaves 7 54
(Richard Fahey) *trckd ldrs: effrt and pushed along over 2f out: wknd over 1f out* **20/1**
7 3 ¾ **Action Master**[304] 6375 8-8-9 **62** (t) SeanCorby(7) 8 39
(J J Lambe, Ire) *hld up: pushed along and hung lft over 2f out: sn wknd* **15/2**

2m 9.69s (-2.31) **Going Correction** -0.10s/f (Good)
**WFA** 3 from 4yo+ 11lb 7 Ran SP% **111.0**
Speed ratings (Par 103): **105,103,102,101,96 95,92**
CSF £5.23 CT £34.18 TOTE £1.80: £1.10, £2.10; EX 6.00 Trifecta £48.00.
**Owner** The Dukes of Roxburghe & Devonshire **Bred** Floors Farming & The Duke Of Devonshire **Trained** Middleham Moor, N Yorks

**FOCUS**
Another handicap that was weak for the grade, this time the top weight rated 5lb below the ceiling.

## 4256 BETVICTOR.COM H'CAP 6f
**4:00** (4:03) (Class 5) (0-75,74) 3-Y-O+ £2,911 (£866; £432; £216) Stalls Low

Form RPR
0106 1 **Goninodaethat**[8] 4003 6-9-1 **63** GrahamLee 7 72
(Jim Goldie) *mde all: rdn and edgd lft over 1f out: kpt on wl fnl f* **25/1**
0612 2 1 ¼ **Jinky**[7] 4016 6-9-9 **71** 6ex JoeFanning 4 76
(Linda Perratt) *trckd ldrs: effrt and wnt 2nd over 2f out: sn rdn: kpt on ins fnl f: nt rch wnr* **2/1**[1]
6125 3 nk **Spirit Of Alsace (IRE)**[7] 4017 3-8-6 **65** JackGarritty(5) 3 68
(Jim Goldie) *plld hrd: sn prom: effrt and rdn over 1f out: kpt on ins fnl f* **10/1**
0001 4 nk **Opt Out**[8] 4004 4-9-4 **66** 6ex PJMcDonald 9 69
(Alistair Whillans) *hld up bhd ldng gp: pushed and effrt over 1f out: kpt on fnl f* **16/1**
0053 5 ½ **Sunny Side Up (IRE)**[9] 3954 5-8-10 **63** GemmaTutty(5) 5 64+
(Karen Tutty) *missed break: hld up: gng wl whn nt clr run over 2f out to over 1f out: kpt on fnl f* **8/1**
1446 6 shd **Go Go Green (IRE)**[9] 3952 8-9-7 **72** GaryBartley(3) 8 73
(Jim Goldie) *hld up in midfield: effrt and rdn over 1f out: no imp fnl f* **9/1**
0042 7 shd **Thorntoun Lady (USA)**[8] 4004 4-9-5 **67** DanielTudhope 10 68
(Jim Goldie) *hld up: rdn and effrt 2f out: no imp* **13/2**[3]
2033 8 hd **Tango Sky (IRE)**[16] 3697 5-9-7 **74** SammyJoBell(5) 6 75+
(Richard Fahey) *dwlt: hld up: rdn along over 2f out: no imp fr over 1f out* **9/2**[2]
0004 9 9 **Natures Law (IRE)**[2] 4195 4-8-7 **55** oh1 (b) JasonHart 1 26
(Keith Dalgleish) *taken early to post: t.k.h: chsd ldrs tl rdn and wknd over 1f out* **7/1**
0004 10 7 **L'Ami Louis (IRE)**[8] 4004 6-9-11 **73** (b[1]) TomEaves 2 41
(Ian Semple) *taken early to post: w wnr to 1/2-way: rdn and wknd over 1f out* **25/1**

1m 12.23s (-0.17) **Going Correction** -0.10s/f (Good)
**WFA** 3 from 4yo+ 6lb 10 Ran SP% **121.1**
Speed ratings (Par 103): **97,95,94,94,93 93,93,93,81,80**
CSF £78.12 CT £565.64 TOTE £19.90: £4.40, £1.40, £3.80; EX 105.70 Trifecta £777.50.
**Owner** G E Adams & J S Goldie **Bred** W G H Barrons **Trained** Uplawmoor, E Renfrews

**FOCUS**
A fair handicap in which the outsider of the four Jim Goldie-trained runners came out on top.

## 4257 SPINCAST AT BETVICTOR DOWNLOAD THE NEW APP H'CAP 5f
**4:30** (4:32) (Class 6) (0-65,63) 3-Y-O+ £2,045 (£603; £302) Stalls Low

Form RPR
4600 1 **Tadalavil**[13] 3833 9-8-8 **50** SammyJoBell(5) 13 59
(Linda Perratt) *chsd ldrs: rdn 2f out: kpt on wl fnl f: led cl home* **16/1**
114 2 shd **Classy Anne**[31] 3191 4-9-6 **62** JackGarritty(5) 3 71
(Jim Goldie) *trckd ldrs: rdn to ld over 1f out: kpt on ins fnl f: hdd cl home* **5/1**[2]
0063 3 ½ **Saxonette**[8] 4005 6-8-11 **48** PJMcDonald 2 55
(Linda Perratt) *hld up in midfield: hdwy and ev ch over 1f out to ins fnl f: kpt on same pce nr fin* **9/1**
0000 4 nse **Findog**[13] 3831 4-9-2 **56** ConnorBeasley(3) 4 63
(Linda Perratt) *hld up bhd ldng gp: rdn and hdwy over 1f out: kpt on ins fnl f* **18/1**
0002 5 1 **Black Douglas**[8] 4005 5-9-2 **53** GrahamLee 8 56
(Jim Goldie) *hld up in midfield: effrt and drifted lft over 1f out: no imp fnl f* **7/1**
5611 6 1 **Emily Davison (IRE)**[18] 3609 3-9-2 **63** (p) GemmaTutty(5) 12 60
(Karen Tutty) *hld up in tch: rdn along over 2f out: one pce fr over 1f out* **12/1**
-100 7 shd **Little Eli**[16] 3697 4-9-12 **63** (p) JasonHart 11 62
(Eric Alston) *t.k.h: prom: rdn whn n.m.r briefly over 1f out: one pce fnl f* **10/1**
0400 8 ¾ **Chloe's Dream (IRE)**[2] 4195 4-8-11 **53** KevinStott(5) 5 49
(Linda Perratt) *t.k.h: w ldr tl rdn and no ex ins fnl f* **20/1**
0060 9 1 ½ **Here Now And Why (IRE)**[21] 3530 7-9-1 **52** (p) DanielTudhope 7 43
(Philip Kirby) *in tch: drvn along over 2f out: outpcd over 1f out* **9/1**
5000 10 ½ **Fife Jo**[8] 4004 4-8-1 **45** JoeDoyle(7) 1 34
(Jim Goldie) *fly-jmpd s: bhd: rdn over 2f out: sme late hdwy: nvr on terms* **66/1**
0602 11 4 ½ **Baltic Spirit (IRE)**[2] 4193 3-9-1 **57** (b) JoeFanning 6 28
(Keith Dalgleish) *dwlt: hld up: rdn over 2f out: wknd over 1f out* **9/2**[1]
0541 12 nse **Chosen One (IRE)**[8] 4005 9-9-10 **61** 6ex JamesSullivan 10 34
(Ruth Carr) *led tl rdn and wknd over 1f out* **6/1**[3]

59.09s (-0.31) **Going Correction** -0.10s/f (Good)
**WFA** 3 from 4yo+ 5lb 12 Ran SP% **115.8**
Speed ratings (Par 101): **98,97,97,96,95 93,93,92,90,89 82,81**
CSF £92.02 CT £788.86 TOTE £21.30: £6.20, £1.20, £3.70; EX 108.80 Trifecta £2144.10.
**Owner** Ken McGarrity **Bred** Theakston Stud **Trained** East Kilbride, S Lanarks

**FOCUS**
A modest handicap in which Linda Perratt trained the first, third and fourth.

## 4258 INSTABET APP ONLY AT BETVICTOR H'CAP 7f 50y
**5:00** (5:02) (Class 4) (0-85,86) 3-Y-O+ £5,498 (£1,636; £817; £408) Stalls High

Form RPR
1200 1 **Escape To Glory (USA)**[19] 3573 6-10-0 **82** PaulMulrennan 4 90
(Michael Dods) *hld up in tch: rdn and hdwy to ld over 1f out: kpt on wl fnl f* **6/1**
2003 2 1 **Powerful Presence (IRE)**[7] 4013 8-10-0 **82** (v[1]) DanielTudhope 3 86
(David O'Meara) *dwlt: t.k.h: sn trcking ldrs: edgd lft and ev ch over 1f out: sn rdn: kpt on same pce wl ins fnl f* **6/1**
3041 3 shd **Silver Rime (FR)**[7] 4013 9-10-1 **86** 6ex ConnorBeasley(3) 1 90
(Linda Perratt) *hld up: rdn over 3f out: hdwy over 1f out: kpt on ins fnl f: nrst fin* **9/1**
6-63 4 ¾ **Gatepost (IRE)**[17] 3646 5-10-0 **82** PJMcDonald 7 84
(Richard Fahey) *prom: drvn and outpcd over 2f out: kpt on fnl f: nvr able to chal* **9/2**[2]
-200 5 2 ¾ **Circuitous**[19] 3573 6-9-12 **80** (v) TomEaves 2 75
(Keith Dalgleish) *led: rdn and hdd over 1f out: wknd ins fnl f* **13/2**
2444 6 ½ **King Of Macedon (IRE)**[10] 3910 3-9-0 **76** (b) JoeFanning 5 67
(Mark Johnston) *t.k.h: pressed ldr: rdn over 2f out: carried hd high and wknd over 1f out* **3/1**[1]
512 7 nk **Order Of Service**[8] 4001 4-9-3 **71** GrahamLee 6 64
(Jim Goldie) *hld up in tch: drvn and outpcd over 2f out: n.d after* **11/2**[3]

1m 30.85s (-2.55) **Going Correction** -0.10s/f (Good)
**WFA** 3 from 4yo+ 8lb 7 Ran SP% **110.5**
Speed ratings (Par 105): **110,108,108,107,104 104,103**
CSF £38.21 TOTE £6.60: £3.00, £2.70; EX 52.00 Trifecta £432.70.
**Owner** Pearson, Lamb, Wynn Williams **Bred** Castleton Lyons **Trained** Denton, Co Durham

**FOCUS**
A useful handicap run at a good pace.

## 4259 PLAY ROULETTE & BLACKJACK AT BETVICTOR.COM APPRENTICE H'CAP 1m 5f 13y
**5:30** (5:30) (Class 6) (0-65,63) 4-Y-O+ £2,045 (£603; £302) Stalls Low

Form RPR
3154 1 **Eilean Mor**[7] 4014 6-8-13 **50** MeganCarberry 4 59
(R Mike Smith) *hld up in tch: hdwy to ld over 2f out: sn hrd pressed: edgd lft over 1f out: kpt on wl fnl f: all out* **5/1**[2]
364 2 nse **Wor Lass**[18] 3602 6-8-10 **50** LukeLeadbitter(3) 12 58
(Iain Jardine) *hld up in midfield: hdwy to chal over 2f out: kpt on fnl f: jst hld* **9/1**
0501 3 1 ¾ **Rainford Glory (IRE)**[10] 3912 4-9-8 **59** SammyJoBell 5 64
(Richard Fahey) *t.k.h: trckd ldrs: effrt over 2f out: kpt on ins fnl f* **3/1**[1]
/6-4 4 2 ½ **Hunting Tower**[18] 3605 10-9-9 **63** (t) SeanCorby(3) 8 65
(J J Lambe, Ire) *hld up: rdn over 3f out: hdwy over 1f out: nvr able to chal* **7/1**[3]
4343 5 nk **Grand Diamond (IRE)**[7] 4015 10-9-2 **53** JordanNason 11 54
(Jim Goldie) *stdd in rr: t.k.h: effrt and pushed along over 2f out: kpt on fnl f: nvr able to chal* **7/1**[3]
6034 6 ¾ **Captain Rhyric**[18] 3623 5-8-8 **45** JackGarritty 7 45
(James Moffatt) *led 2f: cl up: led over 3f out to over 2f out: outpcd over 1f out* **12/1**
0540 7 ¾ **Saddlers Mot**[23] 3482 10-9-7 **58** GemmaTutty 1 57
(Karen Tutty) *midfield: effrt and drvn over 2f out: no imp fr over 1f out* **18/1**
5-06 8 1 **Vittachi**[52] 2515 7-9-0 **56** (p) RowanScott(5) 13 53
(Alistair Whillans) *midfield: drvn along over 2f out: outpcd wl over 1f out* **8/1**
-006 9 5 **Jebulani**[18] 3605 4-8-8 **45** JoeDoyle 3 35
(Barry Murtagh) *cl up: led after 2f to over 3f out: rdn and wknd over 2f out* **20/1**
4-00 10 11 **Mystical King**[33] 3103 4-8-3 **45** JoshDoyle(5) 6 18
(Linda Perratt) *trckd ldrs tl rdn and wknd over 2f out* **33/1**
4500 11 3 ¼ **Stormy Morning**[49] 2620 8-9-1 **52** (p) RobJFitzpatrick 2 20
(Philip Kirby) *s.i.s: hld up: struggling over 3f out: sn btn* **20/1**
0-65 12 8 **Inniscastle Boy**[35] 3052 5-8-1 **45** RachaelGrant(7) 9
(Jim Goldie) *hld up on outside: rdn and struggling over 3f out: sn btn* **18/1**

2m 54.58s (0.58) **Going Correction** -0.10s/f (Good) 12 Ran SP% **118.5**
Speed ratings (Par 101): **94,93,92,91,91 90,90,89,86,79 77,72**
CSF £48.14 CT £159.72 TOTE £4.90: £1.60, £3.60, £1.70; EX 49.80 Trifecta £482.50.
**Owner** R Michael Smith **Bred** Triple H Stud Ltd **Trained** Galston, E Ayrshire
■ Stewards' Enquiry : Luke Leadbitter two-day ban: careless riding (28-29 Jul); two-day ban: use of whip (31 Jul & 1st Aug)

**FOCUS**
A modest staying handicap.
T/Plt: £96.50 to a £1 stake. Pool: £65,366.15 - 494.45 winning units. T/Qpdt: £32.10 to a £1 stake. Pool: £6165.44 - 141.82 winning units. RY

# 4079 LINGFIELD (L-H)
Monday, July 14

**OFFICIAL GOING: Standard**
Wind: light, half behind Weather: dry and warm

## 4260 RACING SPECIALS AT 32REDSPORT.COM MAIDEN AUCTION STKS 6f 1y(P)
**5:50** (5:51) (Class 5) 2-Y-O £2,911 (£866; £432; £216) Stalls Low

Form RPR
264 1 **The Dapper Tapper (IRE)**[10] 3934 2-8-13 **0** SilvestreDeSousa 1 68
(Eve Johnson Houghton) *broke fast: mde all: rdn wl over 1f out: r.o wl u.p: holding runner-up cl home* **3/1**[2]
4 2 hd **Bannister Bell (IRE)**[14] 3779 2-8-10 **0** DeclanBates(3) 7 67
(David Evans) *w wnr thrght: rdn 2f out: drvn over 1f out: r.o u.p: hld towards fin* **20/1**

0 **3** 1 **Cartmell Cleave**[19] 3584 2-8-13 0...................................... LukeMorris 4 64
(Stuart Kittow) *s.i.s: racd off the pce in midfield: hdwy over 2f out: swtchd rt and drvn to chse ldng pair over 1f out: clsd u.p 1f out: no imp fnl 100yds* **10/1**

**4** 1 1/2 **Willow Creek** 2-8-12 0...................................... JimCrowley 2 59
(William Haggas) *chsd ldrs: rdn and effrt in 3rd 2f out: 4th and outpcd over 1f out: styd on same pce after* **11/10**[1]

**5** 1/2 **Lady Maesmor** 2-8-7 0 ow1...................................... JohnFahy 8 52
(Martyn Meade) *s.i.s: bhd: clsd over 2f out: rdn and hdwy on inner over 1f out: kpt on ins fnl f: nvr trbld ldrs* **10/1**

0 **6** 3 1/2 **White Vin Jan**[44] 2771 2-8-10 0...................................... TomQueally 5 45
(Michael Bell) *chsd ldrs: 4th and rdn whn wd bnd 2f out and lost pl: wknd 1f out* **9/2**[3]

**7** 6 **Dark Symphony (IRE)** 2-7-13 0...................... CharlotteJenner(7) 6 23
(Mark Usher) *racd off the pce in midfield: rdn and effrt on outer over 2f out: struggling 2f out: sn wknd* **66/1**

**8** 6 **Snappy Mann** 2-8-11 0...................................... ChrisCatlin 3 10
(Willie Musson) *racd off the pce in midfield: dropped to rr and struggling over 2f out: lost tch over 1f out* **33/1**

1m 12.78s (0.88) **Going Correction** 0.0s/f (Stan) **8** Ran SP% **118.2**
Speed ratings (Par 94): **94,93,92,90,89 85,77,69**
CSF £59.41 TOTE £3.70: £1.30, £3.30, £3.70; EX 20.30 Trifecta £140.80.
**Owner** C Whichelow, D Smith & I Mavroleon **Bred** J McCabe **Trained** Blewbury, Oxon

**FOCUS**
Not much strength to this maiden which was run at a sound pace. It paid to race handy. The winner has been rated back to his debut effort.

## 4261 BET NOW AT 32REDSPORT.COM H'CAP 1m 5f (P)
**6:20** (6:21) (Class 6) (0-60,60) 3-Y-O **£2,264** (£673; £336; £168) **Stalls** Low

Form RPR
-005 **1** **Windshield**[13] 3819 3-9-2 **55**...................................... LukeMorris 7 63
(Sir Mark Prescott Bt) *chsd ldr: rdn ent fnl 2f: drvn over 1f out: styd on u.p to ld fnl 100yds: rdn out* **3/1**[1]

0602 **2** 3/4 **Rock Of Leon**[33] 3120 3-8-9 **48**...................................... TomQueally 3 54
(Michael Bell) *t.k.h: hld up wl in tch in midfield: nt clr run over 2f out: rdn to chse ldng pair jst over 2f out: styd on u.p ins fnl f: wnt 2nd towards fin* **4/1**[2]

6165 **3** 1/2 **Chesil Beach**[19] 3567 3-8-13 **59**...................................... RobHornby(7) 8 64
(Andrew Balding) *hld up in tch in midfield: clsd and nt clr run over 2f out: swtchd rt and effrt over 1f out: styd on wl ins fnl f: wnt 3rd nr fin* **8/1**[3]

-024 **4** 3/4 **Maid Of Tuscany (IRE)**[19] 3567 3-8-12 **58**............ CharlotteJenner(7) 1 62
(Mark Usher) *dwlt: sn rcvrd to ld: rdn 2f out: hdd fnl 100yds: no ex: wknd and lost 2 pls towards fin* **8/1**[3]

0000 **5** 2 1/4 **Dark Tsarina (IRE)**[13] 3819 3-8-4 **50**..................(v[1]) KieranShoemark(7) 4 51
(Michael Madgwick) *hld up in tch in midfield: hdwy and n.m.r over 2f out: 4th and drvn over 1f out: no imp: wknd ins fnl f* **50/1**

0054 **6** 3 1/2 **Telegraphy (USA)**[33] 3098 3-9-7 **60**...................................... OisinMurphy 6 55
(Ed Dunlop) *s.i.s: in rr: rdn 3f out: wnt 6th but stl plenty to do 2f out: no imp: n.d* **3/1**[1]

6000 **7** 5 **Harlequin Jinks**[25] 3407 3-8-7 **46** oh1...................................... RobertHavlin 9 34
(Mark Usher) *in tch in last trio: reminders 8f out: hdwy to chse ldrs 7f out: rdn over 3f out: wknd 2f out* **50/1**

-004 **8** 6 **Acquaint (IRE)**[9] 3950 3-9-1 **54**...................................... JimCrowley 2 33
(John Wainwright) *chsd ldrs: rdn over 3f out: lost u.p over 2f out: wknd 2f out* **10/1**

4200 **9** 12 **Flying Author (IRE)**[25] 3391 3-8-7 **46** oh1................ SilvestreDeSousa 5 7
(Phil McEntee) *hld up in last pair: rdn over 3f out: sn struggling: wl bhd 2f out: t.o* **8/1**[3]

2m 46.81s (0.81) **Going Correction** 0.0s/f (Stan) **9** Ran SP% **116.3**
Speed ratings (Par 98): **97,96,96,95,94 92,89,85,78**
CSF £15.20 CT £85.30 TOTE £3.30: £1.60, £1.10, £2.50; EX 17.70 Trifecta £77.30.
**Owner** Cheveley Park Stud **Bred** Cheveley Park Stud Ltd **Trained** Newmarket, Suffolk

**FOCUS**
A modest staying handicap run at a steady pace.

## 4262 32RED CASINO H'CAP 6f 1y(P)
**6:50** (6:50) (Class 4) (0-80,80) 3-Y-O+ **£5,175** (£1,540; £769; £384) **Stalls** Low

Form RPR
10 **1** **Dinneratmidnight**[59] 2317 3-9-6 **80**...................................... JimCrowley 8 88+
(Ralph Beckett) *chsd ldr tl over 4f out: styd chsng ldrs: rdn and effrt over 1f out: led jst ins fnl f: r.o wl* **3/1**[2]

6000 **2** 3/4 **Al's Memory (IRE)**[83] 1630 5-9-1 **72**...................................... DeclanBates(3) 5 79
(David Evans) *in tch in midfield: rdn and effrt wl over 1f out: styd on wl u.p ins fnl f: wnt 2nd last strides* **16/1**

1023 **3** nk **Putin (IRE)**[7] 4024 6-9-1 **69**...................................(bt) LukeMorris 1 75
(Phil McEntee) *led tl 4f out: chsd ldr after: rdn and ev ch over 1f out: led 1f out: sn hdd: kpt on one pce after: lost 2nd last strides* **8/1**[3]

6503 **4** 1 **Thataboy (IRE)**[21] 3522 3-8-8 **75**...................................(tp) JennyPowell(7) 7 77
(Tom Dascombe) *in tch in midfield: effrt and rdr dropped whip over 1f out: hdwy to chse ldrs ins fnl f: kpt on same pce fnl 100yds* **10/1**

-200 **5** hd **Kinglami**[39] 2919 5-9-4 **79**...................................(p) KieranShoemark(7) 3 81
(Brian Gubby) *hld up in tch in rr of main gp: rdn and effrt on outer wl over 1f out: styd on wl u.p ins fnl f: nt rch ldrs* **8/1**[3]

3224 **6** nk **Drive On (IRE)**[117] 1013 3-9-6 **80**...................................(p) SilvestreDeSousa 4 80
(Eve Johnson Houghton) *in tch in midfield: hdwy to chse ldrs over 3f out: rdn and ev ch over 1f out: no ex jst ins fnl f: wknd towards fin* **11/4**[1]

4464 **7** 1 **Honey Meadow**[12] 3855 3-8-6 **66**...................................... ChrisCatlin 2 63
(Robert Eddery) *in tch in midfield: effrt u.p over 1f out: kpt on but no real imp fnl f* **8/1**[3]

0225 **8** 4 1/2 **Outbacker (IRE)**[9] 3956 3-8-11 **74**...................................(b) MichaelJMMurphy(3) 9 57+
(Mark Johnston) *s.i.s: grad rcvrd and hdwy on outer to ld 4f out: rdn 2f out: hdd 1f out: sn btn and fdd ins fnl f* **8/1**[3]

0 **9** 6 **Zarliman (IRE)**[12] 3861 4-9-7 **75**...................................... TomQueally 6 39
(Martyn Meade) *s.i.s: a outpcd in detached last* **10/1**

1m 11.28s (-0.62) **Going Correction** 0.0s/f (Stan)
**WFA** 3 from 4yo+ 6lb **9** Ran SP% **120.2**
Speed ratings (Par 105): **104,103,102,101,101 100,99,93,85**
CSF £51.93 CT £361.65 TOTE £5.10: £1.50, £6.10, £1.70; EX 81.50 Trifecta £1491.80 Part won..
**Owner** The Rat Pack Partnership **Bred** Bumble Bloodstock Ltd **Trained** Kimpton, Hants

**FOCUS**
They went a sound pace for this fair handicap.

## 4263 32RED H'CAP 7f 1y(P)
**7:20** (7:20) (Class 5) (0-75,74) 3-Y-O **£2,911** (£866; £432; £216) **Stalls** Low

Form RPR
-405 **1** **Marmarus**[16] 3709 3-8-4 **60**...................................... RyanTate(3) 8 67
(Clive Cox) *hld up in tch in midfield: hdwy on outer over 2f out: 3rd and edgd lft u.p over 1f out: drvn and str run fnl 100yds to ld nr fin* **12/1**

1220 **2** 1/2 **Chantrea (IRE)**[70] 2024 3-9-2 **72**...................................... AshleyMorgan(3) 9 77
(Lady Cecil) *chsd ldr: rdn to chal wl over 1f out: led ent fnl f: kpt on u.p tl hdd and no ex nr fin* **7/1**

1-00 **3** 1 **Giant Samurai (USA)**[18] 3625 3-9-5 **72**...................................... RaulDaSilva 4 74
(John Quinn) *led: rdn wl over 1f out: drvn and hdd ent fnl f: styd pressing ldr tl no ex and wknd towards fin* **14/1**

415- **4** 1/2 **Punk**[311] 6170 3-9-5 **72**......................................[1] DaneO'Neill 1 73
(George Peckham) *s.i.s: hld up in tch in rr: hdwy u.p on outer to chse ldng trio jst over 1f out: kpt on: nt rch ldrs* **20/1**

2-52 **5** hd **Half Way**[21] 3518 3-8-11 **69**...................................... AmyScott(5) 6 69+
(Henry Candy) *t.k.h: hld up in tch in midfield: swtchd rt and effrt over 1f out: kpt on wl u.p ins fnl f: nt rch ldrs* **7/2**[2]

4261 **6** 2 **Tyrsal (IRE)**[18] 3627 3-8-11 **71**...................................... KieranShoemark(7) 7 66
(Robert Eddery) *t.k.h: chsd ldng trio: rdn and unable qck wl over 1f out: wknd ins fnl f* **8/1**

6145 **7** 3 1/4 **Thanks Harry**[49] 2624 3-9-7 **74**...................................... GeorgeBaker 2 61+
(Gary Moore) *hld up in tch towards rr: effrt but plenty to do whn forced to swtchd rt wl over 1f out: no imp* **2/1**[1]

5600 **8** 1/2 **Crafty Business (IRE)**[33] 3114 3-8-12 **65**...................................... RobertHavlin 3 50
(Mark Hoad) *chsd ldrs tl rdn and unable qck 2f out: wknd fnl f* **33/1**

00-4 **9** 3 **Shaft Of Light**[17] 3677 3-8-9 **62**...................................... LukeMorris 5 40+
(Sir Mark Prescott Bt) *s.i.s: rdn along thrght: in tch towards rr: wd and struggling bnd wl over 1f out: bhd fnl f* **6/1**[3]

1m 25.64s (0.84) **Going Correction** 0.0s/f (Stan) **9** Ran SP% **115.5**
Speed ratings (Par 100): **95,94,93,92,92 90,86,85,82**
CSF £92.95 CT £1202.93 TOTE £17.10: £7.80, £2.80, £2.80; EX 101.00 Trifecta £1144.80.
**Owner** Ms Gillian Khosla **Bred** Vimal And Gillian Khosla **Trained** Lambourn, Berks

**FOCUS**
An open 3yo handicap run at a steady pace. Again it paid to race handy.

## 4264 32RED.COM CLASSIFIED CLAIMING STKS 1m 4f (P)
**7:50** (7:50) (Class 6) 3-Y-O+ **£2,264** (£673; £336; £168) **Stalls** Low

Form RPR
5043 **1** **Elegant Ophelia**[32] 3155 5-9-4 57...................................(t) GeorgeBaker 5 65
(Dean Ivory) *hld up in tch in midfield: clsd to trck ldrs 4f out: wnt 2nd jst over 2f out: rdn to ld over 1f and sn clr: r.o: comf* **3/1**[1]

2224 **2** 5 **Litmus (USA)**[13] 3824 5-9-6 55...................................(b) HayleyTurner 9 59
(Simon Dow) *led after 1f: rdn over 2f out: hdd and brushed aside by wnr over 1f out: no ch w wnr but battled on to hold 2nd fnl f* **8/1**

3054 **3** nk **Cabuchon (GER)**[4] 4107 7-9-0 60...................................(t) DeclanBates(3) 8 56
(David Evans) *in tch in midfield: niggled along 9f out: effrt and wl in tch over 2f out: short of room bnd 2f out: rallied and styd on wl ins fnl f: wnt 3rd last strides* **7/2**[2]

3-06 **4** nk **Green Earth (IRE)**[20] 3553 7-8-13 57...................................... JemmaMarshall(3) 1 54
(Pat Phelan) *s.i.s: in tch in midfield: clsd to chse ldrs over 2f out: 3rd and one pce u.p over 1f out: kpt on: lost 3rd cl home* **16/1**

0602 **5** 3/4 **Illegale (IRE)**[16] 3710 8-9-4 43...................................(bt) OisinMurphy 7 55
(Nikki Evans) *stdd s: t.k.h: hld up in tch towards rr: clsd and n.m.r jst over 2f out: rdn over 1f out: no ch w wnr but kpt on u.p fnl f* **25/1**

0644 **6** 1 1/4 **Ice Tres**[19] 3585 5-9-4 51...................................(p) RobertHavlin 4 53
(Rod Millman) *chsd ldrs: wnt 2nd over 3f out tl jst over 2f out: drvn and unable qck over 1f out: wknd fnl f* **8/1**

/00- **7** 1 1/4 **Rock Band**[307] 6283 5-9-5 50...................................(t) LukeMorris 10 52
(Emmet Michael Butterly, Ire) *in tch in midfield: clsd over 3f out: rdn and effrt ent fnl 2f: outpcd and btn over 1f out: wknd fnl f* **8/1**

5620 **8** 1 **Sutton Sid**[19] 3576 4-8-10 60...................................(vt) DavidParkes(7) 3 48
(Ann Stokell) *s.i.s: rdn along in detached last: clsd to rr of field 7f out: outpcd u.p over 2f out: wl hld after* **9/2**[3]

-043 **9** 13 **Red Willow**[16] 3710 8-9-1 42...................................(p) MichaelJMMurphy(3) 2 28
(John E Long) *led for 1f: chsd ldrs: wnt 2nd 4f out: sn u.p and lost pl: bhd over 1f out* **50/1**

0-10 **10** 7 **Until The Man (IRE)**[102] 1012 7-9-5 49...................................(b) IrineuGoncalves 11 18
(Natalie Lloyd-Beavis) *t.k.h: hdwy to chse ldr after 1f tl 4f out: sn dropped out and bhd: t.o over 1f out* **33/1**

00-0 **11** 17 **Iceman George**[13] 3309 10-8-12 52...................................(v) TimClark(5) 6
(Denis Quinn) *a towards rr: drvn and dropped to last 5f out: lost tch and t.o fnl 3f* **25/1**

2m 30.45s (-2.55) **Going Correction** 0.0s/f (Stan) **11** Ran SP% **117.2**
Speed ratings (Par 101): **108,104,104,104,103 102,102,101,92,88 76**
CSF £26.41 TOTE £4.00: £1.50, £1.40, £1.90; EX 24.70 Trifecta £112.20.
**Owner** World Freight Consultants Ltd **Bred** Newsells Park Stud **Trained** Radlett, Herts

**FOCUS**
The pace was steady for this modest claimer.

## 4265 32RED ON THE APP STORE MEDIAN AUCTION MAIDEN STKS 1m 2f (P)
**8:20** (8:21) (Class 6) 3-4-Y-O **£2,264** (£673; £336; £168) **Stalls** Low

Form RPR
32 **1** **Old Guard**[21] 3537 3-9-3 0...................................... GeorgeBaker 3 78+
(Roger Charlton) *t.k.h: chsd ldr for 2f: styd chsng ldrs: wnt 2nd again over 2f out: rdn 2f out: 3rd and sltly outpcd over 1f out: rallied u.p ins fnl f: styd on to ld last strides* **10/11**[1]

3 **2** hd **Tabjeel**[27] 3332 3-9-3 0...................................... DaneO'Neill 2 76+
(Saeed bin Suroor) *t.k.h: hld up in tch in midfield: hdwy to chse ldng pair over 2f out: rdn and qcknd to ld on inner ent fnl f: hung lft 1f out: drvn fnl 150yds: hdd last strides* **9/4**[2]

3 **3** hd **Kicking The Can (IRE)**[21] 3525 3-9-3 0...................................... RobertHavlin 9 75
(Peter Chapple-Hyam) *led: rdn ent fnl 2f: drvn: hdd and sltly outpcd ent fnl f: kpt on u.p fnl 100yds* **7/2**[3]

**4** 12 **Numrood** 3-9-3 0...................................... LukeMorris 5 52
(George Peckham) *hld up in tch in midfield: rdn and outpcd over 2f out: wnt modest 4th wl over 1f out: no imp* **16/1**

0 **5** 1 3/4 **Perfect Outcome**[29] 3276 3-8-9 0...................................... RyanTate(3) 1 43
(Patrick Chamings) *hld up towards rr: rdn over 3f out: sme hdwy past btn horses over 2f out: wnt modest 5th over 1f out: n.d* **50/1**

0 **6** 4 **Byronegetonefree**[37] 2996 3-9-0 0...................... MichaelJMMurphy(3) 4 41
(John E Long) *chsd ldrs: wnt 2nd 8f out tl rn green u.p over 2f out: 4th and btn 2f out: sn wknd* **66/1**

00U **7** *2 1/4* **Slunovrat (FR)**[40] 2883 3-9-0 0 RobertTart(3) 6 37
(David Menuisier) *in tch in midfield: pushed along 7f out: rdn and outpcd over 3f out: n.d after* **66/1**

**8** *1 1/2* **Deftera Fantutte (IRE)** 3-8-9 0 JemmaMarshall(3) 8 29
(Pat Phelan) *chsd ldrs: rdn and btn 3f out: sn wknd* **66/1**

0-5 **9** *2 3/4* **Born To Reign**[118] 1002 3-9-3 0 TomQueally 10 29
(Michael Bell) *s.i.s: pushed along in last pair thrght: lost tch 3f out* **25/1**

05 **10** *8* **Arryzona**[14] 3796 3-9-3 0 AdamBeschizza 7 13
(Christine Dunnett) *s.i.s: nvr gng wl in rr thrght: lost tch over 3f out: t.o* **66/1**

2m 5.91s (-0.69) **Going Correction** 0.0s/f (Stan) **10** Ran SP% **123.0**
Speed ratings (Par 101): **102,101,101,92,90 87,85,84,82,75**
CSF £3.34 TOTE £1.80: £1.10, £1.20, £1.80; EX 4.10 Trifecta £7.90.
**Owner** Lady Rothschild **Bred** The Rt Hon Lord Rothschild **Trained** Beckhampton, Wilts

**FOCUS**
An uncompetitive maiden run at a steady pace. The front three fought out a thrilling finish.

## 4266 ALL NEW 32REDSPORT.COM H'CAP 1m 1y(P)
8:50 (8:51) (Class 6) (0-60,60) 3-Y-0+ £2,264 (£673; £336; £84; £84) Stalls High

Form RPR

4362 **1** **Cyflymder (IRE)**[6] 4055 8-9-2 **50** OisinMurphy 1 60
(David C Griffiths) *mde all: rdn and qcknd clr over 1f out: in command fnl f: rdn out* **4/1**[1]

5005 **2** *1 1/4* **Plough Boy (IRE)**[25] 3389 3-9-2 **59** ChrisCatlin 2 64
(Willie Musson) *t.k.h: chsd ldng trio: rdn and effrt over 1f out: hdwy to chse clr wnr and shifted lft jst ins fnl f: r.o but no threat to wnr* **4/1**[1]

-300 **3** *1 1/4* **Orders From Rome (IRE)**[32] 3160 5-9-12 **60** (t[1]) DaneO'Neill 7 65
(Charlie Fellowes) *nt best away: pushed along and sn rcvrd to r in midfield: effrt: swtchd rt and nt clr run 1f out: swtchd further rt and hdwy jst ins fnl f: r.o* **14/1**

0534 **4** *1 3/4* **Greek Islands (IRE)**[6] 4056 6-9-7 **55** TomQueally 4 55
(Edward Creighton) *chsd ldrs: rdn and unable qck over 1f out: wl hld and kpt on same pce ins fnl f* **8/1**[3]

4-00 **4** *dht* **Squirrel Wood (IRE)**[21] 3528 6-9-7 **55** GeorgeBaker 3 56
(Mary Hambro) *chsd ldr: rdn and unable qck over 1f out: lost 2nd and hmpd ins fnl f: wl hld and kpt on same pce after* **12/1**

6000 **6** *1* **Divine Rule (IRE)**[19] 3576 6-9-10 **58** (v) AmirQuinn 8 56
(Laura Mongan) *hld up in tch in midfield: effrt u.p over 1f out: styd on ins fnl f: no threat to wnr* **25/1**

4355 **7** *1/2* **Warbond**[19] 3576 6-9-7 **55** (b) LukeMorris 11 52+
(Michael Madgwick) *dwlt: in tch in last trio: effrt towards inner 2f out: sme hdwy and swtchd rt 1f out: kpt on: nvr trbld ldrs* **4/1**[1]

0304 **8** *1* **Bold Ring**[6] 4055 8-9-1 **56** CharlotteJenner(7) 12 50+
(Edward Creighton) *hld up in tch in last trio: swtchd rt and effrt over 1f out: kpt on: nvr trbld ldrs* **20/1**

630/ **9** *2 3/4* **Cahala Dancer (IRE)**[751] 3392 6-9-1 **49** LiamKeniry 10 37
(Roger Teal) *t.k.h: hld up in tch but stuck wd: rdn and hung lft over 1f out: no hdwy and wl hld fnl f: eased cl home* **33/1**

2563 **10** *2 1/4* **Happydoingnothing**[25] 3389 3-9-2 **59** (p) AdamBeschizza 9 40
(Christine Dunnett) *hld up in tch in last trio but stuck wd: rdn over 2f out: no prog and wd bnd 2f out: wl hld after* **10/1**

0540 **11** *nk* **Greensward**[27] 3327 8-9-12 **60** (p) HayleyTurner 5 42
(Conor Dore) *in tch in midfield: rdn and outpcd wl over 1f out: wknd over 1f out* **5/1**[2]

1m 38.08s (-0.12) **Going Correction** 0.0s/f (Stan)
**WFA** 3 from 5yo+ 9lb **11** Ran SP% **122.8**
Speed ratings (Par 101): **100,98,97,95,95 94,94,93,90,88 87**
CSF £20.10 CT £214.63 TOTE £6.40: £1.90, £2.20, £4.60; EX 24.80 Trifecta £566.50.
**Owner** Shaun Humphries & Eros Bloodstock **Bred** Miss Laura G F Ferguson **Trained** Bawtry, S Yorks

**FOCUS**
They went an honest pace for this open handicap. Again the prominent runners were favoured.
T/Plt: £73.60 to a £1 stake. Pool: £68,461.82 - 678.47 winning units. T/Qpdt: £14.60 to a £1 stake. Pool: £7204.65 - 364.10 winning units. SP

# [4024] WINDSOR (R-H)
### Monday, July 14

**OFFICIAL GOING: Good to firm (8.3)**
Wind: Moderate, behind Weather: Fine becoming cloudy, very warm

## 4267 MECCABINGO.COM APPRENTICE H'CAP 5f 10y
6:00 (6:00) (Class 5) (0-75,75) 3-Y-0+ £2,587 (£770; £384; £192) Stalls Low

Form RPR

3442 **1** **Dark Lane**[3] 4151 8-8-9 **60** HollieDoyle(4) 7 68
(David Evans) *chsd ldrs: rdn over 1f out: swtchd between rivals and r.o to ld ins fnl f: styd on* **7/2**[2]

6154 **2** *1/2* **Whitecrest**[10] 3920 6-9-10 **71** PhilipPrince 8 77
(John Spearing) *chsd clr ldng pair: rdn over 1f out: styd on to take 2nd wl ins fnl f: a hld* **8/1**

-000 **3** *1/2* **Tidal's Baby**[30] 3246 5-10-0 **75** GeorgeDowning 4 79
(Tony Carroll) *s.s: sn in tch in last pair: prog and rdn towards outer wl over 1f out: cl up 1f out: styd on same pce* **4/1**[3]

32-3 **4** *1/2* **Joyous**[191] 53 4-8-12 **63** PaulBooth(4) 1 65
(Dean Ivory) *pressed ldr: urged along to try to chal over 1f out: nt qckn and lost 2nd jst ins fnl f* **8/1**

3051 **5** *shd* **The Dandy Yank (IRE)**[9] 3972 3-9-8 **74** (p) CamHardie 2 74
(Jamie Osborne) *led towards nr side rail: rdn over 1f out: hdd and no ex ins fnl f* **11/4**[1]

666 **6** *1 1/2* **Valmina**[91] 1489 7-9-11 **72** (t) LouisSteward 6 69
(Tony Carroll) *hld up and sn in last: stl there over 1f out: shkn up and sme prog on outer sn after: one pce fnl f* **8/1**

022 **7** *1/2* **First In Command (IRE)**[10] 3921 9-9-11 **72** (t) EoinWalsh 5 67
(Daniel Mark Loughnane) *in tch: rdn 2f out: tried to cl on inner over 1f out: keeping on whn nt clr run jst ins fnl f: no ch after* **10/1**

00 **8** *3/4* **Triple Dream**[23] 3470 9-9-8 **71** (tp) RyanWhile(2) 9 63
(Milton Bradley) *chsd ldrs: pushed along and no prog 2f out: steadily lost pl fr over 1f out* **25/1**

58.84s (-1.46) **Going Correction** -0.25s/f (Firm)
**WFA** 3 from 4yo+ 5lb **8** Ran SP% **115.2**
Speed ratings (Par 103): **101,100,99,98,98 96,95,94**
CSF £31.62 CT £116.70 TOTE £4.30: £1.80, £2.10, £1.90; EX 32.00 Trifecta £338.70.
**Owner** Mrs E Evans & C W Racing **Bred** David Jamison Bloodstock **Trained** Pandy, Monmouths

**FOCUS**
Top bend dolled out 8yds from normal inner configuration adding 29yds to races of one mile and beyond. Inner of straight dolled out 5yds at 6f and 2yds at winning post. Dry overnight and quickening ground. Any number were in with a chance a furlong out.

## 4268 ARNOLD SANDERSON MEMORIAL (S) STKS 1m 2f 7y
6:30 (6:30) (Class 6) 3-4-Y-0 £1,940 (£577; £288; £144) Stalls Centre

Form RPR

003 **1** **Exclusive Contract (IRE)**[7] 4026 3-8-5 0 WilliamCarson 8 62
(Jamie Osborne) *trckd ldrs: n.m.r 7f out: prog and rdn to chse ldr 2f out: chal after: kpt on to ld last 75yds* **2/1**[1]

506 **2** *1/2* **Lindart (ITY)**[25] 3382 3-8-10 **48** (b[1]) SeanLevey 3 66
(Richard Hannon) *t.k.h: led 1f: stdd bhd ldrs: rdn to ld again over 2f out: kpt on u.p: worn down last 75yds* **20/1**

0-66 **3** *2 3/4* **Clodoaldo (IRE)**[9] 3978 3-8-7 **62** RyanClark(3) 4 61
(Brian Meehan) *rousted along early: led after 2f: rdn and hanging 3f out: hdd jst over 2f out: nt qckn after* **7/2**[3]

0 **4** *1 3/4* **Deja Bougg**[38] 2946 3-8-0 0 NoelGarbutt(5) 2 53
(David Evans) *taken down early: slowly away: mostly in last pair: rdn 3f out: n.d but plugged on fnl 2f* **40/1**

5003 **5** *2* **Haleo**[5] 4088 3-8-5 **65** (b[1]) CamHardie(5) 5 54
(William Muir) *wl in tch: rdn over 2f out: nt qckn and no imp after* **6/1**

25-0 **6** *9* **Hail To Princess**[81] 1664 4-9-2 **43** DavidProbert 1 32
(Patrick Chamings) *led after 1f tl after 2f: chsd ldr to 3f out: wknd u.p* **10/1**

543 **7** *6* **Stanlow**[13] 3824 4-9-12 **55** (v) ShaneKelly 6 30
(Daniel Mark Loughnane) *hld up in last: rdn over 3f out: no prog and wl btn 2f out: wknd* **3/1**[2]

2m 6.27s (-2.43) **Going Correction** -0.25s/f (Firm)
**WFA** 3 from 4yo 11lb **7** Ran SP% **111.1**
Speed ratings (Par 101): **99,98,96,95,93 86,81**
.Exclusive Contract was bought by Ollie Pears for £10,000. \n\x\x Clodoaldo was claimed by Mr P W Middleton for £6000
**Owner** J A Osborne **Bred** Pat Grogan **Trained** Upper Lambourn, Berks

**FOCUS**
Not a strong race, but a good battle between the first two.

## 4269 REUBEN FOUNDATION BRITISH STALLION STUDS EBF MAIDEN FILLIES' STKS (BOBIS RACE) 5f 10y
7:00 (7:03) (Class 5) 2-Y-0 £2,911 (£866; £432; £216) Stalls Low

Form RPR

3 **1** **War Alert (USA)**[35] 3063 2-9-0 0 JamieSpencer 10 78
(David Brown) *pressed ldr: led 2f out: drvn and hdd 1f out: kpt on wl to ld again nr fin* **5/2**[1]

4 **2** *1/2* **Disprove (IRE)**[17] 3671 2-8-9 0 NoelGarbutt(5) 15 76
(Hugo Palmer) *ponied to s: t.k.h: towards rr: prog on wd outside fr 1/2-way: urged along and clsd to ld 1f out: kpt on but hdd nr fin* **8/1**

**3** *1 3/4* **Effectual** 2-9-0 0 AndreaAtzeni 16 70
(Roger Varian) *t.k.h: hld up on outer but sn chsd ldrs: shkn up and on terms jst over 1f out: styd on same pce* **10/1**

32 **4** *1 1/4* **Robin Hill**[14] 3799 2-9-0 0 SamHitchcott 6 65
(William Muir) *led against nr side rail: hdd 2f out: steadily outpcd* **14/1**

**5** *1 1/4* **Renaissant** 2-9-0 0 RyanMoore 2 68+
(Richard Hannon) *rn v green in rr stl green but styd on fr jst over 1f out: nrst fin* **13/2**[3]

6 **6** *hd* **Emirates Challenge (IRE)**[43] 2800 2-9-0 0 HarryBentley 11 60
(Saeed bin Suroor) *s.i.s: in tch in rr: shkn up wl over 1f out: kpt on same pce: n.d* **14/1**

02 **7** *nse* **Artfilly (IRE)**[30] 3232 2-9-0 0 MartinHarley 14 60
(Ed Walker) *spd fr wd draw to chse ldng trio: shkn up and fdd over 1f out* **11/2**[2]

4 **8** *3/4* **Lady Kyllar**[63] 2220 2-9-0 0 KierenFallon 13 57
(George Margarson) *chsd ldrs but sn pushed along: no prog 2f out: steadily wknd* **16/1**

**9** *3* **Candlelight (IRE)** 2-9-0 0 WilliamBuick 5 46
(Charles Hills) *trckd ldrs: nudged along fr 2f out: steadily wknd* **20/1**

0 **10** *3 1/4* **Gen I Am**[11] 3888 2-9-0 0 SeanLevey 12 35
(Richard Hannon) *prom early: in rr by 1/2-way: no ch over 1f out* **50/1**

**11** *9* **Inspire** 2-9-0 0 DavidProbert 7
(Mark Usher) *rn green and a in rr: shied 1/2-way: wl bhd after* **100/1**

**12** *51* **Some Show** 2-9-0 0 FergusSweeney 4 +
(Henry Candy) *s.i.s: outpcd in last whn bdly hmpd 1/2-way: virtually p.u* **33/1**

4 **F** **Carrot Top**[51] 2557 2-9-0 0 RichardKingscote 8
(Ralph Beckett) *in tch in rr whn stmbld and fell 1/2-way* **8/1**

**B** **Star Fire** 2-9-0 0 JamesDoyle 3
(Roger Charlton) *wl in rr tl b.d 1/2-way* **12/1**

59.46s (-0.84) **Going Correction** -0.25s/f (Firm) **14** Ran SP% **126.2**
Speed ratings (Par 91): **96,95,92,90,88 88,88,86,82,76 62, , ,**
CSF £23.15 TOTE £3.00: £1.70, £2.70, £3.80; EX 26.80 Trifecta £270.50.
**Owner** Qatar Bloodstock Partnership **Bred** Highfield Farm **Trained** Averham Park, Notts

**FOCUS**
Several of the fancied runners in this maiden had double-figure draws, but the first three all overcame that handicap. It's been rated in line with the recent race average for now.

## 4270 BETDAQ £25 NO LOSE FREE BET EBF STALLION MAIDEN STKS 6f
7:30 (7:33) (Class 5) 2-Y-0 £2,911 (£866; £432; £216) Stalls Low

Form RPR

02 **1** **Heartbreak Hero**[18] 3626 2-9-5 0 RyanMoore 8 80+
(William Haggas) *mde all and racd against nr side rail: clr wl over 1f out: comf* **8/11**[1]

**2** *1 3/4* **Accra Beach (USA)** 2-9-5 0 JamesDoyle 16 77+
(Roger Charlton) *s.i.s: towards rr: abt 11th 1/2-way and off the pce: reminder and gd prog on outer fr 2f out: chsd wnr jst ins fnl f: styd on wl and shaped w promise* **8/1**[3]

**3** *2 3/4* **Carnival King (IRE)** 2-9-5 0 JimmyFortune 12 67+
(Brian Meehan) *towards rr: abt 10th 1/2-way and off the pce: pushed along and styd on steadily on outer fr 2f out: tk 3rd cl home* **33/1**

**4** *1/2* **Skate** 2-9-2 0 JoeyHaynes(3) 3 65+
(Roger Charlton) *towards rr: 9th and off the pce 1/2-way: shkn up and prog 2f out: styd on to take 4th nr fin* **33/1**

**5** *1 1/4* **Dunnscotia** 2-9-5 0 WilliamCarson 14 61
(Paul Webber) *prom: chsd wnr 1/2-way to jst ins fnl f: wknd* **66/1**

**6** *3/4* **Crafty Choice** 2-9-5 0 SeanLevey 5 60+
(Richard Hannon) *wl in rr: abt 14th 1/2-way and wl off the pce: pushed along and stdy prog fnl 2f: nrst fin* **8/1**[3]

0 **7** ½ **Classic Seniority**[7] 4025 2-9-5 0 PatDobbs 1 58
(Richard Hannon) *trckd ldrs on inner: pushed along in 3rd fr 2f out to 1f out: steadily fdd* **33/1**

0 **8** 1½ **Arthur's Way (IRE)**[11] 3889 2-9-5 0 MartinLane 10 53
(Paul Cole) *rousted early and sn chsd wnr: lost 2nd 1/2-way: steadily fdd fnl 2f* **66/1**

0 **9** 1 **Starlight June**[20] 3558 2-9-0 0 RichardKingscote 6 45
(Jonathan Portman) *chsd ldrs on inner lost pl 1/2-way but stl in tch: no prog fnl 2f* **66/1**

**10** nse **Hillgrove Angel (IRE)** 2-9-2 0 RyanClark(3) 15 50
(Brian Meehan) *s.i.s: wl in rr: in last quartet 1/2-way and wl off the pce: pushed along and kpt on fnl 2f: nt disgracd* **100/1**

6 **11** ¾ **Able Mate**[38] 2964 2-9-5 0 AdamKirby 13 48
(Clive Cox) *trckd ldrs and travelled wl to 1/2-way: pushed along and steadily wknd jst over 2f out* **6/1**[2]

**12** 1¾ **Snappy Guest** 2-9-5 0 KierenFallon 4 42
(George Margarson) *wl in rr: pushed along bef 1/2-way: sme prog 2f out: no hdwy fnl f* **33/1**

**13** hd **Commodore (IRE)** 2-9-5 0 PatCosgrave 7 42
(George Baker) *in tch in midfield: abt 7th 1/2-way: shkn up and steadily lost pl fr over 2f out* **33/1**

**14** 2 **Fast Dancer (IRE)** 2-9-5 0 JamieSpencer 2 36
(Joseph Tuite) *s.i.s: a wl in rr: no prog fnl 2f* **66/1**

**15** 1 **Sir Henry Raeburn (IRE)** 2-9-5 0 (t) MartinHarley 9 33
(Paul Cole) *prom early: lost pl and wknd fr 1/2-way* **12/1**

**16** 18 **Ocean Bentley (IRE)** 2-9-5 0 DavidProbert 11
(Tony Carroll) *s.i.s: a struggling and bhd: t.o* **100/1**

1m 11.76s (-1.24) **Going Correction** -0.25s/f (Firm) **16** Ran SP% **124.8**
Speed ratings (Par 94): **98,95,92,91,89 88,88,86,84,84 83,81,81,78,77 53**
CSF £6.72 TOTE £1.80: £1.10, £2.40, £4.90; EX 9.10 Trifecta £180.00.
**Owner** J C Smith **Bred** Mrs Johnny Eddis **Trained** Newmarket, Suffolk

**FOCUS**
This proved a straightforward task for the odds-on favourite. The form should be solid enough for the level, and might be a bit better.

## 4271 BETDAQ 3% COMMISSION FILLIES' H'CAP 1m 67y
8:00 (8:00) (Class 4) (0-80,80) 3-Y-O+ £5,175 (£1,540; £769; £384) Stalls Low

Form RPR

102 **1** **Rekdhat (IRE)**[33] 3117 3-9-5 **80** FrederikTylicki 12 90
(Roger Varian) *hld up towards rr: rdn and prog fr 3f out to press ldr 2f out: drvn to ld jst over 1f out: styd on wl* **6/1**[2]

-226 **2** 1 **Joys Of Spring (IRE)**[20] 3560 3-9-3 **78** AndreaAtzeni 9 86
(Luca Cumani) *trckd ldrs: prog gng wl 3f out: led jst over 2f out: drvn and hdd jst over 1f out: nt qckn* **5/1**[1]

5323 **3** 1¼ **Hedge End (IRE)**[5] 4074 3-9-2 **77** PatDobbs 5 82
(Richard Hannon) *settled in midfield: rdn over 2f out: prog to chse ldng pair jst over 1f out: styd on but no imp* **7/1**[3]

1-61 **4** hd **Rayoumti (IRE)**[15] 3760 3-9-0 **75** MartinHarley 11 80
(George Margarson) *hld up towards rr: eased off ins and prog over 2f out: rdn to take 4th fnl f: styd on to press for 3rd nr fin* **9/1**

3312 **5** 2 **Havelovewilltravel (IRE)**[96] 1393 4-9-12 **78** (p) RyanMoore 13 80
(Jeremy Noseda) *sltly awkward s: chsd ldr after 1f to over 2f out: outpcd fnl 2f* **5/1**[1]

5261 **6** 1 **Thankyou Very Much**[7] 4023 4-9-3 **69** 6ex (p) TedDurcan 7 69
(James Bethell) *awkward s: wl in rr: pushed along over 3f out: sme prog on outer over 2f out: no hdwy over 1f out* **17/2**

4-63 **7** ½ **Anya**[35] 3066 5-9-8 **74** FergusSweeney 3 73
(Henry Candy) *trckd ldng trio: rdn wl over 2f out: hanging and lost pl fr wl over 1f out* **16/1**

1550 **8** 1¼ **Al Manaal**[16] 3727 4-9-11 **80** CharlesBishop(3) 10 76
(Mick Channon) *hld up in last: rdn on wd outside over 2f out: no great prog* **33/1**

2006 **9** 3¼ **Flamborough Breeze**[16] 3733 5-9-1 **67** (t) WilliamCarson 14 55
(Ed Vaughan) *hld up in rr on outer: brief effrt 3f out: no prog 2f out: wknd* **25/1**

0442 **10** 2 **Alys Love**[15] 3755 3-9-2 77 DougieCostello 4 59
(William Muir) *t.k.h: trckd ldr 1f: prom tl wknd over 2f out* **16/1**

00-6 **11** 2½ **Celestial Bay**[11] 3887 5-9-1 **67** JimmyFortune 1 45
(Sylvester Kirk) *hld up in midfield: rdn and lost pl over 2f out: sn btn* **33/1**

-236 **12** ½ **Tullia (IRE)**[23] 3476 3-9-2 77 WilliamBuick 2 52
(William Knight) *led to jst over 2f out: wknd qckly* **5/1**[1]

1m 42.16s (-2.54) **Going Correction** -0.25s/f (Firm)
**WFA** 3 from 4yo+ 9lb **12** Ran SP% **118.8**
Speed ratings (Par 102): **102,101,99,99,97 96,96,94,91,89 87,86**
CSF £35.48 CT £218.75 TOTE £6.30: £2.10, £2.00, £2.60; EX 23.10 Trifecta £380.10.
**Owner** Sheikh Ahmed Al Maktoum **Bred** Darley **Trained** Newmarket, Suffolk

**FOCUS**
An open handicap.

## 4272 BETDAQ THE SPORTS BETTING EXCHANGE H'CAP (BOBIS RACE) 1m 3f 135y
8:30 (8:30) (Class 4) (0-85,85) 3-Y-O £5,175 (£1,540; £769; £384) Stalls Low

Form RPR

1242 **1** **Solidarity**[10] 3923 3-9-7 **85** WilliamBuick 2 93
(Charlie Appleby) *trckd ldng pair: wnt 2nd over 2f out: drvn to ld 1f out: styd on wl* **15/8**[1]

5103 **2** 1½ **Barye**[24] 3421 3-8-9 **73** JimCrowley 5 79
(David Simcock) *trckd ldr: led over 3f out: rdn and pressed 2f out: hdd 1f out: kpt on same pce* **6/1**

1-15 **3** 2½ **Tears Of The Sun**[17] 3644 3-9-3 **81** JamieSpencer 1 83
(Roger Varian) *hld up in last: prog to go 3rd wl over 1f out: drvn but nvr able to chal: one pce and eased nr fin* **9/4**[2]

-534 **4** 1 **Ganges (IRE)**[24] 3428 3-8-13 **77** AndreaAtzeni 3 77
(James Toller) *in tch in 4th: hanging and sharp reminders 4f out: sn outpcd and btn: kpt on fr over 1f out* **3/1**[3]

5512 **5** nk **Avocadeau (IRE)**[17] 3683 3-8-5 **69** (p) SamHitchcott 6 69
(William Muir) *led: tried to kick on 4f out but sn hdd: outpcd after: plugged on* **16/1**

2m 28.39s (-1.11) **Going Correction** -0.25s/f (Firm) **5** Ran SP% **110.7**
Speed ratings (Par 102): **93,92,90,89,89**
CSF £13.20 TOTE £3.20: £1.50, £3.00; EX 14.40 Trifecta £28.00.
**Owner** Godolphin **Bred** Darley **Trained** Newmarket, Suffolk

**FOCUS**
This was perhaps not as competitive as it had looked on paper.

## 4273 THYSSENKRUPP AEROSPACE CUP H'CAP 1m 2f 7y
9:00 (9:01) (Class 6) (0-65,71) 4-Y-O+ £1,940 (£577; £288; £144) Stalls Centre

Form RPR

5222 **1** **If I Were A Boy (IRE)**[4] 4105 7-9-2 **60** (p) JimCrowley 7 69
(Dominic Ffrench Davis) *sn trckd ldrs: rdn 3f out: prog u.p 2f out: chsd ldr 1f out: sustained chal to ld post* **7/2**[1]

0-61 **2** nse **Bertie Moon**[7] 4030 4-9-6 **71** 6ex PaddyPilley(7) 14 80
(Geoffrey Deacon) *trckd ldr: led 2f out: urged along and kpt on whn pressed fnl f: hdd post* **6/1**

2044 **3** 2½ **Highlife Dancer**[18] 3617 6-9-2 **63** (v) CharlesBishop(3) 13 67
(Mick Channon) *chsd ldrs in 5th: rdn 3f out: tried to cl 2f out: tk 3rd fnl f: unable to chal* **20/1**

-113 **4** nk **Megalala (IRE)**[54] 2464 13-9-5 **63** WilliamCarson 12 67
(John Bridger) *led: rdn 3f out: hdd 2f out: one pce after* **14/1**

5156 **5** nk **Bennelong**[11] 3878 8-9-2 **60** (b) StevieDonohoe 3 63
(Lee Carter) *chsd ldrs: rdn over 3f out: nt qckn and no imp 2f out: kpt on nr fin* **20/1**

01/0 **6** 1 **Casual Mover (IRE)**[30] 3226 6-9-7 **65** AdamKirby 8 66
(John Best) *hld up in midfield: rdn 3f out: nt qckn and no imp on ldrs 2f out: one pce* **33/1**

0500 **7** nk **Treasure The Ridge (IRE)**[46] 1941 5-9-7 **65** (b) DougieCostello 16 66
(Brett Johnson) *hld up towards rr on outer: rdn 3f out: kpt on same pce fnl 2f: nvr a threat* **20/1**

6236 **8** shd **Emman Bee (IRE)**[6] 4045 5-9-3 **61** (p) FergusSweeney 11 61
(Luke Dace) *chsd ldng pair: rdn 3f out: hanging and nt qckn 2f out: fdd* **10/1**

5306 **9** nk **Chapter And Verse (IRE)**[27] 3335 8-9-6 **64** ShaneKelly 6 64
(Mike Murphy) *hld up in last trio: pushed along over 2f out: stdy prog over 1f out but nowhere nr ldrs: reminder fnl f: nvr involved* **7/1**

0412 **10** 4½ **Minstrel Lad**[41] 2875 6-9-3 **64** SimonPearce(3) 5 55
(Lydia Pearce) *hld up in midfield: rdn 3f out: no prog 2f out: wknd* **11/2**[3]

0000 **11** 2 **Duke Of Destiny (IRE)**[24] 3427 5-9-6 **64** (p) WilliamBuick 1 51
(Ed Walker) *dwlt: hld up in last: shkn up over 2f out: no prog and nvr involved* **5/1**[2]

0-00 **12** 1½ **Bridge That Gap**[20] 3556 6-9-4 **62** (p) KierenFallon 10 47
(Roger Ingram) *hld up in last trio: pushed along on outer wl over 2f out: no prog: eased fnl f* **33/1**

-005 **13** 4½ **It's Taboo**[16] 3733 4-9-5 **63** DavidProbert 15 39
(Mark Usher) *nvr beyond midfield: shkn up and no prog 3f out: wknd 2f out* **20/1**

2m 5.63s (-3.07) **Going Correction** -0.25s/f (Firm) **13** Ran SP% **121.7**
Speed ratings (Par 101): **102,101,99,99,99 98,98,98,98,94 92,91,88**
CSF £21.77 CT £371.98 TOTE £5.10: £1.60, £2.90, £5.90; EX 14.30 Trifecta £698.50.
**Owner** R F Haynes **Bred** Kilco Builders **Trained** Lambourn, Berks

**FOCUS**
It paid not to be held up too far off the pace here.
T/Jkpt: £469.30 to a £1 stake. Pool: £33,183.31 - 50.20 winning units. T/Plt: £38.10 to a £1 stake. Pool: £93,381.33 - 1788.56 winning units. T/Qpdt: £10.80 to a £1 stake. Pool: £8875.90 - 603.08 winning units. JN

# 2238 KILLARNEY (L-H)
Monday, July 14

**OFFICIAL GOING: Flat course - good; hurdle course - good (good to firm in places)**

## 4276a IRISH STALLION FARMS EUROPEAN BREEDERS FUND CAIRN ROUGE STKS (LISTED RACE) (F&M) 1m 100y
6:40 (6:41) 3-Y-O+ £27,083 (£7,916; £3,750; £1,250)

RPR

**1** **Palace (IRE)**[19] 3593 3-9-0 102 SeamieHeffernan 5 99+
(A P O'Brien, Ire) *chsd ldrs: 6th 1/2-way: rdn under 3f out and wnt 4th u.p 1 1/2f out: styd on wl ins fnl f to ld cl home: readily* **11/8**[1]

**2** ½ **Dalkova**[19] 3595 5-9-9 90 NGMcCullagh 8 100
(J P Murtagh, Ire) *disp early: sn settled bhd ldrs: 3rd 1/2-way: tk clsr order on outer 2f out: rdn to ld ins fnl f: strly pressed ins fnl 150yds and hdd cl home: no ex* **14/1**

**3** ¾ **Beyond Brilliance (IRE)**[19] 3593 3-9-0 93 AnaO'Brien 6 96+
(A P O'Brien, Ire) *hld up: 9th 1/2-way: hdwy u.p to chse ldrs in 5th ent fnl f: kpt on wl towards fin into 3rd cl home: nt trble principals* **16/1**

**4** nk **Califante**[12] 3864 4-9-9 97 RonanWhelan 7 98+
(T Hogan, Ire) *towards rr: last 1/2-way: no imp u.p in rr 1 1/2f out: r.o wl ins fnl f: nrst fin: nt trble principals* **25/1**

**5** nk **Sparkle Factor (IRE)**[16] 3742 3-9-0 90 PatSmullen 4 95
(D K Weld, Ire) *disp early: sn settled bhd ldrs: 4th 1/2-way: gd hdwy travelling wl into 2nd over 2f out: rdn to ld 1 1/2f out: sn hdd and no ex u.p: wknd towards fin* **5/1**[3]

**6** ¾ **Whimsical (IRE)**[12] 3864 5-9-9 89 (p) WayneLordan 9 95
(P D Deegan, Ire) *hld up in tch: 8th 1/2-way: prog fr 2f out to chse ldrs in 6th ins fnl f: kpt on same pce* **50/1**

**7** 1¼ **Exactement (IRE)**[12] 3864 4-9-9 95 GaryCarroll 10 93
(Sabrina J Harty, Ire) *hld up: 10th 1/2-way: rdn under 3f out and no imp on ldrs ent fnl f: kpt on* **33/1**

**8** ¾ **Terrific (IRE)**[25] 3376 3-9-0 97 (b) ColmO'Donoghue 1 89
(A P O'Brien, Ire) *sn led: extended advantage and wnt over 3 l clr 1/2-way: reduced advantage over 2f out and hdd 1 1/2f out: wknd ins fnl f* **4/1**[2]

**9** 1¾ **Achnaha (IRE)**[29] 3288 3-9-0 90 (p) LeighRoche 13 85
(P D Deegan, Ire) *towards rr: 11th 1/2-way: rdn and no imp 3f out: sn one pce* **25/1**

**10** 1¼ **Shanooan (USA)**[19] 3593 3-9-0 88 BillyLee 2 82
(George Kent, Ire) *trckd ldrs: 2nd 1/2-way: rdn and dropped to 4th over 1 1/2f out: wknd ins fnl f* **33/1**

**11** 1¾ **Colour Blue (IRE)**[5] 4095 3-9-0 93 ConnorKing 11 79
(W McCreery, Ire) *hld up: tk clsr order bhd ldrs after 2f: 5th 1/2-way: rdn over 2f out and no imp on ldrs over 1f out: wknd and eased* **8/1**

**12** 4½ **Talitha Kum (IRE)**[16] 3741 4-9-9 90 ChrisHayes 3 71
(P D Deegan, Ire) *hld up: clsr in 7th 1/2-way: rdn and no imp 3f out: wknd and eased fnl f* **16/1**

1m 40.9s (-6.20)
**WFA** 3 from 4yo+ 9lb **12** Ran SP% **123.8**
CSF £24.23 TOTE £2.40: £1.02, £2.70, £5.20; DF 32.50 Trifecta £302.00.

**Owner** Michael Tabor & Derrick Smith & Mrs John Magnier **Bred** Whisperview Trading Ltd **Trained** Cashel, Co Tipperary

**FOCUS**
Favourite backers had more than a few moments of worry but they collected in the end. There was a solid gallop set by her stablemate Terrific.

4277 - (Foreign Racing) - See Raceform Interactive

## 3806 CHANTILLY (R-H)
Monday, July 14

**OFFICIAL GOING: Turf: very soft**

### 4278a PRIX JEAN PRAT (GROUP 1) (3YO COLTS & FILLIES) (TURF) 1m
1:50 (12:00) 3-Y-O £190,466 (£76,200; £38,100; £19,033; £9,533)

RPR

1 **Charm Spirit (IRE)**[37] 3028 3-9-2 0 OlivierPeslier 2 117+
(F Head, France) *midfield on inner: rdn 2f out: angled off rail ent fnl f: r.o strly between rivals and grad reeled in ldr: led cl home: shade cosily* **5/2**[1]

2 ¾ **Shifting Power**[51] 2571 3-9-2 0 RichardHughes 7 115
(Richard Hannon) *t.k.h: trckd ldr on outer: rdn 2f out: kpt on same pce fr over 1f out and nvr quite able to chal: fin 3rd: plcd 2nd* **5/2**[1]

3 nk **La Hoguette (FR)**[43] 2817 3-8-13 0 GregoryBenoist 1 111
(J-C Rouget, France) *t.k.h: trckd ldr on inner: rdn over 1f out: abt to chal whn hmpd on rail ent fnl f: lost momentum and dropped to 4th: kpt on wl but nt rcvr: fin 4th: plcd 3rd* **10/1**

4 nk **Yuften**[27] 3320 3-9-2 0 AndreaAtzeni 5 116
(William Haggas) *led: rdn over 1f out: edgd rt to rail and hmpd rival ent fnl f: r.o wl but grad reeled in and hdd cl home: fin 2nd, nk: disq and plcd 4th* **9/1**

5 1 ¾ **Muwaary**[26] 3352 3-9-2 0 PaulHanagan 6 110
(John Gosden) *plld hrd: hld up in last pair on outer: rdn in last ent fnl f: kpt on and wnt 5th cl home but nvr a factor* **5/1**[3]

6 snk **Calling Out (FR)**[14] 3807 3-9-2 0 AntoineHamelin 3 110
(J-P Gauvin, France) *hld up in last pair on inner: angled out and rdn over 1f out: outpcd fnl f: nvr a factor* **33/1**

7 hd **Prestige Vendome (FR)**[43] 2818 3-9-2 0 (p) ThierryThulliez 4 109
(N Clement, France) *restrained early: sn midfield on outer: rdn over 1f out: outpcd and wl hld fnl f: dropped to last cl home* **9/2**[2]

1m 41.01s (3.01) 7 Ran SP% **114.0**
WIN (incl. 1 euro stake): 3.00. PLACES: 1.80, 1.60. SF: 8.10.
**Owner** H H Sheikh Abdulla Bin Khalifa Al Thani **Bred** Ecurie Des Monceaux **Trained** France

**FOCUS**
The Jean Prat is usually an ordinary Group 1 and the first three past the post this time had all earlier finished well behind Kingman. The winner can probably improve again.

## 4101 BATH (L-H)
Tuesday, July 15

**OFFICIAL GOING: Firm (11.1)**
Wind: Mild breeze; across Weather: Sunny

### 4279 SHAWBROOK BANK H'CAP 1m 3f 144y
2:15 (2:15) (Class 6) (0-60,60) 3-Y-O+ £1,940 (£577; £288; £144) Stalls Low

Form RPR

0-50 1 **Sweeping Rock (IRE)**[62] 2252 4-9-6 52 (t) MartinDwyer 3 65
(Marcus Tregoning) *trckd ldrs: led over 2f out: rdn clr over 1f out: wl in command fnl f* **9/2**[3]

600- 2 3 ¼ **Wintour Leap**[230] 8066 3-8-7 57 DanielMuscutt(5) 8 65
(Robert Stephens) *trckd ldrs: rdn over 2f out: chsd wnr ent fnl f: styd on but a being comf hld* **9/2**[3]

6334 3 2 **Fair Comment**[14] 3818 4-9-12 58 RobertHavlin 5 62
(Michael Blanshard) *led: rdn and hdd over 2f out: hld by wnr over 1f out: lost 2nd ent fnl f: kpt on same pce* **7/2**[1]

-005 4 hd **Sir Tyto (IRE)**[14] 3824 6-8-8 47 (p) ChrisMeehan(7) 1 51
(Peter Makin) *w ldr tl over 3f out: sn rdn to chse ldrs: kpt on same pce fnl 2f* **10/1**

6-20 5 2 ¾ **Walter De La Mare (IRE)**[29] 3309 7-8-9 46 CamHardie(5) 6 45
(Anabel K Murphy) *mid-div: rdn wl over 2f out: nvr any imp* **5/1**

0206 6 ½ **Jumbo Prado (USA)**[31] 3233 5-9-11 57 WilliamTwiston-Davies 2 56
(John Stimpson) *hld up: hdwy 3f out: sn rdn: wknd ent fnl f* **20/1**

-214 7 5 **Captain Oats (IRE)**[13] 3852 11-9-11 60 RosieJessop(3) 7 50
(Pam Ford) *s.i.s: bhd: hdwy on outer fr 4f out: rdn over 2f out: nvr threatened: wknd over 1f out* **4/1**[2]

000- 8 42 **Actonetaketwo**[229] 8082 4-9-0 47 oh1 DavidProbert 4
(Ron Hodges) *mid-div tl pushed along over 4f out: rdn 3f out: wknd 2f out: t.o* **20/1**

2m 28.34s (-2.26) **Going Correction** -0.075s/f (Good)
**WFA** 3 from 4yo+ 13lb 8 Ran SP% **113.9**
Speed ratings (Par 101): **104,101,100,100,98 98,94,66**
CSF £24.80 CT £76.99 TOTE £6.00: £2.10, £1.80, £1.50; EX 32.90 Trifecta £113.40.
**Owner** Jas Singh **Bred** John & Dermot Dwan **Trained** Whitsbury, Hants

**FOCUS**
False rail around bottom bend and up to 3f and races incorporating bottom bend increased in distance by about 25yds. An extremely moderate, but equally competitive opener with less than two points covering the first five in the market. The third has been rated to her recent best.

### 4280 CARTER JONAS LETTINGS H'CAP 1m 5y
2:45 (2:46) (Class 4) (0-80,78) 3-Y-O+ £4,690 (£1,395; £697; £348) Stalls Low

Form RPR

5212 1 **Sonnetation (IRE)**[10] 3971 4-9-2 68 GeorgeBaker 4 75
(Jim Boyle) *mde all: rdn whn hrd pressed fr over 2f out: 1 l clr ent fnl f: jst hld on* **3/1**[3]

3122 2 shd **Sahra Al Khadra**[18] 3670 3-9-2 77 DaneO'Neill 1 82
(Charles Hills) *trckd ldng pair: rdn over 2f out: no imp tl r.o ins fnl f: jst failed* **7/4**[1]

5222 3 1 ¼ **Fleckerl (IRE)**[24] 3468 4-9-11 77 MartinDwyer 2 81
(William Muir) *trckd wnr: rdn and ev ch over 2f out tl no ex ent fnl f* **5/2**[2]

114- 4 2 ¾ **Chinese Jade**[319] 5952 3-9-0 78 RosieJessop(3) 3 74
(Sir Mark Prescott Bt) *stdd s: racd in 4th: rdn wl over 2f out: nvr finding pce to get on terms* **6/1**

1m 41.31s (0.51) **Going Correction** -0.075s/f (Good)
**WFA** 3 from 4yo 9lb 4 Ran SP% **104.2**
Speed ratings (Par 105): **94,93,92,89**
CSF £7.98 TOTE £3.40; EX 6.80 Trifecta £9.40.
**Owner** The 'In Recovery' Partnership **Bred** Dr Dean Harron **Trained** Epsom, Surrey

■ Acclio was withdrawn. Price at time of withdrawal 16-1. Rule 4 does not apply.

**FOCUS**
The third has been rated close to his non-claiming best.

### 4281 WESTERN DAILY PRESS H'CAP (BOBIS RACE) 5f 161y
3:15 (3:15) (Class 3) (0-95,95) 3-Y-O £7,439 (£2,213; £1,106; £553) Stalls Centre

Form RPR

2620 1 **Speed Hawk (USA)**[3] 4179 3-9-5 93 GeorgeBaker 6 101
(Robert Cowell) *prom: led narrowly jst over 3f out: drifted lft but r.o fnl f: rdn out* **8/11**[1]

32-1 2 1 ½ **Jacob's Pillow**[33] 3156 3-8-5 84 NathanAlison(5) 4 87
(William Haggas) *led tl narrowly hdd jst over 3f out: rdn 2f out: hld ent fnl f: kpt on same pce: sltly hmpd nring fin* **9/4**[2]

130- 3 nk **Umneyati**[283] 7011 3-9-6 94 JimCrowley 2 96
(James Tate) *trckd ldrs: rdn wl over 1f out: kpt on same pce fnl f* **20/1**

40-6 4 6 **Bahamian Heights**[45] 2767 3-9-2 95 (b) DannyBrock(5) 5 77
(Clive Brittain) *trckd ldrs: rdn over 2f out: wknd ins fnl f* **10/1**[3]

1200 5 ½ **Harwoods Volante (IRE)**[52] 2556 3-9-1 89 RobertHavlin 3 70
(Amanda Perrett) *trckd ldrs: rdn wl over 2f out: sn one pce* **12/1**

1m 10.03s (-1.17) **Going Correction** -0.075s/f (Good) 5 Ran SP% **110.2**
Speed ratings (Par 104): **104,102,101,93,92**
CSF £2.57 TOTE £1.80: £1.10, £1.40; EX 3.00 Trifecta £7.40.
**Owner** Khalifa Dasmal **Bred** Santa Rosa Partners **Trained** Six Mile Bottom, Cambs

**FOCUS**
The runner-up has been rated to his maiden figure, and the third to her 2yo form.

### 4282 BRISTOL POST FILLIES' H'CAP 5f 161y
3:45 (3:46) (Class 5) (0-75,75) 3-Y-O+ £2,587 (£770; £384; £192) Stalls Centre

Form RPR

0513 1 **Verus Delicia (IRE)**[13] 3848 5-8-11 65 EoinWalsh(5) 5 75
(Daniel Mark Loughnane) *chsd ldrs: rdn and ev ch 2f out: led jst ins fnl f: r.o wl to assert fnl 120yds: rdn out* **9/4**[1]

3200 2 1 ½ **Dangerous Age**[80] 1742 4-9-12 75 GeorgeBaker 4 80
(B W Hills) *chsd ldrs: rdn and ev ch 2f out tl jst ins fnl f: kpt on but nt pce of wnr* **9/4**[1]

2545 3 hd **Catalinas Diamond (IRE)**[7] 4049 6-8-2 56 (t) CamHardie(5) 3 60
(Pat Murphy) *awkwardly away: last but in tch: hdwy 3f out: rdn into narrow advantage 2f out: hdd jst ins fnl f: no ex* **7/2**[2]

2150 4 4 **A Legacy Of Love (IRE)**[11] 3936 3-9-4 73 JimCrowley 1 63
(Amanda Perrett) *prom: rdn and ev ch 2f out tl no ex ent fnl f* **11/2**[3]

0100 5 10 **Baytown Kestrel**[20] 3571 3-9-6 75 (p) SeanLevey 2 32
(Brian Ellison) *led: rdn: edgd lft and hdd 2f out: sn btn* **8/1**

1m 10.45s (-0.75) **Going Correction** -0.075s/f (Good)
**WFA** 3 from 4yo+ 6lb 5 Ran SP% **110.3**
Speed ratings (Par 100): **102,100,99,94,81**
CSF £7.53 TOTE £3.20: £1.30, £1.20; EX 9.00 Trifecta £17.10.
**Owner** R M Brilley **Bred** R Fagan **Trained** Baldwin's Gate, Staffs

**FOCUS**
They went a good pace, the time was all right and the third has been rated a little off her spring form.

### 4283 DPS NURSERY H'CAP 5f 11y
4:15 (4:15) (Class 5) 2-Y-O £2,587 (£770; £384; £192) Stalls Centre

Form RPR

1 1 **Dittander**[79] 1764 2-9-7 75 SeanLevey 4 80+
(Richard Hannon) *slowly away: sn trcking ldrs: led ent fnl f: edgd lft u.p: kpt on wl* **10/11**[1]

6001 2 ¾ **Multi Quest**[14] 3813 2-7-13 58 PhilipPrince(5) 2 58
(Jo Hughes) *led: rdn 2f out: hdd ent fnl f kpt on but no ex fnl 120yds* **9/2**[2]

5143 3 1 ¼ **River Spirit**[11] 3937 2-8-4 65 DanielCremin(7) 5 63
(Mick Channon) *trckd ldrs: rdn whn swtchd lft over 1f out: running on whn short of room on far rails and snatched up fnl 175yds: kpt on whn swtchd rt sn after but no ch after* **6/1**[3]

0344 4 2 **Surrey Pink (FR)**[6] 4083 2-8-4 58 MartinDwyer 6 46
(William Muir) *trckd ldrs: rdn over 2f out: nt pce to chal: no ex ins fnl f* **13/2**

3661 5 nk **Diminutive (IRE)**[10] 3967 2-8-7 61 StevieDonohoe 3 48
(Grace Harris) *trckd ldrs: rdn whn outpcd over 2f out: kpt on but no ch fnl f* **10/1**

6306 6 5 **Hell For Leather**[18] 3658 2-7-9 54 oh1 (p) NoelGarbutt(5) 1 23
(Bill Turner) *sn pushed along to chse ldrs: rdn wl over 2f out: wknd jst over 1f out* **33/1**

1m 3.0s (0.50) **Going Correction** -0.075s/f (Good) 6 Ran SP% **110.2**
Speed ratings (Par 94): **93,91,89,86,86 78**
CSF £5.07 TOTE £1.50: £1.40, £1.50; EX 4.90 Trifecta £12.90.
**Owner** Rockcliffe Stud **Bred** Rockcliffe Stud **Trained** East Everleigh, Wilts

■ Stewards' Enquiry : Philip Prince two-day ban; careless riding (29th-31st July)

**FOCUS**
The winner had a class edge against these rivals. The form is rated around the second to her C&D form. The runner-up has been rated to her C&D maiden form.

### 4284 NEW HORSERACING ODDS AT UNIBET.CO.UK H'CAP 5f 11y
4:45 (4:45) (Class 4) (0-85,84) 3-Y-O+ £4,690 (£1,395; £697; £348) Stalls Centre

Form RPR

0015 1 **Extrasolar**[11] 3927 4-9-12 84 (t) PatDobbs 3 92
(Amanda Perrett) *in tch: pushed along wl over 2f out: hdwy whn swtchd lft jst over 1f out: r.o wl to ld fnl 120yds: rdn out* **15/8**[1]

153 2 ¾ **Monumental Man**[18] 3676 5-9-9 81 (p) DaneO'Neill 2 86
(James Unett) *chsd ldr: rdn over 2f out: r.o to hold ev ch fnl 120yds: no ex nring fin* **13/2**[3]

321 3 hd **Secret Millionaire (IRE)**[16] 3749 7-9-2 77 MichaelJMMurphy(3) 4 82
(Luke Dace) *chsd ldrs: rdn wl over 2f out: kpt on ins fnl f* **11/4**[2]

1360 4 1 ½ **Dreams Of Glory**[31] 3213 6-9-1 73 OisinMurphy 7 72
(Ron Hodges) *in tch: rdn over 2f out: no imp tl r.o ins fnl f* **7/1**

0001 5 2 ½ **Powerful Wind (IRE)**[21] 3551 5-9-10 82 DavidProbert 5 72
(Ronald Harris) *set str pce: 2 l clr 2f out: sn rdn: hdd fnl 120yds: wknd* **8/1**

0046 6 1 **Swendab (IRE)**[15] 3783 6-9-3 75 (v) FergusSweeney 6 62
(John O'Shea) *s.i.s: rdn wl over 2f out: nvr gng pce to get on terms* **25/1**

235 7 1 ¾ **Arctic Lynx (IRE)**[26] 3386 7-9-8 80 JimCrowley 1 60
(Robert Cowell) *chsd ldrs: rdn over 2f out: wknd ent fnl f* **11/1**

1m 1.01s (-1.49) **Going Correction** -0.075s/f (Good) 7 Ran SP% **110.6**
Speed ratings (Par 105): **108,106,106,104,100 98,95**
CSF £13.57 TOTE £2.30: £1.50, £3.00; EX 11.80 Trifecta £48.30.
**Owner** Odile Griffith & John Connolly **Bred** Brook Stud Bloodstock Ltd **Trained** Pulborough, W Sussex

■ Stewards' Enquiry : Dane O'Neill four-day ban; used whip above the permitted level (4th-7th Aug)

**FOCUS**
Another strongly run race and another winning favourite on the card. A small pb from the winner and the runner-up has been rated to form.

## 4285 DOWNLOAD THE UNIBET PRO APP H'CAP — 5f 11y

5:15 (5:16) (Class 6) (0-65,63) 3-Y-O+ — £1,940 (£577; £288; £144) Stalls Centre

Form — RPR

035 **1** **Spray Tan**[5] [4102] 4-9-2 53 — DavidProbert 1 — 63
(Tony Carroll) *little slowly away: in tch in last pair: hdwy over 2f out: led over 1f out: r.o wl: rdn out* 9/2[3]

-001 **2** *1* **Burnt Cream**[12] [3896] 7-9-6 57 — (t) RobertHavlin 4 — 63
(Martin Bosley) *trckd ldrs: rdn to chse wnr ent fnl f: kpt on but a being hld* 8/1

6261 **3** *1/2* **Molly Jones**[5] [4101] 5-9-0 51 6ex — JohnFahy 7 — 55+
(Derek Haydn Jones) *hld up last: hdwy 2f out: nt clr run and swtchd rt over 1f out: sn rdn: r.o ins fnl f* 13/8[1]

4064 **4** *2 1/4* **Mossgo (IRE)**[28] [3323] 4-9-5 56 — (t) GeorgeBaker 2 — 52
(John Best) *disp ld: rdn over 2f out: hdd over 1f out: kpt on same pce fnl f* 7/1

0-06 **5** *3/4* **Baby Queen (IRE)**[10] [3954] 8-9-8 62 — MatthewLawson(3) 5 — 55
(Brian Baugh) *disp ld: rdn over 2f out: hdd over 1f out: kpt on same pce fnl f* 10/1

0420 **6** *2 1/4* **Volcanic Dust (IRE)**[4] [4151] 6-8-13 53 — (t) MichaelJMMurphy(3) 3 — 38
(Milton Bradley) *trckd ldrs: rdn over 2f out: wknd fnl f* 16/1

4221 **7** *13* **Douneedahand**[94] [1449] 3-9-2 63 — CamHardie(5) 6
(Seamus Mullins) *trckd ldrs: rdn over 2f out: wknd over 1f out* 4/1[2]

1m 2.05s (-0.45) **Going Correction** -0.075s/f (Good)
**WFA** 3 from 4yo+ 5lb — 7 Ran SP% **114.9**
Speed ratings (Par 101): **100,98,97,94,92 89,68**
CSF £39.48 TOTE £6.20: £2.80, £2.90; EX 33.90 Trifecta £135.60.
**Owner** Silks Racing Partnership **Bred** Lady Whent **Trained** Cropthorne, Worcs

**FOCUS**
Another race where Bath form came to the fore. The third, who didn't have the best of runs, has been rated close to last week's win.
T/Plt: £60.10 to a £1 stake. Pool: £68,543.44 - 831.83 winning units T/Qpdt: £5.10 to a £1 stake. Pool: £5,826.13 - 833.92 winning units TM

# 3945 BEVERLEY (R-H)

Tuesday, July 15

**OFFICIAL GOING: Good (good to firm in places back straight)**
Wind: Light; against Weather: Cloudy with sunny periods

## 4286 RACING UK PROFITS ALL RETURNED TO RACING MAIDEN AUCTION STKS — 5f

2:00 (2:02) (Class 5) 2-Y-O — £3,234 (£962; £481; £240) Stalls Low

Form — RPR

2 **1** **Gerry The Glover (IRE)**[17] [3713] 2-8-13 0 — TomEaves 13 — 75+
(Brian Ellison) *trckd ldrs on outer: hdwy over 1f out: rdn to chse clr ldr jst ins fnl f: styd on wl to ld last 50yds* 6/4[1]

0 **2** *1 1/2* **Dad's Girl**[50] [2615] 2-8-4 0 — IanBrennan 6 — 60
(Ollie Pears) *sn led: qcknd clr over 2f out: rdn ent fnl f: hdd and no ex last 50yds* 20/1

2 **3** *1* **Eye Glass (IRE)**[50] [2615] 2-8-6 0 — DuranFentiman 4 — 59+
(Tim Easterby) *in rr: pushed along 1/2-way: swtchd lft and hdwy wl over 1f out: styd on strly fnl f: nrst fin* 3/1[2]

00 **4** *1 1/4* **Maid In Rome (IRE)**[10] [3947] 2-8-6 0 — AndrewElliott 8 — 54
(Tim Easterby) *chsd ldrs: rdn along to chse ldng pair ent fnl f: kpt on same pce* 100/1

05 **5** *1/2* **Mister York**[58] [2358] 2-8-9 0 — PJMcDonald 14 — 55
(Mel Brittain) *sn outpcd in rr: hdwy on outer wl over 1f out: styd on fnl f: nrst fin* 100/1

0 **6** *nk* **Zipedeedodah (IRE)**[8] [4025] 2-8-11 0 — GrahamLee 11 — 56
(Joseph Tuite) *prom: rdn along wl over 1f out: wknd appr fnl f* 7/1

56 **7** *nk* **Perfect Girl (IRE)**[10] [3975] 2-8-8 0 — SilvestreDeSousa 12 — 52
(Tim Easterby) *midfield: effrt 2f out: sn rdn and kpt on fnl f: nrst fin* 20/1

**8** *1* **Thorkhill Star (IRE)** 2-8-11 0 — TonyHamilton 1 — 51
(Richard Fahey) *midfield: effrt 2f out: sn rdn along and no imp* 9/2[3]

**9** *2 1/4* **Unforgettable You (IRE)** 2-8-4 0 — JasonHart 5 — 36
(Declan Carroll) *cl up: rdn along over 2f out: wknd over 1f out* 25/1

0 **10** *4 1/2* **Farang Jai Dee (IRE)**[4] [4170] 2-8-8 0 — NeilFarley(3) 9 — 27
(Declan Carroll) *prom: rdn along wl over 1f out: sn wknd* 25/1

**11** *1/2* **Reckless Blue** 2-8-4 0 — JamesSullivan 7 — 18
(Michael Easterby) *dwlt: a towards rr* 50/1

0 **12** *shd* **Lady Jade**[10] [3947] 2-8-6 0 — AndrewMullen 3 — 20
(Nigel Tinkler) *a towards rr* 100/1

6 **13** *4* **Prince Of Clowns (IRE)**[26] [3394] 2-8-13 0 — PhillipMakin 17 — 13
(John Quinn) *dwlt and swtchd rt to inner s: sn outpcd and bhd fr 1/2-way* 33/1

**14** *11* **Ted Larkin (IRE)** 2-8-13 0 — RobertWinston 10
(Richard Guest) *a towards rr* 33/1

1m 3.87s (0.37) **Going Correction** -0.025s/f (Good) — 14 Ran SP% **123.7**
Speed ratings (Par 94): **96,93,92,90,89 88,88,86,83,75 75,74,68,50**
CSF £40.73 TOTE £2.30: £1.10, £5.10, £1.70; EX 42.40 Trifecta £163.90.
**Owner** Mrs J A Martin **Bred** Aidan Fogarty **Trained** Norton, N Yorks

**FOCUS**
Rail around bottom bend at innermost position and distances as advertised. Little strength in depth to an ordinary maiden auction event. The gallop was sound and this form should prove reliable. The winner didn't have to replicate his pre-race form to win, and the form could be rated 7lb higher through the third.

## 4287 100% RACING UK PROFITS RETURNED TO RACING H'CAP (DIV I) — 5f

2:30 (2:30) (Class 6) (0-60,60) 3-Y-O+ — £2,264 (£673; £336; £168) Stalls Low

Form — RPR

505 **1** **Mey Blossom**[6] [4069] 9-9-0 52 — (b) ConnorBeasley(3) 5 — 62
(Richard Whitaker) *hld up in tch: trckd ldrs 2f out: swtchd rt to inner and hdwy jst over 1f out: rdn to chal ent fnl f: led last 100yds: kpt on* 5/1[3]

1526 **2** *1/2* **Lucky Mark (IRE)**[67] [2127] 5-9-3 52 — DanielTudhope 1 — 60
(John Balding) *sn led: rdn along and edgd lft over 1f out: drvn and edgd lft again ins fnl f: hdd last 100yds* 7/1

4404 **3** *nk* **Hazard Warning (IRE)**[11] [3913] 4-9-6 55 — (b) GrahamLee 7 — 62+
(James Given) *dwlt and in rr: hdwy 2f out: effrt to chse ldrs whn nt clr run and swtchd lft ent fnl f: sn rdn and kpt on strly towards fin* 7/2[1]

2350 **4** *1 1/4* **Windforpower (IRE)**[10] [3954] 4-9-11 60 — (p) JoeFanning 2 — 62
(Tracy Waggott) *trckd ldrs: hdwy 2f out: rdn wl over 1f out: kpt on fnl f* 4/1[2]

6036 **5** *nk* **Classical Diva**[6] [4071] 3-8-9 49 — (b) AndrewMullen 3 — 48
(Declan Carroll) *dwlt and reminders s: sn trcking ldrs on inner: swtchd lft and effrt over 1f out: sn rdn and one pce fnl f* 16/1

0000 **6** *3 3/4* **Red Cape (FR)**[22] [3530] 11-9-3 52 — (b) JamesSullivan 4 — 40
(Ruth Carr) *cl up: rdn along over 2f out: sn drvn and wknd* 16/1

0000 **7** *2 1/4* **Lord Buffhead**[43] [2831] 5-8-13 48 — (v) RobbieFitzpatrick 10 — 28
(Richard Guest) *towards rr: hdwy on outer over 2f out: rdn to chse ldrs over 1f out: sn no imp* 20/1

-425 **8** *1 1/4* **Spoken Words**[14] [3833] 5-8-10 50 — KevinStott(5) 6 — 25
(John David Riches) *chsd ldrs: rdn along bef 1/2-way: sn outpcd* 6/1

6-00 **9** *nk* **Lizzy's Dream**[63] [2232] 6-9-2 54 — NeilFarley(3) 12 — 28
(Robin Bastiman) *a towards rr* 20/1

5460 **10** *1 3/4* **Busy Bimbo (IRE)**[11] [3913] 5-8-12 47 — (b) PatrickMathers 8 — 15
(Alan Berry) *in tch: rdn along over 2f out: sn drvn and wknd* 25/1

3003 **11** *2* **Major Muscari (IRE)**[7] [4055] 6-9-5 54 — BenCurtis 11 — 15
(Shaun Harris) *dwlt: towards rr: hdwy on outer and in tch 1/2-way: sn rdn along and wknd wl over 1f out* 10/1

1m 3.27s (-0.23) **Going Correction** -0.025s/f (Good)
**WFA** 3 from 4yo+ 5lb — 11 Ran SP% **119.9**
Speed ratings (Par 101): **100,99,98,96,96 90,86,84,84,81 78**
CSF £39.56 CT £143.71 TOTE £5.60: £1.90, £2.50, £1.80; EX 32.50 Trifecta £156.20.
**Owner** Waz Developments Ltd **Bred** Hellwood Stud Farm **Trained** Scarcroft, W Yorks
■ Lees Anthem was withdrawn. Price at time of withdrawal 5-1. Rule 4 applies to bets struck before withdrawal but not to SP bets - deduction 15p in the pound. New market formed.

**FOCUS**
Division one of a moderate sprint. The gallop was fair. The winner, running off a career-low mark, has been rated to his best form since last August.

## 4288 100% RACING UK PROFITS RETURNED TO RACING H'CAP (DIV II) — 5f

3:00 (3:00) (Class 6) (0-60,60) 3-Y-O+ — £2,264 (£673; £336; £168) Stalls Low

Form — RPR

6360 **1** **Pearl Noir**[11] [3913] 4-8-12 52 — (b) MatthewHopkins(5) 7 — 62
(Scott Dixon) *qckly away: mde all: rdn over 1f out: drvn ins fnl f: kpt on wl towards fin* 10/1

0054 **2** *3/4* **Nelson's Pride**[22] [3530] 3-8-12 57 — (b) KevinStott(5) 8 — 62
(Kevin Ryan) *midfield: hdwy 2f out: rdn and edgd lft appr fnl f: sn chsng wnr: drvn and kpt on towards fin* 9/2[2]

0010 **3** *2* **Ichimoku**[21] [3548] 4-9-3 52 — RoystonFfrench 9 — 52
(Bryan Smart) *in tch: pushed along and sltly outpcd 1/2-way: hdwy whn swtchd rt over 1f out: sn rdn and styd on fnl f: nrst fin* 20/1

0044 **4** *1* **Two Turtle Doves (IRE)**[9] [4005] 8-9-3 52 — SilvestreDeSousa 12 — 49
(Michael Mullineaux) *towards rr: hdwy on outer 2f out: rdn wl over 1f out: chsd ldrs ent fnl f: no imp* 16/1

2305 **5** *hd* **Captain Scooby**[11] [3913] 8-9-1 50 — (v) AmyRyan 10 — 46
(Richard Guest) *in rr: pushed along and hdwy 2f out: rdn and styng on whn n.m.r and swtchd rt over 1f out: kpt on fnl f: nrst fin* 8/1

1110 **6** *3/4* **Fathom Five (IRE)**[22] [3530] 10-9-4 60 — JoshQuinn(7) 2 — 53
(Shaun Harris) *chsd ldrs: rdn along wl over 1f out: wknd ent fnl f* 8/1

-663 **7** *1 3/4* **Singing Star (IRE)**[34] [3093] 3-8-10 50 — PJMcDonald 1 — 35
(Mel Brittain) *cl up: rdn along 2f out: sn drvn and wknd* 4/1[1]

-202 **8** *1/2* **Knockamany Bends (IRE)**[25] [3440] 4-9-4 53 — PaddyAspell 5 — 38
(John Wainwright) *chsd ldrs: rdn along over 2f out: drvn and edgd rt wl over 1f out: sn wknd* 20/1

0502 **9** *1 1/2* **Argent Touch**[7] [4059] 3-9-4 58 — DaleSwift 6 — 36
(Derek Shaw) *dwlt and towards rr: effrt and sme hdwy wl over 1f out: sn rdn and n.d* 7/1[3]

2420 **10** *1/2* **Novalist**[34] [3099] 6-8-12 47 — (b) JasonHart 11 — 25
(Robin Bastiman) *a in rr* 20/1

0312 **11** *nk* **Choc'A'Moca (IRE)**[11] [3913] 7-9-7 56 — (v) PaulMulrennan 13 — 33
(Paul Midgley) *racd wd: a in rr* 8/1

000- **12** *18* **Sharp Shoes**[286] [6944] 7-8-11 46 — TomEaves 3
(Christopher Wilson) *cl up: rdn along over 2f out: drvn wl over 1f out: sn wknd and eased ins fnl f* 50/1

4241 **13** *2 3/4* **Alpha Tauri (USA)**[110] [1127] 8-8-11 46 — (t) RobbieFitzpatrick 4
(Charles Smith) *dwlt: hdwy on inner over 2f out: rdn along wl over 1f out: sn btn and eased fnl f* 16/1

1m 3.25s (-0.25) **Going Correction** -0.025s/f (Good)
**WFA** 3 from 4yo+ 5lb — 13 Ran SP% **121.1**
Speed ratings (Par 101): **101,99,96,95,94 93,90,89,87,86 86,57,53**
CSF £52.61 CT £906.85 TOTE £16.90: £4.40, £2.40, £6.40; EX 66.90 Trifecta £2888.90 Part won..
**Owner** P J Dixon & Partners **Bred** Mrs Yvette Dixon **Trained** Babworth, Notts

**FOCUS**
The second division of a moderate sprint. The gallop was sound but very few figured. The runner-up has been rated to her 2yo form.

## 4289 129TH YEAR OF THE WATT MEMORIAL H'CAP — 2m 35y

3:30 (3:31) (Class 4) (0-85,85) 3-Y-O+ — £6,469 (£1,925; £962; £481) Stalls Low

Form — RPR

52-0 **1** **Stopped Out**[32] [3204] 9-9-9 80 — (p) JoeFanning 6 — 88
(Philip Kirby) *led and sn clr: pushed along over 3f out: rdn clr again 2f out: drvn ins fnl f: hld on wl towards fin* 8/1

0-65 **2** *nk* **Almagest**[6] [4068] 6-10-0 85 — (p) DanielTudhope 5 — 92
(David O'Meara) *hld up in rr: hdwy on inner 2f out: rdn to chse wnr jst over 1f out: swtchd lft and drvn ins fnl f: kpt on wl towards fin: jst hld* 6/1[3]

2060 **3** *6* **Ebony Express**[45] [2787] 5-9-8 79 — BenCurtis 7 — 79
(Alan Swinbank) *hld up in rr: hdwy on outer over 3f out: rdn over 2f out: drvn wl over 1f out and sn one pce* 14/1

2311 **4** *2 1/4* **Longshadow**[18] [3661] 4-9-0 74 — (v) JoeyHaynes(3) 4 — 71
(Jason Ward) *trckd ldrs: smooth hdwy to cl up on wnr over 4f out: effrt wl over 2f out: sn rdn along: drvn wl over 1f out and sn one pce* 4/1[2]

2223 **5** *2 3/4* **New Tarabela**[34] [3110] 3-8-4 80 — (p) SilvestreDeSousa 2 — 73
(James Tate) *chsd wnr: tk clsr order on wnr over 4f out: rdn along 3f out: drvn over 2f out and grad wknd* 5/4[1]

6132 **6** *26* **Rosairlie (IRE)**[23] [3501] 6-9-10 81 — PJMcDonald 1 — 65
(Micky Hammond) *trckd ldng pair on inner: pushed along 4f out: rdn 3f out: wknd wl over 1f out* 6/1[3]

3m 34.01s (-5.79) **Going Correction** -0.325s/f (Firm)
**WFA** 3 from 4yo+ 19lb — 6 Ran SP% **110.8**
Speed ratings (Par 105): **101,100,97,96,95 82**
CSF £51.45 TOTE £10.00: £4.50, £3.40; EX 45.50 Trifecta £435.40.
**Owner** The Well Oiled Partnership **Bred** J And T Shally **Trained** Middleham, N Yorks

**FOCUS**
A useful handicap but a stop-start gallop means the bare form isn't reliable. The first two pulled clear. The runner-up has been rated back to last August's C&D win off the same mark.

## 4290 IRISHBIGRACETRENDS.COM H'CAP — 1m 100y
4:00 (4:01) (Class 4) (0-80,79) 3-Y-O+ £4,690 (£1,395; £697; £348) Stalls Low

Form RPR
1316 1 **Border Bandit (USA)**[20] 3572 6-9-9 **74**....................(p) RobertWinston 6 85
(Tracy Waggott) *trckd ldrs: hdwy over 2f out: led jst over 1f out: sn rdn and clr ins fnl f: kpt on strly* **5/1**[3]
1 2 3 **Sophisticated Heir (IRE)**[43] 2841 4-9-12 **77**.................. DanielTudhope 3 81
(David O'Meara) *trckd ldrs on inner: hdwy over 2f out: n.m.r and swtchd lft over 1f out: sn rdn: chsd wnr ins fnl f: no imp* **6/1**
-145 3 ½ **Eeny Mac (IRE)**[11] 3910 7-9-10 **75**..................... AndrewElliott 8 78
(Neville Bycroft) *set gd pce: rdn along 2f out: drvn: edgd rt and hdd jst over 1f out: kpt on same pce u.p fnl f* **12/1**
2-21 4 nk **Extraterrestrial**[17] 3703 10-9-9 **79**.................. SammyJoBell(5) 10 81
(Richard Fahey) *hld up towards rr: hdwy on outer over 2f out: rdn over 1f out: kpt on u.p fnl f: nrst fin* **9/1**
1510 5 nse **Ellaal**[15] 3791 5-9-3 **68**........................................ PaulMulrennan 9 70
(Ruth Carr) *trckd ldrs on outer: hdwy 3f out: rdn wl over 1f out: sn drvn and kpt on same pce* **20/1**
-112 6 ¾ **Jacbequick**[10] 3946 3-8-10 **75**..................... JacobButterfield(5) 1 73
(Ollie Pears) *cl up on inner: effrt over 2f out: rdn whn nt clr run and swtchd lft over 1f out: n.m.r and swtchd rt to inner jst ins fnl f: sn n.m.r and kpt on same pce* **9/2**[2]
3532 7 1¼ **Potent Embrace (USA)**[11] 3925 3-9-0 **74**.................. JoeFanning 2 70
(Mark Johnston) *in rr: swtchd to outer and hdwy over 2f out: rdn wl over 1f out: sn no imp* **3/1**[1]
5601 8 shd **Shadowtime**[15] 3791 9-9-10 **78**........................ ConnorBeasley(3) 5 75
(Tracy Waggott) *midfield: hdwy over 2f out: rdn along wl over 1f out: drvn and wknd appr fnl f* **11/1**
2435 9 1¼ **Hydrant**[10] 3977 8-9-4 **76**.............................. LukeLeadbitter(7) 11 70
(Richard Guest) *prom: chsd ldr 1/2-way: rdn along over 2f out: sn drvn and grad wknd* **28/1**
414- 10 nk **Chevalgris**[403] 3067 4-9-13 **78**.................... SilvestreDeSousa 4 72
(Alan Swinbank) *dwlt: a in rr* **12/1**
1m 44.28s (-3.32) **Going Correction** -0.325s/f (Firm)
**WFA** 3 from 4yo+ 9lb 10 Ran SP% **116.1**
Speed ratings (Par 105): **103,100,99,99,99 98,97,97,95,95**
CSF £34.94 CT £342.44 TOTE £6.00: £1.60, £2.60, £3.90; EX 33.60 Trifecta £417.40.
**Owner** Elsa Crankshaw Gordon Allan **Bred** Darley **Trained** Spennymoor, Co Durham

**FOCUS**
A fair handicap featuring a couple of unexposed sorts. The gallop was no more than fair but the winner won with a bit in hand. The third has been rated close to his form.

## 4291 SANDRA EVISON MEMORIAL H'CAP — 7f 100y
4:30 (4:30) (Class 5) (0-75,75) 3-Y-O+ £3,234 (£962; £481; £240) Stalls Low

Form RPR
2011 1 **Kimbali (IRE)**[11] 3908 5-9-2 **70**.................. LukeLeadbitter(7) 10 79+
(Declan Carroll) *hld up in midfield: swtchd lft to outer and gd hdwy wl over 2f out: swtchd rt 2f out and sn chal: led over 1f out: rdn ins fnl f: kpt on wl* **9/1**
0040 2 ½ **Mishaal (IRE)**[18] 3660 4-9-4 **70**......................... PaulMulrennan 8 78
(Michael Herrington) *s.i.s and bhd: stdy hdwy on inner over 2f out: rdn over 1f out: styd on strly ent fnl f: sn ev ch: kpt on* **25/1**
1635 3 2 **Real Tigress (IRE)**[22] 3533 5-9-11 **72**........................ GrahamLee 6 75
(Les Eyre) *in tch: hdwy over 2f out: rdn over 1f out: chal and ev ch ent fnl f: sn drvn and kpt on same pce* **7/2**[2]
2206 4 hd **Al Muheer (IRE)**[10] 3955 9-10-0 **75**.................(e) JamesSullivan 7 78+
(Ruth Carr) *hld up towards rr: hdwy on wd outside 2f out: sn rdn: styd on strly fnl f: nrst fin* **8/1**
3442 5 ¾ **Whispered Times (USA)**[11] 3908 7-8-12 **59**..............(p) JoeFanning 11 60
(Tracy Waggott) *trckd ldrs: effrt over 2f out: rdn over 1f out: chal ent fnl f: sn drvn and one pce* **6/1**
2061 6 1¾ **Relight My Fire**[11] 3910 4-9-6 **74**.....................(b) RachelRichardson(7) 9 70
(Tim Easterby) *hld up towards rr: hdwy over 2f out: rdn along wl over 1f out: kpt on same pce fnl f* **5/1**[3]
00-0 7 2¼ **Dennis**[66] 2169 4-9-4 **65**.................................. SilvestreDeSousa 4 56
(Tim Easterby) *dwlt and in rr: hdwy on outer over 2f out: chsd ldrs wl over 1f out: sn rdn and no imp* **25/1**
5013 8 12 **Zaitsev (IRE)**[11] 3910 4-10-0 **75**........................ RobertWinston 3 36
(Ollie Pears) *led: pushed along 3f out: rdn over 2f out: drvn and hdd over 1f out: sn wknd* **11/4**[1]
4040 9 1¼ **Llewellyn**[10] 3955 6-9-5 **69**................................. NeilFarley(3) 13 27
(Declan Carroll) *chsd ldrs: rdn along 3f out: sn wknd* **25/1**
0210 10 3¼ **Smalljohn**[22] 3533 8-9-2 **68**.............................(v) AdamCarter(5) 16 17
(Bryan Smart) *cl up on outer: rdn along wl over 2f out: drvn and hld whn n.m.r and hmpd wl over 1f out: wknd after* **40/1**
-004 11 14 **Majestic Dream (IRE)**[10] 3979 6-9-7 **68**..............(b) BarryMcHugh 14
(Michael Easterby) *cl up: rdn along wl over 2f out: wkng whn n.m.r and hmpd wl over 1f out* **20/1**
1m 31.82s (-1.98) **Going Correction** -0.325s/f (Firm) 11 Ran SP% **119.7**
Speed ratings (Par 103): **98,97,95,94,94 92,89,75,74,70 54**
CSF £217.81 CT £944.46 TOTE £11.90: £3.80, £7.10, £1.50; EX 226.80 Trifecta £851.30.
**Owner** Mrs Sarah Bryan **Bred** P Kelly **Trained** Sledmere, E Yorks

**FOCUS**
Mainly exposed sorts in a fair handicap. The gallop was decent and the leaders not surprisingly failed to get home. The runner-up is the key to the form.

## 4292 KCOM GROUP H'CAP — 1m 1f 207y
5:00 (5:01) (Class 6) (0-65,65) 3-Y-O £2,385 (£704; £352) Stalls Low

Form RPR
-002 1 **Archduchess**[24] 3471 3-9-3 **61**..........................(b) SilvestreDeSousa 13 71
(Rae Guest) *prom: chsd ldr after 3f: hdwy over 2f out: led wl over 1f out: sn rdn and edgd rt: clr ent fnl f: rdn out* **12/1**
2163 2 3¼ **Trinity Star (IRE)**[29] 3303 3-9-5 **63**.................... PaulMulrennan 4 68
(Michael Dods) *in rr: hdwy on inner whn hmpd over 2f out: chsd ldrs whn n.m.r wl over 1f out: squeezed through on inner ent fnl f: sn rdn and kpt on* **3/1**[1]
3-00 3 1¼ **Bertha Burnett (IRE)**[10] 3950 3-8-1 **50**...................... JackGarritty(5) 6 51
(Brian Rothwell) *hld up in rr: swtchd lft to outer and hdwy wl over 2f out: chsd ldrs wl over 1f out: rdn to chse wnr ent fnl f: sn drvn and one pce* **11/1**
06-0 4 1¼ **Darling Boyz**[27] 3362 3-8-11 **55**.................................. IanBrennan 7 54
(John Quinn) *sn led and edgd rt to rails after 1f: hdd 7f out: chsd ldrs: rdn along: sltly outpcd and edgd rt over 2f out: plugged on u.p appr fnl f* **16/1**
-520 5 4½ **Victory Danz (IRE)**[11] 3912 3-9-2 **60**.......................... DanielTudhope 8 51
(David O'Meara) *chsd ldrs: effrt 3f out: rdn along 2f out: sn drvn and one pce* **7/2**[2]
0052 6 ½ **Belle Peinture (FR)**[10] 3973 3-8-2 **46**......................... DuranFentiman 12 36
(Alan Lockwood) *cl up: edgd rt after 1f: led over 7f out: rdn along 3f out: drvn 2f out: hdd wl over 1f out and sn wknd* **22/1**
5623 7 1 **Moving Waves (IRE)**[11] 3912 3-8-11 **55**................(p) RobertWinston 2 43
(Ollie Pears) *chsd ldrs whn hmpd after 1f and again over 8f out: sn towards rr: sme hdwy wl over 2f out: rdn wl over 1f out: sn no imp* **7/2**[2]
5550 8 6 **Running Wolf (IRE)**[15] 3789 3-9-2 **65**......................(p) KevinStott(5) 3 41
(Michael Dods) *trckd ldrs: hmpd after 1f: in tch: rdn along 3f out: wknd over 2f out* **7/1**[3]
5135 9 2½ **It's All A Game**[18] 3662 3-8-11 **62**........................(b) LukeLeadbitter(7) 9 34
(Richard Guest) *in tch: rdn along 3f out: wknd over 2f out* **12/1**
-005 10 nse **Miguela McGuire**[27] 3362 3-8-3 **47**.............................. PatrickMathers 5 18
(Eric Alston) *a towards rr* **40/1**
2m 4.08s (-2.92) **Going Correction** -0.325s/f (Firm) 10 Ran SP% **118.3**
Speed ratings (Par 98): **98,95,94,93,89 89,88,83,81,81**
CSF £48.77 CT £421.56 TOTE £9.30: £2.60, £1.10, £3.10; EX 39.10 Trifecta £490.80.
**Owner** Miss K Rausing **Bred** Miss K Rausing **Trained** Newmarket, Suffolk
■ Stewards' Enquiry : Ian Brennan three-day ban; careless riding (29th July-1st Aug).

**FOCUS**
A modest handicap run at an even tempo. The runner-up has been rated close to form, with the third close to her C&D latest.

## 4293 DOROTHY LAIRD MEMORIAL TROPHY H'CAP (LADIES RACE) — 1m 1f 207y
5:30 (5:31) (Class 6) (0-65,65) 4-Y-O+ £2,385 (£704; £352) Stalls Low

Form RPR
015 1 **Valantino Oyster (IRE)**[21] 3546 7-10-4 **62**....................(p) MrsCBartley 6 73
(Tracy Waggott) *chsd ldr: tk clsr order over 4f out: led over 2f out: sn rdn clr and edgd rt over 1f out: kpt on strly* **8/1**
-032 2 3¼ **City Ground (USA)**[39] 2963 7-10-7 **65**.................... MissSBrotherton 13 70
(Michael Easterby) *trckd ldng pair on inner: hdwy 3f out: chsd wnr 2f out: rdn over 1f out: hung bdly lft ins fnl f: sn no imp* **11/4**[1]
0/03 3 2½ **Snow Dancer (IRE)**[17] 3705 10-10-2 **60**.................... LucyAlexander 10 60
(John David Riches) *hld up towards rr: hdwy wl over 2f out: swtchd lft and effrt wl over 1f out: sn rdn and styd on fnl f: nrst fin* **16/1**
4414 4 nk **Amazing Blue Sky**[11] 3912 8-9-10 **54**.......................... GemmaTutty 16 54
(Ruth Carr) *hld up: hdwy 1/2-way: chsd ldrs 3f out: rdn along 2f out: one pce appr fnl f* **7/1**
-056 5 hd **Kheskianto (IRE)**[21] 3546 8-9-2 **46** oh1.....................(t) MissAliceMills 4 45
(Michael Chapman) *towards rr: hdwy on wd outside over 2f out: rdn along wl over 1f out: kpt on fnl f: nrst fin* **14/1**
0000 6 1¼ **Sophie's Beau (USA)**[21] 3548 7-8-13 **48**..................... MissLWilson(5) 11 45
(Michael Chapman) *t.k.h early: stdd s and hld up in rr: hdwy over 2f out: rdn along wl over 1f out: kpt on fnl f: nrst fin* **40/1**
0000 7 ½ **Valentine's Gift**[11] 3912 6-9-12 **56**................................... JulieBurke 2 52
(Neville Bycroft) *hld up in rr: sme hdwy over 2f out: sn rdn along and n.d* **14/1**
6330 8 ¾ **Tinseltown**[7] 4058 8-10-7 **65**....................................... ShirleyTeasdale 1 59
(Brian Rothwell) *led: clr 1/2-way: pushed along 3f out: hdd over 2f out and sn rdn: drvn wl over 1f out and sn wknd* **13/2**[3]
5302 9 3½ **Outlaw Torn (IRE)**[3] 4197 5-10-2 **65**.....................(e) ClaireMurray(5) 14 53
(Richard Guest) *in tch: hdwy on outer wl over 2f out: rdn wl over 1f out: sn wknd* **9/2**[2]
4550 10 1½ **Poor Duke (IRE)**[4] 4156 4-10-6 **64**..................(p) MissMMullineaux 17 49
(Michael Mullineaux) *chsd ldng pair: rdn along over 3f out: drvn wl over 2f out and sn wknd* **16/1**
0/0- 11 ½ **Tri Nations (UAE)**[279] 5168 9-9-12 **56**...................(bt) MissHBethell 7 40
(Brian Ellison) *in tch: pushed along 4f out: rdn along 3f out: sn wknd* **10/1**
000- 12 15 **Landesherr (GER)**[344] 5050 7-9-2 **46** oh1...................[1] MissHCuthbert 8
(Thomas Cuthbert) *chsd ldrs: rdn along 3f out: sn wknd* **50/1**
00-0 13 hd **Speedy Star (IRE)**[24] 3482 5-9-2 **46** oh1................... MissJoannaMason 3
(Tina Jackson) *towards rr: pushed along whn n.m.r and stmbld over 3f out: bhd after* **50/1**
2m 4.24s (-2.76) **Going Correction** -0.325s/f (Firm) 13 Ran SP% **122.3**
Speed ratings (Par 101): **98,95,93,93,93 92,91,91,88,87 86,74,74**
CSF £30.66 CT £356.87 TOTE £9.50: £2.10, £1.50, £3.80; EX 35.20 Trifecta £407.90.
**Owner** Steve Sawley **Bred** Des Vere Hunt Farm Co And Jack Ronan **Trained** Spennymoor, Co Durham

**FOCUS**
A modest handicap in which a reasonable gallop steadied around 4f out and not many figured. The winner is better than ever.
T/Jkpt: Not won. T/Plt: £304.40 to a £1 stake. Pool: £87,926.21 - 210.86 winning units T/Qpdt: £214.40 to a £1 stake. Pool: £5,708.25 - 19.70 winning units JR

# 3529 THIRSK (L-H)
Tuesday, July 15

**OFFICIAL GOING: Good to firm (9.4)**
Wind: Almost nil Weather: Fine and sunny; very warm

## 4294 LIVE RACING AND BETTING - RACING UK IPAD APP FILLIES' H'CAP — 7f
6:10 (6:12) (Class 5) (0-70,70) 3-Y-O+ £2,587 (£770; £384; £192) Stalls Low

Form RPR
45-0 1 **Sugar Town**[34] 3096 4-8-6 **51** oh4..................................... SamJames(3) 5 60
(Peter Niven) *led after 1f: mde rest: hld on towards fin* **33/1**
1521 2 nk **Grace Hull**[113] 1082 4-9-9 **65**.........................................(p) JasonHart 4 73+
(Garry Moss) *hld up in rr: effrt over 3f out: swtchd ins over 2f out: chsd wnr last 100yds: no ex nr fin* **11/2**[2]
0-0 3 1¼ **Genax (IRE)**[22] 3528 3-7-8 **51**...................................... JoeDoyle(7) 7 53
(John Wainwright) *chsd ldrs: chalng whn hit over hd by winning rdr's whip appr fnl f: styd on same pce* **10/1**
0203 4 2 **Gladsome**[10] 3956 6-8-10 **55**................................... ConnorBeasley(3) 2 55
(Michael Herrington) *chsd ldrs: effrt over 2f out: kpt on same pce over 1f out* **15/2**
4-60 5 2 **Dream Scenario**[5] 4108 4-9-12 **68**..........................(v) PJMcDonald 6 63
(Mel Brittain) *trckd ldrs: t.k.h: effrt over 2f out: one pce* **11/2**[2]
0042 6 ½ **Les Gar Gan (IRE)**[10] 3956 3-9-6 **70**...........................(b) TomEaves 1 60
(Keith Dalgleish) *in rr: effrt over 3f out: hung lft over 1f out: nvr a factor* **7/2**[1]

0006 **7** 1 1/4 **See Clearly**[10] 3956 5-8-11 **53**..........(p) TonyHamilton 8 43
(Tim Easterby) *chsd ldrs: one pce fnl 2f* **8/1**
0000 **8** 3/4 **Classy Lassy (IRE)**[11] 3913 3-7-13 **52**..........JoeyHaynes(3) 11 37
(Brian Ellison) *rr-div: drvn over 4f out: kpt on fnl 2f: nvr a factor* **16/1**
0046 **9** 1 1/2 **Just The Tonic**[13] 3844 7-9-7 **70**.......... MeganCarberry(7) 10 54
(Marjorie Fife) *s.i.s: in rr: hdwy over 3f out: lost pl over 1f out* **7/1**[3]
0346 **10** 2 3/4 **Graceful Act**[13] 3846 6-8-13 **55**.......... AndrewElliott 9 32
(Ron Barr) *led 1f: chsd ldrs on outer: lost pl over 1f out* **16/1**
5040 **P** **Spinner Lane**[25] 3440 3-8-2 **52** oh6 ow1..........(p) FrannyNorton 3
(Richard Whitaker) *uns rdr leaving padock and rn loose: led rdrless to s: mid-div: lost pl over 4f out: eased over 3f out: sn t.o: p.u over 2f out* **50/1**

1m 26.61s (-0.59) **Going Correction** +0.025s/f (Good)
**WFA** 3 from 4yo+ 8lb **11** Ran SP% **114.1**
Speed ratings (Par 100): **104,103,102,99,97 97,95,94,93,89**
CSF £200.62 CT £1971.06 TOTE £35.10: £6.80, £2.30, £2.80; EX 293.50 Trifecta £1959.70 Part won..
**Owner** Stuart Barker **Bred** Mrs S M Roy **Trained** Barton-le-Street, N Yorks

**FOCUS**
This handicap was weakened by the withdrawal of two of the likely market leaders. They went a steady pace and not many got involved behind the front-running winner.Tom Eaves reported that the ground was on the faster side. The first, second and third are far from solid and had the run of things.

## 4295 RACING UK ANYWHERE AVAILABLE NOW MAIDEN STKS 5f
**6:40** (6:45) (Class 5) 3-4-Y-O **£2,726** (£805; £402) **Stalls** High

Form RPR
4266 **1** **Fredricka**[24] 3487 3-9-0 61.......... JasonHart 2 65
(Garry Moss) *trckd ldrs: upsides 2f out: shkn up to ld appr fnl f: drvn out* **2/1**[2]
02 **2** 1 **Oasis Mirage**[18] 3677 3-9-0 0.......... JoeFanning 7 61
(Robert Cowell) *led: rdn 2f out: hdd appr fnl f: styd on same pce* **7/4**[1]
330- **3** 3/4 **Resist**[256] 7665 3-9-0 57.......... GrahamLee 5 59
(James Given) *w ldr: rdn over 1f out: kpt on one pce* **7/1**[3]
52 **4** 2 3/4 **Procurer (FR)**[50] 2619 3-9-5 0.......... TomEaves 8 54
(Scott Dixon) *trckd ldrs: t.k.h: drvn 2f out: wknd fnl f* **12/1**
**5** 1 1/2 **Slick Indian** 3-8-12 0.......... AnnaHesketh(7) 3 48
(Michael Easterby) *s.s: a outpcd and in last* **33/1**

59.05s (-0.55) **Going Correction** -0.15s/f (Firm) **5** Ran SP% **92.8**
Speed ratings (Par 103): **98,96,95,90,88**
CSF £4.01 TOTE £2.10: £1.40, £1.20; EX 3.90 Trifecta £6.90.
**Owner** Ron Hull **Bred** J C Parsons & J J Gilmartin **Trained** Tickhill, S Yorks
■ Bifocal and Blaze It were withdrawn. Prices at time of withdrawal 11-2 and 20-1 respectively. Rule 4 applies to all bets - deduction 15p in the pound.

**FOCUS**
An ordinary maiden. Bifocal and Blaze It gave trouble at the start and were withdrawn. Weak form but it makes sense.

## 4296 RACINGUK.COM/ANYWHERE: 3 DEVICES, 1 PRICE H'CAP 2m
**7:10** (7:11) (Class 5) (0-70,70) 4-Y-O+ **£2,587** (£770; £384; £192) **Stalls** Low

Form RPR
-112 **1** **Maoi Chinn Tire (IRE)**[24] 3482 7-8-9 **65**..........(t) JoeDoyle(7) 6 77+
(Jennie Candlish) *hld up in mid-div: t.k.h: smooth hdwy to ld over 2f out: sn jnd: rdn and styd on fnl f* **9/2**[3]
23-0 **2** 1 1/4 **Chant (IRE)**[32] 3205 4-9-7 **70**.......... PJMcDonald 9 80
(Ann Duffield) *mid-div: hdwy to trck ldrs 6f out: effrt over 2f out: sn upsides: rdn and nt qckn ins fnl f* **7/1**
6454 **3** 8 **Kastela Stari**[28] 3336 7-8-5 **54**..........(t) JamesSullivan 11 54
(Tim Fitzgerald) *s.i.s: in rr: hdwy over 3f out: chsng ldrs over 2f out: kpt on take 3rd appr fnl f: one pce* **16/1**
2531 **4** nk **My Destination (IRE)**[5] 4115 5-8-12 **68** 6ex..........(b) LukeLeadbitter(7) 7 68
(Declan Carroll) *hld up in rr: hdwy 3f out: styd on to take 4th last 50yds* **10/3**[1]
-350 **5** 2 1/2 **Uganda Glory (USA)**[15] 3803 4-9-0 **63**..........(v) TomEaves 3 60
(George Baker) *trckd ldrs: effrt over 2f out: wknd fnl f* **9/1**
342 **6** 7 **Mason Hindmarsh**[18] 3661 7-9-2 **65**.......... GrahamLee 1 54
(Karen McLintock) *w ldr: led over 3f out: hdd over 2f out: wknd over 1f out* **7/2**[2]
0524 **7** 4 1/2 **Petella**[38] 2980 8-7-13 **55**..........(p) KieranSchofield(7) 12 38
(George Moore) *s.i.s: in rr: drvn 7f out: sn bhd: kpt on fnl 2f* **14/1**
63-6 **8** 1 1/4 **Indepub**[18] 3661 5-8-11 **60**..........(b) PaulMulrennan 10 42
(Martin Todhunter) *chsd ldrs: drvn over 4f out: lost pl over 1f out* **25/1**
40-5 **9** 16 **Carthaginian (IRE)**[25] 3438 5-9-2 **65**.......... PhillipMakin 2 28
(Martin Todhunter) *in rr: drvn over 5f out: lost pl over 3f out: sn bhd: eased over 1f out: t.o* **33/1**
061 **10** 3/4 **Dabuki (FR)**[13] 3843 4-9-6 **69**..........(p) SilvestreDeSousa 8 31
(Geoffrey Harker) *led: hdd over 3f out: lost pl over 2f out: sn eased and bhd: t.o* **7/1**

3m 29.08s (0.78) **Going Correction** +0.025s/f (Good) **10** Ran SP% **117.8**
Speed ratings (Par 103): **99,98,94,94,92 89,87,86,78,78**
CSF £36.52 CT £466.95 TOTE £6.10: £2.00, £2.90, £7.20; EX 38.30 Trifecta £651.50.
**Owner** The Best Club In The World **Bred** Mrs E Thompson **Trained** Basford Green, Staffs

**FOCUS**
They went a fair pace in this handicap and the first two pulled a long way clear. The runner-up is unexposed as a stayer and has been rated back to his 3yo form.

## 4297 DOWNLOAD NEW RACING UK IPAD APP CLASSIFIED STKS 6f
**7:40** (7:42) (Class 5) 3-Y-O **£2,587** (£770; £384; £192) **Stalls** High

Form RPR
21-6 **1** **Angel Flores (IRE)**[20] 3575 3-9-0 70.......... TonyHamilton 4 78+
(Richard Fahey) *trckd ldrs: led on bit over 2f out: hdd over 1f out: styd on to ld last 50yds* **11/4**[2]
-164 **2** 1 **Castorienta**[14] 3821 3-9-0 66.......... TomEaves 2 75
(George Baker) *trckd ldrs: rdn to ld narrowly over 1f out: hdd and no ex wl ins fnl f* **20/1**
6250 **3** 2 1/2 **Disclosure**[8] 4019 3-9-0 70.......... GrahamLee 6 67
(Les Eyre) *chsd ldrs: drvn over 2f out: kpt on to take 3rd last 100yds* **6/1**
3-13 **4** 1 1/4 **Thornaby Princess**[19] 3600 3-9-0 68.......... DanielTudhope 7 63
(Marjorie Fife) *in rr: hdwy on outside over 2f out: chsng ldrs over 1f out: fdd last 50yds* **9/2**[3]
0122 **5** 1/2 **Native Falls (IRE)**[9] 4003 3-9-0 68.......... SilvestreDeSousa 5 61
(Alan Swinbank) *led: hdd over 2f out: fdd last 150yds* **5/4**[1]
2060 **6** 20 **False Witness (IRE)**[18] 3650 3-8-7 62..........(v[1]) AnnaHesketh(7) 3
(David Nicholls) *in rr: swtchd outside and drvn over 2f out: sn lost pl: bhd and eased ins fnl f: t.o* **33/1**

1m 11.14s (-1.56) **Going Correction** -0.15s/f (Firm) **6** Ran SP% **111.3**
Speed ratings (Par 100): **104,102,99,97,97 70**
CSF £46.73 TOTE £4.00: £2.20, £5.70; EX 58.30 Trifecta £232.30.
**Owner** Richard Fahey Ebor Racing Club Ltd **Bred** Pier House Stud **Trained** Musley Bank, N Yorks

**FOCUS**
The favourite was disappointing in this classified but the first two pulled clear. The runner-up has been rated as running a 5lb pb.

## 4298 JW 4X4 NORTHALLERTON H'CAP (BOBIS RACE) 1m 4f
**8:10** (8:10) (Class 4) (0-80,80) 3-Y-O **£4,851** (£1,443; £721) **Stalls** High

Form RPR
0124 **1** **Penhill**[32] 3200 3-9-4 **77**.......... PJMcDonald 3 89
(James Bethell) *trckd ldr: chal over 2f out: led over 1f out: drvn clr* **5/4**[2]
-61 **2** 3 3/4 **Galactic Heroine**[18] 3653 3-9-7 **80**.......... GrahamLee 2 86
(James Given) *led: drvn 3f out: hdd over 1f out: kpt on same pce* **10/11**[1]
0504 **3** 3 1/4 **Mariners Moon (IRE)**[11] 3911 3-8-13 **72**.......... DanielTudhope 4 74
(David O'Meara) *hld up in last: hdwy 3f out: chsng ldrs over 1f out: one pce: eased whn wl hld nr fin* **8/1**[3]

2m 35.61s (-0.59) **Going Correction** +0.025s/f (Good) **3** Ran SP% **107.9**
Speed ratings (Par 102): **102,99,97**
CSF £2.79 TOTE £2.70; EX 2.40 Trifecta £2.20.
**Owner** Clarendon Thoroughbred Racing **Bred** Newsells Park Stud & Equity Bloodstock **Trained** Middleham Moor, N Yorks

**FOCUS**
There were only three runners but they went a fair pace and the winner scored in good style. The unexposed runner-up had the run of things, so every chance the form is this good.

## 4299 BET ON THE MOVE - RACING UK'S APP MAIDEN STKS 1m
**8:40** (8:41) (Class 5) 3-Y-O+ **£2,587** (£770; £384; £192) **Stalls** Low

Form RPR
-222 **1** **Musaddas**[20] 3577 4-9-13 84.......... KierenFallon 3 89+
(Saeed bin Suroor) *trckd ldrs: drvn over 3f out: led 2f out: clr 1f out: heavily eased clsng stages* **1/6**[1]
5- **2** 7 **Iftikaar (IRE)**[392] 4-9-13 74.......... PhillipMakin 4 69
(Philip Kirby) *trckd ldr: led 3f out: hdd 2f out: no ch w wnr* **4/1**[2]
**3** 1 3/4 **Glasgow Kiss (IRE)** 3-8-13 0.......... RonanWhelan 5 58
(John Patrick Shanahan, Ire) *mid-div: drvn to chse ldrs 3f out: one pce and 3rd 1f out* **6/1**[3]
6-4 **4** 3 **Blue Sonic**[19] 3607 4-9-8 0.......... GrahamLee 1 53
(Jim Goldie) *t.k.h in mid-div: outpcd over 2f out: edgd rt and kpt on ins fnl f* **12/1**
00 **5** 3/4 **Wilful Minx (FR)**[18] 3652 3-8-13 0.......... JamesSullivan 2 49
(James Given) *led: hdd 3f out: fdd appr fnl f* **50/1**
40 **6** 3/4 **Cayjo**[34] 3097 3-9-4 0.......... FrannyNorton 6 52
(Mark Johnston) *chsd ldrs: drvn 3f out: one pce* **14/1**
5 **7** 2 3/4 **Legal Advisor**[19] 3602 3-9-4 0.......... JoeFanning 7 46
(Philip Kirby) *wnt rt s: in rr: sme hdwy 4f out: sn wknd* **16/1**
0 **8** 11 **Red Legacy**[18] 3652 6-9-8 0.......... MichaelStainton 8 16
(Sean Regan) *in rr: drvn over 4f out: sn bhd* **100/1**

1m 40.59s (0.49) **Going Correction** +0.025s/f (Good)
**WFA** 3 from 4yo+ 9lb **8** Ran SP% **143.2**
Speed ratings (Par 103): **98,91,89,86,85 84,82,71**
CSF £2.64 TOTE £1.10: £1.02, £1.70, £1.90; EX 3.00 Trifecta £3.20.
**Owner** Godolphin **Bred** Highbury Stud Ltd **Trained** Newmarket, Suffolk

**FOCUS**
The hot favourite powered clear in this ordinary maiden. Weak form, with the runner-up yet to prove as good as he was in France.

## 4300 DON'T MISS ANYTHING WITH RACING UK ANYWHERE H'CAP 1m
**9:10** (9:10) (Class 5) (0-75,75) 3-Y-O **£2,587** (£770; £384; £192) **Stalls** Low

Form RPR
221 **1** **Green Zone (IRE)**[7] 4063 3-8-11 **65** 6ex..........(p) SilvestreDeSousa 4 73
(Nigel Tinkler) *trckd ldrs: chal over 2f out: led over 1f out: drvn out* **2/1**[1]
1203 **2** 1 1/4 **Alquimia (IRE)**[18] 3663 3-9-7 **75**.......... TonyHamilton 7 80
(Richard Fahey) *hld up in mid-div: effrt over 2f out: styd on to take 2nd ins fnl f* **5/1**[3]
2624 **3** 3/4 **Baltic Fire (IRE)**[25] 3430 3-8-4 **61**.......... JoeyHaynes(3) 6 64
(K R Burke) *chsd ldrs: chal over 2f out: kpt on same pce to take 3rd ins fnl f* **7/1**
0006 **4** 1 1/2 **Syros (IRE)**[11] 3911 3-8-13 **67**.......... BarryMcHugh 8 67
(Michael Easterby) *s.i.s: swtchd lft sn after s: in rr: hdwy on ins over 2f out: swtchd rt and kpt on same pce ins fnl f* **16/1**
0055 **5** 3/4 **Edward Elgar**[7] 4063 3-8-2 **56** oh1..........(p) FrannyNorton 9 54
(Richard Whitaker) *chsd ldrs: drvn over 3f out: edgd lft and one pce over 1f out* **25/1**
5511 **6** 1/2 **In Focus (IRE)**[6] 4067 3-9-2 **70** 6ex.......... BenCurtis 2 67
(Alan Swinbank) *led: hdd over 1f out: wknd towards fin* **5/2**[2]
35-0 **7** 1 3/4 **Scots Law (IRE)**[29] 3300 3-9-1 **69**.......... JoeFanning 1 62
(Keith Dalgleish) *chsd ldrs: drvn over 2f out: wknd towards fin* **16/1**
3000 **8** 7 **Kraka Gym (IRE)**[11] 3911 3-8-3 **57**..........(b) JamesSullivan 5 33
(Michael Easterby) *dwlt: sn mid-div: drvn over 3f out: lost pl over 1f out* **28/1**
0120 **9** 3 1/4 **Kisanji**[10] 3946 3-9-1 **69**.......... KierenFallon 3 37
(Alan McCabe) *s.i.s: t.k.h in rr: drvn 3f out: nvr on terms: eased nr fin* **12/1**

1m 39.96s (-0.14) **Going Correction** +0.025s/f (Good) **9** Ran SP% **117.8**
Speed ratings (Par 100): **101,99,99,97,96 96,94,87,84**
CSF £12.80 CT £59.43 TOTE £3.10: £1.10, £1.60, £2.40; EX 13.30 Trifecta £59.60.
**Owner** Sunrise **Bred** Incense Partnership **Trained** Langton, N Yorks

**FOCUS**
The pace was not very strong but the well-backed favourite delivered in decent style. The runner-up is progressing, while the third helps set the level.
T/Plt: £184.40 to a £1 stake. Pool: £63,917.28 - 252.90 winning units T/Qpdt: £28.80 to a £1 stake. Pool: £5,216.64 - 133.95 winning units WG

# 4087 YARMOUTH (L-H)
Tuesday, July 15

**OFFICIAL GOING: Good to firm**
Wind: Light; half against Weather: Dry and quite warm

## 4301 BRITISH STALLION STUDS EBF MAIDEN STKS 7f 3y
**5:50** (5:50) (Class 5) 2-Y-O **£3,234** (£962; £481; £240) **Stalls** Centre

Form RPR
04 **1** **Orlando Rogue (IRE)**[36] 3063 2-9-5 0.......... PatCosgrave 5 76
(George Baker) *chsd ldr: upsides and gng best ent fnl 2f: rdn to ld jst over 1f out: in command and edgd rt ins fnl f: rdn out* **11/4**[1]

2 **2** *2* **Berland (IRE)** 2-9-5 0 TomQueally 2 71
(Michael Bell) *t.k.h: hld up in tch in midfield: rdn and effrt to chse ldng trio over 1f out: styd on to chse wnr fnl 75yds: kpt on but no imp* **6/1³**

5 **3** *¾* **Mountainside**[20] 3578 2-9-5 0 MartinLane 7 69
(Charlie Appleby) *in tch in midfield: effrt and rdn to chse ldng pair 2f out: keeping on same pce whn swtchd lft ins fnl f: kpt on* **6/1³**

00 **4** *nk* **My Mate (IRE)**[32] 3194 2-9-5 0 AdamKirby 3 68
(Clive Brittain) *led: rdn ent fnl 2f: drvn and hdd jst over 1f out: plugged on same pce and lost 2 pls fnl 75yds* **12/1**

**5** *6* **Giannizzero (IRE)** 2-9-5 0 MartinHarley 4 52
(Marco Botti) *in tch in midfield: rdn and effrt over 2f out: no ex and btn over 1f out: wknd fnl f* **10/1**

04 **6** *1½* **Goolagong Girl (IRE)**[26] 3381 2-9-0 0 JimmyQuinn 8 43
(Jane Chapple-Hyam) *dwlt: hld up in tch in rr: rdn 3f out: btn and hung lft u.p over 1f out: sn wknd* **33/1**

**7** *18* **Bow And Arrow** 2-9-5 0 WilliamBuick 1
(Charlie Appleby) *dwlt: rn green and nvr travelling wl: pushed along and hdwy into midfield after 3f: lost pl qckly over 2f out: t.o and eased ins fnl f* **3/1²**

0 **8** *1¾* **Andretti**[24] 3474 2-9-5 0 (v¹) RyanMoore 6
(Sir Michael Stoute) *chsd ldrs: rdn 3f out: lost pl qckly and btn ent fnl 2f: sn lost tch: t.o and eased ins fnl f* **7/1**

1m 27.29s (0.69) **Going Correction** +0.075s/f (Good) **8 Ran SP% 112.5**
Speed ratings (Par 94): **99,96,95,95,88 86,66,64**
CSF £18.95 TOTE £2.20: £1.10, £2.40, £1.90; EX 21.60 Trifecta £156.80.
**Owner** Mr & Mrs J Pittam **Bred** Barbara Prendergast **Trained** Manton, Wilts

**FOCUS**
Bottom bend dolled out 1.5m and races on Round course increased by 7m. An ordinary maiden run at a modest pace. The fourth was well placed throughout and has been rated a minor improver.

## 4302 AUGUST MUSIC NIGHTS AT YARMOUTH RACECOURSE (S) NURSERY H'CAP 7f 3y
**6:20** (6:21) (Class 6) 2-Y-O **£1,940** (£577; £288; £144) **Stalls** Centre

Form RPR

0602 **1** **Ciaras Cookie (IRE)**[10] 3967 2-9-7 **54** AdamKirby 5 62
(David Evans) *mde all: rdn over 2f out: drvn and wnt clr over 1f out: in command fnl f: styd on: comf* **10/11¹**

4040 **2** *8* **Penalty Scorer**[11] 3937 2-9-1 **53** (e¹) DuilioDaSilva⁽⁵⁾ 2 39
(Richard Guest) *stdd s and short of room leaving stalls: t.k.h: hld up in rr: hdwy 1/2-way: 3rd and rdn 2f out: btn but wnt 2nd and edgd rt ins fnl f: wknd but hld on for 2nd after* **7/1³**

5044 **3** *2* **Reet Petite (IRE)**[25] 3435 2-9-4 **51** (p) PaulHanagan 7 32
(Michael Dods) *in tch in midfield: chsd wnr 1/2-way: rdn over 2f out: no ex over 1f out: wl btn and lost 2nd whn sltly hmpd ins fnl f: wknd* **9/4²**

0000 **4** *2¾* **Sarah Catherine**[10] 3967 2-8-7 **47** (v¹) CharlotteJenner⁽⁷⁾ 6 20
(Mark Usher) *in tch: dropped to last 4f out: rdn and btn 1/2-way: no ch after: wnt modest 4th ins fnl f: plugged on* **25/1**

4406 **5** *2* **Marti Ella**[10] 3967 2-8-4 **44** JosephineGordon⁽⁷⁾ 1 12
(J S Moore) *chsd ldrs: pushed along and outpcd over 2f out: 4th and wl btn over 1f out* **20/1**

6050 **6** *12* **Mary Ann Bugg (IRE)**[10] 3967 2-9-0 **47** (t) WilliamCarson 3
(Phil McEntee) *chsd ldr tl 1/2-way: sn struggling u.p: wl bhd over 1f out* **16/1**

1m 29.34s (2.74) **Going Correction** +0.075s/f (Good) **6 Ran SP% 110.1**
Speed ratings (Par 92): **87,77,75,72,70 56**
CSF £7.76 TOTE £1.70: £1.30, £3.00; EX 9.20 Trifecta £12.60.There was no bid for the winner.
**Owner** Mrs Emma Ambrose **Bred** River Downs Stud **Trained** Pandy, Monmouths

**FOCUS**
In a poor seller run at a medium pace, the winner was, and remains, the only runner with any obvious prospects. Perhaps she was the only one that got home.

## 4303 ASCO AND PERENCO H'CAP 1m 3f 101y
**6:50** (6:50) (Class 5) (0-70,70) 3-Y-O+ **£2,911** (£866; £432; £216) **Stalls** Low

Form RPR

312 **1** **Giantstepsahead (IRE)**[29] 3308 5-9-11 **67** JackMitchell 5 79
(Denis Quinn) *mde all: clr and rdn 2f out: styd on wl: in command whn flashed tail u.p wl ins fnl f* **4/1²**

4502 **2** *2¼* **Sweetheart Abbey**[17] 3711 3-8-11 **65** TomQueally 2 72
(William Knight) *taken down early: hld up in rr: hdwy 3f out: edgd lft but styd on to chse clr wnr jst over 1f out: kpt on but a hld* **9/2³**

3102 **3** *4½* **Corn Maiden**[12] 3899 5-9-6 **62** MartinHarley 7 62
(Lydia Pearce) *chsd ldrs: wnt 2nd 4f out: drvn and no imp over 1f out: 3rd and wknd ins fnl f* **7/1**

0033 **4** *10* **Semaral (IRE)**[30] 3268 3-9-2 **70** TedDurcan 6 60
(Chris Wall) *hld up in tch: hdwy to chse ldrs 3f out: rdn and no rspnse 2f out: wknd over 1f out* **2/1¹**

0024 **5** *16* **Magnolia Ridge (IRE)**[11] 3919 4-9-11 **67** (p) ShaneKelly 1 24
(Kristin Stubbs) *in tch in midfield: sme hdwy 5f out: lost pl and rdn 3f out: sn bhd: t.o* **5/1**

-203 **6** *8* **Armourer (IRE)**[22] 3541 3-9-0 **68** (b¹) DougieCostello 4 11
(William Muir) *dwlt: sn rcvrd to chse wnr: lost 2nd 4f out: sn dropped out: lost tch 3f out: t.o* **8/1**

2m 28.69s (-0.01) **Going Correction** +0.075s/f (Good)
**WFA** 3 from 4yo+ 12lb **6 Ran SP% 111.8**
Speed ratings (Par 103): **103,101,98,90,79 73**
CSF £21.69 CT £118.24 TOTE £4.90: £1.30, £3.10; EX 24.20 Trifecta £50.30.
**Owner** K Hills **Bred** Darragh O'Reilly **Trained** Newmarket, Suffolk
■ Stewards' Enquiry : Jack Mitchell three-day ban; careless riding (29th July-1st Aug)

**FOCUS**
The winner made all at a routine pace until applying pressure 3f out, with only the runner-up ever threatening to make a race of it. Consequently, it didn't look a competitive race. The runner-up has been rated to her AW latest.

## 4304 INSPECTION VERIFICATION BUREAU H'CAP 1m 1f
**7:20** (7:22) (Class 6) (0-55,55) 3-Y-O **£1,940** (£577; £288; £144) **Stalls** Low

Form RPR

3002 **1** **Tete Orange**[6] 4092 3-9-1 **49** MartinHarley 14 67+
(Stuart Williams) *nt best away and rdn along to cl and chse ldrs after 1f: jnd ldr and gng best 3f out: led wl over 1f out: sn rdn and clr: drew wl clr fnl f: readily* **13/8¹**

6304 **2** *8* **Lynngale**[27] 3362 3-9-5 **53** ShaneKelly 13 54
(Kristin Stubbs) *led and crossed to rail: rdn over 2f out: hdd wl over 1f out: no ch w wnr but battled on to hold 2nd fnl f* **20/1**

05-5 **3** *nk* **Bushy Glade (IRE)**[24] 3477 3-8-13 **52** ShelleyBirkett⁽⁵⁾ 12 54+
(Julia Feilden) *hld up in midfield: nt clr run and shuffled bk 3f out: hdwy and switching lft over 1f out: battling for 2nd ins fnl f: kpt on: no ch w wnr* **33/1**

4006 **4** *1¼* **Marphilly (IRE)**[42] 2878 3-8-12 **46** oh1 (v¹) LiamJones 5 44
(John Best) *s.i.s: hld up in last trio: rdn and hdwy on outer over 3f out: plugged on to go 4th ins fnl f: no ch w wnr* **33/1**

-000 **5** *1½* **Venus Marina**[26] 3389 3-9-0 **51** AshleyMorgan⁽³⁾ 8 46
(Chris Wall) *t.k.h: chsd ldrs: rdn over 2f out: 3rd and outpcd over 1f out: wknd ins fnl f* **8/1³**

3500 **6** *2¼* **Sexy Secret**[10] 3971 3-9-4 **55** SimonPearce⁽³⁾ 11 45
(Lydia Pearce) *in tch in midfield: rdn 3f out: no ch w wnr and plugged on same pce fnl 2f* **12/1**

0045 **7** *2* **Fickle Feelings (IRE)**[21] 3545 3-9-4 **52** GrahamGibbons 3 38
(David Barron) *wl in tch in midfield: switching rt 3f out: rdn and btn wl over 1f out: sn wknd* **4/1²**

3664 **8** *1¼* **Honiton Lace**[8] 4026 3-9-5 **53** ¹ AdamKirby 1 36
(Phil McEntee) *chsd ldrs: drvn and unable qck 2f out: wknd over 1f out* **12/1**

003- **9** *1* **Ohio (IRE)**[342] 5151 3-9-7 **55** (b¹) J-PGuillambert 10 36
(Nick Littmoden) *t.k.h: hld up in tch in midfield: rdn and effrt 3f out: no imp and wknd wl over 1f out* **20/1**

5054 **10** *hd* **Moonwood**[8] 4017 3-9-4 **52** (v) PaulHanagan 9 33
(Ollie Pears) *in tch in midfield: hdwy to chse ldrs and rdn 3f out: btn 2f out: sn wknd* **14/1**

6500 **11** *2¾* **Water For Life**[42] 2878 3-8-12 **46** oh1 TomQueally 7 21
(Dave Morris) *t.k.h: hld up in tch in midfield: rdn 3f out: sn struggling and wknd 2f out* **25/1**

6300 **12** *6* **Trinity Lorraine (IRE)**[42] 2878 3-8-7 **46** oh1 TimClark⁽⁵⁾ 2 8
(Alan Bailey) *in tch towards rr: rdn 3f out: sn btn: wl bhd over 1f out* **33/1**

5004 **13** *16* **Va Benny**[16] 3756 3-9-4 **52** (p) FrederikTylicki 4
(J R Jenkins) *a bhd: lost tch over 3f out: t.o* **33/1**

-000 **14** *1½* **Haaffa Sovereign**[49] 2643 3-8-5 **46** oh1 JordanVaughan⁽⁷⁾ 6
(George Margarson) *a towards rr: lost tch over 3f out: t.o* **66/1**

1m 56.68s (0.88) **Going Correction** +0.075s/f (Good) **14 Ran SP% 117.9**
Speed ratings (Par 98): **99,91,91,90,89 87,85,84,83,83 80,75,61,59**
CSF £42.46 CT £693.00 TOTE £2.50: £1.10, £3.20, £8.30; EX 32.80 Trifecta £544.70.
**Owner** J W Parry **Bred** The National Stud **Trained** Newmarket, Suffolk

**FOCUS**
This was a low-grade race dominated by fillies and run at a solid gallop. It rarely pays to get excited about a horse rated 49, but the winner is undoubtedly going in the right direction. She has been rated close to last week's effort.

## 4305 HI-SPAN.COM H'CAP 6f 3y
**7:50** (7:50) (Class 3) (0-90,90) 3-Y-O+ **£7,762** (£2,310; £1,154; £577) **Stalls** Centre

Form RPR

10-2 **1** **Tanzeel (IRE)**[24] 3479 3-9-3 **87** (t) PaulHanagan 3 101
(Charles Hills) *chsd ldr: rdn to ld and hung rt over 1f out: clr fnl f: r.o wl: comf* **11/8¹**

2014 **2** *3¼* **Peace Seeker**[44] 2803 6-9-12 **90** (t) WilliamCarson 5 94
(Anthony Carson) *led: rdn and hung lft wl over 1f out: hdd: hmpd and swtchd lft over 1f out: no ch w wnr but battled on to hold 2nd ins fnl f* **12/1**

0-54 **3** *hd* **Mississippi**[17] 3714 5-9-7 **85** GrahamGibbons 4 88
(David Barron) *hld up in tch: rdn and effrt to go 3rd jst over 1f out: no ch w wnr but battling for 2nd ins fnl f: kpt on* **2/1²**

0000 **4** *nk* **Picture Dealer**[4] 4146 5-9-7 **88** SimonPearce⁽³⁾ 1 90
(Lydia Pearce) *v.s.a: detached in last: clsd 4f out: rdn and effrt whn swtchd lft over 1f out: no ch w wnr but styd on ins fnl f* **6/1³**

0210 **5** *14* **Green Monkey**[17] 3702 4-9-2 **80** ShaneKelly 2 38
(James Fanshawe) *chsd ldrs: rdn over 1f out: lost 3rd jst over 1f out: sn btn and eased ins fnl f* **6/1³**

1m 13.81s (-0.59) **Going Correction** +0.075s/f (Good)
**WFA** 3 from 4yo+ 6lb **5 Ran SP% 111.7**
Speed ratings (Par 107): **106,101,101,101,82**
CSF £17.46 TOTE £2.10: £1.20, £3.00; EX 13.00 Trifecta £28.30.
**Owner** Hamdan Al Maktoum **Bred** Norelands Stallions **Trained** Lambourn, Berks

**FOCUS**
This was contested by some useful sprinters and the lightly raced winner can go on to better things. Unconvincing form, with the runner-up rated to form.

## 4306 FUSION HAIR AND BEAUTY CONSULTANTS LTD H'CAP 6f 3y
**8:20** (8:20) (Class 6) (0-60,60) 3-Y-O+ **£1,940** (£577; £288; £144) **Stalls** Centre

Form RPR

4212 **1** **Refuse Colette (IRE)**[18] 3678 5-9-4 **54** PaoloSirigu 2 75
(Mick Quinn) *in tch: rdn and hdwy to ld 2f out: sn drew clr 1f out and styd on wl: readily* **3/1¹**

-356 **2** *7* **See Vermont**[11] 3913 6-8-11 **47** (p) TomQueally 8 46
(Robin Bastiman) *chsd ldr tl 2f out: outpcd and btn over 1f out: kpt on to chse clr wnr again 1f out: no imp* **14/1**

6-03 **3** *2* **Roring Samson (IRE)**[7] 4048 3-9-4 **60** PatCosgrave 7 51
(George Baker) *chsd ldrs: rdn and effrt over 2f out: chsd wnr 2f out: sn drvn and outpcd 3rd and wl hld fnl f* **4/1²**

0004 **4** *¾* **Swiss Lait**[20] 3588 3-9-4 **60** LiamKeniry 5 49
(David Elsworth) *s.i.s: hld up in tch in rr: rdn over 2f out: hdwy u.p and swtchd lft ins fnl f: styd on: nvr trbld ldrs* **8/1³**

000- **5** *shd* **Magic Ice**[306] 6345 4-8-13 **49** PaddyAspell 9 38
(John Berry) *stdd s: t.k.h: hld up in tch in rr: sme hdwy over 1f out: plugged on ins fnl f: nvr trbld ldrs* **25/1**

63-0 **6** *hd* **Pieman's Girl**[172] 311 3-9-3 **59** WilliamCarson 12 47
(Anthony Carson) *racd nr stands' rail: in tch in midfield overall: rdn and hdwy 3f out: chsd ldrs and drvn 2f out: sn outpcd and btn: plugged on* **33/1**

52-5 **7** *3½* **Aaranyow (IRE)**[19] 3630 6-8-12 **51** RobertTart⁽³⁾ 1 29
(Clifford Lines) *in tch in midfield: rdn and hdwy over 2f out: outpcd and btn over 1f out: wknd fnl f* **10/1**

00-6 **8** *½* **Hazza The Jazza**[43] 2844 4-8-12 **53** (b) DuilioDaSilva⁽⁵⁾ 3 29
(Richard Guest) *in tch in midfield: rdn and effrt over 2f out: struggling 2f out and sn wknd* **8/1³**

45-0 **9** *2* **Port Lairge**[79] 1771 4-9-2 **57** LouisSteward⁽⁵⁾ 6 27
(John Gallagher) *chsd ldrs tl rdn and lost pl 1/2-way: wknd wl over 1f out* **20/1**

3-06 **10** *hd* **Celestial Knight**[17] 3700 3-9-4 **60** ShaneKelly 4 28
(James Fanshawe) *s.i.s: in tch towards rr: rdn and effrt wl over 1f out: no prog and sn btn: wknd* **10/1**



The Form Book, Raceform Ltd, Newbury, RG14 5SJ

0340 11 nk **Magical Rose (IRE)**[43] 2843 4-9-9 **59**..........................(p) JimmyQuinn 10 27
(Conrad Allen) *hld up in tch: rdn and struggling ent fnl 2f: sn btn and wknd* **8/1**[3]
0260 12 3 1/4 **Homeboy (IRE)**[5] 4101 6-8-11 **47**..........................(b) GrahamGibbons 11
(David Evans) *led and racd nr stands' rail: drvn and hdd 2f out: sn btn and wknd: bhd fnl f* **20/1**
1m 14.11s (-0.29) **Going Correction** +0.075s/f (Good)
**WFA** 3 from 4yo+ 6lb **12** Ran SP% **119.5**
Speed ratings (Par 101): **104,94,92,91,90 90,85,85,82,82 81,77**
CSF £44.72 CT £176.69 TOTE £3.10: £1.20, £2.20, £2.70; EX 25.50 Trifecta £206.70.
**Owner** YNWA Partnership **Bred** Patrick O'Reilly **Trained** Newmarket, Suffolk
**FOCUS**
The winner has been campaigned at 7f-plus since her early days but looked much better over 6f here. Unexposed at this trip, she appeared to be well handicapped against some modest but largely unexposed rivals. Not much solid here.

## 4307 INSPECTION VERIFICATION BUREAU PLATE H'CAP 5f 43y
**8:50** (8:50) (Class 5) (0-70,70) 3-Y-O **£2,587** (£770; £384; £192) **Stalls** Centre

Form RPR
-264 1 **Rozene (IRE)**[18] 3669 3-9-7 **70**.......................... GrahamGibbons 5 77
(David Barron) *chsd ldrs: wnt 2nd 3f out: shkn up to ld over 1f out: sn rdn and hung lft: fnd ex and asserted ins fnl f: r.o* **1/1**[1]
5320 2 1 **Champagne Charley**[17] 3707 3-8-13 **62**.......................... ShaneKelly 2 64
(Des Donovan) *dropped in bhd after s: hld up in rr: hdwy 2f out: swtchd rt and effrt over 1f out: pressed wnr and drvn and ins fnl f: fnd little and btn fnl 100yds: wnt 2nd cl home* **11/2**[3]
1222 3 hd **Gulland Rock**[16] 3756 3-9-4 **67**.......................... DougieCostello 4 69
(William Muir) *stdd and rrd as stalls opened: chsd ldr for 2f: styd handy: drvn and pressing wnr 1f out: styd on same pce fnl 100yds: lost 2nd cl home* **7/4**[2]
450- 4 11 **Anytimeatall (IRE)**[217] 8228 3-8-8 **62**.......................... NatashaEaton(5) 3 24
(Alan Bailey) *restless in stalls: awkward as stalls opened: sn led: rdn and hdd over 1f out: wknd fnl f* **14/1**
1m 4.07s (1.37) **Going Correction** +0.075s/f (Good) **4** Ran SP% **108.4**
Speed ratings (Par 100): **92,90,90,72**
CSF £6.67 TOTE £1.70; EX 7.10 Trifecta £7.60.
**Owner** Twinacre Nurseries Ltd **Bred** M Downey & John Osborne **Trained** Maunby, N Yorks
■ Stewards' Enquiry : Graham Gibbons six-day ban; excessive use of whip (29th July-3rd Aug)
**FOCUS**
The first three are all solid performers at a realistic level and the pace was good. The winner has been rated as running a small pb, while the third helps set the level.
T/Plt: £19.50 to a £1 stake. Pool: £75,652.94 - 2,824.92 winning units T/Qpdt: £7.30 to a £1 stake. Pool: £7,364.03 - 745.50 winning units SP

# 3597 COMPIEGNE (L-H)
Tuesday, July 15

**OFFICIAL GOING: Turf: heavy**

## 4312a PRIX DE FRANCIERES (CONDITIONS) (2YO) (TURF) 7f
**11:45** (12:00) 2-Y-O **£12,083** (£4,833; £3,625; £2,416; £1,208)

RPR
1 **Nucifera (USA)**[25] 2-9-0 0.......................... StephanePasquier 4
(J E Pease, France) **3/5**[1]
2 snk **Red Tornado (FR)**[43] 2829 2-8-13 0 ow2.......... ChristopheSoumillon 5
(Harry Dunlop) *dwlt sltly: sn led on rail: shkn up and lened 2f out: hdd 1 1/2f out: swtchd outside as wnr moved on to rail: rdn and r.o fnl f: nt quite get bk up* **18/5**[2]
3 2 **Fleur De Printemps**[12] 2-8-8 0.......................... CristianDemuro 1
(F Vermeulen, France) **175/10**
4 1 3/4 **Kailong (FR)** 2-8-10 0.......................... TonyPiccone 8
(E Leenders, France) **49/10**[3]
5 snk **Konigin Ricke (GER)**[38] 2-8-8 0.......................... FilipMinarik 7
(M Figge, Germany) **108/10**
6 2 **Maui (FR)**[22] 2-8-8 0.......................... RonanThomas 3
(Mlle V Dissaux, France) **185/10**
1m 33.06s (93.06) **6** Ran SP% **120.2**
PARI-MUTUEL (all including 1 euro stake): WIN 1.60; PLACE 1.10, 1.10, 1.20; DF 2.40; SF 4.20.
**Owner** Flaxman Stables Ireland Ltd **Bred** Flaxman Holdings Limited **Trained** Chantilly, France

# 4065 CATTERICK (L-H)
Wednesday, July 16

**OFFICIAL GOING: Good to firm (9.2)**
Wind: Stiff breeze across Weather: Cloudy

## 4313 DOWNLOAD THE RACING UK IPAD APP NURSERY H'CAP (BOBIS RACE) 5f 212y
**2:00** (2:02) (Class 4) 2-Y-O **£4,204** (£1,251; £625; £312) **Stalls** Low

Form RPR
442 1 **Izzthatright (IRE)**[33] 3201 2-9-7 **74**.......................... TonyHamilton 4 76
(Richard Fahey) *slt ld: rdn along wl over 1f out: drvn ins fnl f: edgd lft and kpt on wl towards fin* **11/4**[2]
414 2 3/4 **Madamoiselle Bond**[58] 2403 2-8-12 **70**.......................... KevinStott(5) 3 70
(William Jarvis) *trckd ldrs: hdwy wl over 1f out: effrt and nt clr run ent fnl f: sn swtchd rt and rdn: kpt on towards fin: tk 2nd on line* **13/2**[3]
3331 3 nse **Miami Carousel (IRE)**[8] 4057 2-9-5 **79** 6ex.......................... JoeDoyle(7) 2 80
(John Quinn) *cl up on inner: effrt 2f out: sn rdn: n.m.r over 1f out and ins fnl f: hld whn sddle slipped towards fin* **1/1**[1]
5046 4 2 1/2 **Foxtrot Knight**[12] 3937 2-8-12 **65**.......................... JoeFanning 8 57
(Olly Stevens) *trckd ldng pair: hdwy and cl up on outer 2f out: sn rdn: drvn ent fnl f: sn one pce* **10/1**
060 5 1 **Secret Of Dubai**[20] 3620 2-7-12 **56**.......................... JackGarritty(5) 6 45
(Brian Ellison) *in tch: hdwy over 2f out: rdn to chse ldrs over 1f out: sn drvn and one pce* **16/1**
215 6 20 **Cabbies Lou**[54] 2521 2-9-2 **72**.......................... JoeyHaynes(3) 7
(Noel Wilson) *a in rr: rdn along over 2f out: sn outpcd and bhd* **25/1**
1m 12.55s (-1.05) **Going Correction** -0.30s/f (Firm) **6** Ran SP% **108.8**
Speed ratings (Par 96): **95,94,93,90,89 62**
CSF £18.98 CT £24.63 TOTE £3.20: £1.70, £4.00; EX 18.10 Trifecta £28.10.
**Owner** The Go 90 Partnership **Bred** Patrick Cummins **Trained** Musley Bank, N Yorks
**FOCUS**
Officially good to firm ground on which 12mm of water had been applied since Monday. Following the first race, winning jockey Tony Hamilton confirmed that the ground was as stated, and Joe Fanning agreed that it was "good, fast ground." An ordinary nursery. They went quick, recording a time 1.25 seconds outside of standard, and it produced a close finish. The runner-up helps set the level.

## 4314 YORKSHIRE-OUTDOORS.CO.UK (S) STKS 5f 212y
**2:30** (2:30) (Class 6) 3-Y-O+ **£2,385** (£704; £352) **Stalls** Low

Form RPR
-620 1 **Logans Lad (IRE)**[14] 3848 4-9-0 61..........................(vt[1]) FrankieMcDonald 1 67
(Daniel Mark Loughnane) *cl up on inner: led 1/2-way: rdn clr wl over 1f out: kpt on* **11/2**[3]
0400 2 3 1/4 **Tuibama (IRE)**[12] 3913 5-9-0 52..........................(p) DaleSwift 6 59
(Tracy Waggott) *bhd: hdwy 2f out: swtchd rt to outer and rdn wl over 1f out: styd on fnl f* **16/1**
-030 3 2 1/4 **Greenbury (IRE)**[15] 3833 3-8-9 50..........................(p) PJMcDonald 11 50
(Ann Duffield) *chsd ldng pair: rdn along 2f out: drvn over 1f out: kpt on one pce fnl f* **33/1**
00-0 4 hd **Sherry For Nanny (IRE)**[16] 3792 3-8-4 47..........................(p) IanBrennan 5 44
(Marjorie Fife) *in tch: hdwy 1/2-way: rdn to chse ldrs 2f out: drvn and kpt on one pce fnl f* **100/1**
-305 5 hd **A J Cook (IRE)**[10] 4005 4-8-9 55.......................... ShirleyTeasdale(5) 4 49
(Ron Barr) *chsd ldrs: rdn along over 2f out: sn one pce* **33/1**
5333 6 2 **Sewn Up**[6] 4101 4-9-6 50..........................(p) RoystonFfrench 8 49
(Andrew Hollinshead) *towards rr: effrt and sme hdwy whn n.m.r wl over 1f out: n.d* **8/1**
0406 7 hd **Dodina (IRE)**[21] 3571 4-8-8 62..........................(b) MeganCarberry(7) 10 44
(Brian Ellison) *slt ld: hdd 1/2-way: rdn along 2f out: sn drvn and wknd* **10/3**[1]
0000 8 1/2 **The Strig**[6] 4114 7-9-0 63..........................(v) AndrewMullen 7 41
(Nigel Tinkler) *dwlt: sn rdn along: a in rr* **11/1**
5304 9 1 1/4 **Thrust Control (IRE)**[7] 4069 7-9-0 51..........................(p) JoeFanning 12 37
(Tracy Waggott) *in tch: rdn along over 2f out: sn drvn and wknd* **11/2**[3]
0560 10 1 3/4 **Lady Montenegro**[22] 3548 3-7-11 46..........................(p) RowanScott(7) 3 26
(Ann Duffield) *a towards rr* **28/1**
3305 11 7 **Casper Lee (IRE)**[16] 3793 3-8-6 51..........................(b) ConnorBeasley(3) 9 10
(Michael Herrington) *dwlt: sn rdn along and a bhd* **25/1**
3R-R R **Defence Council (IRE)**[108] 1191 6-8-9 74.......... JacobButterfield(5) 2
(Ollie Pears) *ref to r: tk no part* **4/1**[2]
1m 11.78s (-1.82) **Going Correction** -0.30s/f (Firm)
**WFA** 3 from 4yo+ 5lb **12** Ran SP% **113.3**
Speed ratings (Par 101): **100,95,92,92,92 89,89,88,86,84 75,**
CSF £79.75 TOTE £4.60: £2.50, £4.40, £5.90; EX 111.10 Trifecta £1694.90 Part won. Pool of £2259.89 - 0.37 winning units..There was no bid for winner. Sewn Up was claimed by K Dalgleish for £5000.
**Owner** Ian O'Connor **Bred** Tally-Ho Stud **Trained** Baldwin's Gate, Staffs
**FOCUS**
A weak seller in which few got involved. There was a good early pace and they were soon strung out. The third has been rated pretty much to form.

## 4315 ABF THE SOLDIERS' CHARITY H'CAP 5f
**3:00** (3:00) (Class 5) (0-75,75) 3-Y-O **£2,911** (£866; £432; £216) **Stalls** Low

Form RPR
4-43 1 **Innocently (IRE)**[17] 3756 3-9-7 **75**.......................... DanielTudhope 7 84
(David O'Meara) *qckly away: mde all: rdn clr wl over 1f out: readily* **3/1**[2]
3133 2 2 3/4 **Noble Asset**[19] 3669 3-9-6 **74**..........................[1] PhillipMakin 6 73
(John Quinn) *prom: chsd wnr fr 1/2-way: rdn along wl over 1f out: drvn and no imp fnl f* **2/1**[1]
430 3 1 1/4 **Fuel Injection**[11] 3959 3-8-10 **64**..........................(p) GrahamLee 3 59
(Paul Midgley) *trckd ldrs: hdwy over 2f out: rdn wl over 1f out: drvn and kpt on same pce fnl f* **9/2**[3]
1550 4 1 1/4 **Red Forever**[4] 4186 3-8-11 **65**.......................... PatrickMathers 5 55
(Alan Berry) *in tch: sme hdwy over 2f out: sn rdn and no imp* **16/1**
0506 5 2 3/4 **De Repente (IRE)**[12] 3921 3-8-8 **62**.......................... RaulDaSilva 1 42
(Paul Green) *towards rr: rdn along 1/2-way: n.d* **10/1**
5-01 6 2 1/4 **Lexington Rose**[20] 3600 3-9-6 **74**.......................... RoystonFfrench 2 46
(Bryan Smart) *trckd wnr on inner: rdn along 2f out: sn wknd* **11/2**
0000 7 3/4 **Lorimer's Lot (IRE)**[6] 4114 3-9-2 **70**.......................... DuranFentiman 4 39
(Mark Walford) *awkward and dwlt s: a in rr* **22/1**
58.41s (-1.39) **Going Correction** -0.30s/f (Firm) **7** Ran SP% **111.2**
Speed ratings (Par 100): **99,94,92,90,86 82,81**
CSF £8.87 TOTE £2.50: £2.30, £1.10; EX 7.70 Trifecta £24.10.
**Owner** Hollowdean **Bred** Longfort Stud **Trained** Nawton, N Yorks
**FOCUS**
A run-of-the-mill sprint handicap. Once again you wanted to be right on the pace and there was little change in the positions throughout the race.

## 4316 RACING UK ANYWHERE AVAILABLE NOW H'CAP (QUALIFIER FOR THE CATTERICK TWELVE FURLONG SERIES FINAL) 1m 3f 214y
**3:30** (3:30) (Class 5) (0-70,65) 3-Y-O **£3,881** (£1,155; £577; £288) **Stalls** Low

Form RPR
4330 1 **Indira**[30] 3316 3-9-3 **61**.......................... RobertWinston 7 71
(John Berry) *trckd ldr: cl up 1/2-way: chal over 3f out: led over 2f out: rdn wl over 1f out: kpt on wl fnl f* **7/2**[2]
6300 2 1 **Flying Cape (IRE)**[34] 3146 3-9-7 **65**.......................... RoystonFfrench 1 73
(Andrew Hollinshead) *trckd ldng pair: hdwy over 2f out: rdn to chse wnr over 1f out: sn drvn: edgd lft ins fnl f: kpt on same pce* **7/1**
-215 3 2 1/4 **Chivers (IRE)**[19] 3655 3-9-4 **62**.......................... TonyHamilton 4 66
(Tim Easterby) *trckd ldrs: hdwy wl over 2f out: rdn to chse ldng pair appr fnl f: sn drvn and one pce* **9/2**[3]
0345 4 3 1/2 **Stout Cortez**[24] 3498 3-9-7 **65**.......................... JoeFanning 2 64
(Mark Johnston) *led: pushed along over 3f out: rdn and hdd over 2f out: sn wknd* **9/4**[1]
2635 5 2 1/4 **Coin Broker (IRE)**[11] 3950 3-9-4 **62**.......................... DanielTudhope 6 57
(David O'Meara) *hld up in rr: niggled along 7f out: rdn along over 4f out: nvr a factor* **7/2**[2]
4450 6 6 **Arianrhod (IRE)**[19] 3644 3-9-6 **64**..........................[1] GrahamLee 5 50
(Donald McCain) *in rr: sme hdwy over 4f out: rdn along over 3f out: sn btn* **20/1**
2m 34.96s (-3.94) **Going Correction** -0.30s/f (Firm) **6** Ran SP% **110.7**
Speed ratings (Par 100): **101,100,98,96,95 91**
CSF £26.15 TOTE £7.20: £2.40, £3.00; EX 23.80 Trifecta £145.70.
**Owner** Severn Crossing Partnership **Bred** Mrs M L Parry & P M Steele-Mortimer **Trained** Newmarket, Suffolk

**FOCUS**
Only one of these had previously managed to win, so this is modest form at best. With the topweight 5lb below the ceiling, it was effectively a 0-65. The runner-up has been rated to his turf best.

## 4317 CATTERICKBRIDGE.CO.UK H'CAP 5f 212y
**4:00** (4:01) (Class 4) (0-85,85) 3-Y-0+ **£6,817** (£2,013; £1,007) **Stalls** Low

Form RPR
0053 **1** **Lady Frances**[8] 4053 3-9-1 **79** JoeFanning 9 89
(Mark Johnston) *qckly away: mde all: rdn clr 2f out: kpt on strly fnl f* **8/1**
0344 **2** 2 **Go Far**[6] 4128 4-9-5 **78** (b) RoystonFfrench 2 83
(Alan Bailey) *chsd wnr: hdwy over 2f out: rdn wl over 1f out: drvn and no imp fnl f* **9/2**[2]
424 **3** 1 **Dark Castle**[18] 3702 5-9-11 **84** PJMcDonald 4 86
(Micky Hammond) *in tch: hdwy on inner 2f out: rdn to chse ldng pair over 1f out: drvn and one pce ins fnl f* **3/1**[1]
4532 **4** 2 **Solar Spirit (IRE)**[14] 3844 9-9-2 **75** RobertWinston 3 71
(Tracy Waggott) *trckd ldrs: effrt over 2f out: sn rdn along and one pce* **13/2**
-400 **5** hd **Bop It**[18] 3702 5-9-10 **83** (p) DanielTudhope 1 78
(David O'Meara) *chsd wnr: rdn along over 2f out: sn drvn and grad wknd* **13/2**
2041 **6** 1 **Thatcherite (IRE)**[11] 3948 6-9-2 **75** (t) BarryMcHugh 6 71+
(Tony Coyle) *dwlt and sltly hmpd s: in rr: sme hdwy on inner wl over 1f out: sn rdn and n.d* **10/1**
2235 **7** 1 **Avon Breeze**[21] 3571 5-9-9 **82** AmyRyan 7 71
(Richard Whitaker) *a towards rr* **6/1**[3]
0-00 **8** 1 **Nameitwhatyoulike**[18] 3714 5-9-12 **85** PhillipMakin 8 71
(Michael Easterby) *in tch: rdn along 1/2-way: sn outpcd* **14/1**

1m 10.81s (-2.79) **Going Correction** -0.30s/f (Firm)
**WFA** 3 from 4yo+ 5lb **8 Ran SP% 111.0**
Speed ratings (Par 105): **106,103,102,99,99 97,96,95**
CSF £41.16 CT £128.82 TOTE £6.50: £1.10, £2.30, £1.50; EX 46.00 Trifecta £355.80.
**Owner** Sheikh Hamdan bin Mohammed Al Maktoum **Bred** Darley **Trained** Middleham Moor, N Yorks

**FOCUS**
A decent contest and a case could have been made for all of these. However, yet again it proved almost impossible to make up any ground and there was another all-the-way winner. The time was half a second inside of standard.

## 4318 GO RACING IN YORKSHIRE SUMMER FESTIVAL MEDIAN AUCTION MAIDEN STKS 7f
**4:30** (4:31) (Class 6) 3-5-Y-0 **£2,385** (£704; £352) **Stalls** Low

Form RPR
44-0 **1** **Rust (IRE)**[23] 3535 4-9-12 56 (p) PJMcDonald 2 62
(Ann Duffield) *trckd ldrs: hdwy 2f out: effrt and nt clr run over 1f out: swtchd lft and rdn ent fnl f: sn drvn on inner and styd wl to ld nr fin* **7/1**[3]
55 **2** nk **Showtime Star**[20] 3601 4-9-12 0 BenCurtis 3 61
(Alan Swinbank) *slt ld: rdn along wl over 1f out: drvn ent fnl f: hdd and no ex towards fin* **4/1**[2]
6233 **3** 1 **Irondale Express**[9] 4023 3-9-0 69 BarryMcHugh 6 50
(Tony Coyle) *trckd ldng pair: hdwy on outer over 2f out: chal wl over 1f out: sn rdn and ev ch tl drvn ins fnl f and kpt on same pce* **8/13**[1]
0005 **4** 8 **Princess Myla (IRE)**[8] 4059 3-9-0 52 GrahamLee 7 29
(Paul Midgley) *hld up: hdwy wl over 2f out: sn rdn and nvr nr ldrs* **12/1**
**5** 2 1/4 **Say Something** 3-8-7 0 RowanScott[(7)] 1 23
(Ann Duffield) *cl up on inner: rdn along over 2f out: drvn wl over 1f out and grad wknd* **40/1**
-40 **6** 2 **Bon Chance**[12] 3914 3-9-5 0 PhillipMakin 4 22
(Michael Easterby) *chsd ldrs: rdn along 1/2-way: sn wknd* **20/1**
000 **7** 2 1/4 **King Couture (IRE)**[8] 4062 3-9-5 0 AndrewElliott 5 16
(Michael Easterby) *a in rr: outpcd and bhd fr 1/2-way* **150/1**

1m 25.63s (-1.37) **Going Correction** -0.30s/f (Firm)
**WFA** 3 from 4yo 7lb **7 Ran SP% 110.0**
Speed ratings (Par 101): **95,94,93,84,81 79,76**
CSF £31.78 TOTE £7.10: £3.00, £1.80; EX 29.90 Trifecta £51.60.
**Owner** Evelyn Duchess Of Sutherland **Bred** Redmyre Bloodstock & John Cullinan **Trained** Constable Burton, N Yorks

**FOCUS**
This weak maiden took very little winning. The runner-up has been rated as running a minor pb.

## 4319 BETFAIR NOVICE FLAT AMATEUR RIDERS' H'CAP (FOR NOVICE AMATEUR RIDERS) 1m 3f 214y
**5:00** (5:01) (Class 6) (0-65,65) 4-Y-0+ **£2,183** (£677; £338; £169) **Stalls** Low

Form RPR
20-0 **1** **Hyperlink (IRE)**[40] 2963 5-11-7 **65** MrAlexFerguson 3 77
(Michael Bell) *prom on inner: led after 1 1/2f: pushed clr 2f out: rdn ins fnl f: kpt on strly* **8/1**[3]
3203 **2** 5 **Merchant Of Medici**[5] 4175 7-10-13 **60** (p) DylanMcDonagh[(3)] 12 64
(Micky Hammond) *trckd ldrs: pushed along and hdwy on wd outside over 2f out: rdn to chse wnr appr fnl f: sn edgd lft and no imp* **11/2**[2]
6363 **3** 3 3/4 **Rockabilly Riot (IRE)**[14] 3843 4-11-2 **60** MrHStock 7 58
(Martin Todhunter) *in tch: hdwy on inner 3f out: rdn to chse ldrs wl over 1f out: kpt on one pce appr fnl f* **12/1**
6626 **4** 3/4 **Monzino (USA)**[6] 4115 6-10-5 **49** MissJWalton 10 48+
(Michael Chapman) *hld up: hdwy 3f out: rdn 2f out: styd on fnl f: nrst fin* **16/1**
6050 **5** 1 **Al Furat (USA)**[10] 4000 6-10-7 **54** MissEmilyBullock[(3)] 6 49
(Ron Barr) *trckd ldrs on inner: hdwy to chse wnr 3f out: rdn over 2f out: sn one pce* **18/1**
-063 **6** 3/4 **Monthly Medal**[20] 3623 11-10-2 **47** oh1 (t) MissLWilson 1 40+
(Wilf Storey) *hld up towards rr: stdy hdwy on inner 4f out: rdn along over 2f out: kpt on u.p: nvr nr ldrs* **25/1**
30-6 **7** 1 **Weybridge Light**[14] 3843 9-10-6 **50** (b) MrWHRReed 8 42
(David Thompson) *hld up: hdwy on outer to trck ldrs over 5f out: effrt over 3f out: rdn along over 2f out: sn wknd* **50/1**
-030 **8** shd **Silver Tigress**[12] 3912 6-10-0 **47** MissKMabon[(3)] 2 39
(Iain Jardine) *hld up in rr: hdwy on outer 2f out: sn rdn and plugged on: n.d* **12/1**
4142 **9** 10 **Rocky Two (IRE)**[19] 3657 4-10-11 **55** PhillipDennis 14 31
(Philip Kirby) *nvr bttr than midfield* **8/1**[3]
3040 **10** 1/2 **Pertemps Networks**[6] 4115 10-11-6 **64** MissETodd 11 39
(Michael Easterby) *prom: rdn along over 3f out: wknd wl over 2f out* **28/1**
3/5- **11** 1 3/4 **Schelm (GER)**[59] 5734 12-10-5 **52** (p) MrOJPimlott[(3)] 4 25
(John Quinn) *dwlt: a in rr* **20/1**
12 **14** **Gios Last (GER)**[44] 4-10-9 **53** (p) MrDGNoonan 9
(Keith Dalgleish) *led 1 1/2f: prom: rdn along 4f out: sn lost pl and bhd fr wl over 2f out* **11/4**[1]
2-00 **13** 6 **Dan Emmett (USA)**[57] 2424 4-11-6 **64** MrKWood 13 5
(John Wainwright) *prom: pushed along 7f out: sn lost pl and bhd over 4f out: t.o fnl 3f* **14/1**
63-0 **U** **Sheila's Castle**[22] 3546 10-10-6 **53** MissRHorne[(3)] 5
(Sean Regan) *a towards rr: bhd whn sddle slipped 3f out: uns rdr ins fnl f* **33/1**

2m 36.8s (-2.10) **Going Correction** -0.30s/f (Firm) **14 Ran SP% 114.4**
Speed ratings (Par 101): **95,91,89,88,88 87,86,86,80,79 78,69,65,**
CSF £45.69 CT £526.55 TOTE £8.10: £2.20, £1.80, £3.00; EX 45.20 Trifecta £469.00.
**Owner** Mrs John Ferguson **Bred** Airlie Stud **Trained** Newmarket, Suffolk

**FOCUS**
Just modest form. The runner-up and third suggest this could be rated three or four pounds higher.
T/Plt: £1,450.90 to a £1 stake. Pool of £51576.86 - 25.95 winning tickets. T/Qpdt: £39.80 to a £1 stake. Pool of £4051.95 - 75.20 winning tickets. JR

# 4260 LINGFIELD (L-H)
Wednesday, July 16

**OFFICIAL GOING: Standard**
Wind: virtually nil Weather: warm and mainly sunny

## 4320 BRITISH STALLION STUDS EBF MAIDEN FILLIES' STKS (BOBIS RACE) 6f 1y(P)
**2:10** (2:11) (Class 5) 2-Y-O **£2,911** (£866; £432; £216) **Stalls** Low

Form RPR
**1** **L'Addition** 2-9-0 0 TedDurcan 1 71+
(William Jarvis) *chsd ldrs: swtchd lft and effrt over 1f out: led fnl 100yds: sn in command: r.o wl: readily* **16/1**
3 **2** 1 1/4 **Primrose Valley**[67] 2151 2-8-9 0 (p[1]) CamHardie[(5)] 6 67
(Ed Vaughan) *dwlt: hld up wl in tch towards rr: hdwy over 1f out: r.o wl ins fnl f: wnt 2nd last strides* **3/1**[2]
0 **3** nk **Its Lady Mary**[13] 3888 2-9-0 0 JimCrowley 8 66
(Paul Cole) *chsd ldr: rdn and qcknd to ld ent fnl 2f: drvn over 1f out: hdd and one pce fnl 100yds: lost 2nd last strides* **50/1**
**4** 2 1/2 **Local Time** 2-9-0 0 AndreaAtzeni 5 59+
(Saeed bin Suroor) *dwlt: hld up wl in tch: rdn and hdwy over 1f out: styd on ins fnl f: nvr trbld ldrs* **5/4**[1]
00 **5** 3/4 **Recover (USA)**[12] 3933 2-9-0 0 (b[1]) JimmyFortune 2 56
(Brian Meehan) *led: rdn and hdd ent fnl 2f: 3rd and outpcd 1f out: wknd ins fnl f* **50/1**
**6** 2 1/2 **Fleetwood Poppy** 2-9-0 0 RobertHavlin 4 49
(Michael Attwater) *wl in tch in midfield: rdn and effrt ent fnl 2f: outpcd and btn over 1f out: wl hld whn sltly hmpd ins fnl f* **66/1**
**7** 3/4 **With Charm (USA)** 2-9-0 0 AdamKirby 7 47
(Charlie Appleby) *in tch towards rr: rdn and outpcd ent fnl 2f: wknd over 1f out* **8/1**
6 **8** 1 1/4 **Gumhrear (IRE)**[21] 3563 2-9-0 0 SilvestreDeSousa 10 43
(James Tate) *chsd ldrs: rdn and lost pl whn wd bnd 2f out: sn wknd* **14/1**
**9** 37 **Malarkey (IRE)** 2-9-0 0 WilliamBuick 12
(John Gosden) *s.i.s: detached in last: clsd but stl last 3f out: lost tch 2f out and sn eased: t.o* **4/1**[3]

1m 12.57s (0.67) **Going Correction** -0.075s/f (Stan) **9 Ran SP% 118.5**
Speed ratings (Par 91): **92,90,89,86,85 82,81,79,30**
CSF £65.37 TOTE £27.90: £3.70, £1.90, £6.70; EX 75.20 Trifecta £2229.40 Part won. Pool of £2972.66 - 0.59 winning units..
**Owner** Clive Washbourn **Bred** Laundry Cottage Stud Farm **Trained** Newmarket, Suffolk

**FOCUS**
Some powerful stables were represented in this maiden, which was run at a fair pace. The fifth probably anchors the form.

## 4321 INTEGRO INSURANCE BROKERS H'CAP 1m 4f (P)
**2:40** (2:40) (Class 6) (0-60,60) 3-Y-O **£2,264** (£673; £336; £168) **Stalls** Low

Form RPR
66-2 **1** **Leaderene**[7] 4084 3-8-11 **50** SilvestreDeSousa 6 71+
(Mark Johnston) *mde virtually all: wnt clr wl over 2f out: in n.d after and r.o wl: unchal* **4/9**[1]
0222 **2** 8 **Whispering Star (USA)**[85] 1632 3-9-7 **60** [1] JamieSpencer 4 67
(David Simcock) *awkward leaving stalls and s.i.s: in rr: rdn and hdwy on outer to chse clr ldr over 2f out: no imp: eased towards fin* **7/2**[2]
004 **3** 2 1/4 **Sound Of Life (IRE)**[41] 2926 3-8-8 **47** (p) ChrisCatlin 1 48
(Rae Guest) *pushed along leaving stalls: hdwy to chse wnr 9f out tl over 2f out: 3rd and wl btn over 1f out: plugged on* **10/1**[3]
000 **4** 7 **Oakbank (USA)**[18] 3712 3-8-2 **47** oh1 DanielMuscutt[(5)] 7 36
(Brett Johnson) *chsd ldr for 3f: styd chsng ldrs: rdn and struggling over 3f out: 4th and lost tch over 2f out* **50/1**
0330 **5** 1/2 **Lochalsh (IRE)**[18] 3711 3-9-7 **60** AndreaAtzeni 2 49
(William Knight) *chsd ldrs for 4f: in midfield after: dropped to last and struggling u.p over 3f out: lost tch over 2f out* **14/1**
0005 **6** 15 **French Accent**[48] 2694 3-8-7 **47** oh1 RobertHavlin 5 11
(John Best) *s.i.s: grad rcvrd: hdwy into midfield 8f out: rdn over 3f out: lost tch over 2f out: t.o* **50/1**

2m 30.36s (-2.64) **Going Correction** -0.075s/f (Stan) **6 Ran SP% 111.2**
Speed ratings (Par 98): **105,99,98,93,93 83**
CSF £2.23 TOTE £1.80: £1.30, £1.10; EX 2.40 Trifecta £5.50.
**Owner** Miss K Rausing **Bred** Miss K Rausing **Trained** Middleham Moor, N Yorks

**FOCUS**
An uncompetitive handicap run at a steady pace. The runner-up, who was eased off late, has been rated a minor improver.

## 4322 HENRY STREETER H'CAP 1m 7f 169y(P)
**3:10** (3:10) (Class 5) (0-75,72) 3-Y-O+ **£3,234** (£962; £481; £240) **Stalls** Low

Form RPR
320- **1** **Mick Duggan**[210] 8337 4-9-11 **69** JimCrowley 4 80
(Ralph Beckett) *chsd ldrs: rdn and effrt to chse ldr over 1f out: drvn and styd on to chal ins fnl f: led cl home* **7/2**[3]
2216 **2** hd **Bold Runner**[19] 3673 3-8-10 **71** SilvestreDeSousa 2 82
(Jose Santos) *in tch in midfield: hdwy to chse ldr over 5f out: rdn to ld ent fnl 2f: drvn and hrd pressed ins fnl f: kpt on: hdd and no ex cl home* **7/4**[1]
3511 **3** 8 **Annaluna (IRE)**[14] 3851 5-9-0 **58** (v) AdamKirby 6 59
(David Evans) *chsd ldr tl led 7f out: rdn and hdd 2f out: 3rd and wknd jst over 1f out* **7/2**[3]

4006 **4** 2 ¼ **Admirable Duque (IRE)**[46] 2774 8-9-9 **72**............ JoshBaudains(5) 1 71
(Dominic Ffrench Davis) *hld up in tch in midfield: hdwy to chse ldrs 3f out: 4th and wknd u.p over 1f out* **25/1**

300 **5** 2 ¾ **Storm Hawk (IRE)**[14] 3859 7-9-10 **68**............(b) TomQueally 7 65
(Pat Eddery) *v.s.a: rcvrd and wl in tch after 2f: rdn over 3f out: sn outpcd: wknd 2f out* **25/1**

2-42 **6** 4 ½ **Aiyana**[36] 3078 4-9-9 **67**............ JimmyFortune 5 57
(Hughie Morrison) *led tl 7f out: chsd ldr tl over 5f out: chsd ldrs after: rdn and outpcd whn short of room bnd ent fnl 2f: sn wknd* **3/1**[2]

1106 **7** 14 **Fire In Babylon (IRE)**[134] 829 6-9-1 **64**............(b) TobyAtkinson(5) 3 37
(Noel Quinlan) *hld up in tch in last pair: rdn over 3f out: sn struggling: wknd over 2f out* **25/1**

3m 23.36s (-2.34) **Going Correction** -0.075s/f (Stan)
**WFA** 3 from 4yo+ 17lb **7** Ran SP% **117.3**
Speed ratings (Par 103): **102,101,97,96,95 93,86**
CSF £10.30 TOTE £6.10: £3.10, £2.30; EX 15.20 Trifecta £87.50.
**Owner** Mark Muddiman **Bred** Pendley Farm **Trained** Kimpton, Hants
■ Stewards' Enquiry : Silvestre De Sousa two-day ban: use of whip (31 Jul- 1 Aug)

**FOCUS**
A steadily run staying handicap. The front two pulled a long way clear. The form could be rated a few lengths higher or lower.

## 4323 PAUL KELLEWAY MEMORIAL CLASSIFIED STKS — 1m 1y(P)
3:40 (3:40) (Class 3) 3-Y-0+ — £7,956 (£2,367; £1,183; £591) Stalls High

Form RPR

641 **1** **Tenor (IRE)**[14] 3861 4-9-6 **90**............(t) AdamKirby 7 97
(John Ryan) *chsd ldrs: dropped to midfield and pushed along briefly 5f out: rdn and hdwy to chal 2f out: drvn to ld over 1f out: r.o wl fnl f* **11/4**[2]

-044 **2** 1 ¼ **Monsieur Chevalier (IRE)**[34] 3152 7-9-3 **87**............ RobertTart(3) 5 94
(P J O'Gorman) *s.i.s: bhd: rdn and hdwy on outer bnd 2f out: styd on wl ins fnl f: wnt 2nd cl home* **6/1**[3]

-265 **3** ½ **Snow Trouble (USA)**[54] 2502 3-8-12 **88**............ JimCrowley 1 91
(Marcus Tregoning) *dwlt: hdwy into midfield after 1f: nt clr run and shuffled bk to last ent fnl 2f: rdn over 1f out: stl last ent fnl f: str run fnl f: wnt 3rd last stride* **6/1**[3]

13 **4** shd **Knavery (USA)**[19] 3651 3-8-12 **90**............ JamieSpencer 4 91
(Roger Varian) *chsd ldrs: rdn to ld and edgd lft u.p ent fnl f: hdd and hrd drvn over 1f out: styd on same pce after: lost 2 pls cl home* **9/4**[1]

1220 **5** nk **High Time Too (IRE)**[21] 3573 4-8-12 **84**............ NoelGarbutt(5) 11 89
(Hugo Palmer) *hld up in tch towards rr: hdwy over 2f out: rdn to chse ldrs over 1f out: kpt on u.p but nvr quite gng pce to chal* **25/1**

4203 **6** ¾ **Fashion Line (IRE)**[37] 3055 4-8-12 **88**............ LouisSteward(5) 10 88
(Michael Bell) *racd in last pair: pushed along 6f out: nt clr run jst over 2f out: hdwy u.p over 1f out: kpt on but no threat to wnr* **12/1**

0415 **7** 2 ¼ **Born To Surprise**[44] 2849 5-9-6 **90**............ AmirQuinn 9 85
(Lee Carter) *hld up in tch towards rr: hdwy over 2f out: rdn to chse ldrs over 1f out: no ex 1f out: wknd ins fnl f* **25/1**

0 **8** ¾ **Tellovoi (IRE)**[17] 3753 6-9-6 **90**............(v) TomQueally 3 83+
(Ann Stokell) *racd keenly: w ldr tl led over 2f out: sn hdd and carried lft bnd 2f out: no ex and btn over 1f out: wknd ins fnl f* **33/1**

3003 **9** 1 ¼ **Act Of Charity (IRE)**[18] 3719 3-8-12 **85**............(b) KierenFallon 6 80
(Gay Kelleway) *dwlt: pushed along and hdwy on inner to chse ldr over 5f out: rdn and short of room ent fnl 2f: wknd over 1f out* **14/1**

1100 **10** 1 ½ **Alumina (IRE)**[18] 3724 3-8-9 **90**............ DavidProbert 8 72
(Andrew Balding) *hld up in tch towards rr: nt clr run bhd wkng rival ent fnl 2f: no hdwy over 1f out: nvr trbld ldrs* **25/1**

0050 **11** 4 ½ **Dubawi Fun**[27] 3378 3-8-5 **89**............ AhmadAlSubousi(7) 2 65+
(Ismail Mohammed) *led tl hdd and rdn over 2f out: lost pl qckly bnd ent fnl 2f: bhd fnl f* **25/1**

1m 35.65s (-2.55) **Going Correction** -0.075s/f (Stan)
**WFA** 3 from 4yo+ 8lb **11** Ran SP% **118.7**
Speed ratings (Par 107): **109,107,107,107,106 106,103,103,101,100 95**
CSF £18.35 TOTE £3.70: £1.60, £2.90, £1.90; EX 26.00 Trifecta £204.00.
**Owner** Kilco (International) Ltd **Bred** Epona Bloodstock Ltd And P A Byrne **Trained** Newmarket, Suffolk

**FOCUS**
A tight classified stakes with only 6lb covering the 11 runners. The fifth limits the form somewhat.

## 4324 PMSG 50TH ANNIVERSARY H'CAP — 6f 1y(P)
4:10 (4:12) (Class 6) (0-65,64) 3-Y-0 — £2,264 (£673; £336; £168) Stalls Low

Form RPR

3-65 **1** **Majestic Song**[58] 2384 3-9-4 **64**............ RobertTart(3) 11 75+
(James Toller) *wnt rt s: racd in last quartet: rdn and hdwy to chse ldrs over 1f out: str run to ld fnl 75yds: sn in command and gng away at fin* **8/1**

0002 **2** 2 ¾ **Mimi Luke (USA)**[19] 3679 3-8-10 **58**............(v) TimClark(5) 7 60
(Alan Bailey) *wl in tch in midfield: hdwy on inner to chse ldrs 2f: wnt 2nd over 1f out: ev ch ins fnl f: outpcd by wnr fnl 75yds: kpt on: regained 2nd last stride* **16/1**

2152 **3** shd **Kodafine (IRE)**[4] 4186 3-9-6 **63**............ AdamKirby 2 65
(David Evans) *broke fast: led: drvn 2 l clr ent fnl 2f: wandered rt 1f out: sn hrd pressed: hdd and brushed aside by wnr fnl 75yds: lost 2nd last stride* **5/4**[1]

524 **4** 1 ¾ **Lead A Merry Dance**[21] 3586 3-9-7 **64**............ JamesDoyle 3 61
(Sylvester Kirk) *chsd ldr: 3rd and sltly outpcd over 1f out: rallied and kpt on ins fnl f: keeping on same pce whn nt clr run and eased towards fin* **3/1**[2]

000- **5** 1 ¼ **Risk 'N' Reward (IRE)**[197] 8451 3-8-12 **55**............ PatCosgrave 6 48+
(Michael Murphy) *stdd s: t.k.h: hld up in rr: effrt and racing awkwardly bnd 2f out: kpt on ins fnl f: nvr trbld ldrs* **33/1**

4600 **6** ¾ **Monashka Bay (IRE)**[50] 2647 3-9-0 **57**............ DavidProbert 5 48
(Michael Blanshard) *in tch towards rr: effrt u.p over 2f out: kpt on u.p but no real imp* **6/1**[3]

0035 **7** ½ **Orlando Star (CAN)**[15] 3821 3-8-9 **57**............(v) DannyBrock(5) 10 46
(Roger Teal) *chsd ldrs but a stuck wd: rdn and hung rt bnd 2f out: lost any ch and one pce after* **16/1**

0222 **8** 5 **Meebo (IRE)**[16] 3792 3-9-5 **62**............(vt) NickyMackay 8 36
(J R Jenkins) *t.k.h: chsd ldrs: rdn and outpcd ent fnl 2f: wknd jst over 1f out* **10/1**

-563 **9** 80 **Loot**[15] 3816 3-8-6 **54**............ RyanWhile(5) 9
(Bill Turner) *in tch towards rr: rdn over 2f out: sn lost tch: t.o and virtually p.u fnl f* **33/1**

1m 11.57s (-0.33) **Going Correction** -0.075s/f (Stan) **9** Ran SP% **121.6**
Speed ratings (Par 98): **99,95,95,92,91 90,89,82,**
CSF £131.40 CT £268.56 TOTE £9.90: £2.50, £2.80, £1.10; EX 99.40 Trifecta £629.90.
**Owner** P C J Dalby & R D Schuster **Bred** Newsells Park Stud & Cannon Bloodstock **Trained** Newmarket, Suffolk

**FOCUS**
A modest contest run at a sound pace. The form could be rated up to 4lb higher.

## 4325 FREDDIE FARMER FOUNDATION MAIDEN STKS — 1m 4f (P)
4:40 (4:40) (Class 5) 3-4-Y-0 — £2,587 (£770; £384; £192) Stalls Low

Form RPR

3 **1** **Clear Mind**[61] 2310 3-8-11 **0**............ WilliamBuick 6 83+
(John Gosden) *chsd ldrs: effrt to chse ldr and switching rt wl over 1f out: rdn to ld ins fnl f: sn clr: readily* **1/1**[1]

4-54 **2** 2 ¾ **Courageous Rock (USA)**[26] 3432 3-9-2 **77**............ SilvestreDeSousa 8 82
(Ed Vaughan) *led: rdn jst over 2f out: clr w wnr jst over 1f out: hdd ins fnl f: sn brushed aside by wnr but kpt on for clr 2nd* **10/1**

6-5 **3** 2 ¾ **Robertson (IRE)**[14] 3857 4-10-0 **0**............ JamesDoyle 14 77
(James Fanshawe) *chsd ldrs: rdn over 2f out: 3rd and outpcd over 1f out: no threat to wnr but kpt on again ins fnl f* **25/1**

0 **4** 6 **Upper Street (IRE)**[27] 3385 3-8-11 **0**............(v[1]) ShaneKelly 4 63+
(Sir Michael Stoute) *v.s.a: rcvrd and tagged on to bk of field 9f out: hdwy on inner 3f out: 4th and no imp over 1f out: wknd fnl f* **33/1**

030 **5** ¾ **Mawaseel**[32] 3248 3-9-2 **72**............ PaulHanagan 7 66
(B W Hills) *in tch in midfield: nt clr run over 2f out: rdn and swtchd lft over 1f out: plugged on but no imp* **20/1**

4- **6** ¾ **Sagua La Grande (IRE)**[396] 3343 4-9-11 **0**............(t) AshleyMorgan(3) 10 65
(Lady Cecil) *t.k.h: hld up towards rr: hdwy over 3f out: nt clr run over 2f out: hdwy over 1f out: no ch w wnr but kpt on ins fnl f* **20/1**

22 **7** 1 ¾ **Perspicace**[20] 3631 3-9-2 **0**............ GeorgeBaker 12 62
(Roger Charlton) *chsd ldr tl wl over 1f out: sn rdn and btn: fdd fnl f* **6/1**[3]

0-0 **8** 9 **Sarpech (IRE)**[14] 3857 3-9-2 **0**............ JamieSpencer 2 48
(Sir Mark Prescott Bt) *s.i.s: hld up towards rr: struggling 3f out: no ch whn rn wd bnd 2f out* **25/1**

4 **9** 1 ½ **Absolute Sway**[26] 3434 3-9-2 **0**............ AdamKirby 11 46
(Charlie Appleby) *s.i.s: hdwy into midfield after 2f: clsd to chse ldrs 5f out: rdn and btn over 2f out: wknd 2f out* **7/2**[2]

00 **10** 2 **Rideonastar (IRE)**[47] 2746 3-9-2 **0**............ JimCrowley 5 42
(Ralph Beckett) *hld up in tch: rdn and outpcd 3f out: no ch 2f out* **33/1**

**11** ¾ **Knife Point (GER)** 3-8-11 **0**............ NoelGarbutt(5) 3 41+
(Hugo Palmer) *v.s.a: clsd on to bk of field 8f out: rdn over 3f out: sn bhd* **66/1**

00 **12** 26 **Il Gran Capo (IRE)**[16] 3804 3-9-2 **0**............ RobertHavlin 13
(Roger Ingram) *in tch in midfield: rdn 4f out: sn lost pl: t.o and eased ins fnl f* **100/1**

0 **13** 3 ½ **Mountain River (IRE)**[18] 3712 3-9-2 **0**............ LiamKeniry 9
(J S Moore) *in tch in midfield: rdn and lost pl 5f out: lost tch over 3f out: t.o and eased ins fnl f* **100/1**

2m 29.73s (-3.27) **Going Correction** -0.075s/f (Stan)
**WFA** 3 from 4yo 12lb **13** Ran SP% **122.2**
Speed ratings (Par 103): **107,105,103,99,98 98,97,91,90,88 88,71,68**
CSF £11.35 TOTE £2.40: £1.10, £2.30, £5.60; EX 16.00 Trifecta £247.80.
**Owner** P Stokes & S Krase **Bred** Millsec Limited **Trained** Newmarket, Suffolk

**FOCUS**
They went a steady pace for this fair maiden and the pace held up.

## 4326 INDUS CATERING AMATEUR RIDERS' H'CAP (DIV I) — 1m 2f (P)
5:10 (5:10) (Class 6) (0-60,60) 3-Y-0+ — £2,183 (£677; £338; £169) Stalls Low

Form RPR

6121 **1** **Glennten**[35] 3115 5-10-8 **59**............ MrWillPettis(5) 6 68
(Jose Santos) *chsd ldrs: wnt 2nd 4f out: wnt clr w ldr 3f out: rdn to ld wl over 1f out: kpt on and in command after* **7/4**[1]

0U25 **2** 1 **Flag Of Glory**[11] 3973 7-10-7 **58**............ MissMEdden(5) 1 65
(Peter Hiatt) *led for 2f: chsd ldr after tl led again 5f out: wnt clr w wnr 3f out: rdn and hdd wl over 1f out: kpt on but a hld after* **7/1**[3]

0-05 **3** 4 **Estibdaad (IRE)**[65] 2212 4-10-1 **52**............(t) MissMBryant(5) 2 52
(Paddy Butler) *hld up towards rr: clsd 5f out: nudged along and hdwy to chse clr ldng pair wl over 1f out: kpt on but nvr able to chal* **25/1**

510/ **4** 3 ¼ **Lord Of The Storm**[728] 4219 6-10-5 **54**............ MrChrisMartin(3) 5 47
(Bill Turner) *towards rr: rdn and effrt 3f out: no ch w ldng pair and kpt on same pce fnl 2f* **16/1**

06-5 **5** 1 **Capitol Gain (IRE)**[37] 14 5-10-9 **60**............(p) MrORJSangster(5) 9 51
(George Baker) *dwlt: styd wd and hld up towards rr: rdn and effrt wl over 2f out: no threat to ldrs but kpt on ins fnl f* **8/1**

0000 **6** 7 **Mists Of Time (IRE)**[23] 3528 4-10-0 **46** oh1............ MrRBirkett 4 24
(Pat Eddery) *in tch in midfield but niggled along: chsd ldrs and rdn 3f out: sn wknd* **33/1**

5060 **7** 3 ½ **Berkeley Street (USA)**[20] 3632 4-9-7 **46** oh1............ MissGFriswell(7) 3 17
(Jane Chapple-Hyam) *bhd: rdn over 2f out: sme hdwy past btn horse over 1f out: n.d* **16/1**

200 **8** 9 **Salient**[25] 3473 10-10-1 **47**............ MrSWalker 8
(Michael Attwater) *in tch in midfield: rdn over 4f out: sn struggling: lost tch wl over 1f out* **11/4**[2]

000 **9** 5 **Femme De Menage**[23] 3537 3-8-13 **46** oh1............ MrHHunt(5) 10
(Andrew Balding) *pushed along early to go prom: chsd ldrs: rdn over 3f out: sn btn: wl bhd over 1f out: t.o* **12/1**

02-0 **10** 2 **Dreamy Ciara**[40] 2963 4-10-4 **57**............ MissKARandall(7) 11
(Raymond York) *styd wd thrght: towards rr: hdwy into midfield 6f out: wknd 4f out: wl bhd and drifting lft over 2f out: t.o* **50/1**

00-0 **11** 16 **Jack Firefly**[35] 3123 5-10-0 **46** oh1............(b[1]) MissAliceMills 7
(Michael Murphy) *t.k.h: hdwy to clr 8f out tl 5f out: lost 2nd and dropped out rapidly: t.o fnl 2f* **50/1**

2m 7.78s (1.18) **Going Correction** -0.075s/f (Stan)
**WFA** 3 from 4yo+ 10lb **11** Ran SP% **116.8**
Speed ratings (Par 101): **92,91,88,85,84 79,76,69,65,63 50**
CSF £14.09 CT £224.42 TOTE £2.60: £1.10, £2.60, £8.30; EX 11.70 Trifecta £174.70.
**Owner** Bob Cooper & Val Dean **Bred** The Hon Mrs R Pease **Trained** Upper Lambourn, Berks

**FOCUS**
A modest handicap, confined to amateur riders, run at a sound pace. The runner-up should support the level and it could be 5lb higher.

## 4327 INDUS CATERING AMATEUR RIDERS' H'CAP (DIV II) — 1m 2f (P)
5:45 (5:46) (Class 6) (0-60,60) 3-Y-0+ — £2,183 (£677; £338; £169) Stalls Low

Form RPR

3041 **1** **Edgware Road**[11] 3973 6-10-4 **55**............ MissBHampson(5) 6 68+
(Andy Turnell) *chsd clr ldr: clsd 4f out: rdn to ld ent fnl 2f: styd on wl and clr fnl f: readily* **3/1**[2]

6126 **2** 3 ½ **Olivers Mount**[50] 2646 4-10-13 **59**............(t) MrSWalker 3 63
(Ed Vaughan) *hld up in midfield: clsd on ldr 4f out: clr in ldng quartet 3f out: swtchd out rt and effrt to chse wnr wl over 1f out: no imp: kpt on* **7/4**[1]

00-0 **3** *4* **Rock Band**[2] 4264 5-10-4 **50**....................(t) MrHAABannister 10 47
(Emmet Michael Butterly, Ire) *prom in main gp: clsd on ldr 4f out: clr in ldng quartet 3f out: rdn and chsd wnr briefly 2f out: sn outpcd: plugged on* **4/1**

2205 **4** *shd* **Super Duplex**[102] 1302 7-10-5 **58**....................(t) MissLWilliams(7) 1 55
(Roger Teal) *led: sn clr: rdn and hdd ent fnl 2f: outpcd and btn over 1f out: battling for 3rd fnl f: plugged on* **7/2**[3]

/0-0 **5** *15* **Swords**[58] 2396 12-9-7 **46** oh1.................... MissSPeacock(7) 2 14
(Ray Peacock) *hld up in rr: lost tch w ldrs but sme hdwy 3f out: modest 6th and no ch 2f out* **66/1**

-000 **6** *¾* **Heading To First**[23] 3521 7-9-11 **48** oh1 ow2..........[1] MissMBryant(5) 7 15
(Paddy Butler) *t.k.h: hld up off the pce in midfield: 5th and outpcd 3f out: no ch after* **50/1**

6/0- **7** *13* **Cunning Plan (IRE)**[238] 7984 7-9-7 **46** oh1.......... MissKARandall(7) 9
(Raymond York) *prom in main gp: rdn and lost pl 5f out: t.o fnl 2f* **50/1**

-066 **8** *1* **Somerton Star**[113] 1088 4-10-0 **46** oh1.................... MrRBirkett 5
(Pat Eddery) *racd in midfield: rdn and lost pl over 3f out: lost tch over 2f out: t.o* **33/1**

4000 **9** *1* **Wings Of Fire (IRE)**[102] 1302 4-10-1 **54**.................... MrAGuerrini(7) 8
(Denis Quinn) *hld up in rr but v wd thrght: effrt 4f out: sn btn and lost tch 3f out: t.o* **25/1**

2m 7.29s (0.69) **Going Correction** -0.075s/f (Stan) **9** Ran SP% **115.8**
Speed ratings (Par 101): **94,91,88,87,75 75,64,64,63**
CSF £8.43 CT £20.27 TOTE £5.00: £1.70, £1.20, £1.60; EX 10.60 Trifecta £36.20.
**Owner** Power Bloodstock Ltd **Bred** Juddmonte Farms Ltd **Trained** Broad Hinton, Wilts

**FOCUS**
The second division of the amateur riders' handicap was run at a fair pace. The runner-up is consistent and has been rated pretty much to his recent best.
T/Plt: £39.90 to a £1 stake. Pool of £71899.18 - 1313.89 winning tickets. T/Qpdt: £10.80 to a £1 stake. Pool of £6074.95 - 415.22 winning tickets. SP

## 3980 SANDOWN (R-H)
Wednesday, July 16

**OFFICIAL GOING: Good to firm (sprint 8.5, rnd 8.6)**
Wind: Light, against Weather: Cloudy, very warm

### 4328 XL GROUP H'CAP (BOBIS RACE) 5f 6y
**6:00** (6:01) (Class 4) (0-85,85) 3-Y-O **£5,175** (£1,540; £769; £384) **Stalls** Low

Form RPR

3132 **1** **Royal Brave (IRE)**[8] 4043 3-8-4 **68**.................... MartinDwyer 1 77
(William Muir) *trckd ldrs and racd against far rail: clsd and eased out over 1f out: rdn to ld last 150yds: styd on wl* **8/1**

2322 **2** *1½* **Amahoro**[6] 4133 3-8-13 **80**.................... CharlesBishop(3) 2 84
(Mick Channon) *taken down early: t.k.h: hld up bhd ldrs: eased to outer and prog wl over 1f out: chal fnl f: styd on but outpcd by wnr* **7/2**[2]

0616 **3** *1½* **Mr Dandy Man (IRE)**[6] 4133 3-8-12 **76**.................... DavidProbert 3 75
(Ronald Harris) *led and racd against far rail: rdn and hdd last 150yds: outpcd after* **16/1**

604 **4** *2* **National Service (USA)**[26] 3433 3-8-6 **70**..........(t) AndreaAtzeni 5 61
(Stuart Williams) *dwlt: hld up in last trio: styd on against far rail fr over 1f out: tk 4th nr fin but nvr any ch* **7/1**

15-0 **5** *hd* **Autumns Blush (IRE)**[37] 3068 3-9-1 **79**.................... KierenFallon 4 70
(Jeremy Noseda) *dwlt: hld up in last pair: pushed along and taken to outer over 1f out: kpt on but nvr in it* **33/1**

0331 **6** *½* **Red Lady (IRE)**[15] 3817 3-8-13 **77**.................... JimmyFortune 6 66
(Brian Meehan) *pressed ldr to over 1f out: wknd* **8/1**

2121 **7** *nk* **Groundworker (IRE)**[17] 3756 3-9-0 **78**.................... RyanMoore 7 66
(Sylvester Kirk) *mostly in last trio and racd on outer: rdn 2f out: no prog and btn over 1f out: kpt on ins fnl f* **3/1**[1]

331 **8** *2¾* **Al Senad**[11] 3951 3-9-7 **85**.................... SeanLevey 9 63
(Peter Chapple-Hyam) *pressed ldrs but racd four off far rail: rdn over 2f out: lost pl and struggling over 1f out* **9/2**[3]

6023 **9** *1¼* **Touch The Clouds**[26] 3433 3-8-10 **74**.................... FrederikTylicki 8 47+
(William Stone) *pressed ldr but racd three off far rail: rdn over 2f out: lost pl and struggling over 1f out* **16/1**

1m 1.33s (-0.27) **Going Correction** -0.125s/f (Firm) **9** Ran SP% **114.8**
Speed ratings (Par 102): **97,94,92,89,88 87,87,83,81**
CSF £35.95 CT £360.04 TOTE £9.80: £2.50, £1.70, £3.80; EX 38.00 Trifecta £313.90.
**Owner** Muir Racing Partnership - Ascot **Bred** M Fahy **Trained** Lambourn, Berks

**FOCUS**
Round course at innermost configuration and distances as advertised. An open looking sprint handicap on paper but the first three home came from stalls 1, 2 and 3, and it proved hard to get into this down the middle of the track. The runner-up is consistent and could support the race being rated slightly higher.

### 4329 BERRYLANDS H'CAP 7f 16y
**6:35** (6:36) (Class 5) (0-70,70) 3-Y-O **£3,234** (£962; £481; £240) **Stalls** Low

Form RPR

1232 **1** **Biotic**[14] 3855 3-9-0 **63**.................... AndreaAtzeni 4 73+
(Rod Millman) *chsd ldrs in 5th: rdn over 2f out: wnt 2nd over 1f out: styd on wl fnl f to ld last stride* **5/1**[1]

-040 **2** *nse* **White Russian**[34] 3154 3-9-0 **63**.................... DaneO'Neill 3 72
(Henry Candy) *led: rdn 2 l clr wl over 1f out: styd on fnl f: hdd last stride* **12/1**

5-00 **3** *1¾* **Ajig**[57] 2433 3-9-2 **65**.................... JohnFahy 5 69
(Eve Johnson Houghton) *wl in tch in midfield: shkn up and prog on outer 2f out: wnt 3rd 1f out: styd on same pce after* **25/1**

5303 **4** *2¼* **Penny's Boy**[15] 3821 3-9-6 **69**....................(t) PatDobbs 1 67
(Sylvester Kirk) *chsd ldng pair: rdn to chse ldr briefly wl over 1f out: fdd fnl f* **9/1**[3]

636 **5** *1* **Djinni (IRE)**[13] 3890 3-9-5 **68**....................(b[1]) SeanLevey 16 63+
(Richard Hannon) *forced to r on outer fr wdst draw: in tch in midfield: shkn up over 2f out: prog to take 5th ins fnl f: n.d* **20/1**

-042 **6** *¾* **Chutney (IRE)**[18] 3708 3-9-2 **70**.................... CamHardie(5) 11 63+
(Richard Hannon) *racd wd in last quartet: shkn up over 2f out: prog over 1f out: styd on fnl f: no ch* **9/1**[3]

2230 **7** *¾* **Jersey Brown (IRE)**[38] 3037 3-9-3 **66**.......... WilliamTwiston-Davies 7 58+
(Mick Channon) *stdd s: hld up towards rr: prog over 2f out: chsd ldrs over 1f out: no hdwy fnl f* **12/1**

-064 **8** *¾* **Canova (IRE)**[23] 3516 3-9-4 **67**....................(bt[1]) JamesDoyle 13 56+
(Roger Charlton) *stdd s: hld up in last quartet: pushed along over 2f out: sme prog over 1f out: rdn and kpt on same pce fnl f: nvr involved* **13/2**[2]

1-04 **9** *½* **Encore Encore (FR)**[79] 1786 3-9-2 **65**.................... JimmyFortune 14 53
(Harry Dunlop) *chsd ldr to wl over 1f out: wknd* **25/1**

3-53 **10** *¾* **Goodwood Storm**[50] 2647 3-9-7 **70**.................... MartinDwyer 12 56+
(William Knight) *stdd s: hld up in last: prog on inner fr 3f out: chsd ldrs over 1f out: shkn up and no hdwy fnl f: fdd* **9/1**[3]

0610 **11** *8* **Adore**[11] 3946 3-9-5 **68**....................(p) RyanMoore 8 32
(Sir Michael Stoute) *a towards rr: shkn up over 2f out: sn wknd* **5/1**[1]

-303 **12** *hd* **What A Dandy (IRE)**[22] 3559 3-9-1 **64**.................... PatCosgrave 6 28
(Jim Boyle) *free to post: t.k.h: chsd ldng trio: wknd wl over 1f out* **10/1**

0-00 **13** *3¼* **Stapleford Lad**[18] 3709 3-8-13 **62**.................... KierenFox 10 17
(Stuart Williams) *settled in rr: pushed along 3f out: no prog and sn btn* **100/1**

00-0 **14** *9* **Luna Sunrise**[17] 3755 3-8-12 **61**.................... KierenFallon 2
(Timothy Jarvis) *t.k.h in midfield: wknd over 2f out: t.o* **25/1**

1m 27.99s (-1.51) **Going Correction** -0.175s/f (Firm) **14** Ran SP% **118.4**
Speed ratings (Par 100): **101,100,98,96,95 94,93,92,92,91 82,81,78,67**
CSF £60.33 CT £946.98 TOTE £5.40: £2.10, £5.10, £8.80; EX 59.70 Trifecta £989.70.
**Owner** Mrs Mette Campbell-Andenaes **Bred** Mette Campbell-Andenaes **Trained** Kentisbeare, Devon

**FOCUS**
A wide open handicap on paper but once again low-drawn runners dominated and not many got into it. The runner-up had a good trip and has been rated as putting up an improved effort first time on fast ground, while the third has been rated back to some form.

### 4330 RAYNES PARK MAIDEN AUCTION STKS 7f 16y
**7:10** (7:12) (Class 5) 2-Y-O **£3,234** (£962; £481; £240) **Stalls** Low

Form RPR

2 **1** **Taper Tantrum (IRE)**[25] 3467 2-9-1 0.................... RyanMoore 13 79+
(Michael Bell) *rousted fr wdst draw: led and crossed to inner: mde all: shkn up over 1f out: in command fnl f: rdn out* **10/11**[1]

060 **2** *2¾* **Clever Love (FR)**[40] 2944 2-8-12 0.................... PhilipPrince(5) 2 74
(Jo Hughes) *chsd wnr: rdn and no imp over 1f out: kpt on wl to hold on for 2nd* **66/1**

5 **3** *½* **Red Rebel**[33] 3181 2-8-10 0.................... RyanTate(3) 4 68
(Clive Cox) *chsd ldng pair: rdn and nt qckn 2f out: one pce after* **5/2**[2]

**4** *nse* **Lear's Rock (IRE)** 2-8-13 0.................... JimCrowley 10 68+
(Ralph Beckett) *slowly away: wl in rr to 1/2-way: pushed along and prog 3f out: stl pushed and styd on fnl f to dispute 3rd nr fin* **16/1**

0 **5** *1¼* **Berkshire Beauty**[22] 3557 2-8-12 0.................... DavidProbert 9 64
(Andrew Balding) *mostly in 6th: shkn up and one pce fnl 2f* **16/1**

002 **6** *nk* **Playboy Bay**[11] 3945 2-8-11 0.................... SamHitchcott 8 62
(Mick Channon) *chsd ldrs: rdn wl over 2f out: hanging bdly rt after and wouldn't r in a st line: kpt on fnl f* **9/1**[3]

04 **7** *5* **Mistral**[22] 3542 2-8-6 0.................... HayleyTurner 5 43
(Steph Hollinshead) *trckd ldrs: pushed along 3f out: rdn and no prog 2f out: wknd over 1f out* **20/1**

**8** *3½* **Diamond Runner (IRE)** 2-8-8 0....................(v[1]) NoelGarbutt(5) 3 41+
(Hugo Palmer) *slowly away: sn pushed along in rr: nvr a factor but only wknd over 1f out* **33/1**

0 **9** *6* **Quae Supra**[17] 3748 2-9-3 0.................... SeanLevey 7 29
(Richard Hannon) *sn pushed along in rr: no prog 3f out: wknd 2f out* **50/1**

0 **10** *1* **Emperors Warrior (IRE)**[26] 3429 2-8-13 0.................... PatDobbs 11 22
(Richard Hannon) *hung lft bnd 5f out: wl in rr and rdn after: nvr a factor* **33/1**

**11** *4* **Senor Firecracker (IRE)** 2-8-11 0.......... WilliamTwiston-Davies 12 9
(Brett Johnson) *s.v.s: a in last and wl bhd* **50/1**

1m 30.02s (0.52) **Going Correction** -0.175s/f (Firm) **11** Ran SP% **118.8**
Speed ratings (Par 94): **90,86,86,86,84 84,78,74,67,66 62**
CSF £112.31 TOTE £2.00: £1.10, £7.10, £1.20; EX 77.10 Trifecta £250.50.
**Owner** Secular Stagnation **Bred** Philip Newton **Trained** Newmarket, Suffolk

**FOCUS**
Probably not the strongest of maidens for the track, certainly in terms of depth, and the horse with the best form got the job done in straightforward style. The gelded runner-up has been rated as leaving his pre-race form well behind.

### 4331 RYMAN THE STATIONER H'CAP 1m 14y
**7:40** (7:41) (Class 3) (0-90,89) 3-Y-O+ **£7,439** (£2,213; £1,106; £553) **Stalls** Low

Form RPR

-531 **1** **Billingsgate (IRE)**[31] 3273 3-9-4 **88**.................... WilliamBuick 5 95+
(Charlie Appleby) *trckd ldng pair: rdn to chal and upsides over 1f out: chsd new ldr after: drvn to ld last 100yds: hld on wl* **85/40**[2]

4341 **2** *nk* **George Cinq**[5] 4148 4-9-3 **84**.................... LouisSteward(5) 7 92
(Michael Bell) *hld up in last: smooth prog on outer over 2f out: shkn up to ld over 1f out: drvn and hdd last 100yds: nt qckn* **6/4**[1]

1220 **3** *¾* **Tigers Tale (IRE)**[40] 2959 5-9-12 **88**....................(v) JamesDoyle 1 95
(Roger Teal) *led but pressed: rdn jst over 2f out: hdd and nt qckn over 1f out: styd on again last 100yds* **8/1**

-006 **4** *1* **Directorship**[17] 3753 8-9-13 **89**.................... GeorgeBaker 8 93
(Patrick Chamings) *hld up in last trio: clsd 2f out: already outpcd whn rdn fnl f: styd on nr fin but no ch* **7/1**[3]

144- **5** *¾* **Maverik**[198] 8445 6-9-11 **87**.................... JimCrowley 6 90
(William Knight) *pressed ldr: rdn over 2f out: upsides over 1f out: grad outpcd* **16/1**

430- **6** *7* **Purple 'n Gold (IRE)**[24] 7121 5-9-2 **78**....................(b) RyanMoore 2 65
(David Pipe) *trckd ldng pair: shkn up and no rspnse over 2f out: wknd over 1f out* **16/1**

1500 **7** *nk* **Birdman (IRE)**[11] 3982 4-9-12 **88**.................... MartinLane 4 75
(David Simcock) *hld up in last trio: rdn wl over 2f out: wknd wl over 1f out* **25/1**

1m 40.49s (-2.81) **Going Correction** -0.175s/f (Firm)
**WFA** 3 from 4yo+ 8lb **7** Ran SP% **111.2**
Speed ratings (Par 107): **107,106,105,104,104 97,96**
CSF £5.34 CT £17.30 TOTE £2.70: £1.30, £1.60; EX 5.90 Trifecta £35.60.
**Owner** Godolphin **Bred** Darley **Trained** Newmarket, Suffolk

**FOCUS**
The strongest race of the evening and the pace looked reasonable, although nothing more than that, to the the eye. Straightforward form, with the third back to his July 2013 form here.

### 4332 GRANBY H'CAP 1m 2f 7y
**8:15** (8:17) (Class 4) (0-80,80) 3-Y-O **£4,690** (£1,395; £697; £348) **Stalls** Low

Form RPR

043 **1** **High Church (IRE)**[17] 3750 3-9-3 **76**.................... JamesDoyle 9 87+
(Roger Charlton) *hld up in last pair: pushed along and prog on outer over 2f out: pressed ldr jst over 1f out: drvn to ld narrowly last 100yds: hld on wl* **5/1**[2]

3332 **2** *shd* **Loving Home**[26] 3432 3-9-7 **80**.................... WilliamBuick 11 90+
(John Gosden) *pressed ldr after 2f: led over 2f out: drvn over 1f out: narrowly hdd last 100yds: styd on wl: jst failed* **11/2**[3]

0041 **3** 3 **Beakers N Num Nums (IRE)**[13] 3898 3-9-1 **74**............ MartinDwyer 6 78
(William Jarvis) *racd freely: led: rdn and hdd over 2f out: kpt pressing ldr to jst over 1f out: one pce* **10/1**

2244 **4** 2 ½ **Cotton Club (IRE)**[21] 3587 3-8-12 **78**.................... PatMillman(7) 4 77+
(Rod Millman) *hld up in last pair: several reminders fr wl over 2f out: sme prog fr over 1f out: nvr threatened* **8/1**

5553 **5** hd **Best Kept**[11] 3986 3-9-3 **76**.......................................(b¹) AndreaAtzeni 8 75
(Amanda Perrett) *trckd ldr 2f: styd prom: rdn over 2f out: stl pressing over 1f out: wknd fnl f* **12/1**

6-01 **6** 1 ¼ **Golden Journey (IRE)**[26] 3421 3-8-13 **75**........................ RyanTate(3) 7 71
(Clive Cox) *hld up in midfield: shkn up over 2f out: no prog or imp on ldrs over 1f out* **8/1**

3053 **7** ½ **Arcamante (ITY)**[37] 3064 3-8-13 **72**..........................(e¹) FrederikTylicki 3 68
(K R Burke) *hld up in rr: shkn up and hanging 2f out: no prog: nudged along and kpt on fnl f* **25/1**

2-41 **8** 1 ¼ **Rapid Advance**[40] 2968 3-9-7 **80**....................................... RyanMoore 1 82+
(Sir Michael Stoute) *trckd ldrs: shkn up over 2f out: cl enough wl over 1f out: sn wknd u.p* **9/4¹**

006 **9** 2 ¾ **Cobham's Circus (IRE)**[39] 2996 3-8-8 **67**...................... ShaneKelly 10 55
(Marcus Tregoning) *nvr bttr than midfield: rdn and struggling over 2f out: wl btn over 1f out* **20/1**

2m 7.77s (-2.73) **Going Correction** -0.175s/f (Firm) **9** Ran SP% **110.4**
Speed ratings (Par 102): **103,102,100,98,98 97,96,95,93**
CSF £30.33 CT £247.63 TOTE £5.20: £1.50, £1.60, £2.80; EX 25.00 Trifecta £316.20.
**Owner** Lady Rothschild **Bred** The Rt Hon Lord Rothschild **Trained** Beckhampton, Wilts
■ Mr Greenspan was withdrawn. Price at time of withdrawal 16/1. Rule 4 does not apply.

**FOCUS**
Two pulled clear to fight out this 3yo contest. and the form looks decent.

## 4333 MOLESEY H'CAP 1m 6f
**8:50** (8:50) (Class 5) (0-70,69) 3-Y-O **£3,234** (£962; £481; £240) **Stalls** Low

Form RPR

3066 **1** **Needless Shouting (IRE)**[15] 3818 3-9-3 **65**.................. SamHitchcott 9 75
(Mick Channon) *mde all: kicked on 3f out: jnd ins fnl f: hld on gamely last 75yds* **16/1**

6015 **2** hd **Frederic Chopin**[15] 3823 3-8-13 **61**.................................(t) HarryBentley 1 70
(Stuart Williams) *trckd ldng pair: gap appeared and pushed through to go 2nd jst over 1f out: str chal and upsides ins fnl f: styd on but outbattled nr fin* **14/1**

3005 **3** 4 ½ **Peacemaker (IRE)**[11] 3978 3-9-0 **62**............................(p) JimmyFortune 2 65+
(Eve Johnson Houghton) *hld up in midfield: rdn over 2f out: styd on fr over 1f out to take 3rd fnl f: no ch w ldng pair* **8/1**

5004 **4** 1 ½ **Hallbeck**[16] 3789 3-9-4 **66**................................................ DaneO'Neill 6 67
(Henry Candy) *trckd ldrs: rdn over 2f out: cl up but nt qckn wl over 1f out: fdd fnl f* **11/4¹**

0-00 **5** 1 **Mr Smith**[47] 2746 3-9-2 **64**..............................................(p) WilliamBuick 8 64+
(John Gosden) *hld up in last pair: shkn up and no rspnse 3f out: n.d after: styd on fr over 1f out: nrst fin* **11/2³**

4042 **6** ½ **Majestic Sun (IRE)**[12] 3912 3-9-3 **65**............................... ShaneKelly 10 64
(Peter Chapple-Hyam) *free to post: t.k.h: hld up in 8th: eased to outer 2f out and shuffled along: v modest prog and reminder fnl f: nvr involved* **11/2³**

3103 **7** 1 **Jarlath**[27] 3391 3-9-7 **69**................................................... RyanMoore 7 67
(Seamus Mullins) *trckd wnr: rdn and tried to chal over 2f out: lost 2nd and wknd jst over 1f out* **3/1²**

0643 **8** 6 **Drifter (IRE)**[35] 3120 3-9-1 **63**....................................... StephenCraine 4 53
(Tom Dascombe) *tk fierce hold: hld up in midfield: cl enough over 2f out: wknd wl over 1f out* **16/1**

0663 **9** 1 **Zephyr**[26] 2679 3-9-0 **62**................................................(p) FrederikTylicki 5 51
(Jamie Snowden) *wl in tch in midfield: rdn and wknd over 2f out* **33/1**

0-65 **10** 8 **Hiorne Tower (FR)**[41] 2924 3-9-6 **68**................................... GeorgeBaker 3 46
(John Best) *s.v.s: a detached in last: shkn up and no prog over 2f out* **25/1**

3m 3.96s (-0.54) **Going Correction** -0.175s/f (Firm) **10** Ran SP% **118.8**
Speed ratings (Par 100): **94,93,91,90,89 89,89,85,85,80**
CSF £223.11 CT £1932.92 TOTE £16.60: £4.20, £3.10, £3.60; EX 238.10 Trifecta £1597.80.
**Owner** Lord Ilsley Racing (Russell Syndicate) **Bred** John Connaughton **Trained** West Ilsley, Berks

**FOCUS**
A modest handicap in which it proved hard to get in a serious blow from off the pace. Most of these look far from straightforward. The winner was given a good ride to see off the runner-up and it looks ordinary form.
T/Jkpt: Not won. T/Plt: £588.90 to a £1 stake. Pool of £100445.98 - 124.50 winning units.
T/Qpdt: £54.80 to a £1 stake. Pool of £10,071.54 - 136.00 winning units. JN

# 4042 BRIGHTON (L-H)
Thursday, July 17

**OFFICIAL GOING: Good to firm (firm in places; 8.0)**
Wind: virtually nil Weather: sunny and warm

## 4337 ISE LANGUAGE SCHOOL AT ISEHOVE.COM H'CAP 5f 59y
**2:05** (2:05) (Class 6) (0-55,53) 3-Y-O+ **£1,940** (£577; £288; £144) **Stalls** Low

Form RPR

2062 **1** **Johnny Splash (IRE)**[16] 3820 5-9-3 **49**..........................(v) GeorgeBaker 3 61
(Roger Teal) *broke sharply: mde all: sn clr: shkn up over 1f out: unchal* **5/2¹**

3562 **2** 2 ¾ **See Vermont**[2] 4306 6-9-1 **47**......................................(p) AdamBeschizza 6 49
(Robin Bastiman) *sn pushed along in tch: hdwy to chse wnr wl over 1f out: nvr threatened: kpt on same pce fnl f* **9/2²**

0602 **3** 3 ¼ **Tiger's Home**[9] 4042 4-9-0 **51**................................ ShelleyBirkett(5) 2 42
(Julia Feilden) *outpcd in rr after 1f: hdwy 2f out: wnt 3rd over 1f out: nvr threatened: fdd fnl 120yds* **5/2¹**

0303 **4** 2 **Spic 'n Span**[17] 3784 9-9-0 **46**.......................................(p) SteveDrowne 4 30
(Ronald Harris) *chsd wnr tl wl over 1f out: fdd ins fnl f* **11/1**

4650 **5** ¾ **Interakt**[22] 3589 7-8-6 **45**............................................(b) NoraLooby(7) 8 26
(Joseph Tuite) *chsd wnr: rdn over 2f out: sn one pce* **8/1³**

3060 **6** ¾ **Back On Baileys**[7] 4101 3-8-6 **45**.................................(v) RyanPowell(3) 1 23
(John Ryan) *s.i.s: in last pair: nvr gng pce to get involved* **33/1**

-403 **7** 2 ¼ **Astral Rose**[20] 3679 3-9-2 **52**......................................(b) OisinMurphy 7 22
(Jonathan Portman) *s.i.s: a in rr* **14/1**

0-06 **8** 21 **Diamond Solitaire (IRE)**[17] 3801 3-9-3 **53**.................... SamHitchcott 5
(Timothy Jarvis) *chsd ldrs: rdn over 2f out: wknd over 1f out: eased whn no ch* **8/1³**

1m 2.06s (-0.24) **Going Correction** -0.10s/f (Good)
**WFA** 3 from 4yo+ 4lb **8** Ran SP% **115.5**
Speed ratings (Par 101): **97,92,87,84,83 81,78,44**
CSF £14.16 CT £30.33 TOTE £2.30: £1.10, £1.80, £1.60; EX 10.60 Trifecta £25.30.
**Owner** Barry Kitcherside **Bred** J Connolly **Trained** Ashtead, Surrey

**FOCUS**
All races on inner line and distances as advertised. Recent winning form was non-existent in this opener and it really isn't a race to dwell on. A length best from the winner.

## 4338 BIBBY FINANCIAL SERVICES MEDIAN AUCTION MAIDEN STKS 5f 213y
**2:35** (2:35) (Class 6) 2-Y-O **£1,940** (£577; £288; £144) **Stalls** Low

Form RPR

5 **1** **Jargon (FR)**[24] 3536 2-9-5 0.............................................. GeorgeBaker 9 81+
(Michael Bell) *trckd ldr: mounting chal on rails whn bdly hmpd and dropped to 3rd jst over 1f out: swtchd rt: r.o strly whn rdn: led nr fin: readily* **2/1¹**

6323 **2** 1 **Amber Crystal**[33] 3211 2-8-9 0...................................... LouisSteward(5) 2 63
(John Gallagher) *led: drifted bdly lft u.p over 1f out: no ex whn hdd nr fin* **6/1**

35 **3** 1 ½ **Burning The Clocks (IRE)**[36] 3119 2-9-5 0......................... ShaneKelly 5 64
(Peter Chapple-Hyam) *trckd ldrs: effrt on outer over 2f out: lft 2nd jst over 1f out: kpt on but nvr able to chal: no ex whn lost 2nd towards fin* **3/1²**

265 **4** 2 ¼ **Aevalon**[13] 3933 2-9-0 0...................................................... PatDobbs 4 52
(Eve Johnson Houghton) *towards rr: rdn over 3f out: styd on fnl f but nvr gng pce to get on terms* **10/1**

6 **5** nk **First Class Mail**[19] 3728 2-9-5 0................... WilliamTwiston-Davies 8 56
(Mick Channon) *s.i.s: last and sn pushed along: looked to be hanging lft fnl 2f: styd on but no ch fnl f* **4/1³**

0 **6** nk **Toast Of Newbury (IRE)**[10] 4025 2-9-5 0.......................... OisinMurphy 6 55
(Jamie Osborne) *in tch: pushed along over 3f out: nvr gng pce to get on terms* **14/1**

04 **7** 1 ¾ **Spirit In Time (IRE)**[16] 3813 2-9-0 0............................ FergusSweeney 7 45
(Malcolm Saunders) *little slowly away: sn trcking ldr: rdn over 2f out: hld over 1f out: wknd ins fnl f* **100/1**

02 **8** ½ **Lady Charlie**[21] 3606 2-8-9 0...................................... PhilipPrince(5) 1 43
(Jo Hughes) *in last pair: sn pushed along: hdwy over 2f out: nvr threatened: wknd fnl f* **33/1**

0 **8** dht **Activation**[10] 4025 2-9-5 0............................................ HayleyTurner 3 48
(Hughie Morrison) *mid-div: pushed along over 4f out: wknd jst over 1f out* **50/1**

1m 10.24s (0.04) **Going Correction** -0.10s/f (Good) **9** Ran SP% **114.3**
Speed ratings (Par 92): **95,93,91,88,88 87,85,84,84**
CSF £14.38 TOTE £2.90: £1.40, £1.40, £1.60; EX 13.20 Trifecta £46.50.
**Owner** The Royal Ascot Racing Club **Bred** S C E A Haras Du Ma **Trained** Newmarket, Suffolk
■ Stewards' Enquiry : Louis Steward two-day ban: careless riding (31st Jul & 1st Aug)

**FOCUS**
It's unlikely this was the strongest of juvenile races. Ordinary form rated around the runner-up.

## 4339 TM LEWIN H'CAP 5f 213y
**3:05** (3:06) (Class 4) (0-80,85) 3-Y-O+ **£4,690** (£1,395; £697; £348) **Stalls** Low

Form RPR

3344 **1** **Ginzan**[18] 3749 6-9-1 **68**................................................ FergusSweeney 4 76
(Malcolm Saunders) *trckd ldrs: rdn 2f out: str run to ld fnl 140yds: a holding on* **15/2**

4052 **2** ¾ **Noverre To Go (IRE)**[18] 3749 8-9-10 **77**.......................(p) SteveDrowne 6 83
(Ronald Harris) *hld up bhd ldrs: rdn and hanging sltly lft over 1f out: r.o fnl f: fin strly to snatch 2nd nring fin but nvr quite rching wnr* **4/1²**

0155 **3** ½ **Storm Lightning**[19] 3697 5-9-4 **71**.................................. GeorgeBaker 1 75
(Mark Brisbourne) *prom: led 2f out: sn rdn: hdd fnl 140yds: kpt on but sn hld by wnr: lost 2nd nring fin* **9/2³**

1421 **4** nse **Iseemist (IRE)**[7] 4121 3-9-8 **85**6ex........................ LouisSteward(5) 3 88
(John Gallagher) *trckd ldrs: rdn to chse ldr briefly jst over 1f out: kpt on disputing hld 2nd tl no ex fnl 100yds* **1/1¹**

5600 **5** 6 **Lionheart**[14] 3879 4-9-3 **70**................................................ ShaneKelly 5 55
(Peter Crate) *led tl rdn 2f out: sn hld: wknd ins fnl f* **12/1**

1m 9.28s (-0.92) **Going Correction** -0.10s/f (Good)
**WFA** 3 from 4yo+ 5lb **5** Ran SP% **107.6**
Speed ratings (Par 105): **102,101,100,100,92**
CSF £34.13 TOTE £11.70: £3.70, £1.80; EX 32.00 Trifecta £82.60.
**Owner** Paul Nicholas **Bred** Hedsor Stud **Trained** Green Ore, Somerset

**FOCUS**
This was steadily run and that was the catalyst for an upset. The winner was on a good mark on her best form, and she has been rated as running only slightly better than her recent efforts.

## 4340 HARRINGTONS LETTINGS H'CAP 1m 1f 209y
**3:35** (3:35) (Class 5) (0-70,70) 3-Y-O+ **£2,587** (£770; £384; £192) **Stalls** High

Form RPR

4066 **1** **Secular Society**[20] 3681 4-9-13 **69**..............................(p) PatCosgrave 4 79
(George Baker) *chsd clr ldr in clr 2nd: rdn to cl on ldr over 2f out: led over 1f out: kpt on wl* **5/1³**

0130 **2** 2 **Gabrial The Terror (IRE)**[5] 4190 4-9-12 **68**...................... LiamKeniry 5 74
(David Simcock) *chsd clr ldrs in 3rd: rdn to cl on ldrs 2f out: edgd lft over 1f out: wnt 2nd ent fnl f: kpt on same pce* **11/4¹**

6655 **3** 6 **Tunnel Tiger (IRE)**[16] 3814 3-7-12 **57**..................... CallumShepherd(7) 6 52
(William Knight) *hld up wl off pce: wnt 4th wl over 3f out: sn rdn: wnt 3rd wl ins fnl f: nvr any ch w ldrs* **6/1**

6302 **4** ¾ **Nubar Boy**[21] 3616 7-9-9 **70**.................................(p) GeorgeDowning(5) 7 63
(Ian Williams) *led: sn clr: rdn over 2f out: hdd over 1f out: fdd ins fnl f* **5/1³**

3053 **5** 3 ¾ **Whitby Jet (IRE)**[16] 3825 6-9-9 **70**.............................. CamHardie(5) 1 56
(Ed Vaughan) *hld up wl off pce: rdn 3f out: nvr any imp* **3/1²**

-500 **6** 11 **Third Strike**[19] 3711 3-8-10 **62**.................................. FergusSweeney 2 27
(Gary Moore) *stdd s wl off pce: rdn 3f out: nvr any imp: eased whn no ch fnl f* **7/1**

-50B **7** 1 **Permsiri (IRE)**[18] 3754 3-8-0 **52** oh7................................ KieranO'Neill 3 15
(Malcolm Saunders) *trckd ldrs tl over 3f out: sn struggling in rr* **66/1**

2m 1.78s (-1.82) **Going Correction** -0.10s/f (Good)
**WFA** 3 from 4yo+ 10lb **7** Ran SP% **113.3**
Speed ratings (Par 103): **103,101,96,96,93 84,83**
CSF £18.77 TOTE £5.40: £2.70, £1.80; EX 22.30 Trifecta £137.70.
**Owner** Mrs Sue Head **Bred** Aston Mullins Stud **Trained** Manton, Wilts

**FOCUS**
Not many got into this and it was won in dour style. The runner-up has been rated to form.

## 4341 BIBBY FINANCIAL SERVICES SOUTH COAST H'CAP 6f 209y
**4:05** (4:06) (Class 6) (0-55,55) 3-Y-0+ **£1,940** (£577; £288; £144) **Stalls** Low

Form RPR
5-13 **1** **Royal Caper**[16] 3820 4-9-5 **53** StevieDonohoe 1 64
(Miss Joey Ellis) *chsd ldrs: rdn over 2f out: led over 1f out: kpt on wl* **7/2**[1]
002 **2** *1 3/4* **Big City Boy (IRE)**[9] 4056 6-8-12 **46** oh1 OisinMurphy 9 52
(Phil McEntee) *led: rdn 2f out: hdd over 1f out: kpt on same pce fnl f* **10/1**
0046 **3** *1* **Anginola (IRE)**[8] 4080 5-9-3 **51** (v) AmirQuinn 10 55
(Laura Mongan) *s.i.s: towards rr: stdy prog fr 3f out: wnt 4th over 1f out: styd on to go 3rd fnl 100yds but nvr threatening to rch ldrs* **9/1**
2540 **4** *1 1/4* **Mill I Am (USA)**[28] 3384 4-9-7 **55** AdamBeschizza 7 56
(Stuart Williams) *mid-div: hdwy over 2f out: sn rdn: wnt 3rd ent fnl f tl no ex fnl 100yds* **8/1**[3]
0044 **5** *2 1/2* **Dancing Sal (IRE)**[9] 4048 3-9-0 **55** ShaneKelly 8 46
(Gary Moore) *mid-div: rdn on outer 3f out: no imp tl styd on ins fnl f: nvr trbld ldrs* **6/1**[2]
-043 **6** *1/2* **Dark Phantom (IRE)**[18] 3754 3-8-8 **49** (t) MartinLane 4 39
(Peter Makin) *hld up bhd: sme prog u.p over 2f out but nvr gng pce to get involved* **6/1**[2]
2606 **7** *nk* **High On The Hog (IRE)**[9] 4042 6-8-12 **46** oh1 JimmyQuinn 6 38
(Mark Brisbourne) *chsd ldrs: rdn over 2f out: wknd over 1f out* **16/1**
3456 **8** *1/2* **Jazz Bay**[16] 3820 3-8-6 **47** (p) WilliamCarson 2 35
(John Bridger) *trckd ldr: rdn wl over 2f out: wknd over 1f out* **10/1**
0/0- **9** *1* **Buxton**[558] 80 10-9-0 **55** (t) RhiainIngram(7) 5 43
(Roger Ingram) *hld up towards rr: rdn 3f out: nvr threatened: wknd ins fnl f* **40/1**
5066 **10** *19* **Lady Rain**[7] 4101 5-8-12 **46** oh1 SteveDrowne 3
(Ronald Harris) *mid-div tl wknd over 2f out* **33/1**
-002 **U** **Copper To Gold**[21] 3630 5-8-7 **46** CamHardie(5) 11
(Robin Bastiman) *rrd bdly as stalls were abt to open and uns rdr* **6/1**[2]
1m 21.79s (-1.31) **Going Correction** -0.10s/f (Good)
**WFA** 3 from 4yo+ 7lb **11** Ran SP% **115.6**
Speed ratings (Par 101): **103,101,99,98,95 95,94,94,92,71**
CSF £38.85 CT £295.58 TOTE £4.20: £2.30, £4.10, £4.20; EX 46.90 Trifecta £350.20.
**Owner** Mrs Angela Ellis **Bred** P And Mrs A G Venner **Trained** Newmarket, Suffolk

**FOCUS**
The runner-up confirmed his AW latest.

## 4342 GATWICK AIRPORT H'CAP 7f 214y
**4:35** (4:35) (Class 5) (0-75,74) 3-Y-0+ **£2,587** (£577; £577; £192) **Stalls** Low

Form RPR
4003 **1** **Siouxperhero (IRE)**[17] 3805 5-9-3 **63** (b) DougieCostello 4 72
(William Muir) *trckd ldr: rdn to ld wl over 1f out: drifted lft: r.o wl and in command fnl f* **8/1**
1663 **2** *1 3/4* **Welsh Inlet (IRE)**[9] 4047 6-9-1 **61** WilliamCarson 7 66
(John Bridger) *in tch: rdn wl over 2f out: hdwy ent fnl f: kpt on wl towards fin* **8/1**
4122 **2** *dht* **Picks Pinta**[6] 4161 3-8-13 **72** PhilipPrince(5) 5 75
(Jo Hughes) *chsd ldrs: chal 2f out tl edgd lft whn rdn: kpt on but nt pce of wnr fnl f* **11/10**[1]
0-64 **4** *3 1/2* **Just Isla**[23] 3555 4-8-11 **57** (p) SteveDrowne 2 54
(Peter Makin) *in tch: pushed along and hdwy over 2f out: rdn over 1f out in disp 3rd: fdd fnl 100yds* **7/1**[3]
6044 **5** *1 1/4* **Jonnie Skull (IRE)**[14] 3895 8-9-4 **64** (vt) OisinMurphy 1 58
(Phil McEntee) *led: rdn and hdd wl over 1f out: wknd fnl f* **9/1**
2004 **6** *16* **Sword Of The Lord**[17] 3791 4-10-0 **74** WilliamTwiston-Davies 6 49
(George Margarson) *stdd s: last: swtchd rt over 2f out: sn rdn: no imp: eased whn btn 1f out* **4/1**[2]
6260 **7** *2 1/2* **Sebs Sensei (IRE)**[33] 3229 3-8-11 **65** (p) RobertHavlin 3 15
(Mark Hoad) *trckd ldr: rdn over 2f out: wknd over 1f out* **40/1**
1m 33.56s (-2.44) **Going Correction** -0.10s/f (Good)
**WFA** 3 from 4yo+ 8lb **7** Ran SP% **114.8**
Speed ratings (Par 103): **108,106,106,102,101 85,83**
TOTE WIN: £10.20; PL: Picks Pinta £0.70, Welsh Inlet £1.50, Siouxperhero £4.10; EX: S/PP £14.50, S/WI £26.80; CSF: S/PP £8.74, S/WI £34.18; Trifecta: S/PP/WI £79.00, S/WI/PP £80.00.00.
**Owner** Muir Racing Partnership - Bath **Bred** J & J Waldron **Trained** Lambourn, Berks

**FOCUS**
The third has been rated close to her latest form.

## 4343 STREAMLINE TAXIS APPRENTICE H'CAP 1m 3f 196y
**5:05** (5:05) (Class 6) (0-60,60) 4-Y-0+ **£1,940** (£577; £288; £144) **Stalls** High

Form RPR
0-60 **1** **Elsie Bay**[17] 3803 5-9-0 **60** (p) HectorCrouch(7) 6 66
(Gary Moore) *mde all: rdn whn strly chal fr 2f out: kpt on gamely to assert fnl 120yds* **16/1**
0054 **2** *3/4* **Sir Tyto (IRE)**[2] 4279 6-8-8 **47** (p) OisinMurphy 3 52
(Peter Makin) *cl up: rdn over 2f out: edgd lft over 1f out: kpt on ins fnl f to chse wnr fnl 120yds but a being hld* **4/1**[3]
301 **3** *hd* **Poste Restante**[20] 3682 4-8-8 **52** LewisWalsh(5) 1 57
(David Simcock) *hld up: pushed along over 3f out: no imp tl over 1f out: styd on fnl f but nvr gng pce to chal* **9/4**[1]
3022 **4** *3 1/2* **Cherry Princess**[16] 3824 4-8-7 **53** AaronJones(7) 5 53
(Stuart Williams) *racd keenly: trcking ldrs: rdn for str chal fr 2f out: cl 4th but hld whn short of room fnl 100yds* **3/1**[2]
0500 **5** *nk* **Mazij**[36] 3115 6-8-4 **46** oh1 ShelleyBirkett(3) 4 45
(Peter Hiatt) *trckd wnr tl rdn 2f out: sn one pce* **12/1**
6234 **6** *4 1/2* **Indian Scout**[12] 3973 6-8-5 **47** (b) CamHardie(3) 7 38
(Anabel K Murphy) *cl up: rdn over 2f out: short of room on rails briefly over 1f out: fdd fnl 120yds* **4/1**[3]
04-6 **7** *25* **No Compromise**[132] 872 5-8-7 **53** (p) KieranShoemark(7) 2 4
(Richard Phillips) *hld up last: struggling 3f out: sn lost tch: t.o* **33/1**
2m 34.17s (1.47) **Going Correction** -0.10s/f (Good) **7** Ran SP% **112.3**
Speed ratings (Par 101): **91,90,90,88,87 84,68**
CSF £75.43 TOTE £23.00: £9.20, £2.40; EX 115.40 Trifecta £533.30.
**Owner** Mrs J Gawthorpe **Bred** Mrs J A Gawthorpe **Trained** Lower Beeding, W Sussex

**FOCUS**
A moderate finale. The runner-up has a shaky profile but this is rated as his best turf run to date.
T/Plt: £39.50 to a £1 stake. Pool: £68,616.31 - 1267.74 winning units. T/Qpdt: £30.70 to a £1 stake. Pool: £4364.35 - 105.00 winnning units. TM

# 4108 DONCASTER (L-H)
### Thursday, July 17

**OFFICIAL GOING: Good to firm (9.2)**
Wind: Light behind Weather: Fine and dry

## 4344 CROWNHOTEL-BAWTRY.COM APPRENTICE H'CAP 5f
**5:55** (5:55) (Class 5) (0-70,69) 3-Y-0+ **£2,587** (£770; £384; £192) **Stalls** Low

Form RPR
-200 **1** **Pastureyes**[50] 2677 4-9-6 **61** (p) MatthewHopkins 5 69
(Scott Dixon) *cl up: led jst over 2f out: rdn wl over 1f out: kpt on wl towards fin* **15/2**
2043 **2** *nk* **Dancing Maite**[7] 4131 9-8-12 **53** (b) AlistairRawlinson 2 60
(Roy Bowring) *cl up: slt ld 31/2f out: rdn and hdd jst over 2f out: cl up and drvn over 1f out: kpt on wl u.p towards fin* **11/4**[2]
0503 **3** *2 3/4* **Burren View Lady (IRE)**[13] 3920 4-9-11 **69** (e) RachelRichardson(3) 3 66
(Tim Easterby) *trckd ldrs: hdwy over 2f out: sn chsng ldng pair: rdn over 1f out and kpt on same pce* **6/4**[1]
3625 **4** *1* **Your Gifted (IRE)**[119] 1030 7-8-9 **55** ClaireMurray(5) 6 48
(Lisa Williamson) *dwlt and in rr: pushed along and hdwy 1/2-way: rdn 2f out: chsd ldrs over 1f out: sn no imp* **20/1**
1106 **5** *2* **Fathom Five (IRE)**[2] 4288 10-9-0 **60** JoshQuinn(5) 1 46
(Shaun Harris) *led 1 1/2f: cl up on inner: rdn along 1/2-way: sn wknd* **5/1**[3]
5400 **6** *2* **Kuanyao (IRE)**[15] 3854 8-10-0 **69** (b) JordanVaughan 8 48
(Conor Dore) *sn outpcd and a in rr* **9/1**
59.02s (-1.48) **Going Correction** -0.30s/f (Firm) **6** Ran SP% **109.9**
Speed ratings (Par 103): **99,98,94,92,89 86**
CSF £27.07 CT £43.66 TOTE £5.80: £3.10, £1.90; EX 29.00 Trifecta £74.90.
**Owner** Paul J Dixon & Mrs Jayne Jackson **Bred** Mrs Yvette Dixon **Trained** Babworth, Notts

**FOCUS**
Round course railed out from 1m2f to where it joins the straight and races of 1m2f and over increased by 10yds. Warm, bright and a light breeze. The ground rode as advertised. A modest sprint handicap for apprentice riders. The gallop was sound but few got into it. There's no depth to the form and the runner-up has been rated to his recent level.

## 4345 D C TRAINING AND DEVELOPMENT SERVICES LTD FILLIES' NURSERY H'CAP (BOBIS RACE) 6f
**6:30** (6:33) (Class 4) 2-Y-0 **£3,881** (£1,155; £577; £288) **Stalls** Low

Form RPR
1 **1** **New Providence**[19] 3706 2-9-4 **75** RyanMoore 5 85+
(Hugo Palmer) *hld up in tch: hdwy 1/2-way: led wl over 1f out: rdn ins fnl f: kpt on strly* **2/1**[1]
0100 **2** *2 1/2* **Cajoling (IRE)**[19] 3721 2-9-7 **78** JamieSpencer 7 80
(Jonathan Portman) *hld up in rr: swtchd lft to outer and hdwy over 2f out: rdn jst over 1f out: drvn to chse wnr ins fnl f: sn no imp* **12/1**
210 **3** *nk* **Polar Vortex (IRE)**[29] 3353 2-9-4 **75** AdamKirby 3 76
(Clive Cox) *led: rdn along wl over 2f out: hdd wl over 1f out: sn drvn and kpt on same pce fnl f* **4/1**[3]
4466 **4** *1 3/4* **Jersey Belle**[42] 2928 2-7-13 **63** PaddyPilley(7) 1 59
(Mick Channon) *cl up: rdn along wl over 2f out: wknd over 1f out* **25/1**
043 **5** *3/4* **Tarando**[61] 2349 2-8-8 **65** AndreaAtzeni 2 59
(Michael Bell) *trckd ldrs: rdn along and outpcd wl over 2f out: kpt on fnl f* **11/4**[2]
010 **6** *3 1/4* **Gold Waltz**[27] 3415 2-8-9 **66** IanBrennan 4 50
(Ralph Beckett) *in tch: rdn along over 2f out: sn one pce* **7/1**
216 **7** *4 1/2* **Mecca's Mirage (IRE)**[13] 3922 2-8-13 **73** ConnorBeasley(3) 6 43
(Michael Dods) *chsd ldng pair: shkn up 1/2-way: sn rdn and wknd* **12/1**
1m 11.39s (-2.21) **Going Correction** -0.30s/f (Firm) **7** Ran SP% **111.7**
Speed ratings (Par 93): **102,98,98,95,94 90,84**
CSF £25.54 TOTE £2.90: £1.60, £2.70; EX 25.10 Trifecta £90.20.
**Owner** Chris Humber **Bred** James Ortega Bloodstock **Trained** Newmarket, Suffolk

**FOCUS**
The early pace was not particularly strong in this fillies' nursery, and the form is fair. The runner-up and third help set the opening level.

## 4346 ALL NEW AYGO @ BURROWS TOYOTA EBF STALLIONS MAIDEN FILLIES' STKS (BOBIS RACE) 7f
**7:00** (7:02) (Class 5) 2-Y-0 **£2,911** (£866; £432; £216) **Stalls** Low

Form RPR
5 **1** **Adelasia (IRE)**[32] 3267 2-9-0 0 WilliamBuick 5 78+
(Charlie Appleby) *set stdy pce: qcknd 1/2-way: rdn and qcknd clr wl over 1f out: kpt on strly* **9/2**[2]
03 **2** *2 3/4* **Astrelle (IRE)**[32] 3267 2-9-0 0 MartinHarley 7 71
(Marco Botti) *trckd wnr: effrt 2f out: sn rdn: drvn and no imp fnl f* **15/2**
5 **3** *1/2* **Hoorayforhollywood**[48] 2744 2-9-0 0 RyanMoore 9 69
(Sir Michael Stoute) *trckd ldng pair: effrt over 2f out: rdn wl over 1f out: kpt on same pce fnl f* **5/1**[3]
6 **4** *1/2* **Lashkaal**[48] 2744 2-9-0 0 PaulHanagan 1 68
(John Gosden) *trckd ldrs: effrt over 2f out: sn rdn along and kpt on same pce* **5/4**[1]
**5** *3/4* **Mahsooba (USA)** 2-9-0 0 DaneO'Neill 10 66+
(Ed Dunlop) *towards rr: swtchd rt and rdn 2f out: styd on wl fnl f: nrst fin* **20/1**
0 **6** *2 1/2* **Mikandy (IRE)**[23] 3558 2-8-11 0 RyanTate(3) 12 59+
(Clive Cox) *in rr tl styd on fnl 2f: nrst fin* **80/1**
33 **7** *1/2* **Three Robins**[22] 3584 2-9-0 0 SeanLevey 8 58
(Richard Hannon) *chsd ldrs: rdn along over 2f out: sn wknd* **8/1**
**8** *2* **Roxie Lot** 2-9-0 0 JohnFahy 6 52+
(Pam Sly) *towards rr: hdwy wl over 2f out: rdn to chse ldrs wl over 1f out: sn wknd* **66/1**
**9** *2 1/4* **Chanson De Marins (FR)** 2-8-11 0 ConnorBeasley(3) 2 46+
(John Holt) *dwlt: green and a in rr* **200/1**
**10** *4 1/2* **Lady D's Rock (IRE)** 2-9-0 0 AdamKirby 3 34
(Clive Cox) *midfield: hdwy to chse ldrs wl over 2f out: sn rdn and wknd wl over 1f out* **25/1**
**11** *2 1/4* **Meadow Cross (IRE)** 2-9-0 0 AndrewElliott 11 28
(Tim Easterby) *midfield: rdn along 3f out: sn outpcd* **100/1**
**12** *3 1/4* **Anniversarie** 2-8-9 0 JacobButterfield(5) 4 19
(John Norton) *dwlt and awkward s: green and a in rr* **200/1**
1m 25.47s (-0.83) **Going Correction** -0.30s/f (Firm) **12** Ran SP% **115.5**
Speed ratings (Par 91): **92,88,88,87,86 84,83,81,78,73 70,67**
CSF £35.72 TOTE £5.30: £1.60, £2.00, £2.80; EX 27.40 Trifecta £122.90.
**Owner** Godolphin **Bred** J O'Connor **Trained** Newmarket, Suffolk


The Form Book, Raceform Ltd, Newbury, RG14 5SJ

**FOCUS**
An interesting maiden for juvenile fillies and a lacklustre early pace. They finished quite strung out and, the winner aside, the form looks ordinary. The runner-up has been rated to her debut figure.

## 4347 TERRY BELLAS MEMORIAL CLASSIFIED STKS 7f
7:35 (7:36) (Class 3) 4-Y-O+ £7,762 (£2,310; £1,154; £577) Stalls Low

Form RPR
0-11 **1** **King Torus (IRE)**[44] 2869 6-9-3 90 JamesSullivan 8 98
(Ruth Carr) *trckd ldr: hdwy over 2f out: rdn to ld appr fnl f: kpt on strly* **10/3**[2]

00-0 **2** *2* **Jammy Guest (IRE)**[27] 3420 4-9-3 88 MartinHarley 7 93
(George Margarson) *trckd ldrs: hdwy 2f out: n.m.r and rdn over 1f out: styd on wl fnl f: nrst fin* **16/1**

2553 **3** *hd* **Apostle (IRE)**[6] 4169 5-9-3 89 JamieSpencer 6 93
(David Simcock) *set stdy pce: qcknd 3f out: rdn 2f out: hdd and drvn appr fnl f: kpt on same pce* **3/1**[1]

164- **4** *nse* **Badr Al Badoor (IRE)**[126] 948 4-9-0 90 TomQueally 5 90
(James Fanshawe) *t.k.h: hld up: hdwy over 2f out: rdn to chse ldrs over 1f out: drvn and kpt on wl fnl f* **10/1**

11-0 **5** *2* **Pipers Note**[19] 3714 4-9-3 90 RyanMoore 1 88
(Richard Whitaker) *stdd s and sltly hmpd ins first f: trckd ldrs: hdwy on inner to chse ldrs 2f out: sn rdn: drvn ent fnl f and sn one pce* **7/2**[3]

-006 **6** *1* **Smarty Socks (IRE)**[19] 3716 10-9-3 89 DanielTudhope 4 86
(David O'Meara) *in rr: effrt and sme hdwy over 2f out: sn rdn and btn* **8/1**

2650 **7** *1 1/2* **Corporal Maddox**[14] 3876 7-9-3 87 (p) AdamKirby 2 82
(Ronald Harris) *prom: rdn along over 2f out: sn drvn and wknd* **25/1**

2210 **U** **Johnny Cavagin**[34] 3202 5-9-3 85 (t) PaulHanagan 3
(Richard Guest) *rrd s and uns rdr stalls* **13/2**

1m 25.84s (-0.46) **Going Correction** -0.30s/f (Firm) **8** Ran SP% **113.6**
Speed ratings (Par 107): **90,87,87,87,85 84,82,**
CSF £52.74 TOTE £3.60: £1.90, £4.20, £1.10; EX 52.00 Trifecta £112.50.
**Owner** Sprint Thoroughbred Racing **Bred** Whisperview Trading Ltd **Trained** Huby, N Yorks

**FOCUS**
The pace was solid for this useful Classified event although a loose horse caused an anxious moment or two. The runner-up has been rated back to form, with the third a little off.

## 4348 188BET NOVICE STKS (BOBIS RACE) 6f
8:10 (8:10) (Class 4) 2-Y-O £6,469 (£1,925; £962; £481) Stalls Low

Form RPR
25 **1** **Osaila (IRE)**[27] 3415 2-8-9 0 FrankieDettori 5 95+
(Richard Hannon) *trckd ldr: hdwy over 2f out: cl up over 1f out: rdn and qcknd to ld ent fnl f: sn clr: readily* **10/11**[1]

21 **2** *3* **Surewecan**[16] 3827 2-9-7 0 FrannyNorton 3 96+
(Mark Johnston) *led: qcknd over 2f out: rdn wl over 1f out: hdd and drvn ent fnl f: kpt on: no ch w wnr* **4/1**[2]

12 **3** *3 3/4* **Geordie George (IRE)**[21] 3619 2-9-0 0 JoeDoyle(7) 4 85
(John Quinn) *trckd ldrs: hdwy over 2f out: rdn wl over 1f out: kpt on same pce* **11/2**

610 **4** *6* **Billyoakes (IRE)**[5] 4218 2-9-7 0 MartinHarley 2 67
(Mick Channon) *chsd ldng pair: rdn along over 2f out: sn outpcd* **40/1**

2201 **5** *1/2* **Commander Patten (IRE)**[8] 4079 2-9-4 0 RyanMoore 1 62
(Alan Bailey) *trckd ldrs: hdwy on inner 3f out: rdn along 2f out: sn drvn and wknd* **9/2**[3]

1m 11.52s (-2.08) **Going Correction** -0.30s/f (Firm) **5** Ran SP% **108.4**
Speed ratings (Par 96): **101,97,92,84,83**
CSF £4.68 TOTE £1.80: £1.10, £2.30; EX 4.90 Trifecta £11.00.
**Owner** Al Shaqab Racing **Bred** Mennetou Syndicate **Trained** East Everleigh, Wilts

**FOCUS**
They raced up the far rail and the early pace was modest for this decent novices' sprint. They finished well strung out and the form looks solid. It's been rated as a good renewal, with the third rated a length off his best.

## 4349 188BET CASINO H'CAP 1m 2f 60y
8:40 (8:40) (Class 4) (0-85,85) 4-Y-O+ £5,175 (£1,540; £769; £384) Stalls Low

Form RPR
40/ **1** **Gabrial The Hero (USA)**[698] 5366 5-9-2 80 JamieSpencer 6 89+
(David Simcock) *stdd s: hld up and bhd: stdy hdwy on wd outside over 2f out: rdn over 1f out: styd on strly fnl f: to ld last 75yds* **16/1**

0162 **2** *1 1/4* **Kingscroft (IRE)**[12] 3955 6-8-11 80 JacobButterfield(5) 5 86
(Michael Herrington) *trckd ldrs: hdwy 2f out: rdn to ld ent fnl f: drvn and hdd last 75yds: sn no ex* **12/1**

11-5 **3** *1 3/4* **Odin (IRE)**[190] 85 6-9-6 84 DaneO'Neill 12 86
(Don Cantillon) *hld up in rr: hdwy wl over 2f out: sn rdn: styd on wl fnl f: nrst fin* **33/1**

3-00 **4** *nk* **Endless Credit (IRE)**[22] 3574 4-9-5 83 AndreaAtzeni 3 84
(Luca Cumani) *trckd ldng pair on inner: smooth hdwy to ld over 2f out: rdn over 1f out: hdd ent fnl f: sn one pce* **15/8**[1]

1065 **5** *nk* **Correggio**[25] 3499 4-8-12 76 FrannyNorton 1 77
(Micky Hammond) *led: rdn along over 3f out: hdd over 2f out: sn drvn and grad wknd appr fnl f* **9/1**

0040 **6** *1* **Prophesy (IRE)**[34] 3205 5-8-7 71 (p) AndrewElliott 11 70
(Tim Easterby) *cl up: rdn along over 3f out: drvn 2f out: grad wknd* **14/1**

311 **7** *1* **Perfect Cracker**[17] 3802 6-8-13 80 RyanTate(3) 7 77
(Clive Cox) *hld up towards rr: hdwy 3f out: chsd ldrs 2f out: sn rdn and n.m.r over 1f out: grad wknd* **4/1**[2]

4022 **8** *hd* **Icebuster**[18] 3752 6-8-11 82 PatMillman(7) 2 78
(Rod Millman) *t.k.h: trckd ldrs on inner: hdwy wl over 3f out: rdn along over 2f out: sn drvn and wknd* **11/1**

2200 **9** *1 1/2* **Kashmir Peak (IRE)**[62] 2314 5-9-7 85 IanBrennan 10 78
(John Quinn) *hld up: hdwy on outer over 3f out: chsd ldrs over 2f out: sn rdn and wknd* **7/1**[3]

6405 **10** *1 1/4* **Karam Albaari (IRE)**[17] 3802 6-9-1 79 FrederikTylicki 9 70
(J R Jenkins) *midfield: hdwy and in tch 4f out: effrt to chse ldrs over 2f out: sn rdn and n.m.r over 1f out: sn wknd* **16/1**

2m 9.79s (0.39) **Going Correction** -0.175s/f (Firm) **10** Ran SP% **114.7**
Speed ratings (Par 105): **91,90,88,88,88 87,86,86,85,84**
CSF £190.04 CT £6096.71 TOTE £7.00: £3.20, £1.10, £3.90; EX 33.40 Trifecta £39.70.
**Owner** Dr Marwan Koukash **Bred** Kirk Wycoff & Deby Wycoff **Trained** Newmarket, Suffolk

**FOCUS**
Bereft of early tempo, this useful and competitive handicap turned into something of a sprint from 3f out and the winner came from last to first. The winner looks capable of better, the runner-up continues his recent revival, while the third, who didn't pick up anything like so well as the winner, at least confirmed his AW winter improvement back on turf.

## 4350 188BET H'CAP 1m 2f 60y
9:10 (9:12) (Class 5) (0-70,70) 3-Y-O £2,587 (£770; £384; £192) Stalls Low

Form RPR
0-44 **1** **Lil Rockerfeller (USA)**[24] 3537 3-9-7 70 SeanLevey 8 78
(Richard Hannon) *awkward s: sn pushed along to chse ldng pair: led after 1f: jnd 3f out and sn rdn: drvn wl over 1f out: edgd rt and hdd briefly ins fnl f: rallied and sn led again: kpt on gamely* **11/1**

3233 **2** *1/2* **Interconnection**[17] 3789 3-9-2 65 (b[1]) RichardKingscote 6 72
(Ed Vaughan) *led 1f: trckd ldr: hdwy and cl up 3f out: chal 2f out: sn rdn: drvn to ld briefly ins fnl f: sn hdd and no ex* **7/2**[3]

6612 **3** *2* **Charlie Wells (IRE)**[15] 3850 3-9-6 69 JohnFahy 1 72
(Eve Johnson Houghton) *trckd ldrs: pushed along over 3f out: sn rdn and outpcd: styd on u.p to chse ldng pair appr fnl f: no imp* **9/4**[2]

12 **4** *9* **Derbyshire (IRE)**[14] 3897 3-9-6 69 JamieSpencer 2 62
(Kevin Ryan) *trckd ldng pair: tk clsr order 3f out: rdn along 2f out: sn wknd: eased fnl f* **11/8**[1]

6006 **5** *13* **Ofelia (IRE)**[12] 3950 3-7-11 51 oh3 JackGarritty(5) 3 18
(Brian Ellison) *hld up in rr: hdwy over 4f out: rdn along 3f out: sn drvn and btn: bhd and eased fnl f* **20/1**

2m 9.14s (-0.26) **Going Correction** -0.175s/f (Firm) **5** Ran SP% **108.2**
Speed ratings (Par 100): **94,93,92,84,74**
CSF £45.75 TOTE £4.50: £6.90, £1.10; EX 17.50 Trifecta £96.60.
**Owner** Middleham Park Racing XLV **Bred** Brushwood Stable **Trained** East Everleigh, Wilts

**FOCUS**
A modest 3yo handicap run at a fair pace for the paucity of runners and it produced a protracted dual up the centre of the track. The third has been rated a length off his latest.
T/Jkpt: Not won. T/Plt: £390.90 to a £1 stake. Pool: £79,011.15 - 147.55 winning units. T/Qpdt: £60.70 to a £1 stake. Pool: £7998.32 - 97.38 winning units. JR

# 4116 EPSOM (L-H)
Thursday, July 17

**OFFICIAL GOING: Good to firm (8.5)**
Wind: virtually nil Weather: warm and sunny

## 4351 LADIES' DERBY H'CAP (FOR LADY AMATEUR RIDERS) 1m 4f 10y
6:10 (6:12) (Class 4) (0-80,79) 4-Y-O+ £4,991 (£1,548; £773; £387) Stalls Centre

Form RPR
533 **1** **Nave (USA)**[7] 4119 7-9-11 71 MissMeganNicholls(5) 7 80
(David Simcock) *hld up wl off the pce in midfield: clsd 6f out: rdn and hdwy to chse clr ldr ent fnl 2f: no imp tl clsd and swtchd rt ins fnl f: styd on to ld last strides* **5/1**

3052 **2** *nk* **Echo Brava**[7] 4104 4-10-4 76 MissHayleyMoore(3) 6 84
(Luke Dace) *chsd ldrs and clr in ldng quartet: hdwy to join ldr over 4f out: led over 3f out and kicked clr: stl clr but edging lft u.p ins fnl f: worn down and hdd last strides* **4/1**[3]

1411 **3** *1 1/4* **Last Minute Lisa (IRE)**[7] 4116 4-9-5 60 oh2 MrsCBartley 10 66+
(Sylvester Kirk) *hld up wl off the pce in last pair: swtchd lft and hdwy towards inner 3f out: 5th and swtchd rt over 2f out: chsd ldng pair and rdn over 1f out: styd on but nvr gng to rch ldrs* **9/4**[1]

6-05 **4** *6* **Tapis Libre**[34] 3192 6-9-12 70 (p) MissJoannaMason(3) 2 66
(Michael Easterby) *pressed ldng pair and clr in ldng quartet: rdn and struggling to qckn 3f out: 4th and wl hld over 1f out* **14/1**

-353 **5** *4 1/2* **Hi Note**[9] 4045 6-10-7 79 MissSMDoolan(3) 8 68
(Sheena West) *chsd ldr and clr in ldng quartet: led 5f out tl 4f out: rdn and outpcd by ldr over 3f out: wknd wl over 1f out* **16/1**

2161 **6** *3 1/2* **Jewelled**[9] 4045 8-10-1 75 6ex MissEllaSmith(5) 9 58
(Ralph J Smith) *stdd after s: hld up wl off the pce in last pair: pushed along and hdwy over 2f out: no imp: n.d* **16/1**

2054 **7** *2* **Super Duplex**[1] 4327 7-8-12 60 oh2 (t) MissLWilliams(7) 1 40
(Roger Teal) *racd in midfield but nvr on terms w ldrs: rdn and struggling 3f out: wl btn fnl 2f* **50/1**

6215 **8** *4 1/2* **Pertuis (IRE)**[17] 3785 8-10-3 72 (p) MissCWalton 5 45
(Micky Hammond) *racd wl off the pce in midfield: short-lived effrt 3f out: sn struggling and bhd fnl 2f* **20/1**

5332 **9** *25* **Sagesse**[9] 4045 4-10-6 75 (b) MissSBrotherton 4 8
(Sir Mark Prescott Bt) *led tl 5f out: rdn and dropped out qckly over 3f out: bhd fnl 2f: t.o* **3/1**[2]

2m 38.5s (-0.40) **Going Correction** -0.125s/f (Firm) **9** Ran SP% **117.6**
Speed ratings (Par 105): **96,95,94,90,87 85,84,81,64**
CSF £25.85 CT £57.58 TOTE £6.60: £2.20, £1.60, £1.40; EX 26.10 Trifecta £121.20.
**Owner** Anthony Hogarth **Bred** Mineola Farm II Llc Et Al **Trained** Newmarket, Suffolk

**FOCUS**
Rail at innermost position and distances as advertised. On a hot day the ground had dried out to good to firm. A fair handicap and a chance for lady amateurs to compete over the full Derby distance. The runner-up has been rated a little off his AW best.

## 4352 TATTENHAM CORNER CLAIMING STKS 7f
6:45 (6:47) (Class 5) 3-Y-O+ £3,234 (£962; £481; £240) Stalls Low

Form RPR
2303 **1** **Aqua Ardens (GER)**[27] 3438 6-9-4 74 (t) PatCosgrave 5 71
(George Baker) *chsd ldng pair: wnt 2nd jst over 2f out: shkn up and qcknd to ld over 1f out: clr and rdn ins fnl f: kpt on: eased cl home* **9/4**[2]

0115 **2** *1* **Conry (IRE)**[20] 3645 8-9-4 85 StevieDonohoe 4 68
(Ian Williams) *in tch in last pair: swtchd rt and effrt over 2f out: hdwy to go 3rd jst over 1f out: r.o wl ins fnl f: wnt 2nd fnl 50yds: nvr gng to rch wnr* **5/4**[1]

5303 **3** *1 1/2* **Bayleyf (IRE)**[14] 3879 5-9-10 66 (p) KierenFox 1 70
(Lee Carter) *led: hdd and drvn over 1f out: styd on same pce after and lost 2nd fnl 50yds* **7/1**

06-0 **4** *6* **Chelwood Gate (IRE)**[15] 3861 4-9-6 78 LiamKeniry 6 50
(Patrick Chamings) *dwlt: in tch in midfield: rdn and effrt over 2f out: struggling and btn whn hung lft ent fnl f: wknd* **6/1**[3]

-604 **5** *4 1/2* **Fiducia**[24] 3526 4-8-11 62 HarryBentley 2 30
(Simon Dow) *s.i.s: hld up in tch in last pair: rdn and hdwy to chse ldrs 2f out: no imp: wknd over 1f out* **16/1**

4000 6 1 **Speed Society**[9] 4055 3-8-5 59 (b[1]) WilliamCarson 3 25
(Jim Boyle) *chsd ldr tl jst over 2f out: sn wknd and bhd over 1f out* 33/1
1m 21.7s (-1.60) **Going Correction** -0.125s/f (Firm)
**WFA** 3 from 4yo+ 7lb 6 Ran SP% **110.8**
Speed ratings (Par 103): **104,102,101,94,89 88**
CSF £5.28 TOTE £2.90: £1.50, £1.30; EX 5.50 Trifecta £14.00.
**Owner** M Khan X2 & G Baker **Bred** Gestut Karlshof **Trained** Manton, Wilts

**FOCUS**
A typical claimer featuring runners of mixed ability. It has been rated around the front-running third in line with his C&D handicap latest.

## 4353 IRISH STALLION FARMS EBF MAIDEN STKS 7f
7:15 (7:15) (Class 5) 2-Y-O £3,881 (£1,155; £577; £288) Stalls Low

| Form | | | | RPR |
|---|---|---|---|---|
| 04 | 1 | | **Faithful Creek (IRE)**[26] 3474 2-9-5 0 GeorgeBaker 5<br>(Brian Meehan) *hld up in tch in rr: hdwy in centre over 2f out: rdn to chse ldr over 1f out: clsd to chal and bmpd ins fnl f: sn led: r.o wl and gng away at fin* 10/1 | 86+ |
| 362 | 2 | 1 3/4 | **Silver Ranger**[32] 3279 2-9-5 0 PatDobbs 4<br>(Richard Hannon) *bmpd s: reminders sn after s: chsd ldr tl led 5f out: racd awkwardly bnd 4f out: rdn over 2f out: hung rt 1f out: bmpd wnr ins fnl f: sn hdd and outpcd* 5/6[1] | 81 |
| | 3 | 8 | **Water Thief (USA)** 2-9-5 0 MartinLane 3<br>(Mark Johnston) *rn green: wnt rt s: chsd ldrs: rdn to chse ldr 3f out tl wandered rt and lft and dropped to 3rd 2f out: wknd over 1f out* 8/1[3] | 60 |
| 33 | 4 | 2 1/2 | **Red Rubles (IRE)**[26] 3474 2-9-5 0 DavidProbert 6<br>(Andrew Balding) *in tch: hdwy to chse ldr over 4f out tl 3f out: sn rdn and lost pl: bhd over 1f out* 2/1[2] | 53 |
| 66 | 5 | shd | **Tumut (IRE)**[9] 4044 2-9-2 0 CharlesBishop(3) 1<br>(Mick Channon) *led for 2f: shuffled bk to cl 4th 4f out: hdwy on inner to chse clr ldr ent fnl 2f tl over 1f out: wkng whn hmpd jst over 1f out* 20/1 | 53 |

1m 22.61s (-0.69) **Going Correction** -0.125s/f (Firm) 5 Ran SP% **112.9**
Speed ratings (Par 94): **98,96,86,84,83**
CSF £19.77 TOTE £10.10: £3.40, £1.10; EX 20.00 Trifecta £71.00.
**Owner** Decadent Racing **Bred** Tally-Ho Stud **Trained** Manton, Wilts

**FOCUS**
A fair maiden run 0.91secs slower than the preceding claimer and something of an upset. The first two finished well clear and the form is hopefully okay.

## 4354 ASHTEAD H'CAP 1m 2f 18y
7:50 (7:51) (Class 4) (0-80,80) 3-Y-O+ £5,822 (£1,732; £865; £432) Stalls Low

| Form | | | | RPR |
|---|---|---|---|---|
| 1164 | 1 | | **Compton Bird**[12] 3968 5-9-6 72 FergusSweeney 5<br>(Paul Fitzsimons) *stdd after s: hld up in rr: swtchd lft and hdwy to chse ldrs ent fnl 2f: rdn and qcknd to ld over 1f out: in command fnl f: r.o* 10/1 | 83 |
| -332 | 2 | 3 1/2 | **Dalgig**[7] 4116 4-9-4 75 CamHardie(5) 3<br>(Jamie Osborne) *broke fast: led and racd keenly: rdn over 2f out: hdd over 1f out: no ch w wnr but battled on to hold 2nd fnl f* 11/4[2] | 79 |
| 6323 | 3 | 1 | **Loch Ma Naire (IRE)**[28] 3396 3-8-11 73 (b) OisinMurphy 1<br>(Ed Dunlop) *chsd ldr: rdn to press ldr ent fnl 2f: 3rd and styd on same pce fr over 1f out* 6/1 | 75 |
| 3163 | 4 | 1/2 | **Starwatch**[22] 3582 7-9-11 77 WilliamCarson 2<br>(John Bridger) *chsd ldrs: effrt u.p over 2f out: 4th and kpt on same pce fr over 1f out* 8/1 | 79 |
| 6012 | 5 | 8 | **Jacob Cats**[16] 3815 5-10-0 80 (v) GeorgeBaker 7<br>(William Knight) *in tch towards rr: hdwy into midfield 8f out: rdn over 2f out: fnd nil and sn btn: hung lft over 1f out: eased wl ins fnl f* 9/4[1] | 66 |
| 1313 | 6 | 10 | **Stockhill Diva**[24] 3540 4-9-5 71 LiamKeniry 6<br>(Brendan Powell) *hld up in tch: rdn and dropped to rr over 2f out: sn wl btn: wl bhd and eased ins fnl f* 9/2[3] | 38 |
| 2000 | 7 | 35 | **Munsarim (IRE)**[14] 3878 7-9-3 69 (b) AmirQuinn 4<br>(Lee Carter) *bustled along leaving stalls: stdd bk towards rr after 2f: rdn and lost tch 3f out: wl t.o and virtually p.u ins fnl f* 33/1 | |

2m 6.41s (-3.29) **Going Correction** -0.125s/f (Firm)
**WFA** 3 from 4yo+ 10lb 7 Ran SP% **113.0**
Speed ratings (Par 105): **108,105,104,104,97 89,61**
CSF £36.81 TOTE £9.10: £4.30, £2.10; EX 47.40 Trifecta £224.30.
**Owner** Erik Penser **Bred** Whitsbury Manor Stud **Trained** Upper Lambourn, Berks

**FOCUS**
Quite a competitive handicap but they seemed to go a good gallop and were well strung out at the finish. The runner-up has been rated close to his C&D latest, and the third close to form.

## 4355 COLLECT TOTEPOOL WINNINGS AT BETFRED SHOPS H'CAP 7f
8:25 (8:26) (Class 4) (0-85,85) 3-Y-O+ £6,469 (£1,925; £962; £481) Stalls Low

| Form | | | | RPR |
|---|---|---|---|---|
| 0 | 1 | | **Dr Red Eye**[54] 2548 6-9-8 79 (p[1]) OisinMurphy 2<br>(Scott Dixon) *mde all: pressed and rdn ent fnl 2f: battled on gamely and forged ahd ins fnl f: styd on wl* 9/2[2] | 88 |
| 1321 | 2 | 1 1/4 | **Shifting Star (IRE)**[17] 3805 9-8-12 69 (vt) WilliamCarson 6<br>(John Bridger) *chsd wnr: rdn and effrt to chal ent fnl 2f: no ex and styd on same pce ins fnl f* 10/1 | 75 |
| 6212 | 3 | 1 1/4 | **Intomist (IRE)**[14] 3879 5-8-8 72 (p) DanielCremin(7) 5<br>(Jim Boyle) *in tch in midfield: clsd to trck ldrs and nt clr run 2f out: swtchd lft and rdn 1f out: r.o same pce u.p* 5/1[3] | 75 |
| 1302 | 4 | hd | **Compton**[12] 3969 5-9-13 84 (t) HarryBentley 7<br>(Stuart Williams) *dwlt: hld up in tch in last trio: rdn and effrt 2f out: no imp tl styd on u.p ins fnl f: no threat to wnr* 6/1 | 86 |
| 323 | 5 | shd | **Related**[12] 3969 4-9-7 83 (v[1]) CamHardie(5) 8<br>(David Simcock) *t.k.h: chsd ldrs: effrt and edgd lft 2f out: fnd little for press and styd on same pce after* 9/4[1] | 85 |
| 6105 | 6 | 3/4 | **Amadeus Wolfe Tone (IRE)**[7] 4121 5-10-0 85 (b) GeorgeBaker 3<br>(Jamie Osborne) *hld up in tch in last trio: clsd 2f out: nt clr run over 1f out: swtchd lft jst ins fnl f: kpt on same pce after* 6/1 | 85 |
| 1062 | 7 | 2 | **Rogue Wave (IRE)**[20] 3667 3-9-3 81 SamHitchcott 1<br>(Timothy Jarvis) *wl in tch in midfield: rdn and effrt on inner 2f out: no prog 1f out: wknd ins fnl f* 16/1 | 73 |
| 0000 | 8 | 1 1/4 | **Brocklebank (IRE)**[18] 3753 5-9-6 77 WilliamTwiston-Davies 4<br>(Simon Dow) *hld up in last: effrt 2f out: no prog over 1f out: wknd fnl f* 16/1 | 69 |

1m 21.95s (-1.35) **Going Correction** -0.125s/f (Firm)
**WFA** 3 from 4yo+ 7lb 8 Ran SP% **115.0**
Speed ratings (Par 105): **102,100,99,98,98 97,95,94**
CSF £48.27 CT £234.36 TOTE £6.50: £2.30, £2.60, £2.00; EX 45.60 Trifecta £120.00.
**Owner** The Red Eye Partnership **Bred** G E Amey **Trained** Babworth, Notts

**FOCUS**
The feature race and a good contest on paper, although the time was 0.25secs slower than the earlier claimer over the trip. The first two held those positions throughout. The runner-up was well placed and has been rated as matching last year's best.

## 4356 BURGH HEATH H'CAP 1m 114y
8:55 (8:58) (Class 5) (0-75,72) 3-Y-O £4,528 (£1,347; £673; £336) Stalls Low

| Form | | | | RPR |
|---|---|---|---|---|
| 040 | 1 | | **Inspector Norse**[31] 3315 3-9-3 68 LiamKeniry 2<br>(Sylvester Kirk) *mde all: rdn ent fnl 2f: styd on strly: rdn out* 4/1[2] | 75 |
| 53-0 | 2 | 1 3/4 | **This Is The Day**[35] 3159 3-9-5 70 TedDurcan 1<br>(Charlie Fellowes) *chsd ldng pair: clsd and nt clr run 2f out: swtchd rt and rdn to chse wnr over 1f out: r.o but no imp fnl f* 10/1[3] | 73 |
| 005 | 3 | 1 1/4 | **Capmonde (IRE)**[24] 3537 3-8-13 64 MartinDwyer 5<br>(William Knight) *chsd wnr: rdn and effrt ent fnl f: 3rd and styd on same pce fr over 1f out* 10/1[3] | 64 |
| 1031 | 4 | nk | **Comanchero (IRE)**[5] 4191 3-8-12 63 OisinMurphy 6<br>(Andrew Balding) *t.k.h: hld up in 5th: plenty to do and swtchd rt over 2f out: sn rdn: wnt 4th over 1f out: styd on u.p but nvr gng to rch ldrs* 1/2[1] | 62+ |
| 00-0 | 5 | 3 | **Always Resolute**[79] 1847 3-8-10 61 SamHitchcott 4<br>(Timothy Jarvis) *t.k.h: hld up in tch in midfield: rdn 3f out: unable qck u.p 2f out: wknd 1f out* 33/1 | 54 |
| -230 | 6 | 8 | **Dynamic Ranger (USA)**[58] 2418 3-9-7 72 GeorgeBaker 7<br>(Gary Moore) *stdd and dropped in bhd after s: hld up in detached last: rdn and effrt over 2f out: no prog: wknd over 1f out* 14/1 | 46 |

1m 45.42s (-0.68) **Going Correction** -0.125s/f (Firm) 6 Ran SP% **114.5**
Speed ratings (Par 100): **98,96,95,95,92 85**
CSF £41.16 TOTE £7.70: £3.30, £3.10; EX 62.20 Trifecta £24.30.
**Owner** J C Smith **Bred** Littleton Stud **Trained** Upper Lambourn, Berks

**FOCUS**
A two-horse race according to the market, although it didn't work out that way, as the pace was steady early and it turned into a sprint. The third has been rated to her maiden form.
T/Plt: £204.00 to a £1 stake. Pool: £57,730.19 - 206.49 winning units. T/Qpdt: £199.00 to a £1 stake. Pool: £4411.92 - 16.40 winning units. SP

# 4192 HAMILTON (R-H)
Thursday, July 17
**OFFICIAL GOING: Good (good to firm in places; 7.7)**
Wind: Almost nil Weather: Overcast

## 4357 IRISH CHAMPIONS WEEKEND EBF MAIDEN STKS 5f 4y
2:15 (2:17) (Class 5) 2-Y-O £3,408 (£1,006; £503) Stalls Centre

| Form | | | | RPR |
|---|---|---|---|---|
| | 1 | | **Enlace** 2-9-0 0 JoeFanning 5<br>(Mark Johnston) *w ldr: led gng wl 1/2-way: shkn up and qcknd over 1f out: rdn out fnl f: readily* 5/2[2] | 84+ |
| | 2 | 3 | **Gurkha Friend** 2-9-5 0 GrahamLee 7<br>(Karen McLintock) *dwlt: t.k.h and sn in tch: hdwy to chse wnr 1f out: kpt on: nt pce to chal* 18/1 | 76+ |
| 4 | 3 | 1/2 | **Dark Reckoning**[20] 3656 2-9-0 0 PJMcDonald 3<br>(Ann Duffield) *in tch: effrt and pushed along 2f out: kpt on same pce ins fnl f* 8/1 | 69+ |
| 30 | 4 | 4 | **Westhoughton**[7] 4110 2-9-5 0 PaulMulrennan 1<br>(David O'Meara) *dwlt: hld up in tch: pushed along 2f out: sn outpcd* 22/1 | 60 |
| 3 | 5 | 1 | **Caigemdar (IRE)**[13] 3933 2-9-0 0 GrahamGibbons 2<br>(David Barron) *t.k.h early: cl up tl rdn and wknd appr fnl f* 11/8[1] | 51 |
| 642 | 6 | 2 1/2 | **Danot (IRE)**[8] 4065 2-9-5 0 TomEaves 4<br>(Keith Dalgleish) *led to 1/2-way: cl up tl rdn and wknd over 1f out* 6/1[3] | 47 |
| 30 | 7 | 7 | **Show Spirit**[58] 2436 2-8-9 0 ShaneGray(5) 8<br>(Kevin Ryan) *prom tl rdn and wknd over 1f out* 25/1 | 17 |
| | 8 | hd | **Caties Do Dah** 2-9-0 0 PatrickMathers 6<br>(Alan Berry) *dwlt: bhd and outpcd: nvr on terms* 200/1 | 16 |

58.88s (-1.12) **Going Correction** -0.35s/f (Firm) 8 Ran SP% **110.0**
Speed ratings (Par 94): **94,89,88,82,80 76,65,64**
CSF £39.93 TOTE £4.20: £1.70, £6.90, £2.90; EX 34.40 Trifecta £346.50.
**Owner** Sheikh Hamdan bin Mohammed Al Maktoum **Bred** Darley **Trained** Middleham Moor, N Yorks

**FOCUS**
Fresh ground around the loop and all distances as advertised. After 12mm of rain over the previous four days, the ground was on the quick side of good. Previous form was thin on the ground and the first two were newcomers.

## 4358 ROA OWNERS JACKPOT CLAIMING STKS 6f 5y
2:45 (2:45) (Class 6) 3-Y-O+ £2,045 (£603; £302) Stalls High

| Form | | | | RPR |
|---|---|---|---|---|
| 4-00 | 1 | | **Fast Finian (IRE)**[17] 3795 5-9-2 82 (p) JoeFanning 3<br>(Ann Stokell) *cl up: chal over 1f out: sn rdn: led ins fnl f: kpt on wl* 4/1[3] | 71 |
| 0-00 | 2 | nk | **Waffle (IRE)**[45] 2849 8-9-4 93 GrahamGibbons 6<br>(David Barron) *led: rdn over 1f out: edgd rt and hdd ins fnl f: kpt on: hld nr fin* 8/11[1] | 72 |
| 01-0 | 3 | 3/4 | **Milly's Secret (IRE)**[100] 1358 3-8-10 76 (p) PJMcDonald 1<br>(Ann Duffield) *prom: drvn and outpcd after 2f: rallied fnl f: nrst fin* 3/1[2] | 65 |
| 0400 | 4 | 1 | **Bapak Muda (USA)**[5] 4195 4-8-13 60 (p) KevinStott(5) 5<br>(Kevin Ryan) *cl up: rdn and edgd rt 2f out: kpt on same pce fnl f* 22/1 | 66 |
| 100 | 5 | 8 | **Absolute Bearing (IRE)**[24] 3530 5-9-0 48 (p) PaulMulrennan 2<br>(Tim Etherington) *in tch: drvn and outpcd 1/2-way: sn btn* 66/1 | 36 |
| 0056 | 6 | 2 1/2 | **Bix (IRE)**[5] 4195 4-8-13 46 (b) GrahamLee 4<br>(Alan Berry) *s.s: a outpcd and bhd* 66/1 | 27 |

1m 10.77s (-1.43) **Going Correction** -0.35s/f (Firm)
**WFA** 3 from 4yo+ 5lb 6 Ran SP% **110.2**
Speed ratings (Par 101): **95,94,93,92,81 78**
CSF £7.13 TOTE £4.30: £2.40, £1.10; EX 10.90 Trifecta £18.70.
**Owner** Martyn Elvin **Bred** N Hartery **Trained** Lincoln, Lincolnshire

**FOCUS**
As is often the case, official ratings went out of the window in this Class 6 claimer. It has been rated cautiously with the fourth to this year's form.

## 4359 TOTEPOOL HOME OF POOL BETTING H'CAP 1m 1f 36y
3:15 (3:16) (Class 4) (0-80,80) 3-Y-O+ £5,175 (£1,540; £769; £384) Stalls Low

| Form | | | | RPR |
|---|---|---|---|---|
| 661P | 1 | | **Incurs Four Faults**[5] 4196 3-8-0 61 oh1 JoeFanning 3<br>(Keith Dalgleish) *t.k.h early: mde all: pushed along over 2f out: drew clr fnl f* 7/2[1] | 69 |

1244 **2** *3* **Lord Franklin**[9] 4058 5-9-6 **72** JasonHart 7 75
(Eric Alston) *chsd ldrs: drvn and outpcd over 2f out: rallied to take 2nd cl home: no ch w wnr* **12/1**

-420 **3** *nse* **Red Charmer (IRE)**[62] 2293 4-9-9 **75** PJMcDonald 8 78
(Ann Duffield) *pressed wnr: drvn over 2f out: edgd rt over 1f out: kpt on same pce fnl f: lost 2nd cl home* **15/2**

4331 **4** *3 1/4* **Hard Core Debt**[5] 4197 4-9-4 **70** 6ex BenCurtis 4 66
(Brian Ellison) *hld up: hdwy on outside to chse ldrs over 3f out: rdn over 2f out: outpcd fnl f* **4/1**[2]

-240 **5** *1 1/2* **Dancing Cosmos (IRE)**[29] 3361 4-9-13 **79** GrahamLee 9 72
(John Patrick Shanahan, Ire) *hld up in tch: effrt over 2f out: edgd rt and wknd over 1f out* **7/1**[3]

0236 **6** *3 1/2* **Argaki (IRE)**[11] 3999 4-9-13 **79** TomEaves 1 65
(Keith Dalgleish) *hld up in tch: nt clr run and swtchd lft 2f out: sn no imp* **8/1**

-162 **7** *13* **Champagne Rules**[45] 2839 3-9-5 **80** PaddyAspell 6 37
(Sharon Watt) *dwlt: bhd: shortlived effrt over 3f out: btn fnl 2f* **12/1**

5-55 **8** *33* **Almerzem (USA)**[15] 3856 3-9-0 **75** (t) KierenFallon 2
(Saeed bin Suroor) *plld hrd: in tch: rdn and outpcd over 3f out: btn and eased fnl 2f* **4/1**[2]

1m 54.56s (-5.14) **Going Correction** -0.525s/f (Hard)
**WFA** 3 from 4yo+ 9lb **8** Ran SP% **113.0**
Speed ratings (Par 105): **101,98,98,95,94 90,79,50**
CSF £44.23 CT £293.38 TOTE £4.60: £1.70, £2.80, £2.90; EX 50.50 Trifecta £437.50.
**Owner** J S Morrison **Bred** Baldernock Bloodstock Ltd **Trained** Carluke, S Lanarks

**FOCUS**
A sound gallop and only the first four home were seriously involved. The runner-up has been rated to form.

## 4360 RACING UK CLUB DAY MAIDEN STKS 1m 3f 16y
**3:45** (3:46) (Class 5) 3-Y-O+ **£3,234** (£962; £481; £240) **Stalls** Low

Form RPR

30 **1** **Another Lincolnday**[58] 2422 3-9-3 0 GrahamGibbons 3 75
(David Barron) *hld up and wl bhd: plenty to do whn n.m.r briefly over 2f out: chsd clr ldng pair over 1f out: kpt on to ld wl ins fnl f: sn clr* **14/1**[3]

-522 **2** *2 1/2* **Legal Waves (IRE)**[11] 3998 4-10-0 80 BenCurtis 6 71
(Alan Swinbank) *led at decent gallop: jnd 1/2-way: rdn over 3f out: no ex and hdd wl ins fnl f* **1/1**[1]

0003 **3** *hd* **Dolce N Karama (IRE)**[11] 3998 3-9-3 93 GrahamLee 1 70
(John Patrick Shanahan, Ire) *t.k.h: cl up: chal 1/2-way: rdn over 3f out: no ex wl ins fnl f* **11/10**[2]

46 **4** *23* **Hatton Springs (IRE)**[12] 3953 3-8-7 0 GarryWhillans(5) 2 26
(Stuart Coltherd) *hld up: rdn and struggling 3f out: n.d after* **125/1**

0 **5** *10* **Pal Ella**[31] 3302 3-8-12 0 TomEaves 4 9
(Keith Dalgleish) *chsd clr ldng trio tl rdn and wknd 2f out* **66/1**

0 **6** *99* **Reeflex**[75] 1962 3-9-3 0 JasonHart 5
(Eric Alston) *upset in stalls: t.k.h: struggling 1/2-way: sn lost tch* **50/1**

2m 21.07s (-4.53) **Going Correction** -0.525s/f (Hard)
**WFA** 3 from 4yo 11lb **6** Ran SP% **108.5**
Speed ratings (Par 103): **95,93,93,76,69**
CSF £27.29 TOTE £12.00: £5.40, £1.10; EX 28.40 Trifecta £43.40.
**Owner** J D Spensley & Mrs M A Spensley **Bred** J D Spensley & Mrs M A Spensley **Trained** Maunby, N Yorks

**FOCUS**
The first two in the betting went head-to-head in the final 4f and set themselves up to be vulnerable to a closer. The runner-up and third set a good standard but neither is straightforward and the form is not solid.

## 4361 INJURED JOCKEYS FUND 50TH ANNIVERSARY H'CAP 1m 5f 9y
**4:15** (4:15) (Class 4) (0-85,83) 3-Y-O+ **£6,469** (£1,925; £962; £481) **Stalls** Low

Form RPR

6564 **1** **Snow Squall**[6] 4160 3-8-8 **76** PaulMulrennan 2 91
(Mark Johnston) *prom gng wl: smooth hdwy to ld over 1f out: pushed clr* **3/1**[1]

-110 **2** *2 3/4* **Piton**[47] 2761 3-8-8 **76** JoeFanning 6 87
(Mark Johnston) *led: rdn and hdd over 1f out: kpt on same pce fnl f* **9/2**[3]

3141 **3** *5* **Aleksandar**[16] 3829 5-9-4 **73** GrahamLee 1 76
(Jim Goldie) *cl up: rdn over 3f out: edgd rt 2f out: sn outpcd by first two* **4/1**[2]

-135 **4** *3/4* **A Southside Boy (GER)**[33] 3240 6-8-9 **64** TomEaves 7 66
(Jim Goldie) *hld up: rdn over 3f out: kpt on fnl f: nvr able to chal* **12/1**

-020 **5** *3/4* **O Ma Lad (IRE)**[64] 2259 6-9-13 **82** PhillipMakin 3 83
(John Quinn) *hld up in tch: stdy hdwy 3f out: drvn and wknd wl over 1f out* **5/1**

3230 **6** *11* **High Office**[22] 3574 8-9-8 **80** GeorgeChaloner(3) 4 65
(Richard Fahey) *pressed ldr: rdn over 3f out: wknd 2f out* **7/1**

15-6 **7** *21* **Emirates Galloper (IRE)**[34] 3182 3-9-1 **83** (p) KierenFallon 5 36
(Saeed bin Suroor) *dwlt: t.k.h and sn midfield: rdn over 5f out: struggling 3f out: sn btn* **7/1**

2m 45.32s (-8.58) **Going Correction** -0.525s/f (Hard)
**WFA** 3 from 5yo+ 13lb **7** Ran SP% **112.5**
Speed ratings (Par 105): **105,103,100,99,99 92,79**
CSF £16.09 CT £52.73 TOTE £3.70: £2.20, £3.50; EX 18.30 Trifecta £69.30.
**Owner** Sheikh Hamdan bin Mohammed Al Maktoum **Bred** Darley **Trained** Middleham Moor, N Yorks

**FOCUS**
They went a sound gallop and 3yos finished first and second, both trained by Mark Johnston. The winning time was just outside a record that has stood for 19 years. The form makes sense.

## 4362 HORSE COMES FIRST H'CAP 5f 4y
**4:45** (4:46) (Class 6) (0-60,60) 3-Y-O+ **£1,940** (£577; £288; £144) **Stalls** Centre

Form RPR

00-4 **1** **Mandy Layla (IRE)**[93] 1500 4-9-8 **58** PaulMulrennan 7 68
(Bryan Smart) *cl up: rdn to ld over 1f out: hdd ins fnl f: rallied to regain ld nr fin* **7/2**[1]

4600 **2** *hd* **Busy Bimbo (IRE)**[2] 4287 5-8-8 **47** (b) GeorgeChaloner(3) 9 56
(Alan Berry) *prom: effrt and rdn over 1f out: led ins fnl f: hdd and no ex towards fin* **9/1**[2]

646 **3** *4* **Pull The Pin (IRE)**[21] 3609 5-9-2 **57** (bt) ShirleyTeasdale(5) 6 52
(Ann Stokell) *led tl rdn and hdd over 1f out: outpcd by first two ins fnl f* **7/2**[1]

600- **4** *2* **Stoneacre Oskar**[209] 8371 5-8-13 **49** GrahamLee 10 36
(Peter Grayson) *bhd and sn outpcd: hdwy over 1f out: kpt on: nvr able to chal* **12/1**[3]

3515 **5** *nk* **Rock Canyon (IRE)**[5] 4195 5-9-2 **52** PJMcDonald 3 38
(Linda Perratt) *towards rr: drvn and outpcd 1/2-way: kpt on fnl f: nvr able to chal* **7/2**[1]

4000 **6** *3/4* **Chloe's Dream (IRE)**[3] 4257 4-8-12 **53** KevinStott(5) 8 37
(Linda Perratt) *dwlt: t.k.h and sn prom: drvn over 2f out: wknd over 1f out* **7/2**[1]

-000 **7** *1/2* **Fol Hollow (IRE)**[12] 3954 9-9-0 **55** GarryWhillans(5) 4 37
(Stuart Coltherd) *chsd ldrs tl edgd rt and wknd over 1f out* **20/1**

-000 **8** *3/4* **Wicked Wilma (IRE)**[11] 4005 10-8-10 **46** oh1 PatrickMathers 5 25
(Alan Berry) *prom: drvn 1/2-way: rdn and wknd wl over 1f out* **50/1**

5250 **9** *shd* **Ishetoo**[21] 3609 10-8-10 **46** oh1 TomEaves 1 25
(Peter Grayson) *bhd and outpcd: nvr on terms* **50/1**

59.01s (-0.99) **Going Correction** -0.35s/f (Firm) **9** Ran SP% **115.3**
Speed ratings (Par 101): **93,92,86,83,82 81,80,79,79**
CSF £37.13 CT £116.45 TOTE £4.70: £1.70, £3.20, £1.50; EX 36.40 Trifecta £171.60.
**Owner** Mrs V Smart & Miss C Derighetti **Bred** Mrs E J O'Grady **Trained** Hambleton, N Yorks

**FOCUS**
A low-grade sprint handicap and it paid to be close to the pace. The winner didn't show much last year, but is now a stone lower than her opening 3yo mark and this is rated her best race since her 2yo days. The runner-up has been rated back to her May C&D win.

## 4363 RACING UK ON SKY 432 H'CAP 1m 65y
**5:15** (5:16) (Class 6) (0-65,65) 3-Y-O **£1,940** (£577; £288; £144) **Stalls** Low

Form RPR

5002 **1** **Her Red Devil (IRE)**[16] 3828 3-8-7 **54** GeorgeChaloner(3) 3 59
(Richard Fahey) *hld up in tch: effrt and rdn over 2f out: kpt on wl fnl f to ld cl home* **9/2**[2]

5000 **2** *nk* **Torridon**[36] 3105 3-8-2 **46** JoeFanning 8 50
(Mark Johnston) *led at modest gallop: rdn 2f out: kpt on wl fnl f: hdd cl home* **28/1**

6-05 **3** *nk* **Paddy's Rock (IRE)**[15] 3846 3-8-10 **54** PJMcDonald 6 57+
(Ann Duffield) *s.i.s: bhd: hdwy on outside 2f out: styd on strly fnl f: nrst fin* **5/1**[3]

4 **4** *1 1/4* **Shiftin Bobbins**[62] 2322 3-8-8 **52** PaulMulrennan 4 52
(Michael Dods) *pressed ldr: rdn and ev ch over 2f out: kpt on same pce fnl f* **12/1**

-0 **5** *3/4* **Helen's Armada (IRE)**[29] 3360 3-9-7 **65** GrahamLee 7 64
(John Patrick Shanahan, Ire) *hld up in tch: effrt and rdn over 2f out: edgd rt and no imp over 1f out* **8/1**

4141 **6** *1 1/4* **Dark Crystal**[3] 4254 3-9-2 **65** 6ex KevinStott(5) 2 61
(Linda Perratt) *t.k.h: cl up: rdn over 2f out: no ex over 1f out* **5/2**[1]

053 **7** *3* **Archie's Advice**[36] 3103 3-9-4 **62** TomEaves 1 51
(Keith Dalgleish) *dwlt: t.k.h early: hld up in tch: rdn and outpcd 3f out: n.d after* **13/2**

0332 **8** *hd* **Street Boss (IRE)**[13] 3911 3-8-12 **56** (p) DuranFentiman 5 44
(Tim Easterby) *prom: rdn over 3f out: edgd rt and wknd 2f out* **11/2**

1m 46.24s (-2.16) **Going Correction** -0.525s/f (Hard) **8** Ran SP% **114.4**
Speed ratings (Par 98): **89,88,88,87,86 85,82,81**
CSF £111.12 CT £655.10 TOTE £3.80: £1.10, £8.30, £4.20; EX 104.00 Trifecta £580.10.
**Owner** Dr Marwan Koukash **Bred** Seamus Phelan **Trained** Musley Bank, N Yorks

**FOCUS**
A modest 3yo handicap run at a steady pace until the final 4f. The third has been rated to his 2yo form.
T/Plt: £75.90 to a £1 stake. Pool: £52,294.82 - 502.86 winning units. T/Qpdt: £14.20 to a £1 stake. Pool: £3964.45 - 206.35 winning units. RY

# 3966 LEICESTER (R-H)
Thursday, July 17

**OFFICIAL GOING: Good to firm (good in places; 7.8)**
Wind: Nil Weather: Fine

## 4364 AT THE RACES VIRGIN 534 NURSERY H'CAP 7f 9y
**2:25** (2:26) (Class 5) 2-Y-O **£2,587** (£770; £384; £192) **Stalls** High

Form RPR

560 **1** **Mr Shekells**[27] 3429 2-8-0 **61** ow1 DannyBrock(5) 4 63
(Philip McBride) *hld up: racd keenly: hdwy over 4f out: shkn up to ld over 1f out: edgd rt: rdn out* **10/1**

000 **2** *1/2* **Groor**[26] 3448 2-9-7 **77** RyanMoore 7 78
(James Tate) *trckd ldrs: rdn over 2f out: hung rt fr over 1f out: ev ch ins fnl f: styd on* **7/4**[1]

01 **3** *1/2* **Cafe Cortado (IRE)**[35] 3157 2-7-11 **56** oh1 JoeyHaynes(3) 2 56
(K R Burke) *chsd ldr: rdn over 2f out: ev ch fr over 1f out: edgd lft ins fnl f: unable qck towards fin* **10/1**

0006 **4** *3 3/4* **Framley Garth (IRE)**[19] 3720 2-8-3 **59** PaoloSirigu 5 49
(David Elsworth) *trckd ldrs: plld hrd: rdn over 2f out: styd on same pce fnl f* **11/1**

0134 **5** *2 1/4* **Mylaporyours (IRE)**[55] 2521 2-9-5 **75** AndreaAtzeni 3 58
(Rod Millman) *led: rdn and hdd over 1f out: hmpd and wknd ins fnl f* **8/1**[3]

450 **6** *6* **Go White Lightning (IRE)**[23] 3558 2-8-1 **62** NoelGarbutt(5) 6 29
(David Evans) *sn pushed along and a in rr: wknd over 1f out* **50/1**

4352 **7** *2 1/2* **British Embassy (IRE)**[9] 4057 2-8-12 **68** JimmyFortune 1 29
(Eve Johnson Houghton) *hld up: rdn over 2f out: wknd over 1f out: eased* **15/8**[2]

1m 24.55s (-1.65) **Going Correction** -0.20s/f (Firm) **7** Ran SP% **110.7**
Speed ratings (Par 94): **101,100,99,95,93 86,83**
CSF £26.24 TOTE £18.80: £7.80, £1.30; EX 34.70 Trifecta £246.80.
**Owner** Nigel Davies & P J McBride **Bred** Warwick Stud **Trained** Newmarket, Suffolk

**FOCUS**
Quick ground, as per the official description. A modest nursery, and questionable form with the second favourite not running his race. They came down the centre.

## 4365 COMPARE PRICES AT ATTHERACES.COM/ODDS (S) STKS 7f 9y
**2:55** (2:55) (Class 6) 3-Y-O **£1,940** (£577; £288; £144) **Stalls** High

Form RPR

-304 **1** **Bishan Bedi (IRE)**[35] 3158 3-9-3 62 MartinDwyer 4 65
(William Jarvis) *s.i.s: hld up: hdwy over 2f out: sn rdn: led ins fnl f: styd on* **3/1**[2]

-503 **2** *1 3/4* **Chess Valley**[6] 4152 3-9-4 70 TomQueally 5 61
(Rae Guest) *a.p: jnd ldr 1/2-way: led on bit over 1f out: hdd ins fnl f: styd on same pce* **8/11**[1]

005 **3** *4 1/2* **Vodka Time (IRE)**[63] 2281 3-9-9 67 AdamKirby 1 55
(David Evans) *chsd ldr tl led 4f out: rdn and hdd over 1f out: wknd ins fnl f* **7/2**[3]

4404 4 13 **El Duque**[9] 4042 3-9-4 59 (tp) RyanWhile(5) 3 21
(Bill Turner) *led 3f: sn rdn: wknd 2f out* **33/1**
5 5 **Good To Remember** 3-8-12 0 JamesSullivan 2
(Ruth Carr) *chsd ldrs tl rdn and wknd over 2f out* **100/1**
1m 24.93s (-1.27) **Going Correction** -0.20s/f (Firm) **5** Ran SP% **109.1**
Speed ratings (Par 98): **99,97,91,77,71**
.Bishan Bedi was bought in for 6000gns.\n\x\x Chess Valley was claimed by Willie Musson for £6,000.
**Owner** William Jarvis **Bred** Holborn Trust Co **Trained** Newmarket, Suffolk
**FOCUS**
A very ordinary seller. Again they raced down the middle. There's a chance the form could be a bit better than this.

## 4366 AT THE RACES SKY 415 CONDITIONS STKS (BOBIS RACE) 1m 1f 218y
**3:25** (3:25) (Class 3) 3-Y-O **£7,561** (£2,263; £1,131) **Stalls** Low

Form RPR
-124 1 **Arod (IRE)**[40] 2990 3-9-3 109 JamieSpencer 1 113+
(Peter Chapple-Hyam) *trckd ldr: racd keenly: led over 1f out: sn clr: easily* **2/9**[1]
1-16 2 9 **Spark Plug (IRE)**[28] 3375 3-9-3 102 JimmyFortune 3 100
(Brian Meehan) *hld up: pushed along over 3f out: styng on same pce whn lft 2nd over 1f out* **9/2**[2]
-006 3 21 **Sir Jack Layden**[7] 4127 3-9-3 105 RyanMoore 2 56
(David Brown) *led: pushed along over 4f out: rdn and hdd over 1f out: sn eased* **16/1**[3]
2m 6.96s (-0.94) **Going Correction** -0.20s/f (Firm) **3** Ran SP% **105.9**
Speed ratings (Par 104): **95,87,71**
CSF £1.51 TOTE £1.30; EX 1.10 Trifecta £1.60.
**Owner** Qatar Racing Limited **Bred** Kabansk Ltd & Rathbarry Stud **Trained** Newmarket, Suffolk
**FOCUS**
An interesting conditions race run at what looked a reasonable clip, and all eyes were on Derby fourth Arod. The winner has been rated as running a pb.

## 4367 EBF STALLIONS BREEDING WINNERS/AT THE RACES FILLIES' H'CAP (BOBIS RACE) 7f 9y
**3:55** (3:55) (Class 4) (0-80,80) 3-Y-O **£6,301** (£1,886; £943; £472; £235) **Stalls** High

Form
421 1 **Laftah (IRE)**[22] 3586 3-9-6 79 PaulHanagan 3 87
(Roger Varian) *mde all: racd keenly: rdn over 1f out: styd on: edgd lft towards fin* **9/2**[2]
21-3 2 ½ **Perfect Persuasion**[36] 3117 3-9-7 80 RyanMoore 7 86
(William Haggas) *trckd ldrs: rdn over 2f out: r.o* **4/6**[1]
5210 3 ½ **Relation Alexander (IRE)**[19] 3724 3-9-1 74 MartinHarley 4 79
(Paul D'Arcy) *hld up in tch: chsd wnr 2f out: sn rdn: unable qck wl ins fnl f* **20/1**
-006 4 3½ **Valen (IRE)**[48] 2745 3-9-5 78 TomQueally 2 74
(Michael Bell) *hld up: racd keenly: hdwy over 2f out: rdn over 1f out: styd on same pce ins fnl f* **8/1**[3]
2144 5 ¾ **Joie De Reve (IRE)**[22] 3581 3-9-1 74 [1] JamieSpencer 5 68
(David Simcock) *stdd s: hld up: pushed along 1/2-way: hdwy u.p over 1f out: no ex ins fnl f* **11/1**
54-0 6 6 **Redinha**[18] 3755 3-9-4 77 AdamKirby 1 55
(Clive Cox) *trckd ldrs: plld hrd: rdn over 2f out: wknd over 1f out* **20/1**
2-65 7 1¾ **Threetimesalady**[12] 3957 3-9-4 80 RosieJessop(3) 6 54
(Sir Mark Prescott Bt) *w wnr tl rdn over 2f out: sn hung lft: wknd over 1f out* **20/1**
1m 23.42s (-2.78) **Going Correction** -0.20s/f (Firm) **7** Ran SP% **111.9**
Speed ratings (Par 99): **107,106,105,101,101 94,92**
CSF £7.54 TOTE £8.30: £2.70, £1.10; EX 10.30 Trifecta £42.00.
**Owner** Hamdan Al Maktoum **Bred** Bernard Cooke **Trained** Newmarket, Suffolk
**FOCUS**
A fair fillies' handicap and, as expected, the quickest of the C&D times. They split into two groups, both near the centre. The third has been rated in line with the best view of her Yarmouth win.

## 4368 ATTHERACES/EBF MAIDEN STKS 1m 1f 218y
**4:25** (4:25) (Class 5) 3-Y-O **£3,881** (£1,155; £577; £288) **Stalls** Low

Form RPR
423 1 **Mustadaam (IRE)**[13] 3923 3-9-5 82 PaulHanagan 5 83
(Brian Meehan) *trckd ldrs: wnt 2nd 6f out: led over 2f out: sn rdn: styd on* **1/1**[1]
2-36 2 ¾ **Conquerant**[49] 2696 3-9-5 84 (p) WilliamBuick 3 82
(Charlie Appleby) *hld up in tch: jnd wnr over 1f out: sn rdn: nt run on* **11/4**[2]
-240 3 7 **Moontown**[33] 3248 3-9-5 75 RobertWinston 4 69
(Charles Hills) *chsd ldr 4f: remained handy: rdn over 2f out: sn outpcd* **12/1**
4 shd **Haydn's Lass** 3-9-0 0 MartinDwyer 2 64
(Marcus Tregoning) *s.s: sn pushed along in rr: outpcd over 3f out: styd on ins fnl f* **16/1**
0 5 1 **Crowded**[13] 3925 3-9-5 0 AdamKirby 6 67
(Charlie Appleby) *sn led: rdn over 3f out: hdd over 2f out: wknd over 1f out* **9/2**[3]
00 6 2 **Bowberry**[35] 3142 3-8-11 0 RyanTate(3) 1 58
(Clive Cox) *sn pushed along in rr: nvr on terms* **66/1**
2m 4.59s (-3.31) **Going Correction** -0.20s/f (Firm) **6** Ran SP% **109.9**
Speed ratings (Par 100): **105,104,98,98,97 96**
CSF £3.73 TOTE £2.10: £1.10, £1.60; EX 4.10 Trifecta £18.00.
**Owner** Hamdan Al Maktoum **Bred** Shadwell Estate Company Limited **Trained** Manton, Wilts
**FOCUS**
A reasonable maiden run in a time 2.37sec quicker than Arod recorded in the three-runner conditions event. The winner has been rated to form.

## 4369 READ WILLIAM BUICK'S BLOG AT ATTHERACES.COM H'CAP 1m 3f 183y
**4:55** (4:55) (Class 5) (0-75,72) 4-Y-O+ **£2,587** (£770; £384; £192) **Stalls** Low

Form RPR
5013 1 **Royal Marskell**[8] 4093 5-9-5 70 JamesSullivan 3 76
(Alison Hutchinson) *trckd ldrs: n.m.r over 3f out: led over 2f out: rdn and edgd lft ins fnl f: jst hld on* **7/1**[3]
065 2 hd **Saint Thomas (IRE)**[21] 3616 7-8-12 63 FrannyNorton 5 68
(John Mackie) *trckd ldr: ev ch over 2f out: sn rdn: r.o* **7/1**[3]
-024 3 ¾ **Wall Street Boss (USA)**[19] 3699 4-9-7 72 (p) FrederikTylicki 6 76
(James Fanshawe) *hld up: hdwy u.p over 1f out: r.o towards fin* **6/5**[1]
-314 4 1½ **Atalanta Bay (IRE)**[26] 3472 4-9-1 66 MartinDwyer 1 67
(Marcus Tregoning) *led at stdy pce: edgd lft almost thrght: qcknd over 3f out: hdd over 2f out: sn rdn: styd on same pce ins fnl f* **11/4**[2]
0-50 5 1½ **Guilded Spirit**[23] 3556 4-8-13 67 MichaelJMMurphy(3) 2 66
(Stuart Kittow) *prom: racd keenly: rdn over 2f out: styd on same pce fr over 1f out* **10/1**
0-00 6 ¾ **Dougal Philps**[8] 3177 5-8-12 70 PatMillman(7) 4 68
(Dr Richard Newland) *s.s: hld up: rdn over 2f out: nt trble ldrs* **20/1**
2m 33.64s (-0.26) **Going Correction** -0.20s/f (Firm) **6** Ran SP% **111.0**
Speed ratings (Par 103): **92,91,91,90,89 88**
CSF £50.92 TOTE £5.60: £2.60, £4.50; EX 43.70 Trifecta £138.70.
**Owner** Miss Chantal Wootten **Bred** Miss V Woodward **Trained** Exning, Suffolk
**FOCUS**
A very ordinary handicap run at just a fair pace. Muddling form, with the third rated to his latest.

## 4370 FOLLOW @ATTHERACES ON TWITTER APPRENTICE H'CAP 5f 218y
**5:25** (5:25) (Class 6) (0-65,65) 3-Y-O+ **£1,940** (£577; £288; £144) **Stalls** High

Form RPR
4233 1 **Consistant**[15] 3848 6-9-5 56 JoeDoyle 8 65
(Brian Baugh) *hld up in tch: rdn to ld ins fnl f: r.o* **5/2**[2]
0564 2 ½ **Haadeeth**[6] 4151 7-9-0 54 (bt) HollieDoyle(3) 3 61
(David Evans) *chsd ldr: edgd lft and led 1/2-way: rdn and hdd ins fnl f: styd on* **7/1**[3]
036/ 3 1 **Avertor**[190] 8-9-13 64 RobJFitzpatrick 13 68
(Robert Stephens) *s.i.s: hdwy 2f out: rdn and edgd lft over 1f out: r.o* **20/1**
200 4 1¼ **Divertimenti (IRE)**[7] 4131 10-9-2 53 (b) GemmaTutty 10 53
(Roy Bowring) *hld up: rdr dropped whip 1/2-way: r.o ins fnl f: nvr nrr* **20/1**
5203 5 4½ **Penina (IRE)**[20] 3668 3-9-9 65 MeganCarberry 1 49
(Brian Ellison) *s.i.s: sn prom: rdn and hung lft over 1f out: styd on same pce* **15/8**[1]
100 6 1 **Minty Jones**[14] 3882 5-8-13 55 (v) LewisStones(5) 4 37
(Michael Mullineaux) *led to 1/2-way: rdn and wknd over 1f out* **22/1**
0000 7 1¼ **New Rich**[15] 3848 4-9-9 60 (p) RyanWhile 9 38
(Eve Johnson Houghton) *sn pushed along in rr: sme hdwy over 1f out: nvr on terms* **7/1**[3]
35-0 8 1 **Noble Reach**[13] 3916 3-8-9 51 JordanNason 7 25
(Deborah Sanderson) *chsd ldrs to 1/2-way* **20/1**
20-0 9 hd **Monte Viso**[19] 3709 3-9-6 62 PatMillman 5 35
(Stuart Kittow) *s.i.s: sn prom: wknd 1/2-way* **20/1**
1m 12.18s (-0.82) **Going Correction** -0.20s/f (Firm)
**WFA** 3 from 4yo+ 5lb **9** Ran SP% **111.7**
Speed ratings (Par 101): **97,96,95,93,87 86,84,83,82**
CSF £16.78 CT £276.43 TOTE £3.30: £1.20, £2.00, £5.70; EX 16.20 Trifecta £110.70.
**Owner** Miss J A Price **Bred** Bearstone Stud **Trained** Audley, Staffs
**FOCUS**
A low-grade apprentice handicap. Little solid, but the winner has been rated to his best form over the past year.
T/Plt: £28.40 to a £1 stake. Pool: £41,570.06 - 1066.61 winning units. T/Qpdt: £7.90 to a £1 stake. Pool: £2696.35 - 251.95 winning units. CR

# 4135 LEOPARDSTOWN (L-H)
Thursday, July 17
**OFFICIAL GOING: Good to firm**

## 4379a IRISH STALLION FARMS EUROPEAN BREEDERS FUND "NASRULLAH" H'CAP (PREMIER HANDICAP) 1m 2f
**8:30** (8:30) 3-Y-O+
**£50,000** (£15,833; £7,500; £2,500; £1,666; £833)

RPR
1 **Chance To Dance (IRE)**[16] 3838 4-9-12 102 (t) KevinManning 7 108
(J S Bolger, Ire) *racd in mid-div tl tk clsr order 3f out: led over 1f out and sn rdn clr: kpt on wl though advantage reduced cl home* **5/1**[2]
2 ½ **Magnolia Beach (IRE)**[26] 3491 3-8-13 99 (p) ColinKeane 3 104+
(G M Lyons, Ire) *hld up in rr tl prog on inner under 2f out: wnt 4th 1f out: styd on strly into 2nd fnl 100yds: nt rch wnr* **5/2**[1]
3 ¾ **Ned's Indian (IRE)**[20] 3689 6-8-3 82 oh4 ow2 LeighRoche(3) 5 86
(Sabrina J Harty, Ire) *chsd ldrs in 4th tl prog to press ldr in 2nd 2f out: led briefly under 2f out: sn hdd and no ex fnl 100yds where dropped to 3rd* **14/1**
4 nk **Spirit Of The Law (IRE)**[33] 3251 5-8-12 88 TonyHamilton 2 91
(Richard Fahey) *racd in mid-div tl tk clsr order 3f out: rdn and nt qckn 2f out in 6th: styd on wl into 4th ins fnl f* **5/1**[2]
5 2½ **Vastonea (IRE)**[20] 3689 6-8-13 89 ChrisHayes 6 87
(Kevin Prendergast, Ire) *hld up towards rr tl prog on outer under 2f out: no imp ent fnl f: kpt on one pce* **10/1**
6 ½ **Defining Year (IRE)**[20] 3687 6-9-4 94 PatSmullen 1 91
(D K Weld, Ire) *hld up: sme hdwy 3f out: nt qckn and dropped to rr 2f out: kpt on again ins fnl f* **11/2**[3]
7 hd **Eighteen Summers (USA)**[16] 3838 7-8-10 86 WayneLordan 10 83
(Edward Lynam, Ire) *sn led tl hdd under 2f out: wknd appr fnl f* **8/1**
8 ½ **Long Journey Home (IRE)**[35] 3169 6-8-13 92 (t) ConnorKing(3) 8 88
(Daniel William O'Sullivan, Ire) *trckd ldr in 2nd early: t.k.h in 3rd tl nt qckn over 1f out: sn no ex* **16/1**
9 16 **Castle Guest (IRE)**[20] 3689 5-9-10 100 (t) ShaneFoley 9 64
(M Halford, Ire) *sn trckd ldr in 2nd: rdn and nt qckn over 2f out: sn no ex: eased fnl f* **10/1**
2m 2.63s (-5.57) **Going Correction** -0.30s/f (Firm)
**WFA** 3 from 4yo+ 10lb **9** Ran SP% **119.1**
Speed ratings: **110,109,109,108,106 106,106,105,93**
CSF £18.54 CT £167.95 TOTE £6.10: £1.30, £1.80, £3.50; DF 12.30 Trifecta £1391.80.
**Owner** Mrs J S Bolger **Bred** J S Bolger **Trained** Coolcullen, Co Carlow
**FOCUS**
Smart form.

4380 - (Foreign Racing) - See Raceform Interactive

# [4357] HAMILTON (R-H)

Friday, July 18

**OFFICIAL GOING: Good to firm (good in places; 7.5)**

Wind: 1st three races: breezy, across, last four races, light, half against Weather: Cloudy, bright

## 4381 SUPERSEAL SUPER SIX APPRENTICE SERIES H'CAP (ROUND THREE OF HAMILTON PARK APPRENTICE RIDER SERIES) 1m 65y

**6:10** (6:10) (Class 6) (0-60,60) 4-Y-O+ **£2,045** (£603; £302) **Stalls** Low

Form RPR

3445 **1** **Dansili Dutch (IRE)**[22] 3604 5-9-2 **60**........................ JoshDoyle(5) 1 69
(David O'Meara) *hld up: rdn 4f out: hdwy on outside 2f out: led wl ins fnl f: pushed out* **9/2**[2]

2/00 **2** *1 ¾* **Rocky's Pride (IRE)**[14] 3908 8-8-7 **46** oh1........... GeorgeChaloner 2 51+
(Richard Whitaker) *mde most tl rdn and hdd wl ins fnl f: kpt on same pce* **10/1**

0314 **3** *6* **Indian Giver**[6] 4197 6-9-4 **57**................................ IanBrennan 6 48
(John David Riches) *chsd ldrs: drvn over 2f out: one pce fr over 1f out* **9/2**[2]

054- **4** *½* **Meydan Style (USA)**[500] 884 8-8-0 **46** oh1.......... JordanSwarbrick(7) 4 36
(Brian Baugh) *towards rr: rdn over 3f out: kpt on fr over 1f out: nvr able to chal* **66/1**

3455 **5** *2 ½* **Buzz Law (IRE)**[8] 4116 6-8-12 **56**........................(v) PeterSword(5) 9 40
(K R Burke) *dwlt: sn prom: drvn over 2f out: wknd over 1f out* **6/1**[3]

6400 **6** *3 ¼* **Cabal**[29] 3398 7-8-8 **47**..........................................(b) NeilFarley 5 24
(Andrew Crook) *hld up: stdy hdwy over 3f out: rdn and wknd fr 2f out* **25/1**

4051 **7** *1 ½* **Hayek**[18] 3798 7-8-8 **50**.................................(b) RachelRichardson(3) 3 23
(Tim Easterby) *hld up: pushed along over 3f out: n.m.r wl over 2f out: sn n.d* **8/1**

042 **8** *1* **Gadobout Dancer**[30] 3364 7-8-8 **47**........................ ConnorBeasley 7 18
(Keith Dalgleish) *sn w ldr: rdn over 3f out: wknd over 1f out* **7/2**[1]

0550 **9** *1 ¼* **Taxiformissbyron**[12] 4000 4-8-7 **46** oh1....................(p) JoeyHaynes 8 14
(Iain Jardine) *hld up in tch: effrt and pushed along 3f out: wknd wl over 1f out* **6/1**[3]

1m 44.88s (-3.52) **Going Correction** -0.45s/f (Firm) 9 Ran SP% **112.7**

Speed ratings (Par 101): **99,97,91,90,88 85,83,82,81**

CSF £47.15 CT £225.26 TOTE £5.90: £2.10, £4.20, £1.30; EX 86.10 Trifecta £484.00.

**Owner** Direct Racing **Bred** Castlefarm Stud **Trained** Nawton, N Yorks

**FOCUS**

Fresh ground around the loop and all distances as advertised. They went a decent pace in this modest handicap and the first two pulled clear. The time was 0.12 seconds faster than Racing Post standard and Ian Brennan reported that the ground was very fast. The winner is rated to her winter AW best.

## 4382 BRITISH STALLION STUDS EBF MAIDEN STKS 6f 5y

**6:40** (6:40) (Class 5) 2-Y-O **£3,881** (£1,155; £577; £288) **Stalls** High

Form RPR

23 **1** **Publilia**[8] 4117 2-9-0 0........................................ JoeFanning 10 86+
(Mark Johnston) *mde virtually all: shkn up and drew clr fr over 1f out: readily* **10/11**[1]

33 **2** *4 ½* **You're My Cracker**[21] 3642 2-9-0 0........................ GrahamLee 6 72
(Donald McCain) *w wnr to over 2f out: rdn and kpt on same pce over 1f out* **6/1**[3]

24 **3** *2* **Split The Atom (IRE)**[30] 3358 2-9-5 0..................... RonanWhelan 9 71
(John Patrick Shanahan, Ire) *dwlt: sn in tch: drvn along over 2f out: kpt on same pce appr fnl f* **10/1**

52 **4** *¾* **Battleranger (IRE)**[17] 3827 2-9-5 0..................... SilvestreDeSousa 2 68
(Keith Dalgleish) *prom on outside: drvn along over 2f out: outpcd appr fnl f* **7/2**[2]

6 **5** *3 ½* **Shortmile Lady (IRE)**[46] 2824 2-8-11 0.................. ConnorBeasley(3) 4 53
(Michael Dods) *bhd and sn outpcd: hdwy over 1f out: kpt on fnl f: nvr able to chal* **20/1**

0 **6** *¾* **Sir Acclam (IRE)**[27] 3454 2-9-5 0.........................(p) JamesSullivan 5 56
(Keith Dalgleish) *prom: drvn along over 2f out: wknd over 1f out* **25/1**

0 **7** *3* **Tecumseh (IRE)**[27] 3454 2-9-5 0............................ DanielTudhope 7 47
(K R Burke) *plld hrd: hld up bhd ldng gp: rdn over 2f out: edgd rt and wknd over 1f out* **16/1**

**8** *2 ½* **A Lovable Rogue** 2-9-2 0.......................................... NeilFarley(3) 8 39
(Ian Semple) *t.k.h: prom tl rdn and wknd over 2f out* **22/1**

00 **9** *16* **Douglas Bank (IRE)**[46] 2837 2-9-2 0..................... GeorgeChaloner(3) 1
(Richard Fahey) *dwlt: sn pushed along bhd ldng gp on outside: struggling over 2f out: sn lost tch* **33/1**

1m 10.17s (-2.03) **Going Correction** -0.20s/f (Firm) 9 Ran SP% **119.8**

Speed ratings (Par 94): **105,99,96,95,90 89,85,82,61**

CSF £6.81 TOTE £1.70: £1.10, £2.00, £3.00; EX 7.60 Trifecta £32.70.

**Owner** Abdulla Al Mansoori **Bred** Mrs F S Williams **Trained** Middleham Moor, N Yorks

**FOCUS**

This maiden was weakened by the withdrawal of leading form contender Songye but the favourite scored in emphatic style.

## 4383 JOHN SMITH'S EXTRA SMOOTH H'CAP 6f 5y

**7:10** (7:10) (Class 5) (0-70,76) 3-Y-O+ **£3,234** (£962; £481; £240) **Stalls** Centre

Form RPR

0003 **1** **Baron Run**[37] 3102 4-9-8 **69**.................................. JoeyHaynes(3) 2 79
(K R Burke) *mde all: rdn along over 2f out: kpt on gamely fnl f: jst hld on* **5/2**[1]

0230 **2** *nse* **Layla's Hero (IRE)**[43] 2914 7-9-6 **64**....................(v) PaulMulrennan 6 73
(David Nicholls) *slowly away: racd towards stands' side away fr main gp: hdwy over 1f out: kpt on wl: jst hld* **13/2**

-622 **3** *¾* **Kirtling Belle**[21] 3669 3-9-6 **69**........................... SilvestreDeSousa 5 74
(Keith Dalgleish) *t.k.h early: trckd ldrs: effrt and rdn over 2f out: kpt on ins fnl f* **4/1**[3]

0351 **4** *1* **Gold Beau (FR)**[6] 4194 4-9-13 **76** 6ex........................(p) ShaneGray(5) 8 79
(Kristin Stubbs) *prom: effrt and drvn over 2f out: kpt on same pce ins fnl f* **11/4**[2]

5556 **5** *½* **Bunce (IRE)**[12] 4004 6-9-12 **70**................................ JoeFanning 7 72
(Linda Perratt) *hld up in tch: rdn over 2f out: hdwy over 1f out: nt pce to chal ins fnl f* **12/1**

6466 **6** *½* **Bonnie Charlie**[8] 4131 8-9-7 **65**.............................. PaulQuinn 4 65
(David Nicholls) *dwlt: hld up bhd ldng gp: rdn and edgd rt over 2f out: hdwy over 1f out: no imp fnl f* **9/1**

0-10 **7** *hd* **Mandalay King (IRE)**[22] 3599 9-9-7 **70**.................(p) ShirleyTeasdale(5) 1 69
(Marjorie Fife) *trckd ldrs: drvn along over 2f out: no ex ins fnl f* **16/1**

1-02 **8** *7* **Chookie's Lass**[112] 1149 3-9-7 **70**............................ TomEaves 3 46
(Keith Dalgleish) *trckd ldrs tl rdn and wknd over 1f out* **25/1**

1m 10.46s (-1.74) **Going Correction** -0.20s/f (Firm)

**WFA** 3 from 4yo+ 5lb 8 Ran SP% **116.0**

Speed ratings (Par 103): **103,102,101,100,99 99,99,89**

CSF £19.67 CT £63.63 TOTE £3.40: £1.90, £1.90, £1.50; EX 25.10 Trifecta £137.90.

**Owner** Mrs Elaine M Burke **Bred** Mrs D Hughes **Trained** Middleham Moor, N Yorks

**FOCUS**

They went a fair pace and there was a tight finish in this sprint handicap. The form is rated around the third and fourth.

## 4384 JOHN SMITH'S SCOTTISH STEWARDS' CUP (H'CAP) 6f 5y

**7:40** (7:41) (Class 2) (0-105,105) 3-Y-O+

**£20,542** (£6,151; £3,075; £1,537; £768; £386) **Stalls** Centre

Form RPR

530U **1** **Blaine**[6] 4188 4-9-3 **96**..........................................(b) AmyRyan 11 106
(Kevin Ryan) *prom: rdn to ld over 1f out: sn hrd pressed: hld on wl fnl f* **6/1**

-531 **2** *nk* **Tatlisu (IRE)**[20] 3714 4-8-9 **88**................................ TomEaves 15 97
(Richard Fahey) *hld up in tch: hdwy and edgd lft 2f out: chsd wnr appr fnl f: kpt on: hld nr fin* **8/1**

0022 **3** *hd* **Out Do**[27] 3483 5-8-13 **92**...................................... DanielTudhope 13 100
(David O'Meara) *hld up: stdy hdwy whn n.m.r briefly over 1f out: effrt stands' side over 1f out: kpt on wl fnl f: hld nr fin* **9/2**[2]

0020 **4** *1 ¾* **Sir Reginald**[28] 3420 6-8-11 **93**......................... GeorgeChaloner(3) 3 95
(Richard Fahey) *taken early to post: hld up bhd ldng gp: rdn over 2f out: kpt on fnl f: nt pce to chal* **10/1**

0050 **5** *½* **Hitchens (IRE)**[6] 4188 9-9-5 **98**........................ SilvestreDeSousa 4 99
(David Barron) *prom: effrt and rdn 2f out: kpt on same pce fnl f* **8/1**

2030 **6** *shd* **Yeeoow (IRE)**[20] 3737 5-8-11 **93**............................ JoeyHaynes(3) 16 93
(K R Burke) *hld up: rdn over 2f out: hdwy towards stands' side over 1f out: kpt on: no imp* **4/1**[1]

030 **7** *2* **Stonefield Flyer**[27] 3456 5-8-7 **86** oh3....................... DavidProbert 5 80
(Keith Dalgleish) *cl up: rdn over 2f out: no ex over 1f out* **40/1**

0000 **8** *½* **Doc Hay (USA)**[21] 3666 7-8-12 **91**.............................. IanBrennan 7 83
(Brian Ellison) *hld up: effrt and hung rt 2f out: no imp appr fnl f* **20/1**

0030 **9** *nk* **Cosmic Chatter**[20] 3716 4-9-0 **93**............................ JoeFanning 12 85
(David Barron) *t.k.h: hld up bhd ldng gp: rdn 2f out: no imp fnl f* **14/1**

0501 **10** *1 ¼* **Hopes N Dreams (IRE)**[17] 3830 6-9-1 **94**................. PaulMulrennan 2 82
(Kevin Ryan) *taken early to post: led tl rdn and hdd over 1f out: wknd ins fnl f* **5/1**[3]

1140 **11** *nse* **Victoire De Lyphar (IRE)**[20] 3716 7-9-1 **94**..............(e) JamesSullivan 9 81
(Ruth Carr) *taken early to post: in tch: rdn over 2f out: sn outpcd* **28/1**

1421 **12** *½* **Khelman (IRE)**[22] 3610 4-8-7 **86** oh2.......................... PatrickMathers 8 72
(Richard Fahey) *chsd ldrs: drvn and outpcd 2f out: n.d after* **16/1**

1303 **13** *½* **Barkston Ash**[13] 3960 6-9-4 **97**................................(p) JasonHart 1 81
(Eric Alston) *dwlt: bhd: outpcd whn hmpd over 2f out: sn n.d* **20/1**

1m 9.64s (-2.56) **Going Correction** -0.20s/f (Firm) 13 Ran SP% **128.4**

Speed ratings (Par 109): **109,108,108,106,105 105,102,101,101,99 99,99,98**

CSF £55.15 CT £207.88 TOTE £8.70: £2.60, £3.10, £2.20; EX 73.90 Trifecta £324.10.

**Owner** Matt & Lauren Morgan **Bred** Toby Barker **Trained** Hambleton, N Yorks

■ Stewards' Enquiry : Amy Ryan four-day ban: use of whip (1, 3, 4, 5 Aug)

**FOCUS**

A hot sprint handicap. There didn't seem to be much track bias, with most of the runners racing up the centre to stands' side. The winner built on his penultimate run.

## 4385 EBF STALLIONS GLASGOW STKS (LISTED RACE) 1m 3f 16y

**8:10** (8:10) (Class 1) 3-Y-O

**£22,684** (£8,600; £4,304; £2,144; £1,076; £540) **Stalls** Low

Form RPR

-343 **1** **Postponed (IRE)**[29] 3375 3-9-3 104........................ AndreaAtzeni 4 111
(Luca Cumani) *hld up: smooth hdwy on outside over 3f out: led over 2f out: sn pushed along and edgd rt: qckn clr fnl f: readily* **4/5**[1]

-300 **2** *3 ½* **Double Bluff (IRE)**[41] 2986 3-9-3 95........................ JoeFanning 7 105
(Mark Johnston) *led at ordinary gallop: rdn and hdd over 2f out: kpt on ins fnl f: no ch w wnr* **16/1**

1-20 **3** *nse* **Impulsive Moment (IRE)**[41] 2990 3-9-3 97................ DavidProbert 1 105
(Andrew Balding) *dwlt: hld up in tch: stdy hdwy whn n.m.r over 3f out and over 2f out: kpt on fnl f* **5/1**[3]

-140 **4** *1 ¾* **Odeon**[28] 3417 3-9-3 105........................................ GrahamLee 3 102
(James Given) *t.k.h: trckd ldrs: drvn over 2f out: no ex fr over 1f out* **9/2**[2]

-130 **5** *nk* **Sudden Wonder (IRE)**[41] 2990 3-9-3 105............... SilvestreDeSousa 5 101
(Charlie Appleby) *prom: wnt 2nd after 4f: drvn and ev ch over 2f out: wknd over 1f out* **7/1**

4240 **6** *8* **Nancy From Nairobi**[29] 3376 3-8-12 95..................... TomEaves 6 83
(Mick Channon) *prom: drvn along 3f out: wknd fr 2f out* **25/1**

2m 18.66s (-6.94) **Going Correction** -0.45s/f (Firm) 6 Ran SP% **112.6**

Speed ratings (Par 108): **107,104,104,103,102 97**

CSF £15.75 TOTE £1.60: £1.10, £4.20; EX 13.20 Trifecta £62.00.

**Owner** Sheikh Mohammed Obaid Al Maktoum **Bred** St Albans Bloodstock Llp **Trained** Newmarket, Suffolk

**FOCUS**

Once a Derby Trial, this race looked more of a testing ground for the St Leger this year. The pace was not strong but the odds-on favourite was impressive under a waiting ride and broke the track record by 0.65 seconds. A length best from the winner.

## 4386 PATERSONS OF GREENOAKHILL H'CAP 1m 3f 16y

**8:45** (8:45) (Class 6) (0-65,65) 3-Y-O **£2,587** (£770; £384; £192) **Stalls** Low

Form RPR

-422 **1** **Mister Uno (IRE)**[32] 3303 3-8-13 **57**........................(p) GrahamLee 3 65
(Ann Duffield) *chsd clr ldr: clsd 1/2-way: drvn to ld over 1f out: hld on wl fnl f* **9/4**[1]

6003 **2** *nk* **Keep To The Beat**[13] 3950 3-8-9 **58**........................(p) ShaneGray(5) 1 65
(Kevin Ryan) *led and clr to 1/2-way: rdn and hdd over 1f out: rallied: kpt on same pce wl ins fnl f* **9/1**

4-00 **3** *2 ¾* **Modify**[29] 3407 3-8-3 **50**....................................... JulieBurke(3) 2 52
(David O'Meara) *trckd ldrs: rdn over 2f out: hung lft ent fnl f: kpt on same pce* **28/1**

-040 **4** *hd* **In Vino Veritas (IRE)**[63] 2319 3-9-7 **65**.......................[1] PaulMulrennan 7 67
(Ann Duffield) *hld up in tch: drvn and outpcd 3f out: rallied fnl f: nvr able to chal* **17/2**

3454 **5** *1 ½* **Stout Cortez**[2] 4316 3-9-7 **65**................................ JoeFanning 6 66
(Mark Johnston) *plld hrd: in tch: stdy hdwy 1/2-way: effrt and hung rt over 2f out: one pce whn hmpd ent fnl f* **11/4**[2]

5550 **6** *nk* **Unfinishedbusiness**[18] 3789 3-8-10 **57**................. GeorgeChaloner(3) 4 56
(Richard Fahey) *dwlt: hld up: rdn over 3f out: no imp tl styd on fnl f: nvr able to chal* **7/2**[3]
-050 **7** *10* **Heartstrings**[13] 3950 3-9-7 **65**................................................ TomEaves 8 47
(Mick Channon) *prom: drvn over 3f out: wknd over 2f out* **15/2**
2m 23.92s (-1.68) **Going Correction** -0.45s/f (Firm) **7** Ran SP% **115.4**
Speed ratings (Par 98): **88,87,85,85,84 84,77**
CSF £23.61 CT £446.29 TOTE £2.50: £1.40, £3.90; EX 17.40 Trifecta £228.70.
**Owner** John Gatenby **Bred** R A Major **Trained** Constable Burton, N Yorks
**FOCUS**
They went a stop-start gallop in this minor handicap and the first two pulled clear. The winner is progressing again.

## 4387 JOHN SMITH'S H'CAP 1m 1f 36y
**9:15** (9:16) (Class 5) (0-70,70) 3-Y-0+ **£3,234** (£962; £481; £240) **Stalls** Low

Form RPR
6051 **1** **Bahamian C**[21] 3662 3-9-3 **68**........................................ PatrickMathers 1 76
(Richard Fahey) *chsd ldrs: drvn and outpcd over 3f out: rallied and edgd lft 2f out: led wl ins fnl f: kpt on wl* **6/1**
3252 **2** *nk* **Call Of Duty (IRE)**[12] 4000 9-8-5 **52** ow1...................(b) EmmaSayer(5) 7 60
(Dianne Sayer) *hld up: stdy hdwy over 3f out: blkd 2f out: rdn and ev ch wl ins fnl f: jst hld* **11/2**
3150 **3** *½* **Cameroonеy**[23] 3572 11-9-7 **68**...........................(p) ShirleyTeasdale(5) 9 75
(Marjorie Fife) *led: rdn over 3f out: edgd lft and hdd wl ins fnl f: kpt on same pce* **4/1**[3]
**4** *4 ½* **Quick Succession (USA)**[76] 3-9-1 **66**.............................. JoeFanning 3 63
(Keith Dalgleish) *prom: rdn and lost pl over 4f out: n.d after* **12/1**
3042 **5** *1* **Sakhalin Star (IRE)**[8] 4108 3-9-0 **70**........................... DuilioDaSilva(5) 8 64+
(Richard Guest) *in tch: smooth hdwy 4f out: rdn over 2f out: edgd rt and outpcd over 1f out* **7/2**[2]
6616 **6** *1* **Rasselas (IRE)**[14] 3908 7-9-5 **68**............................(b) AnnaHesketh(7) 11 61
(David Nicholls) *pressed ldr: drvn and lost pl over 2f out: n.d after* **14/1**
-034 **7** *2* **Royal Straight**[4] 4255 9-9-8 **64**.............................................(t) GrahamLee 2 53
(Linda Perratt) *hld up: stdy hdwy over 3f out: rdn and wknd over 1f out* **8/1**
2233 **8** *1 ¼* **Tectonic (IRE)**[6] 4197 5-10-0 **70**.....................................(p) TomEaves 10 57
(Keith Dalgleish) *hld up: stdy hdwy over 3f out: rdn and wknd over 1f out* **3/1**[1]
00-0 **9** *51* **Idarose (IRE)**[15] 3880 5-8-9 **51** oh6.......................................(p) IanBrennan 6
(John David Riches) *walked to s: s.i.s: hld up: stdy hdwy over 4f out: rdn and wknd fnl 3f: eased whn no ch fr 2f out* **80/1**
1m 56.54s (-3.16) **Going Correction** -0.45s/f (Firm)
**WFA** 3 from 5yo+ 9lb **9** Ran SP% **123.6**
Speed ratings (Par 103): **96,95,95,91,90 89,87,86,41**
CSF £41.87 CT £152.82 TOTE £7.90: £2.40, £1.90, £1.50; EX 32.90 Trifecta £323.30.
**Owner** S & G Clayton **Bred** Giles Wates **Trained** Musley Bank, N Yorks
■ Stewards' Enquiry : Shirley Teasdale four-day ban: use of whip (1, 3, 4, 5 Aug)
**FOCUS**
They went a decent pace and there was a tight finish between the first three, who pulled clear. The winner backed up his latest form.
T/Plt: £32.00 to a £1 stake. Pool: £50206.04 - 1144.29 winning tickets T/Qpdt: £10.60 to a £1 stake. Pool: £4983.10 - 345.90 winning tickets RY

# 3959 HAYDOCK (L-H)
Friday, July 18
**OFFICIAL GOING: Good to firm (9.3)**
Wind: fresh, half behind Weather: Warm but cloudy

## 4388 RACING UK ANYWHERE AVAILABLE NOW H'CAP (BOBIS RACE) 1m 2f 95y
**2:10** (2:10) (Class 4) (0-85,85) 3-Y-0 **£5,175** (£1,540; £769; £384) **Stalls** Centre

Form RPR
041 **1** **New Story**[19] 3750 3-9-7 **85**........................................ DanielTudhope 3 102+
(Ismail Mohammed) *trckd ldng pair: led gng wl 2f out: pushed clr fr over 1f out: eased nr fin: impressive* **11/8**[1]
1-54 **2** *5* **Idder (IRE)**[33] 3273 3-9-2 **80**.............................................(p) AndreaAtzeni 2 85
(Roger Varian) *trckd ldng pair: rdn 3f out: kpt on same pce: wnt 2nd ins fnl f: no ch w wnr* **2/1**[2]
2031 **3** *¾* **Watersmeet**[15] 3880 3-8-12 **76**........................................ FrannyNorton 7 80
(Mark Johnston) *w ldr: led 4f out: rdn whn hdd 2f out: one pce and sn no ch w wnr: lost 2nd ins fnl f* **9/2**[3]
6001 **4** *hd* **Rising Breeze (FR)**[13] 3974 3-8-11 **78**......................... JoeyHaynes(3) 6 81
(K R Burke) *dwlt: hld up in rr: rdn over 2f out: kpt on fr over 1f out* **14/1**
5115 **5** *14* **Fitzgerald (IRE)**[73] 2060 3-9-6 **84**.................................... MartinHarley 5 61
(Marco Botti) *hld up in tch: hdwy and briefly chsd ldr 2f out: wknd over 1f out* **9/1**
4-45 **6** *6* **Aristocracy**[13] 3986 3-8-2 **66**............................................... LukeMorris 4 31
(Mick Channon) *led narrowly: rdn whn hdd 4f out: wknd over 2f out* **33/1**
2m 8.39s (-7.11) **Going Correction** -0.625s/f (Hard) **6** Ran SP% **113.2**
Speed ratings (Par 102): **103,99,98,98,87 82**
CSF £4.44 CT £8.22 TOTE £2.30: £1.30, £1.50; EX 5.50 Trifecta £13.20.
**Owner** Sultan Ali **Bred** Chancery Bourse Investments Ltd **Trained** Newmarket, Suffolk
**FOCUS**
6f races on stands' side track, all others on inner track and races on Round course increased by 1yd. A decent 3yo handicap run at a sound pace, with the winning time dipping under standard. The winner is rated value for 6l.

## 4389 BRITISH STALLION STUDS EBF MAIDEN STKS 6f
**2:40** (2:40) (Class 5) 2-Y-0 **£2,911** (£866; £432; £216) **Stalls** High

Form RPR
222 **1** **Mattmu**[53] 2601 2-9-5 0.............................................. DavidAllan 8 82
(Tim Easterby) *trckd ldrs: rdn to ld over 1f out: kpt on: jst hld on* **3/1**[2]
**2** *hd* **Excilly** 2-9-0 0........................................................ RichardKingscote 11 76+
(Tom Dascombe) *midfield: pushed along and hdwy 2f out: rdn to chse ldr appr fnl f: kpt on: jst hld* **13/8**[1]
0 **3** *1* **Dark Profit (IRE)**[48] 2776 2-9-5 0.................................... AndreaAtzeni 1 78
(Charles Hills) *trckd ldrs: rdn and upsides over 1f out: no ex towards fin* **9/2**[3]
**4** *3 ¼* **Brindle** 2-9-0 0........................................................... TonyHamilton 4 64
(Richard Fahey) *dwlt: sn prom: rdn and upsides over 1f out: edgd lft and no ex ins fnl f* **16/1**
6 **5** *1 ½* **Fast Magic (IRE)**[31] 3330 2-9-5 0........................................ TomEaves 7 64
(Kevin Ryan) *led narrowly: rdn whn hdd over 1f out: wknd ins fnl f* **50/1**
**6** *1 ¼* **Jolievitesse (FR)** 2-9-5 0............................................. DanielTudhope 12 60
(K R Burke) *hld up: pushed along 1/2-way: kpt on fnl f* **9/1**
**7** *¾* **Our Time Will Come (IRE)** 2-9-0 0...................................... PhillipMakin 5 53+
(John Quinn) *slowly away: hld up: pushed along over 2f out: kpt on fnl f* **14/1**
**8** *1 ½* **Yukon Gold** 2-9-5 0.................................................. SilvestreDeSousa 9 54
(Charlie Appleby) *dwlt: sn pushed along towards rr: nvr threatened* **8/1**
**9** *4 ½* **Dylan's Storm (IRE)** 2-9-5 0............................................. LukeMorris 3 40
(David Dennis) *hld up: rdn over 3f out: sn struggling* **50/1**
5 **10** *29* **Tuebrook**[79] 1889 2-9-5 0............................................. GrahamGibbons 2
(Michael Easterby) *w ldr: rdn 1/2-way: sn wknd* **80/1**
1m 11.39s (-2.41) **Going Correction** -0.475s/f (Firm) **10** Ran SP% **120.1**
Speed ratings (Par 94): **97,96,95,91,89 87,86,84,78,39**
CSF £8.51 TOTE £3.30: £1.20, £1.30, £1.70; EX 11.50 Trifecta £45.00.
**Owner** James Bowers **Bred** J Bowers **Trained** Great Habton, N Yorks
**FOCUS**
An interesting juvenile maiden which has been won by smart performers such as Zarwaan, Professor and Shropshire in recent seasons.

## 4390 AMITY FINANCIAL SOLUTIONS FOR LIFE INSURANCE H'CAP (BOBIS RACE) 6f
**3:15** (3:18) (Class 4) (0-85,85) 3-Y-0 **£5,175** (£1,540; £769; £384) **Stalls** High

Form RPR
143 **1** **Captain Myles (IRE)**[13] 3959 3-9-1 **79**......................(p) StevieDonohoe 11 90
(Tim Pitt) *mde all: rdn over 1f out: kpt on wl* **7/1**[3]
10-4 **2** *nk* **Fast Track**[27] 3478 3-9-7 **85**.......................................... GrahamGibbons 3 95+
(David Barron) *hld up in tch: rdn and hdwy to chse ldng pair over 1f out: kpt on: wnt 2nd 75yds out* **5/2**[2]
122 **3** *1* **Double Up**[37] 3114 3-8-13 **77**............................................. AndreaAtzeni 9 84
(Roger Varian) *racd keenly: pressed ldr: rdn 2f out: lost 2nd 75yds out: no ex* **13/8**[1]
1402 **4** *¾* **Elusive George (IRE)**[34] 3225 3-8-12 **76**........................... PhillipMakin 12 80
(John Quinn) *trckd ldng pair: rdn 2f out: one pce* **10/1**
4024 **5** *2 ½* **Signore Piccolo**[13] 3959 3-9-4 **82**...................................... JasonHart 8 78
(Eric Alston) *in tch on outer: rdn 2f out: no ex fnl f* **7/1**[3]
6-33 **6** *2 ¼* **Withernsea (IRE)**[20] 3693 3-9-3 **81**............................... TonyHamilton 6 70
(Richard Fahey) *hld up: rdn over 2f out: nvr threatened* **12/1**
4-21 **7** *11* **Epic Voyage (USA)**[17] 3832 3-9-0 **78**.................................. TomEaves 1 32
(Brian Ellison) *dwlt: hld up in rr: a bhd* **20/1**
1m 10.43s (-3.37) **Going Correction** -0.475s/f (Firm) **7** Ran SP% **113.2**
Speed ratings (Par 102): **103,102,101,100,96 93,79**
CSF £24.37 CT £41.66 TOTE £7.80: £3.80, £1.60; EX 24.80 Trifecta £102.50.
**Owner** Paul Wildes **Bred** Burgage Stud And Partners **Trained** Market Drayton, Shropshire
**FOCUS**
A competitive 3yo sprint handicap before the field was reduced by almost half due to withdrawals. It was run 0.96secs faster than the preceding maiden and the form seems sound.

## 4391 FAMILY FUN DAY HERE 7TH AUGUST H'CAP 5f
**3:50** (3:50) (Class 4) (0-80,80) 3-Y-0+ **£5,175** (£1,540; £769; £384) **Stalls** Centre

Form RPR
-304 **1** **Rich Again (IRE)**[15] 3882 5-8-9 **63**...........................(b[1]) AndreaAtzeni 11 72
(James Bethell) *slowly away: sn rcvrd to chse ldrs: rdn 2f out: kpt on to ld 75yds out: jst hld on* **9/2**[2]
303 **2** *nse* **Cruise Tothelimit (IRE)**[19] 3749 6-9-11 **79**............. SilvestreDeSousa 1 88
(Ian Williams) *midfield: rdn and hdwy to chse ldrs over 1f out: kpt on: jst failed* **9/2**[2]
4002 **3** *¾* **Flash City (ITY)**[8] 4114 6-8-11 **65**...................................... PJMcDonald 3 71+
(Ruth Carr) *rrd s and slowly away: hld up in rr: stl last over 1f out: rdn and kpt on wl fnl f* **4/1**[1]
1000 **4** *nse* **Little Eli**[4] 4257 4-8-9 **63**..............................................(p) FrannyNorton 12 69
(Eric Alston) *w ldr: led over 1f out: rdn and hung lft ins fnl f: hdd 75yds out: no ex* **10/1**
3312 **5** *1* **Tyfos**[15] 3887 9-9-10 **78**.............................................. RichardKingscote 10 80
(Brian Baugh) *led narrowly: rdn whn hdd over 1f out: one pce* **6/1**[3]
0506 **6** *½* **Waseem Faris (IRE)**[11] 4027 5-9-10 **78**..........................(v) BrianHughes 2 79
(Mick Channon) *hld up: stl on bit over 1f out: rdn and one pce fnl f* **16/1**
005 **7** *hd* **Sleepy Blue Ocean**[13] 3948 8-9-6 **74**.............................(p) LukeMorris 15 74
(John Balding) *midfield: rdn 2f out: one pce and nvr threatened ldrs* **7/1**
0454 **8** *3 ¼* **Beau Mistral (IRE)**[14] 3921 5-9-0 **68**................................... RaulDaSilva 5 56
(Paul Green) *hld up: rdn 1/2-way: nvr threatened* **20/1**
155 **9** *hd* **Perfect Blossom**[11] 4016 7-9-4 **75**.................................... SladeO'Hara(3) 13 62
(Alan Berry) *chsd ldrs: wknd over 1f out* **25/1**
00/6 **10** *1 ¾* **Living It Large (FR)**[19] 3749 7-9-2 **77**........................ MeganCarberry(7) 7 58
(Ed de Giles) *chsd ldrs: rdn 2f out: wknd over 1f out* **14/1**
4000 **11** *1* **Rusty Rocket (IRE)**[13] 3948 5-9-7 **80**............................. JackGarritty(5) 9 58
(Paul Green) *midfield: rdn 1/2-way: sn wknd* **12/1**
58.93s (-1.87) **Going Correction** -0.475s/f (Firm) **11** Ran SP% **121.1**
Speed ratings (Par 105): **95,94,93,93,92 91,90,85,85,82 81**
CSF £25.95 CT £91.32 TOTE £5.10: £1.40, £2.00, £2.10; EX 28.70 Trifecta £96.50.
**Owner** Clarendon Thoroughbred Racing **Bred** Mrs Sandra Maye **Trained** Middleham Moor, N Yorks
**FOCUS**
A fair sprint handicap that produced a good finish. The winner is rated back to his turf best.

## 4392 BROWN SHIPLEY WEALTH WELL MANAGED H'CAP (BOBIS RACE) 1m 6f
**4:25** (4:25) (Class 4) (0-85,85) 3-Y-0 **£5,175** (£1,540; £769; £384) **Stalls** Low

Form RPR
1113 **1** **Maid In Rio (IRE)**[6] 4183 3-9-7 **85**................................... FrannyNorton 2 97+
(Mark Johnston) *trckd ldr: led over 2f out: pushed clr fr over 1f out: eased fnl 50yds* **11/8**[1]
5213 **2** *2 ¼* **Gallic Destiny (IRE)**[56] 2530 3-8-8 **72**............................(p) LiamKeniry 4 78
(Andrew Balding) *in tch: rdn over 2f out: kpt on same pce: wnt 2nd 75yds out: no threat to eased wnr* **16/1**
2262 **3** *½* **Mr Gallivanter (IRE)**[8] 4113 3-9-4 **82**............................... PhillipMakin 7 87
(John Quinn) *led: rdn whn hdd over 2f out: one pce: lost 2nd 75yds out* **7/2**[2]
4-06 **4** *1* **Intense Tango**[70] 2109 3-8-1 **72**............................ RobJFitzpatrick(7) 9 76
(K R Burke) *hld up: pushed along over 2f out: one pce: n.m.r towards inner fnl 110yds* **7/1**
0221 **5** *½* **The Kid**[17] 3818 3-8-11 **75**..........................................(tp) RichardKingscote 5 78
(Tom Dascombe) *hld up: rdn over 2f out: hung persistently lft and nvr threatened* **4/1**[3]
543 **6** *13* **Shadows Ofthenight (IRE)**[15] 3877 3-8-9 **73**. WilliamTwiston-Davies 1 58
(Mick Channon) *in tch: pushed along over 3f out: wknd over 2f out* **11/1**
2m 58.85s (-3.15) **Going Correction** -0.625s/f (Hard) **6** Ran SP% **111.0**
Speed ratings (Par 102): **84,82,82,81,81 74**
CSF £24.00 CT £62.41 TOTE £2.10: £1.60, £4.50; EX 27.50 Trifecta £63.90.
**Owner** The New Fairyhouse Partnership **Bred** Miss Susan Bates And Suzannah Dwyer **Trained** Middleham Moor, N Yorks


The Form Book, Raceform Ltd, Newbury, RG14 5SJ

**FOCUS**
Colour Vision won this staying handicap for 3yos the season before taking the Gold Cup, while last year's winner Hawk High later scored at the Cheltenham festival. It was run in a modest time but the form is taken at face value.

## 4393 LANCASHIRE LIFE MAIDEN STKS 1m
**4:55** (4:55) (Class 5) 3-Y-O+ **£2,587** (£770; £384; £192) **Stalls** Low

Form RPR
2- **1** **Elsiniaar**[400] 3250 4-9-13 0 JackMitchell 9 87+
(Roger Varian) *trckd ldr: led gng wl over 1f out: rdn ins fnl f: reduced advantage towards fin but a holding on* **5/4**[1]
422 **2** ½ **Taqneen (IRE)**[27] 3465 3-9-5 80 FrannyNorton 7 81
(Ed Dunlop) *in tch: t.k.h early: pushed along over 3f out: drvn over 2f out: kpt on ins fnl f: wnt 2nd 50yds out* **11/4**[2]
-53 **3** ¾ **The Character (IRE)**[14] 3925 3-8-12 0 JennyPowell(7) 3 79
(Tom Dascombe) *led: rdn over 2f out: hdd over 1f out: one pce: lost 2nd 50yds out* **7/2**[3]
3-0 **4** 2 ¾ **Ghosting (IRE)**[72] 2075 3-9-5 0 (t) RichardKingscote 5 73
(Tom Dascombe) *hld up: rdn over 2f out: kpt on fnl f: nvr threatened* **11/2**
0 **5** 2 ¾ **Trimoulet**[14] 3925 5-9-10 0 ThomasBrown(3) 2 68
(Daniel Kubler) *trckd ldr: rdn over 2f out: wknd fnl f* **50/1**
4 **6** 6 **French Flirt**[21] 3664 3-9-0 0 WilliamTwiston-Davies 4 47
(Timothy Jarvis) *hld up: rdn over 2f out: sn btn* **33/1**

1m 39.16s (-4.54) **Going Correction** -0.625s/f (Hard)
**WFA** 3 from 4yo+ 8lb 6 Ran SP% **113.6**
Speed ratings (Par 103): **97,96,95,93,90 84**
CSF £5.09 TOTE £1.90: £1.40, £1.50; EX 3.80 Trifecta £9.20.
**Owner** Hamdan Al Maktoum **Bred** Floors Farming & The Duke Of Devonshire **Trained** Newmarket, Suffolk

**FOCUS**
Maidens for older horses at this time of year are not often that strong, and this one was weakened by late absentees, including one rated in the 80s. The form makes sense.

## 4394 BETDAQ HAYDOCK PARK APPRENTICE TRAINING SERIES H'CAP (PART OF THE RACING EXCELLENCE INITIATIVE) 1m
**5:25** (5:26) (Class 5) (0-75,73) 4-Y-O+ **£2,587** (£770; £384; £192) **Stalls** Low

Form RPR
0641 **1** **Kuwait Star**[13] 3958 5-9-7 **68** JacobButterfield 1 76
(Michael Herrington) *mde all: strly pressed fr over 2f out: hld on wl* **2/1**[2]
0553 **2** *nse* **Janaab (IRE)**[18] 3791 4-8-11 **61** (t) JackGarritty(3) 3 68
(Tim Easterby) *trckd ldr: rdn to chal strly fr over 2f out: kpt on but a jst hld* **5/1**[3]
1-41 **3** 1 ½ **Big Storm Coming**[21] 3667 4-9-9 **73** MeganCarberry(3) 2 77+
(Brian Ellison) *trckd ldr: rdn over 2f out: kpt on same pce* **15/8**[1]
0306 **4** 2 ½ **Day Of The Eagle (IRE)**[13] 3949 8-9-0 **66** DanielleMooney(5) 4 64
(Michael Easterby) *hld up: rdn over 2f out: one pce and nvr threatened* **10/1**
1465 **5** 1 ¼ **Exclusive Waters (IRE)**[63] 2301 4-8-11 **65** (b) JackBudge(7) 9 60
(Charles Hills) *slowly away: hld up in rr: rdn over 2f out: one pce and nvr threatened* **7/1**
650 **6** 2 ¼ **Kay Gee Be (IRE)**[43] 2911 10-8-5 **57** (p) JordanHibberd(5) 5 47
(Alan Berry) *in tch: rdn over 2f out: wknd over 1f out* **20/1**
6360 **P** **Lucky Dan (IRE)**[36] 3138 8-8-5 **59** JamesKendrick(7) 6
(Paul Green) *hld up: tk str hold and sddle sn slipped: in tch on outer over 5f out: eased over 2f out: p.u ins fnl f* **28/1**

1m 40.04s (-3.66) **Going Correction** -0.625s/f (Hard) 7 Ran SP% **114.6**
Speed ratings (Par 103): **93,92,91,88,87 85,**
CSF £12.59 CT £20.68 TOTE £2.80: £2.00, £3.10; EX 14.20 Trifecta £36.00.
**Owner** Miss Vivian Pratt **Bred** H & V Pratt **Trained** Cold Kirby, N Yorks

**FOCUS**
This modest apprentices' handicap was run 0.88secs slower than the preceding maiden. The winner was a bit closer to his last year's best.
T/Jkpt: £10,040.00 to a £1 stake. Pool: £42422.75 - 3.00 winning tickets T/Plt: £8.20 to a £1 stake. Pool: £68132.41 - 6010.06 winning tickets T/Qpdt: £5.40 to a £1 stake. Pool: £4114.60 - 561.65 winning tickets AS

# 3887 NEWBURY (L-H)
Friday, July 18
**OFFICIAL GOING: Good to firm (good in places; 6.8)**
Wind: virtually nil Weather: sunny and warm

## 4395 HIGHCLERE THOROUGHBRED RACING EBF STALLIONS MAIDEN STKS (BOBIS RACE) 7f (S)
**2:00** (2:03) (Class 4) 2-Y-O **£6,469** (£1,925; £962; £481) **Stalls** Centre

Form RPR
4 **1** **Nafaqa (IRE)**[27] 3448 2-9-5 0 PaulHanagan 7 85+
(B W Hills) *a.p: rdn ent fnl f: led fnl 120yds: kpt on wl* **8/11**[1]
2 **2** ½ **Marshall Jennings (IRE)**[35] 3194 2-9-5 0 RichardHughes 15 84
(Richard Hannon) *led: rdn over 1f out: hdd fnl 120yds: kpt on* **3/1**[2]
**3** ½ **Prince Gagarin (IRE)** 2-9-5 0 AdamKirby 8 82+
(Ed Dunlop) *mid-div: hdwy 3f out: sn rdn to chse ldrs: kpt on ins fnl f: wnt 3rd fnl stride* **14/1**
**4** *nse* **Lethal Legacy (IRE)** 2-9-5 0 PatDobbs 16 82+
(Richard Hannon) *chsd ldng pair: pushed along 2f out: nt clrest of runs fnl f: swtchd lft grad: kpt on nicely wout threatening* **33/1**
**5** 2 **Dissolution** 2-9-5 0 JamesDoyle 5 79+
(Sir Michael Stoute) *hld up towards rr: rdn over 2f out: stdy prog over 1f out: styd on fnl f* **10/1**[3]
**6** 2 **Fieldsman (USA)** 2-9-5 0 OisinMurphy 3 71
(Ed Dunlop) *in tch: rdn to chse ldrs 2f out: kpt on same pce fnl f* **33/1**
**7** 1 ¾ **Mickey Haller (IRE)** 2-9-5 0 JimmyFortune 11 67+
(Brian Meehan) *trckd ldng pair: rdn over 2f out: fdd ins fnl f* **33/1**
**8** 3 **The Twisler** 2-9-5 0 WilliamBuick 14 59+
(Charles Hills) *mid-div: pushed along over 2f out: nvr any imp: hung lft fnl f* **50/1**
**9** 4 ½ **Call Out Loud** 2-9-5 0 RyanMoore 2 46
(Sir Michael Stoute) *hld up towards rr: sme minor prog past btn horses: nvr a factor* **20/1**
**10** 3 ¼ **Marma's Boy** 2-9-5 0 JimCrowley 9 38+
(Ralph Beckett) *mid-div tl wknd 2f out* **33/1**
**11** 7 **Titian Lord (IRE)** 2-9-5 0 GeorgeBaker 1 19
(Charles Hills) *a towards rr: wknd 2f out* **66/1**
**12** 1 ¼ **Beijing Star** 2-9-5 0 WilliamCarson 10 15
(Charles Hills) *mid-div: rdn over 2f out: wknd over 1f out* **100/1**
**13** 11 **Beauchamp Fire** 2-9-5 0 JohnFahy 4
(Paul Fitzsimons) *mid-div tl wknd 2f out* **150/1**
**14** 29 **Victoriously** 2-9-5 0 TomQueally 12
(Brian Meehan) *a towards rr: wknd and eased fr over 1f out* **66/1**

1m 27.09s (1.39) **Going Correction** -0.075s/f (Good) **14** Ran SP% **121.8**
Speed ratings (Par 96): **89,88,87,87,85 83,81,77,72,68 60,59,46,13**
CSF £2.58 TOTE £2.10: £1.10, £1.10, £3.00; EX 4.00 Trifecta £20.90.
**Owner** Hamdan Al Maktoum **Bred** Shadwell Estate Company Limited **Trained** Upper Lambourn, Berks

**FOCUS**
Rail out between 1m and 5f on Round course and distances on Round course increased by 18yds. There was a 3m cut-off at 1m1f leading into bend to give fresh ground. Quick ground despite a little overnight rain. The last half-dozen winners of this maiden have gone on to make an impact in stakes company, most recently Jersey Stakes runner-up Muwaary. Only two of these had run previously, and the pair dominated the market and the race itself. There were several promising performances in behind.

## 4396 AL BASTI EQUIWORLD EBF STALLIONS MAIDEN FILLIES' STKS (BOBIS RACE) 6f 8y
**2:30** (2:37) (Class 4) 2-Y-O **£6,469** (£1,925; £962; £481) **Stalls** Centre

Form RPR
3 **1** **Taaqah (USA)**[34] 3223 2-9-0 0 RyanMoore 5 81+
(James Tate) *mid-div: pushed along and hdwy 2f out: rdn to ld ent fnl f: kpt on strly to assert fnl 120yds* **5/2**[2]
63 **2** 1 ½ **Zifena**[23] 3583 2-9-0 0 JimmyFortune 2 77
(Eve Johnson Houghton) *mid-div: hdwy 2f out: ev ch whn rdn ent fnl f: kpt on but nt pce of wnr fnl 120yds* **16/1**
5 **3** 1 **Black Cherry**[21] 3671 2-9-0 0 RichardHughes 11 74
(Richard Hannon) *led: rdn and hdd 2f out: sn sltly outpcd: kpt on again ins fnl f* **2/1**[1]
**4** 2 ½ **Evening Rain (USA)** 2-8-11 0 MatthewLawson(3) 7 66+
(Saeed bin Suroor) *trckd ldrs: led narrowly 2f out: sn rdn: hdd ent fnl f: kpt on same pce* **7/1**
0 **5** *hd* **Angels Wings (IRE)**[21] 3648 2-9-0 0 JamesDoyle 3 65
(Charles Hills) *trckd ldrs: rdn and ev ch 2f out tl no ex ins fnl f* **7/1**
4 **6** ½ **Finial**[34] 3223 2-9-0 0 JohnFahy 16 64
(Clive Cox) *mid-div: rdn 2f out: kpt on fnl f but nt pce to get onterms* **6/1**[3]
**7** ¾ **Fret** 2-9-0 0 HarryBentley 8 62
(Henry Candy) *mid-div: rdn 2f out: nvr gng pce to get involved* **20/1**
**8** *shd* **Belle Dormant (IRE)** 2-9-0 0 WilliamCarson 14 61
(Seamus Durack) *rdn 2f out: a mid-div* **20/1**
**9** *hd* **Kipuka** 2-9-0 0 JimCrowley 4 61+
(Paul Cole) *hld up towards rr: hdwy over 2f out into midfield: looked to be hanging lft and no further imp fr over 1f out* **20/1**
**10** 2 **Margot Rose** 2-9-0 0 OisinMurphy 1 55
(Harry Dunlop) *prom: rdn and ev ch 2f out: wknd jst over 1f out* **50/1**
4 **11** 1 **Piping Dream (IRE)**[23] 3583 2-9-0 0 PatDobbs 9 52+
(Richard Hannon) *rrd leaving stalls: towards rr: sme hdwy over 2f out: sn rdn: wknd jst over 1f out* **25/1**
**12** 2 **Montalcino (IRE)** 2-9-0 0 SamanthaSpratt 12 46
(Brian Meehan) *dwlt: a towards rr* **50/1**
**13** 1 ¼ **Escrick (IRE)** 2-9-0 0 TomQueally 10 42
(David Simcock) *a towards rr* **20/1**
**14** 4 ½ **Catharina** 2-9-0 0 KieranO'Neill 13 29
(Richard Hannon) *a towards rr* **33/1**
**15** 1 **Where's Sue (IRE)** 2-9-0 0 WilliamBuick 6 26
(Charles Hills) *chsd ldrs: rdn over 2f out: wknd over 1f out* **14/1**

1m 13.8s (0.80) **Going Correction** -0.075s/f (Good) **15** Ran SP% **143.5**
Speed ratings (Par 93): **91,89,87,84,84 83,82,82,82,79 78,75,73,67,66**
CSF £46.49 TOTE £3.10: £1.10, £6.30, £1.30; EX 76.10 Trifecta £255.40.
**Owner** Sheikh Juma Dalmook Al Maktoum **Bred** Bruce Berenson & Laurie Berenson **Trained** Newmarket, Suffolk

**FOCUS**
Subsequent Group winners J Wonder and Amazing Maria finished first and third in this event last year. The late withdrawal of favourite Sulaalaat took away some of the interest in this renewal. Five of the first six had run previously.

## 4397 AL BASTI EQUIWORLD TBA FILLIES' H'CAP (BOBIS RACE) 1m 2f 6y
**3:05** (3:07) (Class 3) (0-90,88) 3-Y-O **£9,703** (£2,887; £1,443; £721) **Stalls** Centre

Form RPR
5413 **1** **Cay Dancer**[19] 3758 3-9-3 **84** RichardHughes 1 93+
(Richard Hannon) *in last pair: travelling wl on heels of ldrs w nt clr run fr 2f out tl jst over 1f out: led ent fnl f: kpt on wl: pushed out: comf* **11/4**[2]
2411 **2** ¾ **Miss Lucy Jane**[13] 3950 3-8-8 **75** JamesDoyle 5 81
(Richard Fahey) *slowly away: in last pair: pushed along and hdwy over 3f out: kpt on to chse wnr ins fnl f but a being hld* **12/1**
3143 **3** 1 ½ **Rosehill Artist (IRE)**[6] 4211 3-9-7 **88** WilliamBuick 7 91
(Charles Hills) *trckd ldrs: rdn and ev ch 2f out tl ent fnl f: kpt on same pce* **6/1**
2310 **4** 1 ¼ **Polar Eyes**[30] 3357 3-8-7 **81** JordanNason(7) 4 82
(Peter Chapple-Hyam) *racd keenly: trckd ldr: rdn 2f out: sn edgd rt: led over 1f out: hdd ent fnl f: no ex fnl 120yds* **14/1**
-231 **5** 3 ¾ **Sea The Bloom**[13] 3953 3-8-8 **75** RyanMoore 2 69
(Sir Michael Stoute) *racd keenly: trckd ldrs: pushed along over 3f out: nvr gng pce to get on terms* **5/2**[1]
561 **6** 3 **Wojha (IRE)**[46] 2842 3-8-9 **76** PaulHanagan 6 64
(William Haggas) *led: rdn 2f out: hdd over 1f out: wknd ins fnl f* **9/2**[3]
-361 **7** 3 **Baynunah (USA)**[28] 3430 3-8-9 **76** TomQueally 3 58
(James Fanshawe) *trckd ldrs: rdn over 2f out: wknd ent fnl f* **10/1**

2m 7.7s (-1.10) **Going Correction** -0.075s/f (Good) 7 Ran SP% **111.2**
Speed ratings (Par 101): **101,100,99,98,95 92,90**
CSF £32.21 TOTE £3.00: £1.70, £3.70; EX 32.70 Trifecta £129.10.
**Owner** R Barnett **Bred** W And R Barnett Ltd **Trained** East Everleigh, Wilts

**FOCUS**
The race distance was 18m longer than advertised. They went what appeared to be an ordinary gallop in this fair fillies' handicap, but the first two came from the rear. The winner rates better than the bare form, with the third and fourth the best guides.

## 4398 ROSE BOWL STKS - SPONSORED BY COMPTON BEAUCHAMP ESTATES LTD (LISTED RACE) 6f 8y
**3:40** (3:40) (Class 1) 2-Y-O **£14,461** (£5,482; £2,743; £1,366; £685) **Stalls** Centre

Form RPR
11 **1** **Limato (IRE)**[23] 3580 2-9-0 0 JamesDoyle 5 111+
(Henry Candy) *travelled wl: trckd ldrs: pushed along ent fnl f: qcknd up wl to ld fnl 100yds: readily* **11/8**[2]

061 **2** *1 ¼* **Cotai Glory**[8] 4103 2-9-0 0 GeorgeBaker 4 106
(Charles Hills) *led: rdn over 1f out: drifted lft whn hdd fnl 100yds: nt pce of wnr* **7/1**[3]
110 **3** *4 ½* **Adaay (IRE)**[31] 3318 2-9-0 0 PaulHanagan 2 93
(William Haggas) *little slowly away: trckd ldrs: rdn to chse ldr over 1f out: unable to mount chal: outpcd by front pair ins fnl f* **5/4**[1]
311 **4** *2 ¾* **Step To The Shears**[19] 3751 2-9-0 0 PatDobbs 3 84
(Richard Hannon) *trckd ldr: rdn over 2f out: one pce fnl f* **10/1**
0 **5** *3 ½* **Fast Romance (USA)**[15] 3888 2-8-9 0 JimCrowley 1 69
(Paul Cole) *trckd ldrs: rdn over 2f out: outpcd over 1f out* **100/1**
1m 11.21s (-1.79) **Going Correction** -0.075s/f (Good) **5** Ran SP% **109.1**
Speed ratings (Par 102): **108,106,100,96,92**
CSF £10.73 TOTE £2.70: £1.10, £4.10; EX 5.40 Trifecta £23.00.
**Owner** Paul G Jacobs **Bred** Seamus Phelan **Trained** Kingston Warren, Oxon
**FOCUS**
This is not always a strong Listed race, but the time was quick and there was a lot to like about the winner's performance.

## 4399 R & M ELECTRICAL GROUP H'CAP 5f 34y
**4:15** (4:15) (Class 5) (0-75,76) 3-Y-0+ **£2,911** (£866; £432; £216) **Stalls** Centre

Form RPR
6026 **1** **Flying Bear (IRE)**[8] 4121 3-9-2 **74** RyanMoore 5 82
(Jeremy Gask) *chsd ldrs: pushed along over 3f out: rdn over 2f out: stdy run fr over 1f out to ld nring fin: drvn rt out* **7/4**[1]
0466 **2** *nk* **Swendab (IRE)**[3] 4284 6-9-7 **75** (v) RichardHughes 2 83
(John O'Shea) *bmpd and wnt lft s: chsd ldr: rdn to ld 2f out: kpt on: hdd nring fin* **5/1**[3]
1542 **3** *4* **Whitecrest**[4] 4267 6-8-12 **71** PhilipPrince(5) 1 65
(John Spearing) *s.i.s and hmpd s: chsd ldrs: rdn over 2f out: kpt on to go 3rd fnl 120yds but nt pce to trble front pair* **7/2**[2]
5601 **4** *1 ¼* **Edged Out**[7] 4151 4-9-6 **74** 6ex OisinMurphy 6 63
(Christopher Mason) *chsd ldr: rdn and ev ch 2f out tl jst over 1f out: fdd fnl 120yds* **7/2**[2]
041 **5** *1 ½* **Ask The Guru**[8] 4102 4-9-3 **76** 6ex (v) LouisSteward(5) 3 60
(Michael Attwater) *wnt sltly lft s: led tl rdn 2f out: sn hld: wknd fnl f* **7/1**
1m 1.13s (-0.27) **Going Correction** -0.075s/f (Good)
**WFA** 3 from 4yo+ 4lb **5** Ran SP% **110.0**
Speed ratings (Par 103): **99,98,92,90,87**
CSF £10.69 TOTE £2.40: £1.10, £3.10; EX 12.30 Trifecta £30.60.
**Owner** Flying Bear Partnership **Bred** Joseph Flanagan & Jarlath Fahey **Trained** Sutton Veny, Wilts
**FOCUS**
All five of the runners in this modest sprint handicap had run within the last eight days. They went a decent gallop but this is slightly unconvincing form.

## 4400 TKP SURFACING H'CAP 1m 2f 6y
**4:45** (4:45) (Class 3) (0-95,94) 3-Y-0+
**£7,158** (£2,143; £1,071; £535; £267; £134) **Stalls** Centre

Form RPR
-334 **1** **Border Legend**[20] 3730 5-9-12 **92** GeorgeBaker 2 103+
(Roger Charlton) *travelled wl most of way: trckd ldr: led over 2f out: rdn 3 l clr over 1f out: only jst hld on* **11/4**[1]
3-60 **2** *nse* **Ajman Bridge**[20] 3730 4-9-9 **89** PatDobbs 4 99
(Luca Cumani) *untidy and hmpd leaving stalls: sn trcking ldrs: rdn over 1f out: 3 l 2nd ent fnl f: str run fnl 120yds: jst failed* **7/1**
0-04 **3** *2 ¼* **Enobled**[34] 3244 4-9-4 **84** RyanMoore 7 90
(Sir Michael Stoute) *hld up: hdwy 3f out: sn rdn: swtchd rt wl over 1f out: wnt 3rd jst ins fnl f: styd on* **4/1**[3]
0440 **4** *nk* **Pasaka Boy**[20] 3730 4-9-4 **84** TomQueally 5 89
(Jonathan Portman) *wnt sltly lft s: hld up: hdwy 3f out: sn rdn: disp 3rd ent fnl f: styd on but no ex nring fin* **12/1**
0000 **5** *2 ¾* **Burano (IRE)**[13] 3982 5-10-0 **94** (b) JimmyFortune 3 94
(Brian Meehan) *led: rdn whn hdd wl over 2f out: kpt chsng ldrs tl no ex fnl 140yds* **7/1**
1151 **6** *7* **Insaany**[21] 3675 3-8-9 **85** PaulHanagan 9 79
(Mark Johnston) *trckd ldrs: pushed along to chal 3f out: sn rdn: hld over 1f out: wknd fnl f* **3/1**[2]
2120 **7** *3 ½* **Kastini**[35] 3196 4-8-11 **77** (v) RichardHughes 6 64
(Denis Coakley) *hld up: hdwy 3f out: sn rdn: nt pce to quite get on terms: wknd fnl f* **10/1**
2m 6.05s (-2.75) **Going Correction** -0.075s/f (Good)
**WFA** 3 from 4yo+ 10lb **7** Ran SP% **113.4**
Speed ratings (Par 107): **108,107,106,105,103 98,95**
CSF £21.88 CT £75.11 TOTE £3.00: £2.10, £4.60; EX 20.50 Trifecta £101.30.
**Owner** The Queen **Bred** The Queen **Trained** Beckhampton, Wilts
**FOCUS**
The race distance was 18m longer than advertised. This decent handicap was run in a time 1.65sec quicker than the earlier fillies' race. The form is rated slightly positively.

## 4401 RONNIE COOK MEMORIAL APPRENTICE H'CAP 6f 8y
**5:15** (5:15) (Class 5) (0-75,80) 4-Y-0+ **£2,911** (£866; £432; £216) **Stalls** Centre

Form RPR
4044 **1** **Panther Patrol (IRE)**[15] 3887 4-8-10 **64** (v) KieranShoemark(5) 4 76
(Eve Johnson Houghton) *trckd ldrs: led over 1f out: kpt on wl: cosily* **7/2**[1]
3501 **2** *¾* **Chevise (IRE)**[28] 3422 6-8-5 **59** (b) HectorCrouch(5) 7 68
(Steve Woodman) *mid-div: hdwy 2f out: sn rdn: chsd wnr jst ins fnl f: kpt on but a being hld* **10/1**
0300 **3** *4 ½* **Generalyse**[15] 3882 5-9-9 **75** PaulBooth(3) 1 69
(Ben De Haan) *racd keenly: prom: led 2f out: rdn and hdd over 1f out: no ex fnl f* **25/1**
4314 **4** *nk* **Ada Lovelace**[28] 3422 4-8-10 **66** EilishMcCall(7) 9 59
(John Gallagher) *mid-div: hdwy wl over 2f out: led briefly over 1f out: sn rdn: no ex fnl f* **8/1**
1524 **5** *1 ¾* **Pettochside**[7] 4146 5-9-9 **75** RobHornby(3) 6 63
(Chris Gordon) *hld up: styd on fnl f but nvr gng pce to rch ldrs* **7/2**[1]
2242 **6** *3 ¼* **Ray Of Joy**[11] 4024 8-9-1 **67** (v) CharlieBennett(3) 2 44
(J R Jenkins) *stdd s: swtchd lft 3f out: sn rdn: nvr any imp on ldrs* **11/2**[2]
430 **7** *1 ¼* **Jontleman (IRE)**[11] 4024 4-9-5 **73** PaddyPilley(5) 8 46
(Mick Channon) *in tch: rdn over 3f out: nvr threatened: wknd over 1f out* **7/1**[3]
3000 **8** *1 ½* **Prince Regal**[49] 2732 4-9-5 **75** PaulCooley(7) 5 43
(Timothy Jarvis) *led tl rdn 2f out: wknd over 1f out* **14/1**
00 **9** *7* **Salvado (IRE)**[32] 3313 4-9-6 **69** SeanBowen 10 15
(Tony Carroll) *v awkwardly away: a in rr* **7/1**[3]
1m 12.19s (-0.81) **Going Correction** -0.075s/f (Good) **9** Ran SP% **115.5**
Speed ratings (Par 103): **102,101,95,94,92 87,86,84,74**
CSF £39.91 CT £759.81 TOTE £4.50: £1.60, £3.70, £6.20; EX 46.10 Trifecta £1269.90.
**Owner** G C Stevens **Bred** Kilfrush Stud **Trained** Blewbury, Oxon

**FOCUS**
A modest apprentice handicap in which the first two finished clear. The winner is rated similar to last August's C&D form.
T/Plt: £41.30 to a £1 stake. Pool: £64916.80 - 1146.69 winning tickets T/Qpdt: £30.00 to a £1 stake. Pool: £3552.94 - 87.40 winning tickets TM

# 4198 NEWMARKET (R-H)
### Friday, July 18
**OFFICIAL GOING: Good changing to good to firm after race 1 (5:45)**
Wind: Light half-behind Weather: Fine

## 4402 NEWMARKETRACECOURSES.CO.UK H'CAP (JOCKEY CLUB GRASSROOTS FLAT MIDDLE DISTANCE SERIES QUALIIFER) 1m 2f
**5:45** (5:45) (Class 5) (0-75,74) 3-Y-0+ **£3,881** (£1,155; £577; £288) **Stalls** Centre

Form RPR
3243 **1** **Excellent Puck (IRE)**[133] 870 4-9-10 **70** JamesDoyle 3 78
(Shaun Lycett) *hld up in tch: shkn up and hung lft over 1f out: rdn to ld ins fnl f: styd on* **11/4**[1]
1000 **2** *½* **Indian Trifone (IRE)**[34] 3254 4-9-8 **68** WilliamBuick 6 75
(Ed Walker) *trckd ldr 6f: remained handy: rdn over 1f out: edgd lft ins fnl f: r.o* **4/1**[2]
13-6 **3** *1 ¼* **Tucson Arizona**[51] 2685 3-9-4 **74** AdamKirby 4 79
(Anthony Carson) *trckd ldrs: led over 2f out: rdn and hdd ins fnl f: styd on same pce* **11/4**[1]
-054 **4** *nk* **Little Buxted (USA)**[9] 4077 4-9-6 **73** GeorgeBuckell(7) 2 77
(Robert Mills) *trckd ldrs: racd keenly: rdn over 2f out: hung lft and outpcd over 1f out: r.o ins fnl f* **8/1**[3]
-045 **5** *5* **Dolphin Rock**[30] 3368 7-9-13 **73** DaneO'Neill 7 68
(Brian Ellison) *led: rdn and hdd over 2f out: wknd ins fnl f* **10/1**
4120 **6** *½* **Minstrel Lad**[4] 4273 6-9-1 **64** SimonPearce(3) 5 58
(Lydia Pearce) *hld up: hdwy 2f out: sn carried lft and hmpd: no ex fnl f* **8/1**[3]
0066 **7** *27* **Archie Rice (USA)**[27] 3475 8-9-0 **63** RyanTate(3) 1 5
(Tom Keddy) *hld up: hdwy over 3f out: wknd 2f out* **33/1**
-110 **8** *hd* **The Ginger Berry**[34] 3226 4-8-13 **59** ChrisCatlin 8
(Dr Jon Scargill) *trckd ldrs: wnt 2nd 4f out tl wknd over 2f out* **25/1**
2m 7.39s (1.89) **Going Correction** +0.125s/f (Good)
**WFA** 3 from 4yo+ 10lb **8** Ran SP% **111.4**
Speed ratings (Par 103): **97,96,95,95,91 90,69,69**
CSF £13.09 CT £30.62 TOTE £3.70: £1.50, £1.80, £1.40; EX 17.30 Trifecta £38.80.
**Owner** Exors of the Late P Grocott **Bred** Swersky & Associates **Trained** Clapton-on-the-Hill, Gloucs
**FOCUS**
Stands' side track used with stalls on far side, except 1m2f: centre. The ground was changed to good to firm after this contest despite the time of this opener being fairly slow. The pace looked steady enough but the winner has beaten a couple of unexposed types in second and third so the form might not be too bad for the grade.

## 4403 PLACE UK 60TH ANNIVERSARY MAIDEN FILLIES' STKS (BOBIS RACE) 7f
**6:20** (6:21) (Class 4) 2-Y-O **£3,881** (£1,155; £577; £288) **Stalls** High

Form RPR
**1** **Efflorescence (USA)** 2-9-0 0 AdamKirby 7 90+
(Charlie Appleby) *plld hrd: mde all: rdn clr fr over 1f out* **13/2**
**2** *2 ¾* **Good Place (USA)** 2-9-0 0 HarryBentley 2 83+
(Saeed bin Suroor) *mid-div: hdwy to chse wnr over 2f out: rdn over 1f out: styd on same pce ins fnl f* **4/1**[2]
**3** *2* **Vesnina** 2-9-0 0 SteveDrowne 4 77+
(Richard Hannon) *s.s: hld up: hdwy over 1f out: nt rch ldrs* **14/1**
**4** *1 ¾* **Rastanora (USA)** 2-9-0 0 WilliamBuick 9 72+
(John Gosden) *mid-div: outpcd 1/2-way: shkn up and r.o ins fnl f: nt trble ldrs* **10/1**
6 **5** *3 ¼* **On High**[21] 3671 2-9-0 0 PatCosgrave 3 64
(Richard Hannon) *mid-div: hdwy 1/2-way: rdn over 1f out: wknd fnl f* **33/1**
5 **6** *½* **Star Of Spring (IRE)**[24] 3558 2-9-0 0 ChrisCatlin 11 62
(Charles Hills) *hld up: hdwy 1/2-way: rdn and wknd over 1f out* **9/2**[3]
300 **7** *3 ¾* **Ocean Crystal**[6] 4202 2-8-7 0 JordonMcMurray(7) 5 52
(John Ryan) *hld up: styd on appr fnl f: nvr nr to chal* **100/1**
0 **8** *1* **Decibelle**[21] 3671 2-9-0 0 HayleyTurner 12 50
(Jane Chapple-Hyam) *chsd ldrs tl rdn and wknd over 1f out* **100/1**
60 **9** *¾* **All My Love (IRE)**[24] 3558 2-9-0 0 KieranO'Neill 1 47
(Richard Hannon) *chsd ldrs: rdn over 2f out: wknd over 1f out* **40/1**
3 **10** *1 ¼* **All Rounder (USA)**[24] 3558 2-9-0 0 JamesDoyle 10 44
(John Gosden) *prom: rdn over 2f out: wknd over 1f out* **5/4**[1]
00 **11** *nk* **Auld Fyffee (IRE)**[6] 4202 2-8-11 0 RyanPowell(3) 13 43
(John Ryan) *hld up: a in rr* **100/1**
24 **12** *4* **Shahralasal (IRE)**[21] 3648 2-9-0 0 DaneO'Neill 8 32
(Roger Varian) *prom over 4f* **8/1**
**13** *10* **Todegica** 2-9-0 0 JimCrowley 6 5
(Ralph Beckett) *prom to 1/2-way: eased fnl 2f* **20/1**
1m 27.2s (1.50) **Going Correction** +0.125s/f (Good) **13** Ran SP% **118.2**
Speed ratings (Par 93): **96,92,90,88,84 84,80,78,78,76 76,71,60**
CSF £31.11 TOTE £8.10: £2.40, £2.20, £3.40; EX 22.20 Trifecta £512.30.
**Owner** Godolphin **Bred** Darley **Trained** Newmarket, Suffolk
**FOCUS**
An open-looking maiden on paper but the two fillies with the best form both ran disappointingly and were beaten some way out. The first four home were all newcomers.

## 4404 NGK SPARK PLUGS H'CAP (BOBIS RACE) 7f
**6:50** (6:51) (Class 4) (0-85,85) 3-Y-O **£5,175** (£1,540; £769; £384) **Stalls** High

Form RPR
2212 **1** **Baltic Brave (IRE)**[27] 3480 3-9-1 **79** (t) RyanMoore 10 91
(Hughie Morrison) *hld up: hdwy and n.m.r wl over 1f out: led sn after: rdn out* **7/2**[2]
3-53 **2** *3* **Dutch Art Dealer**[7] 4147 3-8-13 **77** JimCrowley 9 81
(Paul Cole) *trckd ldrs: rdn and n.m.r over 1f out: sn ev ch: styd on same pce ins fnl f* **9/4**[1]
-135 **3** *2* **Pactolus (IRE)**[21] 3672 3-8-10 **74** AdamBeschizza 4 73
(Stuart Williams) *hld up: hdwy and nt clr run over 1f out: styd on to go 3rd wl ins fnl f: nt trble ldrs* **11/1**
6000 **4** *1 ¼* **Mawfoor (IRE)**[13] 3980 3-9-7 **85** (b[1]) PaulHanagan 5 81
(Brian Meehan) *a.p: rdn whn hmpd over 2f out: ev ch over 1f out: no ex ins fnl f* **12/1**

-052 **5** 1/2 **Constantine**[15] 3882 3-9-3 **81** ... KieranO'Neill 2 75
(Richard Hannon) *sn led: racd keenly: rdn: edgd and hdd over 1f out: no ex ins fnl f* **16/1**

025 **6** *shd* **Pennine Warrior**[39] 3067 3-8-3 **72** ...(p) MatthewHopkins(5) 8 66
(Scott Dixon) *trckd ldrs: plld hrd: rdn and hung rt fr over 2f out: ev ch over 1f out: no ex fnl f* **20/1**

1- **7** *45* **About Turn**[367] 4379 3-9-4 **82** ... WilliamBuick 1
(Charlie Appleby) *hld up: wknd 2f out: eased* **4/1**[3]

-103 **8** 1/2 **Battle Command (USA)**[21] 3672 3-9-1 **79** ... MartinHarley 7
(Peter Chapple-Hyam) *chsd ldr: rdn: edgd rt and ev ch over 1f out: wknd and eased ins fnl f* **6/1**

1m 26.59s (0.89) **Going Correction** +0.125s/f (Good) **8** Ran SP% **113.9**
Speed ratings (Par 102): **99,95,93,91,91 91,39,39**
CSF £11.72 CT £76.01 TOTE £3.30: £1.30, £1.20, £3.90; EX 11.00 Trifecta £91.70.
**Owner** The Brave Partnership **Bred** Tally-Ho Stud **Trained** East Ilsley, Berks

**FOCUS**
Some unexposed/progressive types in this handicap. The form is rated around the runner-up.

## 4405 OAKMONT CONSTRUCTION CONDITIONS STKS 5f
**7:20** (7:20) (Class 3) 3-Y-O+ **£8,715** (£2,609; £1,304; £652) **Stalls** High

Form RPR

-406 **1** **Move In Time**[6] 4215 6-8-9 **102** ... JimCrowley 6 106
(David O'Meara) *mde all: rdn over 1f out: r.o wl: eased nr fin* **13/8**[1]

5021 **2** 3 1/2 **Swiss Cross**[15] 3876 7-8-9 **89** ...(bt) MartinHarley 3 93
(Phil McEntee) *trckd wnr: ev ch wl over 1f out: sn rdn: styd on same pce ins fnl f* **6/1**[3]

11-0 **3** 4 1/2 **Strategical (USA)**[34] 3245 3-8-6 **102** ow1 ... WilliamBuick 2 77
(Charlie Appleby) *trckd ldrs: rdn and edgd lft over 1f out: wknd fnl f* **13/8**[1]

0-06 **4** *shd* **Simple Magic (IRE)**[34] 3245 3-8-0 **92** ... NickyMackay 5 71
(John Gosden) *s.i.s: hld up: rdn and hung rt over 1f out: sn wknd* **5/1**[2]

58.63s (-0.47) **Going Correction** +0.125s/f (Good)
**WFA** 3 from 6yo+ 4lb **4** Ran SP% **107.1**
Speed ratings (Par 107): **108,102,95,95**
CSF £10.75 TOTE £3.10; EX 10.70 Trifecta £15.30.
**Owner** A Turton, J Blackburn & R Bond **Bred** Bond Thoroughbred Corporation **Trained** Nawton, N Yorks

**FOCUS**
A disappointing turnout for what is often a good-quality sprint. It became even less competitive when both 3yos, Strategical and Simple Magic, ran some way below their capabilities. The winner is rated close to his best.

## 4406 32RED H'CAP (JOCKEY CLUB GRASSROOTS FLAT SPRINT SERIES QUALIFIER) 6f
**7:50** (7:50) (Class 4) (0-80,80) 3-Y-O+ **£5,175** (£1,540; £769; £384) **Stalls** High

Form RPR

0623 **1** **Light From Mars**[7] 4154 9-9-5 **80** ...(p) MikeyEnnis(7) 4 88
(Ronald Harris) *a.p: chsd ldr over 1f out: rdn and edgd lft ins fnl f: r.o to ld nr fin* **7/1**[3]

6626 **2** *nk* **Atlantis Crossing (IRE)**[11] 4024 5-9-0 **68** ... PatCosgrave 9 75
(Jim Boyle) *hld up: hdwy over 2f out: led over 1f out: sn rdn: hdd nr fin* **9/1**

602 **3** *1* **Vincentti (IRE)**[9] 4078 4-9-10 **78** ... AdamKirby 8 82
(Ronald Harris) *s.i.s: hld up: pushed along over 2f out: rdn and r.o wl ins fnl f: nt rch ldrs* **8/1**

3-10 **4** 1 1/4 **Tychaios**[15] 3887 4-8-11 **65** ... RyanMoore 7 65
(Stuart Williams) *chsd ldrs: rdn and ev ch over 1f out: styd on same pce ins fnl f* **9/2**[1]

001 **5** 2 1/2 **Diamond Lady**[32] 3305 3-9-7 **80** ... FrederikTylicki 6 71
(William Stone) *mid-div: hdwy over 2f out: rdn over 1f out: no ex fnl f* **5/1**[2]

00-0 **6** *nk* **Rocket Rob (IRE)**[16] 3854 8-9-7 **75** ... ChrisCatlin 11 66
(Willie Musson) *hld up: racd keenly: hdwy over 1f out: no ex fnl f* **16/1**

1502 **7** 1 1/4 **Powerful Pierre**[101] 1368 7-9-5 **78** ...(b) TobyAtkinson(5) 1 65
(Noel Quinlan) *sn chsng ldr: rdn and ev ch over 1f out: wknd ins fnl f* **33/1**

0265 **8** 2 1/4 **Commanche**[8] 4128 5-9-5 **78** ... MarcMonaghan(5) 2 58
(Chris Dwyer) *prom: rdn over 2f out: wknd fnl f* **5/1**[2]

0233 **9** 1 1/4 **Putin (IRE)**[4] 4262 6-9-1 **69** ...(bt) MartinHarley 10 45
(Phil McEntee) *broke wl and sn clr: rdn and hdd over 1f out: wknd ins fnl f* **8/1**

4230 **10** 2 3/4 **Jay Bee Blue**[11] 4024 5-9-6 **74** ...(bt) JamesDoyle 5 41
(Sean Curran) *hld up: rdn over 2f out: wknd over 1f out* **9/1**

1m 12.59s (0.09) **Going Correction** +0.125s/f (Good)
**WFA** 3 from 4yo+ 5lb **10** Ran SP% **115.1**
Speed ratings (Par 105): **104,103,102,100,97 96,95,92,90,86**
CSF £67.40 CT £529.07 TOTE £6.30: £2.40, £2.90, £2.80; EX 101.00 Trifecta £1283.90 Part won..
**Owner** Mrs N Macauley **Bred** Harts Farm And Stud **Trained** Earlswood, Monmouths
■ A first Flat winner for Mikey Ennis.

**FOCUS**
An exposed bunch, most of whom find winning difficult and not form to spend a great deal of time over. The form is rated around the runner-up.

## 4407 ALL NEW 32REDSPORT.COM MAIDEN STKS 1m
**8:25** (8:27) (Class 5) 3-Y-O **£3,881** (£1,155; £577; £288) **Stalls** High

Form RPR

**1** **Rapprochement (IRE)** 3-9-5 0 ...[1] AdamKirby 15 96
(Charlie Appleby) *mde all: racd keenly: rdn clr fr over 1f out: easily* **11/2**

**2** *11* **Momayyaz (IRE)** 3-9-0 0 ... FrederikTylicki 7 66+
(Saeed bin Suroor) *hld up: rdn over 2f out: hdwy and nt clr run over 1f out: styd on to go 2nd nr fin: no ch w wnr* **14/1**

**3** *shd* **Glorious Sun** 3-9-5 0 ... HayleyTurner 16 70
(Ed Walker) *chsd wnr over 4f: remained handy: rdn to go 2nd again over 1f out: sn outpcd* **16/1**

552- **4** *1* **Soviet Courage (IRE)**[260] 7646 3-9-5 76 ... RyanMoore 2 68
(William Haggas) *hld up: hdwy over 3f out: sn rdn: styd on same pce fr over 1f out* **7/4**[1]

**5** 1 1/4 **Lord Empire (IRE)** 3-9-5 0 ... JimCrowley 9 65+
(David Simcock) *prom: rdn over 2f out: styd on same pce fr over 1f out* **33/1**

2 **6** 1 1/2 **Dreaming Beauty**[35] 3184 3-9-0 0 ... JamesDoyle 5 57
(Jeremy Noseda) *prom: rdn over 2f out: wknd fnl f* **4/1**[2]

0 **7** *nk* **Tasaaboq**[28] 3432 3-9-5 0 ...(t) PaddyAspell 14 61
(Phil McEntee) *trckd ldrs: wnt 2nd over 3f out: rdn over 1f out: hung lft and wknd fnl f* **100/1**

**8** 2 1/4 **Gold Run** 3-9-5 0 ... HarryBentley 1 56
(Olly Stevens) *hld up: rdn and hung lft over 1f out: n.d* **66/1**

**9** 1 1/4 **Frederic** 3-9-5 0 ... LemosdeSouza 12 53
(Luca Cumani) *s.i.s: hld up: hdwy over 3f out: wknd over 1f out* **33/1**

**10** *5* **Royal Battalion** 3-9-5 0 ... JamieSpencer 11 42
(Olly Stevens) *s.s: hld up: swtchd rt over 1f out: nvr on terms* **5/1**[3]

**11** *2* **Absolute (IRE)** 3-9-5 0 ... MartinHarley 10 37
(Marco Botti) *s.i.s: hld up: rdn over 2f out: sn wknd* **16/1**

0-P **12** *9* **Fennann**[46] 2850 3-9-5 0 ...(p) AdamBeschizza 3 16
(Gary Moore) *s.s: sn pushed along in rr: rdn and wknd over 2f out* **100/1**

1m 39.21s (-0.79) **Going Correction** +0.125s/f (Good) **12** Ran SP% **116.2**
Speed ratings (Par 100): **108,97,96,95,94 93,92,90,89,84 82,73**
CSF £75.32 TOTE £8.10: £2.40, £4.60, £2.90; EX 60.60 Trifecta £991.60.
**Owner** Godolphin **Bred** Darley **Trained** Newmarket, Suffolk

**FOCUS**
Most likely this was not a strong maiden for the track and, winner aside, not many shaped with too much promise. Tricky form to pin down.

## 4408 MARITIME CARGO SERVICES H'CAP 7f
**8:55** (8:55) (Class 5) (0-75,75) 4-Y-O+ **£3,881** (£1,155; £577; £288) **Stalls** High

Form RPR

2134 **1** **Athletic**[9] 4078 5-8-7 **66** ...(v) DannyBrock(5) 4 81+
(Andrew Reid) *s.s: racd centre: hld up: hdwy to ld that trio over 1f out: led overall ins fnl f: qcknd clr* **11/4**[1]

1361 **2** *7* **Botanist**[13] 3971 7-8-7 **61** ... JimmyQuinn 6 58
(Shaun Harris) *racd towards stands' side: chsd ldr tl led overall over 1f out: rdn and hdd ins fnl f: sn hung lft and btn* **9/2**[3]

3310 **3** *6* **Sheikh The Reins (IRE)**[21] 3646 5-9-2 **70** ...(v) RobertHavlin 9 51
(John Best) *racd alone far side: up w the pce: rdn and ev ch over 1f out: wknd fnl f* **8/1**

30-5 **4** 1 1/4 **Lunette (IRE)**[27] 3476 4-9-4 **72** ... JimCrowley 8 50
(Ralph Beckett) *racd centre: led that trio tl rdn and hdd over 1f out: wknd fnl f* **11/4**[1]

3-00 **5** *9* **Duke Of Grazeon (IRE)**[79] 1881 4-9-0 **68** ... FrederikTylicki 7 23
(Mrs Ilka Gansera-Leveque) *racd centre: chsd ldr: rdn over 2f out: wknd over 1f out* **4/1**[2]

3325 **6** 1 1/2 **Amosite**[37] 3125 8-9-2 **70** ...(v) HayleyTurner 1 21
(J R Jenkins) *racd towards stands' side: led overall tl rdn: hdd & wknd over 1f out* **11/1**

1m 25.63s (-0.07) **Going Correction** +0.125s/f (Good) **6** Ran SP% **111.0**
Speed ratings (Par 103): **105,97,90,88,78 76**
CSF £14.96 CT £81.68 TOTE £3.80: £2.30, £1.90; EX 12.90 Trifecta £123.40.
**Owner** A S Reid **Bred** A S Reid **Trained** Mill Hill, London NW7

**FOCUS**
A modest heat in which the field raced across the track. There seemed plenty of pace on. The winner is rated in line with his AW form.
T/Plt: £291.30 to a £1 stake. Pool: £66486.87 - 166.60 winning tickets T/Qpdt: £131.40 to a £1 stake. Pool: £5061.16 - 28.50 winning tickets CR

# 4129 NOTTINGHAM (L-H)
Friday, July 18

**OFFICIAL GOING: Good to firm (8.5)**
Wind: Light, half-behind Weather: Fine and dry

## 4409 IRISH STALLION FARMS EBF MAIDEN STKS 6f 15y
**1:50** (1:51) (Class 5) 2-Y-O **£3,234** (£962; £481; £240) **Stalls** Centre

Form RPR

5 **1** **Inniscastle Lad**[20] 3728 2-9-5 0 ... DougieCostello 9 81
(William Muir) *cl up on outer: slt ld 1/2-way: pushed along and hdd narrowly wl over 1f out: sn rdn: drvn to ld last 100yds: kpt on wl* **10/1**

3 **2** *hd* **Cool Strutter (IRE)**[8] 4109 2-9-5 0 ... JamieSpencer 1 80
(Richard Hannon) *cl up: slt ld wl over 1f out: sn rdn: drvn and edgd lft ins fnl f: hdd last 100yds: no ex towards fin* **11/8**[1]

**3** 4 1/2 **Toocoolforschool (IRE)** 2-9-5 0 ... BenCurtis 3 67
(K R Burke) *dwlt and in rr: sn swtchd lft and hdwy to trck ldrs 1/2-way: effrt 2f out: sn rdn and kpt on same pce appr fnl f* **7/1**[3]

**4** *1* **Hatchet Harry (IRE)** 2-9-5 0 ... JFEgan 5 64
(David Evans) *a.p: cl up over 2f out: sn rdn and ev ch: drvn and wknd appr fnl f* **16/1**

2 **5** 3/4 **La Estatua**[16] 3847 2-9-0 0 ... JimmyQuinn 8 57
(James Tate) *chsd ldrs: pushed along over 2f out: sn rdn and one pce* **11/4**[2]

66 **6** 1 3/4 **Black Granite (IRE)**[37] 3119 2-9-5 0 ... RobertHavlin 6 56
(Jeremy Noseda) *in rr: hdwy over 2f out: sn rdn along and kpt on same pce fnl f* **20/1**

**7** *4* **Lopito De Vega (IRE)** 2-9-5 0 ... DaleSwift 4 44
(James Given) *t.k.h: slt ld: hdd 1/2-way: sn rdn along and wknd* **50/1**

0 **8** 1 3/4 **Presto Boy**[22] 3626 2-9-5 0 ... ShaneKelly 2 39
(James Fanshawe) *a towards rr* **20/1**

1m 12.74s (-1.96) **Going Correction** -0.475s/f (Firm) **8** Ran SP% **107.7**
Speed ratings (Par 94): **94,93,87,86,85 83,77,75**
CSF £21.45 TOTE £11.40: £2.70, £1.10, £3.20; EX 25.10 Trifecta £221.30.
**Owner** The Lavelle Family **Bred** G Doyle & Lord Margadale **Trained** Lambourn, Berks

**FOCUS**
Races on Outer track and rail out 2m on home bend increased distances on Round course by 6yds. The ground was officially described as good to firm for the first of seven races. The whole course had been watered. The front pair pulled clear in this maiden, of which Dream Ahead is the standout winner in recent years.

## 4410 NOTTINGHAM RACECOURSE SUPPORTS NOTTINGHAM MEANS BUSINESS NURSERY H'CAP 6f 15y
**2:20** (2:20) (Class 5) 2-Y-O **£3,234** (£962; £481; £240) **Stalls** Centre

Form RPR

000 **1** **Alpine Affair**[36] 3136 2-8-12 **66** ...(b[1]) MartinLane 7 77
(Brian Meehan) *trckd ldrs: hdwy over 2f out: rdn to ld appr fnl f: sn clr* **7/2**[3]

0464 **2** 4 1/2 **Lady Zodiac (IRE)**[14] 3937 2-8-0 **54** oh3 ... AndrewMullen 8 51
(Tim Pitt) *wnt bdly rt s: sn chsng ldr: hdwy to ld wl over 2f out: rdn over 1f out: hdd appr fnl f: sn drvn and kpt on: no ch w wnr* **16/1**

0431 **3** 1 1/4 **Baileys Pursuit**[15] 3894 2-8-8 **62** ... JimmyQuinn 6 55
(Christine Dunnett) *hld up: hdwy 1/2-way: chsd ldrs 2f out: sn rdn and kpt on fnl f* **16/1**

433 **4** 1 1/4 **Simply Magic (IRE)**[45] 2859 2-8-13 **67** ... KierenFallon 4 57
(Richard Hannon) *in tch: niggled along bef 1/2-way: rdn over 2f out: drvn wl over 1f out and sn one pce* **3/1**[2]

050 5 shd **Verchild Lad (IRE)**[48] 2756 2-8-2 **56** ow2.................... RoystonFfrench 9 47+
(David Evans) *carried bdly rt and hmpd s: towards rr: hdwy over 2f out: sn rdn along and plugged on one pce fnl f* **12/1**

5533 6 11 **Emef Rock (IRE)**[18] 3779 2-9-2 **70**.............................. RobertWinston 5 38
(Mick Channon) *trckd ldrs: rdn along wl over 2f out: sn outpcd* **11/4**[1]

403 7 9 **Elizabeth Ernest**[22] 3606 2-8-1 **60**.................................. CamHardie(5) 1
(Richard Fahey) *sn led: pushed along 1/2-way: hdd wl over 2f out: sn rdn and wknd* **12/1**

3444 8 4 ½ **Celestial Vision (USA)**[14] 3922 2-9-7 **75**...................... StephenCraine 2
(Tom Dascombe) *awkward s and s.i.s: a in rr* **7/1**

1m 13.01s (-1.69) **Going Correction** -0.475s/f (Firm) 8 Ran SP% **113.5**
Speed ratings (Par 94): **92,86,84,82,82 67,55,49**
CSF £55.17 CT £784.59 TOTE £6.90: £2.30, £6.10, £3.20; EX 88.80 Trifecta £1062.80.
**Owner** Longview Stud & Bloodstock Ltd **Bred** Longview Stud & Bloodstock Ltd **Trained** Manton, Wilts

**FOCUS**
The pace was sound.

## 4411 PAUL SMITH FASHION H'CAP 6f 15y
2:55 (2:56) (Class 5) (0-70,69) 3-Y-O £3,234 (£962; £481; £240) Stalls Centre

Form RPR

3400 1 **Inciting Incident (IRE)**[21] 3669 3-9-3 **65**.................(p[1]) RobertWinston 8 75
(Ed McMahon) *qckly away and swtchd rt to stands' rail: mde all: rdn clr over 1f out: drvn and kpt on wl towards fin* **4/1**[2]

5114 2 ¾ **Shades Of Silk**[29] 3406 3-8-10 **58**.................................... DaleSwift 12 66+
(James Given) *racd nr stands' rail: trckd ldrs: hdwy over 1f out: rdn to chse wnr and hung bdly lft jst ins fnl f: kpt on* **10/1**

10-0 3 3 ½ **Alderley**[20] 3733 3-9-4 **66**............................................... FrederikTylicki 9 62
(Martyn Meade) *trckd wnr nr stands' rail: rdn along wl over 1f out: drvn and sltly hmpd ins fnl f: sn one pce* **20/1**

0500 4 nk **He's My Boy (IRE)**[13] 3972 3-8-11 **59**............................(v[1]) ShaneKelly 4 54
(James Fanshawe) *trckd ldrs towards stands' rail: effrt wl over 1f out: rdn and no imp ent fnl f* **14/1**

0-34 5 1 ¼ **Shilla (IRE)**[17] 3817 3-9-7 **69**...................................... FergusSweeney 10 60+
(Henry Candy) *racd nr stands' rail: in rr: effrt 2f out: n.m.r wl over 1f out: sn swtchd lft and rdn: kpt on fnl f: nrst fin* **6/1**[3]

-230 6 ½ **Royal Encounter**[46] 2847 3-9-3 **65**.................................. JamieSpencer 6 55
(Ed Vaughan) *racd towards stands' rail: hld up in tch: effrt over 2f out: sn rdn and n.d* **7/1**

-064 7 1 ¾ **Pensax Lad (IRE)**[13] 3972 3-9-7 **69**................................ SteveDrowne 7 53
(Ronald Harris) *trckd ldrs nr stands' rail: effrt 2f out: sn rdn and wknd over 1f out* **8/1**

5030 8 nk **Look Here's Al**[21] 3650 3-9-3 **65**................................ RoystonFfrench 11 48
(Andrew Hollinshead) *racd nr stands' rail: trckd ldrs: rdn along over 2f out: drvn and wknd over 1f out* **10/1**

1002 9 7 **Le Laitier (FR)**[8] 4131 3-9-6 **68**........................................ KierenFallon 1 29
(Scott Dixon) *racd centre: chsd ldrs: rdn along over 2f out: sn btn* **3/1**[1]

0060 10 ½ **Walta (IRE)**[21] 3650 3-8-6 **57**..............................(b) AshleyMorgan(3) 13 16
(Roy Bowring) *dwlt: racd towards stands' rail and in rr: swtchd lft and effrt over 2f out: sn rdn and nvr a factor* **20/1**

0000 11 9 **Hickster (IRE)**[29] 3405 3-8-9 **57**.......................................(vt) JimmyQuinn 5
(Roy Bowring) *racd towards centre: in tch: rdn along 1/2-way: sn outpcd and bhd* **33/1**

0606 12 29 **False Witness (IRE)**[3] 4297 3-9-0 **62**........................(b[1]) AdrianNicholls 2
(David Nicholls) *wnt rt and awkward s: racd towards centre: a in rr: bhd and eased fnl 2f* **33/1**

1m 12.04s (-2.66) **Going Correction** -0.475s/f (Firm) 12 Ran SP% **123.2**
Speed ratings (Par 100): **98,97,92,91,90 89,87,86,77,76 64,26**
CSF £43.39 CT £727.54 TOTE £5.40: £1.80, £2.60, £6.30; EX 60.10 Trifecta £1742.50.
**Owner** The W H O Society **Bred** Yeomanstown Stud **Trained** Lichfield, Staffs

**FOCUS**
A competitive 3yo sprint handicap, although none of the runners looked to be progressing rapidly coming into this. Nothing got into it from off the pace. the winner is rated back to his best.

## 4412 GATELEY H'CAP 5f 13y
3:30 (3:30) (Class 2) (0-100,95) 3-Y-O+ £12,938 (£3,850; £1,924; £962) Stalls Centre

Form RPR

1034 1 **Taurus Twins**[11] 4027 8-8-12 **81**.................................(b) RobertWinston 9 91
(Richard Price) *qckly away and sn swtchd rt to stands' rail racd alone after and sn clr: rdn over 1f out: drvn ins fnl f: kpt on wl towards fin* **12/1**

4602 2 nk **Megaleka**[8] 4128 4-8-10 **82**.............................................. RobertTart(3) 6 91+
(Alan Bailey) *towards rr: pushed along and hdwy over 2f out: chsd ldrs over 1f out: rdn to chal ent fnl f: sn hung bdly lft to far rail: kpt on: jst hld* **7/1**[3]

0041 3 1 ¾ **Forest Edge (IRE)**[13] 3969 5-9-6 **89**.................................(b) JFEgan 1 92
(David Evans) *in tch on outer: hdwy over 2f out: rdn over 1f out: sltly hmpd ins fnl f: kpt on same pce* **10/1**

0002 4 ¾ **Inxile (IRE)**[29] 3395 9-9-4 **87**.......................................(p) AdrianNicholls 10 87
(David Nicholls) *prom on stands' rail whn hmpd after 1f: sn swtchd lft to centre and prom: rdn along wl over 1f out: drvn appr fnl f and kpt on same pce* **22/1**

1466 5 1 ½ **Doctor Parkes**[14] 3927 8-9-1 **84**.................................... FrederikTylicki 4 79
(Stuart Williams) *chsd ldrs: rdn along wl over 1f out: one pce appr fnl f* **7/1**[3]

00 6 shd **Secret Asset (IRE)**[27] 3452 9-9-12 **95**.............................(p) RobertHavlin 7 89
(Jane Chapple-Hyam) *towards rr centre: hdwy wl over 1f out: sn rdn and kpt on fnl f: nrst fin* **10/1**

1122 7 ¾ **Random Success (IRE)**[14] 3920 4-8-2 **76** oh4.............. CamHardie(5) 2 67+
(Roger Charlton) *hmpd s and in rr: rdn and sme hdwy wl over 1f out: n.d* **9/2**[2]

4001 8 1 ½ **Gladiatrix**[11] 4027 5-9-8 **91** 6ex..........................................(b) KierenFallon 3 77
(Rod Millman) *wnt lft s: a towards rr* **12/1**

0-10 9 nk **Barracuda Boy (IRE)**[27] 3452 4-9-12 **95**......................(p) HayleyTurner 5 80
(Tom Dascombe) *chsd ldrs: rdn along over 2f out: sn wknd* **10/3**[1]

5-00 10 13 **Excel's Beauty**[34] 3219 3-9-2 **89**....................................(p) JamieSpencer 8 26
(James Tate) *prom: rdn along over 2f out: sn edgd rt and wknd qckly: bhd and eased fnl f* **8/1**

58.05s (-3.45) **Going Correction** -0.475s/f (Firm) course record
**WFA** 3 from 4yo+ 4lb 10 Ran SP% **115.3**
Speed ratings (Par 109): **108,107,104,103,101 100,99,97,96,76**
CSF £92.32 CT £901.11 TOTE £16.50: £3.00, £2.60, £5.70; EX 102.30 Trifecta £657.80.
**Owner** G E Amey & G D Bailey **Bred** G E Amey **Trained** Ullingswick, H'fords

**FOCUS**
Not a strong contest for the prize money, with the top weight rated 5lb below the ceiling. Another to make all on the rail. The winner is rated to his best, but there are obvious doubts.

## 4413 JIM TAYLOR MEMORIAL MAIDEN FILLIES' STKS (BOBIS RACE) 1m 2f 50y
4:05 (4:07) (Class 5) 3-Y-O £3,234 (£962; £481; £240) Stalls Low

Form RPR

3-30 1 **Momentus (IRE)**[42] 2960 3-9-0 99................................ FergusSweeney 3 95+
(David Simcock) *mde all: pushed clr over 2f out: easily* **1/2**[1]

0- 2 4 ½ **Allegation (FR)**[336] 5472 3-9-0 0.......................................... TedDurcan 4 79
(David Lanigan) *trckd ldrs: hdwy 3f out: rdn to chse wnr fr wl over 1f out: kpt on fnl f: no ch w wnr* **33/1**

3 ½ **Long View (IRE)** 3-9-0 0.............................................(v[1]) ShaneKelly 2 78
(Sir Michael Stoute) *trckd ldrs on inner: pushed along and outpcd 3f out: swtchd rt over 2f out: kpt on appr fnl f* **10/1**

4 8 **Bright Beacon** 3-9-0 0................................................... MartinLane 1 63
(Charlie Appleby) *towards rr: hdwy over 4f out: effrt to chse ldrs 3f out: sn rdn and one pce* **5/1**[2]

5 1 ½ **Sona** 3-9-0 0.................................................................. RobertHavlin 8 60
(John Gosden) *dwlt and in rr: j. path after 3f: pushed along and green over 3f out: sme late hdwy* **7/1**[3]

4 6 2 ¼ **Emily Yeats**[36] 3142 3-9-0 0............................................ MartinDwyer 6 56
(Paul Webber) *cl up: rdn along over 3f out: drvn over 2f out: sn wknd* **25/1**

0 7 26 **Endless Seas**[14] 3925 3-9-0 0.......................................... AndrewMullen 5 6
(Michael Appleby) *chsd ldrs: rdn along 5f out: sn lost pl and bhd* **50/1**

2m 10.64s (-3.66) **Going Correction** -0.475s/f (Firm) 7 Ran SP% **113.7**
Speed ratings (Par 97): **95,91,91,84,83 81,60**
CSF £25.79 TOTE £1.50: £1.10, £14.90; EX 26.70 Trifecta £96.60.
**Owner** Andrew Whitlock & Mark Hitchcroft **Bred** Lorgnette Bloodstock **Trained** Newmarket, Suffolk

**FOCUS**
A strong 3yo fillies' maiden. The winner stood out on pre-race form and was value for 8l.

## 4414 COMPLIANCE SURVEYS ONLINE H&S TRAINING H'CAP 1m 75y
4:35 (4:36) (Class 4) (0-85,84) 3-Y-O+ £5,175 (£1,540; £769; £384) Stalls Centre

Form RPR

5003 1 **Shahdaroba (IRE)**[20] 3703 4-9-13 **83**..........................(p) JamieSpencer 5 91
(Micky Hammond) *set gd pce: pushed along over 4f out: rdn along and hdd 2f out: cl up and drvn ent fnl f: kpt on gamely to ld again last 50yds* **4/1**[3]

4102 2 shd **Self Employed**[14] 3917 7-9-6 **76**.................................... RobertWinston 6 83
(Garry Woodward) *sn trcking wnr: smooth hdwy and cl up 3f out: slt ld 2f out: sn rdn: drvn and edgd lft ins fnl f: hdd last 50yds: kpt on: jst hld* **3/1**[2]

4244 3 4 **Showpiece**[27] 3480 3-8-13 **82**........................................(b[1]) CamHardie(5) 1 78
(Richard Hannon) *trckd ldrs: hdwy 3f out: shkn up 2f out: sn rdn and no imp appr fnl f* **6/4**[1]

4242 4 1 **Caramack**[18] 3782 4-9-7 **77**.............................................. FergusSweeney 4 73
(Richard Lee) *trckd ldng pair: effrt over 3f out: rdn along over 2f out: drvn over 1f out and kpt on one pce* **10/1**

3-62 5 7 **Black Dave (IRE)**[7] 4154 4-8-10 **66**.......................................... JFEgan 3 45
(David Evans) *t.k.h: hld up: a in rr: b.b.v* **5/1**

1m 44.93s (-4.07) **Going Correction** -0.475s/f (Firm)
**WFA** 3 from 4yo+ 8lb 5 Ran SP% **110.8**
Speed ratings (Par 105): **101,100,96,95,88**
CSF £16.18 TOTE £3.80: £1.90, £2.50; EX 16.20 Trifecta £26.30.
**Owner** Barlow Racing Partnership **Bred** Tinnakill Bloodstock & Forenaghts Stud **Trained** Middleham, N Yorks

**FOCUS**
A run-of-the-mill handicap for the grade, featuring a good tussle in the final 1f. The winner is rated to this year's best.

## 4415 WATCH RACING UK ON CHANNEL 432 H'CAP 1m 75y
5:05 (5:05) (Class 6) (0-65,64) 3-Y-O+ £2,045 (£603; £302) Stalls Centre

Form RPR

0-01 1 **Hostile Fire (IRE)**[85] 1683 3-9-6 **64**.................................... JamieSpencer 1 76+
(Ed de Giles) *dwlt and hld up in rr: hdwy 3f out: swtchd lft over 2f out and sn trcking ldrs: n.m.r and swtchd rt to outer over 1f out: rdn to ld ent fnl f: sn edgd lft: styd on* **7/2**[1]

4023 2 1 ¾ **Greyemkay**[8] 4105 6-8-5 **46**.......................................... DanielMuscutt(5) 11 53
(Richard Price) *trckd ldrs: hdwy 4f out: sn chsng ldrs: cl up over 2f out: sn rdn and ev ch: drvn ent fnl f and kpt on same pce* **7/1**

5130 3 ¾ **Dutch Lady**[17] 3828 3-9-1 **59**.......................................... RobertHavlin 3 62
(John Holt) *trckd ldng pair: hdwy over 3f out: led over 2f out: rdn wl over 1f out: drvn and hdd ent fnl f: kpt on same pce* **14/1**

4352 4 2 ¼ **Living Leader**[7] 4153 5-9-13 **63**......................................(p) PaddyAspell 5 63
(Grace Harris) *trckd ldrs: effrt 3f out: rdn along and sltly outpcd over 2f out: swtchd rt and drvn over 1f out: kpt on one pce fnl f* **4/1**[2]

0133 5 2 **Caledonia Laird**[22] 3618 3-9-1 **59**.................................... MartinDwyer 7 53
(Jo Hughes) *midfield: hdwy 4f out: trckd ldrs 3f out: effrt 2f out: sn rdn and hld whn n.m.r over 1f out: sn one pce* **7/1**

1250 6 2 ½ **Khajaaly (IRE)**[29] 3402 7-8-12 **55**...................(vt) AlistairRawlinson(7) 6 45
(Michael Appleby) *midfield: effrt 3f out: sn rdn along and plugged on one pce* **11/2**[3]

5200 7 ½ **Master Of Song**[13] 3971 7-8-12 **51**........................(b) AshleyMorgan(3) 14 40
(Roy Bowring) *cl up: slt ld 3f out: sn hdd and rdn: grad wknd fnl 2f* **25/1**

-500 8 2 **Assembly**[16] 3848 4-9-10 **60**.......................................... DougieCostello 2 44
(Mark Rimell) *dwlt and in rr: sme hdwy over 3f out: sn rdn along and n.d* **33/1**

-656 9 hd **Tony Hollis**[34] 3242 6-8-11 **47**........................................(t[1]) AndrewMullen 8 31
(Michael Appleby) *set gd pce: rdn along and hdd 3f out: sn wknd* **12/1**

02-6 10 3 ½ **Flying Applause**[198] 7 9-9-0 **50**.................................(b) JimmyQuinn 9 25
(Roy Bowring) *a towards rr* **22/1**

/000 11 7 **Audacious**[10] 3155 6-9-2 **55**.................................... NataliaGemelova(3) 12 14
(Charles Pogson) *chsd ldrs: hdwy 1/2-way: rdn along over 3f out: sn wknd* **25/1**

-240 12 1 ¼ **Aureolin Gulf**[148] 676 5-8-9 **45**.................................... RoystonFfrench 10 2
(Andrew Hollinshead) *t.k.h: a towards rr* **40/1**

0064 13 31 **Woolston Ferry (IRE)**[9] 4073 8-9-10 **60**.................(b[1]) FergusSweeney 16
(Henry Candy) *dwlt: a in rr: bhd and eased wl over 1f out* **14/1**

1m 44.34s (-4.66) **Going Correction** -0.475s/f (Firm)
**WFA** 3 from 4yo+ 8lb 13 Ran SP% **121.1**
Speed ratings (Par 101): **104,102,101,99,97 94,94,92,92,88 81,80,49**
CSF £26.61 CT £323.57 TOTE £3.90: £1.70, £3.10, £4.20; EX 33.10 Trifecta £455.50.
**Owner** Ali Mortazavi **Bred** Thomas Hassett **Trained** Ledbury, H'fords

**FOCUS**
An open handicap to close. The pace was strong. The winner is value for further, with the next two to form.

T/Plt: £509.10 to a £1 stake. Pool: £45541.37 - 65.30 winning tickets T/Qpdt: £49.50 to a £1 stake. Pool: £4349.35 - 65.00 winning tickets JR

# 4057 PONTEFRACT (L-H)

Friday, July 18

**OFFICIAL GOING: Good to firm (good in places; 7.8)**

Wind: light 1/2 against Weather: fine

## 4416 COUNTRYWIDE FREIGHT MAIDEN AUCTION STKS (BOBIS RACE) 6f

**6:30** (6:31) (Class 4) 2-Y-O **£4,528** (£1,347; £673; £336) **Stalls** Low

Form RPR

1 **George Dryden (IRE)** 2-8-13 0 PJMcDonald 7 94+
(Ann Duffield) *trckd ldrs: led 2f out: styd on strly to go clr fnl f: impressive* **8/1**[3]

20 **2** 6 **Caprior Bere (FR)**[27] 3448 2-8-13 0 BenCurtis 4 76
(K R Burke) *trckd ldrs: t.k.h: chsd wnr over 1f out: kpt on same pce* **5/4**[1]

50 **3** 3 **Summer Stroll (IRE)**[21] 3648 2-8-6 0 ow1 SamJames(3) 8 63
(David O'Meara) *chsd ldrs: kpt on one pce to take modest 3rd last 50yds* **50/1**

42 **4** 1 1/2 **Oregon Gift**[10] 4044 2-8-12 0 MichaelJMMurphy(3) 5 65
(Mark Johnston) *led: hdd 2f out: wknd last 100yds* **4/1**[2]

**5** 2 **Red Harry (IRE)** 2-9-1 0 AndrewElliott 1 59+
(Tom Tate) *s.i.s: mid-div: outpcd over 2f out: hdwy over 1f out: kpt on* **25/1**

44 **6** nk **Black Pudding (IRE)**[13] 3947 2-8-4 0 RowanScott(7) 10 54
(Ann Duffield) *chsd ldrs: outpcd over 2f out: kpt on fnl f* **50/1**

4 **7** hd **Stolen Story (IRE)**[11] 4025 2-9-4 0 KierenFallon 2 60
(George Margarson) *s.i.s: in rr and sn drvn along: eged lft and sme hdwy appr fnl f: nvr on terms* **4/1**[2]

0 **8** 7 **Youonlyliveonce (IRE)**[27] 3481 2-8-8 0 JoeDoyle(7) 11 36
(John Quinn) *racd wd: chsd ldrs: lost pl over 2f out* **66/1**

03 **9** 1 1/4 **Cisco Boy**[44] 2895 2-9-1 0 DavidAllan 9 32
(Tim Easterby) *mid-div: drvn and lost pl over 2f out* **16/1**

5 **10** 2 1/4 **Proud Of You (IRE)**[45] 2866 2-8-10 0 ShelleyBirkett(5) 3 26
(Nigel Tinkler) *s.i.s: in rr: bhd fnl 2f* **16/1**

1m 17.99s (1.09) **Going Correction** +0.25s/f (Good) **10 Ran SP% 116.6**
Speed ratings (Par 96): **102,94,90,88,85 84,84,75,73,70**
CSF £18.14 TOTE £10.80: £2.80, £1.10, £9.10; EX 29.60 Trifecta £792.90.
**Owner** S Bradley **Bred** Ms Nicola Kent **Trained** Constable Burton, N Yorks

**FOCUS**
A dry, warm 24 hours although a shade overcast. Few got into it after a lack of early pace and while probably ordinary form, the winner looks useful.

## 4417 TOTEPOOL FILLIES' H'CAP 1m 4f 8y

**7:00** (7:00) (Class 4) (0-85,79) 3-Y-O+ **£5,175** (£1,540; £769; £384) **Stalls** Low

Form RPR

21 **1** **Hoop Of Colour (USA)**[36] 3141 3-9-2 79 PhillipMakin 5 91+
(Lady Cecil) *hld up in last: nt clr run over 2f out tl over 1f out: chsd ldr 1f out: swtchd rt: r.o to ld nr fin* **9/4**[2]

0235 **2** nk **Vicky Valentine**[20] 3698 4-9-0 65 PJMcDonald 4 69
(Alistair Whillans) *w ldr: led over 8f out: qcknd pce 4f out: over 2 l clr 1f out: hdd and no ex nr fin* **20/1**

0342 **3** 4 1/2 **Dark Amber**[18] 3803 4-9-4 69 KierenFallon 1 64
(Brendan Powell) *reluctant ldr: hdd over 8f out: chsd ldr: edgd lft over 1f out: one pce* **10/3**[3]

6-31 **4** 3 1/2 **Some Site (IRE)**[37] 3103 3-9-1 78 MartinLane 2 67
(David Simcock) *trckd ldrs: effrt over 3f out: fdd over 1f out* **6/4**[1]

0002 **5** 1 3/4 **Bayan Kasirga (IRE)**[18] 3787 4-9-5 70 TonyHamilton 3 55
(Richard Fahey) *s.i.s: sn chsng ldrs: hmpd 2f out: wknd over 1f out* **8/1**

2m 45.67s (4.87) **Going Correction** +0.25s/f (Good)
**WFA** 3 from 4yo 12lb **5 Ran SP% 109.7**
Speed ratings (Par 102): **93,92,89,87,86**
CSF £34.44 TOTE £2.90: £1.60, £4.00; EX 21.70 Trifecta £70.00.
**Owner** Niarchos Family **Bred** Flaxman Holdings Limited **Trained** Newmarket, Suffolk

**FOCUS**
A fillies' handicap run at a dawdling early pace. The winner is better than the bre form, the runner-up the key.

## 4418 BETFRED H'CAP 5f

**7:30** (7:30) (Class 3) (0-95,90) 3-Y-O+
**£9,337** (£2,796; £1,398; £699; £349; £175) **Stalls** Low

Form RPR

3120 **1** **Another Wise Kid (IRE)**[7] 4174 6-9-12 90 PhillipMakin 5 100
(Paul Midgley) *w ldr: led over 1f out: drvn out* **5/1**[3]

0440 **2** 1 1/2 **Normal Equilibrium**[14] 3927 4-9-7 88 (p) MichaelJMMurphy(3) 4 93
(Robert Cowell) *chsd ldrs: effrt over 2f out: chsd wnr jst ins fnl f: styd on same pce* **7/2**[1]

-010 **3** 3/4 **Bispham Green**[27] 3458 4-9-7 85 DavidNolan 6 87
(David O'Meara) *chsd ldrs: drvn over 2f out: edgd lft and kpt on fnl f: tk 3rd nr fin* **7/1**

0036 **4** 1 **Fitz Flyer (IRE)**[7] 4174 8-9-5 83 (v) AdrianNicholls 3 81
(David Nicholls) *in rr: hdwy 2f out: kpt on same pce* **6/1**

3560 **5** 2 **Singeur (IRE)**[21] 3666 7-9-7 85 KierenFallon 9 76
(Robin Bastiman) *chsd ldrs on outer: one pce fnl 2f* **11/2**

3310 **6** 1/2 **Adam's Ale**[13] 3948 5-9-1 79 TonyHamilton 1 68
(Paul Midgley) *led: hdd over 1f out: wknd last 100yds* **4/1**[2]

42-1 **7** 2 1/4 **Zac Brown (IRE)**[25] 3531 3-9-4 86 GrahamGibbons 7 66
(David Barron) *dwlt: effrt over 2f out: fdd appr fnl f* **15/2**

0402 **8** nse **Oldjoesaid**[20] 3697 10-9-0 78 PJMcDonald 8 59
(Paul Midgley) *chsd ldrs on outer: lost pl over 1f out* **12/1**

1m 3.57s (0.27) **Going Correction** +0.25s/f (Good)
**WFA** 3 from 4yo+ 4lb **8 Ran SP% 114.7**
Speed ratings (Par 107): **107,104,103,101,98 97,94,94**
CSF £22.94 CT £228.58 TOTE £6.80: £2.20, £1.70, £3.30; EX 29.50 Trifecta £432.00.
**Owner** Michael Ng **Bred** Paul Kavanagh **Trained** Westow, N Yorks

**FOCUS**
A decent sprint handicap but not impressive form for the grade. Those racing prominently did best and few got into it. The winner is better than ever.

## 4419 COLSTROPE CUP H'CAP (BOBIS RACE) 1m 4y

**8:00** (8:00) (Class 4) (0-85,82) 3-Y-O **£6,469** (£1,925; £962; £481) **Stalls** Low

Form RPR

5042 **1** **Imshivalla (IRE)**[15] 3885 3-8-9 70 TonyHamilton 2 75+
(Richard Fahey) *stmbld s: sn trckling ldrs: swtchd ins 1f out: styd on to ld clsng stages* **6/1**[3]

-410 **2** 1/2 **Mayfield Boy**[33] 3273 3-9-1 76 PJMcDonald 1 79
(Mel Brittain) *swvd rt s: sn led: narrowly hdd appr fnl f: rallied and ld last 100yds: hdd and no ex clsng stages* **7/2**[2]

21-3 **3** 1/2 **El Beau (IRE)**[27] 3464 3-9-1 76 PhillipMakin 4 78
(John Quinn) *trckd ldrs: narrow ld appr fnl f: hdd and no ex last 100yds* **7/2**[2]

61-5 **4** 6 **Ryeolliean**[20] 3719 3-9-3 78 DavidNolan 3 66
(David O'Meara) *led early: w ldr: wknd over 1f out* **8/1**

-031 **5** 5 **Elusive Guest (FR)**[18] 3804 3-9-7 82 KierenFallon 5 59
(George Margarson) *swvd rt s: in rr: drvn over 3f out: outpcd over 2f out: edgd rt and wknd over 1f out: eased towards fin* **6/4**[1]

1m 46.74s (0.84) **Going Correction** +0.25s/f (Good) **5 Ran SP% 109.8**
Speed ratings (Par 102): **105,104,104,98,93**
CSF £26.16 TOTE £7.20: £2.30, £2.00; EX 25.70 Trifecta £73.00.
**Owner** Pow Partnership **Bred** M Fahy & Rathbarry Stud **Trained** Musley Bank, N Yorks

**FOCUS**
A somewhat tactical affair but the pace was sound enough and there was a tight finish to this 3yo handicap. Fairly useful form, rated around the second and third.

## 4420 CRABBIE'S ALCOHOLIC GINGER BEER MAIDEN H'CAP 1m 2f 6y

**8:35** (8:36) (Class 5) (0-70,69) 3-Y-O+ **£3,234** (£962; £481; £240) **Stalls** Low

Form RPR

40-4 **1** **Nakeeta**[22] 3603 3-9-1 66 DavidNolan 7 76
(Iain Jardine) *mid-div: hdwy over 2f out: chsng ldrs whn swtchd rt over 1f out: styd on to ld clsng stages* **8/1**

054 **2** 1/2 **Kinema (IRE)**[36] 3135 3-9-1 66 LukeMorris 10 75
(Ed Walker) *w ldr: effrt over 2f out: led over 1f out: hdd and no ex clsng stages* **9/2**[1]

502 **3** 3 1/2 **Frosty The Snowman (IRE)**[13] 3978 3-8-11 62 PJMcDonald 12 64
(Ruth Carr) *in rr: hdwy over 1f out: styd on to take 3rd last 75yds* **11/2**[2]

6333 **4** 3 3/4 **Nam Ma Prow**[37] 3098 3-8-1 52 (v[1]) DuranFentiman 8 47
(Simon West) *led: drvn over 2f out: wknd fnl 150yds* **12/1**

0-56 **5** 3/4 **Cape Summit**[28] 3421 3-9-3 68 PhillipMakin 5 62
(Ed Dunlop) *trckd ldrs: effrt over 2f out: one pce whn hmpd over 1f out* **13/2**

-000 **6** hd **Shades Of Silver**[47] 2801 4-9-3 58 WilliamTwiston-Davies 6 51
(Michael Scudamore) *chsd ldrs on outside: drvn over 3f out: outpcd over 2f out: kpt on fnl 150yds* **17/2**

0545 **7** nk **Mendelita**[29] 3396 3-8-10 61 TonyHamilton 4 54
(Richard Fahey) *chsd ldrs: drvn 3f out: sn outpcd: kpt on fnl 150yds* **15/2**

5050 **8** 1 1/4 **Buy Out Boy**[10] 4063 3-8-11 62 (p) AndrewMullen 2 52
(Michael Appleby) *mid-div: drvn over 4f out: wknd over 1f out* **16/1**

-032 **9** 3/4 **Solid Justice (IRE)**[30] 3362 3-9-4 69 AndrewElliott 3 58
(Jason Ward) *in rr: sme hdwy over 1f out: nvr on terms* **6/1**[3]

60-0 **10** 1 1/2 **Rosy Ryan (IRE)**[43] 2937 4-8-9 50 oh5 DavidAllan 13 36
(Tina Jackson) *hld up in rr: sme hdwy 4f out: outpcd over 2f out: nt clr run over 1f out: sn wknd* **50/1**

050 **11** 18 **I Am Not Here (IRE)**[18] 3804 3-9-0 65 KierenFallon 11 17
(Timothy Jarvis) *dwlt: in rr: sme hdwy on outside over 2f out: sn wknd: bhd whn eased ins fnl f: t.o* **12/1**

2m 15.3s (1.60) **Going Correction** +0.25s/f (Good)
**WFA** 3 from 4yo 10lb **11 Ran SP% 117.8**
Speed ratings (Par 103): **103,102,99,96,96 96,95,94,94,93 78**
CSF £43.98 CT £218.78 TOTE £9.60: £3.00, £1.90, £2.50; EX 46.60 Trifecta £116.80.
**Owner** Alex and Janet Card **Bred** Mike Channon Bloodstock Ltd **Trained** Bonchester Bridge, Borders

**FOCUS**
A modest handicap and they sprinted for home a little too early, which played into the hands of the winner. He's rated to form.

## 4421 INJURED JOCKEYS FUND 50TH ANNIVERSARY H'CAP 6f

**9:05** (9:05) (Class 5) (0-75,80) 3-Y-O+ **£3,234** (£962; £481; £240) **Stalls** Low

Form RPR

-042 **1** **Jamesbo's Girl**[13] 3952 4-9-4 67 GrahamGibbons 6 80
(David Barron) *w ldrs: led and edgd lft over 1f out: rdn rt out* **9/2**[2]

5051 **2** 2 1/2 **Bajan Bear**[8] 4131 6-9-11 74 6ex AdrianNicholls 5 79
(David Nicholls) *hld up in rr: effrt and swtchd outside 2f out: styd on to take 2nd last 150yds: no imp* **5/1**[3]

214 **3** 3/4 **Al Khan (IRE)**[13] 3952 5-9-7 75 (p) JacobButterfield(5) 8 78
(Ollie Pears) *w ldrs: led over 2f out: sn hdd: swtchd rt over 1f out: kpt on same pce* **15/2**

4303 **4** 1/2 **Lucky Lodge**[36] 3149 4-9-0 63 (b) DavidAllan 1 64
(Mel Brittain) *led tl over 2f out: led 2f out: sn hdd: kpt on same pce fnl f* **17/2**

2022 **5** 1/2 **Diamond Blue**[21] 3668 6-9-2 65 (p) TonyHamilton 7 64
(Richard Fahey) *in rr: hdwy and swtchd outside over 1f out: kpt on same pce* **7/1**

5324 **6** 1 1/4 **Solar Spirit (IRE)**[2] 4317 9-9-12 75 RobertWinston 9 70
(Tracy Waggott) *t.k.h in midfield: effrt over 2f out: wl hld whn eased towards fin* **7/1**

0001 **7** nk **Dream Ally (IRE)**[6] 4195 4-9-2 65 6ex PJMcDonald 3 59
(Micky Hammond) *chsd ldrs: fdd last 150yds* **10/1**

321 **8** 6 **Makin The Rules (IRE)**[9] 4071 3-9-5 80 6ex JoeDoyle(7) 4 54
(John Quinn) *dwlt: sn trcking ldrs: lost pl over 1f out* **4/1**[1]

1m 17.26s (0.36) **Going Correction** +0.25s/f (Good)
**WFA** 3 from 4yo+ 5lb **8 Ran SP% 111.2**
Speed ratings (Par 103): **107,103,102,102,101 99,99,91**
CSF £25.63 CT £157.75 TOTE £6.60: £1.60, £2.20, £2.50; EX 24.80 Trifecta £287.00.
**Owner** Hardisty Rolls **Bred** Lady Juliet Tadgell **Trained** Maunby, N Yorks

**FOCUS**
A genuine pace and it paid to race handily. The winner was very well treated on 2yo form.
T/Plt: £253.60 to a £1 stake. Pool: £42431.29 - 122.10 winning tickets T/Qpdt: £51.90 to a £1 stake. Pool: £4728.75 - 67.40 winning tickets WG

## 4388 HAYDOCK (L-H)

Saturday, July 19

**OFFICIAL GOING: Good to soft (good in places; 9.1)**

Wind: Mainly fine Weather: Sunny Intervals

### 4422 CELEBRATE 10 YEARS WITH RACING UK NURSERY H'CAP — 5f

**6:25** (6:27) (Class 5) 2-Y-O — **£3,881** (£1,155; £577; £288) **Stalls** Centre

Form — RPR

61 **1** **Rise Up Lotus (IRE)**[75] 2022 2-9-2 **74** ............ DaneO'Neill 4 — 78
(Charles Hills) *dwlt: hld up in rr: hdwy 2f out: led over 1f out: rdn ins fnl f: kpt on wl: in command fnl 100yds* — **8/13**[1]

0363 **2** *1* **Midnight Destiny (IRE)**[10] 4083 2-8-0 **58** oh1 ............ RaulDaSilva 5 — 57
(Derek Shaw) *racd freely: led: rdn 2f out: hdd over 1f out: stl ev ch ins fnl f: hld fnl 100yds* — **12/1**

4165 **3** *2* **Low Cut Affair (IRE)**[76] 1982 2-9-1 **73** ............ JFEgan 2 — 65
(David Evans) *w ldr: rdn 2f out: nt qckn u.p over 1f out: kpt on same pce ins fnl f* — **11/2**[3]

420 **4** *4 1/2* **Macarthurs Park (IRE)**[72] 2089 2-7-7 **58** oh1 ............ (p) JoeDoyle(7) 7 — 34
(Tom Dascombe) *trckd ldrs: tail flashed whn rdn over 2f out: nt pick-up u.p: continued to flash tail and lft bhd fnl f* — **3/1**[2]

1m 2.5s (1.70) **Going Correction** +0.275s/f (Good) — **4** Ran SP% **110.0**

Speed ratings (Par 94): **97,95,92,85**

CSF £8.42 TOTE £1.40; EX 10.40 Trifecta £31.90.

**Owner** Hamdan Al Maktoum **Bred** Tally-Ho Stud **Trained** Lambourn, Berks

**FOCUS**

All races on Inner track and races on Round course increased by 1yd. All races on Inner track and races on Round course increased by 1yd. The ground had eased with 12mm of rain in 18 hours and three non-runners left a quartet of fillies, turning this into no more than a modest sprint nursery. They came up the centre of the track and the ground rode dead.

### 4423 BOOK YOUR CHRISTMAS PARTY AT HAYDOCK PARK H'CAP — 1m 6f

**7:00** (7:00) (Class 4) (0-80,79) 4-Y-O+ — **£5,175** (£1,540; £769; £384) **Stalls** Low

Form — RPR

0136 **1** **Precision Strike**[21] 3699 4-8-7 **65** ............ (v) JFEgan 11 — 72
(Richard Guest) *dwlt: swtchd lft s: hld up: smooth hdwy 3f out: led over 1f out: sn rdn: kpt on and a doing enough towards fin* — **20/1**

2213 **2** *1/2* **English Summer**[8] 4160 7-9-7 **79** ............ (t) DavidNolan 2 — 88+
(Richard Fahey) *chsd ldrs: denied a run whn snatched up and stmbld over 1f out: sn rdn: nt clr run ins fnl f: r.o to take 2nd fnl 75yds: clsd on wnr nr fin* — **5/1**[2]

-210 **3** *3/4* **Perfect Summer (IRE)**[49] 2782 4-9-7 **79** ............ JamieSpencer 6 — 84
(Lady Cecil) *hld up: no bttr than midfield tl swtchd rt over 2f out: hdwy over 1f out: sn rdn to chse ldrs: hung lft and wnt 2nd ins fnl f: lost 2nd and nt qckn fnl 75yds: styd on same pce* — **2/1**[1]

0/05 **4** *2* **Nafaath (IRE)**[27] 3501 8-9-2 **74** ............ GrahamLee 3 — 76
(Donald McCain) *in tch: hdwy to go prom 8f out: led over 2f out: rdn and hdd over 1f out: kpt on u.p: one pce fnl 75yds* — **14/1**

0033 **5** *4* **Cloud Monkey (IRE)**[31] 3371 4-8-13 **71** ............ PhillipMakin 9 — 68
(Martin Todhunter) *hld up: hdwy gng wl on inner 3f out: chalng over 1f out: no ex fnl 100yds: eased after* — **14/1**

5-53 **6** *6* **Kleitomachos (IRE)**[81] 1848 6-9-5 **77** ............ SeanLevey 5 — 65
(Stuart Kittow) *prom: lost pl 6f out: sn pushed along: outpcd 3f out: kpt on u.p ins fnl f: eased whn no imp towards fin* — **6/1**[3]

32-3 **7** *1 1/4* **Highway Code (USA)**[21] 3699 8-9-1 **73** ............ (t) PatCosgrave 8 — 60
(Richard Lee) *midfield: rdn and outpcd 3f out: no imp after* — **8/1**

3623 **8** *6* **Lineman**[14] 3976 4-8-12 **70** ............ RobertWinston 7 — 48
(Andrew Hollinshead) *midfield: hdwy to go prom after 6f: chalng over 2f out: wknd over 1f out* — **8/1**

/0-6 **9** *2 3/4* **Mafeteng**[15] 3918 6-8-8 **66** ............ RaulDaSilva 1 — 40
(David Thompson) *led: hdd 12f out: dropped to midfield after 4f: rdn and wknd 2f out* — **40/1**

5610 **10** *1* **Aldborough (IRE)**[17] 3860 4-9-4 **76** ............ (p) DougieCostello 10 — 49
(Ralph Beckett) *s.i.s: bustled along and hdwy to ld over 12f out: rdn and hdd over 2f out: sn wknd* — **9/1**

2m 59.55s (-2.45) **Going Correction** -0.05s/f (Good) — **10** Ran SP% **117.0**

Speed ratings (Par 105): **105,104,104,103,100 97,96,93,91,91**

CSF £117.63 CT £295.96 TOTE £19.00: £4.70, £2.20, £1.30; EX 174.80 Trifecta £313.20.

**Owner** Resdev **Bred** Mickley Stud **Trained** ingmanthorpe, W Yorks

**FOCUS**

An open staying handicap. They went hard up front and the first two came from well off the pace. Fair form.

### 4424 BRITISH STALLION STUDS EBF MAIDEN STKS — 7f

**7:30** (7:31) (Class 5) 2-Y-O — **£2,911** (£866; £432; £216) **Stalls** Low

Form — RPR

02 **1** **Medrano**[37] 3136 2-9-5 0 ............ GrahamLee 11 — 83
(David Brown) *chsd ldr: rdn over 2f out: styd on ins fnl f: led nr fin* — **6/1**[3]

3 **2** *nk* **Salateen**[28] 3454 2-9-5 0 ............ JamieSpencer 9 — 82
(Kevin Ryan) *led: rdn over 2f out: kpt on willingly tl hdd and hld nr fin* **6/1**[3]

4 **3** *3* **Maftoon (IRE)**[29] 3429 2-9-5 0 ............ DaneO'Neill 2 — 74+
(Richard Hannon) *missed break: sn in tch: rdn over 2f out: sn hung lft: styd on to chse ldrs ins fnl f: sn no imp on front pair: eased whn hld nr fin* — **3/1**[1]

**4** *3 1/2* **Lord Ben Stack (IRE)** 2-9-5 0 ............ DanielTudhope 6 — 65+
(K R Burke) *dwlt and carried rt s: in tch: rdn over 2f out: nt qckn: one pce ins fnl f* — **7/1**

3 **5** *shd* **Here Now**[15] 3924 2-9-5 0 ............ AhmedAjtebi 4 — 64
(Charlie Appleby) *chsd ldrs: rdn over 2f out: nt qckn ins fnl f: no ex fnl 150yds* — **7/2**[2]

32 **6** *1/2* **Critical Risk (IRE)**[30] 3381 2-9-5 0 ............ SeanLevey 8 — 63+
(Brian Meehan) *dwlt: hld up: pushed along and outpcd 3f out: styd on u.p wl ins fnl f: nvr trble ldrs* — **7/1**

5 **7** *2 1/2* **Mywayalways (IRE)**[10] 4079 2-9-5 0 ............ JFEgan 3 — 56+
(David Evans) *hld up: outpcd u.p over 2f out: nvr a threat* — **33/1**

**8** *1* **Amazour (IRE)** 2-9-5 0 ............ TomQueally 1 — 54
(Ismail Mohammed) *chsd ldrs: rdn over 1f out: wknd ins fnl f* — **40/1**

4 **9** *2 1/4* **Loom Of Life (IRE)**[21] 3701 2-9-5 0 ............ TonyHamilton 5 — 47
(Richard Fahey) *awkward s and wnt rt: midfield: rdn over 3f out: sn wknd* — **12/1**

**10** *11* **Pumaflor (IRE)** 2-9-0 0 ............ DuilioDaSilva(5) 7 — 18+
(Richard Guest) *wnt rt s: racd keenly: hld up: rdn 3f out: outpcd: nvr a threat* — **80/1**

1m 30.02s (-0.68) **Going Correction** -0.05s/f (Good) — **10** Ran SP% **115.1**

Speed ratings (Par 94): **101,100,97,93,93 92,89,88,85,73**

CSF £40.85 TOTE £6.60: £1.40, £2.20, £1.60; EX 40.80 Trifecta £139.80.

**Owner** Peter Onslow & Mr & Mrs Gary Middlebrook **Bred** Peter Onslow **Trained** Averham Park, Notts

**FOCUS**

The gallop was fair and the ground appeared very loose on top but this looked a reasonable maiden and a few winners might come out of it.

### 4425 ABACUS SECURITIES 11TH YEAR CONDITIONS STKS — 7f

**8:00** (8:00) (Class 3) 3-Y-O+ — **£8,086** (£2,406; £1,202; £601) **Stalls** Low

Form — RPR

3220 **1** **Professor**[7] 4200 4-9-1 111 ............ SeanLevey 4 — 114
(Richard Hannon) *trckd ldrs: pushed along over 2f out: rdn to chal over 1f out: led ins fnl f: kpt on wl towards fin* — **13/8**[1]

0240 **2** *1/2* **Trade Storm**[112] 1181 6-9-1 113 ............ JamieSpencer 1 — 113
(David Simcock) *led after 1f: rdn whn pressed ins fnl f: sn hdd: kpt on u.p: hld towards fin* — **2/1**[2]

16-0 **3** *nse* **Rerouted (USA)**[191] 111 6-9-1 113 ............ PatCosgrave 7 — 113
(M F De Kock, South Africa) *led for 1f: chsd ldr after: effrt to chal fr over 1f out: kpt on ins fnl f: hld towards fin* — **10/1**

4002 **4** *3 3/4* **Morache Music**[14] 3960 6-9-1 104 ............ TomQueally 6 — 103
(Peter Makin) *hld up: pushed along over 2f out: rdn and no imp over 1f out: one pce fnl f and no ch* — **6/1**

112- **5** *13* **Diescentric (USA)**[350] 5013 7-9-1 108 ............ PaulMulrennan 2 — 76
(Julie Camacho) *hld up in rr: outpcd over 1f out: sn lft bhd* — **5/1**[3]

1m 29.23s (-1.47) **Going Correction** -0.05s/f (Good) — **5** Ran SP% **111.5**

Speed ratings (Par 107): **106,105,105,101,86**

CSF £5.26 TOTE £2.70: £1.60, £1.70; EX 5.50 Trifecta £28.40.

**Owner** Mrs P Good **Bred** Exors Of The Late J R Good **Trained** East Everleigh, Wilts

**FOCUS**

A select field for this useful minor event but a genuine pace for the ground and a tight finish ensued. They came up the centre of the track.

### 4426 DOWNLOAD NEW RACING UK IPAD APP H'CAP — 1m

**8:30** (8:30) (Class 5) (0-75,75) 3-Y-O — **£2,911** (£866; £432; £216) **Stalls** Low

Form — RPR

-263 **1** **Arable**[60] 2432 3-9-7 **75** ............ TomQueally 7 — 87
(Charles Hills) *hld up in rr: hdwy over 2f out: led over 1f out: r.o wl to draw clr ins fnl f* — **11/2**

2143 **2** *6* **Starlight Serenade**[9] 4112 3-9-5 **73** ............ GrahamGibbons 9 — 72
(Ralph Beckett) *in tch: effrt 3f out: kpt on u.p to take 2nd ins fnl f: no imp on wnr* — **6/4**[1]

0444 **3** *1* **Rangi Chase (IRE)**[8] 4161 3-9-4 **72** ............ DavidNolan 5 — 68
(Richard Fahey) *in tch: rdn and outpcd over 2f out: kpt on u.p ins fnl f: nvr able to mount serious chal* — **5/1**[3]

3052 **4** *nk* **Rocksee (IRE)**[21] 3733 3-9-0 **68** ............ (p) StephenCraine 1 — 63
(Tom Dascombe) *chsd ldr: led 3f out: rdn over 2f out: hdd over 1f out: no ex fnl 150yds* — **16/1**

0322 **5** *1 1/2* **Company Secretary (USA)**[52] 2679 3-8-5 **59** ............ (b) FrannyNorton 8 — 51
(Jo Hughes) *in rr: rdn and outpcd over 3f out: nvr a threat* — **14/1**

4130 **6** *1 3/4* **Know Your Name**[8] 4161 3-9-7 **75** ............ (v) JFEgan 10 — 63
(David Evans) *led: hdd 3f out: rdn over 2f out: wknd fnl f* — **17/2**

-621 **U** **Dream Impossible (IRE)**[19] 3781 3-8-6 **60** ............ BenCurtis 3
(Peter Makin) *racd keenly: prom on outer: sddle sn slipped: effrt and cl 3rd whn uns rdr jst over 3f out* — **9/2**[2]

1m 43.21s (-0.49) **Going Correction** -0.05s/f (Good) — **7** Ran SP% **113.3**

Speed ratings (Par 100): **100,94,93,92,91 89,**

CSF £13.95 CT £43.07 TOTE £7.80: £3.50, £1.60; EX 17.10 Trifecta £66.70.

**Owner** K Abdullah **Bred** Juddmonte Farms Ltd **Trained** Lambourn, Berks

**FOCUS**

Mainly exposed sorts in a fair handicap. The gallop was strong and it played into the hands of an unexposed improver who came from off the pace.

### 4427 TOM JONES HERE 9TH AUGUST H'CAP — 1m 2f 95y

**9:00** (9:01) (Class 5) (0-75,75) 3-Y-O+ — **£2,911** (£866; £432; £216) **Stalls** Centre

Form — RPR

3354 **1** **Evervescent (IRE)**[16] 3880 5-9-0 **68** ............ JoeDoyle(7) 5 — 76
(Graeme McPherson) *chsd ldrs: wnt 2nd over 3f out: rdn over 2f out: led narrowly over 1f out: kpt on u.p: jst hld on* — **9/1**

-055 **2** *shd* **Rex Whistler (IRE)**[15] 3919 4-9-4 **65** ............ PaulMulrennan 1 — 73
(Julie Camacho) *midfield: hdwy 3f out: effrt to chse ldrs over 2f out: r.o towards fin: jst failed* — **5/1**[3]

0423 **3** *1/2* **Artful Prince**[14] 3977 4-10-0 **75** ............ (b) DaleSwift 10 — 82
(James Given) *w ldr: led 4f out: rdn over 2f out: hdd narrowly over 1f out: continued to chal ins fnl f: hld nr fin* — **9/2**[2]

-15 **4** *3* **Frosty Berry**[68] 2213 5-9-4 **65** ............ RobertWinston 8 — 66
(Paul Midgley) *midfield: rdn and hdwy over 2f out: sn chsd ldrs: no ex fnl 100yds* — **9/1**

0320 **5** *2 1/4* **Engrossing**[13] 3999 5-9-10 **71** ............ (e) JamesSullivan 11 — 68
(Ruth Carr) *hld up: pushed along over 4f out: hdwy u.p over 2f out: chsd ldrs over 1f out: one pce ins fnl f* — **7/1**

0323 **6** *1 3/4* **Ferdy (IRE)**[17] 3845 5-8-10 **57** ............ RaulDaSilva 9 — 51
(Paul Green) *in rr: rdn and hdwy over 2f out: no imp over 1f out* — **16/1**

-403 **7** *4 1/2* **Tiptree Lace**[21] 3712 3-8-13 **70** ............ TomQueally 3 — 55
(William Knight) *midfield: pushed along and outpcd over 4f out: nt clr run under 3f out: plugged on ins fnl f: n.d* — **12/1**

100 **8** *2 3/4* **Equitable**[49] 2781 3-9-1 **72** ............ (t) PhillipMakin 4 — 52
(Lady Cecil) *in tch: rdn over 2f out: sn wknd* — **3/1**[1]

34/3 **9** *4 1/2* **Kudu Country (IRE)**[37] 3139 8-8-9 **69** ............ DougieCostello 6 — 40
(Tom Tate) *in tch: pushed along over 4f out: sn lost pl: n.d after* — **8/1**

4056 **10** *1 3/4* **Gioia Di Vita**[15] 3919 4-9-3 **64** ............ (p) GrahamLee 2 — 32
(David Thompson) *led: hdd 4f out: sn rdn: wknd 2f out* — **16/1**

2m 13.76s (-1.74) **Going Correction** -0.05s/f (Good)

**WFA** 3 from 4yo+ 10lb — **10** Ran SP% **122.9**

Speed ratings (Par 103): **104,103,103,101,99 97,94,92,88,87**

CSF £56.62 CT £237.16 TOTE £9.90: £2.80, £2.70, £1.90; EX 85.90 Trifecta £557.30.

**Owner** Ever Equine **Bred** Keogh Family **Trained** Upper Oddington, Gloucs

**FOCUS**

The pace was honest enough and not many got into this modest handicap. The winner came up the far rail.

T/Plt: £19.40 to a £1 stake. Pool: £72,582.05 - 2,730.74 winning tickets. T/Qpdt: £3.70 to a £1 stake. Pool: £1,263.36 - 6,423.37 winning tickets. DO

# 4320 LINGFIELD (L-H)

Saturday, July 19

**OFFICIAL GOING: Turf course - good (good to firm in places; goingstick 7.2); all-weather - standard**

Wind: virtually nil Weather: sunny and warm

## 4428 LADBROKES H'CAP 7f

**5:30** (5:31) (Class 6) (0-65,65) 3-Y-O+ **£2,587** (£770; £384; £192) **Stalls** Centre

Form RPR

2165 **1** **Belle Bayardo (IRE)**[25] 3549 6-9-6 **57**........................ AdamKirby 11 68
(Tony Carroll) *t.k.h early: chsd ldrs: hmpd after 1f: wnt 2nd 4f out: drvn to ld 2f out: clr ins fnl f: r.o* **7/2**[1]

2221 **2** *2 1/2* **Byrd In Hand (IRE)**[11] 4046 7-9-8 **59**........................ WilliamCarson 7 63
(John Bridger) *led and grad crossed to r against stands' rail: rdn and hdd 2f out: styd on same pce after* **6/1**

1643 **3** *1/2* **My Manekineko**[10] 4073 5-9-11 **62**........................ FergusSweeney 4 65
(J R Jenkins) *chsd ldrs: drvn ent fnl 2f: styd on same pce u.p fnl f* **12/1**

-032 **4** *1 1/4* **Lady Crossmar (IRE)**[8] 4155 3-9-0 **65**........................ JoshQuinn(7) 2 61+
(Richard Hannon) *awkward leaving stalls and v.s.a: wl off the pce in rr: rdn and hdwy over 1f out: kpt on wl to go 4th ins fnl f: nvr trbld ldrs* **12/1**

6350 **5** *1* **The Happy Hammer (IRE)**[24] 3589 8-8-11 **51**..........(b) RobertTart(3) 8 48
(Eugene Stanford) *in tch in rr of main gp: rdn over 2f out: no real imp tl swtchd rt and styd on ins fnl f* **8/1**

-045 **6** *2 1/4* **Eager To Bow (IRE)**[32] 3328 8-9-8 **62**..........(p) ThomasBrown(3) 6 53
(Patrick Chamings) *wl in tch in midfield: rdn 3f out: no ex and outpcd over 1f out: wknd fnl f* **8/1**

-514 **7** *nk* **Strike A Light**[46] 2878 3-8-8 **57**........................ DannyBrock(5) 1 44+
(Rae Guest) *s.i.s: wl off the pce in last pair: sme hdwy u.p over 1f out: styd on past btn horses fnl f: nvr trbld ldrs* **4/1**[2]

2000 **8** *2* **Encapsulated**[28] 3470 4-8-12 **56**..........(p) RhiainIngram(7) 3 41
(Roger Ingram) *in tch towards rr of main gp: rdn and no prog over 1f out: wknd fnl f* **40/1**

0445 **9** *4 1/2* **Dancing Sal (IRE)**[2] 4341 3-8-11 **55**........................ PaddyAspell 10 25
(Gary Moore) *led for 1f: chsd ldrs tl rdn and lost pl 1/2-way: bhd 1f out* **14/1**

003 **10** *11* **Popping Candy**[24] 3588 3-9-2 **60**........................ JackMitchell 12 2
(Roger Varian) *chsng ldrs whn bdly hmpd after 1f: lost pl and nvr on terms after* **5/1**[3]

1m 22.41s (-0.89) **Going Correction** -0.075s/f (Good)
**WFA** 3 from 4yo+ 7lb **10** Ran SP% **119.9**
Speed ratings (Par 101): **102,99,98,97,96 93,93,90,85,73**
CSF £25.52 CT £236.93 TOTE £5.30: £1.40, £1.60, £4.70; EX 20.60 Trifecta £181.20.
**Owner** Richard Ward **Bred** L Mulryan **Trained** Cropthorne, Worcs
■ Stewards' Enquiry : Paddy Aspell two-day ban: careless riding (2-3 Aug)

**FOCUS**
9.4mm of overnight rain eased the ground to good, good to firm in places. A weak affair featuring mainly exposed sorts.

## 4429 LADBROKES/BRITISH STALLION STUDS EBF MAIDEN STKS 7f

**6:00** (6:02) (Class 5) 2-Y-O **£2,911** (£866; £432; £216) **Stalls** Centre

Form RPR

0 **1** **Pasticcio**[11] 4044 2-9-5 0........................ AdamKirby 2 77
(Charlie Appleby) *mde all and crossed to r against stands' rail: rdn ent fnl 2f: looked in command 1f out: hrd pressed towards fin: a jst lasting home* **5/1**[3]

3 **2** *shd* **Al Bandar (IRE)**[9] 4129 2-9-5 0........................ RichardHughes 5 77
(Richard Hannon) *t.k.h: chsd ldrs: hdwy to go 2nd ent fnl f: drvn 1f out: r.o u.p and clsd fnl 100yds: jst failed* **7/4**[1]

**3** *3 1/4* **Swaheen** 2-9-2 0........................ RobertTart(3) 1 68+
(Sir Michael Stoute) *s.i.s: in tch towards rr: rdn over 2f out: hdwy under hands and heels riding over 1f out: wnt 3rd fnl 150yds: sn outpcd but kpt on for clr 3rd* **8/1**

**4** *6* **Amadeity (IRE)** 2-9-5 0........................ SteveDrowne 9 52+
(Jo Hughes) *s.i.s: rn green in rr: shifting lft 1/2-way: hdwy past btn horses over 1f out: styd on but no ch w ldrs* **50/1**

5 **5** *2 3/4* **New Brunswick (GER)**[15] 3929 2-9-5 0........................ WilliamBuick 4 45
(John Gosden) *chsd ldrs: effrt in cl 3rd wl over 1f out: btn and lost 3rd ins fnl f: fdd fnl 100yds* **2/1**[2]

**6** *nk* **Who'Sthedude (IRE)** 2-9-5 0........................ JimCrowley 7 44
(Ralph Beckett) *chsd ldrs tl shuffled bk into midfield: rdn and outpcd whn swtchd rt over 1f out: sn wknd* **8/1**

00 **7** *nse* **Moonadee (IRE)**[7] 4207 2-8-12 0........................ TylerSaunders(7) 8 44
(B W Hills) *hld up in tch in rr: pushed along and switching lft 2f out: no imp: wknd fnl f* **16/1**

00 **8** *4* **Striking Stone**[40] 3063 2-9-5 0..........(p) LiamJones 3 33
(Jo Hughes) *t.k.h: chsd ldr tl jst over 2f out: sn rdn and lost pl: bhd 1f out* **80/1**

60 **9** *12* **Pyrocumulus (IRE)**[15] 3934 2-8-12 0........................ JoshuaBrowning(7) 6
(Jo Hughes) *dwlt: in tch towards rr: rdr wout irons over 4f out: dropped to rr over 2f out: wl bhd fnl f* **66/1**

1m 22.89s (-0.41) **Going Correction** -0.075s/f (Good) **9** Ran SP% **119.2**
Speed ratings (Par 94): **99,98,95,88,85 84,84,80,66**
CSF £14.67 TOTE £6.40: £1.60, £1.10, £2.70; EX 9.20 Trifecta £140.80.
**Owner** Godolphin **Bred** Hascombe And Valiant Studs **Trained** Newmarket, Suffolk

## 4430 LADBROKES NURSERY H'CAP 6f

**6:35** (6:35) (Class 5) 2-Y-O **£3,105** (£924; £461; £230) **Stalls** Centre

Form RPR

3102 **1** **Fuwairt (IRE)**[8] 4150 2-9-11 **86**........................ RichardHughes 5 90
(Richard Hannon) *racd in last pair: stmbld bdly 4f out: swtchd lft and clsd 2f out: chal jst ins fnl f: shkn up to ld wl ins fnl f: faltered towards fin and jst hld on* **5/2**[1]

1550 **2** *nse* **Lightning Stride**[9] 4123 2-9-2 **80**........................ RyanClark(3) 2 83
(Brian Meehan) *hld up in tch: clsd to chse ldrs 2f out: rdn and chal over 1f out: drvn to ld jst ins fnl f: rallied cl home: jst failed* **6/1**

421 **3** *2 1/4* **Latch Onto Blue**[12] 4011 2-9-1 **76**........................ JamesDoyle 6 72
(Charles Hills) *chsd ldr tl over 4f out: shuffled bk and n.m.r 2f out: swtchd lft and hdwy jst over 1f out: kpt on same pce ins fnl f* **7/2**[2]

354 **4** *1 1/2* **Designate (IRE)**[75] 2007 2-8-10 **71**..........(b[1]) JimCrowley 4 63
(Ralph Beckett) *led: rdn 2f out: pressed and drvn over 1f out: hdd ins fnl f: wknd fnl 75yds* **5/1**[3]

465 **5** *6* **The Paco Kid**[36] 3194 2-9-4 **79**........................ WilliamBuick 1 53
(Olly Stevens) *sn dropped to last pair and outpcd: swtchd lft and clsd 2f out: rdn and hdwy to chse ldrs over 1f out: btn ins fnl f: eased fnl 100yds* **5/1**[3]

0401 **6** *2 1/2* **Zebs Lad (IRE)**[15] 3937 2-9-0 **75**........................ SteveDrowne 3 41
(Ronald Harris) *t.k.h: chsd ldrs: wnt 2nd over 4f out tl over 1f out: sn lost pl: wknd fnl f* **5/1**[3]

1m 10.87s (-0.33) **Going Correction** -0.075s/f (Good) **6** Ran SP% **115.1**
Speed ratings (Par 94): **99,98,95,93,85 82**
CSF £18.37 TOTE £3.20: £2.60, £2.30; EX 9.70 Trifecta £31.40.
**Owner** Al Shaqab Racing **Bred** Tommy Burns **Trained** East Everleigh, Wilts

**FOCUS**
A nursery dominated by the two with the highest official ratings.

## 4431 DOWNLOAD THE NEW LADBROKES APP H'CAP 6f

**7:10** (7:10) (Class 6) (0-65,65) 3-Y-O+ **£2,587** (£770; £384; £192) **Stalls** Centre

Form RPR

4605 **1** **Top Offer**[24] 3589 5-9-9 **62**........................ ShaneKelly 3 73
(Peter Crate) *wl in tch in midfield: clsd to chal over 1f out: rdn to ld ins fnl f: r.o wl* **8/1**

523 **2** *1 1/4* **Assertive Agent**[21] 3734 4-9-6 **59**........................ LukeMorris 11 66
(Tony Carroll) *chsd ldrs: swtchd lft and hdwy u.p over 1f out: pressing ldrs and wnt 2nd ins fnl f: no ex and outpcd towards fin* **7/2**[1]

0-02 **3** *1 1/4* **Saskia's Dream**[16] 3895 6-9-6 **59**..........(v) RichardHughes 6 62
(Jane Chapple-Hyam) *in tch towards rr: effrt and drifting lft over 1f out: styd on ins fnl f: wnt 3rd last strides* **9/2**[2]

0020 **4** *hd* **Only Ten Per Cent (IRE)**[25] 3561 6-9-11 **64**..........(v) FergusSweeney 8 66
(J R Jenkins) *chsd ldr: rdn to ld and edgd rt over 1f out: drvn and hdd ins fnl f: wknd fnl 50yds* **16/1**

1000 **5** *1* **Night Trade (IRE)**[12] 4024 7-9-1 **54**..........(p) SteveDrowne 7 53
(Ronald Harris) *in tch in midfield: swtchd lft and hdwy u.p in centre over 1f out: kpt on same pce ins fnl f* **25/1**

3000 **6** *shd* **Commandingpresence (USA)**[11] 4049 8-9-6 **59**........ WilliamCarson 9 58
(John Bridger) *led: rdn and hdd over 1f out: sn hmpd: swtchd lft and no ex ent fnl f* **12/1**

-066 **7** *2 1/4* **Tregereth (IRE)**[14] 3966 4-9-0 **56**........................ MatthewLawson(3) 12 48
(Jonathan Portman) *in tch towards rr: rdn and struggling over 2f out: swtchd lft and tried to rally over 1f out: no threat to ldrs* **5/1**[3]

0-30 **8** *1 1/4* **Hit The Lights (IRE)**[30] 3392 4-9-5 **61**........................ ThomasBrown(3) 2 49
(Patrick Chamings) *racd alone on far side: chsd ldrs overall: rdn 2f out: wknd ins fnl f* **8/1**

4305 **9** *13* **New Leyf (IRE)**[38] 3118 8-9-12 **65**..........(b) AdamKirby 5 11
(Jeremy Gask) *hld up in last pair: rdn 1/2-way: wknd over 1f out: wl bhd fnl f* **9/2**[2]

-240 **10** *4* **Yankee Red**[45] 2886 3-9-2 **60**........................ LiamJones 4
(John Best) *s.i.s: a bhd: rdn over 2f out: wl bhd fnl f* **25/1**

1m 10.54s (-0.66) **Going Correction** -0.075s/f (Good)
**WFA** 3 from 4yo+ 5lb **10** Ran SP% **118.7**
Speed ratings (Par 101): **101,99,97,97,96 95,92,91,73,68**
CSF £36.86 CT £145.82 TOTE £11.10: £3.80, £2.00, £2.10; EX 46.10 Trifecta £405.40.
**Owner** Peter Crate **Bred** Juddmonte Farms Ltd **Trained** Newdigate, Surrey

**FOCUS**
Weak handicap form.

## 4432 LADBROKES CLAIMING STKS 1m 1y(P)

**7:45** (7:45) (Class 6) 3-5-Y-O **£2,587** (£770; £384; £192) **Stalls** High

Form RPR

5110 **1** **Tee It Up Tommo (IRE)**[115] 1103 5-9-9 80........................ JimCrowley 3 85+
(Michael Wigham) *hld up off the pce in midfield: clsd to chse ldrs and carried wd bnd 2f out: rdn and rallied to chse ldr over 1f out: str run to ld fnl 50yds: sn in command* **5/4**[1]

3266 **2** *3/4* **Inkerman (IRE)**[17] 3850 4-9-3 74........................ RichardHughes 5 77
(Jamie Osborne) *hld up off the pce in midfield: clsd over 2f out: swtchd lft and gd hdwy on inner to ld wl over 1f out: sn clr: drvn 1f out: hdd fnl 50yds: sn btn* **5/2**[2]

056 **3** *6* **Harry Bosch**[9] 4118 4-9-6 78........................[1] RyanClark(3) 2 69
(Brian Meehan) *w ldr and sn clr of field: led over 2f out: rdn and edgd rt bnd 2f out: sn hdd: 3rd and wknd 1f out* **5/1**[3]

4303 **4** *hd* **Nothing Special**[38] 3105 3-8-8 60..........(p) RichardKingscote 1 60
(Tom Dascombe) *chsd clr ldng pair: clsd and chsng ldrs whn carried rt bnd 2f out: 4th and outpcd over 1f out: wknd* **5/1**[3]

0430 **5** *7* **Dividend Dan (IRE)**[26] 3527 4-8-10 55........................ SladeO'Hara(3) 7 43
(Mike Murphy) *led and sn clr w rival: hdd and rdn over 2f out: carried rt bnd 2f out: sn wknd* **20/1**

- **6** *25* **Speedy Rio (IRE)** 3-8-9........................ LukeMorris 4
(Luke Dace) *s.i.s: a bhd: t.o fnl 3f* **33/1**

06 **7** *9* **Planet Rock**[26] 3517 3-8-0 0..........(b[1]) CamHardie(5) 6
(Keiran Burke) *sn outpcd in last pair: t.o fnl 3f* **66/1**

1m 36.82s (-1.38) **Going Correction** -0.05s/f (Stan)
**WFA** 3 from 4yo+ 8lb **7** Ran SP% **115.5**
Speed ratings (Par 101): **104,103,97,97,90 65,56**
CSF £4.64 TOTE £2.20: £1.30, £2.00; EX 5.30 Trifecta £21.40.
**Owner** Palatinate Thoroughbred Racing Limited **Bred** Oghill House Stud **Trained** Newmarket, Suffolk

**FOCUS**
This looked a competitive little claimer on paper but two drew clear.

## 4433 LADBROKES (S) H'CAP 1m 2f (P)

**8:15** (8:15) (Class 6) (0-65,65) 3-Y-O+ **£2,587** (£770; £384; £192) **Stalls** Low

Form RPR

5000 **1** **Treasure The Ridge (IRE)**[5] 4273 5-10-0 **65**.....(b) SilvestreDeSousa 13 76
(Brett Johnson) *chsd ldr: rdn and ev ch 2f out: led over 1f out: r.o wl and drew clr fnl f* **4/1**[2]

3633 **2** *2 3/4* **Gift Of Silence**[22] 3678 5-9-11 **62**........................ PaddyAspell 11 68
(John Berry) *in tch in midfield: effrt but wdst bnd 2f out: styd on wl u.p ins fnl f: wnt 2nd last strides: no threat to wnr* **12/1**

/-52 **3** *nk* **Tin Pan Alley**[28] 3473 6-10-0 **65**........................ AdamKirby 5 70
(Andy Turnell) *led: rdn 2f out: hdd over 1f out: outpcd by wnr fnl f: lost 2nd last strides* **2/1**[1]

-400 **4** *nk* **Precision Five**[24] 3585 5-9-11 **62**..........(p) JimCrowley 6 67
(Jeremy Gask) *hld up in tch in rr of main gp: swtchd rt and effrt on outer over 1f out: styd on wl ins fnl f: no threat to wnr* **7/1**

2066 **5** *3/4* **Jumbo Prado (USA)**[4] 4279 5-9-6 **57**........................ ShaneKelly 14 60
(John Stimpson) *chsd ldrs: 3rd and rdn ent fnl 2f: styd on same pce fr over 1f out* **20/1**

4105 **6** *1 ½* **Anjuna Beach (USA)**[25] 3553 4-9-13 **64** .......... JamesDoyle 2 64
(Gary Moore) *t.k.h: hld up in tch in midfield: rdn and hdwy to chse ldrs over 1f out: no ex and outpcd fnl 150yds* **6/1**[3]

2060 **7** *hd* **Silvee**[18] 3824 7-8-10 **47** .......... (p) WilliamCarson 1 47
(John Bridger) *chsd ldrs: rdn and lost pl over 2f out: rallied on inner u.p over 1f out: styd on same pce fnl f* **25/1**

000- **8** *½* **Berwin (IRE)**[390] 3635 5-9-9 **60** .......... RichardHughes 7 59
(Sylvester Kirk) *wnt lft s and slowly away: hld up in detached last: clsd over 2f out: pushed along and sme hdwy over 1f out: kpt on same pce ins fnl f* **16/1**

546 **9** *¾* **Claude Greenwood**[35] 3230 4-8-4 **46** .......... (b) CamHardie(5) 9 44
(Linda Jewell) *t.k.h: hld up in tch in rr of main gp: rdn and effrt wl over 1f out: kpt on but n.d* **16/1**

0003 **10** *2 ¼* **Monsieur Chabal**[28] 3471 3-8-5 **52** .......... LukeMorris 3 45
(Jamie Osborne) *in tch in midfield: hdwy to chse ldrs 2f out: sn drvn and edging lft: wknd ins fnl f* **8/1**

2m 6.5s (-0.10) **Going Correction** -0.05s/f (Stan)
**WFA** 3 from 4yo+ 10lb **10** Ran SP% **119.3**
Speed ratings (Par 101): **98,95,95,95,94 93,93,92,92,90**
CSF £52.57 CT £124.59 TOTE £6.10: £2.10, £2.30, £1.10; EX 54.90 Trifecta £246.90.Treasure The Ridge was bought by Andrew Reid for £6,600.
**Owner** Mrs A M Upsdell **Bred** S Coughlan **Trained** Epsom, Surrey

**FOCUS**
As weak handicap form as you could find.

## 4434 LADBROKES FILLIES' H'CAP 1m 2f (P)
**8:45** (8:47) (Class 5) (0-75,75) 3-Y-O+ £3,557 (£1,058; £529; £264) **Stalls** Low

Form RPR

1-10 **1** **Grasped**[75] 2016 4-9-13 **74** .......... [1] JamesDoyle 3 83
(Lady Cecil) *chsd ldr: rdn to ld wl over 1f out: asserted ins fnl f: r.o wl* **7/2**[2]

0254 **2** *¾* **Red Velour**[47] 2847 3-9-1 **72** .......... ChrisCatlin 12 80
(Jeremy Noseda) *in tch in midfield: hdwy on outer to chse ldrs jst over 2f out: chsd wnr ins fnl f: kpt on but a hld* **14/1**

65-5 **3** *nk* **Super Moment (IRE)**[22] 3653 3-8-11 **68** .......... SilvestreDeSousa 2 75
(Saeed bin Suroor) *led: rdn ent fnl 2f: hdd wl over 1f out: styd on same pce ins fnl f* **5/1**[3]

4-00 **4** *nk* **Shining Glitter (IRE)**[38] 3106 3-8-5 **67** .......... CamHardie(5) 11 73
(James Fanshawe) *in tch in midfield: hdwy and swtchd lft over 1f out: styd on strly fnl 100yds: nt rch ldrs* **16/1**

3344 **5** *¾* **Tilstarr (IRE)**[16] 3874 4-9-10 **71** .......... GeorgeBaker 4 76
(Roger Teal) *t.k.h: pushed rt s: chsd ldrs: rdn and unable qck wl over 1f out: kpt on same pce u.p ins fnl f* **8/1**

0-22 **6** *½* **Dalmatia (IRE)**[20] 3750 3-9-3 **74** .......... ShaneKelly 10 78
(Sir Michael Stoute) *chsd ldrs: 4th and unable qck over 1f out: pushed along and styd on same pce ins fnl f* **2/1**[1]

-444 **7** *1 ¼* **Lyric Ballad**[24] 3582 4-9-11 **72** .......... (b[1]) RichardHughes 7 74
(Hughie Morrison) *led rdrless to s: s.i.s: in tch in rr: effrt u.p over 2f out: no imp: bhd fnl f* **25/1**

3213 **8** *shd* **Starlit Cantata**[16] 3897 3-9-0 **71** .......... JohnFahy 13 72
(Eve Johnson Houghton) *in tch in midfield: effrt but stuck wd bnd 2f out: kpt on but no imp fr over 1f out* **12/1**

5313 **9** *1* **Oratorio's Joy (IRE)**[12] 4030 4-9-11 **72** .......... WilliamCarson 9 72
(Jamie Osborne) *dwlt and rdn leaving stalls: in tch towards rr: clrest of runs over 2f out: swtchd rt and drvn over 1f out: kpt on but no threat to ldrs* **25/1**

4342 **10** *8* **Swiss Kiss**[12] 4029 3-9-4 **75** .......... WilliamBuick 6 59
(John Gosden) *t.k.h early: chsd ldrs tl settled bk into midfield after 2f: rdn and lost pl bnd 2f out: n.d after* **8/1**

004- **11** *3 ½* **Pearlofthequarter**[245] 7934 3-8-7 **64** .......... LukeMorris 5 42
(Jonathan Portman) *short of room sn after s: in tch in midfield: wknd u.p over 1f out* **50/1**

2m 5.19s (-1.41) **Going Correction** -0.05s/f (Stan)
**WFA** 3 from 4yo+ 10lb **11** Ran SP% **124.3**
Speed ratings (Par 100): **103,102,102,101,101 100,99,99,99,92 89**
CSF £54.05 CT £255.08 TOTE £5.00: £2.00, £3.40, £2.10; EX 71.80 Trifecta £313.70.
**Owner** K Abdullah **Bred** Juddmonte Farms Ltd **Trained** Newmarket, Suffolk

T/Plt: £9.40 to a £1 stake. Pool: £64,670.10 - 5,016.89 winning tickets. T/Qpdt: £3.70 to a £1 stake. Pool: £6,423.37 - 1,263.36 winning tickets. SP

# [4395] NEWBURY (L-H)
Saturday, July 19

**OFFICIAL GOING: Good (good to firm in places; 6.6)**
Wind: mild breeze behind in relation to stright Weather: overcast, hot

## 4435 COMPTON BEAUCHAMP ESTATES LTD MAIDEN STKS (BOBIS RACE) 1m 2f 6y
**1:35** (1:35) (Class 4) 3-Y-O £4,513 (£1,351; £675; £337; £168; £84) **Stalls** Centre

Form RPR

-265 **1** **Saab Almanal**[50] 2746 3-9-5 **95** .......... TomQueally 1 92+
(James Fanshawe) *trckd ldrs: pushed along to chal wl over 1f out: led fnl 120yds: styd on wl: asserting at fin: pushed out* **10/3**[2]

322 **2** *¾* **Smiling Stranger (IRE)**[27] 3498 3-9-5 **82** .......... OisinMurphy 3 91
(Andrew Balding) *led: rdn whn strly chal 2f out: hdd fnl 120yds: styd on* **4/1**

5 **3** *3 ½* **Deuce Again**[37] 3141 3-9-0 **0** .......... SteveDrowne 11 79
(John Gosden) *hld up towards rr: pushed along and hdwy over 2f out: wnt 3rd ent fnl f: styd on but nt pce to trble front pair* **14/1**

**4** *shd* **Long Cross** 3-9-5 **0** .......... WilliamBuick 9 84
(John Gosden) *hld up towards rr: pushed along and stdy prog fr 3f out: wnt 4th ent fnl f: styd on nicely wout ever threatening* **7/2**[3]

-256 **5** *3 ¼* **Automated**[72] 2087 3-9-5 **88** .......... RichardHughes 4 78
(Clive Brittain) *mid-div: hdwy over 3f out: rdn in disp 3rd 2f out: nt pce to chal: wknd fnl 120yds* **3/1**[1]

3-4 **6** *1* **Skilled**[58] 2485 3-9-5 **0** .......... JamesDoyle 2 76
(Roger Charlton) *mid-div: hdwy over 2f out: sn rdn in disp 3rd: nvr trbld ldng pair: wknd fnl 140yds* **14/1**

50 **7** *2 ½* **Cabin Fever**[33] 3315 3-9-0 **0** .......... RichardKingscote 7 66+
(Ralph Beckett) *hld up towards rr: hdwy over 2f out where nt clrest of runs: styd on same pce fnl f: nvr any danger* **25/1**

53-0 **8** *5* **Tinga (IRE)**[99] 1424 3-9-0 **82** .......... JimCrowley 10 57
(Ralph Beckett) *mid-div: rdn over 2f out: nvr any imp: wknd over 1f out* **16/1**

0 **9** *3 ¾* **Saturation Point**[21] 3712 3-9-0 **0** .......... AndreaAtzeni 5 50
(James Toller) *s.i.s: a towards rr* **66/1**

00 **10** *14* **En Reve**[11] 4052 3-9-0 **0** .......... FergusSweeney 6 23
(Seamus Durack) *trckd ldr tl rdn over 2f out: sn wknd* **200/1**

0 **11** *13* **Beauchamp Kite**[45] 2881 3-9-5 **0** .......... (b[1]) DavidProbert 8 3
(Paul Fitzsimons) *chsd ldrs tl lost pl 4f out: sn rdn: wknd over 2f out* **200/1**

2m 9.39s (0.59) **Going Correction** +0.25s/f (Good) **11** Ran SP% **115.9**
Speed ratings (Par 102): **107,106,103,103,100 100,98,94,91,79 69**
CSF £16.71 TOTE £4.80: £1.70, £1.40, £3.70; EX 13.80 Trifecta £138.40.
**Owner** Mohamed Obaida **Bred** Rabbah Bloodstock Limited **Trained** Newmarket, Suffolk

**FOCUS**
Rail out between 1m and 5f on Round course and distances on Round course increased by 18yds. There was a 3m cut-off at 1m1f leading into bend to give fresh ground. There was 5mm of rain overnight, which left the ground officially good, good to firm in places, although the jockeys thought it was more like good, or on the easy side of good. A decent enough maiden, featuring four horses with official marks of 82 plus. The winner did it well even if his bare form was 10lb+ off his York figure.

## 4436 AL BASTI EQUIWORLD EBF BREEDING WINNERS FILLIES' H'CAP 1m (S)
**2:05** (2:07) (Class 2) (0-100,96) 3-Y-O+
£12,450 (£3,728; £1,864; £932; £466; £234) **Stalls** Centre

Form RPR

4411 **1** **Kosika (USA)**[16] 3879 4-9-5 **87** .......... FrannyNorton 5 101
(Mark Johnston) *mde all: qcknd clr over 1f out: unchal* **8/1**

231 **2** *3 ¼* **Token Of Love**[28] 3476 3-8-12 **88** .......... MartinHarley 8 93+
(William Haggas) *hld up towards rr: hdwy jst over 2f out: sn rdn and looking to be hanging lft: styd on to chse wnr jst ins fnl f but nvr any ch* **9/4**[1]

-060 **3** *¾* **Oxsana**[31] 3357 3-9-0 **90** .......... LiamJones 6 93
(William Haggas) *mid-div: hdwy over 2f out: sn rdn: disp 2nd briefly ent fnl f: styd on* **20/1**

621- **4** *1 ½* **Enraptured (IRE)**[330] 5716 3-8-10 **86** .......... WilliamBuick 3 85
(John Gosden) *trckd ldrs: rdn to chse wnr 2f out tl no ex ent fnl f* **7/1**[3]

-200 **5** *1 ¼* **Jordan Princess**[37] 3143 3-8-12 **88** .......... AndreaAtzeni 2 84
(Luca Cumani) *hld up towards rr: rdn 2f out: no imp tl styd on wl ent fnl f* **11/2**[2]

-000 **6** *2 ¼* **Folk Melody (IRE)**[21] 3727 3-9-2 **92** .......... SilvestreDeSousa 4 83
(Charlie Appleby) *mid-div: rdn 2f out: nvr any real imp* **20/1**

326 **7** *6* **Feedyah (USA)**[31] 3357 3-9-6 **96** .......... AdamKirby 11 74
(Charlie Appleby) *trckd ldrs: rdn 2f out: wknd jst over 1f out* **7/1**[3]

0046 **8** *6* **Miss Lillie**[11] 4053 3-8-2 **78** .......... (p) WilliamCarson 9 42
(Roger Teal) *mid-div: pushed along 4f out: sn lost pl: wknd over 1f out* **33/1**

0-22 **9** *nse* **Gown (IRE)**[8] 4163 3-8-4 **80** .......... JimmyQuinn 7 44
(Charles Hills) *trckd wnr tl rdn 2f out: sn wknd* **16/1**

5-06 **10** *2* **Ligeia**[21] 3727 3-8-4 **80** .......... KieranO'Neill 1 39
(Richard Hannon) *a towards rr* **50/1**

-110 **11** *3 ½* **Aertex (IRE)**[35] 3247 3-8-11 **87** .......... RichardHughes 10 38
(Richard Hannon) *hld up towards rr: rdn over 2f out: nvr any imp: wknd fnl f* **7/1**[3]

1m 36.46s (-3.24) **Going Correction** -0.20s/f (Firm)
**WFA** 3 from 4yo 8lb **11** Ran SP% **115.1**
Speed ratings (Par 96): **108,104,104,102,101 99,93,87,86,84 81**
CSF £24.60 CT £352.55 TOTE £8.70: £2.90, £1.30, £4.90; EX 26.70 Trifecta £439.10.
**Owner** Sheikh Hamdan bin Mohammed Al Maktoum **Bred** Betz Thoroughbred Et Al **Trained** Middleham Moor, N Yorks

**FOCUS**
Older fillies have held a significant edge over the 3yos in this race in recent times, and the only 4yo in the field this year enhanced that statistic further with a commanding, all-the-way win. Another step up from the winner.

## 4437 DOOM BAR STKS (REGISTERED AS THE STEVENTON STAKES) (LISTED RACE) 1m 2f 6y
**2:40** (2:40) (Class 1) 3-Y-O+
£20,982 (£7,955; £3,981; £1,983; £995; £499) **Stalls** Centre

Form RPR

362 **1** **Amralah (IRE)**[15] 3930 4-9-4 **103** .......... AndreaAtzeni 2 111
(Mick Channon) *racd keenly: led for 2f: trckd ldr: led over 2f out: sn rdn: kpt on gamely: jst hld on: all out* **16/1**

0-20 **2** *shd* **Vancouverite**[112] 1183 4-9-4 **115** .......... (b[1]) JamieSpencer 3 111+
(Charlie Appleby) *hld up: hdwy 2f out: nt clrest of runs and sn swtchd rt and rdn: str run fr jst ins fnl f: edged lft: fin wl: jst failed* **10/1**[3]

11-3 **3** *1 ½* **Nabucco**[56] 2554 5-9-7 **109** .......... WilliamBuick 4 111
(John Gosden) *in tch: tk clsr order 3f out: rdn 2f out: chsd wnr over 1f out: styd on but no ex fnl f* **7/1**[2]

326- **4** *2 ¼* **Al Kazeem**[286] 7058 6-9-4 **124** .......... JamesDoyle 10 105
(Roger Charlton) *mid-div: hdwy over 2f out: rdn to dispute 2nd over 1f out tl no ex ent fnl f: hld in 4th whn leaned on fnl 130yds* **11/10**[1]

10-5 **5** *nk* **Out Of Bounds (USA)**[68] 2223 5-9-4 **105** .......... SilvestreDeSousa 8 104
(Saeed bin Suroor) *racd keenly trcking ldrs: rdn over 2f out: edgd lft jst over 1f out: styd on same pce* **25/1**

**6** *1 ¼* **Sir Walter Scott (IRE)**[279] 7229 4-9-4 **0** .......... AdamKirby 6 101
(Luca Cumani) *hld up towards rr: sme hdwy 2f out: sn rdn: styd on fnl f but nt gng pce to get involved* **12/1**

0-30 **7** *4* **Triple Threat (FR)**[83] 1783 4-9-4 **111** .......... MaximeGuyon 7 93
(A Fabre, France) *trckd ldrs early: midfield after 2f: rdn over 2f out: nvr finding pce to get on terms* **7/1**[2]

42 **8** *11* **Baltic Knight (IRE)**[21] 3731 4-9-4 **107** .......... RichardHughes 1 72
(Richard Hannon) *hld up towards rr: effrt over 3f out: wknd over 1f out* **14/1**

0-00 **9** *6* **Battle Of Marengo (IRE)**[133] 900 4-9-4 **113** .......... [1] JimCrowley 9 61
(David Simcock) *mid-div: rdn over 3f out: wknd 2f out* **12/1**

0- **10** *8* **Zaidiyn (FR)**[66] 4-9-4 **94** .......... PaulHanagan 5 46
(Brian Ellison) *s.i.s: in rr tl swtchd out and hdwy after 1f: led after 2f: rdn and hdd over 2f out: sn btn* **50/1**

2m 8.59s (-0.21) **Going Correction** +0.25s/f (Good) **10** Ran SP% **115.5**
Speed ratings (Par 111): **110,109,108,106,106 105,102,93,88,82**
CSF £164.33 TOTE £21.30: £4.30, £3.20, £2.20; EX 226.20 Trifecta £927.00.
**Owner** Prince A A Faisal **Bred** Nawara Stud Co Ltd **Trained** West Ilsley, Berks

**FOCUS**
The time only comes out the same as the opening maiden. The winenr showed his Sandown form doesn't flatter him and the third helps set the standard.

## 4438 AL BASTI EQUIWORLD HACKWOOD STKS (GROUP 3) 6f 8y
**3:15** (3:15) (Class 1) 3-Y-O+
**£34,026** (£12,900; £6,456; £3,216; £1,614; £810) **Stalls** Centre

Form RPR
-164 **1** **Music Master**[28] 3451 4-9-4 112 FergusSweeney 10 115+
(Henry Candy) *racd centre: hld up towards rr: hdwy fr wl over 1f out: gap appeared kindly ent fnl f: rdn and r.o strly fnl 140yds: led fnl strides* **3/1**[1]
4-50 **2** *nk* **Heeraat (IRE)**[66] 2256 5-9-4 108 PaulHanagan 1 114
(William Haggas) *racd centre: broke wl: stdd sn after towards rr: hdwy over 2f out: sn rdn: str chal jst ins fnl f: led narrowly towards fin: hdd fnl strides* **11/1**
2300 **3** *shd* **Es Que Love (IRE)**[28] 3451 5-9-4 107 AdamKirby 6 114
(Clive Cox) *racd centre: chsd ldrs: rdn 2f out: led over 1f out: kpt on: hdd nring fin* **17/2**
-322 **4** *2 ½* **Naadirr (IRE)**[35] 3253 3-8-13 108 MartinHarley 8 105
(Marco Botti) *racd centre: mid-div: rdn and hdwy over 1f out: kpt on ins fnl f but nt pce to rch ldrs* **13/2**[3]
1110 **5** *hd* **That Is The Spirit**[31] 3352 3-8-13 106 DanielTudhope 5 104
(David O'Meara) *racd centre: led: rdn and hdd over 1f out: kpt on but no ex fnl f* **10/1**
-016 **6** *1 ¾* **Rocky Ground (IRE)**[28] 3452 4-9-4 113 AndreaAtzeni 14 99
(Roger Varian) *racd stands' side w one other: hld up towards rr: hdwy to ld gp but mid-div overall: sn rdn: kpt on but nt pce to get on terms* **5/1**[2]
30-5 **7** *½* **Hallelujah**[56] 2564 6-9-1 102 (t) HayleyTurner 9 95
(James Fanshawe) *racd centre: chsd ldrs: rdn over 2f out: kpt on same pce fnl f* **22/1**
1233 **8** *2 ½* **Rivellino**[28] 3452 4-9-4 105 JimCrowley 11 90
(K R Burke) *racd centre: mid-div: rdn 2f out: nt pce to chal: fdd fnl f* **9/1**
2250 **9** *shd* **Ahtoug**[14] 3981 6-9-4 113 WilliamBuick 2 90
(Charlie Appleby) *racd centre: chsd ldrs: rdn over 2f out: wknd fnl f* **11/1**
3304 **10** *1 ½* **Complicate (AUS)**[14] 3960 5-9-4 107 SilvestreDeSousa 7 85
(Saeed bin Suroor) *racd centre: chsd ldr: rdn over 2f out: wknd ent fnl f* **25/1**
0402 **11** *1 ¼* **Trader Jack**[8] 4146 5-9-4 83 JimmyFortune 12 81
(David Flood) *racd centre: a towards rr* **100/1**
-454 **12** *nk* **Highland Colori (IRE)**[21] 3723 6-9-4 108 DavidProbert 13 80
(Andrew Balding) *racd stands' side w one other: overall mid-div: rdn over 2f out: sn btn* **14/1**

1m 11.38s (-1.62) **Going Correction** -0.20s/f (Firm)
**WFA** 3 from 4yo+ 5lb **12** Ran SP% **117.1**
Speed ratings (Par 113): **102,101,101,98,97 95,94,91,91,89 87,87**
CSF £36.18 TOTE £3.60: £1.50, £3.80, £2.80; EX 36.20 Trifecta £276.00.
**Owner** Godfrey Wilson **Bred** Mrs C R D Wilson **Trained** Kingston Warren, Oxon

**FOCUS**
A good, competitive Group 3 sprint, and a three-way photo at the line. The winner ran as well as ever.

## 4439 WEATHERBYS SUPER SPRINT (BOBIS RACE) 5f 34y
**3:50** (3:52) (Class 2) 2-Y-O
**£122,925** (£52,275; £24,600; £14,750; £9,825; £7,375) **Stalls** Centre

Form RPR
1212 **1** **Tiggy Wiggy (IRE)**[31] 3353 2-9-1 104 RichardHughes 14 117+
(Richard Hannon) *mde all: qcknd clr over 1f out: v impressive* **5/2**[1]
2135 **2** *6* **Haxby (IRE)**[32] 3322 2-8-10 93 AndreaAtzeni 10 90
(Roger Varian) *chsd wnr: rdn whn readily outpcd by wnr over 1f out: kpt on but sn no ch* **10/1**
51 **3** *1 ¼* **Fast Act (IRE)**[24] 3570 2-8-8 0 JamieSpencer 3 84
(Kevin Ryan) *chsd wnr: rdn whn readily outpcd by wnr over 1f out: kpt pressing for 2nd tl no ex cl home* **12/1**
110 **4** *1* **Bond's Girl**[29] 3415 2-8-0 88 PatrickMathers 16 72+
(Richard Fahey) *s.i.s: sn mid-div: rdn and hdwy over 1f out: r.o ins fnl f: wnt 4th fnl 100yds* **10/1**
2212 **5** *shd* **Realtra (IRE)**[47] 2856 2-8-0 92 SilvestreDeSousa 5 72
(Richard Fahey) *mid-div: hdwy over 3f out: rdn to chse ldrs 2f out: kpt on same pce fnl f* **6/1**[3]
2124 **6** *¾* **Parsley (IRE)**[8] 4164 2-8-2 93 KieranO'Neill 19 71
(Richard Hannon) *chsd ldrs: rdn over 2f out: drifted lft fr 2f out: kpt on same pce fnl f* **16/1**
01 **7** *nk* **Pillar Box (IRE)**[35] 3210 2-8-9 0 LiamJones 13 77
(William Haggas) *chsd ldrs: rdn over 2f out: drifted lft but kpt on fnl f* **20/1**
10 **8** *1 ½* **Harry's Dancer (IRE)**[31] 3353 2-8-0 0 JimmyQuinn 18 62
(John Quinn) *mid-div: rdn over 2f out: nvr any real imp* **5/1**[2]
1615 **9** *¾* **Diamond Creek (IRE)**[8] 4164 2-8-1 81 PaulHanagan 17 61
(Richard Fahey) *chsd ldrs: rdn over 2f out: one pce fnl f* **22/1**
4140 **10** *nse* **Prince Bonnaire**[32] 3322 2-8-6 82 OisinMurphy 23 65
(David Brown) *sn pushed along towards rr: r.o ent fnl f but nvr any ch* **100/1**
1230 **11** *½* **Roudee**[32] 3322 2-8-13 95 RichardKingscote 7 71
(Tom Dascombe) *mid-div: hdwy over 2f out: sn rdn: one pce fnl f* **25/1**
6442 **12** *¾* **Brazen Spirit**[24] 3584 2-8-8 80 JohnFahy 2 63
(Clive Cox) *wnt rt s: towards rr: sme late prog: n.d* **80/1**
3320 **13** *shd* **Harry Hurricane**[32] 3322 2-9-0 81 (p) JamesDoyle 6 69
(George Baker) *mid-div: keeping on at same pce whn hmpd ins fnl f* **66/1**
2110 **14** *nk* **Midterm Break (IRE)**[32] 3322 2-8-13 92 AndrewMullen 15 67
(David Barron) *chsd ldrs tl lost pl after 1f: mid-div and nt a threat after* **33/1**
2135 **15** *¾* **Charlie's Star**[8] 4150 2-8-1 78 ow1 DavidProbert 20 52
(David Evans) *sn pushed along towards rr: nvr any danger* **66/1**
0621 **16** *½* **Magical Memory (IRE)**[23] 3613 2-8-11 88 WilliamBuick 24 60
(Charles Hills) *s.i.s: towards rr: hdwy 3f out: sn rdn: wknd fnl f* **12/1**
631 **17** *nse* **Tachophobia**[17] 3842 2-8-11 83 TonyHamilton 4 60
(Richard Fahey) *nvr bttr than mid-div* **66/1**
62 **18** *¾* **Spirit Of Zeb (IRE)**[9] 4129 2-8-8 0 JamesSullivan 1 54
(Richard Fahey) *nvr bttr than mid-div* **66/1**
62 **19** *1 ½* **Grey Zeb (IRE)**[36] 3188 2-8-10 0 JimCrowley 8 51
(Keith Dalgleish) *chsd ldrs: rdn over 2f out: wknd ent fnl f* **100/1**
14 **20** *2 ½* **Captain Colby (USA)**[66] 2258 2-8-3 83 (p) FrannyNorton 21 35
(Kevin Ryan) *wnt rt s and bmpd: sn mid-div: wknd jst over 1f out* **20/1**
32 **21** *1 ½* **Secret Spirit**[25] 3557 2-8-6 0 RyanTate 22 32
(Clive Cox) *bmpd s: a towards rr* **40/1**
33 **22** *¾* **Eastern Racer (IRE)**[7] 4185 2-8-8 0 StevieDonohoe 25 32
(Brian Ellison) *a towards rr* **66/1**
5212 **23** *4* **Be Bold**[7] 4205 2-8-8 85 (b) SteveDrowne 12 17
(Richard Hannon) *s.i.s: sn mid-div: wknd over 1f out* **66/1**
521 **24** *2 ¼* **L'Etacq**[26] 3524 2-8-11 75 JimmyFortune 9 12
(Richard Hannon) *in tch: rdn over 2f out: wknd ent fnl f* **100/1**

59.85s (-1.55) **Going Correction** -0.20s/f (Firm) **24** Ran SP% **135.2**
Speed ratings (Par 100): **104,94,92,90,90 89,88,86,85,85 84,83,83,82,81 80,80,79,76,72 70,69,62,59**
CSF £26.43 TOTE £3.50: £1.50, £3.60, £4.60; EX 34.00 Trifecta £565.10.
**Owner** Potensis Ltd C Giles Merriebelle Stables **Bred** Cbs Bloodstock **Trained** East Everleigh, Wilts
■ Flyball (66-1) was withdrawn. Rule 4 does not apply.

**FOCUS**
The usual mix of ability on show here, and a runaway winner. The winner rates as good a 5f juvenile filly as we have seen for quite a while. The runner-up and third have been rated to their pre-race marks.

## 4440 LUCK GREAYER BLOODSTOCK SHIPPING CONDITIONS STKS (BOBIS RACE) 7f (S)
**4:25** (4:26) (Class 3) 2-Y-O
**£7,470** (£2,236; £1,118; £559) **Stalls** Centre

Form RPR
01 **1** **Stec (IRE)**[15] 3924 2-8-8 77 JennyPowell(7) 3 90
(Tom Dascombe) *racd centre: mde all: drifted lft whn rdn 2f out: strly pressed ent fnl f: kpt on v gamely: on top at fin* **7/1**[3]
**2** *nk* **Time Test** 2-8-9 0 JamesDoyle 4 83+
(Roger Charlton) *racd centre: trckd wnr: chal wnr ent fnl f: sn rdn: nt qckn: hld nring fin* **8/11**[1]
**3** *12* **Stealing Thunder (IRE)** 2-8-9 0 JamieSpencer 1 51
(Eve Johnson Houghton) *racd far side: trckd ldr: rdn over 2f out: sn outpcd: wnt btn 3rd ent fnl f* **10/1**
03 **4** *12* **Lwah (IRE)**[16] 3875 2-8-12 0 RichardHughes 2 33
(Richard Hannon) *racd far side: led: overall trckd wnr: rdn 2f out: wknd jst over 1f out* **9/4**[2]

1m 26.63s (0.93) **Going Correction** -0.20s/f (Firm) **4** Ran SP% **110.3**
Speed ratings (Par 98): **86,85,71,58**
CSF £13.18 TOTE £8.20; EX 11.50 Trifecta £35.00.
**Owner** D Ward **Bred** D G Iceton **Trained** Malpas, Cheshire
■ Stewards' Enquiry : Jenny Powell two-day ban: use of whip (3-6 Aug)

**FOCUS**
An interesting conditions race but somewhat unsatisfactory, in that for some reason they split into two pairs. Tricky to pin down, but the form has to be given a chance.

## 4441 OAKLEY COACHBUILDERS H'CAP 2m
**5:00** (5:00) (Class 4) (0-85,85) 4-Y-O+
**£4,690** (£1,395; £697; £348) **Stalls** Centre

Form RPR
4114 **1** **See And Be Seen**[15] 3932 4-8-6 69 ow1 (p) RenatoSouza 8 80
(Sylvester Kirk) *trckd ldr: led over 2f out: sn rdn: strly chal ent fnl f: styd on wl to assert fnl 75yds* **14/1**
-000 **2** *2* **Romeo Montague**[28] 3453 6-9-5 83 OisinMurphy 10 91+
(Ed Dunlop) *mid-div: rdn over 3f out: hdwy over 1f out: styd on fnl f: wnt 2nd nring fin* **12/1**
212 **3** *nk* **Ivanhoe**[58] 2490 4-8-5 69 DavidProbert 3 76
(Michael Blanshard) *mid-div: gd hdwy 2f out: rdn and ev ch ent fnl f: no ex fnl 75yds: lost 2nd nring fin* **8/1**
2411 **4** *2 ½* **Manomine**[41] 3032 5-8-11 75 SilvestreDeSousa 4 79
(Clive Brittain) *mid-div: hdwy 3f out: sn rdn to chse ldrs: kpt on tl no ex fnl 120yds* **8/1**
2103 **5** *1* **Story Writer**[17] 3859 5-9-1 79 AndreaAtzeni 7 82
(William Knight) *mid-div: rdn 2f out: styd on fnl f: nvr trbld ldrs* **9/2**[3]
-020 **6** *1 ¼* **Bohemian Rhapsody (IRE)**[12] 3204 5-9-7 85 (p) MartinHarley 9 87
(Seamus Durack) *trckd ldrs: rdn 3f out: styd on same pce fnl 2f* **4/1**[2]
0/0- **7** *1 ¼* **Bilidn**[55] 6750 6-8-13 80 (t) RyanTate(3) 2 80
(Ben De Haan) *trckd ldrs: rdn over 3f out: fdd fnl 120yds* **33/1**
55 **8** *3 ¼* **Desert Recluse (IRE)**[17] 3851 7-8-8 72 StevieDonohoe 1 68
(Ian Williams) *sn led: rdn and hdd over 2f out: wknd fnl f* **20/1**
-600 **9** *6* **Riptide**[27] 3501 8-8-6 75 (v) NoelGarbutt(5) 5 64
(Michael Scudamore) *hld up towards rr: rdn over 3f out: nvr any imp* **25/1**
-650 **10** *23* **Saborido (USA)**[35] 3249 8-8-6 77 KieranShoemark(7) 11 38
(Amanda Perrett) *a towards rr: eased whn btn over 1f out* **25/1**
3416 **11** *1 ½* **Number One London (IRE)**[28] 3453 4-9-5 83 (p) JimmyFortune 12 43
(Brian Meehan) *towards rr of midfield: sme hdwy 4f out: sn rdn: eased whn appeared to lose action wl over 1f out* **3/1**[1]
242/ **12** *24* **Zakatal**[139] 8235 8-8-11 78 RyanPowell(3) 13 9
(Simon Earle) *a towards rr: eased whn btn over 1f out* **40/1**
/0-0 **13** *11* **War Singer (USA)**[17] 3860 7-9-3 81 (t) HayleyTurner 6
(Johnny Farrelly) *a towards rr: eased whn btn over 1f out* **33/1**

3m 33.49s (1.49) **Going Correction** +0.25s/f (Good) **13** Ran SP% **120.5**
Speed ratings (Par 105): **106,105,104,103,103 102,101,100,97,85 84,72,67**
CSF £157.46 CT £1450.37 TOTE £13.50: £3.40, £4.10, £2.30; EX 196.60 Trifecta £1796.20 Part won..
**Owner** Timothy Pearson **Bred** Exors Of The Late T E Pocock **Trained** Upper Lambourn, Berks

**FOCUS**
A fair staying handicap. Another personal best from the winner.
T/Plt: £196.30 to a £1 stake. Pool: £138194.61 - 513.66 winning tickets T/Qpdt: £65.40 to a £1 stake. Pool: £8227.19 - 93.00 winning tickets TM

# 4402 NEWMARKET (R-H)
Saturday, July 19

**OFFICIAL GOING: Good to firm (good in places)**
Wind: Nil Weather: Fine

## 4442 32REDSPORT.COM H'CAP 1m
**1:50** (1:52) (Class 2) (0-105,103) 3-Y-O+
**£28,012** (£8,388; £4,194; £2,097; £1,048; £526) **Stalls** High

Form RPR
0150 **1** **Balty Boys (IRE)**[14] 3962 5-9-7 97 (b) PaulPickard 13 106
(Brian Ellison) *a.p: rdn over 3f out: r.o to ld wl ins fnl f* **16/1**
1312 **2** *1* **Johnno**[8] 4169 5-9-1 91 (b) PaddyAspell 14 98
(David Nicholls) *hld up in tch: led over 2f out: sn rdn: hdd wl ins fnl f* **7/1**
0121 **3** *2* **Llanarmon Lad (IRE)**[21] 3726 5-9-0 95 CamHardie(5) 10 97
(Brian Ellison) *chsd ldrs: rdn over 3f out: styd on same pce ins fnl f* **9/2**[1]
-040 **4** *¾* **Fury**[35] 3251 6-9-2 92 (b) RyanMoore 7 93
(William Haggas) *hld up: rdn over 3f out: hdwy over 1f out: styd on* **6/1**[2]

-155 **5** *5* **Boonga Roogeta**[11] 4060 5-8-11 **90**....................(v[1]) RosieJessop(3) 11 79
(Peter Charalambous) *chsd ldr: rdn and ev ch over 2f out: wknd fnl f* **40/1**

60-4 **6** *3 ½* **Albaqaa**[8] 4169 9-8-2 **83**.............................ShelleyBirkett(5) 6 64
(P J O'Gorman) *hld up: hdwy over 2f out: rdn: edgd lft and wknd over 1f out* **20/1**

4131 **7** *2 ½* **Balducci**[16] 3886 7-9-7 **97**....................(v) DavidNolan 1 72
(David O'Meara) *led and sn clr: rdn and hdd over 2f out: wknd over 1f out* **10/1**

2420 **8** *3 ¾* **Busatto (USA)**[14] 3982 4-8-13 **92**....................MichaelJMMurphy(3) 2 59
(Mark Johnston) *chsd ldrs: rdn and carried rt over 2f out: wknd over 1f out* **13/2**[3]

02 **9** *2 ¾* **Tanseeb**[35] 3244 3-8-2 **86**....................JoeFanning 3 44
(Mark Johnston) *chsd ldrs: rdn over 2f out: sn edgd lft and wknd* **6/1**[2]

14-0 **10** *10* **Common Touch (IRE)**[51] 2707 6-9-4 **94**....................KierenFallon 5 31
(Willie Musson) *hld up: pushed along over 3f out: wknd over 1f out* **25/1**

113- **11** *nk* **Music Theory (IRE)**[322] 5999 3-9-5 **103**....................MartinLane 12 38
(Charlie Appleby) *hld up: hdwy 1/2-way: hung rt fr over 3f out: wknd over 1f out* **10/1**

1m 40.71s (0.71) **Going Correction** +0.20s/f (Good)
**WFA** 3 from 4yo+ 8lb **11** Ran SP% **107.7**
Speed ratings (Par 109): **104,103,101,100,95 91,89,85,82,72 72**
CSF £100.27 CT £443.97 TOTE £17.40: £4.30, £1.90, £2.00; EX 119.10 Trifecta £1301.90 Part won..
**Owner** Koo's Racing Club, Carr & Jacobs **Bred** Lynn Lodge Stud **Trained** Norton, N Yorks
■ Rule 4 of 10p in the pound applies to all bets; Withdrawn: Prince Of Johanne
■ Stewards' Enquiry : Paul Pickard four-day ban: use of whip (3-6 Aug)

**FOCUS**
Stands' side track used with stalls on far side, except 1m2f & 1m4f: centre. The meeting started with what looked a fiendishly difficult handicap to work out, but it's easy to pick holes in the result. Prince Of Johanne refused to go in the stalls, Music Theory unshipped his rider on the way to the start (before being quickly caught) and ran moderately, Balducci went off far too quickly and coming up the far rail proved to be an advantage in this.

## 4443 NEWSELLS PARK STUD STKS (REGISTERED AS THE APHRODITE STAKES) (LISTED RACE) (F&M) 1m 4f

**2:25** (2:25) (Class 1) 3-Y-0+

**£22,684** (£8,600; £4,304; £2,144; £1,076; £540) **Stalls** Centre

Form RPR

-512 **1** **Noble Protector**[77] 1942 4-9-2 90....................ShelleyBirkett 2 108
(Stuart Kittow) *a.p: nt clr run and swtchd lft over 2f out: led over 1f out: rdn and edgd lft ins fnl f: r.o wl* **12/1**

3123 **2** *5* **Criteria (IRE)**[30] 3376 3-8-4 104....................NickyMackay 5 100
(John Gosden) *a.p: chsd ldr over 2f out: ld over 1f out: sn rdn and hdd: styd on same pce ins fnl f* **3/1**[1]

1205 **3** *9* **Groovejet**[37] 3143 3-8-7 88 ow3....................RobertHavlin 6 89
(Peter Chapple-Hyam) *hld up: nt clr run over 3f out: hdwy 2f out: sn rdn: styd on same pce: wnt 3rd wl ins fnl f* **66/1**

-153 **4** *½* **Queen Of Ice**[37] 3143 3-8-4 93....................MartinDwyer 14 85+
(William Haggas) *chsd ldr tl led over 9f out: rdn and hdd over 1f out: wknd ins fnl f* **9/1**[3]

-460 **5** *½* **Astonishing (IRE)**[14] 3961 4-9-2 101....................RyanMoore 11 84
(Sir Michael Stoute) *hld up: swtchd lft and hdwy over 2f out: sn rdn: wknd fnl f* **7/2**[2]

1606 **6** *½* **Flemish School**[15] 3930 4-9-2 90....................(p) GrahamLee 8 84
(David Elsworth) *hld up: nt clr run over 2f out: rdn over 1f out: n.d* **33/1**

-500 **7** *3 ¼* **Khione**[49] 2764 5-9-2 103....................LukeMorris 13 78
(Luca Cumani) *hld up: hdwy over 4f out: rdn whn hmpd over 2f out: wknd over 1f out* **10/1**

311- **8** *shd* **Speckled (USA)**[261] 7650 4-9-2 95....................MartinLane 4 78
(Charlie Appleby) *mid-div: hdwy over 4f out: rdn over 2f out: wknd over 1f out* **12/1**

3155 **9** *2 ¼* **Special Meaning**[49] 2764 4-9-5 93....................JoeFanning 9 78+
(Mark Johnston) *led: hdd over 9f out: chsd ldr tl rdn over 2f out: wknd over 1f out* **9/1**[3]

14 **10** *1* **Kallisha**[70] 2152 3-8-4 90....................CamHardie 1 73
(Ralph Beckett) *s.i.s: sn rcvrd into mid-div: rdn over 2f out: wknd over 1f out* **14/1**

1110 **11** *10* **Anipa**[43] 2960 3-8-7 98....................HarryBentley 7 60
(Roger Varian) *mid-div: hdwy over 4f out: rdn and wknd 2f out* **14/1**

-466 **12** *10* **Uchenna (IRE)**[37] 3143 3-8-4 88....................AdamBeschizza 10 41
(David Simcock) *mid-div: hdwy over 4f out: rdn and wknd over 1f out* **50/1**

**13** *32* **Dame Lucy (IRE)**[266] 7553 4-9-2 0....................KierenFallon 3
(Michael Murphy) *hld up: pushed along over 3f out: sn wknd and eased* **33/1**

5-05 **14** *47* **Rock Choir**[33] 3307 4-9-2 93....................SebSanders 12
(William Haggas) *chsd ldrs tl rdn and wknd 3f out: eased* **16/1**

2m 29.4s (-3.50) **Going Correction** -0.025s/f (Good)
**WFA** 3 from 4yo+ 12lb **14** Ran SP% **120.2**
Speed ratings (Par 111): **110,106,100,100,100 99,97,97,95,95 88,81,60,29**
CSF £46.89 TOTE £13.70: £4.20, £1.60, £12.40; EX 60.90 Trifecta £2305.20 Part won..
**Owner** The Black Type Partnership III **Bred** D R Tucker **Trained** Blackborough, Devon
■ Stewards' Enquiry : Ryan Moore three-day ban: careless riding (6, 7, 8 Aug) £290 fine: left course within five mins of weighed in announcement

**FOCUS**
Plenty of these had met before, and it didn't look that strong for the grade. That said, the pace seemed sound. The winner posted a clear personal best.

## 4444 LETTERGOLD MAIDEN AUCTION FILLIES' STKS (BOBIS RACE) 7f

**3:05** (3:09) (Class 5) 2-Y-0 **£3,881** (£1,155; £577; £288) **Stalls** High

Form RPR

2 **1** **Arethusa**[17] 3858 2-8-9 0....................KierenFallon 14 79
(Ed Dunlop) *a.p: chsd ldr 1/2-way: shkn up to ld over 1f out: r.o* **11/4**[1]

**2** *2 ¼* **Thunder In Myheart (IRE)** 2-8-8 0....................LouisSteward(5) 1 77+
(Michael Bell) *a.p: rdn over 1f out: r.o to go 2nd nr fin* **10/1**

5 **3** *1* **What A Party (IRE)**[16] 3893 2-8-6 0....................HarryBentley 4 67
(Gay Kelleway) *chsd ldr to 1/2-way: rdn over 1f out: styd on* **100/1**

5 **4** *shd* **Multi Grain**[27] 3497 2-8-9 0....................JoeFanning 11 70
(Brian Ellison) *led: hdd over 5f out: chsd ldrs: rdn over 1f out: styd on* **6/1**

00 **5** *2 ½* **Lady Mascot (IRE)**[25] 3557 2-8-6 0....................CamHardie(5) 6 65
(Richard Hannon) *led over 5f out: rdn and hdd over 1f out: wknd ins fnl f* **20/1**

6 **6** *2 ¾* **Zubaidah**[25] 3558 2-8-13 0....................PatCosgrave 5 60
(George Baker) *chsd ldrs: rdn over 2f out: wknd fnl f* **4/1**[2]

**7** *hd* **Titled Lady** 2-8-8 0....................LiamKeniry 13 54+
(David Elsworth) *hld up: styd on appr fnl f: nvr nrr* **25/1**

**8** *¾* **Ickymasho** 2-8-8 0....................LukeMorris 16 52
(Jonathan Portman) *hld up: hdwy 1/2-way: rdn and wknd over 1f out* **50/1**

**9** *2* **Theydon Bois** 2-8-3 0....................RosieJessop(3) 12 45
(Peter Charalambous) *s.s: hdwy over 4f out: rdn and wknd over 1f out* **66/1**

**10** *½* **Tinkers Kiss (IRE)** 2-8-2 0....................DannyBrock(5) 8 44
(Philip McBride) *mid-div: rdn over 2f out: wknd fnl f* **33/1**

**11** *5* **Jellwa (IRE)** 2-9-0 0....................WilliamTwiston-Davies 10 38
(Mick Channon) *prom: rdn over 2f out: wknd over 1f out* **11/2**[3]

6 **12** *nk* **Stamp Of Approval (IRE)**[30] 3387 2-8-6 0....................AshleyMorgan(3) 7 32
(Chris Wall) *hld up: rdn over 2f out: wknd over 1f out* **40/1**

**13** *nk* **Pisces** 2-8-4 0....................SimonPearce(3) 3 29
(David Elsworth) *sn pushed along and a in rr* **20/1**

0 **14** *½* **Happy Pursuit**[54] 2612 2-8-11 0....................AdamBeschizza 9 32
(Stuart Williams) *hld up: rdn over 2f out: a in rr* **66/1**

**15** *7* **Vivo Per Lei (IRE)** 2-8-5 0....................DanielMuscutt(5) 15 12
(Marco Botti) *prom: rdn over 2f out: sn wknd* **50/1**

**16** *20* **Colours Of Glory (IRE)** 2-8-9 0....................TedDurcan 2
(Charles Hills) *s.s: a in rr: wknd over 2f out* **20/1**

**17** *10* **Snow Cover** 2-8-9 0....................NickyMackay 17
(Roger Varian) *prom: lost pl over 4f out: bhd fr 1/2-way* **10/1**

1m 28.41s (2.71) **Going Correction** +0.20s/f (Good) **17** Ran SP% **125.9**
Speed ratings (Par 91): **92,89,88,88,85 82,81,81,78,78 72,72,71,71,63 40,28**
CSF £28.58 TOTE £3.20: £1.70, £3.30, £11.30; EX 45.50 Trifecta £2351.10 Part won..
**Owner** The Serendipity Partnership **Bred** Highbury Stud & John Troy **Trained** Newmarket, Suffolk

**FOCUS**
Probably not a strong contest. They got racing a long way out.

## 4445 EBF STALLIONS 32RED FILLIES' H'CAP 6f

**3:40** (3:41) (Class 3) (0-95,95) 3-Y-0+

**£8,715** (£2,609; £1,304; £652; £326; £163) **Stalls** High

Form RPR

144- **1** **Athenian (IRE)**[234] 8064 5-9-9 **92**....................LukeMorris 1 100
(Sir Mark Prescott Bt) *stmbld s: sn trcking ldrs: rdn to ld over 1f out: edgd lft ins fnl f: styd on* **5/1**[3]

1-06 **2** *½* **Artistic Charm**[22] 3674 3-8-9 **83**....................HarryBentley 6 88
(David Simcock) *s.i.s: hld up: hdwy and nt clr run 1f out: sn rdn: r.o* **12/1**

1322 **3** *nk* **Lady Horatia**[19] 3788 3-8-10 **84**....................MartinDwyer 2 88+
(William Muir) *trckd ldrs: rdn over 1f out: edgd lft ins fnl f: r.o* **3/1**[1]

-250 **4** *¾* **Mar Mar (IRE)**[36] 3203 4-9-11 **94**....................[1] KierenFallon 10 97
(Saeed bin Suroor) *w ldr: rdn and ev ch over 1f out: edgd lft ins fnl f: styd on same pce* **7/1**

0015 **5** *4 ½* **Baby Bush (IRE)**[29] 3425 3-8-2 **81**....................CamHardie(5) 5 69
(Richard Hannon) *chsd ldrs: rdn over 1f out: no ex ins fnl f* **8/1**

1-21 **6** *½* **Souville**[36] 3185 3-8-10 **84**....................TedDurcan 8 70
(Chris Wall) *trckd ldrs: rdn over 1f out: eased whn btn ins fnl f* **9/2**[2]

3062 **7** *nk* **Jillnextdoor (IRE)**[21] 3693 4-9-4 **87**....................WilliamTwiston-Davies 7 73
(Mick Channon) *hld up: effrt over 1f out: no ex fnl f* **20/1**

4-62 **8** *hd* **Holley Shiftwell**[22] 3676 4-8-12 **81**....................AdamBeschizza 3 66
(Stuart Williams) *led: rdn and hdd over 1f out: wknd ins fnl f* **12/1**

440- **9** *2 ½* **Sound Of Guns**[372] 4260 4-9-12 **95**....................GeorgeBaker 9 72
(Ed Walker) *hld up: effrt over 2f out: edgd lft and wknd over 1f out* **14/1**

6306 **P** **Kyleakin Lass**[48] 2803 5-9-5 **88**....................JoeFanning 4
(Jonathan Portman) *hld up: p.u and dismntd wl over 2f out: lame* **16/1**

1m 13.5s (1.00) **Going Correction** +0.20s/f (Good)
**WFA** 3 from 4yo+ 5lb **10** Ran SP% **116.2**
Speed ratings (Par 104): **101,100,99,98,92 92,91,91,88,**
CSF £63.09 CT £215.50 TOTE £5.60: £2.30, £4.10, £1.40; EX 66.50 Trifecta £276.20.
**Owner** Axom (XXXI) **Bred** Keatly Overseas Ltd **Trained** Newmarket, Suffolk

**FOCUS**
For some reason most of the jockeys didn't seem to want to go on in this sprint, so the early part of the contest was moderately run. Personal bests from the first two.

## 4446 PETER ALLUM MAIDEN STKS 7f

**4:15** (4:15) (Class 5) 3-Y-0 **£3,881** (£1,155; £577; £288) **Stalls** High

Form RPR

4-32 **1** **Marmoom**[9] 4111 3-9-5 80....................GeorgeBaker 2 90+
(Charles Hills) *chsd ldr tl led over 2f out: shkn up over 1f out: r.o: eased nr fin* **7/4**[1]

2 **2** *¾* **Cloud Line**[22] 3664 3-9-0 0....................HarryBentley 5 83
(William Haggas) *a prominengt: rdn to chse wnr over 1f out: r.o* **9/4**[2]

06- **3** *6* **Purple Lane (IRE)**[229] 8124 3-9-5 0....................MartinLane 4 72
(David Simcock) *hld up: hdwy 1/2-way: rdn over 1f out: styd on same pce* **16/1**

63 **4** *¾* **Venturous Spirit (IRE)**[20] 3755 3-9-0 0....................NickyMackay 10 66
(John Gosden) *chsd ldrs: shkn up over 1f out: styd on same pce* **14/1**

4 **5** *¾* **Lockhart (IRE)**[12] 4022 3-9-5 0....................JoeFanning 6 69
(Mark Johnston) *led over 4f: sn rdn: wknd ins fnl f* **4/1**[3]

**6** *2 ¾* **Quaintrelle (IRE)** 3-9-0 0....................LukeMorris 3 56
(Ed Vaughan) *chsd ldrs: rdn over 2f out: hung lft and wknd over 1f out* **50/1**

**7** *shd* **Crysdal** 3-9-0 0....................TedDurcan 12 56
(David Lanigan) *s.i.s: hld up: rdn over 2f out: wknd over 1f out* **25/1**

**8** *4* **Gharaaneej (IRE)** 3-9-0 0....................RobertHavlin 7 46
(John Gosden) *s.i.s: hld up: nvr nr to chal* **12/1**

0- **9** *6* **Sybilicious**[270] 7448 3-8-7 0....................AaronJones(7) 9 30
(Stuart Williams) *prom: racd keenly: rdn and wknd over 1f out* **66/1**

0- **10** *1* **Gracefilly**[270] 7435 3-8-7 0....................BradleyBosley(7) 8 28
(Ed Walker) *s.i.s: hld up: plld hrd: wknd over 2f out* **40/1**

1m 26.22s (0.52) **Going Correction** +0.20s/f (Good) **10** Ran SP% **117.1**
Speed ratings (Par 100): **105,104,97,96,95 92,92,87,80,79**
CSF £5.66 TOTE £2.60: £1.10, £1.50, £4.90; EX 6.60 Trifecta £68.90.
**Owner** Hamdan Al Maktoum **Bred** Hellwood Stud Farm **Trained** Lambourn, Berks

**FOCUS**
Some ordinary horses have taken this in the past, but Penitent proved in 2009 that a late-maturing type can take this maiden and go on to better things, as did Lay Time in 2011. The first two finished clear and the form is rated slightly positively.

## 4447 NEWMARKET EQUINE HOSPITAL H'CAP 7f

**4:50** (4:50) (Class 3) (0-90,89) 3-Y-0+ **£7,762** (£2,310; £1,154; £577) **Stalls** High

Form RPR

2364 **1** **Liberty Jack (IRE)**[9] 4118 4-9-1 **76**....................(p[1]) KierenFallon 6 87
(Jim Boyle) *a.p: shkn up to ld over 1f out: sn hung lft: r.o* **7/1**

0343 **2** *3 ¼* **Ansaab**[15] 3917 6-9-6 **86**....................(t) CamHardie(5) 7 91
(Alan McCabe) *chsd ldr: rdn and ev ch over 1f out: hmpd ins fnl f: styd on same pce* **7/2**[1]

3024 **3** *1* **Compton**[2] 4355 5-9-9 **84**.....(t) WilliamTwiston-Davies 9 84
(Stuart Williams) *prom: rdn and nt clr run over 1f out: styd on* **5/1**[3]

100 **4** *1 ½* **Skaters Waltz (IRE)**[28] 3480 3-9-0 **82**.....(b[1]) LukeMorris 5 75
(Paul Cole) *s.i.s: sn pushed along in rr: hdwy u.p over 1f out: styd on same pce fnl f* **25/1**

2410 **5** *nk* **Crowdmania**[30] 3378 3-9-6 **88**..... JoeFanning 8 80
(Mark Johnston) *led: rdn and hdd over 1f out: wknd ins fnl f* **9/2**[2]

-060 **6** *1* **Crew Cut (IRE)**[42] 2992 6-9-5 **80**.....(p) AdamBeschizza 10 73
(Stuart Williams) *chsd ldrs: rdn over 2f out: wknd ins fnl f* **8/1**

0434 **7** *9* **Nonno Giulio (IRE)**[22] 3651 3-9-5 **87**.....[1] RobertHavlin 3 53
(John Gosden) *hld up: rdn and wknd over 1f out* **10/1**

6004 **8** *14* **Forceful Appeal (USA)**[16] 3879 6-9-6 **81**..... GeorgeBaker 4 14
(Simon Dow) *hld up in tch: wknd over 1f out* **8/1**

1624 **9** *15* **Mac's Superstar (FR)**[21] 3703 4-9-2 **77**..... ShaneKelly 1
(James Fanshawe) *hld up: pushed along 1/2-way: wknd over 2f out* **8/1**

1m 25.85s (0.15) **Going Correction** +0.20s/f (Good)
**WFA** 3 from 4yo+ 7lb **9** Ran SP% **115.8**
Speed ratings (Par 107): **107,103,102,100,100 98,88,72,55**
CSF £31.84 CT £134.88 TOTE £7.80: £1.90, £1.50, £2.80; EX 37.50 Trifecta £362.10.
**Owner** M Fitzgerald **Bred** D J And Mrs Deer **Trained** Epsom, Surrey
■ Stewards' Enquiry : Kieren Fallon two-day ban: careless riding (3-4 Aug)

**FOCUS**
A decent handicap run at just an ordinary gallop early. The form is rated around the second.

## 4448 £10 FREE BET AT 32REDSPORT.COM H'CAP (BOBIS RACE) 1m 2f
**5:20** (5:21) (Class 2) (0-100,98) 3-Y-O
**£12,450** (£3,728; £1,864; £932; £466; £234) **Stalls** Centre

Form RPR

41 **1** **Winter Thunder**[29] 3432 3-8-12 **89**..... KierenFallon 5 111
(Saeed bin Suroor) *hld up: hdwy over 2f out: led over 1f out: shkn up and r.o strly* **5/2**[1]

-230 **2** *12* **Gold Trail (IRE)**[30] 3379 3-8-12 **89**..... MartinLane 3 88
(Charlie Appleby) *chsd ldr tl led 6f out: hdd over 3f out: led again over 2f out tl rdn and hdd over 1f out: wknd ins fnl f* **4/1**[3]

1210 **3** *1 ¼* **Chatez (IRE)**[30] 3378 3-9-7 **98**..... GeorgeBaker 1 95
(Alan King) *stdd s: hld up: hdwy over 2f out: rdn over 1f out: wknd ins fnl f* **7/2**[2]

3-1 **4** *½* **Earl Of Menteith (IRE)**[13] 3998 3-8-6 **83**..... JoeFanning 9 79
(Mark Johnston) *led: hdd 6f out: led again over 3f out tl over 2f out: rdn and ev ch over 1f out: wknd ins fnl f* **8/1**

-610 **5** *6* **Zee Zeely**[30] 3379 3-8-9 **86**.....(p) HarryBentley 6 70
(William Haggas) *prom: rdn over 2f out: wknd over 1f out* **8/1**

6414 **6** *4 ½* **Stampede (IRE)**[54] 2617 3-7-13 **81**..... CamHardie[(5)] 2 57
(Sir Michael Stoute) *chsd ldrs tl rdn and wknd over 1f out* **8/1**

0500 **7** *nk* **Lyn Valley**[14] 3982 3-8-12 **92**..... MichaelJMMurphy[(3)] 8 67
(Mark Johnston) *chsd ldrs: rdn over 3f out: wknd over 2f out* **9/1**

2m 5.15s (-0.35) **Going Correction** -0.025s/f (Good) **7** Ran SP% **114.1**
Speed ratings (Par 106): **100,90,89,89,84 80,80**
CSF £12.64 CT £33.91 TOTE £2.70: £2.20, £2.50; EX 13.30 Trifecta £39.30.
**Owner** Godolphin **Bred** Darley **Trained** Newmarket, Suffolk

**FOCUS**
The favourite won by a long way and showed smart form, but nothing else ran its race.
T/Jkpt: Not won. T/Plt: £15.90 to a £1 stake. Pool: £112785.07 - 5147.46 winning tickets T/Qpdt: £5.40 to a £1 stake. Pool: £6468.51 - 875.11 winning tickets CR

# 4018 RIPON (R-H)
### Saturday, July 19

**OFFICIAL GOING: Good (good to firm in places) changing to good to soft after race 2 (2:35) changing to soft after race 3 (3:10)**
Wind: Light across Weather: Heavy cloud and rain showers, warm

## 4449 DOBSONS GASKETS (S) STKS 6f
**2:00** (2:00) (Class 6) 2-Y-O **£3,234** (£962; £481; £240) **Stalls** High

Form RPR

020 **1** **Shamrock Sheila (IRE)**[21] 3744 2-8-3 0..... JoeyHaynes[(3)] 6 59+
(J S Moore) *trckd ldrs: swtchd rt and hdwy 2f out: rdn to chal and edgd lft jst over 1f out: led ent fnl f: rdn out* **2/1**[2]

6022 **2** *1 ¾* **Wink Oliver**[12] 4012 2-8-6 60..... NathanAlison[(5)] 3 59
(Marjorie Fife) *dwlt: hdwy on outer and cl up 4f out: led jst over 2f out: sn rdn: hdd ent fnl f: kpt on same pce* **11/8**[1]

6034 **3** *2 ¼* **Astrea**[14] 3967 2-8-6 53.....(v[1]) AdrianNicholls 1 47
(Nigel Tinkler) *cl up: rdn to ld briefly wl over 2f out: sn hdd: drvn and hld whn sltly hmpd appr fnl f: one pce after* **16/1**

6055 **4** *3* **Autumn Revue**[29] 3435 2-8-6 53.....(b) DuranFentiman 2 38
(Tim Easterby) *cl up: led after 1f: hdd wl over 2f out and sn rdn along: wknd fnl 2f* **20/1**

**5** *3 ¼* **Proved You Wrong (IRE)** 2-8-11 0..... BenCurtis 7 33
(Jo Hughes) *qckly away and led 1f: prom: rdn along bef 1/2-way: sn wknd* **15/2**[3]

1644 **6** *hd* **Tagtale (IRE)**[16] 3894 2-8-8 54..... GeorgeChaloner[(3)] 5 33
(Richard Fahey) *chsd ldrs: rdn along wl over 2f out: sn btn* **8/1**

00 **7** *1 ½* **Secret House**[26] 3529 2-8-6 0..... BarryMcHugh 4 23
(Michael Easterby) *dwlt: a in rr* **66/1**

1m 14.16s (1.16) **Going Correction** +0.125s/f (Good) **7** Ran SP% **110.5**
Speed ratings (Par 92): **97,94,91,87,83 83,81**
CSF £4.71 TOTE £2.70: £1.40, £1.70; EX 6.10 Trifecta £31.90.There was no bid for winner. Wink Oliver claimed by K Stubbs for £6,000.
**Owner** Mrs T Burns & J S Moore **Bred** Rathasker Stud **Trained** Upper Lambourn, Berks

**FOCUS**
Rail from back straight to home straight moved out 3yds and distances on Round course increased by about 7yds. The opening contest on the seven-race card was a moderate juvenile seller in which they went a respectable gallop on ground officially described as good, good to firm in places.

## 4450 EBF STALLIONS YORKSHIRE.COM MAIDEN STKS (BOBIS RACE) 5f
**2:35** (2:36) (Class 4) 2-Y-O **£5,175** (£1,540; £769; £384) **Stalls** High

Form RPR

36 **1** **Rocking The Boat (IRE)**[54] 2612 2-9-0 0..... RobertWinston 11 75
(Charles Hills) *qckly away: mde all: rdn over 1f out: kpt on strly fnl f* **12/1**

023 **2** *1 ¾* **Khawaater**[35] 3232 2-9-0 70..... DaneO'Neill 3 69
(Roger Varian) *trckd ldrs: hdwy to chse ldng pair 2f out: rdn over 1f out: drvn to chse wnr ins fnl f: sn no imp* **2/1**[1]

30 **3** *nk* **Magic Time (IRE)**[74] 2051 2-9-0 0..... PJMcDonald 9 68
(Ann Duffield) *cl up: rdn 2f out and ev ch tl drvn and one pce ent fnl f* **11/2**[3]

**4** *3 ¼* **Pacngo** 2-9-0 0..... DavidAllan 8 56+
(Tim Easterby) *dwlt and towards rr: hdwy 1/2-way: shkn up and styd on fr over 1f out: nrst fin* **7/1**

**5** *3 ¼* **Handsome Dude** 2-9-5 0..... GrahamGibbons 7 49
(David Barron) *in tch: effrt over 2f out: sn rdn along and kpt on one pce* **9/4**[2]

0 **6** *shd* **Ryedale Mist**[22] 3648 2-9-0 0..... AndrewElliott 6 44
(Tim Easterby) *chsd ldng pair: rdn along over 2f out: sn wknd* **33/1**

**7** *1 ¼* **Time Continuum** 2-9-0 0..... JasonHart 10 39
(Eric Alston) *green: a towards rr* **50/1**

45 **8** *3 ¼* **Secret Friend (IRE)**[63] 2349 2-9-0 0..... DuranFentiman 5 28
(Tim Easterby) *midfield: rdn along and edgd rt over 2f out: sn outpcd* **33/1**

**9** *2 ¼* **Moon Arc (IRE)** 2-9-5 0..... TomEaves 2 25
(Keith Dalgleish) *wnt rt s: a towards rr* **20/1**

**10** *¾* **Double K** 2-9-5 0..... PaulMulrennan 4 22
(Paul Midgley) *dwlt: green and a in rr* **50/1**

1m 0.32s (0.32) **Going Correction** +0.125s/f (Good) **10** Ran SP% **114.2**
Speed ratings (Par 96): **102,99,98,93,88 88,86,80,77,76**
CSF £34.29 TOTE £11.30: £2.90, £1.10, £1.70; EX 33.80 Trifecta £85.30.
**Owner** Hon Mrs J M Corbett, D M James, C Wright **Bred** Wardstown Stud Ltd **Trained** Lambourn, Berks

**FOCUS**
A fair juvenile sprint maiden in which they went a proper gallop on ground that was changed to good to soft after this race following steady rain.

## 4451 VW VAN CENTRE (WEST YORKSHIRE) H'CAP 1m
**3:10** (3:11) (Class 4) (0-85,82) 3-Y-O+
**£7,470** (£2,236; £1,118; £559; £279; £140) **Stalls** Low

Form RPR

3161 **1** **Border Bandit (USA)**[4] 4290 6-9-12 **80** 6ex.....(p) RobertWinston 4 88
(Tracy Waggott) *hld up towards rr: hdwy 3f out: cl up 2f out: rdn to ld jst over 1f out: drvn ins fnl f: kpt on wl towards fin* **6/4**[1]

3635 **2** *½* **Shouranour (IRE)**[8] 4175 4-9-1 **76**.....(p) JoshDoyle[(7)] 8 83+
(David O'Meara) *trckd ldrs: pushed along over 2f out: swtchd rt to inner 1 1/2f out: sn rdn: swtchd lft ins fnl f: drvn and kpt on wl towards fin* **11/2**[2]

0350 **3** *nse* **Fazza**[24] 3572 7-9-1 **74**..... KevinStott[(5)] 7 81
(Edwin Tuer) *hld up towards rr: hdwy 3f out: cl up 2f out: sn rdn and ev ch tl drvn ins fnl f and no ex last 75yds* **6/1**[3]

0002 **4** *1 ½* **Wannabe King**[15] 3915 8-10-0 **82**.....(p) PJMcDonald 5 86
(Geoffrey Harker) *trckd ldr on inner: rdn along over 2f out: drvn over 1f out: kpt on same pce* **12/1**

0316 **5** *1 ¾* **Ralphy Boy (IRE)**[8] 4161 5-9-6 **77**..... JulieBurke[(3)] 6 77
(Alistair Whillans) *led: pushed along 3f out: jnd and rdn 2f out: drvn and hdd appr fnl f: grad wknd* **10/1**

0605 **6** *5* **Lilac Lace (IRE)**[43] 2954 4-9-9 **77**.....[1] DavidAllan 1 65
(Tim Easterby) *dwlt: in rr whn n.m.r and hmpd on inner after 1f: hdwy 3f out: rdn along over 2f out: sn btn* **7/1**

0516 **7** *11* **Space War**[25] 3547 7-9-0 **68**..... GrahamGibbons 3 31
(Michael Easterby) *t.k.h early: hld up: hdwy on inner over 2f out: rdn along whn hmpd 1 1/2f out: sn wknd* **17/2**

64/0 **8** *12* **Take It To The Max**[49] 2763 7-9-9 **77**.....(p) AndrewElliott 2 12
(George Moore) *sn trcking ldr: slipped bnd over 4f out: rdn along 3f out: sn wknd* **28/1**

1m 43.77s (2.37) **Going Correction** +0.425s/f (Yiel) **8** Ran SP% **112.9**
Speed ratings (Par 105): **105,104,104,102,101 96,85,73**
CSF £9.61 CT £37.87 TOTE £1.90: £1.10, £2.30, £1.90; EX 9.20 Trifecta £34.10.
**Owner** Elsa Crankshaw Gordon Allan **Bred** Darley **Trained** Spennymoor, Co Durham
■ Stewards' Enquiry : Josh Doyle two-day ban: careless riding (3-4 Aug)

**FOCUS**
A decent handicap in which they went a good gallop on ground changed once again to soft from good to soft after this race.

## 4452 RIPON BELL-RINGER H'CAP (BOBIS RACE) 1m 4f 10y
**3:45** (3:46) (Class 2) (0-100,89) 3-Y£15,562 (£4,660; £2,330; £1,165; £582) **Stalls** Low

Form RPR

1241 **1** **Penhill**[4] 4298 3-9-1 **83** 6ex..... PJMcDonald 1 96
(James Bethell) *hld up in rr: smooth hdwy on outer 3f out: trckd ldrs 2f out: shkn up to ld ent fnl f: sn clr: readily* **9/4**[2]

3100 **2** *6* **Notarised**[28] 3491 3-8-13 **81**..... RoystonFfrench 5 84
(Mark Johnston) *slt ld: pushed along over 3f out: rdn over 2f out: drvn over 1f out: hdd ent fnl f: kpt on: no ch w wnr* **4/1**[3]

4405 **3** *2 ¼* **Fire Fighting (IRE)**[14] 3965 3-9-0 **82**..... AdrianNicholls 3 81
(Mark Johnston) *trckd ldng pair on inner: swtchd lft and hdwy over 3f out: sn cl up: rdn to dispute ld 2f out and ev ch tl drvn and one pce ent fnl f* **11/1**

221 **4** *7* **Desert Snow**[17] 3857 3-9-3 **85**..... FrederikTylicki 2 73+
(Saeed bin Suroor) *trckd ldrs: hdwy 3f out: chal 2f out: sn rdn and ev ch tl drvn: edgd rt and wknd over 1f out* **2/1**[1]

-310 **5** *9* **Gold Approach**[29] 3419 3-9-7 **89**..... GrahamGibbons 4 63
(William Haggas) *cl up: rdn along 4f out: n.m.r over 3f out: sn wknd and bhd* **6/1**

2m 39.62s (2.92) **Going Correction** +0.425s/f (Yiel) **5** Ran SP% **106.7**
Speed ratings (Par 106): **107,103,101,96,90**
CSF £10.61 TOTE £3.00: £3.30, £2.70; EX 17.30 Trifecta £67.40.
**Owner** Clarendon Thoroughbred Racing **Bred** Newsells Park Stud & Equity Bloodstock **Trained** Middleham Moor, N Yorks

**FOCUS**
The feature contest was a good 3yo middle-distance handicap in which they went a sensible even gallop on ground decribed as soft.

## 4453 SKYBET SUPPORTING THE YORKSHIRE RACING SUMMER FESTIVAL H'CAP 1m 1f 170y
**4:20** (4:20) (Class 4) (0-85,83) 3-Y-O+
**£7,470** (£2,236; £1,118; £559; £279; £140) **Stalls** Low

Form RPR

1323 **1** **Bureau (IRE)**[8] 4162 3-9-2 **82**..... AdrianNicholls 1 91
(Mark Johnston) *mde all: rdn along over 2f out: drvn and jnd ent fnl f: edgd lft last 100yds: kpt on gamely* **15/2**

1-14 **2** *nk* **Calm Attitude (IRE)**[52] 2670 4-9-6 **76** DavidAllan 5 84
(Rae Guest) *hld up towards rr: stdy hdwy wl over 2f out: swtchd lft and effrt over 1f out: sn rdn and chal ins fnl f: ev ch tl drvn and no ex towards fin* **8/1**

-044 **3** *2 ¼* **Jodies Jem**[15] 3931 4-9-12 **82** PaulMulrennan 4 86
(William Jarvis) *trckd ldrs on inner: hdwy over 2f out: effrt wl over 1f out: sn rdn and kpt on same pce* **3/1**[1]

02 **4** *nse* **Muffin McLeay (IRE)**[31] 3368 6-9-12 **82** GrahamGibbons 2 86
(David Barron) *trckd ldrs: hdwy 3f out: rdn along 2f out: drvn and one pce fnl f* **4/1**[2]

0662 **5** *4* **Berlusca (IRE)**[15] 3910 5-9-8 **81** SamJames(3) 8 76
(David O'Meara) *in tch: hdwy on outer 3f out: chsd ldrs 2f out: sn rdn and one pce fr over 1f out* **14/1**

034 **6** *hd* **Arantes**[36] 3183 3-8-13 **82** CharlesBishop(3) 9 77
(Mick Channon) *trckd ldrs: hdwy 3f out: rdn along to chse ldrs 2f out: sn drvn and wknd over 1f out* **9/2**[3]

1453 **7** *1* **Eeny Mac (IRE)**[4] 4290 7-9-5 **75** AndrewElliott 3 68
(Neville Bycroft) *chsd wnr: rdn along wl over 2f out: grad wknd* **9/1**

2566 **8** *1 ¼* **Ginger Jack**[24] 3573 7-9-13 **83** PJMcDonald 7 73
(Geoffrey Harker) *hld up: a towards rr* **6/1**

2m 8.54s (3.14) **Going Correction** +0.425s/f (Yiel)
**WFA** 3 from 4yo+ 10lb **8** Ran SP% **117.0**
Speed ratings (Par 105): **104,103,101,101,98 98,97,96**
CSF £66.66 CT £221.26 TOTE £6.30: £1.90, £2.30, £1.30; EX 45.00 Trifecta £512.00.
**Owner** Sheikh Hamdan bin Mohammed Al Maktoum **Bred** Darley **Trained** Middleham Moor, N Yorks

**FOCUS**
A decent handicap in which they went a sensible gallop.

## 4454 YORKSHIRE RACING SUMMER FESTIVAL H'CAP — 1m 4f 10y
**4:55** (4:56) (Class 4) (0-80,78) 3-Y-O+ **£5,175** (£1,540; £769; £384) **Stalls** Low

Form RPR

-021 **1** **Only Orsenfoolsies**[19] 3787 5-9-11 **75** PJMcDonald 11 87
(Micky Hammond) *mde all: jnd and rdn along 1 1/2f out: styd on strly fnl f* **2/1**[1]

1-60 **2** *3 ¼* **Satanic Beat (IRE)**[24] 3574 5-10-0 **78** RussKennemore 10 85
(Jedd O'Keeffe) *a chsng wnr: rdn to chal 1 1/2f out: drvn appr fnl f: kpt on same pce* **8/1**[3]

5131 **3** *2* **Maybeme**[31] 3368 8-9-10 **74** (p) AndrewElliott 4 78+
(Neville Bycroft) *blind removed late: hld up and bhd: hdwy on wd outside 3f out: rdn along 2f out: styd on wl appr fnl f: nrst fin* **4/1**[2]

1440 **4** *1* **Choisan (IRE)**[35] 3240 5-9-9 **73** (tp) DuranFentiman 2 75
(Tim Easterby) *in tch on inner: pushed along over 4f out: rdn and outpcd wl over 3f out: drvn and plugged on fr over 1f out: n.d* **4/1**[2]

6-20 **5** *½* **Bright Applause**[21] 3699 6-9-6 **70** BarryMcHugh 7 71
(Tracy Waggott) *trckd ldrs on inner: swtchd lft and hdwy to chse ldng pair 3f out: rdn along over 2f out: drvn and wknd over 1f out* **9/1**

10-0 **6** *2 ¾* **Jan De Heem**[11] 4058 4-9-2 **66** (v) GrahamGibbons 8 63
(Tina Jackson) *trckd ldrs: hdwy 4f out: rdn along 3f out: drvn 2f out: sn wknd* **25/1**

4540 **7** *2 ¼* **King Of Paradise (IRE)**[18] 3829 5-9-7 **71** JasonHart 9 64
(Eric Alston) *hld up: hdwy on outer 5f out: effrt to chse ldrs 3f out: rdn along over 2f out: wknd over 1f out* **9/1**

0/0- **8** *62* **Lucky Windmill**[462] 1538 7-9-6 **70** RobertWinston 3
(Tracy Waggott) *towards rr: hdwy on outer to chse ldrs after 3f: rdn along 4f out: lost pl 3f out: sn bhd* **20/1**

241- **9** *28* **Crow Down (IRE)**[55] 8298 5-9-9 **73** (b) RoystonFfrench 5
(Simon Waugh) *in tch: niggled along 7f out: rdn and lost pl 5f out: sn bhd: t.o fnl 3f* **25/1**

2m 41.77s (5.07) **Going Correction** +0.425s/f (Yiel) **9** Ran SP% **116.9**
Speed ratings (Par 105): **100,97,96,95,95 93,92,50,32**
CSF £18.73 CT £57.76 TOTE £3.00: £1.10, £3.80, £1.10; EX 27.50 Trifecta £119.30.
**Owner** Foolsies **Bred** Redmyre Bloodstock & Newhall Farm Estate **Trained** Middleham, N Yorks

**FOCUS**
A fair middle-distance handicap in which they went an even gallop.

## 4455 GO RACING IN YORKSHIRE MAIDEN H'CAP — 6f
**5:25** (5:35) (Class 5) (0-70,64) 3-Y-O+ **£3,234** (£962; £481; £240) **Stalls** High

Form RPR

0043 **1** **Bearskin (IRE)**[17] 3846 3-8-11 **54** (v) PJMcDonald 2 65
(Ann Duffield) *trckd ldrs: hdwy and cl up 1/2-way: chal 2f out: rdn and led appr fnl f: sn clr and kpt on strly* **4/1**[2]

6222 **2** *3 ½* **Margrets Gift**[44] 2910 3-9-7 **64** DavidAllan 12 65
(Tim Easterby) *led: rdn along 2f out: drvn and hdd appr fnl f: one pce* **9/2**[3]

-340 **3** *1 ½* **Ty Cobb (IRE)**[12] 4019 3-8-12 **55** IanBrennan 11 51
(John Quinn) *cl up: rdn along 1/2-way: drvn and kpt on same pce appr fnl f* **10/1**

3023 **4** *1 ¾* **McCarthy Mor (IRE)**[22] 3650 3-8-12 **58** (v) GeorgeChaloner(3) 7 49
(Richard Fahey) *dwlt and hmpd s: in rr: hdwy to trck ldrs 1/2-way: effrt and n.m.r 2f out: sn swtchd rt and rdn wl over 1f out: sn no imp* **7/2**[1]

0204 **5** *2 ¼* **Lexi's Beauty (IRE)**[15] 3938 4-8-10 **48** JasonHart 9 33
(Brian Baugh) *in tch on inner: hdwy 1/2-way: rdn along 2f out: sn no imp* **16/1**

504 **6** *7* **Patron Of Explores (USA)**[14] 3951 3-8-9 **52** DuranFentiman 1 15
(Patrick Holmes) *chsd ldrs: rdn along 1/2-way: sn outpcd* **28/1**

0-50 **7** *18* **Bay Street Belle**[15] 3916 3-9-5 **62** GrahamGibbons 3
(David Barron) *wnt lft s: prom: pushed along after 2f: sn lost pl and bhd fr 1/2-way* **11/1**

1m 13.33s (0.33) **Going Correction** +0.125s/f (Good)
**WFA** 3 from 4yo+ 5lb **7** Ran SP% **87.2**
Speed ratings (Par 103): **102,97,95,93,90 80,56**
CSF £12.52 CT £62.09 TOTE £5.20: £1.70, £2.00; EX 12.30 Trifecta £45.70.
**Owner** Evelyn Duchess Of Sutherland **Bred** T Kenny & P Byrne **Trained** Constable Burton, N Yorks
■ Rule 4 of 25p in the pound applies to all bets; Withdrawn: Traditionelle

**FOCUS**
A modest maiden sprint handicap concluded the card in which they went a contested gallop.
T/Plt: £11.20 to a £1 stake. Pool: £57505.67 - 3716.80 winning tickets T/Qpdt: £5.90 to a £1 stake. Pool: £3679.87 - 458.80 winning tickets JR

# [3762] CURRAGH (R-H)
Saturday, July 19
**OFFICIAL GOING: Good to firm (firm in places)**

## 4459a MICHAEL MURPHY HOME FURNISHINGS MINSTREL STKS (GROUP 3) — 7f
**4:40** (4:40) 3-Y-O+ **£32,500** (£9,500; £4,500; £1,500)

RPR

**1** **Ansgar (IRE)**[32] 3317 6-9-9 108 (t) PatSmullen 4 111
(Sabrina J Harty, Ire) *mde all: rdn under 2f out: hung lft ins fnl f: styd on wl* **8/1**

**2** *1* **Darwin (USA)**[6] 4235 4-9-12 112 (b[1]) JosephO'Brien 8 111+
(A P O'Brien, Ire) *trckd ldrs in 3rd tl prog into 2nd 2f out: sn rdn and no imp on wnr fnl 100yds where sltly hmpd: kpt on same pce* **6/4**[1]

**3** *nk* **Eastern Rules (IRE)**[30] 3412 6-9-9 108 ShaneFoley 6 107+
(M Halford, Ire) *hld up in rr: stl last 2f out: swtchd to far side 1f out in 6th: styd on strly into 3rd cl home: nrst fin* **10/3**[2]

**4** *½* **Intensical (IRE)**[21] 3737 3-9-2 99 KevinManning 2 103
(J S Bolger, Ire) *trckd ldr in 2nd tl rdn along in 3rd 2f out: no imp ent fnl f: kpt on same pce and dropped to 4th cl home* **12/1**

**5** *¾* **Waltzing Matilda (IRE)**[31] 3352 3-8-13 104 WayneLordan 7 98+
(T Stack, Ire) *hld up: rdn along over 2f out in 5th: no imp ent fnl f: kpt on same pce* **4/1**[3]

**6** *nk* **Michaelmas (USA)**[31] 3352 3-9-2 100 (b[1]) SeamieHeffernan 3 100+
(A P O'Brien, Ire) *hld up: nt qckn appr fnl f: kpt on one pce* **16/1**

**7** *4 ¼* **Shining Emerald**[31] 3352 3-9-2 103 (b) ChrisHayes 1 89+
(P D Deegan, Ire) *hld up towards rr: rdn over 2f out and dropped to rr 1f out: sn no ex* **14/1**

**8** *¾* **Exactement (IRE)**[5] 4276 4-9-6 94 GaryCarroll 5 87+
(Sabrina J Harty, Ire) *chsd ldrs on far side early: nt qckn 2f out: sn no ex and dropped to rr* **50/1**

1m 23.11s (-7.69) **Going Correction** -0.80s/f (Hard)
**WFA** 3 from 4yo+ 7lb **8** Ran SP% **116.4**
Speed ratings: **111,109,109,108,108 107,102,102**
CSF £20.87 TOTE £8.90: £2.10, £1.02, £1.10; DF 35.00 Trifecta £108.00.
**Owner** Mrs Chynel Phelan/Shane Fox **Bred** Miss Chynel Phelan **Trained** Newbridge, Co Kildare

**FOCUS**
Last year's winner was back to defend his crown but the standard of opposition didn't appear to be as strong as 12 months ago. The winner made all under a canny ride from Pat Smullen, who stacked them up in behind 3f out. The winning time was 1.12 second quicker than the 7f handicap that preceded it.

## 4460a JEBEL ALI RACECOURSE & STABLES ANGLESEY STKS (GROUP 3) — 6f 63y
**5:10** (5:12) 2-Y-O **£35,208** (£10,291; £4,875; £1,625)

RPR

**1** **Dick Whittington (IRE)**[28] 3448 2-9-3 101 JosephO'Brien 1 107
(A P O'Brien, Ire) *chsd ldrs in 3rd: strly rdn 1f out: styd on wl to ld fnl 100yds: kpt on wl* **2/1**[1]

**2** *½* **Toscanini (IRE)**[28] 3448 2-9-3 101 ShaneFoley 6 106
(M Halford, Ire) *trckd ldr in 2nd on stands' side tl led 1f out: sn strly pressed and hdd fnl 100yds: kpt on wl* **2/1**[1]

**3** *¾* **Rapid Applause**[21] 3738 2-9-3 100 FergalLynch 5 103
(M D O'Callaghan, Ire) *hld up in rr: prog whn short of room ent fnl f: squeezed through into 3rd fnl 100yds: nt rch principals* **10/1**[3]

**4** *1 ¼* **Itorio (IRE)**[16] 3901 2-9-3 90 WayneLordan 2 100
(Ms Sheila Lavery, Ire) *broke wl and led tl hdd 1f out: no ex and wknd fnl 150yds* **20/1**

**5** *1 ½* **Newsletter (IRE)**[31] 3353 2-9-0 102 (t) PatSmullen 3 92
(K J Condon, Ire) *hld up in 4th tl rdn and nt qckn under 1f out: sn one pce* **9/4**[2]

1m 15.33s (-3.77) **Going Correction** -0.525s/f (Hard) **5** Ran SP% **111.3**
Speed ratings: **104,103,102,100,98**
CSF £6.44 TOTE £2.30: £1.30, £1.20; DF 5.30 Trifecta £19.90.
**Owner** Michael Tabor & Derrick Smith & Mrs John Magnier **Bred** Swordlestown Stud **Trained** Cashel, Co Tipperary
■ Stewards' Enquiry : Fergal Lynch one-day ban: careless riding (TBA)

**FOCUS**
Small in numbers but no shortage of quality. This was a proper Group 3. Both the winner and the second had solid Group form having contested the Chesham Stakes at Royal Ascot, and the form has been given a chance despite the compressed nature of the finish.

## 4461a DARLEY IRISH OAKS (GROUP 1) (FILLIES) — 1m 4f
**5:45** (6:06) 3-Y-O
**£193,333** (£63,333; £30,000; £10,000; £6,666; £3,333)

RPR

**1** **Bracelet (IRE)**[30] 3376 3-9-0 107 ColmO'Donoghue 3 112+
(A P O'Brien, Ire) *sn settled in mid-div: tk clsr order in 3rd 2f out: styd on wl to ld 1f out: drvn out cl home: hld on wl* **10/1**

**2** *nk* **Tapestry (IRE)**[29] 3418 3-9-0 108 JosephO'Brien 10 111+
(A P O'Brien, Ire) *hld up: rdn along in 6th 2f out: gd prog into 3rd ent fnl f: styd on strly into 2nd clsng strides: nrst fin* **13/2**

**3** *nk* **Volume**[43] 2960 3-9-0 111 KevinManning 2 111
(Luca Cumani) *led and sn 4 l clr: advantage reduced 2f out: hdd 1f out: rallied wl tl no ex and dropped to 3rd clsng strides* **4/1**[3]

**4** *4 ¾* **Beyond Brilliance (IRE)**[5] 4276 3-9-0 95 AnaO'Brien 7 103
(A P O'Brien, Ire) *hld up in rr: last 2f out: styd on wl on outer in 7th 1f out: kpt on strly into 4th clsng stages* **80/1**

**5** *1* **Tarfasha (IRE)**[43] 2960 3-9-0 111 PatSmullen 4 102
(D K Weld, Ire) *t.k.h early and trckd ldrs in 3rd: chsd ldr in 2nd 3f out tl no imp in 3rd over 1f out: sn one pce: dropped to 5th cl home* **7/4**[1]

**6** *¾* **Maid Of The Glens (IRE)**[23] 3607 3-9-0 79 RonanWhelan 8 101
(John Patrick Shanahan, Ire) *racd in mid-div: rdn along under 2f out: no imp ent fnl f: kpt on one pce* **100/1**

**7** *1* **Lustrous**[30] 3376 3-9-0 104 PatDobbs 11 99
(Richard Hannon) *hld up towards rr: c wd fr over 2f out: no imp ent fnl f* **20/1**

**8** *½* **Marvellous (IRE)**[43] 2960 3-9-0 116 (b[1]) RyanMoore 5 98
(A P O'Brien, Ire) *chsd ldrs: pushed along 3f out: no imp appr fnl f* **7/2**[2]

9 1 1/2 **Ballybacka Queen (IRE)**[55] 2581 3-9-0 100 FMBerry 6 96
(P A Fahy, Ire) *hld up towards rr: rdn 2f out: no imp appr fnl f: kpt on one pce* **50/1**
10 7 **Palace (IRE)**[5] 4276 3-9-0 102 SeamieHeffernan 1 85
(A P O'Brien, Ire) *sn chsd ldr in 2nd: rdn along in 3rd 3f out: sn wknd* **12/1**
2m 33.68s (-4.82) **Going Correction** -0.125s/f (Firm) **10** Ran SP% **117.6**
Speed ratings: **111,110,110,107,106 106,105,105,104,99**
CSF £72.35 CT £307.72 TOTE £11.70: £2.20, £2.40, £1.60; DF 54.40 Trifecta £342.20.
**Owner** Michael Tabor & Derrick Smith & Mrs John Magnier **Bred** Roncon & Chelston **Trained** Cashel, Co Tipperary
**FOCUS**
Epsom Oaks winner Taghrooda missed the race to wait for the King George at Ascot. There was a delay of 21 minutes from the official start time. Volume was to blame for the wait as she had to have a protrusion from her shoes removed as they are deemed illegal in Irish racing. Quite a few suffered as a result, none more so than the runner-up Tapestry, who was a lather of sweat beforehand. The aforementioned Volume set a brisk tempo from the outset and ensured that it was a truly-run affair. The first three finished clear and the form is rated around the third.

# DIEPPE (R-H)
## Saturday, July 19
**OFFICIAL GOING: Turf: good to soft**

## 4464a PRIX JEHAN ANGO (CLAIMER) (3YO FILLIES) (TURF) 7f
**5:38** (12:00) 3-Y-O £6,250 (£2,500; £1,875; £1,250; £625)

RPR
1 **Sunstream (FR)** 3-9-0 0 (b) FlavienPrat 7 84
(M Munch, Germany) **42/10**[2]
2 4 **Baracoa**[29] 3-9-0 0 (b) LouisBeuzelin 14 73
(H-F Devin, France) **67/10**
3 1 1/2 **Pan Di Stelle (FR)**[10] 3-9-2 0 (b) MllePaulineDominois(5) 6 76
(C Lerner, France) **18/5**[1]
4 2 **Maruschka (IRE)**[101] 3-9-0 0 TheoBachelot 4 64
(V Luka Jr, Czech Republic) **203/10**
5 1/2 **Easy Risk (FR)**[96] 3-9-0 0 FabriceVeron 10 62
(Yannick Fouin, France) **193/10**
6 2 **Conquete (FR)**[31] 3372 3-8-13 0 StephanePasquier 3 56
(P Bary, France) **13/2**
7 1 **Sissi Pompon (IRE)**[17] 3-8-6 0 KorentinNaimi(8) 9 54
(M Boutin, France) **30/1**
8 1 1/2 **Serena (FR)**[10] 3-9-2 0 (p) AnthonyCrastus 1 52
(N Minner, Belgium) **73/10**
9 3/4 **Feen Melody (FR)**[44] 3-8-13 0 (p) EddyHardouin 8 47
(P Demercastel, France) **30/1**
10 2 1/2 **Stella D'Oro (FR)**[36] 3-8-13 0 AlexandreRoussel 5 40
(Mlle S-V Tarrou, France) **84/1**
11 hd **Romantic Bliss (IRE)**[10] 4067 3-9-0 0 (b) AntoineHamelin 2 41
(K R Burke) *chsd ldrs on inner: 3rd and pushed along over 2f out: sn rdn and nt qckn: wknd appr fnl f* **47/10**[3]
12 6 **Amistades (IRE)**[75] 3-8-7 0 NicolasLarenaudie(6) 13 24
(F-X De Chevigny, France) **35/1**
13 1 1/2 **Lady Dam's (FR)**[17] 3-9-0 0 (p) JimmyTastayre 12 20
(C Boutin, France) **36/1**
1m 22.8s (82.80) **13** Ran SP% **119.6**
WIN (incl. 1 euro stake): 5.20. PLACES: 1.90, 2.20, 1.80. DF: 18.70. SF: 36.30.
**Owner** MM Racing **Bred** H Wirth **Trained** Germany

## 4465a PRIX SICKERT (CLAIMER) (3YO COLTS & GELDINGS) (TURF) 7f
**6:45** (12:00) 3-Y-O £6,250 (£2,500; £1,875; £1,250; £625)

RPR
1 **Little Big Shot (IRE)**[14] 3997 3-9-3 0 (b) Christophe-PatriceLemaire 3 80
(F-H Graffard, France) **33/10**[2]
2 4 **Color Code (FR)**[10] 3-8-10 0 KorentinNaimi(8) 6 70
(M Boutin, France) **211/10**
3 hd **Balfour (FR)**[21] 3-9-5 0 Georges-AntoineAnselin(6) 10 76
(P Nicot, France) **107/10**
4 3/4 **We'll Shake Hands (FR)**[47] 2828 3-9-11 0 AntoineHamelin 4 74
(K R Burke) *pressed ldr on inner: outpcd by ldrs 2 1/2f out: rdn 1 1/2f out: kpt on gamely fnl f to hold on to 4th* **83/10**
5 snk **Arpegio (FR)**[15] 3-8-9 0 (b[1]) TheoBachelot 8 58
(S Wattel, France) **27/10**[1]
6 snk **Freedom Tales (FR)**[60] 3-9-0 0 (p) GuillaumeAmbrosioni(7) 12 70
(M Boutin, France) **238/10**
7 nk **Boogy Man (ITY)**[13] 3-9-11 0 (p) MickaelBarzalona 5 73
(C Boutin, France) **5/1**[3]
8 9 **Appiano (FR)**[17] 3-9-2 0 (b) MorganDelalande 1 40
(Y Barberot, France) **168/10**
9 20 **Manchu (FR)**[17] 3-8-13 0 (b) TonyPiccone 7
(F Chappet, France) **186/10**
10 10 **Bechir (FR)** 3-9-2 0 JeromeCabre 2
(P Van De Poele, France) **35/1**
11 6 **Vicosoprano (IRE)**[74] 3-9-1 0 (b) NicolasLarenaudie(5) 9
(M Nigge, France) **34/1**
12 3/4 **Grey Frost (FR)**[20] 3-9-0 0 (b) FabriceVeron 11
(G Lassaussaye, France) **112/10**
1m 29.3s (89.30) **12** Ran SP% **119.4**
WIN (incl. 1 euro stake): 4.30. PLACES: 2.10, 3.00, 2.80. DF: 43.30. SF: 57.60.
**Owner** H H Sheikh Mohammed Bin Khalifa Al Thani **Bred** Ballylinch Stud **Trained** France

# 3481 REDCAR (L-H)
## Sunday, July 20
**OFFICIAL GOING: Good (good to firm in places; 8.0)**
Wind: light half behind Weather: mixture of sunshine and cloud

## 4467 BRITISH STALLION STUDS EBF YORKSHIRE REGIMENT MAIDEN STKS 7f
**2:10** (2:12) (Class 5) 2-Y-O £3,234 (£962; £481; £240) Stalls Centre

Form RPR
3 1 **Spring Offensive (IRE)**[19] 3827 2-9-5 0 TonyHamilton 2 79+
(Richard Fahey) *hld up: gd hdwy 2f out: rdn to ld ins fnl f: kpt on wl* **3/1**[2]
6 2 1 1/2 **Indelible Ink (IRE)**[30] 3429 2-9-5 0 ShaneKelly 6 75
(Sir Michael Stoute) *hld up: hdwy over 2f out: rdn to ld appr fnl f: hdd ins fnl f: kpt on but a hld* **2/1**[1]
4 3 3 3/4 **Al Rayyan (IRE)**[60] 2450 2-9-5 0 SilvestreDeSousa 13 65
(Kevin Ryan) *midfield: pushed along 1/2-way: hdwy to chal over 1f out: wandered u.p ent fnl f: no ex ins fnl f* **9/2**
0 4 3 **Sovereign Bounty**[25] 3569 2-9-5 0 RussKennemore 1 57
(Jedd O'Keeffe) *in tch: rdn 2f out: edgd lft appr fnl f: wknd ins fnl f* **125/1**
5 1 1/2 **Bread** 2-9-5 0 JasonHart 8 53
(Garry Moss) *led: rdn over 2f out: hdd appr fnl f: wknd* **80/1**
6 2 **Dew Pond** 2-9-5 0 DavidAllan 11 47
(Tim Easterby) *hld up: rdn 3f out: kpt on ins fnl f* **66/1**
7 1/2 **Baron Spikey (IRE)** 2-9-5 0 PJMcDonald 3 46
(Ann Duffield) *in tch: rdn and outpcd over 2f out: plugged on ins fnl f* **25/1**
34 8 nk **Forgiving Glance**[20] 3794 2-8-9 0 ShirleyTeasdale(5) 12 40
(Philip Kirby) *in tch: rdn and hung rt 2f out: sn wknd* **80/1**
06 9 5 **Cheeky Chapman**[15] 3947 2-9-5 0 TomEaves 5 32
(Clive Mulhall) *racd keenly in tch: rdn over 2f out: sn wknd* **100/1**
2 10 nk **Pensax Boy**[22] 3701 2-9-5 0 RobertWinston 10 31
(Ian Williams) *prom: rdn 3f out: hung lft and wknd fnl 2f* **10/3**[3]
11 2 1/4 **Poet Mark (IRE)** 2-9-5 0 DuranFentiman 9 25
(Tim Easterby) *slowly away: a towards rr* **80/1**
402 12 1 1/2 **Our Kylie (IRE)**[26] 3542 2-9-0 63 BarryMcHugh 4 16
(Tony Coyle) *prom: wknd fnl 2f* **20/1**
1m 26.55s (2.05) **Going Correction** +0.275s/f (Good) **12** Ran SP% **115.2**
Speed ratings (Par 94): **99,97,93,89,87 85,85,84,78,78 76,74**
CSF £8.73 TOTE £2.80: £1.10, £1.70, £2.30; EX 11.90 Trifecta £31.30.
**Owner** A Rhodes Haulage And P Timmins **Bred** J Hanly **Trained** Musley Bank, N Yorks
**FOCUS**
After 3mm of rain overnight and a further 10mm in the morning the going was good, good to firm in places. They were tightly bunched for a long way in this maiden but finished quite well strung out and the two market leaders filled the first two places. More to come from the winner.

## 4468 REDCAR CRICKET CLUB H'CAP (DIV I) 1m 1f
**2:40** (2:41) (Class 6) (0-60,60) 3-Y-O+ £2,587 (£770; £384; £192) Stalls Low

Form RPR
3006 1 **Pim Street (USA)**[13] 4014 4-9-4 55 SamJames(3) 9 66
(David O'Meara) *midfield: pushed along and hdwy 3f out: swtchd rt over 1f out: r.o wl: led 110yds out* **12/1**
-440 2 3 1/2 **Yorksters Prince (IRE)**[24] 3623 7-9-4 57 (b) ShirleyTeasdale(5) 7 61
(Marjorie Fife) *led: rdn over 3f out: drvn over 1f out: kpt on: hdd 110yds out* **9/1**
600/ 3 3 1/2 **Zelos Dream (IRE)**[7] 4238 7-8-13 47 (p) AdrianNicholls 2 43
(Seamus G O'Donnell, Ire) *trckd ldrs: rdn over 3f out: chsd ldr 2f out: no ex fnl f* **17/2**
041 4 nk **Dandarrell**[131] 910 7-9-12 60 PaulMulrennan 3 56
(Julie Camacho) *midfield: rdn over 3f out: hdwy on outer over 2f out: chal over 1f out: wknd ins fnl f* **13/2**[3]
0255 5 2 1/2 **Shearian**[20] 3791 4-9-11 59 JoeFanning 8 49
(Tracy Waggott) *in tch: rdn over 2f out: wknd ins fnl f* **11/2**[2]
0000 6 3 **Mcmonagle (USA)**[16] 3908 6-9-2 55 (tp) JacobButterfield(5) 12 39
(Alan Brown) *prom: rdn over 3f out: wknd over 1f out* **14/1**
-000 7 2 3/4 **Bitusa (USA)**[61] 2426 4-8-12 46 oh1 RobertWinston 4 24
(Karen Tutty) *s.i.s: hld up: rdn over 3f out: nvr threatened* **25/1**
2622 8 1 **Tukitinyasok (IRE)**[15] 3949 7-9-10 58 TomEaves 5 34
(Clive Mulhall) *in tch: rdn over 3f out: wknd 2f out* **9/2**[1]
35-6 9 7 **War Lord (IRE)**[45] 2913 4-9-9 60 JulieBurke(3) 13 22
(Philip Kirby) *dwlt: hld up in rr: rdn over 3f out: nvr threatened* **22/1**
-050 10 1 3/4 **Eium Mac**[33] 3339 5-8-7 46[1] AdamCarter(5) 10 4
(Neville Bycroft) *dwlt: hld up in midfield: rdn over 3f out: nvr threatened* **16/1**
4055 11 1 **Slinky McVelvet**[31] 3382 3-9-3 60 (p) JasonHart 1 15
(Garry Moss) *trckd ldrs: rdn over 4f out: wknd 2f out* **10/1**
-026 12 12 **Slingsby**[12] 4063 3-8-10 53 GrahamGibbons 14
(Michael Easterby) *in tch on outer: lost footing on bnd over 5f out: sn lost pl and btn* **16/1**
4060 13 4 **Barbara Elizabeth**[15] 3950 3-8-7 50 BarryMcHugh 6
(Tony Coyle) *hld up: wknd over 3f out* **20/1**
1m 54.51s (1.51) **Going Correction** +0.10s/f (Good)
**WFA** 3 from 4yo+ 9lb **13** Ran SP% **115.6**
Speed ratings (Par 101): **97,93,90,90,88 85,83,82,76,74 73,62,59**
CSF £108.89 CT £1004.96 TOTE £14.80: £3.50, £3.00, £3.20; EX 95.90 Trifecta £595.10.
**Owner** Dundalk Racing Club **Bred** Mr & Mrs D Probert, R Cowley & Darley **Trained** Nawton, N Yorks
■ Stewards' Enquiry : Shirley Teasdale 11-day ban: use of whip (6 - 16 Aug)
Joe Fanning one-day ban: careless riding (3 Aug)
**FOCUS**
The winner scored in good style from off the decent pace in this minor handicap.

## 4469 INFINITY TYRES H'CAP 5f
**3:10** (3:12) (Class 5) (0-70,69) 3-Y-O £3,234 (£962; £481; £240) Stalls Centre

Form RPR
3120 1 **Bashiba (IRE)**[15] 3972 3-8-6 54 (t) SilvestreDeSousa 8 69
(Nigel Tinkler) *midfield: rdn 1/2-way: hdwy over 1f out: led ins fnl f: kpt on wl* **17/2**
0-30 2 2 1/2 **Monarch Maid**[26] 3561 3-9-3 65 RobertWinston 6 71
(Peter Hiatt) *w ldr: rdn to ld over 1f out: hdd ins fnl f: kpt on but no ch w wnr* **7/2**[1]
216 3 1/2 **Orient Class**[12] 4059 3-9-7 69 (v) PaulMulrennan 5 73
(Paul Midgley) *chsd ldrs: rdn 1/2-way: kpt on* **5/1**[3]
0030 4 nk **Tweety Pie (IRE)**[13] 4019 3-9-1 66 (b[1]) NeilFarley(3) 1 69
(Declan Carroll) *prom: rdn 2f out: one pce fnl f* **13/2**
-326 5 2 1/4 **White Flag**[26] 3548 3-7-13 54 RachelRichardson(7) 4 49
(Tim Easterby) *in tch: rdn 1/2-way: plugged on fnl f* **12/1**
4140 6 1 **Storyline (IRE)**[12] 4059 3-9-3 65 DavidAllan 12 56
(Tim Easterby) *led narrowly: rdn whn hdd over 1f out: wknd fnl f* **9/2**[2]
5546 7 1 **Madagascar Moll (IRE)**[24] 3600 3-8-10 65 JoshDoyle(7) 2 53
(David O'Meara) *s.i.s: hld up: rdn 1/2-way: nvr threatened* **9/1**
0605 8 2 1/4 **Khalice**[11] 4071 3-9-5 67 GrahamLee 9 47
(James Given) *hld up: nvr threatened* **11/1**
1503 9 11 **Biscuiteer**[36] 3228 3-8-11 59 (b) LukeMorris 11
(Scott Dixon) *midfield: rdn 1/2-way: sn wknd* **16/1**
000 10 6 **Kaytom**[15] 3951 3-8-7 55 PaulPickard 7
(John Wainwright) *s.i.s: hld up: a bhd* **66/1**
59.46s (0.86) **Going Correction** +0.275s/f (Good) **10** Ran SP% **114.3**
Speed ratings (Par 100): **104,100,99,98,95 93,91,88,70,61**
CSF £37.57 CT £166.09 TOTE £7.80: £2.50, £3.30, £1.70; EX 40.80 Trifecta £251.70.

**Owner** Y T Szeto **Bred** John T Heffernan & Grainne Dooley **Trained** Langton, N Yorks
**FOCUS**
They leaders set a good pace and the winner forged clear under a hold-up ride in this handicap.

## 4470 DOWNLOAD THE RACING UK IPAD APP CLASSIFIED CLAIMING STKS 1m 2f
**3:40** (3:40) (Class 6) 3-Y-O+ **£2,726** (£805; £402) **Stalls** Low

Form RPR
0000 **1** **Le Deluge (FR)**[71] 2169 4-9-0 69 GrahamGibbons 2 73
(Michael Easterby) *mde all: clr over 3f out: rdn over 2f out: kpt on* **8/1**
4-50 **2** *6* **Mixed Message (IRE)**[56] 1356 4-9-4 67 DaleSwift 8 66
(Brian Ellison) *trckd ldr on outer: rdn over 3f out: edgd lft over 1f out: kpt on same pce: no threat to wnr* **18/1**
3024 **3** *2* **Matraash (USA)**[11] 4080 8-9-2 68 (p) StephenCraine 3 60
(Daniel Mark Loughnane) *midfield: rdn and hdwy 4f out: wnt 3rd over 1f out: plugged on* **6/1**
0505 **4** *½* **Al Furat (USA)**[4] 4319 6-8-11 51 ShirleyTeasdale(5) 1 59
(Ron Barr) *trckd ldr: rdn over 3f out: jst dropped to 4th whn briefly n.m.r over 1f out: plugged on* **66/1**
-020 **5** *1 ½* **Juvenal (IRE)**[57] 2546 5-9-3 68 (p) SilvestreDeSousa 9 57
(Geoffrey Harker) *s.i.s: swtchd lft: hld up in rr: rdn over 3f out: plugged on fnl f: nvr threatened* **9/1**
5012 **6** *½* **Gabrial's Hope (FR)**[24] 3623 5-9-5 64 RobertWinston 4 58
(Tracy Waggott) *hld up: rdn 4f out: nvr threatened* **9/2**[2]
0113 **7** *18* **Gabrial The Duke (IRE)**[17] 3898 4-9-6 73 (p) TomEaves 7 25
(David Simcock) *in tch: rdn over 4f out: sn wknd* **15/8**[1]
0-64 **8** *14* **Gala Casino Star (IRE)**[30] 3436 9-8-10 66 JordanNason(7) 5
(Deborah Sanderson) *hld up: a bhd* **5/1**[3]
000/ **9** *17* **Takaatuf (IRE)**[274] 6100 8-9-6 72 JoeFanning 6
(Tina Jackson) *trckd ldrs: rdn over 4f out: wknd over 4f out: t.o* **40/1**

2m 7.01s (-0.09) **Going Correction** +0.10s/f (Good) 9 Ran SP% **114.2**
Speed ratings (Par 101): **104,99,97,97,96 95,81,70,56**
CSF £136.42 TOTE £10.00: £2.70, £6.70, £1.70; EX 264.40 Trifecta £732.50.Le Deluge was claimed by Miss A Stokell for £4000
**Owner** Mrs Jean Turpin **Bred** J F Gribomont **Trained** Sheriff Hutton, N Yorks
**FOCUS**
The market leaders were disappointing but winner scored in emphatic style under a prominent ride in this claimer.

## 4471 SKYBET SUPPORTING THE YORKSHIRE SUMMER RACING FESTIVAL H'CAP 6f
**4:10** (4:12) (Class 4) (0-85,85) 3-Y-O+ **£6,469** (£1,925; £962; £481) **Stalls** Centre

Form RPR
0416 **1** **See The Storm**[18] 3848 6-8-10 69 LukeMorris 6 78
(Ian Williams) *midfield: rdn and hdwy over 1f out: kpt on wl: led 50yds out* **12/1**
6521 **2** *nk* **Gran Canaria Queen**[15] 3952 5-9-5 78 DavidAllan 10 86
(Tim Easterby) *w ldr: rdn to ld ent fnl f: kpt on: hdd 50yds out* **10/1**
4336 **3** *nse* **Jack Luey**[22] 3714 7-9-7 85 JoeDoyle(5) 11 93
(Lawrence Mullaney) *led narrowly: rdn 2f out: hdd ent fnl f: kpt on* **17/2**[3]
5330 **4** *1 ½* **Hadaj**[12] 4061 5-9-11 84 (b) GrahamLee 17 86
(Ruth Carr) *hld up: rdn 1/2-way: kpt on wl fnl f: nrst fin* **10/1**
5-41 **5** *shd* **Duke Cosimo**[64] 2332 4-9-10 83 (b) GrahamGibbons 2 85
(David Barron) *in tch: rdn to chse ldrs over 1f out: kpt on* **7/2**[1]
3120 **6** *nk* **Mercers Row**[26] 3547 7-8-13 72 JoeFanning 3 73
(Karen Tutty) *hld up: hdwy over 1f out: sn rdn: kpt on* **25/1**
0006 **7** *1* **Polski Max**[33] 3342 4-9-5 83 JackGarritty(5) 4 80
(Richard Fahey) *chsd ldrs: rdn 1/2-way: one pce* **9/1**
0420 **8** *shd* **Eland Ally**[17] 3882 6-8-11 70 AndrewElliott 15 67
(Tom Tate) *hld up: rdn 1/2-way: kpt on fnl f* **20/1**
4010 **9** *nk* **Bachotheque (IRE)**[36] 3256 4-9-3 76 SilvestreDeSousa 14 72
(Tim Easterby) *chsd ldrs: rdn 1/2-way: grad wknd fnl f* **20/1**
113 **10** *½* **Avonmore Star**[26] 3549 6-8-7 66 BenCurtis 7 60
(Alan McCabe) *midfield: rdn 2f out: no imp* **25/1**
-126 **11** *1* **Adiator**[33] 3338 6-8-7 66 AndrewMullen 13 56
(Neville Bycroft) *chsd ldrs: rdn 1/2-way: wknd ins fnl f* **16/1**
061- **12** *shd* **Woodland Girl**[380] 4019 3-8-1 70 SammyJoBell(5) 16 59
(Richard Fahey) *slowly away: hld up in rr: rdn 2f out: sme late hdwy: nvr threatened* **25/1**
140- **13** *shd* **Barney McGrew (IRE)**[324] 5974 11-9-5 78 PaulMulrennan 18 68
(Michael Dods) *hld up in rr: sme late hdwy: nvr threatened* **50/1**
5451 **14** *½* **Head Space (IRE)**[10] 4114 6-9-6 79 (v) JamesSullivan 1 67
(Ruth Carr) *hld up: rdn and sme hdwy over 1f out: wknd ins fnl f* **4/1**[2]
3165 **15** *3 ¼* **Foreign Rhythm (IRE)**[31] 3395 9-8-2 66 oh4 ShirleyTeasdale(5) 5 42
(Ron Barr) *s.i.s: hld up: nvr threatened* **100/1**
6-00 **16** *1 ¼* **Enderby Spirit (GR)**[64] 2332 8-8-13 72 PaddyAspell 12 44
(Bryan Smart) *s.i.s: sn midfield: rdn 1/2-way: wknd over 1f out* **20/1**
4000 **17** *3 ¾* **Tax Free (IRE)**[25] 3571 12-9-4 77 AdrianNicholls 9 35
(David Nicholls) *prom: rdn 1/2-way: wknd over 1f out* **25/1**

1m 12.42s (0.62) **Going Correction** +0.275s/f (Good)
**WFA** 3 from 4yo+ 5lb 17 Ran SP% **124.8**
Speed ratings (Par 105): **106,105,105,103,103 103,101,101,101,100 99,99,98,98,93 92,87**
CSF £114.05 CT £1097.44 TOTE £12.90: £2.60, £2.30, £2.50, £3.70; EX 129.50 Trifecta £1725.60 Part won..
**Owner** Keating Bradley Fold Ltd **Bred** D R Botterill **Trained** Portway, Worcs
**FOCUS**
A competitive sprint handicap.

## 4472 FIRST WORLD WAR 100TH ANNIVERSARY FILLIES' H'CAP 1m
**4:40** (4:41) (Class 5) (0-75,75) 3-Y-O+ **£3,234** (£962; £481; £240) **Stalls** Centre

Form RPR
5225 **1** **Maiden Approach**[15] 3974 3-9-1 70 TonyHamilton 11 78
(Richard Fahey) *mde all: rdn over 2f out: jnd over 1f out: kpt on: jst hld on* **9/2**[3]
1532 **2** *nse* **Push Me (IRE)**[30] 3439 7-9-11 72 GrahamLee 4 82
(Iain Jardine) *trckd ldrs: rdn and upsides over 1f out: kpt on: jst failed* **7/2**[1]
-160 **3** *hd* **Ivy Port**[15] 3979 4-8-10 57 AndrewMullen 7 66
(Michael Appleby) *trckd ldrs: rdn over 2f out: upsides over 1f out: edgd rt ins fnl f: kpt on: jst hld* **16/1**
02-6 **4** *1 ¾* **Arabian Beauty (IRE)**[21] 3750 3-9-6 75 (b[1]) SilvestreDeSousa 2 78
(Saeed bin Suroor) *prom: rdn over 2f out: one pce fnl f* **9/2**[3]
4030 **5** *nk* **No Poppy (IRE)**[10] 4112 6-9-10 71 DavidAllan 3 76
(Tim Easterby) *in tch: rdn over 2f out: one pce* **4/1**[2]
1653 **6** *¾* **Dalmarella Dancer (IRE)**[17] 3885 3-9-3 72 (v[1]) BenCurtis 9 74
(K R Burke) *hld up: racd keenly: sme hdwy over 2f out: rdn over 1f out: hung lft ins fnl f: one pce and nvr threatened* **9/2**[3]
553 **7** *12* **Harboured (USA)**[150] 675 3-8-8 63 LukeMorris 8 36
(Sir Mark Prescott Bt) *midfield: rdn 1/2-way: sn struggling* **7/2**[1]
600 **8** *¾* **Yawail**[16] 3916 3-8-3 58 JamesSullivan 10 30
(Brian Rothwell) *wnt lft s: hld up: a bhd* **80/1**
56-0 **9** *1* **Thundering Cloud (IRE)**[65] 2296 3-8-8 63 [1] RoystonFfrench 5 32
(Simon Waugh) *hld up: a bhd* **50/1**

1m 40.47s (3.87) **Going Correction** +0.275s/f (Good)
**WFA** 3 from 4yo+ 8lb 9 Ran SP% **128.1**
Speed ratings (Par 100): **91,90,90,89,88 87,75,75,74**
CSF £23.22 CT £247.62 TOTE £5.90: £2.80, £1.40, £4.10; EX 20.70 Trifecta £160.00.
**Owner** Middleham Park Racing LXVII **Bred** Westminster Race Horses Gmbh **Trained** Musley Bank, N Yorks
**FOCUS**
The pace was not strong and there was tight finish to this handicap.

## 4473 REDCAR CRICKET CLUB H'CAP (DIV II) 1m 1f
**5:10** (5:11) (Class 6) (0-60,60) 3-Y-O+ **£2,587** (£770; £384; £192) **Stalls** Low

Form RPR
5505 **1** **Diletta Tommasa (IRE)**[34] 3308 4-9-7 60 (p) EoinWalsh(5) 13 69
(John Stimpson) *hld up on inner: rdn and gd hdwy 2f out: sn chsd ldr: kpt on: led towards fin* **14/1**
4032 **2** *1* **Sicilian Bay (IRE)**[12] 4063 3-8-8 51 PJMcDonald 6 57
(Paul Midgley) *led for 1f: trckd ldr: led again 3f out: sn rdn: kpt on: hdd towards fin* **9/2**[1]
063- **3** *1 ¼* **Cherry Tiger**[128] 7610 4-9-4 57 JoeDoyle(5) 14 61
(Graeme McPherson) *midfield on inner: hdwy over 2f out: sn chsd ldr: kpt on* **16/1**
6200 **4** *1* **Sutton Sid**[6] 4264 4-9-12 60 (b) JoeFanning 11 62
(Ann Stokell) *slowly away: hld up in rr: rdn over 4f out: hdwy over 2f out: kpt on fnl f* **10/1**
0350 **5** *½* **Severiano (USA)**[39] 3123 4-9-0 55 (be) AlistairRawlinson(7) 3 56
(Alan McCabe) *midfield: rdn over 2f out: kpt on* **25/1**
4000 **6** *shd* **Midnight Warrior**[11] 4069 4-8-7 46 oh1 ShirleyTeasdale(5) 4 47
(Ron Barr) *racd keenly: trckd ldr: rdn over 2f out: wknd ins fnl f* **50/1**
-630 **7** *½* **Qibtee (FR)**[87] 1660 4-9-9 57 [1] DavidAllan 8 57
(Les Eyre) *hld up in midfield: pushed along and sme hdwy over 3f out: rdn over 2f out: one pce* **8/1**
0-06 **8** *6* **My New Angel (IRE)**[20] 3781 5-9-6 54 (e) SilvestreDeSousa 7 41
(Daniel Mark Loughnane) *trckd ldr: rdn over 3f out: wknd over 1f out* **17/2**
0006 **9** *hd* **Wyldfire (IRE)**[14] 4000 4-9-4 52 JamesSullivan 10 39
(Ruth Carr) *hld up: rdn over 3f out: nvr threatened* **5/1**[2]
-006 **10** *7* **Secret Kode (IRE)**[11] 4066 3-8-7 50 (p) RoystonFfrench 2 21
(Simon Waugh) *dwlt: pushed along to ld after 1f: rdn whn hdd 3f out: sn wknd* **100/1**
2600 **11** *3 ½* **Nelson's Bay**[13] 4023 5-9-10 58 GrahamLee 12 23
(Wilf Storey) *midfield: rdn over 3f out: wknd 2f out* **12/1**
-003 **12** *4 ½* **Prostate Awareness (IRE)**[23] 3662 3-8-9 57 (p) JackGarritty(5) 1 11
(Patrick Holmes) *trckd ldrs: lost pl over 3f out: wknd 2f out* **6/1**[3]
0505 **13** *4* **Mary's Prayer**[54] 2655 3-8-11 54 PatrickMathers 5
(John Holt) *midfield: rdn over 3f out: wknd over 2f out* **33/1**
1000 **14** *3 ¼* **Medecis Mountain**[16] 3908 5-8-12 46 (p) PaulPickard 15
(John Wainwright) *hld up: a bhd* **66/1**
6560 **15** *18* **Tony Hollis**[2] 4415 6-8-13 47 (t) AndrewMullen 9
(Michael Appleby) *trckd ldrs towards outer: rdn and edgd rt over 2f out: sn lost pl: eased over 1f out* **12/1**

1m 54.16s (1.16) **Going Correction** +0.10s/f (Good)
**WFA** 3 from 4yo+ 9lb 15 Ran SP% **119.0**
Speed ratings (Par 101): **98,97,96,95,94 94,94,88,88,82 79,75,71,68,52**
CSF £72.54 CT £1069.05 TOTE £15.30: £3.20, £1.60, £4.00; EX 98.00 Trifecta £884.10 Part won..
**Owner** J T Stimpson **Bred** Ms Sheila Lavery **Trained** Butterton, Staffs
**FOCUS**
The winner came from off the pace to reel in the favourite in this minor handicap.

## 4474 GO RACING IN YORKSHIRE FUTURE STARS APPRENTICE H'CAP (ROUND 5) 1m 6f 19y
**5:40** (5:40) (Class 5) (0-70,71) 4-Y-O+ **£3,234** (£962; £481; £240) **Stalls** Low

Form RPR
0054 **1** **Madrasa (IRE)**[29] 3482 6-9-11 64 (b) JoeDoyle 9 73
(Keith Reveley) *hld up in tch: rdn 3f out: chsd ldng pair over 1f out: led ins fnal f: kpt on* **9/4**[1]
0-31 **2** *1* **Underwritten**[11] 4082 5-8-12 56 AaronJones(5) 7 64
(Shaun Harris) *trckd ldr: rdn to ld narrowly over 3f out: strly pressed 2f out: hdd ins fnl f: one pce* **11/4**[2]
-544 **3** *½* **Beat The Shower**[27] 3532 8-9-3 56 AlistairRawlinson 3 63
(Peter Niven) *in tch: smooth hdwy 3f out: rdn to press ldr 2f out: no ex towards fin* **3/1**[3]
0644 **4** *10* **Blue Top**[12] 3535 5-9-3 59 (p) RachelRichardson(3) 2 52
(Mark Walford) *hld up in tch: rdn over 3f out: sn struggling* **13/2**
5000 **5** *hd* **Time Of My Life (IRE)**[14] 4000 5-9-0 53 (p) JackGarritty 4 46
(Patrick Holmes) *in tch: rdn over 3f out: wknd over 2f out* **12/1**
1400 **6** *4* **Dubara Reef (IRE)**[33] 3336 7-8-8 47 (p) JordanNason 6 34
(Paul Green) *led: rdn whn hdd over 3f out: sn wknd* **9/1**

3m 8.28s (3.58) **Going Correction** +0.10s/f (Good) 6 Ran SP% **113.5**
Speed ratings (Par 103): **93,92,92,86,86 84**
CSF £8.90 CT £17.54 TOTE £2.50: £1.70, £2.10; EX 8.50 Trifecta £22.10.
**Owner** M W Joyce **Bred** Paget Bloodstock **Trained** Lingdale, Redcar & Cleveland
■ Stewards' Enquiry : Jack Garritty four-day-ban: failed to ride out to fourth place (3-6 Aug)
**FOCUS**
There was a tight finish between the three market leaders in this staying handicap.

T/Jkpt: Not won. T/Plt: £632.50 to a £1 stake. Pool: £92,938.76 - 107.25 winning units. T/Qpdt: £66.10 to a £1 stake. Pool: £7042.38 - 78.80 winning units. AS

## 4456 CURRAGH (R-H)

Sunday, July 20

**OFFICIAL GOING: Straight course - good; round course - good to firm**

**4477a** **MELD STKS (FOR THE DEFENCE FORCES CUP) (GROUP 3)** **1m 2f**
**3:15** (3:15) 3-Y-O+ **£32,500** (£9,500; £4,500; £1,500)

RPR

1 **Parish Hall (IRE)**[21] 3765 5-9-12 112..........................(t) KevinManning 4 107+
(J S Bolger, Ire) *hld up in rr: rdn to take clsr order under 2f out: chsd ldr in 2nd over 1f out: styd on wl to ld cl home* **11/8**[1]

2 ½ **Afternoon Sunlight (IRE)**[70] 2186 3-8-13 102.................. PatSmullen 3 103
(D K Weld, Ire) *led: qcknd 2f out: strly pressed fnl 150yds: kpt on wl tl hdd cl home* **10/3**[3]

3 3 **Ponfeigh (IRE)**[22] 3739 3-8-13 102.......................... DeclanMcDonogh 2 97
(John M Oxx, Ire) *hld up in 3rd: rdn along 2f out and no imp appr fnl f: kpt on same pce* **11/4**[2]

4 9 ½ **Festive Cheer (FR)**[113] 1182 4-9-9 114........................... JosephO'Brien 1 78
(A P O'Brien, Ire) *chsd ldr in 2nd tl nt qckn over 1f out: sn no ex: eased* **9/2**

2m 13.77s (4.47) **Going Correction** +0.20s/f (Good)
**WFA** 3 from 4yo+ 10lb **4** Ran SP% **110.0**
Speed ratings: **90,89,87,79**
CSF £6.26 TOTE £2.20; DF 6.10.
**Owner** Mrs J S Bolger **Bred** J S Bolger **Trained** Coolcullen, Co Carlow

**FOCUS**
A decent race for the level, but the time was slow.

**4478a** **KILBOY ESTATE STKS (GROUP 2) (FILLIES)** **1m 1f**
**3:45** (3:48) 3-Y-O+ **£54,166** (£15,833; £7,500; £2,500)

RPR

1 **Mango Diva**[44] 2956 4-9-9 106.......................................... RyanMoore 1 105+
(Sir Michael Stoute) *chsd ldrs in 3rd towards inner: n.m.r 2f out: chsd ldr in 2nd over 1f out: styd on strly to ld on line* **9/2**[2]

2 shd **Lahinch Classics (IRE)**[65] 2299 3-9-0 96.................. WayneLordan 4 104
(David Wachman, Ire) *chsd ldr in 2nd tl led 2f out: strly pressed ins fnl 100yds: hdd on line* **5/1**[3]

3 ½ **My Titania (IRE)**[30] 3418 3-9-0 107..................... DeclanMcDonogh 3 103+
(John M Oxx, Ire) *hld up in 5th: swtchd lft to outer under 2f out in 6th: prog into 5th 1f out: styd on strly into 3rd cl home: nvr nrr* **1/1**[1]

4 hd **Odeliz (IRE)**[44] 2956 4-9-9 106..................................... DanielTudhope 2 104+
(K R Burke) *chsd ldrs in 4th: rdn along in 3rd appr fnl f: kpt on wl: dropped to 4th cl home* **8/1**

5 1 ¼ **Peace Burg (FR)**[9] 4165 4-9-9 110..............................(t) JosephO'Brien 6 101
(A P O'Brien, Ire) *chsd ldr in rr tl gd prog on inner under 2f out in 4th: no imp fnl 150yds: kpt on same pce* **6/1**

6 4 ½ **Wannabe Better (IRE)**[18] 3864 4-9-9 106........................... BillyLee 7 91
(T Stack, Ire) *hld up towards rr: nt qckn over 1f out: sn one pce* **20/1**

7 6 ½ **Indigo Lady**[42] 3041 4-9-9 96.................................. SeamieHeffernan 5 78
(W McCreery, Ire) *led tl hdd 2f out: sn wknd and eased* **50/1**

1m 55.62s (0.72) **Going Correction** +0.20s/f (Good)
**WFA** 3 from 4yo 9lb **7** Ran SP% **117.0**
Speed ratings: **104,103,103,103,102 98,92**
CSF £28.02 TOTE £5.30: £2.50, £2.90; DF 32.20 Trifecta £76.00.
**Owner** Antoniades Family **Bred** A G Antoniades **Trained** Newmarket, Suffolk
■ Stewards' Enquiry : Ryan Moore one-day ban: use of whip (TBA)

**FOCUS**
A decent race for the grade.

**4480a** **ROCKINGHAM H'CAP** **5f**
**4:45** (4:46) 3-Y-O+
**£50,000** (£15,833; £7,500; £2,500; £1,666; £833)

RPR

1 **Sir Maximilian (IRE)**[19] 3830 5-9-6 96.......................... StevieDonohoe 8 106+
(Tim Pitt) *chsd ldrs in 4th in centre of trck: prog into 3rd 1f out: styd on strly to ld ins fnl 100yds: hld on wl* **11/1**

2 1 **Caspian Prince (IRE)**[36] 3241 5-9-11 **101**.......................(t) AdamKirby 3 107
(Tony Carroll) *broke smartly and led in centre of trck: crossed to stands' side under 2f out: kpt on wl tl hdd ins fnl 100yds* **8/1**[3]

3 2 **My Good Brother (IRE)**[35] 3284 5-9-12 **102**...........(v[1]) RonanWhelan 10 101
(T G McCourt, Ire) *chsd ldr in 2nd on stands' side: crossed sltly under 2f out: rdn in 3rd ins fnl f and nt match principals: kpt on same pce* **33/1**

4 ½ **Lady Mega (IRE)**[23] 3686 3-7-11 **84** oh1................. RobbieDowney[(7)] 11 80
(Edward Lynam, Ire) *racd in mid-div: prog in 7th 1f out: styd on wl into 4th ins fnl f: nvr on terms w principals* **11/2**[1]

5 nse **Yulong Baoju (IRE)**[11] 4095 4-9-7 **97** 5ex..................(vt[1]) FergalLynch 13 94
(Edward Lynam, Ire) *racd in mid-div: prog in 8th 1f out: edgd lft ins fnl f: kpt on wl: nvr on terms* **10/1**

6 1 ¼ **Shipyard (USA)**[22] 3737 5-8-12 **88**............................. GaryCarroll 12 80
(A Oliver, Ire) *racd in mid-div: prog over 1f out in 5th: kpt on same pce fnl f: no imp fnl 100yds* **10/1**

7 1 ¾ **Bubbly Bellini (IRE)**[30] 3420 7-9-2 **99**...........................(b) SeanCorby[(7)] 2 85
(Adrian McGuinness, Ire) *chsd ldrs in 6th on far side: rdn and no imp ent fnl f: kpt on one pce* **25/1**

8 nk **Calm Bay (IRE)**[8] 4219 8-7-8 **80** oh6........................ KeithMoriarty[(10)] 1 65
(H Rogers, Ire) *chsd ldrs in 5th on far side: rdn in 4th over 1f out: sn no imp: kpt on one pce* **33/1**

9 nk **Kernoff (IRE)**[23] 3686 3-9-3 **97**.................................(p) ShaneFoley 5 80
(M Halford, Ire) *sn towards rr: 15th 1f out: styd on wl ins fnl f: nvr nrr* **8/1**[3]

10 hd **Master Speaker (IRE)**[35] 3284 4-9-4 **97**...........................(t) SJHassett[(3)] 4 80
(Martin Hassett, Ire) *racd in mid-div: rdn in 6th over 1f out: sn no imp: kpt on one pce* **16/1**

11 1 ½ **Whozthecat (IRE)**[8] 4215 7-9-1 **98**.......................(v) LukeLeadbitter[(7)] 14 76
(Declan Carroll) *trckd ldrs in 3rd on stands' side tl wknd under 2f out* **10/1**

12 hd **Masai (IRE)**[45] 2939 3-9-1 **95**....................................(t) JosephO'Brien 6 71
(A P O'Brien, Ire) *hld up on far side: sme prog 2f out: no imp appr fnl f* **12/1**

13 1 ½ **Wind Inher Sleeves (USA)**[36] 3258 3-8-3 **86**............ ConorHoban[(3)] 7 57
(M Halford, Ire) *hld up: nt qckn under 2f out: sn no imp* **16/1**

14 1 **Green Door (IRE)**[9] 4158 3-9-11 **105**..............................(b) ColinKeane 16 72
(Olly Stevens) *upset in stalls: racd in mid-div on stands' side tl rdn and nt qckn under 2f out: sn no ex* **6/1**[2]

15 2 ½ **More Questions (IRE)**[36] 3258 4-8-13 **92**..................(p) LeighRoche[(3)] 15 51
(Edward Lynam, Ire) *hld up on stands' side: no imp 2f out* **9/1**

16 5 **Harry Trotter (IRE)**[22] 3737 5-8-13 **92**..........................(b[1]) ConnorKing[(3)] 9 33
(David Marnane, Ire) *lft in stalls and lost considerable grnd: a bhd* **12/1**

57.79s (-5.11) **Going Correction** -0.75s/f (Hard)
**WFA** 3 from 4yo+ 4lb **16** Ran SP% **134.4**
Speed ratings: **110,108,105,104,102 102,99,99,98,98 95,95,93,91,87 79**
CSF £104.46 CT £2982.73 TOTE £18.60: £4.00, £1.60, £6.40, £1.60; DF 156.20 Trifecta £5448.40.
**Owner** Paul Wildes **Bred** Holborn Trust Co **Trained** Market Drayton, Shropshire

**FOCUS**
They went a real rattle in this sprint handicap and very few had the ability to come from off the pace and trouble the principals.

4479 - 4481a (Foreign Racing) - See Raceform Interactive

## 4008 MAISONS-LAFFITTE (R-H)

Sunday, July 20

**OFFICIAL GOING: Turf: very soft**

**4482a** **PRIX ROBERT PAPIN (GROUP 2) (2YO COLTS & FILLIES) (TURF)** **5f 110y**
**1:30** (12:00) 2-Y-O **£61,750** (£23,833; £11,375; £7,583; £3,791)

RPR

1 **Kool Kompany (IRE)**[22] 3738 2-9-2 0.......................... RichardHughes 3 110
(Richard Hannon) *disp ld on inner: hdd after 1f and pressed ldr on outer: shkn up sn after 1/2-way and led ins fnl 2f: r.o u.p fnl f* **9/4**[2]

2 ½ **Strath Burn**[17] 3889 2-9-2 0......................................... JamieSpencer 1 108
(Charles Hills) *chsd ldrs on inner: swtchd outside and hdwy over 1 1/2f out: r.o fnl f to go 2nd fnl strides: nvr quite on terms w wnr* **8/1**

3 hd **Lehaim (FR)**[20] 3806 2-9-2 0...................................... TheoBachelot 5 108
(M Nigge, France) *wnt sltly rt leaving stalls: settled in last wl in tch: rdn and hdwy on outer over 1 1/2f out: r.o fnl f to chal wnr 110yds out: sn no ex and lost 2nd fnl strides* **28/1**

4 1 **Goken (FR)**[20] 3806 2-9-2 0.......................................... FabriceVeron 4 104
(H-A Pantall, France) *disp ld on outer: led after 1f and swtchd to rail: hdd ins fnl 2f: remained prom tl no ex fnl 100yds* **11/10**[1]

5 1 ¼ **South Bank (USA)**[24] 3641 2-8-13 0................... ChristopheSoumillon 2 97
(Mme C Head-Maarek, France) *chsd ldrs on outer: rdn and nt qckn over 1 1/2f out: grad outpcd fnl f and nt given a hrd time whn btn* **4/1**[3]

1m 5.6s (-1.70) **5** Ran SP% **112.9**
WIN (incl. 1 euro stake): 3.60. PLACES: 1.80, 4.00. SF: 12.60.
**Owner** Middleham Park Racing LXXXVI **Bred** Miss Imelda O'Shaughnessy **Trained** East Everleigh, Wilts

**FOCUS**
A tight renewal of this event, up to scratch compared with recent renewals.

**4483a** **PRIX EUGENE ADAM (GRAND PRIX DE MAISONS-LAFFITTE) (GROUP 2) (3YO) (TURF)** **1m 2f (S)**
**2:40** (12:00) 3-Y-O **£61,750** (£23,833; £11,375; £7,583; £3,791)

RPR

1 **Western Hymn**[43] 2990 3-8-11 0.................................... WilliamBuick 6 114+
(John Gosden) *w.w in rr: crept clsr on outer 2f out: qcknd to ld 150yds out: drvn clr: comf* **6/4**[2]

2 3 **Army Bulletin (IRE)**[20] 3807 3-8-11 0........................... MaximeGuyon 3 108
(A Fabre, France) *trckd ldr: rdn 1 1/2f out: disp ld appr fnl f: hdd 150yds out: kpt on u.p: nt pce of wnr* **14/1**

3 1 ½ **Master Carpenter (IRE)**[20] 3807 3-8-11 0 Christophe-PatriceLemaire 5 105
(Rod Millman) *w.w: hdwy to dispute ld appr fnl f: hdd 150yds out: no ex* **7/1**[3]

4 1 ¼ **Shamkiyr (FR)**[49] 2818 3-8-11 0....................... ChristopheSoumillon 1 103
(A De Royer-Dupre, France) *trckd ldrs: smooth prog 2f out: shkn up to ld briefly 1 1/2f out: hdd sn after: grad outpcd by ldrs fnl f* **6/5**[1]

5 6 **Norse Prize (FR)**[35] 3290 3-8-11 0................................... AlexisBadel 4 91
(Mme M Bollack-Badel, France) *settled in 4th: last and rdn over 1 1/2f out: no imp: wknd fnl f* **16/1**

6 2 **Ashkannd (FR)**[21] 3-8-11 0........................................ FreddyDiFede 2 87
(A De Royer-Dupre, France) *led: qcknd 3 l clr over 3f out: rdn and hdd 1 1/2f out: sn wknd* **66/1**

2m 7.9s (5.50) **6** Ran SP% **112.0**
WIN (incl. 1 euro stake): 2.60. PLACES: 1.60, 3.30. SF: 24.00.
**Owner** RJH Geffen and Rachel Hood **Bred** Newsells Park Stud **Trained** Newmarket, Suffolk

4484 - 4485a (Foreign Racing) - See Raceform Interactive

## 4253 AYR (L-H)

Monday, July 21

**OFFICIAL GOING: Good to soft (good in places; 8.8) changing to good (good to soft in places) after race 2 (2.45) changing to good after race 4 (3.50)**
Straights in 4m, Home bend in 6m, Rothesay bend in 4m and consequently races between 7f-10f increased by about 18yds and 13f race by 30yds.
Wind: Breezy; half against Weather: Sunny; hot

**4486** **SUNDAY MAIL CENTENARY FUND MAIDEN STKS** **6f**
**2:15** (2:15) (Class 5) 2-Y-O **£2,587** (£770; £384; £192) **Stalls** Low

Form RPR

1 **Glenalmond (IRE)** 2-9-5 0.......................................... DanielTudhope 4 79+
(K R Burke) *t.k.h early: trckd ldrs: smooth hdwy to ld over 1f out: sn hrd pressed: pushed out to assert last 75yds* **11/8**[1]

2 2 ½ **My Dream Boat (IRE)**[33] 3358 2-9-5 0........................ PJMcDonald 1 78+
(Donald McCain) *sn pushed along in tch: swtchd rt and hdwy to chal over 1f out: hld last 75yds* **14/5**[3]

6 3 5 **Spirit Of The Sea (IRE)**[30] 3454 2-9-0 0.......................... GrahamLee 3 58
(Jim Goldie) *prom: effrt and rdn wl over 1f out: outpcd by first two fnl f* **9/1**

4 6 **Prince Of Time** 2-9-5 0............................................. FrannyNorton 6 45+
(Mark Johnston) *green in preliminaries: led at ordinary gallop: rdn and hdd over 1f out: sn btn* **11/4**[2]

5 12 **Disushe Star** 2-9-5 0...................................................... TomEaves 2 9
(Keith Dalgleish) *dwlt: t.k.h and sn chsng ldr: rdn and wknd wl over 1f out* **33/1**

1m 13.76s (1.36) **Going Correction** 0.0s/f (Good) **5** Ran SP% **108.0**
Speed ratings (Par 94): **90,89,82,74,58**
CSF £5.26 TOTE £2.70: £1.30, £1.50; EX 3.90 Trifecta £14.60.
**Owner** Mrs Melba Bryce **Bred** Laundry Cottage Stud Farm **Trained** Middleham Moor, N Yorks

**FOCUS**
Straights in 4m, Home bend in 6m, Rothesay bend in 4m and consequently races between 7f-10f increased by about 18yds and 13f race by 30yds. The ground was drying out all the time and the meeting started on going officially described as good to soft, good in places. The stalls were on the far side on the sprint track. The first two pulled clear in this maiden and, despite the small field, this is probably fair form. The winner looks sure to rate higher.

## 4487 AYRSHIRE POST H'CAP (A QUALIFIER FOR THE £15000 BETFAIR SCOTTISH SPRINT SERIES FINAL) 6f
**2:45** (2:46) (Class 5) (0-75,75) 3-Y-O+ **£2,911** (£866; £432; £216) **Stalls** Low

Form RPR
2302 **1** **Layla's Hero (IRE)**[3] 4383 7-9-1 **64**..........................(v) PaulMulrennan 3 79+
(David Nicholls) *in tch gng wl: smooth hdwy whn n.m.r briefly over 1f out: led appr fnl f: pushed out: comf* **3/1**[1]
0014 **2** *1 1/4* **Opt Out**[7] 4256 4-8-11 **63**.......................... ConnorBeasley(3) 1 70
(Alistair Whillans) *s.i.s: bhd and sn struggling: hdwy on outside over 1f out: chsd wnr ins fnl f: no imp* **8/1**
6122 **3** *1 1/2* **Jinky**[7] 4256 6-9-9 **72**.......................... TomEaves 4 75
(Linda Perratt) *in tch: effrt and rdn over 1f out: chsd wnr briefly ent fnl f: kpt on same pce* **5/1**[2]
0466 **4** *1 1/2* **Klynch**[14] 4013 8-9-12 **75**..........................(v) PJMcDonald 8 73
(Ruth Carr) *trckd ldrs: effrt and drvn 2f out: kpt on same pce fnl f* **5/1**[2]
1061 **5** *3/4* **Goninodaethat**[7] 4256 6-9-5 **68** 6ex.......................... GrahamLee 6 64
(Jim Goldie) *mde most tl rdn and hdd appr fnl f: sn outpcd* **7/1**
0610 **6** *6* **Take The Lead**[45] 2951 4-8-12 **68**.......................... AnnaHesketh(7) 10 46
(David Nicholls) *w ldrs on outside: pushed along and hung lft over 1f out: wknd fnl f* **25/1**
5-60 **7** *3* **Red Cobra (IRE)**[35] 3298 4-8-7 **56**.......................... DavidAllan 9 25
(Tim Easterby) *hld up bhd ldng gp: drvn over 2f out: btn over 1f out* **7/1**
0420 **8** *8* **Thorntoun Lady (USA)**[7] 4256 4-9-3 **69**.......................... GaryBartley(3) 2 14
(Jim Goldie) *hld up bhd ldng gp: drvn along over 2f out: sn struggling* **14/1**
0064 **9** *3* **Lightnin Hopkins (IRE)**[19] 3844 4-9-12 **75**..........................(v[1]) DanielTudhope 5 11
(David O'Meara) *w ldrs tl rdn and wknd fr 2f out* **13/2**[3]

1m 11.89s (-0.51) **Going Correction** 0.0s/f (Good) **9** Ran SP% **118.3**
Speed ratings (Par 103): **103,101,99,97,96 88,84,73,69**
CSF £28.59 CT £118.30 TOTE £4.60: £1.60, £2.60, £1.80; EX 34.30 Trifecta £229.00.
**Owner** Hart Inn I **Bred** Epona Bloodstock Ltd **Trained** Sessay, N Yorks

**FOCUS**
An ordinary sprint handicap and several of these know each other quite well. The front five pulled clear. The winner rated a fair bit higher in the past.

## 4488 POLYFLOR H'CAP 5f
**3:20** (3:20) (Class 4) (0-85,86) 3-Y-O+ **£5,498** (£1,636; £817; £408) **Stalls** Low

Form RPR
5565 **1** **Bunce (IRE)**[3] 4383 6-8-12 **69**.......................... PJMcDonald 3 78
(Linda Perratt) *hld up in tch: pushed along and hdwy on outside to ld over 1f out: kpt on ins fnl f* **15/2**[3]
0045 **2** *1 1/2* **Midnight Dynamo**[15] 4003 7-8-13 **70**.......................... GrahamLee 8 74
(Jim Goldie) *hld up: pushed along and hdwy on outside over 1f out: chsd wnr ins fnl f: kpt on* **16/1**
-032 **3** *1 1/4* **Gowanharry (IRE)**[44] 3006 5-9-3 **77**..........................(tp) ConnorBeasley(3) 5 77
(Michael Dods) *t.k.h: trckd ldrs: shkn up and chsd wnr over 1f out: edgd lft and no ex ins fnl f* **7/2**[2]
0341 **4** *1 1/4* **Taurus Twins**[3] 4412 8-9-8 **86** 6ex..........................(b) AlistairRawlinson(7) 4 81
(Richard Price) *led: rdn and hdd over 1f out: kpt on same pce fnl f* **10/3**[1]
00-0 **5** *nk* **Hazelrigg (IRE)**[39] 3138 9-9-3 **74**..........................(e) DavidAllan 7 68
(Tim Easterby) *t.k.h: chsd ldrs: outpcd and carried hd high over 1f out: kpt on towards fin: no imp* **16/1**
-602 **6** *1 1/2* **Corncockle**[32] 3386 3-9-3 **78**..........................[1] DanielTudhope 2 66
(David O'Meara) *hld up in tch: effrt and rdn wl over 1f out: sn no imp* **8/1**
6033 **7** *hd* **Alaskan Bullet (IRE)**[24] 3659 5-9-5 **76**.......................... TomEaves 6 67
(Brian Ellison) *taken early to post: stdd s: hld up: effrt against far rail wl over 1f out: no imp whn n.m.r briefly ins fnl f* **17/2**
6304 **8** *shd* **Imperial Legend (IRE)**[10] 4174 5-9-12 **83**..........................(p) PaulMulrennan 1 70
(David Nicholls) *pressed ldr: drvn and ev ch over 1f out: wknd ins fnl f* **10/3**[1]

58.57s (-0.83) **Going Correction** 0.0s/f (Good)
**WFA** 3 from 5yo+ 4lb **8** Ran SP% **113.5**
Speed ratings (Par 105): **106,103,101,99,99 96,96,96**
CSF £113.11 CT £496.86 TOTE £7.00: £1.90, £5.00, £1.30; EX 115.60 Trifecta £868.20.
**Owner** Peter Tsim & Helen Perratt **Bred** John Doyle **Trained** East Kilbride, S Lanarks

**FOCUS**
A fair sprint handicap and they went a decent pace. The winner's best effort since 2012.

## 4489 KILMARNOCK STANDARD H'CAP 7f 50y
**3:50** (3:50) (Class 6) (0-65,65) 3-Y-O+ **£1,940** (£577; £288; £144) **Stalls** High

Form RPR
-033 **1** **Gambino (IRE)**[9] 4195 4-8-11 **55**..........................(p) AlistairRawlinson(7) 2 64
(John David Riches) *in tch: hdwy on outside to ld over 1f out: sn hrd pressed: hld on wl fnl f* **10/1**
002- **2** *3/4* **Royal Duchess**[284] 7148 4-8-9 **53** ow2.......................... MeganCarberry(7) 10 60
(Lucy Normile) *s.i.s: hld up on outside: hdwy on outside over 2f out: led briefly over 1f out: kpt on same pce wl ins fnl f* **20/1**
3260 **3** *3/4* **Clumber Place**[11] 4108 8-9-5 **56**.......................... JasonHart 4 61
(Shaun Harris) *led: rdn over 2f out: hdd over 1f out: kpt on same pce ins fnl f* **7/1**[3]
0403 **4** *hd* **Surround Sound**[16] 3949 4-9-10 **61**.......................... DavidAllan 5 66
(Tim Easterby) *hld up: rdn and hdwy 2f out: kpt on wl fnl f: nvr able to chal* **9/4**[1]
4000 **5** *2 1/2* **New Lease Of Life**[16] 3952 5-9-2 **53**.......................... DanielTudhope 1 51
(Jim Goldie) *hld up in tch: effrt and rdn 2f out: edgd lft and no imp over 1f out* **17/2**
4525 **6** *2 3/4* **Viking Warrior (IRE)**[12] 4070 7-8-11 **51**..........................(p) NeilFarley(3) 6 42
(Shaun Harris) *t.k.h: trckd ldrs: effrt and rdn 2f out: wknd ent fnl f* **17/2**
-000 **7** *2 1/4* **Mystical King**[7] 4259 4-8-6 **46** oh1.......................... ConnorBeasley(3) 7 31
(Linda Perratt) *hld up: drvn and outpcd over 3f out: carried hd high: no imp fr 2f out* **50/1**
0040 **8** *2 1/2* **Natures Law (IRE)**[7] 4256 4-9-2 **53**..........................(p) GrahamLee 9 32
(Keith Dalgleish) *taken early to post: hld up in tch: effrt and rdn over 2f out: wknd over 1f out* **8/1**
0003 **9** *2 1/2* **Locky Taylor (IRE)**[20] 3833 3-9-2 **60**..........................(p) TomEaves 8 29
(Kevin Ryan) *cl up tl rdn and wknd wl over 1f out* **11/1**
1-00 **10** *1 1/4* **Toboggan Star**[79] 1940 3-9-7 **65**.......................... PJMcDonald 3 31
(Ann Duffield) *t.k.h: hld up: drvn over 2f out: sn btn* **5/1**[2]

1m 31.56s (-1.84) **Going Correction** -0.275s/f (Firm)
**WFA** 3 from 4yo+ 7lb **10** Ran SP% **116.2**
Speed ratings (Par 101): **99,98,97,97,94 91,88,85,82,81**
CSF £188.76 CT £1533.21 TOTE £8.60: £2.10, £5.70, £2.50; EX 282.70 Trifecta £980.10.
**Owner** J D Riches **Bred** Messrs M Quinn & P Slattery **Trained** Pilling, Lancashire

**FOCUS**
A moderate handicap but the form seems sound.

## 4490 HAPPY 60TH BIRTHDAY IAIN FERGUSON H'CAP 1m
**4:25** (4:25) (Class 5) (0-70,70) 3-Y-O **£2,911** (£866; £432; £216) **Stalls** Low

Form RPR
4140 **1** **Porthos Du Vallon**[17] 3911 3-9-6 **69**..........................(p) TomEaves 1 74
(Keith Dalgleish) *hld up: hdwy on outside over 2f out: led 1f out: drvn out fnl f* **6/1**[3]
54-2 **2** *1/2* **Real Jazz (IRE)**[10] 4152 3-8-11 **60**..........................(b) LukeMorris 5 64
(Sir Mark Prescott Bt) *sn pushed along and prom: drvn along fr 1/2-way: hung lft and hdwy to chal over 1f out: sn hrd rdn: no ex wl ins fnl f* **2/1**[1]
0530 **3** *1 1/4* **Archie's Advice**[4] 4363 3-8-13 **62**.......................... DanielTudhope 7 63
(Keith Dalgleish) *s.i.s: bhd: drvn and outpcd over 2f out: kpt on strly fnl f: nt rch first two* **7/1**
-612 **4** *1/2* **Next Stop**[75] 2080 3-9-7 **70**.......................... FrannyNorton 3 70
(David Nicholls) *hld up in tch: drvn and outpcd 2f out: kpt on fnl f: no imp* **5/2**[2]
-454 **5** *shd* **Notts So Blue**[32] 3407 3-7-11 **51** oh6.......................... JackGarritty(5) 2 51
(Shaun Harris) *trckd ldrs: drvn over 2f out: no ex over 1f out* **33/1**
060 **6** *hd* **Uplifted (IRE)**[54] 2674 3-8-9 **58**..........................(b) PaulMulrennan 4 58
(Kevin Ryan) *led: rdn over 2f out: hdd 1f out: no ex whn lost several pls nr fin* **8/1**
5-00 **7** *8* **Scots Law (IRE)**[6] 4300 3-9-6 **69**..........................[1] GrahamLee 6 50
(Keith Dalgleish) *taken early to post: trckd ldrs tl rdn and wknd fr 2f out* **9/1**

1m 41.25s (-2.55) **Going Correction** -0.275s/f (Firm) **7** Ran SP% **112.7**
Speed ratings (Par 100): **101,100,99,98,98 98,90**
CSF £17.92 TOTE £5.40: £3.20, £1.40; EX 21.70 Trifecta £83.70.
**Owner** Lamont Racing **Bred** Aiden Murphy **Trained** Carluke, S Lanarks

**FOCUS**
An ordinary handicap, but they seemed to go a reasonable pace. Slightly unconvincing form.

## 4491 DAILY RECORD H'CAP 1m
**4:55** (4:56) (Class 2) (0-100,95) 3-Y-O+
**£14,006** (£4,194; £2,097; £1,048; £524; £263) **Stalls** Low

Form RPR
0-14 **1** **Muharrer**[30] 3457 5-9-3 **87**.......................... ConnorBeasley(3) 9 96
(Michael Dods) *hld up: gd hdwy on outside over 2f out: led appr fnl f: drvn and hld on wl* **7/1**[2]
2000 **2** *nk* **Ingleby Angel (IRE)**[9] 4214 5-10-0 **95**.......................... DanielTudhope 4 103
(David O'Meara) *hld up: rdn over 2f out: hdwy on outside over 1f out: chsd wnr ins fnl f: kpt on: hld towards fin* **7/1**[2]
6145 **3** *1 1/2* **Dubai Hills**[23] 3703 8-9-4 **88**.......................... SamJames(3) 10 93
(David O'Meara) *in tch: effrt and pushed along over 2f out: kpt on ins fnl f* **16/1**
1233 **4** *hd* **Dubai Dynamo**[15] 4002 9-9-8 **89**.......................... PJMcDonald 3 93
(Ruth Carr) *hld up in midfield: rdn and effrt over 2f out: kpt on same pce ins fnl f* **8/1**[3]
221 **5** *1 1/4* **Sound Advice**[15] 4002 5-9-11 **92**.......................... TomEaves 6 93
(Keith Dalgleish) *t.k.h: led and clr w one other: drvn and hdd appr fnl f: kpt on same pce* **9/1**
3-21 **6** *1* **Le Chat D'Or**[42] 3050 6-9-10 **91**..........................(bt) PaulMulrennan 1 95+
(Michael Dods) *hld up and bhd: stdy hdwy over 1f out: styng on whn no room ins fnl f: nt rcvr* **11/4**[1]
0315 **7** *3/4* **Another For Joe**[16] 3955 6-8-13 **80**.......................... GrahamLee 5 77
(Jim Goldie) *pressed ldr and sn clr of rest: drvn and outpcd over 2f out: n.d after* **10/1**
0102 **8** *1* **Ifwecan**[16] 3982 3-9-5 **94**.......................... FrannyNorton 7 87
(Mark Johnston) *chsd clr ldng pair: drvn over 2f out: wknd over 1f out* **11/4**[1]
0 **9** *10* **Secret Recipe**[38] 3202 4-9-11 **92**.......................... DavidAllan 8 64
(David Nicholls) *midfield on outside: struggling 3f out: sn btn* **66/1**

1m 39.82s (-3.98) **Going Correction** -0.275s/f (Firm)
**WFA** 3 from 4yo+ 8lb **9** Ran SP% **115.9**
Speed ratings (Par 109): **108,107,106,106,104 103,103,102,92**
CSF £55.27 CT £763.98 TOTE £7.10: £2.20, £1.80, £4.90; EX 52.10 Trifecta £812.20.
**Owner** Andrew Tinkler **Bred** Shadwell Estate Company Limited **Trained** Denton, Co Durham

**FOCUS**
A valuable handicap for a Monday and, with two soon tearing off into a clear lead, there was never any danger of a falsely run race. The form looks solid, with a personal best from the winner.

## 4492 IRVINE HERALD APPRENTICE H'CAP 1m 5f 13y
**5:25** (5:25) (Class 6) (0-65,65) 4-Y-O+ **£1,940** (£577; £288; £144) **Stalls** Low

Form RPR
3642 **1** **Wor Lass**[7] 4259 6-8-8 **50**.......................... LukeLeadbitter(3) 6 58
(Iain Jardine) *hld up: stdy hdwy over 4f out: rdn to ld over 1f out: edgd lft ins fnl f: hld on wl* **11/4**[1]
622 **2** *3/4* **Rowlestone Lass**[19] 3852 4-8-12 **51**.......................... AlistairRawlinson 7 57
(Richard Price) *hld up towards rr: hdwy to ld over 2f out: hdd over 1f out: rallied: no ex wl ins fnl f* **10/3**[3]
3435 **3** *hd* **Grand Diamond (IRE)**[7] 4259 10-8-6 **52**.......................... RachaelGrant(7) 5 58
(Jim Goldie) *hld up and bhd: stdy hdwy gng wl to chse clr ldng trio over 2f out: nudged along and kpt on strly fnl f* **9/1**
5220 **4** *3/4* **Latin Rebel (IRE)**[33] 3365 7-9-2 **55**.......................... JackGarritty 2 60
(Jim Goldie) *led 1f: cl up: led over 3f out to over 2f out: rallied: one pce whn n.m.r briefly ins fnl f* **6/1**
5165 **5** *13* **Father Shine (IRE)**[11] 4115 11-8-9 **53**.......................... AlexHopkinson(5) 1 39
(Shaun Harris) *in tch: outpcd over 5f out: n.d after* **12/1**
0-02 **6** *2 1/2* **Harrison's Cave**[25] 3605 6-9-2 **62**.......................... JamieGormley(7) 8 44
(Keith Dalgleish) *chsd ldrs: drvn and hung lft over 2f out: sn btn* **3/1**[2]
500/ **7** *9* **Top Billing**[64] 5796 5-9-12 **65**.......................... MeganCarberry 3 33
(Nicky Richards) *hld up: rdn fr 1/2-way: wknd fr 3f out* **14/1**
0000 **8** *1 1/2* **Roc Fort**[35] 3301 5-8-2 **46** oh1..........................(b) JoshDoyle(5) 4 12
(James Moffatt) *t.k.h: led tl rdn and hdd over 3f out: sn wknd* **80/1**

2m 52.55s (-1.45) **Going Correction** -0.275s/f (Firm) **8** Ran SP% **114.6**
Speed ratings (Par 101): **93,92,92,91,83 82,76,75**
CSF £12.25 CT £70.57 TOTE £3.00: £1.10, £1.90, £1.90; EX 11.30 Trifecta £47.20.
**Owner** Les Dodds **Bred** L Dodds **Trained** Bonchester Bridge, Borders



The Form Book, Raceform Ltd, Newbury, RG14 5SJ

**FOCUS**
A moderate apprentice handicap in which the front four pulled miles clear of the others. The winner confirmed last week's run here.
T/Plt: £426.90 to a £1 stake. Pool: £60,853.79 - 104.06 winning units T/Qpdt: £155.80 to a £1 stake. Pool: £4,886.52 - 23.20 winning units RY

## 4286 BEVERLEY (R-H)
Monday, July 21

**OFFICIAL GOING: Good**
Inside rail in 5f chute in 3m. Round course rail off bend into straight moved in adding 5yds to races on RC. False rail in straight with a drop in at 2.5f.
Wind: Light; half behind Weather: Fine, warm and dry

### 4493 TRIBFEST MUSIC FESTIVAL CLAIMING STKS 5f
6:15 (6:15) (Class 6) 2-Y-O £2,385 (£704; £352) Stalls Low

Form RPR
6426 1 **Danot (IRE)**[4] 4357 2-9-5 74 JoeFanning 2 70
(Keith Dalgleish) *trckd ldng pair: chsd ldr 2f out: rdr lost iron briefly 1 1/2f out: sn rcvrd and rdn: swtchd rt jst ins fnl f: styd on to ld last 75yds* 9/4[2]
1560 2 nk **Elizabeth Flynn (IRE)**[13] 4057 2-8-2 73 RobJFitzpatrick(7) 1 59
(K R Burke) *cl up: led after 1 1/2f: pushed clr over 1f out: rdn and hung lft ent fnl f: sn drvn: hdd and no ex last 75yds* 5/4[1]
554 3 1 1/2 **Poolstock**[14] 4011 2-9-5 60 DavidNolan 3 64
(David O'Meara) *trckd ldrs: hdwy 2f out: sn rdn and kpt on same pce fnl f* 9/1
30 4 2 1/2 **Studio Star**[38] 3201 2-8-7 0 (p) JacobButterfield(5) 6 48
(Ollie Pears) *qckly away: led for 1 1/2f: rdn along and sltly outpcd 1/2-way: sn drvn and kpt on one pce fnl f* 9/2[3]
5 4 **Aneto Peak** 2-9-2 0 HayleyTurner 5 37
(Nigel Tinkler) *dwlt: green and a in rr* 20/1
1m 3.72s (0.22) **Going Correction** -0.075s/f (Good) 5 Ran SP% **108.2**
Speed ratings (Par 92): **95,94,92,88,81**
CSF £5.25 TOTE £2.50: £1.30, £1.10; EX 5.80 Trifecta £17.10.Poolstock was claimed by Mr J L Eyre for £15,000
**Owner** Equus Syndicate **Bred** Tally-Ho Stud **Trained** Carluke, S Lanarks
**FOCUS**
Inside rail in 5f chute moved in 3m for entire length of chute. Round course inside rail off bend into home straight moved in and 5yds added to all races on Round course. There was a trial of a false running rail in the home straight around two and a half furlongs out, in a bid to reduce interference. A modest 2yo claimer run at a sound pace. The winner is rated to his mark.

### 4494 RICHARD AND CAROL HUDSON H'CAP 5f
6:45 (6:45) (Class 5) (0-75,74) 3-Y-O+ £3,234 (£962; £481; £240) Stalls Low

Form RPR
0003 1 **Mister Manannan (IRE)**[11] 4114 7-9-8 70 AdrianNicholls 4 81+
(David Nicholls) *t.k.h early: sn in tch: hdwy 1/2-way: chsd ldrs and swtchd lft over 1f out: rdn to ld jst ins fnl f: kpt on strly* 10/3[1]
5604 2 1/2 **Medici Time**[20] 3831 9-9-1 63 (v) TonyHamilton 7 72
(Tim Easterby) *towards rr: hdwy 2f out: rdn over 1f out: swtchd lft and drvn ent fnl f: fin strly* 18/1
051 3 1 **Mey Blossom**[6] 4287 9-8-6 57 6ex (b) GeorgeChaloner(3) 2 62+
(Richard Whitaker) *in tch: rdn along 2f out: swtchd rt and drvn ent fnl f: kpt on wl towards fin* 8/1
1201 4 nse **Cadeaux Pearl**[17] 3913 6-9-1 63 MartinLane 1 68
(Scott Dixon) *chsd ldrs: swtchd lft wl over 1f out: sn rdn: styd on wl fnl f: nrst fin* 7/1[3]
0005 5 3/4 **Bronze Beau**[11] 4114 7-9-7 72 (t) NataliaGemelova(3) 10 74
(Kristin Stubbs) *cl up: rdn wl over 1f out: led jst over 1f out: drvn and hdd jst ins fnl f: kpt on same pce* 10/1
6346 6 1 1/2 **Haajes**[11] 4114 10-9-3 70 (v) ShirleyTeasdale(5) 9 67
(Paul Midgley) *towards rr: pushed along and outpcd 1/2-way: sn rdn and hdwy wl over 1f out: kpt on ins fnl f: nrst fin* 16/1
0320 7 shd **Boxing Shadows**[16] 3948 4-9-0 67 JacobButterfield(5) 13 64
(Les Eyre) *in tch on outer: hdwy 1/2-way: rdn and edgd lft wl over 1f out: sn drvn and kpt on one pce* 12/1
0220 8 3/4 **Noodles Blue Boy**[16] 3948 8-9-9 71 (b) JoeFanning 8 65+
(Ollie Pears) *dwlt and sltly hmpd s: towards rr: rdn along and sme hdwy 2f out: sn drvn and n.d* 8/1
/51- 9 1 1/4 **Boris Grigoriev (IRE)**[305] 6547 5-9-11 73 (b) GrahamGibbons 3 62
(Michael Easterby) *led: rdn along wl over 1f out: drvn and hdd appr fnl f: sn wknd* 5/1[2]
315 10 shd **Incomparable**[27] 3548 9-8-2 55 oh1 (p) MatthewHopkins(5) 6 44
(Scott Dixon) *prom: rdn along 2f out: sn drvn and wknd* 20/1
0000 11 4 1/2 **Red Explorer (USA)**[21] 3795 4-8-9 60 MichaelJMMurphy(3) 14 33
(Ann Stokell) *a in rr* 50/1
1213 12 59 **Amenable (IRE)**[13] 4050 7-9-12 74 (p) HayleyTurner 15
(Conor Dore) *stmbld s and s.i.s: a bhd: eased fr 1/2-way* 12/1
1m 2.59s (-0.91) **Going Correction** -0.075s/f (Good) 12 Ran SP% **116.8**
Speed ratings (Par 103): **104,103,101,101,100 97,97,96,94,94 87,**
CSF £66.68 CT £449.56 TOTE £3.90: £1.30, £5.30, £4.20; EX 58.90 Trifecta £1310.20.
**Owner** Dubelem (Racing) Limited **Bred** Mull Enterprises Ltd **Trained** Sessay, N Yorks
**FOCUS**
This open sprint handicap was run at a decent pace. The winner was basicaly back to his best form of the past year.

### 4495 SKYBET SUPPORTING THE YORKSHIRE RACING SUMMER FESTIVAL H'CAP 7f 100y
7:15 (7:17) (Class 6) (0-55,65) 3-Y-O £2,264 (£673; £336; £168) Stalls Low

Form RPR
23-4 1 **Heska (IRE)**[16] 3970 3-9-7 65 (tp) AndrewMullen 3 71
(Michael Appleby) *v s.i.s and bhd: hdwy over 2f out: rdn along wl over 1f out: drvn and styd on strly ins fnl f: led last 40yds* 5/1[3]
30-6 2 nk **Strictly Glitz (IRE)**[16] 3946 3-8-10 54 IanBrennan 12 59
(John Quinn) *rrd s and slowly away: sn swtchd rt towards inner: in rr tl hdwy whn swtchd lft wl over 2f out: rdn along wl over 1f out: drvn on outer and styd on wl fnl f: jst hld* 25/1
22 3 3/4 **Blue Bounty**[43] 3037 3-9-6 64 JoeFanning 13 67+
(Mark H Tompkins) *trckd ldrs: hdwy 3f out: trckd ldr 2f out: sn chal: rdn to ld ent fnl f: sn drvn: hdd and no ex last 40yds* 4/1[2]
0-53 4 1 **Vale Mentor (IRE)**[14] 4017 3-8-6 50 AndrewElliott 8 51
(Tim Easterby) *trckd ldrs: pushed along 2f out: effrt whn n.m.r over 1f out: sn swtchd lft and kpt on u.p fnl f* 10/1
-333 5 hd **Ice Mayden**[16] 3946 3-8-8 55 GeorgeChaloner(3) 2 55+
(Bryan Smart) *led and set str pce: rdn along wl over 1f out: sn jnd: hdd ent fnl f: kpt on same pce* 5/2[1]
555 6 3 1/4 **Libra Romana (IRE)**[13] 4048 3-8-6 50 ChrisCatlin 9 42
(Sir Mark Prescott Bt) *towards rr: hdwy 3f out: rdn along 2f out: sn drvn and edgd rt: kpt on one pce* 10/1
0440 7 shd **Marlismamma (FR)**[16] 3946 3-8-2 49 (p) JulieBurke(3) 1 41
(David O'Meara) *chsd ldng pair: rdn along over 2f out: drvn wl over 1f out: grad wknd* 16/1
-000 8 3/4 **Moxey**[52] 2742 3-7-11 46 NoelGarbutt(5) 6 36
(John Davies) *towards rr: hdwy over 2f out: rdn along wl over 1f out: kpt on one pce* 40/1
-502 9 2 1/2 **Irene Hull (IRE)**[32] 3407 3-9-1 59 RobertWinston 7 43+
(Garry Moss) *cl up: rdn along wl over 2f out: drvn and wknd over 1f out* 6/1
50-0 10 6 **Different Scenario**[34] 3343 3-8-4 48 oh1 ow2 MartinLane 10 17
(Mel Brittain) *a in rr* 50/1
6260 11 6 **No Refund (IRE)**[44] 2997 3-9-4 62 GrahamGibbons 4 16
(Martin Smith) *chsd ldrs on inner: wandered over 3f out: rdn along and n.m.r whn lost action wl over 2f out: sn in rr* 20/1
6-00 12 10 **Arabian Sunset (IRE)**[20] 3828 3-8-3 47 oh1 ow1..(b[1]) RoystonFfrench 5
(Simon Waugh) *chsd ldrs: rdn along 1/2-way: sn wknd* 50/1
0304 13 12 **Roomie**[21] 3792 3-8-5 49 (be) DuranFentiman 11
(Tim Easterby) *a towards rr: hung lft bnd over 4f out: nvr a factor* 25/1
1m 33.79s (-0.01) **Going Correction** -0.075s/f (Good) 13 Ran SP% **122.4**
Speed ratings (Par 98): **97,96,95,94,94 90,90,89,86,80 73,61,48**
CSF £134.53 CT £573.27 TOTE £5.70: £1.90, £5.20, £1.70; EX 213.30 Trifecta £1902.50 Part won..
**Owner** Dennis & Andy Deacon **Bred** Mrs E Henry **Trained** Danethorpe, Notts
**FOCUS**
A modest 3yo handicap run at a sound pace, and the first two came from the back. The winner could do better than this.

### 4496 WEATHERBYS STALLION BOOK H'CAP (BOBIS RACE) 7f 100y
7:45 (7:45) (Class 4) (0-80,77) 3-Y-O £6,469 (£1,925; £962; £481) Stalls Low

Form RPR
1126 1 **Jacbequick**[6] 4290 3-9-0 75 (p) JacobButterfield(5) 3 82
(Ollie Pears) *trckd ldng pair on inner: swtchd lft to outer over 2f out: effrt to chal wl over 1f out: rdn to ld appr fnl f: styd on strly* 5/2[2]
6235 2 2 1/2 **Heroique (IRE)**[21] 3788 3-9-3 73 (e) DuranFentiman 6 73
(Tim Easterby) *led: pushed along and jnd 2f out: rdn over 1f out: hdd appr fnl f: sn drvn and kpt on same pce* 8/1
012 3 hd **Mr McLaren**[24] 3663 3-9-6 76 DavidNolan 2 76
(David O'Meara) *hld up in rr: hdwy on outer 2f out: sn rdn: styd on ins fnl f: nrst fin* 9/4[1]
2431 4 2 1/2 **Tamayuz Magic (IRE)**[47] 2896 3-8-6 62 (b) BarryMcHugh 5 55
(Michael Easterby) *trckd ldr: cl up over 2f out: rdn wl over 1f out: sn drvn and wknd* 6/1
213 5 1 1/4 **Moonlight Venture**[86] 1714 3-9-7 77 TonyHamilton 4 67
(Kevin Ryan) *t.k.h: trckd ldrs on outer: hung lft bnd over 4f out: rdn along wl over 2f out: drvn and one pce over 1f out* 3/1[3]
0030 6 2 **Whitby High Light**[37] 3243 3-9-0 70 RoystonFfrench 1 55
(Andrew Hollinshead) *hld up: a in rr* 16/1
1m 32.9s (-0.90) **Going Correction** -0.075s/f (Good) 6 Ran SP% **115.6**
Speed ratings (Par 102): **102,99,98,96,94 92**
CSF £22.76 TOTE £2.70: £2.50, £4.00; EX 27.90 Trifecta £93.40.
**Owner** Cherry Garth Racing **Bred** Russ Wake **Trained** Norton, N Yorks
**FOCUS**
They went a decent pace for this fair handicap. The winner resumed his progress back at this C&D.

### 4497 SPS GROUP MAIDEN H'CAP 2m 35y
8:15 (8:15) (Class 6) (0-65,60) 3-Y-O £2,264 (£673; £336; £168) Stalls Low

Form RPR
-622 1 **Kirkman (IRE)**[21] 3796 3-9-7 60 JoeFanning 6 74+
(James Bethell) *trckd ldr: lft in ld over 10f out: pushed along 3f out: rdn clr wl over 1f out: styd on strly* 3/1[2]
3540 2 6 **Bentons Lad**[56] 2616 3-8-10 49 AndrewMullen 5 53
(George Moore) *trckd ldrs: hdwy over 3f out: swtchd ins and rdn 2f out: styd on u.p to chse wnr ent fnl f: sn no imp* 8/1
0-06 3 2 **Little Bruv**[11] 4134 3-8-6 45 IanBrennan 2 47
(Tim Easterby) *t.k.h: trckd ldrs: hdwy to chse wnr 3f out: rdn along 2f out: sn drvn and kpt on one pce* 5/2[1]
0-04 4 hd **Major Rowan**[12] 4066 3-8-5 47 (b) GeorgeChaloner(3) 7 48
(Bryan Smart) *t.k.h: hld up in rr: hdwy on outer 3f out: rdn along over 2f out: drvn and kpt appr fnl f: nrst fin* 8/1
0546 5 2 1/4 **Telegraphy (USA)**[7] 4261 3-9-7 60 (b) PhillipMakin 10 59
(Ed Dunlop) *hld up in rr: hdwy on inner over 4f out: rdn along to chse ldrs over 2f out: drvn wl over 1f out: sn no imp* 9/2[3]
466 6 1 1/4 **My Escapade (IRE)**[66] 2292 3-8-13 52 RoystonFfrench 3 49
(Simon Waugh) *chsd ldrs: rdn along 3f out: drvn 2f out: sn wknd* 25/1
-305 7 14 **Kaizen Factor**[68] 2247 3-8-13 52 MichaelStainton 11 32
(Micky Hammond) *in tch: pushed along 4f out: rdn 3f out: sn wknd* 25/1
0040 8 13 **To Begin**[21] 3789 3-8-8 47 DuranFentiman 9 12
(Tim Easterby) *hld up towards rr: rdn along over 3f out: sn outpcd and bhd* 16/1
0040 9 26 **Acquaint (IRE)**[7] 4261 3-9-1 54 (p) PaulPickard 1
(John Wainwright) *t.k.h: led tl hung bdly lft path over 10f out: sn rallied and cl up: rdn along wl over 3f out: wknd qckly wl over 2f out: sn bhd* 20/1
6000 P **Pindora (GER)**[12] 4085 3-8-10 49 (t) BenCurtis 4
(Noel Quinlan) *in tch on inner whn lost action and p.u over 6f out* 16/1
3m 37.94s (-1.86) **Going Correction** -0.075s/f (Good) 10 Ran SP% **118.2**
Speed ratings (Par 98): **101,98,97,96,95 95,88,81,68,**
CSF £26.96 CT £67.35 TOTE £3.40: £1.20, £1.90, £1.90; EX 26.00 Trifecta £117.90.
**Owner** M J Dawson **Bred** B Kennedy & Mrs Ann Marie Kennedy **Trained** Middleham Moor, N Yorks
**FOCUS**
A weak contest for the grade with the top-weights 5lb below the ceiling. It was sound run and the winner produced a step up.

### 4498 BARRY PARKER MEMORIAL H'CAP 1m 1f 207y
8:45 (8:45) (Class 5) (0-75,75) 3-Y-O+ £3,234 (£962; £481; £240) Stalls Low

Form RPR
-323 1 **Rainbow Rock (IRE)**[38] 3187 3-8-13 70 JoeFanning 9 82+
(Mark Johnston) *hld up in tch: hdwy wl over 2f out: sn trcking ldrs: rdn to ld jst over 1f out: edgd rt and clr ins fnl f: styd on strly* 7/4[1]

-065 **2** *3 1/4* **Duke Of Yorkshire**[44] 2980 4-9-6 **67**.......... DuranFentiman 7 72
(Tim Easterby) *trckd ldrs: hdwy over 2f out: rdn wl over 1f out: n.m.r appr fnl f: sn drvn and kpt on: no ch w wnr* **33/1**

2234 **3** *1* **Ocean Applause**[9] 4190 4-9-7 **75**.......... (t) JordonMcMurray(7) 8 78
(John Ryan) *hld up in rr: hdwy on wd outside wl over 1f out: sn rdn and styd on wl fnl f: nrst fin* **10/1**

2343 **4** *nse* **New Colours**[11] 4120 3-8-10 **67**.......... (v) BenCurtis 10 70
(Marcus Tregoning) *trckd ldr: led over 7f out: rdn along over 2f out: drvn and hdd jst over 1f out: sn n.m.r and swtchd lft ent fnl f: one pce* **4/1**[2]

0004 **5** *nse* **Warlu Way**[10] 4175 7-9-13 **74**.......... GrahamGibbons 4 77
(Michael Easterby) *dwlt and towards rr: hdwy whn n.m.r bnd over 4f out: hdwy on inner wl over 2f out: rdn to chse ldrs over 1f out: drvn and no imp fnl f* **5/1**[3]

-035 **6** *2 1/4* **Quite Sparky**[17] 3912 7-8-6 **58**.......... (p) JacobButterfield(5) 6 56
(Mike Sowersby) *chsd ldrs: rdn along over 2f out: drvn wl over 1f out: kpt on one pce* **25/1**

26 **7** *1 1/4* **Checkpoint**[10] 4156 5-9-4 **65**.......... BarryMcHugh 5 61
(Tony Coyle) *hld up towards rr: hdwy over 3f out: chsd ldrs on outer over 2f out: rdn and edgd rt over 1f out: sn drvn and wknd* **9/1**

00-6 **8** *1* **It's A Mans World**[23] 3718 8-9-8 **69**.......... PaulPickard 2 63
(Brian Ellison) *hld up: a towards rr* **33/1**

4206 **9** *1 3/4* **King Of The Celts (IRE)**[27] 3544 6-9-8 **69**.......... TonyHamilton 3 59
(Tim Easterby) *led over 2f: cl up: rdn along over 2f out: drvn and hld whn n.m.r over 1f out: wknd qckly* **9/1**

6166 **10** *1 1/4* **Rasselas (IRE)**[3] 4387 7-9-7 **68**.......... (v) AdrianNicholls 1 56
(David Nicholls) *trckd ldng pair: hdwy on inner whn n.m.r and hmpd over 2f out: swtchd lft over 1f out and sn rdn: drvn whn n.m.r over 1f out: sn wknd* **16/1**

2m 6.04s (-0.96) **Going Correction** -0.075s/f (Good)
**WFA** 3 from 4yo+ 10lb **10 Ran SP% 117.7**
Speed ratings (Par 103): **100,97,96,96,96 94,93,92,91,90**
CSF £77.17 CT £461.38 TOTE £2.60: £1.20, £5.50, £1.70; EX 74.30 Trifecta £321.40.
**Owner** P D Savill **Bred** P D Savill **Trained** Middleham Moor, N Yorks

**FOCUS**
An open contest run at a fair pace. The winner could leave this form well behind in time.
T/Plt: £76.10 to a £1 stake. Pool: £57,071.96 - 547.14 winning units T/Qpdt: £25.10 to a £1 stake. Pool: £4,700.97 - 138.34 winning units JR

# 4267 WINDSOR (R-H)
## Monday, July 21

**OFFICIAL GOING: Good to firm (good in places; 8.7)**
Top bend out 8yds adding 29yds to races of 1m+. Inner of Straight out 5yds at 6f and 2yds at WP.
Wind: Almost nil Weather: Fine, very warm

## 4499 BETDAQ 3% COMMISSION RATE BRITISH STALLION STUDS EBF MAIDEN FILLIES' STKS (BOBIS RACE) 6f
**6:25** (6:27) (Class 5) 2-Y-O **£2,911** (£866; £432; £216) **Stalls** Low

Form RPR

00 **1** **Pixeleen**[23] 3728 2-9-0 0.......... OisinMurphy 3 66
(Malcolm Saunders) *mde virtually all: rdn over 1f out: kpt on wl ins fnl f* **25/1**

4 **2** *1/2* **Mystic And Artist**[65] 2348 2-9-0 0.......... MartinHarley 8 64+
(K R Burke) *chsd ldrs: rdn 2f out: styd on to take 2nd ins fnl f: a hld* **5/2**[1]

**3** *1/2* **Majestic Manner** 2-9-0 0.......... RyanMoore 6 63+
(William Haggas) *in tch in midfield: outpcd fr 1/2-way: clsd over 1f out: shkn up and styd on to take 3rd nr fin* **9/2**[3]

0 **4** *1* **Piccadillo**[16] 3975 2-8-11 0.......... ThomasBrown(3) 2 60
(Daniel Kubler) *w wnr: rdn over 1f out: lost 2nd and no ex ins fnl f* **66/1**

5 **5** *nk* **Sallabeh**[48] 2873 2-9-0 0.......... TomQueally 11 59
(George Margarson) *in tch in midfield: pushed along and outpcd 1/2-way: shkn up and styd on again fr over 1f out: nrst fin* **20/1**

**6** *nk* **Camagueyana** 2-9-0 0.......... JimCrowley 12 58+
(Ralph Beckett) *hld up wl in rr: prog fr 2f out: swtchd to outer and styd on fnl f: nrst fin* **12/1**

**7** *1* **Alhella** 2-9-0 0.......... JamieSpencer 7 55+
(Kevin Ryan) *hld up in rr: pushed along and no prog 2f out: styd on fr jst over 1f out: nrst fin* **16/1**

5 **8** *1/2* **Moon River (IRE)**[18] 3888 2-9-0 0.......... (b1) JimmyFortune 14 53
(Brian Meehan) *chsd ldng pair: rdn 2f out: no imp over 1f out: wknd ins fnl f* **11/4**[2]

0 **9** *3/4* **Seebeedee**[17] 3933 2-9-0 0.......... SamHitchcott 1 51
(Harry Dunlop) *s.i.s and pushed along early: sn in tch: outpcd 1/2-way: n.d after: kpt on fnl f* **100/1**

00 **10** *1 3/4* **Papier**[19] 3858 2-9-0 0.......... SeanLevey 5 46
(Richard Hannon) *trckd ldrs: shkn up over 1f out: wknd and eased ins fnl f* **50/1**

**11** *4* **Hey You (IRE)** 2-9-0 0.......... RichardHughes 9 34+
(Richard Hannon) *s.s: mostly in last pair and pushed along: nvr a factor* **6/1**

0 **12** *2 1/4* **Gipsy Doll**[11] 4126 2-9-0 0.......... PatCosgrave 4 27
(Paul Cole) *chsd ldrs tl wknd qckly wl over 1f out* **66/1**

00 **13** *2* **Celestine Abbey**[38] 3194 2-8-9 0.......... ShelleyBirkett(5) 10 21
(Julia Feilden) *hld up and a towards rr: no prog 2f out* **100/1**

**14** *13* **Gogglebox** 2-9-0 0.......... RichardKingscote 15
(Tom Dascombe) *s.s: a in last pair: t.o* **25/1**

1m 12.53s (-0.47) **Going Correction** -0.15s/f (Firm) **14 Ran SP% 120.7**
Speed ratings (Par 91): **97,96,95,94,93 93,92,91,90,88 82,79,77,59**
CSF £84.53 TOTE £36.50: £7.80, £1.60, £1.50; EX 140.80 Trifecta £381.40.
**Owner** Biddestone Racing Partnership IX 1 **Bred** Glebe Farm Stud **Trained** Green Ore, Somerset

**FOCUS**
The inner of the straight was dolled out 5yds at 6f and 2yds at the winning post. The top bend was dolled out 8yds from its normal inner configuration, adding 29yds to race distances of 1m+. The course had missed the rain in the previous 24 hours, and with warm sunshine during the day the ground had dried to ride faster than when declarations were made. Consequently there were plenty of withdrawals during the evening. Jockeys reported the ground was on the fast side of good, but perfectly safe after this opening contest. The newcomers were not particularly strong in the market, suggesting this wasn't too strong an affair. A number should improve on the bare form.

## 4500 BETDAQ £25 NO LOSE FREE BET MAIDEN STKS 1m 2f 7y
**6:55** (6:56) (Class 5) 3-4-Y-O **£2,587** (£770; £384; £192) **Stalls** Centre

Form RPR

2 **1** **Mythical Madness**[31] 3434 3-9-3 0.......... AdamKirby 2 79+
(Charlie Appleby) *trckd ldrs in 5th: gng easily whn nt clr run over 2f out: swtchd to outer and prog to ld 1f out: pushed along and qckly drew clr* **6/5**[1]

4 **2** *3* **Ronnie Rockcake**[28] 3517 4-9-13 0.......... (p) SebSanders 10 73
(Ben Pauling) *trckd ldrs in 6th: shkn up and prog on outer over 2f out: led briefly jst over 1f out: styd on but outpcd by wnr fnl f* **66/1**

0-6 **3** *1 1/4* **Sealed With A Kiss**[24] 3653 3-8-12 0.......... FrederikTylicki 6 66
(James Fanshawe) *trckd ldrs in 4th: wnt 2nd 2f out to over 1f out: one pce after* **33/1**

2- **4** *2* **Tornesel**[355] 4896 3-9-3 0.......... (t) WilliamBuick 5 67
(John Gosden) *trckd ldng pair: shkn up over 2f out: nt qckn over 1f out: hung lft fnl f* **2/1**[2]

5 **5** *hd* **Dalasi (IRE)**[21] 3804 3-8-12 0.......... DaneO'Neill 3 62
(Henry Candy) *led: sent for home over 3f out: styd on inner after: hdd & wknd jst over 1f out* **10/1**

4-3 **6** *2 1/2* **Steppe Daughter (IRE)**[70] 2211 3-8-12 0.......... OisinMurphy 14 57
(Denis Coakley) *hld up and detached in last trio early: in tch over 3f out but nt wl plcd whn pce lifted sn after: no ch over 2f out: pushed along and kpt on steadily fr over 1f out* **12/1**

0-0 **7** *1* **Aurora Borealis (IRE)**[55] 2649 3-8-12 0.......... JimmyFortune 1 57
(Ed Dunlop) *hld up in 7th: in tch over 3f out but nt wl plcd whn pce lifted sn after: pushed along and no imp on ldrs 2f out: eased nr fin* **33/1**

5 **8** *14* **Opus Too (IRE)**[49] 2842 3-8-12 0.......... ShelleyBirkett(5) 7 34
(Julia Feilden) *hld up in last trio and detached early: in tch 4f out: sn lft bhd: t.o* **100/1**

33 **9** *1/2* **Mr Greenspan (USA)**[65] 2346 3-9-3 77.......... RichardHughes 4 33
(Richard Hannon) *chsd ldr: shkn up 3f out: lost 2nd and wknd 2f out: eased fnl f* **6/1**[3]

**10** *hd* **Moojaned (IRE)** 3-9-3 0.......... SamHitchcott 13 32
(Dai Burchell) *dwlt: hld up and detached in last early: in tch 4f out and appeared to be gng wl enough: lft bhd fr 3f out: t.o* **100/1**

2m 6.49s (-2.21) **Going Correction** -0.15s/f (Firm)
**WFA** 3 from 4yo 10lb **10 Ran SP% 119.2**
Speed ratings (Par 103): **102,99,98,97,96 94,94,82,82,82**
CSF £113.39 TOTE £2.00: £1.10, £7.20, £6.30; EX 46.90 Trifecta £1168.90.
**Owner** Godolphin **Bred** Highbank Stud **Trained** Newmarket, Suffolk

**FOCUS**
Half a dozen withdrawals took some of the depth out of this maiden, and the gallop was not particularly searching. The overall time was quicker than the 0-75 handicap, though. The winner didn't need to match his debut effort.

## 4501 TRAILFINDERS WORLDWIDE FLY DRIVE EXPERTS H'CAP 1m 2f 7y
**7:25** (7:26) (Class 5) (0-75,75) 3-Y-O+ **£2,911** (£866; £432; £216) **Stalls** Centre

Form RPR

4121 **1** **Balmoral Castle**[45] 2963 5-9-5 **73**.......... NedCurtis(7) 8 82+
(Jonathan Portman) *hld up in last pair: swtchd to outer and prog over 2f out: led wl over 1f out: edgd lft but clr fnl f: eased 75yds out and nrly plld himself up: ld dwindling fast at fin* **6/1**[3]

21-0 **2** *nk* **Billy Blue (IRE)**[38] 3197 3-9-4 **75**.......... WilliamBuick 2 80+
(John Gosden) *trckd ldng trio: nt clr run briefly wl over 2f out: racd awkwardly and sn dropped to last: drvn and rallied jst over 1f out: r.o to take 2nd nr fin where gaining fast on eased wnr* **4/1**[1]

636 **3** *1/2* **Choral Festival**[21] 3803 8-9-5 **66**.......... WilliamCarson 9 70
(John Bridger) *hld up towards rr: prog on inner over 2f out: tried to chal wl over 1f out: sn outpcd by wnr and edgd lft: kpt on* **12/1**

0226 **4** *1/2* **Gang Warfare**[12] 4077 3-9-2 **73**.......... JamieSpencer 6 77
(Olly Stevens) *trckd ldrs in 5th: drvn over 2f out: disp 2nd over 1f out: a hld but kpt on* **5/1**[2]

646 **5** *3 1/2* **Carraig Rock**[19] 3856 4-9-9 **70**.......... OisinMurphy 4 67
(Hughie Morrison) *hld up in last: swtchd to wd outside and effrt over 2f out: no prog and btn over 1f out* **22/1**

5-06 **6** *nse* **Flashheart (IRE)**[16] 3977 4-10-0 **75**.......... (t) JimCrowley 10 72
(Marcus Tregoning) *mostly in same pl: pushed along 4f out w others stl to be asked: no prog 2f out: wl btn after* **5/1**[2]

024 **7** *4* **Nubar Boy**[4] 4340 7-9-4 **70**.......... (p) GeorgeDowning(5) 7 59
(Ian Williams) *hld up tl quick move to press ldng pair after 1f: rdn 3f out: steadily wknd fnl 2f* **12/1**

-000 **8** *2 1/2* **Couloir Extreme (IRE)**[18] 3874 4-9-9 **70**.......... (v1) RyanMoore 5 54
(Gary Moore) *pressed ldr: urged along briefly wl over 2f out: lost pl steadily sn after: eased ins fnl f* **8/1**

5006 **9** *3 1/2* **Malachim Mist (IRE)**[9] 4208 3-9-2 **73**.......... RichardHughes 1 51
(Richard Hannon) *led: tried to kick on over 3f out: styd towards inner: drvn and hdd wl over 1f out: sn btn: eased fnl f* **6/1**[3]

2m 6.8s (-1.90) **Going Correction** -0.15s/f (Firm)
**WFA** 3 from 4yo+ 10lb **9 Ran SP% 112.7**
Speed ratings (Par 103): **101,100,100,99,97 97,93,91,89**
CSF £29.39 CT £276.25 TOTE £5.40: £1.80, £2.40, £1.30; EX 32.70 Trifecta £231.60.
**Owner** J G B Portman **Bred** Springcombe Park Stud **Trained** Upper Lambourn, Berks
■ Stewards' Enquiry : William Carson one-day ban: careless riding (4 Aug)

**FOCUS**
A competitive handicap, and a solid enough gallop throughout. The winner improved again from Goodwood.

## 4502 TRAILFINDERS WHICH? BEST HOLIDAY COMPANY H'CAP 6f
**7:55** (7:56) (Class 4) (0-85,85) 3-Y-O+ **£4,851** (£1,443; £721; £360) **Stalls** Low

Form RPR

515 **1** **Polybius**[28] 3539 3-9-5 **83**.......... TedDurcan 9 99+
(David Lanigan) *hld up in last pair: prog on wd outside over 2f out: led over 1f out: sn dashed clr: eased last 75yds* **3/1**[2]

0-00 **2** *3 1/2* **La Tinta Bay**[13] 4053 3-8-9 **78**.......... CamHardie(5) 6 78
(Richard Hannon) *w ldr: upsides wl over 1f out: sn outpcd by wnr: kpt on to win battle for 2nd* **20/1**

3-23 **3** *shd* **Mission Approved**[23] 3702 4-9-12 **85** RyanMoore 1 86
(Luca Cumani) *trckd ldrs: rdn to chal towards inner wl over 1f out: sn outpcd by wnr: kpt on* **6/5**[1]
4210 **4** *nse* **Tagula Night (IRE)**[17] 3927 8-9-9 **82** (bt) AdamKirby 8 83
(Dean Ivory) *trckd ldrs: pushed along wl over 2f out: rdn and nt qckn over 1f out: kpt on again fnl f* **6/1**[3]
30 **5** *hd* **Shushu Sugartown (IRE)**[61] 2470 3-8-4 **68** MartinDwyer 2 67
(Ian Williams) *hld up in last pair: rdn and nt qckn 2f out: styd on fnl f to press for a pl nr fin* **33/1**
4616 **6** *2 1/4* **Sarangoo**[10] 4154 6-9-5 **78** FergusSweeney 4 71
(Malcolm Saunders) *led: styd on inner fr 1/2-way: hdd and btn over 1f out* **16/1**
1000 **7** *3 1/4* **Sacha Park (IRE)**[45] 2962 3-9-4 **82** RichardHughes 5 63
(Richard Hannon) *trckd ldrs: shkn up and no prog 2f out: eased whn no ch fnl f* **13/2**
1m 11.1s (-1.90) **Going Correction** -0.15s/f (Firm)
**WFA** 3 from 4yo+ 5lb **7** Ran SP% **111.7**
Speed ratings (Par 105): **106,101,101,101,100 97,93**
CSF £53.09 CT £104.22 TOTE £3.90: £2.40, £8.60; EX 77.10 Trifecta £133.80.
**Owner** Niarchos Family **Bred** Niarchos Family **Trained** Upper Lambourn, Berks
**FOCUS**
What looked a competitive handicap beforehand produced a runaway winner, who was value for further. However there is still some doubt over the bare form.

## 4503 WIN £10,000,000 ON BETDAQ COLOSSUS H'CAP 1m 67y
8:25 (8:25) (Class 5) (0-75,75) 3-Y-O+ £2,911 (£866; £432) Stalls Low

Form RPR
1-03 **1** **Tides Reach (IRE)**[23] 3733 3-9-3 **72** JamesDoyle 7 81
(Roger Charlton) *trckd ldr: led 5f out: shkn up over 2f out: rdn and in command 1f out: lft clr last 100yds* **4/6**[1]
2241 **2** *8* **Royal Connection**[13] 4047 3-9-2 **71** RichardHughes 4 74
(Richard Hannon) *led stdd pce after 2f: hdd 5f out: styd on inner and rdn over 2f out: 2 l down and hld whn heavily eased last 100yds* **7/4**[2]
0500 **3** *6* **Keene's Pointe**[12] 4072 4-8-5 **59** TylerSaunders(7) 6 50
(B W Hills) *awkward s and immediately bhd: ct up as pce slackened 5f out: lft bhd again sn after 1/2-way* **7/1**[3]
1m 43.66s (-1.04) **Going Correction** -0.15s/f (Firm)
**WFA** 3 from 4yo 8lb **3** Ran SP% **108.9**
Speed ratings (Par 103): **99,91,85**
CSF £2.17 TOTE £1.80; EX 1.90 Trifecta £1.90.
**Owner** D J Deer **Bred** D J And Mrs Deer **Trained** Beckhampton, Wilts
**FOCUS**
This race was decimated by the six non-runners. The winner confirmed recent C&D form with the runner-up.

## 4504 LOVE TRAVEL, LOVE TRAILFINDERS FILLIES' H'CAP (BOBIS RACE) 1m 3f 135y
8:55 (8:55) (Class 4) (0-80,77) 3-Y-O £4,851 (£1,443; £721; £360) Stalls Centre

Form RPR
060 **1** **Sleeper**[14] 4029 3-8-5 **61** AndreaAtzeni 10 68+
(Ralph Beckett) *hld up tl prog to join ldng pair 1/2-way: disp ld jst over 3f out tl drvn to ld over 1f out: styd on* **8/1**
0604 **2** *2* **High Love (IRE)**[21] 3803 3-8-7 **63** (p) WilliamCarson 5 67
(Tom Dascombe) *pressed ldr: disp ld w wnr fr jst over 3f out to over 1f out: one pce u.p* **14/1**
-113 **3** *1 1/2* **Nyanza (GER)**[39] 3146 3-9-3 **73** FergusSweeney 3 75
(Alan King) *trckd ldrs: wnt 3rd 3f out: hanging lft and nt qckn fr 2f out: one pce* **7/1**[3]
034 **4** *nk* **Strawberry Martini**[29] 3498 3-9-3 **73** MartinDwyer 4 74
(William Muir) *chsd ldrs: u.p fr 4f out: nvr able to chal but kpt on to press for 3rd nr fin* **20/1**
-242 **5** *1 3/4* **Shama's Song (IRE)**[39] 3154 3-9-3 **73** RyanMoore 8 71
(Sir Michael Stoute) *wl in tch: rdn 3f out: no imp on ldrs fr 2f out: one pce* **9/4**[1]
3251 **6** *2 1/2* **Yeah Baby (IRE)**[21] 3803 3-9-4 **74** TomQueally 7 68
(Charles Hills) *dwlt: hld up in last pair: rdn over 3f out: no prog and wl btn 2f out: passed a few late on* **9/1**
1-25 **7** *2* **Gay Marriage (IRE)**[27] 3560 3-9-6 **76** WilliamBuick 9 67
(John Gosden) *hld up in tch: drvn 3f out: no prog and wl btn 2f out* **7/1**[3]
-314 **8** *1 3/4* **Crystal Nymph (IRE)**[41] 3085 3-9-7 **77** RichardHughes 6 65
(Richard Hannon) *dwlt: hld up in last pair: shkn up and no prog over 2f out: no ch whn rdn over 1f out* **6/1**[2]
423 **9** *35* **Colourful**[24] 3653 3-9-6 **76** JamesDoyle 1 6
(Lady Cecil) *led to jst over 3f out: wknd rapidly: t.o* **7/1**[3]
2m 26.84s (-2.66) **Going Correction** -0.15s/f (Firm) **9** Ran SP% **115.1**
Speed ratings (Par 99): **102,100,99,99,98 96,95,94,70**
CSF £111.47 CT £822.15 TOTE £8.10: £3.10, £3.60, £2.30; EX 130.60 Trifecta £1701.30 Part won..
**Owner** The Millennium Madness Partnership **Bred** Miss A Gibson Fleming **Trained** Kimpton, Hants
**FOCUS**
A competitive fillies' handicap, but a slight question mark over the bare form as the fancied runners failed to give their running and were not involved at the finish.
T/Jkpt: Not won. T/Plt: £304.70 to a £1 stake. Pool: £94,812.66 - 227.08 winning units T/Qpdt: £96.90 to a £1 stake. Pool: £6,980.26 - 53.30 winning units JN

4505 - 4509a (Foreign Racing) - See Raceform Interactive

# 3952 CARLISLE (R-H)
Tuesday, July 22

**OFFICIAL GOING: Good to firm (7.5)**
Old Stable bend moved out 2yds and distances on Round course increased by 2yds.
Wind: virtually nil Weather: Hot and sunny

## 4510 JESSIE J HERE THIS SUNDAY MAIDEN STKS 5f
6:10 (6:10) (Class 5) 2-Y-O £2,587 (£770; £384; £192) Stalls Low

Form RPR
2 **1** **Teruntum Star (FR)**[11] 4170 2-9-5 0 PaulMulrennan 1 83+
(Kevin Ryan) *mde all: rdn over 1f out: kpt on* **1/4**[1]
**2** *1 1/2* **Chances Are (IRE)** 2-9-0 0 TomEaves 7 73+
(Keith Dalgleish) *dwlt: sn chsd ldr: rdn 2f out: kpt on* **7/1**[3]
**3** *1* **Signoret (IRE)** 2-9-0 0 TonyHamilton 2 69+
(Richard Fahey) *chsd ldr: rdn 2f out: edgd rt and one pce ins fnl f* **4/1**[2]
03 **4** *6* **Crystal Wish**[20] 3841 2-8-9 0 KevinStott(5) 8 47
(Kevin Ryan) *chsd ldr on outer: rdn 1/2-way: wknd fnl f* **7/1**[3]
0 **5** *1* **Invincible Wish (IRE)**[27] 3570 2-9-5 0 PaulPickard 4 49
(Brian Ellison) *chsd ldr: rdn 1/2-way: wknd over 1f out* **33/1**
06 **6** *1 3/4* **Yukos Flyer (IRE)**[17] 3945 2-9-0 0 DavidNolan 6 38
(Richard Fahey) *hld up: rdn and outpce 1/2-way: nvr threatened* **66/1**
**7** *1/2* **Ty Ty** 2-9-5 0 GrahamGibbons 3 41
(Michael Easterby) *slowly away: hld up: pushed along 1/2-way: nvr threatened* **22/1**
**8** *11* **Ship Canal** 2-9-5 0 BarryMcHugh 9
(Michael Easterby) *slowly away: a bhd* **50/1**
1m 0.49s (-0.31) **Going Correction** -0.10s/f (Good) **8** Ran SP% **135.7**
Speed ratings (Par 94): **98,95,94,84,82 80,79,61**
CSF £4.48 TOTE £1.10: £1.02, £2.70, £2.10; EX 7.50 Trifecta £32.70.
**Owner** T A Rahman **Bred** Petra Bloodstock Agency **Trained** Hambleton, N Yorks
**FOCUS**
Old Stable bend moved out 2yds and distances on Round course increased by 2yds. The opening contest on an ordinary seven-race card was a fair juvenile sprint maiden in which they went a proper gallop on good to firm ground. Quite a taking debut from the winner.

## 4511 WET WET WET LIVE 4TH AUGUST H'CAP 5f
6:40 (6:41) (Class 5) (0-70,69) 3-Y-O+ £2,587 (£770; £384; £192) Stalls Low

Form RPR
0-00 **1** **Slim Chance (IRE)**[20] 3844 5-9-5 **62** AndrewElliott 5 70
(Simon West) *in tch on inner: n.m.r over 1f out: swtchd lft ent fnl f: r.o to ld nr fin* **66/1**
5-50 **2** *hd* **Bosham**[17] 3948 4-9-11 **68** GrahamGibbons 4 75
(Michael Easterby) *led narrowly: rdn over 1f out: kpt on: hdd nr fin* **5/2**[1]
-053 **3** *1* **Passionada**[18] 3921 5-9-5 **62** RobertWinston 2 65
(Ed McMahon) *w ldr: rdn 2f out: one pce ins fnl f* **5/1**
1260 **4** *3/4* **Amis Reunis**[10] 4194 5-8-9 **52** (p) PatrickMathers 8 53
(Alan Berry) *chsd ldng pair: rdn 2f out: one pce* **9/1**
0000 **5** *2 1/4* **The Nifty Fox**[16] 4005 10-9-2 **59** (p) DanielTudhope 7 52
(Tim Easterby) *hld up: rdn 2f out: sn no imp on ldrs* **14/1**
6223 **6** *1 3/4* **Kirtling Belle**[4] 4383 3-9-8 **69** TomEaves 3 54
(Keith Dalgleish) *chsd ldng pair: rdn 2f out: wknd fnl f* **3/1**[2]
05U3 **7** *35* **Manatee Bay**[18] 3913 4-9-6 **63** AdrianNicholls 1
(David Nicholls) *v.s.a: a wl bhd* **7/2**[3]
1m 0.55s (-0.25) **Going Correction** -0.10s/f (Good)
**WFA** 3 from 4yo+ 4lb **7** Ran SP% **110.6**
Speed ratings (Par 103): **98,97,96,94,91 88,32**
CSF £211.91 CT £970.81 TOTE £35.30: £8.40, £2.20; EX 260.50 Trifecta £2152.60.
**Owner** Mrs Barbara Hothersall **Bred** David Brickley **Trained** Middleham Moor, N Yorks
**FOCUS**
A modest sprint handicap in which they went a contested gallop. The winner was down at a career-low mark.

## 4512 WATCH RACING ON SKY 432 H'CAP 5f 193y
7:10 (7:10) (Class 5) (0-75,72) 3-Y-O £2,587 (£770; £384; £192) Stalls Low

Form RPR
-064 **1** **Centre Haafhd**[25] 3663 3-9-7 **72** GrahamGibbons 4 78
(David Barron) *little s.i.s: rdn up to ld after 110yds: mde rest: rdn 2f out: edgd lft appr fnl f: a doing jst enough* **6/4**[1]
0566 **2** *1/2* **Secret Applause**[15] 4019 3-8-7 **58** AndrewMullen 2 62
(Michael Dods) *dwlt: hld up in tch: rdn 1/2-way: hdwy to chse wnr jst ins fnl f: kpt on but a hld* **4/1**[2]
54-6 **3** *1/2* **La Havrese (FR)**[25] 3664 3-8-9 **60**[1] PJMcDonald 6 62
(Ann Duffield) *hld up in tch: rdn and hdwy on outer 2f out: kpt on fnl f* **11/2**[3]
0632 **4** *hd* **Another Royal**[13] 4071 3-8-4 **55** (b) DuranFentiman 1 56
(Tim Easterby) *trckd ldr: rdn to chal over 1f out: carried lft and sltly hmpd appr fnl f: swtchd rt: one pce ins fnl f* **4/1**[2]
1303 **5** *7* **Raise A Billion**[13] 4071 3-8-4 **55** oh1 ow2 PatrickMathers 3 34
(Alan Berry) *trckd ldr: rdn over 2f out: wknd over 1f out* **12/1**
6064 **6** *7* **Princess Rose**[13] 4071 3-8-2 **56** (b) JoeyHaynes(3) 7 13
(John Weymes) *trckd ldr on outer: rdn over 2f out: wknd over 1f out* **12/1**
1m 13.04s (-0.66) **Going Correction** -0.10s/f (Good) **6** Ran SP% **110.8**
Speed ratings (Par 100): **100,99,98,98,89 79**
CSF £7.47 TOTE £2.60: £1.50, £1.60; EX 10.50 Trifecta £51.40.
**Owner** D G Pryde, Jim Beaumont & James Callow **Bred** Shadwell Estate Company Limited **Trained** Maunby, N Yorks
**FOCUS**
A fair 3yo sprint handicap in which they went a decent pace. The form makes sense.

## 4513 EBF BREEDERS BACKING RACING SWIFT MAIDEN FILLIES' STKS 7f 200y
7:40 (7:40) (Class 5) 3-Y-O+ £3,881 (£1,155; £577; £288) Stalls Low

Form RPR
-422 **1** **Muhawalah (IRE)**[14] 4052 3-9-0 **76** (b) FrederikTylicki 1 81
(Roger Varian) *trckd ldr: rdn 2f out: led ins fnl f: carried hd high and looked bit awkward but sn in command* **5/4**[1]
5320 **2** *2 1/2* **Potent Embrace (USA)**[7] 4290 3-9-0 **74** JoeFanning 5 75
(Mark Johnston) *led: rdn 2f out: hdd ins fnl f: one pce* **11/8**[2]
**3** *6* **Lady Bingo (IRE)** 3-9-0 0 HarryBentley 3 61
(Sir Mark Prescott Bt) *dwlt: sn in tch in 3rd: rdn over 2f out: outpcd by ldng pair fr over 1f out* **8/1**[3]
20 **4** *1 1/2* **Gotcha**[25] 3664 3-9-0 0 PJMcDonald 4 58
(James Bethell) *hld up: rdn over 2f out: sn btn* **10/1**
46 **5** *2 1/4* **Fillydelphia (IRE)**[15] 4022 3-9-0 0 AndrewMullen 6 53
(Patrick Holmes) *dwlt: hld up: rdn over 3f out: sn btn* **66/1**
1m 38.55s (-1.45) **Going Correction** -0.10s/f (Good) **5** Ran SP% **108.2**
Speed ratings (Par 100): **103,100,94,93,90**
CSF £3.12 TOTE £2.50: £1.30, £1.10; EX 3.00 Trifecta £8.50.
**Owner** Hamdan Al Maktoum **Bred** Shadwell Estate Company Limited **Trained** Newmarket, Suffolk
**FOCUS**
A fair small-field fillies' maiden in which they raced in single file at a decent tempo. The first two were clear and the winner is rated to form.

## 4514 JOIN REWARDS4RACING H'CAP 7f 200y
8:10 (8:11) (Class 4) (0-85,81) 3-Y-O+ £4,690 (£1,395; £697; £348) Stalls Low

Form RPR
20-1 **1** **Jacob Black**[34] 3362 3-9-1 **76** TomEaves 5 83+
(Keith Dalgleish) *mde all: rdn and strly pressed over 2f out: kpt on wl and a in command fnl 110yds* **7/2**[2]
2110 **2** *1* **True Pleasure (IRE)**[39] 3202 7-9-12 **79** PJMcDonald 7 86
(James Bethell) *hld up: rdn and hdwy on outside over 1f out: kpt on: wnt 2nd 110yds out* **5/1**[3]

2/ **3** 1 1/4 **Naoise (IRE)**[30] 3508 6-9-2 **74**......(t) JacobButterfield(5) 2 78
(Ollie Pears) *hld up on inner: racd keenly: rdn 2f out: kpt on fnl f: wnt 3rd nr fin* **5/1**[3]
0505 **4** 1/2 **Skytrain**[10] 4190 4-9-11 **78**......(b1) JoeFanning 6 81
(Mark Johnston) *prom: rdn to press ldr over 2f out: no ex and lost 2 pls fnl 110yds* **13/2**
6404 **5** 3 **Toto Skyllachy**[17] 3955 9-10-0 **81**...... DanielTudhope 4 77
(David O'Meara) *trckd ldng pair: rdn over 3f out: lost pl over 2f out and sn btn* **10/3**[1]
3314 **6** 2 1/4 **Hard Core Debt**[5] 4359 4-9-1 **68**...... BenCurtis 3 59
(Brian Ellison) *trckd ldng pair: rdn over 3f out: wknd over 1f out* **7/2**[2]
1m 38.14s (-1.86) **Going Correction** -0.10s/f (Good)
**WFA** 3 from 4yo+ 8lb 6 Ran SP% **114.2**
Speed ratings (Par 105): **105,104,102,102,99 97**
CSF £21.40 TOTE £3.80: £3.50, £2.30; EX 14.90 Trifecta £42.70.
**Owner** Redgate Bloodstock **Bred** Miss Emma Foley **Trained** Carluke, S Lanarks
**FOCUS**
A fairly decent handicap in which they went an even gallop. The form is rated around the second.

## 4515 BOOK YOUR CHRISTMAS PARTY 2014 FILLIES' H'CAP 6f 192y
**8:40** (8:41) (Class 5) (0-70,70) 3-Y-O+ **£2,587** (£770; £384; £192) **Stalls** Low

Form RPR
1056 **1** **Alexandrakollontai (IRE)**[10] 4194 4-9-8 **67**......(b) JulieBurke(3) 1 78
(Alistair Whillans) *hld up: rdn over 3f out: hdwy over 1f out: led jst ins fnl f: kpt on wl* **8/1**
5-01 **2** 3 **Sugar Town**[7] 4294 4-8-8 **53** 6ex...... SamJames(3) 3 56+
(Peter Niven) *led: rdn over 2f out: edgd rt appr fnl f: sn hdd: one pce and no ch w wnr* **4/1**[2]
1-05 **3** 2 1/4 **An Chulainn (IRE)**[56] 2639 3-9-7 **70**...... JoeFanning 8 64
(Mark Johnston) *hld up: rdn over 2f out: carried hd high but kpt on to take modest 3rd 110yds out* **4/1**[2]
-516 **4** 1 **Heidi's Delight (IRE)**[13] 4070 5-8-10 **52**......(b) PJMcDonald 6 47
(Ann Duffield) *hld up: rdn over 2f out: hdwy on outer over 1f out: one pce fnl f* **33/1**
0221 **5** 2 **Mrs Warren**[35] 3328 4-9-13 **69**...... PaulMulrennan 5 59
(George Baker) *trckd ldr: rdn 2f out: wknd ins fnl f* **2/1**[1]
0426 **6** 2 1/4 **Les Gar Gan (IRE)**[7] 4294 3-9-7 **70**......(p) TomEaves 4 51
(Keith Dalgleish) *trckd ldr towards outer: rdn over 2f out: wknd over 1f out* **5/1**[3]
2034 **7** 5 **Gladsome**[7] 4294 6-8-8 **55**...... JacobButterfield(5) 7 26
(Michael Herrington) *trckd ldr: rdn 3f out: wknd 2f out* **10/1**
1m 26.02s (-1.08) **Going Correction** -0.10s/f (Good)
**WFA** 3 from 4yo+ 7lb 7 Ran SP% **113.1**
Speed ratings (Par 100): **102,98,96,94,92 90,84**
CSF £38.85 CT £147.04 TOTE £9.50: £2.60, £1.90; EX 48.60 Trifecta £161.80.
**Owner** Chris Spark & William Orr **Bred** Sean O'Sullivan **Trained** Newmill-On-Slitrig, Borders
**FOCUS**
A modest fillies' handicap in which they went a respectable gallop. The winner is rated to form.

## 4516 ULTIMATE LADIES' NIGHT 4TH AUGUST H'CAP (BOBIS RACE) 1m 1f 61y
**9:10** (9:10) (Class 4) (0-80,78) 3-Y-O **£5,038** (£1,744) **Stalls** Low

Form RPR
-634 **1** **Alpine Storm (IRE)**[18] 3923 3-8-12 **69**...... JoeFanning 4 79
(Mark Johnston) *mde all: tk str hold: rdn clr fnl 2f: eased nr fin* **7/2**[3]
61P1 **2** 5 **Incurs Four Faults**[5] 4359 3-8-9 **66** 6ex...... JasonHart 1 66
(Keith Dalgleish) *slowly away: lft 2nd over 7f out: rdn over 3f out: hrd drvn over 2f out: sn no imp and btn: eased ins fnl f* **10/11**[1]
5533 **U** **Lilly Junior**[13] 4090 3-9-1 **72**......(p) GrahamGibbons 3
(William Haggas) *trckd ldr: racd keenly: lost footing on bnd over 7f out: rdr lost balance and uns* **2/1**[2]
1m 57.3s (-0.30) **Going Correction** -0.10s/f (Good) 3 Ran SP% **107.9**
Speed ratings (Par 102): **97,92,**
CSF £7.08 TOTE £3.20; EX 6.50 Trifecta £7.00.
**Owner** Sheikh Hamdan bin Mohammed Al Maktoum **Bred** Darley **Trained** Middleham Moor, N Yorks
**FOCUS**
A fair small-field 3yo handicap concluded the card, but it was an eventful race which produced an understandably modest comparative winning time. Hard form to gauge.
T/Jkpt: £45,293.80 to a £1 stake. Pool: £95,691.27 - 1.50 winning tickets. T/Plt: £61.90 to a £1 stake. Pool: £66,280.59 - 780.94 winning tickets. T/Qpdt: £21.40 to a £1 stake. Pool: £5,794.21 - 200.32 winning tickets. AS

# 3656 MUSSELBURGH (R-H)
Tuesday, July 22
**OFFICIAL GOING: Good to firm (7.9)**
Wind: Light, half behind Weather: Sunny, warm

## 4517 ARTHUR MCKAY H'CAP 1m 1f
**2:00** (2:00) (Class 5) (0-70,68) 4-Y-O+ **£3,234** (£962; £481; £240) **Stalls** Low

Form RPR
3603 **1** **Staffhoss**[15] 4014 4-8-13 **60**...... JoeFanning 4 69
(Mark Johnston) *trckd ldr: rdn over 2f out: led over 1f out: kpt on wl* **9/2**[3]
5105 **2** 1 1/4 **Ellaal**[7] 4290 5-9-7 **68**...... PaulMulrennan 1 74
(Ruth Carr) *led: rdn over 2f out: hdd over 1f out: rallied: kpt on same pce last 100yds* **10/3**[2]
0340 **3** nk **Royal Straight**[4] 4387 9-8-12 **64**......(t) SammyJoBell(5) 5 69
(Linda Perratt) *hld up: hdwy on outside over 2f out: edgd rt and chsd ldrs 1f out: kpt on towards fin* **12/1**
-461 **4** 3 **Testa Rossa (IRE)**[16] 4000 4-8-12 **59**...... GrahamLee 3 58
(Jim Goldie) *prom: pushed along fr 1/2-way: rallied: drvn over 2f out: edgd rt and outpcd over 1f out* **7/4**[1]
4330 **5** 1 1/2 **Violent Velocity (IRE)**[15] 4023 11-8-8 **60**...... JackGarritty(5) 2 56
(John Quinn) *trckd ldrs: drvn over 3f out: wknd ins fnl f* **11/2**
6-00 **6** 5 **Declamation (IRE)**[16] 4001 4-9-6 **67**...... PJMcDonald 6 52
(Alistair Whillans) *hld up: shkn up over 3f out: wknd fr 2f out* **25/1**
0006 **7** 9 **Act Your Shoe Size**[26] 3608 5-9-4 **65**...... TomEaves 7 32
(Keith Dalgleish) *in tch: pushed along over 3f out: wknd fr 2f out* **14/1**
1m 51.15s (-2.75) **Going Correction** -0.225s/f (Firm) 7 Ran SP% **111.2**
Speed ratings (Par 103): **103,101,101,98,97 93,85**
CSF £18.71 CT £159.53 TOTE £4.40: £2.50, £1.90; EX 15.00 Trifecta £84.00.
**Owner** Emjayaarrghh Syndicate **Bred** Mark Johnston Racing Ltd **Trained** Middleham Moor, N Yorks

**FOCUS**
A low-key opening to proceedings but a game effort from the winner who was gaining his first turf success at the 11th attempt. Sound form.

## 4518 BRITISH STALLION STUDS EBF MAIDEN STKS (BOBIS RACE) 7f 30y
**2:30** (2:31) (Class 4) 2-Y-O **£4,204** (£1,251; £625; £312) **Stalls** Low

Form RPR
5 **1** **Moonlightnavigator (USA)**[10] 4216 2-9-5 0...... PhillipMakin 3 83+
(John Quinn) *t.k.h: mde virtually all: hrd pressed fr over 2f out: hld on wl towards fin* **9/4**[2]
3 **2** nk **Henrytheaeroplane (USA)**[19] 3883 2-9-5 0...... TonyHamilton 2 82+
(Richard Fahey) *pressed ldr: rdn to chal over 2f out: kpt on u.p fnl f: hld nr fin* **8/11**[1]
**3** 9 **Bizzario** 2-9-5 0...... JoeFanning 4 58
(Mark Johnston) *in tch: pushed along and rn green over 2f out: sn outpcd: edgd rt and no imp over 1f out* **6/1**[3]
**4** 8 **Little Houidini** 2-9-5 0...... TomEaves 1 36
(Keith Dalgleish) *dwlt: t.k.h and sn chsng ldrs: rdn and wknd fr 3f out* **40/1**
1m 28.47s (-0.53) **Going Correction** -0.225s/f (Firm) 4 Ran SP% **105.4**
Speed ratings (Par 96): **94,93,83,74**
CSF £4.11 TOTE £2.50; EX 4.40 Trifecta £6.20.
**Owner** Malcolm Walker **Bred** Highfield Farm **Trained** Settrington, N Yorks
**FOCUS**
Only four runners but the two with experience provided a cracking finish and they both have plenty to recommend them going forward. However, the bare form has its limitations. The pace was sedate in the early stages.

## 4519 HAPPY 40TH BIRTHDAY MARK BEMROSE H'CAP (QUALIFIER FOR BETFAIR SCOTTISH SPRINT SERIES FINAL) 5f
**3:00** (3:00) (Class 6) (0-65,63) 3-Y-O+ **£2,587** (£770; £384; £192) **Stalls** High

Form RPR
3504 **1** **Windforpower (IRE)**[7] 4287 4-9-9 **60**......(p) JoeFanning 7 69
(Tracy Waggott) *trckd ldrs: effrt and rdn over 1f out: led ins fnl f: hld on wl* **5/2**[1]
6000 **2** hd **Pavers Star**[18] 3913 5-8-5 **45**...... JoeyHaynes(3) 6 53
(Noel Wilson) *t.k.h: led: rdn 2f out: edgd rt and hdd ins fnl f: hld cl home* **16/1**
0006 **3** 2 1/4 **Chloe's Dream (IRE)**[5] 4362 4-8-9 **51**...... KevinStott(5) 3 51
(Linda Perratt) *trckd ldr: drvn along 2f out: kpt on same pce fnl f* **8/1**
0025 **4** 1 1/4 **Black Douglas**[8] 4257 5-9-2 **53**...... GrahamLee 5 49
(Jim Goldie) *in tch: rdn over 2f out: kpt on ins fnl f: no imp* **3/1**[2]
0004 **5** nk **Findog**[8] 4257 4-9-2 **56**...... GeorgeChaloner(3) 2 51
(Linda Perratt) *taken early to post: dwlt: sn pushed along bhd ldng gp: effrt on outside over 2f out: no imp over 1f out* **7/2**[3]
0000 **6** 2 1/4 **Wicked Wilma (IRE)**[5] 4362 10-8-8 **45**...... PatrickMathers 1 32
(Alan Berry) *prom: rdn over 2f out: wknd appr fnl f* **40/1**
6020 **7** 18 **Baltic Spirit (IRE)**[8] 4257 3-9-2 **57**......(b) JasonHart 8
(Keith Dalgleish) *taken early to post: s.v.s: t.o thrght* **5/1**
59.15s (-1.25) **Going Correction** -0.225s/f (Firm)
**WFA** 3 from 4yo+ 4lb 7 Ran SP% **111.9**
Speed ratings (Par 101): **101,100,97,95,94 91,62**
CSF £39.89 CT £274.93 TOTE £2.90: £1.30, £8.10; EX 40.40 Trifecta £582.70.
**Owner** David Tate **Bred** Tally-Ho Stud **Trained** Spennymoor, Co Durham
**FOCUS**
A low-grade sprint which was weakened by the absence of the previous day's runner-up Opt Out. The winner sets the standard.

## 4520 DOWNLOAD THE RACING UK IPAD APP H'CAP (QUALIFIER FOR £15,000 BETFAIR SCOTTISH STAYERS SERIES FNL) 1m 4f 100y
**3:30** (3:30) (Class 5) (0-70,68) 4-Y-O+ **£5,175** (£1,540; £769; £384) **Stalls** Centre

Form RPR
151 **1** **Valantino Oyster (IRE)**[7] 4293 7-9-11 **68** 6ex......(p) DaleSwift 2 77
(Tracy Waggott) *mde all: stdd after 2f: rdn over 2f out: edgd lft and hld on wl fnl f* **4/1**[2]
6352 **2** 3/4 **Dhaular Dhar (IRE)**[8] 4254 12-8-11 **57**...... GaryBartley(3) 5 65
(Jim Goldie) *hld up: stdy hdwy over 2f out: rdn to chse wnr ins fnl f: kpt on: hld nr fin* **13/2**
2000 **3** 2 **Hunting Ground (USA)**[15] 4015 4-9-6 **63**......(v1) JoeFanning 1 68
(Mark Johnston) *t.k.h: prom: effrt and chsd wnr wl over 1f out to ins fnl f: one pce* **9/2**[3]
1541 **4** 3/4 **Eilean Mor**[8] 4259 6-8-2 **50**...... NoelGarbutt(5) 7 54
(R Mike Smith) *prom: drvn and outpcd over 2f out: rallied and edgd lft over 1f out: sn no imp* **5/2**[1]
5522 **5** 1 **Geanie Mac (IRE)**[15] 4015 5-8-12 **55**......(p) PJMcDonald 4 57
(Linda Perratt) *pressed wnr: drvn over 2f out: outpcd wl over 1f out* **9/2**[3]
060 **6** 4 1/2 **Vittachi**[8] 4259 7-8-13 **56**......(p) JasonHart 6 51
(Alistair Whillans) *hld up: hdwy on outside to chse ldrs 1/2-way: drvn and wknd fr over 2f out* **8/1**
2m 42.9s (0.90) **Going Correction** -0.225s/f (Firm) 6 Ran SP% **109.4**
Speed ratings (Par 103): **88,87,86,85,85 82**
CSF £27.37 TOTE £4.50: £2.20, £3.40; EX 22.30 Trifecta £136.90.
**Owner** Steve Sawley **Bred** Des Vere Hunt Farm Co And Jack Ronan **Trained** Spennymoor, Co Durham
**FOCUS**
A small field but a few of them came into the race in good order and a game front-running display from the winner, who's in the form of his life.

## 4521 RACINGUK.COM/ANYWHERE, 3 DEVICES, 1 PRICE H'CAP 5f
**4:00** (4:00) (Class 4) (0-80,76) 3-Y-O+ **£5,175** (£1,540; £769; £384) **Stalls** High

Form RPR
-560 **1** **Space Artist (IRE)**[66] 2352 4-9-11 **76**...... PhillipMakin 2 86
(Bryan Smart) *mde all: rdn and edgd lft ins fnl f: kpt on strly* **7/2**[3]
0023 **2** hd **Flash City (ITY)**[4] 4391 6-9-2 **67**...... PJMcDonald 4 76
(Ruth Carr) *trckd ldrs: effrt and rdn over 1f out: chsd wnr ins fnl f: kpt on: hld nr fin* **6/4**[1]
2312 **3** 4 1/2 **Salvatore Fury (IRE)**[10] 4194 4-9-6 **71**......(p) JoeFanning 1 64
(Keith Dalgleish) *t.k.h: trckd wnr: rdn and effrt over 1f out: outpcd ins fnl f* **10/3**[2]
1550 **4** hd **Perfect Blossom**[4] 4391 7-9-6 **74**...... GeorgeChaloner(3) 3 66
(Alan Berry) *propped as stalls opened: in tch: rdn 1/2-way: effrt over 1f out: no ex ins fnl f* **10/1**
6024 **5** 4 **Jumbo Steps (IRE)**[16] 4003 7-9-3 **68**...... GrahamLee 8 46
(Jim Goldie) *bhd and outpcd: pushed along and no imp fr 2f out* **7/1**

2-00 **6** *7* **Gottcher**[26] 3611 6-9-6 **71** .......... JasonHart 6 24
(Ian Semple) *t.k.h: cl up tl rdn and wknd fr 2f out* **16/1**

58.62s (-1.78) **Going Correction** -0.225s/f (Firm) **6** Ran SP% **112.8**
Speed ratings (Par 105): **105,104,97,97,90 79**
CSF £9.30 CT £17.55 TOTE £8.20: £2.50, £1.30; EX 12.30 Trifecta £37.50.
**Owner** The Smart Dame Laura Partnership **Bred** Rathasker Stud **Trained** Hambleton, N Yorks

**FOCUS**
Another small field but a well-handicapped pair fought out the finish in a truly run sprint. The winner is rated to his best.

## 4522 DOWNLOAD NEW RACING UK IPAD APP H'CAP — 2m

**4:30** (4:30) (Class 6) (0-65,71) 4-Y-O+ **£3,234** (£962; £481; £240) **Stalls** Low

Form RPR

5-56 **1** **La Bacouetteuse (FR)**[21] 3829 9-9-7 **65** ..........(b) DavidAllan 6 76
(Iain Jardine) *hld up: pushed along 6f out: hdwy u.p 3f out: chal and edgd lft over 1f out: led and edgd rt ins fnl f: styd on wl* **4/1**[3]

1121 **2** *2¾* **Maoi Chinn Tire (IRE)**[7] 4296 7-9-6 **71** 6ex..........(t) MeganCarberry[(7)] 7 79
(Jennie Candlish) *t.k.h: hld up: hdwy to chse ldrs 1/2-way: led gng wl over 2f out: rdn and edgd rt over 1f out: hdd and one pce ins fnl f* **5/4**[1]

0/60 **3** *7* **Claude Carter**[16] 3302 10-7-11 **46** .......... SammyJoBell[(5)] 1 45
(Alistair Whillans) *hld up in tch: drvn along and outpcd 4f out: kpt on fr 2f out: nt rch first two* **12/1**

0/0- **4** *5* **Jim Tango (FR)**[16] 3625 10-8-2 **46** ..........(p) JamesSullivan 5 39
(Karen McLintock) *chsd ldrs: rdn and outpcd over 4f out: no imp fr 2f out* **66/1**

0/44 **5** *6* **Strobe**[19] 3661 10-8-2 **46** oh1..........(p) JoeFanning 8 32
(Lucy Normile) *pressed ldr: led over 4f out to over 2f out: rdn and wknd over 1f out* **6/1**

6015 **6** *10* **Voice From Above (IRE)**[25] 3661 5-8-2 **51** .......... JackGarritty[(5)] 3 25
(Patrick Holmes) *led to over 4f out: rallied and ev ch over 2f out: sn rdn and btn* **7/2**[2]

0060 **7** *45* **Jebulani**[8] 4259 4-8-2 **46** oh1.......... IanBrennan 4
(Barry Murtagh) *in tch: drvn along over 6f out: wknd over 3f out: btn and eased fnl 2f* **20/1**

3m 26.23s (-7.27) **Going Correction** -0.225s/f (Firm) course record **7** Ran SP% **114.9**
Speed ratings (Par 101): **109,107,104,101,98 93,71**
CSF £9.52 CT £53.04 TOTE £4.60: £2.10, £1.40; EX 13.30 Trifecta £62.50.
**Owner** Miss S A Booth **Bred** Sarl Classic Breeding & Maria R Mendes **Trained** Bonchester Bridge, Borders

**FOCUS**
Not many of these made much appeal beforehand and the pair at the head of the weights dominated the finish. The winner is related to his best when non-claimer ridden.

## 4523 WATCH MUSSELBURGH ON RACING UK ANYWHERE TODAY H'CAP — 7f 30y

**5:00** (5:00) (Class 5) (0-70,69) 3-Y-O+ **£3,234** (£962; £481; £240) **Stalls** Low

Form RPR

0044 **1** **Shamaheart (IRE)**[15] 4023 4-10-0 **69** ..........(p) DavidAllan 5 77
(Geoffrey Harker) *hld up in tch: hdwy over 1f out: led ins fnl f: styd on wl* **11/2**[3]

1013 **2** *nk* **Orwellian**[47] 2914 5-9-9 **64** .......... PhillipMakin 7 71
(Bryan Smart) *hld up: hdwy on outside 2f out: kpt on fnl f: tk 2nd towards fin* **15/2**

-154 **3** *½* **Ixelles Diamond (IRE)**[17] 3956 3-9-3 **68** .......... GeorgeChaloner[(3)] 3 71
(Richard Fahey) *cl up: rdn to ld over 1f out: hdd ins fnl f: no ex and lost 2nd towards fin* **9/2**[2]

3554 **4** *4* **Live Dangerously**[8] 4254 4-9-12 **67** .......... JoeFanning 6 63
(Keith Dalgleish) *t.k.h: cl up: led over 2f out to over 1f out: wknd ins fnl f* **7/2**[1]

3432 **5** *1¼* **Running Reef (IRE)**[13] 4070 5-9-7 **62** .......... IanBrennan 8 54
(Tracy Waggott) *in tch: drvn along over 2f out: wknd over 1f out* **7/2**[1]

44-6 **6** *¾* **Berbice (IRE)**[8] 4254 9-8-4 **50** oh5.......... SammyJoBell[(5)] 4 40
(Linda Perratt) *dwlt: hld up: hdwy whn nt clr run over 2f out: nt clr run and swtchd twice over 1f out: no imp fnl f* **33/1**

5040 **7** *3¾* **Mysterial**[17] 3949 4-9-11 **66** .......... JamesSullivan 1 47
(Ruth Carr) *t.k.h early: in tch: rdn over 2f out: wknd over 1f out* **6/1**

660 **8** *3¼* **Rioja Day (IRE)**[8] 4254 4-9-7 **62** ..........(b) GrahamLee 2 34
(Jim Goldie) *led tl rdn and hdd over 2f out: wknd over 1f out* **12/1**

1m 26.96s (-2.04) **Going Correction** -0.225s/f (Firm)
**WFA** 3 from 4yo+ 7lb **8** Ran SP% **114.7**
Speed ratings (Par 103): **102,101,101,96,95 94,89,86**
CSF £45.95 CT £201.71 TOTE £9.10: £2.90, £3.80, £1.50; EX 46.60 Trifecta £288.30.
**Owner** A S Ward **Bred** Gus Roche **Trained** Thirkleby, N Yorks

**FOCUS**
A competitive enough finale run at a strong pace, Rioja Day being bustled along to lead and taking no prisoners. The winner was close to this year's best.
T/Plt: £173.10 to a £1 stake. Pool: £46,614.74 - 196.53 winning tickets. T/Qpdt: £16.40 to a £1 stake. Pool: £5,468.72 - 246.52 winning tickets. RY

# 3293 COLOGNE (R-H)

Tuesday, July 22

**OFFICIAL GOING: Turf: soft**

## 4524a CAGLIOSTRO ZWEIJAHRIGEN TROPHY (LISTED RACE) (2YO) (TURF) — 7f

**5:10** (12:00) 2-Y-O **£11,666** (£5,416; £2,500; £1,250)

RPR

**1** **Palace Prince (GER)** 2-8-11 0.......... AHelfenbein 2 95
(Frau R Weissmeier, Germany) **119/10**

**2** *2½* **Sign Your Name (GER)**[26] 3641 2-8-8 0.......... StefanieHofer 4 86
(Mario Hofer, Germany) **32/5**[3]

**3** *2* **Assault On Rome (IRE)**[10] 4178 2-8-13 0.......... FrannyNorton 6 86
(Mark Johnston) *dwlt: pushed along and sn led: c wd into st: hdd 3f out: dropped to 4th and scrubbed along to chse ldr 2f out: sn rdn: edgd lft and no imp: kpt on ins fnl f but wl hld by front two* **3/1**[2]

**4** *1½* **Aspasius (GER)** 2-8-11 0.......... SHellyn 1 80
(K Demme, Germany) **45/1**

**5** *¾* **Banana Split** 2-8-13 0.......... AdriedeVries 8 80
(P Harley, Germany) **2/1**[1]

**6** *4* **Nabhan** 2-9-2 0.......... EPedroza 5 73
(A Wohler, Germany) **2/1**[1]

**7** *1½* **Laleh (GER)** 2-8-13 0.......... FilipMinarik 7 67
(Mario Hofer, Germany) **84/10**

**8** *6* **Meqlaam (GER)** 2-8-11 0.......... MaximPecheur 9 50
(K Demme, Germany) **46/1**

**9** *19* **Lady Simpatico** 2-8-8 0.......... BGanbat 3
(Frau S Weis, Germany) **50/1**

1m 24.73s (84.73) **9** Ran SP% **129.8**
WIN (incl. 10 euro stake): 129. PLACES 30, 26, 24. SF: 1,077.
**Owner** Gestut Hony-Hof **Bred** Gestut Hony-Hof **Trained** Germany

# 4313 CATTERICK (L-H)

Wednesday, July 23

**OFFICIAL GOING: Good to firm (8.7)**
Wind: Light hal;f against Weather: Fine and dry

## 4527 BRITISH STALLION STUDS EBF MAIDEN STKS — 5f 212y

**2:20** (2:22) (Class 5) 2-Y-O **£2,911** (£866; £432; £216) **Stalls** Low

Form RPR

**1** **Kayo Koko (IRE)** 2-9-0 0.......... PJMcDonald 7 71+
(Ann Duffield) *trckd ldrs: hdwy over 2f out: rdn to ld over 1f out: kpt on wl fnl f* **10/1**[2]

6 **2** *2* **Muhaarib Al Emarat (IRE)**[12] 4170 2-9-5 0.......... TonyHamilton 5 70
(Richard Fahey) *prom on outer: effrt and hdwy 2f out: rdn and ev ch over 1f out: kpt on fnl f* **12/1**[3]

2 **3** *hd* **Summer Times**[21] 3842 2-9-5 0.......... JoeFanning 1 69
(Mark Johnston) *sn pushed along on inner to chse ldng pair: niggled along 1/2-way: effrt 2f out and sn rdn: n.m.r on inner and nt clr run over 1f out: kpt on same pce ins fnl f* **2/5**[1]

0 **4** *2¾* **Keen Move**[34] 3381 2-9-5 0.......... DanielTudhope 9 63+
(Ismail Mohammed) *dwlt and in rr: pushed along 1/2-way: hdwy on inner whn n.m.r wl over 1f out: sn rdn and kpt on: nrst fin* **25/1**

00 **5** *¾* **Bombay Mix**[13] 4126 2-9-0 0.......... FrederikTylicki 4 54
(Charlie Fellowes) *led: rdn along over 2f out: hdd over 1f out and wkng whn n.m.r on inner ins fnl f* **14/1**

50 **6** *2* **Strategise (IRE)**[23] 3799 2-9-0 0.......... RichardKingscote 6 48
(Tom Dascombe) *chsd ldrs: rdn along 1/2-way: wknd over 2f out* **20/1**

6 **7** *2½* **Elevator Action (IRE)**[75] 2134 2-8-11 0.......... GeorgeChaloner[(3)] 3 40
(Richard Fahey) *sn rdn along and a outpcd in rr* **16/1**

**8** *1¼* **My Specialbru** 2-9-5 0.......... PaulPickard 8 42
(Tracy Waggott) *dwlt and sn pushed along: sn outpcd and bhd* **66/1**

1m 13.31s (-0.29) **Going Correction** -0.10s/f (Good) **8** Ran SP% **110.9**
Speed ratings (Par 94): **97,94,94,90,89 86,83,81**
CSF £83.32 TOTE £16.70: £1.40, £2.80, £1.02; EX 107.80 Trifecta £227.30.
**Owner** John Dance **Bred** Tally-Ho Stud **Trained** Constable Burton, N Yorks
■ Siren's Cove (4-1) was withdrawn. Rule 4 applies to all bets. Deduction - 20p in the pound.

**FOCUS**
It was dry overnight and the going had quickened up to good to firm, good in places (GoingStick 8.7). This looked a modest maiden and the form is rated in line with the race average.

## 4528 DOWNLOAD THE RACING UK IPAD APP (S) STKS — 7f

**2:50** (2:57) (Class 6) 2-Y-O **£2,385** (£704; £352) **Stalls** Low

Form RPR

06 **1** **Stardrifter**[19] 3924 2-8-11 0.......... TonyHamilton 7 75+
(Richard Fahey) *cl up: led 1/2-way: rdn clr 2f out: unchal* **10/11**[1]

0443 **2** *8* **Reet Petite (IRE)**[8] 4302 2-8-6 **52** ..........(v[1]) AndrewMullen 5 46
(Michael Dods) *chsd ldng pair: rdn along to chse wnr 2f out: sn drvn and no imp* **15/2**

050 **3** *3¼* **Rutland Panther**[18] 3945 2-8-5 **57** ow1.......... LukeLeadbitter[(7)] 10 43
(Declan Carroll) *chsd ldrs: rdn along over 2f out: drvn wl over 1f out: kpt on one pce appr fnl f* **7/2**[2]

00 **4** *1* **Hafina**[34] 3394 2-8-6 0.......... GrahamGibbons 1 39+
(Michael Easterby) *dwlt and bhd: hdwy 2f out: styng on whn n.m.r ent fnl f and again last 100yds: nrst fin* **50/1**

0665 **5** *¾* **Sunhill Lodge Lady**[14] 4065 2-8-6 **39** .......... PJMcDonald 11 33
(Ann Duffield) *chsd ldrs on outer: hdwy 1/2-way: rdn along over 2f out: sn drvn and one pce* **22/1**

0 **6** *hd* **Seraffimo**[13] 4109 2-8-11 0.......... PaddyAspell 8 37
(Sharon Watt) *a towards rr* **100/1**

50 **7** *1¼* **Regal Accolade**[18] 3945 2-8-8 0.......... SamJames[(3)] 4 34+
(David O'Meara) *dwlt: a towards rr* **20/1**

5 **8** *1½* **Proved You Wrong (IRE)**[4] 4449 2-8-11 0.......... FrannyNorton 3 30
(Jo Hughes) *led: rdn along and hdd 1/2-way: sn drvn and wknd over 2f out* **6/1**[3]

000 **9** *3¾* **Esk Valley Lady**[90] 1656 2-8-6 **34** .......... JoeFanning 2 14
(Philip Kirby) *trckd ldrs on inner whn n.m.r and hit rail after 2f: sn in rr* **28/1**

1m 27.39s (0.39) **Going Correction** -0.10s/f (Good) **9** Ran SP% **116.2**
Speed ratings (Par 92): **93,83,80,79,78 77,76,74,70**
CSF £8.05 TOTE £2.20: £1.10, £2.90, £1.10; EX 8.40 Trifecta £23.10.Winner bought in for £12,000.
**Owner** Mrs H Steel **Bred** Bugley Stud (alchemilla) Partnership **Trained** Musley Bank, N Yorks

**FOCUS**
This looked quite a weak juvenile seller. The winner was value for extra.

## 4529 PIN POINT RECRUITMENT NURSERY H'CAP — 7f

**3:20** (3:22) (Class 5) 2-Y-O **£2,911** (£866; £432; £216) **Stalls** Low

Form RPR

233 **1** **Kylach Me If U Can**[66] 2358 2-8-9 **68** .......... TomEaves 10 77
(Kevin Ryan) *trckd ldng pair: hdwy to ld 1 1/2f out: sn pushed clr: readily* **6/1**[2]

056 **2** *3¾* **Chester Deal**[84] 1872 2-8-0 **59** oh2.......... FrannyNorton 4 58
(Jo Hughes) *in rr whn n.m.r after 1f: hdwy 1/2-way: rdn along to chse ldrs wl over 1f out: kpt on to chse wnr fnl f: no imp* **7/1**

0560 **3** *1* **Mountain Man**[15] 4057 2-8-6 **65** .......... GrahamGibbons 9 61
(Michael Easterby) *towards rr: hdwy over 2f out: rdn along wl over 1f out: kpt on fnl f: nrst fin* **33/1**

0652 **4** *3* **Dragline**[18] 3963 2-8-0 **59** .......... DuranFentiman 5 47
(Tim Easterby) *cl up: led 2f out: sn rdn and hdd 1 1/2f out: one pce* **13/2**[3]

335 **5** *1* **Flatcapper (IRE)**[18] 3945 2-8-5 **64** .......... PatrickMathers 2 50+
(Richard Fahey) *rrd s and s.i.s: bhd tl sme hdwy fnl 2f: nvr a factor* **8/1**

0540 **6** *5* **Seamoor Secret**[39] 3223 2-8-2 **61** .......... AndrewMullen 8 33
(Alex Hales) *chsd ldng pair on inner: rdn along 2f out: sn drvn and grad wknd* **20/1**

226 **7** *1¾* **Midlander (IRE)**[11] 4185 2-9-7 **80** .......... JoeFanning 3 47
(Mark Johnston) *slt ld on inner: rdn along and hdd 2f out: sn wknd* **1/1**[1]

0063 **8** *30* **Blazing Rose (IRE)**[16] 4018 2-8-0 **62**.......................... JulieBurke(3) 7
(David O'Meara) *a in rr: outpcd and bhd fnl 3f* **22/1**

1m 26.69s (-0.31) **Going Correction** -0.10s/f (Good) 8 Ran SP% **113.3**
Speed ratings (Par 94): **97,92,91,88,87 81,79,45**
CSF £44.84 CT £1274.08 TOTE £7.20: £2.20, £2.40, £7.70; EX 35.20 Trifecta £712.40.
**Owner** Geoff & Sandra Turnbull **Bred** Wellsummers Stud **Trained** Hambleton, N Yorks

**FOCUS**
A few of these had the potential to do better over this longer trip. The winner resumed his progress.

## 4530 RADIOYORKSHIRE.CO.UK YOUR LOCAL SPORTS STATION CLAIMING STKS 7f
**3:50** (3:51) (Class 6) 3-4-Y-O **£2,385** (£704; £352) **Stalls** Low

Form RPR

4642 **1** **Cape Of Hope (IRE)**[27] 3609 4-9-1 63.......................(v) AdrianNicholls 8 69+
(David Nicholls) *t.k.h: hld up and bhd: gd hdwy over 2f out: swtchd wd and chsd ldrs over 1f out: rdn to chal ins fnl f: led last 50yds: kpt on* **11/4**[2]

0564 **2** *½* **Patrona Ciana (FR)**[27] 3608 4-9-5 76.......................... DanielTudhope 3 72+
(David O'Meara) *hld up towards rr: hdwy on inner 3f out: sn chsng ldng pair: effrt to chal over 1f out: led jst ins fnl f: sn jnd and drvn: hdd and no ex last 50yds* **7/4**[1]

5000 **3** *7* **Mount Cheiron (USA)**[16] 4014 3-8-7 51..................(p) EmmaSayer(5) 1 50
(Dianne Sayer) *chsd clr ldr: tk clsr order over 2f out: rdn to chal over 1f out: sn drvn and one pce fnl f* **14/1**

0400 **4** *nse* **Mysterial**[1] 4523 4-9-5 66..........................(b) JamesSullivan 5 53
(Ruth Carr) *qckly away and sn clr ldr: pushed along over 2f out: rdn wl over 1f out: drvn and hdd ins fnl f: wknd* **4/1**[3]

-006 **5** *1 ½* **Scrutiny**[26] 3651 3-8-9 78.......................................... SamJames(3) 6 46+
(David O'Meara) *hld up towards rr: hdwy over 2f out: rdn along wl over 1f out: sn no imp* **13/2**

4-00 **6** *hd* **Rosie Hall (IRE)**[48] 2937 4-8-7 41.......................... RoystonFfrench 2 36
(Les Eyre) *chsd ldrs: rdn along wl over 2f out: sn wknd* **66/1**

0000 **7** *nk* **Bitusa (USA)**[3] 4468 4-9-1 45.......................................... JoeFanning 9 43
(Karen Tutty) *dwlt and awkward s: hdwy on outer and in tch 1/2-way: sn rdn and n.d* **16/1**

0450 **8** *29* **Lady Dancer (IRE)**[35] 3366 3-7-7 34..............(b) KieranSchofield(7) 4
(George Moore) *chsd ldrs: rdn along 1/2-way: sn wknd and bhd fnl 2f* **100/1**

1m 25.36s (-1.64) **Going Correction** -0.10s/f (Good)
**WFA** 3 from 4yo 7lb 8 Ran SP% **111.4**
Speed ratings (Par 101): **105,104,96,96,94 94,94,60**
CSF £7.49 TOTE £3.60: £1.70, £1.50, £2.10; EX 10.50 Trifecta £69.40.Cape of Hope was the subject of a friendly claim for £6,000.
**Owner** Middleham Park Racing LIII & Partners **Bred** Pendley Farm **Trained** Sessay, N Yorks

**FOCUS**
The pace was strong and the winner came from well back. He looks to be returning to form.

## 4531 SKYBET SUPPORTING THE YORKSHIRE RACING SUMMER FESTIVAL H'CAP 5f
**4:20** (4:20) (Class 4) (0-85,85) 3-Y-O+ **£6,469** (£1,925; £962; £481) **Stalls** Low

Form RPR

2002 **1** **Silvanus (IRE)**[12] 4174 9-9-12 **85**.......................... PJMcDonald 2 98
(Paul Midgley) *trckd ldng pair: hdwy over 1f out: swtchd rt and chal ent fnl f: sn led: rdn and kpt on strly* **9/2**[3]

032 **2** *1 ½* **Cruise Tothelimit (IRE)**[5] 4391 6-9-6 **79**.......................... GrahamLee 4 86
(Ian Williams) *trckd ldrs: hdwy 2f out: sn rdn: chsd wnr ins fnl f: no imp* **11/4**[1]

6051 **3** *1 ¾* **Mutafaakir (IRE)**[16] 4016 5-9-9 **82**..........................(b[1]) JamesSullivan 7 83
(Ruth Carr) *cl up: led 2f out: sn rdn: hdd jst ins fnl f: sn drvn and kpt on same pce* **11/2**

4000 **4** *¾* **Saffire Song**[13] 4128 3-8-3 **66**.......................................... JoeFanning 1 63
(Alan Bailey) *chsd ldrs: rdn along 2f out: drvn over 1f out: sn one pce* **22/1**

6020 **5** *½* **Red Baron (IRE)**[26] 3666 5-9-9 **85**..........................(p) NeilFarley(3) 6 82
(Eric Alston) *slt ld: rdn along 1/2-way: hdd 2f out: sn drvn: cl up tl grad wknd fnl f* **8/1**

3010 **6** *hd* **Lady Poppy**[19] 3920 4-8-0 **66** oh2.......................... KieranSchofield(7) 3 64
(George Moore) *hld up towards rr: gd hdwy on inner 2f out: chsd ldrs and n.m.r over 1f out: swtchd rt and effrt whn n.m.r ins fnl f: no imp after* **16/1**

6022 **7** *1 ¼* **Megaleka**[5] 4412 4-9-7 **85**.......................................... TimClark(5) 5 76
(Alan Bailey) *hld up: a towards rr* **7/2**[2]

5503 **8** *3 ¾* **Economic Crisis (IRE)**[22] 3831 5-8-11 **70**.......................... TomEaves 8 48
(Alan Berry) *in tch on wd outside: effrt over 2f out: sn rdn along and wknd* **25/1**

/004 **9** *¾* **Blue Bullet (IRE)**[54] 2727 4-8-9 **68**.......................... PaulPickard 9 43
(Brian Ellison) *dwlt and swtchd lft s to rails: a in rr* **22/1**

58.46s (-1.34) **Going Correction** -0.10s/f (Good)
**WFA** 3 from 4yo+ 4lb 9 Ran SP% **112.0**
Speed ratings (Par 105): **106,103,100,99,98 98,96,90,89**
CSF £16.20 CT £67.92 TOTE £8.20: £2.30, £1.90, £1.20; EX 21.00 Trifecta £112.90.
**Owner** Colin Alton **Bred** Barronstown Stud And Mrs T Stack **Trained** Westow, N Yorks

**FOCUS**
This race worked out very nicely for the winner, who is rated back to his best. The pace was good.

## 4532 AUGUST 15TH IS LADIES' EVENING H'CAP 5f 212y
**4:50** (4:51) (Class 6) (0-60,59) 3-Y-O+ **£2,264** (£673; £336; £168) **Stalls** Low

Form RPR

6242 **1** **Goadby**[18] 3966 3-9-5 **59**.......................................... GrahamGibbons 8 66
(John Holt) *qckly away: mde all: jnd and rdn 2f out: drvn over 1f out: kpt on gamely towards fin: jst hld on* **6/1**[3]

0006 **2** *nse* **Red Cape (FR)**[8] 4287 11-9-3 **52**..........................(b) JamesSullivan 10 60
(Ruth Carr) *cl up: chal 2f out: sn rdn: drvn ins fnl f and ev ch: jst hld* **16/1**

3055 **3** *1 ½* **A J Cook (IRE)**[7] 4314 4-8-13 **53**..........................(v[1]) ShirleyTeasdale(5) 6 57
(Ron Barr) *trckd ldrs: hdwy to chse ldng pair 2f out: rdn and n.m.r on inner jst over 1f out: kpt on same pce* **12/1**

3630 **4** *1* **Red Shadow**[22] 3833 5-8-10 **45**..........................(p) JoeFanning 12 46
(Alan Brown) *racd wd: chsd ldrs: rdn along 2f out: sn drvn and kpt on same pce* **16/1**

4250 **5** *¾* **Spoken Words**[8] 4287 5-8-8 **50**.......................... AlistairRawlinson(7) 9 49
(John David Riches) *towards rr: hdwy over 2f out: sn rdn and kpt on appr fnl f: nrst fin* **10/1**

-060 **6** *nse* **Shikari**[16] 4019 3-8-9 **49**.......................................... JasonHart 4 46
(Robin Bastiman) *midfield: hdwy 1/2-way: rdn to chse ldrs wl over 1f out: sn drvn: n.m.r and no imprtession* **10/1**

5000 **7** *1 ½* **Card High (IRE)**[27] 3604 4-8-6 **46** ow1..........................(t) EmmaSayer(5) 2 40
(Wilf Storey) *towards rr: sme hdwy over 2f out: sn rdn and n.d* **80/1**

4043 **8** *hd* **Hazard Warning (IRE)**[8] 4287 4-9-6 **55**..........................(b) GrahamLee 7 48+
(James Given) *s.i.s: a in rr* **2/1**[1]

4554 **9** *1 ½* **Cahal (IRE)**[16] 4019 3-9-2 **56**.......................................... AdrianNicholls 1 46
(David Nicholls) *trckd ldrs on inner: hdwy over 2f out: rdn wl over 1f out: hld whn n.m.r on inner jst ins fnl f: wknd* **5/2**[2]

U0-0 **10** *8* **Fair Bunny**[42] 3093 7-8-10 **45**..........................(b) PaulPickard 5 10
(Alan Brown) *a towards rr* **100/1**

1m 12.97s (-0.63) **Going Correction** -0.10s/f (Good)
**WFA** 3 from 4yo+ 5lb 10 Ran SP% **116.1**
Speed ratings (Par 101): **100,99,97,96,95 95,93,93,91,80**
CSF £96.15 CT £1115.31 TOTE £6.50: £2.50, £4.50, £3.10; EX 49.40 Trifecta £885.80.
**Owner** Cleartherm Glass Sealed Units Ltd **Bred** D R Botterill **Trained** Peckleton, Leics

**FOCUS**
A very ordinary contest in which few got involved, the pace holding up well.

## 4533 CATTERICKBRIDGE.CO.UK APPRENTICE TRAINING SERIES H'CAP (PART OF THE RACING EXCELLENCE INITIATIVE) 1m 3f 214y
**5:20** (5:21) (Class 6) (0-65,64) 4-Y-O+ **£2,385** (£704; £352) **Stalls** Low

Form RPR

3300 **1** **Tinseltown**[8] 4293 8-9-12 **64**.......................................... JoeDoyle 7 71
(Brian Rothwell) *mde all: rdn along over 2f out: clr over 1f out: styd on strly* **2/1**[1]

1060 **2** *2 ½* **Charles De Mille**[19] 3919 6-9-2 **59**.......................... KieranSchofield(5) 4 62
(George Moore) *in tch: hdwy to trck ldrs 5f out: effrt to chse wnr over 2f out: rdn and ch wl over 1f out: drvn and kpt on same pce fnl f* **8/1**

1216 **3** *1 ¼* **Elizabeth Coffee (IRE)**[18] 3973 6-9-11 **63**.......................... JordanNason 3 64
(John Weymes) *t.k.h: trckd ldrs: swtchd wd and rdn over 2f out: drvn over 1f out: no imp ins fnl f* **9/2**[3]

-005 **4** *5* **Maillot Jaune (IRE)**[21] 3843 4-8-7 **45**..........................(p) JackGarritty 5 38
(Patrick Holmes) *prom: pushed along over 3f out: rdn over 2f out: drvn wl over 1f out and sn one pce* **8/1**

-000 **5** *1 ¼* **Royal Trooper (IRE)**[34] 3398 8-9-3 **58**..........................(t) BeckyBrisbourne(3) 1 49
(Mark Brisbourne) *dwlt and towards rr: hdwy on outer 5f out: chsd ldrs 3f out: rdn over 2f out: sn one pce* **12/1**

-543 **6** *2* **Woodstock (IRE)**[9] 4255 4-9-6 **63**.......................... RowanScott(5) 8 51
(Alistair Whillans) *in tch: pushed along over 4f out: sn lost pl and bhd fr over 2f out* **7/2**[2]

6/0- **7** *8* **Sea Cliff (IRE)**[98] 2120 10-8-7 **45**.......................... AlistairRawlinson 6 20
(Andrew Crook) *a in rr: bhd fnl 3f* **33/1**

5/0- **8** *28* **Ely Valley**[546] 336 4-8-4 **45**.......................... RachelRichardson(3) 2
(Ron Barr) *chsd wnr: rdn along 5f out: sn lost pl and bhd fnl 3f* **12/1**

2m 36.75s (-2.15) **Going Correction** -0.10s/f (Good) 8 Ran SP% **114.3**
Speed ratings (Par 101): **103,101,100,97,96 95,89,71**
CSF £18.94 CT £64.27 TOTE £3.30: £1.10, £3.00, £1.40; EX 26.00 Trifecta £74.00.
**Owner** Tony Arnott **Bred** Biddestone Stud **Trained** Norton, N Yorks

**FOCUS**
An ordinary race, but another course win, his fourth from ten starts, for the favourite. Very straightforward form.
T/Plt: £29.50 to a £1 stake. Pool: £56,096.86 - 1,386.26 winning tickets. T/Qpdt: £28.40 to a £1 stake. Pool: £3,722.85 - 96.86 winning tickets. JR

# 4364 LEICESTER (R-H)
### Wednesday, July 23

**OFFICIAL GOING: Good to firm (good in places; watered; 7.8)**
Wind: Light across Weather: Fine

## 4534 BETFAIR AMATEUR H'CAP (FOR NOVICE AMATEUR RIDERS) 7f 9y
**5:45** (5:46) (Class 6) (0-60,60) 4-Y-O+ **£1,871** (£580; £290; £145) **Stalls** High

Form RPR

0006 **1** **Sophie's Beau (USA)**[8] 4293 7-10-9 **48**.......................... MissJWalton 9 55
(Michael Chapman) *mde all: rdn over 1f out: styd on* **12/1**

6060 **2** *1 ¾* **High On The Hog (IRE)**[6] 4341 6-10-7 **46** oh1.... MissMeganNicholls 2 48
(Mark Brisbourne) *a.p: rdn over 2f out: styd on to go 2nd wl ins fnl f: nt rch wnr* **5/1**[3]

0030 **3** *½* **Burnhope**[41] 3149 5-11-0 **53**..........................[1] MrKLocking 3 54
(Scott Dixon) *a.p: chsd wnr 2f out: rdn and styd on same pce wl ins fnl f* **4/1**[2]

-035 **4** *1 ¼* **Zainda (IRE)**[42] 3097 4-10-8 **50**.......................... MrAFrench(3) 1 48
(Paul Midgley) *chsd ldrs: outpcd over 2f out: rallied over 1f out: styd on* **5/1**[3]

0330 **5** *½* **Eastlands Lad (IRE)**[16] 4023 5-10-6 **48**..........[1] DylanMcDonagh(3) 11 44
(Micky Hammond) *prom: rdn over 2f out: hung rt over 1f out: styd on same pce fnl f* **7/2**[1]

0500 **6** *nk* **Sairaam (IRE)**[34] 3384 8-10-7 **46** oh1..........................(p) MissPFuller 7 41
(Charles Smith) *s.i.s: sn prom: chsd wnr 4f out tl pushed along 2f out: no ex ins fnl f* **12/1**

6350 **7** *3 ¼* **Upper Lambourn (IRE)**[35] 3366 6-10-4 **46** oh1....(t) MissKatyLyons(3) 6 33
(Christopher Kellett) *in rr: styd on appr fnl f: nvr nrr* **50/1**

50-0 **8** *nk* **Carazam (IRE)**[65] 2381 7-11-4 **60**..........................(t) MrJPWilliams(3) 4 46
(Bernard Llewellyn) *sn pushed along in rr: hdwy over 1f out: nvr nrr* **10/1**

2600 **9** *4* **Homeboy (IRE)**[8] 4306 6-10-4 **46**..........................(b) MissKFBegley(3) 10 21
(David Evans) *chsd wnr 3f: sn rdn: wknd 2f out* **16/1**

0-00 **10** *4 ½* **Gifted Heir (IRE)**[145] 783 10-10-4 **46** oh1.......................... MissSPeacock(3) 5 9
(Ray Peacock) *s.s: outpcd* **100/1**

5605 **11** *10* **Alberto**[22] 3820 4-10-7 **46** oh1.......................... MrJamesHughes 12
(Jo Hughes) *prom: drvn along 1/2-way: sn wknd* **20/1**

0-00 **12** *6* **Finn Mac**[33] 3439 4-10-4 **46** oh1.......................... MrPHardy(3) 13
(John Norton) *sn outpcd* **66/1**

1m 28.03s (1.83) **Going Correction** -0.075s/f (Good) 12 Ran SP% **115.1**
Speed ratings (Par 101): **86,84,83,82,81 81,77,77,72,67 55,49**
CSF £67.63 CT £289.68 TOTE £15.00: £4.20, £2.00, £1.80; EX 90.50 Trifecta £487.50.
**Owner** Mrs M Chapman **Bred** Steve C Snowden & Doug Wilson **Trained** Market Rasen, Lincs

**FOCUS**
A moderate handicap restricted to novice amateur riders in which they went an honest gallop on good to firm ground. Limited form, rated around the principals.

## 4535 MOLYNEUX H'CAP 5f 218y
**6:15** (6:15) (Class 5) (0-70,69) 3-Y-O **£2,587** (£770; £384; £192) **Stalls** High

Form RPR

3156 **1** **First Experience**[19] 3936 3-9-6 **68**.......................... KierenFallon 6 80
(Rae Guest) *sn pushed along and prom: chsd ldr over 1f out: r.o to ld wl ins fnl f* **7/1**



The Form Book, Raceform Ltd, Newbury, RG14 5SJ

0424 **2** *1* **Faure Island**[19] 3936 3-9-6 **68** FergusSweeney 4 77
(Henry Candy) *w ldr tl led over 3f out: rdn edgd lft and hdd wl ins fnl f* **3/1**[2]

0542 **3** *9* **Nelson's Pride**[8] 4288 3-8-9 **57** (b) JamieSpencer 7 39
(Kevin Ryan) *hld up: rdn over 1f out: wnt 3rd ins fnl f: nvr on terms* **7/4**[1]

6343 **4** *3 ¾* **Coiste Bodhar (IRE)**[12] 4155 3-9-1 **63** (p) RobertWinston 1 46+
(Joseph Tuite) *led: hdd over 3f out: sn rdn: wknd and eased fnl f: sddle slipped* **6/1**[3]

0-46 **5** *1 ¼* **Maymyo (IRE)**[43] 3083 3-8-7 **60** JoshBaudains(5) 2 27
(Sylvester Kirk) *hld up: rdn over 2f out: n.d* **12/1**

343- **6** *1* **Cockney Belle**[336] 5634 3-9-2 **69** MarcMonaghan(5) 3 33
(Marco Botti) *chsd ldrs: rdn over 2f out: edgd lft and wknd over 1f out* **8/1**

-560 **7** *8* **Quantum Dot (IRE)**[11] 4186 3-8-13 **64** GeorgeChaloner(3) 5
(Lisa Williamson) *awkward leaving stalls: chsd ldrs: rdn over 2f out: wkng whn n.m.r over 1f out* **40/1**

1m 11.34s (-1.66) **Going Correction** -0.075s/f (Good) **7** Ran SP% **109.4**
Speed ratings (Par 100): **108,106,94,89,88 86,76**
CSF £25.78 TOTE £8.00: £4.90, £2.80; EX 28.30 Trifecta £46.00.
**Owner** Fitorfat Racing & Guy Carstairs **Bred** Northmore Stud **Trained** Newmarket, Suffolk

**FOCUS**
A modest 3yo sprint handicap in which they went a contested gallop. The first two are rated slightly above their pre-race bests.

## 4536 SUTTON (S) STKS — 1m 60y
**6:45** (6:45) (Class 6) 3-Y-O — **£1,940** (£577; £288; £144) **Stalls** Low

Form — RPR

4600 **1** **Kalon Brama (IRE)**[33] 3433 3-8-6 55 [1] ChrisCatlin 4 63+
(Peter Charalambous) *hld up: hdwy over 2f out: shkn up to ld over 1f out: sn clr* **6/1**[3]

053 **2** *6* **Vodka Time (IRE)**[6] 4365 3-8-8 67 DeclanBates(3) 6 54
(David Evans) *hld up: racd keenly: hdwy over 2f out: rdn over 1f out: edgd rt and kpt on to go 2nd wl ins fnl f* **9/4**[1]

5500 **3** *nk* **Running Wolf (IRE)**[8] 4292 3-8-11 65 (v[1]) AndrewMullen 8 54
(Michael Dods) *sn trcking ldr: rdn over 2f out: sn hung rt: styd on same pce fr over 1f out* **11/4**[2]

364 **4** *¾* **Chanceuse**[14] 4088 3-8-12 50 (v[1]) RobertWinston 7 53
(Gay Kelleway) *sn led: rdn and hdd over 1f out: wknd ins fnl f* **16/1**

0160 **5** *1 ½* **Sweet Alibi (IRE)**[12] 4152 3-8-7 64 PhilipPrince(5) 5 49
(J S Moore) *hld up: hdwy u.p over 2f out: no ex fnl f* **13/2**

404- **6** *6* **Tara's Treasure (IRE)**[215] 8367 3-8-11 51 SamHitchcott 2 35
(Gary Moore) *hld up in tch: plld hrd: riddem over 3f out: wknd over 1f out* **10/1**

50-0 **7** *¾* **Enfys Hud**[26] 3643 3-8-1 58 NoelGarbutt(5) 3 28
(David Evans) *hld up: hdwy u.p over 4f out: wknd 3f out* **8/1**

06-4 **8** *12* **L'Es Fremantle (FR)**[10] 543 3-8-4 17 PaulBooth(7) 1
(Michael Chapman) *chsd ldrs: rdn 4f out: wknd wl over 2f out* **150/1**

1m 44.88s (-0.22) **Going Correction** -0.075s/f (Good) **8** Ran SP% **111.8**
Speed ratings (Par 98): **98,92,91,90,89 83,82,70**
CSF £19.00 TOTE £6.40: £1.70, £1.30, £1.30; EX 25.60 Trifecta £106.60.Winner bought in for 7,500gns.
**Owner** pcracing.co.uk **Bred** Tally-Ho Stud **Trained** Newmarket, Suffolk

**FOCUS**
A very modest 3yo seller in which there was a contested gallop. The easy winner and the fourth set the level.

## 4537 GALLOPING GARRATT'S 21ST H'CAP — 7f 9y
**7:20** (7:21) (Class 4) (0-80,78) 3-Y-O+ — **£4,690** (£1,395; £697; £348) **Stalls** High

Form — RPR

4-20 **1** **Bold Lass (IRE)**[42] 3117 3-9-6 **77** TedDurcan 6 87+
(David Lanigan) *hld up: hdwy 1/2-way: led over 1f out: rdn ins fnl f: r.o wl* **2/1**[2]

0031 **2** *2 ¼* **Red Paladin (IRE)**[13] 4108 4-9-7 **71** JamieSpencer 1 78
(Kevin Ryan) *sn pushed along in rr: hdwy to have ev ch fr over 1f out tl rdn and no ex wl ins fnl f* **11/2**[3]

243 **3** *½* **Available (IRE)**[13] 4132 5-10-0 **78** (tp) FrannyNorton 8 84
(John Mackie) *racd alone tl wnt towards centre 1/2-way: overall ldr: rdn: hdd and edgd lft over 1f out: styd on same pce fnl f* **11/2**[3]

5501 **4** *1 ¾* **Pearl Nation (USA)**[27] 3628 5-9-13 **77** AndrewMullen 5 78
(Michael Appleby) *trckd ldrs: rdn over 2f out: ev ch over 1f out: no ex ins fnl f* **15/8**[1]

-006 **5** *9* **Footstepsintherain (IRE)**[32] 3479 4-10-0 **78** KierenFallon 7 55
(David Dennis) *chsd ldr: rdn over 2f out: ev ch over 1f out: wknd fnl f* **14/1**

4224 **6** *2 ¾* **Great Expectations**[51] 2833 6-9-12 **76** FergusSweeney 3 45
(J R Jenkins) *hld up: hdwy over 2f out: rdn over 1f out: sn wknd* **16/1**

51-3 **7** *5* **Kingswinford (IRE)**[19] 3915 8-9-2 **66** PaddyAspell 4 22
(John Norton) *chsd ldrs: rdn 1/2-way: wknd over 2f out* **50/1**

1m 24.78s (-1.42) **Going Correction** -0.075s/f (Good)
**WFA** 3 from 4yo+ 7lb **7** Ran SP% **113.4**
Speed ratings (Par 105): **105,102,101,99,89 86,80**
CSF £13.25 CT £51.04 TOTE £3.30: £2.50, £2.00; EX 10.70 Trifecta £38.00.
**Owner** B E Nielsen **Bred** Bjorn E Nielsen **Trained** Upper Lambourn, Berks

**FOCUS**
A fair handicap in which there was a slight difference of opinion, and the third horse home set a decent tempo initially isolated on the stands' rail, whereas the remainder raced more towards the centre. The second and third set the level.

## 4538 KEITH ORCHARD OF ATHERSTONE 70TH BIRTHDAY H'CAP — 1m 3f 183y
**7:55** (7:55) (Class 4) (0-85,85) 4-Y-O+ — **£4,690** (£1,395; £697; £348) **Stalls** Low

Form — RPR

5-01 **1** **Dolphin Village (IRE)**[36] 3341 4-9-1 **82** GeorgeChaloner(3) 3 91
(Richard Fahey) *racd keenly: sn led: hdd over 10f out: trckd ldr tl over 5f out: remained handy: rdn to ld over 1f out: styd on wl* **6/4**[1]

0-05 **2** *2* **Monsieur Rieussec**[44] 3065 4-9-3 **81** TedDurcan 4 87
(Jonathan Portman) *hld up: hdwy over 2f out: rdn and ev ch over 1f out: styd on same pce ins fnl f* **2/1**[2]

0-30 **3** *1 ¾* **Kuda Huraa (IRE)**[46] 2991 6-9-7 **85** FergusSweeney 1 88
(Alan King) *trckd ldrs: wnt 2nd over 5f out tl led over 2f out: rdn and hdd over 1f out: no ex ins fnl f* **5/1**[3]

0224 **4** *1 ¾* **Tepmokea (IRE)**[25] 3696 8-9-2 **80** (b) PaddyAspell 7 80
(Conor Dore) *led at stdy pce over 10f out: qcknd over 3f out: rdn and hdd over 2f out: no ex fnl f* **8/1**

214 **5** *2* **Incendo**[21] 3860 8-8-12 **76** (v) HayleyTurner 2 73
(Conor Dore) *s.i.s: hld up: shkn up over 2f out: hung rt over 1f out: nt trble ldrs* **9/1**

2m 33.64s (-0.26) **Going Correction** -0.075s/f (Good) **5** Ran SP% **111.1**
Speed ratings (Par 105): **97,95,94,93,92**
CSF £4.83 TOTE £1.80: £1.10, £2.60; EX 6.30 Trifecta £17.30.
**Owner** Y Nasib **Bred** Gerrardstown House Stud **Trained** Musley Bank, N Yorks

**FOCUS**
A decent middle-distance handicap in which they went an, at best, even gallop at single file for much of the journey. The winner continued his quietly progressive profile.

## 4539 BREEDERS BACKING RACING EBF MAIDEN STKS — 5f 2y
**8:30** (8:31) (Class 5) 3-Y-O+ — **£3,881** (£1,155; £577; £288) **Stalls** High

Form — RPR

03-5 **1** **Cordial**[19] 3916 3-9-0 74 HarryBentley 3 71+
(Stuart Williams) *mde all: shkn up and c clr fnl f: easily* **1/2**[1]

0-5 **2** *3 ¼* **Plauseabella**[23] 3801 3-8-11 0 MichaelJMMurphy(3) 4 52
(Stuart Kittow) *chsd wnr: rdn 1/2-way: styd on same pce fnl f* **6/1**[3]

**3** *¾* **Satellite Express (IRE)** 3-8-11 0 DeclanBates(3) 5 49
(David Evans) *s.i.s: sn prom: rdn 1/2-way: no ex fnl f* **7/2**[2]

**4** *5* **Altjira** 3-9-0 0 (v[1]) MatthewHopkins(5) 2 36
(Scott Dixon) *s.i.s: sn chsng ldrs: rdn 1/2-way: wknd over 1f out* **20/1**

1m 1.49s (1.49) **Going Correction** -0.075s/f (Good) **4** Ran SP% **107.9**
Speed ratings (Par 103): **85,79,78,70**
CSF £3.94 TOTE £1.40; EX 3.30 Trifecta £5.40.
**Owner** D A Shekells **Bred** Juddmonte Farms Ltd **Trained** Newmarket, Suffolk

**FOCUS**
A poor small-field maiden which proved as one-sided as the market suggested. The form has been given a token rating through the winner.

## 4540 MELTON MOWBRAY H'CAP — 1m 1f 218y
**9:00** (9:00) (Class 5) (0-70,68) 3-Y-O — **£3,234** (£962; £481; £240) **Stalls** Low

Form — RPR

-354 **1** **Final Countdown**[24] 3760 3-9-4 **65** WilliamCarson 6 73+
(Anthony Carson) *trckd ldrs: led over 2f out: rdn and edgd rt over 1f out: hung lft ins fnl f: styd on u.p* **11/2**

0501 **2** *½* **Pink Diamond**[11] 4210 3-9-1 **62** KierenFallon 4 69
(Eve Johnson Houghton) *hld up: pushed along over 4f out: hdwy over 1f out: r.o to go 2nd wl ins fnl f: nt quite rch wnr* **7/2**[2]

6-45 **3** *1* **Scoppio Del Carro**[33] 3421 3-9-6 **67** (t) LiamKeniry 3 72
(Andrew Balding) *hld up: hdwy over 4f out: rdn over 1f out: nt clr run and edgd lft ins fnl f: swtchd rt: styd on* **4/1**[3]

3535 **4** *2 ½* **Opera Fan (FR)**[34] 3391 3-9-7 **68** FrannyNorton 2 68
(Mark Johnston) *led 1f: chsd ldrs: rdn over 1f out: n.m.r and styd on same pce fnl f* **11/4**[1]

66-5 **5** *6* **Tipsy Star**[25] 3712 3-9-3 **64** FergusSweeney 5 53
(Jonathan Geake) *hld up: hdwy over 2f out: rdn over 1f out: nt clr run and wknd ins fnl f* **25/1**

4302 **6** *7* **Black Label**[25] 3712 3-9-7 **68** (p) JamieSpencer 1 44
(Harry Dunlop) *led 9f out: rdn and hdd over 2f out: wknd over 1f out* **5/1**

0500 **7** *1 ½* **Buy Out Boy**[5] 4420 3-8-12 **59** (v[1]) AndrewMullen 8 32
(Michael Appleby) *prom: racd keenly: trckd ldr over 7f out tl rdn over 3f out: wknd over 2f out* **12/1**

2m 6.77s (-1.13) **Going Correction** -0.075s/f (Good) **7** Ran SP% **112.5**
Speed ratings (Par 100): **101,100,99,97,93 87,86**
CSF £24.13 CT £84.02 TOTE £7.80: £3.30, £1.30; EX 32.20 Trifecta £102.00.
**Owner** Christopher Wright & Minster Stud **Bred** Stratford Place Stud & Minster Stud **Trained** Newmarket, Suffolk

**FOCUS**
The concluding contest was a modest 3yo handicap in which they went a contested gallop.
T/Plt: £43.60 to a £1 stake. Pool: £56,596.53 - 947.31 winning tickets. T/Qpdt: £5.00 to a £1 stake. Pool: £5,610.12 - 819.97 winning tickets. CR

# 4428 LINGFIELD (L-H)
### Wednesday, July 23

**OFFICIAL GOING: Standard**
Wind: light, half against Weather: warm and sunny

## 4541 188BET MAIDEN AUCTION STKS — 7f 1y(P)
**2:00** (2:00) (Class 6) 2-Y-O — **£2,264** (£673; £336; £168) **Stalls** Low

Form — RPR

0 **1** **Ragtime Dancer**[29] 3557 2-8-10 0 OisinMurphy 9 68+
(Jonathan Portman) *s.i.s: grad rcvrd to chse ldrs after 2f: rdn to chal over 1f out: led 1f out: r.o wl: rdn out* **10/1**

**2** *1 ½* **Edge Of Heaven** 2-8-6 0 LukeMorris 5 60+
(Jonathan Portman) *dwlt: in tch in rr of main gp: hdwy and drvn over 1f out: styd on wl to go 2nd ins fnl f: no threat to wnr* **33/1**

4 **3** *¾* **Saumur**[32] 3467 2-8-3 0 CamHardie(5) 4 60
(Denis Coakley) *trckd ldng trio: nt clr run 2f out: swtchd lft and effrt on inner to chse ldrs 1f out: kpt on same pce ins fnl f* **2/1**[2]

06 **4** *1 ½* **Toast Of Newbury (IRE)**[6] 4338 2-9-5 0 JamesDoyle 2 67
(Jamie Osborne) *led: rdn wl over 1f out: hdd 1f out: no ex: wknd and lost 2 pls ins fnl f* **8/1**

3 **5** *3 ½* **Little Miss Mighty**[19] 3934 2-8-8 0 JackMitchell 1 46
(Nick Littmoden) *bustled along early: chsd ldrs tl shuffled bk into midfield after 2f out: effrt u.p 2f out: outpcd over 1f out: swtchd rt and kpt on same pce fnl f* **7/1**[3]

0 **6** *2 ¼* **New Abbey Dancer (IRE)**[76] 2089 2-8-8 0 DavidProbert 6 40+
(Gay Kelleway) *in tch in rr of main gp: outpcd and wd bnd 2f out: n.d and plugged on same pce fr over 1f out* **66/1**

42 **7** *½* **Bannister Bell (IRE)**[9] 4260 2-9-3 0 AdamKirby 3 48
(David Evans) *w ldr: rdn and ev ch ent fnl 2f: outpcd and btn over 1f out: wknd fnl f* **6/4**[1]

6 **8** *13* **Cahar Fad (IRE)**[15] 4054 2-8-13 0 HayleyTurner 8 9
(Steph Hollinshead) *dwlt: pushed along early: in tch in rr: struggling over 2f out: wknd 2f out* **20/1**

0 **9** *26* **Cool Choice**[58] 2612 2-9-1 0 (e[1]) J-PGuillambert 7
(Nick Littmoden) *in tch in rr: rdn and lost tch 5f out: t.o 2f out* **50/1**

1m 26.3s (1.50) **Going Correction** +0.05s/f (Slow) **9** Ran SP% **117.2**
Speed ratings (Par 92): **93,91,90,88,84 82,81,66,37**
CSF £279.43 TOTE £16.60: £3.10, £6.70, £1.20; EX 295.20 Trifecta £2475.00 Part won..
**Owner** Mrs Hugh Maitland-Jones **Bred** Mrs Hugh Maitland-Jones **Trained** Upper Lambourn, Berks

**FOCUS**
A modest juvenile maiden, with improvement from the winner.

## 4542 188BET CLAIMING STKS 6f 1y(P)
2:30 (2:31) (Class 6) 2-Y-O £2,134 (£635; £317; £158) Stalls Low

Form RPR
0201 1 **Shamrock Sheila (IRE)**[4] 4449 2-8-0 0 JoeyHaynes(3) 8 61
(J S Moore) *chsd ldrs and travelled strly: rdn and effrt over 1f out: chal 1f out: pushed along to ld fnl 75yds: r.o wl: comf* 4/5[1]
6615 2 3/4 **Diminutive (IRE)**[8] 4283 2-8-4 62 (p) DavidProbert 2 58
(Grace Harris) *pressed ldr: drvn to ld over 1f out: clr w wnr ins fnl f: hdd and styd on same pce after* 7/2[2]
6644 3 2 **Itsindebag**[29] 3550 2-7-10 53 ow1 JosephineGordon(7) 6 51
(J S Moore) *dwlt: in tch in last pair: swtchd rt over 2f out: wd bnd and lost grnd 2f out: rallied and styd on fnl f: no threat to ldrs* 14/1
4 1/2 **Paris Carver (FR)** 2-8-7 0 LukeMorris 5 53
(Jonathan Portman) *s.i.s: in tch in rr: nt clr run 2f out: rdn and hdwy on inner to chse ldrs over 1f out: wknd ins fnl f* 7/1[3]
0 5 6 **Dark Symphony (IRE)**[9] 4260 2-8-4 0 HayleyTurner 4 32
(Mark Usher) *chsd ldrs: rdn and lost pl over 1f out: wknd fnl f* 25/1
0 6 nk **Blackasyourhat (IRE)**[30] 3536 2-8-7 0 (t) MartinLane 1 34
(Roger Ingram) *led: rdn wl over 1f out: sn hdd and btn: wknd fnl f* 14/1
00 7 3/4 **Tribal Diamond**[20] 3889 2-8-3 0 JimmyQuinn 7 28
(Edward Creighton) *t.k.h: hld up in tch in midfield: effrt and drvn over 1f out: no rspnse and sn btn: wknd fnl f* 33/1

1m 13.94s (2.04) **Going Correction** +0.05s/f (Slow) 7 Ran SP% **110.4**
Speed ratings (Par 92): **88,87,84,83,75 75,74**
CSF £3.42 TOTE £1.70: £1.10, £3.10; EX 5.50 Trifecta £18.00.
**Owner** Mrs T Burns & J S Moore **Bred** Rathasker Stud **Trained** Upper Lambourn, Berks

**FOCUS**
No great gallop on here and the two with the most obvious claims came clear. The second and third help with the ordinary level.

## 4543 ALDERMORE BLOCK DISCOUNTING MAIDEN STKS 1m 4f (P)
3:00 (3:01) (Class 5) 3-Y-O+ £2,587 (£770; £384; £192) Stalls Low

Form RPR
5524 1 **Fiery Sunset**[19] 3918 3-8-10 78 RichardHughes 5 85
(Michael Bell) *in tch: hdwy to chse ldrs 7f out: wnt 2nd 5f out tl led over 2f out: rdn clr wl over 1f out: eased towards fin* 6/1[3]
-222 2 1 1/4 **Button Down**[16] 4020 3-8-10 83 JamesDoyle 9 83
(Lady Cecil) *chsd ldrs: effrt in 4th 2f out: chsd clr wnr over 1f out: styd on and clsd ins fnl f: a hld* 3/1[2]
303 3 6 **Saarrem (USA)**[48] 2917 3-9-1 80 PaulHanagan 3 78
(John Gosden) *led for over 1f: steadily dropped bk and in midfield 9f out: hdwy 4f out: 6th and plenty to do whn effrt 2f out: kpt on to take 3rd ins fnl f: no ch w wnr* 11/4[1]
6 4 3/4 **Jonny Rae**[53] 2773 3-9-1 0 DavidProbert 16 77
(Andrew Balding) *t.k.h: chsd ldrs tl led over 10f out: rdn and hdd over 2f out: 3rd and btn over 1f out: wknd ins fnl f* 3/1[2]
0-0 5 6 **Summerling (IRE)**[112] 1233 3-8-10 0 OisinMurphy 15 63
(Jonathan Portman) *t.k.h: chsd ldrs: wnt 2nd 10f out tl 5f out: chsd ldrs after tl rdn and btn 2f out: sn wknd* 100/1
04 6 1 1/4 **Upper Street (IRE)**[7] 4325 3-8-10 0 (v) ShaneKelly 6 61
(Sir Michael Stoute) *dwlt: in tch in midfield: hdwy to chse ldrs 4f out: 3rd and drvn 2f out: sn outpcd and btn: wknd over 1f out* 14/1
04 7 6 **Soundtrack (IRE)**[25] 3712 3-9-1 0 AdamKirby 10 56
(William Knight) *hld up in tch in last quartet: hmpd bnd 9f out: hdwy 5f out: rdn and btn over 2f out: wknd 2f out* 20/1
033 8 9 **Prairie Rose (GER)**[47] 2967 3-8-10 78 [1] HarryBentley 11 37
(Olly Stevens) *t.k.h: chsd ldr tl 9f out: in tch after tl rdn and btn over 2f out: sn dropped out* 12/1
04 9 1/2 **Deja Bougg**[9] 4268 3-8-10 0 SilvestreDeSousa 12 36
(David Evans) *taken down early: stdd and swtchd lft s: hld up in rr: rdn and struggling over 4f out: no ch but plugged on past btn horses fnl f* 66/1
00 10 8 **Silken Waters**[24] 3750 3-8-10 0 DaneO'Neill 2 23
(Eve Johnson Houghton) *in tch in midfield: rdn and btn ent fnl 3f: sn wl btn: eased fnl f: t.o* 100/1
06 11 17 **Greatday Allweek (IRE)**[7] 2924 5-9-1 0 LamornaBardwell(7) 1
(Seamus Mullins) *in tch in midfield: stmbld and lost pl bnd 9f out: bhd after: lost tch 5f out: t.o over 3f out* 100/1
12 nk **Bo Peep (IRE)**[154] 4-9-8 0 KieranO'Neill 14
(Seamus Mullins) *s.i.s: hld up towards rr: rdn over 4f out: sn struggling: t.o over 2f out* 100/1
13 2 **Battle Group**[102] 9-9-13 0 LiamKeniry 13
(Johnny Farrelly) *racd in last quartet: rdn and dropped away tamely over 5f out: t.o over 3f out* 33/1
0-0 14 8 **Hopeigetlucky**[24] 3750 3-9-1 0 PatCosgrave 7
(Stuart Kittow) *in tch in midfield: reminders 6f out: lost tch u.p 3f out: t.o fnl 2f* 100/1

2m 30.74s (-2.26) **Going Correction** +0.05s/f (Slow)
**WFA** 3 from 4yo+ 12lb 14 Ran SP% **119.5**
Speed ratings (Par 103): **109,108,104,103,99 98,94,88,88,83 71,71,70,64**
CSF £23.50 TOTE £8.20: £2.70, £2.10, £1.40; EX 24.90 Trifecta £64.80.
**Owner** The Queen **Bred** The Queen **Trained** Newmarket, Suffolk

**FOCUS**
A fair maiden, albeit it was run at a steady pace, and a pair of fillies drew clear. The fifth looks the key to the form.

## 4544 ALDERMORE BANK PLC H'CAP 7f 1y(P)
3:30 (3:32) (Class 5) (0-70,70) 3-Y-O+ £3,234 (£962; £481; £240) Stalls Low

Form RPR
6021 1 **Exceedexpectations (IRE)**[15] 4055 5-10-0 70 (v) StevieDonohoe 4 77
(Lee Carter) *chsd ldr after 2f: rdn to ld 2f out: sustained duel u.p w runner-up after: forged ahd ins fnl f: styd on: rdn out* 6/1[3]
2000 2 1 **Where's Reiley (USA)**[15] 4042 8-9-3 59 (v) AdamKirby 3 63
(Michael Attwater) *rdn along early: hdwy to ld and edgd lft 5f out: drvn and hdd 2f out: clr w wnr and sustained dual after: no ex and btn fnl 100yds* 33/1
0324 3 5 **Kakapuka**[12] 4156 7-9-12 68 MartinHarley 8 59
(Anabel K Murphy) *chsd ldng trio: wnt 3rd wl over 2f out: styd on same pce u.p fr over 1f out* 10/1
2301 4 1 1/2 **Misstemper (IRE)**[23] 3792 3-9-4 67 (p) SilvestreDeSousa 2 51
(Jose Santos) *led tl hdd and hmpd bnd 5f out: chsd ldrs after: 4th and no imp u.p wl over 2f out: n.d and plugged on same pce after* 6/1[3]
1500 5 1 1/4 **Passing By**[11] 4211 3-9-7 70 RichardHughes 5 50
(Richard Hannon) *dwlt and niggled along early: in tch towards rr: outpcd whn rdn and wd bnd 2f out: n.d after: plugged on ins fnl f* 9/2[2]
00-6 6 1 1/2 **Presidente**[19] 3914 3-9-7 70 GeorgeBaker 1 46
(Ed Walker) *hld up in last trio: outpcd ent fnl 2f: swtchd lft and sme hdwy over 1f out: no ch w ldrs: wknd ins fnl f* 6/4[1]
5522 7 1 1/2 **Mister Mayday (IRE)**[29] 3559 3-9-2 65 (b) PatCosgrave 6 37
(George Baker) *taken down early: in tch towards rr: rdn and outpcd over 2f out: n.d after: wknd ins fnl f* 6/1[3]
-500 8 15 **Tevez**[49] 2884 9-9-12 68 (p) DavidProbert 7 3
(Des Donovan) *s.i.s: nvr gng wl and detached last thrght: eased fnl f* 33/1

1m 25.04s (0.24) **Going Correction** +0.05s/f (Slow)
**WFA** 3 from 5yo+ 7lb 8 Ran SP% **116.0**
Speed ratings (Par 103): **100,98,93,91,90 88,86,69**
CSF £165.76 CT £1937.66 TOTE £6.20: £1.90, £3.50, £2.40; EX 96.20 Trifecta £792.50.
**Owner** Clear Racing **Bred** R S Cockerill (farms) Ltd & Peter Dodd **Trained** Epsom, Surrey

**FOCUS**
A strange race, with little getting into it. The winner maintained his resurgence for new connections.

## 4545 188BET CASINO H'CAP 6f 1y(P)
4:00 (4:02) (Class 5) (0-70,69) 3-Y-O+ £3,234 (£962; £481; £240) Stalls Low

Form RPR
0441 1 **Panther Patrol (IRE)**[5] 4401 4-9-11 68 (v) JohnFahy 2 84+
(Eve Johnson Houghton) *mde all: readily wnt clr ent fnl 2f: wl clr and in n.d 1f out: eased towards fin* 5/4[1]
0665 2 3 **Dominium (USA)**[16] 4024 7-9-12 69 (b) RichardHughes 1 76
(Jeremy Gask) *hld up in midfield: hmpd bnd 5f out and dropped to rr: rdn and hdwy on outer: styd on to go 2nd ins fnl f: no ch w wnr* 7/2[2]
060 3 3/4 **Pabusar**[34] 3402 6-9-3 60 OisinMurphy 3 62
(Ann Stokell) *t.k.h: hld up in tch in midfield: nt clr run jst over 2f out: swtchd rt over 1f out: hdwy to chse clr wnr jst ins fnl f: kpt on but n.d: lost 2nd fnl 50yds* 5/1[3]
3006 4 2 1/2 **Dream Catcher (FR)**[19] 3935 6-9-8 65 DaneO'Neill 9 60
(Henry Candy) *in tch towards rr: hdwy into midfield 4f out: drvn ent fnl 2f: hdwy and wnt 2nd briefly 1f out: sn outpcd* 16/1
0504 5 3 **Khelfan**[30] 3522 3-8-5 53 NickyMackay 4 40
(Martin Smith) *s.i.s: bhd: no ch w wnr but hdwy on inner and nt clr run 1f out: swtchd rt and then bk lft: styd on: n.d* 20/1
0403 6 1 1/4 **Lady Phill**[11] 4206 4-9-9 66 KierenFox 8 48
(Michael Attwater) *dwlt and sn bustled along: stuck wd but hdwy to chse ldrs 4f out: rdn over 2f out: chsd clr wnr 2f out: lost 2nd 1f out and wknd fnl f* 12/1
3030 7 1 1/4 **What A Dandy (IRE)**[7] 4329 3-9-6 68 [1] PatCosgrave 7 47
(Jim Boyle) *chsd ldrs: hung lft over 2f out: outpcd by wnr 2f out: wknd u.p ent fnl f* 6/1
060- 8 1 3/4 **Forest Glen (IRE)**[303] 6690 3-8-10 58 LiamKeniry 6 30
(Sylvester Kirk) *pressed wnr tl rdn and outpcd ent fnl 2f: lost 2nd over 1f out: sn wknd* 66/1
6000 9 3/4 **Crafty Business (IRE)**[9] 4263 3-9-3 65 (v[1]) RobertHavlin 5 35
(Mark Hoad) *in tch in midfield: rdn and lost pl over 4f out: n.d after: drvn and btn over 2f out: bhd fnl f* 66/1

1m 12.22s (0.32) **Going Correction** +0.05s/f (Slow)
**WFA** 3 from 4yo+ 5lb 9 Ran SP% **118.9**
Speed ratings (Par 103): **99,95,94,90,86 85,83,81,80**
CSF £5.82 CT £16.33 TOTE £2.30: £1.50, £1.40, £2.30; EX 6.70 Trifecta £28.90.
**Owner** G C Stevens **Bred** Kilfrush Stud **Trained** Blewbury, Oxon

**FOCUS**
This proved straightforward for the winner, who is better on this surface.

## 4546 TBA NEXT GENERATION CLUB H'CAP 5f 6y(P)
4:30 (4:31) (Class 6) (0-65,65) 3-Y-O+ £2,587 (£770; £384; £192) Stalls Low

Form RPR
5030 1 **Dishy Guru**[25] 3707 5-9-12 65 (b) LiamKeniry 3 77
(Michael Blanshard) *s.i.s: bhd: hdwy u.p over 1f out: chsd clr ldng pair 1f out: str run to ld fnl 50yds: sn in command* 4/1[2]
0013 2 1 **Billy Red**[22] 3826 10-9-7 65 (b) DannyBrock(5) 7 73
(J R Jenkins) *pressed ldr and sn clr of field: led 2f out and sn rdn: forged ahd ins fnl f: hdd and no ex fnl 50yds* 8/1
2-50 3 2 **Aaranyow (IRE)**[8] 4306 6-8-7 51 (p) NathanAlison(5) 1 52
(Clifford Lines) *led and sn clr w rival: hdd 2f out: sn drvn: ev ch after tl no ex ins fnl f: wknd towards fin* 14/1
4210 4 4 **College Doll**[20] 3896 5-9-2 60 (t) EoinWalsh(5) 2 46
(Christine Dunnett) *racd off the pce in midfield: effrt u.p 2f out: no real imp: plugged on to go modest 4th ins fnl f* 33/1
6524 5 3/4 **Artemis (IRE)**[26] 3679 3-8-13 56 JimmyQuinn 6 39
(Conrad Allen) *dwlt: racd off the pce in midfield: plenty to do and effrt wl over 1f out: no imp: wl hld and hung rt towards fin* 16/1
3202 6 1 **Champagne Charley**[8] 4307 3-9-5 62 (t) ShaneKelly 9 41
(Des Donovan) *a in rr and stuck wd: rdn over 1f out: no hdwy: wl btn and eased towards fin* 7/1[3]
0644 7 3/4 **Mossgo (IRE)**[8] 4285 4-9-3 56 (t) LukeMorris 5 33
(John Best) *chsd clr ldng pair for 1f: 4th and struggling u.p 2f out: wknd over 1f out* 8/1
1- 8 2 1/2 **Greek Spirit (IRE)**[284] 7197 4-9-12 65 MartinHarley 8 33
(Alan McCabe) *pushed along leaving stalls: chsd clr ldng pair after 1f: rdn and no hdwy wl over 1f out: wknd 1f out* 5/4[1]

59.59s (0.79) **Going Correction** +0.05s/f (Slow)
**WFA** 3 from 4yo+ 4lb 8 Ran SP% **114.7**
Speed ratings (Par 101): **95,93,90,83,82 81,79,75**
CSF £35.72 CT £408.07 TOTE £4.50: £1.50, £3.10, £2.60; EX 36.60 Trifecta £814.30.
**Owner** Clifton Partners **Bred** J W Ford **Trained** Upper Lambourn, Berks

**FOCUS**
This run-of-the-mill sprint handicap was run at a solid pace but few managed to play a serious part. The winner has not rated this high for a while.

## 4547 188BET GREAT IN PLAY H'CAP 1m 4f (P)
5:00 (5:00) (Class 5) (0-75,74) 3-Y-O £3,234 (£962; £481; £240) Stalls Low

Form RPR
2356 1 **Gavlar**[23] 3789 3-9-0 67 (v[1]) TomQueally 4 76
(William Knight) *s.i.s: racd in last pair: clsd and nt clr run over 2f out: swtchd rt and hdwy u.p 2f out: swtchd lft and drvn to chal fnl 150yds: led fnl 75yds: styd on* 8/1
042 2 1 1/4 **Fort Berkeley (IRE)**[21] 3856 3-9-5 72 JimCrowley 7 79
(Paul Cole) *chsd ldr tl over 9f out: styd chsng ldrs: rdn to chse ldr again jst over 2f out: ev ch over 1f out: led ins fnl f: sn hdd and one pce* 5/1[3]


The Form Book, Raceform Ltd, Newbury, RG14 5SJ

-023 **3** *3* **Oyster (IRE)**[18] 3978 3-8-11 **64**..............................(b) J-PGuillambert 6 66
(Nick Littmoden) *s.i.s: bhd and rn in snatches: rdn 5f out: hdwy 3f out: chsd ldrs whn hung lft and swtchd rt over 1f out: kpt on same pce ins fnl f* **14/1**

0-12 **4** *3* **Red Passiflora**[22] 3823 3-9-4 **71**..............................(p) LukeMorris 9 68
(Sir Mark Prescott Bt) *sn led: rdn over 2f out: drvn and hrd pressed over 1f out: hdd ins fnl f: wknd fnl 100yds* **11/4**[1]

-465 **5** *9* **Mairise**[33] 3428 3-9-4 **71**.............................. ShaneKelly 3 54
(Sir Michael Stoute) *chsd ldrs: rdn over 2f out: btn whn wd bnd 2f out: sn wknd* **6/1**

2200 **6** *3* **Template (IRE)**[33] 3421 3-9-3 **70**..............................(b[1]) RobertHavlin 5 48
(Amanda Perrett) *wl in tch in midfield: rdn over 3f out: sn btn: wl bhd over 1f out* **33/1**

-442 **7** *1 ½* **Spirit Or Soul (FR)**[42] 3116 3-9-1 **68**..............................(p) MartinHarley 1 44
(Marco Botti) *in tch in midfield: rdn 3f out: sn btn: bhd over 1f out* **7/1**

-344 **8** *3* **Grand Meister**[34] 3396 3-9-7 **74**.............................. RichardHughes 8 45
(Michael Bell) *chsd ldrs: wnt 2nd over 9f out tl over 2f out: sn rdn and btn: wknd over 1f out: eased ins fnl f* **7/2**[2]

-425 **9** *99* **Gift Of Rain (IRE)**[47] 2948 3-9-3 **70**.............................. AdamKirby 2
(Ed Dunlop) *in tch in last trio: rdn 8f out: sn dropped to last and struggling: lost tch 5f out: sn wl t.o and eased* **33/1**

2m 31.12s (-1.88) **Going Correction** +0.05s/f (Slow) **9** Ran SP% **116.0**
Speed ratings (Par 100): **108,107,105,103,97 95,94,92,26**
CSF £47.91 CT £549.75 TOTE £12.40: £2.20, £2.30, £4.80; EX 62.30 Trifecta £2859.40 Part won..
**Owner** Chasemore Farm **Bred** A Black **Trained** Patching, W Sussex

**FOCUS**
A modest 3yo handicap and straightforward enough form. The third helps with the level.
T/Jkpt: Not won. T/Plt: £73.40 to a £1 stake. Pool: £48,295.53 - 479.78 winning tickets. T/Qpdt: £19.90 to a £1 stake. Pool: £6,052.81 - 224.44 winning tickets. SP

## 4328 SANDOWN (R-H)

### Wednesday, July 23

**OFFICIAL GOING: Good to firm (good in places; watered; 8.4)**
Sprint course at full width. Round course railed out 4yds from 9f to Winning Post and distances increased by 5yds on Round course.
Wind: Moderate, behind Weather: Fine, hot

### 4548 BROOKLANDS APPRENTICE H'CAP 1m 2f 7y
**6:05** (6:05) (Class 5) (0-70,70) 4-Y-O+ **£3,234** (£962; £481; £240) **Stalls** Low

Form RPR

3064 **1** **Hallingham**[21] 3853 4-8-12 **56**..............................(b) CamHardie 3 67+
(Jonathan Portman) *trckd ldng trio: clsd over 2f out: led wl over 1f out and sn rdn clr: 5 l ahd fnl f: idled last 100yds* **14/1**

321 **2** *2 ½* **Who's That Chick (IRE)**[22] 3825 5-9-11 **69**.............................. OisinMurphy 9 75+
(Ralph J Smith) *hld up in rr: prog wl over 2f out: drvn wl over 1f out: tk 2nd ins fnl f: kpt on but no ch to chal* **4/1**[1]

0443 **3** *nk* **Highlife Dancer**[9] 4273 6-9-0 **63**..............................(v) PaddyPilley(5) 10 68
(Mick Channon) *led after 1f: stretched on 1/2-way: rdn and hdd wl over 1f out: no ch w wnr after: lost 2nd ins fnl f: kpt on* **12/1**

332 **4** *4* **Vodka Wells (FR)**[14] 4066 4-9-12 **70**.............................. MeganCarberry 5 68+
(Brian Ellison) *hld up in rr: rdn 3f out: kpt on fr 2f out to take 4th ins fnl f: nvr a threat* **7/1**[2]

3302 **5** *¾* **Enriching (USA)**[20] 3898 6-9-0 **65**.............................. JackOsborn(7) 14 61
(Nick Littmoden) *chsd ldr after 3f to jst over 2f out: steadily fdd* **16/1**

-544 **6** *1 ¼* **Beep**[30] 3540 4-9-2 **60**.............................. NedCurtis 8 54+
(Lydia Richards) *hld up in rr: rdn on outer over 2f out: hung rt fnl f but kpt on: no ch* **12/1**

0/35 **7** *1* **Cappielow Park**[36] 3336 5-8-7 **51**..............................(p) RobJFitzpatrick 13 43+
(Ali Stronge) *slowly away: hld up in last: rdn and sme prog fr 3f out: no imp on ldrs over 1f out* **10/1**[3]

0046 **8** *nk* **Speedy Writer**[16] 4030 4-9-9 **67**.............................. CharlotteJenner 12 59
(Henry Candy) *hld up and sn in last trio: nt clr run over 2f out: swtchd rt and bmpd rival: plugged on fnl f* **12/1**

0016 **9** *½* **Roxy Lane**[26] 3678 5-8-9 **53**.............................. CharlesBishop 2 44
(Peter Hiatt) *led 1f: prom tl wknd wl over 1f out* **20/1**

3013 **10** *1 ½* **Automotive**[27] 3616 6-9-7 **65**.............................. ShelleyBirkett 1 53
(Julia Feilden) *hld up in midfield: shkn up and nt qckn on outer over 2f out: no prog after: fdd fnl f* **7/1**[2]

1210 **11** *nk* **Nelson Quay (IRE)**[54] 2720 4-8-12 **59**.............................. DavidParkes(3) 11 46
(Jeremy Gask) *tk fierce hold: hld up in midfield: no prog over 2f out: wl btn over 1f out* **14/1**

000- **12** *12* **Mad About Harry (IRE)**[299] 6810 4-9-0 **58**..............................(b[1]) DanielCremin 6 22
(Linda Jewell) *a in rr: pushed along and no ch whn bdly bmpd jst over 2f out: wknd* **50/1**

0/10 **13** *30* **Black Minstrel (IRE)**[15] 4051 5-9-5 **63**.............................. RyanTate 7
(Amanda Perrett) *t.k.h: prom: stmbld after 2f: wknd 3f out: wl t.o* **7/1**[2]

2m 8.47s (-2.03) **Going Correction** -0.05s/f (Good) **13** Ran SP% **115.6**
Speed ratings (Par 103): **106,104,103,100,99 98,98,97,97,96 96,86,62**
CSF £66.89 CT £704.82 TOTE £22.50: £5.90, £1.40, £4.00; EX 105.10 Trifecta £1303.10.
**Owner** The Ladies Of The Manor Syndicate **Bred** John W Ford And Peter J Skinner **Trained** Upper Lambourn, Berks

**FOCUS**
Sprint course at full width .Round course railed out 4yds from 9f to Winning Post and distances increased by 5yds on Round course. An open-looking handicap, confined to apprentice riders. The third limits the form.

### 4549 WISHING I WAS LUCKY H'CAP 1m 14y
**6:35** (6:36) (Class 4) (0-85,81) 3-Y-O+ **£5,175** (£1,540; £769; £384) **Stalls** Low

Form RPR

0215 **1** **Ogbourne Downs**[16] 4028 4-10-0 **81**.............................. SteveDrowne 8 88
(Charles Hills) *hld up and sn in last: prog on outer over 2f out: jnd ldr over 1f out: gd battle after and drew wl clr of rest: won on the nod* **5/1**[3]

4534 **2** *shd* **Jack Of Diamonds (IRE)**[32] 3468 5-9-4 **71**.............................. JamesDoyle 3 78
(Roger Teal) *led: shkn up over 2f out: jnd and drvn over 1f out: gd battle after and clr of rest: r.o but pipped on the nod* **11/2**

3650 **3** *5* **Gracious George (IRE)**[40] 3180 4-8-12 **70**..............................(p) CamHardie(5) 2 65
(Jimmy Fox) *in tch: rdn and nt qckn jst over 2f out: wnt 3rd over 1f out but lft bhd by ldng pair after* **12/1**

6604 **4** *hd* **Life And Times (USA)**[14] 4091 6-9-4 **71**.............................. SilvestreDeSousa 6 66
(Mark Johnston) *slowly away and lft abt 6 l: rcvrd to trck ldng pair after 3f: drvn and nt qckn 2f out: sn btn: plugged on to press for 3rd again nr fin* **7/1**

-601 **5** *1 ¾* **Matravers**[18] 3970 3-8-12 **73**.............................. RyanMoore 5 62
(Sir Michael Stoute) *sn trckd ldr: rdn to chal over 2f out: lost 2nd and fdd wl over 1f out* **7/2**[2]

6-41 **6** *8* **Alketios (GR)**[32] 3465 3-9-6 **81**.............................. AndreaAtzeni 1 51
(Luca Cumani) *prom early: shuffled bk and in last pair 1/2-way: rdn and no prog 3f out: wknd 2f out: eased fnl f* **15/8**[1]

1m 44.02s (0.72) **Going Correction** -0.05s/f (Good)
**WFA** 3 from 4yo+ 8lb **6** Ran SP% **109.2**
Speed ratings (Par 105): **94,93,88,88,86 78**
CSF £29.78 CT £281.49 TOTE £3.70: £2.60, £4.60; EX 40.40 Trifecta £112.10.
**Owner** S W Group Logistics Limited **Bred** Bumble Bloodstock & Mrs S Nicholls **Trained** Lambourn, Berks

■ Stewards' Enquiry : James Doyle two-day ban: use of whip (6-7 Aug)

**FOCUS**
The first pair totally dominated the finish of this fair handicap, in which the market leaders produced tame efforts. The winner is consistent.

### 4550 BRITISH STALLION STUDS EBF MAIDEN STKS 7f 16y
**7:10** (7:10) (Class 5) 2-Y-O **£3,881** (£1,155; £577; £288) **Stalls** Low

Form RPR

2 **1** **Darshini**[19] 3929 2-9-5 0.............................. RyanMoore 9 78+
(Sir Michael Stoute) *mde virtually all: pushed along over 2f out: pressed but a in control: punched out firmly fnl f* **11/8**[1]

**2** *1* **Farham (USA)** 2-9-5 0.............................. FrankieDettori 5 75+
(Richard Fahey) *prom: trckd wnr 1/2-way: pushed along over 2f out: tried to chal and styd on but a wl hld* **12/1**

0 **3** *1* **Cahill (IRE)**[19] 3929 2-9-5 0.............................. WilliamTwiston-Davies 7 73
(Alan King) *wl in tch: shkn up 2f out: kpt on to take 3rd ins fnl f: nvr gng pce to chal* **33/1**

**4** *nse* **Bollihope** 2-9-5 0.............................. WilliamBuick 8 72+
(John Gosden) *dwlt: hld up in last trio: pushed along 3f out: shkn up and sme prog over 1f out: styd on fnl f: nrly tk 3rd* **12/1**

**5** *½* **Dance Of Fire** 2-9-5 0.............................. DavidProbert 2 71+
(Andrew Balding) *green preliminaries: t.k.h early: wl in tch: pushed along over 2f out: styd on fnl f: nrst fin* **33/1**

4 **6** *shd* **Landwade Lad**[25] 3720 2-9-5 0.............................. ShaneKelly 3 71
(James Fanshawe) *t.k.h: w wnr to 1/2-way: lost pl wl over 1f out: kpt on after but no real danger* **16/1**

2 **7** *¾* **Azmaam (IRE)**[32] 3474 2-9-5 0.............................. PaulHanagan 10 69+
(Richard Hannon) *dwlt and then s.i.s: mostly last to 1/2-way: pushed along 3f out: kpt on fr over 2f out but nvr gng pce to threaten ldrs* **7/4**[2]

0 **8** *½* **Best Endeavour**[47] 2964 2-9-5 0.............................. MartinDwyer 4 67
(William Muir) *t.k.h early: trckd ldrs: pushed along over 2f out: wnt 3rd over 1f out and cl enough: one pce after tl wknd ins fnl f* **66/1**

0 **9** *23* **Virtualise**[34] 3381 2-9-5 0.............................. TomQueally 6 5
(John Gallagher) *a in rr: wknd 1/2-way: t.o* **100/1**

**10** *5* **Malimbi (IRE)** 2-9-5 0.............................. SilvestreDeSousa 1
(Mark Johnston) *in tch but rn green: wknd 3f out: eased and t.o* **10/1**[3]

1m 30.57s (1.07) **Going Correction** -0.05s/f (Good) **10** Ran SP% **117.2**
Speed ratings (Par 94): **91,89,88,88,88 87,87,86,60,54**
CSF £19.48 TOTE £2.50: £1.20, £3.00, £7.10; EX 21.30 Trifecta £224.70.
**Owner** Robert Ng **Bred** Bluehills Racing Limited **Trained** Newmarket, Suffolk

**FOCUS**
Probably just a fair juvenile maiden and, certainly not for the first time here this tern, it paid to race handily.

### 4551 TEDDINGTON H'CAP (BOBIS RACE) 7f 16y
**7:45** (7:46) (Class 3) (0-90,87) 3-Y-O **£7,439** (£2,213; £1,106; £553) **Stalls** Low

Form RPR

13 **1** **Provenance**[62] 2495 3-9-4 **84**..............................[1] RyanMoore 4 93+
(Sir Michael Stoute) *hld up in last: prog on outer wl over 1f out: drvn fnl f: r.o wl to ld post* **11/4**[2]

5-40 **2** *shd* **Mezel**[67] 2333 3-8-9 **75**.............................. PaulHanagan 3 84
(B W Hills) *led: kicked on over 2f out and sn 2 l clr: drvn over 1f out: styd on wl but hdd post* **12/1**

-1 **3** *1 ½* **Zain Empire**[27] 3601 3-8-9 **75**.............................. JamesDoyle 2 80
(Robert Cowell) *rrd bef stalls opened: hld up in last pair: prog over 2f out: chsd ldr jst over 1f out: styd on but no imp: lost 2nd ins fnl f* **9/2**[3]

1135 **4** *2 ¾* **Crystal Lake (IRE)**[11] 4198 3-9-5 **85**.............................. JimCrowley 5 83
(Ralph Beckett) *in tch: nt best plcd wl whn kick for home sed over 2f out: last wl over 1f out: kpt on ins fnl f: no ch* **9/4**[1]

1215 **5** *1* **Regiment**[26] 3651 3-9-7 **87**.............................. AndreaAtzeni 6 82
(Richard Fahey) *trckd ldrs: rdn to chse ldr 2f out to jst over 1f out: wknd fnl f* **8/1**

54-1 **6** *2 ¼* **Pageant Belle**[19] 3916 3-8-9 **80**.............................. CamHardie(5) 1 69
(Roger Charlton) *t.k.h: trckd ldrs: shkn up to dispute 2nd 2f out: edgd lft over 1f out: wknd sn after* **10/1**

1-04 **7** *15* **Monsea (IRE)**[46] 2983 3-9-7 **87**.............................. RichardHughes 7 35
(Richard Hannon) *trckd ldr to 2f out: wkng whn short of room over 1f out: eased and t.o* **9/1**

1m 28.2s (-1.30) **Going Correction** -0.05s/f (Good) **7** Ran SP% **113.5**
Speed ratings (Par 104): **105,104,103,100,98 96,79**
CSF £33.69 TOTE £4.60: £2.30, £5.10; EX 36.70 Trifecta £258.20.
**Owner** Cheveley Park Stud **Bred** Cheveley Park Stud Ltd **Trained** Newmarket, Suffolk

**FOCUS**
The pace began to get serious 2f out in this fair 3yo handicap and those given waiting rides had more to do as a result. The form is rated towards the positive side.

### 4552 TOM JONES HERE 30 JULY H'CAP 1m 6f
**8:20** (8:20) (Class 4) (0-80,80) 4-Y-O+ **£4,690** (£1,395; £697; £348) **Stalls** Low

Form RPR

131 **1** **Meetings Man (IRE)**[32] 3475 7-9-0 **78**..............................(p) CamHardie(5) 4 85
(Ali Stronge) *t.k.h: trckd ldr: rdn to ld jst over 2f out: edgd rt over 1f out: pressed fnl f: hld on wl* **2/1**[2]

0031 **2** *½* **Gambol (FR)**[19] 3919 4-9-3 **76**.............................. PaulHanagan 6 82
(B W Hills) *hld up in last: pushed along and prog wl over 2f out: drvn to chse wnr over 1f out: tried to chal fnl f: nt qckn and a hld* **5/4**[1]

5563 **3** *1 ½* **Poitin**[14] 4076 4-8-11 **70**.............................. JamesDoyle 3 74
(Harry Dunlop) *hld up in last pair: prog 2f out but hanging: tk 3rd 1f out and looked a threat: nt qckn after* **10/1**

6301 **4** *2 ¾* **Angus Glens**[14] 4088 4-8-9 **68**..............................(p) SilvestreDeSousa 5 69
(David Dennis) *pushed up to ld and set str pce early: drvn and hdd jst over 2f out: hld whn short of room over 1f out: one pce* **9/1**[3]

0000 **5** *¾* **Azrag (USA)**[12] 4144 6-9-2 **75**..............................(p) RobertHavlin 2 75
(Michael Attwater) *walked to post: trckd ldng pair: rdn and nt qckn over 2f out: wl hld after* **16/1**

10/0 6 16 **Figaro**62 2482 6-9-7 80.....(t) DavidProbert 1 59
(Tim Vaughan) *trckd ldng pair: rdn over 2f out: wknd qckly over 1f out: t.o* 9/1³

3m 1.87s (-2.63) **Going Correction** -0.05s/f (Good) 6 Ran SP% **112.8**
Speed ratings (Par 105): **105,104,103,102,101 92**
CSF £4.92 TOTE £2.70: £1.10, £1.90; EX 5.50 Trifecta £21.50.
**Owner** Mrs Bettine Evans **Bred** Hakan Keles **Trained** Eastbury, Berks

**FOCUS**
A fair handicap that was run at a decent gallop. The winner has got back to his best of late.

## 4553 JESSIE J HERE 7 AUGUST H'CAP 5f 6y
8:50 (8:50) (Class 4) (0-80,80) 3-Y-0+ £4,690 (£1,395; £697; £348) Stalls Low

Form RPR
-221 1 **Perfect Muse**29 3561 4-9-5 73.....AdamKirby 5 82+
(Clive Cox) *trckd ldrs: rdn to take 2nd 1f out: chal on ins of ldr: drvn to ld last 50yds* 7/4¹

0552 2 ½ **Alpha Delta Whisky**19 3939 6-9-2 70.....(v) TomQueally 1 77
(John Gallagher) *trckd ldr: led on inner over 3f out: hung lft off rail fr 2f out: kpt on but hdd last 50yds* 11/2³

5000 3 2¼ **Jiroft (ITY)**16 4027 7-9-12 80.....¹ OisinMurphy 7 79
(Ann Stokell) *prom on outer: chsd ldr jst over 2f out: tried to chal over 1f out: nt qckn and lost 2nd 1f out: one pce* 20/1

221- 4 hd **Stellarta**302 6718 3-8-12 70.....PaulHanagan 2 67
(Michael Blanshard) *in tch: prog on inner 2f out: chsd ldrs 1f out: nt qckn and no imp after* 13/2

-155 5 3 **Aye Aye Digby (IRE)**24 3749 9-9-7 75.....GeorgeBaker 4 63
(Patrick Chamings) *led to over 3f out: chsd ldr to jst over 2f out: sn wknd* 8/1

6415 6 ½ **Lujeanie**83 1893 8-9-2 70.....ShaneKelly 3 56
(Peter Crate) *hld up in last pair: pushed along and no prog 2f out: nvr in it* 20/1

1-02 7 1 **Tom Sawyer**22 3831 6-9-0 75.....(b) MeganCarberry(7) 8 57
(Julie Camacho) *s.i.s: tried to cl on ldrs 1/2-way: hanging rt and no prog over 1f out: wl btn after* 4/1²

2531 8 1 **Welease Bwian (IRE)**22 3826 5-8-9 70.....(t) AaronJones(7) 6 49
(Stuart Williams) *hld up in last pair: pushed along and no prog 2f out: nvr in it* 10/1

1m 0.33s (-1.27) **Going Correction** -0.125s/f (Firm)
**WFA** 3 from 4yo+ 4lb 8 Ran SP% **114.8**
Speed ratings (Par 105): **105,104,100,100,95 94,93,91**
CSF £11.74 CT £137.87 TOTE £2.30: £1.10, £2.10, £4.50; EX 11.80 Trifecta £117.20.
**Owner** R J Vines **Bred** R J Vines **Trained** Lambourn, Berks

**FOCUS**
A fair sprint handicap and the winner has more to offer.
T/Plt: £191.90 to a £1 stake. Pool: £76,322.30 - 290.20 winning tickets. T/Qpdt: £5.90 to a £1 stake. Pool: £7,756.93 - 972.11 winning tickets. JN

4554 - 4555a (Foreign Racing) - See Raceform Interactive

# 4094 NAAS (L-H)
Wednesday, July 23

**OFFICIAL GOING: Good to firm**

## 4556a ISS RECRUITMENT & TRAINING H'CAP 6f
6:55 (6:55) 3-Y-0+ £5,175 (£1,200; £525; £300)

RPR
1 **Almadaa**11 4219 7-9-8 67.....(b) ConnorKing(3) 5 74
(David Marnane, Ire) *hld up far side: gd hdwy in 11th bef 1/2-way to chse ldrs in 3rd ent fnl f: kpt on wl u.p to ld cl home* 9/1

2 hd **Kimbay (IRE)**222 8284 4-8-4 49.....ConorHoban(3) 13 55
(S M Duffy, Ire) *trckd ldrs nr side: rdn to ld over 1f out: strly pressed u.p ins fnl f and hdd cl home* 25/1

3 ½ **Doonard Prince (IRE)**24 3769 5-9-5 66.....RossCoakley(5) 14 70+
(Miss Elizabeth Doyle, Ire) *towards rr nr side: hdwy in 10th bef 1/2-way to chse ldrs in 4th wl ins fnl f: kpt on wl into 3rd towards fin: nvr on terms* 7/4¹

4 1½ **Above The Law (IRE)**11 4219 5-9-9 72.....(v) SeanCorby(7) 9 72
(A Oliver, Ire) *on toes befhand: prom nr side and disp bef 1/2-way travelling wl: narrow advantage 2f out tl hdd u.p over 1f out: kpt on one pce and dropped to 4th nr fin* 8/1³

5 3¾ **Jembatt (IRE)**12 4244 7-9-8 64.....(p) JosephO'Brien 10 52
(Michael Mulvany, Ire) *hld up towards rr: rdn fr after 1/2-way and sme hdwy whn swtchd lft ent fnl f: clsd u.p into nvr nrr 5th* 11/2²

6 1 **Copper Dock (IRE)**18 3990 10-8-0 49.....KarenKenny(7) 3 33
(T G McCourt, Ire) *trckd ldrs far side: rdn over 2f out and dropped to 5th u.p 1f out where edgd sltly rt: kpt on one pce* 20/1

7 ¾ **Katie Hall (IRE)**11 4222 3-9-3 64.....RonanWhelan 2 45
(C W J Farrell, Ire) *sn led far side tl jnd bef 1/2-way: rdn and hdd under 2f out: sn wknd* 20/1

8 ¾ **Regal Power**24 3769 5-9-0 66.....CarolineMurtagh(10) 1 46
(J P Murtagh, Ire) *in rr: last 1/2-way: sn rdn and sme late hdwy u.p fnl 2f: nvr nrr* 12/1

9 1¾ **Too Many Diamonds (IRE)**11 4222 3-8-4 51 oh4.....(v) RoryCleary 12 24
(Damian Joseph English, Ire) *hld up in tch nr side: rdn and no imp 2f out: one pce fnl f* 25/1

10 nk **Lager Time (IRE)**26 3686 4-9-11 70.....RichardEvans(3) 6 43
(David Evans) *hld up in tch: hdwy in 9th down centre of trck fr bef 1/2-way to chse ldrs in 6th under 2f out: rdn and no ex 1f out where sltly hmpd: wknd* 10/1

11 ¾ **Lady Ranger (IRE)**12 4243 3-8-8 58.....LeighRoche(3) 11 28
(Adrian Paul Keatley, Ire) *chsd ldrs nr side: rdn and no ex fr 1/2-way: one pce fnl 2f* 9/1

12 3¾ **La Canaada (IRE)**12 4244 6-8-5 47.....(t) ChrisHayes 8 6
(H Rogers, Ire) *chsd ldrs: rdn and wknd fr 2f out* 9/1

13 4½ **Russian Roulette (IRE)**21 3865 3-8-9 56.....MichaelHussey 7
(Charles O'Brien, Ire) *hld up towards rr: rdn bef 1/2-way and no imp: wknd* 33/1

14 3½ **Si Seulement (IRE)**33 3441 3-7-11 51 oh4.....(p) IanQueally(7)
(T G McCourt, Ire) *chsd ldrs far side: racd keenly: rdn fr 1/2-way and sn no ex u.p: wknd fnl 2f* 25/1

1m 9.55s (-3.65)
**WFA** 3 from 4yo+ 5lb 14 Ran SP% **133.6**
CSF £234.45 CT £604.65 TOTE £16.40: £3.40, £10.60, £1.60; DF 492.70 Trifecta £1603.10.
**Owner** Western Partnership **Bred** Shadwell Estate Company **Trained** Bansha, Co Tipperary
■ Stewards' Enquiry : Richard Evans caution: used whip above shoulder height.

**FOCUS**
A first win in almost a year for Almadaa, although he has remained fairly consistent in that time without really running near his best. They went a reasonable clip but everything remained in contention well into the contest.

## 4557a YEOMANSTOWN & MORRISTOWN LATTIN STUDS EUROPEAN BREEDERS FUND STKS (LISTED RACE) (F&M) 6f
7:30 (7:30) 3-Y-0+ £29,250 (£8,550; £4,050; £1,350)

RPR
1 **Minalisa**38 3278 5-9-5 97.....FMBerry 5 102+
(Rae Guest) *trckd ldrs on outer far side: cl 3rd 1/2-way: impr into 2nd travelling wl 1 1/2f out: sn rdn and qcknd to ld fnl 100yds: extended advantage towards fin* 3/1¹

2 1½ **Tobann (IRE)**21 3864 4-9-10 102.....(t) KevinManning 1 102
(J S Bolger, Ire) *sn led far side: narrow advantage bef 1/2-way: extended advantage over 2f out: rdn over 1f out and sn strly pressed: hdd fnl 100yds and no ex* 3/1¹

3 ¾ **Gathering Power (IRE)**41 3167 4-9-5 101.....FergalLynch 4 95+
(Edward Lynam, Ire) *hld up in rr: rdn over 2f out and sn swtchd to outer: hung lft in 7th over 1f out: kpt on again u.p into nvr threatening 3rd nr fin: nvr nrr* 5/1²

4 1 **Yulong Baoju (IRE)**3 4480 4-9-5 97.....(vt) ColmO'Donoghue 6 92
(Edward Lynam, Ire) *hld up bhd ldrs: rdn in 6th over 2f out and sme hdwy u.p between horses into 4th ins fnl f: sn no imp on ldrs in 3rd and dropped to 4th nr fin* 3/1¹

5 ¾ **Floating Along (IRE)**300 6768 4-9-5 83.....ColinKeane 8 89
(G M Lyons, Ire) *trckd ldrs nr side: cl 4th 1/2-way: rdn and no ex fr under 2f out: kpt on one pce in 5th between horses ins fnl f* 16/1

6 1 **Flic Flac (IRE)**20 3902 6-9-5 93.....(v) PatSmullen 10 86
(D K Weld, Ire) *hld up towards rr: hdwy over 2f out on outer to chse ldrs in 3rd briefly ins fnl f: no ex and wknd towards fin* 14/1

7 1¾ **Seas Of Wells (IRE)**21 3864 3-9-0 91.....DeclanMcDonogh 9 79
(John M Oxx, Ire) *chsd ldrs: 6th 1/2-way: rdn over 2f out and sn no imp on ldrs: one pce fnl f* 10/1³

8 nse **Dark Skies (IRE)**38 3282 3-9-0 80.....(p) WayneLordan 3 79
(David Wachman, Ire) *cl up far side: cl 2nd bef 1/2-way: rdn and no ex on ldr 2f out: sn wknd* 50/1

9 nk **Sassaway (IRE)**90 1687 7-9-5 86.....ChrisHayes 7 79
(Eamonn O'Connell, Ire) *broke wl tout: dispute early: sn settled bhd ldrs: 5th 1/2-way: sn rdn and wknd* 33/1

1m 8.03s (-5.17)
**WFA** 3 from 4yo+ 5lb 9 Ran SP% **118.2**
CSF £12.11 TOTE £4.50: £1.02, £1.10, £2.40; DF 15.00 Trifecta £62.30.
**Owner** C J Mills **Bred** C J Mills **Trained** Newmarket, Suffolk

**FOCUS**
A possibly unlucky second in this race last year, this looked a slightly easier proposition for Minalisa and she took full advantage.

4558 - 4560a (Foreign Racing) - See Raceform Interactive

# VICHY
Wednesday, July 23

**OFFICIAL GOING: Turf: very soft**

## 4561a GRAND PRIX DE VICHY-AUVERGNE (GROUP 3) (3YO+) (TURF) 1m 2f
7:40 (12:00) 3-Y-0+ £33,333 (£13,333; £10,000; £6,666; £3,333)

RPR
1 **Hippy (FR)**39 3265 6-8-13 0.....Pierre-CharlesBoudot 7 101
(E Libaud, France) *cl up in 4th: rdn to chal appr fnl f: led under 1f out: r.o to win a shade cosily* 92/10

2 ½ **Ipswich (IRE)**41 3171 4-8-13 0.....GeraldMosse 8 100
(A De Royer-Dupre, France) *hld up towards rr: rdn and hdwy 1 1/2f out: r.o u.p fnl f: a hld by wnr* 42/10²

3 ¾ **Vif Monsieur (GER)**24 3770 4-9-2 0.....KClijmans 3 102
(S Smrczek, Germany) *trckd ldr on outer: led after 3f: tk field stands's side into st: rdn 1 1/2f out: hdd under 1f out: kpt on gamely u.p* 68/10³

4 nk **Gaga A (URU)**38 5-8-13 0.....GregoryBenoist 2 98
(D Smaga, France) *settled in 3rd: chsd ldng gp fr 1/2-way: hrd rdn over 1f out: one pce fnl f* 203/10

5 shd **Onedargent (FR)**14 4-9-2 0.....UmbertoRispoli 4 100
(J-P Gallorini, France) *midfield on inner: dropped towards rr 1/2-way: rdn 2f out and effrt to chse ldrs 1 1/2f out: btn appr fnl f: fin 6th: plcd 5th* 36/1

6 nk **Satanicjim (IRE)**44 5-9-2 0.....AdrienFouassier 6 99?
(Alain Couetil, France) *sn pushed along in rr: hdwy 2 1/2f out: hrd rdn to chse ldrs over 1f out: sn btn: fin 7th: plcd 6th* 137/10

7 dist **Ocovango**41 3171 4-9-2 0.....MaximeGuyon 1
(A Fabre, France) *led: hdd after 3f: 2nd and no imp u.p 2 1/2f out: hrd rdn 2f out: wknd qckly and heavily eased: fin 8th: plcd 7th* 1/1¹

D ½ **Orator (IRE)**23 3811 4-9-2 0.....(p) RonanThomas 9 100
(F-H Graffard, France) *wnt rt s: drifted rt again sn after and caused vally jem to fall: racd in midfield: rdn and no real imp fr 2f out: plugged on at same pce fnl f: fin 5th: disqualified and plcd last* 101/10

F **Vally Jem (FR)**28 3598 5-8-13 0.....(p) IoritzMendizabal 5
(D Sepulchre, France) *settled towards rr: clipped heels of rival and fell after 1f* 185/10

2m 10.18s (1.58) 9 Ran SP% **120.2**
WIN (incl. 1 euro stake): 10.20. PLACES: 3.30, 1.80, 3.80. DF: 20.30. SF: 51.50.
**Owner** Jacques Seror **Bred** Jacques Seror **Trained** France

# 4279 BATH (L-H)
Thursday, July 24

**OFFICIAL GOING: Firm (10.3)**
False rail around bottom bend and up to 3f marker and races incorporating bottom bend increased in distance by about 25yds.
Wind: Mild breeze; across Weather: Sunny

## 4562 ROYAL BRITISH LEGION KEYNSHAM MEMORIAL H'CAP 1m 2f 46y
2:20 (2:20) (Class 6) (0-60,56) 3-Y-0 £1,940 (£577; £288; £144) Stalls Low

Form RPR
3042 1 **Lynngale**9 4304 3-9-4 53.....TomEaves 7 66
(Kristin Stubbs) *mde all: kicked clr 3f out: unchal* 9/2³



The Form Book, Raceform Ltd, Newbury, RG14 5SJ

4341 **2** *2* **King Calypso**[15] 4085 3-8-8 **48** CamHardie(5) 3 57
(Denis Coakley) *in tch: rdn 3f out: styd on to chse wnr over 1f out: a being comf hld fnl f* **15/8**[1]

00-0 **3** *8* **Alba Verde**[24] 3781 3-8-10 **45** LukeMorris 6 39
(Sir Mark Prescott Bt) *hld up: rdn 3f out: stdy prog whn hanging lft fr 2f out: wnt 3rd ins fnl f: nvr any threat to ldng pair* **4/1**[2]

3664 **4** *1 1/4* **Stoneham**[12] 4210 3-9-4 **56** CharlesBishop(3) 2 48
(Mick Channon) *s.i.s: sn chsng wnr: rdn 3f out: sn hld by wnr: keeping on at same pce whn lost 2nd over 1f out: no ex whn lost 3rd ins fnl f* **7/1**

-000 **5** *5* **Cadmium**[16] 4055 3-9-6 **55** GeorgeBaker 5 37
(Harry Dunlop) *hld up: plld wd and rdn 3f out: sme hdwy over 2f out: no further imp fr wl over 1f out* **16/1**

0060 **6** *2 3/4* **Mystical Maze**[19] 3950 3-8-3 **45** (p) KieranShoemark(7) 8 22
(Mark Brisbourne) *in tch: rdn 3f out: wknd 2f out* **17/2**

00-0 **7** *4 1/2* **Sir Percy Blakeney**[15] 4084 3-9-0 **49** MartinDwyer 4 17
(Marcus Tregoning) *trckd wnr tl rdn 3f out: edgd lft and wknd 2f out* **10/1**

0000 **8** *1 1/4* **Harlequin Jinks**[10] 4261 3-8-10 **45** (v[1]) SteveDrowne 1 11
(Mark Usher) *in tch tl rdn 3f out: qckly btn* **66/1**

2m 8.9s (-2.10) **Going Correction** -0.20s/f (Firm) **8** Ran SP% **112.5**
Speed ratings (Par 98): **100,98,92,91,87 84,81,80**
CSF £12.89 CT £35.06 TOTE £4.60: £1.10, £1.30, £1.80; EX 11.80 Trifecta £56.60.
**Owner** Mrs Lynn Gale **Bred** Kumari Puran **Trained** Norton, N Yorks

**FOCUS**
False rail around bottom bend and up to 3f marker and races incorporating bottom bend increased in distance by about 25yds. Rattling firm ground, but that wouldn't have been a surprise to anyone so it was disappointing that there were no so many non-runners through the card. A weak handicap won by a canny front-running ride from Tom Eaves. The time was relatively good.

## 4563 TRENT SERVICES FILLIES' H'CAP 1m 2f 46y
**2:50** (2:50) (Class 5) (0-70,67) 3-Y-O **£2,587** (£770; £384; £192) **Stalls** Low

Form RPR

0333 **1** **Assoluta (IRE)**[12] 4210 3-8-6 **52** RenatoSouza 4 58
(Sylvester Kirk) *trckd ldr: jnd ldr 4f out: led wl over 2f out: pushed clr over 1f out: comf* **9/4**[1]

4050 **2** *3 1/2* **Mary Le Bow**[24] 3803 3-8-7 **60** (p) KieranShoemark(7) 2 59
(Karen George) *hld up in tch: rdn wl over 2f out: styd on to chse wnr ent fnl f but a being hld* **9/1**

00-0 **3** *2 1/4* **Soiree D'Ete**[14] 4105 3-8-6 **52** LukeMorris 1 47
(Sir Mark Prescott Bt) *trckd ldr: rdn over 3f out: chsd wnr 2f out tl no ex ent fnl f* **9/2**[3]

-000 **4** *3/4* **Pink And Black (IRE)**[24] 3803 3-9-5 **65** [1] MartinDwyer 5 59
(William Muir) *hld up last but wl in tch: rdn 3f out: nvr gng pce to get involved but styd on fnl f* **6/1**

3604 **5** *nk* **Habdab**[17] 4029 3-9-2 **67** CamHardie(5) 6 60
(Richard Hannon) *trckd ldrs: rdn over 3f out: styd on fnl f but nvr gng pce to get on terms* **5/2**[2]

-300 **6** *8* **Rio Yuma (ITY)**[87] 1794 3-9-0 **60** TomEaves 3 38
(Kristin Stubbs) *led tl rdn wl over 2f out: wknd over 1f out* **14/1**

2m 10.42s (-0.58) **Going Correction** -0.20s/f (Firm) **6** Ran SP% **108.5**
Speed ratings (Par 97): **94,91,89,88,88 82**
CSF £20.55 TOTE £3.20: £1.90, £4.70; EX 20.80 Trifecta £76.30.
**Owner** M Nicolson, G Doran, A Wilson **Bred** Laundry Cottage Stud Farm **Trained** Upper Lambourn, Berks

**FOCUS**
A weak fillies' handicap won in emphatic style by a horse who was 0-14 coming into this contest. Not form to dwell on, with the time slow.

## 4564 DAVID AND JANE WARD'S 25TH ANNIVERSARY H'CAP 5f 161y
**3:25** (3:26) (Class 6) (0-65,64) 3-Y-O+ **£1,940** (£577; £288; £144) **Stalls** Centre

Form RPR

053 **1** **Mambo Spirit (IRE)**[37] 3328 10-9-4 **56** MartinDwyer 5 70
(Tony Newcombe) *hld up: hmpd after 2f: gd hdwy on inner 3f out to trck ldrs: led over 1f out: rdn clr: easily* **4/1**[2]

0644 **2** *5* **Annes Rocket (IRE)**[12] 4206 9-9-7 **64** (p) CamHardie(5) 7 62
(Jimmy Fox) *hld up: rdn and hdwy over 1f out: r.o ins fnl f: wnt 2nd fnl strides: no ch w wnr* **9/1**

4041 **3** *nk* **Bajan Story**[41] 3178 5-8-12 **50** LukeMorris 6 47
(Michael Blanshard) *hld up: swtchd rt and rdn over 2f out: stdy prog to chse wnr ent fnl f but no ch: lost 2nd fnl strides* **4/1**[2]

0654 **4** *1* **Comptonspirit**[14] 4102 10-9-7 **62** (p) MatthewLawson(3) 3 55
(Brian Baugh) *chsd ldr: led over 2f out: rdn: edgd rt and hdd over 1f out: no ex fnl f* **10/1**

5453 **5** *1* **Catalinas Diamond (IRE)**[9] 4282 6-9-4 **56** (t) SteveDrowne 1 46
(Pat Murphy) *hld up: nt clrest of runs fr 2f out tl jst ins fnl f: kpt on but no ch* **6/1**[3]

-000 **6** *2 1/4* **Lucky Surprise**[16] 4056 3-8-12 **55** (b) HarryBentley 11 36
(Jeremy Gask) *in tch: rdn over 2f out: nvr threatened: wknd fnl f* **25/1**

6312 **7** *3/4* **Birdie Queen**[14] 4101 4-9-9 **61** GeorgeBaker 2 41
(Gary Moore) *racd keenly: in tch: rdn wl over 1f out: nvr threatened: wknd fnl f* **9/4**[1]

10/4 **8** *3 3/4* **Under Review (IRE)**[18] 4038 8-8-13 **56** (t) PhilipPrince(5) 8 24
(Liam Corcoran) *chsd ldr: rdn over 2f out: sn btn* **22/1**

400- **9** *6* **Saxony**[302] 6746 3-7-9 **45** BradleyBosley(7) 12
(Paul Morgan) *led tl rdn over 2f out: wknd over 1f out* **80/1**

1m 9.5s (-1.70) **Going Correction** -0.425s/f (Firm)
**WFA** 3 from 4yo+ 5lb **9** Ran SP% **113.6**
Speed ratings (Par 101): **94,87,86,85,84 81,80,75,67**
CSF £37.83 CT £151.50 TOTE £7.70: £2.60, £2.40, £1.60; EX 41.00 Trifecta £184.00.
**Owner** Nigel Hardy **Bred** R Warren **Trained** Yarnscombe, Devon

**FOCUS**
Quite a competitive sprint for the grade. However, it's not often you see handicaps over this sort of distance won by 5l. The form is not that solid.

## 4565 RAWLINGS BROTHERS 40TH BIRTHDAY CELEBRATIONS H'CAP 5f 11y
**4:00** (4:00) (Class 5) (0-75,74) 3-Y-O **£2,587** (£770; £384; £192) **Stalls** Centre

Form RPR

4305 **1** **Searchlight**[24] 3790 3-9-6 **73** TomEaves 4 83
(Kevin Ryan) *mde all: rdn ent fnl f: kpt on strly and a in command* **10/3**

2012 **2** *2 1/4* **Vodka Chaser (IRE)**[19] 3972 3-8-11 **69** TimClark(5) 1 71
(Alison Hutchinson) *chsd wnr: rdn over 2f out: kpt on but nt pce to chal* **3/1**[3]

3504 **3** *3/4* **Gold Club**[16] 4059 3-8-11 **64** SteveDrowne 2 63
(Ed McMahon) *pushed along to chse ldng trio after 1f: rdn over 2f out: kpt on to go 3rd ent fnl f but nt pce to get on terms* **5/2**[2]

0515 **4** *2* **The Dandy Yank (IRE)**[10] 4267 3-9-2 **74** (p) CamHardie(5) 5 66
(Jamie Osborne) *chsd wnr: rdn over 2f out: no ex ent fnl f* **9/4**[1]

1m 0.25s (-2.25) **Going Correction** -0.425s/f (Firm) **4** Ran SP% **107.4**
Speed ratings (Par 100): **101,97,96,93**
CSF £12.75 TOTE £3.70; EX 12.60 Trifecta £23.50.
**Owner** Elite Racing Club **Bred** Elite Racing Club **Trained** Hambleton, N Yorks

**FOCUS**
The combination of a drop back to the minimum trip and a positive ride proved just the ticket for the winner, who is rated to his turf best.

## 4566 BATHWICK CAR AND VAN HIRE EBF NOVICE STKS (BOBIS RACE) 5f 11y
**4:35** (4:35) (Class 4) 2-Y-O **£6,469** (£1,925) **Stalls** Centre

Form RPR

143 **1** **Snap Shots (IRE)**[20] 3928 2-9-0 94 JennyPowell(7) 4 94
(Tom Dascombe) *sn pushed along to press ldr: rdn 2f out: led jst ins fnl f: kpt on wl to assert fnl 75yds* **11/8**[2]

514 **2** *1* **Zeb Un Nisa**[26] 3721 2-8-11 90 CamHardie(5) 1 85
(Roger Charlton) *broke wl: racd freely: led: rdn and hdd jst ins fnl f: no ex fnl 75yds* **4/7**[1]

1m 0.9s (-1.60) **Going Correction** -0.425s/f (Firm) **2** Ran SP% **105.8**
Speed ratings (Par 96): **95,93**
TOTE £1.60; EX 1.50.
**Owner** True Reds **Bred** Tally-Ho Stud **Trained** Malpas, Cheshire

**FOCUS**
Just two runners for the strongest race on the card, but they raced hard from the start with both seemingly wanting to lead. The winner gave another boost to Beacon's form.

## 4567 GLOBAL FURNITURE ALLIANCE H'CAP 5f 11y
**5:10** (5:11) (Class 6) (0-55,57) 3-Y-O+ **£1,940** (£577; £288; £144) **Stalls** Centre

Form RPR

2613 **1** **Molly Jones**[9] 4285 5-8-12 **51** TimClark(5) 10 61
(Derek Haydn Jones) *hld up: hdwy over 2f out: rdn over 1f out: str run ins fnl f: led nring fin* **9/4**[1]

5642 **2** *nk* **Haadeeth**[7] 4370 7-8-11 **52** (bt) HollieDoyle(7) 4 61
(David Evans) *prom: rdn to ld over 1f out: kpt on: hdd nring fin* **11/2**

-655 **3** *3 1/2* **Captain Ryan**[24] 3784 3-8-13 **54** DeclanBates(3) 9 49
(Peter Makin) *racd keenly: trckd ldrs: effrt 2f out: kpt on same pce fnl f* **5/1**[3]

0444 **4** *2* **Two Turtle Doves (IRE)**[9] 4288 8-8-10 **51** LewisStones(7) 5 40
(Michael Mullineaux) *in tch: rdn over 2f out to chse ldrs: kpt on same pce fr over 1f out* **20/1**

4-00 **5** *nk* **Spider Lily**[40] 3214 3-8-7 **48** oh1 ow2 MichaelJMMurphy(3) 7 35+
(Peter Makin) *s.i.s: bhd: swtchd to centre wl over 2f out: sn rdn: r.o ent fnl f but nt any danger* **66/1**

0300 **6** *1 1/2* **Elite Freedom (IRE)**[14] 4101 3-9-2 **54** (p) SamHitchcott 2 36
(Brian Baugh) *chsd ldrs: rdn over 2f out: fdd ins fnl f* **20/1**

0351 **7** *1 1/2* **Spray Tan**[9] 4285 4-9-6 **57** 6ex JoeyHaynes(3) 11 34
(Tony Carroll) *towards rr: hdwy over 2f out: sn rdn: nvr threatened: wknd fnl f* **4/1**[2]

3034 **8** *shd* **Spic 'n Span**[7] 4337 9-8-12 **46** (p) SteveDrowne 8 23
(Ronald Harris) *prom: led over 2f out: sn rdn: hdd over 1f out: sn wknd* **16/1**

0060 **9** *1 1/2* **Arch Walker (IRE)**[14] 4101 7-9-0 **48** (b) TomEaves 1 20
(John Weymes) *led tl over 2f out: sn rdn: wknd fnl f* **12/1**

0-00 **10** *1/2* **Hares Grove (IRE)**[20] 3938 5-8-7 **46** oh1 PhilipPrince(5) 6 16
(Richard Price) *s.i.s: a towards rr* **66/1**

0606 **11** *1* **Trending (IRE)**[13] 4151 5-9-7 **55** (bt) HarryBentley 12 21
(Jeremy Gask) *mid-div: rdn over 2f out: sn btn* **9/1**

1m 0.8s (-1.70) **Going Correction** -0.425s/f (Firm)
**WFA** 3 from 4yo+ 4lb **11** Ran SP% **118.9**
Speed ratings (Par 101): **96,95,89,86,86 83,81,81,78,78 76**
CSF £14.36 CT £57.45 TOTE £4.70: £2.10, £1.90, £1.70; EX 17.20 Trifecta £69.40.
**Owner** Mrs E M Haydn Jones **Bred** Mrs M L Parry & P M Steele-Mortimer **Trained** Efail Isaf, Rhondda C Taff

**FOCUS**
Not many of these came here in great form, but one notable exception was the winner, who posted his best run since she was a 2yo.

## 4568 SATELLITE INFORMATION SERVICES H'CAP 1m 5f 22y
**5:40** (5:40) (Class 6) (0-65,65) 4-Y-O+ **£1,940** (£577; £288; £144) **Stalls** High

Form RPR

4005 **1** **Freddy Q (IRE)**[29] 3585 5-8-9 **56** MichaelJMMurphy(3) 1 63
(Tony Newcombe) *trckd ldr: rdn over 2f out: led over 1f out: styd on: all out to jst hold on* **11/4**[2]

0543 **2** *shd* **Cabuchon (GER)**[10] 4264 7-8-8 **59** (vt[1]) HollieDoyle(7) 4 66
(David Evans) *stdd s: last: tk clsr order over 3f out: swtchd rt over 2f out: sn rdn and drifted rt: ev ch ent fnl f: kpt on: fin stands' side: jst hld* **6/1**

-000 **3** *3* **Bondi Mist (IRE)**[22] 3853 5-8-3 **52** (v) PhilipPrince(5) 3 54
(Jonathan Geake) *sn pushed into ld: clr after 2f tl rdn over 2f out: hdd over 1f out: kpt on same pce* **20/1**

4433 **4** *3 3/4* **Arlecchino (IRE)**[20] 3919 4-9-7 **65** (b) RoystonFfrench 2 62
(Ed McMahon) *trckd ldrs: rdn over 2f out: nvr quite gng pce to threaten: kpt on same pce* **5/2**[1]

4105 **5** *2* **Glens Wobbly**[14] 4107 6-8-5 **52** RyanTate(3) 6 46
(Jonathan Geake) *hld up in last pair: rdn whn swtchd lft over 2f out: nvr gng the pce to get on terms* **4/1**[3]

0002 **6** *6* **Kelpie Blitz (IRE)**[24] 3778 5-9-2 **65** (p) CamHardie(5) 5 50
(Paul Morgan) *trckd ldrs: rdn 3f out: sn btn* **4/1**[3]

2m 49.9s (-2.10) **Going Correction** -0.20s/f (Firm) **6** Ran SP% **114.3**
Speed ratings (Par 101): **98,97,96,93,92 88**
CSF £19.63 TOTE £2.70: £1.40, £6.30; EX 24.40 Trifecta £334.70.
**Owner** I R Newman **Bred** John Martin McLoughney **Trained** Yarnscombe, Devon

■ Stewards' Enquiry : Michael J M Murphy two-day ban: use of whip (7-8 Aug)

**FOCUS**
Another weak handicap, but the pace looked reasonable and it threw up a good finish as the front pair, wide apart, hit the line together. The winner's best form for this yard.

T/Plt: £97.30 to a £1 stake. Pool: £50,644.26 - 379.82 winning units T/Qpdt: £41.40 to a £1 stake. Pool: £3,136.14 - 56.00 winning units TM

# [4344]DONCASTER (L-H)
Thursday, July 24

**OFFICIAL GOING: Good (good to firm in places; 8.4)**
Round course railed out from 10f to where it joins the straight and races of 10f and over increased by 10yds.
Wind: Moderate behind Weather: Fine and dry

## 4569 OWLERTON GREYHOUND STADIUM @OWLERTONSTADIUM.CO.UK MAIDEN STKS 7f
5:45 (5:48) (Class 4) 3-Y-0+ £5,175 (£1,540; £769; £384) Stalls High

Form RPR
1 **Synergise** 3-9-5 0 AndreaAtzeni 3 89+
(Roger Varian) *s.i.s: in tch after 2f: hdwy to trck ldrs 1/2-way: pushed along to chse ldng pair and green over 2f out: chal and sltly hmpd ent fnl f: sn led and rdn: kpt on strly* 5/1[3]

4 2 2 ½ **Inflection (IRE)**[57] 2682 3-9-0 0 JamesDoyle 4 74
(Hugo Palmer) *trckd ldrs: hdwy and cl up 1/2-way: led 3f out: pushed along over 2f out: jnd and rdn whn hung lft ent fnl f: sn hdd and kpt on same pce* 5/2[1]

-325 3 3 ¼ **Bold Spirit**[43] 3114 3-9-5 72 PatDobbs 5 71
(Richard Hannon) *led: pushed along and hdd 3f out: rdn 2f out: wknd appr fnl f* 7/2[2]

0 4 2 ¾ **Bond Empire**[26] 3700 4-9-12 0 BarryMcHugh 11 66
(Geoffrey Oldroyd) *chsd ldrs: pushed along and sltly outpcd over 2f out: kpt on fnl f* 100/1

5 ½ **Katie Taylor (IRE)** 4-9-7 0 MartinLane 6 60
(Rae Guest) *chsd ldrs: rdn along over 2f out: sn one pce* 14/1

5- 6 3 ½ **Country Drive (USA)**[341] 5529 3-9-0 0 PaulMulrennan 8 48
(Ed Dunlop) *towards rr tl sme late hdwy* 7/2[2]

0 7 1 **Asha**[17] 4022 3-9-0 0 DavidProbert 9 45
(David C Griffiths) *prom: rdn along wl over 2f out: grad wknd* 100/1

03 8 2 **Mad Endeavour**[22] 3849 3-9-5 0 PaulHanagan 1 45
(Stuart Kittow) *a in rr* 8/1

5 9 2 **Norfolk Sound**[37] 3332 3-8-11 0 AshleyMorgan(3) 7 35
(Chris Wall) *a towards rr* 25/1

0 10 4 **Tiger Heights**[14] 4111 3-9-2 0 GaryBartley(3) 2 30
(Jim Goldie) *in tch on outer: rdn along 1/2-way: sn outpcd* 100/1

1m 23.42s (-2.88) **Going Correction** -0.40s/f (Firm)
**WFA** 3 from 4yo 7lb 10 Ran SP% 114.3
Speed ratings (Par 105): **100,97,93,90,89 85,84,82,80,75**
CSF £17.39 TOTE £7.80: £2.40, £1.60, £2.10; EX 25.20 Trifecta £73.20.
**Owner** Miss Emma O'Gorman **Bred** Fittocks Stud Ltd **Trained** Newmarket, Suffolk

**FOCUS**
Round course railed out from 1m2f to where it joins the straight and races of 1m2f and over increased by 10yds. An ordinary maiden and one in which they went a decent gallop. The third set an unexacting standard and the winner was well on top.

## 4570 PARK HILL HOSPITAL MAIDEN STKS (BOBIS RACE) 7f
6:15 (6:19) (Class 3) 2-Y-0 £7,115 (£2,117; £1,058; £529) Stalls High

Form RPR
3 1 **Basateen (IRE)**[13] 4167 2-9-5 0 PaulHanagan 5 99+
(Richard Hannon) *prom: cl up 1/2-way: led wl over 2f out: pushed clr appr fnl f: styd on strly* 5/6[1]

2 8 **Mulzamm (IRE)** 2-9-5 0 JamesDoyle 7 77+
(Charlie Appleby) *hld up towards rr: hdwy 1/2-way: chsd ldrs over 2f out: rdn wl over 1f out: edgd lft appr fnl f: kpt on: no ch w wnr* 13/2[2]

3 1 **Best Dressed** 2-9-5 0 SeanLevey 10 75+
(David Brown) *trckd ldrs: hdwy 3f out: cl up over 2f out: rdn and edgd lft over 1f out: kpt on same pce* 40/1

4 5 **Hail Clodius (IRE)** 2-9-5 0 PatDobbs 8 61+
(Richard Hannon) *dwlt and in rr: hdwy 3f out: pushed along and styd on fnl 2f: nrst fin* 13/2[2]

5 5 1 ½ **Giantouch (USA)**[26] 3720 2-9-5 0 MartinHarley 9 57
(Marco Botti) *trckd ldrs: hdwy 1/2-way: sn chsng ldng trio: effrt over 2f out: sn rdn and grad wknd* 28/1

0 6 4 **Milady Eileen (IRE)**[12] 4216 2-9-0 0 TonyHamilton 1 41
(Richard Fahey) *chsd ldrs: rdn along wl over 2f out: sn outpcd* 50/1

0 7 1 ½ **Eben Dubai (IRE)**[29] 3578 2-9-5 0 ShaneKelly 6 42
(Sir Michael Stoute) *midfield: rdn along 1/2-way: sn outpcd* 14/1

02 8 hd **Biting Bullets (USA)**[14] 4103 2-9-5 0 GrahamGibbons 4 42
(Jo Hughes) *n.m.r s: sn t.k.h and chsd ldrs: rdn along over 3f out: sn wknd* 12/1[3]

6 9 ½ **Digital Rebellion (IRE)**[33] 3474 2-9-5 0 MartinLane 2 40
(Charlie Appleby) *led: rdn along 1/2-way: hdd wl over 2f out and sn wknd* 16/1

10 3 **Shamazing** 2-9-0 0 PaulMulrennan 3 27
(Kevin Ryan) *prom: pushed along 1/2-way: sn rdn and wknd* 25/1

11 1 ¾ **Phantasmo (IRE)** 2-9-5 0 PhillipMakin 12 28
(John Quinn) *a in rr* 66/1

12 ¾ **Full Of Speed (USA)** 2-9-5 0 FrederikTylicki 11 26
(James Fanshawe) *dwlt: a in rr* 40/1

1m 22.78s (-3.52) **Going Correction** -0.40s/f (Firm) 2y crse rec 12 Ran SP% 117.1
Speed ratings (Par 98): **104,94,93,88,86 81,80,79,79,75 73,72**
CSF £5.73 TOTE £3.10: £1.80, £1.50, £11.20; EX 7.60 Trifecta £248.80.
**Owner** Hamdan Al Maktoum **Bred** Forenaghts Stud **Trained** East Everleigh, Wilts

**FOCUS**
A fair juvenile maiden in which they went an honest gallop. The winner looks a pattern performer and the time was very good.

## 4571 ESQUIRES COFFEE H'CAP 6f
6:45 (6:47) (Class 5) (0-70,70) 4-Y-0+ £3,881 (£1,155; £577; £288) Stalls High

Form RPR
1003 1 **Ace Master**[87] 1803 6-9-1 67 (b) AshleyMorgan(3) 11 78
(Roy Bowring) *prom: hdwy wl over 2f out and sn cl up: rdn over 1f out: drvn ins fnl f: kpt on wl to ld nr fin* 25/1

5065 2 hd **Clubland (IRE)**[14] 4131 5-8-12 68 AlistairRawlinson(7) 1 78
(Roy Bowring) *prom: hdwy to ld wl over 2f out: rdn and edgd rt over 1f out: drvn ins fnl f: hdd and no ex nr fin* 7/1[2]

3021 3 1 ¼ **Layla's Hero (IRE)**[3] 4487 7-9-7 70 6ex (v) PaulMulrennan 15 76
(David Nicholls) *trckd ldrs: hdwy 1/2-way: rdn to chal over 1f out: ev ch tl drvn and no ex last 100yds* 2/1[1]

0442 4 6 **Shillito**[15] 4069 4-8-13 62 BarryMcHugh 4 49
(Tony Coyle) *chsd ldr: cl up 1/2-way: rdn along over 2f out: sn drvn and kpt on same pce appr fnl f* 14/1

5002 5 nk **Monsieur Royale**[12] 4195 4-8-1 55 (b) JackGarritty(5) 5 41
(Geoffrey Oldroyd) *in tch: rdn along wl over 2f out: drvn wl over 1f out: sn one pce* 12/1

4146 6 2 ½ **Prigsnov Dancer (IRE)**[42] 3150 9-8-6 62 DavidParkes(7) 18 40
(Deborah Sanderson) *nvr bttr than midfield* 12/1

2203 7 ¾ **Niceonemyson**[42] 3150 5-8-7 61 KevinStott(5) 10 36
(Christopher Wilson) *bhd tl styd on fnl 2f: n.d* 10/1

4560 7 dht **It Must Be Faith**[16] 4061 4-9-6 69 (p) AndrewMullen 2 44
(Michael Appleby) *led: rdn along 1/2-way: sn hdd & wknd* 10/1

4-01 9 1 ¼ **Uprise**[28] 3630 5-9-2 68 (t) RyanPowell(3) 7 39
(George Margarson) *dwlt: a in rr* 16/1

-030 10 ½ **Abraham Monro**[15] 4069 4-8-3 52 DuranFentiman 17 22
(Ruth Carr) *chsd ldrs: rdn along 1/2-way: sn outpcd* 8/1[3]

1130 11 1 **Avonmore Star**[4] 4471 6-9-3 66 MartinHarley 6 33
(Alan McCabe) *a in rr* 8/1[3]

06-0 12 31 **Dr Victoria**[20] 3916 5-8-2 51 oh6 AndreaAtzeni 9
(John Norton) *a in rr: bhd 1/2-way: eased wl over 1f out* 100/1

1m 10.68s (-2.92) **Going Correction** -0.40s/f (Firm) 12 Ran SP% 119.0
Speed ratings (Par 103): **103,102,101,93,92 89,88,88,86,86 84,43**
CSF £192.14 CT £525.90 TOTE £25.00: £11.10, £3.10, £2.30; EX 108.80 Trifecta £249.80.
**Owner** S R Bowring **Bred** S R Bowring **Trained** Edwinstowe, Notts

**FOCUS**
A modest sprint handicap in which they went a contested gallop right across the track with the serious action unfolding centrally. The first three finished clear.

## 4572 SIG INSULATION H'CAP (BOBIS RACE) 6f
7:20 (7:20) (Class 4) (0-80,80) 3-Y-0 £5,175 (£1,540; £769; £384) Stalls High

Form RPR
4024 1 **Elusive George (IRE)**[6] 4390 3-9-3 76 PhillipMakin 3 83
(John Quinn) *cl up: rdn to take narrow advantage over 1f out: drvn ins fnl f: hld on gamely nr line* 6/1[3]

4111 2 nse **Syrian Pearl**[19] 3966 3-9-1 77 AshleyMorgan(3) 7 85+
(Chris Wall) *trckd ldrs: hdwy 2f out: rdn to chal ins fnl f: sn drvn and ev ch: jst failed* 6/1[3]

1242 3 nk **Khatiba (IRE)**[14] 4132 3-9-5 78 AndreaAtzeni 4 84
(Roger Varian) *in tch: niggled along 1/2-way: hdwy to chse ldrs wl over 1f out: drvn to chal ent fnl f: ev ch tl edgd lft and no ex towards fin* 3/1[2]

0303 4 2 ½ **Munfallet (IRE)**[26] 3704 3-9-4 77 SeanLevey 6 75
(David Brown) *led: rdn along and jnd 2f out: narrowly hdd and drvn over 1f out: ev ch tl wknd ins fnl f* 15/2

6-35 5 ¾ **Fair Ranger**[16] 4043 3-8-13 72 PatDobbs 8 67
(Richard Hannon) *in rr: rdn along and detached 1/2-way: hdwy wl over 1f out: styd on fnl f: nrst fin* 20/1

0521 6 ¾ **Maraayill (IRE)**[42] 3145 3-9-6 79 (tp) MartinHarley 2 72
(Marco Botti) *in rr: rdn along 1/2-way: hdwy 2f out: drvn to chse ldrs over 1f out: sn no imp* 5/2[1]

-404 7 shd **Comino (IRE)**[12] 4191 3-9-2 75 AmyRyan 1 68
(Kevin Ryan) *racd wd: cl up: rdn along over 2f out: drvn wl over 1f out and grad wknd* 10/1

0054 8 3 ½ **Westminster (IRE)**[49] 2921 3-9-1 74 (p) RobertHavlin 5 56
(John Gosden) *prom: rdn along wl over 2f out: sn wknd* 14/1

1m 11.08s (-2.52) **Going Correction** -0.40s/f (Firm) 8 Ran SP% 114.4
Speed ratings (Par 102): **100,99,99,96,95 94,94,89**
CSF £41.58 CT £129.68 TOTE £5.90: £2.00, £2.10, £1.70; EX 43.40 Trifecta £376.30.
**Owner** S A T Quinn **Bred** H Etreham,Vision Bloods,Pontchartrain S **Trained** Settrington, N Yorks

**FOCUS**
A fair 3yo sprint handicap in which they went a good gallop. The winner is rated up a length.

## 4573 SKY BET SUPPORTING YORKSHIRE RACING SUMMER FESTIVAL FILLIES' H'CAP 7f
7:55 (7:56) (Class 3) (0-90,90) 3-Y-0+ £8,409 (£2,502; £1,250; £625) Stalls High

Form RPR
11 1 **Etaab (USA)**[42] 3159 3-9-3 86 PaulHanagan 3 95+
(William Haggas) *trckd ldr: niggled along over 2f out: rdn over 1f out: chal ins fnl f: led last 100yds* 8/13[1]

-206 2 1 **Tight Fit**[24] 3788 4-9-10 86 JamesDoyle 2 93
(Henry Candy) *set stdy pce: qcknd over 2f out: rdn over 1f out: edgd lft ins fnl f: hdd and no ex last 100yds* 5/1[3]

5130 3 ½ **Dusky Queen (IRE)**[12] 4212 4-9-11 90 GeorgeChaloner(3) 5 96
(Richard Fahey) *trckd ldr: hdwy 2f out: sn rdn: drvn and ev ch ent fnl f: drvn kpt on same pce last 100yds* 11/4[2]

2013 4 19 **Dorraar (IRE)**[26] 3708 3-8-10 79 AndreaAtzeni 1 32
(Roger Varian) *hld up: effrt wl over 2f out: sn rdn and no imp: outpcd and eased over 1f out* 9/1

1m 24.03s (-2.27) **Going Correction** -0.40s/f (Firm)
**WFA** 3 from 4yo 7lb 4 Ran SP% 115.3
Speed ratings (Par 104): **96,94,94,72**
CSF £4.64 TOTE £1.30; EX 4.70 Trifecta £14.80.
**Owner** Hamdan Al Maktoum **Bred** Shadwell Farm LLC **Trained** Newmarket, Suffolk

**FOCUS**
The feature race was a decent small-field fillies' handicap in which they went quite steady early on. The winner continued her steady progress.

## 4574 SAINT GOBAIN H'CAP 1m 2f 60y
8:30 (8:30) (Class 5) (0-75,75) 3-Y-0 £3,234 (£962; £481; £240) Stalls Low

Form RPR
3210 1 **Tower Power**[16] 4058 3-9-7 75 MartinHarley 8 84+
(Ismail Mohammed) *sn led and set stdy pce: qcknd 3f out: rdn clr over 1f out: kpt on strly* 7/4[1]

040 2 1 ¼ **Artistic Muse (IRE)**[31] 3537 3-8-13 67 PaulHanagan 7 73
(B W Hills) *hld up in rr: str run on outer 2f out: rdn and hung bdly lft appr fnl f: chsng wnr whn hung lft ins fnl f: sn no imp* 6/1

1260 3 2 **Kantara Castle (IRE)**[39] 3273 3-9-1 69 (t) FrannyNorton 4 71
(John Mackie) *trckd wnr: cl up 3f out: rdn along 2f out: drvn and sltly hmpd jst ins fnl f: kpt on same pce after* 11/1

023 4 ¾ **Frosty The Snowman (IRE)**[6] 4420 3-8-8 62 PJMcDonald 3 64
(Ruth Carr) *hld up in tch: hdwy on outer 4f out: rdn along to chse ldrs 2f out: drvn and hmpd appr fnl f: one pce after* 3/1[2]

402 5 4 ½ **Far Ranging (USA)**[30] 3543 3-8-7 61 BarryMcHugh 6 53
(Julie Camacho) *hld up towards rr: hdwy over 4f out: chsd ldrs and rdn along over 2f out: sn wknd* 20/1

0-50 6 ½ **Attenzione (IRE)**[19] 3977 3-9-2 75........................(tp) MarcMonaghan(5) 2 66
(Marco Botti) *prom: hdwy and cl up 3f out: rdn along 2f out: drvn and hmpd appr fnl f: sn wknd* 20/1

-640 7 2½ **Strait Run (IRE)**[13] 4147 3-9-6 74.................................. PatDobbs 5 60
(Richard Hannon) *in tch on outer: rdn along 3f out: sn wknd* 5/1[3]

003 8 nse **King's Prospect**[19] 3953 3-8-11 65.......................... PaulMulrennan 1 51
(Tracy Waggott) *trckd ldrs on inner: hdwy 3f out: rdn along 2f out: sn drvn and wknd appr fnl f* 22/1

2m 9.88s (0.48) **Going Correction** +0.075s/f (Good) **8** Ran SP% **114.5**
Speed ratings (Par 100): **101,100,98,97,94 93,91,91**
CSF £12.36 CT £87.91 TOTE £2.60: £1.10, £3.00, £2.50; EX 11.00 Trifecta £119.20.
**Owner** Abdulla Al Mansoori **Bred** Sir Eric Parker **Trained** Newmarket, Suffolk

**FOCUS**
Modest handicap form. The winner made all at a steady pace and could do better.

## 4575 1STSECURITYSOLUTIONS.CO.UK H'CAP 1m 6f 132y
9:00 (9:01) (Class 4) (0-80,80) 4-Y-0+ £5,175 (£1,540; £769; £384) Stalls Low

Form RPR

0-04 1 **Nanton (USA)**[14] 4113 12-8-13 72................................ DanielTudhope 11 80
(Jim Goldie) *hld up in rr: hdwy on outer over 2f out: str run fr over 1f out: rdn to ld last 100yds: sn edgd lft and styd on strly* 7/2[1]

5235 2 1¾ **Deepsand (IRE)**[14] 4113 5-9-3 76....................................(p) DavidAllan 9 82
(Tim Easterby) *hld upon inner: swtchd rt and hdwy 3f out: trckd ldrs 2f out: rdn to ld over 1f out: edgd lft jst ins fnl f: hdd and kpt on same pce last 100yds* 9/2[2]

-223 3 1 **Merchant Of Dubai**[12] 4204 9-8-9 73............................. JackGarritty(5) 6 78
(Jim Goldie) *trckd ldr: hdwy and cl up over 4f out: led 3f out: rdn along over 2f out: drvn and hdd appr fnl f: kpt on same pce* 8/1

06/ 4 1¼ **Tindaro (FR)**[38] 6439 7-9-7 80............................................(t) PatDobbs 5 83
(Paul Webber) *hld up in tch: hdwy 4f out: chsd ldrs over 2f out: sn rdn and n.m.r wl over 1f out: swtchd rt and styd on fnl f: nrst fin* 12/1

0341 5 shd **Hurry Home Poppa (IRE)**[19] 3976 4-8-4 63.................. JimmyQuinn 10 68+
(John Mackie) *trckd ldng pair: hdwy 3f out: rdn along over 2f out: drvn and hld whn sltly hmpd ins fnl f: one pce* 5/1[3]

-044 6 3¾ **Snowy Dawn**[13] 4144 4-9-3 76...........................................(p) ShaneKelly 8 74
(Andrew Hollinshead) *hld up in rr: hdwy on outer to trck ldrs 6f out: effrt 3f out: rdn along 2f out: sn one pce* 9/2[2]

0015 7 ¾ **Royal Alcor (IRE)**[19] 3976 7-9-3 76..............................(t) DavidProbert 1 73
(Gay Kelleway) *trckd ldrs on inner: hdwy over 3f out: rdn along over 2f out: sn wknd* 25/1

2600 8 1¼ **Singzak**[26] 3699 6-8-12 71.................................. GrahamGibbons 3 66
(Michael Easterby) *led: pushed along 4f out: rdn and hdd 3f out: drvn over 2f out: sn wknd* 33/1

0043 9 7 **Keep Calm**[42] 3151 4-8-5 64..........................................(b) FrannyNorton 2 50
(John Mackie) *trckd ldrs on inner: hdwy 4f out: rdn along 3f out: sn wknd* 10/1

/51- 10 7 **Bradbury (IRE)**[509] 378 6-8-13 72...................................(p) JasonHart 4 49
(Eric Alston) *t.k.h: hld up: pushed along 4f out: rdn 3f out: sn wknd* 12/1

3m 8.36s (0.96) **Going Correction** +0.075s/f (Good) **10** Ran SP% **117.6**
Speed ratings (Par 105): **100,99,98,97,97 95,95,94,91,87**
CSF £19.23 CT £118.56 TOTE £5.10: £1.80, £2.10, £3.40; EX 21.20 Trifecta £155.00.
**Owner** Johnnie Delta Racing **Bred** Samuel H And Mrs Rogers, Jr **Trained** Uplawmoor, E Renfrews

**FOCUS**
They went a fair gallop and the first two came from the back. The form makes sense.
T/Jkpt: £14,330.60 to a £1 stake. Pool: £20,184.00 - 0.50 winning units. T/Plt: £11.60 to a £1 stake. Pool: £76,918.76 - 4,835.64 winning units T/Qpdt: £7.40 to a £1 stake. Pool: £7,365.71 - 726.96 winning units JR

# 4541 LINGFIELD (L-H)
Thursday, July 24

**OFFICIAL GOING: Standard**
Wind: Light; half against Weather: Warm and sunny

## 4576 ALL NEW 32REDSPORT.COM NURSERY H'CAP 5f 6y(P)
5:30 (5:30) (Class 6) 2-Y-O £2,264 (£673; £336; £168) Stalls Low

Form RPR

062 1 **Somedaysrdiamonds**[15] 4087 2-8-8 57............................ LiamJones 2 59
(J S Moore) *taken down early: mde all: rdn and wnt clr over 1f out: tiring towards fin but a holding rivals: rdn out* 25/1

055 2 nk **Lyfka**[37] 3330 2-8-5 59.......................................... LouisSteward(5) 4 60+
(Paul Cole) *s.i.s: hld up in last pair: effrt over 1f out: hdwy ins fnl f: r.o strly to snatch 2nd on post: nt quite rch wnr* 6/1

41 3 shd **Loumarin (IRE)**[15] 4087 2-9-1 64................................ RichardHughes 3 65
(Martyn Meade) *chsd ldrs: wnt 2nd over 2f out: outpcd and rdn over 1f out: styd on u.p and grad clsd on wnr: lost 2nd last stride* 2/1[1]

503 4 ¾ **Lady Marita (IRE)**[29] 3757 2-8-12 61............................ RobertWinston 8 59
(J S Moore) *in tch in midfield: hdwy u.p to chse ldrs ent fnl f: kpt on steadily but nvr gng pce to chal wnr* 7/1

3220 5 3¼ **One Moment**[29] 3583 2-9-7 70.........................................[1] JamieSpencer 5 56
(Robert Cowell) *in tch in midfield: hung rt bnd 2f out: sn rdn and no imp* 7/2[2]

532 6 3¼ **Clodovil Doll (IRE)**[57] 2666 2-9-7 70............................ GrahamLee 7 44
(James Tate) *t.k.h: hld up in tch in midfield: rdn and wd bnd 2f out: no imp and wl hld after* 5/1[3]

4560 7 1 **Toytown (IRE)**[20] 3937 2-8-9 58.................................. RaulDaSilva 1 29
(Derek Shaw) *bustled along leaving stalls and sn pressing wnr: lost 2nd over 2f out: rdn and btn over 1f out: fdd fnl f* 14/1

646 8 7 **Tommys Geal**[64] 2460 2-7-8 50 oh4 ow1.................... HectorCrouch(7) 6
(Michael Madgwick) *a in rr: rdn and struggling 1/2-way: bhd over 1f out* 66/1

1m 0.38s (1.58) **Going Correction** +0.10s/f (Slow) **8** Ran SP% **111.0**
Speed ratings (Par 92): **91,90,90,89,83 78,77,65**
CSF £157.15 CT £428.89 TOTE £16.20: £3.90, £1.40, £2.00; EX 164.50 Trifecta £943.60 Part won..
**Owner** G V March & J S Moore **Bred** Manor Farm Stud (rutland) **Trained** Upper Lambourn, Berks

**FOCUS**
An ordinary nursery, run at a decent pace.

## 4577 32RED/BRITISH STALLION STUDS EBF MAIDEN STKS 5f 6y(P)
6:00 (6:00) (Class 5) 2-Y-O £2,911 (£866; £432; £216) Stalls Low

Form RPR

4302 1 **Magic Florence (IRE)**[22] 3841 2-9-0 70........................ GrahamLee 3 68+
(James Given) *led for 1f: chsd ldr and clr of field after: pushed along over 1f out: led jst ins fnl f: r.o* 30/100[1]

0 2 1¼ **Candlelight (IRE)**[10] 4269 2-9-0 0............................ RobertWinston 2 64
(Charles Hills) *nt best away: sn rcvrd and led after 1f: sn clr w wnr: rdn over 1f out: hdd jst ins fnl f: one pce after* 4/1[2]

0 3 10 **Prince Rofan (IRE)**[70] 2288 2-9-5 0............................ RaulDaSilva 4 39
(Derek Shaw) *a off the pce in last trio: rdn and effrt over 1f out: wnt rt u.p 1f out: wnt 3rd ins fnl f: nvr trbld ldrs* 25/1

0 4 2¾ **Cape Point**[29] 3584 2-9-5 0...................................... LiamKeniry 6 31
(Michael Blanshard) *chsd ldrs: hung rt bnd 4f out: stl in tch whn hung bdly rt and lost any ch bnd 2f out: lost 3rd ins fnl f* 16/1[3]

0 5 nse **Noble Cause**[24] 3799 2-9-0 0.................................. FergusSweeney 1 26
(Luke Dace) *s.i.s: a off the pce in last trio: n.d* 33/1

0 6 11 **Blue Amazon (IRE)**[26] 3728 2-9-0 0.......................... StevieDonohoe 5
(Lee Carter) *s.i.s: outpcd in last trio thrght* 20/1

1m 0.69s (1.89) **Going Correction** +0.10s/f (Slow) **6** Ran SP% **114.4**
Speed ratings (Par 94): **88,86,70,65,65 47**
CSF £1.86 TOTE £1.10: £1.02, £2.70; EX 2.20 Trifecta £10.60.
**Owner** The Cool Silk Partnership **Bred** Pat Beirne **Trained** Willoughton, Lincs

**FOCUS**
The first pair completely dominated.

## 4578 BET NOW AT 32REDSPORT.COM H'CAP 7f 1y(P)
6:30 (6:31) (Class 6) (0-65,65) 4-Y-0+ £2,264 (£673; £336; £168) Stalls Low

Form RPR

3012 1 **For Shia And Lula (IRE)**[31] 3526 5-9-7 65.............. FrankieMcDonald 4 75
(Daniel Mark Loughnane) *hld up wl in tch in midfield: rdn and effrt to chal between horses 1f out: led ins fnl f: r.o wl: rdn out* 5/1[2]

0634 2 1 **Darnathean**[37] 3328 5-9-3 61....................................(p) RichardHughes 14 68+
(Paul D'Arcy) *taken down early: hld up in tch in towards rr: rdn and effrt wl over 1f out: r.o wl ins fnl f: wnt 2nd cl home* 8/1

6525 3 ¾ **Parisian Pyramid (IRE)**[16] 4050 8-9-2 60........................(v) AmirQuinn 8 65
(Lee Carter) *pressed ldr: rdn and ev ch 2f out: unable qck 1f out: styd on same pce fnl f* 20/1

-004 4 nse **Wotalad**[24] 3798 4-8-7 51.............................................. HayleyTurner 5 56
(Richard Whitaker) *led: rdn wl over 1f out: hdd ins fnl f: no ex: wknd towards fin and lost 2 pls cl home* 16/1

5104 5 1¾ **Perfect Pastime**[31] 3528 6-9-1 59....................................(b) AdamKirby 1 59
(Jim Boyle) *restless in stalls: in tch in midfield on inner: clsd to chse ldrs and swtchd rt 1f out: hrd drvn and no imp ins fnl f* 4/1[1]

3621 6 ½ **Cyflymder (IRE)**[10] 4266 8-8-12 56 6ex.......................... OisinMurphy 10 55
(David C Griffiths) *in tch in midfield but stuck wd: rdn wl over 1f out: kpt on but no real imp* 6/1[3]

2615 7 ¾ **Ishi Honest**[16] 4056 4-8-13 57.................................. SilvestreDeSousa 2 54
(Mark Usher) *chsd ldrs: drvn and clsd over 1f out: no ex 1f out: wknd ins fnl f* 10/1

0060 8 1 **Officer In Command (USA)**[24] 3795 8-8-9 60........(p) GeorgiaCox(7) 13 55
(John Butler) *v.s.a: detached last and nudged along: clsd and in tch 3f out: stl nudged along hdwy past btn horses over 1f out: styd on: n.d* 66/1

3344 9 nk **Bertie Blu Boy**[110] 1297 6-9-1 59.................................(p) GrahamLee 11 53
(Lisa Williamson) *wl in tch in midfield: rdn and unable qck over 1f out: wknd fnl f* 5/1[2]

4064 10 2 **Blazing Knight (IRE)**[17] 4024 4-9-4 62...........................(b) JimCrowley 6 51
(Chris Gordon) *s.i.s: bhd and sn pushed along: sme hdwy wl over 1f out: n.d* 12/1

/00- 11 1 **Duke Of Aricabeau (IRE)**[505] 898 5-8-10 57........... SimonPearce(3) 7 43
(Lydia Pearce) *in tch towards rr: drvn and effrt over 1f out: wknd fnl f* 66/1

0650 12 5 **Royal College**[15] 4073 4-9-5 63.................................. GeorgeBaker 9 36
(Gary Moore) *in tch towards rr: effrt ent fnl f: kpt on but nvr trbld ldrs* 8/1

0-00 R **My Gigi**[51] 2864 4-9-0 58.................................................[1] LiamJones 12
(Laura Mongan) *reluctant to go to s and led rdrless to s: ref to r: tk no part* 50/1

1m 25.65s (0.85) **Going Correction** +0.10s/f (Slow) **13** Ran SP% **122.2**
Speed ratings (Par 101): **99,97,97,96,94 94,93,92,92,89 88,82,**
CSF £44.91 CT £771.02 TOTE £4.60: £1.60, £6.10, £12.30; EX 63.70 Trifecta £1034.20.
**Owner** Over The Moon Racing IV **Bred** A M F Persse **Trained** Baldwin's Gate, Staffs

**FOCUS**
This looked wide open. They went a fair pace but it did pay to sit prominently. The winner is rated back to his old best.

## 4579 32RED CASINO MAIDEN H'CAP 1m 1y(P)
7:05 (7:06) (Class 6) (0-65,65) 3-Y-0+ £2,264 (£673; £336; £168) Stalls High

Form RPR

4023 1 **Fruit Pastille**[28] 3614 3-9-3 65.................................. RichardHughes 1 74
(Hughie Morrison) *nt best away and sn rdn along: chsd ldrs after 1f: wnt 2nd over 4f out: rdn to ld over 1f out: hdd ins fnl f: battled bk and sn led again: styd on* 5/1[2]

0422 2 nk **Celestial Ray**[24] 3805 5-9-6 60.................................. KierenFallon 2 70
(Linda Jewell) *dwlt: sn pushed along and rcvrd to r in midfield: hdwy to chse ldrs 2f: rdn to chal over 1f out: led ins fnl f: sn hdd: kpt on but a jst hld* 4/1[1]

-230 3 8 **Harwoods Star (IRE)**[24] 3805 4-9-8 62.......................... AdamKirby 10 54
(Amanda Perrett) *rdn to ld and crossed to inner rail: rdn and hdd over 1f out: 3rd and btn 1f out: wknd ins fnl f: hung on for 3rd cl home* 8/1

0460 4 nk **Pendo**[65] 2429 3-9-2 64.............................................. GrahamLee 6 53
(Paul Cole) *dwlt: in tch in rr: rdn and outpcd over 2f: shifting rt ent fnl f: styd on and pressing for 3rd cl home: nvr trbld ldrs* 20/1

4305 5 ½ **Coillte Cailin (IRE)**[26] 3705 4-9-11 65.................(b[1]) FrankieMcDonald 4 55
(Daniel Mark Loughnane) *hld up in tch towards rr: rdn ent fnl 2f: swtchd lft and sme hdwy over 1f out: styd on: nvr trbld ldrs* 16/1

-003 6 ½ **Sweet Marwell (IRE)**[31] 3526 4-9-5 59........................ FergusSweeney 9 48
(Jo Crowley) *in tch in midfield: rdn and effrt to chse clr ldng trio over 1f out: no prog* 33/1

-044 7 2¼ **Anjin (IRE)**[27] 3683 3-9-2 64.......................................... LukeMorris 3 46
(Sir Mark Prescott Bt) *s.i.s and rdn along early: hdwy to r in midfield after 2f: rdn over 2f out: sme hdwy over 1f out: btn 1f out: wknd ins fnl f* 5/1[2]

0-00 8 3½ **Fiftyshadesdarker (IRE)**[38] 3315 3-9-3 65..............(tp) PatCosgrave 11 38
(George Baker) *chsd ldr tl over 4f out: 4th and struggling u.p 2f out: wknd over 1f out* 25/1

000 **9** ½ **Varsovian**[14] 4130 4-9-5 **59** JimCrowley 7 33
(Dean Ivory) *s.i.s: bhd: outpcd over 2f out: u.p and wd bnd 2f out: no hdwy: wknd over 1f out* **7/1**

2206 **10** 1½ **Midaz**[24] 3795 4-9-11 **65** GeorgeBaker 12 36
(Hughie Morrison) *dwlt: rcvrd and in tch in midfield: rdn and struggling over 2f out: lost pl and bhd whn hmpd wl over 1f out* **6/1**[3]

4656 **11** 5 **Tax Reform (IRE)**[31] 3526 4-9-3 **62** (b) LouisSteward(5) 5 21
(Mark Hoad) *sn dropped to rr and rdn along: lost tch u.p 2f out* **25/1**

-424 **12** 6 **Nixyba**[135] 914 3-9-2 **64** OisinMurphy 8 8
(Tim Vaughan) *a towards rr and nvr gng wl: rdn 4f out: lost tch ent fnl 2f* **16/1**

1m 37.32s (-0.88) **Going Correction** +0.10s/f (Slow)
**WFA** 3 from 4yo+ 8lb **12** Ran SP% **118.4**
Speed ratings (Par 101): **108,107,99,99,98 98,96,92,92,90 85,79**
CSF £23.97 CT £161.89 TOTE £4.00: £1.20, £1.50, £3.50; EX 15.40 Trifecta £97.20.
**Owner** The Caledonian Racing Society **Bred** M E Broughton **Trained** East Ilsley, Berks

**FOCUS**
A typically weak maiden handicap and most were off the bridle around halfway, but the form makes sense with the first pair coming clear. The winner rates a small personal best.

## 4580 32RED.COM H'CAP — 1m 1y(P)
**7:40** (7:40) (Class 4) (0-85,85) 3-Y-0+ **£5,175** (£1,540; £769; £384) **Stalls High**

Form RPR

1- **1** **Maverick Wave (USA)**[317] 6277 3-9-5 **84** WilliamBuick 6 97
(John Gosden) *dwlt: towards rr early: hdwy to chse ldrs over 5f out: rdn and effrt jst over 1f out: qckn to ld ins fnl f: r.o strly: easily* **5/4**[1]

1-43 **2** 4 **My Target (IRE)**[22] 3861 3-8-12 **84** ow2 AhmadAlSubousi(7) 4 88
(Saeed bin Suroor) *in tch in midfield: n.m.r on inner 2f out: rdn and hdwy over 1f out: styd on to go 2nd wl ins fnl f: no ch w wnr* **6/1**

-061 **3** nk **Mister Musicmaster**[13] 4153 5-8-13 **77** JennyPowell(7) 2 82
(Ron Hodges) *led tl over 5f out: styd upsides ldr tl rdn to ld again ent fnl 2f: hdd ins fnl f: outpcd by wnr and kpt on same pce after: lost 2nd wl ins fnl f* **20/1**

4506 **4** 1½ **Dullingham**[31] 3538 3-9-4 **83** AdamKirby 7 83
(Charlie Appleby) *rdn along early: chsd ldrs: effrt u.p wl over 1f out: swtchd rt over 1f out: styd on same pce fnl f* **5/1**[3]

0100 **5** nk **Tasrih (USA)**[49] 2922 5-9-12 **83** BenCurtis 1 84
(Alan McCabe) *taken down early: w ldr: led and stdd gallop over 5f out: hdd and rdn 2f out: no ex ins fnl f: wknd fnl 100yds* **20/1**

5120 **6** 4½ **Kung Hei Fat Choy (USA)**[22] 3844 5-10-0 **85** (b) GrahamLee 5 76
(James Given) *racd in midfield: rdn over 4f out: nvr gng wl after: drvn and no hdwy over 2f out: wknd over 1f out* **20/1**

1165 **7** 3¾ **Reedcutter**[19] 3980 3-9-4 **83** RichardHughes 8 63
(James Toller) *stdd and dropped in bhd after s: hld up in rr: clsd after 2f: effrt u.p over 1f out: no hdwy and sn wknd: eased towards fin* **3/1**[2]

4625 **8** 7 **Pashan Garh**[27] 3646 5-8-9 **66** StevieDonohoe 3 32
(Pat Eddery) *dwlt: dropped to rr and u.p 5f out: nvr travelling after: lost tch over 2f out* **33/1**

1m 36.57s (-1.63) **Going Correction** +0.10s/f (Slow)
**WFA** 3 from 5yo 8lb **8** Ran SP% **117.6**
Speed ratings (Par 105): **112,108,107,106,105 101,97,90**
CSF £9.10 CT £104.05 TOTE £4.10: £2.70, £1.20, £4.90; EX 10.50 Trifecta £90.50.
**Owner** HRH Princess Haya Of Jordan **Bred** Jim Plemmons & Darley **Trained** Newmarket, Suffolk
■ Stewards' Enquiry : Ahmad Al Subousi nine-day ban: use of whip (7-15 Aug)

**FOCUS**
The pace looked good and the form has been given a chance with the winner unexposed.

## 4581 32RED ON THE APP STORE H'CAP — 6f 1y(P)
**8:10** (8:10) (Class 5) (0-75,75) 3-Y-0+ **£2,911** (£866; £432; £216) **Stalls Low**

Form RPR

3046 **1** **Langley Vale**[21] 3879 5-9-6 **72** SebSanders 2 82
(Roger Teal) *chsd ldrs: wnt 2nd over 3f out: rdn and ev ch 2f out: sustained duel w ldr tl forged ahd ins fnl f: rdn out* **7/1**

01-0 **2** 1 **Brother Tiger**[21] 3882 5-9-7 **73** OisinMurphy 8 80
(David C Griffiths) *sn pushed along to press ldrs: led over 4f out and crossed to inner rail: rdn and hrd pressed 2f out: hdd ins fnl f: no ex* **9/2**[3]

1403 **3** 1 **Seek The Fair Land**[22] 3854 8-9-8 **74** (b) AmirQuinn 5 78
(Lee Carter) *hld up in tch in rr: hdwy u.p on inner over 1f out: styd on to go 3rd wl ins fnl f: nvr enough pce to rch ldrs* **16/1**

0602 **4** 1 **Top Cop**[31] 3519 5-9-1 **74** (p) MikeyEnnis(7) 1 75
(Ronald Harris) *led for over 1f: chsd ldrs after: rdn wl over 1f out: hung rt and one pce fnl f: lost 3rd wl ins fnl f* **14/1**

5034 **5** ½ **Thataboy (IRE)**[10] 4262 3-9-4 **75** (p) RichardKingscote 7 73
(Tom Dascombe) *hld up in tch in rr: rdn and hdwy ent fnl f: kpt on u.p: nvr trbld ldrs* **6/1**

6141 **6** ¾ **Dissent (IRE)**[16] 4049 5-9-7 **73** (b) GrahamLee 6 70
(James Given) *chsd ldrs but stuck wd: sltly hmpd over 5f out: rdn and no rspnse over 1f out: wl hld fnl f* **3/1**[1]

0362 **7** 7 **Rigolleto (IRE)**[20] 3935 6-9-6 **72** RichardHughes 3 46
(Anabel K Murphy) *in tch in midfield: effrt u.p jst over 2f out: wknd over 1f out: eased wl ins fnl f* **8/1**

0030 **8** 1¼ **Multitask**[47] 2995 4-9-9 **75** LiamKeniry 4 45
(Michael Madgwick) *short of room and hmpd sn after s: in tch in midfield: rdn and no hdwy wl over 1f out: sn wknd: bhd and eased wl ins fnl f* **4/1**[2]

1m 11.69s (-0.21) **Going Correction** +0.10s/f (Slow)
**WFA** 3 from 4yo+ 5lb **8** Ran SP% **113.6**
Speed ratings (Par 103): **105,103,102,101,100 99,90,88**
CSF £37.91 CT £488.41 TOTE £15.00: £4.40, £1.30, £6.60; EX 43.20 Trifecta £451.10.
**Owner** Dr G F Forward & F C Taylor **Bred** Miss Brooke Sanders **Trained** Ashtead, Surrey

**FOCUS**
A very tight-looking sprint handicap where the pace held up.

## 4582 RACING SPECIALS AT 32REDSPORT.COM H'CAP — 1m 5f (P)
**8:45** (8:45) (Class 6) (0-65,65) 4-Y-0+ **£2,264** (£673; £336; £168) **Stalls Low**

Form RPR

0340 **1** **Honourable Knight (IRE)**[13] 4149 6-9-5 **60** (v) LiamKeniry 2 66
(Mark Usher) *chsd ldrs tl hdwy to ld after 2f: mde rest: rdn 2 l clr over 1f out: hrd pressed ins fnl f: fnd ex and forged ahd fnl 50yds* **16/1**

1211 **2** ¾ **Glennten**[8] 4326 5-9-10 **65** 6ex SilvestreDeSousa 7 70
(Jose Santos) *chsd ldr for 2f: styd chsng ldrs tl wnt 2nd again 7f out: rdn over 2f out: hrd drvn and rallied to chal ins fnl f: no ex and btn fnl 50yds* **4/5**[1]

1565 **3** 1½ **Bennelong**[10] 4273 8-9-7 **62** (b) StevieDonohoe 1 65
(Lee Carter) *hld up in tch in last pair: effrt 2f out: drvn over 1f out: wnt 3rd over 1f out: styd on same pce ins fnl f* **7/1**[3]

600/ **4** 1¼ **Giant Sequoia (USA)**[45] 6255 10-8-9 **50** (t) AdamBeschizza 6 51
(Des Donovan) *stdd and awkward leaving stalls: hld up in tch in last: rdn wl over 1f out: hdwy to go 4th 1f out: styd on same pce after* **14/1**

2430 **5** 5 **Tracks Of My Tears**[24] 3803 4-9-6 **61** GrahamLee 4 54
(Giles Bravery) *led for 2f: chsd ldr tl 7f out: 3rd and rdn 2f out: outpcd and btn over 1f out: wknd fnl f* **9/4**[2]

2m 51.05s (5.05) **Going Correction** +0.10s/f (Slow) **5** Ran SP% **111.4**
Speed ratings (Par 101): **88,87,86,85,82**
CSF £30.51 TOTE £10.10: £6.50, £1.10; EX 21.90 Trifecta £133.70.
**Owner** Mrs T Channing-Williams **Bred** Mohammed Al Sulaim **Trained** Upper Lambourn, Berks

**FOCUS**
A moderate staying handicap, run at an uneven pace. Muddling form.
T/Plt: £70.90 to a £1 stake. Pool: £53,639.42 - 552.22 winning units T/Qpdt: £46.20 to a £1 stake. Pool: £5,934.98 - 95.06 winning units SP

# [4548] SANDOWN (R-H)
### Thursday, July 24

**OFFICIAL GOING: Good to firm (8.7)**
Sprint course at full width. Round course railed out 4yds from 9f to Winning Post and distances increased by 5yds on Round course.
Wind: Moderate; behind Weather: Fine, hot

## 4583 MOLSON COORS / IRISH STALLION FARMS EBF MAIDEN STKS — 5f 6y
**2:00** (2:01) (Class 5) 2-Y-O **£3,881** (£1,155; £577; £288) **Stalls Low**

Form RPR

3 **1** **Profitable (IRE)**[21] 3889 2-9-5 0 AdamKirby 2 81+
(Clive Cox) *racd against rail: trckd ldr: led wl over 1f out: shkn up and sn clr: styd on* **2/5**[1]

5 **2** 2¾ **Equally Fast**[38] 3311 2-9-5 0 DougieCostello 1 71
(William Muir) *racd against rail: chsd ldrs: shkn up over 2f out: kpt on fr over 1f out: snatched 2nd last stride* **14/1**

5 **3** nse **Renaissant**[10] 4269 2-9-0 0 RichardHughes 3 66
(Richard Hannon) *led but racd off far rail: hdd wl over 1f out: shkn up and no ch w wnr fnl f: lost 2nd last stride* **7/2**[2]

5 **4** ¾ **The Wispe**[29] 3563 2-9-0 0 JamieSpencer 4 63
(Robert Cowell) *racd on outer: chsd ldrs: shkn up 2f out: kpt on fnl f to press for a pl nr fin* **33/1**

**5** 6 **Torridonian** 2-9-0 0 RyanMoore 6 42
(James Tate) *s.i.s: a last: pushed along over 2f out: wknd and eased fnl f* **12/1**[3]

1m 0.32s (-1.28) **Going Correction** -0.30s/f (Firm) **5** Ran SP% **111.0**
Speed ratings (Par 94): **98,93,93,92,82**
CSF £7.62 TOTE £1.30: £1.10, £3.90; EX 6.00 Trifecta £17.50.
**Owner** A D Spence **Bred** Con Harrington **Trained** Lambourn, Berks

**FOCUS**
The rail was moved out 4yds from the 1m1f marker to the winning post, adding 5yds to the Round Course distances. The ground would have been drying all the time on a hot, sunny day, and was changed to good to firm prior to racing. Both Adam Kirby and Richard Hughes reported it to be fine with no jar. Little depth to this juvenile maiden, but a potentially useful winner who can rate higher.

## 4584 WEATHERBYS STALLION BOOK H'CAP (BOBIS RACE) — 1m 6f
**2:30** (2:30) (Class 3) (0-90,88) 3-Y-O **£7,762** (£2,310; £1,154; £577) **Stalls Low**

Form RPR

-106 **1** **Purple Spectrum**[21] 3892 3-8-11 **78** (p) RyanMoore 7 90+
(William Haggas) *led: hdd 8f out to over 4f out: urged along wl over 2f out: clr and drvn over 1f out: styd on strly* **11/2**[3]

2-14 **2** 3½ **Devilment**[55] 2748 3-9-7 **88** WilliamBuick 6 95
(Charlie Appleby) *hld up in last: prog to chse wnr wl over 1f out: drvn and styd on but no imp fnl f* **4/1**[2]

160 **3** 7 **Belfilo (IRE)**[69] 2319 3-8-10 **77** JimCrowley 4 74
(Andrew Balding) *hld up in tch: rdn 3f out: sn lft wl bhd: poor 5th over 1f out: kpt on to take modest 3rd last strides* **8/1**

5641 **4** ½ **Snow Squall**[7] 4361 3-9-0 **81** 6ex SilvestreDeSousa 1 78
(Mark Johnston) *hld up in tch: rdn to take 2nd briefly 2f out: sn btn: wknd fnl f* **6/5**[1]

2104 **5** 2 **Norse Star (IRE)**[29] 3587 3-8-12 **79** LiamKeniry 2 73
(Sylvester Kirk) *trckd ldng pair: chsd wnr 4f out to 2f out: steadily wknd* **11/1**

3522 **6** 33 **Samtu (IRE)**[19] 3986 3-8-4 **71** RoystonFfrench 3 19
(Clive Brittain) *sddle slipped sn after s: t.k.h: pressed wnr: led 8f out to over 4f out racing v wd: dropped away over 3f out* **8/1**

2m 58.87s (-5.63) **Going Correction** -0.225s/f (Firm) **6** Ran SP% **111.4**
Speed ratings (Par 104): **107,105,101,100,99 80**
CSF £26.82 TOTE £6.10: £3.10, £2.60; EX 24.60 Trifecta £140.30.
**Owner** The Queen **Bred** The Queen **Trained** Newmarket, Suffolk

**FOCUS**
A fair staying handicap for 3yos, but little depth. A clear best from the winner.

## 4585 IRISH CHAMPIONS WEEKEND EBF STALLIONS STAR STKS (LISTED RACE) (FILLIES) — 7f 16y
**3:05** (3:05) (Class 1) 2-Y-O
**£17,013** (£6,450; £3,228; £1,608; £807; £405) **Stalls Low**

Form RPR

1 **1** **Alonsoa (IRE)**[30] 3558 2-9-0 0 DaneO'Neill 7 96+
(Henry Candy) *sn trckd ldr: shkn up 2f out: rdn to ld jst over 1f out: styd on wl* **5/6**[1]

1 **2** ¾ **Pack Together**[44] 3076 2-9-0 78 RichardHughes 4 94+
(Richard Hannon) *hld up in last pair: prog on inner wl over 1f out: drvn and r.o to take 2nd last 100yds: tried to cl on wnr but no imp nr fin* **10/3**[2]

146 **3** 1¾ **Bonnie Grey**[26] 3721 2-9-0 82 SilvestreDeSousa 6 89
(Rod Millman) *hld up in last pair: rdn wl over 2f out: sn struggling: kpt on fr over 1f out to take 3rd last strides* **14/1**

12 **4** ½ **Russian Punch**[27] 3649 2-9-0 77 GrahamLee 5 88
(James Given) *led: rdn 2f out: hdd jst over 1f out: steadily fdd* **33/1**

221 **5** 1 **Lady Moscou (IRE)**[14] 4129 2-9-0 76 RyanMoore 2 85
(James Tate) *trckd ldng pair: rdn and outpcd 2f out: no imp after* **8/1**[3]

4 **6** 5 **Teosroyal (IRE)**[21] 3888 2-9-0 0 WilliamBuick 8 72
(Clive Brittain) *trckd ldrs: shkn up over 2f out: wknd over 1f out* **20/1**

021 **7** ¾ **Mary McPhee**[20] 3933 2-9-0 82 JamieSpencer 3 70
(Charles Hills) *t.k.h: hld up in tch: rdn over 2f out: wknd over 1f out* **11/1**

1m 27.98s (-1.52) **Going Correction** -0.225s/f (Firm) **7** Ran SP% **111.4**
Speed ratings (Par 99): **99,98,96,95,94 88,87**
CSF £3.50 TOTE £1.90: £1.10, £2.10; EX 4.40 Trifecta £29.10.
**Owner** Mrs Patricia J Burns **Bred** Lodge Park Stud **Trained** Kingston Warren, Oxon

**FOCUS**
Not a particularly strong fillies' Listed event, although the two at the head of the market came to the fore. It was run at a steady gallop early. Improvement from several but the principals finished compressed.

## 4586 ODGERS BERNDTSON H'CAP 1m 2f 7y
**3:40** (3:41) (Class 4) (0-85,85) 3-Y-O+ **£5,175** (£1,540; £769; £384) **Stalls** Low

Form RPR
31-4 **1** **Alex Vino (IRE)**[111] 1279 3-8-13 **80**................................ RyanMoore 1 92+
(Sir Michael Stoute) *hld up in last pair: urged along to make prog on outer over 2f out: tk 2nd jst over 1f out: drvn and surged into ld last 100yds* **1/1**[1]

-012 **2** 1 ½ **Qanan**[29] 3582 5-9-11 **82**................................ TedDurcan 6 91
(Chris Wall) *trckd ldr after 3f: led over 2f out: rdn and styd on fr over 1f out: hdd and outpcd last 100yds* **9/2**[3]

2010 **3** 5 **Epic Battle (IRE)**[12] 4184 4-10-0 **85**................................ KierenFallon 2 85
(George Margarson) *hld up in last pair: shkn up and no real prog over 2f out: kpt on to take 3rd ins fnl f: n.d* **6/1**

0411 **4** 6 **Dandy (GER)**[14] 4104 5-9-8 **79**................................(v) JimmyFortune 3 67
(Andrew Balding) *trckd ldr 3f: settled in 3rd after: chsd ldr over 2f out and tried to chal: lost 2nd and wknd qckly jst over 1f out* **7/2**[2]

00-4 **5** 15 **Robin Hood (IRE)**[17] 4030 6-8-10 **67**................................ JackMitchell 9 27
(Philip Mitchell) *pushed up to ld at decent pce: hdd over 2f out: immediately btn: wknd over 1f out: t.o* **16/1**

2m 7.51s (-2.99) **Going Correction** -0.225s/f (Firm)
**WFA** 3 from 4yo+ 10lb **5** Ran SP% **110.6**
Speed ratings (Par 105): **102,100,96,92,80**
CSF £5.92 TOTE £1.80: £1.90, £1.50; EX 5.10 Trifecta £15.20.
**Owner** Nurlan Bizakov **Bred** Hesmonds Stud Ltd **Trained** Newmarket, Suffolk

**FOCUS**
This was run at a fair gallop. The winner was unexposed.

## 4587 KINGSWAY CLAIMS MAIDEN STKS 1m 14y
**4:15** (4:16) (Class 5) 3-4-Y-O **£3,234** (£962; £481; £240) **Stalls** Low

Form RPR
0 **1** **Tercel (IRE)**[98] 1529 3-9-3 0................................ RyanMoore 5 83+
(Sir Michael Stoute) *t.k.h: hld up in 6th: prog on outer over 2f out: clsd to ld jst ins fnl f and pushed along firmly: rdn out to make sure nr fin* **9/2**[3]

-422 **2** nk **Hesbaan (IRE)**[17] 4022 3-9-3 74................................ DaneO'Neill 6 82
(Marcus Tregoning) *trckd ldr: shkn up to ld 2f out: rdn and hdd jst ins fnl f: tried to rally but hld last 75yds* **7/4**[2]

-362 **3** 3 ¼ **Conquerant**[7] 4368 3-9-3 84................................(v[1]) WilliamBuick 3 74
(Charlie Appleby) *trckd ldng pair: covered up bhd them 2f out: wnr sn wnt past: nt qckn over 1f out: styd on to take 3rd ins fnl f* **13/8**[1]

4 **4** 3 ½ **Esteban**[20] 3925 3-9-3 0................................ AdamKirby 1 66
(Marco Botti) *mde most to 2f out: nt qckn and sn btn* **6/1**

00- **5** 2 ¾ **Stilla Afton**[234] 8124 3-8-5 0................................ CharlotteJenner[(7)] 7 55
(Marcus Tregoning) *chsd ldng trio: pushed along over 3f out: rdn and steadily outpcd fr over 2f out* **66/1**

**6** 1 ¼ **Arquimedes (IRE)** 3-9-3 0................................ JimCrowley 8 57
(Charles Hills) *s.s: hld up in last pair: pushed along and outpcd fr 3f out: kpt on one pce* **20/1**

00- **7** 4 ½ **Steve Rogers (IRE)**[260] 7774 3-9-3 0................................ JackMitchell 2 46
(Roger Varian) *dwlt: hld up in last pair: lft bhd fr 3f out: pushed along after and no prog: nvr involved* **20/1**

0 **8** 14 **Praise N Glory**[17] 4029 3-8-12 0................................ LiamKeniry 4 9
(Linda Jewell) *wl in tch tl wknd qckly jst over 2f out: t.o* **100/1**

1m 41.48s (-1.82) **Going Correction** -0.225s/f (Firm) **8** Ran SP% **118.9**
Speed ratings (Par 103): **100,99,96,92,90 88,84,70**
CSF £13.08 TOTE £5.30: £1.60, £1.20, £1.10; EX 14.80 Trifecta £29.50.
**Owner** Ballymacoll Stud **Bred** Ballymacoll Stud Farm Ltd **Trained** Newmarket, Suffolk

**FOCUS**
An ordinary maiden for the track, not up to the race standard. Improvement from the winner.

## 4588 LUBRICATORS H'CAP 7f 16y
**4:50** (4:50) (Class 5) (0-75,75) 3-Y-O+ **£3,234** (£962; £481; £240) **Stalls** Low

Form RPR
3221 **1** **Global Leader (IRE)**[15] 4090 4-9-10 **71**................................ RyanMoore 1 84+
(Paul D'Arcy) *hld up and sn in last: prog to chse ldr over 1f out: cajoled along firmly to cl fnl f: narrow but decisive ld last 100yds* **8/11**[1]

200- **2** nk **Wordismybond**[238] 8087 5-9-2 **63**................................ SilvestreDeSousa 6 75
(Peter Makin) *t.k.h: led after 1f: drvn over 1f out: hdd last 100yds: styd on but a hld* **14/1**

5433 **3** 6 **My Son Max**[24] 3795 6-9-11 **72**................................ AdamKirby 2 68
(Michael Blake) *cl up: trckd ldr 1/2-way: drvn and nt qckn 2f out: lost 2nd over 1f out: wknd fnl f* **10/1**

1153 **4** 3 ½ **Eastern Dragon (IRE)**[14] 4121 4-9-7 **75**................................ MikeyEnnis[(7)] 3 62
(Michael Scudamore) *trckd ldrs: shkn up and no rspnse jst over 2f out: wknd over 1f out* **6/1**[3]

2123 **5** ¾ **Intomist (IRE)**[7] 4355 5-9-4 **72**................................(p) DanielCremin[(7)] 4 57
(Jim Boyle) *led 1f: chsd ldr to 1/2-way: shkn up over 2f out: sn wknd* **4/1**[2]

1m 27.2s (-2.30) **Going Correction** -0.225s/f (Firm) **5** Ran SP% **107.9**
Speed ratings (Par 103): **104,103,96,92,91**
CSF £11.19 TOTE £1.70: £1.20, £4.20; EX 9.20 Trifecta £37.90.
**Owner** Dr J S Kinnear **Bred** Thomas J Murphy **Trained** Newmarket, Suffolk

**FOCUS**
They appeared to go a fair enough gallop. There was little depth to this.
T/Plt: £13.80 to a £1 stake. Pool: £54,396.19 - 2,875.65 winning units T/Qpdt: £2.20 to a £1 stake. Pool: £4,269.74 - 1,405.35 winning units JN

# 4301 YARMOUTH (L-H)
### Thursday, July 24

**OFFICIAL GOING: Good to firm**
Bottom bend dolled out 1.5m and races on Round course increased by 7m.
Wind: Light breeze Weather: Hot and sunny; 24 degrees

## 4589 INJURED JOCKEYS SUPPORT JACK BERRY HOUSE MAIDEN AUCTION STKS 6f 3y
**2:10** (2:10) (Class 5) 2-Y-O **£2,911** (£866; £432; £216) **Stalls** Centre

Form RPR
2 **1** **Felix Leiter**[12] 4192 2-9-0 0................................ BenCurtis 3 74
(K R Burke) *plld hrd: mde all: rdn over 2f out: drvn out to hold sustained chal of rival ins fnl f* **15/8**[1]

533 **2** ¾ **Red Perdita (IRE)**[22] 3858 2-8-13 67................................ PatCosgrave 4 71
(George Baker) *dwlt: bhd tl rdn and effrt over 2f out: wnt 2nd 1f out: ev ch but drvn and edging lft after: hld fnl 75yds* **7/1**

5 **3** 4 ½ **Lady Maesmor**[10] 4260 2-8-6 0................................ JoeFanning 2 51
(Martyn Meade) *chsd ldrs: rdn over 2f out: outpcd over 1f out: wnt mod 3rd ins fnl f* **6/1**

0302 **4** ½ **York Express**[15] 4079 2-8-13 74................................ TomQueally 1 56
(Ismail Mohammed) *pressed wnr: rdn over 2f out: ev ch 1f out: sn wknd: lost 3rd cl home* **7/2**[2]

3 **5** 2 **Scent Of Power**[23] 3813 2-8-6 0................................ WilliamCarson 6 43
(Anthony Carson) *plld hrd: prom: rdn over 2f out: wknd over 1f out* **8/1**

**6** 4 ½ **Park Glen (IRE)** 2-8-6 0................................ StevieDonohoe 5 30
(Noel Quinlan) *t.k.h towards rr: rdn and btn wl over 1f out: sn edgd rt* **5/1**[3]

00 **7** 13 **Sky Steps (IRE)**[34] 3429 2-8-6 0................................ DannyBrock[(5)] 7
(Philip McBride) *s.s: a struggling in rr: t.o over 1f out: eased* **66/1**

1m 13.78s (-0.62) **Going Correction** -0.15s/f (Firm) **7** Ran SP% **113.1**
Speed ratings (Par 94): **98,97,91,90,87 81,64**
CSF £15.40 TOTE £2.60: £1.20, £5.00; EX 11.90 Trifecta £80.10.
**Owner** T Dykes & Mrs E Burke **Bred** Tibthorpe Stud **Trained** Middleham Moor, N Yorks

**FOCUS**
The bottom bend had been dolled out by 1.5m, adding 7m to all race distances of 1m1f and above. After the first, jockey Pat Cosgrave said the ground was "a bit slow on top if anything", while Joe Fanning reported "It's lovely ground." This looked a modest but competitive event and the winner showed a good attitude.

## 4590 GREENE KING FESTIVAL AT GREAT YARMOUTH RACECOURSE MAIDEN FILLIES' STKS 6f 3y
**2:40** (2:43) (Class 5) 3-4-Y-O **£2,911** (£866; £432; £216) **Stalls** Centre

Form RPR
0223 **1** **Miss Brazil (IRE)**[29] 3586 3-9-0 75................................ KieranO'Neill 3 76
(Richard Hannon) *led briefly: cl 2nd tl led again wl over 2f out: rdn over 1f out: hrd pressed fnl 100yds: all out* **10/11**[1]

4-2 **2** nse **Anna's Vision (IRE)**[26] 3729 3-9-0 0................................ TomQueally 7 75
(Jeremy Noseda) *pressed ldng pair: wnt 2nd 2f out: rdn and sustained chal fr over 1f out: carried hd high: ev ch fnl 100yds: jst hld* **2/1**[2]

**3** 3 **Capelita** 3-9-0 0................................ JoeFanning 6 65+
(Clive Brittain) *s.s: plld v hrd: effrt over 2f out: drvn and racing awkwardly and hanging lft fr over 1f out: nvr looked like getting in a blow* **7/1**[3]

**4** 3 **Apparatchika** 3-9-0 0................................ PatCosgrave 1 56+
(M F De Kock, South Africa) *s.s: bhd tl rdn and effrt over 2f out: racing awkwardly whn wl hld over 1f out* **10/1**

0050 **5** 1 **Ellingham (IRE)**[21] 3896 3-8-9 50................................ EoinWalsh[(5)] 5 52?
(Christine Dunnett) *t.k.h and sn led: rdn and hdd wl over 2f out: sn lost pl: btn wl over 1f out* **150/1**

0-0 **6** 3 ½ **Sybilicious**[5] 4446 3-8-7 0................................ AaronJones[(7)] 4 41
(Stuart Williams) *dwlt: a bhd: rdn and btn over 2f out* **66/1**

0 **7** 11 **Lucky Stars**[73] 2211 4-9-0 0................................ ShelleyBirkett[(5)] 2 7
(Gay Kelleway) *dwlt: nvr bttr than midfield: rdn and struggling bdly wl over 2f out: t.o* **100/1**

1m 13.73s (-0.67) **Going Correction** -0.15s/f (Firm)
**WFA** 3 from 4yo 5lb **7** Ran SP% **110.5**
Speed ratings (Par 100): **98,97,93,89,88 83,69**
CSF £2.67 TOTE £1.70: £1.10, £2.20; EX 3.20 Trifecta £9.70.
**Owner** Saeed Manana **Bred** M Morrissey **Trained** East Everleigh, Wilts

**FOCUS**
The betting suggested this was between just two of these, and they fought out the finish. The form is far from solid.

## 4591 INJURED JOCKEYS FUND 50TH ANNIVERSARY H'CAP 1m 3f 101y
**3:15** (3:15) (Class 5) (0-70,70) 3-Y-O+ **£2,587** (£770; £384; £192) **Stalls** Low

Form RPR
6-21 **1** **Leaderene**[8] 4321 3-8-8 **61** 6ex................................ JoeFanning 2 76+
(Mark Johnston) *sn led and set brisk gallop: pushed along 3f out: a gng best: clr 2f out: eased cl home* **4/6**[1]

1023 **2** 2 ¾ **Corn Maiden**[9] 4303 5-9-6 **62**................................ WilliamTwiston-Davies 4 67
(Lydia Pearce) *3rd tl last 6f out: rdn and outpcd over 4f out: rallied 2f out to go 2nd jst ins fnl f but nvr any threat to wnr* **14/1**

4341 **3** nk **The Ducking Stool**[15] 4093 7-9-6 **67**................................ ShelleyBirkett[(5)] 5 72
(Julia Feilden) *pressed wnr: rdn over 3f out: 3rd and outpcd over 2f out: hld after: ev ch of wl hld 2nd 1f out: no ex* **9/2**[3]

2310 **4** 6 **Loving Your Work**[34] 3419 3-9-3 **70**................................ PatCosgrave 6 65
(George Baker) *last tl 3rd 6f out: pushed along 5f out: drvn into 2nd over 2f out: hd high and nt striding out: lost two pls 1f out and fdd* **3/1**[2]

2m 27.74s (-0.96) **Going Correction** -0.05s/f (Good)
**WFA** 3 from 4yo+ 11lb **4** Ran SP% **109.8**
Speed ratings (Par 103): **101,99,98,94**
CSF £9.97 TOTE £1.50; EX 7.90 Trifecta £15.40.
**Owner** Miss K Rausing **Bred** Miss K Rausing **Trained** Middleham Moor, N Yorks

**FOCUS**
A weak handicap and the winner had an easy time in front.

## 4592 JME LTD H'CAP 1m 2f 21y
**3:50** (3:50) (Class 6) (0-60,60) 3-Y-O+ **£1,940** (£577; £288; £144) **Stalls** Low

Form RPR
056 **1** **Nifty Kier**[19] 3971 5-8-9 **46**................................ DannyBrock[(5)] 6 55
(Phil McEntee) *mde all: wnt 3 l clr 5f out: rdn over 1f out: a gamely holding chalr after* **10/1**

6553 **2** ¾ **Tunnel Tiger (IRE)**[7] 4340 3-8-8 **57**................................ CallumShepherd[(7)] 2 64
(William Knight) *t.k.h: wnt 2nd 7f out: rdn over 2f out: sustained chal thrght fnl f but nvr really looked getting up* **4/1**[3]

5333 **3** 8 **Bethan**[15] 4092 5-9-4 **55**................................(p) ShelleyBirkett[(5)] 9 47
(Julia Feilden) *trckd ldrs: pushed along and outpcd briefly over 4f out: wnt 3rd over 2f out: v one pce: wl hld whn rdr lost whip over 1f out* **11/4**[1]

2004 **4** 2 ½ **Sutton Sid**[4] 4473 4-10-0 **60**................................(b) JoeFanning 3 47
(Ann Stokell) *s.i.s: towards rr: rdn 4f out: 4th and struggling to get on terms over 2f out* **7/2**[2]

0050 **5** 2 **Mr Chocolate Drop (IRE)**[27] 3678 10-8-11 **46** oh1(t) RossAtkinson[(3)] 8 29
(Mandy Rowland) *plld hrd in rr: rdn over 3f out: sn wl btn* **25/1**

3645 **6** 5 **Loucal**[27] 3678 4-9-2 **53**................................ TobyAtkinson[(5)] 1 27
(Noel Quinlan) *prom: drvn over 4f out: sn lost pl: struggling bdly over 2f out* **7/2**[2]

0064 **7** *12* **Marphilly (IRE)**[9] 4304 3-8-4 **46** oh1..............................(v) JimmyQuinn 7
(John Best) *s.i.s: towards rr: shkn up over 4f out: immediately fnd nil: t.o and eased 1f out* **14/1**

2m 10.11s (-0.39) **Going Correction** -0.05s/f (Good)
**WFA** 3 from 4yo+ 10lb **7 Ran SP% 110.7**
Speed ratings (Par 101): **99,98,92,90,88 84,74**
CSF £46.25 CT £134.77 TOTE £9.10: £4.60, £1.70; EX 66.70 Trifecta £230.40.
**Owner** Mrs Rebecca McEntee **Bred** Mrs S H Jones **Trained** Newmarket, Suffolk

**FOCUS**
This is poor form whichever way you look at it. The first two were always to the fore.

## 4593 RACING WELFARE H'CAP 1m 1f
**4:25** (4:25) (Class 5) (0-75,75) 3-Y-O+ **£2,749** (£818; £408; £204) **Stalls** Low

Form RPR
2343 **1** **Ocean Applause**[3] 4498 4-9-9 **75**..............................(t) JoeDoyle(5) 4 84+
(John Ryan) *settled in 3rd pl: wnt 2nd 4f out: led over 2f out: pushed along to go clr ins fnl f: readily* **9/4**[1]

3126 **2** *1 ½* **Frontline Phantom (IRE)**[28] 3623 7-8-10 **64**............... PeterSword(7) 7 70
(K R Burke) *midfield: pushed along over 2f out: 5th whn n.m.r and swtchd rt over 1f out: styd on gamely to go 2nd ins fnl f but no match for wnr* **6/1**

0355 **3** *1 ½* **Sbraase**[27] 3667 3-9-5 **75**..............................(p) JohnFahy 5 76
(James Tate) *settled towards rr: effrt 2f out: rdn in 2nd and ev ch over 1f out: sn outpcd by wnr and lost 2nd ins fnl f* **7/2**[3]

1022 **4** *nk* **Hot Mustard**[15] 4090 4-9-0 **61**.............................. TomQueally 2 63
(Michael Bell) *t.k.h: trckd ldrs: rdn over 3f out: sn outpcd: rallied and sme prog ins fnl f* **10/3**[2]

0445 **5** *¾* **Jonnie Skull (IRE)**[7] 4342 8-8-12 **64**......................(vt) DannyBrock(5) 3 64
(Phil McEntee) *led: rdn over 3f out: hdd over 2f out: no ex fnl f* **16/1**

-345 **6** *½* **Guaracha**[20] 3923 3-9-2 **72**..............................(p) JoeFanning 6 70
(Clive Brittain) *2nd much of way: ev ch tl drvn and no ex over 1f out* **16/1**

3/3 **7** *½* **Don't Be**[28] 3628 4-9-9 **70**.............................. ChrisCatlin 8 68
(Sir Mark Prescott Bt) *hld up last: rdn 4f out: sn outpcd: n.d after* **8/1**

1m 55.31s (-0.49) **Going Correction** -0.05s/f (Good)
**WFA** 3 from 4yo+ 9lb **7 Ran SP% 113.2**
Speed ratings (Par 103): **100,98,97,97,94 93,93**
CSF £15.94 CT £44.88 TOTE £4.50: £2.30, £1.60; EX 18.70 Trifecta £71.10.
**Owner** W McLuskey **Bred** R G Levin **Trained** Newmarket, Suffolk

**FOCUS**
A few of these had a chance inside the 2f marker. The winner is rated to last year's best.

## 4594 SCOOTER RALLY AT GREAT YARMOUTH RACECOURSE H'CAP 6f 3y
**5:00** (5:00) (Class 4) (0-85,84) 3-Y-O+ **£4,690** (£1,395; £697; £348) **Stalls** Centre

Form RPR
5400 **1** **Decent Fella (IRE)**[43] 3096 8-8-7 **65**..............................(t) JoeFanning 5 74
(Ann Stokell) *towards rr: rdn to cl over 1f out: led ins fnl f: kpt on steadily* **20/1**

5665 **2** *¾* **Jungle Bay**[22] 3854 7-8-9 **74**..............................(b) LewisWalsh(7) 3 81
(Jane Chapple-Hyam) *t.k.h: sn cl up: rdn 1/2-way: led 2f out: hdd ins fnl f: nt qckn* **5/1**[3]

-245 **3** *1 ½* **Honeymoon Express (IRE)**[26] 3708 4-8-11 **74**.....(p) ShelleyBirkett(5) 1 77
(Julia Feilden) *led: rdn over 2f out: hdd 2f out: kpt on same pce* **7/1**

1-00 **4** *nk* **Kaab (IRE)**[26] 3704 3-9-5 **82**.............................. TomQueally 2 83
(Ed Dunlop) *pressed ldr: rdn 2f out: sn outpcd: nvr making any imp after* **10/1**

-303 **5** *nk* **Port Alfred**[17] 4027 4-9-12 **84**.............................. AhmedAjtebi 6 86
(Charlie Appleby) *plld hrd: chsd ldrs: drvn and racd awkwardly and outpcd 2f out: sme prog ins fnl f but nvr gng wl enough* **3/1**[1]

-226 **6** *2 ¼* **Tidentime (USA)**[27] 3646 5-9-11 **83**............... WilliamTwiston-Davies 4 79
(Mick Channon) *bhd: drvn and struggling over 2f out* **3/1**[1]

4662 **7** *9* **Swendab (IRE)**[6] 4399 6-8-12 **75**..............................(v) JoeDoyle(5) 7 47
(John O'Shea) *pressed ldr tl rdn and dropped out qckly over 2f out* **9/2**[2]

1m 12.55s (-1.85) **Going Correction** -0.15s/f (Firm)
**WFA** 3 from 4yo+ 5lb **7 Ran SP% 111.2**
Speed ratings (Par 105): **106,105,103,102,102 99,87**
CSF £108.78 TOTE £19.90: £11.10, £2.30; EX 174.60 Trifecta £419.00.
**Owner** Stephen Arnold **Bred** Michael Dalton **Trained** Lincoln, Lincolnshire

**FOCUS**
Just fair form, the winner back from the wilderness.

## 4595 MUSIC NIGHTS AT GREAT YARMOUTH RACECOURSE H'CAP 6f 3y
**5:35** (5:35) (Class 6) (0-60,60) 3-Y-O+ **£1,940** (£577; £288; £144) **Stalls** Centre

Form RPR
2121 **1** **Refuse Colette (IRE)**[9] 4306 5-9-10 **60** 6ex..................... PaoloSirigu 8 78+
(Mick Quinn) *hld up: clsd to ld wl over 2f out: rdn clr and in full command over 1f out: eased fnl 75yds* **1/2**[1]

2-50 **2** *2 ½* **High Tone**[23] 3820 4-8-13 **49**.............................. JoeFanning 6 56
(Dean Ivory) *prom: chsd wnr and rdn fr wl over 2f out: easily hld fr over 1f out* **9/1**[3]

0350 **3** *11* **Gung Ho Jack**[16] 4049 5-9-9 **59**.............................. WilliamCarson 9 31
(John Best) *struggling bdly in last and rdn early: passed fading rivals to go remote 3rd 1f out* **6/1**[2]

4450 **4** *4 ½* **Danzoe (IRE)**[16] 4049 7-9-4 **54**..................... WilliamTwiston-Davies 5 11
(Christine Dunnett) *drvn and struggling bdly after 2f: t.o* **12/1**

6000 **5** *1 ¼* **Loma Mor**[92] 1642 3-8-8 **52**.............................. BillyCray(3) 3 4
(Alan McCabe) *led tl rdn and hdd wl over 2f out: edging lft after and sn dropped rt out: t.o* **50/1**

-006 **6** *4* **Irish Boy (IRE)**[28] 3612 6-9-4 **59**..............................(tp) EoinWalsh(5) 2
(Christine Dunnett) *cl up tl rdn and fdd bdly 1/2-way: t.o* **25/1**

400 **7** *10* **Notgordonitsrodger (IRE)**[57] 2682 4-9-5 **60**............. DannyBrock(5) 1
(Phil McEntee) *s.s: sn dashed up to ldrs: ev ch 1/2-way: fdd bdly over 2f out: hopelessly t.o and eased* **10/1**

1m 12.41s (-1.99) **Going Correction** -0.15s/f (Firm)
**WFA** 3 from 4yo+ 5lb **7 Ran SP% 113.5**
Speed ratings (Par 101): **107,103,89,83,81 76,62**
CSF £5.91 CT £14.08 TOTE £1.30: £1.02, £3.20; EX 6.80 Trifecta £15.10.
**Owner** YNWA Partnership **Bred** Patrick O'Reilly **Trained** Newmarket, Suffolk

**FOCUS**
Some of these aren't going to be winning anytime soon, but the first two were clear and the winner showed form a bit better than the grade.

T/Plt: £597.30 to a £1 stake. Pool: £44,664.81 - 54.58 winning units T/Qpdt: £902.10 to a £1 stake. Pool: £2,877.26 - 2.36 winning units IM

4596 - 4597a (Foreign Racing) - See Raceform Interactive

# 4374 LEOPARDSTOWN (L-H)
Thursday, July 24

**OFFICIAL GOING: Good to firm**

## 4598a JOCKEY CLUB OF TURKEY SILVER FLASH STKS (GROUP 3) (FILLIES) 7f
**6:25** (6:26) 2-Y-O **£32,500** (£9,500; £4,500; £1,500)

RPR
**1** **Jack Naylor**[17] 4031 2-9-0.............................. FMBerry 8 102
(Mrs John Harrington, Ire) *dwlt: sn chsd ldrs: 5th 1/2-way: hdwy on outer fr 2f out to chse ldrs in 3rd ent fnl f where edgd sltly lft: kpt on wl to ld ins fnl 75yds: readily* **14/1**

**2** *1 ½* **Agnes Stewart (IRE)**[22] 3863 2-9-0.............................. BillyLee 2 98
(Edward Lynam, Ire) *settled towards rr: 7th 1/2-way: hdwy on outer fr under 2f out: rdn in 6th 1 1/2f out and r.o wl into nvr threatening 2nd fnl strides: nt trble wnr* **11/2**

**3** *hd* **Qualify (IRE)**[27] 3684 2-9-0.............................. SeamieHeffernan 1 97
(A P O'Brien, Ire) *trckd ldr tl led after 1f: 1 l clr 1/2-way: extended advantage into st: strly pressed wl ins fnl f and hdd ins fnl 75yds: no ex and denied 2nd fnl strides* **8/1**

**4** *hd* **Raydara (IRE)**[7] 4375 2-9-0.............................. ShaneFoley 3 97
(M Halford, Ire) *sn led tl hdd after 1f: 2nd 1/2-way: rdn over 1 1/2f out and sn no imp on ldr: dropped to 3rd u.p ins fnl 100yds: denied 3rd fnl strides* **3/1**[2]

**5** *2 ¾* **New Alliance (IRE)**[4] 4475 2-9-0.............................. KevinManning 5 89
(J S Bolger, Ire) *hld up in tch: 6th 1/2-way: sme hdwy far side fr 2f out into 5th: rdn and no ex ent fnl f: kpt on one pce* **14/1**

**6** *1 ¼* **As Good As Gold (IRE)**[4] 4476 2-9-0 **80**............... ColmO'Donoghue 6 86
(A P O'Brien, Ire) *settled in rr: last 1/2-way: rdn into st and clsd u.p into mod 7th over 1f out: kpt on one pce* **33/1**

**7** *nk* **Marsali (USA)**[43] 3126 2-9-0.............................. PatSmullen 4 85
(D K Weld, Ire) *settled bhd ldrs: 4th 1/2-way: rdn into st and wnt rt into 3rd briefly over 1 1/2f out: sn no ex whn sltly hmpd and wknd ins fnl f* **11/4**[1]

**8** *16* **Cocoon (IRE)**[27] 3684 2-9-1 ow1.............................. JosephO'Brien 7 53
(A P O'Brien, Ire) *chsd ldrs: 3rd 1/2-way: rdn 2f out and no imp on ldr whn sn sltly hmpd: wknd and eased 1 1/2f out* **4/1**[3]

1m 28.48s (-0.22) **Going Correction** -0.10s/f (Good) **8 Ran SP% 114.4**
Speed ratings: **97,95,95,94,91 90,89,71**
CSF £88.49 TOTE £6.10: £1.70, £1.40, £2.70; DF 53.30 Trifecta £377.00.
**Owner** Gerard Byrne **Bred** Oliver Costello **Trained** Moone, Co Kildare
■ Stewards' Enquiry : Pat Smullen two-day ban: careless riding (tbn)

**FOCUS**
An intriguing Group 3, even if it was without an apparent embryo star. The pace was fair.

## 4599a JAPANESE RACING AUTHORITY TYROS STKS (GROUP 3) 7f
**6:55** (6:57) 2-Y-O **£32,500** (£9,500; £4,500)

RPR
**1** **Gleneagles (IRE)**[25] 3762 2-9-3.............................. JosephO'Brien 1 105+
(A P O'Brien, Ire) *w.w in rr of trio: hdwy on outer fr 2f out: rdn to ld 1f out and kpt on wl u.p ins fnl f* **4/7**[1]

**2** *¾* **Tombelaine (USA)**[42] 3164 2-9-3.............................. PatSmullen 2 103
(D K Weld, Ire) *trckd ldr in 2nd: pushed along into st and clsd u.p to chal between horses over 1f out: kpt on wl in cl 2nd ins fnl f: a hld* **7/4**[2]

**3** *hd* **Convergence (IRE)**[48] 2969 2-9-3.............................. ColinKeane 3 102
(G M Lyons, Ire) *led: 1 l clr 1/2-way: rdn and strly pressed fr 2f out: hdd u.p 1f out: dropped to cl 3rd ins fnl f and kpt on wl towards fin: a hld* **10/1**[3]

1m 29.92s (1.22) **Going Correction** -0.10s/f (Good) **3 Ran SP% 109.1**
Speed ratings: **89,88,87**
CSF £1.92 TOTE £1.50; DF 1.90 Trifecta £2.00.
**Owner** Michael Tabor & Mrs John Magnier & Derrick Smith **Bred** You'resothrilling Syndicate **Trained** Cashel, Co Tipperary

**FOCUS**
A fascinating race with a potential Classic contender sent off favourite. Any race in which Colin Keane dictates the pace can be deemed a bit suspect form-wise, and it is testament to his tactical acumen that so little split the three at the finish. The fillies' Group 3 had a faster time.

4600 - 4602a (Foreign Racing) - See Raceform Interactive

# 4561 VICHY
Thursday, July 24

**OFFICIAL GOING: Turf: soft**

## 4603a PRIX DES REVES D'OR - JACQUES BOUCHARA (LISTED RACE) (2YO) (TURF) 5f
**1:20** (12:00) 2-Y-O **£22,916** (£9,166; £6,875; £4,583; £2,291)

RPR
**1** **Kenouska (FR)**[31] 2-8-10 0.............................. FabriceVeron 3 99
(H-A Pantall, France) **3/1**[2]

**2** *5* **Dikta Del Mar (SPA)**[47] 3027 2-8-10 0.............................. J-LMartinez 2 81
(T Martins, Spain) **58/10**[3]

**3** *nk* **Country Gorl (FR)**[47] 3027 2-8-10 0.............................. GregoryBenoist 4 80
(P Sogorb, France) **105/10**

**4** *1* **Pierre Precieuse (FR)**[20] 2-8-10 0.............................. SebastienMaillot 5 76
(E Caroux, France) **31/1**

**5** *nk* **Adulation (IRE)**[22] 3841 2-8-10 0.............................. GeraldMosse 8 75
(William Haggas) *broke wl and led: pushed along 2f out: rdn and hdd appr 1f out: one pce fnl f* **11/10**[1]

**6** *1 ½* **Loose Cannon (FR)**[14] 2-8-10 0..............................(b) MickaelBarzalona 6 70
(D Windrif, France) **73/10**

**7** *10* **Cisca Bere (FR)**[69] 2-8-10 0..............................(b[1]) FranckBlondel 1 34
(M Pimbonnet, France) **191/10**

**8** *1* **Dame Des Lys (FR)**[30] 2-8-10 0.............................. IoritzMendizabal 7 30
(J Heloury, France) **215/10**

1m 1.0s (61.00) **8 Ran SP% 120.6**
WIN (incl. 1 euro stake): 4.00. PLACES: 1.60, 2.10, 2.40. DF: 8.40. SF: 17.20.
**Owner** Guy Pariente **Bred** Guy Pariente Holding **Trained** France

# 4178 ASCOT (R-H)

Friday, July 25

**OFFICIAL GOING: Good to firm changing to good after race 2 (2:45) changing to good to soft after race 4 (3:55)**

Wind: Light, half behind Weather: Heavy rain for 50 minutes from start of meeting; becoming dry.

## 4604 JOHN GUEST EBF STALLIONS MAIDEN FILLIES' STKS (BOBIS RACE) 7f

**2:10** (2:11) (Class 4) 2-Y-O **£6,469** (£1,925; £962; £481) **Stalls** Centre

Form RPR

24 **1** **Malabar**[35] 3415 2-9-0 0 WilliamTwiston-Davies 2 89+
(Mick Channon) *lw: trckd ldrs: clsd to ld 2f out: edgd rt and jnd over 1f out: drvn and asserted last 150yds* **8/15**[1]

**2** *1 3/4* **Mistrusting (IRE)** 2-9-0 0 WilliamBuick 3 86+
(Charlie Appleby) *lengthy: str: lw: dwlt: hld up in rr: prog over 2f out: jnd wnr over 1f out: upsides ins fnl f: one pce last 150yds* **11/2**[2]

0 **3** *1* **Sister Of Mercy (IRE)**[22] 3888 2-9-0 0 DavidProbert 9 81+
(Roger Charlton) *leggy: athletic: in tch: shkn up and prog over 2f out: sn outpcd by ldrs: styd on to take 3rd ins fnl f: gng on at fin* **33/1**

**4** *1 3/4* **What Say You (IRE)** 2-9-0 0 MartinHarley 6 77+
(K R Burke) *unf: scope: pressed ldrs: shkn up over 2f out: chsd ldng pair over 1f out but nt qckn: one pce and lost 3rd ins fnl f* **8/1**[3]

3 **5** *5* **Jillanar (IRE)**[15] 4126 2-9-0 0 TomQueally 8 63
(George Margarson) *swtg: pressed ldr to over 2f out: steadily outpcd and fdd* **16/1**

**6** *6* **Tatiani** 2-9-0 0 SilvestreDeSousa 10 47
(Jose Santos) *leggy: a in rr: pushed along 1/2-way: bhd over 1f out* **50/1**

**7** *nk* **Royal Party** 2-9-0 0 LukeMorris 7 46
(William Knight) *unf: bit bkwd: slowly away: a in rr: urged along 1/2-way: no prog* **50/1**

**8** *1/2* **La Donacella** 2-9-0 0 JimmyFortune 5 45
(Daniel Kubler) *w'like: slowly away: a in rr: lft bhd fr over 2f out* **66/1**

54 **9** *hd* **Rosie Royale (IRE)**[16] 4075 2-9-0 0 OisinMurphy 1 44
(Roger Teal) *w'like: w ldrs tl wknd rapidly jst over 2f out* **33/1**

322 **10** *2* **Crystal Malt (IRE)**[22] 3888 2-9-0 0 RichardHughes 4 39
(Richard Hannon) *leggy: led to 2f out: wknd: wl btn 6th whn heavily eased fnl f* **11/2**[2]

1m 26.55s (-1.05) **Going Correction** -0.10s/f (Good) 2y crse rec **10** Ran SP% **124.3**
Speed ratings (Par 93): **102,100,98,96,91 84,83,83,83,80**
CSF £4.33 TOTE £1.50: £1.10, £1.90, £7.70; EX 5.10 Trifecta £122.20.
**Owner** Jon and Julia Aisbitt **Bred** Woodcote Stud Ltd **Trained** West Ilsley, Berks

**FOCUS**
Follwing a dry night, the going was given as good to firm, but rain began to fall just before the first race. That didn't stop the juvenile course record from being lowered by 0.21sec, however.

## 4605 MITIE TOTAL SECURITY MANAGEMENT NURSERY H'CAP (BOBIS RACE) 6f

**2:45** (2:48) (Class 4) 2-Y-O **£6,469** (£1,925; £962; £481) **Stalls** Centre

Form RPR

4332 **1** **Bronze Maquette (IRE)**[14] 4143 2-9-5 **83** JimmyFortune 4 87+
(Gary Moore) *trckd ldrs: prog against nr side rail to ld wl over 1f out: sn jnd: gd battle after: gained upper hand last 75yds* **3/1**[2]

545 **2** *nk* **Anastazia**[15] 4126 2-8-4 **68** LukeMorris 2 71+
(Paul D'Arcy) *lw: swtchd to join main gp after 1f: wl in tch: prog to chal over 1f out: gd battle after: jst hld last 75yds* **8/1**

0001 **3** *2 3/4* **Alpine Affair**[7] 4410 2-8-8 **72** 6ex (b) JamieSpencer 1 70+
(Brian Meehan) *awkward s: swtchd sharply to join main gp sn after: shkn up in last over 4f out: prog 2f out: chsd ldng pair jst over 1f out: clsng whn nowhere to go jst ins fnl f: nt rcvr* **15/8**[1]

630 **4** *5* **Dubai Breeze (IRE)**[15] 4126 2-8-11 **75** WilliamBuick 5 62+
(Clive Brittain) *trckd ldr: chalng whn stmbld and rdr lost an iron briefly 2f out: nt really rcvr: wknd fnl f* **5/1**[3]

2255 **5** *3/4* **Arlecchino's Leap**[14] 4143 2-8-6 **70** (v) DavidProbert 3 48
(Mark Usher) *racd alone in centre: on terms tl wknd over 1f out* **14/1**

2120 **6** *7* **Be Bold**[6] 4439 2-9-7 **85** (b) RichardHughes 6 48
(Richard Hannon) *lw: led to wl over 1f out: eased whn btn fnl f* **5/1**[3]

1m 16.7s (2.20) **Going Correction** +0.40s/f (Good) **6** Ran SP% **110.9**
Speed ratings (Par 96): **101,100,96,90,89 79**
CSF £25.19 TOTE £3.70: £1.80, £3.10; EX 26.10 Trifecta £77.30.
**Owner** R A Green **Bred** Rosetown Bloodstock Ltd **Trained** Lower Beeding, W Sussex

**FOCUS**
Run in heavy rain, this looked a competitive little nursery on paper. The winner has solid C&D form while the runner-up has been rated as improving.

## 4606 JOHN GUEST BROWN JACK STKS (H'CAP) 2m

**3:20** (3:20) (Class 2) (0-100,99) 3-Y-O+ **£19,407** (£5,775; £2,886; £1,443) **Stalls** Low

Form RPR

1131 **1** **Maid In Rio (IRE)**[7] 4392 3-8-5 **93** 6ex SilvestreDeSousa 2 106
(Mark Johnston) *mde all: set average pce: nudged along and drew clr over 2f out: extended advantage after: easily* **5/2**[1]

1161 **2** *9* **Hassle (IRE)**[14] 4144 5-9-7 **92** (p) AdamKirby 9 94
(Clive Cox) *swtg: hld up in last trio: prog on outer fr 3f out: rdn to go 2nd wl over 1f out but wnr already gone: clr of rest fnl f but no imp* **7/2**[2]

2221 **3** *3 1/2* **Kashgar**[27] 3698 5-8-12 **83** LukeMorris 6 83+
(Bernard Llewellyn) *hld up in midfield: urged along over 2f out: n.m.r sn after: drvn and kpt on fr over 1f out to take 3rd nr fin* **12/1**

-134 **4** *nk* **Elidor**[34] 3449 4-10-0 **99** RichardHughes 8 96
(Mick Channon) *lw: hld up in last trio: shkn up and prog over 2f out: chsd clr ldng pair jst over 1f out: jst pushed along and lost 3rd nr fin* **4/1**[3]

4115 **5** *1* **Spice Fair**[23] 3859 7-8-13 **84** SeanLevey 10 80
(Mark Usher) *trckd ldrs: rdn and outpcd over 2f out: one pce and steadily lft bhd* **25/1**

3362 **6** *2 1/2* **Entihaa**[29] 3622 6-8-10 **81** ow1 TomQueally 5 74
(Alan Swinbank) *hld up in last: rdn and struggling to stay in tch fr 7f out: detached over 2f out: styd on past wkng rivals fr over 1f out* **10/1**

3204 **7** *3/4* **Arty Campbell (IRE)**[35] 3424 4-8-4 **80** oh5 DanielMuscutt(5) 3 72
(Bernard Llewellyn) *t.k.h: trckd wnr: easily lft bhd over 2f out: lost 2nd and wknd wl over 1f out* **33/1**

30-0 **8** *1 1/2* **Boite (IRE)**[27] 3717 4-9-10 **95** RobertHavlin 4 86
(Peter Chapple-Hyam) *hld up towards rr: rdn and struggling wl over 2f out: sn no ch* **20/1**

0101 **9** *2 3/4* **Sir Frank Morgan (IRE)**[16] 4068 4-8-12 **83** WilliamBuick 7 70
(Mark Johnston) *trckd wnr: drvn 3f out: lost pl and wknd 2f out* **10/1**

0-50 **10** *hd* **Eshtiaal (USA)**[34] 3449 4-9-5 **90** (tp) JimmyFortune 1 77
(Brian Meehan) *lw: trckd ldrs: shkn up 4f out: tried to mount an effrt over 2f out: wknd over 1f out: eased* **12/1**

3m 35.05s (6.05) **Going Correction** +0.40s/f (Good)
**WFA** 3 from 4yo+ 17lb **10** Ran SP% **115.9**
Speed ratings (Par 109): **100,95,93,93,93 91,91,90,89,89**
CSF £10.68 CT £86.65 TOTE £2.90: £1.60, £1.90, £3.70; EX 11.30 Trifecta £57.70.
**Owner** The New Fairyhouse Partnership **Bred** Miss Susan Bates And Suzannah Dwyer **Trained** Middleham Moor, N Yorks

**FOCUS**
With the rain continuing to fall the going was changed to good prior to this race. The winner had an easy time of it up front.

## 4607 WOODCOTE STUD EBF STALLIONS VALIANT STKS (LISTED RACE) (F&M) 1m (R)

**3:55** (3:57) (Class 1) 3-Y-O+

**£22,684** (£8,600; £4,304; £2,144; £1,076; £540) **Stalls** Low

Form RPR

1253 **1** **Euro Charline**[35] 3418 3-8-7 109 AndreaAtzeni 1 110
(Marco Botti) *led at gd pce: jnd and shkn up jst over 2f out: narrowly hdd briefly wl over 1f out: drvn and grad asserted last 150yds* **1/1**[1]

3-06 **2** *1 1/2* **Kiyoshi**[14] 4165 3-8-7 105 JamieSpencer 6 107
(Charles Hills) *lw: trckd ldrs: prog to go 2nd 1/2-way: jnd wnr jst over 2f out: narrow ld briefly wl over 1f out: drvn fnl f: no ex last 150yds* **5/1**[3]

-100 **3** *1 3/4* **Zurigha (IRE)**[49] 2956 4-9-5 105 RichardHughes 3 109
(Richard Hannon) *hld up in tch: trckd ldng pair over 3f out: rdn over 2f out: nvr able to threaten but kpt on u.p fnl f* **14/1**

-300 **4** *3/4* **Gifted Girl (IRE)**[37] 3355 5-9-1 105 TomQueally 4 103
(Paul Cole) *pushed along early in last pair: shkn up and prog to take 4th over 2f out: nvr able to threaten ldngpair but kpt on fr over 1f out* **10/1**

6-24 **5** *6* **Veiled Intrigue**[20] 3983 3-8-7 101 DavidProbert 7 87
(Henry Candy) *trapped out wd: chsd ldrs: lost pl and struggling bdly over 3f out: no ch after: plugged on* **16/1**

1004 **6** *31* **Amulet**[17] 4060 4-9-1 89 JimmyFortune 5 18
(Eve Johnson Houghton) *reluctant to enter stalls: chsd wnr to 1/2-way: lost pl and struggling 3f out: sn wknd: t.o and eased* **20/1**

60-6 **7** *9* **Woodland Aria**[37] 3355 4-9-1 104 WilliamBuick 2
(John Gosden) *dwlt: mostly in last pair: rdn and brief effrt over 3f out: sn wknd: t.o and eased* **4/1**[2]

1m 41.88s (1.18) **Going Correction** +0.40s/f (Good)
**WFA** 3 from 4yo+ 8lb **7** Ran SP% **113.1**
Speed ratings (Par 111): **110,108,106,106,100 69,60**
CSF £6.20 TOTE £1.80: £1.50, £2.50; EX 5.80 Trifecta £43.70.
**Owner** Team Valor **Bred** Brian Liversage **Trained** Newmarket, Suffolk

**FOCUS**
This race looked up to standard, and the highest-rated filly in the line-up came out on top. The third has been rated back to her best.

## 4608 JOHN GUEST H'CAP 1m 2f

**4:30** (4:31) (Class 2) (0-100,98) 3-Y-O+

**£18,675** (£5,592; £2,796; £1,398; £699; £351) **Stalls** Low

Form RPR

10-0 **1** **Forgotten Hero (IRE)**[20] 3962 5-9-6 **90** JamieSpencer 5 99
(Charles Hills) *trckd ldng trio: clsd over 2f out: hd high but urged into ld jst over 1f out: styd on* **6/1**

3145 **2** *1 3/4* **Hit The Jackpot (IRE)**[13] 4212 5-9-12 **96** SilvestreDeSousa 9 102
(David O'Meara) *trckd ldr after 3f and t.k.h: rdn to ld wl over 1f out: drvn and hdd jst over 1f out: kpt on* **11/2**

0151 **3** *1* **Presburg (IRE)**[21] 3931 5-9-7 **91** OisinMurphy 3 95
(Joseph Tuite) *hld up in 5th: shkn up and sme prog on outer over 2f out: rdn and kpt on to take 3rd ins fnl f: no threat* **5/1**[3]

1622 **4** *1 1/2* **Kingscroft (IRE)**[8] 4349 6-8-5 **80** JacobButterfield(5) 6 81
(Michael Herrington) *trckd ldr 3f: styd cl up: tried to chal on inner over 2f out: nt qckn wl over 1f out: one pce after* **11/1**

2-42 **5** *2 1/2* **Zain Eagle**[13] 4214 4-9-13 **97** RichardHughes 8 94
(Robert Cowell) *swtg: led: stdd pce after 3f: tried to kick on 3f out: hdd wl over 1f out: grad wknd* **5/2**[1]

6001 **6** *2 3/4* **Charles Camoin (IRE)**[13] 4184 6-9-5 **89** JimmyFortune 7 80
(Sylvester Kirk) *s.i.s: hld up in last pair: rdn and no prog wl over 2f out: sn no ch* **3/1**[2]

3000 **7** *21* **Rebellious Guest**[35] 3416 5-9-12 **96** TomQueally 4 47
(George Margarson) *hld up in last pair: shkn up and no prog 3f out: wknd 2f out: t.o* **20/1**

2m 10.27s (2.87) **Going Correction** +0.40s/f (Good) **7** Ran SP% **113.0**
Speed ratings (Par 109): **104,102,101,100,98 96,79**
CSF £37.39 CT £175.77 TOTE £8.40: £3.40, £2.90; EX 36.50 Trifecta £198.10.
**Owner** Mrs Julie Martin And David R Martin **Bred** James Burns And A Moynan **Trained** Lambourn, Berks

**FOCUS**
The going was changed once again prior to this race, with the rain having eased it further to good to soft. This was a bit of a muddling affair.

## 4609 VARTAN RAVENSCROFT OCTOBER CLUB CHARITY H'CAP 5f

**5:00** (5:03) (Class 4) (0-85,85) 3-Y-O+ **£6,469** (£1,925; £962; £481) **Stalls** Centre

Form RPR

4131 **1** **Iffranesia (FR)**[21] 3920 4-9-7 **82** AdamBeschizza 1 93
(Robert Cowell) *trckd ldr: shkn up to ld 1f out: drvn out and styd on wl* **13/2**

3635 **2** *1* **Secret Missile**[16] 4078 4-9-3 **78** (b) MartinDwyer 4 85
(William Muir) *racd keenly: led at mod pce: wound it up fr 1/2-way: shkn up and hdd 1f out: nt qckn* **16/1**

6262 **3** *1* **Atlantis Crossing (IRE)**[7] 4406 5-8-5 **71** ow3 JacobButterfield(5) 7 74
(Jim Boyle) *lw: hld up in tch: rdn over 1f out: prog to go 3rd jst ins fnl f: styd on but unable to chal* **11/2**[3]

-665 **4** *3/4* **Gabbiano**[14] 4146 5-9-10 **85** DavidProbert 6 86
(Jeremy Gask) *swtg: hld up in rr: prog wl over 1f out: rdn to dispute 3rd jst ins fnl f: one pce after* **9/4**[1]

0500 **5** *shd* **Outer Space**[14] 4146 3-9-5 **84** WilliamTwiston-Davies 3 83
(Jamie Osborne) *s.s: r in last tl rdn and prog over 1f out: styd on wl fnl f: nrst fin* **10/1**

0512 **6** *4* **Bajan Bear**[7] 4421 6-8-12 **73** AdrianNicholls 8 59
(David Nicholls) *chsd ldrs: rdn 1/2-way: wnt 3rd over 1f out tl jst ins fnl f: wknd* **5/1**[2]

0000 **7** 2½ **Lupo D'Oro (IRE)**15 4128 5-8-12 **73**.......................... JamieSpencer 10 50
(John Best) *dwlt: sn chsd ldng pair: lost 3rd and wknd over 1f out* **14/1**
0103 **8** 2¼ **Bispham Green**7 4418 4-9-10 **85**.......................... SilvestreDeSousa 12 54
(David O'Meara) *lw: dwlt: a in rr: shkn up wl over 1f out: sn wknd* **7/1**
1500 **9** 6 **Go Nani Go**15 4128 8-9-10 **85**.......................... OisinMurphy 13 32
(Ed de Giles) *in tch: shkn up 2f out: sn wknd qckly* **12/1**
1m 1.69s (1.19) **Going Correction** +0.40s/f (Good)
**WFA** 3 from 4yo+ 4lb **9** Ran SP% **118.0**
Speed ratings (Par 105): **106,104,102,101,101 95,91,87,77**
CSF £104.89 CT £619.19 TOTE £6.20: £2.20, £5.60, £2.10; EX 99.60 Trifecta £415.80.
**Owner** Cyril Humphris **Bred** Cyril Humphris **Trained** Six Mile Bottom, Cambs
**FOCUS**
They went no pace and the first two filled those positions virtually throughout. Questionable form.
T/Plt: £225.40 to a £1 stake. Pool: £100245.26 - 324.54 winning tickets T/Qpdt: £91.70 to a £1 stake. Pool: £7534.67 - 60.80 winning tickets JN

## 4576 LINGFIELD (L-H)
Friday, July 25

**OFFICIAL GOING: Standard**
This fixture was switched from Chepstow.
Wind: virtually nil Weather: warm, light cloud

### 4610 INDUS CATERING MAIDEN AUCTION FILLIES STKS (BOBIS RACE) 6f 1y(P)
5:15 (5:17) (Class 5) 2-Y-0 £2,587 (£770; £384; £192) Stalls Low

Form RPR
42 **1** **Prize Exhibit**30 3583 2-8-10 0..........................1 FergusSweeney 6 89+
(Jamie Osborne) *chsd ldr: rdn and qcknd to ld over 1f out: awkward hd carriage and edging lft but drew wl clr fnl f: easily* **8/13**1
03 **2** 9 **Its Lady Mary**9 4320 2-8-13 0.......................... LukeMorris 2 65
(Paul Cole) *led: clr w wnr over 2f out: rdn and hdd over 1f out: sn outpcd and btn: wknd fnl f but stl clr 2nd* **4/1**2
020 **3** 4 **Artfilly (IRE)**11 4269 2-8-3 72.......................... CliffordLee(7) 8 50
(Ed Walker) *chsd ldrs: 3rd and outpcd u.p jst over 2f out: no ch after: plugged on* **5/1**3
06 **4** 1½ **White Vin Jan**11 4260 2-8-1 0.......................... MichaelKenneally(7) 3 44
(Michael Bell) *chsd ldrs: 4th and outpcd jst over 2f out: no ch after* **16/1**
0 **5** ½ **Freedom Rose (IRE)**16 4075 2-8-6 0.......................... RaulDaSilva 4 40
(Derek Shaw) *in tch in midfield: rdn over 3f out: outpcd and edgd lft over 2f out: no ch fnl 2f* **25/1**
**6** 2¼ **Onelastfling** 2-8-1 0.......................... CamHardie(5) 1 33
(Sylvester Kirk) *s.i.s: detached in last and niggled along: nvr on terms: plugged on past rivals ins fnl f* **20/1**
06 **7** 2 **Lady Ballantrae (IRE)**15 4117 2-8-10 0.......................... HayleyTurner 5 31
(Simon Dow) *s.i.s: a last trio: rdn and btn over 2f out: sn lost tch* **50/1**
**8** 1½ **Pudding (IRE)** 2-8-7 0.......................... AshleyMorgan(3) 7 27
(Lady Cecil) *s.i.s: a towards rr and stuck wd: rdn and btn over 2f out: sn lost tch* **8/1**
1m 12.03s (0.13) **Going Correction** 0.0s/f (Stan) **8** Ran SP% **126.1**
Speed ratings (Par 94): **99,87,81,79,79 76,73,71**
CSF £4.02 TOTE £1.60: £1.02, £1.20, £2.10; EX 3.80 Trifecta £11.30.
**Owner** M Buckley Mrs P Shanahan M V Magnier **Bred** Mrs R F Johnson Houghton **Trained** Upper Lambourn, Berks
**FOCUS**
A moderate fillies' maiden, but an impressive winner.

### 4611 SHOVELSTRODE RACING FILLIES H'CAP 7f 1y(P)
5:50 (5:50) (Class 5) (0-70,69) 3-Y-0+ £2,587 (£770; £384; £192) Stalls Low

Form RPR
3410 **1** **Medam**30 3575 5-9-8 63.......................... RobertWinston 5 71
(Shaun Harris) *mde all: rdn over 1f out: 2 l clr ins fnl f: idling fnl 100yds: jst hld on* **8/1**
0623 **2** shd **Invoke (IRE)**20 3966 3-9-7 69.......................... LukeMorris 6 74+
(Michael Bell) *t.k.h early: hld up in tch in midfield: rdn over 1f out: swtchd rt and hdwy ins fnl f: hrd drvn and r.o strly fnl 100yds: jst failed* **4/1**2
044 **3** ¾ **Marydale**25 3801 3-9-3 65.......................... FergusSweeney 8 68
(Henry Candy) *dwlt: sn bustled along and rcvrd to chse wnr: drvn over 2f out: styd on same pce fnl 2f* **3/1**1
-400 **4** ¾ **See No Ships**20 3966 3-8-2 50 oh2.......................... KieranO'Neill 9 51
(Mark Usher) *hld up in tch in midfield: rdn over 1f out: styd on wl ins fnl f: nvr enough pce to rch ldrs* **25/1**
6365 **5** hd **Djinni (IRE)**9 4329 3-9-0 67..........................(b) CamHardie(5) 4 67
(Richard Hannon) *wl in tch in midfield: rdn ent fnl 2f: drvn and r.o same pce fr over 1f out* **5/1**3
-452 **6** nse **Golly Miss Molly**32 3528 3-8-2 50 oh2.......................... HayleyTurner 2 50
(Jeremy Gask) *chsd ldrs: rdn 2f out: r.o same pce u.p fnl f* **12/1**
1240 **7** ½ **Tortoise**31 3545 3-8-2 55..........................(b) PhilipPrince(5) 3 54
(Richard Guest) *taken down early: rdn along early: hld up in tch in midfield: hdwy on inner over 1f out: no ex 1f out: wknd towards fin* **16/1**
6-00 **8** 1¾ **Queen Hermione (IRE)**43 3150 6-9-0 55..........................(v) RaulDaSilva 1 52
(Derek Shaw) *taken down early: hld up in tch in last pair: rdn over 2f out: no real imp and one pce fr over 1f out* **14/1**
-600 **9** nk **Footsieonehundred (IRE)**16 4074 3-8-3 58..........................(t) JackGilligan(7) 7 51
(Patrick Gilligan) *s.i.s: bhd and swtchd rt and wd: hdwy into midfield over 3f out: rdn and btn whn drifted lft over 1f out: sn wknd* **5/1**3
000 **10** 7 **Sterling Kate**25 3801 3-8-2 50 oh2.......................... NickyMackay 10 25
(Roger Ingram) *racd in last pair: rdn over 2f out: sn struggling: wknd over 1f out* **50/1**
1m 25.23s (0.43) **Going Correction** 0.0s/f (Stan)
**WFA** 3 from 5yo+ 7lb **10** Ran SP% **115.5**
Speed ratings (Par 103): **97,96,96,95,94 94,94,92,91,83**
CSF £39.64 CT £118.82 TOTE £7.80: £2.80, £1.60, £2.10; EX 30.70 Trifecta £100.60.
**Owner** Burton Agnes Bloodstock **Bred** Burton Agnes Stud Co Ltd **Trained** Carburton, Notts
**FOCUS**
An ordinary fillies' handicap that seemed wide open. It was run at an average pace and threw up a tight finish, but the form looks a bit shaky.

### 4612 PORTO RACING H'CAP 7f 1y(P)
6:20 (6:21) (Class 5) (0-75,74) 3-Y-0 £2,587 (£770; £384; £192) Stalls Low

Form RPR
0-00 **1** **Orion's Bow**15 4130 3-9-7 74..........................(bt1) NickyMackay 5 82
(John Gosden) *dwlt: hld up in tch in last pair: rdn over 2f out: drvn over 1f out: styd on wl and edgd lft ins fnl f: led fnl 50yds: gng away at fin* **9/2**3
4051 **2** 1 **Marmarus**11 4263 3-8-4 64.......................... JennyPowell(7) 1 69
(Clive Cox) *w ldr tl led after 1f: rdn and c towards centre wl over 1f out: kpt on gamely tl hdd and outpcd fnl 50yds* **7/4**1
3304 **3** nk **Spreadable (IRE)**17 4043 3-9-5 72.......................... LukeMorris 4 76
(Nick Littmoden) *dwlt and pushed along early: in tch in midfield: drvn and hdwy to chal over 1f out: ev ch tl outpcd fnl 50yds* **9/2**3
2202 **4** 1½ **Chantrea (IRE)**11 4263 3-9-4 74.......................... AshleyMorgan(3) 3 75
(Lady Cecil) *chsd ldng pair: wnt 2nd briefly 2f out: 3rd and rdn over 1f out: r.o same pce: stl pressing ldrs but hld whn hmpd wl ins fnl f* **7/2**2
3662 **5** 1½ **Persian Bolt (USA)**20 3970 3-9-3 70..........................(b) FergusSweeney 2 66
(Eve Johnson Houghton) *led tl faltered and hdd: w ldr after tl rdn and dropped to 4th 2f out: wknd 1f out* **10/1**
1350 **6** 2¾ **It's All A Game**10 4292 3-8-2 60..........................(b) PhilipPrince(5) 6 49
(Richard Guest) *dwlt: in tch in last pair: rdn over 3f out: wknd u.p over 1f out* **16/1**
1m 24.61s (-0.19) **Going Correction** 0.0s/f (Stan) **6** Ran SP% **109.9**
Speed ratings (Par 100): **101,99,99,97,96 92**
CSF £12.29 TOTE £5.70: £2.30, £2.80; EX 14.00 Trifecta £70.30.
**Owner** Cheveley Park Stud **Bred** Cheveley Park Stud Ltd **Trained** Newmarket, Suffolk
■ Stewards' Enquiry : Nicky Mackay one-day ban: careless riding (Aug 8)
**FOCUS**
Not the worst 3yo handicap for the class and they went a sound pace.

### 4613 LINGFIELD PARK SUPPORTS YOUNG EPILEPSY H'CAP 1m 1y(P)
6:50 (6:52) (Class 5) (0-70,70) 3-Y-0+ £2,587 (£770; £384; £192) Stalls Low

Form RPR
1-35 **1** **Bon Port**81 2027 3-8-5 62.......................... CharlieBennett(7) 7 70
(Hughie Morrison) *hld up in tch: rdn and hdwy to chse ldrs wl over 1f out: chal 1f out: led fnl 100yds: pushed along and r.o wl after* **20/1**
0314 **2** 1 **Comanchero (IRE)**8 4356 3-9-5 69.......................... OisinMurphy 9 75
(Andrew Balding) *hld up in tch: rdn and hdwy to chse ldrs over 1f out: ev ch 1f out: styd on same pce fnl 100yds* **6/1**2
6463 **3** hd **Fiftyshadesfreed (IRE)**27 3709 3-9-1 65..........................(p) PatCosgrave 1 71+
(George Baker) *dwlt and rdn along early: sn in midfield: short of room and shuffled bk 5f out: nt clr run and switching rt jst over 2f out: shifting lft and r.o strly ins fnl f* **7/4**1
3400 **4** nk **Boogangoo (IRE)**23 3850 3-9-6 70.......................... DavidProbert 3 75
(Grace Harris) *wl in tch in midfield: switching rt over 1f out: styd on wl u.p ins fnl f* **7/1**3
2-05 **5** 1 **Lacock**26 3760 3-9-4 68.......................... FergusSweeney 6 71
(Henry Candy) *sn pushed along to ld: rdn 2f out: drvn and hrd pressed over 1f out: hdd ins fnl f: wknd towards fin* **8/1**
-005 **6** 1¾ **Duke Of Grazeon (IRE)**7 4408 4-9-9 65..........................(b) RaulDaSilva 11 66
(Mrs Ilka Gansera-Leveque) *in tch in midfield: rdn and hdwy over 2f out: chsd ldr wl over 1f out tl ins fnl f: wknd fnl 100yds* **8/1**
0000 **7** ½ **Isabella Beeton**15 4120 3-8-11 64.......................... JemmaMarshall(3) 10 61
(Pat Phelan) *stdd and dropped in bhd after s: rdn and hdwy on outer over 1f out: styd on steadily ins fnl f: nvr trbld ldrs* **25/1**
5540 **8** 2¾ **Rouge Nuage (IRE)**13 4181 4-9-12 68.......................... LukeMorris 8 61
(Conrad Allen) *chsd ldrs: rdn over 2f out: no ex u.p over 1f out: wknd ins fnl f* **8/1**
010 **9** 1¾ **Wellesinthewater (IRE)**36 3402 4-9-8 64..........................(v) HayleyTurner 5 53
(Derek Shaw) *pressed ldr on inner: rdn and lost pl ent fnl 2f: wknd jst over 1f out* **33/1**
3 **10** 1½ **Polar Forest**56 2730 4-9-12 68..........................(e) RobertWinston 4 54
(Richard Guest) *chsd ldrs: rdn and losing pl whn hmpd jst over 2f out: bhd over 1f out* **8/1**
1m 37.14s (-1.06) **Going Correction** 0.0s/f (Stan)
**WFA** 3 from 4yo+ 8lb **10** Ran SP% **119.1**
Speed ratings (Par 103): **105,104,103,103,102 100,100,97,95,94**
CSF £135.74 CT £331.95 TOTE £29.00: £4.10, £2.10, £1.60; EX 100.70 Trifecta £645.10 Part won..
**Owner** A C Pickford & Partners **Bred** Llety Stud **Trained** East Ilsley, Berks
■ Stewards' Enquiry : Raul Da Silva three-day ban: careless riding (Aug 8-10)
**FOCUS**
A run-of-the-mill handicap.

### 4614 LINGFIELD PARK OWNERS GROUP H'CAP 5f 6y(P)
7:20 (7:22) (Class 5) (0-70,70) 3-Y-0+ £2,587 (£770; £384; £192) Stalls Low

Form RPR
-106 **1** **Clearing**30 3581 4-9-12 70.......................... PatCosgrave 1 81
(Jim Boyle) *mde all: shkn up and qcknd clr over 1f out: drvn 1f out: kpt on: eased nr fin* **1/1**1
0621 **2** 2 **Johnny Splash (IRE)**8 4337 5-8-13 57..........................(v) OisinMurphy 6 61
(Roger Teal) *chsd wnr thrght: rdn and outpcd over 1f out: kpt on again ins fnl f* **5/2**2
-060 **3** 2¼ **Senator Bong**173 451 4-9-8 66.......................... FergusSweeney 7 62
(Peter Grayson) *chsd ldrs: effrt in 3rd wl over 1f out: sn outpcd and wl hld fnl f* **7/1**3
5300 **4** 2 **Rosie Prospects**28 3679 3-8-3 51 oh1..........................(p) NickyMackay 5 39
(Roger Ingram) *chsd ldrs: drvn and struggling 2f out: 4th and wl hld fnl f* **25/1**
034- **5** 9 **Caesars Gift (IRE)**228 8222 3-9-0 62..........................(v) TomQueally 2 17
(Derek Shaw) *s.i.s: sn outpcd and a wl bhd: wnt 5th and eased towards fin* **8/1**
-000 **6** 1½ **My Time**19 4005 5-8-3 54 ow3.......................... JennyPowell(7) 4 5
(Michael Mullineaux) *awkward leaving stalls: nvr gng wl and nvr on terms w ldrs: eased ins fnl f* **20/1**
59.41s (0.61) **Going Correction** 0.0s/f (Stan)
**WFA** 3 from 4yo+ 4lb **6** Ran SP% **110.8**
Speed ratings (Par 103): **95,91,88,85,70 68**
CSF £3.54 CT £8.65 TOTE £1.50: £1.10, £2.00; EX 3.20 Trifecta £7.90.
**Owner** The Paddock Space Partnership **Bred** Paddock Space **Trained** Epsom, Surrey
**FOCUS**
Straightforward sprint form for the class with the well-backed winner making all.

### 4615 LINGFIELD EQUINE VETS H'CAP 1m 7f 169y(P)
7:50 (7:52) (Class 6) (0-60,60) 3-Y-0+ £1,940 (£577; £288; £144) Stalls Low

Form RPR
-312 **1** **Underwritten**5 4474 5-9-10 56.......................... RobertWinston 3 70
(Shaun Harris) *led: rdn over 2f out: c towards centre wl over 1f out: hrd pressed 1f out: drvn and hdd briefly ins fnl f: sn led again and styd on wl* **2/1**2
0051 **2** 1¼ **Windshield**11 4261 3-8-10 59.......................... LukeMorris 4 72
(Sir Mark Prescott Bt) *chsd wnr: rdn 3f out: swtchd lft wl over 1f out: hrd drvn and ev ch 1f out: led ins fnl f: sn hdd and no ex* **6/4**1

1653 **3** 1 1/4 **Chesil Beach**[11] 4261 3-8-11 60 DavidProbert 1 71
(Andrew Balding) *chsd ldrs: rdn and outpcd wl over 1f out: styd on again ins fnl f* **9/2**[3]

0004 **4** 7 **Oakbank (USA)**[9] 4321 3-8-0 49 oh4 KieranO'Neill 8 52
(Brett Johnson) *t.k.h: wl in tch in midfield: rdn and outpcd over 2f out: no ch w ldrs but kpt on to go 4th last stride* **50/1**

-002 **5** shd **Epsom Salts**[16] 4082 9-9-11 60 JemmaMarshall(3) 9 62
(Pat Phelan) *hld up in tch: hdwy to chse ldrs 1/2-way: 4th and outpcd u.p 2f out: wknd ins fnl f: lost 4th last stride* **14/1**

3-46 **6** 2 1/2 **Wasabi (IRE)**[25] 3780 5-9-3 49 OisinMurphy 2 48
(John Berry) *hld up in tch in midfield: rdn and outpcd over 2f out: wknd 2f out* **12/1**

3135 **7** 11 **Galiotto (IRE)**[17] 842 8-9-12 58 (v) FergusSweeney 6 44
(Noel Williams) *in tch in last trio: rdn 5f out: struggling over 3f out: bhd over 2f out* **25/1**

5005 **8** 5 **Rollin 'n Tumblin**[74] 2207 10-9-0 46 KierenFox 7 26
(Michael Attwater) *stdd s: t.k.h: hld up in tch in last trio: rdn over 2f out: sn btn: no ch and heavily eased ins fnl f* **33/1**

6000 **9** 3 3/4 **Storm Of Choice**[53] 2850 3-7-9 49 oh4 CamHardie(5) 5 25
(Michael Attwater) *in tch: rdn and lost pl 4f out: wl bhd 2f out: t.o* **66/1**

3m 26.82s (1.12) **Going Correction** 0.0s/f (Stan)
**WFA** 3 from 5yo+ 17lb **9** Ran SP% **116.1**
Speed ratings (Par 101): **97,96,95,92,92 90,85,82,81**
CSF £5.25 CT £10.84 TOTE £4.10: £1.70, £1.20, £1.10; EX 7.40 Trifecta £20.10.
**Owner** W A Robinson **Bred** W And R Barnett Ltd **Trained** Carburton, Notts

**FOCUS**
They went a routine gallop in this modest staying handicap and the market leaders, who dominated in the home straight, were always handy.

## 4616 BREATHE SPA AT LINGFIELD MARRIOTT H'CAP 1m 4f (P)
**8:20** (8:22) (Class 6) (0-65,70) 3-Y-O+ **£1,940** (£577; £288; £144) **Stalls** Low

Form RPR

0001 **1** **Treasure The Ridge (IRE)**[6] 4433 5-9-12 70 (b) JennyPowell(7) 3 85
(Andrew Reid) *hld up in tch in last trio: clsd to trck ldrs over 2f out: rdn to chal over 1f out: led ins fnl f: r.o wl: rdn out* **5/2**[2]

5022 **2** 1/2 **Sweetheart Abbey**[10] 4303 3-9-3 66 (p) TomQueally 2 80
(William Knight) *taken down early: hld up in rr: clsd and wl in tch 3f out: rdn and effrt to chal 1f out: ev ch tl no ex fnl 50yds* **3/1**[3]

0021 **3** 1 1/4 **Archduchess**[10] 4292 3-9-4 67 (b) SilvestreDeSousa 6 79
(Rae Guest) *led for 2f: keen whn hdd and dropped bk to 3rd: wnt 2nd again over 6f out: rdn to ld 2f out: drvn and hdd ins fnl f: wknd towards fin* **7/4**[1]

2104 **4** 8 **Passionate Affair (IRE)**[15] 4106 3-9-2 65 (tp) FergusSweeney 4 64
(Jamie Osborne) *hld up in tch in last trio: rdn and effrt on outer over 3f out: drvn and chsd ldrs over 2f out: wknd fnl f* **10/1**

0244 **5** 1 3/4 **Maid Of Tuscany (IRE)**[11] 4261 3-8-2 58 CharlotteJenner(7) 5 54
(Mark Usher) *t.k.h: in tch: hdwy to chse ldr 9f out tl over 6f out: styd chsng ldrs: rdn and effrt on inner wl over 1f out: wknd fnl f* **16/1**

5344 **6** 2 1/2 **Greek Islands (IRE)**[11] 4266 6-8-10 54 RhiainIngram(7) 7 46
(Edward Creighton) *t.k.h: dashed up to ld after 2f: settled bttr in front: hdd and rdn 2f out: wknd fnl f* **33/1**

302- **7** 56 **The Wallace Line (IRE)**[235] 8131 3-8-8 57 (p) OisinMurphy 1
(Tim Vaughan) *chsd ldr for 2f: nvr gng wl and niggled along: chsd ldrs tl dropped to rr u.p 4f out: t.o and eased fnl 2f* **16/1**

2m 31.07s (-1.93) **Going Correction** 0.0s/f (Stan)
**WFA** 3 from 5yo+ 12lb **7** Ran SP% **113.7**
Speed ratings (Par 101): **106,105,104,99,98 96,59**
CSF £10.35 TOTE £4.00: £1.90, £3.10; EX 14.40 Trifecta £29.50.
**Owner** A S Reid **Bred** S Coughlan **Trained** Mill Hill, London NW7

**FOCUS**
An ordinary 3yo handicap, run at a fair enough pace.
T/Plt: £6.30 to a £1 stake. Pool: £50,299.01 - 5754.66 winning tickets T/Qpdt: £3.20 to a £1 stake. Pool: £4,098.51 - 941.20 winning tickets SP

# 4442 NEWMARKET (R-H)
Friday, July 25

**OFFICIAL GOING: Good to firm (7.1)**
Far side track used with Stalls on Far side except 10f &12: Centre.
Wind: Light across Weather: Cloudy with sunny spells

## 4617 ADNAMS LONGSHORE VODKA FILLIES' H'CAP 1m 2f
**5:35** (5:35) (Class 5) (0-70,70) 3-Y-O+ **£3,881** (£1,155; £577; £288) **Stalls** Centre

Form RPR

055 **1** **Dubai Hadeia**[26] 3755 3-9-3 69 MartinLane 9 79
(Charlie Appleby) *hld up: hdwy over 4f out: rdn to ld over 2f out: hung rt wl over 1f out: styd on* **4/1**[2]

0342 **2** 1 1/2 **Thatchereen (IRE)**[29] 3614 3-8-11 68 LouisSteward(5) 7 77
(Michael Bell) *hld up: hdwy over 2f out: sn rdn: hmpd wl over 1f out: styd on to go 2nd nr fin* **11/4**[1]

60-3 **3** nk **Russian Royale**[30] 3585 4-9-7 70 MikeyEnnis(7) 6 76
(Stuart Kittow) *s.i.s: hdwy over 8f out: chsd ldr 6f out: rdn over 2f out: sn edgd rt: styd on same pce ins fnl f* **6/1**

0-06 **4** 4 1/2 **Sheer Poetry (IRE)**[28] 3652 3-8-2 54 (e) RoystonFfrench 2 52
(Mike Murphy) *prom: racd keenly: rdn over 2f out: no ex fnl f* **16/1**

-234 **5** 17 **Pink Lips**[28] 3682 6-9-6 62 (p) FrederikTylicki 8 28
(J R Jenkins) *hld up: shkn up over 3f out: wknd over 2f out: eased* **7/1**

652 **6** 2 1/4 **Cape Mystery**[43] 3142 3-9-2 68 JamesDoyle 3 29
(Peter Chapple-Hyam) *led: rdn and hdd over 2f out: wknd over 1f out* **9/2**[3]

0565 **7** 3/4 **Kheskianto (IRE)**[10] 4293 8-8-2 51 oh6 (t) PaulBooth(7) 1 11
(Michael Chapman) *chsd ldrs: rdn over 4f out: wknd over 2f out* **9/1**

0-14 **8** 5 **Panettone (IRE)**[17] 4045 5-9-9 68 RossAtkinson(3) 4 18
(Roger Varian) *sn pushed along to chse ldr: lost 2nd 6f out: rdn and wknd 3f out* **9/1**

0504 **9** 29 **Satin Waters**[48] 2997 3-8-0 52 oh4 (v[1]) JimmyQuinn 5
(Peter Charalambous) *prom tl rdn and wknd over 3f out* **33/1**

2m 8.15s (2.65) **Going Correction** +0.35s/f (Good)
**WFA** 3 from 4yo+ 10lb **9** Ran SP% **113.4**
Speed ratings (Par 100): **103,101,101,97,84 82,81,77,54**
CSF £15.10 CT £62.88 TOTE £5.10: £2.20, £1.40, £2.20; EX 17.30 Trifecta £168.20.
**Owner** Godolphin **Bred** D J And Mrs Deer **Trained** Newmarket, Suffolk
■ Stewards' Enquiry : Martin Lane two-day ban: careless riding (Aug 8-9)

**FOCUS**
Far side track used with stalls on far side except 1m2f and 1m4f: centre. Despite the presence of a Godolphin winner, this was an unremarkable race by Newmarket standards, with the first four finishing a long way clear. The third has been rated close to form.

## 4618 ADNAMS COPPER HOUSE GIN MEDIAN AUCTION MAIDEN STKS 6f
**6:10** (6:11) (Class 5) 2-Y-O **£3,881** (£1,155; £577; £288) **Stalls** High

Form RPR

2 **1** **Home Of The Brave (IRE)**[27] 3728 2-9-5 0 JamesDoyle 11 94+
(Hugo Palmer) *mde all: shkn up and hung rt ins fnl f: r.o wl: comf* **10/11**[1]

2 **2** 4 **Atletico (IRE)**[18] 4025 2-9-5 0 FrederikTylicki 2 80
(Roger Varian) *a.p: chsd wnr 1/2-way: rdn over 1f out: styd on same pce ins fnl f* **9/4**[2]

**3** 9 **State Of The Union (IRE)** 2-9-5 0 FrankieDettori 4 53+
(Richard Hannon) *trckd wnr 5f out tl 1/2-way: shkn up over 1f out: wknd fnl f* **12/1**[3]

**4** 4 1/2 **Astrophysics** 2-9-5 0 LiamKeniry 14 40+
(David Elsworth) *hld up: nt clr run: edgd rt and hmpd over 2f out: r.o ins fnl f: nvr nrr* **16/1**

65 **5** 1/2 **First Class Mail**[8] 4338 2-9-2 0 CharlesBishop(3) 1 38+
(Mick Channon) *s.i.s: hld up: hdwy over 2f out: rdn: edgd lft and wknd over 1f out* **33/1**

**6** 1 **Zamperini (IRE)** 2-9-5 0 ShaneKelly 5 39+
(Mike Murphy) *s.i.s: hmpd over 2f out: styd on towards fin: nvr nrr* **66/1**

00 **7** nk **Father Stone**[34] 3474 2-9-5 0 TedDurcan 13 34
(David Elsworth) *chsd ldrs tl rdn and wknd over 1f out* **50/1**

**8** 1 3/4 **Zigayani (IRE)** 2-9-5 0 RyanMoore 12 29
(Sir Michael Stoute) *hld up: effrt whn hmpd over 2f out: n.d* **12/1**[3]

**9** hd **Yorkshire (IRE)** 2-9-5 0 PaulHanagan 10 28
(Kevin Ryan) *hld up in tch: plld hrd: rdn and wknd over 1f out* **16/1**

00 **10** 8 **Ralph McTell**[87] 1859 2-8-12 0 JordanVaughan(7) 8
(Alan Coogan) *prom: pushed along over 3f out: edgd lft and hmpd over 2f out: sn wknd* **150/1**

**11** 1 3/4 **Wisewit** 2-9-5 0 SebSanders 7
(James Toller) *chsd ldrs: rdn 1/2-way: wknd over 1f out* **33/1**

**12** 68 **Avenue Des Champs** 2-9-0 0 NoelGarbutt(5) 6
(Jane Chapple-Hyam) *s.s: a bhd* **66/1**

00 **13** hd **Julia Stardust**[89] 1764 2-9-0 0 MartinLane 9
(Alan Coogan) *chsd ldrs tl wknd over 3f out: eased* **150/1**

1m 12.55s (0.05) **Going Correction** +0.10s/f (Good) **13** Ran SP% **122.5**
Speed ratings (Par 94): **103,97,85,79,79 77,77,74,74,64 61, ,**
CSF £2.90 TOTE £2.00: £1.10, £1.10, £3.30; EX 3.80 Trifecta £19.20.
**Owner** Flemington Bloodstock Partnership **Bred** Earl Ecurie Du Grand Chene **Trained** Newmarket, Suffolk

**FOCUS**
The first two home set a decent standard and they went a good gallop thanks to the all-the-way winner.

## 4619 WILD DUCK NORFOLK WOODLAND RETREAT NURSERY H'CAP (BOBIS RACE) 7f
**6:40** (6:40) (Class 4) 2-Y-O **£5,175** (£1,540; £769; £384) **Stalls** High

Form RPR

633 **1** **Guilty (IRE)**[17] 4044 2-9-1 72 JamesDoyle 3 77
(Richard Hannon) *trckd ldrs: rdn to ld over 1f out: r.o* **11/2**[2]

21 **2** 1 1/4 **Panda Spirit (USA)**[23] 3858 2-9-7 78 RyanMoore 2 80
(Sir Michael Stoute) *led: shkn up and hdd over 1f out: no ex towards fin* **4/7**[1]

5601 **3** 2 1/4 **Mr Shekells**[8] 4364 2-8-3 65 6ex DannyBrock(5) 4 61
(Philip McBride) *hld up: hdwy over 1f out: sn rdn: styd on same pce ins fnl f* **8/1**

01 **4** 1 1/2 **Scutum (IRE)**[22] 3875 2-9-7 78 FrankieDettori 1 70
(Brian Meehan) *hld up: hdwy over 2f out: rdn over 1f out: no ex ins fnl f* **13/2**[3]

3441 **5** 1 **No One Knows**[21] 3922 2-9-7 78 MartinLane 5 67
(B W Hills) *w ldr tl rdn over 2f out: no ex fnl f* **14/1**

642 **6** 11 **Ho Yam Lay**[22] 3894 2-7-10 58 NoelGarbutt(5) 6 17
(Nick Littmoden) *chsd ldrs: rdn over 2f out: wknd over 1f out* **50/1**

1m 28.0s (2.30) **Going Correction** +0.10s/f (Good) **6** Ran SP% **112.1**
Speed ratings (Par 96): **90,88,86,84,83 70**
CSF £9.10 TOTE £5.60: £2.10, £1.10; EX 10.10 Trifecta £37.90.
**Owner** Mrs J K Powell **Bred** John Doyle **Trained** East Everleigh, Wilts

**FOCUS**
This was a middling nursery handicap in which all the runners were in good form beforehand. The form looks straightforward.

## 4620 NGK SPARK PLUGS H'CAP 1m
**7:10** (7:10) (Class 5) (0-75,81) 3-Y-O+ **£3,881** (£1,155; £577; £288) **Stalls** High

Form RPR

4221 **1** **Specialty (IRE)**[28] 3678 4-9-6 67 AdamKirby 8 76
(Pam Sly) *racd far side: overall ldr: rdn and hung rt fr over 2f out: hdd over 1f out: rallied to ld nr fin: 1st of 4 in gp* **3/1**[2]

1341 **2** 1/2 **Athletic**[7] 4408 5-9-6 72 6ex (v) DannyBrock(5) 10 83+
(Andrew Reid) *hld up: racd far side: hdwy over 2f out: overall ldr over 1f out: sn rdn and hung rt: hdd nr fin: 2nd of 4 in gp* **2/1**[1]

306 **3** 2 1/2 **Emperatriz**[14] 4153 4-9-6 67 RobertHavlin 1 69
(John Holt) *racd centre: chsd ldrs: rdn to ld that gp over 1f out: styd on same pce ins fnl f: 1st of 6 in gp* **25/1**

3431 **4** hd **Ocean Applause**[1] 4593 4-9-13 81 6ex (t) JordonMcMurray(7) 3 83
(John Ryan) *s.i.s: racd centre: hld up: hdwy over 2f out: rdn over 1f out: styd on same pce ins fnl f: 2nd of 6 in gp* **6/1**

3612 **5** 3 3/4 **Botanist**[7] 4408 7-9-0 61 BenCurtis 9 54
(Shaun Harris) *racd far side: prom: chsd ldr 1/2-way tl rdn and edgd rt over 1f out: wknd ins fnl f: 3rd of 4 in gp* **8/1**

6015 **6** 6 **Tanawar (IRE)**[19] 4001 4-9-2 63 PaulHanagan 6 41
(Ruth Carr) *racd centre: prom: rdn over 1f out: wknd fnl f: 3rd of 6 in gp* **5/1**[3]

6401 **7** 3 1/4 **Meridius (IRE)**[45] 3088 4-9-5 66 (p) JamesDoyle 4 36
(Nick Littmoden) *racd centre: chsd ldr tl led that gp over 3f out: rdn and hdd over 1f out: wknd fnl f: 4th of 6 in gp* **14/1**

6000 **8** 6 **Berrahri (IRE)**[28] 3643 3-9-4 73 TedDurcan 7 27
(John Best) *racd far side: chsd ldr to 1/2-way: rdn over 2f out: wknd over 1f out: last of 4 in gp* **25/1**

34-0 **9** nk **Volcanic Jack (IRE)**[25] 3785 6-8-4 58 PaulBooth(7) 5 13
(Michael Chapman) *led centre gp tl rdn and hdd over 3f out: wknd over 2f out: 5th of 6 in gp* **50/1**

000- **10** ½ **West Leake Diman (IRE)**[260] 7792 5-10-0 **75**................ PaddyAspell 2 29
(Mrs Ilka Gansera-Leveque) *s.i.s: racd centre: hld up: rdn and wknd over 2f out: last of 6 in gp* **33/1**

1m 39.96s (-0.04) **Going Correction** +0.10s/f (Good)
**WFA** 3 from 4yo+ 8lb **10** Ran SP% **119.7**
Speed ratings (Par 103): **104,103,101,100,97 91,87,81,81,81**
CSF £9.35 CT £129.13 TOTE £3.90: £1.50, £1.30, £6.50; EX 7.20 Trifecta £247.30.

**Owner** Michael H Sly Dr T Davies Mrs Pam Sly **Bred** M H Sly, Dr T Davies & Mrs P Sly **Trained** Thorney, Cambs

**FOCUS**
The field in this competitive handicap split into two groups leaving the stalls, with the first two home both showing speed in the far-side quartet.

## 4621 MK SHIPPING MAIDEN STKS 1m 4f
**7:40** (7:40) (Class 5) 3-Y-O **£3,881** (£1,155; £577; £288) **Stalls** Centre

| Form | | | | RPR |
|---|---|---|---|---|
| 52 | **1** | | **Gwafa (IRE)**[22] 3891 3-9-5 0 ... MartinHarley 4 (Marco Botti) *awkward leaving stalls: hld up: hdwy to chse ldr over 3f out: led on bit over 2f out: clr over 1f out: easily* **5/6**[1] | 92 |
| 0- | **2** | *19* | **Almuhalab**[336] 5718 3-9-5 0 ... PaulHanagan 3 (Charles Hills) *led: racd freely: rdn and hdd over 2f out: wknd over 1f out* **8/1** | 62 |
| 00-6 | **3** | *9* | **Hoist The Colours (IRE)**[39] 3315 3-9-5 0 ... TedDurcan 1 (David Lanigan) *trckd ldrs: rdn over 4f out: wknd 2f out: eased* **10/3**[2] | 55 |
| 0 | **4** | *23* | **Undress (IRE)**[28] 3653 3-9-0 0 ... RyanMoore 2 (William Haggas) *trckd ldr: shkn up and hung lft 4f out: wknd 3f out: eased* **4/1**[3] | |

2m 34.86s (1.96) **Going Correction** +0.35s/f (Good) **4** Ran SP% **108.7**
Speed ratings (Par 100): **107,94,88,73**
CSF £7.64 TOTE £1.60; EX 6.90 Trifecta £10.40.

**Owner** Saleh Al Homaizi & Imad Al Sagar **Bred** Kenilworth House Stud **Trained** Newmarket, Suffolk

**FOCUS**
In theory, these were all horses of some quality, but it didn't work out like that and in the event there was no opposition to the easy winner. The pace was modest, and when it quickened 3f out all the runners apart from the winner were in trouble.

## 4622 32RED H'CAP 1m 4f
**8:10** (8:13) (Class 3) (0-90,90) 3-Y-O+ **£7,762** (£2,310; £1,154; £577) **Stalls** Centre

| Form | | | | RPR |
|---|---|---|---|---|
| 311 | **1** | | **Connecticut**[42] 3200 3-9-1 **89** ... AndreaAtzeni 6 (Luca Cumani) *a.p: chsd ldr over 1f out: shkn up to ld over 1f out: r.o wl: readily* **8/11**[1] | 102+ |
| 212 | **2** | *2 ½* | **Xinbama (IRE)**[14] 4160 5-9-5 **81** ... FrankieDettori 2 (B W Hills) *hld up: hdwy over 2f out: rdn to chse wnr over 1f out: styd on same pce ins fnl f* **8/1**[2] | 90 |
| 0610 | **3** | *7* | **Linguine (FR)**[14] 4173 4-10-0 **90** ... AdamKirby 1 (Paul Midgley) *led: qcknd over 3f out: rdn and hdd over 1f out: wknd ins fnl f* **14/1** | 88 |
| -32 | **4** | *1* | **Missed Call (IRE)**[41] 3218 4-9-9 **85** ... RyanMoore 4 (Martyn Meade) *chsd ldrs: rdn over 1f out: wknd ins fnl f* **9/1**[3] | 81 |
| 0/00 | **5** | *2 ¾* | **Buthelezi (USA)**[20] 3962 6-9-12 **88** ... BenCurtis 5 (Brian Ellison) *hld up: shkn up over 1f out: nvr on terms* **20/1** | 80 |
| 1200 | **6** | *1 ¼* | **Thecornishcowboy**[13] 4204 5-9-2 **85** ...(t) JordonMcMurray(7) 3 (John Ryan) *prom: rdn over 3f out: wknd over 1f out* **33/1** | 75 |
| -053 | **7** | *6* | **Buckland (IRE)**[23] 3860 6-9-7 **90** ... KieranShoemark(7) 8 (Charlie Fellowes) *hld up: hdwy over 3f out: wknd over 1f out* **40/1** | 70 |
| 0104 | **8** | *1 ¾* | **Lady Of Yue**[15] 4119 4-8-9 **71** oh1 ... JimmyQuinn 9 (Eugene Stanford) *chsd ldr tl rdn 3f out: wknd over 1f out* **40/1** | 48 |

2m 35.67s (2.77) **Going Correction** +0.35s/f (Good)
**WFA** 3 from 4yo+ 12lb **8** Ran SP% **98.3**
Speed ratings (Par 107): **104,102,97,97,95 94,90,89**
CSF £4.13 CT £19.59 TOTE £1.30: £1.10, £1.50, £2.20; EX 4.00 Trifecta £19.70.

**Owner** Sheikh Mohammed Obaid Al Maktoum **Bred** Whatton Manor Stud **Trained** Newmarket, Suffolk

■ Warrior Of Light was withdrawn. Rule 4 applies to all bets - deduction 20p in the pound.

**FOCUS**
This was a good handicap and it provided a winner to match.

## 4623 ALL NEW 32REDSPORT.COM H'CAP (LONDON MILE SERIES QUALIFIER) 1m
**8:45** (8:45) (Class 5) (0-75,75) 3-Y-O **£3,881** (£1,155; £577; £288) **Stalls** High

| Form | | | | RPR |
|---|---|---|---|---|
| 01- | **1** | | **Fray**[275] 7466 3-9-6 **74** ... JamesDoyle 5 (Roger Charlton) *trckd ldrs: shkn up to ld ins fnl f: r.o wl* **5/2**[1] | 86+ |
| 0420 | **2** | *3 ¼* | **Cornish Path**[16] 4074 3-9-7 **75** ... BenCurtis 7 (Henry Candy) *sn led: rdn over 1f out: hdd and unable qck ins fnl f* **11/4**[2] | 80 |
| -630 | **3** | *1 ½* | **Hala Hala (IRE)**[29] 3608 3-8-12 **73** ... AhmadAlSubousi(7) 3 (Michael Bell) *hld up: swtchd lft and hdwy over 1f out: rdn and hung lft fnl f: styd on same pce* **12/1** | 75 |
| 510 | **4** | *1 ½* | **Betty Bere (FR)**[20] 3978 3-9-1 **69** ... MartinHarley 4 (K R Burke) *chsd ldrs: rdn and ev ch over 1f out: no ex ins fnl f* **6/1**[3] | 67 |
| -503 | **5** | *1 ¾* | **Dynaglow (USA)**[29] 3615 3-9-7 **75** ... WilliamBuick 6 (John Gosden) *chsd ldr: rdn and ev ch over 1f out: wknd ins fnl f* **5/2**[1] | 69 |
| 40-0 | **6** | *1 ¼* | **Crown Pleasure (IRE)**[66] 2431 3-8-9 **68** ... DannyBrock(5) 1 (Willie Musson) *hld up: effrt over 2f out: wknd fnl f* **33/1** | 59 |
| 05-6 | **7** | *6* | **Vied (USA)**[43] 3158 3-8-6 **60** ...[1] AdamBeschizza 2 (Robert Cowell) *hld up: pushed along 1/2-way: wknd over 1f out* **40/1** | 37 |

1m 40.24s (0.24) **Going Correction** +0.10s/f (Good) **7** Ran SP% **111.2**
Speed ratings (Par 100): **102,98,97,95,94 92,86**
CSF £9.11 TOTE £2.70: £1.70, £1.80; EX 11.10 Trifecta £83.80.

**Owner** K Abdullah **Bred** Juddmonte Farms Ltd **Trained** Beckhampton, Wilts

**FOCUS**
This was a routine handicap, but the lightly raced winner is progressive.

T/Plt: £4.20 to a £1 stake. Pool: £63,011.36 - 10,915.86 winning units. T/Qpdt: £2.60 to a £1 stake. Pool: £4677.69 - 1308.21 winning units. CR

# [4294] THIRSK (L-H)
Friday, July 25

**OFFICIAL GOING: Good to firm (9.0)**
Wind: almost nil Weather: fine and sunny, very warm

## 4624 EBFSTALLIONS.COM MAIDEN STKS 5f
**2:00** (2:07) (Class 5) 2-Y-O **£3,234** (£962; £481; £240) **Stalls** High

| Form | | | | RPR |
|---|---|---|---|---|
| 620 | **1** | | **Grey Zeb (IRE)**[6] 4439 2-9-5 0 ... TomEaves 15 (Keith Dalgleish) *trckd ldrs on inner: led jst ins fnl f: sn clr* **4/1**[2] | 78+ |
| 0 | **2** | *5* | **Wiseton (IRE)**[20] 3947 2-9-5 0 ... GrahamGibbons 3 (David Barron) *led: clr over 2f out: hdd jst ins fnl f: kpt on same pce* **33/1** | 60+ |
| 4 | **3** | *1 ½* | **Flicka's Boy**[52] 2866 2-9-5 0 ... BarryMcHugh 2 (Tony Coyle) *mid-div: hdwy over 2f out: kpt on fnl f* **10/1** | 55 |
| | **4** | *shd* | **Colombia (IRE)** 2-9-0 0 ... PJMcDonald 13 (Ann Duffield) *chsd ldrs: upsides over 1f out: kpt on same pce* **16/1** | 49 |
| 0 | **5** | *1 ½* | **Magh Meall**[99] 1536 2-9-0 0 ... PaulQuinn 10 (David Nicholls) *mid-div: hdwy over 2f out: keeping on same pce whn nt clr run last 75yds* **100/1** | 44 |
| | **6** | *½* | **Mighty Zip (USA)** 2-9-5 0 ... HarryBentley 12 (Kevin Ryan) *trckd ldrs: drvn 2f out: sn upsides: edgd lft and fdd fnl f* **5/6**[1] | 47+ |
| | **7** | *nk* | **Star Cracker (IRE)** 2-9-5 0 ... PaulMulrennan 7 (Michael Dods) *s.i.s: in rr: stdy hdwy over 1f out: nt clr run and swtchd lft ins fnl f: styng on nicely at fin: will improve* **11/2**[3] | 49+ |
| | **8** | *hd* | **Normandy Knight** 2-9-5 0 ... TonyHamilton 5 (Richard Fahey) *s.i.s: edgd rt sn after s: in rr: kpt on fnl 2f: nvr a factor* **9/1** | 45 |
| 00 | **9** | *12* | **Ubedizzy (IRE)**[30] 3570 2-9-2 0 ...[1] JoeyHaynes(3) 8 (Noel Wilson) *chsd ldrs on outer: outpcd and hung lft over 2f out: sn bhd: eased clsng stages* **150/1** | |
| | **10** | *11* | **Tagula Nation (IRE)** 2-9-0 0 ... PhillipMakin 4 (Paul Midgley) *dwlt: in rr: wl bhd fnl 2f* **150/1** | |
| 0 | **P** | | **Double K**[6] 4450 2-9-5 0 ... DavidNolan 9 (Paul Midgley) *dwlt: in rr: eased over 3f out: sn p.u* **125/1** | |

1m 0.6s (1.00) **Going Correction** +0.10s/f (Good) **11** Ran SP% **121.0**
Speed ratings (Par 94): **96,88,85,85,83 82,81,81,62,44**
CSF £125.20 TOTE £4.40: £1.90, £4.40, £2.30; EX 80.10 Trifecta £576.80.
**Owner** Straightline Construction Ltd **Bred** Tally-Ho Stud **Trained** Carluke, S Lanarks

■ Alfie Bond and Belle Nellieb were withdrawn. Prices at time of withdrawal 125-1 and 33-1 respectively. Rule 4 does not apply.

**FOCUS**
A routine 2yo maiden to start proceedings and a race where previous experience proved the key.

## 4625 SKYBET SUPPORTING THE YORKSHIRE RACING SUMMER FESTIVAL NURSERY H'CAP (BOBIS RACE) 6f
**2:30** (2:35) (Class 3) 2-Y-O **£7,762** (£2,310; £1,154; £577) **Stalls** High

| Form | | | | RPR |
|---|---|---|---|---|
| 1234 | **1** | | **Vimy Ridge**[29] 3619 2-9-1 **85** ... JackGarritty(5) 5 (Richard Fahey) *in rr: swtchd lft and hdwy over 1f out: led last 150yds: sn clr* **11/2**[3] | 91 |
| 004 | **2** | *2* | **Johnny B Goode (IRE)**[29] 3613 2-8-9 **74** ... TonyHamilton 1 (Richard Fahey) *w ldr: led over 1f out: hdd jst ins fnl f: kpt on same pce* **12/1** | 74 |
| 3313 | **3** | *2 ¼* | **Perardua**[21] 3922 2-8-4 **72** ... GeorgeChaloner(3) 6 (Richard Fahey) *led: hdd over 1f out: one pce* **15/2** | 65 |
| 6102 | **4** | *1 ¼* | **Denzille Lane (IRE)**[13] 4218 2-9-7 **86** ... FrannyNorton 3 (Mark Johnston) *wnt lft s: chsd ldrs: one pce fnl 2f* **7/4**[1] | 76 |
| 1 | **5** | *¾* | **Punk Rocker (IRE)**[15] 4109 2-8-8 **73** ow1 ... PaulMulrennan 4 (Michael Dods) *hld up in mid-div: hdwy on ins 2f out: nt clr run: swtchd lft and one pce ins fnl f* **4/1**[2] | 60 |
| 3313 | **6** | *8* | **Miami Carousel (IRE)**[9] 4313 2-9-2 **81** ... PhillipMakin 2 (John Quinn) *chsd ldrs on outer: drvn over 2f out: lost pl over 1f out: bhd whn eased clsng stages* **4/1**[2] | 44 |

1m 12.82s (0.12) **Going Correction** +0.10s/f (Good) **6** Ran SP% **111.2**
Speed ratings (Par 98): **103,100,97,95,94 84**
CSF £60.77 TOTE £8.90: £3.70, £5.40; EX 79.10 Trifecta £256.90.
**Owner** P Timmins & A Rhodes Haulage **Bred** Mrs Sheila Oakes **Trained** Musley Bank, N Yorks

**FOCUS**
A decent little nursery with an impressive winner and a 1-2-3 for trainer Richard Fahey. The pace didn't look that quick.

## 4626 BRITISH STALLION STUDS EBF MAIDEN FILLIES' STKS (BOBIS RACE) 7f
**3:05** (3:08) (Class 4) 2-Y-O **£4,528** (£1,347; £673; £336) **Stalls** Low

| Form | | | | RPR |
|---|---|---|---|---|
| | **1** | | **Supreme Occasion (IRE)** 2-9-0 0 ... DanielTudhope 9 (David O'Meara) *mid-div: hdwy over 3f out: swtchd rt over 1f out: r.o to ld nr fin* **7/1** | 80+ |
| 54 | **2** | *½* | **Abbey Angel (IRE)**[40] 3267 2-9-0 0 ... TonyHamilton 7 (Richard Fahey) *w ldr: led over 2f out: hdd and no ex nr fin* **9/2**[3] | 79 |
| 56 | **3** | *hd* | **Hollie Point**[28] 3648 2-9-0 ... AhmedAjtebi 10 (Charlie Appleby) *trckd ldrs: chal 1f out: no ex clsng stages* **14/1** | 78 |
| 3 | **4** | *3* | **Encore L'Amour**[28] 3648 2-9-0 0 ... HarryBentley 4 (David Simcock) *led: hdd over 2f out: wknd fnl 75yds* **2/1**[1] | 70 |
| 4 | **5** | *5* | **Romance Story (IRE)**[23] 3858 2-8-11 0 ... MatthewLawson(3) 12 (Saeed bin Suroor) *in rr: hdwy over 3f out: kpt on fnl 2f* **3/1**[2] | 57 |
| 05 | **6** | *2 ½* | **Old Fashion**[23] 3858 2-9-0 0 ... PaulMulrennan 13 (Ed Dunlop) *s.i.s: hdwy over 2f out: keeping on at fin* **66/1** | 50 |
| 0 | **7** | *nk* | **Horsetracker**[22] 3881 2-8-9 0 ... GeorgeDowning(5) 5 (Ian Williams) *mid-div: effrt over 2f out: one pce* **100/1** | 49 |
| 5023 | **8** | *nk* | **Euthenia**[13] 4178 2-9-0 71 ... SamHitchcott 1 (Mick Channon) *trckd ldrs: drvn over 2f out: wknd over 1f out* **14/1** | 48 |
| 00 | **9** | *4* | **Pixey Punk**[18] 4018 2-9-0 0 ... DavidAllan 8 (Tim Easterby) *mid-div: effrt over 2f out: sn wknd* **100/1** | 38 |
| | **10** | *4* | **Heart Of Africa** 2-9-0 0 ... TomEaves 6 (Charlie Appleby) *s.i.s: in rr: detached last over 3f out: sme hdwy over 2f out: hung lft and sn wknd* **16/1** | 27 |
| | **11** | *9* | **The Other Lady** 2-9-0 0 ... GrahamGibbons 2 (Alan McCabe) *s.i.s: in rr: bhd fnl 2f: eased towards fin* **80/1** | |
| | **12** | *½* | **Accra Girl** 2-9-0 0 ... IanBrennan 3 (Marjorie Fife) *s.i.s: sn mid-div: drvn over 2f out: sn lost pl* **100/1** | |

30 **13** *7* **Dancing Moon (IRE)**[51] 2888 2-8-7 0........................ DanielCremin(7) 11 +
(Mick Channon) *t.k.h in mid-div on outer: sddle sn slipped: w ldrs and wd 4f out: lost pl 3f out: eased* **28/1**

1m 28.21s (1.01) **Going Correction** +0.10s/f (Good) **13** Ran SP% **117.4**
Speed ratings (Par 93): **98,97,97,93,88 85,84,84,79,75 65,64,56**
CSF £37.39 TOTE £7.70: £2.00, £2.00, £3.80; EX 45.10 Trifecta £686.10.
**Owner** Hambleton Racing Ltd XXXIII **Bred** Denis Noonan **Trained** Nawton, N Yorks

**FOCUS**
Despite the size of the field, this looked a modest and uncompetitive fillies' maiden and they didn't go that quick. The first four pulled clear.

## 4627 RACING UK ANYWHERE AVAILABLE NOW (S) H'CAP 7f
**3:40** (3:40) (Class 6) (0-65,65) 3-Y-O **£2,587** (£770; £384; £192) **Stalls** Low

Form RPR

3320 **1** **Street Boss (IRE)**[8] 4363 3-8-12 **56**........................(b[1]) GrahamGibbons 11 62
(Tim Easterby) *chsd ldrs: led over 2f out: drvn out* **7/2**[1]

4400 **2** *1 ½* **Marlismamma (FR)**[4] 4495 3-8-2 **49**........................(p) JulieBurke(3) 12 52
(David O'Meara) *chsd ldrs: 2nd over 1f out: kpt on same pce* **7/1**[3]

6P50 **3** *hd* **Jenny Sparks**[93] 1648 3-7-9 **46** oh1........................ PaddyPilley(7) 10 48
(Mick Channon) *in rr: effrt 3f out: chsng ldrs over 1f out: kpt on same pce ins fnl f* **33/1**

0000 **4** *½* **Skinny Latte**[16] 4069 3-8-2 **46** oh1........................(p) PatrickMathers 8 47
(Micky Hammond) *hld up towards rr: hdwy over 2f out: chsng ldrs over 1f out: one pce* **40/1**

0300 **5** *2* **Sandsman's Girl (IRE)**[20] 3972 3-8-9 **53**........................(b) DaleSwift 2 49
(James Given) *mid-div: effrt over 2f out: hung lft over 1f out: one pce* **8/1**

4550 **6** *1* **Henke (IRE)**[18] 4019 3-8-4 **53**........................(p) ShelleyBirkett(5) 4 46
(Nigel Tinkler) *hld up towards rr: hdwy over 2f out: nvr trbld ldrs* **7/2**[1]

00-0 **7** *1* **Red Tide (IRE)**[66] 2433 3-9-7 **65**........................(p) DanielTudhope 9 55
(Marjorie Fife) *led: hdd over 2f out: wknd fnl f* **5/1**[2]

0440 **8** *4* **Molly Ahoy**[17] 4049 3-8-10 **57**........................ BillyCray(3) 1 37
(Alan McCabe) *s.s: drvn over 3f out: lost pl over 1f out* **16/1**

5600 **9** *1 ½* **Lady Montenegro**[9] 4314 3-7-11 **48** ow2........................ RowanScott(7) 6 24
(Ann Duffield) *trckd ldrs: effrt over 3f out: lost pl over 1f out* **9/1**

0000 **10** *2 ¼* **Kaytom**[5] 4469 3-8-11 **55**........................ PaulPickard 3 25
(John Wainwright) *s.i.s: in rr: hdwy over 2f out: wknd over 1f out* **28/1**

0-04 **11** *7* **Sherry For Nanny (IRE)**[9] 4314 3-8-3 **47**........................(p) IanBrennan 5
(Marjorie Fife) *chsd ldrs: drvn over 3f out: lost pl over 2f out: bhd whn eased ins fnl f* **16/1**

1m 28.67s (1.47) **Going Correction** +0.10s/f (Good) **11** Ran SP% **115.3**
Speed ratings (Par 98): **95,93,93,92,90 89,87,83,81,79 71**
CSF £27.15 CT £547.21 TOTE £2.80: £1.10, £2.80, £13.30; EX 25.60 Trifecta £609.30.The winner was sold for 8,000gns to Lime Grove Racing.
**Owner** Habton Farms **Bred** Mark & Pippa Hackett **Trained** Great Habton, N Yorks

**FOCUS**
A moderate selling handicap in which only three of these had tasted success before.

## 4628 RACING UK ANDROID APP RACINGUK.COM/MOBILE H'CAP (BOBIS RACE) 7f
**4:15** (4:16) (Class 4) (0-80,77) 3-Y-O **£6,469** (£1,925; £962; £481) **Stalls** Low

Form RPR

0123 **1** **Mr McLaren**[4] 4496 3-9-6 **76**........................ DanielTudhope 6 85+
(David O'Meara) *trckd ldrs: effrt 3f out: led appr fnl f: kpt on wl* **10/3**[2]

4446 **2** *¾* **King Of Macedon (IRE)**[11] 4258 3-9-6 **76**........................(b) FrannyNorton 5 83
(Mark Johnston) *trckd ldr: t.k.h: narrow ld 2f out: carried hd high: hdd appr fnl f: kpt on same pce* **5/1**[3]

2352 **3** *3* **Heroique (IRE)**[4] 4496 3-9-3 **73**........................(e) DuranFentiman 7 72
(Tim Easterby) *led: hdd 2f out: kpt on one pce* **13/2**

1061 **4** *2* **Desert Ranger (IRE)**[22] 3895 3-9-6 **76**........................ DavidAllan 1 70
(James Tate) *strated slowly: hdwy 5f out: drvn to chse ldrs over 2f out: 4th over 1f out: no threat* **5/1**[3]

1243 **5** *1* **Miaplacidus (IRE)**[16] 4067 3-8-2 **63**........................ SammyJoBell(5) 4 54
(Richard Fahey) *chsd ldrs: drvn over 3f out: fdd appr fnl f* **11/1**

6322 **6** *hd* **Zain Zone (IRE)**[20] 3957 3-9-7 **77**........................ PJMcDonald 2 68
(Ruth Carr) *rrd: s.v.s: hdwy 5f out: chsng ldrs over 2f out: fdd over 1f out* **9/4**[1]

1m 27.43s (0.23) **Going Correction** +0.10s/f (Good) **6** Ran SP% **108.8**
Speed ratings (Par 102): **102,101,97,95,94 94**
CSF £18.64 TOTE £2.90: £1.90, £2.30; EX 17.80 Trifecta £89.90.
**Owner** Middleham Park Racing LXIV & Partner **Bred** R J Cornelius **Trained** Nawton, N Yorks

**FOCUS**
Not a bad 3yo handicap, though the pace wasn't that strong.

## 4629 INFINITY TYRES FILLIES' H'CAP 6f
**4:50** (4:50) (Class 5) (0-70,71) 3-Y-O+ **£3,234** (£962; £481; £240) **Stalls** High

Form RPR

5033 **1** **Burren View Lady (IRE)**[8] 4344 4-9-12 **69**........................(e) DavidAllan 5 78
(Tim Easterby) *chsd ldrs: led wl over 1f out: edgd rt: kpt on towards fin* **5/1**[2]

5131 **2** *¾* **Verus Delicia (IRE)**[10] 4282 5-9-9 **71** 6ex........................ EoinWalsh(5) 6 78
(Daniel Mark Loughnane) *hld up in mid-div: t.k.h: hdwy and nt clr run over 2f out: swtchd lft over 1f out: sn upsides: no ex clsng stages* **5/2**[1]

1650 **3** *4* **Foreign Rhythm (IRE)**[5] 4471 9-9-0 **62**........................ ShirleyTeasdale(5) 8 56
(Ron Barr) *dwlt: hld up in mid-div: hdwy on ins over 2f out: sn chsng ldrs: kpt on same pce to take 3rd last 50yds* **25/1**

060 **4** *1* **Dartrix**[58] 2677 5-9-9 **66**........................ PaulMulrennan 7 57
(Michael Dods) *hld up in rr: hdwy over 2f out: chsng ldrs over 1f out: kpt on one pce* **7/1**

5-40 **5** *nse* **Sakhee's Rose**[28] 3668 4-9-5 **62**........................(b) GrahamGibbons 2 53
(Ed McMahon) *dwlt: wnt rt after s: hdwy over 2f out: sn chsng ldrs: one pce over 1f out* **15/2**

-000 **6** *4* **Charlemagne Diva**[15] 4131 4-8-5 **53**........................(t) DuilioDaSilva(5) 9 31
(Richard Guest) *led: hdd wl over 1f out: sn wknd* **5/1**[2]

2604 **7** *5* **Amis Reunis**[3] 4511 5-8-9 **52**........................(p) PatrickMathers 4 14
(Alan Berry) *half-rrd s: sn chsng ldrs: lost pl over 1f out* **13/2**[3]

-605 **8** *11* **Dream Scenario**[10] 4294 4-9-8 **65**........................(v) DuranFentiman 1
(Mel Brittain) *chsd ldrs on outside: drvn over 2f out: lost pl over 1f out: bhd whn eased ins fnl f* **12/1**

6-04 **9** *2* **Jenny Twigg**[27] 3700 4-8-4 **50** oh5........................ NeilFarley(3) 3
(Chris Fairhurst) *t.k.h: trckd ldrs on outer: hung lft over 2f out: lost pl over 1f out: eased whn bhd clsng stages* **100/1**

1m 12.84s (0.14) **Going Correction** +0.10s/f (Good) **9** Ran SP% **112.0**
Speed ratings (Par 100): **103,102,96,95,95 89,83,68,65**
CSF £17.15 CT £276.86 TOTE £5.30: £1.90, £1.20, £6.50; EX 12.00 Trifecta £254.70.
**Owner** Habton Farms **Bred** L Mulryan **Trained** Great Habton, N Yorks

**FOCUS**
A modest fillies' sprint handicap.

## 4630 RACING EXCELLENCE "HANDS AND HEELS" APPRENTICE SERIES H'CAP 5f
**5:20** (5:23) (Class 5) (0-75,75) 3-Y-O+ **£3,234** (£962; £481; £240) **Stalls** High

Form RPR

0010 **1** **Captain Dunne (IRE)**[15] 4114 9-10-0 **75**........................ RachelRichardson 7 83
(Tim Easterby) *chsd ldrs: led over 3f out: drvn over 1f out: hld on wl clsng stages* **7/2**[3]

5565 **2** *½* **Jofranka**[21] 3920 4-9-10 **74**........................ PaulMcGiff(3) 4 80
(David Barron) *led over 1f: drvn and chal over 1f out: no ex clsng stages* **3/1**[2]

0220 **3** *2 ¾* **First In Command (IRE)**[11] 4267 9-9-6 **72**........................(t) LouiseDay(5) 1 68
(Daniel Mark Loughnane) *chsd ldrs on outside: outpcd and swtchd stands' side over 2f out: kpt on to take 3rd last 75yds* **6/1**

10-0 **4** *3* **Irish Girls Spirit (IRE)**[95] 1604 5-8-7 **57**........................ RowanScott(3) 2 42
(Paul Midgley) *chsd ldrs: drvn 2f out: wknd fnl f* **12/1**

0-05 **5** *5* **Dusty Storm (IRE)**[43] 3138 4-9-12 **73**........................ LewisWalsh 3 40
(Ed McMahon) *chsd ldrs: drvn 2f out: wknd appr fnl f* **9/4**[1]

(0.40) **Going Correction** +0.10s/f (Good) **5** Ran SP% **100.0**
Speed ratings (Par 103): **100,99,94,90,82**
CSF £11.51 TOTE £3.20: £1.50, £1.70; EX 11.30 Trifecta £42.60.
**Owner** Middleham Park Racing XV & Partners **Bred** Ballybrennan Stud Ltd **Trained** Great Habton, N Yorks
■ Perfect Blossom was withdrawn. Price at time of withdrawal 15-2. Rule 4 applies to all bets.
■ Stewards' Enquiry : Rowan Scott seven-day ban: used whip contrary to race rules (tbn)

**FOCUS**
A small field for this modest "hands and heels" apprentice handicap, reduced further when Perfect Blossom was withdrawn after bursting out of the stalls.
T/Plt: £782.60 to a £1 stake. Pool: £52338.17 - 48.82 winning tickets T/Qpdt: £19.40 to a £1 stake. Pool: £4580.84 - 174.00 winning tickets WG

# 4212 YORK (L-H)
### Friday, July 25

**OFFICIAL GOING: Good to firm (round 7.4, home straight: far side 7.3, centre 7.3, stands' side 7.1)**
Rail alignment around home bend to provide fresh ground reduced distances of races of 1m and further by 24yds.
Wind: Light across Weather: Fine and dry

## 4631 DRS TELEVISION APPRENTICE STKS (H'CAP) (BOBIS RACE) 1m
**6:00** (6:00) (Class 4) (0-80,78) 3-Y-O **£5,175** (£1,540; £769; £384) **Stalls** Low

Form RPR

2262 **1** **Joys Of Spring (IRE)**[11] 4271 3-9-7 **78**........................ GianlucaSanna(5) 7 89+
(Luca Cumani) *cl up: led 4f out: rdn clr 2f out: edgd lft ent fnl f: kpt on wl* **5/2**[1]

001 **2** *1 ¼* **Top Of The Glas (IRE)**[28] 3663 3-9-9 **78**........................ MeganCarberry(3) 8 84
(Brian Ellison) *hld up in rr: hdwy on inner 3f out: effrt 2f out: rdn to chse wnr ins fnl f: kpt on* **11/4**[2]

0165 **3** *1 ¼* **Spiceupyourlife (IRE)**[18] 4013 3-9-6 **75**........................ JackGarritty(3) 4 78
(Richard Fahey) *trckd ldrs: hdwy over 3f out: effrt 2f out: sn rdn: kpt on same pce fnl f* **12/1**

0560 **4** *1* **Xanthos**[35] 3428 3-9-5 **76**........................[1] BradleyBosley(5) 5 77
(Ed Walker) *dwlt and towards rr: hdwy on wd outside 3f out: rdn 2f out: kpt on u.p fnl f* **16/1**

0104 **5** *nse* **Sellingallthetime (IRE)**[25] 3797 3-9-1 **70**........................(p) AlistairRawlinson(3) 6 71
(Michael Appleby) *trckd ldrs: hdwy over 3f out: rdn along and outpcd over 2f out: sn drvn and kpt on same pce* **8/1**

4102 **6** *2* **Mayfield Boy**[7] 4419 3-9-10 **76**........................ KevinStott 3 74
(Mel Brittain) *led: hdd 4f out and sn pushed along: rdn 2f out: hld whn stmbld ins fnl f: eased after* **9/2**[3]

2211 **7** *2* **Green Zone (IRE)**[10] 4300 3-9-7 **73** 6ex........................(p) ShelleyBirkett 1 65
(Nigel Tinkler) *trckd ldrs on inner: pushed along wl over 2f out: rdn along wl over 1f out: sn btn* **7/1**

1m 37.68s (-1.32) **Going Correction** -0.10s/f (Good) **7** Ran SP% **110.6**
Speed ratings (Par 102): **102,100,99,98,98 96,94**
CSF £8.93 CT £61.00 TOTE £2.90: £1.80, £2.00; EX 7.30 Trifecta £73.90.
**Owner** Sheikh Mohammed Obaid Al Maktoum **Bred** Paul And Eilidh Hyland **Trained** Newmarket, Suffolk

**FOCUS**
A dry and warm run up to a meeting staged on quick ground. The rail alignment around the home bend on fresh ground reduced distances for races of one mile and over by 24yds. A few in-form types in a fair handicap. A steady gallop means the bare form isn't entirely reliable but the first two are ones to keep onside.

## 4632 TIM BRESNAN TESTIMONIAL SEASON STKS (H'CAP) 6f
**6:30** (6:31) (Class 4) (0-80,79) 4-Y-O+ **£5,175** (£1,540; £769; £384) **Stalls** Low

Form RPR

3046 **1** **Arctic Feeling (IRE)**[15] 4128 6-8-13 **76**........................ SammyJoBell(5) 15 89
(Richard Fahey) *trckd ldrs: hdwy 2f out: rdn to ld jst ins fnl f: kpt on* **9/1**[2]

2130 **2** *1 ¼* **Mon Brav**[27] 3702 7-9-5 **77**........................ DaleSwift 2 86
(Brian Ellison) *swtchd rt s: in rr: pushed along and hdwy 2f out: swtchd rt to stands' rail wl over 1f out: sn drvn: styd on strly fnl f* **8/1**[1]

1635 **3** *1 ½* **Meandmyshadow**[15] 4132 6-8-10 **68**........................ KierenFallon 6 72
(Alan Brown) *stall opened fractionally early: led 2f: cl up: rdn wl over 1f out and ev ch: drvn and kpt on same pce ins fnl f* **12/1**

4200 **4** *nk* **Eland Ally**[5] 4471 6-8-12 **70**........................ AndrewElliott 4 73
(Tom Tate) *sltly hmpd s and towards rr: hdwy wl over 1f out: sn rdn: kpt on fnl f: nrst fin* **8/1**[1]

6024 **5** *¾* **Ypres**[15] 4131 5-8-13 **74**........................ JoeyHaynes(3) 13 75
(Jason Ward) *trckd ldrs: hdwy over 2f out: rdn to chal over 1f out: led briefly ent fnl f: sn hdd and one pce* **20/1**

3134 **6** *nk* **Sunraider (IRE)**[17] 4061 7-9-7 **79**........................ GrahamLee 8 79
(Paul Midgley) *hld up towards rr: hdwy 2f out: rdn over 1f out: swtchd lft ins fnl f: kpt on: nrst fin* **8/1**[1]

-502 **7** *shd* **Bosham**[3] 4511 4-8-10 **68**........................ BarryMcHugh 12 67
(Michael Easterby) *prom: led over 2f out: rdn and hdd over 1f out: grad wknd* **9/1**[2]

2050 **8** *3* **Mayfield Girl (IRE)**[41] 3256 4-9-0 **72**........................ PJMcDonald 3 62
(Mel Brittain) *towards rr: hdwy on outer 1/2-way: trckd ldrs 2f out: rdn to ld over 1f out: hdd and drvn ent fnl f: wknd* **25/1**

6023 **9** *1* **Vincentti (IRE)**[7] 4406 4-9-6 **78**....................................... SteveDrowne 14 65
(Ronald Harris) *trckd ldrs: hdwy and cl up 1/2-way: rdn along wl over 1f out: ev ch tl drvn and wknd ent fnl f* **10/1**[3]

3034 **10** *hd* **Lucky Lodge**[7] 4421 4-7-12 **63**....................(b) RobertDodsworth[(7)] 1 49
(Mel Brittain) *racd alone on far rail: prom: rdn along wl over 2f out: sn outpcd* **14/1**

0040 **11** *2 ¾* **Majestic Dream (IRE)**[10] 4291 6-8-10 **68**............(b) GrahamGibbons 11 45
(Michael Easterby) *cl up: led after 2f: hdd wl over 2f out: sn rdn and grad wknd* **12/1**

6146 **12** *2* **Teetotal (IRE)**[29] 3599 4-8-13 **76**............................. ShelleyBirkett[(5)] 9 47
(Nigel Tinkler) *chsd ldrs: rdn along over 2f out: sn drvn and wknd* **12/1**

0010 **13** *1 ½* **Dream Ally (IRE)**[7] 4421 4-8-4 **67**..............................(p) JackGarritty[(5)] 7 33
(Micky Hammond) *dwlt: sn in tch: rdn along over 2f out: sn wknd* **25/1**

4500 **14** *6* **Trade Secret**[41] 3256 7-9-5 **77**......................................... TomEaves 5 24
(Mel Brittain) *in tch: rdn along wl over 2f out: sn wknd* **25/1**

4241 **15** *½* **Vallarta (IRE)**[13] 4206 4-9-4 **76**...................................(v) FrannyNorton 10 21
(Mick Channon) *chsd ldrs: rein broke wl over 2f out: sn lost pl and bhd fnl f* **8/1**[1]

1m 11.05s (-0.85) **Going Correction** 0.0s/f (Good) **15** Ran SP% **119.6**
Speed ratings (Par 105): **105,103,101,100,99 99,99,95,94,93 90,87,85,77,76**
CSF £73.98 CT £879.85 TOTE £10.00: £3.70, £3.30, £2.60; EX 87.90 Trifecta £722.20.
**Owner** Percy / Green Racing 2 **Bred** John McEnery **Trained** Musley Bank, N Yorks

**FOCUS**
Not many unexposed sorts but a fair and wide-open handicap. The gallop was sound and the majority of the runners bunched in the centre before fanning across the track in the closing stages.

## 4633 BATLEYS CASH AND CARRY MEDIAN AUCTION MAIDEN STKS (BOBIS RACE) 7f

**7:00** (7:07) (Class 4) 2-Y-O **£5,175** (£1,540; £769; £384) **Stalls** Low

Form RPR

**1** **Celestial Path (IRE)** 2-9-5 0....................................... ChrisCatlin 8 85+
(Sir Mark Prescott Bt) *dwlt and in rr: swtchd lft to outer and gd hdwy wl over 2f out: led wl over 1f out: rdn and kpt on strly fnl f* **16/1**

233 **2** *1 ¼* **Intiwin (IRE)**[11] 4253 2-9-2 0.................................. GeorgeChaloner[(3)] 2 82
(Richard Fahey) *slt ld: rdn and hdd over 1f out: sn drvn: kpt on* **4/1**[2]

5 **3** *2 ½* **Dominada (IRE)**[29] 3619 2-9-5 0.................................. PJMcDonald 10 75+
(Brian Ellison) *midfield: rdn along wl over 2f out: drvn over 1f out: styd on fnl f: nrst fin* **8/1**

**4** *nk* **Swift Approval (IRE)** 2-9-5 0....................................... GrahamLee 9 74+
(Kevin Ryan) *trckd ldrs: hdwy 3f out: effrt 2f out: sn rdn and kpt on same pce appr fnl f* **5/1**[3]

3 **5** *2 ¼* **Water Thief (USA)**[8] 4353 2-9-5 0................................ FrannyNorton 13 68
(Mark Johnston) *hld up towards rr: hdwy on outer 3f out: chsd ldrs 2f out: sn rdn and one pce* **11/1**

**6** *3* **Honeysuckle Lil (IRE)** 2-9-0 0......................................... DavidAllan 3 55+
(Tim Easterby) *towards rr: hdwy over 2f out: rdn along wl over 1f out: kpt on fnl f: nvr nr ldrs* **28/1**

6 **7** *1* **Arcano Gold (IRE)**[13] 4216 2-9-5 0.................................. DavidNolan 1 58
(Richard Fahey) *chsd ldrs on outer: rdn along and outpcd 3f out: drvn and edgd lft wl over 1f out: one pce* **6/1**

0 **8** *1 ½* **Thewaythewindblows (IRE)**[21] 3929 2-9-2 0......... ThomasBrown[(3)] 4 54
(Daniel Kubler) *cl up: rdn along 3f out: wknd 2f out* **20/1**

**9** *6* **Philba** 2-9-5 0........................................................... AndrewMullen 6 37
(Michael Appleby) *chsd ldrs: hdwy and prom 1/2-way: rdn and edgd lft wl over 2f out: sn drvn and wknd* **20/1**

5 **10** *6* **Kifaaya**[21] 3924 2-9-5 0.................................................. JoeFanning 11 21
(Mark Johnston) *s.i.s and in0 rr: sme hdwy towards outer whn n.m.r wl over 2f out: sn rdn along and nvr a factor* **11/4**[1]

**11** *¾* **Boldbob (IRE)** 2-9-5 0................................................ TomEaves 7 19
(Micky Hammond) *a in rr* **33/1**

**12** *3* **Hugie Boy (IRE)** 2-9-5 0............................................. DaleSwift 5 11
(Scott Dixon) *cl up: rdn along 1/2-way: wknd wl over 2f out* **40/1**

0 **13** *8* **Hoofithully**[118] 1161 2-8-12 0................................ DanielleMooney[(7)] 12
(Michael Easterby) *a in rr: outpcd and bhd fnl 3f* **50/1**

1m 25.41s (0.11) **Going Correction** 0.0s/f (Good) **13** Ran SP% **123.3**
Speed ratings (Par 96): **99,97,94,94,91 88,87,85,78,71 70,67,58**
CSF £75.92 TOTE £20.70: £5.60, £1.80, £2.90; EX 126.00 Trifecta £1334.50 Part won..
**Owner** G C Woodall **Bred** Miss Catherine Monaghan **Trained** Newmarket, Suffolk

**FOCUS**
A race that has often thrown up a decent type, the pick being subsequent Breeders Cup winner Vale Of York in 2009 and this year's winner looks a potentially smart prospect.

## 4634 BRITISH STALLION STUDS EBF LYRIC FILLIES' STKS (LISTED RACE) (F&M) 1m 2f 88y

**7:30** (7:32) (Class 1) 3-Y-O+

**£22,684** (£8,600; £4,304; £2,144; £1,076; £540) **Stalls** Low

Form RPR

-010 **1** **Tasaday (USA)**[118] 1181 4-9-7 113.................................... KierenFallon 2 104+
(Saeed bin Suroor) *hld up in tch: hdwy 3f out: swtchd rt and chal 1 1/2f out: led ent fnl f: drvn and kpt on wl towards fin* **6/4**[1]

3012 **2** *nk* **Raskova (USA)**[13] 4184 4-9-4 86......................................... JoeFanning 3 100
(William Jarvis) *hld up in rr: hdwy over 2f out: swtchd lft and rdn over 1f out: chal ins fnl f: sn drvn and ev ch tl no ex towards fin* **12/1**

-301 **3** *hd* **Regardez**[28] 3665 3-8-11 104........................................... JimCrowley 6 102
(Ralph Beckett) *cl up: led over 3f out: rdn along over 2f out: drvn and hdd ent fnl f: kpt on wl u.p tl no ex towards fin* **3/1**[2]

-102 **4** *2 ¼* **Wall Of Sound**[39] 3307 4-9-4 96......................... RichardKingscote 5 95
(Tom Dascombe) *led: pushed along and hdd over 3f out: cl up and rdn over 2f out: drvn over 1f out: wknd jst ins fnl f* **7/1**

64-2 **5** *7* **Regal Hawk**[28] 3665 4-9-4 93.......................................... GrahamLee 8 82
(James Tate) *t.k.h: trckd ldng pair: hdwy on outer over 3f out: rdn along 2f out: sn drvn and wknd* **14/1**

4212 **6** *shd* **Flycatcher (IRE)**[29] 3608 3-8-8 83.............................. GeorgeChaloner 4 82
(Richard Fahey) *towards rr: effrt and sme hdwy on outer 3f out: rdn along over 2f out: sn drvn and wknd* **18/1**

020 **7** *3 ¼* **Tahira (GER)**[13] 4214 4-9-4 98..................................... PhillipMakin 1 75
(John Quinn) *trckd ldng pair on inner: effrt over 3f out: sn rdn along: drvn 2f out and sn wknd* **6/1**[3]

2m 9.07s (-3.43) **Going Correction** -0.10s/f (Good)
**WFA** 3 from 4yo+ 10lb **7** Ran SP% **111.4**
Speed ratings (Par 108): **109,108,108,106,101 101,98**
CSF £19.85 TOTE £2.30: £1.60, £4.40; EX 16.80 Trifecta £43.00.
**Owner** Godolphin **Bred** Darley **Trained** Newmarket, Suffolk

**FOCUS**
A couple of smart sorts in the seventh running of this Listed event, but the gallop was only an ordinary one and the proximity of the 86-rated runner-up holds the form down.

## 4635 SKY BET SUPPORTING THE YORKSHIRE RACING FESTIVAL STKS (H'CAP) 1m

**8:00** (8:01) (Class 3) (0-90,89) 3-Y-O+ **£8,086** (£2,406; £1,202; £601) **Stalls** Low

Form RPR

4023 **1** **Anderiego (IRE)**[28] 3667 6-9-8 **81**...............................(v) DanielTudhope 6 90
(David O'Meara) *hld up towards rr: gd hdwy on outer over 2f out: rdn to ld over 1f out: clr ins fnl f: kpt on* **9/2**[2]

5350 **2** *1 ¾* **Green Howard**[21] 3917 6-9-8 **81**........................................ JasonHart 8 86
(Robin Bastiman) *hld up in rr: hdwy over 2f out: rdn to chse wnr ins fnl f: sn drvn and no imp* **16/1**

6625 **3** *nse* **Berlusca (IRE)**[6] 4453 5-9-5 **81**.................................... SamJames[(3)] 1 86
(David O'Meara) *dwlt and in rr: hdwy over 2f out: nt clr run and swtchd lft to outer wl over 1f out: sn rdn and styd on fnl f: nrst fin* **20/1**

1450 **4** *hd* **Barren Brook**[14] 4175 7-9-6 **79**.................................... BarryMcHugh 5 84
(Michael Easterby) *hld up towards rr: hdwy over 2f out: nt clr run and swtchd lft over 1f out: sn rdn and kpt on fnl f: nrst fin* **9/1**

3132 **5** *1 ½* **Bartack (IRE)**[13] 4212 4-9-7 **87**................................(v) JoshDoyle[(7)] 3 88
(David O'Meara) *dwlt: sn trcking ldrs on inner: hdwy 3f out: effrt and ev ch wl over 1f out: sn rdn and kpt on same pce* **10/3**[1]

4203 **6** *¾* **Red Charmer (IRE)**[8] 4359 4-9-2 **75**............................. PJMcDonald 12 74
(Ann Duffield) *trckd ldng pair: hdwy to ld 3f out: rdn along over 2f out: hdd and drvn over 1f out: kpt on same pce fnl f* **14/1**

3302 **7** *1 ¼* **Simply Shining (IRE)**[20] 3979 4-8-10 **74**................... SammyJoBell[(5)] 2 70
(Richard Fahey) *trckd ldr: pushed along 3f out: rdn over 2f out: drvn and grad wknd appr fnl f* **10/1**

0031 **8** *2 ½* **Shahdaroba (IRE)**[7] 4414 4-10-2 **89** 6ex.....................(v) GrahamLee 10 80
(Micky Hammond) *trckd ldrs: effrt over 3f out: sn rdn along and wknd 2f out* **16/1**

-413 **9** *½* **Big Storm Coming**[7] 4394 4-9-0 **73**.................................. DaleSwift 9 63
(Brian Ellison) *midfield: hdwy 3f out: chsd ldrs over 2f out: sn rdn and wknd wl over 1f out* **8/1**

00 **10** *2* **Equity Risk (USA)**[35] 3431 4-9-13 **86**........................... PhillipMakin 7 71
(Kevin Ryan) *chsd ldrs: rdn along 3f out: drvn over 2f out: sn wknd* **16/1**

-403 **11** *nse* **Tiger Twenty Two**[27] 3694 3-8-13 **83**.................. GeorgeChaloner[(3)] 11 66
(Richard Fahey) *led: rdn along and hdd 3f out: drvn over 2f out: grad wknd* **11/2**[3]

1m 36.64s (-2.36) **Going Correction** -0.10s/f (Good)
**WFA** 3 from 4yo+ 8lb **11** Ran SP% **115.9**
Speed ratings (Par 107): **107,105,105,105,103 102,101,99,98,96 96**
CSF £73.05 CT £1326.80 TOTE £5.20: £1.90, £4.90, £5.30; EX 93.30 Trifecta £1038.20 Part won..
**Owner** Ebor Racing Club **Bred** Gerrardstown House Stud **Trained** Nawton, N Yorks

**FOCUS**
A useful handicap featuring exposed sorts in which the gallop wasn't overly strong, but one in which the hold-up horses came to the fore in the closing stages.

## 4636 NOVUS STKS (H'CAP) (BOBIS RACE) 5f 89y

**8:30** (8:30) (Class 4) (0-85,84) 3-Y-O **£5,175** (£1,540; £769; £384) **Stalls** Low

Form RPR

3053 **1** **Meadway**[34] 3484 3-9-1 **78**........................................... PaulMulrennan 3 86
(Bryan Smart) *qckly away: mde all: rdn over 1f out: drvn ins fnl f: hld on wl towards fin* **11/1**

0304 **2** *½* **Tweety Pie (IRE)**[5] 4469 3-8-0 **66**................................. NeilFarley[(3)] 11 72
(Declan Carroll) *towards rr: hdwy 2f out: swtchd rt to stands' rail and rdn to chal whn n.m.r last 100yds: kpt on wl towards fin* **14/1**

6213 **3** *nk* **Dutch Breeze**[18] 4021 3-9-1 **78**...............................(p) DavidAllan 12 83
(Tim Easterby) *trckd ldrs: hdwy on outer 2f out: rdn to chal ent fnl f: sn drvn and ev ch tl edgd rt and no ex last 100yds* **10/3**[1]

5401 **4** *1* **Lexington Abbey**[15] 4133 3-9-2 **84**............................ ShaneGray[(5)] 8 86
(Kevin Ryan) *a.p: rdn 2f out and ev ch tl drvn and one pce ins fnl f* **11/2**[3]

6163 **5** *1 ¾* **Mr Dandy Man (IRE)**[9] 4328 3-8-13 **76**.....................(p) SteveDrowne 1 71
(Ronald Harris) *prom: rdn 2f out: drvn and one pce ent fnl f* **16/1**

-431 **6** *½* **Innocently (IRE)**[9] 4315 3-9-4 **81** 6ex......................... DanielTudhope 10 74
(David O'Meara) *prom: rdn along 2f out: sn drvn and one pce appr fnl f* **4/1**[2]

4054 **7** *1 ¼* **Oriental Relation (IRE)**[15] 4133 3-9-1 **78**......................... GrahamLee 2 67
(James Given) *towards rr: hdwy on outer 2f out: sn rdn and no imp appr fnl f* **16/1**

4303 **8** *2 ¾* **Fuel Injection**[9] 4315 3-7-11 **65** oh1.........................(p) JackGarritty[(5)] 6 44
(Paul Midgley) *midfield: rdn along over 2f out: sn outpcd* **25/1**

4103 **9** *5* **Tinsill**[17] 4059 3-8-4 **67**.............................................(p) AndrewMullen 5 28
(Nigel Tinkler) *towards rr: rdn along 1/2-way: sn outpcd* **25/1**

2250 **10** *1* **Taquka (IRE)**[15] 4133 3-9-2 **79**.................................(b[1]) JimCrowley 7 36
(Ralph Beckett) *chsd ldrs: rdn along 1/2-way: drvn 2f out and sn wknd* **14/1**

-400 **11** *2 ½* **Canyari (IRE)**[27] 3704 3-9-2 **82**............................(v[1]) GeorgeChaloner[(3)] 9 30
(Richard Fahey) *chsd ldrs: rdn along bef 1/2-way: sn outpcd and bhd* **8/1**

044 **12** *9* **National Service (USA)**[9] 4328 3-8-7 **70**.................(t) GrahamGibbons 4
(Stuart Williams) *dwlt: a in rr* **8/1**

1m 4.1s **Going Correction** 0.0s/f (Good) **12** Ran SP% **121.8**
Speed ratings (Par 102): **100,99,98,97,94 93,91,87,79,77 73,59**
CSF £159.82 CT £638.32 TOTE £12.90: £3.30, £3.00, £2.10; EX 189.10 Trifecta £768.20 Part won..
**Owner** Michael Moses & Terry Moses **Bred** Bond Thoroughbred Corporation **Trained** Hambleton, N Yorks

**FOCUS**
A couple of recent winners in a useful handicap. The pace was sound throughout and this form should prove reliable.

T/Jkpt: £12,100.90 to a £1 stake. Pool: £17,043.57 - 1 winning units. T/Plt: £232.80 to a £1 stake. Pool: £102,949.85 - 322.70 winning units. T/Qpdt: £48.30 to a £1 stake. Pool: £8,227.56 - 125.80 winning units. JR

4637 - 4643a (Foreign Racing) - See Raceform Interactive

# 4603 VICHY

Friday, July 25

**OFFICIAL GOING: Turf: good to soft**

## 4644a PRIX JACQUES DE BREMOND (LISTED RACE) (4YO+) (TURF) 1m

3:20 (3:20) 4-Y-0+ **£21,666** (£8,666; £6,500; £4,333; £2,166)

RPR

1 **Roero (FR)**34 5-8-11 0 Francois-XavierBertras 8 109
(F Rohaut, France) **4/1**2

2 1/2 **Boomshackerlacker (IRE)**35 3416 4-8-11 0 (p) MickaelBarzalona 6 108
(George Baker) *t.k.h: hld up bhd hd of main gp as ldr wnt clr: shkn up and tk clsr order over 2f out: rdn to chal over 1f out: edgd rt then carried further rt by eventual wnr fnl 150yds: hdd 50yds out: no ex* **73/10**

3 1 1/2 **Spoil The Fun (FR)**40 3291 5-9-2 0 JulienAuge 5 109
(C Ferland, France) **11/10**1

4 1 1/4 **Pump Pump Boy (FR)**41 6-8-11 0 Pierre-CharlesBoudot 2 102
(J-P Gauvin, France) **49/10**3

5 1 1/2 **Brooklyn Bowl (USA)**32 4-8-11 0 (p) FranckBlondel 7 98
(F Rohaut, France) **43/5**

6 snk **Zayade (FR)**25 3811 5-8-8 0 AlexandreRoussel 4 95
(J Boisnard, France) **14/1**

7 6 1/2 **Far Afield**205 4043 4-8-11 0 AntoineHamelin 9 83
(J-P Gallorini, France) **35/1**

8 2 1/2 **Fanoos**27 3731 5-8-8 0 (p) FabriceVeron 1 74
(Mme G Rarick, France) **213/10**

1m 43.7s (103.70) **8 Ran SP% 121.0**
WIN (incl. 1 euro stake): 5.00. PLACES: 1.50, 1.80, 1.20. DF: 20.10. SF: 36.10.
**Owner** Scea Haras De Saint Pair & F Rohaut **Bred** 6 C Racing Ltd **Trained** Sauvagnon, France

# 4604 ASCOT (R-H)

Saturday, July 26

**OFFICIAL GOING: Good (good to soft in places on round course; straight course: stands' side 8.7, centre 8.7, far side 8.4, round 7.2)**
Wind: Light, across Weather: Fine, very warm

## 4645 TITANIC BELFAST WINKFIELD STKS (LISTED RACE) 7f

1:30 (1:31) (Class 1) 2-Y-0

**£17,013** (£6,450; £3,228; £1,608; £807; £405) **Stalls** Centre

Form RPR

25 1 **Kodi Bear (IRE)**39 3318 2-9-3 0 AdamKirby 4 106+
(Clive Cox) *lw: t.k.h: trckd clr ldr: clsd to ld jst over 2f out: drvn and styd on wl fnl f* **2/1**1

31 2 1 1/2 **Disegno (IRE)**31 3578 2-9-3 0 RyanMoore 1 102
(Sir Michael Stoute) *str: hld up bhd ldrs: shkn up over 2f out: prog over 1f out: drvn to chse wnr fnl f: styd on but no imp* **7/1**3

13 3 3/4 **Muhaarar**16 4123 2-9-3 0 PaulHanagan 6 100
(Charles Hills) *lw: trckd ldng pair: clsd to chal jst over 2f out: sn rdn and nt qckn: wnt 2nd briefly over 1f out: kpt on same pce fnl f* **2/1**1

412 4 1 3/4 **Diaz (IRE)**23 3883 2-9-3 92 JoeFanning 2 95
(Mark Johnston) *wnt rt s: led and clr: rdn and hdd jst over 2f out: lost 2nd over 1f out: steadily fdd* **11/1**

1 5 3/4 **Peacock**56 2776 2-9-3 0 RichardHughes 5 93
(Richard Hannon) *athletic: hld up in last pair: pushed along over 2f out: sn outpcd: rdn over 1f out: kpt on but no ch* **9/2**2

310 6 8 **Ustinov**16 4123 2-9-3 88 JimmyFortune 3 71
(Brian Meehan) *t.k.h: hld up in last pair: brief effrt over 2f out: wknd over 1f out* **33/1**

1m 27.78s (0.18) **Going Correction** +0.05s/f (Good) **6 Ran SP% 108.6**
Speed ratings (Par 102): **100,98,97,95,94 85**
CSF £15.65 TOTE £2.80: £1.50, £3.00; EX 11.90 Trifecta £28.50.
**Owner** Mrs Olive Shaw **Bred** Mrs M Fox **Trained** Lambourn, Berks

**FOCUS**
A hot, drying day following Friday's thunderstorm. Joe Fanning felt the ground on the straight course was still on the easy side of good, but both Ryan Moore and Paul Hanagan described it as good. Group 1 scorers Toronado and Raven's Pass are the best previous winners of this Listed event, which was first run in 2006. This looked an up-to-scratch edition. They went a fair pace, racing down the centre of the track. The third has been rated close to his July Stakes form.

## 4646 PRINCESS MARGARET JUDDMONTE STKS (GROUP 3) (FILLIES) 6f

2:05 (2:05) (Class 1) 2-Y-0

**£28,355** (£10,750; £5,380; £2,680; £1,345; £675) **Stalls** Centre

Form RPR

251 1 **Osaila (IRE)**9 4348 2-9-0 93 FrankieDettori 1 101+
(Richard Hannon) *hld up in last: stdy prog jst over 2f out: rdn to ld jst over 1f out: hung lft ins fnl f: pushed out and readily asserted last 100yds* **7/4**1

502 2 2 **Pastoral Girl**22 3933 2-9-0 82 JoeFanning 6 95
(James Given) *hld up towards rr: prog to chse ldr 2f out: rdn to chal jst over 1f out: pressing wnr whn carried lft ins fnl f: one pce after* **33/1**

1 3 1 1/2 **Explosive Lady (IRE)**21 3975 2-9-0 0 MartinHarley 7 91
(K R Burke) *w'like: hld up in last pair: gng wl enough whn nt clr run 2f out and swtchd rt: drvn and styd on fr over 1f out to take 3rd last strides* **10/1**

1 4 nk **Muraaqaba**29 3671 2-9-0 0 PaulHanagan 5 91
(Mark Johnston) *w'like: str: chsd ldng pair: pushed along bef 1/2-way: struggling to hold pl 2f out: rallied over 1f out: trying to chal but hld whn impeded ins fnl f: fdd* **15/8**2

412 5 nk **Rosie's Premiere (IRE)**15 4159 2-9-0 82 RichardHughes 2 89
(Dean Ivory) *leggy: led: drvn and tried to go clr 2f out: hdd and fdd jst over 1f out* **12/1**

23 6 2 **Tongue Twista**15 4164 2-9-0 0 J-PGuillambert 3 83
(Nick Littmoden) *trckd ldrs: tried to cl 2f out: nt qckn over 1f out: steadily wknd* **25/1**

151 7 2 3/4 **Accipiter**15 4150 2-9-0 88 AshleyMorgan 8 76
(Chris Wall) *str: mounted on crse: hld up towards rr: rdn and no rspnse wl over 1f out: no ch after* **12/1**

01 8 9 **Goldcrest**23 3888 2-9-0 0 DaneO'Neill 4 49
(Henry Candy) *athletic: lw: chsd ldr to 2f out: wknd rapidly* **7/1**3

1m 14.33s (-0.17) **Going Correction** +0.05s/f (Good) **8 Ran SP% 114.9**
Speed ratings (Par 101): **103,100,98,97,97 94,91,79**
CSF £57.71 TOTE £2.80: £1.10, £7.70, £2.10; EX 72.90 Trifecta £695.20.
**Owner** Al Shaqab Racing **Bred** Mennetou Syndicate **Trained** East Everleigh, Wilts

**FOCUS**
The Princess Margaret hasn't been won by an absolute top-class filly since Russian Rhythm in 2002, though Scarlet Runner (2006), Visit (2007), Lady Of The Desert (2009) and Maureen (2012) did all go on to win again in Group company. They appeared to go a fair pace in this year's renewal, but with an 82-rated horse in second it's doubtful this is top-class form. The race has been rated towards the bottom end of the race average.

## 4647 WEATHERBYS PRIVATE BANKING H'CAP (BOBIS RACE) 1m (S)

2:40 (2:43) (Class 2) 3-Y-0

**£28,012** (£8,388; £4,194; £2,097; £1,048; £526) **Stalls** Centre

Form RPR

-315 1 **Mange All**16 4125 3-8-8 86 LiamJones 6 97
(William Haggas) *lw: t.k.h: trckd ldng pair: rdn to chse ldr wl over 1f out: 2 l down fnl f: styd on wl to ld last 2 strides* **10/1**

2346 2 nk **American Hope (USA)**37 3378 3-9-7 99 ShaneKelly 5 109
(Mike Murphy) *lw: t.k.h: trckd ldr: led over 2f out gng strly: drvn 2 l clr over 1f out: styd on but hdd last 2 strides* **11/2**2

3611 3 2 1/2 **Moohaarib (IRE)**29 3651 3-9-1 93 MartinHarley 10 97
(Marco Botti) *swtg: hld up in last trio: stl there 2f out: gd prog to chse ldng pair fnl f: kpt on but no imp* **11/2**2

-101 4 nse **Glorious Empire (IRE)**15 4169 3-9-5 97 GeorgeBaker 7 101
(Ed Walker) *t.k.h: hld up in midfield: prog over 2f out: chsd ldng pair wl over 1f out: no real imp: lost 3rd fnl f but kpt on* **11/2**2

-312 5 2 3/4 **You're Fired (IRE)**14 4198 3-8-11 89 JimCrowley 9 87
(K R Burke) *lw: in tch in midfield: rdn 3f out: lost pl and in last trio 2f out: kpt on u.p fr over 1f out* **9/2**1

5311 6 1 **Billingsgate (IRE)**10 4331 3-9-0 92 WilliamBuick 2 87
(Charlie Appleby) *hld up towards rr: prog over 2f out and disp 2nd briefly wl over 1f out: no hdwy after: fdd fnl f* **8/1**3

2321 7 1 3/4 **Between Wickets**28 3695 3-8-4 82 MartinDwyer 4 73
(Marcus Tregoning) *swtg: hld up towards rr: sme prog over 2f out: no hdwy over 1f out: fdd* **25/1**

215 8 1/2 **Voyageofdiscovery (USA)**15 4147 3-8-4 82 JimmyQuinn 11 72
(Clive Cox) *hld up in last trio: sme prog into midfield over 1f out: no hdwy after: fdd fnl f* **25/1**

2121 9 9 **Baltic Brave (IRE)**8 4404 3-8-9 87 (t) RichardHughes 8 57
(Hughie Morrison) *hld up in last trio: shkn up and no prog over 2f out: wknd over 1f out* **10/1**

1312 10 2 3/4 **Sir Guy Porteous (IRE)**16 4118 3-9-2 94 JoeFanning 3 57
(Mark Johnston) *led at gd pce: hdd over 2f out: wknd qckly over 1f out* **16/1**

-421 11 20 **Kafeel (USA)**26 3782 3-8-9 87 PaulHanagan 1
(Roger Varian) *trckd ldng pair: rdn 3f out: wknd qckly 2f out: virtually p.u nr fin* **8/1**3

1m 39.72s (-1.08) **Going Correction** +0.05s/f (Good) **11 Ran SP% 118.3**
Speed ratings (Par 106): **107,106,104,104,101 100,98,98,89,86 66**
CSF £64.59 CT £342.29 TOTE £12.70: £3.50, £2.10, £2.10; EX 89.50 Trifecta £696.00.
**Owner** B Haggas **Bred** J B Haggas **Trained** Newmarket, Suffolk

**FOCUS**
A red-hot 3yo handicap with more than half the field last-time-out winners, but they didn't include the first two. They went an even pace and the field raced centre-to-far side. Strong form.

## 4648 LONGINES INTERNATIONAL STKS (HERITAGE H'CAP) 7f

3:15 (3:17) (Class 2) 3-Y-0+

**£93,375** (£27,960; £13,980; £6,990; £3,495; £1,755) **Stalls** Centre

Form RPR

2101 1 **Heavy Metal**21 3964 4-8-9 95 3ex JoeFanning 15 106
(Mark Johnston) *wl in tch: prog fr 4f out to trck ldrs over 2f out: led jst over 1f out: drvn and kpt on wl* **33/1**

4030 2 1 **Dont Bother Me (IRE)**35 3452 4-8-12 98 (p) MartinHarley 3 106
(Marco Botti) *chsd ldrs: rdn over 2f out: styd on to chse wnr fnl f: nvr quite able to chal* **16/1**

1343 3 nk **Watchable**36 3420 4-8-10 96 RichardHughes 19 103
(David O'Meara) *lw: wl in tch: rdn and prog over 2f out: disp 2nd fnl f: kpt on but nvr quite able to chal* **10/1**

6001 4 shd **Heaven's Guest (IRE)**14 4200 4-8-12 103 3ex JackGarritty(5) 17 110
(Richard Fahey) *hld up wl in rr: gd prog fr 2f out: styd on to take 4th last strides: nrst fin* **20/1**

2000 5 1/2 **Don't Call Me (IRE)**14 4212 7-8-8 94 (t) OisinMurphy 12 100
(David Nicholls) *hld up in midfield: rdn and prog jst over 2f out: kpt on fnl f: nrst fin* **20/1**

-111 6 1/2 **King Torus (IRE)**9 4347 6-8-7 93 3ex JamesSullivan 26 97
(Ruth Carr) *mostly in midfield: rdn and prog fr 2f out: kpt on fnl f: nrst fin* **25/1**

3100 7 1 **Pacific Heights (IRE)**14 4214 5-9-0 100 DaleSwift 18 102
(Brian Ellison) *mostly in midfield: rdn and prog over 2f out: chsd ldrs over 1f out: kpt on same pce* **50/1**

4064 8 1/2 **Fort Bastion (IRE)**14 4200 5-8-11 97 ow1 RussKennemore 27 98
(Ruth Carr) *lw: wl in rr: stl more in front than bhd whn nt clr run wl over 1f out: styd on fnl f: nrst fin* **33/1**

5000 9 1/2 **Hawkeyethenoo (IRE)**35 3451 8-8-12 101 GaryBartley(3) 22 100
(Jim Goldie) *hld up in rr: rdn and sme prog 2f out: edgd rt over 1f out: kpt on: n.d* **33/1**

0231 10 3/4 **Majestic Moon (IRE)**43 3189 4-8-9 95 PaulHanagan 20 92+
(Richard Fahey) *led: drvn and hung rt to far rail over 1f out: sn hdd & wknd* **25/1**

2010 11 1 **Louis The Pious**14 4200 6-9-5 105 JosephO'Brien 11 100
(David O'Meara) *lw: settled in midfield: rdn over 3f out: nvr gng pce to threaten but kpt on fr over 1f out* **33/1**

-345 12 shd **Ayaar (IRE)**38 3356 4-8-11 97 FrankieDettori 7 91
(Luca Cumani) *lw: dwlt: wl in rr: rdn and prog on far side of gp over 2f out: no hdwy fnl f* **8/1**3

0541 13 1/2 **Bronze Angel (IRE)**14 4212 5-8-11 97 3ex (b) MartinDwyer 28 90
(Marcus Tregoning) *a in midfield: rdn and no imp on ldrs over 2f out: one pce* **9/1**

0510 14 1/2 **Gabriel's Lad (IRE)**28 3723 5-9-10 110 GeorgeBaker 8 102
(Denis Coakley) *s.v.s: mostly in last gp: stl wl in rr 2f out: styd on fnl f: no ch* **20/1**

3-12 15 1 **Horsted Keynes (FR)**36 3420 4-9-3 103 JimCrowley 25 92
(Roger Varian) *lw: wl in rr: rdn 3f out: kpt on fr over 1f out: no ch* **7/1**2

5-40 16 nk **Redvers (IRE)**77 2145 6-8-11 97 (b) FrederikTylicki 21 85
(Ed Vaughan) *mostly in midfield: rdn over 2f out: tried to make hdwy over 1f out: fdd fnl f* **20/1**

0-30 **17** *1* **Belgian Bill**[38] 3356 6-9-2 102.......(tp) RyanMoore 29 88
(George Baker) *rel to r and lft many l: mostly in last pair: late prog fr over 1f out* **6/1**[1]
3160 **18** *nk* **Brazos (IRE)**[21] 3982 3-8-12 105....... WilliamBuick 5 87
(Clive Brittain) *in tch: rdn to chse ldrs over 2f out: wknd over 1f out* **40/1**
2100 **19** *3/4* **Abseil (USA)**[14] 4200 4-8-11 97....... JamesDoyle 24 80
(Sir Michael Stoute) *wl in tch: rdn and nt qckn over 2f out: edgd rt and short of room over 1f out: fdd* **12/1**
0-20 **20** *hd* **Yeager (USA)**[69] 2362 4-8-9 95....... JimmyQuinn 10 78
(Jeremy Noseda) *taken down early: nvr beyond midfield: u.p and no prog over 2f out* **33/1**
1006 **21** *nk* **Georgian Bay (IRE)**[14] 4200 4-8-10 99.......(v) JoeyHaynes(3) 13 81
(K R Burke) *slowly away and drvn early: nvr beyond midfield: no ch whn short of room over 1f out* **25/1**
3060 **22** *1/2* **Santefisio**[14] 4212 8-9-0 100.......(b) JimmyFortune 6 80
(Keith Dalgleish) *nvr beyond midfield: drvn and no imp over 2f out: fdd fnl f* **33/1**
0-60 **23** *2 1/4* **Pastoral Player**[36] 3420 7-8-13 99....... HayleyTurner 1 74
(Hughie Morrison) *taken down early: hld up towards rr: shkn up and no prog over 2f out: wknd fnl f* **25/1**
0262 **24** *3/4* **Dance And Dance (IRE)**[30] 3621 8-8-8 94.......(b) LiamJones 16 67
(Ed Vaughan) *pressed ldng pair: u.p 3f out: wknd 2f out* **33/1**
6320 **25** *6* **My Freedom (IRE)**[28] 3716 6-9-3 103....... AhmedAjtebi 14 60
(Saeed bin Suroor) *trckd ldr 1f: styd prom tl wknd 2f out: eased fnl f* **66/1**
50-1 **26** *2 3/4* **Field Of Dream**[38] 3356 7-9-7 107.......(b) AdamKirby 4 57
(Jamie Osborne) *taken down early: nvr beyond midfield: rdn and no prog over 2f out: wknd and eased over 1f out* **16/1**
0500 **27** *2 1/4* **Racy**[14] 4179 7-8-10 96.......(p) PaulPickard 2 40
(Brian Ellison) *swtg: taken down v early: racd freely: pressed ldr after 1f tl 2f out: wknd rapidly* **66/1**
0303 **28** *nk* **Brae Hill (IRE)**[29] 3645 8-8-9 95....... StevieDonohoe 23 38
(Richard Fahey) *swtg: taken down v early: pressed ldrs tl wknd rapidly sn after 1/2-way* **66/1**
0100 **29** *1/2* **Clockmaker (IRE)**[14] 4188 8-8-8 94....... LiamKeniry 9 36
(Conor Dore) *taken down early: slowly away: a in last pair: wl bhd over 2f out* **100/1**

1m 25.93s (-1.67) **Going Correction** +0.05s/f (Good)
**WFA** 3 from 4yo+ 7lb **29** Ran SP% **141.3**
Speed ratings (Par 109): **111,109,109,109,108 108,107,106,105,105 103,103,103,102,101 101,100,99,98,98 98,97,95,94,87 8**
CSF £435.78 CT £5664.26 TOTE £42.80: £8.40, £5.00, £2.60, £5.30; EX 2264.80 TRIFECTA Not won..
**Owner** Sheikh Hamdan bin Mohammed Al Maktoum **Bred** Darley **Trained** Middleham Moor, N Yorks

**FOCUS**
A valuable and hugely competitive handicap contested by any number who had run well in similar cavalry charges. The field raced in one group down the centre before drifting over to the far side in the latter stages. The draw didn't seem to have a material effect with the pace coming from Majestic Moon, drawn 20, and Racy from stall two. Surprisingly few made their presence felt. The third and fourth have been rated to form.

## 4649 KING GEORGE VI AND QUEEN ELIZABETH STKS (SPONSORED BY QIPCO BRITISH CHAMPIONS SERIES) (GROUP 1) 1m 4f
**3:50** (3:54) (Class 1) 3-Y-O+
**£603,961** (£228,975; £114,594; £57,084; £28,648; £14,377) **Stalls** Low

Form RPR
1-11 **1** **Taghrooda**[50] 2960 3-8-6 116....... PaulHanagan 7 126
(John Gosden) *lw: hld up in 7th: prog 3f out to chse ldng pair jst over 2f out: rdn and clsd over 1f out: led last 150yds: styd on strly and sn clr* **7/2**[2]
-221 **2** *3* **Telescope (IRE)**[35] 3450 4-9-7 123....... RyanMoore 2 124
(Sir Michael Stoute) *trckd ldng pair: wnt 2nd over 2f out: clsd to chal and upsides over 1f out: jst led whn wnr swept past ins fnl f* **5/2**[1]
-241 **3** *shd* **Mukhadram**[21] 3984 5-9-7 121....... DaneO'Neill 1 123
(William Haggas) *lw: trckd clr ldr: clsd to ld wl over 2f out and sent for home: jnd jst over 1f out: hdd last 150yds: battled on wl* **12/1**
141 **4** *1 3/4* **Eagle Top**[36] 3417 3-8-9 118....... WilliamBuick 8 120
(John Gosden) *hld up in last: shkn up 3f out: prog u.p to take 4th over 1f out: no imp on ldrs fnl f tl kpt on cl home* **4/1**[3]
3-32 **5** *6* **Trading Leather (IRE)**[21] 3984 4-9-7 119....... KevinManning 6 110
(J S Bolger, Ire) *hld up in midfield: rdn and no prog wl over 2f out: wl btn sn after: steadily wknd* **8/1**
6122 **6** *3* **Magician (IRE)**[38] 3354 4-9-7 124.......(t) JosephO'Brien 4 106
(A P O'Brien, Ire) *hld up in 6th: rdn 3f out: no prog and btn 2f out: wknd* **9/2**
3123 **7** *9* **Romsdal**[49] 2990 3-8-9 115....... RichardHughes 5 91
(John Gosden) *lw: trckd ldng trio: rdn 3f out: no prog and sn btn: eased over 1f out* **12/1**
-605 **8** *32* **Leitir Mor (IRE)**[37] 3412 4-9-7 107.......(tp) RonanWhelan 3 40
(J S Bolger, Ire) *led at gd pce and sn clr: drvn over 4f out: hdd & wknd rapidly wl over 2f out: virtually p.u* **100/1**

2m 28.13s (-4.37) **Going Correction** +0.225s/f (Good)
**WFA** 3 from 4yo+ 12lb **8** Ran SP% **116.5**
Speed ratings (Par 117): **123,121,120,119,115 113,107,86**
CSF £12.98 CT £93.40 TOTE £4.20: £1.70, £1.20, £3.70; EX 12.60 Trifecta £111.40.
**Owner** Hamdan Al Maktoum **Bred** Shadwell Estate Company Limited **Trained** Newmarket, Suffolk

**FOCUS**
A compelling renewal of this 'Super Group 1', not least due to the trio of 3yos from the John Gosden stable, the largest representation for the age group since Galileo beat three other 3yos in 2001. The defection of Flintshire reduced the international element of a race which had gone to Germany for the last two years. The pace was solid.

## 4650 LONGINES H'CAP (LADIES' RACE) (FOR LADY AMATEUR RIDERS) 7f
**4:25** (4:30) (Class 3) (0-90,90) 3-Y-O+ **£8,110** (£2,515; £1,257; £629) **Stalls** Centre

Form RPR
4161 **1** **See The Storm**[6] 4471 6-9-9 75 6ex....... MissKHarrington 2 85
(Ian Williams) *trckd ldrs: stdy prog to ld jst over 2f out: rdn over 1f out: jst hld on* **14/1**
4150 **2** *shd* **Born To Surprise**[10] 4323 5-10-7 90....... MissHayleyMoore(3) 6 101+
(Lee Carter) *hld up in tch: nt clr run 2f out tl squeezed through to chse ldng pair over 1f out: nt clr run and swtchd rt jst ins fnl f: rdn to chse wnr sn after: clsng at fin: jst failed* **12/1**
2005 **3** *1 1/4* **Kinglami**[12] 4262 5-9-9 78.......(p) MissBAndrews(3) 9 84
(Brian Gubby) *prom: rdn to chse wnr 2f out: kpt on but hld ins fnl f and sn lost 2nd* **8/1**[3]
3364 **4** *1 3/4* **Karaka Jack**[43] 3190 7-9-9 75....... MrsCBartley 11 76
(Jim Goldie) *settled in rr: shkn up over 2f out: prog over 1f out: kpt on but nvr gng pce to threaten* **4/1**[1]
504 **5** *1 1/4* **Jubilee Brig**[45] 3122 4-9-11 82.......(v) MissBHampson(5) 7 80
(Andy Turnell) *trckd ldrs: cl up whn nt clr run and swtchd rt wl over 1f out: kpt on one pce after and no imp* **20/1**
2116 **6** *1/2* **Red Refraction (IRE)**[15] 4146 4-10-4 89....... MissMeganNicholls(5) 8 86
(Richard Hannon) *lw: hld up in tch: shkn up over 2f out: tried to cl over 1f out: one pce after* **4/1**[1]
1152 **7** *3 3/4* **Conry (IRE)**[9] 4352 8-10-5 85....... MissGAndrews 13 72
(Ian Williams) *swtchd to join main gp in centre after 1f: wl in rr: shkn up and no prog 2f out: drvn and passed wkng rivals fnl f* **25/1**
3304 **8** *1 1/2* **Hadaj**[6] 4471 5-10-4 84.......(b) MissSBrotherton 1 67
(Ruth Carr) *pressed ldrs: shkn up and wknd 2f out* **7/1**[2]
0006 **9** *nk* **Tamayuz Star (IRE)**[21] 3969 4-10-2 87....... MissKMargarson(5) 5 69
(George Margarson) *mde most to jst over 2f out: sn wknd* **8/1**[3]
600- **10** *nk* **Ertikaan**[285] 7254 7-9-2 73....... MissJoeyEllis(5) 3 55
(Miss Joey Ellis) *t.k.h: pressed ldr: upsides over 2f out: sn wknd* **33/1**
3103 **11** *4* **Sheikh The Reins (IRE)**[8] 4408 5-9-5 71 oh3.......(v) MissAliceMills 12 42
(John Best) *racd alone against nr side rail: on terms to 3f out: sn btn* **33/1**
0000 **12** *4* **Lord Of The Dance (IRE)**[31] 3573 8-9-8 77....... MissMMullineaux(3) 10 38
(Michael Mullineaux) *taken down early: dwlt: wl in rr: taken to r along against far rail 4f out: nvr on terms* **8/1**[3]
0-02 **13** *10* **Desert Society (IRE)**[29] 3672 3-9-7 80....... MissEJJones 4 12
(Richard Hannon) *lw: lost prom pl after 3f: sn bhd: t.o* **8/1**[3]

1m 28.57s (0.97) **Going Correction** +0.05s/f (Good)
**WFA** 3 from 4yo+ 7lb **13** Ran SP% **125.8**
Speed ratings (Par 107): **96,95,94,92,91 90,86,84,84,83 79,74,63**
CSF £173.22 CT £1501.00 TOTE £14.20: £3.50, £3.50, £3.20; EX 218.60 Trifecta £1472.40.
**Owner** Keating Bradley Fold Ltd **Bred** D R Botterill **Trained** Portway, Worcs

**FOCUS**
One of the highlights of the season for lady amateur riders. The bulk of the field raced as a bunch up the centre. The winner has been rated as running another pb.

## 4651 CANISBAY BLOODSTOCK H'CAP (BOBIS RACE) 1m 4f
**5:00** (5:00) (Class 4) (0-85,84) 3-Y-O **£7,762** (£2,310; £1,154; £577) **Stalls** Low

Form RPR
-006 **1** **Trip To Paris (IRE)**[37] 3379 3-9-7 84.......(b) RyanMoore 9 94
(Ed Dunlop) *hld up towards rr: prog on outer jst over 2f out: rdn to ld jst over 1f out: r.o wl* **7/4**[1]
5012 **2** *1 3/4* **Our Gabrial (IRE)**[15] 4162 3-9-1 83....... JackGarritty(5) 10 90
(Richard Fahey) *hld up in last trio: prog on outer 2f out: drvn and edgd rt fnl f: styd on to take 2nd nr fin: no ch w wnr* **14/1**
01-0 **3** *1/2* **Hooded (USA)**[71] 2303 3-9-2 79....... JamesDoyle 4 85
(Roger Charlton) *lw: trckd ldr after 1f: rdn to ld narrowly 2f out: hdd and outpcd jst over 1f out: lost 2nd nr fin* **8/1**[3]
1100 **4** *3/4* **Anglo Irish**[36] 3419 3-9-3 80....... WilliamBuick 5 85
(John Gosden) *trckd ldrs: prog to go 3rd 4f out: rdn to chal 2f out: hanging and nt qckn but urged upsides jst over 1f out: wnr swept by and one pce after* **14/1**
1002 **5** *3/4* **Notarised**[7] 4452 3-9-3 80....... JoeFanning 6 85
(Mark Johnston) *led 1f: sn settled bhd ldng pair: rdn over 2f out: hanging fr wl over 1f out: keeping on to press for a pl whn squeezed out last 75yds* **4/1**[2]
3-22 **6** *2* **Itsnowcato**[14] 4196 3-8-11 74....... DaneO'Neill 1 75
(Ed Walker) *swtg: pushed up to ld after 1f: rdn and hdd 2f out: steadily lost pls fr over 1f out* **8/1**[3]
0014 **7** *8* **Rising Breeze (FR)**[8] 4388 3-8-12 78....... JoeyHaynes(3) 2 66
(K R Burke) *s.s: hld up in last: rdn and no prog over 2f out: wl btn after* **14/1**
4245 **8** *hd* **Three Peaks**[23] 3891 3-9-2 79.......(p) FrankieDettori 8 66
(Charles Hills) *hld up in last trio: rdn and no prog over 2f out: sn wl btn* **16/1**
2541 **9** *1 1/4* **High Master (IRE)**[45] 3116 3-8-12 75....... JimmyFortune 3 60
(Richard Hannon) *hld up in midfield: rdn wl over 2f out: sn lft bhd and btn* **20/1**
0413 **10** *3 1/4* **Beakers N Num Nums (IRE)**[10] 4332 3-8-12 75....... MartinDwyer 7 55
(William Jarvis) *t.k.h: trckd ldng trio after 3f: wknd 2f out* **10/1**

2m 34.26s (1.76) **Going Correction** +0.225s/f (Good) **10** Ran SP% **118.3**
Speed ratings (Par 102): **103,101,101,101,100 99,93,93,92,90**
CSF £29.89 CT £163.55 TOTE £2.70: £1.20, £3.80, £3.00; EX 29.20 Trifecta £184.80.
**Owner** La Grange Partnership **Bred** Paul Monaghan & T J Monaghan **Trained** Newmarket, Suffolk

**FOCUS**
A good 3yo middle-distance handicap run at a fair pace, even if the time was 6.13sec slower than the King George. The front six pulled well clear. The fifth has been rated to his latest form.
T/Jkpt: Not won. T/Plt: £930.30 to a £1 stake. Pool: £251,724.67 - 197.50 winning units. T/Qpdt: £224.80 to a £1 stake. Pool: £18,961.61 - 62.40 winning units. JN

# 4610 LINGFIELD (L-H)
Saturday, July 26

**OFFICIAL GOING: Turf course - good to firm (watered); all-weather - standard**
Wind: virtually nil Weather: warm and sunny

## 4652 BET NOW AT 32REDSPORT.COM MAIDEN AUCTION STKS 5f
**5:30** (5:30) (Class 6) 2-Y-O **£2,458** (£731; £365; £182) **Stalls** Centre

Form RPR
**1** **Lightscameraction (IRE)** 2-8-12 0....... DanielMuscutt(5) 6 81+
(Gay Kelleway) *chsd ldr tl led 2f out: shkn up and readily wnt clr ent fnl f: eased towards fin: v easily* **3/1**[3]
**2** *2 3/4* **Rock Follies** 2-8-9 0....... MartinHarley 7 59
(Lady Cecil) *dwlt: in tch in last pair: effrt and nt clr run over 1f out: swtchd lft ent fnl f: kpt on wl to snatch 2nd last strides: no ch w wnr* **11/4**[2]
0 **3** *nk* **Frozen Princess**[103] 1488 2-8-8 0....... FergusSweeney 5 57
(Jamie Osborne) *chsd ldrs tl short of room after 1f: in tch in midfield: after: rdn and effrt 2f out: chsd clr wnr jst over 1f out: no imp: lost 2nd last strides* **14/1**
04 **4** *1 1/2* **Freeze The Secret (IRE)**[21] 3975 2-8-8 0....... OisinMurphy 4 52
(David C Griffiths) *hld up in tch in midfield: swtchd lft and effrt u.p over 1f out: styd on same pce fnl f* **16/1**
5 **5** *3* **Mazoula (IRE)**[26] 3799 2-8-3 0....... NoelGarbutt(5) 1 41
(Hugo Palmer) *dwlt: in tch in last pair: rdn 1/2-way: struggling whn sltly hmpd over 1f out: wknd fnl f* **8/1**

62 **6** *1 ½* **Frank The Barber (IRE)**[25] 3813 2-9-0 0................ RussKennemore 2 41
(Steph Hollinshead) *chsd ldrs: rdn and chsd wnr wl over 1f out tl jst over 1f out: sn btn and wknd fnl f* **8/1**

622 **7** *3* **Jimmy's Girl (IRE)**[42] 3210 2-8-9 66................ KieranO'Neill 3 26
(Richard Hannon) *t.k.h: led tl 2f out: sn rdn and lost pl: bhd fnl f* **9/4[1]**

58.0s (-0.20) **Going Correction** -0.275s/f (Firm) 7 Ran SP% **117.2**
Speed ratings (Par 92): **90,85,85,82,77 75,70**
CSF £12.24 TOTE £4.80: £2.20, £2.80; EX 17.00 Trifecta £143.70.
**Owner** LCA Lights Camera Action Ltd **Bred** Timmy & Michael Hillman **Trained** Exning, Suffolk

**FOCUS**
A dry, hot day; 3mm of water was applied to the turf track in the morning. The median RPR of past winners over the last ten years is 70. Two of those with previous form had already bettered that mark, but one of the debutants ran away with this. The first three home raced near the stands' rail. The winner is well regarded but there was more style than substance to this win.

## 4653 ALL NEW 32REDSPORT.COM MEDIAN AUCTION MAIDEN STKS 7f
**6:00** (6:03) (Class 6) 3-5-Y-O £1,940 (£577; £288; £144) **Stalls** Centre

Form RPR

22 **1** **Elizona**[31] 3586 3-9-0 0................ FrederikTylicki 3 62+
(James Fanshawe) *trckd ldng pair: clsd to ld on bit jst over 2f out: rdn over 1f out: in command fnl f: rdn out* **1/20[1]**

05 **2** *4* **Smile For Me (IRE)**[22] 3938 3-9-0 0................ OisinMurphy 7 52+
(Harry Dunlop) *taken down early: dwlt: sn rcvrd and led after 1f: hdd jst over 2f out: wandered u.p and outpcd over 1f out: styd on same pce fnl f* **8/1[2]**

**3** *2 ¾* **Graffiti Art**[119] 5-9-0 0................ JennyPowell(7) 2 48
(Brendan Powell) *s.i.s: bhd and sn rdn along in rr: drifting rt over 1f out: styd on ins fnl f: to snatch 3rd last strides* **14/1[3]**

6003 **4** *nk* **Fleeting Indian (IRE)**[26] 3800 5-9-5 45................(v) CallumShepherd(7) 1 52
(Linda Jewell) *led for 1f: pressed ldr after tl 3rd and rdn 2f out: struggling over 1f out: wknd fnl f: lost 3rd last strides* **33/1**

6 **5** *11* **Adimendis (IRE)**[24] 3849 3-9-5 0................ LiamKeniry 4 20
(J S Moore) *t.k.h: broke wl: stdd and in tch in 4th: rdn jst over 2f out: sn btn and dropped out: eased ins fnl f* **8/1[2]**

1m 23.22s (-0.08) **Going Correction** -0.275s/f (Firm)
**WFA** 3 from 5yo 7lb 5 Ran SP% **127.1**
Speed ratings (Par 101): **89,84,81,80,68**
CSF £2.61 TOTE £1.10: £1.02, £2.60; EX 2.30 Trifecta £7.00.
**Owner** Mrs Alice Cherry **Bred** Mrs Elizabeth Grundy & Mrs Alice Cherry **Trained** Newmarket, Suffolk

**FOCUS**
Eight favourites have obliged in this contest over the past ten years, but none was as short as the good thing in this weak renewal. The poor fourth limits the form.

## 4654 32RED ON THE APP STORE H'CAP 7f
**6:30** (6:31) (Class 5) (0-70,70) 3-Y-O £3,234 (£962; £481; £240) **Stalls** Centre

Form RPR

0-33 **1** **Lady Sparkler (IRE)**[26] 3801 3-9-7 70................ FrederikTylicki 7 77+
(Roger Varian) *s.i.s: in tch in last trio: nt clr run 2f out tl swtchd lft 1f out: hdwy to chal between rivals ins fnl f: r.o wl to ld last stride* **5/2[1]**

-530 **2** *shd* **Goodwood Storm**[10] 4329 3-9-7 70................ LukeMorris 4 76
(William Knight) *t.k.h: chsd ldr: rdn to ld 1f out: hrd pressed ins fnl f: battled on wl but hdd last stride* **4/1[3]**

0042 **3** *hd* **Go For Broke**[33] 3516 3-9-5 68................(b[1]) KieranO'Neill 6 73
(Richard Hannon) *wl in tch in midfield: swtchd lft and effrt to press ldr 1f out: ev ch ins fnl f: kpt on* **7/2[2]**

500- **4** *1 ½* **Berkeley Vale**[283] 7302 3-9-2 65................ SebSanders 8 67
(Roger Teal) *t.k.h: hld up in tch in last pair: nt clr run wl over 1f out: swtchd rt 1f out: kpt on under hands and heels ins fnl f: wnt 4th last strides: nvr threatened ldrs* **20/1**

0525 **5** *hd* **Aristocratic Duty**[15] 4152 3-8-13 62................ LiamKeniry 1 63
(Sylvester Kirk) *dropped in bhd after s: clsd and swtchd lft over 1f out: styd on same pce u.p fnl f* **14/1**

0052 **6** *hd* **Moneypennie**[18] 4048 3-8-2 51 oh1................(tp) JimmyQuinn 2 52
(Marcus Tregoning) *chsd ldrs: rdn and effrt wl over 1f out: kpt on same pce fr over 1f out* **10/1**

4-00 **7** *nk* **Applejack Lad**[17] 4074 3-9-7 70................(t) AdamKirby 5 70
(John Ryan) *led: rdn 2f out: hdd over 1f out: no ex u.p 1f out: wknd ins fnl f* **7/1**

6-51 **8** *nk* **Born To Fly (IRE)**[18] 4048 3-9-0 63................(b) J-PGuillambert 3 62
(Nick Littmoden) *dwlt: sn rcvrd and in tch in midfield: rdn and effrt wl over 1f out: no imp: kpt on same pce fnl f* **8/1**

1m 24.02s (0.72) **Going Correction** -0.275s/f (Firm) 8 Ran SP% **114.9**
Speed ratings (Par 100): **84,83,83,81,81 81,81,80**
CSF £12.70 CT £34.16 TOTE £2.90: £1.10, £2.60, £1.60; EX 18.40 Trifecta £85.30.
**Owner** Sotirios Hassiakos & Maurice Manasseh **Bred** Barouche Stud Ireland Ltd **Trained** Newmarket, Suffolk

**FOCUS**
Quite a competitive handicap. There looked to be little early pace; three horses finished close up a little way clear of the rest. The bare form is ordinary.

## 4655 MARK'S "FINAL FURLONG" H'CAP 7f 140y
**7:00** (7:01) (Class 6) (0-65,65) 3-Y-O+ £2,587 (£770; £384; £192) **Stalls** Centre

Form RPR

0632 **1** **Hawk Moth (IRE)**[18] 4046 6-9-2 53................(p) LukeMorris 8 63
(John Spearing) *hld up in tch in midfield: swtchd lft and shkn up to chal 1f out: rdn to ld ins fnl f: drvn and r.o wl fnl 100yds* **9/2[2]**

0324 **2** *½* **Lady Crossmar (IRE)**[7] 4428 3-9-1 65................ CamHardie(5) 11 72
(Richard Hannon) *chsd ldrs: rdn ent fnl 2f: swtchd arnd 2 rivals ent fnl f: hdwy to chse wnr fnl 75yds: r.o wl* **6/1**

6433 **3** *2* **My Manekineko**[7] 4428 5-9-11 62................ DougieCostello 3 66
(J R Jenkins) *chsd ldrs: rdn and ev ch over 1f out: no ex and outpcd fnl 100yds* **16/1**

0-00 **4** *1 ¼* **Emperor Julius (IRE)**[145] 817 4-10-0 65................ FergusSweeney 1 66
(Jo Crowley) *in tch in midfield: rdn and effrt over 1f out: kpt on u.p fnl 150yds: nvr trbld ldrs* **50/1**

5520 **5** *nk* **Not Rigg (USA)**[21] 3979 4-9-9 60................(p) J-PGuillambert 9 60
(Nick Littmoden) *reminders sn after s: chsd ldr: drvn to ld over 1f out: hdd ins fnl f: wknd fnl 100yds* **8/1**

0046 **6** *shd* **Why Not Now**[18] 4048 3-8-9 54................ OisinMurphy 10 52
(Roger Charlton) *t.k.h: hld up in tch towards rr: rdn and effrt over 1f out: hdwy and swtchd rt ins fnl f: kpt on but enough pce to chal* **5/1[3]**

0510 **7** *2 ¾* **Little Indian**[39] 3327 4-9-6 62................ DannyBrock(5) 6 55
(J R Jenkins) *stdd after s: hld up in last pair: rdn and effrt 2f out: no imp and one pce front over 1f out: nvr trbld ldrs* **10/1**

5150 **8** *nk* **Carrera**[17] 4073 4-9-9 60................ MartinHarley 7 52
(Michael Blanshard) *hld up in last pair: rdn and effrt wl over 1f out: drvn and no imp 1f out: nvr threatened ldrs* **4/1[1]**

022 **9** *1 ¼* **Big City Boy (IRE)**[9] 4341 6-8-10 47................ FrederikTylicki 12 36
(Phil McEntee) *led: rdn and hdd 1f out: wknd fnl f* **8/1**

2411 **10** *½* **Fairy Mist (IRE)**[18] 4042 7-9-3 54................(b) AdamKirby 4 42
(John Bridger) *hld up in tch towards rr: effrt and sme hdwy 2f out: no prog over 1f out: wknd 1f out: eased towards fin* **8/1**

4500 **11** *38* **Rise To Glory (IRE)**[112] 1312 6-9-5 56................ DuranFentiman 2
(Shaun Harris) *in tch in midfield: lost pl and rdn over 2f out: bhd over 1f out: heavily eased ins fnl f: t.o* **25/1**

1m 29.66s (-2.64) **Going Correction** -0.275s/f (Firm)
**WFA** 3 from 4yo+ 8lb 11 Ran SP% **123.2**
Speed ratings (Par 101): **102,101,99,98,97 97,95,94,93,93 55**
CSF £33.49 CT £418.24 TOTE £6.60: £2.00, £2.60, £6.80; EX 36.70 Trifecta £291.60.
**Owner** Kinnersley Partnership **Bred** Dr D Harron **Trained** Kinnersley, Worcs

**FOCUS**
A fairly competitive renewal featuring last year's winner, who won it once again. The third has been rated to his latest form.

## 4656 32RED.COM H'CAP 1m 7f 169y(P)
**7:35** (7:35) (Class 5) (0-70,70) 4-Y-O+ £3,234 (£962; £481; £240) **Stalls** Low

Form RPR

6032 **1** **Mister Bob (GER)**[37] 3404 5-8-8 57................(p) TedDurcan 6 64+
(James Bethell) *hld up in tch in last pair: rdn and effrt ent fnl 2f: drvn over 1f out: styd on strly fnl 100yds to ld cl home* **5/2[1]**

-160 **2** *½* **Conquestadim**[32] 3556 4-9-4 67................ OisinMurphy 4 73
(Hughie Morrison) *led: rdn ent fnl 2f: drvn and kpt on ins fnl f: hdd and no ex cl home* **5/2[1]**

05-4 **3** *1 ¼* **Reggie Perrin**[17] 4076 6-8-11 60................(vt) LukeMorris 1 65
(Pat Phelan) *dwlt and bustled along leaving stalls: in tch towards rr: rdn over 3f out: drvn over 1f out: swtchd lft and styd on u.p ins fnl f* **4/1[3]**

5000 **4** *hd* **Stormy Morning**[12] 4259 8-8-2 51 oh2................(p) DuranFentiman 7 56
(Philip Kirby) *in tch in midfield: effrt u.p 2f out: drvn over 1f out: no ex and kpt on same pce ins fnl f* **20/1**

5465 **5** *½* **Red Dragon (IRE)**[19] 4030 4-9-1 64................ MartinHarley 5 68
(Michael Blanshard) *chsd ldrs: wnt 2nd over 5f out: pressing ldr and rdn 2f out: drvn over 1f out: lost 2nd ins fnl f: wknd towards fin* **7/2[2]**

2400 **6** *3 ¾* **Montjess (IRE)**[23] 3874 4-9-2 65................(p) AmirQuinn 2 65
(Laura Mongan) *chsd ldr tl over 5f out: styd chsng ldrs: rdn and outpcd jst over 2f out: tried to rally over 1f out: wknd ins fnl f* **14/1**

00-P **7** *56* **Kent Ragstone (USA)**[17] 4076 5-9-7 70................ LiamKeniry 3
(Murty McGrath) *in tch in midfield tl lost pl and dropped to rr 6f out: rdn over 4f out: lost tch 3f out: t.o and virtually p.u over 1f out* **20/1**

3m 24.21s (-1.49) **Going Correction** 0.0s/f (Stan) 7 Ran SP% **115.6**
Speed ratings (Par 103): **103,102,102,102,101 99,71**
CSF £9.11 TOTE £4.70: £2.60, £1.40; EX 11.20 Trifecta £37.90.
**Owner** Robert Gibbons **Bred** Newsells Park Stud Ltd **Trained** Middleham Moor, N Yorks

**FOCUS**
Little strength in depth with the market leaders dominating this muddling handicap. The third has been rated close to his latest form.

## 4657 32RED H'CAP 1m 5f (P)
**8:05** (8:07) (Class 5) (0-70,73) 3-Y-O £3,234 (£962; £481; £240) **Stalls** Low

Form RPR

0612 **1** **Daydreamer**[26] 3797 3-9-6 69................ SebSanders 8 84+
(William Haggas) *chsd ldr tl led jst over 2f out: shkn up and qcknd clr 2f out: in n.d after: eased towards fin: v easily* **7/4[1]**

5-62 **2** *8* **Mountain Kingdom (IRE)**[21] 3953 3-9-6 69................ LukeMorris 4 73+
(Sir Mark Prescott Bt) *chsd ldrs: rdn to chse wnr 2f out: no imp u.p over 1f out: clr 2nd but wl hld fnl f: eased towards fin* **11/4[3]**

3561 **3** *2* **Gavlar**[3] 4547 3-9-3 73 6ex................(v) CallumShepherd(7) 5 72
(William Knight) *s.i.s: hld up in tch in last pair: rdn and edgd lft 2f: swtchd rt over 1f out: no ch but kpt on to go 3rd wl ins fnl f* **9/4[2]**

6112 **4** *1 ¼* **Big Kenny**[17] 4088 3-9-3 66................(b) AdamKirby 3 63
(Neil King) *stdd s: t.k.h: hld up in tch in last trio: rdn and effrt jst over 2f out: no ch w wnr over 1f out: wknd ins fnl f* **16/1**

3-05 **5** *½* **Supachap**[86] 1898 3-8-10 64................ CamHardie(5) 9 60
(Hughie Morrison) *chsd ldrs: rdn and outpcd wl over 1f out: 3rd and wl hld 1f out: wknd ins fnl f* **10/1**

044 **6** *14* **Approaching Star (FR)**[31] 3568 3-9-7 70................ MartinHarley 1 45
(Ismail Mohammed) *led tl rdn and hdd jst over 2f out: sn rdn and outpcd: wknd qckly over 1f out: eased ins fnl f* **20/1**

-310 **7** *3* **That Be Grand**[29] 3655 3-8-12 61................ JasonHart 7 32
(Shaun Harris) *in tch in last trio: rdn 3f out: struggling whn hmpd bnd 2f out: sn lost tch: eased ins fnl f* **33/1**

2m 44.5s (-1.50) **Going Correction** 0.0s/f (Stan) 7 Ran SP% **116.5**
Speed ratings (Par 100): **104,99,97,97,96 88,86**
CSF £7.17 CT £10.58 TOTE £4.30: £2.20, £3.90; EX 5.90 Trifecta £22.20.
**Owner** Mr & Mrs R Scott **Bred** Mr & Mrs R & P Scott **Trained** Newmarket, Suffolk

**FOCUS**
An ordinary staying handicap, but run at a sound pace. The fourth was pretty exposed over the winter and limits the form.

## 4658 RACING SPECIALS AT 32REDSPORT.COM H'CAP 1m 2f (P)
**8:35** (8:35) (Class 6) (0-65,66) 3-Y-O+ £2,587 (£770; £384; £192) **Stalls** Low

Form RPR

6003 **1** **Censorius**[28] 3711 3-9-4 65................(v) AdamKirby 5 71
(Ed Walker) *nt best away and bustled along early: in toouch in midfield: switching rt 7f out: hdwy on outer to chse ldr 5f out: rdn and clr w rival 2f out: led ins fnl f: asserted fnl 100yds: eased cl home* **6/4[1]**

606 **2** *½* **Perseverent Pete (USA)**[53] 2875 4-8-10 47 oh2................ LukeMorris 1 51
(Christine Dunnett) *led for 2f: chsd ldr tl 5f out: 3rd and unable qck whn rdr dropped whip 2f out: rallied fnl f: wnt 2nd fnl 75yds: kpt on* **25/1**

5051 **3** *1* **Diletta Tommasa (IRE)**[6] 4473 4-9-10 66 6ex................(p) EoinWalsh(5) 6 68+
(John Stimpson) *stdd s: hld up in tch in last trio: effrt on inner whn nt clr run 2f out: swtchd rt and plenty to do wl over 1f out: swtchd lft 1f out: r.o strly to go 3rd towards fin: no threat to wnr* **4/1[2]**

-000 **4** *½* **Bridge That Gap**[12] 4273 6-9-9 60................(p) JimmyQuinn 10 61+
(Roger Ingram) *hld up in tch in last trio: effrt and wd bnd 2f out: styd on wl u.p ins fnl f: nvr trbld ldrs* **25/1**

5145 **5** *½* **Lily Edge**[17] 4081 5-9-4 60................(v) CamHardie(5) 8 60
(John Bridger) *in tch in midfield: rdn and effrt on outer over 2f out: outpcd 2f out: rallied and kpt on again ins fnl f: no threat to wnr* **7/1**

-003 **6** *shd* **Ede's The Business**[17] 4085 3-8-3 **53**..................(v) JemmaMarshall(3) 4 53
(Pat Phelan) *in tch in midfield: 4th and outpcd u.p 2f out: rallied and kpt on again ins fnl f* **20/1**

0-60 **7** *½* **Severn Crossing**[52] 2883 3-9-3 **64**..............(p) MartinDwyer 11 63
(William Muir) *t.k.h: w ldrs tl led over 8f out: stdd gallop 7f out: rdn and clr w wnr 2f out: hdd ins fnl f: lost 2nd fnl 75yds and wknd towards fin* **14/1**

0006 **8** *shd* **Divine Rule (IRE)**[12] 4266 6-8-12 **56**..................(v) CharlotteJenner(7) 7 55
(Laura Mongan) *in tch in midfield: rdn and outpcd over 2f out: rallied and kpt on ins fnl f: no threat to wnr* **16/1**

5300 **9** *½* **Hurricane Harry**[17] 4077 3-9-3 **64**.............................. OisinMurphy 9 62
(William Knight) *hld up in tch in rr: rdn ent fnl 2f: sme hdwy 1f out: kpt on: nvr trbld ldrs* **6/1**[3]

0-04 **10** *¾* **Danglydontask**[33] 3525 3-8-13 **60**...............................(b) PaddyAspell 2 56
(David Arbuthnot) *in tch in midfield: n.m.r over 2f out: rdn wl over 1f out: kpt on fnl f: no threat to ldrs* **14/1**

1-06 **11** *7* **Reimpose (USA)**[15] 4152 3-9-1 **62**............................ StevieDonohoe 3 44
(Pat Eddery) *restless in stalls: t.k.h: w ldr for 1f: stdd bk and chsd ldrs: rdn and losing pl 2f out: wknd over 1f out* **25/1**

2m 8.17s (1.57) **Going Correction** 0.0s/f (Stan)
**WFA** 3 from 4yo+ 10lb **11** Ran SP% **122.3**
Speed ratings (Par 101): **93,92,91,91,91 90,90,90,90,89 83**
CSF £55.15 CT £130.59 TOTE £2.90: £1.30, £6.50, £1.50; EX 52.90 Trifecta £306.60.
**Owner** Al Ansari, Greenwood, Pegum **Bred** Langham Hall Stud **Trained** Newmarket, Suffolk

**FOCUS**
Despite a large field there was little pace on, so tactics proved crucial in a bunched field. Ordinary form.
T/Plt: £13.70 to a £1 stake. Pool: £65724.67 - 3498.62 winning tickets T/Qpdt: £4.60 to a £1 stake. Pool: £7270.47 - 1153.75 winning tickets SP

# 3713 NEWCASTLE (L-H)
## Saturday, July 26

**OFFICIAL GOING: Good to firm (firm in places on round course; str 7.6; rnd 8.2)**
Rail moved on to fresh ground around back of course.
Wind: light across Weather: Hot and sunny

## 4659 COLLINGWOOD INSURANCE COMPANY MAIDEN AUCTION STKS (BOBIS RACE) 7f
**1:55** (2:04) (Class 4) 2-Y-O £3,881 (£1,155; £577; £288) **Stalls** Centre

Form RPR

434 **1** **Gaudy (IRE)**[12] 4253 2-8-9 77.............................. ShaneGray(5) 5 84+
(Kevin Ryan) *trckd ldr: rdn to ld 2f out: kpt on wl* **9/2**[2]

5322 **2** *3* **Ythan Waters**[12] 4253 2-8-13 83.............................. PhillipMakin 4 74
(Bryan Smart) *led: rdn whn hdd 2f out: one pce and hld by wnr ins fnl f* **6/4**[1]

0 **3** *4½* **Call Me Crockett (IRE)**[16] 4129 2-8-12 0.................... AndrewMullen 2 61
(Richard Guest) *trckd ldrs: rdn and outpcd by ldng pair over 2f out: plugged on fnl f* **80/1**

04 **4** *2¼* **Lord Of Words (IRE)**[21] 3945 2-8-6 0.................. JacobButterfield(5) 9 54
(Brian Ellison) *hld up: rdn over 3f out: plugged on into modest 3rd over 1f out* **25/1**

**5** *shd* **Cosmic Statesman** 2-8-9 0............................. SammyJoBell(5) 7 57
(Richard Fahey) *slowly away: hld up: pushed along and sme hdwy 3f out: one pce fnl 2f* **8/1**[3]

**6** *1* **Lostock Hall (IRE)** 2-9-1 0.............................. PJMcDonald 10 55
(K R Burke) *s.i.s: hld up: rdn and sme hdwy 3f out: no further imp fnl 2f* **9/2**[2]

3305 **7** *3½* **Rose Of Kiev (IRE)**[19] 4018 2-8-6 71.................... RoystonFfrench 12 37
(Mark Johnston) *midfield: rdn and outpcd 4f out: no threat after* **16/1**

**8** *9* **Canny Kool** 2-8-13 0.............................. IanBrennan 3 19
(Brian Ellison) *trckd ldrs: rdn over 2f out: wknd over 1f out* **14/1**

0 **9** *6* **Moon Arc (IRE)**[7] 4450 2-8-13 0.............................. TomEaves 8 3
(Keith Dalgleish) *hld up: rdn 1/2-way: sn wknd* **28/1**

0026 **10** *5* **Playboy Bay**[10] 4330 2-8-11 70..............................(v[1]) SamHitchcott 11
(Mick Channon) *hld up: rdn over 3f out: sn wknd* **16/1**

1m 25.77s (-2.03) **Going Correction** -0.325s/f (Firm) **10** Ran SP% **114.4**
Speed ratings (Par 96): **98,94,89,86,86 85,81,71,64,58**
Sekuras girl was withdrawn. Price at time of withdrawal 20-1 - Rule 4 does not apply. CSF £11.18 TOTE £5.40: £1.80, £1.10, £10.70; EX 14.40 Trifecta £555.90.
**Owner** Qatar Racing Limited **Bred** Mrs Jean Brennan **Trained** Hambleton, N Yorks

**FOCUS**
Rail moved on to fresh ground around back of course. Not much got into this maiden with the front two dominating from the outset.

## 4660 COLLINGWOOD FLEET INSURANCE H'CAP (BOBIS RACE) 6f
**2:30** (2:31) (Class 3) (0-90,87) 3-Y-O £9,056 (£2,695; £1,346; £673) **Stalls** Centre

Form RPR

0-04 **1** **Zaraee (IRE)**[15] 4176 3-9-2 **87**.............................. NathanAlison(5) 6 98
(William Haggas) *trckd ldr: rdn 2f out: kpt on: led 50yds out* **5/2**[1]

2032 **2** *¾* **Lincoln (IRE)**[19] 4021 3-9-6 **86**.............................. TomEaves 4 95
(Mick Channon) *led: rdn 2f out: kpt on: hdd 50yds out* **11/4**[2]

3103 **3** *3¾* **Highland Acclaim (IRE)**[15] 4146 3-9-4 **87**................ SamJames(3) 3 84
(David O'Meara) *s.i.s: hld up in rr: rdn over 2f out: wnt 3rd ins fnl f: one pce and no threat to ldng pair* **5/2**[1]

330 **4** *1¾* **Election Night**[40] 3300 3-8-4 **70**.............................. IanBrennan 2 61
(Tim Easterby) *hld up: racd keenly: rdn over 2f out: sn btn* **11/1**

3105 **5** *4½* **Crisis Averted (IRE)**[35] 3484 3-8-11 **77**................(v) PJMcDonald 5 54
(Richard Fahey) *in tch: rdn over 2f out: wknd fnl f* **4/1**[3]

1m 12.09s (-2.51) **Going Correction** -0.325s/f (Firm) **5** Ran SP% **112.1**
Speed ratings (Par 104): **103,102,97,94,88**
CSF £9.88 TOTE £4.00: £1.90, £1.50; EX 8.40 Trifecta £24.20.
**Owner** Hamdan Al Maktoum **Bred** London Thoroughbred Services Ltd **Trained** Newmarket, Suffolk

**FOCUS**
A fair little 3yo sprint handicap.

## 4661 COLLINGWOOD LEARNER DRIVER INSURANCE "BEESWING" H'CAP 7f
**3:05** (3:06) (Class 3) (0-95,93) 3-Y-O+ £11,644 (£3,465; £1,731; £865) **Stalls** Centre

Form RPR

2565 **1** **Laffan (IRE)**[21] 3964 5-9-11 **90**.............................. RobertWinston 12 102
(Tim Easterby) *prom: led 1/2-way: rdn and hung lft 2f out: kpt on to go clr fnl f* **5/1**[2]

3432 **2** *3¼* **Ansaab**[7] 4447 6-9-3 **89**..............................(t) KieranShoemark(7) 2 93
(Alan McCabe) *midfield on outer: rdn and hdwy 2f out: wnt 2nd ins fnl f: kpt on but no threat wnr* **7/1**

3165 **3** *2* **Ralphy Boy (IRE)**[7] 4451 5-8-6 **76**.............................. GarryWhillans(5) 1 74
(Alistair Whillans) *w ldr: rdn over 2f out: lost 2nd ins fnl f: no ex* **20/1**

0363 **4** *1* **Azagal (IRE)**[15] 4176 3-8-13 **92**.............................. RachelRichardson(7) 8 85
(Tim Easterby) *hld up: rdn over 2f out: hdwy over 1f out: kpt on* **6/1**[3]

1311 **5** *hd* **Repetition**[15] 4161 4-9-6 **85**.............................. TomEaves 4 80
(Kristin Stubbs) *led narrowly: hdd 1/2-way: rdn over 2f out: wknd ins fnl f* **7/2**[1]

1050 **6** *1* **Just Paul (IRE)**[31] 3573 4-8-9 **79**.............................. KevinStott(5) 5 72
(Philip Kirby) *midfield: rdn over 2f out: one pce fnl f* **7/1**

0006 **7** *1¼* **Evanescent (IRE)**[35] 3483 5-8-10 **75**.............................. IanBrennan 11 64
(John Quinn) *trckd ldrs: rdn and outpcd over 2f out: no threat after* **20/1**

1400 **8** *nse* **Victoire De Lyphar (IRE)**[8] 4384 7-9-13 **92**................(e) PJMcDonald 6 81
(Ruth Carr) *trckd ldrs: rdn over 2f out: wknd ins fnl f* **10/1**

0413 **9** *1½* **Silver Rime (FR)**[12] 4258 9-9-4 **86**.............................. ConnorBeasley(3) 9 71
(Linda Perratt) *hld up: rdn over 3f out: nvr threatened* **10/1**

3020 **10** *¾* **Outlaw Torn (IRE)**[11] 4293 5-8-6 **74** oh9..................(e) BillyCray(3) 3 57
(Richard Guest) *midfield: rdn over 2f out: wknd over 1f out* **50/1**

5650 **11** *2½* **Joe Eile (IRE)**[43] 3202 6-9-6 **85**.............................. PhillipMakin 7 62
(John Quinn) *midfield: rdn over 2f out: wknd over 1f out* **12/1**

5040 **12** *¾* **Showboating (IRE)**[14] 4181 6-9-3 **82**..................(vt) StephenCraine 10 57
(Alan McCabe) *slowly away: hld up: rdn over 3f out: a bhd* **14/1**

1m 25.29s (-2.51) **Going Correction** -0.325s/f (Firm)
**WFA** 3 from 4yo+ 7lb **12** Ran SP% **122.2**
Speed ratings (Par 107): **101,97,95,93,93 92,91,91,89,88 85,84**
CSF £40.37 CT £669.84 TOTE £5.80: £1.90, £2.70, £4.20; EX 36.60 Trifecta £806.10.
**Owner** Middleham Park Racing XI & Partners **Bred** Vincent Dunne **Trained** Great Habton, N Yorks

**FOCUS**
A good-quality handicap where racing stands' side proved an advantage.

## 4662 COLLINGWOOD ANNUAL LEARNER DRIVER INSURANCE H'CAP 2m 19y
**3:40** (3:41) (Class 5) (0-75,75) 4-Y-O+ £2,587 (£770; £384; £192) **Stalls** Low

Form RPR

3114 **1** **Longshadow**[11] 4289 4-9-5 **73**..............................(v) PJMcDonald 2 82
(Jason Ward) *trckd ldr: led 4f out: rdn over 2f out: styd on wl* **5/2**[1]

2016 **2** *3¼* **Jan Smuts (IRE)**[33] 3532 6-8-7 **66**..............................(tp) EmmaSayer(5) 4 71
(Wilf Storey) *hld up on inner: angled rt to outer over 2f out: sn hdwy: wnt 2nd appr fnl f: kpt on but no ch w wnr* **11/1**

-046 **3** *1¼* **Bowdler's Magic**[17] 4068 7-9-6 **74**..............................(t) RaulDaSilva 3 78
(David Thompson) *midfield on inner: rdn and hdwy to chse ldr over 2f out: one pce fnl f* **9/1**

0541 **4** *½* **Madrasa (IRE)**[6] 4474 6-8-7 **64**..............................(b) ConnorBeasley(3) 8 67
(Keith Reveley) *hld up: rdn over 2f out: kpt on ins fnl f: nvr threatened* **3/1**[2]

1133 **5** *1¼* **Miss Macnamara (IRE)**[17] 4068 5-9-3 **71**.............................. PhillipMakin 1 72
(Martin Todhunter) *trckd ldrs: rdn over 3f out: wknd ins fnl f* **9/2**[3]

150- **6** *5* **Renegotiate**[20] 5356 5-8-11 **68**..............................(p) SamJames(3) 7 63
(Peter Niven) *led: hdd 4f out: sn rdn: wknd over 2f out* **8/1**

2610 **7** *½* **Flying Power**[28] 3699 6-9-2 **75**.............................. JacobButterfield(5) 5 70
(John Norton) *midfield: rdn over 3f out: wknd over 2f out* **12/1**

02-1 **8** *46* **Rayadour (IRE)**[23] 2900 5-8-12 **66**..............................(v[1]) TomEaves 6 6
(Micky Hammond) *in tch: wknd qckly over 3f out: eased* **8/1**

3m 32.25s (-7.15) **Going Correction** -0.325s/f (Firm) **8** Ran SP% **120.0**
Speed ratings (Par 103): **104,102,101,101,100 98,98,75**
CSF £32.72 CT £221.41 TOTE £2.90: £1.10, £3.30, £3.10; EX 33.90 Trifecta £349.10.
**Owner** David Robertson & J Ward **Bred** Miss K Rausing **Trained** Middleham, N Yorks

**FOCUS**
A modest handicap. The third has been rated to this year's form.

## 4663 COLLINGWOOD TAXI INSURANCE/EBFSTALLIONS.COM FILLIES' H'CAP 1m 4f 93y
**4:15** (4:15) (Class 4) (0-85,81) 4-Y-O+ £6,469 (£1,925; £962; £481) **Stalls** Low

Form RPR

2010 **1** **Wilhana (IRE)**[15] 4160 4-9-7 **81**.............................. StephenCraine 2 89
(Pam Sly) *trckd ldr: rdn 2f out: styd on: led 110yds out* **9/2**

-046 **2** *¾* **Magic Art (IRE)**[42] 3218 4-9-7 **78**.............................. PhillipMakin 1 87
(Marco Botti) *led at stdy pce: rdn over 2f out: hdd 110yds out: no ex* **10/3**[2]

-030 **3** *4½* **A Star In My Eye (IRE)**[43] 3205 4-8-10 **77**.............. AhmadAlSubousi(7) 4 76
(Kevin Ryan) *hld up in tch: rdn over 2f out: no imp: wnt modest 3rd towards fin* **7/2**[3]

2352 **4** *1¼* **Vicky Valentine**[8] 4417 4-8-6 **66**.............................. PJMcDonald 3 63
(Alistair Whillans) *trckd ldr: chal over 2f out: sn rdn: wknd ins fnl f* **9/4**[1]

2163 **5** *54* **Elizabeth Coffee (IRE)**[3] 4533 6-7-13 **66** ow3....... KieranShoemark(7) 5
(John Weymes) *v.s.a: hld up in rr: tk clsr order 1/2-way: wknd over 3f out: eased* **5/1**

2m 39.97s (-5.63) **Going Correction** -0.325s/f (Firm) **5** Ran SP% **110.9**
Speed ratings (Par 102): **105,104,101,100,64**
CSF £19.45 TOTE £7.60: £2.50, £1.80; EX 24.60 Trifecta £67.10.
**Owner** David L Bayliss **Bred** Darley **Trained** Thorney, Cambs

**FOCUS**
A tight fillies' handicap. Muddling form.

## 4664 COLLINGWOOD SHORT TERM LEARNER DRIVER INSURANCE H'CAP 5f
**4:50** (4:50) (Class 6) (0-60,60) 3-Y-O+ £2,587 (£770; £384; £192) **Stalls** Centre

Form RPR

5200 **1** **Spring Bird**[22] 3913 5-9-7 **57**.............................. PaulQuinn 5 68
(David Nicholls) *mde all in centre: rdn clr over 1f out: diminishing advantage fnl 110yds but a holding on* **15/2**

3425 **2** *nk* **Mission Impossible**[40] 3298 9-9-10 **60**..................(p) RobertWinston 12 70
(Tracy Waggott) *racd stands' side: hld up: rdn 1/2-way: r.o wl fr over 1f out: edgd lft ins fnl f: jst hld* **2/1**[1]

0045 **3** *2¼* **Findog**[4] 4519 4-9-4 **57**.............................. SamJames(3) 7 59
(Linda Perratt) *hld up: rdn 1/2-way: kpt on to go 3rd ins fnl f* **11/2**[3]

0500 **4** *2* **Sunrise Dance**[29] 3668 5-9-10 **60**.............................. AndrewMullen 13 55
(Robert Johnson) *led trio stands' side: prom overall: rdn 1/2-way: wknd ins fnl f* **10/1**

4002 **5** *¾* **Tuibama (IRE)**[10] 4314 5-9-5 **55**..............................(p) PhillipMakin 2 47
(Tracy Waggott) *trckd ldr: rdn 2f out: wknd fnl f* **3/1**[2]

0600 **6** *1½* **Arch Walker (IRE)**[2] 4567 7-8-12 **48**..............................(b) TomEaves 4 35
(John Weymes) *trckd ldr: rdn 1/2-way: wknd fnl f* **12/1**

6001 **7** *nse* **Tadalavil**[12] 4257 9-8-12 **53**.............................. SammyJoBell(5) 3 39
(Linda Perratt) *trckd ldr: rdn 2f out: wknd over 1f out* **8/1**

-000 8 8 **Mrs Gorsky**[57] 2738 4-8-3 **46** oh1 RachelRichardson(7) 9 4
(Patrick Holmes) *racd stands' side: hld up: a bhd* **33/1**
000- 9 11 **Liberal Lady**[472] 1467 6-9-3 **56** (t) ConnorBeasley(3) 1
(Robert Johnson) *dwlt: hld up: a bhd* **20/1**
59.53s (-1.57) **Going Correction** -0.325s/f (Firm)
**WFA** 3 from 4yo+ 4lb **9** Ran SP% **121.1**
Speed ratings (Par 101): **99,98,94,91,90 88,88,75,57**
CSF £24.08 CT £93.88 TOTE £7.60: £2.10, £1.60, £2.20; EX 35.00 Trifecta £146.00.
**Owner** D G Clayton **Bred** D G Clayton **Trained** Sessay, N Yorks
**FOCUS**
A weak sprint handicap in which the main body of the field race down the centre while three came up the stands' rail. It's been rated to face value for now.

## 4665 COLLINGWOOD.GI APPRENTICE H'CAP 1m 2f 32y
5:25 (5:25) (Class 6) (0-60,61) 3-Y-O+ £1,940 (£577; £288; £144) Stalls Centre

Form RPR
0300 1 **Silver Tigress**[10] 4319 6-8-11 **46** KieranShoemark(4) 2 53
(Iain Jardine) *trckd ldr: rdn over 2f out: chal strly ins fnl f: kpt on: led post* **10/1**
5500 2 shd **Taxiformissbyron**[8] 4381 4-8-10 **45** RowanScott(4) 10 52
(Iain Jardine) *led at stdy pce: rdn over 2f out: jnd ins fnl f: kpt on: hdd post* **20/1**
2245 3 2 3/4 **Lil Sophella (IRE)**[19] 4023 5-9-8 **57** PeterSword(4) 1 59
(Patrick Holmes) *slowly away: hld up: hdwy on inner over 3f out: rdn 2f out: kpt on* **4/1**[2]
/033 4 4 **Snow Dancer (IRE)**[11] 4293 10-9-12 **59** ChrisMeehan(2) 6 53
(John David Riches) *hld up: rdn over 2f out: nvr threatened* **13/2**
0061 5 3/4 **Pim Street (USA)**[6] 4468 4-9-12 **61** 6ex JoshDoyle(4) 8 54
(David O'Meara) *hld up: rdn over 3f out: sn no imp* **5/4**[1]
0636 6 4 **Monthly Medal**[10] 4319 11-9-0 **45** (t) AnnaHesketh 9 30
(Wilf Storey) *midfield: rdn 3f out: wknd over 1f out* **20/1**
0464 7 1 1/4 **Bold And Free**[21] 3958 4-9-4 **51** (p) JordonMcMurray(2) 3 34
(David Thompson) *trckd ldr: rdn over 2f out: sn wknd* **9/2**[3]
2m 10.67s (-1.23) **Going Correction** -0.325s/f (Firm)
**WFA** 3 from 4yo+ 10lb **7** Ran SP% **114.6**
Speed ratings (Par 101): **91,90,88,85,84 81,80**
CSF £169.98 CT £926.62 TOTE £9.50: £3.20, £6.00; EX 64.60 Trifecta £703.20.
**Owner** John Mabon & I J Jardine **Bred** Mrs J M F Dibben & Mrs Amanda Brudenell **Trained** Bonchester Bridge, Borders
**FOCUS**
A weak handicap for apprentice riders and it paid to be handy.
T/Plt: £60.40 to a £1 stake. Pool: £83,167.30 - 1004.17 winning units. T/Qpdt: £26.10 to a £1 stake. Pool: £4655.98 - 131.56 winning units. AS

# 4617 NEWMARKET (R-H)
Saturday, July 26

**OFFICIAL GOING: Good to firm (7.3)**
Far side track used with Stalls on Far side except 10f & 13f: Centre.
Wind: Light half-behind Weather: Cloudy with sunny spells

## 4666 ADNAMS SOUTHWOLD BITTER EBF STALLIONS MAIDEN STKS (BOBIS RACE) 7f
2:10 (2:10) (Class 4) 2-Y-O £4,528 (£1,347; £673; £336) Stalls Low

Form RPR
1 **Future Empire** 2-9-5 0 HarryBentley 11 85+
(Saeed bin Suroor) *trckd ldrs: rdn to ld over 1f out: r.o* **7/2**[2]
6 2 2 1/2 **Invincible Gold (IRE)**[68] 2380 2-9-5 0 NickyMackay 9 78
(Ed Walker) *chsd ldr: rdn and ev ch over 1f out: styd on same pce ins fnl f* **25/1**
0 3 2 **Space Age (IRE)**[15] 4167 2-9-5 0 SilvestreDeSousa 13 73
(Charlie Appleby) *s.i.s: sn racing keenly and prom: rdn over 1f out: styd on same pce ins fnl f* **9/4**[1]
56 4 nk **Honcho (IRE)**[16] 4109 2-9-5 0 (p) DavidProbert 8 72
(David Elsworth) *led: rdn and hdd over 1f out: styd on same pce ins fnl f* **33/1**
5 hd **Sahaafy (USA)** 2-9-5 0 ChrisHayes 1 72+
(B W Hills) *s.i.s: hld up: swtchd lft over 5f out: hdwy over 2f out: sn rdn: styd on same pce fnl f* **11/2**[3]
6 1 1/2 **Doubly Clever (IRE)** 2-9-5 0 GrahamGibbons 4 67
(Charles Hills) *hld up in tch: rdn over 1f out: no ex fnl f* **28/1**
62 7 1/2 **Steady Major (IRE)**[39] 3324 2-9-5 0 PatCosgrave 7 66
(David Simcock) *trckd ldrs: rdn over 1f out: no ex ins fnl f* **12/1**
8 3/4 **Deerfield** 2-9-5 0 TomQueally 10 64+
(Charlie Appleby) *s.i.s: hld up: shkn up over 2f out: nvr trbld ldrs* **8/1**
9 1 **Belgrade** 2-9-5 0 PatDobbs 12 61
(Richard Hannon) *chsd ldrs: rdn over 1f out: wknd fnl f* **11/2**[3]
00 10 2 3/4 **Happy Pursuit**[7] 4444 2-9-0 0 AdamBeschizza 5 49
(Stuart Williams) *s.i.s: hld up: rdn and wknd over 1f out* **100/1**
11 17 **Shadow Rock (IRE)** 2-9-5 0 TedDurcan 3 8
(Richard Hannon) *s.s: outpcd* **33/1**
12 shd **North America** 2-9-5 0 RobertHavlin 2 8
(Charlie Appleby) *s.i.s: a in rr: bhd fr 1/2-way* **25/1**
1m 26.59s (0.89) **Going Correction** +0.10s/f (Good) **12** Ran SP% **120.6**
Speed ratings (Par 96): **98,95,92,92,92 90,90,89,88,84 65,65**
CSF £97.22 TOTE £5.00: £2.10, £5.50, £1.30; EX 138.60 Trifecta £675.10.
**Owner** Godolphin **Bred** Rabbah Bloodstock Limited **Trained** Newmarket, Suffolk
**FOCUS**
Far side track used with stalls on far side except 1m2f & 1m5f: centre. Quick, watered ground. Far-side track; Stalls 1m2f & 1m5f: Centre, Remainder: Stands' side. The second, third and fourth had already raced, but there were still some interesting newcomers on show, the most obvious among them the winner. They raced stands' side. The runner-up was a notable improver, but the well-backed third did not take much of a step forward.

## 4667 ADNAMS DRY HOPPED LAGER H'CAP 1m 2f
2:45 (2:45) (Class 3) (0-95,95) 3-Y-O+
£9,337 (£2,796; £1,398; £699; £349; £175) Stalls Centre

Form RPR
-330 1 **First Flight (IRE)**[37] 3378 3-9-1 **92** HarryBentley 7 104+
(Saeed bin Suroor) *hld up: hdwy and hmpd over 2f out: rdn to ld ins fnl f: r.o* **7/4**[1]
5-20 2 nk **Ajmany (IRE)**[61] 2618 4-9-9 **95** (b) CamHardie(5) 2 106
(Luca Cumani) *a.p: racd keenly: rdn to ld over 2f out: hdd ins fnl f: r.o* **11/2**[3]
4350 3 1 **Awake My Soul (IRE)**[14] 4212 5-9-12 **93** GrahamGibbons 4 102
(David O'Meara) *hld up: hdwy and nt clr run over 1f out: sn rdn: r.o* **11/2**[3]
31 4 4 1/2 **Tryster (IRE)**[25] 3822 3-8-11 **88** (p) SilvestreDeSousa 8 92
(Charlie Appleby) *hld up: hdwy over 2f out: sn hung rt: rdn and ev ch whn hung lft over 1f out: wknd ins fnl f* **4/1**[2]
6-03 5 1 1/4 **Proud Chieftain**[28] 3726 6-9-13 **94** PatDobbs 3 92
(Clifford Lines) *chsd ldrs: racd away fr main gp over 7f out: rdn over 2f out: wknd ins fnl f* **14/1**
1101 6 9 **San Cassiano (IRE)**[28] 3718 7-9-9 **90** JasonHart 1 71
(Ruth Carr) *led: rdn and hdd over 2f out: wknd over 1f out* **11/1**
3231 7 hd **Bureau (IRE)**[7] 4453 3-8-7 **87** MichaelJMMurphy(3) 6 68
(Mark Johnston) *chsd ldr: rdn whn hmpd over 2f out: wknd over 1f out* **9/1**
2m 5.35s (-0.15) **Going Correction** +0.20s/f (Good)
**WFA** 3 from 4yo+ 10lb **7** Ran SP% **112.1**
Speed ratings (Par 107): **108,107,106,103,102 95,95**
CSF £11.22 CT £42.27 TOTE £2.90: £2.10, £3.20; EX 10.20 Trifecta £59.80.
**Owner** Godolphin **Bred** Darley **Trained** Newmarket, Suffolk
**FOCUS**
A sound pace for this decent handicap and strong form. The main action unfolded on the stands' side. The third has been rated to the same mark as his C&D effort last June.

## 4668 ADNAMS GHOST SHIP FILLIES' H'CAP 7f
3:20 (3:21) (Class 2) (0-100,98) 3-Y-O+ £16,172 (£4,812; £2,405; £1,202) Stalls Low

Form RPR
312 1 **Bragging (USA)**[52] 2892 3-8-10 **87** TedDurcan 4 100+
(Sir Michael Stoute) *trckd ldrs: pushed along over 2f out: rdn to ld ins fnl f: r.o wl* **5/1**[2]
-005 2 3 3/4 **The Gold Cheongsam (IRE)**[43] 3203 4-10-0 **98** (t) SebSanders 2 104
(Jeremy Noseda) *hld up: hdwy over 2f out: rdn over 1f out: styd on to go 2nd wl ins fnl f* **10/1**
4643 3 3/4 **Wedding Ring (IRE)**[15] 4163 3-9-6 **97** SilvestreDeSousa 11 98
(Charlie Appleby) *hld up: hdwy over 1f out: sn rdn: styd on same pce ins fnl f* **7/1**
-012 4 1 **Remember**[15] 4166 3-9-5 **96** KieranO'Neill 3 94+
(Richard Hannon) *trckd ldrs: led over 2f out: rdn and edgd rt over 1f out: hdd and no ex ins fnl f* **13/2**[3]
4211 5 1/2 **Laftah (IRE)**[9] 4367 3-8-1 **83** CamHardie(5) 7 80
(Roger Varian) *trckd ldr: racd keenly: rdn and ev ch over 2f out: no ex ins fnl f* **8/1**
33/5 6 nk **Desert Blossom (IRE)**[54] 2840 4-9-13 **97** RobertHavlin 8 96
(Charlie Appleby) *s.i.s: hld up: hdwy over 2f out: nt clr run over 1f out: styd on same pce ins fnl f* **50/1**
1-32 7 1/2 **Perfect Persuasion**[9] 4367 3-8-5 **82** ChrisHayes 6 77
(William Haggas) *prom: rdn over 2f out: no ex fnl f* **13/2**[3]
-225 8 nse **Musicora**[28] 3724 3-9-1 **92** PatDobbs 10 87
(Richard Hannon) *hld up: rdn over 1f out: nvr trbld ldrs* **20/1**
44-1 9 nk **Athenian (IRE)**[7] 4445 5-9-12 **96** LukeMorris 1 93
(Sir Mark Prescott Bt) *prom: rdn over 2f out: no ex fnl f* **8/1**
4111 10 10 **Kosika (USA)**[7] 4436 4-9-9 **96** MichaelJMMurphy(3) 5 67
(Mark Johnston) *led: rdn and hdd over 2f out: wknd over 1f out* **10/3**[1]
0-01 11 2 1/4 **Stealth Missile (IRE)**[18] 4053 3-8-12 **89** (t) TomQueally 9 51
(Clive Brittain) *mid-div: pushed along and lost pl 1/2-way: wknd 2f out* **33/1**
1m 24.69s (-1.01) **Going Correction** +0.10s/f (Good)
**WFA** 3 from 4yo+ 7lb **11** Ran SP% **119.9**
Speed ratings (Par 96): **109,104,103,102,102 101,101,101,100,89 86**
CSF £54.26 CT £363.65 TOTE £5.60: £2.10, £3.60, £2.20; EX 55.40 Trifecta £577.50.
**Owner** K Abdullah **Bred** Juddmonte Farms Inc **Trained** Newmarket, Suffolk
**FOCUS**
They raced up the middle. This was a very good fillies' handicap, but Bragging murdered them and is probably a Group horse. The runner-up and third have been rated close to their marks.

## 4669 ADNAMS BROADSIDE H'CAP (BOBIS RACE) 6f
3:55 (3:59) (Class 2) (0-105,102) 3-Y-O £32,345 (£9,625; £4,810; £2,405) Stalls Low

Form RPR
0-42 1 **Fast Track**[8] 4390 3-8-6 **87** GrahamGibbons 1 97+
(David Barron) *racd stands' side: trckd ldrs: led overall over 2f out: rdn over 1f out: jst hld on: 1st of 9 in gp* **5/1**[1]
6415 2 nse **Eastern Impact (IRE)**[42] 3253 3-9-1 **96** TonyHamilton 14 106+
(Richard Fahey) *racd far side: hld up: swtchd rt and hdwy over 1f out: rdn to ld that side ins fnl f: r.o: jst failed: 1st of 10 in gp* **10/1**
-305 3 1/2 **Suzi's Connoisseur**[15] 4166 3-9-0 **95** PatDobbs 10 103
(Hugo Palmer) *racd far side: hld up: hdwy over 2f out: rdn over 1f out: r.o: 2nd of 10 in gp* **8/1**[3]
-334 4 3/4 **Our Queenie (IRE)**[15] 4163 3-8-1 **87** CamHardie(5) 5 93
(Richard Hannon) *racd stands' side: prom: pushed along and lost pl over 4f out: hdwy u.p over 1f out: r.o: 2nd of 9 in gp* **16/1**
5-21 5 1 1/4 **Major Jack**[17] 4086 3-8-1 **82** HarryBentley 7 84
(Roger Charlton) *racd stands' side: chsd ldrs: rdn and ev ch over 1f out: styd on same pce ins fnl f: 3rd of 9 in gp* **14/1**
1213 6 1/2 **Golden Steps (FR)**[15] 4166 3-8-11 **92** CraigAWilliams 9 92
(Marco Botti) *racd stands' side: hld up: hdwy over 2f out: rdn and ev ch over 1f out: styd on same pce ins fnl f: 4th of 9 in gp* **8/1**[3]
0531 7 shd **Lady Frances**[10] 4317 3-8-4 **85** SilvestreDeSousa 2 85
(Mark Johnston) *racd stands' side: trckd ldrs: rdn over 1f out: styd on same pce ins fnl f: 5th of 9 in gp* **16/1**
0001 8 3/4 **Deeds Not Words (IRE)**[15] 4166 3-8-13 **97** CharlesBishop(3) 18 95
(Mick Channon) *led far side tl rdn and hdd over 1f out: no ex ins fnl f: 3rd of 10 in gp* **16/1**
-351 9 1/2 **Greeb**[28] 3702 3-8-8 **89** TedDurcan 17 85
(Charles Hills) *racd far side: hld up: rdn 1/2-way: hdwy over 1f out: styd on same pce ins fnl f: 4th of 10 in gp* **8/1**[3]
5211 10 shd **Foxy Clarets (IRE)**[23] 3882 3-8-4 **85** (b) LukeMorris 11 81
(Richard Fahey) *racd far side: sn pushed along in rr: hdwy over 2f out: lost pl over 1f out: styd on ins fnl f: 5th of 10 in gp* **20/1**
-220 11 shd **Toofi (FR)**[38] 3352 3-9-7 **102** TomQueally 19 97
(Roger Varian) *racd far side: trckd ldrs: rdn to ld that side over 1f out: hdd and no ex ins fnl f: 6th of 10 in gp* **6/1**[2]
6144 12 2 3/4 **The Hooded Claw (IRE)**[15] 4166 3-8-6 **87** (p) JasonHart 16 74
(Tim Easterby) *racd far side: prom: drvn along 1/2-way: no ex fnl f: 7th of 10 in gp* **14/1**
6-00 13 1/2 **Sleeper King (IRE)**[42] 3253 3-9-2 **97** (p) DavidProbert 6 82
(Kevin Ryan) *overall ldr stands' side: rdn and hdd over 2f out: wknd ins fnl f: 6th of 9 in gp* **33/1**

3-46 **14** *nk* **Survived**$^{15}$ [4171] 3-8-11 **92** ChrisHayes 12 76
(William Haggas) *racd far side: chsd ldrs: rdn over 2f out: wknd fnl f: 8th of 10 in gp* **16/1**

-100 **15** *1* **Speedfiend**$^{42}$ [3245] 3-9-5 **100** PatCosgrave 8 81
(Noel Quinlan) *racd stands' side: hld up: hdwy over 2f out: rdn and wknd over 1f out: 7th of 9 in gp* **33/1**

0360 **16** *1* **Ventura Mist**$^{15}$ [4171] 3-8-13 **94** (p) DuranFentiman 4 72
(Tim Easterby) *racd stands' side: chsd ldrs tl rdn and wknd over 1f out: 8th of 9 in gp* **33/1**

0-64 **17** *8* **Bahamian Heights**$^{11}$ [4281] 3-8-12 **93** RobertHavlin 15 45
(Clive Brittain) *racd far side: chsd ldrs: rdn over 2f out: edgd rt and wknd over 1f out: 9th of 10 in gp* **33/1**

1001 **18** *½* **Nova Champ (IRE)**$^{33}$ [3539] 3-8-0 **81** oh1 (p) NickyMackay 3 31
(Stuart Williams) *racd stands' side: hld up: rdn over 2f out: wknd over 1f out: last of 9 in gp* **25/1**

00-0 **19** *11* **Oeil De Tigre (FR)**$^{57}$ 3-8-13 **94** SebSanders 13 9
(Tony Carroll) *racd far side: w ldrs tl rdn over 2f out: wknd and eased over 1f out: last of 10 in gp* **66/1**

1m 11.49s (-1.01) **Going Correction** +0.10s/f (Good) **19 Ran SP% 132.1**
Speed ratings (Par 106): **110,109,109,108,106 105,105,104,104,104 103,100,99,99,97 96,85,85,70**
CSF £53.62 CT £425.93 TOTE £5.20: £1.90, £3.30, £2.20, £5.50; EX 63.60 Trifecta £415.70.
**Owner** Raymond Miquel **Bred** Jnp Bloodstock Ltd **Trained** Maunby, N Yorks

**FOCUS**
The 19 runners were spread all the way across the track in this really competitive 3yo sprint handicap, but there was no obvious bias. The first two may both be a bit better than the bare form for different reasons.

## 4670 ADNAMS MOSAIC EBF STALLIONS CONDITIONS STKS (BOBIS RACE) 6f
**4:30** (4:33) (Class 3) 2-Y-O **£8,409** (£2,502; £1,250; £625) **Stalls** Low

Form RPR

100 **1** **Bossy Guest (IRE)**$^{14}$ [4199] 2-9-2 97 CharlesBishop(3) 5 97
(Mick Channon) *led: rdn over 1f out: hdd ins fnl f: rallied to ld last stride* **11/4$^{2}$**

510 **2** *nk* **Portamento (IRE)**$^{39}$ [3318] 2-9-5 95 SilvestreDeSousa 7 96
(Charlie Appleby) *plld hrd and prom: jnd wnr over 3f out: rdn over 1f out: led ins fnl f: hdd last stride* **9/2$^{3}$**

210 **3** *2¼* **Smaih (GER)**$^{14}$ [4199] 2-9-5 85 PatDobbs 6 89
(Richard Hannon) *w wnr 2f: remained handy: rdn over 1f out: styd on same pce ins fnl f* **15/2**

143 **4** *2* **Percy Alleline**$^{27}$ [3751] 2-9-5 91 GrahamGibbons 4 83
(Ralph Beckett) *trckd ldrs: racd keenly: rdn and edgd rt over 1f out: no ex ins fnl f* **8/1**

31 **5** *1* **Fanciful Angel (IRE)**$^{23}$ [3893] 2-9-5 0 LukeMorris 3 80
(Marco Botti) *hld up: hdwy over 2f out: sn rdn: no ex fnl f* **2/1$^{1}$**

**6** *½* **Mukhayyam** 2-8-10 0 TedDurcan 2 70+
(Sir Michael Stoute) *hld up: shkn up over 2f out: nvr trbld ldrs* **15/2**

1m 14.03s (1.53) **Going Correction** +0.10s/f (Good) **6 Ran SP% 112.8**
Speed ratings (Par 98): **93,92,89,86,85 84**
CSF £15.51 TOTE £3.80: £1.70, £2.30; EX 17.30 Trifecta £80.60.
**Owner** John Guest Racing **Bred** Dowager Countess Harrington **Trained** West Ilsley, Berks

**FOCUS**
They raced middle-to-stands' side. Not form to get too excited about. The third has been rated as putting up an improved effort.

## 4671 ADNAMS COPPER HOUSE GIN H'CAP (BOBIS RACE) 1m
**5:05** (5:06) (Class 3) (0-90,86) 3-Y-O
**£9,337** (£2,796; £1,398; £699; £349; £175) **Stalls** Low

Form RPR

5130 **1** **Munaaser**$^{56}$ [2781] 3-9-3 **82** TedDurcan 2 101+
(Sir Michael Stoute) *hld up: swtchd rt over 2f out: hdwy to ld on bit over 1f out: c clr ins fnl f: canter* **7/4$^{1}$**

-633 **2** *3* **Surety (IRE)**$^{53}$ [2879] 3-8-10 **75** TomQueally 5 79
(Clive Brittain) *racd keenly: w ldr: rdn and ev ch over 1f out: styd on same pce fnl f* **12/1**

4105 **3** *¾* **Crowdmania**$^{7}$ [4447] 3-9-7 **86** SilvestreDeSousa 1 88
(Mark Johnston) *chsd ldrs: rdn and ev ch over 1f out: styd on same pce fnl f* **3/1$^{3}$**

621 **4** *1¾* **Doctor Sardonicus**$^{42}$ [3229] 3-9-5 **84** HarryBentley 3 82
(David Simcock) *led: rdn over 2f out: hdd over 1f out: no ex ins fnl f* **10/1**

-401 **5** *½* **Lawyer (IRE)**$^{19}$ [4028] 3-9-1 **85** CamHardie(5) 4 82
(Luca Cumani) *trckd ldrs: plld hrd: rdn over 1f out: no ex fnl f* **9/4$^{2}$**

3346 **6** *2* **Shimba Hills**$^{56}$ [2769] 3-8-5 **73** CharlesBishop(3) 6 65
(Mick Channon) *hld up in tch: rdn over 1f out: wknd fnl f* **16/1**

1m 39.88s (-0.12) **Going Correction** +0.10s/f (Good) **6 Ran SP% 114.8**
Speed ratings (Par 104): **104,101,100,98,98 96**
CSF £23.59 TOTE £3.00: £1.40, £3.80; EX 24.70 Trifecta £80.90.
**Owner** Hamdan Al Maktoum **Bred** Shadwell Estate Company Limited **Trained** Newmarket, Suffolk

**FOCUS**
An ordinary-looking race of its type.

## 4672 ROBERT PALMER MEMORIAL H'CAP (BOBIS RACE) 1m 5f
**5:35** (5:36) (Class 4) (0-80,80) 3-Y-O **£6,469** (£1,925; £962; £481) **Stalls** Centre

Form RPR

2566 **1** **Late Shipment**$^{22}$ [3932] 3-9-1 **74** (p) SilvestreDeSousa 3 86
(Mark Johnston) *mde all: rdn over 2f out: styd on strly* **5/2$^{1}$**

6636 **2** *6* **Race To Glory (FR)**$^{24}$ [3857] 3-9-5 **78** PatDobbs 5 81
(Roger Charlton) *chsd wnr: rdn over 2f out: styd on same pce fnl f* **7/1**

0002 **3** *6* **Injun Sands**$^{29}$ [3655] 3-8-12 **71** RobertHavlin 4 65
(Jane Chapple-Hyam) *s.i.s: hld up: rdn over 2f out: wknd fnl f* **7/2$^{3}$**

02 **4** *¾* **Mymatechris (IRE)**$^{31}$ [3568] 3-9-1 **74** DavidProbert 6 67
(Andrew Balding) *prom: rdn over 2f out: wknd ins fnl f* **11/4$^{2}$**

3-10 **5** *1* **Morning Watch (IRE)**$^{45}$ [3110] 3-9-2 **80** (v$^{1}$) LouisSteward(5) 1 71
(Lady Cecil) *chsd ldrs: rdn over 3f out: wknd over 1f out* **7/2$^{3}$**

2m 47.69s (3.69) **Going Correction** +0.20s/f (Good) **5 Ran SP% 112.2**
Speed ratings (Par 102): **96,92,88,88,87**
CSF £19.37 TOTE £4.30: £2.60, £2.30; EX 18.40 Trifecta £36.90.
**Owner** R Barnett **Bred** W And R Barnett Ltd **Trained** Middleham Moor, N Yorks

**FOCUS**
Uncompetitive stuff with the winner making all under a good front-running ride. It's hard to rate the race more positively as things stand.
T/Plt: £64.20 to a £1 stake. Pool: £88373.87 - 1003.94 winning tickets T/Qpdt: £37.80 to a £1 stake. Pool: £5105.73 - 99.95 winning tickets CR

# 4205 SALISBURY (R-H)
Saturday, July 26

**OFFICIAL GOING: Good to firm (9.1)**
Wind: virtually nil Weather: sunny

## 4673 CPA SCAFFOLDING "CARNARVON" H'CAP (FOR GENTLEMAN AMATEUR RIDERS) 1m
**5:45** (5:45) (Class 5) (0-70,68) 3-Y-O+ **£2,807** (£870; £435; £217) **Stalls** High

Form RPR

3524 **1** **Living Leader**$^{8}$ [4415] 5-10-13 **63** (p) MrMichaelJMurphy(3) 10 74
(Grace Harris) *mid-div: hdwy over 3f out: hanging rt whn ldng wl over 2f out: sn rdn clr: fin on far side rails: easily* **11/2**

620/ **2** *12* **Almaas (USA)**$^{674}$ [6401] 5-10-13 **65** MrAlexFerguson(5) 9 48
(Saeed bin Suroor) *trckd ldr: led over 3f out: hdd whn hmpd wl over 2f out: sn rdn and hld: kpt on same pce* **9/2$^{3}$**

0644 **3** *2* **Masai Moon**$^{17}$ [4072] 10-10-10 **64** (b) MrRTimby(7) 8 43
(Rod Millman) *towards rr: hdwy 4f out: rdn to chse ldrs 3f out: swtchd lft over 2f out: kpt on same pce* **20/1**

1102 **4** *¾* **Hail Promenader (IRE)**$^{31}$ [3589] 8-11-1 **67** (tp) MrGrahamCarson(5) 5 44
(Anthony Carson) *in tch tl lost pl after 1f: sn pushed along in last pair: rdn and stdy prog fr over 2f out: styd on fnl f but nvr any ch* **4/1$^{2}$**

-440 **5** *3* **Candelita**$^{16}$ [4115] 7-10-4 **58** MrStanSheppard(7) 3 28
(Matt Sheppard) *mid-div: struggling in rr over 3f out: sme late prog: nvr any threat* **20/1**

-002 **6** *1¼* **Galatian**$^{17}$ [4073] 7-11-7 **68** MrSWalker 4 35
(Rod Millman) *chsd ldrs: rdn over 3f out: sn one pce* **5/1**

-020 **7** *2½* **Imperial Glance**$^{24}$ [3850] 4-11-2 **68** MrHHunt(5) 6 30
(Andrew Balding) *taken to s early: awkward leaving stalls: sn trcking ldrs: rdn over 3f out: sn btn* **10/3$^{1}$**

6 **8** *11* **City Of Angkor Wat (IRE)**$^{35}$ [3473] 4-10-3 **55** MrJamesHughes(5) 7
(Jo Hughes) *led tl over 3f out: sn wknd* **16/1**

6005 **9** *6* **Lionheart**$^{9}$ [4339] 4-11-1 **67** MrGeorgeCrate(5) 1
(Peter Crate) *mid-div: rdn over 3f out: wknd over 2f out* **16/1**

1m 44.5s (1.00) **Going Correction** +0.05s/f (Good) **9 Ran SP% 114.6**
Speed ratings (Par 103): **97,85,83,82,79 78,75,64,58**
CSF £30.20 CT £366.43 TOTE £4.50: £1.10, £1.80, £4.90; EX 41.30 Trifecta £215.60.
**Owner** Mrs Michelle Harris **Bred** D J And Mrs Deer **Trained** Shirenewton, Monmouthshire

**FOCUS**
The going was officially described as good to firm before the gentleman amateur riders' handicap that got the seven-race card under way. The track had been watered. An open contest on paper but it was turned into a rout. The race fell apart and the winner doesn't look an obvious improver.

## 4674 DORSET SUBARU CLASSIFIED CLAIMING STKS 6f 212y
**6:15** (6:16) (Class 5) 3-4-Y-O **£2,749** (£818; £408; £204) **Stalls** Centre

Form RPR

-404 **1** **Concrete Mac**$^{33}$ [3518] 3-8-4 68 CharlieBennett(7) 6 73
(Hughie Morrison) *chsd ldrs: pushed along over 3f out: rdn over 2f out: led ent fnl f: kpt on wl* **9/1**

6030 **2** *3¼* **Freddy With A Y (IRE)**$^{15}$ [4156] 4-9-4 73 (p) GeorgeBaker 4 68
(Gary Moore) *trckd ldrs: rdn and ev ch over 1f out tl jst ins fnl f: kpt on same pce* **3/1$^{2}$**

1053 **3** *shd* **Rough Courte (IRE)**$^{14}$ [4191] 3-8-4 71 PaddyPilley(7) 5 64
(Mick Channon) *taken to s early: led: rdn over 2f out: hdd ent fnl f: keeping on at same pce whn hung into rails nring fin* **4/1$^{3}$**

0532 **4** *7* **Vodka Time (IRE)**$^{3}$ [4536] 3-7-12 65 PhilipPrince(5) 2 38
(David Evans) *slowly away: nvr travelling in detached last: wnt 4th 2f out but nvr any danger* **13/2**

2662 **5** *29* **Inkerman (IRE)**$^{7}$ [4432] 4-9-0 74 (p) RichardHughes 1
(Jamie Osborne) *trckd ldr: swtchd rt for effrt 3f out: wknd 2f: eased whn btn* **11/8$^{1}$**

1m 28.19s (-0.41) **Going Correction** +0.05s/f (Good)
**WFA** 3 from 4yo 7lb **5 Ran SP% 110.4**
Speed ratings (Par 103): **104,100,100,92,59**
CSF £35.29 TOTE £19.00: £6.80, £1.30; EX 36.70 Trifecta £137.20.Vodka Time was claimed by Mr S. A. Harris for £4,000.
**Owner** Adrian N R Mcalpine & Partners **Bred** Jeremy Green And Sons **Trained** East Ilsley, Berks

**FOCUS**
A small-field classified race featuring some performers who've hardly been pulling up any trees in handicaps. The runner-up and third are not bombproof form-wise.

## 4675 PARTY CONTINUES AT THE CHAPEL NIGHTCLUB H'CAP 5f
**6:45** (6:45) (Class 6) (0-65,65) 3-Y-O+ **£2,587** (£770; £384; £192) **Stalls** High

Form RPR

2-34 **1** **Joyous**$^{12}$ [4267] 4-9-12 **63** RichardHughes 5 71
(Dean Ivory) *led for 1f: chsd ldr: rdn over 2f out: r.o fnl f: led nring fin* **2/1$^{1}$**

3510 **2** *¾* **Picc Of Burgau**$^{24}$ [3848] 4-9-11 **62** GeorgeBaker 3 67
(Geoffrey Deacon) *hld up in tch: hdwy over 2f out: sn rdn: swtchd lft over 1f out: r.o wl ins fnl f: snatched 2nd fnl stride* **2/1$^{1}$**

0204 **3** *nse* **Only Ten Per Cent (IRE)**$^{7}$ [4431] 6-9-12 **63** (v) JimCrowley 9 68
(J R Jenkins) *d after 1f: rdn 2f out: kpt on tl no ex and hdd nring fin: lost 2nd fnl stride* **9/2$^{2}$**

0-00 **4** *4½* **My Meteor**$^{16}$ [4102] 7-9-3 **57** DeclanBates(3) 1 46
(Tony Newcombe) *hld up in tch: rdn wl over 2f out: wnt 4th ent fnl f: nvr gng pce to threaten ldrs* **20/1**

1230 **5** *1¼* **Picansort**$^{28}$ [3707] 7-9-11 **62** (b) ShaneKelly 2 46
(Peter Crate) *chsd ldrs: rdn over 2f out: nt pce to chal: fdd ins fnl f* **6/1$^{3}$**

604 **6** *shd* **Silken Poppy**$^{28}$ [3729] 3-9-1 **59** ThomasBrown(3) 6 42
(Patrick Chamings) *chsd ldrs: rdn over 2f out: nt pce to get on terms: fdd ins fnl f* **12/1**

1m 1.5s (0.50) **Going Correction** +0.05s/f (Good)
**WFA** 3 from 4yo+ 4lb **6 Ran SP% 111.6**
Speed ratings (Par 101): **98,96,96,89,87 87**
CSF £5.93 CT £13.82 TOTE £2.40: £1.10, £2.60; EX 5.90 Trifecta £20.40.
**Owner** K T Ivory **Bred** K T Ivory **Trained** Radlett, Herts

**FOCUS**
Six runners in this sprint handicap and it was the least exposed who was successful. The level is a bit fluid, with the third having something to prove on pre-race turf form.

## 4676 BATHWICK TYRES BRITISH STALLION STUDS EBF MAIDEN STKS (BOBIS RACE) 6f
**7:15** (7:18) (Class 4) 2-Y-O **£4,204** (£1,251; £625; £312) **Stalls** High

Form RPR
**1** **Plymouth Sound** 2-9-5 0 JohnFahy 6 77+
(Eve Johnson Houghton) *mid-div: hdwy 3f out: chal wl over 1f out: shkn up to ld ent fnl f: r.o wl* **12/1**
523 **2** *3/4* **Harlequin Striker (IRE)**[14] 4207 2-9-5 78 JamesDoyle 7 75
(Mick Channon) *led: rdn over 1f out: hdd ent fnl f: kpt on: hld nring fin* **9/4**[2]
0 **3** *1 3/4* **Lysander The Greek**[15] 4142 2-9-5 0 JimCrowley 8 70+
(Ralph Beckett) *trckd ldrs: rdn to chal wl over 1f out: hld jst ins fnl f: kpt on same pce* **11/4**[3]
6 **4** *hd* **Crafty Choice**[12] 4270 2-9-5 0 RichardHughes 2 69
(Richard Hannon) *w ldr tl rdn 2f out: sn hld: kpt on same pce fnl f* **15/8**[1]
**5** *nk* **Illusive Force (IRE)** 2-9-5 0 GeorgeBaker 1 68+
(Charles Hills) *mid-div: swtchd lft over 2f out: sn rdn: kpt on ins fnl f* **10/1**
0 **6** *1/2* **Muzarkash**[98] 1583 2-9-5 0 PaulHanagan 5 67+
(B W Hills) *hmpd sn after s: mid-div: hmpd again after 2f: hdwy 3f out: sn rdn to chse ldrs: kpt on fnl f but nt gng pce to get on terms* **25/1**
50 **7** *1* **Mywayalways (IRE)**[7] 4424 2-9-5 0 JFEgan 3 64
(David Evans) *trckd ldrs: rdn over 2f out: keeping on at same pce whn nt clr run fnl 100yds* **50/1**
**8** *4 1/2* **More Drama (IRE)** 2-9-0 0 ShaneKelly 9 45
(Sylvester Kirk) *little slowly away: a towards rr* **50/1**
0 **9** *8* **Red Renee**[31] 3583 2-8-11 0 DeclanBates(3) 4 21
(Mark Gillard) *mid-div for 2f: sn outpcd in last trio* **100/1**
**10** *4* **Lady Vellyn** 2-9-0 0 [1] AdamBeschizza 10 9
(Paul Morgan) *unsettled stalls: s.i.s: a towards rr* **66/1**

1m 17.51s (2.71) **Going Correction** +0.05s/f (Good) **10** Ran SP% **119.3**
Speed ratings (Par 96): **83,82,79,79,79 78,77,71,60,55**
CSF £39.75 TOTE £9.40: £2.40, £1.10, £1.70; EX 54.10 Trifecta £181.00.
**Owner** T Keane, M Page, D Smith & R Whichelow **Bred** Mrs James Wigan **Trained** Blewbury, Oxon

**FOCUS**
Likely just an average maiden with plenty in with a chance a furlong out. The runner-up helps set the opening level.

## 4677 BATHWICK TYRES MAIDEN STKS 6f
**7:50** (7:51) (Class 5) 3-Y-O+ **£3,234** (£962; £481; £240) **Stalls** High

Form RPR
3034 **1** **Munfallet (IRE)**[2] 4572 3-9-0 77 MarcMonaghan(5) 3 75
(David Brown) *led: rdn and hdd over 1f out: kpt on strly to regain ld fnl 75yds: drvn out* **2/1**[1]
60 **2** *hd* **Tap Your Toes (IRE)**[22] 3914 3-9-5 0 ShaneKelly 10 74
(Luca Cumani) *mid-div on outer: hdwy 3f out: rdn in cl 3rd over 1f out: r.o wl fnl 120yds* **12/1**
-204 **3** *1 1/4* **Suitsus**[28] 3709 3-9-5 68 JimCrowley 9 70
(Peter Makin) *trckd ldr: rdn to ld over 1f out: no ex whn hdd fnl 75yds* **4/1**[3]
32-0 **4** *1 3/4* **Nathr (USA)**[22] 3914 3-9-5 80 PaulHanagan 2 64
(Charles Hills) *s.i.s: towards rr: hdwy 3f out: sn rdn to chse ldrs: kpt on but nt gng pce to get on terms fnl f* **11/4**[2]
**5** *2* **Mon Cigar (IRE)** 3-9-5 0 PatCosgrave 5 58
(Denis Coakley) *mid-div tl outpcd over 3f out: kpt on again but no ch fnl f* **33/1**
23 **6** *2* **Inis Airc (IRE)**[28] 3729 3-9-0 0 RichardHughes 6 47
(Sylvester Kirk) *mid-div: rdn 2f out: nt pce to get involved* **6/1**
-60 **7** *2 1/2* **Simma (IRE)**[19] 4029 3-8-9 0 JoshBaudains(5) 4 39+
(Sylvester Kirk) *mid-div: nt clr run on far rails bhd outpcd horse and lost pl over 3f out: sn rdn towards rr: nvr a danger after* **33/1**
5 **8** *1 1/2* **Unbridled Joy (IRE)**[28] 3729 3-9-0 0 JamesDoyle 7 34+
(Clive Cox) *stmbld leaving stalls and nrly uns rdr: in last pair: hdwy 3f out: sn rdn: wknd fnl f* **10/1**
6- **9** *2 1/2* **Queen Cee**[255] 7860 3-8-11 0 ThomasBrown(3) 8 26
(Simon Hodgson) *trckd ldr tl rdn 3f out: sn wknd* **66/1**
**10** *15* **Out Of Orbit** 3-8-11 0 DeclanBates(3) 1
(Mark Gillard) *chsd ldrs for over 2f: sn bhd* **100/1**

1m 14.8s **Going Correction** +0.05s/f (Good) **10** Ran SP% **119.4**
Speed ratings (Par 103): **102,101,100,97,95 92,89,87,83,63**
CSF £28.38 TOTE £5.70: £1.70, £4.70, £1.30; EX 39.40 Trifecta £185.10.
**Owner** J C Fretwell **Bred** Miss Joann Lyons **Trained** Averham Park, Notts

**FOCUS**
An uninspiring 3yo sprint maiden. The third has been rated to his reappearance C&D handicap form.

## 4678 GINGER GROUSE BY FAMOUS GROUSE H'CAP 1m 6f 21y
**8:20** (8:20) (Class 5) (0-75,73) 3-Y-O+ **£2,911** (£866; £432; £216)

Form RPR
4 **1** **Air Squadron**[26] 3796 4-9-1 60 JimCrowley 2 70+
(Ralph Beckett) *hld up: stdy prog fr 4f out: rdn over 2f out: led over 1f out: styd on wl* **10/3**[1]
-000 **2** *3 1/2* **Significant Move**[24] 3851 7-9-6 65 (b) PatCosgrave 8 70
(Stuart Kittow) *chsd clr ldr: clsd on ldr 3f out: sn rdn: styd on to go 2nd ins fnl f but a being hld by wnr* **5/1**
0/04 **3** *3/4* **Benbecula**[41] 3274 5-9-6 72 MikeyEnnis(7) 7 76
(Richard Mitchell) *led: sn clr: rdn 2f out: hdd over 1f out: no ex fnl f* **9/2**[3]
4600 **4** *7* **Last Echo (IRE)**[28] 3711 3-7-7 59 oh3 JaneElliott(7) 1 53
(Ralph Beckett) *trckd ldrs: rdn over 4f out: styd on same pce fnl 3f* **10/1**
5004 **5** *22* **Double Dealites**[17] 4082 4-8-11 59 ThomasBrown(3) 6 22
(Jamie Poulton) *chsd clr ldr: rdn over 4f out: btn whn hung lft fr 3f out: t.o* **4/1**[2]
**6** *33* **Polstar (FR)**[20] 5-9-7 73 PaulNO'Brien(7) 5
(Harry Whittington) *chsd clr ldr tl rdn over 4f out: wknd over 2f out: sn eased: t.o* **16/1**
1105 **7** *1* **Newtown Cross (IRE)**[59] 2683 4-8-13 58 RichardHughes 4
(Jimmy Fox) *hld up: struggling over 5f out: eased whn btn 3f out: t.o* **5/1**
5000 **8** *3* **Assembly**[8] 4415 4-8-5 55 MarcMonaghan(5) 3
(Mark Rimell) *racd keenly: a bhd: t.o* **12/1**

3m 4.92s (-2.48) **Going Correction** -0.075s/f (Good)
**WFA** 3 from 4yo+ 14lb **8** Ran SP% **117.3**
Speed ratings (Par 103): **104,102,101,97,85 66,65,63**
CSF £20.85 CT £75.91 TOTE £4.10: £1.90, £2.00, £2.10; EX 23.00 Trifecta £165.20.
**Owner** Lady Cobham **Bred** Lady Cobham **Trained** Kimpton, Hants

**FOCUS**
An average staying handicap for the grade. The runner-up has been rated to this year's form.

## 4679 BATHWICK TYRES H'CAP (BOBIS RACE) 6f 212y
**8:50** (8:50) (Class 4) (0-85,85) 3-Y-O **£6,469** (£1,925; £962; £481) **Stalls** Centre

Form RPR
1155 **1** **Despot (IRE)**[14] 4181 3-9-2 80 GeorgeBaker 7 92
(Charles Hills) *mde all: rdn clr over 1f out: edgd rt: comf* **9/2**[2]
0030 **2** *4 1/2* **Act Of Charity (IRE)**[10] 4323 3-9-5 83 (b) ShaneKelly 2 83
(Gay Kelleway) *hld up: hdwy 2f out: sn rdn: chsd wnr ent fnl f: kpt on same pce* **20/1**
4460 **3** *nk* **Fiftyshadesofgrey (IRE)**[33] 3539 3-9-0 78 PatCosgrave 6 78
(George Baker) *hld up: pushed along and hdwy 2f out: nt clrest of runs over 1f out: kpt on to go 3rd ins fnl f* **8/1**
-660 **4** *2 1/4* **Art Official (IRE)**[50] 2962 3-9-5 83 RichardHughes 4 77
(Richard Hannon) *trckd ldrs: rdn over 2f out: nt pce to chal* **5/1**[3]
0330 **5** *3* **Captain Midnight (IRE)**[15] 4176 3-9-4 82 JimCrowley 5 68
(David Brown) *hld up: rdn over 2f out: nvr gng pce to get on terms* **12/1**
1-1 **6** *3/4* **Alzanti (USA)**[23] 3890 3-9-7 85 JamesDoyle 1 69
(Amanda Perrett) *stmbld bdly leaving stalls: trckd ldrs: swtchd lft over 2f out: rdn to chse wnr over 1f out tl wknd ent fnl f* **1/1**[1]
1602 **7** *1 1/4* **Solo Hunter**[14] 4208 3-8-11 75 (v) JFEgan 3 56
(David Evans) *trckd ldr: rdn over 2f out: sn wknd* **12/1**

1m 27.24s (-1.36) **Going Correction** +0.05s/f (Good) **7** Ran SP% **116.1**
Speed ratings (Par 102): **109,103,103,100,97 96,95**
CSF £82.90 TOTE £5.60: £2.80, £10.40; EX 93.00 Trifecta £1191.00.
**Owner** Hon Mrs Corbett, C Wright, Mrs B W Hills **Bred** Michael G Daly **Trained** Lambourn, Berks

**FOCUS**
With the favourite bombing out the nightcap didn't take as much winning as it looked to on paper. The winner made all in a good time, though.
T/Plt: £68.90 to a £1 stake. Pool: £65930.61 - 697.84 winning tickets T/Qpdt: £5.80 to a £1 stake. Pool: £7486.36 - 948.03 winning tickets TM

# 4631 YORK (L-H)
## Saturday, July 26

**OFFICIAL GOING: Good to firm (7.5; home straight; far side 7.4, centre 7.4, stands' side 7.2)**
Rail alignment around home bend to provide fresh ground reduced distances of races of 1m and further by 24yds.
Wind: light 1/2 behind Weather: fine and sunny, very warm

## 4680 SKYBET MONEY BACK IF FAVOURITE WINS EBF STALLIONS FILLIES' STKS (H'CAP) 1m 2f 88y
**1:50** (1:50) (Class 3) (0-90,87) 3-Y-O+ **£16,172** (£4,812; £2,405; £1,202) **Stalls** Low

Form RPR
3521 **1** **Kleo (GR)**[18] 4052 3-8-13 82 DanielTudhope 8 96+
(Luca Cumani) *hld up in mid-div: effrt on outside over 3f out: led appr fnl f: edgd lft: styd on strly* **2/1**[1]
0555 **2** *3 3/4* **Cosmic Halo**[20] 3999 5-8-12 74 GeorgeChaloner(3) 2 80
(Richard Fahey) *mid-div: hdwy 4f out: sn chsng ldrs: upsides over 2f out: styd on same pce appr fnl f* **7/1**
0204 **3** *1 1/4* **Maven**[29] 3644 6-10-0 87 DavidAllan 1 91
(Tim Easterby) *trckd ldrs: upsides over 2f out: led briefly wl over 1f out: styd on same pce* **8/1**
5620 **4** *3/4* **Yojojo (IRE)**[56] 2783 5-10-0 87 KierenFallon 4 90
(Gay Kelleway) *t.k.h in rr: effrt over 3f out: kpt on fnl 2f: gng on at fin* **16/1**
4231 **5** *nk* **Maracuja**[12] 4255 3-8-11 80 FrannyNorton 5 82
(Mark Johnston) *set modest pce: qcknd gallop 4f out: hdd wl over 1f out: fdd fnl f* **5/1**[3]
1313 **6** *2* **Maybeme**[7] 4454 8-9-1 74 (p) AndrewElliott 7 72
(Neville Bycroft) *dwlt: in rr: sme hdwy on inner over 2f out: sn wknd* **14/1**
-413 **7** *hd* **Carnevale**[21] 3968 3-8-8 77 AndreaAtzeni 3 75
(Ralph Beckett) *sn chsng ldrs: drvn 3f out: wknd 2f out* **7/2**[2]
5500 **8** *1* **Al Manaal**[12] 4271 4-8-12 78 DanielCremin(7) 6 74
(Mick Channon) *trckd ldrs: t.k.h: wknd over 1f out* **33/1**

2m 8.59s (-3.91) **Going Correction** -0.275s/f (Firm)
**WFA** 3 from 4yo+ 10lb **8** Ran SP% **111.3**
Speed ratings (Par 104): **104,101,100,99,99 97,97,96**
CSF £15.68 CT £87.40 TOTE £2.60: £1.20, £2.00, £2.60; EX 17.20 Trifecta £88.40.
**Owner** Mrs M Marinopoulos **Bred** Figaia Stud **Trained** Newmarket, Suffolk

**FOCUS**
Rail alignment around home bend to provide fresh ground reduced distances of races of 1m and further by 24yds. A dry, bright sunny and hot day, with very little breeze. There had been 2.5mm of water applied overnight and the ground rode as advertised. A decent fillies' handicap and for the seventh time in 11 renewals, it went to a progressive 3yo. The gallop was steady until they turned in, they all quickened up at the same time approaching 3f and came up the centre of the track. The second and third have been rated close to their marks.

## 4681 SKYBET BEST ODDS GUARANTEED STKS (H'CAP) 7f
**2:20** (2:20) (Class 2) (0-105,104) 3-Y-O+ **£16,172** (£4,812; £2,405; £1,202) **Stalls** Low

Form RPR
4413 **1** **Alejandro (IRE)**[21] 3964 5-9-4 94 DavidNolan 5 105
(David O'Meara) *led tl over 4f out: led over 2f out: narrowly hdd wl ins fnl f: rallied to regain ld nr line* **15/2**
3554 **2** *nk* **Alfred Hutchinson**[14] 4212 6-8-13 89 BarryMcHugh 3 99
(Geoffrey Oldroyd) *mid-div: hdwy over 2f out: narrow ld last 75yds: hdd and no ex nr fin* **6/1**[3]
0-25 **3** *1 1/4* **Silent Bullet (IRE)**[27] 3753 3-9-3 100 KierenFallon 10 104
(Saeed bin Suroor) *mid-div: drvn over 3f out: styd on fnl f: tk 3rd nr line* **9/1**
5-05 **4** *1* **Short Squeeze (IRE)**[28] 3731 4-10-0 104 GrahamLee 4 108
(Hugo Palmer) *s.i.s: hld up in rr: hdwy over 3f out: upsides and hung rt over 1f out: wknd clsng stages* **4/1**[2]
0204 **5** *2* **Sir Reginald**[8] 4384 6-9-0 93 GeorgeChaloner(3) 7 92
(Richard Fahey) *chsd ldrs: drvn over 2f out: kpt on same pce* **15/2**
0162 **6** *1/2* **Dutch Rose (IRE)**[18] 4060 5-9-12 102 DanielTudhope 1 100
(David O'Meara) *chsd ldrs: drvn over 3f out: one pce fnl 2f* **3/1**[1]
0000 **7** *1 1/4* **Mezzotint (IRE)**[14] 4200 5-9-2 92 (p) PaulMulrennan 6 86
(Stuart Williams) *s.i.s: hdwy and edgd rt over 2f out: one pce over 1f out* **16/1**
2620 **8** *1/2* **Royal Rascal**[14] 4212 4-9-4 94 DavidAllan 9 87
(Tim Easterby) *chsd ldrs: effrt over 3f out: one pce fnl 2f* **12/1**

0306 **9** *6* **Yeeoow (IRE)**[8] 4384 5-9-2 **92** ........ MartinLane 8 70
(K R Burke) *in rr: hdwy whn nt clr run over 2f out: lost pl over 1f out* **10/1**

0310 **10** *7* **Shahdaroba (IRE)**[1] 4635 4-8-11 **87** ........(v) JamieSpencer 11 46
(Micky Hammond) *chsd ldrs: led over 4f out: hdd over 2f out: sn lost pl: eased clsng stages* **20/1**

1m 22.85s (-2.45) **Going Correction** -0.15s/f (Firm)
**WFA** 3 from 4yo+ 7lb 10 Ran SP% **120.2**
Speed ratings (Par 109): **108,107,106,105,102 102,100,100,93,85**
CSF £53.75 CT £427.88 TOTE £9.60: £2.70, £1.80, £2.30; EX 55.70 Trifecta £503.40.
**Owner** Lydonford Ltd **Bred** Yeomanstown Stud **Trained** Nawton, N Yorks
■ Stewards' Enquiry : Barry McHugh four-day ban: used whip above permitted level (Aug 9-12)

**FOCUS**
A strong race in which it was easy to make a solid case for the majority of the field. The pace was true and they all wanted to come up the centre to stands' side.

## 4682 SKYBET YORK STKS (GROUP 2) 1m 2f 88y
**2:55** (2:55) (Class 1) 3-Y-O+
**£56,710** (£21,500; £10,760; £5,360; £2,690; £1,350) **Stalls** Low

Form RPR

6021 **1** **Sheikhzayedroad**[28] 3722 5-9-3 109........ MartinLane 2 115
(David Simcock) *in rr: pushed along over 6f out: drvn and hdwy over 3f out: 3rd over 2f out: hung lft and hdd and kpt on to ld last 50yds* **7/1**

0-21 **2** *nk* **Secret Gesture**[40] 3307 4-9-0 108........ JamieSpencer 1 111
(Ralph Beckett) *led: qcknd pce over 4f out: hdd over 1f out: rallied and tk 2nd nr fin* **6/1**

2231 **3** *nk* **Windhoek**[22] 3930 4-9-3 109........ KierenFallon 3 114+
(Saeed bin Suroor) *trckd ldrs: t.k.h: chal over 2f out: led over 1f out: hdd wl ins fnl f* **6/4**[1]

1-54 **4** *4 ½* **Producer**[14] 4180 5-9-3 114........ SeanLevey 8 105
(Richard Hannon) *dwlt: hld up in rr: effrt over 3f out: kpt on over 1f out: nvr a threat* **12/1**

0005 **5** *hd* **Zambucca (SAF)**[14] 4180 6-9-3 102........ DavidNolan 7 105
(Gay Kelleway) *trckd ldrs: drvn and outpcd over 2f out: kpt on ins fnl f: tk 5th clsng stages* **25/1**

1-63 **6** *1 ¼* **Danadana (IRE)**[79] 2086 6-9-3 113........ AndreaAtzeni 6 103
(Luca Cumani) *trckd ldrs: drvn over 3f out: one pce fnl 2f: fdd nr fin* **4/1**[2]

-163 **7** *1 ¾* **Long John (AUS)**[14] 4180 4-9-1 114........(b) GrahamLee 4 97
(Charlie Appleby) *hld up in mid-div: reminders over 3f out: drvn and hdwy over 2f out: wknd over 1f out* **5/1**[3]

2m 6.26s (-6.24) **Going Correction** -0.275s/f (Firm) 7 Ran SP% **115.0**
Speed ratings (Par 115): **113,112,112,108,108 107,106**
CSF £48.12 TOTE £7.50: £3.40, £2.50; EX 43.40 Trifecta £108.30.
**Owner** Mohammed Jaber **Bred** Rabbah Bloodstock Limited **Trained** Newmarket, Suffolk

**FOCUS**
Sadly no 3yo took their chance in a decent renewal of this Group 2, which was full of horses who were up to the required level. The pace was quick and it was a race of changing fortunes in the last half furlong with the tactics playing right into the winner's hands. Ordinary form for the grade.

## 4683 SKYBET DASH (H'CAP) 6f
**3:30** (3:33) (Class 2) (0-105,104) 3-Y-O+
**£31,125** (£9,320; £4,660; £2,330; £1,165; £585) **Stalls** Low

Form RPR

-2 **1** **Muthmir (IRE)**[28] 3714 4-8-13 **93**........ GrahamLee 12 107+
(William Haggas) *dwlt: hdwy to trck ldrs over 3f out: led jst ins fnl f: styd on strly: readily* **4/1**[1]

-143 **2** *1 ½* **Goldream**[22] 3927 5-9-2 **96**........(p) SeanLevey 18 105
(Robert Cowell) *chsd ldrs: upsides over 1f out: kpt on to take 2nd clsng stages* **12/1**

2-10 **3** *¾* **Rene Mathis (GER)**[36] 3420 4-9-0 **94**........ DavidNolan 20 101
(Richard Fahey) *in rr-div: hdwy over 2f out: styd on strly fnl f: fin wl* **16/1**

0-2 **4** *shd* **Zalty (FR)**[28] 3737 4-8-10 **93**........(b) ConnorKing(3) 2 99
(David Marnane, Ire) *in rr-div: hdwy over 2f out: kpt on wl fnl f* **8/1**[2]

0223 **5** *shd* **Out Do**[8] 4384 5-9-0 **94**........ DanielTudhope 8 100
(David O'Meara) *in rr: hdwy over 2f out: edgd lft over 1f out: styd on same pce ins fnl f* **10/1**[3]

2416 **6** *1* **See The Sun**[15] 4166 3-8-12 **97**........ DavidAllan 3 99
(Tim Easterby) *led: hung rt over 1f out: hdd jst ins fnl f: wknd towards fin* **12/1**

0631 **7** *1* **Kimberella**[14] 4188 4-9-2 **96**........ AdrianNicholls 11 96
(David Nicholls) *chsd ldrs: kpt on same pce fnl f* **12/1**

0111 **8** *3* **Line Of Reason (IRE)**[15] 4174 4-9-5 **99**........ PaulMulrennan 13 89
(Paul Midgley) *carried lft s: in rr: hdwy over 1f out: nvr a factor* **8/1**[2]

0-60 **9** *nk* **Secretinthepark**[14] 4188 4-8-13 **93**........ SteveDrowne 14 82
(Ed McMahon) *wnt lft s: in rr: kpt on fnl 2f: nvr a factor* **12/1**

0-00 **10** *¾* **Bogart**[14] 4179 5-9-3 **97**........ AmyRyan 4 84
(Kevin Ryan) *chsd ldrs: drvn over 2f out: wknd appr fnl f* **20/1**

0000 **11** *½* **Ancient Cross**[56] 2786 10-8-7 **94**........(t) DanielleMooney(7) 5 79
(Michael Easterby) *mid-div: edgd rt over 2f out: kpt on fnl f* **40/1**

0505 **12** *shd* **Hitchens (IRE)**[8] 4384 9-9-2 **96**........ FrannyNorton 9 81
(David Barron) *chsd ldrs: drvn over 2f out: wknd over 1f out* **20/1**

0004 **13** *1 ¼* **Picture Dealer**[11] 4305 5-8-4 **87**........ SimonPearce(3) 1 68
(Lydia Pearce) *s.i.s: in rr: sme hdwy over 1f out: nvr on terms* **25/1**

-330 **14** *hd* **Hoof It**[35] 3452 7-9-10 **104**........ KierenFallon 16 84
(Michael Easterby) *in rr: sme hdwy over 1f out: nvr a factor* **12/1**

162 **15** *½* **Bondesire**[43] 3203 4-9-0 **97**........ JulieBurke(3) 15 75
(David O'Meara) *chsd ldrs: fdd appr fnl f* **25/1**

2221 **16** *½* **Mappin Time (IRE)**[91] 1742 6-8-10 **90**........(be) AndrewElliott 6 67
(Tim Easterby) *mid-div: lost pl 2f out* **33/1**

-000 **17** *1 ½* **Whozthecat (IRE)**[6] 4480 7-8-8 **95**........(b) LukeLeadbitter(7) 19 67
(Declan Carroll) *mid-div: drvn over 2f out: sn lost pl* **33/1**

3-00 **18** *2* **Morawij**[14] 4179 4-9-9 **103**........(p) AndreaAtzeni 7 69
(Roger Varian) *chsd ldrs: lost pl over 1f out: eased clsng stages* **25/1**

6523 **19** *2* **Foxtrot Romeo (IRE)**[28] 3716 5-8-11 **91**........(tp) PaddyAspell 10 50
(Marco Botti) *in rr: bhd whn eased clsng stages* **14/1**

1m 9.42s (-2.48) **Going Correction** -0.15s/f (Firm)
**WFA** 3 from 4yo+ 5lb 19 Ran SP% **131.7**
Speed ratings (Par 109): **110,108,107,106,106 105,104,100,99,98 98,97,96,95,95 94,92,89,87**
CSF £48.80 CT £755.25 TOTE £4.60: £1.80, £3.20, £4.70, £2.70; EX 59.60 Trifecta £1178.60.
**Owner** Hamdan Al Maktoum **Bred** Sunderland Holdings Ltd **Trained** Newmarket, Suffolk

**FOCUS**
Very few got into this decent sprint, previously won by smart sprinter Hoof It (who won the Stewards' Cup a week later) in 2011 and Hawkeyethenoo the year previously. This year's renewal was won by a 4yo who looks certain to go on to better things. The runner-up has been rated as running as well as ever.

## 4684 SPORTINGLIFE.COM MY STABLE TRACKING SERVICE MEDIAN AUCTION MAIDEN STKS (BOBIS RACE) 6f
**4:05** (4:06) (Class 4) 2-Y-O
**£6,469** (£1,925; £962; £481) **Stalls** Low

Form RPR

**1** **Valley Of Fire** 2-9-5 0........ AndreaAtzeni 8 79
(William Haggas) *dwlt: in rr: hdwy over 2f out: swtchd lft over 1f out: r.o to ld last stride* **9/2**[3]

32 **2** *nse* **Fingal's Cave (IRE)**[15] 4142 2-9-5 0........ WilliamTwiston-Davies 1 79
(Mick Channon) *trckd ldrs: led over 2f out: hdd post* **9/4**[1]

2 **3** *nse* **Gurkha Friend**[9] 4357 2-9-5 0........ GrahamLee 9 79
(Karen McLintock) *t.k.h: led tl over 2f out: rallied ins fnl f: jst hld* **17/2**

**4** *1 ¾* **Must Have (FR)** 2-9-5 0........ SteveDrowne 2 74
(William Jarvis) *s.i.s: hdwy over 2f out: chsng ldrs over 1f out: kpt on same pce* **20/1**

3 **5** *1* **Third Time Lucky (IRE)**[30] 3620 2-9-2 0........ GeorgeChaloner(3) 10 71
(Richard Fahey) *trckd ldrs: effrt and hung lft over 1f out: kpt on same pce* **9/2**[3]

0 **6** *6* **Pumaflor (IRE)**[7] 4424 2-9-0 0........ DuilioDaSilva(5) 3 53
(Richard Guest) *mid-div: lost pl over 4f out: sme hdwy over 1f out: nvr a factor* **50/1**

055 **7** *2 ½* **Mister York**[11] 4286 2-9-5 62........ DavidAllan 4 45
(Mel Brittain) *chsd ldrs: wknd over 1f out* **25/1**

**8** *4 ½* **Mercury** 2-9-5 0........ JamieSpencer 5 32
(Kevin Ryan) *s.i.s: hdwy over 2f out: sn chsng ldrs: wknd over 1f out: eased clsng stages* **10/3**[2]

**9** *6* **Phoenix Storm (IRE)** 2-9-5 0........ DavidNolan 6 14
(Richard Fahey) *in rr: drvn 3f out: sn bhd* **12/1**

1m 11.83s (-0.07) **Going Correction** -0.15s/f (Firm) 9 Ran SP% **119.0**
Speed ratings (Par 96): **94,93,93,91,90 82,78,72,64**
CSF £15.26 TOTE £6.00: £1.70, £1.20, £2.40; EX 21.50 Trifecta £70.00.
**Owner** Sheikh Juma Dalmook Al Maktoum **Bred** Bearstone Stud **Trained** Newmarket, Suffolk

**FOCUS**
Probably just an ordinary maiden for the course and a three-way photo ensued. The second and third are both improving.

## 4685 SKYBET SUPPORTING YORKSHIRE AIR AMBULANCE STKS (H'CAP) 2m 88y
**4:40** (4:40) (Class 3) (0-90,87) 4-Y-O+ **£8,409** (£2,502; £1,250; £625) **Stalls** Low

Form RPR

1305 **1** **Itlaaq**[15] 4173 8-9-3 **83**........(t) KierenFallon 1 91
(Michael Easterby) *hld up towards rr: hdwy 10f out: chsng ldr over 2f out: led last 150yds: edgd rt: jst hld on* **3/1**[1]

1141 **2** *shd* **See And Be Seen**[7] 4441 4-8-8 **74**........(p) RenatoSouza 5 82
(Sylvester Kirk) *chsd ldrs: drvn 4f out: styd on over 1f out: hrd rdn and upsides last 100yds: jst failed* **4/1**[2]

0640 **3** *nk* **Grandorio (IRE)**[15] 4173 4-9-7 **87**........ DanielTudhope 4 95
(David O'Meara) *hld up in rr: brought v wd and hdwy over 3f out: edgd lft and styd on wl fnl f* **4/1**[2]

-652 **4** *nk* **Almagest**[11] 4289 6-9-5 **85**........(p) DavidNolan 7 92
(David O'Meara) *trckd ldrs: swtchd rt 4f out: hung lft over 1f out: styd on ins fnl f* **9/1**

0313 **5** *2* **Ex Oriente (IRE)**[22] 3932 5-8-12 **78**........ AndreaAtzeni 3 83
(Stuart Williams) *hld up in rr: t.k.h: hdwy over 3f out: one pce over 1f out* **6/1**

1000 **6** *3 ¼* **Be Perfect (USA)**[91] 1735 5-9-6 **86**........ AdrianNicholls 6 87
(David Nicholls) *set stdy pce: qcknd gallop over 4f out: hdd & wknd jst ins fnl f* **12/1**

6605 **7** *1* **Argent Knight**[35] 3453 4-9-6 **86**........(v) SteveDrowne 2 86
(William Jarvis) *hld up in mid-div: hdwy over 3f out: chsng ldrs over 1f out: sn wknd* **9/2**[3]

3m 40.03s (5.53) **Going Correction** -0.275s/f (Firm) 7 Ran SP% **115.2**
Speed ratings (Par 107): **75,74,74,74,73 72,71**
CSF £15.41 TOTE £3.70: £2.20, £2.20; EX 9.20 Trifecta £46.70.
**Owner** Wh & Mrs Ja Tinning, M Cox, E Grant **Bred** Shadwell Estate Company Limited **Trained** Sheriff Hutton, N Yorks

**FOCUS**
Another tight finish to a good staying handicap, where most had solid claims. The early pace was modest and two of the seven came up the stands' rail, with the remainder towards the centre and far side. The winner didn't need to find much on his recent solid runs in better grade to take this.

## 4686 SKYBET SUPPORTING NEW BEGINNINGS STKS (NURSERY H'CAP) (BOBIS RACE) 5f
**5:15** (5:15) (Class 3) 2-Y-O **£7,762** (£2,310; £1,154; £577) **Stalls** Low

Form RPR

6134 **1** **Indescribable (IRE)**[15] 4172 2-8-10 **77**........ FrannyNorton 1 81
(Mark Johnston) *led 2f: w ldrs: led 1f out: hld on wl* **15/2**

002 **2** *½* **Miss Mullberry**[29] 3656 2-8-4 **71**........[1] AndreaAtzeni 8 73
(David O'Meara) *dwlt: in rr: hdwy on outside over 1f out: styd on wl to take 2nd nr fin* **7/1**[3]

415 **3** *½* **Olivia Fallow (IRE)**[26] 3786 2-7-12 **68** ow2........ ShirleyTeasdale(5) 3 70
(Paul Midgley) *trckd ldrs: effrt over 1f out: kpt on same pce last 50yds* **11/1**

6521 **4** *1* **Ventura Shadow**[15] 4172 2-8-6 **73**........ PatrickMathers 5 69
(Richard Fahey) *rr-div: hdwy 2f out: chsng ldrs over 1f out: edgd rt and kpt on same pce ins fnl f* **8/1**

010 **5** *1 ¼* **Pillar Box (IRE)**[7] 4439 2-9-0 **88**........ GeorgiaCox(7) 4 80
(William Haggas) *w ldrs: led over 3f out: hdd 1f out: kpt on one pce* **11/4**[1]

433 **6** *1 ½* **Golden Zephyr (IRE)**[28] 3706 2-8-5 **72**........ RoystonFfrench 6 60
(B W Hills) *sn trcking ldrs: t.k.h: one pce whn hmpd wl ins fnl f* **8/1**

6104 **7** *1 ¼* **Billyoakes (IRE)**[9] 4348 2-8-12 **79**........ WilliamTwiston-Davies 2 61
(Mick Channon) *chsd ldrs: wknd fnl f* **16/1**

2623 **8** *2* **Stanghow**[15] 4172 2-8-4 **71**........ MartinLane 9 46
(Mel Brittain) *chsd ldrs: upsides 3f out: wknd over 1f out* **25/1**

1104 **9** *2 ½* **Clouds Rest**[15] 4159 2-8-12 **82**........ GeorgeChaloner(3) 10 48
(Richard Fahey) *hld up in rr: hdwy to join ldrs 3f out: wknd over 1f out* **7/1**[3]

102 **10** *2* **Secret Liaison (IRE)**[17] 4083 2-8-12 **79**........ GrahamLee 7 38
(James Tate) *a towards rr* **5/1**[2]

58.5s (-0.80) **Going Correction** -0.15s/f (Firm) 10 Ran SP% **120.4**
Speed ratings (Par 98): **100,99,98,96,94 92,90,87,83,80**
CSF £61.13 CT £598.58 TOTE £8.50: £2.70, £2.10, £3.90; EX 55.20 Trifecta £427.10.


The Form Book, Raceform Ltd, Newbury, RG14 5SJ

**Owner** Sheikh Hamdan bin Mohammed Al Maktoum **Bred** Darley **Trained** Middleham Moor, N Yorks
■ Stewards' Enquiry : Shirley Teasdale three-day ban: weighed-in 2lb heavy (Aug 17-19)

**FOCUS**
Juvenile handicap form is difficult to fathom for certain at this stage of the season. The third has been rated as posting an effort in keeping with her maiden win.
T/Plt: £202.80 to a £1 stake. Pool: £183,276.91 - 659.41 winning units. T/Qpdt: £37.00 to a £1 stake. Pool: £9068.14 - 181.02 winning units. WG

4687 - 4694a (Foreign Racing) - See Raceform Interactive

4645
## ASCOT (R-H)
Sunday, July 27

**OFFICIAL GOING: Good to firm (good in places on round course; straight course: stands' side 8.9, centre 9.1, far side 8.6; round course 7.9)**
Wind: Almost nil Weather: Fine, warm

### 4695 ANDERS FOUNDATION EBF STALLIONS CROCKER BULTEEL MAIDEN STKS (C&G) (BOBIS RACE) 6f
2:30 (2:31) (Class 2) 2-Y-O £12,938 (£3,850; £1,924; £962) Stalls Centre

| Form | | | | RPR |
|---|---|---|---|---|
| | 1 | | **Growl** 2-9-0 0 JimmyFortune 4 | 88+ |
| | | | (Brian Meehan) *trckd ldrs: clsd fr 2f out to ld jst over 1f out: pushed along and sn clr: eased nr fin* **10/1** | |
| 2 | 2 | 2 | **Auspicion** 2-9-0 0 RyanMoore 2 | 78+ |
| | | | (William Haggas) *slowly away: in tch in last: pushed along firmly fr 2f out: styd on fnl f to take 2nd last strides* **13/8**[2] | |
| | 3 | hd | **Flash Fire (IRE)** 2-9-0 0 JoeFanning 3 | 77 |
| | | | (Mark Johnston) *led: shkn up over 2f out: hdd jst over 1f out: one pce and lost 2nd last strides* **9/1**[3] | |
| | 4 | 2 ½ | **Desert Force** 2-9-0 0 RichardHughes 1 | 70 |
| | | | (Richard Hannon) *pressed ldr: shkn up over 2f out: chal over 1f out: fdd fnl f* **5/4**[1] | |
| | 5 | ¾ | **Pressure** 2-9-0 0 AdamKirby 5 | 68 |
| | | | (Clive Cox) *pressed ldrs: rdn 2f out: sn lost pl and btn* **14/1** | |

1m 16.69s (2.19) **Going Correction** +0.075s/f (Good) 5 Ran SP% **108.3**
Speed ratings (Par 100): **88,85,85,81,80**
CSF £25.96 TOTE £9.10: £3.80, £1.10; EX 28.50 Trifecta £187.70.
**Owner** Lady Rothschild **Bred** Kincorth Investments Inc **Trained** Manton, Wilts

**FOCUS**
This valuable maiden for unraced juvenile males attracted disappointingly few runners, but the first two are entered in Group company. They all raced up the middle of the track. The race average sets the level.

### 4696 GL EVENTS OWEN BROWN STKS (H'CAP) 1m 4f
3:05 (3:06) (Class 2) (0-105,103) 3-Y-O+
£18,675 (£5,592; £2,796; £1,398; £699; £351) Stalls Low

| Form | | | | RPR |
|---|---|---|---|---|
| 35-2 | 1 | | **Pallasator**[22] 3962 5-10-0 103 LukeMorris 7 | 115 |
| | | | (Sir Mark Prescott Bt) *hld up in 5th: urged along 3f out: prog 2f out to chse ldr over 1f out: drvn ahd last 150yds: styd on strly* **3/1**[2] | |
| 3002 | 2 | 2 | **Double Bluff (IRE)**[9] 4385 3-8-10 97 JoeFanning 6 | 106 |
| | | | (Mark Johnston) *led: kicked on 3f out: hrd pressed 2f out: hdd last 150yds: styd on but readily outpcd by wnr* **4/1**[3] | |
| 5003 | 3 | 3 ¾ | **Glenard**[16] 4144 4-9-2 91 GeorgeBaker 8 | 94 |
| | | | (Charles Hills) *hld up in last pair: prog on outer over 2f out gng wl: shkn up and nt qckn over 1f out: tk 3rd fnl f: no ch w ldng pair* **7/1** | |
| 11-0 | 4 | 1 ¾ | **Retirement Plan**[106] 1444 4-9-6 95 RyanMoore 2 | 95 |
| | | | (Lady Cecil) *trckd ldng trio: rdn and nt qckn 2f out: outpcd after and n.d* **5/2**[1] | |
| 2-01 | 5 | nk | **Expert Fighter (USA)**[25] 3860 5-9-7 96 KierenFallon 1 | 96 |
| | | | (Saeed bin Suroor) *t.k.h: trckd ldr: rdn to chal 2f out: nt qckn and lost 2nd over 1f out: wknd* **20/1** | |
| 3004 | 6 | 1 | **Swivel**[15] 4183 3-8-2 89 NickyMackay 9 | 87 |
| | | | (Mark Johnston) *trckd ldng pair: rdn over 2f out: losing pl whn n.m.r wl over 1f out: no ch after* **9/1** | |
| 2035 | 7 | ¾ | **Chancery (USA)**[15] 4214 6-9-11 100 DanielTudhope 5 | 97 |
| | | | (David O'Meara) *hld up in last pair: rdn and no prog over 2f out: wl btn over 1f out* **8/1** | |

2m 31.61s (-0.89) **Going Correction** +0.20s/f (Good)
**WFA** 3 from 4yo+ 12lb 7 Ran SP% **111.9**
Speed ratings (Par 109): **110,108,106,105,104 104,103**
CSF £14.71 CT £74.19 TOTE £4.00: £1.70, £3.10; EX 15.80 Trifecta £87.80.
**Owner** Baxter, Gregson, Jenkins & Warman **Bred** Newsells Park Stud **Trained** Newmarket, Suffolk
■ Stewards' Enquiry : Luke Morris caution: careless riding.

**FOCUS**
A decent handicap with an impressive winner. He looks Group class in the making, with solid formlines in behind.

### 4697 WATCH ON 3 DEVICES RACINGUK.COM/ANYWHERE H'CAP (BOBIS RACE) 6f
3:40 (3:41) (Class 4) (0-85,89) 3-Y-O £6,469 (£1,925; £962; £481) Stalls Centre

| Form | | | | RPR |
|---|---|---|---|---|
| 0-21 | 1 | | **Fyrecracker (IRE)**[26] 3816 3-8-13 75 WilliamBuick 8 | 85 |
| | | | (Marcus Tregoning) *trckd ldrs: shkn up to cl fr over 1f out: led jst ins fnl f: styd on wl* **7/1**[3] | |
| 6602 | 2 | 1 ¼ | **Smart Salute**[15] 4206 3-8-11 73 (b[1]) LukeMorris 9 | 79 |
| | | | (Ed Walker) *in tch: rdn over 2f out: no prog tl styd on wl fr over 1f out: tk 2nd nr fin: no threat to wnr* **25/1** | |
| 2323 | 3 | ¾ | **Newton's Law (IRE)**[19] 4043 3-8-11 73 (t) MartinLane 10 | 77 |
| | | | (Brian Meehan) *sltly awkward s: sn prom: led 1/2-way: rdn 2f out: hdd and one pce jst ins fnl f: lost 2nd nr fin* **8/1** | |
| 5-05 | 4 | 1 ½ | **Autumns Blush (IRE)**[11] 4328 3-8-13 75 KierenFallon 6 | 75 |
| | | | (Jeremy Noseda) *hld up in rr: shkn up over 2f out: styd on fr over 1f out: nrst fin* **20/1** | |
| 5151 | 5 | ½ | **Polybius**[6] 4502 3-9-13 89 6ex TedDurcan 2 | 87 |
| | | | (David Lanigan) *hld up in rr: shkn up and prog jst over 2f out: rdn to chse ldrs 1f out: one pce after and no imp* **5/4**[1] | |
| 5354 | 6 | 1 ¾ | **Royal Warrior**[15] 4186 3-9-4 80 MartinHarley 4 | 72 |
| | | | (Alan McCabe) *led 2f: styd prom: rdn over 2f out: fdd fnl f* **33/1** | |
| 0364 | 7 | shd | **Meritocracy (IRE)**[27] 3809 3-9-1 82 CamHardie(5) 11 | 74 |
| | | | (Paul Cole) *pressed ldr: led after 2f tl 1/2-way: chsd ldr to over 1f out: fdd* **10/1** | |
| 1340 | 8 | 1 ½ | **Strategic Force (IRE)**[34] 3539 3-9-5 81 AdamKirby 1 | 68 |
| | | | (Clive Cox) *in tch: rdn wl over 2f out: no prog wl over 1f out: wl btn after* **16/1** | |
| -033 | 9 | ¾ | **Dutch Interior**[18] 4078 3-9-2 78 RyanMoore 7 | 62 |
| | | | (Gary Moore) *hld up in rr: rdn and no prog over 2f out: last and wl btn over 1f out* **5/1**[2] | |
| 0155 | 10 | 2 ½ | **Baby Bush (IRE)**[8] 4445 3-9-4 80 RichardHughes 5 | 56 |
| | | | (Richard Hannon) *a towards rr: rdn and no prog over 2f out: wknd fnl f* **16/1** | |

1m 14.21s (-0.29) **Going Correction** +0.075s/f (Good) 10 Ran SP% **117.1**
Speed ratings (Par 102): **104,102,101,99,98 96,96,94,93,89**
CSF £168.73 CT £1010.91 TOTE £6.30: £1.90, £6.60, £2.70; EX 97.70 Trifecta £592.30.
**Owner** Mrs Lynn Turner & Guy Brook **Bred** Miss Nicola Cullen **Trained** Whitsbury, Hants

**FOCUS**
They raced up the middle of the track in this fair sprint handicap. The third helps set the standard.

### 4698 MITIE EVENTS & LEISURE H'CAP (BOBIS RACE) 1m 2f
4:15 (4:15) (Class 3) (0-95,89) 3-Y-O
£9,337 (£2,796; £1,398; £699; £349; £175) Stalls Low

| Form | | | | RPR |
|---|---|---|---|---|
| 1 | 1 | | **Redkirk**[31] 3631 3-9-6 88 SebSanders 5 | 101+ |
| | | | (William Haggas) *t.k.h: hld up in 5th: clr run through on inner fr 2f out: led jst over 1f out: pushed out firmly and styd on wl* **4/1**[3] | |
| 11 | 2 | ¾ | **Agent Murphy**[43] 3243 3-9-7 89 JimmyFortune 4 | 99+ |
| | | | (Brian Meehan) *led: shkn up over 2f out: sn hrd pressed: drvn and hdd jst over 1f out: styd on but readily outpointed by wnr* **15/8**[1] | |
| 6431 | 3 | 3 ½ | **Raise Your Gaze**[22] 3986 3-9-5 87 AdamKirby 1 | 90 |
| | | | (Clive Cox) *trckd ldng pair: waiting for room 2f out: rdn and nt qckn over 1f out: sn lft bhd* **11/2** | |
| 1226 | 4 | nk | **Good Value**[15] 4183 3-9-1 83 RyanMoore 2 | 85 |
| | | | (Sir Michael Stoute) *trckd ldr: shkn up to chal over 2f out: upsides over 1f out: sn lost pl and wknd* **11/4**[2] | |
| 151 | 5 | nk | **Lungarno Palace (USA)**[37] 3428 3-9-2 84 (bt) MartinHarley 3 | 86 |
| | | | (Marco Botti) *trckd ldng trio: shkn up and tried to cl on outer 2f out: sn rdn and nt qckn: wl btn fnl f* **12/1** | |
| 063 | 6 | nk | **Mantou (IRE)**[23] 3914 3-8-9 77 TomQueally 6 | 78 |
| | | | (Michael Bell) *slowly away and pushed along briefly: hld up in last: rdn 3f out: sn detached: kpt on nr fin* **12/1** | |

2m 9.19s (1.79) **Going Correction** +0.20s/f (Good) 6 Ran SP% **112.2**
Speed ratings (Par 104): **100,99,96,96,96 95**
CSF £11.95 TOTE £5.50: £2.80, £1.30; EX 11.10 Trifecta £50.80.
**Owner** Scotney/Symonds/Fisher Partnership **Bred** Mrs R D Peacock **Trained** Newmarket, Suffolk

**FOCUS**
Good-looking form with a couple of previously unbeaten horses pulling a little way clear. It's hard to have the form rated any higher than it is.

### 4699 ANTIDOTE MAIDEN FILLIES' STKS (BOBIS RACE) 1m (S)
4:50 (4:52) (Class 4) 3-Y-O £6,469 (£1,925; £962; £481) Stalls Centre

| Form | | | | RPR |
|---|---|---|---|---|
| 43 | 1 | | **Solar Magic**[88] 1868 3-9-0 0 WilliamBuick 4 | 90 |
| | | | (John Gosden) *cl up: led 2f out and sn in command: pushed out fnl f: comf* **4/9**[1] | |
| 2 | 2 | 3 ¼ | **Blue Waltz**[42] 3277 3-9-0 0 AdamKirby 1 | 82 |
| | | | (Luca Cumani) *led 1f: cl up: chal 2f out: chsd wnr after: styd on but no real ch* **11/2**[3] | |
| | 3 | 1 ¼ | **Zora Seas (IRE)** 3-9-0 0 JimmyFortune 3 | 79 |
| | | | (Brian Meehan) *hld up in tch: pushed along 2f out: tk 3rd over 1f out: styd on but n.d* **20/1** | |
| 4-30 | 4 | 5 | **Brown Diamond (IRE)**[81] 2072 3-9-0 78 RyanMoore 5 | 67 |
| | | | (Charles Hills) *led after 1f: shkn up and hdd 2f out: sn wknd* **5/1**[2] | |
| - | 5 | 18 | **Mississippi Queen (USA)** 3-8-9 0 [1] LouisSteward(5) 2 | 24 |
| | | | (Michael Bell) *in tch in rr: shkn up and wknd rapidly jst over 2f out: rn green and t.o* **33/1** | |

1m 41.66s (0.86) **Going Correction** +0.075s/f (Good) 5 Ran SP% **109.0**
Speed ratings (Par 99): **98,94,93,88,70**
CSF £3.27 TOTE £1.60: £1.10, £2.00; EX 3.10 Trifecta £14.30.
**Owner** Cheveley Park Stud **Bred** Cheveley Park Stud Ltd **Trained** Newmarket, Suffolk

**FOCUS**
Not many runners, but still an above-average fillies' maiden. The winner didn't have to run to her best to win.

### 4700 SIS LIVE H'CAP 5f
5:20 (5:21) (Class 2) 3-Y-O+
£28,012 (£8,388; £4,194; £2,097; £787; £787) Stalls Centre

| Form | | | | RPR |
|---|---|---|---|---|
| 5000 | 1 | | **Racy**[1] 4648 7-9-1 95 (p) PaulPickard 9 | 105 |
| | | | (Brian Ellison) *taken down early: hld up wl in rr: cajoled along and gd prog fr 2f out: led ins fnl f: r.o wl* **20/1** | |
| 4666 | 2 | 1 ½ | **Barnet Fair**[15] 4179 6-8-5 90 CamHardie(5) 14 | 95 |
| | | | (David Nicholls) *taken down early: hld up in tch: prog over 1f out: drvn and styd on fnl f to take 2nd last stride* **9/2**[3] | |
| 0151 | 3 | nse | **Peterkin (IRE)**[16] 4158 3-8-8 92 JoeFanning 18 | 95 |
| | | | (Mark Johnston) *prom: led over 1f out: rdn and hdd ins fnl f: kpt on but lost 2nd last stride* **8/1** | |
| 1503 | 4 | hd | **Piazon**[16] 4158 3-8-3 87 HayleyTurner 6 | 90 |
| | | | (Michael Bell) *taken down early: pressed ldr: upsides fr 2f out to over 1f out: hanging lft after: nt qckn fnl f* **25/1** | |
| 2025 | 5 | 1 ½ | **Masamah (IRE)**[15] 4179 8-9-8 102 (p) MartinHarley 7 | 100 |
| | | | (Marco Botti) *mde most to over 1f out: fdd fnl f* **14/1** | |
| 2113 | 5 | dht | **Robot Boy (IRE)**[15] 4179 4-9-8 102 GrahamGibbons 1 | 100 |
| | | | (David Barron) *swtchd to join main gp after 1f: in rr: prog 1/2-way: chsd ldrs over 1f out: one pce fnl f* **7/2**[1] | |
| 0033 | 7 | 1 | **Monsieur Joe (IRE)**[15] 4215 7-9-10 104 TomQueally 12 | 99 |
| | | | (Paul Midgley) *wl in tch: effrt 2f out: rdn and kpt on same pce fr over 1f out: n.d* **14/1** | |
| 0205 | 8 | ½ | **Rasaman (IRE)**[36] 3458 10-7-12 83 DannyBrock(5) 4 | 76 |
| | | | (Jim Goldie) *hld up in rr: swtchd rt 2f out: hung rt towards far side after: plugged on* **40/1** | |
| 0413 | 9 | ½ | **Forest Edge (IRE)**[9] 4412 5-8-9 89 (b) JFEgan 5 | 80 |
| | | | (David Evans) *prom but sn rdn: lost pl and wl hld whn n.m.r over 1f out: one pce* **25/1** | |
| 0-00 | 10 | ¾ | **Free Zone**[50] 2989 5-9-3 97 GeorgeBaker 3 | 85 |
| | | | (Robert Cowell) *racd alone towards far side after 1f: nvr quite on terms fr 1/2-way: fdd fnl f* **33/1** | |

4012 **11** *nk* **Milly's Gift**[15] 4179 4-9-1 **95**.......... AdamKirby 15 82
(Clive Cox) *taken down early: dwlt: sn wl in tch: chsd ldrs 2f out: nt qckn whn short of room over 1f out: wl hld fnl f* **4/1**[2]

-602 **12** *2 ½* **Ajjaadd (USA)**[23] 3927 8-8-13 **93**.......... WilliamTwiston-Davies 10 71
(Ted Powell) *hld up in tch: n.m.r 1/2-way and dropped to rr: nvr on terms after* **10/1**

1014 **13** *2 ¼* **Rothesay Chancer**[20] 4016 6-7-10 **81**.......... JackGarritty(5) 2 51
(Jim Goldie) *swtchd to join main gp after 1f: a in rr: struggling wl over 1f out* **40/1**

-060 **14** *3* **New Fforest**[23] 3927 4-8-9 **89**.......... KierenFallon 17 48
(Andrew Balding) *dwlt and s.i.s: hld up in rr: brief effrt 2f out: wknd over 1f out: eased* **16/1**

0000 **15** *8* **Taajub (IRE)**[23] 3927 7-8-7 **87**.......... ShaneKelly 11 18
(Peter Crate) *hld up in midfield: impeded 1/2-way and lost pl: wknd over 1f out and eased* **25/1**

59.59s (-0.91) **Going Correction** +0.075s/f (Good)
**WFA** 3 from 4yo+ 4lb **15** Ran SP% **123.9**
Speed ratings (Par 109): **110,107,107,107,104 104,103,102,101,100 99,95,92,87,74**
CSF £103.91 CT £821.94 TOTE £23.60: £5.90, £2.60, £2.90; EX 146.80 Trifecta £1888.80.
**Owner** Koo's Racing Club **Bred** Cheveley Park Stud Ltd **Trained** Norton, N Yorks
■ Stewards' Enquiry : J F Egan two-day ban: careless riding (Aug 10-11)

**FOCUS**
A red-hot sprint handicap in which Free Zone raced on his own for much of the way, towards the far side, and was joined by the wandering Rasaman late on, while Rothesay Chancer was a bit wide of the main group of runners, who gradually edged towards the stands' rail. The runner-up has been rated 8lb off his winning figure in this race last year.
T/Jkpt: Not won. T/Plt: £130.90 to a £1 stake. Pool: £151,324.97 - 843.45 winning units. T/Qpdt: £24.60 to a £1 stake. Pool: £9303.30 - 279.35 winning units. JN

# 4510 CARLISLE (R-H)

Sunday, July 27

**OFFICIAL GOING: Good (good to firm in places) changing to good after race 3 (3.15)**
Rail around Old Stable bend and home straight moved out 2yds and distances on Round course increased by 2yds.
Wind: Fresh, half against Weather: Overcast

## 4701 TRAVIS PERKINS FAMILY FUN DAY MAIDEN AUCTION STKS 5f 193y
**2:10** (2:12) (Class 5) 2-Y-O **£2,587** (£770; £384; £192) **Stalls** Low

Form RPR

22 **1** **Gleneely Girl (IRE)**[20] 4018 2-8-4 0.......... ChrisCatlin 8 66
(Rae Guest) *towards rr: pushed along over 2f out: hdwy over 1f out: kpt on wl fnl f to ld post* **6/5**[1]

332 **2** *shd* **You're My Cracker**[9] 4382 2-8-10 72.......... GrahamLee 4 72
(Donald McCain) *t.k.h. early: pressed ldr: led over 1f out: sn rdn: kpt on wl fnl f: hdd post* **15/8**[2]

**3** *1* **Mythmaker** 2-8-9 0.......... PaulMulrennan 6 68+
(Bryan Smart) *in tch on outside: rdn over 2f out: rallied and edgd rt whn checked ent fnl f: kpt on wl towards fin* **50/1**

03 **4** *¾* **Indian Champ**[15] 4192 2-8-4 0..........(b) ShaneGray(5) 3 66
(Kevin Ryan) *t.k.h: led to over 1f out: hung lft ent fnl f: kpt on same pce* **20/1**

4 **5** *4* **Intruder**[15] 4192 2-8-6 0.......... GeorgeChaloner(3) 5 54
(Richard Fahey) *prom: drvn over 2f out: wknd appr fnl f* **9/1**[3]

65 **6** *8* **Sandgate**[36] 3454 2-8-12 0.......... TonyHamilton 2 33
(Richard Fahey) *n.m.r s: bhd: shortlived effrt over 2f out: wknd over 1f out* **28/1**

**7** *4 ½* **Grey Sensation (IRE)** 2-9-1 0.......... BenCurtis 7 22
(K R Burke) *s.i.s: rn green in rr: no ch fr 2f out* **16/1**

**8** *6* **Hey Bob (IRE)** 2-8-12 0.......... TomEaves 1 1
(Keith Dalgleish) *prom tl rdn and wknd qckly 2f out* **20/1**

1m 14.93s (1.23) **Going Correction** +0.225s/f (Good) **8** Ran SP% **111.1**
Speed ratings (Par 94): **100,99,98,97,92 81,75,67**
CSF £3.19 TOTE £2.10: £1.02, £1.10, £7.20; EX 3.80 Trifecta £76.10.
**Owner** Shannon & Guest **Bred** John & Anne-Marie O'Connor **Trained** Newmarket, Suffolk

**FOCUS**
The riders said the ground was basically good but a bit loose on top after a shower before racing. This looked just an average juvenile maiden with the two at the head of the market dominating the finish. The winner was fully entitled to win at these weights.

## 4702 KNAUF PARTNERED WITH TRAVIS PERKINS NURSERY H'CAP 5f
**2:40** (2:40) (Class 5) 2-Y-O **£2,587** (£770; £384; £192) **Stalls** Low

Form RPR

016 **1** **Just The Tip (IRE)**[31] 3619 2-9-7 **72**.......... TomEaves 2 76
(Keith Dalgleish) *mde all: shkn up and qcknd clr wl over 1f out: rdn out fnl f* **9/2**

1433 **2** *3 ½* **River Spirit**[12] 4283 2-8-7 **65**.......... DanielCremin(7) 6 56
(Mick Channon) *chsd wnr thrght: drvn along wl over 1f out: kpt on: no imp* **7/2**[3]

342 **3** *nk* **Ocean Sheridan (IRE)**[22] 3947 2-9-2 **70**.......... ConnorBeasley(3) 3 60
(Michael Dods) *in tch: drvn and outpcd over 1f out: kpt on ins fnl f: nvr able to chal* **5/2**[1]

0343 **4** *1* **Bahango (IRE)**[20] 4011 2-9-2 **67**.......... GrahamLee 5 53
(Kristin Stubbs) *t.k.h: prom on outside: rdn along and effrt over 1f out: one pce fnl f* **11/4**[2]

0402 **5** *1 ¼* **Penalty Scorer**[12] 4302 2-8-2 **53**..........(e) RaulDaSilva 4 35
(Richard Guest) *plld hrd: hld up: rdn and swtchd lft over 1f out: no imp fnl f* **20/1**

5361 **6** *2* **Millar Rose (IRE)**[18] 4065 2-9-5 **70**.......... BenCurtis 1 45
(K R Burke) *plld hrd: trckd ldrs: drvn along 2f out: wknd fnl f* **8/1**

1m 2.69s (1.89) **Going Correction** +0.225s/f (Good) **6** Ran SP% **111.5**
Speed ratings (Par 94): **93,87,86,85,83 80**
CSF £20.11 TOTE £6.70: £2.00, £1.90; EX 18.30 Trifecta £43.50.
**Owner** Straightline Construction Ltd **Bred** Knocklong House Stud **Trained** Carluke, S Lanarks

**FOCUS**
A fair nursery, but one in which a steady gallop saw several fail to settle and this bare form may not be entirely reliable. It's possible the form could be rated 4 or 5lb higher.

## 4703 BRITISH GYPSUM PARTNERED WITH TRAVIS PERKINS CLAIMING STKS 7f 200y
**3:15** (3:16) (Class 5) 3-Y-O+ **£3,234** (£962; £481; £240) **Stalls** Low

Form RPR

0402 **1** **Mishaal (IRE)**[12] 4291 4-9-7 73.......... PaulMulrennan 1 85
(Michael Herrington) *mde all: pushed clr over 1f out: kpt on wl fnl f: unchal* **7/2**[3]

2/3 **2** *6* **Naoise (IRE)**[5] 4514 6-9-4 74..........(t) JacobButterfield(5) 4 73
(Ollie Pears) *t.k.h: chsd ldrs: wnt 2nd after 3f: effrt and ch over 2f out: no ex fr over 1f out* **13/8**[1]

-504 **3** *7* **King Pin**[17] 4108 9-9-2 65..........(p) DaleSwift 2 50
(Tracy Waggott) *s.i.s and sn outpcd: hdwy to take modest 3rd 2f out: no ch w first two* **7/1**

2064 **4** *3 ½* **Al Muheer (IRE)**[12] 4291 9-9-5 75..........(e) GrahamLee 5 45
(Ruth Carr) *chsd wnr 3f: cl up tl rdn and wknd fr 2f out* **15/8**[2]

1m 39.62s (-0.38) **Going Correction** +0.225s/f (Good) **4** Ran SP% **107.6**
Speed ratings (Par 103): **110,104,97,93**
CSF £9.46 TOTE £3.90; EX 10.50 Trifecta £42.00.
**Owner** Kelvyn Gracie & Lawrence McCaughey **Bred** Darley **Trained** Cold Kirby, N Yorks

**FOCUS**
Something of a tactical race with no obvious front-runner and the form is unlikely to prove reliable.

## 4704 WAVIN PARTNERED WITH TRAVIS PERKINS H'CAP 1m 3f 107y
**3:50** (3:51) (Class 4) (0-85,79) 3-Y-O+ **£5,822** (£1,732; £865; £432) **Stalls** High

Form RPR

3314 **1** **Corton Lad**[26] 3829 4-10-0 **79**..........(tp) TomEaves 2 89
(Keith Dalgleish) *trckd ldr: rdn to ld over 2f out: clr over 1f out: kpt on strly fnl f* **7/1**

3-02 **2** *4* **Chant (IRE)**[12] 4296 4-9-8 **73**.......... GrahamLee 5 76
(Ann Duffield) *t.k.h: hld up in tch: hdwy to chse wnr over 2f out: sn rdn: kpt on fnl f: nt pce to chal* **9/4**[1]

60 **3** *nk* **Love Marmalade (IRE)**[16] 4160 4-9-8 **78**.......... GarryWhillans(5) 1 81
(Alistair Whillans) *trckd ldrs: drvn and effrt over 2f out: one pce fr over 1f out* **10/1**

3124 **4** *1 ½* **Zanouska (USA)**[15] 4196 3-8-5 **67**.......... ChrisCatlin 4 67
(Mark Johnston) *in tch: drvn and outpcd 4f out: rallied wl over 1f out: nvr able to chal* **3/1**[2]

-335 **5** *1 ¾* **Discovery Bay**[8] 3466 6-9-6 **71**.......... DougieCostello 6 68
(Brian Ellison) *s.i.s: hld up: rdn over 2f out: edgd rt and sn no imp* **10/1**

0230 **6** *14* **Right Of Appeal**[15] 4189 3-8-5 **70**.......... MichaelJMMurphy(3) 3 44
(Mark Johnston) *t.k.h early: led: stdd pce after 2f: rdn and hdd over 2f out: sn btn* **10/3**[3]

2m 25.25s (2.15) **Going Correction** +0.225s/f (Good)
**WFA** 3 from 4yo+ 11lb **6** Ran SP% **109.5**
Speed ratings (Par 105): **101,98,97,96,95 85**
CSF £22.00 TOTE £7.00: £3.30, £2.40; EX 21.50 Trifecta £64.30.
**Owner** J Hutton **Bred** Frank Brady And Brian Scanlon **Trained** Carluke, S Lanarks

**FOCUS**
The ground was changed to good after the previous race. This featured a couple of in-form types in a fair handicap, with the gallop steadying after a couple of furlongs before picking up again early in the straight. The runner-up has been rated to last year's form and the third to his recent form.

## 4705 TRAVIS PERKINS TOOL HIRE MAIDEN STKS 1m 1f 61y
**4:25** (4:25) (Class 5) 3-Y-O+ **£2,587** (£770; £384; £192) **Stalls** Low

Form RPR

2 **1** **Law Keeper (IRE)**[31] 3602 3-9-0 0.......... GrahamLee 3 76+
(James Tate) *mde all at ordinary gallop: shkn up to go clr over 2f out: kpt on strly fnl f: unchal* **6/5**[1]

0 **2** *4 ½* **Gleese The Devil (IRE)**[17] 4130 3-9-2 0.......... GeorgeChaloner(3) 1 72
(Richard Fahey) *t.k.h early: trckd ldrs: effrt and wnt 2nd over 2f out: kpt on fnl f: nt rch wnr* **18/1**

44 **3** *7* **Spot The Pro (IRE)**[19] 4062 5-10-0 0.......... DougieCostello 2 58
(Rebecca Menzies) *hld up in tch: rdn and outpcd 3f out: plugged on fnl f: no ch w first two* **28/1**

22-0 **4** *2 ¾* **Pressure Point**[46] 3103 4-10-0 76.......... TomEaves 6 52
(Keith Dalgleish) *t.k.h early: chsd wnr to over 2f out: sn rdn and wknd over 1f out* **10/3**[3]

5 **5** *½* **Chilly Miss**[22] 3953 5-9-9 0.......... BrianHughes 4 46
(Malcolm Jefferson) *t.k.h: hld up in tch on outside: rdn and outpcd 3f out: n.d after* **16/1**

**6** *1 ½* **Classical Duet (USA)** 3-9-2 0.......... MichaelJMMurphy(3) 5 47
(Mark Johnston) *slowly away: bhd: rdn and rn green over 4f out: btn fnl 2f* **11/4**[2]

1m 58.7s (1.10) **Going Correction** +0.225s/f (Good)
**WFA** 3 from 4yo+ 9lb **6** Ran SP% **109.8**
Speed ratings (Par 103): **104,100,93,91,90 89**
CSF £23.10 TOTE £2.20: £1.60, £7.20; EX 18.70 Trifecta £183.00.
**Owner** Saif Ali **Bred** Old Carhue Stud **Trained** Newmarket, Suffolk

**FOCUS**
Probably just an ordinary maiden. The level is fluid.

## 4706 LAFARGE PARTNERED WITH TRAVIS PERKINS H'CAP 1m 1f 61y
**5:00** (5:00) (Class 5) (0-70,65) 3-Y-O **£2,587** (£770; £384; £192) **Stalls** Low

Form RPR

5303 **1** **Archie's Advice**[6] 4490 3-9-2 **60**.......... TomEaves 1 66+
(Keith Dalgleish) *trckd ldrs: outpcd and hung rt fr 2f out: gd hdwy and led last 75yds: kpt on wl* **11/4**[2]

2100 **2** *1* **Suni Dancer**[24] 3885 3-8-10 **54**.......... RaulDaSilva 5 58
(Paul Green) *trckd ldrs: led and rdn over 2f out: hdd appr fnl f: rallied: kpt on: hld nr fin* **12/1**

0021 **3** *½* **Her Red Devil (IRE)**[10] 4363 3-8-9 **56**.......... GeorgeChaloner(3) 6 59+
(Richard Fahey) *hld up in tch: stdy hdwy whn n.m.r and stmbld over 3f out: sn drvn and outpcd: kpt on wl fnl f: nrst fin* **7/4**[1]

0003 **4** *½* **Mount Cheiron (USA)**[4] 4530 3-8-0 **51**..........(p) RachelRichardson(7) 3 53
(Dianne Sayer) *pressed ldr: led briefly 3f out: rallied and regained ld appr fnl f to last 75yds: one pce* **9/1**

5205 **5** *8* **Victory Danz (IRE)**[12] 4292 3-8-11 **58**.......... SamJames(3) 2 43
(David O'Meara) *led at ordinary gallop: rdn and hdd 3f out: wknd fr 2f out* **9/2**[3]

0030 **6** *7* **King's Prospect**[3] 4574 3-9-4 **65**.............................. ConnorBeasley(3) 4 35
(Tracy Waggott) *hld up on ins: struggling over 2f out: sn btn* **9/1**

1m 59.8s (2.20) **Going Correction** +0.225s/f (Good) **6** Ran SP% **108.9**
Speed ratings (Par 100): **99,98,97,97,90 83**
CSF £30.60 TOTE £3.60: £2.20, £3.70; EX 27.90 Trifecta £101.30.
**Owner** G L S Partnership **Bred** G L S Partnership **Trained** Carluke, S Lanarks

**FOCUS**
A modest handicap in which the gallop was no more than fair. The runner-up and fourth were well placed and have been rated pretty much to form.

## 4707 TRAVIS PERKINS YOUR LOCAL BUILDERS MERCHANT H'CAP 6f 192y
**5:30** (5:30) (Class 5) (0-75,75) 3-Y-O+ **£2,587** (£770; £384; £192) **Stalls** Low

Form RPR
143 **1** **Al Khan (IRE)**[9] 4421 5-9-9 **75**.............................(p) JacobButterfield(5) 6 83
(Ollie Pears) *trckd ldr: rdn to ld over 1f out: edgd lft: rdn out fnl f* **7/2**[2]
4425 **2** *1 1/4* **Whispered Times (USA)**[12] 4291 7-8-9 **59**.........(p) ConnorBeasley(3) 4 64
(Tracy Waggott) *stdd s: hld up: stdy hdwy over 2f out: effrt and ev ch over 1f out: hung rt and no ex ins fnl f* **9/2**[3]
1-51 **3** *nk* **Hanalei Bay (IRE)**[21] 4001 4-9-10 **71**.............................. TomEaves 1 75
(Keith Dalgleish) *t.k.h early: trckd ldrs: effrt and drvn 2f out: kpt on same pce ins fnl f* **11/2**
0132 **4** *2* **Orwellian**[5] 4523 5-9-3 **64**.............................. PaulMulrennan 2 63
(Bryan Smart) *trckd ldrs: drvn and outpcd over 2f out: rallied appr fnl f: no imp* **7/4**[1]
5301 **5** *4* **Imperator Augustus (IRE)**[18] 4069 6-9-0 **68**..... RachelRichardson(7) 3 56
(Patrick Holmes) *dwlt: hld up in tch: struggling 2f out: hld whn rdr dropped whip 1f out* **6/1**
0506 **6** *16* **Baltic Prince (IRE)**[31] 3604 4-8-9 **56** oh1.............................. RaulDaSilva 5 3
(Paul Green) *led: rdn over 2f out: hdd over 1f out: sn btn: eased whn no ch fnl f* **20/1**

1m 27.97s (0.87) **Going Correction** +0.225s/f (Good) **6** Ran SP% **111.2**
Speed ratings (Par 103): **104,102,102,99,95 77**
CSF £18.88 TOTE £3.60: £2.20, £2.80; EX 16.50 Trifecta £70.30.
**Owner** Richard Walker **Bred** Galadari Sons Stud Company Limited **Trained** Norton, N Yorks

**FOCUS**
A fair pace to this 7f handicap. The runner-up has been rated a length off his recent form.
T/Plt: £175.20 to a £1 stake. Pool: £64,091.72 - 266.97 winning units. T/Qpdt: £61.10 to a £1 stake. Pool: £3447.58 - 41.70 winning units. RY

# 4416 PONTEFRACT (L-H)
Sunday, July 27

**OFFICIAL GOING: Good to firm (7.9)**
False rail removed and distances as advertised.
Wind: light 1/2 behind Weather: fine and sunny

## 4708 YOUR GUIDE TO PONTEFRACT AT PONTEFRACTRACECOURSETIPS.CO.UK MAIDEN STKS (BOBIS RACE) 5f
**2:20** (2:20) (Class 4) 2-Y-O **£6,469** (£1,925; £962; £481) **Stalls** Low

Form RPR
43 **1** **Dark Reckoning**[10] 4357 2-9-0 0.............................. JamieSpencer 1 75
(Ann Duffield) *sn led: drvn 2f out: kpt on wl* **2/1**[1]
**2** *1 1/2* **Charlie Croker (IRE)** 2-9-0 0.............................. KevinStott(5) 4 74
(Kevin Ryan) *chsd ldrs on outer: effrt 2f out: chsd wnr 1f out: kpt on same pce* **9/4**[2]
**3** *1/2* **Doppler Effect** 2-9-5 0.............................. PJMcDonald 2 73
(Ann Duffield) *chsd ldrs on inner: nt clr run and swtchd rt over 1f out: kpt on same pce* **13/2**
**4** *3 1/2* **Never Easy (IRE)** 2-9-5 0.............................. PaulHanagan 5 63+
(Richard Fahey) *swvd rt s: sn chsng ldrs: outpcd and swtchd lft over 3f out: chsd ldrs over 2f out: wknd and eased last 100yds* **5/2**[3]
0 **5** *5* **Smart Stepper (IRE)**[17] 4110 2-9-5 0.............................. AndrewMullen 3 42
(Michael Dods) *led early: chsd ldrs: wknd over 1f out* **25/1**

1m 4.34s (1.04) **Going Correction** -0.10s/f (Good) **5** Ran SP% **109.9**
Speed ratings (Par 96): **87,84,83,78,70**
CSF £6.80 TOTE £2.40: £1.20, £2.40; EX 8.10 Trifecta £28.50.
**Owner** Qatar Racing Limited **Bred** Newsells Park Stud **Trained** Constable Burton, N Yorks

**FOCUS**
False rail removed and distances as advertised. Not a bad little 2yo maiden.

## 4709 MOOR TOP FARM SHOP HEMSWORTH H'CAP 1m 4f 8y
**2:55** (2:55) (Class 5) (0-70,70) 3-Y-O+ **£4,528** (£1,347; £673; £336) **Stalls** Low

Form RPR
0641 **1** **El Bravo**[27] 3785 8-9-10 **69**.............................. NeilFarley(3) 3 74
(Shaun Harris) *chsd ldr: led on ins and rdr dropped whip 1f out: hld on towards fin* **7/1**
6300 **2** *1/2* **Qibtee (FR)**[7] 4473 4-9-1 **57**.............................. DavidAllan 6 61
(Les Eyre) *mid-div: t.k.h: hdwy on outer over 2f out: sn chsng ldrs: cl 2nd 1f out: no ex clsng stages* **7/1**
3002 **3** *1/2* **Flying Cape (IRE)**[11] 4316 3-9-0 **68**.........................(p) RoystonFfrench 2 75+
(Andrew Hollinshead) *trckd ldrs: t.k.h: nt clr run fr over 2f out tl swtchd rt ins fnl f: styd on wl* **7/2**[2]
1411 **4** *1 1/4* **Men Don't Cry (IRE)**[27] 3778 5-9-7 **70**.............................. MeganCarberry(7) 1 71
(Ed de Giles) *hld up in rr: nt clr run on ins fr over 2f out tl jst ins fnl f: styd on same pce* **3/1**[1]
4144 **5** *2 1/4* **Amazing Blue Sky**[12] 4293 8-8-11 **53**.............................. PaulHanagan 7 51
(Ruth Carr) *led: drvn over 2f out: hdd 1f out: wknd fnl 75yds* **6/1**
0404 **6** *1 1/2* **In Vino Veritas (IRE)**[9] 4386 3-8-11 **65**.............................. PJMcDonald 5 60
(Ann Duffield) *chsd ldrs: upsides and reminders over 5f out: sn drvn: wknd fnl f* **5/1**[3]
2032 **7** *hd* **Merchant Of Medici**[11] 4319 7-9-4 **65**.........................(p) KevinStott(5) 4 60
(Micky Hammond) *dwlt: hld up in rr: effrt over 2f out: chsng ldrs on outer over 1f out: fdd jst ins fnl f* **9/1**

2m 41.28s (0.48) **Going Correction** -0.10s/f (Good)
**WFA** 3 from 4yo+ 12lb **7** Ran SP% **113.2**
Speed ratings (Par 103): **94,93,93,92,91 90,89**
CSF £52.61 TOTE £5.90: £2.50, £4.40; EX 61.80 Trifecta £385.20.
**Owner** www.nottinghamshireracing.co.uk (2) **Bred** D J And Mrs Deer **Trained** Carburton, Notts

**FOCUS**
A moderate handicap, run at an average pace and they were well bunched leaving the back straight. The first two have been rated to form.

## 4710 GRAHAM ROCK MEMORIAL H'CAP 1m 2f 6y
**3:30** (3:30) (Class 4) (0-80,80) 3-Y-O+ **£7,115** (£2,117; £1,058; £529) **Stalls** Low

Form RPR
0105 **1** **Dance King**[16] 4144 4-9-7 **75**.............................. DavidAllan 4 85
(Tim Easterby) *mid-div: hdwy over 2f out: 3rd over 1f out: styd on to ld last 100yds* **11/1**
0003 **2** *1 1/2* **Sky Khan**[29] 3718 5-9-11 **79**.............................. IanBrennan 1 86
(John Wainwright) *chsd ldrs: drvn over 4f out: 2nd 2f out: led 1f out: hung rt and hdd ins fnl f: styd on same pce* **11/2**[3]
6004 **3** *1 3/4* **Croquembouche (IRE)**[17] 4104 5-9-5 **80**.............................. MeganCarberry(7) 6 84
(Ed de Giles) *led: hdd 1f out: kpt on same pce* **8/1**
-053 **4** *2 3/4* **Eltheeb**[32] 3574 7-9-9 **77**.............................(p) PhillipMakin 12 76
(Philip Kirby) *in rr: hdwy over 2f out: styd on fnl f: tk 4th nr fin* **12/1**
0655 **5** *1/2* **Correggio**[10] 4349 4-9-7 **75**.............................(p) PJMcDonald 9 73
(Micky Hammond) *in rr: hdwy over 2f out: kpt on same pce over 1f out* **9/1**
2140 **6** *4 1/2* **Honoured (IRE)**[100] 1553 7-9-9 **77**.............................(t) AndrewMullen 3 66
(Michael Appleby) *chsd ldrs: sn drvn along: one pce fnl 2f* **22/1**
00 **7** *5* **Good Speech (IRE)**[29] 3699 4-9-2 **70**.............................. AndrewElliott 5 50
(Tom Tate) *in rr: sn drvn along: sme hdwy on wd outside 2f out: nvr on terms* **16/1**
0 **8** *2 1/2* **Guising**[44] 3196 5-9-11 **79**.............................. RobertWinston 8 54
(David Brown) *in rr: hdwy over 1f out: nvr on terms* **20/1**
6352 **9** *1 1/2* **Shouranour (IRE)**[8] 4451 4-9-9 **77**.........................(p) SilvestreDeSousa 11 49
(David O'Meara) *chsd ldr: upsides 5f out: wknd over 1f out* **9/2**[1]
0001 **10** *5* **Le Deluge (FR)**[7] 4470 4-9-4 **75** 6ex.............................. ConnorKing(3) 10 38
(Ann Stokell) *chsd ldrs: upsides 5f out: lost pl over 2f out* **25/1**
21 **11** *9* **Spanish Plume**[15] 4190 6-9-3 **76**.............................(p) KevinStott(5) 2 21
(Andrew Hollinshead) *trckd ldrs: drvn over 2f out: lost pl over 1f out: bhd whn eased clsng stages* **15/2**
2-60 **12** *1/2* **Aneedh**[44] 3205 4-9-5 **73**.............................(p) RussKennemore 13 17
(Jedd O'Keeffe) *mid-div: effrt on outside 4f out: lost pl over 2f out: bhd whn eased clsng stages* **50/1**
513 **13** *4* **Wahgah (USA)**[33] 3560 3-9-2 **80**.............................. PaulHanagan 7 17
(Saeed bin Suroor) *prom: lost pl after 2f: sme hdwy over 3f out: lost pl over 2f out: bhd whn eased clsng stages* **5/1**[2]

2m 10.96s (-2.74) **Going Correction** -0.10s/f (Good)
**WFA** 3 from 4yo+ 10lb **13** Ran SP% **119.9**
Speed ratings (Par 105): **106,104,103,101,100 97,93,91,90,86 78,78,75**
CSF £67.61 CT £522.88 TOTE £14.40: £4.60, £1.90, £2.00; EX 87.30 Trifecta £716.10.
**Owner** Ambrose Turnbull **Bred** Meon Valley Stud **Trained** Great Habton, N Yorks

**FOCUS**
This looked wide open and it proved hard to make an impact from behind. The third has been rated to this year's form.

## 4711 SKYBET SUPPORTING THE YORKSHIRE RACING SUMMER FESTIVAL POMFRET STKS (LISTED RACE) 1m 4y
**4:05** (4:07) (Class 1) 3-Y-O+
**£25,519** (£9,675; £4,842; £2,412; £1,210; £607) **Stalls** Low

Form RPR
2031 **1** **Custom Cut (IRE)**[29] 3731 5-9-9 108.............................. DavidNolan 2 117
(David O'Meara) *led early: w ldr: led 2f out: drvn and styd on gamely* **9/2**
6411 **2** *1 1/2* **Tenor (IRE)**[11] 4323 4-9-5 91.............................(t) RobertWinston 1 110
(John Ryan) *drvn along to sn ld: hdd 2f out: styd on same pce fnl f* **15/2**
10 **3** *3 1/2* **The Rectifier (USA)**[15] 4180 7-9-5 106.............................(t) FergusSweeney 6 102
(Seamus Durack) *chsd ldrs: kpt on same pce fnl 2f* **10/1**
3020 **4** *1/2* **Artigiano (USA)**[39] 3356 4-9-5 107.............................. SilvestreDeSousa 4 100
(Charlie Appleby) *dwlt: in rr: hdwy 6f out: drvn 3f out: sn outpcd: hdwy over 1f out: keeping on at fin* **5/2**[1]
1004 **5** *1 1/2* **Elleval (IRE)**[28] 3765 4-9-5 108.............................. JamieSpencer 3 97
(David Marnane, Ire) *hld up in rr: effrt 3f out: sn outpcd: hdwy u.p over 1f out: nvr a threat* **7/2**[2]
6660 **6** *4* **Edu Querido (BRZ)**[37] 3416 5-9-5 99.............................(b) CraigAWilliams 5 88
(Marco Botti) *reluctant to go bhd stalls: dwlt: in rr: nvr on terms* **33/1**
6246 **7** *4 1/2* **Highland Knight (IRE)**[15] 4180 7-9-5 109.............................(t) DavidProbert 7 77
(Andrew Balding) *chsd ldrs: drvn over 2f out: lost pl over 1f out: eased clsng stages* **4/1**[3]

1m 42.06s (-3.84) **Going Correction** -0.10s/f (Good)
**WFA** 3 from 4yo+ 8lb **7** Ran SP% **112.8**
Speed ratings (Par 111): **115,113,110,109,108 104,99**
CSF £36.09 TOTE £4.70: £2.30, £4.30; EX 39.30 Trifecta £190.00.
**Owner** Gary Douglas & Pat Breslin **Bred** Moyglare Stud Farm Ltd **Trained** Nawton, N Yorks

**FOCUS**
This was a tight Listed contest. The winner has been rated to form.

## 4712 TIESPLANET.COM - TIES FOR EVERY OCCASION H'CAP 6f
**4:40** (4:40) (Class 3) (0-90,88) 3-Y-O+
**£9,337** (£2,796; £1,398; £699; £349; £175) **Stalls** Low

Form RPR
1/40 **1** **Compton Park**[101] 1538 7-9-4 **80**.............................(t) DavidAllan 6 90
(Les Eyre) *chsd ldrs: swtchd rt appr fnl f: styd on to ld last 75yds* **20/1**
2141 **2** *nk* **Boy In The Bar**[27] 3790 3-9-4 **85**.............................(b) RobertWinston 5 93+
(David Barron) *t.k.h: w ldr: led over 1f out: hdd and no ex ins fnl f* **9/4**[1]
1346 **3** *1 3/4* **Sunraider (IRE)**[2] 4632 7-9-3 **79**.............................. PhillipMakin 4 82
(Paul Midgley) *mid-div: drvn and outpcd over 2f out: hdwy over 1f out: styd on to take 3rd nr fin* **13/2**
1454 **4** *1/2* **Ruby's Day**[17] 4132 5-9-0 **76**.............................. JamieSpencer 2 78
(David Brown) *led: hdd over 1f out: hung lft and fdd last 50yds* **10/1**
-000 **5** *hd* **Twenty One Choice (IRE)**[29] 3737 5-9-6 **82**.............................. OisinMurphy 3 83
(Ed de Giles) *mid-div: outpcd over 2f out: hdwy over 1f out: kpt on one pce* **9/2**[2]
0416 **6** *2 3/4* **Thatcherite (IRE)**[11] 4317 6-8-13 **75**.............................(t) BarryMcHugh 1 67
(Tony Coyle) *s.i.s: hdwy over 1f out: nvr nr ldrs* **14/1**
00 **7** *2 3/4* **Tellovoi (IRE)**[11] 4323 6-9-9 **88**.............................(v) ConnorKing(3) 7 72
(Ann Stokell) *s.i.s: in rr: sme hdwy over 1f out: nvr a factor* **11/1**
1005 **8** *1 3/4* **Ben Hall (IRE)**[22] 3969 3-9-6 **87**.............................. FergusSweeney 10 64
(Mike Murphy) *in rr: sme hdwy on outer over 2f out: nvr a factor* **33/1**
4243 **9** *2 1/4* **Dark Castle**[11] 4317 5-9-7 **83**.............................. PJMcDonald 9 54
(Micky Hammond) *chsd ldrs: dropped bk over 4f out: sme hdwy over 2f out: sn lost pl* **5/1**[3]

1-00 **10** ½ **Can You Conga**[104] 1484 4-9-11 **87** JasonHart 8 56
(Michael Easterby) *chsd ldrs on outer: rdn and lost pl over 2f out* **20/1**

1m 15.22s (-1.68) **Going Correction** -0.10s/f (Good)
**WFA** 3 from 4yo+ 5lb **10** Ran SP% **115.5**
Speed ratings (Par 107): **107,106,104,103,103 99,96,93,90,90**
CSF £63.10 CT £339.42 TOTE £26.30: £3.60, £1.30, £1.90; EX 105.50 Trifecta £993.50.
**Owner** Billy Parker **Bred** David Jamison Bloodstock **Trained** Catton, North Yorkshire

**FOCUS**
A modest but competitive sprint handicap. The runner-up has been rated as running a pb.

## 4713 FLY HIGH FAYE NICKELS MAIDEN STKS — 1m 4y
5:10 (5:10) (Class 5) 3-4-Y-O — £3,881 (£1,155; £577; £288) Stalls Low

Form — RPR

45 **1** **Lockhart (IRE)**[8] 4446 3-9-5 0 SilvestreDeSousa 3 82+
(Mark Johnston) *chsd ldrs: drvn over 2f out: led 1f out: edgd lft: styd on* **13/8**[2]

-423 **2** 1¾ **Hanno (USA)**[44] 3184 3-9-5 79 PaulHanagan 2 77
(Ed Dunlop) *trckd ldr: led gng best appr fnl 2f: hung lft and hdd 1f out: fnd little* **10/11**[1]

465 **3** 6 **Cliff (IRE)**[20] 4022 4-9-8 68 ShelleyBirkett(5) 9 65
(Nigel Tinkler) *mid-div: effrt over 3f out: 3rd over 1f out: one pce* **7/1**[3]

00 **4** 1¾ **Lacerta**[20] 4022 3-9-5 0 PJMcDonald 5 58?
(Micky Hammond) *mid-div: effrt over 2f out: kpt on one pce over 1f out* **33/1**

**5** 3 **Justcallhimbilly**[102] 4-9-10 0 NeilFarley(3) 8 53?
(Shaun Harris) *in rr: drvn 4f out: outpcd over 2f out: sme hdwy fnl f* **25/1**

00 **6** 1½ **Endless Seas**[9] 4413 3-9-0 0 AndrewMullen 1 43
(Michael Appleby) *led: hdd appr fnl 2f: wknd appr fnl f* **25/1**

50 **7** 1 **Legal Advisor**[12] 4299 3-9-5 0 RoystonFfrench 6 45
(Philip Kirby) *s.i.s: a in rr* **25/1**

1m 44.99s (-0.91) **Going Correction** -0.10s/f (Good)
**WFA** 3 from 4yo 8lb **7** Ran SP% **117.5**
Speed ratings (Par 103): **100,98,92,90,87 86,85**
CSF £3.36 TOTE £2.70: £1.30, £1.10; EX 3.00 Trifecta £7.80.
**Owner** Sheikh Hamdan bin Mohammed Al Maktoum **Bred** Old Carhue Stud **Trained** Middleham Moor, N Yorks
■ Mr Gatsby was withdrawn. Price at time of withdrawal 12-1. Rule 4 applies to all bets - deduction 5p in the pound.

**FOCUS**
This was an uncompetitive maiden and the two market leaders dominated the finish. Muddling form.

## 4714 INFINITY TYRES H'CAP — 5f
5:40 (5:44) (Class 5) (0-70,68) 3-Y-0+ — £3,881 (£1,155; £577; £288) Stalls Low

Form — RPR

6065 **1** **Majestic Manannan (IRE)**[22] 3952 5-9-6 **62** AdrianNicholls 2 72
(David Nicholls) *mde virtually all: fnd ex ins fnl f* **7/2**[2]

603 **2** 1 **Pabusar**[4] 4545 6-9-1 **60** (t) ConnorKing(3) 1 66
(Ann Stokell) *dwlt: swtchd rt after 1f: sn chsng wnr: upsides over 1f out: kpt on same pce last 100yds* **5/2**[1]

3200 **3** shd **Boxing Shadows**[6] 4494 4-9-11 **67** DavidAllan 8 73
(Les Eyre) *in rr: hdwy and nt clr run 2f out: swtchd rt jst ins fnl f: styd on wl* **6/1**

513 **4** 1¼ **Mey Blossom**[6] 4494 9-8-9 **56** (b) KevinStott(5) 3 57
(Richard Whitaker) *chsd ldrs: 3rd over 1f out: one pce* **5/1**[3]

-001 **5** 2¾ **Slim Chance (IRE)**[5] 4511 5-9-12 **68** 6ex AndrewElliott 6 59
(Simon West) *led to s: dwlt: t.k.h in rr: swtchd lft sn after s: sme hdwy on outside 2f out: nvr a factor* **10/1**

5410 **6** 1¼ **Chosen One (IRE)**[13] 4257 9-9-5 **61** PJMcDonald 5 48
(Ruth Carr) *mid-div: effrt over 2f out: one pce* **14/1**

6340 **7** 2½ **Bosun Breese**[17] 4114 9-9-10 **66** PhillipMakin 7 44
(Paul Midgley) *mid-div: outpcd over 2f out: kpt on over 1f out* **33/1**

0365 **8** 3½ **Classical Diva**[12] 4287 3-8-3 **49** oh1 (b) AndrewMullen 9 13
(Declan Carroll) *chsd ldrs on outer: lost pl over 1f out* **40/1**

3601 **9** shd **Pearl Noir**[12] 4288 4-8-9 **56** (b) MatthewHopkins(5) 4 21
(Scott Dixon) *chsd ldrs on outer: wknd 2f out* **17/2**

0210 **10** ¾ **Mr Mo Jo**[22] 3948 6-9-12 **68** (b) RoystonFfrench 10 30
(Les Eyre) *awkward at s: in rr: bhd over 2f out: nvr on terms* **20/1**

1m 2.69s (-0.61) **Going Correction** -0.10s/f (Good)
**WFA** 3 from 4yo+ 4lb **10** Ran SP% **118.2**
Speed ratings (Par 103): **100,98,98,96,91 89,85,80,80,78**
CSF £12.61 CT £52.08 TOTE £5.00: £1.80, £1.60, £2.20; EX 17.10 Trifecta £77.70.
**Owner** Dubelem (Racing) Limited **Bred** Curlew Partnership **Trained** Sessay, N Yorks

**FOCUS**
This ordinary sprint handicap saw few land a blow and only two mattered from a fair way out.
T/Plt: £833.50 to a £1 stake. Pool: £96,545.78 - 84.55 winning units. T/Qpdt: £32.40 to a £1 stake. Pool: £8392.75 - 191.50 winning units. WG

# 4038 LES LANDES
Sunday, July 27
**OFFICIAL GOING: Good to firm (firm in places)**

## 4715a LIBERATION BREWERY H'CAP — 7f
3:05 (3:06) 3-Y-0+ — £1,460 (£525; £315)

RPR

**1** **Pas D'Action**[37] 6-10-0 (p) JemmaMarshall 1 49
(Mrs A Malzard, Jersey) **3/1**[3]

**2** 1 **Chester'slittlegem (IRE)**[21] 4038 5-9-10 (p) PhilipPrince 4 42
(Mrs A Corson, Jersey) **13/2**

**3** 3 **Spanish Bounty**[37] 9-10-12 MattieBatchelor 5 50
(Mrs A Malzard, Jersey) **11/4**[2]

**4** 1 **Country Blue (FR)**[21] 4038 5-9-13 TimClark 9 35
(Mrs A Malzard, Jersey) **5/1**

**5** nk **Clear Focus (IRE)**[17] 4102 3-9-8 (v) BrendanPowell 7 33
(Brendan Powell) **1/1**[1]

**6** 8 **Purley Queen (IRE)**[21] 4038 5-10-10 (p) MrFTett 6 23
(Mrs C Gilbert, Jersey) **10/3**

**7** 3 **Lively Little Lady**[21] 4039 4-8-5 (p) NoraLooby 8
(Mrs A Corson, Jersey) **20/1**

**8** 8 **Copper Falls**[21] 4038 5-9-12 MarkQuinlan 2
(Mrs A Malzard, Jersey) **9/2**

1m 30.0s
**WFA** 3 from 4yo+ 7lb **8** Ran SP% **177.7**

**Owner** J Jamouneau **Bred** Jenny Hall Bloodstock Ltd **Trained** St Ouen, Jersey

## 4716a 2014 JERSEY DERBY — 1m 4f
3:40 (3:40) 3-Y-0+ — £1,905 (£685; £410)

RPR

**1** **Rossetti**[21] 4040 6-10-2 (p) CraigWalker 6 69
(Mrs A Malzard, Jersey) **5/2**[2]

**2** 7 **Midnight Sequel**[53] 2594 5-9-13 (tp) MarkQuinlan 7 55
(Neil Mulholland) **5/2**[2]

**3** 2 **I'm Harry**[20] 4030 5-10-2 (vt) MattieBatchelor 5 55
(George Baker) **4/5**[1]

**4** 2½ **Sworn Mammy (GER)**[21] 4041 7-9-13 PhilipPrince 4 48
(R Storp, Germany) **4/1**[3]

**5** nk **King Kenny**[21] 4041 9-10-2 (p) NoraLooby 2 50
(Mrs A Corson, Jersey) **9/2**

**6** 4 **Sweet Liberta (IRE)**[21] 4041 5-9-13 TimClark 1 41
(T Le Brocq, Jersey) **15/2**

2m 52.0s (2.00) **6** Ran SP% **162.6**

**Owner** Sheikh A'Leg Racing **Bred** Bricklow Ltd **Trained** St Ouen, Jersey

## 4717a ANIMAL HEALTH TRUST CELEBRATION MILE — 1m 1f
4:15 (4:15) 3-Y-0+ — £1,460 (£525; £315)

RPR

**1** **First Cat**[37] 7-9-11 PhilipPrince 8 54
(K Kukk, Jersey) **10/3**[2]

**2** nk **Herbalist**[43] 3208 4-10-4 DavidBass 1 60
(Sean Curran) **5/2**[1]

**3** 3 **George Baker (IRE)**[18] 4072 7-10-12 MattieBatchelor 2 62
(George Baker) **5/2**[1]

**4** 1 **Lucifers Shadow (IRE)**[21] 4039 5-9-0 (v) MrFTett 7 34
(Mrs C Gilbert, Jersey) **7/2**[3]

**5** 7 **Beck's Bolero (IRE)**[21] 4040 8-9-11 ow4 (p) MarkQuinlan 3 30
(Mrs A Corson, Jersey) **9/2**

**6** 2 **Jackpot**[21] 4039 4-8-5 JemmaMarshall 4 6
(Mrs A Malzard, Jersey) **13/2**

**7** ½ **Rebel Woman**[21] 4040 8-8-5 (p) NoraLooby 5 5
(Mrs A Corson, Jersey) **8/1**

**8** 4½ **Fast Freddie**[21] 4038 10-9-5 (p) BrendanPowell 9 10
(Mrs A Corson, Jersey) **5/1**

**9** 2 **Grey Panel (FR)**[21] 4040 6-9-1 TimClark 6 1
(T Le Brocq, Jersey) **5/1**

2m 2.0s (122.00) **9** Ran SP% **178.4**

**Owner** Mrs E C Roberts **Bred** W And R Barnett Ltd **Trained** Jersey

## 4718a "BUILDING A BETTER WORKING WORLD" H'CAP — 1m 6f
4:50 (4:50) (0-55,) 3-Y-0+ — £1,460 (£525; £315)

RPR

**1** **Agapanthus (GER)**[17] 4107 9-10-2 (b) MarkQuinlan 5 50
(Neil Mulholland) **5/2**[2]

**2** 8 **Lady Petrus**[37] 9-8-5 PhilipPrince 1 14
(K Kukk, Jersey) **11/2**

**3** ¾ **Mr Opulence**[21] 5-10-6 MrRHodson 2 42
(T Le Brocq, Jersey) **5/2**[2]

**4** 10 **Up In Flames (IRE)**[21] 4041 5-10-4 (p) MattieBatchelor 3 26
(Mrs A Malzard, Jersey) **3/1**[3]

**5** 2 **Rocquaine (IRE)**[37] 5-8-5 (p) NoraLooby 8
(Mrs A Malzard, Jersey) **17/2**

**6** dist **River Du Nord (FR)**[21] 4041 7-9-11 JemmaMarshall 7
(Sue Gardner) **9/4**[1]

**7** dist **Constanzina (FR)**[21] 3048 5-10-7 MrFTett 6
(Mrs A Malzard, Jersey) **10/1**

**8** 15 **Transluscent (IRE)**[59] 3903 4-10-12 (t) BrendanPowell 4
(Sue Gardner) **7/1**

3m 19.0s (199.00) **8** Ran SP% **160.4**

**Owner** Stuart K Brown **Bred** Gestut Schlenderhan **Trained** Limpley Stoke, Wilts

4719 - (Foreign Racing) - See Raceform Interactive

# 3073 MUNICH (L-H)
Sunday, July 27
**OFFICIAL GOING: Turf: soft**

## 4720a GROSSER DALLMAYR-PREIS - BAYERISCHES ZUCHTRENNEN (GROUP 1) (3YO+) (TURF) — 1m 2f
4:05 (12:00) 3-Y-0+ — £83,333 (£25,000; £12,500; £5,833; £2,500)

RPR

**1** **Lucky Lion**[21] 4007 3-8-10 0 IoritzMendizabal 6 117
(Andreas Lowe, Germany) *t.k.h: hld up in midfield: pushed along 3 1/2f out: 6th and rdn 2 1/2f out: chsd ldrs fr over 1 1/2f out: edgd lft appr fnl f: r.o to ld 75yds out: drvn out* **7/2**[2]

**2** ½ **Noble Mission**[28] 3774 5-9-6 0 JamesDoyle 12 116
(Lady Cecil) *broke wl fr wd draw: midfield and forced wd first bnd: moved up to trck ldr on outer ent bk st: led over 2 1/2f out: rdn appr fnl f and edgd lft fr 150yds out: hdd 75yds out: no ex* **3/5**[1]

**3** 3 **Calyxa**[25] 3873 4-9-3 0 RobertHavlin 8 107
(Ferdinand J Leve, Germany) *towards rr: tk clsr order over 3f out: hdwy on outer 2 1/2f out: sn rdn and a styng-on 5th 1 1/2f out: kpt on ins fnl f but no real imp on front two* **242/10**

**4** 1 **Magic Artist (IRE)**[21] 4007 3-8-10 0 ASuborics 10 108
(W Figge, Germany) *midfield on inner: dropped towards rr 1/2-way: short of room over 2f out: swtchd outside and styd on fr 1 1/2f out: wnt 4th ins fnl f: run flattened out ins fnl 100yds* **153/10**

**5** 1½ **Polish Vulcano (GER)**[14] 6-9-6 0 EPedroza 2 105
(H-J Groschel, Germany) *towards rr: last and rdn 2 1/2f out and nt qckn immediately: styd on wl fnl f: nrest at fin* **51/1**

**6** ½ **Nausica Time (GER)**[21] 4006 4-9-3 0 BGanbat 7 101
(S Smrczek, Germany) *led: rdn and hdd over 2 1/2f out: sn outpcd by ldrs: wknd u.p fnl f* **42/1**

**7** ½ **Mr Pommeroy (FR)**[27] 3807 3-8-10 0............................ FabriceVeron 1 103
(H-A Pantall, France) *t.k.h: restrained in midfield on inner: rdn and nt qckn fr 2 1/2f out: one pce fnl f* **99/10**

**8** *hd* **Zazou (GER)**[84] 7-9-6 0............................ APietsch 9 103
(Waldemar Hickst, Germany) *w.w in rr: gd hdwy on inner over 2 1/2f out: 4th and hrd rdn appr fnl f: wknd fr under 1f out* **31/1**

**9** 1 ½ **Night Wish (GER)**[14] 4-9-6 0............................ SHellyn 11 100
(W Figge, Germany) *towards rr on outer: hdwy into midfield over 3f out: rdn and wknd under 2f out* **34/1**

**10** 4 **Move Your Vision (IRE)**[49] 5-9-6 0............................ JBojko 5 92
(Zuzana Kubovicova, Salvador) *trckd ldrs on outer: rdn and nt qckn over 2f out: wknd fnl 1 1/2f* **47/1**

**11** 9 **Bermuda Reef (IRE)**[21] 4006 4-9-6 0............................ AdriedeVries 3 74
(P Schiergen, Germany) *trckd ldr on inner: rdn to hold pl fr 3f out: wknd 2f out: eased ins fnl f* **78/10**[3]

2m 7.52s (-1.45)
**WFA** 3 from 4yo+ 10lb **11 Ran SP% 127.7**
WIN (incl. 10 euro stake): 45. PLACES: 12, 12, 23. SF: 69.
**Owner** Gestut Winterhauch **Bred** Stall Parthenaue **Trained** Germany

# 4482 MAISONS-LAFFITTE (R-H)

## Sunday, July 27

**OFFICIAL GOING: Turf: good**

## 4721a PRIX DE BAGATELLE (LISTED RACE) (3YO FILLIES) (STRAIGHT) (TURF) 1m (S)

**2:40** (12:00) 3-Y-O **£22,916** (£9,166; £6,875; £4,583; £2,291)

RPR

**1** **Bawina (IRE)**[42] 3289 3-8-11 0............................ OlivierPeslier 9 110
(C Laffon-Parias, France) **9/10**[1]

**2** 3 **Oh Star (USA)**[18] 4089 3-8-11 0............................ GeraldMosse 8 103
(John Gosden) *broke wl fr wd draw: w ldrs and moved towards inner: led after 1 1/2f: rdn 1 1/2f out: hdd ent fnl f: kpt on u.p but readily outpcd by wnr* **47/10**[2]

**3** ½ **So In Love**[29] 3-8-11 0............................ MaximeGuyon 6 102
(A Fabre, France) **144/10**

**4** *snk* **Dancing Sands (IRE)**[21] 4009 3-8-11 0............................ MickaelBarzalona 3 102
(H-A Pantall, France) *w.w in rr: rdn and hdwy over 1 1/2f out: styd on u.p fnl f: nvr on terms w ldrs* **162/10**

**5** 3 **Double Diamond (FR)**[36] 3-8-11 0............................ JulienAuge 2 95
(C Ferland, France) **214/10**

**6** 1 **Graceful Grit (IRE)**[39] 3357 3-8-11 0......... Christophe-PatriceLemaire 7 92
(F-H Graffard, France) **123/10**

**7** 1 ¼ **Galaxe (FR)**[54] 2880 3-8-11 0............................ StephanePasquier 4 90
(Rod Collet, France) **87/10**[3]

**8** 2 **Stormyra (FR)**[21] 4009 3-9-2 0............................(p) UmbertoRispoli 5 90
(J-P Gallorini, France) **125/10**

**9** 3 ½ **Starflower**[54] 2880 3-8-11 0............................ GregoryBenoist 1 77
(D Smaga, France) **25/1**

**10** 3 ½ **Local Hero (FR)**[42] 3289 3-8-11 0............................ JohanVictoire 10 69
(Y Durepaire, France) **27/1**

1m 34.2s (-8.10) **10 Ran SP% 119.6**
WIN (incl. 1 euro stake): 1.90. PLACES: 1.20, 1.60, 2.20. DF: 5.30. SF: 6.30.
**Owner** Wertheimer & Frere **Bred** Wertheimer Et Frere **Trained** Chantilly, France

## 4722a PRIX DU CARROUSEL (LISTED RACE) (4YO+) (RIGHT-HANDED) (TURF) 1m 7f 110y

**3:10** (12:00) 4-Y-O+ **£21,666** (£8,666; £6,500; £4,333; £2,166)

RPR

**1** **High Jinx (IRE)**[59] 2704 6-9-1 0............................ ChristopheSoumillon 9 108
(James Fanshawe) *w ldrs: led after 2f: jnd jst past 1/2-way: rdn: hdd and sltly outpcd over 1 1/2f out: rallied u.p to ld 100yds out: hld on gamely* **1/1**[1]

**2** *hd* **Trip To Rhodos (FR)**[34] 5-9-1 0............................ CristianDemuro 3 108
(Pavel Tuma, Czech Republic) **91/10**

**3** 1 ¾ **Biladi (FR)**[28] 5-8-11 0............................ MaximeGuyon 7 102
(X Thomas-Demeaulte, France) **56/1**

**4** 1 **Ederan (IRE)**[34] 4-8-11 0............................ Pierre-CharlesBoudot 11 100
(Rod Collet, France) **23/5**[2]

**5** 1 ¼ **Lucky Look (FR)**[39] 4-8-8 0............................ GregoryBenoist 1 96
(D Smaga, France) **157/10**

**6** 2 **West Of Venus (USA)**[34] 4-8-8 0............................ StephanePasquier 2 94
(J E Pease, France) **129/10**

**7** *hd* **Tres Rock Danon (FR)**[77] 2229 8-8-11 0............................(p) UmbertoRispoli 5 96
(Gerald Geisler, Germany) **233/10**

**8** 5 **Zack Hope**[25] 6-8-11 0............................ TonyPiccone 6 90
(N Caullery, France) **44/1**

**9** *nk* **Achtung (SPA)**[28] 6-8-11 0............................ FranckBlondel 10 90
(J Lopez Sanchez, Spain) **30/1**

**10** 12 **Casar (IRE)**[21] 6-8-11 0............................ AlexisBadel 13 76
(M Delcher Sanchez, France) **78/10**[3]

**11** 4 ½ **Technokrat (IRE)**[24] 6-8-11 0............................ AntoineHamelin 8 70
(S Smrczek, Germany) **269/10**

**12** *dist* **Burggraf**[24] 4-8-11 0............................ OlivierPeslier 12
(J D Hillis, Germany) **53/1**

3m 25.0s (205.00) **12 Ran SP% 119.1**
WIN (incl. 1 euro stake): 2.00. PLACES: 1.40, 2.50, 8.50. DF: 8.10. SF: 10.10.
**Owner** Mr & Mrs W J Williams **Bred** Haras De La Perelle **Trained** Newmarket, Suffolk

# 4486 AYR (L-H)

## Monday, July 28

**OFFICIAL GOING: Good to firm (9.3)**
Wind: Fresh, half against Weather: Fine, dry

## 4723 PLAY BETVICTOR CASINO ON YOUR MOBILE MEDIAN AUCTION MAIDEN STKS 6f

**2:00** (2:02) (Class 5) 2-Y-O **£3,234** (£962; £481; £240) **Stalls** Centre

Form RPR

23 **1** **Polarisation**[16] 4216 2-9-5 0............................ JoeFanning 8 82+
(Mark Johnston) *trckd ldrs: rdn to ld over 1f out: edgd lft: styd on wl fnl f* **5/6**[1]

0 **2** 4 **Baron Spikey (IRE)**[8] 4467 2-9-5 0............................ PJMcDonald 5 70
(Ann Duffield) *in tch: hdwy and ev ch over 1f out: kpt on ins fnl f: nt gng pce of wnr* **22/1**

34 **3** ¾ **Scarlet Bounty (IRE)**[18] 4129 2-9-0 0............................ TonyHamilton 6 63
(Richard Fahey) *hld up in tch: stdy hdwy over 2f out: rdn over 1f out: kpt on same pce fnl f* **3/1**[2]

524 **4** 6 **Battleranger (IRE)**[10] 4382 2-9-5 72............................ TomEaves 4 50
(Keith Dalgleish) *led tl rdn and hdd over 1f out: sn wknd* **10/3**[3]

50 **5** 6 **Go On Chas**[14] 4253 2-9-0 0............................ GarryWhillans(5) 3 32
(Ian Semple) *cl up: drvn over 2f out: wknd over 1f out* **100/1**

0 **6** 13 **Sabbra Cadabra**[14] 4253 2-9-5 0............................ DuranFentiman 2
(Philip Kirby) *t.k.h: cl up tl rdn and wknd over 2f out* **125/1**

1m 13.66s (1.26) **Going Correction** +0.175s/f (Good) **6 Ran SP% 108.8**
Speed ratings (Par 94): **98,92,91,83,75 58**
CSF £17.43 TOTE £1.40: £1.10, £9.20; EX 15.70 Trifecta £38.50.
**Owner** Sheikh Hamdan bin Mohammed Al Maktoum **Bred** Darley **Trained** Middleham Moor, N Yorks

**FOCUS**
A modest 2yo maiden and the third helps with the level. Straights in 8m, Home bend in 6m, Rothesay bend in 4m and consequently races between 7f-10f increased by about 18yds and 13f race by 30yds.

## 4724 DOWNLOAD THE BETVICTOR APP NOW H'CAP 6f

**2:30** (2:31) (Class 5) (0-75,75) 3-Y-O+ **£3,234** (£962; £481; £240) **Stalls** Centre

Form RPR

3514 **1** **Gold Beau (FR)**[10] 4383 4-9-7 75............................(p) JacobButterfield(5) 8 83
(Kristin Stubbs) *mde all: rdn along 2f out: kpt on wl fnl f* **11/4**[2]

2 **2** ½ **Calling You (IRE)**[44] 3260 5-8-9 58............................(b) PJMcDonald 7 64
(S Donohoe, Ire) *prom: effrt and drvn 2f out: chsd wnr fnl f: kpt on fin* **6/1**

414 **3** 1 ¾ **Sleeper Class**[37] 3460 3-8-8 65............................ GaryBartley(3) 1 64
(Jim Goldie) *s.i.s: in tch: effrt and rdn over 1f out: hung lft: one pce ins fnl f* **12/1**

1223 **4** *hd* **Jinky**[7] 4487 6-9-9 72............................ JoeFanning 4 72
(Linda Perratt) *propped and s.s: sn rcvrd to chse wnr: rdn and ev ch over 1f out: outpcd ins fnl f* **15/8**[1]

1253 **5** 1 ¾ **Spirit Of Alsace (IRE)**[14] 4256 3-8-6 65............................ JackGarritty(5) 6 58
(Jim Goldie) *t.k.h: in tch: effrt and rdn over 1f out: no imp fnl f* **5/1**[3]

0040 **6** 3 ¾ **L'Ami Louis (IRE)**[14] 4256 6-9-7 70............................ TomEaves 5 52
(Ian Semple) *s.i.s: hld up in tch: rdn over 2f out: wknd over 1f out* **12/1**

1m 14.07s (1.67) **Going Correction** +0.175s/f (Good)
**WFA** 3 from 4yo+ 5lb **6 Ran SP% 107.8**
Speed ratings (Par 103): **95,94,92,91,89 84**
CSF £17.47 CT £141.88 TOTE £3.30: £2.10, £1.90; EX 22.00 Trifecta £106.80.
**Owner** D Arundale **Bred** Haras Du Quesnay **Trained** Norton, N Yorks

**FOCUS**
A moderate sprint handicap run in a relativel slow time. The winner was allowed an easy lead but is accorded a pb.

## 4725 DOWNLOAD THE INSTABET APP FROM BETVICTOR H'CAP 5f

**3:00** (3:02) (Class 6) (0-65,64) 3-Y-O+ **£2,264** (£673; £336; £168) **Stalls** Centre

Form RPR

2661 **1** **Fredricka**[13] 4295 3-9-7 63............................ JasonHart 8 71
(Garry Moss) *hld up in tch: stdy hdwy over 2f out: effrt and rdn over 1f out: edgd lft and led ins fnl f: hld on wl* **5/1**[3]

1142 **2** *hd* **Classy Anne**[14] 4257 4-9-7 64............................ JackGarritty(5) 10 72
(Jim Goldie) *prom: drvn and outpcd over 1f out: rallied: edgd lft and ev ch ins fnl f: kpt on: jst hld* **5/2**[1]

0633 **3** ½ **Saxonette**[14] 4257 6-8-11 49............................ JoeFanning 13 55
(Linda Perratt) *hld up: rdn and hdwy over 1f out: kpt on ins fnl f: nrst fin* **4/1**[2]

0063 **4** *hd* **Chloe's Dream (IRE)**[6] 4519 4-8-8 51............................ KevinStott(5) 4 56
(Linda Perratt) *led: rdn: edgd lft and hdd ins fnl f: kpt on same pce* **10/1**

0453 **5** 2 **Findog**[2] 4664 4-9-0 57............................ SammyJoBell(5) 7 55
(Linda Perratt) *dwlt: hld up: rdn and effrt whn n.m.r briefly wl over 1f out: kpt on ins fnl f: nvr able to chal* **13/2**

0303 **6** 1 ¼ **Greenbury (IRE)**[12] 4314 3-8-8 50............................(p) PJMcDonald 3 43
(Ann Duffield) *prom: effrt and drvn wl over 1f out: outpcd fnl f* **10/1**

6002 **7** 1 **Busy Bimbo (IRE)**[11] 4362 5-8-8 49............................(b) GeorgeChaloner(3) 6 39
(Alan Berry) *prom tl rdn: edgd lft and wknd over 1f out* **11/1**

0006 **8** 4 **Wicked Wilma (IRE)**[6] 4519 10-8-7 45............................ JamesSullivan 12 21
(Alan Berry) *midfield: drvn along over 2f out: hung lft and wknd wl over 1f out* **66/1**

0200 **9** 7 **Baltic Spirit (IRE)**[6] 4519 3-9-1 57............................ GrahamLee 9 6
(Keith Dalgleish) *taken early to post: sed extremely slowly: nvr on terms* **14/1**

0000 **10** 2 ¾ **Fife Jo**[14] 4257 4-8-9 47 ow2............................(v) TomEaves 2
(Jim Goldie) *prom tl rdn and wknd fr 2f out* **80/1**

59.97s (0.57) **Going Correction** +0.175s/f (Good)
**WFA** 3 from 4yo+ 4lb **10 Ran SP% 114.5**
Speed ratings (Par 101): **102,101,100,100,97 95,93,87,76,71**
CSF £17.50 CT £54.26 TOTE £6.90: £1.60, £1.60, £2.30; EX 12.50 Trifecta £68.10.
**Owner** Ron Hull **Bred** J C Parsons & J J Gilmartin **Trained** Tickhill, S Yorks

**FOCUS**
A modest handicap, but sound form, rated around the third..

## 4726 DOWNLOAD THE BETVICTOR SPINCAST APP H'CAP 1m 5f 13y

**3:30** (3:31) (Class 5) (0-75,70) 3-Y-O+ **£3,234** (£962; £481; £240) **Stalls** Low

Form RPR

2-42 **1** **Thorntoun Care**[14] 4255 3-8-12 67............................ GrahamLee 1 77
(Jim Goldie) *trckd ldrs: effrt and swtchd rt over 1f out: rdn to ld ins fnl f: styd on strly* **11/4**[1]

4221 **2** 1 3/4 **Mister Uno (IRE)**[10] 4386 3-8-8 **63**..........(p) PJMcDonald 4 70
(Ann Duffield) *t.k.h: pressed ldr: drvn to ld over 1f out: hdd ins fnl f: kpt on same pce towards fin* **7/2**[2]

5225 **3** 2 1/2 **Geanie Mac (IRE)**[6] 4520 5-8-8 **55**..........(p) SammyJoBell(5) 5 58
(Linda Perratt) *in tch: effrt and pushed along over 2f out: edgd lft over 1f out: chsd first two ins fnl f: kpt on: no imp* **11/1**

6045 **4** 1 1/2 **Cavalieri (IRE)**[30] 3699 4-10-0 **70**.......... PhillipMakin 6 71
(Philip Kirby) *hld up: hdwy on outside 3f out: rdn and hung lft wl over 1f out: kpt on ins fnl f: nvr able to chal* **5/1**

3355 **5** 1 **Mambo Rhythm**[16] 4189 3-8-10 **65**.......... JoeFanning 3 64
(Mark Johnston) *led at ordinary gallop: rdn over 2f out: hdd over 1f out: no ex and lost two pls last 100yds* **4/1**[3]

6061 **6** 1 1/2 **Gold Chain (IRE)**[9] 4015 4-9-4 **65**.......... EmmaSayer(5) 7 62
(Dianne Sayer) *hld up and bhd: rdn over 3f out: no imp fr 2f out* **8/1**

0-50 **7** 18 **Rock A Doodle Doo (IRE)**[45] 3205 7-9-13 **69**..........(p) TomEaves 2 39
(Sally Hall) *in tch: rdn over 3f out: wknd over 2f out: t.o* **14/1**

2m 55.57s (1.57) **Going Correction** -0.025s/f (Good)
**WFA** 3 from 4yo+ 13lb 7 Ran SP% **111.7**
Speed ratings (Par 103): **94,92,91,90,89 88,77**
CSF £11.89 TOTE £4.20: £2.10, £1.60; EX 12.10 Trifecta £65.10.
**Owner** W M Johnstone **Bred** W M Johnstone **Trained** Uplawmoor, E Renfrews

**FOCUS**
A modest staying handicap in which they went quite a steady pace in the formative stages. The first two progressed.

## 4727 SPINCAST AT BETVICTOR DOWNLOAD THE NEW APP H'CAP (DIV I) 7f 50y
**4:00** (4:01) (Class 6) (0-65,64) 3-Y-O+ **£2,264** (£673; £336; £168) **Stalls High**

Form RPR

0212 **1** **The Dukkerer (IRE)**[26] 3846 3-9-5 **64**.......... JasonHart 3 69
(Garry Moss) *prom: hdwy to ld over 2f out: sn edgd lft: rdn over 1f out: keeping on wl whn pricked ears and veered rt nr fin* **11/8**[1]

4-66 **2** 1 3/4 **Berbice (IRE)**[6] 4523 9-8-2 **45**.......... SammyJoBell(5) 8 48
(Linda Perratt) *hld up: smooth hdwy on outside over 2f out: edgd lft and chsd wnr over 1f out: sn rdn: kpt on same pce ins fnl f* **12/1**

0-60 **3** 3/4 **Hazza The Jazza**[13] 4306 4-8-8 **51**..........(b) DuilioDaSilva(5) 2 54
(Richard Guest) *t.k.h: hld up: effrt and hdwy whn hmpd and swtchd rt over 1f out: kpt on ins fnl f: nrst fin* **11/1**

0-3 **4** 2 3/4 **Erelight (IRE)**[41] 3347 6-8-11 **49**.......... JamesSullivan 6 43
(S Donohoe, Ire) *t.k.h: chsd ldrs: rdn and outpcd 2f out: kpt on ins fnl f: no imp* **11/2**[3]

0030 **5** 1/2 **Jack Barker**[18] 4101 5-8-4 **45**.......... NeilFarley(3) 9 38
(Robin Bastiman) *led and sn crossed to ins rail: rdn and hdd over 2f out: no ex over 1f out* **28/1**

0000 **6** 1 **Medecis Mountain**[8] 4473 5-8-9 **47** ow1..........(v) TomEaves 5 37
(John Wainwright) *sn pressing ldr: drvn and ev ch over 2f out: edgd rt wl over 1f out: wknd fnl f* **33/1**

4-01 **7** 1 3/4 **Rust (IRE)**[12] 4318 4-9-10 **62**..........(p) PJMcDonald 1 47
(Ann Duffield) *prom: drvn and outpcd 2f out: sn btn* **9/4**[2]

1m 33.1s (-0.30) **Going Correction** -0.025s/f (Good)
**WFA** 3 from 4yo+ 7lb 7 Ran SP% **110.7**
Speed ratings (Par 101): **100,98,97,94,93 92,90**
CSF £18.02 CT £121.79 TOTE £1.70: £1.10, £5.10; EX 18.10 Trifecta £83.60.
**Owner** Willam G Pett & Ron Hull **Bred** Mrs Sarah Maccann **Trained** Tickhill, S Yorks

**FOCUS**
The first division of a modest 7f handicap in which they went an ordinary gallop. Weak form, the winner finding a little on recent efforts.

## 4728 SPINCAST AT BETVICTOR DOWNLOAD THE NEW APP H'CAP (DIV II) 7f 50y
**4:30** (4:31) (Class 6) (0-65,64) 3-Y-O+ **£2,264** (£673; £336; £168) **Stalls High**

Form RPR

5003 **1** **Secret City (IRE)**[19] 4070 8-8-12 **53**..........(p) NeilFarley(3) 9 63
(Robin Bastiman) *prom: hdwy to ld over 2f out: pushed out ins fnl f* **7/2**[3]

6-44 **2** 2 3/4 **Blue Sonic**[13] 4299 4-9-1 **53**.......... GrahamLee 8 56
(Jim Goldie) *t.k.h early: pressed ldr: ev ch over 2f out to over 1f out: kpt on same pce ins fnl f* **7/1**

4040 **3** 1 **Starlite Jewel**[39] 3389 3-8-7 **52**.......... JasonHart 5 49
(Stuart Coltherd) *dwlt: hld up: stdy hdwy on outside over 2f out: rdn and chsng ldrs over 1f out: one pce ins fnl f* **20/1**

3336 **4** 1 1/4 **Sewn Up**[12] 4314 4-8-12 **50**..........(p) TomEaves 7 47
(Keith Dalgleish) *t.k.h: hld up in tch: effrt and edgd lft over 1f out: one pce ins fnl f* **10/3**[2]

4-06 **5** 2 3/4 **Saranta**[37] 3486 3-9-2 **64**.......... GeorgeChaloner(3) 4 51
(Richard Fahey) *hld up: pushed along over 2f out: sme late hdwy: nvr able to chal* **3/1**[1]

0000 **6** 1 3/4 **Mystical King**[7] 4489 4-8-4 **45**.......... ConnorBeasley(3) 1 30
(Linda Perratt) *in tch: drvn and outpcd over 2f out: n.d after* **25/1**

0002 **7** nk **Torridon**[11] 4363 3-8-2 **47**.......... JoeFanning 3 28
(Mark Johnston) *led: rdn and hdd over 1f out: sn btn* **4/1**

**8** hd **All Gone (IRE)**[329] 6055 5-8-4 **45**..........(b) JoeyHaynes(3) 6 29
(S Donohoe, Ire) *t.k.h: trckd ldrs tl rdn and wknd over 1f out* **33/1**

1m 33.7s (0.30) **Going Correction** -0.025s/f (Good)
**WFA** 3 from 4yo+ 7lb 8 Ran SP% **114.4**
Speed ratings (Par 101): **97,93,92,91,88 86,85,85**
CSF £27.03 CT £424.68 TOTE £4.30: £1.60, £2.10, £5.00; EX 31.10 Trifecta £280.90.
**Owner** Ms M Austerfield **Bred** Miss Karen Theobald **Trained** Cowthorpe, N Yorks

**FOCUS**
The second division of an ordinary 7f handicap. The winner built on his latest effort.

## 4729 FOLLOW US ON TWITTER @BETVICTORRACING H'CAP 1m
**5:00** (5:00) (Class 5) (0-75,73) 3-Y-O+ **£3,234** (£962; £481; £240) **Stalls Low**

Form RPR

5322 **1** **Push Me (IRE)**[8] 4472 7-9-13 **72**.......... GrahamLee 6 84
(Iain Jardine) *hld up in tch: shkn up briefly over 3f out: smooth hdwy to ld over 1f out: pushed clr* **5/4**[1]

600- **2** 6 **Brooke's Bounty**[396] 3730 4-9-7 **69**.......... GeorgeChaloner(3) 8 66
(Richard Fahey) *pressed ldr: rdn over 2f out: chsd (clr) wnr ins fnl f: kpt on: no imp* **17/2**

2330 **3** 1 3/4 **Tectonic (IRE)**[10] 4387 5-9-10 **69**..........(p) TomEaves 3 62
(Keith Dalgleish) *led: qcknd over 3f out: rdn over 2f out: hdd over 1f out: sn no ex* **7/2**[3]

120 **4** 3/4 **Order Of Service**[14] 4258 4-9-11 **73**.......... GaryBartley(3) 2 64
(Jim Goldie) *trckd ldrs: drvn along over 2f out: outpcd over 1f out* **5/2**[2]

1m 42.74s (-1.06) **Going Correction** -0.025s/f (Good)
**WFA** 3 from 4yo+ 8lb 4 Ran SP% **105.8**
Speed ratings (Par 103): **104,98,96,95**
CSF £10.45 TOTE £1.50; EX 11.60 Trifecta £17.20.
**Owner** Alex and Janet Card **Bred** Mrs Dolores Gleeson **Trained** Bonchester Bridge, Borders

**FOCUS**
A modest little handicap. The winner ran a 4lb pesonal best, but this is shaky form.

## 4730 PLAY AT BETVICTOR'S LIVE CASINO APPRENTICE H'CAP 1m
**5:30** (5:30) (Class 6) (0-60,60) 3-Y-O+ **£2,045** (£603; £302) **Stalls Low**

Form RPR

0-33 **1** **Joyful Sound (IRE)**[31] 3660 6-10-0 **58**..........(p) MeganCarberry 5 65
(Brian Ellison) *hld up: hdwy 3f out: rdn and chsd ldr over 1f out: led wl ins fnl f: drvn out* **15/8**[1]

0331 **2** nk **Gambino (IRE)**[7] 4489 4-10-2 **60** 6ex..........(p) AlistairRawlinson 3 66
(John David Riches) *in tch: hdwy to chse ldng pair 1/2-way: led and rdn over 2f out: hdd wl ins fnl f: r.o* **7/2**[2]

0-03 **3** 1 3/4 **Rock Band**[12] 4327 5-9-5 **50**..........(bt[1]) RobJFitzpatrick 7 51
(Emmet Michael Butterly, Ire) *slowly away: t.k.h in rr: smooth hdwy over 3f out: effrt and chsng ldrs over 1f out: kpt on same pce ins fnl f* **8/1**[3]

5-00 **4** nk **Eretara (IRE)**[41] 3350 5-9-0 **48**..........(b) JoshDoyle(4) 8 49
(S Donohoe, Ire) *hld up: rdn and hdwy on outside over 2f out: kpt on fnl f: nrst fin* **40/1**

0005 **5** 2 1/2 **New Lease Of Life**[7] 4489 5-9-9 **53**.......... JackGarritty 6 48
(Jim Goldie) *chsd clr ldng pair to 1/2-way: effrt and rdn over 2f out: no imp over 1f out* **9/1**

5002 **6** 3 3/4 **Taxiformissbyron**[2] 4665 4-8-11 **45**.......... DanielleMooney(4) 1 31
(Iain Jardine) *led: jnd after 1f and maintained decent gallop: hdd over 2f out: wknd over 1f out* **7/2**[2]

64-0 **7** 1 **Conjuror's Bluff**[66] 2518 6-9-1 **47**..........(p) RachelRichardson(2) 4 31
(Frederick Watson) *hld up: rdn and hdwy over 2f out: wknd over 1f out* **33/1**

0 **8** 2 **Erwhons Gift (IRE)**[85] 1995 3-8-8 **47**.......... SammyJoBell 10 23
(S Donohoe, Ire) *prom tl rdn and lost pl over 3f out: sn btn* **50/1**

0166 **9** 1 1/4 **Look On By**[16] 4197 4-9-11 **55**.......... GemmaTutty 9 31
(Ruth Carr) *dwlt: hdwy on outside to join ldr after 1f: rdn and wknd over 2f out* **16/1**

1m 43.41s (-0.39) **Going Correction** -0.025s/f (Good)
**WFA** 3 from 4yo+ 8lb 9 Ran SP% **113.6**
Speed ratings (Par 101): **100,99,97,97,95 91,90,88,87**
CSF £8.15 CT £40.56 TOTE £3.00: £1.30, £1.10, £2.40; EX 9.70 Trifecta £44.10.
**Owner** Mr & Mrs E J Dolan-Abrahams **Bred** Rathbarry Stud **Trained** Norton, N Yorks

**FOCUS**
A moderate apprentice riders' handicap in which they went a contested gallop. Weak form, but a small personal best from the winner.
T/Plt: £157.80 to a £1 stake. Pool of £66780.52 - 308.89 winning tickets. T/Qpdt: £11.20 to a £1 stake. Pool of £6467.20 - 427.16 winning tickets. RY

# 4652 LINGFIELD (L-H)
## Monday, July 28

**OFFICIAL GOING: Standard**
Wind: light, half against Weather: slightly overcast, bright spells, showers Race 3

## 4731 32RED NOVICE MEDIAN AUCTION STKS 7f 1y(P)
**2:15** (2:16) (Class 5) 2-Y-O **£2,587** (£770; £384; £192) **Stalls Low**

Form RPR

51 **1** **Jargon (FR)**[11] 4338 2-9-2 82.......... GeorgeBaker 5 82
(Michael Bell) *chsd ldr: rdn jst over 2f out: drvn over 1f out: styd on u.p fnl 100yds to ld nr fin* **4/5**[1]

61 **2** hd **Thecornishassassin**[20] 4054 2-9-2 0.......... AdamKirby 1 81
(Robert Eddery) *led: rdn ent fnl 2f: drvn ins fnl f: kpt on but worn down and hdd nr fin* **6/4**[2]

**3** 2 1/4 **Gild Master** 2-9-0 0.......... FergusSweeney 3 73+
(Alan King) *chsd ldng pair: effrt and rdn over 1f out: kpt on same pce under hands and heels riding fnl f* **25/1**

35 **4** 2 1/4 **Golden Wedding (IRE)**[16] 4207 2-9-0 0.......... TomQueally 6 67
(Eve Johnson Houghton) *t.k.h: hld up in tch in last pair: effrt and wd bnd 2f out: sn outpcd and btn* **16/1**[3]

**5** 2 **Cosmic Ray** 2-9-0 0.......... DavidProbert 4 62
(Andrew Balding) *s.i.s: rn green: in tch in rr: rdn wl over 1f out: sn outpcd and btn* **25/1**

1m 25.19s (0.39) **Going Correction** +0.025s/f (Slow) 5 Ran SP% **109.1**
Speed ratings (Par 94): **98,97,95,92,90**
CSF £2.16 TOTE £1.40: £1.10, £1.60; EX 2.30 Trifecta £11.70.
**Owner** The Royal Ascot Racing Club **Bred** S C E A Haras Du Ma **Trained** Newmarket, Suffolk

**FOCUS**
A couple of previous winners on show and they fought out a good finish. The form could be worrth a bit more.

## 4732 32RED CASINO H'CAP (DIV I) 7f 1y(P)
**2:45** (2:46) (Class 6) (0-55,55) 3-Y-O+ **£1,940** (£577; £288; £144) **Stalls Low**

Form RPR

2033 **1** **Alfresco**[20] 4056 10-9-5 **53**..........(b) RobertHavlin 3 60
(Martin Bosley) *wl in tch in midfield: effrt on inner to chse ldr 1f out: styd on to ld wl ins fnl f: jst hld on: all out* **10/1**[3]

-104 **2** nse **True Spirit**[56] 2844 4-9-7 **55**.......... SeanLevey 1 62
(Paul D'Arcy) *bustled along leaving stalls and sn pressing ldrs: rdn to ld 2f out: edgd rt u.p ins fnl f: hdd wl ins fnl f: rallied u.p towards fin: jst hld* **9/4**[1]

2423 **3** hd **Bladewood Girl**[59] 2722 6-9-6 **54**.......... FrederikTylicki 10 60+
(J R Jenkins) *dwlt: in tch in rr: effrt on outer over 2f out: hdwy u.p 1f out: styd on strly: nt quite rch ldrs* **9/2**[2]

/0-0 **4** 3/4 **Buxton**[11] 4341 10-8-12 **46**..........(t) MartinLane 5 51
(Roger Ingram) *hld up in tch in rr of main gp: hdwy between horses over 1f out: drvn and chsd ldrs 1f out: keeping on but hld whn n.m.r towards fin* **20/1**

-002 **5** 3/4 **Proper Charlie**[20] 4049 6-9-4 **52**..........(v) StevieDonohoe 13 55
(Lee Carter) *chsd ldrs: drvn and hdwy to chse ldng pair 1f out: styd on same pce ins fnl f: short of room towards fin* **10/1**[3]

-036 **6** nk **Silvala Dance**[20] 4056 4-9-2 **50**.......... TedDurcan 8 52
(Chris Wall) *hld up wl in tch in midfield: nt clr run 2f out tl hdwy between horses over 1f out: kpt on same pce ins fnl f* **9/2**[2]

-400 **7** 1 1/4 **Cueca (FR)**[33] 3588 3-8-11 **52**........................................ OisinMurphy 9 48
(Jonathan Portman) *in tch in midfield: rdn and effrt over 2f out: kpt on same pce ins fnl f* **14/1**

6665 **8** 2 **Hinton Admiral**[20] 4055 10-8-12 **47** oh1........................ TomQueally 12 44
(Pat Eddery) *stdd and dropped in bhd after s: hld up in rr of main gp: hdwy ent fnl f: stl plenty to do whn nt clr run and swtchd rt ins fnl f: kpt on: nvr trbld ldrs* **14/1**

600 **9** 1 **The Boss Of Me**[20] 4056 3-8-3 **49**..............................(t) CamHardie(5) 14 37
(Sean Curran) *led: rdn and hdd 2f out: sn drvn and lost 2nd 1f out: wknd ins fnl f* **25/1**

6000 **10** 1 **Confiture**[19] 4084 3-8-7 **48**..........................................(b[1]) DavidProbert 4 33
(Michael Blanshard) *t.k.h: hld up in tch towards rr: hdwy u.p on inner over 1f out: no imp 1f out: sn wknd* **20/1**

0-06 **11** 7 **Bridge Valley**[53] 2937 7-8-12 **45**..............................(be) HayleyTurner 6 16
(Alan McCabe) *nvr travelling: immediately rdn and detached in last: n.d* **50/1**

-000 **12** 1 1/2 **Ellen May**[19] 4092 4-8-13 **47**..........................................(b[1]) J-PGuillambert 7 13
(Nick Littmoden) *t.k.h: w ldrs tl rdn and struggling ent fnl 2f: lost pl over 1f out: fdd fnl f* **10/1**[3]

1m 25.79s (0.99) **Going Correction** +0.025s/f (Slow)
**WFA** 3 from 4yo+ 7lb **12** Ran SP% **123.1**
Speed ratings (Par 101): **95,94,94,93,93 92,91,88,87,86 78,76**
CSF £32.56 CT £124.58 TOTE £9.00: £2.70, £1.70, £1.70; EX 35.50 Trifecta £59.60.
**Owner** Mrs A M Riney **Bred** Usk Valley Stud **Trained** Chalfont St Giles, Bucks

**FOCUS**
The first division of a low-grade handicap saw an exciting finish. Slightly the slower division, and the winner's best form sicne June last year.

## 4733 32RED CASINO H'CAP (DIV II) 7f 1y(P)
**3:15** (3:15) (Class 6) (0-55,55) 3-Y-0+ **£1,940** (£577; £288; £144) **Stalls** Low

Form RPR

5540 **1** **Blue Clumber**[20] 4046 4-8-12 **46**.......................................... JimmyQuinn 7 55
(Shaun Harris) *chsd ldr: rdn over 2f out: drvn and styd on wl fnl f to ld nr fin* **16/1**

220 **2** 1/2 **Chapellerie (IRE)**[111] 1369 5-9-0 **55**......................(b) JennyPowell(7) 12 63
(Brendan Powell) *wnt lft s: sn in tch in midfield on outer: sddle slipped and hdwy over 4f out: swtchd lft to chse ldrs on inner 2f out: rdn to ld over 1f out: drvn fnl f: hdd and no ex nr fin* **14/1**

0006 **3** 2 **Reginald Claude**[20] 4049 6-9-6 **54**..............................(be[1]) LiamKeniry 1 57
(Mark Usher) *broke wl: grad stdd bk and towards rr 4f out: hdwy jst over 2f out: wnt 3rd and effrt jst ins fnl f: one pce and no imp fnl 100yds* **12/1**

-006 **4** 1/2 **Jersey Cream (IRE)**[34] 3554 3-8-11 **52**...................... FergusSweeney 4 51
(Gary Moore) *hld up in tch in rr: rdn and hdwy over 1f out: swtchd rt ins fnl f: styd on wl fnl 100yds: nvr trbld ldrs* **8/1**

/04 **5** 1/2 **Tamujin (IRE)**[59] 2722 6-8-12 **46** oh1.................................. PatDobbs 5 46
(Ken Cunningham-Brown) *hld up in tch in rr: hdwy over 2f out: kpt on u.p fnl f: nvr quite pce to threaten ldrs* **25/1**

0600 **6** 3/4 **Lewamy (IRE)**[20] 4056 4-8-8 **47**.................................. CamHardie(5) 13 45
(John Best) *hld up in tch in rr: last and switching lft to inner 2f out: hdwy u.p over 1f out: kpt on fnl f: nvr trbld ldrs* **16/1**

50 **7** 1 **First Rebellion**[34] 3561 5-9-4 **52**..........................................(b) AdamKirby 6 48
(Tony Carroll) *sn led: rdn over 2f out: drvn and hdd over 1f out: 3rd and btn 1f out: wknd fnl 100yds: eased nr fin* **6/1**[3]

0344 **8** 2 **Trigger Park (IRE)**[26] 3849 3-8-8 **49** ow1...................... SteveDrowne 2 36
(Ronald Harris) *in tch in midfield: nt clr run on inner over 2f out: effrt u.p over 1f out: wknd ins fnl f* **8/1**

00-5 **9** nse **Risk 'N' Reward (IRE)**[12] 4324 3-8-11 **52**...................... KierenFallon 10 39+
(Michael Murphy) *dwlt and bmpd s: towards rr: sme hdwy whn hmpd over 4f out: effrt but wd bnd 2f out: kpt on but n.d* **3/1**[1]

0-06 **10** 3/4 **Pacific Trip**[29] 3754 3-8-11 **52**..........................................(v[1]) DavidProbert 3 37
(Andrew Balding) *in tch in midfield: rdn over 2f out: no hdwy: plugged on same pce fr over 1f out* **4/1**[2]

2-54 **11** 5 **Twilight Angel**[52] 2946 6-9-2 **50**.......................................... TomQueally 8 25
(Pat Eddery) *t.k.h: chsd ldrs: losing pl u.p 2f out: wknd over 1f out* **7/1**

000 **12** 2 1/4 **Phantom Spirit**[24] 3916 3-8-5 **46** oh1..............................(p) MartinLane 14 13
(George Baker) *chsd ldrs on outer: struggling ent fnl 2f: wknd over 1f out* **33/1**

1m 25.35s (0.55) **Going Correction** +0.025s/f (Slow)
**WFA** 3 from 4yo+ 7lb **12** Ran SP% **126.9**
Speed ratings (Par 101): **97,96,94,93,93 92,91,88,88,87 82,79**
CSF £237.15 CT £2838.92 TOTE £26.30: £7.70, £2.40, £4.10; EX 445.20 Trifecta £1231.60.
**Owner** Miss H Ward **Bred** Worksop Manor Stud **Trained** Carburton, Notts

**FOCUS**
The second division of the 0-55 handicap was run in a quicker time than the first, but it was a messy race and might not prove that reliable. The winner had only shown her form once in the past year, and is rated back to that.

## 4734 ALL NEW 32REDSPORT.COM H'CAP 1m 4f (P)
**3:45** (3:45) (Class 6) (0-60,60) 3-Y-0+ **£1,940** (£577; £288; £144) **Stalls** Low

Form RPR

0431 **1** **Elegant Ophelia**[14] 4264 5-10-0 **60**..............................(t) GeorgeBaker 5 69+
(Dean Ivory) *in tch in midfield: clsd and gng wl upsides ldr over 2f out: shkn up to ld over 1f out: in command and doing little in front fnl f: comf* **7/4**[1]

-003 **2** 1 1/4 **Give Us A Reason**[19] 4081 4-9-10 **56**.......................... TomQueally 4 63
(James Toller) *stdd s: hld up in tch in rr: swtchd rt over 2f out: effrt and swtchd wd bnd 2f out: hdwy 1f out: hung lft fnl f but styd on wl to go 2nd fnl 75yds: no real threat to wnr* **6/1**

3405 **3** 1 3/4 **Zinnobar**[35] 3540 4-9-2 **48**..........................................(p) OisinMurphy 2 52
(Jonathan Portman) *chsd ldr for 2f: wnt 2nd again 8f out tl short of room and lost 2nd over 2f out: effrt in 3rd over 1f out: one pce* **12/1**

600 **4** 1 **Lola Montez (IRE)**[29] 3750 3-8-13 **57**.......................... TedDurcan 6 60
(David Lanigan) *in tch in last pair: rdn and hdwy on outer 3f out: rdr dropped whip ent fnl f: carried lft and kpt on same pce ins fnl f* **5/1**[3]

422 **5** 5 **Mr Lando**[68] 2464 5-10-0 **60**.......................................... AdamKirby 1 55
(Tony Carroll) *led: rdn and hdd over 1f out: sn btn: wknd fnl f* **9/4**[2]

05-0 **6** 2 1/2 **Bright Society (IRE)**[15] 3567 3-7-13 **48** oh1 ow2......(b) PhilipPrince(5) 7 39
(Sean Curran) *chsd ldrs: wnt 2nd 10f out tl 8f: chsd ldrs after tl lost pl u.p over 2f out: wknd 1f out* **66/1**

6524 **7** nk **Isdaal**[19] 4081 7-9-4 **55**..........................................(p) CamHardie(5) 3 45
(Kevin Morgan) *hld up in tch in midfield: n.m.r and shuffled bk to last over 2f out: wknd u.p over 1f out* **12/1**

2m 32.27s (-0.73) **Going Correction** +0.025s/f (Slow)
**WFA** 3 from 4yo+ 12lb **7** Ran SP% **115.0**
Speed ratings (Par 101): **103,102,101,100,97 95,95**
CSF £13.13 TOTE £3.30: £1.60, £4.00; EX 11.30 Trifecta £75.10.
**Owner** World Freight Consultants Ltd **Bred** Newsells Park Stud **Trained** Radlett, Herts

**FOCUS**
A run-of-the-mill handicap most notable for half-sisters filling the first two positions. The pace was sound and the winner got a bit closer to her 3yo form.

## 4735 DAVID ROYLE 60TH BIRTHDAY MAIDEN STKS 5f 6y(P)
**4:15** (4:16) (Class 5) 3-Y-0+ **£3,072** (£914; £456; £228) **Stalls** High

Form RPR

022 **1** **Oasis Mirage**[13] 4295 3-9-0 **60**.......................................... FrederikTylicki 8 71
(Robert Cowell) *mde all: rdn and qcknd clr over 1f out: r.o strly: readily* **5/4**[1]

352 **2** 5 **Narborough**[57] 2802 3-9-2 **60**.......................................... CharlesBishop(3) 5 58
(Mick Channon) *taken down early: hld up in tch in midfield: hdwy on inner to chse wnr over 1f out: sn rdn and outpcd: wl hld but clr 2nd fnl f* **9/4**[2]

**3** 2 3/4 **Quick Touch** 3-9-5 **0**.......................................... PatDobbs 3 48+
(Robert Cowell) *dwlt: sn rcvrd to chse ldrs after 1f: widish and lost pl bnd 2f out: rallied to go modest 3rd 1f out: no imp* **3/1**[3]

-6 **4** 1 3/4 **Speedy Rio (IRE)**[9] 4432 3-9-2 **0**.......................... MichaelJMMurphy(3) 1 42
(Luke Dace) *dwlt: pushed along in rr: rdn and sme hdwy over 1f out: wnt modest 4th jst ins fnl f: nvr trbld ldrs* **50/1**

60 **5** 2 1/4 **Spider Bay**[56] 2846 5-9-4 **0**..........................................(e[1]) RobertHavlin 4 30
(Lydia Richards) *t.k.h: chsd wnr hmpd after 1f: lost 2nd and btn over 1f out: wknd fnl f* **100/1**

50 **6** hd **Nora Batty**[28] 3801 3-8-9 **0**.......................................... RyanWhile(5) 2 28
(Bill Turner) *in tch in midfield: hmpd after 1f: drvn and no hdwy over 1f out: sn wknd* **16/1**

0/3 **7** 1 1/2 **Lady Cooper**[19] 4086 4-9-4 **0**.......................................... ChrisCatlin 7 24
(Willie Musson) *sn outpcd in rr and stuck wd: n.d* **16/1**

59.89s (1.09) **Going Correction** +0.025s/f (Slow)
**WFA** 3 from 4yo+ 4lb **7** Ran SP% **114.9**
Speed ratings (Par 103): **92,84,79,76,73 72,70**
CSF £4.36 TOTE £2.20: £1.10, £1.80; EX 4.40 Trifecta £8.30.
**Owner** Cheveley Park Stud **Bred** Cheveley Park Stud Ltd **Trained** Six Mile Bottom, Cambs

**FOCUS**
A weak maiden but the winner proved in a class of her own, making the running and coming home clear. Unconvincing form.

## 4736 RACING SPECIALS AT 32REDSPORT.COM H'CAP 1m 4f (P)
**4:45** (4:45) (Class 4) (0-80,80) 4-Y-0+ **£4,690** (£1,395; £697; £348) **Stalls** Low

Form RPR

4503 **1** **Red Runaway**[30] 3696 4-9-4 **77**.......................................... GeorgeBaker 12 86
(Ed Dunlop) *led tl 7f out: chsd ldrs after: drvn to chal on inner over 1f out: led ins fnl f: r.o wl: rdn out* **5/1**[3]

0544 **2** 1/2 **Little Buxted (USA)**[10] 4402 4-9-1 **74**..............................(p) DavidProbert 8 82
(Robert Mills) *chsd ldr: rdn and ev ch 2f out: drvn and led over 1f out: hdd ins fnl f: kpt on wl but a jst hld* **14/1**

5132 **3** 2 **Barwick**[8] 4119 6-9-0 **78**.......................................... CamHardie(5) 11 83
(Lady Herries) *in tch in midfield: hdwy to ld over 7f out: rdn and hrd pressed 2f out: hdd over 1f out: styd on same pce and n.m.r ins fnl f* **10/1**

-236 **4** hd **Mystery Drama**[48] 3085 4-9-3 **76**.......................................... FergusSweeney 3 81+
(Alan King) *hld up in tch in midfield: clsd to trck ldrs but wdst of ldng gp bnd 2f out: rdn and effrt over 1f out: kpt on fnl 100yds: nvr enough pce to chal* **12/1**

-002 **5** hd **Rosslyn Castle**[16] 4204 5-8-12 **76**.......................................... DannyBrock(5) 5 80
(Philip McBride) *s.i.s: hld up towards rr: hdwy into midfield 5f out: hdwy u.p over 1f out: kpt on ins fnl f: nt enough pce to chal* **12/1**

2112 **6** nk **Ifan (IRE)**[31] 3681 6-8-12 **76**.......................................... DanielMuscutt(5) 4 80
(Tim Vaughan) *t.k.h: chsd ldrs: rdn over 1f out: drvn and kpt on same pce fnl f* **8/1**

4050 **7** 2 1/4 **Karam Albaari (IRE)**[11] 4349 6-9-4 **77**.......................................... OisinMurphy 10 77
(J R Jenkins) *s.i.s: hld up in rr: hdwy and rdn over 1f out: kpt on fnl f: nvr trbld ldrs* **20/1**

0-00 **8** 1/2 **Cousin Khee**[19] 4077 7-9-3 **76**.......................................... PatDobbs 7 75
(Hughie Morrison) *hld up in tch in rr: hdwy on outer 2f out: no imp and hung lft fnl f* **16/1**

5/36 **9** 7 **Putra Eton (IRE)**[79] 2162 4-9-4 **77**.......................................... FrederikTylicki 9 65
(Roger Varian) *chsd ldrs: rdn and struggling over 2f out: wknd over 1f out* **3/1**[1]

0000 **10** 1 3/4 **Resurge (IRE)**[17] 4175 9-9-7 **80**..........................................(t) TomQueally 6 65
(Stuart Kittow) *hld up in tch in midfield: dropped towards rr but stl in tch 5f out: rdn and no hdwy over 2f out: wknd over 1f out* **25/1**

-005 **11** 1 1/4 **Mallory Heights (IRE)**[16] 4209 4-9-5 **78**.......................................... AdamKirby 2 61
(Luca Cumani) *in tch in midfield: rdn over 2f out: lost pl 2f out and sn struggling: wknd over 1f out* **7/2**[2]

610- **12** 3 1/4 **Jimmy Sewell (IRE)**[271] 7635 5-9-5 **78**.......................................... AndrewMullen 1 56
(Michael Appleby) *t.k.h: hld up in tch towards rr: reminders 3f out: rdn and btn 2f out: sn wknd* **33/1**

2m 30.34s (-2.66) **Going Correction** +0.025s/f (Slow) **12** Ran SP% **123.6**
Speed ratings (Par 105): **109,108,107,107,107 106,105,105,100,99 98,96**
CSF £74.49 CT £692.56 TOTE £6.70: £2.40, £5.20, £3.40; EX 91.70 Trifecta £874.60.
**Owner** The Hon R J Arculli **Bred** Lofts Hall, M Philipson & Cheveley Park **Trained** Newmarket, Suffolk

**FOCUS**
A competitive contest but the early pace was steady and not much got into the race. The form is taken at face value.

## 4737 MALCOLM STANLEY EVERETT 70TH BIRTHDAY CELEBRATION H'CAP 1m 5f (P)
**5:15** (5:17) (Class 6) (0-60,59) 4-Y-0+ **£2,587** (£770; £384; £192) **Stalls** Low

Form RPR

63-6 **1** **Hell Hath No Fury**[32] 3632 5-8-8 **46**.......................................... AndrewMullen 4 61
(Michael Appleby) *chsd ldrs: rdn over 3f out: led over 2f out and sn clr w runner-up: asserted ent fnl f: styd on wl* **9/2**[2]

46/0 **2** 5 **Black Iceman**[31] 3682 6-8-11 **52**.......................................... SimonPearce(3) 2 58
(Lydia Pearce) *hld up in tch in midfield: hdwy on outer to join ldrs 3f out: clr w wnr and rdn over 2f out: no ex 1f out: wknd fnl 100yds but hld on for 2nd cl home* **33/1**

0246 **3** 3/4 **Ice Apple**[19] 4082 6-8-9 **47**..........................................(b[1]) JimmyQuinn 7 52
(John E Long) *in tch in midfield: rdn and effrt over 2f out: chsd clr ldng pair over 1f out: kpt on and pressing for 2nd towards fin: no ch w wnr* **10/1**

400- **4** 3 1/4 **Richo**[5] 6518 8-8-2 **45**..........................................(b) CamHardie(5) 12 45
(Shaun Harris) *s.i.s: bhd: clsd and in tch 10f out: nt clr run over 2f out: styd on wl u.p fr over 1f out: wnt 4th cl home: nvr trbld ldrs* **25/1**

0542 **5** 1/2 **Ogaritmo**[69] 2419 5-9-5 **57**..........................................(t) LiamJones 3 56
(Alex Hales) *chsd ldrs: wnt 2nd 6f out tl led over 3f out: rdn and hdd over 2f out: sn outpcd: 4th and btn over 1f out: wknd ins fnl f* **7/1**

3116 **6** 1 **Novel Dancer**$^{34}$ [3552] 6-8-10 **55**................................(e) JennyPowell$^{(7)}$ 13 53
(Lydia Richards) *hld up towards rr: rdn and hdwy on outer over 2f out: 5th and stl plenty to do 2f out: no imp* **4/1**$^{1}$

00-0 **7** 1 1/2 **Berwin (IRE)**$^{9}$ [4433] 5-9-4 **56**............................... RenatoSouza 9 52
(Sylvester Kirk) *v.s.a: bhd: clsd and tagged onto bk of field after 3f: stl bhd and shkn up over 1f out: no ch but kpt on ins fnl f* **16/1**

5063 **8** 1/2 **Sawwala**$^{25}$ [3899] 4-9-6 **58**............................... OisinMurphy 11 53
(J R Jenkins) *in tch in midfield: rdn and no imp in 6th 2f out: wknd fnl f* **5/1**$^{3}$

4-00 **9** 1 1/4 **Pahente**$^{34}$ [3556] 6-9-7 **59**............................... AdamKirby 1 52
(Tony Carroll) *in tch in midfield: rdn and over 4f out: lost pl and in rr over 2f out: sn drvn and no prog* **7/1**

50-5 **10** 1 **Helamis**$^{31}$ [3682] 4-8-6 **49**...............................(p) TimClark$^{(5)}$ 8 40
(Denis Quinn) *led tl over 3f out: sn u.p: lost pl and btn over 2f out: fdd over 1f out* **12/1**

040 **11** 7 **Hammered Silver (IRE)**$^{42}$ [3315] 4-9-4 **56**............................... ShaneKelly 10 37
(Mike Murphy) *chsd ldr tl 6f out: rdn over 3f out: sn struggling and lost pl over 2f out: bhd fnl f* **8/1**

500/ **12** 6 **Delagoa Bay (IRE)**$^{707}$ [5430] 6-8-10 **48**............................... LiamKeniry 6 20
(Sylvester Kirk) *in tch in midfield: hdwy to chse ldrs 5f out tl 3f out: sn dropped out: wl bhd fnl f* **50/1**

2m 46.08s (0.08) **Going Correction** +0.025s/f (Slow) **12** Ran SP% **122.4**
Speed ratings (Par 101): **100,96,96,94,94 93,92,92,91,90 86,82**
CSF £152.89 CT £1439.46 TOTE £4.80: £2.20, £8.20, £2.70; EX 286.80 Trifecta £1979.90.
**Owner** C L Bacon **Bred** K F Fallon **Trained** Danethorpe, Notts
■ Stewards' Enquiry : Renato Souza ten-day ban: failed to take all reasonable and permissable measures to obtain best possible placing (Aug 18-27)

**FOCUS**
Another low-grade contest. Limited form ,but the winner could well progress again.

## 4738 BET NOW AT 32REDSPORT.COM H'CAP 1m 2f (P)
5:45 (5:49) (Class 6) (0-55,55) 3-Y-0+ £2,587 (£770; £384; £192) **Stalls** Low

Form RPR

053 **1** **Estibdaad (IRE)**$^{12}$ [4326] 4-9-3 **51**...............................(t) MartinLane 9 59
(Paddy Butler) *led tl over 7f out: chsd ldr after tl led again over 2f out: drvn over 1f out: in command whn drifted rt ins fnl f: kpt on* **20/1**

041 **2** 3/4 **With Hindsight (IRE)**$^{37}$ [3473] 6-9-1 **54**............................... CamHardie$^{(5)}$ 6 60
(John Spearing) *t.k.h: in tch in midfield: effrt u.p to chse ldng pair over 2f out: chsd wnr wl ins fnl f: kpt on* **8/1**

0505 **3** 3/4 **Copperwood**$^{87}$ [1923] 9-9-7 **55**...............................(v) AmirQuinn 8 60
(Lee Carter) *hld up in tch towards rr: hdwy on outer over 3f out: drvn to chse ldng trio 2f out: styd on fnl 100yds: snatched 3rd nr fin* **20/1**

4023 **4** 1/2 **Abigails Angel**$^{20}$ [4046] 7-9-2 **50**............................... WilliamCarson 5 54
(Brett Johnson) *in tch in midfield: hdwy to chse ldr over 2f out: drvn and unable qck wl over 1f out: no ex and lost 2 pls wl ins fnl f* **16/1**

320 **5** 1 **Polydamos**$^{33}$ [3576] 5-9-4 **52**............................... AdamKirby 13 54
(Tony Carroll) *stdd s: hld up in tch in rr: rdn and effrt on outer over 2f out: styd on u.p ins fnl f: nvr trbld ldrs* **10/1**

-040 **6** shd **Youm Jamil (USA)**$^{26}$ [3853] 7-8-9 **48** ow2............... GeorgeDowning$^{(5)}$ 10 49
(Tony Carroll) *stdd s: hld up in tch in rr: swtchd lft and hdwy over 2f out: kpt on u.p fnl f: nvr trbld ldrs* **16/1**

4061 **7** 2 1/2 **Benoordenhout (IRE)**$^{19}$ [4084] 3-8-11 **55**...............................(p) OisinMurphy 2 51
(Jonathan Portman) *in toouch in midfield: nt clr run and swtchd lft jst over 2f out: sme hdwy u.p over 1f out: no imp fnl f and hung rt towards fin* **6/4**$^{1}$

3435 **8** 1 3/4 **Petersboden**$^{18}$ [4105] 5-8-12 **46**............................... LiamKeniry 11 39
(Michael Blanshard) *hld up in tch in midfield: effrt u.p 2f out: no real imp: nvr trbld ldrs* **20/1**

2364 **9** 4 **Bourbon Prince**$^{19}$ [4085] 3-8-8 **52**...............................(v$^{1}$) StevieDonohoe 3 37
(Michael Bell) *hld up in tch in midfield: n.m.r over 2f out: rdn and no prog wl over 1f out: wknd fnl f* **6/1**$^{3}$

0561 **10** 7 **Nifty Kier**$^{4}$ [4592] 5-8-13 **52** 6ex............................... DannyBrock$^{(5)}$ 12 23
(Phil McEntee) *chsd ldrs tl hdwy to ld over 7f out: rdn and hdd over 2f out: losing pl and btn 2f out: wknd and eased ins fnl f* **16/1**

05-6 **11** 4 **Urban Sanctuary**$^{41}$ [3333] 3-8-5 **49**............................... HayleyTurner 1 12
(Ed Walker) *s.i.s: rdn along and towards rr thrght: lost tch over 2f out* **4/1**$^{2}$

**12** 1 1/2 **Arcas (IRE)**$^{46}$ 5-9-4 **52**...............................(p) PaddyAspell 14 12
(Alan Jones) *chsd ldr tl over 7f out: styd chsng ldrs tl rdn and struggling over 3f out: dropping towards rr whn hmpd over 2f out: wl bhd over 1f out* **50/1**

500 **13** 8 **Crazy Train**$^{42}$ [3315] 5-8-6 **47**............................... DavidParkes$^{(7)}$ 4
(Keiran Burke) *in tch towards rr: rdn over 5f out: lost tch 3f out: t.o* **66/1**

2m 5.12s (-1.48) **Going Correction** +0.025s/f (Slow)
**WFA** 3 from 4yo+ 10lb **13** Ran SP% **129.9**
Speed ratings (Par 101): **106,105,104,104,103 103,101,100,96,91 88,86,80**
CSF £177.52 CT £3295.76 TOTE £27.20: £5.80, £2.70, £3.80; EX 370.00 Trifecta £1958.00.
**Owner** Miss M Bryant **Bred** John O'Connor **Trained** East Chiltington, E Sussex

**FOCUS**
Another 0-55 handicap and a welcome Flat winner for Paddy Butler. The time wasn't bad and the winner is rated back to last autumn's form.
T/Plt: £46.80 to a £1 stake. Pool of £65276.17 - 1016.78 winning tickets. T/Qpdt: £32.00 to a £1 stake. Pool of £4614.04 - 106.55 winning tickets. SP

# 4499 WINDSOR (R-H)
Monday, July 28

**OFFICIAL GOING: Good to soft (soft in places; 6.2)**
Wind: Almost nil Weather: Overcast

## 4739 UNIBET.CO.UK DAILY ENHANCED ODDS MAIDEN STKS 5f 10y
6:00 (6:04) (Class 5) 2-Y-0 £2,587 (£770; £384; £192) **Stalls** Low

Form RPR

4 **1** **Hatchet Harry (IRE)**$^{10}$ [4409] 2-9-5 0...............................(t) JFEgan 3 75
(David Evans) *mde virtually all: rdn to assert over 1f out: styd on* **3/1**$^{2}$

53 **2** 2 1/2 **Henley**$^{17}$ [4170] 2-9-5 0............................... RichardHughes 5 66
(William Jarvis) *in tch: pushed along to chse ldng pair 1/2-way: drvn and nt qckn over 1f out: tk 2nd ins fnl f: no threat to wnr* **4/11**$^{1}$

00 **3** 3/4 **Tecumseh (IRE)**$^{10}$ [4382] 2-9-5 0............................... MartinHarley 2 63
(K R Burke) *w wnr to 2f out: rdn and one pce over 1f out: lost 2nd ins fnl f* **10/1**$^{3}$

000 **4** 32 **Majenski (IRE)**$^{63}$ [2622] 2-8-12 0............................... RobHornby$^{(7)}$ 1
(Jamie Osborne) *uns rdr and bolted to post: w ldrs 2f: wknd: t.o and eased over 1f out* **33/1**

1m 1.19s (0.89) **Going Correction** +0.15s/f (Good) **4** Ran SP% **110.3**
Speed ratings (Par 94): **98,94,92,41**
CSF £4.70 TOTE £3.90; EX 4.50 Trifecta £10.10.
**Owner** D O'Callaghan **Bred** Richard Frayne **Trained** Pandy, Monmouths

**FOCUS**
Following 21mm of rain the already watered ground was much softer than at the declaration stage. It was officially described as good to soft, soft in places (GoingStick 6.2), and neither John Egan nor Richard Hughes was in much disagreement with that description after the first. The rail was dolled out 11yds at the 6f point and 5yds at the winning post. The top bend was dolled out 11yds, adding 42yds to race distances of 1m plus. This was a weak maiden, especially with the favourite running below form, but it could be rated up to 10lb better.

## 4740 NEW HORSE RACING ODDS AT UNIBET.CO.UK MAIDEN STKS 6f
6:35 (6:36) (Class 5) 2-Y-0 £2,587 (£770; £384; £192) **Stalls** Low

Form RPR

5 **1** **Typhoon Season**$^{17}$ [4167] 2-9-5 0............................... RichardHughes 8 77+
(Richard Hannon) *w ldrs: chalng whn lft disputing ld over 1f out: drvn and narrow ld fnl f: styd on* **11/8**$^{1}$

54 **2** 1/2 **Ghost Cat**$^{18}$ [4117] 2-9-5 0............................... JimmyFortune 7 75
(Brian Meehan) *w ldr: drvn and upsides over 1f out: pressed wnr fnl f: hld last 100yds* **16/1**

43 **3** 3/4 **Drumkilbo**$^{25}$ [3893] 2-9-5 0............................... RobertHavlin 1 73
(Lady Cecil) *mde most to 2f out: upsides over 1f out: kpt on same pce u.p fnl f* **8/1**$^{3}$

**4** 3 1/2 **King Jerry (IRE)** 2-9-5 0............................... SteveDrowne 14 63
(Ralph Beckett) *in tch: rdn in midfield 1/2-way: nvr on terms but kpt on fr over 1f out* **16/1**

**5** nk **Little Riggs** 2-8-12 0............................... BradleyBosley$^{(7)}$ 6 62
(Ed Walker) *t.k.h: trckd ldrs: urged along over 2f out: steadily wknd over 1f out* **66/1**

**6** 1 1/2 **Q Twenty Girl (IRE)** 2-8-7 0...............................$^{1}$ CharlotteJenner$^{(7)}$ 10 52
(Mark Usher) *sn rdn in rr: nvr on terms: kpt on fr over 1f out: nrst fin* **66/1**

**7** 1 3/4 **Glasgow Gailes (USA)** 2-9-5 0............................... MartinHarley 3 52
(K R Burke) *wl in rr: pushed along over 2f out: nvr on terms but modest late prog* **8/1**$^{3}$

**8** 1/2 **Wesie's Dream** 2-8-9 0............................... PhilipPrince$^{(5)}$ 12 45
(Mark Usher) *trckd ldrs: gng wl enough 1/2-way: rdn and wknd 2f out* **100/1**

0 **9** 1 **Dutch Falcon**$^{30}$ [3728] 2-9-5 0............................... MartinDwyer 5 47
(William Muir) *chsd ldrs: rdn 1/2-way: wknd 2f out* **33/1**

0 **10** 1 3/4 **Picket Line**$^{20}$ [4054] 2-9-5 0............................... JohnFahy 9 42
(Geoffrey Deacon) *slowly away: wl in rr: sme prog 1/2-way: wknd over 1f out* **100/1**

0 **11** 5 **That Man Of Mine (IRE)**$^{16}$ [4207] 2-8-12 0............................... RobHornby$^{(7)}$ 2 27
(Jamie Osborne) *slowly away: a wl in rr: bhd fr 1/2-way* **66/1**

**12** 68 **Invisible Eye** 2-9-2 0............................... CharlesBishop$^{(3)}$ 16 52+
(Mick Channon) *in tch: shkn up in abt 6th whn bdly hmpd and brought to a stand stl over 1f out: walked in* **33/1**

42 **P** **Songye**$^{33}$ [3569] 2-9-5 0............................... JamieSpencer 13
(Kevin Ryan) *w ldrs but sn pushed along: drvn to ld narrowly 2f out: broke down and p.u over 1f out* **9/4**$^{2}$

1m 14.05s (1.05) **Going Correction** +0.15s/f (Good) **13** Ran SP% **119.2**
Speed ratings (Par 94): **99,98,97,92,92 90,87,87,85,83 76, ,**
CSF £26.67 TOTE £2.60: £1.10, £4.90, £3.10; EX 25.20 Trifecta £136.30.
**Owner** Rockcliffe Stud **Bred** Rockcliffe Stud **Trained** East Everleigh, Wilts

**FOCUS**
They drifted over towards the far side in this maiden, which was run in an ordinary time. The form is rated as straightforward through the placed horses.

## 4741 DOWNLOAD THE UNIBET PRO APP FILLIES' H'CAP 6f
7:05 (7:05) (Class 4) (0-80,80) 3-Y-0+ £4,851 (£1,443; £721; £360) **Stalls** Low

Form RPR

3-21 **1** **Mia San Triple**$^{28}$ [3801] 3-9-6 **77**............................... RichardHughes 1 87
(Jeremy Noseda) *mde all: clr 1/2-way: drvn and pressed over 1f out: hld on wl fnl f* **6/4**$^{1}$

3441 **2** 1/2 **Ginzan**$^{11}$ [4339] 6-9-5 **71**............................... FergusSweeney 9 80
(Malcolm Saunders) *mostly chsd wnr: rdn over 2f out: clsd over 1f out: chal fnl f: nt qckn last 100yds* **7/1**$^{3}$

4316 **3** 1 1/2 **Serenity Spa**$^{24}$ [3920] 4-9-12 **78**............................... GeorgeBaker 2 80
(Tony Carroll) *hld up in rr: shkn up 2f out: tried to cl but no imp on ldrs over 1f out: kpt on: fin 4th: plcd 3rd* **5/1**$^{2}$

4210 **4** 1/2 **Backstage Gossip**$^{33}$ [3581] 3-8-10 **67**............................... RobertHavlin 5 66
(Hughie Morrison) *in tch: rdn over 2f out: chsd ldng pair wl over 1f out: no imp and lost 3rd ins fnl f: fin 5th: plcd 4th* **7/1**$^{3}$

4-21 **5** 7 **Byron's Gold**$^{70}$ [2384] 3-9-2 **73**............................... JamesDoyle 10 50
(Ben De Haan) *prom: rdn over 2f out: wknd sn after: fin 6th: plcd 5th* **7/1**$^{3}$

5415 **6** 6 **Hannahs Turn**$^{21}$ [4027] 4-9-7 **80**............................... JoshCrane$^{(7)}$ 4 39
(Chris Dwyer) *taken down early: prom to 1/2-way: wknd qckly over 2f out: fin 7th: plcd 6th* **11/1**

141 **D** 3/4 **Spiraea**$^{24}$ [3935] 4-9-4 **70**............................... JamieSpencer 8 73
(Mark Rimell) *s.i.s: in rr: pushed along 1/2-way: prog 2f out: chsd ldng pair ins fnl f: styd on but nvr able to chal: fin 3rd: disqualified and plcd last - jockey weighed-in light* **8/1**

1m 13.06s (0.06) **Going Correction** +0.15s/f (Good)
**WFA** 3 from 4yo+ 5lb **7** Ran SP% **113.6**
Speed ratings (Par 102): **105,104,101,100,91 83,103**
CSF £12.44 CT £41.82 TOTE £2.20: £1.30, £2.90; EX 14.00 Trifecta £44.40.
**Owner** Gute Freunde Partnership **Bred** Aiden Murphy **Trained** Newmarket, Suffolk

**FOCUS**
This rates the runner-up's best effort since her pb over this C&D last August. The winner built on her C&D maiden win.

## 4742 DAILY UNIBET EARLY PRICES FROM 9AM H'CAP 1m 67y
7:35 (7:35) (Class 5) (0-70,70) 3-Y-0 £2,587 (£770; £384; £192) **Stalls** Low

Form RPR

-011 **1** **Hostile Fire (IRE)**$^{10}$ [4415] 3-9-7 **70**............................... JamieSpencer 5 78+
(Ed de Giles) *hld up in midfield: shkn up over 2f out: prog over 1f out: hrd drvn and r.o wl fnl f to ld last strides* **9/4**$^{1}$

621U **2** nk **Dream Impossible (IRE)**$^{9}$ [4426] 3-8-11 **60**............................... SteveDrowne 4 67
(Peter Makin) *led 1f: chsd ldr: rdn 3f out: clsd to ld over 1f out: drvn and styd on but hdd last strides* **7/2**$^{2}$

0640 **3** 1 1/4 **Canova (IRE)**$^{12}$ [4329] 3-9-4 **67**...............................(bt) JamesDoyle 8 71
(Roger Charlton) *s.i.s: rapid prog to ld after 1f: drvn 2f out: hdd and nt qckn over 1f out: kpt on ins fnl f* **5/1**$^{3}$

0500 **4** 2 1/4 **Heartstrings**$^{10}$ [4386] 3-9-0 **63**...............................(v$^{1}$) MartinHarley 10 62
(Mick Channon) *trckd ldrs: effrt to dispute 2nd 3f out: nt qckn wl over 1f out: one pce after* **12/1**

005 **5** 5 **Purple Spot**$^{21}$ [4029] 3-9-0 **63**............................... RobertHavlin 9 50
(Rod Millman) *sn towards rr: rdn and no prog wl over 2f out: no ch over 1f out* **16/1**

0103 **6** 2 1/4 **Choice Of Destiny**[20] 4063 3-9-3 **66**........................ RichardHughes 11 48
(Philip McBride) *trckd ldrs: shkn up over 2f out: no prog and wl btn over 1f out: eased* **7/2**[2]

-301 **7** 6 **Soul Of Motion**[132] 1002 3-9-5 **68**........................ DavidProbert 3 36
(Gay Kelleway) *detached in last early and pushed along: rdn 3f out: no prog and wl btn fnl 2f* **16/1**

600 **8** 3 1/2 **Nouvelle Ere**[72] 2329 3-8-9 **58**........................ LukeMorris 6 18
(Tony Carroll) *plld hrd early and restrained in last pair: rdn 3f out: sn wknd* **33/1**

1m 45.84s (1.14) **Going Correction** +0.225s/f (Good) **8** Ran SP% **114.3**
Speed ratings (Par 100): **103,102,101,99,94 91,85,82**
CSF £10.20 CT £34.39 TOTE £2.80: £1.50, £1.80, £1.50; EX 6.90 Trifecta £28.40.
**Owner** Ali Mortazavi **Bred** Thomas Hassett **Trained** Ledbury, H'fords

**FOCUS**
Just a modest handicap. Muddling form, with the second and third up there throughout. It's been rated around the third.

## 4743 UNIBET OFFER DAILY JOCKEY & TRAINER SPECIALS H'CAP 1m 2f 7y
**8:05** (8:05) (Class 5) (0-75,75) 3-Y-O+ **£2,587** (£770; £384; £192) **Stalls** Centre

Form RPR

-612 **1** **Bertie Moon**[14] 4273 4-10-0 **75**........................ GeorgeBaker 4 83
(Geoffrey Deacon) *mde all: hld together tl pressed and drvn jst over 1f out: styd on wl nr fin* **9/4**[1]

363 **2** 1 **Choral Festival**[7] 4501 8-9-5 **66**........................ WilliamCarson 6 72
(John Bridger) *cl up: chsd wnr over 2f out: drvn to chal over 1f out: kpt on but no imp last 75yds* **4/1**[3]

2005 **3** 1 1/4 **Triple Chief (IRE)**[16] 4208 3-9-4 **75**........................ RobertHavlin 8 79
(Rod Millman) *trckd ldrs: looked to be gng wl 3f out and sn disp 2nd: nt qckn wl over 1f out: one pce after* **7/2**[2]

3332 **4** 2 3/4 **St Paul De Vence (IRE)**[21] 4028 4-9-7 **68**........................ LukeMorris 7 66
(Paul Cole) *hld up in 5th: urged along over 3f out: hrd rdn and nt qckn 2f out: no imp after* **9/4**[1]

20-0 **5** 5 **Mr Wickfield**[46] 3146 3-8-8 **65**........................ MartinDwyer 3 54
(John Best) *s.i.s but pushed up to chse wnr: rdn 3f out: sn lost pl qckly: wl in rr over 1f out* **25/1**

1110 **6** 1/2 **Kindlelight Storm (USA)**[23] 3977 4-9-10 **71**...........(b) J-PGuillambert 5 59
(Nick Littmoden) *urged along and reminders early in last: brief effrt over 2f out: sn no prog and btn: wknd over 1f out* **20/1**

2m 10.88s (2.18) **Going Correction** +0.225s/f (Good)
**WFA** 3 from 4yo+ 10lb **6** Ran SP% **112.4**
Speed ratings (Par 103): **100,99,98,96,92 91**
CSF £11.70 CT £29.11 TOTE £3.00: £2.70, £2.20; EX 6.90 Trifecta £29.90.
**Owner** Jim Kelly **Bred** M E Wates **Trained** Compton, Berks

**FOCUS**
Not a strong race with the winner enjoying an easy lead. The runner-up has been rated to this year's form.

## 4744 UNIBET - BY PLAYERS FOR PLAYERS H'CAP 1m 3f 135y
**8:35** (8:35) (Class 5) (0-70,67) 4-Y-O+ **£2,587** (£770; £384; £192) **Stalls** Centre

Form RPR

3401 **1** **Honourable Knight (IRE)**[4] 4582 6-9-3 **63** 6ex.............(v) LiamKeniry 5 69
(Mark Usher) *trckd ldng pair: narrow ld fr 3f out: hrd pressed and drvn fnl 2f: hld on wl* **13/2**[3]

/00- **2** 1/2 **Shot In The Dark (IRE)**[33] 7305 5-7-13 **50**........................ PhilipPrince(5) 3 55
(Jonathan Geake) *pressed ldr: chal over 3f out: pressed new ldr and wnr wl over 2f out: upsides over 1f out: nt qckn last 150yds: kpt on* **33/1**

0123 **3** 3/4 **Ferryview Place**[23] 3973 5-8-4 **50**........................ LukeMorris 2 54
(Ian Williams) *led: rdn and hdd 3f out: styd w ldng pair: hrd rdn and chal over 1f out: no ex fnl f* **2/1**[1]

5-03 **4** 1 1/4 **On Stage**[26] 3852 5-8-4 **57**........................ JennyPowell(7) 7 59
(Brendan Powell) *hld up in last pair: trckd ldrs 3f out: rdn over 2f out: nt qckn and wandered over 1f out: one pce* **2/1**[1]

515 **5** 1 **Layline (IRE)**[19] 4093 7-9-2 **67**........................ DanielMuscutt(5) 4 67
(Gay Kelleway) *trckd ldrs: rdn and nt qckn over 2f out: wl hld over 1f out: plugged on* **5/1**[2]

00- **6** 4 **Rajeh (IRE)**[343] 5592 11-8-3 **49** oh3 ow1........................ DavidProbert 6 43
(Peter Grayson) *hld up in last pair: rdn and struggling 3f out: n.d fnl 2f* **20/1**

0/-0 **7** 1 1/4 **Carrowbeg (IRE)**[49] 3064 6-9-1 **61**...........(vt) DaneO'Neill 1 53
(Lawney Hill) *trckd ldrs: rdn and cl up over 2f out: wknd qckly over 1f out* **14/1**

2m 34.36s (4.86) **Going Correction** +0.225s/f (Good) **7** Ran SP% **111.0**
Speed ratings (Par 103): **92,91,91,90,89 87,86**
CSF £153.47 TOTE £6.00: £3.30, £5.00; EX 43.20 Trifecta £436.10.
**Owner** Mrs T Channing-Williams **Bred** Mohammed Al Sulaim **Trained** Upper Lambourn, Berks

**FOCUS**
They went a steady early pace here. The joint-favourites were a bit disappointing and the winner has been nominally rated to his turf best.
T/Jkpt: £5,242.10 to a £1 stake. Pool of £125515.56 - 17.0 winning tickets. T/Plt: £261.80 to a £1 stake. Pool of £100354.91 - 279.78 winning tickets. T/Qpdt: £18.80 to a £1 stake. Pool of £9195.51 - 360.26 winning tickets. JN

# GALWAY (R-H)
Monday, July 28

**OFFICIAL GOING: Good**

## 4746a CONNACHT HOTEL (Q.R.) H'CAP 2m
**6:45** (6:46) (70-100,97) 4-Y-O+
**£35,000** (£11,083; £5,250; £1,750; £1,166; £583)

RPR

**1** **Quick Jack (IRE)**[184] 7723 5-10-11 **85**........................[1] MrSClements(5) 14 94+
(A J Martin, Ire) *hld up: gd prog to trck ldrs 3f out: wnt 2nd over 1f out and led 1f out: sn pushed clr: styd on wl* **4/1**[1]

**2** 3 **Grecian Tiger (IRE)**[26] 3867 5-10-6 **78**...........(v) MrRPQuinlan(3) 3 84
(D K Weld, Ire) *chsd ldrs: 5th 1/2-way: led 2f out: strly pressed over 1f out and sn hdd: kpt on same pce: no imp on wnr* **7/1**[2]

**3** 1 1/2 **Fire Fighter (IRE)**[13] 4311 6-10-2 **78**...........(t) MrFMaguire(7) 15 82
(Adrian Maguire, Ire) *hld up tl tk clsr order on inner under 2f out: gd run through on rails home turn into 3rd 1f out: kpt on same pce: no imp fnl 100yds* **14/1**

**4** 1 1/4 **Spacious Sky (USA)**[18] 4139 5-10-7 **83**...........(t) MissMO'Sullivan(7) 13 86
(A J Martin, Ire) *hld up: plenty to do 2f out: gd prog on inner into 5th over 1f out: kpt on wl into 4th ins fnl f* **20/1**

**5** 1/2 **Swnymor (IRE)**[58] 2760 5-12-0 **97**........................ MrJJCodd 17 99
(John Quinn) *hld up towards rr: plenty to do on inner 2f out: swtchd lft on home turn: 14th 1f out: styd on strly ins fnl f into 5th in clsng stages: nrst fin* **16/1**

**6** 1 3/4 **Moon Dice (IRE)**[30] 3740 9-9-13 **75**........................ MrHDDunne(7) 12 76
(Paul W Flynn, Ire) *hld up towards rr: stl last 3f out: swtchd to outer appr home turn and styd on wl into 6th in clsng stages: nvr nrr* **20/1**

**7** 1 **Streets Of Newyork**[33] 3574 7-10-13 **82**........................ MrMJO'Connor 1 81
(Brian Ellison) *chsd ldrs: 8th 1/2-way: nt qckn over 1f out: kpt on one pce* **10/1**[3]

**8** hd **Digeanta (IRE)**[23] 3993 7-11-7 **90**...........(t) MrPWMullins 16 89
(W P Mullins, Ire) *hld up: gd hdwy to chse ldrs under 2f out: kpt on one pce fr 1f out* **16/1**

**9** 3/4 **Kalann (IRE)**[16] 4223 7-10-2 **74**........................ MrCMotherway(3) 2 72
(Sabrina J Harty, Ire) *nvr bttr than mid-div: hmpd under 3f out: kpt on fr over 1f out: nvr nrr* **16/1**

**10** 2 1/4 **Fosters Cross (IRE)**[13] 4311 12-10-4 **80**........................ MrDJMullins(7) 6 76
(Thomas Mullins, Ire) *trckd ldr in 2nd tl led 1/2-way: hdd 2f out: wknd fnl f* **33/1**

**11** 1/2 **Massini's Trap (IRE)**[11] 4373 5-10-5 **74**........................ MsKWalsh 18 69
(J A Nash, Ire) *hld up in rr: sme prog appr home turn: kpt on wout ever threatening* **20/1**

**12** 1/2 **Taglietelle**[57] 2812 5-11-1 **84**........................ MsNCarberry 8 79
(Gordon Elliott, Ire) *racd in mid-div tl chsd ldrs 1/2-way: rdn to press ldrs in 5th 3f out: nt qckn under 2f out and sn no ex* **16/1**

**13** nk **Gambling Girl (IRE)**[13] 4311 5-10-3 **79**........................ MissKHarrington(7) 11 73
(Mrs John Harrington, Ire) *chsd ldrs: clsd to trck ldrs in 3rd 1/2-way: wnt 2nd 6f out: wknd off home turn over 1f out* **14/1**

**14** 1 3/4 **Wither Hills (IRE)**[8] 4479 8-10-6 **80**...........(p) MrNMcParlan(5) 7 73
(B R Hamilton, Ire) *racd in mid-div tl prog to trck ldrs 3f out: wnt 5th 2f out: no ex and wknd appr fnl f* **12/1**

**15** 1 **Marchese Marconi (IRE)**[38] 3447 5-10-13 **89**.......... MissSO'Brien(7) 19 80
(A P O'Brien, Ire) *hld up towards rr tl tk clsr order 2f out on outer: no imp whn squeezed for room over 1f out* **14/1**

**16** 4 1/2 **Saint Gervais (IRE)**[29] 3768 9-11-0 **83**........................ MrDerekO'Connor 20 69
(John E Kiely, Ire) *hld up towards rr tl gd hdwy to chse ldrs 3f out: nt qckn 2f out and sn no ex* **16/1**

**17** 6 1/2 **Storm Away (IRE)**[51] 3020 5-10-3 **79**........................ MrPPower(7) 10 58
(Patrick J Flynn, Ire) *hld up tl gd hdwy to press ldrs on outer 3f out: nt qckn 2f out and sn no ex: eased* **12/1**

**18** 24 **Dalasiri (IRE)**[15] 4239 5-10-13 **85**........................ MissJMMangan(3) 4 38
(Sabrina J Harty, Ire) *led to 1/2-way: trckd ldrs tl wknd under 3f out* **25/1**

**19** 2 1/2 **Alhellal (IRE)**[70] 7230 8-10-7 **81**........................ MrDLQueally(5) 9 31
(M Phelan, Ire) *chsd ldrs in 4th tl wknd qckly under 3f out* **50/1**

**20** 39 **Pay Day Kitten (USA)**[46] 3169 4-11-7 **90**........................ RobbieMcNamara 5
(D K Weld, Ire) *chsd ldrs early: mid-div after 1/2-way: dropped away qckly under 2f out and sn eased* **14/1**

3m 39.02s (-5.78) **20** Ran SP% **136.1**
CSF £28.73 CT £388.86 TOTE £5.10: £2.10, £2.10, £3.70, £4.60; DF 35.10 Trifecta £368.80.
**Owner** John Breslin **Bred** Newtown Anner Stud **Trained** Summerhill, Co. Meath

**FOCUS**
An ordinary renewal of this big handicap run on ground praised by the riders. The pace was strong. The winner and runner-up have been rated as running personal bests.

4747 - 4748a (Foreign Racing) - See Raceform Interactive

# 4493 BEVERLEY (R-H)
Tuesday, July 29

**OFFICIAL GOING: Good to firm**
Wind: Light; against Weather: Cloudy with sunny periods

## 4749 HAPPY 80TH BIRTHDAY LENNY SAIT (S) H'CAP 1m 4f 16y
**2:20** (2:20) (Class 6) (0-65,60) 3-Y-O+ **£2,587** (£770; £384; £192) **Stalls** Low

Form RPR

5005 **1** **Mazij**[12] 4343 6-8-13 **45**........................ PaulMulrennan 2 51
(Peter Hiatt) *mde all: pushed along wl over 2f out: rdn wl over 1f out: drvn ins fnl f: hld on gamely towards fin* **14/1**

0555 **2** hd **Impeccability**[43] 3309 4-8-13 **45**...........(p) FrannyNorton 4 51
(John Mackie) *hld up towards rr: hdwy over 3f out: rdn to chse ldng pair and edgd rt over 1f out: drvn ins fnl f: styd on strly towards fin: jst failed* **6/1**[2]

5013 **3** nk **Rainford Glory (IRE)**[15] 4259 4-9-11 **60**........................ GeorgeChaloner(3) 7 65
(Richard Fahey) *trckd wnr: hdwy 3f out: pushed along 2f out: sn rdn to chal and ev ch tl drvn ins fnl f and no ex towards fin* **10/11**[1]

0065 **4** 3 **Ofelia (IRE)**[12] 4350 3-7-13 **48**........................[1] JackGarritty(5) 6 48
(Brian Ellison) *hld up in rr: sme hdwy wl over 2f out: rdn wl over 1f out: kpt on: nrst fin* **8/1**[3]

0600 **5** 2 **Barbara Elizabeth**[9] 4468 3-8-6 **50**........................ PatrickMathers 3 47
(Tony Coyle) *towards rr on inner: swtchd lft and rdn wl over 2f out: plugged on: nrst fin* **50/1**

6264 **6** shd **Monzino (USA)**[13] 4319 6-9-1 **47**........................ GrahamLee 1 44
(Michael Chapman) *trckd ldrs: effrt 3f out: sn rdn along: drvn 2f out: sn no imp* **6/1**[2]

60-0 **7** 3 3/4 **Let's Go Live**[25] 3908 4-10-0 **60**........................ BarryMcHugh 9 51
(Tony Coyle) *a towards rr* **40/1**

5400 **8** 1 1/2 **Saddlers Mot**[15] 4259 10-9-4 **55**...........(b) GemmaTutty(5) 5 43
(Karen Tutty) *trckd ldrs: hdwy 3f out: rdn over 2f out: sn drvn and wknd* **12/1**

2-60 **9** 11 **Flying Applause**[11] 4415 9-9-1 **47**...........(bt) RussKennemore 8 18
(Roy Bowring) *chsd ldrs on outer: pushed along over 4f out: rdn wl over 3f out: sn lost pl and bhd* **22/1**

2m 36.86s (-2.94) **Going Correction** -0.225s/f (Firm)
**WFA** 3 from 4yo+ 12lb **9** Ran SP% **115.2**
Speed ratings (Par 101): **100,99,99,97,96 96,93,92,85**
CSF £93.25 CT £154.44 TOTE £18.10: £4.60, £1.70, £1.10; EX 94.00 Trifecta £361.80.There was no bid for the winner. Rainford Glory was claimed for £6,000 by Tony Coyle.
**Owner** Phil Kelly **Bred** The Hill Stud **Trained** Hook Norton, Oxon
■ Stewards' Enquiry : Franny Norton two-day ban: used whip above permitted level (Aug 12-13)

**FOCUS**
Low-grade fare to kick things off but it provided a good finish. The winner dictated a gallop which steadied in the back straight and the runner-up can rate better than the bare result. The form is best rated around the third. Inside rail in 5f chute moved in 3m for entire length of chute. Round course inside rail around bottom bend moved in and 19yds added to all races on Round course. False rail in home straight with a 'drop in' at 2.5f.

## 4750 IRISH STALLION FARMS HOLDERNESS PONY CLUB EBF MAIDEN STKS 7f 100y
**2:50** (2:52) (Class 5) 2-Y-O **£3,234** (£962; £481; £240) **Stalls** Low

Form RPR
0002 1 **Groor**[12] 4364 2-9-5 78 GrahamLee 6 79
(James Tate) *cl up: effrt to chal jst over 2f out: rdn to take slt advantage wl over 1f out: sn edging rt: drvn ent fnl f: kpt on wl towards fin* **6/4**[1]
2 ½ **Manshaa (IRE)** 2-9-5 0 FrannyNorton 2 78+
(Mark Johnston) *qckly away and led: jnd and rdn over 2f out: hdd narrowly and drvn wl over 1f out: ev ch insiude fnl f tl no ex last 50yds* **9/2**[3]
503 3 9 **Summer Stroll (IRE)**[11] 4416 2-9-0 69 DanielTudhope 5 51
(David O'Meara) *chsd ldrs: rdn along wl over 2f out: kpt on same pce u.p appr fnl f: n.d* **8/1**
0 4 ½ **Austin Friars**[31] 3720 2-9-5 0 MartinLane 1 55
(Charlie Appleby) *dwlt: sn trcking ldrs on inner: effrt over 2f out: rdn wl over 1f out: sn drvn and one pce* **7/1**
4 5 hd **Saltarello (IRE)**[19] 4110 2-9-5 0 PhillipMakin 8 54
(John Quinn) *chsd ldrs: rdn along over 2f out: drvn wl over 1f out: sn one pce* **8/1**
00 6 2¾ **North Bay Lady (IRE)**[32] 3648 2-9-0 0 PaulPickard 3 43
(John Wainwright) *towards rr: effrt and sme hdwy wl over 2f out: sn rdn along and n.d* **50/1**
0 7 1½ **Debt Free Dame**[96] 1656 2-9-0 0 JamesSullivan 9 39+
(Michael Easterby) *wnt bdly lft s: sn outpcd and hanging bdly lft on wd outside: bhd after 2f: hdwy wl over 2f out: rdn and styd on fnl f: nvr a factor* **50/1**
0 8 3¼ **Kopassus (IRE)**[18] 4167 2-9-5 0 PaulMulrennan 7 36
(Peter Chapple-Hyam) *a towards rr* **4/1**[2]
0 9 29 **Related To Ewe (IRE)**[87] 1955 2-9-5 0 DavidAllan 4
(Tim Easterby) *a towards rr: outpcd and bhd fr 1/2-way: eased wl over 1f out* **66/1**

1m 32.84s (-0.96) **Going Correction** -0.225s/f (Firm) **9 Ran SP% 118.3**
Speed ratings (Par 94): **96,95,85,84,84 81,79,75,42**
CSF £8.71 TOTE £2.00: £1.10, £1.90, £2.00; EX 11.30 Trifecta £46.20.
**Owner** Sheikh Juma Dalmook Al Maktoum **Bred** Miss K Rausing **Trained** Newmarket, Suffolk

**FOCUS**
A maiden which lacked depth, with the leading pair finishing well clear. The winner probably stepped forward.

## 4751 100% RACING UK PROFITS RETURNED TO RACING MAIDEN AUCTION FILLIES' STKS (BOBIS RACE) 5f
**3:25** (3:27) (Class 5) 2-Y-O **£3,234** (£962; £481; £240) **Stalls** Low

Form RPR
5235 1 **Horsforth**[21] 4057 2-8-7 66 BarryMcHugh 10 65
(Tony Coyle) *cl up: led 2f out: rdn clr over 1f out: hld on wl towards fin* **7/2**[2]
2 nk **Paco's Sunshine (IRE)** 2-8-7 0 PJMcDonald 2 64+
(Brian Ellison) *trckd ldrs on inner: hdwy 2f out: swtchd lft and rdn over 1f out: styd on strly fnl f* **25/1**
3 1¾ **Sweet Missi (IRE)** 2-8-4 0 PaulPickard 1 55+
(Brian Ellison) *dwlt and bhd: hdwy wl over 1f out: swtchd lft and rdn ent fnl f: styd on strly: nrst fin* **33/1**
0 4 nk **Poppy In The Wind**[27] 3841 2-8-4 0 JamesSullivan 6 54+
(Alan Brown) *towards rr: hdwy 2f out: n.m.r and swtchd rt ent fnl f: sn rdn to chse ldng pair: no ex and lost 3rd nr fin* **66/1**
502 5 nk **June's Moon**[24] 3975 2-8-11 0 GrahamLee 8 59
(Jonathan Portman) *trckd ldrs: hdwy 2f out: sn rdn: kpt on same pce fnl f* **8/1**
3 6 hd **Percy's Lass**[24] 3975 2-8-2 0 JackGarritty(5) 9 55
(Brian Ellison) *towards rr: pushed along after 2f: swtchd lft and rdn wl over 1f out: edgd lft ins fnl f: kpt on: nrst fin* **2/1**[1]
7 2 **Zaza Zest (IRE)** 2-8-7 0 PatrickMathers 7 48
(Richard Fahey) *dwlt and towards rr: hdwy on outer whn edgd lft 2f out: sn rdn: keeping on whn green and shied at opponents whip and edgd lft over 1f out: one pce after* **14/1**
8 4 **My Girl Jo (FR)** 2-8-11 0 DanielTudhope 4 37
(David O'Meara) *a towards rr* **4/1**[3]
06 9 2¾ **Ryedale Mist**[10] 4450 2-8-7 0 DavidAllan 3 23
(Tim Easterby) *slt ld: rdn along 1/2-way: hdd 2f out: sn drvn and wknd over 1f out* **20/1**
10 2¼ **Ruby Rose (IRE)** 2-8-11 0 TonyHamilton 5 19
(Kevin Ryan) *cl up: rdn along over 2f out: wkng whn hmpd over 1f out* **9/1**
11 1¾ **Valentine Belle** 2-7-13 0 ShirleyTeasdale(5) 11 6
(Paul Midgley) *dwlt and wnt lft s: a in rr* **66/1**

1m 4.21s (0.71) **Going Correction** -0.025s/f (Good) **11 Ran SP% 117.9**
Speed ratings (Par 91): **93,92,89,89,88 88,85,78,74,70 68**
CSF £94.13 TOTE £3.60: £1.40, £5.50, £8.90; EX 107.30 Trifecta £2565.10.
**Owner** Morecool Racing **Bred** Laundry Cottage Stud Farm **Trained** Norton, N Yorks

**FOCUS**
Just ordinary form at best in this maiden, but there was promise from a few in behind the winner, particularly the Ellison-trained pair in second and third.

## 4752 RACING UK PROFITS ALL RETURNED TO RACING H'CAP 5f
**4:00** (4:00) (Class 5) (0-75,76) 3-Y-O+ **£3,234** (£962; £481; £240) **Stalls** Low

Form RPR
0031 1 **Mister Manannan (IRE)**[8] 4494 7-9-13 76 6ex AdrianNicholls 4 89
(David Nicholls) *t.k.h: towards rr: gd hdwy 2f out: rdn to ld ins fnl f: kpt on strly* **9/2**[3]
0232 2 1¾ **Flash City (ITY)**[7] 4521 6-9-4 67 PJMcDonald 6 74
(Ruth Carr) *cl up: rdn to ld 1 1/2f out: drvn and hdd ins fnl f: kpt on same pce* **4/1**[2]
0-54 3 shd **Emjayem**[19] 4114 4-9-9 72 RobertWinston 9 79
(Ed McMahon) *wnt lft s and in rr: hdwy 2f out: rdn over 1f out: kpt on fnl f* **7/2**[1]
5134 4 ½ **Mey Blossom**[2] 4714 9-8-4 56 (b) ConnorBeasley(3) 2 63+
(Richard Whitaker) *hld up in tch: hdwy whn n.m.r over 1f out: rdn and styng on whn nt clr run wl ins fnl f: no imp after* **8/1**

6003 5 ½ **Lady Ibrox**[71] 2398 4-9-12 75 (t) DaleSwift 8 78
(Alan Brown) *chsd ldrs: rdn along 2f out: drvn and one pce ent fnl f* **20/1**
3041 6 nk **Rich Again (IRE)**[11] 4391 5-9-3 66 (b) DavidAllan 5 68
(James Bethell) *dwlt and in rr: hdwy and n.m.r on inner wl over 1f out: swtchd lft jst ins fnl f: rdn and kpt on: nrst fin* **4/1**[2]
0031 7 4 **Ace Master**[5] 4571 6-9-7 73 6ex (b) BillyCray(3) 3 61
(Roy Bowring) *chsd ldrs on inner: effrt and n.m.r wl over 1f out: sn rdn and wknd* **7/1**
4060 8 ¾ **Dodina (IRE)**[13] 4314 4-8-8 62 (b) JackGarritty(5) 1 47
(Brian Ellison) *led: rdn along 2f out: edgd rt: hit ins rail and hdd 1 1/2f out: drvn and wkng whn edgd rt and hit rail again jst ins fnl f* **16/1**
000 9 11 **Lost In Paris (IRE)**[24] 3948 8-9-3 66 BarryMcHugh 7 11
(Tony Coyle) *cl up: rdn along over 2f out: sn wknd* **50/1**

1m 2.84s (-0.66) **Going Correction** -0.025s/f (Good) **9 Ran SP% 116.6**
Speed ratings (Par 103): **104,101,101,100,99 98,92,91,73**
CSF £23.13 CT £70.83 TOTE £5.50: £1.80, £1.30, £2.10; EX 24.60 Trifecta £97.20.
**Owner** Dubelem (Racing) Limited **Bred** Mull Enterprises Ltd **Trained** Sessay, N Yorks

**FOCUS**
A fair sprint which was soundly run. Sound form, the winner building on his back to form C&D win.

## 4753 WILFORD WATTS MEMORIAL H'CAP 1m 100y
**4:35** (4:35) (Class 4) (0-85,84) 3-Y-O+ **£6,469** (£1,925; £962; £481) **Stalls** Low

Form RPR
6010 1 **Shadowtime**[14] 4290 9-9-7 77 DaleSwift 3 85
(Tracy Waggott) *in tch: hdwy over 3f out: rdn to ld wl over 1f out: drvn and hdd jst over 1f out: rallied gamely to ld again last 75yds* **12/1**
0000 2 nk **Rocket Ronnie (IRE)**[29] 3791 4-9-1 71 AdrianNicholls 7 78
(David Nicholls) *hld up and bhd: hdwy 3f out: trckd ldrs 2f out: rdn to ld jst over 1f out: drvn ins fnl f: hdd and no ex last 75yds* **12/1**
0111 3 3½ **Kimbali (IRE)**[14] 4291 5-8-13 76 LukeLeadbitter(7) 5 75
(Declan Carroll) *hld up towards rr: hdwy over 3f out: chsd ldrs 2f out: sn rdn and kpt on same pce appr fnl f* **15/2**
0430 4 2 **Talented Kid**[18] 4148 5-9-11 81 FrannyNorton 2 76
(Mark Johnston) *sn chsng ldng pair: tk clsr order over 3f out: effrt over 2f out and sn rdn: drvn over 1f out and sn one pce* **7/2**[3]
13 5 hd **Fajry (USA)**[17] 4208 3-9-6 84 HarryBentley 8 76
(Saeed bin Suroor) *chsd ldr: cl up whn hung lft and rn wd bnd at 1/2-way: hdwy to ld 3f out: rdn over 2f out: hdd wl over 1f out: sn drvn and grad wknd* **5/2**[1]
6253 6 3 **Berlusca (IRE)**[4] 4635 5-9-11 81 DanielTudhope 6 68
(David O'Meara) *hld up towards rr: hdwy over 3f out: rdn to chse ldrs on outer 2f out: sn drvn and btn* **11/4**[2]
4530 7 2½ **Eeny Mac (IRE)**[10] 4453 7-9-5 75 (p) AndrewElliott 1 57
(Neville Bycroft) *led: rdn along and hdd 3f out: drvn over 2f out: sn wknd* **10/1**

1m 44.43s (-3.17) **Going Correction** -0.225s/f (Firm)
**WFA** 3 from 4yo+ 8lb **7 Ran SP% 113.7**
Speed ratings (Par 105): **106,105,102,100,100 97,94**
CSF £135.85 CT £1152.32 TOTE £16.00: £5.00, £5.80; EX 213.00 Trifecta £797.70.
**Owner** H Conlon **Bred** Darley **Trained** Spennymoor, Co Durham

**FOCUS**
The leaders went hard here and the pace collapsed in the straight, the race ending up being uncompetitive. The winner's highest figure for four years, with the form rated cautiously.

## 4754 BEVERLEY MIDDLE DISTANCE SERIES H'CAP 1m 4f 16y
**5:10** (5:12) (Class 5) (0-75,73) 3-Y-O+ **£3,234** (£962; £481; £240) **Stalls** Low

Form RPR
0016 1 **Special Fighter (IRE)**[19] 4120 3-9-1 72 FrannyNorton 2 86+
(Mark Johnston) *set stdy pce: qcknd 3f out: rdn clr over 1f out: unchal* **5/4**[1]
5043 2 7 **Mariners Moon (IRE)**[14] 4298 3-9-1 72 DanielTudhope 3 74
(David O'Meara) *trckd wnr on inner: effrt wl over 2f out and snc hasing wnr: rdn wl over 1f out and kpt on same pce* **3/1**[2]
0131 3 1½ **Royal Marskell**[12] 4369 5-10-0 73 JamesSullivan 5 73
(Alison Hutchinson) *trckd ldrs: hdwy to chse ldng pair 1/2-way: effrt on outer 3f out: rdn along 2f out: sn drvn and kpt on one pce* **6/1**
546- 4 ¾ **Mojolika**[80] 5879 6-9-5 69 JackGarritty(5) 6 68
(Patrick Holmes) *hld up in rr: hdwy on outer 4f out: rdn along to chse ldrs 2f out: sn drvn and no imp* **8/1**
60-0 5 20 **Saythatagain (IRE)**[22] 4022 3-8-4 61 DuranFentiman 4 28
(Tim Easterby) *trckd ldrs: pushed along over 3f out: rdn along wl over 2f out: sn outpcd* **20/1**
4046 6 8 **In Vino Veritas (IRE)**[2] 4709 3-8-8 65 PJMcDonald 1 19
(Ann Duffield) *trckd ldrs: pushed along wl over 3f out: rdn wl over 2f out: sn btn and eased* **5/1**[3]

2m 38.06s (-1.74) **Going Correction** -0.225s/f (Firm)
**WFA** 3 from 5yo+ 12lb **6 Ran SP% 116.3**
Speed ratings (Par 103): **96,91,90,89,76 71**
CSF £5.53 TOTE £2.20: £1.10, £1.80; EX 8.00 Trifecta £21.40.
**Owner** Sheikh Hamdan bin Mohammed Al Maktoum **Bred** Darley **Trained** Middleham Moor, N Yorks

**FOCUS**
A one-sided handicap with a step forward from the winner. The pace looked steady until past halfway.

## 4755 LADY JANE BETHELL MEMORIAL LADY RIDERS' H'CAP (FOR LADY AMATEUR RIDERS) 1m 1f 207y
**5:45** (5:46) (Class 6) (0-65,65) 3-Y-O+ **£2,634** (£810; £405) **Stalls** Low

Form RPR
4053 1 **Unex Michelangelo (IRE)**[24] 3958 5-10-6 61 MissHBethell 8 76
(Michael Easterby) *hld up towards rr: hdwy to trck ldrs 4f out: effrt over 2f out: rdn to ld over 1f out: sn edgd lft and clr ins fnl f* **7/2**[2]
0322 2 6 **City Ground (USA)**[14] 4293 7-10-10 65 MissSBrotherton 9 69
(Michael Easterby) *t.k.h: sn led: hdd over 7f out: cl up: led again 1/2-way: hdd and rdn over 2f out: drvn wl over 1f out: kpt on same pce* **9/4**[1]
5650 3 hd **Kheskianto (IRE)**[4] 4617 8-9-5 46 oh1 (t) MissAliceMills 5 49
(Michael Chapman) *dwlt: sn trcking ldrs on inner: hdwy 5f out: led wl over 2f out: sn rdn: hdd over 1f out: kpt on same pce* **9/1**[3]
0006 4 1½ **Midnight Warrior**[9] 4473 4-8-12 46 oh1 MissEmilyBullock(7) 10 46
(Ron Barr) *hld up: hdwy 4f out: chsd ldrs over 2f out: sn rdn: kpt on same pce fnl f* **20/1**
0356 5 ¾ **Quite Sparky**[8] 4498 7-9-12 58 (b) MissPFuller(5) 7 57
(Mike Sowersby) *hld up in rr: hdwy over 3f out: chsd ldrs over 2f out: sn rdn and no imp* **16/1**
-650 6 11 **District Attorney (IRE)**[27] 3843 5-9-0 46 oh1(v) MissMeganNicholls(5) 4 24
(Chris Fairhurst) *chsd ldrs: rdn along over 3f out: sn wknd* **20/1**

U252 **7** *3* **Flag Of Glory**[13] 4326 7-10-0 **60**.................................. MissMEdden(5) 2 32
(Peter Hiatt) *cl up: rdn along 4f out: wknd 3f out* **9/1**[3]

0411 **8** *11* **Edgware Road**[13] 4327 6-10-1 **61**.................................. MissBHampson(5) 3 12
(Andy Turnell) *chsd ldrs: rdn along over 3f out: sn wknd* **9/4**[1]

050- **9** *4 1/2* **Freddie Bolt**[391] 3947 8-9-5 **46** oh1.................................. MissADeniel 1
(Frederick Watson) *prom: led over 7f out: hdd 1/2-way: rdn along and lost pl over 3f out: sn bhd* **100/1**

2m 4.37s (-2.63) **Going Correction** -0.225s/f (Firm) **9** Ran SP% **120.2**
Speed ratings (Par 101): **101,96,96,94,94 85,83,74,70**
CSF £12.12 CT £66.62 TOTE £5.30: £2.00, £1.10, £3.20; EX 11.40 Trifecta £116.40.
**Owner** S Hull, D Swales & M Metcalfe **Bred** Chenchikova Syndicate **Trained** Sheriff Hutton, N Yorks

**FOCUS**
A fair contest for amateur riders, the Mick Easterby yard continuing its fine record in these events here. The form is rated around the second and third.
T/Plt: £511.20 to a £1 stake. Pool: £57,575.69 - 82.20 winning units T/Qpdt: £136.40 to a £1 stake. Pool: £3,448.96 - 18.70 winning units JR

## 3421 GOODWOOD (R-H)

### Tuesday, July 29

**OFFICIAL GOING: Good (good to firm in places on round course; watered; straight course 7.8, round course 8.8, average 8.4) changing to good to firm after race 1 (1.55)**
Wind: Light; half against Weather: Sunny; light cloud

### 4756 BET365.COM STKS (H'CAP) 1m 1f 192y
**1:55** (1:55) (Class 2) 4-Y-O+

**£31,125** (£9,320; £4,660; £2,330; £1,165; £585) **Stalls** Low

Form RPR

0406 **1** **Sennockian Star**[17] 4214 4-9-6 **101**..................................(v) JoeFanning 5 110
(Mark Johnston) *broke fast: sn settled in 3rd: rdn and effrt 2f out: drvn over 1f out: styd on wl ins fnl f to ld fnl 50yds* **14/1**

602 **2** *1/2* **Ajman Bridge**[11] 4400 4-8-10 **91**.................................. WilliamBuick 18 99+
(Luca Cumani) *wl in tch in midfield: wd on bnd 5f out and lost pl: gd hdwy u.p over 1f out: str chal wl ins fnl f: r.o* **8/1**

402 **3** *1/2* **Salutation (IRE)**[38] 3449 4-9-0 **98**.................................. MichaelJMMurphy(3) 16 105
(Mark Johnston) *chsd ldr: rdn over 2f out: upsides ldr 2f out: sustained duel w ldr tl forged ahd wl ins fnl f: sn hdd and no ex* **8/1**

4200 **4** *3/4* **Busatto (USA)**[10] 4442 4-8-9 **90**.................................. RoystonFfrench 12 96
(Mark Johnston) *sn led: jnd and rdn 2f out: sustained duel w rival after tl hdd and no ex wl ins fnl f* **25/1**

0016 **5** *2 1/4* **Charles Camoin (IRE)**[4] 4608 6-8-8 **89**.................................. LiamKeniry 8 90
(Sylvester Kirk) *hld up in midfield: effrt on inner and nt clr run over 1f out: hdwy u.p 1f out: styd on wl fnl f: nvr trbld ldrs* **20/1**

2430 **6** *3/4* **Blue Surf**[24] 3962 5-9-3 **98**..................................(p) PatDobbs 1 98
(Amanda Perrett) *chsd ldng trio: rdn over 2f out: drvn and outpcd 2f out: kpt on but no imp fr over 1f out* **16/1**

4513 **7** *3/4* **Tha'ir (IRE)**[25] 3930 4-9-10 **105**.................................. SilvestreDeSousa 2 104
(Saeed bin Suroor) *wl in tch in midfield: hdwy to chse ldrs 4f out: rdn and outpcd ent fnl 2f: kpt on same pce after* **12/1**

-412 **8** *hd* **Stomachion (IRE)**[52] 2991 4-8-11 **92**.................................. RyanMoore 13 90
(Sir Michael Stoute) *hld up in last quartet: rdn over 2f out: stl plenty to do and swtchd lft over 1f out: styd on under hands and heels riding fnl f: nvr trbld ldrs* **7/1**[2]

5113 **9** *nk* **Magic Hurricane (IRE)**[24] 3962 4-9-1 **96**.................................. FrederikTylicki 6 94
(James Fanshawe) *wl in tch in midfield: rdn and effrt over 2f out: edging rt and no imp over 1f out* **13/2**[1]

0-10 **10** *nk* **Niceofyoutotellme**[41] 3356 5-9-2 **97**.................................. JimCrowley 3 94
(Ralph Beckett) *hld up in last quartet: rdn and effrt over 2f out: sme hdwy over 1f out: swtchd rt and drvn 1f out: kpt on: nvr trbld ldrs* **12/1**

16-6 **11** *1 1/2* **Cameron Highland (IRE)**[31] 3722 5-9-5 **105**........(p) LouisSteward(5) 15 97
(Roger Varian) *hld up in midfield: rdn and no hdwy over 2f out: plugged on: n.d: fin 12th: plcd 11th* **25/1**

411- **12** *2 1/2* **I'm Fraam Govan**[223] 8327 6-8-12 **93**..................................(t) PatCosgrave 4 80
(George Baker) *wl in tch in midfield: rdn and effrt over 2f out: sn outpcd: wknd ent fnl f: fin 13th: plcd 12th* **16/1**

-600 **13** *hd* **Wigmore Hall (IRE)**[24] 3962 7-9-2 **97**.................................. JamieSpencer 14 84
(Michael Bell) *stdd s: hld up in last pair: effrt ent fnl 2f: plugged on but nvr threatened ldrs: fin 14th: plcd 13th* **25/1**

-114 **14** *1 3/4* **Sea Shanty (USA)**[41] 3356 4-9-3 **98**.................................. RichardHughes 9 82
(Richard Hannon) *chsd ldrs: rdn jst over 2f out: sn struggling: wknd over 1f out: fin 15th: plcd 14th* **15/2**[3]

0406 **15** *9* **Hi There (IRE)**[53] 2957 5-9-0 **95**.................................. TomEaves 10 62
(Richard Fahey) *dwlt: bustled along leaving stalls: a towards rr: swtchd rt and effrt on inner over 2f out: no prog: bhd fnl f: fin 16th: plcd 15th* **33/1**

0204 **16** *5* **Gworn**[53] 2957 4-8-7 **88**.................................. PaulHanagan 7 45
(Ed Dunlop) *hld up towards rr: rdn and no hdwy over 2f out: wl bhd and eased ins fnl f: fin 17th: plcd 16th* **20/1**

0040 **17** *6* **Tobacco Road (IRE)**[17] 4184 4-8-7 **88**.................................. SeanLevey 11 34
(Richard Hannon) *stdd after s: hld up in last pair: short-lived effrt over 2f out: sn lost tch and eased over 1f out: t.o: fin 18th: plcd 17th* **33/1**

1006 **D** *1 1/4* **Viewpoint (IRE)**[31] 3730 5-8-7 **93**.................................. CamHardie(5) 17 91
(Richard Hannon) *in tch in midfield: effrt u.p 2f out: styng on same pce whn sddle slipped ent fnl f: rdr almost uns and lost weigh cloth ins fnl f: fin 11th: disqualified (nt draw correct weight)* **16/1**

2m 2.84s (-5.26) **Going Correction** -0.275s/f (Firm) **18** Ran SP% **126.5**
Speed ratings (Par 109): **110,109,109,108,106 106,105,105,105,104 102,100,100,99,92 88,83,103**
CSF £113.42 CT £979.43 TOTE £15.50: £3.80, £2.60, £2.10, £6.90; EX 168.00 Trifecta £1106.70.
**Owner** The Vine Accord **Bred** Cheveley Park Stud Ltd **Trained** Middleham Moor, N Yorks

**FOCUS**
The opening time dipped inside the standard and was just three hundredths of a second off the track record. Joe Fanning said: "It's on the quick side. Good, fast ground", and the official going was amended to good to firm after the first race. Lower bend dolled out 5yds from 6f to 3f marker in the straight and distances utilising that bend increased by 10yds. Top bend dolled out 3yds increasing distances using that bend by 10yds. This was a competitive edition of this high-class handicap, which was traditionally known as the Chesterfield Cup. Despite the brisk gallop the pace held up well and nothing became involved from the rear. Mark Johnston has now won this race four times in the last nine years, and for good measure he had the third and fourth here too. The winner found some improvement from somewhere.

### 4757 BET365 MOLECOMB STKS (GROUP 3) 5f
**2:30** (2:30) (Class 1) 2-Y-O

**£28,355** (£10,750; £5,380; £2,680; £1,345; £675) **Stalls** High

Form RPR

0612 **1** **Cotai Glory**[11] 4398 2-9-1 104.................................. GeorgeBaker 2 107
(Charles Hills) *mde all: shkn up ent fnl f: pressed thrght fnl f: kpt on and a holding runner-up: pushed out towards fin* **3/1**[2]

513 **2** *1/2* **Fast Act (IRE)**[10] 4439 2-9-1 88.................................. JamieSpencer 1 105
(Kevin Ryan) *sn bustled along in midfield: rdn 2f out: hdwy to chse wnr over 1f out: drvn and pressing wnr whn edgd lft ins fnl f: kpt on u.p but a hld* **10/1**

4111 **3** *hd* **Beacon**[25] 3928 2-9-1 107.................................. RichardHughes 4 104
(Richard Hannon) *in tch in midfield: swtchd rt and effrt over 1f out: clsd and chsng ldrs whn hmpd and swtchd rt again fnl 150yds: pressing ldrs and drvn fnl 75yds: kpt on* **10/11**[1]

1162 **4** *1 1/2* **Mukhmal (IRE)**[25] 3928 2-9-1 97..................................[1] PaulHanagan 7 99
(Mark Johnston) *in tch in midfield: rdn 2f out: drvn ent fnl f: kpt on to go 4th wl ins fnl f: nvr enough pce to chal* **7/1**[3]

1324 **5** *1* **Union Rose**[25] 3928 2-9-1 96..................................(p) WilliamTwiston-Davies 5 95
(Ronald Harris) *chsd wnr tl over 1f out: sn drvn: edgd rt and wknd ins fnl f* **25/1**

1346 **6** *1 1/4* **Spirit Of Xian (IRE)**[29] 3806 2-8-12 0..................................(b[1]) PatDobbs 3 88
(Richard Hannon) *chsd ldrs: rdn and no ex over 1f out: btn 1f out: wknd ins fnl f* **25/1**

2110 **7** *1 3/4* **Dougal (IRE)**[19] 4123 2-9-1 99.................................. RyanMoore 6 85
(Richard Hannon) *a in rr: rdn 1/2-way: no imp* **8/1**

353 **8** *2 1/4* **Burning The Clocks (IRE)**[12] 4338 2-9-1 79.................................. RobertHavlin 8 77
(Peter Chapple-Hyam) *a in last pair: rdn and no hdwy ent fnl 2f: nvr on terms* **100/1**

57.3s (-2.90) **Going Correction** -0.475s/f (Firm) 2y crse rec **8** Ran SP% **118.8**
Speed ratings (Par 104): **104,103,102,100,98 96,94,90**
CSF £32.95 TOTE £3.40: £1.10, £2.40, £1.10; EX 34.60 Trifecta £73.70.
**Owner** Ms A A Yap & F Ma **Bred** Glebe Stud, J F Dean & Lady Trenchard **Trained** Lambourn, Berks

**FOCUS**
This looked no more than an average Molecomb Stakes and it threw up a messy finish, but the strong early fractions resulted in a 2yo course record time. The form is straightforward, possibly worth a shade more than rated. The fourth, fifth and race average help.

### 4758 BET365 LENNOX STKS (GROUP 2) 7f
**3:05** (3:05) (Class 1) 3-Y-O+

**£85,065** (£32,250; £16,140; £8,040; £4,035; £2,025) **Stalls** Low

Form RPR

3003 **1** **Es Que Love (IRE)**[10] 4438 5-9-3 110.................................. AdamKirby 5 116
(Clive Cox) *hld up in tch in midfield: gng wl and nt clr run over 1f out: swtchd lft and shkn up to chal 1f out: carried lft but drvn to ld fnl 100yds: r.o and a doing enough after* **7/1**[3]

-106 **2** *nk* **Toormore (IRE)**[42] 3320 3-8-10 115.................................. RichardHughes 6 112
(Richard Hannon) *racd keenly: chsd ldr: upsides ldr and gng wl 2f out: rdn to ld over 1f out: hung lft ins fnl f: hdd fnl 100yds: kpt on but a hld after* **5/6**[1]

4-50 **3** *1/2* **Anjaal**[41] 3352 3-8-10 109.................................. PaulHanagan 4 111
(Richard Hannon) *stdd and short of room sn after s: hld up in tch in rr: rdn over 2f out: no imp tl str run on outer fnl f: wnt 3rd ins fnl f: nt quite rch ldrs* **25/1**

-542 **4** *1 3/4* **Garswood**[31] 3723 4-9-3 113..................................(v[1]) RyanMoore 8 109
(Richard Fahey) *in toouch in midfield: rdn over 1f out: drvn and wnt 3rd 1f out: styd on same pce after and lost 3rd ins fnl f* **4/1**[2]

0-10 **5** *1* **Amarillo (IRE)**[28] 5-9-3 112.................................. AdriedeVries 1 107
(P Schiergen, Germany) *stdd after s: hld up in last pair: clsd and nt clr run over 1f out: sn swtchd lft: no threat to ldrs but r.o ins fnl f* **8/1**

001 **6** *1/2* **Glory Awaits (IRE)**[17] 4187 4-9-3 110..................................(b) JamieSpencer 9 105
(Kevin Ryan) *racd keenly: in tch in midfield on outer: rdn over 2f out: chsng ldrs but keeping on same pce whn hung rt over 1f out: 5th and outpcd 1f out: one pce after* **16/1**

-06 **7** *1 3/4* **Boom And Bust (IRE)**[17] 4187 7-9-3 103..................................(p) MartinDwyer 3 101
(Marcus Tregoning) *led: rdn ent fnl 2f: hdd over 1f out: 4th and btn 1f out: wknd ins fnl f* **20/1**

1m 24.55s (-2.45) **Going Correction** -0.275s/f (Firm)
**WFA** 3 from 4yo+ 7lb **7** Ran SP% **112.7**
Speed ratings (Par 115): **103,102,102,100,98 98,96**
CSF £12.91 TOTE £6.30: £2.90, £1.30; EX 14.10 Trifecta £174.80.
**Owner** The Es Que Love Partnership **Bred** Newhall Ltd **Trained** Lambourn, Berks
■ Stewards' Enquiry : Adam Kirby 19-day ban (6 days deferred): used whip with excessive frequency (5th offence in past 6 months) (Aug 15-27)

**FOCUS**
Not the most competitive Group 2 and it was run at a modest early tempo. The principals were clear at the finish but the form is ordinary for the grade.

### 4759 BET365 SUMMER STKS (H'CAP) 1m 6f
**3:40** (3:42) (Class 2) 3-Y-O+

**£49,800** (£14,912; £7,456; £3,728; £1,864; £936) **Stalls** Low

Form RPR

1510 **1** **Lord Van Percy**[31] 3717 4-9-2 **95**.................................. DavidProbert 14 104
(Andrew Balding) *hld up in tch: hdwy u.p to chal ent fnl f: drvn and drew clr w ldr ins fnl f: led fnl 75yds: kpt on* **8/1**[3]

3-36 **2** *nk* **Havana Cooler (IRE)**[24] 3962 4-9-5 **98**.................................. AdamKirby 13 106
(Luca Cumani) *dwlt: pushed along early and sn rcvrd to r in midfield: hdwy on outer over 2f out: rdn to ld 2f out: hung rt after: drvn and clr w wnr ins fnl f: hdd fnl 75yds: kpt on wl but a jst hld* **5/2**[1]

414 **3** *2 1/4* **Noble Silk**[31] 3717 5-9-2 **95**..................................(p) OisinMurphy 3 100
(Lucy Wadham) *dwlt: pushed along early and rcvrd to r in midfield: hdwy u.p to chse ldrs whn nt clr run and hmpd ent fnl f: swtchd lft and styd on u.p to 3rd wl ins fnl f* **10/1**

-454 **4** ½ **Dashing Star**[24] 3962 4-9-6 **99** .......... WilliamBuick 8 104
(David Elsworth) *led: rdn over 2f out: hdd 2f out: drvn over 1f out: outpcd whn nt clr run and swtchd lft ent fnl f: no threat to ldrs and kpt on same pce ins fnl f* **11/2**[2]

0-00 **5** ½ **Boite (IRE)**[4] 4606 4-9-2 **95** .......... RobertHavlin 6 99
(Peter Chapple-Hyam) *chsd ldrs: rdn and pressing ldrs whn squeezed for room over 1f out: 3rd and outpcd ins fnl f: plugged on same pce and lost 2 pls wl ins fnl f* **50/1**

4401 **6** *hd* **Continuum**[17] 4213 5-9-5 **98** .......... (p) JoeFanning 7 101
(Peter Hedger) *stmbld leaving stalls: hld up towards rr: pushed along 4f out: hdwy whn carried lft and hmpd ent fnl f: pushed along and kpt on despite being impeded ins fnl f* **9/1**

51-0 **7** 1¼ **Big Thunder**[31] 3717 4-9-4 **97** .......... LukeMorris 5 99
(Sir Mark Prescott Bt) *chsd ldr: drvn and pressing ldrs 2f out: no ex u.p and btn 1f out: wknd ins fnl f* **12/1**

6305 **8** 1½ **Kelinni (IRE)**[31] 3730 6-9-4 **97** .......... (p) CraigAWilliams 1 96
(Marco Botti) *t.k.h: chsd ldrs: rdn over 2f out: struggling whn sltly hmpd ent fnl f: wknd fnl 150yds* **16/1**

204 **9** 3¼ **Mirsaale**[37] 3500 4-9-5 **98** .......... TomEaves 10 93
(Keith Dalgleish) *chsd ldrs: rdn and lost pl over 2f out: btn whn sltly hmpd over 1f out: wknd ent fnl f* **50/1**

6562 **10** *nk* **Saptapadi (IRE)**[45] 3250 8-8-11 **90** .......... (t) SilvestreDeSousa 2 85
(Brian Ellison) *hld up towards rr: hmpd bnd 11f out: rdn over 2f out: drvn and no imp whn hmpd over 1f out: plugged on same pce after* **16/1**

0632 **11** 3½ **Repeater**[24] 3985 5-9-9 **102** .......... RyanMoore 9 92
(David O'Meara) *stdd s: hld up in rr: shkn up 2f out: no rspnse: n.d* **12/1**

3151 **12** *8* **Kings Bayonet**[18] 4160 7-8-8 **87** .......... HayleyTurner 4 65
(Alan King) *t.k.h: hld up in last trio: rdn and hdwy on inner over 2f out: no imp wl over 1f out: sn wknd* **14/1**

6300 **13** *8* **Shwaiman (IRE)**[17] 4213 4-9-10 **103** .......... (b1) TomQueally 12 70
(James Fanshawe) *s.i.s: a bhd: rdn and no hdwy ent fnl 2f: bhd and eased ins fnl f* **20/1**

1600 **S** **White Nile (IRE)**[51] 3034 5-8-9 **88** .......... PaulHanagan 11
(Ed Dunlop) *hld up in midfield tl slipped up bnd 11f out* **25/1**

2m 58.5s (-5.10) **Going Correction** -0.275s/f (Firm) **14** Ran SP% **120.5**
Speed ratings (Par 109): **103,102,101,101,100 100,100,99,97,97 95,90,86,**
CSF £27.17 CT £208.75 TOTE £8.60: £3.20, £1.40, £3.50; EX 33.60 Trifecta £323.40.
**Owner** OTI Racing/Mrs L E Ramsden/R Morecombe **Bred** Mr & Mrs A E Pakenham **Trained** Kingsclere, Hants

**FOCUS**
A warm staying handicap in which they didn't go a great pace. The first two defied stalls 14 and 13. All but two of this field hold the Ebor engagement, with Mephisto in 2004 the last horse to win both races. The first two continue to progress.

## 4760 BET365 EBF MAIDEN STKS (BOBIS RACE) (C&G) 6f
**4:15** (4:17) (Class 2) 2-Y-O **£12,938** (£3,850; £1,924; £962) **Stalls** High

Form RPR

**1** **Misleading** 2-9-0 0 .......... WilliamBuick 5 78+
(Peter Chapple-Hyam) *chsd ldrs: wnt 2nd over 3f out: rdn and ev ch over 1f out: led ins fnl f: styd on wl: rdn out* **13/2**[3]

23 **2** 1½ **Aussie Ruler (IRE)**[22] 4025 2-9-0 0 .......... SteveDrowne 3 73
(Ronald Harris) *racd out in centre: wl in tch in midfield: rdn 1/2-way: hdwy u.p to press ldrs 1f out: battling for 2nd and kpt on same pce fnl 100yds: wnt 2nd on post* **12/1**

03 **3** *nse* **Dark Profit (IRE)**[11] 4389 2-9-0 0 .......... JimCrowley 4 73
(Charles Hills) *hld up in tch and travelled strly: clsd and effrt ent fnl 2f: drvn and chsd wnr ins fnl f: kpt on same pce fnl 100yds: lost 2nd on post* **5/2**[1]

**4** *nk* **Koptoon** 2-9-0 0 .......... RichardKingscote 9 72+
(Tom Dascombe) *led and racd against stands' rail: rdn over 1f out: hdd ins fnl f: edgd rt: kpt on same pce and lost 2 pls after* **12/1**

**5** ½ **Deluxe** 2-9-0 0 .......... PatDobbs 11 71+
(Richard Hannon) *in tch in last quartet: rdn 1/2-way: hdwy ent fnl f: kpt on wl: swtchd lft towards fin: nvr trbld ldrs* **20/1**

05 **6** *nk* **Mutafarrej**[18] 4142 2-9-0 0 .......... JoeFanning 1 70
(Mark Johnston) *racd out in centre: wl in tch in midfield: rdn and hdwy to press ldrs 1f out: no ex and outpcd fnl 75yds* **8/1**

3322 **7** 1¼ **Winstanley (IRE)**[29] 3786 2-9-0 84 .......... RyanMoore 13 66+
(Richard Fahey) *chsd ldr tl over 3f out: styd chsng ldrs: rdn and unable qck over 1f out: wknd ins fnl f* **10/3**[2]

**8** *nk* **Lackaday** 2-9-0 0 .......... WilliamTwiston-Davies 6 65+
(Mick Channon) *rrd and uns rdr bef s: in tch in midfield: rdn and outpcd wl over 1f out: no threat to ldrs but kpt on again ins fnl f* **25/1**

**9** *nse* **Sirdaab (USA)** 2-9-0 0 .......... (t) TomQueally 15 65+
(B W Hills) *s.i.s: bhd: pushed along and hdwy ent fnl f: rdn and styd on wl fnl 150yds: n.m.r towards fin* **20/1**

**10** ½ **Harbour Patrol (IRE)** 2-9-0 0 .......... SeanLevey 7 63
(Richard Hannon) *chsd ldrs: rdn 2f out: hung rt: nt moving wl and btn ent fnl f: nt given a hrd time and one pce after* **25/1**

**11** 3¼ **Moodrick (FR)** 2-9-0 0 .......... JamieSpencer 12 54+
(Olly Stevens) *s.i.s: hld up towards rr: effrt ent fnl 2f: rn green and shifting rt fr over 1f out: no ex 1f out: no hdwy 1f out* **16/1**

6 **12** 2¼ **Indian Joe**[57] 2829 2-9-0 0 .......... LiamJones 10 47+
(J S Moore) *s.i.s: hdwy into midfield after 2f: rdn and effrt ent fnl 2f: sn struggling: wknd over 1f out* **100/1**

4 **13** 1¾ **Bouncing Czech**[19] 4103 2-9-0 0 .......... AdamKirby 2 42
(Amanda Perrett) *stdd s: hld up in rr: hdwy and rdn over 1f out: no prog 1f out: sn wknd* **33/1**

1m 11.99s (-0.21) **Going Correction** -0.475s/f (Firm) **13** Ran SP% **118.5**
Speed ratings (Par 100): **82,80,79,79,78 78,76,76,76,75 71,68,66**
CSF £73.13 TOTE £9.10: £2.60, £2.90, £1.50; EX 86.10 Trifecta £308.30.
**Owner** Mrs Fitri Hay **Bred** G B Partnership **Trained** Newmarket, Suffolk

**FOCUS**
A fair 2yo maiden, but they finished compressed and the form is rated a bit below the race average. They went a routine sort of pace and the main action came down the centre. Previous experience had been a pre-requisite to success in this maiden for the past decade, but not this time.

## 4761 BET365 STKS (H'CAP) 1m
**4:50** (4:52) (Class 3) (0-90,90) 3-Y-O+ **£11,320** (£3,368; £1,683; £841) **Stalls** Low

Form RPR

0123 **1** **Extremity (IRE)**[24] 3980 3-9-0 **84** .......... (p) RyanMoore 1 95
(Hugo Palmer) *hld up in midfield: swtchd lft and effrt 2f out: drvn and chal jst ins fnl f: sn clr w runner-up: r.o wl and led towards fin* **3/1**[1]

-021 **2** *shd* **Buckstay (IRE)**[34] 3577 4-9-10 **86** .......... JimCrowley 12 98
(Peter Chapple-Hyam) *hld up towards rr: rdn and gd hdwy on outer over 1f out: led jst ins fnl f: sn clr w wnr: r.o wl but hjeaded towards fin* **7/1**[3]

5054 **3** 3¾ **Skytrain**[7] 4514 4-9-2 **78** .......... (b) JoeFanning 8 81
(Mark Johnston) *chsd ldng pair: rdn to chse ldr over 2f out: led 2f out: edging rt over 1f out: hdd jst ins fnl f: immediately outpcd by ldng pair: tiring but hld on for 3rd* **12/1**

1606 **4** ½ **Secret Art (IRE)**[24] 3982 4-10-0 **90** .......... GeorgeBaker 14 92
(William Knight) *in tch in midfield: rdn and effrt 2f out: outpcd jst over 1f out: no threat to ldng pair but kpt on ins fnl f: wnt 4th nr fin* **12/1**

3300 **5** *nk* **Moonday Sun (USA)**[102] 1558 5-10-0 **90** .......... PatDobbs 11 92
(Amanda Perrett) *in tch in midfield: rdn and effrt ent fnl 2f: chsd ldrs and edging rt over 1f out: outpcd by ldng pair fnl 150yds: kpt on same pce* **25/1**

0064 **6** ¾ **Directorship**[13] 4331 8-9-12 **88** .......... LiamKeniry 10 89
(Patrick Chamings) *hld up in tch in midfield: nt clr run and shuffled bk 2f out: swtchd lft and hdwy u.p jst over 1f out: styd on: no threat to ldrs* **20/1**

0536 **7** ½ **Cool Bahamian (IRE)**[18] 4147 3-8-5 **80** .......... LouisSteward(5) 18 77
(Eve Johnson Houghton) *stdd and dropped in bhd after s: hld up in last pair: n.m.r jst over 2f out: gap opened and hdwy 2f out: no imp 1f out: wl hld and one pce fnl f* **16/1**

2151 **8** ¾ **Ogbourne Downs**[6] 4549 4-9-6 **87** 6ex .......... CamHardie(5) 17 84
(Charles Hills) *in tch in midfield: effrt and short of room jst over 2f out: nt clr run tl gap opened and sme hdwy over 1f out: kpt on fnl f: no threat to ldrs* **12/1**

1214 **9** 1¾ **Lesha (IRE)**[17] 4198 3-9-1 **85** .......... JamieSpencer 4 79
(Kevin Ryan) *wl in tch in midfield: rdn and effrt to chse ldr 2f out: keeping on same pce whn carried rt and hmpd 1f out: wknd and eased wl ins fnl f* **6/1**[2]

5220 **10** 1¼ **Lord Ofthe Shadows (IRE)**[18] 4148 5-9-6 **82** .......... SeanLevey 15 72
(Richard Hannon) *hld up in midfield: rdn over 2f out: lost pl and n.m.r 2f out: wl hld whn hmpd and swtchd lft over 1f out: plugged on but wl hld fnl f* **33/1**

4000 **11** ¾ **Rakaan (IRE)**[22] 4028 7-8-6 **75** .......... JennyPowell(7) 20 63
(Brendan Powell) *stdd s: hld up off the pce in last pair: clsd but nt clr run 2f out: pushed along and kpt on fr over 1f out: n.d* **66/1**

2443 **12** ½ **Showpiece**[11] 4414 3-8-11 **81** .......... (b) RichardHughes 5 71
(Richard Hannon) *s.i.s: sn in tch in midfield: nt clr run and swtchd rt 2f out: no prog 1f out: btn whn nt clr run and eased ins fnl f* **12/1**

2366 **13** *nk* **Argaki (IRE)**[12] 4359 4-9-0 **76** .......... (p) TomEaves 3 62
(Keith Dalgleish) *chsd ldrs: rdn 3f out: carried rt and btn over 1f out: wknd fnl f* **25/1**

4064 **14** *nk* **Commissar**[17] 4184 5-8-11 **73** .......... StevieDonohoe 9 59
(Ian Williams) *stdd s: hld up in last quartet: clsd but stuck bhd a wall of horses 2f out: stl bhd whn nt clr run and swtchd lft 1f out: n.d* **25/1**

5311 **15** ¾ **Bountybeamadam**[27] 3850 4-9-2 **78** .......... (p) PatCosgrave 6 62
(George Baker) *chsd ldr tl rdn to ld over 2f out: hdd 2f out: sn struggling u.p: wknd over 1f out* **25/1**

2223 **16** *hd* **Fleckerl (IRE)**[14] 4280 4-9-0 **76** .......... MartinDwyer 7 60
(William Muir) *hld up towards rr: effrt over 2f out: stl plenty to do whn nt clr run and swtchd lft over 1f out: n.d* **16/1**

4261 **17** 2¾ **Sheila's Buddy**[28] 3815 5-9-4 **80** .......... AdamKirby 13 57
(J S Moore) *hld up in last quartet: rdn and effrt on outer 2f: no hdwy: n.d* **25/1**

44-5 **18** ½ **Maverik**[13] 4331 6-9-11 **87** .......... TomQueally 2 63
(William Knight) *chsd ldrs: rdn over 2f out: struggling and losing pl whn n.m.r wl over 1f out: sn wknd* **25/1**

4512 **19** *18* **Sandra's Diamond (IRE)**[20] 4067 3-8-10 **80** .......... SilvestreDeSousa 16 13
(Keith Dalgleish) *taken down early and walked to s: led and grad crossed to inner: rdn and hdd over 2f out: sn dropped out: t.o and eased ins fnl f* **33/1**

1m 35.82s (-4.08) **Going Correction** -0.275s/f (Firm)
**WFA** 3 from 4yo+ 8lb **19** Ran SP% **129.5**
Speed ratings (Par 107): **109,108,105,104,104 103,103,102,100,99 98,98,97,97,96 96,93,93,75**
CSF £19.99 CT £243.40 TOTE £3.30: £1.80, £1.60, £2.80, £3.20; EX 26.50 Trifecta £394.30.
**Owner** Kremlin Cottage II **Bred** B Holland, S Hillen & J Cullinan **Trained** Newmarket, Suffolk

**FOCUS**
Although this didn't appear the most competitive of handicaps for such a meeting, it was run at a decent early pace and the form should be viewed positively with two in-form horses coming clear late on. The winner resumed his progress.

## 4762 CASINO AT BET365 STKS (H'CAP) 5f
**5:20** (5:23) (Class 3) (0-90,90) 4-Y-O+ **£11,320** (£3,368; £1,683; £841) **Stalls** High

Form RPR

0024 **1** **Inxile (IRE)**[11] 4412 9-9-3 **86** .......... (p) TomQueally 1 96
(David Nicholls) *mde all: edgd lft u.p ent fnl f: styd on wl: rdn out* **25/1**

-616 **2** ¾ **Cheworee**[17] 4188 5-8-13 **82** .......... (tp) RichardKingscote 4 89
(Tom Dascombe) *chsd wnr: rdn over 1f out: pressing wnr but kpt on same pce u.p ins fnl f* **25/1**

123 **3** ½ **Salvatore Fury (IRE)**[7] 4521 4-8-2 **71** .......... (p) AndrewMullen 17 76
(Keith Dalgleish) *t.k.h: hld up in tch in midfield: hdwy 1/2-way: chsd ldrs and rdn whn hmpd 1f out: hrd drvn and kpt on same pce ins fnl f* **25/1**

0220 **4** ½ **Megaleka**[6] 4531 4-8-12 **86** .......... TimClark(5) 14 89
(Alan Bailey) *chsd ldrs: drvn and pressing ldrs 1f out: no ex and styd on same pce fnl 100yds* **33/1**

4-11 **5** 1¾ **Daylight**[52] 2995 4-9-2 **85** .......... (t) OisinMurphy 16 82
(Andrew Balding) *hld up towards rr: swtchd rt 2f out: hdwy u.p jst over 1f out: styd on ins fnl f: nvr enough pce to rch ldrs* **13/2**[1]

5110 **6** *shd* **Sandfrankskipsgo**[17] 4179 5-9-7 **90** .......... GeorgeBaker 3 87
(Peter Crate) *hld up in tch: effrt and rdn jst over 1f out: fnd little and one pce ins fnl f* **25/1**

5066 **7** *nk* **Waseem Faris (IRE)**[11] 4391 5-8-7 **76** .......... (v) MartinDwyer 15 72
(Mick Channon) *hld up towards rr: hdwy u.p ent fnl f: styng on whn n.m.r ins fnl f: kpt on wl but nvr trbld ldrs* **25/1**

1000 **8** *hd* **Apricot Sky**[25] 3927 4-8-13 **82** .......... FergusSweeney 23 77
(Henry Candy) *in tch in midfield: rdn and effrt over 1f out: styd on ins fnl f: nvr enough pce to rch ldrs* **10/1**

0 **9** *hd* **Stone Of Folca**[18] 4174 6-8-13 **82** .......... LukeMorris 2 76
(John Best) *stmbld leaving stalls: sn rcvrd and chsd ldrs: no ex u.p ent fnl f: wknd fnl 100yds* **16/1**

1532 **10** *hd* **Monumental Man**[14] 4284 5-8-13 **82** .......... (p) HayleyTurner 22 76
(James Unett) *in tch: rdn 2f out: unable qck over 1f out: styd on same pce and edgd rt ins fnl f* **25/1**

5120 **11** *nk* **Slip Sliding Away (IRE)**[18] 4146 7-9-1 **84** .......... AdamKirby 24 76
(Peter Hedger) *hld up in rr: rdn and effrt wl over 1f out: sme hdwy over 1f out: kpt on same pce ins fnl f* **13/2**[1]

213 **12** *hd* **Secret Millionaire (IRE)**[14] 4284 7-8-6 **78**........ MichaelJMMurphy(3) 7 70
(Luke Dace) *restless in stalls: hld up towards rr: hdwy u.p 2f out: no prog 1f out: kpt on same pce after* **20/1**

-000 **13** *nk* **Threes Grand**[25] 3920 4-8-4 **73**........ NickyMackay 20 64
(Scott Dixon) *wl in tch in midfield: rdn and unable qck over 1f out: wknd ins fnl f* **50/1**

4511 **14** *3/4* **Dawn Catcher**[26] 3887 4-8-7 **76**........ SteveDrowne 18 64
(Geoffrey Deacon) *in tch in midfield: drvn and unable qck over 1f out: wknd ins fnl f: eased towards fin* **33/1**

0620 **15** *shd* **Jillnextdoor (IRE)**[10] 4445 4-9-3 **86**........(v) RichardHughes 6 74
(Mick Channon) *hld up in rr: stl bhd and hmpd 2f out: swtchd lft and sme hdwy ins fnl f: nvr much room fnl 100yds: eased towards fin* **14/1**

2024 **16** *shd* **Lexi's Hero (IRE)**[17] 4188 6-9-2 **85**........(v) RyanMoore 10 72
(Richard Fahey) *hld up towards rr: pushed along over 1f out: sme hdwy jst ins fnl f: no imp fnl 100yds* **15/2**[2]

0364 **17** *1/2* **Fitz Flyer (IRE)**[11] 4418 8-8-13 **82**........(b) JoeFanning 9 67
(David Nicholls) *hld up in rr: effrt whn hmpd and veered sharply rt 2f out: swtchd lft and sme hdwy 1f out: n.d whn nt clr run and eased ins fnl f* **10/1**

0003 **18** *1/2* **Tidal's Baby**[15] 4267 5-8-7 **76**........ RaulDaSilva 5 60
(Tony Carroll) *s.i.s: bhd and bustled along: hdwy u.p 2f out: wknd fnl f* **8/1**[3]

0212 **19** *1 3/4* **Swiss Cross**[11] 4405 7-9-6 **89**........(bt) SilvestreDeSousa 21 66
(Phil McEntee) *in tch in midfield: rdn and struggling 1/2-way: lost pl 2f out: bhd fnl f* **12/1**

0015 **20** *2 1/4* **Powerful Wind (IRE)**[14] 4284 5-8-13 **82**........ DavidProbert 26 51
(Ronald Harris) *midfield: rdn and btn over 1f out: wknd 1f out* **33/1**

666 **21** *1 1/2* **Valmina**[15] 4267 7-7-13 **71** oh1........(t) JoeyHaynes(3) 25 35
(Tony Carroll) *s.i.s: a bhd: rdn whn hung rt and hmpd over 2f out: nvr on terms* **20/1**

56.83s (-3.37) **Going Correction** -0.475s/f (Firm) **21** Ran SP% **132.3**
Speed ratings (Par 107): **107,105,105,104,101 101,100,100,100,99 99,99,98,97,97 97,96,95,92,89 86**
CSF £440.77 CT £12071.80 TOTE £20.30: £4.20, £7.80, £7.90, £8.20; EX 618.90 TRIFECTA Not won..
**Owner** D Nicholls & Mrs J Love **Bred** Denis And Mrs Teresa Bergin **Trained** Sessay, N Yorks
■ Stewards' Enquiry : Oisin Murphy two-day ban: careless riding (Aug 12-13)

**FOCUS**
A big field for this fairly ordinary sprint handicap, and surprisingly few got into the race. The winner arrested his slide, with the runner-up rated to form.
T/Jkpt: Not won. T/Plt: £18.30 to a £1 stake. Pool: £330,657.69 - 13,182.81 winning units
T/Qpdt: £7.40 to a £1 stake. Pool: £16,690.61 - 1,657.70 winning units SP

## 4589 YARMOUTH (L-H)
### Tuesday, July 29

**OFFICIAL GOING: Good to firm**
Wind: Light; behind Weather: Fine

### 4763 VIKING FAMILY SUPPORT GROUP H'CAP — 1m 2f 21y
**2:10** (2:10) (Class 6) (0-65,66) 3-Y-O+ **£2,587** (£770; £384; £192) **Stalls** Low

Form RPR

0513 **1** **Diletta Tommasa (IRE)**[3] 4658 4-9-10 **66** 6ex........(p) EoinWalsh(5) 4 75
(John Stimpson) *hld up: hdwy over 3f out: led over 2f out: sn rdn: edgd lft ins fnl f: styd on* **9/2**[2]

6332 **2** *1 3/4* **Gift Of Silence**[10] 4433 5-9-11 **62**........ PaddyAspell 5 68
(John Berry) *hld up: hdwy over 2f out: chsd wnr over 1f out: edgd lft and styd on same pce ins fnl f* **7/1**

0224 **3** *1 1/2* **Cherry Princess**[12] 4343 4-9-2 **53**........ MartinHarley 6 56
(Stuart Williams) *led: rdn and hdd over 2f out: styd on same pce ins fnl f* **6/1**[3]

0-44 **4** *1/2* **Sequester**[35] 3545 3-9-3 **64**........ TedDurcan 3 66
(David Lanigan) *trckd ldrs: hung lft over 4f out: sn rdn: styd on same pce fr over 1f out* **5/2**[1]

0403 **5** *1 1/2* **Lifejacket (IRE)**[20] 4084 3-8-8 **55**........ KierenFallon 7 54
(Ed Dunlop) *prom: chsd ldr over 7f out tl rdn over 2f out: no ex fnl f* **9/2**[2]

3025 **6** *10* **Enriching (USA)**[6] 4548 6-10-0 **65**........ J-PGuillambert 2 45
(Nick Littmoden) *prom: pushed along over 4f out: wknd wl over 2f out* **6/1**[3]

14 **7** *1/2* **Nellie The Elegant**[125] 1116 3-8-13 **65**........ DanielMuscutt(5) 1 44
(Tim Vaughan) *w ldr over 2f: remained handy: rdn over 3f out: wknd over 2f out* **20/1**

2m 11.13s (0.63) **Going Correction** +0.125s/f (Good)
**WFA** 3 from 4yo+ 10lb **7** Ran SP% **110.8**
Speed ratings (Par 101): **102,100,99,99,97 89,89**
CSF £32.90 TOTE £4.30: £2.50, £2.60; EX 23.50 Trifecta £105.70.
**Owner** J T Stimpson **Bred** Ms Sheila Lavery **Trained** Butterton, Staffs
■ Stewards' Enquiry : Eoin Walsh caution: care3less riding.

**FOCUS**
A modest handicap in which they went an ordinary gallop on good to firm ground. The winner is in the form of her life. Bottom bend dolled out 1.5m and races on Round course increased by 7m.

### 4764 GRANGE FREEHOUSE AT ORMESBY MAIDEN AUCTION STKS — 7f 3y
**2:40** (2:40) (Class 6) 2-Y-O **£2,846** (£847; £423; £211) **Stalls** Centre

Form RPR

53 **1** **What A Party (IRE)**[10] 4444 2-8-1 0........ ShelleyBirkett(5) 6 75+
(Gay Kelleway) *a.p: chsd ldr 1/2-way: shkn up to ld and hung lft fr over 1f out: styd on* **10/11**[1]

**2** *1 1/4* **My Sebastian** 2-8-9 0........ DannyBrock(5) 4 79
(Philip McBride) *led: rdn and hdd over 1f out: styd on same pce ins fnl f* **11/4**[2]

**3** *4 1/2* **Jen Jos Enigma (IRE)** 2-8-9 0........ MartinHarley 5 61
(Noel Quinlan) *hld up: hdwy 1/2-way: rdn over 1f out: styd on same pce* **9/2**[3]

0064 **4** *7* **Framley Garth (IRE)**[12] 4364 2-9-0 **59**........(v[1]) PaoloSirigu 1 48
(David Elsworth) *chsd ldr tl drvn along 1/2-way: wknd 2f out* **10/1**

**5** *3 1/4* **Shimmering Silver (IRE)** 2-8-9 0[1] FrankieMcDonald 2 34
(Daniel Mark Loughnane) *rn green and hung lft in rr: rdn and wknd 1/2-way* **33/1**

1m 26.54s (-0.06) **Going Correction** -0.15s/f (Firm) **5** Ran SP% **109.3**
Speed ratings (Par 92): **94,92,87,79,75**
CSF £3.57 TOTE £1.70: £1.10, £4.40; EX 5.00 Trifecta £10.10.
**Owner** M M Foulger **Bred** Martyn J McEnery **Trained** Exning, Suffolk

**FOCUS**
A modest juvenile maiden in which they went an honest gallop. The form could be rated 5lb better.

### 4765 MARTIN FOULGER MEMORIAL H'CAP — 6f 3y
**3:15** (3:16) (Class 3) (0-95,94) 3-Y-O+ **£8,409** (£2,502; £1,250; £625) **Stalls** Centre

Form RPR

3442 **1** **Go Far**[13] 4317 4-8-11 **79**........(v) MartinHarley 8 97
(Alan Bailey) *trckd ldr stands' side: edgd towards centre gp over 3f out: led overall over 1f out: rdn clr fnl f: 1st of 2 that side* **7/2**[2]

-000 **2** *5* **Zanetto**[39] 3420 4-9-9 **94**........ ThomasBrown(3) 1 96
(Andrew Balding) *racd centre: sn pushed along to chse ldrs: rdn to ld that gp and chse wnr over 1f out: styd on same pce fnl f: 1st of 6 in gp* **9/4**[1]

0142 **3** *1 3/4* **Peace Seeker**[14] 4305 6-9-8 **90**........(t) WilliamCarson 7 86
(Anthony Carson) *overall ldr stands' side: edgd lft over 3f out: rdn: hung lft and hdd over 1f out: no ex fnl f: last of two that side* **5/1**[3]

350 **4** *1* **Arctic Lynx (IRE)**[14] 4284 7-8-11 **79**........ AdamBeschizza 4 72
(Robert Cowell) *racd centre: sn pushed along in rr: rdn and r.o ins fnl f: nvr nrr: 2nd of 6 in gp* **20/1**

006 **5** *3/4* **Secret Asset (IRE)**[11] 4412 9-9-3 **92**........(p) LewisWalsh(7) 2 83
(Jane Chapple-Hyam) *racd centre: chsd ldr tl led that gp 4f out: rdn and hdd over 2f out: no ex: 3rd of 6 in gp* **10/1**

2453 **6** *1/2* **Honeymoon Express (IRE)**[5] 4594 4-8-2 **75** oh1..(p) ShelleyBirkett(5) 6 64
(Julia Feilden) *led centre 2f: chsd ldr tl led again over 2f out: rdn and hdd over 1f out: no ex fnl f: 4th of 6 in gp* **10/1**

-000 **7** *2 3/4* **Nezar (IRE)**[40] 3378 3-9-5 **92**........ KierenFallon 3 71
(George Margarson) *racd centre: s.i.s: outpcd: 5th of 6 in gp* **7/1**

2650 **8** *4* **Commanche**[11] 4406 5-8-7 **75**........ JimmyQuinn 5 43
(Chris Dwyer) *racd centre: promimnent: pushed along 1/2-way: wknd over 2f out: last of 6 in gp* **12/1**

1m 12.18s (-2.22) **Going Correction** -0.15s/f (Firm)
**WFA** 3 from 4yo+ 5lb **8** Ran SP% **112.8**
Speed ratings (Par 107): **108,101,99,97,96 96,92,87**
CSF £11.45 CT £37.51 TOTE £3.60: £2.20, £1.20, £1.40; EX 16.90 Trifecta £59.60.
**Owner** R West **Bred** Michael Turner **Trained** Newmarket, Suffolk

**FOCUS**
The feature race on the card was a decent sprint handicap in which they went a contested gallop spread across the track. Clearly a step up from the winner.

### 4766 SHIRLEY GILL MEMORIAL H'CAP — 7f 3y
**3:50** (3:51) (Class 4) (0-80,77) 3-Y-O+ **£5,433** (£1,617; £808; £404) **Stalls** Centre

Form RPR

0004 **1** **Tommy's Secret**[17] 4181 4-8-12 **68**........ LewisWalsh(7) 6 81
(Jane Chapple-Hyam) *trckd ldrs: wnt upsides over 2f out: sn rdn: edgd lft and styd on u.p to ld wl ins fnl f* **5/1**[2]

-361 **2** *nk* **Mr Win (IRE)**[31] 3709 3-9-4 **77**........ AshleyMorgan(3) 3 86+
(Chris Wall) *sn trcking ldr: led over 2f out: rdn and hdd wl ins fnl f* **1/2**[1]

-010 **3** *7* **Uprise**[5] 4571 5-9-2 **68**........(t) RyanPowell(3) 7 62
(George Margarson) *prom: rdn over 2f out: styd on same pce fr over 1f out* **16/1**

-440 **4** *1 3/4* **Exceeder**[36] 3539 3-9-7 **77**........ MartinHarley 5 63
(Marco Botti) *hld up: rdn over 2f out: nvr on terms* **7/1**[3]

2616 **5** *1/2* **Tyrsal (IRE)**[15] 4263 3-8-8 **71**........ KieranShoemark(7) 2 56
(Robert Eddery) *sn led: rdn and hdd over 2f out: wknd over 1f out* **12/1**

0-00 **6** *2 1/2* **Someone's Darling**[22] 4024 4-9-1 **67**........ SimonPearce(3) 4 49
(Lydia Pearce) *hld up in tch: rdn over 2f out: wknd over 1f out* **33/1**

1m 25.64s (-0.96) **Going Correction** -0.15s/f (Firm)
**WFA** 3 from 4yo+ 7lb **6** Ran SP% **112.3**
Speed ratings (Par 105): **99,98,90,88,88 85**
CSF £7.96 TOTE £4.90: £2.50, £1.10; EX 13.20 Trifecta £60.20.
**Owner** J Chapple-Hyam & Victory Bloodstock Ltd **Bred** Henry And Mrs Rosemary Moszkowicz **Trained** Dalham, Suffolk
■ Stewards' Enquiry : Lewis Walsh one-day ban: careless riding (Aug 12)

**FOCUS**
A fair 7f handicap in which they went an even gallop. The winner is rated to last year's form.

### 4767 WELL BALANCED LEDGER AT J & H SIMPSON H'CAP — 1m 3y
**4:25** (4:25) (Class 5) (0-75,75) 3-Y-O+ **£3,622** (£1,078; £538; £269) **Stalls** Low

Form RPR

0031 **1** **Siouxperhero (IRE)**[12] 4342 5-9-2 **68**........(b) DanielMuscutt(5) 3 79
(William Muir) *chsd ldrs centre: rdn to ld and hung rt over 2f out: styd on* **9/2**[3]

4455 **2** *1 1/2* **Jonnie Skull (IRE)**[5] 4593 8-9-1 **62**........(vt) WilliamCarson 4 70
(Phil McEntee) *racd alone stands' side: led overall: clr 5f out tl rdn and hdd over 2f out: edgd lft over 1f out: styd on same pce ins fnl f* **10/1**

-614 **3** *2 1/4* **Rayoumti (IRE)**[15] 4271 3-9-6 **75**........ MartinHarley 1 76
(George Margarson) *led centre gp tl rdn and hdd over 2f out: no ex ins fnl f* **2/1**[2]

0-42 **4** *2* **Nabeel (IRE)**[19] 4130 3-9-6 **75**........ KierenFallon 2 71
(Saeed bin Suroor) *s.i.s: sn pushed along to chse ldr centre: rdn over 2f out: styd on same pce fr over 1f out* **11/10**[1]

1m 40.54s (-0.06) **Going Correction** -0.15s/f (Firm)
**WFA** 3 from 5yo+ 8lb **4** Ran SP% **108.2**
Speed ratings (Par 103): **94,92,90,88**
CSF £33.67 TOTE £3.90; EX 15.30 Trifecta £60.80.
**Owner** Muir Racing Partnership - Bath **Bred** J & J Waldron **Trained** Lambourn, Berks

**FOCUS**
A modest small-field handicap in which the 3yos disappointed. The winner was not an obvious improver.

### 4768 FOLLOW US ON TWITTER GREAT YARMOUTH H'CAP — 5f 43y
**5:00** (5:02) (Class 5) (0-70,70) 3-Y-O+ **£3,622** (£1,078; £538; £269) **Stalls** Centre

Form RPR

3256 **1** **Amosite**[11] 4408 8-9-10 **68**........(v) PaddyAspell 5 76
(J R Jenkins) *mde virtually all: rdn over 1f out: styd on wl* **12/1**

-104 **2** *2 1/4* **Tychaios**[11] 4406 4-9-6 **64**........ MartinHarley 6 64
(Stuart Williams) *trckd ldrs: rdn 1/2-way: styd on same pce ins fnl f: wnt 2nd nr fin* **1/2**[1]

6330 **3** *nk* **Imaginary Diva**[98] 1639 8-8-5 **56**........ JordanVaughan(7) 2 55
(George Margarson) *chsd wnr: rdn over 1f out: no ex ins fnl f: lost 2nd nr fin* **12/1**

2330 **4** *3 1/2* **Putin (IRE)**[11] 4406 6-9-7 **70**........(bt) ShelleyBirkett(5) 1 56
(Phil McEntee) *prom: racd alone in centre tl jnd main gp 1/2-way: sn rdn: wknd fnl f* **5/1**[2]

0200 5 21 **Royal Acquisition**[38] 3470 4-9-11 **69**......................(p) AdamBeschizza 3
(Robert Cowell) *awkward leaving stalls: outpcd* **8/1[3]**
1m 3.04s (0.34) **Going Correction** -0.15s/f (Firm) **5** Ran SP% **109.8**
Speed ratings (Par 103): **91,87,86,81,47**
CSF £19.03 TOTE £5.80: £2.80, £1.10; EX 22.20 Trifecta £69.10.
**Owner** Mrs Claire Goddard **Bred** Richard Kent **Trained** Royston, Herts
**FOCUS**
A weak sprint handicap. The winner is rated to her turf best.

## 4769 GREENE KING FESTIVAL AT GREAT YARMOUTH H'CAP — 2m
5:30 (5:31) (Class 6) (0-65,71) 4-Y-0+ **£2,587** (£770; £384; £192) **Stalls** Low

Form — RPR
0-12 **1** **Ninfea (IRE)**[20] 4093 6-8-12 **56**.......................... MartinHarley 7 63
(Neil King) *mde all: set stdy pce tl qcknd over 3f out: rdn over 1f out: styd on* **9/2[3]**
-612 **2** ½ **Lucky Diva**[19] 4107 7-8-8 **57**..........................(v) RyanWhile(5) 5 63
(Bill Turner) *chsd ldrs: wnt 2nd over 2f out: rdn and ev ch fr over 1f out: unable qck towards fin* **7/1**
-561 **3** 4½ **La Bacouetteuse (FR)**[7] 4522 9-9-13 **71** 6ex..................(b) ShaneKelly 3 72
(Iain Jardine) *hld up: hdwy to chse ldr 13f out: rdn over 2f out: styd on same pce fnl f* **5/2[1]**
2642 **4** shd **No Such Number**[19] 4115 6-9-2 **65**.......................... ShelleyBirkett(5) 2 65
(Julia Feilden) *prom: outpcd over 2f out: styd on ins fnl f* **7/2[2]**
4330 **5** 4 **Dr Finley (IRE)**[20] 4082 7-8-7 **54**.......................... SimonPearce(3) 4 50
(Lydia Pearce) *chsd ldr 3f: remained handy: rdn over 3f out: styd on same pce fnl 2f* **8/1**
0605 **6** 6 **Roy Rocket (FR)**[45] 3209 4-8-2 **46** oh1.......................... JimmyQuinn 8 34
(John Berry) *hld up: effrt over 2f out: wknd over 1f out* **8/1**
-540 **7** 5 **Flamingo Beat**[28] 1374 4-9-3 **61**.......................... AdamBeschizza 6 43
(Christine Dunnett) *hld up: hdwy over 2f out: rdn and wknd over 1f out* **14/1**
3m 37.8s (5.40) **Going Correction** +0.125s/f (Good) **7** Ran SP% **110.4**
Speed ratings (Par 101): **91,90,88,88,86 83,80**
CSF £32.65 CT £88.84 TOTE £3.80: £2.60, £3.50; EX 35.30 Trifecta £112.70.
**Owner** The St Gatien Racing For Fun Partnership **Bred** Kilco Builders **Trained** Newmarket, Suffolk
**FOCUS**
The concluding contest was an ordinary staying handicap for older horses in which they went a steady gallop. Unconvincing form.
T/Plt: £22.00 to a £1 stake. Pool: £46,780.20 - 1,549.46 winning units T/Qpdt: £7.10 to a £1 stake. Pool: £3,791.41 - 392.10 winning units CR

4770 - (Foreign Racing) - See Raceform Interactive

# 4745 GALWAY (R-H)
Tuesday, July 29
**OFFICIAL GOING: Good (good to firm in places on jumps course)**

## 4771a TOPAZ MILE H'CAP — 1m 100y
6:40 (6:41) 3-Y-0+
**£57,500** (£18,208; £8,625; £2,875; £1,916; £958)

RPR
**1** **Vastonea (IRE)**[12] 4379 6-8-5 **89**.......................... GaryHalpin(7) 10 97
(Kevin Prendergast, Ire) *towards rr: 13th 1/2-way: hdwy in 11th over 2f out and clsd u.p on outer ins fnl f to ld cl home* **12/1**
**2** ¾ **Piri Wango (IRE)**[57] 2853 5-9-11 **102**.......................... ColinKeane 5 108
(G M Lyons, Ire) *attempted to make all: narrow advantage 1/2-way: rdn into st and extended advantage: strly pressed wl ins fnl f and hdd cl home: no ex* **9/1**
**3** nk **Baraweez (IRE)**[33] 3621 4-9-0 **91**.......................... ColmO'Donoghue 13 96
(Brian Ellison) *hld up in mid-div: hdwy in 10th over 2f out to chse ldrs ent fnl f: wnt 3rd u.p wl ins fnl f and kpt on wl towards fin: hld* **9/1**
**4** nse **Defining Year (IRE)**[12] 4379 6-9-2 **93**..........................(b[1]) PatSmullen 6 98
(D K Weld, Ire) *towards rr: 14th 1/2-way: nt clr run on inner appr st: sn rdn in 12th and clsd u.p far side ins fnl f: nrst fin* **6/1[2]**
**5** ¾ **Jack's Revenge (IRE)**[39] 3420 6-9-4 **95**..................(bt) JosephO'Brien 4 99
(George Baker) *racd in mid-div: rdn in 10th 2f out and n.m.r on inner into st: clsd u.p far side ins fnl f: nvr on terms* **13/2[3]**
**6** 1¼ **Hint Of A Tint (IRE)**[341] 5688 4-9-9 **100**..........................(p) FMBerry 1 101
(David Wachman, Ire) *on toes befhand: chsd ldrs: 4th 1/2-way: rdn 2f out and sn no imp on ldr in 2nd: wknd towards fin* **12/1**
**7** 1½ **General Brook (IRE)**[47] 3169 4-9-1 **92**.......................... WayneLordan 2 90
(David Wachman, Ire) *chsd ldrs: 7th 1/2-way: rdn in 5th into st and no ex u.p whn hmpd ins fnl f and dropped to 7th: kpt on one pce* **12/1**
**8** shd **Maskoon**[32] 3687 3-8-9 **94**.......................... ChrisHayes 7 89
(Kevin Prendergast, Ire) *trckd ldrs: cl 3rd 1/2-way: rdn into st and sn no imp on ldr: wknd 1f out* **5/1[1]**
**9** 1¾ **Intensical (IRE)**[10] 4459 3-9-6 **105**.......................... RonanWhelan 8 96
(J S Bolger, Ire) *chsd ldrs: rdn in 5th under 3f out and no imp on ldrs into st: one pce fnl 2f* **20/1**
**10** nk **Pintura**[59] 2784 7-9-3 **94**..........................(p) DeclanMcDonogh 9 87
(Kevin Ryan) *chsd ldrs: rdn in 7th under 3f out and no imp on ldrs into st: one pce fnl 2f* **16/1**
**11** 7 **Bold Thady Quill (IRE)**[6] 4560 7-9-11 **102**..........................(p) ShaneFoley 15 79
(K J Condon, Ire) *hooded to load: s.i.s: last 1/2-way: sme late hdwy fnl 2f* **20/1**
**12** ½ **Croi An Or (IRE)**[44] 3286 5-9-6 **97**..........................(b) BillyLee 14 73
(T Stack, Ire) *towards rr: rdn and sme hdwy u.p under 2f out: one pce fnl f* **40/1**
**13** nk **Shamar (FR)**[32] 3689 6-8-8 **88**.......................... ConorHoban(3) 17 64
(W P Mullins, Ire) *towards rr: pushed along bef 1/2-way and no imp appr st: one pce fnl 2f* **33/1**
**14** ½ **Lean And Keen (IRE)**[67] 2535 4-8-7 **84**.......................... LeighRoche 16 59
(Sean Byrne, Ire) *cl up: cl 2nd 1/2-way: rdn into st and sn wknd* **20/1**
**15** ¾ **Balty Boys (IRE)**[10] 4442 5-9-12 **103**..................(b) SeamieHeffernan 11 76
(Brian Ellison) *a towards rr: 15th 1/2-way: rdn and no imp under 3f out: one pce fnl 2f* **20/1**
**16** 1½ **Specific Gravity (FR)**[10] 4462 6-8-11 **95**.......................... SeanCorby(7) 3 65
(Adrian McGuinness, Ire) *in tch: 7th 1/2-way: rdn and wknd over 2f out* **14/1**
**17** 1¾ **Seanie (IRE)**[16] 4234 5-8-10 **90**..........................(b) ConnorKing(3) 12 56
(David Marnane, Ire) *racd in mid-div: 12th 1/2-way: rdn and no imp 2f out: wknd fnl f* **20/1**
**18** 2 **Lucky Bridle (IRE)**[31] 3717 5-9-7 **98**.......................... NGMcCullagh 18 59
(W P Mullins, Ire) *in tch: 8th 1/2-way: rdn on outer 3f out and tk clsr order briefly: wknd qckly appr st* **25/1**
1m 45.83s (-4.37)
**WFA** 3 from 4yo+ 8lb **18** Ran SP% **132.9**
CSF £109.99 CT £1055.89 TOTE £11.90: £3.10, £3.10, £2.50, £1.90; DF 142.20 Trifecta £2017.10.
**Owner** Mrs Kevin Prendergast **Bred** Eyrefield Lodge Stud **Trained** Friarstown, Co Kildare
**FOCUS**
A couple of notable features here, with Vastonea becoming the second horse to win this race twice since its inception in 1971, Pinch Hitter having gained back-to-back victories in 1981 and 1982.. This repeat of the gelding's 2012 success was also Kevin Prendergast's sixth in the race. The winner has been rated back to his best.

# 4278 CHANTILLY (R-H)
Tuesday, July 29
**OFFICIAL GOING: Turf: soft**

## 4775a PRIX DE LAIGNEVILLE (CONDITIONS) (3YO) (TURF) — 1m 2f
1:20 (12:00) 3-Y-0 **£14,166** (£5,666; £4,250; £2,833)

RPR
**1** **Dominandros (FR)**[27] 3869 3-9-0 0.......................... Pierre-CharlesBoudot 3 92
(Gay Kelleway) *mde all: set stdy gallop: shkn up and qcknd 1 1/2f out: clr ent fnl f: r.o under hands and heels: a holding runner-up* **59/10[3]**
**2** nk **Pitch (FR)**[102] 3-9-0 0.......................... FranckBlondel 1 91
(F Rossi, France) **17/10[2]**
**3** 1¾ **Dauran (IRE)**[47] 3-9-0 0.......................... ChristopheSoumillon 4 88
(A De Royer-Dupre, France) **3/5[1]**
**4** 7 **Azucardel (FR)**[105] 3-8-10 0.......................... Christophe-PatriceLemaire 2 70
(T Lallie, France) **143/10**
2m 10.39s (5.59) **4** Ran SP% **120.6**
WIN (incl. 1 euro stake): 6.90. PLACES: 3.00, 1.70. SF: 13.80.
**Owner** Winterbeck Manor Stud & Partners **Bred** S C E A Haras De La Perelle **Trained** Exning, Suffolk

## 4776a PRIX DE LA BUTTE AUX GENS D'ARMES (CLAIMER) (4YO+) (TURF) — 1m 1f
3:25 (12:00) 4-Y-0+ **£7,916** (£3,166; £2,375)

RPR
**1** **Roseal Des Bois (FR)**[40] 7-8-8 0.......................... StephanePasquier 8 62
(R Chotard, France) **113/10**
**2** ¾ **Theo Danon (GER)**[44] 6-9-4 0.......................... ChristopheSoumillon 1 70
(Mario Hofer, Germany) **1/1[1]**
**3** hd **Royal Talisman**[41] 3373 6-9-4 0.......................... MickaelBarzalona 3 70
(Jo Hughes) **181/10**
**4** 2½ **Perfect Son**[15] 7-9-1 0.......................... EddyHardouin 4 62
(C Zeitz, Germany) **113/10**
**5** ¾ **Eragons Dream (IRE)**[25] 7-8-11 0..........................(b) ClementCadel 5 56
(F Sanchez, France) **31/1**
**6** 1¼ **Tianjin City (FR)**[15] 4-9-3 0.......................... NicolasLarenaudie(5) 6 65
(A Bonin, France) **192/10**
**7** 2 **Sumatra Tiger (GER)**[54] 9-9-2 0.......................... UmbertoRispoli 2 54
(W Mongil, Germany) **11/1[3]**
**8** 3 **Schimea (IRE)**[30] 4-9-1 0.......................... GeraldMosse 9 47
(S Smrczek, Germany) **9/2[2]**
**9** 10 **Taweel (FR)**[41] 3373 4-8-11 0.......................... StephaneLaurent 10 22
(Mlle B Renk, France) **62/1**
**10** 1¼ **Samuraj (FR)**[75] 4-8-11 0.......................... FlavienPrat 11 19
(M Munch, Germany) **173/10**
**11** dist **Solyway (FR)**[150] 4-9-2 0..........................(p) FabriceVeron 7
(H-A Pantall, France) **152/10**
1m 50.37s (-0.73) **11** Ran SP% **119.3**
WIN (incl. 1 euro stake):12.30. PLACES: 3.00, 1.50, 4.80. DF: 12.60. SF: 39.60.
**Owner** G Luyckx & J Phelippon **Bred** Joelle Brillet **Trained** France

# 4756 GOODWOOD (R-H)
Wednesday, July 30
**OFFICIAL GOING: Good to firm (watered; straight 7.9; round 8.7; average 8.3)**
Wind: Light, Half Against Weather: sunny and warm

## 4777 GOODWOOD STKS (H'CAP) — 2m 5f
1:55 (1:55) (Class 2) (0-95,96) 3-Y-0+
**£24,900** (£7,456; £3,728; £1,864; £932; £468)

Form — RPR
2130 **1** **Teak (IRE)**[18] 4217 7-8-6 **74**..........................(p) SilvestreDeSousa 3 85
(Ian Williams) *hld up towards rr: rdn 4f out: hdwy u.p to chse ldrs over 1f out: chal 1f out: led ins fnl f: styd on strly and gng away at fin* **33/1**
-006 **2** 1¼ **Ray Ward (IRE)**[43] 3321 4-9-7 **89**.......................... JimCrowley 13 99
(David Simcock) *hld up in rr: travelling strly and nt clr run 4f out: sn swtchd lft and smooth hdwy: rdn to go 3rd and bandage flapping over 1f out: drvn to ld ent fnl f: hdd ins fnl f: no ex fnl 75yds* **6/1[2]**
1141 **3** 6 **Longshadow**[4] 4662 4-8-8 **76** 3ex..........................(v) PJMcDonald 15 80
(Jason Ward) *t.k.h: stl tanking along and hdwy to chse ldrs 8f out: wnt 2nd over 6f out: rdn and ev ch over 2f out tl 1f out: sn outpcd* **12/1**
0403 **4** 3 **Brockwell**[18] 4217 5-9-3 **85**.......................... GeorgeBaker 2 88
(Tom Dascombe) *t.k.h: wl in tch in midfield: nt clr run and shuffled bk 6f out: rallied u.p 2f out: styd on but nvr a threat to ldng pair* **8/1**
1/14 **5** ½ **Solar View (IRE)**[28] 3851 5-8-13 **81**.......................... LukeMorris 4 81
(Sir Mark Prescott Bt) *hld up in midfield: pushed along 7f out: hdwy to chse ldrs 5f out: 5th and drvn over 2f out: no hdwy and btn over 1f out: plugged on* **12/1**
1451 **6** 5 **Presto Volante (IRE)**[28] 3859 6-9-3 **85**..........................(p) JamesDoyle 10 80
(Amanda Perrett) *chsd ldrs: lost pl over 5f out: drvn and sltly hmpd 4f out: sme hdwy over 2f out: no hdwy and wl hld fnl 2f* **25/1**
1311 **7** hd **Maid In Rio (IRE)**[5] 4606 3-8-6 **96** 3ex.......................... JoeFanning 7 90
(Mark Johnston) *hld up in tch in midfield: hdwy to chse ldrs over 5f out: jnd ldrs and travelling strly over 3f out: rdn to ld over 2f out: drvn and hdd ent fnl f: sn btn and fdd fnl f* **11/8[1]**

0114 **8** *29* **Sunny Future (IRE)**[18] 4209 8-8-9 **77** .......... MartinLane 1 43
(Malcolm Saunders) *hld up in last pair: rdn and short-lived effrt 3f out: sn wl btn: t.o and eased ins fnl f* **50/1**

2-01 **9** *1* **Stopped Out**[15] 4289 9-8-13 **81** .......... (p) TomEaves 8 46
(Philip Kirby) *led tl rdn and hdd over 2f out: sn dropped and wl btn: t.o and eased ins fnl f* **25/1**

2361 **10** *2 3/4* **Lion Beacon**[40] 3424 4-9-4 **86** .......... SebSanders 12 48
(Amanda Perrett) *chsd ldr tl over 6f out: wd and lost pl bnd over 5f out: rdn and no hdwy whn wandered 2f out: sn bhd: t.o and eased ins fnl f* **25/1**

2-60 **11** *69* **Ballinderry Boy**[43] 3321 4-9-7 **92** .......... ThomasBrown(3) 11
(Andrew Balding) *t.k.h: chsd ldrs tl 8f out: rdn and losing pl 6f out: bhd 3f out: sn t.o: eased fnl f* **20/1**

23-0 **P** **Lieutenant Miller**[43] 3321 8-9-10 **92** .......... RyanMoore 5
(Nicky Henderson) *hld up in last pair: rdn and effrt 4f out: sme hdwy 2f out: 8th and no threat to ldrs whn edgd rt over 1f out: eased and p.u ins fnl f* **15/2[3]**

4m 25.85s (-5.15) **Going Correction** -0.025s/f (Good)
**WFA** 3 from 4yo+ 22lb **12** Ran SP% **115.9**
Speed ratings (Par 109): **108,107,105,104,103 102,101,90,90,89 63,**
CSF £202.69 CT £2537.45 TOTE £47.00: £8.90, £2.00, £2.80; EX 358.00 Trifecta £5324.50 Part won..
**Owner** Farranamanagh **Bred** Michael Morrissey **Trained** Portway, Worcs

**FOCUS**
The lower bend was dolled out 5yds from the 6f marker to the 3f marker, increasing race distances by 10yds. A total of 5mm of water had been applied overnight, but the ground would have been drying all the time on a warm, sunny day and jockeys still felt it was a quick surface. The strongest stayers came to the fore in this marathon handicap, which was run at a reasonable gallop given the distance. The shock winner limits the form, which is pretty straightforward.

## 4778 NEPTUNE INVESTMENT MANAGEMENT GORDON STKS (GROUP 3) 1m 4f
**2:30** (2:32) (Class 1) 3-Y-O
**£45,368** (£17,200; £8,608; £4,288; £2,152; £1,080) **Stalls** High

Form RPR

-214 **1** **Snow Sky**[40] 3417 3-9-1 **108** .......... JamesDoyle 7 112
(Sir Michael Stoute) *t.k.h: hld up in tch in last trio: hdwy over 3f out: rdn to ld over 1f out: wnt rt 1f out and then wnt bk lft u.p ins fnl f: forged ahd again fnl 75yds: r.o* **9/2[3]**

1222 **2** *nk* **Windshear**[20] 4122 3-9-1 **103** .......... RichardHughes 8 111
(Richard Hannon) *in tch in midfield: nt clr run and shuffled bk over 2f out: rdn over 1f out: cl 6th and swtchd lft jst ins fnl f: str run fnl 100yds: wnt 2nd nr fin: nvr quite getting to wnr* **13/2**

5303 **3** *hd* **Somewhat (USA)**[25] 3984 3-9-1 **115** .......... JoeFanning 6 110
(Mark Johnston) *led: rdn over 2f out: hdd over 1f out: ev ch after and kpt on wl u.p: no ex and lost 2nd nr fin* **7/2[2]**

1524 **4** *1* **Cloudscape (IRE)**[41] 3375 3-9-1 **104** .......... (t) WilliamBuick 2 109
(John Gosden) *hld up in tch in rr: effrt 2f out: hdwy u.p over 1f out: chsd ldng pair ins fnl f: styd on but nvr quite enough pce to chal* **9/2[3]**

-433 **5** *3/4* **Scotland (GER)**[40] 3417 3-9-1 **109** .......... JimCrowley 3 107
(Andrew Balding) *chsd ldrs: rdn over 2f out: styd on same pce u.p fnl f* **9/1**

2-21 **6** *3 1/4* **Observational**[68] 2502 3-9-1 **103** .......... GeorgeBaker 1 102
(Roger Charlton) *urged along leaving stalls: chsd ldr tl jst over 2f out: stl chsng ldrs and unable qck over 1f out: wknd ins fnl f* **10/3[1]**

-465 **7** *44* **Red Galileo**[53] 2990 3-9-1 **107** .......... RyanMoore 5 32
(Ed Dunlop) *t.k.h: hld up in tch in last trio: rdn over 2f out: sn btn: lost tch and eased fnl f: t.o* **17/2**

2m 33.08s (-5.32) **Going Correction** -0.025s/f (Good) **7** Ran SP% **115.5**
Speed ratings (Par 110): **116,115,115,115,114 112,83**
CSF £33.85 TOTE £4.60: £2.80, £2.90; EX 32.10 Trifecta £90.70.
**Owner** K Abdullah **Bred** Juddmonte Farms Ltd **Trained** Newmarket, Suffolk
■ Stewards' Enquiry : Joe Fanning two-day ban: used whip above permitted level (Aug 13-14)
Ryan Moore trainer said colt was unsuited by the good to firm ground

**FOCUS**
Each of these runners holds a St Leger entry, and this looked a really competitive Group 3 race. With just two lengths covering the first five, though, it's hard to think this is strong form. The race is rated at the mid-point of the possibilities.

## 4779 QIPCO SUSSEX STKS (BRITISH CHAMPIONS SERIES) (GROUP 1) 1m
**3:05** (3:05) (Class 1) 3-Y-O+ **£170,130** (£64,500; £32,280; £16,080) **Stalls** Low

Form RPR

1211 **1** **Kingman**[43] 3320 3-9-0 **126** .......... JamesDoyle 4 123+
(John Gosden) *hld up in tch in last: wnt 3rd and shkn up jst over 1f out: stl over 1 l down and reminder ins fnl f: qcknd v smartly fnl 110yds and swept past rivals to ld wl ins fnl f: eased cl home* **2/5[1]**

16-1 **2** *1* **Toronado (IRE)**[43] 3317 4-9-8 **125** .......... RichardHughes 5 120
(Richard Hannon) *t.k.h: pressed ldr tl led 2f out: immediately rdn and qcknd: drvn and a jst holding 3rd fr 1f out tl hdd and brushed aside by wnr wl ins fnl f* **11/4[2]**

-602 **3** *hd* **Darwin (USA)**[11] 4459 4-9-8 **112** .......... JosephO'Brien 2 119
(A P O'Brien, Ire) *led and set v stdy gallop: rdn and hdd 2f out: sustained duel w rival and kpt on wl u.p tl brushed aside by wnr wl ins fnl f* **25/1**

1-03 **4** *1 3/4* **Outstrip**[43] 3320 3-9-0 **118** .......... WilliamBuick 1 113
(Charlie Appleby) *trckd ldng pair: rdn whn gallop qcknd 2f out: nt enough room over 1f out: outpcd jst ins fnl f: swtchd lft and kpt on towards fin* **20/1[3]**

1m 41.75s (1.85) **Going Correction** -0.025s/f (Good)
**WFA** 3 from 4yo 8lb **4** Ran SP% **106.7**
Speed ratings (Par 117): **89,88,87,86**
CSF £1.69 TOTE £1.30; EX 1.70 Trifecta £4.40.
**Owner** K Abdullah **Bred** Juddmonte Farms Ltd **Trained** Newmarket, Suffolk

**FOCUS**
The big clash of the week, but it was an unsatisfactory race, with them dawdling through the early stages and it developed into a dash for the line from the 2f marker. We didn't really learn a lot about Kingman, but Toronado was a bit disappointing.

## 4780 VEUVE CLICQUOT VINTAGE STKS (GROUP 2) 7f
**3:40** (3:40) (Class 1) 2-Y-O
**£45,368** (£17,200; £8,608; £4,288; £2,152; £1,080) **Stalls** Low

Form RPR

**1** **Highland Reel (IRE)**[29] 3834 2-9-1 **0** .......... JosephO'Brien 6 110+
(A P O'Brien, Ire) *t.k.h: hld up in tch in midfield: rdn and effrt to chal over 1f out: led ent fnl f: r.o strly: readily* **10/11[1]**

1 **2** *2 1/4* **Tupi (IRE)**[47] 3194 2-9-1 **0** .......... RichardHughes 5 102+
(Richard Hannon) *hld up in tch in last trio: rdn and effrt over 1f out: hdwy to chse clr wnr and edgd rt fnl 100yds: no imp* **13/2**

12 **3** *3/4* **Room Key**[31] 3751 2-9-1 **85** .......... DaneO'Neill 1 101
(Eve Johnson Houghton) *t.k.h: chsd ldrs: nt clr run and shuffled bk over 1f out: swtchd lft 1f out: wnt between horses and wnt 3rd fnl 100yds: no imp* **20/1**

132 **4** *1* **Ahlan Emarati (IRE)**[32] 3738 2-9-1 **0** .......... JamieSpencer 2 97
(Peter Chapple-Hyam) *stdd after s: hld up in last trio: swtchd ins over 2f out: nt clr run 2f out: swtchd bk lft and hdwy between horses over 1f out: one pce fnl f* **5/1[2]**

311 **5** *3/4* **Pallister**[30] 3786 2-9-1 **89** .......... JoeFanning 8 95
(Mark Johnston) *chsd ldr tl led after 1f: rdn ent fnl 2f: hdd and no ex ent fnl f: lost 2nd and wknd ins fnl f* **10/1**

021 **6** *hd* **Chadic**[16] 4253 2-9-1 **88** .......... SilvestreDeSousa 3 95
(Mark Johnston) *led for 1f: sn swtchd lft and chsd ldr: rdn over 2f out: kpt on but unable qck 1f out: wnt 2nd again briefly ins fnl f: wknd fnl 100yds* **20/1**

041 **7** *hd* **Faithful Creek (IRE)**[13] 4353 2-9-1 **89** .......... JimmyFortune 7 94+
(Brian Meehan) *hld up in rr: rdn over 2f out: no prog tl styd on ins fnl f: nvr trbld ldrs* **33/1**

510 **8** *2 1/4* **Dr No**[43] 3318 2-9-1 **103** .......... RyanMoore 4 90
(Richard Hannon) *in tch in midfield: rdn 2f out: keeping on same pce and hld whn squeezed for room jst ins fnl f: sn wknd* **6/1[3]**

1m 26.81s (-0.19) **Going Correction** -0.025s/f (Good) **8** Ran SP% **118.2**
Speed ratings (Par 106): **100,97,96,95,94 94,94,91**
CSF £7.56 TOTE £2.00: £1.20, £1.80, £3.90; EX 7.30 Trifecta £204.90.
**Owner** Derrick Smith & Mrs John Magnier & Michael Tabor **Bred** Hveger Syndicate **Trained** Cashel, Co Tipperary
■ Stewards' Enquiry : Joseph O'Brien He has a lot of speed - he could have gone for a winners' race at Naas over six next week even though he won over a mile last time. He is not short of pace and only ran over a mile last time because it fitted in well. He's a horse who learns quick and he will have learnt a lot today. He travelled well, quickened and went through the line strong. Joseph (O'Brien, jockey) said it was hard to pull him up. He could go to the Futurity or National Stakes, all off those races, and Joseph said he will get further next. He could be anything and everything is an option.-Aidan O'Brien, trainer.

**FOCUS**
A race that throws up a really good horse on a fairly regular basis, and there's a decent chance it did so again. The winner more than confirmed the excellent impression of his latest start.

## 4781 MARKEL INSURANCE MAIDEN FILLIES' STKS (BOBIS RACE) 6f
**4:15** (4:15) (Class 2) 2-Y-O **£12,938** (£3,850; £1,924; £962) **Stalls** High

Form RPR

02 **1** **Royal Razalma (IRE)**[26] 3934 2-9-0 **0** .......... RichardKingscote 1 88+
(Jonathan Portman) *chsd ldr: rdn to ld over 1f out: sn hung lft: in command and r.o wl fnl f: quite comf* **10/1**

0 **2** *2 3/4* **Hundi (IRE)**[33] 3671 2-9-0 **0** .......... JamesDoyle 8 80
(Charles Hills) *pushed rt s and s.i.s: in last quartet early: hdwy at 1/2-way: clsd to chse ldng trio over 1f out: swtchd rt and chsd wnr 1f out: r.o but no imp* **4/1[2]**

2 **3** *2 1/4* **Shahah**[33] 3648 2-9-0 **0** .......... FrankieDettori 11 73
(Richard Hannon) *taken down early: chsd ldrs: clsd and pressing ldng pair whn squeezed for room and swtchd rt over 1f out: 3rd and no ex 1f out: wknd ins fnl f* **7/4[1]**

**4** *3/4* **Bright Flash** 2-9-0 **0** .......... SeanLevey 10 71+
(David Brown) *wnt sharply rt s: sn rcvrd and in tch in midfield: rdn and hung rt over 1f out: kpt on but no threat to ldrs after* **5/1**

50 **5** *4 1/2* **Moon River (IRE)**[9] 4499 2-9-0 **0** .......... (b) JimmyFortune 13 57
(Brian Meehan) *led: rdn and hdd over 1f out: 4th and btn 1f out: sn wknd: lost 4th and eased towards fin* **25/1**

04 **6** *nse* **Piccadillo**[9] 4499 2-9-0 **0** .......... ThomasBrown 7 57
(Daniel Kubler) *in tch in midfield: rdn and edging rt ent fnl 2f: sn outpcd 2f and no threat to ldrs fr over 1f out* **50/1**

**7** *shd* **Touchline** 2-9-0 **0** .......... RyanMoore 5 57
(Michael Bell) *sn bustled along and outpcd in midfield: sme hdwy fnl f: n.d* **9/2[3]**

**8** *5* **Inauguration (IRE)** 2-9-0 **0** .......... JimCrowley 6 42
(Charles Hills) *s.i.s: racd off the pce in last trio: rdn and sme hdwy over 2f out: sn btn and wknd* **25/1**

**9** *nse* **Avenue Du Monde (FR)** 2-9-0 **0** .......... RichardHughes 9 42
(Richard Hannon) *bmpd leaving stalls and slowly away: nvr rcvrd and a bhd* **12/1**

**10** *3 1/2* **Follow The Faith** 2-9-0 **0** .......... CharlesBishop 4 31+
(Mick Channon) *s.i.s: sn swtchd lft: a bhd* **33/1**

1m 11.18s (-1.02) **Going Correction** -0.15s/f (Firm) **10** Ran SP% **120.6**
Speed ratings (Par 97): **100,96,93,92,86 86,86,79,79,74**
CSF £49.93 TOTE £11.50: £2.80, £1.50, £1.10; EX 58.70 Trifecta £205.70.
**Owner** David & Gwyn Joseph **Bred** Miss Eileen Farrelly **Trained** Upper Lambourn, Berks
■ Stewards' Enquiry : Richard Kingscote one-day ban: careless riding (Aug 13)

**FOCUS**
No more than fair maiden form but the winner was quite impressive.

## 4782 EBF STALLIONS BREEDING WINNERS FILLIES' STKS (H'CAP) 1m 1f
**4:50** (4:50) (Class 3) (0-95,95) 3-Y-O+
**£10,893** (£3,262; £1,631; £815; £407; £204) **Stalls** Low

Form RPR

-235 **1** **Magique (IRE)**[32] 3727 4-8-10 **77** .......... JimmyFortune 8 88
(Jeremy Noseda) *mde all: drvn over 1f out: gng clr whn wandered lft and rt ent fnl f: styd on wl: rdn out* **25/1**

3233 **2** *1 3/4* **Hedge End (IRE)**[16] 4271 3-7-10 **77** .......... CamHardie(5) 16 84
(Richard Hannon) *hld up in tch in last quartet: rdn and hdwy wl over 1f out: 4th and styng on ins fnl f: wnt 2nd towards fin: no threat to wnr* **12/1**

51 **3** *1/2* **Patterned**[23] 4029 3-8-3 **79** .......... MartinLane 13 85
(Luca Cumani) *chsd wnr tl 5f out: rdn to chse wnr again and edgd rt wl over 1f out: kpt on same pce u.p fr over 1f out: lost 2nd towards fin* **7/1[3]**

2315 **4** *3/4* **Running Deer (IRE)**[18] 4211 5-9-4 **90** .......... LouisSteward(5) 1 95
(Eve Johnson Houghton) *t.k.h: chsd ldrs: rdn and effrt over 2f out: drvn and styd on same pce fr over 1f out* **12/1**

0504 **5** *3/4* **Auction (IRE)**[33] 3665 4-9-10 **91** .......... RyanMoore 7 97
(Ed Dunlop) *stdd after s: t.k.h: hld up in tch in last trio: clsd and nt clr run 2f out: swtchd lft and hdwy over 1f out: kpt on wl ins fnl f: nvr trbld ldrs* **9/1**

3405 **6** *shd* **Hot Coffee (IRE)**[19] 4163 3-8-11 **87** .......... RichardKingscote 14 93
(Tom Dascombe) *dwlt: hld up in last pair: clsd but stuck bhd and wall of horses 2f out: nvr much room tl swtchd lft jst ins fnl f: r.o wl fnl 100yds: nvr trbld ldrs* **14/1**

2-01 **7** ½ **Hiking (USA)**[18] 4208 3-8-8 **84** JamesDoyle 3 85
(Roger Charlton) *wl in tch in midfield: effrt whn carried rt and unable qck wl over 1f out: no imp: pushed along and one pce fnl f* **11/2**[2]

1124 **8** ¾ **Lady Tiana**[18] 4182 3-8-7 **83** LukeMorris 12 83
(Lucy Wadham) *hld up in tch in midfield: hdwy u.p and edgd rt wl over 1f out: wknd ins fnl f* **12/1**

031 **9** ¾ **Palerma**[45] 3277 3-8-2 **78** MartinDwyer 4 76
(Mick Channon) *t.k.h: hld up in tch in midfield: effrt u.p wll over 1f out: no imp: hld whn swtchd lft ins fnl f: kpt on* **10/1**

2032 **10** 1 ½ **Alquimia (IRE)**[15] 4300 3-7-10 **77** JackGarritty(5) 2 72
(Richard Fahey) *in tch in midfield: effrt on inner 2f out: no hdwy and btn ent fnl f: wknd ins fnl f* **12/1**

0-00 **11** ¾ **Agent Allison**[160] 683 4-10-0 **95** FrankieDettori 6 90
(Peter Chapple-Hyam) *stdd s: hld up in last pair: effrt on inner but nt enough room 2f out: pushed along and sme hdwy jst over 1f out: n.d and eased ins fnl f* **14/1**

221 **12** 3 ¼ **Principle Equation (IRE)**[31] 3755 3-8-5 **81** SilvestreDeSousa 9 74
(Ralph Beckett) *t.k.h: chsd ldrs early: rdn and lost pl over 2f out: wknd over 1f out: bhd and eased ins fnl f* **5/1**[1]

1203 **13** 2 ½ **Saltwater Creek (IRE)**[18] 4182 3-8-1 **77** HarryBentley 5 63
(Michael Bell) *dwlt: sn rcvrd and in tch in midfield on outer: rdn dropped to rr over 2f out: edgd rt and jst over 1f out and sn wknd: eased ins fnl f* **16/1**

4660 **14** ½ **Uchenna (IRE)**[11] 4443 3-8-12 **88** JamieSpencer 10 71
(David Simcock) *in tch in midfield but stuck wd: hdwy to chse ldr 5f out: lost 2nd and dropping out whn hmpd wl over 1f out: wknd 1f out: eased ins fnl f* **25/1**

1m 54.17s (-2.13) **Going Correction** -0.025s/f (Good)
**WFA** 3 from 4yo+ 9lb **14** Ran SP% **121.3**
Speed ratings (Par 104): **108,106,106,105,104 104,104,103,102,101 100,97,95,95**
CSF £302.31 CT £2393.07 TOTE £34.40: £8.20, £2.70, £3.30; EX 425.60 Trifecta £3019.40.

**Owner** Miss Yvonne Jacques **Bred** Mrs Cherry Faeste **Trained** Newmarket, Suffolk

**FOCUS**
It paid to sit handily in a race run at a steady early gallop. The form has been given a chance, with a personal best from the winner.

## 4783 TURF CLUB STKS (H'CAP) 7f
**5:25** (5:25) (Class 3) (0-90,89) 3-Y-O+ **£11,320** (£3,368; £1,683; £841) **Stalls** Low

Form RPR

3235 **1** **Related**[13] 4355 4-9-6 **83** (b[1]) RichardKingscote 1 93
(David Simcock) *mde virtually all: rdn and fnd ex over 1f out: drvn and styd wl on fnl f* **6/1**[3]

5212 **2** 1 ½ **Lulu The Zulu (IRE)**[18] 4181 6-9-5 **82** AndrewMullen 5 88
(Michael Appleby) *awkward leaving stalls: in tch in midfield: n.m.r and swtchd rt over 1f out: hdwy u.p 1f out: chsd wnr ins fnl f: kpt on* **11/2**[2]

2133 **3** 1 ½ **George Rooke (IRE)**[25] 3955 4-9-4 **81** (p) RyanMoore 7 83+
(Keith Dalgleish) *hld up towards rr: plenty to do and rdn 2f out: hdwy ent fnl f: styd on wl u.p to go 3rd towards fin: no threat to wnr* **9/2**[1]

-441 **4** ½ **Accession (IRE)**[63] 2684 5-9-5 **82** MartinLane 12 83
(Charlie Fellowes) *stdd s: hld up in last pair: effrt on outer 2f out: drifting rt and hdwy over 1f out: styd on wl ins fnl f: no threat to wnr* **20/1**

0316 **5** *nse* **Gravitational (IRE)**[28] 3861 4-9-2 **82** AshleyMorgan(3) 6 82
(Chris Wall) *chsd ldrs: rdn and effrt 2f out: chsd wnr jst over 1f out: no imp and lost 2nd ins fnl f: lost 2 pls towards fin* **16/1**

6500 **6** 1 **Corporal Maddox**[13] 4347 7-9-8 **85** (p) SteveDrowne 3 83
(Ronald Harris) *s.i.s: hdwy into midfield on inner 5f out: hmpd sn after: n.m.r 2f out: hdwy u.p over 1f out: kpt on but no threat to wnr* **33/1**

3641 **7** ½ **Liberty Jack (IRE)**[11] 4447 4-9-6 **83** (p) PatCosgrave 10 79
(Jim Boyle) *t.k.h: hld up in tch in midfield: hmpd and stmbld bnd 5f out: n.m.r jst over 2f: sn drvn and fnd little: styd on same pce fnl f* **6/1**[3]

3616 **8** 1 **Little Shambles**[19] 4163 3-9-2 **86** JoeFanning 19 77
(Mark Johnston) *broke wl to cross to inner and chsd wnr: rdn 2f out: lost 2nd jst over 1f out: edgd rt and wknd ins fnl f* **12/1**

0-00 **9** 1 ¼ **Valais Girl**[31] 3753 4-9-8 **85** (p) HarryBentley 9 75
(Marcus Tregoning) *chsd ldrs: rdn and unable qck 2f out: lost pl over 1f out: btn whn n.m.r and wknd ins fnl f* **33/1**

-634 **10** 1 **Gatepost (IRE)**[16] 4258 5-8-13 **81** JackGarritty(5) 2 70
(Richard Fahey) *hld up in midfield: rdn and effrt 2f out: n.m.r and swtchd lft over 1f out: no imp and n.m.r ins fnl f* **8/1**

4-50 **11** 1 ¼ **The Confessor**[52] 3036 7-9-9 **86** DaneO'Neill 8 72
(Henry Candy) *hld up in last quartet: rdn over 2f out: sme hdwy over 1f out: no prog 1f out: wknd and eased wl ins fnl f* **8/1**

1-60 **12** 2 ½ **Obliteright (IRE)**[18] 4181 5-9-3 **80** (v[1]) GeorgeBaker 20 60
(William Knight) *stdd and dropped in bhd s: hld up wl in rr: swtchd lft and effrt 2f out: hung rt and no hdwy after: bhd and eased ins fnl f* **16/1**

3-04 **13** 3 **Bluegrass Blues (IRE)**[102] 1576 4-9-7 **84** (t) LukeMorris 11 63+
(Paul Cole) *in tch in midfield rdn over 2f out: no hdwy and nt clr run 2f out: lost pl and bhd whn hmpd again over 1f out: no ch and eased ins fnl f* **16/1**

3443 **14** *shd* **Kakatosi**[18] 4181 7-9-5 **82** JimmyFortune 17 51
(Mike Murphy) *towards rr: hdwy on outer 5f out: rdn and struggling 2f out: wkng and wl hld whn hmpd jst over 1f out* **20/1**

300 **15** 2 ¼ **Stonefield Flyer**[12] 4384 5-9-6 **83** TomEaves 15 46
(Keith Dalgleish) *in tch in midfield: rdn and unable qck 3f out: wknd over 1f out: bhd and eased wl ins fnl f* **33/1**

1m 25.58s (-1.42) **Going Correction** -0.025s/f (Good)
**WFA** 3 from 4yo+ 7lb **15** Ran SP% **128.0**
Speed ratings (Par 107): **107,105,103,103,102 101,101,100,98,97 96,93,89,89,87**
CSF £38.66 CT £167.21 TOTE £7.30: £2.40, £2.50, £2.40; EX 44.80 Trifecta £185.60.

**Owner** J Barnett & M Caine **Bred** Laundry Cottage Stud Farm **Trained** Newmarket, Suffolk

**FOCUS**
This looked fairly open on paper, but the race was taken apart by the well backed winner. He is related back to earlier C&D form.

T/Jkpt: Not won. T/Plt: £188.70 to a £1 stake. Pool: £247444.94 - 957.12 winning tickets T/Qpdt: £8.10 to a £1 stake. Pool: £16764.65 - 1531.51 winning tickets SP

# [4534] LEICESTER (R-H)
Wednesday, July 30

**OFFICIAL GOING: Good to firm (8.0)**
Wind: Almost nil Weather: Cloudy with sunny spells

## 4784 EBF STALLIONS MEDIAN AUCTION MAIDEN FILLIES' STKS (BOBIS RACE) 5f 218y
**6:00** (6:01) (Class 5) 2-Y-O **£3,881** (£1,155; £577; £288) **Stalls** High

Form RPR

3 **1** **Stroll Patrol**[18] 4202 2-9-0 0 KierenFallon 14 84+
(Philip McBride) *a.p: chsd ldr over 3f out: shkn up over 1f out: led ins fnl f: r.o wl: comf* **2/1**[1]

32 **2** 2 ½ **Primrose Valley**[14] 4320 2-9-0 0 (p) FrederikTylicki 11 77
(Ed Vaughan) *chsd ldrs: led over 3f out: rdn over 1f out: hdd and unable qck ins fnl f* **8/1**[3]

0 **3** 3 ½ **Some Show**[16] 4269 2-9-0 0 FergusSweeney 6 66+
(Henry Candy) *chsd ldr tl over 3f out: remained handy: rdn over 1f out: styd on same pce* **40/1**

0 **4** 1 ½ **Aqlette**[53] 2979 2-9-0 0 MartinHarley 13 62
(Marco Botti) *hld up: hdwy u.p over 1f out: no ex ins fnl f* **14/1**

**5** *nk* **Solstalla** 2-9-0 0 GrahamLee 5 61+
(William Jarvis) *mid-div: pushed along over 2f out: hdwy and nt clr run over 1f out: nt trble ldrs* **8/1**[3]

3 **6** 3 ½ **Dolorous**[27] 3888 2-9-0 0 RobertHavlin 1 50
(John Gosden) *led: racd keenly: hdd over 3f out: wknd over 1f out* **9/4**[2]

06 **7** *shd* **Right Madam (IRE)**[20] 4129 2-9-0 0 RoystonFfrench 2 50
(Andrew Hollinshead) *mid-div: hdwy over 2f out: sn rdn: wknd fnl f* **50/1**

0 **8** 2 **Prima Pagina**[41] 3387 2-8-11 0 RobertTart(3) 10 44
(Dr Jon Scargill) *sn outpcd: nvr nrr* **66/1**

**9** ½ **Run By Faith** 2-9-0 0 HayleyTurner 4 42
(Roger Charlton) *chsd ldrs: pushed along over 3f out: wknd 2f out* **33/1**

40 **10** ¾ **Piping Dream (IRE)**[12] 4396 2-9-0 0 KieranO'Neill 8 40
(Richard Hannon) *prom: rdn 1/2-way: wknd over 1f out* **50/1**

**11** *hd* **Bobbie's Girl (IRE)** 2-9-0 0 ShaneKelly 3 39
(William Haggas) *s.i.s: sn pushed along in rr: nvr on terms* **12/1**

**12** 2 ¼ **Stellar Jet (IRE)** 2-9-0 0 JackMitchell 9 33
(Roger Varian) *s.i.s: sn mid-div: pushed along and edgd rt over 3f out: sn wknd* **20/1**

**13** ¾ **Red Words (IRE)** 2-9-0 0 JimmyQuinn 7 30
(George Margarson) *s.s: outpcd* **66/1**

0 **14** 27 **The Other Lady**[5] 4626 2-9-0 0 JohnFahy 12
(Alan McCabe) *sn outpcd* **100/1**

1m 10.79s (-2.21) **Going Correction** -0.25s/f (Firm) **14** Ran SP% **118.7**
Speed ratings (Par 91): **104,100,96,94,93 88,88,86,85,84 84,81,80,44**
CSF £17.38 TOTE £2.60: £1.20, £2.40, £11.50; EX 15.00 Trifecta £452.10.

**Owner** PMRacing **Bred** Boyce Bloodstock & Mrs C E Percival **Trained** Newmarket, Suffolk

**FOCUS**
A fair fillies' maiden taking place on watered good to firm ground. They went just outside of standard, the winner building on a good debut effort.

## 4785 ROTHLEY (S) STKS 7f 9y
**6:30** (6:30) (Class 6) 3-Y-O **£1,940** (£577; £288; £144) **Stalls** High

Form RPR

5506 **1** **Henke (IRE)**[5] 4627 3-8-12 53 (p) AdrianNicholls 4 54
(Nigel Tinkler) *mid-div: hdwy u.p over 2f out: led over 1f out: all out* **9/2**[3]

3644 **2** *nk* **Chanceuse**[7] 4536 3-8-12 50 (v) ShaneKelly 6 53
(Gay Kelleway) *chsd ldr tl led 1/2-way: rdn and hdd over 1f out: ev ch wl ins fnl f: nt qckn towards fin* **8/1**

00 **3** 2 **Tasaaboq**[12] 4407 3-8-12 0 (t) PaddyAspell 2 48
(Phil McEntee) *chsd ldrs: rdn over 2f out: ev ch over 1f out: styd on same pce ins fnl f* **7/4**[1]

2150 **4** 7 **Romantic Bliss (IRE)**[11] 4464 3-8-12 57 (b) MartinHarley 5 29
(K R Burke) *led to 1/2-way: rdn and ev ch over 1f out: sn wknd* **11/4**[2]

40 **5** 1 **Dandys Perier (IRE)**[50] 3087 3-9-3 57 GrahamLee 3 31
(Ronald Harris) *hld up: rdn and wknd over 2f out* **6/1**

-000 **6** 6 **Stream Of Light**[30] 3792 3-8-7 43 JimmyQuinn 1 5
(John Mackie) *hld up: bhd fr 1/2-way* **50/1**

00 **7** 38 **Beauchamp Kite**[11] 4435 3-8-12 0 (v[1]) FergusSweeney 7
(Paul Fitzsimons) *sn outpcd* **33/1**

1m 24.73s (-1.47) **Going Correction** -0.25s/f (Firm) **7** Ran SP% **111.5**
Speed ratings (Par 98): **98,97,95,87,86 79,35**
CSF £37.13 TOTE £5.10: £2.40, £1.70; EX 44.20 Trifecta £160.90.

**Owner** Wildcard Racing Syndicate **Bred** Ann Foley & J C Bloodstock **Trained** Langton, N Yorks

**FOCUS**
A very weak seller, rated around the front pair.

## 4786 JO DAVIS LIFE BEGINS BIRTHDAY H'CAP 1m 1f 218y
**7:05** (7:07) (Class 4) (0-80,80) 3-Y-O+ **£4,851** (£1,443; £721; £360) **Stalls** Low

Form RPR

3060 **1** **Chapter And Verse (IRE)**[16] 4273 8-8-11 **63** ShaneKelly 5 72
(Mike Murphy) *led after 1f: clr 4f out: drvn out* **8/1**

0644 **2** 2 ½ **Silver Dixie (USA)**[19] 4148 4-9-3 **76** (p) JordanNason(7) 1 80
(Peter Hedger) *hld up in tch: plld hrd: rdn over 2f out: chsd wnr over 1f out: no imp ins fnl f* **4/1**[2]

0313 **3** 2 **Watersmeet**[12] 4388 3-9-0 **76** FrannyNorton 4 76
(Mark Johnston) *chsd wnr after 1f: rdn and hung rt over 2f out: lost 2nd over 1f out: no ex ins fnl f* **4/5**[1]

222- **4** 5 **Response**[323] 6272 4-9-9 **75** GrahamLee 2 66
(Steve Gollings) *led 1f: sn std: rdn over 3f out: outpcd fr over 2f out* **14/1**

0-46 **5** ¾ **Albaqaa**[11] 4442 9-9-11 **80** RobertTart(3) 3 70
(P J O'Gorman) *hld up in tch: racd keenly: rdn over 2f out: sn outpcd* **6/1**[3]

2m 5.45s (-2.45) **Going Correction** -0.125s/f (Firm)
**WFA** 3 from 4yo+ 10lb **5** Ran SP% **107.6**
Speed ratings (Par 105): **104,102,100,96,95**
CSF £36.33 TOTE £7.70: £2.00, £2.00; EX 48.20 Trifecta £132.30.

**Owner** D J Ellis **Bred** Stuart Weld **Trained** Westoning, Beds

■ Stewards' Enquiry : Jordan Nason two-day ban: used whip above permitted level (Aug 13-14)



The Form Book, Raceform Ltd, Newbury, RG14 5SJ

**FOCUS**
Despite the small field for this fair handicap, it still had the look of an interesting affair, but tactics played a part in determining the result. Not form to take too literally.

## 4787 BRITISH STALLION STUDS EBF MAIDEN STKS (BOBIS RACE) 5f 218y
7:40 (7:41) (Class 4) 2-Y-O £4,204 (£1,251; £625; £312) Stalls High

Form RPR
403 1 **Speedy Move (IRE)**[27] 3881 2-9-5 74 MartinHarley 2 84+
(Ismail Mohammed) *led: hdd over 3f out: led again over 2f out: shkn up and hung lft ins fnl f: r.o wl* **10/3**[2]
4 2 3 ¼ **Skate**[16] 4270 2-9-5 0 HayleyTurner 7 74
(Roger Charlton) *chsd ldrs: shkn up over 1f out: styd on same pce ins fnl f* **5/2**[1]
5 3 nk **Rio Ronaldo (IRE)**[23] 4025 2-9-5 0 ShaneKelly 4 73
(Mike Murphy) *trckd ldrs: racd keenly: rdn and ev ch over 1f out: styd on same pce ins fnl f* **7/2**[3]
4 4 7 **Dear Bruin (IRE)**[26] 3933 2-9-0 0 FrannyNorton 1 47
(John Spearing) *trckd ldrs: racd keenly: rdn over 1f out: hung lft and wknd fnl f* **9/2**
5 ½ **Red Unico (IRE)** 2-9-5 0 SeanLevey 8 51
(Alan McCabe) *in rr tl styd on ins fnl f: nvr nrr* **50/1**
0 6 1 **Lopito De Vega (IRE)**[12] 4409 2-9-5 0 DaleSwift 9 48
(James Given) *stdd s: hdwy 2f out: sn rdn: wknd fnl f* **50/1**
50 7 nk **Roman De Brut (IRE)**[32] 3701 2-9-0 0 GeorgeDowning(5) 3 47
(Ian Williams) *s.i.s: hdwy over 4f out: rdn and wknd over 1f out* **66/1**
5 8 1 ¾ **Creative Genius**[32] 3706 2-9-5 0 GrahamLee 6 42
(Ed Walker) *w ldr tl led over 3f out: hdd over 2f out: sn rdn: wknd fnl f* **25/1**
00 9 2 ¼ **Total Demolition (IRE)**[23] 4025 2-9-5 0 ChrisCatlin 10 35
(Olly Stevens) *hld up: nt clr run over 2f out: shkn up over 1f out: nvr nr to chal* **50/1**
10 1 ¼ **Red Majesty** 2-9-5 0 DavidNolan 5 31
(Kevin Ryan) *chsd ldrs: pushed along 1/2-way: rdn and wknd over 1f out* **15/2**

1m 11.85s (-1.15) **Going Correction** -0.25s/f (Firm) 10 Ran SP% **115.0**
Speed ratings (Par 96): **97,92,92,82,82 80,80,78,75,73**
CSF £11.57 TOTE £4.20: £1.80, £1.60, £1.30; EX 13.70 Trifecta £56.80.
**Owner** Dr Ali Ridha **Bred** Rabbah Bloodstock Limited **Trained** Newmarket, Suffolk

**FOCUS**
An ordinary maiden that was a second slower than the opening fillies' maiden over the same trip. This may underplay the winner's improvement.

## 4788 ROTHLEY H'CAP 5f 218y
8:10 (8:12) (Class 5) (0-70,70) 3-Y-O+ £3,234 (£962; £481; £240) Stalls High

Form RPR
1 1 **Sleep Walk**[93] 1790 3-9-2 65 MartinHarley 10 81+
(Roger Charlton) *hld up: plld hrd: hdwy over 1f out: edgd rt ins fnl f: r.o to ld nr fin: easily* **4/5**[1]
1642 2 nk **Castorienta**[15] 4297 3-9-6 69 KierenFallon 3 78+
(George Baker) *hld up: hdwy over 2f out: led over 1f out: rdn and hdd nr fin* **6/1**[2]
1006 3 2 ¾ **Minty Jones**[13] 4370 5-8-6 53 (b) RobertTart(3) 8 55
(Michael Mullineaux) *chsd ldrs: rdn over 2f out: edgd rt and styd on same pce ins fnl f* **33/1**
6032 4 1 **Lucky Di**[28] 3854 4-9-5 70 JordanNason(7) 11 69
(Peter Hedger) *hld up: rdn and hdwy over 1f out: hung rt ins fnl f: r.o* **8/1**[3]
1001 5 2 **Euroquip Boy (IRE)**[28] 3848 7-8-12 61 NoelGarbutt(5) 7 54
(Michael Scudamore) *hld up in tch: plld hrd: rdn over 1f out: wknd ins fnl f* **9/1**
004 6 nse **Divertimenti (IRE)**[13] 4370 10-8-5 52 (b) BillyCray(3) 1 45
(Roy Bowring) *led 5f out: rdn and hdd over 1f out: wknd ins fnl f* **33/1**
-345 7 2 ½ **Shilla (IRE)**[12] 4411 3-9-4 67 FergusSweeney 9 51
(Henry Candy) *mid-div: rdn over 2f out: n.m.r over 1f out: wknd fnl f* **11/1**
1404 8 1 **Clock Opera (IRE)**[25] 3966 4-9-3 61 FrederikTylicki 6 43
(William Stone) *led 1f: w ldr: rdn over 2f out: wknd fnl f* **12/1**
0605 9 ½ **Chester Deelyte (IRE)**[146] 858 6-8-7 51 oh6 (v) RoystonFfrench 4 32
(Lisa Williamson) *chsd ldrs: rdn over 2f out: wknd fnl f* **66/1**
4-5 10 3 **Aya's Gift**[18] 4193 3-8-13 62 GrahamLee 5 33
(Ed Walker) *mid-div: rdn over 2f out: wknd over 1f out* **20/1**

1m 11.82s (-1.18) **Going Correction** -0.25s/f (Firm)
**WFA** 3 from 4yo+ 5lb 10 Ran SP% **119.1**
Speed ratings (Par 103): **97,96,92,91,88 88,85,84,83,79**
CSF £5.81 CT £96.74 TOTE £1.60: £1.02, £1.90, £13.60; EX 7.60 Trifecta £141.60.
**Owner** K Abdullah **Bred** Juddmonte Farms Ltd **Trained** Beckhampton, Wilts

**FOCUS**
Only a modest handicap but an interesting contest nonetheless with the favourite, well backed throughout the day before drifting on course, running out an easy winner. The runner-up helps with the level.

## 4789 SHANGTON H'CAP 1m 60y
8:45 (8:45) (Class 6) (0-65,65) 3-Y-O £2,587 (£770; £384; £192) Stalls Low

Form RPR
00-2 1 **Daisy Boy (IRE)**[55] 2927 3-9-2 60 MartinHarley 4 69+
(Stuart Williams) *mde all: rdn over 1f out: r.o: eased nr fin* **6/4**[1]
003 2 nk **Ajig**[14] 4329 3-9-7 65 JohnFahy 3 71
(Eve Johnson Houghton) *trckd ldrs: rdn over 2f out: sn outpcd: rallied fnl f: r.o towards fin* **11/4**[2]
6001 3 shd **Kalon Brama (IRE)**[7] 4536 3-9-3 61 6ex JimmyQuinn 1 67
(Peter Charalambous) *hld up: hdwy over 2f out: chsd wnr over 1f out: sn rdn and ev ch: kpt on* **7/2**[3]
4506 4 6 **Arianrhod (IRE)**[14] 4316 3-9-3 61 GrahamLee 2 53
(Donald McCain) *hld up in tch: racd keenly: nt clr run over 2f out: sn rdn: styd on same pce fr over 1f out* **20/1**
0005 5 ½ **La Napoule**[31] 3754 3-8-11 55 SeanLevey 6 45
(Richard Hannon) *trckd ldrs: rdn over 2f out: styd on same pce fr over 1f out* **16/1**
2600 6 1 ¾ **No Refund (IRE)**[9] 4495 3-9-4 62 KierenFallon 5 48
(Martin Smith) *s.i.s: hld up: hdwy to chse wnr over 3f out: ev ch fr over 2f out tl rdn over 1f out: wknd ins fnl f* **12/1**
0-30 7 6 **Essanar**[20] 4130 3-9-0 58 RoystonFfrench 7 30
(Andrew Hollinshead) *chsd wnr tl rdn over 3f out: wknd 2f out* **22/1**

1m 46.6s (1.50) **Going Correction** -0.125s/f (Firm) 7 Ran SP% **111.6**
Speed ratings (Par 98): **87,86,86,80,80 78,72**
CSF £5.44 TOTE £2.50: £2.50, £1.50; EX 6.60 Trifecta £20.70.
**Owner** G Johnson **Bred** Shadwell Estate Company Limited **Trained** Newmarket, Suffolk

**FOCUS**
Moderate fare, but the winner will have more to offer next time.

T/Plt: £82.80to a £1 stake. Pool: £59,259 - 522.25 winning tickets T/Qpdt: £8.70 to a £1 stake. Pool: £6,957 - 590.25 winning tickets CR

# 4467 REDCAR (L-H)
### Wednesday, July 30

**OFFICIAL GOING: Good to firm (8.8)**
Wind: fresh across Weather: Cloudy

## 4790 BRITISH STALLION STUDS EBF MAIDEN STKS 6f
2:05 (2:17) (Class 5) 2-Y-O £3,067 (£905; £453) Stalls Centre

Form RPR
60 1 **Savannah Beau**[28] 3841 2-9-0 0 DavidNolan 10 61
(Marjorie Fife) *trckd ldrs: rdn over 2f out: led over 1f out: kpt on* **66/1**
04 2 nk **Sovereign Bounty**[10] 4467 2-9-5 0 RussKennemore 6 65
(Jedd O'Keeffe) *midfield: rdn over 2f out: hdwy over 1f out: chsd wnr jst ins fnl f: kpt on: jst hld* **10/1**
3 1 ¼ **Rahmah (IRE)** 2-8-12 0 AhmadAlSubousi(7) 9 62+
(Robert Cowell) *slowly away: hld up: pushed along 1/2-way: kpt on wl fr over 1f out: wnt 3rd 110yds out* **18/1**
4 ¾ **Racing Knight (IRE)** 2-9-5 0 PhillipMakin 7 59+
(John Quinn) *sn pushed along in midfield: kpt on fnl f* **8/1**
5 1 ½ **Crikey (IRE)** 2-9-0 0 ShaneGray(5) 4 55+
(Kevin Ryan) *prom: rdn and outpcd 1/2-way: plugged on fnl f* **9/4**[1]
0 6 1 ¼ **Oricano**[37] 3529 2-8-9 0 GemmaTutty(5) 3 46
(Karen Tutty) *dwlt: sn pushed along in midfield: kpt on ins fnl f* **33/1**
4 7 ½ **Crosse Fire**[65] 2612 2-9-5 0 DaleSwift 11 50
(Scott Dixon) *prom: pressed ldr 1/2-way: sn rdn: wknd ins fnl f* **9/2**[2]
04 8 ½ **Little Sista**[28] 3841 2-9-0 0 PaulMulrennan 8 43
(Bryan Smart) *led: jnd 1/2-way: rdn and hung lft 2f out: hdd over 1f out: wknd* **5/1**[3]
9 1 ½ **Rose Acclaim (IRE)** 2-9-0 0 DanielTudhope 12 39+
(David O'Meara) *hld up: rdn over 2f out: nvr threatened* **8/1**
0 10 9 **What Usain**[46] 3255 2-9-5 0 BarryMcHugh 1 17
(Geoffrey Oldroyd) *sn outpcd in rr: a bhd* **33/1**
11 3 ¾ **Ventura Canyon (IRE)** 2-9-5 0 JasonHart 13
(Keith Dalgleish) *midfield: rdn 1/2-way: sn wknd* **15/2**

1m 12.94s (1.14) **Going Correction** -0.15s/f (Firm) 11 Ran SP% **121.3**
Speed ratings (Par 94): **86,85,83,82,80 79,78,77,75,63 58**
CSF £645.10 TOTE £28.60: £7.00, £3.20, £5.30; EX 357.80 Trifecta £1987.30.
**Owner** Market Avenue Racing Club Ltd **Bred** P Scholes **Trained** Stillington, N Yorks
■ Star Of The Stage was withdrawn. Price at time of withdrawal 11-4. Rule 4 applies to bets placed prior to withdrawal but not to SP bets - deduction 25p in the pound. New market formed.

**FOCUS**
There was drama beforehand with the heavily backed Star Of The Stage breaking through the stalls and running loose. A modest maiden to open the card and won by a horse who had shown little on her first two starts. The pace looked strong and those racing off it dominated the finish. The bare form has a very ordinary feel.

## 4791 RACING UK ANYWHERE AVAILABLE NOW MAIDEN STKS 7f
2:40 (2:49) (Class 5) 3-Y-O+ £2,726 (£805; £402) Stalls Centre

Form RPR
1 **Ribblehead (USA)** 3-9-5 0 DavidAllan 14 76
(Tim Easterby) *midfield: smooth hdwy 3f out: rdn to chse ldrs over 1f out: kpt on: led towards fin* **8/1**
55 2 nk **Duelling Dragon (USA)**[26] 3914 3-9-5 0 PhillipMakin 5 75
(David Barron) *prom: rdn 2f out: led 1f out: wandered: kpt on: hdd towards fin* **7/2**[3]
66-0 3 ¾ **Abbotsfield (IRE)**[204] 76 4-9-2 55 KevinStott(5) 9 71
(Ben Haslam) *prom: led 3rd out: rdn over 2f out: hdd 1f out: no ex towards fin* **20/1**
F6 4 3 ¼ **Heavenly River (FR)**[116] 1303 3-9-0 0 DanielTudhope 6 59
(K R Burke) *dwlt: hld up: rdn and hdwy over 1f out: kpt on fnl f* **14/1**
05 5 1 ¼ **Blue Army**[20] 4130 3-9-5 0 RoystonFfrench 7 61
(Saeed bin Suroor) *in tch: rdn 2f out: wknd ins fnl f* **5/2**[1]
50-0 6 5 **Sweet Lily Pea (USA)**[22] 4056 3-8-11 55 MatthewLawson(3) 11 42
(Mrs Ilka Gansera-Leveque) *midfield: rdn over 2f out: no imp on ldrs* **33/1**
0-3 7 shd **Maggie's Diamond**[49] 3097 3-9-0 0 TonyHamilton 10 42
(Richard Fahey) *led narrowly: hdd 3f out: sn rdn: wknd over 1f out* **3/1**[2]
8 2 ¾ **Soviet Union (IRE)** 3-9-0 0 JasonHart 13 35
(Mark Walford) *hld up: sn pushed along: minor late hdwy: nvr threatened* **33/1**
9 2 **Highfield Lass** 3-9-0 0 MichaelStainton 1 29
(Chris Fairhurst) *slowly away: sn pushed along in rr: nvr threatened* **125/1**
50 10 nk **Wild Hill Boy**[20] 4130 4-9-12 0 FrannyNorton 2 36
(David C Griffiths) *chsd ldrs: rdn 1/2-way: sn lost pl* **100/1**
-245 11 nk **Playtothewhistle**[146] 861 3-9-5 65 PaulMulrennan 8 33
(Bryan Smart) *midfield: rdn 1/2-way: wknd over 1f out* **12/1**
-06 12 1 **Bond's Gift**[26] 3916 4-9-7 0 BarryMcHugh 4 28
(Geoffrey Oldroyd) *hld up: rdn 1/2-way: nvr threatened* **20/1**
13 2 ¾ **Byronaissance** 5-9-12 0 AndrewElliott 12 26
(Neville Bycroft) *chsd ldrs: wknd over 2f out* **50/1**
/0-0 14 19 **Ely Valley**[7] 4533 4-9-0 35 RachelRichardson(7) 3
(Ron Barr) *w ldr: rdn over 4f out: sn wknd* **200/1**

1m 24.58s (0.08) **Going Correction** -0.15s/f (Firm)
**WFA** 3 from 4yo+ 7lb 14 Ran SP% **120.9**
Speed ratings (Par 103): **93,92,91,88,86 80,80,77,75,75 74,73,70,48**
CSF £34.29 TOTE £7.70: £3.70, £1.80, £5.70; EX 37.80 Trifecta £1237.10.
**Owner** Clipper Logistics **Bred** Machmer Hall & Haymarket Farm **Trained** Great Habton, N Yorks

**FOCUS**
The standard set by the experienced runners in this maiden was undemanding and probably no surprise that a newcomer was able to make a winning start. There's every chance he can do a good bit better.

## 4792 DOWNLOAD THE RACING UK IPAD APP (S) STKS 1m 2f
3:15 (3:16) (Class 6) 3-Y-O+ £2,045 (£603; £302) Stalls Low

Form RPR
-502 1 **Mixed Message (IRE)**[10] 4470 4-9-1 67 DaleSwift 7 62
(Brian Ellison) *trckd ldr: rdn over 3f out: led over 2f out: kpt on: edgd lft ins fnl f* **9/4**[1]
0243 2 1 ¼ **Matraash (USA)**[10] 4470 8-9-11 68 (be) StephenCraine 4 69
(Daniel Mark Loughnane) *midfield on inner: rdn over 3f out: chsd ldrs over 1f out: kpt on: wnt 2nd 75yds out* **7/1**

0006 **3** *1* **Mcmonagle (USA)**[10] 4468 6-9-1 55..................(tp) JacobButterfield(5) 3 62
(Alan Brown) *trckd ldr: rdn over 2f out: l down whn sltly hmpd by wnr ins fnl f: no ex and lost 2nd fnl 75yds out* **40/1**

0005 **4** *½* **Destiny Blue (IRE)**[5] 3035 7-9-6 60..................................(t) BenCurtis 8 61
(Brian Ellison) *s.i.s: hld up: rdn over 2f out: kpt on fnl f: nrst fin* **12/1**

-006 **5** *nk* **Dougal Philps**[13] 4369 5-8-13 65.................................. MikeyEnnis(7) 6 60
(Dr Richard Newland) *in tch on outer: rdn over 2f out: plugged on fnl f* **7/1**

4402 **6** *1 ¾* **Yorksters Prince (IRE)**[10] 4468 7-9-1 57...........(b) ShirleyTeasdale(5) 2 57
(Marjorie Fife) *led: rdn whn hdd over 2f out: wknd ins fnl f* **9/2**[3]

4640 **7** *1 ¾* **Bold And Free**[4] 4665 4-9-6 51...................................... RaulDaSilva 9 54
(David Thompson) *hld up: rdn over 3f out: sn btn* **33/1**

50-0 **8** *4* **Tenhoo**[27] 3880 8-9-6 68................................................... JasonHart 5 46
(Eric Alston) *t.k.h in midfield: rdn over 3f out: sn wknd* **4/1**[2]

/0-0 **9** *3 ½* **Lucky Windmill**[11] 4454 7-9-3 65..........................[1] ConnorBeasley(3) 1 41
(Tracy Waggott) *slowly away: sn in tch: hmpd and lost pl over 3f out: wknd over 1f out* **16/1**

2m 6.54s (-0.56) **Going Correction** -0.075s/f (Good) 9 Ran SP% **112.9**
Speed ratings (Par 101): **99,98,97,96,96 95,93,90,87**
CSF £18.11 TOTE £2.80: £1.10, £1.70, £7.50; EX 19.60 Trifecta £450.50.There was no bid for the winner.
**Owner** W I Bloomfield **Bred** J Costello **Trained** Norton, N Yorks
■ Stewards' Enquiry : Dale Swift one-day ban: careless riding (Aug 13)
Raul Da Silva two-day ban: used whip above permitted level (Aug 13-14)

**FOCUS**
Plenty of the usual suspects for a Redcar seller and a comfortable win for the favourite in an uneventful race. She did not even need to reproduce her recent form.

## 4793 MARKET CROSS JEWELLERS H'CAP 1m 2f
3:50 (3:51) (Class 5) (0-75,74) 3-Y-0+ **£2,587** (£770; £384; £192) **Stalls** Low

Form RPR
00-4 **1** **Quest Of Colour (IRE)**[83] 2095 3-8-0 **56** oh1.............. PatrickMathers 3 63+
(Richard Fahey) *in tch: lost pl and dropped to rr over 5f out: rdn over 3f out: r.o strly fr over 1f out: led towards fin* **10/1**

3543 **2** *½* **The Firm (IRE)**[18] 4190 5-9-6 **66**.............................. FrankieMcDonald 4 72
(Daniel Mark Loughnane) *hld up: n.m.r over 3f out: swtchd rt over 2f out: sn rdn and hdwy: kpt on to ld 75yds out: hdd towards fin* **4/1**[1]

0032 **3** *1* **Keep To The Beat**[12] 4386 3-8-1 **62**..........................(p) ShaneGray(5) 10 66
(Kevin Ryan) *prom: led over 5f out: rdn over 3f out: briefly 3 l clr over 2f out: hdd 75yds out: no ex* **17/2**

0406 **4** *1 ½* **Prophesy (IRE)**[13] 4349 5-9-8 **68**..............................(p) AndrewElliott 9 69
(Tim Easterby) *in tch on outer: rdn over 3f out: kpt on* **9/2**[2]

3600 **5** *¾* **Power Up**[36] 3545 3-8-6 **62**............................................ FrannyNorton 7 62
(Mark Johnston) *trckd ldrs: rdn over 3f out: no ex fnl f* **8/1**

00-2 **6** *3 ¼* **Mighty Missile (IRE)**[56] 2896 3-8-5 **61**........................ JamesSullivan 2 55
(Tom Tate) *hld up: rdn over 3f out: nvr threatened* **11/2**[3]

0-06 **7** *7* **Jan De Heem**[11] 4454 4-9-3 **63**.........................................(v) DavidAllan 8 43
(Tina Jackson) *hld up: rdn over 3f out: sn struggling* **25/1**

4-00 **8** *7* **Enzaal (USA)**[19] 4175 4-10-0 **74**.....................................(p) PhillipMakin 1 41
(Philip Kirby) *led narrowly: hdd over 5f out: rdn 4f out: sn wknd* **16/1**

2442 **S** **Lord Franklin**[13] 4359 5-9-11 **71**..................................... JasonHart 5
(Eric Alston) *s.i.s: hld up in rr: racd keenly: slipped up on bnd over 5f out* **4/1**[1]

2m 5.22s (-1.88) **Going Correction** -0.075s/f (Good)
**WFA** 3 from 4yo+ 10lb 9 Ran SP% **114.0**
Speed ratings (Par 103): **104,103,102,101,101 98,92,87,**
CSF £49.16 CT £357.69 TOTE £15.50: £3.80, £1.10, £2.60; EX 55.20 Trifecta £1005.30.
**Owner** Havelock Racing 2 **Bred** Awbeg Stud **Trained** Musley Bank, N Yorks

**FOCUS**
A run-of-the-mill handicap that went the way of the least-exposed runner in the field. The winner is entitled to do better.

## 4794 RACINGUK.COM/ANYWHERE: 3DEVICES, 1PRICE H'CAP (STRAIGHT-MILE CHAMPIONSHIP QUALIFIER) (BOBIS RACE) 1m
4:25 (4:26) (Class 4) (0-85,85) 3-Y-0 **£6,469** (£1,925; £962; £481) **Stalls** Centre

Form RPR
-161 **1** **Brown Eyed Honey**[21] 4074 3-9-0 **83**........................ NathanAlison(5) 2 96+
(William Haggas) *hld up: smooth hdwy to ld over 1f out: pushed out fnl f: comf* **11/8**[1]

021 **2** *2* **Jailawi (IRE)**[26] 3914 3-9-2 **85**.................................... TimClark(5) 3 91+
(Ismail Mohammed) *trckd ldr: rdn to ld over 2f out: hdd over 1f out: kpt on but no ch w wnrnne* **5/2**[2]

1261 **3** *6* **Jacbequick**[9] 4496 3-8-12 **81** 6ex......................(p) JacobButterfield(5) 4 73
(Ollie Pears) *trckd ldr: pushed along and outpcd over 3f out: rdn over 2f out: wknd fnl f* **3/1**[3]

1026 **4** *nk* **Mayfield Boy**[5] 4631 3-8-13 **77**............................................ DavidAllan 5 68
(Mel Brittain) *led: rdn whn hdd over 2f out: wknd fnl f* **7/1**

1m 36.4s (-0.20) **Going Correction** -0.15s/f (Firm) 4 Ran SP% **108.2**
Speed ratings (Par 102): **95,93,87,86**
CSF £5.04 TOTE £1.70; EX 6.10 Trifecta £8.20.
**Owner** M S Bloodstock Ltd **Bred** Mike Smith **Trained** Newmarket, Suffolk

**FOCUS**
A disappointing turnout for the best race on the card, but another step up the ladder for the ready winner. Probably not a race to take too literally.

## 4795 RACING UK IPAD APP RACINGUK.COM/MOBILE H'CAP (DIV I) 6f
5:00 (5:01) (Class 6) (0-65,65) 3-Y-0+ **£1,940** (£577; £288; £144) **Stalls** Centre

Form RPR
3120 **1** **Choc'A'Moca (IRE)**[15] 4288 7-9-3 **56**.........................(v) PaulMulrennan 4 65
(Paul Midgley) *chsd ldrs: rdn 1/2-way: kpt on fnl f: led post* **12/1**

6304 **2** *nse* **Red Shadow**[7] 4532 5-8-7 **46** oh1............................(p) PaulPickard 14 55
(Alan Brown) *chsd ldrs: rdn 1/2-way: led ins fnl f: kpt on: hdd post* **20/1**

0062 **3** *½* **Red Cape (FR)**[7] 4532 11-8-12 **51**.............................(b) JamesSullivan 15 58
(Ruth Carr) *hld up: rdn and hdwy over 1f out: kpt on* **6/1**[2]

0010 **4** *1* **Almanack**[21] 4078 4-9-7 **65**.................................... NathanAlison(5) 7 73+
(Ian Williams) *hld up: rdn and outpcd 1/2-way: kpt on fr over 1f out: briefly short of room 75yds out* **15/2**

/406 **5** *nk* **Spowarticus**[64] 2658 5-8-8 **47**.........................................(v) IanBrennan 1 50
(Scott Dixon) *led: rdn 1/2-way: hdd ins fnl f: no ex* **33/1**

4424 **6** *1 ¼* **Shillito**[6] 4571 4-9-9 **62**............................................. BarryMcHugh 8 62
(Tony Coyle) *midfield: rdn 1/2-way: one pce fnl f* **15/2**

0535 **7** *hd* **Sunny Side Up (IRE)**[16] 4256 5-9-5 **63**.................. GemmaTutty(5) 11 62
(Karen Tutty) *midfield: rdn over 2f out: one pce and nt rch ldrs* **9/2**[1]

2505 **8** *hd* **Spoken Words**[7] 4532 5-8-10 **49**.................................... RaulDaSilva 10 48
(John David Riches) *hld up: rdn over 3f out: swtchd rt 2f out: kpt on fnl f* **20/1**

2035 **9** *1 ¾* **Penina (IRE)**[13] 4370 3-9-7 **65**.........................................(p) BenCurtis 12 57
(Brian Ellison) *prom: rdn 1/2-way: wknd fnl f* **7/1**[3]

5046 **10** *3 ½* **Patron Of Explores (USA)**[11] 4455 3-8-6 **50**............. DuranFentiman 6 32
(Patrick Holmes) *in tch: rdn 1/2-way: wknd over 1f out* **100/1**

3460 **11** *nk* **Graceful Act**[15] 4294 6-8-9 **53**................................. ShirleyTeasdale(5) 3 35
(Ron Barr) *hld up: a bhd* **25/1**

0626 **12** *3 ¾* **Stroll On (IRE)**[25] 3970 3-9-7 **65**.................................... DavidAllan 5 35
(Rae Guest) *midfield: rdn 1/2-way: wknd fnl f* **8/1**

0-46 **13** *nk* **Foxtrot Pearl (IRE)**[18] 4186 3-9-7 **65**......................... StevieDonohoe 13 34
(John Holt) *chsd ldrs: wknd over 2f out* **10/1**

-040 **14** *1* **Wolfwood**[36] 3547 3-8-2 **46** oh1.................................(p) PatrickMathers 9 12
(John Davies) *hld up: a towards rr* **66/1**

40P **15** *2* **Spinner Lane**[15] 4294 3-8-2 **46** oh1........................................(b[1]) PaulQuinn 2 6
(Richard Whitaker) *hld up on outer: rdn over 3f out: sn struggling* **66/1**

1m 10.52s (-1.28) **Going Correction** -0.15s/f (Firm)
**WFA** 3 from 4yo+ 5lb 15 Ran SP% **116.7**
Speed ratings (Par 101): **102,101,101,99,99 97,97,97,95,90 89,84,84,83,80**
CSF £231.98 CT £1614.54 TOTE £12.90: £4.30, £5.90, £2.50; EX 266.00 Trifecta £2094.80.
**Owner** John Milburn - Andrew Stephenson **Bred** Yeomanstown Stud **Trained** Westow, N Yorks
■ Stewards' Enquiry : Paul Pickard two-day ban: used whip above permitted level (Aug 13-14)
Raul Da Silva jockey said mare slipped on leaving stalls
Nathan Alison jockey said gelding was denied a clear run
Stevie Donohoe jockey said filly lost its action

**FOCUS**
A field full of exposed sprinters and only modest form, with a compressed finish.

## 4796 RACING UK IPAD APP RACINGUK.COM/MOBILE H'CAP (DIV II) 6f
5:35 (5:38) (Class 6) (0-65,65) 3-Y-0+ **£1,940** (£577; £288; £144) **Stalls** Centre

Form RPR
030 **1** **Wimboldsley**[26] 3914 3-8-2 **46** oh1.................................... IanBrennan 5 56
(Scott Dixon) *hld up: rdn and hdwy over 2f out: chsd ldrs over 1f out: kpt on to ld 50yds out* **40/1**

4252 **2** *1* **Mission Impossible**[4] 4664 9-9-7 **60**.......................(p) RobertWinston 11 68
(Tracy Waggott) *w ldr: rdn 1/2-way: led over 1f out: kpt on: hdd 50yds out* **10/3**[1]

6116 **3** *1 ¼* **Emily Davison (IRE)**[16] 4257 3-8-13 **62**...................(p) GemmaTutty(5) 9 65
(Karen Tutty) *chsd ldrs: rdn over 2f out: kpt on* **12/1**

552 **4** *½* **Showtime Star**[14] 4318 4-9-8 **61**........................................ BenCurtis 7 64
(Alan Swinbank) *led narrowly: rdn 1/2-way: hdd over 1f out: no ex ins fnl f* **6/1**[3]

0600 **5** *1 ¼* **Here Now And Why (IRE)**[16] 4257 7-8-7 **51**....(p) JacobButterfield(5) 13 50
(Philip Kirby) *midfield: rdn 1/2-way: one pce and nvr threatened ldrs* **16/1**

046 **6** *1 ½* **Tell Me When**[33] 3650 3-8-9 **53**.................................... JamesSullivan 2 47
(Brian Rothwell) *dwlt: outpcd in rr tl kpt on fnl f* **14/1**

0553 **7** *¾* **A J Cook (IRE)**[7] 4532 4-8-7 **51**..........................(v) ShirleyTeasdale(5) 1 43
(Ron Barr) *prom: rdn over 2f out: wknd ins fnl f* **10/1**

00-4 **8** *¾* **Pink Cadillac (IRE)**[204] 76 4-8-7 **46** oh1.......................... AndrewElliott 8 36
(Ben Haslam) *chsd ldrs: rdn 1/2-way: wknd fnl f* **80/1**

5662 **9** *½* **Secret Applause**[8] 4512 3-8-11 **58**........................(p) ConnorBeasley(3) 4 46
(Michael Dods) *prom: rdn 1/2-way: wknd fnl f* **6/1**[3]

**10** *11* **Silver Lightening (IRE)**[284] 7391 4-9-12 **65**.......................... DavidAllan 6 21
(Eric Alston) *chsd ldrs: lost pl 1/2-way: sn wknd* **14/1**

4666 **U** **Bonnie Charlie**[12] 4383 8-9-10 **63**......................................(v) PaulQuinn 10
(David Nicholls) *stmbld and uns rdr leaving stalls* **9/2**[2]

6630 **U** **Singing Star (IRE)**[15] 4288 3-7-12 **49**............... RobertDodsworth(7) 14
(Mel Brittain) *dwlt: hld up: rdn 1/2-way: towards rr whn hmpd by loose horse and stmbld and uns rdr over 1f out* **18/1**

1m 10.89s (-0.91) **Going Correction** -0.15s/f (Firm)
**WFA** 3 from 4yo+ 5lb 12 Ran SP% **114.8**
Speed ratings (Par 101): **100,98,97,96,94 92,91,90,90,75 ,**
CSF £165.19 CT £1767.48 TOTE £61.50: £11.20, £1.40, £4.60; EX 259.50 Trifecta £1739.30.
**Owner** Paul J Dixon And The Chrystal Maze Ptn **Bred** Paul Dixon & Crystal Maze Partnership **Trained** Babworth, Notts

**FOCUS**
An eventful sprint with second-favourite Bonnie Charlie unseating his rider leaving the stalls and then clipping heels with Singing Star 2f out, causing that rival to come down. Ordinary form, and an unexposed winner.

## 4797 BETFAIR NOVICE FLAT AMATEUR RIDERS' H'CAP (FOR NOVICE AMATEUR RIDERS) 1m
6:10 (6:13) (Class 6) (0-65,71) 4-Y-0+ **£1,871** (£580; £290; £145) **Stalls** Centre

Form RPR
-000 **1** **Sky Crossing**[183] 366 5-10-2 **46** oh1...................................... MrHStock 5 56
(Tom Tate) *mde all: rdn: over 2f out: kpt on* **8/1**

005 **2** *2 ¾* **Acton Gold**[95] 1745 5-10-2 **46** oh1.....................................(p) MissPFuller 7 49
(Brian Baugh) *chsd ldr: rdn 3f out: kpt on but a hld* **20/1**

0044 **3** *¾* **Sutton Sid**[6] 4592 4-10-12 **59**...............................(v) MrRobertHooper(3) 2 61+
(Ann Stokell) *v.s.a: hld up and bhd: stl detached over 2f out: r.o fr over 1f out* **7/2**[1]

5054 **4** *3 ¾* **Al Furat (USA)**[10] 4470 6-10-4 **51**.......................... MissEmilyBullock(3) 14 44
(Ron Barr) *hld up in rr: sn pushed along: kpt on fr over 1f out: nvr threatened ldrs* **5/1**[3]

65-0 **5** *¾* **Chosen Forever**[56] 2901 9-10-9 **53**...........................................(t) MrKWood 6 44
(Lee James) *midfield: hdwy to chse ldr over 2f out: no ex fnl f* **16/1**

-060 **6** *1 ¾* **Magical Mischief**[26] 3908 4-9-13 **46** oh1............... DylanMcDonagh(3) 8 33
(Chris Fairhurst) *midfield: rdn 1/2-way: one pce and nvr threatened* **22/1**

-006 **7** *1 ¼* **Echologic**[39] 3465 4-10-2 **47** oh1.............................(p) MrJamesHughes 12 30
(Brian Baugh) *chsd ldr: wknd 2f out* **50/1**

3040 **8** *hd* **Thrust Control (IRE)**[14] 4314 7-10-6 **50**.......................(p) MrJohnWilley 3 33
(Tracy Waggott) *chsd ldr: rdn 1/2-way: wknd over 1f out* **7/1**

0061 **9** *¾* **Sophie's Beau (USA)**[7] 4534 7-10-10 **54** 6ex............... MissJWalton 13 35
(Michael Chapman) *chsd ldr: wknd over 1f out* **8/1**

-005 **10** *2 ½* **The Blue Banana (IRE)**[25] 3949 5-11-2 **60**...............(b) PhillipDennis 4 35
(Edwin Tuer) *midfield: rdn over 3f out: wknd over 2f out* **4/1**[2]

-000 **11** *12* **Gifted Heir (IRE)**[7] 4534 10-9-13 **47** oh1.................. MissSPeacock(3) 1
(Ray Peacock) *slowly away: hld up: a bhd* **100/1**

0-00 **12** *2* **Jewelled Dagger (IRE)**[97] 1674 10-9-13 **46** oh1...(t) MissCWatling(3) 11
(Sharon Watt) *hld up: a bhd* **20/1**

1m 37.9s (1.30) **Going Correction** -0.15s/f (Firm) 12 Ran SP% **116.3**
Speed ratings (Par 101): **87,84,83,79,79 77,76,75,75,72 60,58**
CSF £160.28 CT £670.32 TOTE £5.50: £3.70, £6.70, £2.30; EX 146.00 Trifecta £893.00.
**Owner** T T Racing **Bred** Bolton Grange **Trained** Tadcaster, N Yorks

**FOCUS**
A low-grade amateur handicap saw a gamble landed, the winner making all the running. The form makes some sense.
T/Plt: £5,730.00 to a £1 stake. Pool: £58870.32 - 7.50 winning tickets T/Qpdt: £23.00 to a £1 stake. Pool: £5104.58 - 164.10 winning tickets AS

# 4583 SANDOWN (R-H)

Wednesday, July 30

**OFFICIAL GOING: Good to firm (8.7)**

Wind: Light, against Weather: Fine, very warm

## 4798 SLUG AND LETTUCE 2-4-1 COCKTAILS APPRENTICE H'CAP 1m 14y

5:50 (5:51) (Class 5) (0-70,69) 4-Y-0+ £3,234 (£962; £481; £240) Stalls Low

Form RPR

3212 1 **Who's That Chick (IRE)**7 4548 5-9-12 69 OisinMurphy 9 76
(Ralph J Smith) *trckd ldr after 2f: led over 2f out and drvn for home: 2 l clr over 1f out: looked vulnerable ins fnl f: hld on* 3/1[2]

5620 2 ½ **Lady Sylvia**33 3678 5-9-3 65 JennyPowell(5) 1 71+
(Joseph Tuite) *hld up in last trio: stdy prog on inner fr 2f out: r.o to take 2nd cl home: clsd on wnr but nvr quite got there* 9/1

205 3 ½ **Polydamos**2 4738 5-8-4 52 JordanVaughan(5) 7 57
(Tony Carroll) *trckd ldng trio: prog to go 2nd over 1f out: grad clsd on wnr but lost 2nd nr fin* 9/1

0-60 4 ½ **Celestial Bay**16 4271 5-9-3 63 DannyBrock(3) 5 67
(Sylvester Kirk) *hld up in midfield: drvn over 2f out: prog over 1f out: wnt 3rd briefly fnl f: one pce last 100yds* 25/1

0352 5 ¾ **Appyjack**35 3576 6-8-9 52 JoeyHaynes 8 54
(Tony Carroll) *hld up in last pair: rdn on wd outside over 2f out: kpt on fr over 1f out: nvr gng pce to threaten* 16/1

2212 6 1 **Byrd In Hand (IRE)**11 4428 7-9-0 60 ShelleyBirkett(3) 2 60
(John Bridger) *trckd ldr 2f: styd cl up: nt qckn 2f out: rdn and kpt on same pce fnl f* 8/1[3]

5241 7 ¾ **Living Leader**4 4673 5-9-5 69 6ex (p) RobHornby(7) 6 67
(Grace Harris) *settled in midfield: shkn up wl over 1f out w wnr already gone: kpt on fnl f: n.d* 9/4[1]

0-16 8 2 **Overrider**89 1923 4-9-0 57 (t) WilliamTwiston-Davies 3 50
(Paul Cole) *led: rdn and hdd over 2f out: lost 2nd over 1f out: fdd fnl f* 25/1

310U 9 2¼ **Mitchell**39 3485 4-8-11 59 (p) RobJFitzpatrick(5) 10 47
(K R Burke) *hld up in midfield on outer: rdn over 2f out: wknd and edgd rt over 1f out* 8/1[3]

146 10 5 **Supa Seeker (USA)**60 2770 8-8-1 51 RussellHarris(7) 4 28
(Tony Carroll) *t.k.h: restrained into last and sn detached: pushed along and no prog over 2f out* 33/1

1m 42.38s (-0.92) **Going Correction** -0.025s/f (Good) 10 Ran SP% 114.5
Speed ratings (Par 103): **103,102,102,101,100 99,99,97,94,89**
CSF £28.83 CT £222.80 TOTE £2.90: £1.50, £3.50, £2.40; EX 34.00 Trifecta £418.80.
**Owner** Piper, Churchill, Hirschfeld **Bred** T Hirschfeld **Trained** Epsom, Surrey

**FOCUS**
Some consistent, if only moderate performers on show. Straightforward form. Sprint course at full width. Round course railed out 4yds from 9f to Winning Post and distances increased by 8yds on Round course.

## 4799 SLUG AND LETTUCE BOOK FOR CHRISTMAS H'CAP 1m 2f 7y

6:25 (6:28) (Class 5) (0-75,75) 4-Y-0+ £3,234 (£962; £481; £240) Stalls Low

Form RPR

3304 1 **Play Street**20 4116 5-8-10 71 NedCurtis(7) 3 78
(Jonathan Portman) *trckd ldr: led 2f out: hrd pressed fnl f: jst hld on* 4/1

6632 2 hd **Ashkalara**28 3853 7-7-13 56 oh7 JoeyHaynes(3) 7 63
(Stuart Howe) *cl up in 4th: shkn up to chal 2f out: edgd lft and nt qckn sn after: renewed effrt fnl f: clsd on wnr fin: jst failed* 10/1

5105 3 1 **Taro Tywod (IRE)**22 4045 5-9-6 74 TomQueally 4 79
(Mark Brisbourne) *trckd ldng pair to over 2f out: nt qckn and lost pl: rallied u.p 1f out: kpt on but no real imp nr fin* 10/1

1031 4 ½ **Cataria Girl (USA)**20 4105 5-8-3 64 (t) JordanVaughan(7) 5 68
(Marcus Tregoning) *fractious bef ent stalls: hld up in last pair: tried to make prog on inner fr 2f out but nt enough room: kpt on whn in the clr fnl f: no ch* 11/4[1]

30-6 5 1 **Purple 'n Gold (IRE)**14 4331 5-9-7 75 (b) JimCrowley 6 77
(David Pipe) *hld up in last pair: cl enough and pushed along 2f out: drvn and nt qckn jst over 1f out* 10/3[2]

3445 6 nk **Tilstarr (IRE)**11 4434 4-9-3 71 OisinMurphy 1 72
(Roger Teal) *led to 2f out: steadily lost pl fr over 1f out* 7/2[3]

2m 9.23s (-1.27) **Going Correction** -0.025s/f (Good) 6 Ran SP% 110.1
Speed ratings (Par 103): **104,103,103,102,101 101**
CSF £38.59 TOTE £4.60: £2.40, £4.20; EX 44.00 Trifecta £246.10.
**Owner** Anthony Boswood **Bred** The Hon Mrs R Pease **Trained** Upper Lambourn, Berks

**FOCUS**
A trappy middle-distance handicap with only 1.25 points separating the first four in the betting. Very ordinary form.

## 4800 SLUG AND LETTUCE/BRITISH STALLION STUDS EBF MAIDEN STKS 7f 16y

6:55 (6:58) (Class 5) 2-Y-0 £3,881 (£1,155; £577; £288) Stalls Low

Form RPR

4 1 **Latharnach (USA)**19 4167 2-9-5 0 WilliamBuick 6 88+
(Charlie Appleby) *trckd ldr: upsides 2f out gng wl: led 1f out: nudged along to assert last 100yds* 8/15[1]

43 2 2½ **Tom Hark (FR)**26 3929 2-9-5 0 PatDobbs 7 79
(Richard Hannon) *led: jnd and shkn up 2f out: hdd 1f out: no ch w wnr but kpt on* 7/2[2]

3 2¾ **Elm Park** 2-9-5 0 DavidProbert 2 74+
(Andrew Balding) *trckd ldrs: shkn up 2f out: rn green after tl picked up fnl f and r.o to take 3rd nr fin* 7/1[3]

4 1 **Able Spirit** 2-9-5 0 MartinDwyer 3 69+
(Brian Meehan) *trckd ldng pair: shkn up 2f out: rn green and no imp after: lost 3rd nr fin* 20/1

5 2¾ **Master Zephyr** 2-9-5 0 JamesDoyle 4 61+
(Roger Charlton) *slowly away: mostly in last trio: effrt on outer over 2f out: no hdwy over 1f out: fdd* 33/1

6 6 3 **Duc De Seville (IRE)**41 3381 2-9-5 0 AdamKirby 9 53
(Clive Cox) *green preliminaries: trckd ldrs: shkn up and wknd 2f out* 25/1

7 nk **Referendum (IRE)** 2-9-5 0 JimCrowley 1 53
(Sir Michael Stoute) *slowly away: hld up in rr: reminder over 2f out: last sn after: nvr a factor* 10/1

8 1 **Memories Galore (IRE)** 2-9-5 0 TedDurcan 5 50
(Harry Dunlop) *green preliminaries: slowest away: hld up in last: outpcd fr over 2f out* 33/1

1m 31.65s (2.15) **Going Correction** -0.025s/f (Good) 8 Ran SP% 123.5
Speed ratings (Par 94): **86,83,80,78,75 72,71,70**
CSF £2.92 TOTE £1.70: £1.02, £1.10, £3.30; EX 3.10 Trifecta £13.50.
**Owner** Godolphin **Bred** Darley **Trained** Newmarket, Suffolk

**FOCUS**
A fair maiden in which the pace held up. The winner built on his good debut.

## 4801 SLUG AND LETTUCE TUESDAYS 2-4-1 CURRIES H'CAP (BOBIS RACE) 1m 14y

7:30 (7:30) (Class 3) (0-90,88) 3-Y-0 £7,439 (£2,213; £1,106; £553) Stalls Low

Form RPR

2121 1 **Halation (IRE)**32 3719 3-9-4 85 JamieSpencer 5 94
(David Simcock) *hld up in last: shkn up over 2f out: prog on outer wl over 1f out: drvn to ld jst ins fnl f: styd on* 2/1[1]

2106 2 1 **Bowie Boy (IRE)**21 4074 3-8-11 78 (p) JimCrowley 3 84
(Ralph Beckett) *trckd ldr: rdn wl over 2f out: grad clsd u.p over 1f out: upsides jst ins fnl f: chsd wnr after: kpt on* 14/1

0036 3 1½ **Master The World (IRE)**18 4198 3-9-7 88 (v1) LiamKeniry 1 91
(David Elsworth) *sn led and racd freely at gd pce: had rest at work whn 2 l clr 2f out: drvn over 1f out: hdd and no ex jst ins fnl f* 3/1[2]

2321 4 1 **Biotic**14 4329 3-8-2 69 oh1 DavidProbert 6 70
(Rod Millman) *hld up in 5th: rdn over 2f out: sme prog and cl up over 1f out: no ex fnl f* 4/1[3]

3635 5 1¾ **Carthage (IRE)**31 3750 3-8-12 79 (b1) PatDobbs 2 76
(Richard Hannon) *in tch: rdn and nt qckn over 2f out: nvr any imp on ldrs: one pce* 10/1

1100 6 2 **Zerfaal**19 4147 3-9-3 84 (b1) DaneO'Neill 8 76
(John Gosden) *trckd ldng pair: rdn over 2f out: lost pl wl over 1f out: wknd fnl f* 6/1

1m 41.73s (-1.57) **Going Correction** -0.025s/f (Good) 6 Ran SP% 108.4
Speed ratings (Par 104): **106,105,103,102,100 98**
CSF £27.17 CT £71.24 TOTE £2.90: £1.80, £3.10; EX 19.90 Trifecta £64.70.
**Owner** Qatar Racing Limited **Bred** Sheikh Sultan Bin Khalifa Al Nayhan **Trained** Newmarket, Suffolk

**FOCUS**
A strong staying effort from the progressive winner. The second and fourth help with the level.

## 4802 SLUG AND LETTUCE WEDNESDAY WINEDOWN £11.45 FILLIES' H'CAP 1m 1f

8:00 (8:01) (Class 5) (0-75,75) 3-Y-0+ £3,881 (£1,155; £577; £288) Stalls Low

Form RPR

-403 1 **Special Miss**30 3803 3-8-9 65 JimCrowley 3 70
(Ali Stronge) *sn trckd ldr: led 2f out: rdn and in command jst over 1f out: ld shortening at fin but nvr seriously threatened* 11/4[2]

3-04 2 ¾ **Dianora**40 3423 3-9-4 74 TedDurcan 6 78
(Sir Michael Stoute) *hld up in last pair: rdn and prog 2f out: chsd wnr fnl f: styd on but nvr able to chal* 6/1

6536 3 1 **Dalmarella Dancer (IRE)**10 4472 3-8-13 72 (v) JoeyHaynes(3) 2 75
(K R Burke) *sn hld up in 3rd: tried for a run on inner and nt clr run wl over 1f out: kpt on again fnl f: nvr able to chal* 11/2

042 4 nse **Petticoat Lane**21 4089 3-9-0 70 AdamKirby 1 72+
(Luca Cumani) *hld up in last pair: tried to make prog on inner jst over 2f out but nowhere to go: nt clr run over 1f out and swtchd lft: threatened to cl fnl f: one pce last 100yds* 5/2[1]

2-36 5 4 **Song Of Norway**71 2431 3-9-5 75 SteveDrowne 5 68
(Peter Makin) *led: rdn: hdd and edgd rt 2f out: wknd jst over 1f out* 3/1[3]

1m 56.11s (0.41) **Going Correction** -0.025s/f (Good) 5 Ran SP% 109.9
Speed ratings (Par 100): **97,96,95,95,91**
CSF £18.21 TOTE £2.80: £2.20, £3.30; EX 18.40 Trifecta £54.50.
**Owner** Tim Dykes **Bred** Team Valor **Trained** Eastbury, Berks

■ Stewards' Enquiry : Joey Haynes one-day ban: careless riding (Aug 13)
Steve Drowne one-day ban: careless riding (Aug 13)

**FOCUS**
Only a handful of runners but this developed into a messy, tactical affair. Ordinary form.

## 4803 DEVINE HOMES H'CAP (BOBIS RACE) 1m 6f

8:35 (8:35) (Class 4) (0-80,80) 3-Y-0 £4,851 (£1,443; £721; £360) Stalls Low

Form RPR

2135 1 **Sebastian Beach (IRE)**27 3892 3-9-7 80 PatDobbs 6 87
(Richard Hannon) *led 1f: 4th 1/2-way: prog to ld over 2f out: hrd pressed on both sides fr over 1f out: edgd rt last 100yds: hld on gamely* 10/3[2]

1352 2 ¾ **Cosette (IRE)**18 4209 3-9-3 76 DaneO'Neill 1 82
(Henry Candy) *hld up in tch: rdn and prog over 2f out: chal and upsides wnr jst over 1f out: nt qckn ins fnl f* 9/2[3]

0102 3 ½ **Taws**20 4134 3-8-5 64 JoeFanning 7 70
(Rod Millman) *led after 1f to 9f out: drvn over 2f out: rallied over 1f out: pressed wnr fnl f: stl trying to chal but hld whn hmpd last 50yds* 9/2[3]

0530 4 1¼ **Arcamante (ITY)**14 4332 3-8-4 70 (e) RobJFitzpatrick(7) 4 74
(K R Burke) *reluctant to go to s: hld up in last: nt clr run on inner over 2f out: swtchd lft and edgd lft sn after: fnlly mde prog to take 4th fnl f: no imp last 75yds* 16/1

4131 5 ¾ **Spectator**18 4189 3-9-3 76 (p) OisinMurphy 2 78
(Andrew Balding) *hld up in tch: effrt on outer over 2f out: nt qckn wl over 1f out: one pce after* 5/2[1]

0152 6 9 **Frederic Chopin**14 4333 3-8-6 65 (t) DavidProbert 9 55
(Stuart Williams) *cl up: led 9f out to over 2f out: wknd qckly jst over 1f out* 8/1

1353 7 10 **Ujagar (IRE)**27 3884 3-9-3 76 (b) RichardKingscote 10 52
(Tom Dascombe) *t.k.h: prog to chse ldr 8f out to over 2f out: wknd qckly: t.o* 14/1

3m 5.61s (1.11) **Going Correction** -0.025s/f (Good) 7 Ran SP% 111.7
Speed ratings (Par 102): **95,94,94,93,93 88,82**
CSF £17.71 CT £64.99 TOTE £4.50: £1.90, £2.60; EX 20.20 Trifecta £129.60.
**Owner** Justin Dowley & Michael Pescod **Bred** Conor Murphy & Rathmore Stud **Trained** East Everleigh, Wilts

■ Stewards' Enquiry : Pat Dobbs two-day ban: careless riding (Aug 13-14)

**FOCUS**
Another steadily run race on the card and another close finish. The form is rated as straightforward.

T/Plt: £171.90 to a £1 stake. Pool: £59,800 - 253.83 winning tickets T/Qpdt: £13.00 to a £1 stake. Pool: £7,487 - 424.50 winning tickets JN

4804 - (Foreign Racing) - See Raceform Interactive

## 4770 GALWAY (R-H)

### Wednesday, July 30

**OFFICIAL GOING: Good (good to firm in places nh course)**

## 4805a TOTE TRIFECTA ROLLOVER H'CAP — 1m 100y
**6:05** (6:08) (50-70,70) 4-Y-O+ — **£7,187** (£1,666; £729; £416)

RPR

1 **Cairdiuil (IRE)**[21] 4100 8-9-9 **65** ... WayneLordan 6 73
(I Madden, Ire) *chsd ldrs: rdn into 2nd 2f out and clsd u.p to ld fnl 100yds: kpt on wl towards fin* **9/1**[3]

2 1 1/4 **Tahaf (IRE)**[20] 4136 4-9-2 **58** ...(bt[1]) SeamieHeffernan 16 63
(Denis Gerard Hogan, Ire) *tacked over to trck ldr in 2nd: led 2f out: nt helped by loose horse and swtchd rt 1 1/2f out: sn strly pressed u.p and hdd fnl 100yds: sn no ex* **16/1**

3 5 1/2 **Prime Exhibit**[19] 4156 9-9-11 **67** ...(t) FMBerry 3 60
(Daniel Mark Loughnane) *hld up towards rr: rdn in 13th over 2f out and r.o wl ins fnl f: nrst fin* **10/1**

4 nk **Truly Delightful (IRE)**[9] 4507 4-9-12 **68** ... RoryCleary 11 60
(Thomas Cleary, Ire) *hld up in rr of mid-div: rdn into mod 6th over 2f out and wnt mod 4th u.p ins fnl f: kpt on same pce* **12/1**

5 3/4 **Al Fahidi (IRE)**[180] 417 4-9-3 **62** ...(p) ConorHoban[(3)] 2 53
(A Oliver, Ire) *chsd ldrs: rdn in 5th over 2f out and no imp on ldrs into st: kpt on one pce* **25/1**

6 1 1/4 **Longfield Lad (IRE)**[68] 2536 4-9-5 **61** ... RonanWhelan 8 49
(John J Walsh, Ire) *chsd ldrs: rdn in 7th over 2f out and no imp on ldrs into st: kpt on one pce* **14/1**

7 1 1/4 **Badger Daly (IRE)**[29] 3836 8-9-5 **66** ...(p) RossCoakley[(5)] 18 51
(J R Hagan, Ire) *sn led: hdd 2f out and sn dropped to 3rd: wknd fnl f* **14/1**

8 1/2 **Mizyen (IRE)**[22] 2970 4-9-11 **67** ... EmmetMcNamara 14 51
(D T Hughes, Ire) *towards rr: rdn and sme hdwy on outer fr over 2f out: kpt on one pce ins fnl f* **14/1**

9 1 3/4 **Postillion (IRE)**[13] 4372 6-9-3 **62** ...(b[1]) ShaneGorey[(3)] 4 42
(J F O'Shea, Ire) *hld up: rdn and no imp towards rr over 2f out: mod 12th into st: kpt on one pce fnl f* **50/1**

10 2 1/2 **Connacht Council (IRE)**[41] 3411 4-9-11 **70** ...(bt) LeighRoche[(3)] 1 45
(W McCreery, Ire) *chsd ldrs: rdn in 4th over 2f out and sn no ex u.p: wknd fnl f* **10/1**

11 2 **The Black Devil (IRE)**[12] 1254 5-10-0 **70** ...(p) ColinKeane 17 40
(Gerard Keane, Ire) *chsd ldrs: pushed along in 7th 5f out and no ex over 2f out: wknd* **16/1**

12 4 1/4 **Danseur De Feu (IRE)**[16] 4275 4-9-13 **69** ...(t) ChrisHayes 13 30
(Kevin Prendergast, Ire) *racd in mid-div: rdn in 8th and no imp 2f out: wknd* **20/1**

13 2 1/2 **Moonbi Creek (IRE)**[46] 3260 7-9-9 **65** ... PatSmullen 15 20
(D K Weld, Ire) *hld up: rdn in 11th over 2f out and no imp into st: one pce fnl f* **11/2**[2]

14 3 1/4 **Sister Slew (IRE)**[26] 3942 4-9-11 **67** ... DavyCondon 12 15
(Gordon Elliott, Ire) *hld up: pushed along in 12th over 2f out and no imp into st* **7/2**[1]

15 4 1/2 **Halul**[29] 3837 4-9-9 **65** ... GaryCarroll 10
(A Oliver, Ire) *a towards rr: nt clr run appr st: one pce* **25/1**

16 4 1/2 **Hughies Bay (IRE)**[51] 3069 4-8-12 **59** ... GaryPhillips[(5)] 5
(Garvan Donnelly, Ire) *chsd ldrs: rdn in 5th 3f out and sn wknd* **40/1**

U **Cool Athlete (IRE)**[7] 4559 8-9-5 **64** ...(b) ConnorKing[(3)] 9
(David Marnane, Ire) *in rr of mid-div: short of room clipped heels and stmbld between horses 5f out and uns rdr* **12/1**

U **Victor's Beach (IRE)**[13] 4372 4-9-4 **60** ...(tp) ShaneFoley 7
(M Halford, Ire) *rrd and uns rdr in stall* **16/1**

1m 49.36s (-0.84) — **18 Ran SP% 135.7**
CSF £151.55 CT £1516.56 TOTE £11.50: £2.50, £4.40, £3.00, £2.10; DF 283.30 Trifecta £4195.80.
**Owner** Ms S V Kempe & Rodney Schofield & Miss K Wilson & **Bred** J S Bolger **Trained** Castlegar, Co Galway

**FOCUS**
They went off at a good clip in a typical Galway handicap where luck in running was at a premium. The first two have been rated close to their best.

4806 - 4807a (Foreign Racing) - See Raceform Interactive

## 4351 EPSOM (L-H)

### Thursday, July 31

**OFFICIAL GOING: Good to firm**
Wind: Moderate, across Weather: Fine, very warm

## 4808 EPSOM BUTTERFIELD APPRENTICE H'CAP — 1m 2f 18y
**5:55** (5:55) (Class 5) (0-70,70) 4-Y-O+ — **£3,881** (£1,155; £577; £288) **Stalls Low**

Form — RPR

2243 1 **Cherry Princess**[2] 4763 4-8-9 **53** ... RobertTart 7 61
(Stuart Williams) *trckd ldng pair: brought towards nr side in st and lost pl 3f out: rallied 2f out: rdn to ld ins fnl f: hung lft but hld on* **5/2**[2]

340/ 2 hd **Marzante (USA)**[1156] 2607 6-9-12 **70** ... AshleyMorgan 1 77
(Roger Charlton) *led: hrd pressed over 2f out: fought on wl but hdd ins fnl f: rallied nr fin* **5/1**[3]

4113 3 1 1/2 **Last Minute Lisa (IRE)**[14] 4351 4-9-5 **63** ... RossAtkinson 8 68
(Sylvester Kirk) *hld up in last: prog over 2f out: rdn to chal over 1f out: nt qckn ins fnl f* **5/4**[1]

463 4 nk **Anginola (IRE)**[14] 4341 5-8-2 **51** ...(p) CharlotteJenner[(5)] 2 55
(Laura Mongan) *trckd ldng trio: prog to chse ldr 2f out: chal and upsides over 1f out tl nt qckn last 100yds* **10/1**

6-55 5 2 1/4 **Young Dottie**[21] 4118 8-9-0 **65** ... PaddyBradley[(7)] 6 65
(Pat Phelan) *hld up in 5th: shkn up over 2f out: chsd ldrs after but no imp: fdd last 150yds* **8/1**

0060 6 2 1/4 **Divine Rule (IRE)**[5] 4658 6-8-0 **51** oh2 ... SophieRalston[(7)] 4 46
(Laura Mongan) *hld up in 6th: prog to press ldr briefly over 2f out: wknd over 1f out* **20/1**

0-00 7 11 **Market Puzzle (IRE)**[80] 2212 7-8-0 **51** oh6 ... GaryMahon[(7)] 5 26
(Mark Brisbourne) *trckd ldr: upsides jst over 3f out: wknd qckly over 2f out* **33/1**

2m 8.34s (-1.36) **Going Correction** -0.15s/f (Firm) — **7 Ran SP% 117.6**
Speed ratings (Par 103): **99,98,97,97,95 93,85**
CSF £16.19 CT £22.01 TOTE £3.30: £2.40, £2.50; EX 17.00 Trifecta £39.70.
**Owner** B Piper & D Shekells **Bred** Old Mill Stud **Trained** Newmarket, Suffolk

**FOCUS**
This modest apprentice riders' handicap was a very messy affair. Just about a personal best from the winner. Rail dolled out up to 6yds from 1m to Winning Post adding 20yds to race distances.

## 4809 IRISH CHAMPIONS WEEKEND EBF MAIDEN STKS — 7f
**6:25** (6:27) (Class 5) 2-Y-O — **£3,881** (£1,155; £577; £288) **Stalls Low**

Form — RPR

1 **Make It Up** 2-9-2 0 ... ThomasBrown[(3)] 3 82+
(Andrew Balding) *w ldr: led 3f out: sent for home jst over 2f out: styd on fnl f and a holding on* **6/1**[3]

3622 2 1/2 **Silver Ranger**[14] 4353 2-9-5 85 ... RichardHughes 5 81
(Richard Hannon) *trckd ldrs in 5th: plld out wd and asked for effrt over 1f out: r.o to take 2nd ins fnl f: clsd on wnr fin but too much to do* **1/1**[1]

632 3 1 1/2 **Big Chill (IRE)**[19] 4207 2-9-2 81 ... RobertTart[(3)] 9 77
(Charles Hills) *pressed ldr on outer: wnt 2nd jst over 2f out: rdn and no imp on wnr over 1f out: lost 2nd ins fnl f: kpt on* **11/4**[2]

6 4 6 **Rocky Desert (IRE)**[33] 3701 2-9-0 0 ... DanielMuscutt[(5)] 2 61
(Marco Botti) *dwlt: sn trckd ldng trio: shkn up and nt qckn over 2f out: lost grnd fr over 1f out* **20/1**

0 5 3 1/4 **Colours Of Glory (IRE)**[12] 4444 2-9-0 0 ... WilliamCarson 7 47+
(Charles Hills) *dwlt: in tch: cl 6th st: wknd over 2f out* **33/1**

0 6 nk **Hillgrove Angel (IRE)**[17] 4270 2-9-2 0 ... RyanClark[(3)] 1 51
(Brian Meehan) *led to 3f out: wknd wl over 1f out* **20/1**

0 7 1/2 **Yukon Gold**[13] 4389 2-9-5 0 ... MartinLane 4 50
(Charlie Appleby) *awkward s: a in last pair and hanging downhill: detached last st: nvr a factor* **7/1**

6 8 1 1/4 **Prince Of Paris**[36] 3578 2-9-5 0 ... ChrisCatlin 8 46
(Roger Ingram) *sn in last pair and nt travel wl downhill: detached in 7th st: bhd after* **33/1**

1m 24.14s (0.84) **Going Correction** -0.15s/f (Firm) — **8 Ran SP% 118.9**
Speed ratings (Par 94): **89,88,86,79,76 75,75,73**
CSF £12.55 TOTE £10.30: £2.60, £1.02, £1.20; EX 15.60 Trifecta £54.70.
**Owner** George Strawbridge **Bred** George Strawbridge **Trained** Kingsclere, Hants

**FOCUS**
With the principals coming well clear this looks straightforward enough maiden form, rated around the second.

## 4810 TOTEPOOL BET ON UK RACING H'CAP — 1m 114y
**6:55** (6:56) (Class 4) (0-80,80) 3-Y-O+ — **£6,469** (£1,925; £962; £481) **Stalls Low**

Form — RPR

315 1 **Potentate (IRE)**[20] 4169 3-9-2 **77** ... RichardHughes 6 84
(Richard Hannon) *hld up: last st: sn pushed along: struggling over 1f out: r.o wl fnl f to ld last strides* **3/1**[2]

-341 2 1/2 **Express Himself (IRE)**[27] 3925 3-9-5 **80** ... SteveDrowne 5 86
(Ed McMahon) *hld up: 5th st: prog 2f out: rdn to ld jst ins fnl f: styd on but hdd last strides* **6/1**[3]

0032 3 1/2 **Al Mukhdam**[19] 4190 4-9-10 **76** ... JamieSpencer 2 82
(Ed de Giles) *led: shkn up over 2f out: hdd jst ins fnl f: styd on but outpcd nr fin* **7/1**

6644 4 1/2 **Mime Dance**[40] 3455 3-8-13 **74** ... DavidProbert 4 78
(Andrew Balding) *trckd ldr: chal 2f out upsides 1f out: nt qckn last 150yds* **3/1**[2]

4462 5 3/4 **King Of Macedon (IRE)**[6] 4628 3-9-0 **75** ...(v[1]) JoeFanning 1 80+
(Mark Johnston) *trckd ldng pair: gng wl bhd them over 2f out tl nowhere to go over 1f out and again jst ins fnl f: no ch to rcvr* **5/2**[1]

3033 6 1 1/2 **Bayleyf (IRE)**[14] 4352 5-8-7 **66** ...(p) CharlotteJenner[(7)] 3 66
(Lee Carter) *t.k.h: hld up in 4th: shkn up over 2f out: nt qckn wl over 1f out: one pce* **12/1**

1m 43.57s (-2.53) **Going Correction** -0.15s/f (Firm)
**WFA** 3 from 4yo+ 9lb — **6 Ran SP% 113.0**
Speed ratings (Par 105): **105,104,104,103,103 101**
CSF £21.02 TOTE £3.40: £1.50, £3.20; EX 17.00 Trifecta £53.60.
**Owner** Saleh Al Homaizi & Imad Al Sagar **Bred** Mrs Celine Collins **Trained** East Everleigh, Wilts

**FOCUS**
This tricky looking handicap was run at a fair pace and it saw changing fortunes inside the final furlong. The third sets the standard.

## 4811 EBF STALLIONS BREEDING WINNERS FILLIES' H'CAP — 7f
**7:30** (7:30) (Class 4) (0-80,80) 3-Y-O+ — **£6,469** (£1,925; £962; £481) **Stalls Low**

Form — RPR

3242 1 **Lady Crossmar (IRE)**[5] 4655 3-8-6 **65** ... KieranO'Neill 3 71
(Richard Hannon) *hld up in 4th: clsd on ldrs 2f out and pushed along: rdn to chal fnl f: narrow ld last 75yds: styd on* **5/2**[2]

1561 2 hd **First Experience**[8] 4535 3-9-1 **74** 6ex ... KierenFallon 2 80
(Rae Guest) *t.k.h: hld up in last: clsd on ldrs and pushed along 2f out: nvr much room but urged along to chal fnl f: upsides 100yds out: jst hld nr fin* **5/4**[1]

3 3/4 **Amygdala (USA)**[46] 3282 3-9-7 **80** ... JamieSpencer 5 84
(Stuart Williams) *trckd ldr: led 2f out gong strly: shkn up over 1f out: hdd and nt qckn last 75yds* **7/2**[3]

6632 4 1 1/2 **Welsh Inlet (IRE)**[14] 4342 6-8-10 **62** ... WilliamCarson 1 65
(John Bridger) *trckd ldng pair: dropped to last over 2f out and pushed along: nvr on terms w ldrs after: kpt on ins fnl f* **7/1**

4036 5 1 3/4 **Lady Phill**[8] 4545 4-9-0 **66** ... JoeFanning 4 65
(Michael Attwater) *led to 2f out: wknd fnl f* **14/1**

1m 24.05s (0.75) **Going Correction** -0.15s/f (Firm)
**WFA** 3 from 4yo+ 7lb — **5 Ran SP% 114.4**
Speed ratings (Par 102): **89,88,87,86,84**
CSF £6.36 TOTE £3.80: £2.10, £1.20; EX 7.80 Trifecta £17.60.
**Owner** Middleham Park Racing Vi **Bred** Scuderia San Pancrazio **Trained** East Everleigh, Wilts

**FOCUS**
A modest little fillies' handicap, run at a steady early pace. The form is not sure to prove solid.

## 4812 SHIRLEY INGRAM MEMORIAL H'CAP — 1m 4f 10y
**8:05** (8:06) (Class 5) (0-75,74) 3-Y-O+ — **£4,204** (£1,251; £625; £312) **Stalls Centre**

Form — RPR

4-06 1 **Mustamir (IRE)**[40] 3466 3-8-13 **71** ...(b[1]) KierenFallon 2 82
(James Tate) *trckd ldng pair after 5f: clsd fr 3f out to ld wl over 1f out: sn pushed clr: comf* **7/1**

331 2 4 1/2 **Nave (USA)**[14] 4351 7-10-0 **74** ... MartinLane 1 78
(David Simcock) *hld up in last: wnt 4th st: sn rdn and nt qckn: kpt on fnl 2f to take 2nd last 75yds: no ch w wnr* **2/1**[1]

3233 3 1 1/4 **Loch Ma Naire (IRE)**[14] 4354 3-9-1 **73** ...(b) RichardHughes 5 75
(Ed Dunlop) *led at gd pce: tried to kick on over 3f out: hdd wl over 1f out: no ch w wnr after: fdd and lost 2nd last 75yds* **5/2**[3]

2543 **4** 4 **Castle Combe (IRE)**[30] 3814 3-9-2 **74**......................(v) MartinDwyer 3 70
(Marcus Tregoning) *chsd ldr to jst over 2f out: sn wknd* **9/4**[2]

6505 **5** 6 **Softly She Treads (IRE)**[56] 2927 3-8-0 **58** oh2...........(v) KieranO'Neill 4 44
(Pat Phelan) *chsd ldng pair 5f: dropped to last st: sn btn* **14/1**

2m 37.94s (-0.96) **Going Correction** -0.15s/f (Firm)
**WFA** 3 from 7yo 12lb **5** Ran SP% **111.8**
Speed ratings (Par 103): **97,94,93,90,86**
CSF £21.70 TOTE £9.80: £2.80, £1.60; EX 29.30 Trifecta £89.40.
**Owner** Sheikh Rashid Dalmook Al Maktoum **Bred** Shadwell Estate Company Limited **Trained** Newmarket, Suffolk

**FOCUS**
This moderate handicap was a muddling affair, and the form is not entirely convincing.

## 4813 HEADLEY COURT H'CAP 7f
**8:35** (8:36) (Class 5) (0-75,73) 3-Y-O **£4,204** (£1,251; £625; £312) **Stalls** Low

Form RPR

0-33 **1** **Weekendatbernies (IRE)**[31] 3804 3-9-7 **73**.................. JamieSpencer 8 79
(Ed de Giles) *trckd ldr: chal 2f out: drvn over 1f out: sustained effrt to ld last 100yds* **7/4**[1]

2412 **2** ½ **Royal Connection**[10] 4503 3-9-5 **71**.......................... RichardHughes 1 75
(Richard Hannon) *led: shkn up whn pressed 2f out: drvn and kpt on fr over 1f out: hdd and hld last 100yds* **3/1**[2]

3-32 **3** 1 ¼ **Hipz (IRE)**[31] 3800 3-8-12 **64**.................................. LiamJones 6 65
(Laura Mongan) *chsd ldrs: 4th st: rdn and nt qckn jst over 2f out: kpt on fnl f to take 3rd nr fin* **10/1**

2300 **4** ¾ **Jersey Brown (IRE)**[15] 4329 3-8-11 **66**.................. CharlesBishop(3) 2 65
(Mick Channon) *t.k.h: trckd ldrs: 3rd st: chal jst over 2f out: upsides over 1f out: nt qckn fnl f* **6/1**

3041 **5** 1 ¼ **Bishan Bedi (IRE)**[14] 4365 3-9-2 **68**.............................. MartinDwyer 7 64
(William Jarvis) *dwlt: hld up: 5th st: shkn up over 2f out: hanging and nt qckn over 1f out: one pce* **4/1**[3]

5546 **6** ½ **Spinning Cobblers**[48] 3198 3-8-6 **58**.............................. HarryBentley 5 52
(Stuart Williams) *hld up: last st: rdn 3f out: no imp after: one pce* **10/1**

1m 23.94s (0.64) **Going Correction** -0.15s/f (Firm) **6** Ran SP% **113.8**
Speed ratings (Par 100): **90,89,88,87,85 85**
CSF £7.39 CT £37.95 TOTE £2.70: £1.20, £2.20; EX 9.40 Trifecta £33.30.
**Owner** Alex Ridgers & Robert Jones **Bred** Catesby W Clay **Trained** Ledbury, H'fords

**FOCUS**
Straightforward form for the class. The first pair were always prominent.
T/Plt: £33.10 to a £1 stake. Pool: £60,642.55 - 1335.31 winning units. T/Qpdt: £6.90 to a £1 stake. Pool: £5791.93 - 614.10 winning units. JN

# 3778 FFOS LAS (L-H)
### Thursday, July 31

**OFFICIAL GOING: Good to firm (8.7)**
Wind: fresh half against Weather: overcast

## 4814 32RED PAYS THE LEVY/EBF STALLIONS MAIDEN STKS 5f
**5:40** (5:44) (Class 5) 2-Y-O **£2,911** (£866; £432) **Stalls** Centre

Form RPR

2 **1** **Judicial (IRE)**[28] 3889 2-9-5 0.................................. GeorgeBaker 1 83+
(Roger Charlton) *broke smartly: racd keenly: mde all: briefly jnd 2f out: shkn up appr fnl f: qckly c clr: easily* **1/10**[1]

**2** 3 ½ **Robin Park** 2-9-0 0.............................................. AdamKirby 4 58+
(Clive Cox) *v reluctant to enter stalls: dwlt sltly: sn trcking rivals: rdn and sltly outpcd over 1f out: r.o ins fnl f: tk 2nd fnl 50yds* **7/1**[2]

**3** 1 ½ **Copleys Walk (IRE)** 2-9-5 0.................................. JohnFahy 3 58
(John Joseph Murphy, Ire) *chsd wnr: rdn to chal briefly 2f out: sn brushed aside: one pce after and lost 2nd fnl 50yds* **20/1**[3]

59.49s (1.19) **Going Correction** +0.125s/f (Good) **3** Ran SP% **108.2**
Speed ratings (Par 94): **95,89,87**
CSF £1.39 TOTE £1.10; EX 2.20 Trifecta £1.80.
**Owner** Elite Racing Club **Bred** Elite Racing Club **Trained** Beckhampton, Wilts

**FOCUS**
A dry run up to a meeting staged on watered ground. A most uncompetitive maiden in which the gallop was only fair. The easy winner was value for extra and the second can leave this form behind.

## 4815 CLOGAU WELSH GOLD NURSERY H'CAP 5f
**6:15** (6:17) (Class 5) 2-Y-O **£2,587** (£770; £384; £192) **Stalls** Centre

Form RPR

41 **1** **Indaria**[36] 3583 2-9-7 **78**........................................ TedDurcan 6 82
(Rod Millman) *sn led: rdn wl over 1f out: drvn out to hold on ins fnl f* **7/4**[1]

1653 **2** nk **Low Cut Affair (IRE)**[12] 4422 2-8-5 **69**.......................... HollieDoyle(7) 5 72
(David Evans) *qckly taken to r alone against stands' rail: pushed along over 1f out: sn ev ch: drifted away fr rail fnl f: jst hld* **8/1**

2320 **3** 2 ¼ **Ar Colleen Aine**[23] 4057 2-8-13 **70**.................. WilliamTwiston-Davies 3 65
(Mick Channon) *sltly outpcd in rr: rdn over 2f out: r.o u.p ins fnl f: wnt 3rd cl home* **8/1**

4640 **4** hd **Fujiano**[41] 3415 2-8-3 **65**............................................ TimClark(5) 4 59
(Derek Haydn Jones) *t.k.h: trckd ldrs: rdn 2f out: unable qck: lost 3rd cl home* **14/1**

0552 **5** 1 ¼ **Lyfka**[7] 4576 2-7-13 **59**.......................................... RyanPowell(3) 2 49
(Paul Cole) *trckd ldrs: rdn 2f out: fdd fnl f* **3/1**[2]

4016 **6** ½ **Zebs Lad (IRE)**[12] 4430 2-9-4 **75**.................................. AdamKirby 1 63
(Ronald Harris) *led early: chsd ldrs: rdn 2f out: n.m.r over 1f out: fdd fnl f* **7/2**[3]

58.92s (0.62) **Going Correction** +0.125s/f (Good) **6** Ran SP% **112.5**
Speed ratings (Par 94): **100,99,95,95,93 92**
CSF £16.43 TOTE £2.70: £1.70, £2.80; EX 17.50 Trifecta £55.00.
**Owner** K L Dare **Bred** Poulton Farm Stud **Trained** Kentisbeare, Devon

**FOCUS**
An ordinary nursery in which the gallop was sound throughout and this form should prove reliable. All bar the runner-up raced in the centre and the first two pulled a couple of lengths clear.

## 4816 TIP TOP TOILETS/EBF STALLIONS MAIDEN STKS 6f
**6:45** (6:45) (Class 5) 3-Y-O **£3,881** (£1,155; £577; £288) **Stalls** Centre

Form RPR

**1** **Shingle** 3-9-2 0.............................................. DeclanBates(3) 4 77+
(Ed de Giles) *s.i.s: trckd ldrs: wnt 2nd 2f out: sn shkn up to ld: bounded clr fnl f: eased nr fin* **3/1**[2]

5224 **2** 8 **Go Charlie**[21] 4101 3-9-5 49.......................................... AdamKirby 5 51
(Ronald Harris) *wnt to post early: t.k.h: trckd ldr tl led after 1f: rdn over 2f out: hdd over 1f out: sn no ch w wnr: wknd towards fin but hld on for 2nd* **12/1**

45-0 **3** ½ **Wedding Wish (IRE)**[105] 1534 3-9-0 85........ WilliamTwiston-Davies 2 44
(Michael Bell) *led 1f: trckd ldr: rdn over 2f out: unable qck and sn lost 2nd: wknd fnl f* **8/13**[1]

30- **4** ½ **Retrofit**[366] 4858 3-9-5 0............................................[1] DougieCostello 1 48
(William Muir) *wnt to post early: t.k.h: last but wl in tch: rdn over 2f out: sn outpcd: styd on fnl f* **6/1**[3]

1m 10.48s (0.48) **Going Correction** +0.125s/f (Good) **4** Ran SP% **108.9**
Speed ratings (Par 100): **101,90,89,89**
CSF £26.06 TOTE £4.20; EX 15.90 Trifecta £36.20.
**Owner** T Gould **Bred** Juddmonte Farms Ltd **Trained** Ledbury, H'fords

**FOCUS**
A race that took little winning with two of the three market leaders bombing out and this is best rated round the 49-rated runner-up, but the winner impressed. The gallop was reasonable.

## 4817 CLOGAU TREE OF LIFE H'CAP 1m 2f (R)
**7:15** (7:15) (Class 5) (0-70,70) 3-Y-O **£2,587** (£770; £384; £192) **Stalls** Low

Form RPR

3034 **1** **Penny's Boy**[15] 4329 3-9-5 **68**.................................(t) LiamKeniry 5 76
(Sylvester Kirk) *racd in 5th: rdn over 2f out: chsd ldr appr fnl f: led 110yds out: r.o* **7/1**

-456 **2** 1 ¼ **Aristocracy**[13] 4388 3-8-6 **62**.............................. DanielCremin(7) 6 67
(Mick Channon) *led: rdn 3f out: kpt on gamely u.p: hdd 110yds out: no ex* **16/1**

5125 **3** 2 **Avocadeau (IRE)**[17] 4272 3-9-5 **68**........................(p) DougieCostello 2 69
(William Muir) *prom: rdn to chse ldr 3f out: unable qck and lost 2nd appr fnl f: one pce* **7/1**

6123 **4** ½ **Charlie Wells (IRE)**[14] 4350 3-9-6 **69**............................(p) JohnFahy 8 69
(Eve Johnson Houghton) *s.i.s: mid-div: rdn 4f out: styd on one pce: nvr able to chal* **2/1**[1]

1554 **5** ½ **Khee Society**[19] 4208 3-9-2 **65**.................................... AdamKirby 4 64
(David Evans) *dwlt: hld up in rr: rdn and effrt on outside over 2f out: one pce and no real imp* **3/1**[2]

5226 **6** 1 ¾ **Distant High**[19] 4191 3-8-13 **62**.................. WilliamTwiston-Davies 3 58
(Richard Price) *hld up in rr: effrt on ins over 2f out: no real imp on ldrs: fdd over 1f out* **8/1**

0162 **7** 13 **Eugenic**[19] 4210 3-8-8 **57**.......................................... TedDurcan 7 28
(Rod Millman) *trckd ldr: pushed along and lost 2nd 3f out: wknd 2f out* **6/1**[3]

2m 9.14s (-0.26) **Going Correction** -0.025s/f (Good) **7** Ran SP% **114.6**
Speed ratings (Par 100): **100,99,97,97,96 95,84**
CSF £103.15 CT £811.11 TOTE £7.30: £3.70, £10.80; EX 163.30 Trifecta £647.00.
**Owner** Malcolm Brown & Mrs Penny Brown **Bred** Peter Webb **Trained** Upper Lambourn, Berks

**FOCUS**
A modest handicap in which the gallop was on the steady side and this bare form may not be reliable. The runner-up is the best guide.

## 4818 RED LION AT LLANDYFAELOG H'CAP 2m (R)
**7:45** (7:46) (Class 4) (0-80,78) 4-Y-O+ **£4,690** (£1,395; £697; £348) **Stalls** Low

Form RPR

6000 **1** **Riptide**[12] 4441 8-9-2 **73**.......................(v) WilliamTwiston-Davies 2 81
(Michael Scudamore) *mde all: rdn along briefly 1/2-way: drvn 3f out: sn jnd: hld on gamely* **8/1**

5113 **2** ½ **Annaluna (IRE)**[15] 4322 5-8-4 **64**........................(v) DeclanBates(3) 5 72
(David Evans) *trckd wnr: pushed along over 3f out: sn ev ch: rdn on u.p: jst hld* **3/1**[2]

-252 **3** 4 **Our Folly**[29] 3851 6-9-3 **74**..................................(t) AdamKirby 1 77
(Stuart Kittow) *chsd ldng pair virtually thrght: rdn 3f out: kpt on one pce fnl 2f* **6/4**[1]

/0-0 **4** 2 ¼ **Bilidn**[12] 4441 6-9-7 **78**......................................(t) GeorgeBaker 6 78
(Ben De Haan) *hld up in last: shkn up over 2f out: unable qck: styd on fnl f: wnt 4th post* **5/1**[3]

4124 **5** hd **Taste The Wine (IRE)**[17] 3698 8-8-2 **64**................(t) PhilipPrince(5) 4 64
(Bernard Llewellyn) *s.i.s: hld up: sme hdwy over 3f out: rdn over 2f out: one pce* **6/1**

1543 **6** 5 **Captain Sharpe**[31] 3780 6-7-11 **59**..................(t) NoelGarbutt(5) 3 53
(Bernard Llewellyn) *racd mainly in 4th: pushed along 5f out: drvn over 2f out: wknd over 1f out* **14/1**

3m 34.85s (4.85) **Going Correction** -0.025s/f (Good) **6** Ran SP% **113.7**
Speed ratings (Par 105): **86,85,83,82,82 80**
CSF £32.62 TOTE £10.10: £4.20, £1.30; EX 46.30 Trifecta £344.30.
**Owner** Middletons & Robert Cocks **Bred** D Robb **Trained** Bromsash, H'fords

**FOCUS**
A fair handicap in which the gallop was a modest one to the home straight. The first two pulled clear in the closing stages. The form is rated around the second and third.

## 4819 CLOGAU 25TH ANNIVERSARY H'CAP 1m 4f (R)
**8:20** (8:20) (Class 3) (0-90,90) 3-Y-O+ **£7,439** (£2,213; £1,106; £553) **Stalls** Low

Form RPR

-252 **1** **Warrior Of Light (IRE)**[48] 3182 3-9-2 **90**...................... TedDurcan 3 103
(David Lanigan) *mde all: pushed along and qcknd pce over 3f out: styd on wl: comf* **7/4**[2]

3-31 **2** 2 **Quest For More (IRE)**[21] 4113 4-9-7 **83**..................(b[1]) GeorgeBaker 1 92
(Roger Charlton) *trckd wnr: relegated to 3rd over 5f out: wnt 2nd again over 2f out: hung lft u.p after: styd on but a being hld* **7/2**[3]

0145 **3** 6 **Shavansky**[29] 3860 10-9-6 **89**.................................. PatMillman(7) 2 88
(Rod Millman) *t.k.h: hld up: rdn over 2f out: kpt on to go 3rd 1f out: no ch w ldng pair* **16/1**

003- **4** 1 ¼ **Solaras Exhibition (IRE)**[75] 6434 6-9-2 **78**.................. DougieCostello 5 75
(Tim Vaughan) *hld up: rdn 3f out: one pce* **25/1**

12 **5** 2 **Arabian Revolution**[28] 3892 3-8-13 **87**..................(p) FergusSweeney 4 81
(Saeed bin Suroor) *trckd wnr: wnt 2nd over 5f out: hung lft u.p and lost 2nd over 2f out: wknd over 1f out* **5/4**[1]

2m 38.61s (1.21) **Going Correction** -0.025s/f (Good)
**WFA** 3 from 4yo+ 12lb **5** Ran SP% **112.8**
Speed ratings (Par 107): **94,92,88,87,86**
CSF £8.47 TOTE £3.40: £2.00, £3.10; EX 7.40 Trifecta £21.90.
**Owner** Niarchos Family **Bred** Peter Anastasiou **Trained** Upper Lambourn, Berks

**FOCUS**
A very useful handicap in which an ordinary gallop increased before the 3f pole. The first two pulled clear and the form has been rated positively.

## 4820 32RED SPONSOR OF 1000 RACES ANNUALLY H'CAP 6f
8:50 (8:50) (Class 6) (0-60,60) 3-Y-O £1,940 (£577; £288; £144) Stalls Centre

Form RPR
000 1 **Razin' Hell**[42] 3380 3-9-2 60 (v) DannyBrock(5) 4 66
(Alan McCabe) *mde virtually all: rdn 2f out: sn hung rt: drvn out* 7/1
00-0 2 1 1/2 **Ignight**[41] 3426 3-8-2 46 PhilipPrince(5) 8 47
(Mark Usher) *disp ld 1f: chsd wnr: carried rt over 1f out: swtchd lft early ins fnl f: hung lft after and a being hld* 25/1
60-0 3 nk **Forest Glen (IRE)**[8] 4545 3-9-5 58 LiamKeniry 1 58+
(Sylvester Kirk) *hld up in rr: rdn 2f out: r.o u.p fnl f to go 3rd cl home* 16/1
-014 4 1/2 **Connaught Water (IRE)**[36] 3564 3-9-4 60 MatthewLawson(3) 7 59
(Jonathan Portman) *s.i.s: in rr: hdwy over 3f out: rdn 2f out: kpt on same pce: lost 3rd cl home* 2/1[1]
4 5 3 1/4 **Ever Yours (IRE)**[26] 3990 3-9-0 53 (b) AdamKirby 6 41
(John Joseph Murphy, Ire) *chsd ldrs: rdn over 2f out: wknd fnl f* 11/4[2]
5000 6 6 **Telegraph (IRE)**[64] 2667 3-9-0 60 HollieDoyle(7) 2 29
(David Evans) *in tch tl rdn and hung lft 1/2-way: one pce and no ch after* 10/1
0050 7 5 **Sutton Sioux**[23] 4055 3-8-7 46 oh1 (t) RenatoSouza 3
(Jeremy Gask) *s.i.s: in rr: rdn 1/2-way: no real imp: edgd lft and wknd over 1f out* 33/1
0000 8 3/4 **Song Of Rowland (IRE)**[37] 3549 3-9-4 57 WilliamTwiston-Davies 5 8
(John Spearing) *chsd ldrs: rdn 1/2-way: wknd wl over 1f out* 3/1[3]

1m 10.94s (0.94) **Going Correction** +0.125s/f (Good) 8 Ran SP% **119.3**
Speed ratings (Par 98): **98,96,95,94,90 82,75,74**
CSF £158.78 CT £2720.19 TOTE £9.00: £3.20, £2.60, £6.40; EX 72.50 Trifecta £1348.40.
**Owner** Timms, Timms, McCabe & Warke **Bred** Alan J McCabe **Trained** Averham Park, Notts

**FOCUS**
A moderate handicap run at a sound pace throughout and another winner on the card that made all the running. A clear turf best from the winner.
T/Plt: £402.20 to a £1 stake. Pool: £37,465.24 - 68.00 winning units. T/Qpdt: £180.00 to a 31 stake. Pool: £5135.10 - 21.10 winning units. RL

# 4777 GOODWOOD (R-H)
## Thursday, July 31

**OFFICIAL GOING: Good to firm (8.0)**
Wind: Light; half against Weather: Mainly sunny

## 4821 FAIRMONT STKS (H'CAP) (BOBIS RACE) 1m 1f 192y
2:05 (2:05) (Class 2) 3-Y-O £31,125 (£9,320; £4,660; £2,330; £1,165; £585) Stalls Low

Form RPR
5000 1 **Lyn Valley**[12] 4448 3-8-9 90 JoeFanning 6 100
(Mark Johnston) *chsd ldrs: rdn and effrt 2f out: swtchd lft over 1f out: styd on wl u.p to ld fnl 75yds: edgd lft towards fin* 14/1
3231 2 1/2 **Rainbow Rock (IRE)**[10] 4498 3-7-9 81 6ex oh5 CamHardie(5) 3 90+
(Mark Johnston) *s.i.s: bustled along: detached in last: clsd onto field 4f out: hdwy u.p 2f out: swtchd lft over 1f out: str run fnl f: pressing wnr whn carried lft and sltly hmpd towards fin* 6/1[2]
1-60 3 1/2 **Madeed**[42] 3378 3-8-8 89 (t) KierenFallon 14 97
(Brian Meehan) *t.k.h: w ldr 3f: chsd ldrs after tl rdn and effrt to ld 2f out: sustained duel w rival after: forged ahd fnl 100yds: sn hdd and one pce towards fin* 15/2
0226 4 3/4 **Braidley (IRE)**[19] 4212 3-8-6 87 PJMcDonald 1 94
(James Bethell) *in tch in midfield: rdn and effrt over 2f out: hdwy u.p to chse ldrs over 1f out: kpt on steadily ins fnl f* 14/1
1516 5 1 1/2 **Insaany**[13] 4400 3-8-4 85 FrannyNorton 15 89
(Mark Johnston) *chsd ldrs: hdwy to join ldr after 3f: led 1/2-way: rdn and hdd 2f out: battled on wl and sustained duel w rival tl no ex fnl 100yds: wknd towards fin* 16/1
3111 6 2 **Roseburg (IRE)**[26] 3965 3-9-7 102 RichardHughes 11 102+
(Luca Cumani) *t.k.h: in tch in midfield: rdn and unable qck over 2f out: rallied and kpt on again ins fnl f: no threat to ldrs* 4/1[1]
602 7 1/2 **Pupil (IRE)**[20] 4147 3-8-9 90 JamesDoyle 12 89
(Richard Hannon) *t.k.h: chsd ldrs early: settled bk and in tch in midfield after 2f: effrt u.p 2f out: no ex 1f out: wknd ins fnl f* 16/1
021 8 3/4 **Astronereus (IRE)**[20] 4168 3-8-6 87 JimCrowley 7 85+
(Amanda Perrett) *hld up towards rr: rdn and no hdwy over 2f out: hdwy ent fnl f: styd on and swtchd rt ins fnl f: no threat to ldrs* 7/1[3]
-552 9 1 **Erroneous (IRE)**[33] 3719 3-8-4 85 HarryBentley 5 81
(David Simcock) *t.k.h: led tl 1/2-way: cl 3rd and rdn ent fnl 2f: struggling and btn over 1f out: wknd ins fnl f* 12/1
1443 10 1 1/4 **Examiner (IRE)**[19] 4198 3-8-5 86 LiamJones 4 80
(William Haggas) *hld up in last quartet: effrt over 2f out: no imp and kpt on same pce after: nvr trbld ldrs* 10/1
2631 11 3/4 **Arable**[12] 4426 3-8-4 85 MartinLane 2 77
(Charles Hills) *s.i.s: t.k.h: hld up in last quartet: rdn and effrt over 2f out: no real hdwy: nvr trbld ldrs* 25/1
4624 12 hd **Donny Rover (IRE)**[20] 4147 3-8-4 85 AndrewMullen 9 77
(Michael Appleby) *s.i.s: niggled along towards rr: rdn 3f out: no prog and plugged on same pce after: nvr trbld ldrs* 16/1
6252 13 4 1/2 **Ventura Quest (USA)**[21] 4125 3-7-13 85 JackGarritty(5) 10 68
(Richard Fahey) *in tch in midfield: rdn 3f out: struggling and lost pl jst over 2f out: bhd ins fnl f: no ch after* 16/1
250 14 7 **Collaboration**[54] 3003 3-8-0 81 (t) DavidProbert 8 51
(Andrew Balding) *hld up in rr: last and rdn 3f out: no rspnse: lost tch 2f out* 18/1

2m 4.49s (-3.61) **Going Correction** -0.10s/f (Good) 14 Ran SP% **121.3**
Speed ratings (Par 106): **110,109,109,108,107 105,105,104,104,103 102,102,98,93**
CSF £96.47 CT £692.62 TOTE £17.60: £5.40, £2.50, £3.20; EX 85.10 Trifecta £2009.90.
**Owner** J Barson **Bred** Highclere Stud And Floors Farming **Trained** Middleham Moor, N Yorks

**FOCUS**
Around 7mm of water had been applied to the track overnight, resulting in a GoingStick reading of 8.0. Lower bend dolled out 5yds from 6f to 3f marker in the straight and distances utilising that bend increased by 10yds. Top bend dolled out 3yds increasing distances using that bend by 10yds. Fresh ground last 3 furlongs of the straight. A hot handicap to start the card in which they went something of a stop/start gallop, but the winning time was still decent. Mark Johnston had taken three of the previous eight runnings of the race and his three challengers this year finished first, second and fifth.

## 4822 QATAR BLOODSTOCK RICHMOND STKS (GROUP 2) (C&G) 6f
2:35 (2:35) (Class 1) 2-Y-O £45,368 (£17,200; £8,608; £4,288; £2,152; £1,080) Stalls High

Form RPR
11 1 **Ivawood (IRE)**[21] 4123 2-9-3 0 RichardHughes 5 117+
(Richard Hannon) *pressed ldr and a travelling wl: led over 1f out: shkn up and readily asserted 1f out: r.o strly: easily: impressive* 2/5[1]
11 2 4 1/2 **Louie De Palma**[20] 4143 2-9-0 0 AdamKirby 2 101
(Clive Cox) *in tch in last pair: rdn and effrt 2f out: drvn 1f out: kpt on wl fnl 100yds to go 2nd towards fin: no ch w wnr* 14/1
3132 3 nk **Jungle Cat (IRE)**[21] 4123 2-9-0 106 JoeFanning 8 100
(Mark Johnston) *led: rdn over 1f out: sn hdd: outpcd by wnr and kpt on same pce fnl f: lost 2nd towards fin* 5/1[2]
1 4 shd **Fox Trotter (IRE)**[21] 4110 2-9-0 0 JimmyFortune 6 100
(Brian Meehan) *dwlt: bhd: rdn over 2f out: styd on past btn horses ins fnl f: almost snatched 3rd but no ch w wnr* 10/1
212 5 1 1/4 **Surewecan**[14] 4348 2-9-0 96 FrannyNorton 3 96
(Mark Johnston) *in tch in midfield: rdn over 2f out: drvn and unable qck over 1f out: no ch w wnr and kpt on same pce fnl f* 20/1
21 6 shd **Sixty (IRE)**[46] 3279 2-9-0 0 PatDobbs 9 96
(Richard Hannon) *chsd ldrs: lost pl 1/2-way: edging rt ent fnl f: kpt on: no ch w wnr* 25/1
1 7 nse **Moonraker**[82] 2146 2-9-0 0 RyanMoore 1 96
(Mick Channon) *t.k.h: hld up in tch: hdwy to chse ldrs 1/2-way: 3rd and no ex u.p 1f out: wknd fnl 75yds* 7/1[3]
21 8 14 **Doc Charm**[52] 3049 2-9-0 0 TomEaves 4 54
(Keith Dalgleish) *in tch: rdn over 2f out: sn struggling: bhd fnl f* 33/1

1m 10.09s (-2.11) **Going Correction** -0.20s/f (Firm) 8 Ran SP% **127.9**
Speed ratings (Par 106): **106,100,99,99,97 97,97,78**
CSF £10.08 TOTE £1.40: £1.10, £3.20, £1.70; EX 10.70 Trifecta £32.10.
**Owner** Carmichael Jennings **Bred** Ms M Davison & Ms D Kitchin **Trained** East Everleigh, Wilts

**FOCUS**
They raced away from the stands' rail in a Group 2 lacking depth. Ivawood impresed, building on his July Stakes win, and arguably value for a little extra. Louie De Palma progressed from his nursery win.

## 4823 ARTEMIS GOODWOOD CUP (BRITISH CHAMPIONS SERIES) (GROUP 2) 2m
3:10 (3:10) (Class 1) 3-Y-O+ £68,052 (£25,800; £12,912; £6,432; £3,228; £1,620) Stalls Low

Form RPR
-121 1 **Cavalryman**[21] 4124 8-9-8 115 KierenFallon 10 118
(Saeed bin Suroor) *hld up in tch in rr: rdn and hdwy over 2f out: led 2f out: sn hung rt but clr over 1f out: kpt on and a doing enough ins fnl f* 5/1[3]
0-60 2 nk **Ahzeemah (IRE)**[42] 3377 5-9-8 110 (p) HarryBentley 3 117
(Saeed bin Suroor) *chsd ldrs: rdn and effrt over 2f out: chsd clr wnr over 1f out: kpt on and grad clsd ins fnl f: nvr quite getting to wnr* 12/1
1142 3 4 1/2 **Brown Panther**[18] 4250 6-9-8 114 RichardKingscote 9 111
(Tom Dascombe) *nt best away: t.k.h: in tch in midfield: chsd ldrs 12f out: rdn to join ldrs and edgd rt over 2f out: 3rd and outpcd over 1f out: kpt on same pce after* 11/4[2]
1553 4 7 **Brass Ring**[40] 3453 4-9-8 103 JamesDoyle 1 103
(John Gosden) *hld up in tch in last trio: last and rdn 3f out: no prog and wl btn over 1f out: styd on past btn horses fnl f* 20/1
4121 5 1 1/2 **Angel Gabrial (IRE)**[33] 3717 5-9-8 106 GeorgeChaloner 7 101
(Richard Fahey) *t.k.h: hld up in tch in midfield: rdn over 2f out: 4th and wl btn over 1f out: wknd ins fnl f* 8/1
1105 6 3 3/4 **Excellent Result (IRE)**[21] 4124 4-9-8 112 JamieSpencer 6 97
(Saeed bin Suroor) *led and set stdy gallop: rdn over 2f out: hdd 2f out and sn btn: wknd fnl f* 28/1
4-24 7 1 1/4 **Forgotten Voice (IRE)**[40] 3450 9-9-8 110 RichardHughes 8 95
(Nicky Henderson) *hld up in rr: quick move to chse ldrs 7f out: rdn over 2f out: short of room and dropped out 2f out: no ch after: eased wl ins fnl f* 7/1
10-2 8 1 1/4 **Estimate (IRE)**[42] 3377 5-9-5 112 RyanMoore 4 91
(Sir Michael Stoute) *chsd ldr: rdn wl over 2f out: no rspnse and losing pl whn short of room ent fnl 2f: sn wl btn: bhd and eased ins fnl f* 2/1[1]

3m 27.07s (-1.93) **Going Correction** -0.10s/f (Good) 8 Ran SP% **116.2**
Speed ratings (Par 115): **100,99,97,94,93 91,90,90**
CSF £62.72 TOTE £5.80: £1.70, £2.90, £1.50; EX 67.10 Trifecta £262.00.
**Owner** Godolphin **Bred** Darley **Trained** Newmarket, Suffolk

**FOCUS**
This year's Goodwood Cup looked well up to standard with a previous Ascot Gold Cup winner in the field, while last year's winner was back to defend his crown, but with the pace moderate until around halfway this wasn't the test of stamina that perhaps it should have been and the time was modest. The favourite running so badly also casts a shadow over the form, but it was still a triumph for Godolphin with a 1-2. Cavalryman is rated in line with his better form since he was a 3yo.

## 4824 STERLING INSURANCE LILLIE LANGTRY STKS (GROUP 3) (F&M) 1m 6f
3:45 (3:45) (Class 1) 3-Y-O+ £34,026 (£12,900; £6,456; £3,216; £1,614; £810) Stalls Low

Form RPR
3-43 1 **Missunited (IRE)**[42] 3377 7-9-6 114 JimCrowley 4 102
(Michael Winters, Ire) *sn pushed up to ld: hdd after 1f: chsd ldr tl rdn to ld again 3f out: hrd pressed over 2f out: battled on v gamely u.p: edgd lft ins fnl f: hld on cl home: all out: dismntd after fin* 3/1[1]
1131 2 1/2 **Arabian Comet (IRE)**[20] 4145 3-8-6 89 JoeFanning 9 101
(William Haggas) *hld up off the pce in last pair: clsd and n.m.r over 2f out: rdn and hdwy over 1f out: chsng ldrs and n.m.r 1f out: r.o strly fnl 100yds: wnt 2nd last strides* 7/1
-422 3 hd **Waila**[19] 4213 4-9-6 100 RyanMoore 10 100
(Sir Michael Stoute) *t.k.h: chsd ldrs: rdn to chse wnr over 2f out: ev ch 2f out: sustained duel w wnr after: battled on wl u.p tl no ex towards fin: lost 2nd last strides* 6/1

3-53 **4** 1 1/4 **Talent**[26] 3961 4-9-6 109 RichardHughes 7 99
(Ralph Beckett) *t.k.h: hld up off the pce in last quartet: stdy hdwy over 2f out: drvn and chsd ldrs 1f out: kpt on same pce ins fnl f* **9/2**[3]

2053 **5** 1/2 **Groovejet**[12] 4443 3-8-6 88 FrannyNorton 8 98
(Peter Chapple-Hyam) *racd off the pce in last quartet and niggled along at times: n.m.r and moved rt over 2f out: hdwy u.p over 1f out: swtchd rt 1f out: kpt on ins fnl f* **33/1**

1 **6** 6 **Stella Bellissima (IRE)**[28] 3891 3-8-6 82 WilliamBuick 6 90
(John Gosden) *awkward leaving stalls: sn rcvrd and hld up in midfield: rdn over 2f out: unable qck: wknd and edgd rt over 1f out* **4/1**[2]

-160 **7** 3/4 **Beacon Lady**[40] 3449 5-9-6 94 TomQueally 1 89
(William Knight) *hld up off the pce in last pair: rdn jst over 3f out: no imp: kpt on past btn horses fnl f: nvr trbld ldrs* **25/1**

1104 **8** 1 1/4 **Honor Bound**[21] 4122 3-8-6 94 DavidProbert 2 87
(Ralph Beckett) *hld up in tch in midfield: rdn and effrt 2f out: sn btn: wknd over 1f out* **33/1**

0-35 **9** 3 3/4 **Nymphea (IRE)**[32] 3770 5-9-6 110 AdriedeVries 5 89
(P Schiergen, Germany) *chsd ldr tl led after 1f: hdd and rdn 3f out: no ex u.p over 1f out: sn wknd* **8/1**

**10** 13 **Baroness Daniela**[28] 4-9-6 96 JamesDoyle 3 63
(H-A Pantall, France) *chsd ldrs: rdn and lost pl 3f out: bhd over 1f out* **25/1**

2m 59.27s (-4.33) **Going Correction** -0.10s/f (Good)
**WFA** 3 from 4yo+ 14lb **10** Ran SP% **114.7**
Speed ratings (Par 113): **108,107,107,106,106 103,102,102,99,92**
CSF £22.90 TOTE £3.80: £1.50, £2.50, £2.20; EX 28.50 Trifecta £72.20.
**Owner** Mrs Vanessa Hutch **Bred** Mrs Vanessa Hutch **Trained** Kanturk, Co Cork
■ Stewards' Enquiry : Jim Crowley two-day ban: used whip above permitted level (Aug 14-15)

**FOCUS**
Run at a reasonable gallop, the race set up for the closers, with the second, third and fourth being in the last quartet early. Missunited is rated a stone off her Gold Cup figure.

## 4825 EBF BRITISH STALLION STUDS NEW HAM MAIDEN FILLIES' STKS (BOBIS RACE) 7f
**4:20** (4:23) (Class 2) 2-Y-O **£12,938** (£3,850; £1,924; £962) **Stalls Low**

Form RPR

42 **1** **Shagah (IRE)**[19] 4202 2-9-0 0 RichardHughes 6 83+
(Richard Hannon) *t.k.h: hld up in tch in midfield: clsd to press ldrs and gng wl 2f out: rdn to ld 1f out: edgd rt but sn qcknd clr: comf* **15/8**[1]

**2** 1 **Kodiva (IRE)** 2-9-0 0 JamesDoyle 4 81+
(Charles Hills) *s.i.s: hld up in tch in rr: rn green bnd over 4f out: rdn and effrt 2f out: hdwy u.p over 1f out: chsd wnr ins fnl f: r.o* **6/1**[3]

02 **3** 2 1/2 **Runner Runner (IRE)**[23] 4054 2-9-0 0 KierenFallon 5 74
(George Baker) *in tch in midfield: shkn up ent fnl 2f: ev ch u.p over 1f out: chsd wnr but unable qck 1f out: lost 2nd and outpcd ins fnl f* **14/1**

53 **4** 2 **Hoorayforhollywood**[14] 4346 2-9-0 0 RyanMoore 9 69+
(Sir Michael Stoute) *in tch in rr and stuck wd: rdn 2f out: kpt on ins fnl f: wnt 4th towards fin: no threat to wnr* **8/1**

05 **5** 1 1/2 **Fast Romance (USA)**[13] 4398 2-9-0 0 JimCrowley 10 65
(Paul Cole) *chsd ldrs: rdn to ld wl over 1f out: hdd and no ex 1f out: 3rd and btn whn hmpd ins fnl f: wknd fnl 100yds* **25/1**

2 **6** 3 **Thunder In Myheart (IRE)**[12] 4444 2-9-0 0 JamieSpencer 8 56
(Michael Bell) *led: rdn and hdd wl over 1f out: no ex and btn ent fnl f: wknd* **3/1**[1]

**7** 1 3/4 **Cassandane (IRE)** 2-9-0 0 JoeFanning 3 52
(Mark Johnston) *chsd ldrs: rdn and lost pl ent fnl 2f: wknd u.p over 1f out* **16/1**

**8** 2 1/4 **World Fair (IRE)** 2-9-0 0 WilliamBuick 7 46
(Charlie Appleby) *dwlt: in tch in rr: sme hdwy u.p over 2f out: wknd over 1f out* **14/1**

**9** 1 1/4 **Perfect Orange** 2-9-0 0 MartinDwyer 2 42
(Marcus Tregoning) *rn green and a towards rr: rdn ent fnl 2f: sn struggling and btn over 1f out* **20/1**

6 **10** 3 1/2 **Nelsons Trick**[29] 3858 2-9-0 0 DavidProbert 1 33
(Rod Millman) *nt best away: sn rcvrd and in tch in midfield: rdn and lost pl jst over 2f out: wknd and bhd over 1f out* **16/1**

1m 28.21s (1.21) **Going Correction** -0.10s/f (Good) **10** Ran SP% **118.9**
Speed ratings (Par 97): **89,87,85,82,81 77,75,73,71,67**
CSF £13.88 TOTE £2.60: £1.30, £2.00, £2.60; EX 18.30 Trifecta £187.30.
**Owner** Al Shaqab Racing **Bred** Irish National Stud **Trained** East Everleigh, Wilts

**FOCUS**
The previous ten runnings of this maiden had all been won by fillies with previous racecourse experience and that trend continued. Improvement from the winner.

## 4826 TATLER STKS (H'CAP) (BOBIS RACE) 7f
**4:50** (4:54) (Class 2) (0-105,103) 3-Y-O
**£15,562** (£4,660; £2,330; £1,165; £582; £292) **Stalls Low**

Form RPR

2400 **1** **Safety Check (IRE)**[19] 4198 3-9-0 96 WilliamBuick 3 104
(Charlie Appleby) *chsd ldrs: switching lft and effrt u.p over 1f out: r.o wl u.p to ld fnl 50yds: drvn out* **14/1**

123- **2** 1/2 **Day Of Conquest**[278] 7534 3-9-2 98 SeanLevey 7 105+
(Richard Hannon) *stdd after s: hld up in last quartet: effrt but forced to switch lft arnd many horses over 1f out: str run ins fnl f: wnt 2nd towards fin: nvr quite getting to wnr* **22/1**

0010 **3** 3/4 **Almargo (IRE)**[20] 4166 3-8-12 94 JoeFanning 5 99
(Mark Johnston) *chsd ldrs: upsides and rdn 2f out: sustained duel w rival tl forged ahd ins fnl f: edgd rt and no ex fnl 50yds* **4/1**[1]

1020 **4** 1/2 **Ifwecan**[10] 4491 3-8-12 94 FrannyNorton 1 98
(Mark Johnston) *led: jnd and rdn 2f out: sustained duel w rival tl hdd ins fnl f: no ex fnl 75yds* **6/1**[2]

1120 **5** 1/2 **Passing Star**[43] 3352 3-9-7 103 RobertWinston 4 105
(Charles Hills) *hld up in tch in midfield: n.m.r over 2f out: swtchd lft 2f out: hdwy u.p to chse ldrs 1f out: kpt on same pce ins fnl f* **8/1**

6-56 **6** 3/4 **Almuheet**[40] 3480 3-8-2 84 [1] HarryBentley 2 84
(Brian Ellison) *hld up in tch in midfield: n.m.r on inner 2f out: rdn and hdwy over 1f out: swtchd lft and kpt on same pce ins fnl f* **20/1**

4501 **7** shd **Nakuti (IRE)**[20] 4163 3-8-2 89 CamHardie(5) 9 89
(Sylvester Kirk) *hld up in tch in midfield: hdwy u.p over 1f out: styd on same pce ins fnl f* **16/1**

-632 **8** 3/4 **Championship (IRE)**[34] 3651 3-8-11 93 RichardHughes 10 91
(Richard Hannon) *hld up in rr: effrt over 1f out: swtchd lft jst over 1f out: r.o wl ins fnl f: nvr trbld ldrs* **8/1**

1610 **9** 1 **Royal Seal**[20] 4166 3-8-9 91 RyanMoore 8 87
(Sir Michael Stoute) *stdd after s: hld up in last quartet: rdn and effrt on outer over 2f out: hdwy u.p over 1f out: wknd ins fnl f* **13/2**[3]

2046 **10** 3/4 **Shot In The Sun (IRE)**[20] 4176 3-7-11 84 JackGarritty(5) 13 78
(Richard Fahey) *stdd and dropped in bhd after s: hld up wl off the pce in rr: clsd 3f out: rdn over 1f out: styd on ins fnl f: nvr trbld ldrs* **16/1**

1-10 **11** 2 3/4 **Magnus Maximus**[42] 3378 3-9-4 100 PatDobbs 11 87
(Richard Hannon) *wl in tch in midfield: rdn and unable qck ent fnl 2f: lost pl over 1f out: wknd fnl f* **14/1**

3-1 **12** 3/4 **Secret Hint**[21] 4111 3-8-2 84 oh4 DavidProbert 12 69
(Andrew Balding) *t.k.h: chsd ldrs: rdn and unable qck ent fnl 2f: lost pl u.p over 1f out: wknd fnl f* **7/1**

-020 **13** 7 **Jallota**[124] 1178 3-9-4 100 JimCrowley 6 66
(Charles Hills) *in tch in midfield: rdn over 2f out: lost pl 2f out: sn wknd and bhd 1f out* **16/1**

1m 25.82s (-1.18) **Going Correction** -0.10s/f (Good) **13** Ran SP% **122.4**
Speed ratings (Par 106): **102,101,100,100,99 98,98,97,96,95 92,91,83**
CSF £295.80 CT £1474.33 TOTE £14.50: £4.00, £4.90, £2.40; EX 300.30 Trifecta £780.30.
**Owner** Godolphin **Bred** Malih Al Basti **Trained** Newmarket, Suffolk

**FOCUS**
They didn't go a mad gallop and it paid to race handily. The third and fourth help with the standard.

## 4827 QIPCO APPRENTICE STKS (H'CAP) 1m 1f
**5:25** (5:25) (Class 3) (0-90,90) 4-Y-O+ **£9,703** (£2,887; £1,443; £721) **Stalls Low**

Form RPR

303 **1** **Angelic Upstart (IRE)**[21] 4118 6-8-9 80 KieranShoemark(7) 12 90
(Andrew Balding) *broke fast: sn restrained and hld up in midfield: hdwy u.p over 1f out: chal 1f out: r.o wl u.p to ld towards fin* **12/1**

0443 **2** nk **Jodies Jem**[12] 4453 4-9-4 82 CharlesBishop 3 91
(William Jarvis) *chsd ldrs: wnt 2nd over 2f and sn upsides ldrs and gng wl: rdn to ld wl over 1f out: hrd pressed 1f out: kpt on wl u.p tl hdd and no ex towards fin* **8/1**[3]

3412 **3** 3 **George Cinq**[15] 4331 4-9-7 88 CamHardie(3) 11 91
(Michael Bell) *stdd s: hld up in rr: clsd and nt clr run over 2f out: swtchd rt 2f out: rdn and hdwy over 1f out: wnt 3rd ins fnl f: no imp* **6/1**[1]

2203 **4** 1 **Tigers Tale (IRE)**[15] 4331 5-9-10 88 (v) OisinMurphy 7 89
(Roger Teal) *sn led: rdn ent fnl 2f: hdd wl over 1f out: unable qck and btn 3rd 1f out: wknd ins fnl f* **6/1**[1]

0125 **5** 3 3/4 **Jacob Cats**[14] 4354 5-9-1 79 (v) MichaelJMMurphy 6 72
(William Knight) *t.k.h: hld up in tch in midfield: drvn 3f out: no ex and btn ent fnl f: wknd fnl f* **14/1**

5000 **6** 3 1/4 **Mabait**[19] 4212 8-9-7 90 (p) GeorgeBuckell(5) 2 76
(David Simcock) *stdd after s: t.k.h: hld up in last pair: effrt on inner 2f out: no prog u.p over 1f out: wknd 1f out* **14/1**

3141 **7** 1/2 **Corton Lad**[4] 4704 4-9-7 85 6ex (tp) JasonHart 14 70
(Keith Dalgleish) *sn chsng ldr: drvn 3f out: sn lost 2nd and struggling: wknd over 1f out* **7/1**[2]

2133 **8** 1/2 **Saucy Minx (IRE)**[33] 3727 4-9-0 83 (b) JennyPowell(5) 10 67
(Amanda Perrett) *chsd ldrs: rdn and no rspnse ent fnl 2f: wknd over 1f out* **8/1**[3]

0156 **9** 1 1/4 **Las Verglas Star (IRE)**[20] 4175 6-9-6 84 GeorgeChaloner 4 65
(Richard Fahey) *rrd as stalls opened: s.i.s: sn bustled along: a towards rr: drvn and no real imp whn hmpd 2f out: wl hld after* **20/1**

005 **10** 3 1/2 **Weapon Of Choice (IRE)**[19] 4184 6-9-8 86 JoeyHaynes 9 60
(Stuart Kittow) *hld up in tch in last quartet: rdn and no hdwy over 2f out: bhd over 1f out* **14/1**

3660 **11** 1/2 **Argaki (IRE)**[2] 4761 4-8-9 76 (p) MarcMonaghan(3) 1 49
(Keith Dalgleish) *in tch in midfield: rdn over 2f out: losing pl and rdn 2f out: wknd over 1f out* **28/1**

1m 53.69s (-2.61) **Going Correction** -0.10s/f (Good) **11** Ran SP% **99.2**
Speed ratings (Par 107): **107,106,104,103,99 96,96,96,94,91 91**
CSF £71.85 CT £345.05 TOTE £10.70: £3.00, £2.30, £2.30; EX 65.20 Trifecta £492.80.
**Owner** Barry Burdett **Bred** Swordlestown Stud **Trained** Kingsclere, Hants
■ Balmoral Castle was withdrawn. Price at time of withdrawal 4-1F. Rule 4 applies to all bets - deduction 20p in the pound.
■ Stewards' Enquiry : Kieran Shoemark four-day ban: used whip above permitted level (Aug 14-17)

**FOCUS**
A decent apprentice handicap, but weakened significantly when the bang-in-form Balmoral Castle was withdrawn just before the start. The pace looked solid and the winner posted a personal best.
T/Jkpt: Part won. £67,098.00 to a £1 stake. Pool: £94,504.28 - 0.50 winning units. T/Plt: £75.10 to a £1 stake. Pool: £306,589.45 - 2978.86 winning units. T/Qpdt: £24.20 to a £1 stake. Pool: £17,982.35 - 549.56 winning units. SP

# 4409 NOTTINGHAM (L-H)
Thursday, July 31

**OFFICIAL GOING: Good to firm (8.4)**
Wind: Light against Weather: Cloudy

## 4828 EBF STALLIONS MAIDEN FILLIES' STKS (BOBIS RACE) 6f 15y
**2:25** (2:28) (Class 5) 2-Y-O **£3,234** (£962; £481; £240) **Stalls Centre**

Form RPR

2 **1** **Sulaalaat**[51] 3076 2-9-0 0 PaulMulrennan 5 90+
(Brian Meehan) *mde all: qcknd clr over 1f out: easily* **1/3**[1]

**2** 4 **March On (USA)** 2-9-0 0 MartinHarley 4 75+
(William Haggas) *dwlt and wnt lft s: sn in tch: hdwy wl over 2f out: pushed along wl over 1f out: rdn to chse wnr ins fnl f: sn no imp* **16/1**

**3** 1 **Ceaseless (IRE)** 2-9-0 0 GrahamLee 7 72+
(James Tate) *in tch: pushed along 1/2-way: rdn and edgd lft wl over 1f out: kpt on same pce fnl f* **10/1**[3]

2 **4** 2 1/4 **Free To Love**[61] 2771 2-9-0 0 SteveDrowne 3 65
(Charles Hills) *dwlt and sltly hmpd s: sn trcking wnr: effrt over 2f out and sn rdn along: wknd appr fnl f* **6/1**[2]

**5** 2 1/2 **Queen's Pearl (IRE)** 2-9-0 0 FrederikTylicki 8 58
(Roger Varian) *dwlt: sn trcking wnr: rdn along wl over 2f out: sn wknd* **16/1**

06 **6** 45 **Rosie Crowe (IRE)**[21] 4110 2-9-0 0 LukeMorris 2
(David C Griffiths) *chsd ldrs: pushed along after 2f: sn rdn and lost pl: bhd fr wl over 2f out: eased* **100/1**

1m 12.83s (-1.87) **Going Correction** -0.225s/f (Firm) **6** Ran SP% **111.2**
Speed ratings (Par 91): **103,97,96,93,90 30**
CSF £7.35 TOTE £1.50: £1.10, £5.90; EX 7.50 Trifecta £31.40.
**Owner** Hamdan Al Maktoum **Bred** Watership Down Stud **Trained** Manton, Wilts

**FOCUS**
The rail was stepped out 4m around the whole track, increasing round course distances by 24 yards. An uncompetitive maiden run at a decent pace. The winner did it easily.

## 4829 BRITISH STALLION STUDS EBF MAIDEN STKS 6f 15y
2:55 (2:57) (Class 5) 2-Y-O £3,234 (£962; £481; £240) Stalls Centre

Form RPR
1 **Uptight (FR)** 2-9-5 0 PaulMulrennan 8 76+
(Kevin Ryan) *wnt lft s: prom: cl up over 3f out: led wl over 2f out: rdn clr and edgd lft ent fnl f: kpt on* **9/2**
5 2 2 1/2 **Giannizzero (IRE)**[16] 4301 2-9-5 0 MartinHarley 6 64
(Marco Botti) *trckd ldrs: green: pushed along and outpcd 1/2-way: sn rdn: styd on wl appr fnl f: nrst fin* **8/1**
3 *shd* **Bridgekeeper** 2-9-5 0 LukeMorris 3 63
(James Eustace) *in tch: green and pushed along 1/2-way: sn rdn: styd on appr fnl f: nrst fin* **20/1**
6 4 3/4 **Dark Wonder (IRE)**[28] 3881 2-9-5 0 GrahamLee 1 61
(James Given) *cl up: pushed along 1/2-way: rdn 2f out: sn one pce* **7/2**[2]
4 5 1 **Prince Of Time**[10] 4486 2-9-5 0 AdrianNicholls 9 58
(Mark Johnston) *slt ld: rdn along 1/2-way: sn hdd and drvn: wknd ins fnl f* **4/1**[3]
04 6 1 3/4 **Duke Of North (IRE)**[21] 4109 2-9-5 0 ShaneKelly 5 53
(James Fanshawe) *in tch: hdwy 1/2-way: sn chsng ldng pair: rdn along wl over 1f out: grad wknd* **10/3**[1]
7 1/2 **Dark Wave** 2-9-5 0 HayleyTurner 2 51
(Ed Walker) *dwlt and bhd: green and rdn along over 2f out: kpt on fnl f: nrst fin* **18/1**
8 2 **Yeah Cool** 2-9-5 0 DanielTudhope 4 45
(Peter Chapple-Hyam) *dwlt: a in rr* **14/1**
9 3/4 **Lady Atlas** 2-9-0 0 MichaelStainton 7 38
(David Brown) *dwlt and sltly hmpd s: sn pushed along: hdwy to chse ldrs on outer 1/2-way: sn rdn and wknd* **25/1**

1m 15.08s (0.38) **Going Correction** -0.225s/f (Firm) 9 Ran SP% **115.1**
Speed ratings (Par 94): **88,84,84,83,82 79,79,76,75**
CSF £40.06 TOTE £4.70: £2.00, £2.70, £3.80; EX 45.50 Trifecta £460.30.
**Owner** Matt & Lauren Morgan **Bred** Madame Antonia Devin **Trained** Hambleton, N Yorks
**FOCUS**
Little form for this maiden which was run at a fair pace. Those in behind the winner are the key to the level.

## 4830 BDN MEDIAN AUCTION MAIDEN STKS 1m 75y
3:30 (3:30) (Class 6) 3-4-Y-O £2,587 (£770; £384; £192) Stalls Centre

Form RPR
0 1 **Hannington**[38] 3525 3-8-12 0 RobHornby(7) 9 67
(Andrew Balding) *hld up in rr on inner: swtchd rt to outer 3f out and gd hdwy over 2f out: rdn to chal over 1f out: led jst ins fnl f: in command whn jinked and rdr lost irons cl home* **16/1**
004 2 1 1/2 **Captain George (IRE)**[27] 3914 3-9-5 76 ShaneKelly 1 64
(James Fanshawe) *trckd ldrs: effrt 3f out and sn pushed along: swtchd rt and rdn 2f out: drvn to chal over 1f out: ev ch tl one pce ins fnl f* **8/11**[1]
6006 3 1 3/4 **Buckland Beau**[42] 3389 3-9-5 57 FrederikTylicki 4 60
(Charlie Fellowes) *cl up: led 3f out: rdn 2f out: sn drvn: hdd ent fnl f: kpt on same pce* **12/1**
4 2 1/4 **Archipeligo** 3-9-5 0 [1] MartinHarley 7 55
(Lady Cecil) *trckd ldrs: hdwy 3f out: rdn to chal wl over 1f out: ev ch tl drvn and one pce ent fnl f* **9/2**[2]
05 5 3/4 **Eloquence**[23] 4052 3-9-0 0 GrahamLee 3 48
(Tom Dascombe) *slt ld: rdn along and hdd 3f out: drvn over 2f out and grad wknd* **8/1**
0-50 6 1 **Born To Reign**[17] 4265 3-9-5 0 HayleyTurner 5 51
(Michael Bell) *in tch: rdn along over 3f out: sn outpcd* **50/1**
0 7 3 3/4 **William Of Orange**[21] 4130 3-9-5 0 LukeMorris 2 42
(Sir Mark Prescott Bt) *dwlt: a in rr* **13/2**[3]
400 8 19 **Gaelic O'Reagan**[75] 2346 3-9-5 0 JimmyQuinn 6
(Robert Eddery) *a towards rr: outpcd and bhd fnl 3f* **100/1**

1m 47.23s (-1.77) **Going Correction** -0.10s/f (Good)
**WFA** 3 from 4yo 8lb 8 Ran SP% **117.1**
Speed ratings (Par 101): **104,102,100,98,97 96,93,74**
CSF £29.04 TOTE £26.60: £5.60, £1.10, £2.50; EX 77.40 Trifecta £607.00.
**Owner** I A Balding **Bred** Bearstone Stud **Trained** Kingsclere, Hants
**FOCUS**
They went an honest pace for this weak maiden. The winner showed big improvement.

## 4831 32RED PAYS THE LEVY H'CAP 1m 75y
4:05 (4:09) (Class 5) (0-75,75) 3-Y-O+ £3,234 (£962; £481) Stalls Centre

Form RPR
0311 1 **Siouxperhero (IRE)**[2] 4767 5-9-13 74 6ex (b) GrahamLee 3 79
(William Muir) *trckd ldng pair on inner: swtchd rt to outer over 2f out: rdn to chal over 1f out: drvn ins fnl f: kpt on wl to ld nr fin* **10/11**[1]
0323 2 1/2 **Celtic Sixpence (IRE)**[20] 4161 6-10-0 75 MichaelStainton 2 79
(Nick Kent) *set stdy pce: qcknd over 2f out: rdn over 1f out: drvn ent fnl f: hdd and no ex towards fin* **3/1**[2]
05-5 3 6 **Skyfire**[57] 2894 7-8-12 62 NataliaGemelova(3) 4 52
(Nick Kent) *trckd ldr: cl up 3f out: rdn along over 2f out: sn drvn and outpcd* **9/1**[3]

1m 47.96s (-1.04) **Going Correction** -0.10s/f (Good) 3 Ran SP% **87.4**
Speed ratings (Par 103): **101,100,94**
CSF £2.24 TOTE £1.20; EX 2.20 Trifecta £2.30.
**Owner** Muir Racing Partnership - Bath **Bred** J & J Waldron **Trained** Lambourn, Berks
■ Piddie's Power was withdrawn. Price at time of withdrawal 4-1. Rule 4 applies to all bets - deduction 20p in the pound.
**FOCUS**
Not much pace for this handicap and there are obvious doubts, but the winner seems better than ever.

## 4832 BDN CONSTRUCTION H'CAP 1m 2f 50y
4:40 (4:40) (Class 4) (0-85,85) 3-Y-O+ £6,469 (£1,925; £962; £481) Stalls Low

Form RPR
2213 1 **No Win No Fee**[20] 4148 4-8-11 75 AlistairRawlinson(7) 4 83+
(Michael Appleby) *trckd ldr: tk cl order over 2f out: rdn to ld over 1f out: hdd ent fnl f: sn drvn and rallied gamely to ld again nr fin* **2/1**[2]
-004 2 *nse* **Endless Credit (IRE)**[14] 4349 4-9-10 81 DanielTudhope 2 89
(Luca Cumani) *trckd ldng pair: smooth hdwy over 2f out: sn cl up: rdn over 1f out: slt ld ent fnl f: sn drvn: hdd and no ex nr fin* **7/4**[1]
52-0 3 *shd* **Saoi (USA)**[19] 4184 7-10-0 85 FrederikTylicki 5 92
(William Knight) *hld up in rr on inner: swtchd rt to outer wl over 1f out: sn rdn and str run to chal ins fnl f: ev ch tl no ex nr fin* **8/1**
6341 4 6 **Alpine Storm (IRE)**[9] 4516 3-8-8 75 6ex AdrianNicholls 1 71
(Mark Johnston) *plld hrd: led and sn clr: pushed along and jnd over 2f out: rdn and hdd over 1f out: wknd ent fnl f* **9/2**[3]
4224 5 3 1/2 **Oddysey (IRE)**[21] 4112 5-9-9 83 ConnorBeasley(3) 3 72
(Michael Dods) *dwlt: hld up in rr: effrt 3f out: rdn along over 2f out: sn outpcd* **17/2**

2m 11.6s (-2.70) **Going Correction** -0.10s/f (Good)
**WFA** 3 from 4yo+ 10lb 5 Ran SP% **109.5**
Speed ratings (Par 105): **106,105,105,101,98**
CSF £5.84 TOTE £3.20: £1.40, £1.10; EX 7.50 Trifecta £14.70.
**Owner** Stephen Almond **Bred** Bearstone Stud **Trained** Danethorpe, Notts
**FOCUS**
A fair handicap for the grade run at a sound pace. The winner matched his penultimate C&D win.

## 4833 MIA LONG RUN HOME H'CAP 5f 13y
5:10 (5:12) (Class 5) (0-75,74) 3-Y-O+ £2,587 (£770; £384; £192) Stalls Centre

Form RPR
2322 1 **Flash City (ITY)**[2] 4752 6-9-5 67 JamesSullivan 6 77
(Ruth Carr) *trckd ldrs: hdwy and nt clr run over 1f out: sn swtchd rt: rdn and qcknd to ld jst ins fnl f: sn hung rt and kpt on towards fin* **7/2**[2]
050 2 3/4 **Sleepy Blue Ocean**[13] 4391 8-9-11 73 (p) DanielTudhope 8 80
(John Balding) *dwlt and sltly hmpd s: towards rr: swtchd rt to stands' rail and hdwy over 1f out: squeezed through to chal ent fnl f: sn rdn and ev ch tl drvn and nt qckn last 50yds* **7/1**[3]
013 3 1 1/2 **Poyle Vinnie**[28] 3887 4-9-9 71 RaulDaSilva 9 73
(Michael Appleby) *wnt lft s: trckd ldrs: hdwy and cl up 2f out: rdn to ld over 1f out: hdd jst ins fnl f: hld whn n.m.r sn after* **2/1**[1]
0440 4 *shd* **Ubetterbegood (ARG)**[32] 3749 6-9-9 71 (v) FrederikTylicki 2 73
(Robert Cowell) *hld up: swtchd lft to outer and rdn over 1f out: kpt on fnl f: nrst fin* **14/1**
2003 5 *shd* **Bilash**[21] 4102 7-8-13 61 (p) ShaneKelly 7 62
(Andrew Hollinshead) *towards rr: hdwy wl over 1f out: rdn and styd on fnl f: nrst fin* **14/1**
0055 6 1/2 **Bronze Beau**[10] 4494 7-9-7 72 (t) NataliaGemelova(3) 5 71
(Kristin Stubbs) *sn led: rdn 2f out: hdd over 1f out: one pce ins fnl f* **8/1**
6014 7 1 3/4 **Edged Out**[13] 4399 4-9-12 74 LukeMorris 1 67
(Christopher Mason) *prom on wd outside: rdn along 2f out: grad wknd* **25/1**
-503 8 1 **Aaranyow (IRE)**[8] 4546 6-8-2 50 (p) NathanAlison(5) 10 44
(Clifford Lines) *cl up: rdn along 2f out: wknd over 1f out* **25/1**
0200 9 1 1/2 **Moorhouse Lad**[21] 4114 11-9-7 72 BillyCray(3) 3 56
(Garry Moss) *prom: rdn along 2f out: sn wknd* **10/1**
6060 10 4 **Royal Bajan (USA)**[21] 4114 6-9-8 70 (p) GrahamLee 4 40
(James Given) *prom: rdn along over 2f out: sn drvn and wknd* **14/1**

59.84s (-1.66) **Going Correction** -0.225s/f (Firm) 10 Ran SP% **115.9**
Speed ratings (Par 103): **104,102,100,100,100 99,96,94,92,86**
CSF £28.19 CT £59.76 TOTE £4.40: £1.80, £2.10, £1.70; EX 24.60 Trifecta £90.70.
**Owner** S R Jackson **Bred** G Riccioni Et Al **Trained** Huby, N Yorks
**FOCUS**
A fair sprint handicap run at a sound pace. The action unfolded up the stands' rail and this could help the winner's confidence.

## 4834 32RED SPONSOR OF 1000 RACES ANNUALLY H'CAP 2m 9y
5:45 (5:46) (Class 6) (0-65,63) 3-Y-O £1,940 (£577; £288; £144) Stalls Low

Form RPR
00-5 1 **Moscato**[21] 4106 3-9-5 61 LukeMorris 4 69+
(Sir Mark Prescott Bt) *chsd ldrs on outer: led over 12f out: rn in snatches and rdn along bef 1/2-way: pushed along over 5f out: rdn 3f out: drvn and wandered over 1f out: jnd ent fnl f: kpt on wl towards fin* **7/2**[1]
6533 2 3/4 **Chesil Beach**[6] 4615 3-8-11 60 RobHornby(7) 2 67
(Andrew Balding) *trckd ldrs: hdwy 3f out: effrt wl over 1f out: rdn to chal ent fnl f: ev ch tl no ex last 100yds* **7/2**[1]
6022 3 2 1/4 **Rock Of Leon**[17] 4261 3-8-8 50 (p) FrederikTylicki 3 54
(Michael Bell) *in tch: hdwy on inner 4f out: chsd ldrs 3f out: rdn to chse ldng pair over 1f out: sn drvn and kpt on same pce* **11/2**
-005 4 1 1/4 **Mr Smith**[15] 4333 3-9-7 63 (p) NickyMackay 1 66
(John Gosden) *led over 3f: trckd wnr: cl up over 3f out: rdn along over 2f out: drvn wl over 1f out: kpt on one pce* **9/2**[3]
6042 5 *nk* **High Love (IRE)**[10] 4504 3-9-7 63 (p) GrahamLee 5 65
(Tom Dascombe) *hld up in rr: hdwy over 3f out: chsd ldrs 2f out: sn swtchd rt and rdn: swtchd lft and drvn ins fnl f: sn no imp* **4/1**[2]
3050 6 26 **Kaizen Factor**[10] 4497 3-8-10 52 MichaelStainton 6 23
(Micky Hammond) *in tch: hdwy to chse ldrs over 4f out: rdn along over 3f out: sn wknd and bhd* **66/1**
0053 7 10 **Peacemaker (IRE)**[15] 4333 3-9-1 62 (p) GeorgeDowning(5) 8 21
(Eve Johnson Houghton) *v awkward and hung bdly lft s: rel to r and lost many l: hdwy to join field after 6f: rdn along wl over 3f out: sn wknd and bhd* **7/1**
060 8 24 **Enniscorthy Myles (USA)**[85] 2075 3-8-3 49 oh4 (p) JimmyQuinn 7
(Tim Pitt) *chsd ldrs: rdn along 4f out: sn outpcd and bhd* **50/1**

3m 32.75s (-1.75) **Going Correction** -0.10s/f (Good) course record 8 Ran SP% **114.0**
Speed ratings (Par 98): **100,99,98,97,97 84,79,67**
CSF £15.82 CT £64.63 TOTE £4.40: £2.00, £1.40, £1.30; EX 20.10 Trifecta £74.40.
**Owner** The Green Door Partnership **Bred** Miss K Rausing **Trained** Newmarket, Suffolk
**FOCUS**
Plenty of unexposed types in this staying handicap which was run at a steady pace.
T/Plt: £21.20 to a £1 stake. Pool: £43,794.35 - 1507.09 winning units. T/Qpdt: £3.00 to a £1 stake. £2508.71 - 612.83 winning units. JR

# 3907 DEAUVILLE (R-H)
Thursday, July 31
**OFFICIAL GOING: Turf: good: polytrack: standard**

## 4838a PRIX DE LA VERONNE (CLAIMER) (3YO) (POLYTRACK) 7f 110y
11:45 (12:00) 3-Y-O £9,583 (£3,833; £2,875; £1,916; £958)

RPR
1 **Skaters Waltz (IRE)**[12] 4447 3-9-8 0 (b) JohanVictoire 7 88
(Paul Cole) *trckd ldr on outer: shkn up to ld 2f out: drvn clr fr 1 1/2f out: easily* **41/10**[3]

2 7 **Ragazzo (FR)**29 3870 3-9-8 0 (p) AntoineCoutier 3 71
(Mario Hofer, Germany) **21/10**1

3 2 1/2 **Vim (FR)**58 3-9-1 0 (p) WilliamsSaraiva 5 57
(C Boutin, France) **242/10**

4 snk **Balfour (FR)**12 4465 3-8-11 0 JulienGrosjean 1 53
(P Nicot, France) **66/10**

5 3/4 **Ar Poulgwenn (IRE)**35 3-9-1 0 (p) JeffersonSmith 2 55
(J-C Rouget, France) **23/10**2

6 1/2 **Vicosoprano (IRE)**12 4465 3-8-11 0 (b) NicolasLarenaudie 6 50
(M Nigge, France) **35/1**

7 1 3/4 **Got Breizh (FR)**28 3-8-11 0 FredericChampagne 4 45
(J Heloury, France) **19/2**

8 2 **Serene Abella**239 3-8-8 0 CesarPasserat 8 37
(Rod Collet, France) **104/10**

1m 29.04s (89.04) **8** Ran SP% **120.4**
WIN (incl. 1 euro stake): 5.10. PLACES: 2.00, 1.50, 4.10. DF: 6.80. SF: 11.70.
**Owner** Sir George Meyrick **Bred** Patrick A Cluskey **Trained** Whatcombe, Oxon

## 4839a PRIX DE LISIEUX (MAIDEN) (UNRACED 2YO FILLIES) (TURF) 6f
12:15 (12:00) 2-Y-O £10,416 (£4,166; £3,125; £2,083; £1,041)

RPR

1 **Rafaadah** 2-9-0 0 ChristopheSoumillon 1 83
(J-C Rouget, France) **16/5**2

2 2 1/2 **Rose Et Or (IRE)** 2-9-0 0 MaximeGuyon 5 76
(A Fabre, France) **13/10**1

3 2 **If I Do (FR)** 2-9-0 0 Christophe-PatriceLemaire 3 70
(P Bary, France) **91/10**

4 1 1/4 **Reprint (IRE)** 2-9-0 0 OlivierPeslier 2 66
(C Laffon-Parias, France) **51/10**3

5 1 **Easy Feeling (USA)** 2-9-0 0 IoritzMendizabal 7 63
(J-C Rouget, France) **14/1**

6 shd **Dulciadargent (FR)** 2-9-0 0 ThierryThulliez 9 62
(N Clement, France) **118/10**

7 3/4 **Road To Damascus (FR)** 2-9-0 0 AlexisBadel 8 60
(F Sanchez, France) **46/1**

8 1/2 **Pretty Picture** 2-9-0 0 Pierre-CharlesBoudot 6 59
(Gay Kelleway) *broke wl and w ldrs on outer: pushed along to hold pl 2f out: fdd and nt given a hrd time ins fnl f* **17/1**

9 6 **Black Bird Runs (FR)** 2-9-0 0 MickaelBarzalona 4 41
(F-H Graffard, France) **26/1**

1m 12.56s (1.56) **9** Ran SP% **119.4**
WIN (incl. 1 euro stake): 4.20. PLACES: 1.40, 1.20, 1.80. DF: 3.80. SF: 7.10.
**Owner** Hamdan Al Maktoum **Bred** Shadwell Estate Co Ltd **Trained** Pau, France

## 4840a PRIX DE PSYCHE (GROUP 3) (3YO FILLIES) (TURF) 1m 2f
1:20 (12:00) 3-Y-O £33,333 (£13,333; £10,000; £6,666; £3,333)

RPR

1 **Be My Gal**31 3808 3-8-11 0 FrankieDettori 4 107+
(Roger Charlton) *pressed ldr between horses: led 2 1/2f out: kicked 1 1/2 l clr under 2f out: rdn 1f out and r.o: won a shade cosily* **12/5**1

2 1 1/2 **Anahita (FR)**31 3808 3-8-11 0 (p) ChristopheSoumillon 7 104
(J-C Rouget, France) *missed break: racd in rr: hdwy on inner under 2f out: 3rd and hrd rdn 1f out: r.o u.p: nvr on terms w wnr* **23/5**3

3 1 **Royalmania**31 3808 3-8-11 0 OlivierPeslier 1 102
(F Head, France) *trckd ldr on inner: effrt to chal on rail 2 1/2f out: swtchd outside 2f out: kpt on at once pce u.p fnl f* **27/10**2

4 2 **No Wind No Rain**28 3-8-11 0 MaximeGuyon 6 98
(Yves de Nicolay, France) *tk a t.k.h: restrained bhd ldng trio on outer: outpcd over 2f out: effrt on outer appr fnl f: kpt on wout threatening ldrs* **47/10**

5 1 **Bocaiuva (IRE)**46 3289 3-8-11 0 Christophe-PatriceLemaire 5 96
(F Chappet, France) *pressed ldr on outer: rdn and outpcd over 1 1/2f out: wknd ins fnl f* **34/1**

6 3/4 **Hug And A Kiss (USA)**32 3773 3-8-11 0 Pierre-CharlesBoudot 3 95
(A Fabre, France) *w.w bhd ldng trio between horses: 5th and rdn 2 1/2f out: short of room and shuffled bk to last 2f out: kpt on again fnl f but nt pce to chal* **58/10**

7 9 **Hualapai (IRE)**33 3745 3-8-11 0 (p) DavidBreux 2 77
(G Botti, France) *led on inner: hdd 2 1/2f out: rdn and styd prom tl wknd fr 1 1/2f out: eased ins fnl f* **83/10**

2m 3.87s (-6.33) **7** Ran SP% **120.2**
WIN (incl. 1 euro stake): 3.40. PLACES: 2.10, 2.60. SF: 12.30.
**Owner** D J Deer **Bred** D J And Mrs Deer **Trained** Beckhampton, Wilts

## 4841a PRIX DU CERCLE (LISTED RACE) (3YO+) (TURF) 5f
2:20 (12:00) 3-Y-O+ £21,666 (£8,666; £6,500; £4,333; £2,166)

RPR

1 **Mirza**54 3030 7-9-2 0 (p) FrankieDettori 2 109
(Rae Guest) *broke wl: trckd ldng pair on outer: rdn to chal 1 1/2f out: r.o u.p to ld 150yds out: wl on top cl home* **12/5**2

2 1/2 **Son Cesio (FR)**54 3030 3-9-2 0 FabriceVeron 4 110
(H-A Pantall, France) **9/5**1

3 3/4 **Caledonia Lady**82 2161 5-9-3 0 AlexisBadel 1 105
(Mme M Bollack-Badel, France) **113/10**

4 1 1/4 **Spirit Quartz (IRE)**298 7054 6-9-2 0 (p) ThomasMessina 5 100
(X Nakkachdji, France) **78/10**3

5 snk **Myasun (FR)**33 3746 7-9-2 0 GregoryBenoist 9 99
(C Baillet, France) **79/10**

6 nse **Frascata (FR)**64 5-9-2 0 Pierre-CharlesBoudot 7 99
(Yves de Nicolay, France) **87/10**

7 2 **Baiadera (GER)**30 7-9-3 0 CristianDemuro 6 93
(R Dzubasz, Germany) **133/10**

8 snk **Best Regards (IRE)**46 4-8-13 0 OlivierPeslier 3 88
(P Harley, Germany) **125/10**

57.33s (-0.17)
**WFA** 3 from 4yo+ 4lb **8** Ran SP% **120.6**
WIN (incl. 1 euro stake): 3.40. PLACES: 1.50, 1.40, 2.30. DF: 3.90. SF: 9.90.
**Owner** C J Mills **Bred** C J Mills **Trained** Newmarket, Suffolk

# 4562 BATH (L-H)
### Friday, August 1

**OFFICIAL GOING: Firm (10.9)**
Wind: mild breeze against Weather: rain

## 4842 PEOPLEAGAINSTPOVERTY.COM FILLIES' H'CAP 1m 5y
5:30 (5:31) (Class 4) (0-80,80) 3-Y-O+ £5,175 (£1,540; £769) Stalls Low

Form RPR

066 1 **Stosur (IRE)**66 2639 3-9-2 **80** (b1) DanielMuscutt(5) 3 88
(Gay Kelleway) *mde all: rdn 2f out: tended to edge rt: styd on strly to assert fnl furlong* **15/2**3

2121 2 5 **Sonnetation (IRE)**17 4280 4-9-3 **69** SteveDrowne 4 67
(Jim Boyle) *trckd wnr: rdn over 2f out: nvr quite finding pce to mount chal: no ex ent fnl f* **8/13**1

3-0 3 21 **Flora Medici**20 4191 3-9-3 **76** LukeMorris 5 54
(Sir Mark Prescott Bt) *slowly away: pushed along early: chsd ldng pair: rdn 4f out: btn over 2f out: eased ins fnl f* **2/1**2

1m 40.44s (-0.36) **Going Correction** -0.15s/f (Firm)
**WFA** 3 from 4yo 7lb **3** Ran SP% **107.0**
Speed ratings (Par 102): **95,90,69**
CSF £12.80 TOTE £6.60; EX 15.10 Trifecta £12.60.
**Owner** Brian C Oakley **Bred** Mervyn Stewkesbury **Trained** Exning, Suffolk

**FOCUS**
The going was firm as is often the case here, despite afternoon rain, and the fields were small. A fair fillies' handicap that was weakened by the absence of the likely favourite, and it produced a turn-up. False rail around bottom bend and up to 3f marker and races incorporating bottom bend increased in distance by about 25yds. The winner seemed to confirm her 2yo form, but it's hard to be confident.

## 4843 SYMONDS FOUNDERS RESERVE H'CAP 2m 1f 34y
6:00 (6:00) (Class 5) (0-70,64) 4-Y-O+ £2,587 (£770; £384; £192) Stalls Low

Form RPR

55 1 **Quadriller (FR)**31 3818 7-9-3 **60** (t) LukeMorris 2 70+
(Philip Hobbs) *travelled wl: trckd ldng pair: wnt 2nd travelling best over 3f out: led jst over 2f out: rdn clr: eased ins fnl f* **7/2**

-121 2 1 3/4 **Ninfea (IRE)**3 4769 6-9-0 **62** 6ex CamHardie(5) 3 65
(Neil King) *trckd ldr tl rdn over 3f out: sn outpcd: styd on again to go 2nd jst ins fnl f: no ch w wnr* **2/1**1

1132 3 2 1/4 **Annaluna (IRE)**1 4818 5-9-4 **64** (v) DeclanBates(3) 1 65
(David Evans) *stmbld leaving stalls: sn led: rdn and hdd jst over 2f out: sn hld: no ex whn lost 2nd jst ins fnl f* **5/2**2

12-2 4 5 **Speed Steed (IRE)**18 2885 7-9-3 **63** (v) ThomasBrown(3) 4 58
(Tim Vaughan) *trckd ldng trio: niggled along over 6f out: drvn over 4f out: nvr any threat: styd on same pce fnl 2f* **3/1**3

3m 48.41s (-3.49) **Going Correction** -0.15s/f (Firm) **4** Ran SP% **109.1**
Speed ratings (Par 103): **102,101,100,97**
CSF £10.74 TOTE £5.10; EX 10.70 Trifecta £26.40.
**Owner** Michelle Ryan **Bred** Brian Moran **Trained** Withycombe, Somerset

**FOCUS**
The pace was sound in this moderate stayers' handicap. Weak form and the winner has been rated to his old French form.

## 4844 BULMERS LIVE COLOURFUL H'CAP 1m 3f 144y
6:35 (6:35) (Class 6) (0-60,59) 3-Y-O £1,940 (£577; £288; £144) Stalls Low

Form RPR

0512 1 **Windshield**7 4615 3-9-7 **59** LukeMorris 2 70+
(Sir Mark Prescott Bt) *sn pushed into ld: nudged along over 6f out: rdn wl over 2f out: idling but enough in hand fnl f: pushed out fnl 120yds: a looking to be holding on* **11/10**1

3412 2 hd **King Calypso**8 4562 3-8-5 **48** CamHardie(5) 4 57
(Denis Coakley) *trckd ldrs: rdn over 2f out: wnt 2nd over 1f out: styd on wl to cl on idling wnr towards fin* **15/8**2

3331 3 7 **Assoluta (IRE)**8 4563 3-9-6 **58** 6ex RenatoSouza 3 55
(Sylvester Kirk) *trckd wnr: racd keenly after 2f: rdn 3f out: nt pce to chal: lost 2nd over 1f out: no ex fnl f* **8/1**

0004 4 5 **Little Flo**31 3819 3-9-1 **53** LiamKeniry 1 42
(Brendan Powell) *trckd ldrs: racd keenly: rdn 3f out: sn dropped to 4th and hld* **6/1**3

2m 29.81s (-0.79) **Going Correction** -0.15s/f (Firm) **4** Ran SP% **107.8**
Speed ratings (Par 98): **96,95,91,87**
CSF £3.40 TOTE £2.00; EX 3.90 Trifecta £6.60.
**Owner** Cheveley Park Stud **Bred** Cheveley Park Stud Ltd **Trained** Newmarket, Suffolk

**FOCUS**
A low-grade 3yo handicap and a close finish. The runner-up has been rated as running a small personal best.

## 4845 FOSTERS RADLER MODERATION H'CAP (BOBIS RACE) 1m 2f 46y
7:10 (7:10) (Class 4) (0-80,78) 3-Y-O £5,175 (£1,540; £769; £384) Stalls Low

Form RPR

-431 1 **Serena Grae**21 4152 3-8-13 **73** MichaelJMMurphy(3) 6 81
(Marcus Tregoning) *led: rdn whn v narrowly hdd jst over 2f out: battled on gamely: led again ent fnl f: styd on strly to draw clr: drvn out* **7/2**3

14-4 2 3 1/4 **Chinese Jade**17 4280 3-9-7 **78** LukeMorris 4 79
(Sir Mark Prescott Bt) *trckd wnr: rdn to take v narrow advantage jst over 2f out tl ent fnl f: sn no ex: jst hld on for 2nd* **11/4**2

3-00 3 shd **Tinga (IRE)**13 4435 3-9-7 **78** (t) SteveDrowne 3 79
(Ralph Beckett) *s.i.s: last of 4: drvn wl over 2f out: no imp tl styd on ins fnl f: wnt 3rd and nrly snatched 2nd fnl strides* **12/1**

0-03 4 nk **Eye Contact**22 4130 3-9-4 **75** TedDurcan 1 75
(Sir Michael Stoute) *trckd ldrs: rdn to chal over 2f out tl wl over 1f out: styd on same pce fnl f: lost 3rd fnl strides* **10/11**1

2m 9.07s (-1.93) **Going Correction** -0.15s/f (Firm) **4** Ran SP% **109.0**
Speed ratings (Par 102): **101,98,98,98**
CSF £12.86 TOTE £4.20; EX 10.30 Trifecta £32.10.
**Owner** Mrs Heather Raw **Bred** Heather Raw **Trained** Whitsbury, Hants

**FOCUS**
The feature contest and quite competitive despite the paper favourite's absence. The runner-up has been rated back to his 2yo form.

## 4846 CHARLES SAUNDERS LTD MAIDEN AUCTION STKS 5f 161y
**7:40** (7:42) (Class 5) 2-Y-O **£2,587** (£770; £384; £192) **Stalls** Centre

Form RPR
00 **1** **Classic Seniority**[18] 4270 2-8-13 0 CamHardie(5) 5 69
(Richard Hannon) *sltly outpcd in last pair over 3f out: drvn over 2f out: no imp unti; str run jst ins fnl f: led fnl 20yds* **11/8**[1]
0 **2** ½ **Margot Rose**[14] 4396 2-8-6 0 LukeMorris 2 55
(Harry Dunlop) *broke best: led briefly: chsd ldrs after 1f: rdn wl over 2f out: hung lft u.p sn after: led ent fnl f: hdd fnl 20yds* **2/1**[2]
033 **3** 1½ **Fast Scat (USA)**[23] 4079 2-8-5 59 DeclanBates(3) 3 52
(David Evans) *s.i.s: led briefly ins 1st f: chsd ldr: rdn wl over 2f out: cl 3rd whn hmpd jst ins fnl f: and again fnl 100yds: kpt on but a being hld after* **5/1**[3]
**4** ¾ **John Joiner** 2-8-8 0 ow2 (b[1]) ChrisMeehan(7) 1 57
(Peter Makin) *awkward leaving stalls: racd keenly: led after 1f: clr over 2f out: sn rdn: hdd ent fnl f: no ex* **12/1**
00 **5** *shd* **Activation**[15] 4338 2-8-13 0 RobertHavlin 4 55
(Hughie Morrison) *hld up in last pair: rdn over 2f out: kpt on but nt pce to get on terms fnl f* **8/1**

1m 11.83s (0.63) **Going Correction** -0.20s/f (Firm) **5 Ran SP% 110.9**
Speed ratings (Par 94): **87,86,84,83,83**
CSF £4.43 TOTE £2.40: £1.80, £1.20; EX 4.60 Trifecta £12.70.
**Owner** Middleham Park Racing LXIII & B Bull **Bred** E Cantillon, D Cantillon & A Driver **Trained** East Everleigh, Wilts

**FOCUS**
Moderate form among those with experience in this maiden and a messy race. It's been rated as ordinary form.

## 4847 GENTING CASINO BRISTOL PLATINUM H'CAP 5f 11y
**8:10** (8:10) (Class 5) (0-75,79) 3-Y-O **£2,587** (£770; £384; £192) **Stalls** Centre

Form RPR
3051 **1** **Searchlight**[8] 4565 3-9-7 79 6ex ShaneGray(5) 4 90
(Kevin Ryan) *mde all: clr after 1f: rdn 2f out: drifted sltly rt: r.o strly: pushed out fnl 120yds: comf* **13/8**[1]
5154 **2** 2½ **The Dandy Yank (IRE)**[8] 4565 3-9-2 74 (v[1]) CamHardie(5) 2 76
(Jamie Osborne) *pressed wnr for 1f: chsd wnr: rdn over 2f out: kpt on but nt pce to get bk on terms: jst hld on for 2nd* **5/1**
6553 **3** *shd* **Captain Ryan**[8] 4567 3-8-2 55 oh1 LukeMorris 3 57
(Peter Makin) *trckd ldng pair: rdn to dispute 2nd over 2f out tl ent fnl f: kpt on again towards fin: nrly snatched 2nd fnl stride* **9/4**[2]
1523 **4** 1 **Kodafine (IRE)**[16] 4324 3-8-4 64 HollieDoyle(7) 5 62
(David Evans) *rrd and slowly away: chsd ldrs: rdn wl over 2f out: kpt on ins fnl f but nvr gng pce to get on terms* **3/1**[3]

1m 1.22s (-1.28) **Going Correction** -0.20s/f (Firm) **4 Ran SP% 110.5**
Speed ratings (Par 100): **102,98,97,96**
CSF £9.61 TOTE £2.30; EX 7.50 Trifecta £10.80.
**Owner** Elite Racing Club **Bred** Elite Racing Club **Trained** Hambleton, N Yorks

**FOCUS**
A fair 3yo sprint and a repeat performance from the winner. There's a chance the form could be rated higher, but there are doubts.

## 4848 SHARES IN SHADARPOUR H'CAP 5f 11y
**8:40** (8:40) (Class 6) (0-60,60) 4-Y-O+ **£1,940** (£577; £288; £144) **Stalls** Centre

Form RPR
6131 **1** **Molly Jones**[8] 4567 5-8-13 57 6ex TimClark(5) 5 70
(Derek Haydn Jones) *blindfold got hung up in reins but sn rcvrd: trckd ldrs: led 2f out: rdn clr: readily* **13/8**[1]
0012 **2** 2 **Burnt Cream**[17] 4285 7-9-6 59 (t) RobertHavlin 7 65
(Martin Bosley) *s.i.s: sn in tch: hdwy wl over 1f out: rdn to dispute 2nd ent fnl f: kpt on but nt pce of wnr* **7/2**[3]
6422 **3** 1¼ **Haadeeth**[8] 4567 7-8-10 56 (bt) HollieDoyle(7) 1 57
(David Evans) *chsd ldr: led briefly over 2f out: sn rdn to chse wnr tl no ex ent fnl f* **11/4**[2]
-065 **4** 2½ **Baby Queen (IRE)**[17] 4285 8-9-2 60 EoinWalsh(5) 3 52
(Brian Baugh) *v awkwardly away: sn chsng ldrs: rdn over 1f out: nt pce to get involved* **6/1**
2500 **5** 5 **Ishetoo**[15] 4362 10-8-2 46 oh1 PhilipPrince(5) 6 20
(Peter Grayson) *led tl rdn over 2f out: sn hld* **20/1**
0066 **6** 72 **Irish Boy (IRE)**[8] 4595 6-9-6 59 (tp) LukeMorris 2
(Christine Dunnett) *dwlt bdly: nvr rcvrd: a bhd* **12/1**

1m 2.07s (-0.43) **Going Correction** -0.20s/f (Firm) **6 Ran SP% 113.7**
Speed ratings (Par 101): **95,91,89,85,77**
CSF £7.84 TOTE £2.40: £1.10, £2.90; EX 7.20 Trifecta £14.70.
**Owner** Mrs E M Haydn Jones **Bred** Mrs M L Parry & P M Steele-Mortimer **Trained** Efail Isaf, Rhondda C Taff
■ Stewards' Enquiry : Hollie Doyle four-day ban: use of whip (15-18 Aug)

**FOCUS**
This moderate older horse sprint was run 0.85sec slower than the preceding contest. The runner-up has been rated close to form.
T/Plt: £3,032.20 to a £1 stake. Pool: £30239.43 - 7.28 winning tickets T/Qpdt: £49.20 to a £1 stake. Pool: £4183.09 - 62.81 winning tickets TM

# 4821 GOODWOOD (R-H)
Friday, August 1

**OFFICIAL GOING: Good to firm (8.1)**
Wind: light, half against Weather: bright spells, light cloud

## 4849 COUTTS GLORIOUS STKS (GROUP 3) 1m 4f
**1:55** (1:57) (Class 1) 4-Y-O+
**£34,026** (£12,900; £6,456; £3,216; £1,614; £810) **Stalls** High

Form RPR
2233 **1** **Pether's Moon (IRE)**[22] 4124 4-9-1 112 RichardHughes 5 111
(Richard Hannon) *chsd ldrs: rdn over 4f out: hdwy on inner to ld wl over 1f out: hung lft but forged clr 1f out: drvn but in command ins fnl f: eased cl home* **11/10**[1]
231/ **2** 1¼ **Encke (USA)**[685] 6245 5-9-1 120 WilliamBuick 1 108
(Charlie Appleby) *chsd ldr: rdn 4f out: clsd to ld ent fnl 2f: hdd wl over 1f out: unable qck ent fnl f: styd on same pce after* **6/1**[3]
-613 **3** 1 **Cafe Society (FR)**[42] 3416 4-9-1 97 JimCrowley 2 106
(David Simcock) *stdd and dropped in bhd after s: hld up in rr: clsd 3f out: shifting rt and hdwy u.p over 1f out: wandering arnd u.p ins fnl f: kpt on to go 3rd towards fin* **6/1**[3]
650 **4** *nk* **Aussie Reigns (IRE)**[41] 3449 4-9-1 99 (v) AdamKirby 7 106
(William Knight) *t.k.h: hld up in tch in midfield: rdn over 3f out: hdwy on inner over 2f out: kpt on same pce u.p fnl f* **20/1**
/00- **5** ¾ **Quest For Peace (IRE)**[272] 7700 6-9-1 109 AndreaAtzeni 6 105
(Luca Cumani) *hld up in tch in last pair: rdn over 3f out: hdwy and pressed ldng pair over 1f out: no ex 1f out: wknd fnl 100yds: lost 2 pls towards fin* **7/1**
-120 **6** 6 **Songcraft (IRE)**[125] 1177 6-9-1 112 (p) SilvestreDeSousa 4 95
(Saeed bin Suroor) *t.k.h: hld up in tch in midfield: nt clrest of runs over 2f out: rdn and effrt over 1f out: btn 1f out: wknd* **11/2**[2]
-000 **7** 13 **Battle Of Marengo (IRE)**[13] 4437 4-9-1 110 JamieSpencer 8 74
(David Simcock) *led: reminder and qcknd gallop over 4f out: hdd ent fnl 2f: sn struggling: bhd 1f out* **25/1**

2m 35.63s (-2.77) **Going Correction** -0.05s/f (Good) **7 Ran SP% 112.7**
Speed ratings (Par 113): **107,106,105,105,104 100,92**
CSF £7.93 TOTE £2.30: £1.30, £2.90; EX 7.50 Trifecta £34.90.
**Owner** John Manley **Bred** Michael G Daly **Trained** East Everleigh, Wilts

**FOCUS**
After another 7mm of water was applied overnight the ground remained officially good to firm (GoingStick 8.1). The pushed-out rail on the lower bend between the 6f marker and 3f pole had been taken down to provide fresh ground on the inside. After the opener, the jockeys variously described conditions as "firm", "fast" and "fast, very fast". This Group 3 was weakened by the absence of Hillstar, but it was still a fascinating race nonetheless. The pace was an even one resulting in a time 1.63sec outside standard. Ordinary form for the level, with the third rated as having run a small personal best.

## 4850 BONHAMS THOROUGHBRED STKS (GROUP 3) 1m
**2:30** (2:30) (Class 1) 3-Y-O
**£34,026** (£12,900; £6,456; £3,216; £1,614; £810) **Stalls** Low

Form RPR
3-11 **1** **Wannabe Yours (IRE)**[55] 2983 3-9-1 100 WilliamBuick 3 114+
(John Gosden) *chsd ldrs: nt clr run ent fnl 2f: swtchd lft and effrt wl over 1f out: hdwy to chse clr wnr ins fnl f: str run fnl 100yds to ld cl home* **7/1**
-513 **2** *nk* **Hors De Combat**[43] 3378 3-9-1 99 FrederikTylicki 7 113
(James Fanshawe) *hld up in tch in rr: rdn and effrt over 2f out: hdwy to ld but drifting rt 2f out: clr over 1f out: drvn ins fnl f: hdd cl home* **9/2**[3]
1522 **3** 3½ **Bow Creek (IRE)**[43] 3378 3-9-1 108 JoeFanning 4 104
(Mark Johnston) *hld up in tch: clsd and nt clr run ent fnl 2f: swtchd lft and effrt wl over 1f out: kpt on to go 3rd ins fnl f: no threat to ldrs* **4/1**[2]
-034 **4** 1½ **Windfast (IRE)**[44] 3352 3-9-1 108 JimmyFortune 6 101
(Brian Meehan) *chsd ldrs: effrt to press ldrs whn carried rt ent fnl 2f: hmpd but chsd wnr over 1f out: no ex: wknd and lost 2 pls ins fnl f* **11/1**
1423 **5** 8 **Shifting Power**[18] 4278 3-9-1 115 RichardHughes 5 83
(Richard Hannon) *chsd ldr: led ent fnl 2f: sn rdn: hung rt and hdd: btn over 1f out: sn wknd and eased wl ins fnl f* **6/4**[1]
1 **6** 22 **Rapprochement (IRE)**[14] 4407 3-9-1 0 AdamKirby 8 32
(Charlie Appleby) *taken down early: led tl rdn and hdd ent fnl 2f: losing pl whn bdly hmpd wl over 1f out: bhd and eased after: t.o* **8/1**

1m 36.1s (-3.80) **Going Correction** -0.05s/f (Good) **6 Ran SP% 110.1**
Speed ratings (Par 110): **117,116,113,111,103 81**
CSF £36.08 TOTE £6.60: £2.50, £2.50; EX 36.70 Trifecta £142.80.
**Owner** Normandie Stud Ltd **Bred** Normandie Stud Ltd **Trained** Newmarket, Suffolk
■ Stewards' Enquiry : Frederik Tylicki four-day ban: 15-18 Aug)

**FOCUS**
A messy race with Rapprochement not settling in front and the field well bunched entering the straight, but the time was 1.30secs quicker than the following Betfred Mile. It's been rated towards the top of the race standard.

## 4851 BETFRED MILE (HERITAGE H'CAP) 1m
**3:05** (3:07) (Class 2) 3-Y-O+
**£80,925** (£24,232; £12,116; £6,058; £3,029; £1,521) **Stalls** Low

Form RPR
0300 **1** **Red Avenger (USA)**[20] 4214 4-8-13 96 (b[1]) JimmyFortune 5 105
(Ed Dunlop) *hld up towards rr: swtchd lft 2f out: rdn and hdwy over 1f out: drvn and str chal fnl 100yds: r.o to ld last stride* **12/1**
1011 **2** *shd* **Heavy Metal**[6] 4648 4-9-0 97 3ex JoeFanning 11 106
(Mark Johnston) *chsd ldrs: chsd ldr and clsd over 2f out: drvn to ld over 1f out: battled on gamely u.p: hdd last stride* **6/1**[1]
0042 **3** *nk* **Magic City (IRE)**[33] 3753 5-9-0 97 RichardHughes 8 105
(Richard Hannon) *hld up towards rr: swtchd lft and hdwy ent fnl f: r.o strly ins fnl f: nt quite rch ldrs* **7/1**[2]
4503 **4** *nk* **Steeler (IRE)**[44] 3356 4-9-9 106 WilliamBuick 17 113
(Charlie Appleby) *chsd ldrs: rdn and effrt to chal 2f out: drvn and kpt on wl fr over 1f out: no ex cl home* **14/1**
-300 **5** *hd* **Belgian Bill**[6] 4648 6-9-5 102 (tp) GeorgeBaker 1 109
(George Baker) *hld up in tch in midfield: pushed rt and nt clr run over 1f out: swtchd lft 1f out: hdwy and swtchd lft again ins fnl f: r.o: nt clr run cl home* **8/1**[3]
0640 **6** ½ **Fort Bastion (IRE)**[6] 4648 5-8-12 95 JamesSullivan 3 101
(Ruth Carr) *hld up in tch: pushed rt and hdwy over 1f out: swtchd rt ins fnl f: r.o wl: nt rch ldrs* **11/1**
5410 **7** ½ **Bronze Angel (IRE)**[6] 4648 5-9-0 97 3ex (v[1]) MartinDwyer 22 101
(Marcus Tregoning) *stdd and dropped in bhd: nt clr run ent fnl 2f: swtchd lft jst over 1f out: r.o u.p fnl f: nt rch ldrs* **11/1**
-102 **8** *hd* **Our Channel (USA)**[20] 4230 3-8-11 101 SilvestreDeSousa 18 104
(William Haggas) *taken down early: broke fast to ld and crossed to inner: 5 l clr 1/2-way: rdn and pressed 2f out: hdd over 1f out: kpt on and stl pressing ldrs tl wknd fnl 50yds* **11/1**
4310 **9** *hd* **Two For Two (IRE)**[20] 4214 6-9-4 101 DanielTudhope 13 104
(David O'Meara) *s.i.s: hld up in rr: hdwy on inner and nt clr run jst over 1f out: swtchd lft jst ins fnl f: r.o ins fnl f: nt rch ldrs* **25/1**
0014 **10** 1½ **Heaven's Guest (IRE)**[6] 4648 4-9-6 103 3ex RyanMoore 12 103
(Richard Fahey) *hld up towards rr: rdn 2f out: styd on steadily ins fnl f: nvr trbld ldrs* **12/1**
-401 **11** 1¾ **Velox**[27] 3982 4-9-0 97 AndreaAtzeni 10 93
(Luca Cumani) *wl in tch in midfield: rdn and effrt 2f out: unable qck and drifting rt over 1f out: stl hanging rt and wknd ins fnl f* **6/1**[1]
-600 **12** ½ **Pastoral Player**[6] 4648 7-8-9 99 CharlieBennett(7) 2 93
(Hughie Morrison) *taken down early: stdd s: hld up towards rr: gd hdwy on inner 2f out: no hdwy u.p over 1f out: wknd ins fnl f* **22/1**

160 **13** ½ **Capo Rosso (IRE)**[20] 4212 4-8-12 **95**....................(t) RichardKingscote 7 88
(Tom Dascombe) *hld up in midfield: n.m.r 2f out: sme hdwy 1f out: kpt on fnl f: n.d* **25/1**

-502 **14** 2¾ **Boomshackerlacker (IRE)**[7] 4644 4-9-6 **103**..............(p) AdamKirby 20 90
(George Baker) *in tch in midfield but stuck wd: rdn and 2f out: no ex over 1f out: wknd fnl f* **33/1**

-120 **15** 2 **Horsted Keynes (FR)**[6] 4648 4-9-6 **103**........................ JimCrowley 14 85
(Roger Varian) *in tch in midfield: rdn wl over 1f out: carried rt and no hdwy ent fnl f: wknd fnl 150yds* **17/2**

464 **16** 1¾ **Askaud (IRE)**[60] 2840 6-8-10 **93**................................(p) FrederikTylicki 16 71
(Scott Dixon) *chsd ldr tl over 2f out: lost pl u.p wl over 1f out: wknd over 1f out* **66/1**

5326 **17** ¾ **George Guru**[48] 3244 7-8-13 **96**....................................... RobertHavlin 4 72
(Michael Attwater) *t.k.h: hld up in tch: lost pl and drvn 2f out: wknd over 1f out* **22/1**

1m 37.4s (-2.50) **Going Correction** -0.05s/f (Good)
**WFA** 3 from 4yo+ 7lb **17** Ran SP% **130.6**
Speed ratings (Par 109): **110,109,109,109,109 108,108,107,107,106 104,103,103,100,98 96,96**
CSF £81.14 CT £568.25 TOTE £16.80: £3.90, £1.80, £2.00, £3.70; EX 125.50 Trifecta £733.30.
**Owner** The Hon R J Arculli **Bred** Wedgewood Farm **Trained** Newmarket, Suffolk
■ Stewards' Enquiry : Jimmy Fortune nine-day ban: use of whip (15-23 Aug); £2300 fine: use of whip

**FOCUS**
A red-hot handicap in which seven of the 17 remaining runners had contested the International Handicap at Ascot the previous weekend. Eight of the last ten winners were been drawn eight or lower (a trend that continued), but although 3yos had won four of the last six runnings, there was only one representative from that age-group this year. The race was weakened slightly when the fancied top-weight Captain Cat was unable to take part due to transport problems, but it was still a most-competitive event in which Our Channel made sure there was no hanging about. Sound form with the third close to last year's best.

## 4852 BETFRED KING GEORGE STKS (GROUP 2) 5f
**3:40** (3:41) (Class 1) 3-Y-O+

**£56,710** (£21,500; £10,760; £5,360; £2,690; £1,350) **Stalls High**

Form RPR

2-01 **1** **Take Cover**[20] 4215 7-9-1 109........................................... AndreaAtzeni 4 116
(David C Griffiths) *taken down early and led to s: led for 1f: chsd ldr tl rdn to ld again over 1f out: edgd rt but hld on wl ins fnl f: all out* **6/1**[3]

0121 **2** nk **Extortionist (IRE)**[27] 3981 3-8-12 113.............................. RyanMoore 8 114
(Olly Stevens) *hld up in rr: swtchd rt and hdwy over 1f out: ev ch 100yds: r.o wl: wnt 2nd nr fin* **5/1**[2]

-500 **3** shd **Moviesta (USA)**[20] 4201 4-9-1 111.............................. PaulMulrennan 5 115
(Bryan Smart) *hld up off the pce in midfield: hdwy over 1f out: chsd wnr 1f out: edgd lft: ev ch fnl 100yds: r.o: lost 2nd nr fin* **9/2**[1]

3426 **4** 1½ **Stepper Point**[27] 3981 5-9-1 113..............................(p) MartinDwyer 15 109
(William Muir) *racd along against stands' rail: off the pce in midfield: rdn 2f out: styd on wl ins fnl f: nt rch ldrs* **12/1**

1132 **5** ½ **G Force (IRE)**[20] 4215 3-8-12 105.............................. DanielTudhope 10 106
(David O'Meara) *hld up in tch in midfield: rdn and effrt wl over 1f out: styd on same pce u.p fnl f* **7/1**

6100 **6** hd **Hamza (IRE)**[41] 3452 5-9-1 109..............................(v[1]) RichardHughes 3 107
(Kevin Ryan) *chsd ldrs: rdn 2f out: drvn over 1f out: kpt on same pce ins fnl f* **10/1**

0414 **7** hd **Wind Fire (USA)**[27] 3981 3-8-9 103.............................. JamieSpencer 12 102
(David Brown) *off the pce in midfield: rdn 1/2-way: hdwy and drifing rt over 1f out: swtchd lft ins fnl f: kpt on wl: no threat to ldrs* **14/1**

2324 **8** 1 **Kingsgate Native (IRE)**[20] 4215 9-9-1 112.............................. JimCrowley 2 102
(Robert Cowell) *hld up in tch in midfield: rdn and effrt jst over 1f out: no prog and btn fnl 150yds: wknd towards fin* **9/1**

6210 **9** 1¼ **Hay Chewed (IRE)**[27] 3981 3-8-9 99..............................[1] TomEaves 1 94
(Conrad Allen) *in tch in midfield: rdn and hdwy 1/2-way: chsd wnr jst over 1f out tl 1f out: sn btn and wknd fnl 150yds* **50/1**

5101 **10** 1 **Ladies Are Forever**[21] 4171 6-8-12 108...............(b) SilvestreDeSousa 9 91
(Geoffrey Oldroyd) *wnt lft s: bhd: sme hdwy u.p 2f out: no imp fnl f: n.d* **14/1**

1-14 **11** hd **Demora**[20] 4179 5-8-12 102.............................. AndrewMullen 7 91
(Michael Appleby) *chsd ldrs: rdn 2f out: drvn and btn over 1f out: wknd ins fnl f* **16/1**

-235 **12** ½ **Reroute (IRE)**[20] 4215 3-8-9 97..............................(b[1]) WilliamBuick 11 88
(Ed Walker) *chsd ldrs: rdn and effrt 2f out: no ex and btn over 1f out: wknd ins fnl f* **50/1**

0330 **13** shd **Monsieur Joe (IRE)**[5] 4700 7-9-1 104.............................. TomQueally 16 91
(Paul Midgley) *a towards rr: swtchd to centre and rdn over 3f out: nvr trbld ldrs* **33/1**

510- **14** ½ **Brown Sugar (IRE)**[293] 7191 3-8-12 111.............................. PatDobbs 13 89
(Richard Hannon) *s.i.s: a bhd: n.d* **25/1**

2162 **15** 1¾ **Caspian Prince (IRE)**[12] 4480 5-9-1 100..............................(t) AdamKirby 6 83
(Tony Carroll) *nt best away: rdn and rcvrd to ld after 1f: rdn and hdd over 1f out: lost 2nd jst over 1f out: fdd fnl f* **20/1**

56.47s (-3.73) **Going Correction** -0.35s/f (Firm)
**WFA** 3 from 4yo+ 3lb **15** Ran SP% **123.1**
Speed ratings (Par 115): **115,114,114,111,111 110,110,108,106,105 105,104,104,103,100**
CSF £34.70 TOTE £7.10: £2.60, £2.20, £2.20; EX 40.40 Trifecta £231.20.
**Owner** Norcroft Park Stud **Bred** Norcroft Park Stud **Trained** Bawtry, S Yorks

**FOCUS**
A well up-to-scratch running of this Group 2 sprint - competitive as ever - even in the absence of July Cup second Tropics. They were spread all the way across the track in the closing stages. The third has been rated to last year's winning mark.

## 4853 BETFRED SUPPORTS JACK BERRY HOUSE NURSERY STKS (H'CAP) (BOBIS RACE) 6f
**4:15** (4:17) (Class 2) 2-Y-O **£12,938** (£3,850; £1,924; £962) **Stalls High**

Form RPR

16 **1** **Son Of Africa**[32] 3786 2-9-1 **83**.............................. JamesDoyle 3 87+
(Henry Candy) *chsd ldr tl led 4f out: mde rest: rdn over 1f out: drifting lft wl fnl f: r.o and a holding rivals* **7/1**

641 **2** ½ **Markaz (IRE)**[21] 4142 2-9-3 **85**.............................. GeorgeBaker 6 88+
(B W Hills) *hld in tch in rr: rdn and hdwy in centre over 1f out: chsd wnr ins fnl f: ev ch fnl 50yds: r.o but hld towards fin* **11/4**[1]

521 **3** ½ **Sunset Sail (IRE)**[46] 3311 2-9-4 **86**.............................. RichardHughes 9 88+
(Richard Hannon) *hld up in last quartet: clsng whn nt clr run and swtchd lft ent fnl f: r.o wl ins fnl f: wnt 3rd cl home: nvr quite getting to ldrs* **9/2**[2]

51 **4** ½ **Inniscastle Lad**[14] 4409 2-8-12 **80**.............................. MartinDwyer 5 80
(William Muir) *chsd ldrs: rdn and sltly outpcd over 1f out: ralllied and kpt on u.p ins fnl f* **10/1**

10 **5** ¾ **George Bowen (IRE)**[22] 4123 2-9-2 **84**.............................. TonyHamilton 13 81+
(Richard Fahey) *t.k.h: hld up in tch in midfield: effrt 2f out: nt clr run and swtchd rt 1f out: styd on u.p ins fnl f: nvr quite enough pce to rch ldrs* **12/1**

6210 **6** 2 **Magical Memory (IRE)**[13] 4439 2-9-6 **88**.............................. RyanMoore 7 79
(Charles Hills) *in tch in midfield: rdn and effrt 2f out: chsd wnr 1f out: no ex: lost 2nd and wknd ins fnl f* **7/1**

1 **7** ¾ **Great Park (IRE)**[36] 3620 2-8-12 **80**.............................. DavidProbert 2 69
(Martyn Meade) *in tch in midfield: rdn and unable qck over 1f out: wknd ins fnl f* **25/1**

4133 **8** 1½ **Red Icon (IRE)**[32] 3786 2-9-7 **89**.............................. RichardKingscote 8 74
(Tom Dascombe) *in tch in midfield: effrt 2f out: lost pl whn short of room over 1f out: no imp u.p fnl f* **16/1**

2341 **9** 1 **Vimy Ridge**[7] 4625 2-9-2 **89** 6ex.............................. JackGarritty[(5)] 12 71+
(Richard Fahey) *hld up in last quartet: effrt 2f out: stl plenty to do whn pushed lft ent fnl f: no imp* **13/2**[3]

4420 **10** 3¼ **Brazen Spirit**[13] 4439 2-8-12 **80**.............................. HarryBentley 1 52
(Clive Cox) *in tch in midfield: rdn 2f out: lost pl u.p over 1f out: wknd fnl f* **25/1**

3346 **11** ½ **Dominic Cork**[21] 4172 2-8-1 **69** ow1.............................. SilvestreDeSousa 14 39
(Kevin Ryan) *led tl 4f out: chsd wnr tl drvn and btn 1f out: sn wknd* **40/1**

510 **12** 2¼ **Showcard**[42] 3415 2-8-10 **78**.............................. AndreaAtzeni 10 42+
(Gary Moore) *lost a shoe bef r: a bhd: rdn and no hdwy 2f out: wknd over 1f out* **33/1**

1m 10.92s (-1.28) **Going Correction** -0.35s/f (Firm) **12** Ran SP% **118.9**
Speed ratings (Par 100): **94,93,92,92,91 88,87,85,84,79 79,76**
CSF £25.61 CT £100.73 TOTE £8.30: £2.50, £1.30, £2.20; EX 29.40 Trifecta £141.90.
**Owner** One Too Many Partners **Bred** Mrs P A Clark **Trained** Kingston Warren, Oxon

**FOCUS**
This looks strong nursery form, the winner and second both holding Group-race entries. They raced middle to stands' side. The runner-up is progressing.

## 4854 L'ORMARINS QUEENS PLATE STKS (REGISTERED AS THE OAK TREE STAKES) (GROUP 3) (F&M) 7f
**4:50** (4:51) (Class 1) 3-Y-O+

**£34,026** (£12,900; £6,456; £3,216; £1,614; £810) **Stalls Low**

Form RPR

-100 **1** **J Wonder (USA)**[42] 3418 3-8-13 104.............................. JimmyFortune 10 110+
(Brian Meehan) *stdd s and dropped in bhd: t.k.h: swtchd lft and effrt over 1f out: str run to chse ldr ins fnl f: r.o to ld cl home* **7/1**

-111 **2** nk **Muteela**[44] 3357 3-8-10 100.............................. JoeFanning 5 106
(Mark Johnston) *led: rdn wl over 1f out: battled on wl u.p tl hdd and no ex cl home* **7/4**[1]

013 **3** ¾ **Indignant**[21] 4171 4-9-2 102.............................. PatDobbs 3 106
(Richard Hannon) *chsd ldr tl 1/2-way: stydchsng ldrs: rdn 2f out: kpt on same pce u.p ins fnl f* **16/1**

-035 **4** ½ **Valonia**[41] 3459 3-8-10 97.............................. HarryBentley 6 103
(Henry Candy) *t.k.h: chsd ldrs: wnt 2nd 1/2-way: rdn ent fnl 2f: kpt on: lost 2nd and one pce ins fnl f* **33/1**

-462 **5** hd **This Time (FR)**[26] 4009 3-8-10 104.............................. FabriceVeron 8 102
(H-A Pantall, France) *in tch in midfield: clsd and chsng ldrs whn nt clr run and switching lft and rt over 1f out: rdn 1f out: nvr enough room after: kpt on cl home* **12/1**

5025 **6** 1½ **Queen Catrine (IRE)**[27] 3983 3-8-10 105.............................. JamieSpencer 2 98
(Charles Hills) *stdd and dropped in bhd s: hld up in rr: effrt on outer 2f out: rdn and no imp ent fnl f* **4/1**[2]

2132 **7** ½ **Wee Jean**[27] 3983 3-8-10 103.............................. RyanMoore 4 97
(Mick Channon) *in tch in midfield: stuck on inner and nvr enough room fr 2f out: nvr able to cl and dropped bk ins fnl f* **6/1**[3]

0052 **8** hd **The Gold Cheongsam (IRE)**[6] 4668 4-9-2 98..............(tp) SebSanders 9 99
(Jeremy Noseda) *in tch in midfield: rdn to chse ldrs 2f out: no ex u.p ins fnl f: wknd towards fin* **12/1**

5410 **9** 23 **Manderley (IRE)**[34] 3724 3-8-10 109.............................. RichardHughes 7 34
(Richard Hannon) *in tch in last trio: effrt over 1f out: sn btn and sltly hmpd over 1f out: heavily eased ins fnl f* **14/1**

1m 25.09s (-1.91) **Going Correction** -0.05s/f (Good)
**WFA** 3 from 4yo 6lb **9** Ran SP% **114.0**
Speed ratings (Par 113): **108,107,106,106,106 104,103,103,77**
CSF £19.37 TOTE £7.90: £2.30, £1.10, £4.50; EX 24.30 Trifecta £225.30.
**Owner** Andrew Rosen **Bred** Canterbury Lace Syndicate **Trained** Manton, Wilts
■ Stewards' Enquiry : Seb Sanders three-day ban: used whip without time to respond

**FOCUS**
A Group 3 fillies' event in which 3yos had just held sway in the previous ten runnings. The pace looked modest, which makes the winner's effort all the more creditable. Mudding form rated through the third.

## 4855 BETFRED MOBILE STKS (H'CAP) (BOBIS RACE) 1m 3f
**5:25** (5:25) (Class 3) (0-90,89) 3-Y-O

**£10,893** (£3,262; £1,631; £815; £407; £204) **Stalls High**

Form RPR

-452 **1** **Tall Ship (IRE)**[22] 4120 3-8-6 **74**.............................. DavidProbert 3 84
(Gary Moore) *chsd ldrs and effrt on inner 2f out: chal 1f out: led ins fnl f: r.o wl and wl in command at fin* **10/1**

2352 **2** 1½ **Artful Rogue (IRE)**[23] 4077 3-8-7 **75**....................(p) SilvestreDeSousa 4 82
(Amanda Perrett) *chsd ldr tl led 8f out: rdn over 2f out: hdd over 1f out: kpt on u.p and led again jst ins fnl f: sn hdd and one pce* **13/2**

4053 **3** 1 **Fire Fighting (IRE)**[13] 4452 3-8-12 **80**.............................. JoeFanning 6 85
(Mark Johnston) *hld up in tch in midfield: clsd to press ldr ent fnl 2f: rdn and led over 1f out: drvn and hdd jst ins fnl f: outpcd fnl 100yds* **4/1**[1]

4413 **4** ½ **Rydan (IRE)**[28] 3931 3-9-4 **86**.............................. TomQueally 9 90
(Robert Mills) *dwlt: hld up in last pair: hdwy u.p and drifting rt over 1f out: styd on same pce fnl f* **9/2**[2]

4134 **5** 1 **Cape Caster (IRE)**[29] 3892 3-8-13 **81**.............................. JimCrowley 8 84
(Ralph Beckett) *hld up in tch in midfield: swtchd effrt u.p and carried rt over 1f out: styd on same pce fnl f* **6/1**[3]

346 **6** ½ **Arantes**[13] 4453 3-8-13 **81**..............................(v[1]) CraigAWilliams 11 83
(Mick Channon) *stdd s: hld up in rr: clsd over 2f out: rdn and effrt over 1f out: kpt on u.p ins fnl f: nvr trbld ldrs* **16/1**

1-40 **7** ½ **Festival Theatre (IRE)**[85] 2087 3-9-1 **83**.............................. RyanMoore 2 84
(Sir Michael Stoute) *in tch in last quartet: swtchd lft jst over 2f out: n.m.r wl over 1f out: rdn hands and heels over 1f out: n.d but kpt on steadily ins fnl f* **6/1**[3]

1444 **8** 2¾ **Cameo Tiara (IRE)**[21] 4145 3-8-12 **80**.............................. RichardHughes 1 76
(Richard Hannon) *led for 3f: chsd ldr tl ent fnl 2f: lost pl and hmpd over 1f out: wknd 1f out* **8/1**

336 **9** *6* **Stormardal (IRE)**[22] 4125 3-9-7 **89** DanielTudhope 7 75
(Ismail Mohammed) *t.k.h: chsd ldrs: short of room 2f out: sn lost pl wknd ent fnl f* **14/1**

-310 **10** *17* **Art Of War (IRE)**[43] 3379 3-9-5 **87** RichardKingscote 10 44
(Tom Dascombe) *in tch in midfield on outer: rdn and dropped to rr whn hmpd over 2f out: wknd wl over 1f out: eased ins fnl f* **16/1**

2m 25.31s (-1.19) **Going Correction** -0.05s/f (Good) **10** Ran SP% **118.7**
Speed ratings (Par 104): **102,100,100,99,99 98,98,96,92,79**
CSF £74.91 CT £308.60 TOTE £13.30: £3.40, £1.70, £1.90; EX 64.30 Trifecta £247.20.
**Owner** R A Green **Bred** Kincorth Investments Inc **Trained** Lower Beeding, W Sussex

**FOCUS**
A fair 3yo handicap. There was a muddling pace and the first two were always well placed.
T/Jkpt: Not won. T/Plt: £70.00 to a £1 stake. Pool: £304367.00 - 3171.14 winning tickets T/Qpdt: £6.60 to a £1 stake. Pool: £22622.09 - 2512.72 winning tickets SP

# 4517 MUSSELBURGH (R-H)
Friday, August 1

**OFFICIAL GOING: Good to firm (7.7)**
Wind: Almost nil Weather: Overcast

## 4856 REBECCA WILSON HEN PARTY AMATEUR RIDERS' H'CAP 1m 5f
6:10 (6:10) (Class 5) (0-70,67) 4-Y-0+ **£3,119** (£967; £483; £242) **Stalls** Centre

Form RPR

603 **1** **Giovanni Jack**[23] 4066 4-9-5 **49** MissMeganNicholls(5) 3 64
(Alan Swinbank) *hld up towards rr: gd hdwy on outside to ld over 2f out: edgd rt over 1f out: sn clr* **17/2**

2253 **2** *8* **Geanie Mac (IRE)**[4] 4726 5-9-11 **55** (p) PhillipDennis(5) 7 58
(Linda Perratt) *t.k.h: cl up: chal after 2f: rdn over 2f out: kpt on fnl f: no ch w wnr* **13/2**[2]

4353 **3** *nk* **Grand Diamond (IRE)**[11] 4492 10-9-13 **52** MrsCBartley 6 55
(Jim Goldie) *hld up: pushed along and outpcd over 3f out: rallied over 1f out: kpt on fnl f: nvr able to chal* **7/1**[3]

-060 **4** *3/4* **Golden Future**[26] 3482 11-9-8 **50** MissJoannaMason(3) 4 51
(Peter Niven) *chsd ldrs: drvn along over 2f out: one pce over 1f out* **16/1**

-026 **5** *1* **Harrison's Cave**[11] 4492 6-10-8 **61** MissADeniel 5 61
(Keith Dalgleish) *hld up: rdn along on outside over 3f out: no imp fr 2f out* **8/1**

5414 **6** *nk* **Eilean Mor**[10] 4520 6-9-12 **54** MrTHamilton(3) 1 53
(R Mike Smith) *led: jnd after 2f: hung lft and hdd over 2f out: sn outpcd* **7/1**[3]

1226 **7** *2 1/4* **Ballyheigue (IRE)**[26] 4041 5-10-0 **58** (p) MissHHeal(5) 8 54
(Liam Corcoran) *in tch: pushed along over 2f out: sn outpcd* **8/1**

0652 **8** *1 1/2* **Duke Of Yorkshire**[11] 4498 4-10-11 **67** MrWEasterby(3) 9 61
(Tim Easterby) *t.k.h: trckd ldrs on outside: rdn and outpcd over 2f out: sn btn* **15/8**[1]

2m 54.35s (2.35) **Going Correction** +0.125s/f (Good) **8** Ran SP% **111.7**
Speed ratings (Par 103): **97,92,91,91,90 90,89,88**
CSF £59.27 CT £402.71 TOTE £10.10: £3.40, £2.70, £2.00; EX 77.70 Trifecta £708.40.
**Owner** Mrs Lizzy Wilson **Bred** Juddmonte Farms Ltd **Trained** Melsonby, N Yorks

**FOCUS**
A weak handicap for amatuer riders. The runner-up has been rated close to her recent form.

## 4857 WILKINSON & ASSOCIATES NURSERY H'CAP 5f
6:45 (6:45) (Class 6) (0-65,64) 2-Y-0 **£3,234** (£962; £481; £120; £120) **Stalls** High

Form RPR

4055 **1** **Bowson Fred**[21] 4172 2-9-4 **61** BarryMcHugh 5 65
(Michael Easterby) *pressed ldr: led gng wl over 1f out: sn rdn: kpt on wl fnl f* **11/4**[2]

304 **2** *1 1/2* **Westhoughton**[15] 4357 2-9-5 **62** DavidNolan 6 61
(David O'Meara) *in tch: effrt and rdn over 1f out: kpt on fnl f: wnt 2nd cl home* **2/1**[1]

4025 **3** *nk* **Penalty Scorer**[5] 4702 2-8-5 **53** (e) DuilioDaSilva(5) 3 51
(Richard Guest) *hld up in tch: hdwy to chse wnr over 1f out: kpt on fnl f: lost 2nd cl home* **16/1**

3444 **4** *1* **Surrey Pink (FR)**[17] 4283 2-8-11 **54** PhillipMakin 2 48
(William Muir) *dwlt: bhd and sn outpcd: hdwy on outside over 1f out: kpt on ins fnl f* **7/1**

005 **5** *dht* **Recover (USA)**[16] 4320 2-9-3 **60** (b) StevieDonohoe 4 54
(Brian Meehan) *cl up: rdn over 1f out: no ex ins fnl f* **11/2**[3]

0304 **6** *6* **Pickle Lilly Pearl**[25] 4018 2-9-3 **60** (p) JasonHart 7 32
(David C Griffiths) *led against stands' rail: rdn over 2f out: hdd over 1f out: sn btn* **7/1**

0443 **7** *2 3/4* **On Appro**[23] 4065 2-8-6 **49** DuranFentiman 8 11
(Tim Easterby) *dwlt: sn in tch: rdn 2f out: wknd appr fnl f* **18/1**

1m 1.18s (0.78) **Going Correction** +0.025s/f (Good) **7** Ran SP% **111.5**
Speed ratings (Par 92): **94,91,91,89,89 79,75**
CSF £8.21 CT £66.38 TOTE £3.20: £1.90, £2.30; EX 9.20 Trifecta £73.70.
**Owner** Mrs A Jarvis **Bred** Mrs A Jarvis **Trained** Sheriff Hutton, N Yorks

**FOCUS**
An ordinary nursery. The modest third has been rated to her mark.

## 4858 PMD LTD H'CAP 1m 1f
7:20 (7:20) (Class 5) (0-70,70) 3-Y-0+ **£5,175** (£1,540; £769; £384) **Stalls** Low

Form RPR

1503 **1** **Camerooney**[14] 4387 11-9-7 **70** (p) JordanNason(7) 2 78
(Marjorie Fife) *mde all: qcknd over 3f out: rdn 2f out: hld on wl fnl f* **4/1**[2]

1052 **2** *1/2* **Ellaal**[10] 4517 5-9-12 **68** DaleSwift 3 75
(Ruth Carr) *trckd ldrs: effrt and rdn over 2f out: chsd wnr over 1f out: kpt on: hld nr fin* **7/2**[1]

2522 **3** *1 3/4* **Call Of Duty (IRE)**[14] 4387 9-8-8 **55** (p) EmmaSayer(5) 4 58
(Dianne Sayer) *dwlt: bhd: outpcd 1/2-way: hdwy on outside wl over 1f out: kpt on fnl f: nrst fin* **13/2**[3]

5532 **4** *1/2* **Janaab (IRE)**[14] 4394 4-9-8 **64** (t) DavidAllan 8 66
(Tim Easterby) *trckd wnr: rdn over 2f out: edgd rt over 1f out: sn one pce* **7/2**[1]

3522 **5** *1/2* **Dhaular Dhar (IRE)**[10] 4520 12-9-0 **59** GaryBartley(3) 1 60
(Jim Goldie) *hld up in tch: pushed along over 2f out: no imp fr over 1f out* **8/1**

3403 **6** *4* **Royal Straight**[10] 4517 9-9-1 **62** (t) SammyJoBell(5) 6 55
(Linda Perratt) *hld up in tch: stdy hdwy over 2f out: rdn and one pce whn n.m.r briefly over 1f out: sn btn* **15/2**

0200 **7** *1 1/4* **Outlaw Torn (IRE)**[6] 4661 5-9-4 **65** (e) DuilioDaSilva(5) 7 55
(Richard Guest) *t.k.h: hld up: rdn and effrt over 2f out: wknd over 1f out* **8/1**

1m 54.2s (0.30) **Going Correction** +0.125s/f (Good) **7** Ran SP% **111.8**
Speed ratings (Par 103): **103,102,101,100,100 96,95**
CSF £17.49 CT £85.65 TOTE £4.90: £2.30, £2.80; EX 19.80 Trifecta £60.80.
**Owner** Mrs Jean Stapleton **Bred** Miss Dianne Hill **Trained** Stillington, N Yorks

**FOCUS**
A modest handicap. The runner-up has been rated as improving marginally on his latest C&D form.

## 4859 MABANAFT MABA-DASH H'CAP 5f
7:50 (7:50) (Class 3) (0-90,90) 3-Y-0+ **£7,762** (£2,310; £1,154; £577) **Stalls** High

Form RPR

1533 **1** **Algar Lad**[21] 4174 4-9-3 **86** SamJames(3) 7 95
(David O'Meara) *cl up: led over 1f out: edgd rt and hrd pressed ins fnl f: hld on wl u.p* **2/1**[1]

5651 **2** *shd* **Bunce (IRE)**[11] 4488 6-8-9 **75** 6ex PJMcDonald 2 83
(Linda Perratt) *bhd and sn outpcd: gd hdwy on outside over 1f out: kpt on wl fnl f: jst failed* **10/1**

3316 **3** *1 1/4* **Red Lady (IRE)**[16] 4328 3-8-8 **77** StevieDonohoe 6 79
(Brian Meehan) *cl up: effrt and rdn over 1f out: kpt on same pce ins fnl f* **8/1**

0330 **4** *1/2* **Alaskan Bullet (IRE)**[11] 4488 5-8-10 **76** (p) PaulPickard 3 77
(Brian Ellison) *dwlt: hld up: rdn and hdwy over 1f out: kpt on fnl f: no imp* **13/2**[3]

3040 **5** *nk* **Imperial Legend (IRE)**[11] 4488 5-9-3 **83** (v) PaulQuinn 1 83
(David Nicholls) *dwlt: hld up in tch on outside: smooth hdwy 1/2-way: rdn over 1f out: one pce whn hmpd ins fnl f* **13/2**[3]

5652 **6** *1/2* **Jofranka**[7] 4630 4-8-8 **74** (b[1]) DavidAllan 8 72
(David Barron) *t.k.h: led tl rdn and hdd over 1f out: sn no ex* **9/2**[2]

1030 **7** *5* **Bispham Green**[7] 4609 4-9-4 **84** (b[1]) DavidNolan 9 64
(David O'Meara) *prom: drvn over 2f out: wknd over 1f out* **7/1**

59.68s (-0.72) **Going Correction** +0.025s/f (Good)
**WFA** 3 from 4yo+ 3lb **7** Ran SP% **110.9**
Speed ratings (Par 107): **106,105,103,103,102 101,93**
CSF £21.55 CT £124.40 TOTE £2.80: £1.70, £3.80; EX 16.60 Trifecta £131.60.
**Owner** Great Northern Partnership **Bred** Highclere Stud **Trained** Nawton, N Yorks

**FOCUS**
Not a bad sprint handicap. The winner has been rated as recording a small pb, while the runner-up has run his best race since his 2yo days.

## 4860 WILKINSON & ASSOCIATES H'CAP 5f
8:20 (8:20) (Class 6) (0-65,63) 3-Y-0+ **£3,234** (£962; £481; £240) **Stalls** High

Form RPR

2150 **1** **Scoreline**[27] 3972 3-9-4 **63** SamJames(3) 6 71
(David O'Meara) *prom: rdn 2f out: hdwy to ld ins fnl f: pushed out* **4/1**[2]

0010 **2** *3/4* **Tadalavil**[6] 4664 9-8-9 **53** SammyJoBell(5) 2 59
(Linda Perratt) *hld up in tch: hdwy on outside over 1f out: chsd wnr ins fnl f: r.o* **9/1**

0002 **3** *nk* **Pavers Star**[10] 4519 5-8-3 **45** (p) JoeyHaynes(3) 5 50
(Noel Wilson) *led: rdn over 1f out: hdd ins fnl f: kpt on same pce* **4/1**[2]

0-41 **4** *3/4* **Mandy Layla (IRE)**[15] 4362 4-9-8 **61** PhillipMakin 4 63
(Bryan Smart) *chsd ldr: rdn and edgd rt over 1f out: rallied and ev ch briefly ins fnl f: one pce last 100yds* **2/1**[1]

6254 **5** *1* **Your Gifted (IRE)**[15] 4344 7-9-1 **54** (v) PJMcDonald 3 53
(Lisa Williamson) *dwlt: hld up: hdwy over 1f out: rdn and no imp fnl f* **11/2**[3]

4020 **6** *2 1/4* **I'll Be Good**[45] 3338 5-9-4 **60** (t) SladeO'Hara(3) 7 51
(Alan Berry) *cl up tl rdn and wknd over 1f out* **7/1**

1m 0.47s (0.07) **Going Correction** +0.025s/f (Good)
**WFA** 3 from 4yo+ 3lb **6** Ran SP% **111.2**
Speed ratings (Par 101): **100,98,98,97,95 91**
CSF £36.32 TOTE £4.20: £1.60, £3.80; EX 41.90 Trifecta £104.30.
**Owner** K Nicholson & Partners **Bred** Mickley Stud **Trained** Nawton, N Yorks

**FOCUS**
A modest handicap, run at a strong pace. The runner-up has been rated to his Ayr win.

## 4861 THOMSON ANNIVERSARY H'CAP (QUALIFIER FOR THE £15,000 BETFAIR SCOTTISH MILE SERIES FINAL) 7f 30y
8:50 (8:50) (Class 5) (0-75,75) 3-Y-0+ **£3,234** (£962; £481; £240) **Stalls** Low

Form RPR

3123 **1** **Strong Man**[119] 1286 6-9-10 **73** BarryMcHugh 3 81
(Michael Easterby) *stdd in rr: shkn up and plenty to do 3f out: hdwy against far rail over 1f out: kpt on wl to ld nr fin* **8/1**

-550 **2** *nk* **Smart Alec (IRE)**[44] 3360 3-8-1 **56** DuranFentiman 1 60
(Alan Swinbank) *in tch: effrt over 2f out: led against far rail over 1f out: kpt on fnl f: hdd nr fin* **10/1**

0142 **3** *shd* **Opt Out**[11] 4487 4-9-2 **65** PJMcDonald 2 71
(Alistair Whillans) *dwlt: hld up: hdwy on outside 2f out: kpt on ins fnl f* **9/2**[2]

265 **4** *2* **Funding Deficit (IRE)**[26] 4004 4-8-7 **63** JordanNason(7) 6 64
(Jim Goldie) *awkward s: sn prom: rdn over 2f out: edgd rt wl over 1f out: one pce fnl f* **10/1**

1314 **5** *1 1/2* **Mowhoob**[25] 4013 4-9-6 **72** GaryBartley(3) 8 69
(Jim Goldie) *w ldr: led over 2f out to over 1f out: outpcd fnl f* **13/2**

2142 **6** *2* **Cara's Request (AUS)**[21] 4156 9-9-7 **75** KevinStott(5) 5 67
(Michael Dods) *trckd ldrs: effrt and rdn over 2f out: wknd appr fnl f* **2/1**[1]

0002 **7** *1/2* **Snow Bay**[39] 3533 8-9-11 **74** PhillipMakin 4 64
(Paul Midgley) *led at decent gallop: hdd over 2f out: rallied and ev ch over 1f out: sn btn* **5/1**[3]

-020 **8** *2 1/2* **Chookie's Lass**[14] 4383 3-8-12 **67** JasonHart 7 49
(Keith Dalgleish) *s.i.s: t.k.h in rr: struggling 1/2-way: nvr on terms* **25/1**

1m 29.17s (0.17) **Going Correction** +0.125s/f (Good)
**WFA** 3 from 4yo+ 6lb **8** Ran SP% **114.7**
Speed ratings (Par 103): **104,103,103,101,99 97,96,93**
CSF £83.40 CT £329.28 TOTE £9.90: £2.80, £2.70, £1.90; EX 96.60 Trifecta £312.40.
**Owner** Mrs Jean Turpin **Bred** Mrs Jean Turpin **Trained** Sheriff Hutton, N Yorks

**FOCUS**
A modest handicap, run at a strong pace. The runner-up has been rated as running his best race since his 2yo days.
T/Plt: £526.60 to a £1 stake. Pool: £46,437 - 64.36 winning tickets T/Qpdt: £60.80 to a £1 stake. Pool: £4,923 - 59.90 winning tickets RY

4666 **NEWMARKET** (R-H)

Friday, August 1

**OFFICIAL GOING: Good to firm (7.5)**
Wind: Light half-behind Weather: Cloudy

## 4862 JUST RECRUITMENT H'CAP — 6f
5:20 (5:20) (Class 5) (0-75,75) 3-Y-O — £3,881 (£1,155; £577; £288) Stalls High

Form — RPR

5004 1 **He's My Boy (IRE)**[14] 4411 3-8-3 **57** ....(v) HayleyTurner 8 69
(James Fanshawe) *hld up: hdwy over 2f out: rdn to ld ins fnl f: r.o wl* **5/1**[3]

6401 2 2 **Poetic Choice**[37] 3588 3-9-7 **75** .... J-PGuillambert 2 81
(Nick Littmoden) *led: rdn over 1f out: hdd and unable qck ins fnl f* **9/2**[2]

-136 3 2 3/4 **Costa Filey**[24] 4043 3-9-4 **72** .... JimmyQuinn 5 69
(Ed Vaughan) *hood removed late and s.s: hld up: plld hrd: hdwy over 1f out: sn rdn and edgd lft: styd on same pce ins fnl f* **16/1**

-054 4 3/4 **Autumns Blush (IRE)**[5] 4697 3-9-7 **75** .... ShaneKelly 4 70
(Jeremy Noseda) *trckd ldrs: rdn over 1f out: no ex ins fnl f* **11/4**[1]

1130 5 2 1/2 **Moonspring (IRE)**[22] 4132 3-9-4 **72** .... OisinMurphy 6 59
(Robert Cowell) *hld up: hdwy over 1f out: sn rdn: wknd ins fnl f* **15/2**

0004 6 1/2 **Saffire Song**[9] 4531 3-8-12 **66** .... MartinHarley 7 51
(Alan Bailey) *w ldr tl rdn over 2f out: wknd fnl f* **8/1**

0230 7 3/4 **Touch The Clouds**[16] 4328 3-8-12 **73** .... JordonMcMurray[(7)] 3 56
(William Stone) *chsd ldrs: rdn over 2f out: wknd fnl f* **12/1**

-555 8 12 **Finflash (IRE)**[20] 4186 3-9-4 **72** .... WilliamTwiston-Davies 1 16
(Mick Channon) *prom: rdn over 2f out: wknd over 1f out* **13/2**

1m 12.82s (0.32) **Going Correction** +0.125s/f (Good) — 8 Ran SP% **111.3**
Speed ratings (Par 100): **102,99,95,94,91 90,89,73**
CSF £26.16 CT £324.01 TOTE £5.00: £1.70, £1.60, £4.50; EX 23.70 Trifecta £274.90.
**Owner** P S Ryan **Bred** Rossenarra Bloodstock Limited **Trained** Newmarket, Suffolk

**FOCUS**
Not a bad sprint handicap for the class. Stands side track used with Stalls on Far side except 12: Centre. The winner has been rated back to his 2yo level.

## 4863 MURKETTS VAUXHALL H'CAP — 1m 4f
5:50 (5:51) (Class 5) (0-70,75) 3-Y-O — £3,881 (£1,155; £577; £288) Stalls Centre

Form — RPR

0031 1 **Statsminister**[22] 4106 3-9-6 **68** .... FergusSweeney 2 79
(Luke Dace) *s.i.s: rcvrd to ld after 1f: rdn over 2f out: styd on gamely* **16/1**

3301 2 nk **Indira**[16] 4316 3-9-4 **66** .... MartinLane 7 76
(John Berry) *hld up: hdwy 4f out: rdn and hung lft over 1f out: ev ch ins fnl f: styd on* **13/2**[2]

0-44 3 3/4 **Mishko (IRE)**[36] 3631 3-8-12 **67** .... MikeyEnnis[(7)] 1 76
(Steve Gollings) *led 1f: chsd wnr tl wnt upsides over 4f out: rdn over 2f out: stl ev ch ins fnl f: unable qck towards fin* **10/1**

0233 4 6 **Oyster (IRE)**[9] 4547 3-9-2 **64** ....(b) J-PGuillambert 9 63
(Nick Littmoden) *hld up: rdn over 3f out: hdwy over 2f out: hung lft over 1f out: no ex* **14/1**

6121 5 9 **Daydreamer**[6] 4657 3-9-13 **75** 6ex .... MartinHarley 8 60
(William Haggas) *trckd ldrs: racd keenly: rdn and wknd over 1f out* **8/11**[1]

5464 6 2 1/2 **Alphabetique**[23] 4092 3-9-5 **67** .... ShaneKelly 6 48
(Peter Chapple-Hyam) *hld up: hdwy over 3f out: sn rdn: wknd over 1f out* **10/1**

2213 7 30 **Bishop Wulstan (IRE)**[22] 4106 3-9-0 **62** .... SeanLevey 4
(Richard Hannon) *chsd ldrs tl rdn and wknd over 3f out* **9/1**[3]

2m 32.33s (-0.57) **Going Correction** +0.125s/f (Good) — 7 Ran SP% **112.0**
Speed ratings (Par 100): **106,105,105,101,95 93,73**
CSF £108.34 CT £1094.50 TOTE £14.60: £5.40, £2.80; EX 87.00 Trifecta £505.60.
**Owner** Mrs Charles Cyzer **Bred** C A Cyzer **Trained** Okehurst Lane, W Sussex
■ Stewards' Enquiry : Fergus Sweeney two-day ban: use of whip (15-16 Aug)

**FOCUS**
A modest 3yo handicap for the class, the pace was indifferent and a tight finish ensued. The form is hard to rate with the favourite disappointing.

## 4864 FRESH LINEN EBF STALLIONS MAIDEN STKS (BOBIS RACE) — 6f
6:25 (6:25) (Class 4) 2-Y-O — £4,528 (£1,347; £673; £336) Stalls High

Form — RPR

1 **Sawaahel** 2-9-5 0 .... SeanLevey 6 74+
(Richard Hannon) *s.i.s: sn rcvrd to ld: rdn and edgd lft over 1f out: r.o* **7/2**[2]

2 shd **Swot** 2-9-5 0 .... WilliamBuick 5 74+
(John Gosden) *trckd ldrs: shkn up over 2f out: chsd wnr and edgd lft ins fnl f: sn rdn and ev ch: r.o* **9/4**[1]

3 1 1/4 **Steal The Scene (IRE)** 2-9-5 0 .... PatCosgrave 3 70+
(Richard Hannon) *w wnr: rdn: edgd lft and ev ch over 1f out: n.m.r wl ins fnl f: styd on same pce* **5/1**[3]

0 4 nse **Red Tycoon (IRE)**[53] 3063 2-9-5 0 .... ShaneKelly 1 70+
(Ed Dunlop) *hld up: hdwy over 1f out: nt clr run ins fnl f: r.o* **20/1**

04 5 nk **Gea And Tea**[20] 4207 2-9-5 0 .... JimmyQuinn 7 69
(Robert Eddery) *trckd ldrs: rdn and edgd lft over 1f out: styd on* **8/1**

6 3/4 **Dutch Garden** 2-9-5 0 .... MartinHarley 2 67
(David Brown) *prom: racd keenly: shkn up over 2f out: styd on same pce ins fnl f* **10/1**

0 7 6 **Senor Firecracker (IRE)**[16] 4330 2-9-5 0 .... WilliamTwiston-Davies 9 49
(Brett Johnson) *hld up: shkn up over 1f out: wknd fnl f* **28/1**

8 nk **Longside** 2-9-5 0 .... JamesDoyle 4 48+
(Charles Hills) *dwlt: hld up: shkn up and hung lft over 1f out: wknd fnl f* **5/1**[3]

1m 15.45s (2.95) **Going Correction** +0.125s/f (Good) — 8 Ran SP% **114.7**
Speed ratings (Par 96): **85,84,83,83,82 81,73,73**
CSF £11.86 TOTE £4.50: £1.50, £1.30, £1.90; EX 10.20 Trifecta £70.60.
**Owner** Hamdan Al Maktoum **Bred** Heather Raw **Trained** East Everleigh, Wilts

**FOCUS**
Usually a decent 2yo maiden but they finished in a heap. It's difficult to rate this, with the pace holding up well and nothing solid to hang the form on.

## 4865 AMP SILVER JUBILEE NOVICE STKS (BOBIS RACE) — 7f
7:00 (7:00) (Class 4) 2-Y-O — £6,469 (£1,925; £962) Stalls High

Form — RPR

3 1 **Prince Gagarin (IRE)**[14] 4395 2-9-0 0 .... RyanMoore 3 90+
(Ed Dunlop) *trckd ldr tl qcknd to ld 2f out: sn shkn up: r.o wl* **6/5**[1]

1 2 2 1/4 **Zephuros (IRE)**[34] 3720 2-9-7 0 .... WilliamBuick 1 91
(Charlie Appleby) *hld up in tch: tk clsr order over 2f out: rdn and hung lft fr over 1f out: styd on same pce ins fnl f: wnt 2nd post* **15/8**[2]

21 3 nk **Lexington Times (IRE)**[21] 4167 2-9-7 0 .... SeanLevey 2 90
(Richard Hannon) *led: rdn and hdd 2f out: styd on same pce ins fnl f* **11/4**[3]

1m 28.25s (2.55) **Going Correction** +0.125s/f (Good) — 3 Ran SP% **106.9**
Speed ratings (Par 96): **90,87,87**
CSF £3.62 TOTE £2.10; EX 3.80 Trifecta £3.00.
**Owner** Windflower Overseas & J L Dunlop OBE **Bred** Windflower Overseas **Trained** Newmarket, Suffolk

**FOCUS**
A good-quality novice stakes. The second and third have been rated as running similar races to their maiden clash, but the form could be rated higher.

## 4866 NGK SPARK PLUGS H'CAP — 7f
7:30 (7:30) (Class 4) (0-85,83) 4-Y-O+ — £5,175 (£1,540; £769; £384) Stalls High

Form — RPR

2110 1 **Meet Me Halfway**[29] 3879 4-9-3 **82** .... AshleyMorgan[(3)] 12 90
(Chris Wall) *hld up in tch: shkn up over 1f out: r.o to ld wl ins fnl f: comf* **7/1**[2]

4101 2 1 **Secret Success**[23] 4072 4-8-8 **70** ....(t) MartinLane 10 75
(Paul Cole) *led: rdn over 1f out: hdd and unable qck wl ins fnl f* **10/1**

3412 3 nk **Athletic**[7] 4620 5-8-8 **75** ....(v) DannyBrock[(5)] 4 87+
(Andrew Reid) *dwlt and hld up: swtchd lft over 1f out: gd hdwy fnl f: full of running whn rn out of room wl ins fnl f: swtchd rt and r.o: nvr able to chal* **13/8**[1]

0605 4 1/2 **Spiritual Star (IRE)**[33] 3759 5-9-7 **83** ....(t) WilliamCarson 8 86
(Anthony Carson) *chsd ldr: rdn over 2f out: edgd rt over 1f out: styd on same pce ins fnl f* **10/1**

2100 5 1/2 **Firmdecisions (IRE)**[29] 3879 4-9-6 **82** ....(v) PatCosgrave 11 84
(Brett Johnson) *trckd ldrs: rdn over 2f out: edgd lft and no ex ins fnl f* **16/1**

240 6 2 1/2 **Azrur (IRE)**[21] 4146 4-9-7 **83** .... SeanLevey 1 79
(David Brown) *racd alone stands' side: up w the pce: rdn and hung lft fr over 2f out: styd on same pce fnl f* **8/1**[3]

000- 7 2 1/4 **Yair Hill (IRE)**[294] 7176 6-9-6 **82** .... MartinHarley 3 72
(Geoffrey Deacon) *hld up: effrt over 1f out: nvr trbld ldrs* **8/1**[3]

1040 8 shd **Front Page News**[24] 4053 4-9-2 **78** .... JimmyQuinn 9 67
(Robert Eddery) *prom: rdn over 2f out: wknd ins fnl f* **8/1**[3]

004- 9 3/4 **Red Aggressor (IRE)**[342] 5750 5-8-12 **74** .... HarryBentley 7 61
(Clive Brittain) *prom: rdn over 1f out: wknd fnl f* **25/1**

5020 10 3 3/4 **Powerful Pierre**[14] 4406 7-8-8 **75** ....(b) TobyAtkinson[(5)] 6 53
(Noel Quinlan) *hld up: rdn and wknd over 1f out* **33/1**

-005 11 2 1/4 **Lunar Deity**[54] 3036 5-8-10 **79** .... AaronJones[(7)] 2 51
(Stuart Williams) *hld up: rdn over 2f out: hung lft and wknd over 1f out* **8/1**[3]

1m 25.52s (-0.18) **Going Correction** +0.125s/f (Good) — 11 Ran SP% **125.9**
Speed ratings (Par 105): **106,104,104,103,103 100,97,97,96,92 90**
CSF £80.63 CT £174.29 TOTE £7.80: £2.30, £3.20, £1.30; EX 80.90 Trifecta £138.80.
**Owner** Des Thurlby **Bred** Stratford Place Stud And Watership Down **Trained** Newmarket, Suffolk

**FOCUS**
The pace was honest for this fairly useful handicap and all bar one raced towards the far rail. Questionable form with doubts over most of the runners.

## 4867 32RED PAYS THE LEVY MAIDEN FILLIES' STKS — 7f
8:00 (8:00) (Class 5) 3-Y-O+ — £3,881 (£1,155; £577; £288) Stalls High

Form — RPR

22 1 **Cloud Line**[13] 4446 3-9-0 0 .... RyanMoore 3 82+
(William Haggas) *trckd ldrs: wnt 2nd over 2f out: rdn over 1f out: r.o u.p to ld post* **8/15**[1]

2 shd **Batrana** 3-9-0 0 .... PatCosgrave 9 81+
(M F De Kock, South Africa) *led: racd freely: shkn up: qcknd and edgd rt over 2f out: rdn over 1f out: r.o: hdd post* **14/1**

6-3 3 5 **Spellbind**[62] 2780 3-9-0 0 .... MartinLane 4 68
(Charlie Appleby) *hld up: rdn over 2f out: hdwy over 1f out: styd on same pce ins fnl f* **3/1**[2]

4 3 1/4 **Rectitude** 3-9-0 0 .... WilliamBuick 5 59
(John Gosden) *s.i.s: hld up: hdwy over 3f out: rdn over 1f out: wknd ins fnl f* **8/1**[3]

0 5 24 **Focail Mear**[36] 3631 3-8-11 0 .... RyanPowell[(3)] 8
(John Ryan) *chsd ldr tl rdn over 2f out: wknd over 1f out* **25/1**

1m 27.08s (1.38) **Going Correction** +0.125s/f (Good)
**WFA** 3 from 4yo 6lb — 5 Ran SP% **111.9**
Speed ratings (Par 100): **97,96,91,87,60**
CSF £9.71 TOTE £1.40: £1.50, £3.50; EX 10.90 Trifecta £27.50.
**Owner** Lael Stable **Bred** Lael Stables **Trained** Newmarket, Suffolk

**FOCUS**
Not a bad fillies' maiden where two came clear. Muddling form, with the winner rated to her C&D latest.

## 4868 32RED SPONSOR OF 1000 RACES ANNUALLY H'CAP — 1m
8:30 (8:30) (Class 4) (0-80,80) 3-Y-O+ — £5,175 (£1,540; £769; £384) Stalls High

Form — RPR

1222 1 **Sahra Al Khadra**[17] 4280 3-9-4 **77** .... WilliamBuick 6 84
(Charles Hills) *mde all: rdn over 1f out: edgd rt ins fnl f: all out* **5/6**[1]

0013 2 nk **Kalon Brama (IRE)**[2] 4789 3-8-2 **61** 6ex .... JimmyQuinn 4 67
(Peter Charalambous) *hld up: hdwy: nt clr run and swtchd rt 2f out: chsd wnr over 1f out: sn rdn: r.o* **4/1**[2]

6000 3 6 **Vainglory (USA)**[48] 3244 10-9-12 **78** .... MartinLane 5 71
(David Simcock) *chsd ldrs: rdn over 1f out: styd on same pce* **9/2**[3]

-000 4 3/4 **Applejack Lad**[6] 4654 3-8-11 **70** ....(tp) PatCosgrave 1 60
(John Ryan) *chsd wnr tl rdn over 1f out: no ex ins fnl f* **6/1**

0-0 5 14 **Game Mascot**[33] 3759 4-10-0 **80** .... ChrisCatlin 2 39
(Peter Hiatt) *hld up: hdwy over 3f out: wknd over 1f out* **12/1**

1m 40.02s (0.02) **Going Correction** +0.125s/f (Good)
**WFA** 3 from 4yo+ 7lb — 5 Ran SP% **114.7**
Speed ratings (Par 105): **104,103,97,96,82**
CSF £4.86 TOTE £1.60: £1.10, £2.20; EX 4.40 Trifecta £7.40.
**Owner** Hamdan Al Maktoum **Bred** Sheikh Hamdan Bin Maktoum Al Maktoum **Trained** Lambourn, Berks

**FOCUS**
A modest handicap. The winner has been rated as running a small pb.

T/Plt: £133.00 to a £1 stake. Pool: £43009.53 - 235.94 winning tickets T/Qpdt: £6.10 to a £1 stake. Pool: £5539.84 - 662.68 winning tickets CR

# 4624 THIRSK (L-H)

Friday, August 1

**OFFICIAL GOING: Good to firm changing to good to firm (good in places) after race 1 (1:45)**

Wind: Light across Weather: Overcast and humid

## 4869 EMMA STOTHARD, SCULPTOR - FILLIES' NURSERY H'CAP (BOBIS RACE) 5f

**1:45** (1:47) (Class 4) (0-85,85) 2-Y-O **£6,469** (£1,925; £962; £481) **Stalls** High

Form RPR

2201 **1** **Al Ghuwariyah (IRE)**[20] 4185 2-8-3 **72** ShaneGray(5) 3 79
(Kevin Ryan) *cl up: slt ld over 2f out: rdn over 1f out: drvn and edgd rt ins fnl f: kpt on* **8/1**[3]

100 **2** *1* **Harry's Dancer (IRE)**[13] 4439 2-9-7 **85** PhillipMakin 7 88
(John Quinn) *slt ld on inner: hdd 1/2-way: rdn wl over 1f out: drvn whn n.m.r on inner ins fnl f: kpt on same pce* **11/8**[1]

4153 **3** *1 1/4* **Olivia Fallow (IRE)**[6] 4686 2-8-1 **68** ConnorBeasley(3) 1 67
(Paul Midgley) *trckd ldrs: hdwy 2f out: rdn to chse ldng pair ent fnl f: kpt on same pce* **4/1**[2]

611 **4** *3/4* **Rise Up Lotus (IRE)**[13] 4422 2-8-13 **77** GrahamLee 4 73
(Charles Hills) *dwlt and wnt lft s: in rr: pushed along 1/2-way: rdn to chse ldrs wl over 1f out: sn hanging lft and no imp fnl f* **4/1**[2]

303 **5** *4* **Magic Time (IRE)**[13] 4450 2-8-8 **72** PJMcDonald 6 54
(Ann Duffield) *trckd ldng pair: effrt over 2f out: rdn along wl over 1f out: wknd appr fnl f* **9/1**

233 **6** *6* **Lily Moreton (IRE)**[48] 3236 2-8-3 **67** DuranFentiman 2 27
(Noel Wilson) *chsd ldrs: rdn along over 2f out: sn edgd lft and wknd* **28/1**

59.06s (-0.54) **Going Correction** -0.025s/f (Good) **6 Ran SP% 106.7**
Speed ratings (Par 93): **103,101,99,98,91 82**
CSF £17.66 CT £41.44 TOTE £7.40: £3.60, £1.10; EX 29.60 Trifecta £106.80.

**Owner** Mubarak Al Naemi **Bred** Sean Gorman **Trained** Hambleton, N Yorks

**FOCUS**
A fair fillies' nursery which the leading pair dominated throughout. Both bends dolled out for fresh ground and races of 7f & 8f increased by 8yds and 12f and 2m races by 12yds. The runner-up has been rated back to her earlier form.

## 4870 BOOK FOR LADIES' DAY SATURDAY 6TH SEPTEMBER CLAIMING STKS 7f

**2:20** (2:20) (Class 5) 2-Y-O **£3,234** (£962; £481; £240) **Stalls** Low

Form RPR

5033 **1** **Summer Stroll (IRE)**[3] 4750 2-9-5 69 SamJames(3) 2 65
(David O'Meara) *in rr: pushed along over 3f out: hdwy over 2f out: rdn to chse ldng pair jst over 1f out: styd on wl to ld ins fnl f: r.o* **11/4**[2]

013 **2** *1* **Cafe Cortado (IRE)**[15] 4364 2-8-13 56 JoeyHaynes(3) 3 56
(K R Burke) *trckd ldr: hdwy 3f out: cl up over 2f out and sn rdn: led wl over 1f out: drvn ent fnl f: sn hdd and kpt on same pce* **11/8**[1]

0503 **3** *3 3/4* **Rutland Panther**[9] 4528 2-8-9 57 LukeLeadbitter(7) 4 46
(Declan Carroll) *led: rdn along over 2f out: hdd wl over 1f out: drvn appr fnl f: grad wknd* **25/1**

6053 **4** *1 1/4* **Fazenda's Girl**[42] 3435 2-8-12 53 BarryMcHugh 6 39
(Michael Easterby) *in tch: hdwy over 2f out: rdn along wl over 1f out: sn no imp* **14/1**

244 **5** *4* **Strategic Order (IRE)**[32] 3786 2-9-13 73 GrahamLee 1 43
(Paul Midgley) *hld up: hdwy to trck ldrs 3f out: pushed along over 2f out: sn rdn and btn* **3/1**[3]

0630 **6** *3/4* **Blazing Rose (IRE)**[9] 4529 2-9-0 62 (v[1]) DavidNolan 5 28
(David O'Meara) *chsd ldng pair: hdwy 3f out: rdn along over 2f out: sn drvn and wknd over 1f out* **16/1**

1m 29.17s (1.97) **Going Correction** +0.20s/f (Good) **6 Ran SP% 110.2**
Speed ratings (Par 94): **96,94,90,89,84 83**
CSF £6.66 TOTE £4.40: £2.10, £1.10; EX 6.70 Trifecta £49.80.Cafe Cortado was claimed by Mr Claes Bjorling £12,000.

**Owner** Middleham Park Racing XXXVIII & Partners **Bred** M Phelan **Trained** Nawton, N Yorks

**FOCUS**
A modest claimer. Solid form and could be rated 3lb higher.

## 4871 MARKET CROSS JEWELLERS H'CAP 1m

**2:55** (2:56) (Class 5) (0-70,68) 3-Y-O **£3,234** (£962; £481; £240) **Stalls** Low

Form RPR

0064 **1** **Syros (IRE)**[17] 4300 3-9-6 **67** KierenFallon 4 73+
(Michael Easterby) *trckd ldrs: hdwy wl over 2f out: sn chsng ldng pair: rdn along wl over 1f out: styd on wl appr fnl f: led nr fin* **3/1**[2]

003 **2** *1/2* **Bertha Burnett (IRE)**[17] 4292 3-8-1 **51** ow2 ConnorBeasley(3) 2 56
(Brian Rothwell) *led: pushed clr 1/2-way: rdn 2f out: drvn ent fnl f: hdd and no ex towards fin* **6/1**[3]

6243 **3** *1* **Baltic Fire (IRE)**[17] 4300 3-8-11 **61** JoeyHaynes(3) 9 64+
(K R Burke) *chsd ldr: rdn along over 2f out: drvn over 1f out: kpt on same pce fnl f* **9/4**[1]

600- **4** *5* **Lady Bubbles**[273] 7664 3-7-12 **52** ow2 DanielleMooney(7) 5 44
(Michael Easterby) *dwlt and in rr: hdwy over 2f out: rdn along wl over 1f out: sn no imp* **80/1**

1303 **5** *3/4* **Dutch Lady**[14] 4415 3-8-12 **59** GrahamLee 7 49
(John Holt) *trckd ldrs on outer: pushed along 1/2-way: rdn 3f out: drvn over 2f out: n.d* **9/4**[1]

1200 **6** *1 1/2* **Kisanji**[17] 4300 3-9-7 **68** (p) BenCurtis 10 54
(Alan McCabe) *dwlt: hld up: a in rr* **20/1**

046 **7** *18* **Quasqazah**[28] 3925 3-9-6 **67** DaleSwift 3 12
(Ruth Carr) *t.k.h: chsd ldng pair: pushed along 3f out: rdn over 2f out: sn wknd* **16/1**

1m 41.68s (1.58) **Going Correction** +0.20s/f (Good) **7 Ran SP% 112.7**
Speed ratings (Par 100): **100,99,98,93,92 91,73**
CSF £20.50 CT £46.13 TOTE £3.30: £1.90, £2.70; EX 19.80 Trifecta £74.50.

**Owner** S Chappell **Bred** Lynn Lodge Stud **Trained** Sheriff Hutton, N Yorks

**FOCUS**
Modest fare and not even a particularly strong race for the level. The pace was steady until past halfway, the leader slipping the field at the top of the straight and nearly holding on. The third has been rated a length off his C&D latest.

## 4872 BREEDERS BACKING RACING EBF CONDITIONS STKS 7f

**3:30** (3:30) (Class 3) 3-Y-O+ **£9,703** (£2,887; £1,443; £721) **Stalls** Low

Form RPR

-263 **1** **Mushir**[20] 4187 3-9-5 101 GrahamLee 2 104
(Roger Varian) *mde all: jnd over 2f out and sn rdn: drvn ins fnl f: hld on gamely towards fin* **11/8**[1]

2610 **2** *nk* **Free Wheeling (AUS)**[34] 3731 6-9-4 108 (t) KierenFallon 3 98
(Saeed bin Suroor) *t.k.h early: trckd wnr: pushed along to take clsr order over 2f out: rdn to chal wl over 1f out: carried hd high: drvn and ev ch ins fnl f tl no ex nr fin* **6/4**[2]

-001 **3** *3/4* **Big Johnny D (IRE)**[35] 3645 5-9-4 96 FrannyNorton 4 96
(David Barron) *hld up in rr: swtchd rt to outer and hdwy whn bmpd 2f out: sn rdn to chse ldng pair: kpt on fnl f: nrst fin* **4/1**[3]

02-0 **4** *5* **Invincible Strike (IRE)**[48] 3253 3-8-12 95 PaddyAspell 1 81
(James Tate) *dwlt and sn pushed along to trck ldng pair on inner: t.k.h after: effrt and swtchd rt to outer 2f out: sn rdn and btn* **16/1**

1m 26.64s (-0.56) **Going Correction** +0.20s/f (Good)
**WFA** 3 from 5yo+ 6lb **4 Ran SP% 108.0**
Speed ratings (Par 107): **111,110,109,104**
CSF £3.75 TOTE £1.90; EX 3.50 Trifecta £3.80.

**Owner** Hamdan Al Maktoum **Bred** Shadwell Estate Company Limited **Trained** Newmarket, Suffolk

■ Stewards' Enquiry : Paddy Aspell one-day ban: careless riding (15 Aug)

**FOCUS**
A small field but it featured a couple of smart performers. The winner dictated just a modest gallop. Muddling form.

## 4873 YORKSHIRE OUTDOORS MAIDEN STKS 5f

**4:05** (4:06) (Class 5) 3-4-Y-O **£3,408** (£1,006; £503) **Stalls** High

Form RPR

2-33 **1** **Kommander Kirkup**[22] 4111 3-9-2 79 (b) ConnorBeasley(3) 7 74
(Michael Dods) *racd nr stands' rail: prom: hdwy to ld 2f out: carried hd high: sn rdn clr: kpt on* **2/5**[1]

**2** *3 3/4* **Our Grey Lady** 3-8-9 0 RyanWhile(5) 8 56
(Bill Turner) *dwlt and green in rr: hdwy wl over 1f out: sn rdn and edgd lft: styd on wl fnl f* **10/1**

30-3 **3** *1 1/2* **Resist**[17] 4295 3-9-0 57 GrahamLee 5 50
(James Given) *prom: hdwy to chse wnr 2f out: sn rdn: drvn ent fnl f: sn wknd* **7/2**[2]

5 **4** *2* **Slick Indian**[17] 4295 3-8-12 0 AnnaHesketh(7) 4 48
(Michael Easterby) *dwlt and in rr: rdn 2f out: styd on fnl f: nrst fin* **20/1**

0 **5** *hd* **Aphrilis (IRE)**[81] 2217 3-9-0 0 BenCurtis 1 42
(Brian Ellison) *wnt lft s and bhd tl styd on appr fnl f: nrst fin* **25/1**

-006 **6** *nk* **Kalani's Diamond**[27] 3951 4-8-12 36 [1] AdamCarter(5) 6 42
(Bryan Smart) *led: rdn along 1/2-way: hdd 2f out: sn drvn and wknd appr fnl f* **66/1**

50 **7** *3* **Smart Dj**[22] 4111 3-9-5 0 FrannyNorton 3 35
(Andrew Hollinshead) *chsd ldrs: rdn along over 2f out: sn outpcd* **25/1**

0430 **8** *1 3/4* **Fujin**[61] 2802 3-9-2 63 JoeyHaynes(3) 2 29
(Noel Wilson) *chsd ldrs on outer: rdn along 2f out: sn wknd* **8/1**[3]

59.11s (-0.49) **Going Correction** -0.025s/f (Good)
**WFA** 3 from 4yo 3lb **8 Ran SP% 127.8**
Speed ratings (Par 103): **102,96,93,90,90 89,84,82**
CSF £6.99 TOTE £1.40: £1.02, £2.30, £1.40; EX 8.00 Trifecta £21.80.

**Owner** Kevin Kirkup **Bred** W M Lidsey **Trained** Denton, Co Durham

**FOCUS**
A weak maiden and favourite backers had few worrying moments. The third has been rated a little off her C&D latest.

## 4874 TOMRODS STEEL H'CAP 2m

**4:40** (4:40) (Class 5) (0-75,75) 4-Y-O+ **£3,234** (£962; £481; £240) **Stalls** Low

Form RPR

4110 **1** **Hot Spice**[20] 4217 6-9-4 **72** KierenFallon 2 81
(Michael Easterby) *set stdy pce: qcknd over 3f out: rdn along wl over 1f out: drvn and edgd rt ins fnl f: hld on gamely towards fin* **7/4**[2]

-532 **2** *1/2* **Beat The Tide**[39] 3532 4-9-4 **75** (p) ConnorBeasley(3) 3 83
(Michael Dods) *hld up in rr: hdwy over 2f out: swtchd rt and rdn to chse wnr ent fnl f: sn drvn and edgd sltly lft: kpt on* **5/4**[1]

1124 **3** *4 1/2* **Hallstatt (IRE)**[23] 4068 8-9-4 **72** (t) FrannyNorton 4 75
(John Mackie) *trckd ldng pair: hdwy wl over 2f out: chsd wnr wl over 1f out: sn rdn and kpt on same pce* **5/1**[3]

120- **4** *14* **Kodicil (IRE)**[151] 7280 6-9-1 **69** PaddyAspell 1 55
(Mark Walford) *trckd wnr: pushed along over 3f out: rdn wl over 2f out: sn wknd* **11/1**

3m 36.64s (8.34) **Going Correction** +0.20s/f (Good) **4 Ran SP% 105.8**
Speed ratings (Par 103): **87,86,84,77**
CSF £4.14 TOTE £2.20; EX 4.10 Trifecta £5.30.

**Owner** S Hull, D Swales, A Turton & J Blackburn **Bred** J L Dunlop **Trained** Sheriff Hutton, N Yorks

**FOCUS**
An uncompetitive staying handicap, the winner taking full advantage of being able to dictate. Straightforward form to rate.

## 4875 GO RACING IN YORKSHIRE FUTURE STARS APPRENTICE H'CAP (ROUND 6) 6f

**5:10** (5:15) (Class 5) (0-70,69) 3-Y-O+ **£3,234** (£962; £481; £240) **Stalls** High

Form RPR

0652 **1** **Clubland (IRE)**[8] 4571 5-10-0 **68** AlistairRawlinson 7 81
(Roy Bowring) *cl up: led over 4f out: rdn and edgd rt over 1f out: sn clr: readily* **11/8**[1]

4246 **2** *5* **Shillito**[2] 4795 4-9-6 **62** LauraBarry(2) 9 59
(Tony Coyle) *cl up: lost pl after 1f: pushed along 1/2-way: rdn and hdwy to chse ldng pair 2f out: sn drvn: hung lft ent fnl f: sn hrd drvn and wandered: hung rt nr fin* **5/2**[2]

6421 **3** *1* **Cape Of Hope (IRE)**[9] 4530 4-9-13 **69** 6ex (v) AnnaHesketh(2) 4 66
(David Nicholls) *sltly hmpd s: hld up towards rr: hdwy on inner over 2f out: effrt and nt clr run wl over 1f out: swtchd lft ent fnl f: swtchd rt and nt clr run and hmpd ins fnl f: kpt on nr fin* **7/2**[3]

0000 **4** *nk* **The Strig**[16] 4314 7-9-3 57 (v) HectorCrouch 10 50
(Nigel Tinkler) *led 1 1/2f: cl up: rdn along whn n.m.r wl over 1f out: sn one pce* **16/1**

-006 5 3 1/4 **Rosie Hall (IRE)**[9] 4530 4-8-9 **49** oh4 GaryMahon 8 31
(Les Eyre) *rrd and wnt lft s: in rr: rdn along 1/2-way: plugged on fnl f: n.d* **33/1**

2045 6 5 **Lexi's Beauty (IRE)**[13] 4455 4-8-4 **49** oh2 (p) JordanSwarbrick(5) 6 15
(Brian Baugh) *awkward s: prom: rdn along over 2f out: sn wknd* **25/1**

0-00 7 1 1/2 **Connexion Francais**[35] 3653 3-8-5 **49** oh4 DanielleMooney 3 10
(Tim Etherington) *dwlt and sltly hmpd s: a in rr* **100/1**

0006 8 3/4 **Charlemagne Diva**[7] 4629 4-8-13 **53** (vt1) LukeLeadbitter 1 12
(Richard Guest) *chsd ldrs on wd outside: rdn along over 2f out: sn wknd* **12/1**

1m 13.2s (0.50) **Going Correction** -0.025s/f (Good)
**WFA** 3 from 4yo+ 4lb **8** Ran SP% **114.3**
Speed ratings (Par 103): **95,88,87,86,82 75,73,72**
CSF £4.88 CT £9.11 TOTE £2.20: £1.10, £1.90, £1.50; EX 5.90 Trifecta £9.40.
**Owner** S R Bowring **Bred** Mrs Sharon Slattery **Trained** Edwinstowe, Notts
■ Stewards' Enquiry : Laura Barry four-day ban: use of whip (17-19, 23 Aug)
Anna Hesketh two-day ban: careless riding (15-16 Aug)

**FOCUS**
Uncompetitive by sprint handicap standards and very few ever threatened a serious blow. The third has been rated close to his latest effort in a claimer.
T/Plt: £81.60 to a £1 stake. Pool: £40948.83 - 365.89 winning tickets T/Qpdt: £15.40 to a £1 stake. Pool: £3011.45 - 144.10 winning tickets JR

## 3691 CLAIREFONTAINE (R-H)
Friday, August 1

**OFFICIAL GOING: Turf: good to soft**

### 4881a PRIX LA CONFRERIE DES CHEVALIERS DU PONT L'EVEQUE (CLAIMER) (2YO COLTS & GELDINGS) (TURF) 7f
1:15 (12:00) 2-Y-O £7,916 (£3,166; £2,375; £1,583; £791)

RPR

1 **Monsieur Royal (FR)**[22] 2-9-2 0 (p) JulienGrosjean 1 71
(C Plisson, France) **13/1**

2 3/4 **Mount Isa (IRE)**[67] 2623 2-8-13 0 IoritzMendizabal 9 66
(J S Moore) *midfield: pushed along fr bef 1/2-way: rdn to chal and crossed to nr side rail in st: kpt on wl and pressed wnr fnl f: hld towards fin* **27/10**[1]

3 1 1/4 **Beaubec (FR)** 2-9-6 0 (b) DavyBonilla 4 70
(M Boutin, France) **33/10**[2]

4 1 1/4 **Rivolochop (FR)**[22] 2-9-2 0 AnthonyCrastus 8 62
(C Boutin, France) **59/10**[3]

5 2 1/2 **Atlas Royal (FR)** 2-9-2 0 UmbertoRispoli 2 55
(Mario Hofer, Germany) **33/10**[2]

6 1/2 **Mr Bright Eyes (FR)**[30] 3871 2-8-13 0 (b) MickaelBarzalona 5 51
(D Windrif, France) **105/10**

7 5 **Hilton Jelois (FR)**[97] 2-8-10 0 (p) MathieuPelletan(6) 6 41
(J-L Pelletan, France) **32/1**

8 1 3/4 **Tiramisu (FR)**[12] 2-8-13 0 CristianDemuro 7 33
(G Botti, France) **14/1**

9 4 **Camden Market (FR)**[30] 3871 2-8-10 0 (p) MickaelBerto(6) 3 25
(F Vermeulen, France) **164/10**

1m 26.9s (86.90) **9** Ran SP% **119.3**
WIN (incl. 1 euro stake): 14.00. PLACES: 2.70, 1.60, 1.70. DF: 25.90. SF: 82.90.
**Owner** Christophe Plisson **Bred** C Plisson **Trained** France

### 4882a PRIX DE LA CONFRERIE DES CHEVALIERS DU CAMEMBERT (CLAIMER) (2YO FILLIES) (TURF) 7f
1:45 (12:00) 2-Y-O £7,916 (£3,166; £2,375; £1,583; £791)

RPR

1 **Dayaday (FR)**[34] 3744 2-9-2 0 StephanePasquier 5 66
(M Delcher Sanchez, France) **102/10**

2 1 **Snow Guest (FR)**[22] 2-9-2 0 (p) MickaelBarzalona 1 63
(D Windrif, France) **57/10**[3]

3 1/2 **Sulphur (FR)**[34] 3744 2-8-9 0 (p) UmbertoRispoli 6 55
(Mario Hofer, Germany) **137/10**

4 nk **Fly Grazer (IRE)**[42] 3435 2-8-9 0 ThierryJarnet 7 54
(J S Moore) *midfield in tch: clsd and pushed along to chal into st: rdn over 1f out: kpt on same pce and hld fnl f* **13/2**

5 snk **Boann (IRE)**[30] 3872 2-8-13 0 (b1) IoritzMendizabal 13 57
(J S Moore) *t.k.h: trckd ldr: rdn to chal into st: sltly outpcd whn short of room fnl f: kpt on wl towards fin but hld* **83/10**

6 3/4 **Qoosine (FR)**[30] 3872 2-8-10 0 MllePaulineDominois(6) 11 58
(Rod Collet, France) **9/1**

7 hd **Who Knows (IRE)**[30] 3872 2-8-9 0 MarcLerner 3 51
(C Lerner, France) **7/2**[1]

8 2 **Sister Love (FR)**[30] 3872 2-8-9 0 DavyBonilla 10 45
(L Baudron, France) **58/1**

9 1 **Rue Du Temple (IRE)** 2-9-2 0 (b1) DavidBreux 12 50
(F Vermeulen, France) **29/1**

10 2 **Salut Lilly (FR)** 2-8-8 0 (p) NathanKasztelan(8) 2 44
(S Jesus, France) **67/1**

11 3 **Komtess Ka (FR)**[76] 2-8-4 0 MlleZoePfeil(5) 14 29
(A Junk, France) **78/1**

12 1/2 **Golfa (SPA)** 2-8-4 0 MickaelBerto(5) 8 28
(R Avial Lopez, Spain) **146/10**

13 1 1/4 **Princesse Rebelle (FR)**[56] 2976 2-8-13 0 MaximeGuyon 4 29
(M Nigge, France) **5/1**[2]

14 4 **Be Mine (FR)**[15] 2-8-9 0 (b1) StephaneLaurent 9 14
(S Jeddari, France) **71/1**

1m 26.05s (86.05) **14** Ran SP% **119.2**
WIN (incl. 1 euro stake): 11.20. PLACES: 3.90, 2.60, 4.50. DF: 40.00. SF: 53.80.
**Owner** Safsaf Canarias Srl **Bred** S.C.E.A. Des Prairies **Trained** France

## 4252 SAINT-MALO (L-H)
Friday, August 1

**OFFICIAL GOING: Turf: good**

### 4883a PRIX GEORGES CREIS (MAIDEN) (2YO) (TURF) 5f 110y
11:00 (12:00) 2-Y-O £6,250 (£2,500; £1,875; £1,250; £625)

RPR

1 1 **Modern Family (FR)**[45] 2-8-13 0 MorganDelalande 3 70+
(Y Barberot, France) *fin 2nd: awrdd the r* **14/5**[2]

2 shd **Jimmy's Hall**[30] 3871 2-9-2 0 MatthiasLauron 6 69
(J S Moore) *chsd ldrs: rdn to chal 2f out: kpt on wl but jst hld whn sltly impeded by wnr cl home: fin 3rd: plcd 2nd* **143/10**

3 **Something Lucky (IRE)**[12] 2-9-2 0 TonyPiccone 9 73+
(Matthieu Palussiere, France) *fin 1st: disqualified for causing interference: plcd 3rd* **9/5**[1]

4 2 **Sourdeval** 2-8-8 0 AurelienLemaitre 4 55
(C Lerner, France) **97/10**

5 shd **Hypothese (IRE)** 2-8-13 0 EddyHardouin 5 59
(Matthieu Palussiere, France) **241/10**

6 1/2 **Evasion Des Mottes (FR)**[22] 2-8-13 0 (b1) MickaelForest 7 58
(Mme A-M Poirier, France) **30/1**

7 4 **The Iron Man (FR)**[85] 2-9-2 0 LouisBeuzelin 2 48
(H-F Devin, France) **7/2**[3]

8 1 1/2 **A Ma Reine (FR)** 2-8-8 0 TheoBachelot 1 35
(S Wattel, France) **114/10**

9 2 **Key Code** 2-8-11 0 MatthieuAutier 8 31
(E J O'Neill, France) **204/10**

1m 4.5s (64.50) **9** Ran SP% **120.1**
WIN (incl. 1 euro stake): 3.80. PLACES: 1.20, 2.20, 1.10. DF: 26.20. SF: 59.50.
**Owner** Ecurie Ascot **Bred** Ecurie Ascot **Trained** France

## 4569 DONCASTER (L-H)
Saturday, August 2

**OFFICIAL GOING: Good to firm (good in places; 8.7) (watered)**
Wind: Moderate across Weather: Cloudy with sunny periods

### 4884 UNISON FIGHTING FOR BETTER PAY MAIDEN AUCTION STKS (BOBIS RACE) (DIV I) 7f
2:15 (2:18) (Class 4) 2-Y-O £5,175 (£1,540; £769; £384) Stalls High

Form RPR

032 1 **Astrelle (IRE)**[16] 4346 2-8-10 **76** PaoloSirigu 4 75
(Marco Botti) *cl up: led wl over 2f out: rdn wl over 1f out: hdd and edgd lft ent fnl f: rallied wl and sn led again: drvn out* **5/1**

042 2 1/2 **Pivot Point (IRE)**[23] 4109 2-8-11 **75** SamanthaSpratt 9 75
(Brian Meehan) *trckd ldrs: hdwy and cl up over 2f out: rdn to take slt ead ent fnl f: sn edgd lft and hdd: hung lft and no ex last 100* **9/2**[3]

6 3 1 **Servery**[21] 4207 2-9-4 0 GeorgeBaker 1 79
(Richard Hannon) *trckd ldrs: effrt over 2f out: rdn over 1f out: drvn and kpt on same pce fnl f* **6/1**

3 4 nk **Bizzario**[11] 4518 2-8-10 0 MichaelJMMurphy(3) 8 74
(Mark Johnston) *sn slt ld: pushed along 3f out: hdd over 2f out: rdn wl over 1f out: one pce ins fnl f and hld whn n.m.r and hmpd towards fin* **4/1**[2]

30 5 1 **Laidback Romeo (IRE)**[37] 3613 2-9-1 0 JohnFahy 2 72
(Clive Cox) *hld up towards rr: hdwy 3f out: chsd ldrs 2f out: rdn wl over 1f out: styng on same pce whn n.m.r and hmpd towards fin* **7/2**[1]

6 6 **Comanche Chieftain (CAN)** 2-8-13 0 AndrewMullen 6 54
(Michael Appleby) *dwlt: sn chsng ldrs and t.k.h: pushed along 3f out: rdn wl over 2f out: sn outpcd* **25/1**

7 1 1/4 **Blythe Star (IRE)** 2-9-1 0 DougieCostello 3 53
(Danielle McCormick) *s.i.s and in rr: hdwy 3f out: chsd ldrs 2f out: sn rdn and no imp* **25/1**

8 3 3/4 **Sonar (IRE)** 2-9-1 0 JamieSpencer 10 43
(Michael Bell) *dwlt: a towards rr* **8/1**

00 9 11 **Flying Grange**[47] 3296 2-8-11 0 AndrewElliott 11 9
(Tim Easterby) *chsd ldrs on outer: rdn along 1/2-way: sn wknd* **100/1**

10 5 **Ponty Grigio (IRE)** 2-8-13 0 DuranFentiman 5
(Tim Easterby) *chsd ldrs: pushed along 1/2-way: sn rdn and wknd* **25/1**

1m 27.33s (1.03) **Going Correction** -0.15s/f (Firm) **10** Ran SP% **115.0**
Speed ratings (Par 96): **88,87,86,85,84 77,76,72,59,53**
CSF £26.30 TOTE £5.30: £1.50, £2.10, £2.00; EX 11.20 Trifecta £45.70.
**Owner** Sheikh Mohammed Bin Khalifa Al Maktoum **Bred** Azienda Agricola Gennaro Stimola **Trained** Newmarket, Suffolk
■ Stewards' Enquiry : Samantha Spratt three-day ban: careless riding (Aug 16-18)

**FOCUS**
John Fahy said of the ground "It's loose on top but quite firm underneath". Round course railed out from 10f to where it joins the straight and races of 10f and over increased by 10yds. They raced centre-field in what was an ordinary maiden and the pace was a steady one. Straightforward form to rate.

### 4885 UNISON FIGHTING FOR BETTER PAY MAIDEN AUCTION STKS (BOBIS RACE) (DIV II) 7f
2:50 (2:52) (Class 4) 2-Y-O £5,175 (£1,540; £769; £384) Stalls High

Form RPR

63 1 **Gregoria (IRE)**[64] 2716 2-8-13 0 LiamJones 8 79
(William Haggas) *mde all: rdn wl over 1f out: kpt on strly fnl f* **12/1**

0 2 2 1/4 **Crack Shot (IRE)**[42] 3474 2-9-1 0 AndreaAtzeni 4 75
(Clive Brittain) *trckd ldng pair: hdwy 3f out: rdn to chal 2f out: drvn and kpt on same pce fnl f* **20/1**

4 3 1 3/4 **Hail Clodius (IRE)**[9] 4570 2-9-1 0 PatCosgrave 1 70
(Richard Hannon) *trckd ldng pair: hdwy 1/2-way: cl up over 2f out: sn rdn and ch tl drvn and sltly outpcd over 1f out: kpt on towards fin* **11/8**[1]

4 1 1/2 **Nobbly Bobbly (IRE)** 2-9-1 0 JamieSpencer 5 66+
(James Bethell) *dwlt: sn in tch: hdwy 1/2-way: chsd ldrs over 2f out: rdn to chse ldng pair over 1f out: green and edgd rt ins fnl f: wknd* **7/2**[2]

424 5 3 3/4 **Oregon Gift**[15] 4416 2-8-10 **73** MichaelJMMurphy(3) 9 54
(Mark Johnston) *chsd wnr: rdn along wl over 2f out: sn wknd* **7/2**[2]

00 6 1 3/4 **Arthur's Way (IRE)**[19] 4270 2-9-1 0 IrineuGoncalves 7 51
(Paul Cole) *nvr bttr than midfield* **50/1**

7 1 1/4 **Overlord** 2-9-1 0 ChrisCatlin 2 48
(Sir Mark Prescott Bt) *dwlt and a towards rr* **8/1**[3]

0 8 *hd* **Poet Mark (IRE)**[13] 4467 2-8-11 0 (b[1]) AndrewElliott 10 43
(Tim Easterby) *dwlt: a in rr* **50/1**

00 9 2 1/2 **Youonlyliveonce (IRE)**[15] 4416 2-8-13 0 IanBrennan 6 39
(John Quinn) *chsd ldrs: rdn along 1/2-way: sn wknd* **50/1**

1m 27.34s (1.04) **Going Correction** -0.15s/f (Firm) **9 Ran SP% 116.0**
Speed ratings (Par 96): **88,85,83,81,77 75,74,73,70**
CSF £207.49 TOTE £9.20: £2.70, £3.80, £1.30; EX 121.20 Trifecta £486.20.
**Owner** Chris Humber & Amanda Brudenell **Bred** Kabansk Ltd & Rathbarry Stud **Trained** Newmarket, Suffolk

**FOCUS**
Time may show this was the stronger of the two divisions and, in contrast to the first race, they raced against the stands' rail. Fluid form. The pace held up well with the winner improving up in trip.

## 4886 UNISON ESSENTIAL PROTECTION FOR WORKERS MAIDEN STKS (BOBIS RACE) 1m 2f 60y
**3:25** (3:26) (Class 4) 3-Y-O **£5,175** (£1,540; £769; £384) **Stalls** Low

Form RPR

033 1 **Pleasant Valley (IRE)**[30] 3891 3-9-0 78 AndreaAtzeni 6 80+
(Luca Cumani) *mde all: jnd and pushed along wl over 2f out: rdn wl over 1f out: styd on strly fnl f* **11/8**[1]

2 1 1/2 **Shama's Crown (IRE)** 3-9-0 0 JamieSpencer 4 77+
(Jeremy Noseda) *dwlt: rapid hdwy on outer to trck wnr after 2f: clsd up 3f out: chal over 2f out: sn rdn and ev ch tl kpt on same pce ins fnl f* **7/1**

5344 3 1 **Ganges (IRE)**[19] 4272 3-9-2 76 (v[1]) RobertTart(3) 7 80
(James Toller) *hld up: hdwy 1/2-way: trckd ldrs on outer 4f out: effrt 3f out: rdn along and sltly outpcd over 2f out: kpt on u.p fnl f* **11/2**[3]

346 4 1 3/4 **Hatsaway (IRE)**[43] 3419 3-9-5 87 LiamJones 3 77
(Clive Brittain) *prom: effrt over 3f out: rdn along wl over 2f out: sn drvn and kpt on one pce* **11/4**[2]

5 11 **Mistiroc** 3-9-5 0 IanBrennan 1 56
(Jim Goldie) *trckd ldrs on inner: pushed along over 4f out: rdn 3f out: sn outpcd* **66/1**

0 6 23 **House Captain**[40] 3537 3-9-5 0 SteveDrowne 9 12
(Richard Hannon) *in tch: rdn along over 4f out: outpcd over 3f out and sn bhd* **33/1**

03 7 55 **Pas De Cheval (IRE)**[25] 4062 3-9-5 0 (v) GeorgeBaker 2
(Sir Michael Stoute) *unruly stalls: dwlt: a in rr: detached and bhd fr 1/2-way* **15/2**

2m 11.55s (2.15) **Going Correction** -0.075s/f (Good) **7 Ran SP% 112.9**
Speed ratings (Par 102): **88,86,86,84,75 57,13**
CSF £11.60 TOTE £2.30: £1.80, £2.70; EX 13.70 Trifecta £40.70.
**Owner** Wildenstein Stables Limited **Bred** Dayton Investments Ltd **Trained** Newmarket, Suffolk

**FOCUS**
A fair maiden. The winner has been rated as running a small pb.

## 4887 UNISON AND UIA INSURANCE H'CAP (BOBIS RACE) 1m 4f
**4:00** (4:00) (Class 4) (0-85,85) 3-Y-O **£5,175** (£1,154; £1,154; £384) **Stalls** Low

Form RPR

41 1 **Mizzou (IRE)**[25] 4062 3-9-7 85 AndreaAtzeni 3 95
(Luca Cumani) *hld up in rr: niggled along 4f out: rdn and hdwy on outer wl over 2f out: drvn to chse ldng pair ins fnl f: styd on wl to ld on line* **5/2**[2]

5312 2 *shd* **Innocent Touch (IRE)**[21] 4189 3-9-1 79 PatrickMathers 5 88
(Richard Fahey) *awkward s and rdr briefly lost iron: trckd ldng pair: hdwy and cl up over 3f out: led wl over 2f out: sn rdn and hdd over 1f out: drvn and rallied to ld again ins fnl f: hdd on line* **6/1**

41 2 *dht* **Wakea (USA)**[31] 3856 3-9-5 83 JamieSpencer 1 92
(Jeremy Noseda) *trckd ldrs: hdwy 3f out: cl up 2f out: rdn to take slt ld over 1f out: drvn and hdd ins fnl f: rallied nr fin* **6/5**[1]

5413 4 6 **Allegria (IRE)**[29] 3918 3-9-7 85 NickyMackay 4 84
(John Gosden) *stmbld sltly s: led 1f: trckd ldr: hdwy and cl up 4f out: led briefly over 3f out: rdn and hdd wl over 2f out: sn drvn and grad wknd* **11/2**[3]

5-14 5 *nk* **Dalaki (IRE)**[76] 2363 3-8-6 70 (b) LiamJones 7 69
(Clive Brittain) *prom: led after 1f: rdn along 4f out: hdd wl over 2f out: sn drvn and grad wknd* **16/1**

2m 33.0s (-1.90) **Going Correction** -0.075s/f (Good) **5 Ran SP% 109.6**
Speed ratings (Par 102): **103,102,102,98,98**
WIN: 3.70 Mizzou; PL: 1.80 Mizzou, 0.90 Innocent Touch, 0.60 Wakea; EX: 3.00, 7.40; CSF: 8.29, 2.93; TC: ; TF: 8.00, 1340.00;.
**Owner** Jon S Kelly **Bred** Matrix Bloodstock **Trained** Newmarket, Suffolk

**FOCUS**
A decent handicap, dominated by the right horses, and it threw up a cracking finish. The pace and time were all right and three came clear. The fourth has been rated 3lb off her C&D latest.

## 4888 UNISON DEFENDING OUR NHS H'CAP 1m 2f 60y
**4:35** (4:35) (Class 2) (0-100,95) 3-Y-O+
**£12,450** (£3,728; £1,864; £932; £466; £234) **Stalls** Low

Form RPR

0663 1 **Whispering Warrior (IRE)**[22] 4173 5-9-10 91 AndreaAtzeni 4 101+
(David Simcock) *hld up towards rr: hdwy wl over 2f out: rdn to chse ldrs over 1f out: drvn ent fnl f: styd on wl to ld last 50yds* **9/2**[3]

0014 2 3/4 **Spirit Of The Law (IRE)**[16] 4379 5-9-6 87 PatrickMathers 2 95
(Richard Fahey) *trckd ldng pair: hdwy and cl up 3f out: rdn to ld 2f out: drvn ins fnl f: hdd and no ex last 50yds* **8/1**

4421 3 1 3/4 **Yenhaab (IRE)**[22] 4162 3-9-2 92 JamieSpencer 1 97
(William Haggas) *cl up: led after 1f: pushed along 3f out: hdd 2f out and sn rdn: drvn ent fnl f: sn one pce* **11/8**[1]

3341 4 2 **Border Legend**[15] 4400 5-10-0 95 GeorgeBaker 7 96
(Roger Charlton) *hld up in tch: hdwy 3f out: rdn to chse ldng pair whn hung lft over 1f out: sn btn* **11/4**[2]

1016 5 *nk* **San Cassiano (IRE)**[7] 4667 7-9-9 90 IanBrennan 5 90
(Ruth Carr) *led 1f: trckd ldr: rdn along 3f out: wknd 2f out* **20/1**

/005 6 1 3/4 **Buthelezi (USA)**[8] 4622 6-9-5 86 (p) DuranFentiman 6 83
(Brian Ellison) *hld up: a in rr* **33/1**

-305 7 4 1/2 **Storm King**[30] 3886 5-9-8 89 (p) SteveDrowne 3 77
(David C Griffiths) *in tch: pushed along 4f out: rdn 3f out: sn btn* **25/1**

2m 9.61s (0.21) **Going Correction** -0.075s/f (Good)
**WFA** 3 from 5yo+ 9lb **7 Ran SP% 109.6**
Speed ratings (Par 109): **96,95,94,92,92 90,87**
CSF £34.62 TOTE £4.30: £2.50, £2.90; EX 29.30 Trifecta £79.70.
**Owner** Daniel Pittack **Bred** Epona Bloodstock Ltd **Trained** Newmarket, Suffolk

**FOCUS**
A good-quality handicap, run at a fair clip. The third has been rated to form.

## 4889 UNISON DEFENDING PUBLIC SERVICES CONDITIONS STKS 6f
**5:10** (5:10) (Class 3) 3-Y-O+
**£8,715** (£2,609; £1,304; £652; £326; £163) **Stalls** High

Form RPR

-666 1 **Justineo**[62] 2820 5-9-2 107 AndreaAtzeni 1 110
(Roger Varian) *mde all: rdn and qcknd clr wl over 1f out: readily* **11/10**[1]

0-30 2 3 **Royal Rock**[80] 2254 10-9-2 100 GeorgeBaker 2 100
(Chris Wall) *dwlt: hld up in rr: hdwy 2f out: rdn to chse wnr ins fnl f: sn no imp* **11/2**[3]

5300 3 1 3/4 **Secret Witness**[35] 3732 8-8-13 92 (b) SteveDrowne 5 92
(Ronald Harris) *trckd ldrs: hdwy over 2f out: rdn along wl over 1f out: kpt on same pce* **10/1**

-000 4 1 3/4 **Langavat (IRE)**[28] 3960 3-8-9 92 ChrisCatlin 9 85
(Richard Hannon) *chsd ldrs: rdn along and outpcd over 2f out: plugged on fnl f* **25/1**

0100 5 1 1/4 **Burning Thread (IRE)**[21] 4179 7-8-13 92 (b) IanBrennan 3 82
(Tim Etherington) *sn chsng ldrs: rdn along over 2f out: sn drvn and wknd* **16/1**

2200 6 4 **Annunciation**[28] 3960 4-8-13 102 PatCosgrave 4 69
(Richard Hannon) *prom: rdn along over 2f out: sn drvn and wknd* **5/2**[2]

1m 11.51s (-2.09) **Going Correction** -0.15s/f (Firm)
**WFA** 3 from 4yo+ 4lb **6 Ran SP% 110.4**
Speed ratings (Par 107): **107,103,100,98,96 91**
CSF £7.43 TOTE £1.70: £1.30, £2.20; EX 6.50 Trifecta £26.70.
**Owner** Saleh Al Homaizi & Imad Al Sagar **Bred** Saleh Al Homaizi & Imad Al Sagar **Trained** Newmarket, Suffolk

**FOCUS**
A good opportunity for the favourite and he duly obliged. The winner has been rated back to his best.

## 4890 THOMPSONS SOLICITORS ACTING FOR UNISON MEMBERS H'CAP 5f
**5:40** (5:41) (Class 5) (0-70,70) 3-Y-O **£3,881** (£1,155; £577; £288) **Stalls** High

Form RPR

-146 1 **Where The Boys Are (IRE)**[42] 3462 3-8-12 64 RobertTart(3) 5 71
(Ed McMahon) *trckd ldrs: hdwy 2f out: rdn to chal over 1f out: led ent fnl f: drvn out* **7/1**[3]

0026 2 *nk* **Jamboree Girl**[28] 3959 3-9-7 70 DuranFentiman 12 76
(Tim Easterby) *trckd ldrs: hdwy 2f out: sn rdn and ev ch ent fnl f: drvn and no ex last 50yds* **8/1**

0551 3 3/4 **Classic Pursuit**[31] 3855 3-9-7 70 (p) SteveDrowne 10 73
(Ronald Harris) *towards rr: hdwy over 2f out: rdn wl over 1f out: styd on wl fnl f: nrst fin* **4/1**[1]

0122 4 *nk* **Vodka Chaser (IRE)**[9] 4565 3-9-1 69 PhilipPrince(5) 1 71
(Alison Hutchinson) *chsd ldrs on wd outside: hdwy whn edgd lft 2f out: sn rdn: chal and ev ch over 1f out: sn drvn and no ex wl ins fnl f* **7/1**[3]

-302 5 *nk* **Monarch Maid**[13] 4469 3-9-2 65 ChrisCatlin 2 66
(Peter Hiatt) *sn led: rdn along 2f out: drvn and hdd ent fnl f: kpt on same pce* **5/1**[2]

134 6 1 **Thornaby Princess**[18] 4297 3-9-4 67 AndrewElliott 8 65
(Marjorie Fife) *towards rr: hdwy 2f out: sn rdn to chse ldrs over 1f out: kpt on same pce fnl f* **8/1**

1030 7 1 1/2 **Tinsill**[8] 4636 3-9-4 67 AndreaAtzeni 3 59
(Nigel Tinkler) *in rr: pushed along 1/2-way: swtchd wd to outer and rdn 2f out: styd on fnl f: nrst fin* **9/1**

2356 8 3/4 **Diamondsinthesky (IRE)**[28] 3972 3-8-5 54 (v) RaulDaSilva 6 43
(Derek Shaw) *dwlt: a towards rr* **16/1**

625- 9 4 1/2 **Simply Black (IRE)**[267] 7804 3-8-9 65 JoshDoyle(7) 7 38
(David O'Meara) *chsd ldrs: rdn along over 2f out: sn wknd* **8/1**

5030 10 3 3/4 **Biscuiteer**[13] 4469 3-8-8 57 (b) IanBrennan 4 17
(Scott Dixon) *cl up: rdn along 1/2-way: sn wknd* **28/1**

-536 11 4 1/2 **Reet Thicknstrong**[58] 2932 3-8-4 58 AdamCarter(5) 9
(Bryan Smart) *cl up: disp ld 1/2-way: sn rdn along and wknd wl over 1f out* **14/1**

59.37s (-1.13) **Going Correction** -0.15s/f (Firm) **11 Ran SP% 121.0**
Speed ratings (Par 100): **103,102,101,100,100 98,96,95,87,81 74**
CSF £63.91 CT £263.68 TOTE £8.20: £2.40, £4.10, £2.00; EX 105.60 Trifecta £1392.90 Part won. Pool: £1,857.21 - 0.96 winning units..
**Owner** Philip Wilkins **Bred** Neville O'Byrne **Trained** Lichfield, Staffs
■ Stewards' Enquiry : Duran Fentiman four-day ban: used whip above permitted level (Aug 16-19)

**FOCUS**
Several had their chance in what was a modest sprint handicap. Sound form, but lacking improvers. The runner-up has been rated as running a small pb.

## 4891 UNISON AND LV=LIVERPOOL VICTORIA CAR INSURANCE FILLIES' H'CAP 6f
**6:10** (6:12) (Class 5) (0-70,75) 3-Y-O+ **£3,881** (£1,155; £577; £288) **Stalls** High

Form RPR

0415 1 **Fever Few**[23] 4108 5-9-7 68 AshleyMorgan(3) 2 82
(Chris Wall) *prom: cl up 1/2-way: led wl over 1f out: rdn ins fnl f: kpt on wl* **9/2**[2]

0225 2 2 1/4 **Diamond Blue**[15] 4421 6-9-6 64 (p) PatrickMathers 14 71
(Richard Fahey) *towards rr: hdwy 2f out: rdn over 1f out: styd on to chse wnr ins fnl f: edgd lft and kpt on* **8/1**

530 3 1 1/2 **Koala Bear**[44] 3384 4-9-1 62 [1] MichaelJMMurphy(3) 15 64
(James Fanshawe) *chsd ldrs: hdwy 2f out: rdn wl over 1f out: chsd wnr ent fnl f: sn n.m.r: kpt on same pce* **7/1**

1312 4 1 3/4 **Verus Delicia (IRE)**[8] 4629 5-9-12 75 EoinWalsh(5) 1 72
(Daniel Mark Loughnane) *towards rr: pushed along on outer 1/2-way: rdn over 2f out: styd on fnl f: nrst fin* **4/1**[1]

5522 5 1/2 **Traditionelle**[26] 4019 3-8-13 61 AndrewElliott 10 55
(Tim Easterby) *cl up: led 1/2-way: rdn 2f out: hdd wl over 1f out: wknd ent fnl f* **5/1**[3]

2421 6 3/4 **Goadby**[10] 4532 3-9-0 62 ChrisCatlin 6 54
(John Holt) *slt ld: hdd 1/2-way: sn rdn along: drvn and grad wknd fr over 1f out* **14/1**

3130 7 1/2 **Betty Boo (IRE)**[31] 3846 4-8-9 60 AlexHopkinson(7) 13 51
(Shaun Harris) *cl up: rdn along wl over 2f out: sn drvn and wknd* **12/1**

3042 8 *nk* **Tweety Pie (IRE)**[8] 4636 3-9-4 69 NeilFarley(3) 9 58
(Declan Carroll) *a towards rr* **8/1**

06-0 9 *hd* **Dont Tell Nan**[28] 3972 3-8-3 47 RaulDaSilva 7 39
(Derek Shaw) *t.k.h: chsd ldrs: rdn along 1/2-way: sn wknd* **40/1**

4-46 **10** ¾ **Go Glamorous (IRE)**[32] 3817 3-9-8 **70**............................ SteveDrowne 3 56
(Ronald Harris) *chsd ldrs: rdn along over 2f out: sn drvn and wknd over 1f out* **33/1**

5460 **11** 1¼ **Madagascar Moll (IRE)**[13] 4469 3-8-8 **63**.......................... JoshDoyle(7) 8 45
(David O'Meara) *dwlt and towards rr: hdwy into midfield 1/2-way: rdn along wl over 1f out: sn edgd lft and wknd* **20/1**

3006 **12** *shd* **Elite Freedom (IRE)**[9] 4567 3-8-4 **52**..........................(p) AndrewMullen 11 34
(Brian Baugh) *a towards rr* **50/1**

1-0 **13** *52* **Greek Spirit (IRE)**[10] 4546 4-9-0 **65**..................(t) CallumShepherd(7) 12
(Alan McCabe) *rrd at s: fly-leaping and virtually ref to r: a t.o* **16/1**

1m 11.99s (-1.61) **Going Correction** -0.15s/f (Firm)
**WFA** 3 from 4yo+ 4lb **13** Ran SP% **121.9**
Speed ratings (Par 100): **104,101,99,96,96 95,94,93,93,92 91,90,21**
CSF £39.98 CT £264.04 TOTE £5.00: £2.00, £2.80, £2.40; EX 56.90 Trifecta £966.90.
**Owner** Mrs C A Wall & R Wayman **Bred** Redgate Bloodstock Ltd & Mrs Z Wise **Trained** Newmarket, Suffolk

**FOCUS**
An open sprint. It was soundly run and the winner has been rated as running a clear personal best.
T/Plt: £46.90 to a £1 stake. Pool: £73,179.50 - 1,138.25 winning tickets. T/Qpdt: £13.50 to a £1 stake. Pool: £4,193.25 - 229.62 winning tickets. JR

# 4849 GOODWOOD (R-H)

## Saturday, August 2

**OFFICIAL GOING: Good to firm (8.2; watered)**
Wind: medium, half against Weather: mainly dry, light drizzly rain showers

## 4892 32REDSPORT.COM H'CAP (CONSOLATION RACE FOR THE 32RED CUP) (HERITAGE HANDICAP) 6f

**2:05** (2:05) (Class 2) 3-Y-0+

**£24,900** (£7,456; £3,728; £1,864; £932; £468) **Stalls** High

Form RPR

6662 **1** **Barnet Fair**[6] 4700 6-9-1 **90**............................ CamHardie(5) 5 101+
(David Nicholls) *wnt to s early: racd far side: mid-div: hdwy 2f out: sn rdn: swtchd lft ent fnl f: led fnl 120yds: drifted rt: r.o wl* **7/1**[2]

-233 **2** *shd* **Mission Approved**[12] 4502 4-9-1 **85**.......................... ShaneKelly 18 94
(Luca Cumani) *racd stands' side: hld up: smooth hdwy 2f out: sn rdn: r.o strly ins fnl f: ev ch fnl 120yds: kpt on: jst hld* **20/1**

5312 **3** *shd* **Tatlisu (IRE)**[15] 4384 4-9-4 **88**.......................... RyanMoore 17 97+
(Richard Fahey) *racd stands' side: trckd ldr: rdn whn drfiting rt and chalng ent fnl f: kpt on wl w ev ch: jst hld* **11/2**[1]

1200 **4** 1¾ **Slip Sliding Away (IRE)**[4] 4762 7-8-12 **85**............. ThomasBrown(3) 11 88
(Peter Hedger) *racd stands' side to centre: hld up: hdwy over 2f out: sn rdn: mounting chal whn carried rt ent fnl f: kpt on but no ex fnl 75yds* **12/1**

0-06 **5** *shd* **Humidor (IRE)**[35] 3732 7-9-10 **94**.......................... AdamKirby 4 97
(George Baker) *wnt to s early: racd farside: overall ldr: rdn 2f out: kpt on gamely but no ex hdd fnl 120yds* **20/1**

1603 **6** *nk* **Huntsmans Close**[30] 3876 4-9-3 **87**.......................... WilliamBuick 23 92
(Roger Charlton) *racd stands' side: mid-div: hdwy 2f out: sn rdn: cl up and running on whn squeezed out and snatched up ent fnl f: kpt on but no ch after* **16/1**

5042 **7** ¾ **Confessional**[21] 4188 7-9-8 **92**..........................(e) GrahamLee 6 91
(Tim Easterby) *racd far side: chsd ldrs: rdn 2f out: kpt on tl no ex fnl 120yds* **12/1**

0053 **7** *dht* **Kinglami**[7] 4650 5-8-9 **79**..........................(p) CraigAWilliams 2 78
(Brian Gubby) *racd far side: mid-div: rdn over 2f out: no imp tl r.o wl fnl f* **12/1**

-115 **9** *hd* **Daylight**[4] 4762 4-9-1 **85**..........................(t) OisinMurphy 1 84
(Andrew Balding) *got wound up behand and wnt to s early: racd far side: hld up: rdn and hdwy fr 2f out: kpt on fnl f but nvr quite gng pce to get on terms* **8/1**

50-4 **10** 1¼ **School Fees**[23] 4121 5-8-12 **82**.......................... RichardHughes 12 77
(Olly Stevens) *racd stands' side: outpcd in rr and detached 1st 3f: stdy prog fr 2f out: r.o fnl f but nvr any ch* **16/1**

2-00 **11** *2* **Secondo (FR)**[48] 3271 4-9-7 **91**.......................... JamesDoyle 20 79
(Roger Charlton) *racd stands' side: hld up: hdwy over 2f out: sn rdn: chsd ldrs over 1f out: hld whn briefly short of rooom ent fnl f: sn wknd* **8/1**

5010 **12** ½ **Hopes N Dreams (IRE)**[15] 4384 6-9-10 **94**.......................... JimmyFortune 3 81
(Kevin Ryan) *wnt to s early: racd far side: trckd ldrs: rdn 2f out: wknd ent fnl f* **25/1**

0065 **13** *2* **El Viento (FR)**[35] 3732 6-9-2 **89**..........................(v) GeorgeChaloner(3) 28 69
(Richard Fahey) *racd stands' side: mid-div: rdn 3f out: wknd over 1f out* **14/1**

-011 **14** *hd* **Stepping Out (IRE)**[33] 3788 3-9-4 **92**.......................... RichardKingscote 14 71
(Tom Dascombe) *led stands' side gp: overall chsng ldr: rdn and hdd 2f out: sn btn* **15/2**[3]

0003 **15** 1¾ **Regal Parade**[56] 2992 10-9-3 **87**..........................(t) WilliamCarson 25 61
(Milton Bradley) *racd stands' side: mid-div: rdn over 2f out: wknd over 1f out* **25/1**

1114 **16** ¾ **Ladweb**[44] 3386 4-9-1 **85**.......................... TomQueally 15 57
(John Gallagher) *racd stands' side: trckd ldrs: rdn over 2f out: wknd over 1f out* **33/1**

3210 **17** 1½ **Shaolin (IRE)**[22] 4146 4-9-0 **84**..........................(t) KierenFallon 10 51
(Seamus Durack) *racd farside: mid-div: rdn over 2f out: wknd over 1f out* **33/1**

6365 **18** *14* **Noble Deed**[51] 3152 4-9-4 **88**.......................... JoeFanning 26 10
(Michael Attwater) *wnt to s early: racd stands' side: a outpcd in rr* **25/1**

1m 10.48s (-1.72) **Going Correction** -0.025s/f (Good)
**WFA** 3 from 4yo+ 4lb **18** Ran SP% **130.3**
Speed ratings (Par 109): **110,109,109,107,107 106,105,105,105,103 101,100,97,97,95 94,92,73**
CSF £150.09 CT £870.77 TOTE £7.80: £2.00, £4.80, £2.00, £4.20; EX 291.60 Trifecta £927.20.
**Owner** Donald Wheatley **Bred** Mrs J M Russell **Trained** Sessay, N Yorks

**FOCUS**
Ten non-runners in this consolation handicap, but the remaining 18 still split into two groups. The groups merged centre to far side from around 2f out and there was no discernible bias. All rail removed fresh ground on top bend and distances as advertised. Straightforward form and the winner has been rated close to his best.

## 4893 JAGUAR STKS (H'CAP) (BOBIS RACE) 1m 4f

**2:40** (2:41) (Class 2) (0-105,97) 3-Y-0

**£31,125** (£9,320; £4,660; £2,330; £1,165; £585) **Stalls** High

Form RPR

0022 **1** **Double Bluff (IRE)**[6] 4696 3-9-7 **97**.......................... JoeFanning 4 110
(Mark Johnston) *chsd ldr tl led and travelling strly 3f out: rdn clr ent fnl 2f: styd on wl and in command fr over 1f out: rdn out* **7/1**[3]

411 **2** *3* **Kings Fete**[22] 4173 3-9-6 **96**.......................... JamesDoyle 11 104
(Sir Michael Stoute) *stdd s: hld up in rr: rdn and effrt on outer over 2f out: edging rt but hdwy over 1f out: chsd wnr ins fnl f: styd on but nvr threatened wnr* **3/1**[1]

2-11 **3** 1¼ **Second Step (IRE)**[30] 3892 3-9-2 **92**.......................... AdamKirby 15 98
(Luca Cumani) *hld up in midfield: effrt jst over 2f out: edging rt but hdwy u.p over 1f out: chsd clr wnr 1f out: kpt on same pce and lost 2nd ins fnl f* **7/1**[3]

6212 **4** 2½ **Oasis Fantasy (IRE)**[21] 4183 3-8-11 **87**.......................... RyanMoore 7 89
(Ed Dunlop) *t.k.h: hld up in tch in midfield: rdn and hdwy ent fnl 2f: chsd clr wnr over 1f out: no imp and lost 2nd 1f out: wknd fnl 100yds* **4/1**[2]

150 **5** ¾ **Fun Mac (GER)**[30] 3892 3-8-5 **81**.......................... CraigAWilliams 5 82
(Hughie Morrison) *t.k.h: hld up in tch in midfield: n.m.r and swtchd lft ent fnl 2f: rdn and effrt over 1f out: kpt on steadily ins fnl f: nvr trbld ldrs* **20/1**

4-51 **6** 1¼ **Adventure Seeker (IRE)**[78] 2319 3-8-13 **89**.......................... KierenFallon 8 88
(Ed Vaughan) *hld up towards rr: effrt 2f out: sme hdwy u.p over 1f out: plugged on same pce fnl f: nvr threatened ldrs* **7/1**[3]

3222 **7** 1½ **Smiling Stranger (IRE)**[14] 4435 3-8-9 **85**.......................... OisinMurphy 3 81
(Andrew Balding) *led tl 3f out: sn rdn and outpcd by wnr ent fnl 2f: btn over 1f out: wknd ins fnl f* **16/1**

4336 **8** 4½ **Karraar**[29] 3931 3-8-9 **85** ow1..........................(p) DaneO'Neill 14 74
(Richard Hannon) *in tch in midfield: rdn 2f out: unable qck u.p and btn over 1f out: wknd fnl f* **25/1**

1623 **9** *1* **Master Of Finance (IRE)**[41] 3512 3-8-13 **89**.......................... WilliamBuick 1 77
(Mark Johnston) *chsd ldrs: effrt on inner 3f out: struggling and outpcd wl over 1f out: wknd jst over 1f out* **12/1**

-212 **10** *1* **Black Shadow**[56] 2986 3-9-5 **95**.......................... TomQueally 16 81
(Amanda Perrett) *stdd after s: hld up towards rr: rdn ent fnl 2f: no prog and wknd over 1f out* **14/1**

-612 **11** *9* **Galactic Heroine**[18] 4298 3-8-8 **84** ow1.......................... GrahamLee 12 56
(James Given) *in tch in midfield: lost pl and bhd 3f out: losing tch and edging rt over 1f out: bhd and eased ins fnl f* **33/1**

-212 **12** 2¼ **Pack Leader (IRE)**[38] 3587 3-9-0 **90**.......................... RichardKingscote 6 58
(Amanda Perrett) *rrd as stalls opened: hld up towards rr: rdn and effrt ent fnl 2f: wknd and edgd rt over 1f out: bhd and eased ins fnl f* **20/1**

1045 **13** 3¼ **Norse Star (IRE)**[9] 4584 3-7-11 **78** ow1.......................... DannyBrock(5) 2 41
(Sylvester Kirk) *hld up towards rr: rdn and effrt on inner over 3f out: no prog u.p 2f out and sn btn: bhd and eased ins fnl f: t.o* **50/1**

2m 35.13s (-3.27) **Going Correction** +0.025s/f (Good) **13** Ran SP% **121.0**
Speed ratings (Par 106): **111,109,108,106,106 105,104,101,100,99 93,92,90**
CSF £26.71 CT £158.33 TOTE £7.70: £2.50, £1.70, £2.00; EX 34.80 Trifecta £334.50.
**Owner** R W Huggins **Bred** Michael G Daly **Trained** Middleham Moor, N Yorks

**FOCUS**
Traditionally a strong handicap and, although the top weight came in 8lb below the ceiling this year, the form should once again prove reliable. Sound form. The winner stretched clear and has been rated as running a pb.

## 4894 MARKEL INSURANCE NASSAU STKS (BRITISH CHAMPIONS SERIES) (GROUP 1) (F&M) 1m 1f 192y

**3:15** (3:17) (Class 1) 3-Y-0+

**£113,420** (£43,000; £21,520; £10,720; £5,380; £2,700) **Stalls** Low

Form RPR

112 **1** **Sultanina**[28] 3961 4-9-7 105.......................... WilliamBuick 2 116
(John Gosden) *stmbld s: chsd ldr for 2f: chsd ldrs after: rdn 2f out: chsd wnr 1f out: drvn and str run to ld fnl 75yds: sn in command and gng away at fin* **11/2**

1-14 **2** 1½ **Narniyn (IRE)**[34] 3774 4-9-7 112.......................... ChristopheSoumillon 5 113
(A De Royer-Dupre, France) *hld up in last pair: clsd on inner 3f out: rdn to ld 2f out: edgd lft u.p 1f out: hdd and one pce fnl 75yds* **7/4**[1]

0-12 **3** *3* **Venus De Milo (IRE)**[34] 3766 4-9-7 112.......................... JosephO'Brien 1 107
(A P O'Brien, Ire) *taken down early: led: hdd and rdn 2f out: keeping on same pce whn lost 2nd and swtchd rt 1f out: plugged on same pce fnl f* **5/2**[2]

-221 **4** ½ **Eastern Belle**[51] 3143 3-8-12 99.......................... JimmyFortune 7 106
(John Gosden) *stdd and dropped in bhd after s: hld up in rr: swtchd rt and effrt 2f out: no imp 1f out: plugged on same pce fnl f* **16/1**

5120 **5** *1* **Lustrous**[14] 4461 3-8-12 104.......................... RichardHughes 3 104
(Richard Hannon) *chsd ldrs: wnt 2nd 6f out tl 2f out: sn rdn and unable qck: outpcd and btn 1f out: plugged on* **16/1**

-451 **6** *13* **Mango Diva**[13] 4478 4-9-7 108.......................... RyanMoore 6 80
(Sir Michael Stoute) *hld up in tch in midfield: effrt 2f out: no rspnse and btn whn edgd rt over 1f out: bhd and eased ins fnl f* **4/1**[3]

2m 6.58s (-1.52) **Going Correction** +0.025s/f (Good)
**WFA** 3 from 4yo 9lb **6** Ran SP% **112.1**
Speed ratings (Par 117): **107,105,103,103,102 91**
CSF £15.57 TOTE £6.00: £2.60, £1.40; EX 17.80 Trifecta £47.60.
**Owner** Normandie Stud Ltd **Bred** Normandie Stud Ltd **Trained** Newmarket, Suffolk

**FOCUS**
A weak running of the Nassau although it did go to the least exposed of these, Sultanina battling on well to complete a hat-trick in the race for trainer John Gosden, who won the 2012 edition with The Fugue and last year's race with Winsili. The winner continues to progress and the form has been rated around the runner-up.

## 4895 32RED CUP (STEWARDS' CUP) (HERITAGE H'CAP) 6f

**3:50** (3:54) (Class 2) 3-Y-0+

**£62,250** (£18,640; £9,320; £4,660; £2,330; £1,170) **Stalls** High

Form RPR

1-11 **1** **Intrinsic**[71] 2503 4-8-11 **95**.......................... RichardHughes 22 106+
(Robert Cowell) *hld up in tch in midfield: clsd and carried rt over 1f out: chal 1f out: rdn to ld and hung bdly lft ins fnl f: stened and r.o strly towards fin: comf* **6/1**[2]

0-30 **2** *1* **Ninjago**[42] 3452 4-9-5 **103** RyanMoore 15 111
(Richard Hannon) *hld up in rr: effrt and hdwy ent fnl f: drvn and r.o strly fnl 100yds: wnt 2nd last strides* **10/1**

4044 **3** *nk* **Alben Star (IRE)**[35] 3737 6-9-4 **105** GeorgeChaloner(3) 19 112
(Richard Fahey) *taken down early: chsd ldrs: chsd ldr jst over 2f out: rdn to ld over 1f out: drvn and hdd ins fnl f: no ex fnl 75yds: lost 2nd last strides* **8/1**[3]

1022 **4** *¾* **Ruwaiyan (USA)**[35] 3715 5-9-5 **103** (p) GrahamLee 8 108
(James Tate) *stdd s: t.k.h: hld up in rr: swtchd rt and clsd over 1f out: rdn and hdwy 1f out: r.o wl ins fnl f: wnt 4th last strides* **25/1**

21 **5** *nk* **Muthmir (IRE)**[7] 4683 4-9-0 **98** 6ex DaneO'Neill 2 102+
(William Haggas) *stdd after s: hld up in tch in midfield: hdwy and chse ldrs and rdn jst over 1f out: drvn and styd on same pce fnl 150yds* **5/2**[1]

31 **6** *½* **Discussiontofollow (IRE)**[21] 4179 4-9-0 **98** 6ex ShaneKelly 23 100+
(Mike Murphy) *stdd s: t.k.h: hld up towards rr: clsd 2f out: swtchd lft and effrt over 1f out: keeping on whn sltly impeded ins fnl f: kpt on towards fin* **10/1**

1631 **7** *½* **Sir Maximilian (IRE)**[13] 4480 5-9-4 **102** 6ex StevieDonohoe 11 102
(Tim Pitt) *in tch in midfield: rdn 2f out: drvn and hdwy to chse ldrs 1f out: edgd lft and kpt on same pce ins fnl f* **25/1**

2201 **8** *1* **Joey's Destiny (IRE)**[51] 3152 4-8-11 **95** MartinDwyer 20 92
(George Baker) *stdd s: t.k.h: hld up in midfield: hdwy u.p: over 1f out: keeping on whn bmpd ins fnl f: no imp fnl 100yds* **25/1**

0-50 **9** *½* **Hallelujah**[14] 4438 6-9-4 **102** (t) HayleyTurner 14 98
(James Fanshawe) *sn bustled along in midfield: sme hdwy u.p ent fnl f: styd on but nvr gng pce to chal* **20/1**

020 **10** *¾* **Seeking Magic**[42] 3452 6-9-3 **101** (t) AdamKirby 28 94
(Clive Cox) *racd along nr stands' rail: pressed ldr tl led ent fnl 2f: hung bdly rt after and hdd 1f out: wknd fnl 100yds* **16/1**

0035 **11** *1* **Arnold Lane (IRE)**[21] 4188 5-9-2 **100** CraigAWilliams 25 90
(Mick Channon) *in tch in midfield: rdn and effrt over 1f out: kpt on same pce ins fnl f: nvr enough pce to threaten ldrs* **33/1**

-223 **12** *nk* **Hoodna (IRE)**[21] 4200 4-9-2 **100** KierenFallon 5 89
(Saeed bin Suroor) *hld up towards rr: swtchd rt and hdwy over 1f out: drvn and no prog jst ins fnl f: sn btn and eased wl ins fnl f* **12/1**

2504 **13** *nk* **Mar Mar (IRE)**[14] 4445 4-8-10 **94** OisinMurphy 24 82
(Saeed bin Suroor) *hld up in midfield: rdn over 1f out: unable qck u.p over 1f out: kpt on same pce ins fnl f* **50/1**

4210 **14** *nse* **Ashpan Sam**[35] 3732 5-9-7 **105** JimmyFortune 21 93
(John Spearing) *chsd ldrs: rdn 2f out: carried rt and unable qck over 1f out: btn and bmpd ins fnl f: sn wknd: eased towards fin* **25/1**

4010 **15** *1* **Clear Spring (IRE)**[35] 3714 6-8-10 **99** CamHardie(5) 7 84
(John Spearing) *in tch in midfield: rdn 2f out: no hdwy u.p over 1f out: wknd ins fnl f* **50/1**

5256 **15** *dht* **Expert (IRE)**[77] 2344 3-8-12 **100** PatDobbs 27 84
(Richard Hannon) *towards rr: rdn 2f out: kpt on past btn horses ins fnl f: nvr trbld ldrs* **50/1**

3-10 **17** *1¾* **Flyman**[84] 2145 4-8-9 **98** (b) JackGarritty(5) 16 77
(Richard Fahey) *dwlt: rdn along early and sn rcvrd to r in midfield: struggling u.p over 1f out: wknd fnl f* **50/1**

2005 **18** *1* **Borderlescott**[22] 4174 12-8-11 **95** TomQueally 12 71
(Robin Bastiman) *in tch in midfield: lost pl 2f out: trying to rally u.p whn short of room 1f out: no imp after* **40/1**

-000 **19** *2½* **York Glory (USA)**[21] 4215 6-9-9 **107** (b) JamesDoyle 3 75
(Kevin Ryan) *t.k.h: hld up in midfield: swtchd rt 2f out: hdwy and drvnto chse ldrs over 1f out: no ex 1f out: wknd ins fnl f* **33/1**

100 **20** *nk* **Barracuda Boy (IRE)**[15] 4412 4-8-11 **95** (v[1]) RichardKingscote 6 62
(Tom Dascombe) *chsd ldrs: rdn 2f out: struggling and btn over 1f out: wknd fnl f* **40/1**

1220 **21** *2¾* **Bear Behind (IRE)**[28] 3960 5-8-4 **95** JennyPowell(7) 4 53
(Tom Dascombe) *taken down early: chsd ldrs: rdn 2f out: wknd over 1f out: bhd ins fnl f* **40/1**

-000 **22** *¾* **Zero Money (IRE)**[21] 4179 8-8-11 **95** (b) JoeFanning 17 51
(Hugo Palmer) *led tl jst over 2f out: sn lost pl: wkng whn squeezed for room over 1f out: sn bhd* **66/1**

30U1 **23** *4½* **Blaine**[15] 4384 4-9-4 **102** 6ex (b) AmyRyan 13 43
(Kevin Ryan) *restless in stalls: a towards rr: rdn 2f out: lost tch over 1f out and wl bhd fnl f* **33/1**

-200 **24** *19* **Rex Imperator**[21] 4201 5-9-10 **108** (p) JosephO'Brien 26
(William Haggas) *hld up in tch in midfield: rdn and effrt 2f out: sn btn and lost tch: heavily eased ins fnl f: t.o* **16/1**

1m 10.27s (-1.93) **Going Correction** -0.025s/f (Good)
**WFA** 3 from 4yo+ 4lb **24** Ran SP% **137.2**
Speed ratings (Par 109): **111,109,109,108,107 107,106,105,104,103 102,101,101,101,100 100,97,96,93,92 88,87,81,56**
CSF £59.39 CT £513.74 TOTE £6.70: £2.00, £3.40, £2.70, £5.80; EX 94.70 Trifecta £384.80.
**Owner** Malih Lahej Al Basti **Bred** Cheveley Park Stud Ltd **Trained** Six Mile Bottom, Cambs

**FOCUS**
Despite the usual big field the betting was largely concentrated on a few towards the head of the market, and the right horses came to the fore. It looks solid form and the time was 0.21sec quicker than the consolation race. They split into two groups initially but soon merged and there was no bias. Another step forward from the progressive winner, and the runner-up has been rated as running as well as ever.

## 4896 NATWEST AHEAD FOR BUSINESS EBF STALLIONS MAIDEN STKS (BOBIS RACE) (C&G) 7f

4:25 (4:28) (Class 2) 2-Y-O **£12,938** (£3,850; £1,924; £962) **Stalls** Low

Form RPR

32 **1** **Dutch Connection**[30] 3881 2-9-0 0 WilliamBuick 5 88+
(Charles Hills) *trckd ldrs: jnd ldrs travelling best 2f out: shkn up to ld ent fnl f: r.o wl: rdn out* **9/2**[3]

63 **2** *2½* **Rotherwick (IRE)**[22] 4142 2-9-0 0 MartinLane 6 80
(Paul Cole) *w ldr: rdn to ld 2f out: hdd ent fnl f: kpt on but nt pce of wnr* **10/1**

6 **3** *½* **Fieldsman (USA)**[15] 4395 2-9-0 0 RyanMoore 1 79
(Ed Dunlop) *mid-div: hdwy over 2f out: sn rdn: swtchd lft over 1f out: wnt 3rd ent fnl f: kpt on same pce* **11/2**

5 **4** *1¼* **Dance Of Fire**[10] 4550 2-9-0 0 OisinMurphy 7 75
(Andrew Balding) *wnt lft and slowly away: midfield after 1f: pushed along over 2f out: rdn and hdwy over 1f out: wnt 4th ins fnl f: kpt on* **14/1**

43 **5** *nk* **Maftoon (IRE)**[14] 4424 2-9-0 0 DaneO'Neill 3 74
(Richard Hannon) *mid-div: rdn whn swtchd lft wl over 2f out: kpt on fnl 120yds but nvr gng pce to get involved* **12/1**

3 **6** *2¼* **Secret Brief (IRE)**[76] 2359 2-9-0 0 JoeFanning 2 68
(Mark Johnston) *led: rdn and hdd 2f out: kpt pressing ldrs tl hung lft and wknd ins fnl f* **10/3**[2]

04 **7** *2* **Silver Quay (IRE)**[29] 3929 2-9-0 0 JimmyFortune 11 63
(Richard Hannon) *hld up towards rr: pushed along fr over 2f out: sme minor late prog: nvr threatened* **33/1**

4 **8** *6* **Lethal Legacy (IRE)**[15] 4395 2-9-0 0 RichardHughes 10 47
(Richard Hannon) *trckd ldrs: pushed along to hold pl over 3f out: rdn over 2f out: wknd over 1f out* **5/2**[1]

**9** *1¼* **Jolie De Vivre (IRE)** 2-9-0 0 ShaneKelly 4 43
(Sylvester Kirk) *rn green: sn struggling in rr* **66/1**

**10** *2* **Heatstroke (IRE)** 2-9-0 0 JamesDoyle 8 38+
(Charles Hills) *towards rr of mid-div: effrt 3f out where bmpd: wknd over 1f out* **20/1**

1m 27.25s (0.25) **Going Correction** +0.025s/f (Good) **10** Ran SP% **117.9**
Speed ratings (Par 100): **99,96,95,94,93 91,88,82,80,78**
CSF £48.33 TOTE £4.70: £1.70, £3.00, £1.70; EX 47.20 Trifecta £313.80.
**Owner** Mrs Susan Roy **Bred** Mrs S M Roy **Trained** Lambourn, Berks

**FOCUS**
Six of the last ten winners of this maiden were subsequently successful at Listed level or higher, most notably Jukebox Jury (2008), who later added the Irish St Leger. The second has been rated to form.

## 4897 TELEGRAPH NURSERY STKS (H'CAP) (BOBIS RACE) 7f

5:00 (5:00) (Class 2) 2-Y-O **£12,938** (£3,850; £1,924; £962) **Stalls** Low

Form RPR

300 **1** **Grigolo**[22] 4167 2-8-8 **72** JoeFanning 6 77
(Mark Johnston) *stdd s: t.k.h: hld up in tch in rr: hdwy on inner 3f out: chsd ldrs 2f out and sn swtchd lft: rdn over 1f out: r.o to ld fnl 100yds: rdn out* **6/1**[3]

641 **2** *1½* **Special Venture (IRE)**[39] 3542 2-8-11 **75** GrahamLee 2 76
(Tim Easterby) *t.k.h: sn led: rdn 2f out: battled on wl u.p tl hdd and no ex fnl 100yds: hung on for 2nd cl home* **16/1**

543 **3** *nk* **Grand Proposal**[28] 3945 2-8-6 **70** CraigAWilliams 9 70
(Kevin Ryan) *t.k.h: stdd and dropped in bhd over 5f out: hung rt 3f out: rdn and hdwy on inner over 1f out: swtchd lft 1f out: kpt on u.p fnl 100yds: no threat to wnr* **25/1**

311 **4** *nk* **When Will It End (IRE)**[21] 4203 2-9-2 **80** RichardHughes 7 81
(Richard Hannon) *hld up in tch in last trio: shkn up and effrt whn nt clr run and swtchd rt 2f out: hdwy whn squeezed for room and pushed lft 1f out: kpt on fnl 100yds: no threat to wnr* **5/2**[1]

01 **5** *nse* **Shaakis (IRE)**[25] 4044 2-8-10 **74** DaneO'Neill 5 73
(Marcus Tregoning) *in tch in midfield: rdn and effrt on outer over 1f out: styd on u.p ins fnl f: no threat to wnr* **7/1**

13 **6** *¾* **Muqaawel (USA)**[28] 3963 2-9-0 **78** AdamKirby 1 75
(Mark Johnston) *chsd ldrs: wnt 2nd over 2f out: rdn to chal over 1f out: drvn and no ex 1f out: wknd fnl 100yds* **4/1**[2]

004 **7** *5* **My Mate (IRE)**[18] 4301 2-7-12 **67** CamHardie(5) 10 51
(Clive Brittain) *t.k.h: chsd ldrs but stuck wd: rdn 2f out: struggling over 1f out: wknd fnl f* **8/1**

01 **8** *6* **Guiding Light (IRE)**[31] 3847 2-9-4 **82** JimmyFortune 4 49
(Andrew Balding) *t.k.h: hld up in tch in midfield: lost pl and pushed rt 2f out: sn btn: eased ins fnl f* **8/1**

011 **9** *1¾* **Stec (IRE)**[14] 4440 2-8-12 **83** JennyPowell(7) 8 46
(Tom Dascombe) *chsd ldr tl over 2f out: sn rdn and lost pl 2f out: wknd over 1f out: bhd and eased ins fnl f* **8/1**

1m 27.82s (0.82) **Going Correction** +0.025s/f (Good) **9** Ran SP% **118.4**
Speed ratings (Par 100): **96,94,93,93,93 92,86,80,78**
CSF £97.62 CT £2250.79 TOTE £6.80: £2.40, £4.40, £6.80; EX 95.50 Trifecta £1711.40.
**Owner** Sheikh Hamdan bin Mohammed Al Maktoum **Bred** Darley **Trained** Middleham Moor, N Yorks

**FOCUS**
An interesting nursery run in a time 0.57secs slower than the preceding maiden. On-screen sectionals showed the early gallop was slightly slower in this contest, but a split of 11.46 between 3f and 2f out was the quickest in either race (from leader), before they slowed up again. Another step forward from the progressive runner-up.

## 4898 SEAMUS BUCKLEY'S 20TH GLORIOUS STKS (H'CAP) (BOBIS RACE) 5f

5:35 (5:36) (Class 3) (0-95,92) 3-Y-O
**£10,893** (£3,262; £1,631; £815; £407; £204) **Stalls** High

Form RPR

0-42 **1** **Online Alexander (IRE)**[42] 3484 3-9-1 **86** AmyRyan 6 100
(Kevin Ryan) *chsd ldr and travelled strly: led over 1f out: rdn and asserted 1f out: edgd rt but r.o strly ins fnl f: readily* **8/1**

0261 **2** *2¾* **Flying Bear (IRE)**[15] 4399 3-8-2 **78** (b[1]) CamHardie(5) 1 84
(Jeremy Gask) *stdd s: t.k.h and sn in tch in midfield: effrt over 1f out: kpt on u.p to go 2nd nr fin: no threat to wnr* **12/1**

1513 **3** *nk* **Peterkin (IRE)**[6] 4700 3-9-7 **92** JoeFanning 2 97
(Mark Johnston) *t.k.h: led: rdn and hdd over 1f out: outpcd and swtchd lft jst ins fnl f: hung lft u.p and lost 2nd nr fin* **3/1**[1]

431 **4** *¾* **Captain Myles (IRE)**[15] 4390 3-8-13 **84** (p) StevieDonohoe 3 86
(Tim Pitt) *chsd ldrs: rdn and effrt over 1f out: drifted rt and r.o same pce ins fnl f* **10/1**

1321 **5** *nk* **Royal Brave (IRE)**[17] 4328 3-8-4 **75** MartinDwyer 7 76
(William Muir) *in tch in midfield: effrt over 1f out: drvn and kpt on same pce ins fnl f* **20/1**

0011 **6** *nk* **Desert Ace (IRE)**[38] 3565 3-9-6 **91** (tp) AdamKirby 9 91
(Clive Cox) *restless in stalls: chsd ldrs: riidden 2f out: unable qck and outpcd over 1f oui: kpt on same pce ins fnl f* **20/1**

5005 **7** *½* **Outer Space**[8] 4609 3-8-12 **83** JamesDoyle 8 81
(Jamie Osborne) *bmpd at s: hld up in tch in last quartet: effrt and nt clrest of runs wl over 1f out: kpt on ins fnl f: nvr trbld ldrs* **12/1**

3111 **8** *1¾* **War Spirit**[28] 3959 3-8-13 **84** RichardHughes 5 76
(Richard Hannon) *hld up in tch in midfield: effrt and unable qck over 1f out: btn 1f out: wknd ins fnl f* **7/2**[2]

5-11 **9** *2* **Money Team (IRE)**[42] 3484 3-9-2 **87** RyanMoore 11 72
(David Barron) *hld up in tch in last quartet: effrt 2f out: no hdwy: wl hld and edging rt ins fnl f: nvr trbld ldrs* **5/1**[3]

2-10 **10** *½* **Zac Brown (IRE)**[15] 4418 3-9-0 **85** JimmyFortune 12 68
(David Barron) *hld up in rr: shkn up wl over 1f out: hung rt and no hdwy over 1f out: nvr trbld ldrs* **33/1**

1-61 **11** *3¾* **Angel Flores (IRE)**[18] 4297 3-7-11 **73** oh1 JackGarritty(5) 10 42
(Richard Fahey) *bhd: rdn 2f out: no hdwy: bhd fnl f* **14/1**

57.66s (-2.54) **Going Correction** -0.375s/f (Firm) **11** Ran SP% **118.6**
Speed ratings (Par 104): **105,101,100,99,99 98,97,95,91,91 85**
CSF £97.68 CT £356.44 TOTE £9.10: £2.80, £3.20, £1.80; EX 133.40 Trifecta £708.60.
**Owner** Noel O'Callaghan **Bred** Deer Forest Stud **Trained** Hambleton, N Yorks

**FOCUS**
A decent enough 3yo sprint handicap. The main action was up the middle. The runner-up, who won a 6f nursery here last year, has been rated as running a small pb.
T/Jkpt: Not won. T/Plt: £827.20 to a £1 stake. Pool: £320,494.88 - 282.81 winning tickets.
T/Qpdt: £150.60 to a £1 stake. Pool: £13,405.55 - 65.87 winning tickets. SP

4381 **HAMILTON** (R-H)
Saturday, August 2

**OFFICIAL GOING: Good (7.9)**
Wind: Almost nil Weather: Overcast, raining

## 4899 MARGARET SMITH MEMORIAL NURSERY H'CAP 6f 5y
**6:15** (6:17) (Class 6) (0-65,63) 2-Y-0 **£2,587** (£770; £384; £192) **Stalls** High

Form RPR
6446 1 **Tagtale (IRE)**[14] 4449 2-8-7 **52**.............................. GaryBartley(3) 4 63
(Richard Fahey) *cl up: led over 2f out: rdn clr fnl f* **14/1**
0253 2 4 1/2 **Penalty Scorer**[1] 4857 2-8-6 **53**.............................(e) DuilioDaSilva(5) 6 50
(Richard Guest) *dwlt: t.k.h in tch: effrt and ev ch whn hung rt over 1f out: no ex ins fnl f* **11/2**[3]
055 3 6 **Triggers Broom (IRE)**[38] 3569 2-7-13 **46**.................. SammyJoBell(5) 1 25
(Richard Fahey) *prom: effrt on outside over 2f out: outpcd by first two over 1f out* **7/1**
6655 4 2 **Sunhill Lodge Lady**[10] 4528 2-7-12 **51** oh4 ow2.......(p) RowanScott(7) 2 20
(Ann Duffield) *led to over 2f out: rdn and wknd over 1f out* **25/1**
446 5 1 3/4 **Black Pudding (IRE)**[15] 4416 2-9-7 **63**.............................. PJMcDonald 7 31
(Ann Duffield) *sn cl up: rdn over 2f out: outpcd whn rdr dropped whip over 1f out: sn btn* **6/4**[1]
5423 6 4 **Ingleby Spring (IRE)**[26] 4012 2-9-7 **63**........................ LucyAlexander 5 19
(Richard Fahey) *t.k.h early: cl up tl rdn and wknd fr 2f out* **3/1**[2]
300 7 6 **Show Spirit**[16] 4357 2-8-8 **55**.......................................(b[1]) ShaneGray(5) 3
(Kevin Ryan) *s.i.s: bhd and outpcd: no ch fr 1/2-way* **12/1**
1m 13.15s (0.95) **Going Correction** +0.025s/f (Good) 7 Ran SP% **111.1**
Speed ratings (Par 92): **94,88,80,77,75 69,61**
CSF £82.40 TOTE £8.80: £3.90, £3.10; EX 98.20 Trifecta £362.60.
**Owner** Richard Fahey Ebor Racing Club Ltd **Bred** Sean O'Sullivan **Trained** Musley Bank, N Yorks

**FOCUS**
Far side rail in straight dolled out to preserve ground and all distances as advertised. A poor race in which the winner showed surprise improvement with the two market principals proving disappointing. It rained heavily pre-racing and the going had eased considerably from the good to firm that these horses would have been declared to run on. Gary Bartley, the winning jockey in the first, said in his post-race interview that it rode as good to soft ground. The winner was a surprise improver.

## 4900 ALEA CASINO OPEN MAIDEN STKS 6f 5y
**6:45** (6:47) (Class 5) 3-Y-0+ **£3,234** (£962; £481; £240) **Stalls** High

Form RPR
1 **Ridge Ranger (IRE)** 3-9-0 0.............................................. JasonHart 3 80+
(Eric Alston) *dwlt: hld up: hdwy 1/2-way: led centre over 1f out: drew clr fnl f: comf* **14/1**[3]
3- 2 3 1/4 **Cagoule**[261] 7889 3-9-5 0........................................ DanielTudhope 2 74
(David O'Meara) *t.k.h: led towards far side after 1f: rdn and hdd over 1f out: one pce ins fnl f* **1/3**[1]
0030 3 4 1/2 **Locky Taylor (IRE)**[12] 4489 3-9-0 59.............................(p) ShaneGray(5) 4 60
(Kevin Ryan) *led 1f: cl up: rdn along 1/2-way: outpcd by first two fr over 1f out* **7/1**[2]
60-0 4 3 **Llandanwg**[71] 2524 3-9-0 45............................................ PhillipMakin 7 45
(Bryan Smart) *hld up in tch: rdn over 2f out: no imp fr over 1f out* **20/1**
5 5 12 **Say Something**[17] 4318 3-9-0 0............................................ PJMcDonald 5 7
(Ann Duffield) *towards rr: effrt and pushed along over 2f out: wknd over 1f out* **20/1**
00 6 4 **Bannock Town**[52] 3103 3-9-2 0.......................................... GaryBartley(3) 6
(Linda Perratt) *bhd and sn drvn along: nvr on terms* **50/1**
7 1/2 **Katies Joy (IRE)** 3-8-9 0.............................................. GarryWhillans(5) 1
(Ian Semple) *green in preliminaries: prom tl hung rt and wknd over 2f out* **14/1**[3]
1m 12.27s (0.07) **Going Correction** +0.025s/f (Good) 7 Ran SP% **112.3**
Speed ratings (Par 103): **100,95,89,85,69 64,63**
CSF £18.88 TOTE £15.80: £4.10, £1.10; EX 29.10 Trifecta £87.60.
**Owner** Con Harrington **Bred** Con Harrington **Trained** Longton, Lancs

**FOCUS**
A weak maiden in which the favourite disappointed. The form could be worth 5-6lb more.

## 4901 CAESARS ENTERTAINMENT H'CAP 5f 4y
**7:15** (7:15) (Class 5) (0-75,75) 3-Y-0+ **£3,381** (£1,155; £577; £288) **Stalls** High

Form RPR
1422 1 **Classy Anne**[5] 4725 4-8-12 **64**.......................................... GaryBartley(3) 6 76+
(Jim Goldie) *t.k.h early: mde all: rdn over 1f out: edgd lft ins fnl f: kpt on wl* **7/4**[1]
0200 2 1 1/4 **Captain Royale (IRE)**[23] 4114 9-9-3 **71**...............(p) JacobButterfield(5) 8 78
(Tracy Waggott) *cl up: effrt and rdn over 1f out: kpt on ins fnl f: nt rch wnr* **14/1**
0015 3 1 1/4 **Slim Chance (IRE)**[6] 4714 5-9-2 **65**................................... JasonHart 7 68
(Simon West) *t.k.h: hld up: rdn and hdwy over 1f out: kpt on to take 3rd cl home* **9/1**
6042 4 nse **Medici Time**[12] 4494 9-9-3 **66**...................................(v) DanielTudhope 5 68
(Tim Easterby) *hld up: rdn and hdwy over 1f out: kpt on same pce wl ins fnl f* **6/1**[3]
6512 5 1/2 **Bunce (IRE)**[1] 4859 6-9-7 **75**........................................ GemmaTutty(5) 2 76
(Linda Perratt) *prom: effrt and drvn 2f out: kpt on same pce ins fnl f* **9/2**[2]
5041 6 1 3/4 **Windforpower (IRE)**[11] 4519 4-9-2 **65**..........................(p) FrannyNorton 4 59
(Tracy Waggott) *prom: rdn over 2f out: no ex over 1f out* **12/1**
0-05 7 2 **Hazelrigg (IRE)**[12] 4488 9-9-10 **73**..................................(e) DavidAllan 10 60
(Tim Easterby) *in tch: outpcd and hung rt 2f out: sn btn* **9/1**
6565 8 nk **Ingenti**[28] 3954 6-9-1 **64**............................................... PJMcDonald 3 50
(Christopher Wilson) *hld up: rdn over 2f out: btn over 1f out* **10/1**
59.75s (-0.25) **Going Correction** +0.025s/f (Good) 8 Ran SP% **112.3**
Speed ratings (Par 103): **103,101,99,98,98 95,92,91**
CSF £27.64 CT £171.93 TOTE £2.30: £1.50, £3.20, £3.40; EX 25.30 Trifecta £141.90.
**Owner** The Vital Sparks **Bred** Jonayro Investments **Trained** Uplawmoor, E Renfrews

**FOCUS**
A reasonable little heat for the grade. The first two domianted and the winner doesn't look finished yet.

## 4902 TBA/EBF STALLIONS BREEDING WINNERS FILLIES' H'CAP 6f 5y
**7:45** (7:45) (Class 3) (0-90,85) 3-Y-O+ **£9,703** (£2,887; £1,443; £721) **Stalls** Centre

Form RPR
0421 1 **Jamesbo's Girl**[15] 4421 4-9-1 **74**.................................... PhillipMakin 2 87
(David Barron) *trckd ldrs gng wl: led and rdn over 1f out: kpt on strly fnl f* **2/1**[1]
0561 2 1 1/4 **Alexandrakollontai (IRE)**[11] 4515 4-8-12 **74**..............(b) JulieBurke(3) 4 82
(Alistair Whillans) *s.i.s: bhd: rdn along 1/2-way: gd hdwy to chse wnr ins fnl f: no imp* **6/1**
5212 3 2 **Gran Canaria Queen**[13] 4471 5-9-7 **80**................................ DavidAllan 8 82
(Tim Easterby) *cl up: rdn and ev ch wl over 1f out: no ex and lost 2nd ins fnl f* **7/2**[2]
1-03 4 1/2 **Milly's Secret (IRE)**[16] 4358 3-8-6 **76**..........................(p) RowanScott(7) 9 75
(Ann Duffield) *prom: rdn and outpcd 2f out: edgd lft and kpt on ins fnl f: no imp* **14/1**
-430 5 2 1/2 **Augusta Ada**[33] 3788 3-8-10 **78**................................ JacobButterfield(5) 1 69
(Ollie Pears) *dwlt: sn pushed along and in tch on outside: effrt over 2f out: hung rt and wknd appr fnl f* **5/1**[3]
5030 6 3 **Economic Crisis (IRE)**[10] 4531 5-8-10 **69**........................ PJMcDonald 6 51
(Alan Berry) *led tl rdn: hdd & wknd over 1f out* **10/1**
0452 7 1/2 **Midnight Dynamo**[12] 4488 7-8-12 **71**............................ DanielTudhope 3 52
(Jim Goldie) *in tch: rdn and edgd rt wl over 1f out: wknd fnl f* **12/1**
1m 11.58s (-0.62) **Going Correction** +0.025s/f (Good)
**WFA** 3 from 4yo+ 4lb 7 Ran SP% **110.0**
Speed ratings (Par 104): **105,103,100,100,96 92,92**
CSF £13.21 CT £35.33 TOTE £3.20: £1.60, £3.40; EX 15.00 Trifecta £43.00.
**Owner** Hardisty Rolls **Bred** Lady Juliet Tadgell **Trained** Maunby, N Yorks

**FOCUS**
The best race on the card but, with Lady Frances coming out, that left Gran Canaria Queen as top weight with an official rating 10lb below the ceiling for the grade, so this is not strong form for the level.

## 4903 BOOK NOW FOR SILVER BELL RACENIGHT H'CAP (QUALIFIER FOR THE £15,000 BETFAIR SCOTTISH MILE) 1m 65y
**8:15** (8:15) (Class 5) (0-75,75) 3-Y-O+ **£3,881** (£1,155; £577; £288) **Stalls** Low

Form RPR
-513 1 **Hanalei Bay (IRE)**[6] 4707 4-9-10 **71**................................ PhillipMakin 8 79
(Keith Dalgleish) *w ldr: led gng wl over 2f out: sn rdn: hrd pressed wl ins fnl f: hld on wl* **7/2**[1]
-053 2 nk **An Chulainn (IRE)**[11] 4515 3-9-0 **68**............................(b[1]) FrannyNorton 7 74
(Mark Johnston) *t.k.h: hld up in midfield: pushed along whn edgd rt and carried hd high over 3f out: hdwy wl over 1f out: chal and carried hd even higher wl ins fnl f: nt go past* **11/2**[3]
4034 3 6 **Surround Sound**[12] 4489 4-9-0 **61**........................................ DavidAllan 6 55
(Tim Easterby) *prom: effrt and rdn over 2f out: outpcd by first two fnl f* **7/2**[1]
2000 4 2 1/4 **Outlaw Torn (IRE)**[1] 4858 5-8-13 **65**...........................(e) DuilioDaSilva(5) 3 53
(Richard Guest) *chsd ldrs: rdn over 3f out: outpcd over 1f out* **10/1**
4416 5 hd **Ted's Brother (IRE)**[21] 4196 6-9-9 **75**............................(e[1]) ShaneGray(5) 2 63
(Richard Guest) *hld up: outpcd and hung rt over 3f out: kpt on wl fnl f: nrst fin* **7/1**
0060 6 nk **Silver Duke (IRE)**[64] 2737 3-9-0 **68**................................ DanielTudhope 1 54
(Jim Goldie) *bhd: struggling over 4f out: kpt on wl fnl f: nvr able to chal* **20/1**
3303 7 nk **Tectonic (IRE)**[5] 4729 5-9-8 **69**.............................................(p) TomEaves 5 55
(Keith Dalgleish) *hld up: stdy hdwy over 2f out: rdn over 1f out: wknd fnl f* **9/1**
2233 8 4 **Ewell Place (IRE)**[19] 4254 5-8-12 **64**........................(p) SammyJoBell(5) 4 41
(Richard Fahey) *led to over 2f out: rdn and wknd over 1f out* **4/1**[2]
1m 47.25s (-1.15) **Going Correction** -0.10s/f (Good)
**WFA** 3 from 4yo+ 7lb 8 Ran SP% **116.2**
Speed ratings (Par 103): **101,100,94,92,92 91,91,87**
CSF £23.45 CT £71.87 TOTE £4.50: £1.60, £2.10, £1.70; EX 24.20 Trifecta £120.70.
**Owner** Mrs Francesca Mitchell **Bred** Holborn Trust Co **Trained** Carluke, S Lanarks

**FOCUS**
A modest heat in which two pulled clear. The winner continued his good recent run.

## 4904 GBX ANTHEMS HERE ON 28 AUGUST H'CAP (QUALIFIER FOR THE £15,000 BETFAIR SCOTTISH STAYERS FINAL) 1m 3f 16y
**8:45** (8:45) (Class 5) 3-Y-O+ **£3,881** (£1,155; £577; £288) **Stalls** Low

Form RPR
4346 1 **Clear Spell (IRE)**[47] 3303 3-8-12 **66**............................... PJMcDonald 2 73
(Alistair Whillans) *hld up in tch: stdy hdwy over 2f out: effrt and swtchd lft over 1f out: kpt on to ld towards fin* **2/1**[1]
2204 2 nk **Latin Rebel (IRE)**[12] 4492 7-8-8 **55**..........................(p) GaryBartley(3) 9 61
(Jim Goldie) *t.k.h: hld up in tch: rdn and edgd rt over 2f out: hdwy on outside over 1f out: kpt on wl to take 2nd towards fin* **5/2**[2]
511 3 1/2 **Valantino Oyster (IRE)**[11] 4520 7-10-0 **72**..............(p) LucyAlexander 3 77
(Tracy Waggott) *led at stdy pce: qcknd over 3f out: rdn over 2f out: kpt on fnl f: hdd and no ex towards fin* **5/1**
0 4 3/4 **Polar Forest**[8] 4613 4-9-3 **66**...................................(e) DuilioDaSilva(5) 1 70
(Richard Guest) *trckd ldrs: wnt 2nd over 2f out: rdn and ev ch over 1f out: one pce ins fnl f* **7/1**
4 5 8 **Quick Succession (USA)**[15] 4387 3-8-12 **66**........................ TomEaves 4 56
(Keith Dalgleish) *chsd ldr: rdn over 3f out: hung rt and wknd over 2f out* **7/2**[3]
2m 23.32s (-2.28) **Going Correction** -0.10s/f (Good)
**WFA** 3 from 4yo+ 10lb 5 Ran SP% **113.3**
Speed ratings (Par 103): **104,103,103,102,97**
CSF £7.56 TOTE £3.20: £1.40, £2.50; EX 7.40 Trifecta £22.00.
**Owner** Still Game Racing Syndicate **Bred** Mrs T Mahon **Trained** Newmill-On-Slitrig, Borders

**FOCUS**
Just five runners and Valentino Oyster was allowed to dictate at what looked very steady fractions, so hard to be excited about the form.
T/Plt: £61.20 to a £1 stake. Pool: £57,794.00 - 688.66 winning tickets. T/Qpdt: £5.70 to a £1 stake. Pool: £8,040.00 - 1,030.75 winning tickets. RY

## 4731 LINGFIELD (L-H)

Saturday, August 2

**OFFICIAL GOING: Turf course - good to firm (watered; 8.9); awt - standard**

Wind: Moderate, behind Weather: Fine

### 4905 INJURED JOCKEYS FUND 50TH ANNIVERSARY APPRENTICE H'CAP 7f 140y

5:30 (5:30) (Class 6) (0-65,65) 3-Y-0+ £2,587 (£770; £384; £192) **Stalls** Centre

Form RPR

00-2 1 **Wordismybond**[9] 4588 5-9-12 65 ChrisMeehan(2) 1 75
(Peter Makin) *mde virtually all and sn crossed to nr side rail: pressed 2f out: shkn up over 1f out: readily asserted fnl f* 11/4[1]

556 2 1 ¾ **Libra Romana (IRE)**[12] 4495 3-8-0 48 JackGilligan(4) 2 53
(Sir Mark Prescott Bt) *t.k.h: racd on outer: trckd clr ldng pair: clsd to go 2nd jst over 2f out and pressed wnr: drvn over 1f out: one pce* 5/1[3]

1500 3 3 **Carrera**[7] 4655 4-9-3 58 KieranShoemark(4) 7 57
(Michael Blanshard) *rdn in 5th pl after 3f: prog u.p to chse ldng pair 2f out: no imp after* 4/1[2]

3040 4 hd **Bold Ring**[19] 4266 8-8-13 54 RhiainIngram(4) 3 52
(Edward Creighton) *trckd ldng pair: rdn and nt qckn over 2f out: no imp after tl kpt on fnl f to press for 3rd nr fin* 20/1

0060 5 1 ½ **Flamborough Breeze**[19] 4271 5-9-10 65 (t) HectorCrouch(4) 8 59
(Ed Vaughan) *dwlt: sn wl bhd in last pair: shoved along after 3f: hung lft fr 2f out and ended on wd outside: kpt on fr over 1f out: no ch* 7/1

0000 6 nse **Rio Cobolo (IRE)**[39] 3547 8-9-2 57 (v) PeterSword(4) 4 51
(Philip Kirby) *awkward s: a towards rr: rdn and tried to cl over 2f out: no hdwy fnl f* 12/1

0340 7 2 ½ **Delightful Sleep**[22] 4153 6-9-3 56 HollieDoyle(2) 6 44
(David Evans) *hld up in last pair and wl bhd: pushed along and sme prog over 1f out: no ch and fdd fnl f* 8/1

1651 8 ½ **Belle Bayardo (IRE)**[14] 4428 6-9-13 64 DavidParkes 5 51
(Tony Carroll) *taken down early: stdd s: t.k.h and sn w wnr: rdn 3f out: wknd jst over 2f out* 9/2[3]

1m 29.85s (-2.45) **Going Correction** -0.25s/f (Firm)
**WFA** 3 from 4yo+ 7lb 8 Ran SP% 113.4
Speed ratings (Par 101): **102,100,97,97,95 95,93,92**
CSF £22.10 CT £75.62 TOTE £3.50: £1.60, £2.10, £1.50; EX 23.90 Trifecta £98.90.
**Owner** T W Wellard & Partners **Bred** Henry And Mrs Rosemary Moszkowicz **Trained** Ogbourne Maisey, Wilts
■ Stewards' Enquiry : Kieran Shoemark one-day ban: careless riding (Aug 18)

**FOCUS**
The official going on the turf course was good to firm. A modest handicap for apprentice riders. The form is not bombproof but the runner-up has been rated as running about her best race.

### 4906 188BET MEDIAN AUCTION MAIDEN STKS 7f 140y

6:00 (6:01) (Class 6) 2-Y-0 £2,134 (£635; £317; £158) **Stalls** Centre

Form RPR

53 1 **Red Rebel**[17] 4330 2-9-5 0 LukeMorris 6 73
(Clive Cox) *mde virtually all and racd against nr side rail: drvn and hung lft off rail over 1f out: hld on ins fnl f* 5/1[3]

64 2 1 **Nufooth (IRE)**[21] 4202 2-9-0 0 PatDobbs 10 66
(Richard Hannon) *trckd ldng pair: rdn jst over 2f out: wnt 2nd over 1f out: chal fnl f: nt qckn last 100yds* 4/6[1]

0 3 hd **Victoriously**[15] 4395 2-9-5 0 JackMitchell 4 70+
(Brian Meehan) *sn off the pce: rdn and prog on outer over 2f out: clsd on ldrs over 1f out: kpt on fnl f to press for 2nd nr fin* 33/1

24 4 ¾ **Paddys Motorbike (IRE)**[34] 3751 2-9-2 0 DeclanBates(3) 3 69
(David Evans) *dwlt and vigorously pushed along early: nvr gng wl in midfield: rdn and prog over 2f out: kpt on u.p fnl f: nrst fin* 7/2[2]

60 5 1 ½ **Francis Scott Key (IRE)**[23] 4109 2-9-2 0 RyanClark(3) 2 66
(Brian Meehan) *w wnr to over 2f out: drvn and lost 2nd wl over 1f out: one pce* 12/1

6 1 **Haarib** 2-9-5 0 HayleyTurner 1 64
(Ed Walker) *green preliminaries: gd spd to trck ldng pair: rn green whn reminder jst over 2f out: lost pl and steadily fdd over 1f out: nt disgracd* 16/1

7 16 **Alexi (IRE)** 2-9-0 0 WilliamTwiston-Davies 5 25
(Harry Dunlop) *sn detached in last pair: shoved along by 1/2-way: t.o* 33/1

0 8 1 **Titian Lord (IRE)**[15] 4395 2-9-5 0 KierenFallon 8 28
(Charles Hills) *s.s: mostly detached in last pair and rdn by 1/2-way: t.o* 16/1

1m 30.89s (-1.41) **Going Correction** -0.25s/f (Firm) 8 Ran SP% 124.2
Speed ratings (Par 92): **97,96,95,95,93 92,76,75**
CSF £9.53 TOTE £5.30: £1.60, £1.10, £9.00; EX 14.80 Trifecta £278.20.
**Owner** P Bamford **Bred** D R Tucker **Trained** Lambourn, Berks

**FOCUS**
Just an ordinary maiden. The fourth helps set the standard.

### 4907 188BET H'CAP 7f

6:30 (6:31) (Class 5) (0-75,77) 3-Y-0+ £3,234 (£962; £481; £240) **Stalls** Centre

Form RPR

0402 1 **White Russian**[17] 4329 3-9-0 67 HayleyTurner 3 75
(Henry Candy) *trckd ldng pair: pushed along 3f out: clsd 2f out: rdn to ld jst over 1f out: drvn out and hld on nr fin* 3/1[1]

U6-3 2 nk **Ziggy's Secret**[52] 3125 4-9-12 73 DougieCostello 9 82
(Lucy Wadham) *walked to post early: trckd ldng trio: swtchd lft wl over 1f out: drvn and prog to takew 2nd ins fnl f clsd on wnr fin* 8/1

0002 3 1 ¾ **Al's Memory (IRE)**[19] 4262 5-9-10 74 DeclanBates(3) 10 78
(David Evans) *led and racd against nr side rail: drvn 2f out: hdd jst over 1f out: one pce and lost 2nd ins fnl f* 7/1

0515 4 ½ **Perfect Mission**[22] 4154 6-8-11 65 (v) KieranShoemark(7) 7 68
(Andrew Balding) *in tch: rdn and prog over 2f out: tried to chal over 1f out: nt qckn* 6/1[3]

4300 5 1 ½ **Jontleman (IRE)**[15] 4401 4-9-6 70 CharlesBishop(3) 5 69
(Mick Channon) *stdd s: hld up in last pair: shkn up on outer 2f out: styd on steadily after: nvr able to chal* 10/1

3212 6 ½ **Shifting Star (IRE)**[16] 4355 9-9-11 72 (vt) WilliamCarson 8 70
(John Bridger) *pressed ldr to 2f out: steadily wknd u.p* 9/2[2]

2245 7 shd **Sakash**[22] 4148 4-9-9 70 OisinMurphy 2 67
(J R Jenkins) *racd on outer: towards rr: clsd grad over 2f out: drvn over 1f out: no prog fnl f* 6/1[3]

325 8 11 **Polar Kite (IRE)**[123] 1217 6-10-0 75 [1] JackMitchell 6 43
(Roger Ingram) *stdd s: hld up in last pair: in tch 2f out: wknd rapidly sn after* 20/1

0620 9 19 **Llyrical**[40] 3518 3-8-5 63 TimClark(5) 4
(Derek Haydn Jones) *in tch tl wknd rapidly wl over 2f out: wl t.o* 14/1

1m 21.04s (-2.26) **Going Correction** -0.25s/f (Firm)
**WFA** 3 from 4yo+ 6lb 9 Ran SP% 115.9
Speed ratings (Par 103): **102,101,99,99,97 96,96,84,62**
CSF £27.74 CT £156.08 TOTE £3.50: £1.90, £3.10, £2.10; EX 34.10 Trifecta £64.10.
**Owner** Six Too Many **Bred** Trebles Holford Farm Thoroughbreds **Trained** Kingston Warren, Oxon

**FOCUS**
A fair handicap. The front-running third has been rated close to his AW latest.

### 4908 SPEEDY ANTON CHARLES GORDON MARGUET-BALL H'CAP 6f

7:00 (7:00) (Class 6) (0-65,65) 3-Y-0+ £2,587 (£770; £384; £192) **Stalls** Centre

Form RPR

03-0 1 **Maria Montez**[21] 4206 5-9-12 65 KierenFallon 7 77
(B W Hills) *trckd ldng pair: quick move to ld jst over 2f out: rdn clr over 1f out: drvn out* 6/1[3]

232 2 2 ¾ **Assertive Agent**[14] 4431 4-9-7 60 LukeMorris 2 63
(Tony Carroll) *pushed along early in midfield: rdn and prog over 2f out: drvn to go 2nd ins fnl f: no threat to wnr* 4/1[2]

5002 3 ½ **Divine Call**[31] 3848 7-9-8 61 (v) WilliamTwiston-Davies 4 62
(Milton Bradley) *trckd ldrs gng wl: pushed along whn nt clr run 2f out: rdn and trying to make prog whn nt clr run 1f out: styd on to take 3rd nr fin* 8/1

300 4 nk **Hit The Lights (IRE)**[14] 4431 4-9-7 60 OisinMurphy 11 60
(Patrick Chamings) *taken down early: led against nr side rail: rdn and hdd jst over 2f out: one pce and lost 2 pls ins fnl f* 7/2[1]

0000 5 nk **Encapsulated**[14] 4428 4-9-1 54 (p) WilliamCarson 3 53
(Roger Ingram) *racd on outer: chsd ldrs: drvn over 2f out: tried to cl over 1f out: nt qckn and wl hld after* 25/1

2045 6 ¾ **Indian Affair**[40] 3519 4-9-3 61 TimClark(5) 10 58
(Milton Bradley) *trckd ldrs: rdn jst over 2f out: nt qckn and hld whn nt clr run briefly ins fnl f: kpt on* 7/1

0000 7 1 **New Rich**[16] 4370 4-9-0 58 (p) GeorgeDowning(5) 9 52
(Eve Johnson Houghton) *s.s: hld up in last trio: swtchd out wd and rdn 2f out: kpt on but nvr gng pce to threaten* 8/1

0006 8 1 ¾ **Commandingpresence (USA)**[14] 4431 8-9-5 58 KieranO'Neill 8 46
(John Bridger) *taken down early: chsd ldr to over 2f out: wknd u.p* 16/1

0616 9 2 ¾ **Caminel (IRE)**[35] 3709 3-9-6 63 MartinLane 5 41
(Jeremy Gask) *stdd s: hld up in last trio: off the pce whn swtchd out wd 1/2-way: shkn up briefly 2f out: no prog and nvr involved* 12/1

0413 10 7 **Bajan Story**[9] 4564 5-8-11 50 LiamKeniry 1 18
(Michael Blanshard) *a in last trio: wknd 2f out: eased over 1f out* 10/1

1m 9.39s (-1.81) **Going Correction** -0.25s/f (Firm)
**WFA** 3 from 4yo+ 4lb 10 Ran SP% 117.7
Speed ratings (Par 101): **102,98,97,97,96 95,94,92,88,79**
CSF £30.57 CT £196.04 TOTE £7.30: £1.70, £1.70, £2.60; EX 23.30 Trifecta £136.50.
**Owner** John M Cole **Bred** D R Tucker **Trained** Upper Lambourn, Berks

**FOCUS**
A competitive handicap for the grade, but the winner won unchallenged. The runner-up has been rated to her C&D latest, with the third close to his recent turf form.

### 4909 CORE GROUP/BRITISH STALLION STUDS EBF MAIDEN STKS 5f 6y(P)

7:30 (7:30) (Class 5) 2-Y-0 £2,911 (£866; £432; £216) **Stalls** High

Form RPR

22 1 **Burnt Sugar (IRE)**[23] 4110 2-9-5 0 PatDobbs 1 86+
(Richard Hannon) *disp ld tl def advantage over 2f out: drew clr wl over 1f out: pushed out to the fin* 1/8[1]

06 2 6 **Zipedeedodah (IRE)**[18] 4286 2-9-5 0 OisinMurphy 3 64
(Joseph Tuite) *disp ld to over 2f out: easily lft bhd wl over 1f out* 6/1[2]

06 3 1 **Fine Judgment**[33] 3799 2-9-0 0 MartinDwyer 4 56
(William Muir) *disp ld on outer 2f: hung rt bnd 2f out: sn lft bhd* 7/1[3]

5 4 2 ½ **Ms Eboracum (IRE)**[66] 2680 2-9-0 0 AdamBeschizza 2 47
(Edward Creighton) *cl up bhd ldrs to jst over 2f out: sn lft bhd* 20/1

53 5 7 **Perfect Concord**[23] 4103 2-9-0 0 LiamKeniry 5 22
(Michael Blanshard) *cl up bhd ldrs to jst over 2f out: wknd over 1f out: eased* 33/1

58.47s (-0.33) **Going Correction** 0.0s/f (Stan) 5 Ran SP% 123.4
Speed ratings (Par 94): **102,92,90,86,75**
CSF £2.35 TOTE £1.10: £1.02, £2.20; EX 2.30 Trifecta £4.40.
**Owner** De La Warr Racing **Bred** Ballylinch Stud **Trained** East Everleigh, Wilts

**FOCUS**
The pace was decent and the winner looks to have improved slightly.

### 4910 188BET CASINO H'CAP 1m 4f (P)

8:00 (8:01) (Class 5) (0-70,70) 3-Y-0+ £3,234 (£962; £481; £240) **Stalls** Low

Form RPR

-002 1 **Secure Cloud (IRE)**[23] 4106 3-8-12 65 KierenFallon 1 78+
(B W Hills) *trckd ldng pair after 2f: wnt 2nd 2f out: pushed into ld jst ins fnl f: cosily* 5/4[2]

4114 2 1 **Men Don't Cry (IRE)**[6] 4709 5-10-0 70 OisinMurphy 5 80
(Ed de Giles) *trckd ldr: led over 2f out: drvn and hdd jst ins fnl f: kpt on wl but readily hld* 11/10[1]

2006 3 9 **Rookery (IRE)**[28] 3986 3-9-1 68 MartinLane 6 64?
(Roger Ingram) *sn led: rdn and hdd over 2f out: sn lost 2nd and wl btn after* 14/1

6004 4 3 **Sparkling Ice (IRE)**[30] 3898 3-8-7 65 (b) GeorgeDowning(5) 3 56
(Eve Johnson Houghton) *trckd ldng pair 2f: rdn 4f out: easily lft bhd fr 2f out* 12/1[3]

1060 5 1 ½ **Fire In Babylon (IRE)**[17] 4322 6-9-0 61 (b) TobyAtkinson(5) 4 49
(Noel Quinlan) *hld up in last: urged along 3f out: no prog: wl btn over 1f out* 20/1

2m 33.09s (0.09) **Going Correction** 0.0s/f (Stan)
**WFA** 3 from 5yo+ 11lb 5 Ran SP% 111.2
Speed ratings (Par 103): **99,98,92,90,89**
CSF £2.99 TOTE £2.30: £1.20, £1.20; EX 2.70 Trifecta £12.50.
**Owner** Prolinx Limited **Bred** Padraic Connolly **Trained** Upper Lambourn, Berks

**FOCUS**
As the betting suggested, the two market leaders pulled well clear. There's a chance the form could be rated a little higher.

## 4911 188BET GREAT IN PLAY H'CAP 1m 2f (P)
8:30 (8:32) (Class 6) (0-60,60) 3-Y-O+ £2,587 (£770; £384; £192) Stalls Low

Form RPR
030 1 **Fresh Kingdom (IRE)**[47] 3315 3-9-1 **58**........................(p) ShaneKelly 6 67
(James Fanshawe) *wl plcd: trckd ldr 5f out: led over 2f out and sent for home: drvn and kpt on fnl f* **4/1**[2]
3003 2 1 ½ **Orders From Rome (IRE)**[19] 4266 5-9-12 **60**............(t) KierenFallon 13 66
(Charlie Fellowes) *forced to r wd early: chsd ldrs: prog 4f out: drvn to chse wnr wl over 1f out: kpt on but no imp fnl f* **4/1**[2]
1032 3 1 **Sandy Cove**[24] 4085 3-9-1 **58**.................................... LukeMorris 5 62
(James Eustace) *in tch: prog over 3f out: rdn over 2f out: chsd ldng pair over 1f out: kpt on same pce* **3/1**[1]
-016 4 ¾ **Oly'Roccs (IRE)**[40] 3534 3-8-8 **51**................................ OisinMurphy 3 54
(Philip Kirby) *led 4f: chsd ldr to 5f out: styd cl up: rdn over 2f out: effrt on inner over 1f out: kpt on same pce* **8/1**[3]
0305 5 3 ½ **Capers Royal Star (FR)**[33] 3805 3-9-3 **60**.............. MartinLane 4 56
(Paul Cole) *chsd ldr 2f: styd prom: rdn 3f out: fdd over 1f out* **8/1**[3]
0004 6 *nse* **Bridge That Gap**[7] 4658 6-9-12 **60**.........................(p) JimmyQuinn 11 55
(Roger Ingram) *slowly away then squeezed out: mostly in last trio: sme prog over 2f out: drvn and kpt on one pce fr over 1f out: no ch* **8/1**[3]
000 7 ¾ **Bison Grass**[58] 2930 4-9-9 **57**................................. AdamBeschizza 8 51
(Giles Bravery) *dwlt: wl in rr: prog over 3f out to rch 7th over 2f out: rdn and no hdwy after* **25/1**
0-04 8 1 ½ **Lingfield Lupus (IRE)**[24] 4084 3-8-3 **49** oh4...............(v) MartinDwyer 9 37
(John Best) *dwlt: frntically rdn to chse ldr after 2f: led after 4f: hdd & wknd over 2f out* **16/1**
0000 9 8 **Wings Of Fire (IRE)**[17] 4327 4-8-7 **46** oh1.................. TimClark(5) 1 21
(Denis Quinn) *dwlt: a towards rr: lost tch w ldrs fr 3f out* **66/1**
0/02 10 *shd* **Medal Of Valour (JPN)**[24] 3035 6-9-9 **57**....................(tp) LiamKeniry 10 32
(Mark Gillard) *blindfold off fraction late and dwlt: a in rr: rdn and no prog over 2f out* **25/1**
0600 11 1 ¾ **Silvee**[14] 4433 7-8-12 **46** oh1.......................................(p) WilliamCarson 2 17
(John Bridger) *nvr beyond midfield: drvn over 4f out: struggling 3f out* **25/1**
6000 12 1 ½ **Spirited Silver**[24] 4084 3-8-3 **56** oh11.......................... KieranO'Neill 7 14
(John Bridger) *dwlt: nvr beyond midfield: struggling over 3f out* **66/1**
5000 13 16 **Crazy Train**[5] 4738 5-8-6 **47**....................................(b[1]) DavidParkes(7) 12
(Keiran Burke) *awkward s: racd wd: nvr beyond midfield: wknd over 3f out: t.o* **50/1**

2m 6.12s (-0.48) **Going Correction** 0.0s/f (Stan)
**WFA** 3 from 4yo+ 9lb **13** Ran SP% **120.7**
Speed ratings (Par 101): **101,99,99,98,95 95,94,93,87,87 85,84,71**
CSF £19.37 CT £55.29 TOTE £5.70: £2.20, £1.90, £1.50; EX 25.00 Trifecta £89.90.
**Owner** Cheng Wai Tao **Bred** Graiguelin Stud **Trained** Newmarket, Suffolk

**FOCUS**
A modest but tight handicap for the grade. Typically muddling form. It's been rated around the runner-up.
T/Plt: £8.00 to a £1 stake. Pool: £59,592.55 - 5,370.69 winning tickets. T/Qpdt: £3.60 to a £1 stake. Pool: £6,242.15 - 1,250.82 winning tickets.

# 4862 NEWMARKET (R-H)
Saturday, August 2

**OFFICIAL GOING: Firm (8.4)**
Wind: Light across Weather: Cloudy

## 4912 MATTIOLI WOODS SUPPORTING ALZHEIMER'S RESEARCH UK H'CAP (BOBIS RACE) 7f
2:20 (2:20) (Class 3) (0-90,90) 3-Y-O £12,938 (£3,850; £1,924; £962) Stalls Low

Form RPR
-215 1 **Outback Traveller (IRE)**[29] 3917 3-9-6 **89**............. SilvestreDeSousa 2 99
(Jeremy Noseda) *racd stands' side: a.p: chsd ldr over 2f out: rdn to ld and hung rt over 1f out: r.o: 1st of 5 in gp* **9/4**[2]
6031 2 1 ¾ **Ticking Katie (IRE)**[22] 4176 3-9-0 **90**....................(p) RobJFitzpatrick(7) 1 95
(K R Burke) *racd stands' side: a.p: swtchd lft over 2f out: rdn over 1f out: chsd wnr wl ins fnl f: r.o: 2nd of 5 in gp* **11/2**
1543 3 1 ¾ **Ixelles Diamond (IRE)**[11] 4523 3-8-2 **71** oh3.................. JimmyQuinn 4 71
(Richard Fahey) *w ldr stands' side tl pushed along over 2f out: rdn and nt clr run over 1f out: styd on same pce ins fnl f: 3rd of 5 in gp* **20/1**
-321 4 1 ½ **Marmoom**[14] 4446 3-8-13 **82**........................................... TedDurcan 3 79
(Charles Hills) *overall ldr stands' side: rdn and hdd over 1f out: no ex ins fnl f* **15/8**[1]
2105 5 3 ¾ **Galvanize**[26] 4021 3-9-0 **83**.......................................... DavidProbert 8 70
(Kevin Ryan) *trckd ldr centre tl rdn to ld that pair over 1f out: wknd ins fnl f: 1st of 2 in gp* **20/1**
1 6 2 ¼ **Mr Bossy Boots (IRE)**[182] 423 3-8-8 **77**........................ JimCrowley 5 58
(Ralph Beckett) *racd stands' side: s.s: hld up: effrt over 2f out: wknd over 1f out: last of 5 in gp* **5/1**[3]
2005 7 1 ¼ **Harwoods Volante (IRE)**[18] 4281 3-9-2 **85**...............(p) RobertHavlin 6 63
(Amanda Perrett) *led centre pair tl rdn and hdd over 1f out: wknd fnl f: last of 2 in gp* **33/1**

1m 24.79s (-0.91) **Going Correction** +0.125s/f (Good) **7** Ran SP% **110.1**
Speed ratings (Par 104): **110,108,106,104,100 97,96**
CSF £13.47 CT £176.06 TOTE £3.50: £1.80, £3.00; EX 14.90 Trifecta £95.10.
**Owner** Saeed Suhail **Bred** Tally-Ho Stud **Trained** Newmarket, Suffolk

**FOCUS**
Stands' side track used with Stalls on Stands side except 10f & 12f: Centre. This was a fair 3yo handicap. They went an average pace with two keeping mid-track away from the main group, and the stands' side proved the place to be. The runner-up has been rated as running a small pb.

## 4913 CHEVELEY PARK STUD SUPPORTING ALZHEIMER'S RESEARCH UK FILLIES' NURSERY H'CAP (BOBIS RACE) 6f
2:55 (2:57) (Class 2) 2-Y-O £25,876 (£7,700; £3,848; £1,924) Stalls Low

Form RPR
632 1 **Zifena**[15] 4396 2-8-12 **77**........................................... JimCrowley 12 89
(Eve Johnson Houghton) *hld up: hdwy over 2f out: rdn over 1f out: r.o to ld nr fin* **20/1**
1 2 *hd* **Enlace**[16] 4357 2-9-1 **80**.............................................. SilvestreDeSousa 10 91+
(Mark Johnston) *w ldr tl rdn to ld over 1f out: wandered ins fnl f: hdd nr fin* **13/8**[1]
11 3 1 ¾ **New Providence**[16] 4345 2-9-0 **84**................................ NoelGarbutt(5) 1 90
(Hugo Palmer) *hld up in tch: rdn over 1f out: r.o* **15/2**[2]
421 4 1 ¾ **Prize Exhibit**[8] 4610 2-9-6 **85**................................. FergusSweeney 6 86
(Jamie Osborne) *chsd ldrs: rdn and ev ch over 1f out: styd on same pce ins fnl f* **9/1**[3]
032 5 1 ¾ **Lady Gemini**[21] 4216 2-9-5 **84**.................................. ThomasHenderson 4 79
(Jo Hughes) *led: rdn and hdd over 1f out: no ex ins fnl f* **20/1**
1 6 ¾ **L'Addition**[17] 4320 2-8-5 **70**........................................ DavidProbert 18 63+
(William Jarvis) *hld up: hdwy over 2f out: rdn over 1f out: styd on same pce fnl f* **11/1**
032 7 ¾ **Lacing**[23] 4126 2-8-10 **75**.............................................. JimmyQuinn 7 66
(Richard Fahey) *chsd ldrs: rdn over 1f out: styd on same pce fnl f* **18/1**
212 8 ¾ **Panda Spirit (USA)**[8] 4619 2-9-2 **81**............................ TedDurcan 9 70
(Sir Michael Stoute) *prom: rdn over 2f out: no ex fnl f* **9/1**[3]
4322 9 2 ½ **Indian Keys**[37] 3620 2-8-7 **72**...................................... RobertHavlin 20 53
(Kevin Ryan) *chsd ldrs: rdn over 1f out: wknd ins fnl f* **33/1**
11 10 1 **Dittander**[18] 4283 2-9-1 **80**........................................... SeanLevey 8 58
(Richard Hannon) *hmpd s: hld up: hdwy and hung lft over 2f out: wknd over 1f out* **20/1**
4142 11 1 **Madamoiselle Bond**[17] 4313 2-8-2 **72**........................ ShelleyBirkett(5) 17 47
(William Jarvis) *chsd ldrs: rdn over 2f out: wknd fnl f* **33/1**
1002 12 2 ¾ **Cajoling (IRE)**[16] 4345 2-9-0 **79**................................. HarryBentley 5 46
(Jonathan Portman) *hld up: rdn over 2f out: wknd over 1f out* **25/1**
324 13 3 ½ **Robin Hill**[19] 4269 2-8-4 **69**....................................... SamHitchcott 14 25
(William Muir) *hld up: hdwy over 2f out: rdn and wknd over 1f out* **33/1**
011 14 *nk* **Feeling Easy (IRE)**[21] 4205 2-8-12 **84**..................... KieranShoemark(7) 3 39
(Robert Eddery) *chsd ldrs tl rdn and wknd over 2f out* **33/1**
31 15 1 ¾ **East Coast Lady (IRE)**[23] 4126 2-9-6 **85**.................... FrederikTylicki 11 35
(Robert Eddery) *prom: rdn over 2f out: wknd over 1f out* **9/1**[3]
330 16 *nk* **Three Robins**[16] 4346 2-8-4 **69**..................................... KieranO'Neill 15 18
(Richard Hannon) *chsd ldrs: rdn over 2f out: hmpd and wknd sn after* **50/1**
00 17 ¾ **Ocean Crystal**[15] 4403 2-7-11 **65** oh3............................. RyanPowell(3) 19 12
(John Ryan) *prom: lost pl 1/2-way: hung lft and wknd over 2f out* **100/1**

1m 12.42s (-0.08) **Going Correction** +0.125s/f (Good) **17** Ran SP% **126.3**
Speed ratings (Par 97): **105,104,102,100,97 96,95,94,91,90 88,85,80,80,77 77,76**
CSF £49.81 CT £308.92 TOTE £36.20: £5.30, £1.10, £1.60, £2.50; EX 100.10 Trifecta £1499.30.
**Owner** Dr Philip Brown **Bred** Dr Philip J Brown **Trained** Blewbury, Oxon

**FOCUS**
This was a warm fillies' nursery, run at a sound pace, and the form should work out well. Strong form with the fifth rated pretty much to her latest form.

## 4914 ALZHEIMER'S RESEARCH UK EBF MAIDEN FILLIES' STKS (BOBIS RACE) 7f
3:30 (3:32) (Class 4) 2-Y-O £5,175 (£1,540; £769; £384) Stalls Low

Form RPR
5 1 **Mahsooba (USA)**[16] 4346 2-9-0 0.................................. DavidProbert 13 79+
(Ed Dunlop) *hld up: nt clr ruin over 2f out: hdwy over 1f out: r.o to ld wl ins fnl f* **3/1**[2]
0 2 *nk* **Titled Lady**[14] 4444 2-9-0 0........................................... LiamKeniry 10 79
(David Elsworth) *hld up: hdwy over 1f out: rdn and ev ch wl ins fnl f: r.o* **33/1**
44 3 *hd* **Tohfa (IRE)**[22] 4170 2-9-0 0.......................................... LukeMorris 12 78
(Richard Hannon) *prom: chsd ldr over 5f out: rdn to ld over 1f out: hdd wl ins fnl f* **16/1**
4 1 ½ **Stay Silent (IRE)** 2-8-11 0......................................... MatthewLawson(3) 9 74+
(Saeed bin Suroor) *slowly into stirde: hld up: hdwy over 2f out: rdn and hung lft over 1f out: styd on* **8/1**
5 *hd* **Endless Time (IRE)** 2-9-0 0.................................... SilvestreDeSousa 6 74+
(Charlie Appleby) *s.i.s: sn prom: rdn over 1f out: kpt on* **9/2**[3]
6 *nse* **Sandy Cay (USA)** 2-9-0 0............................................. TedDurcan 15 73+
(Sir Michael Stoute) *s.i.s: rn green in rr: nt clr run and swtchd rt over 1f out: r.o ins fnl f: nt trble ldrs* **11/1**
4 7 1 ¼ **Rastanora (USA)**[15] 4403 2-9-0 0.................................. RobertHavlin 3 70
(John Gosden) *led: rdn and hdd over 1f out: hung lft and no ex ins fnl f* **9/4**[1]
8 ½ **Almaardiyah (IRE)** 2-9-0 0........................................... SeanLevey 1 69
(Richard Hannon) *prom: rdn and edgd lft over 1f out: styd on same pce fnl f* **18/1**
9 4 ½ **Bling Ring (USA)** 2-9-0 0............................................. HarryBentley 2 57+
(Charles Hills) *trckd ldrs: rdn and ev ch over 1f out: wknd ins fnl f* **16/1**
0 10 *shd* **Pisces**[14] 4444 2-8-11 0............................................... SimonPearce(3) 8 56
(David Elsworth) *prom: rdn over 2f out: wknd over 1f out* **66/1**
11 ¾ **Lexi's Red Devil (IRE)** 2-9-0 0................................... MartinHarley 7 54
(Marco Botti) *a in rr: n.m.r over 5f out: wknd over 1f out* **33/1**
0 12 4 **With Charm (USA)**[17] 4320 2-9-0 0................................... JimmyQuinn 11 43
(Charlie Appleby) *s.i.s: a in rr: wknd over 1f out* **50/1**

1m 27.21s (1.51) **Going Correction** +0.125s/f (Good) **12** Ran SP% **119.8**
Speed ratings (Par 93): **96,95,95,93,93 93,92,91,86,86 85,80**
CSF £108.16 TOTE £5.00: £1.80, £6.80, £2.60; EX 131.30 Trifecta £1463.10.
**Owner** Hamdan Al Maktoum **Bred** Shadwell Farm LLC **Trained** Newmarket, Suffolk

**FOCUS**
There wasn't much pace on in this interesting fillies' maiden, which resulted in a bunch finish and it was a muddling race.

## 4915 BARCLAYS BANK SUPPORTING ALZHEIMERS'S RESEARCH UK H'CAP 1m 2f
4:05 (4:05) (Class 3) (0-90,90) 3-Y-O+ £9,703 (£2,887; £1,443; £721) Stalls Centre

Form RPR
0-35 1 **Lady Pimpernel**[22] 4145 4-9-11 **87**............................. FergusSweeney 3 96
(Henry Candy) *chsd ldr: rdn over 2f out: led 1f out: styd on wl* **7/2**[2]
20 2 1 ½ **Tanseeb**[14] 4442 3-9-1 **86**......................................... FrederikTylicki 6 92
(Mark Johnston) *chsd ldrs: rdn to ld over 1f out: sn hdd: styd on same pce ins fnl f* **7/2**[2]
2310 3 5 **Bureau (IRE)**[7] 4667 3-9-2 **87**.................................... AdrianNicholls 1 83
(Mark Johnston) *led: qcknd over 2f out: rdn and hdd over 1f out: wknd ins fnl f* **8/1**[3]
101 4 3 ½ **Mindurownbusiness (IRE)**[23] 4118 3-9-5 **90**............... JimCrowley 5 79
(David Simcock) *hld up: rdn over 1f out: wknd fnl f* **5/6**[1]

2m 6.57s (1.07) **Going Correction** +0.125s/f (Good)
**WFA** 3 from 4yo 9lb **4** Ran SP% **110.1**
Speed ratings (Par 107): **100,98,94,92**
CSF £14.98 TOTE £4.20; EX 15.80 Trifecta £55.50.
**Owner** Henry Candy & Partners II **Bred** Harts Farm Stud **Trained** Kingston Warren, Oxon

**FOCUS**
A good-quality little handicap. The sound early pace seemed to steady around 1m out but it was fair overall. The runner-up has been rated as high as ever.

## 4916 STANDARD LIFE INVESTMENTS SUPPORTING ARUK H'CAP 7f
4:40 (4:41) (Class 2) (0-112,106) 3-Y-O+ £16,172 (£4,812; £2,405) Stalls Low

Form RPR
6260 1 **Noble Citizen (USA)**[81] 2245 9-9-2 98........(b) JimCrowley 2 99
(David Simcock) *chsd ldr: rdn to ld 1f out: r.o u.p* 9/2[2]
-651 2 ½ **Golden Town (IRE)**[21] 4198 3-9-0 102........(v) SilvestreDeSousa 3 100
(Saeed bin Suroor) *hld up in tch: racd keenly: rdn over 1f out: ev ch whn hung lft ins fnl f: r.o* 1/3[1]
0-00 3 1½ **Excellent Guest**[43] 3420 7-8-9 98........ JordanVaughan(7) 1 94?
(George Margarson) *led at stdy pce tl qcknd over 2f out: hdd 1f out: styd on same pce* 7/1[3]

1m 27.1s (1.40) **Going Correction** +0.125s/f (Good)
**WFA** 3 from 4yo+ 6lb 3 Ran SP% 105.7
Speed ratings (Par 109): **97,96,94**
CSF £6.72 TOTE £3.20; EX 6.50 Trifecta £7.20.
**Owner** Khalifa Dasmal **Bred** Don M Robinson **Trained** Newmarket, Suffolk

**FOCUS**
There were two defeections from this valuable handicap. There was no pace and this is weak form for the level.

## 4917 REG DAY MEMORIAL SUPPORTING ARUK H'CAP 1m 4f
5:15 (5:15) (Class 4) (0-85,84) 4-Y-O+ £7,762 (£2,310; £1,154; £577) Stalls Centre

Form RPR
0/1 1 **Gabrial The Hero (USA)**[16] 4349 5-9-7 84........ FergusSweeney 4 92+
(David Simcock) *s.i.s: hld up: hdwy over 1f out: r.o u.p to ld wl ins fnl f: jst hld on* 5/2[2]
06/4 2 nse **Tindaro (FR)**[9] 4575 7-9-2 79........(t) SeanLevey 3 87
(Paul Webber) *a.p: led 3f out: rdn over 1f out: hdd wl ins fnl f: r.o* 10/1
3-11 3 2¾ **Nullarbor Sky (IRE)**[51] 3161 4-9-7 84........[1] FrederikTylicki 6 88
(Lucy Wadham) *led 9f: rdn over 1f out: styd on same pce ins fnl f* 3/1[3]
4404 4 3 **Pasaka Boy**[15] 4400 4-9-6 83........ MartinHarley 7 82
(Jonathan Portman) *chsd ldr: rdn and ev ch over 1f out: hung lft and no ex ins fnl f* 9/4[1]
1-53 5 6 **Odin (IRE)**[16] 4349 6-9-5 82........ DavidProbert 1 71
(Don Cantillon) *chsd ldrs: rdn over 2f out: wknd and eased fnl f* 5/1

2m 33.87s (0.97) **Going Correction** +0.125s/f (Good) 5 Ran SP% 110.1
Speed ratings (Par 105): **101,100,99,97,93**
CSF £24.06 TOTE £2.70: £1.20, £4.30; EX 23.10 Trifecta £71.50.
**Owner** Dr Marwan Koukash **Bred** Kirk Wycoff & Deby Wycoff **Trained** Newmarket, Suffolk
■ Stewards' Enquiry : Fergus Sweeney seven-day ban: used whip above permitted level (Aug 17-23)

**FOCUS**
A tight middle-distance handicap. They went a modest pace until around 3f out. Muddling form rated through the third to form.

## 4918 ALZHEIMER'S RESEARCH UK H'CAP 6f
5:45 (5:46) (Class 3) (0-90,90) 3-Y-O+ £9,703 (£2,887; £1,443; £721) Stalls Low

Form RPR
1033 1 **Highland Acclaim (IRE)**[7] 4660 3-9-2 87........ SamJames(3) 1 100+
(David O'Meara) *hld up in tch: plld hrd: shkn up over 1f out: qcknd to ld ins fnl f: sn clr* 11/2
015 2 2¾ **Diamond Lady**[15] 4406 3-8-12 80........ FrederikTylicki 9 84
(William Stone) *hmpd at s: sn w ldr: rdn and ev ch fr over 1f out: styd on same pce ins fnl f* 12/1
3442 3 ¾ **Jazz (IRE)**[26] 4013 3-9-3 85........ JimCrowley 5 87
(Charles Hills) *led: rdn over 1f out: edgd lft and hdd ins fnl f: no ex* 5/1[3]
2623 4 1 **Atlantis Crossing (IRE)**[8] 4609 5-8-7 71........ SilvestreDeSousa 2 70
(Jim Boyle) *s.i.s: hld up: hung lft fr over 2f out: rdn over 1f out: styd on ins fnl f: nt trble ldrs* 3/1[1]
0405 5 hd **Joe Packet**[42] 3479 7-9-5 83........ MartinHarley 12 82
(Jonathan Portman) *chsd ldrs: rdn and ev ch over 1f out: no ex ins fnl f* 7/2[2]
3240 6 nk **Chilworth Icon**[22] 4146 4-9-12 90........ SamHitchcott 8 88
(Mick Channon) *bmpd s: hld up: rdn over 1f out: no imp ins fnl f* 8/1
03-0 7 1¼ **Wahaab (IRE)**[70] 2556 3-9-7 89........ SeanLevey 11 82
(Richard Hannon) *edgd rt s: trckd ldrs: rdn and hung lft over 1f out: wknd wl ins fnl f* 8/1
1260 8 nk **Welsh Sunrise**[106] 1554 4-8-10 74........ HarryBentley 4 67
(Stuart Williams) *prom: rdn over 2f out: nt clr run over 1f out: wknd ins fnl f* 16/1

1m 12.07s (-0.43) **Going Correction** +0.125s/f (Good)
**WFA** 3 from 4yo+ 4lb 8 Ran SP% 115.1
Speed ratings (Par 107): **107,103,102,101,100 100,98,98**
CSF £67.97 CT £353.13 TOTE £9.10: £2.00, £2.40, £2.00; EX 63.90 Trifecta £311.50.
**Owner** Evan M Sutherland **Bred** Rathbarry Stud **Trained** Nawton, N Yorks

**FOCUS**
This looked an open handicap and there was a tight finish. The third continues to run well in defeat and is the best guide.
T/Plt: £2,433.40 to a £1 stake. Pool: £80,671.84 - 24.20 winning tickets T/Qpdt: £486.20 to a £1 stake. Pool: £4,139.94 - 6.30 winning tickets CR

# 4869 THIRSK (L-H)
Saturday, August 2

**OFFICIAL GOING: Good to soft (good in places) changing to soft (heavy in places) after race 3 (3.05) changing to heavy after race 6 (4.50)**
Wind: moderate 1/2 behind Weather: overcast becoming sunny and warm, thunder storm race 2, heavy showers

## 4919 EBF STALLIONS MAIDEN STKS (BOBIS RACE) 5f
1:55 (1:57) (Class 4) 2-Y-O £4,851 (£1,443; £721; £360) Stalls High

Form RPR
2 1 **Chances Are (IRE)**[11] 4510 2-9-0 0........ TomEaves 7 74+
(Keith Dalgleish) *mde all: edgd lft 1f out: kpt on wl* 5/4[1]
0 2 2 **Thorkhill Star (IRE)**[18] 4286 2-9-5 0........ TonyHamilton 3 72
(Richard Fahey) *dwlt: in rr: hdwy stands' side over 1f out: fin wl to take 2nd last 50yds* 16/1
4 3 2¼ **Pacngo**[14] 4450 2-9-0 0........ DavidAllan 11 59
(Tim Easterby) *trckd ldrs: chal over 1f out: wknd fnl 75yds* 2/1[2]
4 4 3 **Colombia (IRE)**[8] 4624 2-9-0 0........ PJMcDonald 6 48
(Ann Duffield) *hld up in mid-div: hdwy over 2f out: chsng ldrs over 1f out: edgd rt ins fnl f: one pce* 12/1
65 5 1 **Fast Magic (IRE)**[15] 4389 2-9-0 0........ KevinStott(5) 4 49
(Kevin Ryan) *mid-div: effrt over 2f out: one pce* 7/1[3]
00 6 1½ **Hoofithully**[8] 4633 2-9-5 0........ JamesSullivan 9 45
(Michael Easterby) *chsd ldrs: wknd over 1f out: hmpd ins fnl f* 100/1
6 7 shd **Ya Halla (IRE)**[37] 3626 2-8-7 0........ AhmadAlSubousi(7) 5 39
(Robert Cowell) *mid-div: swtchd to wd outside over 1f out: nvr a factor* 40/1
05 8 ½ **Invincible Wish (IRE)**[11] 4510 2-9-7 0 ow2........ PaulPickard 1 44
(Brian Ellison) *dwlt: in rr: sme hdwy whn hung lft over 1f out: nvr a factor: weighed in 2lb heavy* 66/1
9 1½ **The Fulwell End** 2-9-2 0........ JoeyHaynes(3) 10 36
(Noel Wilson) *dwlt: sn chsng ldrs: lost pl 2f out* 25/1
10 2¾ **Myboydaniel** 2-9-0 0 ow2........ MeganCarberry(7) 8 26
(Brian Ellison) *mid-div: effrt over 2f out: lost pl over 1f out* 22/1
0 11 1 **Valentine Belle**[4] 4751 2-9-0 0........ PaulMulrennan 2 18
(Paul Midgley) *sn chsng ldrs on outer: lost pl over 1f out* 100/1

1m 1.35s (1.75) **Going Correction** +0.125s/f (Good) 11 Ran SP% 118.0
Speed ratings (Par 96): **91,87,84,79,77 75,75,74,72,67 66**
CSF £22.84 TOTE £2.20: £1.10, £3.70, £1.90; EX 19.50 Trifecta £54.90.
**Owner** Steve Macdonald **Bred** Piercetown Stud **Trained** Carluke, S Lanarks
■ Stewards' Enquiry : P J McDonald two-day ban: careless riding (Aug 16-17)
Megan Carberry one-day ban: weighed-in 2lb heavy (Aug 16)

**FOCUS**
After riding in the opener Tony Hamilton and Tom Eaves both said: "It is a bit on the dead side," Paul Mulrennan said: "It is just a fraction on the easy side" but James Sullivan said: "It is good, maybe a bit on the quick side." The first race was won in a time 3.35sec over standard, which suggests that the ground was certainly no quicker than good. Both bends dolled out for fresh ground and races of 7f & 8f increased by 8yds and 12f and 2m races by 12yds. Fairly modest maiden form. The stands' rail was the place to be, with the first three all racing there. The third and fourth help set the level.

## 4920 THIRSK LADIES' DAY SATURDAY 6TH SEPTEMBER NURSERY H'CAP (BOBIS RACE) 5f
2:30 (2:32) (Class 3) (0-95,82) 2-Y-O £9,703 (£2,887; £1,443; £721) Stalls High

Form RPR
0022 1 **Miss Mullberry**[7] 4686 2-8-13 74........ DanielTudhope 2 81
(David O'Meara) *hld up in rr: hdwy and swtchd lft over 1f out: led jst ins fnl f: all out* 6/1
2011 2 shd **Shamrock Sheila (IRE)**[10] 4542 2-7-10 64........ JosephineGordon(7) 1 71
(J S Moore) *mid-div: hdwy on outside over 2f out: upsides over 1f out: styd on towards fin: jst failed* 16/1
31 3 nk **She's A Worldie (IRE)**[29] 3909 2-9-5 80........ PaulMulrennan 6 86
(Bryan Smart) *led after 1f: wandered and hdd jst ins fnl f: kpt on towards fin* 7/2[2]
0621 4 1½ **Somedaysrdiamonds**[9] 4576 2-8-0 61 oh1........ JamesSullivan 7 61
(J S Moore) *led 1f: chsd ldrs: kpt on same pce fnl f* 20/1
6150 5 2 **Diamond Creek (IRE)**[14] 4439 2-9-6 81........ TonyHamilton 5 74
(Richard Fahey) *chsd ldrs: upsides over 1f out: wknd last 150yds* 4/1[3]
6116 6 6 **Honest Bob'S**[21] 4218 2-9-0 82........ MeganCarberry(7) 3 53
(Brian Ellison) *dwlt: hdwy over 2f out: lost pl over 1f out* 9/1
1341 7 1 **Indescribable (IRE)**[7] 4686 2-9-7 82........ FrannyNorton 9 50
(Mark Johnston) *chsd ldrs: drvn and outpcd over 2f out: sn lost pl* 2/1[1]
5602 8 8 **Elizabeth Flynn (IRE)**[12] 4493 2-8-3 67........ JoeyHaynes(3) 4 6
(K R Burke) *w ldrs: wknd over 1f out: eased whn bhd clsng stages* 25/1

1m 0.72s (1.12) **Going Correction** +0.125s/f (Good) 8 Ran SP% 114.3
Speed ratings (Par 98): **96,95,95,92,89 80,78,65**
CSF £92.83 CT £387.87 TOTE £5.10: £1.80, £3.30, £1.60; EX 51.70 Trifecta £280.10.
**Owner** MiddlehamParkRacingXXXVII,CTasker&P'tner **Bred** Dachel Stud **Trained** Nawton, N Yorks

**FOCUS**
Quite a valuable sprint nursery, run in a time 0.63sec quicker than the maiden. Ordinary but sound form.

## 4921 JAYNE AND JOE PARKER'S BIRTHDAY CELEBRATION H'CAP 1m 4f
3:05 (3:06) (Class 4) (0-80,77) 3-Y-O+ £4,851 (£1,443; £721; £360) Stalls High

Form RPR
3362 1 **Epsom Hill (SWE)**[25] 4058 3-9-1 75........(p) PaulMulrennan 5 91
(Charlie Fellowes) *trckd ldrs: led 3f out: styd on strly to forge clr fnl f* 11/2[3]
60-0 2 10 **Next Edition (IRE)**[63] 2790 6-9-10 76........ JoeyHaynes(3) 10 77
(Philip Kirby) *mid-div: hdwy to chse ldrs over 4f out: 2nd over 2f out: styd on same pce appr fnl f* 28/1
-064 3 5 **Rochambeau (IRE)**[44] 3391 3-8-7 67........ JamesSullivan 9 61
(Ruth Carr) *in rr: drvn and reluctant over 7f out: hdwy to chse ldrs 4f out: 3rd and one pce 1f out* 18/1
001 4 3 **Craggaknock**[33] 3789 3-8-11 71........ JasonHart 7 60
(Mark Walford) *trckd ldrs: drvn over 4f out: wknd over 1f out: eased in clsng stages* 15/8[1]
-211 5 20 **Leaderene**[9] 4591 3-8-8 68........ FrannyNorton 3 39
(Mark Johnston) *t.k.h: led: hdd 3f out: sn lost pl: bhd whn eased ins fnl f: t.o* 11/4[2]
2553 6 13 **Save The Bees**[23] 4113 6-9-11 77........ NeilFarley(3) 4 17
(Declan Carroll) *t.k.h w ldrs: drvn and lost pl over 5f out: sn bhd: t.o whn eased over 1f out* 12/1
0025 7 20 **Bayan Kasirga (IRE)**[15] 4417 4-9-4 67........ TonyHamilton 2
(Richard Fahey) *mid-div: lost pl 7f out: sn bhd: hopelessly t.o 4f out: eased over 1f out* 20/1
0335 8 1¾ **Cloud Monkey (IRE)**[14] 4423 4-9-7 70........ PhillipMakin 6
(Martin Todhunter) *in rr: bhd fnl 6f: eased over 1f out: t.o* 14/1
0045 9 ½ **Warlu Way**[12] 4498 7-9-11 74........ BarryMcHugh 1
(Michael Easterby) *reluctant and v.s.a: bhd: hopelessly t.o 4f out: eased over 1f out: virtually p.u* 8/1

2m 42.63s (6.43) **Going Correction** +0.675s/f (Yiel)
**WFA** 3 from 4yo+ 11lb 9 Ran SP% 115.8
Speed ratings (Par 105): **105,98,95,93,79 71,57,56,56**
CSF £139.79 CT £2569.78 TOTE £4.70: £1.30, £11.00, £5.60; EX 203.80 Trifecta £2673.30 Part won. Pool: £3,564.47 - 0.77 winning units..
**Owner** The Epsom Hill Partnership **Bred** Ms K Jacobson **Trained** Newmarket, Suffolk



The Form Book, Raceform Ltd, Newbury, RG14 5SJ

**FOCUS**
This ordinary handicap was run in a heavy downpour, and they finished well strung out. The form may not prove wholly reliable.

## 4922 TOTEPOOL THIRSK SUMMER CUP (H'CAP) 1m
**3:40** (3:42) (Class 3) (0-90,91) 3-Y-O+ **£19,407** (£5,775; £2,886; £1,443) **Stalls** Low

Form RPR

0060 **1** **Osteopathic Remedy (IRE)**[21] 4212 10-9-4 **84**..........(t) PhillipMakin 12 94
(Michael Dods) *prom: chsd ldrs over 3f out: 2nd over 1f out: styd on to ld nr fin* **8/1**[3]

2042 **2** *nk* **Kiwi Bay**[27] 4002 9-8-13 **79**.............................. PaulMulrennan 15 88
(Michael Dods) *trckd ldrs: led over 2f out: hdd and no ex in clsng stages* **20/1**

6224 **3** *2 ¾* **Kingscroft (IRE)**[8] 4608 6-9-0 **80**.............................. RobertWinston 17 83
(Michael Herrington) *in rr: hdwy over 4f out: 3rd over 1f out: kpt on same pce* **14/1**

1325 **4** *¾* **Bartack (IRE)**[8] 4635 4-9-0 **87**..............................(v) JoshDoyle(7) 16 88+
(David O'Meara) *in rr: hdwy on outside over 2f out: styd on fnl f* **6/1**[1]

3202 **5** *1 ¼* **Potent Embrace (USA)**[11] 4513 3-8-1 **74**................ RoystonFfrench 18 71
(Mark Johnston) *w ldr: led over 4f out: hdd over 2f out: kpt on same pce* **20/1**

-141 **6** *¾* **Muharrer**[12] 4491 5-9-8 **91**.............................. ConnorBeasley(3) 1 87
(Michael Dods) *mid-div: kpt on fnl 2f: nvr a threat* **9/1**

3503 **7** *2 ½* **Fazza**[14] 4451 7-8-9 **75**.............................. JamesSullivan 6 66+
(Edwin Tuer) *in rr: hdwy over 2f out: edgd lft over 1f out: one pce* **12/1**

0354 **8** *½* **Farlow (IRE)**[35] 3716 6-9-10 **90**.............................. TonyHamilton 3 79
(Richard Fahey) *mid-div: effrt over 3f out: chsng ldrs over 2f out: eased whn wl hld towards fin* **6/1**[1]

3-50 **9** *hd* **Beaumont's Party (IRE)**[42] 3457 7-9-2 **89**............. MeganCarberry(7) 2 78
(Brian Ellison) *chsd ldrs: one pce fnl 2f* **16/1**

1453 **10** *3 ¾* **Dubai Hills**[12] 4491 8-9-8 **88**.............................. DavidNolan 10 68
(David O'Meara) *chsd ldrs: drvn over 2f out: fdd appr fnl f* **18/1**

1113 **11** *2 ½* **Kimbali (IRE)**[4] 4753 5-8-3 **76**.............................. LukeLeadbitter(7) 14 51
(Declan Carroll) *mid-div: effrt over 2f out: wl hld whn eased in clsng stages* **20/1**

0231 **12** *nk* **Anderiego (IRE)**[8] 4635 6-9-6 **86**..............................(v) DanielTudhope 7 60
(David O'Meara) *mid-div: effrt over 2f out: wl hld whn eased ins fnl f* **7/1**[2]

0030 **13** *9* **Trail Blaze (IRE)**[21] 4212 5-9-5 **90**..............................(p) KevinStott(5) 9 43
(Kevin Ryan) *led: hdd over 4f out: wknd over 2f out: eased fnl f* **9/1**

013- **14** *¾* **Altharoos (IRE)**[318] 6537 4-9-10 **90**.............................. TomEaves 11 42
(Sally Hall) *hld up in rr: bhd whn eased over 1f out* **25/1**

1520 **15** *1 ¾* **Conry (IRE)**[7] 4650 8-9-3 **83**.............................. BenCurtis 8 30
(Ian Williams) *t.k.h in rr: bhd fnl 3f: eased over 1f out* **25/1**

1053 **16** *½* **Crowdmania**[7] 4671 3-8-12 **85**.............................. FrannyNorton 5 30
(Mark Johnston) *in rr: drvn over 3f out: bhd whn eased over 1f out* **10/1**

/64- **U** **Red Inca**[423] 2976 6-8-9 **75**.............................. PaulPickard 4
(Brian Ellison) *ducked down and uns rdr s* **20/1**

1m 46.07s (5.97) **Going Correction** +0.925s/f (Soft)
**WFA** 3 from 4yo+ 7lb **17** Ran SP% **133.5**
Speed ratings (Par 107): **107,106,103,103,101 101,98,98,98,94 91,91,82,81,79 79,**
CSF £173.27 CT £1371.84 TOTE £12.60: £2.60, £4.70, £4.00, £1.90; EX 162.30 Trifecta £2038.10 Part won. Pool: £2,717.57 - 0.97 winning units..
**Owner** Kevin Kirkup **Bred** Airlie Stud **Trained** Denton, Co Durham

**FOCUS**
The official going was changed before this race to Soft, heavy in places. This was won in a time 10.2sec over Racing Post standard, which suggests the rain had slowed the ground significantly. A competitive edition of this handicap, Thirsk's most valuable race of the year. They came down the middle in the home straight and high numbers dominated, with a pair of old-timers from the Michael Dods stable contesting the finish. The winner bounced back to form with the ground turning in his favour.

## 4923 PETER BELL MEMORIAL STKS (H'CAP) 7f
**4:15** (4:19) (Class 3) (0-90,85) 3-Y-O+ **£9,703** (£2,887; £1,443; £721) **Stalls** Low

Form RPR

-212 **1** **Wilde Inspiration (IRE)**[21] 4191 3-9-0 **80**............... ConnorBeasley(3) 8 91
(Julie Camacho) *s.i.s: in rr: hdwy over 3f out: chsng ldrs 2f out: chal over 1f out: styd on to ld nr fin* **9/4**[1]

20P0 **2** *hd* **Our Boy Jack (IRE)**[22] 4156 5-9-7 **78**.............................. TonyHamilton 10 90
(Richard Fahey) *trckd ldrs: drvn over 3f out: led over 1f out: hdd and no ex clsng stages* **8/1**

2001 **3** *7* **Escape To Glory (USA)**[19] 4258 6-10-0 **85**.............................. PaulMulrennan 2 79
(Michael Dods) *in rr: drvn over 4f out: hdwy over 1f out: kpt on to take modest 3rd last 75yds* **7/1**

0110 **4** *1 ¼* **Mu'Ajiza**[25] 4060 4-9-11 **82**.............................. RobertWinston 5 73
(Paul Midgley) *s.i.s: hdwy on outside 3f out: 3rd over 1f out: one pce* **10/1**

662 **5** *3 ¼* **Fieldgunner Kirkup (GER)**[61] 2841 6-8-13 **77**............. PaulMcGiff(7) 1 59
(David Barron) *sn chsng ldrs: drvn and outpcd over 3f out: wknd over 1f out* **7/1**

0616 **6** *nk* **Relight My Fire**[18] 4291 4-9-3 **74**..............................(b) BarryMcHugh 9 55
(Tim Easterby) *led early: w ldrs: led over 3f out: hdd over 1f out: sn wknd* **20/1**

0 **7** *1* **Earth Drummer (IRE)**[35] 3737 4-10-0 **85**.............................. DavidNolan 7 64
(David O'Meara) *chsd ldrs: drvn over 2f out: wknd over 1f out* **13/2**[3]

-000 **8** *3 ¼* **Nameitwhatyoulike**[17] 4317 5-9-4 **82**.............................. DanielleMooney(7) 12 52
(Michael Easterby) *t.k.h: w ldrs: wknd over 1f out* **14/1**

3115 **9** *5* **Repetition**[7] 4661 4-10-0 **85**.............................. TomEaves 4 42
(Kristin Stubbs) *sn led: hdd over 3f out: lost pl over 1f out: eased whn bhd clsng stages* **9/2**[2]

1m 32.79s (5.59) **Going Correction** +0.925s/f (Soft)
**WFA** 3 from 4yo+ 6lb **9** Ran SP% **118.9**
Speed ratings (Par 107): **105,104,96,95,91 91,90,86,80**
CSF £21.88 CT £113.15 TOTE £3.60: £1.50, £2.30, £2.70; EX 19.80 Trifecta £96.70.
**Owner** Judy & Richard Peck **Bred** Pier House Stud **Trained** Norton, N Yorks
■ Favourite Treat was withdrawn. Price at time of withdrawal 18/1. Rule 4 does not apply.

**FOCUS**
An ordinary handicap run at a modest gallop. Again they took the centre-course route down the straight, and the first two finished clear. The runner-up has been rated back to the level of his C&D effort in soft ground last September.

## 4924 TOTEPOOL SUPPORTING THE SPORT YOU LOVE MAIDEN STKS 1m
**4:50** (4:50) (Class 4) 3-Y-O+ **£4,851** (£1,443; £721; £360) **Stalls** Low

Form RPR

4222 **1** **Taqneen (IRE)**[15] 4393 3-9-5 79..............................(b[1]) PaulMulrennan 5 82
(Ed Dunlop) *mde all: rdn over 1f out: kpt on: unchal* **10/11**[1]

3630 **2** *3 ½* **Millkwood**[38] 3572 4-9-12 76..............................(b) RobertWinston 1 75
(John Davies) *sn trcking ldrs: t.k.h: 2nd over 2f out: hung rt and fnd little* **2/1**[2]

4- **3** *7* **Medicine Hat**[291] 7276 3-9-5 0.............................. JamesSullivan 7 58
(George Moore) *chsd ldrs: pushed along over 3f out: edgd lft and wknd over 1f out* **20/1**

5-2 **4** *9* **Iftikaar (IRE)**[18] 4299 4-9-12 70.............................. RoystonFfrench 2 38
(Philip Kirby) *chsd wnr: pushed along over 3f out: wknd over 1f out* **8/1**

**5** *4 ½* **Guesshowmuchiloveu (IRE)** 3-9-5 0.............................. TomEaves 6 27
(Charlie Fellowes) *dwlt: in rr: drvn over 4f out: lost pl over 2f out* **15/2**[3]

1m 52.54s (12.44) **Going Correction** +1.175s/f (Soft)
**WFA** 3 from 4yo 7lb **5** Ran SP% **113.4**
Speed ratings (Par 105): **84,80,73,64,60**
CSF £3.10 TOTE £1.90: £1.10, £1.70; EX 3.20 Trifecta £22.40.
**Owner** Hamdan Al Maktoum **Bred** Corduff Bloodstock Ltd & David Egan **Trained** Newmarket, Suffolk

**FOCUS**
Conditions were testing by this stage and the runners splashed through puddles as they came down the middle of the home straight. Weak form. The winner has been rated to form.

## 4925 COLLECT TOTEPOOL WINNINGS AT BETFRED SHOPS H'CAP 6f
**5:20** (5:20) (Class 4) (0-85,86) 3-Y-O+ **£4,851** (£1,443; £721; £360) **Stalls** High

Form RPR

0300 **1** **We'll Deal Again**[37] 3599 7-8-10 **69**.............................. BarryMcHugh 11 79
(Michael Easterby) *chsd ldrs: led jst ins fnl f: hld on towards fin* **14/1**

04-0 **2** *nk* **Half A Billion (IRE)**[91] 1938 5-9-1 **77**.............................. ConnorBeasley(3) 10 86
(Michael Dods) *led tl over 1f out: kpt on ins fnl f: no ex towards fin* **8/1**

6056 **3** *1 ¾* **Lilac Lace (IRE)**[14] 4451 4-8-7 **73**.............................. RachelRichardson(7) 5 76
(Tim Easterby) *in rr: hdwy and edgd lft over 2f out: upsides 1f out: kpt on same pce* **8/1**

0000 **4** *4* **Lastchancelucas**[22] 4174 4-8-12 **78**....................(v[1]) LukeLeadbitter(7) 12 69
(Declan Carroll) *chsd ldrs on inner: wknd appr fnl f* **10/1**

322 **5** *1* **Cruise Tothelimit (IRE)**[10] 4531 6-9-7 **80**.............................. BenCurtis 4 67
(Ian Williams) *w ldr: led over 1f out: hdd jst ins fnl f: sn wknd* **9/1**

3363 **6** *¾* **Jack Luey**[13] 4471 7-9-10 **86**.............................. JoeyHaynes(3) 7 71
(Lawrence Mullaney) *chsd ldrs: one pce fnl 2f* **7/2**[1]

0100 **7** *¾* **Bachotheque (IRE)**[13] 4471 4-9-2 **75**.............................. TonyHamilton 14 58
(Tim Easterby) *s.i.s: sn drvn along in rr: sme hdwy over 1f out: nvr a factor* **5/1**[2]

4510 **8** *2 ¾* **Head Space (IRE)**[13] 4471 6-9-6 **79**..............................(v) JamesSullivan 3 53
(Ruth Carr) *in rr: hdwy over 2f out: lost pl over 1f out* **9/1**

5605 **9** *1* **Singeur (IRE)**[15] 4418 7-9-11 **84**.............................. PaulMulrennan 1 55
(Robin Bastiman) *chsd ldrs on outer: effrt over 2f out: wknd fnl f* **13/2**[3]

1 **10** *12* **Ella's Delight (IRE)**[77] 2329 4-9-4 **77**.............................. DavidNolan 9 9
(Martin Todhunter) *in rr: lost pl 2f out: bhd whn eased ins fnl f* **8/1**

30/0 **11** *19* **Two Pancakes**[23] 4111 4-8-9 **68**.............................. PaulPickard 2
(Declan Carroll) *dwlt: sn detached in last: eased whn t.o* **33/1**

1m 16.8s (4.10) **Going Correction** +0.85s/f (Soft) **11** Ran SP% **124.3**
Speed ratings (Par 105): **106,105,103,97,96 95,94,90,89,73 48**
CSF £128.29 CT £980.69 TOTE £19.50: £6.00, £4.90, £4.20; EX 142.20 Trifecta £926.80 Part won. Pool: £1,235.74 - 0.01 winning units..
**Owner** K Wreglesworth **Bred** K Wreglesworth **Trained** Sheriff Hutton, N Yorks

**FOCUS**
The official going became heavy all round before this ordinary sprint handicap. The winner has been in patchy form for the past year, but he was close to his old turf best here, while the runner-up has been rated close to his best.
T/Plt: £156.80 to a £1 stake. Pool of £71323.89 - 332.03 winning tickets. T/Qpdt: £53.70 to a £1 stake. Pool of £3888.15 - 53.55 winning tickets. WG

4926 - 4929a (Foreign Racing) - See Raceform Interactive

# 4838 DEAUVILLE (R-H)
### Saturday, August 2
**OFFICIAL GOING: Turf: good to soft; polytrack: standard**

## 4930a PRIX DE TOURGEVILLE (LISTED RACE) (3YO COLTS & GELDINGS) (TURF) 1m (R)
**12:00** (12:00) 3-Y-O **£22,916** (£9,166; £6,875; £4,583; £2,291)

RPR

**1** **Luannan (IRE)**[37] 3-8-11 0.............................. ChristopheSoumillon 8 105
(J-C Rouget, France) **6/5**[1]

**2** *½* **Chameur (FR)**[56] 3028 3-9-2 0.............................. AlexisBadel 3 108
(Mme M Bollack-Badel, France) **84/10**

**3** *1 ½* **Complicit (IRE)**[44] 3378 3-8-11 0..................(b[1]) Pierre-CharlesBoudot 5 100
(Paul Cole) *t.k.h: a.p: w ldr over 3f out: rdn 2f out: dropped to 3rd and nt pce of front pair fnl f: kpt on* **165/10**

**4** *1 ¼* **Redbrook (IRE)**[45] 3352 3-9-2 0.............................. FrankieDettori 6 102
(A De Royer-Dupre, France) **33/10**[2]

**5** *1* **Zlatan In Paris (FR)**[50] 3-8-11 0.............................. IoritzMendizabal 7 95
(J-C Rouget, France) **84/10**

**6** *snk* **Kenbest (FR)**[13] 3-8-11 0.............................. ThierryJarnet 4 94
(H-A Pantall, France) **229/10**

**7** *1* **Age Of Innocence**[24] 3-8-11 0.............................. MaximeGuyon 1 92
(A Fabre, France) **107/10**

**8** *2* **No Mood**[31] 3870 3-8-11 0.............................. OlivierPeslier 2 88
(C Laffon-Parias, France) **15/2**[3]

1m 41.33s (0.53) **8** Ran SP% **120.2**
WIN (incl. 1 euro stake): 2.20. PLACES: 1.40, 2.30, 3.40. DF: 9.90. SF: 12.90.
**Owner** H H Aga Khan **Bred** Haras De Son Altesse L'Aga Khan Scea **Trained** Pau, France

## 4931a PRIX SIX PERFECTIONS (LISTED RACE) (2YO FILLIES) (TURF) 7f
**1:30** (12:00) 2-Y-O **£22,916** (£9,166; £6,875; £4,583; £2,291)

RPR

**1** **Tigrilla (IRE)**[35] 3721 2-9-0 0.............................. OlivierPeslier 2 103+
(Roger Varian) *trckd ldr: pushed along to chal 2f out: led over 1f out: drew clr under hand ride fnl f: easily* **7/2**[3]

**2** *3 ½* **My Year Is A Day (FR)**[29] 2-9-0 0.............................. MaximeGuyon 3 94
(J-C Rouget, France) **3/1**[2]

**3** *1 ¾* **Malicieuse (IRE)**[39] 2-9-0 0.............................. StephanePasquier 1 89
(J E Pease, France) **13/10**[1]

**4** *½* **Queen Bee (FR)**[33] 3806 2-9-0 0.............................. GregoryBenoist 4 88
(E Lellouche, France) **47/10**

**5** *hd* **Raison D'Etre (FR)**[37] 3640 2-9-0 0.............................. AnthonyCrastus 5 88
(F Vermeulen, France) **26/1**

6 4 **Power Of The Moon (IRE)**37 3641 2-9-0 0................ TheoBachelot 6 77
(M Nigge, France) **105/10**

1m 27.17s (-1.13) 6 Ran SP% **120.6**
WIN (incl. 1 euro stake): 4.50. PLACES: 2.60, 2.30. SF: 15.80.
**Owner** Cheveley Park Stud **Bred** Old Carhue Stud **Trained** Newmarket, Suffolk

## 4932a PRIX D'ETREHAM (CONDITIONS) (2YO COLTS & GELDINGS) (TURF) 7f 110y
**2:40** (12:00) 2-Y-O **£14,166** (£5,666; £4,250; £2,833; £1,416)

RPR
1 *shd* **Medley Chic (IRE)**15 2-8-10 0................ MickaelBarzalona 5 81
(F Head, France) *fin 2nd: awrdd the r* **5/1**3
2 *hd* **Desmios (FR)**30 2-8-10 0................ OlivierPeslier 10 80
(C Laffon-Parias, France) *fin 3rd: plcd 2nd* **7/2**2
3 **Zeppelin (FR)**16 2-8-10 0................ Pierre-CharlesBoudot 1 80
(H-F Devin, France) *fin 1st: disqualified and plcd 3rd* **29/10**1
4 *snk* **Patong (FR)**16 2-8-10 0................ ThierryJarnet 9 80
(Y Gourraud, France) **213/10**
5 ½ **Speed Machine (IRE)**37 3640 2-9-0 0................ IoritzMendizabal 2 83
(Paul Cole) *sn led: rdn 2f out: r.o wl but hdd towards fin: no ex and dropped to 5th* **51/10**
6 2 **El Valle (FR)**20 4248 2-8-10 0................ CristianDemuro 3 74
(Mlle V Dissaux, France) **141/10**
7 ½ **Chambois (FR)**43 2-8-10 0................ GregoryBenoist 7 73
(M Delzangles, France) **91/10**
8 *snk* **Sombre Heros (FR)**39 2-8-10 0................ ThierryThulliez 4 72
(Mlle H Mennessier, France) **25/1**
9 *hd* **Portenio (FR)**36 3691 2-9-0 0................ MarcLerner 8 76
(C Lerner, France) **124/10**
10 *dist* **Max Attack (FR)**77 2-8-10 0................(p) MaximeGuyon 6
(A Junk, France) **147/10**

1m 36.61s (8.21) 10 Ran SP% **119.6**
WIN (incl. 1 euro stake): 6.00. PLACES: 2.00, 1.70, 1.70. DF: 10.60. SF: 25.80.
**Owner** Olivier Thomas **Bred** Petra Bloodstock Agency Ltd **Trained** France

4933 - 4934a (Foreign Racing) - See Raceform Interactive

# 4185 CHESTER (L-H)
Sunday, August 3

**OFFICIAL GOING: Good to soft (6.5)**
Wind: Fresh, half behind Weather: Cloudy, fine

## 4935 MBNA / EBF STALLIONS MAIDEN STKS (BOBIS RACE) 7f 2y
**2:00** (2:00) (Class 4) 2-Y-O **£6,469** (£1,925; £962; £481) **Stalls** Low

Form RPR
32 1 **Salateen**15 4424 2-9-5 0................ PaulMulrennan 1 90+
(Kevin Ryan) *mde all: shkn up and qcknd clr over 1f out: pushed out fnl f: easily* **5/4**1
32 2 7 **Al Bandar (IRE)**15 4429 2-9-5 0................ SeanLevey 5 72
(Richard Hannon) *sn cl up on outside: wnt 2nd after 2f: drvn and ev ch over 2f out: outpcd by wnr fr over 1f out* **3/1**3
00 3 2 **Horsetracker**9 4626 2-8-9 0................ GeorgeDowning(5) 2 62
(Ian Williams) *sn outpcd and bhd: sme hdwy over 1f out: kpt on fnl f: nvr able to chal* **40/1**
32 4 1½ **Henrytheaeroplane (USA)**12 4518 2-9-5 0................ TonyHamilton 3 63
(Richard Fahey) *t.k.h: chsd wnr tl checked and pushed along after 2f: rallied over 2f out: btn over 1f out* **2/1**2
5 5 3½ **Joshua Potman (IRE)**31 3883 2-9-5 0................ RichardKingscote 4 54
(Tom Dascombe) *bhd and outpcd: nvr on terms* **25/1**

1m 31.26s (4.76) **Going Correction** +0.65s/f (Yiel) 5 Ran SP% **109.1**
Speed ratings (Par 96): **98,90,87,86,82**
CSF £5.27 TOTE £1.90: £1.20, £2.00; EX 4.70 Trifecta £46.40.
**Owner** Sheikh Abdullah Almalek Alsabah **Bred** Mrs Janis Macpherson **Trained** Hambleton, N Yorks

**FOCUS**
The ground was on the soft side and the rail was out, adding 39yds to the first five races, 60yds to the 1m4f race and 41yds to the 1m2f race. After riding in the first Sean Levey said the ground was "sticky" while Tony Hamilton said it was "on the soft side". Three of these had run to a decent standard already so it was going to require a good performance to score.

## 4936 MBNA/EBF STALLIONS STKS (BOBIS RACE) 6f 18y
**2:30** (2:30) (Class 2) 2-Y-O **£12,606** (£3,772; £1,886; £944; £470) **Stalls** Low

Form RPR
2221 1 **Mattmu**16 4389 2-9-1 90................ DavidAllan 3 94+
(Tim Easterby) *pressed ldr: led 2f out: sn pushed along and edgd lft: rdn out fnl f* **7/2**3
2411 2 1½ **Kibaar**22 4218 2-9-1 87................ TomQueally 5 90+
(B W Hills) *awkward s: hld up last but in tch: effrt and hdwy to chse wnr ins fnl f: kpt on: nt pce to chal* **13/2**
41 3 2 **Ticks The Boxes (IRE)**27 4025 2-9-1 0................ MartinHarley 2 84
(Clive Cox) *trckd ldrs: effrt and wnt 2nd briefly over 1f out: outpcd ins fnl f* **11/4**2
2300 4 4½ **Roudee**15 4439 2-9-1 92................ RichardKingscote 1 70
(Tom Dascombe) *led: rdn and hdd 2f out: wknd 1f out* **7/4**1
123 5 1¼ **Steve Prescott**23 4159 2-9-1 87................ DavidNolan 4 66
(Richard Fahey) *prom: drvn and outpcd over 2f out: btn over 1f out* **7/1**

1m 18.55s (4.75) **Going Correction** +0.65s/f (Yiel) 5 Ran SP% **111.1**
Speed ratings (Par 100): **94,92,89,83,81**
CSF £24.40 TOTE £4.50: £1.60, £2.20; EX 13.00 Trifecta £53.00.
**Owner** James Bowers **Bred** J Bowers **Trained** Great Habton, N Yorks

**FOCUS**
A competitive little nursery.

## 4937 MBNA QUEENSFERRY STKS (LISTED RACE) 6f 18y
**3:05** (3:05) (Class 1) 3-Y-O+
**£20,982** (£7,955; £3,981; £1,983; £995; £499) **Stalls** Low

Form RPR
6304 1 **Intransigent**22 4187 5-9-0 102................ OisinMurphy 11 112
(Andrew Balding) *hld up: gd hdwy on outside to ld over 1f out: pushed out fnl f: comf* **10/1**
-100 2 2 **Coulsty (IRE)**24 4127 3-9-0 103................ SeanLevey 1 108
(Richard Hannon) *t.k.h: trckd ldrs: effrt and rdn over 1f out: kpt on to take 2nd cl home: nt rch wnr* **14/1**
1105 3 *shd* **Ertijaal (IRE)**22 4200 3-9-0 104................(b) PaulMulrennan 4 108
(William Haggas) *t.k.h: hld up bhd ldng gp: no room tl gd hdwy on ins over 1f out: sn chsng wnr: kpt on fnl f: lost 2nd cl home* **2/1**1
6360 4 2¾ **Ballista (IRE)**22 4188 6-9-0 98................ RichardKingscote 3 96
(Tom Dascombe) *led: rdn and hdd over 1f out: outpcd fnl f* **12/1**
0633 5 ½ **Dinkum Diamond (IRE)**29 3981 6-9-4 107................ BenCurtis 6 99
(Henry Candy) *t.k.h: cl up on outside tl rdn and wknd over 1f out* **5/1**
0244 6 ½ **Body And Soul (IRE)**36 3715 4-8-9 101................ DavidAllan 8 88
(Tim Easterby) *prom: pushed along 1/2-way: rdn and wknd over 1f out* **9/2**3
0053 7 ½ **Boomerang Bob (IRE)**22 4188 5-9-0 98................ SebSanders 5 91
(B W Hills) *cl up: rdn over 2f out: wknd over 1f out* **7/2**2

1m 16.23s (2.43) **Going Correction** +0.65s/f (Yiel)
**WFA** 3 from 4yo+ 4lb 7 Ran SP% **113.9**
Speed ratings (Par 111): **109,106,106,102,101 101,100**
CSF £128.85 TOTE £10.70: £3.90, £5.30; EX 120.30 Trifecta £512.50.
**Owner** Kingsclere Racing Club **Bred** Kingsclere Stud **Trained** Kingsclere, Hants

**FOCUS**
Plenty of pace on here, and the race was set up for a closer.

## 4938 MBNA MILE (H'CAP) 7f 122y
**3:40** (3:42) (Class 3) (0-95,98) 3-Y-O+ **£8,409** (£2,502; £1,250; £625) **Stalls** Low

Form RPR
5533 1 **Apostle (IRE)**17 4347 5-9-7 88................ MartinHarley 1 97
(David Simcock) *hld up in midfield: stdy hdwy over 2f out: rdn to ld ent fnl f: drvn out* **4/1**1
4021 2 1¼ **Mishaal (IRE)**7 4703 4-8-12 79 6ex................ PaulMulrennan 9 85
(Michael Herrington) *taken early to post: pressed ldr: led briefly 2f out: ev ch to ent fnl f: kpt on fin* **10/1**
3201 3 *hd* **My Single Malt (IRE)**23 4156 6-8-6 76 oh1................(p) ConnorBeasley(3) 8 81
(Julie Camacho) *in tch: rdn and hdwy to ld over 1f out: hdd ent fnl f: kpt on u.p* **14/1**
0024 4 4½ **Postscript (IRE)**23 4154 6-9-4 85................ StevieDonohoe 3 79
(David Simcock) *hld up: hdwy on outside over 2f out: no imp over 1f out* **16/1**
1630 5 1½ **Verse Of Love**22 4188 5-9-1 85................ DeclanBates(3) 11 75
(David Evans) *midfield: drvn along over 2f out: hdwy over 1f out: kpt on: nvr able to chal* **25/1**
1 6 1 **Dr Red Eye**17 4355 6-9-4 85................(p) OisinMurphy 6 73
(Scott Dixon) *led tl rdn and hdd 2f out: sn btn* **8/1**
-600 7 *shd* **Deauville Prince (FR)**44 3420 4-9-12 93................(t) RichardKingscote 4 81
(Tom Dascombe) *dwlt: bhd: pushed along 3f out: hdwy over 1f out: kpt on: nt pce to chal* **7/1**
2130 8 *nk* **Chosen Character (IRE)**22 4187 6-9-13 94................(vt) StephenCraine 2 81
(Tom Dascombe) *prom: drvn along 3f out: wknd over 1f out* **16/1**
1000 9 2¾ **Clockmaker (IRE)**8 4648 8-9-11 92................ HayleyTurner 14 72
(Conor Dore) *taken early to post: hld up: rdn 3f out: nvr able to chal* **25/1**
-314 10 1 **Knight Owl**64 2772 4-9-4 85................ ShaneKelly 10 63+
(James Fanshawe) *stmbld bdly leaving stalls: bhd: pushed along over 2f out: nvr on terms* **5/1**2
11 2¾ **Piceno (IRE)**50 3221 6-8-8 80................(p) MatthewHopkins(5) 13 51
(Scott Dixon) *prom on outside: struggling over 2f out: sn btn* **16/1**
-005 12 2½ **Unsinkable (IRE)**28 4002 4-9-3 84................ TomEaves 12 48
(Ian Semple) *taken early to post: bhd: struggling over 3f out: btn fnl 2f* **50/1**
3120 13 13 **Sir Guy Porteous (IRE)**8 4647 3-9-6 94................ FrannyNorton 5 25
(Mark Johnston) *chsd ldrs: rdn over 3f out: wknd over 2f out* **6/1**3

1m 37.3s (3.50) **Going Correction** +0.65s/f (Yiel)
**WFA** 3 from 4yo+ 7lb 13 Ran SP% **117.6**
Speed ratings (Par 107): **108,106,106,102,100 99,99,99,96,95 92,90,77**
CSF £42.67 CT £530.80 TOTE £6.90: £2.00, £3.20, £4.00; EX 49.50 Trifecta £343.70.
**Owner** Dr Marwan Koukash **Bred** Mrs Eleanor Kent **Trained** Newmarket, Suffolk

**FOCUS**
A competitive handicap.

## 4939 RACING UK NURSERY H'CAP (BOBIS RACE) 6f 18y
**4:15** (4:15) (Class 4) (0-85,78) 2-Y-O **£6,469** (£1,925; £962; £481) **Stalls** Low

Form RPR
2422 1 **Don Sigfredo (IRE)**22 4185 2-9-5 76................(p) RichardKingscote 6 84
(Tom Dascombe) *trckd ldrs: effrt and rdn over 1f out: led ins fnl f: kpt on wl towards fin* **3/1**2
4421 2 ½ **Izzthatright (IRE)**18 4313 2-9-7 78................ TonyHamilton 4 85
(Richard Fahey) *pressed ldr: led over 2f out: rdn over 1f out: hdd ins fnl f: kpt on: hld nr fin* **3/1**2
5324 3 2¼ **Anonymous John (IRE)**22 4185 2-8-12 72................(v) DeclanBates(3) 2 72
(David Evans) *in tch: sn pushed along: hdwy to chse ldrs whn edgd lft over 1f out: no imp fnl f* **7/1**3
1350 4 8 **Charlie's Star**15 4439 2-9-5 76................(v1) BenCurtis 5 52
(David Evans) *s.i.s: bhd and outpcd: sme late hdwy: nvr on terms* **8/1**
2641 5 *nk* **The Dapper Tapper (IRE)**20 4260 2-8-11 68................ FrannyNorton 1 43
(Eve Johnson Houghton) *chsd ldrs: rdn over 2f out: edgd lft and wknd over 1f out* **11/4**1
0464 6 5 **Sportlobster (IRE)**23 4157 2-8-9 66................(v) HayleyTurner 3 26
(Tom Dascombe) *led to over 2f out: rdn and wknd over 1f out* **17/2**

1m 18.39s (4.59) **Going Correction** +0.65s/f (Yiel) 6 Ran SP% **110.8**
Speed ratings (Par 96): **95,94,91,80,80 73**
CSF £12.04 TOTE £3.60: £1.60, £2.20; EX 10.70 Trifecta £48.00.
**Owner** Coxon Dascombe Lowe Pritchard **Bred** John Hutchinson **Trained** Malpas, Cheshire

**FOCUS**
With the top weight rated 7lb below the ceiling this was just a fair nursery.

## 4940 HALLIWELL JONES H'CAP 1m 4f 66y
**4:45** (4:46) (Class 4) (0-85,85) 3-Y-O+ **£6,469** (£1,925; £962; £481) **Stalls** Low

Form RPR
2132 1 **English Summer**15 4423 7-9-6 80................(t) GeorgeChaloner(3) 2 89
(Richard Fahey) *trckd ldrs: hdwy to ld over 1f out: sn rdn and edgd lft: hrd pressed ins fnl f: hld on wl* **15/8**2
0025 2 *nk* **Notarised**8 4651 3-8-11 79................ FrannyNorton 1 87
(Mark Johnston) *led at modest gallop: rdn: edgd rt and hdd over 1f out: rallied and ev ch ins fnl f: kpt on: hld nr fin* **5/4**1
210 3 9 **Spanish Plume**7 4710 6-9-5 76................(p) DavidNolan 4 69
(Andrew Hollinshead) *chsd ldr 4f: cl up: rdn and outpcd over 2f out: sn no imp w first two* **14/1**
26-0 4 4½ **Rio's Rosanna (IRE)**64 2787 7-9-11 85................ ConnorBeasley(3) 3 71
(Richard Whitaker) *s.i.s: sn prom: hdwy to chse ldr after 4f out to over 2f out: sn wknd* **13/2**3



The Form Book, Raceform Ltd, Newbury, RG14 5SJ

451- **5** 2 **Cool Sky**[88] 3344 5-9-13 **84** ........ StevieDonohoe 6 67
(Ian Williams) *hld up in tch: drvn and outpcd over 4f out: n.d after* **11/1**
2m 46.87s (8.37) **Going Correction** +0.65s/f (Yiel)
**WFA** 3 from 5yo+ 11lb **5** Ran SP% **107.6**
Speed ratings (Par 105): **98,97,91,88,87**
CSF £4.35 TOTE £1.90: £1.10, £1.80; EX 5.90 Trifecta £15.70.
**Owner** Dr Marwan Koukash **Bred** Juddmonte Farms Ltd **Trained** Musley Bank, N Yorks

**FOCUS**
They went fairly steady here and the first two pulled well clear.

## 4941 WAR HORSE AT THE LOWRY SALFORD H'CAP (BOBIS RACE) 1m 2f 75y
**5:15** (5:16) (Class 4) (0-80,79) 3-Y-O **£6,469** (£1,925; £962; £481) **Stalls** High

Form RPR
-330 **1** **Roskilly (IRE)**[108] 1530 3-9-3 **75** ........ OisinMurphy 3 84
(Andrew Balding) *t.k.h early: hld up in tch: hdwy to ld 2f out: rdn and edgd lft over 1f out: kpt on wl fnl f* **4/1**[3]
-012 **2** 1 1/4 **Empress Ali (IRE)**[37] 3643 3-9-7 **79** ........ JamesSullivan 1 85
(Tom Tate) *led to over 4f out: sn rdn: rallied to chse wnr over 1f out: kpt on ins fnl f* **11/8**[1]
0-41 **3** 1 3/4 **Nakeeta**[16] 4420 3-8-13 **71** ........ DavidNolan 4 74
(Iain Jardine) *hld up in tch: pushed along over 2f out: hdwy over 1f out: kpt on ins fnl f* **7/2**[2]
1234 **4** 2 **Charlie Wells (IRE)**[3] 4817 3-8-11 **69** ........(b[1]) JohnFahy 5 68
(Eve Johnson Houghton) *s.i.s: t.k.h and sn cl up: led and rdn over 4f out: hdd 2f out: wknd ins fnl f* **13/2**
4443 **5** 9 **Rangi Chase (IRE)**[15] 4426 3-8-9 **70** ........ GeorgeChaloner(3) 6 52
(Richard Fahey) *t.k.h early: prom: checked after 2f: rdn and outpcd wl over 2f out: sn btn* **10/1**
0306 **6** 23 **Whitby High Light**[13] 4496 3-8-9 **67** ........[1] RoystonFfrench 2 5
(Andrew Hollinshead) *t.k.h: cl up tl rdn and wknd over 3f out: sn btn* **16/1**
2m 18.16s (6.96) **Going Correction** +0.65s/f (Yiel) **6** Ran SP% **112.6**
Speed ratings (Par 102): **98,97,95,94,86 68**
CSF £10.04 TOTE £4.30: £2.40, £1.50; EX 10.40 Trifecta £28.90.
**Owner** Mick and Janice Mariscotti **Bred** Gigginstown House Stud **Trained** Kingsclere, Hants

**FOCUS**
They seemed to get racing some way out here and that suited the two who were held up off the pace.
T/Plt: £285.90 to a £1 stake. Pool: £73102.75 - 186.64 winning tickets T/Qpdt: £69.90 to a £1 stake. Pool: £6821.67 - 72.20 winning tickets RY

# 4435 NEWBURY (L-H)
## Sunday, August 3

**OFFICIAL GOING: Good to soft changing to good after race 3 (3.15)**
Wind: mild half-across Weather: cloudy with sunny periods

## 4942 DAISYS DREAM AMATEUR RIDERS' H'CAP 1m 2f 6y
**2:10** (2:13) (Class 5) (0-70,69) 3-Y-O+ **£2,495** (£774; £386; £193) **Stalls** Centre

Form RPR
40 **1** **Victor's Bet (SPA)**[74] 2471 5-10-9 **69** ........ MissEllaSmith(5) 10 77
(Ralph J Smith) *hld up bhd: gd hdwy in centre 3f out: led 2f out: styd on wl: pushed out* **20/1**
154 **2** 1 1/4 **Frosty Berry**[15] 4427 5-10-2 **64** ........ MrAFrench(7) 6 70
(Paul Midgley) *hld up: hdwy over 3f out: rdn over 2f out: chsd wnr wl over 1f out: styd on but a being comf hld* **6/1**
2360 **3** 1 **Emman Bee (IRE)**[20] 4273 5-9-12 **60** ........ MrJDoe(7) 5 64
(Luke Dace) *racd keenly: trckd ldrs: rdn and ev ch briefly wl over 2f out: kpt chsng wnr tl wl over 1f out: styd on same pce* **12/1**
4134 **4** 3 1/2 **Allergic Reaction (IRE)**[24] 4120 3-9-13 **63** ........ MrSWalker 9 60
(William Knight) *taken to s early: trckd ldrs: rdn wl over 2f out: nvr threatened: styd on same pce* **2/1**[1]
3014 **5** 3 3/4 **Angus Glens**[11] 4552 4-10-5 **67** ........(p) MissGFriswell(7) 4 57
(David Dennis) *t.k.h: led for 1f: trckd ldr: led over 4f out: rdn and hdd over 2f out: grad fdd* **10/1**
0005 **6** 3 **Hill Fort**[41] 3515 4-10-12 **67** ........ MrMarioBaratti 7 52
(Ronald Harris) *mid-div: rdn 3f out: nvr threatened* **33/1**
421 **7** 1 3/4 **Raamz (IRE)**[46] 3363 7-10-7 **62** ........ MissSBrotherton 3 43
(Kevin Morgan) *trckd ldrs: rdn and ev ch over 3f out: wknd over 1f out* **5/1**[3]
5454 **8** 4 1/2 **Petrify**[23] 4149 4-9-4 **52** oh6........(tp) MrJPWilliams(7) 8 25
(Bernard Llewellyn) *s.i.s: sn mid-div: rdn over 3f out: wknd over 2f out* **18/1**
0130 **9** 1 1/4 **Automotive**[11] 4548 6-10-8 **63** ........ MrRBirkett 2 33
(Julia Feilden) *mid-div: hdwy 4f out: rdn 3f out where nt clr run briefly: wknd wl over 1f out* **9/2**[2]
/3-0 **10** 22 **Eseej (USA)**[51] 3179 9-10-0 **60** ........ MissPFuller(5) 1
(Geoffrey Deacon) *led after 1f: rdn and hdd over 4f out: sn btn: t.o* **50/1**
2m 11.62s (2.82) **Going Correction** +0.20s/f (Good)
**WFA** 3 from 4yo+ 9lb **10** Ran SP% **114.2**
Speed ratings (Par 103): **96,95,94,91,88 86,84,81,80,62**
CSF £130.92 CT £1515.68 TOTE £31.00: £8.20, £2.40, £3.20; EX 167.40 Trifecta £1630.70.
**Owner** Homecroft Wealth & Jayne Smith **Bred** Jose Simo Vazquez **Trained** Epsom, Surrey

**FOCUS**
There was 26.3mm of rain in the 24 hours before racing and the ground was given as good to soft. The rail had been moved out since the last meeting, meaning all races were 33 metres longer, but the cutoff at the 1m1f point remained in place. The visual impression was of an overly strong pace, with the winner (detached at one point) and runner-up filling the last two spots for much of the way before staying on down the outside of runners in the straight.

## 4943 ACADEMY INSURANCE EBF STALLIONS MAIDEN STKS (BOBIS RACE) 6f 8y
**2:40** (2:43) (Class 4) 2-Y-O **£4,075** (£1,212; £606; £303) **Stalls** High

Form RPR
**1** **Carry On Deryck** 2-9-5 0........ LiamKeniry 3 80+
(Sylvester Kirk) *hld up: gng wl but nt clr run twice fr 2f out: pushed along and hdwy ent fnl f: fin strly on stands' side rails to ld fnl 20yds: readily* **25/1**
2 **2** 3/4 **Accra Beach (USA)**[20] 4270 2-9-5 0........ JamesDoyle 1 75
(Roger Charlton) *trckd ldrs: chal jst over 2f out: sn rdn: edgd ahd fnl 100yds: hdd fnl 20yds: nt gng pce of wnr* **1/4**[1]
0 **3** nk **Galago (IRE)**[31] 3889 2-9-5 0........ JimmyFortune 6 74
(Sylvester Kirk) *prom: rdn and ev ch fr 2f out: edgd lft u.p fnl f: kpt on* **16/1**
6 **4** shd **Chevallier**[23] 4142 2-9-5 0........ RichardHughes 4 74
(Richard Hannon) *prom: led 2f out: rdn and strly pressed: narrowly hdd fnl 100yds: kpt on but lost 2 pls nring fin* **9/2**[2]
0 **5** 2 1/2 **Invisible Eye**[6] 4740 2-9-5 0........ WilliamTwiston-Davies 8 66
(Mick Channon) *little slowly away: hld up: hdwy to chse ldrs 2f out: sn rdn: kpt on same pce fnl f* **14/1**[3]
**6** shd **Finton Friend (IRE)** 2-9-5 0........ SteveDrowne 7 66
(Charles Hills) *s.i.s: towards rr: pushed along and stdy prog fr over 1f out: nvr threatened ldrs but styd on fnl f* **14/1**[3]
**7** 1 1/4 **Imperial Link** 2-9-0 0........ LukeMorris 5 57
(Paul Cole) *trckd ldrs: rdn 2f out: sn one pce* **20/1**
5 **8** 9 **Orobas (IRE)**[69] 2622 2-9-5 0........ DavidProbert 2 35
(Harry Whittington) *mid-div: rdn over 2f out: wknd over 1f out* **16/1**
05 **9** 21 **Blue Eyed Boy**[24] 4103 2-9-0 0........ DannyBrock(5) 9
(Roy Brotherton) *racd keenly: sn led: rdn and hdd 2f out: sn hung lft and wknd* **66/1**
1m 15.75s (2.75) **Going Correction** +0.30s/f (Good) **9** Ran SP% **133.4**
Speed ratings (Par 96): **93,92,91,91,88 88,86,74,46**
CSF £36.50 TOTE £42.80: £7.10, £1.02, £5.40; EX 115.60 Trifecta £1563.00.
**Owner** Walters Plant Hire Spiers & Hartwell **Bred** Landmark Racing Limited **Trained** Upper Lambourn, Berks

**FOCUS**
They raced stands' side. The straight course this time, but the favourite was laboured and again the pace looked overly fast.

## 4944 GRUNDON RECYCLE NURSERY H'CAP (BOBIS RACE) 7f (S)
**3:15** (3:16) (Class 4) (0-85,83) 2-Y-O **£3,881** (£1,155; £577; £288) **Stalls** High

Form RPR
5213 **1** **Power Play (IRE)**[22] 4203 2-9-7 **83** ........ RichardHughes 2 88
(Richard Hannon) *trckd ldr: led jst over 1f out: r.o fnl f: rdn out* **2/1**[1]
4353 **2** 1/2 **Popeswood (IRE)**[23] 4157 2-8-9 **74** ........ CharlesBishop(3) 3 79
(Mick Channon) *cl up: rdn over 1f out: r.o ins fnl f: pressed wnr fnl 100yds: hld nring fin* **7/1**
035 **3** nk **Outback Ruler (IRE)**[24] 4129 2-8-9 **71** ........ HarryBentley 5 74
(Clive Cox) *cl up: rdn to chse wnr jst over 1f out tl fnl 100yds: kpt on* **6/1**[3]
4251 **4** 2 1/2 **Buckleberry**[43] 3467 2-8-10 **72** ........ JamesDoyle 7 71
(Jonathan Portman) *trckd ldrs: nt clrest of runs 2f out: rdn ent fnl f: kpt on same pce* **4/1**[2]
014 **5** shd **Scutum (IRE)**[9] 4619 2-9-1 **77** ........ JimmyFortune 6 75
(Brian Meehan) *s.i.s: last but wl in tch: nt clr run 2f out: rdn ent fnl f: kpt on but nt grnd pce to get involved* **6/1**[3]
304 **6** 3 **Agadoo**[57] 2979 2-8-6 **68** ........ JimmyQuinn 4 56
(Shaun Harris) *led: rdn and hdd jst over 1f out: fdd ins fnl f* **20/1**
1m 29.36s (3.66) **Going Correction** +0.30s/f (Good) **6** Ran SP% **99.2**
Speed ratings (Par 96): **91,90,90,87,87 83**
CSF £12.32 TOTE £2.90: £1.90, £3.20; EX 10.70 Trifecta £48.40.
**Owner** Mohamed Saeed Al Shahi **Bred** Barnane Stud **Trained** East Everleigh, Wilts
■ Tumut was withdrawn. Price at time of withdrawal 8-1. Rule 4 applies to all bets - deduction 10p in the pound.

**FOCUS**
The going was changed to good after this nursery. Just an ordinary contest and, despite there being only six runners, a few found trouble with the action again unfolding stands' side.

## 4945 BRITISH STALLION STUDS EBF CHALICE STKS (LISTED RACE) (F&M) 1m 4f 5y
**3:50** (3:51) (Class 1) 3-Y-O+
**£22,684** (£8,600; £4,304; £2,144; £1,076; £540) **Stalls** Centre

Form RPR
-135 **1** **Silk Sari**[29] 3961 4-9-4 **99** ........ AndreaAtzeni 8 101
(Luca Cumani) *mid-div: hdwy wl over 2f out: sn rdn: led over 1f out: edgd lft and styd on: rdn out* **9/4**[1]
0064 **2** nk **Moment In Time (IRE)**[22] 4213 5-9-4 **98** ........ JamieSpencer 3 100
(David Simcock) *hld up: swtchd to centre and hdwy wl over 2f out: sn rdn: hung lft jst over 1f out: r.o ins fnl f: wnt 2nd towards fin* **10/1**
2451 **3** 1/2 **Cascading**[31] 3877 3-8-7 **83** ........ RobertHavlin 9 99
(Hughie Morrison) *led: rdn jst ins 2f out: hdd over 1f out: battling on whn carried sltly lft fnl 120yds: hefty bump fnl 75yds: kpt on but hld after* **33/1**
316 **4** 1 3/4 **Wonderstruck (IRE)**[45] 3376 3-8-7 **99** ........ WilliamBuick 7 96
(William Haggas) *stmbld sltly leaving stalls: sn trcking ldr: rdn wl over 2f out: styd on but nvr finding pce to chal: gifted 4th fnl 75yds* **9/4**[1]
0045 **5** 3/4 **Quiz Mistress**[29] 3962 6-9-4 **99** ........ RichardHughes 1 100+
(Hughie Morrison) *mid-div: hdwy over 2f out: rdn 2f out: running on on far side rails and nt wout ch whn bdly hmpd fnl 75yds: lost 4th sn after: nt time to rcvr* **7/1**[2]
00-1 **6** 1/2 **Alwilda**[30] 3932 4-9-4 **88** ........ LukeMorris 6 94
(Sir Mark Prescott Bt) *trckd ldrs: pushed along to hold pce over 4f out: rdn over 3f out: hld wl over 1f out: r.o again fnl 120yds* **28/1**
2121 **7** nk **Cosseted**[37] 3644 4-9-4 **91** ........ JimCrowley 5 97+
(James Fanshawe) *hld up: hdwy over 3f out: rdn over 2f out: no further imp tl r.o ent fnl f: hld in disp 4th whn bdly squeezed out fnl 120yds: nt rcvr* **8/1**[3]
51-0 **8** nse **Lady Tyne**[88] 2072 3-8-7 **86** ........ JamesDoyle 2 93?
(Roger Charlton) *hld up: rdn over 2f out: styd on fnl f but nvr gng pce to threaten* **12/1**
5000 **9** 4 **Khione**[15] 4443 5-9-4 **101** ........(b[1]) AdamKirby 4 87
(Luca Cumani) *trckd ldr tl rdn wl over 2f out: wknd over 1f out* **14/1**
2m 34.93s (-0.57) **Going Correction** +0.20s/f (Good)
**WFA** 3 from 4yo+ 11lb **9** Ran SP% **115.0**
Speed ratings (Par 111): **109,108,108,107,106 106,106,106,103**
CSF £27.17 TOTE £3.90: £1.50, £1.10, £4.00; EX 22.60 Trifecta £349.30.
**Owner** Fittocks Stud & Andrew Bengough **Bred** Fittocks Stud Ltd & Arrow Farm Stud **Trained** Newmarket, Suffolk
■ Stewards' Enquiry : Andrea Atzeni three-day ban: careless riding (Aug 17-19)

**FOCUS**
An ordinary Listed contest. Last year's race was won by Seal Of Approval, who later added the Group 1 Fillies & Mares Stakes on British Champions Day.

## 4946 BATHWICK TYRES H'CAP 5f 34y
**4:25** (4:27) (Class 4) (0-85,84) 3-Y-O+ **£4,690** (£1,395; £697; £348) **Stalls** High

Form RPR
1220 **1** **Random Success (IRE)**[16] 4412 4-9-0 **72** ........ JamesDoyle 12 89+
(Roger Charlton) *stdd s: last: swtchd lft and hdwy 2f out: led jst ins fnl f: qcknd clr: drifted rt: pushed out* **10/3**[1]

6352 **2** *2 3/4* **Secret Missile**[9] 4609 4-9-8 **80**......(b) MartinDwyer 2 87
(William Muir) *led: rdn wl over 1f out: hdd jst ins fnl f: kpt on but nt pce of wnr* **9/2**[3]

0302 **3** *1 3/4* **Ziggy Lee**[27] 4027 8-9-5 **84**...... JordanNason(7) 5 85
(Peter Hedger) *in tch: rdn 2f out: kpt on same pce fnl f* **6/1**

21-4 **4** *1/2* **Stellarta**[11] 4553 3-8-9 **70**...... LiamKeniry 4 68
(Michael Blanshard) *trckd ldrs: rdn 2f out: kpt on same pce fnl f* **10/1**

030- **5** *3/4* **Cheveton**[236] 8232 10-9-9 **81**...... JimCrowley 9 78
(Richard Price) *chsd ldr: riddn 2f out: nt pce to get on terms* **20/1**

-000 **6** *hd* **Steel Rain**[63] 2803 6-9-1 **73**...... DavidProbert 10 69
(Nikki Evans) *hld up: rdn over 1f out: kpt on fnl f but nt pce to get on terms* **25/1**

4020 **7** *6* **Rebecca Romero**[23] 4146 7-9-0 **77**...... CamHardie(5) 3 52
(Denis Coakley) *in tch: rdn wl over 2f out: wknd ent fnl f* **11/2**

-050 **8** *7* **Exceptionelle**[43] 3458 4-9-12 **84**......(p[1]) AndreaAtzeni 1 34
(Roger Varian) *wnt lft s: racd alone in centre for 2f: chsd ldrs: rdn 3f out: wknd ent fnl f* **7/2**[2]

1m 2.08s (0.68) **Going Correction** +0.30s/f (Good)
**WFA** 3 from 4yo+ 3lb **8** Ran SP% **110.9**
Speed ratings (Par 105): **106,101,98,98,96 96,86,75**
CSF £17.38 CT £80.95 TOTE £3.20: £1.40, £1.70, £2.80; EX 16.00 Trifecta £108.40.
**Owner** Paul Inglett **Bred** M Smith & Grennanstown Stud **Trained** Beckhampton, Wilts

**FOCUS**
They raced stands' side in this ordinary sprint handicap.

## 4947 AL BASTI EQUIWORLD FILLIES' H'CAP — 1m 2f 6y
**4:55** (4:56) (Class 5) (0-75,73) 3-Y-O — **£2,587** (£770; £384; £192) **Stalls** Centre

Form RPR

3422 **1** **Thatchereen (IRE)**[9] 4617 3-8-12 **69**...... LouisSteward(5) 3 79
(Michael Bell) *hld up in last pair: hdwy 3f out: led 2f out: rdn clr: comf* **2/1**[1]

065 **2** *3 3/4* **Bright Cecily (IRE)**[29] 3968 3-9-7 **73**......(p) AdamKirby 5 75
(Clive Cox) *racd keenly early: trckd ldrs: rdn and ev ch 2f out: sn hld by wnr: kpt on same pce fnl f* **4/1**[2]

2130 **3** *hd* **Starlit Cantata**[15] 4434 3-9-5 **71**...... JimmyFortune 1 73
(Eve Johnson Houghton) *in tch: rdn and ev ch 2f out: sn hld by wnr: kpt on same pce fnl f* **8/1**

1600 **4** *3/4* **Full Moon Fever (IRE)**[21] 4249 3-9-7 **73**...... WilliamBuick 6 73
(Ed Walker) *hld up last: rdn whn outpcd 2f out: styd on wl fnl f but nvr any ch* **4/1**[2]

6526 **5** *17* **Cape Mystery**[9] 4617 3-9-2 **68**...... JamieSpencer 7 36
(Peter Chapple-Hyam) *sn led: rdn and hdd 2f out: eased whn btn ent fnl f* **14/1**

3623 **6** *10* **Cincinnati Girl (IRE)**[38] 3631 3-9-3 **69**...... PatCosgrave 4 18
(Denis Coakley) *trckd ldr: rdn over 3f out: wknd 2f out* **9/2**[3]

2m 10.29s (1.49) **Going Correction** +0.20s/f (Good) **6** Ran SP% **109.3**
Speed ratings (Par 97): **102,99,98,98,84 76**
CSF £9.58 TOTE £2.30: £1.70, £2.80; EX 9.50 Trifecta £56.30.
**Owner** T Redman And P Philipps **Bred** Norman Orminston **Trained** Newmarket, Suffolk

**FOCUS**
They came up the middle of the track in this weak fillies' handicap. The pace, set by Cape Mystery, looked steady.

## 4948 AJC PREMIER H'CAP — 1m 4f 5y
**5:25** (5:27) (Class 5) (0-70,70) 3-Y-O+ — **£2,587** (£770; £384; £192) **Stalls** Centre

Form RPR

1030 **1** **Jarlath**[18] 4333 3-9-1 68......(b[1]) SteveDrowne 10 81
(Seamus Mullins) *mid-div: rdn and hdwy jst over 2f out: led ent fnl f: styd on strly fnl 140yds* **12/1**

00U0 **2** *2* **Slunovrat (FR)**[20] 4265 3-8-1 54...... RaulDaSilva 1 63
(David Menuisier) *trckd ldrs: rdn over 3f out: ev ch ent fnl f: hld fnl 140yds: styd on* **66/1**

5355 **3** *2 3/4* **Cinnilla**[24] 4134 3-9-0 67......(v[1]) JimCrowley 7 72
(Ralph Beckett) *led: rdn 2f out: hdd ent fnl f: styd on but sn no ex* **6/1**[3]

4433 **4** *6* **Highlife Dancer**[11] 4548 6-9-5 64......(v) CharlesBishop(3) 2 59
(Mick Channon) *in tch: rdn 3f out: styd on same pce fnl 2f: nvr threatened ldrs* **10/1**

5-20 **5** *2 3/4* **Shades Of Grey**[54] 3086 7-9-12 68...... AdamKirby 3 59
(Clive Cox) *mid-div: rdn 3f out: wnt 5th over 1f out but nvr any ch w ldrs* **6/1**[3]

2036 **6** *6* **Armourer (IRE)**[19] 4303 3-8-13 66...... MartinDwyer 12 47
(William Muir) *rdn 3f out: nvr bttr than mid-div* **20/1**

2403 **7** *nk* **Moontown**[17] 4368 3-9-3 70...... RobertHavlin 5 51
(Charles Hills) *mid-div: rdn 3f out: nvr any imp on ldrs* **8/1**

600 **8** *2 3/4* **Vedani (IRE)**[30] 3932 5-9-12 68...... DavidProbert 6 45
(Tony Carroll) *towards rr: sme late prog past btn horses: nvr a factor* **40/1**

-550 **9** *1/2* **Ganymede**[108] 1530 3-9-0 67...... JimmyFortune 9 43
(Eve Johnson Houghton) *trckd ldrs: rdn 3f out: wknd over 1f out* **16/1**

0166 **10** *hd* **Graphene**[24] 4106 3-8-2 60...... CamHardie(5) 14 35
(Rod Millman) *rdn over 2f out: a towards rr* **10/1**

610 **11** *2 1/4* **Westerly**[27] 4020 3-9-3 70...... JamesDoyle 13 42
(William Haggas) *hld up towards rr: rdn 3f out: nvr any imp* **4/1**[1]

-210 **12** *7* **L'Avenue (IRE)**[109] 1509 3-9-3 70...... AndreaAtzeni 8 31
(James Tate) *pushed along in midfield early: rdn 3f out: wknd over 1f out* **11/2**[2]

0040 **13** *3/4* **Bold Cross (IRE)**[24] 4105 11-8-12 57...... ThomasBrown(3) 11 16
(Edward Bevan) *a towards rr* **33/1**

2010 **14** *1/2* **April Ciel**[22] 4209 5-9-11 67......(p) LukeMorris 4 26
(Ronald Harris) *trckd ldr tl rdn over 3f out: wknd 2f out* **25/1**

2m 36.79s (1.29) **Going Correction** +0.20s/f (Good)
**WFA** 3 from 5yo+ 11lb **14** Ran SP% **122.3**
Speed ratings (Par 103): **103,101,99,95,94 90,89,87,87,87 86,81,80,80**
CSF £671.32 CT £5149.97 TOTE £12.50: £3.90, £14.80, £2.90; EX 1802.80 Trifecta £3275.10 Part won..
**Owner** Phoenix Bloodstock **Bred** D & C Bloodstock **Trained** Wilsford-Cum-Lake, Wilts
■ Stewards' Enquiry : Raul Da Silva four-day ban: used whip above permitted level (Aug 17-19,23)

**FOCUS**
Not many got into this.
T/Jkpt: Part won. T/Plt: £73.10 to a £1 stake. Pool: £97062.26 - 969.05 winning tickets T/Qpdt: £8.00 to a £1 stake. Pool: £6750.45 - 622.70 winning tickets TM

# [4926] GALWAY (R-H)
Sunday, August 3

**OFFICIAL GOING: Flat course - soft; jumps courses - yielding to soft changing to yielding to soft all over after race 5 (4.30)**

## 4949a IRISH STALLION FARMS EUROPEAN BREEDERS FUND "AHONOORA" H'CAP — 7f
**4:30** (4:30) 3-Y-O+
**£50,000** (£15,833; £7,500; £2,500; £1,666; £833)

RPR

**1** **Baraweez (IRE)**[5] 4771 4-9-2 **91**...... ColmO'Donoghue 11 98
(Brian Ellison) *settled towards rr: impr into 6th 1/2-way: rdn into 4th 2f out and clsd on outer to ld jst ins fnl f: kpt on wl* **4/1**[1]

**2** *1/2* **Jack's Revenge (IRE)**[5] 4771 6-9-6 **95**......(bt) JosephO'Brien 12 101+
(George Baker) *s.i.s and racd in rr: last 1/2-way: hdwy on outer appr st to chse ldrs in 3rd 1f out: kpt on wl in 2nd towards fin: a hld* **9/2**[2]

**3** *1 1/2* **Pacific Heights (IRE)**[8] 4648 5-9-11 **100**......(v[1]) ChrisHayes 1 102
(Brian Ellison) *sn led tl jnd 1/2-way: rdn w narrow advantage over 2f out: strly pressed into st and hdd jst ins fnl f: sn no ex in 3rd: kpt on same pce* **4/1**[1]

**4** *2 1/4* **Have A Nice Day**[15] 4457 4-8-4 **79** oh7...... WayneLordan 10 75
(Sabrina J Harty, Ire) *chsd ldrs: 3rd 1/2-way: rdn 2f out and outpcd into st: no imp in 6th 1f out: kpt on u.p into 4th cl home* **16/1**

**5** *hd* **Fastidious**[91] 1996 5-8-13 **88**...... FergalLynch 8 83
(M D O'Callaghan, Ire) *hooded to load: sn trckd ldr in 2nd tl disp 1/2-way: rdn in cl 2nd over 2f out and no imp on ldrs in 3rd over 1f out: one pce fnl f* **14/1**[3]

**6** *3/4* **Oor Jock (IRE)**[5] 4773 6-8-4 **79** oh3......(b) RoryCleary 6 72
(Adrian McGuinness, Ire) *hld up in tch: 8th 1/2-way: rdn 2f out and no imp over 1f out: kpt on one pce towards fin* **16/1**

**7** *1* **Northern Rocked (IRE)**[3] 4835 8-8-12 **87**......(b) PatSmullen 2 78
(D K Weld, Ire) *chsd ldrs: 5th 1/2-way: rdn 2f out and no ex u.p in 4th over 1f out: wknd* **9/2**[2]

**8** *4 1/2* **Hidden Oasis (IRE)**[53] 3127 3-9-10 **105**...... FMBerry 4 81
(David Wachman, Ire) *prom: sn chsd ldrs: racd keenly: 4th 1/2-way: rdn and no imp fr 2f out: wknd and eased fnl f* **9/2**[2]

**9** *1* **Knights Templar (IRE)**[5] 4773 7-8-4 **79**...... DannyGrant 3 55
(Patrick J Flynn, Ire) *hld up in tch: racd keenly: 7th 1/2-way: rdn 2f out and no imp far side into st: wknd fnl f* **33/1**

1m 28.11s (-3.49)
**WFA** 3 from 4yo+ 6lb **9** Ran SP% **115.9**
CSF £22.19 CT £76.28 TOTE £4.90: £1.50, £1.50, £1.60; DF 16.60 Trifecta £47.90.
**Owner** A Barnes **Bred** Sunderland Holdings Inc **Trained** Norton, N Yorks

**FOCUS**
The second and fourth have been rated to their best.

## 4950a GALWAY SHOPPING CENTRE H'CAP — 7f
**5:00** (5:01) (50-75,78) 3-Y-O+ — **£6,037** (£1,400; £612; £350)

RPR

**1** **Beau Satchel**[63] 2809 4-9-4 **64** ow1...... JosephO'Brien 4 77+
(Adrian McGuinness, Ire) *chsd ldrs: 5th 1/2-way: tk clsr order in 3rd over 2f out: rdn to ld ent fnl f and kpt on wl* **11/2**[2]

**2** *1* **Prime Exhibit**[4] 4805 9-9-6 **67**......(t) FMBerry 6 76+
(Daniel Mark Loughnane) *hld up in tch: hdwy in 4th under 2f out and rdn into 2nd ins fnl f: kpt on wl towards fin: nvr on terms* **11/2**[2]

**3** *2 3/4* **Cairdiuil (IRE)**[4] 4805 8-9-9 **70** 5ex...... WayneLordan 3 72
(I Madden, Ire) *sn led: rdn w narrow advantage into st: hdd u.p ent fnl f and sn no ex u.p in 3rd: kpt on one pce* **4/1**[1]

**4** *4 1/4* **Almosthaditall (USA)**[17] 4377 3-9-0 **67**...... DannyGrant 5 55
(Patrick J Flynn, Ire) *chsd ldrs: 4th 1/2-way: rdn and outpcd in 6th over 2f out: kpt on u.p ins fnl f into mod 4th nr fin* **33/1**

**5** *1/2* **Kanes Pass (IRE)**[5] 4773 5-9-11 **75**......(t) LeighRoche(3) 2 64
(W McCreery, Ire) *prom: settled bhd ldr in cl 2nd: rdn almost on terms into st and no imp on wnr in 3rd ent fnl f: wknd towards fin* **11/2**[2]

**6** *2 3/4* **Elusive Prince**[5] 4773 6-10-0 **75**......(bt) RonanWhelan 9 56
(T Hogan, Ire) *hld up: pushed along in 10th fr 1/2-way and no imp over 2f out: rdn into mod 5th 1 1/2f out: one pce fnl f: lame* **20/1**

**7** *nk* **Lake George (IRE)**[5] 4773 6-9-5 **73**...... DylanRobinson(7) 14 54
(James M Barrett, Ire) *hld up: 9th 1/2-way: rdn in 10th 2f out and no imp: kpt on one pce ins fnl f* **22/1**

**8** *hd* **Northern Surprise (IRE)**[22] 4227 3-9-2 **69**...... BillyLee 13 47
(Timothy Doyle, Ire) *hld up in tch: rdn in 8th 2f out and no imp on ldrs over 1f out: kpt on one pce* **9/1**

**9** *7 1/2* **Togoville (IRE)**[27] 4034 4-9-6 **67**......(b) ColinKeane 11 27
(Patrick Martin, Ire) *hld up: swtchd rt bef 1/2-way: rdn in 7th over 2f out and sn no imp on ldrs: one pce fnl f* **10/1**

**10** *2 1/4* **Moonbi Creek (IRE)**[4] 4805 7-9-4 **65**......(v) PatSmullen 1 19
(D K Weld, Ire) *sn chsd ldrs: 3rd 1/2-way: dropped to 4th over 2f out and sn no ex u.p: wknd fnl f* **10/1**

**11** *4 1/4* **Tom Dooley (IRE)**[6] 4747 3-9-0 **67**......(t) DeclanMcDonogh 10 7
(Michael Mulvany, Ire) *towards rr thrght: rdn and no imp over 2f out* **16/1**

**12** *23* **Dean Deifir (IRE)**[49] 3287 3-8-5 **65**......[1] GaryHalpin(7) 16
(David Peter Nagle, Ire) *towards rr thrght: rdn and no imp fr 1/2-way: t.o* **50/1**

**P** **Le Cheile (IRE)**[10] 4597 3-8-13 **66**...... KevinManning 8
(Brendan W Duke, Ire) *chsd ldrs in 3rd early: wknd qckly and p.u injured bef 1/2-way* **8/1**[3]

1m 28.18s (-3.42)
**WFA** 3 from 4yo+ 6lb **13** Ran SP% **125.3**
CSF £36.24 CT £139.75 TOTE £6.30: £2.50, £1.90, £1.80; DF 54.80 Trifecta £182.80.
**Owner** Total Recall Racing Club **Bred** Advantage Chemicals Holdings Ltd **Trained** Lusk, Co Dublin

**FOCUS**
The runner-up has been rated in line with his recent best.

## 4951a TRAPPERS INN H'CAP — 1m 4f
**5:30** (5:30) (50-80,79) 3-Y-O+ — **£7,762** (£1,800; £787; £450)

RPR

**1** **Pyromaniac (IRE)**[14] 3131 4-9-8 **73**......(t) FMBerry 9 80
(A J Martin, Ire) *hld up in tch: 7th 1/2-way: hdwy bhd ldrs into 4th 2f out: rdn in 2nd 1 1/2f out and clsd u.p to ld narrowly ins fnl f: strly pressed and all out towards fin to jst hold on* **5/2**[1]

2 shd **Pivot Bridge**[60] 1415 6-9-7 72 RonanWhelan 14 79+
(Adrian McGuinness, Ire) *w.w towards rr: 8th 1/2-way: hdwy to chse ldrs in 6th 2f out: clsd u.p to chal in cl 2nd ins fnl f and ev ch: jst hld* **9/2**[2]

3 2 **What Lies Ahead (IRE)**[13] 4505 4-9-8 73 WayneLordan 5 77
(W McCreery, Ire) *chsd ldrs: 4th 1/2-way: hdwy on outer over 3f out to ld over 2f out: rdn into st and hdd ins fnl f: sn no ex u.p in 3rd: kpt on one pce* **7/1**

4 2 **Landau (IRE)**[10] 4600 4-9-10 75 (t) JosephO'Brien 2 76
(Gordon Elliott, Ire) *chsd ldrs: 5th 1/2-way: hdwy on inner fr 3f out: n.m.r appr st: rdn 1 1/2f out and no imp on ldrs in 4th ins fnl f: kpt on one pce* **7/1**

5 2 3/4 **Solar Focus (IRE)**[24] 4138 3-8-10 72 KevinManning 8 68
(J S Bolger, Ire) *chsd ldrs: 3rd 1/2-way: rdn in 2nd over 2f out and no ex whn short of room on inner into st: dropped to 6th ins fnl f and kpt on again towards fin* **6/1**[3]

6 1 1/2 **Weld Arab (IRE)**[19] 4308 3-8-1 66 (b[1]) LeighRoche(3) 13 60
(D K Weld, Ire) *hld up in tch: 6th 1/2-way: hdwy bhd ldrs into 3rd over 2f out: rdn into st and sn no ex u.p in 5th: wknd* **9/2**[2]

7 9 1/2 **Louisville Lip (IRE)**[103] 7280 7-9-13 78 DannyGrant 3 57
(Patrick J Flynn, Ire) *towards rr: 9th 1/2-way: rdn in 8th 2f out and no imp on ldrs into st: one pce* **20/1**

8 shd **Time To Work (IRE)**[274] 5021 6-9-4 76 (b) AnaO'Brien(7) 12 55
(Gordon Elliott, Ire) *dwlt and racd in rr for most: pushed along early: last 1/2-way: rdn and no imp bef st: kpt on one pce fnl f* **14/1**

9 nk **Achtung**[53] 3133 4-8-4 55 RoryCleary 6 33
(Luke Comer, Ire) *sn led: 1 l clr 1/2-way: rdn 3f out and strly pressed: hdd over 2f out and wknd qckly bef st* **28/1**

10 27 **Love Tangle (IRE)**[15] 3110 3-8-8 70 (v[1]) ColmO'Donoghue 11
(Anthony Middleton) *settled bhd ldr: 2nd 1/2-way: rdn over 3f out and sn no ex u.p: wknd qckly bef st and eased: t.o* **20/1**

2m 40.02s (-3.08)
**WFA** 3 from 4yo+ 11lb **10** Ran SP% **123.9**
CSF £14.25 CT £73.74 TOTE £3.70: £2.00, £2.50, £1.70; DF 22.60 Trifecta £110.80.
**Owner** Newtown Anner Stud Farm Ltd **Bred** Mr Maurice Regan **Trained** Summerhill, Co. Meath

**FOCUS**
The runner-up has been rated close to his best.

# [4930]DEAUVILLE (R-H)
Sunday, August 3
**OFFICIAL GOING: Turf: soft; polytrack: standard**

## 4952a PRIX DE LA PEGASERIE (CLAIMER) (3YO) (POLYTRACK) 1m 1f 110y
12:30 (12:00) 3-Y-O £11,250 (£4,500; £3,375; £2,250; £1,125)

RPR

1 **Tarnag (FR)**[67] 3-8-5 0 MllePaulineDominois(8) 3 91
(E Lellouche, France) **91/10**

2 2 **Star Dolois (FR)**[25] 3-8-11 0 (b) RonanThomas 14 85
(A Bonin, France) **162/10**

3 1 3/4 **Elector Of Saxony (USA)**[17] 3-9-2 0 MaximeGuyon 11 86
(Z Hegedus, Hungary) **54/10**[2]

4 snk **Grace Of Love (IRE)**[155] 3-8-11 0 IoritzMendizabal 8 81
(J-C Rouget, France) **92/10**

5 1 1/2 **Le Bandit (FR)** 3-9-1 0 (p) TonyPiccone 4 82
(J Rossi, France) **23/1**

6 hd **Bushido (FR)**[61] 3-8-11 0 (b) Christophe-PatriceLemaire 5 78
(P Bary, France) **193/10**

7 1 1/4 **Villanueva (IRE)**[32] 3-8-8 0 ThierryThulliez 13 72
(C Laffon-Parias, France) **76/10**

8 3 **Take The Crown (FR)**[45] 3-9-2 0 ChristopheSoumillon 10 74
(J-C Rouget, France) **41/10**[1]

9 3/4 **Vesly (FR)**[21] 4252 3-8-8 0 GregoryBenoist 2 64
(Y Barberot, France) **50/1**

10 nse **Gulfstream Kitten (USA)**[17] 3-9-1 0 UmbertoRispoli 7 71
(Gianluca Bietolini, Italy) **171/10**

11 2 1/2 **Geonpi (IRE)** 3-9-4 0 FranckBlondel 6 69
(F Rossi, France) **59/10**[3]

12 hd **Starlight Princess (IRE)**[36] 3745 3-8-8 0 (b) MickaelBarzalona 9 59
(J S Moore) *hld up towards rr on inner: rdn and effrt to improve 2f out: no ex and btn fnl f: wknd* **34/1**

13 1 **Collani (IRE)**[32] 3-9-1 0 GeraldMosse 12 64
(M Nigge, France) **222/10**

14 nk **After Math (FR)**[112] 3-9-1 0 DavidMorrison 1 63
(C Gourdain, France) **105/10**

1m 57.77s (117.77) **14** Ran SP% **119.3**
WIN (incl. 1 euro stake): 8.40 (Tarnag coupled with Vesly). PLACES: 3.40, 4.80, 2.50. DF: 96.40. SF: 168.10.
**Owner** Gerard Augustin-Normand **Bred** Ecurie Jarlan **Trained** Lamorlaye, France

## 4953a PRIX DE CABOURG JOCKEY CLUB DE TURQUIE (GROUP 3) (2YO) (TURF) 6f
2:40 (12:00) 2-Y-O £33,333 (£13,333; £10,000; £6,666; £3,333)

RPR

1 **Ervedya (FR)**[40] 2-8-8 0 ThierryJarnet 3 108+
(J-C Rouget, France) *trckd ldr: chal 2f out: rdn to ld over 1f out: r.o strly and asserted fnl f: pushed out: comf* **6/1**[3]

2 2 **City Money (IRE)**[30] 2-8-11 0 StephanePasquier 6 102
(M Delcher Sanchez, France) *t.k.h: bmpd s: midfield in tch: rdn and effrt over 1f out: outpcd by wnr fnl f: kpt on and jst hld on for 2nd* **14/1**

3 nse **El Suizo (FR)**[57] 3027 2-8-11 0 FabriceVeron 2 102
(H-A Pantall, France) *midfield in tch: rdn 2f out: kpt on steadily fnl f and wnt 3rd cl home: almost snatched 2nd post but no ch w wnr* **7/2**[2]

4 nk **Ride Like The Wind (IRE)**[28] 2-8-11 0 MickaelBarzalona 1 101
(F Head, France) *t.k.h: dwlt sltly and hld up towards rr: swtchd rt and rdn over 1f out: kpt on same pce and nvr able to chal fnl f: dropped to 4th cl home* **3/1**[1]

5 1 1/4 **Mindsomer (FR)**[41] 2-8-11 0 CristianDemuro 8 97
(F Chappet, France) *trckd ldr: rdn and outpcd over 1f out: kpt on for wl hld 5th fnl f* **20/1**

6 1 1/2 **Mocklershill (FR)**[38] 3641 2-8-11 0 Christophe-PatriceLemaire 4 93
(F Chappet, France) *led: rdn and hdd over 1f out: sn outpcd by wnr: no ex and fdd fnl f* **14/1**

7 shd **Courtofversailles (USA)**[16] 2-8-11 0 Pierre-CharlesBoudot 7 93
(A Fabre, France) *bmpd s: hld up and a towards rr: rdn over 2f out: outpcd fnl f: kpt on but nvr threatened* **3/1**[1]

8 1/2 **Kenouska (FR)**[10] 4603 2-8-8 0 OlivierPeslier 5 88
(H-A Pantall, France) *plld hrd: wnt rt s: hld up and a in rr: rdn 2f out: sn outpcd: kpt on fnl f but nvr threatened* **9/1**

1m 10.29s (-0.71) **8** Ran SP% **114.6**
WIN (incl. 1 euro stake): 7.30. PLACES: 1.80, 3.50, 1.80. DF: 48.50. SF: 72.70.
**Owner** H H Aga Khan **Bred** S.A. Aga Khan **Trained** Pau, France

## 4954a PRIX ROTHSCHILD (GROUP 1) (3YO+ FILLIES & MARES) (STRAIGHT) (TURF) 1m (R)
3:10 (12:00) 3-Y-O+ £142,850 (£57,150; £28,575; £14,275)

RPR

1 **Esoterique (IRE)**[46] 3355 4-9-2 0 Pierre-CharlesBoudot 2 118
(A Fabre, France) *hld up in tch in centre: tacked across to join remainder after 3f: last but gng much the best over 1f out: angled lft and rdn ent fnl f: r.o strly and chal fnl 150yds: led towards fin: pushed out: cosily* **12/1**

2 3/4 **Miss France (IRE)**[49] 3289 3-8-9 0 MaximeGuyon 1 115
(A Fabre, France) *prom in centre: tacked across to join remainder after 3f and trckd ldr: rdn to chal 2f out: w ldrs ent fnl f and led briefly 100yds out: sn hdd: kpt on but hld* **5/2**[2]

3 1 3/4 **Integral**[23] 4165 4-9-2 0 RyanMoore 4 112
(Sir Michael Stoute) *trckd ldr on far side: rdn to chal 2f out: w ldrs ent fnl f: hdd fnl 120yds and sn no ex in wl hld 3rd* **8/13**[1]

4 3/4 **L'Amour De Ma Vie (USA)**[46] 3355 5-9-2 0 ChristopheSoumillon 3 111
(Mme Pia Brandt, France) *led on far side: rdn and strly pressed fr 2f out: jnd ent fnl f: hdd fnl 120yds: no ex and dropped to wl hld 4th* **7/1**[3]

1m 37.86s (-2.94)
**WFA** 3 from 4yo+ 7lb **4** Ran SP% **110.7**
WIN (incl. 1 euro stake): 9.20. PLACES: 2.60, 2.00. SF: 21.00.
**Owner** Baron Edouard De Rothschild **Bred** Societe Civile De L'Ecurie De Meautry **Trained** Chantilly, France

**FOCUS**
A messy race, with the four runners splitting into two pairs early (the Andre Fabre runners, who finished first and second, racing more centre-to-stands' side) and them going a steady gallop. They all ended up racing near to the far rail and there was a bit of a turn up really.

# [2584]DUSSELDORF (R-H)
Sunday, August 3
**OFFICIAL GOING: Turf: good to soft**

## 4955a 156TH HENKEL-PREIS DER DIANA - DEUTSCHES STUTEN-DERBY (GROUP 1) (3YO FILLIES) (TURF) 1m 3f
4:10 (12:00) 3-Y-O
£250,000 (£83,333; £41,666; £22,500; £10,833; £8,333)

RPR

1 **Feodora (GER)**[49] 3289 3-9-2 0 MircoDemuro 2 111+
(A Wohler, Germany) *w.w in midfield: gd hdwy on inner 2 1/2f out: rdn to chal on rail under 1 1/2f out: r.o to ld ins fnl f: asserted fnl 110yds: comf* **26/1**

2 2 1/2 **Diamond Dove (GER)**[32] 3873 3-9-2 0 FrederikTylicki 1 106
(Andreas Lowe, Germany) *midfield on inner: tk clsr order 3 1/2f out: chsd ldrs 2 1/2f out: chal outside two rivals: edgd rt and bmpd Wunder 1 1/2f out: hrd rdn and led appr fnl f: sn hdd: styd on but nt pce of wnr fnl 110yds* **96/10**

3 3 **Longina (GER)**[56] 3046 3-9-2 0 AdriedeVries 9 101
(P Schiergen, Germany) *led after 1f: hdd appr fnl f: plugged on at one pce u.p* **27/10**[2]

4 2 1/2 **Lacy (GER)**[26] 4064 3-9-2 0 SilvestreDeSousa 4 96
(Waldemar Hickst, Germany) *dwlt: waited in bk three: hdwy on outer 3f out: rdn 1 1/2f out: styd on u.p fnl f to grab 4th cl home: nvr threatened ldrs* **136/10**

5 shd **Wunder (GER)**[34] 3808 3-9-2 0 AHelfenbein 7 96
(Markus Klug, Germany) *tk v t.k.h: reluctant ldr tl hdd after 1f: swtchd out and effrt between horses 1 1/2f out whn hmpd and lost pl: swtchd outside and rdn appr fnl f but no imp: plugged on: lost 4th cl home* **13/10**[1]

6 2 **Oriental Magic (GER)**[26] 4064 3-9-2 0 FilipMinarik 3 92
(J Hirschberger, Germany) *towards rr: rdn and effrt to chse ldng gp 2f out: sn outpcd by ldrs and one pce fnl f* **37/1**

7 7 **Tanamia (GER)**[43] 3-9-2 0 JBojko 5 80
(A Wohler, Germany) *midfield on outer: rdn to hold pl over 3f out: wl btn fnl 1 1/2f* **33/1**

8 5 **Papagena Star (IRE)**[26] 4064 3-9-2 0 MartinSeidl 11 71
(Markus Klug, Germany) *chsd ldng trio on outer: rdn to hold pl 3f out: wknd u.p fr 1 1/2f out* **129/10**

9 7 **Ajaxana (GER)**[21] 4247 3-9-2 0 AnthonyCrastus 10 58
(Waldemar Hickst, Germany) *chsd ldr on outer: rdn and hmpd over 1 1/2f out: sn btn and eased ins fnl f* **63/10**[3]

10 6 **World's Dream (GER)**[21] 3-9-2 0 FabienLefebvre 12 47
(Markus Klug, Germany) *dwlt: towards rr: rdn and outpcd in last 3f out: nvr in contention* **41/1**

11 nse **Ninfea (GER)**[21] 3-9-2 0 (p) EPedroza 8 47
(A Wohler, Germany) *midfield: rdn and lost pl 3f out: sn btn* **9/1**

12 hd **Ninas Terz (GER)**[21] 3-9-2 0 DanielePorcu 6 47
(P Schiergen, Germany) *midfield: dropped towards rr 5f out: nvr rcvrd* **38/1**

2m 15.35s (135.35) **12** Ran SP% **131.9**
WIN (incl. 10 euro stake): 269. PLACES: 50, 26, 18. SF: 2,421.
**Owner** Gestut Etzean **Bred** Gestut Etzean **Trained** Germany

# OVREVOLL (R-H)

Thursday, July 31

**OFFICIAL GOING: Turf: good**

## 4956a WABA GRUPPEN OSLO CUP (GROUP 3) (3YO+) (TURF) 1m 4f
**6:25** (12:00) 3-Y-O+ **£29,850** (£14,925; £7,164; £4,776; £2,985)

RPR

1 **Without Fear (FR)**[32] 3772 6-9-6 0 RafaelSchistl 1 99
(Niels Petersen, Norway) *mde all: rdn over 2f out: styd on wl: strly pressed towards fin: jst hld on* **7/4**[2]

2 *hd* **Energia El Gigante (BRZ)**[51] 3090 5-9-4 0 RafaeldeOliveira 3 97
(Fabricio Borges, Sweden) *trckd ldr: rdn over 2f out: styd on wl fnl f and chal towards fin: jst hld* **69/10**[3]

3 *3 3/4* **Fearless Hunter (GER)**[32] 3772 4-9-4 0 PatCosgrave 4 91
(Rune Haugen, Norway) *t.k.h: midfield in tch: rdn to chal over 2f out: outpcd by wnr and dropped to 3rd over 1f out: plugged on but wl hld* **185/10**

4 *1/2* **Lindenthaler (GER)**[32] 3772 6-9-4 0 (b) ValmirDeAzeredo 2 90
(Fredrik Reuterskiold, Sweden) *midfield: shuffled bk 1/2-way: rdn in last and outpcd over 2f out: plugged on and tk wl hld 4th towards fin* **26/1**

5 *1 1/2* **Bank Of Burden (USA)**[32] 3772 7-9-6 0 Per-AndersGraberg 7 90
(Niels Petersen, Norway) *hld up in rr early: clsd and prom 1/2-way: rdn over 2f out: sn outpcd: fdd and dropped to 5th towards fin* **7/10**[1]

6 *3 1/4* **Diamant (GER)**[301] 4-9-4 0 Jan-ErikNeuroth 5 83
(Wido Neuroth, Norway) *hld up and a towards rr: rdn and no imp fnl 2f: sn dropped to last and btn* **11/1**

2m 32.7s (-1.40) **6** Ran SP% **125.0**
PARI-MUTUEL (including 1 unit stake): WIN 2.74; PLACE 1.27, 1.30, 1.71; SF 23.03.
**Owner** Stall Bonne Nuit **Bred** Zamim Ralphy Meahjohn **Trained** Norway

## 4957a POLAR CUP (GROUP 3) (3YO+) (TURF) 6f 187y
**7:15** (12:00) 3-Y-O+ **£29,850** (£9,950; £4,975; £2,985; £1,990)

RPR

1 **Ragazzo (NOR)**[26] 3996 5-9-8 0 JacobJohansen 1 102
(Annike Bye Hansen, Norway) *pressed ldr on inner: rdn to ld over 1f out: r.o and asserted fnl f: eased down at fin: readily* **19/20**[1]

2 *1* **Giftorm (USA)**[354] 5326 4-9-4 0 ValmirDeAzeredo 2 95
(Fredrik Reuterskiold, Sweden) *dwlt: sn pushed along in detached last: stl in rr whn rdn 2f out: r.o fnl f and wnt 2nd cl home: nrst fin but no threat to wnr* **139/10**

3 *1/2* **Liber**[35] 4-9-4 0 (p) OliverWilson 9 94
(Bent Olsen, Denmark) *led: rdn and hdd over 1f out: kpt on but nt pce of wnr fnl f: dropped to 3rd cl home* **148/10**

4 *nk* **Easy Road**[35] 4-9-4 0 ElioneChaves 5 93
(Cathrine Erichsen, Norway) *midfield: rdn and effrt to chal 2f out: kpt on but nt pce of wnr fnl f: jst lost out for 3rd* **215/10**

5 *1* **Energia Dust (BRZ)**[26] 3996 6-9-4 0 RafaeldeOliveira 7 90
(Fabricio Borges, Sweden) *midfield in tch: rdn over 2f out: kpt on same pce and nvr able to chal* **58/10**[3]

6 *1* **Over The Ocean (USA)**[26] 3996 4-9-4 0 Per-AndersGraberg 8 87
(Niels Petersen, Norway) *chsd ldrs: rdn over 2f out: sn outpcd: fdd fnl f* **15/2**

7 *1* **Avon Pearl**[18] 4247 5-9-8 0 (b) PatCosgrave 12 88
(Rune Haugen, Norway) *towards rr: rdn over 2f out: kpt on same pce and nvr threatened* **47/10**[2]

8 *3/4* **Govinda (USA)**[26] 3996 7-9-4 0 ManuelSantos 4 82
(Hans-Inge Larsen, Sweden) *t.k.h: in tch: rdn 2f out: outpcd and btn fnl f: fdd* **39/1**

9 *2 1/4* **Proud Possibility (USA)**[26] 3996 4-9-4 0 RafaelSchistl 6 75
(Niels Petersen, Norway) *hld up: rdn and no imp in st: eased fnl f: nvr a factor* **269/10**

10 *1* **Silver Ocean (USA)**[63] 6-9-4 0 RobertHavlin 10 72
(Niels Petersen, Norway) *dwlt and a towards rr: rdn and no imp in st: last and wl btn whn eased fnl f: nvr a factor* **139/10**

1m 20.6s (80.60) **10** Ran SP% **125.6**
PARI-MUTUEL (including 1 unit stake): WIN 1.95; PLACE 1.42, 3.10, 2.59; SF 24.26.
**Owner** Stall Trotting **Bred** Johan C Loken **Trained** Norway

# 4701 CARLISLE (R-H)

Monday, August 4

**OFFICIAL GOING: Good (6.6)**
Wind: Fresh, half against Weather: Sunny

## 4958 LONGINES WORLD FEGENTRI CHAMPIONSHIP H'CAP (LADY AMATEUR RIDERS') 1m 1f 61y
**5:45** (5:45) (Class 6) (0-65,57) 4-Y-O+ **£3,119** (£967; £483; £242) **Stalls** Low

Form RPR

0064 **1** **Midnight Warrior**[6] 4755 4-9-9 **45** MissCBuesa 3 52
(Ron Barr) *trckd ldrs: led over 3f out: pushed along and edgd lft over 1f out: kpt on fnl f: all out* **11/2**

030- **2** *shd* **Hail Bold Chief (USA)**[255] 8006 7-10-2 **52** MissMeganNicholls 1 59
(Alan Swinbank) *hld up: hdwy on wd outside 3f out: effrt and rdn over 1f out: styng on whn edgd rt wl ins fnl f: jst hld* **9/4**[1]

-055 **3** *2* **Edas**[39] 3605 12-9-13 **49** MissHCuthbert 2 52
(Thomas Cuthbert) *prom: ev ch over 2f out to over 1f out: kpt on same pce fnl f* **25/1**

43 **4** *hd* **Diddy Eric**[47] 3363 4-9-13 **49** (b) MissAliceMills 9 51
(Micky Hammond) *towards rr: pushed along over 3f out: rallied over 1f out: kpt on ins fnl f* **5/1**[3]

0-00 **5** *3 3/4* **Rosy Ryan (IRE)**[17] 4420 4-9-9 **45** MissAYeager 6 39
(Tina Jackson) *t.k.h: chsd ldrs: rdn over 2f out: outpcd over 1f out* **33/1**

506 **6** *2 3/4* **Kay Gee Be (IRE)**[17] 4394 10-10-4 **54** (p) MissEALalor 8 43
(Alan Berry) *in tch: outpcd over 2f out: sme late hdwy: nvr rchd ldrs* **12/1**

544 **7** *2 3/4* **Spokesperson (USA)**[29] 4000 6-9-9 **45** (p) MissSiljaStoren 5 28
(Frederick Watson) *led 1f: chsd ldrs tl rdn and wknd 2f out* **9/2**[2]

660 **8** *1 1/4* **Remix (IRE)**[42] 3540 5-10-7 **57** (p) MissMBlumenauer 7 37
(Ian Williams) *dwlt: bhd: shortlived effrt over 2f out: sn btn* **6/1**

0-66 **9** *34* **Heart Beat Song**[98] 1813 6-9-9 **45** MissNPSchlatter 4
(James Moffatt) *t.k.h: led after 1f to over 3f out: wknd over 2f out* **16/1**

2m 0.25s (2.65) **Going Correction** +0.30s/f (Good) **9** Ran SP% **115.7**
Speed ratings (Par 101): **100,99,98,97,94 92,89,88,58**
CSF £18.30 CT £285.88 TOTE £5.20: £2.00, £1.40, £4.70; EX 20.50 Trifecta £368.00.
**Owner** K Trimble **Bred** Tarworth Bloodstock Investments Ltd **Trained** Seamer, N Yorks
■ Stewards' Enquiry : Miss A Yeager three-day ban: used whip without giving filly time to respond (Aug 18,20,21)
Miss Alice Mills two-day ban: used whip above permitted level (Aug 18,20)

**FOCUS**
Rail at innermost position and all distances as advertised. A weak handicap to open lady riders' evening, with the winner scraping home. The runner-up ran to his form of last year in a light campaign.

## 4959 CFM CASH 4 KIDS CLAIMING STKS (PRO-AM LADY RIDERS' RACE) 1m 1f 61y
**6:15** (6:15) (Class 5) 4-Y-O+ **£3,234** (£962; £481; £240) **Stalls** Low

Form RPR

1660 **1** **Rasselas (IRE)**[14] 4498 7-9-10 66 (b) AnnaHesketh 6 64
(David Nicholls) *prom: hdwy to ld over 1f out: pushed out fnl f* **7/1**

5223 **2** *2 1/2* **Call Of Duty (IRE)**[3] 4858 9-9-11 55 (b) EmmaSayer 2 60
(Dianne Sayer) *hld up in tch: hdwy over 2f out: rdn and edgd rt over 1f out: sn chsng wnr: kpt on same pce fnl f* **11/2**[3]

5200 **3** *2 1/4* **Conry (IRE)**[2] 4922 8-10-6 83 HayleyTurner 1 64
(Ian Williams) *missed break: hld up: effrt and hdwy over 2f out: kpt on same pce appr fnl f* **13/8**[1]

5001 **4** *4* **Well Painted (IRE)**[26] 4080 5-9-13 81 (bt) MissBHampson(5) 4 54
(Andy Turnell) *dwlt: t.k.h and led after 1f: rdn and drifted to stands' rail ent st: hdd over 1f out: sn btn* **5/2**[2]

5500 **5** *3/4* **Poor Duke (IRE)**[20] 4293 4-9-13 60 (p) MissMMullineaux 7 47
(Michael Mullineaux) *t.k.h: cl up tl rdn and outpcd fr 2f out* **33/1**

1250 **6** *6* **Licence To Till (USA)**[24] 4156 7-10-2 77 LucyAlexander 3 37
(Alan Berry) *led 1f: chsd ldrs tl rdn and wknd over 2f out* **15/2**

1m 58.7s (1.10) **Going Correction** +0.30s/f (Good) **6** Ran SP% **109.3**
Speed ratings (Par 103): **107,104,102,99,98 93**
CSF £41.21 TOTE £9.10: £4.50, £2.50; EX 42.30 Trifecta £73.70.
**Owner** J P Honeyman **Bred** Lynch Bages Ltd **Trained** Sessay, N Yorks

**FOCUS**
A moderate claimer. The winner didn't need to match his June win at this track.

## 4960 COMPARE BOOKIES ODDS AT BOOKIES.COM H'CAP (PRO-AM LADY RIDERS' RACE) 5f
**6:45** (6:46) (Class 6) (0-65,63) 4-Y-O+ **£3,234** (£962; £360; £360) **Stalls** Low

Form RPR

-004 **1** **My Meteor**[9] 4675 7-9-13 **55** HayleyTurner 7 64
(Tony Newcombe) *trckd ldrs gng wl: led over 1f out: sn rdn: hld on wl fnl f* **8/1**[3]

0102 **2** *3/4* **Tadalavil**[3] 4860 9-9-11 **53** SammyJoBell 13 59
(Linda Perratt) *hld up in midfield: rdn and hdwy over 1f out: kpt on ins fnl f* **12/1**

3055 **3** *nk* **Captain Scooby**[20] 4288 8-9-2 **49** (v) MelissaThompson(5) 11 54
(Richard Guest) *hld up in midfield: rdn and hdwy over 1f out: kpt on fnl f: nrst fin* **12/1**

463 **3** *dht* **Pull The Pin (IRE)**[18] 4362 5-10-0 **56** (bt) LucyAlexander 3 61
(Ann Stokell) *cl up: rdn and ev ch over 1f out: kpt on ins fnl f* **6/1**[2]

4444 **5** *nse* **Two Turtle Doves (IRE)**[11] 4567 8-9-8 **50** MissMMullineaux 14 55
(Michael Mullineaux) *in midfield on outside: rdn over 2f out: kpt on wl fnl f* **25/1**

5350 **6** *nk* **Sunny Side Up (IRE)**[5] 4795 5-10-7 **63** (p) GemmaTutty 4 67
(Karen Tutty) *dwlt: towards rr: rdn and hdwy over 1f out: kpt on ins fnl f: nt gng pce to chal* **9/2**[1]

0254 **7** *1* **Black Douglas**[13] 4519 5-9-10 **52** MrsCBartley 6 52
(Jim Goldie) *midfield: pushed along over 2f out: no imp whn n.m.r over 1f out: kpt on ins fnl f* **12/1**

6544 **8** *nk* **Comptonspirit**[11] 4564 10-10-5 **61** (p) MissSBrotherton 12 60
(Brian Baugh) *hld up: rdn over 2f out: hdwy on outside over 1f out: kpt on: nvr able to chal* **14/1**

155 **9** *hd* **Rock Canyon (IRE)**[18] 4362 5-9-9 **51** MeganCarberry 15 49
(Linda Perratt) *in tch: rdn and edgd rt wl over 1f out: sn outpcd* **22/1**

6660 **10** *nk* **Thewestwalian (USA)**[24] 4153 6-8-12 **47** oh2 MissMollyKing(5) 2 42
(Peter Hiatt) *bhd: rdn 1/2-way: hdwy over 1f out: nrst fin* **50/1**

0634 **11** *1* **Chloe's Dream (IRE)**[7] 4725 4-9-4 **51** MissMeganNicholls(5) 10 45
(Linda Perratt) *dwlt: sn trcking ldrs: rdn over 2f out: no ex over 1f out* **9/1**

5354 **12** *1 1/2* **Greenhead High**[39] 3609 6-9-12 **54** (v) AnnaHesketh 16 42
(David Nicholls) *led: swtchd rt over 3f out: rdn and hdd over 1f out: sn btn* **9/2**[1]

5530 **12** *dht* **A J Cook (IRE)**[5] 4796 4-9-5 **52** (v) MissLWilson(5) 1 40
(Ron Barr) *in tch: drvn over 1f out: sn btn* **16/1**

530 **14** *1 1/2* **Rutterkin (USA)**[40] 3562 6-9-3 **45** RachelRichardson 5 43
(James Moffatt) *hld up: pushed along whn n.m.r over 1f out: nvr on terms* **33/1**

0060 **15** *3/4* **Wicked Wilma (IRE)**[7] 4725 10-9-3 **47** oh2 EmmaSayer 9 25
(Alan Berry) *prom: rdn over 2f out: wknd over 1f out* **66/1**

1m 3.0s (2.20) **Going Correction** +0.35s/f (Good) **15** Ran SP% **122.0**
Speed ratings (Par 101): **96,94,94,94,94 93,92,91,91,90 89,86,86,84,83**
PLACE: £1.30 Captain Scooby, £1.10 Pull The Pin; EX: £207.40; CSF: £96.31; TC: MM&TD&PTP £320.28, MM&TD&CS £581.42; TF: 528.70 TOTE £10.70: £3.30, £5.20 TRIFECTA Part won..
**Owner** A G Newcombe **Bred** M P B Bloodstock Ltd **Trained** Yarnscombe, Devon

**FOCUS**
A messy bunch finish to this weak sprint handicap, which is rated around the runner-up.

## 4961 LLOYD CARLISLE BMW H'CAP (PRO-AM LADY RIDERS' RACE) 5f 193y
**7:15** (7:17) (Class 5) (0-75,75) 4-Y-O+ **£3,234** (£962; £481; £240) **Stalls** Low

Form RPR

5126 **1** **Bajan Bear**[10] 4609 6-10-7 **75** AnnaHesketh 9 84
(David Nicholls) *hld up: stdy hdwy 1/2-way: effrt whn n.m.r briefly and swtchd rt over 1f out: led ins fnl f: edgd lft: kpt on wl* **7/1**[3]

6040 **2** *1 3/4* **Amis Reunis**[10] 4629 5-9-2 **56** oh6 (p) EmmaSayer 8 59
(Alan Berry) *prom: effrt and rdn over 1f out: kpt on to take 2nd cl home: nt rch wnr* **40/1**

0153 **3** *nk* **Slim Chance (IRE)**[2] 4901 5-9-11 **65** MissCWalton 3 67
(Simon West) *hld up in midfield on ins: hdwy to ld over 1f out: hdd ins fnl f: one pce and lost 2nd cl home* **8/1**

0245 **4** *1* **Jumbo Steps (IRE)**[13] 4521 7-9-13 **67** MrsCBartley 12 66
(Jim Goldie) *trckd ldrs: effrt and ev ch over 1f out: kpt on same pce ins fnl f* **20/1**

4664 **5** *shd* **Klynch**[14] 4487 8-10-6 **74**.....................(b) MissSBrotherton 6 72
(Ruth Carr) *midfield: rdn along 2f out: kpt on ins fnl f* **8/1**

0U01 **6** *nk* **Iceblast**[26] 4070 6-9-10 **64**.....................(b) MissJoannaMason 14 62
(Michael Easterby) *missed break: bhd: hdwy over 1f out: kpt on fnl f: nrst fin* **14/1**

1455 **7** *shd* **De Lesseps (USA)**[98] 1819 6-9-2 **56** oh7..................... MeganCarberry 13 53
(James Moffatt) *midfield: rdn 2f out: no imp fnl f* **66/1**

4001 **8** *4* **Decent Fella (IRE)**[11] 4594 8-10-3 **71**.....................(t) LucyAlexander 10 55
(Ann Stokell) *hld up: rdn 2f out: nvr able to chal* **18/1**

1653 **9** *1* **Lothair (IRE)**[23] 4194 5-9-11 **70**..................... MissMeganNicholls(5) 7 51
(Alan Swinbank) *led ttl rdn and hdd over 1f out: sn btn* **3/1**[1]

1206 **10** *1 1/2* **Mercers Row**[15] 4471 7-10-3 **71**..................... GemmaTutty 5 47
(Karen Tutty) *in tch: effrt over 2f out: wknd over 1f out* **7/1**[3]

5600 **11** *hd* **Methaaly (IRE)**[54] 3099 11-9-2 **56** oh10.....................(be) MissMMullineaux 2 32
(Michael Mullineaux) *s.i.s: bhd: pushed along 1/2-way: nvr on terms* **66/1**

531 **12** *7* **Mambo Spirit (IRE)**[11] 4564 10-9-12 **66**..................... HayleyTurner 11 19
(Tony Newcombe) *t.k.h: cl up tl lost pl over 2f out: sn btn: eased whn no ch fnl f* **9/2**[2]

2424 **R** **Caramack**[17] 4414 4-10-7 **75**..................... MlleBarbaraGuenet 4
(Richard Lee) *ref to r* **10/1**

1m 15.1s (1.40) **Going Correction** +0.35s/f (Good) **13 Ran SP% 121.6**
Speed ratings (Par 103): **104,101,101,99,99 99,99,93,92,90 90,81,**
CSF £272.96 CT £2370.58 TOTE £8.10: £2.80, £8.80, £3.40; EX 286.80 Trifecta £1192.80 Part won..
**Owner** C McKenna **Bred** Mr And Mrs C McKenna **Trained** Sessay, N Yorks

**FOCUS**
A modest sprint handicap and another bunch finish. The winner is in top form but the runner-up was running from 6lb out of the handicap.

## 4962 LLOYD CARLISLE MINI H'CAP (PRO-AM LADY RIDERS' RACE) 2m 1f 52y
**7:45** (7:47) (Class 5) (0-70,66) 4-Y-0+ **£3,234** (£962; £481; £240) **Stalls Low**

Form RPR

**1** **Point The Toes (IRE)**[41] 2797 9-10-2 **66**..................... MissNFahey(5) 8 75
(Mark Fahey, Ire) *hld up: hdwy and prom over 3f out: led over 1f out: pushed clr fnl f* **20/1**

46 **2** *5* **Zarosa (IRE)**[76] 2424 5-9-11 **56**..................... ShelleyBirkett 4 59
(John Berry) *prom: smooth hdwy to ld over 2f out: hdd over 1f out: kpt on: nt pce of wnr* **16/1**

0162 **3** *hd* **Jan Smuts (IRE)**[9] 4662 6-10-7 **66**.....................(tp) MissSMDoolan 6 69
(Wilf Storey) *hld up in midfield: hdwy and ev ch wl over 1f out: kpt on same pce ins fnl f* **9/1**

1354 **4** *2* **A Southside Boy (GER)**[18] 4361 6-10-4 **63**..................... MrsCBartley 11 64
(Jim Goldie) *hld up: niggled along and hdwy over 3f out: ev ch 2f out: one pce fnl f* **4/1**[2]

0616 **5** *shd* **Gold Chain (IRE)**[7] 4726 4-10-6 **65**..................... EmmaSayer 12 65
(Dianne Sayer) *bhd: hdwy and cl up wl over 1f out: outpcd appr fnl f* **12/1**

00-4 **6** *2 1/4* **Sendiym (FR)**[14] 3051 7-9-5 **50**.....................(p) MlleBarbaraGuenet 2 48
(Dianne Sayer) *t.k.h: hld up: pushed along and effrt on wd outside over 2f out: kpt on fnl f: no imp* **66/1**

5031 **7** *7* **Scribe (IRE)**[25] 4107 6-10-0 **64**.....................(bt) MissBHampson(5) 3 54
(Andy Turnell) *t.k.h: in tch: hdwy and ev ch over 2f out: wknd over 1f out* **14/1**

4-34 **8** *16* **Danceintothelight**[33] 3845 7-9-9 **54**..................... MissCWalton 5 27
(Micky Hammond) *cl up: led after 5f and sn clr: rdn and hdd over 2f out: sn btn* **9/1**

4543 **9** *6* **Kastela Stari**[20] 4296 7-9-8 **53**.....................(t) MissSBrotherton 7 19
(Tim Fitzgerald) *hld up: stdy hdwy 1/2-way: rdn and wknd over 3f out* **7/1**[3]

265/ **10** *5* **Maybe I Wont**[16] 6957 9-9-12 **62**..................... MissAlexandraWilson(5) 9 23
(James Moffatt) *chsd ldrs tl rdn and wknd over 4f out* **33/1**

3-60 **11** *2* **Indepub**[20] 4296 5-9-12 **57**.....................(p) LucyAlexander 10 15
(Martin Todhunter) *prom tl drvn and wknd fr 3f out* **16/1**

/0-6 **12** *10* **Pindar (GER)**[14] 3785 10-9-9 **54**.....................(v[1]) MissJoannaMason 1
(Joanne Foster) *bhd: struggling over 5f out: nvr on terms* **66/1**

21-0 **13** *99* **Goldan Jess (IRE)**[16] 4076 10-10-6 **65**..................... HayleyTurner 13
(Philip Kirby) *led 5f: cl up: drvn and lost pl qckly after 7f: sn eased: t.o* **7/4**[1]

3m 55.11s (2.11) **Going Correction** +0.30s/f (Good) **13 Ran SP% 125.7**
Speed ratings (Par 103): **107,104,104,103,103 102,99,91,88,86 85,80,34**
CSF £315.99 CT £3088.65 TOTE £27.10: £6.10, £5.20, £3.40; EX 281.60 Trifecta £1171.30 Part won..
**Owner** Mrs Maureen Fahey **Bred** Edward Sexton **Trained** Cloneygath, Co Kildare

**FOCUS**
An ordinary staying handicap and form to be cautious about. The favourite was beaten by halfway.

## 4963 WISHING I WAS LUCKY STKS (PRO-AM LADY RIDERS' H'CAP) 7f 200y
**8:15** (8:16) (Class 4) (0-85,85) 4-Y-0+ **£6,469** (£1,925; £962; £481) **Stalls Low**

Form RPR

4130 **1** **Silver Rime (FR)**[9] 4661 9-10-7 **85**..................... SammyJoBell 6 94
(Linda Perratt) *hld up: hdwy over 2f out: effrt and chsd ldr over 1f out: styd on wl to ld cl home* **7/1**

0001 **2** *hd* **Talent Scout (IRE)**[30] 3955 8-10-4 **82**..................... GemmaTutty 2 90
(Karen Tutty) *t.k.h: led: rdn 2f out: kpt on fnl f: hdd cl home* **11/4**[1]

6411 **3** *3 1/4* **Kuwait Star**[17] 4394 5-9-8 **72**..................... HayleyTurner 4 73
(Michael Herrington) *trckd ldr: rdn 3f out: lost 2nd over 1f out: kpt on same pce fnl f* **4/1**[2]

063 **4** *3/4* **Emperatriz**[10] 4620 4-9-2 **66** oh1..................... ShelleyBirkett 3 65
(John Holt) *trckd ldrs: rdn over 2f out: one pce over 1f out* **5/1**[3]

0000 **5** *1 1/4* **Lord Of The Dance (IRE)**[9] 4650 8-9-10 **74**..................... MissMMullineaux 5 70
(Michael Mullineaux) *s.i.s: bhd: hdwy on outside over 2f out: edgd rt and one pce fnl f* **16/1**

3150 **6** *8* **Another For Joe**[14] 4491 6-10-2 **80**..................... MrsCBartley 7 58
(Jim Goldie) *prom: rdn over 2f out: wknd over 1f out* **5/1**[3]

045 **7** *nk* **Jubilee Brig**[9] 4650 4-9-13 **82**.....................(v) MissBHampson(5) 9 59
(Andy Turnell) *t.k.h: hld up in tch: stdy hdwy 1/2-way: rdn and wknd 2f out* **9/1**

235- **8** *2* **On The Hoof**[542] 563 5-9-8 **72**..................... MissJoannaMason 1 44
(Michael Easterby) *hld up: shkn up and outpcd over 2f out: sn btn* **33/1**

-001 **9** *5* **Fast Finian (IRE)**[18] 4358 5-10-4 **82**..................... LucyAlexander 8 43
(Ann Stokell) *plld hrd: hld up: rdn over 2f out: sn btn* **14/1**

1m 41.12s (1.12) **Going Correction** +0.30s/f (Good) **9 Ran SP% 118.0**
Speed ratings (Par 105): **106,105,102,101,100 92,92,90,85**
CSF £27.21 CT £90.06 TOTE £8.60: £2.20, £1.60, £1.30; EX 32.20 Trifecta £95.50.
**Owner** Ken McGarrity **Bred** Jean-Philippe Dubois **Trained** East Kilbride, S Lanarks

**FOCUS**
A modest handicap, run at a decent clip. The winner was held up and matched his best form from the past.

## 4964 WET WET WET HERE LIVE AFTER RACING H'CAP (PRO-AM LADY RIDERS' RACE) 1m 3f 107y
**8:45** (8:46) (Class 5) (0-70,70) 4-Y-0+ **£3,234** (£962; £481; £240) **Stalls High**

Form RPR

4003 **1** **Sergeant Pink (IRE)**[14] 3365 8-9-2 **51** oh1..................... EmmaSayer 10 61
(Dianne Sayer) *mde all: rdn over 2f out: kpt on wl fnl f* **22/1**

00-2 **2** *nk* **Thackeray**[56] 3052 7-9-7 **56**..................... RachelRichardson 2 65+
(Chris Fairhurst) *s.i.s: hld up: hdwy whn n.m.r briefly 2f out: gd hdwy fnl f: wnt 2nd cl home: jst hld* **16/1**

0051 **3** *shd* **Freddy Q (IRE)**[11] 4568 5-9-9 **58**..................... HayleyTurner 1 67
(Tony Newcombe) *prom: rdn over 2f out: chsd wnr briefly wl ins fnl f: hld cl home* **6/1**[3]

6031 **4** *1/2* **Giovanni Jack**[3] 4856 4-9-1 **55** 6ex..................... MissMeganNicholls(5) 9 63
(Alan Swinbank) *cl up: chsd wnr over 3f out: rdn over 2f out: no ex and lost two pls wl ins fnl f* **6/4**[1]

2042 **5** *2 1/4* **Latin Rebel (IRE)**[2] 4904 7-9-6 **55**.....................(p) MrsCBartley 14 59
(Jim Goldie) *hld up: effrt whn edgd rt wl over 1f out: kpt on fnl f: nvr able to chal* **5/1**[2]

1335 **6** *1 3/4* **Miss Macnamara (IRE)**[9] 4662 5-10-7 **70**..................... LucyAlexander 15 72
(Martin Todhunter) *in tch on outside: rdn over 2f out: edgd rt and sn one pce* **10/1**

-054 **7** *nk* **Tapis Libre**[18] 4351 6-10-4 **67**.....................(p) MissJoannaMason 11 68
(Michael Easterby) *trckd ldrs: drvn along over 3f out: rallied: outpcd over 1f out* **14/1**

1-60 **8** *3 1/4* **Waahej**[36] 3761 8-9-9 **58**..................... ShelleyBirkett 4 54
(Peter Hiatt) *hld up midfield: rdn over 2f out: outpcd over 1f out* **66/1**

440/ **9** *nk* **Smart Ruler (IRE)**[16] 6615 8-10-2 **70**..................... MissAlexandraWilson(5) 7 65
(James Moffatt) *hld up midfield: effrt and rdn over 3f out: no imp fr 2f out* **33/1**

0210 **10** *1 1/2* **Kathlatino**[50] 3269 7-9-10 **59**.....................(v) MissCWalton 3 52
(Micky Hammond) *hld up midfield on inisde: rdn and no imp whn nt clr run briefly over 2f out: sn btn* **22/1**

606/ **11** *1* **Muwalla**[14] 4455 7-9-8 **62** ow2.....................(tp) MissKRowntree(5) 12 53
(Chris Grant) *s.i.s: bhd: rdn over 3f out: nvr able to chal* **66/1**

0-00 **12** *5* **Spin Cast**[62] 2540 6-10-6 **69**..................... MissHBethell 6 52
(Brian Ellison) *cl up tl rdn and wknd wl over 1f out* **9/1**

0245 **13** *1 1/4* **Magnolia Ridge (IRE)**[20] 4303 4-10-2 **65**.....................(p) NataliaGemelova 8 46
(Kristin Stubbs) *cl up: drvn over 3f out: sn lost pl and struggling* **20/1**

-523 **14** *3 1/2* **Tin Pan Alley**[16] 4433 6-9-11 **65**..................... MissBHampson(5) 13 40
(Andy Turnell) *dwlt: t.k.h in rr: rdn over 3f out: sn btn* **25/1**

00-0 **15** *nk* **Landesherr (GER)**[20] 4293 7-9-2 **51** oh11..................... MissHCuthbert 5 26
(Thomas Cuthbert) *t.k.h: hld up: rdn over 3f out: sn btn* **100/1**

2m 30.26s (7.16) **Going Correction** +0.30s/f (Good) **15 Ran SP% 126.8**
Speed ratings (Par 103): **85,84,84,84,82 81,81,78,78,77 76,73,72,69,69**
CSF £329.40 CT £2400.10 TOTE £14.80: £3.90, £4.70, £1.90; EX 449.70 Trifecta £1427.00 Part won..
**Owner** Andrew Sayer **Bred** Ring Pink Partnership **Trained** Hackthorpe, Cumbria

**FOCUS**
A moderate handicap, in which the game winner, a 120-rated chaser, made all. The favourite ran below his recent wide-margin Musselburgh success.
T/Jkpt: Not won. T/Plt: £1,748.50 to a £1 stake. Pool: £80,360.63 - 33.55 winning tickets T/Qpdt: £63.90 to a £1 stake. Pool: £8,896.45 - 102.90 winning tickets RY

# 4072 KEMPTON (A.W) (R-H)
Monday, August 4

**OFFICIAL GOING: Standard**
Wind: virtually nil Weather: sunny, light cloud

## 4965 £25 FREE BET AT BETVICTOR.COM MEDIAN AUCTION MAIDEN STKS 6f (P)
**2:15** (2:16) (Class 5) 2-Y-O **£2,587** (£770; £384; £192) **Stalls Low**

Form RPR

4 **1** **Spring Loaded (IRE)**[26] 4087 2-9-5 0..................... SeanLevey 10 73
(Paul D'Arcy) *chsd ldr: rdn to chal over 1f out: led ins fnl f: styd on wl: drvn out* **10/1**

3 **2** *3/4* **State Of The Union (IRE)**[10] 4618 2-9-5 0..................... RichardHughes 6 71
(Richard Hannon) *led: rdn and qcknd 2f out: drvn and hdd ins fnl f: styd on same pce after* **5/6**[1]

53 **3** *hd* **Rockaroundtheclock (IRE)**[26] 4087 2-9-5 0..................... LukeMorris 3 70
(Paul Cole) *chsd ldrs: rdn and sltly outpcd 2f out: rallied u.p ins fnl f: swtchd lft and kpt on towards fin* **7/2**[2]

20 **4** *1* **Stinky Socks (IRE)**[87] 2107 2-9-0 0..................... TomQueally 9 62
(Charles Hills) *t.k.h: chsd ldrs: effrt ent fnl 2f: styd on same pce fnl f* **9/2**[3]

0 **5** *4 1/2* **Retro Valley (IRE)**[32] 3881 2-9-5 0..................... FergusSweeney 4 54
(David Dennis) *wl in tch in midfield: rdn and outpcd 2f out: wknd over 1f out* **50/1**

**6** *nk* **Tangramm** 2-9-5 0..................... SebSanders 1 53
(Simon Dow) *s.i.s: bhd rdn 1/2-way: styd on ins fnl f: nvr trbld ldrs* **25/1**

5 **7** *3* **King's Bond**[34] 3813 2-9-5 0..................... RobertHavlin 11 44+
(Ronald Harris) *wnt lft s and v.s.a: hdwy into midfield 4f out: rdn and rn green over 2f out: wknd 2f out* **100/1**

63 **8** *nk* **Theydon Thunder**[35] 3794 2-9-5 0..................... JimmyQuinn 8 43
(Peter Charalambous) *racd in midfield but nvr on terms: rdn over 2f out: wknd 2f out* **50/1**

00 **9** *12* **That Man Of Mine (IRE)**[7] 4740 2-8-12 0..................... RobHornby(7) 5 7
(Jamie Osborne) *sn outpcd in last trio: lost tch over 2f out* **100/1**

**10** *6* **Double Bronze** 2-9-5 0..................... RichardKingscote 7
(Milton Bradley) *dwlt: midfield tl dropped to last after 2f: lost tch over 2f out* **50/1**

1m 14.7s (1.60) **Going Correction** +0.075s/f (Slow) **10 Ran SP% 115.8**
Speed ratings (Par 94): **92,91,90,89,83 83,79,78,62,54**
CSF £18.64 TOTE £15.00: £2.60, £1.10, £1.40; EX 23.30 Trifecta £97.50.
**Owner** Rowley Racing **Bred** Swordlestown Little **Trained** Newmarket, Suffolk

**FOCUS**
Not the strongest 2yo maiden Kempton will ever stage and all of these were making their Polytrack debuts. The principals were up with the pace throughout and the first four came clear.

## 4966 PLAY ROULETTE & BLACKJACK AT BETVICTOR.COM MAIDEN FILLIES' STKS 1m 4f (P)
**2:45** (2:49) (Class 5) 3-Y-0+ **£2,587** (£770; £384; £192) **Stalls** Centre

Form RPR
5 **1** **Sona**[17] 4413 3-9-0 0 .................... WilliamBuick 8 84
(John Gosden) *chsd ldrs: rdn and effrt to chal 2f out: led over 1f out: rn green u.p ins fnl f: hrd drvn and hld on towards fin* **9/2**[3]
0-2 **2** *hd* **Allegation (FR)**[17] 4413 3-9-0 0 .................... TedDurcan 12 83
(David Lanigan) *chsd ldrs: wnt 2nd over 8f out: rdn 3f out: ev ch u.p fr 2f out: kpt on but unable qck fnl 100yds* **11/4**[2]
3 **3** *2* **Long View (IRE)**[17] 4413 3-9-0 0 ....................(v) ShaneKelly 9 80
(Sir Michael Stoute) *led after 2f: rdn ent 2f out: hdd over 1f out: sn outpcd in 3rd: plugged on same pce after* **7/4**[1]
5 **4** *3 ½* **Gale Force**[38] 3652 3-9-0 0 .................... FrederikTylicki 7 74
(James Fanshawe) *in tch in midfield: rdn over 2f out: sn struggling and outpcd: no threat to ldrs but plugged on fnl f* **5/1**
0 **5** *3 ¾* **Curved**[52] 3174 3-9-0 0 .................... JamesDoyle 4 68
(Lady Cecil) *led for 2f: chsd ldrs after: rdn ent fnl 2f: sn outpcd: 4th and no ch 1f out: wknd fnl f* **20/1**
00 **6** *5* **Tribulina**[33] 3857 3-9-0 0 .................... MircoMimmocchi 3 60
(Marco Botti) *in tch in midfield: rdn and struggling ent fnl 3f: sn outpcd and n.d fr over 2f out* **100/1**
5 **7** *8* **May Hay**[52] 3174 4-9-11 0 .................... WilliamCarson 2 47
(Anthony Carson) *off the pce in last quartet: hdwy and in tch in midfield 1/2-way: rdn wl over 2f out: sn btn: bhd over 1f out* **20/1**
**8** *20* **Madame Rouge** 3-9-0 0 .................... DavidProbert 5 15
(David Evans) *sn in rr: rdn 1/2-way: lost tch 3f out: t.o and eased ins fnl f* **66/1**
06 **9** *shd* **Mikey Miss Daisy**[52] 3174 3-9-0 0 .................... StevieDonohoe 6 15
(Martin Hill) *racd off the pce in last quartet: reminder over 5f out: lost tch 3f out: t.o and eased ins fnl f* **100/1**
**10** *4* **Bally Broadwell**[237] 4-9-11 0 .................... LiamKeniry 13 9
(Michael Madgwick) *v.s.a: a in rr: rdn over 5f out: lost tch 3f out: t.o and eased ins fnl f* **100/1**

2m 34.25s (-0.25) **Going Correction** +0.075s/f (Slow)
**WFA** 3 from 4yo+ 11lb **10** Ran SP% **111.9**
Speed ratings (Par 100): **103,102,101,99,96 93,88,74,74,71**
CSF £15.78 TOTE £5.10: £1.40, £1.60, £1.20; EX 17.60 Trifecta £40.20.
**Owner** Lady Bamford **Bred** Newsells Park Stud **Trained** Newmarket, Suffolk

**FOCUS**
A modest fillies' maiden in which they bet 20-1 bar four. The first three home had run against each other in a 1m2f Nottingham maiden 17 days ago. The winner clearly improved from that debut.

## 4967 DOWNLOAD THE BETVICTOR APP NOW NURSERY H'CAP 7f (P)
**3:15** (3:17) (Class 5) (0-70,70) 2-Y-0 **£2,587** (£770; £384; £192) **Stalls** Low

Form RPR
544 **1** **Muradif (IRE)**[27] 4044 2-9-7 70 .................... SebSanders 2 81+
(William Haggas) *t.k.h: hld up in tch in midfield on inner: swtchd lft over 2f out: rdn and hdwy to ld 1f out: edgd lft but r.o wl: gng away at fin* **1/1**[1]
4334 **2** *2 ¼* **Simply Magic (IRE)**[17] 4410 2-9-2 65 .................... RichardHughes 10 68
(Richard Hannon) *dwlt: rcvrd and in tch in midfield after 2f: rdn ent fnl 2f: hdd 1f out: outpcd and btn ins fnl f: kpt on for clr 2nd* **8/1**
0562 **3** *2 ¼* **Chester Deal**[12] 4529 2-8-6 60 .................... PhilipPrince(5) 9 56
(Jo Hughes) *t.k.h: chsd ldrs on outer: rdn ent fnl 2f: no ch w ldng pair but hld on to 3rd fnl f* **20/1**
050 **4** *¾* **Jet Mate (IRE)**[77] 2380 2-8-9 58 .................... MartinDwyer 4 52
(William Muir) *t.k.h: hld up in last trio: rdn and outpcd ent fnl 2f: rallied and styd on wl ins fnl f: no threat to ldrs* **25/1**
6360 **5** *¾* **Chetan**[31] 3934 2-8-12 61 .................... RichardKingscote 6 53
(Milton Bradley) *led and set stdy gallop: rdn and qcknd ent fnl 2f: hdd over 1f out: sn outpcd and btn wknd ins fnl f* **50/1**
206 **6** *1 ¼* **Secret Lightning (FR)**[32] 3888 2-9-5 68 .................... LiamKeniry 8 57
(Sylvester Kirk) *chsd ldr: rdn ent fnl 2f: outpcd and wl btn over 1f out: plugged on same pce fnl f* **6/1**[2]
064 **7** *½* **Toast Of Newbury (IRE)**[12] 4541 2-9-4 67 ....................(t) JamesDoyle 3 54
(Jamie Osborne) *chsd ldrs: effrt on inner ent fnl 2f: outpcd and btn over 1f out: wknd fnl f* **7/1**[3]
065 **8** *½* **Chilworth Bells**[32] 3875 2-8-7 56 .................... LukeMorris 7 42
(Mick Channon) *hld up in tch in midfield: rdn and outpcd ent fnl 2f: n.d after: plugged on ins fnl f* **25/1**
0505 **9** *½* **Verchild Lad (IRE)**[17] 4410 2-8-5 54 .................... SilvestreDeSousa 5 38
(David Evans) *hld up in last pair: rdn over 2f out: outpcd ent fnl 2f: n.d but plugged on fnl f* **8/1**
5646 **10** *3* **Invincible Zeb (IRE)**[32] 3875 2-9-7 70 .................... RobertHavlin 1 46
(Ronald Harris) *hld up in tch in rr: rdn over 2f out: sn outpcd and struggling: wknd over 1f out* **33/1**

1m 28.74s (2.74) **Going Correction** +0.075s/f (Slow) **10** Ran SP% **116.4**
Speed ratings (Par 94): **87,84,81,81,80 78,78,77,77,73**
CSF £8.73 CT £104.43 TOTE £1.90: £1.10, £1.90, £4.40; EX 9.70 Trifecta £49.10.
**Owner** Sheikh Ahmed Al Maktoum **Bred** Mrs Adelaide Doran **Trained** Newmarket, Suffolk

**FOCUS**
A modest nursery, though several of these had the potential to improve for the different surface and/or switch to handicapping and the winner was one of those. The pace was ordinary and the winner was heavily backed.

## 4968 DOWNLOAD THE BETVICTOR INSTABET APP H'CAP 1m (P)
**3:45** (3:45) (Class 5) (0-75,75) 3-Y-0+ **£2,587** (£770; £384; £192) **Stalls** Low

Form RPR
6432 **1** **Messila Star**[33] 3861 4-9-12 73 ....................(v) WilliamBuick 4 85
(Jeremy Noseda) *chsd ldng trio: rdn and effrt to ld over 1f out: clr and drvn ins fnl f: styd on: drvn out* **11/8**[1]
-630 **2** *2* **Anya**[21] 4271 5-9-11 72 .................... FergusSweeney 6 79
(Henry Candy) *in tch in midfield: effrt to chse ldrs over 1f out: kpt on to chse wnr ins fnl f: no imp* **8/1**
0532 **3** *¾* **Warfare**[35] 3795 5-9-2 63 .................... RichardHughes 8 69
(Kevin Ryan) *wl in tch in midfield: effrt to chse ldrs over 1f out: kpt on same pce and wnt 3rd ins fnl f* **9/2**[2]
6115 **4** *1* **Barnmore**[33] 3861 6-9-6 74 .................... RobHornby(7) 2 77
(Peter Hedger) *hld up in tch in last trio: clsng whn hmpd over 2f out: sn swtchd lft: rallied over 1f out: kpt on wl ins fnl f: snatched 4th last stride: no threat to wnr* **8/1**
6110 **5** *shd* **Zed Candy Girl**[24] 4153 4-8-6 58 ....................(p) TimClark(5) 10 61+
(Dai Burchell) *chsd ldrs: rdn to ld 2f out: sn hung lft and hdd over 1f out: no ex and btn 1f out: lost 3 pls ins fnl f* **16/1**
-330 **6** *3* **Dana's Present**[33] 3861 5-9-9 70 .................... PatCosgrave 7 66
(George Baker) *dwlt: rcvrd and in midfield after 2f: rdn and effrt wl over 1f out: unable qck and btn 1f out: wknd ins fnl f* **12/1**
625 **7** *4* **Black Dave (IRE)**[17] 4414 4-9-0 68 .................... HarryBurns(7) 9 55
(David Evans) *t.k.h: hdwy into midfield but stuck wd after 2f: rdn 3f out: sn struggling and wknd 2f out* **33/1**
0000 **8** *1 ¼* **Munsarim (IRE)**[18] 4354 7-9-6 67 ....................(p) AmirQuinn 3 51
(Lee Carter) *in tch towards rr: short-lived effrt on inner 2f out: wknd over 1f out* **33/1**
4004 **9** *2* **Boogangoo (IRE)**[10] 4613 3-9-2 70 .................... DavidProbert 1 49
(Grace Harris) *led: rdn and hdd 2f out: outpcd and btn over 1f out: wknd 1f out: eased wl ins fnl f* **12/1**
0-40 **10** *¾* **Captain Starlight (IRE)**[170] 627 4-9-11 72 .................... LiamKeniry 11 50
(Jo Crowley) *stdd after s: t.k.h: hld up in tch in rr: riddn and over 2f out: sn btn* **33/1**
3324 **11** *7* **St Paul De Vence (IRE)**[7] 4743 4-9-7 68 ....................(p) LukeMorris 5 30
(Paul Cole) *chsd ldrs: rdn and lost pl over 2f out: drvn and wknd 2f out: bhd 1f out* **6/1**[3]
-000 **12** *5* **Snow King (USA)**[31] 3931 4-9-11 72 .................... WilliamTwiston-Davies 13 22
(Ted Powell) *stdd after s: hld up in tch in last pair: rdn over 2f out: sn btn: bhd over 1f out* **50/1**

1m 39.57s (-0.23) **Going Correction** +0.075s/f (Slow)
**WFA** 3 from 4yo+ 7lb **12** Ran SP% **128.8**
Speed ratings (Par 103): **104,102,101,100,100 97,93,91,89,89 82,77**
CSF £14.50 CT £46.45 TOTE £2.10: £1.20, £2.90, £2.10; EX 15.90 Trifecta £98.80.
**Owner** Sheikh Khaled Duaij Al Sabah **Bred** Cheveley Park Stud Ltd **Trained** Newmarket, Suffolk
■ Equitable was withdrawn. Price at time of withdrawal 12-1. Rule 4 applies to bets placed prior to withdarwal but not to SP bets - deduction 5p in the pound. New market formed.

**FOCUS**
An ordinary handicap. The first three came from midfield to beat the leading trio.

## 4969 GERRY KERR HAPPY RETIREMENT H'CAP (DIV I) 1m (P)
**4:15** (4:15) (Class 6) (0-60,60) 3-Y-0 **£1,940** (£577; £288; £144) **Stalls** Low

Form RPR
-046 **1** **Windy Citi**[64] 2805 3-9-7 60 .................... GeorgeBaker 6 83+
(Chris Wall) *led for over 1f: chsd ldr after and t.k.h: led on bit over 2f out: effrtlessly strode clr over 1f out: unextended* **2/1**[1]
2362 **2** *5* **Choral Clan (IRE)**[46] 3389 3-9-6 59 ....................(t) JackMitchell 2 63
(Philip Mitchell) *broke wl: grad stdd bk: in tch in last trio 5f out: rdn and hdwy on outer over 1f out: chsd clr wnr over 1f out: kpt on but no ch* **4/1**[2]
0-50 **3** *2 ¼* **Risk 'N' Reward (IRE)**[7] 4733 3-8-13 52 ....................(v[1]) PatCosgrave 7 51
(Michael Murphy) *t.k.h: hld up in tch: hdwy into midfield: drvn and hdwy on inner to go 2nd 2f out: no ch w wnr lost 2nd over 1f out: plugged on* **9/2**[3]
0442 **4** *1* **Mercury Magic**[36] 3754 3-9-4 60 .................... RobertTart(3) 5 57
(David Menuisier) *in tch: dropped to last and rdn along over 4f out: styd on and past btn horses over 1f out: no ch w wnr* **12/1**
1055 **5** *1 ¼* **Intense Feeling (IRE)**[42] 3523 3-9-2 60 .................... DannyBrock(5) 1 54
(Lee Carter) *t.k.h: chsd ldrs: rdn ent fnl 2f: outpcd and no ch over 1f out: plugged on* **10/1**
24U **6** *8* **Dylan's Centenary**[36] 3754 3-8-11 57 .................... SophieKilloran(7) 11 32
(Rod Millman) *s.i.s: hdwy on outer to chse ldrs after 3f: rdn over 2f out: sn btn: wknd wl over 1f out* **11/1**
04-0 **7** *1* **Dark Reality (IRE)**[55] 3083 3-9-7 60 ....................(v[1]) HarryBentley 10 33
(Ralph Beckett) *s.i.s: hdwy on outer to chse ldrs 5f out: rdn over 2f out: sn btn: wknd wl over 1f out* **10/1**
1564 **8** *3* **Royal Bushida**[124] 1235 3-8-8 47 ....................(v) MartinLane 4 13
(Derek Shaw) *hld up in tch in midfield: rdn over 2f out: sn btn: bhd over 1f out* **25/1**
5006 **9** *1 ¾* **Third Strike**[18] 4340 3-9-7 60 ....................(b[1]) FergusSweeney 9 22
(Gary Moore) *led tl hung rt and hdd over 2f out: sn btn and wknd: bhd 1f out* **16/1**
4526 **10** *12* **Golly Miss Molly**[10] 4611 3-8-3 49 ow1 .................... DavidParkes(7) 3
(Jeremy Gask) *chsd ldrs: lost pl and rdn 1/2-way: in last 3f out: sn lost tch: t.o* **20/1**

1m 40.58s (0.78) **Going Correction** +0.075s/f (Slow) **10** Ran SP% **120.2**
Speed ratings (Par 98): **99,94,91,90,89 81,80,77,75,63**
CSF £10.07 CT £34.07 TOTE £3.00: £1.40, £2.20, £2.20; EX 12.10 Trifecta £69.00.
**Owner** Scuderia Giocri **Bred** Scuderia Giocri **Trained** Newmarket, Suffolk

**FOCUS**
A weak handicap, in which only two of these had tasted success before, and it turned into a one-sided contest due to a big improver. The time was a bit slower than the second division.

## 4970 GERRY KERR HAPPY RETIREMENT H'CAP (DIV II) 1m (P)
**4:45** (4:46) (Class 6) (0-60,60) 3-Y-0 **£1,940** (£577; £288; £144) **Stalls** Low

Form RPR
0052 **1** **Plough Boy (IRE)**[21] 4266 3-9-7 60 .................... ChrisCatlin 6 74
(Willie Musson) *t.k.h: hld up in tch in midfield: hdwy to join ldrs over 2f out: rdn to ld over 1f out: hld on wl ins fnl f* **11/4**[1]
-060 **2** *shd* **Celestial Knight**[20] 4306 3-9-4 57 ....................(v[1]) ShaneKelly 2 71
(James Fanshawe) *in tch in midfield: swtchd lft and effrt to chal 2f out: ev ch after: kpt on: jst hld towards fin* **10/1**
55-5 **3** *2 ¼* **Palace Dragon (IRE)**[26] 4085 3-9-6 59 .................... LukeMorris 8 68+
(Sir Mark Prescott Bt) *in tch in midfield but stuck wd: rdn and effrt 3f out: hdwy to chse ldrs over 1f out: styd on fnl f but nvr enough pce to chal ldrs* **4/1**[2]
0005 **4** *7* **Venus Marina**[20] 4304 3-8-7 49 .................... AshleyMorgan(3) 3 42
(Chris Wall) *led: rdn ent fnl 2f: hdd over 1f out: wknd 1f out* **8/1**
0000 **5** *2 ¼* **Isabella Beeton**[10] 4613 3-9-4 60 .................... JemmaMarshall(3) 4 48
(Pat Phelan) *chsd ldrs: wnt 2nd over 3f out tl 2f out: sn wknd* **13/2**
0044 **6** *2 ¾* **Swiss Lait**[20] 4306 3-9-7 60 .................... LiamKeniry 7 41
(David Elsworth) *hld up in tch in midfield: rdn and no hdwy over 2f out: wknd 2f out* **14/1**
5630 **7** *1 ¾* **Happydoingnothing**[21] 4266 3-9-5 58 .................... AdamBeschizza 10 35
(Christine Dunnett) *hld up in tch in rr: effrt u.p over 2f: no prog: wknd 2f out* **20/1**
0-00 **8** *½* **Exceed Policy**[42] 3528 3-8-7 49 oh4 .................... MartinLane 1 22
(David Dennis) *chsd ldrs: drvn and struggling over 2f out: sn lost pl and wknd wl over 1f out* **66/1**
600 **9** *nse* **Pendley Legacy**[38] 3652 3-9-7 60 .................... AdamKirby 9 36
(Clive Cox) *t.k.h: hld up in tch in rr: effrt and rdn over 2f out: sn btn* **11/2**[3]

4000 **10** *6* **Cueca (FR)**[7] 4732 3-8-13 **52**................................ RichardKingscote 5 14
(Jonathan Portman) *hld up in rr: rdn and over 2f out: sn btn: bhd fnl 2f* **33/1**

1200 **11** *6* **Cascadia (IRE)**[46] 3407 3-9-0 **53**................................ OisinMurphy 11
(Alison Hutchinson) *chsd ldrs tl lost pl qckly over 2f out: wl bhd fnl f* **20/1**

1m 40.37s (0.57) **Going Correction** +0.075s/f (Slow) **11** Ran SP% **116.2**
Speed ratings (Par 98): **100,99,97,90,88 85,83,83,83,77 71**
CSF £29.54 CT £112.03 TOTE £3.00: £1.10, £5.80, £1.10; EX 35.90 Trifecta £150.60.
**Owner** K A Cosby & Partners **Bred** J P Keappock **Trained** Newmarket, Suffolk

**FOCUS**
This division of the handicap contained three previous winners. The winning time was 0.21sec faster than the first leg and and the front three pulled well clear.

## 4971 BETVICTOR.COM FILLIES' H'CAP 6f (P)
**5:15** (5:15) (Class 4) (0-85,85) 3-Y-0+ **£5,175** (£1,540; £769; £384) **Stalls** Low

Form RPR

-112 **1** **Johara (IRE)**[37] 3704 3-9-7 **84**................................ TedDurcan 6 100+
(Chris Wall) *hld up in tch in midfield: swtchd lft and rdn over 2f out: qcknd to ld over 1f out: in command and edgd rt 1f out: r.o: comf* **7/4**[1]

30 **2** *3* **Marjong**[32] 3876 4-9-2 **75**................................ SebSanders 1 79
(Simon Dow) *t.k.h: hld up in tch in last trio: swtchd rt and hdwy over 1f out: chsd clr wnr 1f: kpt on but no imp* **8/1**[3]

3223 **3** *½* **Lady Horatia**[16] 4445 3-9-8 **85**................................ MartinDwyer 3 86
(William Muir) *t.k.h: led tl over 4f out: chsd ldr after: rdn over 2f out: drvn and unable qck over 1f out: no ch w wnr and one pce fnl f* **4/1**[2]

-651 **4** *1 ½* **Majestic Song**[19] 4324 3-8-7 **73**................................ RobertTart(3) 5 70
(James Toller) *rrd as stalls opened and s.i.s: in tch in rr: hdwy u.p over 1f out: kpt on but no ch w wnr fnl f* **10/1**

6026 **5** *3* **Bowstar**[23] 4182 5-9-4 **77**................................(b) RobertHavlin 2 65
(Michael Attwater) *bustled along leaving stalls: hdwy to ld over 4f out: rdn and hdd over 1f out: sn btn: wknd 1f out* **20/1**

1150 **6** *6* **Dreams Of Reality**[23] 4186 3-8-11 **74**................................ RichardKingscote 7 42
(Tom Dascombe) *hld up in last trio but stuck wd: rdn over 2f out: sn btn* **9/1**

0144 **7** *13* **Nova Princesse (GER)**[27] 4053 3-8-11 **74**................................(tp) LukeMorris 4
(Marco Botti) *chsd ldrs tl rdn and lost pl over 2f out: wl bhd and heavily eased ins fnl f* **9/1**

0001 **8** *3 ½* **Dancealot**[31] 3936 3-9-0 **82**................................ DannyBrock(5) 8
(Clive Brittain) *in tch in midfield: rdn and lost pl over 2f out: sn wl btn: bhd and heavily eased ins fnl f* **8/1**[3]

1m 12.67s (-0.43) **Going Correction** +0.075s/f (Slow)
**WFA** 3 from 4yo+ 4lb **8** Ran SP% **112.4**
Speed ratings (Par 102): **105,101,100,98,94 86,69,64**
CSF £15.89 CT £48.65 TOTE £2.10: £1.10, £2.60, £1.80; EX 13.70 Trifecta £71.70.
**Owner** Mrs Claude Lilley **Bred** Tribesmen Syndicate **Trained** Newmarket, Suffolk

**FOCUS**
This fillies' sprint handicap was the best race on the card and they went a strong pace from the off, perhaps too strong as it turned out. The winner resumed her progress after slightly disappointing turf effort.

## 4972 KEMPTON LIVE WITH DIZZEE RASCAL 06.09.14 H'CAP 6f (P)
**5:50** (5:53) (Class 6) (0-65,64) 3-Y-0 **£1,940** (£577; £288; £144) **Stalls** Low

Form RPR

4-45 **1** **Tahchee**[46] 3406 3-9-1 **58**................................ FrederikTylicki 1 70
(James Fanshawe) *chsd ldrs: rdn and effrt to ld over 1f out: clr and r.o wl fnl f: rdn out* **4/1**[1]

0022 **2** *2* **Mimi Luke (USA)**[19] 4324 3-9-2 **59**................................(v) SilvestreDeSousa 10 65
(Alan Bailey) *chsd ldrs: rdn and ev ch over 2f out: led 2f out: hdd over 1f out: styd on same pce after* **15/2**

244 **3** *2 ¾* **Lead A Merry Dance**[19] 4324 3-9-6 **63**................................ MartinDwyer 2 60
(Sylvester Kirk) *hld up in tch in midfield: hdwy u.p on inner over 1f out: wnt 3rd ins fnl f: r.o but no ch w ldrs* **6/1**[3]

4640 **4** *nk* **Honey Meadow**[21] 4262 3-9-7 **64**................................ OisinMurphy 12 60
(Robert Eddery) *hld up in tch in midfield: rdn and effrt whn hung rt over 2f out: hdwy between horses ins fnl f: r.o: no threat to ldrs* **8/1**

5-56 **5** *1 ¼* **Tolly McGuiness**[26] 4089 3-8-5 **48**................................ WilliamCarson 5 40
(Julia Feilden) *t.k.h: rdn ent fnl 2f: outpcd and btn over 1f out: kpt on same pce fnl f* **14/1**

2356 **6** *¾* **Baars Causeway (IRE)**[40] 3588 3-9-6 **63**................................ AdamKirby 9 53
(Timothy Jarvis) *led: rdn and hdd 2f out: 3rd and outpcd over 1f out: wknd ins fnl f* **9/1**

5045 **7** *nk* **Khelfan**[12] 4545 3-8-6 **52**................................ NathanAlison(3) 11 41
(Martin Smith) *awkward leaving stalls and s.i.s: t.k.h: hdwy to chse ldrs 5f out: rdn and unable qck 2f out: wl hld 1f out* **12/1**

530 **8** *3* **Ecliptic Sunrise**[25] 4111 3-8-11 **57**................................(t) ThomasBrown(3) 8 36
(Des Donovan) *s.i.s: in tch in midfield: rdn and unable qck over 2f out: sn outpcd and btn 2f out* **12/1**

3644 **9** *1 ½* **Dancing Angel**[27] 4049 3-9-1 **58**................................ LukeMorris 6 32
(James Eustace) *hld up in tch in last trio: rdn and effrt over 2f out: no prog: nvr trbld ldrs* **5/1**[2]

0505 **10** *½* **Ellingham (IRE)**[11] 4590 3-8-7 **50**................................ JimmyQuinn 4 23
(Christine Dunnett) *hld up in tch in midfield: rdn over 2f out: sn outpcd: towards rr and wl hld fnl 2f* **50/1**

3305 **11** *2 ½* **Wedgewood Estates**[24] 4155 3-8-10 **53**................................ DavidProbert 7 18
(Tony Carroll) *hld up in tch in last trio: rdn and no hdwy over 2f out: bhd fnl 2f* **8/1**

5306 **12** *10* **Dove Mountain (IRE)**[42] 3522 3-9-5 **62**................................ TedDurcan 3
(Gary Brown) *hld up in rr: effrt over 2f out: sn btn: bhd and eased ins fnl f* **66/1**

1m 13.86s (0.76) **Going Correction** +0.075s/f (Slow) **12** Ran SP% **120.4**
Speed ratings (Par 98): **97,94,90,90,88 87,87,83,81,80 77,63**
CSF £34.54 CT £185.05 TOTE £4.60: £1.40, £1.40, £2.30; EX 22.60 Trifecta £107.00.
**Owner** Chris Van Hoorn **Bred** F Stribbling **Trained** Newmarket, Suffolk

**FOCUS**
A moderate handicap with 11 of the 12 runners maidens coming into it. They didn't go much of a pace, and the winner was among the least exposed.
T/Plt: £2.80 to a £1 stake. Pool: £55718.09 - 14469.19 winning tickets T/Qpdt: £1.90 to a £1 stake. Pool: £3981.61 - 1508.58 winning tickets SP

# 4449 RIPON (R-H)
Monday, August 4

**OFFICIAL GOING: Good (8.0)**
Wind: fresh half behind Weather: mixture of sunshine and cloud

## 4973 BRITISH STALLION STUDS EBF MAIDEN FILLIES' STKS (BOBIS RACE) 6f
**2:00** (2:00) (Class 5) 2-Y-0 **£3,881** (£1,155; £577; £288) **Stalls** High

Form RPR

0 **1** **Little Lady Katie (IRE)**[63] 2824 2-8-11 0................................ JoeyHaynes(3) 12 72
(K R Burke) *in tch: outpcd and dropped to midfield over 3f out: rdn and hdwy over 1f out: chal strly ins fnl f: kpt on: led post* **50/1**

0 **2** *hd* **Stocking**[38] 3671 2-9-0 0................................ AndreaAtzeni 2 71
(Roger Varian) *s.i.s: sn pushed along towards rr: swtchd lft over 2f out: sn gd hdwy: led ins fnl f: flashed tail: kpt on: hdd post* **8/1**[3]

33 **3** *3* **Faraajh (IRE)**[30] 3947 2-9-0 0................................ PaulMulrennan 4 62
(James Tate) *w ldr: rdn to ld over 1f out: hdd ins fnl f: no ex* **11/4**[2]

6 **4** *2 ¼* **Honeysuckle Lil (IRE)**[10] 4633 2-9-0 0................................ DavidAllan 13 55
(Tim Easterby) *trckd ldrs: rdn 2f out: one pce* **9/4**[1]

0 **5** *2 ¾* **My Girl Jo (FR)**[6] 4751 2-9-0 0................................ DanielTudhope 14 47+
(David O'Meara) *hld up: rdn 1/2-way: kpt on fnl f* **14/1**

**6** *1 ¾* **Yat Ding Yau (FR)** 2-9-0 0................................ JoeFanning 11 42
(William Jarvis) *s.i.s: sn pushed along towards rr: kpt on fnl f: nrst fin* **28/1**

63 **7** *½* **Spirit Of The Sea (IRE)**[14] 4486 2-9-0 0................................ GrahamLee 1 40
(Jim Goldie) *midfield towards outer: pushed along 1/2-way: nvr threatened ldrs* **9/1**

006 **8** *1 ¼* **Sparkling Sapphire**[31] 3909 2-8-11 36................................ GeorgeChaloner(3) 5 37
(Richard Whitaker) *chsd ldrs: rdn over 2f out: wknd over 1f out* **150/1**

60 **9** *2 ¾* **Elevator Action (IRE)**[12] 4527 2-9-0 0................................ TonyHamilton 9 28
(Richard Fahey) *hld up: pushed along over 3f out: nvr threatened* **50/1**

**10** *1* **Anneani (IRE)** 2-9-0 0................................ PJMcDonald 15 25+
(Paul Green) *s.i.s: sn pushed along in rr: nvr threatened* **100/1**

65 **11** *1* **Shortmile Lady (IRE)**[17] 4382 2-8-11 0................................ ConnorBeasley(3) 10 22
(Michael Dods) *led: rdn whn hdd over 1f out: wknd* **16/1**

**12** *nse* **The Wee Barra (IRE)** 2-9-0 0................................ TomEaves 7 22
(Kevin Ryan) *sn pushed along towards rr: a bhd* **10/1**

0 **13** *8* **Where's Sue (IRE)**[17] 4396 2-9-0 0................................ RobertWinston 6
(Charles Hills) *prom: rdn over 2f out: wknd over 1f out: eased* **14/1**

**14** *6* **Lydiate Lady** 2-9-0 0................................ RaulDaSilva 8
(Paul Green) *midfield: rdn 1/2-way: sn wknd* **100/1**

1m 12.73s (-0.27) **Going Correction** -0.175s/f (Firm) **14** Ran SP% **116.9**
Speed ratings (Par 91): **94,93,89,86,83 80,80,78,74,73 72,72,61,53**
CSF £401.64 TOTE £44.70: £16.50, £4.10, £1.50; EX 537.70 Trifecta £2222.50 Not won..
**Owner** Ontoawinner 5, M Hulin & Mrs E Burke **Bred** Roger K Lee **Trained** Middleham Moor, N Yorks

**FOCUS**
Rail on bend from back straight to home straight moved out 3m and distances increased by about 7yds on Round course. A moderate 2yo maiden, as the third did not set a high standard.

## 4974 STUDLEY (S) H'CAP 5f
**2:30** (2:30) (Class 6) (0-65,65) 3-Y-0 **£2,587** (£770; £384; £192) **Stalls** High

Form RPR

3265 **1** **White Flag**[15] 4469 3-8-2 **53**................................ RachelRichardson(7) 1 60
(Tim Easterby) *prom towards outer: rdn 2f out: led ins fnl f: kpt on: rdr dropped whip 40yds out* **15/2**

3601 **2** *nk* **Camanche Grey (IRE)**[31] 3938 3-9-7 **65**................................ GrahamLee 2 71
(Ben Haslam) *w ldr: rdn 2f out: kpt on* **7/2**[1]

4004 **3** *2* **Lady Mai (IRE)**[32] 3896 3-8-2 **51**................................ SammyJoBell(5) 8 57+
(Richard Fahey) *chsd ldrs: pushed along 1/2-way: n.m.r over 1f out tl 110yds out: kpt on* **11/2**[3]

0500 **4** *nk* **Danfazi (IRE)**[39] 3600 3-9-6 **64**................................(p) JamesSullivan 4 62
(Kristin Stubbs) *led narrowly: rdn 1/2-way: hdd ins fnl f: no ex* **12/1**

3000 **5** *1* **Chuckamental**[23] 4193 3-8-4 **48**................................ JoeFanning 6 42
(Bryan Smart) *prom: rdn 1/2-way: wknd ins fnl f* **7/1**

0054 **6** *1 ½* **Princess Myla (IRE)**[19] 4318 3-8-6 **50**................................ BarryMcHugh 7 39
(Paul Midgley) *dwlt: hld up: rdn and sme hdwy over 1f out: wknd ins fnl f* **12/1**

3036 **7** *¾* **Greenbury (IRE)**[7] 4725 3-8-6 **50**................................(v[1]) PJMcDonald 10 36
(Ann Duffield) *chsd ldrs: pushed along 1/2-way: wknd ins fnl f* **6/1**

-440 **8** *1 ½* **Lunesdale Buddy**[44] 3486 3-8-2 **46** oh1................................ PatrickMathers 3 27
(Alan Berry) *hld up: rdn 1/2-way: nvr threatened* **50/1**

6433 **9** *6* **Soul Instinct**[119] 1343 3-8-9 **58**................................ ShaneGray(5) 5 17
(Kevin Ryan) *dwlt: hld up: pushed 1/2-way: sn btn* **5/1**[2]

0000 **10** *2* **Cool Reception**[39] 3601 3-8-2 **46** oh28................................ IanBrennan 9
(Ollie Pears) *hld up: outpcd and bhd fr 1/2-way* **33/1**

59.49s (-0.51) **Going Correction** -0.175s/f (Firm) **10** Ran SP% **113.1**
Speed ratings (Par 98): **97,96,93,92,91 88,87,85,75,72**
CSF £32.85 CT £159.75 TOTE £10.00: £3.30, £1.50, £1.40; EX 41.10 Trifecta £154.30.There was no bid for the winner.
**Owner** Habton Farms **Bred** Exors Of The Late T E Pocock **Trained** Great Habton, N Yorks

**FOCUS**
A typically weak selling handicap, but well run. The winner was back to her best, and runner-up showed that his Warwick maiden success is possibly a bit better than it seemed.

## 4975 RIPON REMEMBERS THE GREAT WAR H'CAP 1m 1f 170y
**3:00** (3:00) (Class 4) (0-85,82) 4-Y-0+ **£4,725** (£1,414; £707; £354; £176) **Stalls** Low

Form RPR

0-41 **1** **Woodacre**[27] 4058 7-8-3 **67**................................ GeorgeChaloner(3) 2 74+
(Richard Whitaker) *dwwlt: hld up in tch: swtchd lft to outer wl over 2f out: sn rdn and hdwy: led wl over 1f out: pressed ins fnl f: kpt on to assert fnl 110yds* **5/4**[1]

1-20 **2** *1* **Miguel Grau (USA)**[159] 744 4-9-2 **77**................................ AndreaAtzeni 1 82+
(Roger Varian) *hld up in tch: rdn and hdwy to chal over 1f out: pressed ldr ins fnl f: one pce and hld in 2nd fnl 110yds* **9/2**[3]

5300 **3** *1* **Eeny Mac (IRE)**[6] 4753 7-9-0 **75**................................(p) AndrewElliott 5 78
(Neville Bycroft) *led: rdn whn hdd over 1f out: one pce: hld in 3rd whn n.m.r on inner 50yds out* **16/1**

2060 **4** *1 ¾* **King Of The Celts (IRE)**[14] 4498 6-8-6 **67**................................ PJMcDonald 3 67
(Tim Easterby) *trckd ldr on inner: rdn 2f out: one pce* **9/1**

024 **5** *¾* **Muffin McLeay (IRE)**[16] 4453 6-9-7 **82**................................ GrahamGibbons 4 81
(David Barron) *trckd ldr: rdn to chal 2f out: grad wknd fr appr fnl f* **3/1**[2]

6044 **6** *19* **Life And Times (USA)**[12] 4549 6-8-9 **70**........................ JoeFanning 6 39
(Mark Johnston) *hld up in tch: racd keenly: rdn 3f out: sn wknd* **11/1**

2m 5.04s (-0.36) **Going Correction** 0.0s/f (Good) **6** Ran SP% **111.8**
Speed ratings (Par 105): **101,100,99,98,97 82**
CSF £7.21 TOTE £2.80: £1.20, £3.50; EX 7.30 Trifecta £93.10.
**Owner** Mrs R M Whitaker **Bred** Hellwood Stud Farm **Trained** Scarcroft, W Yorks

**FOCUS**
A modest handicap run at a muddling pace. The winner can do a bit better in the future, while the runner-up was making his turf debut. The front-running third is rated as running to form.

## 4976 WEATHERBYS STALLION BOOK SUMMER SPRINT TROPHY (H'CAP) 6f
**3:30** (3:30) (Class 3) (0-95,95) 3-Y-0+
**£7,470** (£2,236; £1,118; £559; £279; £140) **Stalls** High

Form RPR

1-05 **1** **Pipers Note**[18] 4347 4-9-3 **89**........................ GeorgeChaloner(3) 3 99
(Richard Whitaker) *trckd ldng pair: rdn to ld narrowly over 1f out: strly pressed thrght fnl f: kpt on wl* **5/1**[3]

1201 **2** *shd* **Another Wise Kid (IRE)**[17] 4418 6-9-12 **95**........................ GrahamLee 9 104
(Paul Midgley) *pressed ldr: rdn 2f out: upsides thrght fnl f: kpt on wl: jst hld* **11/1**

2235 **3** *2* **Out Do**[9] 4683 5-9-11 **94**........................ DanielTudhope 4 95
(David O'Meara) *midfield: rdn and hdwy over 1f out: chsd ldng pair ins fnl f: kpt on* **5/2**[1]

1101 **4** *2 ½* **My Name Is Rio (IRE)**[27] 4061 4-9-2 **85**........................ PaulMulrennan 11 77
(Michael Dods) *led narrowly: rdn over 2f out: hdd over 1f out: grad wknd* **4/1**[2]

0130 **5** *1 ¼* **So Beloved**[45] 3431 4-9-9 **92**........................ JamesSullivan 6 80
(Ruth Carr) *stdd s: hld up: pushed along over 2f out: kpt on fnl f* **11/1**

0-02 **6** *½* **Secret Look**[27] 4061 4-9-7 **90**........................ RobertWinston 1 76
(Ed McMahon) *trckd ldng pair: rdn over 2f out: grad wknd over 1f out* **8/1**

544 **7** *1* **Ruby's Day**[8] 4712 5-8-0 **76**........................ ClaireMurray(7) 10 59
(David Brown) *chsd ldng pair: rdn over 2f out: wknd over 1f out* **14/1**

-002 **8** *1 ¾* **Waffle (IRE)**[18] 4358 8-9-2 **85**........................ PhillipMakin 5 61
(David Barron) *hld up: rdn over 2f out: nvr threatened* **16/1**

0300 **9** *1 ¾* **Cosmic Chatter**[17] 4384 4-9-8 **91**........................ GrahamGibbons 8 61
(David Barron) *dwlt: hld up: rdn over 2f out: sn btn* **11/1**

2210 **10** *hd* **Mappin Time (IRE)**[9] 4683 6-9-4 **87**........................(be) DavidAllan 7 56
(Tim Easterby) *hld up: pushed along 1/2-way: sn btn* **25/1**

1m 10.63s (-2.37) **Going Correction** -0.175s/f (Firm) **10** Ran SP% **117.7**
Speed ratings (Par 107): **108,107,105,101,100 99,98,95,93,93**
CSF £59.39 CT £173.43 TOTE £5.70: £2.50, £3.60, £1.30; EX 70.00 Trifecta £300.80.
**Owner** Six Iron Partnership & Partner **Bred** Wadacre Stud **Trained** Scarcroft, W Yorks

**FOCUS**
This event, formerly the Armstrong Memorial, was won in 2011 by Pepper Lane, who went on to take the Great St Wilfrid over C&D, while last year's winner Spinatrix was runner-up in the big sprint. The winner was a dual CD winner and the runner-up more than confirmed his latest run at Pontefract as being reliable form.

## 4977 CITY WELTER H'CAP (BOBIS RACE) 5f
**4:00** (4:00) (Class 4) (0-85,84) 3-Y-0 **£4,851** (£1,443; £721; £360) **Stalls** High

Form RPR

4316 **1** **Innocently (IRE)**[10] 4636 3-9-4 **81**........................ DanielTudhope 4 90
(David O'Meara) *prom: led 2f out: sn rdn: kpt on wl* **7/1**

4014 **2** *1 ½* **Lexington Abbey**[10] 4636 3-9-7 **84**........................ TomEaves 2 88
(Kevin Ryan) *chsd ldrs: rdn over 2f out: kpt on* **15/2**

0013 **3** *½* **Pushkin Museum (IRE)**[23] 4186 3-8-12 **78**........ GeorgeChaloner(3) 1 80
(Richard Fahey) *s.i.s: hld up: sn pushed along: hdwy on outer over 1f out: kpt on fnl f: wnt 3rd post* **4/1**[2]

2133 **4** *nse* **Dutch Breeze**[10] 4636 3-9-3 **80**........................(p) DavidAllan 5 82
(Tim Easterby) *in tch: rdn over 3f out: chsd ldr over 1f out: one pce fnl f: lost 3rd post* **9/4**[1]

5504 **5** *2 ¼* **Red Forever**[19] 4315 3-8-2 **65** oh2........................ PatrickMathers 9 59
(Alan Berry) *hld up: rdn 1/2-way: kpt on fnl f: nvr threatened* **40/1**

3030 **6** *3* **Fuel Injection**[10] 4636 3-8-2 **65** oh3........................(p) JamesSullivan 6 48
(Paul Midgley) *chsd ldrs: rdn 1/2-way: wknd fnl f* **22/1**

1332 **7** *1 ¾* **Noble Asset**[19] 4315 3-8-11 **74**........................ PhillipMakin 7 50
(John Quinn) *chsd ldrs: shuffled bk and lost pl over 1f out: no threat after* **5/1**[3]

310- **8** *¾* **Omaha Gold (IRE)**[303] 7026 3-8-12 **75**........................ PaulMulrennan 8 49
(Bryan Smart) *t.k.h to post: led: rdn whn hdd 2f out: wknd* **8/1**

6026 **9** *2* **Corncockle**[14] 4488 3-8-11 **77**........................ SamJames(3) 3 44
(David O'Meara) *hld up: pushed along 1/2-way: nvr threatened* **16/1**

58.76s (-1.24) **Going Correction** -0.175s/f (Firm) **9** Ran SP% **115.5**
Speed ratings (Par 102): **102,99,98,98,95 90,87,86,83**
CSF £58.29 CT £239.29 TOTE £9.30: £2.90, £1.90, £1.70; EX 39.80 Trifecta £140.90.
**Owner** Hollowdean **Bred** Longfort Stud **Trained** Nawton, N Yorks

**FOCUS**
A fair sprint handicap, and the time was alright compared to the earlier selling handicap. The winner is speedy, while runner-up ran a small personal best.

## 4978 SIS LIVE MAIDEN STKS 1m 4f 10y
**4:30** (4:31) (Class 5) 3-Y-0+ **£3,234** (£962; £481; £240) **Stalls** Low

Form RPR

0-2 **1** **Spiritoftheunion**[61] 2899 3-8-12 0........................ PaulMulrennan 6 83+
(Michael Bell) *mde all: pushed clr over 2f out: rdn out fnl f: comf* **5/4**[1]

4 **2** *7* **Haydn's Lass**[18] 4368 3-8-12 0........................ BenCurtis 7 72
(Marcus Tregoning) *chsd ldr: rdn 4f out: outpcd by wnr over 3f out: plugged on: no ch w wnr* **9/4**[2]

62 **3** *nk* **Di's Gift**[27] 4062 5-10-0 0........................ RobertWinston 2 77
(Richard Guest) *hld up in rr: rdn over 5f out: hdwy into 3rd 4f out: kpt on* **5/1**[3]

4 **4** *12* **Braes Of Lochalsh**[29] 3998 3-9-3 0........................ GrahamLee 4 57
(Jim Goldie) *hld up: rdn over 6f out: plugged on past tiring rivals into poor 4th 3f out: nvr threatened* **16/1**

4-6 **5** *26* **Hope For Glory**[27] 4062 5-9-11 0........................ JoeyHaynes(3) 3 16
(Jason Ward) *hld up: rdn 5f out: sn wknd* **80/1**

0 **6** *38* **Shaf (IRE)**[25] 4130 3-9-3 0........................ JoeFanning 5
(Ed Dunlop) *dwlt: sn in tch in 3rd: rdn over 5f out: wknd 4f out: t.o* **15/2**

6 **7** *27* **Big Fortune**[35] 3796 4-10-0 0........................ StephenCraine 1
(David C Griffiths) *in tch: rdn 6f out: sn wknd: t.o* **66/1**

2m 34.39s (-2.31) **Going Correction** 0.0s/f (Good)
**WFA** 3 from 4yo+ 11lb **7** Ran SP% **112.3**
Speed ratings (Par 103): **107,102,102,94,76 51,33**
CSF £4.05 TOTE £3.00: £1.40, £1.50; EX 5.00 Trifecta £13.40.
**Owner** Ahmad Abdulla Al Shaikh **Bred** Horizon Bloodstock Limited **Trained** Newmarket, Suffolk

**FOCUS**
An uncompetitive maiden. The nicely bred winner made all in a time faster than the following handicap over the same trip.

## 4979 FOSSGATE H'CAP 1m 4f 10y
**5:00** (5:00) (Class 5) (0-75,72) 3-Y-0+ **£3,234** (£962; £481; £240) **Stalls** Low

Form RPR

5354 **1** **Opera Fan (FR)**[12] 4540 3-8-11 **66**........................ JoeFanning 5 83+
(Mark Johnston) *trckd ldng pair: led over 2f out: sn rdn clr: eased fnl 50yds* **9/4**[1]

-040 **2** *6* **Grand Liaison**[26] 4081 5-9-2 **60**........................ GrahamLee 6 64
(James Given) *hld up in tch: pushed along 4f out: n.m.r 2f out: angled lft to outer over 1f out: styd on: wnt 2nd ins fnl f: no ch w easy wnr* **22/1**

5113 **3** *3 ¼* **Valantino Oyster (IRE)**[2] 4904 7-10-0 **72**........................(p) DaleSwift 3 71
(Tracy Waggott) *pressed ldr: rdn to ld 4f out: hdd over 2f out: one pce and sn no ch w wnr: lost 2nd ins fnl f* **7/2**[2]

000 **4** *¾* **Good Speech (IRE)**[8] 4710 4-9-12 **70**........................ JamesSullivan 2 68
(Tom Tate) *led narrowly: rdn whn hdd 4f out: plugged on* **4/1**[3]

-205 **5** *½* **Bright Applause**[16] 4454 6-9-10 **68**........................ BarryMcHugh 1 65
(Tracy Waggott) *hld up in tch: rdn over 3f out: one pce and no imp* **6/1**

0610 **6** *3* **Dabuki (FR)**[20] 4296 4-9-9 **67**........................(p) PJMcDonald 7 59
(Geoffrey Harker) *midfield: rdn 4f out: sn no imp: wknd fnl f* **14/1**

004 **7** *10* **Two B'S**[86] 2170 3-8-7 **62**........................ DuranFentiman 4 38
(Tim Easterby) *hld up in rr: rdn 5f out: sn btn* **7/1**

2m 35.43s (-1.27) **Going Correction** 0.0s/f (Good)
**WFA** 3 from 4yo+ 11lb **7** Ran SP% **110.8**
Speed ratings (Par 103): **104,100,97,97,97 95,88**
CSF £47.96 TOTE £2.70: £1.40, £7.30; EX 18.70 Trifecta £128.80.
**Owner** Sheikh Majid bin Mohammed Al Maktoum **Bred** T , D & A De La Heronniere **Trained** Middleham Moor, N Yorks

**FOCUS**
A moderate little handicap, and time was slower than the preceding maiden. The winner's improvement had seemed to level out, but he clearly improved here to win easily.
T/Plt: £27.40 to a £1 stake. Pool: £62316.84 - 1659.03 winning tickets T/Qpdt: £9.00 to a £1 stake. Pool: £5398.72 - 440.55 winning tickets AS

# 4739 WINDSOR (R-H)
Monday, August 4

**OFFICIAL GOING: Good to firm (good in places)**
Wind: Moderate, behind Weather: Fine but cloudy

## 4980 BRITISH STALLION STUDS EBF MAIDEN FILLIES' STKS (BOBIS RACE) 6f
**6:00** (6:02) (Class 5) 2-Y-0 **£2,911** (£866; £432; £216) **Stalls** Low

Form RPR

55 **1** **Sallabeh**[14] 4499 2-9-0 0........................ TomQueally 11 73
(George Margarson) *trckd ldrs: pushed along over 2f out: shkn up to ld wl over 1f out: in command fnl f: pushed out* **8/1**

**2** *1 ¾* **Penny Pepper (IRE)** 2-9-0 0........................ JohnFahy 4 67+
(Eve Johnson Houghton) *hld up in rr: gng wl 2f out: prog and pushed along over 1f out: reminders and styd on to take 2nd nr fin* **4/1**[3]

**3** *½* **Lolita** 2-9-0 0........................ PaddyAspell 7 65
(J R Jenkins) *pressed ldr: chalng whn wnr wl by wl over 1f out: chsng after: no imp and lost 2nd nr fin* **50/1**

00 **4** *1* **Gen I Am**[21] 4269 2-9-0 0........................ SeanLevey 5 62
(Richard Hannon) *led: rdn and hdd wl over 1f out: fdd ins fnl f* **66/1**

**5** *¾* **Cascading Stars (IRE)** 2-9-0 0........................ StevieDonohoe 12 60
(J S Moore) *settled in last trio: pushed along over 2f out: prog and reminder over 1f out: kpt on: nrst fin* **33/1**

0 **6** *nk* **Tamarin**[38] 3671 2-9-0 0........................ PatDobbs 9 59
(Sir Michael Stoute) *trckd ldrs: shkn up and nt qckn wl over 1f out: one pce after* **13/8**[1]

**7** *1* **Kizingo (IRE)** 2-9-0 0........................ MartinLane 8 56
(Charles Hills) *slowly away: sn in midfield: pushed along over 2f out: no hdwy over 1f out* **7/2**[2]

**8** *3 ¾* **Kyllarney** 2-9-0 0........................ JimCrowley 6 45
(Charles Hills) *slowly away: mostly in last trio: pushed along and no prog fr 2f out* **20/1**

0 **9** *¾* **Catharina**[17] 4396 2-9-0 0........................ RichardHughes 3 43+
(Richard Hannon) *trckd ldrs: pushed along over 2f out: lost grnd over 1f out: eased fnl f* **10/1**

0 **10** *1 ¼* **More Drama (IRE)**[9] 4676 2-9-0 0........................ LiamKeniry 1 39
(Sylvester Kirk) *a in rr: nudged along 2f out: str reminder and veered lft fnl f* **25/1**

1m 12.05s (-0.95) **Going Correction** -0.275s/f (Firm) **10** Ran SP% **115.5**
Speed ratings (Par 91): **95,92,92,90,89 89,87,82,81,80**
CSF £37.62 TOTE £8.90: £1.80, £1.70, £7.10; EX 44.90 Trifecta £1353.70 Part won..
**Owner** Salem Rashid **Bred** Jeremy Green And Sons **Trained** Newmarket, Suffolk

**FOCUS**
The inner of the straight was dolled out 11yds at 6f and 5yds at the winning post. Top bend dolled out 11yds from normal inner configuration, adding 42yds to race distances of a mile and over. An average maiden for the track, but the winner was well on top.

## 4981 SPORTSABLE - GRASSROOTS TO PARALYMPIC SPORTS CLUB H'CAP 5f 10y
**6:30** (6:30) (Class 5) (0-70,70) 3-Y-0+ **£2,911** (£866; £432; £216) **Stalls** Low

Form RPR

0053 **1** **Come On Dave (IRE)**[25] 4128 5-9-4 **70**........................ DanielMuscutt(5) 2 84
(John Butler) *taken down early: mde all: urged along over 1f out: clr fnl f: rdn out* **10/3**[3]

0230 **2** *1 ¾* **Silverrica (IRE)**[28] 4027 4-9-9 **70**........................ FergusSweeney 7 77
(Malcolm Saunders) *chsd wnr: rdn over 1f out: one pce and no imp fnl f* **8/1**

421 **3** *1 ¾* **Dark Lane**[21] 4267 8-8-13 **65**........................ NoelGarbutt(5) 8 65
(David Evans) *rrd s: pushed along in last trio: rdn 2f out: prog on fr over 1f out to take 3rd ins fnl f* **6/1**

5-45 **4** *1 ¼* **Oscars Journey**[59] 2951 4-9-5 **66**........................ PaddyAspell 4 61
(J R Jenkins) *chsd ldng trio: shkn up wl over 1f out: one pce and no prog* **16/1**

5102 **5** *3 ½* **Picc Of Burgau**[9] 4675 4-9-2 **63**........................ GeorgeBaker 5 44
(Geoffrey Deacon) *hld up in last trio: pushed along and no prog 2f out: reminder 1f out: nvr in it* **3/1**[2]

-341 6 *hd* **Joyous**[9] 4675 4-9-6 **67** RichardHughes 3 55
(Dean Ivory) *chsd ldng pair: pushed along 1/2-way: no prog over 1f out: lost pl fnl f: heavily eased last 75yds: dismntd after fin* **11/4**[1]
0643 7 *17* **West Coast Dream**[41] 3561 7-9-0 **64** DeclanBates(3) 6
(Roy Brotherton) *stmbld bdly s: a last and nvr able to rcvr: t.o* **14/1**
58.16s (-2.14) **Going Correction** -0.275s/f (Firm) 7 Ran SP% **112.7**
Speed ratings (Par 103): **106,103,100,98,92 92,65**
CSF £28.54 CT £151.16 TOTE £4.70: £2.60, £4.30; EX 31.00 Trifecta £117.10.
**Owner** Wildcard Racing Syndicate **Bred** Mrs Eithne Hamilton **Trained** Newmarket, Suffolk
**FOCUS**
Little got into this modest sprint. The winner made all in a fast time off his lowest turf mark for two years.

## 4982 FEXCO COMMERCIAL FX SERVICES H'CAP 1m 67y
**7:00** (7:00) (Class 4) (0-85,85) 3-Y-0+ **£4,851** (£1,443; £721; £360) **Stalls** Low

Form RPR
1354 1 **Crystal Lake (IRE)**[12] 4551 3-9-6 **84** JimCrowley 7 95
(Ralph Beckett) *trckd ldr: shkn up to ld over 2f out: rdn clr over 1f out: in n.d after* **11/10**[1]
0000 2 *4 ½* **Set The Trend**[30] 3969 8-9-9 **85** GeorgeDowning(5) 5 87
(David Dennis) *chsd ldng pair: rdn over 2f out: kpt on to take 2nd 1f out but wnr already clr* **10/1**[3]
5000 3 *¾* **Al Manaal**[9] 4680 4-9-2 **76** CharlesBishop(3) 6 76
(Mick Channon) *t.k.h early: trckd ldng pair: shkn up 2f out: nvr any ch but kpt on to take 3rd ins fnl f* **16/1**
0413 4 *½* **Craftsmanship (FR)**[53] 3144 3-8-13 **77** (p) FrederikTylicki 8 75
(Robert Eddery) *hld up in last: pushed along 5f out and struggling after: looked like fining wl btn 2f out: fnlly r.o fnl f* **7/2**[2]
5-00 5 *¾* **Mezmaar**[32] 3886 5-9-11 **85** RyanClark(3) 4 82
(Kevin Morgan) *taken steadily to post: hld up in 5th: pushed along fr 1/2-way: no imp on ldrs 2f out: plugged on* **50/1**
3104 6 *4* **After The Goldrush**[28] 4028 3-8-12 **76** (b) RichardHughes 3 63
(Richard Hannon) *led at str pce: rdn and hdd over 2f out: no ch w wnr over 1f out: wknd rapidly fnl f* **7/2**[2]
1m 42.45s (-2.25) **Going Correction** -0.125s/f (Firm)
**WFA** 3 from 4yo+ 7lb 6 Ran SP% **109.0**
Speed ratings (Par 105): **106,101,100,100,99 95**
CSF £12.49 CT £97.75 TOTE £1.90: £1.10, £4.50; EX 11.00 Trifecta £83.60.
**Owner** The Pickford Hill Partnership **Bred** B Holland, S Hillen & J Cullinan **Trained** Kimpton, Hants
**FOCUS**
They got racing from a fair way out in what was a fair handicap. The first couple home sat just behind the early leader.

## 4983 ROYAL BERKSHIRE ODD FELLOWS H'CAP 6f
**7:30** (7:30) (Class 4) (0-85,85) 3-Y-0+ **£4,851** (£1,443; £721; £360) **Stalls** Low

Form RPR
6440 1 **Triple Chocolate**[63] 2849 4-8-12 **71** JimmyQuinn 9 80
(Roger Ingram) *hld up wl off the pce: prog fr 2f out: wnt 2nd over 1f out: led jst ins fnl f: drvn out* **8/1**
2410 2 *1 ½* **Vallarta (IRE)**[10] 4632 4-9-3 **76** (v) WilliamTwiston-Davies 10 80
(Mick Channon) *dwlt: hld up wl off the pce: rdn over 2f out: styd on fr over 1f out to take 2nd ins fnl f* **8/1**
0000 3 *1 ¼* **Sacha Park (IRE)**[14] 4502 3-9-2 **79** RichardHughes 8 78
(Richard Hannon) *dwlt: hld up in last pair and wl off the pce: crept clsr fr 2f out: hrd rdn and prog to take 3rd ins fnl f: unable to threaten* **20/1**
06 4 *1 ½* **Breccbennach**[38] 3676 4-9-7 **80** (tp) GeorgeBaker 7 75
(Seamus Durack) *led at furious pce: clr 1/2-way: wknd and hdd jst ins fnl f* **11/2**[3]
1452 5 *¾* **Desert Command**[25] 4121 4-9-11 **84** DavidProbert 12 77
(Andrew Balding) *pressed ldr at str pce and clr of rest: unable to sustain press fr 1/2-way: sn rdn: lost 2nd and wknd over 1f out* **2/1**[1]
015- 6 *nse* **Shamahan**[320] 6526 5-9-1 **77** MichaelJMMurphy(3) 11 70
(Luke Dace) *chsd clr ldng pair: drvn over 2f out: no imp over 1f out: fdd* **25/1**
1056 7 *¾* **Amadeus Wolfe Tone (IRE)**[18] 4355 5-9-11 **84** (b) AdamKirby 1 74+
(Jamie Osborne) *hld up in last pair and wl off the pce: clsd fr 2f out: possible threat whn stuck bhd rival jst over 1f out: no ch after* **5/1**[2]
6161 8 *31* **Role Player**[26] 4078 4-9-12 **85** TomQueally 3
(Michael Bell) *chsd clr ldrs: wknd rapidly over 2f out: virtually p.u fnl f* **5/1**[2]
1m 10.42s (-2.58) **Going Correction** -0.275s/f (Firm)
**WFA** 3 from 4yo+ 4lb 8 Ran SP% **112.9**
Speed ratings (Par 105): **106,104,102,100,99 99,98,56**
CSF £67.50 CT £1225.18 TOTE £8.30: £1.80, £2.80, £4.00; EX 69.60 Trifecta £455.30.
**Owner** Fahed Al Dabbous **Bred** Lael Stables **Trained** Epsom, Surrey
**FOCUS**
They went tearing off in this sprint and it played right into the hands of the hold-up horses.

## 4984 GETREADING.CO.UK MAIDEN STKS 1m 2f 7y
**8:00** (8:02) (Class 5) 3-4-Y-O **£2,726** (£805; £402) **Stalls** Centre

Form RPR
2406 1 **Nancy From Nairobi**[17] 4385 3-8-13 **94** RichardHughes 10 75+
(Mick Channon) *mde all: shkn up 2f out: rdn and styd on fnl f* **5/4**[1]
4 2 *1 ¼* **Past Forgetting (IRE)**[36] 3755 3-8-13 0 LemosdeSouza 9 73+
(Luca Cumani) *hld up: shkn up and prog on outer over 2f out: tk 2nd jst over 1f out: styd on but nvr really threatened wnr* **5/1**[3]
0 3 *1* **Lu's Buddy (GR)**[51] 3248 3-9-4 0 PatDobbs 2 76
(Amanda Perrett) *chsd wnr to 1/2-way: rdn over 2f out: rallied to dispute 2nd and edgd lft whn jockey dropped whip 1f out: kpt on* **33/1**
05 4 *2* **Crowded**[18] 4368 3-9-4 0 MartinLane 1 72
(Charlie Appleby) *hld up towards rr: clsd on ldrs over 2f out gng wl enough: jst pushed along and nvr really threatened: hld whn short of room jst over 1f out* **12/1**
3 5 *1 ¼* **Le Maitre Chat (USA)**[114] 1438 3-9-4 0 AdamKirby 3 70
(Clive Cox) *t.k.h early: hld up in 4th: rdn 3f out: tried to cl over 2f out: racd awkwardly and no headway over 1f out* **15/8**[2]
55 6 *1 ¼* **Dalasi (IRE)**[14] 4500 3-8-13 0 FergusSweeney 11 62
(Henry Candy) *prom: trckd wnr 1/2-way: chal 3f out: btn off over 1f out: short of room sn after: jst pushed along and fdd* **10/1**
6- 7 *9* **Grey Odyssey**[370] 8312 3-9-4 0 TomQueally 6 50
(Dean Ivory) *a in last: shoved along bef 1/2-way: no prog and wl btn 3f out* **50/1**
06- 8 *16* **Rock Charm**[276] 7654 3-8-11 0 AaronJones(7) 8 20
(Stuart Williams) *hld up towards rr: lost tch over 3f out: t.o* **66/1**
2m 9.39s (0.69) **Going Correction** -0.125s/f (Firm) 8 Ran SP% **119.1**
Speed ratings (Par 103): **92,91,90,88,87 86,79,66**
CSF £8.65 TOTE £2.20: £1.10, £1.80, £4.60; EX 11.40 Trifecta £138.10.
**Owner** Norman Court Stud **Bred** Norman Court Stud **Trained** West Ilsley, Berks

■ Stewards' Enquiry : Pat Dobbs caution: careless riding.
Lemos de Souza one-day ban: careless riding (Aug 18)
**FOCUS**
A fair maiden, and the winner was the form pick even if her Pattern form was a bit flattering. She got an uncomplicated ride from the front. The runner-up shaped okay from off the pace, while the third was a big improver from his debut.

## 4985 COWORTH PARK ROYAL WINDSOR LADIES NIGHT AMATEUR RIDERS' H'CAP 1m 3f 135y
**8:30** (8:31) (Class 5) (0-75,81) 3-Y-0+ **£2,807** (£870; £435; £217) **Stalls** Centre

Form RPR
0000 1 **Couloir Extreme (IRE)**[14] 4501 4-10-3 **67** (v) MissHayleyMoore(3) 6 79
(Gary Moore) *hld up in 4th: quick move up inner to ld jst over 4f out and dashed for home: rdn over 2f out: kpt on wl fnl f* **14/1**
0064 2 *6* **Admirable Duque (IRE)**[19] 4322 8-9-8 **58** (b) MrChrisMartin(3) 2 63
(Dominic Ffrench Davis) *hld up and sn in last: rdn and prog over 3f out: chsd clr wnr over 2f out: tried to cl over 1f out: no imp after* **20/1**
-615 3 *7* **Aldwick Bay (IRE)**[59] 2963 6-10-9 **75** MissCAGreenway(5) 4 65
(Tom Dascombe) *hld up in rr: rdn and prog over 3f out: tk modest 3rd over 1f out: no ch w ldng pair* **11/4**[1]
0353 4 *3 ¼* **Royal Etiquette (IRE)**[53] 3147 7-9-4 **56** oh1 (tp) MrAlexFerguson(5) 10 41
(Lawney Hill) *dwlt: sn in tch: rdn and effrt over 3f out: no real imp on ldrs after* **9/1**
-205 5 *nse* **Urban Space**[36] 3761 8-9-9 **56** oh3 (t) MrMichaelJMurphy 8 41
(John Flint) *hld up in rr: rdn and sme prog over 3f out: urged along and one pce fnl 2f* **7/1**
6121 6 *1 ¼* **Bertie Moon**[7] 4743 4-11-1 **81** 6ex MissPFuller(5) 1 64
(Geoffrey Deacon) *fast away: led but hdd after 1f: tried to ld again 7f out but had to chse new ldr: chal over 4f out but wnr sn swept past: wkng whn rdr dropped whip 2f out* **7/2**[2]
0324 7 *14* **Norse Light**[23] 4189 3-9-12 **75** (b) MrHHunt(5) 7 35
(Ralph Beckett) *led after 1f to 7f out: wknd 5f out: t.o* **9/2**[3]
3146 8 *8* **Pandorica**[38] 3644 6-10-2 **70** (p) MrJPWilliams(7) 5 17
(Bernard Llewellyn) *in tch: struggling and pushed along 1/2-way: wknd over 3f out: t.o* **25/1**
2263 9 *½* **My Lord**[15] 2774 6-10-1 **69** MrJDoe(7) 3 15
(Luke Dace) *sn chsd ldng pair: clsd qckly to ld 7f out: hdd & wknd rapidly jst over 4f out: t.o* **8/1**
2m 27.62s (-1.88) **Going Correction** -0.125s/f (Firm)
**WFA** 3 from 4yo+ 11lb 9 Ran SP% **116.0**
Speed ratings (Par 103): **101,97,92,90,90 89,79,74,74**
CSF £254.93 CT £999.70 TOTE £12.20: £2.60, £5.30, £1.60; EX 88.60 Trifecta £1103.90 Part won..
**Owner** C E Stedman **Bred** Irish National Stud **Trained** Lower Beeding, W Sussex
**FOCUS**
No hanging around here and those held up off the gallop prospered. Hayley Moore made a race-winning move more than 3f out.
T/Plt: £2,390.20 to a £1 stake. Pool: £93,842 - 28.66 winning tickets T/Qpdt: £122.40 to a £1 stake. Pool: £12,158 - 73.45 winning tickets JN

# 4527 CATTERICK (L-H)
### Tuesday, August 5
**OFFICIAL GOING: Good to firm (good in places; 8.6)**
Wind: Moderate across Weather: Cloudy with sunny periods

## 4993 BETFRED SUPPORTS JACK BERRY HOUSE EBF MAIDEN STKS 7f
**2:15** (2:17) (Class 5) 2-Y-O **£2,911** (£866; £432; £216) **Stalls** Low

Form RPR
2 1 **Berland (IRE)**[21] 4301 2-9-5 0 JoeFanning 7 78+
(Michael Bell) *sn trcking ldng pair: hdwy on outer to ld 2f out: rdn and edgd lft to inner rail wl over 1f out: kpt on* **30/100**[1]
25 2 *2* **La Estatua**[18] 4409 2-9-0 0 GrahamLee 3 67
(James Tate) *slt ld for 1f: cl up on inner: rdn along over 2f out: chsd wnr over 1f out: sn drvn and no imp* **4/1**[2]
0 3 *3* **Grey Sensation (IRE)**[9] 4701 2-9-5 0 DanielTudhope 8 64+
(K R Burke) *towards rr: pushed along 1/2-way: hdwy 2f out: kpt on to take 3rd wl ins fnl f* **33/1**
034 4 *1 ¼* **Indian Champ**[9] 4701 2-9-0 0 ShaneGray(5) 5 61
(Kevin Ryan) *cl up: slt ld after 1f: pushed along over 2f out: sn hdd and rdn: drvn and wknd over 1f out* **10/1**[3]
0 5 *3 ¾* **Phantasmo (IRE)**[12] 4570 2-9-5 0 PhillipMakin 4 50
(John Quinn) *chsd ldrs: rdn along wl over 2f out: sn one pce* **28/1**
4 6 *3* **Little Houdini**[14] 4518 2-9-5 0 TomEaves 2 42
(Keith Dalgleish) *a towards rr* **66/1**
004 7 *14* **Hafina**[13] 4528 2-9-0 0 GrahamGibbons 6
(Michael Easterby) *a in rr* **66/1**
1m 25.85s (-1.15) **Going Correction** -0.325s/f (Firm) 7 Ran SP% **115.4**
Speed ratings (Par 94): **93,90,87,85,81 78,62**
CSF £1.88 TOTE £1.30: £1.02, £2.40; EX 2.30 Trifecta £11.90.
**Owner** Sheikh Marwan Al Maktoum **Bred** Darley **Trained** Newmarket, Suffolk
**FOCUS**
Rail in home straight moved out 3yds to provide fresh ground. After a dry night, the ground was changed to good to firm, good in places. An uncompetitive maiden to open proceedings and the heavily backed favourite landed the odds in comfortable fashion.

## 4994 BETFRED RACING FOLLOW US ON TWITTER H'CAP 5f
**2:45** (2:46) (Class 6) (0-60,60) 3-Y-0+ **£2,385** (£704; £352) **Stalls** Low

Form RPR
6030 1 **Perfect Words (IRE)**[60] 2955 4-9-2 **55** (p) IanBrennan 6 67
(Marjorie Fife) *mde all: jnd and rdn over 1f out: kpt on wl fnl f* **11/4**[2]
0-04 2 *2 ½* **Irish Girls Spirit (IRE)**[11] 4630 5-9-2 **55** (v[1]) GrahamLee 7 58
(Paul Midgley) *cl up: effrt to chal over 1f out and sn rdn: drvn ins fnl f and kpt on same pce* **15/2**
5262 3 *2 ¼* **Lucky Mark (IRE)**[21] 4287 5-9-1 **54** DanielTudhope 1 49
(John Balding) *trckd ldng pair on inner: pushed along 1/2-way: rdn wl over 1f out: sn drvn and one pce* **2/1**[1]
6505 4 *½* **Fizzolo**[98] 1860 3-8-2 **49** GemmaTutty(5) 3 41
(Karen Tutty) *towards rr: hdwy over 2f out: sn rdn and chsd ldrs over 1f out: no imp fnl f* **33/1**
1466 5 *1* **Prigsnov Dancer (IRE)**[12] 4571 9-9-0 **60** DavidParkes(7) 5 50
(Deborah Sanderson) *a in rr* **5/1**[3]
0206 6 *½* **I'll Be Good**[4] 4860 5-9-4 **60** (t) SladeO'Hara(3) 2 48
(Alan Berry) *chsd ldrs on inner: rdn along 2f out: grad wknd* **15/2**

5065 7 10 **De Repente (IRE)**[20] 4315 3-9-3 **59** ........ JoeFanning 9 10
(Paul Green) *chsd ldrs: rdn along 1/2-way: outpcd fnl 2f* **14/1**

58.0s (-1.80) **Going Correction** -0.325s/f (Firm)
**WFA** 3 from 4yo+ 3lb 7 Ran SP% **109.8**
Speed ratings (Par 101): **101,97,93,92,91 90,74**
CSF £21.34 CT £44.34 TOTE £4.70: £1.50, £2.90; EX 23.60 Trifecta £47.60.
**Owner** Green Lane **Bred** Rathasker Stud **Trained** Stillington, N Yorks

**FOCUS**
A low-grade sprint but a tidy performance from the winner who, off a career-low mark, got off the mark at the 27th attempt. The winning time was fast.

## 4995 BETFRED EXCLUSIVE COMPETITIONS ON FACEBOOK H'CAP 1m 5f 175y
**3:15** (3:22) (Class 4) (0-85,85) 3-Y-O+ **£6,469** (£1,925; £962; £481) **Stalls** Low

Form RPR
0161 1 **Special Fighter (IRE)**[7] 4754 3-8-8 **78** 6ex ........ JoeFanning 3 91
(Mark Johnston) *trckd ldr: cl up over 4f out: led over 2f out: sn rdn clr: kpt on strly fnl f* **6/4**[1]

0312 2 3 1/2 **Gambol (FR)**[13] 4552 4-9-7 **78** ........ GeorgeBaker 5 86
(B W Hills) *trckd ldrs: hdwy to chse wnr 2f out: rdn wl over 1f out: kpt on same pce fnl f* **11/4**[2]

0603 3 5 **Ebony Express**[21] 4289 5-9-7 **78** ........ BenCurtis 7 79
(Alan Swinbank) *hld up in tch: hdwy on outer wl over 2f out: rdn to chse ldng pair wl over 1f out: drvn and no imp fnl f* **12/1**

0-30 4 3/4 **Kiwayu**[25] 4173 5-10-0 **85** ........ PhillipMakin 1 85
(Philip Kirby) *trckd ldrs on inner: pushed along over 3f out: rdn over 2f out: sn drvn and one pce* **7/1**

/345 5 3/4 **Local Hero (GER)**[30] 3204 7-9-2 **80** ........(p) MikeyEnnis(7) 6 79
(Steve Gollings) *hld up in rr: hdwy 3f out: effrt on inner 2f out and sn nt clr run: swtchd rt and rdn wl over 1f out: sn drvn and no imp* **6/1**[3]

-060 6 3 1/2 **Tappanappa (IRE)**[24] 4217 7-9-1 **72** ........(p[1]) AndrewMullen 2 66
(Michael Appleby) *dwlt and reminders in rr after 1f: pushed along after 4f: hdwy u.p on outer to chse ldrs 1/2-way: rdn over 4f out: sn drvn and outpcd* **12/1**

3001 7 1 **Tinseltown**[13] 4533 8-8-11 **68** ........ TomEaves 4 61
(Brian Rothwell) *led: pushed along over 3f out: rdn and hdd over 2f out: sn drvn and wknd* **33/1**

2m 56.95s (-6.65) **Going Correction** -0.325s/f (Firm)
**WFA** 3 from 4yo+ 13lb 7 Ran SP% **111.8**
Speed ratings (Par 105): **106,104,101,100,100 98,97**
CSF £5.42 TOTE £2.50: £1.40, £1.40; EX 6.50 Trifecta £32.70.
**Owner** Sheikh Hamdan bin Mohammed Al Maktoum **Bred** Darley **Trained** Middleham Moor, N Yorks

**FOCUS**
The feature race on the card saw an authoritative performance from the only 3yo in the line-up, who was defying a penalty. The runner-up probably improved again in defeat.

## 4996 BETFRED CALL US ON 0800221221 CLASSIFIED CLAIMING STKS (QUALIFIER FOR 2014 CATTERICK 12F SERIES) 1m 3f 214y
**3:45** (3:45) (Class 6) 3-Y-O+ **£3,408** (£1,006; £503) **Stalls** Centre

Form RPR
2145 1 **Incendo**[13] 4538 8-9-3 73 ........(v) PaulMulrennan 5 68+
(Conor Dore) *hld up in rr: smooth hdwy 3f out: trckd ldr 2f out: clsd up on bit over 1f out: shkn up to ld last 100yds: readily* **10/11**[1]

0205 2 1 1/4 **Juvenal (IRE)**[16] 4470 5-9-3 66 ........(p) DavidAllan 2 66
(Geoffrey Harker) *trckd ldng pair: hdwy 4f out: led over 2f out: rdn wl over 1f out: jnd appr fnl f and sn drvn: hdd and no ex last 100yds* **3/1**[3]

3322 3 8 **Gift Of Silence**[7] 4763 5-9-4 62 ........ PaddyAspell 6 55
(John Berry) *hld up in tch: hdwy wl over 3f out: effrt to chse ldng pair 2f out: sn rdn and one pce* **11/4**[2]

2646 4 3 1/2 **Monzino (USA)**[7] 4749 6-8-12 47 ........ MikeyEnnis(7) 1 50
(Michael Chapman) *trckd ldr: cl up after 5f: led 4f out: rdn along and hdd over 2f out: sn drvn and outpcd* **28/1**

6-40 5 34 **L'Es Fremantle (FR)**[13] 4536 3-7-13 19 ........ JoeyHaynes(3) 4
(Michael Chapman) *led: jnd after 5f: rdn along and hdd 4f out: drvn and lost pl 3f out: sn bhd* **150/1**

2m 37.28s (-1.62) **Going Correction** -0.325s/f (Firm)
**WFA** 3 from 5yo+ 11lb 5 Ran SP% **108.2**
Speed ratings (Par 101): **92,91,85,83,60**
CSF £3.81 TOTE £1.80: £1.10, £1.70; EX 3.90 Trifecta £5.80.
**Owner** Mrs Louise Marsh **Bred** London Thoroughbred Services Ltd **Trained** Hubbert's Bridge, Lincs

**FOCUS**
Uncompetitive fare. The winner did it nicely but still off his recent turf best, as the runner-up had question marks hanging over him.

## 4997 BETFRED WATCH FRED'S PUSHES ON BETFRED TV H'CAP 5f 212y
**4:15** (4:15) (Class 5) (0-75,73) 3-Y-O+ **£2,911** (£866; £432; £216) **Stalls** Low

Form RPR
3246 1 **Solar Spirit (IRE)**[18] 4421 9-9-12 **73** ........ RobertWinston 7 81
(Tracy Waggott) *stdd and swtchd lft to inner s: sn trcking ldrs: hdwy 2f out: rdn jst over 1f out and squeezed through to chal ins fnl f: edgd rt and styd on to ld nr fin* **7/2**[2]

5524 2 shd **Showtime Star**[6] 4796 4-9-0 **61** ........ BenCurtis 2 68
(Alan Swinbank) *cl up: effrt 2f out: rdn to take slt ld appr 1f out: sn drvn: hdd and no ex nr fin* **3/1**[1]

0623 3 1 **Red Cape (FR)**[6] 4795 11-8-7 **54** ........(b) JamesSullivan 1 58
(Ruth Carr) *slt ld: rdn along over 2f out: drvn and hdd 1f out: ev ch: hld whn nt much rr nr fin* **5/1**[3]

0234 4 1 **McCarthy Mor (IRE)**[17] 4455 3-8-6 **57** ........ PatrickMathers 3 56
(Richard Fahey) *chsd ldrs: hdwy over 2f out: swtchd rt to outer and rdn wl over 1f out: drvn and no imp ins fnl f* **17/2**

2250 5 4 1/2 **Outbacker (IRE)**[22] 4262 3-9-0 **65** ........ JoeFanning 8 50
(Mark Johnston) *chsd ldrs: effrt on outer over 2f out: sn rdn and wknd over 1f out* **8/1**

0100 6 3/4 **Dream Ally (IRE)**[11] 4632 4-9-4 **65** ........ PJMcDonald 5 48
(Micky Hammond) *a towards rr* **14/1**

2014 7 nk **Cadeaux Pearl**[15] 4494 6-9-2 **63** ........ TomEaves 4 46
(Scott Dixon) *a towards rr* **6/1**

360P 8 2 1/4 **Lucky Dan (IRE)**[18] 4394 8-8-12 **59** ........ RaulDaSilva 6 34
(Paul Green) *a towards rr* **25/1**

1m 12.13s (-1.47) **Going Correction** -0.325s/f (Firm)
**WFA** 3 from 4yo+ 4lb 8 Ran SP% **110.3**
Speed ratings (Par 103): **96,95,94,93,87 86,85,82**
CSF £13.35 CT £47.45 TOTE £3.90: £1.40, £1.30, £2.00; EX 16.20 Trifecta £71.50.
**Owner** Elsa Crankshaw Gordon Allan **Bred** Paul Hensey **Trained** Spennymoor, Co Durham

**FOCUS**
A modest race for a 0-75 with only the winner having a rating in the 70s, but there were some in-form sorts on display and it looks a solid enough piece of form despite the steady pace.

## 4998 BETFRED RACING LIKE US ON FACEBOOK H'CAP 7f
**4:45** (4:45) (Class 6) (0-65,64) 3-Y-O **£2,385** (£704; £352) **Stalls** Low

Form RPR
4-63 1 **La Havrese (FR)**[14] 4512 3-9-3 **60** ........ PJMcDonald 4 71
(Ann Duffield) *trckd ldrs on inner: hdwy over 2f out: rdn to chal over 1f out: led ins fnl f: r.o* **5/1**[2]

0034 2 1/2 **Mount Cheiron (USA)**[9] 4706 3-8-4 **52** ow1 ........(p) EmmaSayer(5) 14 61+
(Dianne Sayer) *towards rr: hdwy on outer over 2f out: rdn to chse ldng pair over 1f out: swtchd lft ins fnl f: styng on whn n.m.r fnl 75yds* **16/1**

2550 3 1/2 **Armelle (FR)**[92] 2020 3-8-1 **49** ........ MatthewHopkins(5) 5 57
(Scott Dixon) *slt ld: rdn 2f out: drvn and edgd rt ent fnl f: sn hdd: kpt on gamely u.p towards fin* **14/1**

0004 4 5 **Skinny Latte**[11] 4627 3-8-2 **45** ........(p) PatrickMathers 9 40
(Micky Hammond) *chsd ldrs: rdn on outer over 2f out: drvn wl over 1f out: kpt on same pce* **14/1**

5540 5 2 1/2 **Cahal (IRE)**[13] 4532 3-8-13 **56** ........ AdrianNicholls 6 45
(David Nicholls) *cl up: rdn over 2f out: drvn wl over 1f out: grad wknd* **4/1**[1]

3403 6 1 **Ty Cobb (IRE)**[17] 4455 3-8-11 **54** ........(p) IanBrennan 8 40
(John Quinn) *chsd ldrs: rdn over 2f out: sn drvn and no imp* **8/1**

3201 7 3/4 **Street Boss (IRE)**[11] 4627 3-9-2 **59** ........(b) RussKennemore 11 43
(Jedd O'Keeffe) *in tch: rdn over 2f out: sn drvn and no imp* **11/1**

4002 8 3/4 **Marlismamma (FR)**[11] 4627 3-8-2 **48** ........(p) JulieBurke(3) 2 30
(David O'Meara) *in tch on inner: rdn over 2f out: no hdwy* **8/1**

5230 9 3 **Rockie Road (IRE)**[33] 3880 3-8-9 **52** ........ RaulDaSilva 10 26
(Paul Green) *dwlt and towards rr: hdwy into midfield 1/2-way: rdn over 2f out: n.d* **6/1**[3]

-510 10 6 **Born To Fly (IRE)**[10] 4654 3-9-6 **63** ........(b) SebSanders 1 22
(Nick Littmoden) *dwlt: a in rr* **9/1**

0255 11 1 **Under Approval**[36] 3792 3-8-8 **56** ........ GemmaTutty(5) 13 12
(Karen Tutty) *a towards rr* **40/1**

005- 12 1 1/2 **Annie's Rose**[234] 8300 3-8-4 **47** ........ JoeFanning 12
(Bryan Smart) *prom on outer: pushed along bef 1/2-way: sn rdn and wknd wl over 2f out* **20/1**

0030 13 1/2 **Prostate Awareness (IRE)**[16] 4473 3-9-0 **57** ........(p) AndrewElliott 15
(Patrick Holmes) *a towards rr* **14/1**

1m 25.13s (-1.87) **Going Correction** -0.325s/f (Firm) 13 Ran SP% **120.4**
Speed ratings (Par 98): **97,96,95,90,87 86,85,84,81,74 73,71,70**
CSF £81.56 CT £1090.97 TOTE £8.40: £1.90, £5.00, £7.50; EX 99.60 Trifecta £3160.60.
**Owner** Jimmy Kay **Bred** S C A Elevage De La Croix De Place **Trained** Constable Burton, N Yorks

**FOCUS**
The pace held up on the fast ground. A big field but not many improvers on show, the winner the glaring exception. The runner-up did well having been held up from a wide draw.
T/Plt: £33.00 to a £1 stake. Pool: £56,516.36 - 1,248.91 winning tickets. T/Qpdt: £10.70 to a £1 stake. Pool: £4,936.81 - 341.26 winning tickets. JR

# 4814 FFOS LAS (L-H)
Tuesday, August 5

**OFFICIAL GOING: Good to soft (7.1)**
Wind: moderate half against Weather: sunny

## 4999 BRITISH STALLION STUDS EBF MEDIAN AUCTION MAIDEN FILLIES' STKS (BOBIS RACE) 6f
**2:00** (2:05) (Class 5) 2-Y-O **£2,911** (£866; £432; £216) **Stalls** Centre

Form RPR
4050 1 **As A Dream (IRE)**[50] 3312 2-9-0 53 ........ DavidProbert 6 68
(David Evans) *t.k.h early: hld up: clsd 1/2-way: rdn over 1f out: r.o wl fnl f to ld fnl 50yds* **25/1**

0 2 1 **Escrick (IRE)**[18] 4396 2-9-0 0 ........ FergusSweeney 8 65
(David Simcock) *trckd ldrs: pushed along to ld appr fnl f: sn edgd lft and drvn: hdd and no ex fnl 50yds* **3/1**[2]

00 3 1 **Seebeedee**[15] 4499 2-9-0 0 ........ SamHitchcott 4 62
(Harry Dunlop) *trckd ldrs tl rdn along and lost pl over 3f out: swtchd rt over 1f out: r.o wl fnl f: wnt 3rd post* **8/1**

0232 4 hd **Khawaater**[17] 4450 2-9-0 72 ........ AndreaAtzeni 1 61
(Roger Varian) *cl up: led over 2f out: sn rdn: hdd appr fnl f: one pce and lost 3rd post* **4/6**[1]

5 hd **Rictrude (FR)** 2-9-0 0 ........ RichardKingscote 5 61
(Tom Dascombe) *s.i.s: towards rr: rdn 2f out and sltly outpcd by ldrs: r.o wl ins fnl f* **7/1**[3]

6 8 **Mandria (IRE)** 2-8-11 0 ........ ThomasBrown(3) 2 37
(Daniel Kubler) *s.i.s: sn in tch on outer: rdn over 2f out: hung lft and wknd over 1f out* **16/1**

60 7 9 **Emilys Girl (IRE)**[32] 3933 2-9-0 0 ........ SteveDrowne 7
(Ronald Harris) *led tl rdn and hdd over 2f out: wknd qckly* **66/1**

1m 13.38s (3.38) **Going Correction** +0.35s/f (Good) 7 Ran SP% **119.8**
Speed ratings (Par 91): **91,89,88,88,87 77,65**
CSF £104.43 TOTE £15.60: £6.50, £2.50; EX 115.60 Trifecta £623.30.
**Owner** A Morgans & Mrs E Evans **Bred** E Glanville **Trained** Pandy, Monmouths
■ Lady Vellyn (66-1) was withdrawn. Rule 4 does not apply.

**FOCUS**
A modest and uncompetitive fillies' maiden with the field reduced by one when Lady Vellyn had to be withdrawn after going down in her stall. The winner was back in ground with some ease in it for the first time since its debut.

## 5000 BRAND NEW 32RED SPORT.COM H'CAP 6f
**2:30** (2:33) (Class 6) (0-60,56) 3-Y-O+ **£1,940** (£577; £288; £144) **Stalls** Centre

Form RPR
0-50 1 **Gracie's Games**[32] 3935 8-8-13 **45** ........(v) WilliamTwiston-Davies 11 58
(John Spearing) *cl up tl led after 1f: 3 l clr 1/2-way: drvn 2f out: r.o strly* **12/1**

6545 2 3 1/4 **Diamond Vine (IRE)**[34] 3848 6-8-13 **45** ........(p) LukeMorris 6 48
(Ronald Harris) *towards rr: drvn 1/2-way: r.o fnl f: wnt 2nd nr fin* **8/1**

0005 3 3/4 **Night Trade (IRE)**[17] 4431 7-9-7 **53** ........(p) SteveDrowne 9 54
(Ronald Harris) *towards rr: hdwy 1/2-way: rdn 2f out: chsd wnr 1f out: no imp: lost 2nd nr fin* **8/1**

0-00 4 1/2 **Almax**[56] 3074 3-9-0 **55** ........ CamHardie(5) 5 53
(Michael Bell) *s.s: in rr: rdn and hdwy over 2f out: r.o u.p fnl f* **7/1**

00 **5** *1 ¼* **First Rebellion**[8] 4733 5-9-6 **52**.................................. DavidProbert 3 48
(Tony Carroll) *prom: chsd wnr 1/2-way: rdn 2f out: lost 2nd 1f out: fdd* **12/1**

-044 **6** *¾* **Angels Calling**[67] 2726 4-8-13 **52**.................................. PeterSword(7) 1 45
(K R Burke) *s.i.s: sn chsd ldrs on outer: drvn over 1f out: one pce* **9/2**[1]

4130 **7** *3 ½* **Bajan Story**[3] 4908 5-9-4 **50**.................................. FergusSweeney 4 33
(Michael Blanshard) *in tch: rdn over 3f out: wknd fnl f* **5/1**[2]

6043 **8** *2* **Lucky Clover**[32] 3938 3-8-12 **48**.................................. RichardKingscote 8 24
(Malcolm Saunders) *led 1f: styd prom: rdn over 2f out: wknd over 1f out* **6/1**[3]

-000 **9** *nk* **Hares Grove (IRE)**[12] 4567 5-8-10 **45**.................................. DeclanBates(3) 7 21
(Richard Price) *mid-div: rdn 1/2-way: wknd over 1f out* **66/1**

4223 **10** *1* **Haadeeth**[4] 4848 7-9-10 **56**..................................(vt) AndreaAtzeni 10 29
(David Evans) *racd keenly: prom: chsd wnr after 2f to 1/2-way: sn rdn and wknd* **5/1**[2]

1m 12.1s (2.10) **Going Correction** +0.35s/f (Good)
**WFA** 3 from 4yo+ 4lb **10** Ran SP% **117.4**
Speed ratings (Par 101): **100,95,94,94,92 91,86,84,83,82**
CSF £105.03 CT £838.77 TOTE £17.90: £3.80, £2.10, £2.70; EX 92.70 Trifecta £912.40.
**Owner** David Prosser & Keith Warrington **Bred** David Prosser & Keith Warrington **Trained** Kinnersley, Worcs

**FOCUS**
A moderate sprint handicap and it was noticeable that the first three home all raced closer to the stands' side of the track. The winner is in foal.

## 5001 32RED CASINO H'CAP — 1m 6f (R)
**3:00** (3:00) (Class 6) (0-60,60) 4-Y-O+ **£1,940** (£577; £288; £144) **Stalls** Low

Form RPR

6434 **1** **Grayswood**[27] 4093 4-9-7 **60**..................................(p) MartinDwyer 2 69
(William Muir) *hld up towards rr: clsd over 3f out: rdn over 2f out: r.o u.p to ld fnl 50yds* **5/1**[3]

6222 **2** *nk* **Rowlestone Lass**[15] 4492 4-8-10 **52**.................................. DeclanBates(3) 9 60
(Richard Price) *mid-div: stdy hdwy 4f out: led gng wl over 1f out: sn rdn and wandered: hdd fnl 50yds* **9/2**[2]

-501 **3** *½* **Sweeping Rock (IRE)**[21] 4279 4-9-4 **60**..................................(t) MichaelJMMurphy(3) 8 67
(Marcus Tregoning) *t.k.h early: chsd ldrs: drvn 3f out: hmpd 2f out: styd on fnl f* **9/2**[2]

0500 **4** *2* **Medburn Cutler**[35] 3824 4-8-8 **47**..................................(p) RenatoSouza 4 51
(Paul Henderson) *towards rr: rdn and hdwy 3f out: sn began to hang lft: styd on fnl f* **20/1**

/540 **5** *½* **Just Duchess**[26] 4107 4-8-5 **47** oh1 ow1.................. ThomasBrown(3) 10 50
(Michael Blanshard) *chsd ldrs: effrt 4f out: rdn to ld over 2f out: hdd over 1f out: fdd fnl f* **14/1**

00-4 **6** *5* **Jawinski (IRE)**[36] 3778 4-8-8 **47**.................................. DavidProbert 3 43
(David Evans) *trckd ldrs tl led 6f out: rdn 3f out: sn hdd: wknd over 1f out* **10/1**

6025 **7** *1* **Illegale (IRE)**[22] 4264 8-8-11 **50**..................................(bt) LukeMorris 6 45
(Nikki Evans) *mid-div: rdn 3f out: wknd 2f out* **25/1**

013 **8** *1 ¼* **Poste Restante**[19] 4343 4-8-6 **52**.................................. LewisWalsh(7) 5 45
(David Simcock) *hld up: rdn 4f out: no real imp: wknd over 1f out* **7/2**[1]

0/52 **9** *4 ½* **Surprise Us**[25] 4149 7-8-2 **46**..................................(p) TimClark(5) 1 33
(Mark Gillard) *led to 6f out: styd prom tl drvn and wknd over 3f out* **8/1**

420 **10** *30* **Innoko (FR)**[34] 3852 4-9-7 **60**..................................(t) WilliamTwiston-Davies 7
(Tony Carroll) *hld up in rr: rdn 4f out: wknd over 2f out: t.o* **20/1**

3m 13.87s (10.07) **Going Correction** +0.35s/f (Good) **10** Ran SP% **115.5**
Speed ratings (Par 101): **85,84,84,83,83 80,79,78,76,59**
CSF £26.62 CT £108.41 TOTE £4.30: £1.70, £1.90, £2.20; EX 24.40 Trifecta £133.50.
**Owner** C L A Edginton **Bred** Car Colston Hall Stud **Trained** Lambourn, Berks
■ Stewards' Enquiry : Declan Bates one-day ban; careless riding (19th Aug)

**FOCUS**
A modest staying handicap and there wasn't much pace on until after turning in. The winner's best figures had come on the AW, so this was in line with his turf best. The runner-up travelled bit better but tired late on.

## 5002 BARRY WALTERS CATERING H'CAP — 1m 2f (R)
**3:30** (3:30) (Class 5) (0-75,72) 3-Y-O+ **£2,587** (£770; £384; £192) **Stalls** Low

Form RPR

4602 **1** **Golden Jubilee (USA)**[40] 3617 5-9-6 **64**......(v) WilliamTwiston-Davies 3 74
(Nigel Twiston-Davies) *mde all: drvn 3f out: styd on strly: hld on wl towards fin* **11/1**

-453 **2** *½* **Scoppio Del Carro**[13] 4540 3-9-0 **67**..................................(t) DavidProbert 2 76
(Andrew Balding) *wnt lft s: hld up in last: rdn and hdwy over 3f out: chsd wnr ins fnl f: clsng towards fin* **5/2**[2]

6422 **3** *1 ¼* **Light Of Asia (IRE)**[48] 3360 3-9-3 **70**.................................. RichardKingscote 4 77
(Ed Dunlop) *hld up in 4th: hdwy over 3f out: chsd wnr over 2f out: one pce u.p and lost 2nd ins fnl f* **6/4**[1]

60-2 **4** *11* **Miss Blakeney**[41] 3585 5-9-12 **70**..................................(vt) MartinDwyer 1 56
(Marcus Tregoning) *bmpd s: racd in 3rd: effrt and briefly chsd wnr 3f out: wknd wl over 1f out* **9/2**[3]

1130 **5** *4 ½* **Gabrial The Duke (IRE)**[16] 4470 4-10-0 **72**.................................. LukeMorris 5 49
(David Simcock) *trckd wnr: rdn along over 5f out: lost 2nd 3f out: wknd 2f out* **8/1**

2m 14.55s (5.15) **Going Correction** +0.35s/f (Good)
**WFA** 3 from 4yo+ 9lb **5** Ran SP% **106.2**
Speed ratings (Par 103): **93,92,91,82,79**
CSF £35.49 TOTE £8.00: £3.70, £1.90; EX 32.00 Trifecta £74.40.
**Owner** Mrs J K Powell **Bred** Dixiana Farms Llc **Trained** Naunton, Gloucs

**FOCUS**
Just the five runners in this ordinary handicap, which became tactical. The winner had an easy lead and is now 2-2 over CD.

## 5003 EBF STALLIONS BREEDING WINNERS FILLIES' H'CAP — 1m 4f (R)
**4:00** (4:00) (Class 4) (0-85,85) 3-Y-O+ **£6,469** (£1,925; £962; £481) **Stalls** Low

Form RPR

0402 **1** **Artistic Muse (IRE)**[12] 4574 3-8-2 **70**.................................. RoystonFfrench 4 81
(B W Hills) *hld up in rr: niggled along over 5f out: hdwy on outer 3f out: sn hung lft: led over 1f out: drvn out* **20/1**

4122 **2** *2 ¼* **Reesha**[32] 3918 3-9-3 **85**.................................. AndreaAtzeni 5 92
(Roger Varian) *trckd ldrs: briefly wnt 2nd over 3f out: swtchd rt over 1f out: chsd wnr ins fnl f: styd on but a being hld* **9/4**[2]

-452 **3** *2 ¼* **By Jupiter**[27] 4081 3-7-13 **72**.................................. CamHardie(5) 6 75
(Michael Bell) *led: drvn over 2f out: hdd over 1f out: one pce and lost 2nd ins fnl f* **7/1**

-543 **4** *1 ½* **Micras**[39] 3655 3-8-8 **76**.................................. DavidProbert 1 77
(Andrew Balding) *trckd ldr 2f: styd prom: rdn over 3f out: kpt on same pce* **10/1**

356 **5** *6* **Astra Hall**[26] 4113 5-9-11 **82**.................................. RichardKingscote 2 73
(Ralph Beckett) *s.i.s: in rr: effrt and clsd 3f out: sn one pce: wknd fnl f* **9/2**[3]

-213 **6** *32* **Swan Lakes (IRE)**[25] 4145 3-8-10 **78**.................................. FergusSweeney 3 18
(David Simcock) *prom: trckd ldr after 2f tl over 3f out: wknd qckly: t.o* **7/4**[1]

2m 40.15s (2.75) **Going Correction** +0.35s/f (Good)
**WFA** 3 from 5yo 11lb **6** Ran SP% **111.7**
Speed ratings (Par 102): **104,102,101,100,96 74**
CSF £64.27 TOTE £17.10: £5.80, £1.80; EX 62.60 Trifecta £446.00.
**Owner** Miss Emily Asprey & Christopher Wright **Bred** Tullamaine Castle Stud **Trained** Upper Lambourn, Berks

**FOCUS**
The best race on the card, run at an even gallop, but another surprising winner with the complete outsider of the sextet coming out on top. The favourite ran poorly, and was beaten 2f out.

## 5004 £10 FREE BET AT 32RED.COM H'CAP — 1m (R)
**4:30** (4:30) (Class 5) (0-75,75) 3-Y-O **£2,587** (£770; £384; £192) **Stalls** Low

Form RPR

3466 **1** **Shimba Hills**[10] 4671 3-8-13 **70**.................................. CharlesBishop(3) 3 77
(Mick Channon) *mde all: styd hrd on ins rail st: qcknd 3f out: edgd rt 2f out: drvn out* **6/1**[3]

2360 **2** *1 ¼* **Tullia (IRE)**[22] 4271 3-9-7 **75**.................................. AndreaAtzeni 1 79
(William Knight) *trckd ldrs: chsd wnr over 2f out: kpt on u.p: nvr quite able to chal* **7/2**[2]

3-04 **3** *1 ¼* **Ghosting (IRE)**[18] 4393 3-9-6 **74**..................................(t) RichardKingscote 4 75
(Tom Dascombe) *hld up: effrt on outer 3f out: sn edgd lft: styd on to go 3rd last strides* **6/1**[3]

2266 **4** *nse* **Distant High**[5] 4817 3-8-5 **62**.................................. DeclanBates(3) 5 63
(Richard Price) *mid-div: rdn unable qck over 2f out: rdr dropped hands ins fnl f: r.o nr fin: tk 4th post* **8/1**

06-3 **5** *shd* **Purple Lane (IRE)**[17] 4446 3-9-1 **69**.................................. FergusSweeney 7 70
(David Simcock) *s.s: in rr: hdwy 3f out: sn swtchd lft and chsd ldrs: unable qck: lost 2 pls last strides* **9/4**[1]

-323 **6** *nk* **On Demand**[132] 1112 3-9-1 **69**.................................. DavidProbert 2 69
(Andrew Balding) *mid-div: drvn 3f out: styd on same pce fnl 2f* **8/1**

210- **7** *8* **Sweet P**[263] 7892 3-8-13 **67**.................................. MartinDwyer 6 49
(Marcus Tregoning) *t.k.h: trckd wnr: pushed along 3f out: sn lost 2nd: grad wknd* **10/1**

1m 44.25s (3.25) **Going Correction** +0.35s/f (Good) **7** Ran SP% **112.9**
Speed ratings (Par 100): **97,95,94,94,94 94,86**
CSF £26.46 TOTE £8.20: £4.10, £2.10; EX 30.00 Trifecta £79.20.
**Owner** Dave and Gill Hedley **Bred** G Hedley & Mike Channon Bloodstock Limited **Trained** West Ilsley, Berks
■ Stewards' Enquiry : Declan Bates seven-day ban; failing to ride out (20th-26th Aug)

**FOCUS**
A modest handicap and another all-the-way winner, who was down in grade and in the weights. He probably ran to his best. The runner-up ran closer to her spring form in easy ground.

## 5005 32RED.COM H'CAP — 1m (R)
**5:00** (5:03) (Class 6) (0-55,54) 3-Y-O+ **£1,940** (£577; £288; £144) **Stalls** Low

Form RPR

3525 **1** **Appyjack**[6] 4798 6-9-0 **52**.................................. CamHardie(5) 13 63
(Tony Carroll) *dropped in last fr wd draw: gd hdwy on outer 3f out: chsd ldr over 1f out: led ins fnl f: rdn out* **6/1**[3]

60-5 **2** *1* **Flipping**[36] 3781 7-9-1 **48**.................................. WilliamTwiston-Davies 15 57
(Stuart Kittow) *towards rr: hdwy over 4f out: led 2f out tl ins fnl f: no ex* **8/1**

000- **3** *1 ¼* **Jay Kay**[377] 4621 5-8-9 **46** oh1..............................[1] MichaelJMMurphy(3) 6 51
(K R Burke) *chsd ldrs: n.m.r over 2f out: sn swtchd rt: one pce after* **8/1**

0232 **4** *1 ¼* **Greyemkay**[18] 4415 6-8-9 **47**.................................. DanielMuscutt(5) 8 50
(Richard Price) *mid-div: hdwy 4f out: rdn 2f out: kpt on same pce* **5/2**[1]

-005 **5** *7* **Cameley Dawn**[43] 3518 3-9-0 **54**.................................. RichardKingscote 5 40
(Malcolm Saunders) *chsd ldrs: rdn over 3f out: sltly hmpd over 2f out: styd on same pce after* **16/1**

-060 **6** *½* **Pacific Trip**[8] 4733 3-8-12 **52**..................................(v) DavidProbert 2 37
(Andrew Balding) *hld up in rr: sme hdwy 3f out: styd on same pce fnl 2f* **33/1**

5-60 **7** *3* **Rapunzal**[85] 2221 3-9-0 **54**.................................. FergusSweeney 10 32
(Henry Candy) *chsd ldrs tl n.m.r and shuffled bk bnd after 2f: rdn 3f out: no real imp* **6/1**[3]

6644 **8** *2 ¼* **Stoneham**[12] 4562 3-8-9 **52**..................................(v[1]) CharlesBishop(3) 9 25
(Mick Channon) *led to 2f out: sn rdn and one pce* **6/1**[3]

0065 **9** *2 ¾* **The Name Is Frank**[28] 4046 9-8-9 **45**..................................(bt) DeclanBates(3) 1 13
(Mark Gillard) *chsd ldr tl over 3f out: wknd over 2f out* **25/1**

0-03 **10** *2* **Alba Verde**[12] 4562 3-8-5 **48** oh3.................................. LukeMorris 11 7
(Sir Mark Prescott Bt) *prom: chsd ldr over 3f out tl over 2f out: drvn and sn wknd* **5/1**[2]

0005 **11** *2 ¾* **Cadmium**[12] 4562 3-8-10 **50**..................................(p) SamHitchcott 3 6
(Harry Dunlop) *mid-div tl n.m.r and dropped to rr bnd after 2f: effrt 3f out: wknd 2f out* **50/1**

00/0 **12** *9* **Rockinit (IRE)**[36] 3781 8-8-13 **53**.................................. SeanBowen(7) 7
(Peter Bowen) *mid-div tl rdn and wknd over 3f out* **50/1**

00-0 **13** *5* **Saxony**[12] 4564 3-7-12 **50** oh5.................................. BradleyBosley(7) 12
(Paul Morgan) *mid-div: rdn 4f out: wknd 2f out* **66/1**

1m 42.4s (1.40) **Going Correction** +0.35s/f (Good)
**WFA** 3 from 5yo+ 7lb **13** Ran SP% **128.4**
Speed ratings (Par 101): **107,106,104,103,96 96,93,90,88,86 83,74,69**
CSF £55.86 CT £417.30 TOTE £9.00: £2.60, £2.80, £3.00; EX 57.60 Trifecta £893.50.
**Owner** Mayden Stud **Bred** Mayden Stud, J A And D S Dewhurst **Trained** Cropthorne, Worcs

**FOCUS**
Big on numbers but short on quality in this moderate handicap. The pace was honest, though, and first four pulled well clear, with the winner coming from last.

T/Plt: £1,901.10 to a £1 stake. Pool: £60,028.14 - 23.50 winning tickets. T/Qpdt: £39.80 to a £1 stake. Pool: £7,507.19 - 139.46 winning tickets. RL

# 4965 KEMPTON (A.W) (R-H)

Tuesday, August 5

**OFFICIAL GOING: Standard**

Wind: virtually nil Weather: overcast, dry

## 5006 KEMPTON LIVE WITH DIZZEE RASCAL 06.09.14 CLASSIFIED STKS 1m (P)

**6:00** (6:00) (Class 6) 3-Y-O+ **£1,940** (£577; £288; £144) **Stalls** Low

| Form | | | | RPR |
|---|---|---|---|---|
| 0032 | 1 | | **Ajig**[6] 4789 3-8-11 65 JohnFahy 8 (Eve Johnson Houghton) *s.i.s and rdn along early: in rr: drvn wl over 2f out: hdwy 2f out: led fnl 150yds: r.o wl: eased cl home* **5/1**[2] | 71 |
| 2023 | 2 | 1 ½ | **Two In The Pink (IRE)**[27] 4072 4-9-4 62 AdamKirby 5 (Ralph J Smith) *hld up in tch in midfield: swtchd rt and hdwy 2f out: drvn to ld over 1f out: hdd fnl 150yds: one pce* **8/1** | 68 |
| 2342 | 3 | 2 ½ | **Plucky Dip**[27] 4074 3-8-11 62 WilliamBuick 7 (John Ryan) *in tch in midfield: rdn and effrt 2f out: pressed ldrs and drvn over 1f out: outpcd fnl 150yds* **11/8**[1] | 61 |
| -236 | 4 | nk | **Stybba**[40] 3603 3-8-11 62 (p) JamieSpencer 11 (Andrew Balding) *chsd ldrs: wnt 2nd 5f out tl rdn to ld ent fnl 2f: hdd over 1f out: outpcd fnl f* **15/2**[3] | 60 |
| 5400 | 5 | 4 ½ | **Rouge Nuage (IRE)**[11] 4613 4-9-4 65 (p) RichardHughes 3 (Conrad Allen) *t.k.h: hld up in rr: effrt and hung rt 2f out: styd on past btn horses fnl f: nvr trbld ldrs* **15/2**[3] | 51 |
| 005 | 6 | hd | **Classic Mission**[42] 3559 3-8-11 61 (p) ShaneKelly 1 (Jonathan Portman) *hld up in tch in midfield: rdn ent fnl 2f: sn outpcd and btn over 1f out: wknd fnl f* **33/1** | 49 |
| 5-00 | 7 | nk | **Calrissian (IRE)**[70] 2647 3-8-11 65 JimCrowley 4 (Timothy Jarvis) *chsd ldrs: lost pl u.p over 2f out: wl hld over 1f out* **20/1** | 49 |
| -000 | 8 | 2 ½ | **Fiftyshadesdarker (IRE)**[12] 4579 3-8-11 62 (tp) PatCosgrave 9 (George Baker) *led tl rdn and hdd ent fnl 2f: wknd u.p over 1f out* **40/1** | 43 |
| 04-6 | 9 | 2 ¼ | **Marishi Ten (IRE)**[108] 853 4-9-4 63 RobertHavlin 10 (Jo Davis) *stdd s: t.k.h: hld up in rr: hdwy on outer to chse ldrs 5f out: rdn and btn over 2f out: sn wknd* **40/1** | 39 |
| -600 | 10 | 14 | **Severn Crossing**[10] 4658 3-8-11 62 (p) OisinMurphy 2 (William Muir) *w ldr for 3f: rdn and lost pl over 3f out: bhd over 1f out* **14/1** | 5 |

1m 39.15s (-0.65) **Going Correction** 0.0s/f (Stan)
**WFA** 3 from 4yo 7lb **10** Ran **SP%** **112.7**
Speed ratings (Par 101): **103,101,99,98,94 94,93,91,88,74**
CSF £40.89 TOTE £5.90: £2.00, £2.30, £1.10; EX 30.60 Trifecta £79.60.
**Owner** Eden Racing Club **Bred** Southcourt Stud **Trained** Blewbury, Oxon

**FOCUS**

These low-60s types were well matched, so it was a competitive race. The early pace was good but slackened after 2f, and the winner had been running well in handicaps.

## 5007 BETVICTOR.COM MAIDEN FILLIES' STKS 1m (P)

**6:30** (6:32) (Class 5) 3-Y-O+ **£2,587** (£770; £384; £192) **Stalls** Low

| Form | | | | RPR |
|---|---|---|---|---|
| 2 | 1 | | **Momayyaz (IRE)**[18] 4407 3-8-7 0 AhmadAlSubousi(7) 4 (Saeed bin Suroor) *chsd ldrs: rdn and outpcd wl over 1f out: swtchd lft and wnt 3rd 1f out: reminder and qcknd ins fnl f: led fnl 75yds: gng away at fin* **4/1**[2] | 85+ |
| 34 | 2 | 1 ½ | **Moonvoy**[78] 2389 3-9-0 0 RichardHughes 12 (Jeremy Noseda) *chsd ldrs: rdn to chal 2f out: led over 1f out but hrd pressed: hdd fnl 75yds: no ex* **9/4**[1] | 80 |
| | 3 | ¾ | **Emirates Joy (USA)** 3-9-0 0 WilliamBuick 13 (Charlie Appleby) *chsd ldrs: rdn and effrt to chal over 1f out: ev ch tl no ex fnl 75yds* **6/1** | 78 |
| 42 | 4 | 7 | **Inflection (IRE)**[12] 4569 3-8-9 0 (t) NoelGarbutt(5) 7 (Hugo Palmer) *chsd ldrs: rdn ent fnl 2f: outpcd and btn over 1f out: plugged on to go modest 4th ins fnl f* **11/2**[3] | 62 |
| 46 | 5 | ¾ | **French Flirt**[18] 4393 3-9-0 0 JimCrowley 6 (Timothy Jarvis) *led: hung rt and hdd over 1f out: sn btn: wknd fnl f* **33/1** | 60 |
| 3 | 6 | 2 | **Lady Bingo (IRE)**[14] 4513 3-9-0 0 JamieSpencer 2 (Sir Mark Prescott Bt) *in tch in midfield: 6th and outpcd over 2f out: n.d after* **9/1** | 56 |
| | 7 | nk | **Perfect Rhythm** 3-9-0 0 LiamKeniry 8 (Patrick Chamings) *pushed along leaving stalls: hld up towards rr and t.k.h after 1f: switching lft and rdn over 2f out: sn outpcd and wl btn* **100/1** | 55 |
| 3/ | 8 | hd | **Precinct**[640] 7553 4-9-7 0 MartinLane 9 (James Eustace) *v.s.a: bhd: shkn up ent fnl 2f: no ch but kpt on past btn horses fr over 1f out* **20/1** | 56 |
| 03 | 9 | nk | **Executrix**[35] 3822 3-9-0 0 ShaneKelly 1 (Sir Michael Stoute) *t.k.h: hld up in tch: rdn and outpcd jst over 2f out: no ch over 1f out* **25/1** | 54 |
| | 10 | ½ | **Jethou Island** 3-9-0 0 HayleyTurner 10 (Henry Candy) *t.k.h: hld up in tch in midfield: rdn over 2f out: sn outpcd and wl btn over 1f out* **40/1** | 53 |
| | 11 | 3 | **Keeper's Ring (USA)** 3-9-0 0 FrederikTylicki 11 (Roger Varian) *in tch in midfield on outer: rdn and struggling over 2f out: bhd fnl 2f* **16/1** | 46 |
| | 12 | 3 ¾ | **Lostintheclouds** 3-9-0 0 PatDobbs 14 (Mike Murphy) *s.i.s: a bhd* **66/1** | 37 |
| 0- | 13 | 16 | **Cape Castle (IRE)**[276] 7693 3-9-0 0 SilvestreDeSousa 5 (Clive Brittain) *in tch in midfield: rdn and losing pl 1/2-way: bhd over 2f out: t.o* **50/1** | |
| | 14 | 12 | **Touig** 3-9-0 0 JimmyQuinn 3 (Stuart Howe) *s.i.s: rn green and a bhd: t.o fnl 2f* **100/1** | |

1m 40.21s (0.41) **Going Correction** 0.0s/f (Stan)
**WFA** 3 from 4yo 7lb **14** Ran **SP%** **115.7**
Speed ratings (Par 100): **97,95,94,87,87 85,84,84,84,83 80,76,60,48**
CSF £11.90 TOTE £5.50: £1.60, £1.30, £2.30; EX 13.60 Trifecta £48.80.
**Owner** Godolphin **Bred** Darley **Trained** Newmarket, Suffolk

**FOCUS**

There should be a number of future winners in this solidly run maiden, although those outside the first three are probably waiting for handicaps. That said, it was the slowest of the three CD races on the night. The runner-up set a decent standard considering her Wood Ditton effort.

## 5008 FOLLOW @BETVICTORRACING ON TWITTER H'CAP 1m (P)

**7:00** (7:01) (Class 5) (0-75,75) 3-Y-O **£2,587** (£770; £384; £192) **Stalls** Low

| Form | | | | RPR |
|---|---|---|---|---|
| 4-13 | 1 | | **Si Senor (IRE)**[91] 2058 3-9-1 69 OisinMurphy 8 (Ed Vaughan) *hld up in tch in midfield: effrt on inner 2f out: qcknd to ld over 1f out: sn clr: easily* **4/1**[2] | 87+ |
| 6-36 | 2 | 5 | **Swordbearer**[26] 4130 3-9-2 70 FrederikTylicki 10 (James Fanshawe) *stdd s: hld up in tch in last trio: swtchd lft and effrt over 2f out: hdwy over 1f out: styd on to go 2nd ins fnl f: no ch w ldrs* **9/1** | 76 |
| 634 | 3 | 1 | **Venturous Spirit (IRE)**[17] 4446 3-9-4 72 WilliamBuick 9 (John Gosden) *stdd s: hld up in tch in last trio: rdn and effrt 2f out: styd on ins fnl f: wnt 3rd towards fin: no ch w wnr* **13/2** | 76 |
| -060 | 4 | 1 | **Ligeia**[17] 4436 3-9-7 75 (p) RichardHughes 2 (Richard Hannon) *sn led: rdn ent fnl 2f: hdd over 1f out: sn brushed aside by wnr: plugged on: lost 2 pls ins fnl f* **10/1** | 76 |
| 6332 | 5 | nse | **Surety (IRE)**[10] 4671 3-9-7 75 SilvestreDeSousa 4 (Clive Brittain) *chsd ldr: rdn over 2f out: 3rd and outpcd u.p over 1f out: plugged on: lost 2 pls ins fnl f* **5/1**[3] | 76 |
| 0401 | 6 | 4 | **Inspector Norse**[19] 4356 3-9-3 71 LiamKeniry 7 (Sylvester Kirk) *t.k.h: chsd ldrs on outer: rdn and no rspnse jst over 2f out: wknd over 1f out* **12/1** | 63 |
| 5535 | 7 | 1 ½ | **Best Kept**[20] 4332 3-9-6 74 (tp) PatDobbs 1 (Amanda Perrett) *chsd ldrs on inner: rdn and no rspnse jst over 2f out: sn btn* **5/2**[1] | 63 |
| 5032 | 8 | 9 | **Chess Valley**[19] 4365 3-8-12 66 ChrisCatlin 6 (Willie Musson) *stdd s: hld up in rr: lost tch 2f out* **40/1** | 34 |
| 0004 | 9 | 6 | **Applejack Lad**[4] 4868 3-9-0 68 (tp) AdamKirby 5 (John Ryan) *led early: sn hdd and chsd ldrs after: rdn and lost pl qckly over 2f out: bhd over 1f out* **16/1** | 22 |

1m 38.8s (-1.00) **Going Correction** 0.0s/f (Stan) **9** Ran **SP%** **113.7**
Speed ratings (Par 100): **105,100,99,98,97 93,92,83,77**
CSF £38.98 CT £193.95 TOTE £4.60: £1.50, £3.00, £1.80; EX 40.30 Trifecta £248.80.
**Owner** A E Oppenheimer **Bred** Hascombe And Valiant Studs **Trained** Newmarket, Suffolk

**FOCUS**

This was the fastest of the three CD races on the night. The winner did well to win this middling handicap so impressively off just a medium gallop. The first three home were in the last four early.

## 5009 BRITISH STALLION STUDS EBF MAIDEN STKS (BOBIS RACE) 7f (P)

**7:30** (7:30) (Class 4) 2-Y-O **£4,075** (£1,212; £606; £303) **Stalls** Low

| Form | | | | RPR |
|---|---|---|---|---|
| 0 | 1 | | **Bow And Arrow**[21] 4301 2-9-5 0 AdamKirby 4 (Charlie Appleby) *in tch in midfield: swtchd lft and effrt 2f out: str run to ld 1f out: drew clr fnl f: readily* **12/1** | 82+ |
| 0 | 2 | 3 ¼ | **Dutch Portrait**[81] 2298 2-9-5 0 SilvestreDeSousa 12 (Paul Cole) *chsd ldrs: rdn over 2f out: drvn over 1f out: wnt 2nd ins fnl f: styd on but no ch w wnr* **20/1** | 73 |
| 00 | 3 | 2 ¼ | **Ghalib (IRE)**[29] 4025 2-9-5 0 MartinHarley 7 (Marco Botti) *chsd ldrs: drvn and ev ch over 1f out: 3rd and outpcd fnl f* **6/1**[3] | 67 |
| | 4 | 1 | **Equitanus (IRE)** 2-9-5 0 JimCrowley 1 (Andrew Balding) *hld up wl in tch in midfield: effrt on inner 2f out: no imp over 1f out: wnt 4th ins fnl f* **11/4**[1] | 64+ |
| | 5 | ¾ | **Mecado (IRE)** 2-9-5 0 RichardHughes 2 (Richard Hannon) *led: pushed along ent fnl 2f: hdd 1f out: sn outpcd: wknd and lost 4th ins fnl f* **10/1** | 62 |
| | 6 | 4 | **Muntadab (IRE)** 2-9-5 0 ShaneKelly 11 (Sir Michael Stoute) *t.k.h: hld up in tch in midfield: shkn up jst over 2f out: sn outpcd and btn* **9/1** | 52 |
| 55 | 7 | 2 ½ | **New Brunswick (GER)**[17] 4429 2-9-5 0 WilliamBuick 3 (John Gosden) *t.k.h: w ldr: rdn ent fnl 2f: ev ch tl btn over 1f out: fdd fnl f* **3/1**[2] | 45 |
| | 8 | ¾ | **Directional** 2-9-5 0 MartinLane 10 (Charlie Appleby) *s.i.s: rdn along in last trio: bhd 2f out* **9/1** | 43 |
| | 9 | 2 ½ | **Light Breaks (IRE)** 2-9-5 0 ChrisCatlin 8 (Sir Mark Prescott Bt) *sn dropped to rr and rn green: rdn along thrght: lost tch 2f out* **25/1** | 36 |
| | 10 | 2 ¼ | **Devilution (IRE)** 2-9-5 0 FrannyNorton 6 (Derek Shaw) *wnt sharply rt s: t.k.h and sn in midfield: rdn and dropped out over 2f out: sn bhd* **50/1** | 30+ |
| 600 | 11 | 2 ½ | **Pyrocumulus (IRE)**[17] 4429 2-8-12 0 JoshuaBrowning(7) 5 (Jo Hughes) *hmpd s: a bhd* **100/1** | 23+ |

1m 26.74s (0.74) **Going Correction** 0.0s/f (Stan) **11** Ran **SP%** **114.3**
Speed ratings (Par 96): **95,91,88,87,86 82,79,78,75,73 70**
CSF £224.31 TOTE £12.50: £3.70, £7.20, £2.90; EX 263.70 Trifecta £1194.30.
**Owner** Godolphin **Bred** Darley **Trained** Newmarket, Suffolk

**FOCUS**

Run at a fair pace, this maiden contained some expensive and good-looking juveniles, so they should improve on what they have achieved so far.

## 5010 DOWNLOAD THE BETVICTOR INSTABET APP MEDIAN AUCTION MAIDEN STKS 1m 3f (P)

**8:00** (8:01) (Class 6) 3-5-Y-O **£1,940** (£577; £288; £144) **Stalls** Low

| Form | | | | RPR |
|---|---|---|---|---|
| 3 | 1 | | **Elbereth**[34] 3856 3-8-12 0 OisinMurphy 8 (Andrew Balding) *chsd ldrs: upsides ldr 3f out: rdn over 2f out: led over 1f out: r.o wl and drew clr fnl f* **5/2**[2] | 78 |
| 3302 | 2 | 2 ¼ | **Invasor Luck (USA)**[28] 4051 3-9-3 80 TomQueally 4 (James Fanshawe) *led: jnd 3f out: rdn: unable qck and hdd over 1f out: one pce fnl f* **4/5**[1] | 79 |
| 050 | 3 | 2 ½ | **Sir Rosco**[36] 3804 3-9-3 72 ShaneKelly 9 (Sir Michael Stoute) *in tch in midfield: effrt and wnt 3rd jst over 2f out: sn outpcd: pushed along and no imp after* **7/1**[3] | 75 |
| 5 | 4 | 2 ½ | **Roxy Hart**[40] 3631 3-8-12 0 JimmyQuinn 2 (Ed Vaughan) *stdd s: hld up in last pair: shkn up and hdwy jst over 2f out: wnt modest 4th over 1f out: styd on but no threat to ldrs* **20/1** | 66 |
| 05 | 5 | 6 | **Perfect Outcome**[22] 4265 3-8-12 0 LiamKeniry 7 (Patrick Chamings) *chsd ldng pair tl 4th and btn jst over 2f out: wknd over 1f out* **33/1** | 56 |
| 4 | 6 | 5 | **Numrood**[22] 4265 3-9-3 0 FrederikTylicki 1 (George Peckham) *in tch in midfield: rdn 1/2-way: wknd u.p over 2f out: sn bhd* **10/1** | 52 |

7 ½ **Golden Bird (IRE)** 3-9-3 0 ChrisCatlin 5 51
(Dean Ivory) *wnt lft s and s.i.s: hld up in last pair: rdn over 2f out: sn bhd* **50/1**

8 6 **Lady Sorento** 3-8-12 0 StevieDonohoe 6 36
(Tim Pitt) *hmpd s and slowly away: rdn and no rspnse over 2f out: wl bhd over 1f out* **33/1**

2m 22.32s (0.42) **Going Correction** 0.0s/f (Stan) 8 Ran SP% **118.3**
Speed ratings (Par 101): **98,96,94,92,88 84,84,80**
CSF £4.88 TOTE £4.10: £1.10, £1.10, £2.20; EX 5.00 Trifecta £14.20.
**Owner** David Taylor **Bred** David Taylor **Trained** Kingsclere, Hants

**FOCUS**
An ordinary gallop favoured those who raced handily, with the front-runners successfully quickening it up off the home turn. The winner improved from her debut, while the runner-up was a little disappointing.

## 5011 PLAY ROULETTE & BLACKJACK AT BETVICTOR.COM H'CAP 1m 4f (P)
8:30 (8:31) (Class 6) (0-65,65) 3-Y-O+ £1,940 (£577; £288; £144) Stalls Centre

Form RPR

45-0 1 **Ragged Robbin (FR)**[59] 2998 3-8-13 **61** (t) TedDurcan 4 75+
(David Lanigan) *chsd ldr unitl 8f out: chsd ldrs after: rdn to go 2nd again 2f out: led over 1f out: r.o strly and drew clr fnl f: readily* **12/1**

1100 2 4½ **The Ginger Berry**[18] 4402 4-9-10 **64** RobertTart(3) 5 71+
(Dr Jon Scargill) *t.k.h: hld up in tch in midfield: effrt and hung rt over 2f out: swtchd lft and rdn 2f out: hdwy over 1f out: chsd wnr fnl 150yds: no imp* **9/2[2]**

2550 3 1¼ **Citizen Kaine (IRE)**[34] 3850 3-9-1 **63** J-PGuillambert 10 68
(Jo Hughes) *hld up towards rr: hdwy on outer to chse ldrs 6f out: rdn over 3f out: styd on same pce u.p fnl 2f: wnt 3rd ins fnl f* **8/1**

066 4 2 **Nelson Of The Nile**[38] 3712 3-9-1 **63** ShaneKelly 3 65
(Jonathan Portman) *in tch in midfield: rdn over 2f out: drvn and outpcd 2f out: no ch w wnr but kpt on ins fnl f* **8/1**

210 5 1 **Hamble**[42] 3552 5-9-7 **58** PatrickDonaghy 9 58
(Giles Bravery) *t.k.h: hld up in midfield: hdwy to chse ldr 8f out: led over 3f out: rdn and hdd over 1f out: sn outpcd: lost 2nd and wknd ins fnl f* **14/1**

000 6 ½ **Dire Straits (IRE)**[36] 3804 3-8-12 **63** AshleyMorgan(3) 6 62+
(Chris Wall) *chsd ldrs: rdn and lost pl over 3f out: n.d but plugged on fnl f* **3/1[1]**

0440 7 2 **Olymnia**[55] 3120 3-9-0 **62** JimmyQuinn 1 58
(Robert Eddery) *hld up in tch towards rr: effrt on inner 2f out: drvn and no hdwy over 1f out: sn wknd* **20/1**

0-00 8 1½ **Passion Play**[28] 4051 6-9-12 **63**[1] JimCrowley 11 57
(Bill Turner) *led tl rdn and hdd over 3f out: wknd u.p 2f out* **33/1**

0600 9 hd **Ophir**[38] 3711 3-9-1 **63** DougieCostello 12 56
(William Muir) *dropped in bhd after s: hld up in rr: rdn over 2f out: no hdwy* **7/1[3]**

-650 10 4 **Hiorne Tower (FR)**[20] 4333 3-9-3 **65** HayleyTurner 8 52
(John Best) *stdd s: hld up in last pair: rdn over 2f out: no hdwy: bhd over 1f out* **25/1**

6440 11 4 **Zaeem**[157] 801 5-9-13 **64** AdamKirby 7 44
(Dean Ivory) *in tch in midfield: rdn and no rspnse over 2f out: sn btn and bhd* **12/1**

5530 12 17 **Wildomar**[27] 4077 5-9-11 **62** ChrisCatlin 2 15
(Peter Hiatt) *hld up in rr: rdn and c wd 3f out: sn lost tch: t.o* **20/1**

2m 37.48s (2.98) **Going Correction** 0.0s/f (Stan)
**WFA** 3 from 4yo+ 11lb 12 Ran SP% **116.3**
Speed ratings (Par 101): **90,87,86,84,84 83,82,81,81,78 76,64**
CSF £60.75 CT £466.33 TOTE £14.80: £4.00, £1.40, £3.80; EX 63.20 Trifecta £839.30 Part won. Pool: £1,119.19 - 0.50 winning units..
**Owner** Niarchos Family **Bred** Famille Niarchos **Trained** Upper Lambourn, Berks

**FOCUS**
This was a modest handicap run at a muddling pace, but the winner was likely to be better than he showed in previous races. A positive view is taken about the form.

## 5012 DOWNLOAD THE BETVICTOR APP NOW H'CAP (BOBIS RACE) 6f (P)
9:00 (9:00) (Class 4) (0-85,85) 3-Y-O £4,690 (£1,395; £697; £348) Stalls Low

Form RPR

2500 1 **Taquka (IRE)**[11] 4636 3-8-5 **76** PatrickO'Donnell(7) 11 84
(Ralph Beckett) *hld up in last trio: nt clr run 2f out: stl 10th over 1f out: rdn and str run fnl f: to ld cl home* **33/1**

2246 2 ¾ **Drive On (IRE)**[22] 4262 3-9-1 **79** (p) JohnFahy 3 85
(Eve Johnson Houghton) *in tch in midfield: effrt u.p 2f out: chsd cllear wnr jst over 1f out: kpt on* **12/1**

3640 3 ¾ **Meritocracy (IRE)**[9] 4697 3-9-4 **82** MartinLane 7 86
(Paul Cole) *led: rdn and clr over 1f out: drvn and tiring fnl 100yds: hdd and lost 2 pls towards fin* **16/1**

11 4 nk **Sleep Walk**[6] 4788 3-8-7 **71** 6ex MartinHarley 8 74
(Roger Charlton) *t.k.h: hld up in tch in last trio: rdn and effrt wl over 1f out: styd on u.p fnl f: nvr enough pce to chal* **11/10[1]**

0500 5 1 **Dubawi Fun**[20] 4323 3-9-0 **85** AhmadAlSubousi(7) 6 84
(Ismail Mohammed) *chsd ldrs: rdn and unable qck 2f out: rallied and styd on ins fnl f* **50/1**

1-0 6 1¼ **Furas (IRE)**[41] 3577 3-9-6 **84** (b[1]) SilvestreDeSousa 5 79
(Saeed bin Suroor) *in tch in midfield: rdn over 2f out: styd on same pce fr over 1f out* **7/2[2]**

145 7 nse **Willy Brennan (IRE)**[73] 2556 3-9-6 **84** RichardHughes 9 79
(Andrew Balding) *hld up in rr: rdn and effrt jst over 2f out: no prog tl styd on ins fnl f: nvr trbld ldrs* **6/1[3]**

0010 8 ¾ **Nova Champ (IRE)**[10] 4669 3-9-2 **80** (p) JamieSpencer 2 73
(Stuart Williams) *chsd ldr: rdn 2f out: unable qck over 1f out: lost 2nd jst over 1f out: wknd fnl f* **8/1**

1353 9 1¾ **Dynamo Walt (IRE)**[34] 3855 3-8-4 **68** FrannyNorton 1 55
(Derek Shaw) *t.k.h: chsd ldrs: drvn and btn over 1f out: wknd fnl f* **16/1**

1m 12.2s (-0.90) **Going Correction** 0.0s/f (Stan) 9 Ran SP% **119.6**
Speed ratings (Par 102): **106,105,104,103,102 100,100,99,97**
CSF £389.00 CT £6486.26 TOTE £20.10: £6.40, £3.20, £3.40; EX 162.90 Trifecta £1178.10.
**Owner** The Pickford Hill Partnership **Bred** Tally-Ho Stud **Trained** Kimpton, Hants

**FOCUS**
A strong gallop by the third set up a close finish, with one of the finishers just snatching it. The winner was back to his best, and the runner-up ran a small personal best for a yard going well.
T/Jkpt: £63,312.10 to a £1 stake. Pool: £936,306.29 - 10.50 winning tickets. T/Plt: £56.50 to a £1 stake. Pool: £82,553.20 - 1,062 winning tickets. T/Qpdt: £34.00 to a £1 stake. Pool: £5,413.56 - 117.60 winning tickets. SP

# 4973 RIPON (R-H)
Tuesday, August 5

**OFFICIAL GOING: Good (8.2)**
Wind: light 1/2 behind Weather: fine, showers after race 2

## 5013 SILKS AND SADDLES BAR MAIDEN STKS 6f
6:15 (6:17) (Class 5) 2-Y-O £3,234 (£962; £481; £240) Stalls High

Form RPR

3 1 **Toocoolforschool (IRE)**[18] 4409 2-9-5 0 BenCurtis 9 86+
(K R Burke) *mde all: drvn over 1f out: styd on wl ins fnl f* **2/1[1]**

23 2 1¼ **Summer Times**[13] 4527 2-9-5 0 JoeFanning 1 81
(Mark Johnston) *chsd ldrs: 2nd over 1f out: styd on same pce* **5/2[2]**

43 3 5 **Flicka's Boy**[11] 4624 2-9-5 0 BarryMcHugh 7 66
(Tony Coyle) *w wnr: t.k.h: one pce over 1f out* **14/1**

2 4 2½ **Fullon Clarets**[60] 2949 2-9-5 0 TonyHamilton 4 59
(Richard Fahey) *chsd ldrs: swtchd lft to stands' side rail over 3f out: one pce fnl 2f* **11/2[3]**

0 5 7 **A Lovable Rogue**[18] 4382 2-9-5 0 TomEaves 6 38
(Ian Semple) *mid-div: sme hdwy over 2f out: lost pl over 1f out* **80/1**

6 6 1¼ **Aprovado (IRE)**[40] 3620 2-9-5 0 PaulMulrennan 3 34
(Michael Dods) *mid-div: sme hdwy over 2f out: wknd over 1f out* **25/1**

5 7 3¼ **Gideon Jukes**[77] 2428 2-9-2 0 GeorgeChaloner(3) 5 24
(Richard Fahey) *mid-div: sn pushed along: outpcd and lost pl over 4f out: sme hdwy over 2f out: sn wknd* **11/1**

8 6 **Juncart** 2-9-5 0 GrahamLee 8
(Kevin Ryan) *dwlt: in rr and drvn along: bhd fnl 2f* **11/2[3]**

9 15 **Pancake Day** 2-9-5 0 AndrewElliott 2
(Jason Ward) *dwlt and wnt rt s: in rr: sme hdwy on outside over 2f out: sn lost pl and bhd: eased clsng stages* **100/1**

1m 11.37s (-1.63) **Going Correction** -0.275s/f (Firm) 9 Ran SP% **113.7**
Speed ratings (Par 94): **99,97,90,87,78 76,72,64,44**
CSF £6.91 TOTE £4.50: £1.40, £1.30, £2.30; EX 7.80 Trifecta £37.80.
**Owner** Ontoawinner 6, M Hulin, E Burke **Bred** Mark Salmon **Trained** Middleham Moor, N Yorks

**FOCUS**
A dry run up to a meeting at which the rail on the bend from the back straight to the home straight was moved out, adding 7 yards to the distances on the round track. Tom Eaves and Andrew Elliott both called the ground good but Barry McHugh described it as "a little bit quick". A fair maiden in which the first two pulled clear in the closing stages.

## 5014 CONSTANT SECURITY SERVICES NURSERY H'CAP 5f
6:45 (6:46) (Class 5) (0-75,77) 2-Y-O £3,234 (£962; £481; £240) Stalls High

Form RPR

3133 1 **Perardua**[11] 4625 2-9-2 **70** GeorgeChaloner(3) 1 79+
(Richard Fahey) *mde all: styd on strly to forge clr fnl f* **3/1[2]**

045 2 3½ **Classic Flyer**[31] 3947 2-8-9 **63** SamJames(3) 5 59
(David O'Meara) *dwlt: hdwy to chse ldrs over 3f out: 2nd jst ins fnl f: no imp* **5/1**

2160 3 ½ **Mecca's Mirage (IRE)**[19] 4345 2-9-1 **69** ConnorBeasley(3) 6 64
(Michael Dods) *outpcd and lost pl over 3f out: hdwy over 1f out: swtchd rt and styd on ins fnl f* **9/1**

626 4 2¼ **Frank The Barber (IRE)**[10] 4652 2-8-12 **63** GrahamGibbons 4 50
(Steph Hollinshead) *chsd ldrs: fdd fnl f* **14/1**

0161 5 3¾ **Just The Tip (IRE)**[9] 4702 2-9-12 **77** 5ex TomEaves 2 50
(Keith Dalgleish) *dwlt: sn chsing ldrs: wknd over 1f out* **11/4[1]**

034 6 1¼ **Crystal Wish**[14] 4510 2-8-7 **63** (t) KevinStott(5) 3 32
(Kevin Ryan) *chsd ldrs: wknd fnl f* **4/1[3]**

054 7 2 **Ripon Rose**[60] 2949 2-8-9 **60** PaulMulrennan 7 21
(Paul Midgley) *outpcd and in rr: nvr on terms* **9/1**

58.6s (-1.40) **Going Correction** -0.275s/f (Firm) 7 Ran SP% **115.0**
Speed ratings (Par 94): **100,94,93,90,84 82,78**
CSF £18.55 TOTE £3.30: £1.60, £5.30; EX 16.80 Trifecta £140.40.
**Owner** Diamond Racing Ltd **Bred** Diamond Racing Ltd **Trained** Musley Bank, N Yorks

**FOCUS**
A fair nursery in which the gallop was reasonable but once again those up with the pace were favoured. The impressive winner is possibly value for a bit more than the winning margin.

## 5015 WASHROOM COMPANY H'CAP (BOBIS RACE) 1m 1f 170y
7:15 (7:15) (Class 4) (0-80,76) 3-Y-O £4,851 (£1,443; £721; £360) Stalls Low

Form RPR

3411 1 **Truancy (IRE)**[26] 4120 3-9-2 **74** (p) JoeyHaynes(3) 2 84+
(K R Burke) *t.k.h: trckd ldr: led over 6f out: drvn 3f out: over 3 l clr 1f out: lasted home* **13/8[1]**

3-43 2 1 **Stanarley Pic**[84] 2235 3-8-12 **67** BenCurtis 3 73
(Alan Swinbank) *awkward s: hld up in rr: drvn over 4f out: hdwy over 3f out: end over 2f out: styd on fnl f: nt quite trble wnr* **4/1**

1-54 3 4½ **Ryeolliean**[18] 4419 3-9-6 **75** DanielTudhope 1 74
(David O'Meara) *hld up in rr: effrt over 4f out: hdwy over 3f out: 3rd 2f out: kewpt on same pce: eased towards fin* **10/3[3]**

62-1 4 25 **Bold Captain (IRE)**[29] 4022 3-9-7 **76** PhillipMakin 4 22
(John Quinn) *led: hdd over 6f out: drvn over 3f out: wknd 2f out: eased whn bhd ins fnl f: t.o* **11/4[2]**

2m 2.5s (-2.90) **Going Correction** -0.275s/f (Firm) 4 Ran SP% **107.8**
Speed ratings (Par 102): **100,99,95,75**
CSF £8.02 TOTE £2.00; EX 5.80 Trifecta £24.00.
**Owner** Market Avenue Racing Club Ltd **Bred** Keogh Family **Trained** Middleham Moor, N Yorks

**FOCUS**
Not a competitive race for the money but a decent gallop throughout and the winner is value for a bit more than the winning margin.

## 5016 DAVID CHAPMAN MEMORIAL H'CAP 5f
7:45 (7:45) (Class 3) (0-95,92) 3-Y-O- £7,561 (£2,263; £1,131; £566; £282) Stalls High

Form RPR

0021 1 **Silvanus (IRE)**[13] 4531 9-9-10 **90** PaulMulrennan 6 99
(Paul Midgley) *chsd ldrs: led ins fnl f: hld on nr fin* **17/2**

3106 2 hd **Adam's Ale**[18] 4418 5-8-12 **78** GrahamLee 4 86
(Paul Midgley) *chsd ldrs: rdn over 2f out: styd on wl ins fnl f: jst hld* **9/2[2]**

4402 3 ½ **Normal Equilibrium**[18] 4418 4-9-5 **88** (p) ConnorBeasley(3) 2 94
(Robert Cowell) *chsd ldrs: ev ch ins fnl f: no ex* **7/2[1]**

2204 4 ½ **Megaleka**[7] 4762 4-9-0 **85** DannyBrock(5) 10 90
(Alan Bailey) *w ldrs stands' side: led over 2f out: hdd ins fnl f: kpt on same pce* **15/2**

0513 5 1 **Mutafaakir (IRE)**[13] 4531 5-9-2 **82** (b) JamesSullivan 5 83
(Ruth Carr) *led: edgd rt and hdd over 2f out: fdd last 50yds* **8/1**

3605 **6** *1* **Jamaican Bolt (IRE)**[52] 3239 6-9-10 **90**........................ BarryMcHugh 3 87
(Geoffrey Oldroyd) *in rr: hdwy over 1f out: kpt on: nt rch ldrs* **7/1**[3]
4020 **7** *1¼* **Oldjoesaid**[18] 4418 10-8-11 **77**.......................................... PJMcDonald 11 70
(Paul Midgley) *dwlt: in rr: kpt on fnl f: nvr a factor* **25/1**
0241 **8** *shd* **Inxile (IRE)**[7] 4762 9-9-12 **92** 6ex.................................(p) AdrianNicholls 7 85
(David Nicholls) *mid-div: effrt over 2f out: edgd lft over 1f out: nvr trbld ldrs* **8/1**
0101 **9** *1¼* **Captain Dunne (IRE)**[11] 4630 9-8-7 **80**............(p) RachelRichardson(7) 1 68
(Tim Easterby) *wnt rt s: racd alone far side: w ldrs: wknd fnl 75yds* **20/1**
0000 **10** *¾* **Chooseday (IRE)**[28] 4061 5-8-13 **84**........................ ShaneGray(5) 8 69
(Kevin Ryan) *a in rr* **10/1**

57.61s (-2.39) **Going Correction** -0.275s/f (Firm) **10** Ran SP% **115.1**
Speed ratings (Par 107): **108,107,106,106,104 102,100,100,98,97**
CSF £45.98 CT £160.27 TOTE £9.00: £2.60, £2.30, £1.60; EX 53.00 Trifecta £252.10.
**Owner** Colin Alton **Bred** Barronstown Stud And Mrs T Stack **Trained** Westow, N Yorks

**FOCUS**
Mainly exposed sorts in a solid handicap. The gallop was sound and those held up didn't figure. The bulk of the runners raced stands' side.

## 5017 THEAKSTON TERRACE BAR H'CAP — 2m
**8:15** (8:16) (Class 4) (0-85,85) 3-Y-0+ **£4,851** (£1,443; £721; £360) **Stalls** High

Form RPR
6524 **1** **Almagest**[10] 4685 6-10-0 **85**..........................................(p) DanielTudhope 4 93
(David O'Meara) *hld up in rr: t.k.h: effrt over 4f out: nt clr run over 2f out: handy 3rd over 1f out: styd on to ld last strides* **3/1**[1]
1010 **2** *hd* **Sir Frank Morgan (IRE)**[11] 4606 4-9-11 **82**........................ JoeFanning 1 89
(Mark Johnston) *trckd ldr: led over 2f out: edgd rt over 1f out: hdd fnl strides* **4/1**[2]
426 **3** *nk* **Mason Hindmarsh**[21] 4296 7-8-6 **66** oh2................. ConnorBeasley(3) 6 72
(Karen McLintock) *led: hdd over 2f out: rallied and swtchd rt ins fnl f: styd on: no ex clsng stages* **14/1**
2352 **4** *4½* **Deepsand (IRE)**[12] 4575 5-9-5 **76**.......................................(p) DavidAllan 9 77
(Tim Easterby) *hld up in rr: effrt 4f out: one pce fnl 2f* **9/2**[3]
5622 **5** *½* **Dr Irv**[27] 4068 5-9-3 **74**........................................................ GrahamLee 3 74
(Philip Kirby) *trckd ldrs: effrt 3f out: one pce over 1f out* **4/1**[2]
1326 **6** *3* **Rosairlie (IRE)**[21] 4289 6-9-8 **79**........................................ PJMcDonald 2 76
(Micky Hammond) *mid-div: drvn over 3f out: sn chsng ldrs: wknd fnl f* **9/1**
6050 **7** *¾* **Argent Knight**[10] 4685 4-9-13 **84**........................................(v) TomEaves 5 80
(William Jarvis) *s.i.s: reminders after s: sn chsng ldrs: drvn over 3f out: wknd fnl f* **16/1**
3-63 **8** *7* **Perennial**[15] 3192 5-9-10 **81**................................................ PhillipMakin 8 69
(Philip Kirby) *mid-div: hdwy on outer 10f out: chsng ldrs 6f out: drvn over 3f out: wknd over 1f out* **10/1**

3m 30.01s (-1.79) **Going Correction** -0.275s/f (Firm) **8** Ran SP% **114.8**
Speed ratings (Par 105): **93,92,92,90,90 88,88,84**
CSF £15.14 CT £142.64 TOTE £4.40: £1.20, £2.50, £5.30; EX 16.30 Trifecta £269.40.
**Owner** The Marooned Crew **Bred** Juddmonte Farms Ltd **Trained** Nawton, N Yorks

**FOCUS**
Probably just ordinary form and the gallop was on the steady side until passing the 3f marker. The first three finished clear and the winner is better than the bare facts.

## 5018 SIS LIVE MAIDEN STKS — 1m 1f 170y
**8:45** (8:45) (Class 5) 3-4-Y-O **£3,234** (£962; £481; £240) **Stalls** Low

Form RPR
62 **1** **Mount Shamsan**[67] 2733 4-9-12 83........................................ GrahamLee 5 83
(William Haggas) *trckd ldr: chal over 3f out: drvn and narrow advantage over 2f out: forged clr ins fnl f* **1/2**[1]
6 **2** *3* **Classical Duet (USA)**[9] 4705 3-9-3 0................................ JoeFanning 1 77
(Mark Johnston) *sn led: hdd narrowly over 2f out: kpt on same pce appr fnl f* **6/1**[3]
0- **3** *nse* **Magic Music Man**[319] 6581 3-9-3 0................................ PJMcDonald 3 77
(K R Burke) *chsd ldng pair: modest 3rd 2f out: styd on fnl f* **20/1**
566 **4** *3* **Cape Karli (IRE)**[41] 3568 3-8-12 67................................ PaulMulrennan 6 66
(Kevin Ryan) *chsd ldrs: drvn 4f out: kpt on one pce fnl 3f* **14/1**
**5** *½* **Encountering (IRE)** 3-9-3 0.............................................. DanielTudhope 8 70
(James Fanshawe) *in rr: hdwy over 3f out: hung rt: kpt on same pce* **10/1**
42 **6** *31* **Dancin Alpha**[50] 3302 3-9-3 0.............................................. BenCurtis 7 6
(Alan Swinbank) *in rr and sn drvn along: bhd 7f out: t.o* **7/2**[2]
5 **7** *19* **Joyful Star**[30] 3998 4-9-12 0.............................................. JasonHart 2
(Frederick Watson) *dwlt: sn mid-div: lost pl over 3f out: sn bhd: t.o* **66/1**
**8** *55* **Bahama Dancer** 3-8-12 0.............................................. AndrewElliott 4
(Jason Ward) *reluctant leaving paddock and briefly uns rdr: s.i.s: sn bhd: t.o 4f out: eventually completed* **50/1**

2m 4.0s (-1.40) **Going Correction** -0.275s/f (Firm)
**WFA** 3 from 4yo 9lb **8** Ran SP% **127.1**
Speed ratings (Par 103): **94,91,91,89,88 63,48,4**
CSF £5.22 TOTE £1.30: £1.02, £2.40, £7.10; EX 5.30 Trifecta £51.80.
**Owner** Abdulla Al Khalifa **Bred** Sheikh Abdulla Bin Isa Al-Khalifa **Trained** Newmarket, Suffolk

**FOCUS**
An uncompetitive maiden in which the gallop was no more than fair. The time was modest when compared to the earlier handicap. Winner did not need to improve to win, but second and third big improvers from debut.
T/Plt: £33.60 to a £1 stake. Pool: £73,549.67 - 1,596.64 winning tickets. T/Qpdt: £6.90 to a £1 stake. Pool: £5,926.75 - 630.55 winning tickets. WG

5019 - 5023a (Foreign Racing) - See Raceform Interactive

# 3282 CORK (R-H)
Tuesday, August 5

**OFFICIAL GOING: Good changing to yielding on the sprint course and yielding to soft on the round course after race 1 (5.25)**

## 5024a IRISH STALLION FARMS EUROPEAN BREEDERS FUND GIVE THANKS STKS (GROUP 3) (F&M) — 1m 4f
**7:55** (7:56) 3-Y-0+ **£40,625** (£11,875; £5,625; £1,875)

RPR
**1** **Edelmira (IRE)**[51] 3285 3-8-12 ........................................ PatSmullen 7 106+
(D K Weld, Ire) *hld up towards rr: pushed along under 3f out: n.m.r and swtchd lft in 8th 2f out: qcknd wl on outer to ld 1f out and sn clr* **6/1**[2]
**2** *3¼* **Dark Crusader (IRE)**[38] 3717 4-9-9 94.................................. FMBerry 1 101
(A J Martin, Ire) *hld up towards rr: prog under 3f out: wnt 3rd under 2f out: kpt on wl into 2nd ins fnl f: no match for wnr* **9/1**
**3** *1¼* **Shell House (IRE)**[11] 4641 3-8-12 91........................ SeamieHeffernan 12 99
(A P O'Brien, Ire) *racd in mid-div tl hdwy over 2f out: on terms appr fnl f but sn hdd and dropped to 3rd: kpt on same pce* **12/1**
**4** *1½* **Tarana (IRE)**[37] 3764 4-9-9 101............................(b[1]) DeclanMcDonogh 13 97
(John M Oxx, Ire) *trckd ldrs in 3rd tl led after 5f: qcknd clr 3f out: advantage reduced and hdd 1f out: sn no ex and dropped to 4th: kpt on one pce* **9/4**[1]
**5** *¾* **Circling (IRE)**[41] 3593 3-8-12 100........................................(p) ConnorKing 9 95
(David Wachman, Ire) *chsd ldrs: rdn briefly into 3rd over 2f out: nt qckn 1f out: kpt on one pce* **8/1**[3]
**6** *6½* **Just Gorgeous (IRE)**[52] 3263 3-8-12 84...........(b[1]) ColmO'Donoghue 11 85
(A P O'Brien, Ire) *chsd ldrs: prog into 2nd 1/2-way: rdn along 4f out: no ex in 6th appr fnl f* **14/1**
**7** *2* **Fastnet Mist (IRE)**[41] 3593 3-8-12 96........................................ BillyLee 8 82
(David Wachman, Ire) *racd in mid-div: rdn along in 5th 3f out: no imp under 2f out: sn one pce* **20/1**
**8** *1¾* **Leaf (IRE)**[35] 3840 3-8-12 ..............................................(p) WayneLordan 3 79
(David Wachman, Ire) *t.k.h and trckd ldr in 2nd: 3rd 1/2-way tl nt qckn over 2f out: sn no ex* **12/1**
**9** *3½* **Tarziyna (IRE)**[20] 4335 3-8-12 96.................................. NGMcCullagh 10 73
(John M Oxx, Ire) *hld up towards rr: kpt on one pce fnl 2f: nvr on terms* **6/1**[2]
**10** *5½* **Coolibah (IRE)**[60] 2973 4-9-9 93........................................ JosephO'Brien 6 65
(Charles O'Brien, Ire) *a in rr: nvr a factor* **25/1**
**11** *11* **Dance With Another (IRE)**[20] 4335 3-8-12 84.......(v[1]) MichaelHussey 2 47
(A P O'Brien, Ire) *led for 5f: rdn in 4th 1/2-way: wknd qckly under 4f out* **33/1**
**12** *¾* **Beyond Brilliance (IRE)**[17] 4461 3-8-12 101........................ AnaO'Brien 5 46
(A P O'Brien, Ire) *racd in mid-div tl no imp under 2f out and sn eased* **8/1**[3]

2m 41.22s (-6.68)
**WFA** 3 from 4yo 11lb **12** Ran SP% **125.2**
CSF £61.23 TOTE £8.80: £2.60, £2.90, £3.70; DF 92.60 Trifecta £833.10.
**Owner** H H Aga Khan **Bred** His Highness The Aga Khan's Studs S C **Trained** Curragh, Co Kildare

**FOCUS**
The runner-up helps to set the standard, and is rated to her best.

5025 - (Foreign Racing) - See Raceform Interactive

# 4952 DEAUVILLE (R-H)
Tuesday, August 5

**OFFICIAL GOING: Polytrack: standard; turf: good**

## 5026a PRIX DE LA BIENNE (CLAIMER) (2YO FILLIES) (POLYTRACK) — 7f 110y
**11:45** (12:00) 2-Y-0 **£9,583** (£3,833; £2,875; £1,916; £958)

RPR
**1** **Kunst Basel (FR)** 2-8-7 0........................... Georges-AntoineAnselin(6) 1 65
(Mario Hofer, Germany) **29/10**[2]
**2** *½* **Chefchaouen (IRE)**[42] 3557 2-8-13 0................................ ThierryJarnet 5 64
(J S Moore) *tk a t.k.h: w ldrs: cl 3rd on outer 1/2-way: shkn up 2f out: rdn appr fnl f: r.o u.p: nvr quite on terms w wnr* **152/10**
**3** *½* **Who Knows (IRE)**[4] 4882 2-8-4 0.................... MllePaulineDominois(5) 7 59
(C Lerner, France) **36/5**
**4** *shd* **Whole Lotta Love (FR)**[26] 2-8-9 0........................... MickaelBarzalona 8 58
(Y Barberot, France) **71/10**
**5** *1¾* **Beauty Traou Land (FR)** 2-8-13 0.................... ChristopheSoumillon 2 58
(B De Montzey, France) **58/10**[3]
**6** *hd* **Melchope (FR)**[26] 2-9-0 0............................................(p) CristianDemuro 4 59
(E J O'Neill, France) **5/2**[1]
**7** *1¼* **Lyavenita (FR)** 2-9-2 0...................................................... UmbertoRispoli 9 58
(J-V Toux, France) **25/1**
**8** *6* **Morning (GER)** 2-9-2 0........................................... StephanePasquier 3 43
(M Delcher Sanchez, France) **84/10**
**9** *6* **All Blues (FR)**[34] 3872 2-8-10 0 ow1.................. Pierre-CharlesBoudot 6 23
(M Boutin, France) **154/10**

1m 31.43s (91.43) **9** Ran SP% **120.2**
WIN (incl. 1 euro stake): 3.90. PLACES: 1.90, 4.60, 2.30. DF: 39.50. SF: 52.80.
**Owner** Manfred Hofer & Michael Motschmann **Bred** Razza Della Sila Srl **Trained** Germany

## 5027a PRIX D'HEURTEVENT (MAIDEN) (3YO COLTS & GELDINGS) (YOUNG JOCKEYS & APPRENTICES) (POLYTRACK) — 1m 1f 110y
**1:50** (12:00) 3-Y-0 **£10,416** (£4,166; £3,125; £2,083; £1,041)

RPR
**1** **Saane (FR)**[60] 3-8-8 0.............................................. JeffersonSmith(8) 7 87
(J-C Rouget, France) **41/10**[2]
**2** *10* **Prometheus (IRE)**[78] 3-8-10 0........................... VincentCheminaud(6) 3 67
(A De Royer-Dupre, France) **61/10**
**3** *½* **Diyoudar (FR)**[34] 3869 3-8-10 0.................. Georges-AntoineAnselin(6) 5 65
(Rod Collet, France) **43/5**
**4** *1¾* **Dakota City**[27] 3-8-10 0.............................................. SoufyaneMoulin(6) 4 62
(P Bary, France) **6/4**[1]
**5** *snk* **Company Secretary (USA)**[17] 4426 3-9-2 0................(p) PhilipPrince 2 62
(Jo Hughes) *led on inner: hdd after 1f and trckd ldr: rdn over 3f out and no imp on 3 l ldr: hrd rdn and nt qckn 1 1/2f out: kpt on at one pce tl fdd fnl half f* **96/10**
**6** *1¼* **Rochefort (FR)**[34] 3869 3-8-10 0.............................................. MlleZoePfeil(6) 6 59
(Mme C Head-Maarek, France) **233/10**
**7** *snk* **Labaik (FR)**[34] 3869 3-8-10 0........................................ ThibaultSpeicher(6) 8 59
(J E Hammond, France) **23/5**[3]
**8** *6* **Ambrass (GER)** 3-8-9 0.............................................. ValentinSeguy(4) 1 43
(W Mongil, Germany) **221/10**

1m 59.24s (119.24) **8** Ran SP% **119.8**
WIN (incl. 1 euro stake): 5.10. PLACES: 2.20, 2.20, 2.50. DF: 17.70. SF: 40.30.
**Owner** Gerard Augustin-Normand **Bred** Franklin Finance S.A. **Trained** Pau, France

4337 **BRIGHTON** (L-H)

Wednesday, August 6

**OFFICIAL GOING: Good (good to soft in places) changing to good after race 1 (2.20)**

Wind: Moderate, across away from stands Weather: Sunny

## 5028 HILLS PROSPECTS NURSERY H'CAP 5f 59y

**2:20** (2:20) (Class 5) (0-75,75) 2-Y-O **£2,587** (£770; £384; £192) **Stalls** Centre

Form RPR

5210 **1** **L'Etacq**[18] 4439 2-9-5 **73**........ RichardHughes 2 75
(Richard Hannon) *cl up: hmpd on rail after 1f: effrt and n.m.r over 1f out: rdn to ld fnl 50yds* **5/4**[1]

3232 **2** ½ **Amber Crystal**[20] 4338 2-9-1 **69**........ FergusSweeney 5 68
(John Gallagher) *led: hrd rdn over 1f out: hdd and unable qck fnl 50yds* **3/1**[2]

2216 **3** 1 ¾ **Brown Velvet**[38] 3751 2-9-5 **73**........(v) MartinDwyer 6 66
(Hugo Palmer) *in tch: drvn along and outpcd 2f out: styd on fnl f* **8/1**

4332 **4** 1 ¾ **River Spirit**[10] 4702 2-8-4 **65**........ DanielCremin(7) 4 52
(Mick Channon) *in rr: rdn over 2f out: no imp* **7/1**

2555 **5** 1 ¾ **Arlecchino's Leap**[12] 4605 2-8-13 **67**........(v) DavidProbert 8 47
(Mark Usher) *chsd ldr tl wknd 1f out* **5/1**[3]

1m 5.4s (3.10) **Going Correction** +0.15s/f (Good) **5 Ran SP% 109.7**

Speed ratings (Par 94): **81,80,77,74,71**

CSF £5.16 TOTE £2.10: £1.20, £2.00; EX 5.40 Trifecta £19.60.

**Owner** Coriolan Partnership **Bred** Mrs S M Mitchell **Trained** East Everleigh, Wilts

■ Stewards' Enquiry : Fergus Sweeney two-day ban: careless riding (Aug 24-25)

**FOCUS**

The ground was changed from good to firm, good in places to good, good to soft in places following 13mm of overnight rain. That then changed to just good after one race. Rail dolled out 3yds between 6f and 2.5f and distances increased by about 6yds. Just an ordinary handicap. The winner was the narrow pick of the weights.

## 5029 EBF / LAINES BEST MAIDEN STKS 6f 209y

**2:50** (2:50) (Class 5) 2-Y-O **£2,911** (£866; £432; £216) **Stalls** Centre

Form RPR

64 **1** **Crafty Choice**[11] 4676 2-9-5 0........ RichardHughes 3 77+
(Richard Hannon) *trckd ldr: sltly outpcd 2f out: rallied and led ins fnl f: rdn out* **1/1**[1]

0 **2** 1 ¾ **Grand Spirit (IRE)**[27] 4129 2-9-5 0........ LemosdeSouza 1 71
(Luca Cumani) *chsd ldng pair: led and qcknd 2f out: hdd and no ex ins fnl f* **7/2**[2]

6 **3** 1 ¼ **Natural Charm (IRE)**[28] 4075 2-9-0 0........ AndreaAtzeni 4 63
(Roger Varian) *in tch in 4th: rdn 2f out: one pce* **9/2**

6 **4** 17 **Beauchamp Ace**[67] 2777 2-9-5 0........ FergusSweeney 2 20
(Paul Fitzsimons) *led tl wknd 2f out* **4/1**[3]

1m 26.41s (3.31) **Going Correction** +0.15s/f (Good) **4 Ran SP% 110.4**

Speed ratings (Par 94): **87,85,83,64**

CSF £4.89 TOTE £1.90; EX 5.10 Trifecta £13.10.

**Owner** Middleham Park Racing CIII **Bred** Pevens Racing **Trained** East Everleigh, Wilts

■ Stewards' Enquiry : Lemos de Souza caution: careless riding

**FOCUS**

Not easy to work out the value of this form. The winner probably only needed minor progress to win, but all of these could be a bit better than they showed here.

## 5030 THORLEY TAVERNS (S) H'CAP 1m 3f 196y

**3:20** (3:21) (Class 6) (0-55,56) 3-Y-O+ **£1,940** (£577; £288; £144) **Stalls** High

Form RPR

04-0 **1** **Unidexter (IRE)**[57] 2465 4-9-1 **46**........(t) RichardHughes 7 51
(Sheena West) *restless in stalls: hld up in rr: swtchd to centre 3f out: hdwy over 1f out: led ins fnl f: rdn out* **6/1**[2]

5006 **2** 1 **Sexy Secret**[22] 4304 3-8-11 **53**........[1] RobertHavlin 3 56
(Lydia Pearce) *chsd ldrs: hrd rdn over 2f out: led over 1f out edgd rt and tl ins fnl f: one pce* **7/2**[1]

500/ **3** 3 ¼ **Safe Investment (USA)**[24] 749 10-9-2 **47**.(tp) WilliamTwiston-Davies 8 45
(Lawney Hill) *towards rr: rdn 4f out: styd on u.p fnl 2f: nvr nrr* **12/1**

0600 **4** 2 ½ **Royal Mizar (SPA)**[44] 3521 4-9-5 **50**........ OisinMurphy 4 44
(Ralph J Smith) *prom tl outpcd fnl 2f* **7/2**[1]

0005 **5** 4 ½ **Royal Trooper (IRE)**[14] 4533 8-9-4 **56** ow1........(t) BeckyBrisbourne(7) 6 43
(Mark Brisbourne) *s.s and rdn early: bhd: sme hdwy 3f out: nvr able to chal* **8/1**

0606 **6** nk **Mystic Angel (IRE)**[28] 4084 3-8-8 **50**........(p) MartinDwyer 5 37
(William Muir) *chsd clr ldr: clsd and chal 2f out: wknd qckly over 1f out* **7/2**[1]

3250 **7** 20 **Banreenahreenkah (IRE)**[37] 3798 4-9-4 **54**........ HarryPoulton(5) 1 9
(Paul Fitzsimons) *led: sn 7 l clr: hdd & wknd rapidly over 1f out: wl btn and eased fnl f* **7/1**[3]

400- **8** 13 **Play Tiger (FR)**[382] 4521 5-9-2 **47**........ ChrisCatlin 10
(Peter Hiatt) *mid-div: wknd 4f out: sn bhd* **20/1**

2m 37.81s (5.11) **Going Correction** +0.15s/f (Good)

**WFA** 3 from 4yo+ 11lb **8 Ran SP% 117.0**

Speed ratings (Par 101): **88,87,85,83,80 80,66,58**

CSF £27.99 CT £247.12 TOTE £7.70: £2.70, £1.50, £4.60; EX 21.30 Trifecta £337.80.

**Owner** The Cheapskates **Bred** Pat Fullam **Trained** Falmer, E Sussex

■ Stewards' Enquiry : Robert Havlin four-day ban: used whip above permitted level (Aug 23-26)

**FOCUS**

This looked a weak event, with not one of the runners finishing closer than fifth in either of its previous two starts. The first three came from off the gallop.

## 5031 JOHN SMITH'S BRIGHTON MILE CHALLENGE TROPHY (H'CAP) 7f 214y

**3:50** (3:52) (Class 4) (0-80,80) 3-Y-O+

**£12,450** (£3,728; £1,864; £932; £466; £234) **Stalls** Centre

Form RPR

6444 **1** **Mime Dance**[6] 4810 3-8-11 **74**........(p) OisinMurphy 13 83
(Andrew Balding) *outpcd towards rr: effrt in centre over 2f out: styd on to ld ins fnl f* **5/1**[1]

0 **2** ½ **Piceno (IRE)**[3] 4938 6-9-5 **80**........(p) MatthewHopkins(5) 11 89
(Scott Dixon) *fast away: led tl ins fnl f: rallied wl: jst hld* **14/1**

3441 **3** 4 ½ **Scottish Glen**[25] 4181 8-9-7 **77**........ DavidProbert 5 76
(Patrick Chamings) *towards rr: drvn along and styd on fnl 2f: nvr nrr* **8/1**

4045 **4** 3 **Good Luck Charm**[34] 3879 5-9-7 **77**........ GeorgeBaker 3 70
(Gary Moore) *towards rr tl styd on u.p fnl 2f* **8/1**

0216 **5** nk **Luhaif**[26] 4148 4-9-10 **80**........(b) AdamBeschizza 12 71
(Julia Feilden) *chsd ldrs tl outpcd 2f out* **20/1**

5360 **6** 4 ½ **Cool Bahamian (IRE)**[8] 4761 3-8-12 **80**........ LouisSteward(5) 1 60
(Eve Johnson Houghton) *mid-div: hdwy over 2f out: hrd rdn over 1f out: wknd fnl f* **5/1**[1]

0046 **7** ¾ **Sword Of The Lord**[20] 4342 4-9-4 **74**........ AndreaAtzeni 9 53
(George Margarson) *mid-div: outpcd and struggling over 2f out: sme late hdwy* **16/1**

-150 **8** nse **Realize**[25] 4181 4-8-13 **76**........(p) CharlieBennett(7) 4 55
(Hughie Morrison) *chsd ldrs tl wknd over 1f out* **33/1**

0661 **9** ¾ **Secular Society**[20] 4340 4-9-3 **73**........(p) PatCosgrave 2 50
(George Baker) *dwlt: sn in midfield: rdn and btn over 2f out* **16/1**

0543 **10** 9 **Skytrain**[8] 4761 4-9-4 **77**........(b) MichaelJMMurphy(3) 7 33
(Mark Johnston) *nvr gng wl: last and drvn along: a bhd* **6/1**[2]

-020 **11** 1 **Desert Society (IRE)**[11] 4650 3-9-3 **80**........(b[1]) RichardHughes 6 56
(Richard Hannon) *chsd ldr tl hrd rdn and wknd over 2f out: no ch whn eased over 1f out* **13/2**[3]

-410 **12** 7 **Rapid Advance**[21] 4332 3-9-3 **80**........(p) ShaneKelly 10 17
(Sir Michael Stoute) *chsd ldrs tl wknd over 2f out* **8/1**

1m 36.11s (0.11) **Going Correction** +0.15s/f (Good)

**WFA** 3 from 4yo+ 7lb **12 Ran SP% 120.4**

Speed ratings (Par 105): **105,104,100,97,96 92,91,91,90,81 80,73**

CSF £77.62 CT £569.24 TOTE £5.70: £2.00, £3.50, £2.70; EX 97.10 Trifecta £913.00.

**Owner** David Brownlow **Bred** The Stanley Estate And Stud Company **Trained** Kingsclere, Hants

**FOCUS**

This was the most competitive race on the card and it was run at a sound pace. The runner-up set a decent pace and the winner, first run since gelded and fitted with cheekpieces for the first time, came from the rear.

## 5032 EBF / STAR GREAT PUBS & BARS FILLIES' H'CAP 6f 209y

**4:20** (4:21) (Class 4) (0-85,85) 3-Y-O+ **£6,301** (£1,886; £943; £472) **Stalls** Centre

Form RPR

5310 **1** **Lady Frances**[11] 4669 3-9-3 **85**........ MichaelJMMurphy(3) 1 93
(Mark Johnston) *mde all: hrd rdn and edgd rt ins fnl f: hld on gamely* **10/3**[3]

0-22 **2** hd **Meeting Waters**[29] 4053 3-9-5 **84**........ JohnFahy 2 91
(William Haggas) *chsd wnr: drvn to chal ins fnl f: r.o: jst hld* **2/1**[2]

2423 **3** 1 ¾ **Khatiba (IRE)**[13] 4572 3-9-1 **80**........(p[1]) AndreaAtzeni 4 83
(Roger Varian) *chsd ldng pair: drvn along and styd on same pce fnl 2f* **15/8**[1]

-002 **4** 4 ½ **La Tinta Bay**[16] 4502 3-8-13 **78**........ RichardHughes 6 74
(Richard Hannon) *stdd s: hld up in rr: effrt and hrd rdn over 1f out: wknd fnl f* **5/1**

1m 25.02s (1.92) **Going Correction** +0.15s/f (Good)

**WFA** 3 from 4yo 6lb **4 Ran SP% 107.9**

Speed ratings (Par 102): **95,94,92,87**

CSF £10.13 TOTE £3.90; EX 9.40 Trifecta £12.00.

**Owner** Sheikh Hamdan bin Mohammed Al Maktoum **Bred** Darley **Trained** Middleham Moor, N Yorks

■ Stewards' Enquiry : John Fahy two-day ban: used whip above permitted level (Auf 23-24)

**FOCUS**

Ordinary fillies form. The winner dictated and got the better of an honest battle with the runner-up.

## 5033 MAISON MAURICE H'CAP 1m 1f 209y

**4:50** (4:51) (Class 6) (0-55,68) 3-Y-O+ **£1,940** (£577; £288; £144) **Stalls** High

Form RPR

0542 **1** **Sir Tyto (IRE)**[20] 4343 6-9-2 **47**........(p) RichardHughes 5 54
(Peter Makin) *mde all: qcknd over 2f out: hrd rdn ins fnl f: a in control* **2/1**[1]

-000 **2** 2 ½ **Market Puzzle (IRE)**[6] 4808 7-8-11 **45**........ MichaelJMMurphy(3) 9 47
(Mark Brisbourne) *in tch: drvn and hung lft 2f out: styd on to take 2nd nr fin* **33/1**

460 **3** ½ **Supa Seeker (USA)**[7] 4798 8-9-6 **51**........ LiamKeniry 7 52
(Tony Carroll) *disp 2nd: chsd wnr over 1f out: one pce: lost 2nd nr fin* **16/1**

053 **4** ¾ **Polydamos**[7] 4798 5-9-0 **52**........ JordanVaughan(7) 2 52
(Tony Carroll) *chsd ldrs: rdn and outpcd over 2f out: kpt on fnl f* **11/4**[2]

460 **5** ¾ **Claude Greenwood**[18] 4433 4-9-0 **46** oh1........ RobertHavlin 6 43
(Linda Jewell) *disp 2nd tl no ex 1f out* **16/1**

0004 **6** ¾ **Up Hill Battle's**[69] 2694 3-8-5 **45**........ FrankieMcDonald 8 42
(Daniel Mark Loughnane) *hld up towards rr: effrt in centre 3f out: sn rdn: nvr able to chal* **5/1**[3]

00/4 **7** hd **Giant Sequoia (USA)**[13] 4582 10-9-0 **45**........(t) AdamBeschizza 4 42
(Des Donovan) *towards rr: rdn over 2f out: n.d* **8/1**

5-60 **8** hd **Urban Sanctuary**[9] 4738 3-8-9 **49**........(b[1]) HayleyTurner 1 47
(Ed Walker) *s.s: bhd: styng on to chse ldrs whn nt clr run on rail ins fnl f: nt rcvr* **17/2**

2m 9.11s (5.51) **Going Correction** +0.15s/f (Good)

**WFA** 3 from 4yo+ 9lb **8 Ran SP% 113.0**

Speed ratings (Par 101): **83,81,80,80,79 78,78,78**

CSF £66.59 CT £827.69 TOTE £2.60: £1.50, £5.50, £2.10; EX 44.30 Trifecta £365.00.

**Owner** WH And Mrs Jennifer Simpson **Bred** Michael Conlon **Trained** Ogbourne Maisey, Wilts

**FOCUS**

A good tactical ride from the front by Richard Hughes. There is possibly a bit better to come from the winner but the race lacked any depth, so it's not form to be taking any chances with.

## 5034 OLD MOUT H'CAP 5f 213y

**5:25** (5:26) (Class 6) (0-55,55) 3-Y-O **£1,940** (£577; £288; £144) **Stalls** Centre

Form RPR

300 **1** **Lunarian**[37] 3801 3-9-2 **53**........ CharlesBishop(3) 1 61
(Mick Channon) *mde all: hard rdn and r.o wl fnl 2f: readily* **7/2**[3]

60-0 **2** 2 ¼ **Posh Bounty**[61] 2946 3-8-12 **46** oh4........ OisinMurphy 3 47
(Joseph Tuite) *chsd wnr thrght: one pce appr fnl f: jst hld on for 2nd nr fin* **8/1**

2242 **3** hd **Go Charlie**[6] 4816 3-9-1 **49**........ SteveDrowne 8 50+
(Ronald Harris) *stdd s: plld hrd in rr: hdwy in centre over 1f out: disp 2nd ins fnl f: one pce nr fin* **3/1**[2]

-000 **4** 3 **Stapleford Lad**[21] 4329 3-9-7 **55**........ KierenFox 7 47
(Stuart Williams) *towards rr: effrt over 2f out: styd on same pce* **6/1**

0-03 **5** shd **Forest Glen (IRE)**[6] 4820 3-9-7 **55**........ LiamKeniry 4 46
(Sylvester Kirk) *dwlt: in tch: rdn over 2f out: sn btn* **9/4**[1]

3004 **6** 7 **Rosie Prospects**[12] 4614 3-9-1 **49**........(p) NickyMackay 5 19
(Roger Ingram) *chsd ldrs: rdn 3f out: wknd 2f out* **16/1**

5000 **7** *1 ¾* **Paradise Child**[42] 3564 3-8-7 **46** oh4 RyanWhile(5) 2 11
(Bill Turner) *dwlt: prom tl hrd rdn and wknd wl over 1f out* **40/1**
1m 13.29s (3.09) **Going Correction** +0.15s/f (Good) **7** Ran SP% **111.7**
Speed ratings (Par 98): **85,82,81,77,77 68,65**
CSF £29.34 CT £90.32 TOTE £5.80: £2.80, £3.40; EX 26.90 Trifecta £97.10.
**Owner** Mrs Ann C Black **Bred** R J Cornelius **Trained** West Ilsley, Berks
**FOCUS**
A moderate handicap, and the first two were having their first start in that company. The third sets the standard.
T/Plt: £194.30 to a £1 stake. Pool: £64,829.62 - 243.51 winning units. T/Qpdt: £98.50 to a £1 stake. Pool: £4820.51 - 36.20 winning units. LM

# 5006 KEMPTON (A.W) (R-H)
Wednesday, August 6

**OFFICIAL GOING: Standard**
Wind: Moderate, across (away from stands) Weather: Fine, very warm

## 5035 BETDAQ NO PREMIUM CHARGE APPRENTICE H'CAP (LONDON MIDDLE DISTANCE SERIES QUALIFIER) 1m 3f (P)
**6:10** (6:10) (Class 4) (0-85,82) 4-Y-0+ **£4,690** (£1,395; £697; £348) **Stalls** Low

Form RPR
0011 **1** **Treasure The Ridge (IRE)**[12] 4616 5-9-4 **75** (b) DannyBrock 3 83
(Andrew Reid) *hld up bhd ldng pair: prog on inner and drvn to ld over 1f out: hrd pressed fnl f: jst hld on* **3/1**[2]
-101 **2** *shd* **Grasped**[18] 4434 4-9-5 **76** CamHardie 1 84
(Lady Cecil) *trckd ldr: shkn up over 2f out: nt qckn and sn dropped to 3rd: chsd wnr over 1f out: sustained chal fnl f: jst failed* **4/5**[1]
0060 **3** *2 ½* **Aviator (GER)**[28] 4077 6-9-2 **73** (b) MarcMonaghan 2 77
(James Eustace) *led at mod pce: kicked on 3f out: rdn and hdd over 1f out: wandered and looked awkward: sn btn* **13/2**[3]
1330 **4** *3 ½* **Back Burner (IRE)**[42] 3582 6-9-4 **75** TimClark 5 73
(Dai Burchell) *hld up in last: shkn up jst over 2f out: no real rspnse* **12/1**
2006 **5** *2* **Thecornishcowboy**[12] 4622 5-9-6 **82** (t) JoshQuinn(5) 4 77
(John Ryan) *trckd ldng pair: rdn over 2f out: no prog: wknd jst over 1f out* **12/1**
2m 25.04s (3.14) **Going Correction** +0.075s/f (Slow) **5** Ran SP% **109.3**
Speed ratings (Par 105): **91,90,89,86,85**
CSF £5.74 TOTE £4.70: £2.40, £1.10; EX 6.00 Trifecta £15.40.
**Owner** A S Reid **Bred** S Coughlan **Trained** Mill Hill, London NW7
**FOCUS**
A disappointing turnout numerically for this opener but the finish was played out by two progressive individuals and it's likely this represents strong handicap form.

## 5036 BETDAQ £25 NO LOSE FREE BET FILLIES' H'CAP 1m 4f (P)
**6:40** (6:41) (Class 5) (0-70,69) 3-Y-0+ **£2,587** (£770; £384; £192) **Stalls** Centre

Form RPR
0601 **1** **Sleeper**[16] 4504 3-9-0 **66** AndreaAtzeni 7 76+
(Ralph Beckett) *trckd ldr 3f: nt gng sweetly fr a m out: drvn over 3f out: prog to ld over 1f out: kpt finding enough fnl f* **6/4**[1]
-004 **2** *1* **Shining Glitter (IRE)**[18] 4434 3-8-11 **68** CamHardie(5) 3 76
(James Fanshawe) *hld up in midfield: nt clr run over 2f out: drvn and prog over 1f out: tk 2nd ins fnl f: kpt on but no imp on wnr last 75yds* **7/2**[2]
255 **3** *2* **Elpida (USA)**[34] 3877 3-9-2 **68** JimCrowley 8 73
(David Simcock) *hld up in last pair: rdn 3f out: detached in last over 2f out: styd on wl fr over 1f out: tk 3rd last strides* **14/1**
4311 **4** *hd* **Elegant Ophelia**[9] 4734 5-9-11 **66** 6ex (t) GeorgeBaker 4 70
(Dean Ivory) *hld up in midfield: prog over 2f out: pushed up to chal over 1f out: sn rdn and fnd nil: one pce after* **10/1**
0044 **5** *1 ¾* **Hallbeck**[21] 4333 3-8-13 **65** FergusSweeney 2 67
(Henry Candy) *prom: rdn to ld 2f out to over 1f out: fdd ins fnl f* **7/1**[3]
41 **6** *nk* **Bella Varenna (IRE)**[28] 4081 3-9-3 **69** AdamKirby 9 70
(Marco Botti) *settled in 7th: rdn and prog on inner over 2f out: cl up over 1f out: fdd fnl f* **10/1**
046 **7** *3 ¾* **Upper Street (IRE)**[14] 4543 3-9-1 **67** ShaneKelly 6 62
(Sir Michael Stoute) *prog to trck ldr after 3f: led briefly over 2f out: wknd over 1f out* **14/1**
0-00 **8** *2 ¼* **Berwin (IRE)**[9] 4737 5-8-10 **56** RenatoSouza(5) 1 48
(Sylvester Kirk) *v.s.a and shkn up to catch up in last pair: drvn and effrt on inner over 2f out: wknd over 1f out* **50/1**
0435 **9** *¾* **Ana Shababiya (IRE)**[28] 4092 4-9-8 **68** TimClark(5) 10 58
(Ismail Mohammed) *racd freely: led to over 2f out: wknd* **25/1**
2m 34.75s (0.25) **Going Correction** +0.075s/f (Slow)
**WFA** 3 from 4yo+ 11lb **9** Ran SP% **112.0**
Speed ratings (Par 100): **102,101,100,99,98 98,96,94,94**
CSF £6.19 CT £48.24 TOTE £2.30: £1.10, £1.40, £3.40; EX 8.70 Trifecta £71.10.
**Owner** The Millennium Madness Partnership **Bred** Miss A Gibson Fleming **Trained** Kimpton, Hants
**FOCUS**
A fair race for the grade. The winner was less exposed than most.

## 5037 BRITISH STALLION STUDS EBF MAIDEN FILLIES' STKS (BOBIS RACE) 7f (P)
**7:10** (7:11) (Class 4) 2-Y-0 **£4,075** (£1,212; £606; £303) **Stalls** Low

Form RPR
4 **1** **Local Time**[21] 4320 2-9-0 0 HarryBentley 10 87+
(Saeed bin Suroor) *sn trckd ldr: rdn to chal 2f out: led jst over 1f out: styd on wl and drew clr* **7/1**
2 **2** *4* **Turning Times (IRE)**[60] 2979 2-9-0 0 AdamKirby 7 76
(Charlie Appleby) *led: kicked on over 2f out: drvn and hdd jst over 1f out: one pce* **3/1**[2]
**3** *1* **Rock Kristal (IRE)** 2-9-0 0 WilliamBuick 11 74+
(John Gosden) *dwlt: wl in rr on outer: shkn up 3f out: prog over 1f out: styd on to take 3rd ins fnl f: nrst fin* **8/1**
2 **4** *1* **Ajaadat**[42] 3563 2-9-0 0 AndreaAtzeni 1 71+
(Roger Varian) *trckd ldrs: shkn up over 2f out: nt qckn wl over 1f out: kpt on fnl f to take 4th nr fin* **11/4**[1]
**5** *¾* **Silver Rainbow (IRE)** 2-9-0 0 KierenFallon 3 69+
(B W Hills) *dwlt: in tch towards rr: shkn up and prog wl over 2f out: tk 3rd jst over 1f out tl ins fnl f: fdd* **14/1**
3 **6** *5* **Vesnina**[19] 4403 2-9-0 0 RichardHughes 4 55
(Richard Hannon) *trckd ldrs: effrt 2f out: nt qckn and reminder on inner over 1f out: wknd and eased* **4/1**[3]
30 **7** *½* **All Rounder (USA)**[19] 4403 2-9-0 0 RobertHavlin 6 54
(John Gosden) *prom tl shkn up and wknd over 2f out* **14/1**
5 **8** *2 ¼* **Candle Of The Sea (IRE)**[60] 2979 2-9-0 0 JamieSpencer 2 48
(Ed Vaughan) *dwlt: swtchd lft and bmpd rival after 150yds: a in rr: pushed along on inner 2f out: sn wknd* **16/1**
40 **9** *½* **Winter Queen**[52] 3267 2-9-0 0 MartinLane 9 47
(Charlie Appleby) *dwlt: bmpd by rival after 150yds: mostly in last: no prog over 2f out* **66/1**
00 **10** *3 ½* **Eileen Gray (IRE)**[52] 3267 2-9-0 0 JimCrowley 12 37
(Charles Hills) *t.k.h: racd wd: prog to go 3rd briefly 3f out: wknd over 2f out* **100/1**
1m 26.78s (0.78) **Going Correction** +0.075s/f (Slow) **10** Ran SP% **117.0**
Speed ratings (Par 93): **98,93,92,91,90 84,84,81,80,76**
CSF £28.38 TOTE £9.90: £2.20, £1.70, £2.60; EX 42.60 Trifecta £407.50.
**Owner** Godolphin **Bred** Darley **Trained** Newmarket, Suffolk
**FOCUS**
Some big yards represented and the likelihood is this was an above-average performance by the winner.

## 5038 BETDAQ 3% COMMISSION H'CAP (BOBIS RACE) (LONDON MIDDLE DISTANCE SERIES QUALIFIER) 1m 3f (P)
**7:40** (7:40) (Class 4) (0-80,78) 3-Y-O **£4,690** (£1,395; £697; £348) **Stalls** Low

Form RPR
0626 **1** **Masterpaver**[24] 3643 3-9-0 **71** AdamKirby 7 82+
(Alan Bailey) *hld up: prog to trck ldng pair 7f out: chal on wd outside 4f out: drvn over 2f out: led over 1f out: styd on and drew clr* **11/1**
1-02 **2** *4* **Billy Blue (IRE)**[16] 4501 3-9-5 **76** WilliamBuick 2 81
(John Gosden) *trckd ldrs: lost pl 7f out: pushed along over 3f out: drvn and limited rspnse over 2f out: kpt on fr over 1f out to take 2nd ins fnl f* **5/2**[1]
4 **3** *¾* **Gangster Squad (FR)**[34] 3897 3-9-2 **78** CamHardie(5) 4 81
(Martyn Meade) *hld up in last pair: rdn over 3f out: struggling after tl styd on fnl f to take 3rd last strides* **33/1**
1032 **4** *nk* **Barye**[23] 4272 3-9-4 **75** JimCrowley 5 78
(David Simcock) *trckd ldr: led 8f out to 5f out: drvn to ld over 2f out: hdd over 1f out: wknd ins fnl f* **5/1**[3]
3-21 **5** *nk* **Bishop Of Ruscombe**[154] 839 3-9-7 **78** DavidProbert 1 80
(Andrew Balding) *t.k.h: trckd ldrs: tried to mount an effrt over 2f out: nt qckn wl over 1f out: no hdwy after* **11/4**[2]
0031 **6** *¾* **Censorius**[11] 4658 3-8-12 **69** (v) PatCosgrave 6 70
(Ed Walker) *shoved along leaving stalls to get gng: in rr: rdn 4f out: struggling after: plugged on fnl f* **10/1**
1064 **7** *shd* **Ice Slice (IRE)**[28] 4074 3-9-7 **78** PaddyAspell 9 79
(James Eustace) *trckd ldrs after 4f: rdn over 2f out: no imp on ldrs over 1f out: fdd* **16/1**
-506 **8** *57* **Attenzione (IRE)**[13] 4574 3-9-2 **73** (vt[1]) AndreaAtzeni 8
(Marco Botti) *hld up in last pair: rdn 5f out: sn lost tch: wl t.o* **20/1**
03-0 **P** **Arbaab**[120] 1357 3-8-12 **69** ShaneKelly 3
(Sir Michael Stoute) *led 3f: led 5f out: drvn and hdd over 2f out: broke down and p.u over 1f out* **5/1**[3]
2m 21.43s (-0.47) **Going Correction** +0.075s/f (Slow) **9** Ran SP% **119.6**
Speed ratings (Par 102): **104,101,100,100,100 99,99,58,**
CSF £40.20 CT £915.14 TOTE £10.00: £2.30, £1.70, £7.00; EX 43.40 Trifecta £1973.40 Part won..
**Owner** Mrs A M Riney **Bred** Mrs A M Riney **Trained** Newmarket, Suffolk
**FOCUS**
This was very steadily run in the early stages but they quickened up with fully a half-mile to run and it took plenty of getting. The winner was something of a surprising improver but did it well.

## 5039 HBAA WHO CARES WINS MAIDEN STKS 1m (P)
**8:10** (8:12) (Class 5) 3-Y-O+ **£2,587** (£770; £384; £192) **Stalls** Low

Form RPR
**1** **Unforgiving Minute** 3-9-5 0 AdamKirby 8 86+
(Clive Cox) *t.k.h early: hld up in midfield disputing 7th: shkn up whn ldr wnt for home over 2f out: prog to go 2nd jst over 1f out: styd on to ld last 60yds* **4/1**[3]
3- **2** *nk* **Royal Flag**[447] 2384 4-9-12 0 AndreaAtzeni 6 86+
(Saeed bin Suroor) *trckd ldrs disputing 5th: shkn up over 2f out: prog over 1f out: styd on to take 2nd last strides: nt rch wnr* **13/8**[1]
52 **3** *½* **Above The Rest (IRE)**[37] 3804 3-9-5 0 JimCrowley 4 84
(Timothy Jarvis) *disp ld tl drew clr over 2f out: 4 l up over 1f out: wknd and hung lft fnl f: hdd last 60yds* **8/1**
**4** *1 ¼* **Golden Emerald** 3-9-5 0 HayleyTurner 3 81+
(James Fanshawe) *dwlt: sn in tch disputing 5th: shkn up and prog on inner 2f out: clsd w others 1f out: kpt on same pce fnl f* **20/1**
45 **5** *½* **Savant (IRE)**[51] 3315 3-9-5 0 ShaneKelly 9 80+
(Sir Michael Stoute) *settled in midfield disputing 7th: pushed along and outpcd fr over 2f out: styd on steadily fr over 1f out: do bttr* **10/1**
44 **6** *3 ½* **Esteban**[13] 4587 3-9-0 0 MarcMonaghan(5) 1 71
(Marco Botti) *trckd ldng pair: rdn to chse clr ldr over 2f out to jst over 1f out: wknd* **33/1**
**7** *2* **Kubeba (IRE)** 3-9-5 0 MartinLane 14 67
(Paul Cole) *trckd ldng pair: rdn over 2f out: no prog over 1f out: wknd* **50/1**
5 **8** *3* **Lord Empire (IRE)**[19] 4407 3-9-5 0 PatCosgrave 13 59
(David Simcock) *dwlt: wl in rr: pushed along wl over 2f out: kpt on steadily fr over 1f out: nt disgracd* **25/1**
0 **9** *2* **Jack Bear**[39] 3712 3-9-0 0 NedCurtis(5) 12 55
(Jonathan Portman) *in rr: pushed along 3f out: sn lft bhd: plugged on fr over 1f out* **66/1**
0 **10** *3 ½* **Frankie**[57] 3083 3-9-0 0 CamHardie(5) 7 46
(Jimmy Fox) *dwlt: in rr: pushed along and lft bhd fr over 2f out* **100/1**
00 **11** *1* **William Of Orange**[6] 4830 3-9-5 0 ChrisCatlin 10 44
(Sir Mark Prescott Bt) *dwlt: a wl in rr: drvn in last pair 3f out: nvr a factor* **100/1**
02 **12** *¾* **Fallen In Line (IRE)**[86] 2201 3-9-5 0 WilliamBuick 2 42
(John Gosden) *towards rr: pushed along 1/2-way: no prog over 2f out: wknd over 1f out* **10/3**[2]
0 **13** *nk* **Moojaned (IRE)**[16] 4500 3-9-0 0 TimClark(5) 5 41
(Dai Burchell) *disp ld to over 2f out: wknd rapidly* **100/1**
- **14** *1 ½* **Euroquip Susie** 6-9-2 0 NoelGarbutt(5) 11 34
(Michael Scudamore) *slowly away: rn green and rousted in last pair: u.p and no prog 3f out* **100/1**
1m 40.46s (0.66) **Going Correction** +0.075s/f (Slow)
**WFA** 3 from 4yo+ 7lb **14** Ran SP% **120.3**
Speed ratings (Par 103): **99,98,98,96,96 92,90,87,85,82 81,80,80,78**
CSF £10.29 TOTE £5.60: £1.70, £1.80, £2.30; EX 14.30 Trifecta £86.40.
**Owner** P W Harris **Bred** Equine Breeding Ltd **Trained** Lambourn, Berks

**FOCUS**
A hugely encouraging start to the career of Unforgiving Minute.

## 5040 WIN BIG ON THE BETDAQ COLOSSUS H'CAP (LONDON MILE SERIES QUALIFIER) 1m (P)
**8:40** (8:40) (Class 4) (0-85,85) 3-Y-0+ **£4,690** (£1,395; £697; £348) **Stalls** Low

Form RPR
0-31 **1** **Bombardment (USA)**[27] 4130 3-9-0 **78** WilliamBuick 11 86
(Charlie Appleby) *led after 2f: mde rest: tending to hang lft whn rdn over 2f out: jnd over 1f out: fended off rival sn after: drvn out* **6/1**[2]
2221 **2** ½ **Musaddas**[22] 4299 4-9-13 **84** KierenFallon 7 92
(Saeed bin Suroor) *hld up in midfield on outer: shkn up wl over 2f out: prog over 1f out: nvr really pce to chal but styd on to take 2nd last stride* **5/4**[1]
2220 **3** *hd* **Rome**[56] 3118 4-9-6 **77** GeorgeBaker 1 85
(Gary Moore) *led 2f: trckd wnr: chal over 2f out: upsides over 1f out: nt qckn and hld ins fnl f: lost 2nd last stride* **14/1**
2205 **4** 1 ¾ **High Time Too (IRE)**[21] 4323 4-9-13 **84** MartinDwyer 8 87
(Hugo Palmer) *hld up in last trio: nt clr run briefly over 2f out: prog to chse ldng pair over 1f out: kpt on but lost 3rd ins fnl f* **10/1**
1-50 **5** 1 ¼ **Killing Time (IRE)**[105] 1655 3-9-0 **78** RichardHughes 6 77
(Ralph Beckett) *hld up in last pair swtchd to outer over 2f out and pushed along: reminder over 1f out: kpt on but nvr involved* **7/1**[3]
4314 **6** ½ **Ocean Applause**[12] 4620 4-9-7 **78** (t) AdamKirby 10 77
(John Ryan) *hld up and sn in last: pushed along over 2f out: reminder over 1f out: kpt on but nvr involved* **20/1**
4041 **7** *nse* **Aomen Rock**[28] 4073 4-9-4 **75** (v) ShaneKelly 5 74
(James Fanshawe) *wl in tch: rdn to chse ldrs wl over 1f out: no imp after: wknd ins fnl f* **10/1**
5342 **8** *nk* **Jack Of Diamonds (IRE)**[14] 4549 5-9-12 **83** JimCrowley 9 81
(Roger Teal) *trckd ldrs: short of room over 2f out and lost pl: tried to rally over 1f out: wknd fnl f* **12/1**
5000 **9** 5 **Birdman (IRE)**[21] 4331 4-10-0 **85** (be) MartinLane 3 71
(David Simcock) *hld up in midfield: effrt on inner over 2f out: no prog over 1f out: wknd* **16/1**
5-00 **10** 7 **Al Jamal**[37] 3802 4-9-8 **79** [1] HarryBentley 4 48
(Jeremy Gask) *trckd ldrs: lost pl over 2f out: sn wknd* **50/1**

1m 39.45s (-0.35) **Going Correction** +0.075s/f (Slow)
**WFA** 3 from 4yo+ 7lb **10** Ran SP% **116.4**
Speed ratings (Par 105): **104,103,103,101,100 99,99,99,94,87**
CSF £13.78 CT £106.12 TOTE £7.00: £2.60, £1.10, £3.40; EX 17.10 Trifecta £238.40.
**Owner** Godolphin **Bred** Pontchartrain Stud **Trained** Newmarket, Suffolk
**FOCUS**
A competitive race, won in gutsy fashion by handicap debutant Bombardment.

## 5041 VISIT AND DINE IN THE PANORAMIC H'CAP 1m (P)
**9:10** (9:10) (Class 6) (0-65,65) 3-Y-0+ **£1,940** (£577; £288; £144) **Stalls** Low

Form RPR
5653 **1** **Bennelong**[13] 4582 8-8-11 **60** (v) PaigeBolton(7) 6 68
(Lee Carter) *hld up in rr: stdy prog on inner fr 2f out gng wl: couple of reminders and r.o to ld last 100yds: readily* **16/1**
2500 **2** 1 ½ **Princess Spirit**[28] 4073 5-9-2 **58** (p) ShaneKelly 7 62
(Edward Creighton) *trckd ldrs: rdn and prog over 1f out: styd on to take 2nd last 50yds: nt pce of wnr* **10/1**
4560 **3** 1 **El Mirage (IRE)**[53] 3231 4-9-4 **60** JimCrowley 9 62
(Dean Ivory) *hld up in last trio: rdn over 2f out: prog over 1f out: styd on u.p to take 3rd last stride* **33/1**
1105 **4** *shd* **Zed Candy Girl**[2] 4968 4-8-11 **58** (p) TimClark(5) 10 60
(Dai Burchell) *prom: trckd ldr over 3f out: rdn to ld over 2f out and sent for home: floundered over 1f out: hdd and btn last 100yds* **13/2**[3]
2034 **5** 1 ½ **Substantivo (IRE)**[42] 3589 4-9-4 **60** KierenFallon 12 59
(Timothy Jarvis) *racd wd early: prom 1/2-way: drvn to chse ldr over 1f out to jst ins fnl f: no ex and wl hld whn hmpd nr fin* **4/1**[1]
1-30 **6** 3 ¾ **Kingswinford (IRE)**[14] 4537 8-9-8 **64** (p) PaddyAspell 5 53
(John Norton) *trckd ldrs: drvn over 2f out: sn lost pl: looked like dropping rt away over 1f out: plugged on again fnl f* **25/1**
5000 **7** *nk* **Tevez**[14] 4544 9-9-2 **65** (p) HollieDoyle(7) 3 53
(Des Donovan) *slowly away: hld up in last pair: swtchd to inner and sme prog 2f out: no hdwy jst over 1f out: wknd* **7/1**
2303 **8** 2 ½ **Harwoods Star (IRE)**[13] 4579 4-9-5 **61** (t) AdamKirby 1 43
(Amanda Perrett) *led 2f: styd prom: wknd fr 2f out* **6/1**[2]
1065 **9** ¾ **Shahrazad (IRE)**[28] 4073 5-8-12 **61** (t) JackGilligan(7) 13 42
(Patrick Gilligan) *sn hld up in last pair: tried to make prog on inner 2f out: no hdwy over 1f out: wknd* **12/1**
0000 **10** 4 ½ **Spirit Of Gondree (IRE)**[28] 4073 6-9-7 **63** (p) PatCosgrave 8 33
(Milton Bradley) *hld up in midfield: lost pl and last over 2f out: shkn up over 1f out: no prog* **25/1**
0640 **11** 2 ¾ **Woolston Ferry (IRE)**[19] 4415 8-9-2 **58** FergusSweeney 2 21
(Henry Candy) *dwlt: pushed up into midfield: lost pl over 2f out: wknd* **8/1**
4333 **12** 2 **My Manekineko**[11] 4655 5-9-5 **61** RichardHughes 11 19
(J R Jenkins) *led after 2f: hdd over 2f out: sn btn: wknd and heavily eased fnl f* **4/1**[1]

1m 39.81s (0.01) **Going Correction** +0.075s/f (Slow) **12** Ran SP% **124.5**
Speed ratings (Par 101): **102,100,99,99,97 94,93,91,90,86 83,81**
CSF £171.80 CT £5182.08 TOTE £15.60: £4.80, £3.80, £8.50; EX 144.70 Trifecta £2240.30 Part won..
**Owner** John Joseph Smith **Bred** The National Stud **Trained** Epsom, Surrey
**FOCUS**
A moderate finale. There was a decent pace and the first three all came from the rear.
T/Jkpt: Not won. T/Plt: £11.60 to a £1 stake. Pool: £65,549.36 - 4097.99 winning units. T/Qpdt: £10.20 to a £1 stake. Pool: £6132.09 - 441.86 winning units. JN

# 4905 LINGFIELD (L-H)
## Wednesday, August 6

**OFFICIAL GOING: Standard**
Wind: brisk across Weather: sunny with some cloud

## 5042 200 DEPOSIT BONUS AT WINNER.COM MAIDEN FILLIES' STKS (BOBIS RACE) 5f 6y(P)
**2:00** (2:00) (Class 5) 2-Y-0 **£2,587** (£770; £384; £192) **Stalls** High

Form RPR
220 **1** **Al Fareej (IRE)**[49] 3353 2-9-0 **80** KierenFallon 2 79+
(James Tate) *trckd ldrs: qcknd up to ld jst ins fnl f: r.o strly* **2/5**[1]
53 **2** 1 ½ **Renaissant**[13] 4583 2-9-0 0 PatDobbs 5 72+
(Richard Hannon) *trckd ldrs: sltly outpcd over 1f out: r.o wl ins fnl f: wnt 2nd fnl 75yds* **6/1**[3]
02 **3** 2 **Candlelight (IRE)**[13] 4577 2-9-0 0 WilliamBuick 4 64
(Charles Hills) *led: rdn over 1f out: hdd jst ins fnl f: sn outpcd by wnr: no ex whn lost 2nd fnl 75yds* **4/1**[2]
54 **4** ¾ **The Wispe**[13] 4583 2-9-1 0 ow1 AdamKirby 7 63
(Robert Cowell) *trckd ldrs: rdn wl over 1f out: kpt on but nt pce to get on terms* **14/1**
**5** 4 **Medicean Bliss (IRE)** 2-9-0 0 MartinLane 3 47
(Jeremy Gask) *dwlt: rn green and sn outpcd in detached last: sme late prog but nvr gng pce to get on terms* **33/1**
**6** 5 **Rubheira** 2-8-9 0 RyanWhile(5) 1 29
(Hugo Froud) *s.i.s: sn chsng ldrs: rdn 2f out: wknd ent fnl f* **66/1**
05 **7** ½ **Noble Cause**[13] 4577 2-8-9 0 CamHardie(5) 6 28
(Luke Dace) *s.i.s: in last pair: rdn over 2f out: nvr threatened* **66/1**

59.31s (0.51) **Going Correction** -0.025s/f (Stan) **7** Ran SP% **118.3**
Speed ratings (Par 91): **94,91,88,87,80 72,72**
CSF £3.86 TOTE £1.30: £1.10, £3.10; EX 3.90 Trifecta £8.10.
**Owner** Saif Ali **Bred** Tinnakill Bloodstock **Trained** Newmarket, Suffolk
**FOCUS**
An uncompetitive fillies' maiden and this proved very straightforward for the hot favourite. She was arguably value for further.

## 5043 DOWNLOAD THE WINNER.COM APP NOW NURSERY H'CAP 6f 1y(P)
**2:30** (2:30) (Class 5) (0-75,75) 2-Y-0 **£2,587** (£770; £384; £192) **Stalls** Low

Form RPR
0106 **1** **Gold Waltz**[20] 4345 2-8-10 **64** PatDobbs 2 67
(Ralph Beckett) *squeezed up s: sn trcking ldrs: str run on inner turning in: led jst over 1f out: r.o: rdn out* **8/1**[3]
060 **2** *nk* **Western Playboy (IRE)**[55] 3140 2-8-3 **62** CamHardie(5) 5 64
(Sylvester Kirk) *chsd ldrs: rdn 2f out: r.o wl to go 2nd ins fnl f: clsng on wnr nring fin* **3/1**[1]
6532 **3** 2 ¼ **Low Cut Affair (IRE)**[6] 4815 2-9-1 **69** AdamKirby 1 64
(David Evans) *led: rdn and hdd jst over 1f out: no ex whn lost 2nd ins fnl f* **9/2**[2]
6304 **4** 1 ¾ **Dubai Breeze (IRE)**[12] 4605 2-9-4 **72** WilliamBuick 6 62+
(Clive Brittain) *hld up bhd ldrs: rdn 2f out: kpt on wl ins fnl f but nt pce to rch ldrs* **3/1**[1]
1345 **5** *shd* **Mylaporyours (IRE)**[20] 4364 2-9-2 **70** HarryBentley 3 60
(Rod Millman) *trckd ldr: mounting chal whn hung bdly rt turning in: no ch after: fin on stands' side rail* **8/1**[3]
4213 **6** 5 **Latch Onto Blue**[18] 4430 2-9-7 **75** KierenFallon 4 62
(Charles Hills) *cl up: rdn wl over 2f out: btn wl over 1f out: wknd ent fnl f* **3/1**[1]

1m 12.83s (0.93) **Going Correction** -0.025s/f (Stan) **6** Ran SP% **115.4**
Speed ratings (Par 94): **92,91,88,86,86 79**
CSF £33.11 TOTE £9.60: £5.10, £2.10; EX 35.80 Trifecta £361.10.
**Owner** Sutong Pan **Bred** David Jamison Bloodstock **Trained** Kimpton, Hants
**FOCUS**
A modest nursery with five of the six runners having their first experience of Polytrack. A minor best from the winner.

## 5044 BET & WATCH AT WINNER.COM MAIDEN STKS 7f 1y(P)
**3:00** (3:03) (Class 5) 3-Y-0+ **£2,587** (£770; £384; £192) **Stalls** Low

Form RPR
-525 **1** **Half Way**[23] 4263 3-9-0 **69** AmyScott(5) 6 74
(Henry Candy) *mde all: 4 l clr 2f out: sn rdn: wl in command fnl f: unchal* **5/1**
2 **2** 4 **Childesplay**[117] 1422 3-9-0 0 AdamKirby 4 58+
(Heather Main) *trckd ldrs: rdn over 2f out: r.o to go 2nd ins fnl f: no ch w wnr* **2/1**[1]
46 **3** 5 **Four Cheers (IRE)**[37] 3804 3-9-5 0 KierenFallon 2 50
(Clive Brittain) *trckd wnr: rdn 2f out: nt pce to get on terms: no ex whn lost 2nd ins fnl f* **6/1**
0 **4** 2 ¼ **Gharaaneej (IRE)**[18] 4446 3-9-0 0 WilliamBuick 9 39
(John Gosden) *mid-div: pushed along on outer over 3f out: styd on fr 1f out but nvr gng pce to get involved* **9/2**[3]
5 **5** 1 **Oskar Denarius (IRE)**[93] 2031 3-9-5 0 PatDobbs 7 41
(Marcus Tregoning) *s.i.s: in last pair: sme minor late prog: n.d* **16/1**
2 **6** ¾ **Better Chance (IRE)**[33] 3916 3-9-0 0 AhmedAjtebi 3 34
(Saeed bin Suroor) *trckd wnr: rdn 2f out: wknd jst over 1f out* **5/2**[2]
**7** 1 ½ **Heinrich (USA)** 3-9-0 0 RenatoSouza(5) 8 35
(Sylvester Kirk) *s.i.s: a towards rr* **33/1**
**8** *nk* **Tsarglas** 3-9-5 0 HarryBentley 1 34
(Stuart Williams) *mid-div: rdn over 3f out: nvr any imp: wknd 1f out* **50/1**
-64 **9** 1 ¼ **Speedy Rio (IRE)**[9] 4735 3-9-0 0 CamHardie(5) 5 31
(Luke Dace) *s.i.s: mid-div for over 2f: sn struggling in last trio: nt a danger after* **66/1**

1m 23.76s (-1.04) **Going Correction** -0.025s/f (Stan) **9** Ran SP% **123.3**
Speed ratings (Par 103): **104,99,93,91,90 89,87,87,85**
CSF £16.52 TOTE £6.70: £2.70, £1.10, £1.80; EX 20.40 Trifecta £93.30.
**Owner** Henry Candy **Bred** Shadwell Estate Company Limited **Trained** Kingston Warren, Oxon
**FOCUS**
There were a couple of interesting types in this 3yo maiden, but the winner turned it into a procession. This was out of line with his profile and there are reservations over the form.

## 5045 HORSE RACING LOYALTY BONUS AT WINNER.COM H'CAP 5f 6y(P)
**3:30** (3:31) (Class 5) (0-70,74) 3-Y-0+ **£2,587** (£770; £384; £192) **Stalls** High

Form RPR
0531 **1** **Come On Dave (IRE)**[2] 4981 5-9-11 **74** 6ex DanielMuscutt(5) 3 87
(John Butler) *dismntd and walked to s early: mde all: 3 l clr 2f out: r.o strly whn rdn: unchal* **11/10**[1]
0132 **2** 3 **Billy Red**[14] 4546 10-9-5 **68** (b) DannyBrock(5) 4 70
(J R Jenkins) *chsd wnr: rdn over 2f out: outpcd by wnr over 1f out: kpt on fnl f* **10/1**
6212 **3** 2 **Johnny Splash (IRE)**[12] 4614 5-8-13 **57** (v) WilliamBuick 6 52
(Roger Teal) *chsd ldrs: rdn over 2f out: r.o to go 3rd ent fnl f but nvr a threat* **3/1**[2]
035 **4** 3 ½ **Rylee Mooch**[34] 3887 6-9-8 **66** (be[1]) KierenFallon 1 48
(Richard Guest) *chsd ldrs: pushed along over 3f out: rdn over 2f out: no ex whn lost 3rd ent fnl f* **4/1**[3]
0040 **5** 3 **Scruffy Tramp (IRE)**[64] 2879 3-9-2 **70** KieranShoemark(7) 2 41+
(John Butler) *s.i.s: sn outpcd in last: nvr on terms* **14/1**

0603 **6** *1* **Senator Bong**[12] 4614 4-9-6 64 AdamKirby 5 32
(Peter Grayson) *in tch: rdn 3f out: wknd over 1f out* **12/1**
58.01s (-0.79) **Going Correction** -0.025s/f (Stan)
**WFA** 3 from 4yo+ 3lb **6** Ran SP% **116.1**
Speed ratings (Par 103): **105,100,97,91,86 85**
CSF £14.20 TOTE £2.10: £1.10, £3.70; EX 15.50 Trifecta £44.30.
**Owner** Wildcard Racing Syndicate **Bred** Mrs Eithne Hamilton **Trained** Newmarket, Suffolk

**FOCUS**
There was always likely to be plenty of pace on here and it was a question of which of the established trailblazers would be able to dominate. Another all-the-way winner but the form is taken at face value.

## 5046 WINNER.COM FILLIES' HORSERACING H'CAP 1m 1y(P)
**4:00** (4:00) (Class 5) (0-75,72) 3-Y-O+ **£2,587** (£770; £384; £192) **Stalls** High

Form RPR
3420 **1** **Swiss Kiss**[18] 4434 3-9-5 70 WilliamBuick 7 79
(John Gosden) *racd keenly: mde all: rdn clr wl over 1f out: readily* **3/1**[2]
0532 **2** *2* **An Chulainn (IRE)**[4] 4903 3-9-3 68 (b) FrannyNorton 4 71
(Mark Johnston) *hld up bhd ldng quartet: cl up 4f out: rdn whn briefly hmpd wl over 1f out: r.o ins fnl f: snatched 2nd fnl stride: no ch w wnr* **7/4**[1]
6232 **3** *nse* **Invoke (IRE)**[12] 4611 3-9-7 72 AdamKirby 1 75
(Michael Bell) *trckd ldrs: rdn 3f out: wnt 2nd over 1f out: a being readily hld by wnr: lost 2nd fnl stride* **4/1**
5246 **4** *shd* **Heho**[55] 3159 3-9-7 72 (v[1]) KierenFallon 6 75
(Sir Michael Stoute) *trckd ldrs: rdn to chse wnr over 2f out tl over 1f out: kpt on again fnl 120yds* **7/2**[3]
0426 **5** *6* **Chutney (IRE)**[21] 4329 3-9-4 69 PatDobbs 2 57
(Richard Hannon) *trckd ldrs: rdn over 3f out: outpcd 2f out: no threat after* **8/1**
1m 37.31s (-0.89) **Going Correction** -0.025s/f (Stan)
**WFA** 3 from 4yo 7lb **5** Ran SP% **114.7**
Speed ratings (Par 100): **103,101,100,100,94**
CSF £9.13 TOTE £5.30: £1.70, £1.40; EX 10.30 Trifecta £29.30.
**Owner** Lordship Stud **Bred** Lordship Stud **Trained** Newmarket, Suffolk

**FOCUS**
A modest fillies' handicap and another all-the-way winner. She could have lots more to offer but the form has been rated cautiously.

## 5047 WINNER.CO.UK HORSERACING H'CAP 1m 7f 169y(P)
**4:30** (4:31) (Class 4) (0-85,81) 4-Y-O+ **£4,690** (£1,395; £697; £348) **Stalls** Low

Form RPR
1035 **1** **Story Writer**[18] 4441 5-9-4 78 AdamKirby 3 86
(William Knight) *trckd ldrs: rdn over 3f out: chal ent fnl f: led fnl 100yds: pushed out* **5/4**[1]
3121 **2** *3/4* **Underwritten**[12] 4615 5-8-2 62 JimmyQuinn 5 69
(Shaun Harris) *led: rdn whn strly chal fr 3f out: battled on gamely to edge bk ahd over 1f out: hdd fnl 100yds: styd on* **6/1**
311 **3** *3 1/4* **Meetings Man (IRE)**[14] 4552 7-9-2 81 (p) CamHardie(5) 2 84
(Ali Stronge) *racd keenly: trckd ldrs: chal 3f out: rdn 2f out: hld ent fnl f: no ex* **3/1**[2]
0642 **4** *2* **Admirable Duque (IRE)**[2] 4985 8-8-11 71 (be) MartinLane 1 72
(Dominic Ffrench Davis) *hld up in cl 5th: pushed along over 3f out: rdn over 2f out: nvr threatened: wnt 4th nr fin* **12/1**
2334 **5** *nk* **Rosie Rebel**[35] 3859 4-9-2 76 [1] WilliamBuick 4 76
(Rae Guest) *trckd ldrs: rdn 2f out: ch over 1f out: fdd fnl 120yds: lost 4th nr fin* **7/2**[3]
3m 24.62s (-1.08) **Going Correction** -0.025s/f (Stan) **5** Ran SP% **113.6**
Speed ratings (Par 105): **101,100,99,98,97**
CSF £9.66 TOTE £2.20: £1.90, £2.50; EX 8.70 Trifecta £25.40.
**Owner** The Pheasant Rew Partnership **Bred** Oakhill Stud **Trained** Patching, W Sussex

**FOCUS**
This small-field staying handicap was run at an early dawdle and the pace didn't increase until entering the last half-mile. Muddling form, the winner basically to his recent course level.

## 5048 PLAY BLACKJACK AND ROULETTE AT WINNER.COM H'CAP 1m 4f (P)
**5:00** (5:00) (Class 6) (0-60,60) 3-Y-O **£1,940** (£577; £288; £144) **Stalls** Low

Form RPR
6000 **1** **Topaling**[28] 4085 3-8-10 49 TedDurcan 2 52
(Mark H Tompkins) *hld up: pushed along and hdwy over 2f out: c wdst and lost pl turning in: sn drvn: str run ins fnl f: led fnl strides* **8/1**
00-2 **2** *nk* **Wintour Leap**[22] 4279 3-9-2 60 DanielMuscutt(5) 1 63
(Robert Stephens) *trckd ldr: rdn over 2f out: led narrowly ent fnl f: kpt on: hdd fnl strides* **3/1**[2]
0005 **3** *nk* **Dark Tsarina (IRE)**[23] 4261 3-8-3 49 (p) KieranShoemark(7) 3 51
(Michael Madgwick) *cl up: rdn 3f out: ev ch ent fnl f: kpt on* **12/1**
-040 **4** *1 1/2* **Lingfield Lupus (IRE)**[4] 4911 3-8-7 49 oh4 (v) JimmyQuinn 5 46
(John Best) *trckd ldrs: jnd ldr 7f out: rdn to ld 3f out: edgd rt and hdd ent fnl f: no ex* **8/1**
2445 **5** *1 1/4* **Maid Of Tuscany (IRE)**[12] 4616 3-8-12 58 CharlotteJenner(7) 6 56
(Mark Usher) *cl up: rdn whn lft 3rd over 2f out: kpt on same pce fr over 1f out* **5/1**[3]
006 **6** *6* **Bowberry**[20] 4368 3-9-6 59 AdamKirby 8 47
(Clive Cox) *s.i.s: towards rr: struggling over 3f out: short-lived effrt 2f out: nvr threatened* **5/2**[1]
0-05 **7** *20* **Escarlata Rossa**[28] 4088 3-8-4 48 oh3 RossAtkinson(3) 4 18
(J S Moore) *led: rdn and hdd 3f out: cl 3rd whn squeezed up on inner sn after: sn hld: wknd over 1f out* **25/1**
0030 **8** *70* **Monsieur Chabal**[18] 4433 3-8-9 48 KierenFallon 7
(Jamie Osborne) *s.i.s: bhd: effrt over 3f out: qckly btn: eased over 2f out* **5/1**[3]
2m 32.99s (-0.01) **Going Correction** -0.025s/f (Stan) **8** Ran SP% **120.7**
Speed ratings (Par 98): **99,98,98,97,96 92,79,32**
CSF £34.18 CT £297.41 TOTE £11.50: £4.40, £1.10, £3.10; EX 48.80 Trifecta £430.90.
**Owner** M P Bowring **Bred** Dullingham Park Stud & M P Bowring **Trained** Newmarket, Suffolk

**FOCUS**
A poor handicap with a tight three-way finish. The form is rated a little negatively.
T/Plt: £48.10 to a £1 stake. Pool: £50,102.25 - 759.35 winning units. T/Qpdt: £8.00 to a £1 stake. Pool: £3967.51 - 362.59 winning units. TM

# 4708 PONTEFRACT (L-H)
Wednesday, August 6

**OFFICIAL GOING: Good to firm (firm in places; 8.2)**
Wind: Moderate half behind Weather: Cloudy with sunny periods and heavy showers

## 5049 RICHARD KENDALL ESTATE AGENT NEW PONTEFRACT OFFICE H'CAP (FOR GENTLEMAN AMATEUR RIDERS) 1m 2f 6y
**2:10** (2:10) (Class 5) (0-75,74) 3-Y-O+ **£3,119** (£967; £483; £242) **Stalls** Low

Form RPR
0163 **1** **Silver Alliance**[27] 4116 6-11-7 74 (p) MrRBirkett 4 82
(Julia Feilden) *trckd ldrs: hdwy to chse ldr 3f out: chal over 1f out: rdn to ld ent fnl f: kpt on wl towards fin* **6/1**
4/30 **2** *1 1/2* **Kudu Country (IRE)**[18] 4427 8-10-8 66 MrHStock(5) 6 71
(Tom Tate) *cl up: led after 1f: rdn along 2f out: hdd and drvn ent fnl f: kpt on u.p towards fin* **4/1**[3]
-145 **3** *hd* **Obboorr**[29] 4058 5-10-7 65 MrKWood(5) 1 70
(John Wainwright) *hld up in rr: smooth hdwy on outer over 2f out: chsd ldng pair ent fnl f: sn rdn and edgd lft: kpt on same pce towards fin* **3/1**[2]
-531 **4** *18* **Poetic Verse**[18] 3699 4-11-7 74 MrSWalker 7 44
(John Quinn) *trckd ldrs: hdwy 3f out: effrt to chse ldng pair over 2f out: sn rdn and wknd wl over 1f out: bhd and eased fnl f* **6/5**[1]
0-00 **5** *20* **Carazam (IRE)**[14] 4534 7-9-12 58 (tp) MrJPWilliams(7) 5
(Bernard Llewellyn) *led 1f: chsd ldr on inner: rdn along 4f out: sn lost pl and bhd fnl 2f* **25/1**
2m 13.43s (-0.27) **Going Correction** -0.35s/f (Firm) **5** Ran SP% **108.6**
Speed ratings (Par 103): **87,85,85,71,55**
CSF £27.99 TOTE £4.60: £1.60, £2.40; EX 28.90 Trifecta £55.90.
**Owner** In It To Win Partnership **Bred** Peter Harris **Trained** Exning, Suffolk

**FOCUS**
Course officials understandably elected not to water but somehow the course missed the downpours and, despite 4mm falling overnight, it was the quickest ground here so far in 2014. This was a typically moderate handicap of its type, run at a fair pace.

## 5050 FRIENDS OF FRANCIS HAMILTON MEMORIAL EBF STALLIONS MAIDEN STKS (BOBIS RACE) 6f
**2:40** (2:40) (Class 4) 2-Y-O **£6,469** (£1,925; £962; £481) **Stalls** Low

Form RPR
2 **1** **Maftool (USA)**[27] 4117 2-9-5 0 SilvestreDeSousa 8 89+
(Saeed bin Suroor) *trckd ldrs: hdwy to chse ldr wl over 1f out: rdn: green and wandered over 1f out: styd on u.p ins fnl f: led last 100yds* **10/11**[1]
3 **2** *1 1/2* **Flash Fire (IRE)**[10] 4695 2-9-5 0 JoeFanning 5 85
(Mark Johnston) *led: rdn along wl over 1f out: drvn ent fnl f: hdd and no ex last 100yds* **3/1**[2]
0 **3** *7* **Zigayani (IRE)**[12] 4618 2-9-5 0 GrahamLee 1 64
(Sir Michael Stoute) *cl up on inner: rdn along over 2f out: grad wknd appr fnl f* **7/1**
**4** *2 1/4* **Properus (IRE)** 2-9-5 0 TomEaves 3 57+
(Kevin Ryan) *in tch: hdwy on inner over 2f out: swtchd rt to outer and rdn wl over 1f out: sn no imp* **14/1**
3 **5** *10* **Best Dressed**[13] 4570 2-9-5 0 SeanLevey 9 27
(David Brown) *chsd ldrs on outer: rdn along over 2f out: sn wknd* **11/2**[3]
**6** *3/4* **Cape Hideaway** 2-9-5 0 JasonHart 6 25
(Mark Walford) *in tch: rdn along 1/2-way: sn outpcd and rr* **50/1**
0 **7** *25* **Edie White**[32] 3947 2-9-0 0 DuranFentiman 7
(Lawrence Mullaney) *prom: rdn along whn n.m.r wl over 2f out: sn wknd* **100/1**
**P** **Secret Pattern** 2-9-5 0 PaulMulrennan 2
(Ollie Pears) *dwlt and hmpd s: green and in rr: hung rt 1/2-way: sn unbalanced and hung bdly rt and rn v wd home turn: lost action and t.o whn p.u ins fnl f* **33/1**
1m 14.65s (-2.25) **Going Correction** -0.35s/f (Firm) **8** Ran SP% **117.8**
Speed ratings (Par 96): **101,99,89,86,73 72,39,**
CSF £3.96 TOTE £2.20: £1.10, £1.10, £2.20; EX 4.30 Trifecta £15.50.
**Owner** Godolphin **Bred** C Kidder & J K & Linda Griggs **Trained** Newmarket, Suffolk

**FOCUS**
This looked a fair 2yo maiden and the form appears solid with the two market leaders dominating the finish.

## 5051 JAYNE AND STEVE ROBINSON - YOUR LOCAL BOOKMAKER H'CAP (BOBIS RACE) 1m 4y
**3:10** (3:11) (Class 4) (0-80,80) 3-Y-O **£6,469** (£1,925; £962; £481) **Stalls** Low

Form RPR
0421 **1** **Imshivalla (IRE)**[19] 4419 3-8-13 72 TonyHamilton 6 80
(Richard Fahey) *mde all: rdn wl over 1f out: drvn ins fnl f: styd on wl towards fin* **6/4**[1]
3005 **2** *1 1/4* **Emef Diamond**[34] 3897 3-9-2 75 TomEaves 5 79
(Mick Channon) *prom: trckd wnr after 2f: effrt 2f out: rdn to chal jst over 1f out: ev ch tl drvn and kpt on same pce wl ins fnl f* **5/1**[3]
1-33 **3** *nk* **El Beau (IRE)**[19] 4419 3-9-3 76 PhillipMakin 4 79
(John Quinn) *trckd wnr 2f: prom: rdn along and sltly outpcd wl over 1f out: drvn and kpt on u.p ins fnl f: hld whn n.m.r towards fin* **13/8**[2]
3305 **4** *6* **Captain Midnight (IRE)**[11] 4679 3-9-4 80 ConnorBeasley(3) 7 69
(David Brown) *hld up: effrt 2f out: sn rdn and btn wl over 1f out* **7/1**
1m 43.06s (-2.84) **Going Correction** -0.35s/f (Firm) **4** Ran SP% **107.3**
Speed ratings (Par 102): **100,98,98,92**
CSF £8.58 TOTE £1.70; EX 8.70 Trifecta £11.10.
**Owner** Pow Partnership **Bred** M Fahy & Rathbarry Stud **Trained** Musley Bank, N Yorks

**FOCUS**
A modest little handicap run at a true pace. The winner was given a good front-running ride.

## 5052 TIESPLANET.COM - LADIES LOVE GUYS IN TIES H'CAP 1m 4f 8y
**3:40** (3:40) (Class 3) (0-95,88) 3-Y-O **£9,337** (£2,796; £1,398; £699; £349) **Stalls** Low

Form RPR
2221 **1** **Rocket Ship**[28] 4066 3-8-11 82 JoeFanning 2 92+
(Sir Michael Stoute) *mde all: rdn clr wl over 1f out: styd on strly* **5/4**[1]
101 **2** *4* **Hidden Gold (IRE)**[33] 3918 3-9-1 86 SilvestreDeSousa 8 89
(Saeed bin Suroor) *trckd ldrs: hdwy over 2f out: rdn to chse wnr over 1f out: sn drvn and no imp fnl f* **5/2**[2]
5222 **3** *4* **Legal Waves (IRE)**[20] 4360 4-9-5 79 BenCurtis 5 75
(Alan Swinbank) *trckd ldng pair: hdwy on inner to chse wnr over 2f out: rdn along wl over 1f out: sn one pce* **7/1**

0534 **4** ½ **Eltheeb**[10] 4710 7-9-3 **77**......(p) TomEaves 4 72
(Philip Kirby) *hld up in rr: effrt over 2f out: sn rdn and no imp* **5/1**[3]
1342 **5** 7 **Brigadoon**[33] 3926 7-9-8 **82**...... AndrewMullen 7 66
(Michael Appleby) *cl up: rdn along 3f out: drvn over 2f out and sn wknd* **12/1**

2m 34.54s (-6.26) **Going Correction** -0.35s/f (Firm)
**WFA** 3 from 4yo+ 11lb 5 Ran SP% **109.9**
Speed ratings (Par 107): **106,103,100,100,95**
CSF £4.57 TOTE £1.60: £1.10, £2.20; EX 4.00 Trifecta £9.40.
**Owner** K Abdullah **Bred** Juddmonte Farms Ltd **Trained** Newmarket, Suffolk
**FOCUS**
The feature handicap was an interesting affair and the form looks solid. The winner won in the style of a horse that could rate higher.

## 5053 CHAPLINS CLUB H'CAP 5f
**4:10** (4:10) (Class 5) (0-75,81) 3-Y-0+ **£3,234** (£962; £481; £240) **Stalls** Low

Form RPR
133 **1** **Poyle Vinnie**[6] 4833 4-9-6 **71**...... AndrewMullen 5 85
(Michael Appleby) *cl up: rdn to chal wl over 1f out: drvn ins fnl f: kpt on wl to ld nr fin* **4/1**[2]
2200 **2** *nse* **Noodles Blue Boy**[16] 4494 8-9-5 **70**......(p) RobertWinston 4 83
(Ollie Pears) *qckly away and wnt rt s: led: jnd and rdn wl over 1f out: drvn ins fnl f: edgd rt last 75yds: hdd nr fin* **16/1**
2003 **3** 3½ **Boxing Shadows**[10] 4714 4-9-1 **66**...... DavidAllan 2 66
(Les Eyre) *t.k.h: trckd ldrs: hdwy to chse ldng pair over 2f out: rdn wl over 1f out: kpt on same pce fnl f* **7/2**[1]
0245 **4** 1¾ **Ypres**[12] 4632 5-9-7 **72**...... PJMcDonald 8 66
(Jason Ward) *trckd ldrs: hdwy 2f out: rdn along wl over 1f out: drvn and no imp fnl f* **7/1**[3]
0311 **5** 2¼ **Mister Manannan (IRE)**[8] 4752 7-9-11 **81** 6ex...... KevinStott[(5)] 6 67+
(David Nicholls) *dwlt and sltly hmpd s: in rr and t.k.h: hdwy to trck ldrs 1/2-way: rdn along on inner over 1f out: sn no imp* **7/2**[1]
0416 **6** ¾ **Windforpower (IRE)**[4] 4901 4-9-0 **65**......(p) JoeFanning 1 48
(Tracy Waggott) *trckd ldrs on inner: pushed along and outpcd 1/2-way: rdn and sme hdwy wl over 1f out: sn drvn and wknd* **8/1**
1460 **7** *nk* **Teetotal (IRE)**[12] 4632 4-9-9 **74**...... SilvestreDeSousa 9 56
(Nigel Tinkler) *t.k.h: hld up in rr: effrt and sme hdwy 2f out: sn rdn and btn* **8/1**
3506 **8** 1½ **Sunny Side Up (IRE)**[2] 4960 5-8-7 **63**......(p) GemmaTutty[(5)] 11 40
(Karen Tutty) *chsd ldrs on outer: rdn along over 2f out: sn wknd* **12/1**

1m 1.54s (-1.76) **Going Correction** -0.35s/f (Firm) 8 Ran SP% **112.7**
Speed ratings (Par 103): **100,99,94,91,87 86,86,83**
CSF £61.60 CT £242.22 TOTE £5.60: £1.60, £3.80, £1.30; EX 63.30 Trifecta £378.10.
**Owner** Dallas Racing & C L Bacon **Bred** Cecil And Miss Alison Wiggins **Trained** Danethorpe, Notts
**FOCUS**
This appeared to be a competitive sprint handicap for the class, but the first pair dominated the home straight.

## 5054 MATTY BOWN VETERANS H'CAP 1m 4y
**4:40** (4:41) (Class 4) (0-80,83) 6-Y-0+ **£5,175** (£1,540; £769; £384) **Stalls** Low

Form RPR
0422 **1** **Kiwi Bay**[4] 4922 9-9-6 **79**...... PaulMulrennan 3 87
(Michael Dods) *trckd ldrs on outer: hdwy and cl up 2f out: rdn to chal ent fnl f: drvn to ld last 100yds: r.o* **3/1**[1]
0101 **2** 1¼ **Shadowtime**[8] 4753 9-9-10 **83** 6ex...... DaleSwift 1 88
(Tracy Waggott) *trckd ldrs on inner: hdwy wl over 1f out: rdn to chal end edgd rt ins fnl f: sn drvn and kpt on wl towards fin* **11/1**
2243 **3** *hd* **Kingscroft (IRE)**[4] 4922 6-9-7 **80**...... RobertWinston 2 85
(Michael Herrington) *trckd ldrs: hdwy 2f out: rdn over 1f out: tk slt ld ent fnl f: sn drvn: hdd kpt on same pce last 100yds* **3/1**[1]
0536 **4** 1¾ **Icy Blue**[30] 4023 6-8-2 **61**......(p) JoeFanning 7 61
(Richard Whitaker) *trckd ldr: cl up 3f out: led wl over 1f out and sn rdn: drvn and hdd ent fnl f: kpt on same pce* **14/1**
5030 **5** ½ **Fazza**[4] 4922 7-8-11 **75**...... KevinStott[(5)] 8 74
(Edwin Tuer) *hld up in rr: hdwy wl over 1f out: rdn and styng on strly whn nt clr run and hmpd ins fnl f: sn swtchd lft: kpt on* **6/1**[3]
1102 **6** 4½ **True Pleasure (IRE)**[15] 4514 7-9-7 **80**...... PJMcDonald 6 68
(James Bethell) *hld up: a towards rr* **9/2**[2]
2/32 **7** 17 **Naoise (IRE)**[10] 4703 6-8-10 **74**......(t) JacobButterfield[(5)] 9 22
(Ollie Pears) *dwlt and towards rr: rdn along on outer over 2f out: sn outpcd and bhd* **11/1**
4045 **8** 9 **Toto Skyllachy**[15] 4514 9-9-6 **79**...... DanielTudhope 5 5
(Marjorie Fife) *led: rdn along wl over 2f out: hdd & wknd wl over 1f out* **14/1**

1m 42.68s (-3.22) **Going Correction** -0.35s/f (Firm) 8 Ran SP% **112.5**
Speed ratings (Par 103): **102,100,100,98,98 93,76,67**
CSF £35.97 CT £103.53 TOTE £3.50: £1.40, £2.20, £1.30; EX 34.60 Trifecta £170.00.
**Owner** Kiwi Racing **Bred** Templeton Stud **Trained** Denton, Co Durham
**FOCUS**
A modest handicap for veterans and it proved a tight betting heat. There was a decent enough pace.

## 5055 KEITH HAMMILL MEMORIAL H'CAP 6f
**5:10** (5:10) (Class 5) (0-75,75) 3-Y-0 **£3,234** (£962; £481; £240) **Stalls** Low

Form RPR
0020 **1** **Le Laitier (FR)**[19] 4411 3-9-0 **68**...... TomEaves 1 75
(Scott Dixon) *qckly away: mde all: rdn over 1f out: drvn ins fnl f: kpt on wl towards fin* **12/1**
-200 **2** ¾ **Two Smart (IRE)**[67] 2768 3-9-7 **75**......[1] PJMcDonald 4 79
(K R Burke) *chsd wnr: cl up 2f out: rdn over 1f out: drvn and kpt on fnl f* **8/1**
4242 **3** 1¾ **Faure Island**[14] 4535 3-9-4 **72**...... BenCurtis 8 71
(Henry Candy) *trckd ldrs on outer: effrt over 2f out: rdn along wl over 1f out: drvn and kpt on same pce ins fnl f* **2/1**[1]
0233 **4** 1¾ **Percy's Gal**[30] 4019 3-8-13 **72**...... GemmaTutty[(5)] 7 65
(Karen Tutty) *hld up: hdwy wl over 1f out: rdn to chse ldrs ent fnl f: sn drvn and no imp* **4/1**[2]
0641 **5** 6 **Centre Haafhd**[15] 4512 3-9-7 **75**......(b) GrahamGibbons 5 55
(David Barron) *chsd ldrs: sltly hmpd after 2f: effrt over 2f out: sn rdn along and wknd wl over 1f out* **4/1**[2]
4434 **6** 8 **Alpine Flower (IRE)**[28] 4067 3-8-9 **63**......(t) DavidAllan 2 26
(Tim Easterby) *hmpd s: a in rr* **8/1**
-061 **7** 9 **Sartori**[30] 4019 3-9-0 **68**...... RobertWinston 9
(Marjorie Fife) *hld up: rdn along over 2f out: sn outpcd and bhd* **7/1**[3]

1m 14.88s (-2.02) **Going Correction** -0.35s/f (Firm) 7 Ran SP% **115.7**
Speed ratings (Par 100): **99,98,95,93,85 74,62**
CSF £102.67 CT £274.20 TOTE £13.90: £4.80, £4.00; EX 104.90 Trifecta £595.10.

**Owner** P J Dixon & Partners **Bred** J Vittori & Mme Y Dixon **Trained** Babworth, Notts
**FOCUS**
An ordinary 3yo sprint handicap. The winner was quickly away and made all.
T/Plt: £31.80 to a £1 stake. Pool: £62,167.21 - 1423.15 winning units. T/Qpdt: £6.60 to a £1 stake. Pool: £4817.39 - 534.66 winning units. JR

# 4763 YARMOUTH (L-H)
### Wednesday, August 6
**OFFICIAL GOING: Good to soft (good in places)**
Wind: Light across Weather: Cloudy with sunny spells until heavy rain between races 5 and 6

## 5056 GEORGE DARLING MEMORIAL MAIDEN AUCTION STKS 7f 3y
**5:20** (5:21) (Class 6) 2-Y-0 **£2,458** (£731; £365; £182) **Stalls** Centre

Form RPR
53 **1** **Lady Maesmor**[13] 4589 2-8-8 0...... JackMitchell 1 68
(Martyn Meade) *w ldr tl led over 2f out: rdn over 1f out: jst hld on* **5/2**[1]
**2** *shd* **Fidelma Moon (IRE)** 2-8-5 0...... JoeyHaynes[(3)] 4 68+
(K R Burke) *hld up in tch: shkn up over 1f out: r.o u.p ins fnl f: jst failed* **4/1**[2]
**3** ¾ **Spring Dixie (IRE)** 2-8-9 0...... FrederikTylicki 5 67+
(Rae Guest) *chsd ldrs: n.m.r and lost pl over 4f out: hdwy over 1f out: r.o* **4/1**[2]
**4** 3 **Everyday (IRE)** 2-8-12 0...... WilliamCarson 6 62+
(George Baker) *s.i.s: plld hrd in rr: hdwy over 4f out: rdn and ev ch 2f out: wknd ins fnl f* **4/1**[2]
60 **5** 4½ **Cahar Fad (IRE)**[14] 4541 2-8-6 0......(p) PaddyPilley[(7)] 2 50
(Steph Hollinshead) *led: rdn and hdd over 2f out: wknd over 1f out* **33/1**
06 **6** 6 **New Abbey Dancer (IRE)**[14] 4541 2-8-3 0...... ShelleyBirkett[(5)] 7 29
(Gay Kelleway) *chsd ldrs to 1/2-way* **20/1**
**7** 3½ **Norfolk Sunset** 2-8-7 0...... LukeMorris 3 19
(Ed Vaughan) *s.i.s: sn prom: pushed along and lost pl over 4f out: sn bhd* **8/1**[3]
**8** 2¾ **Indomitable Spirit** 2-8-13 0...... LiamJones 8 17
(Martin Smith) *s.i.s: outpcd* **16/1**

1m 32.87s (6.27) **Going Correction** +0.20s/f (Good) 8 Ran SP% **113.3**
Speed ratings (Par 92): **72,71,71,67,62 55,51,48**
CSF £12.34 TOTE £2.80: £1.70, £1.70, £1.70; EX 14.10 Trifecta £40.70.
**Owner** Dr Graham Jackson **Bred** D P Martin **Trained** Newmarket, Suffolk
**FOCUS**
Bottom bend dolled out 1.5m and races on Round course increased by 7m. Although a total of 12mm of morning rain, there was a drying wind and the ground rode as advertised. There was a genuine pace, although they ran into a stiff headwind. A maiden with little apparent strength in depth and one with more experience beat three newcomers. The form does not look up to much.

## 5057 MOULTON NURSERIES FILLIES' H'CAP 7f 3y
**5:50** (5:50) (Class 5) (0-70,66) 3-Y-0+ **£2,587** (£770; £384; £192) **Stalls** Centre

Form RPR
5140 **1** **Strike A Light**[18] 4428 3-8-11 **57**...... LukeMorris 3 74+
(Rae Guest) *trckd ldrs: led wl over 1f out: sn rdn clr: easily* **9/4**[1]
6504 **2** 8 **Mendacious Harpy (IRE)**[43] 3559 3-9-6 **66**......(b) WilliamCarson 2 60
(George Baker) *s.i.s: sn prom: led overall over 2f out: rdn and hdd wl over 1f out: sn outpcd* **3/1**[2]
0-03 **3** 1 **Alderley**[19] 4411 3-9-5 **65**...... FrederikTylicki 4 57
(Martyn Meade) *led main gp tl rdn and hdd over 2f out: styd on same pce fr over 1f out* **6/1**[3]
5006 **4** ¾ **Sairaam (IRE)**[14] 4534 8-8-4 **47** oh2......(p) BillyCray[(3)] 5 39
(Charles Smith) *racd alone stands' side: led overall tl rdn: hung lft and hdd over 2f out: styd on same pce fr over 1f out* **33/1**
4001 **5** 2½ **Ermine Ruby**[29] 4056 3-9-0 **60**...... CraigAWilliams 6 43
(Charles Hills) *chsd ldrs: rdn over 2f out: wknd over 1f out* **9/4**[1]
5404 **6** 34 **Mill I Am (USA)**[20] 4341 4-8-7 **54**...... AaronJones[(7)] 1
(Stuart Williams) *s.v.s: a wl bhd* **14/1**

1m 29.58s (2.98) **Going Correction** +0.20s/f (Good)
**WFA** 3 from 4yo+ 6lb 6 Ran SP% **110.4**
Speed ratings (Par 100): **90,80,79,78,76 37**
CSF £8.97 TOTE £4.00: £1.60, £1.90; EX 9.30 Trifecta £24.50.
**Owner** Trevor Benton **Bred** Cheveley Park Stud Ltd **Trained** Newmarket, Suffolk
**FOCUS**
The pace was genuine for a relatively modest fillies' handicap.

## 5058 GREAT YARMOUTH & CAISTER GOLF CLUB MERCHANTS H'CAP 1m 3y
**6:20** (6:20) (Class 5) (0-75,74) 4-Y-0+ **£2,587** (£770; £384; £192) **Stalls** Centre

Form RPR
3404 **1** **Handheld**[64] 2876 7-9-2 **73**......(p) ShelleyBirkett[(5)] 6 81
(Julia Feilden) *a.p: chsd ldr over 3f out: led over 1f out: sn rdn: styd on* **7/2**[2]
4552 **2** 1¼ **Jonnie Skull (IRE)**[8] 4767 8-8-9 **61**......(vt) WilliamCarson 1 66
(Phil McEntee) *led: clr 7f out tl over 2f out: rdn and hdd over 1f out: styd on* **7/1**
02 **3** *nse* **Ela Goog La Mou**[39] 3705 5-8-3 **58**...... RosieJessop[(3)] 4 63
(Peter Charalambous) *hld up: hdwy over 3f out: rdn over 1f out: ev ch ins fnl f: styd on same pce* **9/2**[3]
5455 **4** 1¾ **Peak Storm**[26] 4153 5-9-1 **67**......(v) LukeMorris 5 68
(John O'Shea) *hld up: hung lft over 3f out: sn rdn: hdwy u.p over 1f out: no imp ins fnl f* **12/1**
0041 **5** 41 **Tommy's Secret**[8] 4766 4-9-1 **74** 6ex...... LewisWalsh[(7)] 2
(Jane Chapple-Hyam) *chsd ldr to 1/2-way: sn rdn: wknd over 2f out* **3/1**[1]
1314 **6** *hd* **Pretty Bubbles**[34] 3890 5-9-5 **71**...... FrederikTylicki 3
(J R Jenkins) *prom: shkn up over 2f out: wknd wl over 1f out* **3/1**[1]

1m 43.92s (3.32) **Going Correction** +0.20s/f (Good) 6 Ran SP% **110.6**
Speed ratings (Par 103): **91,89,89,87,46 46**
CSF £26.12 TOTE £3.80: £1.80, £3.10; EX 28.30 Trifecta £178.80.
**Owner** Newmarket Equine Tours Racing Club **Bred** Juddmonte Farms Ltd **Trained** Exning, Suffolk
**FOCUS**
An uncompetitive handicap for the class and the pace was just fair.

## 5059 CUSTOM KITCHENS OF LOWESTOFT H'CAP 6f 3y
**6:50** (6:51) (Class 5) (0-70,70) 3-Y-0+ **£2,587** (£770; £384; £192) **Stalls** Centre

Form RPR
1211 **1** **Refuse Colette (IRE)**[13] 4595 5-9-11 **69**...... PaoloSirigu 3 80
(Mick Quinn) *trckd ldrs tl led over 2f out: shkn up over 1f out: styd on wl: eased towards fin* **4/5**[1]

2426 **2** 1/2 **Ray Of Joy**[19] 4401 8-9-12 **70**....................(v) FrederikTylicki 4 76
(J R Jenkins) *hmpd after s: sn prom: rdn over 1f out: styd on* **9/2**[2]

0-00 **3** 2 **Aye Aye Skipper (IRE)**[27] 4131 4-9-9 **67**.................... SebSanders 1 67
(Dean Ivory) *w ldr tl rdn over 2f out: styd on same pce ins fnl f* **12/1**

0103 **4** 5 **Uprise**[8] 4766 5-9-7 **68**....................(t) RyanPowell(3) 5 53
(George Margarson) *hld up: rdn over 1f out: wknd fnl f* **8/1**

4504 **5** nk **Danzoe (IRE)**[13] 4595 7-8-7 **51**.................... LukeMorris 2 35
(Christine Dunnett) *led: rdn and hdd over 2f out: wknd ins fnl f* **25/1**

1040 **6** 1 **Sweet Talking Guy (IRE)**[28] 4078 4-9-2 **63**..........(t) SimonPearce(3) 6 44
(Lydia Pearce) *hld up: rdn and wknd over 1f out* **7/1**[3]

1m 17.05s (2.65) **Going Correction** +0.20s/f (Good) **6** Ran SP% **108.9**
Speed ratings (Par 103): **90,89,86,80,79 78**
CSF £4.31 TOTE £1.40: £1.20, £1.70; EX 3.70 Trifecta £32.80.
**Owner** YNWA Partnership **Bred** Patrick O'Reilly **Trained** Newmarket, Suffolk

**FOCUS**
They decided to come up the centre of the track for this modest handicap and the pace was reasonable.

## 5060 BANHAM POULTRY H'CAP 5f 43y
**7:20** (7:20) (Class 4) (0-80,80) 3-Y-0+ **£5,045** (£1,501; £750; £375) **Stalls** Centre

Form RPR

3424 **1** **Indian Tinker**[39] 3707 5-8-11 **67**.................... LiamJones 8 79
(Robert Cowell) *hld up in tch: led and hung lft fr over 1f out: drvn out* **9/2**[2]

5600 **2** 1 1/4 **It Must Be Faith**[13] 4571 4-8-6 **67**....................(p) AlistairRawlinson(5) 3 75
(Michael Appleby) *awkward leaving stalls: hld up: hdwy 1/2-way: rdn over 1f out: styd on to go 2nd wl ins fnl f: nt rch wnr* **9/2**[2]

1224 **3** 1 1/4 **Vodka Chaser (IRE)**[4] 4890 3-8-5 **69**.................... PhilipPrince(5) 1 71
(Alison Hutchinson) *w ldrs tl led 3f out: rdn and hdd over 1f out: styd on same pce ins fnl f* **4/1**[1]

6500 **4** 2 1/2 **Commanche**[8] 4765 5-9-0 **75**.................... ShelleyBirkett(5) 2 69
(Chris Dwyer) *prom: rdn over 1f out: styd on same pce* **13/2**

23 **5** 1 3/4 **Cardinal**[71] 2637 9-8-12 **68**.................... FrederikTylicki 5 56
(Robert Cowell) *led 2f: rdn over 1f out: wknd fnl f* **11/2**

6620 **6** 3 **Swendab (IRE)**[13] 4594 6-9-8 **78**....................(v) LukeMorris 7 55
(John O'Shea) *prom: rdn 1/2-way: wknd over 1f out* **15/2**

-020 **7** 2 1/4 **Tom Sawyer**[14] 4553 6-9-2 **75**....................(b) JoeyHaynes(3) 6 44
(Julie Camacho) *w ldrs tl rdn 1/2-way: wknd over 1f out* **5/1**[3]

1m 3.18s (0.48) **Going Correction** +0.20s/f (Good)
**WFA** 3 from 4yo+ 3lb **7** Ran SP% **113.5**
Speed ratings (Par 105): **104,102,100,96,93 88,84**
CSF £24.48 CT £86.31 TOTE £5.70: £1.90, £5.40; EX 31.70 Trifecta £155.50.
**Owner** J Sargeant **Bred** R S Cockerill (farms) Ltd **Trained** Six Mile Bottom, Cambs

**FOCUS**
No more than a fair sprint for the class and those at the foot of the weights filled the first three places. They raced up the middle.

## 5061 GREENE KING FESTIVAL AT YARMOUTH RACECOURSE H'CAP 5f 43y
**7:50** (7:52) (Class 6) (0-60,66) 3-Y-0 **£1,940** (£577; £288; £144) **Stalls** Centre

Form RPR

3-06 **1** **Pieman's Girl**[22] 4306 3-9-4 **57**.................... WilliamCarson 4 65
(Anthony Carson) *sn pushed along and prom: led 2f out: rdn and hung lft ins fnl f: styd on* **14/1**

153 **2** 1 1/4 **Dancing Juice**[25] 4193 3-8-13 **55**....................(v) JoeyHaynes(3) 6 58
(K R Burke) *sn led: rdn and hdd 2f out: edgd lft ins fnl f: styd on same pce* **9/2**[3]

0221 **3** 1 1/4 **Oasis Mirage**[9] 4735 3-9-13 **66** 6ex.................... FrederikTylicki 5 65
(Robert Cowell) *w ldr tl pushed along 1/2-way: rdn over 1f out: edgd lft and no ex ins fnl f* **4/5**[1]

0-46 **4** 2 3/4 **Reaffirmed (IRE)**[41] 3627 3-9-6 **59**.................... LukeMorris 3 48+
(Ed Vaughan) *prom: rdn over 1f out: hung lft fnl f: styd on same pce* **10/3**[2]

50-4 **5** 11 **Anytimeatall (IRE)**[22] 4307 3-9-4 **60**.................... RobertTart(3) 2 9
(Alan Bailey) *awkward leaving stalls: chsd ldrs: rdn 1/2-way: sn wknd* **20/1**

1m 6.7s (4.00) **Going Correction** +0.20s/f (Good) **5** Ran SP% **108.2**
Speed ratings (Par 98): **76,74,72,67,50**
CSF £68.48 TOTE £15.20: £4.80, £2.30; EX 89.00 Trifecta £115.40.
**Owner** W H Carson **Bred** Minster Stud **Trained** Newmarket, Suffolk

**FOCUS**
A sharp shower arrived before the start of this moderate sprint handicap in which there was an upset.

## 5062 FAMILY FUNDAY AT GREAT YARMOUTH RACECOURSE H'CAP 1m 6f 17y
**8:20** (8:20) (Class 5) (0-75,72) 3-Y-0+ **£2,587** (£770; £384; £192) **Stalls** Low

Form RPR

0661 **1** **Needless Shouting (IRE)**[21] 4333 3-8-13 **70**.................... SamHitchcott 5 81
(Mick Channon) *sn led at stdy pce: qcknd over 3f out: rdn over 1f out: styd on* **9/2**[3]

-622 **2** 3/4 **Mountain Kingdom (IRE)**[11] 4657 3-9-0 **71**.................... LukeMorris 1 81
(Sir Mark Prescott Bt) *a.p: chsd wnr over 2f out: rdn over 1f out: styd on* **11/8**[1]

3413 **3** 10 **The Ducking Stool**[13] 4591 7-9-4 **67**.................... ShelleyBirkett(5) 2 64
(Julia Feilden) *chsd wnr tl rdn over 2f out: styd on same pce fr over 1f out* **9/2**[3]

0243 **4** 36 **Wall Street Boss (USA)**[20] 4369 4-10-0 **72**..........(v[1]) FrederikTylicki 3 22
(James Fanshawe) *hld up: pushed along 6f out: rdn and wknd 3f out* **11/4**[2]

0-05 **5** 15 **Mr Wickfield**[9] 4743 3-8-8 **65**.................... LiamJones 4
(John Best) *chsd ldrs tl rdn and wknd over 3f out* **25/1**

3m 14.64s (7.04) **Going Correction** +0.35s/f (Good)
**WFA** 3 from 4yo+ 13lb **5** Ran SP% **109.0**
Speed ratings (Par 103): **93,92,86,66,57**
CSF £10.98 TOTE £6.10: £2.00, £1.40; EX 11.60 Trifecta £17.70.
**Owner** Lord Ilsley Racing (Russell Syndicate) **Bred** John Connaughton **Trained** West Ilsley, Berks

**FOCUS**
The pace was sedate for this modest and poorly contested handicap, the form of which may prove unreliable. The front two drew well clear.

T/Plt: £358.80 to a £1 stake. Pool: £47,557.79 - 96.74 winning units. T/Qpdt: £48.80 to a £1 stake. Pool: £4749.49 - 71.95 winning units. CR

# 5028 BRIGHTON (L-H)
Thursday, August 7

**OFFICIAL GOING: Good to firm (good in places; 7.5)**
Wind: Light; against Weather: Dry and sunny

## 5070 CHOICEBET.NET MONEY BACK SHORT HEAD LOSERS H'CAP 5f 59y
**2:20** (2:20) (Class 5) (0-75,74) 4-Y-0+ **£2,587** (£770; £384; £192) **Stalls** Centre

Form RPR

3144 **1** **Ada Lovelace**[20] 4401 4-8-12 **65**.................... RichardHughes 3 76
(John Gallagher) *chsd ldrs: clsd and swtchd rt 2f out: led and travelling strly over 1f out: nudged along and in command fnl f: easily* **9/4**[1]

5423 **2** 2 1/4 **Whitecrest**[20] 4399 6-9-7 **74**.................... WilliamTwiston-Davies 7 77
(John Spearing) *racd off the pce in midfield: clsd to chse ldrs 2f out: chsd wnr and drvn over 1f out: kpt on for clr 2nd but no threat to wnr* **8/1**

1553 **3** 3 1/2 **Storm Lightning**[21] 4339 5-9-4 **71**.................... GeorgeBaker 4 62
(Mark Brisbourne) *stdd after s: hld up wl off the pce in rr: rdn over 1f out: r.o fnl f to snatch 3rd cl home: nvr trbld ldrs* **5/2**[2]

5310 **4** 1/2 **Welease Bwian (IRE)**[15] 4553 5-8-10 **70**..........(t) AaronJones(7) 5 59
(Stuart Williams) *racd off the pce in 5th: sme hdwy over 1f out: wnt 3rd fnl 100yds tl cl home: nvr a threat to ldrs* **12/1**

3604 **5** 2 1/4 **Dreams Of Glory**[23] 4284 6-9-4 **71**.................... DavidProbert 1 52
(Ron Hodges) *pressed ldr and clr of field tl 2f out: 3rd and btn over 1f out: wknd fnl f* **7/2**[3]

0/60 **6** 3 **Living It Large (FR)**[20] 4391 7-9-7 **74**.................... OisinMurphy 6 45
(Ed de Giles) *sn bustled up to ld and clr w rival: rdn and hdd over 1f out: sn btn and wknd fnl f* **13/2**

1m 2.76s (0.46) **Going Correction** +0.075s/f (Good) **6** Ran SP% **113.7**
Speed ratings (Par 103): **99,95,89,89,85 80**
CSF £20.63 TOTE £2.80: £2.10, £2.90; EX 19.50 Trifecta £45.10.
**Owner** D A Clark **Bred** D A Clark **Trained** Chastleton, Oxon

**FOCUS**
Rail on apex of bend moved after racing on Wednesday and dolled out 3yds between 6f and 2.5f and distances increased by about 9yds. An ordinary little handicap. The winner was well backed on her first try over 5f for John Gallagher, while the runner-up can be rated up to his recent best.

## 5071 HOWARD EDUCATION LTD (S) H'CAP 6f 209y
**2:50** (2:50) (Class 6) (0-60,60) 3-Y-0+ **£1,940** (£577; £288; £144) **Stalls** Centre

Form RPR

2214 **1** **Clapperboard**[49] 3389 3-9-4 **60**....................(b) FergusSweeney 11 66
(Paul Fitzsimons) *mde all: rdn over 1f out: hrd pressed ins fnl f: battled on gamely: all out* **6/1**[3]

4046 **2** shd **Mill I Am (USA)**[1] 5057 4-9-4 **54**.................... RichardHughes 12 61
(Stuart Williams) *chsd ldng trio: rdn and effrt over 1f out: chsd wnr 1f out: str chal fnl 100yds: r.o: jst hld* **5/1**[2]

4110 **3** nk **Fairy Mist (IRE)**[12] 4655 7-9-4 **54**....................(v) WilliamCarson 8 60
(John Bridger) *t.k.h: hld up in tch in midfield: swtchd rt and rdn over 1f out: styd on wl u.p fnl 100yds: nt quite rch ldng pair* **9/2**[1]

5256 **4** 1 **Viking Warrior (IRE)**[17] 4489 7-8-13 **49**.................... OisinMurphy 1 54
(Shaun Harris) *in tch in midfield: effrt on inner 2f out: chsd ldrs and short of room whn hmpd ins fnl f: nvr enough room fnl 150yds and coasted home* **8/1**

353- **5** 1/2 **Ding Ding**[303] 7110 3-8-9 **54**.................... CharlesBishop(3) 2 54
(Mick Channon) *hld up towards rr: rdn and effrt 2f out: hdwy u.p and swtchd rt ins fnl f: styd on wl towards fin: nt rch ldrs* **14/1**

00-6 **6** nse **Stonecrabstomorrow (IRE)**[44] 3555 11-9-2 **55** MichaelJMMurphy(3) 3 57
(Michael Attwater) *s.i.s: bhd: stl in rr and swtchd rt over 1f out: hdwy 1f out: styd on strly ins fnl f: nt rch ldrs* **25/1**

00-0 **7** nse **Actonetaketwo**[23] 4279 4-8-10 **46** oh1.................... DavidProbert 15 48
(Ron Hodges) *nt best away: sn rcvrd to chse ldr: unable qck u.p over 1f out: one pce ins fnl f* **33/1**

0602 **8** 2 **High On The Hog (IRE)**[15] 4534 6-8-5 **46**.................... CamHardie(5) 14 43
(Mark Brisbourne) *in tch in midfield: rdn and no imp over 1f out: kpt on same pce ins fnl f* **8/1**

1040 **9** 1 1/2 **Katmai River (IRE)**[38] 3781 7-8-10 **53**..........(v) CharlotteJenner(7) 6 46
(Mark Usher) *t.k.h: hld up towards rr: rdn over 2f out: no hdwy tl kpt on ins fnl f: nvr trbld ldrs* **10/1**

6150 **10** 1 1/2 **Ishi Honest**[14] 4578 4-9-6 **56**.................... SilvestreDeSousa 7 58
(Mark Usher) *chsd ldrs: rdn 2f out: drvn and short of room ent fnl f: looked to be struggling whn squeezed for room and hmpd ins fnl f: no ch and nt pushed after* **8/1**

3-00 **11** 2 **Holli Deya**[134] 1105 4-8-3 **46** oh1....................(v) AaronJones(7) 9 30
(Andi Brown) *dwlt: hld up towards rr: rdn and effrt ent fnl 2f: lost pl over 1f out: wl hld after* **50/1**

0643 **12** hd **Little Choosey**[30] 4042 4-8-10 **46**.................... JohnFahy 10 29
(Anabel K Murphy) *hld up towards rr: hdwy into midfield on outer 1/2-way: rdn and btn 2f out: wknd over 1f out* **8/1**

1m 24.46s (1.36) **Going Correction** +0.075s/f (Good)
**WFA** 3 from 4yo+ 6lb **12** Ran SP% **118.1**
Speed ratings (Par 101): **95,94,94,93,92 92,92,90,88,87 84,84**
CSF £35.35 CT £149.75 TOTE £6.60: £2.10, £2.50, £1.90; EX 38.70 Trifecta £136.90.The winner was bought in for 8,800gns
**Owner** Saxon Gate Bloodstock (Helene Moller) **Bred** Theakston Stud **Trained** Upper Lambourn, Berks

**FOCUS**
A weak handicap in which they finished in a bit of a heap. The runner-up ran a personal best on turf.

## 5072 TM LEWIN SHIRTS, SUITS AND MORE MAIDEN AUCTION STKS 7f 214y
**3:20** (3:20) (Class 5) 2-Y-0 **£2,587** (£770; £384; £192) **Stalls** Centre

Form RPR

0 **1** **Percy Veer**[39] 3748 2-9-0 0.................... SilvestreDeSousa 7 62
(Sylvester Kirk) *chsd ldr tl led over 2f out: rdn and hdd over 1f out: led again ins fnl f: r.o wl* **16/1**

0 **2** 1/2 **Diamond Runner (IRE)**[22] 4330 2-8-8 0....................(v) NoelGarbutt(5) 8 60
(Hugo Palmer) *dwlt and rdn along early: in tch: hdwy to press ldrs 1/2-way: rdn to ld over 1f out: hld hd high and immediately hung lft: stl racing awkwardly and hdd ins fnl f: hld towards fin* **33/1**

006 **3** 1/2 **Arthur's Way (IRE)**[5] 4885 2-9-3 0.................... GeorgeBaker 3 63
(Paul Cole) *led: hdd over 2f out: rdn 2f out: 3rd and stl pressing ldrs 1f out: unable qck fnl 100yds* **8/1**[3]

4 **4** 3 1/2 **Lear's Rock (IRE)**[22] 4330 2-8-13 0.................... AndreaAtzeni 4 51
(Ralph Beckett) *in tch: effrt in 4th ent fnl 2f: rdn and no imp over 1f out: one pce and wl hld fnl f* **5/4**[2]

643 **5** *8* **Hawkmeister (IRE)**[30] 4054 2-9-0 75...(b[1]) RichardHughes 5 32
(Richard Hannon) *stdd s: hld up in tch: rdn 3f out: drvn and no hdwy wl over 1f out: wl btn 1f out: eased ins fnl f* **6/5**[1]

1m 38.78s (2.78) **Going Correction** +0.075s/f (Good) 5 Ran SP% **109.8**
Speed ratings (Par 94): **89,88,88,84,76**
CSF £250.81 TOTE £16.60: £6.10, £3.90; EX 108.80 Trifecta £323.10.
**Owner** Mr & Mrs M Crow **Bred** Miss K Rausing **Trained** Upper Lambourn, Berks

**FOCUS**
A modest 2yo maiden.

## 5073 FROSTS4CARS.CO.UK BRIGHTON CHALLENGE CUP (H'CAP) 1m 3f 196y
3:50 (3:50) (Class 4) (0-80,79) 3-Y-O+

**£12,450** (£3,728; £1,864; £932; £466; £234) **Stalls** High

Form RPR

1323 **1** **Barwick**[10] 4736 6-9-4 **78**... CamHardie(5) 13 88
(Lady Herries) *stdd s: in tch in midfield: effrt in 3rd over 1f out: drvn and ev ch 1f out: led fnl 100yds: styd on wl: rdn out* **10/1**

00-0 **2** *3/4* **Laser Blazer**[18] 2774 6-9-2 **71**...(p) FergusSweeney 1 80
(Alan King) *stdd s: t.k.h: hld up in rr: hdwy 4f out: rdn and effrt to chse ldrs 1f out: kpt on wl towards fin: wnt 2nd last strides* **10/1**

0522 **3** *hd* **Echo Brava**[21] 4351 4-9-6 **78**... MichaelJMMurphy(3) 5 87
(Luke Dace) *in tch in midfield: swtchd rt and effrt to chse ldr 2f out: ev ch and drvn 1f out: kpt on same pce fnl 100yds* **10/1**

0252 **4** *hd* **Notarised**[4] 4940 3-8-13 **79**... SilvestreDeSousa 7 87
(Mark Johnston) *led: rdn ent fnl 2f: hrd drvn over 1f out: hdd fnl 100yds: no ex: kpt on same pce after: lost 2 pls nr fin* **5/4**[1]

3421 **5** *hd* **Ethics Girl (IRE)**[28] 4119 8-9-0 **69**...(bt) JimCrowley 9 77
(John Berry) *hld up in tch towards rr: hdwy over 2f out: drvn to chse ldrs 1f out: pressing ldrs ins fnl f: one pce towards fin* **14/1**

0016 **6** *6* **Whinging Willie (IRE)**[28] 4119 5-8-7 **69**...(p) HectorCrouch(7) 12 67
(Gary Moore) *in tch in midfield: hdwy to chse ldr 8f out tl 2f out: btn over 1f out: wknd fnl f* **28/1**

0150 **7** *5* **Royal Alcor (IRE)**[14] 4575 7-9-5 **74**...(t) DavidProbert 6 64
(Gay Kelleway) *hld up in tch towards rr: hdwy over 2f out: no hdwy and edgd lft over 1f out: wknd fnl f* **50/1**

3535 **8** *1 1/2* **Hi Note**[21] 4351 6-9-5 **77**... CharlesBishop(3) 4 65
(Sheena West) *chsd ldrs: rdn and unable qck over 2f out: lost pl and btn wl over 1f out: wknd fnl f* **33/1**

1641 **9** *3* **Compton Bird**[21] 4354 5-9-10 **79**... AndreaAtzeni 14 62
(Paul Fitzsimons) *stdd s: hld up in tch towards rr: short-lived effrt 2f out: sn btn and wknd over 1f out* **7/1**[2]

6411 **10** *19* **El Bravo**[11] 4709 8-9-3 **75** 6ex... NeilFarley(3) 3 28
(Shaun Harris) *chsd ldrs early: steadily lost pl: towards rr and drvn over 2f out: wknd 2f out: wl bhd and eased fnl f: t.o* **33/1**

1142 **11** *1 3/4* **Men Don't Cry (IRE)**[5] 4910 5-9-1 **70**... OisinMurphy 2 20
(Ed de Giles) *in tch in midfield: pushed along 1/2-way: dropped to rr and rdn over 2f out: sn btn: bhd and eased fnl f: t.o* **15/2**[3]

6413 **12** *3 1/4* **The Holyman (IRE)**[30] 4051 6-9-5 **74**... RichardHughes 11 19
(Jo Crowley) *chsd ldr for 4f: styd chsng ldrs tl rdn and lost pl ent fnl 2f: bhd and eased fnl f: t.o* **20/1**

2m 31.81s (-0.89) **Going Correction** +0.075s/f (Good)
**WFA** 3 from 4yo+ 11lb 12 Ran SP% **118.7**
Speed ratings (Par 105): **105,104,104,104,104 100,96,95,93,81 79,77**
CSF £99.50 CT £1035.88 TOTE £10.60: £2.20, £4.30, £2.70; EX 153.50 Trifecta £1156.90.
**Owner** Seymour Bloodstock (uk) Ltd **Bred** Dullingham Park **Trained** Patching, W Sussex
■ Stewards' Enquiry : Michael J M Murphy two-day ban: used whip above permitted level (Aug 23-24)

**FOCUS**
A competitive handicap run at what looked a reasonable gallop and no reason why this form shouldn't be taken seriously.

## 5074 OVER 300 USED CARS AT FROSTS FILLIES' H'CAP 1m 1f 209y
4:20 (4:21) (Class 4) (0-85,85) 3-Y-O+ **£4,690** (£1,395; £697; £348) **Stalls** High

Form RPR

2121 **1** **Who's That Chick (IRE)**[8] 4798 5-8-13 **70**... OisinMurphy 2 80
(Ralph J Smith) *t.k.h: chsd ldng pair: rdn and effrt over 1f out: chsd ldr 1f out: led and drifted lft fnl 75yds: r.o* **7/2**[3]

1-13 **2** *2* **Sequined (USA)**[47] 3476 3-9-2 **82**... SilvestreDeSousa 4 89
(Charlie Appleby) *t.k.h: chsd ldr tl led over 1f out: sn rdn and wnt lft: hit rail jst ins fnl f: hdd fnl 75yds: no ex and btn whn hmpd towards fin* **11/4**[2]

1053 **3** *2 1/4* **Taro Tywod (IRE)**[8] 4799 5-8-12 **74**... CamHardie(5) 5 76
(Mark Brisbourne) *in tch in last pair: rdn over 2f out: no imp tl styd on ins fnl f: wnt 3rd fnl 75yds: no threat to ldrs* **12/1**

6204 **4** *1 1/2* **Yojojo (IRE)**[12] 4680 5-10-0 **85**... DavidProbert 1 84
(Gay Kelleway) *hld up in tch in rr: rdn over 2f out: no imp on ldrs: clsng on 3rd whn nt clr run and swtchd rt ins fnl f: wnt 4th nr finsh: nvr trbld ldrs* **6/1**

1-51 **5** *1/2* **Ejadah (IRE)**[35] 3885 3-9-3 **83**... AndreaAtzeni 3 81
(Roger Varian) *taken down early: led but nvr settled: hdd and rdn over 1f out: 3rd and btn 1f out: wknd and lost 2 pls fnl 75yds* **13/8**[1]

2m 4.12s (0.52) **Going Correction** +0.075s/f (Good)
**WFA** 3 from 5yo 9lb 5 Ran SP% **109.0**
Speed ratings (Par 102): **100,98,96,95,95**
CSF £13.06 TOTE £3.50: £1.60, £1.90; EX 12.00 Trifecta £67.70.
**Owner** Piper, Churchill, Hirschfeld **Bred** T Hirschfeld **Trained** Epsom, Surrey
■ Stewards' Enquiry : Andrea Atzeni two-day ban: failed to take all reasonable and permissable measures to ride out for 4th (Aug 23-24)

**FOCUS**
Not a bad little fillies' handicap, but the form may not be too strong considering the favourite was too keen.

## 5075 HARRINGTONS LETTINGS H'CAP 7f 214y
4:50 (4:50) (Class 6) (0-60,60) 3-Y-O+ **£1,940** (£577; £288; £144) **Stalls** Centre

Form RPR

3603 **1** **Emman Bee (IRE)**[4] 4942 5-9-9 **60**... MichaelJMMurphy(3) 3 73
(Luke Dace) *chsd ldng trio: effrt to chse ldr 2f out: led over 1f out: clr 1f out: r.o wl: comf* **9/2**[2]

6321 **2** *4* **Hawk Moth (IRE)**[12] 4655 6-9-9 **57**...(p) RichardHughes 5 62
(John Spearing) *hld up in tch in midfield: rdn and effrt wl over 1f out: chsd clr wnr jst over 1f out: no imp* **11/4**[1]

3014 **3** *1* **Elle Rebelle**[44] 3554 4-8-13 **52**... CamHardie(5) 2 54
(Mark Brisbourne) *stdd s: hld up in last trio: rdn and effrt 2f out: hdwy 1f out: styd on on fnl 100yds to snatch 3rd last strides: nvr trbld ldrs* **13/2**

2126 **4** *hd* **Byrd In Hand (IRE)**[8] 4798 7-9-12 **60**... WilliamCarson 11 61
(John Bridger) *t.k.h: chsd ldrs tl led over 2f out: drvn and hdd over 1f out: 3rd and btn 1f out: kpt on same pce: lost 3rd last strides* **6/1**[3]

-060 **5** *4* **My New Angel (IRE)**[18] 4473 5-9-3 **51**...(be) FrankieMcDonald 4 43
(Daniel Mark Loughnane) *fly-jmpd leaving stalls: stdd after s: hld up towards rr: effrt u.p jst over 2f out: plugged on but no threat to ldrs fnl f* **25/1**

0-00 **6** *nk* **Clock On Tom**[48] 3439 4-9-8 **56**... SamHitchcott 1 47
(Michael Easterby) *chsd ldrs: rdn 2f out: outpcd and btn over 1f out: wknd fnl f* **25/1**

6125 **7** *1 1/4* **Botanist**[13] 4620 7-9-9 **60**... NeilFarley(3) 6 48
(Shaun Harris) *in tch in midfield: rdn and effrt to chse ldrs jst over 2f out: btn over 1f out: wknd fnl f* **6/1**[3]

6000 **8** *1 3/4* **Sarlat**[33] 3950 3-8-0 **49** oh4... NatashaEaton(5) 10 29
(Mark Brisbourne) *led tl over 2f out: 4th and btn over 1f out: wknd fnl f* **66/1**

0060 **9** *3 1/2* **Hejaz (IRE)**[101] 1819 4-8-11 **50**...(e[1]) GeorgeDowning(5) 9 26
(John Butler) *hld up in tch in rr: plenty to do and drvn wl over 1f out: sn hung lft and wl btn* **10/1**

0000 **10** *nk* **Ishisoba**[92] 2069 4-8-9 **49**... CharlesBishop(3) 7 22
(Mark Hoad) *in tch: rdn and no hdwy jst over 2f out: bhd ent fnl f* **66/1**

5205 **11** *56* **Not Rigg (USA)**[12] 4655 4-9-7 **58**...(p) RyanPowell(3) 8
(Nick Littmoden) *in tch in midfield: sddle slipped after 2f: wd and lost pl bnd 4f out: t.o fnl 2f* **11/1**

1m 36.19s (0.19) **Going Correction** +0.075s/f (Good)
**WFA** 3 from 4yo+ 7lb 11 Ran SP% **114.9**
Speed ratings (Par 101): **102,98,97,96,92 92,91,89,86,85 29**
CSF £16.32 CT £78.48 TOTE £4.70: £1.60, £1.80, £2.30; EX 20.80 Trifecta £80.70.
**Owner** Mark Benton **Bred** O Bourke **Trained** Okehurst Lane, W Sussex

**FOCUS**
A moderate handicap, rated around the second. The winner is in foal.

## 5076 FROST4CARS.CO.UK ON YOUR MOBILE LADY AMATEUR RIDERS' H'CAP 1m 1f 209y
5:20 (5:21) (Class 5) (0-70,68) 3-Y-O+ **£2,495** (£774; £386; £193) **Stalls** High

Form RPR

3222 **1** **City Ground (USA)**[9] 4755 7-10-7 **65**... MissSBrotherton 7 74
(Michael Easterby) *t.k.h: chsd ldrs: effrt to chse ldr over 2f out: rdn to ld over 1f out: in command fnl f: pushed out* **5/2**[2]

1302 **2** *1 3/4* **Gabrial The Terror (IRE)**[21] 4340 4-10-7 **68**...(p) MissHayleyMoore(3) 5 73
(David Simcock) *hld up in tch: rdn over 2f out: nt clr run and swtchd rt 2f out: drvn to chse wnr and drifting lft 1f out: r.o for clr 2nd but a hld by wnr* **6/4**[1]

134 **3** *6* **Megalala (IRE)**[24] 4273 13-10-5 **63**... MissEJJones 2 57
(John Bridger) *led: rdn and hdd over 1f out: 3rd and btn 1f out: plugged on to hold 3rd fnl f* **8/1**

2520 **4** *nk* **Flag Of Glory**[9] 4755 7-9-11 **60**...(p) MissMEdden(5) 1 53
(Peter Hiatt) *chsd ldr tl over 4f out: squeezed for room bnd 4f out: rdn over 2f out: btn over 1f out: plugged on and battling for 3rd fnl f* **12/1**

0540 **5** *4* **Super Duplex**[21] 4351 7-9-6 **57**...(t) MissLWilliams(7) 4 42
(Roger Teal) *stdd s: hld up in tch: hdwy on inner to chse ldr over 4f out tl over 2f out: sn wknd* **20/1**

6451 **6** *hd* **Crouching Harry (IRE)**[36] 3852 5-9-7 **54**...[1] MissJoannaMason(3) 6 39
(Anabel K Murphy) *stdd after s: hld up in rr: detached last 1/2-way: effrt but stl lots to do wl over 1f out: no hdwy* **6/1**[3]

0600 **7** *22* **Berkeley Street (USA)**[22] 4326 4-9-0 **52** oh7... MissKMargarson(5) 3
(Jane Chapple-Hyam) *in tch in midfield: nudged lft and short of room bnd 4f out: lost pl: bhd over 1f out: t.o* **33/1**

2m 5.0s (1.40) **Going Correction** +0.075s/f (Good) 7 Ran SP% **109.4**
Speed ratings (Par 103): **97,95,90,90,87 87,69**
CSF £6.00 TOTE £3.30: £1.80, £1.60; EX 7.40 Trifecta £26.70.
**Owner** Steve Hull **Bred** Mrs E Scott Jr & Mrs L Macelree **Trained** Sheriff Hutton, N Yorks

**FOCUS**
A typically weak race of its type.
T/Plt: £2,008.10 to a £1 stake. Pool: £63,243.35 - 22.99 winning units T/Qpdt: £390.70 to a £1 stake. Pool: £4,857.62 - 9.20 winning units SP

# 4422 HAYDOCK (L-H)
Thursday, August 7

**OFFICIAL GOING: Good (good to soft in places; 7.6) changing to good to soft after race 2 (2.40)**
Wind: Light; half against Weather: Fine

## 5077 DOWNLOAD NEW RACINGUK IPAD APP H'CAP (JOCKEY CLUB GRASSROOTS MIDDLE DISTANCE SERIES QUALIFIER) 1m 2f 95y
2:10 (2:10) (Class 5) (0-70,69) 3-Y-O+ **£2,587** (£770; £384; £192) **Stalls** Centre

Form RPR

0-05 **1** **Always Resolute**[21] 4356 3-8-8 **58**... MartinLane 11 71
(Timothy Jarvis) *sn trcking ldr: led 2f out: forged clr fnl f* **50/1**

3002 **2** *3 1/2* **Qibtee (FR)**[11] 4709 4-9-0 **55**... RobertWinston 8 61
(Les Eyre) *in rr: swtchd outside 2f out: styd on to take 2nd last 50yds* **11/2**[2]

0265 **3** *1/2* **Where's Tiger**[38] 3789 3-8-7 **57**... PJMcDonald 4 62
(Jedd O'Keeffe) *mid-div: drvn over 4f out: swtchd ins 1f out: styd on to take 3rd nr fin* **8/1**[3]

1262 **4** *nk* **Frontline Phantom (IRE)**[14] 4593 7-9-6 **64**... JoeyHaynes(3) 7 68
(K R Burke) *chsd ldrs: chal over 1f out: kpt on same pce* **8/1**[3]

0552 **5** *nk* **Rex Whistler (IRE)**[19] 4427 4-9-10 **68**... ConnorBeasley(3) 9 72
(Julie Camacho) *mid-div: effrt over 3f out: kpt on one pce over 1f out* **11/4**[1]

4334 **6** *1 1/4* **Arlecchino (IRE)**[14] 4568 4-9-8 **63**...(b) RoystonFfrench 3 64
(Ed McMahon) *wnt lft s: in rr: sme hdwy over 2f out: kpt on: nvr a threat* **8/1**[3]

0334 **7** *2 1/4* **Snow Dancer (IRE)**[12] 4665 10-8-10 **56**... KevinStott(5) 10 53
(John David Riches) *in rr: sme hdwy over 2f out: nvr nr ldrs* **16/1**

0060 **8** *2* **Wyldfire (IRE)**[18] 4473 4-8-9 **50** oh1... JamesSullivan 6 43
(Ruth Carr) *trckd ldrs: fdd over 1f out* **20/1**

5324 **9** *3 3/4* **Janaab (IRE)**[6] 4858 4-9-9 **64**...(t) DavidAllan 5 50
(Tim Easterby) *in rr: hdwy on ins over 2f out: wknd fnl f* **8/1**[3]

5400 **10** *2 1/2* **King Of Paradise (IRE)**[19] 4454 5-10-0 **69**... JasonHart 2 51
(Eric Alston) *hmpd s: a in rr* **14/1**

1002 **11** *4* **Suni Dancer**[11] 4706 3-8-4 **54**.................................. RaulDaSilva 1 28
(Paul Green) *led: hdd 2f out: sn wknd* **12/1**

2m 13.68s (-1.82) **Going Correction** -0.10s/f (Good)
**WFA** 3 from 4yo+ 9lb **11** Ran SP% **113.5**
Speed ratings (Par 103): **103,100,99,99,99 98,96,94,91,89 86**
CSF £298.62 CT £2457.77 TOTE £37.50: £12.70, £2.20, £3.10; EX 512.50 Trifecta £2647.80 Part won..
**Owner** Market Avenue Racing Club & Partners **Bred** Jarvis Associates **Trained** Twyford, Bucks

**FOCUS**
All races on Inner home straight and distances on Round course increased by 3yds. A modest handicap won decisively by the outsider of the field. The winner was a big price but there seemed no fluke, as it was the best time on the card.

## 5078 WATCH ON 3 DEVICES RACINGUK.COM/ANYWHERE MAIDEN STKS 1m

**2:40** (2:40) (Class 5) 2-Y-O **£2,587** (£770; £384; £192) **Stalls** Low

Form RPR

43 **1** **Al Rayyan (IRE)**[18] 4467 2-9-5 0.................................. GrahamLee 9 78
(Kevin Ryan) *mde all: drvn over 2f out: styd on wl fnl f* **9/2**[2]

20 **2** *1 1/4* **Azmaam (IRE)**[15] 4550 2-9-5 0.................................. SeanLevey 6 75
(Richard Hannon) *trckd wnr: chal over 1f out: rdn and styd on same pce last 150yds* **8/11**[1]

**3** *3/4* **The Lampo Genie** 2-9-5 0.................................. DanielTudhope 1 73+
(K R Burke) *s.i.s: in rr: hdwy over 3f out: swtchd rt over 1f out: tk 3rd last 75yds: fin wl* **12/1**

0 **4** *2 1/4* **Bellajeu**[35] 3888 2-9-0 0.................................. HarryBentley 2 63
(Olly Stevens) *trckd ldrs: t.k.h: effrt over 2f out: one pce* **6/1**[3]

45 **5** *nk* **Saltarello (IRE)**[9] 4750 2-9-5 0.................................. PhillipMakin 5 67
(John Quinn) *chsd ldrs: one pce fnl 2f* **20/1**

**6** *7* **Newera** 2-9-5 0.................................. RichardKingscote 4 51
(Tom Dascombe) *in rr-div: hdwy over 5f out: outpcd and lost pl over 2f out* **8/1**

0 **7** *7* **Harps Of Bretagne**[33] 3945 2-9-0 0.................................. RoystonFfrench 7 30
(Lisa Williamson) *chsd ldrs: wknd 2f out* **100/1**

**8** *1 1/2* **Egmont** 2-9-5 0.................................. PJMcDonald 8 32
(George Moore) *s.i.s: in rr and drvn along: bhd fnl 3f* **33/1**

6 **9** *1/2* **Red Stripes (USA)**[70] 2698 2-9-2 0.................................. JoeyHaynes(3) 3 31
(Michael Mullineaux) *in rr-div: sn drvn along: lost pl over 3f out: sn bhd* **100/1**

1m 44.76s (1.06) **Going Correction** -0.10s/f (Good) **9** Ran SP% **118.9**
Speed ratings (Par 94): **90,88,88,85,85 78,71,69,69**
CSF £8.27 TOTE £5.10: £1.50, £1.10, £2.80; EX 10.90 Trifecta £71.10.
**Owner** Mubarak Al Naemi **Bred** Bakewell Bl & Avn **Trained** Hambleton, N Yorks

**FOCUS**
A fair stamina test for these juveniles. The finish was fought out by the form pair.

## 5079 RACINGUK ANYWHERE AVAILABLE NOW FILLIES' H'CAP 1m

**3:10** (3:11) (Class 5) (0-75,73) 3-Y-O+ **£2,587** (£770; £384; £192) **Stalls** Low

Form RPR

0305 **1** **No Poppy (IRE)**[18] 4472 6-9-10 **69**.................................. RobertWinston 11 81
(Tim Easterby) *in rr: hdwy over 2f out: led appr fnl f: kpt on towards fin* **7/1**

2251 **2** *nk* **Maiden Approach**[18] 4472 3-9-5 **71**.................................. TonyHamilton 8 81
(Richard Fahey) *led early: chsd ldr: chal appr fnl f: edgd lft: no ex clsng stages* **6/1**

6353 **3** *6* **Real Tigress (IRE)**[23] 4291 5-9-13 **72**.................................. DavidAllan 5 77+
(Les Eyre) *mid-div: hdwy on inner over 2f out: nt clr run over 1f out: styd on ins fnl f: tk modest 3rd nr fin* **10/3**[1]

0524 **4** *1/2* **Rocksee (IRE)**[19] 4426 3-9-2 **68**..........................(p) RichardKingscote 4 63
(Tom Dascombe) *chsd ldrs: swtchd rt over 1f out: kpt on same pce* **11/1**

053 **5** *3/4* **Piddie's Power**[28] 4108 7-9-13 **72**.................................. StevieDonohoe 6 67
(Kevin Frost) *mid-div: effrt over 3f out: kpt on appr fnl f* **12/1**

2616 **6** *1* **Thankyou Very Much**[24] 4271 4-9-9 **68**..........................(p) PJMcDonald 2 60
(James Bethell) *in rr: hdwy on ins 2f out: nvr trbld ldrs* **4/1**[2]

-300 **7** *1 1/2* **Silver Mirage**[33] 3979 3-9-5 **71**.................................. GrahamLee 1 59
(Michael Bell) *sn led: hdd appr fnl f: sn wknd* **12/1**

5550 **8** *2 1/4* **La Danza**[33] 3971 4-8-9 **54**.................................. JasonHart 3 38
(Lisa Williamson) *chsd ldrs: wknd appr fnl f* **28/1**

00-6 **9** *2 3/4* **Natalia**[54] 3230 5-8-9 **54** oh2.................................. RoystonFfrench 12 31
(Andrew Hollinshead) *in rr: outpcd over 3f out* **25/1**

5642 **10** *4 1/2* **Patrona Ciana (FR)**[15] 4530 4-10-0 **73**.................................. DanielTudhope 7 40
(David O'Meara) *hld up in rr: sme hdwy over 2f out: lost pl over 1f out: eased towards fin* **11/2**[3]

30-0 **11** *12* **Seraphima**[33] 3966 4-8-4 **54** oh3.................................. SammyJoBell(5) 9
(Lisa Williamson) *chsd ldrs: lost pl over 3f out: bhd whn eased ins fnl f* **100/1**

1m 43.25s (-0.45) **Going Correction** +0.05s/f (Good)
**WFA** 3 from 4yo+ 7lb **11** Ran SP% **117.3**
Speed ratings (Par 100): **104,103,97,97,96 95,93,91,88,84 72**
CSF £47.82 CT £170.62 TOTE £9.50: £2.10, £1.70, £2.00; EX 56.70 Trifecta £310.10.
**Owner** J Musgrave **Bred** Michael O'Mahony **Trained** Great Habton, N Yorks

**FOCUS**
The official going was eased to good to soft after the second race, despite it having been warm and sunny since lunchtime. This ordinary fillies' handicap was run at a solid gallop. The first two drew clear.

## 5080 OUR LOCAL HEROES FOUNDATION H'CAP (THE JOCKEY CLUB GRASSROOTS FLAT SPRINT SERIES QUALIFIER) 6f

**3:40** (3:42) (Class 5) (0-70,68) 3-Y-O **£2,587** (£770; £384; £192) **Stalls** Low

Form RPR

2204 **1** **Fantasy Justifier (IRE)**[27] 4155 3-9-6 **67**.................................. ChrisCatlin 1 75
(Ronald Harris) *mid-div: hdwy over 2f out: led appr fnl f: jst hld on* **20/1**

1142 **2** *shd* **Shades Of Silk**[20] 4411 3-9-1 **62**.................................. GrahamLee 7 70
(James Given) *led: hdd appr fnl f: rallied ins fnl f: jst failed* **9/2**[2]

2222 **3** *1 3/4* **Margrets Gift**[19] 4455 3-9-3 **64**..........................(p) RobertWinston 4 66
(Tim Easterby) *mid-div: hdwy over 2f out: chsng ldng pair 1f out: kpt on same pce* **13/2**[3]

2445 **4** *hd* **Injaz**[31] 4019 3-8-9 **61**..........................(b[1]) KevinStott(5) 2 62
(Kevin Ryan) *dwlt: in rr and drvn along: hdwy over 1f out: hung rt and styd on ins fnl f* **13/2**[3]

2535 **5** *1 1/4* **Spirit Of Alsace (IRE)**[10] 4724 3-9-4 **65**.................................. DanielTudhope 3 62
(Jim Goldie) *w ldr: fdd fnl f* **12/1**

2503 **6** *1 3/4* **Disclosure**[23] 4297 3-9-7 **68**.................................. DavidAllan 9 60
(Les Eyre) *chsd ldrs: effrt over 2f out: fdd appr fnl f* **7/1**

0640 **7** *1* **Pensax Lad (IRE)**[20] 4411 3-9-6 **67**.................................. SteveDrowne 10 56
(Ronald Harris) *in rr: effrt over 2f out: fdd appr fnl f* **12/1**

0300 **8** *3/4* **Look Here's Al**[20] 4411 3-9-2 **63**.................................. GrahamGibbons 6 49
(Andrew Hollinshead) *in rr-div: hdwy over 2f out: wknd over 1f out* **12/1**

2043 **9** *6* **Suitsus**[12] 4677 3-9-7 **68**.................................. PatCosgrave 8 35
(Peter Makin) *mid-div: effrt over 2f out: wknd over 1f out* **3/1**[1]

-060 **10** *38* **Diamond Solitaire (IRE)**[21] 4337 3-8-6 **53**.................................. MartinLane 11
(Timothy Jarvis) *wnt rt s: hdwy and in tch over 2f out: sn lost pl and heavily eased: hopelessly t.o* **20/1**

1m 15.3s (1.50) **Going Correction** +0.325s/f (Good) **10** Ran SP% **114.9**
Speed ratings (Par 100): **103,102,100,100,98 96,94,93,85,35**
CSF £106.42 CT £673.61 TOTE £13.30: £4.00, £1.60, £2.50; EX 105.10 Trifecta £255.10.
**Owner** Farley, Fantasy Fellowship B & RHS **Bred** Denis And Mrs Teresa Bergin **Trained** Earlswood, Monmouths

**FOCUS**
Ordinary sprint handicap form. The time was alright compared to the older horse handicaps.

## 5081 ZIP GOES A MILLION H'CAP 6f

**4:10** (4:11) (Class 4) (0-85,86) 3-Y-O+ **£5,175** (£1,540; £769; £384) **Stalls** Low

Form RPR

/401 **1** **Compton Park**[11] 4712 7-9-13 **86** 6ex..........................(t) DavidAllan 1 102
(Les Eyre) *hld up in mid-div: stdy hdwy over 2f out: swtchd lft over 1f out: led last 100yds: styd on wl* **7/1**

0461 **2** *1 3/4* **Arctic Feeling (IRE)**[13] 4632 6-9-4 **82**.................................. SammyJoBell(5) 3 92
(Richard Fahey) *trckd ldrs: led over 1f out: hdd and no ex ins fnl f* **6/1**[3]

-415 **3** *1* **Duke Cosimo**[18] 4471 4-9-10 **83**..........................(b) GrahamGibbons 2 90
(David Barron) *chsd ldrs: upsides 1f out: styd on same pce* **10/3**[1]

4005 **4** *3/4* **Bop It**[22] 4317 5-9-7 **80**.................................. DanielTudhope 11 84
(David O'Meara) *sn trcking ldrs: effrt and hung lft appr fnl f: fdd clsng stages* **7/2**[2]

4466 **5** *2* **Go Go Green (IRE)**[24] 4256 8-8-9 **71**.................................. JoeyHaynes(3) 4 69
(Jim Goldie) *trckd ldrs: effrt 2f out: one pce* **16/1**

0251 **6** *nk* **Supersta**[40] 3729 3-8-10 **73**.................................. ChrisCatlin 5 69
(Ronald Harris) *in rr: hdwy over 2f out: one pce* **16/1**

162- **7** *shd* **Ambitious Boy**[308] 6977 5-9-4 **77**.................................. RoystonFfrench 8 74
(Andrew Hollinshead) *mid-div: outpcd and lost pl over 2f out: kpt on fnl f* **12/1**

5006 **8** *1 3/4* **Corporal Maddox**[8] 4783 7-9-12 **85**..........................(p) SteveDrowne 6 76
(Ronald Harris) *dwlt: in rr: nvr a factor* **14/1**

0525 **9** *1 1/4* **Constantine**[20] 4404 3-9-4 **81**.................................. SeanLevey 7 67
(Richard Hannon) *led: hdd over 2f out: wknd over 1f out* **10/1**

2050 **10** *2 1/4* **Rasaman (IRE)**[11] 4700 10-9-10 **83**.................................. GrahamLee 9 63
(Jim Goldie) *in rr: effrt over 2f out: lost pl over 1f out* **12/1**

1m 14.78s (0.98) **Going Correction** +0.325s/f (Good)
**WFA** 3 from 4yo+ 4lb **10** Ran SP% **115.0**
Speed ratings (Par 105): **106,103,102,101,98 98,98,95,94,91**
CSF £47.94 CT £150.69 TOTE £5.30: £2.10, £2.60, £1.60; EX 34.60 Trifecta £70.50.
**Owner** Billy Parker **Bred** David Jamison Bloodstock **Trained** Catton, North Yorkshire

**FOCUS**
A decent handicap, run slightly quicker than the previous Class 5 event, which was hand-timed. Solid form.

## 5082 RACINGUK IPAD APP RACINGUK.COM/MOBILE H'CAP 6f

**4:40** (4:40) (Class 5) (0-70,69) 4-Y-O+ **£2,587** (£770; £384; £192) **Stalls** Low

Form RPR

2063 **1** **Borough Boy (IRE)**[34] 3935 4-8-7 **55**.................................. FrannyNorton 9 63
(Derek Shaw) *hld up in rr: swtchd lft after 1f: hdwy on ins and n.m.r over 2f out: led last 150yds: r.o* **4/1**[2]

6000 **2** *1* **Methaaly (IRE)**[3] 4961 11-7-13 **50** oh4..........................(b) JoeyHaynes(3) 5 54
(Michael Mullineaux) *chsd ldrs: kpt on to take 2nd last 50yds* **22/1**

-600 **3** *2* **Red Cobra (IRE)**[17] 4487 4-8-6 **54**.................................. JasonHart 3 52
(Tim Easterby) *led: clr 3f out: hdd jst ins fnl f: no ex* **6/1**

035 **4** *nk* **Italian Tom (IRE)**[26] 4206 7-9-7 **69**.................................. SteveDrowne 1 66
(Ronald Harris) *chsd ldrs: 2nd over 1f out: kpt on same pce* **10/1**

6002 **5** *2 1/4* **Koharu**[51] 3329 4-9-0 **62**..........................(t) PatCosgrave 6 52
(Peter Makin) *mid-div: effrt over 2f out: one pce* **5/1**[3]

300 **6** *1* **Rutterkin (USA)**[3] 4960 6-7-11 **50** oh5.................................. SammyJoBell(5) 4 37
(James Moffatt) *mid-div: effrt and edgd lft over 2f out: nvr a threat* **20/1**

2145 **7** *nk* **Hab Reeh**[26] 4194 6-9-3 **65**.................................. GrahamLee 7 51
(Ruth Carr) *mid-div: effrt over 2f out: nvr a factor* **5/2**[1]

044 **8** *19* **Captain Kendall (IRE)**[64] 2890 5-8-9 **62**.................................. LouisSteward(5) 10
(Harry Chisman) *sn detached in last: bhd fnl 3f: eased clsng stages: lame* **6/1**

1m 15.17s (1.37) **Going Correction** +0.325s/f (Good) **8** Ran SP% **112.0**
Speed ratings (Par 103): **103,101,99,98,95 94,93,68**
CSF £78.97 CT £520.08 TOTE £4.40: £1.40, £3.50, £2.60; EX 84.60 Trifecta £753.60.
**Owner** Brian Johnson (Northamptonshire) **Bred** E Kopica And M Rosenfeld **Trained** Sproxton, Leics

**FOCUS**
A modest event run at a strong gallop, courtesy of the third. The possible negative is that the runner-up was 4lb out of the handicap.

## 5083 FOLLOW @HAYDOCKRACES ON TWITTER H'CAP 1m 6f

**5:10** (5:10) (Class 4) (0-80,80) 4-Y-O+ **£5,175** (£1,540; £769; £384) **Stalls** Low

Form RPR

1361 **1** **Precision Strike**[19] 4423 4-8-3 **67**..........................(v) DuilioDaSilva(5) 10 76+
(Richard Guest) *dwlt: hld up in rr: hdwy on outside over 3f out: w ldrs over 1f out: led over 1f out: edgd lft: drvn out* **9/2**[2]

0205 **2** *2 1/4* **O Ma Lad (IRE)**[21] 4361 6-9-7 **80**.................................. PhillipMakin 5 85
(John Quinn) *hld up: effrt over 3f out: chsng ldrs over 2f out: kkpt on same pce fnl f* **9/2**[2]

4661 **3** *shd* **Albonny (IRE)**[29] 4076 5-8-12 **71**.................................. MartinLane 6 76
(Timothy Jarvis) *hld up in rr: hdwy to trck ldrs 10f out: drvn over 3f out: kpt on fnl f* **7/1**

1413 **4** *1 1/4* **Aleksandar**[21] 4361 5-8-13 **72**.................................. GrahamLee 8 75
(Jim Goldie) *led: qcknd pce over 4f out: hdd over 3f out: one pce over 1f out* **4/1**[1]

4404 **5** *1 1/4* **Choisan (IRE)**[19] 4454 5-8-13 **72**..........................(tp) RobertWinston 4 73
(Tim Easterby) *led early: chsd ldrs: drvn upsides 3f out: one pce over 1f out* **5/1**[3]

-342 **6** *3 1/4* **Opera Buff**[63] 2920 5-9-7 **80**..........................(p) RaulDaSilva 1 77
(Jose Santos) *trckd ldrs: drvn over 3f out: wknd clsng stages* **4/1**[1]

1020 **7** *7* **Java Rose**[118] 1418 5-9-2 **75**..........................(p) ChrisCatlin 7 62
(Charlie Longsdon) *sn chsng ldrs: led over 3f out: hdd over 1f out: sn wknd: eased clsng stages* **14/1**

3m 3.23s (1.23) **Going Correction** +0.05s/f (Good) **7** Ran SP% **112.2**
Speed ratings (Par 105): **98,96,96,95,95 93,89**
CSF £23.88 CT £137.00 TOTE £3.10: £1.80, £3.30; EX 25.50 Trifecta £217.90.
**Owner** Resdev **Bred** Mickley Stud **Trained** Ingmanthorpe, W Yorks

**FOCUS**
They went what looked an even gallop in this fair handicap, but the first three all came from the rear.
T/Plt: £70.10 to a £1 stake. Pool: £66,018.24 - 687.22 winning units T/Qpdt: £13.30 to a £1 stake. Pool: £5,920.18 - 328.19 winning units WG

## 4659 NEWCASTLE (L-H)
Thursday, August 7

**OFFICIAL GOING: Good to soft (soft in places; 6.5)**
Wind: Breezy, half against Weather: Sunny, hot

### 5084 PERCY HEDLEY EMPLOYABILITY PROJECT APPRENTICE H'CAP 1m 2f 32y
**5:25** (5:25) (Class 6) (0-60,55) 3-Y-O+ **£2,264** (£673; £336; £168) **Stalls** Centre

Form RPR
34 **1** **Diddy Eric**[3] 4958 4-9-8 **49**.....(b) RobJFitzpatrick 7 58
(Micky Hammond) *dwlt: hld up: shkn up and plenty to do over 2f out: gd hdwy on outside over 1f out: edgd lft and led ins fnl f: pushed out* **5/1**[1]
400 **2** ¾ **Tortoise**[13] 4611 3-9-3 **53**.....(b) GemmaTutty 10 60
(Richard Guest) *t.k.h: hld up: stdy hdwy over 2f out: led over 1f out to ins fnl f: kpt on towards fin* **12/1**
-113 **3** 1 ¾ **Remember Rocky**[50] 3364 5-10-0 **55**.....(p) MeganCarberry 11 59
(Lucy Normile) *hld up in midfield: hdwy over 2f out: chsd ldr over 1f out to ins fnl f: kpt on same pce* **5/1**[1]
00-4 **4** 3 ¾ **Lady Bubbles**[6] 4871 3-8-9 **50**..... DanielleMooney(5) 14 47
(Michael Easterby) *hld up: pushed along over 2f out: hdwy over 1f out: kpt on fnl f: nt rch first three* **16/1**
6253 **5** 1 **Troy Boy**[32] 4000 4-9-2 **46**..... LukeLeadbitter(3) 12 41
(Robin Bastiman) *pressed ldr: rdn and led briefly over 1f out: outpcd fnl f* **8/1**[3]
3001 **6** 1 ½ **Silver Tigress**[12] 4665 6-9-5 **51**..... KieranShoemark(5) 9 43
(Iain Jardine) *hld up: pushed along over 2f out: effrt whn n.m.r and swtchd rt over 1f out: sn no imp* **13/2**[2]
0054 **7** 1 ¾ **Maillot Jaune (IRE)**[15] 4533 4-9-4 **45**.....(p) JackGarritty 6 34
(Patrick Holmes) *midfield: hdwy over 2f out: wknd ent fnl f* **25/1**
-534 **8** ½ **Vale Mentor (IRE)**[17] 4495 3-9-0 **50**..... RachelRichardson 13 38
(Tim Easterby) *t.k.h: prom on outside: rdn over 2f out: no imp whn n.m.r over 1f out* **5/1**[1]
650 **9** nk **Sketch Map (IRE)**[82] 2355 3-9-0 **55**..... RowanScott(5) 3 42
(Jedd O'Keeffe) *in tch: effrt and rdn 2f out: wknd ins fnl f* **12/1**
420 **10** hd **Gadobout Dancer**[20] 4381 7-9-6 **47**..... LauraBarry 1 34
(Keith Dalgleish) *prom: effrt and hdwy over 2f out: wknd over 1f out* **11/1**
0060 **11** ½ **Secret Kode (IRE)**[18] 4473 3-8-9 **45**..... JordanNason 5 31
(Simon Waugh) *t.k.h: led to over 1f out: sn rdn and wknd* **16/1**

2m 14.25s (2.35) **Going Correction** +0.25s/f (Good)
**WFA** 3 from 4yo+ 9lb **11** Ran SP% **113.8**
Speed ratings (Par 101): **100,99,98,95,94 93,91,91,90,90 90**
CSF £63.60 CT £313.56 TOTE £6.70: £2.40, £2.70, £1.80; EX 95.00 Trifecta £130.30.
**Owner** Mrs Rita Butler **Bred** Lady Richard Wellesley **Trained** Middleham, N Yorks

**FOCUS**
A modest apprentice event. The gallop didn't appear strong, and the first four came from off the pace.

### 5085 COQUETVALE HOTEL NURSERY H'CAP (BOBIS RACE) 7f
**6:00** (6:00) (Class 4) (0-85,85) 2-Y-O **£3,881** (£1,155; £577; £288) **Stalls** Centre

Form RPR
1 **1** **Supreme Occasion (IRE)**[13] 4626 2-8-8 **75**..... SamJames(3) 3 84+
(David O'Meara) *t.k.h: trckd ldrs: rdn to ld appr fnl f: styd on wl* **1/1**[1]
215 **2** 1 ¼ **Arabian Bride (IRE)**[27] 4157 2-9-1 **79**..... AdrianNicholls 6 84
(Mark Johnston) *led: rdn over 2f out: hdd appr fnl f: rallied: one pce last 100yds* **14/1**
132 **3** 2 ¼ **Buccaneers Vault (IRE)**[27] 4157 2-9-7 **85**..... PaulMulrennan 2 84
(Michael Dods) *pressed ldr: rdn and ev ch over 2f out: kpt on same pce fnl f* **13/2**
014 **4** 1 ¾ **Sakhee's Return**[30] 4057 2-8-13 **77**..... AndrewElliott 5 72
(Tim Easterby) *hld up: rdn and edgd lft over 2f out: kpt on fnl f: nvr able to chal* **9/2**[2]
2331 **5** 2 ¼ **Kylach Me If U Can**[15] 4529 2-8-13 **77**..... TomEaves 7 66
(Kevin Ryan) *trckd ldrs: ev ch over 2f out: rdn and hung lft over 1f out: sn btn* **11/2**[3]
3514 **6** 2 ½ **Multiplier**[31] 4012 2-8-11 **75**..... JamesSullivan 4 57
(Kristin Stubbs) *hld up: effrt and rdn 2f out: drifted lft ent fnl f: sn btn* **40/1**
3355 **7** 1 ½ **Flatcapper (IRE)**[15] 4529 2-7-9 **64** oh2..... JackGarritty(5) 1 42
(Richard Fahey) *prom tl rdn and wknd 2f out* **20/1**

1m 28.21s (0.41) **Going Correction** +0.05s/f (Good) **7** Ran SP% **110.8**
Speed ratings (Par 96): **99,97,95,93,90 87,85**
CSF £15.93 TOTE £2.10: £1.50, £4.30; EX 14.40 Trifecta £90.50.
**Owner** Hambleton Racing Ltd XXXIII **Bred** Denis Noonan **Trained** Nawton, N Yorks

**FOCUS**
A fairly useful nursery and a progressive winner, who justified market confidence with a bit more up her sleeve than the bare result implies.

### 5086 NORTHUMBRIAN WATER MEDIAN AUCTION MAIDEN STKS 6f
**6:35** (6:35) (Class 6) 2-Y-O **£2,264** (£673; £336; £168) **Stalls** Centre

Form RPR
6 **1** **Park Glen (IRE)**[14] 4589 2-8-11 0..... SamJames(3) 5 72+
(Noel Quinlan) *trckd ldrs: rdn to ld over 1f out: kpt on wl towards fin* **10/1**
3 **2** ½ **Mythmaker**[11] 4701 2-9-5 0..... PaulMulrennan 9 75
(Bryan Smart) *cl up: effrt and ev ch over 1f out: kpt on fnl f: hld nr fin* **11/4**[2]
0 **3** 6 **Yorkshire (IRE)**[13] 4618 2-9-5 0..... TomEaves 4 57+
(Kevin Ryan) *t.k.h: led to over 1f out: wknd ins fnl f* **9/4**[1]
60 **4** ¾ **Charlotte's Secret**[26] 4216 2-9-0 0..... JackGarritty(5) 6 55
(Richard Fahey) *hld up: rdn over 2f out: hdwy over 1f out: kpt on: nvr able to chal* **7/2**[3]
**5** 1 **Coyled Spring (IRE)** 2-9-0 0..... BarryMcHugh 1 47+
(Tony Coyle) *towards rr: pushed along over 2f out: no imp fr wl over 1f out* **25/1**
3 **6** ¾ **Sweet Missi (IRE)**[9] 4751 2-9-0 0..... PaulPickard 8 45
(Brian Ellison) *hld up in tch: drvn and outpcd over 2f out: n.d after* **13/2**
5 **7** 18 **Aneto Peak**[17] 4493 2-9-5 0..... AdrianNicholls 3
(Nigel Tinkler) *prom tl rdn and wknd over 2f out* **66/1**
U **Get Knotted (IRE)** 2-9-2 0..... ConnorBeasley(3) 7
(Michael Dods) *uns rdr and loose to post* **16/1**

1m 15.75s (1.15) **Going Correction** +0.05s/f (Good) **8** Ran SP% **113.3**
Speed ratings (Par 92): **94,93,85,84,83 82,58,**
CSF £37.06 TOTE £15.00: £3.20, £1.50, £1.80; EX 44.70 Trifecta £171.10.
**Owner** Mrs C Cashman **Bred** Rathbarry Stud **Trained** Newmarket, Suffolk

**FOCUS**
No great depth, but the leading pair still deserve some credit for pulling well clear.

### 5087 PERCY HEDLEY SPLASH APPEAL H'CAP 5f
**7:10** (7:10) (Class 5) (0-75,73) 3-Y-O **£2,911** (£866; £432; £216) **Stalls** Centre

Form RPR
0300 **1** **Tinsill**[5] 4890 3-9-1 **67**..... AdrianNicholls 3 76
(Nigel Tinkler) *hld up in tch: pushed along over 2f out: swtchd lft and hdwy over 1f out: led ins fnl f: rdn out* **10/1**
2641 **2** ¾ **Rozene (IRE)**[23] 4307 3-9-6 **72**..... GrahamGibbons 2 78
(David Barron) *led: rdn over 1f out: hdd ins fnl f: kpt on: hld towards fin* **9/2**[3]
5462 **3** 2 ¼ **Distant Past**[33] 3959 3-9-7 **73**..... TomEaves 4 71
(Kevin Ryan) *w ldr: drvn along wl over 1f out: outpcd by first two ins fnl f* **11/8**[1]
5225 **4** 3 **Traditionelle**[5] 4891 3-8-9 **61**..... AndrewElliott 5 48
(Tim Easterby) *taken early to post: t.k.h: trckd ldrs: rdn and edgd lft over 1f out: sn btn* **3/1**[2]
-016 **5** 3 ½ **Lexington Rose**[22] 4315 3-9-7 **73**..... PaulMulrennan 1 48
(Bryan Smart) *prom: drvn over 2f out: wknd wl over 1f out* **7/1**

1m 1.49s (0.39) **Going Correction** +0.05s/f (Good) **5** Ran SP% **106.9**
Speed ratings (Par 100): **98,96,93,88,82**
CSF £48.21 TOTE £6.00: £2.30, £1.90; EX 32.80 Trifecta £92.80.
**Owner** Crawford Society 1 **Bred** L T Roberts **Trained** Langton, N Yorks

**FOCUS**
A fair contest, though not that competitive by usual sprint standards. The winner returned to his best after a couple of lesser efforts on fast ground.

### 5088 PUNTER SOUTHALL FOR PENSIONS H'CAP 7f
**7:45** (7:45) (Class 5) (0-75,75) 3-Y-O+ **£2,911** (£866; £432; £216) **Stalls** Centre

Form RPR
4130 **1** **Big Storm Coming**[13] 4635 4-9-9 **72**..... PaulPickard 6 84+
(Brian Ellison) *dwlt: hld up: gd hdwy on outside to ld over 1f out: idled and hung lft ins fnl f: rdn out* **9/1**
3425 **2** ¾ **Mfiftythreedotcom (IRE)**[26] 4191 3-9-0 **69**.....(p) TonyHamilton 9 74
(Richard Fahey) *hld up: rdn whn n.m.r over 2f out: gd hdwy fnl f: kpt on strly to take 2nd cl home* **6/1**[1]
354 **3** hd **No Quarter (IRE)**[29] 4070 7-8-11 **60**..... RoystonFfrench 14 66
(Tracy Waggott) *cl up: rdn and chsd wnr over 1f out: kpt on fnl f: no ex and lost 2nd cl home* **16/1**
42-4 **4** nse **Tiger Jim**[28] 4111 4-8-13 **65**..... GaryBartley(3) 12 71+
(Jim Goldie) *dwlt: hld up: smooth hdwy over 2f out: rdn over 1f out: kpt on strly towards fin: improve* **6/1**[1]
1206 **5** 7 **Kung Hei Fat Choy (USA)**[14] 4580 5-9-7 **73**.....(b) ConnorBeasley(3) 13 61
(James Given) *cl up: led over 3f out to over 1f out: sn n.m.r and outpcd: no imp fnl f* **7/1**[2]
40-0 **6** ½ **Barney McGrew (IRE)**[18] 4471 11-9-12 **75**..... PaulMulrennan 15 62
(Michael Dods) *trckd ldrs gng wl: effrt and ev ch briefly over 1f out: wknd ins fnl f* **14/1**
-540 **7** 4 **Broctune Papa Gio**[28] 4108 7-9-3 **66**..... TomEaves 8 42
(Keith Reveley) *hld up in midfield: drvn and outpcd over 2f out: n.d after* **25/1**
-010 **8** 1 ¾ **Rust (IRE)**[10] 4727 4-8-13 **62**.....(b[1]) PJMcDonald 3 34
(Ann Duffield) *in tch: rdn 3f out: wknd fr 2f out* **25/1**
0-00 **9** nse **Dennis**[23] 4291 4-9-0 **63**..... AndrewElliott 11 35
(Tim Easterby) *led to over 3f out: rdn and wknd fr 2f out* **20/1**
444 **10** ¾ **Dutch Descent (IRE)**[42] 3601 3-9-1 **70**..... GrahamGibbons 16 38
(David Barron) *racd alone stands' side: prom tl wknd fr 2f out* **7/1**[2]
0000 **11** 1 ½ **Orbit The Moon (IRE)**[28] 4108 6-9-6 **69**.....(tp) DavidNolan 10 35
(Michael Dods) *cl up: drvn along over 2f out: wknd wl over 1f out* **8/1**[3]
0460 **12** 2 ¾ **Just The Tonic**[23] 4294 7-9-5 **68**..... IanBrennan 4 27
(Marjorie Fife) *towards rr: drvn along over 3f out: sn btn* **14/1**
4314 **13** 6 **Tamayuz Magic (IRE)**[17] 4496 3-8-7 **62**.....(p) BarryMcHugh 7 3
(Michael Easterby) *cl up tl lost pl over 3f out: btn fnl 2f* **7/1**[2]

1m 27.37s (-0.43) **Going Correction** +0.05s/f (Good)
**WFA** 3 from 4yo+ 6lb **13** Ran SP% **118.9**
Speed ratings (Par 103): **104,103,102,102,94 94,89,87,87,86 85,81,75**
CSF £60.20 CT £881.92 TOTE £8.80: £2.50, £2.20, £6.20; EX 54.70 Trifecta £579.10.
**Owner** Fishlake Commercial Motors Ltd **Bred** Bearstone Stud **Trained** Norton, N Yorks

**FOCUS**
A fair handicap which was soundly run. The first, second and fourth came from the rear.

### 5089 PERCY HEDLEY FOUNDATION H'CAP 6f
**8:15** (8:18) (Class 6) (0-65,65) 3-Y-O+ **£2,264** (£673; £336; £168) **Stalls** Centre

Form RPR
2522 **1** **Mission Impossible**[8] 4796 9-9-10 **63**.....(p) PaulMulrennan 15 72
(Tracy Waggott) *prom: rdn 2f out: hdwy to ld ins fnl f: hld on wl u.p* **6/1**[3]
6324 **2** hd **Another Royal**[16] 4512 3-8-12 **55**.....(b) TonyHamilton 9 62
(Tim Easterby) *hmpd s: hld up: stdy hdwy 2f out: effrt and ev ch ins fnl f: rdn and kpt on: hld cl home* **12/1**
0340 **3** ¾ **Lucky Lodge**[13] 4632 4-9-8 **61**.....(b) AndrewElliott 10 67
(Mel Brittain) *wnt lft s: sn cl up: led over 2f out to ins fnl f: kpt on: hld towards fin* **17/2**
604 **4** ¾ **Dartrix**[13] 4629 5-9-8 **64**..... ConnorBeasley(3) 5 68
(Michael Dods) *taken early to post: hld up: stdy hdwy and prom over 1f out: sn rdn: kpt on ins fnl f: hld nr fin* **5/1**[2]
5013 **5** 2 ½ **Exotic Guest**[32] 4003 4-9-12 **65**..... JamesSullivan 7 61
(Ruth Carr) *hmpd s: hld up: rdn and hdwy over 1f out: kpt on fnl f: no imp* **9/2**[1]
0431 **6** ½ **Bearskin (IRE)**[19] 4455 3-9-5 **62**.....(p) PJMcDonald 4 55
(Ann Duffield) *prom: drvn and outpcd over 2f out: kpt on fnl f: no imp* **9/2**[1]
5544 **7** ½ **Live Dangerously**[16] 4523 4-9-12 **65**..... TomEaves 1 57
(Keith Dalgleish) *dwlt: sn cl up: ev ch over 2f out to over 1f out: wknd ins fnl f* **7/1**
02-2 **8** 4 ½ **Royal Duchess**[17] 4489 4-8-10 **54**..... JackGarritty(5) 16 32
(Lucy Normile) *towards rr: drvn over 2f out: sn btn* **10/1**
3433 **9** 1 ½ **Lendal Bridge**[46] 3503 3-8-13 **56**..... BarryMcHugh 6 28
(Tony Coyle) *midfield: rdn and outpcd over 2f out: sn btn* **16/1**
6503 **10** 2 ¼ **Foreign Rhythm (IRE)**[13] 4629 9-9-2 **62**..... RachelRichardson(7) 2 28
(Ron Barr) *hld up in tch: rdn over 2f out: btn over 1f out* **40/1**

5004 **11** *2 3/4* **Sunrise Dance**[12] 4664 5-9-5 **58** ............ IanBrennan 13 15
(Robert Johnson) *dwlt: towards rr: rdn along 1/2-way: btn fnl 2f* **25/1**

00-0 **12** *24* **Liberal Lady**[12] 4664 6-9-1 **54** ............(p) DavidNolan 11
(Robert Johnson) *taken early to post: led tl hdd & wknd qckly over 2f out* **80/1**

1m 14.96s (0.36) **Going Correction** +0.05s/f (Good)
**WFA** 3 from 4yo+ 4lb **12** Ran SP% **120.5**
Speed ratings (Par 101): **99,98,97,96,93 92,92,86,84,81 77,45**
CSF £76.30 CT £621.37 TOTE £4.20: £1.60, £4.00, £2.20; EX 99.70 Trifecta £581.60.
**Owner** H Conlon **Bred** Rodney Meredith **Trained** Spennymoor, Co Durham
■ Lees Anthem was withdrawn. Price at time of withdrawal 11/1. Rule 4 applies to all bets struck prior to withdrawal but not to SP bets. Deduct 5p in the pound. New market formed.

**FOCUS**
A run-of-the-mill sprint which was soundly run. The winner was continuing his good run, while the runner-up improved.

## 5090 NCFE H'CAP — 1m 6f 97y
8:45 (8:45) (Class 5) (0-70,67) 3-Y-O+ **£2,911** (£866; £432; £216) **Stalls** Low

Form RPR

0031 **1** **Sergeant Pink (IRE)**[3] 4964 8-8-12 **56** 6ex............ EmmaSayer(5) 7 65
(Dianne Sayer) *t.k.h: hld up in tch: outpcd 1/2-way: stdy hdwy 3f out: effrt over 1f out: pushed along and styd on to ld towards fin* **5/2**[1]

-050 **2** *hd* **Authentication**[69] 2738 5-8-10 **49** ............ PJMcDonald 2 57
(Mel Brittain) *led at modest gallop: rdn and qcknd 2f out: edgd rt u.p ins fnl f: kpt on: hdd towards fin* **4/1**[3]

0560 **3** *2* **Gioia Di Vita**[19] 4427 4-9-7 **60** ............ DavidNolan 5 65
(David Thompson) *in tch: effrt over 2f out: rdn over 1f out: kpt on same pce ins fnl f* **9/1**

5414 **4** *2 1/4* **Madrasa (IRE)**[12] 4662 6-10-0 **67** ............(b) TomEaves 1 69
(Keith Reveley) *t.k.h: trckd ldrs: wnt 2nd over 3f out: rdn over 2f out: outpcd fnl f* **3/1**[2]

6-00 **5** *14* **Thundering Cloud (IRE)**[18] 4472 3-8-7 **59** ............ RoystonFfrench 3 41
(Simon Waugh) *t.k.h: chsd ldrs tl rdn and outpcd over 2f out: sn btn* **33/1**

0000 **6** *11* **Musikhani**[47] 3482 4-9-1 **59** ............(p) JackGarritty(5) 4 26
(Philip Kirby) *pressed ldr: rdn over 3f out: wknd over 2f out* **5/1**

0-60 **7** *6* **Mafeteng**[19] 4423 6-9-9 **62** ............ RaulDaSilva 6 20
(David Thompson) *hld up: rdn and struggling over 3f out: sn btn* **12/1**

3m 15.92s (4.62) **Going Correction** +0.25s/f (Good)
**WFA** 3 from 4yo+ 13lb **7** Ran SP% **110.9**
Speed ratings (Par 103): **96,95,94,93,85 79,75**
CSF £11.96 TOTE £3.10: £1.60, £2.70; EX 13.60 Trifecta £91.00.
**Owner** Andrew Sayer **Bred** Ring Pink Partnership **Trained** Hackthorpe, Cumbria

**FOCUS**
An ordinary staying event which was steadily run. The winner followed up his Carlisle win, but this time after being held up.
T/Jkpt: Not won. T/Plt: £155.60 to a £1 stake. Pool: £54,204.56 - 254.19 winning units T/Qpdt: £42.50 to a £1 stake. Pool: £6,550.05 - 113.98 winning units RY

# [4798]SANDOWN (R-H)
Thursday, August 7

**OFFICIAL GOING: Round course - good to firm (good in places); sprint course - good (good to firm in places)**
Wind: Light, against Weather: Fine, very warm

## 5091 EBFSTALLIONS.COM MAIDEN STKS — 5f 6y
5:40 (5:44) (Class 5) 2-Y-O **£3,881** (£1,155; £577; £288) **Stalls** Low

Form RPR

32 **1** **Cool Strutter (IRE)**[20] 4409 2-9-5 0 ............ JamieSpencer 8 82+
(Richard Hannon) *mde all and sn crossed to far rail: shkn up and in command wl over 1f out: pushed out* **10/11**[1]

4 **2** *3 1/4* **Astrophysics**[13] 4618 2-9-5 0 ............ LiamKeniry 6 70
(David Elsworth) *chsd wnr: rdn 2f out: no imp after: kpt on to hold on for 2nd* **5/1**[2]

**3** *1 1/4* **Excellent George** 2-9-5 0 ............ MartinHarley 4 66+
(Stuart Williams) *racd against far rail: chsd ldng pair: rdn 2f out: kpt on to press for 2nd fnl f: no ch w wnr* **33/1**

**4** *1 3/4* **Manofmanytalents** 2-9-5 0 ............ AdamBeschizza 5 60+
(Michael Squance) *dwlt: sn pushed along in rr: prog against far rail fr 1/2-way: tk 4th over 1f out: kpt on* **66/1**

**5** *5* **Just Us Two (IRE)** 2-9-5 0 ............ PatDobbs 2 42+
(Robert Cowell) *v s.i.s: virtually t.o after 1f: stl last 1/2-way: styd on wl fr over 1f out: tk modest 5th nr fin* **33/1**

**6** *nk* **Gin Trap (USA)** 2-9-5 0 ............ JimCrowley 1 40
(Olly Stevens) *trckd ldng trio: pushed along and lost grnd fr 2f out: wknd fnl f* **14/1**

2425 **7** *3 1/4* **Zuzinia (IRE)**[26] 4185 2-9-0 **69** ............ WilliamTwiston-Davies 3 24
(Mick Channon) *hld up towards rr: tried to make prog 1/2-way: wknd over 1f out* **15/2**[3]

5 **8** *1/2* **Dunnscotia**[24] 4270 2-9-5 0 ............ JimmyFortune 10 27
(Paul Webber) *dwlt: sn chsd ldrs towards outer: shkn up 2f out: wknd over 1f out* **12/1**

40 **9** *1 1/4* **Bouncing Czech**[9] 4760 2-9-5 0 ............ AdamKirby 11 22
(Amanda Perrett) *dwlt: racd wdst of all: wl in tch: lost pl fr 1/2-way: nudged along and wknd over 1f out* **50/1**

0 **10** *4* **Swift Susie**[94] 2022 2-8-7 0 ............ AaronJones(7) 7
(Stuart Williams) *taken v steadily to post: slowly away: a wl in rr* **100/1**

**11** *2 1/4* **Steevo (IRE)** 2-9-5 0 ............ GeorgeBaker 12
(Gary Moore) *taken steadily to post: slowly away: rn green and a wl in rr* **25/1**

1m 2.19s (0.59) **Going Correction** 0.0s/f (Good) **11** Ran SP% **109.3**
Speed ratings (Par 94): **95,89,87,85,77 76,71,70,68,62 58**
CSF £4.28 TOTE £1.60: £1.10, £2.10, £3.70; EX 5.90 Trifecta £64.40.
**Owner** Qatar Racing Limited **Bred** Tally-Ho Stud **Trained** East Everleigh, Wilts
■ Equally Fast was withdrawn. Price at time of withdrawal 12/1. Rule 4 applies to all bets - deduct 5p in the pound.

**FOCUS**
Rail at innermost configuration and all distances as advertised. Sprint course at full width. A modest 2yo maiden with the pre-race pick winning.

## 5092 TELEGRAPH HILL H'CAP — 7f 16y
6:15 (6:16) (Class 4) (0-85,85) 3-Y-O+ **£4,690** (£1,395; £697; £348) **Stalls** Low

Form RPR

-401 **1** **Take A Note**[27] 4154 5-9-8 **81** ............(v) JimCrowley 9 93
(Patrick Chamings) *led after 1f: clr after 3f: hld togther tl rdn out fnl f: unchal* **6/1**[3]

1-50 **2** *2 1/2* **Champagne Sydney (IRE)**[90] 2112 3-9-1 **80** ............ PatDobbs 1 83
(Richard Hannon) *chsd ldng pair: rdn over 2f out: kpt on to take 2nd jst ins fnl f: no ch w wnr* **8/1**

1410 **3** *1* **Bravo Echo**[26] 4181 8-9-7 **80** ............ RobertHavlin 2 82
(Michael Attwater) *led 1f: chsd wnr: rdn over 2f out and no imp: lost 2nd jst ins fnl f* **11/2**[2]

0246 **4** *2 1/2* **Subtle Knife**[49] 3402 5-9-6 **79** ............ PatrickDonaghy 4 75
(Giles Bravery) *hld up and sn wl off the pce in last: rdn and hanging fr 3f out: kpt on fr 2f out to take 4th fnl f: n.d* **14/1**

040- **5** *3 3/4* **Lizzie Tudor**[372] 4897 4-9-12 **85** ............[1] LiamKeniry 6 71
(Andrew Balding) *hld up in 5th: nudged along over 2f out: no prog and wl btn whn rdn over 1f out* **15/2**

2150 **6** *1/2* **Voyageofdiscovery (USA)**[12] 4647 3-9-2 **81** ............ AdamKirby 8 64
(Clive Cox) *stdd s: hld up in 6th and off the pce: pushed along and no prog wl over 2f out: no ch whn rdn over 1f out* **7/4**[1]

5604 **7** *7* **Xanthos**[13] 4631 3-8-9 **74** ............ MartinHarley 3 39
(Ed Walker) *restless stalls: chsd ldng trio tl wknd qckly wl over 1f out* **6/1**[3]

1m 27.67s (-1.83) **Going Correction** -0.10s/f (Good)
**WFA** 3 from 4yo+ 6lb **7** Ran SP% **109.9**
Speed ratings (Par 105): **106,103,102,99,94 94,86**
CSF £47.48 CT £258.27 TOTE £5.20: £2.70, £3.70; EX 22.50 Trifecta £136.00.
**Owner** The Foxford House Partnership **Bred** P J L Wright **Trained** Baughurst, Hants

**FOCUS**
A fair handicap with the winner making most at fait pace. The third sets level.

## 5093 BRITISH STALLION STUDS EBF MAIDEN STKS — 1m 14y
6:50 (6:50) (Class 5) 2-Y-O **£3,881** (£1,155; £577; £288) **Stalls** Low

Form RPR

0 **1** **Snoano**[27] 4167 2-9-5 0 ............ WilliamBuick 5 84+
(John Gosden) *sn trckd ldr: shkn up to chal over 2f out and stl green: rdn to ld over 1f out: steadily asserted* **6/4**[2]

5 **2** *2 1/4* **Deluxe**[9] 4760 2-9-5 0 ............ PatDobbs 6 79+
(Richard Hannon) *sn led sent for home over 2f out: rdn and hdd over 1f out: one pce fnl f* **5/1**[3]

52 **3** *3 1/4* **Ventriloquist**[43] 3578 2-9-5 0 ............ AdamKirby 4 72
(Charlie Appleby) *best away but restrained into 3rd and t.k.h: shkn up over 2f out: tried to cl over 1f out: sn rdn and nt qckn* **11/10**[1]

**4** *2 1/4* **Gold Prince (IRE)** 2-9-5 0 ............ LiamKeniry 3 67+
(Sylvester Kirk) *a last: outpcd over 2f out: no ch after: kpt on nr fin* **20/1**

1m 44.55s (1.25) **Going Correction** -0.10s/f (Good) **4** Ran SP% **109.0**
Speed ratings (Par 94): **89,86,83,81**
CSF £8.68 TOTE £2.20; EX 7.50 Trifecta £9.40.
**Owner** Hamdan Al Maktoum **Bred** Minster Stud **Trained** Newmarket, Suffolk

**FOCUS**
Just the four runners, but those with previous experience had all shown a fair level of ability already. The runner-up is a good guide.

## 5094 COBHAM H'CAP (BOBIS RACE) — 1m 2f 7y
7:25 (7:25) (Class 3) (0-90,86) 3-Y-O **£7,439** (£2,213; £1,106; £553) **Stalls** Low

Form RPR

51 **1** **Prince Of Stars**[92] 2075 3-9-6 **85** ............ WilliamBuick 1 97+
(John Gosden) *trckd ldng pair: nt clr run on inner and dropped to 4th 2f out: swtchd lft over 1f out and drvn: edgd rt but r.o to ld last 100yds* **15/8**[1]

2332 **2** *1* **Hedge End (IRE)**[8] 4782 3-8-7 **77** ............ CamHardie(5) 8 84
(Richard Hannon) *trckd ldr: rdn to chal 2f out: led over 1f out: kpt on but wl hdd and hld last 100yds* **7/1**

2565 **3** *1 1/4* **Automated**[19] 4435 3-9-7 **86** ............ JimmyFortune 3 92
(Clive Brittain) *led at mod pce: kicked on wl over 2f out: drvn and hdd over 1f out: fought on wl but hld in 3rd whn hmpd nr fin* **16/1**

211 **4** *shd* **Hoop Of Colour (USA)**[20] 4417 3-9-6 **85** ............ MartinHarley 9 90
(Lady Cecil) *trckd ldng trio: rdn to chal on outer 2f out: nrly upsides over 1f out: nt qckn after* **5/1**[3]

21 **5** *1 1/2* **Mythical Madness**[17] 4500 3-9-6 **85** ............ AdamKirby 2 87
(Charlie Appleby) *hld up in 6th: shkn up over 2f out: nt qckn whn shied lft over 1f out: one pce after* **4/1**[2]

016 **6** *2 1/2* **Comedy King (IRE)**[46] 3499 3-9-4 **83** ............ AndreaAtzeni 6 80
(Luca Cumani) *cl up: rdn over 2f out: no prog whn bmpd over 1f out: fdd* **13/2**

2444 **7** *1/2* **Cotton Club (IRE)**[22] 4332 3-8-12 **77** ............ OisinMurphy 7 73
(Rod Millman) *hld up in last: shkn up and no prog over 2f out: nvr figured* **14/1**

2m 10.49s (-0.01) **Going Correction** -0.10s/f (Good) **7** Ran SP% **109.8**
Speed ratings (Par 104): **96,95,94,94,92 90,90**
CSF £14.24 CT £143.43 TOTE £3.10: £2.30, £1.70; EX 13.20 Trifecta £167.20.
**Owner** Jaber Abdullah **Bred** Rabbah Bloodstock Limited **Trained** Newmarket, Suffolk

**FOCUS**
They went no gallop, and on a night when it had already been proving difficult to close from off the pace, it was a muddling affair. The third looks best guide.

## 5095 CHRISTMAS PARTIES AT SANDOWN PARK H'CAP — 1m 2f 7y
7:55 (7:56) (Class 4) (0-80,80) 3-Y-O+ **£4,690** (£1,395; £697; £348) **Stalls** Low

Form RPR

0043 **1** **Croquembouche (IRE)**[11] 4710 5-10-0 **80** ............ OisinMurphy 5 88
(Ed de Giles) *led: drvn wl over 2f out: narrowly hdd over 1f out: rallied to ld jst ins fnl f: kpt on gamely* **15/8**[2]

0030 **2** *1/2* **Tinshu (IRE)**[26] 4184 8-9-10 **76** ............(p) AdamKirby 6 83
(Derek Haydn Jones) *trckd wnr: rdn over 2f out: narrow ld over 1f out: hdd and nt qckn jst ins fnl f* **13/2**

5563 **3** *3 3/4* **Fastnet Red**[35] 3892 3-9-2 **77** ............ WilliamBuick 1 77
(John Gosden) *pushed along early to get gng: in tch in last pair: rdn 3f out: no imp on ldrs u.str.p over 1f out* **5/4**[1]

4031 **4** *nk* **Special Miss**[8] 4802 3-8-3 **69** 6ex........................ CamHardie(5) 2 68
(Ali Stronge) *t.k.h: hld up: trckd ldng pair after 4f: plld out and shkn up wl over 1f out: nt qckn and sn btn* **6/1**[3]
2m 9.03s (-1.47) **Going Correction** -0.10s/f (Good)
**WFA** 3 from 4yo+ 9lb **4** Ran SP% **106.8**
Speed ratings (Par 105): **101,100,97,97**
CSF £12.11 TOTE £3.80; EX 13.30 Trifecta £20.80.
**Owner** John Manser **Bred** Ballymacoll Stud Farm Ltd **Trained** Ledbury, H'fords
**FOCUS**
Another where it proved hard to challenge from off the pace. The second helps set the standard.

## 5096 NYMT CHARITY RACEDAY 30TH AUGUST H'CAP 1m 14y
**8:25** (8:25) (Class 5) (0-75,75) 3-Y-O+ **£3,234** (£962; £481; £240) **Stalls** Low

Form RPR
3456 **1** **Guaracha**[14] 4593 3-9-0 **68**........................(p) JimmyFortune 1 74
(Clive Brittain) *led or disp thrght: rdn 2f out: grad asserted ins fnl f: drvn out* **16/1**
2431 **2** *1/2* **Cherry Princess**[7] 4808 4-8-9 **56** oh3........................ OisinMurphy 9 62
(Stuart Williams) *w wnr thrght: rdn 2f out: stl upsides 1f out: kpt on but no ex ins fnl f* **10/3**[2]
6503 **3** *3/4* **Gracious George (IRE)**[15] 4549 4-9-8 **69**........................(p) PatDobbs 5 73
(Jimmy Fox) *hld up in last pair: rdn 2f out: limited imp tl styd on fnl f to take 3rd last strides* **7/1**[3]
3655 **4** *1/2* **Djinni (IRE)**[13] 4611 3-8-7 **66**........................(b) CamHardie(5) 2 68
(Richard Hannon) *trckd ldng pair: rdn 2f out: awkward hd carriage and nt qckn over 1f out: one pce after* **7/1**[3]
-031 **5** *3/4* **Tides Reach (IRE)**[17] 4503 3-9-7 **75**........................ GeorgeBaker 4 75
(Roger Charlton) *trckd ldng pair: rdn 2f out: nt qckn and no imp over 1f out: one pce* **6/5**[1]
2520 **6** *1 1/2* **Benandonner (USA)**[51] 3334 11-8-9 **56** oh1.............. FergusSweeney 7 54
(Mike Murphy) *sn hld up in last pair and t.k.h: shkn up over 2f out: sn outpcd: n.d after* **10/1**
1m 43.8s (0.50) **Going Correction** -0.10s/f (Good)
**WFA** 3 from 4yo+ 7lb **6** Ran SP% **108.5**
Speed ratings (Par 103): **93,92,91,91,90 89**
CSF £63.44 CT £371.07 TOTE £13.00: £7.20, £1.70; EX 77.60 Trifecta £648.50 Part won..
**Owner** C E Brittain **Bred** Michael E Broughton **Trained** Newmarket, Suffolk
■ Stewards' Enquiry : Pat Dobbs four-day ban: used whip above permitted level (Aug 23-26)
George Baker trainer's rep said filly was unsuited by the good to firm (good in places) ground
**FOCUS**
Yet again the pace held up well, the first two holding positions throughout, and the form is worth treating cautiously.
T/Plt: £483.30 to a £1 stake. Pool: £47,934.51 - 72.40 winning units T/Qpdt: £196.40 to a £1 stake. Pool: £4,301.46 - 16.20 winning units JN

# 3792 SOUTHWELL (L-H)
### Thursday, August 7

**OFFICIAL GOING: Standard**
Wind: Light behind Weather: Fine & dry

## 5097 32RED FILLIES' H'CAP 6f (F)
**5:15** (5:15) (Class 5) (0-75,74) 3-Y-O+ **£2,726** (£805; £402) **Stalls** Low

Form RPR
5421 **1** **Guishan**[28] 4132 4-9-5 **66**........................ AndrewMullen 1 80
(Michael Appleby) *awkward and wnt rt s: sn rdn along to join ldrs and slt ld after 2f: rdn 2f out: drvn and wandered ent fnl f: drvn out* **5/2**[1]
0-10 **2** *1* **Musical Molly (IRE)**[41] 3669 3-8-13 **64**........................ DaleSwift 4 74
(Brian Ellison) *cl up: effrt 2f out: rdn to chal over 1f out: drvn and ev ch ent fnl f: no ex last 100yds* **7/2**[2]
2561 **3** *6* **Amosite**[9] 4768 8-9-13 **74** 6ex........................(v) JoeFanning 6 66
(J R Jenkins) *trckd ldrs on outer: wd st riodden 2f out: kpt on same pce appr fnl f* **9/2**[3]
1340 **4** *2* **Solarmaite**[33] 3971 5-8-13 **63**........................(b) BillyCray(3) 5 48
(Roy Bowring) *prom: wd st: rdn 2f out: sn edgd lft and outpcd: kpt on fnl f* **7/2**[2]
6106 **5** *1/2* **Take The Lead**[17] 4487 4-8-13 **67**........................ AnnaHesketh(7) 3 51
(David Nicholls) *dwlt and in rr: hdwy 1/2-way: rdn to chse ldrs 2f out: wknd over 1f out* **10/1**
3523 **6** *1* **Heroique (IRE)**[13] 4628 3-9-8 **73**........................(e) DuranFentiman 2 53
(Tim Easterby) *led 2f: prom: rdn along wl over 2f out: sn wknd* **7/1**
1m 17.74s (1.24) **Going Correction** +0.25s/f (Slow)
**WFA** 3 from 4yo+ 4lb **6** Ran SP% **112.8**
Speed ratings (Par 100): **101,99,91,89,88 87**
CSF £11.58 TOTE £3.20: £1.80, £2.40; EX 16.30 Trifecta £27.20.
**Owner** Brian D Cantle **Bred** B D Cantle **Trained** Danethorpe, Notts
**FOCUS**
There was a fair pace set in this moderate sprint handicap for fillies and the two market leaders pulled clear inside the final 2f.

## 5098 32RED CASINO MEDIAN AUCTION MAIDEN STKS 7f (F)
**5:50** (5:51) (Class 6) 2-Y-O **£2,045** (£603; £302) **Stalls** Low

Form RPR
00 **1** **Thewaythewindblows (IRE)**[13] 4633 2-9-2 0.......(t) ThomasBrown(3) 4 68
(Daniel Kubler) *chsd ldr: rdn along 3f out: sn cl up: led wl over 1f out: edgd lft ins fnl f: styd on* **3/1**[2]
04 **2** *1 3/4* **Keen Move**[15] 4527 2-9-5 0........................ JoeFanning 2 63
(Ismail Mohammed) *led: jnd and rdn along over 2f out: drvn and hanging lft wl over 1f out: sn hdd: kpt on same pce fnl f* **7/4**[1]
**3** *1* **Furiously Fast (IRE)** 2-9-5 0........................ KierenFallon 3 63+
(Clive Brittain) *dwlt and sn pushed along in rr: rdn along 1/2-way: hdwy wl over 2f out: kpt on wl fnl f: nrst fin* **3/1**[2]
6 **4** *4 1/2* **Dew Pond**[18] 4467 2-9-5 0........................ DuranFentiman 5 48
(Tim Easterby) *chsd ldrs on outer: rdn along wl over 2f out: drvn and one pce fnl 2f* **6/1**[3]
00 **5** *8* **Tobougan Run**[42] 3620 2-9-5 0........................ AndrewMullen 1 27
(Michael Appleby) *chsd ldrs on inner: rdn along wl over 2f out: sn drvn and wknd* **16/1**
00 **6** *13* **Hold Firm**[35] 3875 2-9-2 0........................ AshleyMorgan(3) 6
(Mark H Tompkins) *s.i.s: a in rr* **10/1**
1m 34.05s (3.75) **Going Correction** +0.25s/f (Slow) **6** Ran SP% **115.6**
Speed ratings (Par 92): **88,86,84,79,70 55**
CSF £9.07 TOTE £6.40: £2.30, £2.10; EX 17.20 Trifecta £47.80.
**Owner** Who Dares Wins **Bred** J Yeomans, B McGarvey & A Everard **Trained** Whitsbury, Hants

**FOCUS**
An ordinary 2yo maiden, but the winner is improving.

## 5099 ALL NEW 32REDSPORT.COM MAIDEN STKS 6f (F)
**6:25** (6:27) (Class 5) 2-Y-O **£2,587** (£770; £384; £192) **Stalls** Low

Form RPR
542 **1** **Ghost Cat**[10] 4740 2-9-5 0........................ KierenFallon 3 75+
(Brian Meehan) *cl up: slt ld over 2f out: rdn wl over 1f out: drvn and edgd lft ins fnl f: jst hld on* **1/2**[1]
0 **2** *shd* **Captain Revelation**[26] 4185 2-9-5 0........................ RichardKingscote 2 75+
(Tom Dascombe) *slt ld: hdd over 3f out: cl up: rdn wl over 1f out: drvn and ev ch ins fnl f: jst hld* **4/1**[2]
0 **3** *8* **Dark Side Dream**[27] 4167 2-9-5 0........................ JimmyQuinn 4 51
(Chris Dwyer) *towards rr: hdwy on inner wl over 2f out: rdn to chse ldng pair wl over 1f out: sn drvn and kpt on one pce* **33/1**
55 **4** *7* **Monksford Lady**[31] 4011 2-8-11 0........................ GeorgeChaloner(3) 1 25
(Donald McCain) *t.k.h: cl up on inner: slt ld over 3f out: sn rdn and hdd 2f out: sn wknd* **20/1**
03 **5** *2 1/2* **Call Me Crockett (IRE)**[12] 4659 2-9-5 0........................ DuranFentiman 7 22
(Richard Guest) *chsd ldrs: rdn along 1/2-way: sn outpcd* **12/1**[3]
50 **6** *3* **Native Charmer**[51] 3330 2-9-5 0........................ DaleSwift 5 13
(Ed McMahon) *dwlt: a outpcd in rr* **25/1**
540 **7** *nk* **Lucilla Aurelius (IRE)**[33] 3945 2-9-0 **56**........................ PatrickMathers 6 7
(Tony Coyle) *chsd ldrs: rdn along 1/2-way: sn drvn and wknd* **16/1**
1m 17.22s (0.72) **Going Correction** +0.25s/f (Slow) **7** Ran SP% **111.8**
Speed ratings (Par 94): **105,104,94,84,81 77,77**
CSF £2.50 TOTE £1.20: £1.10, £1.90; EX 3.50 Trifecta £35.40.
**Owner** The Pony Club **Bred** Mascalls Stud **Trained** Manton, Wilts
**FOCUS**
A modest 2yo maiden, with the front pair pulling well clear.

## 5100 SHANE W DARBY MEMORIAL H'CAP 1m (F)
**7:00** (7:00) (Class 4) (0-85,82) 3-Y-O+ **£4,690** (£1,395; £697; £348) **Stalls** Low

Form RPR
5014 **1** **Pearl Nation (USA)**[15] 4537 5-9-9 **77**........................ AndrewMullen 9 90
(Michael Appleby) *trckd ldrs on outer: hdwy and wd st: led 2f out: sn jnd and rdn: drvn ent fnl f: edgd rt and kpt on wl towards fin* **6/4**[1]
4600 **2** *1 3/4* **Blazeofenchantment (USA)**[44] 3547 4-8-6 **65**...... JacobButterfield(5) 4 74
(John Wainwright) *chsd ldrs and pushed along after 2f: rdn along 1/2-way: wd st: chal wl over 1f out: sn drvn and ev ch tl no ex wl ins fnl f* **20/1**
2240 **3** *7* **Sofias Number One (USA)**[56] 3155 6-9-2 **73**...............(b) BillyCray(3) 6 66
(Roy Bowring) *chsd ldrs: rdn along and lost pl over 4f out: hdwy on inner u.p wl over 1f out: kpt on fnl f* **6/1**
1-6 **4** *3 3/4* **Dutch Rifle**[76] 2510 3-9-2 **77**........................ KierenFallon 1 60
(James Tate) *sn cl up: led over 3f out: rdn and hdd 2f out: sn drvn and wknd over 1f out* **3/1**[2]
6313 **5** *7* **Mishrif (USA)**[42] 3629 8-9-8 **76**........................(v) PaddyAspell 8 44
(J R Jenkins) *s.i.s: a in rr* **10/1**
0104 **6** *1 1/4* **Patriotic (IRE)**[29] 4090 6-9-13 **81**........................(v[1]) JimmyQuinn 3 46
(Chris Dwyer) *chsd ldrs on inner: hdwy over 3f out: rdn wl over 2f out: sn drvn and grad wknd* **16/1**
0-66 **7** *9* **Mandy The Nag (USA)**[24] 4255 4-8-11 **68**........................ GeorgeChaloner(3) 5 13
(Richard Fahey) *prom: pushed along 1/2-way: sn rdn: lost pl and bhd* **5/1**[3]
4006 **8** *6* **Kuanyao (IRE)**[21] 4344 8-8-12 **66**........................(b) HayleyTurner 7
(Conor Dore) *rdn to ld and sn swtchd lft to inner: rdn along and hdd 3f out: sn wknd* **25/1**
1m 44.14s (0.44) **Going Correction** +0.25s/f (Slow)
**WFA** 3 from 4yo+ 7lb **8** Ran SP% **119.5**
Speed ratings (Par 105): **107,105,98,94,87 86,77,71**
CSF £37.79 CT £153.92 TOTE £2.80: £1.30, £5.80, £2.90; EX 57.40 Trifecta £288.90.
**Owner** Iddon, M&C Dixon, Taylor, Finn, O'Brien **Bred** William A Carl Estate **Trained** Danethorpe, Notts
**FOCUS**
Not a bad handicap for the class.

## 5101 £10 FREE BET AT 32REDSPORT.COM H'CAP 1m 4f (F)
**7:35** (7:36) (Class 5) (0-70,70) 3-Y-O+ **£2,726** (£805; £402) **Stalls** Low

Form RPR
000/ **1** **Steuben (GER)**[653] 7315 8-9-1 **62**........................ RossCoakley(5) 7 79
(J P Murtagh, Ire) *in tch: pushed along 7f out: hdwy and cl up over 4f out: chal wl over 2f out: sn rdn: drvn ent fnl f: kpt on to ld nr fin* **11/10**[1]
0265 **2** *nk* **Master Dan**[38] 3797 3-8-12 **65**........................ DaleSwift 3 81
(James Given) *prom: hdwy and cl up 5f out: slt ld over 3f out: jnd and rdn 2f out: drvn and wandered over 1f out: kpt on tl hdd and no ex nr fin* **20/1**
0356 **3** *25* **Yasir (USA)**[10] 3269 6-9-7 **63**........................(b[1]) HayleyTurner 4 39
(Conor Dore) *bhd: hdwy and in tch 5f out: rdn along to chse ldrs over 3f out: sn drvn and plugged on one pce* **8/1**[3]
516- **4** *3 1/4* **Aryizad (IRE)**[313] 6846 5-10-0 **70**........................ BenCurtis 6 41
(Alan Swinbank) *trckd ldrs: effrt over 4f out: rdn along over 3f out: sn drvn and wknd* **8/1**[3]
2-00 **5** *9* **Princeofthedesert**[13] 4062 8-8-9 **51** oh3........................(p) PaddyAspell 5 7
(Garry Woodward) *cl up: led over 7f out: rdn along over 4f out: hdd over 3f out and sn wknd* **25/1**
340- **6** *10* **Rocked The Boat**[243] 8201 3-8-10 **63**........................ KierenFallon 8
(David O'Meara) *racd wd: hdwy to chse ldrs 4f out: rdn along 3f out: sn drvn and wknd* **5/1**[2]
406 **7** *18* **Cayjo**[23] 4299 3-8-0 **53** oh2........................ JoeFanning 9
(Mark Johnston) *hld up towards rr: hdwy 1/2-way: chsd ldrs 4f out: rdn along on inner over 3f out: sn wknd* **5/1**[2]
00 **8** *36* **Shirocco Passion**[83] 2319 3-9-0 **67**........................ PatrickMathers 2
(Tony Coyle) *prom: rdn along over 5f out: sn wknd and bhd* **20/1**
-006 **9** *5* **Red Pilgrim (IRE)**[30] 4051 4-9-12 **68**........................(t) SebSanders 1
(James Toller) *led over 4f: cl up: rdn along over 5f out: sn wknd and bhd* **20/1**
2m 42.14s (1.14) **Going Correction** +0.25s/f (Slow)
**WFA** 3 from 4yo+ 11lb **9** Ran SP% **121.3**
Speed ratings (Par 103): **106,105,89,86,80 74,62,38,34**
CSF £32.98 CT £136.94 TOTE £3.10: £2.30, £4.70, £1.10; EX 28.30 Trifecta £214.80.
**Owner** B J Lewis **Bred** Gestut Schlenderhan **Trained** Coolaghknock Glebe,Co Kildare
■ Stewards' Enquiry : Ross Coakley four-day ban: used whip above permitted level (Aug 23-26)

**FOCUS**
This weak handicap was yet another affair where two clear clear in the home straight.

## 5102 MACMILLAN ROSELAND BUSINESS PARK AI EASTMIDLANDS H'CAP 1m 6f (F)
**8:05** (8:08) (Class 6) (0-60,58) 3-Y-O £1,940 (£577; £288; £144) **Stalls** Low

Form RPR
6230 **1** **Moving Waves (IRE)**[23] 4292 3-9-4 **55**.....................(p) RobertWinston 5 61
(Ollie Pears) *cl up: led 1/2-way: rdn along wl over 2f out: clr over 1f out: sn drvn and jst hld on* **8/1**[2]
**2** ½ **Bwindi (IRE)**[12] 4690 3-9-6 **57**..................................... KierenFallon 7 62
(J P Murtagh, Ire) *sn pushed along in rr: rn in snatches: rdn along and sme hdwy 4f out: in tch and drvn over 3f out: no prog tl styd on wl fr over 1f out: jst hld* **8/13**[1]
040 **3** *6* **Deja Bougg**[15] 4543 3-9-4 **58**.................................... DeclanBates[(3)] 3 55
(David Evans) *in rr: hdwy 5f out: rdn along to chse ldng pair 3f out: drvn 2f out: kpt on same pce appr fnl f* **33/1**
000 **4** *4 ½* **Prince Of Islay (IRE)**[36] 3856 3-9-4 **55**..................(p) JoeFanning 6 46
(Robert Mills) *a.p: cl up 1/2-way: rdn along 3f out: drvn 2f out and grad wknd* **8/1**[2]
0654 **5** *32* **Ofelia (IRE)**[9] 4749 3-8-11 **48**.................................... DaleSwift 2
(Brian Ellison) *bhd: hdwy and in tch over 5f out: rdn along over 4f out: sn outpcd* **10/1**[3]
5000 **6** *11* **Buy Out Boy**[15] 4540 3-9-4 **55**......................(b[1]) AndrewMullen 4
(Michael Appleby) *led: hdd 1/2-way: rdn along 5f out: sn wknd and bhd* **8/1**[2]
-063 **7** *38* **Little Bruv**[17] 4497 3-8-8 **45**.................................... DuranFentiman 1
(Tim Easterby) *chsd ldrs: rdn along over 6f out: sn lost pl and bhd: t.o fnl 4f* **8/1**[2]

3m 17.26s (8.96) **Going Correction** +0.25s/f (Slow) **7** Ran SP% **118.4**
Speed ratings (Par 98): **84,83,80,77,59 53,31**
CSF £14.13 TOTE £6.00: £2.70, £1.50; EX 17.40 Trifecta £92.80.
**Owner** Mrs Z Wentworth **Bred** J O'Connor **Trained** Norton, N Yorks
■ Stewards' Enquiry : Kieren Fallon four-day ban: used whip above permitted level (Aug 23-26)

**FOCUS**
A very weak 3yo staying handicap that saw a slow-motion finish.

## 5103 RACING SPECIALS AT 32REDSPORT.COM H'CAP 7f (F)
**8:35** (8:36) (Class 6) (0-55,55) 3-Y-O+ £1,940 (£577; £288; £144) **Stalls** Low

Form RPR
0060 **1** **See Clearly**[23] 4294 5-9-3 **51**.........................(p) DuranFentiman 11 65
(Tim Easterby) *cl up: led 1/2-way: rdn clr wl over 1f out: kpt on strly* **25/1**
0400 **2** *3 ¼* **Thrust Control (IRE)**[8] 4797 7-8-11 **50**..............(p) JacobButterfield[(5)] 13 56
(Tracy Waggott) *prom: rdn along over 2f out: sn chsng wnr: drvn appr fnl f: no imp* **10/1**
2000 **3** *nk* **Master Of Song**[20] 4415 7-8-12 **49**.......................(tp) AshleyMorgan[(3)] 10 54
(Roy Bowring) *chsd ldrs: wd st: hdwy over 2f out: rdn wl over 1f out: drvn and kpt on fnl f* **3/1**[1]
-063 **4** *5* **Benidorm**[38] 3798 6-8-7 **46**...........................................(e) DuilioDaSilva[(5)] 8 38
(Richard Guest) *midfield: hdwy over 2f out: sn rdn and kpt on appr fnl f: nrst fin* **12/1**
1042 **5** ½ **True Spirit**[10] 4732 4-9-7 **55**........................................ SeanLevey 6 46
(Paul D'Arcy) *chsd ldrs: rdn along over 2f out: drvn wl over 1f out: sn edgd lft and no imp* **7/2**[2]
0/0- **6** *3 ¾* **Indastar**[414] 3479 4-9-2 **50**........................................ DaleSwift 12 31
(Michael Herrington) *dwlt and in rr tl styd on fnl 2f* **33/1**
0044 **7** *1* **Wotalad**[14] 4578 4-9-0 **51**.........................................(v) GeorgeChaloner[(3)] 3 30
(Richard Whitaker) *qckly away and led: hdd 1/2-way: cl up tl rdn over 2f out and sn wknd* **8/1**
03 **8** *3 ½* **Genax (IRE)**[23] 4294 3-8-11 **51**.................................... PaddyAspell 5 18
(John Wainwright) *dwlt: sn chsng ldrs: rdn along 3f out: sn wknd* **10/1**
0354 **9** ¾ **Zainda (IRE)**[15] 4534 4-9-2 **50**.................................... JoeFanning 14 18
(Paul Midgley) *chsd ldrs on outer: rdn along 1/2-way: sn wknd* **8/1**
350- **10** *3 ½* **Hidden Asset**[345] 5869 4-9-1 **49**.................................(p) AndrewMullen 7 7
(Michael Appleby) *a in rr* **6/1**[3]
2005 **11** *11* **Flying Giant (IRE)**[94] 2597 4-8-12 **51**.......................(t) PhilipPrince[(5)] 2
(Jo Hughes) *swtchd rt to outer sn after s: a in rr* **25/1**
2-60 **12** *9* **Moss Hill**[72] 2658 5-8-12 **49**.......................................[1] JoeyHaynes[(3)] 4
(Jason Ward) *midfield on inner: rdn along 3f out: sn wknd and bhd* **33/1**

1m 31.68s (1.38) **Going Correction** +0.25s/f (Slow)
**WFA** 3 from 4yo+ 6lb **12** Ran SP% **123.2**
Speed ratings (Par 101): **102,98,97,92,91 87,86,82,81,77 64,54**
CSF £257.60 CT £984.25 TOTE £17.90: £7.80, £3.80, £1.90; EX 180.50 Trifecta £801.60 Part won..
**Owner** Ryedale Partners No 4 **Bred** Rabbah Bloodstock Limited **Trained** Great Habton, N Yorks

**FOCUS**
The well-treated winner took this apart off the home turn.
T/Plt: £8.30 to a £1 stake. Pool: £34,105.20 - 2,979.87 winning units T/Qpdt: £4.70 to a £1 stake. Pool: £3,345.23 - 523.33 winning units JR

# 5056 YARMOUTH (L-H)
Thursday, August 7

**OFFICIAL GOING: Good to soft (good in places; 6.6)**
Wind: Fresh; behind Weather: Cloudy with sunny spells

## 5104 BRITISH STALLION STUDS EBF MAIDEN STKS 6f 3y
**2:30** (2:31) (Class 5) 2-Y-O £3,234 (£962; £481; £240) **Stalls** Centre

Form RPR
32 **1** **Arthur MartinLeake (IRE)**[45] 3536 2-9-5 0............................ BenCurtis 2 78
(K R Burke) *chsd ldr tl led over 1f out: sn rdn: edgd lft ins fnl f: styd on* **8/13**[1]
**2** *3* **Quite Smart (IRE)** 2-9-0 0........................................ TedDurcan 1 64+
(Robert Cowell) *prom: pushed along over 3f out: sn outpcd: r.o ins fnl f: nt trble wnr* **25/1**
**3** *2* **Pencil** 2-9-0 0.........................................................[1] PaddyAspell 4 58+
(James Eustace) *prom: outpcd 2f out: styd on fnl f* **33/1**
66 **4** *4 ½* **Emirates Challenge (IRE)**[24] 4269 2-9-0 0.................. FrederikTylicki 3 45
(Saeed bin Suroor) *led: rdn and hdd over 1f out: wknd ins fnl f* **10/1**[3]
**5** *8* **Tadqeeq** 2-9-5 0.................................................. LiamJones 7 26
(William Haggas) *s.i.s: outpcd* **3/1**[2]
0 **6** *20* **Avenue Des Champs**[13] 4618 2-9-5 0............................ CraigAWilliams 5
(Jane Chapple-Hyam) *s.i.s: sn pushed along in rr: bhd fnl 4f* **150/1**
**7** *9* **Bang In Trouble (IRE)** 2-9-0 0.............................. DannyBrock[(5)] 6
(Des Donovan) *chsd ldrs tl rdn: edgd rt and wknd over 2f out* **12/1**

1m 15.11s (0.71) **Going Correction** +0.20s/f (Good) **7** Ran SP% **111.2**
Speed ratings (Par 94): **103,99,96,90,79 53,41**
CSF £20.42 TOTE £1.60: £1.10, £9.90; EX 12.50 Trifecta £119.10.
**Owner** M Charge & Mrs E Burke **Bred** Thomas Hassett **Trained** Middleham Moor, N Yorks

**FOCUS**
Bottom bend dolled out 1.5m and races on Round course increased by 7m. The pace was fair for this uncompetitive maiden.

## 5105 GET £50 FREE TODAY WITH RACEBETS.COM MAIDEN H'CAP 6f 3y
**3:00** (3:01) (Class 6) (0-65,62) 3-Y-O+ £2,458 (£731; £365; £182) **Stalls** Centre

Form RPR
0366 **1** **Silvala Dance**[10] 4732 4-9-0 **50**.................................... TedDurcan 12 63
(Chris Wall) *hld up: hdwy over 2f out: led over 1f out: rdn out* **5/1**[2]
2020 **2** *2* **Knockamany Bends (IRE)**[23] 4288 4-9-2 **52**.................. PaddyAspell 9 59
(John Wainwright) *led: rdn and hdd over 1f out: styd on same pce ins fnl f* **25/1**
220 **3** *2 ¾* **Big City Boy (IRE)**[12] 4655 6-8-6 **47**.......................... DannyBrock[(5)] 5 45
(Phil McEntee) *w ldrs tl rdn over 2f out: styd on same pce fnl f* **12/1**
0222 **4** *1 ¼* **Mimi Luke (USA)**[3] 4972 3-9-2 **59**.......................(v) RobertTart[(3)] 11 52
(Alan Bailey) *hld up: hdwy over 2f out: sn rdn: no ex ins fnl f* **7/2**[1]
0246 **5** ½ **Tubeanie (IRE)**[45] 3518 3-9-1 **60**...............................(p) DanielMuscutt[(5)] 3 52+
(Amy Weaver) *s.i.s: sn pushed along in rr: r.o u.p ins fnl f: nvr nrr* **16/1**
400 **6** ½ **Habeshia**[38] 3798 4-8-11 **47**.......................................(t) LukeMorris 2 38
(John Best) *prom: pushed along and outpcd over 3f out: rallied u.p over 1f out: styd on same pce ins fnl f* **14/1**
030 **7** ½ **Popping Candy**[19] 4428 3-9-6 **60**.................................. FrederikTylicki 8 48
(Roger Varian) *chsd ldrs: rdn 1/2-way: styd on same pce appr fnl f* **8/1**[3]
2026 **8** *4 ½* **Champagne Charley**[15] 4546 3-9-7 **61**..............................(t) BenCurtis 13 35
(Des Donovan) *s.i.s: sn pushed along in rr: rdn over 2f out: nvr on terms* **10/1**
2400 **9** ½ **Yankee Red**[19] 4431 3-9-3 **57**.....................................(b[1]) LiamJones 1 29
(John Best) *sn pushed along to chse ldrs: rdn over 2f out: wknd over 1f out* **33/1**
0600 **10** *nk* **Jalusive (IRE)**[76] 2525 5-8-9 **46** oh1..............................(t) CraigAWilliams 4 17
(Christine Dunnett) *w ldrs to 1/2-way: rdn and wknd over 1f out* **66/1**
-502 **11** ¾ **High Tone**[14] 4595 4-8-6 **49**........................................ PaulBooth[(7)] 6 19
(Dean Ivory) *prom: rdn 1/2-way: wknd over 1f out* **7/2**[1]
42-0 **12** *14* **Tarquin (IRE)**[200] 245 5-9-12 **62**.................................. ShaneKelly 7
(Kristin Stubbs) *hld up: hmpd over 3f out: wknd over 2f out: eased over 1f out* **10/1**

1m 15.41s (1.01) **Going Correction** +0.20s/f (Good)
**WFA** 3 from 4yo+ 4lb **12** Ran SP% **118.9**
Speed ratings (Par 101): **101,98,94,93,92 91,91,85,84,83 82,64**
CSF £126.74 CT £1455.57 TOTE £6.60: £1.90, £6.20, £3.40; EX 105.00 Trifecta £2676.30 Part won..
**Owner** Mrs D A Lochhead **Bred** Mrs Mary Taylor **Trained** Newmarket, Suffolk

**FOCUS**
An open maiden handicap run at a sound pace. It paid to race handy.

## 5106 FOLLOW US ON TWITTER AT GREAT YARMOUTH RACECOURSE (S) H'CAP 1m 3y
**3:30** (3:30) (Class 6) (0-65,52) 3-Y-O £1,940 (£577; £288; £144) **Stalls** Centre

Form RPR
6640 **1** **Honiton Lace**[23] 4304 3-9-1 **51**.................................(tp) DannyBrock[(5)] 1 57
(Phil McEntee) *mde virtually all: rdn over 3f out: clr over 1f out: styd on* **5/1**
5040 **2** *1 ¼* **Satin Waters**[13] 4617 3-9-0 **48**......................................[1] RosieJessop[(3)] 5 50
(Peter Charalambous) *prom: outpcd over 5f out: hdwy to chse wnr over 1f out: styd on* **8/1**
6442 **3** *5* **Chanceuse**[8] 4785 3-9-7 **52**...........................................(v) ShaneKelly 7 43
(Gay Kelleway) *chsd ldrs: lost pl over 6f out: rdn over 4f out: hdwy over 1f out: styd on same pce fnl f* **5/2**[1]
P503 **4** ½ **Jenny Sparks**[13] 4627 3-8-7 **45**.................................... PaddyPilley[(7)] 2 34
(Mick Channon) *s.i.s: sn prom: rdn over 3f out: edgd rt over 2f out: no ex fnl f* **9/2**[3]
5400 **5** *3* **Previous Acclaim (IRE)**[30] 4048 3-8-9 **45**..............(b[1]) ShelleyBirkett[(5)] 4 27
(Julia Feilden) *prom: chsd wnr over 4f: rdn over 2f out: lost 2nd over 1f out: wknd ins fnl f* **12/1**
3640 **6** *17* **Bourbon Prince**[10] 4738 3-9-0 **52**.........................(p) MichaelKenneally[(7)] 3
(Michael Bell) *chsd ldrs: pushed along over 3f out: wknd over 1f out* **3/1**[2]

1m 44.93s (4.33) **Going Correction** +0.20s/f (Good) **6** Ran SP% **107.2**
Speed ratings (Par 98): **86,84,79,79,76 59**
CSF £38.11 TOTE £6.80: £2.80, £4.20; EX 49.40 Trifecta £187.00.There was no bid for the winner. Satin Waters was claimed by Mrs Christine Dunnett for £5,000
**Owner** Eventmaker Racehorses **Bred** Mrs P De W Johnson **Trained** Newmarket, Suffolk

**FOCUS**
A modest selling handicap run at an honest pace.

## 5107 JENNINGSBET.COM FILLIES' H'CAP (BOBIS RACE) 1m 3y
**4:00** (4:02) (Class 4) (0-85,83) 3-Y-O £4,916 (£1,463; £731; £365) **Stalls** Centre

Form RPR
116 **1** **Buredyma**[28] 4112 3-9-3 **79**.......................................... LiamJones 3 86
(William Haggas) *led: pushed along and hdd 2f out: rallied u.p to ld nr fin* **11/4**[2]
6303 **2** *nk* **Hala Hala (IRE)**[13] 4623 3-8-10 **72**.............................. TomQueally 2 78
(Michael Bell) *hld up: hdwy over 3f out: led over 2f out: rdn: edgd lft and flashed tail 1f out: hdd nr fin* **6/1**[3]
2621 **3** *1* **Joys Of Spring (IRE)**[13] 4631 3-9-0 **83**................... GianlucaSanna[(7)] 1 87
(Luca Cumani) *plld hrd: trckd wnr tl over 6f out: remained handy: rdn over 1f out: ev ch ins fnl f: unable qck towards fin* **8/13**[1]
1-00 **4** *4 ½* **Don't**[80] 2383 3-8-4 **71**.............................................. ShelleyBirkett[(5)] 4 64
(Julia Feilden) *s.i.s: plld hrd and sn prom: wnt 2nd over 6f out tl wnt upsides over 3f out: rdn and ev ch over 1f out: no ex ins fnl f* **20/1**

1m 41.77s (1.17) **Going Correction** +0.20s/f (Good) **4** Ran SP% **107.6**
Speed ratings (Par 99): **102,101,100,96**
CSF £16.28 TOTE £3.40; EX 9.50 Trifecta £18.80.
**Owner** Saleh Al Homaizi & Imad Al Sagar **Bred** Pantile Stud **Trained** Newmarket, Suffolk
■ Stewards' Enquiry : Gianluca Sanna one-day ban: careless riding (Aug 23)

**FOCUS**
An uncompetitive fillies' handicap run at a steady pace.

## 5108 INJURED JOCKEYS FUND H'CAP — 1m 2f 21y
4:30 (4:30) (Class 5) (0-70,70) 3-Y-O — £2,846 (£847; £423; £211) Stalls Low

Form — RPR
3541 **1** **Final Countdown**[15] 4540 3-9-5 68 ... CraigAWilliams 1 78+
(Anthony Carson) *hld up in tch: racd keenly: rdn over 2f out: styd on to ld wl ins fnl f* 11/4[2]
4562 **2** 3/4 **Aristocracy**[7] 4817 3-8-6 62 ... DanielCremin(7) 3 70
(Mick Channon) *chsd ldr tl led 3f out: sn rdn: hdd and unable qck wl ins fnl f* 8/1
-415 **3** 1 1/4 **Go Sakhee**[28] 4120 3-9-7 70 ... FrederikTylicki 2 76
(Roger Varian) *chsd ldrs: rdn over 2f out: styd on same pce ins fnl f* 5/2[1]
542 **4** 1 1/4 **Kinema (IRE)**[20] 4420 3-9-7 70 ... LukeMorris 7 73
(Ed Walker) *s.i.s: hld up: hdwy u.p over 2f out: hung lft ins fnl f: styd on same pce* 4/1[3]
5-53 **5** 1 1/2 **Bushy Glade (IRE)**[23] 4304 3-7-10 52 ... PaddyPilley(7) 5 52
(Julia Feilden) *chsd ldrs: rdn over 3f out: no ex fnl f* 16/1
5566 **6** 18 **Lucky Visione**[41] 3683 3-9-5 68 ... (b[1]) ShaneKelly 6 47
(Gay Kelleway) *led 7f: wknd over 1f out* 25/1
3-41 **F** **Heska (IRE)**[17] 4495 3-9-0 68 ... (tp) AlistairRawlinson(5) 4
(Michael Appleby) *s.i.s: hld up: clipped heels and fell over 5f out* 5/1

2m 13.92s (3.42) **Going Correction** +0.35s/f (Good) — **7** Ran SP% **112.7**
Speed ratings (Par 100): **100,99,98,97,96 81,**
CSF £23.84 TOTE £3.60: £2.30, £3.60; EX 20.30 Trifecta £77.50.
**Owner** Christopher Wright & Minster Stud **Bred** Stratford Place Stud & Minster Stud **Trained** Newmarket, Suffolk

**FOCUS**
An open handicap run at a fair pace.

## 5109 CONFERENCES AT GREAT YARMOUTH RACECOURSE H'CAP — 1m 1f
5:00 (5:00) (Class 6) (0-65,61) 3-Y-O+ — £2,199 (£654; £327; £163) Stalls Low

Form — RPR
5610 **1** **Nifty Kier**[10] 4738 5-8-12 50 ... DannyBrock(5) 5 59
(Phil McEntee) *mde all: clr over 4f out: rdn over 2f out: all out* 7/1[3]
0224 **2** nk **Hot Mustard**[14] 4593 4-9-13 60 ... TomQueally 7 68
(Michael Bell) *hld up: hdwy over 3f out: rdn to chse wnr over 1f out: styd on: nt quite get up* 15/8[1]
0421 **3** 4 **Lynngale**[14] 4562 3-9-6 61 ... ShaneKelly 2 61
(Kristin Stubbs) *chsd wnr: rdn over 2f out: lost 2nd over 1f out: no ex ins fnl f* 3/1[2]
0665 **4** 1 1/2 **Jumbo Prado (USA)**[19] 4433 5-9-4 56 ... (b) EoinWalsh(5) 6 53
(John Stimpson) *hld up: pushed along over 4f out: r.o ins fnl f: nvr nrr* 10/1
-056 **5** 4 **Super Cookie**[56] 2750 4-9-13 60 ... FrederikTylicki 4 48
(Anthony Carson) *chsd ldrs: rdn over 2f out: wknd fnl f* 7/1[3]
5530 **6** 5 **Harboured (USA)**[18] 4472 3-9-5 60 ... (b[1]) LukeMorris 1 38
(Sir Mark Prescott Bt) *hld up: pushed along over 3f out: wknd over 2f out* 10/1
062 **7** 2 1/4 **Perseverent Pete (USA)**[12] 4658 4-9-2 49 ... CraigAWilliams 8 22
(Christine Dunnett) *prom: rdn over 3f out: wknd over 2f out* 16/1

2m 0.15s (4.35) **Going Correction** +0.35s/f (Good)
**WFA** 3 from 4yo+ 8lb — **7** Ran SP% **108.8**
Speed ratings (Par 101): **94,93,90,88,85 80,78**
CSF £18.59 CT £42.27 TOTE £7.80: £4.10, £1.40; EX 22.10 Trifecta £68.50.
**Owner** Mrs Rebecca McEntee **Bred** Mrs S H Jones **Trained** Newmarket, Suffolk
■ Stewards' Enquiry : Tom Queally two-day ban: used whip above permitted level (Aug 23-24)

**FOCUS**
They went a sound pace for this modest handicap.

## 5110 GREENE KING FESTIVAL AT GREAT YARMOUTH APPRENTICE H'CAP — 7f 3y
5:30 (5:30) (Class 5) (0-70,63) 4-Y-O+ — £2,587 (£770; £384; £192) Stalls Centre

Form — RPR
5522 **1** **Jonnie Skull (IRE)**[1] 5058 8-9-5 61 ... (vt) JackGilligan(5) 6 70
(Phil McEntee) *overall ldr 1f: stl led main gp: rdn 1/2-way: edgd lft and styd on to ld overall wl ins fnl f* 15/8[1]
0064 **2** 1 1/4 **Sairaam (IRE)**[1] 5057 8-8-3 45 ... (p) PaddyPilley(5) 5 51
(Charles Smith) *racd alone in centre for much of the trip: overall ldr 6f out: clr 1/2-way: rdn over 1f out: hdd and unable qck wl ins fnl f* 16/1
4233 **3** 6 **Bladewood Girl**[10] 4732 6-9-3 54 ... CharlieBennett 2 44
(J R Jenkins) *prom: rdn over 2f out: wknd fnl f* 7/2[3]
0000 **4** 4 1/2 **Duke Of Destiny (IRE)**[24] 4273 5-9-5 63 ... (p) CliffordLee(7) 1 42
(Ed Walker) *s.s: hdwy over 5f out: rdn over 2f out: wknd over 1f out* 13/2
10U0 **5** shd **Mitchell**[8] 4798 4-9-3 59 ... (p) PeterSword(5) 3 37
(K R Burke) *hld up: rdn and edgd rt over 1f out: nvr trbld ldrs* 11/4[2]
6023 **6** 7 **Tiger's Home**[21] 4337 4-9-0 51 ... DavidParkes 4 11
(Julia Feilden) *chsd ldrs: rdn 1/2-way: wknd over 2f out* 14/1

1m 28.84s (2.24) **Going Correction** +0.20s/f (Good) — **6** Ran SP% **109.6**
Speed ratings (Par 103): **95,93,86,81,81 73**
CSF £29.33 TOTE £4.10: £2.70, £4.60; EX 39.50 Trifecta £90.60.
**Owner** Mrs R McEntee & The Guernsey Boys **Bred** Canice Farrell Jnr **Trained** Newmarket, Suffolk

**FOCUS**
A modest handicap, confined to apprentice riders, run at a fair pace. The front two pulled clear.
T/Plt: £1,110.40 to a £1 stake. Pool: £46,196.29 - 30.37 winning units T/Qpdt: £312.60 to a £1 stake. Pool: £2,940.27 - 6.96 winning units CR

5111 - 5114a (Foreign Racing) - See Raceform Interactive

# 4596 LEOPARDSTOWN (L-H)
Thursday, August 7

**OFFICIAL GOING: Yielding**

## 5115a BALLYROAN STKS (GROUP 3) — 1m 4f
7:30 (7:30) 3-Y-O+ — £32,500 (£9,500; £4,500; £1,500)

RPR
**1** **Eye Of The Storm (IRE)**[21] 4380 4-9-9 109 ... JosephO'Brien 5 107
(A P O'Brien, Ire) *chsd ldrs tl led after 2f: jnd briefly over 3f out: narrow advantage into st and sn rdn: pressed clly ins fnl f: kpt on wl* 7/4[1]
**2** 1/2 **Roheryn (IRE)**[62] 2974 3-8-9 96 ... ColinKeane 3 103
(G M Lyons, Ire) *sn led tl hdd after 2f: cl 2nd 1/2-way: disp briefly over 3f out: rdn in cl 2nd into st and pressed wnr ins fnl f: kpt on wl towards fin: a hld* 7/1
**3** 2 **Streetcar To Stars**[41] 3690 3-8-12 100 ... DeclanMcDonogh 2 103
(John M Oxx, Ire) *settled in 2nd under dropped to 3rd after 2f: cl 3rd 1/2-way: pushed along 3f out and no imp on ldrs in 4th over 1f out: kpt on same pce into 3rd ins fnl f: nvr trbld ldrs* 2/1[2]
**4** 2 1/4 **Chance To Dance (IRE)**[15] 4560 4-9-9 108 ... (t) KevinManning 1 99
(J S Bolger, Ire) *hld up in rr: last 1/2-way: pushed along in 4th over 3f out and no imp on ldrs u.p in 3rd over 1f out: one pce ins fnl f and dropped to 4th* 4/1[3]
**5** 7 **El Salvador (IRE)**[6] 4877 5-9-9 103 ... AnaO'Brien 4 88
(A P O'Brien, Ire) *sweated up befhand: hld up bhd ldrs: 4th 1/2-way: pushed along in rr of quintet over 3f out and no imp on ldrs into st: one pce fnl 2f* 10/1

2m 31.94s (-3.36) **Going Correction** 0.0s/f (Good)
**WFA** 3 from 4yo+ 11lb — **5** Ran SP% **111.3**
Speed ratings: **111,110,109,107,103**
CSF £13.98 TOTE £2.80: £1.40, £2.70; DF 14.70 Trifecta £25.40.
**Owner** Michael Tabor & Derrick Smith & Mrs John Magnier **Bred** K Molloy **Trained** Cashel, Co Tipperary

**FOCUS**
There was no great pace on here, and they raced in pretty much the order they finished in.

5116 - 5117a (Foreign Racing) - See Raceform Interactive

# 5026 DEAUVILLE (R-H)
Thursday, August 7

**OFFICIAL GOING: Turf: heavy; polytrack: standard**

## 5118a PRIX DE BAVENT (CLAIMER) (2YO COLTS & GELDINGS) (TURF) — 6f
12:00 (12:00) 2-Y-O — £11,250 (£4,500; £3,375; £2,250; £1,125)

RPR
**1** **Cornwallville (IRE)**[21] 2-9-7 0 ... FlavienPrat 6 86
(D Windrif, France) 11/10[1]
**2** 2 1/2 **Mount Isa (IRE)**[6] 4881 2-8-9 0 ... (p) MickaelBarzalona 1 67
(J S Moore) *hld up in rr: hdwy 1 1/2f out: styd on u.p fnl f: no ch w wnr* 39/10[3]
**3** 1 **Rockaroundtheclock (IRE)**[3] 4965 2-9-2 0 ... OlivierPeslier 3 71
(Paul Cole) *a.p on outer: rdn and nt qckn 1 1/2f out: one pce fnl f* 3/1[2]
**4** 3/4 **Royal Dolois (FR)**[113] 2-8-13 0 ... Pierre-CharlesBoudot 7 65
(J-M Lefebvre, France) 83/10
**5** 2 1/2 **Stocksandshares (IRE)**[21] 2-8-9 0 ... (b) AntoineHamelin 2 54
(Matthieu Palussiere, France) 30/1
**6** 1 1/2 **Jimmy's Hall**[6] 4883 2-8-13 0 ... (p) IoritzMendizabal 5 53
(J S Moore) *chsd ldrs: rdn and nt qckn 1 1/2f out: wknd ins fnl f* 91/10
**7** 10 **Key Code**[6] 4883 2-8-9 0 ... (p) CristianDemuro 4 19
(E J O'Neill, France) 49/1

1m 13.2s (2.20) — **7** Ran SP% **118.9**
WIN (incl. 1 euro stake): 2.10. PLACES: 1.40, 2.00. SF: 9.40.
**Owner** Frederic Sarfati **Bred** Corrin Stud & Blackwater Bloodstock Ltd **Trained** France

## 5119a PRIX D'HEROUVILLE (CLAIMER) (2YO FILLIES) (TURF) — 6f
12:30 (12:00) 2-Y-O — £11,250 (£4,500; £3,375; £2,250; £1,125)

RPR
**1** **Super Eria (FR)**[91] 2-9-2 0 ... ThierryJarnet 2 78
(D Guillemin, France) 41/10[2]
**2** 1 **La Mezcla (FR)**[21] 2-8-13 0 ... TheoBachelot 4 72
(S Wattel, France) 15/2[3]
**3** 1/2 **Join Up (FR)**[40] 3744 2-9-0 0 ... (b) ChristopheSoumillon 1 72
(J-C Rouget, France) 7/5[1]
**4** 3/4 **Seradora (FR)**[18] 2-8-9 0 ... CristianDemuro 6 64
(E J O'Neill, France) 10/1
**5** shd **Pretty Picture**[7] 4839 2-8-13 0 ... Pierre-CharlesBoudot 10 68
(Gay Kelleway) *w ldrs: rdn to hold pl 2f out: styd prom: no ex fnl 75yds* 205/10
**6** snk **Freaky Girl (FR)**[21] 2-8-13 0 ... Christophe-PatriceLemaire 7 68
(Robert Collet, France) 51/1
**7** 2 **Areion (IRE)**[27] 4143 2-9-0 0 ... (b) IoritzMendizabal 5 63
(J S Moore) *w.w in midfield: effrt 1 1/2f out but no real imp: one pce fnl f* 33/1
**8** 1/2 **Multi Quest**[23] 4283 2-9-0 0 ... MickaelBarzalona 8 61
(Jo Hughes) *w ldrs: rdn and nt qckn 2f out: fdd fnl 120yds* 178/10
**9** 1/2 **Loose Cannon (FR)**[14] 4603 2-9-5 0 ... (b) MllePaulineDominois(6) 11 71
(D Windrif, France) 15/2[3]
**10** 2 1/2 **Fly Grazer (IRE)**[6] 4882 2-8-9 0 ... (p) GeraldMosse 9 47
(J S Moore) *w.w in rr: rdn and sme hdwy over 1 1/2f out: nvr in contention* 207/10
**11** 6 **Louve Indienne (FR)**[61] 2-8-9 0 ... UmbertoRispoli 12 29
(N Bertran De Balanda, France) 67/1
**12** 1 1/4 **Tiziana (FR)**[20] 2-8-13 0 ... MaximeGuyon 13 29
(Mario Hofer, Germany) 212/10

1m 13.07s (2.07) — **12** Ran SP% **119.3**
WIN (incl. 1 euro stake): 5.10. PLACES: 1.60, 1.90, 1.30. DF: 16.20. SF: 32.30.
**Owner** Endre Rosjoe **Bred** D Chassagneux, J-P Boin & G Gaboriau **Trained** France

# 5070 BRIGHTON (L-H)
Friday, August 8

**OFFICIAL GOING: Good to firm (8.0)**
Wind: Virtually nil Weather: overcast, dry

## 5120 EBF/VISIT US AT WINNERPLANT.CO.UK MAIDEN STKS — 5f 213y
2:10 (2:10) (Class 5) 2-Y-O — £2,911 (£866; £432; £216) Stalls Centre

Form — RPR
5 **1** **Mecado (IRE)**[3] 5009 2-9-5 0 ... PatDobbs 3 72
(Richard Hannon) *stmbld sn after s: in tch: swtchd rt and hdwy over 2f out: drvn to chse ldr over 1f out: styd on u.p and chal ins fnl f: led fnl 75yds: sn in command* 4/11[1]
03 **2** 1 1/4 **Frozen Princess**[13] 4652 2-9-0 0 ... FergusSweeney 4 63
(Jamie Osborne) *t.k.h: hld up in tch in rr: clsd and led travelling strly ent fnl 2f: rdn over 1f out: drvn and pressed ins fnl f: hdd fnl 75yds: sn btn* 7/1[3]

00 **3** *5* **Gipsy Doll**[18] 4499 2-9-0 0........................................ LukeMorris 5 48
(Paul Cole) *chsd ldng pair: outpcd and dropped to last whn short of room over 2f out: no ch but kpt on fnl f to go 3rd cl home* **25/1**

465 **4** *3/4* **Arizona Snow**[37] 3847 2-9-5 63........................... SteveDrowne 2 51
(Ronald Harris) *racd keenly: chsd ldr tl led over 2f out: 3rd and btn over 1f out: wknd and lost 3rd cl home* **16/1**

420 **5** *2 1/2* **Bannister Bell (IRE)**[16] 4541 2-9-2 67........................ DeclanBates(3) 1 44
(David Evans) *led tl over 2f out: drvn and btn over 1f out: wknd 1f out* **6/1**[2]

1m 12.38s (2.18) **Going Correction** +0.125s/f (Good) **5 Ran SP% 109.8**
Speed ratings (Par 94): **90,88,81,80,77**
CSF £3.50 TOTE £1.50: £1.10, £2.10; EX 3.80 Trifecta £23.00.
**Owner** Potensis Ltd & J Palmer-Brown **Bred** J F Tuthill **Trained** East Everleigh, Wilts

**FOCUS**
Rail dolled out 3yds between 6f and 2.5f and distances increased by about 9yds. This was a moderate 2yo maiden and the first two home had most of the home straight to themselves.

## 5121 VISIT US AT CHECKATRADE.COM H'CAP 1m 3f 196y
**2:40** (2:41) (Class 6) (0-65,65) 3-Y-O+ **£1,940** (£577; £288; £144) **Stalls High**

Form RPR

234- **1** **Sacred Square (GER)**[26] 5218 4-10-0 65........................(b) JimCrowley 3 80
(Donald McCain) *chsd ldng pair: wnt 2nd 3f out: rdn to ld 1f out: hung lft but wnt clr over 1f out: in command but kpt up to work fnl f: rdn out* **2/1**[1]

4516 **2** *13* **Crouching Harry (IRE)**[1] 5076 5-9-3 54................................ JohnFahy 5 48
(Anabel K Murphy) *s.i.s: hld up in tch in last pair: effrt over 2f out: modest 3rd and drvn over 1f out: wnt 2nd fnl 100yds: no ch w wnr* **11/4**[2]

1044 **3** *1* **Passionate Affair (IRE)**[14] 4616 3-9-3 65.............(tp) FergusSweeney 1 58
(Jamie Osborne) *led: rdn and hdd 2f out: sn brushed aside by wnr: lost modest 2nd fnl 100yds* **4/1**

0342 **4** *shd* **Evergreen Forest (IRE)**[10] 4041 6-9-7 58...................(b) SteveDrowne 2 50
(Natalie Lloyd-Beavis) *chsd ldr: rdn 3f out: outpcd and btn 2f out: no ch w wnr after: plugging on whn swtchd rt fnl 100yds* **8/1**

5432 **5** *11* **Cabuchon (GER)**[15] 4568 7-9-6 60............................(vt) DeclanBates(3) 6 43
(David Evans) *hld up in tch in last pair: effrt jst over 2f out: btn 2f out: wl bhd and heavily eased ins fnl f* **7/2**[3]

2m 33.31s (0.61) **Going Correction** +0.125s/f (Good)
**WFA** 3 from 4yo+ 11lb **5 Ran SP% 113.3**
Speed ratings (Par 101): **102,93,92,92,85**
CSF £8.06 TOTE £2.60: £1.40, £1.80; EX 9.90 Trifecta £25.40.
**Owner** Tony Bloom **Bred** Graf And Grafin Von Stauffenberg **Trained** Cholmondeley, Cheshire

**FOCUS**
A weak handicap that proved one-way traffic. The winner was having his first Flat start since being gelded, but hadn't been showing a great deal over hurdles.

## 5122 REDWOOD PARK SCHOOL, COSHAM H'CAP 1m 1f 209y
**3:10** (3:11) (Class 6) (0-60,59) 3-Y-O **£1,940** (£577; £288; £144) **Stalls High**

Form RPR

0055 **1** **Cameley Dawn**[3] 5005 3-9-2 54................................. FergusSweeney 7 61
(Malcolm Saunders) *t.k.h: chsd ldrs tl hdwy to join ldr 7f out: rdn to ld over 1f out: asserted fnl 100yds: styd on wl* **11/4**[3]

3010 **2** *2 1/2* **Prim And Proper**[45] 3559 3-9-7 59........................................ JimCrowley 3 61
(Brendan Powell) *t.k.h: hld up in tch in last pair: effrt nrest inner over 2f out: chsd wnr over 1f out: no ex ins fnl f: wknd towards fin* **2/1**[1]

0500 **3** *1 3/4* **Appellez Baileys (FR)**[42] 3673 3-8-7 45........................ NickyMackay 5 44
(Chris Dwyer) *led and set stdy gallop: jnd 7f out: rdn 2f out: hdd over 1f out: 3rd and one pce fnl f* **12/1**

0-03 **4** *2 3/4* **Soiree D'Ete**[15] 4563 3-8-12 50........................................ LukeMorris 2 44
(Sir Mark Prescott Bt) *t.k.h: chsd ldr tl 7f out: rdn over 2f out: drvn and unable qck over 1f out: wknd ins fnl f* **9/4**[2]

0606 **5** *2 1/2* **Mystical Maze**[15] 4562 3-8-7 45........................................ ChrisCatlin 6 34
(Mark Brisbourne) *stdd after s: t.k.h: hld up in tch in last pair: rdn and effrt over 2f out: btn over 1f out: wknd fnl f* **9/1**

2m 8.54s (4.94) **Going Correction** +0.125s/f (Good) **5 Ran SP% 108.5**
Speed ratings (Par 98): **85,83,81,79,77**
CSF £8.38 TOTE £4.50: £2.20, £1.30; EX 7.40 Trifecta £47.80.
**Owner** Mr & Mrs J Harris **Bred** The Hill Stud **Trained** Green Ore, Somerset

**FOCUS**
An ordinary 3yo handicap, run at a routine pace. The second sets level.

## 5123 HARRY BLOOM MEMORIAL H'CAP (BOBIS RACE) 1m 1f 209y
**3:40** (3:41) (Class 4) (0-80,80) 3-Y-O **£6,301** (£1,886; £943; £472; £235) **Stalls High**

Form RPR

0533 **1** **Fire Fighting (IRE)**[7] 4855 3-9-7 80..............................(b[1]) LukeMorris 2 90
(Mark Johnston) *chsd ldrs: rdn to chal between rivals over 2f out: led 2f out: wnt rt u.p over 1f out: hrd drvn and edgd bk lft u.p ins fnl f: hld on towards fin* **9/4**[1]

4221 **2** *hd* **Muhawalah (IRE)**[17] 4513 3-9-6 79..............................(b) FrederikTylicki 4 88
(Roger Varian) *in tch in last pair: dropped to last and rdn on downhill run 3f out: rallied and hdwy over 1f out: ev ch and faltered fnl 100yds: stl ev ch but nt finding much whn bmpd fnl 50yds: hld towards fin* **7/2**[3]

0323 **3** *2 1/2* **Sandy Cove**[6] 4911 3-8-1 63 oh3 ow2............................ RyanTate(3) 5 67
(James Eustace) *chsd ldr: rdn and ev ch 2f out: 3rd and unable qck 1f out: outpcd fnl 100yds* **10/1**

-605 **4** *3/4* **Laurelita (IRE)**[56] 3195 3-9-6 79....................................... JimCrowley 6 82
(George Baker) *in tch in midfield: effrt to chal and drifted rt 2f out: no ex u.p 1f out: one pce after* **8/1**

4311 **5** *hd* **Serena Grae**[7] 4845 3-9-6 79 6ex........................................ SebSanders 1 81
(Marcus Tregoning) *led tl hdd 2f out: drvn and unable qck over 1f out: one pce fnl f* **3/1**[2]

0341 **6** *1 1/4* **Penny's Boy**[8] 4817 3-9-1 74 6ex..................................(t) PatDobbs 3 74
(Sylvester Kirk) *hld up in tch in last: hdwy on outer to press ldrs whn pushed rt 2f out: btn ent fnl f: wknd fnl 150yds* **11/2**

2m 3.09s (-0.51) **Going Correction** +0.125s/f (Good) **6 Ran SP% 113.6**
Speed ratings (Par 102): **107,106,104,104,104 103**
CSF £10.63 TOTE £3.40: £2.10, £1.70; EX 7.20 Trifecta £63.60.
**Owner** A D Spence **Bred** P Bellaiche **Trained** Middleham Moor, N Yorks
■ Stewards' Enquiry : Luke Morris one-day ban: careless riding (Aug 23)

**FOCUS**
A fair 3yo handicap. They went a sound enough pace and it saw a close two-way finish.

## 5124 £500 MONEY BACKS ONLY AT CHOICEBET.NET H'CAP 5f 213y
**4:10** (4:10) (Class 4) (0-80,78) 3-Y-O-**£7,561** (£2,263; £1,131; £566; £282) **Stalls Centre**

Form RPR

4411 **1** **Panther Patrol (IRE)**[16] 4545 4-9-4 70..............................(v) JohnFahy 8 82
(Eve Johnson Houghton) *chsd ldrs: wnt 2nd over 3f out: rdn and fnd ex to ld over 1f out: r.o wl ins fnl f* **9/4**[1]

4412 **2** *1* **Ginzan**[11] 4741 6-9-5 71........................................ FergusSweeney 2 80
(Malcolm Saunders) *t.k.h: chsd ldrs: hmpd and snatched up bnd 4f out: in tch in midfield after: hdwy u.p 1f out: pressing wnr fnl 100yds: r.o but a hld after* **7/2**[2]

5533 **3** *1/2* **Storm Lightning**[1] 5070 5-9-5 71........................................ JimCrowley 4 78
(Mark Brisbourne) *chsd ldr tl 3f out: drvn and effrt over 1f out: styd on same pce ins fnl f* **7/1**

0461 **4** *1/2* **Langley Vale**[15] 4581 5-9-11 77..........................................(p) SebSanders 7 82
(Roger Teal) *led: rdn and hdd over 1f out: drvn and styd on same pce ins fnl f* **6/1**

2130 **5** *1* **Secret Millionaire (IRE)**[10] 4762 7-9-12 78........................ LukeMorris 5 80
(Luke Dace) *t.k.h: hld up in tch in midfield: rdn and effrt over 1f out: no imp and one pce fnl f* **8/1**

522 **6** *1 1/4* **Noverre To Go (IRE)**[22] 4339 8-9-12 78.....................(p) SteveDrowne 1 76
(Ronald Harris) *stdd s: t.k.h: hld up in tch in last trio: hmpd bnd 4f out: effrt nrest inner wl over 1f out: no imp: wknd ins fnl f* **5/1**[3]

0010 **7** *1/2* **Decent Fella (IRE)**[4] 4961 8-9-2 71............................(t) CharlesBishop(3) 6 68
(Ann Stokell) *stdd s: t.k.h: hld up in tch in last trio: rdn and effrt over 1f out: no prog* **16/1**

4156 **8** *3 1/2* **Lujeanie**[16] 4553 8-9-2 68..........................................(p) PatDobbs 3 53
(Peter Crate) *stdd s: hld up in tch in last trio: rdn and no hdwy over 1f out: wknd ins fnl f* **25/1**

1m 10.61s (0.41) **Going Correction** +0.125s/f (Good) **8 Ran SP% 117.3**
Speed ratings (Par 105): **102,100,100,99,98 96,95,91**
CSF £10.50 CT £47.57 TOTE £3.10: £1.30, £1.80, £2.00; EX 9.30 Trifecta £76.30.
**Owner** G C Stevens **Bred** Kilfrush Stud **Trained** Blewbury, Oxon
■ Stewards' Enquiry : Seb Sanders two-day ban: careless riding (Aug 23-24)

**FOCUS**
A modest yet competitive sprint handicap. Solid form for the class.

## 5125 CHECKATRADE.COM FOUNDATION CHARITY H'CAP 6f 209y
**4:40** (4:40) (Class 5) (0-70,70) 3-Y-O+ **£2,587** (£770; £384; £192) **Stalls Centre**

Form RPR

342 **1** **Darnathean**[15] 4578 5-9-4 62..........................................(p) LukeMorris 4 72
(Paul D'Arcy) *racd in last pair: rdn and clsd on ldr over 2f out: drvn to chse ldr 2f out: led ent fnl f: r.o: rdn out* **11/4**[2]

-644 **2** *1 1/2* **Just Isla**[22] 4342 4-8-8 55..........................................(p) DeclanBates(3) 1 61
(Peter Makin) *hld up in midfield: clsd on ldr over 2f out: rdn to chse ldrs over 1f out: wnt 2nd ins fnl f: one pce fnl 100yds* **2/1**[1]

6324 **3** *2 1/4* **Welsh Inlet (IRE)**[8] 4811 6-9-4 62................................ WilliamCarson 8 62
(John Bridger) *hld up in midfield: rdn and clsd on ldr over 2f out: drvn and no ex 1f out: kpt on same pce after: wnt 3rd last strides* **4/1**[3]

0000 **4** *nk* **Red Explorer (USA)**[18] 4494 4-8-10 57..................(v[1]) CharlesBishop(3) 3 56
(Ann Stokell) *led and sn clr: rdn 2f out: hdd ent fnl f: no ex fnl 150yds: wknd towards fin and lost 3rd last strides* **16/1**

6026 **5** *3/4* **Loud**[35] 3910 4-9-12 70..........................................(b[1]) JimCrowley 5 68
(Amy Weaver) *s.i.s: bhd and niggled along: rdn and clsd on outer over 2f out: no ex u.p over 1f out: one pce after* **8/1**

3243 **6** *3 1/2* **Kakapuka**[16] 4544 7-9-10 68................................................ JohnFahy 7 56
(Anabel K Murphy) *t.k.h: chsd ldr tl 2f out: lost pl u.p over 1f out: wknd 1f out* **6/1**

1m 23.87s (0.77) **Going Correction** +0.125s/f (Good)
**WFA** 3 from 4yo+ 6lb **6 Ran SP% 111.3**
Speed ratings (Par 103): **100,98,95,95,94 90**
CSF £8.52 CT £19.33 TOTE £2.90: £1.80, £1.80; EX 9.20 Trifecta £22.50.
**Owner** K Snell **Bred** K Snell **Trained** Newmarket, Suffolk

**FOCUS**
A moderate handicap, run at a brisk pace. The first two were both previous CD winners.

## 5126 VISIT US AT CHECKATALENT.COM H'CAP 5f 59y
**5:10** (5:10) (Class 6) (0-60,56) 3-Y-O+ **£1,940** (£577; £288; £144) **Stalls Centre**

Form RPR

-005 **1** **Spider Lily**[15] 4567 3-8-4 45........................................ DeclanBates(3) 2 59
(Peter Makin) *chsd ldrs tl over 4f out: swtchd rt over 2f out: swtchd bk lft and rdn to ld over 1f out: r.o wl and drew clr fnl 100yds: comf* **8/1**

2123 **2** *3 3/4* **Johnny Splash (IRE)**[2] 5045 5-9-2 56....................(v) DanielMuscutt(5) 3 58
(Roger Teal) *led: rdn ent fnl 2f: drvn and hdd over 1f out: kpt on same pce ins fnl f* **5/4**[1]

4-00 **3** *2 3/4* **Compton Albion (IRE)**[55] 3231 4-8-9 51........................ DavidParkes(7) 6 43
(Jeremy Gask) *in tch in rr: rdn and effrt to press ldrs over 1f out: no ex and btn 1f out: wknd fnl 100yds* **6/1**[3]

3423 **4** *1/2* **Bubbly Bailey**[36] 3896 4-9-4 53..................................(v) PaddyAspell 4 44
(J R Jenkins) *chsd ldr tl lost pl u.p over 1f out: wl btn and plugged on same pce fnl f* **5/2**[2]

0340 **5** *nk* **Spic 'n Span**[15] 4567 9-8-10 45..................................(b) LukeMorris 7 35
(Ronald Harris) *taken down early: dwlt: rcvrd to chse ldrs over 4f out: rdn and pressed ldrs 2f out: btn over 1f out: bhd 1f out: plugged on* **7/1**

1m 3.91s (1.61) **Going Correction** +0.125s/f (Good)
**WFA** 3 from 4yo+ 3lb **5 Ran SP% 110.9**
Speed ratings (Par 101): **92,86,81,80,80**
CSF £18.86 TOTE £11.60: £4.30, £1.10; EX 17.50 Trifecta £66.10.
**Owner** Hoofbeats Racing Club 1 **Bred** Mrs P J Makin **Trained** Ogbourne Maisey, Wilts

**FOCUS**
This ordinary little sprint handicap, run at a decent pace.
T/Plt: £14.60 to a £1 stake. Pool of £59353.80 - 2951.52 winning tickets. T/Qpdt: £5.90 to a £1 stake. Pool of £4173.30 - 515.25 winning tickets. SP

# 5077 HAYDOCK (L-H)
Friday, August 8

**OFFICIAL GOING: Good changing to good (good to soft in places) after race 3 (6.55)**
Wind: Moderate, half against Weather: Overcast

## 5127 BETDAQ HAYDOCK PARK APPRENTICE TRAINING SERIES H'CAP (PART OF THE RACING EXCELLENCE INITIATIVE) 1m 3f 200y
**5:50** (5:50) (Class 5) (0-75,74) 4-Y-O+ **£2,587** (£770; £384; £192) **Stalls Centre**

Form RPR

6100 **1** **Flying Power**[13] 4662 6-9-9 74................................ JackGarritty(3) 5 81
(John Norton) *mde all: qcknd 4f out: rdn 2f out: kpt on wl fnl f* **11/2**[3]

2-30 **2** *2* **Highway Code (USA)**[20] 4423 8-9-10 72........................(t) EoinWalsh 1 76
(Richard Lee) *hld up: outpcd 3f out: swtchd rt wl over 1f out: prog and r.o ins fnl f: tk 2nd post: no imp on wnr* **10/3**[2]

3541 **3** *shd* **Evervescent (IRE)**[20] 4427 5-9-7 **72** JoeDoyle(3) 4 76
(Graeme McPherson) *in tch: effrt to chse wnr over 1f out: no real imp ins fnl f: lost 2nd post* **15/8**[1]

5030 **4** *7* **Well Owd Mon**[34] 3973 4-8-2 **55** oh5 RobHornby(5) 3 47
(Andrew Hollinshead) *hld up in rr: rdn and outpcd 3f out: kpt on ins fnl f: nt able to trble ldrs* **10/1**

0602 **5** *4* **Charles De Mille**[16] 4533 6-8-6 **59** KieranSchofield(5) 2 45
(George Moore) *racd keenly: prom: chsd wnr 5f out: lost 2nd over 2f out: wknd ins fnl f* **11/2**[3]

3236 **6** *1 ¼* **Ferdy (IRE)**[20] 4427 5-8-8 **56** GeorgeDowning 6 40
(Paul Green) *prom: niggled along 4f out: chsd wnr over 2f out: lost 2nd over 1f out: wknd ins fnl f* **15/2**

2m 33.19s (-0.61) **Going Correction** -0.20s/f (Firm) 6 Ran SP% **109.5**
Speed ratings (Par 103): **94,92,92,87,85 84**
CSF £22.70 TOTE £8.80: £3.70, £2.30; EX 25.40 Trifecta £45.30.
**Owner** Jaffa Racing Syndicate **Bred** Rabbah Bloodstock Limited **Trained** High Hoyland, S Yorks

**FOCUS**
All races on Inner home straight and distances on Round course increased by 3yds. An unconvincing apprentice rider's handicap, rated around the third.

## 5128 BRITISH STALLION STUDS EBF MAIDEN STKS 6f
**6:20** (6:21) (Class 5) 2-Y-O **£2,911** (£866; £432; £216) **Stalls** Low

Form RPR

564 **1** **Honcho (IRE)**[13] 4666 2-9-2 75 JoeyHaynes(3) 9 76
(David Elsworth) *chsd ldrs: led over 2f out: sn rdn: pressed fnl f: hld on wl cl home* **7/1**[2]

**2** *nk* **Opportuna** 2-9-0 0 RichardKingscote 5 70+
(Tom Dascombe) *sn pushed along towards rr: rn green: impr into midfield 4f out: effrt whn swtchd lft wl over 1f out: r.o to chal fnl 100yds: jst hld* **12/1**

22 **3** *3 ¼* **Marshall Jennings (IRE)**[21] 4395 2-9-5 0 SeanLevey 2 65
(Richard Hannon) *racd keenly: w ldr: led over 3f out: hdd over 2f out: stl chalng over 1f out: no ex fnl 75yds* **2/7**[1]

**4** *2* **Emblaze** 2-9-0 0 PhillipMakin 6 54+
(Bryan Smart) *dwlt: sn in midfield: edgd lft 2f out: rdn whn edgd rt over 1f out: styd on same pce ins fnl f* **25/1**

06 **5** *½* **Pumaflor (IRE)**[13] 4684 2-9-0 0 DuilioDaSilva(5) 3 58
(Richard Guest) *towards rr: carried rt over 1f out: styd on ins fnl f: nt trble ldrs: nt pce to chal* **66/1**

06 **6** *3 ½* **Muzarkash**[13] 4676 2-9-5 0 RoystonFfrench 8 47
(B W Hills) *racd keenly: led: hdd over 3f out: rdn over 2f out: wknd ins fnl f* **10/1**[3]

24 **7** *3* **Mighty Warrior**[36] 3893 2-9-5 0 DavidNolan 7 38
(Richard Fahey) *in tch: rdn 1/2-way: wknd over 1f out* **12/1**

**8** *1 ½* **My Mo (FR)** 2-9-0 0 GeorgeDowning(5) 4 34
(David Dennis) *midfield: green and edgd lft over 2f out: sn wknd* **50/1**

**9** *16* **Blythe Prince** 2-9-5 0 DougieCostello 1
(Danielle McCormick) *sn rdn and bhd: a outpcd* **33/1**

1m 15.95s (2.15) **Going Correction** +0.225s/f (Good) 9 Ran SP% **125.0**
Speed ratings (Par 94): **94,93,89,86,85 81,77,75,53**
CSF £87.41 TOTE £4.60: £1.10, £3.10, £1.02; EX 125.80 Trifecta £236.70.
**Owner** D R C Elsworth **Bred** Paul Hancock **Trained** Newmarket, Suffolk

**FOCUS**
A fair maiden.

## 5129 COUNTRYWIDE FREIGHT NURSERY H'CAP (BOBIS RACE) 6f
**6:55** (6:56) (Class 4) (0-80,78) 2-Y-O **£4,528** (£1,347; £673; £336) **Stalls** Low

Form RPR

41 **1** **Lady Desire (IRE)**[51] 3358 2-9-7 **78** PhillipMakin 3 89+
(Keith Dalgleish) *chsd ldrs: chalng over 2f out: led over 1f out: r.o wl to draw clr ins fnl 100yds* **4/1**[3]

2103 **2** *3 ½* **Polar Vortex (IRE)**[22] 4345 2-9-4 **75** AdamKirby 4 75
(Clive Cox) *led: rdn over 2f out: hdd over 1f out: unable to go w wnr fnl 100yds* **2/1**[1]

3203 **3** *1 ¼* **Ar Colleen Aine**[8] 4815 2-8-12 **69** FrannyNorton 1 65
(Mick Channon) *racd keenly: hld up: hdwy over 2f out: chsd ldrs over 1f out: styd on same pce fnl 100yds* **14/1**

320 **4** *1 ½* **War Paint (IRE)**[84] 2313 2-8-10 **67** RichardKingscote 6 59
(Tom Dascombe) *hld up: rdn over 2f out: plugged on fnl f: nvr a threat* **9/2**

0013 **5** *8* **Alpine Affair**[14] 4605 2-9-7 **78** (b) SeanLevey 2 46
(Brian Meehan) *hld up: rdn over 2f out: no imp over 1f out: btn ins fnl f: allowed to coast home fnl 150yds* **7/2**[2]

6524 **6** *1 ¾* **Dragline**[16] 4529 2-8-2 **59** DuranFentiman 5 22
(Tim Easterby) *racd keenly: prom: hung lft and lost pl over 2f out: continued to hang lft over 1f out: bhd after* **9/1**

1m 15.68s (1.88) **Going Correction** +0.225s/f (Good) 6 Ran SP% **110.4**
Speed ratings (Par 96): **96,91,89,87,77 74**
CSF £12.02 TOTE £5.00: £2.90, £1.20; EX 14.10 Trifecta £29.50.
**Owner** G Brogan **Bred** Rockhart Trading Ltd **Trained** Carluke, S Lanarks

**FOCUS**
The first two were up there all the way and sound enough form for class.

## 5130 SUPPLY UK FILLIES' H'CAP 5f
**7:25** (7:25) (Class 5) (0-70,69) 3-Y-O+ **£2,587** (£770; £384; £192) **Stalls** Centre

Form RPR

4445 **1** **Two Turtle Doves (IRE)**[4] 4960 8-8-5 **50** HarryBentley 4 58
(Michael Mullineaux) *chsd ldrs: led over 2f out: rdn ins fnl f: kpt on wl towards fin* **7/2**[2]

0020 **2** *½* **Busy Bimbo (IRE)**[11] 4725 5-8-0 **50** oh1 (b) JoeDoyle(5) 7 56
(Alan Berry) *a.p: rdn over 1f out: chalng ins fnl f: kpt on* **8/1**

2545 **3** *¾* **Your Gifted (IRE)**[7] 4860 7-8-4 **54** (v) JackGarritty(5) 1 57
(Lisa Williamson) *s.i.s: hld up: nt clr run and swtchd rt over 1f out: hdwy after: styd on ins fnl f: nt trble front two* **7/1**

0306 **4** *1 ½* **Economic Crisis (IRE)**[6] 4902 5-9-10 **69** JamesSullivan 3 67
(Alan Berry) *in tch: rdn over 2f out: nt qckn over 1f out: styd on same pce ins fnl f* **6/1**

5540 **5** *1 ¼* **Dark Opal (IRE)**[80] 2421 4-9-5 **67** JoeyHaynes(3) 5 60
(John Weymes) *prom: chalng 2f out: rdn over 1f out: no ex fnl 100yds* **5/1**[3]

0106 **6** *½* **Lady Poppy**[16] 4531 4-9-5 **64** AndrewElliott 6 56
(George Moore) *led: rdn and hdd over 2f out: fdd ins fnl f* **3/1**[1]

45-4 **7** *3 ¼* **Avonvalley**[102] 1814 7-9-3 **62** AdamKirby 8 42
(Peter Grayson) *awkward s: bhd and outpcd: nvr a threat* **10/1**

4/00 **8** *6* **Hollydanfaye**[64] 2909 4-8-5 **50** oh1 RoystonFfrench 2 8
(Paul Green) *in tch: lost pl 3f out: u.p and outpcd after* **33/1**

1m 2.41s (1.61) **Going Correction** +0.40s/f (Good) 8 Ran SP% **113.8**
Speed ratings (Par 100): **103,102,101,98,96 95,90,81**
CSF £31.03 CT £186.05 TOTE £4.40: £2.10, £3.00, £2.70; EX 30.40 Trifecta £217.40.
**Owner** G Cornes **Bred** M Sharkey **Trained** Alpraham, Cheshire

**FOCUS**
The going was eased slightly to good, good to soft in places A modest fillies' handicap, rated around the second.

## 5131 IRISH CHAMPIONS WEEKEND EBF NOVICE STKS (BOBIS RACE) 7f
**8:00** (8:02) (Class 4) 2-Y-O **£6,469** (£1,925; £962; £481) **Stalls** Low

Form RPR

1334 **1** **Sea Wolf (IRE)**[27] 4218 2-9-6 87 PaulMulrennan 1 91
(Michael Dods) *mde all: rdn 2f out: sn edgd lft and strly pressed: kpt on gamely towards fin* **9/4**[2]

16 **2** *½* **Peace And War (USA)**[49] 3415 2-9-1 0 JamieSpencer 3 85
(Olly Stevens) *hmpd s: chsd ldr: rdn to chal strly 2f out: sn edgd lft: no ex towards fin* **4/1**[3]

5100 **3** *1 ¼* **Dr No**[9] 4780 2-9-6 103 SeanLevey 2 86
(Richard Hannon) *wnt rt s: chsd ldrs: effrt to chal 2f out: sn carried lft: nt qckn over 1f out: plld off rail ins fnl f: kpt on towards fin but hld* **5/6**[1]

**4** *10* **Azzir (IRE)** 2-8-10 0 HarryBentley 5 63+
(Timothy Jarvis) *wnt bdly rt s and almost off the crse: rn green: bhd: hdwy 4f out: nvr able to rch others: n.d* **20/1**

1m 30.72s (0.02) **Going Correction** -0.025s/f (Good) 4 Ran SP% **110.1**
Speed ratings (Par 96): **98,97,96,84**
CSF £10.87 TOTE £3.60; EX 10.90 Trifecta £12.20.
**Owner** Mr & Mrs Paul Gaffney **Bred** Irish National Stud **Trained** Denton, Co Durham

**FOCUS**
A decent little novice race. The third was well below best form.

## 5132 CHRIS FAYLE MEMORIAL H'CAP (BOBIS RACE) 1m 3f 200y
**8:30** (8:30) (Class 4) (0-80,84) 3-Y-O **£5,175** (£1,540; £769; £384) **Stalls** Centre

Form RPR

-064 **1** **Intense Tango**[21] 4392 3-8-13 **72** PaulMulrennan 1 81
(K R Burke) *chsd ldrs: led 2f out: rdn over 1f out: all out towards fin: jst hld on* **12/1**

230 **2** *nse* **Latin Charm (IRE)**[62] 3003 3-9-4 **77** (p) AdamKirby 6 86
(Marco Botti) *in tch: rdn 3f out: edgd rt over 2f out: wnt 2nd ins fnl f: r.o for press to press wnr towards fin: jst failed* **4/1**[3]

3121 **3** *4 ½* **Emerahldz (IRE)**[53] 3303 3-8-11 **75** JackGarritty(5) 4 77
(Richard Fahey) *led early: chsd ldr after: led jst over 3f out: rdn over 2f out: sn hdd: lost 2nd ins fnl f: styd on same pce fnl 75yds* **15/2**

66-4 **4** *6* **Captain Swift (IRE)**[180] 551 3-8-11 **70** SeanLevey 3 62
(Brian Meehan) *hld up: rdn over 2f out: no imp on ldrs: one pce fnl f* **33/1**

1611 **5** *2 ½* **Special Fighter (IRE)**[3] 4995 3-9-11 **84** 12ex FrannyNorton 7 72
(Mark Johnston) *racd keenly: sn led: hdd jst over 3f out: rdn over 2f out: wknd ins fnl f* **6/4**[1]

0234 **6** *1 ¾* **Frosty The Snowman (IRE)**[15] 4574 3-8-3 **62** JamesSullivan 2 48
(Ruth Carr) *in tch: pushed along over 4f out: rdn and outpcd 3f out: wl bhd fnl f* **20/1**

542 **7** *19* **Idder (IRE)**[21] 4388 3-9-7 **80** (p[1]) RichardKingscote 5 35
(Roger Varian) *s.i.s: hld up: pushed along and outpcd over 3f out: wl bhd fnl f* **11/4**[2]

2m 31.43s (-2.37) **Going Correction** -0.025s/f (Good) 7 Ran SP% **113.8**
Speed ratings (Par 102): **106,105,102,98,97 96,83**
CSF £58.45 TOTE £16.10: £6.70, £1.40; EX 70.10 Trifecta £212.30.
**Owner** Cedars Two **Bred** Newsells Park Stud **Trained** Middleham Moor, N Yorks

**FOCUS**
An interesting handicap run at a fair gallop. The third ran to form.
T/Plt: £380.50 to a £1 stake. Pool of £55488.99 - 106.45 winning units. T/Qpdt: £58.10 to a £1 stake. Pool of £5056.99 - 64.40 winning units. DO

# 5042 LINGFIELD (L-H)
Friday, August 8

**OFFICIAL GOING: Standard**
Wind: Almost nil Weather: Cloudy, quite humid

## 5133 GREYHOUND FILLIES' (S) STKS 6f 1y(P)
**2:20** (2:20) (Class 6) 2-Y-O **£1,940** (£577; £288; £144) **Stalls** Low

Form RPR

6220 **1** **Jimmy's Girl (IRE)**[13] 4652 2-8-7 65 CamHardie(5) 3 58
(Richard Hannon) *mde all and sn stretched field: only one rival 1/2-way: drew clr wl over 1f out: 4 l up fnl f: tired last 100yds but a holding on* **3/1**[1]

6443 **2** *1 ¼* **Itsindebag**[16] 4542 2-8-5 55 (p) JosephineGordon(7) 2 53
(J S Moore) *hld up in 5th and sn wl off the pce: pushed along 1/2-way: prog to go 2nd jst ins fnl f: clsd on wnr fin but nvr gng to get there* **10/1**

4253 **3** *nk* **Kidmeforever**[34] 3967 2-8-7 59 PhilipPrince(5) 4 52
(J S Moore) *hld up in 4th and sn off the pce: rdn 1/2-way: prog to go 3rd jst ins fnl f: clsd on wnr w runner-up: nrst fin* **5/1**[3]

06 **4** *2 ¼* **Tilly Range (IRE)**[56] 3173 2-8-12 0 JFEgan 1 45
(David Evans) *chsd ldng pair but sn rdn: unable to stay in tch 1/2-way: no imp over 1f out* **33/1**

4 **5** *1 ¾* **Paris Carver (FR)**[16] 4542 2-8-12 0 JimmyFortune 7 40
(Jonathan Portman) *dwlt: wl off the pce in last: taken wd over 3f out: tried to cl over 1f out: no real hdwy* **5/1**[3]

6152 **6** *hd* **Diminutive (IRE)**[16] 4542 2-9-3 62 (p) OisinMurphy 5 45
(Grace Harris) *outpcd in 6th after 2f: n.m.r 1/2-way: no ch whn nt clr run jst over 1f out* **7/2**[2]

35 **7** *2* **Scent Of Power**[15] 4589 2-8-12 0 WilliamCarson 6 34
(Anthony Carson) *chsd wnr: chal 3f out and clr of rest: btn wl over 1f out: wknd rapidly fnl f* **3/1**[1]

1m 12.76s (0.86) **Going Correction** -0.075s/f (Stan) 7 Ran SP% **117.6**
Speed ratings (Par 89): **91,89,88,85,83 83,80**
CSF £34.57 TOTE £4.30: £2.50, £4.40; EX 26.50 Trifecta £118.40.The winner was bought by Chris Dwyer for 5,400gns.
**Owner** Will Mellor & Kevin McMullen **Bred** Laundry Cottage Stud Farm **Trained** East Everleigh, Wilts

■ Stewards' Enquiry : Philip Prince two-day ban: used whip with excessive frequency (Aug 23-24)

**FOCUS**
Early speed won this for the winner.

## 5134 INOX NOVICE STKS (BOBIS RACE) 5f 6y(P)
2:50 (2:50) (Class 4) 2-Y-O **£6,469** (£1,925; £962; £481) **Stalls** High

Form RPR

5102 1 **Portamento (IRE)**[13] 4670 2-9-7 96........................ WilliamBuick 1 93
*(Charlie Appleby) mde virtually all: shkn up to gain decisive ld over 1f out: styd on* **8/13**[1]

5213 2 1 1/2 **Sunset Sail (IRE)**[7] 4853 2-9-2 86........................ CamHardie(5) 2 88
*(Richard Hannon) pressed wnr: stl chalng 2f out: rdn over 1f out: kpt on but no imp fnl f* **7/4**[2]

4101 3 1 **Expensive Date**[30] 4083 2-9-6 81........................ JimmyFortune 3 83
*(Paul Cole) pressed ldng pair but racd wdst of the trio: stl rt there 2f out: wd bnd sn after: rdn and kpt on same pce fr over 1f out* **14/1**[3]

41 4 5 **Hatchet Harry (IRE)**[11] 4739 2-9-7 0........................ JFEgan 4 66
*(David Evans) pressed ldng trio but forced to r wdst of all: dropped to last over 3f out: sn rdn and struggling* **20/1**

58.45s (-0.35) **Going Correction** -0.075s/f (Stan) 4 Ran SP% 109.7
Speed ratings (Par 96): **99,96,95,87**
CSF £1.98 TOTE £1.70; EX 2.10 Trifecta £4.50.
**Owner** Godolphin **Bred** Darley **Trained** Newmarket, Suffolk

**FOCUS**
Just the four runners, but all had shown decent form and it went to the highest-rated runner.

## 5135 PATRICK MCVEIGH MAIDEN STKS 1m 5f (P)
3:20 (3:20) (Class 5) 3-Y-O+ **£2,587** (£770; £384; £192) **Stalls** Low

Form RPR

0-63 1 **Hoist The Colours (IRE)**[14] 4621 3-9-1 74........................(b[1]) TedDurcan 6 89
*(David Lanigan) sn trckd ldr: strly rdn 4f out: led 3f out: drew clr over 1f out: pushed out* **8/1**[3]

3033 2 4 **Saarrem (USA)**[16] 4543 3-9-1 80........................(p) DaneO'Neill 3 83
*(John Gosden) racd on outer: trckd ldrs: cl 3rd over 4f out: chal and looked to be gng best over 3f out: rdn and fnd nil in pursuit of wnr over 2f out* **5/4**[2]

3522 3 1 1/4 **Artful Rogue (IRE)**[7] 4855 3-9-1 75........................(p) WilliamBuick 5 81
*(Amanda Perrett) pushed up to ld: rdn and hdd 3f out: nt qckn and wl hld fnl 2f* **1/1**[1]

0-P0 4 10 **Fennann**[21] 4407 3-9-1 0........................(p) SamHitchcott 1 66
*(Gary Moore) in tch in last pair: rdn 1/2-way and nt keen: lost tch over 4f out: plugged on to claim remote 4th fnl f* **100/1**

0 5 nk **Guard of Honour (IRE)**[36] 3891 3-9-1 0........................ PatCosgrave 4 66
*(Rebecca Curtis) chsd ldrs: rdn 7f out: lost tch 4f out: bhd after* **12/1**

0/ 6 25 **Musical Moon**[645] 7507 4-9-13 0........................ GeorgeBaker 2 28
*(Lady Herries) chsd ldrs: rdn 7f out: lost tch over 4f out: wl t.o* **33/1**

060 7 99 **Planet Rock**[20] 4432 3-8-8 0........................(b) DavidParkes(7) 7
*(Keiran Burke) rdn and lost tch after 4f: sn wl t.o: btn 2f by wnr* **100/1**

2m 42.0s (-4.00) **Going Correction** -0.075s/f (Stan)
**WFA** 3 from 4yo 12lb 7 Ran SP% 118.2
Speed ratings (Par 103): **109,106,105,99,99 84,23**
CSF £19.56 TOTE £11.10: £3.30, £1.60; EX 24.30 Trifecta £39.10.
**Owner** B E Nielsen **Bred** Pier House Stud **Trained** Upper Lambourn, Berks

**FOCUS**
A fair maiden, in which the first three all had headgear on for the first or second time and is rated around the second.

## 5136 TERSUS H'CAP 6f 1y(P)
3:50 (3:50) (Class 6) (0-60,66) 3-Y-O+ **£2,587** (£770; £384; £192) **Stalls** Low

Form RPR

2202 1 **Chapellerie (IRE)**[11] 4733 5-8-12 55........................(b) JennyPowell(7) 1 68
*(Brendan Powell) n.m.r after 1f and dropped to 6th: gd prog over 1f out: rdn to ld ins fnl f: sn clr* **7/4**[1]

0063 2 3 1/4 **Reginald Claude**[11] 4733 6-9-4 54........................(be) LiamKeniry 4 57
*(Mark Usher) hld up in tch: shkn up over 1f out: styd on fnl f to take 2nd nr fin: no threat to wnr* **9/2**[3]

4004 3 1/2 **Microlight**[160] 798 6-8-10 46 oh1........................ JimmyQuinn 8 47
*(John E Long) led 150yds: chsd ldr: drvn 2f out: tried to chal 1f out: sn one pce* **20/1**

0025 4 nk **Proper Charlie**[11] 4732 6-9-2 52........................(v) AmirQuinn 7 52
*(Lee Carter) led after 150yds: rdn 2f out: hdd ins fnl f: no ch w wnr and lost 2 pls nr fin* **4/1**[2]

4030 5 1/2 **Astral Rose**[22] 4337 3-8-7 47........................(b) OisinMurphy 2 44
*(Jonathan Portman) cl up whn n.m.r on inner and lost pl after 1f: cl up again over 2f out: drvn over 1f out: one pce* **12/1**

0050 6 2 3/4 **Triple Star**[36] 3890 3-9-6 60........................[1] JimmyFortune 3 49
*(Hughie Morrison) v.s.a: detached in last and nvr in it: passed one rival fnl f* **5/1**

24-0 7 1 3/4 **Jawking**[35] 3921 5-9-7 57........................ PaoloSirigu 5 41
*(James Unett) sn trckd ldng pair on outer: lost pl fr wl over 2f out: wknd over 1f out* **10/1**

1m 12.69s (0.79) **Going Correction** -0.075s/f (Stan)
**WFA** 3 from 4yo+ 4lb 7 Ran SP% 112.8
Speed ratings (Par 101): **91,86,86,85,84 81,78**
CSF £9.55 CT £111.06 TOTE £2.20: £1.10, £2.60; EX 9.00 Trifecta £64.10.
**Owner** T M Clarke **Bred** Castellane Partnership **Trained** Upper Lambourn, Berks

**FOCUS**
Not much went right for the winner, but she overcame it all and won easily.

## 5137 JACKSONS ESTATE AGENTS H'CAP 1m 7f 169y(P)
4:20 (4:21) (Class 5) (0-75,75) 4-Y-O+ **£3,752** (£1,116; £557; £278) **Stalls** Low

Form RPR

20-1 1 **Mick Duggan**[23] 4322 4-9-7 75........................ OisinMurphy 9 87+
*(Ralph Beckett) trckd ldr: led 1/2-way: rdn clr over 1f out: in n.d after: kpt on* **2/1**[1]

6500 2 1 3/4 **Saborido (USA)**[20] 4441 8-9-6 74........................(b) GeorgeBaker 8 83
*(Amanda Perrett) hld up in rr: stdy prog 5f out: trckd ldng pair on outer over 3f out: rdn and nt qckn over 1f out: sn wnt 2nd: kpt on fnl f* **7/1**

-222 3 3 1/2 **Dumbfounded (FR)**[30] 4076 6-8-8 69........................ KieranShoemark(7) 5 74
*(Lady Herries) in tch: rdn to chse ldng trio over 3f out: no imp over 2f out: kpt on to take 3rd ins fnl f* **3/1**[2]

3-61 4 1 3/4 **Hell Hath No Fury**[11] 4737 5-8-2 56 6ex........................ AndrewMullen 3 59
*(Michael Appleby) cl up: pressed wnr 7f out: drvn over 2f out: nt qckn wl over 1f out: wknd fnl f* **9/2**[3]

1050 5 3 1/4 **Newtown Cross (IRE)**[13] 4678 4-7-12 57........................[1] CamHardie(5) 7 56
*(Jimmy Fox) hld up tl wnt prom after 5f: chal fr 7f out to 5f out: sn rdn and btn* **20/1**

-060 6 4 **Ascendant**[37] 3859 8-8-13 74........................(b) JennyPowell(7) 1 68
*(Andrew Reid) stdd s: hld up in last: shkn up 5f out: no prog and sn lost tch* **7/1**

0005 7 2 3/4 **Azrag (USA)**[16] 4552 6-9-4 72........................(p) RobertHavlin 2 63
*(Michael Attwater) walked to post: led at mod pce to 1/2-way: sn dropped to rr: lost tch 4f out: no ch after* **16/1**

3m 22.25s (-3.45) **Going Correction** -0.075s/f (Stan) 7 Ran SP% 112.2
Speed ratings (Par 103): **105,104,102,101,99 97,96**
CSF £15.97 CT £39.89 TOTE £2.70: £1.60, £3.50; EX 13.20 Trifecta £51.90.
**Owner** Mark Muddiman **Bred** Pendley Farm **Trained** Kimpton, Hants

**FOCUS**
They went steady early, but picked up far enough out and again the runner-up sets level.

## 5138 INDUS CATERING H'CAP 7f 1y(P)
4:50 (4:54) (Class 6) (0-60,60) 3-Y-O+ **£2,587** (£770; £384; £192) **Stalls** Low

Form RPR

3440 1 **Bertie Blu Boy**[15] 4578 6-9-6 59........................(b) GeorgeBaker 6 67
*(Lisa Williamson) fast away: mde all: 2 l clr over 1f out: drvn fnl f: jst lasted* **9/2**[2]

6006 2 shd **Lewamy (IRE)**[11] 4733 4-8-3 47........................ CamHardie(5) 14 55
*(John Best) off the pce in 9th: prog on outer jst over 2f out: drvn and r.o fnl f: tk 2nd last strides: jst failed* **25/1**

5253 3 hd **Parisian Pyramid (IRE)**[15] 4578 8-9-7 60........................(p) AmirQuinn 11 67
*(Lee Carter) prom: rdn over 2f out: edgd rt sn after: chsd wnr fnl f: clsd nr fin but lost 2nd last strides* **10/1**

0-04 4 2 1/2 **Buxton**[11] 4732 10-8-7 46........................(t) NickyMackay 9 47
*(Roger Ingram) slowly away: hld up in last quartet: stl wl in rr over 1f out: rdn and r.o to take 4th nr fin* **12/1**

-033 5 1 **Roring Samson (IRE)**[24] 4306 3-9-1 60........................ PatCosgrave 3 56
*(George Baker) off the pce in midfield: prog on outer over 3f out: 5th whn impeded bnd wl over 1f out: kpt on same pce after* **3/1**[1]

5401 6 1/2 **Blue Clumber**[11] 4733 4-8-13 52 6ex........................ JimmyQuinn 8 49
*(Shaun Harris) chsd wnr: rdn over 2f out: no imp over 1f out: lost 2nd and wknd fnl f* **10/1**

5005 7 3/4 **Ishetoo**[7] 4848 10-8-7 46 oh1........................ FrankieMcDonald 10 41
*(Peter Grayson) chsd ldrs: rdn 3f out: no imp fnl 2f: one pce* **33/1**

4004 8 3/4 **See No Ships**[14] 4611 3-8-4 49........................ KieranO'Neill 2 40
*(Mark Usher) chsd ldng pair: rdn 3f out: wknd on inner jst over 1f out* **6/1**[3]

600 9 3 3/4 **Byrae**[71] 2690 4-9-2 55........................ SamHitchcott 5 38
*(Polly Gundry) slowly away: mostly in last quartet: rdn on inner 2f out: no great prog* **12/1**

64-0 10 1 1/4 **Mack's Sister**[103] 1766 7-8-6 52........................ KieranShoemark(7) 7 32
*(Michael Madgwick) chsd ldrs but sn pushed along: no prog 2f out: wknd fnl f* **25/1**

6006 11 1/2 **No Refund (IRE)**[9] 4789 3-8-13 58........................ TedDurcan 12 35
*(Martin Smith) slowly away: mostly in last quartet: drvn on outer and no prog 2f out* **6/1**[3]

0000 12 3 3/4 **Cuthbert (IRE)**[106] 1668 7-8-7 46 oh1........................ KierenFox 1 15
*(Michael Attwater) in tch in midfield: rdn 3f out: no prog whn hmpd jst over 2f out: wknd* **33/1**

-000 13 4 **Charlies Mate**[64] 2927 3-8-2 47........................(b[1]) PaoloSirigu 13 3
*(John Best) slowly away: a detached in last* **25/1**

1m 24.92s (0.12) **Going Correction** -0.075s/f (Stan)
**WFA** 3 from 4yo+ 6lb 13 Ran SP% 122.7
Speed ratings (Par 101): **96,95,95,92,91 91,90,89,85,83 83,78,74**
CSF £122.84 CT £1114.87 TOTE £6.30: £2.30, £7.20, £2.00; EX 127.00 Trifecta £1141.10.
**Owner** B & B Hygiene Limited **Bred** H Bourchier **Trained** Saighton, Cheshire

■ Stewards' Enquiry : Frankie McDonald one-day ban: careless riding (Aug 23)

**FOCUS**
Ordinary form, rated around the third.

## 5139 HEART FM 97.5 FM H'CAP 1m 2f (P)
5:20 (5:20) (Class 6) (0-65,67) 3-Y-O+ **£2,587** (£770; £384; £192) **Stalls** Low

Form RPR

5-01 1 **Ragged Robbin (FR)**[3] 5011 3-9-7 67 6ex........................(t) TedDurcan 2 76+
*(David Lanigan) trckd ldr after 3f: rdn to ld jst over 2f out: hrd pressed fr over 1f out: hld on wl* **5/4**[1]

0641 2 1/2 **Hallingham**[16] 4548 4-9-9 65........................(b) NedCurtis(5) 5 73
*(Jonathan Portman) pushed along early in last pair: gng bttr whn prog on wd outside 3f out: chsd wnr 2f out: chal and upsides 1f out: nt qckn last 100yds* **7/1**[3]

4004 3 nk **Precision Five**[20] 4433 5-9-11 62........................(p) GeorgeBaker 6 69
*(Jeremy Gask) stdd s: hld up in last pair: stl there 2f out: gd prog on outer over 1f out: edgd lft but styd on fnl f: a jst too much to do* **8/1**

4633 4 1 1/4 **Fiftyshadesfreed (IRE)**[14] 4613 3-9-5 65........................(p) PatCosgrave 3 73+
*(George Baker) hld up in tch: rdn and prog over 2f out: tried to chal on inner fnl f: keeping on whn hmpd nr fin* **11/4**[2]

6216 5 2 **Cyflymder (IRE)**[15] 4578 8-9-3 54........................ OisinMurphy 7 55
*(David C Griffiths) tried to ld but hdd after 1f: styd prom: lost pl on inner over 2f out: n.d after: plugged on* **16/1**

0653 6 hd **Dreaming Again**[133] 1141 4-8-6 48........................ CamHardie(5) 4 48
*(Jimmy Fox) in tch: rdn over 2f out: no prog and btn wl over 1f out* **20/1**

1206 7 1 3/4 **Minstrel Lad**[21] 4402 6-9-8 62........................ SimonPearce(3) 1 59
*(Lydia Pearce) in tch towards rr: dropped to last and rdn over 2f out: no prog after* **16/1**

3000 8 1/2 **Chantecler**[29] 4134 3-9-1 61........................[1] JimmyFortune 8 57
*(Hughie Morrison) pushed up to ld after 1f: rdn and hdd jst over 2f out: hmpd sn after: fdd* **20/1**

2m 5.65s (-0.95) **Going Correction** -0.075s/f (Stan)
**WFA** 3 from 4yo+ 9lb 8 Ran SP% 116.0
Speed ratings (Par 101): **100,99,99,98,96 96,95,94**
CSF £11.11 CT £48.03 TOTE £2.90: £1.20, £1.90, £1.80; EX 11.10 Trifecta £57.30.
**Owner** Niarchos Family **Bred** Famille Niarchos **Trained** Upper Lambourn, Berks

**FOCUS**
This developed into something of a sprint. The third ran close to recent C&D level.

T/Plt: £137.30 to a £1 stake. Pool of £52462.73 - 278.91 winning tickets. T/Qpdt: £21.20 to a £1 stake. Pool of £5484.74 - 190.80 winning tickets. JN

# [4856]MUSSELBURGH (R-H)

Friday, August 8

**OFFICIAL GOING: Good (good to firm in places) changing to good after race 5 (4.00)**

Wind: Light, half behind Weather: Overcast, raining from race 4

## 5140 BRITISH STALLION STUDS EBF STALLIONS CONDITIONS STKS (BOBIS RACE) 5f

**2:00** (2:00) (Class 3) 2-Y-O **£8,086** (£2,406; £1,202; £601) **Stalls** High

Form RPR

1 **1** **Fendale**[34] 3947 2-9-2 0 ........ PaulMulrennan 1 93+
(Bryan Smart) *trckd ldrs: effrt and plld out over 1f out: led ins fnl f: pushed out* **5/4**[2]

21 **2** *1 3/4* **Teruntum Star (FR)**[17] 4510 2-8-11 83 ........ KevinStott[(5)] 5 87
(Kevin Ryan) *led: rdn over 1f out: edgd rt and hdd ins fnl f: kpt on same pce* **10/11**[1]

1615 **3** *2 1/2* **Just The Tip (IRE)**[3] 5014 2-8-8 72 ........ JoeFanning 4 70
(Keith Dalgleish) *w ldr: rdn and outpcd over 1f out: no ex whn edgd lft ins fnl f* **14/1**[3]

04 **4** *13* **Poppy In The Wind**[10] 4751 2-8-6 0 ow1 ........ GeorgeChaloner[(3)] 2 24
(Alan Brown) *dwlt: bhd and outpcd: no ch fr 1/2-way* **50/1**

59.15s (-1.25) **Going Correction** -0.25s/f (Firm) 4 Ran SP% **105.5**
Speed ratings (Par 98): **100,97,93,72**
CSF £2.56 TOTE £2.20; EX 2.60 Trifecta £3.00.
**Owner** Ritchie Fiddes **Bred** Cheveley Park Stud Ltd **Trained** Hambleton, N Yorks

**FOCUS**
A match on paper and the two principals fought out the finish. That said, the winner was impressive off the fast pace.

## 5141 PARTNERSHIP CHALLENGE NURSERY H'CAP 7f 30y

**2:30** (2:30) (Class 5) (0-75,75) 2-Y-O **£3,234** (£962; £481; £240) **Stalls** Low

Form RPR

21 **1** **Alans Pride (IRE)**[34] 3945 2-8-13 70 ........ ConnorBeasley[(3)] 5 78
(Michael Dods) *mde all: qcknd over 3f out: styd on strly fnl f: unchal* **11/4**[2]

0401 **2** *2 1/2* **Binky Blue (IRE)**[49] 3435 2-8-8 62 ........ DaleSwift 4 63
(Brian Ellison) *t.k.h: pressed wnr: rdn over 2f out: kpt on fnl f: nt rch wnr* **11/2**[3]

005 **3** *2 1/4* **Frosty Times (FR)**[67] 2837 2-8-0 54 ........ PatrickMathers 1 49
(Richard Fahey) *t.k.h: prom: rdn over 2f out: edgd rt over 1f out: kpt on ins fnl f: no imp* **7/1**

550 **4** *1/2* **Robben**[35] 3924 2-8-0 59 ........(b[1]) ShaneGray[(5)] 6 53
(Kevin Ryan) *trckd ldrs: effrt and rdn over 2f out: hung rt over 1f out: outpcd fnl f* **7/1**

565 **5** *1 1/2* **Miss Van Gogh**[37] 3841 2-7-11 56 ........(v[1]) SammyJoBell[(5)] 3 46+
(Richard Fahey) *s.i.s: bhd: hdwy 1/2-way: rdn over 2f out: sn outpcd* **5/2**[1]

340 **6** *6* **Forgiving Glance**[19] 4467 2-8-0 54 oh2 ........ DuranFentiman 7 28+
(Philip Kirby) *prom on outside: bmpd and pushed along over 4f out: rdn and wknd over 2f out* **7/1**

1m 29.86s (0.86) **Going Correction** -0.15s/f (Firm) 6 Ran SP% **108.1**
Speed ratings (Par 94): **89,86,83,83,81 74**
CSF £16.45 TOTE £3.00: £1.40, £2.40; EX 9.10 Trifecta £43.70.
**Owner** Alan Henderson & Alan Bolton **Bred** Roundhill Stud **Trained** Denton, Co Durham

**FOCUS**
Just an fair nursery, with the winner building on his latest win.

## 5142 "EME SWEEPSTAKES" H'CAP 1m

**3:00** (3:00) (Class 5) (0-70,68) 3-Y-O+ **£3,234** (£962; £481; £240) **Stalls** Low

Form RPR

0522 **1** **Ellaal**[7] 4858 5-10-0 68 ........ PaulMulrennan 5 79
(Ruth Carr) *mde all: rdn over 2f out: edgd lft ins fnl f: kpt on strly* **5/1**[1]

3312 **2** *2 1/2* **Gambino (IRE)**[11] 4730 4-8-13 58 ........(p) KevinStott[(5)] 3 63
(John David Riches) *dwlt: sn in tch: effrt and chsd wnr 2f out: rdn and kpt on same pce fnl f* **11/2**[2]

1 **3** *5* **Senor George (IRE)**[53] 3299 7-9-13 67 ........ StephenCraine 1 61
(Brian Ellison) *sn chsng ldrs: effrt and rdn over 2f out: outpcd by first two over 1f out* **5/1**[1]

4252 **4** *2 1/4* **Whispered Times (USA)**[12] 4707 7-9-2 59 ........(p) ConnorBeasley[(3)] 11 48
(Tracy Waggott) *hld up: pushed along over 2f out: sme late hdwy: nvr on terms* **7/1**

-366 **5** *nk* **Pat's Legacy (USA)**[31] 4058 8-9-7 61 ........(p) DanielTudhope 10 49
(Marjorie Fife) *s.i.s: hld up: pushed along over 2f out: no imp* **6/1**[3]

-012 **6** *7* **Sugar Town**[17] 4515 4-8-12 55 ........(p) SamJames[(3)] 7 27
(Peter Niven) *cl up: rdn over 2f out: hung rt and wknd wl over 1f out* **6/1**[3]

2555 **7** *1/2* **Shearian**[19] 4468 4-9-4 58 ........ RobertWinston 4 29
(Tracy Waggott) *t.k.h: hld up towards rr: hung lft bnd ent st: sn rdn and outpcd* **8/1**

4266 **8** *3 1/4* **Les Gar Gan (IRE)**[17] 4515 3-9-7 68 ........(p) JoeFanning 8 30
(Keith Dalgleish) *prom on outside: outpcd over 3f out: btn fnl 2f* **14/1**

5160 **9** *2* **Space War**[20] 4451 7-9-13 67 ........(b) GrahamGibbons 6 26
(Michael Easterby) *s.i.s: hld up: rdn over 3f out: nvr on terms* **22/1**

0060 **10** *8* **Act Your Shoe Size**[17] 4517 5-9-8 62 ........ TomEaves 2
(Keith Dalgleish) *in tch: struggling over 3f out: sn wknd* **20/1**

1m 39.36s (-1.84) **Going Correction** -0.15s/f (Firm)
**WFA** 3 from 4yo+ 7lb 10 Ran SP% **116.7**
Speed ratings (Par 103): **103,100,95,93,92 85,85,82,80,72**
CSF £32.29 CT £145.40 TOTE £4.90: £1.30, £1.90, £1.70; EX 22.50 Trifecta £86.20.
**Owner** The Bottom Liners & Paul Saxton **Bred** W And R Barnett Ltd **Trained** Huby, N Yorks

**FOCUS**
A fair handicap in which nothing got seriously involved from off the pace and the winner made all.

## 5143 JONATHON JOYCE STORM ID H'CAP 7f 30y

**3:30** (3:30) (Class 4) (0-85,84) 3-Y-O+ **£6,469** (£1,925; £962; £481) **Stalls** Low

Form RPR

4210 **1** **Khelman (IRE)**[21] 4384 4-9-9 84 ........ GeorgeChaloner[(3)] 4 93
(Richard Fahey) *midfield: rdn and rn wd bnd over 3f out: hdwy over 2f out: led wl ins fnl f: hld on wl* **9/1**

1653 **2** *nk* **Ralphy Boy (IRE)**[13] 4661 5-8-13 76 ........ GarryWhillans[(5)] 1 84
(Alistair Whillans) *prom: rdn to ld appr fnl f: hdd wl ins fnl f: kpt on* **11/1**

4625 **3** *hd* **King Of Macedon (IRE)**[8] 4810 3-9-0 78 ........(b) JoeFanning 9 83
(Mark Johnston) *s.i.s: bhd: hdwy on outside over 3f out: styd on strly fnl f: jst hld* **6/1**[3]

0506 **4** *1* **Just Paul (IRE)**[13] 4661 4-9-5 77 ........ PJMcDonald 10 81
(Philip Kirby) *s.i.s: hld up: hdwy over 2f out: rdn and kpt on ins fnl f* **11/2**[2]

213 **5** *hd* **Red Pike (IRE)**[48] 3480 3-9-6 84 ........ PaulMulrennan 3 86+
(Bryan Smart) *led: rdn along and hdd appr fnl f: rallied: kpt on same pce last 100yds* **15/8**[1]

431 **6** *4* **Al Khan (IRE)**[12] 4707 5-9-4 81 6ex ........(p) JacobButterfield[(5)] 2 74
(Ollie Pears) *sn pushed along towards rr: hdwy over 2f out: rdn and no imp over 1f out* **7/1**

0032 **7** *4 1/2* **Powerful Presence (IRE)**[25] 4258 8-9-10 82 ........(v) DanielTudhope 6 64
(David O'Meara) *chsd ldr: rdn over 2f out: wknd over 1f out* **7/1**

2005 **8** *4* **Circuitous**[25] 4258 6-9-6 78 ........(v) TomEaves 7 49
(Keith Dalgleish) *prom: rdn over 2f out: wknd over 1f out* **33/1**

3145 **9** *13* **Mowhoob**[7] 4861 4-9-0 72 ........ GrahamLee 8 10
(Jim Goldie) *hld up towards rr: rdn over 2f out: nvr able to chal* **22/1**

1m 28.61s (-0.39) **Going Correction** +0.10s/f (Good)
**WFA** 3 from 4yo+ 6lb 9 Ran SP% **115.1**
Speed ratings (Par 105): **106,105,105,104,104 99,94,89,74**
CSF £101.94 CT £645.74 TOTE £11.70: £3.10, £3.20, £2.30; EX 61.30 Trifecta £474.40.
**Owner** S & G Clayton **Bred** Oghill House Stud & Jimmy Hyland **Trained** Musley Bank, N Yorks

**FOCUS**
It started to rain heavily before this race. They went a decent pace, but there still wasn't much covering the first five at the line.

## 5144 ARCHERFIELD CUP (H'CAP) 1m 6f

**4:00** (4:00) (Class 3) (0-95,95) 3-Y-O+ **£16,172** (£4,812; £2,405; £1,202) **Stalls** Centre

Form RPR

2001 **1** **Alex My Boy (IRE)**[36] 3884 3-9-1 95 ........ JoeFanning 10 109+
(Mark Johnston) *cl up: led over 3f out: pushed clr fr over 1f out: readily* **11/8**[1]

23 **2** *4* **Dark Ruler (IRE)**[107] 1651 5-9-2 83 ........ BenCurtis 11 90
(Alan Swinbank) *midfield: smooth hdwy to chal over 3f out: rdn over 2f out: edgd rt ent fnl f: one pce* **8/1**

6-0 **3** *1 1/4* **Lady Kashaan (IRE)**[112] 1562 5-9-8 89 ........ RobertWinston 6 94
(Alan Swinbank) *prom: rdn and effrt over 2f out: one pce fr over 1f out* **7/1**[3]

0006 **4** *3/4* **Be Perfect (USA)**[13] 4685 5-9-2 83 ........ AdrianNicholls 4 88
(David Nicholls) *chsd ldr: rdn over 2f out: one pce fr over 1f out: hld whn checked ent fnl f* **20/1**

1110 **5** *nk* **Saved By The Bell (IRE)**[28] 4173 4-9-7 88 ........ DanielTudhope 1 92
(David O'Meara) *t.k.h: hld up: effrt and pushed along over 2f out: no imp fr over 1f out* **7/2**[2]

03 **6** *1* **Love Marmalade (IRE)**[12] 4704 4-8-11 78 ........ PJMcDonald 3 80
(Alistair Whillans) *midfield: rdn along over 2f out: kpt on same pce over 1f out* **16/1**

3135 **7** *1/2* **Ex Oriente (IRE)**[13] 4685 5-8-10 77 ........ AdamBeschizza 2 79
(Stuart Williams) *s.i.s: hld up: rdn over 2f out: hdwy over 1f out: nvr able to chal* **16/1**

1500 **8** *3/4* **Jonny Delta**[55] 3240 7-8-13 80 ........ GrahamLee 8 81
(Jim Goldie) *hld up: stdy hdwy over 2f out: rdn and outpcd wl over 1f out* **16/1**

-650 **9** *40* **Inniscastle Boy**[25] 4259 5-8-6 76 oh31 ........(p) ConnorBeasley[(3)] 5 21
(Jim Goldie) *led to over 3f out: lost tch fr over 2f out: t.o* **100/1**

0/0- **10** *27* **Thimaar (USA)**[47] 2149 6-10-0 95 ........(p) TomEaves 9
(Donald McCain) *in tch: rdn 1/2-way: lost tch fnl 4f: t.o* **50/1**

3m 5.12s (-0.18) **Going Correction** +0.20s/f (Good)
**WFA** 3 from 4yo+ 13lb 10 Ran SP% **113.3**
Speed ratings (Par 107): **108,105,105,104,104 103,103,103,80,64**
CSF £12.52 CT £56.97 TOTE £2.30: £1.30, £1.80, £1.70; EX 11.90 Trifecta £51.30.
**Owner** Jaber Abdullah **Bred** Orpendale, Chelston & Wynatt **Trained** Middleham Moor, N Yorks

**FOCUS**
A solid contest won easily by a very progressive winner., who was well positioned throughout.

## 5145 BOOGIE IN THE MORNING H'CAP 1m 4f 100y

**4:30** (4:30) (Class 6) (0-65,67) 3-Y-O+ **£3,234** (£962; £481; £240) **Stalls** Centre

Form RPR

00-0 **1** **Titus Bolt (IRE)**[78] 2475 5-9-9 59 ........ GrahamLee 3 63
(Jim Goldie) *w ldr: led over 3f out to wl over 1f out: drvn and rallied to ld ins fnl f: kpt on strly* **3/1**[1]

0031 **2** *1 1/2* **Exclusive Contract (IRE)**[25] 4268 3-9-2 63 ........ PJMcDonald 7 65
(Ollie Pears) *chsd ldrs: effrt and rdn over 2f out: hung rt over 1f out: styd on fnl f: tk 2nd cl home* **4/1**[2]

1420 **3** *hd* **Rocky Two (IRE)**[23] 4319 4-9-4 54 ........ JoeFanning 1 56
(Philip Kirby) *t.k.h: prom: effrt over 2f out: kpt on ins fnl f* **3/1**[1]

4036 **4** *nse* **Royal Straight**[7] 4858 9-9-9 64 ........(t) SammyJoBell[(5)] 6 66
(Linda Perratt) *hld up: shkn up and gd hdwy to ld wl over 1f out: sn rdn: hdd ins fnl f: no ex and lost two pls nr fin* **5/1**[3]

1445 **5** *2 3/4* **Amazing Blue Sky**[12] 4709 8-9-3 53 ........ DaleSwift 5 50
(Ruth Carr) *led: rdn and hdd over 3f out: edgd rt and no ex over 1f out* **6/1**

0-00 **6** *53* **Idarose (IRE)**[21] 4387 5-8-6 45 ........ SamJames[(3)] 4
(John David Riches) *dwlt: in tch: rdn and outpcd over 3f out: sn btn* **66/1**

0 **7** *12* **Gios Last (GER)**[23] 4319 4-9-1 51 ........ TomEaves 2
(Keith Dalgleish) *t.k.h: hld up in tch on ins: rdn over 3f out: sn btn* **10/1**

2m 47.19s (5.19) **Going Correction** +0.30s/f (Good)
**WFA** 3 from 4yo+ 11lb 7 Ran SP% **111.5**
Speed ratings (Par 101): **94,93,92,92,91 55,47**
CSF £14.44 CT £36.57 TOTE £3.60: £2.80, £2.90; EX 16.90 Trifecta £74.10.
**Owner** Ian G M Dalgleish **Bred** Patrick Brady **Trained** Uplawmoor, E Renfrews

**FOCUS**
The going was changed to good all over before this race. An ordinary handicap run at an even tempo.

## 5146 TOM FINDLAY 70TH BIRTHDAY AMATEUR RIDERS' H'CAP 2m

**5:00** (5:01) (Class 5) (0-70,72) 4-Y-O+ **£3,119** (£967; £483; £242) **Stalls** High

Form RPR

5613 **1** **La Bacouetteuse (FR)**[10] 4769 9-11-0 68 ........(b) MissSBrotherton 6 77
(Iain Jardine) *in tch: stdy hdwy 1/2-way: led 3f out: sn pushed clr: kpt on wl fnl f* **11/4**[2]

2532 **2** *3* **Geanie Mac (IRE)**[7] 4856 5-9-10 55 ........(p) PhillipDennis[(5)] 1 59
(Linda Perratt) *led 2f: pressed ldr: ev ch 3f out: kpt on fnl f: nt pce of wnr* **6/1**[3]

0265 **3** *1 1/2* **Harrison's Cave**[7] 4856 6-10-6 60 ........ MissADeniel 4 62
(Keith Dalgleish) *t.k.h: prom: rdn over 2f out: kpt on ins fnl f* **7/1**

00/0 **4** *shd* **Top Billing**[18] 4492 5-10-3 60 ........(b) MissJRRichards[(3)] 7 62
(Nicky Richards) *hld up: outpcd over 4f out: rallied over 2f out: kpt on fnl f: nrst fin* **20/1**

1 **5** ½ **Point The Toes (IRE)**[4] 4962 9-10-13 **72** 6ex............(p) MrBPFahey(5) 3 73
(Mark Fahey, Ire) *hld up: niggled fr 1/2-way: hdwy on wd outside bnd over 3f out: pushed along and no imp fr 2f out* **15/8**[1]
/603 **6** *2* **Claude Carter**[17] 4522 10-9-9 **49** oh4................................ MrsCBartley 2 48
(Alistair Whillans) *chsd ldrs: effrt over 3f out: wknd over 1f out* **16/1**
0604 **7** *9* **Golden Future**[7] 4856 11-9-7 **50**........................ MissJoannaMason(3) 5 38
(Peter Niven) *led after 2f: rdn and hdd 3f out: sn btn* **15/2**

3m 38.97s (5.47) **Going Correction** +0.40s/f (Good) **7** Ran SP% **110.6**
Speed ratings (Par 103): **102,100,99,99,99 98,93**
CSF £18.12 TOTE £3.50: £1.80, £2.70; EX 11.80 Trifecta £102.40.
**Owner** Miss S A Booth **Bred** Sarl Classic Breeding & Maria R Mendes **Trained** Bonchester Bridge, Borders

**FOCUS**
They went no pace in this modest amateurs' staying event.
T/Jkpt: Part won. £14506.60 to a £1 stake. Pool of £20431.86 - 0.50 winning units. T/Plt: £180.20 to a £1 stake. Pool of £63414.81 - 256.77 winning tickets. T/Qpdt: £33.90 to a £1 stake. Pool of £6122.95 - 133.50 winning tickets. RY

## 4912 NEWMARKET (R-H)
Friday, August 8

**OFFICIAL GOING: Soft**
Wind: Light against Weather: Heavy showers

### 5147 FIRESTONE BUILDING PRODUCTS NURSERY H'CAP 7f
**5:40** (5:40) (Class 4) (0-85,79) 2-Y-O **£5,175** (£1,540; £769; £384) **Stalls** High

Form RPR
432 **1** **Azraff (IRE)**[35] 3924 2-9-3 **75**.............................................. MartinHarley 1 85+
(Marco Botti) *trckd ldr tl led over 2f out: rdn over 1f out: r.o: eased nr fin* **11/8**[1]
225 **2** *2* **Persun**[58] 3107 2-9-3 **75**................................................ JamesDoyle 5 79
(Mick Channon) *hld up: hdwy over 1f out: sn rdn and hung lft: chsd wnr fnl f: styd on* **15/2**[3]
6331 **3** *3* **Guilty (IRE)**[14] 4619 2-9-7 **79**..................................... RichardHughes 4 75
(Richard Hannon) *prom: rdn over 1f out: no ex ins fnl f* **7/4**[2]
500 **4** *nse* **Mywayalways (IRE)**[13] 4676 2-8-11 **69**.......................... AndreaAtzeni 6 64
(David Evans) *chsd ldrs: rdn over 1f out: no ex ins fnl f* **14/1**
5116 **5** *nk* **Disavow**[27] 4203 2-9-7 **79**........................................ SilvestreDeSousa 3 74
(Mark Johnston) *led: rdn and hdd over 2f out: no ex ins fnl f* **8/1**

1m 29.52s (3.82) **Going Correction** +0.40s/f (Good) **5** Ran SP% **108.0**
Speed ratings (Par 96): **94,91,88,88,87**
CSF £11.29 TOTE £2.60: £1.60, £2.90; EX 8.50 Trifecta £22.10.
**Owner** Saleh Al Homaizi & Imad Al Sagar **Bred** Lodge Park Stud **Trained** Newmarket, Suffolk

**FOCUS**
Far side track used with Stalls on Far side except 10f: Centre. Bend into home straight realigned and 10f race increased by 18m. Torrential rain before racing changed the ground completely and it was officially soft before the opener. This decent nursery was won in resounding fashion.

### 5148 POSI+IV (S) STKS 7f
**6:10** (6:11) (Class 5) 2-Y-O **£3,881** (£1,155; £577; £288) **Stalls** High

Form RPR
5 **1** **Honey Required**[30] 4075 2-8-8 0.............................................. AndreaAtzeni 6 62+
(William Haggas) *a.p: rdn over 2f out: led ins fnl f: r.o wl* **7/4**[1]
0 **2** *2¾* **Grenade**[59] 3082 2-8-13 0................................................ RichardHughes 3 59
(Richard Hannon) *led to 1/2-way: led again over 1f out: rdn and hdd ins fnl f: wknd towards fin* **9/1**
0644 **3** *nk* **Framley Garth (IRE)**[10] 4764 2-8-13 **59**.................. SilvestreDeSousa 4 58
(David Elsworth) *chsd ldrs: rdn over 1f out: hung lft ins fnl f: styd on: wnt 3rd nr fin* **5/1**[3]
6021 **4** *nk* **Ciaras Cookie (IRE)**[24] 4302 2-8-13 **67**............................ JamesDoyle 2 58
(David Evans) *up w the pce and racd alone towards centre tl shkn up to ld and hung lft over 2f out: rdn and hdd over 1f out: no ex ins fnl f* **10/3**[2]
000 **5** *2* **Father Stone**[14] 4618 2-8-13 **55**.......................................... HayleyTurner 5 53
(David Elsworth) *trckd ldr tl led 1/2-way: hdd over 2f out: rdn and ev ch over 1f out: no ex fnl f* **13/2**
05 **6** *1¾* **Madame Ascension**[34] 3967 2-8-3 0...................................... NoelGarbutt(5) 7 43
(David Evans) *sn pushed along in rr: hdwy 1/2-way: rdn over 2f out: styd on same pce fr over 1f out* **40/1**
**7** *23* **Deeper Magic (IRE)** 2-8-8 0............................................[1] PhilipPrince(5) 8
(J S Moore) *s.s: sn pushed along in rr: sme hdwy 4f out: sn wknd* **22/1**
650 **8** *19* **Endislie (IRE)**[56] 3201 2-8-13 **58**.............................................. LiamJones 1
(J S Moore) *s.i.s: hdwy over 4f out: rdn and wknd over 2f out* **20/1**

1m 29.52s (3.82) **Going Correction** +0.475s/f (Yiel) **8** Ran SP% **111.0**
Speed ratings (Par 94): **97,93,93,93,90 88,62,40**
CSF £17.15 TOTE £2.90: £1.10, £2.20, £2.90; EX 13.60 Trifecta £53.00.
**Owner** M S Bloodstock Ltd **Bred** Mike Smith **Trained** Newmarket, Suffolk

**FOCUS**
A poor race for the track but the winner did it well on this drop in grade.

### 5149 FIRESTONE BUILDING PRODUCTS MAIDEN STKS (BOBIS RACE) 7f
**6:45** (6:46) (Class 4) 2-Y-O **£3,881** (£1,155; £577; £288) **Stalls** High

Form RPR
**1** **Gibeon (IRE)** 2-9-5 0.................................................... JamesDoyle 1 85+
(Richard Hannon) *edgd rt s: hld up: hdwy over 1f out: edgd lft and r.o to ld nr fin* **16/1**
**2** *hd* **Acaster Malbis (FR)** 2-9-5 0........................................ RichardHughes 2 84+
(Richard Hannon) *s.i.s: hld up: pushed along 1/2-way: hdwy over 1f out: rdn to ld and hung lft ins fnl f: hdd nr fin* **10/3**[1]
**3** *1½* **Bartel (IRE)** 2-9-5 0...................................................... JackMitchell 8 80+
(Ed Vaughan) *s.i.s: hld up: hdwy over 1f out: rdn and ev ch ins fnl f: edgd lft: styd on same pce* **33/1**
**4** *3* **Beach Samba (IRE)** 2-9-5 0...................................... FrankieDettori 4 72+
(Ed Dunlop) *sn led: shkn up and edgd lft over 1f out: hdd and no ex ins fnl f* **10/1**
**5** *1* **Banditry (IRE)** 2-9-5 0................................................[1] KierenFallon 10 70
(Michael Bell) *prom: shkn up over 2f out: styd on same pce fr over 1f out* **16/1**
**6** *½* **Voice Control (IRE)** 2-9-5 0............................................ ShaneKelly 5 70+
(Sir Michael Stoute) *dwlt: sn pushed along in rr: r.o ins fnl f: nrst fin* **20/1**
**7** *1½* **Spiriting (IRE)** 2-9-5 0............................................... AndreaAtzeni 3 64+
(Luca Cumani) *prom: rdn and ev ch over 1f out: sn hung lft: wknd ins fnl f* **13/2**
**8** *2¾* **Hills And Dales (IRE)** 2-9-5 0.............................. SilvestreDeSousa 9 57+
(Charlie Appleby) *w ldr tl shkn up over 2f out: wkng whn hmpd over 1f out* **8/1**
**9** *4* **Inshaa** 2-9-5 0................................................................. LiamJones 6 46
(Sir Michael Stoute) *prom tl rdn and wknd over 1f out* **5/1**[3]
**10** *shd* **Forza Blacky** 2-9-0 0........................................... DannyBrock(5) 7 46
(Philip McBride) *prom: rdn over 2f out: wknd over 1f out* **20/1**
**11** *6* **Emirates Skycargo (IRE)** 2-9-5 0.................................... WilliamBuick 11 30
(Charlie Appleby) *chsd ldrs: pushed along 1/2-way: wknd 2f out* **9/2**[2]
**12** *44* **Katniss (IRE)** 2-8-7 0........................................... AaronJones(7) 12
(Stuart Williams) *in rr: hung lft and wknd 1/2-way* **100/1**

1m 29.28s (3.58) **Going Correction** +0.55s/f (Yiel) **12** Ran SP% **116.7**
Speed ratings (Par 96): **101,100,99,95,94 93,92,89,84,84 77,27**
CSF £65.34 TOTE £21.90: £6.20, £2.10, £8.70; EX 65.70 Trifecta £1625.00 Part won. Pool of £2166.74 - 0.36 winning units..
**Owner** Gillian, Lady Howard De Walden **Bred** Avington Manor Stud **Trained** East Everleigh, Wilts
■ Stewards' Enquiry : Andrea Atzeni two-day ban: careless riding (Aug 25-26)

**FOCUS**
A fascinating maiden featuring a whole host of well-bred two-year-old's from top yards and, as is often the case here, they got racing from quite a long way out, setting it up for horses to get involved from off the pace. Richard Hannon's pair dominated the finish but several in behind showed promise and this contest is likely to throw up a raft of future winners.

### 5150 32RED CASINO H'CAP 1m 2f
**7:15** (7:18) (Class 5) (0-75,74) 3-Y-O+ **£3,881** (£1,155; £577; £288) **Stalls** Centre

Form RPR
121 **1** **Giantstepsahead (IRE)**[24] 4303 5-9-13 **73**.................... JackMitchell 9 85
(Denis Quinn) *mde all: rdn over 1f out: hung lft ins fnl f: styd on* **8/1**
2542 **2** *2* **Red Velour**[20] 4434 3-9-4 **73**........................................ WilliamBuick 3 81
(Jeremy Noseda) *a.p: chsd wnr over 3f out: rdn over 1f out: styd on same pce ins fnl f* **9/4**[1]
011/ **3** *9* **Daaree (IRE)**[668] 6972 4-9-9 **69**........................................ DaneO'Neill 4 60
(Saeed bin Suroor) *dwlt: hld up: hdwy over 2f out: wknd over 1f out* **9/4**[1]
0436 **4** *3½* **She's Gorgeous (IRE)**[34] 3974 3-9-3 **72**........................ AndreaAtzeni 6 56
(James Fanshawe) *prom: rdn over 2f out: wknd over 1f out* **9/2**[2]
0450 **5** *5* **Warlu Way**[6] 4921 7-10-0 **74**........................................ KierenFallon 1 49
(Michael Easterby) *s.s: bhd: effrt over 3f out: wknd over 2f out* **12/1**
4-00 **6** *4* **Volcanic Jack (IRE)**[14] 4620 6-8-2 **55**........................ BradleyBosley(7) 11 22
(Michael Chapman) *plld hrd: trckd ldr tl rdn over 3f out: wknd over 2f out* **66/1**
002 **7** *5* **Indian Trifone (IRE)**[21] 4402 4-9-11 **71**............................ JamesDoyle 7 29
(Ed Walker) *hld up: rdn over 3f out: hung lft and wknd over 2f out* **6/1**[3]

2m 10.65s (5.15) **Going Correction** +0.625s/f (Yiel)
**WFA** 3 from 4yo+ 9lb **7** Ran SP% **114.3**
Speed ratings (Par 103): **104,102,95,92,88 85,81**
CSF £26.39 CT £54.37 TOTE £5.90: £2.90, £2.00; EX 22.40 Trifecta £54.10.
**Owner** K Hills **Bred** Darragh O'Reilly **Trained** Newmarket, Suffolk
■ Stewards' Enquiry : Kieren Fallon jockey said colt was slowly away
James Doyle jockey said colt had no more to give

**FOCUS**
The rain was getting heavier and conditions took their toll as they trailed in at long intervals here.

### 5151 THOROUGHBRED BREEDERS' ASSOCIATION EBF STALLIONS FILLIES' H'CAP 1m
**7:50** (7:50) (Class 3) (0-95,89) 3-Y-O+ **£9,703** (£2,887; £1,443; £721) **Stalls** High

Form RPR
21-1 **1** **Water Hole (IRE)**[29] 4112 3-9-5 **87**.................................. WilliamBuick 6 102
(John Gosden) *mde all: rdn over 1f out: r.o* **5/4**[1]
01-1 **2** *2* **Fray**[14] 4623 3-8-13 **81**................................................ JamesDoyle 2 90
(Roger Charlton) *hmpd s: hld up in tch: chsd wnr over 1f out: sn rdn: no imp ins fnl f* **7/4**[2]
1046 **3** *8* **Nirva (IRE)**[42] 3672 3-8-8 **76**........................ SilvestreDeSousa 5 64
(Ralph Beckett) *prom: rdn over 1f out: wknd fnl f* **5/1**[3]
11 **4** *¾* **Etaab (USA)**[15] 4573 3-9-7 **89**........................................ DaneO'Neill 4 75
(William Haggas) *w wnr tl rdn over 1f out: wknd ins fnl f* **13/2**

1m 47.88s (7.88) **Going Correction** +0.70s/f (Yiel) **4** Ran SP% **110.8**
Speed ratings (Par 104): **88,86,78,77**
CSF £3.85 TOTE £2.00; EX 3.30 Trifecta £8.50.
**Owner** W S Farish **Bred** Barronstown Stud **Trained** Newmarket, Suffolk

**FOCUS**
A good quality fillies' handicap featuring at least two fillies that could be well ahead of their marks, but conditions were dreadful and it was a case of who handled them best.

### 5152 £10 FREE BET AT 32REDSPORT.COM H'CAP 6f
**8:20** (8:20) (Class 3) (0-95,94) 3-Y-O+ **£7,762** (£2,310; £1,154; £577) **Stalls** High

Form RPR
4130 **1** **Forest Edge (IRE)**[12] 4700 5-9-7 **89**..............................(b) JFEgan 11 97
(David Evans) *led far side duo tl hdd over 1f out: rallied to ld wl ins fnl f: 1st of 2 that side* **5/1**[2]
1160 **2** *1¼* **Links Drive Lady**[39] 3788 6-9-6 **88**................................ KierenFallon 7 92
(Dean Ivory) *chsd wnr far side tl led overall and hung rt over 1f out: rdn and hdd wl ins fnl f: styd on same pce: last of 2 that side* **13/2**[3]
3003 **3** *1½* **Secret Witness**[6] 4889 8-9-10 **92**..............................(b) SteveDrowne 3 91
(Ronald Harris) *stall opened fractionally early: chsd ldr centre to 1/2-way: rdn and outpcd over 1f out: rallied to ld that gp ins fnl f: r.o: nt rch far side duo: 1st of 4 in gp* **8/1**
0002 **4** *2* **Zanetto**[10] 4765 4-9-12 **94**........................................(v[1]) WilliamBuick 2 87
(Andrew Balding) *s.i.s: sn rcvrd to ld overall in centre: rdn and hdd over 1f out: no ex ins fnl f: 2nd of 4 in gp* **5/2**[1]
3344 **5** *3¼* **Our Queenie (IRE)**[13] 4669 3-9-2 **88**............................ RichardHughes 5 69
(Richard Hannon) *racd centre: hld up: rdn over 1f out: wknd fnl f: 3rd of 4 in gp* **5/2**[1]
-620 **6** *½* **Holley Shiftwell**[20] 4445 4-8-13 **81**............................ AndreaAtzeni 6 62
(Stuart Williams) *racd centre: prom: chsd ldr 1/2-way: rdn over 1f out: wknd ins fnl f: last of 4 in gp* **8/1**

1m 16.02s (3.52) **Going Correction** +0.775s/f (Yiel)
**WFA** 3 from 4yo+ 4lb **6** Ran SP% **109.4**
Speed ratings (Par 107): **107,105,103,100,96 95**
CSF £33.86 CT £231.76 TOTE £5.40: £2.40, £3.10; EX 27.20 Trifecta £133.20.
**Owner** P & K Swinnerton **Bred** Alberto Panetta **Trained** Pandy, Monmouths

**FOCUS**
This might be misleading form as they appeared to go off too fast and the two that stayed on the far rail finished first and second, so there may have been a track bias in play.
T/Plt: £1163.40 to a £1 stake. Pool of £65664.64 - 41.20 winning units. T/Qpdt: £270.40 to a £1 stake. Pool of £6213.37 - 17.00 winning units. CR

5153 - (Foreign Racing) - See Raceform Interactive

## 4226 TIPPERARY (L-H)

Friday, August 8

**OFFICIAL GOING: Good to firm**

### 5154a KILFRUSH STUD ABERGWAUN STKS (LISTED RACE) 5f

**6:05** (6:06) 3-Y-O+ **£27,083** (£7,916; £3,750; £1,250)

RPR

1 **Sir Maximilian (IRE)**[6] 4895 5-9-7 103 StevieDonohoe 7 109
(Tim Pitt) *towards rr early: 6th 1/2-way: swtchd to outer in 4th 1f out: styd on strly to ld in clsng stages* **2/1**[2]

2 ¾ **Abstraction (IRE)**[169] 680 4-9-7 106 SeamieHeffernan 8 106
(Sarah Dawson, Ire) *broke wl and racd in cl 2nd on nr side: led 1/2-way and edgd lft appr fnl f: styd on wl tl hdd in clsng stages* **16/1**

3 nk **Russian Soul (IRE)**[26] 4235 6-9-12 111 (p) ShaneFoley 6 110
(M Halford, Ire) *trckd ldrs in 4th: rdn fr 2f out: chsd ldr in 2nd whn edgd lft 1f out: kpt on same pce and dropped to 3rd in clsng stages* **13/8**[1]

4 2 ¼ **Jamesie (IRE)**[26] 4235 6-9-7 104 ColmO'Donoghue 3 97
(David Marnane, Ire) *hld up in rr: rdn over 2f out: stl last 1f out: kpt on wl ins fnl f into 4th cl home: nvr nrr* **5/1**[3]

5 ½ **One Chance (IRE)**[55] 3245 3-9-0 95 ow1 TomQueally 2 90
(John Butler) *chsd ldrs far side: n.m.r 2f out and sn rdn: kpt on into 5th ins fnl f: nvr on terms* **14/1**

6 1 ¾ **My Good Brother (IRE)**[19] 4480 5-9-7 102 (v) ColinKeane 5 89
(T G McCourt, Ire) *trckd ldrs in 3rd towards far side: wnt 2nd 1/2-way: no imp in 3rd whn squeezed for room and snatched up 1f out: sn no ex* **9/1**

7 4 ¼ **Best Be Careful (IRE)**[3] 5021 6-9-2 65 FMBerry 9 69
(John James Feane, Ire) *broke wl and led to 1/2-way: wknd fnl f* **150/1**

56.5s (-2.50)
**WFA** 3 from 4yo+ 3lb 7 Ran SP% **111.3**
CSF £30.54 TOTE £3.40: £2.20, £4.80; DF 38.20 Trifecta £148.90.
**Owner** Paul Wildes **Bred** Holborn Trust Co **Trained** Market Drayton, Shropshire

**FOCUS**
The winner is well suited to a fast 5f and is on the up. The second and third help to confirm the level.

## 4695 ASCOT (R-H)

Saturday, August 9

**OFFICIAL GOING: Good (good to soft in places)**
Wind: Moderate, half against Weather: Fine

### 5160 DUBAI DUTY FREE SHERGAR CUP DASH (H'CAP) 5f

**12:55** (12:56) (Class 2) (0-105,105) 3-Y-O+

**£19,672** (£6,888; £3,148; £2,456; £2,164; £1,576) **Stalls** High

Form RPR

1432 1 **Goldream**[14] 4683 5-9-3 98 (p) CraigAWilliams 10 107
(Robert Cowell) *prom: effrt over 1f out: chsd ldr jst ins fnl f: drvn and r.o to ld last strides* **7/2**[1]

4061 2 hd **Move In Time**[22] 4405 6-9-5 100 OlivierPeslier 3 108
(David O'Meara) *prom: prog to ld jst over 1f out: drvn and styd on but hdd last strides* **4/1**[2]

000 3 1 ¼ **Ballesteros**[56] 3241 5-9-2 97 HayleyTurner 2 101
(Richard Fahey) *sweating: awkward s: last early: prog fr 1/2-way: drvn to take 2nd briefly 1f out: one pce after* **25/1**

620 4 nk **Bondesire**[14] 4683 4-9-2 97 S'mangaKhumalo 11 99
(David O'Meara) *dwlt: wl in rr: last 2f out: swtchd rt over 1f out and drvn: styd on fnl f: nrst fin* **15/2**

4105 5 ¾ **Swan Song**[63] 2989 5-9-5 100 FrankieDettori 6 100
(Andrew Balding) *trckd ldrs: nt clr run wl over 1f out: rdn and one pce after* **6/1**[3]

0430 6 nk **Addictive Dream (IRE)**[56] 3241 7-9-8 103 RichardHughes 5 102
(David Nicholls) *led to jst over 1f out: fdd* **8/1**

0-66 7 shd **Kingsgate Choice (IRE)**[90] 2197 7-9-10 105 StefanieHofer 1 103
(Ed de Giles) *settled in rr: rdn and tried to make prog over 1f out: no hdwy fnl f* **16/1**

0001 8 ½ **Racy**[13] 4700 7-9-6 101 (p) YuichiFukunaga 12 97
(Brian Ellison) *hld up in rr: rdn over 1f out: one pce and no imp on ldrs* **7/1**

2006 9 ½ **Annunciation**[7] 4889 4-9-6 101 TomQueally 8 96
(Richard Hannon) *in tch: lost pl 2f: last over 1f out: no hdwy after* **16/1**

0255 10 ½ **Masamah (IRE)**[13] 4700 8-9-6 101 (p) Emma-JayneWilson 9 94
(Marco Botti) *trckd ldr to 2f out: sn lost pl u.p* **8/1**

1m 1.27s (0.77) **Going Correction** +0.20s/f (Good) 10 Ran SP% **118.6**
Speed ratings (Par 109): **101,100,98,98,97 96,96,95,94,93**
CSF £17.72 CT £312.17 TOTE £4.40: £2.10, £2.00, £4.60; EX 21.50 Trifecta £576.60.
**Owner** J Sargeant & Mrs J Morley **Bred** Tsega Breeding Limited **Trained** Six Mile Bottom, Cambs

**FOCUS**
Rail on Round course out 3yds at 12f increased to 9yds at bend into home straight. Old Mile increased by 10yds, 12f by 14yds and 2m by 16yds. As ever with this novelty event, the form of the races needs treating with caution. Frankie Dettori and Hayley Turner both described the ground as riding "good" on the straight course. The market leaders came to the fore in this good-quality sprint and the winner recorded a new personal best.

### 5161 DUBAI DUTY FREE SHERGAR CUP STAYERS (H'CAP) 2m

**1:30** (1:30) (Class 2) (0-100,100) 4-Y-O+

**£19,672** (£6,888; £3,148; £2,456; £2,164; £1,576) **Stalls** Low

Form RPR

1-04 1 **Retirement Plan**[13] 4696 4-9-8 94 Emma-JayneWilson 3 103
(Lady Cecil) *led 2f: trckd ldrs: 4th 4f out: rdn to chse clr ldr jst over 2f out: grad clsd u.p: led last 150yds: styd on* **7/1**

0530 2 1 ¼ **Buckland (IRE)**[15] 4622 6-8-12 84 AdriedeVries 7 91
(Charlie Fellowes) *impeded s: rapid prog to ld after 2f: sent for home and clr 2f out: hdd and no ex last 150yds* **25/1**

1612 3 2 ¼ **Hassle (IRE)**[15] 4606 5-9-9 95 (p) OlivierPeslier 1 99+
(Clive Cox) *hld up in last trio: prog whn nt clr run 2f out: hdwy to take 3rd 1f out: styd on but no ch to threaten* **7/2**[1]

1255 4 ½ **Debdebdeb**[28] 4213 4-9-4 90 YuichiFukunaga 6 94+
(Andrew Balding) *v awkward s: t.k.h: hld up in last pair: stl last 3f out: prog on inner fr 2f out: styd on to take 4th nr fin: too much to do* **17/2**

0001 5 nk **Moidore**[71] 2739 5-9-1 87 StefanieHofer 5 90
(John Quinn) *hld up in midfield: pushed along in 7th 4f out: no prog over 2f out: styd on fnl f to take 5th nr fin* **20/1**

1-00 6 ¾ **Big Thunder**[11] 4759 4-9-10 96 S'mangaKhumalo 10 98
(Sir Mark Prescott Bt) *tk fierce hold: hld up in last trio tl plld way through to go 3rd 1/2-way: lost pl 2f out: wknd ins fnl f* **8/1**

2213 7 2 ¼ **Kashgar**[15] 4606 5-8-11 83 RichardHughes 2 83
(Bernard Llewellyn) *mostly in midfield: drvn to dispute 3rd briefly 2f out: wknd fnl f* **8/1**

8 nse **Edge Of Sanity (IRE)**[42] 3740 5-9-11 97 JimmyFortune 11 97
(Brian Ellison) *hld up in last pair: rdn over 3f out: stl last over 1f out: kpt on fnl f: no ch* **5/1**[2]

0-22 9 ¾ **Earth Amber**[101] 1869 5-10-0 100 HayleyTurner 4 99
(Nicky Henderson) *trckd ldrs: rdn in 5th 4f out: tried to make prog 2f out: fdd over 1f out* **6/1**[3]

0102 10 2 **Sir Frank Morgan (IRE)**[4] 5017 4-8-10 82 FrankieDettori 8 78
(Mark Johnston) *prom: trckd ldr 1/2-way: rdn over 3f out: lost pl jst over 2f out: wknd over 1f out* **7/1**

3m 35.46s (6.46) **Going Correction** +0.20s/f (Good) 10 Ran SP% **119.5**
Speed ratings (Par 109): **91,90,89,89,88 88,87,87,86,85**
CSF £167.18 CT £721.39 TOTE £6.30: £2.30, £6.30, £1.40; EX 237.30 Trifecta £1462.20.
**Owner** K Abdullah **Bred** Juddmonte Farms Ltd **Trained** Newmarket, Suffolk

**FOCUS**
They went an average gallop and it paid to race handily, with the first and second up there throughout.

### 5162 DUBAI DUTY FREE SHERGAR CUP CHALLENGE (H'CAP) 1m 4f

**2:05** (2:05) (Class 3) (0-95,94) 4-Y-O+

**£19,726** (£6,942; £3,202; £2,510; £2,218; £1,630) **Stalls** Low

Form RPR

-40 1 **Semeen**[53] 3341 5-9-2 88 TomQueally 7 96
(Luca Cumani) *trckd ldrs: prog over 2f out: shkn up to ld over 1f out: in command fnl f: readily* **6/1**[2]

-035 2 1 ½ **Proud Chieftain**[14] 4667 6-9-6 92 (p) StefanieHofer 6 98
(Clifford Lines) *trckd ldrs: pushed along and lost pl sltly 2f out: styd on fr over 1f out to win battle for 2nd nr fin: no ch w wnr* **20/1**

3433 3 nse **Communicator**[94] 2073 6-9-8 94 AdriedeVries 8 100+
(Andrew Balding) *hld up in rr: prog on inner 2f out: angled out 1f out: shkn up and styd on to dispute 2nd nr fin: no ch to chal* **5/1**[1]

25-0 4 nk **Bantam (IRE)**[70] 2783 4-9-3 89 OlivierPeslier 4 95
(Ed Dunlop) *trckd ldr to 4f out: styd prom: chal on inner 2f out: chsd wnr over 1f out: no imp and lost 2 pls wl ins fnl f* **5/1**[1]

1513 5 ¾ **Presburg (IRE)**[15] 4608 5-9-5 91 CraigAWilliams 2 95
(Joseph Tuite) *hld up in midfield: clsd on ldrs fr 2f out: pressed for a pl 1f out: nt qckn after* **7/1**[3]

0060 6 1 **Viewpoint (IRE)**[11] 4756 5-9-5 91 RichardHughes 11 94
(Richard Hannon) *prom: trckd ldr 4f: rdn to ld 2f out to over 1f out: fdd last 100yds* **7/1**[3]

0165 7 ¾ **Charles Camoin (IRE)**[11] 4756 6-9-3 89 YuichiFukunaga 12 91
(Sylvester Kirk) *hld up in midfield: lost pl and in rr over 4f out: rdn and no real imp on ldrs fnl 2f* **8/1**

101 8 4 **Cashpoint**[37] 3907 9-9-4 90 HayleyTurner 13 85
(Ian Williams) *t.k.h: hld up in last trio: rdn and no prog over 2f out: wknd fnl f* **8/1**

1555 9 19 **Boonga Roogeta**[21] 4442 5-9-3 89 JimmyFortune 10 54
(Peter Charalambous) *led and stretched field out: hdd & wknd rapidly 2f out: t.o* **20/1**

6403 P **Grandorio (IRE)**[14] 4685 4-9-2 88 FrankieDettori 1
(David O'Meara) *nvr gng wl: detached in last after 4f: t.o 4f out: p.u and dismntd nr fin* **7/1**[3]

2m 35.33s (2.83) **Going Correction** +0.20s/f (Good) 10 Ran SP% **116.9**
Speed ratings (Par 107): **98,97,96,96,96 95,95,92,79,**
CSF £117.27 CT £637.28 TOTE £4.70: £2.00, £6.60, £1.90; EX 142.20 Trifecta £737.70.
**Owner** Sheikh Mohammed Obaid Al Maktoum **Bred** Darley **Trained** Newmarket, Suffolk

**FOCUS**
This was run at a fair gallop. The winner enjoyed a nice trip.

### 5163 DUBAI DUTY FREE SHERGAR CUP MILE (H'CAP) 1m (R)

**2:40** (2:40) (Class 2) (0-100,102) 4-Y-O+

**£19,672** (£6,888; £3,148; £2,456; £2,164; £1,576) **Stalls** Low

Form RPR

0005 1 **Don't Call Me (IRE)**[14] 4648 7-9-2 95 (t) Emma-JayneWilson 1 103
(David Nicholls) *trckd ldrs: clsd 2f out: drvn to chal over 1f out: narrow ld jst ins fnl f: hld on wl* **5/1**[2]

4112 2 nk **Tenor (IRE)**[13] 4711 4-9-9 102 (t) S'mangaKhumalo 5 109
(John Ryan) *trckd ldr 2f: styd cl up: rdn to chal over 1f out: pressed wnr fnl f: styd on but a jst hld* **10/1**

0423 3 shd **Magic City (IRE)**[8] 4851 5-9-6 99 TomQueally 3 106
(Richard Hannon) *stdd s and then s.i.s: hld up in last trio: prog on inner over 2f out: chal over 1f out: pressed wnr fnl f: nt qckn last 75yds* **4/1**[1]

1312 4 ½ **Dark Emerald (IRE)**[35] 3964 4-9-5 98 OlivierPeslier 11 104
(Brendan Powell) *trckd ldr after 2f: led over 2f out: drvn and hdd jst ins fnl f: one pce* **11/2**[3]

-450 5 ½ **Bancnuanaheireann (IRE)**[97] 1973 7-9-4 97 YuichiFukunaga 2 101
(Michael Appleby) *hld up in midfield: prog to chse ldng quartet over 1f out: kpt on but nvr able to chal* **14/1**

1452 6 1 ¾ **Hit The Jackpot (IRE)**[15] 4608 5-9-3 96 JimmyFortune 4 96
(David O'Meara) *hld up in last trio: stl there 2f out: rdn over 1f out: kpt on but nvr in it* **5/1**[2]

0002 7 ¾ **Ingleby Angel (IRE)**[19] 4491 5-9-5 98 RichardHughes 10 97
(David O'Meara) *hld up in last trio: rdn and no prog on outer 2f out: one pce after* **9/1**

3100 8 ¾ **Two For Two (IRE)**[8] 4851 6-9-8 101 CraigAWilliams 7 98
(David O'Meara) *hld up in midfield: rdn and no prog 2f out: n.d after* **13/2**

9 ¾ **Energia Flavio (BRZ)**[301] 4-9-7 100 HayleyTurner 12 95
(Marco Botti) *t.k.h: sn trckd ldng trio: rdn over 2f out: wknd over 1f out* **20/1**

0-10 10 12 **Navajo Chief**[28] 4212 7-9-7 100 AdriedeVries 6 68
(Timothy Jarvis) *led to over 2f out: wknd rapidly over 1f out: t.o* **20/1**

1m 42.84s (2.14) **Going Correction** +0.20s/f (Good) 10 Ran SP% **117.3**
Speed ratings (Par 109): **97,96,96,96,95 93,93,92,91,79**
CSF £54.49 CT £216.66 TOTE £5.60: £1.80, £3.30, £1.60; EX 58.60 Trifecta £306.90.
**Owner** Matt & Lauren Morgan **Bred** Darley **Trained** Sessay, N Yorks

**FOCUS**
An open handicap in which several held a chance inside the final furlong.

## 5164 DUBAI DUTY FREE SHERGAR CUP CLASSIC (H'CAP) (BOBIS RACE) 1m 4f
3:15 (3:18) (Class 3) (0-95,93) 3-Y-O

£19,672 (£6,888; £3,148; £2,456; £2,164; £1,576) Stalls Low

Form RPR
0122 1 **Our Gabrial (IRE)**[14] 4651 3-9-5 85 OlivierPeslier 5 95
(Richard Fahey) *hld up in last and detached off str pce: cajoled along and prog on outer over 2f out: jnd ldr fnl f: couple of reminders and won on the nod* 8/1[3]
210 2 nse **Astronereus (IRE)**[9] 4821 3-9-6 86 Emma-JayneWilson 8 96+
(Amanda Perrett) *hld up in midfield: trckd ldrs 4f out: clsd on outer to ld over 1f out: jnd fnl f: disputing ld whn rdr dropped whip 75yds out: jst pipped* 6/1[2]
6414 3 1 1/4 **Snow Squall**[16] 4584 3-9-5 85 AdriedeVries 6 93
(Mark Johnston) *hld up in last pair and detached off str pce early: rdn and prog on outer over 2f out: chal 1f out: nt qckn last 100yds* 10/1
0046 4 2 1/2 **Swivel**[13] 4696 3-9-8 88 JimmyFortune 1 92
(Mark Johnston) *hld up towards rr: in last pair over 2f out: rdn and prog wl over 1f out: kpt on one pce to take 4th ins fnl f* 8/1[3]
4313 5 1 3/4 **Raise Your Gaze**[13] 4698 3-9-7 87 HayleyTurner 9 88
(Clive Cox) *hld up in midfield: clsd on ldrs over 2f out: rdn to ld briefly wl over 1f out: wknd fnl f* 12/1
110 6 3 3/4 **From Frost**[30] 4113 3-9-10 90 (t) StefanieHofer 4 85
(Andrew Balding) *hld up in midfield: towards rr whn shkn up over 2f out: no real prog after* 16/1
2623 7 7 **Mr Gallivanter (IRE)**[22] 4392 3-9-2 82 CraigAWilliams 2 66
(John Quinn) *t.k.h: trckd ldr to 6f out: cl up 2f out: sn wknd* 16/1
2120 8 1 1/2 **Pack Leader (IRE)**[7] 4893 3-9-9 89 TomQueally 3 71
(Amanda Perrett) *prom: trckd ldr 6f out to 5f out: rdn to chal 2f out: wknd over 1f out* 20/1
011 9 10 **Wrangler**[77] 2566 3-9-13 93 FrankieDettori 12 59
(William Haggas) *racd wd: prog fr midfield to trck ldr 5f out: rdn to ld v briefly 2f out but hanging: wknd qckly over 1f out* 2/1[1]
0061 10 1/2 **Trip To Paris (IRE)**[14] 4651 3-9-10 90 (b) S'mangaKhumalo 11 55
(Ed Dunlop) *mde most at str pce: hdd & wknd rapidly 2f out* 6/1[2]

2m 33.06s (0.56) **Going Correction** +0.20s/f (Good) 10 Ran SP% 117.4
Speed ratings (Par 104): **106,105,105,103,102 99,95,94,87,87**
CSF £55.82 CT £490.74 TOTE £8.20: £2.70, £2.40, £3.50; EX 60.70 Trifecta £525.20.
**Owner** Dr Marwan Koukash **Bred** Michael Woodlock & Seamus Kennedy **Trained** Musley Bank, N Yorks

**FOCUS**
Run at a strong gallop, the early leaders fell in a hole over 2f out with the closers dominating.

## 5165 DUBAI DUTY FREE SHERGAR CUP SPRINT (H'CAP) (BOBIS RACE) 6f
3:50 (3:53) (Class 2) (0-100,98) 3-Y-O

£19,672 (£6,888; £3,148; £2,456; £2,164; £1,576) Stalls High

Form RPR
0331 1 **Highland Acclaim (IRE)**[7] 4918 3-9-4 94 RichardHughes 2 104
(David O'Meara) *stdd s: t.k.h: hld up in rr: prog 2f out: rdn over 1f out: clsd to ld last 100yds: jst hld on* 7/2[1]
2136 2 nse **Golden Steps (FR)**[14] 4669 3-9-2 92 JimmyFortune 1 102
(Marco Botti) *hld up towards rr: rdn and prog 2f out: clsd to chal fnl f: w wnr last 100yds: jst pipped* 5/1[2]
0124 3 2 1/4 **Remember**[14] 4668 3-9-6 96 CraigAWilliams 10 99
(Richard Hannon) *trckd ldng pair: led jst over 2f out gng strly: rdn fnl f: hdd and folded last 100yds* 5/1[2]
611 4 1/2 **Telmeyd**[33] 4021 3-9-7 97 StefanieHofer 12 98+
(William Haggas) *completely blew s: detached in last: pushed along 1/2-way: prog on outer 2f out: rdn and kpt on same pce fnl f* 7/2[1]
-450 5 1 1/2 **Sir Robert Cheval**[92] 2111 3-9-3 93 YuichiFukunaga 4 90
(Marco Botti) *trckd ldrs: rdn to dispute 2nd briefly over 1f out: wknd fnl f* 16/1
5520 6 1 1/2 **No Leaf Clover (IRE)**[29] 4166 3-9-2 92 (p) S'mangaKhumalo 9 84
(Ollie Pears) *nvr beyond midfield: rdn and no prog 2f out: hanging and wknd over 1f out* 8/1[3]
0010 7 1 1/2 **Deeds Not Words (IRE)**[14] 4669 3-9-6 96 AdriedeVries 8 83
(Mick Channon) *led to jst over 2f out: wknd over 1f out* 10/1
0300 8 hd **Major Crispies**[29] 4166 3-9-7 97 Emma-JayneWilson 3 83
(James Eustace) *chsd ldrs: rdn 2f out: wknd over 1f out* 16/1
30-3 9 2 1/4 **Umneyati**[25] 4281 3-9-4 94 TomQueally 11 73
(James Tate) *t.k.h: trckd ldrs: lost pl 1/2-way: wl in rr fnl 2f* 20/1
-300 10 6 **Rufford (IRE)**[56] 3253 3-9-8 98 (p) FrankieDettori 13 58
(Richard Fahey) *chsd ldr: rdn 1/2-way: sn lost pl and btn: wknd over 1f out* 12/1

1m 14.23s (-0.27) **Going Correction** +0.20s/f (Good) 10 Ran SP% 122.2
Speed ratings (Par 106): **109,108,105,105,103 101,99,99,96,88**
CSF £22.03 CT £92.10 TOTE £4.40: £1.90, £1.80, £2.10; EX 23.90 Trifecta £116.60.
**Owner** Evan M Sutherland **Bred** Rathbarry Stud **Trained** Nawton, N Yorks
■ Stewards' Enquiry : Richard Hughes two-day ban: used whip above permitted level (Aug 23-24)
Jimmy Fortune two-day ban: used whip above permitted level (Aug 24-25)

**FOCUS**
Run at a sound gallop, the front pair pulled away close home, having come from off the pace, in this decent sprint.
T/Plt: £121.10 to a £1 stake. Pool of £139873.40 - 842.70 winning tickets. T/Qpdt: £25.70 to a £1 stake. Pool of £10001.27 - 287.07 winning tickets. JN

# 4723 AYR (L-H)
Saturday, August 9

**OFFICIAL GOING: Good to soft (good in places; 8.6)**
Wind: Fresh, half against Weather: Cloudy, fine

## 5166 QTS TRAINING LTD APPRENTICE H'CAP 1m
5:40 (5:41) (Class 6) (0-65,65) 3-Y-O+ £2,045 (£603; £302) Stalls Low

Form RPR
2330 1 **Ewell Place (IRE)**[7] 4903 5-9-13 64 (p) JackGarritty 6 73
(Richard Fahey) *prom: hdwy to ld over 1f out: rdn and hld on wl fnl f* 13/2
4451 2 hd **Dansili Dutch (IRE)**[22] 4381 5-9-9 65 JoshDoyle(5) 1 73
(David O'Meara) *hld up in tch: rdn and hdwy over 1f out: chsd wnr wl ins fnl f: r.o* 9/2[2]
1464 3 1 1/4 **Echo Of Lightning**[44] 3604 4-9-6 57 MeganCarberry 10 62
(Brian Ellison) *led: rdn and hdd over 1f out: rallied: lost 2nd and one pce wl ins fnl f* 7/2[1]
-053 4 1 1/2 **Paddy's Rock (IRE)**[23] 4363 3-8-8 55 LukeLeadbitter(3) 8 56
(Ann Duffield) *dwlt: hld up: hdwy on outside over 2f out: edgd lft over 1f out: one pce fnl f* 5/1[3]
4545 5 2 3/4 **Notts So Blue**[19] 4490 3-8-2 46 MatthewHopkins 7 40
(Shaun Harris) *s.i.s: hld up: rdn and hdwy over 1f out: kpt on fnl f: nvr able to chal* 16/1
05 6 1/2 **Helen's Armada (IRE)**[23] 4363 3-9-6 64 LukeDempsey 3 57
(John Patrick Shanahan, Ire) *prom: lost pl over 4f out: struggling over 3f out: rallied over 1f out: kpt on fnl f: no imp* 12/1
-453 7 4 1/2 **Haidees Reflection**[43] 3664 4-8-13 50 JoeDoyle 2 34
(Lucy Normile) *trckd ldrs: rdn over 2f out: wknd over 1f out* 33/1
6031 8 3/4 **Staffhoss**[18] 4517 4-9-5 63 PaulaMuir(7) 4 45
(Mark Johnston) *cl up tl rdn and wknd fr 2f out* 15/2
6/ 9 1/2 **Elusive Gent (IRE)**[36] 3941 7-8-10 47 [1] SeanCorby 5 28
(Adrian Paul Keatley, Ire) *s.i.s: hld up: stdy hdwy over 3f out: rdn and wknd over 2f out* 6/1
200 10 11 **Gadobout Dancer**[2] 5084 7-8-10 47 LauraBarry 9 3
(Keith Dalgleish) *prom tl rdn and wknd over 2f out* 14/1

1m 42.75s (-1.05) **Going Correction** -0.025s/f (Good)
**WFA** 3 from 4yo+ 7lb 10 Ran SP% 119.6
Speed ratings (Par 101): **104,103,102,101,98 97,93,92,92,81**
CSF £36.88 CT £124.23 TOTE £8.40: £2.90, £2.00, £2.00; EX 43.90 Trifecta £203.60.
**Owner** Dr Marwan Koukash **Bred** Peter & Hugh McCutcheon **Trained** Musley Bank, N Yorks

**FOCUS**
Home turn bend in 8m, home straight in 14m. Back straight in 6m Rothesay bend in 6m and 7f-10f races increased by 24yds and 1m 7f race by 42yds. There were various rail movements and the course was at its narrowest. The pace set by the third was sound from the outset.

## 5167 BRITISH STALLION STUDS EBF MAIDEN STKS 7f 50y
6:10 (6:12) (Class 5) 2-Y-O £2,911 (£866; £432; £216) Stalls High

Form RPR
1 **Hernandoshideaway** 2-9-5 0 PaulMulrennan 3 81+
(Michael Dods) *t.k.h: chsd ldng trio: stdy hdwy gng wl whn nt clr run over 2f out tl gap appeared over 1f out: shkn up to ld ent fnl f: nudged out: readily* 8/1
243 2 1 1/4 **Split The Atom (IRE)**[22] 4382 2-9-5 0 RonanWhelan 1 74
(John Patrick Shanahan, Ire) *trckd ldrs: led 3f out: sn rdn: hdd ent fnl f: kpt on: no ch w ready wnr* 15/2[3]
50 3 1 1/4 **Kifaaya**[15] 4633 2-9-2 0 MichaelJMMurphy(3) 6 71
(Mark Johnston) *hld up in tch: rdn over 3f out: effrt and hdwy on outside over 2f out: edgd lft over 1f out: one pce ins fnl f* 4/1[2]
6 4 3 1/4 **Sir Chauvelin**[26] 4253 2-9-5 0 GrahamLee 2 63
(Jim Goldie) *cl up: ev ch 3f out: rdn and outpcd over 1f out* 14/1
5 5 1 3/4 **Cosmic Statesman**[14] 4659 2-9-2 0 GeorgeChaloner(3) 9 59
(Richard Fahey) *hld up: rdn over 2f out: hdwy over 1f out: kpt on fnl f: nvr rchd ldrs* 16/1
4 6 nk **Swift Approval (IRE)**[15] 4633 2-9-5 0 BenCurtis 4 58
(Kevin Ryan) *in tch: n.m.r and pushed along after 150yds: effrt u.p on outside over 2f out: sn no imp: btn over 1f out* 5/6[1]
7 1 1/4 **Bahamian Desert** 2-9-2 0 SamJames(3) 8 55+
(David O'Meara) *led to 3f out: sn rdn: rallied: wknd over 1f out* 25/1
8 1/2 **Sir Lancelott** 2-9-5 0 TomEaves 5 53
(Keith Dalgleish) *towards rr: rdn over 2f out: edgd lft and sn btn* 20/1
6 9 44 **Kepple's Best (IRE)**[113] 1560 2-9-2 0 SladeO'Hara(3) 7
(Alan Berry) *s.i.s: a outpcd: lost tch fr 4f out: t.o* 100/1

1m 34.29s (0.89) **Going Correction** -0.025s/f (Good) 9 Ran SP% 119.6
Speed ratings (Par 94): **93,91,90,86,84 84,82,82,31**
CSF £67.08 TOTE £9.00: £2.00, £2.20, £1.40; EX 62.70 Trifecta £432.40.
**Owner** D C Batey & Foster Watson **Bred** Miss K Rausing **Trained** Denton, Co Durham

**FOCUS**
A fair-looking maiden, run in a time quicker than the following 0-70 handicap.

## 5168 UNISON'S AYRSHIRE & ARRAN HEALTH BRANCH H'CAP (QUALIFIER FOR £15000 BETFAIR SCOTTISH MILE SERIES) 7f 50y
6:40 (6:41) (Class 5) (0-70,70) 3-Y-O+ £2,911 (£866; £432; £216) Stalls High

Form RPR
2603 1 **Clumber Place**[19] 4489 8-8-12 56 BenCurtis 3 64
(Shaun Harris) *mde all at modest gallop: rdn over 1f out: hld on wl fnl f* 4/1[2]
3605 2 1/2 **Kyllachy Star**[56] 3237 8-9-4 65 (v) GeorgeChaloner(3) 2 71
(Richard Fahey) *trckd ldrs: effrt and rdn 2f out: chsd wnr ins fnl f: kpt on towards fin* 11/2
5615 3 1/2 **Orpsie Boy (IRE)**[29] 4156 11-9-10 68 TomEaves 6 73
(Ruth Carr) *hld up: rdn over 2f out: no imp tl swtchd rt and hdwy 1f out: kpt on wl towards fin* 10/1
-406 4 nk **Tiffany Bay (IRE)**[34] 4001 3-9-6 70 [1] RonanWhelan 7 72
(John Patrick Shanahan, Ire) *pressed wnr: ev ch and rdn over 2f out to over 1f out: one pce ins fnl f* 10/1
-442 5 1/2 **Blue Sonic**[12] 4728 4-8-10 54 GrahamLee 4 57
(Jim Goldie) *dwlt: hld up in tch: drvn 2f out: kpt on fnl f: nvr able to chal* 9/2[3]
1416 6 1/2 **Dark Crystal**[23] 4363 3-8-12 65 SamJames(3) 1 65
(Linda Perratt) *trckd ldrs: nt clr run over 2f out: sn rdn: one pce fnl f* 7/2[1]
1423 7 1 3/4 **Opt Out**[8] 4861 4-9-3 66 GarryWhillans(5) 5 63
(Alistair Whillans) *hld up in tch: effrt on outside over 2f out: btn fnl f* 7/2[1]

1m 35.1s (1.70) **Going Correction** -0.025s/f (Good)
**WFA** 3 from 4yo+ 6lb 7 Ran SP% 116.2
Speed ratings (Par 103): **89,88,87,87,86 86,84**
CSF £26.78 TOTE £4.70: £2.50, £3.10; EX 27.60 Trifecta £166.70.
**Owner** Mrs Catherine Stocks **Bred** Worksop Manor Stud **Trained** Carburton, Notts

**FOCUS**
The early gallop didn't look overly strong so Ben Curtis did a good job in setting fractions.

## 5169 GAS SURE & JAMES FREW H'CAP 5f
7:10 (7:11) (Class 6) (0-65,68) 3-Y-O £2,045 (£603; £302) Stalls Low

Form RPR
256- 1 **Autumn Tide (IRE)**[344] 5970 3-7-13 50 (t) SeanCorby(7) 4 56
(Adrian Paul Keatley, Ire) *t.k.h early: cl up: rdn to ld over 1f out: kpt on wl fnl f* 20/1
5045 2 3/4 **Red Forever**[5] 4977 3-9-2 63 SladeO'Hara(3) 1 66
(Alan Berry) *t.k.h: led at decent gallop: rdn and hdd over 1f out: rallied: kpt on fnl f to take 2nd cl home* 13/2[3]

0043 **3** *shd* **Lady Mai (IRE)**[5] 4974 3-8-2 **51**........................ SammyJoBell(5) 3 54
(Richard Fahey) *chsd ldr: hdwy and ev ch over 1f out: sn rdn and chsd wnr: kpt on fnl f: lost 2nd cl home* **3/1**[1]

1501 **4** *2 1/4* **Scoreline**[8] 4860 3-9-7 **68**........................ SamJames(3) 7 63
(David O'Meara) *prom: rdn over 2f out: kpt on same pce fr over 1f out* **7/2**[2]

143 **5** *1 1/2* **Sleeper Class**[12] 4724 3-9-7 **65**........................ GrahamLee 2 54
(Jim Goldie) *hld up in tch: rdn wl over 1f out: sn no imp* **3/1**[1]

1201 **6** *1/2* **Bashiba (IRE)**[20] 4469 3-9-3 **61**........................ PaulMulrennan 5 48
(Nigel Tinkler) *t.k.h: hld up in tch: effrt and rdn over 1f out: sn no imp* **3/1**[1]

1m 0.02s (0.62) **Going Correction** -0.025s/f (Good) **6** Ran SP% **115.3**
Speed ratings (Par 98): **94,92,92,89,86 85**
CSF £139.94 TOTE £12.10: £6.10, £3.80; EX 105.70 Trifecta £211.20.
**Owner** J P H McKeever **Bred** Dr D Crone & P Lafarge & P Johnston **Trained** Dunlavin, Co. Kildare

**FOCUS**
A modest sprint on official ratings, but most of these were in reasonable form coming in to it, so this is probably okay form for the level.

## 5170 QTS LADIES' NIGHT GRAND SPECTACULAR H'CAP 5f
**7:40** (7:40) (Class 4) (0-85,81) 3-Y-0+ **£5,175** (£1,540; £769; £384) **Stalls** Low

Form RPR

-351 **1** **Master Bond**[39] 3831 5-9-3 **77**........................ SamJames(3) 4 88
(David O'Meara) *taken early to post: prom: effrt and rdn 2f out: kpt on wl fnl f to ld nr fin* **4/1**[2]

0323 **2** *3/4* **Gowanharry (IRE)**[19] 4488 5-9-6 **77**..........(tp) PaulMulrennan 7 85
(Michael Dods) *led: rdn over 1f out: kpt on fnl f: hdd nr fin* **6/1**[3]

2234 **3** *1 1/2* **Jinky**[12] 4724 6-9-0 **71**........................ TomEaves 5 74
(Linda Perratt) *trckd ldrs: effrt and chsd ldr over 1f out to ins fnl f: one pce towards fin* **7/1**

4665 **4** *3/4* **Go Go Green (IRE)**[2] 5081 8-8-9 **71**........................ SammyJoBell(5) 3 71
(Jim Goldie) *hld up: rdn along 1/2-way: hdwy over 1f out: kpt on fnl f: nrst fin* **9/1**

0060 **5** *2 1/4* **Polski Max**[20] 4471 4-9-7 **81**..........(p) GeorgeChaloner(3) 10 73
(Richard Fahey) *cl up: drvn along 1/2-way: no ex fr over 1f out* **4/1**[2]

4221 **6** *3/4* **Classy Anne**[7] 4901 4-8-8 **70**........................ JackGarritty(5) 9 59
(Jim Goldie) *cl up: rdn over 2f out: edgd lft and no ex over 1f out* **3/1**[1]

0140 **7** *1/2* **Rothesay Chancer**[13] 4700 6-9-9 **80**........................ GrahamLee 2 68
(Jim Goldie) *bhd and outpcd: rdn along 1/2-way: nvr able to chal* **12/1**

50 **8** *1* **Ambitious Icarus**[39] 3831 5-8-13 **75**..........(e) DuilioDaSilva(5) 11 59
(Richard Guest) *taken early to post: fly-jmpd s: hld up in tch: drvn and outpcd over 2f out: n.d after* **10/1**

58.58s (-0.82) **Going Correction** -0.025s/f (Good) **8** Ran SP% **118.6**
Speed ratings (Par 105): **105,103,101,100,96 95,94,93**
CSF £29.30 CT £165.36 TOTE £5.40: £2.10, £1.70, £2.40; EX 31.10 Trifecta £134.50.
**Owner** Bonded Twentyten Partnership **Bred** Bond Thoroughbred Corporation **Trained** Nawton, N Yorks

**FOCUS**
This looked a difficult puzzle to solve, as plenty of these could be given a decent chance prior to the off.

## 5171 AVESTA SCOTLAND H'CAP (QUALIFIER FOR £15000 BETFAIR SCOTTISH STAYERS SERIES) 1m 7f
**8:10** (8:10) (Class 6) (0-65,65) 4-Y-0+ **£1,940** (£577; £288; £144) **Stalls** Low

Form RPR

15 **1** **Carraroe Flyer (IRE)**[14] 4691 4-8-7 **58**........................ SeanCorby(7) 2 67
(Adrian Paul Keatley, Ire) *hld up: stdy hdwy over 3f out: led over 1f out: sn rdn and edgd lft: kpt on wl fnl f* **5/1**[3]

3533 **2** *2* **Grand Diamond (IRE)**[8] 4856 10-8-4 **53**........................ JackGarritty(5) 6 59
(Jim Goldie) *hld up and bhd: stdy hdwy over 3f out: rdn to chse wnr ent fnl f: r.o* **9/1**

1212 **3** *2* **Underwritten**[3] 5047 5-9-7 **65**........................ BenCurtis 5 68
(Shaun Harris) *chsd clr ldr: hdwy to ld over 2f out: rdn and hdd over 1f out: sn one pce* **9/2**[2]

6421 **4** *3* **Wor Lass**[19] 4492 6-8-9 **53**........................ PaulMulrennan 1 53
(Iain Jardine) *hld up: stdy hdwy after 6f: smooth hdwy and ev ch over 2f out: rdn and outpcd over 1f out* **9/4**[1]

4146 **5** *1/2* **Eilean Mor**[8] 4856 6-8-4 **53**........................ JoeDoyle(5) 4 52
(R Mike Smith) *chsd ldrs: rdn over 2f out: wknd over 1f out* **8/1**

525 **6** *1/2* **Ronald Gee (IRE)**[33] 4015 7-9-6 **64**........................ GrahamLee 3 62
(Jim Goldie) *hld up in tch: stdy hdwy whn n.m.r briefly over 2f out: wknd over 1f out* **8/1**

/022 **7** *3/4* **Cool Baranca (GER)**[10] 2550 8-8-3 **52**........................ EmmaSayer(5) 8 49
(Dianne Sayer) *hld up: stdy hdwy over 3f out: rdn and wknd over 1f out* **13/2**

2-10 **8** *12* **Rayadour (IRE)**[14] 4662 5-9-7 **65**..........(p) TomEaves 7 47
(Micky Hammond) *led and sn clr: hdd over 2f out: sn wknd* **14/1**

3m 27.51s (7.11) **Going Correction** -0.025s/f (Good) **8** Ran SP% **117.8**
Speed ratings (Par 101): **80,78,77,76,76 75,75,68**
CSF £50.17 CT £219.04 TOTE £6.00: £1.80, £2.40, £1.90; EX 76.10 Trifecta £148.10.
**Owner** Liffeydale Syndicate **Bred** Sean Murphy **Trained** Dunlavin, Co. Kildare

**FOCUS**
This staying event was run at a good gallop thanks to Rayadour. It wasn't however surprising to see him drop right out after his early exertions.

## 5172 QTS LADIES' NIGHT H'CAP 1m 2f
**8:40** (8:41) (Class 5) (0-75,74) 3-Y-0+ **£2,911** (£866; £432; £216) **Stalls** Low

Form RPR

3502 **1** **Ingleby Symphony (IRE)**[48] 3502 4-9-9 **72**.......... GeorgeChaloner(3) 1 89
(Richard Fahey) *trckd ldrs: led over 2f out: sn rdn clr: kpt on strly fnl f* **11/4**[2]

4614 **2** *8* **Testa Rossa (IRE)**[18] 4517 4-8-13 **59**........................ GrahamLee 7 61
(Jim Goldie) *hld up in tch: stdy hdwy over 2f out: rdn and chsd (clr) wnr over 1f out: kpt on: no imp* **5/2**[1]

4350 **3** *3* **Hydrant**[25] 4290 8-9-9 **74**........................ DuilioDaSilva(5) 8 70
(Richard Guest) *t.k.h: led: rdn and hdd over 2f out: outpcd over 1f out* **9/2**[3]

-102 **4** *2 1/4* **Dark Ocean (IRE)**[85] 2293 4-9-12 **72**........................ PaulMulrennan 6 64
(Jedd O'Keeffe) *t.k.h: hld up in tch: stdy hdwy 1/2-way: effrt and edgd lft over 2f out: sn outpcd* **9/2**[3]

4204 **5** *2* **I'm Super Too (IRE)**[40] 3785 7-9-12 **72**........................ BenCurtis 5 60
(Alan Swinbank) *hld up: stdy hdwy over 3f out: sn rdn: wknd 2f out* **6/1**

-006 **6** *4 1/2* **Declamation (IRE)**[18] 4517 4-8-11 **62**........................ GarryWhillans(5) 2 41
(Alistair Whillans) *pressed ldr tl rdn and wknd over 2f out* **16/1**

26-0 **7** *2* **Schmooze (IRE)**[99] 1929 5-9-3 **63**........................ TomEaves 4 39
(Linda Perratt) *dwlt: hld up: struggling over 3f out: sn btn* **14/1**

2m 11.48s (-0.52) **Going Correction** -0.025s/f (Good) **7** Ran SP% **118.4**
Speed ratings (Par 103): **101,94,92,90,88 85,83**
CSF £10.68 CT £29.84 TOTE £4.30: £1.50, £3.10; EX 14.20 Trifecta £55.10.
**Owner** Percy Green Racing 4 & Partner **Bred** Sunderland Holdings Inc **Trained** Musley Bank, N Yorks

**FOCUS**
A good race for the level but the early gallop appeared steady.
T/Plt: £902.00 to a £1 stake. Pool: £44,607.93 - 36.10 winning units. T/Qpdt: £208.60 to a £1 stake. Pool: £4510.30 - 16.00 winning units. RY

# 5127 HAYDOCK (L-H)
Saturday, August 9

**OFFICIAL GOING: Good (8.0)**
Wind: Moderate, half against Weather: Fine

## 5173 BETFRED "PLAY TODAYS £1 1/2 MILLION SCOOP6" NURSERY H'CAP (BOBIS RACE) 5f
**1:50** (1:50) (Class 2) 2-Y-O **£9,703** (£2,887; £1,443; £721) **Stalls** Centre

Form RPR

413 **1** **Squats (IRE)**[29] 4143 2-8-7 **87**........................ JoeFanning 1 95+
(William Haggas) *chsd ldr: rdn and r.o to ld narrowly fnl 110yds: pushed out cl home* **3/1**[2]

31 **2** *nk* **Profitable (IRE)**[16] 4583 2-8-0 **83** oh2 ow3.................. RyanTate(3) 5 90+
(Clive Cox) *led: rdn over 1f out: hdd narrowly fnl 110yds: kpt on but a hld* **15/8**[1]

1021 **3** *4* **Fuwairt (IRE)**[21] 4430 2-8-11 **91**........................ RyanMoore 3 84
(Richard Hannon) *hld up: effrt and wnt 3rd 2f out: no imp on ldrs over 1f out: one pce ins fnl f: wl btn fnl 110yds* **13/2**[3]

113 **4** *1 3/4* **Patience Alexander (IRE)**[50] 3415 2-9-7 **101**.................. JimCrowley 4 87
(David Evans) *racd keenly: chsd ldrs: pushed along 2f out: sn outpcd: wl btn ins fnl f* **15/8**[1]

1m 0.17s (-0.63) **Going Correction** -0.125s/f (Firm) **4** Ran SP% **107.9**
Speed ratings (Par 100): **100,99,93,90**
CSF £8.85 TOTE £3.90; EX 9.60 Trifecta £26.50.
**Owner** Sheikh Rashid Dalmook Al Maktoum **Bred** Paul McEnery **Trained** Newmarket, Suffolk

**FOCUS**
All races on Stands side Home straight and distances on Round course increased by about 43yds.
A decent little nursery, run at a solid pace, with the front pair drawing clear.

## 5174 BETFRED GOALS GALORE H'CAP 1m 2f 95y
**2:20** (2:20) (Class 2) (0-105,104) 3-Y-O+
**£28,012** (£8,388; £4,194; £2,097; £1,048; £526) **Stalls** Centre

Form RPR

3564 **1** **Energia Davos (BRZ)**[56] 3217 6-9-1 **98**........................ RyanTate(3) 13 108
(Marco Botti) *hld up in rr: hdwy on outer over 2f out: r.o and edgd lft ins fnl f: led fnl 150yds: in command cl home* **16/1**

1213 **2** *1 1/4* **Llanarmon Lad (IRE)**[21] 4442 5-9-1 **95**........................ HarryBentley 9 103
(Brian Ellison) *midfield: hdwy 3f out: rdn over 2f out: chsd ldrs: chalng wl ins fnl f: wnt 2nd fnl 110yds: kpt on but nt pce of wnr cl home* **8/1**[3]

0-06 **3** *1* **Elhaame (IRE)**[49] 3449 4-8-12 **92**........................ AndreaAtzeni 7 98
(Luca Cumani) *midfield: hdwy over 3f out: led over 2f out: sn rdn: hdd fnl 150yds: styd on same pce cl home* **13/2**[1]

0-0 **4** *2* **Fattsota**[35] 3962 6-9-5 **99**........................ DanielTudhope 14 101
(David O'Meara) *a.p: rdn to chal 3f out: stl there u.p over 1f out: no ex fnl 75yds* **14/1**

1-50 **5** *2 1/2* **Rye House (IRE)**[70] 2779 5-9-4 **98**........................ RyanMoore 12 95
(Sir Michael Stoute) *stdd s: hld up: rdn and hdwy over 2f out: no imp on over 1f out: one pce ins fnl f* **8/1**[3]

-000 **6** *2* **Lahaag**[49] 3449 5-9-0 **94**........................ NickyMackay 1 87
(John Gosden) *racd keenly: in tch: rdn and outpcd over 3f out: styd on same pce and no imp ins fnl f* **9/1**

0-00 **7** *1/2* **Queensberry Rules (IRE)**[28] 4214 4-9-5 **99**..........(t) JimCrowley 11 91
(William Haggas) *midfield: rdn over 1f out: did nt stride out wl: plugged on ins fnl f wout threatening* **9/1**

0350 **8** *nk* **Chancery (USA)**[13] 4696 6-9-3 **97**........................ KierenFallon 5 89
(David O'Meara) *hld up: rdn and hdwy over 2f out: kpt on ins fnl f: nvr able to trble ldrs* **12/1**

2004 **9** *2 1/2* **Busatto (USA)**[11] 4756 4-8-12 **92**........................ JoeFanning 10 79
(Mark Johnston) *prom: chsd ldrs 6f out: led 3f out: rdn and hdd over 2f out: wknd over 1f out* **10/1**

5120 **10** *1 1/2* **Tres Coronas (IRE)**[64] 2957 7-9-10 **104**.................. GrahamGibbons 15 88
(David Barron) *hld up: hdwy into midfield 6f out: rdn and wknd 3f out* **16/1**

0300 **11** *1 1/4* **Trail Blaze (IRE)**[7] 4922 5-8-8 **88**........................ FrannyNorton 6 70
(Kevin Ryan) *prom: rdn 3f out: wknd over 2f out* **33/1**

023 **12** *1 1/4* **Salutation (IRE)**[11] 4756 4-9-4 **101**.................. MichaelJMMurphy(3) 8 81
(Mark Johnston) *led: rdn and hdd 3f out: wknd over 2f out* **15/2**[2]

/12- **13** *1* **Docs Legacy (IRE)**[490] 1391 5-8-5 **85**........................ PatrickMathers 3 63
(Richard Fahey) *midfield tl rdn and wknd over 2f out* **25/1**

0-10 **14** *32* **Groundbreaking**[49] 3449 4-9-8 **102**........................ SeanLevey 2 19
(Charlie Appleby) *s.i.s: in rr: hdwy into midfield 6f out: sn pushed along: wknd over 3f out: wl bhd over 1f out* **9/1**

2m 10.13s (-5.37) **Going Correction** -0.275s/f (Firm)
**WFA** 3 from 4yo+ 9lb **14** Ran SP% **119.3**
Speed ratings (Par 109): **110,109,108,106,104 103,102,102,100,99 98,97,96,70**
CSF £137.55 CT £931.69 TOTE £26.10: £5.40, £2.50, £2.40; EX 199.10 Trifecta £1708.40 Part won..
**Owner** Stefan Friborg **Bred** Haras Estrela Energia **Trained** Newmarket, Suffolk

**FOCUS**
Run at a good pace, the time the winner recorded was a smart one and the form looks sound.

## 5175 BETFRED ROSE OF LANCASTER STKS (GROUP 3) 1m 2f 95y
**2:55** (2:56) (Class 1) 3-Y-O+
**£35,727** (£13,545; £6,778; £3,376; £1,694; £850) **Stalls** Centre

Form RPR

3621 **1** **Amralah (IRE)**[21] 4437 4-9-3 **108**........................ JoeFanning 4 115
(Mick Channon) *mde all: rdn over 2f out: styd on gamely ins fnl f: in contril cl home* **14/1**

222 **2** *1 1/4* **Hillstar**[30] 4124 4-9-3 **113**........................ RyanMoore 6 113
(Sir Michael Stoute) *wore hood in paddock: hld up: hdwy over 2f out: styd on to chse wnr over 1f out: wanted to lug lft: nt quite able to get to wnr ins fnl f: no imp cl home* **3/1**[2]

1305 **3** ¾ **True Story**[35] [3984] 3-8-8 113....................(v) KierenFallon 1 111
(Saeed bin Suroor) *in tch: rdn and outpcd over 3f out: hung lft u.p over 1f out: kpt on but no imp ins fnl f* **9/4**[1]

5044 **4** 3½ **Educate**[28] [4214] 5-9-3 110.................... MartinHarley 2 105
(Ismail Mohammed) *chsd wnr: rdn over 2f out: nt qckn: lost 2nd over 1f out: styd on same pce ins fnl f* **8/1**

-636 **5** *hd* **Danadana (IRE)**[14] [4682] 6-9-3 111.................... AndreaAtzeni 3 104
(Luca Cumani) *midfield: rdn and hdwy over 2f out: styd on same pce ins fnl f and no imp on ldrs* **10/1**

1-33 **6** ½ **Nabucco**[21] [4437] 5-9-3 109.................... NickyMackay 5 103
(John Gosden) *prom: rdn over 2f out: styd on same pce ins fnl f* **6/1**

-202 **7** 4½ **Vancouverite**[21] [4437] 4-9-3 115....................(b) JimCrowley 8 95
(Charlie Appleby) *hld up in rr: rdn and struggling over 2f out: bhd over 1f out* **11/2**[3]

2m 10.96s (-4.54) **Going Correction** -0.275s/f (Firm)
**WFA** 3 from 4yo+ 9lb **7 Ran SP% 112.3**
Speed ratings (Par 113): **107,106,105,102,102 102,98**
CSF £53.76 TOTE £14.20: £4.20, £1.70; EX 54.20 Trifecta £181.80.
**Owner** Prince A A Faisal **Bred** Nawara Stud Co Ltd **Trained** West Ilsley, Berks

**FOCUS**
This looked a strong Group 3 but the winner was allowed too much rope and made all.

## 5176 BETFRED TV/EBF STALLIONS DICK HERN FILLIES' STKS (LISTED RACE) 1m

**3:25** (3:27) (Class 1) 3-Y-0+
**£26,653** (£10,105; £5,057; £2,519; £1,264; £634) **Stalls** Low

Form RPR

2312 **1** **Token Of Love**[21] [4436] 3-8-7 90.................... JoeFanning 7 108
(William Haggas) *chsd ldrs: led 2f out: edgd lft whn asserting 1f out: r.o wl and in command ins fnl f* **9/2**[2]

4035 **2** 2¼ **Lady Lara (IRE)**[52] [3357] 3-8-8 100 ow1.................... KierenFallon 4 103
(Timothy Jarvis) *hld up in rr: stl plenty to do over 3f out: hdwy 2f out: styd on ins fnl f: tk 2nd fnl 110yds: nt rch wnr* **15/2**

4100 **3** 1¾ **Manderley (IRE)**[8] [4854] 3-8-7 107.................... SeanLevey 5 98
(Richard Hannon) *chsd ldr: led over 2f out: sn rdn and hdd: unable to go w wnr ins fnl f: lost 2nd fnl 100yds: kpt on same pce towards fin* **20/1**

-220 **4** 1¼ **Lightning Thunder**[50] [3418] 3-8-7 111.................... HarryBentley 8 95
(Olly Stevens) *midfield: pushed along 3f out: rdn and hung lft fr 2f out: prog ins fnl f: kpt on towards fin: nvr able to chal* **5/4**[1]

-430 **5** 1¼ **Psychometry (FR)**[52] [3357] 3-8-7 88.................... RyanMoore 6 92
(Sir Michael Stoute) *racd keenly in midfield: effrt 2f out: chsd ldrs over 1f out: sn no imp: no ex ins fnl f* **9/1**

431 **6** 5 **Solar Magic**[13] [4699] 3-8-7 91.................... WilliamBuick 2 81
(John Gosden) *midfield: rdn over 2f out: sn wknd* **7/1**[3]

1320 **7** 2¼ **Wee Jean**[8] [4854] 3-8-7 103.................... AndreaAtzeni 9 76
(Mick Channon) *restless in stalls: missed break: in rr: pushed along over 3f out: nvr bttr than midfield over 1f out: no imp: wknd ins fnl f* **7/1**[3]

000 **8** *nse* **Alutiq (IRE)**[40] [3788] 3-8-7 87.................... JoeyHaynes 3 75
(Olly Stevens) *racd keenly: led at str pce: rdn and hdd over 2f out: wknd over 1f out* **50/1**

-400 **9** 2½ **Goldstorm**[55] [3272] 6-9-0 78....................(p) PaddyAspell 1 71
(Brian Baugh) *hld up: struggling 3f out: nvr a threat* **100/1**

1m 41.36s (-2.34) **Going Correction** -0.275s/f (Firm)
**WFA** 3 from 6yo 7lb **9 Ran SP% 117.1**
Speed ratings (Par 108): **100,97,96,94,93 88,86,86,83**
CSF £37.92 TOTE £4.90: £1.70, £2.50, £4.60; EX 53.30 Trifecta £707.50.
**Owner** A E Oppenheimer **Bred** Hascombe And Valiant Studs **Trained** Newmarket, Suffolk

**FOCUS**
A strongly run fillies' Listed race. The winner recorded a clear personal best.

## 5177 BETFRED "DOUBLE DELIGHT" H'CAP (BOBIS RACE) 1m

**4:00** (4:00) (Class 3) (0-95,93) 3-Y-0 **£8,086** (£2,406; £1,202; £601) **Stalls** Low

Form RPR

131 **1** **Provenance**[17] [4551] 3-9-4 90.................... RyanMoore 3 103+
(Sir Michael Stoute) *in tch: effrt whn swtchd rt and sltly inconvenienced over 1f out: r.o ins fnl f: led towards fin* **5/2**[1]

2140 **2** ¾ **Lesha (IRE)**[11] [4761] 3-8-8 85.................... KevinStott(5) 8 93
(Kevin Ryan) *in tch: effrt 2f out: rdn to ld jst over 1f out: hdd towards fin* **9/2**[3]

6320 **3** 2¼ **Championship (IRE)**[9] [4826] 3-9-7 93.................... AndreaAtzeni 7 96
(Richard Hannon) *hld up: hdwy 3f out: rdn whn chsng ldrs and hung rt over 1f out: kpt on and hung lft towards fin whn no imp on front two* **6/1**

2105 **4** 1 **Provident Spirit**[56] [3243] 3-9-1 87.................... WilliamBuick 1 88
(John Gosden) *led after 1f: rdn and hdd jst over 1f out: one pce fnl 100yds* **3/1**[2]

451 **5** ¾ **Lockhart (IRE)**[13] [4713] 3-8-10 82.................... JoeFanning 5 81
(Mark Johnston) *trckd ldrs: rdn 2f out: nt qckn over 1f out: styd on same pce ins fnl f* **7/1**

1055 **6** 2¾ **Galvanize**[7] [4912] 3-8-9 81.................... FrannyNorton 6 74
(Kevin Ryan) *led for 1f: chsd ldr: chalng 2f out: stl ev ch 1f out: no ex fnl 100yds* **14/1**

4430 **7** 14 **Showpiece**[11] [4761] 3-8-8 80....................(b) SeanLevey 4 40
(Richard Hannon) *in rr: pushed along 3f out: bhd over 1f out: eased whn wl btn ins fnl f* **10/1**

1m 41.9s (-1.80) **Going Correction** -0.275s/f (Firm) **7 Ran SP% 114.3**
Speed ratings (Par 104): **98,97,95,94,93 90,76**
CSF £14.08 CT £59.72 TOTE £2.70: £1.90, £2.70; EX 15.30 Trifecta £70.90.
**Owner** Cheveley Park Stud **Bred** Cheveley Park Stud Ltd **Trained** Newmarket, Suffolk

**FOCUS**
A decent 3yo handicap, run at a routine sort of pace and most held a chance at the furlong marker. The form looks sound.

## 5178 BETFRED DUKE OF LANCASTER'S OWN YEOMANRY H'CAP (LONDON MILE SERIES QUALIFIER) 1m

**4:35** (4:37) (Class 3) (0-95,95) 3-Y-0+ **£8,086** (£2,406; £1,202; £601) **Stalls** Low

Form RPR

611- **1** **Cornrow**[320] [6694] 4-9-6 87.................... WilliamBuick 3 102+
(John Gosden) *t.k.h: sn led: rdn and qcknd over 1f out: pushed out fnl f: readily* **4/1**[2]

622 **2** *nk* **Multi Bene**[37] [3886] 5-9-6 92.................... KevinStott(5) 9 100+
(Ed McMahon) *hld up in midfield: stdy hdwy over 2f out: effrt on ins whn hmpd wl over 1f out: kpt on ins fnl f: nrst fin: fin 3rd: plcd 2nd* **9/2**[3]

3160 **3** 3½ **Yourartisonfire**[50] [3437] 4-9-3 87....................(v) JoeyHaynes(3) 4 94
(K R Burke) *trckd ldrs: effrt over 2f out: edgd lft and chsd wnr wl over 1f out: kpt on ins fnl f: fin 2nd: disqualified and plcd 3rd* **7/1**

2-1 **4** 1¾ **Elsiniaar**[22] [4393] 4-9-2 83.................... AndreaAtzeni 7 85
(Roger Varian) *in tch: drvn and outpcd over 3f out: kpt on ins fnl f: nvr able to chal* **3/1**[1]

1166 **5** ½ **Red Refraction (IRE)**[14] [4650] 4-9-7 88.................... RyanMoore 8 89
(Richard Hannon) *pressed wnr: drvn and ch over 2f out: lost 2nd over 1f out: kpt on same pce fnl f* **7/1**

00 **6** 5 **Secret Recipe**[19] [4491] 4-9-6 87.................... PaddyAspell 6 77
(David Nicholls) *s.i.s: hld up: pushed along over 2f out: kpt on fnl f: nvr able to chal* **50/1**

4530 **7** 3 **Dubai Hills**[7] [4922] 8-9-7 88.................... JimCrowley 11 71
(David O'Meara) *prom tl rdn and wknd fr 2f out* **12/1**

1400 **8** 4 **Best Of Order (IRE)**[28] [4200] 7-10-0 95....................(b) GrahamGibbons 10 69
(David O'Meara) *hld up in midfield on outside: rdn over 2f out: sn btn* **25/1**

-214 **9** 10 **Extraterrestrial**[25] [4290] 10-8-12 79....................(p) PatrickMathers 5 30
(Richard Fahey) *t.k.h: hld up in midfield on ins: pushed along whn bdly hmpd bnd over 4f out: sn lost pl and struggling* **20/1**

1130 **10** 11 **St Moritz (IRE)**[35] [3982] 8-9-11 92....................(v) DanielTudhope 1 17
(David O'Meara) *s.i.s: bhd and detached: effrt 3f out: sn n.d: eased whn btn over 1f out* **7/1**

1m 42.09s (-1.61) **Going Correction** -0.275s/f (Firm) **10 Ran SP% 118.9**
Speed ratings (Par 107): **97,93,96,91,90 85,82,78,68,57**
CSF £32.14 CT £127.06 TOTE £5.00: £1.90, £1.80, £2.30; EX 28.10 Trifecta £190.20.
**Owner** HRH Princess Haya Of Jordan **Bred** Darley **Trained** Newmarket, Suffolk
■ Stewards' Enquiry : Joey Haynes two-day ban: careless riding (Aug 23-24)

**FOCUS**
A fair and competitive handicap. Sound form, despite the time being the slowest of the three over C&D.

## 5179 BETFRED "GOALS GALORE EXTRA" LEVY BOARD H'CAP (BOBIS RACE) 1m 3f 200y

**5:05** (5:06) (Class 2) 3-Y-0
**£31,125** (£9,320; £4,660; £2,330; £1,165; £585) **Stalls** Centre

Form RPR

1225 **1** **Montaly**[50] [3419] 3-8-8 92.................... DavidProbert 1 100
(Andrew Balding) *hld up in tch: hdwy and squeezed through over 1f out: led ins fnl f: rdn out* **10/1**

521 **2** ¾ **Gwafa (IRE)**[15] [4621] 3-8-1 85.................... NickyMackay 9 92
(Marco Botti) *prom: rdn over 2f out: led over 1f out to ins fnl f: kpt on same pce* **6/1**

0-13 **3** ½ **Mount Logan (IRE)**[30] [4125] 3-8-11 95.................... AndreaAtzeni 4 101
(Luca Cumani) *hld up in tch: effrt on outside over 2f out: kpt on ins fnl f: nrst fin* **5/1**[3]

516 **4** *nk* **Farquhar (IRE)**[57] [3200] 3-8-6 90.................... FrannyNorton 5 96
(Peter Chapple-Hyam) *s.i.s: hld up: hdwy on outside 3f out: sn rdn: kpt on ins fnl f* **25/1**

142 **5** 1 **Devilment**[16] [4584] 3-8-7 91.................... WilliamBuick 7 95
(Charlie Appleby) *trckd ldrs: effrt whn nt clr run over 2f out to over 1f out: sn rdn and edgd lft: one pce ins fnl f* **12/1**

130 **6** 1½ **Black Schnapps (IRE)**[51] [3379] 3-8-10 94.................... MartinDwyer 10 96
(William Muir) *pressed ldr: rdn and led over 2f out to over 1f out: wknd ins fnl f* **20/1**

142 **7** 3¼ **Satellite (IRE)**[63] [2982] 3-8-11 95.................... RyanMoore 3 91
(William Haggas) *s.i.s: t.k.h in rr: rdn over 2f out: no imp: btn fnl f* **9/4**[1]

0221 **8** 1½ **Double Bluff (IRE)**[7] [4893] 3-9-7 105.................... JoeFanning 8 99
(Mark Johnston) *t.k.h: led to over 2f out: rdn and wknd over 1f out* **7/2**[2]

-120 **9** 1¼ **Personal Opinion**[51] [3379] 3-8-7 91....................(p) JimCrowley 2 83
(Charlie Appleby) *trckd ldrs: rdn whn n.m.r over 2f out: wknd over 1f out* **12/1**

2m 29.07s (-4.73) **Going Correction** -0.275s/f (Firm) **9 Ran SP% 117.0**
Speed ratings (Par 106): **104,103,103,102,102 101,99,98,97**
CSF £69.57 CT £340.55 TOTE £12.00: £3.70, £1.90, £1.40; EX 69.40 Trifecta £761.10.
**Owner** The Farleigh Court Racing Partnership **Bred** Farleigh Court Racing Partnership **Trained** Kingsclere, Hants

**FOCUS**
This was a good-quality 3yo handicap, run at a decent pace, and there were plenty of progressive and unexposed sorts taking part.
T/Jkpt: Not won. T/Plt: £1,074.80 to a £1 stake. Pool of £114128.41 - 77.51 winning tickets.
T/Qpdt: £57.80 to a £1 stake. Pool of £7201.98 - 92.05 winning tickets. DO

# 5133 LINGFIELD (L-H)

### Saturday, August 9

**OFFICIAL GOING: Turf course - good; all weather - standard**
Wind: light Weather: Sunny, light cloud

## 5180 188BET NURSERY H'CAP 6f

**5:20** (5:22) (Class 6) (0-60,60) 2-Y-0 **£2,587** (£770; £384; £192) **Stalls** Centre

Form RPR

064 **1** **White Vin Jan**[15] [4610] 2-8-0 46.................... KieranShoemark(7) 10 54+
(Michael Bell) *broke wl to dispute ld after 1f: led 3f out: kpt on wl fnl f: gng away at fin* **4/1**[2]

4642 **2** 1½ **Lady Zodiac (IRE)**[22] [4410] 2-9-1 54.................... OisinMurphy 2 57
(Andrew Balding) *broke wl to dispute ld after 1f: pushed along 2f out to press ldr: hld fnl 50yds* **7/2**[1]

506 **3** *nse* **Diracan (IRE)**[36] [3933] 2-9-5 58....................(b[1]) GeorgeBaker 12 60
(Nick Littmoden) *trckd ldrs: pushed along 2f out: rdn ent fnl f: styd on: nt pce of wnr* **4/1**[2]

4664 **4** 1¾ **Jersey Belle**[23] [4345] 2-9-0 60.................... PaddyPilley(7) 6 57
(Mick Channon) *hld up in mid-div: pushed along 2f out: styd on same pce fnl f* **5/1**[3]

0506 **5** *nse* **Paco's Dream**[28] [4178] 2-9-2 55.................... PatCosgrave 7 52
(Harry Dunlop) *hld up in rr: rdn 2f out: one pce fnl f* **14/1**

000 **6** 1¼ **Supreme Belle (IRE)**[28] [4202] 2-8-6 45 oh7.................... KieranO'Neill 11 38
(Derek Shaw) *broke wl to dispute ld after 1f: rdn 3f out: hdd 2f out: sn fdd* **25/1**

2533 **7** *nse* **Kidmeforever**[1] [5133] 2-9-1 59.................... PhilipPrince(5) 5 52
(J S Moore) *hld up in mid-div: pushed along 2f out: wknd fnl f* **8/1**

000 **8** 13 **Now Say Boooom**[82] [2402] 2-8-5 47....................[1] RossAtkinson(3) 3
(Luke Dace) *hld up in rr: pushed along 4f out: wknd 2f out* **33/1**

04 **9** ½ **Air Of York (IRE)**[38] [3847] 2-9-2 55.................... SteveDrowne 4 8
(Ronald Harris) *slowly away: sn pushed along: wl btn after* **10/1**

3000 **10** *41* **Sparbrook (IRE)**[54] 3312 2-8-7 **53** TomasHarrigan(7) 8 +
(Simon Dow) *slowly away: sddle slipped after 2f: heavily eased after: virtually p.u* **16/1**
1m 11.43s (0.23) **Going Correction** -0.10s/f (Good) **10** Ran SP% **118.4**
Speed ratings (Par 92): **94,92,91,89,89 87,87,70,69,15**
CSF £18.76 CT £61.47 TOTE £5.10: £2.10, £1.40, £1.80; EX 24.50 Trifecta £111.60.
**Owner** Middleham Park Racing XXIII & Partner **Bred** Redmyre Bloodstock Ltd **Trained** Newmarket, Suffolk
**FOCUS**
Plenty of unexposed types in this nursery, where it paid to race prominently. Low-grade form.

## 5181 188BET MAIDEN STKS 6f
5:50 (5:50) (Class 5) 3-Y-0+ £2,911 (£866; £432; £216) Stalls Centre

Form RPR
**1** **Artistic Queen** 3-8-7 KieranShoemark(7) 6 77
(James Tate) *trckd ldr after 1f: pushed along 2f out: r.o wl fnl f: led fnl stride* **16/1**
4-22 **2** *nse* **Anna's Vision (IRE)**[16] 4590 3-9-0 **74** JamesDoyle 1 76
(Jeremy Noseda) *broke wl to trck ldr after 1f: pushed along 2f out to dispute ld: led ins fnl 100yds: hdd on post* **7/4**[1]
5302 **3** *3/4* **Goodwood Storm**[14] 4654 3-9-0 **72** PatCosgrave 5 74
(William Knight) *broke wl to ld after 1f: rdn and jnd 2f out: hdd ins fnl f* **9/4**[2]
- **4** *3 3/4* **Virile (IRE)** 3-9-5 SteveDrowne 4 67
(Richard Hannon) *towards rr: pushed along 3f out: one pce ins fnl f* **8/1**
23/ **5** *4* **Pearl Bell (IRE)**[750] 4282 4-9-4 OisinMurphy 3 50
(Olly Stevens) *trckd ldrs after 1f: pushed along 3f out: one pce fnl f* **5/1**[3]
6 **6** *6* **John Caesar (IRE)**[30] 4111 3-9-5 (t) ChrisCatlin 2 35
(Jeremy Noseda) *slowly away: towards rr and sn pushed along: wknd 3f out* **12/1**
**7** *4 1/2* **Picnic In The Glen** 3-9-0 SamHitchcott 7 16
(Sylvester Kirk) *slow away: sn pushed along: virtually t.o* **33/1**
1m 10.32s (-0.88) **Going Correction** -0.10s/f (Good)
**WFA** 3 from 4yo 4lb **7** Ran SP% **111.4**
Speed ratings (Par 103): **101,100,99,94,89 81,75**
CSF £42.32 TOTE £14.50: £6.10, £1.90; EX 56.60 Trifecta £148.90.
**Owner** James Tate Racing Limited **Bred** Cothi Bloodstock **Trained** Newmarket, Suffolk
**FOCUS**
A fair maiden run at an honest pace.

## 5182 PF WHITEHEAD LOGISTICS H'CAP 6f
6:20 (6:20) (Class 5) (0-75,75) 3-Y-0+ £3,234 (£962; £481; £240) Stalls Centre

Form RPR
1555 **1** **Aye Aye Digby (IRE)**[17] 4553 9-9-6 **73** GeorgeBaker 4 81
(Patrick Chamings) *trckd ldr after 1f: disp ld 2f out: styd on wl fnl f: jst hld on* **8/1**
6652 **2** *shd* **Dominium (USA)**[17] 4545 7-9-2 **69** (b) JamesDoyle 2 76
(Jeremy Gask) *hld up in mid-div: pushed along to cl 2f out: r.o wl fnl f: jst hld* **3/1**[2]
560 **3** *3/4* **Diamond Charlie (IRE)**[71] 2718 6-9-5 **72** SebSanders 7 76
(Simon Dow) *qckly into stride to ld after 1f: 4 l clr after 2f: rdn and hdd ent fnl 2f: styd on fnl f: nt pce of wnr* **8/1**
2231 **4** *3 1/4* **Miss Brazil (IRE)**[16] 4590 3-9-4 **75** KieranO'Neill 3 68
(Richard Hannon) *s.i.s: pushed along after 1f: sme prog 4f out: one pce fnl f* **6/1**
3003 **5** *6* **Generalyse**[22] 4401 5-9-7 **74** AdamKirby 6 49
(Ben De Haan) *hld up in rr: pushed along 3f out: nvr a factor* **7/2**[3]
3-01 **6** *nk* **Maria Montez**[7] 4908 5-9-5 **72** TomQueally 1 46
(B W Hills) *trckd ldrs after 1f: cl up 3f out: sn rdn: wknd ent fnl 2f* **5/2**[1]
1m 9.86s (-1.34) **Going Correction** -0.10s/f (Good)
**WFA** 3 from 4yo+ 4lb **6** Ran SP% **112.3**
Speed ratings (Par 103): **104,103,102,98,90 90**
CSF £31.99 TOTE £7.90: £3.00, £2.10; EX 35.70 Trifecta £210.80.
**Owner** Trolley Action **Bred** G J King **Trained** Baughurst, Hants
**FOCUS**
A decent contest for the grade run at a sound pace.

## 5183 PHILIP PEARCE 50TH BIRTHDAY CELEBRATION H'CAP 7f 140y
6:50 (6:51) (Class 6) (0-60,60) 3-Y-0 £2,587 (£770; £384; £192) Stalls Centre

Form RPR
-600 **1** **Rapunzal**[4] 5005 3-8-10 **54** AmyScott(5) 5 61
(Henry Candy) *trckd ldrs: prom 3f out: pushed along 2f out to dispute ld: r.o strly fnl f: won wl* **5/1**[3]
0-06 **2** *2 1/2* **Sweet Lily Pea (USA)**[10] 4791 3-8-9 **53** TimClark(5) 8 54
(Mrs Ilka Gansera-Leveque) *trckd ldrs after 1f: led ent fnl 3f: rdn and hdd 2f out: nt pce of wnr* **8/1**[3]
5-46 **3** *2 1/4* **Pelagian (USA)**[50] 3426 3-8-12 **51** SteveDrowne 6 46
(Michael Attwater) *hld up: pushed along 3f out where sme prog: rdn 2f out: styd on same pce fnl f* **25/1**
0436 **4** *1 1/4* **Dark Phantom (IRE)**[23] 4341 3-8-8 **47** (t) OisinMurphy 4 39
(Peter Makin) *hld up towards rr: pushed along and hdwy 2f out: styng on at fin* **5/1**[2]
000 **5** *2* **Marmande (IRE)**[185] 486 3-9-4 **57** GeorgeBaker 1 44
(Daniel Kubler) *hld up in mid-div: pushed along 2f out: rdn fnl f: one pce* **16/1**
5562 **6** *2 1/2* **Libra Romana (IRE)**[7] 4905 3-8-7 **49** RosieJessop(3) 3 30
(Sir Mark Prescott Bt) *dwlt slowly away: pushed along after 1f: sn trcking ldrs: prom tl 2f out where pushed along: wknd fnl f* **5/4**[1]
5600 **7** *13* **Quantum Dot (IRE)**[17] 4535 3-9-2 **60** [1] EoinWalsh(5) 2 8
(Lisa Williamson) *mid-div: rdn 2f out: a bhd* **28/1**
0350 **8** *21* **Orlando Star (CAN)**[24] 4324 3-9-4 **57** (p) AdamKirby 9
(Roger Teal) *broke wl to ld after 1f: rdn and hdd 3f out: sn wknd* **8/1**[3]
1m 31.82s (-0.48) **Going Correction** -0.10s/f (Good) **8** Ran SP% **113.2**
Speed ratings (Par 98): **98,95,93,92,90 87,74,53**
CSF £43.12 CT £900.08 TOTE £6.00: £1.50, £2.20, £4.30; EX 41.50 Trifecta £403.50.
**Owner** Port and Brandy Syndicate **Bred** Newsells Park Stud **Trained** Kingston Warren, Oxon
**FOCUS**
They went a fair pace for this modest handicap.

## 5184 WHITEHEAD FAMILY BRITISH STALLION STUD EBF MAIDEN STKS 1m 1y(P)
7:20 (7:22) (Class 5) 2-Y-0 £2,911 (£866; £432; £216) Stalls High

Form RPR
5 **1** **Sharp Sailor (USA)**[49] 3474 2-9-5 MartinHarley 5 83+
(Marco Botti) *trckd ldr after 1f: disp ld 3f out: led ent fnl 2f: r.o strly fnl f: won gng away* **11/4**[3]
0 **2** *3* **Deerfield**[14] 4666 2-9-5 AdamKirby 1 76
(Charlie Appleby) *led after 1f: set str pce: jnd 3f out: hdd ent fnl 2f: styd on fnl f: no ch w wnr* **5/4**[1]
**3** *3* **Bnedel (IRE)** 2-9-5 FrankieDettori 2 69
(Richard Hannon) *hld up in rr: t.k.h after 1f: trckd ldrs tl pushed along 3f out: styd on same pce fnl f* **2/1**[2]
0 **4** *7* **Overlord**[7] 4885 2-9-5 ChrisCatlin 3 56+
(Sir Mark Prescott Bt) *trckd ldrs after 1f: pushed along after 4f where outpcd: wknd fnl 2f* **14/1**
**5** *99* **Willow Jubilee** 2-9-0 SamHitchcott 4
(John E Long) *hld up: in rr after 1f: bdly outpcd after 3f: sn eased: virtually p.u fnl 2f* **50/1**
1m 39.01s (0.81) **Going Correction** -0.025s/f (Stan) **5** Ran SP% **113.1**
Speed ratings (Par 94): **94,91,88,81,**
CSF £6.86 TOTE £5.20: £2.60, £1.10; EX 6.40 Trifecta £11.20.
**Owner** Robert Ng **Bred** London T'Bred Serv & Derry Meeting Farm **Trained** Newmarket, Suffolk
**FOCUS**
Little form to go on for this maiden, which was run at a steady pace.

## 5185 188BET CASINO H'CAP 1m 4f (P)
7:50 (7:50) (Class 5) (0-75,77) 3-Y-0 £3,234 (£962; £481; £240) Stalls Low

Form RPR
2115 **1** **Leaderene**[7] 4921 3-9-1 **68** DaneO'Neill 4 77
(Mark Johnston) *led after 1f: pushed along 3f out: r.o wl fnl 2f: pressed fnl f: hld on wl* **7/2**[3]
0021 **2** *1/2* **Secure Cloud (IRE)**[7] 4910 3-9-7 **74** KierenFallon 1 82
(B W Hills) *trckd ldrs: pushed along 4f out: r.o fnl 2f to chse ldr: nt quite rch wnr* **5/2**[2]
0440 **3** *1 1/2* **Anjin (IRE)**[16] 4579 3-8-8 **61** ChrisCatlin 6 67
(Sir Mark Prescott Bt) *hld up towards rr: pushed along 3f out: r.o fnl f: tk 3rd cl home* **12/1**
6261 **4** *hd* **Masterpaver**[3] 5038 3-9-10 **77** 6ex AdamKirby 2 82
(Alan Bailey) *hld up: pushed along 3f out: rn wd 2f out where hung bdly rt: sn hld after* **7/4**[1]
646 **5** *4 1/2* **Fighting Back**[29] 4168 3-9-7 **74** TomQueally 5 72
(Amanda Perrett) *trckd ldrs: pushed along 4f out: outpcd 2f out: sn wknd* **8/1**
2516 **6** *8* **Yeah Baby (IRE)**[19] 4504 3-9-5 **72** GeorgeBaker 3 57
(Charles Hills) *hld up towards rr: fdd 2f out* **10/1**
2m 31.67s (-1.33) **Going Correction** -0.025s/f (Stan) **6** Ran SP% **115.1**
Speed ratings (Par 100): **103,102,101,101,98 93**
CSF £13.13 TOTE £5.60: £2.40, £1.80; EX 14.40 Trifecta £190.40.
**Owner** Miss K Rausing **Bred** Miss K Rausing **Trained** Middleham Moor, N Yorks
**FOCUS**
The pace was steady for this fair handicap.

## 5186 188BET GREAT IN PLAY MEDIAN AUCTION MAIDEN STKS 1m 2f (P)
8:20 (8:22) (Class 6) 3-4-Y-0 £2,134 (£635; £317; £158) Stalls Low

Form RPR
22 **1** **Wrood (USA)**[47] 3525 3-8-12 TomQueally 7 80+
(James Fanshawe) *trckd ldrs: pushed along to chse ldr 2f out: hrd rdn fnl f: r.o wl to ld fnl 50yds* **6/4**[1]
04 **2** *nk* **Limousine**[55] 3270 3-8-12 JamesDoyle 2 79
(Charles Hills) *led after 1f: pushed along 2f out: r.o wl: hdd fnl 50yds* **6/1**
32 **3** *1 1/2* **Tabjeel**[26] 4265 3-9-3 (p) DaneO'Neill 4 81
(Saeed bin Suroor) *trckd ldrs: gng wl 3f out: pushed along 2f out: r.o: nt pce of ldrs* **5/2**[2]
33 **4** *4 1/2* **Kicking The Can (IRE)**[26] 4265 3-9-3 RobertHavlin 6 73
(Peter Chapple-Hyam) *hld up in mid-div: pushed along 2f out: r.o fnl f* **9/2**[3]
00 **5** *7* **Saturation Point**[21] 4435 3-8-12 ChrisCatlin 9 54
(James Toller) *hld up: pushed along 3f out: a towards rr* **50/1**
00 **6** *1 1/2* **Champs D'Or**[64] 2967 3-8-12 MartinHarley 8 51
(Marco Botti) *hld up towards rr: outpcd 2f out: r.o past btn horses fnl f* **20/1**
**7** *1* **Perfect Legend** 3-9-3 LiamKeniry 1 55
(Andrew Balding) *trckd ldr after 1f: pushed along 3f out: wknd fnl 2f* **25/1**
06 **8** *nk* **Byronegetonefree**[26] 4265 3-9-3 SamHitchcott 10 54
(John E Long) *trckd ldr after 1f: pushed along after 4f: wknd ent fnl 2f* **100/1**
**9** *12* **Willshebetrying** 3-8-12 KierenFallon 5 26
(Robert Mills) *hld up in rr: pushed along 5f out: lost grnd: t.o fnl f* **14/1**
2m 8.97s (2.37) **Going Correction** -0.025s/f (Stan)
**WFA** 3 from 4yo 9lb **9** Ran SP% **119.3**
Speed ratings (Par 101): **89,88,87,83,78 77,76,76,66**
CSF £11.41 TOTE £2.90: £1.20, £2.50, £1.10; EX 13.30 Trifecta £34.60.
**Owner** Mohamed Obaida **Bred** Rabbah Bloodstock Llc **Trained** Newmarket, Suffolk
**FOCUS**
A steadily run maiden. The front three pulled a long way clear.
T/Plt: £184.90 to a £1 stake. Pool: £43,419.33 - 171.36 winning units. T/Qpdt: £48.80 to a £1 stake. Pool: £3957.30 - 59.90 winning units. NF

# 5147 NEWMARKET (R-H)
Saturday, August 9

**OFFICIAL GOING: Soft (good to soft in places; 5.6)**
Wind: Light half-behind Weather: Fine

## 5187 BBAG-SALES.DE-THE GERMAN BLOODSTOCK SALES MAIDEN FILLIES' STKS (BOBIS RACE) 7f
2:00 (2:03) (Class 4) 2-Y-0 £3,881 (£1,155; £577; £288) Stalls High

Form RPR
**1** **Marsh Hawk** 2-9-0 JamesDoyle 2 90+
(Richard Hannon) *mde all: clr 5f out: shkn up over 1f out: r.o wl* **6/1**[3]
**2** *7* **Fadhayyil (IRE)** 2-9-0 DaneO'Neill 7 73+
(B W Hills) *hld up: hdwy 1/2-way: rdn to chse wnr over 1f out: sn outpcd* **7/2**[1]
**3** *3/4* **Light Fantastic** 2-9-0 PatSmullen 8 71+
(Ed Dunlop) *prom: chsd wnr over 4f out tl rdn over 1f out: styd on same pce* **6/1**[3]
**4** *4* **Rose Above** 2-9-0 OisinMurphy 11 61
(Andrew Balding) *hld up: hdwy over 2f out: nvr trbld ldrs* **8/1**
**5** *1 1/4* **I'm A Butterfly (IRE)** 2-9-0 JohnFahy 4 58
(Eve Johnson Houghton) *hld up: rdn over 2f out: nvr trbld ldrs* **8/1**

6 *nk* **Peeps** 2-9-0 0........ TedDurcan 12 57
(Mark H Tompkins) *prom: pushed along over 2f out: wknd over 1f out* **33/1**

7 *2 1/2* **Cascades (IRE)** 2-9-0 0........ LiamKeniry 6 51
(David Elsworth) *chsd wnr tl over 4f out: remained handy tl wknd over 1f out* **4/1**[2]

8 *9* **Lexi Grady Alice** 2-9-0 0........ JimmyQuinn 5 28
(Mark H Tompkins) *s.i.s: a in rr: wknd 3f out* **66/1**

9 *17* **Signs And Signals (IRE)** 2-9-0 0........ FrederikTylicki 3
(Ed Vaughan) *prom: pushed along and lost pl 4f out: sn bhd* **12/1**

1m 27.61s (1.91) **Going Correction** +0.525s/f (Yiel) **9** Ran SP% **105.1**
Speed ratings (Par 93): **110,102,101,96,95 94,91,81,62**
CSF £22.64 TOTE £6.20: £1.90, £1.30, £2.40; EX 18.30 Trifecta £75.60.
**Owner** Rockcliffe Stud **Bred** Rockcliffe Stud **Trained** East Everleigh, Wilts
■ Spirited Acclaim was withdrawn. Price at time of withdrawal 8-1. Rule 4 applies to all bets - deduction 10p in the pound.

**FOCUS**
Far side track used with Stalls on Far side except 10f, 12f &16f: Centre. Bend into home straight realigned and 10f race increased by 18m. This maiden was won by subsequent Group 1 winners Passage Of Time in 2006 and Winsili in 2012, but although this year's winner was impressive the ground appeared to take its toll on a few and they came home at long intervals. The winning time wasn't at all bad in the conditions, though.

## 5188 RACEBETS.COM H'CAP 1m 2f
**2:30** (2:32) (Class 2) (0-100,97) 3-Y-O+ **£12,938** (£3,850; £1,924; £962) **Stalls** Centre

Form RPR

6443 **1** **Clon Brulee (IRE)**[64] 2957 5-10-0 **97**........ SilvestreDeSousa 8 109
(Saeed bin Suroor) *a.p: chsd ldr over 7f out: shkn up to ld over 1f out: styd on wl* **11/4**[2]

6230 **2** *4 1/2* **Master Of Finance (IRE)**[7] 4893 3-8-5 **88**........ CamHardie(5) 7 91
(Mark Johnston) *led: rdn and hdd over 1f out: no ex ins fnl f* **5/2**[1]

6-05 **3** *3/4* **Tinghir (IRE)**[72] 2707 4-9-9 **92**........ TedDurcan 6 94
(David Lanigan) *hld up: pushed along over 2f out: hdwy u.p over 1f out: hung lft ins fnl f: nt run on* **7/2**[3]

0026 **4** *6* **Nicholascopernicus (IRE)**[29] 4173 5-9-6 **89**........ DaneO'Neill 5 80
(Ed Walker) *pushed along in rr early: hdwy over 6f out: pushed along over 3f out: rdn and wknd over 1f out* **13/2**

-043 **5** *17* **Enobled**[22] 4400 4-9-0 **83**........ ShaneKelly 4 61
(Sir Michael Stoute) *chsd ldr tl over 7f out: remained handy tl rdn and wknd 2f out* **5/1**

2m 9.14s (3.64) **Going Correction** +0.525s/f (Yiel)
**WFA** 3 from 4yo+ 9lb **5** Ran SP% **107.5**
Speed ratings (Par 109): **106,102,101,97,83**
CSF £9.46 TOTE £2.80: £1.50, £1.80; EX 7.80 Trifecta £15.80.
**Owner** Godolphin **Bred** Collette Twomey **Trained** Newmarket, Suffolk

**FOCUS**
The five remaining runners went an even pace in this decent handicap and the field stayed against the nearside rail after turning in. The third is the guide.

## 5189 BUY GERMAN, RACE GERMAN, WIN GERMAN H'CAP 7f
**3:05** (3:06) (Class 2) (0-105,103) 3-Y-O+
**£12,450** (£3,728; £1,864; £932; £466; £234) **Stalls** High

Form RPR

-103 **1** **Rene Mathis (GER)**[14] 4683 4-9-3 **94**........ DavidNolan 9 104
(Richard Fahey) *chsd ldr tl shkn up to ld over 2f out: rdn and hung lft over 1f out: styd on* **7/4**[1]

4000 **2** *2 1/4* **Victoire De Lyphar (IRE)**[14] 4661 7-8-13 **90**........(e) FrederikTylicki 4 94
(Ruth Carr) *led over 4f: sn rdn: styd on same pce fnl f* **15/2**

22 **3** *3/4* **Englishman**[50] 3431 4-8-12 **89**........ JamieSpencer 10 91
(Charles Hills) *chsd ldrs: rdn and hung lft fr over 2f out: no ex wl ins fnl f* **3/1**[2]

0340 **4** *1 1/4* **Gramercy (IRE)**[28] 4212 7-8-5 **87**........ CamHardie(5) 1 86
(David Simcock) *prom: racd keenly: rdn over 1f out: no ex ins fnl f* **11/2**[3]

0000 **5** *1 3/4* **Mezzotint (IRE)**[14] 4681 5-8-11 **88**........ JamesDoyle 8 82
(Stuart Williams) *hld up: hdwy 4f out: rdn over 1f out: wknd ins fnl f* **12/1**

4-00 **6** *4* **Common Touch (IRE)**[21] 4442 6-9-1 **92**........ ChrisCatlin 6 76
(Willie Musson) *hld up: pushed along over 2f out: wknd over 1f out* **20/1**

-003 **7** *5* **Excellent Guest**[7] 4916 7-8-13 **90**........ PaoloSirigu 3 61
(George Margarson) *hld up: rdn and wknd over 1f out* **9/1**

1m 27.95s (2.25) **Going Correction** +0.525s/f (Yiel)
**WFA** 3 from 4yo+ 6lb **7** Ran SP% **111.0**
Speed ratings (Par 109): **108,105,104,103,101 96,90**
CSF £14.60 CT £34.62 TOTE £2.30: £1.30, £6.10; EX 14.70 Trifecta £66.10.
**Owner** Dr Marwan Koukash **Bred** Stall 5-Stars **Trained** Musley Bank, N Yorks

**FOCUS**
This decent handicap had gone to a 4yo seven times in the previous ten runnings and that trend continued. It was a small personal-best from the winner.

## 5190 GERMAN-THOROUGHBRED.COM SWEET SOLERA STKS (GROUP 3) (FILLIES) 7f
**3:35** (3:37) (Class 1) 2-Y-O
**£28,355** (£10,750; £5,380; £2,680; £1,345; £675) **Stalls** High

Form RPR

14 **1** **Muraaqaba**[14] 4646 2-9-0 0........ DaneO'Neill 10 104
(Mark Johnston) *a.p: pushed along over 2f out: rdn to ld and hung rt ins fnl f: r.o* **7/1**

011 **2** *1 3/4* **Calypso Beat (USA)**[42] 3721 2-9-0 95........ PatSmullen 2 100
(Kevin Ryan) *led: rdn over 1f out: hdd and unable qck ins fnl f* **10/1**

1 **3** *1* **Winters Moon (IRE)**[28] 4202 2-9-0 0........ SilvestreDeSousa 6 98+
(Saeed bin Suroor) *hld up: hdwy over 2f out: rdn and hung lft over 1f out: styd on same pce ins fnl f* **15/8**[1]

11 **4** *3/4* **Alonsoa (IRE)**[16] 4585 2-9-0 0........ FergusSweeney 8 96
(Henry Candy) *chsd ldr: rdn over 1f out: styd on same pce fnl f* **7/2**[2]

0161 **5** *hd* **Arabian Queen (IRE)**[29] 4164 2-9-5 100........ LiamKeniry 1 100
(David Elsworth) *trckd ldrs: racd keenly: rdn over 1f out: styd on same pce fnl f* **11/2**[3]

31 **6** *1/2* **Stroll Patrol**[10] 4784 2-9-0 81........ JamieSpencer 7 94
(Philip McBride) *hld up in tch: rdn and ev ch over 1f out: hung lft and no ex ins fnl f* **6/1**

511 **7** *10* **Savoy Showgirl (IRE)**[28] 4178 2-9-0 86........ JamesDoyle 3 73
(Michael Bell) *hld up: wknd 2f out* **25/1**

1m 28.04s (2.34) **Going Correction** +0.525s/f (Yiel) **7** Ran SP% **112.1**
Speed ratings (Par 101): **107,105,103,103,102 102,90**
CSF £68.50 TOTE £8.80: £4.60, £3.20; EX 75.60 Trifecta £277.60.
**Owner** Hamdan Al Maktoum **Bred** Shadwell Estate Company Limited **Trained** Middleham Moor, N Yorks

**FOCUS**
This Group 3 contest has been won by some high-class fillies in recent years, with Rainbow View (2008), White Moonstone (2010) and Certify (2012) all going on to take the Fillies' Mile later in the season. This year's field raced up the centre of the track throughout, but they didn't seem to go much of a pace early (the winning time was the slowest of the three 7f races on the card) and a couple were inclined to take a grip. Probably more to come from the winner.

## 5191 POPPY MAIDEN STKS 1m 4f
**4:10** (4:10) (Class 5) 3-Y-O+ **£3,234** (£962; £481; £240) **Stalls** Centre

Form RPR

54 **1** **Pennine Panther**[37] 3891 3-9-1 0........ FergusSweeney 1 78
(Henry Candy) *mde all: rdn and edgd lft over 1f out: jst hld on* **1/1**[1]

**2** *nk* **Shuriken (IRE)** 3-8-10 0........ RobertHavlin 2 72
(Peter Chapple-Hyam) *dwlt: sn prom: edgd lft over 2f out: rdn to chse wnr over 1f out: styd on* **11/1**

0305 **3** *8* **Mawaseel**[24] 4325 3-9-1 71........ DaneO'Neill 3 64
(B W Hills) *chsd wnr tl rdn over 1f out: hung lft and wknd ins fnl f* **11/4**[2]

**4** *33* **River Glass (IRE)** 3-9-1 0........ JamieSpencer 4 35
(Charles Hills) *s.i.s: hld up: hdwy over 4f out: sn rdn: wknd 3f out: eased over 1f out* **10/3**[3]

2m 44.7s (11.80) **Going Correction** +0.525s/f (Yiel) **4** Ran SP% **108.1**
Speed ratings (Par 103): **81,80,75,53**
CSF £11.02 TOTE £1.90; EX 12.40 Trifecta £21.40.
**Owner** Deal, Lowe, Silver, Woods **Bred** Hermes Services Ltd **Trained** Kingston Warren, Oxon

**FOCUS**
An uncompetitive 3yo maiden and they dawdled. Unlike in the previous race on the round course, the runners made for the centre of the track on turning in.

## 5192 ROYAL BRITISH LEGION H'CAP (BOBIS RACE) 1m
**4:45** (4:45) (Class 2) (0-100,102) 3-Y-O **£12,938** (£3,850; £1,924; £962) **Stalls** High

Form RPR

1 **1** **Dream Spirit (IRE)**[49] 3477 3-8-11 **90**........ LiamJones 5 102
(William Haggas) *trckd ldrs: racd keenly: rdn over 1f out: led ins fnl f: styd on* **9/2**[3]

1-1 **2** *1/2* **Maverick Wave (USA)**[16] 4580 3-9-0 **93**........ RobertHavlin 1 104
(John Gosden) *led: rdn over 1f out: edgd lft and hdd ins fnl f: styd on* **2/1**[1]

11 **3** *3 3/4* **Invincible Fresh (IRE)**[36] 3917 3-9-1 **94**........ FrederikTylicki 4 96
(James Fanshawe) *s.i.s: hld up: effrt over 1f out: no ex fnl f* **5/2**[2]

23-2 **4** *28* **Day Of Conquest**[9] 4826 3-9-4 **102**........ CamHardie(5) 3 80
(Richard Hannon) *plld hrd: trckd ldr tl swtchd to r alone 6f out: up w the pce tl pushed along over 2f out: wknd over 1f out* **5/2**[2]

1m 42.14s (2.14) **Going Correction** +0.525s/f (Yiel) **4** Ran SP% **108.7**
Speed ratings (Par 106): **110,109,105,77**
CSF £13.57 TOTE £4.20; EX 10.30 Trifecta £24.60.
**Owner** Roberts Green Whittall-Williams Savidge **Bred** Tom & Paul Monaghan **Trained** Newmarket, Suffolk

**FOCUS**
An interesting 3yo handicap despite the small field, with three of the four remaining runners defending unbeaten records, but the race was spoiled to an extent by the majority of the field pulling hard early, including the winner.

## 5193 PAMELA HAPPY 80TH BIRTHDAY H'CAP 2m 24y
**5:15** (5:17) (Class 3) (0-90,90) 3-Y-O+ **£9,056** (£2,695; £1,346; £673) **Stalls** Centre

Form RPR

-334 **1** **Rhombus (IRE)**[28] 4217 4-9-9 **90**........ CamHardie(5) 6 101
(Ismail Mohammed) *s.i.s: hld up: hdwy to chse ldr over 3f out: rdn to ld and edgd rt over 1f out: styd on wl* **7/2**[3]

1061 **2** *6* **Purple Spectrum**[16] 4584 3-8-9 **86**........(p) LiamJones 5 90+
(William Haggas) *plld hrd: led: rdn and hdd over 1f out: no ex ins fnl f* **11/10**[1]

325 **3** *3/4* **Nashville (IRE)**[28] 4217 5-9-1 **77**........ DavidNolan 4 80
(Richard Fahey) *chsd ldr: tl rdn over 3f out: styd on same pce fr over 1f out* **8/1**

**4** *1/2* **Money Spider (IRE)**[2] 5116 5-8-13 **75**........ JamieSpencer 2 77
(J F Levins, Ire) *chsd ldrs: rdn over 3f out: no ex fnl f* **3/1**[2]

330/ **5** *64* **Regal Park (IRE)**[152] 6690 7-8-6 **73**........ GeorgeDowning(5) 1
(Miss Imogen Pickard) *hld up: rdn over 3f out: wknd over 2f out: eased* **33/1**

3m 39.5s (12.50) **Going Correction** +0.525s/f (Yiel)
**WFA** 3 from 4yo+ 15lb **5** Ran SP% **108.9**
Speed ratings (Par 107): **89,86,85,85,53**
CSF £7.66 TOTE £4.80: £3.10, £1.10; EX 8.80 Trifecta £37.00.
**Owner** Sheikh Rashid Dalmook Al Maktoum **Bred** Ruskerne Ltd **Trained** Newmarket, Suffolk

**FOCUS**
A modest pace for this staying handicap and the runners raced centre-to-stands' side up the straight.
T/Plt: £718.30 to a £1 stake. Pool of £67947.51 - 69.05 winning tickets. T/Qpdt: £190.40 to a £1 stake. Pool of £3653.83 - 14.20 winning tickets. CR

# 4790 REDCAR (L-H)
Saturday, August 9

**OFFICIAL GOING: Good to soft (good in places; 7.2)**
Wind: fresh 1/2 behind Weather: fine but very breezy

## 5194 RACING UK ANYWHERE AVAILABLE NOW (S) STKS 6f
**2:15** (2:16) (Class 6) 2-Y-O **£2,385** (£704; £352) **Stalls** Centre

Form RPR

05 **1** **Smart Stepper (IRE)**[13] 4708 2-8-8 0........ ConnorBeasley(3) 4 58+
(Michael Dods) *mde all: kpt on wl fnl f* **7/1**[3]

00 **2** *2* **Lady Jade**[25] 4286 2-8-6 0........ JasonHart 3 46
(Nigel Tinkler) *chsd ldrs: kpt on fnl f: tk 2nd nr fin* **25/1**

4465 **3** *1/2* **Black Pudding (IRE)**[7] 4899 2-8-11 62........(b[1]) PJMcDonald 1 50
(Ann Duffield) *chsd wnr: upsides over 2f out: rdn over 1f out: wknd nr fin* **6/4**[1]

50 **4** *1 1/4* **Tuebrook**[22] 4389 2-8-11 0........ JamesSullivan 11 46
(Michael Easterby) *hld up in rr: hdwy over 2f out: edgd rt and kpt on fnl f* **50/1**

0 **5** *1 3/4* **Ship Canal**[18] 4510 2-8-11 0........ DavidAllan 8 41
(Michael Easterby) *dwlt: in rr: hdwy over 2f out: kpt on fnl f* **50/1**

6306 **6** *1 1/4* **Blazing Rose (IRE)**[8] 4870 2-8-6 56........[1] LukeMorris 9 32
(David O'Meara) *s.i.s: sme hdwy over 2f out: nvr nr ldrs* **7/1**[3]

6554 **7** *3/4* **Sunhill Lodge Lady**[7] 4899 2-8-6 38........(v[1]) RoystonFfrench 10 30
(Ann Duffield) *mid-div: rdn over 2f out: wknd over 1f out* **28/1**

4432 **8** *7* **Reet Petite (IRE)**[17] 4528 2-8-6 50..............................(v) AndrewMullen 6 9
(Michael Dods) *chsd ldrs: lost pl over 1f out* **5/1**[2]

60 **9** *3* **Prince Of Clowns (IRE)**[25] 4286 2-8-11 0........................ PhillipMakin 5 5
(John Quinn) *chsd ldrs: lost pl wl over 1f out* **8/1**

0 **10** *12* **Tagula Nation (IRE)**[15] 4624 2-8-6 0.................................... IanBrennan 7
(Paul Midgley) *mid-div: lost pl over 2f out: bhd whn eased* **66/1**

3000 **11** *16* **Show Spirit**[7] 4899 2-8-1 50..........................................(p) ShaneGray(5) 2
(Kevin Ryan) *in rr and sn drvn along: wl bhd whn eased over 1f out: t.o* **12/1**

1m 13.87s (2.07) **Going Correction** +0.075s/f (Good) **11** Ran SP% **113.2**
Speed ratings (Par 92): **89,86,85,84,81 80,79,69,65,49 28**
CSF £166.72 TOTE £9.30: £2.60, £5.80, £1.90; EX 227.20 Trifecta £1727.00 Part won..The winner was bought in for £8,200.
**Owner** Appleton, Davison, Thompson **Bred** Cbs Bloodstock **Trained** Denton, Co Durham

**FOCUS**
A one-sided seller, the winner having things under control a long way out.

## 5195 FOLLOW REDCARRACING ON FACEBOOK & TWITTER MEDIAN AUCTION MAIDEN STKS 7f

**2:50** (2:54) (Class 5) 3-4-Y-O **£2,911** (£866; £432; £216) **Stalls** Centre

Form RPR

552 **1** **Duelling Dragon (USA)**[10] 4791 3-9-5 73........................ PhillipMakin 1 81
(David Barron) *w ldrs: led 1f out: edgd rt: drvn out* **15/8**[2]

3 **2** *1* **Glorious Sun**[22] 4407 3-9-5 0............................................ LukeMorris 10 78
(Ed Walker) *t.k.h: led: hdd 1f out: no ex* **5/4**[1]

4653 **3** *1 3/4* **Cliff (IRE)**[13] 4713 4-9-8 68.......................................... ConnorBeasley(3) 7 75
(Nigel Tinkler) *hld up towards rr: hdwy over 3f out: sn chsng ldrs: one pce whn swtchd lft ins fnl f* **7/1**[3]

04 **4** *10* **Bond Empire**[16] 4569 4-9-6 0........................................ JacobButterfield(5) 9 49
(Geoffrey Oldroyd) *dwlt: t.k.h: sn trcking ldrs: outpcd over 3f out: hung lft and wknd appr fnl f* **16/1**

55 **5** *3/4* **It's A Yes From Me**[30] 4111 3-9-5 0.................................. TonyHamilton 4 45
(James Fanshawe) *hld up in mid-div: outpcd and lost pl over 2f out* **10/1**

6030 **6** *1* **Lady Liz**[32] 4063 3-9-0 50.............................................(b) AndrewMullen 8 37
(George Moore) *chsd ldrs: rdn 3f out: lost pl over 1f out* **50/1**

0 **7** *7* **Soviet Union (IRE)**[10] 4791 3-9-0 0.................................. DuranFentiman 2 19
(Mark Walford) *s.i.s: hdwy to chse ldrs over 4f out: wknd over 2f out* **80/1**

05 **8** *nk* **Pepperello**[46] 3543 3-9-5 0............................................ JamesSullivan 3 23
(Tim Etherington) *in rr: rdn 4f out: sn bhd* **100/1**

**9** *3/4* **Mr Gatsby** 3-9-5 0................................................................ JasonHart 5 22
(Mark Walford) *chsd ldrs: lost pl after 2f: bhd fnl 3f* **33/1**

1m 25.47s (0.97) **Going Correction** +0.075s/f (Good)
**WFA** 3 from 4yo 6lb **9** Ran SP% **113.8**
Speed ratings (Par 103): **97,95,93,82,81 80,72,72,71**
L'inganno Felice was withdrawn. Price at time of withdrawal 40-1. Rule 4 does not apply. CSF £4.41 TOTE £3.10: £1.20, £1.10, £2.10; EX 4.70 Trifecta £13.60.
**Owner** Qatar Racing Limited **Bred** Anthem Bloodstock **Trained** Maunby, N Yorks

**FOCUS**
Fair form from the leading trio, who came clear.

## 5196 DOWNLOAD THE RACINGUK IPAD APP H'CAP (QUALIFIER FOR THE STRAIGHT-MILE CHAMPIONSHIP) 1m

**3:20** (3:22) (Class 4) (0-85,83) 3-Y-O+ **£6,469** (£1,925; £962; £481) **Stalls** Centre

Form RPR

06 **1** **Dual Mac**[59] 3097 7-8-13 70..............................................[1] DaleSwift 5 79
(Neville Bycroft) *trckd ldrs: t.k.h: edgd lft and led last 50yds* **33/1**

4-04 **2** *1/2* **Ready (IRE)**[136] 1103 4-9-9 80........................................ AndrewMullen 3 88
(Garry Moss) *chsd ldrs: led 1f out: carried lft and hdd last 50yds: no ex* **25/1**

3051 **3** *shd* **No Poppy (IRE)**[2] 5079 6-9-4 75 6ex................................. DavidAllan 7 83
(Tim Easterby) *in rr-div: hdwy over 2f out: chsng ldrs over 1f out: carried lft last 50yds: no ex* **6/1**[2]

2025 **4** *1 3/4* **Potent Embrace (USA)**[7] 4922 3-8-9 73.......................... AdrianNicholls 12 76
(Mark Johnston) *led: hdd 1f out: fdd clsng stages* **8/1**

3502 **5** *1* **Green Howard**[15] 4635 6-9-10 81........................................ JasonHart 11 82+
(Robin Bastiman) *dwlt: in rr: hdwy over 2f out: hung lft and one pce appr fnl f* **15/2**

4504 **6** *1/2* **Barren Brook**[15] 4635 7-9-8 79.......................................... JamesSullivan 4 79
(Michael Easterby) *hld up towards rr: hdwy over 2f out: one pce whn hmpd wl ins fnl f* **8/1**

0143 **7** *5* **Hakuna Matata**[50] 3437 7-9-5 79..........................(b) ConnorBeasley(3) 13 68
(Michael Dods) *chsd ldrs: wknd appr fnl f* **8/1**

0024 **8** *1/2* **Wannabe King**[21] 4451 8-9-9 80......................................(p) PJMcDonald 6 67
(Geoffrey Harker) *mid-div: effrt over 2f out: lost pl over 1f out* **16/1**

0640 **9** *6* **Commissar**[11] 4761 5-9-1 72........................................... StevieDonohoe 10 46
(Ian Williams) *racd in last: drvn 3f out: nvr on terms* **16/1**

0060 **10** *2 1/4* **Evanescent (IRE)**[14] 4661 5-9-2 73.................................... IanBrennan 9 42
(John Quinn) *chsd ldrs: lost pl over 1f out* **20/1**

-416 **11** *1/2* **Alketios (GR)**[17] 4549 3-9-3 81.......................................... LukeMorris 2 47
(Luca Cumani) *prom: drvn over 2f out: wknd appr fnl f* **7/1**[3]

-210 **12** *1* **Epic Voyage (USA)**[22] 4390 3-8-9 73...................................[1] PaulPickard 1 37
(Brian Ellison) *mid-div: drvn 3f out: lost pl over 1f out* **20/1**

1611 **U** **Border Bandit (USA)**[21] 4451 6-9-12 83..................(p) RobertWinston 14
(Tracy Waggott) *stmbld and uns rdr s* **11/2**[1]

1m 37.42s (0.82) **Going Correction** +0.075s/f (Good)
**WFA** 3 from 4yo+ 7lb **13** Ran SP% **115.3**
Speed ratings (Par 105): **98,97,97,95,94 94,89,88,82,80 79,78,**
CSF £657.53 CT £5527.50 TOTE £48.20: £13.00, £10.10, £3.20; EX 819.50 Trifecta £1003.50 Part won..
**Owner** Mrs C M Whatley **Bred** N Bycroft **Trained** Norton, N Yorks

**FOCUS**
A fair handicap. The pace appeared sound, but not that many ever threatened to land a serious blow.

## 5197 MARKET CROSS JEWELLERS H'CAP 7f

**3:55** (3:56) (Class 4) (0-80,80) 3-Y-O+ **£6,469** (£1,925; £962; £481) **Stalls** Centre

Form RPR

25 **1** **Fieldgunner Kirkup (GER)**[7] 4923 6-9-9 77................ AndrewMullen 2 87
(David Barron) *w ldr: led ins fnl f: kpt on* **14/1**

0212 **2** *hd* **Mishaal (IRE)**[6] 4938 4-9-9 77........................................... DaleSwift 11 86
(Michael Herrington) *t.k.h: mde most: hdd ins fnl f: no ex* **7/2**[1]

6460 **3** *1* **Instant Attraction (IRE)**[31] 4074 3-9-4 78................ RussKennemore 7 82
(Jedd O'Keeffe) *chsd ldrs: hung rt and kpt on same pce last 150yds* **9/1**[3]

1302 **4** *2 1/4* **Mon Brav**[15] 4632 7-9-12 80................................................ PaulPickard 4 81
(Brian Ellison) *hld up in rr: hdwy over 2f out: kpt on fnl f* **11/1**

6022 **5** *hd* **Smart Salute**[13] 4697 3-9-0 74...........................................(b) LukeMorris 3 72
(Ed Walker) *hld up in mid-div: hdwy to chse ldrs over 1f out: one pce* **10/1**

0412 **6** *2 1/2* **Illustrious Prince (IRE)**[49] 3485 7-9-6 77............ ConnorBeasley(3) 15 71
(Julie Camacho) *towards rr: effrt and hung lft over 2f out: nt clr run over 1f out: swtchd lft and styd on last 75yds* **12/1**

0605 **7** *hd* **Lazarus Bell**[50] 3437 4-9-10 78...................................... RobertWinston 17 71
(Alan Brown) *mid-div: hdwy over 2f out: hung lft: one pce* **9/1**[3]

410- **8** *1 1/2* **Hulcolt (IRE)**[310] 6972 3-8-13 73....................................... JasonHart 14 60
(Garry Moss) *chsd ldrs: one pce fnl 2f* **25/1**

0563 **9** *1/2* **Lilac Lace (IRE)**[7] 4925 4-8-12 73.......................... RachelRichardson(7) 18 61
(Tim Easterby) *chsd ldrs: hung lft over 1f out: fdd* **6/1**[2]

5043 **10** *1* **King Pin**[13] 4703 9-8-10 64.........................................(p) RoystonFfrench 19 49
(Tracy Waggott) *in rr: sn drvn along: kpt on over 1f out: nvr on terms* **20/1**

0020 **11** *3/4* **Snow Bay**[8] 4861 8-9-6 74................................................(p) PhillipMakin 8 57
(Paul Midgley) *chsd ldrs: wknd over 1f out* **25/1**

360- **12** *1* **Chiswick Bey (IRE)**[221] 8454 6-9-2 70.............................. TonyHamilton 10 51
(Richard Fahey) *in rr: nvr on terms* **25/1**

3226 **13** *1 1/2* **Zain Zone (IRE)**[15] 4628 3-9-3 77...............................(e[1]) JamesSullivan 1 52
(Ruth Carr) *mid-div: effrt over 2f out: lost pl over 1f out* **12/1**

5310 **14** *6* **Sleeping Apache (IRE)**[30] 4108 4-9-6 74.......................... DuranFentiman 16 35
(Philip Kirby) *chsd ldrs: lost pl 2f out: heavily eased ins fnl f* **28/1**

5000 **P** **Trade Secret**[15] 4632 7-9-6 74.............................................. DavidAllan 13
(Mel Brittain) *in rr: heavily eased 3f out: sn hopelessly t.o: p.u ins fnl f* **20/1**

1m 24.23s (-0.27) **Going Correction** +0.075s/f (Good)
**WFA** 3 from 4yo+ 6lb **15** Ran SP% **120.5**
Speed ratings (Par 105): **104,103,102,100,99 96,96,95,94,93 92,91,89,82,**
CSF £55.81 CT £493.75 TOTE £12.90: £5.40, £3.30, £4.10; EX 103.90 Trifecta £843.30 Part won..
**Owner** J Sagar **Bred** I And D Meinke **Trained** Maunby, N Yorks

**FOCUS**
A fair handicap. As in the previous race the gallop appeared sound, but nothing ever threatened to get heavily involved from off the pace.

## 5198 REDCAR RACECOURSE WEDDING FAYRE 21ST SEPTEMBER CLAIMING STKS 1m

**4:25** (4:26) (Class 6) 3-Y-O **£2,385** (£704; £352) **Stalls** Centre

Form RPR

0533 **1** **Rough Courte (IRE)**[14] 4674 3-8-7 70........................ CharlesBishop(3) 7 66
(Mick Channon) *mde all: clr after 3f: drvn out* **5/2**[2]

0260 **2** *2* **Slingsby**[20] 4468 3-8-7 51................................................(b) PJMcDonald 6 58
(Michael Easterby) *chsd ldrs: chsd wnr 2f out: hung lft and kpt on same pce ins fnl f* **33/1**

533U **3** *10* **Lilly Junior**[18] 4516 3-8-6 72........................................(p) NathanAlison(5) 2 39
(William Haggas) *sn trcking ldrs: t.k.h: 2nd over 3f out: wknd over 1f out* **1/1**[1]

2000 **4** *1* **Hello Sweetness**[35] 3950 3-8-2 44 ow2...........................[1] AndrewMullen 5 28
(Jason Ward) *awkward s: in rr: drvn and hdwy 4f out: wknd over 1f out* **33/1**

0065 **5** *3/4* **Scrutiny**[17] 4530 3-9-2 68..................................................[1] JulieBurke(3) 4 43
(David O'Meara) *in rr: drvn 4f out: chsng ldrs over 2f out: lost pl over 1f out* **14/1**

0322 **6** *3/4* **Sicilian Bay (IRE)**[20] 4473 3-8-2 53.................................... IanBrennan 3 24
(Paul Midgley) *chsd ldrs: lost pl over 1f out* **9/2**[3]

5 **7** *50* **Good To Remember**[23] 4365 3-8-0 0.............................. JamesSullivan 1
(Ruth Carr) *wnt lft s: in rr: lost pl 4f out: sn bhd: hopelessly t.o: virtually p.u* **100/1**

1m 37.36s (0.76) **Going Correction** +0.075s/f (Good) **7** Ran SP% **110.3**
Speed ratings (Par 98): **99,97,87,86,85 84,34**
.Lilly Junior was claimed by B Ellison for £10,500.\n\x\x
**Owner** Billy Parish **Bred** Futoo Club **Trained** West Ilsley, Berks

**FOCUS**
This ended up being a weak claimer. The favourite was very disappointing.

## 5199 WIN A VIP DAY OUT AT REDCARRACING.CO.UK H'CAP 6f

**4:55** (4:55) (Class 4) (0-85,84) 3-Y-O+ **£6,469** (£1,925; £962; £481) **Stalls** Centre

Form RPR

2350 **1** **Avon Breeze**[24] 4317 5-9-8 80.................................(p) RussKennemore 11 90
(Richard Whitaker) *mid-div: drvn over 2f out: styd on to ld 1f out: kpt on* **9/1**[3]

0256 **2** *1 1/2* **Pennine Warrior**[22] 4404 3-8-8 70..................................(p) LukeMorris 7 74
(Scott Dixon) *chsd ldrs: styd on same pce last 75yds* **14/1**

0331 **3** *3/4* **Burren View Lady (IRE)**[15] 4629 4-9-3 75......................(e) DavidAllan 13 78
(Tim Easterby) *mid-div: drvn and outpcd 3f out: hdwy over 1f out: kpt on wl ins fnl f* **12/1**

3225 **4** *hd* **Cruise Tothelimit (IRE)**[7] 4925 6-9-7 79........................ StevieDonohoe 2 81
(Ian Williams) *w ldr: led 2f out: hdd 1f out: kpt on same pce* **14/1**

5100 **5** *hd* **Head Space (IRE)**[7] 4925 6-9-7 79...................................(v) JamesSullivan 4 81
(Ruth Carr) *dwlt: in rr: hdwy over 1f out: styng on wl at fin* **12/1**

0-20 **6** *1/2* **Personal Touch**[57] 3202 5-9-8 80........................................ TonyHamilton 9 80
(Richard Fahey) *chsd ldrs: one pce over 1f out* **9/1**[3]

62 **7** *1 1/4* **Run With Pride (IRE)**[58] 3152 4-9-10 82................................. DaleSwift 3 78
(Derek Shaw) *hld up in rr: hdwy over 2f out: chsng ldrs over 1f out: wknd last 50yds* **3/1**[1]

-543 **8** *1 1/2* **Mississippi**[25] 4305 5-9-12 84........................................... AndrewMullen 10 75
(David Barron) *sn bhd: kpt on fnl 2f: nvr a factor* **7/1**[2]

040- **9** *1 3/4* **Pea Shooter**[315] 6822 5-9-4 76.......................................... AdrianNicholls 16 62
(David Nicholls) *led: hdd 2f out: wknd appr fnl f* **18/1**

3000 **10** *1* **Lewisham**[29] 4146 4-8-13 78............................................ AnnaHesketh(7) 6 60
(David Nicholls) *in rr: sme hdwy over 2f out: wknd over 1f out* **9/1**[3]

0035 **11** *3 1/4* **Lady Ibrox**[11] 4752 4-9-2 74.........................................(t) RobertWinston 15 46
(Alan Brown) *mid-div: hdwy to chse ldrs 3f out: lost pl 2f out* **25/1**

3463 **12** *8* **Sunraider (IRE)**[13] 4712 7-9-7 79........................................ PhillipMakin 1 25
(Paul Midgley) *slipped and s.s: a detached in last: eased clsng stages* **10/1**

1m 11.24s (-0.56) **Going Correction** +0.075s/f (Good)
**WFA** 3 from 4yo+ 4lb **12** Ran SP% **114.4**
Speed ratings (Par 105): **106,104,103,102,102 101,100,98,95,94 90,79**
CSF £123.93 CT £1510.01 TOTE £10.70: £4.10, £3.40, £3.20; EX 158.10 Trifecta £2093.40 Part won..
**Owner** Grange Park Racing II & Partner **Bred** Hellwood Stud Farm **Trained** Scarcroft, W Yorks

**FOCUS**
A fairly useful sprint which was soundly run and the form should prove solid enough for the level.

## 5200 LADIES' & GENTS' EVENING 23RD AUGUST H'CAP 1m 6f 19y
**5:30** (5:30) (Class 6) (0-65,66) 3-Y-O+ **£2,264** (£673; £336; £168) **Stalls** Low

Form RPR
2153 **1** **Chivers (IRE)**[24] 4316 3-9-0 **64** TonyHamilton 4 74
(Tim Easterby) *chsd ldrs: drvn 4f out: sn outpcd: hdwy over 2f out: edgd rt: styd on to ld fnl strides* **11/4**[2]
6506 **2** *nk* **District Attorney (IRE)**[11] 4755 5-8-9 **46** oh1 MichaelStainton 1 55
(Chris Fairhurst) *mid-div: hdwy on ins over 3f out: chsng ldrs over 1f out: edgd rt: led nr fin: hdd fnl strides* **33/1**
5121 **3** *1 ½* **Windshield**[8] 4844 3-9-2 **66** (p) LukeMorris 3 73
(Sir Mark Prescott Bt) *led 1f: trckd ldrs: led over 2f out: rdn 3 l clr over 1f out: fdd and hdd clsng stages* **2/1**[1]
000P **4** *3 ¾* **Pindora (GER)**[19] 4497 3-8-0 **50** oh1 (t) JamesSullivan 2 52
(Noel Quinlan) *chsd ldrs: edgd lft and one pce over 1f out* **33/1**
0502 **5** *1 ¾* **Authentication**[2] 5090 5-8-12 **49** DavidAllan 12 48
(Mel Brittain) *led after 1f: hdd after 2f: chsd ldrs: led over 3f out: hdd over 2f out: one pce* **6/1**[3]
0245 **6** *2 ¾* **Medieval Bishop (IRE)**[47] 3532 5-9-13 **64** (p) JasonHart 6 59
(Mark Walford) *mid-div: hdwy over 3f out: hung lft and one pce fnl 2f* **15/2**
0503 **7** *½* **Cowslip**[66] 2900 5-8-10 **54** KieranSchofield(7) 7 49
(George Moore) *sn bhd: sme hdwy on outside 4f out: nvr nr ldrs* **16/1**
-550 **8** *4* **Amir Pasha (UAE)**[47] 3532 9-8-9 **46** oh1 (p) PJMcDonald 10 35
(Micky Hammond) *mid-div: effrt over 3f out: nvr a factor* **14/1**
0-40 **9** *5* **Petite Madame (IRE)**[48] 3498 3-8-2 **57** (b[1]) NoelGarbutt(5) 9 39
(David Thompson) *in rr: hdwy 9f out: chsng ldrs 6f out: lost pl over 2f out* **50/1**
-003 **10** *3* **Noosa Sound**[47] 3535 4-8-9 **46** oh1 (t) RoystonFfrench 8 24
(John Davies) *w ldrs: led after 2f: hdd over 3f out: wknd 2f out* **25/1**
0400 **11** *9* **To Begin**[19] 4497 3-8-0 **50** oh6 (b[1]) DuranFentiman 11 15
(Tim Easterby) *dwlt: in rr: bhd fnl 3f: eased clsng stages* **50/1**

3m 4.78s (0.08) **Going Correction** +0.075s/f (Good)
**WFA** 3 from 4yo+ 13lb **11** Ran SP% **112.2**
Speed ratings (Par 101): **102,101,100,98,97 96,95,93,90,89 83**
CSF £96.99 CT £214.28 TOTE £3.30: £1.40, £8.70, £1.10; EX 91.90 Trifecta £482.80.
**Owner** C H Stevens **Bred** Epona Bloodstock Ltd **Trained** Great Habton, N Yorks

**FOCUS**
A modest staying event which was run at a sound pace.
T/Plt: £640.90 to a £1 stake. Pool of £63937.52 - 72.81 winning tickets. T/Qpdt: £169.60 to a £1 stake. Pool of £3520.94 - 15.36 winning tickets. WG

# 4784 LEICESTER (R-H)
Sunday, August 10

**OFFICIAL GOING: Soft**
Wind: Fresh across Weather: Rain clearing

## 5201 BRITISH STALLION STUDS EBF MAIDEN STKS (BOBIS RACE) 7f 9y
**2:00** (2:05) (Class 4) 2-Y-O **£5,175** (£1,540; £769; £384) **Stalls** High

Form RPR
2 **1** **Good Contact (USA)**[30] 4167 2-9-5 0 ChrisCatlin 1 80
(Saeed bin Suroor) *trckd ldrs: racd keenly: wnt 2nd over 4f out: shkn up to ld over 1f out: r.o* **2/5**[1]
3 **2** *1* **Wonder Of Qatar (IRE)**[39] 3847 2-9-5 0 SeanLevey 9 78
(Richard Hannon) *a.p: pushed along over 2f out: rdn to chse wnr ins fnl f: r.o* **8/1**[3]
**3** *1 ¾* **Mutasayyid** 2-9-5 0 TomQueally 6 73+
(Richard Hannon) *s.s: sn pushed along in rr: hdwy over 1f out: r.o to go 3rd wl ins fnl f: nrst fin* **14/1**
0 **4** *¾* **Roxie Lot**[24] 4346 2-9-0 0 StephenCraine 4 66
(Pam Sly) *led: rdn and hdd over 1f out: styd on same pce ins fnl f* **50/1**
00 **5** *3 ¼* **Yukon Gold**[10] 4809 2-9-5 0 AhmedAjtebi 3 63
(Charlie Appleby) *chsd ldrs: pushed along 1/2-way: wknd ins fnl f* **33/1**
00 **6** *1 ¼* **Best Endeavour**[18] 4550 2-9-5 0 MartinDwyer 10 60
(William Muir) *mid-div: hdwy over 2f out: wknd ins fnl f* **25/1**
**7** *2* **Pleiades** 2-9-5 0 RyanMoore 7 55
(Sir Michael Stoute) *s.s: sn pushed along in rr: nvr on terms* **6/1**[2]
60 **8** *4* **Akavit (IRE)**[34] 4025 2-9-5 0 OisinMurphy 8 45
(Ed de Giles) *mid-div: pushed along over 4f out: hdwy 1/2-way: wknd 2f out* **100/1**
60 **9** *1* **Able Mate**[27] 4270 2-9-5 0 AdamKirby 5 43
(Clive Cox) *mid-div: pushed along 1/2-way: wknd wl over 1f out* **25/1**

1m 26.95s (0.75) **Going Correction** -0.10s/f (Good) **9** Ran SP% **117.1**
Speed ratings (Par 96): **91,89,87,87,83 81,79,75,73**
CSF £3.97 TOTE £1.30: £1.02, £1.90, £2.60; EX 5.70 Trifecta £22.30.
**Owner** Godolphin **Bred** Darley **Trained** Newmarket, Suffolk
■ Coolcalmcollected was withdrawn. Price at time of withdrawal 8-1. Rule 4 applies to all bets - deduction 10p in the pound.

**FOCUS**
The rain-softened surface found out the majority in this interesting 2yo maiden and the first pair fought out the final furlong towards the stands' side. Sound form.

## 5202 KUBE EXHIBITION CENTRE (S) STKS 7f 9y
**2:30** (2:30) (Class 5) 3-4-Y-O **£2,587** (£770; £384; £192) **Stalls** High

Form RPR
4213 **1** **Cape Of Hope (IRE)**[9] 4875 4-9-7 69 (v) AdrianNicholls 2 76
(David Nicholls) *trckd ldr tl led over 2f out: rdn clr fr over 1f out* **6/4**[1]
6625 **2** *7* **Inkerman (IRE)**[15] 4674 4-9-2 74 AdamKirby 5 53
(Jamie Osborne) *hld up: tk clsr order 4f out: rdn to chse wnr over 1f out: no ex fnl f* **6/4**[1]
0000 **3** *3 ¾* **Assembly**[15] 4678 4-9-2 49 (b) DougieCostello 1 43
(Mark Rimell) *led and sn clr tl 4f out: rdn and hdd over 2f out: wknd fnl f* **25/1**
5061 **4** *½* **Henke (IRE)**[11] 4785 3-9-1 56 (p) AndrewMullen 4 45
(Nigel Tinkler) *chsd ldrs: rdn 1/2-way: wknd ins fnl f* **5/1**[2]
**5** *4 ½* **Brian The Lion** 3-8-10 0 OisinMurphy 3 28
(Shaun Harris) *s.s: outpcd* **16/1**[3]

1m 25.77s (-0.43) **Going Correction** -0.10s/f (Good)
**WFA** 3 from 4yo 6lb **5** Ran SP% **106.4**
Speed ratings (Par 103): **98,90,85,85,80**
CSF £3.57 TOTE £2.00: £1.40, £1.10; EX 5.00 Trifecta £33.70.Cape Of Hope was bought by Tom Dascombe for 9500gns
**Owner** Middleham Park Racing LIII & Partners **Bred** Pendley Farm **Trained** Sessay, N Yorks

**FOCUS**
A very weak affair and the winner was entitled to win with the runner-up not acting on the ground.

## 5203 DANIEL MOULT 30TH BIRTHDAY H'CAP 1m 1f 218y
**3:00** (3:01) (Class 4) (0-85,85) 3-Y-O+ **£6,301** (£1,886; £943; £472; £235) **Stalls** Low

Form RPR
4204 **1** **Gothic**[36] 3986 3-9-4 **84** RyanMoore 5 93
(Sir Michael Stoute) *a.p: chsd ldr 1/2-way: rdn to ld over 2f out: edgd rt over 1f out: styd on u.p* **11/4**[1]
0355 **2** *½* **Noble Gift**[29] 4204 4-9-11 **82** AdamKirby 7 90
(William Knight) *s.i.s: hld up: hdwy 4f out: rdn to chse wnr over 1f out: ev ch ins fnl f: styd on* **6/1**[2]
**3** *1 ½* **All Talk N No Do (IRE)**[71] 2781 3-8-11 **77** OisinMurphy 9 82
(Seamus Durack) *sn led: rdn and hdd over 2f out: styd on same pce ins fnl f* **9/1**
5-40 **4** *½* **Headline News (IRE)**[29] 4184 5-9-11 **82** ChrisCatlin 6 86
(Rae Guest) *hld up: hdwy over 2f out: rdn and hung rt fr over 1f out: nt rch ldrs* **6/1**[2]
-343 **5** *1* **Don't Stare**[32] 4091 4-9-11 **82** (t[1]) ShaneKelly 8 84
(James Fanshawe) *prom: rdn over 2f out: edgd rt over 1f out: styd on* **6/1**[2]
4233 **6** *21* **Artful Prince**[22] 4427 4-9-6 **77** (b) DaleSwift 3 39
(James Given) *chsd ldrs tl rdn and wknd 3f out* **6/1**[2]
0113 **7** *6* **Martinas Delight (USA)**[37] 3926 4-9-2 **73** RobertWinston 1 24
(Timothy Jarvis) *hld up: hdwy 3f out: sn rdn and wknd* **14/1**
1220 **8** *2 ¼* **Red Warrior (IRE)**[30] 4175 4-9-9 **85** LouisSteward(5) 2 32
(Ismail Mohammed) *chsd ldr to 1/2-way: rdn and wknd over 2f out* **7/1**[3]

2m 9.8s (1.90) **Going Correction** +0.35s/f (Good)
**WFA** 3 from 4yo+ 9lb **8** Ran SP% **113.0**
Speed ratings (Par 105): **106,105,104,104,103 86,81,79**
CSF £18.82 CT £127.80 TOTE £2.50: £1.60, £2.20, £2.50; EX 17.70 Trifecta £190.80.
**Owner** Highclere Thoroughbred Racing -Petrushka **Bred** Mr & Mrs G Middlebrook **Trained** Newmarket, Suffolk

## 5204 COPLOW H'CAP (BOBIS RACE) 5f 218y
**3:30** (3:31) (Class 3) (0-90,100) 3-Y-O£9,451 (£2,829; £1,414; £708; £352) **Stalls** High

Form RPR
1522 **1** **Basil Berry**[30] 4176 3-9-0 **86** ConnorBeasley(3) 1 94
(Chris Dwyer) *chsd ldrs: rdn over 1f out: edgd lft and r.o to ld wl ins fnl f* **6/1**[3]
5034 **2** *1* **Piazon**[14] 4700 3-9-0 **88** LouisSteward(5) 9 93
(Michael Bell) *chsd ldrs: rdn and hung lft over 2f out: ev ch fr over 1f out tl unable qck towards fin* **4/1**[1]
-215 **3** *½* **Major Jack**[15] 4669 3-8-13 **82** OisinMurphy 8 85
(Roger Charlton) *hld up: hdwy over 1f out: rdn: hung lft and nt clr run ins fnl f: swtchd rt: r.o: nt rch ldrs* **4/1**[1]
3-51 **4** *hd* **Cordial**[18] 4539 3-8-5 **74** LukeMorris 7 77
(Stuart Williams) *led: edgd rt over 2f out: rdn over 1f out: hdd and no ex wl ins fnl f* **25/1**
2110 **5** *nk* **Foxy Clarets (IRE)**[15] 4669 3-9-2 **85** (b) TonyHamilton 10 87
(Richard Fahey) *in rr: bhd and drvn along 1/2-way: r.o wl ins fnl f: nt rch ldrs* **8/1**
4500 **6** *1* **Charles Molson**[30] 4166 3-9-5 **88** BenCurtis 5 87
(Henry Candy) *prom: rdn over 2f out: styd on same pce ins fnl f* **9/2**[2]
101 **7** *1 ¾* **Dinneratmidnight**[27] 4262 3-9-2 **85** RyanMoore 6 84
(Ralph Beckett) *in rr: outpcd over 3f out: running on whn nt clr run ins fnl f: nvr trbld ldrs* **4/1**[1]
10 **8** *1 ½* **Groundworker (IRE)**[25] 4328 3-8-3 **77** DannyBrock(5) 3 65
(Sylvester Kirk) *chsd ldr: rdn over 2f out: wknd fnl f* **16/1**

1m 11.77s (-1.23) **Going Correction** -0.10s/f (Good) **8** Ran SP% **113.3**
Speed ratings (Par 104): **104,102,102,101,101 100,97,95**
CSF £29.61 CT £107.33 TOTE £5.90: £1.90, £1.40, £1.10; EX 21.00 Trifecta £160.70.
**Owner** Strawberry Fields Stud **Bred** Strawberry Fields Stud **Trained** Newmarket, Suffolk

**FOCUS**
A fair 3yo sprint handicap where the main action came near the stands' rail.

## 5205 BLABY H'CAP 5f 218y
**4:00** (4:00) (Class 5) (0-70,71) 3-Y-O **£3,234** (£962; £481; £240) **Stalls** High

Form RPR
6422 **1** **Castorienta**[11] 4788 3-9-8 **71** PatCosgrave 8 79+
(George Baker) *chsd ldrs: rdn to ld 1f out: r.o* **13/8**[1]
3253 **2** *nk* **Bold Spirit**[17] 4569 3-9-7 **70** (b[1]) RyanMoore 7 76
(Richard Hannon) *led: edgd rt over 2f out: rdn and hdd 1f out: r.o* **2/1**[2]
6630 **3** *3 ¾* **Two Shades Of Grey (IRE)**[45] 3625 3-9-2 **65** TonyHamilton 6 59
(Richard Fahey) *chsd ldr tl rdn over 1f out: no ex ins fnl f* **4/1**[3]
2005 **4** *1* **Clever Miss**[33] 4047 3-8-12 **66** DannyBrock(5) 9 57
(Alan McCabe) *hld up: rdn over 2f out: no ex fnl f* **8/1**
5300 **5** *4 ½* **Ecliptic Sunrise**[6] 4972 3-8-5 **57** (t) ConnorBeasley(3) 5 33
(Des Donovan) *prom: rdn over 2f out: wknd over 1f out* **16/1**

1m 11.1s (-1.90) **Going Correction** -0.10s/f (Good) **5** Ran SP% **108.4**
Speed ratings (Par 100): **108,107,102,101,95**
CSF £4.98 TOTE £2.40: £1.20, £1.20; EX 5.90 Trifecta £8.20.
**Owner** D P Barrie **Bred** D P Barrie **Trained** Manton, Wilts

**FOCUS**
A modest 3yo handicap, but the winning time was quicker than the preceding 0-90.

## 5206 BOOK YOUR CHRISTMAS PARTY AT LEICESTER H'CAP 1m 60y
**4:30** (4:30) (Class 5) (0-75,75) 3-Y-O+ **£3,234** (£962; £481; £240) **Stalls** Low

Form RPR
1103 **1** **Arrowzone**[69] 2827 3-9-7 **75** AdamKirby 1 83
(Garry Moss) *a.p: rdn to ld 2f out: edgd lft ins fnl f: styd on u.p* **2/1**[1]
1105 **2** *1* **Run Fat Lass Run**[27] 4254 4-9-2 **66** (p) ConnorBeasley(3) 8 73
(Philip Kirby) *hld up: hdwy over 1f out: r.o to go 2nd wl ins fnl f: nt rch wnr* **10/1**
3142 **3** *1* **Comanchero (IRE)**[16] 4613 3-9-1 **69** OisinMurphy 6 73+
(Andrew Balding) *a.p: chsd ldr 6f out: rdn and ev ch 2f out: styd on same pce ins fnl f* **3/1**[2]
**4** *1 ¾* **Sweet Martoni**[43] 3733 4-10-0 **75** TomQueally 7 76
(William Knight) *led: rdn and hdd 2f out: styd on same pce fnl f* **7/2**[3]
3530 **5** *hd* **Argot**[36] 3978 3-8-13 **67** LukeMorris 5 66
(Anthony Carson) *hld up: drvn along over 3f out: hdwy over 2f out: no ex ins fnl f* **5/1**

5-53 **6** *1 ¼* **Skyfire**[10] 4831 7-8-8 **58**............ NataliaGemelova(3) 2 55
(Nick Kent) *chsd ldr 2f: remained handy: rdn and ev ch 2f out: no ex fnl f* **16/1**

1m 48.01s (2.91) **Going Correction** +0.35s/f (Good)
**WFA** 3 from 4yo+ 7lb 6 Ran SP% **112.2**
Speed ratings (Par 103): **99,98,97,95,95 93**
CSF £22.22 CT £57.69 TOTE £3.40: £1.80, £4.40; EX 22.90 Trifecta £82.20.
**Owner** Ron Hull **Bred** J K Beckitt And Son **Trained** Tickhill, S Yorks
■ Stewards' Enquiry : Natalia Gemelova two-day ban: used whip above permitted level (Aug 24-25)

**FOCUS**
A modest handicap that looked tight on paper and it was an open finish.

## 5207 ROTHERBY H'CAP 5f 2y
**5:00** (5:00) (Class 6) (0-65,68) 3-Y-O+ **£2,587** (£770; £384; £192) **Stalls** High

Form RPR
2043 **1** **Only Ten Per Cent (IRE)**[15] 4675 6-9-9 **64**............(v) AdamKirby 1 76
(J R Jenkins) *sn chsng ldr: led over 1f out: rdn and edgd lft ins fnl f: r.o* **4/1**[3]

3150 **2** *1 ½* **Incomparable**[20] 4494 9-8-7 **53**............(p) MatthewHopkins(5) 6 60
(Scott Dixon) *chsd ldrs: pushed along 1/2-way: styd on ins fnl f* **8/1**

633 **3** *¾* **Pull The Pin (IRE)**[6] 4960 5-8-12 **56**............(bt) CharlesBishop(3) 2 60
(Ann Stokell) *led: rdn and hdd over 1f out: no ex wl ins fnl f* **15/8**[1]

0063 **4** *2 ¼* **Minty Jones**[11] 4788 5-8-8 **52**............(b) RobertTart(3) 10 48
(Michael Mullineaux) *prom: hung rt fr 1/2-way: no imp fnl f* **7/2**[2]

300 **5** *1 ¾* **Solemn**[37] 3939 9-9-8 **63**............(b) OisinMurphy 8 53
(Milton Bradley) *sn pushed along in rr: n.d* **5/1**

-50 **6** *2 ½* **Aya's Gift**[11] 4788 3-9-0 **58**............(b[1]) LukeMorris 4 38
(Ed Walker) *s.i.s: sn drvn along and a in rr* **14/1**

405- **7** *1* **Time For Crabbies (IRE)**[326] 6519 4-8-9 **53**............ ConnorBeasley(3) 3 30
(Lisa Williamson) *sn pushed along towards rr: rdn 1/2-way: wknd fnl f* **25/1**

1m 0.58s (0.58) **Going Correction** -0.10s/f (Good)
**WFA** 3 from 4yo+ 3lb 7 Ran SP% **115.3**
Speed ratings (Par 101): **91,88,87,83,81 77,75**
CSF £35.59 CT £78.06 TOTE £3.90: £1.90, £5.50; EX 31.80 Trifecta £100.10.
**Owner** B Silkman **Bred** Sandro Garavelli **Trained** Royston, Herts

**FOCUS**
A moderate sprint handicap, run at a brisk early tempo and only three mattered from 2f out.
T/Jkpt: £606.20 to a £1 stake. Pool: £74,708.44 - 87.50 winning units. T/Plt: £11.90 to a £1 stake. Pool: £94,098.13 - 5768.93 winning units. T/Qpdt: £8.20 to a £1 stake. Pool: £6325.29 - 570.60 winning units. CR

# 4980 WINDSOR (R-H)
Sunday, August 10

**OFFICIAL GOING: Good to soft (good in places; 7.6)**
Wind: blustery, behind Weather: heavy shower before racing, dry

## 5208 BETFAIR NOVICE FLAT AMATEUR RIDERS' H'CAP (FOR NOVICE AMATEUR RIDERS) 1m 3f 135y
**2:15** (2:15) (Class 5) (0-70,65) 4-Y-O+ **£2,495** (£774; £386; £193) **Stalls** Centre

Form RPR
3534 **1** **Royal Etiquette (IRE)**[6] 4985 7-10-4 **55**............(tp) MrAlexFerguson 5 66
(Lawney Hill) *s.i.s: hld up wl in tch: clsd to trck ldrs 3f out: led on bit ent fnl 2f: drew clr over 1f out: rdn out: easily* **3/1**[1]

1245 **2** *5* **Taste The Wine (IRE)**[10] 4818 8-10-8 **62**............(t) MrJPWilliams(3) 3 65
(Bernard Llewellyn) *wl in tch in midfield: hdwy to ld 1/2-way: rdn and hdd ent fnl 2f: sn drvn and outpcd: wnt modest 2nd again 1f out* **5/1**[3]

45-3 **3** *1 ¼* **Bernisdale**[33] 2419 6-10-11 **62**............ MrHHunt 4 63
(John Flint) *led for 2f: chsd ldrs after: effrt u.p 3f out: chsd wnr ent fnl 2f: drvn and btn over 1f out: 3rd and plugged on same pce fnl f* **7/2**[2]

105 **4** *2* **Hamble**[5] 5011 5-10-7 **58**............ MrMJPKendrick 1 55
(Giles Bravery) *s.i.s: in tch in last trio: clsd to chse ldrs 3f out: rdn and effrt over 2f out: drvn and btn over 1f out: wknd* **3/1**[1]

0443 **5** *2 ¾* **Sutton Sid**[11] 4797 4-10-8 **59**............(v) MissMBryant 7 52
(Paddy Butler) *wl in tch in midfield: shkn up and effrt 3f out: little rspnse and sn btn* **6/1**

/-00 **6** *9* **Carrowbeg (IRE)**[13] 4744 6-10-4 **55**............(bt) MissPFuller 9 33
(Lawney Hill) *chsd ldrs: rdn and unable qck over 2f out: drifted lft and wknd 2f out* **12/1**

0-05 **7** *15* **Swords**[25] 4327 12-9-6 **46** oh1............ MissSPeacock(3) 2
(Ray Peacock) *t.k.h: chsd ldrs tl led after 2f: hdd 1/2-way: dropped out qckly over 3f out: t.o fnl 2f* **33/1**

-160 **8** *6* **Gentlemax (FR)**[99] 1941 4-10-11 **65**............ MissTWorsley(3) 8 8
(Jim Boyle) *t.k.h: chsd ldrs tl lost pl and bhd 1/2-way: rdn and lost tch over 3f out: t.o fnl 2f* **12/1**

2m 36.87s (7.37) **Going Correction** +0.50s/f (Yiel) 8 Ran SP% **121.5**
Speed ratings (Par 103): **95,91,90,89,87 81,71,67**
CSF £19.83 CT £56.35 TOTE £3.90: £1.60, £1.60, £1.70; EX 22.00 Trifecta £81.60.
**Owner** Mrs John Ferguson **Bred** Windflower Overseas Holdings Inc **Trained** Aston Rowant, Oxon

**FOCUS**
All inner rails moved to provide fresh ground. Top bend dolled out 14yds from normal inner configuration, adding 53yds to races of one mile and beyond. Inner of sraight dolled out 14yds at 6f and 6yds at winning post. Ground described as good to soft after overnight and morning rain.

## 5209 MACDONALD HOTEL WINDSOR NOVICE AUCTION STKS 5f 10y
**2:45** (2:45) (Class 5) 2-Y-O **£2,587** (£770; £384; £192) **Stalls** Low

Form RPR
1246 **1** **Parsley (IRE)**[22] 4439 2-8-6 91............ CamHardie(5) 2 86
(Richard Hannon) *pressed ldr tl led 1/2-way: rdn hands and heels and jnd over 1f out: drifted lft 1f out: asserted fnl 100yds: pushed out* **1/4**[1]

**2** *½* **Marigot Bay** 2-8-6 0............ DavidProbert 5 79+
(Gay Kelleway) *s.i.s and rn green early: clsd to trck ldrs 1/2-way: rdn and ev ch over 1f out: kpt on but hld fnl 100yds* **10/1**[3]

61 **3** *4 ½* **Ivors Rebel**[97] 2007 2-8-13 74............ LiamKeniry 4 70
(David Elsworth) *chsd ldrs: rdn and wnt to r on far rail 1/2-way: 3rd and btn 1f out: wknd ins fnl f* **3/1**[2]

**4** *2 ¾* **Miss Inga Sock (IRE)** 2-8-6 0............ JohnFahy 3 53
(Eve Johnson Houghton) *s.i.s: rn green and pushed along in detached: nvr on terms: wnt modest 4th ins fnl f* **16/1**

60 **5** *4 ½* **Lady Of Illusion**[36] 3975 2-8-3 0............ RyanTate(3) 1 37
(Mark Usher) *t.k.h: led tl hdd 1/2-way: rdn and btn over 1f out: fdd fnl f* **50/1**

1m 0.16s (-0.14) **Going Correction** -0.025s/f (Good) 5 Ran SP% **121.9**
Speed ratings (Par 94): **100,99,92,87,80**
CSF £5.34 TOTE £1.30: £1.02, £3.80; EX 6.80 Trifecta £10.80.
**Owner** De La Warr Racing **Bred** Thomas Hassett **Trained** East Everleigh, Wilts

**FOCUS**
A modest little novice auction stakes.

## 5210 ROYAL WINDSOR RACECOURSE YOUNG HOOVES CLUB MAIDEN AUCTION STKS 6f
**3:15** (3:15) (Class 5) 2-Y-O **£2,587** (£770; £384; £192) **Stalls** Low

Form RPR
03 **1** **Some Show**[11] 4784 2-8-9 0............ FergusSweeney 7 71
(Henry Candy) *chsd ldng trio: rdn and hdwy to ld over 1f out: kpt on wl fnl f: rdn out* **6/4**[1]

0 **2** *¾* **Ickymasho**[22] 4444 2-8-9 0............ RichardKingscote 9 69
(Jonathan Portman) *hld up in tch in midfield: hdwy 2f out: rdn over 1f out: chsd wnr wl ins fnl f: kpt on but a hld* **3/1**[2]

0 **3** *1* **Flashy Diva**[47] 3557 2-8-8 0............ DavidProbert 13 65+
(Henry Candy) *chsd ldng pair: rdn ent fnl 2f: chsd wnr 1f out: styd on same pce and lost 2nd wl ins fnl f* **8/1**

55 **4** *1 ½* **Mazoula (IRE)**[15] 4652 2-8-2 0............ NoelGarbutt(5) 1 59
(Hugo Palmer) *led: rdn over 2f out: drvn and hdd over 1f out: wknd fnl 100yds* **10/1**

00 **5** *1 ¾* **Mullionheir**[61] 3081 2-9-0 0............ WilliamCarson 4 61
(John Best) *t.k.h: chsd ldr tl over 1f out: no ex u.p 1f out: wknd ins fnl f* **33/1**

**6** *½* **Little Lord Nelson** 2-8-12 0............(t) AdamBeschizza 10 57
(Stuart Williams) *s.i.s: hld up in last trio: pushed along and sme hdwy 2f out: styd on same pce fnl f* **12/1**

6 **7** *1 ¼* **Q Twenty Girl (IRE)**[13] 4740 2-7-13 0............ CharlotteJenner(7) 8 48
(Mark Usher) *in tch in midfield: rdn over 2f out: no ex u.p over 1f out: wknd fnl f* **7/1**[3]

6 **8** *3 ¾* **Onelastfling**[16] 4610 2-8-1 0............ CamHardie(5) 11 36
(Sylvester Kirk) *in tch in midfield: rdn ent fnl 2f: sn btn and wknd over 1f out* **20/1**

**9** *5* **Italian Beauty (IRE)** 2-8-8 0............ SamHitchcott 3 23
(Timothy Jarvis) *s.i.s: rn green in last trio: n.d* **20/1**

**10** *10* **Bounty Bah** 2-9-0 0............ LiamKeniry 2
(Mark Usher) *hld up in tch in midfield: rdn over 2f out: sn btn and wknd: t.o ins fnl f* **20/1**

**11** *2 ¼* **Sleeping Rough** 2-8-9 0............ MichaelJMMurphy(3) 5
(Stuart Kittow) *s.i.s: rn green and a rdn along in rr: lost tch 1/2-way: t.o fnl f* **14/1**

1m 13.11s (0.11) **Going Correction** -0.025s/f (Good) 11 Ran SP% **129.3**
Speed ratings (Par 94): **98,97,95,93,91 90,89,84,77,64 61**
CSF £6.20 TOTE £2.00: £1.10, £1.40, £3.40; EX 8.30 Trifecta £26.50.
**Owner** The Rumble Racing Club **Bred** Lady Hardy **Trained** Kingston Warren, Oxon

**FOCUS**
Probably just ordinary maiden form.

## 5211 OSSIE & HUTCH MEMORIAL FILLIES' H'CAP 6f
**3:45** (3:46) (Class 4) (0-85,85) 3-Y-O+ **£6,469** (£1,925; £962; £481) **Stalls** Low

Form RPR
-100 **1** **Perfect Alchemy (IRE)**[72] 2745 3-9-1 **78**............ RichardKingscote 6 88
(Ralph Beckett) *stdd s: t.k.h: chsd ldrs: effrt to chse ldr over 1f out: drvn to ld 1f out: kpt on wl: drvn out* **9/2**[3]

-211 **2** *hd* **Mia San Triple**[13] 4741 3-9-6 **83**............ SilvestreDeSousa 4 92
(Jeremy Noseda) *in tch in last pair: rdn over 2f out: hdwy u.p over 1f out: ev ch ins fnl f: kpt on but hld towards fin* **10/11**[1]

6166 **3** *2 ¼* **Sarangoo**[20] 4502 6-9-4 **77**............ FergusSweeney 5 80
(Malcolm Saunders) *led: rdn 2f out: hdd and no ex 1f out: wknd fnl 100yds* **8/1**

3 **4** *4* **Amygdala (USA)**[10] 4811 3-9-3 **80**............ GeorgeBaker 3 69
(Stuart Williams) *hld up in rr: short-lived effrt over 1f out: sn btn: wknd ins fnl f* **7/2**[2]

-600 **5** *2 ¼* **Lady Gibraltar**[37] 3927 5-9-11 **84**............ KierenFallon 2 67
(Timothy Jarvis) *chsd ldr tl over 1f out: sn rdn and dropped out: wknd fnl f* **6/1**

1m 11.86s (-1.14) **Going Correction** -0.025s/f (Good)
**WFA** 3 from 4yo+ 4lb 5 Ran SP% **118.2**
Speed ratings (Par 102): **106,105,102,97,94**
CSF £9.91 TOTE £7.00: £3.20, £1.10; EX 10.00 Trifecta £47.50.
**Owner** The Perfect Partnership & D H Caslon **Bred** W Maxwell Ervine **Trained** Kimpton, Hants

**FOCUS**
A reasonable fillies' handicap.

## 5212 UNIBET 90+ INSURANCE MONEY BACK MAIDEN STKS 1m 67y
**4:15** (4:15) (Class 5) 2-Y-O **£2,587** (£770; £384; £192) **Stalls** Low

Form RPR
0 **1** **Glasgow Gailes (USA)**[13] 4740 2-9-5 0............ GeorgeBaker 7 74+
(K R Burke) *mde all: clr whn rn green and pushed along briefly bnd 5f out: jnd and rdn over 1f out: asserted u.p ins fnl f: kpt on: quite comf* **2/1**[1]

40 **2** *½* **Stolen Story (IRE)**[23] 4416 2-9-5 0............ KierenFallon 3 73
(George Margarson) *chsd wnr: drvn and effrt to chal over 1f out: kpt on but hld fnl 75yds* **9/4**[2]

**3** *4 ½* **Blues Dancer** 2-9-5 0............ LiamKeniry 2 63+
(Sylvester Kirk) *in tch: wnt 3rd 6f out: rdn and outpcd over 1f out: clr 3rd but wl hld fnl f* **9/2**

**4** *8* **Sheila Belle (IRE)** 2-9-0 0............ JohnFahy 6 41
(J S Moore) *chsd ldng pair tl 6f out: rdn over 2f out: wknd over 1f out* **12/1**

**5** *½* **Le Torrent** 2-9-5 0............ FergusSweeney 4 44
(Henry Candy) *awkward leaving stalls and s.i.s: rn green and pushed along in rr: rdn 2f out: sn wknd* **11/4**[3]

0 **6** *2 ¾* **Who'Sthedaddy**[29] 4207 2-9-2 0............ ThomasBrown(3) 5 38
(Daniel Kubler) *in tch in last pair: rdn over 2f out: sn btn: bhd over 1f out* **20/1**

1m 48.88s (4.18) **Going Correction** +0.50s/f (Yiel) 6 Ran SP% **121.4**
Speed ratings (Par 94): **99,98,94,86,85 82**
CSF £7.64 TOTE £3.40: £1.20, £1.80; EX 8.70 Trifecta £19.70.
**Owner** The Albatross Club **Bred** Exchange Rate Syndicate & M J Hogan Enterprises IN **Trained** Middleham Moor, N Yorks

**FOCUS**
Likely this is quite weak maiden form with the front two having run to just a modest level prior to this.

## 5213 DOWNLOAD THE UNIBET PRO APP H'CAP — 1m 67y
**4:45** (4:47) (Class 3) (0-90,90) 3-Y-0+ **£9,703** (£2,887; £1,443; £721) **Stalls** Low

Form | | | | RPR
1634 **1** **Starwatch**[24] 4354 7-9-0 **76**...(v) WilliamCarson 4 — 85
(John Bridger) *led: rdn ent fnl 2f: drvn and hdd 1f out: battled bk u.p to ld again fnl 50yds: gng away at fin* **5/1**

5-41 **2** *¾* **Ree's Rascal (IRE)**[71] 2772 6-9-8 **89**... NathanAlison(5) 8 — 96
(Jim Boyle) *chsd ldrs: rdn and effrt 2f out: drvn to chal over 1f out: led 1f out: hdd fnl 50yds: no ex and wkng cl home* **5/2**[1]

2600 **3** *1½* **Whipper Snapper (IRE)**[30] 4148 4-9-4 **80**...(v) GeorgeBaker 2 — 84
(William Knight) *reluctant to go down: eventually led rdrless to s: hld up in tch: styd nr-side and effrt to chse ldrs 2f out: one pce fnl f* **7/1**

015- **4** *1¼* **Mystical Sapphire**[283] 7649 4-10-0 **90**... FergusSweeney 1 — 91
(Jo Crowley) *stdd s: hld up in tch in last trio: rdn and hdwy over 1f out: no imp ins fnl f* **12/1**

0646 **5** *2¼* **Directorship**[12] 4761 8-9-11 **87**... LiamKeniry 10 — 83
(Patrick Chamings) *stdd s: t.k.h: hld up in tch in last trio: swtchd lft and effrt over 1f out: no prog and wl hld fnl f* **9/2**[3]

5 **6** *1¾* **Evident (IRE)**[68] 2876 4-8-13 **75**... SilvestreDeSousa 12 — 66
(Jeremy Noseda) *pressed ldr: rdn over 3f out: stl chsng ldrs and hrd drvn over 1f out: btn 1f out: wknd* **4/1**[2]

6020 **7** *½* **Solo Hunter**[15] 4679 3-8-6 **75**... DavidProbert 3 — 64
(David Evans) *chsd ldrs: effrt u.p over 2f out: lost pl and btn over 1f out: wknd fnl f* **7/1**

4100 **8** *36* **Myboyalfie (USA)**[73] 2707 7-9-10 **86**... AdamBeschizza 7
(J R Jenkins) *in tch in midfield: dropped to last and rdn over 2f out: sn lost tch: t.o fnl f* **10/1**

1m 47.15s (2.45) **Going Correction** +0.50s/f (Yiel)
**WFA** 3 from 4yo+ 7lb — **8** Ran SP% **125.2**
Speed ratings (Par 107): **107,106,104,103,101 99,99,63**
CSF £19.85 CT £93.53 TOTE £6.30: £1.50, £1.10, £2.60; EX 17.10 Trifecta £121.60.
**Owner** J J Bridger **Bred** Mrs J A Chapman **Trained** Liphook, Hants

**FOCUS**
A competitive handicap.

## 5214 ESSENSUALS HAIRDRESSING ROYAL WINDSOR LADIES NIGHT H'CAP — 1m 2f 7y
**5:15** (5:15) (Class 5) (0-70,74) 3-Y-0+ **£2,587** (£770; £384; £192) **Stalls** Centre

Form | | | | RPR
632 **1** **Choral Festival**[13] 4743 8-9-11 **67**... WilliamCarson 6 — 74
(John Bridger) *hld up in tch: wnt 2nd 4f out: rdn to chal over 1f out: drifting lft but led fnl 100yds: styd on* **5/2**[2]

2055 **2** *nk* **Urban Space**[6] 4985 8-8-11 **53**...(t) LiamKeniry 1 — 59
(John Flint) *led: rdn ent fnl 2f: drifting lft over 1f out: drvn and hdd fnl 100yds: battled on gamely but hld towards fin* **6/1**

-055 **3** *8* **Lacock**[16] 4613 3-9-1 **66**... FergusSweeney 5 — 57
(Henry Candy) *broke fast: sn restrained and hld up in last: effrt in 3rd 2f out: no prog and wl btn 1f out* **11/4**[3]

604 **4** *5* **Elite Force (IRE)**[31] 4130 3-9-5 **70**...(t) GeorgeBaker 2 — 52
(Roger Charlton) *sn chsd ldr: hung lft and reminders 4f out: hung bdly lft over 2f out: sn drvn and dropped to last: wl btn 1f out* **5/4**[1]

2m 12.29s (3.59) **Going Correction** +0.50s/f (Yiel)
**WFA** 3 from 8yo 9lb — **4** Ran SP% **114.0**
Speed ratings (Par 103): **105,104,98,94**
CSF £15.78 TOTE £3.20; EX 14.60 Trifecta £39.20.
**Owner** Mrs Liz Gardner **Bred** Cheveley Park Stud Ltd **Trained** Liphook, Hants

**FOCUS**
Form weakened by the dreadful run of hot favourite Elite Force who was in trouble a long way out.
T/Plt: £6.50 to a £1 stake. Pool: £87,390.40 - 9772.71 winning units. T/Qpdt: £2.60 to a £1 stake. Pool: £5203.27 - 1474.00 winning units. SP

# 4475 CURRAGH (R-H)
Sunday, August 10

**OFFICIAL GOING: Yielding changing to soft after race 1 (2.35)**

## 5218a KEENELAND PHOENIX STKS (GROUP 1) (C&F) — 6f
**4:05** (4:05) 2-Y-0
**£96,666** (£31,666; £15,000; £5,000; £3,333; £1,666)

| | | | RPR
**1** **Dick Whittington (IRE)**[22] 4460 2-9-3 105... JosephO'Brien 5 — 114
(A P O'Brien, Ire) *chsd ldrs: 4th 1/2-way: tk clsr order bhd ldrs under 2f out where bmpd: rdn on outer and got on terms ent fnl f: kpt on best u.p to ld nr fin* **6/1**[3]

**2** *½* **Kool Kompany (IRE)**[21] 4482 2-9-3 111... RichardHughes 7 — 112
(Richard Hannon) *trckd ldrs: racd keenly early: 3rd 1/2-way: n.m.r bhd ldrs 2f out and sn swtchd rt: rdn on terms ent fnl f and ev ch between horses: hdd nr fin and jst hld 2nd* **8/11**[1]

**3** *shd* **Cappella Sansevero**[43] 3738 2-9-3 105... ColinKeane 3 — 112
(G M Lyons, Ire) *trckd ldrs: rdn to ld 1 1/2f out: sn strly pressed u.p and jnd ent fnl f: hdd ins fnl 150yds: kpt on wl towards fin in cl 3rd: jst hld for 2nd* **13/2**

**4** *2* **Beach Belle**[69] 2856 2-9-0... JamieSpencer 9 — 103
(Kevin Prendergast, Ire) *dwlt sltly: settled bhd ldrs in 5th: tk clsr order bhd ldrs bef 1/2-way: n.m.r over 2f out: rdn in 4th ent fnl f and kpt on wl towards fin: nvr on terms* **4/1**[2]

**5** *5* **Kasbah (IRE)**[18] 4554 2-9-3 92...(b[1]) NGMcCullagh 2 — 91
(J P Murtagh, Ire) *w.w in rr: rdn on outer over 2f out and no imp on ldrs u.p over 1f out: kpt on one pce* **25/1**

**6** *2* **I Am Beautiful (IRE)**[42] 3763 2-9-0 100... SeamieHeffernan 6 — 82
(A P O'Brien, Ire) *led: 1 l clr 1/2-way: rdn and reduced advantage 2f out: hdd u.p 1 1/2f out and no ex: wknd* **16/1**

1m 14.55s (-0.95) **Going Correction** -0.05s/f (Good) — **6** Ran SP% **115.3**
Speed ratings: **104,103,103,100,93 91**
CSF £11.30 TOTE £5.80: £3.90, £1.02; DF 14.40 Trifecta £51.90.
**Owner** Michael Tabor & Derrick Smith & Mrs John Magnier **Bred** Swordlestown Stud **Trained** Cashel, Co Tipperary
■ Stewards' Enquiry : Richard Hughes caution: careless riding.

**FOCUS**
The defection of three of the declared runners because of the soft ground, most notably the Queen Mary Stakes winner, Anthem Alexander, meant this was not the quality of Group 1 event it had promised, but it produced a tight finish.

## 5219a PHOENIX SPRINT STKS (GROUP 3) — 6f
**4:35** (4:36) 3-Y-0+ **£32,500** (£9,500; £4,500; £1,500)

| | | | RPR
**1** **Scream Blue Murder (IRE)**[43] 3736 4-9-4 100... PatSmullen 5 — 106
(T Stack, Ire) *chsd ldrs: 3rd 1/2-way: rdn into 2nd over 1f out: clsd u.p ins fnl f to ld ins fnl 150yds: kpt on wl* **20/1**

**2** *¾* **Jamesie (IRE)**[2] 5154 6-9-7 104... ColmO'Donoghue 4 — 107
(David Marnane, Ire) *hld up in tch: 6th 1/2-way: sn pushed along: rdn in 5th over 1f out and clsd u.p in 3rd ins fnl f to snatch 2nd fnl strides: nvr on terms* **10/1**

**3** *hd* **Hamza (IRE)**[9] 4852 5-9-10 108...(v) JamieSpencer 6 — 109
(Kevin Ryan) *prom: sn settled bhd ldr in cl 2nd: rdn to ld 2f out: strly pressed ent fnl f and hdd ins fnl 150yds: no ex and lost 2nd fnl strides* **9/2**[2]

**4** *¾* **Flight Risk (IRE)**[315] 6882 3-9-3...(t) KevinManning 2 — 103
(J S Bolger, Ire) *dwlt sltly and settled towards rr: clsr in 5th 1/2-way: rdn 2f out and no imp on ldrs in 4th ins fnl f: kpt on same pce* **25/1**

**5** *2¾* **Maarek**[78] 2570 7-9-12 115... DeclanMcDonogh 7 — 100
(Miss Evanna McCutcheon, Ire) *chsd ldrs: 4th 1/2-way: sn pushed along and no imp on ldrs u.p 1 1/2f out: kpt on one pce in 5th ins fnl f* **1/1**[1]

**6** *nk* **An Saighdiur (IRE)**[56] 3284 7-9-7 106... JosephO'Brien 8 — 94
(Andrew Slattery, Ire) *sn led on nr side: narrow advantage 1/2-way: rdn over 2f out and sn hdd: wknd fnl f* **7/1**[3]

**7** *8½* **Rocky Ground (IRE)**[22] 4438 4-9-7 112... AndreaAtzeni 1 — 67
(Roger Varian) *s.i.s and sltly awkward s: detached in rr early: tk clsr order in rr 1/2-way: rdn and no ex 2f out: wknd and eased* **9/2**[2]

1m 13.61s (-1.89) **Going Correction** -0.05s/f (Good)
**WFA** 3 from 4yo+ 4lb — **7** Ran SP% **116.6**
Speed ratings: **110,109,108,107,104 103,92**
CSF £200.21 TOTE £15.60: £5.90, £4.50; DF 145.10 Trifecta £2531.40.
**Owner** Mrs G A Rupert & Mrs John Magnier **Bred** Annalee Bloodstock & Rockhart Trading Ltd **Trained** Golden, Co Tipperary

**FOCUS**
The favourites disappointed.

# 5118 DEAUVILLE (R-H)
Sunday, August 10

**OFFICIAL GOING: Turf: heavy**

## 5222a PRIX DE L'HIPPODROME DE SAN ISIDRO (CLAIMER) (4YO+) (TURF) — 7f 110y
**1:30** (12:00) 4-Y-0+ **£9,583** (£3,833; £2,875; £1,916; £958)

| | | | RPR
**1** **High Star (FR)**[7] 7-8-7 0... JeffersonSmith(8) 6 — 92
(J-C Rouget, France) **22/5**[3]

**2** *1½* **Kanotier (FR)**[71] 6-9-1 0... AlexisBadel 7 — 88
(Mme M Bollack-Badel, France) **87/10**

**3** *3* **Jack Sparrow (GER)**[447] 5-9-1 0...(b) MaximeGuyon 4 — 81
(Frau C Brandstatter, Germany) **73/10**

**4** *hd* **Silverheels (IRE)**[66] 2922 5-9-8 0... OlivierPeslier 3 — 87
(Paul Cole) *trckd ldrs on inner: cl 3rd and rdn 2f out: kpt on u.p but nt pce of front two fr over 1f out: fdd fnl 75yds and lost 3rd fnl strides* **4/1**[2]

**5** *1½* **Seche (FR)**[7] 4-8-13 0... MllePaulineDominois(5) 2 — 79
(L A Urbano-Grajales, France) **97/10**

**6** *snk* **Meshaheera (FR)**[7] 4-8-8 0... ClementCadel 8 — 69
(F Sanchez, France) **33/1**

**7** *1¼* **Nordic Truce (USA)**[21] 7-9-5 0... UmbertoRispoli 1 — 77
(P Monfort, France) **23/10**[1]

**8** *7* **Kilimandjaro (FR)**[43] 4-8-8 0... ValentinSeguy(3) 9 — 51
(C Gourdain, France) **32/1**

**9** *3* **Orife (IRE)**[70] 7-9-1 0...(p) JulienAuge 5 — 48
(C Ferland, France) **67/10**

1m 37.88s (9.48) — **9** Ran SP% **119.5**
WIN (incl. 1 euro stake): 5.40. PLACES: 2.00, 2.80, 2.50. DF: 24.40. SF: 44.30.
**Owner** Simone Brogi **Bred** Scea De L'Aubay & S Bouvier **Trained** Pau, France

## 5223a LARC PRIX MAURICE DE GHEEST (GROUP 1) (3YO+) (TURF) — 6f 110y(S)
**2:08** (12:00) 3-Y-0+ **£166,658** (£66,675; £33,337; £16,654; £8,341)

| | | | RPR
**1** **Garswood**[12] 4758 4-9-2 0... GeraldMosse 13 — 117
(Richard Fahey) *midfield: pushed along and clsd 2f out: rdn to chal over 1f out: led ent fnl f: r.o strly and a doing enough* **17/2**

**2** *½* **Thawaany (IRE)**[43] 3746 4-8-13 0... OlivierPeslier 15 — 113
(F Head, France) *a.p: pushed along to chal 2f out: rdn over 1f out: r.o and wnt 2nd fnl f: nt quite pce of wnr and a being hld* **5/1**[2]

**3** *1¼* **Fiesolana (IRE)**[53] 3355 5-8-13 0... BillyLee 7 — 109
(W McCreery, Ire) *sn led: pushed along 2f out: rdn and hdd ent fnl f: sn dropped to 3rd and hld: kpt on* **10/1**

**4** *hd* **Zejel**[43] 3746 4-8-13 0... JulienAuge 4 — 109
(C Ferland, France) *towards rr: swtchd rt and pushed along to cl 2f out: rdn over 1f out: kpt on wl for 4th but nt pce to chal* **33/1**

**5** *nk* **Vorda (FR)**[36] 3997 3-8-8 0... Christophe-PatriceLemaire 1 — 107+
(P Sogorb, France) *hld up in rr: smooth hdwy 2f out: rdn and nt qckn over 1f out: kpt on fnl f and wnt 5th towards fin: nvr nrr* **10/1**

**6** *½* **Another Party (FR)**[32] 3-8-11 0... AntoineHamelin 10 — 108
(Matthieu Palussiere, France) *chsd ldrs: rdn 2f out: kpt on same pce and hld fnl f* **33/1**

**7** *snk* **Sommerabend**[36] 3997 7-9-2 0... TheoBachelot 12 — 109
(M Rulec, Germany) *w ldr: rdn 2f out: outpcd and lost pl appr fnl f: kpt on but hld after: dropped to 7th cl home* **9/1**

**8** *2* **So Long Malpic (FR)**[36] 3997 7-8-13 0... Pierre-CharlesBoudot 8 — 100
(T Lemer, France) *midfield: pushed along and lost pl bef 1/2-way: swtchd lft and rdn over 1f out: sn outpcd: wl hld fnl f but kpt on and wnt 8th cl home* **40/1**

**9** *½* **Joyeuse**[30] 4171 3-8-8 0... JamesDoyle 11 — 98
(Lady Cecil) *midfield: rdn 2f out: outpcd over 1f out: kpt on but wl hld fnl f: dropped to 9th cl home* **12/1**

10 1 1/2 **Gregorian (IRE)**[29] 4201 5-9-2 0 ........ WilliamBuick 6 97
(John Gosden) *chsd ldrs: pushed along and effrt 2f out: rdn and outpcd over 1f out: no ex and fdd* **3/1**[1]

11 1 1/2 **Gammarth (FR)**[31] 6-9-2 0 ........ (b) FabriceVeron 14 93
(H-A Pantall, France) *chsd ldrs: rdn 2f out: outpcd but keeping on whn squeezed for room ent fnl f: nt rcvr and fdd* **40/1**

12 4 **Viztoria (IRE)**[78] 2570 4-8-13 0 ........ WayneLordan 3 78
(Edward Lynam, Ire) *hld up in tch: clsd gng strly 1/2-way: rdn 2f out: fnd little and qckly btn: wknd* **11/2**[3]

13 12 **Caspar Netscher**[295] 7366 5-9-2 0 ........ JimCrowley 5 47
(David Simcock) *midfield: rdn over 2f out: lost pl and dropped to rr over 1f out: wl btn and eased fnl f* **16/1**

14 shd **Pinturicchio (IRE)**[56] 3291 6-9-2 0 ........ AnthonyCrastus 2 46
(E Lellouche, France) *a towards rr: rdn in last wl over 2f out: sn btn and eased* **16/1**

1m 19.71s (2.51) **Going Correction** +0.80s/f (Soft)
**WFA** 3 from 4yo+ 4lb **14** Ran SP% **126.0**
Speed ratings: **117,116,115,114,114 113,113,111,110,109 107,102,89,89**
WIN (incl. 1 euro stake): 12.60. PLACES: 3.80, 2.20, 5.30. DF: 23.40. SF: 55.10.
**Owner** D W Armstrong & Cheveley Park Stud **Bred** Cheveley Park Stud Ltd **Trained** Musley Bank, N Yorks

**FOCUS**
This had an open look to it with no proven Group 1 performers and the early gallop was sensible considering the ground. Racing away from the stands' rail was beneficial and the frame horses set the below-par level.

## 5224a OSAF PRIX DE REUX (GROUP 3) (3YO+) (TURF) 1m 4f 110y
**2:40** (12:00) 3-Y-O+ **£33,333** (£13,333; £10,000; £6,666; £3,333)

RPR

1 **Gatewood**[43] 3722 6-9-5 0 ........ WilliamBuick 1 109+
(John Gosden) *trckd ldr: chal over 2f out and sn led: rdn and styd on strly fr over 1f out: asserted fnl f and pushed out towards fin: comf* **13/8**[1]

2 2 **Rio Tigre (IRE)**[41] 3812 3-8-7 0 ........ MickaelBarzalona 5 106
(A Fabre, France) *midfield in tch: rdn 2f out: styd on and wnt 2nd ins fnl f: no imp on wnr and wl hld* **5/2**[2]

3 1 3/4 **Going Somewhere (BRZ)**[28] 4250 5-9-10 0 ........ GregoryBenoist 7 108
(D Smaga, France) *hld up in tch in last: rdn over 2f out: plugged on in st and wnt 3rd cl home: nvr nrr* **11/2**

4 hd **Meleagros (IRE)**[42] 3774 5-9-5 0 ........ AdrienFouassier 4 103
(Alain Couetil, France) *midfield in tch: rdn over 2f out: sn outpcd in rr: plugged on fnl f and tk wl hld 4th cl home* **5/1**[3]

5 hd **Swacadelic (GER)**[35] 4007 3-8-11 0 ........ Pierre-CharlesBoudot 6 106
(Jean-Pierre Carvalho, Germany) *led: rdn and hdd 2f out: no ex fnl f: fdd and dropped to last cl home* **6/1**

2m 52.4s (6.00) **Going Correction** +0.80s/f (Soft)
**WFA** 3 from 4yo+ 11lb **5** Ran SP% **113.0**
Speed ratings: **113,111,110,110,110**
WIN (incl. 1 euro stake): 2.90. PLACES: 1.70, 1.60. SF: 6.10.
**Owner** O T I Racing & G Strawbridge **Bred** George Strawbridge **Trained** Newmarket, Suffolk

## 5225a PRIX DE L'HIPPODROME DE CHILE (CLAIMER) (4YO+) (TURF) 1m 2f
**3:45** (12:00) 4-Y-O+ **£7,916** (£3,166; £2,375; £1,583; £791)

RPR

1 shd **Tianjin City (FR)**[12] 4776 4-9-5 0 ........ UmbertoRispoli 10 84
(A Bonin, France) *fin 2nd: awrdd the r* **137/10**

2 1 **Royal Talisman**[12] 4776 6-9-4 0 ........ MickaelBarzalona 16 83
(Jo Hughes) *w.w in midfield on outer: tk clsr order after 1/2-way: disputing 3rd and gng wl enough 2 1/2f out: rdn to ld 1 1/2f out: drvn ins fnl f: hdd 50yds out: no ex: fin 3rd: plcd 2nd* **31/5**

3 1 1/4 **Idee Libre (FR)**[31] 4-9-1 0 ........ OlivierPeslier 12 78
(Yannick Fouin, France) *fin 4th: plcd 3rd* **144/10**

4 shd **Pivoina (IRE)**[31] 7-8-13 0 ........ (p) StephanePasquier 9 74
(D Prod'Homme, France) *fin 5th: plcd 4th* **17/5**[1]

5 1/2 **Moonyr (FR)**[420] 6-8-11 0 ........ AnthonyCrastus 8 71
(Mlle H Mennessier, France) *fin 6th: plcd 5th* **27/1**

6 **Welcome Sir (FR)**[62] 4-8-4 0 ........ MllePaulineDominois(7) 13 76
(E Lellouche, France) *fin 1st: disqualified and plcd 6th* **73/10**

7 3 **Ironstone (IRE)**[77] 5-9-2 0 ........ MaximeGuyon 5 70
(M Cheno, France) **18/5**[2]

8 snk **Place Des Anges (FR)**[7] 4-8-6 0 ........ MathieuPelletan(5) 11 65
(J-L Pelletan, France) **233/10**

9 10 **Durch Den Monsun (FR)**[14] 6-8-11 0 ........ DavidBreux 4 45
(Mme M-C Chaalon, France) **59/1**

10 nk **River Prince (FR)**[51] 4-8-11 0 ........ RaphaelMarchelli 2 44
(P Adda, France) **236/10**

11 1 1/4 **Touch Of Honour (GER)**[38] 3907 5-8-8 0 ........ AntoineHamelin 1 39
(Yasmin Almenrader, Germany) **59/10**[3]

12 2 1/2 **Bayran (FR)** 4-8-6 0 ........ (b[1]) ThibaultSpeicher(5) 3 37
(G Doleuze, France) **53/1**

13 30 **Willibr (IRE)**[31] 5-9-1 0 ........ (p) IoritzMendizabal 6 1
(P Monfort, France) **158/10**

2m 11.9s (1.70) **13** Ran SP% **119.4**
WIN (incl. 1 euro stake): 14.70. PLACES: 4.00, 2.70, 4.50 DF: 35.90. SF: 79.40.
**Owner** Jean-Francois Vignion **Bred** Haras D'Etreham **Trained** France

# 1620 LE LION-D'ANGERS (R-H)
Sunday, August 10
**OFFICIAL GOING: Turf: very soft**

## 5226a PRIX SEA BIRD (CONDITIONS) (3YO) (TURF) 6f
**10:45** (12:00) 3-Y-O **£7,500** (£3,000; £2,250; £1,500; £750)

RPR

1 **Belletriste (FR)**[41] 3801 3-8-9 0 ow1 ........ JohanVictoire 1 79
(Sylvester Kirk) *t.k.h early: midfield in tch: rdn fnl 2f: 2 l down in 2nd 120yds out: r.o strly and clsd rapidly on ldr towards fin: led last strides* **14/5**[3]

2 hd **Majraa (FR)**[159] 3-8-13 0 ........ MatthiasLauron 3 82
(J-C Rouget, France) **8/5**[1]

3 2 **Full In Have (FR)**[111] 3-8-6 0 ........ (b) YoannBarille(2) 5 71?
(N Leenders, France) **28/1**

4 1 **Spring Carnival (USA)**[155] 3-8-13 0 ........ AntoineWerle 6 73
(H-A Pantall, France) **17/10**[2]

5 hd **Lakmee (FR)** 3-8-9 0 ow1 ........ (b[1]) AnthonyClement 7 68
(A Clement, France) **29/1**

6 2 1/2 **Quiaa Nominoor (FR)**[41] 3810 3-8-8 0 ........ (p) FabriceNicoleau(3) 4 62
(Remy Nerbonne, France) **114/10**

7 20 **Smart Sayaah (FR)**[66] 3-8-3 0 ........ MlleAngelaLeCorre(5) 2
(E Large, France) **38/1**

1m 14.29s (74.29) **7** Ran SP% **119.2**
WIN (INCL. 1 EURO STAKE): 3.80. PLACES: 1.80, 1.70. SF: 11.00.
**Owner** The Hon Mrs J M Corbett & C Wright **Bred** Mathieu Daguzan-Garros Et Al **Trained** Upper Lambourn, Berks

# LE TOUQUET (L-H)
Sunday, August 10
**OFFICIAL GOING: Turf: very soft**

## 5227a PRIX CLINIQUE COTE D'OPALE ST MARTIN LES BOULOGNE (MAIDEN) (3YO) (TURF) 1m 2f 110y
**5:20** (12:00) 3-Y-O **£5,000** (£2,000; £1,500; £1,000; £500)

RPR

1 **Donna Bella (FR)**[118] 3-8-13 0 ........ AntoineCoutier 13 73
(S Smrczek, Germany) **162/10**

2 2 **Zabrov (IRE)**[23] 3-9-2 0 ........ MarcNobili 9 72
(J Phelippon, France) **74/10**

3 2 **Nooshi (GER)** 3-8-8 0 ........ (p) CesarPasserat 8 60
(J Hirschberger, Germany) **18/5**[2]

4 1 3/4 **Nalon** 3-8-10 0 ........ NicolasLarenaudie(6) 7 65
(J-M Lefebvre, France) **42/10**[3]

5 1 **Aposcalivic (FR)** 3-8-8 0 ........ MathieuAndrouin 2 55
(P Lenogue, France) **34/1**

6 6 **Rahlah**[32] 3-8-13 0 ........ FabienLefebvre 11 48
(J E Hammond, France) **7/2**[1]

7 9 **Mizzeni (FR)**[323] 6656 3-8-11 0 ........ DanielMuscutt 5 29
(Gay Kelleway) *t.k.h: restrained bhd ldng pair on inner: outpcd and pushed along over 3f out: sn lost pl: wl btn fnl 1 1/2f* **51/1**

8 nk **Prince Jean D'o**[132] 3-8-11 0 ........ AurelienLemaitre 3 28
(F Head, France) **26/5**

9 1 1/4 **Remember Babi (FR)** 3-8-4 0 ........ SirhanBigot(4) 12 23
(F Vermeulen, France) **54/1**

10 1/2 **All Include (FR)**[39] 3-9-2 0 ........ (p) SebastienMaillot 1 30
(N Milliere, France) **172/10**

11 10 **Emma Dilemma (FR)** 3-8-8 0 ........ NJeanpierre 6
(T Doumen, France) **23/1**

12 1 1/4 **Green Light (FR)**[104] 3-8-11 0 ........ LouisBeuzelin 10
(J E Hammond, France) **154/10**

2m 22.38s (142.38) **12** Ran SP% **119.4**
WIN (incl. 1 euro stake): 17.20. PLACES: 4.80, 2.70, 2.10. DF: 47.10. SF: 197.30.
**Owner** Stall Australia **Bred** G Sindermann **Trained** Germany

# 4715 LES LANDES
Sunday, August 10
**OFFICIAL GOING: Good to firm**

## 5228a LADBROKES LIFE H'CAP 5f 110y
**3:10** (3:10) 3-Y-O+ **£1,460** (£525; £315)

RPR

1 **Purley Queen (IRE)**[14] 4715 5-10-3 ........ MrFTett 4 58
(Mrs C Gilbert, Jersey) **7/2**

2 4 **Chester'slittlegem (IRE)**[14] 4715 5-9-8 ........ (p) PhilipPrince 8 35
(Mrs A Corson, Jersey) **7/1**

3 hd **Kersivay**[35] 4038 8-8-12 ........ (p) JemmaMarshall 6 25
(Mrs A Malzard, Jersey) **3/1**[3]

4 hd **Sister Guru**[211] 141 5-10-12 ........ ColinBolger 2 52
(Peter Hedger) **15/8**[2]

5 3/4 **Spanish Bounty**[14] 4715 9-10-7 ........ CraigWalker 5 44
(Mrs A Malzard, Jersey) **5/1**

6 3/4 **Novabridge**[35] 4038 6-10-12 ........ (b) MarkQuinlan 3 47
(Neil Mulholland) **5/4**[1]

7 4 **Country Blue (FR)**[14] 4715 5-9-8 ........ (p) MattieBatchelor 7 15
(Mrs A Malzard, Jersey) **7/2**

8 8 **Hawaiian Freeze**[171] 671 5-9-3 ........ MatthewCosham 1
(J Moon, Jersey) **16/1**

1m 7.0s (67.00) **8** Ran SP% **183.7**

**Owner** Manor Farm Racing **Bred** Mark & Pippa Hackett **Trained** Jersey

## 5229a COUTTS & CO CHANNEL ISLANDS H'CAP 1m 2f
**3:40** (3:40) (0-45,) 3-Y-O+ **£1,790** (£660; £400)

RPR

1 **Lady Petrus**[14] 4718 9-8-9 ........ PhilipPrince 3 12
(K Kukk, Jersey) **7/2**[3]

2 nk **Jackpot**[14] 4717 4-9-12 ........ (p) MrFTett 4 28
(Mrs A Malzard, Jersey) **4/1**

3 hd **Rebel Woman**[14] 4717 8-9-11 ........ (p) CraigWalker 6 27
(Mrs A Corson, Jersey) **7/2**[3]

4 10 **Rocquaine (IRE)**[14] 4718 5-8-11 ........ (p) JemmaMarshall 5
(Mrs A Malzard, Jersey) **8/1**

5 4 **Athania (IRE)**[14] 4040 8-9-11 ........ (p) MattieBatchelor 1
(Mrs A Corson, Jersey) **9/4**[2]

6 8 **Lisahane Bog**[112] 1012 7-10-12 ........ (bp) ColinBolger 2
(Peter Hedger) **15/8**[1]

2m 18.0s (5.00) **6** Ran SP% **141.1**

**Owner** Mrs E C Roberts **Bred** Sir Tatton Skyes And Lady Legard **Trained** Jersey

**5230a** **LADBROKES CLARITY MACHINE H'CAP** **1m 4f**
**4:50** (4:50) 3-Y-O+ **£1,460** (£525; £315)

| | | | RPR |
|---|---|---|---|
| **1** | | **King Kenny**[14] 4716 9-8-6 ....(p) NoraLooby 2 (Mrs A Corson, Jersey) **11/4** | 42 |
| **2** | *nk* | **Midnight Sequel**[14] 4716 5-9-10 ....(tp) MarkQuinlan 5 (Neil Mulholland) **1/1**[1] | 60 |
| **3** | *18* | **Herbalist**[14] 4717 4-9-13 .... PhilipPrince 1 (K Kukk, Jersey) **5/2**[3] | 34 |
| **4** | *7* | **Rossetti**[14] 4716 6-10-12 ....(p) CraigWalker 3 (Mrs A Malzard, Jersey) **9/4**[2] | 36 |
| **5** | *6* | **Sweet Liberta (IRE)**[14] 4716 5-9-8 .... MatthewCosham 4 (T Le Brocq, Jersey) **7/1** | 8 |

2m 48.0s (-2.00) **5** Ran SP% **148.5**

**Owner** The Crawford Family **Bred** D P Martin **Trained** Jersey

## 3046 HOPPEGARTEN (R-H)

Sunday, August 10

**OFFICIAL GOING: Turf: good**

**5231a** **124TH GROSSER PREIS VON BERLIN (GROUP 1) (3YO+) (TURF)** **1m 4f**
**4:10** (12:00) 3-Y-O+ **£83,333** (£33,333; £16,666; £8,333; £4,166)

| | | | RPR |
|---|---|---|---|
| **1** | | **Sirius (GER)**[42] 3770 3-8-9 0....(b) SHellyn 3 (Andreas Lowe, Germany) *w.w in midfield on outer: pushed along appr 2f out: gd hdwy 1 1/2f out: r.o u.p fnl f to ld 50yds out* **13/5**[2] | 109+ |
| **2** | *½* | **Berlin Berlin**[42] 3770 5-9-3 0.... FrederikTylicki 6 (Markus Klug, Germany) *chsd ldng trio: sltly outpcd after 3f out: drvn along to chal appr 1f out: led narrowly ins fnl f: r.o u.p: hdd 50yds out: no ex* **135/10** | 105+ |
| **3** | *1 ½* | **Lucky Speed (IRE)**[42] 3770 4-9-6 0.... AdriedeVries 1 (P Schiergen, Germany) *a.p on inner: rdn and nt qckn immediately 2 1/2f out: hrd rdn and styd on to ld narrowly and briefly appr 1f out: hdd ins fnl f and fdd last 100yds* **11/5**[1] | 105+ |
| **4** | *shd* | **Earl Of Tinsdal (GER)**[294] 7414 6-9-6 0.... EPedroza 8 (A Wohler, Germany) *a.p on outer: chal ldr over 2 1/2f out: led appr 2f out: sn hrd rdn and hdd appr fnl f: kpt on at one pce u.p* **61/10** | 105 |
| **5** | *¾* | **Hey Little Gorl (GER)**[42] 3770 4-9-3 0.... FranckBlondel 7 (Markus Klug, Germany) *hld up towards rr on outer: rdn and hdwy on outer over 1 1/2f out: styd on wl ins fnl f: nrest at fin* **18/1** | 101+ |
| **6** | *¾* | **Hurricane Red (IRE)**[22] 4-9-6 0.... ElioneChaves 2 (Lennart Reuterskiold Jr, Sweden) *settled in midfield on inner: hrd rdn and no imp over 2f out: styng on whn sltly short of room over 1f out: kpt on ins fnl f: nvr on terms* **146/10** | 103 |
| **7** | *¾* | **Emily Of Tinsdal (GER)**[28] 5-9-3 0.... MartinHarley 5 (P Harley, Germany) *hld up towards rr on inner: rdn and tk clsr order over 2f out: kpt on u.p fnl f: nt pce to chal* **186/10** | 99 |
| **8** | *¾* | **Iniciar (GER)**[57] 3266 4-9-6 0.... FilipMinarik 4 (Jean-Pierre Carvalho, Germany) *led on rail: chal fr over 2 1/2f out: hdd appr 2f out: wknd ins fnl f* **71/10** | 100 |
| **9** | *4* | **Open Your Heart (GER)**[35] 4007 3-8-9 0.... MircoDemuro 9 (R Dzubasz, Germany) *w.w in rr: outpcd and rdn in last fr 3f out: nvr in contention* **41/10**[3] | 94 |

2m 31.5s (2.20)
**WFA** 3 from 4yo+ 11lb **9** Ran SP% **128.7**
WIN (incl. 10 euro stake): 36. PLACES: 16, 27, 14. SF: 934.
**Owner** Stall Molenhof **Bred** Gestut Etzean **Trained** Germany

## 5166 AYR (L-H)

Monday, August 11

**OFFICIAL GOING: Soft (good to soft in places; 8.1)**

Home turn bend in 8m, home straight in 14m. Back straight in 6m Rothesay bend in 6m and 7f-10f races increased by 24yds.
Wind: Fresh, across Weather: Overcast

**5232** **BRITISH STALLION STUDS EBF MAIDEN FILLIES' STKS (BOBIS RACE)** **7f 50y**
**2:30** (2:30) (Class 4) 2-Y-O **£4,204** (£1,251; £625; £312) **Stalls** High

| Form | | | | RPR |
|---|---|---|---|---|
| 42 | **1** | | **Mystic And Artist**[21] 4499 2-9-0 0.... DanielTudhope 6 (K R Burke) *mde virtually all: rdn over 2f out: drew clr fr over 1f out: kpt on strly* **7/2**[2] | 76+ |
| 2 | **2** | *4* | **Kodiva (IRE)**[11] 4825 2-9-0 0.... JoeFanning 8 (Charles Hills) *t.k.h: disp ld: rdn 2f out: sn one pce* **4/5**[1] | 66 |
| | **3** | *hd* | **Sarah Joyce (IRE)** 2-9-0 0.... DeclanMcDonogh 3 (John Patrick Shanahan, Ire) *s.i.s: rn green in rr: effrt over 2f out: no imp tl styd on fnl f: nvr able to chal* **25/1** | 66 |
| 54 | **4** | *2 ¼* | **Multi Grain**[23] 4444 2-8-11 0.... MichaelJMMurphy(3) 7 (Brian Ellison) *prom: rdn over 2f out: hung lft and outpcd wl over 1f out: n.d after* **5/1**[3] | 60 |
| 0 | **5** | *3* | **Alhella**[21] 4499 2-9-0 0.... TomEaves 4 (Kevin Ryan) *dwlt: sn prom: pushed along and outpcd over 2f out: btn over 1f out* **15/2** | 52 |

1m 39.15s (5.75) **Going Correction** +0.65s/f (Yiel) **5** Ran SP% **110.1**
Speed ratings (Par 93): **93,88,88,85,82**
CSF £6.77 TOTE £5.00: £1.90, £1.10; EX 6.90 Trifecta £38.40.
**Owner** Hubert John Strecker **Bred** T A Scothern **Trained** Middleham Moor, N Yorks

**FOCUS**
After steady rain in the past 24 hours, the going was changed to soft, good to soft in places and riders said it was tacky after the first. Three non-runners lessened some of the interest in this maiden but the form looks straightforward, and the winner improved again.

**5233** **DANNY TYSON H'CAP (DIV I)** **7f 50y**
**3:00** (3:01) (Class 6) (0-60,62) 3-Y-O+ **£2,045** (£603; £302) **Stalls** High

| Form | | | | RPR |
|---|---|---|---|---|
| 6031 | **1** | | **Clumber Place**[2] 5168 8-10-0 62 6ex.... JasonHart 6 (Shaun Harris) *mde all at modest gallop: shkn up and qcknd clr 2f out: rdn and flashed tail ins fnl f: kpt on strly* **7/2**[2] | 72 |
| 2-20 | **2** | *3* | **Royal Duchess**[4] 5089 4-9-6 54.... TomEaves 7 (Lucy Normile) *prom: effrt and hung lft over 2f out: chsd (clr) wnr over 1f out: kpt on fnl f: nt pce to chal* **9/1** | 56 |
| 506 | **3** | *2 ¾* | **It's All A Game**[17] 4612 3-8-13 58....(b) DuilioDaSilva(5) 2 (Richard Guest) *t.k.h: trckd ldrs: effrt and chsd wnr over 2f out to over 1f out: sn outpcd* **13/2**[3] | 51 |
| 0000 | **4** | *nk* | **Jebel Tara**[41] 3828 9-9-10 58....(bt) PaulPickard 3 (Alan Brown) *hld up: rdn and hdwy over 2f out: kpt on fnl f: nvr able to chal* **20/1** | 52 |
| 4643 | **5** | *2 ¼* | **Echo Of Lightning**[2] 5166 4-9-2 57.... MeganCarberry(7) 10 (Brian Ellison) *pressed wnr tl rdn and outpcd over 2f out: n.d after* **11/8**[1] | 45 |
| 002U | **6** | *9* | **Copper To Gold**[25] 4341 5-8-9 46.... JoeyHaynes(3) 1 (Robin Bastiman) *dwlt: sn in tch: drvn and outpcd over 2f out: sn btn* **22/1** | 11 |
| 000- | **7** | *2 ½* | **Miss Rebero**[307] 7108 4-8-13 47.... GrahamLee 9 (Tim Fitzgerald) *s.i.s: hld up: struggling over 3f out: sn btn* **33/1** | 5 |
| 0403 | **8** | *6* | **Starlite Jewel**[14] 4728 3-8-11 51.... JoeFanning 4 (Stuart Coltherd) *s.i.s: t.k.h: hld up: struggling over 2f out: sn btn* **8/1** | |
| 006 | **9** | *16* | **Bannock Town**[9] 4900 3-8-5 45.... JamesSullivan 8 (Linda Perratt) *towards rr: drvn along over 2f out: sn struggling: t.o* **66/1** | |

1m 37.25s (3.85) **Going Correction** +0.65s/f (Yiel)
**WFA** 3 from 4yo+ 6lb **9** Ran SP% **112.3**
Speed ratings (Par 101): **104,100,97,97,94 84,81,74,56**
CSF £31.50 CT £194.26 TOTE £5.10: £1.50, £2.80, £1.90; EX 32.70 Trifecta £120.80.
**Owner** Mrs Catherine Stocks **Bred** Worksop Manor Stud **Trained** Carburton, Notts

**FOCUS**
A low-grade handicap but a taking performance from the in-form winner, following up her C&D win two days earlier and rated to her best form since early 2011.

**5234** **DANNY TYSON H'CAP (DIV II)** **7f 50y**
**3:30** (3:31) (Class 6) (0-60,60) 3-Y-O+ **£2,045** (£603; £302) **Stalls** High

| Form | | | | RPR |
|---|---|---|---|---|
| 00-3 | **1** | | **Jay Kay**[6] 5005 5-8-7 46 oh1.... JoeyHaynes(3) 2 (K R Burke) *mde virtually all: drew clr fr over 2f out: unchal* **2/1**[1] | 67 |
| 4 | **2** | *8* | **Shiftin Bobbins**[25] 4363 3-8-9 51.... TomEaves 8 (Michael Dods) *hld up: rdn and hdwy on outside over 2f out: chsd (clr) wnr over 1f out: kpt on fnl f: no imp* **8/1** | 50 |
| 6/0 | **3** | *nk* | **Elusive Gent (IRE)**[2] 5166 7-8-11 47....(p) KieranO'Neill 3 (Adrian Paul Keatley, Ire) *s.i.s: hld up: hdwy over 2f out: disp 2nd pl fr over 1f out: no imp fnl f* **8/1** | 47 |
| 1 | **4** | *6* | **Mr Bounty**[73] 2754 4-9-8 58....(p) FergalLynch 9 (M D O'Callaghan, Ire) *hld up in tch: stdy hdwy 4f out: chsd (clr) wnr over 2f out to over 1f out: sn btn* **7/2**[3] | 43 |
| 1603 | **5** | *8* | **Ivy Port**[22] 4472 4-9-7 57.... AndrewMullen 4 (Michael Appleby) *chsd ldrs: drvn and outpcd over 2f out: sn btn* **10/3**[2] | 22 |
| 4425 | **6** | *1 ¾* | **Blue Sonic**[2] 5168 4-9-4 54.... GrahamLee 7 (Jim Goldie) *reluctant to enter stalls: trckd wnr to over 2f out: sn rdn and btn* **8/1** | 15 |
| 0000 | **7** | *22* | **Mrs Gorsky**[16] 4664 4-8-3 46 oh1.... RachelRichardson(7) 5 (Patrick Holmes) *chsd ldrs: drvn along over 3f out: sn btn: t.o* **66/1** | |

1m 37.11s (3.71) **Going Correction** +0.65s/f (Yiel)
**WFA** 3 from 4yo+ 6lb **7** Ran SP% **113.5**
Speed ratings (Par 101): **104,94,94,87,78 76,51**
CSF £18.65 CT £104.35 TOTE £2.70: £1.40, £5.10; EX 20.00 Trifecta £189.20.
**Owner** John Kenny **Bred** Miss S E Hall **Trained** Middleham Moor, N Yorks

**FOCUS**
The second division of the 0-60 handicap saw an even more impressive winner than the first, the third consecutive on the card from the front. The winner has been rated back in line with his 3yo form.

**5235** **SALT HOUSE H'CAP (A QUALIFIER FOR THE £15,000 BETFAIR SCOTTISH MILE SERIES FINAL)** **1m**
**4:00** (4:00) (Class 5) (0-75,78) 3-Y-O+ **£2,911** (£866; £432; £216) **Stalls** Low

| Form | | | | RPR |
|---|---|---|---|---|
| 5021 | **1** | | **Ingleby Symphony (IRE)**[2] 5172 4-10-0 78 6ex.... GeorgeChaloner(3) 1 (Richard Fahey) *trckd ldrs: rdn over 3f out: rallied to chse ldr over 2f out: led ins fnl f: styd on strly* **13/8**[1] | 89 |
| 3414 | **2** | *2 ¼* | **Alpine Storm (IRE)**[11] 4832 3-9-6 74.... JoeFanning 8 (Mark Johnston) *t.k.h: led: rdn over 2f out: hdd ins fnl f: kpt on same pce* **8/1**[3] | 79 |
| 3644 | **3** | *1* | **Karaka Jack**[16] 4650 7-10-0 75.... GrahamLee 5 (Jim Goldie) *in tch: rdn and outpcd 3f out: rallied over 1f out: kpt on to take 3rd towards fin: nt rch first two* **7/2**[2] | 79 |
| 56 | **4** | *1 ¼* | **Helen's Armada (IRE)**[2] 5166 3-8-10 64.... DeclanMcDonogh 3 (John Patrick Shanahan, Ire) *s.i.s: hld up: stdy hdwy 1/2-way: effrt on outside over 2f out: sn rdn: no imp over 1f out* **16/1** | 64 |
| 0-60 | **5** | *3* | **Falcon's Reign (FR)**[72] 2772 5-9-8 69.... AndrewMullen 10 (Michael Appleby) *cl up: effrt and drvn along over 2f out: wknd over 1f out* **8/1**[3] | 63 |
| 3030 | **6** | *1* | **Tectonic (IRE)**[9] 4903 5-9-6 67....(p) TomEaves 2 (Keith Dalgleish) *t.k.h: hld up bhd ldng gp: effrt over 2f out: wknd over 1f out* **16/1** | 59 |
| 0-60 | **7** | *7* | **It's A Mans World**[21] 4498 8-9-4 65....(p) PaulPickard 6 (Brian Ellison) *s.i.s: bhd and detached: nvr on terms* **8/1**[3] | 41 |
| 4166 | **8** | *4 ½* | **Dark Crystal**[2] 5168 3-8-11 65.... JamesSullivan 9 (Linda Perratt) *chsd ldrs tl rdn and wknd over 2f out* **14/1** | 29 |
| 251- | **9** | *shd* | **Megamunch (IRE)**[349] 5870 4-9-7 73.... JacobButterfield(5) 7 (Kristin Stubbs) *towards rr: drvn and struggling 3f out: sn btn* **25/1** | 38 |

1m 47.86s (4.06) **Going Correction** +0.65s/f (Yiel)
**WFA** 3 from 4yo+ 7lb **9** Ran SP% **115.9**
Speed ratings (Par 103): **105,102,101,100,97 96,89,85,84**
CSF £15.60 CT £41.31 TOTE £3.70: £1.60, £2.30, £1.30; EX 14.40 Trifecta £32.90.
**Owner** Percy Green Racing 4 & Partner **Bred** Sunderland Holdings Inc **Trained** Musley Bank, N Yorks

**FOCUS**
Another handicap in which little got into it from off the pace, and the winner was the second on the card to follow up a win here on Saturday, confirming herself better than ever. The runner-up has been rated to a small personal best.

## 5236 WINTER WIZARD H'CAP (QUALIFIER FOR THE £15,000 BETFAIR SCOTTISH SPRINT SERIES FINAL) 6f
4:30 (4:32) (Class 5) (0-75,74) 3-Y-0+ £2,911 (£866; £432; £216) Stalls Low

Form RPR
6645 1 Klynch[7] 4961 8-9-12 74.......(b) JamesSullivan 10 87
(Ruth Carr) trckd stands' side ldr: led on bit over 1f out: drew clr fnl f: v easily 9/1
1U0 2 5 Lady Ranger (IRE)[19] 4556 3-8-4 56.......(b1) KieranO'Neill 8 53
(Adrian Paul Keatley, Ire) stdd s: hld up centre: hdwy and swtchd lft over 1f out: led that gp ins fnl f: no ch w stands' side wnr 10/1
6654 3 1 1/4 Go Go Green (IRE)[2] 5170 8-9-9 71....... DanielTudhope 2 65
(Jim Goldie) dwlt: hld up in tch centre: effrt and led that gp over 1f out to ins fnl f: kpt on same pce 7/1[3]
2454 4 4 1/2 Jumbo Steps (IRE)[7] 4961 7-9-2 67....... GaryBartley(3) 9 48
(Jim Goldie) hld up in tch centre: effrt and rdn 2f out: no imp fnl f 12/1
0615 5 nse Goninodaethat[21] 4487 6-9-5 67....... GrahamLee 11 48
(Jim Goldie) overall ldr stands' side: rdn and hdd over 1f out: sn outpcd 11/1
2343 6 1 1/2 Jinky[2] 5170 6-9-9 71....... JoeFanning 4 47
(Linda Perratt) prom centre: rdn over 2f out: edgd rt and outpcd over 1f out 4/1[2]
1022 7 2 1/2 Tadalavil[7] 4960 9-8-2 55....... SammyJoBell(5) 5 24
(Linda Perratt) chsd ldrs: rdn over 2f out: wknd over 1f out 16/1
0330 8 2 3/4 Tango Sky (IRE)[28] 4256 5-9-8 73.......(p) GeorgeChaloner(3) 1 33
(Richard Fahey) cl up centre: led that gp over 2f out to over 1f out: sn btn 7/1[3]
4535 9 3 1/2 Findog[14] 4725 4-8-5 58 ow3....... JacobButterfield(5) 7 8
(Linda Perratt) taken early to post: dwlt: hld up bhd ldng gp centre: rdn over 2f out: hung lft and sn btn 22/1
5000 10 9 Rise To Glory (IRE)[16] 4655 6-8-7 55 oh1....... JasonHart 3
(Shaun Harris) led centre gp to over 2f out: sn rdn and btn 18/1
031 11 1 3/4 Baron Run[24] 4383 4-9-6 71....... JoeyHaynes(3) 6
(K R Burke) taken early to post: cl up tl rdn and wknd over 2f out 7/2[1]

1m 15.31s (2.91) **Going Correction** +0.475s/f (Yiel)
**WFA** 3 from 4yo+ 4lb **11** Ran SP% **117.8**
Speed ratings (Par 103): **99,92,90,84,84 82,79,75,70,58 56**
CSF £95.89 CT £684.53 TOTE £10.40: £4.00, £3.50, £2.20; EX 147.00 Trifecta £938.20.
**Owner** Douglas Renton **Bred** J C S Wilson Bloodstock **Trained** Huby, N Yorks

**FOCUS**
A run-of-the-mill sprint but it produced a very easy winner, himself one of just two runners to race up against the stands' rail.

## 5237 WEDDINGS AT WESTERN HOUSE HOTEL H'CAP 5f
5:00 (5:00) (Class 6) (0-65,63) 3-Y-0+ £2,045 (£603; £302) Stalls Low

Form RPR
0000 1 Lord Bufthead[27] 4287 5-8-2 46.......(v) DuilioDaSilva(5) 12 58
(Richard Guest) cl up: led 1/2-way: pushed out fnl f 9/1
550 2 2 3/4 Rock Canyon (IRE)[7] 4960 5-8-9 51.......(p) GeorgeChaloner(3) 5 53
(Linda Perratt) chsd ldrs: effrt and chsd wnr over 1f out: kpt on ins fnl f: nt gng pce to chal 10/1
0600 3 1 1/4 Wicked Wilma (IRE)[7] 4960 10-8-6 45.......(p) IanBrennan 7 43
(Alan Berry) trckd ldrs: effrt and pushed along over 1f out: kpt on ins fnl f 40/1
2540 4 1 1/4 Black Douglas[7] 4960 5-8-10 52....... GaryBartley(3) 9 45
(Jim Goldie) hld up: hdwy and drifted to far rail fr over 1f out: kpt on ins fnl f 7/1
0005 5 1 1/4 The Nifty Fox[20] 4511 10-9-3 56.......(p) JamesSullivan 3 45
(Tim Easterby) hld up: rdn and swtchd to stands' rail over 1f out: nt clr run briefly ins fnl f: no imp 10/1
6333 5 dht Saxonette[14] 4725 6-8-12 51....... JoeFanning 6 40
(Linda Perratt) hld up in tch: effrt and pushed along 2f out: no imp fnl f 5/1[2]
6340 7 1 Chloe's Dream (IRE)[7] 4960 4-8-13 52....... TomEaves 10 37
(Linda Perratt) t.k.h: led to 1/2-way: sn rdn: wknd over 1f out 14/1
56-1 8 3/4 Autumn Tide (IRE)[2] 5169 3-9-0 56 6ex.......(t1) KieranO'Neill 4 37
(Adrian Paul Keatley, Ire) dwlt: hld up: hdwy over 2f out: hung lft: wknd over 1f out 11/2[3]
2654 9 2 3/4 Funding Deficit (IRE)[10] 4861 4-9-9 62....... GrahamLee 11 34
(Jim Goldie) prom tl rdn and wknd over 1f out 9/2[1]
-030 10 3 1/4 Hellolini[36] 4005 4-8-6 45.......(p) JasonHart 8 6
(Robin Bastiman) bhd: rdn and effrt whn carried lft over 1f out: sn btn 33/1
2066 11 2 1/2 I'll Be Good[6] 4994 5-9-6 59.......(t) AndrewMullen 1 11
(Alan Berry) chsd centre ldr: effrt and edgd to outer of stands' side gp over 2f out: sn btn 10/1
0000 12 6 Fol Hollow (IRE)[25] 4362 9-8-11 55....... GarryWhillans(5) 2
(Stuart Coltherd) racd w one other centre: prom tl rdn and wknd over 2f out 33/1

1m 1.49s (2.09) **Going Correction** +0.475s/f (Yiel)
**WFA** 3 from 4yo+ 3lb **12** Ran SP% **115.0**
Speed ratings (Par 101): **102,97,95,93,91 91,90,88,84,79 75,65**
CSF £91.44 CT £3423.14 TOTE £8.60: £2.50, £3.40, £8.50; EX 133.10 Trifecta £2247.30 Part won..
**Owner** Available For Sale Or Lease **Bred** T K & Mrs P A Knox **Trained** Ingmanthorpe, W Yorks

**FOCUS**
The riders were much keener to get to the stands' rail here after the success of Klynch in the previous race and the comfortable winner capitalised on what proved a cracking draw. The runner-up has been rated close to his recent form.

## 5238 PEACOCK SALT H'CAP 1m 2f
5:30 (5:30) (Class 3) (0-95,93) 3-Y-0+ £7,762 (£2,310; £1,154; £577) Stalls Low

Form RPR
3503 1 Awake My Soul (IRE)[16] 4667 5-10-0 93....... DanielTudhope 6 105
(David O'Meara) prom: smooth hdwy to ld over 2f out: pushed clr fr over 1f out: readily 9/4[1]
1560 2 3 1/4 Las Verglas Star (IRE)[11] 4827 6-9-0 82....... GeorgeChaloner(3) 11 87
(Richard Fahey) hld up towards rr: hdwy over 3f out: effrt and chsd wnr over 1f out: kpt on fnl f: nt pce to chal 14/1
-646 3 6 Art Scholar (IRE)[40] 3860 7-8-9 79....... AlistairRawlinson(5) 5 73
(Michael Appleby) hld up: hdwy over 2f out: rdn over 1f out: kpt on same pce 12/1
64-U 4 1/2 Red Inca[9] 4922 6-8-10 75....... PaulPickard 12 68
(Brian Ellison) chsd ldrs: hdwy to ld briefly over 2f out: outpcd over 1f out 20/1
-541 5 hd Noble Alan (GER)[47] 3574 11-9-6 85....... IanBrennan 8 78
(Nicky Richards) hld up: rdn over 3f out: hdwy over 1f out: kpt on: nvr able to chal 14/1
0165 6 1 1/2 San Cassiano (IRE)[9] 4888 7-9-10 89....... JamesSullivan 7 79
(Ruth Carr) early ldr: chsd ldr: rdn and ev ch wl over 2f out: sn outpcd: n.d after 20/1
-500 7 8 Beaumont's Party (IRE)[9] 4922 7-9-5 87....... MichaelJMMurphy(3) 2 63
(Brian Ellison) prom: effrt and styd alone far side ent st: rdn and struggling fr 2f out 8/1
0050 8 10 Unsinkable (IRE)[8] 4938 4-9-5 84.......(b1) TomEaves 10 42
(Ian Semple) t.k.h: sn led: rdn and hdd over 2f out: sn btn 50/1
5-01 9 2 3/4 Hold The Line (IRE)[36] 3999 4-9-12 91....... DeclanMcDonogh 9 44
(John Patrick Shanahan, Ire) hld up in tch: effrt and drvn over 3f out: wknd over 2f out 4/1[3]
2315 10 12 Maracuja[16] 4680 3-8-5 79....... JoeFanning 3 10
(Mark Johnston) s.i.s: hld up: rdn over 3f out: btn fnl 2f 10/3[2]

2m 13.73s (1.73) **Going Correction** +0.375s/f (Good)
**WFA** 3 from 4yo+ 9lb **10** Ran SP% **117.5**
Speed ratings (Par 107): **108,105,100,100,100 98,92,84,82,72**
CSF £35.69 CT £318.31 TOTE £3.30: £1.20, £5.10, £2.80; EX 36.80 Trifecta £291.10.
**Owner** Zaro Srl **Bred** Grundy Bloodstock Srl **Trained** Nawton, N Yorks

**FOCUS**
The feature race on the card and, as with so many others this afternoon, the field finished well strung out. The pace was solid thanks to Unsinkable racing freely in first-time blinkers, and the impressive winner looks better than ever, giving the runner-up a 9lb bigger beating than at Nottingham last October.

## 5239 CONFERENCE AND EVENTS AT AYR RACECOURSE H'CAP 1m 2f
6:05 (6:08) (Class 6) (0-60,58) 3-Y-0 £2,045 (£603; £302) Stalls Low

Form RPR
5455 1 Notts So Blue[2] 5166 3-8-9 46....... JasonHart 2 55
(Shaun Harris) mde all at stdy pce: rdn over 2f out: hld on wl fnl f 3/1[3]
0213 2 1 1/4 Her Red Devil (IRE)[15] 4706 3-9-2 56....... GeorgeChaloner(3) 7 63
(Richard Fahey) hld up in tch: hdwy to chse wnr over 2f out: sn rdn: kpt on ins fnl f 5/2[1]
3450 3 7 Rokeby[34] 4058 3-8-13 50.......(b1) AndrewMullen 5 43
(George Moore) s.i.s: hld up in tch: outpcd over 3f out: rallied fnl f: no ch w first two 12/1
002 4 1/2 Tortoise[4] 5084 3-8-11 53.......(b) DuilioDaSilva(5) 4 45
(Richard Guest) t.k.h and sddle sn slipped forward: sn chsng wnr: rdn over 2f out: wknd over 1f out 11/4[2]
465 5 4 1/2 Fillydelphia (IRE)[20] 4513 3-9-6 57....... DanielTudhope 6 41
(Patrick Holmes) prom: drvn and outpcd over 3f out: btn fnl 2f 10/1
6-30 6 hd Jimmy Crackle (IRE)[49] 3534 3-9-7 58....... TomEaves 3 41
(Brian Ellison) trckd ldrs: drvn and outpcd over 3f out: btn fr 2f out 6/1

2m 17.96s (5.96) **Going Correction** +0.375s/f (Good) **6** Ran SP% **111.3**
Speed ratings (Par 98): **91,90,84,84,80 80**
CSF £10.73 TOTE £5.00: £2.20, £1.80; EX 10.50 Trifecta £67.90.
**Owner** www.nottinghamshireracing.co.uk (2) **Bred** Worksop Manor Stud **Trained** Carburton, Notts

**FOCUS**
Another all-the-way winner in the finale, providing Shaun Harris with a double on the card.
T/Plt: £514.40 to a £1 stake. Pool of £79594.54 - 112.95 winning tickets. T/Qpdt: £268.40 to a £1 stake. Pool of £5768.39 - 15.90 winning tickets. RY

# 4919 THIRSK (L-H)
Monday, August 11

**OFFICIAL GOING: Soft (7.5)**
Wind: fresh 1/2 behind Weather: fine but very breezy

## 5240 BETFAIR NOVICE FLAT AMATEUR H'CAP (FOR NOVICE AMATEUR RIDERS) 2m
5:25 (5:25) (Class 6) (0-65,62) 4-Y-0+ £1,871 (£580; £290; £145) Stalls Low

Form RPR
-000 1 Dan Emmett (USA)[26] 4319 4-11-5 60.......(p) MrKWood 9 75
(John Wainwright) hld up in rr: stdy hdwy 7f out: trcking ldrs over 3f out: rdn to ld 2f out: edgd lft: forged wl clr 14/1
1253 2 12 Anne's Valentino[32] 4115 4-10-11 55....... MrJTeal(3) 4 56
(Malcolm Jefferson) trckd ldrs: upsides 7f out: led over 3f out: hdd 2f out: styd on same pce 4/1[2]
5443 3 1/2 Beat The Shower[22] 4474 8-11-1 56....... PhillipDennis 10 56
(Peter Niven) mid-div: hdwy 4f out: chsng ldrs over 2f out: kpt on same pce 3/1[1]
4 4 1 1/4 Graylyn Ruby (FR)[56] 3309 9-11-0 55....... MrHHunt 12 54
(Robert Eddery) mid-div: hdwy to chse ldrs 7f out: one pce fnl 2f 11/1
2100 5 1 1/2 Kathlatino[7] 4964 7-11-1 59.......(v) DylanMcDonagh(3) 6 56
(Micky Hammond) chsd ldrs: drvn 3f out: one pce 11/1
5436 6 4 1/2 Captain Sharpe[11] 4818 6-10-13 57.......(t) MrJPWilliams(3) 13 49
(Bernard Llewellyn) in rr: kpt on fnl 3f: nvr a factor 9/1[3]
4/6- 7 6 Denison Flyer[296] 7375 7-10-1 45.......(p) MissJMcLernon(3) 8 30
(Lawrence Mullaney) chsd ldr: led 7f out: hdd over 3f out: wknd fnl 2f 25/1
/360 8 1 3/4 Freedom Flying[32] 4115 11-10-1 45.......(tp) MrLHall(3) 3 27
(Lee James) mid-div: sme hdwy 6f out: nvr a factor 33/1
005/ 9 4 1/2 Short Takes (USA)[39] 1997 6-11-7 62.......(p) MrHStock 7 39
(Donald McCain) chsd ldrs: drvn 5f out: lost pl over 3f out 3/1[1]
6540 10 6 Joyful Motive[8] 3682 5-10-4 45....... MissJWalton 11 15
(Michael Chapman) in rr: sn pushed along: bhd fnl 7f 16/1
00-0 11 13 Vogarth[36] 93 10-10-1 45....... MrPhilipThomas(3) 5
(Michael Chapman) in rr: sn drvn along: bhd fnl 7f 66/1
-000 12 60 Jewelled Dagger (IRE)[12] 4797 10-10-1 45.......(tp) MissCWatling(3) 2
(Sharon Watt) led: clr after 2f: wd bnd over 8f out: hdd 7f out: hung bdly rt: sn lost pl: t.o 5f out: eventually completed 33/1

3m 41.09s (12.79) **Going Correction** +0.55s/f (Yiel) **12** Ran SP% **120.4**
Speed ratings (Par 101): **90,84,83,83,82 80,77,76,74,71 64,34**
CSF £68.68 CT £220.48 TOTE £18.50: £3.60, £1.80, £1.90; EX 82.60 Trifecta £495.00.
**Owner** R A Kaye **Bred** Swifty Farms Inc Et Al **Trained** Kennythorpe, N Yorks

**FOCUS**
This ended up being a very one-sided handicap. The tearaway early leader was ignored but the overall pace still looked a good one on ground officially described as soft.

## 5241 RACING UK ANYWHERE AVAILABLE NOW MAIDEN AUCTION STKS 7f
**6:00** (6:05) (Class 5) 2-Y-O **£3,234** (£962; £481; £240) **Stalls** Low

Form RPR
35 1 **Only Joking**[82] 2460 2-8-9 0 RobertWinston 2 78+
(Hugo Palmer) *mde all: shkn up and wnt clr appr fnl f: v readily* **3/1**[1]
2 8 **Devious Spirit (IRE)** 2-9-0 0 TonyHamilton 6 59+
(Richard Fahey) *sn chsng wnr: kpt on same pce over 1f out* **4/1**[3]
044 3 nk **Lord Of Words (IRE)**[16] 4659 2-8-11 59 BenCurtis 5 55
(Brian Ellison) *chsd ldrs: drvn and outpcd over 3f out: kpt on same pce fnl 2f* **14/1**
4 1 1/4 **Maureb (IRE)** 2-8-9 0 PatrickMathers 8 50
(Tony Coyle) *dwlt: sn chsng ldrs: drvn and out;pced over 4f out: kpt on fnl 2f: will improve* **7/2**[2]
5 4 1/2 **Midtech Star (IRE)** 2-9-3 0 DavidNolan 3 46
(Ian Williams) *chsd ldrs: drvn over 3f out: wknd over 1f out* **9/2**
00 6 2 1/4 **Debt Free Dame**[13] 4750 2-7-13 0 DanielleMooney(7) 12 29
(Michael Easterby) *sn chsng ldrs: outpcd over 3f out: wknd 2f out* **33/1**
7 1/2 **Arracourt** 2-9-3 0 DavidAllan 10 39
(Tim Easterby) *dwlt: in rr: sme hdwy over 2f out: sn wknd* **25/1**
8 3/4 **Dynamite Inventor (IRE)** 2-8-9 0 KevinStott(5) 7 34
(Kevin Ryan) *s.i.s: a in rr* **16/1**
000 9 8 **Flying Grange**[9] 4884 2-8-11 41 (b[1]) DuranFentiman 4 10
(Tim Easterby) *a in rr: bhd whn eased in clsng stages* **66/1**

1m 31.14s (3.94) **Going Correction** +0.55s/f (Yiel) **9 Ran SP% 106.2**
Speed ratings (Par 94): **99,89,89,88,82 80,79,78,69**
CSF £12.46 TOTE £4.90: £1.40, £1.50, £2.00; EX 12.70 Trifecta £48.20.
**Owner** Anglia Bloodstock Syndicate V **Bred** Mr & Mrs J Davis & P Mitchell B'Stock **Trained** Newmarket, Suffolk
■ Denton Carnival was withdrawn. Price at time of withdrawal 6/1. Rule 4 applies to all bets - deduct of 10p in the pound.
**FOCUS**
A maiden which lacked depth and it was plain sailing for the favourite with noting much getting into it.

## 5242 BRITISH STALLION STUDS EBF MAIDEN STKS (BOBIS RACE) 5f
**6:30** (6:33) (Class 4) 2-Y-O **£4,204** (£1,251; £625; £312) **Stalls** High

Form RPR
0042 1 **Johnny B Goode (IRE)**[17] 4625 2-9-5 76 TonyHamilton 7 78
(Richard Fahey) *trckd ldr: led over 1f out: drvn out* **9/4**[2]
40 2 2 **Crosse Fire**[12] 4790 2-9-5 0 PaulMulrennan 8 71
(Scott Dixon) *led: hdd over 1f out: kpt on same pce* **11/2**[3]
232 3 3 1/4 **Aussie Ruler (IRE)**[13] 4760 2-9-5 80 SteveDrowne 1 59
(Ronald Harris) *chsd ldrs on outside: rdn 2f out: hung rt: fdd appr fnl f* **1/1**[1]
00 4 2 1/2 **Moon Arc (IRE)**[16] 4659 2-9-5 0 PJMcDonald 3 50
(Keith Dalgleish) *dwlty in rr: kpt on fnl f: tk modest 4th nr fin* **66/1**
5 nk **Named Asset** 2-9-5 0 RussKennemore 10 49
(Jedd O'Keeffe) *dwlt: sn chsng ldrs: fdd over 1f out* **12/1**
05 6 3/4 **Olympic Charm**[32] 4109 2-9-5 0 DaleSwift 2 46
(Derek Shaw) *sn chsng ldrs: wknd over 1f out* **16/1**
006 7 2 **Hoofithully**[9] 4919 2-9-5 50 DavidAllan 5 39
(Michael Easterby) *in rr-div: sn drvn along: kpt on fnl f: nvr a factor* **20/1**
0 8 8 **Ted Larkin (IRE)**[27] 4286 2-9-5 0 RobertWinston 4 10
(Richard Guest) *in rr: drvn over 2f out: bhd whn eased ins fnl f* **50/1**

1m 0.33s (0.73) **Going Correction** +0.10s/f (Good) **8 Ran SP% 117.9**
Speed ratings (Par 96): **98,94,89,85,85 83,80,67**
CSF £15.45 TOTE £3.00: £1.10, £1.50, £1.10; EX 16.80 Trifecta £24.80.
**Owner** Jonathan Gill **Bred** Noel Brosnan **Trained** Musley Bank, N Yorks
■ Alfie Bond was withdrawn. Price at time of withdrawal 100/1. Rule 4 does not apply.
**FOCUS**
Fair efforts from the leading pair in this maiden with the short-priced favourite well below form in third. The winner has been rated as posting a clear personal best.

## 5243 MARKET CROSS JEWELLERS H'CAP (BOBIS RACE) 5f
**7:00** (7:00) (Class 4) (0-85,87) 3-Y-O **£4,851** (£1,443; £721; £360) **Stalls** High

Form RPR
5055 1 **Skye's The Limit**[32] 4133 3-8-12 74 TonyHamilton 6 82
(Richard Fahey) *trckd ldrs: effrt over 2f out: led jst ins fnl f: drvn out* **7/1**
0662 2 2 **One Boy (IRE)**[37] 3948 3-9-3 82 ConnorBeasley(3) 7 83
(Michael Dods) *sn outpcd and in rr: hdwy over 2f out: upsides 1f out: kpt on same pce* **5/1**
0540 3 3 3/4 **Oriental Relation (IRE)**[17] 4636 3-9-0 76 (v[1]) DaleSwift 8 64
(James Given) *led tl over 3f out: wknd fnl 150yds* **9/2**[3]
0531 4 2 **Meadway**[17] 4636 3-9-7 83 PaulMulrennan 5 63
(Bryan Smart) *wnt lft s: w ldrs: led over 3f out: hdd jst ins fnl f: sn wknd* **11/4**[1]
-100 5 1 1/2 **Zac Brown (IRE)**[9] 4898 3-9-6 82 GrahamGibbons 3 57
(David Barron) *bmpd s: chsd ldrs: rdn over 2f out: wknd wl over 1f out* **6/1**
-331 6 1 1/2 **Kommander Kirkup**[10] 4873 3-9-3 79 (b) PJMcDonald 4 49
(Michael Dods) *hmpd s: in rr: nvr wnt pce* **10/3**[2]

59.34s (-0.26) **Going Correction** +0.10s/f (Good) **6 Ran SP% 111.4**
Speed ratings (Par 102): **106,102,96,93,91 88**
CSF £39.89 CT £170.04 TOTE £9.00: £3.60, £2.50; EX 40.20 Trifecta £196.60.
**Owner** The Fairweather Foursome **Bred** Whatton Manor Stud **Trained** Musley Bank, N Yorks
**FOCUS**
A fairly useful sprint, although the form could prove a little misleading as the leaders went too hard and set the race up for those coming from behind.

## 5244 LIVE RACING AND BETTING - RACINGS UK IPAD APP (S) H'CAP 1m
**7:30** (7:30) (Class 6) (0-65,64) 3-Y-O+ **£2,587** (£770; £384; £192) **Stalls** Low

Form RPR
3543 1 **No Quarter (IRE)**[4] 5088 7-9-10 60 RoystonFfrench 7 68
(Tracy Waggott) *trckd ldrs: t.k.h: swtchd lft over 2f out: led 1f out: drvn out* **6/4**[1]
0634 2 1 1/4 **Benidorm**[4] 5103 6-8-10 46 (e) RobertWinston 9 51
(Richard Guest) *stdd s: hdwy on outer to trck ldrs over 4f out: led 2f out: hdd and hung lft 1f out: kpt on same pce* **5/1**[3]
0006 3 3 1/4 **Stream Of Light**[12] 4785 3-7-11 45 JoeDoyle(5) 5 42
(John Mackie) *t.k.h: mid-div: drvn and outpcd over 3f out: kpt on to take modest 3rd 1f out* **50/1**
0-00 4 4 1/2 **Red Tide (IRE)**[17] 4627 3-9-5 62 (p) RussKennemore 10 48
(Marjorie Fife) *set stdy pce: hdd 2f out: wknd appr fnl f* **9/1**
4004 5 1 1/4 **Mysterial**[19] 4530 4-9-9 64 (b) KevinStott(5) 1 48
(Ruth Carr) *chsd ldrs: wknd over 1f out* **8/1**
1005 6 2 **Absolute Bearing (IRE)**[25] 4358 5-8-12 48 DavidAllan 2 28
(Tim Etherington) *in rr: kpt on fnl 2f: nvr a factor: weighed in 2lb heavy* **16/1**
-066 7 1 **Uncle Brit**[61] 3105 8-9-5 55 PJMcDonald 4 33
(Malcolm Jefferson) *mid-div: drvn and outpcd over 3f out: no threat after* **7/2**[2]
5-00 8 2 3/4 **Throwing Roses**[30] 4195 4-8-5 46 JordanNason(5) 3 17
(John Weymes) *dwlt: hld up in rr: drvn and outpcd over 3f out: nvr a factor* **12/1**

1m 45.72s (5.62) **Going Correction** +0.55s/f (Yiel)
**WFA** 3 from 4yo+ 7lb **8 Ran SP% 115.5**
Speed ratings (Par 101): **93,91,88,84,82 80,79,77**
CSF £9.46 CT £254.65 TOTE £2.40: £1.10, £3.10, £8.50; EX 9.00 Trifecta £254.80.There was no bid for winner. Mysterial was claimed by D Carroll for £6000.
**Owner** N Waggott **Bred** Mrs T V Ryan **Trained** Spennymoor, Co Durham
**FOCUS**
A weak handicap. It was steadily run until past halfway and few ever threatened to get involved. The winner is rated back to his best and, while the runner-up is far from solid, he was close to form.

## 5245 CALVERTS CARPETS H'CAP 1m
**8:00** (8:00) (Class 5) (0-75,75) 3-Y-O **£3,234** (£962; £481; £240) **Stalls** Low

Form RPR
0-62 1 **Strictly Glitz (IRE)**[21] 4495 3-7-11 56 JoeDoyle(5) 6 59
(John Quinn) *hld up towards rr: hdwy on outer 3f out: styd on to ld jst ins fnl f: drvn out* **9/2**[3]
10- 2 1 1/2 **Ahoy There (IRE)**[290] 7492 3-8-11 65 AndrewElliott 5 65
(Tom Tate) *chsd ldr: led over 2f out: hdd ins fnl f: no ex* **7/1**
0032 3 1/2 **Bertha Burnett (IRE)**[10] 4871 3-8-2 59 oh3 ow3 ConnorBeasley(3) 3 58
(Brian Rothwell) *trckd ldrs: upsides over 1f out: kpt on one pce* **7/1**
114 4 7 **Eddiemaurice (IRE)**[34] 4063 3-9-7 75 (v) RobertWinston 4 58
(Richard Guest) *dwlt: hdwy over 3f out: drvn and nt clr run 2f out: swtchd rt: wknd fnl f* **7/1**
06 5 12 **Uplifted (IRE)**[21] 4490 3-8-2 56 (v[1]) RoystonFfrench 1 11
(Kevin Ryan) *led: qcknd pce over 3f out: hdd over 2f out: lost pl over 1f out* **7/2**[2]
0112 6 6 **Sheriff Of Nawton (IRE)**[84] 2391 3-9-2 73 SamJames(3) 2 14
(David O'Meara) *hld up towards rr: effrt 3f out: sn lost pl: bhd whn eased ins fnl f* **2/1**[1]

1m 44.3s (4.20) **Going Correction** +0.55s/f (Yiel) **6 Ran SP% 111.2**
Speed ratings (Par 100): **101,99,99,92,80 74**
CSF £33.53 TOTE £5.50: £2.40, £3.30; EX 29.70 Trifecta £127.30.
**Owner** Nigel S Cooper **Bred** Lynn Lodge Stud **Trained** Settrington, N Yorks
**FOCUS**
A muddling handicap. The gallop wasn't overly strong until past halfway. The winner is rated to latest with the runner-up to 2yo form.

## 5246 BET ON THE MOVE - RACING UK'S APP MAIDEN STKS 6f
**8:30** (8:30) (Class 5) 3-4-Y-O **£3,408** (£1,006; £503) **Stalls** High

Form RPR
2623 1 **Royal Connoisseur (IRE)**[37] 3951 3-9-5 74 TonyHamilton 1 74
(Richard Fahey) *trckd ldng pair: effrt over 1f out: led 1f out: hung rt: pushed out* **15/8**[2]
05 2 2 **Aphrilis (IRE)**[10] 4873 3-9-0 0 BenCurtis 5 61
(Brian Ellison) *led: drvn over 2f out: hdd 1f out: kpt on same pce* **12/1**
F64 3 4 1/2 **Heavenly River (FR)**[12] 4791 3-8-11 0 JoeyHaynes(3) 3 46
(K R Burke) *racd in last: drvn over 2f out: tk modest 3rd last 100yds* **9/4**[3]
5 4 2 3/4 **Katie Taylor (IRE)**[18] 4569 4-9-4 0 PaulMulrennan 4 38
(Rae Guest) *w ldr: drvn 2f out: wknd appr fnl f: eased nr fin* **7/4**[1]

1m 13.86s (1.16) **Going Correction** +0.10s/f (Good)
**WFA** 3 from 4yo 4lb **4 Ran SP% 109.6**
Speed ratings (Par 103): **96,93,87,83**
CSF £17.84 TOTE £2.30; EX 16.70 Trifecta £47.00.
**Owner** S & G Clayton, A Blower **Bred** Mrs Sheila Morrissey **Trained** Musley Bank, N Yorks
**FOCUS**
A weak sprint maiden in which the front-running second seemed to improve.
T/Jkpt: Not won. T/Plt: £40.80 to a £1 stake. Pool of £59181.76 - 1056.97 winning tickets.
T/Qpdt: £19.60 to a £1 stake. Pool of £5861.97 - 221.0 winning tickets. WG

# 5208 WINDSOR (R-H)
### Monday, August 11

**OFFICIAL GOING: Good to soft (good in places) changing to soft after race 2 (6.10)**
Top bend out 14yds adding 53yds to races of 1m+. Inner of Straight out 14yds at 6f and 6yds at Winning Post.
Wind: light to medium, behind Weather: overcast, heavy rain during the first

## 5247 188BET APPRENTICE H'CAP 6f
**5:40** (5:40) (Class 5) (0-70,70) 3-Y-O+ **£2,587** (£770; £384; £192) **Stalls** Low

Form RPR
2533 1 **Parisian Pyramid (IRE)**[3] 5138 8-9-4 60 (p) ThomasBrown 6 73
(Lee Carter) *mde all: rdn over 1f out: kpt on and a doing enough fnl f: rdn out* **9/2**[3]
501 2 1 1/2 **Gracie's Games**[6] 5000 8-8-9 51 6ex (v) WilliamTwiston-Davies 10 59
(John Spearing) *chsd wnr thrght: rdn 2f out: drvn and kpt on fnl f: a hld* **7/2**[1]
5062 3 1 3/4 **Lindart (ITY)**[28] 4268 3-9-4 67 (b) CamHardie(3) 11 69
(Richard Hannon) *s.i.s: rdn along in rr: hdwy over 2f out: chsd ldng pair wl over 1f out: kpt on but nvr enough pce to chal* **14/1**
4262 4 1 3/4 **Ray Of Joy**[5] 5059 8-9-11 70 (v) DannyBrock(3) 1 67
(J R Jenkins) *s.i.s: hld up in last trio: rdn and hdwy 2f out: plugged on same pce ins fnl f* **4/1**[2]
213 5 3/4 **Dark Lane**[7] 4981 8-9-4 65 HollieDoyle(5) 9 60
(David Evans) *t.k.h: hld up in tch in midfield: effrt to u.p to chse ldrs 2f out: no imp over 1f out* **9/2**[3]
0064 6 3 **Dream Catcher (FR)**[19] 4545 6-9-2 63 CharlotteJenner(5) 4 48
(Henry Candy) *t.k.h: chsd ldrs: rdn and lost pl over 2f out: wl hld and one pce fr over 1f out* **6/1**

6443 **7** *4* **Masai Moon**[16] 4673 10-9-0 61.......................(b) PatMillman(5) 7 33
(Rod Millman) *in tch in midfield: rdn and effrt to chse ldrs 1/2-way tl lost pl qckly ent fnl 2f: wl btn and hung lft fnl f* **14/1**

0300 **8** *2 ¼* **What A Dandy (IRE)**[19] 4545 3-8-11 62....................... DanielCremin(5) 8 26
(Jim Boyle) *stdd s: t.k.h: hld up in last trio: rdn over 2f out: sn struggling: bhd over 1f out* **10/1**

004 **9** *3 ½* **Studfarmer**[38] 3939 4-8-6 51 oh4.......................(p) NoelGarbutt(3) 2 5
(John Panvert) *in tch in midfield: rdn and lost pl 1/2-way: bhd over 1f out* **16/1**

1m 12.56s (-0.44) **Going Correction** +0.025s/f (Good)
**WFA** 3 from 4yo+ 4lb 9 Ran SP% **121.2**
Speed ratings (Par 103): **103,101,98,96,95 91,86,83,78**
CSF £21.82 CT £211.10 TOTE £5.80: £1.90, £1.50, £3.00; EX 28.40 Trifecta £669.60.
**Owner** John Joseph Smith **Bred** Illuminatus Investments **Trained** Epsom, Surrey

**FOCUS**
This was run in torrential rain and it appeared to favour those who raced up with the pace. The winner is rated to his AW winter form and the runner-up matched her recent Ffos Las run, while the third is hard to read.

## 5248 188BET MAIDEN STKS 6f
**6:10** (6:10) (Class 5) 2-Y-O **£2,587** (£770; £384; £192) **Stalls** Low

Form RPR
3 **1** **Steal The Scene (IRE)**[10] 4864 2-9-5 0....................... RichardHughes 9 74+
(Richard Hannon) *dwlt: sn rcvrd and led over 4f out: rdn 2f out: edging lft onto far rail over 1f out: forged ahd 1f out: pushed out towards fin* **6/5**[1]

0 **2** *nk* **Lackaday**[13] 4760 2-9-5 0....................... WilliamTwiston-Davies 8 74+
(Mick Channon) *in tch in midfield: effrt to chse ldrs 2f out: cl 3rd whn bdly hmpd: snatched up and stmbld jst over 1f out: swtchd rt and chsd wnr fnl 100yds: r.o wl* **5/1**[3]

0 **3** *1 ¼* **Wet Sail (USA)**[99] 1977 2-9-5 0....................... FrederikTylicki 6 69+
(Charlie Fellowes) *t.k.h: prom tl stdd bk into midfield after 1f out: swtchd rt 1f out: styd on to go 3rd wl ins fnl f: no threat to ldrs* **4/1**[2]

**4** *1 ¾* **Burauq** 2-9-5 0....................... MartinDwyer 1 63
(William Muir) *chsd ldrs: wnt 2nd 1/2-way: rdn 2f out: no ex and lost 2nd fnl 100yds: wknd towards fin* **33/1**

04 **5** *¾* **Red Tycoon (IRE)**[10] 4864 2-9-5 0....................... ShaneKelly 5 61
(Ed Dunlop) *dwlt: hld up in tch: clsd to join ldrs and looked to be travelling best 2f out: rdn and fnd little over 1f out: wknd ins fnl f* **4/1**[2]

50 **6** *8* **Orobas (IRE)**[8] 4943 2-9-2 0....................... RyanTate(3) 2 35
(Harry Whittington) *led tl over 4f out: lost pl u.p over 2f out: bhd over 1f out* **33/1**

**7** *shd* **Shamiya (IRE)** 2-9-0 0....................... TedDurcan 7 30
(J S Moore) *in tch in last trio: rdn and struggling over 2f out: bhd over 1f out* **25/1**

**8** *5* **Always Be Ready** 2-9-5 0....................... MartinHarley 4 19
(Lady Cecil) *dwlt: a in rr: lost tch over 1f out* **20/1**

1m 14.79s (1.79) **Going Correction** +0.15s/f (Good) 8 Ran SP% **116.6**
Speed ratings (Par 94): **94,93,91,89,88 77,77,71**
CSF £7.46 TOTE £2.00: £1.10, £1.40, £1.60; EX 8.10 Trifecta £34.60.
**Owner** Ms Elaine Chivers & Potensis Ltd **Bred** Shane Doyle **Trained** East Everleigh, Wilts
■ Stewards' Enquiry : Richard Hughes two-day ban: careless riding ( 25-26 Aug)

**FOCUS**
The pace was steady and the time was slow compared to the earlier handicap. The winner didn't improve much on his debut run, even though he beat the fifth further this time. The runner-up and third have both progressed.

## 5249 RACEBETS.COM NOW BEST ODDS GUARANTEED MAIDEN STKS 5f 10y
**6:40** (6:41) (Class 5) 3-4-Y-O **£2,587** (£770; £384; £192) **Stalls** Low

Form RPR
-325 **1** **My Inspiration (IRE)**[50] 3503 3-9-0 73....................... PatCosgrave 1 74
(Jim Boyle) *mde all: in last of field to go towards far side: rdn over 1f out: kpt on u.p and holding runner-up towards fin: rdn out* **6/1**[3]

3233 **2** *¾* **Newton's Law (IRE)**[15] 4697 3-9-5 73.......................(t) RichardHughes 4 76
(Brian Meehan) *hld up in tch in midfield: effrt u.p over 1f out: styd on and drvn to press wnr wl ins fnl f: edgd towards rival and fnd nil fnl 50yds* **8/11**[1]

233 **3** *½* **Eternitys Gate**[54] 3370 3-9-5 70....................... JimCrowley 6 74
(Peter Chapple-Hyam) *pressed wnr: rdn and ev ch 2f out: no ex and one pce ins fnl f* **4/1**[2]

0-6 **4** *2 ¼* **Findhorn Magic**[66] 2946 3-9-0 0....................... TedDurcan 3 61
(Peter Makin) *chsd ldrs: rdn over 1f out: 4th and no ex jst ins fnl f: wknd fnl 100yds* **10/1**

5 **5** *5* **Mon Cigar (IRE)**[16] 4677 3-9-5 0....................... MartinHarley 7 48
(Denis Coakley) *in tch in midfield: rdn and btn over 1f out: wknd fnl f* **10/1**

00 **6** *8* **Praise N Glory**[18] 4587 3-9-0 0....................... SebSanders 5 14
(Linda Jewell) *dwlt: a in last pair: rdn and struggling over 2f out: lost tch over 1f out* **66/1**

**7** *11* **Windy Miller** 3-9-5 0....................... WilliamCarson 2
(Robin Dickin) *s.i.s: rn green and a in rr: lost tch 2f out: t.o* **33/1**

1m 0.85s (0.55) **Going Correction** +0.15s/f (Good) 7 Ran SP% **114.8**
Speed ratings (Par 103): **101,99,99,95,87 74,57**
CSF £10.89 TOTE £5.70: £2.70, £1.20; EX 12.50 Trifecta £18.60.
**Owner** David F Powell **Bred** M Duffy **Trained** Epsom, Surrey

**FOCUS**
A modest sprint maiden in which the winner is rated to this year's form, with the runner-up a shade off.

## 5250 GHOST NURSERY H'CAP 1m 67y
**7:10** (7:10) (Class 4) (0-80,78) 2-Y-O **£4,851** (£1,443; £721; £360) **Stalls** Low

Form RPR
21 **1** **Taper Tantrum (IRE)**[26] 4330 2-9-5 76....................... RyanMoore 5 82
(Michael Bell) *led: qcknd 3f out: drvn and hrd pressed jst over 1f out: hdd ins fnl f: battled on wl to ld again nr fin: rdn out* **8/11**[1]

3532 **2** *shd* **Popeswood (IRE)**[8] 4944 2-9-0 74....................... CharlesBishop(3) 4 79
(Mick Channon) *hld up in tch: clsd 2f out: rdn to chal jst over 1f out: drvn to ld ins fnl f: kpt on u.p: hdd nr fin* **4/1**[3]

0230 **3** *8* **Euthenia**[17] 4626 2-9-0 71....................... WilliamTwiston-Davies 1 58
(Mick Channon) *t.k.h: chsd ldr tl over 3f out: rdn 3f out: btn over 1f out: wknd fnl f* **12/1**

0331 **4** *4* **Divine Law**[37] 3963 2-9-7 78....................... RichardHughes 6 55
(Richard Hannon) *chsd ldrs: wnt 2nd over 3f out: sn rdn: btn over 1f out: fdd ins fnl f* **7/2**[2]

460 **5** *2 ¼* **Vita Mina**[30] 4207 2-8-3 65....................... NoelGarbutt(5) 3 37
(David Evans) *rn in snatches: in tch in last pair: drvn 1/2-way: btn 2f out: sn wknd* **20/1**

1m 48.61s (3.91) **Going Correction** +0.40s/f (Good) 5 Ran SP% **112.6**
Speed ratings (Par 96): **96,95,87,83,81**
CSF £4.19 TOTE £1.60: £1.10, £2.20; EX 4.20 Trifecta £12.70.
**Owner** Secular Stagnation **Bred** Philip Newton **Trained** Newmarket, Suffolk

**FOCUS**
The front two were clear and the winner got a good front-running ride to build on his Sandown win, with the runner-up backing up his Newbury personal best.

## 5251 188BET CASINO H'CAP 1m 2f 7y
**7:40** (7:40) (Class 3) (0-90,89) 3-Y-O+ **£8,086** (£2,406; £1,202; £601) **Stalls** Centre

Form RPR
0264 **1** **Nicholascopernicus (IRE)**[2] 5188 5-10-0 89....................... RyanMoore 6 98
(Ed Walker) *s.i.s and drvn along early: rcvrd to ld after 1f out: mde rest: rdn and qcknd wl over 2f out: clr and in command 1f out: rdn out* **11/4**[3]

1530 **2** *3 ¼* **Hymenaios (IRE)**[47] 3587 3-9-3 87....................... RichardHughes 5 90+
(Richard Hannon) *stdd s: in tch in last pair: rdn and effrt over 2f out: chsd clr wnr jst over 1f out: no imp* **5/2**[2]

**3** *1 ¾* **First Post (IRE)**[59] 3196 7-9-2 77....................... HayleyTurner 1 77
(Derek Haydn Jones) *in tch in last pair: effrt and rdn wl over 2f out: chsd clr wnr and edgd lft over 1f out: no imp: 3rd and one pce fnl f* **10/1**

0500 **4** *4 ½* **Karam Albaari (IRE)**[14] 4736 6-9-0 75....................... FrederikTylicki 4 66
(J R Jenkins) *led for 1f: chsd wnr: rdn wl over 1f out: lost 2nd and btn over 1f out: wknd fnl f* **16/1**

**5** *43* **L'Orfeo**[338] 4-9-10 85....................... KierenFallon 3
(Saeed bin Suroor) *chsd ldrs: rdn and immediately outpcd wl over 2f out: lost tch 2f out: t.o and eased fnl f* **6/4**[1]

2m 10.78s (2.08) **Going Correction** +0.40s/f (Good)
**WFA** 3 from 4yo+ 9lb 5 Ran SP% **110.2**
Speed ratings (Par 107): **107,104,103,99,65**
CSF £9.99 TOTE £3.50: £1.60, £1.70; EX 8.50 Trifecta £35.70.
**Owner** Greenwood, Halsall and Pegum **Bred** Mrs E J O'Grady **Trained** Newmarket, Suffolk

**FOCUS**
Another good front-running ride and the winner is rated to last year's best.

## 5252 188BET GREAT IN PLAY H'CAP 1m 67y
**8:10** (8:10) (Class 5) (0-70,65) 3-Y-O+ **£2,587** (£770; £384; £192) **Stalls** Low

Form RPR
5220 **1** **Mister Mayday (IRE)**[19] 4544 3-9-3 63.......................(b) PatCosgrave 5 69
(George Baker) *taken down early: in tch in midfield: hdwy to join ldr and edgd rt 1f out: drvn fnl 100yds: fnd enough and r.o to ld wl ins fnl f* **7/1**[3]

0336 **2** *½* **Bayleyf (IRE)**[11] 4810 5-9-12 65.......................(p) StevieDonohoe 2 71
(Lee Carter) *led: rdn over 2f out: drvn over 1f out: kpt on u.p tl hdd and no ex wl ins fnl f* **7/1**[3]

4655 **3** *¾* **Exclusive Waters (IRE)**[24] 4394 4-9-10 63.......................(b) KierenFallon 4 67
(Charles Hills) *s.i.s: in tch in rr: rdn 4f out: swtchd lft and hdwy u.p 1f out: kpt on to go 3rd nr fin* **6/1**[2]

3243 **4** *nk* **Welsh Inlet (IRE)**[3] 5125 6-9-9 62....................... WilliamCarson 3 66
(John Bridger) *in tch in midfield: rdn to chse ldr wl over 2f out: drvn and ev ch over 1f out: 3rd and unable qck whn short of room jst ins fnl f: swtchd lft and one pce fnl 100yds* **6/1**[2]

5004 **5** *3 ¼* **Heartstrings**[14] 4742 3-8-12 61.......................(v) CharlesBishop(3) 1 56
(Mick Channon) *chsd ldrs: nt clr run on inner and shuffled bk 2f out swtchd lft and rdn over 1f out: no hdwy* **8/1**

21U2 **6** *4 ½* **Dream Impossible (IRE)**[14] 4742 3-9-3 63....................... RichardHughes 7 48
(Peter Makin) *chsd ldr: rdn and sltly outpcd wl over 2f out: trying to rally whn jostled and swtchd lft over 1f out: btn 1f out: eased ins fnl f* **5/4**[1]

0050 **7** *2* **It's Taboo**[28] 4273 4-9-7 60....................... JimCrowley 6 41
(Mark Usher) *in tch in last pair: u.p and1 no hdwy 3f out: wknd over 1f out: bhd and eased ins fnl f* **14/1**

1m 48.59s (3.89) **Going Correction** +0.40s/f (Good)
**WFA** 3 from 4yo+ 7lb 7 Ran SP% **115.8**
Speed ratings (Par 103): **96,95,94,94,91 86,84**
CSF £55.07 TOTE £8.40: £3.50, £3.30; EX 46.30 Trifecta £666.10.
**Owner** Asprey, Kane & Thomas **Bred** David Allan & Barnane Stud **Trained** Manton, Wilts
■ Stewards' Enquiry : Stevie Donohoe two-day ban: use of whip (25-26 Aug)

**FOCUS**
A muddling race in which the winner earned a small personal-best rating, and the third was close to his turf best, but not entirely convincing overall.
T/Plt: £134.80 to a £1 stake. Pool of £73710.54 - 399.13 winning tickets. T/Qpdt: £32.80 to a £1 stake. Pool of £7253.17 - 163.40 winning tickets. SP

# 1852 WOLVERHAMPTON (A.W) (L-H)
Monday, August 11

**OFFICIAL GOING: Tapeta: standard**
No speed figures will be produced until revised median times can be calculated. The comparisons shown are to the existing medians for the previous surface.
Wind: Strong behind Weather: Cloudy with sunny spells

## 5253 32RED CASINO MEDIAN AUCTION MAIDEN STKS (TAPETA) 5f 20y
**2:15** (2:17) (Class 6) 2-Y-O **£2,264** (£673; £336; £168) **Stalls** Low

Form RPR
322 **1** **Primrose Valley**[12] 4784 2-9-0 72.......................(p) FrederikTylicki 2 82
(Ed Vaughan) *mde all: rdn clr fr over 1f out: eased nr fin* **13/8**[1]

3322 **2** *6* **You're My Cracker**[15] 4701 2-8-9 75....................... JackGarritty(5) 3 60
(Donald McCain) *chsd wnr: rdn over 1f out: sn outpcd* **4/1**[3]

36 **3** *1* **Dolorous**[12] 4784 2-9-0 0....................... WilliamBuick 1 57
(John Gosden) *trckd ldrs: racd keenly: rdn over 1f out: styd on same pce* **5/2**[2]

45 **4** *shd* **Intruder**[15] 4701 2-9-5 0....................... DavidNolan 8 61
(Richard Fahey) *sn pushed along in rr: hdwy 1/2-way: rdn and swtchd rt over 1f out: styd on same pce* **16/1**

0203 **5** *hd* **Artfilly (IRE)**[17] 4610 2-9-0 69....................... RichardKingscote 6 56
(Ed Walker) *chsd ldrs: pushed along 1/2-way: styd on same pce fr over 1f out* **6/1**

0 **6** *8* **Ruby Rose (IRE)**[13] 4751 2-8-9 0....................... ShaneGray(5) 7 27
(Kevin Ryan) *prom: pushed along 1/2-way: sn wknd* **33/1**

03 **7** *½* **Prince Rofan (IRE)**[18] 4577 2-9-5 0....................... FrannyNorton 4 30
(Derek Shaw) *outpcd* **40/1**

0 **8** *21* **Cap la Nna**[93] 2173 2-9-0 0 ... DavidProbert 5
(David C Griffiths) *s.i.s: outpcd* **80/1**

1m 3.0s (1.10) **Going Correction** +0.35s/f (Slow) **8** Ran SP% **113.4**
Speed ratings (Par 92): **105,95,93,93,93 80,79,46**
CSF £8.35 TOTE £2.40: £1.10, £1.30, £1.40; EX 7.10 Trifecta £15.10.
**Owner** A M Pickering **Bred** Alan Pickering CBE **Trained** Newmarket, Suffolk

**FOCUS**
The first meeting to take place at Wolverhampton since the end of April and the very first fixture to take place on its new Tapeta, the initial time the surface has been used for racing in this country. The most notable aspect of the first race, a modest juvenile sprint maiden, was that unlike on the old surface here where the runners usually fanned out after turning for home, this time the field stayed tight against the inside rail. The winning time was quite slow, which probably isn't a surprise for the first meeting on a new surface. The winner is rated in line with better view of her Leicester second.

## 5254 WOLVERHAMPTON HOLIDAY INN CLAIMING STKS (TAPETA) 5f 20y
2:45 (2:47) (Class 6) 2-Y-O **£2,264** (£673; £336; £168) **Stalls** Low

Form RPR
5323 **1** **Low Cut Affair (IRE)**[5] 5043 2-8-8 72 ... DeclanBates(3) 4 72
(David Evans) *mde all: edgd lft over 3f out: shkn up over 1f out: clr fnl f: eased nr fin* **8/13**[1]

6020 **2** *4* **Elizabeth Flynn (IRE)**[9] 4920 2-8-11 70 ... (v[1]) HarryBentley 2 58
(K R Burke) *chsd wnr tl hmpd and lost 2nd over 3f out: rdn to chse wnr again over 1f out: styd on same pce fnl f* **7/4**[2]

0250 **3** *hd* **Johnny Sorrento**[59] 3201 2-8-1 60 ... (tp) PatrickO'Donnell(7) 3 54
(Tim Pitt) *s.i.s: sn prom: chsd wnr over 3f out tl rdn over 1f out: styd on same pce fnl f* **11/1**[3]

U000 **4** *1¾* **Saphira Silver (IRE)**[47] 3563 2-7-13 0 ow3 ... PhilipPrince(5) 1 44
(Nikki Evans) *sn outpcd* **100/1**

1m 4.72s (2.82) **Going Correction** +0.35s/f (Slow) **4** Ran SP% **107.6**
Speed ratings (Par 92): **91,84,84,81**
CSF £1.91 TOTE £1.50; EX 1.90 Trifecta £2.20.
**Owner** Mrs T Burns **Bred** D Donegan **Trained** Pandy, Monmouths
■ Stewards' Enquiry : Declan Bates one-day ban: careless riding (27 Aug)

**FOCUS**
A weak 2yo claimer and another winner to make all. The time was 1.72sec slower than the opener. The winner is rated to form.

## 5255 BRITISH STALLION STUDS EBF MAIDEN FILLIES' STKS (BOBIS RACE) (TAPETA) 5f 216y
3:15 (3:18) (Class 5) 2-Y-O **£3,234** (£962; £481; £240) **Stalls** Low

Form RPR
05 **1** **Angels Wings (IRE)**[24] 4396 2-9-0 0 ... JamesDoyle 4 79
(Charles Hills) *a.p: shkn up to chse ldr over 1f out: rdn to ld wl ins fnl f: r.o* **4/1**[3]

22 **2** *½* **Free Entry (IRE)**[70] 2824 2-9-0 0 ... KierenFallon 1 77
(James Tate) *led: shkn up over 1f out: rdn and hdd wl ins fnl f* **5/6**[1]

04 **3** *3½* **Aqlette**[12] 4784 2-9-0 0 ... MartinHarley 8 66
(Marco Botti) *sn chsng ldr: rdn and ev ch 2f out: no ex ins fnl f* **7/2**[2]

**4** *6* **Codger's Gift (IRE)** 2-8-9 0 ... JackGarritty(5) 6 47+
(Richard Fahey) *s.i.s: styd on appr fnl f: nvr nrr* **14/1**

05 **5** *7* **Freedom Rose (IRE)**[17] 4610 2-9-0 0 ... FrannyNorton 2 24
(Derek Shaw) *sn pushed along in rr: wknd wl over 2f out* **66/1**

00 **6** *1¾* **Wiggle**[95] 2089 2-9-0 0 ... StevieDonohoe 7 19
(Tim Pitt) *prom tl rdn and wknd over 2f out* **100/1**

6 **7** *2½* **Fast Lola**[59] 3199 2-9-0 0 ... HarryBentley 5 11
(Olly Stevens) *prom tl rdn and wknd over 1f out* **15/2**

**8** *21* **Auntie Dif** 2-8-7 0 ... AdamMcLean(7) 3
(Derek Shaw) *s.s: hdwy over 3f out: sn wknd* **80/1**

1m 17.19s (2.69) **Going Correction** +0.35s/f (Slow) **8** Ran SP% **118.9**
Speed ratings (Par 91): **96,95,90,82,73 71,67,39**
CSF £8.10 TOTE £4.90: £1.50, £1.10, £1.20; EX 9.00 Trifecta £26.10.
**Owner** Lady Bamford **Bred** Leinster Syndicate **Trained** Lambourn, Berks

**FOCUS**
A couple of interesting fillies lined up for this maiden and it resulted in the first reverse at the meeting for favourite backers. The winner was an improver after fair efforts in maidens, with the runner-up rated to latest.

## 5256 ALL NEW 32REDSPORT.COM FILLIES' H'CAP (TAPETA) 7f 32y
3:45 (3:45) (Class 5) (0-75,74) 3-Y-O+ **£2,911** (£866; £432; £216) **Stalls** High

Form RPR
2230 **1** **Imaginary World (IRE)**[32] 4112 6-9-2 69 ... (e) ShaneGray(5) 3 80
(John Balding) *hld up: hdwy over 2f out: nt clr run over 1f out: led ins fnl f: r.o wl* **7/2**[2]

4101 **2** *3¾* **Medam**[17] 4611 5-9-2 67 ... NeilFarley(3) 8 68
(Shaun Harris) *chsd ldr over 5f out tl led over 2f out: rdn over 1f out: hdd and unable qck ins fnl f* **13/2**

1-24 **3** *nse* **Bint Malyana (IRE)**[187] 487 3-8-13 67 ... (p) PatrickDonaghy 7 66
(Paul D'Arcy) *trckd ldr tl over 5f out: remained handy: wnt 2nd again over 2f out: rdn and edgd lft over 1f out: styd on same pce ins fnl f* **3/1**[1]

4-06 **4** *¾* **Redinha**[25] 4367 3-9-6 74 ... AdamKirby 2 71
(Clive Cox) *s.i.s: hld up: pushed along and hdwy over 2f out: sn rdn and outpcd: styd on u.p wl ins fnl f* **7/1**

5064 **5** *4* **Arianrhod (IRE)**[12] 4789 3-7-12 61 oh4 ... JackGarritty(5) 5 44
(Donald McCain) *hld up: pushed along 1/2-way: outpcd fnl 2f* **25/1**

-040 **6** *2¾* **Encore Encore (FR)**[26] 4329 3-8-9 63 ... LukeMorris 1 42
(Harry Dunlop) *chsd ldrs: pushed along 1/2-way: wknd 2f out* **6/1**[3]

0650 **7** *9* **Shahrazad (IRE)**[5] 5041 5-8-13 61 ... (t) SilvestreDeSousa 4 19
(Patrick Gilligan) *led: hdd over 2f out: rdn and wknd over 1f out* **3/1**[1]

1m 30.89s (2.09) **Going Correction** +0.35s/f (Slow)
**WFA** 3 from 5yo+ 6lb **7** Ran SP% **116.2**
Speed ratings (Par 100): **102,97,97,96,92 89,78**
CSF £26.93 CT £75.75 TOTE £4.20: £3.30, £2.00; EX 19.70 Trifecta £45.00.
**Owner** Hairy Gorrilaz **Bred** Denis McDonnell **Trained** Scrooby, S Yorks
■ Stewards' Enquiry : Patrick Donaghy four-day ban: use of whip (25, 26, 27, 28 Aug)

**FOCUS**
An ordinary fillies' handicap, but there was no hanging about.

## 5257 BET NOW AT 32REDSPORT.COM H'CAP (TAPETA) 7f 32y
4:15 (4:18) (Class 6) (0-65,65) 3-Y-O **£2,264** (£673; £336; £168) **Stalls** High

Form RPR
6056 **1** **Madame Mirasol (IRE)**[55] 3344 3-9-7 65 ... (p) JamesDoyle 6 76
(Kevin Ryan) *hld up: pushed along and hdwy over 2f out: rdn to ld 1f out: sn clr: eased nr fin* **3/1**[1]

-600 **2** *3¾* **Simma (IRE)**[16] 4677 3-9-3 61 ... LiamKeniry 10 61
(Sylvester Kirk) *s.i.s: sn prom: outpcd 3f out: hdwy over 1f out: r.o u.p to go 2nd post* **20/1**

0020 **3** *nk* **Torridon**[14] 4728 3-8-3 47 ... (b[1]) FrannyNorton 7 46
(Mark Johnston) *trckd ldrs: wnt 2nd 1/2-way: led over 2f out: sn rdn: hdd 1f out: no ex* **6/1**[3]

5-60 **4** *2¾* **Vied (USA)**[17] 4623 3-8-11 55 ... AdamBeschizza 2 47
(Robert Cowell) *prom: rdn over 2f out: styd on same pce fr over 1f out* **25/1**

0006 **5** *2½* **Speed Society**[25] 4352 3-8-10 54 ... (p[1]) LukeMorris 1 40
(Jim Boyle) *led: hdd over 6f out: led again over 5f out: rdn and hdd over 2f out: wknd fnl f* **5/1**[2]

3005 **6** *¾* **Sandsman's Girl (IRE)**[17] 4627 3-8-7 51 ... (b) HarryBentley 5 35
(James Given) *hld up: hdwy over 2f out: rdn and wknd over 1f out* **12/1**

5640 **7** *12* **Royal Bushida**[7] 4969 3-8-3 47 ... (v) SilvestreDeSousa 4
(Derek Shaw) *hld up: rdn over 2f out: wknd and eased over 1f out* **8/1**

0340 **8** *9* **Border Guard**[49] 3518 3-9-4 62 ... [1] AdamKirby 3
(Milton Bradley) *s.i.s: sn pushed along in rr: wknd over 2f out* **25/1**

-322 **9** *17* **Bereka**[41] 3821 3-9-2 65 ... JackGarritty(5) 9
(Richard Fahey) *led over 6f out tl over 5f out: rdn 1/2-way: wknd over 2f out* **3/1**[1]

1m 31.99s (3.19) **Going Correction** +0.35s/f (Slow) **9** Ran SP% **112.2**
Speed ratings (Par 98): **95,90,90,87,84 83,69,59,40**
CSF £66.63 CT £335.00 TOTE £3.40: £1.60, £4.60, £2.90; EX 64.70 Trifecta £271.90.
**Owner** Mrs Margaret Forsyth **Bred** John Cullinan **Trained** Hambleton, N Yorks
■ Stewards' Enquiry : Jack Garritty trainer's representative could off no explanation for the filly's performance

**FOCUS**
A modest handicap, but another example that come-from-behind horses can win here too. The winner was on a fair mark judged on her AW best and is rated in line with better view, and the runner-up matched her maiden form despite wide trip.

## 5258 32RED H'CAP (TAPETA) 1m 141y
4:45 (4:45) (Class 4) (0-85,85) 3-Y-O+ **£5,175** (£1,540; £769; £384) **Stalls** Low

Form RPR
0-04 **1** **Mazaaher**[57] 3272 4-9-0 71 ... DaneO'Neill 2 81
(B W Hills) *s.i.s: hld up: hdwy over 2f out: rdn over 1f out: styd on u.p to ld wl ins fnl f* **8/1**

0530 **2** *1* **Crowdmania**[9] 4922 3-9-5 84 ... FrannyNorton 8 92
(Mark Johnston) *chsd ldr tl led 3f out: rdn over 1f out: hdd wl ins fnl f* **7/2**[2]

135 **3** *nk* **Fajry (USA)**[13] 4753 3-9-5 84 ... SilvestreDeSousa 4 91
(Saeed bin Suroor) *hld up in tch: rdn over 2f out: nt clr run and swtchd rt ins fnl f: r.o nr fin* **9/2**[3]

-001 **4** *1¼* **Orion's Bow**[17] 4612 3-9-0 79 ... (bt) WilliamBuick 9 83
(John Gosden) *chsd ldrs: rdn over 1f out: ev ch ins fnl f: no ex towards fin* **9/2**[3]

4015 **5** *8* **Lawyer (IRE)**[16] 4671 3-9-6 85 ... AndreaAtzeni 6 71
(Luca Cumani) *s.i.s: hdwy over 6f out: rdn over 2f out: wknd fnl f* **10/3**[1]

2065 **6** *6* **Kung Hei Fat Choy (USA)**[4] 5088 5-9-13 84 ... (b) RichardKingscote 5 56
(James Given) *led: rdn and hdd 3f out: wknd wl over 1f out* **16/1**

5203 **7** *21* **Tatting**[35] 4028 5-9-10 81 ... LiamKeniry 1 5
(Chris Dwyer) *prom tl rdn and wknd over 2f out: eased* **11/1**

60-1 **8** *79* **Classic Colori (IRE)**[19] 3915 7-9-9 80 ... (p) AdamKirby 7
(Martin Keighley) *hld up: rdn 1/2-way: sn lost tch: virtually p.u* **20/1**

1m 52.12s (2.02) **Going Correction** +0.35s/f (Slow)
**WFA** 3 from 4yo+ 8lb **8** Ran SP% **111.8**
Speed ratings (Par 105): **105,104,103,102,95 90,71,1**
CSF £34.46 CT £140.89 TOTE £8.90: £2.70, £1.40, £1.90; EX 39.70 Trifecta £263.90.
**Owner** Hamdan Al Maktoum **Bred** Shadwell Estate Company Limited **Trained** Upper Lambourn, Berks

**FOCUS**
The feature race, but they didn't go a great pace with the early leader anchored in front. Again the winner came from behind. The winner is rated back to his 3yo best, and the runner-up at least as good as ever.

## 5259 RACING SPECIALS AT 32REDSPORT.COM H'CAP (TAPETA) 1m 4f 50y
5:15 (5:17) (Class 5) (0-75,74) 3-Y-O+ **£2,911** (£866; £432; £216) **Stalls** Low

Form RPR
2323 **1** **Warrigal (IRE)**[43] 3761 4-9-12 72 ... (v[1]) WilliamBuick 8 86+
(Jeremy Noseda) *hld up in tch: rdn to ld and hung lft over 1f out: styd on u.p* **3/1**[1]

-000 **2** *¾* **Cousin Khee**[14] 4736 7-10-0 74 ... JamesDoyle 3 86
(Hughie Morrison) *a.p: rdn over 2f out: ev ch and hung lft over 1f out: styd on same pce ins fnl f* **4/1**[3]

3322 **3** *6* **Dalgig**[25] 4354 4-9-12 72 ... AdamKirby 9 74
(Jamie Osborne) *chsd ldr tl led over 2f out: rdn and hdd over 1f out: wknd ins fnl f* **5/1**

3066 **4** *2¾* **Whitby High Light**[8] 4941 3-9-0 71 ... LiamKeniry 5 69
(Andrew Hollinshead) *hld up: hdwy over 1f out: wknd fnl f* **28/1**

024 **5** *shd* **Mymatechris (IRE)**[16] 4672 3-9-2 73 ... (t) DavidProbert 6 71
(Andrew Balding) *chsd ldrs: rdn over 2f out: wknd fnl f* **11/2**

5102 **6** *5* **All The Winds (GER)**[33] 2966 9-9-12 72 ... (t) LukeMorris 7 62
(Shaun Lycett) *hld up: rdn over 2f out: nvr on terms* **16/1**

2306 **7** *nk* **Right Of Appeal**[15] 4704 3-8-11 68 ... FrannyNorton 1 57
(Mark Johnston) *led: rdn and hdd over 2f out: wknd over 1f out* **10/3**[2]

0605 **8** *18* **Fire In Babylon (IRE)**[9] 4910 6-8-12 58 ... (b) AdamBeschizza 4 19
(Noel Quinlan) *hld up: rdn over 3f out: sn wknd* **40/1**

446- **P** **Blizzard Blues (USA)**[74] 563 8-9-2 67 ... (b) EoinWalsh(5) 2
(Aytach Sadik) *s.s: a in rr: rdn and wknd over 4f out: bhd whn p.u and dismntd over 2f out: fatally injured* **80/1**

2m 44.95s (4.15) **Going Correction** +0.35s/f (Slow)
**WFA** 3 from 4yo+ 11lb **9** Ran SP% **113.1**
Speed ratings (Par 103): **100,99,95,93,93 90,90,78,**
CSF £14.73 CT £56.29 TOTE £3.60: £1.30, £1.90, £1.90; EX 16.40 Trifecta £80.40.
**Owner** Miss Yvonne Jacques **Bred** Newsells Park Stud **Trained** Newmarket, Suffolk

**FOCUS**
The first staying event on Tapeta and they seemed to go an ordinary pace. A personal best from the winner.

T/Plt: £20.60 to a £1 stake. Pool of £77631.96 - 2747.19 winning tickets. T/Qpdt: £11.30 to a £1 stake. Pool of £5900.01 - 384.94 winning tickets. CR

5260 - 5262a (Foreign Racing) - See Raceform Interactive

# 4881 CLAIREFONTAINE (R-H)

Monday, August 11

**OFFICIAL GOING: Turf: heavy**

## 5263a PRIX DU DEFI DU GALOP - DREAM WELL (CONDITIONS) (4YO+) (TURF) 1m 1f

**1:20** (1:20) 4-Y-0+ **£18,750** (£7,500; £5,625; £3,750; £1,875)

RPR

1 **Solow**78 2588 4-8-11 0 OlivierPeslier 4 110
(F Head, France) **3/1**1

2 3 **Maningrey (GER)**22 5-8-11 0 MaximeGuyon 6 104
(Waldemar Hickst, Germany) **79/10**

3 2 1/2 **My Stone (FR)**22 6-8-11 0 (b) FredericSpanu 7 99
(Mme C Barande-Barbe, France) **106/10**

4 2 1/2 **Frankyfourfingers (FR)**47 3598 4-8-11 0 StephanePasquier 8 94
(C Delcher-Sanchez, France) **43/10**3

5 1 1/4 **Generalissime (FR)**29 4-8-11 0 Pierre-CharlesBoudot 9 91
(A De Royer-Dupre, France) **18/5**2

6 3 **Empire Storm (GER)**30 4180 7-9-4 0 RobertHavlin 5 92
(Michael Attwater) *pressed ldr: led over 2f out: sn rdn and hdd 1 1/2f out: wknd ins fnl f* **26/1**

7 2 **Gas Total (BRZ)**37 5-8-8 0 (b1) GregoryBenoist 2 77
(D Smaga, France) **151/10**

8 7 **Spirit's Revench (FR)**25 4-8-11 0 ThierryJarnet 1 66
(P Demercastel, France) **164/10**

9 3 **Sahawar (FR)**79 2576 4-8-11 0 (p) JulienAuge 3 59
(C Ferland, France) **9/2**

1m 52.6s (112.60) **9 Ran SP% 119.3**
PARI-MUTUEL (all including 1 euro stake): WIN 4.00 PLACE 1.90, 2.50, 3.40 DF 15.70 SF 27.30.
**Owner** Wertheimer & Frere **Bred** Wertheimer Et Frere **Trained** France

# 4958 CARLISLE (R-H)

Tuesday, August 12

**OFFICIAL GOING: Soft (good to soft in places; 6.2)**

Inside rail from Old Stable bend and up the straight moved out 5yds and distances increased by 2yds.
Wind: Fresh, half against Weather: Overcast

## 5264 APOLLOBET £50 FREE BETS MEDIAN AUCTION MAIDEN STKS 5f 193y

**2:15** (2:19) (Class 5) 2-Y-0 **£2,911** (£866; £432; £216) **Stalls** Low

Form RPR

1 **X Raise (IRE)** 2-9-0 0 GrahamLee 11 66+
(David Brown) *s.i.s: hdwy on outside whn carried lft 1/2-way: effrt and pushed along over 1f out: kpt on wl fnl f to ld cl home* **12/1**

2 hd **Jewelled Prince** 2-9-2 0 GeorgeChaloner(3) 10 71
(Richard Fahey) *trckd ldrs: rdn along 1/2-way: hdwy to ld ins fnl f: edgd lft: kpt on: hdd cl home* **10/1**

2 3 1/2 **Cumbrianna**77 2652 2-9-0 0 PaulMulrennan 7 64
(Bryan Smart) *t.k.h: led: drifted lft fr over 1f out: hdd ins fnl f: kpt on same pce towards fin* **7/2**3

0 4 2 3/4 **Mercury**17 4684 2-9-5 0 DanielTudhope 1 60+
(Kevin Ryan) *prom: rdn over 3f out: effrt on outside of gp over 1f out: kpt on ins fnl f* **3/1**2

0 5 3/4 **Ventura Canyon (IRE)**13 4790 2-9-5 0 TomEaves 12 58+
(Keith Dalgleish) *t.k.h: w ldr: rdn over 2f out: no ex fr over 1f out* **50/1**

62 6 5 **Muhaarib Al Emarat (IRE)**20 4527 2-9-5 0 TonyHamilton 5 42
(Richard Fahey) *trckd ldrs: rdn along and effrt over 2f out: wknd over 1f out* **9/4**1

7 1/2 **Pafiya** 2-9-0 0 JacobButterfield(5) 8 40
(Kristin Stubbs) *uns rdr on way to s: s.i.s: bhd and outpcd: nvr on terms* **40/1**

8 3 3/4 **Choppy Water (IRE)** 2-9-5 0 DavidAllan 4 28
(Tim Easterby) *dwlt: bhd and sn pushed along: nvr on terms* **20/1**

0 9 3/4 **Caties Do Dah**26 4357 2-9-0 0 PatrickMathers 6 21
(Alan Berry) *in tch: rdn and edgd lft over 3f out: sn lost pl and struggling* **250/1**

10 2 3/4 **Geology** 2-9-5 0 IanBrennan 9 17
(Kevin Ryan) *s.i.s: bhd and green: a struggling* **9/1**

1m 17.9s (4.20) **Going Correction** +0.525s/f (Yiel) **10 Ran SP% 114.3**
Speed ratings (Par 94): **93,92,92,88,87 80,80,75,74,70**
CSF £118.58 TOTE £12.30: £3.40, £2.40, £1.40; EX 137.40 Trifecta £470.20.
**Owner** Onslow Hughlock Brooke & Brown **Bred** Peter Onslow & T Whelan **Trained** Averham Park, Notts

**FOCUS**
After 8mm of overnight rain conditions were quite testing, especially with a strong, almost head-on wind against the runners in the home straight. The first four in this modest median auction maiden race ended up towards the stands' rail, and the first two were newcomers. The level is fluid.

## 5265 APOLLOBET BEST ODDS GUARANTEED H'CAP 5f 193y

**2:45** (2:47) (Class 5) (0-70,70) 3-Y-0+ **£2,911** (£866; £432; £216) **Stalls** Low

Form RPR

000- 1 **Seal Rock**52 3488 6-9-10 68 (b) PhillipMakin 7 77
(John Quinn) *trckd ldrs gng wl: rdn to ld over 1f out: kpt on wl towards fin* **4/1**1

-000 2 3/4 **Enderby Spirit (GR)**23 4471 8-9-10 68 PaulMulrennan 10 75
(Bryan Smart) *cl up: swtchd to stands' rail and led over 2f out: hdd over 1f out: kpt on ins fnl f* **12/1**

0402 3 nk **Amis Reunis**8 4961 5-8-7 51 oh1 (p) PatrickMathers 9 57
(Alan Berry) *led to over 2f out: rallied: kpt on u.p ins fnl f* **7/1**

2516 4 1/2 **Bond Club**62 3093 4-9-2 65 (b) JacobButterfield(5) 5 69
(Geoffrey Oldroyd) *s.i.s: bhd and drvn along: hdwy and swtchd lft over 1f out: n.m.r briefly ins fnl f: nudged along and kpt on strly towards fin* **5/1**2

3364 5 nse **Sewn Up**15 4728 4-8-4 51 oh2 (p) JoeyHaynes(3) 3 55
(Keith Dalgleish) *in tch: drvn along over 2f out: rallied: kpt on same pce ins fnl f* **9/1**

1533 6 hd **Slim Chance (IRE)**8 4961 5-9-7 65 AndrewElliott 2 68
(Simon West) *t.k.h: cl up: rdn over 2f out: no ex fnl f* **12/1**

0416 7 3 1/2 **Rich Again (IRE)**14 4752 5-9-8 66 (b) JoeFanning 6 58
(James Bethell) *t.k.h: hld up in tch: effrt over 1f out: one pce whn n.m.r briefly ins fnl f* **7/1**

61-0 8 1 1/2 **Woodland Girl**23 4471 3-9-5 70 GeorgeChaloner(3) 8 56
(Richard Fahey) *trckd ldrs: drvn over 2f out: wknd over 1f out* **9/1**

5221 9 20 **Mission Impossible**5 5089 9-9-11 69 6ex (p) RobertWinston 1
(Tracy Waggott) *t.k.h: in tch: drvn and outpcd over 2f out: btn and eased fr over 1f out* **11/2**3

1m 16.47s (2.77) **Going Correction** +0.525s/f (Yiel)
**WFA** 3 from 4yo+ 4lb **9 Ran SP% 112.4**
Speed ratings (Par 103): **102,101,100,99,99 99,94,92,66**
CSF £50.71 CT £321.84 TOTE £4.80: £1.60, £4.40, £2.00; EX 61.50 Trifecta £462.90.
**Owner** The Seal Pups **Bred** Mrs A D Bourne **Trained** Settrington, N Yorks

**FOCUS**
Again they migrated toward the stands' side rail. The winner used to be rated a lot higher, and the runner-up was formerly much better as well.

## 5266 APOLLOBET ENCHANCED RACING SPECIALS NURSERY H'CAP 5f

**3:20** (3:20) (Class 5) (0-75,72) 2-Y-0 **£3,234** (£962; £481; £240) **Stalls** Low

Form RPR

513 1 **Showstoppa**39 3909 2-9-7 72 JoeFanning 1 77
(Mark Johnston) *mde virtually all: rdn centre over 1f out: edgd lft ins fnl f: r.o strly* **10/3**3

004 2 1/2 **Penny Royale**54 3394 2-9-0 65 DavidAllan 4 68
(Tim Easterby) *s.i.s: in tch: effrt and drvn over 1f out: chsd wnr fnl f: kpt on* **11/4**2

3042 3 1 **Westhoughton**11 4857 2-8-13 64 DanielTudhope 5 63
(David O'Meara) *t.k.h: cl up: rdn and edgd rt over 1f out: kpt on same pce ins fnl f* **13/8**1

3434 4 shd **Bahango (IRE)**16 4702 2-9-0 65 (p) GrahamLee 6 64
(Kristin Stubbs) *w ldrs: rdn and c to stands' rail over 2f out: kpt on same pce fnl f* **15/2**

4261 5 8 **Danot (IRE)**22 4493 2-9-7 72 TomEaves 2 42
(Keith Dalgleish) *t.k.h: cl up tl rdn and wknd fr 2f out* **14/1**

1m 4.51s (3.71) **Going Correction** +0.525s/f (Yiel) **5 Ran SP% 106.3**
Speed ratings (Par 94): **91,90,88,88,75**
CSF £11.82 TOTE £3.50: £1.80, £1.90; EX 13.20 Trifecta £27.60.
**Owner** Hot To Trot & Whitsbury Manor Stud **Bred** Whitsbury Manor Stud **Trained** Middleham Moor, N Yorks

**FOCUS**
A straightforward nursery, the runner-up through to the fourth all to their pre-race marks.

## 5267 APOLLOBET FREE DOWNLOAD APP CLAIMING STKS 1m 1f 61y

**3:50** (3:51) (Class 5) 3-Y-0+ **£2,911** (£866; £432; £216) **Stalls** Low

Form RPR

4240 1 **The Osteopath (IRE)**35 4058 11-9-5 73 PhillipMakin 4 65
(John Davies) *hld up: stdy hdwy over 3f out: sn pushed along: led and edgd rt appr fnl f: kpt on strly* **3/1**1

4-65 2 2 1/4 **Hope For Glory**8 4978 5-9-2 0 JoeyHaynes(3) 2 60
(Jason Ward) *prom: rdn over 3f out: rallied to chse wnr ins fnl f: kpt on: nt pce to chal* **80/1**

0310 3 1 1/2 **Staffhoss**3 5166 4-9-5 63 AdrianNicholls 7 57
(Mark Johnston) *prom: drvn and outpcd over 3f out: rallied fnl f: kpt on: no imp* **5/1**2

0501 4 nk **Gold Class**54 3407 3-8-11 62 (b) PaulMulrennan 5 56
(Ed McMahon) *pressed ldr: ev ch and rdn over 2f out: sn outpcd: rallied whn hmpd appr fnl f: sn no ex* **12/1**

6-00 5 2 3/4 **Greeleys Love (USA)**31 4204 4-9-9 76 (v) JoeFanning 3 54
(Mark Johnston) *led at modest gallop: rdn over 1f out: sn hdd and fnd little* **3/1**1

6601 6 4 1/2 **Rasselas (IRE)**8 4959 7-8-12 66 (b) AnnaHesketh(7) 1 41
(David Nicholls) *in tch: drvn and outpcd over 3f out: btn fnl 2f* **3/1**1

0-4 7 11 **Dream And Hope**42 3822 3-8-6 0 ow1 GeorgeChaloner(3) 8 16
(Philip McBride) *s.i.s: hld up on outside: shortlived effrt wl over 3f out: sn btn* **10/1**3

2m 2.5s (4.90) **Going Correction** +0.525s/f (Yiel)
**WFA** 3 from 4yo+ 8lb **7 Ran SP% 109.7**
Speed ratings (Par 103): **99,97,95,95,92 88,79**
CSF £153.23 TOTE £3.50: £1.80, £11.70; EX 142.00 Trifecta £631.70.
**Owner** Kevin Kirkup **Bred** Joe Rogers **Trained** Piercebridge, Durham

**FOCUS**
A shaky claimer, the winner more reliable than most and stone off this year's best in success with the other form horses not at best.

## 5268 APOLLOBET IN PLAY BETTING H'CAP 1m 1f 61y

**4:25** (4:25) (Class 5) (0-70,75) 3-Y-0+ **£2,911** (£866; £432; £216) **Stalls** Low

Form RPR

41 1 **Diddy Eric**5 5084 4-8-2 50 oh1 (b) RobJFitzpatrick(7) 5 59
(Micky Hammond) *hld up in last pl: stdy hdwy 4f out: rdn and chsd ldr over 1f out: styd on wl fnl f: led nr fin* **2/1**1

6050 2 nk **Moccasin (FR)**32 4175 5-9-12 67 DavidAllan 3 75
(Geoffrey Harker) *chsd ldr: rdn over 2f out: led over 1f out: kpt on fnl f: edgd rt and hdd nr fin* **10/3**2

5221 3 4 1/2 **Ellaal**4 5142 5-10-6 75 6ex PaulMulrennan 8 74
(Ruth Carr) *led: rdn and hdd over 1f out: sn outpcd by first two* **2/1**1

2232 4 4 1/2 **Call Of Duty (IRE)**8 4959 9-8-9 55 (b) EmmaSayer(5) 6 44
(Dianne Sayer) *in tch: rdn towards far side over 2f out: no imp wl over 1f out* **9/1**3

0510 5 2 3/4 **Hayek**25 4381 7-8-9 50 (b) AndrewElliott 2 34
(Tim Easterby) *chsd ldrs: drvn over 3f out: wknd fr 2f out* **20/1**

45 6 3 3/4 **Quick Succession (USA)**10 4904 3-8-13 62 TomEaves 7 38
(Keith Dalgleish) *t.k.h: hld up: rdn over 3f out: btn fnl 2f* **20/1**

2m 1.23s (3.63) **Going Correction** +0.525s/f (Yiel)
**WFA** 3 from 4yo+ 8lb **6 Ran SP% 109.3**
Speed ratings (Par 103): **104,103,99,95,93 89**
CSF £8.46 CT £12.17 TOTE £3.80: £1.80, £2.30; EX 11.10 Trifecta £33.00.
**Owner** Mrs Rita Butler **Bred** Lady Richard Wellesley **Trained** Middleham, N Yorks

■ Stewards' Enquiry : David Allan two-day ban: used whip above permitted level (Aug 26-27)
Rob J Fitzpatrick two-day ban: used whip above permitted level (Aug 26-27)

**FOCUS**
The time was okay compared to the earlier claimer and the winner backed up his Newcastle success (when perhaps a bit better than bare form from rear) and may progress again. The runner-up was close to this year's form.

## 5269 APOLLOBET FOLLOW ON TWITTER AND FACEBOOK H'CAP 7f 200y
**5:00** (5:00) (Class 5) (0-70,69) 3-Y-O+ **£2,911** (£866; £432; £216) **Stalls** Low

Form RPR
5323 **1** **Warfare**[8] 4968 5-9-8 63 PaulMulrennan 1 71
(Kevin Ryan) *chsd ldrs: rdn to ld over 1f out: edgd lft ins fnl f: hld on wl* **4/1**[2]
-215 **2** *1* **World Record (IRE)**[31] 4197 4-10-0 69 PhillipMakin 8 75
(John Quinn) *t.k.h: cl up: effrt and ev ch over 1f out: kpt on ins fnl f: hld cl home* **6/1**
3031 **3** *shd* **Archie's Advice**[16] 4706 3-9-0 62 TomEaves 2 67
(Keith Dalgleish) *in tch: rdn over 3f out: rallied over 1f out: disp 2nd pl ins fnl f: kpt on: hld nr fin* **6/1**
3500 **4** *nk* **Royal Holiday (IRE)**[36] 4023 7-9-10 65 (p) DanielTudhope 5 70
(Marjorie Fife) *led: rdn and hdd over 1f out: rallied: no ex ins fnl f* **3/1**[1]
0000 **5** *1 1/4* **Card High (IRE)**[20] 4532 4-8-4 50 oh5 (t) EmmaSayer(5) 6 52
(Wilf Storey) *hld up: rdn and outpcd over 3f out: rallied over 1f out: kpt on fnl f: nvr able to chal* **66/1**
4325 **6** *2 1/2* **Running Reef (IRE)**[21] 4523 5-9-7 62 RobertWinston 3 58
(Tracy Waggott) *hld up: rdn over 2f out: no imp fr over 1f out* **5/1**[3]
400- **7** *3 1/2* **Last Supper**[285] 7639 5-8-11 52 (p) JoeFanning 4 40
(James Bethell) *cl up: ev ch over 2f out: sn rdn: wknd over 1f out* **20/1**
3260 **8** *1 1/2* **Petergate**[38] 3946 3-8-7 58 (p) ConnorBeasley(3) 9 42
(Brian Rothwell) *hld up: rdn and hdwy wl over 2f out: wknd over 1f out* **8/1**
0-05 **9** *11* **Saythatagain (IRE)**[14] 4754 3-8-7 55 DavidAllan 7 21
(Tim Easterby) *in tch: outpcd over 3f out: btn and eased over 1f out* **16/1**

1m 43.68s (3.68) **Going Correction** +0.525s/f (Yiel)
**WFA** 3 from 4yo+ 7lb 9 Ran SP% **113.5**
Speed ratings (Par 103): **102,101,100,100,99 96,93,91,80**
CSF £27.69 CT £141.50 TOTE £3.90: £1.40, £2.20, £2.00; EX 30.50 Trifecta £78.60.
**Owner** Guy Reed Racing **Bred** G Reed **Trained** Hambleton, N Yorks

**FOCUS**
A modest handicap run at a sound pace in driving rain and four almost in a line inside the final furlong. The winner was off a career-low mark and the second has been rated to his best.

## 5270 APOLLOBET ONLINE GAMES & CASINO H'CAP 1m 3f 107y
**5:30** (5:31) (Class 5) (0-70,67) 3-Y-O+ **£2,911** (£866; £432; £216) **Stalls** High

Form RPR
5450 **1** **Mendelita**[25] 4420 3-8-9 58 TonyHamilton 7 65
(Richard Fahey) *mde virtually all: jnd after 2f: rdn 2f out: hld on gamely fnl f* **8/1**
3555 **2** *1/2* **Mambo Rhythm**[15] 4726 3-9-1 64 (b[1]) JoeFanning 5 70
(Mark Johnston) *prom: stdy hdwy over 2f out: rdn over 1f out: wnt 2nd wl ins fnl f: r.o* **6/1**[3]
0311 **3** *1 1/2* **Sergeant Pink (IRE)**[5] 5090 8-9-4 62 12ex EmmaSayer(5) 6 66
(Dianne Sayer) *t.k.h: cl up: chal after 2f: rdn 2f out: kpt on same pce ins fnl f* **8/1**
3524 **4** *3/4* **Vicky Valentine**[17] 4663 4-9-7 65 GarryWhillans(5) 1 67
(Alistair Whillans) *trckd ldrs: drvn and ev ch over 1f out: kpt on same pce ins fnl f* **8/1**
0-22 **5** *2* **Thackeray**[8] 4964 7-9-3 56 MichaelStainton 8 55
(Chris Fairhurst) *hld up: stdy hdwy over 4f out: rdn 3f out: c stands' side wl over 1f out: edgd lft and no imp fnl f* **11/4**[1]
3324 **6** *3/4* **Vodka Wells (FR)**[20] 4548 4-10-0 67 BenCurtis 3 65
(Brian Ellison) *hld up: rdn and hdwy over 2f out: c stands' side over 1f out: sn rdn and no imp* **3/1**[2]
443 **7** *hd* **Spot The Pro (IRE)**[16] 4705 5-9-11 64 BrianHughes 9 62
(Rebecca Menzies) *hld up bhd ldng gp: stdy hdwy and prom over 3f out: rdn and outpcd 2f out: n.d after* **10/1**
3-4 **8** *17* **Painted Tail (IRE)**[47] 3624 7-9-11 64 DavidAllan 4 48
(Alan Swinbank) *hld up: rdn and struggling over 4f out: btn and eased wl over 1f out* **20/1**

2m 33.91s (10.81) **Going Correction** +0.525s/f (Yiel)
**WFA** 3 from 4yo+ 10lb 8 Ran SP% **113.1**
Speed ratings (Par 103): **81,80,79,79,77 77,76,64**
CSF £53.72 CT £395.94 TOTE £8.40: £3.40, £1.50, £2.50; EX 61.50 Trifecta £644.40.
**Owner** The G-Guck Group **Bred** Avenue Farm Stud **Trained** Musley Bank, N Yorks

**FOCUS**
The rain continued to fall. Just a steady gallop for the first mile and the two who came widest of all in the home straight failed to land a telling blow. The first four home were in the first four throughout. This was a small personal best from the winner, with the second running as well as ever.
T/Plt: £149.30 to a £1 stake. Pool: £75,490.77 - 369.06 winning tickets. T/Qpdt: £22.30 to a £1 stake. Pool: £5,883.29 - 194.80 winning tickets. RY

# 4999 FFOS LAS (L-H)
Tuesday, August 12
**OFFICIAL GOING: Good to soft (soft in places)**
Wind: Strong against Weather: Cloudy with sunny spells

## 5271 HEINEKEN MEDIAN AUCTION MAIDEN STKS 6f
**2:30** (2:31) (Class 5) 2-Y-O **£2,587** (£770; £384; £192) **Stalls** Centre

Form RPR
**1** **Elysian Flyer (IRE)** 2-9-5 0 RichardHughes 1 85+
(Richard Hannon) *led: hdd over 3f out: led again over 2f out: rdn and edgd rt over 1f out: r.o wl* **3/1**[2]
322 **2** *2 3/4* **Fingal's Cave (IRE)**[17] 4684 2-9-5 79 WilliamTwiston-Davies 7 76
(Mick Channon) *a.p: rdn to chse wnr over 1f out: styd on same pce ins fnl f* **5/4**[1]
630 **3** *2 1/4* **Goring (GER)**[56] 3322 2-9-5 79 JimmyFortune 6 69
(Eve Johnson Houghton) *s.i.s: hld up: rdn over 2f out: styd on to go 3rd ins fnl f: nt trble ldrs* **8/1**
22 **4** *1/2* **Little Palaver**[63] 3081 2-9-5 0 AdamKirby 2 67
(Clive Cox) *chsd ldrs: rdn over 2f out: styd on same pce fnl f* **9/2**[3]
0 **5** *1* **Dylan's Storm (IRE)**[25] 4389 2-9-0 0 GeorgeDowning(5) 4 64
(David Dennis) *chsd wnr tl led over 3f out: hdd over 2f out: sn rdn: wknd ins fnl f* **66/1**
**6** *1/2* **Code Red** 2-9-5 0 MartinDwyer 5 62
(William Muir) *s.i.s: sn pushed along in rr: rdn over 2f out: sn outpcd* **7/1**

1m 12.62s (2.62) **Going Correction** +0.45s/f (Yiel) 6 Ran SP% **112.7**
Speed ratings (Par 94): **100,96,93,92,91 90**
CSF £7.24 TOTE £4.60: £1.90, £1.30; EX 8.70 Trifecta £56.90.
**Owner** The Low Flyers **Bred** Tom Shirley **Trained** East Everleigh, Wilts

**FOCUS**
A good start from the winner and worth taking at face value with the second, third and fourth to their marks. The fifth was a big improver, but cost a few quid.

## 5272 FOSTERS MEDIAN AUCTION MAIDEN STKS 1m (R)
**3:00** (3:00) (Class 6) 3-4-Y-O **£1,940** (£577; £288; £144) **Stalls** Low

Form RPR
0- **1** **Scottish Strand**[425] 3245 3-9-5 0 KierenFallon 4 80+
(James Tate) *hld up: hdwy over 2f out: rdn to join ldr over 1f out: styd on to ld wl ins fnl f* **7/2**[2]
3 **2** *1/2* **Zora Seas (IRE)**[16] 4699 3-9-0 0 JimmyFortune 3 74+
(Brian Meehan) *s.i.s: hld up: hdwy over 2f out: led over 1f out: sn rdn: hdd and unable qck wl ins fnl f* **4/6**[1]
-430 **3** *9* **Jessy Mae**[110] 1684 3-8-9 50 TimClark(5) 6 53
(Derek Haydn Jones) *trckd ldrs: racd keenly: chsd ldr over 3f out: led over 2f out: rdn and hdd over 1f out: wknd ins fnl f* **33/1**
65 **4** *2* **Avon Scent**[41] 3849 4-9-7 0 DavidProbert 5 50
(Christopher Mason) *chsd ldr tl led over 3f out: rdn and hdd over 2f out: wknd over 1f out* **16/1**
5- **5** *12* **Bookmaker**[309] 7073 4-9-12 0 RichardHughes 1 36
(Olly Stevens) *prom: pushed along over 2f out: wknd and eased over 1f out* **6/1**[3]
**6** *1 1/2* **Desperado Dancer** 3-9-5 0 IrineuGoncalves 2 23
(Natalie Lloyd-Beavis) *led: rdn and hdd over 3f out: sn wknd* **50/1**

1m 46.32s (5.32) **Going Correction** +0.375s/f (Good)
**WFA** 3 from 4yo 7lb 6 Ran SP% **107.3**
Speed ratings (Par 101): **88,87,78,76,64 63**
CSF £5.63 TOTE £4.60: £2.40, £1.10; EX 6.40 Trifecta £42.20.
**Owner** Saif Ali **Bred** Miss K Rausing **Trained** Newmarket, Suffolk

**FOCUS**
A weak maiden in which the third and fourth limit the level. The winner found loads of improvement from his only 2yo start, with the runner-up off his Ascot debut figure.

## 5273 STRONGBOW H'CAP 1m (R)
**3:35** (3:35) (Class 6) (0-60,58) 3-Y-O+ **£1,940** (£577; £288; £144) **Stalls** Low

Form RPR
2324 **1** **Greyemkay**[7] 5005 6-8-10 47 DanielMuscutt(5) 8 58
(Richard Price) *a.p: chsd ldr over 4f out: led 2f out: sn rdn: jst hld on* **5/4**[1]
0323 **2** *hd* **Schottische**[59] 3230 4-9-5 51 (v) RichardHughes 5 62
(Derek Haydn Jones) *hld up: hdwy 1/2-way: rdn to chse wnr over 1f out: r.o* **7/2**[2]
3400 **3** *11* **Delightful Sleep**[10] 4905 6-9-9 55 AdamKirby 9 40
(David Evans) *hld up: hdwy over 2f out: wknd fnl f* **9/2**[3]
450/ **4** *4* **Lion Court (IRE)**[1002] 7418 6-9-12 58 DavidProbert 3 34
(Dai Burchell) *prom: pushed along and lost pl 1/2-way: sn bhd: mod late prog* **7/1**
0-00 **5** *1 1/4* **Sir Percy Blakeney**[19] 4562 3-8-6 45 (b[1]) MartinDwyer 7 17
(Marcus Tregoning) *led 7f out: rdn: edgd lft and hdd 2f out: sn wknd* **16/1**
0600 **6** *8* **Ficelle (IRE)**[71] 2838 5-9-1 47 (p) JimmyFortune 6
(Nikki Evans) *sn led: hdd 7f out: remained handy: rdn over 3f out: wknd 2f out* **25/1**
6000 **7** *1 1/2* **Hidden Talent**[34] 4072 4-8-10 49 PaddyPilley(7) 4
(Steph Hollinshead) *hld up: rdn and wknd over 2f out* **20/1**

1m 42.58s (1.58) **Going Correction** +0.375s/f (Good)
**WFA** 3 from 4yo+ 7lb 7 Ran SP% **111.8**
Speed ratings (Par 101): **107,106,95,91,90 82,81**
CSF £5.44 CT £13.50 TOTE £3.20: £1.60, £1.50; EX 4.90 Trifecta £11.90.
**Owner** Richard Price & Maria Slade **Bred** Shade Oak Stud **Trained** Ullingswick, H'fords

**FOCUS**
Weak form but the front two were clear and the race is rated around the winner with his recent C&D fourth working out well. There was a small personal best on turf from the second.

## 5274 BULMERS CIDER H'CAP 1m (R)
**4:05** (4:05) (Class 4) (0-85,90) 3-Y-O+ **£4,690** (£1,395; £697; £348) **Stalls** Low

Form RPR
2 **1** **Unison (IRE)**[32] 4148 4-9-1 72 SteveDrowne 2 83
(Peter Makin) *hld up: hdwy over 4f out: led over 1f out: sn rdn: styd on* **5/1**[3]
5545 **2** *1/2* **Khee Society**[12] 4817 3-8-3 67 oh1 ow1 DavidProbert 10 76
(David Evans) *hld up: hdwy over 2f out: rdn to chse wnr and edgd lft over 1f out: styd on* **10/1**
0002 **3** *6* **Set The Trend**[8] 4982 8-9-9 85 GeorgeDowning(5) 8 81
(David Dennis) *hld up: hdwy over 3f out: rdn over 1f out: styd on same pce fnl f* **20/1**
330 **4** *3 1/4* **Prairie Rose (GER)**[20] 4543 3-8-13 77 RichardHughes 7 65
(Olly Stevens) *led: rdn and hdd over 1f out: wknd fnl f* **7/1**
1420 **5** *1/2* **Swift Cedar (IRE)**[31] 4190 4-9-6 77 AdamKirby 9 64
(David Evans) *chsd ldr tl rdn over 2f out: wknd over 1f out* **9/2**[2]
5133 **6** *1 1/4* **Tenbridge**[32] 4153 5-8-4 66 oh5 (v) TimClark(5) 6 51
(Derek Haydn Jones) *prom: chsd ldr over 2f out tl rdn over 1f out: wknd fnl f* **16/1**
10 **7** *1 1/4* **Space Walker (IRE)**[41] 3861 3-8-11 75 WilliamTwiston-Davies 4 56
(Harry Dunlop) *chsd ldrs: lost pl 5f out: sn rdn: wknd 2f out* **10/1**
000 **8** *1/2* **Eurato (FR)**[75] 2699 4-8-7 72 KieranShoemark(7) 3 53
(John Spearing) *sn pushed along and a in rr* **10/1**
3541 **9** *20* **Crystal Lake (IRE)**[8] 4982 3-9-5 90 6ex PatrickO'Donnell(7) 1 24
(Ralph Beckett) *prom: rdn over 3f out: wknd and eased over 2f out* **7/4**[1]

1m 42.62s (1.62) **Going Correction** +0.375s/f (Good)
**WFA** 3 from 4yo+ 7lb 9 Ran SP% **121.6**
Speed ratings (Par 105): **106,105,99,96,95 94,93,92,72**
CSF £56.79 CT £942.31 TOTE £6.90: £2.10, £3.80, £3.40; EX 60.70 Trifecta £849.70.
**Owner** J P Carrington **Bred** Alan Dargan **Trained** Ogbourne Maisey, Wilts

**FOCUS**
A competitive handicap on paper but it concerned only two in the final furlong, and they both found a bit of improvement.

## 5275 DAVIES CHEMISTS H'CAP 5f
4:40 (4:42) (Class 5) (0-75,75) 3-Y-0+ £2,587 (£770; £384; £192) Stalls Centre

Form RPR
2203 1 **First In Command (IRE)**[18] 4630 9-9-6 71 ..........(t) FrankieMcDonald 7 80
(Daniel Mark Loughnane) *hld up in tch: rdn to ld ins fnl f: jst hld on* **6/1**
040- 2 *nk* **Threave**[286] 7633 6-9-7 72 .......... AdamKirby 6 80
(Jo Crowley) *w ldrs: led 2f out: rdn and hung lft fr over 1f out: hdd ins fnl f: styd on* **9/2**[3]
36/3 3 3 ¼ **Avertor**[26] 4370 8-8-8 64 .......... DanielMuscutt(5) 2 60
(Robert Stephens) *prom: rdn over 1f out: styd on same pce fnl f* **8/1**
0140 4 ½ **Edged Out**[12] 4833 4-9-8 73 .......... DavidProbert 4 68
(Christopher Mason) *w ldr tl led over 3f out: hdd 2f out: no ex ins fnl f* **8/1**
0660 5 ½ **Waseem Faris (IRE)**[14] 4762 5-9-10 75 .......... RichardHughes 5 68
(Mick Channon) *trckd ldrs: racd keenly: rdn over 1f out: no ex ins fnl f* **11/4**[1]
4232 6 ¾ **Whitecrest**[5] 5070 6-9-9 74 .......... WilliamTwiston-Davies 1 64
(John Spearing) *led: hdd over 3f out: rdn over 1f out: no ex fnl f* **7/2**[2]
0006 R **Steel Rain**[9] 4946 6-9-8 73 .......... JimmyFortune 3
(Nikki Evans) *ref to r* **10/1**

1m 0.04s (1.74) **Going Correction** +0.45s/f (Yiel) **7 Ran SP% 112.7**
Speed ratings (Par 103): **104,103,98,97,96 95,**
CSF £31.82 TOTE £7.00: £4.10, £1.80; EX 34.30 Trifecta £256.80.
**Owner** Mrs C Loughnane **Bred** Peter And Mrs McCutcheon **Trained** Baldwin's Gate, Staffs

**FOCUS**
A tight little handicap but a couple of the market principals disappointed and two broke clear in the final furlong, although they ended up wide apart in the closing stages. The winner found a bit of improvement on recent form and the second earned a small personal-best rating.

## 5276 AT THE RACES H'CAP 1m 4f (R)
5:15 (5:16) (Class 4) (0-80,78) 3-Y-0+ £4,690 (£1,395; £697; £348) Stalls Low

Form RPR
5-04 1 **Yaakooum (IRE)**[38] 3974 3-8-12 73 .......... RichardHughes 8 85
(Richard Hannon) *hld up: hdwy 1/2-way: led over 2f out: sn hdd: rallied to ld over 1f out: rdn out* **7/1**[3]
312 2 ½ **Kashmiri Sunset**[82] 2491 3-8-11 75 .......... DeclanBates(3) 7 86
(Ed de Giles) *chsd ldrs: led 2f out: sn rdn: hung rt and hdd: styd on u.p* **7/1**[3]
0/-1 3 1 ¾ **Eye Of The Tiger (GER)**[202] 283 9-9-7 76 .......... RossCoakley(5) 10 84
(J P Murtagh, Ire) *hld up: hdwy over 3f out: hmpd over 1f out: rdn and edgd lft ins fnl f: styd on same pce* **3/1**[2]
-031 4 1 ½ **Classical Art (IRE)**[50] 3541 3-9-1 76 .......... KierenFallon 6 82
(Roger Varian) *hld up: rdn over 3f out: hdwy and nt clr run over 1f out: styd on same pce ins fnl f* **8/1**
2162 5 7 **Bold Runner**[27] 4322 3-9-1 76 .......... FrankieMcDonald 2 71
(Jose Santos) *chsd ldrs: stdd and lost pl after 2f: dropped to rr 5f out: hdwy over 3f out: rdn over 1f out: wknd fnl f* **16/1**
-323 6 *hd* **Curbyourenthusiasm (IRE)**[46] 3673 3-9-0 75 .......... DavidProbert 9 69
(David Simcock) *s.i.s: hld up: hdwy over 3f out: rdn and wknd over 1f out* **9/4**[1]
0516 7 7 **Laughing Jack**[48] 3574 6-9-9 78 .......... GeorgeDowning(5) 1 61
(George Baker) *s.i.s: plld hrd: hdwy 10f out: wnt 2nd 1/2-way: led 4f out: rdn and hdd over 2f out: wknd over 1f out* **16/1**
05- 8 5 **Mr Fitzroy (IRE)**[86] 7257 4-9-8 72 ..........(tp) SteveDrowne 4 47
(Jo Davis) *chsd ldr to 1/2-way: wknd 3f out* **50/1**
611- 9 4 **Bathwick Street**[458] 2284 5-10-0 78 ..........(p) WilliamTwiston-Davies 3 47
(David Pipe) *led at stdy pce tl rdn and hdd 4f out: wknd over 2f out* **25/1**
-254 10 2 ½ **Green Light**[44] 3750 3-9-0 75 .......... JimmyFortune 5 40
(Ralph Beckett) *hld up: hdwy 1/2-way: rdn over 2f out: wknd and eased over 1f out* **7/1**[3]

2m 41.06s (3.66) **Going Correction** +0.375s/f (Good)
**WFA** 3 from 4yo+ 11lb **10 Ran SP% 122.0**
Speed ratings (Par 105): **102,101,100,99,94 94,90,86,84,82**
CSF £57.98 CT £182.54 TOTE £7.50: £2.30, £2.40, £1.90; EX 69.90 Trifecta £356.40.
**Owner** Saeed H Al Tayer **Bred** George Kent **Trained** East Everleigh, Wilts

**FOCUS**
A competitive handicap and the form should work out given some unexposed and in-form horses came to the fore. A few of these were a bit keen. The winner, second and fourth are all progressive/unexposed and the third is still on a good mark judged on his old form.

## 5277 BURNS PET NUTRITION H'CAP 1m 4f (R)
5:45 (5:45) (Class 6) (0-65,64) 3-Y-0+ £1,940 (£577; £288; £144) Stalls Low

Form RPR
3305 1 **Lochalsh (IRE)**[27] 4321 3-8-12 59 .......... RichardHughes 3 73
(William Knight) *chsd ldr tl led 3f out: rdn over 1f out: styd on wl* **3/1**[2]
3453 2 1 ½ **Reach The Beach**[27] 1622 5-8-11 47 oh2 ..........(t) KierenFallon 5 59
(Brendan Powell) *hld up: hdwy over 2f out: rdn to chse wnr over 1f out: styd on same pce ins fnl f* **7/1**
5012 3 6 **Pink Diamond**[20] 4540 3-9-3 64 .......... JimmyFortune 2 66
(Eve Johnson Houghton) *chsd ldrs: rdn over 2f out: no ex fnl f* **7/4**[1]
0-36 4 2 ½ **Acapulco Bay**[41] 3853 10-8-11 47 ..........(p) DavidProbert 4 45
(Dai Burchell) *s.i.s: sn prom: rdn over 2f out: wknd fnl f* **12/1**
4334 5 2 ½ **Highlife Dancer**[9] 4948 6-9-7 64 ..........(v) PaddyPilley(7) 1 58
(Mick Channon) *led and racd alone for much of the trip: clr 7f out: styd far side turning for home: rdn and hdd 3f out: sn hung rt: wknd wl over 1f out* **9/2**[3]
0550 6 2 ½ **Improvized**[45] 3711 3-8-7 54 ..........(b[1]) MartinDwyer 6 44
(William Muir) *hld up: rdn over 2f out: wknd over 1f out* **7/1**

2m 40.94s (3.54) **Going Correction** +0.375s/f (Good)
**WFA** 3 from 5yo+ 11lb **6 Ran SP% 112.2**
Speed ratings (Par 101): **103,102,98,96,94 93**
CSF £23.31 TOTE £3.80: £1.50, £4.40; EX 28.20 Trifecta £56.20.
**Owner** Mrs Melba Bryce **Bred** J & L Young / Darlacher Ltd **Trained** Patching, W Sussex

**FOCUS**
Improved form from the winner, but this has been rated cautiously.
T/Plt: £76.20 to a £1 stake. Pool: £71,236.71 - 682.30 winning tickets. T/Qpdt: £39.70 to a £1 stake. Pool: £5,657.95 - 105.30 winning tickets. CR

# 5180 LINGFIELD (L-H)
Tuesday, August 12

**OFFICIAL GOING: Polytrack: standard**
Wind: Moderate, half behind Weather: Unsettled

## 5278 RACING SPECIALS AT 32REDSPORT.COM MAIDEN STKS 7f 1y(P)
5:05 (5:05) (Class 5) 2-Y-O £2,587 (£770; £384; £192) Stalls Low

Form RPR
3 1 **Indianaughty (USA)**[48] 3578 2-9-5 .......... MartinHarley 3 77+
(Marco Botti) *led 1f: prom and gng wl after: led again 1f out: in control whn lft clr ins fnl f: rdn out* **2/5**[1]
2 5 **Glorious Magic (IRE)** 2-9-5 .......... HarryBentley 2 64
(Olly Stevens) *in tch: rdn 3f out: one pce fnl 2f: lft 2nd ins fnl f* **12/1**[3]
00 3 1 ½ **Wolf Of Windlesham (IRE)**[31] 4207 2-8-12 .......... TylerSaunders(7) 6 60
(B W Hills) *stdd s and dropped in: bhd: plenty to do over 2f out: rdn and styd on fr over 1f out* **33/1**
06 4 7 **Go Gently (IRE)**[94] 2151 2-9-5 .......... FergusSweeney 4 48
(George Baker) *sn chsng ldr: rdn and wknd over 2f out* **20/1**
000 5 6 **Ralph McTell**[18] 4618 2-8-12 .......... JordanVaughan(7) 1 26
(Alan Coogan) *in tch tl wknd 3f out: sn bhd* **100/1**
U **Wentworth Falls** 2-9-5 .......... WilliamBuick 5 72
(Charlie Appleby) *led after 1f: rn green and hdd 1f out: cl 2nd but hld whn jinked rt and uns rdr ins fnl f* **3/1**[2]

1m 25.25s (0.45) **Going Correction** -0.05s/f (Stan) **6 Ran SP% 112.8**
Speed ratings (Par 94): **95,89,87,79,72**
CSF £6.62 TOTE £1.50: £1.10, £6.10; EX 9.00 Trifecta £69.60.
**Owner** Giuliano Manfredini **Bred** Dell Ridge Farm Llc **Trained** Newmarket, Suffolk

**FOCUS**
There was plenty of late drama in this race, when the second favourite unseated his rider. The winner's debut form had already been franked and here he confirmed that promise.

## 5279 £10 FREE BET AT 32REDSPORT.COM FILLIES' NURSERY H'CAP 7f 1y(P)
5:35 (5:36) (Class 5) (0-70,70) 2-Y-O £2,587 (£770; £384; £192) Stalls Low

Form RPR
531 1 **What A Party (IRE)**[14] 4764 2-9-2 70 .......... ShelleyBirkett(5) 3 75+
(Gay Kelleway) *mde virtually all: travelled smoothly in front: shkn up 2f out: a wl in control: comf* **5/2**[2]
056 2 1 **Old Fashion**[18] 4626 2-9-0 63 .......... MartinHarley 1 65
(Ed Dunlop) *towards rr: effrt and wd st: gd hdwy fnl f* **9/4**[1]
000 3 *nk* **Auld Fyffee (IRE)**[25] 4403 2-8-11 63 .......... RyanPowell(3) 5 64
(John Ryan) *chsd ldrs: n.m.r and lost pl over 2f out: rallied and r.o wl fnl f* **12/1**
0501 4 1 **As A Dream (IRE)**[7] 4999 2-8-10 59 6ex .......... FergusSweeney 4 58
(David Evans) *hld up in 6th: rdn over 3f out: drvn to chse ldrs 1f out: one pce ins fnl f* **6/1**
006 5 ½ **Magic Mac**[49] 3557 2-8-0 49 .......... NickyMackay 7 46
(Hughie Morrison) *t.k.h: w wnr tl outpcd over 2f out: lost 2nd and fdd ins fnl f* **10/1**
000 6 1 **Celestine Abbey**[22] 4499 2-8-5 54 .......... LukeMorris 6 49
(Julia Feilden) *prom: rdn over 2f out: wknd fnl f* **50/1**
600 7 ¾ **All My Love (IRE)**[25] 4403 2-8-11 65 .......... CamHardie(5) 2 58
(Richard Hannon) *in tch: effrt over 2f out: wknd fnl f* **9/2**[3]
0000 8 1 **Sparbrook (IRE)**[3] 5180 2-8-4 53 .......... HarryBentley 8 43
(Simon Dow) *s.i.s and dropped in to rail: hld up in rr: rdn 3f out: mod effrt over 1f out: n.d* **20/1**

1m 25.82s (1.02) **Going Correction** -0.05s/f (Stan) **8 Ran SP% 115.3**
Speed ratings (Par 91): **92,90,90,89,88 87,86,85**
CSF £8.65 CT £54.50 TOTE £2.80: £1.10, £1.10, £2.60; EX 9.50 Trifecta £64.10.
**Owner** M M Foulger **Bred** Martyn J McEnery **Trained** Exning, Suffolk

**FOCUS**
A routine fillies' nursery and a winning time nearly 0.6secs slower than that of the opener, but a progressive winner who stepped up on the bare form of her Yarmouth win. The runner-up also improved, with the third rated to her maiden best.

## 5280 GREYHOUND H'CAP 1m 1y(P)
6:05 (6:05) (Class 6) (0-65,64) 3-Y-0+ £1,940 (£577; £288; £144) Stalls Low

Form RPR
5-53 1 **Palace Dragon (IRE)**[8] 4970 3-9-2 59 .......... LukeMorris 7 67
(Sir Mark Prescott Bt) *mde all: hrd rdn and flashed tail 1f out: hld on fnl f* **5/4**[1]
-351 2 1 **Bon Port**[18] 4613 3-9-0 64 .......... CharlieBennett(7) 1 69
(Hughie Morrison) *prom: chsd wnr 3f out: kpt on fnl f* **9/2**[3]
4634 3 ¾ **Anginola (IRE)**[12] 4808 5-8-8 51 ..........(p) CharlotteJenner(7) 6 55
(Laura Mongan) *in tch: effrt and wd 2f out: styd on fnl f* **25/1**
153- 4 ½ **Loraine**[286] 7622 4-9-13 63 .......... GeorgeBaker 2 66
(Jamie Osborne) *hld up in rr: hdwy on inner over 2f out: swtchd rt ins fnl f: styd on* **6/1**
0062 5 6 **Lewamy (IRE)**[4] 5138 4-8-5 46 .......... CamHardie(5) 3 35
(John Best) *dwlt: plld hrd: sn trcking ldrs: rdn and btn 2f out* **7/2**[2]
5100 6 1 **Little Indian**[17] 4655 4-9-6 61 ..........(v[1]) DannyBrock(5) 5 48
(J R Jenkins) *t.k.h: trckd ldrs: n.m.r and lost pl on bnd after 3f: btn over 2f out* **10/1**
0064 7 8 **Jersey Cream (IRE)**[15] 4733 3-8-9 52 .......... FergusSweeney 9 20
(Gary Moore) *chsd wnr tl 3f out: sn rdn and wknd* **14/1**
0-00 8 10 **Foiled**[43] 3781 4-8-6 45 .......... MatthewCosham(3) 8
(Nikki Evans) *towards rr: dropped to last after 2f: drvn along 4f out: sn lost tch and struggling* **100/1**

1m 37.89s (-0.31) **Going Correction** -0.05s/f (Stan)
**WFA** 3 from 4yo+ 7lb **8 Ran SP% 119.7**
Speed ratings (Par 101): **99,98,97,96,90 89,81,71**
CSF £7.75 CT £96.74 TOTE £2.80: £1.10, £1.60, £4.50; EX 10.60 Trifecta £141.60.
**Owner** Palace House Turf Club **Bred** Frank Dunne **Trained** Newmarket, Suffolk

**FOCUS**
Few got into a moderate contest. The winner built on his previous start and the runner-up is rated close to her C&D win.

## 5281 32RED H'CAP 6f 1y(P)
6:35 (6:36) (Class 4) (0-80,80) 3-Y-0+ £5,175 (£1,540; £769; £384) Stalls Low

Form RPR
1416 1 **Dissent (IRE)**[19] 4581 5-9-4 72 ..........(b) TomQueally 11 83
(James Given) *mde all at str pce: sn crossed to inner fr wd stall and wnt 5 l clr: rdn and kpt on fnl 2f: hld on wl* **8/1**

0406 **2** *1 ¼* **Sweet Talking Guy (IRE)**[6] 5059 4-8-11 68.............(t) SimonPearce(3) 8 75
(Lydia Pearce) *chsd clr ldrs: wnt 5 l 2nd over 1f out: kpt on fnl f: a hld*
**16/1**

302 **3** *nk* **Marjong**[8] 4971 4-9-7 75.......................................................... SebSanders 6 81
(Simon Dow) *towards rr: rdn over 2f out: hdwy over 1f out: styd on u.p*
**5/1**[2]

3304 **4** *3 ½* **Putin (IRE)**[14] 4768 6-8-10 69........................................(bt) DannyBrock(5) 1 64
(Phil McEntee) *chsd wnr tl over 1f out: no ex fnl f*
**12/1**

0301 **5** *1 ¼* **Dishy Guru**[20] 4546 5-9-3 71.........................................(b) LiamKeniry 2 62
(Michael Blanshard) *bhd: hdwy and hrd rdn over 1f out: no imp*
**20/1**

04-0 **6** *hd* **Red Aggressor (IRE)**[11] 4866 5-9-12 80...................................... HarryBentley 9 70
(Clive Brittain) *chsd clr ldrs tl fdd fnl 2f*
**12/1**

504 **7** *hd* **Arctic Lynx (IRE)**[14] 4765 7-9-9 77........................................ GeorgeBaker 4 67
(Robert Cowell) *modest 5th tl rdn and btn wl over 1f out*
**6/1**[3]

33 **8** *2 ½* **O'Gorman**[57] 3313 5-9-12 80................................................ LukeMorris 5 62
(Gary Brown) *bhd: rdn over 2f out: n.d*
**5/1**[2]

0023 **9** *½* **Al's Memory (IRE)**[10] 4907 5-9-1 74......................................... NoelGarbutt(5) 3 54
(David Evans) *mid-div: rdn 3f out: sn wknd*
**9/2**[1]

1316 **10** *½* **Spellmaker**[34] 4078 5-9-2 73............................................ MichaelJMMurphy(3) 7 51
(Tony Newcombe) *dwlt: bhd: rdn 3f out: nvr nr ldrs*
**7/1**

0046 **11** *1 ¼* **Saffire Song**[11] 4862 3-9-1 73............................................... MartinHarley 10 46
(Alan Bailey) *mid-div tl wknd 3f out*
**33/1**

1m 10.22s (-1.68) **Going Correction** -0.05s/f (Stan)
**WFA** 3 from 4yo+ 4lb **11** Ran SP% **118.4**
Speed ratings (Par 105): **109,107,106,102,100 100,100,96,96,95 93**
CSF £129.05 CT £724.69 TOTE £9.60: £2.80, £6.50, £2.40; EX 162.00 Trifecta £1191.50.
**Owner** The Cool Silk Partnership **Bred** Corduff Stud Ltd & J Corcoran **Trained** Willoughton, Lincs

**FOCUS**
The tearaway leader never came back to them, and this has been rated around the runner-up and third.

## 5282 32RED CASINO MAIDEN STKS 1m 4f (P)
**7:05** (7:05) (Class 5) 3-Y-0 **£2,587** (£770; £384; £192) **Stalls** Far side

Form RPR

3322 **1** **Loving Home**[27] 4332 3-9-5 85................................................ NickyMackay 3 76+
(John Gosden) *mde all: pushed along and qcknd wl over 1f out: sn drew wl clr*
**1/20**[1]

46 **2** *11* **Numrood**[7] 5010 3-9-5 0....................................................... LukeMorris 2 58
(George Peckham) *chsd wnr 1f: rdn 4f out: regained 2nd over 2f out: no ch w easy wnr in st*
**33/1**[3]

60 **3** *3 ¼* **New Reaction**[41] 3856 3-9-5 0................................................ GeorgeBaker 1 53
(Amanda Perrett) *pressed wnr after 1f: hung rt on bnds: rdn and lost 2nd over 2f out: sn btn*
**14/1**[2]

50 **4** *½* **Opus Too (IRE)**[22] 4500 3-9-0 0............................................. ShelleyBirkett(5) 4 52
(Julia Feilden) *a last: rdn and n.d fnl 4f*
**100/1**

2m 32.37s (-0.63) **Going Correction** -0.05s/f (Stan) **4** Ran SP% **105.8**
Speed ratings (Par 100): **100,92,90,90**
CSF £3.47 TOTE £1.10; EX 3.70 Trifecta £4.60.
**Owner** Normandie Stud Ltd **Bred** Normandie Stud Ltd **Trained** Newmarket, Suffolk

**FOCUS**
A weak maiden, the winner class above these. The level is a bit fluid behind and has been rated around the second to a better view of his previous form.

## 5283 BUTTERFLIES & BOWS VENUE DECORATION H'CAP 1m 4f (P)
**7:35** (7:37) (Class 6) (0-55,55) 3-Y-0+ **£1,940** (£577; £288; £144) **Stalls** Low

Form RPR

4053 **1** **Zinnobar**[15] 4734 4-8-9 48...................................................(p) DannyBrock(5) 2 56
(Jonathan Portman) *prom: led jst over 1f out: drvn clr*
**5/1**[2]

0-6 **2** *1 ½* **Rajeh (IRE)**[15] 4744 11-8-12 46 oh1....................................... FergusSweeney 3 52
(Peter Grayson) *in tch: effrt 3f out: drvn to chse wnr 1f out: kpt on*
**12/1**

/00- **3** *2 ¼* **Ghufa (IRE)**[287] 7612 10-8-13 50............................................. SimonPearce(3) 11 52
(Lydia Pearce) *mid-div: rdn 3f out: styd on fnl f: nvr nrr*
**25/1**

6004 **4** *1 ¾* **Lola Montez (IRE)**[15] 4734 3-8-10 55...................................(b[1]) TedDurcan 1 54
(David Lanigan) *trckd ldrs: chal on bit 3f out: led briefly and rdn over 1f out: hung lft and nt run on*
**6/4**[1]

3540 **5** *hd* **Sixties Queen**[62] 3115 4-9-3 51................................................ MartinHarley 8 50
(Alan Bailey) *hld up towards rr: rdn and sme hdwy fr 2f out: nt rch ldrs*
**6/1**[3]

00-4 **6** *6* **Richo**[15] 4737 8-8-7 46 oh1..................................................(b) CamHardie(5) 7 35
(Shaun Harris) *s.s: bhd: rdn 3f out: sme late hdwy*
**14/1**

0035 **7** *shd* **Beauchamp Melba**[52] 3471 3-8-5 50.................................(p) WilliamCarson 10 39
(Paul Fitzsimons) *led at gd pce tl over 1f out: sn wknd*
**20/1**

0250 **8** *nk* **Illegale (IRE)**[7] 5001 8-9-2 50...........................................(bt) DougieCostello 13 39
(Nikki Evans) *stdd s: hld up in rr: rdn 2f out: nvr trbld ldrs*
**14/1**

0-46 **9** *2 ¾* **Jawinski (IRE)**[7] 5001 4-8-13 47............................................. SamHitchcott 9 31
(David Evans) *in tch on outer: rdn 4f out: wknd wl over 1f out*
**6/1**[3]

0-60 **10** *1 ¾* **Highland Stardust**[31] 4210 3-8-10 55....................................(p) LukeMorris 6 36
(Clive Cox) *in tch: rdn 5f out: wknd 4f out*
**20/1**

0000 **11** *28* **Wings Of Fire (IRE)**[10] 4911 4-8-12 46 oh1............................ LiamKeniry 4
(Denis Quinn) *prom tl wknd over 3f out*
**50/1**

-000 **12** *5* **Lara Lipton (IRE)**[54] 3385 3-7-10 46 oh1.............................. NoelGarbutt(5) 5
(Jane Chapple-Hyam) *mid-div: rdn 5f out: sn struggling*
**33/1**

2m 31.68s (-1.32) **Going Correction** -0.05s/f (Stan)
**WFA** 3 from 4yo+ 11lb **12** Ran SP% **124.5**
Speed ratings (Par 101): **102,101,99,98,98 94,94,93,92,90 72,68**
CSF £61.92 CT £1403.45 TOTE £6.70: £2.00, £3.50, £7.20; EX 64.60 Trifecta £628.90.
**Owner** Prof C D Green **Bred** Llety Farms **Trained** Upper Lambourn, Berks

**FOCUS**
A weak affair but a small personal best from the winner.

## 5284 ALL NEW 32REDSPORT.COM FILLIES' H'CAP 1m 2f (P)
**8:05** (8:05) (Class 5) (0-70,69) 3-Y-0+ **£2,587** (£770; £384; £192) **Stalls** Low

Form RPR

-444 **1** **Sequester**[14] 4763 3-8-13 63.................................................(p) TedDurcan 4 71
(David Lanigan) *trckd ldrs: led over 6f out: kicked on 2f out and qcknd 3 l clr: hrd rdn fnl f: jst hld on*
**4/1**[2]

0533 **2** *nk* **Taro Tywod (IRE)**[5] 5074 5-9-8 68........................................ CamHardie(5) 7 75
(Mark Brisbourne) *chsd ldrs: rdn over 2f out: wnt 3 l 2nd 1f out: r.o wl fnl f: clsng at fin*
**6/1**

0232 **3** *1 ¼* **Two In The Pink (IRE)**[7] 5006 4-9-7 62.................................... MartinHarley 9 67
(Ralph J Smith) *hld up in rr: rdn and styd on wl fnl 2f: nvr nrr*
**9/2**[3]

23-0 **4** *1* **Star Anise (FR)**[43] 3805 3-8-11 61......................................... SamHitchcott 8 64
(Harry Dunlop) *in tch: trckd wnr over 5f out: rdn and outpcd 2f out: lost 2nd and no ex 1f out*
**33/1**

5-53 **5** *hd* **Super Moment (IRE)**[24] 4434 3-9-5 69.................................... HarryBentley 6 71
(Saeed bin Suroor) *prom: lost pl 3f out: sn rdn and btn: styd on same pce*
**7/4**[1]

4000 **6** *½* **Apache Glory (USA)**[89] 2270 6-9-9 69.................................(p) EoinWalsh(5) 3 70
(John Stimpson) *hld up towards rr: rdn over 2f out: styd on fnl f*
**16/1**

4030 **7** *½* **Tiptree Lace**[24] 4427 3-9-4 68................................................. TomQueally 2 68
(William Knight) *in tch: outpcd and dropped to rr over 2f out: styng on at fin*
**7/1**

-350 **8** *¾* **Division Belle**[38] 3968 3-8-8 61.......................................... MichaelJMMurphy(3) 5 60
(William Muir) *led for over 3f: remained prom: outpcd over 2f out: 3rd and btn whn hmpd over 1f out: wknd*
**16/1**

2m 6.99s (0.39) **Going Correction** -0.05s/f (Stan)
**WFA** 3 from 4yo+ 9lb **8** Ran SP% **116.0**
Speed ratings (Par 100): **96,95,94,93,93 93,93,92**
CSF £28.59 CT £112.21 TOTE £4.20: £1.70, £1.50, £1.80; EX 31.40 Trifecta £182.20.
**Owner** B E Nielsen **Bred** Bjorn E Nielsen **Trained** Upper Lambourn, Berks
■ Stewards' Enquiry : Sam Hitchcott one-day ban: careless riding (Aug 26)

**FOCUS**
The absence of If I Were A Boy and the disappointing effort of the favourite rendered this fillies' handicap less competitive than it might have been. The early pace was muddling. This was a personal best from the winner, though not big improver on previous form and was well placed.
T/Plt: £37.70 to a £1 stake. Pool: £58,060.61 - 1,121.75 winning tickets. T/Qpdt: £19.10 to a £1 stake. Pool: £6,248.14 - 241.79 winning tickets. LM

# 4828 NOTTINGHAM (L-H)
### Tuesday, August 12

**OFFICIAL GOING: Good to soft changing to good after race 1 (5.25)**
Outer track used. Rail moved out 4m around whole course increasing distances on Round course by 24yds.
Wind: Fresh half against Weather: Cloudy with sunny periods

## 5285 SIMPLY CARTONS LTD NURSERY H'CAP 6f 15y
**5:25** (5:25) (Class 5) (0-75,75) 2-Y-0 **£3,234** (£962; £481; £240) **Stalls** Centre

Form RPR

21 **1** **Felix Leiter**[19] 4589 2-9-7 75.................................................. PJMcDonald 8 88+
(K R Burke) *trckd ldr centre: smooth hdwy and cl up over 2f out: led wl over 1f out: sn pushed clr: readily*
**4/1**[2]

0344 **2** *5* **Indian Champ**[7] 4993 2-8-10 69......................................(p) ShaneGray(5) 4 67
(Kevin Ryan) *racd centre: led: pushed along over 2f out: rdn and hdd wl over 1f out: drvn and kpt on same pce fnl f*
**33/1**

320 **3** *½* **Secret Spirit**[24] 4439 2-9-4 75................................................ RyanTate(3) 9 72
(Clive Cox) *in tch: hdwy over 2f out: rdn along wl over 1f out: kpt on fnl f*
**7/2**[1]

5334 **4** *¾* **Diatomic (IRE)**[47] 3620 2-8-13 67....................................... RichardKingscote 2 61
(Tom Dascombe) *in rr: hdwy over 2f out: sn rdn: styd on fnl f: nrst fin* **33/1**

6333 **5** *1 ¾* **Atreus**[50] 3529 2-8-10 64...................................................... GrahamGibbons 11 53
(Michael Easterby) *racd nr stands' rail: chsd ldrs: hdwy over 2f out: rdn along wl over 1f out: sn one pce*
**6/1**

005 **6** *nse* **Bombay Mix**[20] 4527 2-8-8 62................................................ AndreaAtzeni 3 51
(Charlie Fellowes) *midfield: rdn along 1/2-way: n.d*
**8/1**

5452 **7** *nse* **Anastazia**[18] 4605 2-9-4 72.................................................... SeanLevey 1 61
(Paul D'Arcy) *towards rr: hdwy to chse ldrs 1/2-way: rdn along over 2f out: grad wknd*
**5/1**[3]

3544 **8** *hd* **Designate (IRE)**[24] 4430 2-9-2 70...............................(t) SilvestreDeSousa 5 61
(Ralph Beckett) *chsd ldrs: rdn along over 2f out: wknd over 1f out* **14/1**

6446 **9** *1* **Alpha Spirit**[54] 3063 2-8-9 66.............................................. CharlesBishop(3) 7 51
(Mick Channon) *t.k.h: a towards rr*
**12/1**

0526 **10** *11* **Thumper (FR)**[61] 3170 2-9-1 69............................................ JamieSpencer 10 21
(Robert Cowell) *racd nr stands' rail: prom: rdn along over 2f out: sn wknd*
**10/1**

1m 15.0s (0.30) **Going Correction** -0.025s/f (Good) **10** Ran SP% **113.6**
Speed ratings (Par 94): **97,90,89,88,86 86,86,85,84,69**
CSF £119.42 CT £498.84 TOTE £3.80: £2.10, £7.60, £1.20; EX 110.70 Trifecta £543.20.
**Owner** T Dykes & Mrs E Burke **Bred** Tibthorpe Stud **Trained** Middleham Moor, N Yorks

**FOCUS**
No rain overnight and a second drying day after 39mm fell in the space of 12 hours two days previously. It left the ground riding dead, although one or two riders described it as 'tacky'. There was a strong headwind into the straight and no surprise the time was ordinary for a fair nursery which lacked any real depth. All bar two came up the centre of the track and few got into it. The winner was impressive in building on his maiden win, with the runner-up rated close to form.

## 5286 EBF STALLIONS NOVICE STKS (BOBIS RACE) 6f 15y
**5:55** (5:56) (Class 4) 2-Y-0 **£6,469** (£1,925; £962; £481) **Stalls** Centre

Form RPR

4214 **1** **Prize Exhibit**[10] 4913 2-8-13 84.............................................. JamieSpencer 6 95+
(Jamie Osborne) *stdd s and hld up: smooth hdwy to trck ldng pair 1/2-way: swtchd lft and cl up wl over 1f out: shkn up to ld appr fnl f: sn clr: readily*
**5/1**[3]

1 **2** *9* **George Dryden (IRE)**[25] 4416 2-9-7 0..................................... PJMcDonald 3 76
(Ann Duffield) *led: rdn along over 2f out: drvn and hdd appr fnl f: sn one pce*
**9/4**[2]

12 **3** *1 ¾* **Enlace**[10] 4913 2-9-2 80...................................................... SilvestreDeSousa 5 66
(Mark Johnston) *cl up: rdn along wl over 2f out: drvn wl over 1f out: sn one pce*
**10/11**[1]

3204 **4** *5* **Red Connect**[70] 2873 2-8-7 79............................................. MeganCarberry(7) 4 49
(Alan McCabe) *chsd ldrs: rdn along and outpcd 1/2-way: sn drvn: plugged on to take remote 4th nr fin*
**50/1**

41 **5** *nk* **Al Gomry**[45] 3713 2-9-7 0...................................................... FrankieDettori 1 55
(Richard Fahey) *chsd ldrs: pushed along bef 1/2-way: sn rdn and btn over 2f out*
**10/1**

1m 15.38s (0.68) **Going Correction** -0.025s/f (Good) **5** Ran SP% **110.9**
Speed ratings (Par 96): **94,82,79,73,72**
CSF £16.67 TOTE £7.70: £2.40, £1.30; EX 17.60 Trifecta £24.10.
**Owner** M Buckley Mrs P Shanahan M V Magnier **Bred** Mrs R F Johnson Houghton **Trained** Upper Lambourn, Berks


The Form Book, Raceform Ltd, Newbury, RG14 5SJ

**FOCUS**
They came up the centre of the track and there was a clear-cut winner of a decent novices' event. A tricky race to rate as the time wasn't great and the second and third probably did too much.

## 5287 RACING UK ANYWHERE AVAILABLE NOW H'CAP 6f 15y
**6:25** (6:25) (Class 6) (0-60,61) 3-Y-O+ **£1,940** (£577; £288; £144) **Stalls** Centre

Form RPR
0046 **1** **Divertimenti (IRE)**[13] 4788 10-8-10 49..........................(b) BillyCray(3) 5 58
(Roy Bowring) *mde all: rdn wl over 1f out: drvn ins fnl f: edgd lft last 50yds: hld on wl towards fin* **25/1**
250 **2** *nk* **Very First Blade**[35] 4055 5-8-9 48...............................(b) RobertTart(3) 6 57
(Michael Mullineaux) *trckd ldrs: hdwy 2f out: rdn ent fnl f: ev ch whn hmpd and swtchd rt last 50yds: kpt on nr line: fin 3rd: plcd 2nd* **20/1**
5635 **3** *nse* **Kiss From A Rose**[39] 3935 3-9-2 56...................... SilvestreDeSousa 17 63
(Rae Guest) *trckd ldrs: swtchd rt and hdwy to chal wl over 1f out: rdn ent fnl f: sn ev ch tl drvn: hung lft and no ex last 50yds: fin 2nd: disqualified and plcd 3rd* **5/2**[1]
0631 **4** *½* **Borough Boy (IRE)**[5] 5082 4-9-11 61 6ex.......................... DaleSwift 7 67
(Derek Shaw) *towards rr: hdwy wl over 2f out: rdn to chse ldrs ent fnl f: styng on wl whn n.m.r towards fin* **9/2**[2]
2605 **5** *¾* **Masked Dance (IRE)**[96] 2094 7-9-6 56......................(p) PJMcDonald 12 59
(Scott Dixon) *dwlt and in rr: hdwy over 2f out: rdn to chse ldrs over 1f out: drvn and kpt on fnl f: nrst fin* **16/1**
0300 **6** *4* **Abraham Monro**[19] 4571 4-9-0 50........................... JamesSullivan 8 39
(Ruth Carr) *trckd ldrs: effrt 2f out: sn rdn and no imp appr fnl f* **8/1**[3]
0004 **7** *hd* **The Strig**[11] 4875 7-9-5 55...................................(v) J-PGuillambert 13 43
(Nigel Tinkler) *cl up: rdn along over 2f out: sn drvn and grad wknd* **10/1**
-000 **8** *½* **Queen Hermione (IRE)**[18] 4611 6-9-7 57......................(vt) SeanLevey 15 43
(Derek Shaw) *in rr and outpcd 1/2-way: sme late hdwy* **10/1**
0456 **9** *nk* **Indian Affair**[10] 4908 4-9-7 60.............................. CharlesBishop(3) 4 45
(Milton Bradley) *chsd ldrs: rdn along 2f out: drvn over 1f out: grad wknd* **10/1**
0006 **10** *½* **My Time**[18] 4614 5-8-9 50.......................................(v[1]) JordanNason(5) 9 33
(Michael Mullineaux) *a in rr* **50/1**
4040 **11** *hd* **Clock Opera (IRE)**[13] 4788 4-9-3 60.................... MeganCarberry(7) 2 42
(William Stone) *chsd ldrs: rdn along over 2f out: sn wknd* **20/1**
4665 **12** *2 ½* **Prigsnov Dancer (IRE)**[7] 4994 9-9-3 60....................(p) DavidParkes(7) 10 33
(Deborah Sanderson) *cl up: rdn along 2f out: sn drvn and wknd* **10/1**

1m 15.14s (0.44) **Going Correction** -0.025s/f (Good)
**WFA** 3 from 4yo+ 4lb **12** Ran SP% **115.4**
Speed ratings (Par 101): **96,95,95,94,93 88,88,87,87,86 86,82**
CSF £431.15 CT £1759.99 TOTE £24.20: £6.50, £3.90, £1.80; EX 239.50 Trifecta £624.30.
**Owner** K Nicholls **Bred** Airlie Stud **Trained** Edwinstowe, Notts
■ Compton Prince (25-1) was withdrawn. Rule 4 does not apply.

**FOCUS**
A weak sprint handicap choc-full of exposed sorts. Five drew clear of the rest and the form is unlikely to amount to much. The winner rolled back the years, rated to best form from past year.

## 5288 DOWNLOAD THE RACINGUK IPAD APP H'CAP 1m 6f 15y
**6:55** (6:55) (Class 3) (0-90,85) 3-Y-O+
**£7,470** (£2,236; £1,118; £559; £279; £140) **Stalls** Low

Form RPR
144 **1** **Tiger Lilly (IRE)**[40] 3884 3-8-0 75............................ JackGarritty(5) 7 87
(Richard Fahey) *hld up in tch: hdwy over 4f out: cl up over 3f out: led wl over 2f out: hdd and sltly hmpd wl over 1f out: sn rdn: styd on wl u.p fnl f to ld nr line* **5/1**
20-5 **2** *nk* **Zipp (IRE)**[94] 2160 4-9-10 81.............................. SilvestreDeSousa 4 93
(Ralph Beckett) *bhd: reminders and hdwy over 4f out: effrt on outer 3f out: chal over 2f out: rdn to ld wl over 1f out and sn edgd lft: clr and drvn ins fnl f: wandered and wknd last 50yds: hdd and no ex nr line* **3/1**[1]
5661 **3** *6* **Late Shipment**[17] 4672 3-8-12 82............................... JimCrowley 8 86
(Mark Johnston) *trckd ldng pair: sn trcking ldr: cl up 4f out: rdn along 3f out: drvn over 2f out and sn one pce* **7/2**[2]
4160 **4** *¾* **Number One London (IRE)**[24] 4441 4-9-11 82.........(p) FrankieDettori 5 85
(Brian Meehan) *led 1f: prom: rdn along over 3f out: drvn 2f out: sn one pce* **7/1**
01 **5** *3 ¾* **Dino Mite**[43] 3796 3-8-10 80...................................... ShaneKelly 3 77
(Peter Chapple-Hyam) *led after 1f: rdn along over 3f out: hdd wl over 2f out: sn drvn and grad wknd* **9/2**[3]
2-00 **6** *3 ½* **Sioux Chieftain (IRE)**[60] 3205 4-9-5 76..................... AndrewMullen 1 68
(Michael Appleby) *in tch: hdwy over 4f out: rdn along over 3f out: sn drvn and outpcd over 2f out* **10/1**
222- **7** *13* **Deficit (IRE)**[302] 7242 4-9-12 83.............................. JamieSpencer 6 57
(Steve Gollings) *trckd ldrs: hdwy 1/2-way: rdn along over 3f out: sn drvn and wknd* **10/1**

3m 4.53s (-2.47) **Going Correction** -0.15s/f (Firm)
**WFA** 3 from 4yo 13lb **7** Ran SP% **112.8**
Speed ratings (Par 107): **101,100,97,96,94 92,85**
CSF £19.77 CT £58.02 TOTE £7.10: £4.00, £3.10; EX 16.70 Trifecta £79.60.
**Owner** Sir Robert Ogden **Bred** Lynch Bages Ltd **Trained** Musley Bank, N Yorks

**FOCUS**
The searching pace and strong headwind played into the hands of an improving duo who came from off the pace.

## 5289 LADIES DAY ON FRIDAY 15TH AUGUST CONDITIONS STKS 5f 13y
**7:25** (7:29) (Class 3) 3-Y-O+
**£8,715** (£2,609; £1,304; £652; £326; £163) **Stalls** Centre

Form RPR
0200 **1** **Judge 'n Jury**[39] 3927 10-8-4 91..............................(t) DavidParkes(7) 11 98
(Ronald Harris) *cl up on stands' rail: led 2f out: rdn clr appr fnl f: kpt on strly* **25/1**
0020 **2** *4* **Green Door (IRE)**[23] 4480 3-9-5 105......................(b) JamieSpencer 4 94
(Olly Stevens) *dwlt and in rr: rdn along bef 1/2-way: swtchd rt to stands' rail and hdwy over 1f out: squeezed through to chse wnr ins fnl f: sn no imp* **6/1**[3]
-000 **3** *1* **Free Zone**[16] 4700 5-8-11 95.................................... FrankieDettori 9 80
(Robert Cowell) *slt ld: pushed along and hdd jst over 2f out: rdn wl over 1f out: drvn ent fnl f: kpt on same pce* **5/1**[2]
0000 **4** *shd* **Dungannon**[31] 4179 7-8-8 95.............................(v) ThomasBrown(3) 1 80
(Andrew Balding) *trckd ldrs: hdwy 1/2-way: rdn to chse ldng pair wl over 1f out: sn rdn and one pce fnl f* **9/2**[1]
1-03 **5** *4* **Strategical (USA)**[25] 4405 3-8-8 97.................... SilvestreDeSousa 2 64
(Charlie Appleby) *in rr and pushed along over 3f out: rdn and sme hdwy on wd outside whn hung lft 2f out: sn drvn and n.d* **6/1**[3]
-000 **6** *6* **Morawij**[17] 4683 4-8-11 99...........................................(b[1]) AndreaAtzeni 7 44
(Roger Varian) *chsd ldng pair: rdn along 1/2-way: drvn over 2f out and sn wknd* **8/1**
600- **7** *2* **Duke Of Firenze**[325] 6623 5-8-11 100............................... JimCrowley 5 36
(Robert Cowell) *chsd ldrs: rdn along 1/2-way: sn wknd* **10/1**

1m 0.04s (-1.46) **Going Correction** -0.025s/f (Good)
**WFA** 3 from 4yo+ 3lb **7** Ran SP% **87.5**
Speed ratings (Par 107): **110,103,102,101,95 85,82**
CSF £94.67 TOTE £19.90: £6.20, £2.90; EX 105.20 Trifecta £291.70.
**Owner** Robert & Nina Bailey **Bred** C A Cyzer **Trained** Earlswood, Monmouths
■ Graphic Quest (3-1F) was withdrawn. Rule 4 applies to all bets. Deduction - 25p in the pound.

**FOCUS**
The winner made all up the stands' rail and everything else was upwards of 10lb below form, unless the winner rediscovered his best, which seems unlikely.

## 5290 BET ON THE MOVE WITH RACING UK H'CAP 5f 13y
**7:55** (7:55) (Class 4) (0-70,70) 3-Y-O+ **£3,234** (£962; £481; £240) **Stalls** Centre

Form RPR
4451 **1** **Two Turtle Doves (IRE)**[4] 5130 8-8-10 56 6ex....... SilvestreDeSousa 4 67
(Michael Mullineaux) *cl up: rdn wl over 1f out: drvn to ld ins fnl f: kpt on* **7/2**[2]
14 **2** *½* **By Rights**[59] 3228 3-8-10 62................................... JoeyHaynes(3) 7 70
(Tony Carroll) *wnt rt s: t.k.h: sn slt ld: rdn wl over 1f out: drvn ent fnl f: sn hdd: kpt on* **6/1**
-454 **3** *3 ¼* **Oscars Journey**[8] 4981 4-9-6 66.............................. PaddyAspell 1 64
(J R Jenkins) *cl up: rdn 2f out: sn ev ch tl drvn ent fnl f and kpt on same pce* **4/1**[3]
2105 **4** *2 ¼* **Backstage Gossip**[15] 4741 3-9-3 66............................. RobertHavlin 5 54
(Hughie Morrison) *cl up: rdn along: n.m.r and outpcd over 2f out: sn swtchd rt and drvn: one pce* **5/2**[1]
5 **5** *2 ¾* **Sir Geoffrey (IRE)**[62] 3092 8-9-2 67...................(p) MatthewHopkins(5) 3 47
(Scott Dixon) *cl up: rdn along jst over 2f out: sn drvn and outpcd* **10/1**
1356 **6** *2 ¾* **Queen Aggie (IRE)**[110] 1665 4-9-9 69.............................. JimCrowley 9 39
(Tony Carroll) *racd towards stands' rail: a towards rr: rdn along over 2f out: sn outpcd* **5/1**

1m 1.54s (0.04) **Going Correction** -0.025s/f (Good)
**WFA** 3 from 4yo+ 3lb **6** Ran SP% **110.8**
Speed ratings (Par 105): **98,97,92,88,84 79**
CSF £23.31 CT £81.82 TOTE £2.70: £1.30, £3.00; EX 19.20 Trifecta £26.80.
**Owner** G Cornes **Bred** M Sharkey **Trained** Alpraham, Cheshire

**FOCUS**
A modest sprint handicap containing plenty out of form. The winner is rated back to last year's best.

## 5291 NEW AWESOME AUTUMN HOSPITALITY PACKAGES AVAILABLE APPRENTICE H'CAP 1m 2f 50y
**8:25** (8:25) (Class 6) (0-60,60) 4-Y-O+ **£1,940** (£577; £288; £144) **Stalls** Low

Form RPR
0006 **1** **Shades Of Silver**[25] 4420 4-9-2 55.................................. JennyPowell 8 66
(Michael Scudamore) *trckd ldrs: hdwy over 4f out: slt ld 3f out: rdn along 2f out: drvn appr fnl f: kpt on strly and sn clr* **11/4**[1]
10/4 **2** *3 ¼* **Lord Of The Storm**[27] 4326 6-8-13 52................................ RyanWhile 3 57
(Bill Turner) *trckd ldrs: hdwy wl over 2f out: rdn wl over 1f out: styd on fnl f: nearest fin* **12/1**
2453 **3** *hd* **Lil Sophella (IRE)**[17] 4665 5-9-4 57.............................. JackGarritty 7 61
(Patrick Holmes) *in tch: hdwy 4f out: cl up 3f out: disp ld over 2f out: sn rdn and ev ch tl drvn and one pce ins fnl f* **4/1**[3]
5251 **4** *2 ¼* **Appyjack**[7] 5005 6-9-5 58 6ex.................................. MeganCarberry 4 58+
(Tony Carroll) *hld up in rr: hdwy wl over 2f out: sn rdn: kpt on appr fnl f: nrst fin* **7/2**[2]
605 **5** *shd* **Claude Greenwood**[6] 5033 4-8-7 46 oh1................. MatthewHopkins 6 46
(Linda Jewell) *chsd clr ldr: hdwy and cl up over 3f out: rdn over 2f out: sn drvn and one pce* **16/1**
2345 **6** *3 ¼* **Pink Lips**[18] 4617 6-9-4 60..................................(p) LukeLeadbitter(3) 5 54
(J R Jenkins) *a towards rr* **9/2**
-600 **7** *nse* **Flying Applause**[14] 4749 9-8-4 46 oh1.........................(bt) RobHornby(3) 1 40
(Roy Bowring) *sn led and clr: rdn along over 3f out: sn hdd & wknd over 2f out* **16/1**
54-4 **8** *4 ½* **Meydan Style (USA)**[25] 4381 8-8-0 46 oh1.......... JordanSwarbrick(7) 2 31
(Brian Baugh) *midfield: rdn along over 3f out: sn outpcd and bhd* **25/1**

2m 12.42s (-1.88) **Going Correction** -0.15s/f (Firm) **8** Ran SP% **110.4**
Speed ratings (Par 101): **101,98,98,96,96 93,93,90**
CSF £33.98 CT £121.81 TOTE £4.10: £1.20, £3.20, £2.00; EX 32.50 Trifecta £148.40.
**Owner** The Champion Family & Michael Scudamore **Bred** Newsells Park Stud **Trained** Bromsash, H'fords

**FOCUS**
The winner was down 13lb since his handicap debut and ran his best maiden race over C&D, while the was on his last winning mark.
T/Jkpt: Not won. T/Plt: £1,321.20 to a £1 stake. Pool: £60,939.51 - 33.67 winning tickets. T/Qpdt: £200.60 to a £1 stake. Pool: £7,131.50 - 26.30 winning tickets. JR

# 5222 DEAUVILLE (R-H)
Tuesday, August 12

**OFFICIAL GOING: Turf: very soft; polytrack: standard**

## 5292a PRIX BEACHCOMBER-HOTELS ROYAL PALM MAURITIUS (MAIDEN) (2YO COLTS & GELDINGS) (TURF) 7f
**11:15** (12:00) 2-Y-0 **£10,416** (£4,166; £3,125; £2,083; £1,041)

RPR
**1** **Bukhari (FR)**[40] 2-9-2 0.......................................... ThierryJarnet 6 76
(J-C Rouget, France) **54/10**[3]
**2** *snk* **Leonida (FR)**[25] 2-9-2 0.......................................... GeraldMosse 1 76
(J-M Beguigne, France) **23/10**[1]
**3** *¾* **Carlo Bay (FR)** 2-9-2 0.......................................... MatthiasLauron 9 74
(J-C Rouget, France) **114/10**
**4** *hd* **Polo Dream (FR)** 2-9-2 0.......................................... MaximeGuyon 5 73
(L A Urbano-Grajales, France) **68/10**
**5** *snk* **Duke Of Ellington (FR)** 2-8-13 0.......................................... FlavienPrat 2 70
(M Figge, Germany) **28/1**
**6** *1 ¼* **Itsinthepost (FR)**[25] 2-9-2 0.......................................... AntoineHamelin 10 70
(Matthieu Palussiere, France) **93/10**
**7** *3 ½* **Kamaran (IRE)** 2-8-13 0.......................................... OlivierPeslier 8 57
(Mario Hofer, Germany) **76/10**

8 ¾ **Magic Frost (FR)**[40] 2-9-2 0 StephanePasquier 7 58
(Y Gourraud, France) **18/5**[2]
9 1 ½ **Frostman (FR)**[62] 3113 2-9-2 0 MickaelBarzalona 4 54
(Jo Hughes) *broke wl: hld up towards rr: rdn appr 2f out and no real imp: eased whn btn ins fnl f* **211/10**
10 *dist* **Eileen Celio (FR)** 2-8-13 0 AnthonyCrastus 3
(B Legros, France) **57/1**
1m 30.66s (2.36) **10** Ran SP% **119.6**
WIN (incl. 1 euro stake): 6.40. PLACES: 1.90, 1.40, 2.70. DF: 8.90. SF: 16.50.
**Owner** H H Aga Khan **Bred** Haras De S.A. Aga Khan Scea **Trained** Pau, France

## 5293a PRIX BEACHCOMBER-HOTELS ROYAL PALM MARAKECH (MAIDEN) (2YO FILLIES) (TURF) 7f
**11:45** (12:00) 2-Y-O **£10,416** (£4,166; £3,125; £2,083; £1,041)

RPR
1 **Mancora (FR)** 2-9-0 0 ThierryJarnet 5 80
(J-C Rouget, France) **22/5**[2]
2 4 **Fleur De Printemps**[28] 4312 2-9-0 0 CristianDemuro 12 69
(F Vermeulen, France) **10/1**
3 *nse* **Sculptured (FR)**[31] 4178 2-9-0 0 MickaelBarzalona 11 69
(Jo Hughes) *broke wl fr wd draw: trckd ldrs but racd wd long bnd into st: 7th and rdn 2f out: styd on u.p fr 1 1/2f out to go 2nd cl home: dropped to 3rd fnl stride* **171/10**
4 *snk* **Malvasia (FR)**[17] 2-9-0 0 MatthiasLauron 1 68
(J-C Rouget, France) **121/10**
5 *nk* **Moonlight Swing (FR)**[26] 2-9-0 0 LouisBeuzelin 9 68
(P Bary, France) **53/1**
6 1 ¼ **Entree Parfaite (FR)** 2-8-11 0 ow1 Pierre-CharlesBoudot 4 61
(Yannick Fouin, France) **233/10**
7 *shd* **Sierra Leona (FR)**[66] 2-9-0 0 GregoryBenoist 10 64
(C Lerner, France) **7/5**[1]
8 6 **Easy Feeling (USA)**[12] 4839 2-9-0 0 IoritzMendizabal 8 48
(J-C Rouget, France) **74/10**[3]
9 ¾ **Morera (IRE)** 2-9-0 0 UmbertoRispoli 3 46
(P Schiergen, Germany) **148/10**
10 ¾ **Vizadora (FR)**[47] 3641 2-9-0 0 ThierryThulliez 7 44
(G Doleuze, France) **35/1**
11 *snk* **Try With Me (IRE)**[17] 2-9-0 0 TheoBachelot 2 43
(Mario Hofer, Germany) **28/1**
12 8 **Konigin Ricke (GER)**[28] 4312 2-9-0 0 MaximeGuyon 6 22
(M Figge, Germany) **139/10**
1m 29.94s (1.64) **12** Ran SP% **119.6**
WIN (incl. 1 euro stake): 5.40. PLACES: 2.20, 2.70, 4.40. DF: 26.30. SF: 49.80.
**Owner** Philippe Segalot **Bred** Haras De Beauvoir **Trained** Pau, France

## 5294a PRIX BEACHCOMBER-HOTELS DINAROBIN HOTEL GOLF & SPA (MAIDEN) (3YO) (POLYTRACK) 6f 110y
**12:15** (12:00) 3-Y-O **£10,416** (£4,166; £3,125; £2,083; £1,041)

RPR
1 **Sailing Club (USA)**[24] 3-9-2 0 GregoryBenoist 6 88
(D Smaga, France) **13/5**[2]
2 ½ **Keena (FR)**[33] 3-8-13 0 ThierryJarnet 5 83
(J-C Rouget, France) **2/1**[1]
3 2 ½ **Palabre (USA)**[24] 3-8-13 0 OlivierPeslier 3 76
(F Head, France) **14/5**[3]
4 ¾ **African Plains**[14] 3-8-13 0 ThierryThulliez 2 74
(Mme C Head-Maarek, France) **31/5**
5 1 ¼ **Zantenor (FR)**[24] 3-9-2 0 (b) Pierre-CharlesBoudot 4 73
(Yves de Nicolay, France) **126/10**
6 2 **Nibbling (IRE)**[80] 2560 3-8-13 0 IoritzMendizabal 1 64
(Paul Cole) *t.k.h: hld up in 5th on rail: rdn and no imp over 1 1/2f out: nt given a hrd time whn btn fnl f* **111/10**
7 5 ½ **Misha (FR)**[113] 3-8-13 0 JeromeCabre 7 48
(D Darlix, France) **37/1**
1m 18.64s (78.64) **7** Ran SP% **119.6**
WIN (incl. 1 euro stake): 2.40 (Sailing Club coupled with African Plains). PLACES: 2.10, 1.80. SF: 11.30.
**Owner** K Abdullah **Bred** Juddmonte Farms **Trained** Lamorlaye, France

# 4749 BEVERLEY (R-H)
Wednesday, August 13

**OFFICIAL GOING: Good to soft (good in places)**
Rail around bottom bend moved and races on Round course increased by 19yds. Rail movement continues into home straight and false rail ends at 2.5f.
Wind: Fresh against Weather: Cloudy, sunny periods

## 5295 JOURNAL CLASSIFIED CLAIMING STKS 7f 100y
**2:00** (2:00) (Class 6) 3-Y-O+ **£2,587** (£770; £384; £192) **Stalls** Low

Form RPR
4333 1 **My Son Max**[20] 4588 6-9-2 71 DanielTudhope 6 67
(Michael Blake) *s.i.s and lost several l s: in tch after 2f: hdwy 3f out: chsd ldrs 2f out and sn rdn: swtchd lft and drvn ent fnl f: styd on wl to ld last 50yds* **4/1**[3]
00-2 2 ½ **Brooke's Bounty**[16] 4729 4-9-5 68 GeorgeChaloner(3) 3 72
(Richard Fahey) *chsd ldng pair: effrt 2f out and sn rdn: edgd rt over 1f out: drvn and kpt on towards fin* **5/1**
0644 3 ½ **Al Muheer (IRE)**[17] 4703 9-9-2 75 (be) JamesSullivan 4 65
(Ruth Carr) *chsd ldr: cl up 1/2-way: chal wl over 2f out: rdn to ld over 1f out: edgd rt ent fnl f: sn drvn: hdd and no ex last 50yds* **11/4**[2]
0655 4 1 ¼ **Scrutiny**[4] 5198 3-9-1 68 SamJames(3) 2 67
(David O'Meara) *chsd ldrs: rdn along wl over 2f out and sn outpcd: styd on u.p fnl f* **11/1**
0130 5 2 ¾ **Zaitsev (IRE)**[29] 4291 4-9-9 75 RobertWinston 5 62
(Ollie Pears) *set str pce: rdn along and jnd wl over 2f out: hdd over 1f out: drvn and hld whn sltly hmpd jst ins fnl f: one pce* **13/8**[1]
0020 6 1 ¼ **Last Destination (IRE)**[39] 3949 6-9-4 52 AndrewMullen 1 53
(Nigel Tinkler) *a towards rr* **25/1**
1m 34.99s (1.19) **Going Correction** +0.15s/f (Good)
**WFA** 3 from 4yo+ 6lb **6** Ran SP% **113.6**
Speed ratings (Par 101): **99,98,97,96,93 91**
CSF £24.15 TOTE £4.70: £2.20, £2.80; EX 17.90 Trifecta £53.50.My Son Max was claimed by R Ford for £6000.
**Owner** Mrs J M Haines **Bred** Mrs Fiona Denniff **Trained** Trowbridge, Wilts
**FOCUS**
The course soaked up 3mm of overnight rain and the ground was described as good to soft, good in places. Rail movements on the bottom bend increased distances on the round course by 19yds. A couple of fair sorts in a race where an ordinary gallop only picked up turning for home and this bare form may not be entirely reliable. The runner-up is key to the form, rated back to his best.

## 5296 HULL DAILY MAIL/BRITISH STALLION STUDS EBF MAIDEN STKS 7f 100y
**2:30** (2:30) (Class 5) 2-Y-O **£3,234** (£962; £481; £240) **Stalls** Low

Form RPR
03 1 **Space Age (IRE)**[18] 4666 2-9-5 0 PhillipMakin 6 84
(Charlie Appleby) *mde all: rdn clr wl over 1f out: kpt on strly* **13/8**[1]
5 2 4 **Pamushana (IRE)**[32] 4202 2-9-0 0 TonyHamilton 5 69
(Richard Fahey) *prom: chsd wnr 1/2-way: rdn along and sltly outpcd over 1f out: styd on ins fnl f: tk 2nd nr fin* **7/4**[2]
0 3 ½ **Fast Charlie (IRE)**[48] 3620 2-9-5 0 PJMcDonald 1 73
(Ann Duffield) *trckd ldng pair on inner: hdwy over 2f out: rdn to chse wnr over 1f out: sn rn green and wandered: kpt on same pce* **18/1**
45 4 2 ½ **Prince Of Time**[13] 4829 2-9-5 0 FrannyNorton 2 67
(Mark Johnston) *t.k.h: chsd ldng pair: rdn along and sltly outpcd wl over 2f out: swtchd rt to inner over 1f out: kpt on: nrst fin* **7/1**[3]
5 2 ¼ **Dubawi Diamond** 2-9-5 0 PaulMulrennan 8 61+
(James Tate) *wnt bdly lft s and in rr: hdwy over 2f out: rdn along over 1f out: kpt on fnl f: nrst fin* **12/1**
4 6 5 **Sweet Talker**[53] 3481 2-9-0 0 DuranFentiman 7 43
(Tim Easterby) *in tch: rdn along wl over 2f out: sn drvn and outpcd* **12/1**
5 7 1 ½ **Stormin Tom (IRE)**[53] 3481 2-9-5 0 DavidAllan 4 45
(Tim Easterby) *a in rr: rdn along over 3f out: sn outpcd* **16/1**
0 8 9 **Devilution (IRE)**[8] 5009 2-9-5 0 TomEaves 3 22
(Derek Shaw) *dwlt: hdwy and in tch on inner after 2f: rdn along 1/2-way: sn outpcd* **50/1**
1m 35.66s (1.86) **Going Correction** +0.15s/f (Good) **8** Ran SP% **115.4**
Speed ratings (Par 94): **95,90,89,87,84 78,77,66**
CSF £4.77 TOTE £2.60: £1.10, £1.40, £4.70; EX 5.00 Trifecta £55.80.
**Owner** Godolphin **Bred** Darley **Trained** Newmarket, Suffolk
**FOCUS**
An uncompetitive event but fair form from the winner. The gallop was a modest one and not many figured.

## 5297 ST STEPHEN'S MAIDEN AUCTION STKS 5f
**3:00** (3:03) (Class 5) 2-Y-O **£3,234** (£962; £481; £240) **Stalls** Low

Form RPR
0 1 **Star Cracker (IRE)**[19] 4624 2-9-3 0 PaulMulrennan 4 75+
(Michael Dods) *trckd ldng pair on inner: swtchd lft and hdwy over 1f out: rdn to chal insidce fnl f: kpt on wl to ld nr fin* **2/1**[1]
56 2 ½ **Jebediah Shine**[42] 2-8-5 0 SamJames(3) 1 64
(David O'Meara) *led: rdn along over 1f out: drvn ins fnl f: hdd and no ex towards fin* **16/1**
2 3 ¾ **Rock Follies**[18] 4652 2-8-10 0 PhillipMakin 9 64
(Lady Cecil) *trckd ldrs: hdwy 2f out: rdn to chal ent fnl f: ev ch tl one pce towards fin* **7/2**[3]
4 1 ¼ **Cabelo (IRE)** 2-8-6 0 BenCurtis 11 55+
(Brian Ellison) *green: sn pushed along and outpcd in rr: gd hdwy on outer over 1f out: styd on fnl f: nrst fin* **20/1**
0 5 ½ **Threatorapromise (IRE)**[42] 3841 2-8-10 0 BarryMcHugh 10 57
(Tony Coyle) *chsd ldrs: hdwy wl over 1f out: sn rdn: kpt on same pce fnl f* **50/1**
0523 6 *nk* **Straightothepoint**[49] 3570 2-9-1 75 RoystonFfrench 14 61
(Bryan Smart) *towards rr: pushed along and hdwy 1/2-way: rdn wl over 1f out: kpt on fnl f: nrst fin* **3/1**[2]
7 ½ **Cloak And Degas (IRE)** 2-9-1 0 TomEaves 7 59
(Scott Dixon) *cl up: rdn along wl over 1f out: grad wknd appr fnl f* **25/1**
50 8 1 ¼ **Aneto Peak**[6] 5086 2-8-13 0 AdrianNicholls 3 53
(Nigel Tinkler) *chsd ldrs on inner: rdn along wl over 1f out: wknd ent fnl f* **50/1**
060 9 *nk* **Cheeky Chapman**[24] 4467 2-9-0 54 GeorgeChaloner(3) 8 56
(Clive Mulhall) *dwlt: a towards rr* **16/1**
0 10 2 ¼ **Pancake Day**[8] 5013 2-8-11 0 AndrewElliott 12 42
(Jason Ward) *midfield: rdn along 1/2-way: n.d* **50/1**
0 11 ¾ **Zaza Zest (IRE)**[15] 4751 2-8-8 0 TonyHamilton 5 36
(Richard Fahey) *midfield on inner: pushed along 1/2-way: sn rdn and n.d* **7/1**
12 3 ½ **Bushtiger (IRE)** 2-9-1 0 GrahamGibbons 6 30
(David Barron) *dwlt: green and a in rr* **12/1**
1m 5.45s (1.95) **Going Correction** +0.275s/f (Good) **12** Ran SP% **127.0**
Speed ratings (Par 94): **95,94,93,91,90 89,88,86,86,82 81,76**
CSF £39.50 TOTE £3.30: £1.40, £6.00, £1.30; EX 47.20 Trifecta £265.60.
**Owner** James McLaren **Bred** James Mc Claren **Trained** Denton, Co Durham
**FOCUS**
A modest maiden in which the gallop was only fair and several finished in a heap. Those held up never figured. The well-backed winner, along with the second, found big improvement.

## 5298 RAWFIELD AND PARAGON DATA H'CAP 5f
**3:35** (3:36) (Class 5) (0-75,75) 3-Y-O+ **£3,234** (£962; £481; £240) **Stalls** Low

Form RPR
2002 1 **Noodles Blue Boy**[7] 5053 8-9-5 70 (p) RobertWinston 1 83
(Ollie Pears) *qckly away and mde all: clr 1/2-way: kpt on strly* **5/2**[1]
00 2 4 **Ambitious Icarus**[4] 5170 5-9-10 75 (e) JasonHart 2 74
(Richard Guest) *trckd ldrs: swtchd lft and hdwy over 1f out: sn rdn: kpt on to chse wnr ins fnl f: no imp* **7/1**
5U30 3 1 **Manatee Bay**[22] 4511 4-8-12 63 FrannyNorton 7 58+
(David Nicholls) *dwlt and in rr: hdwy whn hmpd 2f out and sn swtchd rt: hdwy and rdn over 1f out: swtchd lft ent fnl f: kpt on strly: nrst fin* **14/1**
3064 4 ½ **Economic Crisis (IRE)**[5] 5130 5-9-2 67 PaulMulrennan 6 60
(Alan Berry) *sn chsng wnr: rdn along wl over 1f out: drvn ent fnl f: kpt on same pce* **10/1**
5020 5 1 **Bosham**[19] 4632 4-9-5 70 GrahamGibbons 3 60
(Michael Easterby) *dwlt and towards rr: rdn along 1/2-way: sme hdwy over 1f out: n.d* **7/2**[2]

2454 **6** *hd* **Ypres**[7] 5053 5-9-4 72.......................................(p) JoeyHaynes(3) 4 61
(Jason Ward) *chsd ldrs: hdwy on inner wl over 1f out: sn rdn and no imp* **6/1**[3]

0140 **7** *1 1/4* **Cadeaux Pearl**[8] 4997 6-8-12 63.............................. PJMcDonald 5 47
(Scott Dixon) *chsd ldrs: rdn along over 2f out: sn wknd* **13/2**

050 **8** *1 1/4* **Hazelrigg (IRE)**[11] 4901 9-9-6 71..............................(e) TonyHamilton 8 51
(Tim Easterby) *a towards rr* **16/1**

2100 **9** *1* **Mr Mo Jo**[17] 4714 6-9-2 67..............................(b) DavidAllan 10 43
(Les Eyre) *chsd ldng pair: rdn along 2f out: sn wknd* **16/1**

1m 4.33s (0.83) **Going Correction** +0.275s/f (Good) **9** Ran SP% **118.4**
Speed ratings (Par 103): **104,97,96,95,93 93,91,89,87**
CSF £21.24 CT £209.18 TOTE £2.90: £1.60, £2.60, £4.10; EX 21.20 Trifecta £295.90.
**Owner** K C West **Bred** Fifehead Farms M C Denning **Trained** Norton, N Yorks
■ Stewards' Enquiry : P J McDonald two-day ban: careless riding (Aug 27-28)

**FOCUS**
An open handicap on paper but one turned into a procession by the market leader, who was well in. The gallop seemed reasonable throughout.

## 5299 BRIDGE MCFARLAND SOLICITORS H'CAP 1m 1f 207y
**4:05** (4:05) (Class 4) (0-85,83) 3-Y-O+ **£6,469** (£1,925; £962; £481) **Stalls** Low

Form RPR

12 **1** **Sophisticated Heir (IRE)**[29] 4290 4-9-9 78.................. DanielTudhope 3 86+
(David O'Meara) *trckd ldng pair: hdwy wl over 2f out: rdn to take slt ld jst over 1f out: drvn ins fnl f: jst hld on* **3/1**[1]

-411 **2** *shd* **Woodacre**[9] 4975 7-9-4 76 6ex.............................. GeorgeChaloner(3) 5 83+
(Richard Whitaker) *trckd ldrs on inner: hdwy over 2f out: effrt and nt clr run over 1f out: sn swtchd lft and rdn to chal ins fnl f: sn drvn and kpt on: jst failed* **3/1**[1]

0-21 **3** *1/2* **Sir Charlie Kunz**[198] 357 3-9-1 79.............................. FrannyNorton 4 85
(Mark Johnston) *trckd ldr: hdwy and cl up 3f out: chal over 2f out: rdn over 1f out: drvn ent fnl f and ev ch tl no ex last 40yds* **4/1**[2]

3 **4** *1* **Park Place**[61] 2170 4-9-8 77.............................. PhillipMakin 6 81
(John Quinn) *hld up in tch: hdwy over 2f out: rdn and edgd lft over 1f out: drvn and styd on wl towards fin* **16/1**

6555 **5** *shd* **Correggio**[17] 4710 4-9-5 74..............................(p) PJMcDonald 2 79
(Micky Hammond) *trckd ldrs: effrt on inner 2f out and sn n.m.r: swtchd lft and rdn whn nt clr run ins fnl f: same pce after* **9/1**

3003 **6** *1* **Eeny Mac (IRE)**[9] 4975 7-9-5 74..............................(p) AndrewElliott 1 76
(Neville Bycroft) *led: jnd and pushed along wl over 2f out: rdn wl over 1f out: drvn and hdd appr fnl f: grad wknd* **6/1**[3]

0056 **7** *1 3/4* **Buthelezi (USA)**[11] 4888 6-10-0 83..............................(p) TomEaves 7 82
(Brian Ellison) *hld up in rr: hdwy on outer over 4f out: rdn along 2f out: one pce appr fnl f* **10/1**

20-0 **8** *4* **Topamichi**[121] 1483 4-9-9 78.............................. BenCurtis 8 69
(Mark H Tompkins) *dwlt and t.k.h in rr: sme hdwy over 2f out: sn rdn and btn* **14/1**

2m 8.26s (1.26) **Going Correction** +0.15s/f (Good)
**WFA** 3 from 4yo+ 9lb **8** Ran SP% **115.9**
Speed ratings (Par 105): **100,99,99,98,98 97,96,93**
CSF £12.15 CT £35.68 TOTE £3.80: £2.00, £1.20, £1.10; EX 11.70 Trifecta £27.80.
**Owner** Colne Valley Racing **Bred** J S Bolger & John Corcoran **Trained** Nawton, N Yorks

**FOCUS**
A useful handicap in which the gallop steadied around halfway and, although several finished in a bit of a heap, this race could produce its share of winners. The fourth improved slightly on his maiden win and the fifth helps set the level.

## 5300 INCENTIVE FM H'CAP 1m 1f 207y
**4:40** (4:40) (Class 5) (0-70,69) 3-Y-O+ **£3,234** (£962; £481; £240) **Stalls** Low

Form RPR

2653 **1** **Where's Tiger**[6] 5077 3-8-7 57.............................. PJMcDonald 5 68
(Jedd O'Keeffe) *trckd ldrs: smooth hdwy on outer 3f out: led 2f out: rdn clr ent fnl f: kpt on strly* **7/4**[1]

6520 **2** *4 1/2* **Duke Of Yorkshire**[12] 4856 4-9-13 68.............................. DuranFentiman 8 70
(Tim Easterby) *hld up in rr: hdwy 2f out: rdn over 1f out: styd on to chse wnr ins fnl f: sn no imp* **7/2**[2]

6005 **3** *1 1/4* **Power Up**[14] 4793 3-8-10 60..............................(b[1]) FrannyNorton 3 60
(Mark Johnston) *hld up in tch: hdwy 2f out and sn rdn: drvn ent fnl f: kpt on towards fin* **4/1**[3]

-550 **4** *1 1/4* **Brockfield**[73] 2806 8-9-6 61.............................. DavidAllan 4 59
(Mel Brittain) *trckd ldng pair: hdwy on inner 2f out: squeezed through to chal over 1f out and ev ch: sn drvn and wknd ins fnl f* **5/1**

6220 **5** *6* **Tukitinyasok (IRE)**[24] 4468 7-9-2 57.............................. BarryMcHugh 7 43
(Clive Mulhall) *trckd ldr: effrt over 2f out: sn rdn and wknd over 1f out* **5/1**

0-00 **6** *8* **Fair Bunny**[21] 4532 7-8-9 50 oh5.............................. PaulPickard 1 21
(Alan Brown) *led: rdn along 3f out: hdd 2f out: sn drvn and wknd* **33/1**

2m 7.66s (0.66) **Going Correction** +0.15s/f (Good)
**WFA** 3 from 4yo+ 9lb **6** Ran SP% **114.9**
Speed ratings (Par 103): **103,99,98,97,92 86**
CSF £8.47 CT £20.72 TOTE £2.30: £1.80, £1.50; EX 10.40 Trifecta £27.40.
**Owner** Highbeck Racing **Bred** Michael E Broughton **Trained** Middleham Moor, N Yorks

**FOCUS**
A modest handicap featuring exposed sorts. A steady gallop saw several fail to settle and this bare form doesn't look reliable, although the second is rated close to this year's best.

## 5301 "WOODY" MEMORIAL H'CAP (PART OF THE BEVERLEY MIDDLE DISTANCE SERIES) 1m 4f 16y
**5:10** (5:10) (Class 5) (0-75,74) 3-Y-O+ **£3,234** (£962; £481; £240) **Stalls** Low

Form RPR

**1** **Got To Dream**[32] 4225 3-9-3 74.............................. FrannyNorton 6 85
(Mark Johnston) *t.k.h: led and sn clr: 15 l advantage 4f out: pushed along 2f out: kpt on strly: unchal* **7/4**[1]

652 **2** *9* **Saint Thomas (IRE)**[27] 4369 7-9-4 64.............................. GrahamGibbons 3 61
(John Mackie) *chsd clr ldr: pushed along wl over 2f out: rdn wl over 1f out: kpt on ins fnl f to take modest 2nd nr fin: no ch w wnr* **9/2**

4045 **3** *hd* **Choisan (IRE)**[6] 5083 5-9-5 72..............................(tp) RachelRichardson(7) 4 69
(Tim Easterby) *chsd clr ldr: rdn along wl over 2f out: edgd lft wl over 1f out: sn no imp: lost 2nd nr fin* **3/1**[3]

0022 **4** *2* **Qibtee (FR)**[6] 5077 4-9-0 60.............................. DavidAllan 2 53
(Les Eyre) *hld up in rr: effrt 3f out: sn rdn along and plugged on one pce* **2/1**[2]

2m 40.5s (0.70) **Going Correction** +0.15s/f (Good)
**WFA** 3 from 4yo+ 11lb **4** Ran SP% **112.9**
Speed ratings (Par 103): **103,97,96,95**
CSF £9.74 TOTE £1.80; EX 7.00 Trifecta £13.70.
**Owner** Mrs Lisa Kelly **Bred** Fittocks Stud **Trained** Middleham Moor, N Yorks

**FOCUS**
A very one-sided event after the eased-down winner was allowed to do her own thing in front. The gallop was just an ordinary one. A tricky race to rate but the winner has clearly improved.
T/Plt: £14.90 to a £1 stake. Pool of £63960.87, 3117.05 winning tickets. T/Qpdt: £4.00 to £1 stake. Pool of £4850.46 - 894.25 winning tickets. JR

# 5035 KEMPTON (A.W) (R-H)
Wednesday, August 13

**OFFICIAL GOING: Polytrack: standard**
Wind: Moderate, half against Weather: Fine

## 5302 BETBRIGHT.COM APPRENTICE H'CAP (LONDON MIDDLE DISTANCE SERIES QUALIFIER) (BOBIS RACE) 1m 3f (P)
**6:20** (6:20) (Class 4) (0-80,81) 3-Y-O **£4,690** (£1,395; £697; £348) **Stalls** Low

Form RPR

3440 **1** **Grand Meister**[21] 4547 3-9-4 72.............................. LouisSteward 6 81
(Michael Bell) *hld up in 5th: hdwy 3f out: led over 1f out: rdn clr: comf* **5/2**[2]

1244 **2** *3* **Zanouska (USA)**[17] 4704 3-8-12 66.............................. EoinWalsh 2 70
(Mark Johnston) *t.k.h: prom: sltly lost pl 3f out: drvn and rallied over 1f out: one pce* **5/1**

66 **3** *1 1/4* **Arantes**[12] 4855 3-9-9 80.............................. DanielCremin(3) 5 82
(Mick Channon) *stdd s: hld up in rr: rdn over 2f out: styd on fnl f* **7/2**[3]

0502 **4** *1 1/4* **Mary Le Bow**[20] 4563 3-8-8 65..............................(p) LewisWalsh(3) 4 65
(Karen George) *cl up: trckd ldr 7f out tl wl over 1f out: wknd fnl f* **16/1**

0053 **5** *hd* **Triple Chief (IRE)**[16] 4743 3-9-4 75.............................. PatMillman(3) 3 74
(Rod Millman) *led: hrd rdn over 2f out: hdd & wknd over 1f out* **8/1**

3301 **6** *3/4* **Roskilly (IRE)**[10] 4941 3-9-8 81 6ex.............................. KieranShoemark(5) 1 79
(Andrew Balding) *in tch: lost pl and rdn over 3f out: nvr gng wl enough to rcvr* **9/4**[1]

2m 22.3s (0.40) **Going Correction** +0.05s/f (Slow) **6** Ran SP% **115.2**
Speed ratings (Par 102): **100,97,96,96,95 95**
CSF £15.78 TOTE £3.60: £1.30, £2.40; EX 12.80 Trifecta £73.40.
**Owner** Mrs Doreen Tabor **Bred** Car Colston Hall Stud **Trained** Newmarket, Suffolk

**FOCUS**
Question marks over a few these coming into the race and, coupled with the small field, it looks to be only modest form. The winner is rated to a length personal best, with the runner-up to form.

## 5303 KEMPTON LIVE WITH DIZZEE RASCAL 06.09.14 H'CAP 7f (P)
**6:50** (6:50) (Class 6) (0-65,68) 3-Y-O+ **£1,940** (£577; £288; £144) **Stalls** Low

Form RPR

421 **1** **Darnathean**[5] 5125 5-10-0 68 6ex..............................(p) LukeMorris 1 76
(Paul D'Arcy) *chsd ldrs: led jst ins fnl f: drvn out* **7/1**

-405 **2** *nk* **Sakhee's Rose**[19] 4629 4-9-6 60..............................(b) RichardHughes 9 67
(Ed McMahon) *hld up in rr: rdn and hdwy over 1f out: r.o wl fnl f: clsng at fin* **7/1**

5003 **3** *nk* **Keene's Pointe**[23] 4503 4-9-2 56..............................(b) JamesDoyle 10 62
(B W Hills) *stdd s and dropped in: hld up towards rr: gd hdwy over 1f out: r.o fnl f* **14/1**

0345 **4** *1 1/2* **Substantivo (IRE)**[7] 5041 4-9-6 60.............................. DaneO'Neill 12 62
(Timothy Jarvis) *chsd ldrs: rdn over 2f out: styd on same pce fnl f* **6/1**[3]

0512 **5** *1 1/2* **Marmarus**[19] 4612 3-9-2 65.............................. RyanTate(3) 14 61+
(Clive Cox) *sn led and crossed to inner fr wd stall: hrd rdn and hdd jst ins fnl f: no ex* **5/1**[2]

506- **6** *1/2* **Marengo**[326] 6641 3-9-1 64.............................. DeclanBates(3) 4 59
(Ed de Giles) *hld up in rr: sme hdwy 2f out: nt rch ldrs* **12/1**

0000 **7** *1 1/4* **Varsovian**[20] 4579 4-9-3 57.............................. SebSanders 5 51
(Dean Ivory) *prom on rail tl wknd 1f out* **20/1**

2460 **8** *1/2* **Midnight Feast**[60] 3233 6-9-4 58..............................(b) StevieDonohoe 2 50
(Lee Carter) *in tch tl outpcd fnl 2f* **8/1**

3503 **9** *2 1/4* **Gung Ho Jack**[20] 4595 5-9-3 57.............................. GeorgeBaker 6 44
(John Best) *hld up in rr: shkn up and sme hdwy over 1f out: n.d* **20/1**

-00R **10** *3/4* **My Gigi**[20] 4578 4-9-4 58.............................. FergusSweeney 7 43
(Laura Mongan) *mid-div tl rdn and btn 2f out* **50/1**

0050 **11** *2 3/4* **Rafaaf (IRE)**[42] 3854 6-9-3 57.............................. StephenCraine 8 34
(Richard Phillips) *chsd ldr: chal over 2f out: sn wknd* **33/1**

4222 **12** *13* **Celestial Ray**[20] 4579 5-9-9 63.............................. JimCrowley 3 7
(Linda Jewell) *mid-div: rdn over 3f out: wknd over 2f out: fatally injured* **11/4**[1]

1m 26.57s (0.57) **Going Correction** +0.05s/f (Slow)
**WFA** 3 from 4yo+ 6lb **12** Ran SP% **122.5**
Speed ratings (Par 101): **98,97,97,95,93 93,91,91,88,87 84,69**
CSF £54.85 CT £689.97 TOTE £5.70: £1.60, £3.30, £6.30; EX 57.00 Trifecta £741.00.
**Owner** K Snell **Bred** K Snell **Trained** Newmarket, Suffolk

**FOCUS**
The favourite seemingly had an issue, but otherwise the right horses were involved and this looks sound. The winner is rated close to last year's best.

## 5304 BETBRIGHT MONEYBACK OFFERS H'CAP (LONDON MILE SERIES QUALIFIER) 1m (P)
**7:20** (7:21) (Class 5) (0-70,70) 3-Y-O **£2,587** (£770; £384; £192) **Stalls** Low

Form RPR

0461 **1** **Windy Citi**[9] 4969 3-9-3 66 6ex.............................. GeorgeBaker 1 75+
(Chris Wall) *trckd ldrs on inner: led 1f out: rdn out and a in control* **1/2**[1]

-565 **2** *3/4* **Cape Summit**[26] 4420 3-9-7 70.............................. JamesDoyle 6 77
(Ed Dunlop) *in tch: effrt 2f out: drvn to chal 1f out: kpt on: a jst hld* **7/1**[3]

1 **3** *3/4* **Dream Ruler**[163] 816 3-9-7 70.............................. FergusSweeney 3 75
(Jo Crowley) *hld up in 6th: rdn over 2f out: styd on fnl f* **5/1**[2]

5656 **4** *2* **Tea In Transvaal (IRE)**[39] 3979 3-9-6 69.............................. RichardHughes 8 69
(Richard Hannon) *towards rr: effrt in centre over 2f out: no imp over 1f out* **8/1**

0063 **5** *1 1/2* **Buckland Beau**[13] 4830 3-9-2 65.............................. FrederikTylicki 2 62
(Charlie Fellowes) *led: rdn and hdd 1f out: wknd fnl f* **33/1**

43-6 **6** *2 1/2* **Cockney Belle**[21] 4535 3-9-5 68.............................. MartinHarley 4 59
(Marco Botti) *t.k.h: pressed ldr tl wknd wl over 1f out* **12/1**

0000 **7** *nk* **Berrahri (IRE)**[19] 4620 3-9-5 68.............................. SteveDrowne 5 59
(John Best) *sn bhd* **50/1**

3010 **8** *2 1/4* **Soul Of Motion**[16] 4742 3-9-4 67..............................(v[1]) DavidProbert 7 52
(Gay Kelleway) *prom on outer: wknd 2f out* **25/1**

1m 39.93s (0.13) **Going Correction** +0.05s/f (Slow) **8** Ran SP% **123.4**
Speed ratings (Par 100): **101,100,99,97,96 93,93,90**
CSF £5.51 CT £11.94 TOTE £1.20: £1.02, £2.10, £1.70; EX 5.60 Trifecta £23.00.
**Owner** Scuderia Giocri **Bred** Scuderia Giocri **Trained** Newmarket, Suffolk

**FOCUS**
A modest handicap which proved an ideal opportunity for the favourite to score under a penalty.

## 5305 BRITISH STALLION STUDS EBF MAIDEN FILLIES' STKS (BOBIS RACE) 7f (P)
**7:50** (7:51) (Class 5) 2-Y-O **£2,911** (£866; £432; £216) **Stalls** Low

Form RPR
6 **1** **Sandy Cay (USA)**[11] 4914 2-9-0 ...................................... JamesDoyle 5 83+
(Sir Michael Stoute) *hld up in 5th: effrt 2f out: qcknd to ld ins fnl f: readily* **5/4**[1]
3 **2** *1* **Impressive Victory (USA)**[35] 4075 2-9-0 .................... HarryBentley 3 80
(Saeed bin Suroor) *set modest pce: m most: qcknd 3f out: hdd ins fnl f: kpt on* **4/1**[2]
**3** *2 3/4* **Althania (USA)** 2-9-0 ...................................... DaneO'Neill 6 74+
(John Gosden) *t.k.h towards rr: gd hdwy over 1f out: r.o wl fnl f: promising* **16/1**
**4** *2 1/2* **Tropicana Bay** 2-9-0 ...................................... FrederikTylicki 9 67+
(Roger Varian) *prom tl outpcd fnl 2f* **20/1**
56 **5** *1* **Star Of Spring (IRE)**[26] 4403 2-9-0 .............................. JimCrowley 13 64
(Charles Hills) *chsd ldrs tl outpcd fnl 2f* **12/1**
65 **6** *nk* **On High**[26] 4403 2-8-9 ...................................... CamHardie(5) 1 63
(Richard Hannon) *mid-div: effrt over 2f out: no imp over 1f out* **33/1**
0 **7** *7* **World Fair (IRE)**[13] 4825 2-9-0 .............................. DavidProbert 11 45
(Charlie Appleby) *plld hrd towards rr: mod effrt over 2f out: sn wknd* **16/1**
06 **8** *nk* **Mikandy (IRE)**[27] 4346 2-8-11 .............................. RyanTate(3) 2 44
(Clive Cox) *mid-div: hmpd and carried wd on bend over 3f out: nt rcvr* **66/1**
00 **9** *6* **Catharina**[9] 4980 2-9-0 ...................................... RichardHughes 7 29
(Richard Hannon) *stdd s: t.k.h in rr: rapid hdwy on outer to go prom whn rn wd into st: wknd 2f out: eased* **50/1**
**10** *3 1/2* **Joy Of Being (USA)** 2-9-0 .............................. AdamKirby 14 20
(Charlie Appleby) *s.i.s: a bhd* **14/1**
0 **P** **Fret**[26] 4396 2-9-0 ...................................... JamieSpencer 8
(Henry Candy) *trckd ldrs tl wnt lame p.u over 3f out* **9/2**[3]

1m 26.9s (0.90) **Going Correction** +0.05s/f (Slow) **11 Ran SP% 119.9**
Speed ratings (Par 91): **96,94,91,88,87 87,79,79,72,68**
CSF £6.04 TOTE £2.60: £1.40, £1.10, £3.80; EX 7.70 Trifecta £59.90.
**Owner** K Abdullah **Bred** Juddmonte Farms Inc **Trained** Newmarket, Suffolk
**FOCUS**
Despite the fact they bet double figures bar three, this had the look of a decent fillies' maiden. The pace was modest, before they quickened, and it was slower than the earlier all-age Class 6 handicap. The level is a bit fluid, but the fifth and sixth-place finishers were close to their latest efforts.

## 5306 BETBRIGHT MOBILE NURSERY H'CAP (BOBIS RACE) 7f (P)
**8:20** (8:21) (Class 4) (0-85,79) 2-Y-O **£3,881** (£1,155; £577; £288) **Stalls** Low

Form RPR
4031 **1** **Speedy Move (IRE)**[14] 4787 2-9-7 79 .............................. MartinHarley 5 84
(Ismail Mohammed) *mde all: rdn 2f out: kpt on gamely fnl f: jst hld on* **4/1**[3]
5441 **2** *hd* **Muradif (IRE)**[9] 4967 2-9-4 76 6ex .............................. SebSanders 4 80+
(William Haggas) *towards rr: rdn and hdwy over 1f out: str run fnl f: jst failed* **5/4**[1]
0602 **3** *1/2* **Western Playboy (IRE)**[7] 5043 2-7-13 62 .............................. CamHardie(5) 6 65
(Sylvester Kirk) *trckd ldr: chal over 2f out: kpt on fnl f* **10/1**
632 **4** *1/2* **Rotherwick (IRE)**[11] 4896 2-9-7 79 .............................. LukeMorris 1 80+
(Paul Cole) *in tch: drvn to chse ldrs 2f out: kpt on u.p fnl f* **15/8**[2]
001 **5** *2 1/4* **Classic Seniority**[12] 4846 2-9-1 73 .............................. RichardHughes 3 69
(Richard Hannon) *t.k.h: in tch: chal over 2f out: no ex over 1f out* **20/1**
231 **6** *1 1/2* **Spindle (IRE)**[44] 3794 2-9-1 73 .............................. LiamKeniry 2 65
(Mark Usher) *prom tl outpcd fnl 2f* **10/1**
006 **7** *1 3/4* **Foylesideview (IRE)**[51] 3524 2-8-10 68 .............................. FergusSweeney 8 55
(Luke Dace) *a bhd* **50/1**

1m 27.77s (1.77) **Going Correction** +0.05s/f (Slow) **7 Ran SP% 124.1**
Speed ratings (Par 96): **91,90,90,89,87 85,83**
CSF £10.51 CT £49.91 TOTE £4.90: £1.80, £1.60; EX 11.10 Trifecta £130.50.
**Owner** Dr Ali Ridha **Bred** Rabbah Bloodstock Limited **Trained** Newmarket, Suffolk
**FOCUS**
Despite the topweight being 6lb below the ceiling for this race, it looked a fairly competitive nursery between some improving types with four last-time-out winners taking their chance. The winner is rated a length up on fluid Leicester win, with the third to latest.

## 5307 BETBRIGHT - LIVE THE MOMENT H'CAP 6f (P)
**8:50** (8:52) (Class 6) (0-65,65) 3-Y-O **£1,940** (£577; £288; £144) **Stalls** Low

Form RPR
-451 **1** **Tahchee**[9] 4972 3-9-6 64 6ex .............................. FrederikTylicki 5 74+
(James Fanshawe) *hld up in 5th: effrt over 2f out: led over 1f out: rdn out* **4/5**[1]
-323 **2** *3/4* **Hipz (IRE)**[13] 4813 3-9-5 63 .............................. LiamJones 1 70
(Laura Mongan) *chsd ldrs: wnt cl 2nd over 1f out: unable qck fnl f: a hld* **5/1**[3]
236 **3** *2 1/4* **Inis Airc (IRE)**[18] 4677 3-9-4 62 .............................. JamesDoyle 2 62
(Sylvester Kirk) *pressed ldr: outpcd 2f out: styd on fnl f* **4/1**[2]
2210 **4** *1/2* **Douneedahand**[29] 4285 3-8-12 63 .............................. GaryMahon(7) 3 61
(Seamus Mullins) *led tl over 1f out: one pce* **20/1**
0450 **5** *1 1/4* **Khelfan**[9] 4972 3-8-3 52 .............................. NathanAlison(5) 9 46
(Martin Smith) *stdd s and dropped in: hld up in rr: hdwy 2f out: no ex 1f out* **25/1**
6046 **6** *hd* **Silken Poppy**[18] 4675 3-8-12 56 .............................. DavidProbert 4 50
(Patrick Chamings) *prom tl outpcd 2f out* **33/1**
1235 **7** *5* **Rose Buck**[124] 1425 3-9-6 64 .............................. AdamKirby 7 42
(Giles Bravery) *a towards rr: lost tch 2f out* **10/1**

1m 13.25s (0.15) **Going Correction** +0.05s/f (Slow) **7 Ran SP% 112.9**
Speed ratings (Par 98): **101,100,97,96,94 94,87**
CSF £4.96 CT £9.87 TOTE £2.00: £1.50, £2.90; EX 5.70 Trifecta £10.10.
**Owner** Chris Van Hoorn **Bred** F Stribbling **Trained** Newmarket, Suffolk
**FOCUS**
Little depth, but right trio filled the first three places and the winner progressed again from his recent C&D win. The second was on a good mark judged on 2yo form.

## 5308 BETBRIGHT.COM H'CAP 7f (P)
**9:20** (9:21) (Class 5) (0-75,75) 3-Y-O+ **£2,587** (£770; £384; £192) **Stalls** Low

Form RPR
0026 **1** **Galatian**[18] 4673 7-9-4 67 .............................. GeorgeBaker 1 76
(Rod Millman) *prom: led wl over 1f out: jst hld on: all out* **10/1**
4346 **2** *nse* **Good Authority (IRE)**[32] 4181 7-9-1 71 .............................. KieranShoemark(7) 14 80
(Karen George) *stdd s: bhd: gd hdwy on inner 2f out: str chal ins fnl f: jst failed* **5/1**[3]
3050 **3** *1* **New Leyf (IRE)**[25] 4431 8-9-6 69 .............................. (b) SteveDrowne 2 75
(Jeremy Gask) *mid-div: clsd on ldrs 2f out: kpt on fnl f* **25/1**
32- **4** *1/2* **Charter (IRE)**[429] 3159 4-9-12 75 .............................. JamesDoyle 8 80
(Michael Wigham) *chsd ldrs: effrt over 2f out: one pce fnl f* **4/1**[2]
2421 **5** *nk* **Lady Crossmar (IRE)**[13] 4811 3-9-1 70 .............................. RichardHughes 5 72
(Richard Hannon) *mid-div: effrt over 1f out: r.o* **6/1**
0500 **6** *3/4* **Light Rose (IRE)**[32] 4181 4-9-3 66 .............................. JimCrowley 9 68
(Jeremy Gask) *mid-div on outer: rdn and hdwy 2f out: one pce fnl f* **20/1**
40-P **7** *3/4* **Rizal Park (IRE)**[126] 1390 3-9-6 75 .............................. [1] DavidProbert 6 73
(Andrew Balding) *stdd s: towards rr: hdwy 2f out: no imp* **20/1**
000- **8** *1/2* **Gigawatt**[434] 2984 4-9-9 72 .............................. AdamKirby 10 71
(Jim Boyle) *s.s: bhd tl styd on fnl 2f* **50/1**
2126 **9** *nk* **Shifting Star (IRE)**[11] 4907 9-9-8 71 .............................. (vt) WilliamCarson 4 69
(John Bridger) *chsd ldrs tl wknd over 1f out* **20/1**
5035 **10** *nk* **Dynaglow (USA)**[19] 4623 3-9-5 74 .............................. RobertHavlin 3 70
(John Gosden) *twrds rr: rdn 2f out: n.d* **10/1**
0300 **11** *5* **Wickhambrook (IRE)**[39] 3979 3-9-4 73 .............................. MartinHarley 12 56
(Ismail Mohammed) *led tl hrd rdn and wknd wl over 1f out* **25/1**
4033 **12** *2* **Seek The Fair Land**[20] 4581 8-9-11 74 .............................. (b) StevieDonohoe 7 53
(Lee Carter) *in tch tl wknd 2f out* **14/1**
1012 **13** *17* **Secret Success**[12] 4866 4-9-12 75 .............................. (bt[1]) LukeMorris 11 10+
(Paul Cole) *prom tl rein broke and rn v wd bnd into st: nt rcvr* **11/4**[1]

1m 25.59s (-0.41) **Going Correction** +0.05s/f (Slow)
**WFA** 3 from 4yo+ 6lb **13 Ran SP% 126.4**
Speed ratings (Par 103): **104,103,102,102,101 101,100,99,99,98 93,90,71**
CSF £57.11 CT £1299.23 TOTE £12.50: £3.00, £2.30, £7.20; EX 70.80 Trifecta £1888.90 Part won. Pool of £2518.53 - 0.47 winning units..
**Owner** Tarka Racing **Bred** Mrs B A Matthews **Trained** Kentisbeare, Devon
**FOCUS**
A fair race to close the card and it was competitive enough. It was the quickest of the four 7f races on the card which suggests they went a good pace. The winner is rated up a length on last winter's form, and the third helps set the level.
T/Plt: £20.10 to a £1 stake. Pool of £57,591.15 - 2,090.45 winning units. T/Qpdt: £1.70 to a £1 stake. Pool of £7,832.26 - 3,305.35 winning units. LM

# 4673 SALISBURY (R-H)
## Wednesday, August 13
**OFFICIAL GOING: Good to firm (good in places)**
Wind: Light against Weather: Cloudy with sunny spells

## 5309 BRITISH STALLION STUDS EBF MOLSON COORS MAIDEN (BOBIS RACE) 6f
**2:20** (2:20) (Class 4) 2-Y-O **£4,204** (£1,251; £625; £312) **Stalls** Low

Form RPR
**1** **Twilight Son** 2-9-5 0 .............................. FergusSweeney 3 81+
(Henry Candy) *trckd ldr: swtchd rt to chal over 1f out: led ent fnl f: r.o wl: rdn out* **5/1**[3]
4 **2** *1/2* **Desert Force**[17] 4695 2-9-5 0 .............................. RichardHughes 5 79
(Richard Hannon) *trckd ldr: rdn to ld over 1f out: hdd ent fnl f: no ex fnl 120yds* **2/1**[1]
30 **3** *1 1/2* **Tansfeeq**[62] 3136 2-9-5 0 .............................. GeorgeBaker 1 75
(B W Hills) *taken to s early: racd keenly: led: pushed along and hdd over 1f out: no ex fnl f* **20/1**
0 **4** *shd* **Oriental Splendour (IRE)**[37] 4025 2-9-5 0 .............................. JamesDoyle 6 74
(Roger Charlton) *hld up: nt clr run and swtchd lft over 1f out: r.o wl fnl f: nt rch ldrs* **10/1**
40 **5** *1 1/4* **Hound Music**[50] 3558 2-9-0 0 .............................. MartinHarley 8 65
(Jonathan Portman) *hld up: hdwy 2f out: sn rdn: kpt on same pce fnl f* **25/1**
03 **6** *hd* **Lysander The Greek**[18] 4676 2-9-5 0 .............................. SilvestreDeSousa 7 70
(Ralph Beckett) *mid-div: pushed along whn j. path over 3f out: drvn to chse ldrs over 2f out: one pce fnl f* **11/2**
5232 **7** *1 1/4* **Harlequin Striker (IRE)**[18] 4676 2-9-5 76 .............................. LiamKeniry 9 66
(Mick Channon) *in tch: rdn over 2f out: nt pce to threaten: wknd fnl f* **4/1**[2]
5 **8** *1/2* **Little Riggs**[16] 4740 2-9-5 0 .............................. LukeMorris 10 64
(Ed Walker) *wnt lft s: sn pushed along towards rr: nvr gng pce to get on terms* **12/1**
**9** *3/4* **Awjab (IRE)** 2-9-5 0 .............................. DaneO'Neill 4 62
(Brian Meehan) *sn pushed along in mid-div: nvr treatened: wknd fnl f* **28/1**

1m 15.83s (1.03) **Going Correction** +0.025s/f (Good) **9 Ran SP% 114.2**
Speed ratings (Par 96): **94,93,91,91,89 89,87,86,85**
CSF £14.83 TOTE £5.70: £2.70, £1.10, £5.10; EX 21.40 Trifecta £277.10.
**Owner** Godfrey Wilson **Bred** Mrs C R D Wilson **Trained** Kingston Warren, Oxon
**FOCUS**
The ground had dried out slightly from that forecast and was officially Good to firm, good in places. This is usually a good maiden and it's rated near averages with the fifth and sixth fitting in.

## 5310 S H JONES WINES NURSERY H'CAP (BOBIS RACE) 1m
**2:50** (2:51) (Class 3) (0-95,82) 2-Y-O **£7,115** (£2,117; £1,058; £529) **Stalls** Low

Form RPR
3001 **1** **Grigolo**[11] 4897 2-9-2 78 .............................. SilvestreDeSousa 3 85
(Mark Johnston) *mde all: rdn over 2f out: drifted lft: kpt on strly to assert fnl f* **9/2**[2]
3114 **2** *1 1/2* **When Will It End (IRE)**[11] 4897 2-9-6 82 .............................. RichardHughes 6 85
(Richard Hannon) *little slowly away: in last but in tch: rdn over 2f out: r.o ins fnl f: wnt 2nd fnl 120yds: a bhd: hld* **11/2**
0021 **3** *3/4* **Groor**[15] 4750 2-9-2 78 .............................. KierenFallon 2 80
(James Tate) *cl up: nt clr run and swtchd rt 2f out: sn rdn: kpt on to chse wnr fnl f: lost 2nd fnl 120yds* **5/1**[3]
6323 **4** *3/4* **Big Chill (IRE)**[13] 4809 2-9-3 79 .............................. GeorgeBaker 1 79
(Charles Hills) *trckd ldrs: rdn over 2f out: kpt on same pce fnl f* **16/1**
21 **5** *1/2* **Darshini**[21] 4550 2-9-3 79 .............................. RyanMoore 5 78
(Sir Michael Stoute) *pushed along briefly early: trckd ldrs: rdn 2f out: nvr able to quite chal: no ex fnl f* **10/11**[1]
531 **6** *11* **Red Rebel**[11] 4906 2-9-2 78 .............................. AdamKirby 4 52
(Clive Cox) *trckd wnr: rdn over 2f out: sn drifted lft and btn* **25/1**

1m 45.7s (2.20) **Going Correction** +0.025s/f (Good) **6 Ran SP% 112.3**
Speed ratings (Par 98): **90,88,87,87,86 75**
CSF £28.50 TOTE £4.70: £2.20, £2.20; EX 18.90 Trifecta £85.90.
**Owner** Sheikh Hamdan bin Mohammed Al Maktoum **Bred** Darley **Trained** Middleham Moor, N Yorks

**FOCUS**
Not as strong a nursery as it might have been, with the top weight 13lb below the race ceiling, and they didn't go much of a pace early either. A new trip for all six of these, but not a searching test of stamina, as a Mark Johnston runner was allowed the luxury of a soft lead. The third and fourth have been rated close to their maiden form.

## 5311 GOLDRING SECURITY SERVICES PEMBROKE CUP (H'CAP) (BOBIS RACE) 1m

3:25 (3:30) (Class 4) (0-85,85) 3-Y-O £6,469 (£1,925; £962; £481) Stalls Low

Form RPR

3210 **1** **Between Wickets**[18] 4647 3-9-2 80[1] MartinDwyer 4 91
(Marcus Tregoning) *s.i.s: bhd: hdwy whn nt clr run 2f out: swtchd lft and sn rdn: str run ent fnl f: drifted rt: led fnl 120yds: readily* **8/1**

151 **2** *1 1/4* **Potentate (IRE)**[13] 4810 3-9-1 79 RichardHughes 7 87
(Richard Hannon) *mid-div: rdn and hdwy 2f out: led ent fnl f: hdd fnl 120yds: nt gng pce of wnr* **3/1**[2]

5444 **3** *3* **Grevillea (IRE)**[33] 4162 3-8-13 77 WilliamTwiston-Davies 3 78
(Mick Channon) *taken to s early: mid-div: hdwy 2f out: chsng ldrs whn squeezed up over 1f out: kpt on but hld after* **16/1**

1062 **4** *1/2* **Bowie Boy (IRE)**[14] 4801 3-9-2 80 (p) SilvestreDeSousa 1 80
(Ralph Beckett) *trckd ldrs: led over 2f out: rdn and hung bdly rt over 1f out: sn hdd: no ex fnl f* **7/1**[3]

4603 **5** *2 1/4* **Fiftyshadesofgrey (IRE)**[18] 4679 3-8-12 76 PatCosgrave 5 71
(George Baker) *in tch: nt clr run briefly over 2f out: keeping on at same pce whn short of room briefly over 1f out* **8/1**

4016 **6** *3 1/2* **Inspector Norse**[8] 5008 3-8-7 71 LiamKeniry 9 58
(Sylvester Kirk) *disp ld: rdn and hdd 2f out: looking hld whn hmpd over 1f out: wknd ins fnl f* **25/1**

0620 **7** *hd* **Rogue Wave (IRE)**[27] 4355 3-9-2 80 AdamKirby 2 66
(Timothy Jarvis) *trckd ldrs: nt clr run wl over 1f out: sn rdn: wknd ins fnl f* **25/1**

01 **8** *8* **Tercel (IRE)**[20] 4587 3-8-13 77 RyanMoore 10 45
(Sir Michael Stoute) *hld up: plld hrd: swtchd lft and effrt 2f out: qckly btn and eased* **11/4**[1]

-040 **9** *2 1/4* **Monsea (IRE)**[21] 4551 3-9-4 82 DaneO'Neill 6 45
(Richard Hannon) *disp ld tl rdn 2f out: looking hld whn bdly hmpd over 1f out: no ch and eased fnl f* **33/1**

1m 43.08s (-0.42) **Going Correction** +0.025s/f (Good) **9** Ran SP% **102.9**
Speed ratings (Par 102): **103,101,98,98,96 92,92,84,82**
CSF £25.51 CT £271.86 TOTE £7.80: £2.80, £1.40, £4.20; EX 26.00 Trifecta £224.60.
**Owner** R C C Villers **Bred** Miss K J Keir **Trained** Whitsbury, Hants
■ Jailawi was withdrawn. Price at time of withdrawal 6/1. Rule 4 applies to all bets - deduct 10p in the pound.
■ Stewards' Enquiry : Silvestre De Sousa two-day ban: careless riding (Aug 27-28)

**FOCUS**
A decent 3yo handicap, though weakened a little with the favourite running so badly and Jailawi refusing to enter the stalls. The winner was building on his maiden form and the runner-up is rated slightly up on his Epsom win.

## 5312 EBF STALLIONS UPAVON FILLIES' STKS (LISTED RACE) 1m 1f 198y

3:55 (4:00) (Class 1) 3-Y-O+ £23,251 (£8,815; £4,411; £2,197; £1,102; £553) Stalls Low

Form RPR

-351 **1** **Lady Pimpernel**[11] 4915 4-9-2 89 DaneO'Neill 11 103
(Henry Candy) *slowly away: sn pushed along: led after 1f: rdn clr over 1f out: kpt on wl: comf* **20/1**

3004 **2** *2 1/4* **Gifted Girl (IRE)**[19] 4607 5-9-2 102 (t) TomQueally 8 98
(Paul Cole) *hld up towards rr: travelling wl bhd ldrs but nt clr run fr over 2f out: pushed way through jst over 1f out: r.o strly to chse wnr sn after but no ch* **12/1**

111 **3** *1 3/4* **My Spirit (IRE)**[50] 3560 3-8-8 96 ow1 RyanMoore 9 96
(William Haggas) *mid-div: outpcd in last pair over 2f out: r.o wl ent fnl f: wnt 3rd fnl 120yds* **5/1**[3]

-245 **4** *1/2* **Veiled Intrigue**[19] 4607 3-8-7 99 DavidProbert 4 94
(Henry Candy) *led for 1f: trckd wnr tl rdn over 2f out: kpt on wl fnl f* **25/1**

1625 **5** *1* **Pelerin (IRE)**[47] 3665 3-8-7 96 MartinHarley 6 92
(Marco Botti) *hld up: rdn and hdwy over 2f out: kpt on same pce fnl f* **10/1**

1-53 **6** *nse* **Vanity Rules**[36] 4060 4-9-2 96 FrederikTylicki 1 92
(Ed Vaughan) *trckd ldrs: rdn over 2f out: hmpd over 1f out: no ex fnl f* **18/1**

11 **7** *3/4* **Tearless**[32] 4211 4-9-2 97 AdamKirby 7 91
(Charlie Appleby) *mid-div: hdwy fr 4f out: rdn to chse wnr over 2f out: sn edgd rt: fdd ins fnl f* **4/1**[2]

1103 **8** *nk* **Crowley's Law**[39] 3983 3-8-7 98 RichardKingscote 3 90
(Tom Dascombe) *mid-div: hdwy wl over 2f out: sn rdn: fdd fnl f* **7/1**

-464 **9** *1 1/4* **Mutatis Mutandis (IRE)**[62] 3143 3-8-7 92 LukeMorris 12 88
(Ed Walker) *s.i.s: mid-div after 2f: rdn whn hmpd over 1f out: wknd fnl f* **33/1**

5211 **10** *21* **Kleo (GR)**[18] 4680 3-8-7 90 SilvestreDeSousa 2 84
(Luca Cumani) *hld up: nt travelling fr over 4f out: nvr threatened: wknd and eased fnl f* **7/2**[1]

2m 6.85s (-3.05) **Going Correction** +0.025s/f (Good)
**WFA** 3 from 4yo+ 9lb **10** Ran SP% **105.0**
Speed ratings: **113,111,109,109,108 108,107,107,106,89**
CSF £179.90 TOTE £21.90: £4.80, £3.60, £1.40; EX 192.80 Trifecta £1295.20.
**Owner** Henry Candy & Partners II **Bred** Harts Farm Stud **Trained** Kingston Warren, Oxon
■ Albasharah was withdrawn. Price at time of withdrawal 11/2. Rule 4 applies to all bets - deduct 15p in the pound.
■ Stewards' Enquiry : Tom Queally One-day ban: careless riding (Aug 27)

**FOCUS**
This fillies' Listed event had gone to a 3yo five times in the last seven years, but this was one for the older brigade. Three non-runners were added to when Albasharah refused to enter the stalls. This was a clear personal best from the winner, although this was not a strong race for the grade. It's rated around the balance of the fourth to sixth-placed finishers.

## 5313 CHAMPAGNE JOSEPH PERRIER H'CAP 1m 1f 198y

4:30 (4:31) (Class 5) (0-70,70) 3-Y-O+ £2,911 (£866; £432; £216) Stalls Low

Form RPR

0424 **1** **Petticoat Lane**[14] 4802 3-9-5 70 RyanMoore 2 79+
(Luca Cumani) *trckd ldr: shkn up to ld over 1f out: styd on wl: rdn out* **13/8**[1]

6403 **2** *1 1/4* **Canova (IRE)**[16] 4742 3-9-2 67 (bt) JamesDoyle 5 72
(Roger Charlton) *sn led: rdn and hdd over 1f out: styd on but a bhd hld* **3/1**[2]

2006 **3** *3/4* **Template (IRE)**[21] 4547 3-9-0 65 RobertHavlin 6 69
(Amanda Perrett) *mid-div: nt clr run on rails fr over 2f out tl over 1f out: styd on wl: clsng on ldng pair towards fin* **10/1**

6000 **4** *3 1/4* **Silvee**[11] 4911 7-8-9 51 oh6 (p) WilliamCarson 8 48
(John Bridger) *in tch: rdn over 3f out: edgd lft 2f out: styd on same pce fnl f* **66/1**

050 **5** *1* **Do Wah Diddy Diddy**[74] 2773 3-9-5 70 AdamKirby 7 65
(Clive Cox) *hld up towards rr: struggling 3f out: swtchd rt and styd on fr over 1f out: fin wl but no ch* **9/1**

00-5 **6** *3/4* **Stilla Afton**[20] 4587 3-8-5 56 MartinDwyer 4 50
(Marcus Tregoning) *hmpd sn after s: trckd ldrs: rdn over 2f out: sn one pce* **8/1**[3]

-505 **7** *3 1/2* **Guilded Spirit**[27] 4369 4-9-9 65 KierenFallon 11 52
(Stuart Kittow) *hld up: hdwy over 3f out: rdn over 2f out: wknd over 1f out* **8/1**[3]

000- **8** *hd* **Konzert (ITY)**[282] 7733 4-8-11 58 GeorgeDowning(5) 1 44
(Ian Williams) *towards rr: struggling over 3f out: nvr any danger* **25/1**

**9** *2 1/4* **Victory Rich (IRE)**[298] 7389 3-8-11 67 NedCurtis(5) 9 49
(Roger Curtis) *racd keenly in tch: rdn wl over 2f out: wknd fnl f* **50/1**

6-00 **10** *1 3/4* **Cinnamon Spice**[60] 3248 3-9-0 65 PatCosgrave 12 43
(Harry Dunlop) *mid-div: rdn over 2f out: wknd over 1f out* **25/1**

0500 **11** *1 3/4* **I Am Not Here (IRE)**[26] 4420 3-8-11 62 DaneO'Neill 10 37
(Timothy Jarvis) *s.i.s: mid-div: squeezed out over 3f out: sn btn* **40/1**

2m 10.7s (0.80) **Going Correction** +0.025s/f (Good)
**WFA** 3 from 4yo+ 9lb **11** Ran SP% **118.0**
Speed ratings (Par 103): **97,96,95,92,92 91,88,88,86,85 83**
CSF £6.01 CT £36.39 TOTE £2.60: £1.20, £1.80, £1.70; EX 7.10 Trifecta £46.30.
**Owner** Fittocks Stud **Bred** Fittocks Stud **Trained** Newmarket, Suffolk

**FOCUS**
This looked a weak contest and very few ever got into it. The winning time was nearly four seconds slower than the fillies' Listed event. This was a personal best from the winner.

## 5314 CGA RACING EXCELLENCE APPRENTICE H'CAP (WHIPS SHALL BE CARRIED BUT NOT USED) 6f 212y

5:00 (5:01) (Class 5) (0-70,70) 3-Y-O+ £2,911 (£866; £432; £216) Stalls Centre

Form RPR

-064 **1** **Cincuenta Pasos (IRE)**[61] 3198 3-9-6 68 JennyPowell 2 73
(Joseph Tuite) *cl up: led 2f out: in command fnl f: comf* **11/4**[1]

0050 **2** *1 1/2* **Cadmium**[8] 5005 3-8-0 51 oh1 Leah-AnneAvery(3) 5 52
(Harry Dunlop) *trckd ldrs: chal over 3f out tl drifted lft 2f out: kpt on to regain 2nd towards fin* **33/1**

0423 **3** *nk* **Go For Broke**[18] 4654 3-9-5 70 GaryMahon(3) 7 70
(Richard Hannon) *trckd ldr: jnd ldr over 3f out tl 2f out: kpt on same pce fnl f* **4/1**[3]

-355 **4** *hd* **Fair Ranger**[20] 4572 3-9-5 70 JoshQuinn(3) 1 70
(Richard Hannon) *led tl 2f out: kpt on same pce fnl f* **6/1**

6442 **5** *5* **Just Isla**[5] 5125 4-8-10 55 (p) PaulBooth(3) 8 44
(Peter Makin) *hld up: swtchd rt 3f out: nt pce to get on terms: wknd fnl f* **3/1**[2]

05 **6** *5* **Shushu Sugartown (IRE)**[23] 4502 3-9-6 68 JordanVaughan 4 42
(Ian Williams) *stdd s: effrt over 2f out: wknd fnl f* **7/1**

6442 **7** *23* **Annes Rocket (IRE)**[20] 4564 9-9-5 64 (p) HectorCrouch(3) 3
(Jimmy Fox) *awkwardly away: hld up and t.k.h: eased whn appeared to lose action over 1f out* **8/1**

1m 31.81s (3.21) **Going Correction** +0.025s/f (Good)
**WFA** 3 from 4yo+ 6lb **7** Ran SP% **112.5**
Speed ratings (Par 103): **82,80,79,79,74 68,42**
CSF £76.57 CT £357.99 TOTE £3.40: £2.40, £8.20; EX 70.70 Trifecta £609.40.
**Owner** Mark Wellbelove & Peter Gleeson **Bred** P J Gleeson **Trained** Great Shefford, Berks

**FOCUS**
A modest apprentice handicap, though run at a fair pace with three disputing the advantage as they passed halfway. The winner is rated back to near 2yo form.
T/Jkpt: Not won. T/Plt: £658.10 to a £1 stake. Pool of £69477.01 - 77.06 winning units. T/Qpdt: £46.30 to a £1 stake. Pool of £5892.68 - 94.00 winning units. TM

# 5104 YARMOUTH (L-H)

## Wednesday, August 13

**OFFICIAL GOING: Good (6.6)**
Bottom bend dolled out 3m and races on Round course increased by 17m.
Wind: medium, across Weather: showers

## 5315 BRITISH STALLION STUDS EBF / BET365 MAIDEN STKS 7f 3y

5:05 (5:05) (Class 5) 2-Y-O £3,234 (£962; £481; £240) Stalls Centre

Form RPR

**1** **Johnny Barnes (IRE)** 2-9-5 0 WilliamBuick 1 83+
(John Gosden) *trckd ldrs: clsd to join ldr over 2f out: led 2f out: rdn and asserted ent fnl f: r.o wl: comf* **7/4**[1]

**2** *1 1/2* **Bartholomew Fair** 2-9-5 0 AndreaAtzeni 5 79+
(Luca Cumani) *in tch in last pair: clsd 3f out: chsd wnr and rdn over 1f out: r.o but a hld fnl f* **7/4**[1]

60 **3** *1 3/4* **Digital Rebellion (IRE)**[20] 4570 2-9-5 0 AhmedAjtebi 4 75
(Charlie Appleby) *in tch in midfield: shkn up and effrt 2f out: 3rd over 1f out: styd on same pce fnl f* **10/1**

0 **4** *5* **Referendum (IRE)**[14] 4800 2-9-5 0 ShaneKelly 6 62
(Sir Michael Stoute) *chsd ldr tl over 2f out: rdn 2f out: sn outpcd: 4th and wl hld fnl f* **7/1**[2]

00 **5** *3 3/4* **Prima Pagina**[14] 4784 2-8-11 0 RobertTart(3) 3 47
(Dr Jon Scargill) *hld up in tch in last pair: swtchd lft and hdwy 3f out: rdn 2f out: sn outpcd and wknd* **33/1**

00 **6** *2 1/2* **Kopassus (IRE)**[15] 4750 2-9-5 0 OisinMurphy 2 45
(Peter Chapple-Hyam) *led tl hdd and rdn wl over 1f out: sn outpcd and btn: bhd fnl f* **8/1**[3]

1m 28.35s (1.75) **Going Correction** +0.30s/f (Good) **6** Ran SP% **108.4**
Speed ratings (Par 94): **102,100,98,92,88 85**
CSF £4.40 TOTE £2.30: £1.70, £1.90; EX 4.50 Trifecta £13.60.
**Owner** Bermuda Thoroughbred Racing Limited **Bred** Citadel Stud **Trained** Newmarket, Suffolk

**FOCUS**
A decent little 2yo maiden. The winner and second have the potential to rate a lot higher, and the third posted improved form.

## 5316 BET365 H'CAP — 5f 43y
5:40 (5:40) (Class 6) (0-55,59) 3-Y-O+ **£1,940** (£577; £288; £144) **Stalls** Centre

Form | RPR
---|---
3001 **1** **Lunarian**[7] 5034 3-9-5 59 6ex........ CharlesBishop(3) 1 | 68
(Mick Channon) *chsd ldrs tl outpcd and dropped to rr of main gp over 3f out: shkn up and hdwy over 1f out: rdn to ld ins fnl f: r.o wl* **3/1**[3] |
6006 **2** 1 **Arch Walker (IRE)**[18] 4664 7-8-12 46........(b) JimmyQuinn 8 | 53
(John Weymes) *led: drvn over 1f out: hdd ins fnl f: kpt on same pce after* **20/1** |
0553 **3** 1 ¼ **Captain Scooby**[9] 4960 8-8-10 49........(v) DuilioDaSilva(5) 7 | 51
(Richard Guest) *in tch in rr of main gp: rdn and effrt over 2f out: kpt on same pce fnl f: wnt 3rd towards fin* **5/2**[1] |
4234 **4** ¾ **Bubbly Bailey**[5] 5126 4-9-5 53........(v) OisinMurphy 2 | 52
(J R Jenkins) *chsd ldrs: wnt 2nd and rdn 2f out: no ex 1f out: wknd fnl f* **11/4**[2] |
5045 **5** 3 **Danzoe (IRE)**[7] 5059 7-9-3 51........ AndreaAtzeni 6 | 40
(Christine Dunnett) *in tch: rdn and effrt to chse ldrs 2f out: drvn and btn 1f out: wknd ins fnl f* **10/1** |
-600 **6** 1 ¼ **Miakora**[39] 3966 6-8-13 47........ PaoloSirigu 9 | 31
(Mick Quinn) *v.s.a: wl off the pce in 7th: sme hdwy u.p 1f out: nvr trbld ldrs* **25/1** |
605 **7** 7 **Give Us A Belle (IRE)**[41] 3896 5-9-4 52........(vt) AdamBeschizza 3 | 11
(Christine Dunnett) *chsd ldr: rdn 1/2-way: lost 2nd 2f out and sn struggling u.p: fdd fnl f* **16/1** |
3303 **8** 12 **Imaginary Diva**[15] 4768 8-9-4 55........ RyanPowell(3) 5 |
(George Margarson) *anticipated s and hit front of stall hrd: bounced bk and lost many l s: nvr a ch to rcvr and nt pushed* **8/1** |

1m 4.48s (1.78) **Going Correction** +0.30s/f (Good)
**WFA** 3 from 4yo+ 3lb — **8** Ran SP% **114.9**
Speed ratings (Par 101): **97,95,93,92,87 85,74,55**
CSF £58.79 CT £171.32 TOTE £4.20: £1.10, £6.10, £1.10; EX 76.70 Trifecta £304.60.
**Owner** Mrs Ann C Black **Bred** R J Cornelius **Trained** West Ilsley, Berks

**FOCUS**
A modest sprint handicap. The winner backed up her Brighton win under penalty against exposed rivals.

## 5317 BET365.COM H'CAP — 2m
6:10 (6:10) (Class 5) (0-75,75) 4-Y-O+ **£2,587** (£770; £384; £192) **Stalls** Low

Form | RPR
---|---
0025 **1** **Rosslyn Castle**[16] 4736 5-9-2 75........ DannyBrock(5) 1 | 83
(Philip McBride) *wl in tch in last: hdwy to chal 2f out: rdn to ld over 1f out: in command but racing lazily ins fnl f: rdn out* **13/8**[1] |
4133 **2** 1 **The Ducking Stool**[7] 5062 7-8-8 67........ ShelleyBirkett(5) 5 | 74
(Julia Feilden) *chsd ldrs: clsd to join ldrs 4f out: led wl over 2f out: sn rdn: hdd and hung lft over 1f out: kpt on trying but a hld fnl f* **11/4**[2] |
1212 **3** 5 **Ninfea (IRE)**[12] 4843 6-8-7 61........ JimmyQuinn 4 | 62
(Neil King) *chsd ldr: rdn and ev ch over 2f out: 3rd and outpcd over 1f out: plugged on same pce after* **9/2** |
-000 **4** 3 ¼ **Passion Play**[8] 5011 6-8-4 63........ RyanWhile(5) 2 | 60
(Bill Turner) *led: rdn over 3f out: hdd and immediately lost pl wl over 2f out: 4th and wl hld fnl 2f* **16/1** |
03-4 **5** 3 **Solaras Exhibition (IRE)**[13] 4819 6-9-5 73........ OisinMurphy 3 | 67
(Tim Vaughan) *in tch in last pair: rdn and effrt over 3f out: outpcd and btn 3f out* **4/1**[3] |

3m 37.11s (4.71) **Going Correction** +0.30s/f (Good) — **5** Ran SP% **108.8**
Speed ratings (Par 103): **100,99,97,95,93**
CSF £6.17 TOTE £2.70: £2.50, £1.10; EX 6.30 Trifecta £13.80.
**Owner** P J McBride **Bred** Carwell Equities Ltd **Trained** Newmarket, Suffolk

**FOCUS**
A weak, muddling staying handicap.

## 5318 CASINO AT BET365.COM H'CAP — 1m 3f 101y
6:40 (6:40) (Class 5) (0-70,75) 3-Y-O **£2,587** (£770; £384; £192) **Stalls** Low

Form | RPR
---|---
63-3 **1** **Authorized Too**[35] 4089 3-9-7 70........ AndreaAtzeni 4 | 87+
(William Haggas) *hld up in 3rd: clsd to join ldr 3f out: led on bit 2f out: cruised clr fnl f: v easily: unextended* **1/1**[1] |
6611 **2** 3 ¾ **Needless Shouting (IRE)**[7] 5062 3-9-12 75 6ex........ SamHitchcott 1 | 79
(Mick Channon) *led: jnd and rdn 3f out: hdd and drvn 2f out: no ch w wnr and one pce fnl f* **9/4**[2] |
0001 **3** 21 **Topaling**[7] 5048 3-8-6 55 6ex........ JimmyQuinn 5 | 24
(Mark H Tompkins) *hld up in detached last: rdn and struggling 4f out: lost tch 2f out: wnt poor 3rd wl ins fnl f* **7/1** |
1253 **4** 2 ¼ **Avocadeau (IRE)**[13] 4817 3-9-5 68........(b[1]) DougieCostello 6 | 34
(William Muir) *chsd ldr tl 3f out: sn wl btn: lost poor 3rd wl ins fnl f* **6/1**[3] |

2m 32.4s (3.70) **Going Correction** +0.30s/f (Good) — **4** Ran SP% **107.6**
Speed ratings (Par 100): **98,95,80,78**
CSF £3.45 TOTE £2.10; EX 3.40 Trifecta £5.80.
**Owner** Abdulla Al Mansoori **Bred** Almagro De Actividades Commerciales **Trained** Newmarket, Suffolk

**FOCUS**
This was one-way traffic, impressive stuff from the unexposed winner.

## 5319 POKER AT BET365.COM H'CAP — 1m 1f
7:10 (7:10) (Class 4) (0-80,80) 3-Y-O+ **£4,851** (£1,443; £721; £360) **Stalls** Low

Form | RPR
---|---
-404 **1** **Ski Lift**[73] 2804 3-8-11 71........ WilliamBuick 5 | 82+
(John Gosden) *in tch in midfield: rdn 4f out: hdwy to chse ldrs over 2f out: styd on and chal 1f out: led ins fnl f: sn clr and gng away at fin* **11/4**[1] |
0-00 **2** 2 ¾ **Blighty (IRE)**[88] 2351 4-9-11 77........ OisinMurphy 3 | 82
(Lady Cecil) *t.k.h: hld up in last pair: rdn and hdwy 3f out: chsd ldrs and swtchd lft ent fnl f: ev ch fnl 150yds: sn outpcd by wnr but hld on for 2nd* **9/2**[2] |
003 **3** nk **Vainglory (USA)**[12] 4868 10-9-9 75........ AndreaAtzeni 7 | 79
(David Simcock) *in tch in midfield: rdn over 3f out: no imp tl styd on u.p ins fnl f: wnt 3rd wl ins fnl f: pressing for 2nd cl home: no threat to wnr* **11/2**[3] |
3503 **4** 1 ¼ **Hydrant**[4] 5172 8-9-3 74........ DuilioDaSilva(5) 6 | 76
(Richard Guest) *chsd ldr tl rdn to ld ent fnl 2f: drvn and hrd pressed 1f out: hdd ins fnl f: no ex: wknd fnl 50yds* **15/2** |
5221 **5** 4 ½ **Jonnie Skull (IRE)**[6] 5110 8-8-5 62........(vt) DannyBrock(5) 4 | 54
(Phil McEntee) *led: clr 5f out: rdn and hdd ent fnl 2f: 5th and btn 1f out: wknd* **9/2**[2] |
2165 **6** 14 **Luhaif**[7] 5031 4-9-9 80........(b) ShelleyBirkett(5) 2 | 43
(Julia Feilden) *chsd ldrs: rdn 3f out: sn struggling and dropped to rr over 2f out: lost tch over 1f out* **7/1** |
0 **7** hd **Dame Lucy (IRE)**[25] 4443 4-9-13 79........[1] DougieCostello 1 | 41
(Martin Smith) *hld up in tch in rr: rdn over 3f out: sn btn: lost tch over 2f out* **8/1** |

1m 57.83s (2.03) **Going Correction** +0.30s/f (Good)
**WFA** 3 from 4yo+ 8lb — **7** Ran SP% **113.8**
Speed ratings (Par 105): **102,99,99,98,94 81,81**
CSF £15.07 CT £62.18 TOTE £3.00: £1.30, £2.90; EX 16.70 Trifecta £61.30.
**Owner** K Abdullah **Bred** Juddmonte Farms Ltd **Trained** Newmarket, Suffolk

**FOCUS**
A modest handicap. The winner is going the right way, the second is rated back to something like his best and the third in line with this year's form.

## 5320 BINGO AT BET365.COM H'CAP — 7f 3y
7:40 (7:40) (Class 5) (0-75,75) 3-Y-O+ **£2,587** (£770; £384; £192) **Stalls** Centre

Form | RPR
---|---
1401 **1** **Strike A Light**[7] 5057 3-8-8 63 6ex........ ChrisCatlin 3 | 70+
(Rae Guest) *t.k.h: hld up wl in tch in midfield: rdn over 2f out: hdwy u.p to chal 1f out: led fnl 100yds: r.o wl* **2/1**[1] |
3146 **2** 1 **Pretty Bubbles**[7] 5058 5-9-8 71........ PaddyAspell 2 | 77
(J R Jenkins) *chsd ldrs: wnt 2nd and stl travelling wl 2f out: rdn and ev ch over 1f out: r.o same pce ins fnl f: wnt 2nd on post* **10/1** |
15-4 **3** nse **Punk**[30] 4263 3-9-3 72........ OisinMurphy 5 | 76
(George Peckham) *led: rdn ent fnl 2f: kpt on wl u.p tl hdd and one pce fnl 100yds: lost 2nd on post* **10/1** |
5050 **4** nk **Anton Chigurh**[100] 2034 5-9-7 75........ DannyBrock(5) 1 | 80
(Philip McBride) *hld up in tch towards rr: rdn ent fnl 2f: 5th and outpcd whn swtchd rt over 1f out: styd on wl fnl 100yds* **6/1**[3] |
0064 **5** 1 ¼ **Valen (IRE)**[27] 4367 3-9-3 75........ MichaelJMMurphy(3) 6 | 75
(Michael Bell) *t.k.h: chsd ldr tl unable qck u.p ent fnl 2f: btn and one pce fnl f* **7/1** |
3553 **6** 3 ¼ **Sbraase**[20] 4593 3-9-5 74........(b[1]) AndreaAtzeni 9 | 65
(James Tate) *slowl into stride and swtchd lft after s: in tch in rr: effrt and drvn wl over 1f out: no hdwy over 1f out: wl hld fnl f* **5/1**[2] |
0635 **7** nse **Fantasy Gladiator**[48] 3628 8-9-5 68........(p) IanBrennan 8 | 61
(John Quinn) *t.k.h: hld up in tch towards rr: rdn and outpcd ent fnl 2f: one pce and n.d after* **25/1** |
4165 **8** 2 ½ **Ted's Brother (IRE)**[11] 4903 6-9-6 74........(e) DuilioDaSilva(5) 4 | 61
(Richard Guest) *stdd s: t.k.h: hld up in tch towards rr: rdn over 2f out: outpcd and btn over 1f out* **16/1** |
-610 **9** 1 **Comrade Bond**[70] 2905 6-9-9 72........(p) TedDurcan 7 | 56
(Mark H Tompkins) *t.k.h: chsd ldrs: rdn 2f out: outpcd over 1f out: wknd fnl f* **8/1** |

1m 27.83s (1.23) **Going Correction** +0.30s/f (Good)
**WFA** 3 from 5yo+ 6lb — **9** Ran SP% **115.8**
Speed ratings (Par 103): **104,102,102,102,101 97,97,94,93**
CSF £23.63 CT £163.73 TOTE £2.40: £1.20, £3.10, £1.90; EX 33.80 Trifecta £48.10.
**Owner** Trevor Benton **Bred** Cheveley Park Stud Ltd **Trained** Newmarket, Suffolk

**FOCUS**
A competitive handicap for the class. The runner-up and third set the level.

## 5321 MOBILE AT BET365.COM H'CAP — 7f 3y
8:10 (8:10) (Class 6) (0-55,55) 3-Y-O **£1,940** (£577; £288; £144) **Stalls** Centre

Form | RPR
---|---
0054 **1** **Venus Marina**[9] 4970 3-8-12 49........ AshleyMorgan(3) 8 | 60
(Chris Wall) *stdd s: hld up in tch in midfield: clsd to join ldr and wnt clr 2f out: pushed into ld and flashed tail 1f out: asserted and edgd rt ins fnl f: pushed out* **3/1**[2] |
-503 **2** 1 ¾ **Risk 'N' Reward (IRE)**[9] 4969 3-9-3 51........(v) DougieCostello 6 | 57
(Martin Smith) *chsd ldr tl over 5f out: styd chsng ldrs tl led over 2f out: rdn and clr w wnr 2f out: hdd 1f out: carried rt and no ex ins fnl f: hld whn swtchd lft towards fin* **5/1**[3] |
-346 **3** 8 **Templar Boy**[44] 3792 3-9-5 53........ PaddyAspell 2 | 38
(J R Jenkins) *t.k.h: chsd ldrs: effrt to chse clr ldng pair jst over 2f out: rn green u.p and no imp: plugged on for clr 3rd* **20/1** |
0000 **4** 4 ½ **Reflection**[42] 3849 3-9-1 49........ JimmyQuinn 3 | 23
(Brian Baugh) *racd in midfield: rdn 1/2-way: modest 6th 2f out: 4th and wl hld fr over 1f out* **33/1** |
000- **5** 2 ¾ **Earl's Bridge**[300] 7320 3-8-7 46........ RyanWhile(5) 14 | 12
(Bill Turner) *racd towards stands' side: s.i.s and rdn along early: hdwy after 2f: chsd ldrs and rdn 3f out: 5th and btn 2f out: wknd over 1f out* **40/1** |
2000 **6** 6 **Cascadia (IRE)**[9] 4970 3-9-5 53........(v[1]) OisinMurphy 9 | 4
(Alison Hutchinson) *in tch in midfield: rdn and no hdwy 1/2-way: sn wl outpcd: no ch fnl 2f* **10/1** |
5000 **7** 2 **Water For Life**[29] 4304 3-8-7 46 oh1........(b[1]) DannyBrock(5) 1 |
(Dave Morris) *led: drvn ent fnl 4f: hdd over 2f out: sn btn: wknd qckly over 1f out* **14/1** |
050 **8** ½ **Arryzona**[30] 4265 3-8-12 46 oh1........ AdamBeschizza 5 |
(Christine Dunnett) *sn rdn along: dropped to rr over 5f out: sn wl bhd: plugged on past btn horses fnl f: n.d* **66/1** |
0040 **9** 2 ½ **Va Benny**[29] 4304 3-8-5 46 oh1........(b[1]) VictorSantos(7) 10 |
(J R Jenkins) *nt best away and jostled leaving stalls: t.k.h and rcvrd to chse ldr over 5f out tl over 2f out: sn wknd* **66/1** |
500 **10** 1 **Dorset Gift**[96] 2125 3-8-5 46 oh1........ MichaelKenneally(7) 4 |
(Michael Bell) *stdd s: hld up off pce towards rr: rdn and effrt 3f out: no hdwy: n.d* **20/1** |
5034 **11** hd **Jenny Sparks**[6] 5106 3-8-9 46 oh1........ CharlesBishop(3) 12 |
(Mick Channon) *racd towards stands' side: in tch in midfield: rdn 3f out: sn btn: bhd over 1f out* **8/1** |
-006 **12** 1 ¾ **Oriental Dream (IRE)**[75] 2741 3-8-7 46 oh1........ ShelleyBirkett(5) 7 |
(Nigel Tinkler) *chsd ldrs tl 1/2-way: sn lost pl: bhd fnl f: t.o* **25/1** |
5466 **13** 2 ¼ **Spinning Cobblers**[13] 4813 3-9-7 55........(p) AndreaAtzeni 13 |
(Stuart Williams) *racd towards stands' side: in tch in midfield: effrt 3f out: edgd lft and btn 2f out: wl bhd and eased ins fnl f: t.o* **11/4**[1] |

1m 27.93s (1.33) **Going Correction** +0.30s/f (Good) — **13** Ran SP% **116.9**
Speed ratings (Par 98): **104,102,92,87,84 77,75,74,72,70 70,68,66**
CSF £16.45 CT £261.65 TOTE £4.70: £1.50, £2.70, £4.20; EX 22.20 Trifecta £219.10.
**Owner** Highgrounds Partnership **Bred** Executive Bloodlines **Trained** Newmarket, Suffolk

**FOCUS**
A weak handicap and hard to rate too positively.

T/Plt: £10.90 to a £1 stake. Pool of £46143.45 - 3087.99 winning tickets. T/Qpdt: £7.00 to a £1 stake. Pool of £6251.72 - 653.50 winning ticket. SP

5322 - 5328a (Foreign Racing) - See Raceform Interactive

## 4644 VICHY

Wednesday, August 13

**OFFICIAL GOING: Turf: heavy**

### 5329a GRAND PRIX DE L'UNION DES VIGNERONS (CONDITIONS) (2YO) (TURF) 7f

**3:40** (12:00) 2-Y-O **£11,250** (£4,500; £3,375; £2,250; £1,125)

RPR

1 **Caprior Bere (FR)**[26] 4416 2-8-11 0 ........................ IoritzMendizabal 3 85
(K R Burke) *tk v t.k.h: hld up towards rr but in tch: last and rdn 1 1/2f out: hdwy on outer appr fnl f: r.o u.p to ld last 150yds: hld on gamely* **43/10**[3]

2 1½ **Malandrino (FR)**[66] 2-9-0 0 ........................ TonyPiccone 1 84
(B Goudot, France) *fin 3rd: plcd 2nd* **51/10**

3 nse **Peewave (FR)** 2-9-0 0 ........................ TheoBachelot 6 84
(W Hefter, Germany) *fin 4th: plcd 3rd* **4/1**[2]

4 nse **Cheeky Lady (FR)**[33] 2-8-10 0 ........................ StephaneRichardot 5 80
(T Larriviere, France) *fin 2nd: disqualified and plcd 4th* **157/10**

5 2 **Royal Style (FR)**[11] 4933 2-9-0 0 ........................ AntoineHamelin 4 78
(Matthieu Palussiere, France) **13/10**[1]

6 snk **Albertochop (FR)**[34] 2-9-0 0 ........................ Pierre-CharlesBoudot 2 78
(X Betron, France) **79/10**

7 10 **Ma Ptite Sarah (FR)**[31] 4248 2-8-10 0 ........................ SebastienMaillot 7 47
(E Caroux, France) **29/1**

1m 35.32s (95.32) 7 Ran **SP% 119.3**
PARI-MUTUEL (all including 1 euro stake): WIN 5.30; PLACE 3.60, 2.70; SF 48.10.
**Owner** Mrs Elaine M Burke **Bred** S N C Regnier & San Gabriel **Trained** Middleham Moor, N Yorks

### 5330a PRIX MAURICE DE NEXON (CONDITIONS) (4YO+) (TURF) 1m 4f

**7:25** (12:00) 4-Y-O+ **£11,250** (£4,500; £3,375; £2,250; £1,125)

RPR

1 **Storm River (FR)**[36] 5-8-13 0 ow2 ........................ Pierre-CharlesBoudot 7 101
(J Phelippon, France) **5/2**[2]

2 nk **Skyline Du Casse (FR)**[54] 8-8-11 0 ........................ Jean-BaptisteHamel 2 99
(F Plouganou, France) **23/5**[3]

3 2 **Tara River (FR)**[23] 4509 5-9-2 0 ........................ FranckBlondel 3 101
(F Rossi, France) **21/10**[1]

4 1½ **Dartagnan D'Azur (FR)**[23] 4509 5-9-6 0 ........................ TheoBachelot 6 102
(W Hefter, Germany) **5/1**

5 1¼ **Stepping Ahead (FR)**[79] 2618 4-9-2 0 ........................ AntoineHamelin 1 96
(K R Burke) *t.k.h: led: 3 l clr 2 1/2f out: rdn and hdd 1 1/2f out: outpcd by ldrs appr fnl f: kpt on at same pce* **49/10**

6 2½ **Lilienthal (IRE)**[1389] 7-8-11 0 ........................ AlexisBadel 4 87
(S Kobayashi, France) **165/10**

7 20 **Rocket Dive (JPN)** 7-8-11 0 ........................ SebastienMaillot 5 55
(S Kobayashi, France) **41/1**

2m 43.6s (8.00) 7 Ran **SP% 120.4**
PARI-MUTUEL (all including 1 euro stake): WIN 3.50; PLACE 2.10, 2.20; SF 13.40.
**Owner** Ecurie Foret Jaune & J Phelippon **Bred** Ecurie Biraben **Trained** France

## 5295 BEVERLEY (R-H)

Thursday, August 14

**OFFICIAL GOING: Good changing to good to soft after race 5 (4.45) changing to heavy after race 6 (5.50)**

Rail around bottom bend moved and races on Round course increased by 19yds. Rail movement continues into home straight and false rail ends at 2.5f.
Wind: Moderate against Weather: Sunny periods

### 5331 DOWNLOAD THE FREE RACING UK APP (S) H'CAP 1m 4f 16y

**2:30** (2:30) (Class 6) (0-60,60) 3-Y-O+ **£2,264** (£673; £336; £168) **Stalls** Low

Form RPR

50-0 1 **Moon Over Rio (IRE)**[68] 1303 3-8-12 55 ........................ AndrewElliott 5 63
(Ben Haslam) *hld up: hdwy on outer over 2f out: rdn along wl over 1f out: styd on strly ins fnl f: led nr line* **9/1**

0-00 2 hd **Different Scenario**[24] 4495 3-8-3 46 ........................ DuranFentiman 8 53
(Mel Brittain) *hld up in rr: hdwy on wd outside over 2f out: rdn wl over 1f out: drvn and styd on wl fnl f* **33/1**

5552 3 nse **Impeccability**[16] 4749 4-9-0 46 ........................(p) FrannyNorton 9 53
(John Mackie) *trckd ldrs: hdwy to chse ldng pair over 2f out: rdn to ld jst over 1f out: drvn and edgd lft ins fnl f: hdd and no ex nr line* **3/1**[1]

0051 4 3 **Mazij**[16] 4749 6-9-0 46 ........................ PaulMulrennan 2 48
(Peter Hiatt) *led: pushed along and jnd wl over 2f out: rdn wl over 1f out: drvn and hdd appr fnl f: one pce* **3/1**[1]

4026 5 1 **Yorksters Prince (IRE)**[15] 4792 7-9-6 57 ........................(b) JordanNason(5) 7 58
(Marjorie Fife) *trckd ldr: effrt and cl up wl over 2f out: rdn wl over 1f out: wknd ent fnl f* **8/1**

0054 6 1 **Destiny Blue (IRE)**[15] 4792 7-10-0 60 ........................(t) BenCurtis 3 59
(Brian Ellison) *dwlt and in rr: hdwy on inner 2f out: sn rdn and no imp fnl f* **6/1**[3]

3565 7 2 **Quite Sparky**[16] 4755 7-9-4 55 ........................(p) JackGarritty(5) 1 51
(Mike Sowersby) *trckd ldrs on inner: effrt over 2f out: sn rdn and wknd over 1f out* **4/1**[2]

0600 8 3¼ **Jebulani**[23] 4522 4-9-0 46 ........................(p) PJMcDonald 4 37
(Barry Murtagh) *chsd ldrs: rdn along wl over 2f out: sn wknd* **16/1**

2m 39.42s (-0.38) **Going Correction** -0.125s/f (Firm)
**WFA** 3 from 4yo+ 11lb 8 Ran **SP% 114.2**
Speed ratings (Par 101): **96,95,95,93,93 92,91,89**
CSF £236.44 CT £1095.80 TOTE £10.10: £1.90, £7.20, £2.30; EX 154.90 Trifecta £1460.60.There was no bid for the winner.
**Owner** Blue Lion Racing IX **Bred** Glending Bloodstock **Trained** Middleham Moor, N Yorks
■ Stewards' Enquiry : Andrew Elliott two-day ban: used whip above permitted level (Aug 28-29)

**FOCUS**
A weak selling handicap.

### 5332 EBF WATCH RACING REPLAYS ON RACING UK MAIDEN FILLIES' STKS (BOBIS RACE) 5f

**3:00** (3:01) (Class 5) 2-Y-O **£3,881** (£1,155; £577; £288) **Stalls** Low

Form RPR

1 **Youcouldntmakeitup (IRE)** 2-9-0 0 ........................ DavidAllan 4 75
(Tim Easterby) *mde all: rdn clr ent fnl f: hld on wl towards fin* **14/1**

2 hd **Beau Eile (IRE)** 2-9-0 0 ........................ GrahamGibbons 2 74+
(David Barron) *trckd ldrs on inner: hdwy 2f out: swtchd lft and effrt over 1f out: rdn and edgd lft ins fnl f: kpt on wl towards fin: jst hld* **6/1**[3]

02 3 3½ **Escrick (IRE)**[9] 4999 2-9-0 0 ........................ PaulMulrennan 10 66+
(David Simcock) *trckd ldrs: hdwy wl over 1f out: effrt whn n.m.r and swtchd lft ent fnl f: rdn and kpt on towards fin* **7/2**[2]

4 4 hd **Brindle**[27] 4389 2-9-0 0 ........................ TonyHamilton 7 60
(Richard Fahey) *sn prom: cl up 1/2-way: rdn wl over 1f out: edgd rt and one pce ent fnl f* **1/1**[1]

5 1¾ **Mallymkun** 2-9-0 0 ........................ PJMcDonald 8 54
(K R Burke) *dwlt and in rr: hdwy over 2f out: chsd ldrs and swtchd rt to inner jst over 1f out: sn rdn and no imp fnl f* **16/1**

6 ½ **Taffetta** 2-9-0 0 ........................ BarryMcHugh 1 52
(Tony Coyle) *in tch: hdwy 2f out: rdn along and n.m.r whn swtchd rt over 1f out: kpt on fnl f* **12/1**

36 7 2¼ **Sweet Missi (IRE)**[7] 5086 2-9-0 0 ........................ BenCurtis 11 44
(Brian Ellison) *in tch: rdn along over 2f out: sn wknd* **16/1**

05 8 ½ **Magh Meall**[20] 4624 2-9-0 0 ........................ AdrianNicholls 6 42
(David Nicholls) *ckose up: rdn along 2f out: drvn and wknd appr fnl f* **33/1**

9 18 **Cirtee** 2-9-0 0 ........................[1] JamesSullivan 3
(Tim Etherington) *sn outpcd and bhd fr 1/2-way* **66/1**

1m 2.91s (-0.59) **Going Correction** -0.125s/f (Firm) 9 Ran **SP% 117.1**
Speed ratings (Par 91): **99,98,93,92,89 89,85,84,55**
CSF £96.59 TOTE £12.50: £3.90, £2.50, £1.30; EX 70.30 Trifecta £449.60.
**Owner** Reality Partnerships III **Bred** Patrick J Moloney **Trained** Great Habton, N Yorks

**FOCUS**
A moderate 2yo maiden.

### 5333 BEVERLY GOLF CLUB 125TH ANNIVERSARY FILLIES' H'CAP 5f

**3:35** (3:36) (Class 5) (0-70,70) 3-Y-O+ **£3,234** (£962; £481; £240) **Stalls** Low

Form RPR

2223 1 **Margrets Gift**[7] 5080 3-9-1 64 ........................(p) DavidAllan 11 73
(Tim Easterby) *cl up: chal 2f out: rdn to ld over 1f out: drvn and hung rt to inner ins fnl f: kpt on* **7/1**[2]

1346 2 2¼ **Thornaby Princess**[12] 4890 3-9-3 66 ........................ RussKennemore 9 67
(Marjorie Fife) *midfield: pushed along and hdwy 2f out: swtchd rt and rdn over 1f out: ch whn n.m.r and sltly hmpd ins fnl f: kpt on* **10/1**

4600 3 nk **Madagascar Moll (IRE)**[12] 4891 3-8-5 61 ........................(v[1]) JoshDoyle(7) 1 61
(David O'Meara) *cl up: chal 2f out and ev ch: rdn over 1f out: drvn and ch whn n.m.r and sltly hmpd ins fnl f: kpt on same pce after* **12/1**

5336 4 1¼ **Slim Chance (IRE)**[2] 5265 5-8-12 65 ........................ RowanScott(7) 8 61
(Simon West) *dwlt and swtchd rt to inner s: in rr: hdwy 2f out: chsd ldrs whn n.m.r and swtchd lft jst over 1f out: kpt on fnl f: nrst fin* **7/1**[2]

5405 5 shd **Dark Opal (IRE)**[6] 5130 4-9-4 67 ........................ JoeyHaynes(3) 7 63
(John Weymes) *towards rr: hdwy 2f out: sn rdn: styd on fnl f: nrst fin* **11/1**

5423 6 2 **Nelson's Pride**[22] 4535 3-8-4 58 ........................(b) KevinStott(5) 13 46
(Kevin Ryan) *dwlt and swtchd rt s: bhd: hdwy wl over 1f out: sn rdn and styd on fnl f: nrst fin* **12/1**

-055 7 hd **Dusty Storm (IRE)**[20] 4630 4-9-10 70 ........................ GrahamGibbons 5 58
(Ed McMahon) *chsd ldrs: rdn wl over 1f out: hld whn n.m.r appr fnl f: wknd* **9/1**

60 8 1¼ **Six Wives**[41] 3920 7-8-13 64 ........................(p) MatthewHopkins(5) 6 48
(Scott Dixon) *led: rdn along over 2f out: drvn and hdd over 1f out: wknd* **15/2**[3]

1260 9 3¾ **Adiator**[25] 4471 6-9-5 65 ........................ AndrewElliott 12 35
(Neville Bycroft) *a in rr* **9/1**

0500 10 hd **Mayfield Girl (IRE)**[20] 4632 4-9-10 70 ........................ PJMcDonald 2 39
(Mel Brittain) *a towards rr* **11/4**[1]

6-00 11 1 **Dont Tell Nan**[12] 4891 3-8-2 51 oh4 ........................ FrannyNorton 3 16
(Derek Shaw) *prom: rdn along bef 1/2-way: sn lost pl and bhd* **33/1**

-040 12 1 **Jenny Twigg**[20] 4629 4-8-5 51 oh6 ........................ DuranFentiman 10 13
(Chris Fairhurst) *a in rr* **66/1**

1m 2.31s (-1.19) **Going Correction** -0.125s/f (Firm)
**WFA** 3 from 4yo+ 3lb 12 Ran **SP% 120.7**
Speed ratings (Par 100): **104,100,99,97,97 94,94,92,86,85 84,82**
CSF £76.68 CT £850.20 TOTE £6.10: £1.90, £3.90, £4.10; EX 75.00 Trifecta £1260.80.
**Owner** Margaret's Partnership **Bred** Mrs M Holdcroft And Mrs M Forsyth **Trained** Great Habton, N Yorks

**FOCUS**
Not the worst race for the class.

### 5334 SCULPTURE TO WEAR EQUESTRIAN JEWELLERY H'CAP 2m 35y

**4:10** (4:10) (Class 4) (0-85,85) 3-Y-O+ **£6,469** (£1,925; £962; £481) **Stalls** Low

Form RPR

1155 1 **Spice Fair**[20] 4606 7-9-11 82 ........................ LiamKeniry 3 91
(Mark Usher) *dwlt and in rr: hdwy over 3f out: chsd clr ldr 2f out: sn rdn: styd on strly fnl f: led last 50yds* **12/1**

0064 2 2 **Be Perfect (USA)**[6] 5144 5-9-12 83 ........................ AdrianNicholls 1 90
(David Nicholls) *led: pushed clr 3f out: rdn along wl over 1f out: drvn ins fnl f: hdd and no ex last 50yds* **8/1**

6221 3 10 **Kirkman (IRE)**[24] 4497 3-7-11 72 oh2 ........................ JoeyHaynes(3) 9 67
(James Bethell) *trckd ldrs: hdwy 3f out: sn chsng ldr: rdn along over 2f out: sn drvn and one pce* **9/4**[2]

0463 4 ½ **Bowdler's Magic**[19] 4662 7-9-2 73 ........................(t) RoystonFfrench 6 67
(David Thompson) *in tch: hdwy over 3f out: rdn along over 2f out: plugged on appr fnl f* **25/1**

5322 5 1¾ **Beat The Tide**[13] 4874 4-9-6 77 ........................(p) PaulMulrennan 5 69
(Michael Dods) *hld up in tch: hdwy over 4f out: rdn along 3f out: drvn 2f out: sn one pce* **5/1**[3]

14-2 6 3¼ **Enchanted Garden**[26] 3240 6-8-11 68 ........................ TomEaves 7 56
(Malcolm Jefferson) *trckd ldr: cl up 5f out: rdn along 3f out: sn drvn and wknd* **2/1**[1]

000 7 1 **Agreement (IRE)**[33] 4217 4-9-12 83 ........................ IanBrennan 4 70
(John Quinn) *trckd ldrs on inner: pushed along 4f out: rdn over 3f out: sn wknd* **25/1**

000 **8** 2 3/4 **Waterclock (IRE)**[47] 3717 5-10-0 85........................(b1) RussKennemore 8 69
(Jedd O'Keeffe) *trckd ldrs: hdwy on outer 1/2-way: chsd ldr 3f out: sn rdn along and wknd fnl 2f* **14/1**

3m 35.38s (-4.42) **Going Correction** -0.125s/f (Firm)
**WFA** 3 from 4yo+ 15lb **8** Ran SP% **113.9**
Speed ratings (Par 105): **106,105,100,99,98 97,96,95**
CSF £101.81 CT £294.41 TOTE £13.20: £3.10, £2.20, £1.10; EX 127.90 Trifecta £573.40.
**Owner** Saxon House Racing **Bred** Mrs D Hughes **Trained** Upper Lambourn, Berks

**FOCUS**
A competitive-looking staying event.

## 5335 YORKSHIRE AIR AMBULANCE NURSERY H'CAP 7f 100y
**4:45** (4:46) (Class 5) (0-75,74) 2-Y-O **£3,234** (£962; £481; £240) **Stalls** Low

Form RPR
542 **1** **Abbey Angel (IRE)**[20] 4626 2-9-7 74........................ TonyHamilton 4 83+
(Richard Fahey) *trckd ldrs: hdwy over 2f out: chal over 1f out: rdn to ld and hung rt ent fnl f: drvn out* **2/1**[1]

0260 **2** 2 1/2 **Playboy Bay**[19] 4659 2-8-12 65........................ SamHitchcott 5 68
(Mick Channon) *towards rr: swtchd wd wl over 1f out: sn rdn: styd on wl fnl f: nt rch wnr* **16/1**

0534 **3** 1 **Fazenda's Girl**[13] 4870 2-8-0 53........................(b) JamesSullivan 13 53
(Michael Easterby) *sn led: rdn along over 2f out: drvn over 1f out: hdd ent fnl f: kpt on same pce* **33/1**

5433 **4** 3/4 **Grand Proposal**[12] 4897 2-9-0 72........................ ShaneGray(5) 7 70
(Kevin Ryan) *trckd ldrs: hdwy over 2f out: rdn over 1f out: kpt on same pce fnl f* **11/2**[3]

033 **5** 1 1/4 **Twin Turbo (IRE)**[50] 3569 2-9-3 70........................ FrannyNorton 6 65
(Mark Johnston) *trckd ldr: hdwy and cl up wl over 2f out: rdn and edgd lft wl over 1f out: sn drvn and btn* **4/1**[2]

0331 **6** 1 1/2 **Summer Stroll (IRE)**[13] 4870 2-8-12 68........................ SamJames(3) 2 59
(David O'Meara) *midfield: effrt and sme hdwy over 2f out: sn rdn and no imp* **8/1**

0605 **7** 1/2 **Secret Of Dubai**[29] 4313 2-8-2 55 ow2........................ BenCurtis 8 45
(Brian Ellison) *chsd ldrs: hdwy on outer and cl up 4f out: rdn along wl over 2f out: sn drvn and wknd wl over 1f out* **33/1**

030 **8** 7 **Cisco Boy**[27] 4416 2-9-1 68........................ DavidAllan 10 41
(Tim Easterby) *nvr bttr than midfield* **16/1**

6013 **9** 4 **Mr Shekells**[20] 4619 2-8-6 64........................ DannyBrock(5) 3 27
(Philip McBride) *chsd ldrs: hdwy on inner 3f out: rdn along over 2f out: sn wknd* **4/1**[2]

000 **10** 2 **Chollima**[33] 4216 2-8-0 53 oh3........................(b1) DuranFentiman 1 11
(Tim Easterby) *a in rr: outpcd and bhd fr 3f out* **25/1**

066 **11** 1 1/2 **Yukos Flyer (IRE)**[23] 4510 2-7-9 53 oh2........................ JackGarritty(5) 9 7
(Richard Fahey) *s.i.s: a in rr: bhd fnl 3f* **25/1**

1m 36.79s (2.99) **Going Correction** +0.325s/f (Good) **11** Ran SP% **125.2**
Speed ratings (Par 94): **95,92,91,90,88 87,86,78,73,71 69**
CSF £40.36 CT £868.92 TOTE £3.70: £1.60, £5.10, £6.50; EX 48.40 Trifecta £862.10.
**Owner** Mrs H Steel **Bred** Paul Hyland **Trained** Musley Bank, N Yorks

**FOCUS**
An interesting contest run in driving rain.

## 5336 BET AND WATCH WITH RACINGUK'S APP H'CAP 1m 100y
**5:15** (5:15) (Class 5) (0-70,76) 3-Y-O **£3,234** (£962; £481; £240) **Stalls** Low

Form RPR
-621 **1** **Strictly Glitz (IRE)**[3] 5245 3-8-8 62 6ex........................ JoeDoyle(5) 7 73
(John Quinn) *trckd ldrs: hdwy 1/2-way: led wl over 2f out: rdn clr wl over 1f out: styd on strly* **13/8**[1]

0-21 **2** 3 1/2 **Daisy Boy (IRE)**[15] 4789 3-9-3 66........................ GrahamGibbons 1 69
(Stuart Williams) *chsd ldng pair: effrt over 2f out: rdn to chse wnr over 1f out: drvn and no imp fnl f* **11/4**[2]

-350 **3** 2 1/2 **White Rose Runner**[101] 2020 3-8-13 62........................ DavidAllan 3 59
(Mel Brittain) *prom: cl up 1/2-way: rdn along over 2f out: drvn wl over 1f out and kpt on one pce* **16/1**

4661 **4** 5 **Shimba Hills**[9] 5004 3-9-10 76 6ex........................ CharlesBishop(3) 6 62
(Mick Channon) *sn led: rdn along and hdd wl over 2f out: sn drvn wl over 1f out: wknd* **7/2**[3]

-065 **5** 5 **Saranta**[17] 4728 3-8-12 64........................[1] GeorgeChaloner(3) 5 38
(Richard Fahey) *towards rr: effrt and sme hdwy on outer over 2f out: sn rdn and nvr a factor* **12/1**

0003 **6** 15 **Tawan**[51] 3543 3-8-2 54 oh4 ow3........................(b) ConnorBeasley(3) 2
(Brian Rothwell) *a in rr: bhd and eased fnl 2f* **50/1**

-000 **7** 6 **L'Artiste (IRE)**[40] 3946 3-9-1 64........................ PhillipMakin 4
(John Quinn) *a in rr: bhd and eased fnl 2f* **12/1**

1m 56.59s (8.99) **Going Correction** +0.775s/f (Yiel) **7** Ran SP% **110.2**
Speed ratings (Par 100): **86,82,80,75,70 55,49**
CSF £5.72 TOTE £2.80: £1.40, £2.80; EX 6.70 Trifecta £52.20.
**Owner** Nigel S Cooper **Bred** Lynn Lodge Stud **Trained** Settrington, N Yorks

**FOCUS**
A moderate handicap, run on deteriorating ground.

## 5337 WHITE ROSE SADDLERY AMATEUR RIDERS' H'CAP 1m 100y
**5:50** (5:50) (Class 6) (0-65,64) 4-Y-O+ **£2,183** (£677; £338; £169) **Stalls** Low

Form RPR
-340 **1** **Think**[63] 3155 7-9-9 45........................(p) MrHAABannister 12 51
(Clive Mulhall) *in tch: hdwy to trck ldrs over 3f out: effrt to chse clr ldr wl over 1f out: sn rdn: styd on wl to ld last 110yds* **16/1**

66-3 **2** 3/4 **William Hogarth**[101] 1284 9-9-4 45........................ MissLWilson(5) 10 50
(Brian Ellison) *towards rr: hdwy over 2f out: rdn wl over 1f out: styd on strly fnl f: nrst fin* **5/1**[2]

0156 **3** hd **Tanawar (IRE)**[20] 4620 4-10-12 62........................(b) MissSBrotherton 11 66
(Ruth Carr) *plld hrd: cl up: led over 6f out and sn wl clr: rdn over 1f out: hdd and no ex last 110yds* **4/1**[1]

U016 **4** hd **Iceblast**[10] 4961 6-10-11 64........................(b) MissJoannaMason(3) 4 68
(Michael Easterby) *towards rr: hdwy over 2f out: rdn wl over 1f out: styd on wl fnl f: nrst fin* **6/1**[3]

-005 **5** nk **Rosy Ryan (IRE)**[10] 4958 4-9-6 45........................ MrTHamilton(3) 9 48
(Tina Jackson) *chsd ldrs: rdn along 3f out: drvn wl over 1f out: kpt on same pce u.p appr fnl f* **33/1**

3540 **6** 1 **Zainda (IRE)**[7] 5103 4-9-7 50........................ MrAFrench(7) 7 51
(Paul Midgley) *t.k.h: led 1 1/2f: chsd clr ldr: rdn along over 2f out: drvn wl over 1f out: kpt on same pce* **16/1**

0553 **7** 3/4 **Edas**[10] 4958 12-9-10 49........................ MissHCuthbert(3) 6 48
(Thomas Cuthbert) *towards rr: hdwy on inner over 2f out: rdn along wl over 1f out: kpt on same pce fnl f* **6/1**[3]

6503 **8** 3/4 **Kheskianto (IRE)**[16] 4755 8-9-9 45........................(t) MissAliceMills 5 42
(Michael Chapman) *trckd ldrs: hdwy on inner to chse ldng pair over 3f out: rdn along over 2f out: drvn wl over 1f out: sn one pce* **9/1**

4600 **9** 1 **Graceful Act**[15] 4795 6-10-2 52........................ MissCWalton 8 47
(Ron Barr) *chsd ldrs: rdn along 3f out: sn drvn and plugged on one pce* **16/1**

3305 **10** 2 1/2 **Violent Velocity (IRE)**[23] 4517 11-10-1 58........................ MrOJPimlott(7) 1 47
(John Quinn) *a in rr* **4/1**[1]

5440 **11** 1 **Spokesperson (USA)**[10] 4958 6-9-9 45........................ MissADeniel 3 32
(Frederick Watson) *a towards rr* **16/1**

1m 58.65s (11.05) **Going Correction** +1.225s/f (Soft) **11** Ran SP% **121.7**
Speed ratings (Par 101): **93,92,92,91,91 90,89,89,88,85 84**
CSF £97.50 CT £331.43 TOTE £16.60: £3.20, £3.10, £2.10; EX 149.10 Trifecta £810.50.
**Owner** Mrs C M Mulhall & Carl Chapman **Bred** Mike Channon Bloodstock Ltd **Trained** Scarcroft, W Yorks

**FOCUS**
They finished in a heap here.
T/Jkpt: Not won. T/Plt: £247.80 to a £1 stake. Pool: £68,654.43 - 202.25 winning units. T/Qpdt: £45.90 to a £1 stake. Pool: £5218.05 - 84.10 winning units. JR

# 4149 CHEPSTOW (L-H)
Thursday, August 14

**OFFICIAL GOING: Soft (heavy in places in home straight)**
Wind: Light across Weather: Showers

## 5338 PORSCHE CENTRE BRISTOL LADY RIDERS' H'CAP (FOR LADY AMATEUR RIDERS) 1m 2f 36y
**5:55** (5:55) (Class 6) (0-65,65) 3-Y-O+ **£1,871** (£580; £290; £145) **Stalls** Low

Form RPR
5622 **1** **Aristocracy**[7] 5108 3-9-11 65........................ MissBHampson(5) 8 74
(Mick Channon) *chsd ldr 4f: remained handy: wnt 2nd again over 3f out: rdn to ld over 1f out: styd on* **5/2**[1]

0552 **2** 1 1/4 **Urban Space**[4] 5214 8-9-13 53........................(t) MissEJJones 5 60
(John Flint) *led over 4f: led again over 3f out: rdn and hdd over 1f out: ev ch ins fnl f: styd on same pce towards fin* **11/4**[2]

-135 **3** 3/4 **Belle Park**[43] 3853 7-10-0 59........................ MissMeganNicholls(5) 10 64
(Victor Dartnall) *s.i.s: hld up: hdwy over 3f out: rdn over 1f out: styd on: nt rch ldrs* **11/4**[2]

5204 **4** 5 **Flag Of Glory**[7] 5076 7-10-1 60........................ MissMEdden(5) 9 56
(Peter Hiatt) *prom: lost pl over 6f out: bhd over 4f out: r.o fr over 1f out* **16/1**

50-0 **5** 7 **Having A Ball**[40] 3973 10-9-3 48........................ MissPFuller(5) 2 30
(Geoffrey Deacon) *chsd ldrs: rdn over 3f out: wknd over 2f out* **25/1**

4325 **6** 2 1/4 **Cabuchon (GER)**[6] 5121 7-9-13 60........................(t) MissKFBegley(7) 7 38
(David Evans) *in tch: rdn over 4f out: wknd over 2f out* **16/1**

4540 **7** 5 **Petrify**[11] 4942 4-8-13 46........................(t) MissAWillmott(7) 6 15
(Bernard Llewellyn) *hld up in tch: racd keenly: jnd ldr over 6f out: led over 5f out: hdd over 3f out: wknd over 2f out* **12/1**[3]

0000 **8** 13 **Gifted Heir (IRE)**[15] 4797 10-8-12 45........................ MissSPeacock(7) 1
(Ray Peacock) *s.i.s: hld up: plld hrd: wknd 4f out* **66/1**

-646 **9** 8 **Gravitate**[39] 2916 5-9-13 60........................(t) MissFrancescaNimmo(7) 4
(Paul Webber) *prom: lost pl over 7f out: hdwy over 4f out: wknd over 3f out* **12/1**[3]

2m 17.13s (6.53) **Going Correction** +0.60s/f (Yiel)
**WFA** 3 from 4yo+ 9lb **9** Ran SP% **114.4**
Speed ratings (Par 101): **97,96,95,91,85 84,80,69,63**
CSF £9.46 CT £19.09 TOTE £4.30: £1.10, £2.10, £1.40; EX 13.40 Trifecta £31.10.
**Owner** M Channon **Bred** R F And S D Knipe **Trained** West Ilsley, Berks
■ Stewards' Enquiry : Miss K F Begley 11-day ban: used whip above permitted level (Sep 2,23,Oct 6,7,17,2425,29,Nov 19,25)

**FOCUS**
A weak start to the meeting but they went plenty quick enough in the conditions and the form may well prove strong for the level. The finish was dominated by those towards the head of the market. The winner earned a small personal-best rating, and the second and third were close to their C&D form from May.

## 5339 PARKWAY HOTEL CWMBRAN MEDIAN AUCTION MAIDEN STKS 1m 4f 23y
**6:25** (6:25) (Class 5) 3-5-Y-O **£2,911** (£866; £432; £216) **Stalls** Low

Form RPR
0 **1** **Madame Rouge**[10] 4966 3-8-11 0........................ SilvestreDeSousa 1 78
(David Evans) *led 2f: chsd ldrs: rdn to chse ldr 3f out: led over 1f out: styd on u.p* **10/1**[3]

000 **2** 1/2 **William Of Orange**[8] 5039 3-9-2 0........................ LukeMorris 3 82
(Sir Mark Prescott Bt) *chsd ldr: pushed along at various stages: led over 3f out: sn rdn: hdd over 1f out: ev ch ins fnl f: unable qck nr fin* **6/4**[2]

42 **3** 21 **Ronnie Rockcake**[24] 4500 4-9-13 0........................(p) TomQueally 5 51
(Ben Pauling) *rrd s: hdwy to ld 10f out: rdn and hdd over 3f out: sn wknd* **5/6**[1]

0/50 **4** nk **Swift Act**[45] 3778 5-9-5 46........................ MatthewCosham(3) 2 45
(Nikki Evans) *s.i.s: sn pushed along in rr: rdn and wknd over 3f out* **25/1**

0000 **5** 45 **Premier Jack's**[39] 4041 3-8-11 41........................ DanielMuscutt(5) 4
(Nikki Evans) *prom tl rdn and wknd over 4f out* **33/1**

2m 43.41s (4.41) **Going Correction** +0.60s/f (Yiel)
**WFA** 3 from 4yo+ 11lb **5** Ran SP% **110.4**
Speed ratings (Par 103): **109,108,94,94,64**
CSF £25.75 TOTE £9.50: £3.60, £1.40; EX 21.50 Trifecta £30.20.
**Owner** Wayne Clifford **Bred** Mrs S Clifford **Trained** Pandy, Monmouths
■ Stewards' Enquiry : Silvestre De Sousa two-day ban: used whip above permitted level (Aug 29-30)

**FOCUS**
One of the weakest maidens you'll find and it produced something of an upset. It's been rated cautiously.

## 5340 PORSCHE CENTRE CARDIFF FILLIES' H'CAP 1m 2f 36y
**6:55** (6:56) (Class 5) (0-75,72) 3-Y-O+ **£2,911** (£866; £432; £216) **Stalls** Low

Form RPR
2333 **1** **Loch Ma Naire (IRE)**[14] 4812 3-9-5 72........................(b) GrahamLee 4 83
(Ed Dunlop) *chsd ldrs: shkn up to ld over 1f out: styd on wl* **7/4**[1]

01 **2** 2 3/4 **Koliakhova (FR)**[38] 4026 3-9-5 72........................ TomQueally 3 78
(John Flint) *led: rdn and hdd over 1f out: styd on same pce ins fnl f* **7/1**

0-63 **3** 2 **Sealed With A Kiss**[24] 4500 3-9-2 69........................ FrederikTylicki 2 71
(James Fanshawe) *prom: rdn over 2f out: styd on same pce fnl f* **3/1**[2]

2044 **4** 3/4 **Lady Bayside**[34] 4153 6-9-11 69 OisinMurphy 7 70
(Malcolm Saunders) *chsd ldr tl rdn over 3f out: styd on same pce fr over 1f out* **9/2**[3]

343- **5** 4 1/2 **Society Pearl (IRE)**[349] 5959 4-9-10 68 SilvestreDeSousa 5 60
(David Evans) *hld up in tch: racd keenly: rdn and ev ch over 2f out: wknd fnl f* **16/1**

4536 **6** 2 1/4 **Affaire De Coeur**[33] 4211 3-9-5 72 LukeMorris 6 60
(David Simcock) *s.i.s and flashed tail early on: hld up: hdwy over 2f out: rdn: edgd lft and wknd over 1f out* **6/1**

2m 16.86s (6.26) **Going Correction** +0.60s/f (Yiel)
**WFA** 3 from 4yo+ 9lb 6 Ran SP% **112.2**
Speed ratings (Par 100): **98,95,94,93,90 88**
CSF £14.54 TOTE £2.60: £1.80, £2.30; EX 16.00 Trifecta £66.70.
**Owner** St Albans Bloodstock LLP **Bred** D D & Mrs J P Clee **Trained** Newmarket, Suffolk

**FOCUS**
Modest fillies' form. The runner-up has been rated to her French form.

## 5341 GET FREE BETS AT THEBOOKIESOFFERS.CO.UK H'CAP 2m 49y
**7:25** (7:26) (Class 5) (0-75,75) 3-Y-O+ **£2,911** (£866; £432; £216) **Stalls** Low

Form RPR
-431 **1** **Deauville Dancer (IRE)**[35] 4134 3-8-13 75 LukeMorris 2 87+
(Sir Mark Prescott Bt) *chsd ldr: rdn over 2f out: led over 1f out: edgd rt ins fnl f: styd on u.p* **1/1**[1]

/054 **2** 3/4 **Nafaath (IRE)**[26] 4423 8-9-12 73 GrahamLee 6 83
(Donald McCain) *led: rdn over 2f out: hdd over 1f out: styd on* **4/1**[2]

140- **3** 3 1/2 **Big Time Billy (IRE)**[369] 5288 8-9-6 74 (v) SeanBowen(7) 1 80
(Alan Phillips) *prom: rdn over 3f out: styd on same pce fr over 1f out* **20/1**

2523 **4** 3 1/4 **Our Folly**[14] 4818 6-9-5 73 (t) MikeyEnnis(7) 8 75
(Stuart Kittow) *hld up: hdwy over 3f out: sn rdn: wknd fnl f* **8/1**

123 **5** 15 **Ivanhoe**[26] 4441 4-9-9 70 (b[1]) DavidProbert 4 54
(Michael Blanshard) *chsd ldrs: rdn over 2f out: wknd over 1f out* **9/2**[3]

2040 **6** 12 **Arty Campbell (IRE)**[20] 4606 4-10-0 75 MartinLane 5 45
(Bernard Llewellyn) *hld up: rdn over 3f out: wknd and eased over 2f out* **14/1**

3m 50.15s (11.25) **Going Correction** +0.60s/f (Yiel)
**WFA** 3 from 4yo+ 15lb 6 Ran SP% **110.7**
Speed ratings (Par 103): **95,94,92,91,83 77**
CSF £5.08 CT £40.92 TOTE £2.10: £1.60, £2.00; EX 6.10 Trifecta £64.60.
**Owner** Suffolk Bloodstock **Bred** Ruskerne Ltd **Trained** Newmarket, Suffolk

**FOCUS**
A personal best from the winner. Bit fluid with some doubts over the rest, the second is rated up a bit on recent form (used to be lot better) and the third only 4lb off last year's Flat form.

## 5342 THEBOOKIESOFFERS.CO.UK FOR THE BEST BOOKIES OFFERS MAIDEN H'CAP 2m 2f
**7:55** (7:55) (Class 6) (0-65,64) 3-Y-O+ **£1,940** (£577; £288; £144) **Stalls** Low

Form RPR
5004 **1** **Medburn Cutler**[9] 5001 4-9-0 50 oh3 (p) SilvestreDeSousa 6 53
(Paul Henderson) *hld up: hdwy over 3f out: led over 2f out: sn rdn: styd on wl* **2/1**[1]

-335 **2** 4 **Fuzzy Logic (IRE)**[25] 3780 5-9-0 50 oh5 MartinLane 7 48
(Bernard Llewellyn) *chsd ldr tl led over 7f out: rdn and hdd over 2f out: styd on same pce fnl f* **11/4**[3]

00/0 **3** 2 1/4 **Scotsbrook Cloud**[32] 1740 9-8-13 54 NoelGarbutt(5) 2 49
(David Evans) *s.i.s: sn prom: rdn over 3f out: no ex fnl f: collapsed fatally after r* **6/1**

-466 **4** 34 **Wasabi (IRE)**[20] 4615 5-9-0 50 oh3 (p) GrahamLee 1 8
(John Berry) *trckd ldrs tl rdn over 3f out: sn wknd* **9/4**[2]

40/0 **5** 53 **Bogey Hole (IRE)**[45] 3780 5-9-0 50 oh5 DavidProbert 4
(Nikki Evans) *led: hdd over 7f out: wknd 4f out* **25/1**

4m 16.04s (12.44) **Going Correction** +0.60s/f (Yiel)
**WFA** 3 from 4yo+ 18lb 5 Ran SP% **108.9**
Speed ratings (Par 101): **96,94,93,78,54**
CSF £7.63 TOTE £2.50: £1.40, £1.80; EX 7.90 Trifecta £31.50.
**Owner** Eddie Evans **Bred** Eddie Evans **Trained** Whitsbury, Hants

**FOCUS**
An already weak affair was made even weaker by the absence of likely short-priced favourite Experimentalist. The winner probably didn't have to improve, and the runner-up is rated to this year's form.

## 5343 FREE CASINO BONUSES AT THEBOOKIESOFFERS.CO.UK H'CAP 1m 4f 23y
**8:25** (8:26) (Class 6) (0-60,59) 3-Y-O+ **£1,940** (£577; £288; £144) **Stalls** Low

Form RPR
6004 **1** **Last Echo (IRE)**[19] 4678 3-9-0 56 SilvestreDeSousa 2 67
(Ralph Beckett) *a.p: led over 2f out: rdn clr fr over 1f out: eased nr fin* **11/4**[2]

2140 **2** 5 **Captain Oats (IRE)**[30] 4279 11-9-9 59 RachealKneller(5) 6 63
(Pam Ford) *s.i.s: hld up: hdwy over 2f out: chsd wnr over 1f out: no imp ins fnl f* **12/1**

-364 **3** 7 **Acapulco Bay**[2] 5277 10-8-11 47 (p) AmyScott(5) 5 40
(Dai Burchell) *prom: led 10f out: rdn and hdd over 2f out: wknd fnl f* **10/1**

5465 **4** 2 **Telegraphy (USA)**[24] 4497 3-9-3 59 (b) GrahamLee 8 49
(Ed Dunlop) *hld up: rdn over 3f out: wknd over 2f out* **9/2**[3]

3343 **5** 3/4 **Fair Comment**[30] 4279 4-9-13 58 DavidProbert 1 47
(Michael Blanshard) *led 2f: chsd ldr: rdn and wknd 2f out* **10/1**

2652 **6** 27 **Master Dan**[7] 5101 3-9-2 58 DaleSwift 4 6
(James Given) *prom: rdn over 3f out: wknd over 2f out* **2/1**[1]

000 **7** 37 **Bison Grass**[12] 4911 4-9-9 54 (v[1]) LukeMorris 3
(Giles Bravery) *chsd ldrs: rdn over 3f out: wknd over 2f out* **10/1**

2m 45.69s (6.69) **Going Correction** +0.60s/f (Yiel)
**WFA** 3 from 4yo+ 11lb 7 Ran SP% **113.1**
Speed ratings (Par 101): **101,97,93,91,91 73,48**
CSF £33.46 CT £285.12 TOTE £3.50: £1.90, £4.60; EX 28.00 Trifecta £163.80.
**Owner** R A Farmiloe & Partner **Bred** Ballylinch Stud **Trained** Kimpton, Hants

**FOCUS**
A weak race. The winner had shown a bit of promise in early AW starts and is rated up on that, with the runner-up a bit off.
T/Plt: £63.70 to a £1 stake. Pool: £54,281.51 - 622.05 winning units. T/Qpdt: £15.80 to a £1 stake. Pool: £56,996.07 - 573.70 winning units. CR

# 5187 NEWMARKET (R-H)
Thursday, August 14

**OFFICIAL GOING: Good to soft changing to soft after race 1 (2.10)**
Stands side track used with Stalls on Far side except 10f: Centre.
Wind: light, behind Weather: heavy showers

## 5344 32RED MEDIAN AUCTION MAIDEN FILLIES' STKS (BOBIS RACE) 6f
**2:10** (2:10) (Class 4) 2-Y-O **£3,881** (£1,155; £577; £288) **Stalls** High

Form RPR
**1** **Luna Moon** 2-9-0 0 RyanMoore 9 72+
(Jeremy Noseda) *mde all: rdn over 1f out: drvn and hld on wl fnl f* **9/4**[1]

**2** nk **Cockney Island** 2-9-0 0 MartinHarley 3 71
(Philip McBride) *hld up in tch: rdn and hdwy over 1f out: chsd wnr 1f out: kpt on wl and grad clsng fnl 100yds* **8/1**

60 **3** 1 **Maybe Now Baby (IRE)**[42] 3888 2-9-0 0 JoeFanning 2 68
(David Simcock) *hld up in tch in last pair: rdn and effrt over 1f out: styd on wl fnl 100yds: wnt 3rd last strides* **33/1**

**4** hd **Poyle Jessica** 2-9-0 0 RichardKingscote 10 67+
(Ralph Beckett) *chsd ldrs: effrt over 1f out: 3rd whn rn green and edgd lft 1f out: styd on same pce fnl f: lost 3rd last strides* **11/2**[2]

00 **5** hd **Stone Roses (IRE)**[64] 3119 2-9-0 0 JamieSpencer 4 69+
(Michael Bell) *stdd s: hld up in rr: nt clr run over 1f out: swtchd rt ent fnl f: gap opened and wnt between rivals ins fnl f: nudged along and styd on wl fnl 150yds: nt clr run again and swtchd lft nr fin* **7/1**[3]

0 **6** 3/4 **Theydon Bois**[26] 4444 2-8-11 0 RobertTart(3) 1 64
(Peter Charalambous) *wnt rt s: sn rcvrd to chse ldrs: rdn over 1f out: styd on same pce u.p fnl f* **25/1**

**7** 2 1/4 **Matron** 2-9-0 0 ShaneKelly 6 57+
(James Fanshawe) *chsd ldr: rdn over 1f out: unable qck and lost 2nd 1f out: outpcd ins fnl f* **25/1**

0 **8** 1 1/2 **Avenue Du Monde (FR)**[15] 4781 2-9-0 0 SeanLevey 7 52
(Richard Hannon) *in tch towards rr: sme hdwy u.p ent fnl f: no imp fnl 150yds* **10/1**

**9** 2 1/2 **Gleaming Girl** 2-9-0 0 KierenFallon 12 44
(David Simcock) *rn green: chsd ldrs: pushed along over 2f out: outpcd and lost pl over 1f out: wknd fnl f* **8/1**

0 **10** 1/2 **Pudding (IRE)**[20] 4610 2-8-11 0 AshleyMorgan(3) 8 43
(Lady Cecil) *short of room leaving stalls: in tch: effrt u.p 2f out: no imp over 1f out: wknd 1f out* **66/1**

**11** 1/2 **Courier** 2-9-0 0 WilliamBuick 11 41
(Jeremy Noseda) *in tch in midfield: shkn up and effrt over 2f out: rdn and btn over 1f out: wknd 1f out* **8/1**

1m 18.24s (5.74) **Going Correction** +0.525s/f (Yiel) 11 Ran SP% **113.2**
Speed ratings (Par 93): **82,81,80,80,79 78,75,73,70,69 69**
CSF £18.87 TOTE £2.40: £1.20, £2.70, £4.70; EX 22.70 Trifecta £246.70.
**Owner** Newsells Park Stud **Bred** R Dollar, T Adams & G F Pemberton **Trained** Newmarket, Suffolk
■ Stewards' Enquiry : Joe Fanning one-day ban: careless riding (Aug 28)

**FOCUS**
Those who had run didn't set a high standard so it was no surprise the first two home were newcomers.

## 5345 LYNDSAY WICKS BIRTHDAY MEMORIAL H'CAP (JOCKEY CLUB GRASSROOTS FLAT MIDDLE DISTANCE QUALIFIER) 1m 2f
**2:40** (2:40) (Class 4) (0-85,85) 3-Y-O+ **£5,175** (£1,540; £769; £384) **Stalls** Centre

Form RPR
6240 **1** **Donny Rover (IRE)**[14] 4821 3-9-4 84 AndrewMullen 2 94
(Michael Appleby) *hld up in tch in last pair: rdn over 3f out: hdwy u.p to ld over 1f out: extended advantage 1f out: styd on wl: drvn out* **11/2**[3]

1-44 **2** 1 1/4 **Raven Ridge (IRE)**[90] 2303 3-9-4 84 JamieSpencer 3 92
(Michael Bell) *chsd ldrs: rdn over 3f out: swtchd rt over 1f out: hdwy u.p in 3rd 1f out: kpt on to go 2nd nr fin: no threat to wnr* **6/4**[1]

2431 **3** 1/2 **Excellent Puck (IRE)**[27] 4402 4-9-3 74 KierenFallon 5 81
(Shaun Lycett) *t.k.h: hld up in tch in midfield: rdn and effrt to chse ldr 3f out: ev ch and racing alone on far rail over 1f out: no ex ins fnl f: lost 2nd nr fin* **10/3**[2]

1216 **4** 4 **Bertie Moon**[10] 4985 4-9-7 78 WilliamBuick 4 77
(Geoffrey Deacon) *led: rdn ent fnl 2f: drvn and hdd over 1f out: wknd ins fnl f* **8/1**

1200 **5** 6 **Kastini**[27] 4400 4-9-5 76 (v) MartinHarley 7 64
(Denis Coakley) *hld up in tch in rr: clsd and travelling wl 3f out: effrt to press ldrs 2f out: fnd little for press over 1f out and sn btn: wknd* **16/1**

2-15 **6** 26 **Rasameel (USA)**[62] 3182 3-9-4 84 GeorgeBaker 9 23
(B W Hills) *chsd ldr tl 3f out: sn lost pl: bhd and virtually p.u ins fnl f: t.o* **11/2**[3]

2m 12.32s (6.82) **Going Correction** +0.525s/f (Yiel)
**WFA** 3 from 4yo 9lb 6 Ran SP% **110.8**
Speed ratings (Par 105): **93,92,91,88,83 62**
CSF £13.89 CT £29.41 TOTE £8.00: £2.90, £1.40; EX 14.60 Trifecta £48.20.
**Owner** C L Bacon **Bred** Lynn Lodge Stud **Trained** Danethorpe, Notts
■ Stewards' Enquiry : George Baker jockey said colt stopped quickly

**FOCUS**
An interesting little handicap run at what looked an even enough gallop thanks to habitual front-runner Bertie Moon.

## 5346 £10 FREE BET AT 32REDSPORT.COM H'CAP 7f
**3:15** (3:15) (Class 4) (0-85,84) 3-Y-O+ **£5,175** (£1,540; £769; £384) **Stalls** High

Form RPR
4430 **1** **Kakatosi**[15] 4783 7-9-10 82 ShaneKelly 4 91
(Mike Murphy) *stdd s and swtchd lft: t.k.h: sn in midfield: effrt 2f out: ev ch 1f out: led wl ins fnl f: r.o wl: rdn out* **14/1**

-600 **2** 1 **Obliterieght (IRE)**[15] 4783 5-9-5 77 GeorgeBaker 7 83
(William Knight) *bmpd s: sn stdd and hld up in rr: clsd to trck ldr 2f out: rdn and effrt 1f out: led fnl 100yds: sn hdd and one pce* **7/1**

2246 **3** 3/4 **Great Expectations**[22] 4537 6-9-3 75 (t) PaddyAspell 2 79
(J R Jenkins) *stdd s: hld up in last pair: clsd and nt clr run 2f out: hdwy u.p to chse ldrs and swtchd rt 1f out: kpt on to snatch 3rd last stride* **33/1**

-040 **4** shd **Bluegrass Blues (IRE)**[15] 4783 4-9-12 84 (b[1]) MartinHarley 9 88
(Paul Cole) *chsd ldrs tl led 2f out: sn drvn: hdd fnl 100yds: no ex* **11/1**

02 **5** 3 **Piceno (IRE)**[8] 5031 6-9-8 80 (p) KierenFallon 8 76
(Scott Dixon) *wnt rt s: chsd ldr tl led over 2f out: sn hdd: 5th and btn 1f out: wknd ins fnl f* **9/4**[1]

6 **6** *2 ¼* **Evident (IRE)**[4] 5213 4-9-3 75........................ WilliamBuick 1 66
(Jeremy Noseda) *in tch towards rr: rdn and effrt 2f out: no imp over 1f out: wknd fnl f* **9/2**[2]

0050 **7** *hd* **Lunar Deity**[13] 4866 5-8-11 76........................ AaronJones(7) 3 66
(Stuart Williams) *in tch in midfield: rdn and lost pl over 2f out: no threat to ldrs but plugged on fnl f* **33/1**

-340 **8** *½* **Regal Dan (IRE)**[137] 1191 4-9-6 83........................ CamHardie(5) 6 72
(Charles Hills) *t.k.h: wl in tch in midfield: rdn and unable qck over 2f out: wknd jsut over 1f out* **5/1**[3]

0520 **9** *1 ½* **Afkar (IRE)**[72] 2876 6-8-12 70........................ LiamJones 5 55
(Clive Brittain) *chsd ldrs: u.p over 3f out: wknd over 1f out* **20/1**

6054 **10** *15* **Spiritual Star (IRE)**[13] 4866 5-9-11 83........................(t) WilliamCarson 11 29
(Anthony Carson) *racd alone on far rail: led tl over 2f out: sn dropped out: wl bhd fnl f* **10/1**

1m 28.96s (3.26) **Going Correction** +0.525s/f (Yiel) 10 Ran SP% **112.9**
Speed ratings (Par 105): **102,100,100,99,96 93,93,93,91,74**
CSF £102.54 CT £3208.24 TOTE £17.70: £4.10, £1.80, £5.30; EX 143.40 Trifecta £3168.10 Part won..
**Owner** Robert E Tillett **Bred** T E Pocock **Trained** Westoning, Beds

**FOCUS**
The going description was changed to soft after the previous contest as the rain continued to fall. This wide open handicap was run at what appeared to be a sound gallop and that set things up for the hold-up horses.

## 5347 32RED CASINO MAIDEN STKS 1m 2f
**3:50** (3:53) (Class 5) 3-Y-O **£3,881** (£1,155; £577; £288) **Stalls** Centre

Form RPR

4 **1** **Long Cross**[26] 4435 3-9-5 0........................ WilliamBuick 5 98+
(John Gosden) *chsd ldr: wnt clr w ldr 3f out: upsides over 1f out: pushed into ld ins fnl f: eased nr fin: v easily* **4/7**[1]

52-4 **2** *¾* **Soviet Courage (IRE)**[27] 4407 3-9-5 76........................ JoeFanning 9 91
(William Haggas) *led: qcknd and wnt clr w wnr 3f out: rdn and jnd over 1f out: hdd ins fnl f: one pce and no ch w wnr after* **7/1**[3]

4- **3** *11* **Freemason**[338] 6277 3-9-5 0........................ RyanMoore 7 70
(Sir Michael Stoute) *t.k.h: chsd ldrs 8f out: 3rd and outpcd 3f out: wl btn after: plugged on to hold 3rd fnl f* **4/1**[2]

**4** *¾* **Peril** 3-9-5 0........................ GeorgeBaker 3 69
(Lady Cecil) *hld up in last pair: swtchd rt and hdwy 3f out: 4th and no ch w ldrs 2f out: plugged on* **25/1**

**5** *17* **Well Finished** 3-9-0 0........................ RichardKingscote 6 31
(Ralph Beckett) *in tch in midfield: rdn and immediately struggling whn gallop qcknd 3f out: sn lost tch* **20/1**

3 **6** *12* **Lake Alfred (USA)**[153] 951 3-9-5 0........................ MartinHarley 1 14
(Lady Cecil) *t.k.h early: chsd ldrs: lost pl and rdn over 3f out: sn lost tch: t.o fnl 2f* **12/1**

0 **7** *¾* **Medallero (USA)**[89] 2346 3-9-5 0........................ LiamJones 8 12
(Clive Brittain) *in tch in midfield: rdn 4f out: struggling over 3f out: sn lost tch and t.o fnl 2f* **66/1**

**8** *17* **Kirtling** 3-9-5 0........................ ShaneKelly 2
(Andi Brown) *t.k.h: hld up in tch in midfield: immediately lost tch whn gallop qcknd 3f out: sn t.o* **100/1**

3443 **P** **Ganges (IRE)**[12] 4886 3-9-5 76........................(v) SebSanders 4
(James Toller) *rdn along briefly leaving stalls: hld up in rr: hdwy into midfield 1/2-way: rdn 3f out: sn btn: no ch whn lost action and p.u over 1f out: dismntd* **14/1**

2m 10.96s (5.46) **Going Correction** +0.525s/f (Yiel) 9 Ran SP% **121.6**
Speed ratings (Par 100): **99,98,89,89,75 65,65,51,**
CSF £5.69 TOTE £1.80: £1.10, £1.80, £1.40; EX 6.90 Trifecta £19.30.
**Owner** Jaber Abdullah **Bred** Rabbah Bloodstock Limited **Trained** Newmarket, Suffolk

**FOCUS**
Probably not too much depth to this maiden and they finished well strung out.

## 5348 PREMIER LEAGUE BETTING AT 32REDSPORT.COM H'CAP (BOBIS RACE) 7f
**4:25** (4:25) (Class 2) (0-100,98) 3-Y-O **£12,938** (£3,850; £1,924; £962) **Stalls** High

Form RPR

1014 **1** **Glorious Empire (IRE)**[19] 4647 3-9-6 97........................ GeorgeBaker 4 106
(Ed Walker) *stdd s: hld up in last: effrt and clsd to chal 1f out: rdn and readily fnd enough to ld ins fnl f: pushed out: comf* **5/6**[1]

5302 **2** *1* **Crowdmania**[3] 5258 3-8-7 84........................ JoeFanning 2 90
(Mark Johnston) *chsd ldr: clsd and upsides ldr 2f out: rdn over 1f out: drvn to ld 1f out: hdd ins fnl f: one pce after* **11/2**

1214 **3** *1 ¼* **Captain Bob (IRE)**[40] 3980 3-8-12 89........................ WilliamBuick 3 92
(Charles Hills) *led: rdn wl over 1f out: drvn and hdd 1f out: no ex and one pce ins fnl f* **4/1**[2]

2560 **4** *nk* **Expert (IRE)**[12] 4895 3-9-2 98........................ CamHardie(5) 6 100
(Richard Hannon) *hld up in 3rd: stuck bhd rivals and forced to switch rt 1f out: styd on u.p fnl 100yds: no threat to wnr* **9/2**[3]

1m 28.16s (2.46) **Going Correction** +0.525s/f (Yiel) 4 Ran SP% **108.1**
Speed ratings (Par 106): **106,104,103,103**
CSF £5.65 TOTE £1.90; EX 6.10 Trifecta £10.00.
**Owner** Ms Judy Yap & Ms Salina Yang **Bred** Patrick Grogan **Trained** Newmarket, Suffolk

**FOCUS**
Just four runners but a good quality heat nonetheless and the gallop looked fairly even.

## 5349 32RED.COM H'CAP (BOBIS RACE) 1m
**4:55** (4:56) (Class 4) (0-85,83) 3-Y-O **£5,175** (£1,540; £769; £384) **Stalls** High

Form RPR

2110 **1** **Green Zone (IRE)**[20] 4631 3-9-0 71........................(p) HayleyTurner 2 79
(Nigel Tinkler) *travelled strly: chsd ldrs: clsd to join ldr 2f out: rdn ent fnl f: led fnl 100yds: r.o wl* **10/1**

-13 **2** *¾* **Zain Empire**[22] 4551 3-9-6 77........................ JamieSpencer 3 83
(Robert Cowell) *in tch: rdn 3f out: hdwy u.p to ld jst over 1f out: drifted lft 1f out: hdd fnl 100yds: r.o same pce after* **15/8**[1]

-311 **3** *2 ½* **Bombardment (USA)**[8] 5040 3-9-12 83 6ex........................ WilliamBuick 1 84
(Charlie Appleby) *racd towards centre: pressed ldr: rdn and ev ch 2f out tl no ex 1f out: wknd fnl 100yds* **10/3**[3]

6253 **4** *nk* **King Of Macedon (IRE)**[6] 5143 3-9-7 78........................(b) JoeFanning 5 78
(Mark Johnston) *led: rdn 2f out: drvn and hdd over 1f out: outpcd ins fnl f* **3/1**[2]

0132 **5** *3 ¼* **Kalon Brama (IRE)**[13] 4868 3-8-6 63........................ JimmyQuinn 4 55
(Peter Charalambous) *hld up in tch: swtchd rt and effrt u.p 2f out: no imp: wknd 1f out* **12/1**

10-6 **6** *3* **Zeshov (IRE)**[34] 4169 3-9-6 77........................(p) RyanMoore 6 62
(Jeremy Noseda) *in tch: rdn 2f out: sn struggling and outpcd: wknd ent fnl f* **8/1**

1m 43.25s (3.25) **Going Correction** +0.525s/f (Yiel) 6 Ran SP% **110.8**
Speed ratings (Par 102): **104,103,100,100,97 94**
CSF £28.48 TOTE £9.80: £3.80, £1.50; EX 41.20 Trifecta £87.20.
**Owner** Sunrise **Bred** Incense Partnership **Trained** Langton, N Yorks

**FOCUS**
A competitive little handicap.

## 5350 32RED ON THE APP STORE H'CAP (JOCKEY CLUB GRASSROOTS FLAT SPRINT SERIES QUALIFIER) 5f
**5:25** (5:25) (Class 4) (0-85,84) 3-Y-O+ **£5,175** (£1,540; £769; £384) **Stalls** High

Form RPR

3522 **1** **Secret Missile**[11] 4946 4-9-6 80........................(b) DougieCostello 3 89
(William Muir) *mde all: rdn over 1f out: styd on wl fnl f: rdn out* **13/2**[3]

2300 **2** *1 ¼* **Touch The Clouds**[13] 4862 3-8-9 72........................ PaddyAspell 2 76
(William Stone) *chsd wnr: rdn wl over 1f out: kpt on but a hld ins fnl f* **16/1**

0000 **3** *2 ½* **Apricot Sky**[16] 4762 4-9-7 81........................ WilliamBuick 9 77
(Henry Candy) *t.k.h: hld up in tch in midfield: rdn 2f out: wnt 3rd 1f out: no imp: wknd towards fin* **2/1**[2]

04 **4** *¾* **Pandar**[47] 3697 5-9-9 83........................ KierenFallon 5 76
(Milton Bradley) *in tch in last pair: rdn 1/2-way: sme hdwy 2f out: no imp over 1f out: plugged on same pce fnl f* **7/1**

5000 **5** *1* **Go Nani Go**[20] 4609 8-9-7 84........................ DeclanBates(3) 4 73
(Ed de Giles) *chsd ldrs: rdn and unable qck ent fnl f: wknd ins fnl f* **25/1**

2201 **6** *2 ¼* **Random Success (IRE)**[11] 4946 4-9-4 78 6ex........................ GeorgeBaker 6 59
(Roger Charlton) *stdd s: t.k.h: hld up in rr: rdn and no hdwy over 1f out: wknd 1f out* **6/4**[1]

1m 2.33s (3.23) **Going Correction** +0.80s/f (Soft)
**WFA** 3 from 4yo+ 3lb 6 Ran SP% **108.9**
Speed ratings (Par 105): **106,104,100,98,97 93**
CSF £84.07 CT £253.89 TOTE £7.40: £3.50, £5.40; EX 61.20 Trifecta £253.90.
**Owner** Muir Racing Partnership - Manchester **Bred** Whitsbury Manor Stud **Trained** Lambourn, Berks

**FOCUS**
Deteriorating conditions and it paid to be handy.
T/Plt: £89.70 to a £1 stake. Pool: £60,078.16 - 488.48 winning units. T/Qpdt: £57.00 to a £1 stake. Pool: £4483.59 - 58.20 winning units. SP

# 5309 SALISBURY (R-H)
Thursday, August 14

**OFFICIAL GOING: Good to firm (8.9)**
Rail erected 20ft off permanent far side rail throughout final 6.5f.
Wind: Moderate, against Weather: Changeable with occasional showers

## 5351 BET TOTEJACKPOT AT TOTESPORT.COM MAIDEN AUCTION STKS 6f 212y
**2:20** (2:21) (Class 5) 2-Y-O **£3,234** (£962; £481; £240) **Stalls** Centre

Form RPR

03 **1** **Sister Of Mercy (IRE)**[20] 4604 2-8-8 0........................ JamesDoyle 4 74+
(Roger Charlton) *hld up in midfield: prog 3f out: nt clr run briefly over 2f out: sn shkn up: tk 2nd 1f out: drvn and r.o to ld last strides* **8/11**[1]

6 **2** *nk* **Who'Shedude (IRE)**[26] 4429 2-9-2 0........................ SilvestreDeSousa 2 79
(Ralph Beckett) *led: drvn and hung lft wl over 1f out: hrd pressed after: kpt on wl but hdd last strides* **10/1**

**3** *3 ¼* **Cape Xenia** 2-8-7 0 ow1........................ FergusSweeney 9 61+
(Henry Candy) *hld up in midfield: prog to trck ldrs 2f out: outpcd fnl f* **11/2**[2]

**4** *nse* **Shalimah (IRE)** 2-8-13 0........................ RyanTate(3) 6 70+
(Clive Cox) *settled wl in rr: pushed along and prog over 2f out: shkn up and styd on fr over 1f out: nrly snatched 3rd* **25/1**

5 **5** *½* **Entente**[37] 4054 2-8-13 0........................ SteveDrowne 7 66
(Peter Makin) *prom: chsd ldr 3f out: chal and upsides over 1f out: lost 2nd and fdd fnl f* **12/1**

06 **6** *1* **Hillgrove Angel (IRE)**[14] 4809 2-8-13 0........................ JimmyFortune 12 63
(Brian Meehan) *trckd ldr 3f: losing pl whn squeezed out over 2f out: no ch after: kpt on again fnl f* **33/1**

**7** *hd* **Perceived** 2-8-4 0........................ DavidProbert 11 54+
(Henry Candy) *hld up in rr: pushed along fr 3f out: nvr on terms but kpt on steadily: nt disgracd* **20/1**

**8** *½* **Magical Thomas** 2-8-9 0........................ MartinDwyer 8 58
(Marcus Tregoning) *t.k.h: prom: chsd ldr 4f out to 3f out: shkn up and steadily lost pl* **25/1**

05 **9** *3 ¾* **Berkshire Beauty**[29] 4330 2-8-8 0........................ OisinMurphy 5 47
(Andrew Balding) *wl in tch: rdn over 2f out: wknd over 1f out* **8/1**[3]

66 **10** *6* **Duc De Seville (IRE)**[15] 4800 2-9-2 0........................ AdamKirby 3 39
(Clive Cox) *slowly away: a in last pair: bhd fnl 2f* **50/1**

**11** *23* **Destiny's Shadow (IRE)** 2-9-2 0........................ MartinLane 10
(George Baker) *slowly away: rn green: pushed up and sn prom: wknd 1/2-way: t.o* **50/1**

1m 30.22s (1.62) **Going Correction** +0.025s/f (Good) 11 Ran SP% **120.5**
Speed ratings (Par 94): **91,90,86,86,86 85,84,84,80,73 46**
CSF £8.35 TOTE £1.60: £1.10, £2.30, £2.00; EX 12.20 Trifecta £63.50.
**Owner** Michael Pescod **Bred** Celbridge Estates Ltd **Trained** Beckhampton, Wilts

**FOCUS**
An ordinary maiden auction to start with, but a couple took the eye.

## 5352 MARY WORT MEMORIAL MAIDEN STKS 6f 212y
**2:50** (2:51) (Class 5) 3-4-Y-O **£3,234** (£962; £481; £240) **Stalls** Centre

Form RPR

**1** **Taghreeb** 3-9-5 0........................ DaneO'Neill 6 76+
(Brian Meehan) *dwlt: chsd ldng pair after 3f: pushed along 3f out: rdn and clsd 2f out: narrow ld jst ins fnl f: edgd rt nr fin: jst hld on* **4/1**[2]

6625 **2** *nse* **Persian Bolt (USA)**[20] 4612 3-8-9 70........................(b) GeorgeDowning(5) 3 71
(Eve Johnson Houghton) *led and sn clr: rdn over 2f out: hdd jst ins fnl f: kpt on wl and nudged by rival nr fin: jst failed* **10/1**

342 **3** *shd* **Moonvoy**[9] 5007 3-9-0 0........................ RichardHughes 4 71
(Jeremy Noseda) *chsd clr ldr: pushed along to cl fr 3f out: chal over 1f out but making heavy weather of it: nt qckn ins fnl f: kpt on and n.m.r nr fin* **8/13**[1]


The Form Book, Raceform Ltd, Newbury, RG14 5SJ

-365 **4** *hd* **Song Of Norway**[15] 4802 3-9-0 72 (p) SteveDrowne 7 70
(Peter Makin) *t.k.h: hld up in last pair: prog fr 3f out: rdn over 1f out: chal ins fnl f: nt qckn nr fin* **5/1**[3]

0- **5** *8* **Canary Lad (IRE)**[402] 4121 3-9-5 0 GrahamLee 2 54
(Timothy Jarvis) *chsd clr ldng pair 3f: sn pushed along: no imp 2f out: fdd over 1f out* **40/1**

**6** *34* **Kitty Bequick** 3-9-0 0 JohnFahy 8
(Peter Hedger) *dwlt: t.k.h: hld up in last pair: wknd 1/2-way: t.o* **66/1**

1m 29.23s (0.63) **Going Correction** +0.025s/f (Good)
**WFA** 3 from 4yo 6lb **6** Ran SP% **111.6**
Speed ratings (Par 103): **97,96,96,96,87 48**
CSF £39.61 TOTE £5.20: £2.30, £3.50; EX 34.10 Trifecta £86.40.
**Owner** Hamdan Al Maktoum **Bred** Shadwell Estate Company Limited **Trained** Manton, Wilts

**FOCUS**
The rain started to come down before this race. A modest older-horse maiden, but a thrilling race with four in a line across the track half a furlong from home.

## 5353 £25 FREE BET AT TOTESPORT.COM EBF STALLIONS FILLIES' H'CAP 1m 4f
**3:25** (3:25) (Class 4) (0-80,77) 3-Y-0+ **£6,469** (£1,925; £962; £481) **Stalls** Low

Form RPR
6011 **1** **Sleeper**[8] 5036 3-8-12 72 6ex AndreaAtzeni 7 81
(Ralph Beckett) *trckd ldng trio: pushed along 4f out: rdn and responded wl fr 2f out to ld 1f out: hrd pressed last 100yds: hld on wl* **7/2**[3]

2364 **2** *nk* **Mystery Drama**[17] 4736 4-9-12 75 RichardHughes 5 84
(Alan King) *hld up in detached last: pushed along and no prog 3f out: plld out wd and drvn 2f out: clsd over 1f out to chal ins fnl f: styd on but jst hld* **5/1**

3541 **3** *1 ½* **Opera Fan (FR)**[10] 4979 3-8-12 72 6ex SilvestreDeSousa 1 78
(Mark Johnston) *led: urged along wl over 3f out: kpt on whn pressed fr over 2f out: hdd and one pce fnl f* **9/4**[2]

3522 **4** *nk* **Cosette (IRE)**[15] 4803 3-9-3 77 DaneO'Neill 2 83
(Henry Candy) *trckd ldr: chal fr 3f out: rdn and upsides over 1f out: nt qckn and lost 2nd fnl f* **2/1**[1]

3423 **5** *1* **Dark Amber**[27] 4417 4-9-4 67 GrahamLee 4 71
(Brendan Powell) *trckd ldng pair: appeared gng best fr over 2f out but trapped bhd rivals: swtchd ins over 1f out: nt clr run again and all ch gone* **12/1**

2m 36.93s (-1.07) **Going Correction** +0.025s/f (Good)
**WFA** 3 from 4yo 11lb **5** Ran SP% **110.7**
Speed ratings (Par 102): **104,103,102,102,101**
CSF £20.22 TOTE £4.00: £2.70, £2.00; EX 15.10 Trifecta £33.90.
**Owner** The Millennium Madness Partnership **Bred** Miss A Gibson Fleming **Trained** Kimpton, Hants

**FOCUS**
There wasn't much pace on early in this handicap, but another thrilling race with all five fillies within a length of each other passing the furlong pole.

## 5354 TOTEPOOL SOVEREIGN STKS (GROUP 3) (C&G) 1m
**4:00** (4:00) (Class 1) 3-Y-0+
**£42,532** (£16,125; £8,070; £4,020; £2,017; £1,012) **Stalls** Low

Form RPR
2-21 **1** **Captain Cat (IRE)**[118] 1558 5-9-0 107 JamesDoyle 9 115
(Roger Charlton) *hld up in 6th: gd prog on wd outside 2f out: swept into the ld jst over 1f out: pushed out: decisively* **11/2**

-544 **2** *2 ½* **Producer**[19] 4682 5-9-0 112 RichardHughes 4 109
(Richard Hannon) *trckd ldrs: rdn 2f out: tried to chal over 1f out: bmpd but tk 2nd fnl f: styd on but no ch w wnr* **4/1**[2]

6-03 **3** *2 ¼* **Rerouted (USA)**[26] 4425 6-9-0 112 PatCosgrave 10 104
(M F De Kock, South Africa) *hld up in 5th: clsd on ldrs 2f out: rdn to try to chal over 1f out: edgd rt and bmpd sn after: one pce* **14/1**

-152 **4** *1 ¼* **Yuften**[31] 4278 3-8-7 116 AndreaAtzeni 7 100
(William Haggas) *trckd ldr: led over 2f out: sn rdn: edgd lft over 1f out: nudged rival and hdd: sn btn* **6/4**[1]

-503 **5** *2 ¼* **Anjaal**[16] 4758 3-8-8 111 ow1 DaneO'Neill 11 96+
(Richard Hannon) *s.v.s: grad rcvrd and latched on to bk of field 1/2-way: tried to mount an effrt 2f out: no hdwy fnl f* **5/1**[3]

540 **6** *1 ¼* **Highland Colori (IRE)**[26] 4438 6-9-0 106 DavidProbert 3 93
(Andrew Balding) *led to over 2f out: pressed ldr to over 1f out: wknd* **12/1**

1111 **7** *1* **Genius Boy**[36] 4091 4-9-0 94 GrahamLee 6 91
(James Tate) *trckd ldng pair: rdn and tried to chal fr 2f out: losing pl whn hmpd jst over 1f out: nt rcvr* **12/1**

1m 41.45s (-2.05) **Going Correction** +0.025s/f (Good)
**WFA** 3 from 4yo+ 7lb **7** Ran SP% **114.1**
Speed ratings: **111,108,106,105,102 101,100**
CSF £27.46 TOTE £5.60: £2.30, £2.40; EX 32.80 Trifecta £202.00.
**Owner** Seasons Holidays **Bred** Azienda Agricola Mediterranea **Trained** Beckhampton, Wilts

**FOCUS**
Four non-runners took a little bit away from this Group 3, but it was still a classy contest and the winner was impressive. They appeared to go a solid pace.

## 5355 BILL GARNETT MEMORIAL FILLIES' H'CAP 6f
**4:35** (4:36) (Class 5) (0-70,71) 3-Y-0+ **£3,234** (£962; £481; £240) **Stalls** Low

Form RPR
413 **1** **Spiraea**[17] 4741 4-9-12 70 GrahamLee 1 79+
(Mark Rimell) *trckd ldng pair: rdn over 1f out: r.o wl fnl f to ld nr fin* **11/2**[3]

3450 **2** *nk* **Shilla (IRE)**[15] 4788 3-8-13 66 AmyScott[(5)] 6 73
(Henry Candy) *trckd ldr: led over 1f out: shkn up fnl f styd on but hdd nr fin* **8/1**

0324 **3** *2* **Lucky Di**[15] 4788 4-9-11 69 JohnFahy 8 71+
(Peter Hedger) *hld up in last pair: prog on inner 2f out: rdn over 1f out: styd on fnl f to take 3rd last strides* **10/1**

0365 **4** *nk* **Lady Phill**[14] 4811 4-9-7 65 RobertHavlin 2 66
(Michael Attwater) *led: rdn over 2f out: hdd over 1f out: one pce after* **16/1**

0660 **5** *2* **Tregereth (IRE)**[26] 4431 4-8-11 55 OisinMurphy 3 49
(Jonathan Portman) *chsd ldrs: drvn over 2f out: no imp over 1f out: one pce* **7/1**

0053 **6** *1 ¾* **Night Trade (IRE)**[9] 5000 7-8-9 53 (p) SteveDrowne 5 42
(Ronald Harris) *hld up: nvr beyond midfield: rdn and no prog 2f out: one pce after* **25/1**

1441 **7** *½* **Ada Lovelace**[7] 5070 4-9-13 71 6ex RichardHughes 4 58
(John Gallagher) *stdd s: hld up in midfeld: prog over 2f out: shkn up and nt qckn over 1f out: eased whn btn last 75yds* **9/4**[1]

4535 **8** *¾* **Catalinas Diamond (IRE)**[21] 4564 6-8-12 56 (t) DaneO'Neill 7 41
(Pat Murphy) *awkward s: hld up in last pair: shkn up and no ch whn nt clr run 1f out: no real prog* **16/1**

004 **9** *4 ½* **Jersey Brown (IRE)**[14] 4813 3-9-3 65 WilliamTwiston-Davies 10 34
(Mick Channon) *racd wd early: chsd ldrs: rdn and nt qckn 2f out: wknd qckly fnl f* **11/1**

5303 **10** *3 ½* **Koala Bear**[12] 4891 4-9-4 62 FrederikTylicki 9 21
(James Fanshawe) *t.k.h: hld up: nvr beyond midfield: wknd 2f out* **9/2**[2]

1m 14.44s (-0.36) **Going Correction** +0.025s/f (Good)
**WFA** 3 from 4yo+ 4lb **10** Ran SP% **121.0**
Speed ratings (Par 100): **103,102,99,99,96 94,93,92,86,82**
CSF £51.01 CT £445.82 TOTE £6.40: £2.10, £2.40, £3.40; EX 57.20 Trifecta £320.10.
**Owner** Mark Rimell **Bred** Coln Valley Stud **Trained** Leafield, Oxon

**FOCUS**
A modest fillies' sprint handicap in which those that raced up with the pace were favoured.

## 5356 KEVIN HALL & PAT BOAKES MEMORIAL H'CAP (BOBIS RACE) 1m 6f 21y
**5:05** (5:05) (Class 4) (0-85,83) 3-Y-0 **£4,851** (£1,443; £721; £360)

Form RPR
1023 **1** **Taws**[15] 4803 3-8-4 66 AndreaAtzeni 5 77
(Rod Millman) *trckd ldrs: shkn up 4f out: no prog in 5th 3f out: r.o fr 2f out: clsd to ld last 75yds* **9/2**[3]

0311 **2** *1* **Statsminister**[13] 4863 3-8-11 73 FergusSweeney 7 83
(Luke Dace) *led: drvn over 2f out: kpt on and looked like holding on over 1f out: hdd and outpcd last 75yds* **10/1**

1351 **3** *3 ¼* **Sebastian Beach (IRE)**[15] 4803 3-9-7 83 RichardHughes 6 88
(Richard Hannon) *t.k.h: prom: trckd ldr 1/2-way: rdn over 2f out: no imp over 1f out: one pce and lost 2nd fnl f* **11/4**[1]

2132 **4** *2 ¼* **Gallic Destiny (IRE)**[27] 4392 3-8-11 73 (p) JimmyFortune 3 75
(Andrew Balding) *trckd ldr to 1/2-way: rdn 3f out: disp 2nd again 2f out: wknd over 1f out* **8/1**

2222 **5** *2 ¼* **Button Down**[22] 4543 3-9-7 83 (p) JamesDoyle 4 82
(Lady Cecil) *hld up in last pair: rdn 3f out: no prog and btn 2f out: fdd* **3/1**[2]

0450 **6** *½* **Norse Star (IRE)**[12] 4893 3-8-13 75 (b[1]) PatDobbs 1 73
(Sylvester Kirk) *trckd ldrs: rdn 3f out: no prog 2f out: wknd over 1f out* **16/1**

6222 **7** *¾* **Mountain Kingdom (IRE)**[8] 5062 3-8-9 71 ChrisCatlin 2 68
(Sir Mark Prescott Bt) *slowly away: t.k.h in last pair: stuck bhd rivals fr 4f out to over 1f out: shkn up and no prog after* **9/2**[3]

3m 4.7s (-2.70) **Going Correction** +0.025s/f (Good) **7** Ran SP% **114.1**
Speed ratings (Par 102): **108,107,105,104,103 102,102**
CSF £46.59 TOTE £5.80: £2.90, £5.10; EX 51.50 Trifecta £278.20.
**Owner** R K Arrowsmith **Bred** Harts Farm Stud **Trained** Kentisbeare, Devon

**FOCUS**
This looked a decent staying event for 3yos, with the majority coming into it in good heart, and the form should work out. They appeared to go a solid pace and a pair of fillies dominated the finish.
T/Plt: £898.50 to a £1 stake. Pool: £57,543.09 - 46.75 winning units. T/Qpdt: £150.60 to a £1 stake. Pool: £4,183.10 - 20.55 winning units. JN

5357 - 5360a (Foreign Racing) - See Raceform Interactive

5111
# LEOPARDSTOWN (L-H)
Thursday, August 14

**OFFICIAL GOING: Soft**

## 5361a INVESCO PENSION CONSULTANTS DESMOND STKS (GROUP 3) 1m
**7:15** (7:16) 3-Y-0+ **£33,854** (£9,895; £4,687; £1,562)

RPR
**1** **Custom Cut (IRE)**[18] 4711 5-9-9 109 DanielTudhope 2 116+
(David O'Meara) *chsd ldrs: disp 4th 1/2-way: hdwy bhd ldrs appr st: rdn to ld over 1f out and sn drew clr: comf* **10/3**[2]

**2** *2 ¼* **Brendan Brackan (IRE)**[9] 5022 5-9-9 111 ColinKeane 4 111
(G M Lyons, Ire) *chsd ldrs: 3rd 1/2-way: impr into 2nd over 2f out and sn led: strly pressed and hdd u.p over 1f out: sn no ch w wnr in 2nd: kpt on same pce* **7/4**[1]

**3** *½* **Sruthan (IRE)**[89] 2338 4-9-12 111 ChrisHayes 9 113+
(P D Deegan, Ire) *w.w: last 1/2-way: hdwy in 8th over 2f out on outer to chse ldrs in 3rd wl ins fnl f: kpt on same pce towards fin wout ever troubling wnr* **13/2**[3]

**4** *1* **Palace (IRE)**[26] 4461 3-8-13 102 SeamieHeffernan 8 104
(A P O'Brien, Ire) *dwlt and settled towards rr: clsr in 6th 1/2-way: hdwy u.p into 4th 1 1/2f out: no imp on wnr in 5th ins fnl f: kpt on towards fin* **7/1**

**5** *½* **Harasiya (IRE)**[46] 3766 4-9-6 102 DeclanMcDonogh 7 103
(John M Oxx, Ire) *settled towards rr: 7th 1/2-way: hdwy appr st to chse ldrs in 3rd: rdn and no ex over 1f out: one pce ins fnl f and dropped to 5th nr fin* **20/1**

**6** *2 ½* **Qewy (IRE)**[67] 3041 4-9-9 104 NGMcCullagh 5 101
(John M Oxx, Ire) *in tch: 8th 1/2-way: rdn in rr under 3f out and no imp into st: kpt on into mod 6th ins fnl f: nrst fin* **16/1**

**7** *4 ½* **Ansgar (IRE)**[26] 4459 6-9-12 110 (t) PatSmullen 10 93
(Sabrina J Harty, Ire) *chsd ldrs: disp 4th 1/2-way: rdn in 5th and no ex under 3f out: wknd fnl 2f* **11/1**

**8** *11* **Leitir Mor (IRE)**[19] 4649 4-9-9 107 (tp) KevinManning 1 65
(J S Bolger, Ire) *trckd ldrs tl led narrowly bef 1/2-way: rdn into st and hdd 2f out: sn no ex u.p in 4th: wknd* **16/1**

**9** *16* **Great White Eagle (USA)**[57] 3352 3-9-2 101 JosephO'Brien 6 27
(A P O'Brien, Ire) *led tl hdd narrowly bef 1/2-way: rdn in cl 2nd under 3f out and sn no ex u.p: wknd and eased fnl 2f* **12/1**

1m 43.1s (1.90) **Going Correction** +0.625s/f (Yiel)
**WFA** 3 from 4yo+ 7lb **9** Ran SP% **117.8**
Speed ratings: **115,112,112,111,110 108,103,92,76**
CSF £9.78 TOTE £4.00: £1.40, £1.30, £2.10; DF 8.90 Trifecta £31.40.
**Owner** Gary Douglas & Pat Breslin **Bred** Moyglare Stud Farm Ltd **Trained** Nawton, N Yorks

**FOCUS**
The tough and improved Custom Cut made it a hat-trick of successes as he recorded a convincing success. He was held up off what was quite a strong pace in these conditions. Another clear personal best from the winner, with the placers setting a strong standard.

5362 - 5367a (Foreign Racing) - See Raceform Interactive

5263 **CLAIREFONTAINE** (R-H)

Thursday, August 14

**OFFICIAL GOING: Turf: very soft**

## 5368a PRIX CPM (PRIX DE LA COTE FLEURIE) (H'CAP) (3YO) (TURF) 1m 4f

12:50 (12:00) 3-Y-0

**£23,500** (£9,500; £7,000; £4,500; £2,750; £1,750)

RPR

1 **Le Scribe (FR)**[56] 3-8-10 0 CristianDemuro 15 85
(G Botti, France) **41/5**

2 *3/4* **It's Not It (IRE)**[32] 3-8-10 0 (p) TheoBachelot 10 84
(S Wattel, France) **136/10**

3 *shd* **Tianshan City**[98] 3-9-0 0 (b) JulienAuge 9 88
(C Ferland, France) **12/1**

4 *hd* **Carentan (FR)**[56] 3-8-5 0 MickaelBarzalona 3 79
(P Chatelain, France) **28/1**

5 *1 1/4* **Tres Solid (FR)**[43] 3-8-7 0 Christophe-PatriceLemaire 11 79
(N Caullery, France) **212/10**

6 *1* **Scalambra**[111] 3-8-8 0 (p) Francois-XavierBertras 2 78
(F Rohaut, France) **69/10**[3]

7 *1* **Nahual (FR)**[86] 3-9-4 0 ChristopheSoumillon 13 86
(J Bertran De Balanda, France) **43/10**[1]

8 *1 1/2* **Pink Courageous (FR)**[76] 3-8-10 0 (p) Pierre-CharlesBoudot 4 76
(J-P Gauvin, France) **11/2**[2]

9 *1/2* **Meandra (IRE)**[36] 3-8-2 0 AlexisBadel 6 67
(N Clement, France) **44/5**

10 *3 1/2* **Pleasant Flight (FR)**[28] 3-8-10 0 FlavienPrat 5 70
(D Windrif, France) **244/10**

11 *2* **Isabella Liberty (FR)**[87] 2411 3-8-11 0 IoritzMendizabal 16 67
(Robert Eddery) *sn prom fr wd draw: disp 2nd on outer: cl 3rd and rdn to hold pl fr 2 1/2f out: grad dropped away fnl 1 1/2f* **162/10**

12 *1 1/4* **Trigger Flash (FR)**[75] 3-8-4 0 EddyHardouin 14 58
(N Caullery, France) **41/1**

13 *2* **Peace Mine (CAN)**[50] 1139 3-8-8 0 MllePaulineDominois 12 59
(M Mace, France) **194/10**

14 *1 1/4* **Such Fun (IRE)**[105] 3-8-8 0 UmbertoRispoli 1 57
(F-H Graffard, France) **26/1**

15 *2 1/2* **Firfol (FR)**[114] 3-8-11 0 (b) GregoryBenoist 7 56
(Mme Pia Brandt, France) **25/1**

16 *4* **Icarium (FR)**[46] 3-9-1 0 OlivierPeslier 8 54
(C Laffon-Parias, France) **238/10**

2m 39.9s (2.00) **16 Ran SP% 119.1**
WIN (incl. 1 euro stake): 9.20. PLACES: 3.30, 4.80, 4.10. DF: 57.30. SF: 111.70.
**Owner** Dioscuri Srl & G Botti **Bred** Earl Haras De Magouet **Trained** France

## 5369a PRIX DHEVATARA (PRIX LUTH ENCHANTEE) (LISTED RACE) (4YO+ FILLIES & MARES) (TURF) 1m 1f

1:50 (12:00) 4-Y-0+ **£26,666** (£10,666; £8,000; £5,333; £2,666)

RPR

1 **Gaga A (URU)**[22] 4561 5-8-11 0 GregoryBenoist 4 105
(D Smaga, France) **51/10**[3]

2 *3/4* **Belle De Crecy (IRE)**[63] 3171 5-9-2 0 Christophe-PatriceLemaire 10 108
(Mme C Head-Maarek, France) **41/10**[2]

3 *2 1/2* **Kenbella (FR)**[25] 4484 4-8-11 0 FabriceVeron 6 98
(H-A Pantall, France) *fin 4th: plcd 3rd* **23/1**

4 *nse* **Abilene**[25] 4484 4-8-11 0 Pierre-CharlesBoudot 7 98
(F-H Graffard, France) *fin 5th: plcd 4th* **131/10**

5 *hd* **Abys (FR)**[25] 4484 4-8-11 0 AntoineHamelin 8 98
(Mme Pia Brandt, France) *fin 3rd: disqualified and plcd 5th* **3/1**[1]

6 *2 1/2* **More Than Sotka (FR)**[45] 3811 4-8-11 0 TonyPiccone 9 92
(Matthieu Palussiere, France) **211/10**

7 *2* **Kathinka (GER)**[16] 4-8-11 0 FranckBlondel 1 88
(M Munch, Germany) **43/5**

8 *1 1/2* **Loussia (FR)**[25] 4484 5-8-11 0 StephanePasquier 3 85
(Yannick Fouin, France) **168/10**

9 *5* **Intimhir (IRE)**[25] 4484 4-8-11 0 OlivierPeslier 2 75
(F Head, France) **73/10**

10 *2* **Auction (IRE)**[15] 4782 4-8-11 0 ChristopheSoumillon 11 70
(Ed Dunlop) *chsd ldr: rdn and short of room on rail 1 1/2f out: sn btn and heavily eased fnl f* **99/10**

11 *18* **Akemi (IRE)**[40] 4-8-11 0 MaximeGuyon 5 33
(X Thomas-Demeaulte, France) **192/10**

1m 55.2s (115.20) **11 Ran SP% 119.0**
WIN (incl. 1 euro stake): 6.10. PLACES: 2.40, 2.50, 6.40. DF: 22.40. SF: 35.50.
**Owner** Benjamin Steinbruch **Bred** Haras Phillipson **Trained** Lamorlaye, France

## 5370a PRIX PARI COUPLE (PRIX DES AUBEPINES) (CLAIMER) (3YO) (TURF) 1m 4f

3:25 (12:00) 3-Y-0 **£7,916** (£3,166; £2,375; £1,583; £791)

RPR

1 **Rennsenas (FR)**[82] 3-9-4 0 TonyPiccone 12 73
(C Lotoux, France) **84/10**

2 *1* **Zashka (FR)**[57] 3372 3-8-8 0 GregoryBenoist 7 61
(D Prod'Homme, France) **16/5**[1]

3 *1/2* **L'Indiscrete (FR)**[25] 3-8-6 0 (p) NicolasLarenaudie(5) 14 63
(J Bertran De Balanda, France) **41/1**

4 *1* **Collani (IRE)**[11] 4952 3-9-1 0 GeraldMosse 8 66
(M Nigge, France) **49/10**[2]

5 *1/2* **Martha's Stand (FR)**[27] 3-9-1 0 (p) MaximeGuyon 6 65
(E Libaud, France) **7/1**

6 *3* **Gulfstream Kitten (USA)**[11] 4952 3-9-4 0 UmbertoRispoli 13 63
(Gianluca Bietolini, Italy) **58/10**[3]

7 *1/2* **Paco Keed (FR)**[68] 3-9-1 0 (p) StephanePasquier 5 59
(Y Gourraud, France) **43/5**

8 *1 1/2* **Romina (FR)**[43] 3-8-11 0 MorganDelalande 4 53
(Y Barberot, France) **161/10**

9 *2 1/2* **Voix De La Baie (FR)**[73] 3-9-1 0 AlexandreChampenois(3) 9 56
(Mlle I Gallorini, France) **119/10**

10 *1/2* **Sweet Alibi (IRE)**[22] 4536 3-8-13 0 IoritzMendizabal 2 50
(J S Moore) *hld up in midfield: sltly outpcd 3f out: sn rdn and chsd ldrs over 2f out: plugged on at one pce: eased whn wl hld ins fnl f* **163/10**

11 *10* **Chesieres (FR)**[167] 795 3-8-8 0 (p) EddyHardouin 10 29
(A Le Duff, France) **66/1**

12 *15* **Outback (FR)** 3-8-11 0 (b) AnthonyCrastus 1 8
(D Sepulchre, France) **32/1**

13 *1* **Great Silence (FR)**[244] 3-8-11 0 CristianDemuro 3 7
(F Doumen, France) **41/1**

14 *8* **Victor Springs** 3-8-11 0 AlexisAchard 11
(H Fortineau, France) **67/1**

2m 43.2s (5.30) **14 Ran SP% 119.2**
WIN (incl. 1 euro stake): 9.40. PLACES: 2.90, 1.80, 8.00. DF: 16.40. SF: 39.50.
**Owner** M Delaunay & B Vives **Bred** Haras Du Quesnay **Trained** France

4993 **CATTERICK** (L-H)

Friday, August 15

**OFFICIAL GOING: Good (8.2)**

Wind: Almost nil Weather: Fine

## 5371 PIN POINT RECRUITMENT AMATEUR RIDERS' H'CAP 1m 3f 214y

5:40 (5:40) (Class 5) (0-75,75) 3-Y-0+ **£3,119** (£967; £483; £242) **Stalls** Centre

Form RPR

2-64 1 **Arabian Beauty (IRE)**[26] 4472 3-9-10 73 (p) MrAlexFerguson(5) 3 84+
(Saeed bin Suroor) *hld up in rr: hdwy 4f out: modest 8th 2f out: styd on strly to ld clsng stages* **4/1**[1]

0320 2 *1 1/4* **Merchant Of Medici**[19] 4709 7-9-8 62 (p) DylanMcDonagh(7) 2 68
(Micky Hammond) *trckd ldrs: t.k.h: sddle appeared to sn slip forward: led over 2f out: hdd and no ex nr fin* **12/1**

6153 3 *3/4* **Aldwick Bay (IRE)**[11] 4985 6-10-9 75 MissCAGreenway(5) 1 80
(Tom Dascombe) *led early: chsd ldrs: kpt on same pce fnl f* **5/1**[2]

0045 4 *1/2* **Triple Eight (IRE)**[25] 3958 6-9-13 65 (b) PhillipDennis(5) 13 69
(Philip Kirby) *dwlt: hdwy after 2f: chsng ldrs whn stmbld bnd over 3f out: styd on fnl f* **11/1**

0-51 5 *1 1/2* **Tropical Bachelor (IRE)**[57] 3398 8-9-9 56 MissSBrotherton 5 58
(Brian Baugh) *mid-div: hdwy to chse ldrs over 4f out: kpt on wl ins fnl f* **11/2**[3]

0010 6 *2* **Tinseltown**[10] 4995 8-10-7 68 MissADeniel 12 67
(Brian Rothwell) *sn led: hdd over 2f out: wknd fnl 75yds* **14/1**

123 7 *6* **Northside Prince (IRE)**[34] 4196 8-10-9 75 MissMeganNicholls(5) 6 64
(Alan Swinbank) *mid-div: hdwy to chse ldrs over 5f out: slipped bnd over 3f out: wknd appr fnl f* **5/1**[2]

0531 8 *3* **Unex Michelangelo (IRE)**[17] 4755 5-10-6 70 MissJoannaMason(3) 8 54
(Michael Easterby) *in rr: stmbld bnd over 3f out: sme late hdwy* **5/1**[2]

2150 9 *1 1/2* **Pertuis (IRE)**[29] 4351 8-10-10 71 MrWHogg 4 53
(Micky Hammond) *in rr: hdwy on outside over 5f out: sn chsng ldrs: wknd over 1f out* **33/1**

0000 10 *6* **Jewelled Dagger (IRE)**[4] 5240 10-9-2 56 oh11 (t) MissCWatling(7) 9 28
(Sharon Watt) *in rr: sme hdwy on outer over 5f out: lost pl over 3f out: sn bhd* **125/1**

0/5- 11 *3 3/4* **Anton Dolin (IRE)**[17] 6217 6-10-2 70 (p) MrHFNugent(7) 7 36
(Michael Mullineaux) *a in rr* **50/1**

00/0 12 *13* **Takaatuf (IRE)**[26] 4470 8-10-6 70 MrTHamilton(3) 10 15
(Tina Jackson) *mid-div: slipped bnd after 4f: drvn over 5f out: sn chsng ldrs: lost pl 4f out: sn bhd* **100/1**

2m 39.45s (0.55) **Going Correction** +0.075s/f (Good)
**WFA** 3 from 5yo+ 11lb **12 Ran SP% 114.8**
Speed ratings (Par 103): **101,100,99,99,98 97,93,91,90,86 83,74**
CSF £51.29 CT £244.12 TOTE £4.00: £2.20, £2.10, £2.20; EX 45.60 Trifecta £285.30.
**Owner** Godolphin **Bred** Darley **Trained** Newmarket, Suffolk

**FOCUS**
Mainly exposed sorts in this handicap for amateur riders, which was run at a fair gallop. The winner came from off the pace and is rated a bit better than the bare form.

## 5372 OOPS A DAISY FLORISTS (S) STKS 7f

6:10 (6:11) (Class 6) 2-Y-0 **£2,726** (£805; £402) **Stalls** Low

Form RPR

0053 1 **Frosty Times (FR)**[7] 5141 2-8-11 54 TonyHamilton 4 54
(Richard Fahey) *chsd ldrs: effrt over 2f out: styd on to ld last 100yds: drvn rt out* **6/4**[1]

0650 2 *1 1/2* **Chilworth Bells**[11] 4967 2-8-11 53 JoeFanning 1 50
(Mick Channon) *sn hld up in mid-div: hdwy over 2f out: chsng ldrs whn n.m.r over 1f out: kpt on to take 2nd last 50yds* **4/1**[2]

5400 3 *1* **Lucilla Aurelius (IRE)**[8] 5099 2-8-6 50 (p) BarryMcHugh 5 42
(Tony Coyle) *trckd ldr: led 2f out: hdd ins fnl f: kpt on same pce* **11/2**[3]

0 4 *4* **Arcossi**[111] 1732 2-8-6 0 PJMcDonald 2 32
(Ann Duffield) *s.i.s: in rr: outpcd 3f out: hdwy over 1f out: kpt on to take modest 4th nr fin* **12/1**

4320 5 *hd* **Reet Petite (IRE)**[6] 5194 2-8-9 50 ow3 (v) JasonHart 6 34
(Michael Dods) *t.k.h in rr: effrt on wd outside over 2f out: edgd lft and one pce fnl f* **17/2**

05 6 *2 1/4* **Ship Canal**[6] 5194 2-8-11 0 GrahamGibbons 9 31
(Michael Easterby) *drvn along and swtchd lft after s to ld: hdd 2f out: wknd appr fnl f* **13/2**

500 7 *1 1/4* **Regal Accolade**[23] 4528 2-8-4 46 (v[1]) JoshDoyle(7) 8 27
(David O'Meara) *sn chsng ldrs: drvn over 3f out: edgd lft and wknd over 1f out* **40/1**

06 8 *9* **Sabbra Cadabra**[18] 4723 2-8-8 0 ow2 (b[1]) KevinStott(5) 7 6
(Philip Kirby) *in rr: hdwy over 3f out: sn chsng ldrs: wknd over 1f out: bhd whn eased clsng stages* **66/1**

1m 28.73s (1.73) **Going Correction** +0.075s/f (Good) **8 Ran SP% 110.9**
Speed ratings (Par 92): **93,91,90,85,85 82,81,71**
CSF £6.95 TOTE £1.90: £1.10, £1.60, £2.30; EX 6.50 Trifecta £27.60.There was no bid for the winner
**Owner** Mr And Mrs J D Cotton **Bred** John Dawson Cotton **Trained** Musley Bank, N Yorks

**FOCUS**
Goodish ground here, though loose on top and though several slipped in the first race the home bend proved no problem this time. The first two in this weak seller are rated to form.

## 5373 BE PREMIERE HAIR NURSERY H'CAP (BOBIS RACE) 5f 212y
**6:40** (6:40) (Class 4) (0-85,78) 2-Y-O **£5,175** (£1,540; £769; £384) **Stalls** Low

| Form | | | | RPR |
|---|---|---|---|---|
| 4212 | 1 | | **Izzthatright (IRE)**[12] 4939 2-9-2 78 JackGarritty(5) 3 (Richard Fahey) *mde all: wnt clr over 2f out: styd on strly: unchal* **13/8**[1] | 92 |
| 1420 | 2 | 7 | **Madamoiselle Bond**[13] 4913 2-8-10 72 KevinStott(5) 4 (William Jarvis) *hld up in mid-div: effrt on ins over 2f out: chsd wnr 1f out: no imp* **17/2** | 65 |
| 1040 | 3 | 2 ½ | **Billyoakes (IRE)**[20] 4686 2-9-4 75 GrahamGibbons 2 (Mick Channon) *chsd ldrs: kpt on same pce fnl 2f* **14/1** | 61 |
| 3335 | 4 | 1 ½ | **Atreus**[3] 5285 2-8-7 64 BarryMcHugh 1 (Michael Easterby) *hld up in rr-div: n.m.r on inner and lost pl over 3f out: kpt on one pce fnl 2f* **12/1** | 45 |
| 620 | 5 | shd | **Steady Major (IRE)**[20] 4666 2-9-4 75 DanielTudhope 7 (David Simcock) *s.i.s: in rr: hdwy over 2f out: one pce* **4/1**[2] | 56 |
| 1 | 6 | nse | **Kayo Koko (IRE)**[23] 4527 2-9-4 75 PJMcDonald 6 (Ann Duffield) *trckd ldrs: effrt over 2f out: one pce* **7/1** | 56 |
| 056 | 7 | 10 | **Mutafarrej**[17] 4760 2-9-6 77 JoeFanning 5 (Mark Johnston) *drvn to chse ldrs: lost pl over 1f out: bhd whn eased clsng stages* **5/1**[3] | 28 |

1m 12.93s (-0.67) **Going Correction** +0.075s/f (Good) **7** Ran SP% **112.1**
Speed ratings (Par 96): **107,97,94,92,92 92,78**
CSF £15.73 TOTE £1.90: £1.20, £4.30; EX 13.70 Trifecta £190.20.
**Owner** The Go 90 Partnership **Bred** Patrick Cummins **Trained** Musley Bank, N Yorks
**FOCUS**
Not a particularly strong nursery and something of a tactical affair, but the winner came right away. His Chester run could be rated somehere near this.

## 5374 BLACK BULL INN MOULTON MAIDEN STKS 1m 3f 214y
**7:10** (7:11) (Class 5) 3-Y-O+ **£3,234** (£962; £481; £240) **Stalls** Low

| Form | | | | RPR |
|---|---|---|---|---|
| 0 | 1 | | **Knife Point (GER)**[30] 4325 3-9-2 0 GrahamGibbons 4 (Hugo Palmer) *chsd ldr: drvn and swtchd rt over 2f out: 2nd over 1f out: hung lft and carried hd high: kpt on to ld towards fin* **18/1** | 72+ |
| 0-3 | 2 | nk | **Magic Music Man**[10] 5018 3-9-2 0 DanielTudhope 13 (K R Burke) *chsd ldng pair: 2nd over 5f out: led over 2f out: hdd and no ex towards fin* **9/4**[2] | 71+ |
| 33 | 3 | 5 | **Miss Crystal (IRE)**[104] 1960 3-8-11 0 TonyHamilton 12 (Charles Hills) *led: t.k.h: hdd over 2f out: fdd fnl f* **15/8**[1] | 58+ |
| 0060 | 4 | 2 ¼ | **Primary Route (IRE)**[58] 3363 4-9-5 44 [1] JoeyHaynes(3) 10 (Jason Ward) *mid-div: chsd ldrs over 6f out: one pce fnl 2f* **150/1** | 55 |
| -0 | 5 | 3 ½ | **Nagambie (IRE)**[139] 1166 3-8-11 0 JoeFanning 7 (Mark Johnston) *s.i.s: hdwy after 3f: chsng ldrs 6f out: drvn over 2f out: fdd appr fnl f: eased nr fin* **5/1**[3] | 49 |
| - | 6 | ½ | **Georgian Firebird**[147] 4-9-8 0 DavidAllan 5 (Alan Swinbank) *mid-div: sme hdwy over 3f out: nvr a factor* **6/1** | 48 |
| | 7 | 3 ¼ | **Bulas Belle**[94] 4-9-8 0 PJMcDonald 1 (Edwin Tuer) *strated slowly: in rr and sn drvn along: nvr on terms* **22/1** | 43 |
| -500 | 8 | 2 ½ | **Highway Pursuit**[73] 2867 3-9-2 50 AndrewMullen 6 (George Moore) *s.i.s: in rr: sme hdwy 3f out: wknd over 1f out* **125/1** | 44 |
| - | 9 | 2 ½ | **Rock On Bollinski**[24] 4-9-13 0 BarryMcHugh 9 (Tim Fitzgerald) *s.i.s: in rr: sme hdwy 5f out: lost pl over 2f out: sn bhd* **33/1** | 40 |
| 5 | 10 | 19 | **Justcallhimbilly**[19] 4713 4-9-10 0 NeilFarley(3) 2 (Shaun Harris) *chsd ldrs: drvn 6f out: reminders and lost pl 4f out: sn bhd: t.o* **33/1** | 10 |

2m 39.22s (0.32) **Going Correction** +0.075s/f (Good)
**WFA** 3 from 4yo+ 11lb **10** Ran SP% **113.5**
Speed ratings (Par 103): **101,100,97,95,93 93,91,89,87,75**
CSF £55.94 TOTE £31.20: £5.90, £1.10, £1.70; EX 85.20 Trifecta £382.40.
**Owner** Decadent Racing **Bred** R & B Int **Trained** Newmarket, Suffolk
**FOCUS**
An assorted bunch in this maiden which was dominated by three 3yos, and in all probability just ordinary form. The winner showed big improvement.

## 5375 YORKSHIRE-OUTDOORS.CO.UK H'CAP 5f
**7:45** (7:46) (Class 6) (0-65,64) 3-Y-O+ **£2,726** (£805; £402) **Stalls** Low

| Form | | | | RPR |
|---|---|---|---|---|
| 0301 | 1 | | **Perfect Words (IRE)**[10] 4994 4-9-3 61 6ex (p) JordanNason(5) 9 (Marjorie Fife) *led 1f: w ldr: led over 1f out: kpt on wl* **13/2**[3] | 72 |
| 4166 | 2 | 1 ½ | **Windforpower (IRE)**[9] 5053 4-9-11 64 (p) JoeFanning 4 (Tracy Waggott) *chsd ldrs: kpt on same pce last 150yds* **11/1** | 69 |
| 5300 | 3 | hd | **A J Cook (IRE)**[11] 4960 4-8-13 52 (v) GrahamLee 6 (Ron Barr) *wnt rt s: mid-div: hdwy over 1f out: styd on same pce last 50yds* **16/1** | 56 |
| 2001 | 4 | 1 ¼ | **Spring Bird**[20] 4664 5-9-8 61 AdrianNicholls 1 (David Nicholls) *chsd ldr: led over 3f out: hdd over 1f out: kpt on same pce* **15/2** | 60 |
| 0001 | 5 | 1 | **Lord Buffhead**[4] 5237 5-8-8 52 6ex (v) DuilioDaSilva(5) 3 (Richard Guest) *chsd ldrs: outpcd over 2f out: kpt on fnl f* **4/1**[1] | 48 |
| 5650 | 6 | 1 | **Ingenti**[13] 4901 6-9-4 62 KevinStott(5) 2 (Christopher Wilson) *wnt rt s: chsd ldrs: one pce appr fnl f* **8/1** | 54 |
| 5242 | 7 | 1 ¼ | **Showtime Star**[10] 4997 4-9-8 61 DavidAllan 10 (Alan Swinbank) *mid-div: effrt over 2f out: nvr a threat* **9/2**[2] | 49 |
| 0533 | 8 | nk | **Passionada**[24] 4511 5-9-8 61 DaleSwift 14 (Ed McMahon) *in rr: effrt over 2f out: no imp whn eased clsng stages* **12/1** | 48 |
| 163 | 9 | 1 | **Emily Davison (IRE)**[16] 4796 3-9-1 62 (p) GemmaTutty(5) 7 (Karen Tutty) *squeezed out s: sme hdwy on ins 2f out: nvr a factor* **12/1** | 44 |
| 0546 | 10 | 3 ½ | **Princess Myla (IRE)**[11] 4974 3-8-8 50 PJMcDonald 12 (Paul Midgley) *chsd ldrs: lost pl over 1f out* **66/1** | 19 |
| 25-0 | 11 | 3 ½ | **Simply Black (IRE)**[13] 4890 3-9-7 63 [1] DanielTudhope 5 (David O'Meara) *in rr: sme hdwy over 2f out: no imp whn eased last 100yds* **16/1** | 20 |
| 4106 | 12 | 1 ¼ | **Chosen One (IRE)**[19] 4714 9-9-7 60 JamesSullivan 8 (Ruth Carr) *wnt lft s: a towards rr: nvr on terms* **25/1** | 13 |
| 5054 | 13 | 3 ¾ | **Fizzolo**[10] 4994 3-8-7 49 BarryMcHugh 11 (Karen Tutty) *chsd ldrs: lost pl 2f out* **50/1** | |

1m 0.02s (0.22) **Going Correction** +0.075s/f (Good)
**WFA** 3 from 4yo+ 3lb **13** Ran SP% **117.2**
Speed ratings (Par 101): **101,98,98,96,94 93,91,90,89,83 77,75,69**
CSF £73.71 CT £1099.73 TOTE £8.40: £2.70, £4.20, £7.20; EX 80.50 Trifecta £1104.30 Part won..
**Owner** Green Lane **Bred** Rathasker Stud **Trained** Stillington, N Yorks
**FOCUS**
A modest sprint run and, although the gallop was sound, very few figured. The winner confirmed her C&D latest form.

## 5376 RACING WELFARE DAY ON 27TH AUGUST H'CAP 7f
**8:15** (8:18) (Class 6) (0-60,66) 3-Y-O+ **£2,726** (£805; £402) **Stalls** Low

| Form | | | | RPR |
|---|---|---|---|---|
| 5502 | 1 | | **Smart Alec (IRE)**[14] 4861 3-9-1 57 DuranFentiman 2 (Alan Swinbank) *chsd ldrs: hrd rdn and styd on to ld last 50yds* **11/2**[2] | 68 |
| 2602 | 2 | 1 ½ | **Slingsby**[6] 5198 3-8-9 51 (b) GrahamGibbons 7 (Michael Easterby) *swtchd rt after s: led: hdd and no ex wl ins fnl f* **15/2** | 58 |
| -631 | 3 | ¾ | **La Havrese (FR)**[10] 4998 3-9-10 66 6ex PJMcDonald 5 (Ann Duffield) *chsd ldrs: kpt on to take 3rd nr fin* **4/1**[1] | 71 |
| 6342 | 4 | ¾ | **Benidorm**[4] 5244 6-8-5 46 (e) DuilioDaSilva(5) 15 (Richard Guest) *in rr: hdwy and edgd rt over 2f out: kpt on same pce fnl f* **12/1** | 51 |
| 2564 | 5 | nse | **Viking Warrior (IRE)**[8] 5071 7-8-13 49 JasonHart 3 (Shaun Harris) *mid-div: hdwy on ins over 2f out: kpt on same pce appr fnl f* **6/1**[3] | 54 |
| 4002 | 6 | nk | **Thrust Control (IRE)**[8] 5103 7-8-12 48 (p) JoeFanning 9 (Tracy Waggott) *chsd ldrs: kpt on one pce fnl f* **12/1** | 52 |
| 0013 | 7 | 1 | **Gaelic Wizard (IRE)**[37] 4069 6-9-2 57 GemmaTutty(5) 6 (Karen Tutty) *mid-div: effrt over 2f out: kpt on fnl f* **16/1** | 58 |
| 0050 | 8 | ½ | **The Blue Banana (IRE)**[16] 4797 5-9-2 57 (p) KevinStott(5) 12 (Edwin Tuer) *slowly away: detached in last: styd on fnl 2f: nt rch ldrs* **16/1** | 57 |
| 0U05 | 9 | ¾ | **Mitchell**[8] 5110 4-9-7 57 (v[1]) DanielTudhope 1 (K R Burke) *mid-div: hdwy over 3f out: one pce fnl 2f* **7/1** | 55 |
| 0031 | 10 | 1 ½ | **Secret City (IRE)**[18] 4728 8-9-7 60 (p) NeilFarley(3) 11 (Robin Bastiman) *mid-div: hdwy to chse ldrs over 3f out: one pce fnl 2f* **16/1** | 54 |
| 2010 | 11 | 1 ¾ | **Street Boss (IRE)**[10] 4998 3-9-3 59 (b) RussKennemore 4 (Jedd O'Keeffe) *mid-div: effrt over 2f out: nvr a factor* **22/1** | 47 |
| 6202 | 12 | 6 | **Mitchum**[80] 2653 5-9-6 56 (v) DaleSwift 8 (Ron Barr) *s.i.s: in rr: bhd fnl 2f* **25/1** | 30 |
| 0504 | 13 | ½ | **Ad Vitam (IRE)**[42] 3915 6-8-12 53 (tp) JacobButterfield(5) 14 (Suzzanne France) *in rr: sn drvn along: bhd fnl 2f* **40/1** | 26 |
| 00-0 | 14 | 4 ½ | **Miss Rebero**[4] 5233 4-8-6 47 JackGarritty(5) 13 (Tim Fitzgerald) *in rr and drvn along: sme hdwy 4f out: lost pl over 2f out: sn bhd* **100/1** | 8 |

1m 27.2s (0.20) **Going Correction** +0.075s/f (Good)
**WFA** 3 from 4yo+ 6lb **14** Ran SP% **118.6**
Speed ratings (Par 101): **101,99,98,97,97 97,96,95,94,92 90,84,83,78**
CSF £44.21 CT £185.25 TOTE £6.30: £2.70, £3.00, £1.10; EX 57.30 Trifecta £206.80.
**Owner** Ms A Findlay **Bred** Michael G Daly **Trained** Melsonby, N Yorks
■ Stewards' Enquiry : Duran Fentiman two-day ban: use of whip (29-30 Aug)
**FOCUS**
It paid to race handily in this low-grade handicap which was run at an ordinary gallop and the first three were in the first five from the outset. The form makes sense.
T/Plt: £64.70 to a £1 stake. Pool: £59,895.61 - 675.11 winning units T/Qpdt: £17.90 to a £1 stake. Pool: £6,719.49 - 276.25 winning units WG

# 4942 NEWBURY (L-H)
### Friday, August 15

**OFFICIAL GOING: Soft (6.3)**
Rail movement increased distances on Round course by about 31yds.
Wind: Light; across Weather: Cloudy

## 5377 DON DEADMAN MEMORIAL EUROPEAN BREEDERS' FUND MAIDEN STKS 7f (S)
**2:20** (2:20) (Class 4) 2-Y-O **£4,528** (£1,347; £673; £336) **Stalls** Centre

| Form | | | | RPR |
|---|---|---|---|---|
| 3 | 1 | | **Elm Park**[16] 4800 2-9-5 0 DavidProbert 3 (Andrew Balding) *lengthy: trckd ldr: led over 2f out: rdn clr fnl f: comf* **9/4**[1] | 89+ |
| | 2 | 3 | **Constable Buckley** 2-9-5 0 SamHitchcott 4 (Mick Channon) *unf: mid-div: hdwy over 2f out: rdn to chse wnr over 1f out: kpt on but nt pce of wnr* **28/1** | 80+ |
| | 3 | 1 ¼ | **Acolyte (IRE)** 2-9-5 0 ShaneKelly 7 (Roger Charlton) *unf: scope: mid-div: hdwy over 2f out: rdn over 1f out: kpt on but no ex fnl 120yds* **6/1**[3] | 77 |
| 20 | 4 | 3 ¼ | **Pensax Boy**[26] 4467 2-9-5 0 RobertWinston 14 (Ian Williams) *trckd ldrs: rdn 2f out: kpt on same pce fnl f* **20/1** | 69 |
| | 5 | 1 ¼ | **Manolito** 2-9-5 0 AndreaAtzeni 5 (Hughie Morrison) *unf: trckd ldrs: rdn over 2f out: kpt on same pce fnl f* **10/1** | 65+ |
| | 6 | 4 ½ | **Albecq** 2-9-5 0 SilvestreDeSousa 1 (David Evans) *w'like: hld up: hdwy into midfield over 2f out: sn rdn: styd on but nt pce to get involved* **16/1** | 54 |
| | 7 | 1 ¼ | **Proposed** 2-9-5 0 RichardHughes 10 (Richard Hannon) *str: lw: towards rr: minor late prog: nvr a factor* **8/1** | 50 |
| 00 | 8 | 1 ¼ | **Titian Lord (IRE)**[13] 4906 2-9-5 0 SteveDrowne 8 (Charles Hills) *leggy: mid-div: rdn over 2f out: wknd over 1f out* **100/1** | 47 |
| 00 | 9 | hd | **Soldier Sam (IRE)**[35] 4142 2-9-5 0 [1] SeanLevey 6 (Richard Hannon) *leggy: led: rdn and hdd over 2f out: wknd ent fnl f* **40/1** | 47 |
| | 10 | 8 | **Paddys Runner** 2-9-5 0 WilliamTwiston-Davies 11 (Alan King) *w'like: s.i.s: a towards rr* **33/1** | 26 |
| | 11 | ½ | **St Georges Rock (IRE)** 2-9-2 0 RyanTate(3) 15 (Clive Cox) *w'like: scope: hld up towards rr: effrt 2f out: sn btn* **7/2**[2] | 24 |
| | 12 | 7 | **River Dart (IRE)** 2-9-5 0 BenCurtis 13 (Marcus Tregoning) *w'like: hld up: hdwy into midfield 3f out: wknd 2f out* **12/1** | 6 |
| | 13 | 38 | **Foxy Boris (FR)** 2-8-12 0 JamesMerrett(7) 12 (Paul Cole) *leggy: scope: chsd ldrs 4f: sn wknd: t.o* **66/1** | |

1m 28.59s (2.89) **Going Correction** +0.325s/f (Good) **13** Ran SP% **117.1**
Speed ratings (Par 96): **96,92,91,87,86 80,79,78,77,68 68,60,16**
CSF £80.22 TOTE £3.10: £1.40, £8.70, £2.60; EX 85.50 Trifecta £560.10.
**Owner** Kingsclere Racing Club **Bred** Kingsclere Stud **Trained** Kingsclere, Hants

**FOCUS**

Rail movement increased distances on Round course by about 31yds. The front two in the betting forecast were taken out, so not as strong a maiden as it might have been, and it proved hard to make up ground. They raced up the middle. The winner is rated up a stone on his debut.

## 5378 CHRISTOPHER SMITH ASSOCIATES CLAIMING STKS 7f (S)

2:50 (2:51) (Class 5) 3-Y-0+ £2,587 (£770; £384; £192) Stalls Centre

| Form | | | | RPR |
|---|---|---|---|---|
| 406 | 1 | | **Azrur (IRE)**[14] 4866 4-8-13 82 ............ MarcMonaghan(5) 5 | 85 |
| | | | (David Brown) *mde all: rdn 2f out: kpt on fnl f: drvn out* **10/3**[2] | |
| 0004 | 2 | *nk* | **Langavat (IRE)**[13] 4889 3-8-12 90 ............ RichardHughes 2 | 82 |
| | | | (Richard Hannon) *racd keenly: trckd ldrs: rdn over 2f out: kpt on wl fnl 120yds: clsng on wnr nr fin* **7/2**[3] | |
| 06 | 3 | 1 ½ | **House Captain**[13] 4886 3-8-5 0 ............ MartinDwyer 4 | 71 |
| | | | (Richard Hannon) *hmpd s: sn chsng ldrs: rdn and ev ch 2f out: kpt on tl no ex fnl 120yds* **33/1** | |
| 3500 | 4 | 1 ¾ | **Hagree (IRE)**[51] 3577 3-9-3 82 ............ (p) MartinHarley 3 | 79 |
| | | | (Marco Botti) *trckd ldrs: rdn 2f out: kpt on same pce fnl f* **11/4**[1] | |
| 6-04 | 5 | *nk* | **Chelwood Gate (IRE)**[29] 4352 4-9-3 72 ............ LiamKeniry 1 | 74 |
| | | | (Patrick Chamings) *hld up bhd ldrs: effrt 2f out: kpt on but nt pce to get on terms* **9/1** | |
| 0200 | 6 | 1 ¼ | **Solo Hunter**[5] 5213 3-8-12 75 ............ (b[1]) DavidProbert 8 | 70 |
| | | | (David Evans) *chsd ldrs: rdn over 2f out: edgd lft and one pce fnl f* **8/1** | |
| 00-0 | 7 | 9 | **Yair Hill (IRE)**[14] 4866 6-8-13 80 ............ TedDurcan 6 | 43 |
| | | | (Geoffrey Deacon) *hld up: effrt 2f out: wknd fnl f* **6/1** | |

1m 28.6s (2.90) **Going Correction** +0.325s/f (Good)
**WFA** 3 from 4yo+ 6lb 7 Ran SP% **110.3**
Speed ratings (Par 103): **96,95,93,91,91 90,79**
CSF £14.25 TOTE £4.40: £1.90, £2.20; EX 17.30 Trifecta £199.70.Azrur was claimed by Robert Johnson for £15,000. Langavat was claimed by Nigel Tinkler for £15,000.
**Owner** J C Fretwell **Bred** Kildaragh Stud **Trained** Averham Park, Notts

**FOCUS**

A fair claimer, although like in the opening race it proved hard to make up ground. Again, they raced up the middle. The time was modest compared with the 2yo maiden.

## 5379 PUNTER SOUTHALL TRANSACTION SERVICES H'CAP 1m 5f 61y

3:20 (3:21) (Class 3) (0-90,87) 3-Y-0+ £7,439 (£2,213; £1,106; £533) Stalls Low

| Form | | | | RPR |
|---|---|---|---|---|
| 3621 | 1 | | **Epsom Hill (SWE)**[13] 4921 3-9-0 85 ............ (p) AndreaAtzeni 10 | 100+ |
| | | | (Charlie Fellowes) *trckd ldr: led 2f out: rdn clr ent fnl f: edgd lft: comf* **11/10**[1] | |
| -415 | 2 | 3 | **Mister Fizz**[36] 4119 6-9-7 85 ............ GeorgeDowning(5) 8 | 93 |
| | | | (Miss Imogen Pickard) *led: rdn and hdd 2f out: styd on but sn hld by wnr* **10/1** | |
| 323- | 3 | 1 | **Novirak (IRE)**[420] 3531 6-10-0 87 ............ ShaneKelly 2 | 93+ |
| | | | (James Fanshawe) *mid-div: hdwy to trck ldrs 4f out: rdn in cl 3rd 2f out: styd on same pce* **11/1** | |
| 1453 | 4 | 6 | **Shavansky**[15] 4819 10-9-5 85 ............ PatMillman(7) 9 | 82 |
| | | | (Rod Millman) *dwlt: bhd: gd hdwy over 3f out: rdn and cl up 2f out: fdd fnl f* **14/1** | |
| -303 | 5 | 1 ¾ | **Kuda Huraa (IRE)**[23] 4538 6-9-11 84 ............ PatDobbs 11 | 78 |
| | | | (Alan King) *hld up in last pair: hdwy 4f out: rdn 3f out: wknd over 1f out* **7/1**[2] | |
| -500 | 6 | 2 ¾ | **Eshtiaal (USA)**[21] 4606 4-10-0 87 ............ SeanLevey 5 | 77 |
| | | | (Brian Meehan) *trckd ldrs: rdn over 3f out: wknd 2f out* **8/1**[3] | |
| 4114 | 7 | *nk* | **Manomine**[27] 4441 5-9-2 75 ............ SilvestreDeSousa 7 | 65 |
| | | | (Clive Brittain) *lw: mid-div: rdn 3f out: wknd 2f out* **8/1**[3] | |
| 0/0- | 8 | 23 | **Cyclone**[32] 7229 4-9-12 85 ............ (t) DougieCostello 6 | 40 |
| | | | (Jonjo O'Neill) *mid-div: rdn over 3f out: wknd 2f out: eased fnl f* **33/1** | |
| 0- | 9 | 71 | **Ruggero**[326] 4-9-12 85 ............ TedDurcan 1 | |
| | | | (Roy Brotherton) *trckd ldrs: rdn over 4f out: sn bhd: virtually p.u fnl 2f* **33/1** | |

2m 58.46s (6.46) **Going Correction** +0.675s/f (Yiel)
**WFA** 3 from 4yo+ 12lb 9 Ran SP% **112.3**
Speed ratings (Par 107): **107,105,104,100,99 98,97,83,40**
CSF £12.55 CT £78.65 TOTE £1.90: £1.10, £2.60, £2.70; EX 10.00 Trifecta £69.20.
**Owner** The Epsom Hill Partnership **Bred** Ms K Jacobson **Trained** Newmarket, Suffolk

**FOCUS**

A sound-run handicap. The runner-up is the key to the form.

## 5380 BATHWICK TYRES ST HUGH'S STKS (LISTED RACE) (FILLIES) 5f 34y

3:55 (3:55) (Class 1) 2-Y-0

£14,461 (£5,482; £2,743; £1,366; £685; £344) Stalls Centre

| Form | | | | RPR |
|---|---|---|---|---|
| 3321 | 1 | | **Bronze Maquette (IRE)**[21] 4605 2-9-0 88 ............ ShaneKelly 2 | 103 |
| | | | (Gary Moore) *hld up: hdwy over 1f out: r.o strly to ld fnl 140yds: readily* **10/1** | |
| 2201 | 2 | 1 ¾ | **Al Fareej (IRE)**[9] 5042 2-9-0 80 ............ MartinHarley 3 | 97 |
| | | | (James Tate) *mid-div: hdwy 2f out: rdn to ld over 1f out: hdd and no ex fnl 140yds* **16/1** | |
| 2461 | 3 | 1 | **Parsley (IRE)**[5] 5209 2-9-0 91 ............ PatDobbs 5 | 93 |
| | | | (Richard Hannon) *wnt rt s: chsd ldr: rdn over 1f out: ev ch ent fnl f: kpt on same pce* **4/1**[2] | |
| 1510 | 4 | 2 ¼ | **Accipiter**[20] 4646 2-9-0 88 ............ AshleyMorgan 12 | 85+ |
| | | | (Chris Wall) *mid-div: hdwy 2f out: rdn and ev ch ent fnl f: no ex fnl 120yds* **13/2** | |
| 4125 | 5 | ½ | **Rosie's Premiere (IRE)**[20] 4646 2-9-0 93 ............ RobertWinston 8 | 83 |
| | | | (Dean Ivory) *chsd ldrs: rdn and ev ch over 1f out: fdd fnl 120yds* **11/2**[3] | |
| 310 | 6 | 1 ¼ | **Blue Aegean**[58] 3353 2-9-0 87 ............ SilvestreDeSousa 4 | 79+ |
| | | | (Charlie Appleby) *lw: pushed along towards rr early: swtchd rt 2f out: sn wandered u.p: nvr threatened* **7/2**[1] | |
| 3466 | 7 | 2 | **Spirit Of Xian (IRE)**[17] 4757 2-9-0 91 ............ SeanLevey 11 | 72 |
| | | | (Richard Hannon) *lw: mid-dvision: pushed along over 3f out: drvn 2f out: wknd ent fnl f* **20/1** | |
| 101 | 8 | 1 ½ | **Dangerous Moonlite (IRE)**[47] 3757 2-9-0 96 ............ RichardHughes 7 | 67 |
| | | | (Richard Hannon) *lw: led: rdn and hdd over 1f out: sn wknd* **7/2**[1] | |
| 3021 | 9 | 8 | **Magic Florence (IRE)**[22] 4577 2-9-0 68 ............ TedDurcan 9 | 39 |
| | | | (James Given) *chsd ldr: rdn 2f out: wknd qckly* **40/1** | |

1m 2.76s (1.36) **Going Correction** +0.325s/f (Good) 9 Ran SP% **115.3**
Speed ratings: **102,99,97,94,93 91,88,85,72**
CSF £154.32 TOTE £11.50: £3.10, £5.70, £1.30; EX 139.90 Trifecta £952.80.
**Owner** R A Green **Bred** Rosetown Bloodstock Ltd **Trained** Lower Beeding, W Sussex

**FOCUS**

Again the action was up the middle. Not a good fillies' Listed race on paper, but the form is rated to the pre-race standard, the winner up a stone on her nursery win.

## 5381 KKA - HIGHPOINT H'CAP (BOBIS RACE) 6f 8y

4:30 (4:30) (Class 4) (0-80,80) 3-Y-0 £4,690 (£1,395; £697; £348) Stalls Centre

| Form | | | | RPR |
|---|---|---|---|---|
| 4210 | 1 | | **Katawi**[36] 4131 3-9-2 75 ............ TedDurcan 7 | 92+ |
| | | | (Chris Wall) *lw: trckd ldrs: led over 1f out: qcknd clr: drifted lft: comf* **4/1**[2] | |
| -336 | 2 | 2 | **Withernsea (IRE)**[28] 4390 3-9-5 78 ............ DavidNolan 4 | 85 |
| | | | (Richard Fahey) *in last pair: swtchd rt and short of room 2f out: sn rdn: kpt on to chse wnr jst ins fnl f: no ch* **7/2**[1] | |
| 0341 | 3 | 2 ¼ | **Munfallet (IRE)**[20] 4677 3-8-12 76 ............ MarcMonaghan(5) 8 | 76 |
| | | | (David Brown) *lw: prom: led after 1f: rdn and hdd over 1f out: sn outpcd: no ex whn lost 2nd ins fnl f* **4/1**[2] | |
| 5550 | 4 | 4 ½ | **Finflash (IRE)**[14] 4862 3-8-11 70 ............ WilliamTwiston-Davies 9 | 56 |
| | | | (Mick Channon) *hld up: effrt 2f out: kpt on but no ch fnl f* **14/1** | |
| 5513 | 5 | 3 | **Classic Pursuit**[13] 4890 3-8-12 71 ............ (p) SteveDrowne 1 | 47 |
| | | | (Ronald Harris) *prom: bmpd after 1f: rdn over 2f out: wknd fnl f* **8/1** | |
| 4601 | 6 | 2 ½ | **Double Czech (IRE)**[35] 4155 3-8-13 72 ............ (v) DavidProbert 2 | 40 |
| | | | (Patrick Chamings) *chsd ldrs: hmpd and lost pl after 1f: rdn over 2f out: wknd over 1f out* **13/2**[3] | |
| 0024 | 7 | 1 | **La Tinta Bay**[9] 5032 3-9-5 78 ............ PatDobbs 6 | 43 |
| | | | (Richard Hannon) *led 1f: prom tl wknd over 1f out* **16/1** | |
| 2462 | 8 | 13 | **Drive On (IRE)**[10] 5012 3-9-6 79 ............ (p) SilvestreDeSousa 3 | 2 |
| | | | (Eve Johnson Houghton) *chsd ldrs: edgd lft after 1f: rdn over 2f out: wknd over 1f out* **13/2**[3] | |

1m 14.51s (1.51) **Going Correction** +0.325s/f (Good) 8 Ran SP% **112.5**
Speed ratings (Par 102): **102,99,96,90,86 83,81,64**
CSF £17.79 CT £57.80 TOTE £5.00: £1.60, £2.10, £1.60; EX 21.80 Trifecta £67.00.
**Owner** Moyns Park Stud **Bred** Moyns Park Estate And Stud Ltd **Trained** Newmarket, Suffolk

**FOCUS**

They raced up the middle. The winner impressed and can rate higher again.

## 5382 AL BASTI EQUIWORLD EBF STALLIONS MAIDEN FILLIES' STKS 1m 2f 6y

5:00 (5:00) (Class 5) 3-Y-0+ £5,175 (£1,540; £769; £384) Stalls Low

| Form | | | | RPR |
|---|---|---|---|---|
| 22 | 1 | | **Blue Waltz**[19] 4699 3-9-0 0 ............ ShaneKelly 5 | 79+ |
| | | | (Luca Cumani) *lengthy: trckd ldrs: led over 1f out: sn drifted lft: styd on: pushed out* **11/8**[1] | |
| 4 | 2 | 1 ½ | **Bright Beacon**[28] 4413 3-9-0 0 ............ SilvestreDeSousa 1 | 76 |
| | | | (Charlie Appleby) *lengthy: unf: trckd ldr: rdn over 2f out: ev ch over 1f out: styd on fnl f* **5/1**[3] | |
| 0 | 3 | ½ | **Too The Stars (IRE)**[92] 2279 3-9-0 0 ............ RobertHavlin 2 | 76 |
| | | | (John Gosden) *w'like: led: rdn 2f out: hdd over 1f out: styng on at same pce in disp 2nd whn hmpd fnl 120yds: hld after* **7/1** | |
| | 4 | ¾ | **Seldom Seen** 3-9-0 0 ............ PatDobbs 6 | 74 |
| | | | (Sir Michael Stoute) *unf: scope: trckd ldrs: rdn 2f out: styd on same pce fnl f* **6/1** | |
| 0- | 5 | *shd* | **Rosarina**[239] 8340 3-8-9 0 ............ TimClark(5) 4 | 74 |
| | | | (Jo Crowley) *w'like: in tch: rdn over 2f out: styd on fnl f* **33/1** | |
| | 6 | 2 | **Taweyla (IRE)** 3-9-0 0 ............ AndreaAtzeni 8 | 70 |
| | | | (Roger Varian) *str: in tch: rdn 3f out: one pce fnl 2f* **9/2**[2] | |
| | 7 | 3 ¼ | **Panatella** 3-9-0 0 ............ LiamKeniry 11 | 64 |
| | | | (James Fanshawe) *w'like: hld up: hdwy over 3f out: rdn over 2f out: wknd ent fnl f* **16/1** | |
| 0 | 8 | 19 | **Sirrah Star (IRE)**[44] 3857 6-9-9 0 ............ WilliamCarson 7 | 28 |
| | | | (Neil Mulholland) *slowly away: last: hdwy over 4f out: rdn wl over 2f out: sn wknd* **100/1** | |

2m 14.89s (6.09) **Going Correction** +0.675s/f (Yiel)
**WFA** 3 from 6yo 9lb 8 Ran SP% **113.6**
Speed ratings (Par 100): **102,100,100,99,99 98,95,80**
CSF £8.42 TOTE £1.90: £1.10, £1.50, £1.70; EX 9.50 Trifecta £42.50.
**Owner** Fittocks Stud & Andrew Bengough **Bred** Fittocks Stud **Trained** Newmarket, Suffolk

**FOCUS**

Some slow-maturing fillies, so not form to get carried away with, but the race ought to produce winners. The form is rated at the bottom of the race averages. They edged middle-to-stands' side in the straight.

## 5383 TOM MITCHELL "DIAMOND" BIRTHDAY CELEBRATION APPRENTICE H'CAP (IN SUPPORT OF PROSTATE CANCER UK) 1m 1f

5:30 (5:30) (Class 5) (0-70,70) 4-Y-0+ £2,587 (£770; £384; £192) Stalls Low

| Form | | | | RPR |
|---|---|---|---|---|
| 0-21 | 1 | | **Wordismybond**[13] 4905 5-9-7 70 ............ ChrisMeehan(5) 7 | 77 |
| | | | (Peter Makin) *mde virtually all: jnd 5f out: rdn ahd 3f out: styd on wl fnl f* **13/8**[1] | |
| -604 | 2 | ¾ | **Celestial Bay**[16] 4798 5-8-13 62 ............ DavidParkes(5) 9 | 67 |
| | | | (Sylvester Kirk) *s.i.s: in last pair: hdwy 4f out: rdn to chse wnr wl over 2f out: styd on but a being hld fnl f* **7/1** | |
| 5446 | 3 | ¾ | **Beep**[23] 4548 4-8-12 59 ............ NedCurtis(3) 6 | 62 |
| | | | (Lydia Richards) *trckd ldrs: rdn over 2f out: styd on same pce fnl f* **6/1**[3] | |
| 343 | 4 | ½ | **Megalala (IRE)**[8] 5076 13-9-5 63 ............ ShelleyBirkett 5 | 65 |
| | | | (John Bridger) *fly-leapt leaving stalls: trckd ldrs: jnd wnr 5f out tl rdn 3f out: sn lost pl: styd on again fnl f* **7/2**[2] | |
| 0160 | 5 | ¾ | **Roxy Lane**[23] 4548 5-8-8 52 ............ NoelGarbutt 3 | 52 |
| | | | (Peter Hiatt) *trckd ldr: rdn 3f out: outpcd whn short of room 2f out: styd on again fnl f* **7/1** | |
| 0460 | 6 | 16 | **Speedy Writer**[23] 4548 4-9-2 65 ............ MichaelKenneally(5) 2 | 32 |
| | | | (Henry Candy) *in last pair: effrt 4f out: wknd 2f out* **6/1**[3] | |

2m 1.27s (5.77) **Going Correction** +0.675s/f (Yiel) 6 Ran SP% **113.9**
Speed ratings (Par 103): **101,100,99,99,98 84**
CSF £13.96 CT £54.36 TOTE £2.10: £2.20, £2.50; EX 7.70 Trifecta £38.50.
**Owner** T W Wellard & Partners **Bred** Henry And Mrs Rosemary Moszkowicz **Trained** Ogbourne Maisey, Wilts

**FOCUS**

They finished in a bit of heap and the winner is the best guide to this form.

T/Jkpt: £6,017.00 to a £1 stake. Pool: £46,611.02 - 5.50 winning units T/Plt: £30.50 to a £1 stake. Pool: £77,554.88 - 1,851.12 winning units T/Qpdt: £11.70 to a £1 stake. Pool: £5,465.52 - 345.37 winning units TM

# 5084 NEWCASTLE (L-H)

Friday, August 15

**OFFICIAL GOING: Good to soft (good in places; 6.8)**

Bends moved to fresh ground.

Wind: Breezy; half behind Weather: Cloudy; bright

## 5384 BET365 NURSERY H'CAP — 5f

2:00 (2:00) (Class 6) (0-60,60) 2-Y-O — £1,940 (£577; £288; £144) Stalls Centre

Form — RPR

304 **1** **Studio Star**[25] 4493 2-9-1 59 ....(p) JacobButterfield(5) 3 — 63
(Ollie Pears) *chsd ldrs: hdwy over 1f out: rdn to ld ins fnl f: kpt on wl* **6/1**

3046 **2** *hd* **Pickle Lilly Pearl**[14] 4857 2-9-2 55 .... GrahamGibbons 4 — 58
(David C Griffiths) *led: rdn and edgd rt over 1f out: hdd ins fnl f: kpt on: hld cl home* **16/1**

3632 **3** *1 3/4* **Midnight Destiny (IRE)**[27] 4422 2-9-5 58 .... DaleSwift 5 — 55
(Derek Shaw) *trckd ldrs: effrt and drvn over 1f out: kpt on same pce ins fnl f* **4/1**[2]

2532 **4** *1 1/4* **Penalty Scorer**[13] 4899 2-8-9 53 ....(e) DuilioDaSilva(5) 1 — 45
(Richard Guest) *s.i.s: t.k.h in rr: hdwy 1/2-way: effrt and rdn over 1f out: one pce fnl f* **5/1**[3]

440 **5** *3/4* **Snoway**[34] 4216 2-8-12 51 .... BarryMcHugh 8 — 41
(Tony Coyle) *in tch: drvn and outpcd 2f out: kpt on fnl f: no imp* **9/4**[1]

0540 **6** *1/2* **Ripon Rose**[10] 5014 2-9-7 60 .... PaulMulrennan 6 — 48
(Paul Midgley) *hld up bhd ldng gp: shkn up over 1f out: steadily outpcd fnl f* **12/1**

0040 **7** *nk* **Shamkhani**[48] 3713 2-8-6 45 .... PatrickMathers 11 — 32
(Alan Berry) *hld up: rdn and edgd lft 2f out: sn outpcd* **66/1**

506 **8** *hd* **Strategise (IRE)**[23] 4527 2-9-5 58 .... GrahamLee 10 — 44
(Tom Dascombe) *hld up in tch: drvn and outpcd 2f out: sn btn* **5/1**[3]

1m 1.51s (0.41) **Going Correction** -0.15s/f (Firm) — 8 Ran SP% **113.5**
Speed ratings (Par 92): **90,89,86,84,83 82,82,82**
CSF £91.43 CT £426.96 TOTE £6.30: £2.00, £4.10, £1.20; EX 80.20 Trifecta £487.00.
**Owner** Ownaracehorse Ltd (ownaracehorse.co.uk) **Bred** Elusive Bloodstock **Trained** Norton, N Yorks

**FOCUS**
This was a weak nursery. They went a sound pace down the centre and the first pair were always up there. The winning time suggested good ground. The form makes a lot of sense at face value.

## 5385 BET365 H'CAP — 7f

2:30 (2:30) (Class 4) (0-85,85) 3-Y-O+ — £4,851 (£1,443; £721; £360) Stalls Centre

Form — RPR

2-11 **1** **Shared Equity**[107] 1884 3-9-4 83 .... GrahamLee 6 — 92+
(Jedd O'Keeffe) *hld up in tch: stdy hdwy to ld over 1f out: sn rdn: kpt on strly fnl f* **6/1**[1]

6340 **2** *1 1/4* **Gatepost (IRE)**[16] 4783 5-9-2 80 .... JackGarritty(5) 8 — 88
(Richard Fahey) *dwlt: sn chsng ldrs: effrt and ev ch over 2f out: chsd wnr over 1f out: kpt on: hld last 75yds* **13/2**[2]

-566 **3** *1/2* **Almuheet**[15] 4826 3-9-4 83 .... DaleSwift 4 — 87
(Brian Ellison) *hld up bhd ldng gp: effrt and pushed along over 2f out: hdwy over 1f out: r.o ins fnl f* **12/1**

210U **4** *2 1/2* **Johnny Cavagin**[29] 4347 5-9-12 85 ....(t) TomEaves 10 — 85
(Richard Guest) *t.k.h: hld up in midfield: effrt over 2f out: kpt on fr over 1f out: nt rch first three* **7/1**[3]

/06- **5** *nse* **Reposer (IRE)**[319] 6911 6-9-8 81 .... JoeFanning 9 — 81
(Keith Dalgleish) *t.k.h: led to over 1f out: rdn and wknd ins fnl f* **33/1**

4126 **6** *2* **Illustrious Prince (IRE)**[6] 5197 7-8-13 77 .... JacobButterfield(5) 7 — 72
(Julie Camacho) *chsd ldrs: effrt and rdn 2f out: wknd ins fnl f* **14/1**

0013 **7** *4 1/2* **Escape To Glory (USA)**[13] 4923 6-9-12 85 .... PaulMulrennan 1 — 68
(Michael Dods) *hld up: stdy hdwy over 2f out: sn rdn: no imp fr wl over 1f out* **10/1**

0012 **8** *1 3/4* **Talent Scout (IRE)**[11] 4963 8-9-4 82 ....(p) GemmaTutty(5) 12 — 60
(Karen Tutty) *prom: drvn along over 2f out: wknd over 1f out* **8/1**

6110 **9** *shd* **Lady Artiste (IRE)**[69] 3000 4-9-0 73 .... DavidAllan 14 — 51
(Alan Swinbank) *hld up: drvn along wl over 2f out: sn outpcd: n.d after* **16/1**

0640 **10** *hd* **Lightnin Hopkins (IRE)**[25] 4487 4-8-13 72 ....[1] GrahamGibbons 2 — 50
(David O'Meara) *dwlt: hld up: rdn over 2f out: nvr able to chal* **28/1**

1231 **11** *2 1/2* **Mr McLaren**[21] 4628 3-9-2 81 .... DanielTudhope 3 — 50
(David O'Meara) *prom: rdn over 2f out: wknd over 1f out* **6/1**[1]

4/00 **12** *shd* **Take It To The Max**[27] 4451 7-8-11 70 ....(p) PJMcDonald 5 — 41
(George Moore) *cl up tl rdn and wknd over 2f out* **28/1**

1426 **13** *hd* **Cara's Request (AUS)**[14] 4861 9-8-12 74 .... ConnorBeasley(3) 11 — 44
(Michael Dods) *t.k.h: hld up towards rr: struggling over 2f out: sn btn* **14/1**

0425 **14** *2 1/2* **Sakhalin Star (IRE)**[28] 4387 3-8-5 75 .... DuilioDaSilva(5) 13 — 37
(Richard Guest) *t.k.h: hld up in tch: rdn and outpcd over 2f out: sn btn* **18/1**

1m 25.54s (-2.26) **Going Correction** -0.15s/f (Firm)
**WFA** 3 from 4yo+ 6lb — 14 Ran SP% **116.6**
Speed ratings (Par 105): **106,104,104,101,101 98,93,91,91,91 88,88,88,85**
CSF £41.34 CT £456.20 TOTE £5.20: £2.00, £3.30, £4.20; EX 57.30 Trifecta £659.10.
**Owner** Paul & Dale Chapman Racing **Bred** Trickledown Stud Limited **Trained** Middleham Moor, N Yorks

**FOCUS**
A fair and competiive handicap run at a sound gallop. The winner progressed again.

## 5386 BET365 / EBF MAIDEN STKS — 7f

3:00 (3:03) (Class 5) 2-Y-O — £2,911 (£866; £432; £216) Stalls Centre

Form — RPR

6 **1** **Mukhayyam**[20] 4670 2-9-5 0 .... GrahamLee 5 — 79+
(Sir Michael Stoute) *trckd ldrs: effrt and led over 1f out: hrd pressed ins fnl f: hld on wl towards fin* **5/2**[2]

6 **2** *nk* **Jolievitesse (FR)**[28] 4389 2-9-5 0 .... DanielTudhope 3 — 78
(K R Burke) *trckd ldrs: led over 2f out to over 1f out: rallied: kpt on fnl f: hld nr fin* **5/1**[3]

60 **3** *1 3/4* **Arcano Gold (IRE)**[21] 4633 2-9-5 0 .... TonyHamilton 11 — 74+
(Richard Fahey) *hld up: rdn over 2f out: kpt on wl fnl f: nt rch first two* **10/1**

**4** *hd* **Darrington** 2-9-0 0 .... SammyJoBell(5) 8 — 73+
(Richard Fahey) *hld up in tch: effrt and drvn over 1f out: kpt on same pce ins fnl f* **33/1**

232 **5** *7* **Summer Times**[10] 5013 2-9-5 0 .... JoeFanning 7 — 55
(Mark Johnston) *t.k.h early: cl up: rdn over 2f out: wknd appr fnl f* **15/8**[1]

46 **6** *3 3/4* **Little Houidini**[10] 4993 2-9-5 0 .... TomEaves 4 — 45
(Keith Dalgleish) *led tl rdn and hdd over 2f out: wknd over 1f out* **100/1**

0 **7** *6* **Brightside**[55] 3481 2-9-5 0 .... RoystonFfrench 1 — 30
(Tracy Waggott) *midfield: drvn along 1/2-way: wknd fr 2f out* **150/1**

0 **8** *1* **Molly Approve (IRE)**[69] 2979 2-9-0 0 .... BarryMcHugh 9 — 22
(Tony Coyle) *dwlt: hld up: rdn over 2f out: sn btn* **66/1**

**9** *1 3/4* **Colours Of Victory** 2-9-5 0 .... GrahamGibbons 6 — 22
(Kevin Ryan) *s.i.s: bhd and outpcd: nvr on terms* **25/1**

2 **10** *1 1/2* **Blackfoot Brave (IRE)**[67] 3049 2-9-5 0 .... PaulMulrennan 10 — 19
(Michael Dods) *chsd ldrs tl rdn and wknd over 2f out* **5/1**[3]

06 **11** *5* **Seraffimo**[23] 4528 2-9-5 0 .... PaddyAspell 12 — 6
(Sharon Watt) *midfield: drvn and outpcd 3f out: sn btn* **150/1**

**12** *43* **Gypsy Major** 2-9-5 0 .... JasonHart 2
(John Murray) *missed break: bhd and struggling: lost tch fr 1/2-way* **125/1**

1m 26.72s (-1.08) **Going Correction** -0.15s/f (Firm) — 12 Ran SP% **117.2**
Speed ratings (Par 94): **100,99,97,97,89 85,78,77,75,73 67,18**
CSF £15.00 TOTE £3.50: £1.10, £2.30, £2.20; EX 20.40 Trifecta £130.70.
**Owner** Hamdan Al Maktoum **Bred** Mrs James Wigan **Trained** Newmarket, Suffolk

**FOCUS**
A fair 2yo maiden. The winner built on his debut promise, his cause aided by some others disappointing.

## 5387 BET365.COM H'CAP — 1m 2f 32y

3:35 (3:35) (Class 5) (0-75,75) 3-Y-O — £2,587 (£770; £384; £192) Stalls Centre

Form — RPR

0636 **1** **Mantou (IRE)**[19] 4698 3-9-7 75 .... JoeFanning 3 — 83+
(Michael Bell) *trckd ldr: shkn up to ld over 2f out: edgd lft ins fnl f: hld on wl towards fin* **10/3**[2]

-432 **2** *3/4* **Stanarley Pic**[10] 5015 3-8-13 67 .... DavidAllan 5 — 73
(Alan Swinbank) *hld up: hdwy and swtchd rt over 1f out: chsd wnr appr fnl f: kpt on fin but a hld* **11/4**[1]

3461 **3** *1/2* **Clear Spell (IRE)**[13] 4904 3-9-0 68 .... PJMcDonald 4 — 73
(Alistair Whillans) *hld up in tch: smooth hdwy whn nt clr run briefly over 1f out: effrt whn n.m.r ins fnl f: r.o* **13/2**

1632 **4** *2 1/2* **Trinity Star (IRE)**[31] 4292 3-8-11 65 ....(p) PaulMulrennan 7 — 65
(Michael Dods) *t.k.h: in tch: hdwy to chse wnr wl over 1f out to appr fnl f: no ex last 100yds* **5/1**

-543 **5** *1 1/2* **Ryeolliean**[10] 5015 3-9-7 75 .... DanielTudhope 2 — 72
(David O'Meara) *led at ordinary gallop: rdn and hdd over 2f out: sn outpcd: n.d after* **9/2**[3]

00 **6** *1/2* **Shirocco Passion**[8] 5101 3-8-13 67 .... BarryMcHugh 1 — 64
(Tony Coyle) *dwlt: sn chsng ldrs: rdn over 2f out: wknd over 1f out* **20/1**

0641 **7** *2 3/4* **Syros (IRE)**[14] 4871 3-9-3 71 .... GrahamGibbons 6 — 62
(Michael Easterby) *hld up: drvn and outpcd over 2f out: nvr rchd ldrs* **14/1**

2m 11.69s (-0.21) **Going Correction** +0.025s/f (Good) — 7 Ran SP% **109.4**
Speed ratings (Par 100): **101,100,100,98,96 96,94**
CSF £11.74 CT £48.78 TOTE £3.20: £1.50, £2.20; EX 16.10 Trifecta £84.10.
**Owner** Sheikh Marwan Al Maktoum **Bred** Darley **Trained** Newmarket, Suffolk
■ Stewards' Enquiry : Joe Fanning one-day ban: careless riding (29 Aug)

**FOCUS**
Not a bad 3yo handicap, run at a fair pace. The winner looks the type to progress again.

## 5388 BET365.COM MAIDEN STKS — 1m 2f 32y

4:10 (4:12) (Class 5) 3-Y-O+ — £2,587 (£770; £384; £192) Stalls Centre

Form — RPR

3- **1** **Lobster Pot**[305] 7244 3-8-13 0 .... JoeFanning 9 — 71+
(Hugo Palmer) *mde all: rdn and edgd rt over 1f out: kpt on wl whn pressed ins fnl f* **11/8**[1]

26 **2** *3/4* **Dreaming Beauty**[28] 4407 3-8-13 0 .... GrahamLee 3 — 69
(Jeremy Noseda) *chsd ldrs: wnt 2nd over 3f out: pushed along over 2f out: effrt and clsd ins fnl f: kpt on: hld nr fin* **11/8**[1]

55 **3** *5* **Chilly Miss**[19] 4705 5-9-8 0 .... BrianHughes 2 — 60
(Malcolm Jefferson) *midfield: shkn up over 4f out: rdn and edgd lft over 1f out: chsd clr ldrs ins fnl f: nvr nrr* **16/1**

44 **4** *1* **Braes Of Lochalsh**[11] 4978 3-9-1 0 .... GaryBartley(3) 7 — 64
(Jim Goldie) *hld up: pushed along over 3f out: styng on whn nt clr run over 1f out: kpt on fnl f: nrst fin* **14/1**[3]

4-3 **5** *1/2* **Medicine Hat**[13] 4924 3-9-4 0 .... PJMcDonald 4 — 62
(George Moore) *midfield: effrt over 2f out: hung lft and chsd clr ldrs over 1f out to ins fnl f: sn btn* **14/1**[3]

-000 **6** *2 1/4* **Magic Shoes (IRE)**[85] 2491 3-8-13 0 .... RoystonFfrench 1 — 52?
(Susan Corbett) *prom tl rdn and wknd fr 2f out* **100/1**

00- **7** *8* **Scrafton**[308] 7175 3-9-4 0 .... PaulMulrennan 6 — 42
(James Bethell) *hld up: pushed along over 3f out: struggling fnl 2f* **66/1**

0 **8** *11* **Absolute (IRE)**[28] 4407 3-9-4 0 .... PaddyAspell 10 — 21
(Marco Botti) *trckd wnr to over 3f out: wknd 2f out* **8/1**[2]

00 **9** *1 3/4* **Tiger Heights**[22] 4569 3-9-4 0 .... TomEaves 5 — 18
(Jim Goldie) *hld up: struggling 1/2-way: sn btn* **80/1**

**10** *33* **Teide Mistress (USA)**[33] 4-9-8 0 .... BarryMcHugh 8
(Alistair Whillans) *midfield: struggling 1/2-way: sn btn: t.o* **100/1**

2m 11.7s (-0.20) **Going Correction** +0.025s/f (Good)
**WFA** 3 from 4yo+ 9lb — 10 Ran SP% **119.2**
Speed ratings (Par 103): **101,100,96,95,95 93,87,78,76,50**
CSF £3.24 TOTE £2.20: £1.20, £1.10, £3.10; EX 3.50 Trifecta £24.80.
**Owner** Anglia Bloodstock Syndicate II **Bred** Masaood Al Masaood **Trained** Newmarket, Suffolk

**FOCUS**
The market leaders were always to the fore in this modest maiden, which was steadily run. The winner is entitled to do better.

## 5389 POKER AT BET365 H'CAP — 5f

4:40 (4:40) (Class 5) (0-70,72) 3-Y-O — £2,587 (£770; £384; £192) Stalls Centre

Form — RPR

3230 **1** **Lucky Times**[39] 4019 3-8-12 59 .... DavidAllan 6 — 66+
(Mel Brittain) *in tch: hdwy to ld over 1f out: drvn out fnl f* **14/1**

5014 **2** *1/2* **Scoreline**[6] 5169 3-9-7 68 .... DanielTudhope 8 — 73
(David O'Meara) *hld up: rdn and hdwy over 1f out: chsd wnr ins fnl f: kpt on* **11/2**[2]

3001 **3** *2 1/4* **Tinsill**[8] 5087 3-9-4 72 6ex .... AnnaHesketh(7) 2 — 69
(Nigel Tinkler) *prom: effrt and shkn up over 1f out: kpt on ins fnl f: nt rch first two* **13/2**[3]

4300 **4** *1 1/4* **Fujin**[14] 4873 3-8-10 60 ....(p) JoeyHaynes(3) 5 — 52
(Noel Wilson) *w ldrs: led over 2f out to over 1f out: no ex ins fnl f* **33/1**

630U **5** *shd* **Singing Star (IRE)**[16] 4796 3-8-2 49 .... RoystonFfrench 4 — 41
(Mel Brittain) *led to over 2f out: rdn and no ex fr over 1f out* **12/1**

0452 **6** *nk* **Red Forever**[6] 5169 3-9-2 63 PatrickMathers 9 54
(Alan Berry) *hld up: rdn over 2f out: hung lft over 1f out: kpt on ins fnl f: no imp* **8/1**

0306 **7** *nk* **Fuel Injection**[11] 4977 3-9-1 62 (p) JamesSullivan 1 52
(Paul Midgley) *t.k.h: cl up: rdn and edgd lft over 1f out: no ex ins fnl f* **10/1**

1422 **8** *3/4* **Shades Of Silk**[8] 5080 3-9-1 62 (p) GrahamLee 3 49
(James Given) *cl up: pushed along after 2f: rdn and no ex over 1f out* **11/8**[1]

045- **9** *1 1/4* **Captain Gee**[252] 8188 3-8-8 55 IanBrennan 7 38
(John Quinn) *hld up: rdn 1/2-way: nvr able to chal* **25/1**

1m 0.51s (-0.59) **Going Correction** -0.15s/f (Firm) **9** Ran SP% **112.2**
Speed ratings (Par 100): **98,97,93,91,91 90,90,89,87**
CSF £85.75 CT £553.62 TOTE £14.00: £3.60, £1.50, £2.30; EX 98.10 Trifecta £438.40.
**Owner** Mel Brittain **Bred** Harrowgate Bloodstock Ltd **Trained** Warthill, N Yorks

**FOCUS**
As expected this moderate 3yo sprint handicap was run at a strong pace. The form is rated around the second.

## 5390 CASINO AT BET365 H'CAP 6f
**5:10** (5:12) (Class 6) (0-65,65) 3-Y-O+ **£1,940** (£577; £288; £144) **Stalls** Centre

Form RPR

5503 **1** **Armelle (FR)**[10] 4998 3-8-1 49 MatthewHopkins(5) 2 57
(Scott Dixon) *mde all: rdn 2f out: hld on wl ins fnl f* **13/2**[3]

3042 **2** *nk* **Red Shadow**[16] 4795 5-8-10 49 (p) PaulPickard 11 57
(Alan Brown) *cl up: drvn over 2f out: rallied fnl f: kpt on wl: jst hld* **11/1**

0135 **3** *3/4* **Exotic Guest**[8] 5089 4-9-12 65 JamesSullivan 5 71
(Ruth Carr) *hld up: rdn and gd hdwy over 1f out: kpt on same pce wl ins fnl f* **7/2**[2]

5404 **4** *1* **Black Douglas**[4] 5237 5-8-10 52 GaryBartley(3) 4 54
(Jim Goldie) *dwlt: hld up: pushed along and drifted lft to far rail 2f out: kpt on ins fnl f: nvr able to chal* **15/2**

4004 **5** *1/2* **Bapak Muda (USA)**[29] 4358 4-9-7 60 (p) AmyRyan 8 61
(Kevin Ryan) *hld up: pushed along over 2f out: hdwy over 1f out: kpt on: no imp* **14/1**

6-40 **6** *3/4* **Best Tamayuz**[104] 1939 3-8-9 52 TomEaves 12 49
(Scott Dixon) *t.k.h: in tch: rdn 2f out: no imp fnl f* **40/1**

00-4 **7** *3/4* **Stoneacre Oskar**[29] 4362 5-8-9 48 GrahamLee 10 44
(Peter Grayson) *hld up: rdn over 2f out: hdwy over 1f out: kpt on: nvr able to chal* **22/1**

044 **8** *3/4* **Dartrix**[8] 5089 5-9-8 64 ConnorBeasley(3) 1 58
(Michael Dods) *dwlt: sn midfield: hdwy 2f out: wknd ins fnl f* **10/3**[1]

0000 **9** *1 3/4* **One Kool Dude**[37] 4070 5-8-7 46 oh1 (b) PatrickMathers 6 34
(Micky Hammond) *in tch: rdn over 2f out: wknd over 1f out* **22/1**

0103 **10** *nk* **Ichimoku**[31] 4288 4-8-12 51 RoystonFfrench 7 38
(Bryan Smart) *in tch: drvn and outpcd 1/2-way: no imp fr over 1f out* **12/1**

0040 **11** *1/2* **The Strig**[3] 5287 7-9-2 55 (v) AdrianNicholls 3 40
(Nigel Tinkler) *prom: rdn over 2f out: wknd over 1f out* **11/1**

0440 **12** *4* **Balinka**[77] 2724 4-8-13 52 DavidAllan 14 25
(Mel Brittain) *hld up: rdn over 2f out: sn btn* **20/1**

0050 **13** *5* **Ishetoo**[7] 5138 10-8-7 46 oh1 IanBrennan 13 3
(Peter Grayson) *racd alone nr stands' rail: a bhd: struggling fr 1/2-way* **50/1**

1m 13.37s (-1.23) **Going Correction** -0.15s/f (Firm)
**WFA** 3 from 4yo+ 4lb **13** Ran SP% **119.3**
Speed ratings (Par 101): **102,101,100,99,98 97,96,95,93,92 92,86,80**
CSF £70.48 CT £302.65 TOTE £8.60: £2.90, £3.00, £1.40; EX 60.90 Trifecta £258.80.
**Owner** The Friday Follies **Bred** J Vittori & Mme Y Dixon **Trained** Babworth, Notts

**FOCUS**
The main action developed down the middle of the track in this typically open sprint handicap and the form is straightforward.
T/Plt: £54.50 to a £1 stake. Pool: £77,439.17 - 1,036.73 winning units T/Qpdt: £12.90 to a £1 stake. Pool: £6,930.25 - 394.60 winning units RY

# 5344 NEWMARKET (R-H)
Friday, August 15

**OFFICIAL GOING: Soft (6.1)**
Stands side track used with Stalls on Stands side except 10f: Centre.
Wind: Light; behind Weather: Overcast

## 5391 TONY B CELEBRATION MEDIAN AUCTION MAIDEN STKS (BOBIS RACE) 7f
**5:25** (5:27) (Class 4) 2-Y-O **£3,881** (£1,155; £577; £289) **Stalls** High

Form RPR

43 **1** **Hail Clodius (IRE)**[13] 4885 2-9-5 0 RichardHughes 6 87+
(Richard Hannon) *led tl 3f out: styd upsides ldr and stl travelling strly: shkn up to ld over 1f out: qcknd and gng clr whn flashed tail u.p ins fnl f: easily* **5/2**[2]

63 **2** *5* **Fieldsman (USA)**[13] 4896 2-9-5 0 KierenFallon 4 74
(Ed Dunlop) *chsd ldr tl led 3f out: rdn and hdd over 1f out: outpcd by wnr fnl f: kpt on for clr 2nd* **6/5**[1]

**3** *2 1/4* **Tadpole** 2-9-0 0 LiamJones 2 63
(William Haggas) *chsd ldrs: rdn 3f out: outpcd over 1f out: wl hld and styd on same pce after* **7/2**[3]

**4** *nk* **Le Rouquin (FR)** 2-9-5 0 TomQueally 8 67
(Michael Bell) *chsd ldrs: rdn ent fnl 2f: outpcd over 1f out: battling for modest 3rd and kpt on same pce fnl f* **16/1**

**5** *2 1/4* **Eatsleepracerepeat** 2-9-5 0 ChrisCatlin 1 62
(Lady Cecil) *s.i.s: in tch towards rr: rdn and effrt in 5th over 2f out: sn struggling: wknd over 1f out* **16/1**

**6** *10* **Oakley Girl** 2-9-0 0 HarryBentley 3 31
(Stuart Williams) *s.i.s: in tch in rr: rdn over 2f out: sn btn and lost tch* **33/1**

0 **7** *19* **Katniss (IRE)**[7] 5149 2-9-0 0 AdamBeschizza 7
(Stuart Williams) *s.i.s: in tch in midfield: dropped to rr 1/2-way: sn lost tch: t.o over 1f out* **100/1**

1m 28.54s (2.84) **Going Correction** +0.275s/f (Good) **7** Ran SP% **111.9**
Speed ratings (Par 96): **94,88,85,85,82 71,49**
CSF £5.59 TOTE £3.50: £2.60, £1.20; EX 5.90 Trifecta £11.30.
**Owner** Middleham Park Racing LXXXIV **Bred** Camogue Stud Ltd **Trained** East Everleigh, Wilts

**FOCUS**
Stands' side track used with stalls on stands' side except 10f: Centre. After 11mm of rain had fallen the previous day, the official going was soft. After winning the opener, Richard Hughes described the ground as "tacky". Little depth to this juvenile maiden, in which the two market leaders pulled clear.

## 5392 ANGLIAN HOME IMPROVEMENTS H'CAP 6f
**6:00** (6:00) (Class 4) (0-85,85) 3-Y-O+ **£5,175** (£1,540; £769; £384) **Stalls** High

Form RPR

0030 **1** **Regal Parade**[13] 4892 10-9-12 85 (t) KierenFallon 8 94
(Milton Bradley) *broke wl: sn stdd to chse ldr: rdn to ld over 1f out: r.o wl fnl f* **3/1**[3]

4055 **2** *1/2* **Joe Packet**[13] 4918 7-9-3 81 DannyBrock(5) 7 88
(Jonathan Portman) *stdd after s: t.k.h: hld up in tch: rdn and effrt over 1f out: chsd wnr ins fnl f: r.o but a hld* **2/1**[2]

2-13 **3** *1 1/2* **Sunrise Star**[36] 4133 3-9-3 85 LouisSteward(5) 3 86
(Lady Cecil) *t.k.h: chsd ldng pair: rdn and effrt to chse wnr over 1f out tl ins fnl f: outpcd fnl 100yds* **7/4**[1]

0-06 **4** *3* **Rocket Rob (IRE)**[28] 4406 8-9-0 73 TomQueally 9 66
(Willie Musson) *sn led: rdn and hdd over 1f out: immediately outpcd and btn: wknd ins fnl f* **10/1**

0200 **5** *7* **Powerful Pierre**[14] 4866 7-8-7 71 ow1 TobyAtkinson(5) 6 41
(Noel Quinlan) *stdd after s: t.k.h: hld up in rr: rdn over 1f out: sn btn* **20/1**

1m 14.28s (1.78) **Going Correction** +0.275s/f (Good)
**WFA** 3 from 4yo+ 4lb **5** Ran SP% **108.5**
Speed ratings (Par 105): **99,98,96,92,83**
CSF £9.13 TOTE £4.40: £2.60, £1.20; EX 8.10 Trifecta £11.40.
**Owner** Dab Hand Racing **Bred** Highclere Stud And Harry Herbert **Trained** Sedbury, Gloucs

**FOCUS**
A tight sprint handicap. The winner is rated close to his latter 2013 form.

## 5393 NGK SPARK PLUGS EBF STALLIONS MAIDEN STKS (BOBIS RACE) 1m
**6:30** (6:30) (Class 4) 2-Y-O **£4,528** (£1,347; £673; £336) **Stalls** High

Form RPR

2 **1** **My Sebastian**[17] 4764 2-9-5 0 KierenFallon 2 85
(Philip McBride) *chsd ldrs: effrt and squeezed between rivals to ld 2f out: edgd lft u.p ins fnl f: hld on wl: rdn out* **4/1**[3]

**2** *nk* **Arabian Oasis** 2-9-5 0 WilliamBuick 4 84+
(Charlie Appleby) *t.k.h: hld up in tch: rdn 3f out: hdwy to chse wnr jst over 1f out: str chal ins fnl f: r.o but hld towards fin* **11/4**[2]

**3** *3/4* **Khusoosy (USA)** 2-9-5 0 ChrisCatlin 5 83+
(Saeed bin Suroor) *s.i.s: bhd: hdwy over 1f out: rdn and chsd clr ldng pair 1f out: styd on wl under hands and heels fnl 100yds: nvr quite getting to ldrs* **8/1**

2 **4** *5* **Manshaa (IRE)**[17] 4750 2-9-5 0 DaneO'Neill 6 71
(Mark Johnston) *led tl hdd and rdn 2f out: outpcd and btn ent fnl f: wknd fnl 150yds* **6/4**[1]

63 **5** *3* **Servery**[13] 4884 2-9-5 0 RichardHughes 1 64
(Richard Hannon) *chsd ldr: ev ch and rdn 2f out: sn outpcd and btn 1f out: wknd fnl f* **7/1**

1m 44.88s (4.88) **Going Correction** +0.275s/f (Good) **5** Ran SP% **110.3**
Speed ratings (Par 96): **86,85,84,79,76**
CSF £15.20 TOTE £4.10: £2.00, £1.80; EX 21.00 Trifecta £51.30.
**Owner** Ten Fools & A Horse & Partner **Bred** Wood Farm Stud (Waresley) **Trained** Newmarket, Suffolk

**FOCUS**
Recent winners of this interesting maiden included Frankel in 2010 and subsequent Derby hero Motivator in 2004. This year's winner was the only runner in the field not entered in the Derby. The pair with the best pre-race form disappointed but the winner could be rated higher.

## 5394 32RED CASINO H'CAP 1m
**7:00** (7:01) (Class 5) (0-75,75) 3-Y-O+ **£3,881** (£1,155; £577; £288) **Stalls** High

Form RPR

1245 **1** **Trulee Scrumptious**[43] 3878 5-8-10 59 (v) JimmyQuinn 9 71
(Peter Charalambous) *mde all: clr and rdn 2f out: drvn ent fnl f: styd on wl* **6/1**

1432 **2** *2 1/2* **Starlight Serenade**[27] 4426 3-9-3 73 SilvestreDeSousa 6 78
(Ralph Beckett) *stdd s: t.k.h: hld up in rr: rdn 2f out: hdwy u.p to chse clr wnr ins fnl f: styd on but no imp* **13/8**[1]

634 **3** *2 3/4* **Emperatriz**[11] 4963 4-9-2 65 StevieDonohoe 5 65
(John Holt) *taken down early: chsd wnr: rdn over 2f out: styd on same pce u.p fnl 2f: lost 2nd ins fnl f* **8/1**

4005 **4** *3/4* **Rouge Nuage (IRE)**[10] 5006 4-9-2 65 (p) LiamJones 7 63
(Conrad Allen) *chsd ldng trio: rdn over 2f out: drvn and no imp fr over 1f out* **25/1**

3602 **5** *4* **Tullia (IRE)**[10] 5004 3-9-5 75 AndreaAtzeni 1 63
(William Knight) *chsd ldrs: rdn 3f out: struggling 2f out and sn btn: wknd 1f out* **5/1**[3]

563 **6** *6* **Harry Bosch**[27] 4432 4-9-12 75 TomQueally 3 50
(Gay Kelleway) *hld up in last trio: rdn over 2f out: no prog and sn btn: bhd 1f out* **20/1**

2242 **7** *1 1/4* **Hot Mustard**[8] 5109 4-8-11 60 RichardHughes 8 32
(Michael Bell) *in tch in midfield: rdn 3f out: no prog and btn 1f out: bhd and eased ins fnl f* **7/2**[2]

0-06 **8** *1 3/4* **Crown Pleasure (IRE)**[21] 4623 3-8-10 66 ChrisCatlin 12 33
(Willie Musson) *stdd s: hld up in tch in rr: rdn 3f out: sn btn: bhd 1f out* **50/1**

1m 41.23s (1.23) **Going Correction** +0.275s/f (Good)
**WFA** 3 from 4yo+ 7lb **8** Ran SP% **112.9**
Speed ratings (Par 103): **104,101,98,98,94 88,86,85**
CSF £15.70 CT £78.27 TOTE £7.80: £2.20, £1.10, £2.60; EX 19.50 Trifecta £124.20.
**Owner** pcracing.co.uk **Bred** Dxb Bloodstock Ltd **Trained** Newmarket, Suffolk

**FOCUS**
A fair handicap in which the first four were always prominent and the winner made all. She was close to confirming last year's best figure.

## 5395 £10 FREE BET AT 32REDSPORT.COM H'CAP 1m 2f
**7:35** (7:36) (Class 5) (0-70,68) 3-Y-O+ **£3,881** (£1,155; £577; £288) **Stalls** Centre

Form RPR

2344 **1** **Charlie Wells (IRE)**[12] 4941 3-9-5 68 (b) JohnFahy 5 76
(Eve Johnson Houghton) *t.k.h: hld up in tch towards rr: hdwy over 2f out: rdn to chse clr ldr and edgd rt ent fnl f: styd on u.p to ld fnl 50yds* **9/2**[2]

0-54 **2** *nk* **My Guardian Angel**[33] 3678 5-9-8 62 (p) TedDurcan 1 69
(Mark H Tompkins) *hld up in tch in rr: swtchd lft and hdwy 2f out: chsd ldrs and rdn over 1f out: styd on ins fnl f: wnt 2nd towards fin* **14/1**



The Form Book, Raceform Ltd, Newbury, RG14 5SJ

5010 **3** ½ **Storm Rider (IRE)**[64] 3146 3-9-3 66 RichardHughes 6 72
(Richard Hannon) *chsd ldrs tl 1/2-way: lost pl and rdn 3f out: rallied u.p to chse ldrs 1f out: styd on ins fnl f: wnt 3rd last strides* **7/2**[1]

2060 **4** *hd* **Minstrel Lad**[7] 5139 6-9-5 62 SimonPearce(3) 9 68
(Lydia Pearce) *stdd s: hld up in rr: hdwy 1/2-way: chsd ldr over 2f out: led on bit over 1f out: clr and rdn 1f out: edgd lft u.p ins fnl f: wknd fnl 100yds: hdd and lost 3 pls fnl 50yds* **8/1**[3]

0021 **5** *7* **Tete Orange**[31] 4304 3-9-1 64 AndreaAtzeni 3 57
(Stuart Williams) *in tch in midfield: rdn over 1f out: no rspnse and sn btn: wknd fnl f* **7/2**[1]

**6** *6* **Bosstime (IRE)**[112] 1704 4-9-9 63 StevieDonohoe 8 44
(John Holt) *chsd ldr tl over 2f out: sn hung lft u.p and lost pl 2f out: wknd over 1f out* **12/1**

0-45 **7** 1¼ **Robin Hood (IRE)**[22] 4586 6-9-11 65 JackMitchell 10 44
(Philip Mitchell) *hld up in tch in midfield: rdn 3f out: lost pl and towards rr whn swtchd rt over 1f out: sn wknd u.p* **10/1**

50 **8** 3¾ **L Ge R**[56] 3428 3-8-2 54 RosieJessop(3) 4 26
(Peter Charalambous) *led: rdn and hdd over 1f out: drvn and lost 2nd jst over 1f out: sn btn and fdd fnl f* **8/1**[3]

3606 **9** *21* **Mcbirney (USA)**[57] 3398 7-9-9 63 PatrickDonaghy 2
(Paul D'Arcy) *stdd s: hld up in rr: hdwy into midfield 5f out: rdn 3f out: wknd 2f out: wl bhd fnl f: t.o: lame* **12/1**

2m 10.94s (5.44) **Going Correction** +0.275s/f (Good)
**WFA** 3 from 4yo+ 9lb 9 Ran SP% **116.0**
Speed ratings (Par 103): **89,88,88,88,82 77,76,73,57**
CSF £65.02 CT £245.78 TOTE £5.30: £1.70, £2.50, £1.80; EX 61.30 Trifecta £356.20.
**Owner** Eden Racing **Bred** Carlingford Breeding Syndicate **Trained** Blewbury, Oxon

**FOCUS**
Only a modest handicap. A small personal best from the winner.

## 5396 ENCON GROUP FILLIES' H'CAP 7f
8:05 (8:05) (Class 3) (0-95,89) 3-Y-O+ £7,762 (£2,310; £1,154) Stalls High

Form RPR

5112 **1** **Felwah**[34] 4182 3-9-1 84 DaneO'Neill 3 94
(William Haggas) *mde all: rdn and qcknd 2f out: in command ins fnl f: r.o wl* **8/11**[1]

5612 **2** 2¼ **Alexandrakollontai (IRE)**[13] 4902 4-8-10 76 (b) JulieBurke(3) 8 82
(Alistair Whillans) *wnt sharply lft s: in tch in 3rd: rdn ent fnl 2f: chsd wnr over 1f out: r.o same pce fnl f* **15/8**[2]

010 **3** *7* **Stealth Missile (IRE)**[20] 4668 3-9-6 89 (t) KierenFallon 7 78
(Clive Brittain) *chsd wnr: rdn ent fnl 2f: dropped to 3rd and btn over 1f out: eased wl ins fnl f* **5/1**[3]

1m 32.1s (6.40) **Going Correction** +0.275s/f (Good)
**WFA** 3 from 4yo 6lb 3 Ran SP% **109.4**
Speed ratings (Par 104): **74,71,63**
CSF £2.44 TOTE £1.80; EX 2.30 Trifecta £2.20.
**Owner** Khalil Alsayegh **Bred** Khalil Al Sayegh **Trained** Newmarket, Suffolk

**FOCUS**
The field was depleted after five were withdrawn because of the ground, and the favourite made no mistake. The form is rated around the second.
T/Plt: £49.30 to a £1 stake. Pool: £57,394.64 - 848.93 winning units T/Qpdt: £16.40 to a £1 stake. Pool: £5,311.41 - 239.40 winning units SP

# 5285 NOTTINGHAM (L-H)
Friday, August 15

**OFFICIAL GOING: Good to firm (firm in places in the back straight)**
Outer track used. Rail moved out 4m around whole course increasing distances on Round course by 24yds.
Wind: Light; half behind Weather: Sunny periods

## 5397 JUNCTION 17 PRESTIGE CARS EBF STALLIONS MAIDEN STKS 6f 15y
2:10 (2:10) (Class 5) 2-Y-O £3,234 (£962; £481; £240) Stalls Centre

Form RPR

32 **1** **Flash Fire (IRE)**[9] 5050 2-9-5 0 FrannyNorton 1 88
(Mark Johnston) *mde most: rdn wl over 1f out: drvn ins fnl f: kpt on wl towards fin* **5/6**[1]

**2** ½ **Charming Thought** 2-9-5 0 JamesDoyle 6 86+
(Charlie Appleby) *cl up: chal 2f out: rdn over 1f out: ev ch tl no ex last 75yds* **2/1**[2]

52 **3** *7* **Giannizzero (IRE)**[15] 4829 2-9-0 0 DanielMuscutt(5) 3 64
(Marco Botti) *trckd ldrs: hdwy and cl up on outer 1/2-way: rdn along wl over 1f out: wknd fnl f* **16/1**

5 **4** ½ **Red Harry (IRE)**[28] 4416 2-9-5 0 AndrewElliott 4 62
(Tom Tate) *t.k.h early: cl up: pushed along and outpcd 1/2-way: rdn wl over 1f out: styd on in fnl f: n.m.r and tk modest 3rd nr fin* **40/1**

**5** *nk* **Bamboccianti** 2-9-2 0 GeorgeChaloner(3) 7 61
(Richard Fahey) *cl up: rdn along wl over 1f out: wknd fnl f* **8/1**[3]

06 **6** *4* **Lopito De Vega (IRE)**[16] 4787 2-9-5 0 PhillipMakin 5 48
(James Given) *dwlt and wnt lft s: a towards rr* **100/1**

**7** *18* **Sir Veillance** 2-9-5 0 AndrewMullen 2
(Michael Appleby) *sn pushed along in rr: reminders and edgd lft 1/2-way: sn outpcd and bhd* **66/1**

1m 13.45s (-1.25) **Going Correction** -0.175s/f (Firm) 7 Ran SP% **109.8**
Speed ratings (Par 94): **101,100,91,90,89 84,60**
CSF £2.39 TOTE £1.40: £1.10, £3.70; EX 3.20 Trifecta £16.40.
**Owner** Sheikh Hamdan bin Mohammed Al Maktoum **Bred** Darley **Trained** Middleham Moor, N Yorks

**FOCUS**
No overnight rain, but 5mm of water was put on the bends and on the home straight early in the morning. The going was a little quicker than had been expected. This has proved a good maiden in recent years, and this was perhaps another step up from the winner.

## 5398 EAST MIDLANDS DESIGNER OUTLET FILLIES' H'CAP (JOCKEY CLUB GRASSROOTS SPRINT SERIES QUALIFIER) 6f 15y
2:40 (2:40) (Class 4) (0-80,76) 3-Y-O+ £5,175 (£1,540; £769; £384) Stalls Centre

Form RPR

4211 **1** **Guishan**[8] 5097 4-9-6 72 6ex AndrewMullen 1 85
(Michael Appleby) *wnt lft s: sn cl up and led after 1f: pushed along over 2f out: rdn wl over 1f out: wandered and drvn ent fnl f: kpt on strly* **7/2**[2]

5612 **2** 2¼ **First Experience**[15] 4811 3-9-6 76 LukeMorris 4 81
(Rae Guest) *trckd wnr: hdwy 2f out: rdn over 1f out: drvn and kpt on fnl f* **11/4**[1]

0604 **3** *nk* **Ligeia**[10] 5008 3-9-0 75 CamHardie(5) 7 79
(Richard Hannon) *chsd ldrs on outer: pushed along 1/2-way: rdn 2f out: kpt on u.p fnl f* **6/1**

2111 **4** *hd* **Refuse Colette (IRE)**[9] 5059 5-9-9 75 6ex PaoloSirigu 2 79
(Mick Quinn) *trckd ldrs on outer: hdwy 1/2-way: rdn to chse wnr ent fnl f: edgd lft and one pce last 100yds* **9/2**[3]

3313 **5** 1¼ **Burren View Lady (IRE)**[6] 5199 4-9-9 75 (e) DuranFentiman 6 75
(Tim Easterby) *trckd ldrs: hdwy 1/2-way: rdn along 2f out: drvn and one pce appr fnl f* **8/1**

6353 **6** *3* **Meandmyshadow**[21] 4632 6-9-2 68 JamesDoyle 5 59
(Alan Brown) *slt ld 1f: cl up: rdn over 2f out: drvn wl over 1f out and sn wknd* **5/1**

1m 13.23s (-1.47) **Going Correction** -0.175s/f (Firm)
**WFA** 3 from 4yo+ 4lb 6 Ran SP% **109.1**
Speed ratings (Par 102): **102,99,98,98,96 92**
CSF £12.71 TOTE £3.30: £1.30, £1.70; EX 11.10 Trifecta £54.40.
**Owner** Brian D Cantle **Bred** B D Cantle **Trained** Danethorpe, Notts

**FOCUS**
Some in-form fillies lined up for this handicap. The winner continued her progress.

## 5399 GROSVENOR CASINO NOTTINGHAM H'CAP 5f 13y
3:10 (3:10) (Class 6) (0-60,60) 3-Y-O+ £1,940 (£577; £288; £144) Stalls Centre

Form RPR

0051 **1** **Spider Lily**[7] 5126 3-8-6 51 6ex DeclanBates(3) 2 59+
(Peter Makin) *trckd ldrs: cl up 1/2-way: led ent fnl f and sn rdn: drvn and edgd rt nr fin: hld on wl* **4/1**[1]

0122 **2** *hd* **Burnt Cream**[14] 4848 7-9-6 59 (t) StevieDonohoe 8 67
(Martin Bosley) *hld up: hdwy 2f out: rdn ent fnl f: chal and ev ch last 100yds: no ex nr fin* **5/1**[2]

522 **3** 1½ **Narborough**[18] 4735 3-9-1 60 CharlesBishop(3) 4 62
(Mick Channon) *hld up in tch: smooth hdwy 1/2-way: trckd ldrs on bit and nt clr run wl over 1f out tl checked and swtchd rt ent fnl f: sn rdn and kpt on* **5/1**[2]

0654 **4** ¾ **Baby Queen (IRE)**[14] 4848 8-9-2 58 NeilFarley(3) 3 58
(Brian Baugh) *dwlt: sn cl up: rdn along 2f out: drvn over 1f out: kpt on same pce* **12/1**

2104 **5** ½ **College Doll**[23] 4546 5-8-13 52 (t) JimmyQuinn 1 51
(Christine Dunnett) *led: rdn along wl over 1f out: drvn and hdd ent fnl f: sn one pce* **25/1**

5453 **6** ½ **Your Gifted (IRE)**[7] 5130 7-8-11 53 (v) GeorgeChaloner(3) 9 50
(Lisa Williamson) *chsd ldrs on outer: rdn along 2f out: sn drvn and kpt on same pce* **11/2**[3]

0-00 **7** *3* **Rat Catcher (IRE)**[59] 3338 4-9-0 53 [1] RichardKingscote 10 39
(Lisa Williamson) *chsd ldrs on outer: rdn along 2f out: sn drvn and wknd* **20/1**

6003 **8** 1¼ **Red Cobra (IRE)**[8] 5082 4-9-1 54 DuranFentiman 6 35
(Tim Easterby) *wnt lft and sltly hmpd s: sn swtchd rt to r alone nr stands' rail: a in rr* **4/1**[1]

0-02 **9** *11* **Ignight**[15] 4820 3-8-4 46 AndrewMullen 5
(Mark Usher) *awkward and wnt rt s: t.k.h: chsd ldrs: rdn along 1/2-way: sn wknd* **8/1**

1m 0.32s (-1.18) **Going Correction** -0.175s/f (Firm)
**WFA** 3 from 4yo+ 3lb 9 Ran SP% **116.1**
Speed ratings (Par 101): **102,101,99,98,97 96,91,89,72**
CSF £24.14 CT £102.63 TOTE £4.60: £1.10, £2.10, £1.80; EX 16.70 Trifecta £48.60.
**Owner** Hoofbeats Racing Club 1 **Bred** Mrs P J Makin **Trained** Ogbourne Maisey, Wilts

**FOCUS**
A weak sprint handicap, rated around the third.

## 5400 WATCH RACING UK ANYWHERE MAIDEN STKS 1m 75y
3:45 (3:47) (Class 5) 3-Y-O £2,587 (£770; £384; £192) Stalls Centre

Form RPR

523 **1** **Above The Rest (IRE)**[9] 5039 3-9-5 0 JamesDoyle 4 85
(Timothy Jarvis) *mde most: jnd 1/2-way: pushed along 3f out: rdn clr wl over 1f out: readily* **8/13**[1]

3623 **2** *5* **Conquerant**[22] 4587 3-9-5 82 (p) MartinLane 5 74
(Charlie Appleby) *trckd wnr: cl up 1/2-way: chal 3f out: rdn along over 2f out: drvn wl over 1f out: kpt on same pce* **7/4**[2]

50 **3** 2¼ **Norfolk Sound**[22] 4569 3-8-7 0 SamuelClarke(7) 9 63
(Chris Wall) *trckd ldrs: hdwy to chse ldng pair over 3f out: rdn and edgd lft wl over 1f out: kpt on same pce* **14/1**

0 **4** *10* **Highfield Lass**[16] 4791 3-9-0 0 MichaelStainton 10 40
(Chris Fairhurst) *in tch: rdn along over 3f out: plugged on one pce u.p fnl 2f* **33/1**

05 **5** *1* **Focail Mear**[14] 4867 3-8-11 0 RyanPowell(3) 3 38
(John Ryan) *chsd ldrs: rdn along over 3f out: sn outpcd* **33/1**

**6** 1¾ **Hidden Power** 3-9-5 0 J-PGuillambert 1 39
(Jo Hughes) *in tch: rdn along over 3f out: sn outpcd* **10/1**[3]

60- **7** *17* **Little Miss Becky**[240] 8326 3-9-0 0 PatrickDonaghy 7
(Giles Bravery) *dwlt: a in rr: bhd fnl 3f* **50/1**

0 **8** *27* **Tobago Cays**[46] 3801 3-8-9 0 RyanWhile(5) 2
(Bill Turner) *s.i.s: a in rr: bhd fnl 3f* **66/1**

1m 45.96s (-3.04) **Going Correction** -0.175s/f (Firm) 8 Ran SP% **123.4**
Speed ratings (Par 100): **108,103,100,90,89 88,71,44**
CSF £2.12 TOTE £1.80: £1.02, £1.10, £3.20; EX 1.90 Trifecta £7.90.
**Owner** Cedars Two **Bred** J C Carr **Trained** Twyford, Bucks
■ Three Mmm's was withdrawn. Price at time of withdrawal 25-1. Rule 4 does not apply.

**FOCUS**
This was effectively a two-horse race and, with the Godolphin horse lacking in heart, it probably took little winning. The second is rated close to his latest form.

## 5401 TBA EBF FILLIES' H'CAP (BOBIS RACE) 1m 2f 50y
4:20 (4:20) (Class 3) (0-95,90) 3-Y-O £8,409 (£2,502; £1,250; £625) Stalls Low

Form RPR

21 **1** **Scallop**[50] 3602 3-9-1 84 JamesDoyle 6 90
(Sir Michael Stoute) *trckd ldr: cl up 4f out: effrt to take slt ld 2f out: sn rdn: drvn ins fnl f: kpt on gamely towards fin: jst hld on* **9/4**[1]

4131 **2** *shd* **Cay Dancer**[28] 4397 3-9-2 90 CamHardie(5) 2 95
(Richard Hannon) *trckd ldrs: hdwy on outer 3f out: chsd ldrs and pushed along 2f out: rdn over 1f out: styd on to chal ins fnl f: sn ev ch: jst hld* **9/4**[1]

3103 **3** *hd* **Bureau (IRE)**[13] 4915 3-9-3 86 FrannyNorton 7 91
(Mark Johnston) *set stdy pce: qcknd 4f out: rdn along and jnd 3f out: hdd narrowly 2f out: sn drvn and cl up: ev ch tl no ex nr fin* **8/1**

4221 **4** *hd* **Thatchereen (IRE)**[12] 4947 3-8-1 75 6ex DanielMuscutt(5) 4 79
(Michael Bell) *t.k.h: trckd ldng pair: hdwy over 3f out and sn cl up: chal 2f out: sn rdn and ev ch tl drvn ins fnl f and no ex towards fin* **6/1**[2]

0310 5 1¾ **Palerma**[16] 4782 3-8-6 78 CharlesBishop(3) 1 79
(Mick Channon) *hld up in rr: hdwy over 3f out: trckd ldrs 2f out: sn rdn and kpt on same pce fnl f* **12/1**

4112 6 2¾ **Miss Lucy Jane**[28] 4397 3-8-5 77 GeorgeChaloner(3) 3 73
(Richard Fahey) *trckd ldng pair on inner: pushed along 4f out: rdn 3f out: one pce fnl 2f* **7/1**[3]

2m 12.34s (-1.96) **Going Correction** -0.175s/f (Firm) **6** Ran SP% **107.1**
Speed ratings (Par 101): **100,99,99,99,98 96**
CSF £6.45 TOTE £2.40: £1.20, £1.20; EX 6.50 Trifecta £28.80.
**Owner** K Abdullah **Bred** Juddmonte Farms Ltd **Trained** Newmarket, Suffolk

**FOCUS**
This looked a good handicap, but they didn't go that hard early and it turned into something of a sprint. They finished in a bit of a heap, with the second to form basically rated to form.

## 5402 FREEDMAN AND PARTNERS H'CAP 1m 2f 50y
**4:50** (4:50) (Class 6) (0-65,63) 3-Y-O **£2,045** (£603; £302) **Stalls** Low

Form RPR

0050 1 **Oracle Boy**[45] 3819 3-8-11 53 (p) RichardKingscote 7 64
(William Muir) *cl up: led after 3f: pushed along over 2f out: rdn clr over 1f out: kpt on strly* **4/1**[2]

-300 2 5 **Essanar**[16] 4789 3-8-12 54 FrannyNorton 2 55
(Andrew Hollinshead) *hld up: hdwy 4f out: swtchd rt and effrt over 2f out: sn rdn: drvn and kpt on to take 2nd ins fnl f: no ch w wnr* **14/1**

003 3 ½ **Modify**[28] 4386 3-8-5 50 GeorgeChaloner(3) 5 50
(David O'Meara) *cl up: effrt 3f out: rdn over 2f out: drvn and one pce appr fnl f* **3/1**[1]

000 4 hd **Silken Waters**[23] 4543 3-8-13 55 PhillipMakin 4 55
(Eve Johnson Houghton) *in tch: hdwy 4f out: chsd ldrs over 2f out: rdn wl over 1f out: drvn and kpt on same pce appr fnl f* **6/1**

060- 5 2 **Network Perfection**[398] 4312 3-8-11 53 AndrewElliott 3 49
(Michael Easterby) *t.k.h: slt ld 3f: cl up: rdn along over 3f out: drvn 2f out and grad wknd* **14/1**

030 6 2 **Mad Endeavour**[22] 4569 3-9-7 63 (t) LukeMorris 6 55
(Stuart Kittow) *hld up: hdwy on wd outside 3f out: rdn to chse ldrs 2f out: sn drvn and no imp* **9/2**[3]

0000 7 4 **Moxey**[25] 4495 3-7-12 45 JoeDoyle(5) 9 29
(John Davies) *hld up in rr: hdwy 3f out: rdn along to chse ldrs over 2f out: sn drvn and wknd* **7/1**

-506 8 3 **Born To Reign**[15] 4830 3-8-13 55 HayleyTurner 1 34
(Michael Bell) *chsd ldrs: rdn along wl over 3f out: sn wknd* **10/1**

2m 12.75s (-1.55) **Going Correction** -0.175s/f (Firm) **8** Ran SP% **112.4**
Speed ratings (Par 98): **99,95,94,94,92 91,88,85**
CSF £54.77 CT £187.99 TOTE £4.70: £1.50, £4.60, £1.50; EX 70.80 Trifecta £268.60.
**Owner** The Epicureans **Bred** Newsells Park Stud **Trained** Lambourn, Berks

**FOCUS**
Effectively a maiden handicap. A step up from the winner but the opposition was a bit suspect.

## 5403 BETFAIR NOVICE FLAT AMATEUR RIDERS' H'CAP 1m 6f 15y
**5:20** (5:20) (Class 6) (0-65,71) 4-Y-O+ **£1,871** (£580; £290; £145) **Stalls** Low

Form RPR

4523 1 **Soundbyte**[37] 4082 9-9-11 51 (v) MrMHaddock(3) 3 59
(John Gallagher) *hld up in rr: hdwy on outer over 5f out: wd st: sn chsng ldrs: rdn on wd outside 2f out: styd on ent fnl f: led nr fin* **8/1**[3]

2452 2 hd **Taste The Wine (IRE)**[5] 5208 8-10-8 62 (t) MrJPWilliams(3) 10 69
(Bernard Llewellyn) *trckd ldrs: hdwy over 3f out: led wl over 2f out: rdn wl over 1f out: drvn ins fnl f: hdd nr line* **7/1**[2]

34-1 3 4 **Sacred Square (GER)**[7] 5121 4-11-6 71 6ex (b) MrHStock 9 72
(Donald McCain) *prom: effrt 3f out: sn rdn and sltly outpcd: kpt on u.p fr over 1f out* **4/5**[1]

-006 4 ½ **Volcanic Jack (IRE)**[7] 5150 6-10-4 55 MissJWalton 4 56
(Michael Chapman) *led and sn clr at stdy pce: jnd 6f out: pushed along 4f out: rdn 3f out and sn hdd: drvn and kpt on same pce fnl 2f* **20/1**

4405 5 ½ **Candelita**[20] 4673 7-10-0 54 MrStanSheppard(3) 8 54
(Matt Sheppard) *chsd ldrs on inner: hdwy over 4f out: rdn 3f out: drvn and one pce fnl 2f* **10/1**

5425 6 3½ **Ogaritmo**[18] 4737 5-9-12 52 (t) MrNicholasMeek(3) 2 47
(Alex Hales) *s.i.s and lost several l s: jnd field after 4f: hdwy to chse ldrs over 4f out: rdn along 3f out: sn one pce* **7/1**[2]

500- 7 ½ **Star Of Mayfair (USA)**[259] 7446 4-10-2 56 MissTSutherland(3) 11 50
(Timothy Jarvis) *rrd and lost several l s: jnd field after 4f: cl up 6f out: rdn along 3f out: sn wknd* **25/1**

3m 15.72s (8.72) **Going Correction** -0.175s/f (Firm) **7** Ran SP% **109.4**
Speed ratings (Par 101): **68,67,65,65,65 63,62**
CSF £55.90 CT £84.99 TOTE £10.50: £3.70, £1.40; EX 29.30 Trifecta £54.30.
**Owner** Oliver Parsons **Bred** Mrs R J Gallagher **Trained** Chastleton, Oxon

**FOCUS**
They didn't go much of a pace early and this is ordinary form. The first two are rated to revent levels.
T/Plt: £6.10 to a £1 stake. Pool: £46,496.14 - 5,556.74 winning units T/Qpdt: £3.00 to a £1 stake. Pool: £2,961.39 - 713.40 winning units JR

# 5292 DEAUVILLE (R-H)
Friday, August 15

**OFFICIAL GOING: Turf: heavy; polytrack: standard**

## 5404a PRIX DU PETIT COTIL (CLAIMER) (3YO) (POLYTRACK) 1m 4f 110y
**1:20** (12:00) 3-Y-O **£9,583** (£3,833; £2,875; £1,916; £958)

RPR

1 **Fort Berkeley (IRE)**[23] 4547 3-9-4 0 ChristopheSoumillon 5 85
(Paul Cole) *w ldrs: led after 2f: jnd whn hung on bnd 1/2-way w jockey looking down as if steering broke: wnt on again bef st: rdn whn pressed 2f out: r.o strly and sn asserted: coasted home nring fin: comf* **11/10**[1]

2 1½ **Tahiti Way (FR)**[349] 3-8-11 0 CristianDemuro 6 76
(L A Urbano-Grajales, France) **58/10**[3]

3 ¾ **Handeli (FR)**[71] 3-8-8 0 (b) JohanVictoire 1 72
(Y Durepaire, France) **189/10**

4 hd **Donavista (FR)**[77] 3-8-11 0 GeraldMosse 7 74
(F-H Graffard, France) **78/10**

5 hd **Lady John John (FR)**[44] 3-8-8 0 (p) TheoBachelot 4 71
(S Wattel, France) **71/10**

6 hd **Wadirum (IRE)**[95] 3-9-1 0 JeromeClaudic 2 78
(C Lotoux, France) **3/1**[2]



7 8 **Drole De Mek (FR)**[323] 6785 3-8-11 0 JulienAuge 3 62
(W Walton, France) **231/10**

2m 46.41s (166.41) **7** Ran SP% **120.2**
WIN (incl. 1 euro stake): 2.10. PLACES: 1.50, 2.90. SF: 7.80.
**Owner** Black Run Racing **Bred** Mrs Clodagh McStay **Trained** Whatcombe, Oxon

## 5405a PRIX DE LA VALLEE D'AUGE (LISTED RACE) (2YO) (TURF) 5f
**1:50** (12:00) 2-Y-O **£22,916** (£9,166; £6,875; £4,583; £2,291)

RPR

1 **Souvenir Delondres (FR)**[17] 2-8-10 0 Christophe-PatriceLemaire 8 99+
(J E Pease, France) **7/2**[2]

2 1 **Power Of The Moon (IRE)**[13] 4931 2-8-10 0 TheoBachelot 1 95+
(M Nigge, France) **32/1**

3 ½ **Super Eria (FR)**[8] 5119 2-8-10 0 AnthonyCrastus 5 94
(C Boutin, France) **15/1**

4 1 **Lightscameraction (IRE)**[20] 4652 2-9-0 0 Pierre-CharlesBoudot 6 94
(Gay Kelleway) *w ldrs: rdn to ld narrowly over 1f out: kpt on but strly pressed and hdd fnl f: no ex and dropped to 4th nring fin* **3/1**[1]

5 ½ **Something Lucky (IRE)**[14] 4883 2-9-0 0 Jean-BernardEyquem 11 92
(Matthieu Palussiere, France) **139/10**

6 hd **Loose Cannon (FR)**[8] 5119 2-8-10 0 (b) MickaelBarzalona 4 87
(D Windrif, France) **36/1**

7 2 **Cornwallville (IRE)**[8] 5118 2-9-0 0 JamieSpencer 3 84
(F-H Graffard, France) **7/1**

8 2 **Pierre Precieuse (FR)**[22] 4603 2-8-10 0 SebastienMaillot 10 73
(E Caroux, France) **41/1**

9 ¾ **London Life (IRE)**[35] 4150 2-8-10 0 MaximeGuyon 9 70
(Tom Dascombe) *chsd ldrs: rdn 2f out: outpcd and lost pl over 1f out: wknd and eased fnl f* **7/1**

10 1 **Cheik Bere (FR)**[46] 3806 2-9-0 0 FlavienPrat 2 71
(M Figge, Germany) **48/10**[3]

11 1¾ **Smoke Signals (IRE)**[72] 2-9-0 0 AntoineHamelin 7 64
(Matthieu Palussiere, France) **10/1**

1m 0.91s (3.41) **11** Ran SP% **119.6**
WIN (incl. 1 euro stake): 4.50. PLACES: 2.20, 6.00, 3.70. DF: 65.40. SF: 115.10.
**Owner** Christopher Wright **Bred** Stratford Place Stud **Trained** Chantilly, France

## 5406a PRIX GUILLAUME D'ORNANO - HARAS DU LOGIS SAINT-GERMAIN (GROUP 2) (3YO) (TURF) 1m 2f
**2:50** (12:00) 3-Y-O **£190,000** (£73,333; £35,000; £23,333; £11,666)

RPR

1 **Gailo Chop (FR)**[41] 3994 3-9-2 0 JulienAuge 8 115+
(A De Watrigant, France) *mde all: rdn 2f out: styd on strly and asserted: forged clr fnl f: v readily* **10/1**[3]

2 3½ **Free Port Lux**[33] 4251 3-9-2 0 (b) MickaelBarzalona 2 108+
(F Head, France) *midfield on inner: rdn 2f out: wnt 2nd over 1f out: styd on fnl f but no imp on wnr and wl hld* **10/1**[3]

3 nk **Prince Gibraltar (FR)**[33] 4251 3-9-2 0 ChristopheSoumillon 1 107+
(J-C Rouget, France) *dwlt and hld up in last: rdn 2f out: hung lft u.p but wnt 3rd over 1f out: styd on fnl f but nt qckn so no ch w wnr* **11/8**[2]

4 snk **Western Hymn**[26] 4483 3-9-2 0 WilliamBuick 5 107+
(John Gosden) *dwlt sltly and hld up in last pair: rdn in last over 2f out: styd on in st and wnt 4th fnl f but nvr threatened* **5/4**[1]

5 1¾ **Steaming Kitten (USA)**[47] 3776 3-9-2 0 CristianDemuro 7 104
(Gianluca Bietolini, Italy) *prom: rdn and brief effrt 2f out: sn outpcd by wnr: fdd* **33/1**

6 ½ **Army Bulletin (IRE)**[26] 4483 3-9-2 0 (b[1]) MaximeGuyon 3 103
(A Fabre, France) *trckd wnr on inner: cl up in 2nd 2f out: rdn and fnd little over 1f out: sn btn: fdd fnl f and dropped to 6th towards fin* **16/1**

7 5½ **Nolohay (IRE)**[43] 3-9-2 0 OlivierPeslier 4 92
(C Laffon-Parias, France) *midfield on outer: rdn over 2f out: outpcd and dropped to rr over 1f out: bhd and wl btn fnl f* **18/1**

2m 11.64s (1.44) **7** Ran SP% **118.8**
WIN (incl. 1 euro stake): 11.10. PLACES: 1.40, 1.40, 1.10. DF: 37.20. SF: 74.80.
**Owner** Oti Management Pty Ltd & A Chopard **Bred** A Chopard **Trained** France

## 5407a PRIX DE LIEUREY (GROUP 3) (3YO FILLIES) (ROUND) (TURF) 1m (R)
**3:50** (12:00) 3-Y-O **£33,333** (£13,333; £10,000; £6,666; £3,333)

RPR

1 **Bawina (IRE)**[19] 4721 3-8-11 0 OlivierPeslier 11 112+
(C Laffon-Parias, France) *midfield in tch: pushed along and clsd to chal over 1f out: led ent fnl f: r.o strly and asserted under hands and heels: easily* **11/4**[1]

2 1¾ **Indian Rainbow (IRE)**[44] 3873 3-9-2 0 IoritzMendizabal 12 112
(Andreas Lowe, Germany) *hld up in midfield: rdn fnl 2f: r.o and wnt 2nd fnl 100yds: nt pce of wnr and wl hld* **20/1**

3 1¼ **Visoriyna (FR)**[55] 3-8-11 0 ChristopheSoumillon 8 104
(J-C Rouget, France) *midfield: rdn over 1f out: kpt on fnl f but nt pce to chal and wl hld* **10/3**[2]

4 1 **Kiyoshi**[21] 4607 3-8-11 0 JamieSpencer 9 102
(Charles Hills) *hld up towards rr: swtchd rt and pushed along to cl over 1f out: rdn ent fnl f: kpt on and wnt 4th towards fin: nvr nrr* **7/1**[3]

5 ½ **Amy Eria (IRE)**[40] 4009 3-8-11 0 ThierryThulliez 10 101
(F Rohaut, France) *trckd ldr on outer: pushed along to chal and led 2f out: strly pressed and hdd ent fnl f: sn outpcd by wnr: fdd and dropped to 5th towards fin* **20/1**

6 1 **Kamellata (FR)**[24] 4526 3-8-11 0 FabriceVeron 3 98
(H-A Pantall, France) *hld up in last pair on inner: rdn 2f out: kpt on fnl f and got up to dead-heat for n.d 6th post* **25/1**

6 dht **Evita Peron**[48] 3724 3-8-11 0 WilliamBuick 6 98
(Ralph Beckett) *sn midfield in tch on inner: rdn to chal 2f out: ev ch ent fnl f but sn outpcd by wnr: no ex and fdd: jnd for 6th post* **7/1**[3]

8 1½ **Sarinda**[33] 3-8-11 0 MickaelBarzalona 5 95
(H-A Pantall, France) *hld up in midfield on inner: rdn and effrt over 1f out: outpcd and btn fnl f: fdd and eased* **16/1**

9 1 **Having A Blast (USA)**[32] 3-8-11 0 Christophe-PatriceLemaire 4 93
(M Delzangles, France) *prom: rdn and outpcd 2f out: fdd and eased fnl f* **14/1**

10 2½ **Cladocera (GER)**[46] 3808 3-8-11 0 AntoineHamelin 7 87
(A De Royer-Dupre, France) *dwlt sltly and hld up in last pair: rdn in last 2f out: sn no imp and btn: nvr a factor* **16/1**

11 1¼ **Amazing Maria (IRE)**[70] 2960 3-8-11 0 GeraldMosse 2 84
(Ed Dunlop) *led: rdn and hdd 2f out: qckly btn and wknd: eased fnl f* **7/1**[3]

12 1 1/4 **Delivery**[46] 3808 3-8-11 0 ........ MaximeGuyon 1 81
(A Fabre, France) *trckd ldr on inner: rdn and effrt 2f out: outpcd and wknd over 1f out: eased whn btn fnl f and dropped to last* **7/1**[3]
1m 44.68s (3.88) **12** Ran SP% **131.5**
WIN (incl. 1 euro stake): 3.00. PLACES: 1.40, 3.40, 1.70. DF: 36.80. SF: 45.20.
**Owner** Wertheimer & Frere **Bred** Wertheimer Et Frere **Trained** Chantilly, France

# 4935 CHESTER (L-H)

## Saturday, August 16

**OFFICIAL GOING: Good to soft (soft in places) changing to good to soft after race 1 (2.00)**
Course at normal configuration and all distances as advertised.
Wind: fresh 1/2 against Weather: overcast, breezy

### 5408 CHALICE MAIDEN AUCTION STKS (BOBIS RACE) 7f 2y
**2:00** (2:01) (Class 4) 2-Y-O **£6,469** (£1,925; £962; £481) **Stalls** Low

Form RPR
34 **1** **Bizzario**[14] 4884 2-9-0 0 ........ FrannyNorton 4 79
(Mark Johnston) *mde all: drvn 2f out: styd on wl* **2/1**[1]
3222 **2** 3/4 **Fingal's Cave (IRE)**[4] 5271 2-8-13 79 ........ WilliamTwiston-Davies 5 76
(Mick Channon) *dwlt: hld up in rr: hdwy 4f out: sn trcking ldrs: 2nd 1f out: kpt on same pce* **2/1**[1]
02 **3** 2 1/4 **Grenade**[8] 5148 2-8-13 0 ........ SeanLevey 2 71
(Richard Hannon) *hmpd s: hld up in rr: effrt over 2f out: nt clr run and swtchd rt over 1f out: kpt on to take 3rd in clsng stages* **10/1**[3]
4545 **4** 1 3/4 **Come Uppence**[38] 4083 2-8-12 73 ........ JFEgan 1 65
(David Evans) *wnt rt s: t.k.h: trckd ldrs: drvn over 3f out: kpt on one pce over 1f out* **11/1**
0422 **5** 3/4 **Pivot Point (IRE)**[14] 4884 2-8-13 74 ........ StevieDonohoe 3 64
(Brian Meehan) *chsd ldrs: drvn over 2f out: one pce over 1f out* **11/4**[2]
0 **6** 15 **Blythe Star (IRE)**[14] 4884 2-9-3 0 ........ AndrewElliott 6 29
(Danielle McCormick) *chsd ldrs: drvn 4f out: lost pl over 2f out: sn bhd* **33/1**
1m 27.15s (0.65) **Going Correction** +0.025s/f (Good) **6** Ran SP% **113.7**
Speed ratings (Par 96): **97,96,93,91,90 73**
CSF £6.39 TOTE £3.40: £3.70, £1.40; EX 7.40 Trifecta £29.70.
**Owner** Mrs Jane Newett **Bred** Lady Bamford **Trained** Middleham Moor, N Yorks
**FOCUS**
Franny Norton described the going as 'not too bad, just on the soft side of good'. This was a fair maiden run at a decent pace. The consistent runner-up has been rated a bit off his best.

### 5409 STELLA CIDRE NURSERY H'CAP (BOBIS RACE) 5f 16y
**2:35** (2:36) (Class 4) (0-85,85) 2-Y-O **£6,469** (£1,925; £962; £481) **Stalls** Low

Form RPR
0551 **1** **Bowson Fred**[15] 4857 2-8-3 67 ........ IanBrennan 1 74
(Michael Easterby) *mde all: shkn up 2f out: styd on wl* **11/4**[2]
416 **2** 1 3/4 **Geological (IRE)**[36] 4143 2-9-1 79 ........ SeanLevey 6 80
(Richard Hannon) *chsd ldr: upsides over 2f out: hung rt and styd on same pce last 100yds* **11/2**
110 **3** 1 1/4 **Dittander**[14] 4913 2-9-2 80 ........ PhillipMakin 4 77+
(Richard Hannon) *sn outpcd: hdwy on ins whn nt clr run over 2f out: hung lft and styd on to take 3rd clsng stages* **5/2**[1]
2015 **4** 1 3/4 **Commander Patten (IRE)**[30] 4348 2-9-4 85 ........ RobertTart(3) 10 75
(Alan Bailey) *wnt rt s: chsd ldrs: outpcd over 2f out: kpt on appr fnl f* **15/2**
3231 **5** nk **Low Cut Affair (IRE)**[5] 5254 2-9-0 78 6ex ........ JFEgan 5 67
(David Evans) *chsd ldrs: drvn over 2f out: one pce* **10/1**
361 **6** 1 1/4 **Rocking The Boat (IRE)**[28] 4450 2-8-12 76 ........ OisinMurphy 7 61
(Charles Hills) *chsd ldrs: drvn over 2f out: hung rt and fdd over 1f out* **5/1**[3]
0422 **7** 7 **King Crimson**[98] 2151 2-8-12 76 ........ SamHitchcott 8 49
(Mick Channon) *t.k.h: trckd ldrs: intimdated by rival rdr's whip whn ducked lft 100yds out: sn eased* **14/1**
1m 1.29s (0.29) **Going Correction** +0.025s/f (Good) **7** Ran SP% **114.8**
Speed ratings (Par 96): **98,95,93,90,89 87,76**
CSF £18.36 CT £41.50 TOTE £7.50: £4.00, £1.70; EX 32.30 Trifecta £126.40.
**Owner** Mrs A Jarvis **Bred** Mrs A Jarvis **Trained** Sheriff Hutton, N Yorks
**FOCUS**
A fair nursery which was dominated by the first two. The winner made all from the best draw and next four all had excuses of sorts.

### 5410 STELLA ARTOIS H'CAP (BOBIS RACE) 7f 122y
**3:10** (3:11) (Class 2) 3-Y-O **£48,517** (£14,437; £7,215; £3,607) **Stalls** Low

Form RPR
012 **1** **Top Of The Glas (IRE)**[22] 4631 3-7-9 80 ........ JoeDoyle(5) 6 93+
(Brian Ellison) *s.i.s: sn mid-div: chsng ldrs whn hmpd over 1f out: styd on wl to ld last 50yds* **9/2**[2]
1002 **2** 1 1/2 **Coulsty (IRE)**[13] 4937 3-9-7 101 ........ SeanLevey 7 108
(Richard Hannon) *t.k.h: trckd ldrs: led 1f out: hdd and no ex fnl 50yds* **8/1**[3]
2121 **3** 1 1/2 **Wilde Inspiration (IRE)**[14] 4923 3-8-5 85 ........ IanBrennan 12 88
(Julie Camacho) *mid-div: hdwy 3f out: chsng ldrs over 1f out: kpt on to take 3rd nr fin* **8/1**[3]
0322 **4** 1/2 **Lincoln (IRE)**[21] 4660 3-8-8 88 ........ SamHitchcott 13 90
(Mick Channon) *t.k.h in rr: hdwy on ins whn nt clr run over 2f out and over 1f out: styd on to take 4th post* **11/1**
-502 **5** hd **Champagne Sydney (IRE)**[9] 5092 3-8-0 80 ........ RaulDaSilva 3 82
(Richard Hannon) *chsd ldrs: drvn over 2f out: kpt on same pce fnl f* **10/1**
4441 **6** 3/4 **Mime Dance**[10] 5031 3-8-0 80 oh1 ........(p) PaoloSirigu 14 80
(Andrew Balding) *sn last: hdwy on ins whn nt clr run over 2f out: styd on wl fnl f* **11/1**
6510 **7** hd **Roachdale House (IRE)**[35] 4198 3-8-10 90 ........ DaleSwift 9 89
(Richard Fahey) *mid-div: drvn 3f out: kpt on one pce fnl 2f* **8/1**[3]
0204 **8** 1/2 **Ifwecan**[16] 4826 3-9-1 95 ........ FrannyNorton 2 93
(Mark Johnston) *led: hdd 1f out: wknd fnl 75yds* **7/2**[1]
2155 **9** 1/2 **Regiment**[24] 4551 3-8-5 85 ........ PatrickMathers 15 82
(Richard Fahey) *in rr: sme hdwy on outer over 2f out: nvr trbld ldrs* **25/1**
0100 **10** 3 **Idea (USA)**[35] 4198 3-8-7 87 ........ RoystonFfrench 11 76
(Sir Michael Stoute) *in rr: drvn 3f out: lost pl 2f out* **14/1**
1440 **11** 1 1/4 **The Hooded Claw (IRE)**[21] 4669 3-8-6 86 ........ AndrewElliott 8 72
(Tim Easterby) *chsd ldrs: lost pl over 1f out* **12/1**
6160 **12** 5 **Little Shambles**[17] 4783 3-8-5 85 ........ JFEgan 10 59
(Mark Johnston) *chsd ldrs: drvn 3f out: lost pl over 1f out* **22/1**
1m 32.77s (-1.03) **Going Correction** +0.025s/f (Good) **12** Ran SP% **122.0**
Speed ratings (Par 106): **106,104,103,102,102 101,101,100,100,97 96,91**
CSF £41.90 CT £291.07 TOTE £9.10: £4.10, £2.90, £2.00; EX 45.60 Trifecta £449.00.
**Owner** Market Avenue Racing Club Ltd **Bred** Seamus McConnon **Trained** Norton, N Yorks
**FOCUS**
A competitive handicap run at a strong gallop, which suited those ridden from off the pace. The third, fourth, fifth and sixth have all been rated close to their marks.

### 5411 MINSTRELL RECRUITMENT H'CAP 6f 18y
**3:45** (3:45) (Class 4) (0-85,84) 3-Y-O+ **£6,469** (£1,443; £1,443; £481) **Stalls** Low

Form RPR
0240 **1** **Lexi's Hero (IRE)**[18] 4762 6-9-10 84 ........(v) DavidNolan 4 98
(Richard Fahey) *w ldr: led over 2f out: drvn clr over 1f out: styd on wl* **5/2**[1]
4122 **2** 5 **Ginzan**[8] 5124 6-9-1 75 ........ OisinMurphy 12 73
(Malcolm Saunders) *in rr: nt clr run over 2f out: nt clr run and swtchd rt over 1f: styng on at fin* **4/1**[3]
5060 **2** dht **Smokethatthunders (IRE)**[43] 3939 4-8-1 66 ........ DanielMuscutt(5) 7 64
(James Unett) *in rr: hdwy over 2f out: styng on at fin* **16/1**
2254 **4** nk **Cruise Tothelimit (IRE)**[7] 5199 6-8-11 78 ........ MeganCarberry(7) 5 75
(Ian Williams) *sn trcking ldrs: chsd wnr 2f out: kpt on same pce* **3/1**[2]
1000 **5** 2 1/4 **Bachotheque (IRE)**[14] 4925 4-8-13 73 ........(p) AndrewElliott 2 63
(Tim Easterby) *chsd ldrs on ins: nt clr run over 2f out and over 1f out: one pce* **6/1**
340- **6** 3 1/2 **Hello Beautiful (IRE)**[339] 6295 3-8-4 67 ........ RoystonFfrench 3 46
(Ann Duffield) *t.k.h: led: hdd over 2f out: lost pl over 1f out* **12/1**
3210 **7** 7 **Makin The Rules (IRE)**[29] 4421 3-9-3 74 ........ PhillipMakin 8 36
(John Quinn) *mid-div: effrt on outside over 2f out: wknd over 1f out: sn bhd* **8/1**
1m 13.56s (-0.24) **Going Correction** +0.025s/f (Good)
**WFA** 3 from 4yo+ 3lb **7** Ran SP% **112.5**
Speed ratings (Par 105): **102,95,95,94,91 87,77**
WIN: 4.40 Lexi's Hero; PL: 3.20 Lexi's Hero, 1.70 Smokethatthunders, 1.30 Ginzan; EX: 5.00, 22.60; CSF: 6.18, 20.11; TC: 63.06, 76.97; TF: 32.80, 13690.00;.
**Owner** Dr Marwan Koukash **Bred** T J Pabst **Trained** Musley Bank, N Yorks
**FOCUS**
An ordinary sprint handicap and a one-sided contest. There's a chance the form could be rated a length or so better.

### 5412 STELLA ARTOIS CHALICE MAIDEN STKS 7f 2y
**4:20** (4:21) (Class 4) 3-Y-O+ **£6,469** (£1,925; £962; £481) **Stalls** Low

Form RPR
02 **1** **Enliven**[51] 3601 3-8-12 0 ........ OisinMurphy 4 78+
(Andrew Balding) *hld up: hdwy to trck ldrs 4f out: shkn up to ld over 1f out: styd on wl to go clr* **11/8**[1]
4232 **2** 3 1/4 **Hanno (USA)**[20] 4713 3-9-3 78 ........(p) PhillipMakin 3 73
(Ed Dunlop) *trckd ldr: effrt over 2f out: hung lft over 1f out: no imp* **5/2**[2]
2-04 **3** 1 **Nathr (USA)**[21] 4677 3-9-3 77 ........ FrannyNorton 2 73
(Charles Hills) *trckd ldrs: drvn and outpcd over 2f out: nt clr run on ins over 1f out: swtchd rt: kpt on to take modest 3rd nr fin* **3/1**[3]
6250 **4** 1/2 **Pashan Garh**[23] 4580 5-9-3 67 ........ DanielMuscutt(5) 1 71
(Pat Eddery) *led: drvn over 2f out: hdd over 1f out: one pce* **7/1**
066- **5** 15 **Only For You**[388] 4621 4-9-3 50 ........ DaleSwift 5 27
(Alan Brown) *hld up in last: drvn and lost pl over 2f out: sn bhd* **33/1**
1m 26.45s (-0.05) **Going Correction** +0.025s/f (Good)
**WFA** 3 from 4yo+ 5lb **5** Ran SP% **111.1**
Speed ratings (Par 105): **101,97,96,95,78**
CSF £5.17 TOTE £1.80: £1.10, £1.50; EX 5.50 Trifecta £8.80.
**Owner** The Queen **Bred** The Queen **Trained** Kingsclere, Hants
**FOCUS**
Just a reasonable gallop to this maiden. Neither the runner-up nor third are bombproof and so the level is a bit fluid.

### 5413 BUDWEISER H'CAP 1m 2f 75y
**4:55** (4:55) (Class 4) (0-80,80) 3-Y-O+ **£6,469** (£1,925; £962; £481) **Stalls** High

Form RPR
3564 **1** **Ardmay (IRE)**[59] 3368 5-9-4 76 ........ KevinStott(5) 2 86
(Kevin Ryan) *hld up in mid-div: hdwy over 2f out: led wl over 1f out: edgd rt: drvn out* **8/1**
4042 **2** 1 1/2 **Coincidently**[50] 3644 4-9-3 73 ........ RobertTart(3) 7 80
(Alan Bailey) *mid-div: hdwy over 2f out: sn chsng ldrs: styd on fnl f: tk 2nd post* **4/1**[2]
-533 **3** nse **The Character (IRE)**[29] 4393 3-9-2 77 ........ StephenCraine 10 84
(Tom Dascombe) *swtchd lft after s: hld up in rr: hdwy and nt clr run 2f out: chsng ldrs over 1f out: styd on to take 3rd last 50yds* **7/1**[3]
0455 **4** 4 **Dolphin Rock**[29] 4402 7-9-3 70 ........ DaleSwift 5 69
(Brian Ellison) *led 1f: chsd ldrs: drvn over 3f out: wknd fnl 75yds* **4/1**[2]
2433 **5** 3/4 **Kingscroft (IRE)**[10] 5054 6-9-13 80 ........ FrannyNorton 4 78
(Michael Herrington) *hld up towards rr: effrt over 2f out: sn chsng ldrs: fdd fnl f* **3/1**[1]
5131 **6** 6 **Hanalei Bay (IRE)**[14] 4903 4-9-7 74 ........ PhillipMakin 9 60
(Keith Dalgleish) *hld up in rr: effrt 3f out: lost pl 2f out* **7/1**[3]
4114 **7** 6 **Dandy (GER)**[23] 4586 5-9-12 79 ........(v) OisinMurphy 8 54
(Andrew Balding) *led after 1f: hdd wl over 1f out: sn wknd* **9/1**
0323 **8** 1 3/4 **Al Mukhdam**[16] 4810 4-9-2 76 ........ MeganCarberry(7) 6 48
(Ed de Giles) *s.s: jnd ldr after 2f: lost pl over 2f out: sn bhd* **10/1**
2m 10.85s (-0.35) **Going Correction** +0.025s/f (Good)
**WFA** 3 from 4yo+ 8lb **8** Ran SP% **120.2**
Speed ratings (Par 105): **102,100,100,97,96 92,87,85**
CSF £42.12 CT £241.93 TOTE £10.80: £4.00, £1.90, £4.20; EX 48.40 Trifecta £205.60.
**Owner** A C Henson **Bred** Tom Kelly **Trained** Hambleton, N Yorks
■ Stewards' Enquiry : Stephen Craine two-day ban: used whip above permitted level (Aug 30-31)
**FOCUS**
A slightly stop-start gallop to this handicap after they set off quite fast, then the leaders slowed the pace, but it ended up a fair test. The first two have been rated to this year's form.

### 5414 ANNO 1366 H'CAP 1m 5f 89y
**5:30** (5:30) (Class 4) (0-80,80) 3-Y-O+ **£6,469** (£1,925; £962; £481) **Stalls** Low

Form RPR
0250 **1** **Bayan Kasirga (IRE)**[14] 4921 4-8-12 64 ........ PatrickMathers 2 75
(Richard Fahey) *sn trcking ldrs: cl 2nd 4f out: chal 2f out: led last 75yds: hld on* **16/1**
2524 **2** nk **Notarised**[9] 5073 3-9-2 79 ........ FrannyNorton 1 90
(Mark Johnston) *led: wd bnd over 7f out: drvn over 2f out: hdd and no ex last 75yds* **8/11**[1]

4440 **3** *4 1/2* **Lyric Ballad**[28] 4434 4-9-5 71 (b) JohnFahy 5 75
(Hughie Morrison) *hld up in rr: hdwy 6f out: drvn to chse ldrs 3f out: 3rd over 1f out: one pce* **14/1**

1P12 **4** *2 3/4* **Incurs Four Faults**[25] 4516 3-8-3 66 JFEgan 4 66
(Keith Dalgleish) *sn trcking ldrs: t.k.h: drvn over 2f out: fdd fnl f* **15/2**[3]

0454 **5** *1/2* **Cavalieri (IRE)**[19] 4726 4-9-3 69 (p) PhillipMakin 3 68
(Philip Kirby) *trckd ldrs: drvn over 2f out: one pce* **11/2**[2]

1140 **6** *5* **Sunny Future (IRE)**[17] 4777 8-9-9 75 OisinMurphy 8 67
(Malcolm Saunders) *hld up in rr: effrt over 3f out: lost pl over 2f out* **9/1**

135- **7** *2 1/2* **Don Padeja**[34] 7105 4-9-11 77 RoystonFfrench 9 65
(Jonjo O'Neill) *hld up in rr: effrt over 3f out: wknd over 2f out* **14/1**

2m 55.32s (2.62) **Going Correction** +0.025s/f (Good)
**WFA** 3 from 4yo+ 11lb 7 Ran SP% **114.3**
Speed ratings (Par 105): **92,91,89,87,87 83,82**
CSF £28.43 CT £184.51 TOTE £16.20: £16.30, £1.10; EX 44.50 Trifecta £273.00.
**Owner** Stephen Humphreys **Bred** Lynn Lodge Stud **Trained** Musley Bank, N Yorks

**FOCUS**
Just an ordinary gallop to this handicap and the first two who finished clear were the first two throughout. The runner-up has been rated as running a small personal best.
T/Plt: £75.70 to a £1 stake. Pool: £52,877.86 - 509.67 winning tickets. T/Qpdt: £16.90 to a £1 stake. Pool: £2,661.65 - 116.00 winning tickets. WG

# 4884 DONCASTER (L-H)
### Saturday, August 16

**OFFICIAL GOING: Good (8.2)**
Round course railed out from 10f to where it joins the straight and 10f races increased by 10yds.
Wind: Moderate half against Weather: Cloudy

## 5415 FOLLOW THE SCOOP6 AT TOTEPOOLLIVEINFO.COM H'CAP 7f
**2:30** (2:31) (Class 5) (0-70,70) 3-Y-O+ **£3,234** (£962; £481; £240) **Stalls** High

Form RPR

2-44 **1** **Tiger Jim**[9] 5088 4-9-4 65 GaryBartley(3) 10 76+
(Jim Goldie) *hld up towards rr: stdy hdwy 1/2-way: trckd ldrs over 2f out: effrt over 1f out and sn chal: rdn to ld jst ins fnl f: kpt on* **11/4**[1]

6533 **2** *1 1/2* **Cliff (IRE)**[7] 5195 4-9-10 68 (v[1]) HayleyTurner 12 75
(Nigel Tinkler) *trckd ldrs: hdwy over 2f out: led 1 1/2f out: sn rdn: hdd and drvn jst ins fnl f: edgd lft: kpt on same pce* **12/1**

1210 **3** *3/4* **Reggie Bond**[57] 3439 4-9-9 67 (b) BarryMcHugh 7 72
(Geoffrey Oldroyd) *hld up towards rr: hdwy over 2f out: rdn to chse ldrs over 1f out: kpt on ins fnl f: nrst fin* **11/1**

0311 **4** *4 1/2* **Clumber Place**[5] 5233 8-9-7 65 6ex BenCurtis 11 58
(Shaun Harris) *led: rdn along over 2f out: hdd 1 1/2f out: sn drvn and grad wknd fnl f* **8/1**[3]

210- **5** *1* **Summer Dancer (IRE)**[326] 6721 10-9-7 65 TomQueally 3 56
(Eugene Stanford) *hld up: hdwy on wd outside 1/2-way: chsd ldrs 2f out: rdn over 1f out: one pce fnl f* **20/1**

3143 **6** *nk* **Monel**[41] 4004 6-9-7 65 FergalLynch 2 55
(Jim Goldie) *rrd s and s.i.s: bhd: hdwy wl over 2f out: rdn wl over 1f out: styd on fnl f: nrst fin* **16/1**

3015 **7** *2* **Imperator Augustus (IRE)**[20] 4707 6-9-6 67 DeclanBates(3) 13 52
(Patrick Holmes) *s.i.s and bhd: hdwy wl over 2f out: rdn wl over 1f out: kpt on fnl f: nrst fin* **16/1**

0460 **8** *nk* **Quasqazah**[15] 4871 3-9-2 65 JamesSullivan 9 47
(Ruth Carr) *t.k.h: chsd ldrs: rdn along over 2f out: wknd over 1f out* **50/1**

0343 **9** *shd* **Surround Sound**[14] 4903 4-9-2 60 TedDurcan 8 44
(Tim Easterby) *chsd ldrs: rdn along over 2f out: wknd over 1f out* **9/2**[2]

0-26 **10** *4 1/2* **Mister Marcasite**[103] 2019 4-9-7 65 PaulMulrennan 6 37
(Mel Brittain) *cl up: rdn along over 2f out: sn drvn and wknd* **14/1**

2121 **11** *nk* **The Dukkerer (IRE)**[19] 4727 3-9-2 70 MarcMonaghan(5) 5 39
(Garry Moss) *chsd ldrs: rdn along wl over 2f out: sn wknd* **8/1**[3]

1012 **12** *3/4* **Medam**[5] 5256 5-8-13 60 NeilFarley(3) 1 29
(Shaun Harris) *sn cl up: pushed along 3f out: sn rdn and wknd wl over 1f out* **14/1**

2006 **13** *1 1/2* **Kisanji**[15] 4871 3-8-12 66 (p) AlistairRawlinson(5) 14 29
(Alan McCabe) *in tch: rdn along 3f out: sn lost pl and bhd* **33/1**

1m 27.26s (0.96) **Going Correction** +0.025s/f (Good)
**WFA** 3 from 4yo+ 5lb 13 Ran SP% **117.9**
Speed ratings (Par 103): **95,93,92,87,86 85,83,83,83,77 77,76,75**
CSF £35.92 CT £320.30 TOTE £4.20: £1.30, £2.80, £3.80; EX 47.60 Trifecta £700.90.
**Owner** J S Goldie **Bred** Dunchurch Lodge Stud Co **Trained** Uplawmoor, E Renfrews

**FOCUS**
There was 4mm of rain over the previous 24 hours, the going was given as good, and jockeys riding in the first agreed. The rail was out from the 1m2f point on the Round course to where it joined the straight, adding about ten yards to 1m2f races. Two of the less-exposed runners in the line-up made up the Exacta in this modest handicap. The runner-up has been rated as matching the best view of his maiden form.

## 5416 BETFRED RACING FOLLOW ON TWITTER EBF STALLIONS MAIDEN FILLIES' STKS (BOBIS RACE) 1m (S)
**3:05** (3:08) (Class 5) 2-Y-O **£3,234** (£962; £481; £240) **Stalls** High

Form RPR

0 **1** **Montalcino (IRE)**[29] 4396 2-9-0 0 PaulMulrennan 12 82
(Brian Meehan) *mde all: rdn clr over 1f out: styd on strly* **16/1**

**2** *4* **Shalabina** 2-9-0 0 JamesSullivan 5 73
(Richard Fahey) *towards rr: pushed along 3f out: hdwy wl over 1f out: styd on wl fnl f: nrst fin* **33/1**

**3** *1/2* **Cartier (IRE)** 2-9-0 0 TedDurcan 9 76+
(David Simcock) *midfield on stands' rail: hdwy over 2f out: swtchd lft and rdn over 1f out: styd on wl fnl f: nrst fin* **16/1**

4 **4** *nk* **Ya Latif (IRE)**[53] 3558 2-9-0 0 TomQueally 6 71
(Roger Varian) *trckd ldng trio: smooth hdwy wl over 2f out: chal wl over 1f out and ev ch: sn rdn and wknd ent fnl f* **15/8**[1]

0 **5** *2 1/4* **Lexi's Red Devil (IRE)**[14] 4914 2-8-9 0 MarcMonaghan(5) 11 66
(Marco Botti) *in tch: hdwy to chse ldrs 3f out: rdn along 2f out: kpt on same pce u.p appr fnl f* **33/1**

0 **6** *1* **Almaardiyah (IRE)**[14] 4914 2-9-0 0 RichardKingscote 7 63
(Richard Hannon) *chsd ldrs: rdn along wl over 2f out: sn one pce* **10/1**

02 **7** *1* **Titled Lady**[14] 4914 2-9-0 0 ShaneKelly 8 61
(David Elsworth) *prom: cl up over 3f out: sn rdn along and grad wknd fr over 1f out* **7/2**[2]

**8** *1 3/4* **Thawraat** 2-9-0 0 WilliamCarson 14 57
(Saeed bin Suroor) *chsd ldrs: rdn along over 2f out: drvn wl over 1f out: sn wknd* **15/2**[3]

0 **9** *3* **Strong Flame**[62] 3267 2-9-0 0 SteveDrowne 13 50
(David Brown) *racd nr stands' rail: trckd ldrs: hdwy over 2f out: rdn wl over 1f out: sn wknd* **20/1**

**10** *1 3/4* **Mustique Dancer (IRE)** 2-8-9 0 SammyJoBell(5) 2 46
(Richard Fahey) *s.i.s: a in rr* **33/1**

00 **11** *1 3/4* **Pisces**[14] 4914 2-9-0 0 HayleyTurner 10 42
(David Elsworth) *a towards rr* **40/1**

55 **12** *5* **Super Quick (IRE)**[50] 3642 2-9-0 0 BarryMcHugh 1 31
(Richard Fahey) *a towards rr* **12/1**

**13** *6* **Legerity (IRE)** 2-9-0 0 AhmedAjtebi 4 17
(Charlie Appleby) *a towards rr* **16/1**

**14** *27* **Go Complain** 2-9-0 0 BenCurtis 3
(Alan McCabe) *s.i.s: a in rr: bhd fr 1/2-way* **33/1**

1m 41.75s (2.45) **Going Correction** +0.025s/f (Good) 14 Ran SP% **122.2**
Speed ratings (Par 91): **88,84,83,83,80 79,78,77,74,72 70,65,59,32**
CSF £480.26 TOTE £26.90: £6.40, £12.50, £4.50; EX 686.80 Trifecta £1509.30 Part won..
**Owner** Mrs Emma Capon **Bred** Airlie Stud **Trained** Manton, Wilts

**FOCUS**
A fair standard appeared to be set by the first two in the betting, but with the favourite easily brushed aside and the second-favourite running no sort of race it's questionable what the form is worth. The race has been rated in line with the recent race standard.

## 5417 BETFRED RACING'S BIGGEST SUPPORTER MAIDEN STKS (BOBIS RACE) 6f
**3:40** (3:41) (Class 4) 3-Y-O **£5,175** (£1,540; £769; £348) **Stalls** High

Form RPR

**1** **Crazy Chic (IRE)** 3-9-0 0 MarcMonaghan(5) 5 81
(Marco Botti) *prom: trckd ldng pair fr 1/2-way: hdwy over 1f out: rdn to ld ent fnl f: kpt on wl: readily* **10/1**

602 **2** *2 1/4* **Tap Your Toes (IRE)**[21] 4677 3-9-5 71 ShaneKelly 7 74
(Luca Cumani) *trckd ldr: hdwy to chal 2f out: rdn to ld briefly appr fnl f: sn hdd and drvn: kpt on same pce* **11/8**[1]

00 **3** *3 1/2* **Asha**[23] 4569 3-9-0 0 SteveDrowne 4 58
(David C Griffiths) *chsd ldrs: rdn along 2f out: styd on fnl f* **40/1**

-222 **4** *1/2* **Anna's Vision (IRE)**[7] 5181 3-9-0 74 PaulMulrennan 8 56
(Jeremy Noseda) *led: jnd 2f out: sn rdn and hdd appr fnl f: carried hd high and sn wknd* **7/4**[2]

0 **5** *3 3/4* **Oriental Heights**[37] 4111 3-9-0 0 FergalLynch 3 44
(Jim Goldie) *swtchd rt to stands' rail s: hld up: hdwy to trck ldrs wl over 2f out: rdn along wl over 1f out: sn no imp* **50/1**

54 **6** *9* **Slick Indian**[15] 4873 3-8-12 0 AnnaHesketh(7) 6 20
(Michael Easterby) *hld up: a towards rr* **33/1**

6-64 **7** *3* **Munjally**[82] 2611 3-9-2 75 DeclanBates(3) 1 11
(Patrick Holmes) *racd wd: prom: rdn along wl over 2f out: sn wknd* **4/1**[3]

1m 14.99s (1.39) **Going Correction** +0.025s/f (Good) 7 Ran SP% **114.9**
Speed ratings (Par 102): **91,88,83,82,77 65,61**
CSF £24.70 TOTE £9.60: £3.50, £1.30; EX 30.50 Trifecta £457.00.
**Owner** Scuderia Vittadini Srl **Bred** Scuderia Vittadini Srl **Trained** Newmarket, Suffolk

**FOCUS**
Not a strong maiden. Neither the runner-up nor the fourth are entirely convincing, and the runner-up has been rated a length off his Salisbury run.

## 5418 BETFRED BINGO H'CAP 7f
**4:15** (4:17) (Class 2) (0-105,104) 3-Y-O+ **£12,938** (£3,850; £1,924; £962) **Stalls** High

Form RPR

0024 **1** **Morache Music**[28] 4425 6-9-12 104 TedDurcan 2 111
(Peter Makin) *dwlt and in rr: hdwy over 2f out: chsd ldrs over 1f out: rdn ent fnl f: styd on wl to ld last 50yds* **14/1**

64-4 **2** *hd* **Badr Al Badoor (IRE)**[30] 4347 4-8-11 89 TomQueally 10 95
(James Fanshawe) *hld up in rr: smooth hdwy on inner rail 2f out: effrt to chal over 1f out: rdn to take slt advantage ins fnl f: sn edgd lft: hdd and no ex last 50yds* **14/1**

-600 **3** *hd* **Secretinthepark**[21] 4683 4-8-13 91 SteveDrowne 3 96
(Ed McMahon) *trckd ldrs: hdwy over 2f out: led wl over 1f out: sn rdn: drvn and hdd ins fnl f: kpt on wl u.p towards fin* **5/1**[3]

0005 **4** *3/4* **Mezzotint (IRE)**[7] 5189 5-8-7 85 RichardKingscote 6 91
(Stuart Williams) *dwlt and in rr: hdwy wl over 1f out: rdn and styd on ins fnl f: n.m.r last 100yds and no imp nr fin* **10/1**

1116 **5** *nk* **King Torus (IRE)**[21] 4648 6-9-1 93 JamesSullivan 5 96
(Ruth Carr) *trckd ldrs: hdwy 2f out: sn rdn: drvn and ch ent fnl f: no ex last 100yds* **9/2**[2]

3050 **6** *1/2* **Storm King**[14] 4888 5-8-8 86 (p) FergalLynch 8 87
(David C Griffiths) *cl up: effrt 2f out: sn rdn and ev ch: drvn ent fnl f: hld whn n.m.r last 150yds* **20/1**

0302 **7** *1/2* **Dont Bother Me (IRE)**[21] 4648 4-9-4 101 (p) MarcMonaghan(5) 9 101
(Marco Botti) *trckd ldrs: hdwy over 2f out: sn rdn and ch tl drvn and kpt on same pce fnl f* **2/1**[1]

0002 **8** *nk* **Victoire De Lyphar (IRE)**[7] 5189 7-8-12 90 (e) PaulMulrennan 1 89
(Ruth Carr) *chsd ldrs: hdwy and cl up 1/2-way: rdn along 2f out: sn drvn and grad wknd appr fnl f* **12/1**

4322 **9** *2 1/2* **Ansaab**[21] 4661 6-8-11 89 (t) BenCurtis 4 82
(Alan McCabe) *chsd ldrs on outer: hdwy and cl up 3f out: rdn along over 2f out and wknd over 1f out* **10/1**

640 **10** *nk* **Askaud (IRE)**[15] 4851 6-8-8 91 (p) MatthewHopkins(5) 7 83
(Scott Dixon) *led: rdn along 2f out: sn hdd and drvn: wknd appr fnl f* **20/1**

1m 26.27s (-0.03) **Going Correction** +0.025s/f (Good) 10 Ran SP% **116.9**
Speed ratings (Par 109): **101,100,100,99,99 98,98,97,95,94**
CSF £193.73 CT £1140.12 TOTE £24.10: £4.40, £4.30, £1.50; EX 208.40 Trifecta £1730.40.
**Owner** R P Marchant D M Ahier Mrs E Lee **Bred** Michael E Broughton **Trained** Ogbourne Maisey, Wilts

**FOCUS**
A decent handicap. They went a good clip, it paid to race a little off the gallop and the class horse of the field came through to win. The third has been rated close to form.

## 5419 BETFRED EXCLUSIVE COMPETITIONS FACEBOOK AND TWITTER H'CAP 5f
**4:50** (4:51) (Class 3) (0-95,95) 3-Y-O+ **£8,409** (£2,502; £1,250; £625) **Stalls** High

Form RPR

4421 **1** **Go Far**[18] 4765 4-9-3 88 (v) FergalLynch 8 99
(Alan Bailey) *chsd ldrs: rdn 1 1/2f out: str run to ld jst ins fnl f: drvn out* **12/1**

0 **2** ¾ **Long Awaited (IRE)**[77] 2786 6-9-1 86..........................(b) ShaneKelly 1 94
(David Barron) *hld up in rr: hdwy wl over 1f out: rdn ent fnl f: chsd wnr and drvn last 100yds: no imp towards fin* **12/1**

6056 **3** 1¾ **Jamaican Bolt (IRE)**[11] 5016 6-9-3 88.......................... BarryMcHugh 4 90
(Geoffrey Oldroyd) *towards rr: hdwy wl over 1f out: sn rdn: styd on wl fnl f: nrst fin* **14/1**

-210 **4** nk **Oh So Sassy**[37] 4128 4-9-5 90.......................... TedDurcan 6 91
(Chris Wall) *chsd ldrs: hdwy wl over 1f out: sn rdn and kpt on fnl f* **9/1**[3]

-065 **5** ¾ **Humidor (IRE)**[14] 4892 7-9-9 94.......................... RichardKingscote 17 92+
(George Baker) *racd wd: prom: effrt to chal over 1f out and sn ev ch: drvn: edgd lft and wknd ins fnl f* **4/1**[1]

3636 **6** 1 **Jack Luey**[14] 4925 7-8-9 85.......................... JordanNason(5) 20 79
(Lawrence Mullaney) *towards rr: rdn along wl over 1f out: styd on wl fnl f: nrst fin* **9/1**[3]

33- **7** ¾ **Smart Daisy K**[350] 5991 4-9-1 86.......................... BenCurtis 15 78
(Andrew Hollinshead) *chsd ldrs: rdn along wl over 1f out: sn drvn and kpt on same pce* **16/1**

000 **8** hd **Even Stevens**[70] 2989 6-8-11 87..........................(v) MatthewHopkins(5) 13 78
(Scott Dixon) *led: rdn wl over 1f out: hdd jst ins fnl f: wknd* **20/1**

4023 **9** ½ **Normal Equilibrium**[11] 5016 4-9-2 90..........................(p) MichaelJMMurphy(3) 5 79
(Robert Cowell) *chsd ldrs on outer: rdn along 2f out: grad wknd* **12/1**

1005 **10** ½ **Burning Thread (IRE)**[14] 4889 7-9-6 91..........................(b) JamesSullivan 7 78
(Tim Etherington) *in rr: rdn and hdwy over 1f out: kpt on u.p fnl f: nrst fin* **25/1**

1311 **10** dht **Iffranesia (FR)**[22] 4609 4-9-2 87.......................... AdamBeschizza 12 74
(Robert Cowell) *midfield: effrt 2f out: sn rdn along and no imp* **11/2**[2]

-000 **12** hd **Can You Conga**[20] 4712 4-8-7 85.......................... AnnaHesketh(7) 10 72
(Michael Easterby) *in tch: rdn along 2f out: n.d* **40/1**

0010 **13** ¾ **Gladiatrix**[29] 4412 5-9-0 90..........................(b) MarcMonaghan(5) 16 74
(Rod Millman) *in tch: rdn along 2f out: sn no imp* **33/1**

0010 **14** hd **Sleepy Sioux**[63] 3245 3-8-12 88.......................... SimonPearce(3) 18 71
(David Elsworth) *a towards rr* **16/1**

0033 **15** hd **Secret Witness**[8] 5152 8-9-7 92..........................(b) SteveDrowne 9 74
(Ronald Harris) *dwlt: a in rr* **14/1**

0060 **16** ½ **Riskit Fora Biskit (IRE)**[35] 4179 4-9-7 92.......................... HayleyTurner 2 73
(Michael Bell) *cl up: rdn along 2f out: sn drvn and wknd* **12/1**

2044 **17** ½ **Megaleka**[11] 5016 4-8-10 86.......................... TimClark(5) 3 65
(Alan Bailey) *prom: rdn along wl over 1f out: sn drvn and wknd* **20/1**

59.58s (-0.92) **Going Correction** +0.025s/f (Good)
**WFA** 3 from 4yo+ 2lb **17** Ran SP% **130.0**
Speed ratings (Par 107): **108,106,104,103,102 100,99,99,98,97 97,97,96,95,95 94,93**
CSF £147.65 CT £2142.95 TOTE £13.90: £4.00, £4.20, £3.80, £1.80; EX 247.50 Trifecta £1518.00 Part won..
**Owner** R West **Bred** Michael Turner **Trained** Newmarket, Suffolk

**FOCUS**
Plenty of pace on here. The runner-up has been rated close to form, and the third to this year's form.

## 5420 BETFRED 4X ODDS ON LUCKY 31S H'CAP (BOBIS RACE) 1m 2f 60y
**5:25** (5:26) (Class 4) (0-80,80) 3-Y-O **£5,175** (£1,540; £769; £384) **Stalls** Low

Form RPR

0331 **1** **Pleasant Valley (IRE)**[14] 4886 3-9-5 78.......................... ShaneKelly 3 91+
(Luca Cumani) *trckd ldrs on inner: swtchd rt to outer and gd hdwy over 2f out: led wl over 1f out: rdn clr appr fnl f: comf* **5/2**[2]

0606 **2** 3¼ **Silver Duke (IRE)**[14] 4903 3-8-6 65.......................... HayleyTurner 5 70
(Jim Goldie) *hld up in rr: hdwy over 3f out: chsd ldrs over 2f out: sn rdn: styd on to chse wnr ins fnl f: no imp* **20/1**

1 **3** ¾ **Ribblehead (USA)**[17] 4791 3-9-4 77.......................... TedDurcan 2 81
(Tim Easterby) *hld up on inner towards rr: swtchd rt and hdwy to chse ldrs 2f out: swtchd rt again to outer and rdn over 1f out: kpt on ins fnl f: nrst fin* **5/1**[3]

2603 **4** nk **Kantara Castle (IRE)**[23] 4574 3-8-10 69..........................(t) BenCurtis 7 72
(John Mackie) *trckd ldng pair: hdwy and cl up 4f out: slt ld over 3f out: sn rdn: hdd wl over 1f out: sn drvn and kpt on same pce* **16/1**

124 **5** 4½ **Derbyshire (IRE)**[30] 4350 3-8-5 .......................... ShaneGray(5) 4 64
(Kevin Ryan) *trckd ldr: hdwy and cl up 4f out: sn disp ld: rdn over 2f out: drvn wl over 1f out: wknd appr fnl f* **13/2**

0264 **6** 3½ **Mayfield Boy**[17] 4794 3-9-2 75.......................... PaulMulrennan 6 63
(Mel Brittain) *chsd ldrs: rdn along over 3f out: sn outpcd* **8/1**

2101 **7** 12 **Tower Power**[23] 4574 3-9-7 80.......................... TomQueally 1 54
(Ismail Mohammed) *led: pushed along over 4f out: rdn and hdd over 3f out: sn wknd: bhd and eased wl over 1f out* **9/4**[1]

2m 13.05s (3.65) **Going Correction** +0.425s/f (Yiel) 7 Ran SP% **111.1**
Speed ratings (Par 102): **102,99,98,98,94 92,82**
CSF £44.54 TOTE £2.90: £1.60, £5.10; EX 38.60 Trifecta £352.00.
**Owner** Wildenstein Stables Limited **Bred** Dayton Investments Ltd **Trained** Newmarket, Suffolk

**FOCUS**
They seemed to get racing early in the straight and those held up for a run were the ones to benefit. The runner-up has been rated as running his best race since his debut.

## 5421 BETFRED RACING LIKE US ON FACEBOOK APPRENTICE H'CAP 1m 2f 60y
**6:00** (6:00) (Class 5) (0-75,75) 4-Y-O+ **£3,234** (£962; £481; £240) **Stalls** Low

Form RPR

2624 **1** **Frontline Phantom (IRE)**[9] 5077 7-8-10 64.......................... PeterSword(5) 6 75
(K R Burke) *midfield: smooth hdwy to trck ldrs 4f out: effrt and cl up over 2f out: led wl over 1f out: sn rdn clr: readily* **6/1**[3]

-334 **2** 2½ **Lexington Bay (IRE)**[202] 350 6-9-12 75.......................... SammyJoBell 10 81
(Richard Fahey) *trckd ldr: cl up 3f out: pushed along over 2f out: sn rdn and ev ch: drvn over 1f out and kpt on same pce* **10/1**

2200 **3** 1½ **Missy Wells**[39] 4058 4-8-6 60.......................... AnnaHesketh(5) 3 63
(Mark Walford) *hld up towards rr: hdwy 3f out: rdn along to chse ldrs 2f out: drvn and kpt on same pce fnl f* **12/1**

-041 **4** nk **Nanton (USA)**[23] 4575 12-9-9 75.......................... JordanNason(3) 7 77
(Jim Goldie) *bhd and detached 1/2-way: pushed along over 4f out: swtchd to outer and hdwy wl over 2f out: rdn to chse ldrs over 1f out: no imp fnl f* **6/1**[3]

4064 **5** nse **Prophesy (IRE)**[17] 4793 5-9-1 67..........................(p) RachelRichardson(3) 1 69
(Tim Easterby) *trckd ldng pair on inner: effrt and cl up 3f out: rdn along 2f out: drvn wl over 1f out: kpt on same pce fnl f* **5/1**[2]

5432 **6** 1½ **The Firm (IRE)**[17] 4793 5-9-5 68.......................... EoinWalsh 11 67
(Daniel Mark Loughnane) *hld up in rr: hdwy over 3f out: swtchd lft and pushed along 2f out: sn rdn and kpt on fnl f: nrst fin* **7/2**[1]

010 **7** 1½ **Le Deluge (FR)**[20] 4710 4-9-6 69.......................... ShaneGray 8 66
(Ann Stokell) *led: pushed along 3f out: rdn 2f out: drvn and hdd wl over 1f out: sn wknd* **12/1**

5225 **8** 1¾ **Dhaular Dhar (IRE)**[15] 4858 12-8-3 59.......................... RachaelGrant(7) 2 52
(Jim Goldie) *hld up: a towards rr* **16/1**

6322 **9** 1¼ **Ashkalara**[17] 4799 7-8-9 58.......................... MarcMonaghan 9 49
(Stuart Howe) *sn trcking ldrs: effrt 3f out: rdn along over 2f out: sn wknd* **14/1**

3505 **10** 2 **Severiano (USA)**[27] 4473 4-8-4 56 oh4..........................(be) GemmaTutty(3) 5 43
(Alan McCabe) *hld up towards rr: sme hdwy on outer over 4f out: swtchd lft 3f out: sn rdn and n.d* **20/1**

-000 **11** 2 **Enzaal (USA)**[17] 4793 4-9-4 70..........................(bt[1]) RobJFitzpatrick(3) 12 53
(Philip Kirby) *trckd ldrs: hdwy 3f out: rdn along 2f out: sn drvn and wknd* **25/1**

35-0 **12** ¾ **On The Hoof**[12] 4963 5-9-2 70.......................... JoshDoyle(5) 4 52
(Michael Easterby) *in tch on inner: rdn along over 3f out: sn lost pl and bhd* **14/1**

2m 13.37s (3.97) **Going Correction** +0.425s/f (Yiel) **12** Ran SP% **119.8**
Speed ratings (Par 103): **101,99,97,97,97 96,95,93,92,91 89,88**
CSF £65.59 CT £707.28 TOTE £6.30: £2.50, £3.90, £3.90; EX 72.50 Trifecta £193.10.
**Owner** Ontoawinner & Mrs E Burke **Bred** Joe Rogers **Trained** Middleham Moor, N Yorks

**FOCUS**
A modest contest. The runner-up hadn't run over this short a trip since his 2yo days but was well placed chasing the pace and he's been rated to this year's AW form, while the third has been rated close to her C&D effort in May.
T/Plt: £6,810.90 to a £1 stake. Pool: £70,908.10, 7.60 winning tickets. T/Qpdt: £77.90 to a £1 stake. Pool: £5,131.40 - 48.70 winning tickets. JR

# 5278 LINGFIELD (L-H)
Saturday, August 16

**OFFICIAL GOING: Turf: good; polytrack: standard**
Wind: Light Weather: Sunny light cloud

## 5422 188BET APPRENTICE TRAINING SERIES H'CAP (PART OF THE RACING EXCELLENCE INITIATIVE) 6f
**5:00** (5:00) (Class 5) (0-70,70) 4-Y-O+ **£3,234** (£962; £481; £240) **Stalls** Centre

Form RPR

5331 **1** **Parisian Pyramid (IRE)**[5] 5247 8-9-8 68 6ex..........................(p) JennyPowell 2 77
(Lee Carter) *trckd ldr after 1f: pushed along 2f out to chal: led ent fnl f: r.o wl* **5/2**[2]

6522 **2** 1¼ **Dominium (USA)**[7] 5182 7-9-7 70..........................(b) DavidParkes(3) 3 75
(Jeremy Gask) *trckd ldrs: stl prom 2f out: rdn to chal ent fnl f: hld towards fin* **3/1**[3]

650 **3** 1½ **All Or Nothin (IRE)**[58] 3393 5-9-0 65.......................... CallumShepherd(5) 1 65
(Paddy Butler) *led after 1f: pushed along and pressed ent fnl 2f: hdd ins fnl f: no ex towards fin* **16/1**

6234 **4** 2½ **Atlantis Crossing (IRE)**[14] 4918 5-9-10 70.......................... DanielCremin 7 62
(Jim Boyle) *slowly away: in rr tl 2f out where rdn: r.o fnl f: nvr nrr* **2/1**[1]

6050 **5** ½ **Chester Deelyte (IRE)**[17] 4788 6-8-5 51 oh6..........................(v) AdamMcLean 6 42
(Lisa Williamson) *mid-div: pushed along 2f out: styd on the same pce fnl f* **66/1**

0060 **6** 2½ **Catalyze**[39] 4049 6-8-8 54..........................(t) JordanVaughan 5 37
(Paddy Butler) *hld up in rr: rdn ent fnl 2f f: wknd ins fnl f* **20/1**

4010 **7** ¾ **Meridius (IRE)**[22] 4620 4-9-1 66.......................... JackOsborn(5) 8 46
(Nick Littmoden) *mid-div: pushed along 2f out: one pce ins fnl f* **6/1**

1m 10.64s (-0.56) **Going Correction** -0.125s/f (Firm) 7 Ran SP% **113.3**
Speed ratings (Par 103): **98,96,94,91,90 87,86**
CSF £10.27 CT £93.83 TOTE £4.00: £3.80, £2.70; EX 10.10 Trifecta £75.30.
**Owner** John Joseph Smith **Bred** Illuminatus Investments **Trained** Epsom, Surrey

**FOCUS**
A modest handicap. The runner-up has been rated close to form.

## 5423 188BET (S) STKS 6f
**5:35** (5:35) (Class 6) 3-Y-O+ **£2,264** (£673; £336; £168) **Stalls** Centre

Form RPR

0456 **1** **Eager To Bow (IRE)**[28] 4428 8-9-1 60..........................(p) DavidProbert 1 61
(Patrick Chamings) *mid-div: gd prog 2f out: pushed along to ld ent fnl f: r.o wl* **9/2**[3]

1560 **2** 1 **Lujeanie**[8] 5124 8-9-6 66..........................(p) JimCrowley 9 63
(Peter Crate) *broke wl: restrained in mid-div after 1f: pushed along 2f out: r.o wl fnl f* **3/1**[1]

034 **3** ½ **Fleeting Indian (IRE)**[21] 4653 5-8-8 45..........................(v) DanielCremin(7) 3 56?
(Linda Jewell) *trckd ldrs after 1f: rdn ent fnl 2f: kpt on fnl f: nt gng pce of wnr* **20/1**

0060 **4** 2 **Commandingpresence (USA)**[14] 4908 8-8-7 56.(p) CharlesBishop(3) 7 45
(John Bridger) *disp ld after 1f: rdn ent fnl 2f to dispute ld: no ex ins fnl f* **4/1**[2]

-506 **5** ¾ **Aya's Gift**[6] 5207 3-8-12 58.......................... PatCosgrave 4 47
(Ed Walker) *towards rr: pushed along 2f out: r.o past btn horses fnl f: nvr nrr* **7/1**

555 **6** 1 **Monty Fay (IRE)**[36] 4151 5-8-12 45.......................... RosieJessop(3) 6 44
(Derek Haydn Jones) *mid-div: pushed along 3f out: one pce ins fnl f* **12/1**

5030 **7** 4½ **Aaranyow (IRE)**[16] 4833 6-8-10 50..........................(p) NathanAlison(5) 8 30
(Clifford Lines) *led after 1f: pushed along and hdd 2f out: wknd fnl f* **6/1**

0060 **8** 1¾ **Kuanyao (IRE)**[9] 5100 8-9-3 65..........................(p) RyanPowell(3) 5 29
(Conor Dore) *rdn to trck ldr after 1f: pushed along 3f out: wknd 2f out* **6/1**

000 **9** 99 **Madrinas Prince (IRE)**[147] 1069 5-8-8 0..........................[1] CallumShepherd(7) 2
(Paddy Butler) *slowly away: t.o 3f out: virtually p.u* **100/1**

1m 10.6s (-0.60) **Going Correction** -0.125s/f (Firm)
**WFA** 3 from 5yo+ 3lb **9** Ran SP% **117.7**
Speed ratings (Par 101): **99,97,97,94,93 92,86,83,**
CSF £18.82 TOTE £5.60: £1.50, £1.50, £3.40; EX 14.80 Trifecta £339.60.
**Owner** Mrs J E L Wright **Bred** Stone Ridge Farm **Trained** Baughurst, Hants

**FOCUS**
Weak form, with the poor sixth close up, but they went a good gallop.

## 5424 BRITISH STALLION STUDS EBF NOVICE STKS 7f
**6:05** (6:05) (Class 4) 2-Y-O **£6,469** (£1,925; £962; £481) **Stalls** Centre

Form RPR

2 **1** **Good Place (USA)**[29] 4403 2-8-9 0.......................... RichardHughes 3 86
(Saeed bin Suroor) *hld up and wd after 1f: gd prog 2f out: rdn to ld ins fnl f: r.o wl* **5/4**[1]

1 **2** 2 **Make It Up**[16] 4809 2-9-7 0.......................... DavidProbert 5 93
(Andrew Balding) *led after 1f: pushed along 2f out: hdd ins fnl f: r.o wl: nt gng pce of wnr* **5/1**[3]

12 **3** 3½ **Zephuros (IRE)**[15] 4865 2-9-7 0.......................... WilliamBuick 4 85
(Charlie Appleby) *trckd ldr: pushed along 2f out: no ex ins fnl f* **7/1**

31 **4** 3 1/4 **Winslow (USA)**85 2507 2-9-7 0 JimCrowley 6 75
(Charlie Appleby) *trckd ldr: pushed along and outpcd 3f out: one pce ins fnl f* **7/4**2

1m 22.89s (-0.41) **Going Correction** -0.125s/f (Firm) **4** Ran SP% **110.0**
Speed ratings (Par 96): **97,94,90,87**
CSF £7.63 TOTE £2.10; EX 6.60 Trifecta £17.10.
**Owner** Godolphin **Bred** Darley **Trained** Newmarket, Suffolk

**FOCUS**
A warm little novice stakes featuring four unexposed and promising juveniles. The winner was getting plenty of weight and has only been rated as stepping up slightly on her debut effort.

## 5425 HEART FM 97.5 FM H'CAP 7f 140y
**6:35** (6:36) (Class 6) (0-60,67) 3-Y-O+ **£2,587** (£770; £384; £192) **Stalls** Centre

Form RPR
0 **1** **Chellalla**43 3935 5-9-10 60 StevieDonohoe 6 72
(Ian Williams) *broke wl to ld after 1f: strly pressed ins fnl f: hld on wl: mde all* **7/1**3

5603 **2** 1/2 **El Mirage (IRE)**10 5041 4-9-2 52 JimCrowley 2 63
(Dean Ivory) *hld up in mid-div: gd prog to trck ldr 3f out: rdn to chse ldr ins fnl f: hld towards fin* **8/1**

1264 **3** 3 1/2 **Byrd In Hand (IRE)**9 5075 7-9-9 59 WilliamCarson 8 61
(John Bridger) *trckd ldr after 1f: pushed along 3f out: hrd rdn 2f out: r.o fnl f* **5/1**2

0404 **4** nk **Bold Ring**14 4905 8-9-2 52 PatCosgrave 5 54
(Edward Creighton) *trckd ldrs after 1f: rdn ent fnl 2f: one pce fnl f* **16/1**

6031 **5** nk **Emman Bee (IRE)**9 5075 5-10-3 67 RichardHughes 11 68
(Luke Dace) *trckd ldr after 1f: pushed along to chse ldr 2f out: wknd ins fnl f* **7/4**1

5003 **6** 1 3/4 **Carrera**14 4905 4-9-6 56 (b1) DavidProbert 9 52
(Michael Blanshard) *hld up towards rr: gd prog to trck ldrs 3f out: pushed along 2f out: wknd ins fnl f* **7/1**3

6440 **7** 1 1/2 **Dancing Angel**12 4972 3-8-12 57 RyanTate(3) 7 49
(James Eustace) *hld up in mid-div: pushed along 2f out: styd on same pce ins fnl f* **12/1**

5053 **8** 3/4 **Copperwood**19 4738 9-9-6 56 (v) AmirQuinn 12 47
(Lee Carter) *hld up towards rr: pushed along 2f out: one pce fnl f* **12/1**

0004 **9** 1 1/2 **Silvee**3 5313 7-8-5 46 oh1 (v1) ShelleyBirkett(5) 4 33
(John Bridger) *hld up in last pair after 1f: pushed along 2f: wknd ins fnl f* **20/1**

00-5 **10** 20 **Trust Me Boy**63 3230 6-8-10 46 JimmyQuinn 10
(John E Long) *hld up in last pair after 1f: outpcd and detached 4f out: eased ins fnl 3f: wl btn* **33/1**

1m 30.88s (-1.42) **Going Correction** -0.125s/f (Firm)
**WFA** 3 from 4yo+ 6lb **10** Ran SP% **118.1**
Speed ratings (Par 101): **102,101,98,97,97 95,94,93,91,71**
CSF £62.70 CT £315.59 TOTE £9.50: £3.00, £2.00, £1.30; EX 71.80 Trifecta £260.20.
**Owner** Jamie Robert Roberts **Bred** Azienda Agricola Rosati Colarieti **Trained** Portway, Worcs
■ Stewards' Enquiry : Stevie Donohoe two-day ban: careless riding (Aug 30-31)

**FOCUS**
An open-looking handicap on paper but very few got into it. The runner-up has been rated to her AW latest.

## 5426 INDUS CATERING H'CAP 1m 4f (P)
**7:05** (7:05) (Class 5) (0-70,70) 3-Y-O+ **£3,234** (£962; £481; £240) **Stalls** Low

Form RPR
0222 **1** **Sweetheart Abbey**22 4616 3-9-4 70 (p) RichardHughes 2 79
(William Knight) *t.k.h and hld up in rr: gng wl but short of room 2f out: rdn to ld ins fnl f: r.o wl* **6/4**1

1106 **2** 1 1/4 **Kindlelight Storm (USA)**19 4743 4-9-7 70 (b) JordanVaughan(7) 4 76
(Nick Littmoden) *hld up in last pair: pushed along 2f out to trck ldr: r.o wl ins fnl f: nt gng pce of wnr* **16/1**

6465 **3** 1/2 **Carraig Rock**26 4501 4-9-12 68 JimCrowley 6 73
(Hughie Morrison) *trckd ldr after 1f: pushed along to ld 3f out: rdn and hdd ins fnl f: kpt on same pce* **10/1**

4403 **4** 1 1/2 **Anjin (IRE)**7 5185 3-8-10 62 LukeMorris 1 65
(Sir Mark Prescott Bt) *trckd ldrs after 1f: rdn to chse ldr 2f out: hrd drvn and one pce ins fnl f* **9/4**2

2100 **5** 1 3/4 **Nelson Quay (IRE)**24 4548 4-10-0 70 1 MartinLane 5 70
(Jeremy Gask) *led after 1f: rdn and hdd ent fnl 3f: wknd ins fnl f* **8/1**

**6** 1 **Flowing Air (IRE)**21 4692 4-9-6 67 CamHardie(5) 3 65
(Richard Brabazon, Ire) *hld up in mid-div: rdn and outpcd 2f out: wknd ins fnl f* **5/1**3

2m 30.92s (-2.08) **Going Correction** -0.075s/f (Stan)
**WFA** 3 from 4yo 10lb **6** Ran SP% **113.5**
Speed ratings (Par 103): **103,102,101,100,99 99**
CSF £26.04 TOTE £2.30: £1.30, £3.20; EX 22.60 Trifecta £99.70.
**Owner** Miss S Bannatyne **Bred** Miss S Bannatyne **Trained** Patching, W Sussex

**FOCUS**
They went no gallop early on which holds the form back a touch but the first two home still came from well off the pace. The runner-up has been rated to his spring form.

## 5427 188BET CASINO CLAIMING STKS 1m 1y(P)
**7:35** (7:36) (Class 6) 3-Y-O **£2,264** (£675; £336; £168) **Stalls** High

Form RPR
5331 **1** **Rough Courte (IRE)**7 5198 3-8-9 70 CharlesBishop(3) 9 62+
(Mick Channon) *led after 1f: pushed along 2f out to ld by 2 l: strly pressed ins fnl 50yds: jst hld on* **4/6**1

5100 **2** hd **Born To Fly (IRE)**11 4998 3-8-10 62 (b) JimCrowley 3 59
(Nick Littmoden) *hld up towards rr: short of room ent fnl 2f out: r.o wl ins fnl f to press ldr: jst hld* **8/1**

0 **3** 2 **Kubeba (IRE)**10 5039 3-9-7 0 LukeMorris 2 65
(Paul Cole) *hld up in mid-div: hrd rdn 3f out: r.o wl ins fnl f: nt gng pce of 1st and 2nd* **4/1**2

65 **4** 3/4 **Adimendis (IRE)**21 4653 3-8-9 0 StevieDonohoe 8 51
(J S Moore) *trckd ldrs after 1f: pushed along 3f out: kpt on same pce ins fnl f* **25/1**

2600 **5** 1 **Sebs Sensei (IRE)**30 4342 3-9-2 62 CamHardie(5) 4 61
(Mark Hoad) *trckd ldrs after 1f: pushed along 3f out: one pce ins fnl f* **20/1**

0555 **6** 1/2 **Intense Feeling (IRE)**12 4969 3-8-5 58 KierenFox 7 44
(Lee Carter) *trckd ldr after 1f: pushed along to chse ldr 2f out: wknd ins fnl f* **8/1**

25- **7** 6 **Bush Beauty (IRE)**373 5199 3-8-3 0 DannyBrock(5) 6 33
(Philip McBride) *hld up towards rr: pushed along and wd 2f out: wknd ins fnl f* **6/1**3

0-0 **8** 1 **Emporium**121 1534 3-8-12 0 J-PGuillambert 1 35
(Nick Littmoden) *trckd ldrs after 1f: pushed along 3f out: wknd qckly ins fnl f* **33/1**

00 **9** 3 1/4 **Mountain River (IRE)**31 4325 3-8-6 0 JosephineGordon(7) 5 28
(J S Moore) *slowly away: pushed along after 2f out: a in rr* **50/1**

1m 37.85s (-0.35) **Going Correction** -0.075s/f (Stan) **9** Ran SP% **130.0**
Speed ratings (Par 98): **98,97,95,95,94 93,87,86,83**
CSF £8.42 TOTE £1.70: £1.10, £2.30, £1.90; EX 8.10 Trifecta £29.70.
**Owner** Billy Parish **Bred** Futoo Club **Trained** West Ilsley, Berks
■ Supachap was withdrawn. Price at time of withdrawal 3/1. Rule 4 applies to bets struck prior to withdrawal but not to SP bets. Deduct 25p in the pound. New market formed.

**FOCUS**
A very weak contest. The level is a bit fluid, with some doubts about those down the field, especially the fifth.

## 5428 188BET GREAT IN PLAY H'CAP 1m 2f (P)
**8:05** (8:06) (Class 6) (0-60,64) 3-Y-O+ **£2,587** (£770; £384; £192) **Stalls** Low

Form RPR
1455 **1** **Lily Edge**21 4658 5-9-11 59 (v) WilliamCarson 3 67
(John Bridger) *trckd ldrs after 1f: pushed along 2f out to chse ldr: r.o wl to ld cl home* **10/1**

0531 **2** nk **Estibdaad (IRE)**19 4738 4-9-6 54 (t) MartinLane 9 61
(Paddy Butler) *led after 1f: pushed along 2f out: stl led ent fnl f: hdd fnl 50yds* **7/2**2

0610 **3** 1 1/2 **Benoordenhout (IRE)**19 4738 3-8-13 55 (p) LukeMorris 8 59
(Jonathan Portman) *trckd ldr after 1f: pushed along 2f out: r.o fnl f: nt gng pce of first two* **3/1**1

6531 **4** 1/2 **Bennelong**10 5041 8-9-9 64 (v) PaigeBolton(7) 6 67
(Lee Carter) *hld up in rr: pushed along 3f out: r.o ins fnl f: nvr nrr* **7/1**3

233 **5** 3/4 **Ferryview Place**19 4744 5-9-2 50 (p) StevieDonohoe 2 52
(Ian Williams) *prom and t.k.h after 1f: pushed along 2f out to chse ldrs: styd on the same pce ins fnl f* **8/1**

0030 **6** 3/4 **Rezwaan**56 3473 7-9-4 59 (b) HectorCrouch(7) 1 59
(Murty McGrath) *trckd ldrs in mid-div after 1f: pushed along 2f out: wknd ins fnl f* **20/1**

12 **7** 2 1/4 **With Hindsight (IRE)**19 4738 6-9-3 56 CamHardie(5) 7 52
(John Spearing) *trckd ldrs after 1f: pushed along 3f out: rdn 2f out: one pce ins fnl f* **7/2**2

5405 **8** 1 3/4 **Super Duplex**9 5076 7-9-7 55 (t) JimCrowley 4 47
(Roger Teal) *hld up in rr: pushed along 2f out and wl btn* **8/1**

04-1 **9** 11 **Wicked Tara**41 4039 4-8-5 46 oh1 CharlieBennett(7) 5 16
(Natalie Lloyd-Beavis) *hld up in rr: pushed along and wd 4f out: rdn 3f out: a in rr* **33/1**

2m 6.31s (-0.29) **Going Correction** -0.075s/f (Stan)
**WFA** 3 from 4yo+ 8lb **9** Ran SP% **121.0**
Speed ratings (Par 101): **98,97,96,96,95 94,93,91,82**
CSF £47.23 CT £135.66 TOTE £10.20: £3.00, £1.90, £1.60; EX 72.40 Trifecta £276.10.
**Owner** J J Bridger **Bred** W J Wyatt **Trained** Liphook, Hants

**FOCUS**
The pace was steady throughout and they were well stacked up coming round the home bend. Muddling form. The fourth has been rated close to his recent form despite not having the race run to suit.
T/Plt: £40.10 to £1 stake. Pool of £44924.26 - 817.76 winning tickets. T/Qpdt: £15.50 to a £1 stake. Pool of £6314.19 - 300.62 winning tickets. NF

# 5377 NEWBURY (L-H)
Saturday, August 16

**OFFICIAL GOING: Good to soft (soft in places; 6.1)**
Rail movement increased distances on Round course by about 26yds.
Wind: mild breeze across Weather: sunny

## 5429 PLAY TODAY'S 2M SCOOP6 EBF MAIDEN FILLIES' STKS (BOBIS RACE) 6f 8y
**1:00** (1:00) (Class 4) 2-Y-O **£5,175** (£1,540; £769; £384) **Stalls** Centre

Form RPR
36 **1** **Vesnina**10 5037 2-9-0 0 RichardHughes 3 83
(Richard Hannon) *mde all: kpt on wl fnl f: rdn out* **8/1**

4 **2** 3/4 **Evening Rain (USA)**29 4396 2-9-0 0 JoeFanning 6 82+
(Saeed bin Suroor) *nvr wnr: mounting chal whn sddle slipped briefly wl over 1f out and lost a pl: r.o to regain 2nd nring fin but a being hld* **4/1**2

02 **3** 1/2 **Hundi (IRE)**17 4781 2-9-0 0 WilliamBuick 8 79
(Charles Hills) *mid-div: hdwy over 2f out: rdn to chse wnr over 1f out: kpt on but no ex whn lost 2nd nring fin* **15/8**1

**4** 1 1/2 **Amaze Me** 2-9-0 0 J-PGuillambert 1 74+
(Nick Littmoden) *mid-div: swtchd lft and hdwy 2f out: rdn over 1f out: kpt on same pce fnl f* **33/1**

0 **5** 3/4 **Raspberry Ripple**65 3140 2-9-0 0 JimCrowley 4 72
(Richard Hannon) *s.i.s: sn mid-div: hdwy 2f out: sn rdn: styd on same pce fnl f* **33/1**

02 **6** 3/4 **Stocking**12 4973 2-9-0 0 AndreaAtzeni 10 69
(Roger Varian) *mid-div: hdwy wl over 1f out: sn rdn to chse ldrs: fdd ins fnl f* **11/2**3

**7** 3 3/4 **Tendu** 2-9-0 0 JamesDoyle 12 57+
(John Gosden) *s.i.s: hld up towards rr: pushed along and stdy prog fr over 2f out: no further imp fnl f* **7/1**

**8** 3 1/4 **Forbidden Love** 2-9-0 0 MartinHarley 7 47
(Richard Hannon) *hld up towards rr: pushed along over 3f out: sme hdwy 2f out: wknd fnl f* **16/1**

**9** 2 **Exoplanet Blue** 2-9-0 0 DavidProbert 5 41
(Henry Candy) *s.i.s: a towards rr* **20/1**

**10** 1/2 **Simone On Time (IRE)** 2-9-0 0 LiamKeniry 2 39
(Sylvester Kirk) *trckd ldrs tl rdn over 2f out: sn wknd* **33/1**

6 **11** 6 **Fleetwood Poppy**31 4320 2-9-0 0 KierenFox 11 20
(Michael Attwater) *trckd ldrs: rdn over 2f out: sn wknd* **100/1**

1m 15.71s (2.71) **Going Correction** +0.625s/f (Yiel) **11** Ran SP% **114.2**
Speed ratings (Par 93): **106,105,104,102,101 100,95,91,88,87 79**
CSF £36.96 TOTE £11.70: £3.00, £1.90, £1.10; EX 51.70 Trifecta £124.50.
**Owner** Cheveley Park Stud **Bred** Cheveley Park Stud Ltd **Trained** East Everleigh, Wilts

**FOCUS**
Often an above-average fillies' maiden and was won 12 months earlier by Lightning Thunder. It was a muddling affair this time around, though. The third has been rated close to her Goodwood mark.

## 5430 BETFRED SUPPORTS JACK BERRY HOUSE H'CAP (BOBIS RACE) 1m 2f 6y
1:35 (1:35) (Class 4) (0-85,85) 3-Y-O £4,690 (£1,395; £697; £348) Stalls Low

Form RPR
10 **1** **Flippant (IRE)**[70] 2986 3-9-0 83........ NathanAlison(5) 3 91
(William Haggas) *hld up last but wl in tch: swtchd rt and hdwy fr 3f out: shkn up over 1f out: r.o wl to ld fnl 100yds: pushed out* **10/3**[2]

5331 **2** 1/2 **Fire Fighting (IRE)**[8] 5123 3-9-7 85........(b) JoeFanning 5 92
(Mark Johnston) *cl up: hdwy over 3f out: led wl over 2f out: rdn over 1f out: kpt on tl no ex whn hdd fnl 100yds* **6/1**

215 **3** 1 1/4 **Mythical Madness**[9] 5094 3-9-6 84........ JamesDoyle 2 89
(Charlie Appleby) *hld up bhd ldrs: pushed along over 3f out: rdn: swtchd out and hdwy over 2f out: sn chsng ldrs: styd on same pce fnl f* **4/1**[3]

3140 **4** 1/2 **Crystal Nymph (IRE)**[26] 4504 3-8-12 76........ JimCrowley 6 80
(Richard Hannon) *hld up bhd ldrs: hdwy 4f out: rdn over 2f out: chsd ldr over 1f out tl ins fnl f: styd on same pce* **16/1**

-022 **5** 3/4 **Billy Blue (IRE)**[10] 5038 3-8-12 76........(p) WilliamBuick 1 78
(John Gosden) *trckd ldrs: rdn w awkward hd carriage fr wl over 2f out: short of room briefly whn hld ent fnl f: kpt on but nvr finding pce to chal* **5/1**

-043 **6** 10 **Ghosting (IRE)**[11] 5004 3-8-3 74 ow1........(t) JennyPowell(7) 7 57
(Tom Dascombe) *trckd ldr: led briefly 3f out: sn rdn: kpt chsng ldr tl wknd jst over 1f out* **20/1**

5-13 **7** 20 **Shafrah (IRE)**[63] 3243 3-9-7 85........ RichardHughes 4 30
(Richard Hannon) *led tl 3f out: wknd qckly: eased over 1f out* **11/4**[1]

2m 10.8s (2.00) **Going Correction** +0.275s/f (Good) **7 Ran SP% 111.3**
Speed ratings (Par 102): **103,102,101,101,100 92,76**
CSF £22.06 TOTE £4.80: £2.20, £2.60; EX 27.90 Trifecta £112.00.
**Owner** Bernard Kantor **Bred** Wentworth Racing (pty) Ltd **Trained** Newmarket, Suffolk

**FOCUS**
This was a tight-looking 3yo handicap. It was run at an uneven pace and resulted in a bunched finish, so the form is worth treating with a little caution. The runner-up has been rated back to his best and sets the standard.

## 5431 DENFORD STUD STKS (REGISTERED AS THE WASHINGTON SINGER STAKES) (LISTED RACE) 7f (S)
2:05 (2:06) (Class 1) 2-Y-O £14,461 (£5,482; £2,743; £1,366) Stalls Centre

Form RPR
14 **1** **Belardo (IRE)**[37] 4123 2-9-1 0........ AndreaAtzeni 4 108
(Roger Varian) *travelled wl trcking ldng pair: qcknd up smartly to ld over 1f out: sn in command: readily* **5/4**[1]

21 **2** 3 3/4 **Hawkesbury**[50] 3649 2-9-1 0........ WilliamBuick 3 102
(Charlie Appleby) *stdd into 4th s: swtchd out and hdwy over 2f out: rdn and hung rt fr over 1f out: chsd wnr ent fnl f but nvr finding pce to get on terms* **13/8**[2]

4124 **3** 2 **Diaz (IRE)**[21] 4645 2-9-1 96........[1] JoeFanning 2 93
(Mark Johnston) *led: rdn 2f out: hdd jst over 1f out: sn outpcd by wnr: lost 2nd ent fnl f: no ex fnl 120yds* **6/1**[3]

1 **4** 1/2 **Carry On Deryck**[13] 4943 2-9-1 0........ LiamKeniry 1 92
(Sylvester Kirk) *trckd ldr: pushed along over 3f out: rdn over 2f out: kpt on but sn outpcd and hld: drifted rt fnl f* **8/1**

1m 28.47s (2.77) **Going Correction** +0.625s/f (Yiel) **4 Ran SP% 107.9**
Speed ratings: **109,104,102,101**
CSF £3.55 TOTE £2.20; EX 3.20 Trifecta £6.10.
**Owner** Prince A A Faisal **Bred** Ballylinch Stud **Trained** Newmarket, Suffolk

**FOCUS**
An interesting affair and a taking winner.

## 5432 BETFRED TV GEOFFREY FREER STKS (GROUP 3) 1m 5f 61y
2:40 (2:40) (Class 1) 3-Y-O+ £34,026 (£12,900; £6,456; £3,216; £1,614; £810) Stalls Low

Form RPR
-064 **1** **Seismos (IRE)**[34] 4250 6-9-4 111........ MartinHarley 7 114
(Marco Botti) *trckd ldrs: wnt 2nd after 5f: rdn over 3f out: sltly outpcd whn dropped to 5th: str run ent fnl f: led towards fin: styd on wl* **11/1**

0/1- **2** nk **Willing Foe (USA)**[455] 2443 7-9-4 111........ JamesDoyle 3 113
(Saeed bin Suroor) *trckd ldr for 5f: cl 3rd: led over 2f out: sn rdn: styd on wl: hdd nring fin* **7/1**

1-40 **3** 1 **Seal Of Approval**[42] 3961 5-9-1 110........ GeorgeBaker 9 108
(James Fanshawe) *s.i.s: pushed along in last pair early: swtchd rt to centre whn rdn over 2f out: no prog tl styd on strly ent fnl f but plenty to do: snatched 3rd fnl stride* **6/1**[3]

4-60 **4** nse **Red Cadeaux**[104] 2002 8-9-4 118........ GeraldMosse 2 111
(Ed Dunlop) *in tch: rdn 2f out: trying to mount chal whn short of room over 1f out: kpt on to hold ev ch jst ins fnl f tl no ex nring fin: lost 3rd fnl stride* **7/1**

3033 **5** 1 **Somewhat (USA)**[17] 4778 3-8-7 110........ JoeFanning 8 109
(Mark Johnston) *led: hdd over 2f out: sn rdn: kpt pressing ldrs tl tight for room on rails over 1f out: eased off and swtchd rt: styd on but hld after* **5/1**[2]

5244 **6** nse **Rawaki (IRE)**[49] 3722 6-9-4 107........ LiamKeniry 10 109
(Andrew Balding) *mid-div tl lost pl 3f out: nt clr run over 2f out tl swtchd lft over 1f out: styd on on fnl f but nvr any ch* **16/1**

6133 **7** 1 1/2 **Cafe Society (FR)**[15] 4849 4-9-4 102........ JimCrowley 11 107
(David Simcock) *trckd ldr for 5f: cl 3rd: rdn over 2f out: kpt chsng ldng pair tl ent fnl f: fdd fnl 120yds* **12/1**

-000 **8** 4 **Camborne**[56] 3450 6-9-4 109........(p) WilliamBuick 4 101
(John Gosden) *s.i.s: in last pair: hdwy 4f out into mid-div: rdn 3f out: no further imp fnl 2f* **10/1**

2331 **9** 4 **Pether's Moon (IRE)**[15] 4849 4-9-6 112........(b[1]) RichardHughes 5 97
(Richard Hannon) *hld up towards rr: hdwy into midfield over 5f out: rdn 3f out: sn edgd lft: nvr threatened: wknd over 1f out* **9/2**[1]

3-04 **10** 3 1/4 **Girolamo (GER)**[44] 5-9-4 107........ AdriedeVries 6 90
(P Schiergen, Germany) *mid-div: rdn 3f out: nvr any imp: wknd and eased fnl f* **11/1**

3/2- **11** hd **Triumphant (IRE)**[124] 2105 5-9-4 101........ DavidProbert 1 90
(Gary Moore) *little slowly away: sn mid-div: lost pl over 5f out: rdn 3f out: nvr threatened to get bk on terms* **50/1**

2m 54.77s (2.77) **Going Correction** +0.275s/f (Good)
**WFA** 3 from 4yo+ 11lb **11 Ran SP% 115.4**
Speed ratings: **102,101,101,101,100 100,99,97,94,92 92**
CSF £84.34 TOTE £10.90: £3.50, £2.60, £2.40; EX 110.40 Trifecta £2359.30 Part won..
**Owner** Australian Thoroughbred Bloodstock **Bred** Gestut Karlshof **Trained** Newmarket, Suffolk

■ Stewards' Enquiry : Martin Harley four-day ban: used whip above permitted level (Aug 30-Sep 2)

**FOCUS**
This year's Geoffrey Freer was a tremendously competitive Group 3. They went a sound pace early on but it still paid to be prominent. The runner-up has gone well fresh in the past, he travelled best and has been rated close to last year's C&D win.

## 5433 BETFRED GOALS GALORE LADIES DAY H'CAP 7f (S)
3:15 (3:15) (Class 3) (0-95,95) 3-Y-O+
£12,450 (£3,728; £1,864; £932; £466; £234) Stalls Centre

Form RPR
4414 **1** **Accession (IRE)**[17] 4783 5-8-12 81........ JamesDoyle 4 92
(Charlie Fellowes) *trckd ldrs: led over 2f out: rdn whn strly chal ent fnl f: kpt on wl: asserting nr fin: drvn out* **9/2**[2]

5230 **2** 1/2 **Foxtrot Romeo (IRE)**[21] 4683 5-9-8 91........(tp) MartinHarley 2 101
(Marco Botti) *hld up: hdwy over 2f out: rdn for str chal ent fnl f: kpt on w ev ch tl no ex nring fin* **11/2**[3]

6000 **3** 3 1/2 **Pastoral Player**[15] 4851 7-9-5 95........ CharlieBennett(7) 1 96+
(Hughie Morrison) *hld up: travelling wl whn nt clr run over 2f out: sn rdn: making hdwy whn nt clr run and swtchd rt ent fnl f: r.o to snatch 3rd fnl strides* **7/1**

3540 **4** nk **Farlow (IRE)**[14] 4922 6-9-6 89........[1] RichardHughes 3 89
(Richard Fahey) *led tl over 2f out: sn rdn: kpt chsng wnr tl over 1f out: no ex ins fnl f: lost 3rd fnl strides* **7/2**[1]

2406 **5** hd **Chilworth Icon**[14] 4918 4-9-6 89........ AndreaAtzeni 7 89
(Mick Channon) *mid-div: hdwy over 2f out: sn rdn: hld in 4th whn edgd sltly lft 1f out: kpt on towards fin* **12/1**

0420 **6** 6 **Zacynthus (IRE)**[57] 3431 6-8-13 82........ WilliamBuick 8 66
(Michael Bell) *stmbld leaving stalls: sn prom: rdn and ev ch 2f out: wknd ent fnl f* **10/1**

0530 **7** 7 **Kinglami**[14] 4892 5-8-10 79........(b[1]) JoeFanning 9 45
(Brian Gubby) *racd keenly: trckd ldrs: rdn over 2f out: wknd over 1f out* **7/1**

1611 **8** 2 1/2 **See The Storm**[21] 4650 6-8-6 80........ GeorgeDowning(5) 10 39
(Ian Williams) *racd keenly: hld up: hdwy 1/2-way: sn rdn: wknd over 1f out* **8/1**

4020 **9** 10 **Trader Jack**[28] 4438 5-9-0 83........[1] JimCrowley 5 16
(David Flood) *mid-div: effrt over 2f out: wknd over 1f out* **10/1**

1m 28.63s (2.93) **Going Correction** +0.625s/f (Yiel) **9 Ran SP% 117.8**
Speed ratings (Par 107): **108,107,103,103,102 96,88,85,73**
CSF £30.13 CT £172.81 TOTE £5.40: £1.90, £1.70, £2.70; EX 33.20 Trifecta £250.50.
**Owner** Lady De Ramsey **Bred** Corduff Stud Ltd **Trained** Newmarket, Suffolk

**FOCUS**
A good-quality handicap. It was run at an average pace with those held up at a disadvantage and the trio that initially went back to the centre of the track around 2f out dominated the finish. The winner hs been rated to last year's best.

## 5434 BETFRED HUNGERFORD STKS (GROUP 2) 7f (S)
3:50 (3:50) (Class 1) 3-Y-O+
£56,710 (£21,500; £10,760; £5,360; £2,690; £1,350) Stalls Centre

Form RPR
1312 **1** **Breton Rock (IRE)**[77] 2765 4-9-5 112........ MartinLane 6 116
(David Simcock) *trckd ldrs: led narrowly over 1f out: sn rdn: strly chal but battled on wl fnl f: drifted sltly rt: hld on* **3/1**[2]

5130 **2** shd **Gregorian (IRE)**[6] 5223 5-9-5 116........ WilliamBuick 2 115
(John Gosden) *trckd ldrs: pressed wnr over 1f out: sn rdn: kpt on wl w ev ch fnl f: drifted sltly rt: jst hld on nod* **13/8**[1]

1600 **3** 1 1/2 **Brazos (IRE)**[21] 4648 3-9-0 103........ AndreaAtzeni 7 109
(Clive Brittain) *trckd ldrs: rdn to chse ldng trio wl over 1f out: nt quite pce to get on terms: kpt on to go 3rd ins fnl f* **20/1**

2201 **4** 2 **Professor**[28] 4425 4-9-5 113........ RichardHughes 3 106
(Richard Hannon) *led: rdn and hdd over 1f out: sn hld: no ex whn lost 3rd ins fnl f* **7/1**

0012 **5** 3 3/4 **Chil The Kite**[59] 3356 5-9-5 112........ GeorgeBaker 4 96
(Hughie Morrison) *racd alone nr stands' side rails: prom: rdn over 2f out: hld over 1f out: wknd fnl f* **4/1**[3]

5442 **6** 17 **Producer**[2] 5354 5-9-5 112........ JamesDoyle 1 52
(Richard Hannon) *trckd ldr tl rdn 2f out: qckly btn: eased fnl f* **8/1**

1m 27.18s (1.48) **Going Correction** +0.625s/f (Yiel)
**WFA** 3 from 4yo+ 5lb **6 Ran SP% 111.5**
Speed ratings (Par 115): **116,115,114,111,107 88**
CSF £8.18 TOTE £3.40: £1.70, £1.30; EX 8.60 Trifecta £56.40.
**Owner** John Cook **Bred** George Kent **Trained** Newmarket, Suffolk

**FOCUS**
This Group 2 prize looked a really tight affair and was messy, but the first pair drew away late on. The winner has been rated a length up on his latest Haydock run.

## 5435 BETFRED "RACING'S BIGGEST SUPPORTER" LADIES DERBY H'CAP (FOR LADY AMATEUR RIDERS) 1m 4f 5y
4:25 (4:28) (Class 4) (0-80,75) 3-Y-O+ £4,253 (£1,402; £701; £350) Stalls Low

Form RPR
441 **1** **Lil Rockerfeller (USA)**[30] 4350 3-9-10 73........ MissSBrotherton 8 82
(Richard Hannon) *reluctant to load: nvr looked to be travelling: chsd ldrs: led wl over 2f out: kpt narrow advatage u.p thrght fnl 2f: rdn out* **11/4**[2]

**2** nk **Amanto (GER)**[80] 4-9-8 66........ MissMeganNicholls(5) 3 74
(Paul Nicholls) *trckd ldrs: chal wl over 2f out: sn rdn: kpt on w ev ch tl no ex fnl 75yds* **11/8**[1]

1133 **3** 1/2 **Last Minute Lisa (IRE)**[16] 4808 4-9-10 63........ MissJMMangan 5 70
(Sylvester Kirk) *in tch: smooth hdwy 4f out: chal wl over 2f out: kpt on pressing ldrs tl no ex fnl 100yds* **5/1**[3]

1/0- **4** 12 **Passato (GER)**[34] 22 10-9-8 61........(t) MissEJJones 6 49
(Jo Davis) *chsd clr ldr: clsd on ldr 4f out: led over 3f out tl wl over 2f out: sn one pce* **25/1**

0001 **5** 2 1/4 **Couloir Extreme (IRE)**[12] 4985 4-10-3 75........(v) MissEllaSmith(5) 4 59
(Gary Moore) *s.i.s: nvr travelling: last most of way: nvr threatened* **13/2**

50 **6** 4 1/2 **Desert Recluse (IRE)**[28] 4441 7-10-3 70........(v[1]) MissAliceMills 1 47
(Ian Williams) *led: clr after 2f: hdd over 3f out: wknd 2f out* **12/1**

2m 41.91s (6.41) **Going Correction** +0.275s/f (Good)
**WFA** 3 from 4yo+ 10lb **6 Ran SP% 110.3**
Speed ratings (Par 105): **89,88,88,80,78 75**
CSF £6.68 CT £14.58 TOTE £3.10: £1.70, £1.30; EX 7.40 Trifecta £29.20.
**Owner** Middleham Park Racing XLV **Bred** Brushwood Stable **Trained** East Everleigh, Wilts

**FOCUS**
A fair handicap of its type which provided a decent test and there was a cracking three-way finish. The third looks to have run as well as ever on the face of things.
T/Plt: £68.60 to a £1 stake. Pool: £88,331.09 - 939.59 winning tickets. T/Qpdt: £21.30 to a £1 stake. Pool: £6,380.93 - 221.10 winning tickets. TM

5391 **NEWMARKET** (R-H)

Saturday, August 16

**OFFICIAL GOING: Good to soft (good in places; 6.8)**

Stands side track used with Stalls on Stands Far side except 12f: Centre.
Wind: light, behind Weather: mainly overcast, brighter spells

## 5436 CHEVELEY PARK STUD FILLIES' NURSERY H'CAP (BOBIS RACE) 7f
**1:50** (1:50) (Class 2) 2-Y-O **£12,938** (£3,850; £1,924; £962) **Stalls** Low

Form RPR

0321 **1** **Astrelle (IRE)**[14] 4884 2-8-11 **75**........................ LukeMorris 13 83
(Marco Botti) *chsd ldrs: rdn and effrt to chal over 1f out: drifted rt and led ins fnl f: continuede to edge rt but styd on wl: drvn out* **12/1**

2252 **2** *1* **Persun**[8] 5147 2-8-11 **78**........................ CharlesBishop(3) 6 83
(Mick Channon) *stdd s: hld up in rr: hdwy jst over 2f out: drvn to chse ldng pair 1f out: styd on u.p to go 2nd nr fin* **14/1**

631 **3** *½* **Gregoria (IRE)**[14] 4885 2-8-11 **75**........................ LiamJones 4 79
(William Haggas) *w ldr tl rdn to ld wl over 1f out: drvn over 1f out: hdd ins fnl f: keeping on same pce whn carried rt and sltly hmpd fnl 50yds: lost 2nd nr fin* **9/1**

21 **4** *1* **Home Cummins (IRE)**[56] 3481 2-9-2 **85**........................ JackGarritty(5) 7 86
(Richard Fahey) *t.k.h: hld up in tch in midfield: drvn and drifted lft jst over 1f out: kpt on same pce ins fnl f* **5/1**[2]

01 **5** *1 ½* **Little Lady Katie (IRE)**[12] 4973 2-8-7 **74**........................ JoeyHaynes(3) 9 72
(K R Burke) *in tch in midfield: n.m.r jst over 2f out: swtchd lft and effrt u.p over 1f out: no imp fnl f* **12/1**

532 **6** *3 ¼* **Renaissant**[10] 5042 2-8-1 **70**........................ CamHardie(5) 12 59
(Richard Hannon) *stdd s: t.k.h: sn led: hdd and rdn wl over 1f out: unable qck whn swtchd lft ent fnl f: wknd fnl 150yds* **9/2**[1]

000 **7** *nk* **Ocean Crystal**[14] 4913 2-7-11 **64** oh2........................ RyanPowell(3) 8 52
(John Ryan) *t.k.h: hld up in tch in midfield: sltly hmpd jsut over 2f out: sn rdn and no imp: wknd jst over 1f out* **66/1**

5063 **8** *4 ½* **Diracan (IRE)**[7] 5180 2-7-9 **64** oh4........................(b) NoelGarbutt(5) 5 41
(Nick Littmoden) *s.i.s: rdn along and swtchd lft sn after s: hdwy into midfield 5f out: rdn and no rspnse over 2f out: wknd over 1f out* **50/1**

1 **9** *4* **Sleepy Dust (IRE)**[77] 2771 2-9-1 **79**........................ PatDobbs 1 45
(Sylvester Kirk) *t.k.h: hld up in tch: rdn ent fnl f: sn btn and hung lft: eased ins fnl f* **8/1**[3]

51 **10** *9* **Mahsooba (USA)**[14] 4914 2-8-13 **77**........................ DaneO'Neill 3 20
(Ed Dunlop) *hld up in rr: rdn overv 2f out: no rspnse and sn wl btn: bhd and eased ins fnl f* **9/2**[1]

51 **11** *2* **Adelasia (IRE)**[30] 4346 2-9-4 **82**........................ SilvestreDeSousa 2 20
(Charlie Appleby) *hld up in rr: rdn and no rspnse over 2f out: lost tch over 1f out: bhd and eased ins fnl f* **5/1**[2]

1m 26.03s (0.33) **Going Correction** +0.125s/f (Good) 11 Ran SP% **116.3**
Speed ratings (Par 97): **103,101,101,100,98 94,94,89,84,74 72**
CSF £166.48 CT £1609.95 TOTE £11.90: £2.80, £3.90, £3.30; EX 120.10 Trifecta £416.40.
**Owner** Sheikh Mohammed Bin Khalifa Al Maktoum **Bred** Azienda Agricola Gennaro Stimola **Trained** Newmarket, Suffolk

■ Stewards' Enquiry : Luke Morris one-day ban: careless riding (Aug 30)

**FOCUS**
The ground had dried out to good to soft, good in places and the jockeys reported the ground as sticky and dead. A good prize for this fillies' nursery but the story of the race was the disappointing efforts of the market leaders, who filled the last two places. The third and fifth have been rated close to their maiden wins.

## 5437 BARRY SILKMAN DOUBLE O SEVEN GREY HORSE H'CAP (FOR GREY HORSES ONLY) 6f
**2:20** (2:20) (Class 4) (0-85,85) 3-Y-O+
**£12,450** (£3,728; £1,864; £932; £466; £234) **Stalls** Low

Form RPR

1305 **1** **Moonspring (IRE)**[15] 4862 3-8-7 70........................(e) LiamJones 12 77
(Robert Cowell) *bustled along leaving stalls: sn chsng ldr: drvn and ev ch over 1f out: led 1f out: battled on wl fnl 100yds: drvn out* **20/1**

00 **2** *½* **Baby Strange**[70] 2992 10-8-12 79........................ AdamMcLean(7) 11 84
(Derek Shaw) *hld up in tch in rr: rdn and effrt over 2f out: hdwy u.p over 1f out: ev ch 1f out: kpt on same pce and outbattled by wnr fnl 100yds* **7/1**[3]

6231 **3** *½* **Light From Mars**[29] 4406 9-9-3 84........................(p) MikeyEnnis(7) 9 88
(Ronald Harris) *chsd ldrs: sltly outpcd and swtchd lft 1f out: kpt on wl u.p fnl 100yds* **12/1**

0606 **4** *½* **Crew Cut (IRE)**[28] 4447 6-9-4 78........................ LukeMorris 10 80
(Stuart Williams) *in tch in midfield: rdn over 2f out: drvn and hdwy 1f out: kpt on u.p ins fnl f* **5/1**[2]

2233 **5** *nk* **Lady Horatia**[12] 4971 3-9-8 85........................ MartinDwyer 3 86
(William Muir) *in tch in midfield: rdn and effrt over 1f out: no imp and hung lft 1f out: styd on again fnl 100yds* **9/2**[1]

54 **6** *½* **Rylee Mooch**[10] 5045 6-7-13 64........................(e) PhilipPrince(5) 7 64
(Richard Guest) *led: rdn wl over 1f out: hdd 1f out: wknd ins fnl f* **14/1**

3164 **7** *nk* **Serenity Spa**[19] 4741 4-8-12 77........................ CamHardie(5) 1 76
(Tony Carroll) *in tch towards rr: hdwy and n.m.r over 1f out: rdn and kpt on same pce fnl f* **8/1**

6303 **8** *3 ½* **Two Shades Of Grey (IRE)**[6] 5205 3-7-11 65........(p) JackGarritty(5) 4 52
(Richard Fahey) *in tch in midfield: drvn and struggling whn short of room and swtchd rt over 1f out: wknd fnl f* **9/1**

0424 **9** *nse* **Medici Time**[14] 4901 9-8-6 66........................(v) SilvestreDeSousa 8 53
(Tim Easterby) *s.i.s: bhd: rdn 2f out: hung lft and no hdwy over 1f out: n.d* **10/1**

0605 **10** *½* **Daring Dragon**[63] 3227 4-8-8 68........................(vt¹) AndrewMullen 5 54
(Derek Shaw) *s.i.s: t.k.h: hld up in tch: sme hdwy 1/2-way: rdn and lost pl 2f out: wknd 1f out* **33/1**

1112 **11** *19* **Syrian Pearl**[23] 4572 3-9-0 80........................ AshleyMorgan(3) 6 5
(Chris Wall) *chsd ldrs: rdn 2f out: losing pl whn squeezed for room and hmpd over 1f out: bhd 1f out: sn eased* **5/1**[2]

1m 13.39s (0.89) **Going Correction** +0.125s/f (Good)
**WFA** 3 from 4yo+ 3lb 11 Ran SP% **116.3**
Speed ratings (Par 105): **99,98,97,97,96 95,95,90,90,90 64**
CSF £152.22 CT £1198.78 TOTE £20.60: £5.80, £2.60, £3.10; EX 202.40 Trifecta £681.90.
**Owner** P Foster & Friends **Bred** R N Auld **Trained** Six Mile Bottom, Cambs

**FOCUS**
The annual grey horse handicap and featuring several regulars in the race. Ordinary form with the third rated to form.

## 5438 THAMES MATERIALS STKS (H'CAP) (BOBIS RACE) 6f
**2:55** (2:56) (Class 2) (0-105,100) 3-Y-O
**£31,125** (£9,320; £4,660; £2,330; £1,165; £585) **Stalls** Low

Form RPR

4152 **1** **Eastern Impact (IRE)**[21] 4669 3-9-2 100........................ JackGarritty(5) 5 109
(Richard Fahey) *racd towards nr side: in tch: clsd to chse ldrs whn nt clr run and hmpd over 1f out: sn swtchd rt: str run u.p ins fnl f to ld nr fin* **5/1**[1]

3600 **2** *½* **Ventura Mist**[21] 4669 3-8-13 92........................(p) SilvestreDeSousa 6 99
(Tim Easterby) *racd nr side: chsd ldrs: rdn over 2f out: carried rt and hmpd over 1f out: lost pl and swtchd rt jst over 1f out: r.o strly u.p fnl f: wnt 2nd last strides* **14/1**

412 **3** *nk* **Boy In The Bar**[20] 4712 3-8-11 90........................(b) RobertWinston 1 96
(David Barron) *racd nr side: chsd ldrs: rdn and ev ch over 1f out: hung lft after: racing nr far rail and led ins fnl f: kpt on tl hdd and lost 2 pls nr fin* **6/1**[2]

1232 **4** *1* **Penny Drops**[49] 3724 3-9-0 93........................ LiamJones 10 96+
(William Haggas) *racd towards nr side: in tch: effrt to chse ldrs and carried lft over 1f out: hmpd 1f out: chsd wnr fnl 150yds: kpt on same pce after* **5/1**[1]

3053 **5** *1 ¾* **Suzi's Connoisseur**[21] 4669 3-9-0 98........................(p) NoelGarbutt(5) 12 95+
(Hugo Palmer) *racd in centre: in tch in midfield: rdn over 2f out: chsng ldrs and carried lft over 1f out: hmpd 1f out: styd on same pce after* **6/1**[2]

3140 **6** *1* **Kickboxer (IRE)**[36] 4166 3-9-1 94........................ LukeMorris 3 88
(Mick Channon) *racd towards nr side: bhd: rdn over 3f out: styd on ins fnl f: nvr trbld ldrs* **16/1**

0342 **7** *nse* **Piazon**[6] 5204 3-8-4 88........................ LouisSteward(5) 4 82
(Michael Bell) *racd keenly: led: unsteerable and hung lft across trck fr over 2f out: hdd ins fnl f: sn btn* **7/1**[3]

2612 **8** *½* **Flying Bear (IRE)**[14] 4898 3-7-9 79 oh1........................(b) CamHardie(5) 7 71
(Jeremy Gask) *racd towards nr side: t.k.h: hld up in tch in midfield: effrt and n.m.r over 1f out: kpt on same pce fnl f* **12/1**

3101 **9** *1 ¼* **Lady Frances**[10] 5032 3-8-10 89........................ KierenFallon 8 77
(Mark Johnston) *chsd ldrs tl lost pl 3f out: towards rr whn carried lft over 1f out: no ch whn hmpd and swtchd rt 1f out* **14/1**

1223 **10** *nse* **Double Up**[29] 4390 3-8-0 79........................(t) NickyMackay 9 67
(Roger Varian) *s.i.s: hld up in rr: hdwy into midfield 1/2-way: sltly hmpd jst over 1f out: trying to switch rt but hanging lft ent fnl f: n.d after* **10/1**

100- **11** *2 ¼* **Kaiulani (IRE)**[359] 5680 3-8-8 90........................ CharlesBishop(3) 13 71
(Mick Channon) *stdd s: hld up in rr: hdwy over 2f out: keeping on in midfield but looked btn whn hmpd 1f out: no ch after* **25/1**

0-00 **12** *hd* **Oeil De Tigre (FR)**[21] 4669 3-8-9 91........................ JoeyHaynes(3) 11 71
(Tony Carroll) *racd towards centre: chsd ldr: rdn 2f out: stl pressing ldr whn bmpd and bdly hmpd ent fnl f: lost any ch and bhd after* **40/1**

1m 12.57s (0.07) **Going Correction** +0.125s/f (Good) 12 Ran SP% **116.7**
Speed ratings (Par 106): **104,103,102,101,99 97,97,97,95,95 92,92**
CSF £74.90 CT £431.30 TOTE £6.40: £2.00, £4.90, £2.00; EX 83.30 Trifecta £638.60.
**Owner** Exors of the late D W Barker **Bred** Airlie Stud **Trained** Musley Bank, N Yorks
■ Stewards' Enquiry : Louis Steward four-day ban: careless riding (Aug 30-Sep 2)

**FOCUS**
The feature race and a valuable 3yo sprint handicap. The time was 0.82secs faster than the preceding greys' handicap. Piazon caused mayhem as he hung right across the track after leading on the stands' side and several were impeded. His rider picked up a four-day ban. With the runners splitting into three groups and several getting hampered this is messy form.

## 5439 RACING WELFARE EBF STALLIONS MAIDEN STKS (BOBIS RACE) 6f
**3:25** (3:26) (Class 4) 2-Y-O **£4,528** (£1,347; £673; £336) **Stalls** Low

Form RPR

**1** **Gun Case** 2-9-5 0........................ NickyMackay 8 78+
(Ed Walker) *in tch in midfield: in tch in midfield: rdn and hdwy to chal 1f out: led ins fnl f: r.o wl* **20/1**

64 **2** *¾* **Chevallier**[13] 4943 2-9-5 0........................ PatDobbs 4 76
(Richard Hannon) *led: rdn over 1f out: hdd ins fnl f: kpt on but comf hld fnl 100yds* **4/1**[2]

0 **3** *1 ¾* **Normandy Knight**[22] 4624 2-9-0 0........................ JackGarritty(5) 9 70
(Richard Fahey) *chsd ldr: drvn and ev ch over 1f out: unable qck 1f out: one pce after* **20/1**

5 **4** *shd* **Subversive (IRE)**[78] 2736 2-9-5 0........................ KierenFallon 1 70
(Mark Johnston) *chsd ldrs: rdn and ev ch over 1f out: edgd lft and no ex 1f out: one pce after* **9/1**

**5** *2 ¼* **Qatar Road (FR)** 2-9-5 0........................ LukeMorris 2 63
(Marco Botti) *s.i.s and nudged along in rr: swtchd rt 2f out: sme hdwy over 1f out: hung lft and wknd ins fnl f* **13/2**[3]

4 **6** *¾* **Emirates Airline**[36] 4142 2-9-5 0........................ ChrisCatlin 3 60
(Saeed bin Suroor) *hld up in tch towards rr: effrt 2f out: hung lft and no hdwy 1f out: wknd ins fnl f* **13/8**[1]

**7** *3 ¾* **Je T'Aime Encore** 2-9-0 0........................ HarryPoulton(5) 7 48
(Conrad Allen) *in tch in midfield: rdn and unable qck over 1f out: wknd 1f out* **66/1**

**8** *nk* **Its Gonna Be Me (IRE)** 2-9-5 0........................ DaneO'Neill 6 48
(William Haggas) *s.i.s and wnt lft s: hld up in rr: rdn 2f out: sn outpcd: wknd over 1f out* **10/1**

**9** *2 ¼* **Malvia** 2-9-5 0........................ SilvestreDeSousa 5 40
(Michael Bell) *t.k.h: hld up in tch in midfield: rdn and no hdwy over 1f out: sn wknd* **7/1**

1m 14.06s (1.56) **Going Correction** +0.125s/f (Good) 9 Ran SP% **114.0**
Speed ratings (Par 96): **94,93,90,90,87 86,81,81,78**
CSF £95.49 TOTE £25.30: £5.90, £1.50, £6.20; EX 127.30 Trifecta £1948.10.
**Owner** Sheikh Juma Dalmook Al Maktoum **Bred** Mildmay Bloodstock Ltd **Trained** Newmarket, Suffolk
■ Stewards' Enquiry : Luke Morris jockey said colt hung left; vet said examination failed to reveal any abnormalities.

**FOCUS**
Several well-bred newcomers in this maiden and one of them scored in promising style. It's been rated to the bottom end of the race averages.

## 5440 BETFAIR SUPPORTS RACING WELFARE H'CAP 1m 4f
**3:55** (3:56) (Class 2) (0-112,105) 3-Y-O+**£16,172** (£4,812; £2,405; £1,202) **Stalls** Centre

Form RPR

04 **1** **Fattsota**[7] 5174 6-9-5 98........................ PatDobbs 4 105
(David O'Meara) *chsd ldr: upsides and gng best over 3f out: rdn to ld 2f out: hdd and drvn 1f out: battled bk to ld again wl ins fnl f: styd on* **4/1**[2]

6000 **2** *nk* **Wigmore Hall (IRE)**[18] 4756 7-9-0 98 LouisSteward(5) 5 104
(Michael Bell) *hld up in tch: clsd and rdn 3f out: ev ch over 1f out: drvn to ld 1f out: hdd wl ins fnl f: kpt on* **20/1**
0-00 **3** *6* **Macbeth (IRE)**[56] 3449 5-9-5 98 AndrewMullen 8 94
(Michael Appleby) *chsd ldrs: rdn and clsd over 3f out: pressing ldrs and drvn 2f out: btn over 1f out: hung rt and wknd ins fnl f* **16/1**
45 **4** *6* **Stepping Ahead (FR)**[3] 5330 4-9-2 98 (v[1]) JoeyHaynes(3) 3 85
(K R Burke) *led: sn clr: rdn 4f out: hdd 2f out: 4th and btn whn short of room over 1f out: sn wknd* **8/1[3]**
411 **5** *6* **Winter Thunder**[28] 4448 3-9-2 105 KierenFallon 7 82
(Saeed bin Suroor) *wnt bdly lft and cannoned into rival s: slowly away: nvr travelling wl in rr: rdn 4f out: no hdwy: wl btn and hung lft over 1f out* **4/6[1]**
2001 **6** *7* **Gone Dutch**[52] 3582 4-9-0 98 CamHardie(5) 9 64
(James Fanshawe) *hld up in tch: rdn 4f out: dropped to rr 3f out: sn lost tch* **12/1**

2m 31.13s (-1.77) **Going Correction** +0.125s/f (Good)
**WFA** 3 from 4yo+ 10lb 6 Ran SP% **109.4**
Speed ratings (Par 109): **110,109,105,101,97 93**
CSF £63.32 CT £1048.89 TOTE £4.90: £2.20, £5.50; EX 62.80 Trifecta £355.70.
**Owner** Middleham Park Racing XXVIII & Partner **Bred** Azienda Agricola Francesca **Trained** Nawton, N Yorks

**FOCUS**
Another good prize, but this handicap was weakened by the absence of the three topweights. The winner travelled well and has been rated close to his best.

## 5441 THANK YOU QATAR RACING MARATHON RUNNERS' H'CAP (BOBIS RACE) 7f
4:30 (4:32) (Class 4) (0-80,80) 3-Y-O £5,175 (£1,540; £769; £384) Stalls Low

Form RPR
2131 **1** **Twin Appeal (IRE)**[51] 3625 3-9-7 80 (b) RobertWinston 8 89
(David Barron) *t.k.h: chsd ldr for 2f: styd chsng ldrs: rdn to ld and edgd rt over 1f out: sustained duel w rivals fnl f: styd on wl: bmpd twice nr fin* **9/4[2]**
-532 **2** *hd* **Dutch Art Dealer**[29] 4404 3-9-5 78 LukeMorris 4 86
(Paul Cole) *in tch in midfield: swtchd rt over 1f out: hdwy u.p to chal 1f out: ev ch but hung lft fnl f: bmpd wnr twice nr fin* **2/1[1]**
4021 **3** *2* **White Russian**[14] 4907 3-8-12 71 DaneO'Neill 1 74
(Henry Candy) *led for 2f: chsd ldr after: rdn and ev ch over 1f out tl no ex and crossed wl ins fnl f: wknd towards fin* **10/3[3]**
4250 **4** *7* **Sakhalin Star (IRE)**[1] 5385 3-8-11 75 DuilioDaSilva(5) 6 60
(Richard Guest) *stdd and collided w rival after s: t.k.h: hdwy to ld after 2f: rdn and hdd over 1f out: wknd fnl f* **10/1**
2435 **5** *1 1/4* **Miaplacidus (IRE)**[22] 4628 3-7-11 61 JackGarritty(5) 2 42
(Richard Fahey) *hld up in tch in last pair: rdn and effrt 2f out: sn struggling: wknd over 1f out* **9/1**
50-0 **6** *1* **Storm Trooper (IRE)**[43] 3927 3-9-7 80 PatDobbs 7 59
(Richard Hannon) *stdd and collided w rival s: hld up in tch in rr: rdn 2f out: no hdwy: wknd over 1f out* **14/1**

1m 27.26s (1.56) **Going Correction** +0.125s/f (Good) 6 Ran SP% **112.9**
Speed ratings (Par 102): **96,95,93,85,84 82**
CSF £7.28 CT £13.29 TOTE £3.40: £2.30, £1.50; EX 7.80 Trifecta £12.20.
**Owner** Twinacre Nurseries Ltd **Bred** Glashare House Stud **Trained** Maunby, N Yorks

**FOCUS**
A fair 3yo handicap but the time was over a second slower than the opening nursery. The third has been rated as matching her recent form up in grade.

## 5442 JOCKEY CLUB SUPPORTS RACING WELFARE H'CAP 1m 4f
5:05 (5:05) (Class 4) (0-85,85) 3-Y-O+ £6,469 (£1,925; £962; £481) Stalls Centre

Form RPR
1213 **1** **Emerahldz (IRE)**[8] 5132 3-8-3 75 JackGarritty(5) 3 84
(Richard Fahey) *led for 1f: chsd ldr tl rdn to ld again over 2f out: sustained duel w runner-up fr over 1f out: forged ahd towards fin: all out* **2/1[1]**
1200 **2** *nk* **Galizzi (USA)**[35] 4183 3-9-1 82 KierenFallon 6 90
(Michael Bell) *hld up in tch: clsd on ldr 3f out: rdn and ev ch over 1f out: sustained duel w wnr after: no ex and btn towards fin* **7/2[2]**
0251 **3** *1 1/2* **Rosslyn Castle**[3] 5317 5-9-5 81 6ex DannyBrock(5) 2 86+
(Philip McBride) *stdd s: hld up in rr: clsd 3f out: nt clr run and forced to switch rt over 1f out: hdwy to chse clr ldng pair 1f out: styd on wl u.p fnl 150yds* **4/1[3]**
1350 **4** *5* **Ex Oriente (IRE)**[8] 5144 5-9-5 76 ChrisCatlin 5 73
(Stuart Williams) *t.k.h: hld up in tch: clsd on ldrs 3f out: chsd ldrs and rdn 2f out: wknd over 1f out* **14/1**
5031 **5** *3 1/4* **Red Runaway**[19] 4736 4-9-9 80 DaneO'Neill 1 72
(Ed Dunlop) *chsd ldrs: clsd to press ldrs and rdn 3f out: wknd over 1f out* **5/1**
5442 **6** *3/4* **Little Buxted (USA)**[19] 4736 4-8-13 75 (p) CamHardie(5) 4 66
(Robert Mills) *chsd ldr tl led after 1f: sn clr tl rdn and hdd over 2f out: wknd over 1f out* **7/1**

2m 35.29s (2.39) **Going Correction** +0.125s/f (Good)
**WFA** 3 from 4yo+ 10lb 6 Ran SP% **111.4**
Speed ratings (Par 105): **97,96,95,92,90 89**
CSF £9.03 TOTE £3.20: £1.90, £2.00; EX 10.40 Trifecta £33.70.
**Owner** Mrs H Steel **Bred** D G Iceton **Trained** Musley Bank, N Yorks

**FOCUS**
This ordinary middle-distance handicap was run 4.16secs slower than the earlier Class 2 race over the trip. The 3yos dominated. The winner continues to improve and was always holding the runner-up, who has been rated to his best.
T/Jkpt: Not won. T/Plt: £1,920.30 to a £1 stake. Pool of £108803.30 - 41.36 winning tickets.
T/Qpdt: £52.20 to a £1 stake. Pool of £6846.69 - 97.0 winning tickets. SP

# 5013 RIPON (R-H)
Saturday, August 16
**OFFICIAL GOING: Good (good to soft in places; 8.0)**
Rail at innermost position and distances as advertised.
Wind: Fresh across Weather: CLoudy

## 5443 RIPONBET PLACE 6 MAIDEN AUCTION STKS 6f
2:15 (2:16) (Class 5) 2-Y-O £4,528 (£1,347; £673; £336) Stalls High

Form RPR
**1** **Marsh Pride** 2-8-10 0 PJMcDonald 12 79+
(Ann Duffield) *chsd ldr: rdn over 2f out: kpt on wl: led 110yds out* **20/1**
0 **2** *2 1/2* **Fast Dancer (IRE)**[33] 4270 2-9-5 0 NeilCallan 8 81
(Joseph Tuite) *led: rdn 2f out: kpt on: hdd 100yds out* **13/2[3]**
0 **3** *7* **Tinkers Kiss (IRE)**[28] 4444 2-8-6 0 AdamBeschizza 6 47
(Philip McBride) *chsd ldr: rdn over 2f out: grad wknd over 1f out* **10/1**
423 **4** *2* **Ocean Sheridan (IRE)**[20] 4702 2-8-12 68 ConnorBeasley(3) 2 50
(Michael Dods) *chsd ldr towards outer: rdn over 3f out: wknd over 1f out* **5/1[2]**
02 **5** *3/4* **Thorkhill Star (IRE)**[14] 4919 2-8-13 0 TonyHamilton 1 45
(Richard Fahey) *racd alone far side: prom overall: rdn over 2f out: wknd over 1f out* **6/5[1]**
**6** *2 3/4* **Kelly's Finest (IRE)** 2-8-12 0 GrahamLee 13 36
(James Bethell) *hld up: pushed along 1/2-way: nvr threatened* **20/1**
00 **7** *hd* **Edie White**[10] 5050 2-8-4 0 ow1 JordanNason(5) 3 32
(Lawrence Mullaney) *s.i.s: hld up: nvr threatened* **200/1**
0 **8** *1* **Magic Empress (IRE)**[61] 3296 2-8-6 0 AdrianNicholls 5 26
(Tony Coyle) *dwlt: hld up: nvr threatened* **100/1**
0 **9** *2 1/4* **Bushranger Bay (IRE)**[89] 2386 2-8-13 0 DavidAllan 7 27
(Tim Easterby) *hld up: nvr threatened* **50/1**
0 **10** *1 3/4* **The Fulwell End**[14] 4919 2-9-3 0 JasonHart 11 25
(Noel Wilson) *dwlt: midfield: rdn 1/2-way: sn wknd* **66/1**
5 **11** *4* **Coyled Spring (IRE)**[9] 5086 2-8-9 0 ow1 TomEaves 9 5
(Tony Coyle) *dwlt: midfield: rdn 1/2-way: sn wknd* **40/1**
**12** *1/2* **Splash Of Verve (IRE)** 2-9-5 0 DanielTudhope 4 14
(Philip Kirby) *chsd ldrs: wknd ovre 2f out* **28/1**
43 **P** **Arch Enemy**[77] 2788 2-9-1 0 GrahamGibbons 10
(Michael Easterby) *chsd ldr tl wnt wrong over 3f out: eased and p.u* **8/1**

1m 14.25s (1.25) **Going Correction** +0.225s/f (Good) 13 Ran SP% **116.0**
Speed ratings (Par 94): **100,96,87,84,83 80,79,78,75,73 67,67,**
CSF £134.74 TOTE £21.10: £6.00, £2.40, £2.90; EX 181.00 Trifecta £2005.70.
**Owner** John Dance **Bred** Llety Farms **Trained** Constable Burton, N Yorks

**FOCUS**
A fair juvenile maiden in which the short-priced favourite chose to race in isolation up the far-side rail from his low draw. The contested pace on the stands' side was to produce the winner, though, on ground which appeared to be riding on the good to soft side of the official good, good to soft in places description. The race has a variable race standard and it's questionable how deep this was.

## 5444 WILLIAM HILL SILVER TROPHY H'CAP (CONSOLATION RACE FOR THE WILLIAM HILL GREAT ST WILFRID STKS) 6f
2:50 (2:51) (Class 2) 3-Y-O+
£12,450 (£3,728; £1,864; £932; £466; £234) Stalls High

Form RPR
4153 **1** **Duke Cosimo**[9] 5081 4-9-2 83 (b) GrahamGibbons 2 92
(David Barron) *dwlt: sn chsd ldr far side: rdn over 1f out: kpt on: led nr fin* **13/2[2]**
1665 **2** *shd* **Red Refraction (IRE)**[7] 5178 4-9-6 87 DanielTudhope 9 95
(Richard Hannon) *chsd ldrs far side: rdn 1/2-way: kpt on wl fnl f: jst hld: 2nd of 10 in gp* **10/1[3]**
0000 **3** *shd* **Chooseday (IRE)**[11] 5016 5-9-0 81 (t) NeilCallan 13 89
(Kevin Ryan) *prom stands' side: led gp and overall ldr 2f out: sn rdn: kpt on: hdd towards fin: 1st Of 10 in gp* **33/1**
0605 **4** *1/2* **Polski Max**[7] 5170 4-8-8 78 (p) GeorgeChaloner(3) 16 84
(Richard Fahey) *chsd ldrs stands' side: rdn over 2f out: kpt on: 2nd of 10 in gp* **14/1**
3501 **5** *1/2* **Avon Breeze**[7] 5199 5-9-4 85 (p) RussKennemore 7 89
(Richard Whitaker) *prom far side: led gp over 2f out: sn rdn: edgd lft over 1f out: hdd in gp 110yds out: one pce: 3rd of 10 in gp* **10/1[3]**
3024 **6** *3/4* **Mon Brav**[7] 5197 7-8-8 80 JacobButterfield(5) 1 82
(Brian Ellison) *midfield far side: rdn over 2f out: kpt on: 4th of 10 in gp* **12/1**
4011 **7** *nk* **Compton Park**[9] 5081 7-9-9 90 (t) DavidAllan 10 91
(Les Eyre) *midfield far side: rdn over 2f out: one pce and nvr threatened ldrs: 5th of 10 in gp* **11/2[1]**
2123 **8** *1 1/2* **Gran Canaria Queen**[14] 4902 5-8-6 80 RachelRichardson(7) 19 76
(Tim Easterby) *dwlt: hld up stands' side: rdn 1/2-way: kpt on: nvr threatened ldrs: 3rd of 10 in gp* **20/1**
40-0 **9** *3/4* **Pea Shooter**[7] 5199 5-8-9 76 AdrianNicholls 3 70
(David Nicholls) *hld up far side: rdn 1/2-way: kpt on fnl f: nvr threatened ldrs: 6th of 10 in gp* **25/1**
16 **10** *hd* **Dr Red Eye**[13] 4938 6-9-3 84 (p) GrahamLee 11 77
(Scott Dixon) *led stand's side and overall ldr: rdn whn hdd 2f out: grad wknd: 4th of 10 in gp* **22/1**
0020 **11** *2 1/4* **Waffle (IRE)**[12] 4976 8-9-1 82 PaddyAspell 6 68
(David Barron) *hld up far side: rdn 1/2-way: nvr threatened: 7th of 10 in gp* **40/1**
23 **12** *1/2* **Englishman**[7] 5189 4-9-8 89 (p) HarryBentley 12 73
(Charles Hills) *hld up stands' side: rdn 1/2-way: nvr threatened: 5th of 10 in gp* **11/1**
6000 **13** *2* **Best Trip (IRE)**[63] 3221 7-9-2 83 PaulPickard 15 61
(Brian Ellison) *midfield stands' side: rdn 1/2-way: wknd over 1f out: 6th of 10 in gp* **18/1**
44 **14** *1 1/4* **Pandar**[2] 5350 5-8-13 83 ConnorBeasley(3) 8 57
(Milton Bradley) *midfield far side: rdn 1/2-way: wknd over 1f out: 8th of 10 in gp* **33/1**
1105 **15** *1* **Foxy Clarets (IRE)**[6] 5204 3-9-1 85 TonyHamilton 20 56
(Richard Fahey) *midfield stands' side: rdn 1/2-way: sn wknd: 7th of 10 in gp* **16/1**
0100 **16** *3/4* **Hopes N Dreams (IRE)**[14] 4892 6-9-5 91 ShaneGray(5) 18 59
(Kevin Ryan) *racd stands' side: hld up: rdn 1/2-way: nvr threatened: 8th of 10 in gp* **25/1**
210 **17** *4 1/2* **Soul Brother (IRE)**[56] 3478 3-9-2 86 DeclanMcDonogh 17 40
(Tim Easterby) *hld up stands' side: nvr threatened: 9th of 10 in gp* **14/1**
0050 **18** *1/2* **Circuitous**[8] 5143 6-8-9 76 (v) TomEaves 5 28
(Keith Dalgleish) *a bhd far side: 8th of 10 in gp* **33/1**
000- **19** *3/4* **Rodrigo De Torres**[295] 7495 7-9-8 89 JasonHart 4 39
(John Murray) *led far side: hdd over 2f out: wknd and eased: last of 10 in gp* **28/1**
0000 **20** *2* **Doc Hay (USA)**[29] 4384 7-9-8 89 [1] PJMcDonald 14 33
(Brian Ellison) *s.i.s: hld up stands' side: hung bdly rt fr 1/2-way: ended up on fair rail: a bhd* **10/1[3]**

1m 13.41s (0.41) **Going Correction** +0.225s/f (Good)
**WFA** 3 from 4yo+ 3lb 20 Ran SP% **128.0**
Speed ratings (Par 109): **106,105,105,105,104 103,103,101,100,99 96,96,93,91,90 89,83,82,81,79**
CSF £62.52 CT £2092.20 TOTE £12.70: £2.60, £2.00, £8.50, £4.70; EX 106.00 Trifecta £1919.00 Part won..
**Owner** Mrs Christine Barron **Bred** Cheveley Park Stud Ltd **Trained** Maunby, N Yorks

**FOCUS**
The third running of the consolation race for the Great St Wilfred was predictably competitive with those drawn in stalls 1-10 racing on the far side, and stalls 11-20 competing on the stands' side of the track, but a blanket finish suggested there was no obvious bias. The runner-up has been rated to form.

## 5445 WILLIAM HILL GREAT ST WILFRID STKS (H'CAP) 6f
3:30 (3:30) (Class 2) 3-Y-O+
£43,575 (£13,048; £4,893; £4,893; £1,631; £819) Stalls High

Form RPR
2353 1 **Out Do**12 4976 5-9-1 94 (v1) DanielTudhope 4 104
(David O'Meara) *dwlt: hld up far side: n.m.r towards rail 2f out tl appr fnl f: qcknd up wl: led 75yds out: edgd lft* 7/1[1]
26 2 ½ **Spinatrix**84 2564 6-9-6 102 (p) ConnorBeasley(3) 13 110
(Michael Dods) *prom stands' side: rdn to ld gp wl over 1f out: kpt on wl: 1st of 10 in gp* 10/1[3]
0420 3 nk **Confessional**14 4892 7-8-13 92 (e) DavidAllan 1 99
(Tim Easterby) *trckd ldrs far side: rdn over 2f out: led jst ins fnl f: hdd 75yds out: one pce: 2nd of 9 in gp* 20/1
3123 3 dht **Tatlisu (IRE)**14 4892 4-8-13 92 DeclanMcDonogh 12 99
(Richard Fahey) *midfield stands' side: rdn 1/2-way: kpt on wl fr over 1f out: 2nd of 10 in gp* 8/1[2]
-051 5 shd **Pipers Note**12 4976 4-9-1 94 AmyRyan 17 101
(Richard Whitaker) *chsd ldrs stands' side: rdn over 2f out: kpt on: 3rd of 10 in gp* 12/1
2012 6 shd **Another Wise Kid (IRE)**12 4976 6-9-6 99 GrahamLee 19 105
(Paul Midgley) *racd stands' side: chsd ldrs: rdn over 2f out: kpt on: 4th of 10 in gp* 14/1
6310 7 ½ **Kimberella**21 4683 4-9-2 95 AdrianNicholls 18 100
(David Nicholls) *chsd ldrs stands' side: rdn over 2f out: kpt on: 5th of 10 in gp* 8/1[2]
0100 8 1 **Clear Spring (IRE)**14 4895 6-9-5 98 TomEaves 8 100
(John Spearing) *prom far side: led gp and overall ldr 2f out: sn rdn: hdd jst ins fnl f: no ex: 3rd of 10 in gp* 16/1
0600 9 nk **Supplicant**36 4166 3-9-1 100 GeorgeChaloner(3) 10 101
(Richard Fahey) *chsd ldrs far side: rdn over 2f out: chal over 1f out: no ex ins fnl f: 4th of 9 in gp* 14/1
1140 10 1 **Fast Shot**56 3452 6-8-11 97 RachelRichardson(7) 6 94
(Tim Easterby) *trckd ldrs far side: rdn over 2f out: wknd ins fnl f: 5th of 9 in gp* 16/1
001 11 1¾ **Fairway To Heaven (IRE)**49 3732 5-9-3 96 JackMitchell 14 88
(Michael Wigham) *slowly away: hld up stands' side: rdn over 2f out: nvr threatened: 6th of 10 in gp* 14/1
5050 12 ½ **Hitchens (IRE)**21 4683 9-8-9 95 PaulMcGiff(7) 20 85
(David Barron) *hld up stands' side: rdn over 2f out: nvr threatened: 7th of 10 in gp* 33/1
204 13 shd **Bondesire**7 5160 4-9-1 97 SamJames(3) 11 87
(David O'Meara) *w ldr stands' side: rdn 1/2-way: wknd over 1f out: 8th of 10 in gp* 14/1
1305 14 nk **So Beloved**12 4976 4-8-13 92 PJMcDonald 7 81
(Ruth Carr) *hld up far side: nvr threatened: 6th of 9 in gp* 25/1
204- 15 1¼ **Shropshire (IRE)**337 6352 6-9-10 103 HarryBentley 9 88
(Charles Hills) *hld up far side: rdn 1/2-way: wknd over 1f out: 7th of 9 in gp* 22/1
2310 16 1 **Majestic Moon (IRE)**21 4648 4-9-2 95 TonyHamilton 2 77
(Richard Fahey) *led far side and overall ldr: hdd 2f out: wknd: 8th of 9 in gp* 8/1[2]
0001 17 ¾ **Colonel Mak**73 2898 7-9-2 95 GrahamGibbons 16 74
(David Barron) *led stands' side: hdd wl over 1f out: sn wknd: 9th of 10 in gp* 25/1
4506 18 1½ **Captain Ramius (IRE)**42 3960 8-9-8 101 NeilCallan 3 76
(Kevin Ryan) *slowly away: a bhd far side: last of 9 in gp* 22/1
-100 19 3 **Flyman**14 4895 4-8-12 96 (b) ShaneGray(5) 15 61
(Richard Fahey) *a in rr stands' side* 25/1

1m 12.79s (-0.21) **Going Correction** +0.225s/f (Good)
**WFA** 3 from 4yo+ 3lb 19 Ran SP% **129.0**
Speed ratings (Par 109): **110,109,108,108,108 108,108,106,106,104 102,101,101,101,99 98,97,95,91**
WIN: 7.40 Out Do; PL: 2.50 Spinatrix, 2.20 Tatlisu, 2.60 Out Do, 5.30 Confessional; EX: 70.00; CSF: 69.39; TC: 303.65, 705.51; TF: 1434.80, 406.00;.
**Owner** Evan M Sutherland **Bred** Equibreed S R L **Trained** Nawton, N Yorks

**FOCUS**
The latest renewal of this prestigious 6f sprint handicap produced another blanket finish. There were two distinct groups on opposite sides of the course from the outset. The winner has been rated a length up on his previous form in the first-time visor, with the runner-up rated in line with last year's running, and the third down to the seventh close to their marks.

## 5446 ATTHERACES.COM H'CAP 1m
4:00 (4:01) (Class 3) (0-90,90) 3-Y-O-£9,451 (£2,829; £1,414; £708; £352) Stalls Low

Form RPR
3254 1 **Bartack (IRE)**14 4922 4-9-10 86 (v) DanielTudhope 7 98
(David O'Meara) *prom: led 2f out: sn rdn: kpt on wl* 5/1[1]
5320 2 2½ **Dream Walker (FR)**49 3716 5-9-9 90 JacobButterfield(5) 1 96
(Brian Ellison) *chsd ldrs: rdn over 2f out: kpt on* 15/2[3]
4432 3 ¾ **Jodies Jem**16 4827 4-9-7 86 (p) GeorgeChaloner(3) 14 90
(William Jarvis) *hld up: rdn and hdwy on outer over 2f out: kpt on* 5/1[1]
2334 4 1¼ **Dubai Dynamo**26 4491 9-9-9 88 ConnorBeasley(3) 9 91+
(Ruth Carr) *midfield on inner: n.m.r over 1f out: swtchd lft: sn rdn: kpt on fnl f* 11/1
1333 5 nk **George Rooke (IRE)**17 4783 4-9-5 81 (p) TomEaves 5 82
(Keith Dalgleish) *trckd ldrs: rdn to chse wnr over 1f out: wknd fnl 110yds* 13/2[2]
611U 6 hd **Border Bandit (USA)**7 5196 6-9-7 83 (p) DavidAllan 6 83
(Tracy Waggott) *midfield: rdn over 2f out: one pce* 5/1[1]
0320 7 ½ **Alquimia (IRE)**17 4782 3-8-8 76 TonyHamilton 2 74
(Richard Fahey) *in tch on inner: pushed along over 2f out: nt a much room and nvr threatened ldrs* 12/1
2536 8 1 **Berlusca (IRE)**18 4753 5-9-1 80 SamJames(3) 13 77
(David O'Meara) *dwlt: hld up: rdn over 2f out: nvr threatened* 33/1
13-0 9 hd **Altharoos (IRE)**14 4922 4-9-12 88 DeclanMcDonogh 3 84
(Sally Hall) *dwlt: hld up: rdn 3f out: nvr threatened* 25/1
006 10 1¼ **Secret Recipe**7 5178 4-9-6 82 PaddyAspell 12 75
(David Nicholls) *swtchd rt s: hld up in rr: rdn over 2f out: sn btn* 40/1
2036 11 5 **Red Charmer (IRE)**22 4635 4-8-12 74 PJMcDonald 10 56
(Ann Duffield) *midfield: rdn over 2f out: sn wknd* 14/1
000 12 13 **Equity Risk (USA)**22 4635 4-9-6 82 NeilCallan 11 34
(Kevin Ryan) *chsd ldrs towards outer: rdn over 3f out: wknd 2f out* 20/1
5430 13 ¾ **Skytrain**10 5031 4-9-2 78 (b) AdrianNicholls 4 28
(Mark Johnston) *led: rdn whn hdd 2f out: wknd* 12/1

1m 41.43s (0.03) **Going Correction** +0.225s/f (Good)
**WFA** 3 from 4yo+ 6lb 13 Ran SP% **119.5**
Speed ratings (Par 107): **108,105,104,103,103 103,102,101,101,100 95,82,81**
CSF £40.15 CT £207.70 TOTE £7.80: £2.30, £3.50, £3.60; EX 50.80 Trifecta £258.10.
**Owner** Ebor Racing Club III **Bred** Alberto Panetta **Trained** Nawton, N Yorks

**FOCUS**
A decent handicap in which they went a contested gallop. The third has been rated close to form.

## 5447 RIPON HORN BLOWER CONDITIONS STKS (BOBIS RACE) 6f
4:35 (4:35) (Class 3) 2-Y-O £9,451 (£2,829; £1,414; £708; £352) Stalls High

Form RPR
431 1 **Dark Reckoning**20 4708 2-9-0 81 HarryBentley 1 88
(Ann Duffield) *hld up in tch: pushed along and hdwy 2f out: rdn to ld 110yds out: pushed out and a holding on* 10/1
1400 2 nk **Prince Bonnaire**28 4439 2-9-3 79 GrahamLee 2 90
(David Brown) *led: rdn over 2f out: hdd 110yds out: kpt on but a hld* 7/1[3]
213 3 5 **Lexington Times (IRE)**15 4865 2-9-5 91 DanielTudhope 4 77
(Richard Hannon) *trckd ldr: rdn over 2f out: sn outpcd and lost pl: wnt modest 3rd ins fnl f* 2/1[2]
2125 4 6 **Surewecan**16 4822 2-9-5 99 AdrianNicholls 3 57
(Mark Johnston) *dwlt: sn trckd ldr: rdn over 2f out: wknd over 1f out* 10/11[1]
2445 5 3¾ **Strategic Order (IRE)**15 4870 2-9-0 67 PJMcDonald 5 40
(Paul Midgley) *hld up: rdn over 2f out: sn wknd* 40/1

1m 14.27s (1.27) **Going Correction** +0.225s/f (Good) 5 Ran SP% **109.7**
Speed ratings (Par 98): **100,99,92,84,79**
CSF £68.25 TOTE £9.90: £4.30, £4.10; EX 74.80 Trifecta £135.50.
**Owner** Qatar Racing Limited **Bred** Newsells Park Stud **Trained** Constable Burton, N Yorks

**FOCUS**
A good quality small-field juvenile conditions stakes which was won by the 2012 July Cup-winner Mayson in 2010. The front-running runner-up had faced tough tasks in his previous two starts and has been rated as running a pb here.

## 5448 BRITISH STALLION STUDS EBF FILLIES' H'CAP 1m 1f 170y
5:10 (5:12) (Class 4) (0-80,80) 3-Y-O+ £6,301 (£1,886; £943; £472; £235) Stalls Low

Form RPR
2211 1 **Puzzle Time**143 1099 4-9-12 78 TonyHamilton 4 89
(Giles Bravery) *trckd ldr: led over 2f out: rdn 2f out: hung rt ent fnl f: kpt on* 11/1
210 2 1½ **Principle Equation (IRE)**17 4782 3-9-6 80 GrahamLee 3 88
(Ralph Beckett) *led: rdn whn hdd over 2f out: kpt on but a hld* 3/1[2]
3104 3 7 **Polar Eyes**29 4397 3-9-3 80 GeorgeChaloner(3) 2 74
(Peter Chapple-Hyam) *midfield: rdn 4f out: plugged on and no threat to ldng pair* 8/1
3136 4 shd **Maybeme**21 4680 8-9-7 73 (p) TomEaves 5 66
(Neville Bycroft) *s.i.s: hld up: rdn over 5f out: plugged on fnl f: nvr threatened* 12/1
513 5 ½ **Patterned**17 4782 3-9-6 80 DanielTudhope 7 72
(Luca Cumani) *midfield: rdn over 3f out: sn no imp* 9/4[1]
-042 6 1½ **Dianora**17 4802 3-9-1 75 GrahamGibbons 8 64
(Sir Michael Stoute) *trckd ldr on outer: rdn over 3f out: wknd over 1f out* 9/1
0/01 7 17 **Aseela (IRE)**99 2135 4-8-3 62 KieranSchofield(7) 6 16
(George Moore) *hld up: a bhd* 33/1
5616 8 7 **Wojha (IRE)**29 4397 3-9-1 75 NeilCallan 1 15
(William Haggas) *sn trckd ldr: rdn 4f out: sn wknd* 4/1[3]

2m 6.64s (1.24) **Going Correction** +0.225s/f (Good)
**WFA** 3 from 4yo+ 8lb 8 Ran SP% **115.8**
Speed ratings (Par 102): **104,102,97,97,96 95,81,76**
CSF £44.74 CT £285.27 TOTE £4.80: £2.20, £1.80, £2.40; EX 33.60 Trifecta £124.30.
**Owner** J J May **Bred** Plantation Stud **Trained** Newmarket, Suffolk

**FOCUS**
A fair fillies' handicap in which they went an even gallop. There's little depth to the form with the favourite disappointing.

## 5449 SIS LIVE H'CAP 1m 4f 10y
5:45 (5:46) (Class 5) (0-75,71) 3-Y-O £4,528 (£1,347; £673; £336) Stalls Low

Form RPR
3012 1 **Indira**15 4863 3-9-6 70 GrahamLee 1 80
(John Berry) *trckd ldng pair: n.m.r towards inner over 2f out: angled lft to outer 2f out: sn rdn: led appr fnl f: kpt on: jst hld on* 9/4[1]
0-26 2 hd **Mighty Missile (IRE)**17 4793 3-8-8 58 AdrianNicholls 2 67
(Tom Tate) *dwlt: hld up: drvn over 3f out: styd on wl fr over 1f out: jst failed* 17/2
301 3 2¼ **Another Lincolnday**30 4360 3-9-7 71 GrahamGibbons 5 76
(David Barron) *prom: rdn over 2f out: kpt on same pce* 11/4[2]
-105 4 1 **Lady Yeats**66 3110 3-9-7 71 DeclanMcDonogh 7 74
(George Moore) *trckd ldng pair: rdn to ld 2f out: hdd appr fnl f: no ex* 11/2
2212 5 3½ **Mister Uno (IRE)**19 4726 3-9-2 66 (p) PJMcDonald 6 64
(Ann Duffield) *hld up: rdn over 2f out: no imp* 4/1[3]
0312 6 1¾ **Exclusive Contract (IRE)**8 5145 3-8-13 63 TomEaves 3 58
(Ollie Pears) *led: rdn whn hdd 2f out: sn wknd* 12/1

2m 41.5s (4.80) **Going Correction** +0.225s/f (Good) 6 Ran SP% **111.0**
Speed ratings (Par 100): **93,92,91,90,88 87**
CSF £20.80 TOTE £3.70: £1.40, £4.60; EX 19.20 Trifecta £139.80.
**Owner** Severn Crossing Partnership **Bred** Mrs M L Parry & P M Steele-Mortimer **Trained** Newmarket, Suffolk

**FOCUS**
The concluding contest was a modest middle-distance 3yo handicap in which they went a muddling gallop. The third has been rated as matching his maiden figure, and the fourth helps set the standard.
T/Plt: £6,876.30 to a £1 stake. Pool: £98,226.39 - 10.43 winning tickets. T/Qpdt: £150.10 to a £1 stake. Pool: £8,226.44 - 40.54 winning tickets. AS

5450 - 5455a (Foreign Racing) - See Raceform Interactive

## 5364 TRAMORE (R-H)

Saturday, August 16

**OFFICIAL GOING: Good**

### 5456a DAN COWMAN MEMORIAL H'CAP 2m

7:25 (7:26) 4-Y-0+ £6,037 (£1,400; £612; £350)

RPR

1 **Knight's Parade (IRE)**[16] 4837 4-9-4 **71**.........................(t) WayneLordan 74
(Gordon Elliott, Ire) *towards rr: 5th 1/2-way: hdwy in 4th on inner over 2f out: swtchd lft into 2nd ins fnl f and styd on wl u.p to ld ins fnl 100yds: extended advantage towards fin* **10/3**[2]

2 2 3/4 **Wood Breizh (FR)**[18] 4772 4-9-7 **74**........................................ BillyLee 74
(W P Mullins, Ire) *led tl jnd briefly after 1f: narrow advantage for most tl extended ld 3f out: rdn under 2f out and strly pressed wl ins fnl f: hdd ins fnl 100yds and no ex* **9/4**[1]

3 3 1/4 **Jack Daddy**[37] 4139 5-9-12 **79**........................................ ShaneFoley 75
(Joseph G Murphy, Ire) *trckd ldr in 2nd tl disp briefly after 1f: cl 2nd for most tl pushed along 5f out: no imp on ldr u.p over 1f out and sn dropped to 3rd: kpt on one pce* **8/1**

4 2 3/4 **Bell Weir**[28] 2104 6-9-6 **78**........................................ EmmaSayer(5) 71
(Dianne Sayer) *w.w: rdn and no imp detached in rr 4f out: r.o wl on outer ins fnl f into nvr nrr 4th: nrst fin* **16/1**

5 1/2 **Oneeightofamile (IRE)**[51] 3636 9-9-7 **74**........................ SeamieHeffernan 67
(N Dooly, Ire) *chsd ldrs: 4th 1/2-way: wnt cl 3rd over 4f out: sn rdn and no ex u.p fr 3f out: one pce fnl 2f* **7/2**[3]

6 1 **Foot Soldier (IRE)**[14] 4929 5-8-11 **67**........................(v) ConorHoban(3) 59
(C F Swan, Ire) *chsd ldrs: 3rd 1/2-way: rdn and no ex u.p in 4th under 2f out: wknd fnl f* **9/2**

3m 42.0s (-8.10) **6** Ran SP% **111.2**

Pick Six: 1,521.70. Pool of 25,000.00 - 11.5 winning units. Tote Aggregates: 2013: 93,824.00; 2014: 120,672.00. CSF £11.05 TOTE £3.70: £2.00, £1.70; DF 10.20 Trifecta £59.30.

**Owner** Bodhran Makers Syndicate **Bred** E Heary **Trained** Longwood, Co Meath

**FOCUS**

Knight's Parade can't be accused of winning out of turn as he stayed on strongly for a convincing success.

T/Jkpt: @140.00. Pool of @2,432.94 - 15 winning units. T/Plt: @362.70. Pool of @ 15,533.94 - 29.98 winning units. BF

## 4230 ARLINGTON PARK (L-H)

Saturday, August 16

**OFFICIAL GOING: Turf: firm**

### 5457a AMERICAN ST. LEGER STKS (LISTED RACE) (3YO+) (TURF) 1m 5f 110y

9:45 (12:00) 3-Y-0+

£138,795 (£46,265; £23,132; £11,566; £6,939; £4,626)

RPR

1 **The Pizza Man (USA)**[35] 5-8-11 0........................................ FGeroux 9 111
(Roger Brueggemann, U.S.A) **53/10**

2 1 **Dandino**[37] 4124 7-8-7 0........................................ FrankieDettori 2 106
(Marco Botti) **61/10**

3 1 1/4 **Havana Beat (IRE)**[42] 3985 4-8-9 0........................................ JRosario 6 106
(Andrew Balding) **157/10**

4 1/2 **Moment In Time (IRE)**[13] 4945 5-8-2 0........................................ LSaez 5 98+
(David Simcock) **183/10**

5 7 1/4 **Eye Of The Storm (IRE)**[9] 5115 4-8-9 0........................................ RyanMoore 8 95
(A P O'Brien, Ire) **3/1**[1]

6 2 3/4 **Admiral Kitten (USA)**[35] 4-8-11 0........................(b) JRLeparoux 7 93
(Michael J Maker, U.S.A) **13/2**

7 1 1/4 **Moro Tap (USA)**[35] 4-8-7 0........................(b) RAlbarado 1 88
(Michael J Maker, U.S.A) **36/1**

8 hd **Infinite Magic (USA)**[35] 4-8-7 0........................................ CHill 4 87
(Wayne Catalano, U.S.A) **31/1**

9 6 **Suntracer (USA)**[35] 6-8-7 0........................................ JJCastellano 10 79
(Chris Block, U.S.A) **39/10**[2]

10 17 1/2 **Big Kick (CAN)**[47] 5-8-11 0........................(b) JamesGraham 3 58
(Michael Machowsky, U.S.A) **26/5**[3]

2m 47.44s (167.44) **10** Ran SP% **121.8**

PARI-MUTUEL (all including 2 usd stake): WIN 12.60; PLACE (1-2) 6.40, 8.00; SHOW (1-2-3) 4.20, 5.80, 8.40; SF 65.60.

**Owner** Midwest Thoroughbreds Inc **Bred** Midwest Thoroughbreds **Trained** North America

### 5458a SECRETARIAT STKS (GRADE 1) (3YO) (TURF) 1m 2f

10:15 (12:00) 3-Y-0

£178,915 (£59,638; £29,819; £14,909; £8,945; £5,963)

RPR

1 **Adelaide (IRE)**[42] 3994 3-8-7 0........................................ RyanMoore 5 112
(A P O'Brien, Ire) **11/10**[1]

2 1 1/2 **Tourist (USA)**[29] 3-8-9 0........................(b) JRosario 7 111
(William Mott, U.S.A) **21/10**[2]

3 3 **Sheldon (USA)**[42] 3994 3-8-7 0........................(b) JJCastellano 4 103
(James J Toner, U.S.A) **118/10**

4 1/2 **Global View (USA)**[42] 3994 3-8-11 0........................................ JRLeparoux 1 106+
(Thomas F Proctor, U.S.A) **67/10**[3]

5 1 1/4 **Highball (USA)**[35] 4230 3-8-7 0........................(b1) FrankieDettori 2 100
(Wayne Catalano, U.S.A) **141/10**

6 1/2 **Divine Oath (USA)**[35] 4230 3-8-11 0........................................ FGeroux 6 103
(Todd Pletcher, U.S.A) **133/10**

7 3/4 **General Jack (USA)**[45] 3-8-11 0........................................ RAlbarado 3 101
(Michael J Maker, U.S.A) **113/10**

2m 2.31s (0.67) **7** Ran SP% **122.4**

PARI-MUTUEL (all including 2 usd stake): WIN 4.20; PLACE (1-2) 2.60, 3.40; SHOW (1-2-3) 2.20, 2.60, 3.60; SF 11.60.

**Owner** Derrick Smith & Mrs John Magnier & Michael Tabor E **Bred** Elletelle Syndicate **Trained** Cashel, Co Tipperary

### 5459a BEVERLY D. STKS (GRADE 1) (3YO+ FILLIES & MARES) (TURF) 1m 1f 110y

10:54 (12:00) 3-Y-0+

£257,530 (£85,843; £42,921; £21,460; £12,876; £8,584)

RPR

1 **Euro Charline**[22] 4607 3-8-5 0........................................ RyanMoore 2 112
(Marco Botti) **108/10**

2 3/4 **Stephanie's Kitten (USA)**[28] 4466 5-8-11 0........................ FrankieDettori 5 108+
(Chad C Brown, U.S.A) **29/10**[1]

3 nk **Just The Judge (IRE)**[48] 3766 4-8-11 0........................ JamieSpencer 1 108+
(Charles Hills) **31/5**[3]

4 1/2 **La Tia (USA)**[21] 5-8-11 0........................................ EBaird 7 107
(Armando de la Cerda, U.S.A) **171/10**

5 3/4 **Somali Lemonade (USA)**[28] 4466 5-8-11 0........................(b) LSaez 11 105
(Michael Matz, U.S.A) **32/5**

6 nk **I'm Already Sexy (USA)**[35] 4-8-11 0........................(b) FGeroux 8 105
(Wayne Catalano, U.S.A) **192/10**

7 3/4 **Street Of Gold (USA)**[35] 4-8-11 0........................................ EPrado 3 103
(Eric R Reed, U.S.A) **50/1**

8 nse **Sparkling Beam (IRE)**[27] 4484 4-8-11 0........................ ThierryJarnet 10 103
(J E Pease, France) **197/10**

9 5 **Emollient (USA)**[28] 4466 4-8-11 0........................................ JRosario 4 93
(William Mott, U.S.A) **36/5**

10 3/4 **Tannery (IRE)**[28] 4466 5-8-11 0........................................ RAlbarado 6 91
(Alan E Goldberg, U.S.A) **179/10**

11 nse **Alterite (FR)**[28] 4466 4-8-11 0........................................ JJCastellano 9 91
(Chad C Brown, U.S.A) **3/1**[2]

1m 55.52s (0.05)

**WFA** 3 from 4yo+ 7lb **11** Ran SP% **121.3**

PARI-MUTUEL (all including 2 usd stake): WIN 23.60; PLACE (1-2) 10.60, 4.40; SHOW (1-2-3) 6.20, 3.20, 5.80; SF 131.40.

**Owner** Team Valor International **Bred** Brian Liversage **Trained** Newmarket, Suffolk

### 5460a ARLINGTON MILLION XXXII STKS (GRADE 1) (3YO+) (TURF) 1m 2f

11:36 (12:00) 3-Y-0+

£357,831 (£119,277; £59,638; £29,819; £17,891; £11,927)

RPR

1 **Hardest Core (USA)**[35] 4-9-0 0........................................ EVaz 1 118
(Edward Graham, U.S.A) **115/10**

2 1 **Magician (IRE)**[21] 4649 4-9-0 0........................................ JosephO'Brien 3 116
(A P O'Brien, Ire) **9/5**[1]

3 1 1/4 **Side Glance**[41] 4010 7-9-0 0........................................ JamieSpencer 7 113
(Andrew Balding) **89/10**

4 2 3/4 **Up With The Birds (CAN)**[28] 4-9-0 0........................(b) ERosaDaSilva 5 108+
(Malcolm Pierce, Canada) **61/10**

5 1 **Finnegans Wake (USA)**[35] 5-9-0 0........................................ RyanMoore 4 106+
(Dale Romans, U.S.A) **131/10**

6 2 **Smoking Sun (USA)**[90] 2379 5-9-0 0........................(b) StephanePasquier 2 102+
(P Bary, France) **47/10**[3]

7 3/4 **Real Solution (USA)**[70] 3025 5-9-0 0........................................ JJCastellano 6 100
(Chad C Brown, U.S.A) **12/5**[2]

2m 1.51s (-0.13) **7** Ran SP% **121.9**

PARI-MUTUEL (all including 2 usd stake): WIN 25.00; PLACE (1-2) 10.40, 4.20; SHOW (1-2-3) 6.00, 3.00, 5.00; SF 101.60.

**Owner** Andrew Bentley Stables, Llc **Bred** Mueller Farms Inc **Trained** USA

## 5404 DEAUVILLE (R-H)

Saturday, August 16

**OFFICIAL GOING: Turf: very soft; polytrack: standard**

### 5461a PRIX GONTAUT-BIRON HONG KONG JOCKEY CLUB (GROUP 3) (4YO+) (TURF) 1m 2f

1:30 (12:00) 4-Y-0+ £33,333 (£13,333; £10,000; £6,666; £3,333)

RPR

1 **Cocktail Queen (IRE)**[39] 4-8-6 0........................................ AlexisBadel 4 111+
(Mme M Bollack-Badel, France) *mde all: gng best 2f out: rdn over 1f out: styd on strly and forged clr: coasted home towards fin: v readily* **116/10**

2 3 1/2 **Nicolosio (IRE)**[13] 4-8-9 0........................................ MaximeGuyon 2 107
(Waldemar Hickst, Germany) *trckd wnr on inner: angled out and rdn 2f out: sn outpcd: styd on for wl hld 2nd* **23/10**[2]

3 1 **Pilote (IRE)**[41] 4008 4-8-11 0........................................ OlivierPeslier 1 107
(A Fabre, France) *hld up in last: pushed along 4f out: rdn and sme hdwy 2f out: wnt 3rd ent fnl f: styd on but no threat to wnr* **13/10**[1]

4 1 1/4 **Nabucco**[7] 5175 5-8-9 0........................................ RobertHavlin 5 103
(John Gosden) *dwlt sltly and hld up towards rr: clsd and trckd wnr in 2nd over 3f out: rdn over 2f out: sn outpcd: dropped to 4th ent fnl f and wl hld after: plugged on* **9/2**[3]

5 hd **Neatico (GER)**[41] 4006 7-8-9 0........................................ ThierryThulliez 7 102
(P Schiergen, Germany) *hld up in tch: rdn over 2f out: sn outpcd: plugged on fnl f but nvr a threat* **13/2**

6 13 **Amonit (FR)**[356] 4-8-9 0........................................ AnthonyCrastus 6 76
(J Hirschberger, Germany) *trckd wnr on outer: rdn and lost pl over 2f out: sn toiling in last: eased whn btn and wl bhd fnl f* **18/1**

2m 9.9s (-0.30) **6** Ran SP% **118.5**

WIN (incl. 1 euro stake): 12.60. PLACES: 4.10, 2.10. SF: 41.80.

**Owner** J C Smith **Bred** Littleton Stud **Trained** Lamorlaye, France

### 5462a PRIX DE POMONE (GROUP 2) (3YO+ FILLIES & MARES) (TURF) 1m 4f 110y

2:40 (12:00) 3-Y-0+ £61,750 (£23,833; £11,375; £7,583; £3,791)

RPR

1 **Star Lahib (IRE)**[42] 5-9-4 0........................................ UmbertoRispoli 1 109+
(A Wohler, Germany) *trckd ldr on inner: jnd ldr 5f out and led into st: rdn over 1f out: styd on strly and asserted fnl f: readily* **248/10**

2 2 1/2 **Chalnetta (FR)**[45] 4-9-4 0........................................ JulienAuge 6 105+
(C Ferland, France) *hld up in rr: last 3f out: rdn and hdwy fr 2f out: edgd rt u.p: styd on and wnt 2nd towards fin: no ch w wnr* **9/1**

3 1 **Savanne (IRE)**48 3773 3-8-7 0 ........................ MaximeGuyon 3 104
(A Fabre, France) *restrained and hld up: clsd 1/2-way: rdn and effrt to chal 2f out: styd on but outpcd by wnr fnl f and dropped to wl hld 3rd towards fin* **2/1**2

4 hd **Shared Account**72 4-9-4 0 ........................ ChristopheSoumillon 2 103+
(P Bary, France) *midfield in tch: pushed along 2f out: rdn and outpcd ent fnl f: rallied u.p and styd on strly towards fin: wnt 4th post* **13/1**

5 hd **Frine (IRE)**48 4-9-4 0 ........................ JeremyCrocquevieille 7 103
(J-M Osorio, Spain) *midfield on outer: rdn 2f out: edgd rt: styd on same pce and hld fnl f: dropped to 5th post* **58/10**3

6 3/4 **Kicky Blue (GER)**34 4250 4-9-4 0 ........................ MickaelBarzalona 4 102
(T Clout, France) *led: jnd 5f out and hdd into st: rdn and outpcd by wnr fnl 2f: fdd and dropped to 6th cl home* **15/1**

7 1 1/2 **Generosidade (URU)**26 4509 5-9-4 0 ........................ GregoryBenoist 9 100
(D Smaga, France) *trckd ldr on outer: rdn and brief effrt into st: towards rr and outpcd whn squeezed for room over 1f out: plugged on but wl hld fnl f* **19/1**

8 nk **Shamkala (FR)**62 3289 3-8-7 0 ........................ Christophe-PatriceLemaire 5 99
(A De Royer-Dupre, France) *prom early: stdd and hld up: sn towards rr: rdn and nt qckn fnl 2f: plugged on but wl hld and n.d* **6/4**1

9 4 **Rose Vista (FR)**27 4484 5-9-4 0 ........................ FabriceVeron 8 93
(J-L Guillochon, France) *dwlt and bhd early: hld up in rr: rdn over 2f out: sn no imp and btn: eased fnl f: nvr a factor* **57/1**

2m 50.13s (3.73)
**WFA** 3 from 4yo+ 10lb **9** Ran SP% **122.0**
WIN (incl. 1 euro stake): 25.80. PLACES: 5.10, 2.50, 1.50. DF: 96.90. SF: 266.30.
**Owner** Jaber Abdullah **Bred** Piercetown Stud **Trained** Germany

5463 - (Foreign Racing) - See Raceform Interactive

5049 **PONTEFRACT** (L-H)

Sunday, August 17

**OFFICIAL GOING: Good (7.4)**
Wind: fresh 1/2 behind Weather: changeable, very breezy and light showers

## 5464 BRITISH STALLION STUDS EBF TREVOR WOODS MEMORIAL MAIDEN STKS (BOBIS RACE) 5f
**2:15** (2:18) (Class 4) 2-Y-O **£5,175** (£1,540; £769; £384) **Stalls** Low

Form RPR

1 **Grandad's World (IRE)** 2-9-5 0 ........................ TonyHamilton 3 85+
(Richard Fahey) *trckd ldrs: effrt 2f out: led last 100yds: drew clr* **3/1**1

0 2 3 1/4 **Canny Kool**22 4659 2-9-5 0 ........................ PaulPickard 6 72
(Brian Ellison) *dwlt: sn w ldr: led over 2f out: hdd ins fnl f: no ex* **12/1**

2 3 1 3/4 **Robin Park**17 4814 2-8-11 0 ........................ RyanTate(3) 4 61
(Clive Cox) *t.k.h in rr: outpcd over 2f out: styd on fnl f: tk 3rd clsng stages* **9/2**3

0 4 1 3/4 **Charlie Lad**65 3199 2-9-5 0 ........................ RobertWinston 8 59
(Ollie Pears) *edgd lft after s: led tl over 2f out: one pce over 1f out* **25/1**

0 5 nk **Lady Atlas**17 4829 2-9-0 0 ........................ MichaelStainton 1 53
(David Brown) *in rr: hdwy over 1f out: kpt on* **40/1**

40 6 1 **Charles Messier**62 3296 2-9-5 0 ........................ PaulMulrennan 2 55
(Bryan Smart) *chsd ldrs: outpcd over 2f out: one pce fnl f* **7/1**

03 7 6 **Yorkshire (IRE)**10 5086 2-9-5 0 ........................ SilvestreDeSousa 7 33
(Kevin Ryan) *chsd ldrs on outside: sn drvn along: outpcd over 2f out: wknd over 1f out* **7/2**2

02 8 2 1/2 **Baron Spikey (IRE)**20 4723 2-9-5 0 ........................ GrahamLee 5 24
(Ann Duffield) *chsd ldrs: outpcd and lost pl over 2f out* **7/2**2

1m 2.96s (-0.34) **Going Correction** -0.125s/f (Firm) **8** Ran SP% **114.1**
Speed ratings (Par 96): **97,91,89,86,85 84,74,70**
CSF £39.45 TOTE £2.70: £1.10, £4.50, £2.10; EX 47.20 Trifecta £376.90.
**Owner** Dean Hardman and Stella Hardman **Bred** Colman O'Flynn **Trained** Musley Bank, N Yorks

**FOCUS**
There was strong tailwind and they went a good pace in this maiden. The two main form contenders were low-key but a well-backed newcomer scored in good style. Several of the jockeys reported that the ground was good and the time was 1.16 seconds over Racing Post standard.

## 5465 TOTEPOOL HOME OF POOL BETTING H'CAP 1m 4f 8y
**2:45** (2:46) (Class 3) (0-90,87) 3-Y-O+ **£9,337** (£2,796; £1,398; £699; £349; £175) **Stalls** Low

Form RPR

1150 1 **Aramist (IRE)**37 4160 4-9-7 80 ........................ BenCurtis 1 91
(Alan Swinbank) *trckd ldrs: rdn to chse ldr 2f out: led last 100yds: styd on wl* **7/1**

-231 2 3 **Asteroidea**41 4020 3-8-12 81 ........................ GrahamGibbons 2 89
(Pam Sly) *led: qcknd pce over 2f out: hdd ins fnl f: sn heavily eased* **9/2**3

6-04 3 1 3/4 **Rio's Rosanna (IRE)**14 4940 7-9-5 81 ........................ GeorgeChaloner(3) 3 84
(Richard Whitaker) *s.s: t.k.h in rr: hdwy over 5f out: 3rd over 1f out: kpt on same pce* **10/1**

1-41 4 5 **Alex Vino (IRE)**24 4586 3-9-3 86 ........................ ShaneKelly 8 81
(Sir Michael Stoute) *hld up towards rr: hdwy over 5f out: drvn over 2f out: one pce* **11/4**1

-000 5 2 1/4 **Open Eagle (IRE)**43 3962 5-10-0 87 ........................ DanielTudhope 7 79
(David O'Meara) *mid-div on outer: hdwy 4f out: one pce fnl 2f* **16/1**

14-0 6 7 **Chevalgris**33 4290 4-9-5 78 ........................ DavidAllan 5 59
(Alan Swinbank) *sn drvn along in rr: outpcd over 2f out* **40/1**

211 7 11 **Only Orsenfoolsies**29 4454 5-9-10 83 ........................ GrahamLee 4 46
(Micky Hammond) *trckd ldrs: t.k.h: drvn over 2f out: lost pl over 1f out: eased whn bhd* **7/1**

014 8 4 **Craggaknock**15 4921 3-8-2 71 ........................ SilvestreDeSousa 6 28
(Mark Walford) *chsd ldrs: drvn over 4f out: lost pl 2f out: sn eased* **10/3**2

2m 37.95s (-2.85) **Going Correction** -0.125s/f (Firm)
**WFA** 3 from 4yo+ 10lb **8** Ran SP% **110.3**
Speed ratings (Par 107): **104,102,100,97,96 91,84,81**
CSF £35.67 CT £295.92 TOTE £9.80: £2.50, £1.80, £4.60; EX 47.60 Trifecta £331.00.
**Owner** Pam & Richard Ellis **Bred** Fiona Craig & S Couldridge **Trained** Melsonby, N Yorks

**FOCUS**
A decent handicap involving three last-time-out winners. The pace was not strong but they finished quite well strung out.

## 5466 ST. JOHN AMBULANCE H'CAP 2m 1f 22y
**3:15** (3:15) (Class 5) (0-70,72) 3-Y-O+ **£3,881** (£1,155; £577; £288) **Stalls** Low

Form RPR

4433 1 **Beat The Shower**6 5240 8-9-0 56 ........................ RobertWinston 6 64
(Peter Niven) *hld up towards rr: hdwy 5f out: handy 3rd over 2f out: swtchd rt over 1f out: led jst ins fnl f: styd on* **15/2**

3611 2 2 3/4 **Precision Strike**10 5083 4-9-11 72 ........................(v) DuilioDaSilva(5) 1 77
(Richard Guest) *strated slowly: in last: hdwy and modest 4th over 2f out: swtchd ins over 1f out: disp 2nd last 100yds: kpt on same pce* **3/1**2

41 3 shd **Air Squadron**22 4678 4-9-10 66 ........................ SilvestreDeSousa 5 71
(Ralph Beckett) *trckd ldrs: 2nd over 3f out: drvn to chal 2f out: crowded and led briefly 1f out: lost 2nd post* **11/8**1

20-4 4 4 **Kodicil (IRE)**16 4874 6-9-9 65 ........................(p) PaddyAspell 3 65
(Mark Walford) *drvn to ld: edgd rt and hdd 1f out: wknd last 150yds* **17/2**

0506 5 14 **Kaizen Factor**17 4834 3-7-12 59 oh8 ow3 ........................ JackGarritty(5) 4 44
(Micky Hammond) *w ldr: drvn over 5f out: lost pl over 2f out* **25/1**

2334 6 1 1/4 **Jawaab (IRE)**19 4115 10-8-7 52 ........................(v) JoeyHaynes(3) 2 36
(Philip Kirby) *chsd ldrs: drvn over 5f out: lost pl 3f out* **5/1**3

3m 49.91s (5.31) **Going Correction** -0.125s/f (Firm)
**WFA** 3 from 4yo+ 14lb **6** Ran SP% **109.9**
Speed ratings (Par 103): **82,80,80,78,72 71**
CSF £28.76 TOTE £7.50: £3.70, £1.10; EX 28.80 Trifecta £54.80.
**Owner** Mrs Kate Young **Bred** C P E Brooks **Trained** Barton-le-Street, N Yorks

**FOCUS**
It was raining. They went a fair pace in this staying handicap and the winner beat the two market leaders, who finished clear of rest.

## 5467 EBF HIGHFIELD FARM FLYING FILLIES' STKS (LISTED RACE) 6f
**3:45** (3:45) (Class 1) 3-Y-O+ **£28,355** (£10,750; £5,380; £2,680; £1,345; £675) **Stalls** Low

Form RPR

0354 1 **Valonia**16 4854 3-8-12 101 ........................ HarryBentley 2 104
(Henry Candy) *w ldrs: led over 2f out: fnd ex nr fin* **10/3**2

62 2 nk **Spinatrix**1 5445 6-9-1 102 ........................(p) ConnorBeasley 10 103
(Michael Dods) *w ldrs: upsides 1f out: no ex cl home* **5/1**3

1104 3 1/2 **Mu'Ajiza**15 4923 4-9-1 80 ........................ RobertWinston 1 101
(Paul Midgley) *dwlt: sn chsng ldrs on inner: 3rd over 2f out: upsides last 150yds: no ex clsng stages* **33/1**

1010 4 4 **Ladies Are Forever**16 4852 6-9-8 108 ........................(b) DanielTudhope 9 96
(Geoffrey Oldroyd) *chsd ldrs: 4th over 2f out: one pce* **11/2**

2230 5 1 3/4 **Hoodna (IRE)**15 4895 4-9-1 102 ........................ SilvestreDeSousa 8 83
(Saeed bin Suroor) *chsd ldrs on outer: sn drvn along: kpt on one pce to take 5th nr fin* **9/4**1

4-10 6 1/2 **Athenian (IRE)**22 4668 5-9-1 96 ........................ ChrisCatlin 5 81
(Sir Mark Prescott Bt) *in rr: drvn over 2f out: kpt on: nvr a factor* **8/1**

-460 7 1 1/4 **Survived**22 4669 3-8-12 90 ........................1 GrahamGibbons 11 77
(William Haggas) *swtchd lft after s: in rr: kpt on fnl 2f: nvr a factor* **18/1**

4400 8 11 **Masarah (IRE)**40 4060 4-9-1 98 ........................ FrannyNorton 4 42
(Clive Brittain) *led: hdd over 2f out: sn lost pl: eased whn bhd clsng stages* **22/1**

2103 9 1 **Relation Alexander (IRE)**31 4367 3-8-12 75 ........(b1) PaulMulrennan 7 39
(Paul D'Arcy) *sn chsng ldrs: lost pl over 1f out: eased whn bhd clsng stages* **66/1**

3-00 10 2 **Along Again (IRE)**50 3724 3-8-12 99 ........................ ShaneKelly 12 33
(Sir Michael Stoute) *in rr: drvn over 2f out: sn lost pl: eased whn bhd clsng stages* **33/1**

1m 14.39s (-2.51) **Going Correction** -0.125s/f (Firm)
**WFA** 3 from 4yo+ 3lb **10** Ran SP% **114.0**
Speed ratings: **111,110,109,104,102 101,99,85,83,81**
CSF £19.14 TOTE £5.30: £2.00, £2.10, £8.30; EX 17.20 Trifecta £498.40.
**Owner** Qatar Racing Limited **Bred** Tibthorpe Stud **Trained** Kingston Warren, Oxon

**FOCUS**
Older fillies' had won eight of the last nine runnings of this race but a 3yo landed the prize this time. The pace was not very strong and the first three were always prominent.

## 5468 CGC EVENTS FOR CONFERENCE & BANQUETING H'CAP (BOBIS RACE) 1m 4y
**4:20** (4:20) (Class 3) (0-95,90) 3-Y-O **£9,337** (£2,796; £1,398; £699; £349; £175) **Stalls** Low

Form RPR

4211 1 **Imshivalla (IRE)**11 5051 3-8-6 75 ........................ PaulHanagan 1 84
(Richard Fahey) *mde all: pushed clr over 1f out: unchal* **5/2**2

4515 2 2 1/2 **Lockhart (IRE)**8 5177 3-8-12 81 ........................ FrannyNorton 4 84
(Mark Johnston) *sn chsng ldrs: 3rd over 2f out: chsd wnr over 1f out: no imp* **5/1**3

0603 3 nk **Oxsana**29 4436 3-9-7 90 ........................(p) SilvestreDeSousa 5 93+
(William Haggas) *dwlt: in rr: hdwy over 4f out: 3rd 1f out: kpt on same pce* **9/4**1

2126 4 6 **Flycatcher (IRE)**23 4634 3-8-11 83 ........................ GeorgeChaloner(3) 6 72
(Richard Fahey) *trckd ldrs: 2nd over 2f out: wknd fnl f* **6/1**

400 5 11 **Mr Matthews (IRE)**57 3455 3-8-8 77 ........................(v1) BenCurtis 3 40
(K R Burke) *hld up in mid-div: outpcd over 2f out: lost pl wl over 1f out: sn bhd* **12/1**

5434 6 4 1/2 **Castle Combe (IRE)**17 4812 3-8-5 74 ........................(b1) MartinDwyer 2 27
(Marcus Tregoning) *w wnr: t.k.h: drvn over 2f out: lost pl 2f out: eased whn bhd clsng stages* **15/2**

1m 43.35s (-2.55) **Going Correction** -0.125s/f (Firm) **6** Ran SP% **109.8**
Speed ratings (Par 104): **107,104,104,98,87 82**
CSF £14.44 TOTE £2.50: £1.50, £2.80; EX 12.60 Trifecta £32.10.
**Owner** Pow Partnership **Bred** M Fahy & Rathbarry Stud **Trained** Musley Bank, N Yorks

**FOCUS**
The progressive winner scored with plenty in hand under a front-running ride in this decent handicap.

## 5469 TOTEPOOL SUPPORTING THE SPORT YOU LOVE MAIDEN STKS 1m 4y
**4:50** (4:50) (Class 4) 3-Y-O+ **£5,175** (£1,540; £769; £384) **Stalls** Low

Form RPR

4222 1 **Hesbaan (IRE)**24 4587 3-9-5 75 ........................ PaulHanagan 5 77
(Marcus Tregoning) *led 2f: w ldr: led over 1f out: rdn and drew clr last 75yds* **10/11**1



The Form Book, Raceform Ltd, Newbury, RG14 5SJ

24 **2** 2 1/4 **Flawless Pink**[44] 3916 3-9-0 0 SilvestreDeSousa 1 67
(Jeremy Noseda) *chsd ldrs: led after 2f: drvn over 2f out: hdd over 1f out: kpt on same pce* **9/4**[2]
426 **3** 5 **Dancin Alpha**[12] 5018 3-9-5 73 RobertWinston 7 60
(Alan Swinbank) *chsd ldrs: swtchd lft after 1f: clr 3rd and drvn over 2f out: one pce* **10/1**
**4** 1 1/2 **Tasmanian** 3-9-5 0 FrannyNorton 2 57+
(Mark Johnston) *s.s: in rr: hdwy 2f out: kpt on to take modest 4th nr fin: will improve* **4/1**[3]
0 **5** 2 1/4 **Im Dapper Too**[122] 1542 3-9-5 0 GrahamLee 6 52
(John Davies) *mid-div: drvn over 3f out: hdwy over 1f out: nvr a threat* **40/1**
00 **6** 5 **Soviet Union (IRE)**[8] 5195 3-9-0 0 GrahamGibbons 3 35
(Mark Walford) *in rr: effrt over 2f out: wknd over 1f out: eased nr fin* **50/1**
**7** 5 **Rememberance Day** 3-9-0 0 DavidAllan 8 24
(Les Eyre) *wnt rt s: mid-div: hdwy on outside over 3f out: lost pl 2f out: eased nr fin* **20/1**
0 **8** 46 **Mr Gatsby**[8] 5195 3-9-5 0 JasonHart 4
(Mark Walford) *chsd ldrs: drvn over 4f out: sn lost pl: t.o whn eased over 1f out: eventually completed* **25/1**

1m 45.67s (-0.23) **Going Correction** -0.125s/f (Firm) 8 Ran SP% **125.3**
Speed ratings (Par 105): **96,93,88,87,85 80,75,29**
CSF £3.51 TOTE £2.30: £1.10, £1.20, £2.40; EX 3.70 Trifecta £9.60.
**Owner** Hamdan Al Maktoum **Bred** Miss Audrey F Thompson **Trained** Whitsbury, Hants

**FOCUS**
The leading form contender delivered in this maiden and his main market rival finished a clear second.

## 5470 NOVA DISPLAY H'CAP 6f
5:20 (5:22) (Class 5) (0-75,77) 3-Y-O+ **£3,881** (£1,155; £577; £288) **Stalls** Low

Form RPR
1331 **1** **Poyle Vinnie**[11] 5053 4-10-0 77 AndrewMullen 8 91+
(Michael Appleby) *chsd ldrs on outer: edgd lft and led over 2f out: drvn out* **7/2**[1]
3001 **2** 1 3/4 **We'll Deal Again**[15] 4925 7-9-11 74 GrahamGibbons 3 81
(Michael Easterby) *chsd ldrs: sltly hmpd over 2f out: styd on same pce fnl f* **6/1**[2]
0100 **3** nk **Decent Fella (IRE)**[9] 5124 8-9-4 70 (t) MichaelJMMurphy(3) 10 76
(Ann Stokell) *in rr: hdwy over 1f out: styd on to take 3rd nr fin* **28/1**
6530 **4** 1 1/2 **Lothair (IRE)**[13] 4961 5-9-6 69 BenCurtis 6 70
(Alan Swinbank) *trckd ldrs: t.k.h: bdly hmpd over 2f out: chsd wnr over 1f out: kpt on same pce* **11/1**
-034 **5** nk **Milly's Secret (IRE)**[15] 4902 3-9-2 75 (p) RowanScott(7) 4 75
(Ann Duffield) *mid-div: drvn along 3f out: styd on appr fnl f* **7/1**
0201 **6** 1 **Le Laitier (FR)**[11] 5055 3-9-6 72 TomEaves 7 69
(Scott Dixon) *sn led: hdd over 2f out: wknd last 75yds* **12/1**
4600 **7** 1 1/2 **Teetotal (IRE)**[11] 5053 4-9-9 72 SilvestreDeSousa 11 64+
(Nigel Tinkler) *dwlt: swtchd lft after s: in rr: hdwy on outside over 1f out: nvr nr ldrs* **7/1**
2461 **8** 3/4 **Solar Spirit (IRE)**[12] 4997 9-10-0 77 RobertWinston 1 67
(Tracy Waggott) *hld up in mid-div: effrt over 2f out: chsng ldrs over 1f out: wknd fnl 150yds* **8/1**
1006 **9** 1/2 **Dream Ally (IRE)**[12] 4997 4-9-0 63 MichaelStainton 9 51
(Micky Hammond) *swtchd lft sn after s: in rr: kpt on over 1f out: nvr a factor* **33/1**
5036 **10** 2 **Disclosure**[10] 5080 3-9-0 66 DavidAllan 2 48
(Les Eyre) *chsd ldrs: lost pl over 1f out: eased towards fin* **13/2**[3]
166 **11** 6 **Thatcherite (IRE)**[21] 4712 6-9-11 74 (t) BarryMcHugh 5 37
(Tony Coyle) *dwlt: in rr: hmpd after 100yds: bhd whn eased clsng stages* **12/1**
00-0 **12** 26 **West Leake Diman (IRE)**[23] 4620 5-9-9 72 (v[1]) PaddyAspell 12
(Mrs Ilka Gansera-Leveque) *sn led: hdd over 2f out: wknd rapidly: t.o whn eased ins fnl f* **40/1**

1m 16.14s (-0.76) **Going Correction** -0.125s/f (Firm)
**WFA** 3 from 4yo+ 3lb 12 Ran SP% **118.5**
Speed ratings (Par 103): **100,97,97,95,94 93,91,90,89,87 79,44**
CSF £23.24 CT £520.02 TOTE £4.20: £1.70, £2.20, £8.30; EX 27.50 Trifecta £1369.90.
**Owner** Dallas Racing & C L Bacon **Bred** Cecil And Miss Alison Wiggins **Trained** Danethorpe, Notts
■ Stewards' Enquiry : Silvestre De Sousa one-day ban: careless riding (Aug 31)

**FOCUS**
They went a fair pace and the favourite scored in good style in this sprint handicap.
T/Jkpt: Part won. T/Plt: £121.20 to a £1 stake. Pool: £109,663.53 - 660.03 winning units. T/Qpdt: £10.00 to a £1 stake. Pool: £8,428.86 - 623.15 winning units. WG

5461
# DEAUVILLE (R-H)
Sunday, August 17
**OFFICIAL GOING: Turf: soft; polytrack: standard**

## 5478a PRIX FRANCOIS BOUTIN (LISTED RACE) (2YO) (STRAIGHT) (TURF) 7f
1:30 (12:00) 2-Y-O **£22,916** (£9,166; £6,875; £4,583; £2,291)

RPR
**1** **Nucifera (USA)**[33] 4312 2-9-2 0 Christophe-PatriceLemaire 6 106+
(J E Pease, France) **7/2**[2]
**2** 1/2 **Tupi (IRE)**[18] 4780 2-9-2 0 RichardHughes 1 99
(Richard Hannon) *trckd ldr: pushed along to chal 2f out: hmpd whn short of room on rail jst ins fnl f: kpt on after but nt rcvr and hld: fin 3rd: plcd 2nd* **4/5**[1]
**3** 2 **Iceberg (IRE)**[45] 2-9-2 0 OlivierPeslier 5 99
(C Ferland, France) *fin 2nd: disqualified and plcd 3rd* **23/5**[3]
**4** 1 1/2 **Svoul (FR)**[19] 2-9-2 0 ChristopheSoumillon 4 95
(F-H Graffard, France) **5/1**
**5** 12 **Speed Machine (IRE)**[15] 4932 2-9-2 0 IoritzMendizabal 3 63
(Paul Cole) *hld up in tch: rdn and dropped to last 2f out: sn bhd and btn: eased fnl f* **124/10**

1m 29.11s (0.81) **Going Correction** +0.35s/f (Good) 5 Ran SP% **119.8**
Speed ratings: **109,106,106,104,90**
WIN (incl. 1 euro stake): 4.50. PLACES: 1.30, 1.20. SF: 9.20.
**Owner** Flaxman Stables Ireland Ltd **Bred** Flaxman Holdings Limited **Trained** Chantilly, France

## 5479a PRIX MINERVE (GROUP 3) (3YO FILLIES) (TURF) 1m 4f 110y
2:40 (12:00) 3-Y-O **£33,333** (£13,333; £10,000; £6,666; £3,333)

RPR
**1** **Zarshana (IRE)**[35] 4249 3-8-10 0 ow1 (b[1]) ChristopheSoumillon 4 107+
(A De Royer-Dupre, France) *hld up: pushed along and clsd 2f out: rdn to chal ent fnl f: led fnl 120yds: styd on wl* **2/1**[1]
**2** 1/2 **Game Zone (IRE)**[83] 3-8-9 0 Francois-XavierBertras 6 105
(F Rohaut, France) *dwlt but qckly rcvrd: hld up: c towards nr side rail in st: rdn and clsd over 1f out: chal ent fnl f: styd on wl but nt quite pce of wnr* **8/1**
**3** 1 **Mambomiss (FR)**[25] 3-8-9 0 ThomasHenderson 3 104
(D De Watrigant, France) *restrained and hld up in rr: rdn and hdwy fr 2f out: chal ent fnl f and led narrowly tl hdd fnl 120yds: styd on but sn dropped to 3rd and hld* **25/1**
**4** 3/4 **Criteria (IRE)**[29] 4443 3-8-9 0 WilliamBuick 7 102
(John Gosden) *trckd ldr: pushed along to chal 3f out: rdn and ev ch 2f out: styd on same pce fr over 1f out and hld fnl 150yds* **7/1**
**5** 1 1/2 **Indonesienne (IRE)**[49] 3773 3-8-9 0 OlivierPeslier 1 100
(C Ferland, France) *hld up towards rr: rdn 2f out: clsd and ev ch over 1f out: kpt on same pce and hld fnl f* **4/1**[2]
**6** nk **Marsh Daisy**[72] 2960 3-8-9 0 RyanMoore 5 100
(Hughie Morrison) *prom: rdn to chal 2f out: led over 1f out: strly pressed ent fnl f and sn hdd: outpcd and fdd* **6/1**[3]
**7** 1 **Hand Puppet (IRE)**[45] 3-8-9 0 MaximeGuyon 8 98
(A Fabre, France) *midfield in tch: rdn and outpcd over 2f out: clsd again over 1f out: no ex fnl f and nt given hrd time once hld* **10/1**
**8** 3 **Honor Bound**[17] 4824 3-8-9 0 Christophe-PatriceLemaire 9 93
(Ralph Beckett) *got across fr wdst draw and led: rdn into st: hdd over 1f out: sn btn and wknd* **28/1**
**9** shd **Saraaba (IRE)**[35] 4249 3-8-9 0 ThierryJarnet 2 93
(F Head, France) *t.k.h early: midfield on inner: rdn 2f out: no ex ent fnl f: wknd and sn eased* **6/1**[3]

2m 49.23s (2.83) **Going Correction** +0.35s/f (Good) 9 Ran SP% **121.9**
Speed ratings: **105,104,104,103,102 102,101,100,99**
WIN (incl. 1 euro stake): 3.20. PLACES: 1.50, 1.90, 4.60. DF: 7.30. SF: 15.70.
**Owner** H H Aga Khan **Bred** His Highness The Aga Khan's Studs S C **Trained** Chantilly, France

## 5480a PRIX DU HARAS DE FRESNAY-LE-BUFFARD - JACQUES LE MAROIS (GROUP 1) (3YO+ NO GELDINGS) (STR) (TURF) 1m (R)
3:10 (12:00) 3-Y-O+ **£285,700** (£114,300; £57,150; £28,550; £14,300)

RPR
**1** **Kingman**[18] 4779 3-8-13 0 JamesDoyle 1 125+
(John Gosden) *hld up in rr: pushed along to cl 2f out: chal over 1f out and led ent fnl f: rdn and r.o strly: forged clr: comf* **2/7**[1]
**2** 2 1/2 **Anodin (IRE)**[61] 3317 4-9-4 0 OlivierPeslier 3 119
(F Head, France) *midfield: rdn over 1f out: kpt on steadily and wnt 2nd fnl 100yds: nt pce of wnr* **179/10**[3]
**3** 1 **Olympic Glory (IRE)**[84] 2587 4-9-4 0 (b) FrankieDettori 4 117
(Richard Hannon) *hld up: clsd grad fr 1/2-way: pushed along in 2nd 2f out: chal and w ldr briefly over 1f out: hdd ent fnl f and sn outpcd by wnr: no ex and fdd* **7/2**[2]
**4** snk **Rizeena (IRE)**[37] 4165 3-8-9 0 RyanMoore 6 112
(Clive Brittain) *trckd clr ldr: rdn and effrt over 1f out: kpt on same pce and hld fnl f* **20/1**
**5** nk **Red Dubawi (IRE)**[35] 4247 6-9-4 0 EddyHardouin 5 116
(Frau Erika Mader, Germany) *led and sn clr: reeled in fr 2f out: rdn and hdd over 1f out: no ex and fdd* **80/1**

1m 41.9s (1.10) **Going Correction** +0.35s/f (Good)
**WFA** 3 from 4yo+ 6lb 5 Ran SP% **111.3**
Speed ratings: **108,105,104,104,104**
WIN (incl. 1 euro stake): 1.40. PLACES: 1.10, 1.40. SF: 4.90.
**Owner** K Abdullah **Bred** Juddmonte Farms Ltd **Trained** Newmarket, Suffolk

## 5481a PRIX MICHEL HOUYVET (LISTED RACE) (3YO) (TURF) 1m 7f
3:40 (12:00) 3-Y-O **£22,916** (£9,166; £6,875; £4,583; £2,291)

RPR
**1** **Baino Hope (FR)**[44] 3-8-8 0 IoritzMendizabal 1 103
(J-C Rouget, France) **12/5**[2]
**2** 3 **Doumaran (FR)**[69] 3-8-11 0 ChristopheSoumillon 6 102
(A De Royer-Dupre, France) **7/5**[1]
**3** nk **Auvray (FR)**[35] 4251 3-8-11 0 GregoryBenoist 7 102
(E Lellouche, France) **48/10**[3]
**4** 1 3/4 **Noble Raven (FR)**[23] 3-8-8 0 FabriceVeron 8 96
(Mme A-M Poirier, France) **38/1**
**5** nse **Min Alemarat (IRE)**[80] 2696 3-8-11 0 MartinHarley 4 99
(Marco Botti) *trckd ldr on inner: rdn to chal and w ldrs into st: ev ch 2f out: styd on but outpcd by ldrs and hld fnl f: dropped to 5th post* **111/10**
**6** 1 3/4 **Sailor (FR)**[63] 3290 3-8-11 0 (b) ThierryJarnet 2 97
(J Heloury, France) **28/1**
**7** 20 **Maid In Rio (IRE)**[18] 4777 3-8-8 0 JoeFanning 9 68
(Mark Johnston) *sn led: rdn and hdd into st: qckly btn and wknd: t.o* **36/5**
**8** 1 3/4 **Red Turtle (FR)**[65] 3-8-11 0 MaximeGuyon 5 69
(Mme Pia Brandt, France) **176/10**

3m 21.23s (2.13) **Going Correction** +0.35s/f (Good) 8 Ran SP% **120.2**
Speed ratings: **108,106,106,105,105 104,93,92**
WIN (incl. 1 euro stake): 3.40. PLACES: 1.10, 1.10, 1.30. DF: 2.70. SF: 6.20.
**Owner** Ecurie I M Fares **Bred** Scea Haras De Manneville **Trained** Pau, France

## 5482a PRIX DE BONNEBOSQ (CLAIMER) (3YO) (POLYTRACK) 6f 110y
4:10 (12:00) 3-Y-O **£11,250** (£4,500; £3,375; £2,250; £1,125)

RPR
**1** **Saint Pois (FR)**[50] 3-9-1 0 GregoryBenoist 6 88
(J-C Rouget, France) **8/5**[1]
**2** 3/4 **Tout En Style (FR)**[30] 3-8-11 0 StephanePasquier 5 82
(T Lemer, France) **117/10**
**3** 1 **Sweltering (FR)**[50] 3-8-8 0 IoritzMendizabal 4 76
(P Monfort, France) **269/10**
**4** snk **Meritocracy (IRE)**[12] 5012 3-9-4 0 OlivierPeslier 1 86
(Paul Cole) *led: rdn and strly pressed over 1f out: hdd fnl 150yds: no ex and fdd: dropped to 4th cl home* **53/10**[2]

5 snk **Winshine (FR)**[10] 3-8-13 0 DelphineSantiago 7 80
(S Smrczek, Germany) **68/10**
6 ½ **Oromo (FR)**[17] 3-9-2 0 ChristopheSoumillon 9 82
(J Phelippon, France) **31/5**[3]
7 snk **Sunstream (FR)**[29] 4464 3-8-5 0 (b) PierreBazire(8) 11 78
(P Bary, France) **229/10**
8 1 ½ **Caja (FR)**[58] 3-8-8 0 FabriceVeron 2 69
(H-A Pantall, France) **171/10**
9 3 **Get Lucky (FR)**[19] 3-8-6 0 MllePaulineDominois(5) 8 63
(C Lerner, France) **201/10**
10 1 ½ **Race For Fame (IRE)**[19] 3-9-2 0 GeraldMosse 10 64
(M Boutin, France) **138/10**
11 1 **Marie D'o (FR)**[30] 3-8-13 0 AntoineHamelin 12 58
(J Van Handenhove, France) **25/1**
12 3 **Sakal**[94] 2290 3-8-8 0 (b[1]) EddyHardouin 3 44
(Matthieu Palussiere, France) **50/1**

1m 17.43s (77.43) **12** Ran SP% **119.5**
WIN (incl. 1 euro stake): 2.30.(Saint Pois coupled with Sunstream). PLACES: 1.40, 3.10, 4.00. DF: 13.30. SF: 23.00.
**Owner** Gerard Augustin-Normand **Bred** Franklin Finance S.A. **Trained** Pau, France

5483 - (Foreign Racing) - See Raceform Interactive

## 1781 KREFELD (R-H)
Sunday, August 17

**OFFICIAL GOING: Turf: good**

## 5484a GROSSER PREIS DER SPARKASSE KREFELD (EX FURSTENBERG-RENNEN) (GROUP 3) (3YO) (TURF) 1m 2f 55y
**3:35** (12:00) 3-Y-0 **£26,666** (£9,166; £4,583; £2,500; £1,666)

RPR
1 **Eric (GER)**[42] 4007 3-9-0 0 SHellyn 2 102+
(C Von Der Recke, Germany) *settled in rr: tk clsr order on outer 3f out: styd on to ld 1 1/2f out: drvn and edgd rt ins fnl f: sn in command: comf* **37/10**[3]
2 ¾ **Simba**[28] 3-9-0 0 EPedroza 3 101
(A Wohler, Germany) *trckd ldr: rdn 2f out: chal between horses 1 1/2f out: kpt on u.p fnl f but a wl hld by wnr* **7/10**[1]
3 ½ **Firestorm (GER)**[56] 3512 3-9-0 0 AdriedeVries 1 100
(P Schiergen, Germany) *t.k.h: hld up in 3rd: 4th and hrd rdn 2f out: styd on ins fnl f: nvr quite on terms w ldrs* **11/2**
4 2 ½ **Nordico (GER)**[35] 4247 3-9-2 0 DanielePorcu 5 97
(Mario Hofer, Germany) *led field in single file: rdn on rail 2 1/2f out: hdd 1 1/2f out: fdd ins fnl f* **13/5**[2]
5 1 ¾ **Invador**[35] 3-8-11 0 FilipMinarik 4 88
(Jean-Pierre Carvalho, Germany) *t.k.h: hld up in 4th: last and hrd rdn 2f out: plugged on at same pce: nvr in contention* **44/5**

2m 9.13s (129.13) **5** Ran SP% **133.5**
WIN (incl. 10 euro stake): 47. PLACES: 14, 11. SF: 60.
**Owner** Frau Gabriele Inge Gaul **Bred** Frau Gabriele Inge Gaul **Trained** Weilerswist, Germany

## 5302 KEMPTON (A.W) (R-H)
Monday, August 18

**OFFICIAL GOING: Polytrack: standard**
Wind: light to medium, half against Weather: cloudy, heavy rain races 3 and 4

## 5486 DOWNLOAD THE BETVICTOR APP NOW H'CAP 5f (P)
**2:00** (2:00) (Class 5) (0-70,69) 3-Y-0+ **£2,587** (£770; £384; £192) **Stalls** Low

Form RPR
6430 1 **West Coast Dream**[14] 4981 7-9-2 64 DeclanBates(3) 3 72
(Roy Brotherton) *w ldr: clr of field after 2f: drvn over 1f out: forged ahd ins fnl f: styd on* **6/1**
333 2 ¾ **Pull The Pin (IRE)**[8] 5207 5-9-2 61 (bt) RichardHughes 1 66
(Ann Stokell) *broke fast: led: clr w wnr after 2f: drvn over 1f out: hdd ins fnl f: no ex* **3/1**[2]
2223 3 3 ½ **Gulland Rock**[34] 4307 3-9-5 66 MartinDwyer 2 59
(William Muir) *awkward leaving stalls and s.i.s: bhd: drvn and stl plenty to do over 1f out: wnt 3rd ins fnl f: kpt on but nvr a threat to ldrs* **7/4**[1]
3044 4 nk **Putin (IRE)**[6] 5281 6-9-3 69 (bt) JennyPowell(7) 4 61
(Phil McEntee) *outpcd in last pair: rdn over 1f out: wnt 4th ins fnl f: kpt on but no threat to ldrs* **7/2**[3]
2030 5 7 **Island Legend (IRE)**[56] 3520 8-9-10 69 (b) RyanMoore 5 48
(Milton Bradley) *chsd ldrs: outpcd after 2f out: drvn and no hdwy over 1f out: wknd and lost 2 pls ins fnl f: eased towards fin* **10/1**

1m 0.01s (-0.49) **Going Correction** -0.025s/f (Stan)
**WFA** 3 from 5yo+ 2lb **5** Ran SP% **107.0**
Speed ratings (Par 103): **102,100,95,94,83**
CSF £22.39 TOTE £7.30: £3.40, £2.40; EX 21.80 Trifecta £46.60.
**Owner** Miss Emma Byrd **Bred** Eurostrait Ltd **Trained** Elmley Castle, Worcs

**FOCUS**
This looked a competitive little sprint handicap for the class and there was no hanging about, but the first pair dominated. The winner is rated to his March Wolverhampton win.

## 5487 £25 FREE BET AT BETVICTOR.COM H'CAP 1m 2f (P)
**2:30** (2:30) (Class 4) (0-85,85) 3-Y-0+ **£4,851** (£1,443; £721; £360) **Stalls** Low

Form RPR
5130 1 **Wahgah (USA)**[22] 4710 3-9-1 80 DaneO'Neill 1 101
(Saeed bin Suroor) *led for 1f: settled and chsd ldng pair after: rdn and qcknd to ld over 1f out: sn clr and r.o strly: readily* **6/1**[3]
1012 2 6 **Grasped**[12] 5035 4-9-9 80 JamesDoyle 12 89
(Lady Cecil) *chsd ldr after 1f: rdn and chal over 1f out: wnt 2nd but totally outpcd by wnr jst over 1f out: no ch but kpt on for clr 2nd* **6/1**[3]
0122 3 2 ¼ **Qanan**[25] 4586 5-10-0 85 TedDurcan 13 90
(Chris Wall) *chsd ldng trio: drvn over 2f out: no imp: plugged on to go 3rd wl ins fnl f* **9/2**[2]
6442 4 ¾ **Silver Dixie (USA)**[19] 4786 4-9-2 76 (p) CharlesBishop(3) 8 79
(Peter Hedger) *led after 1f: rdn wl over 1f out: hdd over 1f out: 3rd and btn 1f out: lost 3rd wl ins fnl f* **16/1**
1154 5 nse **Barnmore**[14] 4968 6-8-10 74 RobHornby(7) 5 77
(Peter Hedger) *stdd s: hld up in last quartet: sme hdwy whn nt clr run ent fnl f: weaved through and styd on ins fnl f: nvr trbld ldrs* **14/1**
6021 6 1 **Bishop's Castle (USA)**[38] 4175 5-9-12 83 RyanMoore 6 84
(Brian Ellison) *in tch in midfield: effrt u.p whn hung rt and no imp over 1f out: plugged on same pce and wl hld fnl f* **5/2**[1]
110 7 ½ **Perfect Cracker**[32] 4349 6-9-5 79 RyanTate(3) 7 79
(Clive Cox) *stdd s: hld up in last quartet: rdn and sme hdwy towards inner over 1f out: styd on: nvr trbld ldrs* **8/1**
3146 8 nk **Ocean Applause**[12] 5040 4-9-2 78 (t) ShelleyBirkett(5) 11 77
(John Ryan) *hld up in rr: sme hdwy over 1f out: styd on ins fnl f: nvr trbld ldrs* **20/1**
1216 9 1 ¾ **Like A Diamond (IRE)**[185] 611 4-9-11 82 TomQueally 4 78
(Evan Williams) *t.k.h: hld up in tch in midfield: rdn whn swtchd lft and v wd bnd 2f out: no hdwy: wknd over 1f out* **16/1**
0065 10 nse **Thecornishcowboy**[12] 5035 5-9-2 76 (t) RyanPowell(3) 3 72
(John Ryan) *in tch in midfield: rdn and no hdwy over 2f out: wl btn over 1f out* **50/1**
0014 11 4 **Well Painted (IRE)**[14] 4959 5-9-2 76 (bt) RossAtkinson(3) 2 64
(Andy Turnell) *dwlt and pushed along leaving stalls: a in rr: n.d* **40/1**
2200 12 33 **Red Warrior (IRE)**[8] 5203 4-9-9 85 CamHardie(5) 9
(Ismail Mohammed) *in tch in midfield: rdn and dropped to rr 3f out: sn lost tch: t.o and eased fnl f* **16/1**

2m 5.1s (-2.90) **Going Correction** -0.025s/f (Stan)
**WFA** 3 from 4yo+ 8lb **12** Ran SP% **119.9**
Speed ratings (Par 105): **110,105,103,102,102 101,101,101,99,99 96,70**
CSF £41.72 CT £180.71 TOTE £9.70: £2.60, £1.70, £1.90; EX 60.10 Trifecta £211.50.
**Owner** Godolphin **Bred** Shadwell Farm LLC **Trained** Newmarket, Suffolk

**FOCUS**
The injection of pace 4f out caught out the closers, but it made little difference to the result as the winner was far too good. The form is taken at face value.

## 5488 BRITISH STALLION STUDS EBF MAIDEN STKS 6f (P)
**3:00** (3:00) (Class 5) 2-Y-0 **£2,911** (£866; £432; £216) **Stalls** Low

Form RPR
62 1 **Invincible Gold (IRE)**[23] 4666 2-9-5 0 RyanMoore 11 81+
(Ed Walker) *in tch in midfield: effrt u.p to go 3rd wl over 1f out: drvn 1f out: styd on strly to ld fnl 75yds: rdn out* **8/13**[1]
2 1 **Power Game** 2-9-5 0 HarryBentley 7 78+
(Saeed bin Suroor) *s.i.s: racd in last quartet: swtchd towards inner and gd hdwy 2f out: 4th 1f out: r.o strly to go 2nd fnl 50yds* **3/1**[2]
0 3 1 ¼ **Amazour (IRE)**[30] 4424 2-9-5 0 MartinHarley 1 74
(Ismail Mohammed) *led: rdn and qcknd clr 2f out: drvn 1f out: no ex and hdd fnl 75yds: lost 2nd and wknd fnl 50yds* **16/1**
00 4 2 **Presto Boy**[31] 4409 2-9-5 0 (t) HayleyTurner 4 68
(James Fanshawe) *chsd ldrs: rdn to chse clr wnr 2f out: no imp: lost 2 pls fnl 100yds* **33/1**
5 4 ½ **Shipwright (IRE)** 2-9-5 0 DaneO'Neill 6 55
(Mark Johnston) *chsd ldrs: rdn and unable qck 2f out: 5th and wl hld fnl f* **6/1**[3]
00 6 1 ½ **More Drama (IRE)**[14] 4980 2-9-0 0 LiamKeniry 2 45
(Sylvester Kirk) *s.i.s: off the pce in last quartet: modest late hdwy: nvr trbld ldrs* **66/1**
7 1 ¼ **Rainbow Orse** 2-9-5 0 AdamBeschizza 5 47
(Robert Cowell) *chsd ldr tl 2f out: 6th and btn over 1f out: wknd* **33/1**
00 8 2 **Red Flute**[62] 3330 2-9-2 0 (v[1]) BillyCray(3) 12 41
(Alan McCabe) *grad swtchd towards inner after s: hld up in midfield: rdn over 2f out: sn btn* **100/1**
9 1 **Almoqatel (IRE)** 2-9-5 0 TomQueally 8 38
(James Fanshawe) *a in rr: n.d* **33/1**
0 10 ¾ **Red Springer (IRE)**[68] 3119 2-9-5 0 (p) BenCurtis 10 35
(Alan McCabe) *in tch in midfield: struggling u.p over 3f out: bhd over 1f out* **100/1**
11 ¾ **Purple Surprise** 2-8-7 0 JennyPowell(7) 3 28
(Andrew Reid) *sn pushed along and a outpcd in last quartet* **66/1**

1m 13.35s (0.25) **Going Correction** -0.025s/f (Stan) **11** Ran SP% **120.9**
Speed ratings (Par 94): **97,95,94,91,85 83,81,79,77,76 75**
CSF £2.63 TOTE £1.60: £1.02, £2.20, £3.80; EX 3.40 Trifecta £20.50.
**Owner** John Coleman & Clarence Cheng **Bred** Rockfield Farm **Trained** Newmarket, Suffolk

**FOCUS**
Probably just a fair maiden. The first two are capable of better.

## 5489 FOLLOW @BETVICTORRACING ON TWITTER NURSERY H'CAP 1m (P)
**3:30** (3:33) (Class 6) (0-60,60) 2-Y-0 **£1,940** (£577; £288; £144) **Stalls** Low

Form RPR
003 1 **Seebeedee**[13] 4999 2-9-7 60 SamHitchcott 6 65
(Harry Dunlop) *mde all: rdn ent fnl 2f: battled on gamely u.p fnl f: jst hld on* **7/1**[3]
400 2 nse **Winter Queen**[12] 5037 2-8-12 56 CamHardie(5) 1 61
(Charlie Appleby) *in tch in midfield: effrt u.p to chse ldng pair wl over 1f out: chsd wnr ins fnl f: str chal fnl 50yds: jst hld* **4/1**[2]
0222 3 2 ¼ **Wink Oliver**[30] 4449 2-9-7 60 [1] HayleyTurner 14 60
(Kristin Stubbs) *s.i.s: rcvrd and hdwy on outer to chse ldrs 6f out: rdn and unable qck 2f out: styd on same pce fnl f: wnt 3rd nr fin* **8/1**
5504 4 nk **Robben**[10] 5141 2-9-4 57 (b) MartinHarley 4 56
(Kevin Ryan) *chsd wnr: drvn and ev ch 2f out: 3rd and no ex fnl 150yds: wknd fnl 75yds and lost 3rd nr fin* **7/2**[1]
046 5 1 **Goolagong Girl (IRE)**[34] 4301 2-9-2 55 LukeMorris 2 52
(Jane Chapple-Hyam) *in tch in midfield: effrt u.p over 2f out: no imp tl styd on steadily ins fnl f: nvr enough pce to chal* **8/1**
0566 6 1 ¾ **Smugglers Lane (IRE)**[47] 3847 2-9-3 56 BenCurtis 9 49
(David Evans) *sn towards rr: bhd: hdwy over 1f out: styd on u.p fnl f: nvr trbld ldrs* **14/1**
000 7 ¾ **Hidden Agenda**[41] 4054 2-8-10 49 SteveDrowne 10 40
(Michael Blanshard) *in tch in midfield: rdn and no hdwy over 2f out: rallied ent fnl f: n.d but kpt on* **66/1**
6460 8 1 ¼ **Tommys Geal**[25] 4576 2-8-6 45 WilliamCarson 5 33
(Michael Madgwick) *chsd ldrs: drvn and unable qck ent fnl 2f: btn over 1f out: wknd fnl f* **66/1**
0006 9 8 **Celestine Abbey**[6] 5279 2-8-10 54 ShelleyBirkett(5) 11 24
(Julia Feilden) *in tch in midfield: v wd bnd 3f out: sn rdn and struggling: wknd wl over 1f out* **33/1**
6426 10 2 ¼ **Ho Yam Lay**[24] 4619 2-9-3 56 SebSanders 3 21
(Nick Littmoden) *hld up in midfield: effrt on inner over 2f out: sn btn: wknd over 1f out* **25/1**
005 11 13 **Activation**[17] 4846 2-9-7 60 RichardHughes 12
(Hughie Morrison) *chsd ldrs tl 3f out: sn lost pl: wl btn and eased 1f out: t.o* **4/1**[2]

056 **12** *2 1/4* **Madame Ascension**[10] 5148 2-8-2 46........................ NoelGarbutt(5) 7
(David Evans) *s.i.s: nvr gng wl and a u.p in rr: t.o 2f out* **16/1**
0000 **13** *26* **Now Say Boooom**[9] 5180 2-8-4 46 ow1............. MichaelJMMurphy(3) 8
(Luke Dace) *stdd after s: t.k.h for 2f: sn rdn and detached: t.o over 2f out* **66/1**
1m 42.05s (2.25) **Going Correction** -0.025s/f (Stan) **13** Ran SP% **120.8**
Speed ratings (Par 92): **87,86,84,84,83 81,80,79,71,69 56,54,28**
CSF £34.55 CT £239.57 TOTE £10.20: £2.80, £1.70, £1.90; EX 60.10 Trifecta £754.10.
**Owner** Glanvilles Stud Partners **Bred** R Biggs **Trained** Lambourn, Berks

**FOCUS**
A moderate staying nursery, run in driving rain, in which it paid to race handily. The third looks the best guide.

## 5490 BETVICTOR.COM MAIDEN STKS 1m 4f (P)
**4:00** (4:01) (Class 5) 3-Y-0+ **£2,587** (£770; £384; £192) **Stalls** Centre

Form RPR
62 **1** **Classical Duet (USA)**[13] 5018 3-9-4 0............................ DaneO'Neill 7 82+
(Mark Johnston) *chsd ldrs: rdn and hdwy to ld 2f out: clr whn rn green and hung rt 1f out: r.o wl: readily* **9/4**[2]
3 **2** *5* **Will**[174] 741 3-9-4 0.......................................... SebSanders 1 71
(Nick Littmoden) *chsd ldrs: swtchd rt and effrt on inner 2f out: chsd clr wnr 1f out: no imp but battled on to hold 2nd* **7/1**
44 **3** *hd* **Social Riser (IRE)**[46] 3877 3-8-13 0............................ SteveDrowne 6 66
(Charles Hills) *chsd ldr: rdn and ev ch ent fnl 2f: outpcd by wnr over 1f out: wl btn but battling for placings fnl f: kpt on* **12/1**
030 **4** *nk* **Pas De Cheval (IRE)**[16] 4886 3-9-4 0............................ RyanMoore 2 70
(Sir Michael Stoute) *s.i.s: hld up in last pair: effrt u.p 2f out: no ch w wnr but battling for placings fnl f: kpt on towards fin* **3/1**[3]
5434 **5** *hd* **Micras**[13] 5003 3-8-13 76............................ RichardHughes 4 65
(Andrew Balding) *led: rdn and hdd 2f out: sn outpcd and no ch w wnr 1f out: battling for placings and one pce fnl f* **15/8**[1]
0 **6** *4* **Bally Broadwell**[14] 4966 4-9-9 0............................ LiamKeniry 3 58?
(Michael Madgwick) *in tch in midfield: rdn over 2f out: outpcd 2f out: n.d after* **100/1**
50 **7** *1/2* **May Hay**[14] 4966 4-9-9 0............................ WilliamCarson 8 58
(Anthony Carson) *stdd s: hld up in last pair: rdn over 2f out: drvn and no hdwy 2f out: sn wknd* **66/1**
0 **8** *33* **Battle Group**[26] 4543 9-10-0 0............................(b) SamHitchcott 5 10
(Johnny Farrelly) *s.i.s: bhd: hdwy on outer to chse ldrs 8f out: rdn and dropped out rapidly 4f out: reluctant and lost tch 3f out: t.o* **66/1**
2m 34.62s (0.12) **Going Correction** -0.025s/f (Stan)
**WFA** 3 from 4yo+ 10lb **8** Ran SP% **114.7**
Speed ratings (Par 103): **98,94,94,94,94 91,91,69**
CSF £18.39 TOTE £4.40: £1.20, £1.70, £2.50; EX 19.70 Trifecta £118.30.
**Owner** Sheikh Hamdan bin Mohammed Al Maktoum **Bred** Darley **Trained** Middleham Moor, N Yorks

**FOCUS**
An ordinary maiden but it threw up a taking winner. The form is rated around the second to fourth.

## 5491 KEMPTON LIVE WITH DIZZEE RASCAL 06.09.14 H'CAP 1m 4f (P)
**4:30** (4:30) (Class 6) (0-60,60) 3-Y-O **£1,940** (£577; £288; £144) **Stalls** Centre

Form RPR
4122 **1** **King Calypso**[17] 4844 3-8-6 50............................ CamHardie(5) 8 65+
(Denis Coakley) *hld up in tch: hdwy to chse ldrs 2f out: rdn and qcknd to ld over 1f out: in command but idling ins fnl f: rdn out hands and heels fnl 150yds: a holding on* **4/5**[1]
0-60 **2** *1/2* **Kelamita (IRE)**[54] 3567 3-8-8 47............................ RobertHavlin 7 60
(Hughie Morrison) *pressed ldr: rdn and ev ch 2f out: unable qck w wnr over 1f out: chsd wnr and edgd rt ins fnl f: styd on wl and pressing idling wnr nr fin* **16/1**
03-0 **3** *6* **Ohio (IRE)**[34] 4304 3-8-4 50............................ JordanVaughan(7) 9 54
(Nick Littmoden) *hld up in tch in last pair: hdwy ent fnl 2f: 4th and no imp 1f out: no threat to ldrs but plugged on to snatch 3rd last stride* **16/1**
0044 **4** *shd* **Sparkling Ice (IRE)**[16] 4910 3-9-2 60............................ AmyScott(5) 1 63
(Eve Johnson Houghton) *led: hung lft bnd 3f out: rdn over 2f out: hdd and outpcd over 1f out: 3rd and btn whn hmpd ins fnl f: lost 3rd last stride* **8/1**[2]
3313 **5** *2 1/4* **Assoluta (IRE)**[17] 4844 3-9-5 58............................ LiamKeniry 3 58
(Sylvester Kirk) *hld up in last pair: hdwy over 2f out: drvn and no hdwy wl over 1f out: wknd over 1f out* **8/1**[2]
0053 **6** *4 1/2* **Dark Tsarina (IRE)**[12] 5048 3-8-12 51............................(p) LukeMorris 5 44
(Michael Madgwick) *in tch in midfield: rdn and effrt on inner over 2f out: no prog and btn 2f out: sn wknd* **8/1**[2]
0036 **7** *7* **Ede's The Business**[23] 4658 3-8-11 53............................(v) JemmaMarshall(3) 6 34
(Pat Phelan) *in tch in midfield: struggling u.p over 1f out: wknd wl over 1f out* **10/1**[3]
000- **8** *4 1/2* **Desert Island Dusk**[242] 8340 3-8-7 46 oh1............................ WilliamCarson 4 20
(John Bridger) *dwlt: in tch: rdn over 2f out: sn btn and bhd* **66/1**
0-00 **9** *10* **Zealand (IRE)**[206] 316 3-8-8 47............................(t) SteveDrowne 2
(John Best) *dwlt: sn rcvrd and chsd ldrs: rdn and lost pl over 2f out: sn bhd: t.o* **66/1**
2m 36.79s (2.29) **Going Correction** -0.025s/f (Stan) **9** Ran SP% **112.7**
Speed ratings (Par 98): **91,90,86,86,85 82,77,74,67**
CSF £15.63 CT £118.32 TOTE £1.90: £1.40, £5.00, £4.80; EX 17.10 Trifecta £149.70.
**Owner** Count Calypso Racing **Bred** Miss K Rausing **Trained** West Ilsley, Berks
■ Stewards' Enquiry : Liam Keniry three-day ban: used whip without giving filly time to respond (Sep 1-3)

**FOCUS**
This weak handicap was a steadily run affair. The winner rates a bit better than the bare form and the first two were clear.

## 5492 DOWNLOAD THE BETVICTOR INSTABET APP H'CAP 7f (P)
**5:00** (5:00) (Class 5) (0-70,69) 3-Y-O **£2,587** (£770; £384; £192) **Stalls** Low

Form RPR
0443 **1** **Marydale**[24] 4611 3-9-4 66............................ DaneO'Neill 4 75+
(Henry Candy) *chsd ldrs: rdn to ld ent fnl 2f: styd on wl u.p: clr ins fnl f: rdn out* **7/2**[2]
0041 **2** *1 3/4* **He's My Boy (IRE)**[17] 4862 3-9-3 65............................(v) HayleyTurner 2 69
(James Fanshawe) *hld up in midfield: clsd and travelling wl over 1f out: effrt and rdn to chse wnr over 1f out: r.o same pce fnl f* **6/1**
0641 **3** *1/2* **Cincuenta Pasos (IRE)**[5] 5314 3-9-6 68............................ OisinMurphy 1 71
(Joseph Tuite) *chsd ldrs: effrt and ev ch u.p 2f out: 3rd and unable qck over 1f out: one pce fnl f* **6/4**[1]
0405 **4** *shd* **Scruffy Tramp (IRE)**[12] 5045 3-9-2 69............................ DanielMuscutt(5) 9 71
(John Butler) *hld up in last pair: hdwy and nt clr run 2f out: swtchd lft and hdwy between horses over 1f out: kpt on u.p ins fnl f* **33/1**
0321 **5** *1/2* **Ajig**[13] 5006 3-9-6 68............................ JohnFahy 5 69
(Eve Johnson Houghton) *dwlt and short of room leaving stalls: sn rdn along in rr: hdwy u.p on inner 2f out: keeping on same pce whn swtchd lft and n.m.r towards fin* **5/1**[3]
0040 **6** *11* **Applejack Lad**[13] 5008 3-9-3 65............................(t) MartinLane 7 38
(John Ryan) *w ldr on inner: rdn over 2f out: lost pl rapidly 2f out: sn bhd* **50/1**
-004 **7** *3* **Don't**[11] 5107 3-9-2 69............................ ShelleyBirkett(5) 10 34
(Julia Feilden) *led and grad crossed over towards inner: rdn and hdd 2f out: sn dropped out and bhd* **33/1**
0-40 **8** *1 3/4* **Shaft Of Light**[35] 4263 3-8-11 59............................ LukeMorris 8 19
(Sir Mark Prescott Bt) *in tch in midfield: rdn over 3f out: drvn and lost pl over 2f out: bhd over 1f out* **25/1**
4454 **9** *1 1/4* **Injaz**[11] 5080 3-8-11 59............................(b) MartinHarley 3 16
(Kevin Ryan) *in tch in midfield: hmpd: stmbld and dropped to rr bnd over 4f out: nvr gng wl after: lost tch 2f out* **8/1**
1m 25.07s (-0.93) **Going Correction** -0.025s/f (Stan) **9** Ran SP% **116.0**
Speed ratings (Par 100): **104,102,101,101,100 88,84,82,81**
CSF £23.84 CT £43.62 TOTE £6.60: £1.60, £2.10, £1.10; EX 25.00 Trifecta £87.90.
**Owner** Major M G Wyatt **Bred** Lavington Stud **Trained** Kingston Warren, Oxon
■ Stewards' Enquiry : Luke Morris two-day ban: careless riding (Sep 1-2)

**FOCUS**
Not a bad handicap for the class, run at a god pace. The winner stepped up on her maiden best.
T/Plt: £28.00 to a £1 stake. Pool of £62599.12 - 1627.34 winning tickets. T/Qpdt: £5.10 to a £1 stake. Pool of £6202.75 - 898.90 winning tickets. SP

# 5240 THIRSK (L-H)
### Monday, August 18

**OFFICIAL GOING: Good to soft (soft in places on round course; 7.6)**
Wind: Fresh half behind Weather: Cloudy Rails: Both bends dolled out increasing 7f &8f races by about 10yds and 2m race by 15yds

## 5493 BRITISH STALLION STUDS EBF MAIDEN STKS (BOBIS RACE) 6f
**2:15** (2:17) (Class 4) 2-Y-O **£4,204** (£1,251; £625; £312) **Stalls** High

Form RPR
4 **1** **Caius College Girl (IRE)**[57] 3497 2-9-0 0................ GrahamGibbons 6 78+
(David Barron) *cl up: slt ld wl over 2f out: rdn over 1f out: rdr dropped whip ins fnl f: kpt on wl* **5/1**[3]
35 **2** *2 1/4* **Third Time Lucky (IRE)**[23] 4684 2-9-5 0............................ DavidNolan 1 76
(Richard Fahey) *prom: cl up 1/2-way: rdn 2f out and ev ch: drvn and kpt on same pce fnl f* **5/1**[3]
4 **3** *2 1/4* **Koptoon**[20] 4760 2-9-5 0............................ RichardKingscote 8 70
(Tom Dascombe) *slt ld: pushed along 3f out: sn hdd: drvn wl over 1f out: sn one pce* **7/4**[1]
53 **4** *2 1/4* **Looking Good**[80] 2744 2-9-0 0............................ JamieSpencer 10 58
(David Brown) *chsd ldrs: rdn along 2f out: sn no imp* **11/4**[2]
0 **5** *1* **Ty Ty**[27] 4510 2-9-5 0............................ JamesSullivan 7 60
(Michael Easterby) *wnt lft s: in tch: rdn along over 2f out: sn one pce* **100/1**
0 **6** *hd* **Heading Home (FR)**[58] 3481 2-9-5 0............................ PhillipMakin 4 59
(John Quinn) *dwlt and in rr tl styd on fnl 2f: nrst fin* **25/1**
4 **7** *1 1/2* **Never Easy (IRE)**[22] 4708 2-9-5 0............................ TonyHamilton 2 55
(Richard Fahey) *chsd ldrs: rdn along over 2f out: wknd wl over 1f out* **12/1**
6 **8** *2* **Cape Hideaway**[12] 5050 2-9-5 0............................ JasonHart 9 49+
(Mark Walford) *t.k.h: swvd lft after 1f: a in rr* **100/1**
4 **9** *1 1/2* **Racing Knight (IRE)**[19] 4790 2-9-5 0............................ IanBrennan 3 44
(John Quinn) *towards rr: bmpd and hmpd after 1f: in rr after* **20/1**
05 **10** *1/2* **Phantasmo (IRE)**[13] 4993 2-9-0 0............................ JoeDoyle(5) 5 43
(John Quinn) *chsd ldrs: rdn along 1/2-way: sn wknd* **66/1**
**11** *4* **Lady Cordie** 2-9-0 0............................ GrahamLee 11 26
(Jim Goldie) *in tch on inner: rdn along 1/2-way: sn wknd* **50/1**
1m 12.66s (-0.04) **Going Correction** -0.10s/f (Good) **11** Ran SP% **118.1**
Speed ratings (Par 96): **96,93,90,87,85 85,83,80,78,78 72**
CSF £28.85 TOTE £6.90: £2.30, £2.40, £1.10; EX 26.70 Trifecta £150.60.
**Owner** Clive Washbourn **Bred** Denis McDonnell **Trained** Maunby, N Yorks

**FOCUS**
Probably not a particularly strong maiden for the track, but the winner did it nicely and improved from her debut. The principals dominated from the off, not many threatening a serious blow.

## 5494 BREEDERS BACKING RACING EBF MAIDEN STKS (BOBIS RACE) 1m
**2:45** (2:48) (Class 4) 2-Y-O **£5,498** (£1,636; £817; £408) **Stalls** Low

Form RPR
5 **1** **Banditry (IRE)**[10] 5149 2-9-5 0............................ JamieSpencer 12 77
(Michael Bell) *trckd ldrs: swtchd wd st: led 3f out: rdn and edgd lft 2f out: hung lft to inner rail over 1f out: drvn ins fnl f: hld on wl* **5/4**[1]
**2** *nk* **Adele (GER)** 2-9-0 0............................ JoeFanning 5 73+
(Mark Johnston) *in tch: hdwy over 3f out: rdn and cl up whn hmpd over 2f out: sn swtchd rt and styd on to chal ins fnl f: sn drvn and jst hld* **7/1**[3]
55 **3** *3 3/4* **Joshua Potman (IRE)**[15] 4935 2-9-5 0............................ RichardKingscote 8 68
(Tom Dascombe) *led: pushed along and hdd 3f out: sn rdn and edgd rt: drvn wl over 1f out: kpt on same pce* **33/1**
0 **4** *5* **Boldbob (IRE)**[24] 4633 2-9-5 0............................ GrahamLee 7 56
(Micky Hammond) *chsd ldng pair on inner: rdn along wl over 2f out: sn one pce* **66/1**
**5** *2* **Burneston** 2-9-5 0............................ PJMcDonald 3 52
(James Bethell) *towards rr: hdwy and in tch 1/2-way: rdn along 3f out: sn no imp* **9/1**
**6** *1 1/4* **Convicted (FR)** 2-9-5 0............................ StevieDonohoe 14 49
(Ian Williams) *cl up: pushed along 1/2-way: rdn 3f out: sn wknd* **50/1**
**7** *hd* **Game Show** 2-9-5 0............................ PhillipMakin 4 48+
(Charlie Appleby) *dwlt: in rr and hmpd after 1f: pushed along 4f out: rdn and green 3f out: hdwy wl over 1f out: edgd rt ent fnl f: nrst fin* **7/2**[2]
0 **8** *2 1/2* **Ellerina**[42] 4018 2-9-0 0............................ MichaelStainton 11 38+
(Chris Fairhurst) *in tch on outer: hdwy to chse ldrs 3f out: rdn over 2f out: sn drvn and grad wknd* **100/1**
**9** *hd* **Multellie** 2-9-5 0............................ DavidAllan 15 42+
(Tim Easterby) *s.i.s: a towards rr* **20/1**
00 **10** *1 1/4* **Poet Mark (IRE)**[16] 4885 2-9-5 0............................(b) JasonHart 6 39
(Tim Easterby) *dwlt: a in rr* **100/1**
**11** *6* **La Vien Zen (IRE)** 2-9-0 0............................ PaulMulrennan 13 20+
(Ann Duffield) *racd wd: a towards rr* **12/1**

12 *11* **Xander (IRE)** 2-9-5 0 RobertWinston 1
(Tim Easterby) *midfield: pushed along over 3f out: sn outpcd* **20/1**

1m 46.09s (5.99) **Going Correction** +0.50s/f (Yiel) **12 Ran SP% 114.8**
Speed ratings (Par 96): **90,89,85,80,78 77,77,75,74,73 67,56**
CSF £9.36 TOTE £2.20: £1.10, £2.40, £4.20; EX 10.80 Trifecta £127.20.
**Owner** Sheikh Marwan Al Maktoum **Bred** Darley **Trained** Newmarket, Suffolk
■ Dew Pond and Egmont were withdrawn. Prices at time of withdrawal were 33/1 and 50/1 respectively. Rule 4 does not apply.
■ Stewards' Enquiry : Richard Kingscote caution: careless riding.
**FOCUS**
The leading pair came clear in an ordinary maiden which lacked depth, the majority of those in behind looking more ones for the longer term.

## 5495 RACING UK ANYWHERE AVAILABLE NOW H'CAP 1m 4f
**3:15** (3:15) (Class 6) (0-65,65) 3-Y-0+ **£3,234** (£962; £481; £240) **Stalls Low**

Form RPR

6660 **1** **A Little Bit Dusty**[41] 4058 6-10-0 65 (p) PaulMulrennan 9 74
(Conor Dore) *hld up in rr: stdy hdwy to trck ldrs 1/2-way: cl up 3f out: chal 2f out: sn rdn and edgd sltly lft: drvn ent fnl f: kpt on to ld nr fin* **14/1**

0641 **2** *nk* **Midnight Warrior**[14] 4958 4-8-7 49 JackGarritty(5) 16 58
(Ron Barr) *prom: cl up after 4f: slt ld 3f out: rdn along over 2f out: edgd rt and rdr dropped reins over 1f out: sn drvn: hdd and no ex nr fin* **14/1**

0466 **3** *1 1/2* **In Vino Veritas (IRE)**[20] 4754 3-9-2 63 (v1) PJMcDonald 5 69
(Ann Duffield) *trckd ldrs on inner: hdwy over 3f out: rdn along over 2f out: drvn wl over 1f out: kpt on fnl f* **25/1**

4455 **4** *1 1/2* **Amazing Blue Sky**[10] 5145 8-9-0 51 JamesSullivan 12 55
(Ruth Carr) *hld up towards rr: hdwy over 3f out: rdn over 2f out: drvn over 1f out: kpt on same pce fnl f* **10/1[3]**

4503 **5** *1/2* **Rokeby**[7] 5239 3-8-3 50 AndrewMullen 10 53
(George Moore) *towards rr: hdwy 3f out: rdn along 2f out: kpt on appr fnl f: nrst fin* **18/1**

0402 **6** *1/2* **Grand Liaison**[14] 4979 5-9-11 62 GrahamLee 11 64
(James Given) *in tch: hdwy over 3f out: rdn to chse ldrs over 2f out: drvn along wl over 1f out: sn one pce* **7/1[2]**

/0-4 **7** *1/2* **Oliver's Gold**[30] 959 6-8-4 46 oh1 GemmaTutty(5) 6 47
(Mark Walford) *midfield: effrt and sme hdwy on inner over 2f out: sn rdn along and kpt on fnl f: n.d* **6/1[1]**

0120 **8** *2 1/4* **Sirpertan**[80] 2735 3-8-9 56 IanBrennan 14 54
(Marjorie Fife) *led: rdn along 4f out: hdd 3f out: sn drvn and wknd wl over 1f out* **7/1[2]**

411 **9** *1 1/4* **Diddy Eric**[6] 5268 4-9-7 58 6ex (b) JamieSpencer 8 59
(Micky Hammond) *hld up: a towards rr* **6/1[1]**

0615 **10** *1* **Pim Street (USA)**[23] 4665 4-9-7 61 SamJames(3) 2 55
(David O'Meara) *a towards rr* **16/1**

-002 **11** *1/2* **Different Scenario**[4] 5331 3-8-0 47 oh2 RoystonFfrench 15 40
(Mel Brittain) *chsd ldrs: rdn along over 3f out: wknd over 2f out* **7/1[2]**

2-00 **12** *2 3/4* **Hero's Story**[52] 3661 4-9-0 54 GaryBartley(3) 4 43
(Jim Goldie) *a towards rr* **33/1**

0-50 **13** *3/4* **Carthaginian (IRE)**[34] 4296 5-9-9 60 (p) PhillipMakin 7 48
(Martin Todhunter) *midfield: hdwy and in tch 4f out: effrt on outer 3f out: sn rdn and wknd wl over 1f out* **50/1**

4060 **14** *24* **Cayjo**[11] 5101 3-8-3 50 JoeFanning 3
(Mark Johnston) *chsd ldng pair: rdn along over 3f out: sn wknd* **22/1**

40-6 **15** *2 1/4* **Rocked The Boat**[11] 5101 3-9-2 63 DanielTudhope 13 9
(David O'Meara) *a in rr* **10/1[3]**

2m 42.65s (6.45) **Going Correction** +0.50s/f (Yiel)
**WFA** 3 from 4yo+ 10lb **15 Ran SP% 121.8**
Speed ratings (Par 101): **98,97,96,95,95 95,94,93,92,91 91,89,89,73,71**
CSF £190.90 CT £4800.95 TOTE £16.90: £4.00, £7.70, £12.00; EX 353.40 Trifecta £2570.60 Part won..
**Owner** David Baldwin & Chris Marsh **Bred** T O C S Limited **Trained** Hubbert's Bridge, Lincs
**FOCUS**
A modest handicap. The gallop appeared sound, but not that many ever threatened to land a serious blow. Ordinary form.

## 5496 HERRIOTWORLD.COM H'CAP 1m
**3:45** (3:45) (Class 4) (0-80,80) 3-Y-0+ **£4,851** (£1,443; £721; £360) **Stalls Low**

Form RPR

3520 **1** **Shouranour (IRE)**[22] 4710 4-9-10 76 (p) DanielTudhope 5 94
(David O'Meara) *trckd ldng pair: hdwy 3f out: lft 2nd and cl up over 3f out: led wl over 2f out: rdn clr over 1f out: styd on* **11/2[2]**

0511 **2** *3 3/4* **Bahamian C**[31] 4387 3-9-0 75 GeorgeChaloner(3) 8 83
(Richard Fahey) *hld up towards rr: hdwy over 3f out: sn chsng ldrs: rdn wl over 1f out: sn chsng wnr: drvn and no imp fnl f* **15/2**

4603 **3** *2* **Instant Attraction (IRE)**[9] 5197 3-9-3 80 JackGarritty(5) 9 84
(Jedd O'Keeffe) *chsd ldrs: effrt 3f out: rdn along over 2f out: drvn over 1f out and kpt on one pce* **9/2[1]**

2213 **4** *2* **Ellaal**[6] 5268 5-9-9 75 DaleSwift 4 75
(Ruth Carr) *trckd ldr: lft in ld over 3f out: sn jnd: hdd wl over 2f out: sn rdn and edgd lft: drvn wl over 1f out and grad wknd* **9/1**

5364 **5** *hd* **Icy Blue**[12] 5054 6-8-9 61 oh1 (p) JoeFanning 6 61
(Richard Whitaker) *towards rr: hdwy 3f out: chsd ldrs 2f out: sn rdn and kpt on one pce* **7/1**

6240 **6** *5* **Mac's Superstar (FR)**[30] 4447 4-9-11 77 ShaneKelly 7 65
(James Fanshawe) *hld up: hdwy over 3f out: chsd ldrs over 2f out: sn rdn: drvn wl over 1f out and sn btn* **14/1**

10 **7** *3/4* **Cool Music (IRE)**[65] 3254 4-9-9 75 DavidAllan 11 61
(Mel Brittain) *a towards rr* **25/1**

1430 **8** *1 1/2* **Hakuna Matata**[9] 5196 7-9-13 79 (b) PaulMulrennan 1 62
(Michael Dods) *dwlt and in rr: hdwy 3f out: rdn along over 2f out: sn drvn and n.d* **14/1**

002 **9** *1/2* **Rocket Ronnie (IRE)**[20] 4753 4-9-9 75 AdrianNicholls 13 57
(David Nicholls) *hld up: a towards rr* **6/1[3]**

5120 **10** *1 1/2* **Sandra's Diamond (IRE)**[20] 4761 3-9-8 80 GrahamLee 12 57
(Keith Dalgleish) *led tl hung bdly rt and rn wd bnd over 3f out: sn bhd* **12/1**

3232 **11** *4 1/2* **Celtic Sixpence (IRE)**[18] 4831 6-9-9 75 MichaelStainton 10 43
(Nick Kent) *chsd ldrs on outer: rdn along 3f out: wknd over 2f out* **14/1**

0240 **12** *2 3/4* **Wannabe King**[9] 5196 8-9-13 79 (p) PJMcDonald 3 41
(Geoffrey Harker) *in tch: hdwy on inner over 3f out: sn chsng ldrs: rdn wl over 2f out and sn wknd* **20/1**

5/0- **13** *15* **Cape Explorer**[417] 3729 5-9-4 70 PaulPickard 2
(Brian Ellison) *v.s.a: a wl bhd* **50/1**

1m 42.94s (2.84) **Going Correction** +0.50s/f (Yiel)
**WFA** 3 from 4yo+ 6lb **13 Ran SP% 120.4**
Speed ratings (Par 105): **105,101,99,97,97 92,91,89,89,87 83,80,65**
CSF £45.88 CT £205.11 TOTE £3.70: £1.10, £3.30, £2.40; EX 44.40 Trifecta £153.10.
**Owner** Mrs Lynne Lumley **Bred** His Highness The Aga Khan's Studs S C **Trained** Nawton, N Yorks
**FOCUS**
A one-sided handicap, the winner being much improved and chased home by some in-form horses, so there's no reason to doubt the merit of his effort.

## 5497 BET ON THE MOVE - RACING UK'S APP H'CAP 7f
**4:15** (4:16) (Class 5) (0-75,75) 3-Y-0 **£3,234** (£962; £481; £240) **Stalls Low**

Form RPR

4040 **1** **Comino (IRE)**[25] 4572 3-9-4 72 JamieSpencer 5 80+
(Kevin Ryan) *prom: hdwy and cl up 3f out: chal over 2f out: rdn to ld and hung lft 1 1/2f out: drvn out* **4/1[3]**

514 **2** *1 1/4* **We'll Shake Hands (FR)**[30] 4465 3-9-3 71 DanielTudhope 6 75
(K R Burke) *sn cl up: chal 3f out: rdn and ev ch whn hmpd 1 1/2f out: sn swtchd rt and drvn to chse wnr ins fnl f: kpt on* **11/4[1]**

432 **3** *shd* **Piccadilly Jim (IRE)**[61] 3370 3-8-13 67 TonyHamilton 8 70
(Richard Fahey) *in rr and sn pushed along: rdn and hdwy 2f out: n.m.r and nt clr run ent fnl f: sn swtchd rt and fin strly* **7/2[2]**

5236 **4** *nk* **Heroique (IRE)**[11] 5097 3-9-3 71 (e) RobertWinston 4 74
(Tim Easterby) *led: rdn along and jnd 3f out: cl up on inner whn n.m.r wl over 1f out: drvn and kpt on same pce fnl f* **5/1**

2260 **5** *1/2* **Zain Zone (IRE)**[9] 5197 3-9-7 75 JamesSullivan 10 76
(Ruth Carr) *dwlt and in rr: hdwy 3f out: chsd ldrs 2f out: sn rdn and no imp fnl f* **7/1**

2450 **6** *3/4* **Playtothewhistle**[19] 4791 3-8-9 63 PaulMulrennan 3 62
(Bryan Smart) *hld up towards rr: hdwy on wd outside 3f out: rdn over 2f out: styd on appr fnl f: nrst fin* **25/1**

-006 **7** *4 1/2* **Sleeping Star**[83] 2657 3-8-2 56 oh3 RoystonFfrench 11 44
(Mel Brittain) *chsd ldrs on outer: hdwy to chse ldng pair over 3f out: rdn wl over 2f out: drvn 2f out and sn wknd* **33/1**

1360 **8** *10* **Bajan Rebel**[44] 3950 3-8-4 58 AndrewMullen 2 20
(Michael Easterby) *trckd ldng pair: effrt over 3f out: sn rdn and wknd* **10/1**

030- **9** *4* **Chamberlain**[276] 7902 3-9-1 69 JasonHart 1 20
(John Murray) *in tch: rdn along wl over 2f out: sn wknd* **50/1**

1m 30.93s (3.73) **Going Correction** +0.50s/f (Yiel) **9 Ran SP% 115.9**
Speed ratings (Par 100): **98,96,96,96,95 94,89,78,73**
CSF £15.26 CT £41.70 TOTE £6.10: £2.20, £1.40, £1.40; EX 17.70 Trifecta £56.40.
**Owner** Exors of the late D W Barker **Bred** Tom Twomey **Trained** Hambleton, N Yorks
**FOCUS**
A fair handicap which was soundly run. The winner is rated back to his C&D maiden win form.

## 5498 DOWNLOAD NEW RACING UK IPAD APP H'CAP 5f
**4:45** (4:45) (Class 4) (0-80,80) 4-Y-0+ **£4,851** (£1,443; £721; £360) **Stalls High**

Form RPR

6543 **1** **Go Go Green (IRE)**[7] 5236 8-8-8 70 GaryBartley(3) 5 78
(Jim Goldie) *sltly hmpd s and in rr: hdwy 1/2-way: chsd ldrs over 1f out: sn rdn and str run ent fnl f: led last 100yds: hld on* **14/1**

3466 **2** *nse* **Haajes**[28] 4494 10-8-9 68 (v) GrahamLee 11 76
(Paul Midgley) *in tch: hdwy wl over 1f out: swtchd lft and rdn ent fnl f: drvn and styd on wl towards fin: jst hld* **8/1[3]**

1005 **3** *1/2* **Head Space (IRE)**[9] 5199 6-9-6 79 (v) JamesSullivan 6 85
(Ruth Carr) *towards rr: pushed along 1/2-way: gd hdwy on outer wl over 1f out: rdn and ev ch ins fnl f: no ex towards fin* **11/2[2]**

500 **4** *1/2* **Hazelrigg (IRE)**[5] 5298 9-8-12 71 DavidAllan 7 75
(Tim Easterby) *trckd ldrs: swtchd rt to inner wl over 1f out: rdn and ev ch ent fnl f: nt qckn towards fin* **16/1**

3125 **5** *nk* **Tyfos**[31] 4391 9-9-5 78 JasonHart 14 81
(Brian Baugh) *cl up: rdn to ld wl over 1f out: drvn and hdd ins fnl f: no ex* **11/1**

2002 **6** *1* **Captain Royale (IRE)**[16] 4901 9-8-9 73 (p) JacobButterfield(5) 9 73
(Tracy Waggott) *in tch: hdwy 2f out: sn rdn: kpt on fnl f: nrst fin* **20/1**

0200 **7** *nk* **Oldjoesaid**[13] 5016 10-9-2 75 PhillipMakin 8 73
(Paul Midgley) *towards rr: hdwy 2f out: sn rdn and kpt on fnl f: nrst fin* **12/1**

5 **8** *1 3/4* **Sir Geoffrey (IRE)**[6] 5290 8-8-3 67 (p) MatthewHopkins(5) 15 59
(Scott Dixon) *cl up: rdn along 2f out: sn drvn and grad wknd* **20/1**

0000 **9** *nk* **Tax Free (IRE)**[29] 4471 12-9-2 75 AdrianNicholls 4 66
(David Nicholls) *in tch: rdn along and hdwy to chse ldrs 2f out: sn drvn and no imp appr fnl f* **20/1**

3232 **10** *hd* **Gowanharry (IRE)**[9] 5170 5-9-5 78 (tp) PaulMulrennan 12 68
(Michael Dods) *trckd ldrs: hdwy and cl up 2f out: sn rdn and ev ch tl drvn and wknd appr fnl f* **11/4[1]**

0556 **11** *1 1/4* **Bronze Beau**[18] 4833 7-8-8 70 (t) NataliaGemelova(3) 2 56
(Kristin Stubbs) *cl up on outer: rdn along wl over 1f out: grad wknd* **16/1**

1010 **12** *1 3/4* **Captain Dunne (IRE)**[13] 5016 9-9-0 80 (p) RachelRichardson(7) 13 60
(Tim Easterby) *cl up: led over 3f out: rdn along 2f out: sn hdd and grad wknd appr fnl f* **14/1**

5000 **13** *6* **Mayfield Girl (IRE)**[4] 5333 4-8-11 70 PJMcDonald 3 28
(Mel Brittain) *dwlt: a in rr* **20/1**

2105 **14** *3/4* **Green Monkey**[34] 4305 4-9-6 79 ShaneKelly 10 34
(James Fanshawe) *swtchd rt to stands; rail s: a in rr* **18/1**

59.99s (0.39) **Going Correction** +0.225s/f (Good) **14 Ran SP% 118.6**
Speed ratings (Par 105): **105,104,104,103,102 101,100,97,97,97 95,92,82,81**
CSF £112.48 CT £708.57 TOTE £15.60: £4.50, £3.00, £2.50; EX 165.60 Trifecta £2154.20.
**Owner** Johnnie Delta Racing **Bred** Edmond And Richard Kent **Trained** Uplawmoor, E Renfrews
**FOCUS**
A fair handicap. The leaders went hard, setting it up for those coming from behind. The form makes sense.

## 5499 RACINGUK.COM/ANYWHERE: 3 DEVICES, 1 PRICE LADY AMATEUR RIDERS' H'CAP 6f
**5:15** (5:17) (Class 6) (0-60,60) 3-Y-0+ **£2,495** (£774; £386; £193) **Stalls High**

Form RPR

-060 **1** **Liliargh (IRE)**[74] 2911 5-9-3 45 (v) MissMeganNicholls(5) 5 54
(Ben Haslam) *towards rr: hdwy on outer 2f out: rdn over 1f out: styd on ent fnl f: led last 50yds* **10/1**

5405 **2** *hd* **Cahal (IRE)**[13] 4998 3-9-10 55 MissPFuller(5) 14 63
(David Nicholls) *chsd ldrs: hdwy 2f out: rdn to ld ent fnl f: sn edgd lft: hdd and no ex last 50yds* **7/2[1]**

0055 **3** *2* **New Lease Of Life**[21] 4730 5-10-0 51 (p) MrsCBartley 12 53
(Jim Goldie) *hld up: hdwy 2f out: sn rdn: styd on fnl f: nrst fin* **8/1**

6-06 **4** *3/4* **Old Man Clegg**[111] 1839 4-10-4 58 (t) MissJoannaMason(3) 9 57+
(Michael Easterby) *dwlt and in rr: pushed along 1/2-way: hdwy nr stands' rail wl over 1f out: styd on strly fnl f: nrst fin* **12/1**

4065 **5** *1* **Spowarticus**[19] 4795 5-9-5 47 (b1) MissKMargarson(5) 4 43
(Scott Dixon) *cl up: led over 2f out: rdn wl over 1f out: hdd ent fnl f: one pce* **18/1**

3003 **6** *nk* **A J Cook (IRE)**[3] 5375 4-9-13 50....(v) MissCWalton 8 45
(Ron Barr) *hld up in midfield: hdwy 2f out: rdn to chse ldrs over 1f out: kpt on same pce fnl f* **6/1**[2]

330 **7** *½* **Senora Lobo (IRE)**[53] 3630 4-9-8 45....(p) MissSBrotherton 1 38
(Lisa Williamson) *wnt lft s: sn trcking ldrs on outer: hdwy and cl up 1/2-way: effrt 2f out and sn ev ch tl rdn and wknd ent fnl f* **22/1**

4023 **8** *2½* **Amis Reunis**[6] 5265 5-10-4 55....(p) MissADeniel 3 40
(Alan Berry) *slt ld: rdn along and hdd over 2f out: cl up tl drvn and wknd appr fnl f* **7/1**[3]

0400 **9** *2* **The Strig**[3] 5390 7-9-13 55....(v) MissLWilson(5) 10 34
(Nigel Tinkler) *a towards rr* **14/1**

4511 **10** *nk* **Two Turtle Doves (IRE)**[6] 5290 8-10-6 60 6ex.... MissMMullineaux(3) 7 38
(Michael Mullineaux) *midfield: hdwy over 2f out: sn rdn and n.d* **8/1**

6600 **11** *¾* **Thewestwalian (USA)**[14] 4960 6-9-1 45.... MissMollyKing(7) 2 21
(Peter Hiatt) *sn prom: rdn along wl over 2f out: sn wknd* **33/1**

500 **12** *3¼* **Bay Street Belle**[30] 4455 3-9-13 60.... MissAMKeighley(7) 6 25
(David Barron) *midfield rdn along bef 1/2-way: sn lost pl and bhd* **66/1**

0/40 **13** *9* **Under Review (IRE)**[25] 4564 8-9-11 53....(t) MissHHeal(5) 13
(Liam Corcoran) *chsd ldrs: rdn along 2f out: sn hung lft and wknd* **50/1**

1046 **14** *9* **Red Invader (IRE)**[65] 3231 4-10-0 56.... MrsRWilson(5) 11
(Paul D'Arcy) *chsd ldrs: rdn along 2f out: sn wknd* **8/1**

1m 14.63s (1.93) **Going Correction** +0.225s/f (Good)
**WFA** 3 from 4yo+ 3lb **14** Ran SP% **121.8**
Speed ratings (Par 101): **96,95,93,92,90 90,89,86,83,83 82,77,65,53**
CSF £44.25 CT £313.57 TOTE £13.90: £6.00, £2.10, £3.70; EX 58.20 Trifecta £294.10.
**Owner** Middleham Park Racing XXVII **Bred** Camogue Stud Ltd **Trained** Middleham Moor, N Yorks

**FOCUS**
A run-of-the-mill amateur event. It was run at a good pace. The winner had regressed and took advantage of a weight drop.
T/Jkpt: Not won. T/Plt: £331.30 to a £1 stake. Pool of £80868.86 - 178.17 winning tickets. T/Qpdt: £373.80 to a £1 stake. Pool of £6264.11 - 12.40 winning tickets. JR

## 5247 WINDSOR (R-H)
### Monday, August 18

**OFFICIAL GOING: Good changing to good to soft after race 1 (5.30)**
Wind: Behind, fresh race 1, becoming light Weather: Changeable - shower before race 5 Rails: Top bend dolled out 14yds from normal inner configuration adding 53yds to races of one mile and beyond. Inner of Straight dolled out 14yds at 6f and 6yds at Winning Pos

### 5500 BRITISH STALLION STUDS EBF MAIDEN STKS 6f
**5:30** (5:31) (Class 5) 2-Y-O **£2,911** (£866; £432; £216) **Stalls** Low

Form RPR

**1** **Aces (IRE)** 2-9-5 0.... HarryBentley 4 80+
(Charles Hills) *trckd ldrs: wnt 2nd over 2f out: rdn over 1f out: styd on wl to ld last 75yds* **8/1**

42 **2** *1* **Skate**[19] 4787 2-9-5 0.... JamesDoyle 3 77
(Roger Charlton) *mde most: rdn over 1f out: kpt on but hdd and nt qckn last 75yds* **2/1**[1]

02 **3** *4* **Lackaday**[7] 5248 2-9-5 0.... WilliamTwiston-Davies 11 65
(Mick Channon) *in tch on outer: prog over 2f out: chsd ldng pair over 1f out: outpcd fnl f* **5/1**[3]

**4** *nk* **Royal Rettie** 2-8-11 0....[1] AshleyMorgan(3) 1 59
(Amy Weaver) *hld up in midfield: sme prog 2f out: outpcd by ldng pair but styd on fnl f and nrly snatched 3rd* **66/1**

45 **5** *2½* **Romance Story (IRE)**[24] 4626 2-9-0 0.... ChrisCatlin 8 52
(Saeed bin Suroor) *w ldr: pushed along 1/2-way: lost 2nd over 2f out: steadily fdd* **12/1**

**6** *shd* **Kingston Sassafras** 2-9-5 0.... JackMitchell 12 56
(Ed Walker) *hld up in last trio: pushed along on outer over 2f out: sme prog over 1f out: rn green and no ch but kpt on* **33/1**

3 **7** *1½* **Bridgekeeper**[18] 4829 2-9-2 0.... RyanTate(3) 2 52
(James Eustace) *trckd ldrs: pushed along over 2f out: steadily wknd wl over 1f out* **14/1**

**8** *2* **El Fenix (IRE)** 2-9-5 0.... RyanMoore 9 46
(Gary Moore) *dwlt: hld up in last pair: pushed along and sme prog on outer over 2f out: no hdwy over 1f out: wknd* **5/2**[2]

**9** *shd* **Herecomestheband** 2-9-5 0.... PatCosgrave 6 46
(George Baker) *slowly away: sn pushed along in last trio: nvr on terms* **33/1**

**10** *nk* **Reflation** 2-9-5 0.... RichardHughes 10 45
(Richard Hannon) *trckd ldrs: pushed along 1/2-way: lost pl over 2f out: wknd* **12/1**

05 **11** *hd* **Retro Valley (IRE)**[14] 4965 2-9-5 0.... SebSanders 7 44
(David Dennis) *pushed along in midfield bef 1/2-way: wknd over 1f out* **66/1**

1m 13.11s (0.11) **Going Correction** +0.075s/f (Good) **11** Ran SP% **120.6**
Speed ratings (Par 94): **102,100,95,94,91 91,89,86,86,86 86**
CSF £24.65 TOTE £8.60: £2.30, £1.20, £1.80; EX 28.20 Trifecta £115.10.
**Owner** Qatar Racing & Essafinaat **Bred** Lady Janet Brookeborough **Trained** Lambourn, Berks

**FOCUS**
Ground officially described as good but it was changed to good to soft after this opener. This looked quite a warm maiden with a few of the newcomers looking very interesting on paper. The winner should improve.

### 5501 188BET H'CAP 5f 10y
**6:00** (6:01) (Class 4) (0-85,85) 3-Y-O **£5,175** (£1,540; £769; £384) **Stalls** Low

Form RPR

2332 **1** **Newton's Law (IRE)**[7] 5249 3-8-9 73....(t[1]) RichardHughes 7 82
(Brian Meehan) *pressed ldr: cajoled into ld over 1f out: sn hrd pressed: rdn and fnd enough last 100yds* **15/8**[1]

-514 **2** *½* **Cordial**[8] 5204 3-8-10 74.... HarryBentley 4 81
(Stuart Williams) *trckd ldng trio: rdn and prog to chal jst over 1f out: pressed wnr fnl f: nt qckn last 75yds* **8/1**

4012 **3** *1* **Poetic Choice**[17] 4862 3-8-11 75.... JamesDoyle 1 78
(Nick Littmoden) *trckd ldng pair: waiting for a gap fr 2f out: shkn up and styd on fnl f but too late to threaten* **7/2**[3]

2-12 **4** *1* **Jacob's Pillow**[34] 4281 3-9-7 85....(p) RyanMoore 2 85
(William Haggas) *hld up in 5th: pushed along 2f out: reminder and kpt on same pce fnl f: nvr threatened* **2/1**[2]

3251 **5** *½* **My Inspiration (IRE)**[7] 5249 3-8-10 79 6ex.... NathanAlison(5) 6 77
(Jim Boyle) *v awkward s: in tch in last: effrt on outer 2f out: nt qckn over 1f out: one pce after* **9/1**

635 **6** *2½* **Mr Dandy Man (IRE)**[24] 4636 3-8-10 74....(p) SteveDrowne 3 63
(Ronald Harris) *led to over 1f out: wknd qckly fnl f* **25/1**

1m 0.24s (-0.06) **Going Correction** +0.075s/f (Good) **6** Ran SP% **115.3**
Speed ratings (Par 102): **103,102,100,99,98 94**
CSF £17.76 TOTE £3.30: £1.90, £3.70; EX 17.20 Trifecta £76.60.
**Owner** Bayardo **Bred** Ballylinch Stud **Trained** Manton, Wilts

**FOCUS**
A trappy 3yo handicap. The winner reversed C&D latest with the fifth.

### 5502 WARHORSE FIREWORKS AT ROYAL WINDSOR RACECOURSE (S) STKS 1m 3f 135y
**6:30** (6:30) (Class 6) 3-Y-O+ **£1,940** (£577; £288; £144) **Stalls** Centre

Form RPR

500/ **1** **Nebula Storm (IRE)**[297] 7630 7-9-3 85....(v) HectorCrouch(7) 2 73
(Gary Moore) *trckd ldng pair: chal 3f out: led over 2f out: urged along and drew clr jst over 1f out* **5/1**

3223 **2** *3¼* **Gift Of Silence**[13] 4996 5-9-5 64.... PaddyAspell 1 63
(John Berry) *t.k.h: hld up in 4th: clsd to ld 3f out: hdd over 2f out: steadily lft bhd by wnr over 1f out* **5/2**[2]

1451 **3** *¾* **Incendo**[13] 4996 8-10-1 73....(v) HayleyTurner 5 72
(Conor Dore) *stdd s: hld up in last: in trble once pce lifted 3f out: drvn into 3rd 2f out: nvr able to cl* **5/4**[1]

225 **4** *1½* **Mr Lando**[21] 4734 5-9-10 60.... JimmyQuinn 3 64
(Tony Carroll) *plld hrd: trckd ldr: tried to chal 3f out: sn lft bhd and btn* **9/2**[3]

00/3 **5** *9* **Safe Investment (USA)**[12] 5030 10-9-10 46(tp) WilliamTwiston-Davies 6 49
(Lawney Hill) *led at mod pce: shkn up and hdd 3f out: sn wknd* **33/1**

2m 32.46s (2.96) **Going Correction** +0.15s/f (Good) **5** Ran SP% **110.8**
Speed ratings (Par 101): **96,93,93,92,86**
CSF £17.81 TOTE £6.20: £2.60, £1.40; EX 17.50 Trifecta £32.40.There was no bid for the winner.
**Owner** R Macnabb **Bred** Sunderland Holdings Ltd **Trained** Lower Beeding, W Sussex

**FOCUS**
Modest form, the fourth and fifth giving some perspective.

### 5503 188BET FILLIES' H'CAP 1m 2f 7y
**7:00** (7:00) (Class 5) (0-75,74) 4-Y-O+ **£2,911** (£866; £432; £216) **Stalls** Centre

Form RPR

221 **1** **If I Were A Boy (IRE)**[35] 4273 7-8-13 66....(p) JimCrowley 4 74
(Dominic Ffrench Davis) *trckd ldng quartet: rdn over 2f out: prog over 1f out: r.o to ld last 75yds: jst hld on* **7/1**

34-5 **2** *shd* **Rainbow Beauty**[45] 3918 4-9-0 72....(tp) CamHardie(5) 5 79
(Richard Ford) *dwlt: hld up in last and wl off the pce: shkn up over 3f out: prog on outer over 2f out: clsd to chal and w wnr last 75yds: jst hld* **4/1**[2]

1130 **3** *½* **Martinas Delight (USA)**[8] 5203 4-9-6 73.... JamesDoyle 2 79
(Timothy Jarvis) *led: rdn and sent for home jst over 3f out: hrd drvn over 1f out: hdd and no ex last 75yds* **16/1**

3041 **4** *3½* **Play Street**[19] 4799 5-9-2 74.... NedCurtis(5) 3 73
(Jonathan Portman) *trckd ldrs: rdn over 3f out: hanging lft sn after: wnt 2nd 2f out: no imp on ldr over 1f out: wknd ins fnl f* **10/1**

0444 **5** *1* **Lady Bayside**[4] 5340 6-9-2 69.... RichardHughes 7 66
(Malcolm Saunders) *hld up in 7th and wl off the pce: shkn up over 3f out: clsd over 2f out: rdn over 1f out: wknd fnl f* **6/1**[3]

3136 **6** *2* **Stockhill Diva**[32] 4354 4-9-4 71.... LiamKeniry 1 65
(Brendan Powell) *t.k.h: trckd ldrs: cl up in 3rd 3f out: rdn to dispute 2nd 2f out: nt qckn over 1f out: fdd* **6/1**[3]

2451 **7** *2¼* **Trulee Scrumptious**[3] 5394 5-8-12 65 6ex....(v) JimmyQuinn 9 54
(Peter Charalambous) *s.i.s: sn trckd ldr: tried to chal over 3f out: nt qckn and lost 2nd 2f out: wknd* **7/4**[1]

400- **8** *12* **Hermosa Vaquera (IRE)**[99] 7628 4-8-3 56.... HayleyTurner 8 22
(Anna Newton-Smith) *hld up in 6th and wl off the pce: pushed along over 3f out: sn wknd: t.o* **50/1**

2m 9.1s (0.40) **Going Correction** +0.15s/f (Good) **8** Ran SP% **114.4**
Speed ratings (Par 100): **104,103,103,100,99 98,96,86**
CSF £35.09 CT £432.85 TOTE £4.80: £1.70, £1.90, £3.60; EX 46.80 Trifecta £830.40.
**Owner** R F Haynes **Bred** Kilco Builders **Trained** Lambourn, Berks

**FOCUS**
An open fillies' handicap run at what looked a strong pace and that dragged the closers into the reckoning in the final half furlong. The winner is rated back to her form of two years ago.

### 5504 188BET CASINO MAIDEN STKS 1m 67y
**7:30** (7:34) (Class 5) 3-4-Y-O **£2,911** (£866; £432; £216) **Stalls** Low

Form RPR

2 **1** **Shama's Crown (IRE)**[16] 4886 3-9-0 0.... RyanMoore 7 79+
(Jeremy Noseda) *taken down early: wl in tch in midfield: prog on wd outside over 2f out: shkn up to ld over 1f out and sn in command: rdn out nr fin* **4/5**[1]

33 **2** *2* **Labise (IRE)**[138] 1233 3-9-0 0....(t) OisinMurphy 4 74
(Ralph Beckett) *chsd ldrs: rdn 3f out: prog to go 2nd over 1f out but no ch w wnr: kpt on* **7/1**

2203 **3** *1¼* **Rome**[12] 5040 4-9-11 78.... JamesDoyle 5 77
(Gary Moore) *prom: rdn 3f out: nt qckn and lost pl: styd on again fr over 1f out to take 3rd ins fnl f* **5/1**[2]

4 **4** *1* **Golden Emerald**[12] 5039 3-9-5 0.... HayleyTurner 6 74+
(James Fanshawe) *dwlt: in tch in midfield: pushed along fr 3f out: reminder 2f out: nvr going pce to be on terms but styd on to take 4th last strides* **6/1**[3]

5 **5** *hd* **Guesshowmuchiloveu (IRE)**[16] 4924 3-9-5 0.... MartinLane 13 73
(Charlie Fellowes) *mde most to 3f out: w ldr to 2f out: steadily outpcd* **50/1**

0 **6** *½* **Jethou Island**[13] 5007 3-9-0 0.... DaneO'Neill 11 67
(Henry Candy) *towards rr: pushed along 3f out: reminder and swtchd to outer over 1f out: styd on encouragingly fnl f: nrst fin* **50/1**

03 **7** *hd* **Lu's Buddy (GR)**[14] 4984 3-9-5 0.... PatDobbs 2 72
(Amanda Perrett) *pressed ldr: led 3f out: shkn up and hdd over 1f out: steadily wknd* **14/1**

0 **8** *3* **Keeper's Ring (USA)**[13] 5007 3-9-0 0.... JackMitchell 10 60+
(Roger Varian) *towards rr: pushed along 3f out: nvr on terms but kpt on fnl 2f: nt disgracd* **40/1**

4 **9** *¾* **Rectitude**[17] 4867 3-9-0 0.... WilliamBuick 14 58+
(John Gosden) *dwlt: sn prom: shkn up over 2f out: stl green and steadily wknd* **14/1**

00 **10** *7* **Fly A Kite**[56] 3537 3-9-0 0....(p) NedCurtis(5) 9 47
(Jonathan Portman) *dwlt: a in rr: u.p bef 1/2-way: no prog* **100/1**

5-5 **11** *3* **Bookmaker**[6] 5272 4-9-11 0.... JimCrowley 3 41
(Olly Stevens) *wl in tch tl pushed along and wknd 3f out* **66/1**

0 **12** *4 1/2* **Tsarglas**[12] 5044 3-9-5 0 ........ HarryBentley 12 30
(Stuart Williams) *a in rr: rdn and struggling 3f out* **100/1**

0-5 **13** *3/4* **Percys Princess**[145] 1107 3-9-0 0 ........ SteveDrowne 1 23
(Pat Murphy) *dwlt: a wl in rr: nvr a factor* **100/1**

**14** *17* **Alzarica (IRE)** 3-9-5 0 ........ WilliamTwiston-Davies 8
(Malcolm Saunders) *s.s: a detached in last: t.o* **66/1**

1m 45.96s (1.26) **Going Correction** +0.15s/f (Good)
**WFA** 3 from 4yo 6lb **14** Ran SP% **124.7**
Speed ratings (Par 103): **99,97,95,94,94 94,93,90,90,83 80,75,74,57**
CSF £7.36 TOTE £2.10: £1.10, £2.30, £1.70; EX 9.10 Trifecta £24.30.
**Owner** Saeed Suhail **Bred** Lodge Park Stud **Trained** Newmarket, Suffolk

**FOCUS**
Probably just an ordinary maiden. The winner built on her debut promise and the runner-up fits in.

## 5505 188BET GREAT IN PLAY FILLIES' H'CAP 1m 67y
**8:00** (8:01) (Class 4) (0-85,84) 3-Y-O+ **£5,175** (£1,540; £769; £384) **Stalls** Low

Form RPR

6302 **1** **Anya**[14] 4968 5-9-3 **73** ........ DaneO'Neill 2 82
(Henry Candy) *s.i.s: hld up in last: stl there over 2f out: prog on wd outside over 1f out: drvn to ld ins fnl f: styd on wl* **5/1**[3]

-201 **2** *1* **Bold Lass (IRE)**[26] 4537 3-9-8 **84** ........ TedDurcan 5 90
(David Lanigan) *hld up in tch: prog on outer over 2f out: drvn to ld jst over 1f out: hdd and nt qckn ins fnl f* **6/4**[1]

1-42 **3** *3/4* **History Book (IRE)**[39] 4112 4-9-12 **82** ........ WilliamBuick 1 87
(Charlie Appleby) *hld up in tch: nt clr run briefly wl over 1f out: sn rdn: styd on fnl f to take 3rd nr fin* **7/2**[2]

5363 **4** *1/2* **Dalmarella Dancer (IRE)**[19] 4802 3-8-9 **71** ........ (v) JimCrowley 3 74
(K R Burke) *trckd ldrs: rdn to go 2nd 2f out: nt qckn over 1f out and lost pl: one pce after* **12/1**

3110 **5** *2* **Bountybeamadam**[20] 4761 4-9-8 **78** ........ (p) PatCosgrave 7 77
(George Baker) *pushed up to ld: drvn over 2f out: hdd & wknd jst over 1f out* **16/1**

2030 **6** *3 1/2* **Saltwater Creek (IRE)**[19] 4782 3-8-9 **76** ........ CamHardie(5) 8 66
(Michael Bell) *trckd ldr after 1f to 2f out: sn wknd* **8/1**

3125 **7** *6* **Havelovewilltravel (IRE)**[35] 4271 4-9-8 **78** ........ (p) RyanMoore 4 55
(Jeremy Noseda) *trckd ldr 1f: styd cl up: rdn 2f out: wknd over 1f out: eased* **7/1**

1m 45.37s (0.67) **Going Correction** +0.15s/f (Good)
**WFA** 3 from 4yo+ 6lb **7** Ran SP% **116.1**
Speed ratings (Par 102): **102,101,100,99,97 94,88**
CSF £13.36 CT £29.58 TOTE £6.40: £2.90, £1.20; EX 18.20 Trifecta £48.50.
**Owner** Mrs L Alexander **Bred** Mrs L M Alexander **Trained** Kingston Warren, Oxon

**FOCUS**
A soundly run fillies' handicap and the first three came from the back. The winner is rated to her best.
T/Plt: £41.40 to a £1 stake. Pool of £90304.15 - 1590.71 winning tickets. T/Qpdt: £14.00 to a £1 stake. Pool of £6941.92 - 366.76 winning tickets. JN

# 5253 WOLVERHAMPTON (A.W) (L-H)
### Monday, August 18

**OFFICIAL GOING: Tapeta: standard**
No speed figures will be produced until revised median times for the new Tapeta surface can be calculated.
Wind: Fresh across Weather: Cloudy with sunny spells

## 5506 32RED CASINO NURSERY H'CAP (TAPETA) 5f 20y
**6:20** (6:21) (Class 5) (0-70,69) 2-Y-O **£3,234** (£962; £481; £240) **Stalls** Low

Form RPR

5555 **1** **Arlecchino's Leap**[12] 5028 2-8-10 63 ........ (v) RachealKneller(5) 7 66
(Mark Usher) *sn bhd: str run ins fnl f to ld towards fin* **20/1**

5440 **2** *1/2* **Designate (IRE)**[6] 5285 2-9-7 69 ........ (bt) RichardKingscote 4 70
(Ralph Beckett) *w ldr tl led over 3f out: hung rt fr 1/2-way: rdn and hung bdly rt fnl f: hdd towards fin* **11/4**[2]

3240 **3** *1 3/4* **Robin Hill**[16] 4913 2-9-5 67 ........ MartinDwyer 8 62
(William Muir) *a.p: rdn over 1f out: styd on same pce ins fnl f* **7/2**[3]

1603 **4** *1 1/4* **Mecca's Mirage (IRE)**[13] 5014 2-9-3 68 ........ ConnorBeasley(3) 3 58
(Michael Dods) *chsd ldrs: rdn over 1f out: no ex ins fnl f* **5/2**[1]

3460 **5** *4 1/2* **Dominic Cork**[17] 4853 2-9-2 64 ........ NeilCallan 6 38
(Kevin Ryan) *sn pushed along to ld: hdd over 3f out: rdn 1/2-way: wknd ins fnl f* **9/2**

2201 **6** *1* **Jimmy's Girl (IRE)**[10] 5133 2-8-12 65 ........ MarcMonaghan(5) 2 36
(Chris Dwyer) *chsd ldrs: rdn over 1f out: wknd fnl f* **11/1**

2503 **7** *4 1/2* **Johnny Sorrento**[7] 5254 2-8-5 60 ........ (bt[1]) JennyPowell(7) 1 14
(Tim Pitt) *n.m.r after s: sn pushed along in rr: wknd 1/2-way* **28/1**

1m 3.2s (1.30) **Going Correction** +0.175s/f (Slow) **7** Ran SP% **112.2**
Speed ratings (Par 94): **96,95,92,90,83 81,74**
CSF £71.76 CT £244.10 TOTE £22.00: £11.80, £1.90; EX 89.50 Trifecta £289.50.
**Owner** K Senior **Bred** J K Beckitt And Son **Trained** Upper Lambourn, Berks

**FOCUS**
An ordinary nursery run at a fast tempo, that saw a late twist in the tale. The winner is rated back to his pre-race peak.

## 5507 BOOK HOSPITALITY AT WOLVERHAMPTON RACECOURSE CLAIMING STKS (TAPETA) 5f 216y
**6:50** (6:50) (Class 6) 2-Y-O **£1,940** (£577; £288; £144) **Stalls** High

Form RPR

2315 **1** **Low Cut Affair (IRE)**[2] 5409 2-8-8 72 ........ DeclanBates(3) 2 72
(David Evans) *mde all: pushed clr 2f out: easily* **1/4**[1]

065 **2** *7* **Cupulation**[52] 3658 2-8-7 55 ........[1] LouisSteward(5) 4 50
(Amy Weaver) *chsd wnr: rdn over 2f out: styd on same pce fr over 1f out* **11/1**[3]

504 **3** *4 1/2* **Tuebrook**[9] 5194 2-9-2 50 ........ TomEaves 3 41
(Michael Easterby) *chsd ldrs: drvn along over 2f out: wknd over 1f out* **12/1**

00 **4** *1 3/4* **Cap la Nna**[7] 5253 2-7-13 0 ow1 ........ (p) DannyBrock(3) 5 21
(David C Griffiths) *s.i.s: sn prom: rdn over 2f out: swtchd lft and wknd over 1f out* **50/1**

**5** *10* **Emma Bovary** 2-9-2 0 ........ ConnorBeasley(3) 6 8
(John Norton) *s.i.s: sn pushed along in rr: wknd over 2f out* **20/1**

**6** *2 1/2* **Excelling Oscar (IRE)** 2-9-3 0 ........ RyanPowell(3) 1 2
(Conor Dore) *s.i.s: sn pushed along in rr: wknd over 2f out* **10/1**[2]

1m 16.78s (2.28) **Going Correction** +0.175s/f (Slow) **6** Ran SP% **111.8**
Speed ratings (Par 92): **91,81,75,73,60 56**
CSF £4.07 TOTE £1.30: £1.02, £4.40; EX 4.40 Trifecta £12.30.Low Cut Affair was claimed by C. N. Allen for £8000.
**Owner** Mrs T Burns **Bred** D Donegan **Trained** Pandy, Monmouths

**FOCUS**
An uncompetitive 2yo claimer.

## 5508 ALL NEW 32REDSPORT.COM H'CAP (TAPETA) 1m 5f 194y
**7:20** (7:20) (Class 6) (0-60,60) 3-Y-O+ **£2,264** (£673; £336; £168) **Stalls** Low

Form RPR

3640 **1** **Uncle Bernie (IRE)**[60] 3404 4-9-5 54 ........ (p) RobertTart(3) 3 62
(Andrew Hollinshead) *s.i.s: hld up: hdwy over 2f out: r.o u.p to ld nr fin* **20/1**

0004 **2** *nk* **Stormy Morning**[23] 4656 8-9-5 51 ........ (p) JoeFanning 8 58
(Philip Kirby) *chsd ldrs: led over 2f out: rdn ins fnl f: hdd nr fin* **5/1**[2]

0032 **3** *1/2* **Give Us A Reason**[21] 4734 4-9-12 58 ........ NeilCallan 10 64
(James Toller) *mid-div: hdwy over 2f out: rdn and ev ch ins fnl f: styd on* **9/4**[1]

0/40 **4** *1/2* **Giant Sequoia (USA)**[12] 5033 10-8-13 48 ........ (t) DannyBrock(3) 7 53
(Des Donovan) *s.i.s: hld up: hdwy over 2f out: rdn over 1f out: styd on* **14/1**

0304 **5** *1/2* **Well Owd Mon**[10] 5127 4-8-11 50 ........ RobHornby(7) 9 54
(Andrew Hollinshead) *s.i.s: hld up: hdwy over 3f out: rdn and ev ch 2f out: styd on same pce ins fnl f* **7/1**[3]

3530 **6** *7* **Lacey**[60] 3404 5-9-6 57 ........ KevinStott(5) 6 52
(Andrew Hollinshead) *hld up: hdwy over 2f out: sn rdn: styd on same pce fr over 1f out* **7/1**[3]

3214 **7** *1/2* **Nolecce**[44] 3976 7-9-7 60 ........ AdamMcLean(7) 2 54
(Tony Forbes) *chsd ldrs: nt clr run and lost pl over 2f out: n.d after* **8/1**

2060 **8** *2 1/2* **Royal Defence (IRE)**[54] 3579 8-9-2 51 ........ (t) ConnorBeasley(3) 1 41
(Richard Ford) *led 1f: chsd ldr tl led again over 3f out: hdd over 2f out: wknd fnl f* **16/1**

0553 **9** *2* **Layla's Boy**[60] 3404 7-8-11 46 ........ (t) NeilFarley(3) 5 34
(Simon West) *mid-div: pushed along and lost pl over 3f out: sn wknd* **20/1**

650- **10** *15* **Marlborough House**[84] 5099 4-9-9 55 ........ TomEaves 4 22
(Keith Dalgleish) *led after 1f: drvn along over 7f out: hdd over 3f out: wknd 2f out* **10/1**

3m 8.77s (3.97) **Going Correction** +0.175s/f (Slow) **10** Ran SP% **114.7**
Speed ratings (Par 101): **95,94,94,94,93 89,89,88,87,78**
CSF £115.34 CT £316.77 TOTE £10.00: £2.50, £2.60, £1.30; EX 125.20 Trifecta £868.70.
**Owner** Graham Brothers Racing Partnership **Bred** Roundhill Stud & Gleadhill House Stud Ltd **Trained** Upper Longdon, Staffs

**FOCUS**
A weak staying handicap. The surprise winner is rated to form.

## 5509 MATTHEW CHANEY 21ST BIRTHDAY CELEBRATION MAIDEN AUCTION FILLIES' STKS (BOBIS RACE) (TAPETA) 5f 216y
**7:50** (7:51) (Class 5) 2-Y-O **£2,587** (£770; £384; £192) **Stalls** High

Form RPR

5 **1** **Rictrude (FR)**[13] 4999 2-8-9 0 ........ RichardKingscote 8 68
(Tom Dascombe) *chsd ldr tl led over 1f out: sn rdn: jst hld on* **6/1**[2]

236 **2** *nse* **Tongue Twista**[23] 4646 2-8-12 88 ........ J-PGuillambert 2 71
(Nick Littmoden) *a.p: swtchd rt and chsd wnr over 1f out: sn rdn: r.o* **4/7**[1]

0 **3** *2 1/2* **Conjuring (IRE)**[89] 2460 2-8-9 0 ........ ShaneKelly 7 60
(Mike Murphy) *s.s: in rr: rdn 2f out: edgd lft and r.o ins fnl f: nt rch ldrs* **25/1**

0 **4** *1 1/4* **Wesie's Dream**[21] 4740 2-8-1 0 ........ PhilipPrince(5) 6 54
(Mark Usher) *a.p: rdn over 1f out: styd on same pce fnl f* **16/1**

5 **5** *hd* **Shimmering Silver (IRE)**[20] 4764 2-8-9 0 ........ FrankieMcDonald 3 56
(Daniel Mark Loughnane) *plld hrd and prom: rdn over 1f out: edgd lft and styd on same pce fnl f* **50/1**

**6** *3* **Most Tempting** 2-8-9 0 ........ AdamBeschizza 5 47
(Robert Cowell) *s.s: sn pushed along in rr: rdn over 2f out: nvr on terms* **10/1**[3]

**7** *3* **Perfect Slipper** 2-8-6 0 ........ SamJames(3) 1 38
(Noel Quinlan) *pushed along in rr early: effrt over 2f out: wknd fnl f* **6/1**[2]

54 **8** *6* **Ms Eboracum (IRE)**[16] 4909 2-8-6 0 ........ JoeFanning 4 17
(Edward Creighton) *led: rdn and hdd over 1f out: wknd fnl f* **22/1**

1m 16.41s (1.91) **Going Correction** +0.175s/f (Slow) **8** Ran SP% **117.4**
Speed ratings (Par 91): **94,93,90,88,88 84,80,72**
CSF £9.96 TOTE £8.40: £2.00, £1.02, £8.40; EX 11.80 Trifecta £138.50.
**Owner** Chasemore Farm **Bred** Andrew Black **Trained** Malpas, Cheshire
■ Stewards' Enquiry : J-P Guillambert four-day ban: used whip above permitted level (Sep 1-4)

**FOCUS**
There was a turn-up in this moderate fillies' maiden. The favourite was below form.

## 5510 BOOK HORIZONS RESTAURANT H'CAP (TAPETA) 7f 32y
**8:20** (8:21) (Class 6) (0-60,60) 3-Y-O+ **£2,264** (£673; £336; £168) **Stalls** High

Form RPR

0440 **1** **Wotalad**[11] 5103 4-8-11 50 ........ (p) GeorgeChaloner(3) 8 59
(Richard Whitaker) *mde all: rdn over 1f out: edgd rt ins fnl f: styd on u.p* **7/1**

03 **2** *3/4* **Very First Blade**[6] 5287 5-8-9 48 ........ (b) RobertTart(3) 1 55
(Michael Mullineaux) *a.p: rdn to chse wnr and hung rt ins fnl f: r.o* **3/1**[1]

5500 **3** *1 3/4* **La Danza**[11] 5079 4-8-8 49 ........ (v[1]) TimClark(5) 12 52
(Lisa Williamson) *a.p: rdn over 1f out: styd on same pce ins fnl f* **20/1**

0-00 **4** *2* **Seraphima**[11] 5079 4-8-12 48 ........ (v[1]) RoystonFfrench 4 45
(Lisa Williamson) *hld up: hdwy 1/2-way: rdn over 1f out: styd on same pce ins fnl f* **66/1**

-560 **5** *hd* **Gypsy Rider**[76] 2864 5-9-1 51 ........ ShaneKelly 7 48
(Henry Tett) *a.p: rdn over 2f out: styd on same pce ins fnl f* **8/1**

1500 **6** *1/2* **Ishi Honest**[11] 5071 4-9-6 56 ........ GeorgeBaker 10 51
(Mark Usher) *chsd wnr: rdn over 1f out: hung lft and no ex ins fnl f* **11/2**[3]

-300 **7** *3/4* **Monte Cassino (IRE)**[48] 3833 9-9-2 57 ........ (e) AdamCarter(5) 3 51
(Bryan Smart) *mid-div: rdn over 2f out: nvr trbld ldrs* **14/1**

5050 **8** *1/2* **Spoken Words**[19] 4795 5-8-7 48 ........ AlistairRawlinson(5) 11 40
(John David Riches) *hld up: rdn over 1f out: nvr on terms* **18/1**

0060 **9** *4 1/2* **No Refund (IRE)**[10] 5138 3-8-7 55 ........ NatalieHambling-Yates(7) 6 34
(Martin Smith) *s.s: a in rr* **16/1**

0045 **10** *6* **Bapak Muda (USA)**[3] 5390 4-9-10 60 ........ NeilCallan 2 25
(Kevin Ryan) *sn pushed along in rr: hmpd 6f out: rdn over 2f out: n.d* **7/2**[2]

00-0 **11** 1 ½ **Duke Of Aricabeau (IRE)**[25] 4578 5-9-1 54..........(v¹) SimonPearce(3) 5 15
(Lydia Pearce) *s.s: a in rr* **25/1**
1m 30.64s (1.84) **Going Correction** +0.175s/f (Slow)
**WFA** 3 from 4yo+ 5lb **11** Ran SP% **114.1**
Speed ratings (Par 101): **96,95,93,90,90 90,89,88,83,76 74**
CSF £26.80 CT £407.41 TOTE £11.60: £2.70, £1.30, £8.10; EX 32.80 Trifecta £403.50.
**Owner** Mrs Jill Willows **Bred** Hellwood Stud Farm **Trained** Scarcroft, W Yorks
**FOCUS**
A weak handicap. The winner is rated to his best.

## 5511 32RED NOVICE STKS (BOBIS RACE) (TAPETA) 5f 20y
**8:50** (8:51) (Class 4) 2-Y-0 **£6,469** (£1,925; £962; £481) **Stalls** Low

Form RPR
21 **1** **Judicial (IRE)**[18] 4814 2-9-7 0.......................................... GeorgeBaker 4 83+
(Roger Charlton) *mde all: rdn and edgd rt ins fnl f: r.o* **2/5¹**
1166 **2** 1 ¾ **Honest Bob'S**[16] 4920 2-9-6 79.................................... JackGarritty(5) 3 79
(Brian Ellison) *trckd wnr: wnt upsides 1/2-way: ev ch over 1f out: sn rdn: styd on same pce ins fnl f* **14/1**
6201 **3** 5 **Grey Zeb (IRE)**[24] 4624 2-9-7 78.......................................... TomEaves 1 57
(Keith Dalgleish) *trckd ldrs: rdn over 1f out: no ex fnl f* **6/1³**
**4** 4 **Grumpy Angel** 2-8-6 0..........................................¹ GeorgeChaloner(3) 2 30
(Richard Fahey) *s.s: outpcd* **11/2²**
1m 2.56s (0.66) **Going Correction** +0.175s/f (Slow) **4** Ran SP% **107.8**
Speed ratings (Par 96): **101,98,90,83**
CSF £6.61 TOTE £1.20; EX 7.20 Trifecta £10.60.
**Owner** Elite Racing Club **Bred** Elite Racing Club **Trained** Beckhampton, Wilts
**FOCUS**
Not the most competitive novice event. The winner is rated just to form.

## 5512 £10 FREE BET AT 32REDSPORT.COM H'CAP (TAPETA) 1m 141y
**9:20** (9:28) (Class 6) (0-60,60) 3-Y-0+ **£2,264** (£673; £336; £168) **Stalls** Low

Form RPR
0-52 **1** **Flipping**[13] 5005 7-9-2 50.......................................... NeilCallan 9 66
(Stuart Kittow) *a.p: led over 1f out: rdn clr* **3/1¹**
60 **2** 3 ¾ **City Of Angkor Wat (IRE)**[23] 4673 4-9-0 53...........(t) PhilipPrince(5) 13 60
(Jo Hughes) *a.p: rdn and ev ch over 1f out: styd on same pce ins fnl f* **20/1**
3143 **3** 2 ¼ **Indian Giver**[31] 4381 6-9-3 56.................................... AlistairRawlinson(5) 2 58
(John David Riches) *prom: lost pl 3f out: hdwy over 1f out: styd on* **16/1**
6654 **4** nk **Jumbo Prado (USA)**[11] 5109 5-9-7 55.................................... ShaneKelly 8 56
(John Stimpson) *chsd ldrs: rdn over 2f out: no ex ins fnl f* **16/1**
2050 **5** 1 ¾ **Not Rigg (USA)**[11] 5075 4-9-10 58..........................(p) GeorgeBaker 10 55
(Nick Littmoden) *prom: jnd ldr over 6f out: led wl over 1f out: sn rdn and hdd: wknd ins fnl f* **7/2²**
5005 **6** ½ **Poor Duke (IRE)**[14] 4959 4-9-5 60..........................(p) LewisStones(7) 11 56
(Michael Mullineaux) *hld up: hdwy over 2f out: rdn over 1f out: wknd fnl f* **9/1**
/002 **7** 2 ¼ **Rocky's Pride (IRE)**[31] 4381 8-9-4 55.......................... GeorgeChaloner(3) 4 46
(Richard Whitaker) *led: rdn and hdd wl over 1f out: wknd fnl f* **15/2**
0400 **8** 2 ½ **Katmai River (IRE)**[11] 5071 7-8-11 52.......................... CharlotteJenner(7) 1 37
(Mark Usher) *prom: rdn over 2f out: wknd fnl f* **16/1**
0000 **9** 1 ¼ **Classy Lassy (IRE)**[34] 4294 3-8-5 49..........................(p) ConnorBeasley(3) 7 31
(Brian Ellison) *hld up: rdn over 2f out: n.d* **28/1**
0052 **10** 1 ¾ **Acton Gold**[19] 4797 5-8-12 46..........................(p) PaddyAspell 6 24
(Brian Baugh) *hld up: rdn over 2f out: a in rr* **25/1**
0164 **11** 1 ¼ **Oly'Roccs (IRE)**[16] 4911 3-8-10 51.......................... JoeFanning 3 26
(Philip Kirby) *hld up: rdn over 2f out: a in rr* **6/1³**
04-0 **12** ¾ **Pearlofthequarter**[30] 4434 3-9-5 60.......................... RichardKingscote 5 34
(Jonathan Portman) *s.i.s: rdn over 2f out: a in rr* **28/1**
5200 **13** hd **Aldreth**[49] 3789 3-9-2 57.......................................... TomEaves 12 30
(Michael Easterby) *s.i.s: sn pushed along and a in rr* **16/1**
1m 50.61s (0.51) **Going Correction** +0.175s/f (Slow)
**WFA** 3 from 4yo+ 7lb **13** Ran SP% **126.4**
Speed ratings (Par 101): **104,100,98,98,96 96,94,92,91,89 88,87,87**
CSF £73.34 CT £882.07 TOTE £5.50: £2.10, £6.70, £4.40; EX 115.40 Trifecta £1537.90.
**Owner** Reg Gifford **Bred** D R Tucker **Trained** Blackborough, Devon
**FOCUS**
This was off considerably later than advertised due to the course having to be harrowed. The winner came from a Ffos Las race which is working out really well, but this rates a step up.
T/Plt: £29.90 to a £1 stake. Pool of £63877.09 - 1557.64 winning tickets. T/Qpdt: £3.40 to a £1 stake. Pool of £6836.25 - 1467.00 winning tickets. CR

# 5120 BRIGHTON (L-H)
Tuesday, August 19

**OFFICIAL GOING: Good (good to firm in places; 7.3)**
Wind: Moderate, across away from stands Weather: Sunny spells Rails: Rail dolled out from 6f to 3.5f and distances increased by about 5yds

## 5517 WOLSELEY AND PLUMB CENTER FAVOURITE NURSERY H'CAP 5f 59y
**2:15** (2:16) (Class 6) (0-60,59) 2-Y-0+ **£1,940** (£577; £288; £144) **Stalls** Centre

Form RPR
4654 **1** **Arizona Snow**[11] 5120 2-9-7 59..........................................¹ LukeMorris 2 61
(Ronald Harris) *sn outpcd in rr: rapid hdwy fnl f: led fnl stride* **15/2**
6422 **2** hd **Lady Zodiac (IRE)**[10] 5180 2-9-4 56.......................... DavidProbert 4 57
(Andrew Balding) *slt ld tl wnt on over 1f out: hrd rdn fnl f: ct fnl stride* **5/4¹**
040 **3** 1 **Spirit In Time (IRE)**[33] 4338 2-9-2 54.......................... JimCrowley 6 51
(Malcolm Saunders) *chsd ldng pair: hrd rdn wl over 1f out: kpt on fnl f* **20/1**
4444 **4** 1 ¼ **Surrey Pink (FR)**[18] 4857 2-8-13 51..........................(p) MartinDwyer 3 44
(William Muir) *chsd ldrs: rdn over 2f out: one pce* **13/2³**
204 **5** 2 **Macarthurs Park (IRE)**[31] 4422 2-9-2 54..........................(v¹) RichardKingscote 5 40
(Tom Dascombe) *w ldr tl hung lft over 1f out: hrd rdn and flashed tail: wknd fnl f* **8/1**
400 **U** **Piping Dream (IRE)**[20] 4784 2-8-12 55.......................... CamHardie(5) 1
(Richard Hannon) *rrd in stalls and uns rdr s* **3/1²**
1m 4.05s (1.75) **Going Correction** +0.125s/f (Good) **6** Ran SP% **110.4**
Speed ratings: **91,90,89,87,83**
CSF £16.90 TOTE £7.10: £3.10, £1.30; EX 16.80 Trifecta £141.50.
**Owner** Ridge House Stables Ltd **Bred** Winterbeck Manor Stud **Trained** Earlswood, Monmouths

**FOCUS**
The ground had eased slightly from that previously advertised following 4mm of rain overnight and was officially good, good to firm in places. This moderate nursery was contested by six maidens and it was weakened still further when the second-favourite Piping Dream reared as the stalls opened, unshipping Cam Hardie. Not a race to be taking a positive view of.

## 5518 MEARS PETER BENNION-JONES MEMORIAL H'CAP 5f 213y
**2:45** (2:45) (Class 6) (0-60,58) 3-Y-0+ **£1,940** (£577; £288; £144) **Stalls** Centre

Form RPR
1045 **1** **Perfect Pastime**[26] 4578 6-9-7 58..........................(p) PatCosgrave 4 66
(Jim Boyle) *in tch: nt clr run over 2f out: effrt and swtchd lft over 1f out: led ent fnl f: rdn out* **3/1²**
5533 **2** 1 ¼ **Captain Ryan**[18] 4847 3-9-0 54.......................................... LukeMorris 3 58
(Peter Makin) *chsd ldrs: led over 1f out tl ent fnl f: hrd rdn: one pce* **11/4¹**
3125 **3** shd **Clear Focus (IRE)**[23] 4715 3-8-12 52..........................(v) RichardKingscote 6 56
(Brendan Powell) *led tl over 1f out: kpt on same pce* **3/1²**
0005 **4** 7 **Encapsulated**[17] 4908 4-8-9 53..........................(p) RhiainIngram(7) 5 35
(Roger Ingram) *sn pushed along in 6th: effrt in centre 3f out: outpcd fnl 2f* **8/1**
5306 **5** nk **Zafraaj**[40] 4102 3-9-4 58..........................(p) DavidProbert 1 39
(Ronald Harris) *prom tl wknd over 1f out* **11/1**
0-66 **6** 2 ½ **Stonecrabstomorrow (IRE)**[12] 5071 11-9-1 55....... AshleyMorgan(3) 2 28
(Michael Attwater) *s.i.s: bhd: shkn up 2f out: n.d* **6/1³**
605 **7** 6 **Spider Bay**[22] 4735 5-8-8 45.......................................... RobertHavlin 7
(Lydia Richards) *w ldr tl hung lft and wknd wl over 1f out* **66/1**
1m 10.75s (0.55) **Going Correction** +0.125s/f (Good)
**WFA** 3 from 4yo+ 3lb **7** Ran SP% **111.9**
Speed ratings (Par 101): **101,99,99,89,89 86,78**
CSF £11.16 CT £25.00 TOTE £5.80: £2.30, £2.30; EX 12.60 Trifecta £33.30.
**Owner** The Paddock Space Partnership 2 **Bred** R G & T E Levin **Trained** Epsom, Surrey
**FOCUS**
A moderate sprint handicap in which the three market leaders pulled well clear of the others. It's been a long time since the winner rated any higher.

## 5519 IRISH STALLION FARMS EBF MEDIAN AUCTION MAIDEN STKS 6f 209y
**3:15** (3:15) (Class 5) 2-Y-O **£2,911** (£866; £432; £216) **Stalls** Centre

Form RPR
322 **1** **Al Bandar (IRE)**[16] 4935 2-9-0 77.......................................... CamHardie(5) 5 78
(Richard Hannon) *trckd ldrs: led 2f out: rdn clr fnl f: readily* **8/13¹**
5 **2** 4 ½ **Cosmic Ray**[22] 4731 2-9-5 0.......................................... DavidProbert 3 66
(Andrew Balding) *led tl 2f out: hrd rdn appr fnl f: one pce* **6/1³**
00 **3** 1 ½ **Emperors Warrior (IRE)**[34] 4330 2-9-5 0.......................... PatCosgrave 4 62
(Richard Hannon) *prom tl outpcd fnl 2f* **33/1**
6 **4** ¾ **Haarib**[17] 4906 2-9-5 0.......................................... GeorgeBaker 2 62
(Ed Walker) *dwlt: towards rr: shkn up and styd on steadily fnl 2f: nrest at fin* **7/2²**
**5** 7 **King's Concerto (IRE)** 2-9-5 0.......................................... HayleyTurner 7 41
(Dean Ivory) *in tch: outpcd 4f out: btn over 2f out* **33/1**
02 **6** 2 **Diamond Runner (IRE)**[12] 5072 2-9-5 0..........................(v) RobertHavlin 1 35
(Hugo Palmer) *dwlt: in tch after 2f: rdn and wknd over 2f out* **8/1**
**7** hd **Thanksgiving Day (IRE)** 2-9-5 0.......................................... JimCrowley 8 35
(Jamie Osborne) *dwlt: a bhd* **8/1**
**8** 17 **Kylies Wild Card** 2-9-0 0.......................................... WilliamCarson 6
(Simon Hodgson) *prom tl wknd and hung lft over 2f out* **66/1**
1m 23.71s (0.61) **Going Correction** +0.125s/f (Good) **8** Ran SP% **128.0**
Speed ratings (Par 94): **101,95,94,93,85 83,82,63**
CSF £6.24 TOTE £1.80: £1.02, £2.40, £9.80; EX 5.90 Trifecta £105.10.
**Owner** Ahmad Abdulla Al Shaikh **Bred** Oghill House Stud **Trained** East Everleigh, Wilts
**FOCUS**
An uncompetitive 2yo maiden and a comfortable win for the odds-on favourite. It's possible this was a small step up.

## 5520 TPCT LTD H'CAP 1m 3f 196y
**3:45** (3:45) (Class 5) (0-70,65) 3-Y-0 **£2,587** (£770; £384; £192) **Stalls** High

Form RPR
5332 **1** **Chesil Beach**[19] 4834 3-9-7 65.......................................... DavidProbert 5 73
(Andrew Balding) *hld up in rr: hdwy 4f out: chsd ldr and hung lft wl over 1f out: styd on to ld wl ins fnl f* **5/1²**
3233 **2** nk **Sandy Cove**[11] 5123 3-9-4 62.......................................... LukeMorris 2 69
(James Eustace) *chsd ldrs: qcknd through on inner to ld 2f out: hrd rdn and hdd wl ins fnl f: kpt on wl* **5/1²**
0551 **3** 15 **Cameley Dawn**[11] 5122 3-9-2 60.......................... RichardKingscote 7 43
(Malcolm Saunders) *chsd ldr tl over 2f out: wknd wl over 1f out* **11/2³**
2130 **4** 4 **Bishop Wulstan (IRE)**[18] 4863 3-8-13 62.......................... CamHardie(5) 6 39
(Richard Hannon) *hld up in 5th: outpcd and struggling over 2f out: passed btn horses fnl f* **11/2³**
0366 **5** 4 ½ **Armourer (IRE)**[16] 4948 3-9-7 65.......................................... MartinDwyer 1 34
(William Muir) *led tl 2f out: sn wknd* **11/1**
5552 **6** 3 ¼ **Mambo Rhythm**[7] 5270 3-9-6 64..........................(b) AdrianNicholls 3 28
(Mark Johnston) *in tch: rdn 5f out: wnt prom over 3f out: wknd over 2f out* **3/1¹**
0-00 **7** 3 ½ **Aurora Borealis (IRE)**[29] 4500 3-9-5 63.......................... JimCrowley 4 22
(Ed Dunlop) *towards rr: rdn over 4f out: lost tch over 2f out* **13/2**
2m 34.24s (1.54) **Going Correction** +0.125s/f (Good) **7** Ran SP% **110.8**
Speed ratings (Par 100): **99,98,88,86,83 80,78**
CSF £27.92 TOTE £3.00: £1.50, £3.10; EX 16.10 Trifecta £81.10.
**Owner** Kingsclere Racing Club **Bred** Kingsclere Stud **Trained** Kingsclere, Hants
**FOCUS**
An ordinary 3yo handicap in which they appeared to go an even pace. The front pair pulled a long way clear and were the only ones to show their form.

## 5521 MEARS SERVING OUR COMMUNITY H'CAP 1m 1f 209y
**4:15** (4:17) (Class 5) (0-70,70) 3-Y-0+ **£2,587** (£770; £384; £192) **Stalls** High

Form RPR
0166 **1** **Whinging Willie (IRE)**[12] 5073 5-9-5 68.......................... HectorCrouch(7) 6 75
(Gary Moore) *stdd s: hld up in 5th: hdwy 2f out: drvn to ld ins fnl f: rdn out nr fin: jst prevailed* **7/1**
-145 **2** nse **Dalaki (IRE)**[17] 4887 3-9-5 69..........................(b) HarryBentley 5 76
(Clive Brittain) *pressed ldr: led after 2f tl 3f out: hrd rdn and rallied wl ins fnl f: jst deprived* **5/1**
3-02 **3** nk **This Is The Day**[33] 4356 3-9-6 70.......................................... MartinLane 1 76
(Charlie Fellowes) *led 2f: pressed ldr tl led again 3f out: hdd ins fnl f: kpt on wl* **9/2³**
0231 **4** 2 ¾ **Fruit Pastille**[26] 4579 3-9-5 69.......................................... JimCrowley 2 70
(Hughie Morrison) *trckd ldrs: nt clr run on inner 2f out: one pce appr fnl f* **11/4¹**

3346 **5** 1 1/4 **Arlecchino (IRE)**[12] 5077 4-9-6 62....(b) GeorgeBaker 7 61
(Ed McMahon) *stdd s: hld up in rr: sme hdwy 2f out: no imp over 1f out* **4/1**[2]

5500 **6** *11* **Ganymede**[16] 4948 3-9-1 65.... JohnFahy 3 43
(Eve Johnson Houghton) *plld hrd: prom: rdn and edgd rt 3f out: wknd 2f out* **25/1**

4400 **7** 3 1/4 **Zaeem**[14] 5011 5-9-6 62.... HayleyTurner 9 34
(Dean Ivory) *hld up in rr: rdn and n.d fnl 2f* **16/1**

2432 **8** 3/4 **Matraash (USA)**[20] 4792 8-9-7 68....(p) EoinWalsh(5) 4 38
(Daniel Mark Loughnane) *towards rr: hrd rdn over 2f out: sn struggling* **10/1**

2m 4.81s (1.21) **Going Correction** +0.125s/f (Good)
**WFA** 3 from 4yo+ 8lb **8** Ran SP% **112.8**
Speed ratings (Par 103): **100,99,99,97,96 87,85,84**
CSF £40.58 CT £173.97 TOTE £8.70: £2.50, £3.10, £1.50; EX 52.60 Trifecta £225.70.
**Owner** P B Moorhead **Bred** Joe Rogers **Trained** Lower Beeding, W Sussex

**FOCUS**

A modest handicap and there was no pace on early, which helps explain how the pair that disputed the lead throughout were able to hang in there and involve themselves in a tight three-way finish. Improvement from the first three, but not entirely convincing.

## 5522 LOTHBURY PENDIL FINANCIAL SERVICES H'CAP 7f 214y

**4:45** (4:45) (Class 6) (0-65,65) 3-Y-O **£1,940** (£577; £288; £144) **Stalls** Centre

Form RPR

0466 **1** **Why Not Now**[24] 4655 3-8-7 51.... DavidProbert 1 61
(Roger Charlton) *plld hrd early: hld up in rr: hdwy in centre 2f out: edgd lft and led ins fnl f: rdn out* **5/1**[3]

0004 **2** 3/4 **Patronella (IRE)**[39] 4152 3-8-8 52.... RichardKingscote 4 60
(David Simcock) *hld up in rr: hdwy 2f out: led over 1f out tl ins fnl f: kpt on* **11/1**

2433 **3** *5* **Baltic Fire (IRE)**[18] 4871 3-9-0 61.... JoeyHaynes(3) 2 58
(K R Burke) *in tch: hmpd on inner over 4f out: rdn to press ldrs over 2f out: wknd 1f out* **5/2**[1]

1036 **4** 3 1/2 **Choice Of Destiny**[22] 4742 3-9-2 65.... CamHardie(5) 7 53
(Philip McBride) *in tch: nt clr run over 2f out: swtchd lft and effrt wl over 1f out: no imp* **6/1**

0-00 **5** 1 1/2 **Monte Viso**[33] 4370 3-9-1 59....(t) PatCosgrave 8 44
(Stuart Kittow) *towards rr: rdn over 2f out: nvr able to chal* **66/1**

2141 **6** *nk* **Clapperboard**[12] 5071 3-9-5 63....(b) WilliamCarson 5 47
(Paul Fitzsimons) *t.k.h: prom: led over 2f out tl over 1f out: wknd fnl f* **7/1**

6001 **7** *12* **Rapunzal**[10] 5183 3-8-11 60.... AmyScott(5) 6 17
(Henry Candy) *led at gd pce tl wknd 2f out* **7/2**[2]

0045 **8** 1 3/4 **Heartstrings**[8] 5252 3-9-3 61....(v) SamHitchcott 9 14
(Mick Channon) *rdn up to press ldr after 1f: wknd 2f out* **20/1**

300 **9** *20* **Popping Candy**[12] 5105 3-9-0 58....(p) LukeMorris 3
(Roger Varian) *hld up in 6th: rdn and struggling over 2f out: sn bhd* **16/1**

1m 35.84s (-0.16) **Going Correction** +0.125s/f (Good) **9** Ran SP% **114.7**
Speed ratings (Par 98): **105,104,99,95,94 93,81,80,60**
CSF £57.82 CT £168.36 TOTE £7.10: £1.50, £2.90, £1.90; EX 60.70 Trifecta £398.60.
**Owner** S Emmet And Miss R Emmet **Bred** S Emmet And Miss R Emmet **Trained** Beckhampton, Wilts

**FOCUS**

A moderate 3yo handicap, but this time the leaders may have gone off too quick as the front pair came from last and last-but-one. They are rated around their better earlier efforts.

## 5523 D.E.H ELECTRICAL CONTRACTORS LTD H'CAP 6f 209y

**5:15** (5:15) (Class 5) (0-70,69) 3-Y-O+ **£2,587** (£770; £384; £192) **Stalls** Centre

Form RPR

3212 **1** **Hawk Moth (IRE)**[12] 5075 6-9-0 57.... LukeMorris 3 66
(John Spearing) *towards rr: hdwy over 1f out: str run to ld on line* **11/4**[1]

3005 **2** *shd* **Jontleman (IRE)**[17] 4907 4-9-11 68.... SamHitchcott 6 76
(Mick Channon) *chsd ldrs: led 1f out: hrd rdn fnl f: jst ct* **10/1**

3653 **3** 1 1/4 **Sleipnir**[45] 3970 3-9-7 69....(p) GeorgeBaker 1 72
(Philip Hide) *led: hrd rdn and hdd 1f out: kpt on same pce* **9/2**[3]

2402 **4** 1 1/2 **Hierarch (IRE)**[41] 4072 7-9-5 69....(p) SophieKilloran(7) 5 70
(David Simcock) *bhd: hdwy on inner 2f out: jnd ldrs over 1f out: no ex fnl f* **10/1**

121 **5** *shd* **For Shia And Lula (IRE)**[26] 4578 5-9-12 69.... FrankieMcDonald 8 70
(Daniel Mark Loughnane) *prom tl rdn and btn 1f out* **7/1**

1103 **6** *shd* **Fairy Mist (IRE)**[12] 5071 7-8-12 55....(v) WilliamCarson 4 55
(John Bridger) *chsd ldrs: hrd rdn over 1f out: no ex* **7/1**

-044 **7** 1 1/2 **Buxton**[11] 5138 10-8-2 52....(t) RhiainIngram(7) 7 48
(Roger Ingram) *in tch: effrt in centre over 2f out: btn over 1f out* **25/1**

5154 **8** *7* **Perfect Mission**[17] 4907 6-9-1 65....(v) KieranShoemark(7) 2 43
(Andrew Balding) *prom tl wknd and hung lft over 1f out* **10/3**[2]

1m 24.52s (1.42) **Going Correction** +0.125s/f (Good)
**WFA** 3 from 4yo+ 5lb **8** Ran SP% **115.0**
Speed ratings (Par 103): **96,95,94,92,92 92,90,82**
CSF £31.17 CT £120.89 TOTE £4.60: £1.40, £3.60, £1.40; EX 35.90 Trifecta £122.50.
**Owner** Kinnersley Partnership **Bred** Dr D Harron **Trained** Kinnersley, Worcs

**FOCUS**

A modest handicap and it was noticeable how several of the jockeys decided to fan out wide just after halfway. The result suggests that was an advantage. The winner is getting back to last year's form.

T/Plt: £53.60 to a £1 stake. Pool: £84,538.95 - 1,149.35 winning tickets. T/Qpdt: £18.80 to a £1 stake. Pool: £6,309.55 - 247.40 winning tickets. LM

# 5201 LEICESTER (R-H)

Tuesday, August 19

**OFFICIAL GOING: Good (good to firm in places; 7.7)**

Wind: Light across Weather: Cloudy with sunny spells

## 5524 OLD MOUT MAIDEN AUCTION FILLIES' STKS (BOBIS RACE) 5f 2y

**5:00** (5:00) (Class 5) 2-Y-O **£2,587** (£770; £384; £192) **Stalls** High

Form RPR

2 **1** **Marigot Bay**[9] 5209 2-8-2 0.... DanielMuscutt(5) 1 74
(Gay Kelleway) *w ldr: plld hrd: led over 3f out: edgd rt over 1f out: sn rdn: r.o* **2/7**[1]

**2** *3* **Little** 2-8-7 0.... JoeFanning 4 60
(Jamie Osborne) *s.i.s: hdwy 1/2-way: chsd wnr over 1f out: sn ev ch: no ex ins fnl f* **16/1**

5025 **3** *hd* **June's Moon**[21] 4751 2-8-11 68.... OisinMurphy 2 63
(Jonathan Portman) *led: hdd over 3f out: rdn 1/2-way: outpcd over 1f out: r.o towards fin* **8/1**[3]

**4** 3 1/2 **Picture Postcard** 2-8-9 0.... GrahamGibbons 3 49
(William Haggas) *chsd ldrs: pushed along over 3f out: outpcd 1/2-way: n.d after* **6/1**[2]

1m 1.36s (1.36) **Going Correction** -0.15s/f (Firm) **4** Ran SP% **109.0**
Speed ratings (Par 91): **83,78,77,72**
CSF £6.02 TOTE £1.30; EX 5.30 Trifecta £13.20.
**Owner** Rioja Racing **Bred** R J Cornelius **Trained** Exning, Suffolk

**FOCUS**

A modest fillies' 2yo maiden. The winner was possibly value for a bit more.

## 5525 BULMERS CIDER NURSERY H'CAP 5f 218y

**5:30** (5:31) (Class 6) (0-65,65) 2-Y-O **£2,587** (£770; £384; £192) **Stalls** High

Form RPR

0641 **1** **White Vin Jan**[10] 5180 2-8-4 53.... LouisSteward(5) 7 67+
(Michael Bell) *a.p: chsd ldr over 3f out: led over 2f out: hung rt over 1f out: c clr fnl f* **9/2**[1]

004 **2** 3 1/4 **Gen I Am**[15] 4980 2-9-2 60.... PatDobbs 12 64+
(Richard Hannon) *prom: rdn over 2f out: sn outpcd: r.o to go 2nd wl ins fnl f* **5/1**[2]

021P **3** 2 1/4 **Just Marion (IRE)**[39] 4157 2-9-6 64.... DavidNolan 4 61
(David Evans) *led: rdn and hdd over 2f out: no ex ins fnl f* **16/1**

046 **4** *3* **Piccadillo**[20] 4781 2-8-12 59.... ThomasBrown(3) 3 47
(Daniel Kubler) *prom: pushed along and lost pl 4f out: styd on u.p fr over 1f out* **5/1**[2]

050 **5** 1/2 **Invincible Wish (IRE)**[17] 4919 2-8-12 56.... PaulPickard 6 43
(Brian Ellison) *prom: rdn and outpcd over 2f out: styd on ins fnl f* **7/1**[3]

053 **6** 1 3/4 **Clampdown**[64] 3304 2-9-3 61....(p) KierenFallon 2 43
(James Tate) *s.i.s: hdwy over 4f out: rdn over 1f out: sn wknd* **5/1**[2]

1526 **7** *nk* **Diminutive (IRE)**[11] 5133 2-9-4 62....(p) OisinMurphy 1 43
(Grace Harris) *w ldr tl pushed along over 3f out: rdn and wknd over 1f out* **12/1**

040 **8** 2 1/2 **Air Of York (IRE)**[10] 5180 2-8-9 53.... WilliamTwiston-Davies 14 26
(Ronald Harris) *sn pushed along and a in rr* **33/1**

002 **9** 1 1/2 **Lady Jade**[10] 5194 2-8-5 49.... JasonHart 13 18
(Nigel Tinkler) *prom: rdn over 2f out: wknd over 1f out* **14/1**

655 **10** 3 1/2 **First Class Mail**[25] 4618 2-9-4 65....(v1) CharlesBishop(3) 9 23
(Mick Channon) *s.i.s: sn pushed along: rdn over 2f out: a in rr* **7/1**[3]

1m 12.45s (-0.55) **Going Correction** -0.15s/f (Firm) **10** Ran SP% **116.4**
Speed ratings (Par 92): **97,92,89,85,85 82,82,78,76,72**
CSF £26.78 CT £331.17 TOTE £5.30: £1.80, £1.90, £4.10; EX 29.00 Trifecta £409.10.
**Owner** Middleham Park Racing XXIII & Partner **Bred** Redmyre Bloodstock Ltd **Trained** Newmarket, Suffolk

**FOCUS**

A modest nursery. There's more to come from the winner.

## 5526 STRONGBOW BITTER SWEET CLASSIC H'CAP (BOBIS RACE) 5f 218y

**6:00** (6:00) (Class 4) (0-80,80) 3-Y-O **£4,690** (£1,395; £697; £348) **Stalls** High

Form RPR

6400 **1** **Pensax Lad (IRE)**[12] 5080 3-8-7 66.... BenCurtis 7 74
(Ronald Harris) *a.p: rdn over 2f out: led 1f outm: sn hung rt: styd on* **10/1**

1 **2** *1* **Ridge Ranger (IRE)**[17] 4900 3-9-2 75.... JasonHart 5 80
(Eric Alston) *hld up: hdwy 2f out: led over 1f out: sn rdn and hdd: styd on same pce ins fnl f* **6/1**[3]

2423 **3** 2 3/4 **Faure Island**[13] 5055 3-8-13 72....(b1) DaneO'Neill 3 68
(Henry Candy) *prom: chsd ldr over 3f out: led over 2f out: rdn and hdd over 1f out: styd on same pce fnl f* **11/8**[1]

1 **4** *8* **Shingle**[19] 4816 3-9-7 80.... OisinMurphy 4 50
(Ed de Giles) *chsd ldr tl over 3f out: rdn over 2f out: wknd fnl f* **7/4**[2]

-420 **5** *4* **Three Pips**[188] 573 3-8-10 69....(b1) GrahamGibbons 2 27
(Ed McMahon) *sn led: racd keenly: hdd over 2f out: rdn: hung rt and wknd over 1f out* **16/1**

1m 11.77s (-1.23) **Going Correction** -0.15s/f (Firm) **5** Ran SP% **107.7**
Speed ratings (Par 102): **102,100,97,86,81**
CSF £59.48 TOTE £14.30: £3.40, £2.60; EX 112.80 Trifecta £166.90.
**Owner** S & A Mares **Bred** Seamus And James McMullan **Trained** Earlswood, Monmouths

**FOCUS**

Not a bad 3yo handicap, but the market 1-2 disappointed. The winner is rated to his AW form.

## 5527 FOSTER'S SUPER CHILLED H'CAP 1m 3f 183y

**6:30** (6:31) (Class 5) (0-75,79) 3-Y-O+ **£2,911** (£866; £432; £216) **Stalls** Low

Form RPR

-041 **1** **Yaakooum (IRE)**[7] 5276 3-9-8 79 6ex.... PatDobbs 4 87+
(Richard Hannon) *led at stdy pce: qcknd over 3f out: rdn and hdd over 2f out: rallied to ld over 1f out: styd on wl* **1/1**[1]

6465 **2** 1 3/4 **Fighting Back**[10] 5185 3-9-1 72....(b1) NeilCallan 3 77
(Amanda Perrett) *a.p: rdn over 2f out: r.o to go 2nd nr fin: nt rch wnr* **12/1**

21 **3** 1/2 **Law Keeper (IRE)**[23] 4705 3-9-4 75.... KierenFallon 6 79+
(James Tate) *plld hrd and prom: wnt 2nd 10f out: led over 2f out: rdn and hdd over 1f out: styd on same pce ins fnl f* **9/4**[2]

0023 **4** 1 1/4 **Flying Cape (IRE)**[23] 4709 3-8-13 70....(p) RoystonFfrench 1 72
(Andrew Hollinshead) *chsd wnr 2f: remained handy: rdn over 2f out: styd on same pce ins fnl f* **7/1**[3]

623 **5** 1 3/4 **Di's Gift**[15] 4978 5-9-9 75.... DuilioDaSilva(5) 5 74
(Richard Guest) *s.s: hld up: rdn over 2f out: nvr trbld ldrs* **12/1**

2m 40.25s (6.35) **Going Correction** +0.05s/f (Good)
**WFA** 3 from 5yo 10lb **5** Ran SP% **108.7**
Speed ratings (Par 103): **80,78,78,77,76**
CSF £13.02 TOTE £2.00: £1.50, £4.10; EX 12.80 Trifecta £32.30.
**Owner** Saeed H Al Tayer **Bred** George Kent **Trained** East Everleigh, Wilts

**FOCUS**

A modest 3yo handicap run at a slow pace. The winner has more to offer for a truer test.

## 5528 JOHN SMITH'S EXTRA SMOOTH H'CAP 1m 60y

**7:00** (7:01) (Class 4) (0-85,85) 3-Y-O+ **£4,690** (£1,395; £697; £348) **Stalls** Low

Form RPR

4-50 **1** **Maverik**[21] 4761 6-9-12 85.... NeilCallan 1 93
(William Knight) *mde all: racd keenly: rdn over 1f out: jst hld on* **10/1**

0244 **2** *nk* **Postscript (IRE)**[16] 4938 6-9-11 84.... GrahamGibbons 2 91
(David Simcock) *chsd ldrs: shkn up and nt clr run fr over 1f out tl wl ins fnl f: r.o: nt quite get there* **7/1**

-006 **3** *shd* **Henry The Aviator (USA)**[61] 3383 4-9-10 83.... JoeFanning 4 90
(Mark Johnston) *chsd wnr: ev ch fr over 1f out: r.o* **20/1**

3412 **4** 1/2 **Express Himself (IRE)**[19] 4810 3-9-2 81.... SteveDrowne 3 86+
(Ed McMahon) *s.i.s: hld up: plld hrd: hdwy and hung rt fr over 1f out: r.o* **7/2**[2]



The Form Book, Raceform Ltd, Newbury, RG14 5SJ

3140 **5** 1 1/4 **Knight Owl**[16] 4938 4-9-11 84 ShaneKelly 7 87+
(James Fanshawe) *hld up in tch: racd keenly: lost pl over 2f out: hdwy and nt clr run fr over 1f out tl swtchd lft wl ins fnl f: r.o: nvr able to chal* **5/1**[3]

0042 **6** 2 1/4 **Endless Credit (IRE)**[19] 4832 4-9-8 81 DanielTudhope 9 79
(Luca Cumani) *a.p: rdn and nt clr run over 2f out: styd on same pce fnl f* **7/4**[1]

31-5 **7** 3/4 **Ocean Storm (IRE)**[61] 3383 3-9-3 82 (b[1]) KierenFallon 5 77+
(James Tate) *pushed along in rr early: hmpd 7f out: hld up: hdwy over 3f out: rdn over 1f out: no ex fnl f* **16/1**

3111 **8** 2 **Siouxperhero (IRE)**[19] 4831 5-9-3 76 (b) DougieCostello 6 68
(William Muir) *hld up: hdwy 5f out: rdn over 2f out: no ex fnl f* **16/1**

4000 **9** hd **Goldstorm**[10] 5176 6-9-5 78 (p) PaddyAspell 8 69
(Brian Baugh) *mid-div: hdwy over 2f out: sn rdn: no ex fnl f* **50/1**

1m 44.94s (-0.16) **Going Correction** +0.05s/f (Good)
**WFA** 3 from 4yo+ 6lb **9** Ran SP% **115.3**
Speed ratings (Par 105): **102,101,101,101,99 97,96,94,94**
CSF £77.73 CT £1375.18 TOTE £11.90: £2.50, £2.40, £5.50; EX 60.10 Trifecta £661.30.
**Owner** A Brooks **Bred** J G Davis & Star Pointe Ltd **Trained** Patching, W Sussex

**FOCUS**
A fair handicap and a tight finish. The winner was allowed an easy lead but the form is rated as straightforward.

## 5529 FOSTER'S GOLD H'CAP 1m 1f 218y
**7:30** (7:30) (Class 6) (0-60,60) 3-Y-O+ **£2,264** (£673; £336; £168) **Stalls** Low

Form RPR

0061 **1** **Shades Of Silver**[7] 5291 4-9-7 55 WilliamTwiston-Davies 10 63
(Michael Scudamore) *a.p: chsd ldr over 2f out: rdn over 1f out: styd on u.p to ld nr fin* **6/4**[1]

106 **2** 3/4 **Gabrial The Thug (FR)**[38] 4190 4-9-12 60 (t) DavidNolan 13 66
(Richard Fahey) *chsd ldr tl led over 2f out: rdn over 1f out: hdd nr fin* **8/1**

/045 **3** 1 1/4 **Tamujin (IRE)**[22] 4733 6-8-12 46 oh1 LiamKeniry 11 50
(Ken Cunningham-Brown) *hld up: hdwy over 3f out: rdn over 1f out: styd on* **50/1**

50-0 **4** 1 **Hidden Asset**[12] 5103 4-8-13 47 (p) AndrewMullen 4 49+
(Michael Appleby) *hld up: racd keenly: hdwy over 3f out: rdn over 1f out: styd on same pce ins fnl f* **25/1**

5532 **5** 1 **Tunnel Tiger (IRE)**[26] 4592 3-8-11 60 CallumShepherd(7) 12 60
(William Knight) *a.p: rdn over 2f out: styd on same pce fnl f* **6/1**[2]

-064 **6** 1/2 **Sheer Poetry (IRE)**[25] 4617 3-8-12 54 (e) PatDobbs 5 53
(Mike Murphy) *hld up: hdwy over 2f out: rdn over 1f out: styd on same pce fnl f* **7/1**[3]

4424 **7** nk **Mercury Magic**[15] 4969 3-9-4 60 DaneO'Neill 1 58
(David Menuisier) *hld up: nt clr run over 2f out: styd on ins fnl f: nvr trbld ldrs* **16/1**

2403 **8** nk **Sofias Number One (USA)**[12] 5100 6-8-11 48 (p) BillyCray(3) 9 46
(Roy Bowring) *prom: rdn over 3f out: outpcd over 2f out: r.o towards fin* **12/1**

5030 **9** 1/2 **Kheskianto (IRE)**[5] 5337 8-8-5 46 oh1 (t) PaulBooth(7) 8 43
(Michael Chapman) *s.i.s: hld up: hdwy over 2f out: rdn and hung rt over 1f out: no ex fnl f* **33/1**

0063 **10** 1 1/4 **Mcmonagle (USA)**[20] 4792 6-9-2 55 (tp) JacobButterfield(5) 6 49
(Alan Brown) *led: rdn and hdd over 2f out: no extera fnl f* **20/1**

1600 **11** 3 1/2 **Teide Peak (IRE)**[45] 3971 5-9-12 60 SeanLevey 7 48
(Paul D'Arcy) *hld up: rdn over 2f out: nvr on terms* **8/1**

1200 **12** 8 **My Renaissance**[112] 1836 4-9-5 53 ShaneKelly 2 26
(Ben Case) *prom: rdn over 2f out: wknd over 1f out* **33/1**

600/ **13** 36 **Business Bay (USA)**[891] 4945 7-8-12 46 oh1 PaulQuinn 3
(Patrick Clinton) *hld up: rdn and wknd over 2f out* **100/1**

2m 7.93s (0.03) **Going Correction** +0.05s/f (Good)
**WFA** 3 from 4yo+ 8lb **13** Ran SP% **120.0**
Speed ratings (Par 101): **101,100,99,98,97 97,97,96,96,95 92,86,57**
CSF £12.83 CT £438.63 TOTE £2.50: £1.30, £1.80, £6.20; EX 14.40 Trifecta £531.30.
**Owner** The Champion Family & Michael Scudamore **Bred** Newsells Park Stud **Trained** Bromsash, H'fords

■ Stewards' Enquiry : William Twiston-Davies two-day ban: used whip above permitted level (Sep 2-3)
David Nolan one-day ban: careless riding (Sep 2)

**FOCUS**
A moderate handicap. The winner took advantage of being well in.

## 5530 HEINEKEN EXTRA COLD H'CAP 7f 9y
**8:00** (8:01) (Class 6) (0-65,65) 3-Y-O+ **£2,264** (£673; £336; £168) **Stalls** High

Form RPR

0-31 **1** **Jay Kay**[8] 5234 5-9-0 51 6ex DanielTudhope 11 68
(K R Burke) *chsd ldrs: led 2f out: rdn over 1f out: c clr fnl f: comf* **13/8**[1]

2306 **2** 3 1/2 **Royal Encounter**[32] 4411 3-9-7 63 [1] OisinMurphy 7 68
(Ed Vaughan) *chsd ldr: rdn over 2f out: styd on same pce fnl f* **10/1**

3064 **3** 3/4 **Day Of The Eagle (IRE)**[32] 4394 8-10-0 65 GrahamGibbons 9 70
(Michael Easterby) *hld up: hdwy u.p over 1f out: nt rch ldrs* **3/1**[2]

0003 **4** 2 **Master Of Song**[12] 5103 7-8-9 49 (bt) AshleyMorgan(3) 6 49
(Roy Bowring) *s.i.s: hdwy 1/2-way: rdn over 1f out: styd on same pce fnl f* **25/1**

0610 **5** 1/2 **Sophie's Beau (USA)**[20] 4797 7-8-8 52 BradleyBosley(7) 2 51
(Michael Chapman) *led: rdn and hdd 2f out: styd on same pce fr over 1f out* **33/1**

1250 **6** 1 3/4 **Botanist**[12] 5075 7-9-8 59 BenCurtis 5 53
(Shaun Harris) *hld up: hdwy over 2f out: rdn whn nt clr run over 1f out: swtchd lft and no ex ins fnl f* **6/1**[3]

1335 **7** 5 **Caledonia Laird**[32] 4415 3-9-2 58 KierenFallon 3 37
(Jo Hughes) *prom: rdn and ev ch 2f out: wknd fnl f* **10/1**

3440 **8** 3/4 **Trigger Park (IRE)**[22] 4733 3-8-13 55 WilliamTwiston-Davies 10 32
(Ronald Harris) *hld up: a in rr: rdn and wknd over 2f out* **25/1**

6200 **9** 8 **Llyrical**[17] 4907 3-9-6 62 DaneO'Neill 1 18
(Derek Haydn Jones) *prom: racd keenly: rdn over 2f out: wknd over 1f out* **33/1**

-000 **10** 7 **Exceed Policy**[15] 4970 3-8-4 46 oh1 JoeFanning 8
(David Dennis) *hld up: rdn over 2f out: sn wknd* **50/1**

1m 26.79s (0.59) **Going Correction** -0.15s/f (Firm)
**WFA** 3 from 5yo+ 5lb **10** Ran SP% **118.4**
Speed ratings (Par 101): **90,86,85,82,82 80,74,73,64,56**
CSF £19.19 CT £47.10 TOTE £2.60: £1.30, £2.80, £1.90; EX 19.10 Trifecta £80.90.
**Owner** John Kenny **Bred** Miss S E Hall **Trained** Middleham Moor, N Yorks

**FOCUS**
A modest 7f handicap concluded proceedings in which they went an even gallop spread across the track. The winner backed up his Ayr romp.

T/Jkpt: £9,031.20 to a £1 stake. Pool: £31,800.25 - 2.50 winning tickets. T/Plt: £329.90 to a £1 stake. Pool: £59,657.36 - 131.98 winning tickets. T/Qpdt: £99.40 to a £1 stake. Pool: £5,960.69 - 44.34 winning tickets. CR

# 5315 YARMOUTH (L-H)
### Tuesday, August 19

**OFFICIAL GOING: Good to firm (7.2)**
Wind: fresh, half behind Weather: bright spells Rails: Bottom bend dolled out 3m and races on Round course increased by 18yds

## 5531 FAMILY FUNDAY AT GREAT YARMOUTH RACECOURSE MEDIAN AUCTION MAIDEN STKS 6f 3y
**2:00** (2:00) (Class 6) 3-5-Y-O **£2,328** (£693; £346; £173) **Stalls** Centre

Form RPR

32 **1** **Eleusis**[46] 3938 3-9-0 0 TedDurcan 3 84
(Chris Wall) *fly-leapt as stalls: mde all: rdn and qcknd clr over 1f out: in n.d fnl f: eased towards fin* **4/1**[3]

-536 **2** 6 **Whaleweigh Station**[45] 3980 3-9-5 85 FrederikTylicki 5 70
(J R Jenkins) *plunged forward and awkward leaving stall: chsd ldrs: wnt 2nd 4f out: shkn up and fnd nil over 1f out: clr 2nd but no ch w wnr fnl f* **8/11**[1]

3- **3** 14 **Normanna (IRE)**[243] 8342 3-9-0 0 MartinHarley 1 20
(Marco Botti) *stdd s: plld v hrd in rr: rdn: racd awkwardly and foung nil ent fnl 2f: stl unbalanced and changing legs whn wnt poor 3rd ins fnl f* **11/4**[2]

**4** 7 **Saved My Bacon (IRE)** 3-8-7 0 ThomasHemsley(7) 6
(Chris Dwyer) *chsd wnr for 2f: 3rd and wknd over 1f out: fdd and lost 3rd ins fnl f* **66/1**

**5** 6 **Tilsworth Annalisa** 3-8-7 0 VictorSantos(7) 2
(J R Jenkins) *in tch in last pair: rdn over 3f out: lost tch over 2f out: t.o* **66/1**

1m 14.72s (0.32) **Going Correction** -0.025s/f (Good) **5** Ran SP% **107.6**
Speed ratings (Par 101): **96,88,69,60,52**
CSF £7.06 TOTE £4.00: £1.60, £1.10; EX 7.30 Trifecta £8.60.
**Owner** Lady Juliet Tadgell **Bred** Redland Bs, Baroness Bs & D Redvers **Trained** Newmarket, Suffolk

**FOCUS**
After a dry night, the going was left unchanged. There was a slight surprise in this ordinary maiden as the odds-on favourite was readily turned over. Hard form to pin down, the winner rated up two stone.

## 5532 TRAFALGAR RESTAURANT MAIDEN H'CAP 6f 3y
**2:30** (2:31) (Class 5) (0-70,68) 3-Y-O+ **£2,975** (£885; £442; £221) **Stalls** Centre

Form RPR

2224 **1** **Mimi Luke (USA)**[12] 5105 3-8-13 60 (v) MartinHarley 3 67
(Alan Bailey) *chsd ldrs: jnd ldr and travelling strly 3f out: rdn to ld ent fnl f: kpt on u.p fnl 100yds: a jst holding runner-up: drvn out* **11/4**[1]

36-0 **2** shd **Great Wave (IRE)**[99] 2210 3-9-7 68 JamieSpencer 6 74
(David Simcock) *taken down early: stdd s: hld up in tch in rr: hdwy over 2f out: chsd wnr 1f out: ev ch u.p ins fnl f: kpt on and grad clsng nr fin* **4/1**[3]

3000 **3** 1 1/2 **What A Dandy (IRE)**[8] 5247 3-9-1 62 NickyMackay 9 63
(Jim Boyle) *t.k.h: led: rdn and hdd ent fnl f: kpt on same pce fnl 150yds* **12/1**

5-00 **4** 1 **Port Lairge**[35] 4306 4-8-7 54 (b[1]) MichaelJMMurphy(3) 5 52
(John Gallagher) *chsd ldrs: drvn and ev ch 2f out: no ex 1f out: styd on same pce after* **16/1**

6260 **5** 2 1/2 **Stroll On (IRE)**[20] 4795 3-9-3 64 ChrisCatlin 4 54
(Rae Guest) *taken down early: t.k.h: hld up in tch in midfield: drvn and no hdwy 2f out: plugged on same pce after* **8/1**

-064 **6** hd **Red Cossack (CAN)**[58] 3503 3-9-7 68 [1] FrederikTylicki 8 57
(Paul Webber) *racd alone nr stands' rail: chsd ldrs: rdn 2f out: no ex and btn jst over 1f out: wknd ins fnl f* **3/1**[2]

06 **7** 3 1/4 **Habeshia**[12] 5105 4-8-5 49 oh3 (t) JimmyQuinn 2 28
(John Best) *fly-leapt as stalls opened: chsd ldr tl 1/2-way: lost pl u.p 2f out: wl btn after* **10/1**

4000 **8** 1/2 **Yankee Red**[12] 5105 3-8-8 55 LiamJones 1 32
(John Best) *stdd s: t.k.h: sn rcvrd to chse ldrs: rdn ent fnl 2f: no ex over 1f out: fdd fnl f* **20/1**

0-06 **9** 1 1/2 **Sybilicious**[26] 4590 3-8-2 49 oh3 [1] RoystonFrench 7 21
(Stuart Williams) *in tch in last pair: rdn 1/2-way: wknd and bhd over 1f out* **25/1**

1m 15.18s (0.78) **Going Correction** -0.025s/f (Good)
**WFA** 3 from 4yo 3lb **9** Ran SP% **114.1**
Speed ratings (Par 103): **93,92,90,89,86 85,81,80,78**
CSF £13.78 CT £110.95 TOTE £3.00: £1.10, £2.00, £3.10; EX 12.90 Trifecta £145.20.
**Owner** Dr S P Hargreaves **Bred** Marie Becker & Champions **Trained** Newmarket, Suffolk

**FOCUS**
An ordinary sprint handicap for maidens. The winner is rated to form.

## 5533 DON & SHIRLEY MILLER DIAMOND ANNIVERSARY H'CAP 1m 1f
**3:00** (3:00) (Class 5) (0-75,75) 4-Y-O+ **£2,587** (£770; £384; £192) **Stalls** Low

Form RPR

6241 **1** **Frontline Phantom (IRE)**[3] 5421 7-8-8 64 PeterSword(7) 1 74
(K R Burke) *chsd ldrs: hdwy on inner to chse ldr jst over 2f out: led over 1f out: in command and edgd rt ins fnl f: comf* **4/5**[1]

023 **2** 2 1/2 **Ela Goog La Mou**[13] 5058 5-8-10 59 ChrisCatlin 5 64
(Peter Charalambous) *t.k.h: hld up in tch in midfield: hdwy 4f out: led wl over 2f out: rdn and hdd over 1f out: one pce and readily hld fnl f* **5/1**[2]

033 **3** 9 **Vainglory (USA)**[6] 5319 10-9-12 75 JamieSpencer 3 68
(David Simcock) *led for 1f: chsd ldr tl drvn 4f out: 3rd and no imp over 1f out: wknd 1f out: eased towards fin* **5/1**[2]

3135 **4** 8 **Mishrif (USA)**[12] 5100 8-9-9 75 (v) ConnorBeasley(3) 2 44
(J R Jenkins) *stdd s: hld up in last pair: rdn and struggling over 3f out: no ch fnl 2f: wnt modest 4th nr fin* **16/1**

101 **5** 1/2 **Nifty Kier**[12] 5109 5-8-4 56 oh1 DannyBrock(3) 7 24
(Phil McEntee) *nt best away: rcvrd to ld after 1f: rdn and hdd wl over 1f out: sn rdn and btn: wknd over 1f out: lost modest 4th nr fin* **8/1**[3]

1046 **6** 3/4 **Patriotic (IRE)**[12] 5100 6-9-8 71 (p) JimmyQuinn 4 38
(Chris Dwyer) *stdd s: hld up in rr: rdn over 3f out: sn btn and no ch fnl 2f* **33/1**

1m 57.15s (1.35) **Going Correction** +0.25s/f (Good) **6** Ran SP% **108.8**
Speed ratings (Par 103): **104,101,93,86,86 85**
CSF £4.76 TOTE £2.60: £1.70, £1.20; EX 4.70 Trifecta £12.80.
**Owner** Ontoawinner & Mrs E Burke **Bred** Joe Rogers **Trained** Middleham Moor, N Yorks

**FOCUS**
This was run at a fair pace and it looks straightforward form. A similar effort to Doncaster from the winner.

## 5534 CONFERENCES AT GREAT YARMOUTH RACECOURSE MAIDEN H'CAP 1m 3f 101y
**3:30** (3:30) (Class 5) (0-70,70) 3-Y-0+ **£2,975** (£885; £442; £221) **Stalls** Low

Form RPR
22-0 **1** **Rawoof (IRE)**53 3673 3-9-5 70 ........1 ChrisCatlin 7 86
(Rae Guest) *styd wd early: led after 1f and crossed to inner rail: 4 l clr 5f out: rdn 3f out: styd on strly and wl in command fnl 2f: eased towards fin* **4/1**3

5424 **2** *10* **Kinema (IRE)**12 5108 3-9-5 70 ........(p) MartinHarley 6 70
(Ed Walker) *led for 1f: settled bk into midfield: hdwy in 3rd 4f out: chsd ldr over 3f out: no imp: clr 2nd but no ch over 1f out: plugged on* **3/1**2

2332 **3** *8* **Interconnection**33 4350 3-9-2 67 ........(b) FrederikTylicki 1 54
(Ed Vaughan) *hld up in tch in rr: hdwy in 4th 4f out: wnt 3rd and rdn over 3f out: no prog and wl btn fnl 2f* **9/4**1

4303 **4** *7* **Evacusafe Lady**109 1918 3-8-2 56 ........ RyanPowell(3) 5 32
(John Ryan) *t.k.h: hld up in last pair early: hdwy into midfield 8f out: wnt modest 4th 3f out: sn rdn and btn: bhd fnl 2f* **33/1**

5003 **5** *18* **Appellez Baileys (FR)**11 5122 3-8-0 51 oh6 ........ NickyMackay 3
(Chris Dwyer) *prom early: stdd bk and in last pair after 4f: rdn 4f out: sn lost tch: t.o over 2f out* **66/1**

0323 **6** *8* **Keep To The Beat**20 4793 3-8-11 62 ........(p) JamieSpencer 4
(Kevin Ryan) *t.k.h: hld up in tch: hdwy to chse ldr 8f out tl over 3f out: sn dropped out: rdr looking down and eased over 2f out: t.o over 1f out* **3/1**2

5664 **7** *½* **Cape Karli (IRE)**14 5018 3-8-11 67 ........ ShaneGray(5) 2
(Kevin Ryan) *chsd ldrs tl rdn and lost pl qckly 4f out: t.o over 2f out: eased fnl f* **16/1**

2m 29.8s (1.10) **Going Correction** +0.25s/f (Good) **7** Ran SP% **111.1**
Speed ratings (Par 103): **106,98,92,87,74 68,68**
CSF £15.42 TOTE £5.80: £2.90, £2.00; EX 17.60 Trifecta £66.90.
**Owner** Brook Stud **Bred** Shadwell Estate Company Limited **Trained** Newmarket, Suffolk

**FOCUS**
A typically moderate 3yo maiden handicap in which they finished well strung out. A clear step up from the winner.

## 5535 GEV H'CAP 5f 43y
**4:00** (4:00) (Class 5) (0-75,75) 3-Y-0+ **£2,587** (£770; £384; £192) **Stalls** Centre

Form RPR
2243 **1** **Vodka Chaser (IRE)**13 5060 3-8-10 68 ........ PhilipPrince(5) 2 78
(Alison Hutchinson) *chsd ldrs: rdn and effrt to chal over 1f out: led 1f out: in command and wandered ins fnl f: r.o: comf* **8/1**

6002 **2** *1 ½* **It Must Be Faith**13 5060 4-8-12 68 ........(p) AlistairRawlinson(5) 1 73
(Michael Appleby) *dwlt: in tch in midfield: rdn and hdwy to ld over 1f out: sn drvn and hdd 1f out: styd on same pce fnl f* **15/8**1

4404 **3** *2 ¼* **Ubetterbegood (ARG)**19 4833 6-9-5 70 ........(v) TedDurcan 7 67
(Robert Cowell) *stdd s: t.k.h: hld up in tch in last pair: rdn and effrt over 1f out: drvn and wnt 3rd fnl 150yds: no imp* **9/2**3

0502 **4** *1 ¼* **Sleepy Blue Ocean**19 4833 8-9-5 75 ........(p) ShaneGray(5) 8 67
(John Balding) *dwlt: in tch in last pair: rdn 1/2-way: drvn over 1f out: no imp: wnt 4th ins fnl f* **9/2**3

5522 **5** *2 ¾* **Alpha Delta Whisky**27 4553 6-9-8 73 ........(v) MartinHarley 6 55
(John Gallagher) *chsd ldr tl led 1/2-way: drvn and hdd over 1f out: sn btn: bhd fnl f* **10/3**2

5613 **6** *shd* **Amosite**12 5097 8-9-6 74 ........(v) ConnorBeasley(3) 4 56
(J R Jenkins) *sn bustled along: led tl 1/2-way: 3rd and outpcd u.p over 1f out: wknd fnl f* **16/1**

1m 3.17s (0.47) **Going Correction** -0.025s/f (Good)
**WFA** 3 from 4yo+ 2lb **6** Ran SP% **111.2**
Speed ratings (Par 103): **95,92,89,87,82 82**
CSF £23.06 CT £73.66 TOTE £6.70: £3.30, £1.60; EX 24.10 Trifecta £109.30.
**Owner** Miss A L Hutchinson **Bred** Tally-Ho Stud **Trained** Exning, Suffolk

**FOCUS**
An ordinary sprint handicap run at a solid pace. The winner reversed C&D form with the runner-up.

## 5536 WEDDINGS AT GREAT YARMOUTH RACECOURSE H'CAP 7f 3y
**4:30** (4:30) (Class 4) (0-80,80) 3-Y-0+ **£5,045** (£1,501; £750; £375) **Stalls** Centre

Form RPR
6-32 **1** **Ziggy's Secret**17 4907 4-9-1 76 ........ MikeyEnnis(7) 3 86
(Lucy Wadham) *taken down early: stdd and awkward leaving stall: t.k.h: chsd ldr: nudged along to join ldr 1f out: pushed into ld and reminder ins fnl f: sn in command: pushed out* **2/1**2

104 **2** *1 ¼* **Almanack**20 4795 4-8-11 65 ........ StevieDonohoe 5 72
(Ian Williams) *stdd after s: hld up in last pair: rdn over 1f out: styd on wl u.p fnl 150yds: wnt 2nd towards fin: no threat to wnr* **8/1**

652 **3** *1 ¼* **Jungle Bay**26 4594 7-9-8 76 ........(b) TedDurcan 2 80
(Jane Chapple-Hyam) *led: rdn over 1f out: drvn and hdd ins fnl f: sn brushed aside by wnr: lost 2nd and wknd towards fin* **7/1**3

0312 **4** *1* **Red Paladin (IRE)**27 4537 4-9-4 72 ........ JamieSpencer 7 73
(Kevin Ryan) *stdd s: hld up in last pair: rdn and hdwy to chse ldng pair ent fnl 2f: no imp fnl f* **13/8**1

5-62 **5** *19* **Glanely (IRE)**105 2059 4-9-9 77 ........ JackMitchell 6 29
(Martyn Meade) *chsd ldrs: rdn over 2f out: sn hung lft and btn 2f out: wl bhd fnl f* **8/1**

1m 27.66s (1.06) **Going Correction** -0.025s/f (Good)
**WFA** 3 from 4yo+ 5lb **5** Ran SP% **106.2**
Speed ratings (Par 105): **92,90,89,88,66**
CSF £15.55 TOTE £2.50: £1.90, £3.60; EX 14.60 Trifecta £37.20.
**Owner** Mr And Mrs A E Pakenham **Bred** Honeypuddle Stud **Trained** Newmarket, Suffolk

**FOCUS**
Not the strongest race for the grade, but the pace was honest. The winner is rated up to his best.

## 5537 INJURED JOCKEYS FUND APPRENTICE TRAINING SERIES H'CAP (PART OF THE RACING EXCELLENCE INITIATIVE) 1m 3y
**5:05** (5:05) (Class 6) (0-65,65) 4-Y-0+ **£1,940** (£577; £288; £144) **Stalls** Centre

Form RPR
0054 **1** **Rouge Nuage (IRE)**4 5394 4-9-10 65 ........(b) JordanNason 1 74
(Conrad Allen) *racd keenly: chsd ldrs tl led 1/2-way: rdn 2 l clr over 1f out: drifting lft fnl f: styd on* **7/2**2

04 **2** *2* **Polar Forest**17 4904 4-9-10 65 ........(e) PatMillman 3 69
(Richard Guest) *fly-leapt leaving stalls: in tch in midfield: rdn to chse wnr over 1f out: kpt on but a hld* **5/1**3

0256 **3** *3 ½* **Enriching (USA)**21 4763 6-9-3 63 ........ JackOsborn(5) 5 59
(Nick Littmoden) *in tch in rr: rdn and effrt 2f out: sme hdwy to go 3rd 1f out: no imp* **7/1**

0625 **4** *¾* **Lewamy (IRE)**7 5280 4-8-8 49 ........ JennyPowell 6 44
(John Best) *mostly 2nd tl over 1f out: sn outpcd u.p: lost 3rd and plugged on same pce fnl f* **16/1**

4555 **5** *¾* **Buzz Law (IRE)**32 4381 6-8-7 53 ........(b1) PeterSword(5) 4 46
(K R Burke) *in tch in last pair: rdn over 2f out: no prog: 5th and wl hld over 1f out* **7/2**2

2215 **6** *6* **Jonnie Skull (IRE)**6 5319 8-9-9 64 ........(vt) JoeDoyle 7 43
(Phil McEntee) *led tl 1/2-way: rdn and lost pl over 2f out: bhd over 1f out* **9/4**1

1m 39.98s (-0.62) **Going Correction** -0.025s/f (Good) **6** Ran SP% **110.3**
Speed ratings (Par 101): **102,100,96,95,95 89**
CSF £20.07 TOTE £7.00: £3.40, £1.50; EX 19.80 Trifecta £98.10.
**Owner** sportsdays.co.uk **Bred** Dermot Farrington **Trained** Newmarket, Suffolk

**FOCUS**
A modest but competitive apprentice handicap. The winner is rated to this year's turf form.
T/Plt: £28.40 to a £1 stake. Pool: £60,481.67 - 1,551.58 winning tickets. T/Qpdt: £20.90 to a £1 stake. Pool: £3,990.70 - 140.70 winning tickets. SP

# 5478 DEAUVILLE (R-H)
Tuesday, August 19

**OFFICIAL GOING: Turf: very soft; polytrack: standard**

## 5543a PRIX ETALON MUHTATHIR (CONDITIONS) (2YO) (TURF) 6f 110y(S)
**11:15** (11:15) 2-Y-0 **£14,166** (£5,666; £4,250; £2,833)

RPR
**1** **Smaih (GER)**24 4670 2-9-0 0 ........ FrankieDettori 1 93
(Richard Hannon) *mde all: shkn up and qcknd over 1 1/2f out: drvn ins fnl f: sn in control: comf* **19/10**2

**2** *1 ½* **Rafaadah**19 4839 2-8-10 0 ........ IoritzMendizabal 2 85
(J-C Rouget, France) **1/2**1

**3** *2 ½* **Claudia Eria (FR)**8 2-8-5 0 ........ NicolasLarenaudie(5) 4 78
(P Van De Poele, France) **71/10**3

**4** *3* **Dayaday (FR)**18 4882 2-8-10 0 ........ AnthonyCrastus 3 69
(C Boutin, France) **136/10**

1m 22.54s (5.34) **4** Ran SP% **120.3**
WIN (incl. 1 euro stake): 2.90. PLACES: 1.10, 1.10, SF: 3.50.
**Owner** Al Shaqab Racing **Bred** Stiftung Gestut Fahrhof **Trained** East Everleigh, Wilts

## 5544a PRIX ETALON NAAQOOS (CLAIMER) (2YO) (TURF) 1m (R)
**11:45** (11:45) 2-Y-0 **£11,250** (£4,500; £3,375; £2,250; £1,125)

RPR
**1** **Mount Isa (IRE)**12 5118 2-8-11 0 ........ MaximeGuyon 10 70
(Mme Pia Brandt, France) **49/10**3

**2** *2* **Rocket Bob (FR)**119 2-8-11 0 ........ AnthonyCrastus 11 66
(C Boutin, France) **234/10**

**3** *2* **Ever One (FR)** 2-8-8 0 ........ ValentinSeguy(3) 2 61
(K Borgel, France) **165/10**

**4** *1 ¼* **Safzebos (FR)**11 2-8-9 0 ........ JeffersonSmith(6) 1 62
(C Ferland, France) **37/10**1

**5** *1 ½* **Portenio (FR)**17 4932 2-8-10 0 ........ MllePaulineDominois(6) 14 60
(C Lerner, France) **41/10**2

**6** *nk* **Sparkling Frost (FR)** 2-8-11 0 ........ TheoBachelot 4 54
(S Wattel, France) **34/1**

**7** *3* **Take A Guess (FR)**9 2-9-8 0 ........(b1) AntoineHamelin 3 59
(Matthieu Palussiere, France) **81/10**

**8** *3* **Plume D'Outarde**11 2-8-11 0 ........ CristianDemuro 5 41
(F Doumen, France) **212/10**

**9** *1 ½* **Clown (FR)** 2-8-11 0 ........ AlexisBadel 7 38
(Mme M Bollack-Badel, France) **56/1**

**10** *1 ¾* **Chefchaouen (IRE)**14 5026 2-8-8 0 ........ ThierryJarnet 6 31
(J S Moore) *chsd ldrs: cl 5th and pushed along 2 1/2f out and no imp: wknd fnl f* **74/10**

**11** *1 ¾* **Porto Stephano (IRE)**47 2-9-1 0 ........(p) RaphaelMarchelli 9 34
(T Castanheira, France) **68/1**

**12** *1 ¼* **Snow Guest (FR)**18 4882 2-8-8 0 ........(p) MickaelBarzalona 13 25
(D Windrif, France) **87/10**

**13** *10* **Melchope (FR)**14 5026 2-8-8 0 ........(p) GregoryBenoist 8
(E J O'Neill, France) **233/10**

**14** *10* **Boann (IRE)**18 4882 2-8-8 0 ........(b) IoritzMendizabal 12
(J S Moore) *led: hdd after 2f: remained prom non outer: rdn and wknd qckly 2f out w rdr looking down: heavily eased* **231/10**

1m 46.94s (6.14) **14** Ran SP% **119.7**
WIN (incl. 1 euro stake): 5.90. PLACES; 2,70, 6.40, 5.10. DF: 71.40. SF: 140.80.
**Owner** Mlle Sandra Feret **Bred** Tally-Ho Stud **Trained** France

## 5545a SHADWELL PRIX DE LA NONETTE (GROUP 2) (3YO FILLIES) (TURF) 1m 2f
**1:20** (1:20) 3-Y-0 **£61,750** (£23,833; £11,375; £7,583; £3,791)

RPR
**1** **Avenir Certain (FR)**65 3289 3-9-0 0 ........ GregoryBenoist 2 116+
(J-C Rouget, France) *hld up in midfield: smooth prog 1 1/2f out: led ins fnl f: easily* **3/5**1

**2** *1 ½* **Crisolles (FR)**52 3-9-0 0 ........ IoritzMendizabal 6 110
(J-C Rouget, France) *led: hdd ins fnl f: kpt on gamely u.p: no ch w wnr* **176/10**

**3** *2 ½* **Lavender Lane (IRE)**51 3773 3-9-0 0 ........ GeraldMosse 7 105
(J E Hammond, France) *dwlt: w.w in rr: tk clsr order over 1 1/2f out: 3rd and rdn 1f out: no further imp and nvr on terms w front two* **6/1**

**4** *2* **Vazira (FR)**61 3376 3-9-0 0 ........ Christophe-PatriceLemaire 8 101
(A De Royer-Dupre, France) *disp 3rd on outer: rdn and sltly outpcd under 2f out: kpt on again ins fnl f: n.d* **57/10**3

**5** *¾* **Summer Surprice (FR)**28 4525 3-9-0 0 ........ TheoBachelot 5 100
(F-H Graffard, France) *w.w towards rr: rdn and no imp over 1 1/2f out: kpt on under driving fnl f: nvr in contention* **40/1**

**6** *¾* **Maid Of The Glens (IRE)**31 4461 3-9-0 0 ........ ColmO'Donoghue 1 98
(John Patrick Shanahan, Ire) *disp 3rd on inner: rdn and nt qckn fr 2f out: grad dropped away fnl f* **43/1**

7 1/2 **Be My Gal**[19] 4840 3-9-0 0 FrankieDettori 4 97
(Roger Charlton) *trckd ldr: shkn up and tried to chal fr 2 1/2f out: rdn 1 1/2f out: wknd fnl f* **42/10**[2]

2m 11.18s (0.98) **7** Ran SP% **121.0**
WIN (incl. 1 euro stake): 1.60. PLACES: 1.10, 1.90, 1.40. DF: 14.90. SF: 17.60.
**Owner** A Caro & G Augustin-Normand **Bred** Mme E Vidal **Trained** Pau, France

## 5546a PRIX DERRINSTOWN STUD (CLAIMER) (4YO+) (LADY RIDERS) (TURF) 1m 2f

**2:25** (2:25) 4-Y-0+ **£6,666** (£2,666; £2,000; £1,333; £666)

RPR

1 **Royal Talisman**[9] 5225 6-9-4 0 MlleJessicaMarcialis 4 83
(Jo Hughes) *plld hrd: restrained in prom position bhd ldr: cl 3rd and ev ch over 1 1/2f out: rdn and chsd ldr into fnl f: r.o to ld 120yds out: sn clr: readily* **11/5**[1]

2 2 **Grandezza (GER)**[54] 4-8-13 0 DelphineSantiago 1 74
(K Borgel, France) **26/5**[3]

3 2 **Cellalando (FR)**[61] 4-8-13 0 MlleZoePfeil(5) 2 75
(J E Pease, France) **17/2**

4 1 1/4 **Roi d'Aragon (IRE)**[111] 4-9-8 0 (b) ManonScandella-Lacaille 11 77
(F Rossi, France) **128/10**

5 shd **Usbeke (GER)**[65] 8-8-13 0 MlleSarahCallac(3) 8 70
(R Houthoofd, Belgium) **13/1**

6 1 1/4 **Bizzy Nizzy (FR)**[125] 4-8-11 0 KarenBeaumard 10 63
(P Lenogue, France) **79/1**

7 1 1/4 **Montesquieu (FR)**[119] 4-8-10 0 (p) LauraGrosso(6) 3 65
(C Boutin, France) **146/10**

8 2 1/2 **Golden Club (FR)**[17] 5-8-6 0 (b) MlleMarionLanave(5) 6 55
(N Caullery, France) **36/1**

9 nk **Seyfeddine (IRE)**[46] 4-9-3 0 (p) MllePaulineDominois(5) 9 66
(R Le Gal, France) **29/10**[2]

10 1 3/4 **Mont Athos (FR)**[36] 5-8-6 0 MlleMarylineEon(5) 7 51
(J Van Handenhove, France) **87/10**

11 15 **Lie To Me (FR)**[61] 4-9-2 0 CarlaO'Halloran 5 26
(Mme G Rarick, France) **61/1**

2m 14.28s (4.08) **11** Ran SP% **120.2**
WIN (incl. 1 euro stake): 3.20. PLACES: 1.70, 2.00, 2.40. DF: 12.20. SF: 21.70.
**Owner** R P Phillips **Bred** The National Stud **Trained** Lambourn, Berks

# 5486 KEMPTON (A.W) (R-H)

Wednesday, August 20

**OFFICIAL GOING: Polytrack: standard**
Wind: Moderate, half against Weather: Fine

## 5547 KEMPTON LIVE WITH DIZZEE RASCAL 06.09.14 H'CAP 2m (P)

**6:20** (6:20) (Class 6) (0-65,65) 4-Y-0+ **£1,940** (£577; £288; £144) **Stalls Low**

Form RPR

0321 1 **Mister Bob (GER)**[25] 4656 5-9-2 60 (p) TedDurcan 3 67+
(James Bethell) *hld up: last 4f out: rdn and prog over 2f out: led jst over 1f out: styd on* **1/1**[1]

6424 2 3/4 **No Such Number**[22] 4769 6-8-13 62 ShelleyBirkett(5) 4 68
(Julia Feilden) *hld up in tch: clsd gng wl to chal over 1f out: chsd wnr fnl f: styd on but nt qckn and a hld* **11/2**[3]

3305 3 nk **Dr Finley (IRE)**[22] 4769 7-8-5 52 (v) SimonPearce(3) 8 58
(Lydia Pearce) *trckd ldr: led wl over 2f out: drvn and hdd jst over 1f out: kpt on same pce* **16/1**

0236 4 2 **Jezza**[42] 4076 8-9-0 65 (t) KieranShoemark(7) 7 68
(Karen George) *dwlt: hld up in last pair: rdn over 3f out: bdly outpcd over 2f out: kpt on fr over 1f out to take 4th ins fnl f: nrst fin* **5/1**[2]

2463 5 1 1/2 **Ice Apple**[23] 4737 6-8-2 49 ow2 (b) NataliaGemelova(3) 2 51
(John E Long) *hld up in tch: disp 2nd over 2f out: sn hanging bdly rt and fnd nil: one pce after* **14/1**

0-00 6 2 1/4 **Ermyn Lodge**[67] 3249 8-9-0 65 (vt) PaddyBradley(7) 5 64
(Pat Phelan) *trckd ldng pair to 6f out: rdn over 3f out: styd on inner and no prog 2f out* **7/1**

000 7 7 **Berwin (IRE)**[14] 5036 5-8-10 54 LiamKeniry 1 44
(Sylvester Kirk) *rel to r: ct up as pce modest and sn t.k.h: prog 5f out: wknd qckly 2f out* **25/1**

600 8 16 **Gentlemax (FR)**[10] 5208 4-9-7 65 (b[1]) PatCosgrave 6 36
(Jim Boyle) *t.k.h: led at gentle pce: hdd & wknd rapidly wl over 2f out: t.o* **14/1**

3m 33.49s (3.39) **Going Correction** -0.05s/f (Stan) **8** Ran SP% **117.6**
Speed ratings (Par 101): **89,88,88,87,86 85,82,74**
CSF £7.20 CT £56.41 TOTE £1.60: £1.02, £2.70, £3.70; EX 7.30 Trifecta £44.90.
**Owner** Robert Gibbons **Bred** Newsells Park Stud Ltd **Trained** Middleham Moor, N Yorks

**FOCUS**
The pace was steady, but the favourite scored from some way back in this staying handicap. The form looks ordinary.

## 5548 BETBRIGHT MONEYBACK OFFERS MAIDEN FILLIES' STKS 7f (P)

**6:50** (6:52) (Class 5) 3-Y-0+ **£2,587** (£770; £384; £192) **Stalls Low**

Form RPR

3-3 1 **Aragosta**[89] 2511 4-9-5 0 HayleyTurner 5 75+
(James Fanshawe) *trckd ldr: led wl over 1f out: jst pushed along to draw clr fnl f: comf* **9/4**[2]

0-0 2 4 **Gracefilly**[32] 4446 3-9-0 0 RichardKingscote 6 60
(Ed Walker) *led: rdn and hdd wl over 1f out: no ch w wnr but clung on for 2nd* **33/1**

50 3 nk **Unbridled Joy (IRE)**[25] 4677 3-8-11 0 RyanTate(3) 2 59
(Clive Cox) *in tch in midfield: shkn up and prog 2f out but ldng pair already gone: rdn and styd on fnl f to take 3rd last strides* **16/1**

4 hd **Tayma (IRE)** 3-9-0 0 HarryBentley 12 59+
(Saeed bin Suroor) *dwlt but quick prog to go prom: chsd ldng pair over 2f out but sn outpcd: one pce after: lost 2nd last strides* **7/2**[3]

0- 5 1 1/2 **Heavens Eyes (IRE)**[277] 7934 3-9-0 0 PatCosgrave 4 55
(Jo Hughes) *in tch: shkn up and outpcd over 2f out: kpt on one pce fr over 1f out* **50/1**

0 6 3/4 **Noble Descent**[43] 4052 3-9-0 0 ShaneKelly 10 53
(Sir Michael Stoute) *trckd ldrs: shkn up and outpcd over 2f out: one pce and no imp after* **10/1**

6-33 7 1 1/4 **Spellbind**[19] 4867 3-9-0 78 SilvestreDeSousa 3 50
(Charlie Appleby) *a in rr and nvr gng that wl: no prog whn rdn over 2f out: wl btn after* **15/8**[1]

8 1 **Elhaam (IRE)** 3-9-0 0 TomQueally 8 47+
(George Margarson) *slowest away: mostly in last: pushed along and no prog over 2f out: v modest late hdwy* **14/1**

00 9 nk **Petite Fille**[79] 2846 3-8-11 0 SimonPearce(3) 1 46
(Jeremy Gask) *reluctant to go to post: trckd ldng pair to over 2f out: wknd u.p* **66/1**

10 1 **Famous Tales** 4-8-12 0 [1] RobertPWalsh(7) 11 45
(Edward Creighton) *restless in stalls: dwlt: racd wd in rr: nvr a factor* **66/1**

0000 11 1 **Sterling Kate**[26] 4611 3-9-0 46 RobertHavlin 9 40
(Roger Ingram) *dwlt: a in rr: no ch fnl 2f* **100/1**

1m 26.44s (0.44) **Going Correction** -0.05s/f (Stan)
**WFA** 3 from 4yo 5lb **11** Ran SP% **118.3**
Speed ratings (Par 100): **95,90,90,89,88 87,85,84,84,83 82**
CSF £82.71 TOTE £3.00: £1.30, £10.10, £5.40; EX 117.80 Trifecta £2189.80.
**Owner** Lord Vestey **Bred** Stowell Park Stud **Trained** Newmarket, Suffolk

**FOCUS**
Not many got involved in this slowly run maiden, but the well-backed winner powered clear. The form looks very ordinary in terms of depth.

## 5549 BRITISH STALLION STUDS EBF MAIDEN FILLIES' STKS (BOBIS RACE) 1m (P)

**7:20** (7:22) (Class 5) 2-Y-O **£2,911** (£866; £432; £216) **Stalls Low**

Form RPR

5 1 **Endless Time (IRE)**[18] 4914 2-9-0 0 SilvestreDeSousa 7 77+
(Charlie Appleby) *led after 2f: mde rest: drvn and hrd pressed jst over 1f out: kpt on wl fnl f* **2/1**[2]

3 2 nk **Rock Kristal (IRE)**[14] 5037 2-9-0 0 RobertHavlin 6 76+
(John Gosden) *in tch: prog to chse wnr 2f out: rdn to chal and upsides jst over 1f out: nt qckn and hld last 100yds* **4/6**[1]

3 3 3/4 **Justify** 2-9-0 0 FrederikTylicki 2 68+
(Roger Varian) *in tch: pushed along and outpcd over 2f out: kpt on to take 3rd ins fnl f: n.d* **12/1**[3]

0 4 1 1/2 **Heart Of Africa**[26] 4626 2-9-0 0 AhmedAjtebi 8 64
(Charlie Appleby) *racd wd early: prom: trckd wnr 5f out to 2f out: steadily wknd: lost 3rd ins fnl f* **33/1**

0 5 6 **Vivo Per Lei (IRE)**[32] 4444 2-9-0 0 MartinHarley 4 49
(Marco Botti) *hld up in last: pushed along over 2f out: lost grnd on ldrs over 1f out: nvr involved* **50/1**

00 6 7 **Decibelle**[33] 4403 2-9-0 0 HayleyTurner 1 32
(Jane Chapple-Hyam) *led 100yds: steadily lost pl and pushed along in last pair 1/2-way: wknd 2f out* **100/1**

6 7 3 3/4 **Tatiani**[26] 4604 2-9-0 0 IrineuGoncalves 5 23
(Jose Santos) *taken down early: led after 100yds tl after 2f: wknd qckly 2f out* **33/1**

1m 39.41s (-0.39) **Going Correction** -0.05s/f (Stan) **7** Ran SP% **109.8**
Speed ratings (Par 94): **99,98,94,93,87 80,76**
CSF £3.33 TOTE £3.40: £1.30, £1.10; EX 3.30 Trifecta £14.40.
**Owner** Godolphin **Bred** Mabaki Investments **Trained** Newmarket, Suffolk

**FOCUS**
The two market leaders pulled clear in this fillies' maiden and the winner is likely to rate higher, but there was also promise from a newcomer in third.

## 5550 BETBRIGHT MOBILE H'CAP (BOBIS RACE) (LONDON MILE SERIES QUALIFIER) 1m (P)

**7:50** (7:51) (Class 4) (0-80,80) 3-Y-O **£4,690** (£1,395; £697; £348) **Stalls Low**

Form RPR

131 1 **Si Senor (IRE)**[15] 5008 3-9-6 79 FrederikTylicki 7 91+
(Ed Vaughan) *hld up in rr: smooth prog 2f out: led jst over 1f out: nvr c off the bridle after: easily* **7/4**[1]

-034 2 3/4 **Eye Contact**[19] 4845 3-9-1 74 TedDurcan 6 79
(Sir Michael Stoute) *racd wd: trckd ldrs: moved up to chal over 1f out but wnr sn cruised past: gave chse fnl f but no ch* **6/1**[2]

1506 3 1/2 **Voyageofdiscovery (USA)**[13] 5092 3-9-4 80 RyanTate(3) 9 84
(Clive Cox) *dwlt: hld up in last: prog wl over 1f out: rdn and styd on fnl f to take 3rd last strides: no ch w wnr* **8/1**[3]

6604 4 nk **Art Official (IRE)**[25] 4679 3-9-7 80 SeanLevey 8 83
(Richard Hannon) *t.k.h early: trckd ldr: led wl over 2f out: drvn and hdd jst over 1f out: kpt on same pce after* **20/1**

-463 5 2 1/2 **Master Dancer**[46] 3974 3-9-0 73 LiamKeniry 5 70
(Philip Hide) *s.i.s: hld up in rr: last wl over 1f out: sme prog after: rdn and edgd rt fnl f: no further hdwy* **6/1**[2]

-331 6 3/4 **Weekendatbernies (IRE)**[20] 4813 3-9-4 77 OisinMurphy 3 72
(Ed de Giles) *dwlt: t.k.h early: in tch: drvn on inner 2f out: no prog over 1f out: fdd* **6/1**[2]

062 7 1 1/2 **Incredible Fresh (IRE)**[64] 3343 3-9-2 75 ShaneKelly 2 67
(James Fanshawe) *trckd ldrs: tried to chal 2f out: shkn up and wknd over 1f out* **16/1**

2135 8 1 3/4 **Moonlight Venture**[30] 4496 3-9-4 77 TomQueally 4 65
(Kevin Ryan) *t.k.h early: trckd ldng pair: rdn over 2f out: no prog over 1f out: wknd* **10/1**

1000 9 3 3/4 **Equitable**[32] 4427 3-9-2 75 (vt[1]) MartinHarley 1 54
(Lady Cecil) *taken down early: led to wl over 2f out: sn btn* **14/1**

1m 38.56s (-1.24) **Going Correction** -0.05s/f (Stan) **9** Ran SP% **116.7**
Speed ratings (Par 102): **104,103,102,102,99 99,97,95,92**
CSF £12.54 CT £67.51 TOTE £2.30: £1.40, £2.20, £2.30; EX 22.30 Trifecta £85.50.
**Owner** A E Oppenheimer **Bred** Hascombe And Valiant Studs **Trained** Newmarket, Suffolk

**FOCUS**
The winner was impressive in this fair handicap and is value for a good bit extra.

## 5551 BETBRIGHT.COM FILLIES' H'CAP 1m 4f (P)

**8:20** (8:20) (Class 5) (0-70,70) 4-Y-0+ **£2,587** (£770; £384; £192) **Stalls Centre**

Form RPR

4135 1 **Ssafa**[81] 2774 6-9-7 70 (p) MartinLane 7 81+
(Paul Cole) *hld up: last tl gd prog wl over 2f out: swept into the ld over 1f out: drvn clr* **7/1**

3114 2 3 1/2 **Elegant Ophelia**[14] 5036 5-9-4 67 (t) GeorgeBaker 3 72
(Dean Ivory) *t.k.h: trckd ldrs: gng strly whn brought to chal 2f out: limited rspnse whn wnr surged past over 1f out: kpt on to take 2nd* **4/1**[2]

3144 3 hd **Atalanta Bay (IRE)**[34] 4369 4-9-2 65 [1] ShaneKelly 2 70
(Marcus Tregoning) *prom: chsd ldr wl over 2f out: rdn to chal wl over 1f out: wnr sn swept by: kpt on same pce* **9/2**[3]

4456 **4** 2 1/4 **Tilstarr (IRE)**[21] 4799 4-9-7 70 OisinMurphy 4 71
(Roger Teal) *hld up in rr: prog to chse ldrs 2f out: shkn up and one pce over 1f out* **4/1**[2]

5633 **5** 3 3/4 **Poitin**[28] 4552 4-9-7 70 RichardKingscote 8 65
(Harry Dunlop) *led and crossed fr wd draw: drvn and hdd on inner over 1f out: wknd* **11/4**[1]

2204 **6** nk **Neston Grace**[92] 2419 6-9-4 67 SteveDrowne 6 62
(Simon Hodgson) *hld up and racd wd: rdn over 3f out: sn dropped to last and struggling* **20/1**

5405 **7** 3 1/4 **Sixties Queen**[8] 5283 4-7-11 51 NatashaEaton(5) 1 41
(Alan Bailey) *hld up towards rr: pushed along and no prog over 2f out: sn wknd* **16/1**

3333 **8** 3 1/4 **Bethan**[27] 4592 5-8-1 55 (p) ShelleyBirkett(5) 5 40
(Julia Feilden) *chsd ldr to wl over 2f out: sn wknd* **10/1**

2m 33.03s (-1.47) **Going Correction** -0.05s/f (Stan) **8 Ran SP% 117.1**
Speed ratings (Par 100): **102,99,99,98,95 95,93,91**
CSF £35.98 CT £141.90 TOTE £11.50: £1.60, £1.50, £2.20; EX 36.80 Trifecta £182.70.
**Owner** The What A Mare Partnership **Bred** Newsells Park Stud **Trained** Whatcombe, Oxon

**FOCUS**
The went a fair pace in this handicap and the winner scored in emphatic style from some way back.

## 5552 BETBRIGHT.COM H'CAP (BOBIS RACE) (LONDON MIDDLE DISTANCE SERIES QUALIFIER) 1m 3f (P)
**8:50** (8:51) (Class 4) (0-85,85) 3-Y-O **£4,690** (£1,395; £697; £348) **Stalls** Low

Form RPR

1004 **1** **Anglo Irish**[25] 4651 3-9-2 80 RobertHavlin 1 87
(John Gosden) *trckd ldng pair: chal 2f out: led over 1f out: hrd pressed fnl f: drvn out* **5/1**[3]

2614 **2** nk **Masterpaver**[11] 5185 3-9-3 81 ow1 GeorgeBaker 7 88
(Alan Bailey) *trckd ldr: led over 2f out: sn rdn: hdd over 1f out: pressed wnr after: kpt on but nt qckn ins fnl f* **14/1**

3312 **3** 3/4 **Fire Fighting (IRE)**[4] 5430 3-9-7 85 (b) SilvestreDeSousa 5 92+
(Mark Johnston) *sltly awkward s: t.k.h: hld up in last trio: nt clr run over 2f out and swtchd lft: gd prog u.p over 1f out: wnt 3rd ins fnl f and threatened briefly: no ex last 75yds* **9/4**[1]

-016 **4** 3/4 **Golden Journey (IRE)**[35] 4332 3-8-8 75 RyanTate(3) 4 79
(Clive Cox) *trckd ldrs: pushed along over 3f out: drvn to go 3rd jst over 2f out tl ins fnl f: kpt on same pce* **16/1**

0301 **5** 3/4 **Jarlath**[17] 4948 3-8-12 76 (b) SteveDrowne 2 79
(Seamus Mullins) *trckd ldrs: rdn wl over 2f out: tried to cl over 1f out: kpt on same pce* **12/1**

4401 **6** 1 **Grand Meister**[7] 5302 3-8-1 72 KieranShoemark(7) 8 73
(Michael Bell) *hld up in last trio: rdn wl over 2f out: hanging and racd awkwardly after tl kpt on fnl f: n.d* **11/4**[2]

3022 **7** 1 **Invasor Luck (USA)**[15] 5010 3-9-2 80 TomQueally 6 80
(James Fanshawe) *hld up in last trio: shkn up wl over 2f out: prog over 1f out: effrt petered out fnl f* **12/1**

1 **8** 2 3/4 **Got To Dream**[7] 5301 3-9-2 80 6ex DaneO'Neill 3 75
(Mark Johnston) *led to over 2f out: sn btn: eased whn no ch last 100yds* **8/1**

2m 19.12s (-2.78) **Going Correction** -0.05s/f (Stan) **8 Ran SP% 113.1**
Speed ratings (Par 102): **108,107,107,106,106 105,104,102**
CSF £68.57 CT £197.86 TOTE £5.90: £1.60, £3.40, £1.50; EX 78.90 Trifecta £248.40.
**Owner** George Strawbridge **Bred** George Strawbridge **Trained** Newmarket, Suffolk

**FOCUS**
The pace was not strong in this competitive handicap and they finished in a bunch.

## 5553 BETBRIGHT - LIVE THE MOMENT H'CAP (BOBIS RACE) 6f (P)
**9:20** (9:20) (Class 4) (0-85,84) 3-Y-O **£4,690** (£1,395; £697; £348) **Stalls** Low

Form RPR

0050 **1** **Outer Space**[18] 4898 3-9-4 81 WilliamTwiston-Davies 6 91
(Jamie Osborne) *hld up in last pair: prog on inner 2f out: urged along to ld 1f out: edgd lft fnl f: kpt on* **7/1**[3]

-216 **2** 1/2 **Souville**[32] 4445 3-9-7 84 GeorgeBaker 4 92
(Chris Wall) *led: hdd and shkn up 1f out: rdn and edgd lft fnl f: nt qckn* **11/8**[1]

0003 **3** 2 1/4 **Sacha Park (IRE)**[16] 4983 3-9-0 77 SeanLevey 3 78
(Richard Hannon) *hld up in last pair: prog 2f out: rdn to take 3rd over 1f out: nt qckn and no imp on ldng pair* **7/1**[3]

5001 **4** 3/4 **Taquka (IRE)**[15] 5012 3-8-10 80 PatrickO'Donnell(7) 5 79
(Ralph Beckett) *t.k.h: trckd ldr to 2f out: sn lost pl: one pce after* **3/1**[2]

1-06 **5** 2 3/4 **Furas (IRE)**[15] 5012 3-9-4 81 DaneO'Neill 1 72
(Saeed bin Suroor) *trckd ldng pair: wnt 2nd briefly 2f out: fnd little u.p and sn btn* **7/1**[3]

0345 **6** 2 **Thataboy (IRE)**[27] 4581 3-8-11 74 (p) RichardKingscote 2 59
(Tom Dascombe) *t.k.h: racd on outer: chsd ldng trio: rdn over 2f out: btn wl over 1f out* **10/1**

1m 12.28s (-0.82) **Going Correction** -0.05s/f (Stan) **6 Ran SP% 113.7**
Speed ratings (Par 102): **103,102,99,98,94 92**
CSF £17.57 TOTE £7.90: £3.80, £1.60; EX 23.60 Trifecta £114.80.
**Owner** Tony Taylor & Patrick Gage **Bred** Catridge Farm Stud & B & H Jellett **Trained** Upper Lambourn, Berks

**FOCUS**
The pace was not very strong in this sprint handicap and the winner can be marked up for scoring under a hold-up ride.
T/Plt: £29.50 to a £1 stake. Pool: £64,560.76 - 1596.17 winning units. T/Qpdt: £6.50 to a £1 stake. Pool: £6119.41 - 690.05 winning units. JN

# 5422 LINGFIELD (L-H)
Wednesday, August 20

**OFFICIAL GOING: Polytrack: standard**
Wind: medium to fresh, half behind Weather: cloudy, brighter spells

## 5554 £10 FREE BET AT 32REDSPORT.COM NURSERY H'CAP 7f 1y(P)
**2:20** (2:21) (Class 5) (0-70,70) 2-Y-O **£2,911** (£866; £432; £216) **Stalls** Low

Form RPR

005 **1** **Pinter**[43] 4044 2-9-5 68 SilvestreDeSousa 12 75+
(Charlie Appleby) *s.i.s: sn swtchd lft to inner and in rr: switching rt and effrt in modest 7th 2f out: str run over 1f out: swept into ld fnl 50yds: gng away at fin* **9/2**[2]

3342 **2** 1 1/4 **Simply Magic (IRE)**[16] 4967 2-9-1 69 CamHardie(5) 3 72
(Richard Hannon) *in tch midfield: effrt but stl plenty to do 2f out: swtchd rt and clsd on ldrs ins fnl f: styd on to go 2nd nr fin* **5/1**[3]

016 **3** nk **Dream Approval (IRE)**[40] 4157 2-9-0 66 ThomasBrown(3) 4 68
(Daniel Kubler) *chsd ldr: edgd rt 5f out: rdn ent fnl 2f: drvn 1f out: styd on to ld fnl 100yds: hdd and no ex fnl 50yds: lost 2nd nr fin* **16/1**

003 **4** 3/4 **Ghalib (IRE)**[15] 5009 2-9-4 67 MartinHarley 2 67
(Marco Botti) *chsd ldrs: wnt 3rd 4f out: effrt and swtchd rt over 1f out: pressed ldrs 1f out: styd on same pce fnl 100yds* **6/4**[1]

6415 **5** 2 **The Dapper Tapper (IRE)**[17] 4939 2-9-5 68 (v[1]) DaneO'Neill 5 64
(Eve Johnson Houghton) *led: clr and rdn wl over 1f out: drvn and hdd fnl 100yds: sn wknd* **8/1**

3300 **6** 2 3/4 **Three Robins**[18] 4913 2-9-2 65 SeanLevey 7 54
(Richard Hannon) *chsd ldrs: hmpd 5f out: 4th and outpcd 3f out: drvn and no hdwy 2f out: plugged on same pce after* **16/1**

006 **7** 1 **El Campeon**[42] 4079 2-8-6 55 HarryBentley 8 41
(Simon Dow) *hld up in rr: rdn 4f out: sme hdwy over 1f out: nvr trbld ldrs* **50/1**

0060 **8** 1 1/4 **Foylesideview (IRE)**[7] 5306 2-9-2 68 [1] MichaelJMMurphy(3) 1 51
(Luke Dace) *racd in midfield: 6th and outpcd u.p over 2f out: no threat to ldrs fnl 2f* **33/1**

605 **9** 3 3/4 **Francis Scott Key (IRE)**[18] 4906 2-9-4 70 (b[1]) RyanClark(3) 6 44
(Brian Meehan) *hld up in last quartet: struggling 3f out: bhd fnl 2f* **14/1**

300 **10** hd **All Rounder (USA)**[14] 5037 2-9-7 70 (p) RobertHavlin 9 44
(John Gosden) *in tch in midfield: hmpd and lost pl 5f out: nvr gng wl after: bhd fnl 2f* **8/1**

0214 **11** 13 **Ciaras Cookie (IRE)**[12] 5148 2-8-13 67 NoelGarbutt(5) 10 9
(David Evans) *wnt rt s: t.k.h: hld up in rr: rdn over 3f out: lost tch over 2f out: t.o* **25/1**

1m 24.18s (-0.62) **Going Correction** -0.10s/f (Stan) **11 Ran SP% 124.3**
Speed ratings (Par 94): **99,97,97,96,94 90,89,88,84,83 69**
CSF £28.65 CT £348.90 TOTE £7.30: £2.20, £2.70, £5.70; EX 22.80 Trifecta £511.10.
**Owner** Godolphin **Bred** New England, Mount Coote & P Barrett **Trained** Newmarket, Suffolk

**FOCUS**
An interesting nursery to open proceedings, run at a good gallop, with the complexion changing dramatically inside the final furlong. The winnr looks the type to do better again.

## 5555 RACING SPECIALS AT 32REDSPORT.COM MAIDEN AUCTION STKS 6f 1y(P)
**2:55** (3:01) (Class 6) 2-Y-O **£1,973** (£587; £293; £146) **Stalls** Low

Form RPR

42 **1** **Disprove (IRE)**[37] 4269 2-8-8 0 NoelGarbutt(5) 6 79+
(Hugo Palmer) *taken down early and ponied to s: t.k.h: chsd ldrs: hdwy to ld 2f out: shkn up and qcknd clr over 1f out: r.o wl: comf* **4/9**[1]

**2** 3 1/4 **Frantical** 2-8-11 0 ow3 MichaelJMMurphy(3) 7 70
(Luke Dace) *t.k.h: in tch in midfield on outer: rdn and hdwy over 1f out: kpt on wl to go 2nd fnl 75yds: no threat to wnr* **16/1**

4 **3** 1 1/4 **Miss Inga Sock (IRE)**[10] 5209 2-8-7 0 JohnFahy 10 60
(Eve Johnson Houghton) *led for 1f: chsd ldrs after: outpcd 2f out: swtchd rt over 1f out: kpt on wl ins fnl f: no threat to wnr* **10/1**[3]

**4** nse **Clergyman** 2-9-0 0 JackMitchell 9 66
(Martyn Meade) *s.i.s: in tch in last trio: hdwy 2f out: kpt on wl u.p ins fnl f: no threat to wnr* **10/1**[3]

**5** 1 **Masipa (IRE)** 2-8-11 0 (p[1]) ChrisCatlin 4 60
(Rae Guest) *chsd ldrs: effrt u.p 2f out: chsd clr wnr over 1f out: no imp: lost 2nd fnl 75yds: wknd towards fin* **6/1**[2]

**6** 4 1/2 **Paloma Dancer** 2-8-8 0 SilvestreDeSousa 11 44
(Harry Dunlop) *jnd ldr after 1f: rdn to ld jst over 2f out: sn hdd: 4th and btn 1f out: wknd fnl f* **16/1**

00 **7** 3/4 **Senor Firecracker (IRE)**[19] 4864 2-8-13 0 WilliamTwiston-Davies 3 47
(Brett Johnson) *s.i.s: sn rdn along in rr: n.d* **50/1**

0 **8** 1 1/4 **Bounty Bah**[10] 5210 2-9-1 0 LiamKeniry 1 45
(Mark Usher) *in tch in midfield: rdn and outpcd over 2f out: wknd wl over 1f out* **50/1**

**9** 2 1/2 **Dotties Boy** 2-8-8 0 JemmaMarshall(3) 2 33
(Pat Phelan) *a in rr: bhd fnl 2f* **33/1**

**10** 1 1/2 **Lonely Ranger (USA)** 2-9-1 0 HayleyTurner 5 33
(Amy Weaver) *led after 1f tl rdn and hdd jst over 2f out: wknd qckly over 1f out* **25/1**

1m 13.02s (1.12) **Going Correction** -0.10s/f (Stan) **10 Ran SP% 124.2**
Speed ratings (Par 92): **88,83,82,81,80 74,73,71,68,66**
CSF £11.06 TOTE £1.30: £1.10, £4.80, £2.50; EX 15.50 Trifecta £70.40.
**Owner** Lord Vestey **Bred** M Phelan **Trained** Newmarket, Suffolk

**FOCUS**
A one-sided betting market and the favourite got off the mark with the minimum of fuss.

## 5556 32RED H'CAP 1m 7f 169y(P)
**3:30** (3:30) (Class 6) (0-65,64) 3-Y-O **£2,587** (£770; £384; £192) **Stalls** Low

Form RPR

-P04 **1** **Fennann**[12] 5135 3-9-7 64 (b[1]) SamHitchcott 5 69
(Gary Moore) *t.k.h: hld up in tch in last pair: effrt and switching rt 2f out: styd on u.p 1f out: chal ins fnl f: led last strides* **14/1**

0-22 **2** shd **Wintour Leap**[14] 5048 3-9-0 62 DanielMuscutt(5) 6 66
(Robert Stephens) *in tch in midfield: chsd ldrs 5f out: rdn to chse wnr 2f out: drvn and styd on to chal ins fnl f: kpt on: jst hld* **6/1**

0044 **3** nse **Oakbank (USA)**[26] 4615 3-7-13 47 CamHardie(5) 4 51
(Brett Johnson) *chsd ldr tl led over 2f out: rdn 2f out: drvn jst ins fnl f: kpt in tl hdd and lost 2 pls last strides* **6/1**

0443 **4** 3/4 **Passionate Affair (IRE)**[12] 5121 3-9-6 63 (t) RichardKingscote 8 66
(Jamie Osborne) *stdd s: hld up in tch in last pair: effrt on inner wl over 1f out: chsd ldrs u.p 1f out: styd on same pce fnl 100yds* **3/1**[2]

5503 **5** 7 **Citizen Kaine (IRE)**[15] 5011 3-9-6 63 (p) J-PGuillambert 3 58
(Jo Hughes) *in tch in midfield: cl 4th and rdn ent fnl 2f: drvn and outpcd over 1f out: wknd fnl f* **9/4**[1]

0004 **6** 1 1/2 **Prince Of Islay (IRE)**[13] 5102 3-8-5 55 ow1 (p) GeorgeBuckell(7) 7 48
(Robert Mills) *hld up in tch in midfield: effrt on outer 2f out: no prog and btn over 1f out: wknd fnl f* **5/1**[3]

0403 **7** 3 1/4 **Deja Bougg**[13] 5102 3-9-1 58 SilvestreDeSousa 1 47
(David Evans) *led tl rdn and hdd over 2f out: btn over 1f out: sn wknd* **10/1**

0000 **8** 34 **Lara Lipton (IRE)**[8] 5283 3-7-11 45 (p) NoelGarbutt(5) 2
(Jane Chapple-Hyam) *chsd ldrs: rdn 6f out: lost pl over 3f out: lost tch over 2f out: t.o* **66/1**

3m 25.43s (-0.27) **Going Correction** -0.10s/f (Stan) **8 Ran SP% 118.3**
Speed ratings (Par 98): **96,95,95,95,92 91,89,72**
CSF £97.83 CT £569.33 TOTE £11.60: £4.90, £2.00, £1.70; EX 81.20 Trifecta £407.60.
**Owner** Michael Baldry **Bred** Cheveley Park Stud Ltd **Trained** Lower Beeding, W Sussex

**FOCUS**
A low-grade handicap, but a thrilling finish with three in a line as they passed the post.

## 5557 TERRY STEWART CELEBRATION H'CAP 1m 2f (P)
4:05 (4:05) (Class 5) (0-75,75) 3-Y-O £2,911 (£866; £432; £216) Stalls Low

Form RPR
1-05 1 **Zugzwang (IRE)**[116] 1723 3-9-4 72 PatCosgrave 6 79
(Ed de Giles) *chsd ldrs: effrt and chal 2f out: drvn to ld ins fnl f: styd on: drvn out* 14/1
1303 2 1 1/4 **Starlit Cantata**[17] 4947 3-9-3 71 JohnFahy 7 76
(Eve Johnson Houghton) *in tch in midfield: swtchd lft and hdwy to chal over 1f out: led ins fnl f: sn hdd and one pce fnl 100yds* 8/1
040 3 shd **Soundtrack (IRE)**[28] 4543 3-8-13 67 TomQueally 2 72
(William Knight) *s.i.s: in tch in rr: last: rdn and struggling over 2f out: wd bnd 2f out: hdwy over 1f out: styd on strly ins fnl f: nt rch wnr* 10/1
6100 4 3/4 **Westerly**[17] 4948 3-9-0 68 (p) SebSanders 11 71
(William Haggas) *dwlt and rdn along leaving stalls: hdwy to chse ldr after 1f: rdn to ld over 1f out: hdd ins fnl f: styd on same pce after* 6/1[2]
0042 5 shd **Captain George (IRE)**[20] 4830 3-8-13 72 CamHardie(5) 4 75
(James Fanshawe) *hld up in last quartet: rdn over 2f out: hdwy u.p 1f out: styd on wl ins fnl f: nt rch ldrs* 6/1[2]
6-20 6 shd **Moshe (IRE)**[95] 2334 3-9-7 75 SilvestreDeSousa 3 78+
(Hughie Morrison) *s.i.s: in rr: effrt on outer 3f out: hdwy 1f out: styd on wl ins fnl f: nt rch ldrs* 5/2[1]
3423 7 1 1/2 **Plucky Dip**[15] 5006 3-8-5 62 DannyBrock(3) 9 62
(John Ryan) *chsd ldrs: ev ch and rdn over 2f out: no ex and btn over 1f out: wknd ins fnl f* 8/1
-250 8 1 1/4 **Gay Marriage (IRE)**[30] 4504 3-9-7 75 RobertHavlin 10 73
(John Gosden) *led tl rdn and hdd over 1f out: no ex 1f out: wknd ins fnl f* 7/1[3]
5350 9 6 **Best Kept**[15] 5008 3-9-4 72 SeanLevey 5 58
(Amanda Perrett) *in tch in midfield: hdwy to chse ldrs 7f out: drvn and lost pl ent fnl 2f: wknd over 1f out* 7/1[3]
52-3 10 14 **Rolling Dice**[102] 2163 3-9-5 73 LiamKeniry 1 33
(Dominic Ffrench Davis) *hld up in tch in last quartet: rdn over 2f out: sn btn: bhd over 1f out* 25/1

2m 3.71s (-2.89) **Going Correction** -0.10s/f (Stan) 10 Ran SP% 124.0
Speed ratings (Par 100): **107,106,105,105,105 105,103,102,98,86**
CSF £128.62 CT £1196.64 TOTE £18.20: £7.00, £3.10, £3.50; EX 186.10 Trifecta £1910.70.
**Owner** Simon Treacher **Bred** Mrs C E Norton **Trained** Ledbury, H'fords

**FOCUS**
A competitive handicap run at a decent pace and the form should prove solid.

## 5558 ALL NEW 32REDSPORT.COM H'CAP 1m 4f (P)
4:40 (4:40) (Class 6) (0-55,54) 3-Y-O+ £2,587 (£770; £384; £192) Stalls Low

Form RPR
/404 1 **Giant Sequoia (USA)**[2] 5508 10-8-12 48 (t) DannyBrock(3) 4 64+
(Des Donovan) *stdd after s: hld up in last trio: hdwy to chse ldrs 2f out: shkn up to ld 1f out: sn rdn and qcknd wl clr: easily* 5/1[3]
0-62 2 7 **Rajeh (IRE)**[8] 5283 11-8-12 45 TomQueally 10 50
(Peter Grayson) *in tch in midfield: hdwy to chse ldrs 8f out: rdn and pressed ldrs 2f out: wnt 2nd 1f out: kpt on but no ch w wnr* 7/1
6/02 3 2 1/4 **Black Iceman**[23] 4737 6-9-3 53 SimonPearce(3) 3 54
(Lydia Pearce) *chsd ldrs: stdd bk and in last trio 9f out: rdn and effrt over 2f out: no ch but kpt on ins fnl f: wnt 3rd nr fin* 8/1
0223 4 3/4 **Rock Of Leon**[20] 4834 3-8-9 52 (p) MartinLane 2 52
(Michael Bell) *sn bustled up to ld: rdn over 3f out: hdd 2f out: ev ch tl 1f out: sn outpcd and btn: plugged on* 2/1[1]
5400 5 hd **Highly Likely (IRE)**[60] 3473 5-9-0 52 CamHardie(5) 9 52
(Steve Woodman) *dwlt and short of room leaving stalls: in rr: hdwy to join ldr 9f out: rdn to ld 2f out: hdd 1f out: sn outpcd and btn: plugged on* 12/1
1166 6 4 1/2 **Novel Dancer**[23] 4737 6-9-7 54 RobertHavlin 8 46
(Lydia Richards) *bustled along leaving stalls: in tch in midfield: rdn over 3f out: outpcd and btn over 2f out: no ch fnl 2f* 9/2[2]
0046 7 1/2 **Up Hill Battle's**[14] 5033 3-8-3 46 ow1 FrankieMcDonald 6 38
(Daniel Mark Loughnane) *stdd s: t.k.h: hld up in rr: rdn over 2f out: sn struggling and wl btn over 1f out* 16/1
0/42 8 3/4 **Lord Of The Storm**[8] 5291 6-9-0 52 RyanWhile(5) 1 42
(Bill Turner) *in tch in midfield: rdn over 2f out: sn struggling: wknd wl over 1f out* 7/1
006/ 9 3 1/4 **Supernoverre (IRE)**[52] 3221 8-8-12 45 (p) SteveDrowne 5 30
(Alan Jones) *in tch in midfield: rdn and effrt over 2f out: sn btn: bhd fnl 2f* 50/1
0000 10 14 **Charlies Mate**[12] 5138 3-8-2 45 HayleyTurner 7 8
(John Best) *t.k.h: chsd ldrs tl lost pl 3f out: wl bhd over 1f out: t.o* 66/1

2m 29.91s (-3.09) **Going Correction** -0.10s/f (Stan)
**WFA** 3 from 5yo+ 10lb 10 Ran SP% 121.3
Speed ratings (Par 101): **106,101,99,99,99 96,95,95,93,83**
CSF £41.74 CT £281.74 TOTE £11.40: £2.80, £2.40, £2.50; EX 56.00 Trifecta £1259.90.
**Owner** River Racing **Bred** Strategy Bloodstock **Trained** Newmarket, Suffolk
■ Stewards' Enquiry : Danny Brock used whip when clearly winning, 5th suspension in 6mths, matter referred.

**FOCUS**
Low-grade fare and a winner who was far too good for his rivals.

## 5559 32RED.COM H'CAP 6f 1y(P)
5:15 (5:15) (Class 4) (0-80,80) 3-Y-O+ £5,175 (£1,540; £769; £384) Stalls Low

Form RPR
4111 1 **Panther Patrol (IRE)**[12] 5124 4-9-5 75 (v) JohnFahy 5 85
(Eve Johnson Houghton) *chsd ldr: qcknd clr w ldr over 1f out: sustained chal after: hrd drvn ins fnl f: r.o wl to ld on post* 6/4[1]
603 2 nse **Diamond Charlie (IRE)**[11] 5182 6-9-10 80 SebSanders 2 89
(Simon Dow) *led: rdn and clr w wnr over 1f out: sustained duel w wnr: r.o wl: hdd on post* 6/1
-335 3 2 **Marmalady (IRE)**[85] 2645 4-9-10 80 ShaneKelly 1 83
(Gary Moore) *chsd ldng pair: rdn and outpcd by ldng pair wl over 1f out: kpt on ins fnl f but no threat to ldng pair* 4/1[3]
56 4 2 **Dominate**[48] 3876 4-9-4 79 (b) CamHardie(5) 3 76
(Richard Hannon) *in tch in midfield: rdn and outpcd 2f out: no imp over 1f out* 3/1[2]
226 5 1 **Noverre To Go (IRE)**[12] 5124 8-9-7 77 (p) SteveDrowne 7 71
(Ronald Harris) *t.k.h: hld up in tch in rr: rdn and outpcd after: no imp fr wl over 1f out* 14/1
0330 6 2 1/2 **Seek The Fair Land**[7] 5308 8-9-4 74 (b) AmirQuinn 6 60
(Lee Carter) *in tch: rdn and outpcd ent fnl 2f: no ch after: bhd fnl f* 12/1

1m 11.05s (-0.85) **Going Correction** -0.10s/f (Stan) 6 Ran SP% 113.6
Speed ratings (Par 105): **101,100,98,95,94 90**
CSF £11.38 TOTE £2.60: £1.40, £4.60; EX 12.60 Trifecta £31.50.
**Owner** G C Stevens **Bred** Kilfrush Stud **Trained** Blewbury, Oxon

**FOCUS**
Another bobbing finish, with the favourite landing his four-timer in a race where nothing got into it from behind.

## 5560 32RED CASINO H'CAP 1m 2f (P)
5:50 (5:50) (Class 6) (0-65,65) 4-Y-O+ £2,587 (£770; £384; £192) Stalls Low

Form RPR
2600 1 **Menelik (IRE)**[42] 4080 5-9-6 64 (v) AmirQuinn 4 71
(Lee Carter) *s.i.s: swtchd rt and hdwy to ld after 1f: mde rest: rdn and qcknd jst over 2f out: drvn over 1f out: jst hld on* 8/1
0043 2 shd **Precision Five**[12] 5139 5-9-4 62 (p) MartinLane 1 69+
(Jeremy Gask) *in tch in last pair: effrt on inner over 1f out: r.o wl u.p ins fnl f: jst failed* 9/2[3]
2323 3 1 **Two In The Pink (IRE)**[8] 5284 4-9-4 62 MartinHarley 6 67
(Ralph J Smith) *chsd wnr after 1f: rdn ent fnl 2f: styd on same pce ins fnl f* 4/1[2]
2112 4 1 **Glennten**[27] 4582 5-9-7 65 IrineuGoncalves 8 68
(Jose Santos) *t.k.h: wl in tch in midfield: rdn ent fnl 2f: edgd lft 1f out: styd on same pce ins fnl f* 9/2[3]
0000 5 1 **Munsarim (IRE)**[16] 4968 7-9-6 64 (b) KierenFox 2 65
(Lee Carter) *led for 1f: chsd ldrs: rdn and sltly outpcd jst over 2f out: keeping on when carried lft and hmpd jst ins fnl f: one pce after* 12/1
6536 6 1 1/2 **Dreaming Again**[12] 5139 4-7-12 47 CamHardie(5) 5 45
(Jimmy Fox) *wl in tch in last trio: rdn and outpcd ent fnl 2f: n.d but kpt on ins fnl f* 16/1
0032 7 19 **Orders From Rome (IRE)**[18] 4911 5-9-4 62 (t) DaneO'Neill 3 24+
(Charlie Fellowes) *rrd as stalls opened and v.s.a: sn rcvrd and t.k.h in rr: rdn over 2f out: sn btn: wknd 2f out: wl bhd and eased ins fnl f* 7/4[1]

2m 7.02s (0.42) **Going Correction** -0.10s/f (Stan) 7 Ran SP% 117.4
Speed ratings (Par 101): **94,93,93,92,91 90,75**
CSF £45.16 CT £168.08 TOTE £16.20: £8.20, £1.20; EX 37.20 Trifecta £270.60.
**Owner** John Joseph Smith **Bred** Irish National Stud **Trained** Epsom, Surrey

**FOCUS**
A competitive handicap despite the small field and the winner made most under a well-judged ride.
T/Plt: £208.20 to a £1 stake. Pool: £54,969.85 - 192.67 winning units. T/Qpdt: £64.60 to a £1 stake. Pool: £3849.13 - 44.05 winning units. SP

# 5140 MUSSELBURGH (R-H)
Wednesday, August 20

**OFFICIAL GOING: Good to firm (7.6)**
Wind: light against Weather: overcast

## 5561 BLACKROCK FOR INCOME MAIDEN AUCTION STKS 5f
2:10 (2:10) (Class 6) 2-Y-O £2,587 (£770; £384; £192) Stalls High

Form RPR
02 1 **Dad's Girl**[36] 4286 2-8-6 0 IanBrennan 1 65+
(Ollie Pears) *mde all: rdn appr fnl f: pressed 75yds out: hld on wl* 9/4[2]
2336 2 3/4 **Lily Moreton (IRE)**[19] 4869 2-8-10 65 JasonHart 2 66
(Noel Wilson) *sltly awkward s: hld up in rr: pushed along 1/2-way: rdn and hdwy on outer over 1f out: sn chsd wnr: kpt on but a jst hld* 9/1[3]
3 3 2 **Doppler Effect**[24] 4708 2-9-3 0 PJMcDonald 5 66
(Ann Duffield) *trckd ldr: rdn 2f out: one pce* 13/8[1]
5236 4 1 **Straightothepoint**[7] 5297 2-9-1 75 PhillipMakin 4 61
(Bryan Smart) *chsd ldr: rdn 1/2-way: wknd ins fnl f* 9/4[2]

59.94s (-0.46) **Going Correction** -0.10s/f (Good) 4 Ran SP% 109.6
Speed ratings (Par 92): **99,97,94,93**
CSF £17.64 TOTE £2.80; EX 10.20 Trifecta £26.90.
**Owner** Ownaracehorse Ltd (ownaracehorse.co.uk) **Bred** New China Cherub Partnership **Trained** Norton, N Yorks

**FOCUS**
Hard to get too excited by the form of this poorly contested maiden auction.

## 5562 BREWIN DOLPHIN H'CAP (QUALIFER FOR THE £15,000 BETFAIR SCOTTISH MILE SERIES FINAL) 1m
2:45 (2:45) (Class 5) (0-75,74) 4-Y-O+ £3,234 (£962; £481; £240) Stalls Low

Form RPR
3122 1 **Gambino (IRE)**[12] 5142 4-8-5 63 (p) JoeDoyle(5) 4 73
(John David Riches) *hld up in tch: smooth hdwy on outer 3f out: led on bit over 1f out: rdn ins fnl f: pressed towards fin but a holding on* 11/4[2]
6000 2 nk **Nelson's Bay**[31] 4473 5-8-3 56 IanBrennan 6 65
(Wilf Storey) *trckd ldng pair: rdn over 2f out: chsd wnr over 1f out: kpt on: pressed wnr towards fin but a jst hld* 20/1
5031 3 7 **Camerooney**[19] 4858 11-9-2 74 (p) JordanNason(5) 1 66
(Marjorie Fife) *led: rdn 3f out: hdd over 1f out: sn outpcd and dropped to 4th: plugged on ins fnl f: wnt modest 3rd towards fin* 7/2[3]
0441 4 1/2 **Shamaheart (IRE)**[29] 4523 4-9-4 71 (p) PJMcDonald 2 62
(Geoffrey Harker) *trckd ldng pair: rdn 2f out: outpcd by ldng pair appr fnl f: no ex and lost 3rd towards fin* 9/4[1]
1204 5 3/4 **Order Of Service**[23] 4729 4-9-1 71 GaryBartley(3) 3 60
(Jim Goldie) *dwlt: hld up: rdn over 2f out: one pce and nvr threatened* 8/1
2-04 6 7 **Pressure Point**[24] 4705 4-9-5 72 TomEaves 7 45
(Keith Dalgleish) *pressed ldrs: rdn over 2f out: wknd over 1f out* 14/1
6420 7 5 **Patrona Ciana (FR)**[13] 5079 4-9-2 72 SamJames(3) 5 39
(David O'Meara) *hld up in tch: rdn 3f out: sn btn* 10/1

1m 38.45s (-2.75) **Going Correction** -0.25s/f (Firm) 7 Ran SP% 111.3
Speed ratings (Par 103): **103,102,95,95,94 87,82**
CSF £48.72 TOTE £3.50: £2.10, £7.90; EX 54.20 Trifecta £168.00.
**Owner** J D Riches **Bred** Messrs M Quinn & P Slattery **Trained** Pilling, Lancashire

**FOCUS**
As expected, this was strongly run and it saw a good staying performance from the winner.

## 5563 CMYK DIGITAL SOLUTIONS H'CAP 5f
3:20 (3:21) (Class 4) (0-85,82) 3-Y-O+ £5,175 (£1,540; £769; £384) Stalls High

Form RPR
4520 1 **Midnight Dynamo**[18] 4902 7-9-0 70 FergalLynch 1 81
(Jim Goldie) *stdd s: hld up in rr: nudged along and hdwy 2f out: swtchd lft 1f out: sn rdn: kpt on wl: led 110yds out* 14/1

3511 **2** 1 3/4 **Master Bond**[11] 5170 5-9-8 81 SamJames(3) 5 88
(David O'Meara) *in tch: gng wl whn n.m.r over 1f out: swtchd rt to outside 1f out: kpt on: wnt 2nd post* **3/1**[1]
0200 **3** shd **Tom Sawyer**[14] 5060 6-9-0 73 (b) ConnorBeasley(3) 3 78
(Julie Camacho) *chsd ldrs: rdn 2f out: ev ch ins fnl f: kpt on: lost 2nd post* **14/1**
6050 **4** 1/2 **Singeur (IRE)**[18] 4925 7-9-9 82 (p) NeilFarley(3) 10 85+
(Robin Bastiman) *dwlt: hld up: drvn in rr 2f out: kpt on fnl f: nrst fin* **7/1**
125 **5** nse **Bunce (IRE)**[18] 4901 6-9-8 78 TomEaves 9 83+
(Linda Perratt) *in tch: rdn 1/2-way: one pce and nvr threatened ldrs* **25/1**
0021 **6** 1 1/2 **Noodles Blue Boy**[7] 5298 8-9-11 81 6ex (p) RobertWinston 4 78+
(Ollie Pears) *led narrowly: rdn 1/2-way: hdd 110yds out: wknd* **8/1**
5135 **7** 1 3/4 **Mutafaakir (IRE)**[15] 5016 5-9-11 81 (b) PJMcDonald 11 72+
(Ruth Carr) *prom: rdn 1/2-way: wknd ins fnl f* **5/1**[3]
0405 **8** 4 1/2 **Imperial Legend (IRE)**[19] 4859 5-9-12 82 (v) FrannyNorton 6 63+
(David Nicholls) *prom: rdn 2f out: jst lost pl whn hmpd 1f out: wknd and eased* **4/1**[2]
5601 **9** 4 **Space Artist (IRE)**[29] 4521 4-9-11 81 PhillipMakin 2 41+
(Bryan Smart) *pressed ldr: rdn 1/2-way: wknd fnl f: eased fnl 110yds* **6/1**
59.64s (-0.76) **Going Correction** -0.10s/f (Good) 9 Ran SP% **116.7**
Speed ratings (Par 105): **102,99,99,98,98 95,92,85,79**
CSF £56.59 CT £621.88 TOTE £26.10: £6.20, £2.10, £5.40; EX 89.50 Trifecta £1661.50.
**Owner** Lorimer Racing **Bred** E W Hyslop **Trained** Uplawmoor, E Renfrews
■ Stewards' Enquiry : Fergal Lynch one-day ban: careless riding (Sep 3)
**FOCUS**
A race packed with front-runners, and with the pace collapsing it was those ridden with restraint that benefited.

## 5564 RAY HAWTHORNE MEMORIAL H'CAP 2m
3:55 (3:56) (Class 4) (0-85,81) 4-Y-0+ £6,469 (£1,925; £962; £481) Stalls High

Form RPR
12 **1** **Maoi Chinn Tire (IRE)**[29] 4522 7-8-6 71 (t) JoeDoyle(5) 1 80+
(Jennie Candlish) *midfield: pushed along and hdwy over 2f out: rdn to ld over 1f out: kpt on: edgd lft ins fnl f* **8/1**
3626 **2** 2 1/2 **Entihaa**[26] 4606 6-9-5 79 RobertWinston 9 85
(Alan Swinbank) *slowly away: hld up: rdn and hdwy on outer over 2f out: chsd wnr appr fnl f: kpt on but a hld* **7/2**[2]
1413 **3** 1/2 **Longshadow**[21] 4777 4-9-2 76 PJMcDonald 5 81
(Jason Ward) *trckd ldr: rdn over 3f out: styd on same pce* **5/2**[1]
4134 **4** 3 **Aleksandar**[13] 5083 5-8-12 72 FergalLynch 2 74
(Jim Goldie) *midfield on inner: rdn 3f out: one pce and no imp on ldrs* **13/2**
-010 **5** hd **Stopped Out**[21] 4777 9-9-7 81 (p) FrannyNorton 8 83+
(Philip Kirby) *slowly away: sn rushed up to ld: rdn over 2f out: hdd over 1f out: wknd* **7/1**
6131 **6** 6 **La Bacouetteuse (FR)**[12] 5146 9-8-8 71 (b) ConnorBeasley(3) 4 65
(Iain Jardine) *hld up: rdn over 2f out: sn btn* **12/1**
2233 **7** 2 1/4 **Merchant Of Dubai**[27] 4575 9-8-9 72 GaryBartley(3) 3 65
(Jim Goldie) *trckd ldr: rdn 3f out: wknd over 1f out* **5/1**[3]
1050 **8** 22 **Arr' Kid (USA)**[82] 2739 4-9-1 75 (b) TomEaves 7 40
(Keith Dalgleish) *trckd ldr: lost pl qckly 4f out: sn bhd: eased* **33/1**
3m 27.46s (-6.04) **Going Correction** -0.25s/f (Firm) 8 Ran SP% **115.0**
Speed ratings (Par 105): **105,103,103,102,101 98,97,86**
CSF £36.38 CT £90.93 TOTE £8.50: £2.50, £1.40, £1.20; EX 34.70 Trifecta £65.30.
**Owner** The Best Club In The World **Bred** Mrs E Thompson **Trained** Basford Green, Staffs
**FOCUS**
A strong renewal of this feature. The winner might yet have more to offer.

## 5565 JAMES ROCHE MEMORIAL H'CAP (QUALIFIER FOR THE £15,000 BETFAIR SCOTTISH SPRINT SERIES FINAL) 5f
4:30 (4:30) (Class 6) (0-65,63) 3-Y-0+ £2,587 (£770; £384; £192) Stalls High

Form RPR
3335 **1** **Saxonette**[9] 5237 6-8-6 51 ConnorBeasley(3) 9 60
(Linda Perratt) *midfield towards inner: angled off rail fr 1/2-way: chsd ldrs whn briefly n.m.r over 1f out: swtchd rt: r.o: led 75yds out* **8/1**
0014 **2** 3/4 **Spring Bird**[5] 5375 5-8-12 61 AnnaHesketh(7) 5 67
(David Nicholls) *trckd ldrs: rdn 2f out: briefly upsides ins fnl f: one pce fnl 75yds* **7/2**[1]
0055 **3** nk **The Nifty Fox**[9] 5237 10-9-0 56 (p) PhillipMakin 11 61
(Tim Easterby) *trckd ldrs: rdn to ld narrowly ins fnl f: hdd 75yds out: no ex* **9/1**
3400 **4** 3/4 **Chloe's Dream (IRE)**[9] 5237 4-8-10 52 PJMcDonald 1 54
(Linda Perratt) *prom: rdn to ld over 1f out: hdd ins fnl f: no ex* **20/1**
U303 **5** 3/4 **Manatee Bay**[7] 5298 4-9-7 63 FrannyNorton 3 63
(David Nicholls) *midfield: rdn 1/2-way: one pce and nvr threatened ldrs* **9/2**[2]
4044 **6** 1/2 **Black Douglas**[5] 5390 5-8-4 51 (b) JordanNason(5) 6 49+
(Jim Goldie) *s.i.s: hld up in rr: swtchd lft to rail over 1f out: kpt on fnl f: nvr threatened ldrs* **11/2**[3]
0000 **7** 1 3/4 **Fife Jo**[23] 4725 4-8-7 49 oh4 IanBrennan 8 40
(Jim Goldie) *hld up: rdn 1/2-way: nvr threatened* **66/1**
5004 **8** nk **Danfazi (IRE)**[16] 4974 3-9-4 62 (p) TomEaves 4 52
(Kristin Stubbs) *led: rdn whn hdd over 1f out: sn wknd* **16/1**
6005 **9** 1 **Here Now And Why (IRE)**[21] 4796 7-8-8 50 (p) JasonHart 7 37
(Ian Semple) *hld up: pushed along 1/2-way: sn btn* **7/1**
6540 **10** 2 **Funding Deficit (IRE)**[9] 5237 4-9-6 62 FergalLynch 2 42
(Jim Goldie) *in tch on outside: rdn 1/2-way: wknd fnl f* **8/1**
202 **11** 3/4 **Busy Bimbo (IRE)**[12] 5130 5-8-5 52 (b) JoeDoyle(5) 10 29
(Alan Berry) *sn pushed along towards rr: a bhd* **14/1**
59.63s (-0.77) **Going Correction** -0.10s/f (Good)
**WFA** 3 from 4yo+ 2lb 11 Ran SP% **119.3**
Speed ratings (Par 101): **102,100,100,99,97 97,94,93,92,89 87**
CSF £36.66 CT £269.98 TOTE £9.90: £3.30, £1.90, £3.50; EX 53.90 Trifecta £363.30.
**Owner** John Murphy **Bred** Mike Channon Bloodstock Ltd **Trained** East Kilbride, S Lanarks
**FOCUS**
A return to quicker ground appeared key to the winner.

## 5566 BROWN SHIPLEY WEALTH WELL MANAGED H'CAP (QUALIFIER FOR £15000 BETFAIR SCOTTISH MILE SERIES FINAL) 1m
5:05 (5:06) (Class 5) (0-75,75) 3-Y-0 £3,234 (£962; £481; £240) Stalls Low

Form RPR
5116 **1** **In Focus (IRE)**[36] 4300 3-9-4 72 RobertWinston 3 78
(Alan Swinbank) *prom: rdn over 2f out: led wl over 1f out: jnd 110yds out: fnd bit more nr fin* **7/2**[3]
4142 **2** hd **Alpine Storm (IRE)**[9] 5235 3-9-6 74 FrannyNorton 2 79
(Mark Johnston) *racd keenly: led: rdn whn hdd wl over 1f out: rallied and upsides again 110yds out: jst hld nr fin* **7/4**[1]
1660 **3** 1 3/4 **Dark Crystal**[9] 5235 3-8-10 64 PJMcDonald 7 64
(Linda Perratt) *chsd ldng pair: rdn over 2f out: kpt on but a hld by ldng pair* **14/1**
144 **4** 7 **Eddiemaurice (IRE)**[9] 5245 3-9-2 75 (v) DuilioDaSilva(5) 6 59
(Richard Guest) *hld up: rdn 3f out: sn struggling* **7/1**
6211 **5** 6 **Strictly Glitz (IRE)**[6] 5336 3-8-9 68 12ex JoeDoyle(5) 4 37
(John Quinn) *hld up: rdn 3f out: sn btn* **2/1**[2]
0060 **6** 13 **Bannock Town**[9] 5233 3-8-2 59 oh11 ow3 ConnorBeasley(3) 1
(Linda Perratt) *chsd ldng pair: rdn 3f out: sn wknd* **80/1**
1m 40.1s (-1.10) **Going Correction** -0.25s/f (Firm) 6 Ran SP% **112.3**
Speed ratings (Par 100): **95,94,93,86,80 67**
CSF £10.09 TOTE £4.60: £1.30, £1.30; EX 10.30 Trifecta £73.10.
**Owner** G H Bell **Bred** Century Farms **Trained** Melsonby, N Yorks
**FOCUS**
The market anticipated a big run from the runner-up, but it was heartbreak for her supporters.

## 5567 JET PETROL DIAMOND JUBILEE AMATEUR H'CAP (QUALIFIER FOR £15,000 BETFAIR SCOTTISH STAYERS FINAL) 1m 6f
5:35 (5:35) (Class 6) (0-65,61) 4-Y-0+ £2,495 (£774; £386; £193) Stalls Centre

Form RPR
0314 **1** **Giovanni Jack**[16] 4964 4-10-13 60 MrSWalker 11 73+
(Alan Swinbank) *trckd ldrs: led over 2f out: sn pushed clr: eased towards fin* **9/4**[1]
5322 **2** 5 **Geanie Mac (IRE)**[12] 5146 5-10-3 55 (p) MrHStock(5) 10 59
(Linda Perratt) *w ldr: rdn to ld over 3f out: hdd over 2f out: plugged on but no ch w wnr* **8/1**
5332 **3** 1 **Grand Diamond (IRE)**[11] 5171 10-10-7 54 MissCWalton 3 57
(Jim Goldie) *hld up in midfield: pushed along and hdwy over 2f out: one pce in 3rd fr over 1f out* **17/2**
1465 **4** 1 1/4 **Eilean Mor**[11] 5171 6-10-2 52 MrTHamilton(3) 2 53
(R Mike Smith) *led for 1f: trckd ldrs: rdn 3f out: plugged on* **12/1**
5341 **5** 3/4 **Royal Etiquette (IRE)**[10] 5208 7-10-11 61 6ex (tp) MrAlexFerguson(3) 1 61+
(Lawney Hill) *hld up: stl plenty to do over 2f out: sn rdn: kpt on* **8/1**
0-01 **6** 2 **Titus Bolt (IRE)**[12] 5145 5-11-0 61 MrsCBartley 7 59
(Jim Goldie) *rrd s and slowly away: rcvrd to ld after 1f w pce stdy: rdn whn hdd over 3f out: grad wknd* **11/4**[2]
4203 **7** 2 1/4 **Rocky Two (IRE)**[12] 5145 4-10-2 54 PhillipDennis(5) 6 49
(Philip Kirby) *midfield on inner: rdn over 2f out: wknd over 1f out* **6/1**[3]
-006 **8** 6 **Carrowbeg (IRE)**[10] 5208 6-10-3 55 (bt) MissPFuller(5) 5 42
(Lawney Hill) *hld up: hdwy on outside over 5f out: edgd lft and wknd fr over 2f out* **33/1**
4- **9** 16 **Strikemaster (IRE)**[357] 5885 8-10-1 53 (t) MrAaronJames(5) 4 19
(Lee James) *prom on outer: lost pl 5f out: sn bhd* **25/1**
3m 5.95s (0.65) **Going Correction** -0.25s/f (Firm) 9 Ran SP% **118.9**
Speed ratings (Par 101): **88,85,84,83,83 82,81,77,68**
CSF £21.96 CT £133.41 TOTE £4.80: £1.60, £2.30, £2.00; EX 17.00 Trifecta £92.00.
**Owner** Mrs Lizzy Wilson **Bred** Juddmonte Farms Ltd **Trained** Melsonby, N Yorks
**FOCUS**
A tactically run finale, but the winner might have plenty more to offer.
T/Plt: £94.00 to a £1 stake. Pool: £54,601.49 - 424.01 winning units. T/Qpdt: £8.20 to a £1 stake. Pool: £4517.45 - 406.41 winning units. AS

# 5097 SOUTHWELL (L-H)
Wednesday, August 20

**OFFICIAL GOING: Fibresand: standard**
Wind: Moderate behind Weather: Cloudy

## 5568 BARRY AND PAULINE 42ND WEDDING ANNIVERSARY MAIDEN STKS 5f (F)
5:00 (5:00) (Class 5) 3-Y-0+ £2,587 (£770; £384; £192) Stalls High

Form RPR
2220 **1** **Meebo (IRE)**[35] 4324 3-8-9 61 (vt) JennyPowell(5) 4 69
(J R Jenkins) *led 1f: cl up: led wl over 1f out: rdn clr appr fnl f: kpt on* **9/2**[2]
3-2 **2** 6 **Cagoule**[18] 4900 3-9-5 80 DanielTudhope 5 52
(David O'Meara) *cl up: slt ld after 1f: rdn along 2f out: sn hdd and one pce* **4/11**[1]
-4 **3** 3/4 **Black Widow**[42] 4086 3-9-0 0 StevieDonohoe 1 45
(Pat Eddery) *dwlt and wnt lft s: sn rdn along in rr: hdwy over 1f out: kpt on: nrst fin* **25/1**
3 **4** 1 **Quick Touch**[23] 4735 3-9-5 0 PatDobbs 6 46
(Robert Cowell) *cl up on stands' rail: rdn along 2f out: sn drvn and one pce* **7/1**[3]
3600 **5** 1/2 **Island Express (IRE)**[118] 1677 7-9-2 47 (tp) AnnStokell(5) 3 44
(Ann Stokell) *chsd ldrs: rdn along 1/2-way: sn drvn and outpcd* **100/1**
0 **6** shd **Byronaissance**[21] 4791 5-9-7 0 AndrewElliott 2 44
(Neville Bycroft) *chsd ldrs: rdn along 1/2-way: wkng and hld whn n.m.r over 1f out* **33/1**
1m 0.4s (0.70) **Going Correction** +0.175s/f (Slow)
**WFA** 3 from 5yo+ 2lb 6 Ran SP% **111.8**
Speed ratings (Par 103): **101,91,90,88,87 87**
CSF £6.59 TOTE £5.50: £1.60, £1.10; EX 7.00 Trifecta £37.80.
**Owner** Mrs Wendy Jenkins **Bred** Brian Killeen **Trained** Royston, Herts
**FOCUS**
The Fibresand track was riding deep despite no overnight rain. A weak all-aged sprint maiden and 3yos filled the first four places. Improvement from the winner, helped by his rider's claim.

## 5569 BRITISH STALLION STUDS EBF MAIDEN STKS 5f (F)
5:30 (5:31) (Class 5) 2-Y-O £2,911 (£866; £432; £216) Stalls High

Form RPR
2365 **1** **Rita's Boy (IRE)**[47] 3937 2-9-5 71 DanielTudhope 6 71
(K R Burke) *slt ld: shkn up over 1f out: rdn ins fnl f: edgd lft and kpt on towards fin* **5/4**[2]
4 **2** 1/2 **Field Game**[58] 3536 2-9-5 0 PatDobbs 4 69
(Hughie Morrison) *cl up: ev ch whn rdn jst over 1f out and sn edgd lft: styd on wl towards fin* **11/10**[1]
066 **3** 5 **Rosie Crowe (IRE)**[20] 4828 2-9-0 56 StevieDonohoe 2 46
(David C Griffiths) *sn cl up: rdn along 1/2-way: drvn wl over 1f out: kpt on one pce* **33/1**



The Form Book, Raceform Ltd, Newbury, RG14 5SJ

044 **4** *4* **Poppy In The Wind**[12] 5140 2-8-9 61 KevinStott(5) 5 32
(Alan Brown) *sn rdn along in rr: sme hdwy 2f out: sn drvn and no imp* **20/1**

0200 **5** *4* **Blue Burmese (IRE)**[68] 3173 2-9-0 68 AndrewMullen 3 17
(Mark Usher) *in tch: rdn along over 2f out: sn outpcd* **8/1**[3]

0 **6** *1 1/4* **Auntie Dif**[9] 5255 2-8-7 0 AdamMcLean(7) 9 13
(Derek Shaw) *prom: rdn along over 2f out: sn outpcd* **50/1**

000 **7** *5* **Julia Stardust**[26] 4618 2-8-7 0 JordanVaughan(7) 7
(Alan Coogan) *trckd ldrs: rdn along over 2f out: sn wknd* **100/1**

1m 0.16s (0.46) **Going Correction** +0.175s/f (Slow) 7 Ran SP% **113.8**
Speed ratings (Par 94): **103,102,94,87,81 79,71**
CSF £2.88 TOTE £1.90: £1.10, £1.10; EX 3.60 Trifecta £25.20.
**Owner** Middleham Park Racing CVI & Mrs E Burke **Bred** A M F Persse **Trained** Middleham Moor, N Yorks

**FOCUS**
The market made this modest juvenile sprint maiden a two-horse race and so it proved, with the pair drawing clear of the remainder. This is basically rated as straightforward form.

## 5570 BARKESTONE WEALTH MANAGEMENT MAIDEN STKS 7f (F)
**6:00** (6:00) (Class 5) 3-Y-0+ **£2,587** (£770; £384; £192) **Stalls** Low

Form RPR

235- **1** **Nur Jahan (IRE)**[342] 6319 4-9-5 69 StevieDonohoe 6 67+
(David Lanigan) *dwlt: sn trcking ldrs: hdwy over 2f out: led wl over 1f out: rdn clr ent fnl f: styd on* **7/1**[3]

2464 **2** *2 1/4* **Heho**[14] 5046 3-9-0 72 GrahamLee 7 59
(Sir Michael Stoute) *cl up on outer: effrt to chal over 2f out: sn rdn and ev ch: drvn and edgd lft ent fnl f: one pce* **5/4**[1]

500 **3** *4* **Wild Hill Boy**[21] 4791 4-9-5 44 [1] JacobButterfield(5) 2 55
(David C Griffiths) *led to 1/2-way: cl up on inner: rdn along over 2f out: drvn over 1f out: wandered and one pce ins fnl f* **50/1**

3555 **4** *2 1/4* **Puppet Theatre (IRE)**[51] 3798 4-9-5 43 DanielTudhope 4 44
(David O'Meara) *cl up: led 1/2-way: rdn along over 2f out: hdd wl over 1f out and sn wknd* **8/1**

**5** *5* **Copperbelt** 3-9-5 0 RoystonFfrench 3 34
(Mark Johnston) *s.i.s and in rr: hdwy to chse ldrs on outer 3f out: rdn and edgd lft over 2f out: sn wknd* **6/4**[2]

0 **6** *34* **Windy Miller**[9] 5249 3-9-5 0 WilliamCarson 1
(Robin Dickin) *t.k.h: chsd ldrs: rdn along bef 1/2-way: sn outpcd and bhd* **100/1**

1m 31.04s (0.74) **Going Correction** +0.05s/f (Slow)
**WFA** 3 from 4yo 5lb 6 Ran SP% **111.0**
Speed ratings (Par 103): **97,94,89,87,81 42**
CSF £15.97 TOTE £8.20: £5.70, £1.40; EX 16.10 Trifecta £132.70.
**Owner** B E Nielsen **Bred** The Kathryn Stud **Trained** Upper Lambourn, Berks

**FOCUS**
The pace was steady for this weak maiden. The third and fourth hold down the form.

## 5571 LUCY FLINTHAM BIRTHDAY H'CAP 1m (F)
**6:30** (6:32) (Class 5) (0-70,70) 3-Y-0+ **£2,587** (£770; £384; £192) **Stalls** Low

Form RPR

6002 **1** **Blazeofenchantment (USA)**[13] 5100 4-9-3 66 JacobButterfield(5) 9 82+
(John Wainwright) *dwlt and reminders s: sn pushed along and in tch: hdwy on outer and wd st: sn rdn and led 2f out: drvn clr ent fnl f: kpt on strly* **4/1**[2]

5004 **2** *5* **Royal Holiday (IRE)**[8] 5269 7-9-7 65 (p) DanielTudhope 2 70
(Marjorie Fife) *led: rdn along and hdd 2f out: sn drvn and kpt on same pce appr fnl f* **3/1**[1]

2060 **3** *3 3/4* **Midaz**[27] 4579 4-9-4 62 PatDobbs 3 57
(Hughie Morrison) *trckd ldrs: pushed along and outpcd over 3f out: rdn over 2f out: styd on u.p to take modest 3rd ins fnl f* **9/2**[3]

2100 **4** *5* **Epic Voyage (USA)**[11] 5196 3-9-6 70 (b) DaleSwift 4 53
(Brian Ellison) *hld up in tch: hdwy 3f out: rdn to chse ldrs over 2f out: sn drvn and one pce* **5/1**

0004 **5** *8* **Jebel Tara**[9] 5233 9-8-4 53 (bt) KevinStott(5) 8 18
(Alan Brown) *trckd ldrs: smooth hdwy on outer 3f out: sn cl up: rdn 2f out: sn edgd lft and wknd* **16/1**

0550 **6** *2 1/4* **Slinky McVelvet**[31] 4468 3-9-5 69 GrahamLee 7 28
(Garry Moss) *cl up: rdn along 3f out: sn drvn and wknd* **12/1**

5105 **7** *2 3/4* **Hayek**[8] 5268 7-8-7 51 oh1 (b) AndrewElliott 1
(Tim Easterby) *chsd ldrs on inner: rdn along 1/2-way: sn lost pl and bhd* **20/1**

6035 **8** *hd* **Ivy Port**[9] 5234 4-9-8 66 AndrewMullen 6 20
(Michael Appleby) *cl up: rdn along over 3f out: sn drvn and wknd* **4/1**[2]

1m 43.07s (-0.63) **Going Correction** +0.05s/f (Slow)
**WFA** 3 from 4yo+ 6lb 8 Ran SP% **118.2**
Speed ratings (Par 103): **105,100,96,91,83 81,78,78**
CSF £17.09 CT £57.05 TOTE £5.00: £1.70, £1.70, £2.10; EX 20.10 Trifecta £135.20.
**Owner** J S Wainwright **Bred** Gulf Coast Farms LLC **Trained** Kennythorpe, N Yorks

**FOCUS**
A modest handicap run at a reasonable pace and they finished well strung out. The winner could become a course specialist and this form could easily be significantly better than rated.

## 5572 INJURED JOCKEYS FUND 50TH ANNIVERSARY H'CAP 1m 6f (F)
**7:00** (7:00) (Class 4) (0-85,85) 3-Y-0+ **£4,690** (£1,395; £697; £348) **Stalls** Low

Form RPR

0002 **1** **Cousin Khee**[9] 5259 7-9-3 74 DanielTudhope 4 86
(Hughie Morrison) *trckd ldr: cl up after 6f: led 1/2-way: rdn along over 2f out: clr over 1f out: kpt on strly* **11/4**[1]

1313 **2** *4 1/2* **Royal Marskell**[22] 4754 5-9-1 72 JamesSullivan 6 76
(Alison Hutchinson) *trckd ldrs: hdwy 4f out: effrt 3f out: rdn along over 2f out: swtchd rt towards stands' rail and drvn over 1f out: kpt on to take 2nd ins fnl f: no ch w wnr* **8/1**

1213 **3** *4 1/2* **Windshield**[11] 5200 3-8-0 69 (p) LukeMorris 1 67
(Sir Mark Prescott Bt) *hld up: stdy hdwy 6f out: sn trcking ldrs: effrt to chse wnr 3f out: rdn and edgd lft 2f out: sn drvn and one pce* **6/1**

3530 **4** *16* **Ujagar (IRE)**[21] 4803 3-8-6 75 (p) WilliamCarson 5 53
(Tom Dascombe) *prom: cl up 1/2-way: rdn along 4f out: drvn 3f out and sn outpcd* **7/1**

-006 **5** *2 1/2* **Sioux Chieftain (IRE)**[8] 5288 4-9-5 76 AndrewMullen 2 50
(Michael Appleby) *trckd ldrs: rdn along over 4f out: sn wknd* **10/1**

151/ **6** *11* **Any Given Day (IRE)**[86] 6195 9-10-0 85 GrahamLee 3 45
(Donald McCain) *led: rdn along and hdd 1/2-way: wknd qckly and lost pl over 5f out: sn wl bhd* **4/1**[3]

012 **7** *8* **Dynastic**[77] 2904 5-9-1 72 BarryMcHugh 7 22
(Tony Coyle) *hld up: hdwy to chse ldrs over 5f out: rdn along 4f out: sn wknd and bhd whn eased wl over 1f out* **7/2**[2]

3m 6.87s (-1.43) **Going Correction** +0.05s/f (Slow)
**WFA** 3 from 4yo+ 12lb 7 Ran SP% **115.9**
Speed ratings (Par 105): **106,103,100,91,90 84,79**
CSF £25.87 TOTE £4.80: £1.90, £5.90; EX 52.20 Trifecta £197.80.
**Owner** Raymond Tooth **Bred** Miss B Swire **Trained** East Ilsley, Berks

**FOCUS**
With plenty in form, this looked an open affair but as is so often the case on this surface they finished strung out. No more than a fair handicap for the class. The winner is a useful AW performer on his day.

## 5573 JENNIFER WALLACE MEMORIAL FILLIES' H'CAP 7f (F)
**7:30** (7:30) (Class 5) (0-70,70) 3-Y-0+ **£2,587** (£770; £384; £192) **Stalls** Low

Form RPR

1462 **1** **Pretty Bubbles**[7] 5320 5-9-12 70 PaddyAspell 6 89
(J R Jenkins) *swtchd lft s and sn trcking ldrs on inner: hdwy 3f out: led 2f out: sn rdn clr: styd on* **5/2**[1]

-102 **2** *7* **Musical Molly (IRE)**[13] 5097 3-9-2 65 DaleSwift 4 63
(Brian Ellison) *trckd ldrs: hdwy 3f out: rdn over 2f out: styd on to chse wnr jst ins fnl f: sn drvn and no imp* **9/2**[3]

0601 **3** *3 1/4* **See Clearly**[13] 5103 5-9-0 58 (p) DuranFentiman 7 49
(Tim Easterby) *prom: effrt to chal over 2f out: sn rdn and ev ch: drvn over 1f out and kpt on same pce* **6/1**

-660 **4** *2 1/2* **Mandy The Nag (USA)**[13] 5100 4-9-7 65 DavidNolan 2 50
(Richard Fahey) *cl up: led after 3f: pushed along and hdd 3f out: sn rdn: drvn and one pce fnl 2f* **20/1**

1 **5** *3* **Chellalla**[4] 5425 5-9-8 66 6ex StevieDonohoe 3 42
(Ian Williams) *cl up: led 3f out: rdn and hdd 2f out: sn drvn and wknd* **4/1**[2]

164 **6** *2 1/4* **Heidi's Delight (IRE)**[29] 4515 5-8-1 52 (b) RowanScott(7) 5 22
(Ann Duffield) *a towards rr* **20/1**

5244 **7** *shd* **Rocksee (IRE)**[13] 5079 3-8-12 66 (p) JennyPowell(5) 9 34
(Tom Dascombe) *a in rr* **6/1**

4016 **8** *3 3/4* **Blue Clumber**[12] 5138 4-8-3 52 MatthewHopkins(5) 8 12
(Shaun Harris) *a in rr* **20/1**

0340 **9** *2 1/2* **Gladsome**[29] 4515 6-8-9 53 TonyHamilton 10
(Michael Herrington) *a towards rr* **33/1**

3636 **10** *4 1/2* **Arabian Flight**[130] 1450 5-9-4 62 AndrewMullen 1
(Michael Appleby) *slt ld on inner: rdn along and hdd after 3f: sn lost pl and bhd* **8/1**

1m 29.77s (-0.53) **Going Correction** +0.05s/f (Slow)
**WFA** 3 from 4yo+ 5lb 10 Ran SP% **123.7**
Speed ratings (Par 100): **105,97,93,90,87 84,84,80,77,72**
CSF £13.98 CT £64.43 TOTE £3.00: £1.60, £1.30, £3.30; EX 14.50 Trifecta £76.90.
**Owner** Mark Goldstein **Bred** Southill Stud **Trained** Royston, Herts

**FOCUS**
The pace was true for this modest fillies' handicap and the market got it right. The easy winner built on her recent good turf form.

## 5574 IN MEMORY OF NEV HARDY H'CAP 5f (F)
**8:00** (8:01) (Class 6) (0-55,54) 3-Y-0+ **£1,940** (£577; £288; £144) **Stalls** High

Form RPR

0455 **1** **Danzoe (IRE)**[7] 5316 7-8-12 50 (v) EoinWalsh(5) 1 56
(Christine Dunnett) *chsd ldrs on outer: hdwy over 1f out: sn rdn and styd on wl u.p to ld last 50yds* **8/1**[3]

-000 **2** *1/2* **Dont Tell Nan**[6] 5333 3-8-12 47 DaleSwift 8 51
(Derek Shaw) *cl up: rdn to chal over 1f out: slt ld jst ins fnl f: sn drvn: hdd and no ex last 50yds* **16/1**

2623 **3** *hd* **Lucky Mark (IRE)**[15] 4994 5-9-2 54 (p) ShaneGray(5) 5 57
(John Balding) *led: rdn over 1f out: drvn ent fnl f: sn hdd and kpt on same pce* **11/4**[2]

0030 **4** *2* **Red Cobra (IRE)**[5] 5399 4-9-7 54 TonyHamilton 7 50
(Tim Easterby) *chsd ldrs: hdwy wl over 1f out: rdn and no imp fnl f* **2/1**[1]

6540 **5** *2 1/2* **Waabel**[113] 1838 7-9-2 52 (t) CharlesBishop(3) 6 39
(Ann Stokell) *dwlt and in rr: hdwy 2f out: sn rdn and kpt on fnl f: nrst fin* **20/1**

500 **6** *3 1/2* **Upper Lambourn (IRE)**[28] 4534 6-8-12 45 (t) WilliamCarson 10 20
(Christopher Kellett) *in tch: rdn along 2f out: sn drvn and no imp* **8/1**[3]

6000 **7** *6* **Jalusive (IRE)**[13] 5105 5-8-12 45 AdamBeschizza 2
(Christine Dunnett) *prom: rdn along 1/2-way: sn wknd* **25/1**

524 **8** *shd* **Procurer (FR)**[36] 4295 3-9-0 54 MatthewHopkins(5) 9 7
(Scott Dixon) *dwlt: a towards rr* **8/1**[3]

6105 **9** *3 3/4* **Robbian**[54] 3679 3-8-8 50 PaddyPilley(7) 3
(Charles Smith) *chsd ldrs: rdn along 1/2-way: sn wknd* **16/1**

0005 **10** *24* **Loma Mor**[27] 4595 3-8-10 48 BillyCray(3) 11 +
(Alan McCabe) *dwlt and Monty Roberts rug for stalls entry stl in pl: a bhd: eased wl over 1f out* **20/1**

1m 0.54s (0.84) **Going Correction** +0.175s/f (Slow)
**WFA** 3 from 4yo+ 2lb 10 Ran SP% **118.5**
Speed ratings (Par 101): **100,99,98,95,91 86,76,76,70,31**
CSF £123.71 CT £456.56 TOTE £9.00: £2.70, £6.00, £1.70; EX 172.80 Trifecta £1693.00 Part won..
**Owner** One For All **Bred** Miss Anne Ormsby **Trained** Hingham, Norfolk

**FOCUS**
The leaders went off a shade too quickly in this basement sprint handicap. A minor rise for this should leave the winner competitive.
T/Plt: £7.90 to a £1 stake. Pool: £40,086.36 - 3682.88 winning units. T/Qpdt: £6.50 to a £1 stake. Pool: £5047.94 - 570.30 winning units. JR

## [4680]YORK (L-H)

### Wednesday, August 20

**OFFICIAL GOING: Good to firm (good in places; 7.0)**

Wind: moderate 1/2 behind Weather: changeable, breeze, showers Rails: Races on traditional line and all distances as advertised

### 5575 SYMPHONY GROUP STKS (H'CAP) 5f 89y
**1:55** (1:55) (Class 2) (0-105,105) 3-Y-O+

**£31,125** (£9,320; £4,660; £2,330; £1,165; £585) **Stalls** High

Form RPR

0U10 **1** **Blaine**[18] 4895 4-9-5 100 (b) AmyRyan 15 108
(Kevin Ryan) *lw: racd stands' side: in rr: hdwy over 1f out: styd on wl to ld post* **12/1**

0612 **2** *shd* **Move In Time**[11] 5160 6-9-8 103 DanielTudhope 8 111
(David O'Meara) *racd stands' side: trckd ldrs: styd on to ld that side and overall last 50yds: hdd post* **8/1**[3]

0210 **3** *nk* **B Fifty Two (IRE)**[39] 4179 5-8-13 94 (bt) FrankieDettori 3 101
(Charles Hills) *overall ldr far side: hdd and no ex last 50yds: 1st of 5 that gp* **33/1**

1135 **4** *3/4* **Robot Boy (IRE)**[24] 4700 4-9-7 102 GrahamGibbons 4 106
(David Barron) *lw: dwlt: racd far side: hdwy to chse ldr that side over 1f out: kpt on same pce ins fnl f: 2nd of 5 that gp* **13/2**[1]

2100 **5** *3/4* **Ashpan Sam**[18] 4895 5-9-9 104 RyanMoore 5 105
(John Spearing) *racd far side: chsd ldr: kpt on same pce over 1f out: 3rd of 5 that gp* **12/1**

-000 **6** *shd* **Bogart**[25] 4683 5-8-13 94 NeilCallan 9 95
(Kevin Ryan) *lw: drvn to ld stands' side: led that side tl last 50yds: kpt on same pce* **11/1**

1110 **7** *nse* **Line Of Reason (IRE)**[25] 4683 4-9-4 99 GrahamLee 1 100
(Paul Midgley) *racd far side: hld up towards rr: hdwy over 1f out: kpt on same pce: 4th of 5 in gp* **12/1**

0330 **8** *nk* **Secret Witness**[4] 5419 8-8-11 92 (v) LukeMorris 2 92
(Ronald Harris) *racd far side: outpcd and lost pl over 4f out: hdwy over 1f out: kpt on last of 5 in gp* **20/1**

064 **9** *nse* **Mass Rally (IRE)**[98] 2256 7-9-10 105 (b) PaulMulrennan 17 108
(Michael Dods) *hld up in rr stands' side: hdwy whn nt clr run over 1f out: styd on ins fnl f* **11/1**

4166 **10** *1* **See The Sun**[25] 4683 3-8-13 96 DavidAllan 20 92
(Tim Easterby) *racd stands' side: chsd ldrs: one pce fnl 2f* **8/1**[3]

0000 **11** *3 3/4* **York Glory (USA)**[18] 4895 6-9-8 103 (v[1]) JamieSpencer 11 85
(Kevin Ryan) *racd stands' side: towards rr: hdwy over 2f out: chsng ldrs over 1f out: wknd last 75yds* **12/1**

0010 **12** *1 1/2* **Racy**[11] 5160 7-9-6 101 (p) PaulPickard 14 78
(Brian Ellison) *racd stands' side: towards rr: sme hdwy over 2f out: lost pl over 1f out* **20/1**

5133 **13** *nk* **Peterkin (IRE)**[18] 4898 3-8-10 93 JoeFanning 10 69
(Mark Johnston) *racd stands' side: w ldr: lost pl over 1f out* **12/1**

3100 **14** *3/4* **Kimberella**[4] 5445 4-9-0 95 AdrianNicholls 12 68
(David Nicholls) *racd stands' side: chsd ldrs: lost pl over 1f out* **7/1**[2]

2001 **15** *2 1/2* **Judge 'n Jury**[8] 5289 10-8-9 97 6ex (t) DavidParkes(7) 18 61
(Ronald Harris) *racd stands' side: in rr: bhd fnl 2f* **25/1**

1m 2.74s (-1.36) **Going Correction** -0.175s/f (Firm)
**WFA** 3 from 4yo+ 2lb **15 Ran SP% 119.5**
Speed ratings (Par 109): **103,102,102,101,99 99,99,99,99,97 91,89,88,87,83**
CSF £98.03 CT £3157.57 TOTE £16.10: £5.20, £3.00, £6.10; EX 152.80 Trifecta £4142.40 Part won..
**Owner** Matt & Lauren Morgan **Bred** Toby Barker **Trained** Hambleton, N Yorks
■ Stewards' Enquiry : Jamie Spencer three-day ban: used whip without giving horse time to respond (Sep 3-5)
Amy Ryan four-day ban: used whip above permitted level (Sep 3-5,7)

**FOCUS**
Just 0.2mm of rain overnight, and the ground had quickened up to good to firm, good in places. The jockeys in the first generally agreed that the ground was fast. They split into two groups in this quality sprint handicap and there was nothing between them at the finish. The form looks straightforward.

### 5576 TATTERSALLS ACOMB STKS (GROUP 3) 7f
**2:30** (2:32) (Class 1) 2-Y-O

**£45,368** (£17,200; £8,608; £4,288; £2,152; £1,080) **Stalls** Low

Form RPR

321 **1** **Dutch Connection**[18] 4896 2-9-1 87 WilliamBuick 8 107
(Charles Hills) *mid-div: effrt over 2f out: chsng ldrs over 1f out: edgd lft: styd on to ld nr fin* **16/1**

31 **2** *hd* **Toocoolforschool (IRE)**[15] 5013 2-9-1 82 BenCurtis 1 106
(K R Burke) *w'like: str: led 1f: w ldr: led over 1f out: hdd and no ex clsng stages* **33/1**

31 **3** *1 1/4* **Basateen (IRE)**[27] 4570 2-9-1 0 PaulHanagan 5 103
(Richard Hannon) *str: swtg: trckd ldr: t.k.h: led after 1f: hdd over 1f out: hung lft: kpt on same pce* **6/4**[1]

**4** *3/4* **Jamaica (IRE)**[23] 4745 2-9-1 0 JosephO'Brien 11 101
(A P O'Brien, Ire) *angular: dwlt: sn chsng ldrs: drvn over 2f out: one pce over 1f out* **2/1**[2]

321 **5** *2* **Salateen**[17] 4935 2-9-1 91 NeilCallan 10 96
(Kevin Ryan) *leggy: athletic: mid-div: hdwy to chse ldrs over 3f out: one pce fnl 2f* **25/1**

53 **6** *2 1/2* **Dominada (IRE)**[26] 4633 2-9-1 0 PaulMulrennan 3 89
(Brian Ellison) *rr-div: hdwy 3f out: fdd over 1f out* **100/1**

1 **7** *1/2* **Growl**[24] 4695 2-9-1 0 RichardHughes 4 88
(Brian Meehan) *str: hld up in rr: effrt 3f out: wknd over 1f out* **6/1**[3]

0216 **8** *9* **Chadic**[21] 4780 2-9-1 100 JoeFanning 9 63
(Mark Johnston) *chsd ldrs: drvn over 3f out: sn lost pl: eased whn bhd clsng stages* **33/1**

355 **9** *11* **Danny O'Ruairc (IRE)**[37] 4253 2-9-1 75 (p) DarrenMoffatt 6 34
(James Moffatt) *s.s: in rr and sn drvn along: bhd fnl 2f: eased clsng stages* **100/1**

31 **10** *11* **Prince Gagarin (IRE)**[19] 4865 2-9-1 0 RyanMoore 7 4
(Ed Dunlop) *atr: wnt lft s: in rr: lost pl over 2f out: heavily eased clsng stages* **8/1**

1m 22.32s (-2.98) **Going Correction** -0.175s/f (Firm) 2y crse rec **10 Ran SP% 116.3**
Speed ratings: **110,109,108,107,105 102,101,91,78,66**
CSF £424.75 TOTE £12.90: £3.30, £5.00, £1.10; EX 318.80 Trifecta £1063.90.
**Owner** Mrs Susan Roy **Bred** Mrs S M Roy **Trained** Lambourn, Berks

**FOCUS**
Upgraded to Group 3 status in 2006, The Acomb has proved something of a mixed bag in recent seasons, although does usually throw up at least one classy performer (Dante/French Derby winner The Grey Gatsby second last year). This time around it looked well above-average with seven of the 11-strong field having won last time out, and all bar a pair holding future Group 1 engagements. There was a strong pace on early, resulting in a new juvenile track record, and the main action developed nearer the far side late on as two came clear.

### 5577 NEPTUNE INVESTMENT MANAGEMENT GREAT VOLTIGEUR STKS (GROUP 2) (C&G) 1m 4f
**3:05** (3:07) (Class 1) 3-Y-O

**£85,065** (£32,250; £16,140; £8,040; £4,035; £2,025) **Stalls** Centre

Form RPR

3431 **1** **Postponed (IRE)**[33] 4385 3-9-0 106 AndreaAtzeni 3 121+
(Luca Cumani) *lw: trckd ldrs: smooth hdwy over 2f out: led over 1f out: drvn and edgd rt: styd on wl* **5/2**[1]

2141 **2** *2 1/4* **Snow Sky**[21] 4778 3-9-0 111 JamesDoyle 1 117+
(Sir Michael Stoute) *hld up in rr: stdy hdwy over 3f out: rdn to chse wnr 1f out: kpt on: no imp* **7/2**[2]

1404 **3** *8* **Odeon**[33] 4385 3-9-0 103 GrahamLee 8 104
(James Given) *swtg: t.k.h: led: hdd over 1f out: fdd fnl 150yds* **40/1**

2235 **4** *3/4* **Marzocco (USA)**[38] 4251 3-9-0 107 (b[1]) WilliamBuick 7 103
(John Gosden) *sn chsng ldrs: drvn over 5f out: kpt on one pce fnl 2f* **8/1**

**5** *1 3/4* **Granddukeoftuscany (IRE)**[55] 3637 3-9-0 0 JosephO'Brien 10 100
(A P O'Brien, Ire) *unf: scope: trckd ldr: one pce whn hit overhd by rival rdr's whip over 1f out* **11/2**

5211 **6** *2 3/4* **Hartnell**[41] 4122 3-9-0 110 JoeFanning 4 96
(Mark Johnston) *chsd ldrs: drvn over 3f out: hung lft: wknd last 75yds* **9/2**[3]

-216 **7** *1 1/4* **Observational**[21] 4778 3-9-0 103 GeorgeBaker 2 94
(Roger Charlton) *lw: mid-div: drvn and outpcd 4f out: sme hdwy over 2f out: wknd last 100yds* **14/1**

4650 **8** *3/4* **Red Galileo**[21] 4778 3-9-0 106 (t) OisinMurphy 6 93
(Ed Dunlop) *t.k.h in mid-div: drvn over 4f out: wknd over 1f out* **33/1**

0 **9** *31* **Indian Maharaja (IRE)**[143] 1200 3-9-0 99 SeamieHeffernan 9 43
(A P O'Brien, Ire) *w'like: dwlt: t.k.h in last: bhd and drvn 4f out: eased over 1f out: t.o* **14/1**

2m 27.29s (-5.91) **Going Correction** -0.075s/f (Good) **9 Ran SP% 114.2**
Speed ratings (Par 112): **116,114,109,108,107 105,104,104,83**
CSF £11.04 TOTE £3.30: £1.20, £1.70, £5.00; EX 12.10 Trifecta £774.60.
**Owner** Sheikh Mohammed Obaid Al Maktoum **Bred** St Albans Bloodstock Llp **Trained** Newmarket, Suffolk

**FOCUS**
Traditionally a strong Leger trial, but a Group 2 race in its own right, and some good horses have won it in recent years and skipped the final classic, notably Youmzain and Telescope. The winner is really flourishing now.

### 5578 JUDDMONTE INTERNATIONAL STKS (BRITISH CHAMPIONS SERIES) (GROUP 1) 1m 2f 88y
**3:40** (3:42) (Class 1) 3-Y-O+

**£453,680** (£172,000; £86,080; £42,880; £21,520; £10,800) **Stalls** Low

Form RPR

-311 **1** **Australia**[53] 3739 3-8-12 123 JosephO'Brien 6 129
(A P O'Brien, Ire) *hld up in rr: hdwy over 3f out: rdn to ld over 1f out: drvn out* **8/13**[1]

0116 **2** *2* **The Grey Gatsby (IRE)**[38] 4251 3-8-12 119 RichardHughes 2 125
(Kevin Ryan) *lw: hld up in rr: stdy hdwy over 3f out: styd on appr fnl f: tk 2nd last 75yds: no imp* **12/1**[3]

2212 **3** *2 1/4* **Telescope (IRE)**[25] 4649 4-9-6 123 RyanMoore 5 121
(Sir Michael Stoute) *swtg: trckd ldrs: effrt 3f out: rdn and upsides over 1f out: sn 2nd: kpt on same pce* **5/1**[2]

2413 **4** *3 1/4* **Mukhadram**[25] 4649 5-9-6 122 PaulHanagan 4 115
(William Haggas) *led 1f: t.k.h: rdn to ld over 2f out: hdd over 1f out: wknd last 100yds* **5/1**[2]

1241 **5** *1 1/4* **Arod (IRE)**[34] 4366 3-8-12 109 JamieSpencer 3 112
(Peter Chapple-Hyam) *trckd ldrs: t.k.h: effrt 3f out: hung lft and upsides over 1f out: wknd fnl 150yds* **20/1**

5102 **6** *2 3/4* **Kingfisher (IRE)**[53] 3739 3-8-12 111 SeamieHeffernan 1 107
(A P O'Brien, Ire) *swtg: drvn to ld after 1f: set stdy pce: qckng gallop over 4f out: hdd over 2f: wknd over 1f out: sn eased* **100/1**

2m 7.35s (-5.15) **Going Correction** -0.075s/f (Good)
**WFA** 3 from 4yo+ 8lb **6 Ran SP% 108.7**
Speed ratings (Par 117): **117,115,113,111,110 107**
CSF £8.65 TOTE £1.60: £1.10, £2.90; EX 7.80 Trifecta £28.90.
**Owner** D Smith/Mrs J Magnier/M Tabor/T Ah Khing **Bred** Stanley Estate And Stud Co **Trained** Cashel, Co Tipperary

**FOCUS**
A highly select and absorbing running of the International, featuring winners of this year's Eclipse and Hardwicke Stakes, the Epsom and Irish Derby, as well as the winner of the French equivalent. Once pacemaking Kingfisher established himself in front the pace was sound and it was another boost for the Classic generation as the respective Derby winners, both held up early, filled the first two places.

### 5579 FINE EQUINITY STKS (H'CAP) 2m 88y
**4:20** (4:20) (Class 2) (0-100,97) 4-Y-O+

**£24,900** (£7,456; £3,728; £1,864; £932; £468) **Stalls** Low

Form RPR

0 **1** **Edge Of Sanity (IRE)**[11] 5161 5-9-6 **96** PaulMulrennan 7 105
(Brian Ellison) *hld up in mid-div: hdwy over 3f out: led over 1f out: jnd ins fnl f: fnd ex cl home* **25/1**

-312 **2** *1/2* **Quest For More (IRE)**[20] 4819 4-8-9 **85** (b) JamesDoyle 10 93
(Roger Charlton) *trckd ldrs: t.k.h: effrt and hung lft over 2f out: drvn and upsides ins fnl f: no ex* **10/1**

0-4 **3** *2* **Spacious Sky (USA)**[17] 4746 5-8-8 **84** ow1 (t) RichardHughes 16 90
(A J Martin, Ire) *lw: hld up towards rr: stdy hdwy over 5f out: nt clr run over 2f out: styd on same pce fnl f* **9/2**[1]

0506 **4** *1* **Statutory (IRE)**[39] 4213 4-9-7 **97** AndreaAtzeni 5 101
(Saeed bin Suroor) *lw: trckd ldrs: effrt whn hmpd over 2f out: kpt on same pce appr fnl f* **10/1**

1020 **5** *1/2* **Sir Frank Morgan (IRE)**[11] 5161 4-8-7 **83** JoeFanning 4 87
(Mark Johnston) *led 4f: chsd ldrs: led over 2f out: hdd over 1f out: kpt on one pce* **25/1**

3122 **6** ¾ **Gambol (FR)**[15] 4995 4-8-7 **83** ......... PaulHanagan 3 87
(B W Hills) *hld up in mid-div: hdwy and nt clr run 2f out: kpt on same pce* **12/1**

3216 **7** ¾ **Eagle Rock (IRE)**[39] 4217 6-8-10 **86** .........(p) JamesSullivan 14 88
(Tom Tate) *chsd ldrs: drvn over 3f out: one pce* **12/1**

3051 **8** ½ **Itlaaq**[25] 4685 8-8-9 **85** .........(t) GrahamGibbons 11 86
(Michael Easterby) *mid-div: stdy hdwy over 3f out: nt clr run 2f out: one pce* **11/1**

6-03 **9** hd **Lady Kashaan (IRE)**[12] 5144 5-8-13 **89** ......... BenCurtis 6 90
(Alan Swinbank) *mid-div: drvn and outpcd over 3f out: kpt on fnl 2f* **20/1**

5620 **10** nse **Saptapadi (IRE)**[22] 4759 8-8-13 **89** .........(t) PaulPickard 12 90
(Brian Ellison) *hld up in rr: hdwy on outer 3f out: nvr a factor* **20/1**

-006 **11** 1¼ **Big Thunder**[11] 5161 4-9-5 **95** ......... LukeMorris 9 95+
(Sir Mark Prescott Bt) *hood removed late: s.s: hld up in rr: effrt over 3f out: nvr a factor* **9/1**[3]

-310 **12** 1 **Totalize**[53] 3717 5-8-12 **95** ......... MeganCarberry(7) 13 93
(Brian Ellison) *hld up in rr: hdwy on inner over 3f out: wknd over 1f out* **10/1**

1604 **13** 2¼ **Number One London (IRE)**[8] 5288 4-8-6 **82** .........(p) MartinDwyer 15 78
(Brian Meehan) *trckd ldrs: led after 4f: hdd over 2f out: lost pl over 1f out* **25/1**

1020 **14** shd **Streets Of Newyork**[23] 4746 7-8-0 **81** ......... JackGarritty(5) 17 77
(Brian Ellison) *hld up in rr: sme hdwy on inner 3f out: lost pl over 1f out* **20/1**

3012 **15** hd **Knightly Escapade**[39] 4217 6-8-2 **78** ......... DuranFentiman 1 73
(Brian Ellison) *dwlt: sn mid-div: sme hdwy on inner over 3f out: lost pl over 1f out* **16/1**

5-04 **16** ¾ **Bantam (IRE)**[11] 5162 4-8-13 **89** ......... RyanMoore 2 83
(Ed Dunlop) *mid-div: hdwy to chse ldrs over 3f out: lost pl over 1f out* **6/1**[2]

3m 33.6s (-0.90) **Going Correction** -0.075s/f (Good) **16** Ran SP% **125.2**
Speed ratings (Par 109): **99,98,97,97,97 96,96,96,95,95 95,94,93,93,93 93**
CSF £243.17 CT £1346.07 TOTE £29.40: £6.30, £3.20, £1.90, £2.30; EX 368.10 Trifecta £3008.90.
**Owner** R D Rainey **Bred** J S Bolger **Trained** Norton, N Yorks

**FOCUS**
They didn't go fast here and it paid to race handily. Five of the 16 runners were trained by Brian Ellison, and it was the outsider of his quintet that got the job done for him.

## 5580 STANJAMES.COM STKS (NURSERY H'CAP) (BOBIS RACE) 6f
**4:55** (4:56) (Class 2) 2-Y-O
**£24,900** (£7,456; £3,728; £1,864; £932; £468) **Stalls** High

Form RPR

211 **1** **Felix Leiter**[8] 5285 2-8-7 81 6ex ......... BenCurtis 16 89
(K R Burke) *leggy: w ldrs: edgd lft and styd on fnl f: led last 50yds: hld on wl* **3/1**[1]

4112 **2** hd **Kibaar**[17] 4936 2-9-3 91 ......... PaulHanagan 20 98
(B W Hills) *lw: trckd ldrs: chal 1f out: no ex nr fin* **11/1**

123 **3** nk **Geordie George (IRE)**[34] 4348 2-9-0 88 ......... JamesDoyle 11 95
(John Quinn) *chsd ldrs: led over 1f out: edgd rt: hdd and no ex last 50yds* **16/1**

621 **4** 1¼ **Roossey (IRE)**[62] 3394 2-8-9 83 ......... LiamJones 18 86
(William Haggas) *athletic: lw: hld up in mid-div: hdwy over 1f out: swtchd lft ins fnl f: kpt on* **5/1**[2]

221 **5** 2¾ **Burnt Sugar (IRE)**[18] 4909 2-8-12 86 ......... RichardHughes 1 81
(Richard Hannon) *w ldrs: upsides over 1f out: wknd fnl 75yds* **7/1**[3]

410 **6** 1 **Majestic Hero (IRE)**[64] 3322 2-8-5 79 ......... DavidProbert 14 71
(Ronald Harris) *led: hdd over 1f out: wkng whn hmpd wl ins fnl f* **11/1**

033 **7** hd **Dark Profit (IRE)**[22] 4760 2-8-6 80 ......... JimCrowley 19 71+
(Charles Hills) *lw: s.i.s: hdwy over 2f out: kpt on fnl f: nt rch ldrs* **10/1**

010 **8** nk **Kingsbridge**[40] 4143 2-8-4 78 ......... JimmyQuinn 3 68+
(Rod Millman) *in rr: hdwy over 1f out: nvr a factor* **25/1**

1 **9** nk **Uptight (FR)**[20] 4829 2-8-4 78 ......... MartinDwyer 8 67
(Kevin Ryan) *unf: leggy: chsd ldrs: wknd last 100yds* **12/1**

612 **10** nk **Thecornishassassin**[23] 4731 2-8-10 84 ......... AndreaAtzeni 13 72
(Robert Eddery) *mid-div: hdwy over 2f out: one pce whn hmpd ins fnl f* **33/1**

1445 **11** ½ **Burtonwood**[39] 4203 2-8-8 82 .........(b[1]) TonyHamilton 10 69
(Richard Fahey) *lw: in rr: drvn over 2f out: nvr a factor* **25/1**

5150 **12** 3 **Mignolino (IRE)**[62] 3374 2-8-12 86 ......... GrahamGibbons 6 64
(David Barron) *mid-div: effrt over 2f out: hung lft and lost pl over 1f out* **50/1**

1024 **13** 6 **Denzille Lane (IRE)**[26] 4625 2-8-12 86 ......... RyanMoore 5 46
(Mark Johnston) *chsd ldrs: lost pl over 1f out: bhd whn eased clsng stages* **12/1**

231 **14** 6 **Polarisation**[23] 4723 2-8-8 82 ......... JoeFanning 4 24
(Mark Johnston) *mid-div: outpcd over 2f out: sn lost pl: eased whn bhd clsng stages* **17/2**

1m 10.84s (-1.06) **Going Correction** -0.175s/f (Firm) **14** Ran SP% **124.3**
Speed ratings (Par 100): **100,99,99,97,94 92,92,92,91,91 90,86,78,70**
CSF £37.20 CT £486.31 TOTE £3.80: £1.70, £3.50, £3.60; EX 42.50 Trifecta £623.30.
**Owner** T Dykes & Mrs E Burke **Bred** Tibthorpe Stud **Trained** Middleham Moor, N Yorks

**FOCUS**
It was a shame there were six non-runners, but this was still a warm nursery and the main action happened nearest the stands' side until the principals drifted late in the day. The form looks strong.
T/Jkpt: Not won. T/Plt: £74.30 to a £1 stake. Pool: £324,998.32 - 3191.33 winning units. T/Qpdt: £9.20 to a £1 stake. Pool: £19,291.32 - 1546.22 winning units. WG

5581 - 5587a (Foreign Racing) - See Raceform Interactive

# [5368] CLAIREFONTAINE (R-H)
Wednesday, August 20

**OFFICIAL GOING: Turf: very soft**

## 5588a PRIX AUBERVILLE - ETALON LE HAVRE (MAIDEN) (2YO COLTS & GELDINGS) (TURF) 7f
**11:30** (12:00) 2-Y-O **£10,416** (£4,166; £3,125; £2,083; £1,041)

RPR

**1** **Red Tornado (FR)**[36] 4312 2-9-2 0 ......... GeraldMosse 8 76
(Harry Dunlop) *sn pressing ldr: jnd ldr 1/2-way: rdn 2f out: led over 1f out: r.o: strly pressed towards fin: jst hld on* **13/10**[1]

**2** hd **Parzival (IRE)** 2-9-2 0 ......... CristianDemuro 4 76
(G Botti, France) **44/5**

**3** 3 **Mejaen (FR)** 2-9-2 0 ......... FranckBlondel 10 68
(P Decouz, France) **9/1**

**4** 1 **Naabaha (FR)** 2-9-2 0 .........(b[1]) AurelienLemaitre 12 66
(F Head, France) **26/1**

**5** ¾ **Frostman (FR)**[8] 5292 2-9-2 0 ......... ThomasHenderson 9 64
(Jo Hughes) *led: jnd 1/2-way: rdn 2f out: hdd over 1f out: no ex and fdd fnl f: dropped to 5th cl home* **43/1**

**6** ¾ **Max Attack (FR)**[18] 4932 2-9-2 0 ......... ThierryJarnet 5 62
(A Junk, France) **17/1**

**7** 2 **Clever Love (FR)**[35] 4330 2-9-2 0 ......... MickaelBarzalona 11 57
(Jo Hughes) *trckd ldrs: rdn over 2f out: kpt on same pce against rail in st and sn hld* **20/1**

**8** 2½ **Viva Cuba (FR)** 2-8-13 0 ......... UmbertoRispoli 6 48
(C Scandella, France) **62/1**

**9** 3 **Broadway Boogie (IRE)** 2-9-2 0 ......... IoritzMendizabal 3 43
(J-C Rouget, France) **33/10**[2]

**10** 4½ **Sandy Duke (FR)**[20] 2-9-2 0 ......... GregoryBenoist 2 32
(E Lellouche, France) **17/2**[3]

**11** 4½ **Gwel Stad (FR)** 2-8-13 0 ......... MaximeGuyon 1 18
(E Libaud, France) **20/1**

1m 31.2s (91.20) **11** Ran SP% **120.1**
WIN (incl.1 euro stake): 2.30. PLACES: 1.30, 2.20, 2.20. DF: 12.10. SF: 19.10.
**Owner** Blockley,Cross,Johnson,Whitaker,Woodley **Bred** Jean-Francois Gribomont **Trained** Lambourn, Berks

## 5589a PRIX LE PETIT FUTE (PRIX SANEDTKI) (MAIDEN) (3YO FILLIES) (TURF) 1m
**12:00** (12:00) 3-Y-O **£10,416** (£4,166; £3,125; £2,083; £1,041)

RPR

**1** **Lahqa (IRE)**[12] 3-9-0 0 ......... AurelienLemaitre 4 85
(F Head, France) **9/5**[2]

**2** ½ **She Loves You**[18] 3-9-0 0 ......... StephanePasquier 2 84
(A De Royer-Dupre, France) **1/1**[1]

**3** 8 **Memory Lane (FR)**[18] 3-9-0 0 ......... GeraldMosse 6 65
(J-M Beguigne, France) **7/2**[3]

**4** 3½ **Selma Louise (FR)**[4] 3-9-0 0 ......... OlivierPeslier 5 57
(W Mongil, Germany) **14/1**

**5** 8 **Hortensia Diamond (FR)** 3-8-10 0 ......... AntoineHamelin 3 35
(K R Burke) *midfield early: towards rr fr bef 1/2-way and sn pushed along: rdn in last into st: sn no imp on ldrs and btn: eased fnl f* **14/1**

**6** dist **Mylenis (FR)**[42] 3-8-8 0 ......... FlavienMasse(6) 1
(P Cathelin, France) **27/1**

1m 44.0s (104.00) **6** Ran SP% **124.8**
WIN (incl. 1 euro stake): 2.80. PLACES: 1.30, 1.10. SF: 4.20.
**Owner** Hamdan Al Maktoum **Bred** Shadwell Estate Company Limited **Trained** France

## 5590a PRIX DU 70EME ANNIVERSAIRE DU DEBARQUEMENT (MAIDEN) (2YO FILLIES) (TURF) 7f
**12:30** (12:00) 2-Y-O **£10,416** (£4,166; £3,125; £2,083; £1,041)

RPR

**1** **Bandanetta (FR)**[45] 2-9-0 0 ......... StephanePasquier 7 73
(A Bonin, France) **29/10**[1]

**2** 1 **Sculptured (FR)**[8] 5293 2-9-0 0 ......... ThomasHenderson 9 70
(Jo Hughes) *sn led: rdn and strly pressed 2f out: kpt on gamely u.p but hdd ins fnl f and hld towards fin* **7/1**[3]

**3** nk **Simone Angel (FR)** 2-8-10 0 ......... MaximeGuyon 14 65
(C Scandella, France) **30/1**

**4** ¾ **Liberal Angel (FR)**[83] 2697 2-9-0 0 ......... IoritzMendizabal 4 67
(K R Burke) *midfield: rdn to chse ldrs 2f out: nt clr run ent fnl f: sn swtchd rt: kpt on wl but nt quite pce to chal and hld* **31/1**

**5** ¾ **Impedimanta (IRE)**[25] 2-9-0 0 ......... UmbertoRispoli 3 65
(M Delzangles, France) **5/1**[2]

**6** snk **La Giovanella (FR)** 2-8-10 0 ......... WilliamsSaraiva 8 61
(Alex Fracas, France) **65/1**

**7** ½ **Aratika (FR)** 2-9-0 0 .........(b) TheoBachelot 5 64
(W Walton, France) **8/1**

**8** hd **Pink (FR)**[34] 2-9-0 0 ......... Christophe-PatriceLemaire 11 63
(S Kobayashi, France) **10/1**

**9** 1¼ **Why Whipping (FR)**[12] 2-9-0 0 .........(b[1]) EddyHardouin 2 60
(Robert Collet, France) **47/1**

**10** 3½ **Terra Fina** 2-9-0 0 ......... FabriceVeron 6 50
(H-A Pantall, France) **13/1**

**11** ½ **Jialing River (FR)**[25] 2-9-0 0 ......... MickaelBarzalona 15 49
(R Chotard, France) **16/1**

**12** 1¾ **Nimble (IRE)**[49] 3872 2-9-0 0 ......... GregoryBenoist 16 44
(D Smaga, France) **13/1**

**13** 1½ **Xellent (FR)** 2-8-10 0 ......... ThierryJarnet 10 36
(J Heloury, France) **43/1**

**14** 5 **Belliciosa (FR)** 2-9-0 0 .........(p) EnzoCorallo 12 27
(Christian Le Galliard, France) **31/1**

**15** 3 **Babala (FR)** 2-8-10 0 ......... Pierre-CharlesBoudot 13 15
(A Fabre, France) **8/1**

1m 31.6s (91.60) **15** Ran SP% **121.6**
WIN (incl. 1 euro stake): 3.90. PLACES: 1.60, 2.40, 7.40. DF: 14.70. SF: 23.50.
**Owner** Thierry Corbel **Bred** R Corveller **Trained** France

## 5591a PRIX ECOLE BLONDEAU (PRIX PELLEAS) (LISTED RACE) (3YO COLTS & GELDINGS) (TURF) 1m 1f
**1:05** (12:00) 3-Y-O **£22,916** (£9,166; £6,875; £4,583; £2,291)

RPR

**1** **Planetaire**[69] 3-8-11 0 ......... OlivierPeslier 3 103
(C Laffon-Parias, France) **13/2**

**2** 2 **Earnshaw (USA)**[80] 2818 3-9-2 0 ......... MickaelBarzalona 2 104
(A Fabre, France) *hld up in midfield: rdn and clsd 2f out: styd on fnl f and wnt 2nd nring fin: nt pce of wnr* **23/10**[1]

**3** ½ **Master's Spirit (IRE)**[10] 3-8-11 0 ......... ThierryJarnet 4 98
(P Demercastel, France) **44/5**

**4** shd **Pachadargent (FR)**[29] 4525 3-8-11 0 ......... FranckBlondel 7 98
(F Rossi, France) **11/1**

**5** nk **Nabbaash**[77] 2908 3-8-11 0 ......... IoritzMendizabal 5 97
(J-C Rouget, France) **9/2**[3]

**6** ¾ **Vercingetorix (IRE)**[68] 3-8-11 0 ......... MaximeGuyon 1 96
(A Fabre, France) **17/1**

**7** ½ **Garlingari (FR)**[68] 3-8-11 0 .........(p) FredericSpanu 6 95
(Mme C Barande-Barbe, France) **16/1**

8 3 ½ **Ziriyan (FR)**[31] 3-8-11 0 Christophe-PatriceLemaire 9 87
(M Delzangles, France) **43/10**[2]

9 4 **Dominandros (FR)**[22] 4775 3-8-11 0 Pierre-CharlesBoudot 8 79
(Gay Kelleway) *midfield: rdn and lost pl 2f out: last and btn fnl f: eased* **10/1**

1m 55.6s (115.60) **9** Ran SP% **119.8**
WIN (incl. 1 euro stake): 7.50. PLACES: 2.00, 1.60, 2.20. DF: 11.80. SF: 29.60.
**Owner** Wertheimer & Frere **Bred** Wertheimer & Frere **Trained** Chantilly, France

## 5592a PRIX ASSOCIATION PHILATELIQUE ET CARTOPHILE (CLAIMER) (3YO) (TURF) 1m 6f 110y

**2:05** (12:00) 3-Y-O **£9,583** (£3,833; £2,875; £1,916; £958)

RPR

1 **Baillonette (FR)**[31] 3-8-8 0 NicolasLarenaudie 7 73
(S Kobayashi, France) **57/10**[3]

2 ½ **Zashka (FR)**[6] 5370 3-8-8 0 WilliamsSaraiva 8 72
(J-V Toux, France) **4/5**[1]

3 1 ½ **Lila De Viette (FR)**[65] 3-9-1 0 (p) MatthieuAutier 4 77
(C Plisson, France) **15/2**

4 10 **Sweet Alibi (IRE)**[6] 5370 3-8-13 0 (b[1]) SoufyaneMoulin 1 62
(J S Moore) *t.k.h early: hld up in midfield: rdn into st: sn outpcd by ldrs: plugged on for mod 4th fnl f* **10/1**

5 ½ **Kemosabe (IRE)**[31] 3-8-11 0 (b) AlexisAchard 3 59
(M Delzangles, France) **5/1**[2]

6 7 **Birthday Treat (FR)**[150] 3-8-13 0 ow2 NicolasEven 5 52
(Yannick Fouin, France) **14/1**

7 8 **Reveries D'Avril (FR)**[38] 3-8-8 0 (b) MlleAngelaLeCorre 2 37
(D Sepulchre, France) **22/1**

8 8 **Singapore West (FR)** 3-8-11 0 MlleGwladysFradelin 6 30
(G Pannier, France) **36/1**

3m 22.5s (202.50) **8** Ran SP% **121.7**
WIN (incl. 1 euro stake): 6.70. PLACES: 1.40, 1.10, 1.60. DF: 3.70. SF: 13.20.
**Owner** Satoshi Kobayashi **Bred** O Rauscent, D Uzzan & X Bourget **Trained** France

# 4842 BATH (L-H)

Thursday, August 21

**OFFICIAL GOING: Firm (10.4)**
Wind: Light, across towards stand Weather: Mainly cloudy

## 5593 BONUSNETBETS.COM MEDIAN AUCTION MAIDEN STKS 5f 11y

**2:20** (2:21) (Class 6) 2-Y-O **£2,458** (£731; £365; £182) **Stalls** Centre

Form RPR

4220 1 **King Crimson**[5] 5409 2-9-2 76 CharlesBishop(3) 7 78
(Mick Channon) *mde all at gd pce: rdn and hld on wl fnl 2f* **3/1**[2]

222 2 ¾ **Free Entry (IRE)**[10] 5255 2-9-0 0 LukeMorris 8 70
(James Tate) *prom: drvn to chse wnr over 2f out: grad clsd fnl f: a hld* **1/3**[1]

50 3 4 **Dunnscotia**[14] 5091 2-9-5 0 (t) WilliamCarson 1 61
(Paul Webber) *chsd wnr tl 2f out: hrd rdn: hung lft and btn over 1f out* **6/1**[3]

04 4 1 **Cape Point**[28] 4577 2-9-5 0 LiamKeniry 6 57
(Michael Blanshard) *dwlt: sn pushed into midfield: wnt mod 4th and rdn over 2f out: no imp* **25/1**

50 5 6 **King's Bond**[17] 4965 2-9-5 0 DavidProbert 2 36
(Ronald Harris) *dwlt: bhd and rdn along: nvr trbld ldrs* **20/1**

0 6 ½ **My Mo (FR)**[13] 5128 2-9-0 0 GeorgeDowning(5) 5 34
(David Dennis) *sn outpcd and bhd* **25/1**

065 7 ½ **Cerise Firth**[50] 3842 2-9-0 56 StevieDonohoe 3 27
(Steph Hollinshead) *sn outpcd and bhd* **33/1**

050 8 46 **Blue Eyed Boy**[18] 4943 2-9-0 0 (b[1]) TimClark(5) 4
(Roy Brotherton) *chsd ldrs: rdn and wknd over 2f out: bhd and eased over 1f out: sddle slipped: lame* **33/1**

1m 2.79s (0.29) **Going Correction** +0.10s/f (Good) **8** Ran SP% **132.6**
Speed ratings (Par 92): **101,99,93,91,82 81,80,7**
CSF £4.98 TOTE £4.30: £1.30, £1.02, £1.90; EX 6.60 Trifecta £18.10.
**Owner** Wilde & Webster **Bred** Mickley Stud **Trained** West Ilsley, Berks
■ John Joiner was withdrawn. Price at time of withdrawal 8/1. Rule 4 applies to bets struck prior to withdrawal but not to SP bets. Deduct 10p in the pound. New market formed.

**FOCUS**
Following a dry night the ground remained Firm, good to firm in places and 12yds had been added to all races that included the bottom bend. An uncompetitive maiden to open proceedings and very little got into it with the winner showing good speed.

## 5594 GET YOUR FREE BETS AT BONUSNETBETS.COM H'CAP 5f 11y

**2:55** (2:55) (Class 6) (0-60,59) 4-Y-O+ **£2,264** (£673; £336; £168) **Stalls** Centre

Form RPR

0041 1 **My Meteor**[17] 4960 7-9-2 59 NoelGarbutt(5) 6 69
(Tony Newcombe) *dwlt: bhd: hdwy to ld wl over 1f out: drvn clr and in control ent fnl f: readily* **7/2**[2]

2230 2 ¾ **Haadeeth**[16] 5000 7-8-10 55 (t) HarryBurns(7) 5 61
(David Evans) *in tch on outer: drvn to chse wnr over 1f out: clsd steadily: a hld* **6/1**

0062 3 5 **Arch Walker (IRE)**[8] 5316 7-8-8 46 (b) LukeMorris 3 34
(John Weymes) *prom: squeezed for room after 1f: hrd rdn and btn over 1f out* **4/1**[3]

3405 4 shd **Spic 'n Span**[13] 5126 9-8-8 46 ow1 (p) SteveDrowne 4 34
(Ronald Harris) *led: rdn and hdd wl over 1f out: sn btn* **16/1**

0040 5 4 ½ **Studfarmer**[10] 5247 4-8-9 47 (v) WilliamCarson 1 18
(John Panvert) *prom: bmpd after 1f: wknd over 2f out* **11/1**

1222 6 ¾ **Burnt Cream**[6] 5399 7-9-7 59 (t) StevieDonohoe 2 28
(Martin Bosley) *prom: n.m.r and bmpd after 1f: hrd rdn and wknd over 1f out* **13/8**[1]

1m 2.65s (0.15) **Going Correction** +0.10s/f (Good) **6** Ran SP% **108.8**
Speed ratings (Par 101): **102,100,92,92,85 84**
CSF £22.42 TOTE £5.10: £3.20, £3.30; EX 20.90 Trifecta £55.60.
**Owner** A G Newcombe **Bred** M P B Bloodstock Ltd **Trained** Yarnscombe, Devon

**FOCUS**
A low-grade sprint, but run at a good pace and the winner was enhancing a good record at the track.

## 5595 FOLLOW US ON TWITTER AT BONUSNETBETS H'CAP 5f 161y

**3:30** (3:30) (Class 5) (0-75,75) 3-Y-O+ **£3,557** (£1,058; £529; £264) **Stalls** Centre

Form RPR

2302 1 **Silverrica (IRE)**[17] 4981 4-9-0 70 MarcMonaghan(5) 6 79
(Malcolm Saunders) *pressed ldr: led 2f out: drvn out* **3/1**[1]

02 2 ¾ **Dangerous Age**[37] 4282 4-9-10 75 GeorgeBaker 4 82
(Charles Hills) *in tch and travelling wl: effrt 2f out: drvn to chse wnr over 1f out: kpt on* **9/2**[3]

0035 3 2 ¼ **Generalyse**[12] 5182 5-9-3 71 (b) RyanTate(3) 2 70
(Ben De Haan) *bhd: rdn 3f out: styd on to take 3rd ins fnl f* **11/1**

15-6 4 1 **Shamahan**[17] 4983 5-9-7 75 MichaelJMMurphy(3) 5 71
(Luke Dace) *in tch: rdn over 2f out: one pce* **4/1**[2]

6045 5 1 **Dreams Of Glory**[14] 5070 6-9-5 70 LukeMorris 3 63
(Ron Hodges) *led: rdn and hdd 2f out: wknd over 1f out* **10/1**

1311 6 1 ½ **Molly Jones**[20] 4848 5-8-7 63 TimClark(5) 8 51
(Derek Haydn Jones) *blindfold removed late and s.i.s: towards rr on outer: swtchd ins and hung lft 2f out: hrd rdn: n.d* **9/2**[3]

135 7 shd **Dark Lane**[10] 5247 8-8-7 65 HollieDoyle(7) 1 52
(David Evans) *chsd ldrs on inner: wknd 2f out* **14/1**

6024 8 ¾ **Top Cop**[28] 4581 5-9-1 73 (p) DavidParkes(7) 7 58
(Ronald Harris) *chsd ldrs on outer early: rdn and lost pl 3f out: tried to rally 2f out: sn wknd* **14/1**

1m 11.14s (-0.06) **Going Correction** +0.10s/f (Good) **8** Ran SP% **112.1**
Speed ratings (Par 103): **104,103,100,98,97 95,95,94**
CSF £15.88 CT £127.33 TOTE £5.40: £2.40, £1.60, £2.50; EX 18.40 Trifecta £231.60.
**Owner** Mrs Ginny Nicholas **Bred** Miss A R Byrne **Trained** Green Ore, Somerset

**FOCUS**
Quite a competitive sprint handicap and the form looks solid for the grade.

## 5596 LIKE BONUSNETBETS.COM ON FACEBOOK H'CAP 1m 2f 46y

**4:05** (4:08) (Class 6) (0-55,59) 3-Y-O+ **£2,264** (£673; £336; £168) **Stalls** Low

Form RPR

6056 1 **Kristal Hart**[42] 4105 5-8-13 47 (p) LiamKeniry 13 54
(Neil Mulholland) *mde all: rdn and hung rt 2f out: drvn out* **10/1**

6004 2 1 **Royal Mizar (SPA)**[15] 5030 4-8-11 48 RyanTate(3) 12 53
(Ralph J Smith) *mid-div: rdn and hdwy 2f out: styd on u.p to take 2nd fnl 100yds* **17/2**

0605 3 nk **My New Angel (IRE)**[14] 5075 5-9-1 49 (e) FrankieMcDonald 6 53
(Daniel Mark Loughnane) *towards rr: rdn 3f out: hdwy over 1f out: styd on to take 3rd fnl 100yds* **20/1**

5430 4 ½ **Stanlow**[38] 4268 4-9-7 55 (v) ShaneKelly 14 58
(Daniel Mark Loughnane) *in tch: drvn to press wnr 2f out: lost 2nd fnl 100yds: one pce* **5/1**[2]

/020 5 nk **Medal Of Valour (JPN)**[19] 4911 6-9-6 54 (bt[1]) GeorgeBaker 9 57
(Mark Gillard) *bhd: cajoled along and r.o fnl 2f: nrest at fin* **25/1**

0501 6 ¾ **Oracle Boy**[6] 5402 3-9-3 59 6ex (p) DougieCostello 15 60
(William Muir) *prom: hrd rdn 2f out: one pce* **7/4**[1]

006- 7 5 **First Glance**[264] 8116 5-8-12 46 oh1 AndrewMullen 10 38
(Michael Appleby) *sn towards rr: rdn over 2f out: nvr rchd ldrs* **9/1**

0400 8 5 **Bold Cross (IRE)**[18] 4948 11-9-2 53 ThomasBrown(3) 8 35
(Edward Bevan) *bhd: rdn over 2f out: n.d* **8/1**[3]

/520 9 1 **Surprise Us**[16] 5001 7-8-12 46 oh1 (b[1]) StevieDonohoe 2 27
(Mark Gillard) *chsd ldrs: rdn over 3f out: wknd 2f out* **25/1**

00-0 10 nse **Wannabe Magic**[93] 2432 3-8-8 50 JohnFahy 3 30
(Geoffrey Deacon) *mid-div: rdn and hdwy 3f out: wknd over 1f out* **20/1**

2500 11 1 **Banreenahreenkah (IRE)**[15] 5030 4-9-2 50 WilliamCarson 11 29
(Paul Fitzsimons) *plld hrd: chsd ldrs tl wknd 2f out* **16/1**

00-5 12 10 **Earl's Bridge**[8] 5321 3-7-13 46 NoelGarbutt(5) 1 6
(Bill Turner) *dwlt: hld up in rr: drvn along and mod effrt over 2f out: sn wknd* **66/1**

2m 10.7s (-0.30) **Going Correction** 0.0s/f (Good)
**WFA** 3 from 4yo+ 8lb **12** Ran SP% **118.3**
Speed ratings (Par 101): **101,100,99,99,99 98,94,90,89,89 89,81**
CSF £85.27 CT £1676.80 TOTE £19.70: £4.00, £4.30, £6.90; EX 110.80 Trifecta £2401.30 Part won. Pool of £3201.73 - 0.46 winning units..
**Owner** The White Hart Racing Syndicate **Bred** Carmel Stud **Trained** Limpley Stoke, Wilts

**FOCUS**
A low-grade handicap.

## 5597 FREE HORSE RACING TIPS AT BONUSNETBETS.COM H'CAP 1m 5f 22y

**4:40** (4:40) (Class 5) (0-70,66) 4-Y-O+ **£3,557** (£1,058; £529; £264) **Stalls** High

Form RPR

1055 1 **Glens Wobbly**[28] 4568 6-8-0 50 PhilipPrince(5) 5 58
(Jonathan Geake) *chsd ldr: disp ld after 4f tl 4f out: led 2f out: hrd rdn ins fnl f: styd on* **12/1**

154 2 ½ **Happy Families**[53] 3752 4-9-2 66 NoelGarbutt(5) 2 73
(Heather Main) *t.k.h: cl up: rdn to chse wnr over 1f out: kpt on ins fnl f: jst hld* **3/1**[2]

0002 3 1 ¼ **Significant Move**[26] 4678 7-9-6 65 (b) PatCosgrave 7 70
(Stuart Kittow) *cl up: hrd rdn 3f out: outpcd and hanging over 2f out: styd on again fnl f* **7/2**[3]

5013 4 nk **Sweeping Rock (IRE)**[16] 5001 4-9-2 61 (t) ShaneKelly 1 66
(Marcus Tregoning) *led 4f then disp ld: led again 4f out: hdd 2f out: one pce* **6/4**[1]

4341 5 7 **Grayswood**[16] 5001 4-9-4 63 (p) DougieCostello 3 57
(William Muir) *hld up in rr: rdn over 3f out: sn struggling* **5/1**

2m 52.34s (0.34) **Going Correction** 0.0s/f (Good) **5** Ran SP% **111.6**
Speed ratings (Par 103): **98,97,96,96,92**
CSF £47.16 TOTE £12.30: £5.30, £2.60; EX 43.00 Trifecta £349.60.
**Owner** Glen Symes **Bred** H J Manners **Trained** East Kennett, Wilts

**FOCUS**
Only five runners, a steady pace, and not form to get carried away with.

## 5598 POKER HELP DESK AT BONUSNETBETS.COM H'CAP 1m 5y

**5:15** (5:15) (Class 5) (0-70,69) 3-Y-O **£3,105** (£924; £461; £230) **Stalls** Low

Form RPR

5415 1 **Gratzie**[47] 3946 3-9-3 68 CharlesBishop(3) 5 77
(Mick Channon) *t.k.h: pressed ldr: drvn to ld 1f out: clr ins fnl f: comf* **11/5**[2]

5042 2 3 **Mendacious Harpy (IRE)**[15] 5057 3-9-3 65 (b) PatCosgrave 4 67
(George Baker) *led: hrd rdn and hdd 1f out: no ex ins fnl f: jst hld 2nd* **13/8**[1]

030 **3** *nk* **Executrix**[16] 5007 3-9-1 63 ShaneKelly 8 64
(Sir Michael Stoute) *trckd ldrs: rdn over 2f out: one pce* **7/2**[3]

10-0 **4** *nk* **Sweet P**[16] 5004 3-8-10 65 JordanVaughan(7) 6 66
(Marcus Tregoning) *hld up in 5th: effrt in centre 2f out: hrd rdn over 1f out: styd on same pce* **15/2**

01-5 **5** *16* **Bonnie Fairy**[230] 28 3-8-2 50 AndrewMullen 3 14
(Michael Appleby) *prom tl wknd over 2f out* **20/1**

-000 **6** *3 ¾* **Connexion Francais**[20] 4875 3-7-13 50 oh5 RosieJessop(3) 7 5
(Tim Etherington) *sn bhd* **50/1**

1m 42.74s (1.94) **Going Correction** 0.0s/f (Good) **6** Ran SP% **110.1**
Speed ratings (Par 100): **90,87,86,86,70 66**
CSF £5.90 CT £9.50 TOTE £2.50: £1.10, £1.70; EX 8.10 Trifecta £22.00.
**Owner** C Corbett, David Hudd, Chris Wright **Bred** John Troy & Robert Levitt **Trained** West Ilsley, Berks

**FOCUS**
Two non-runners further weakened a modest handicap, but the winner did it comfortably.

## 5599 SSJ ELECTRICAL LTD APPRENTICE H'CAP 1m 3f 144y
**5:45** (5:46) (Class 6) (0-65,64) 4-Y-0+ **£2,587** (£770; £384; £192) **Stalls** Low

Form RPR

3345 **1** **Highlife Dancer**[9] 5277 6-9-6 63 (v) DanielCremin(5) 1 69
(Mick Channon) *mde all: hrd rdn over 1f out: hld on gamely* **5/1**[3]

0003 **2** *½* **First Sargeant**[81] 2806 4-8-11 54 AlistairRawlinson(5) 5 59
(Michael Appleby) *hld up: rdn and hdwy 2f out: styd on fnl f: jst snatched 2nd but hld by wnr* **10/11**[1]

0314 **3** *hd* **Cataria Girl (USA)**[22] 4799 5-9-7 64 (t) JordanVaughan(5) 6 69
(Marcus Tregoning) *t.k.h: cl up: chsd wnr over 2f out: drvn to chal ins fnl f: r.o: jst hld and lost 2nd on line* **3/1**[2]

3256 **4** *3 ¾* **Cabuchon (GER)**[7] 5338 7-9-1 60 (t) HarryBurns(7) 4 59
(David Evans) *in tch: dropped to last 6f out: rdn and unable to chal fnl 2f* **11/1**

00-0 **5** *4 ½* **Konzert (ITY)**[8] 5313 4-9-3 58 GeorgeDowning(3) 7 49
(Ian Williams) *cl up: chsd wnr after 3f tl over 2f out: sn wknd* **12/1**

2m 34.69s (4.09) **Going Correction** 0.0s/f (Good) **5** Ran SP% **110.1**
Speed ratings (Par 101): **86,85,85,83,80**
CSF £10.13 TOTE £5.30: £1.80, £1.10; EX 9.70 Trifecta £16.70.
**Owner** The Highlife Racing Club **Bred** Imperial & Mike Channon Bloodstock Ltd **Trained** West Ilsley, Berks

**FOCUS**
A modest apprentice handicap.
T/Plt: £307.20 to a £1 stake. Pool of £52020.74 - 123.61 winning tickets. T/Qpdt: £87.80 to a £1 stake. Pool of £3967.25 - 33.40 winning tickets. LM

# 5506 WOLVERHAMPTON (A.W) (L-H)
Thursday, August 21

**OFFICIAL GOING: Tapeta: standard**
No speed figures will be produced until revised median times for the new Tapeta surface can be calculated.
Wind: Fresh behind Weather: Overcast

## 5600 HOLIDAY INN WOLVERHAMPTON AMATEUR RIDERS' H'CAP (TAPETA) 1m 4f 50y
**6:20** (6:20) (Class 5) (0-70,76) 3-Y-0+ **£2,807** (£870; £435; £217) **Stalls** Low

Form RPR

2221 **1** **Sweetheart Abbey**[5] 5426 3-10-10 76 6ex (p) MrSWalker 10 85
(William Knight) *hld up: hdwy 4f out: chsd ldr over 2f out: rdn to ld 1f out: styd on wl: comf* **5/6**[1]

1640 **2** *3* **Oly'Roccs (IRE)**[3] 5512 3-8-8 51 PhillipDennis(5) 8 55
(Philip Kirby) *chsd ldr tl led 3f out: rdn: edgd lft and hdd 1f out: styd on same pce* **14/1**

0540 **3** *2* **Tapis Libre**[17] 4964 6-10-6 65 (v[1]) MissJoannaMason(3) 2 66
(Michael Easterby) *chsd ldrs: outpcd over 2f out: styd on to go 3rd nr fin* **8/1**[2]

3340 **4** *¾* **Snow Dancer (IRE)**[14] 5077 10-9-6 55 MrMEnnis(7) 12 55
(John David Riches) *mid-div: hdwy 1/2-way: rdn over 2f out: no ex fnl f* **25/1**

0050 **5** *¾* **Azrag (USA)**[13] 5137 6-11-0 70 (t) MrRBirkett 6 68
(Michael Attwater) *hld up: rdn over 2f out: styd on ins fnl f: nvr nrr* **11/1**[3]

0050 **6** *nk* **St Ignatius**[42] 4119 7-10-8 64 (v) MrMichaelJMurphy 9 62
(Alan Bailey) *led 9f: sn rdn: no ex fr over 1f out* **12/1**

0-05 **7** *8* **Summerling (IRE)**[29] 4543 3-9-12 67 MrJHarding(3) 11 52
(Jonathan Portman) *chsd ldrs: rdn over 2f out: wknd over 1f out* **8/1**[2]

5236 **8** *1 ¼* **Star Of Namibia (IRE)**[96] 2327 4-10-1 60 MissMMullineaux(3) 5 43
(Michael Mullineaux) *mid-div: pushed along and lost pl over 3f out: wknd over 2f out* **11/1**[3]

-000 **9** *nk* **Spin Cast**[17] 4964 6-10-9 65 MissHBethell 1 48
(Brian Ellison) *hld up: rdn over 2f out: sn wknd* **16/1**

4256 **10** *¾* **Ogaritmo**[6] 5403 5-9-6 55 (t) MrNicholasMeek(7) 7 36
(Alex Hales) *s.s: a in rr* **20/1**

/5-0 **11** *11* **Anton Dolin (IRE)**[6] 5371 6-10-7 70 (p) MrHFNugent(7) 3 34
(Michael Mullineaux) *hld up: rdn over 3f out: sn wknd* **50/1**

2m 41.29s (0.49) **Going Correction** +0.10s/f (Slow)
**WFA** 3 from 4yo+ 10lb **11** Ran SP% **124.3**
Speed ratings (Par 103): **102,100,98,98,97 97,92,91,91,90 83**
CSF £15.70 CT £70.43 TOTE £1.60: £1.10, £6.10, £3.70; EX 17.10 Trifecta £127.20.
**Owner** Miss S Bannatyne **Bred** Miss S Bannatyne **Trained** Patching, W Sussex

**FOCUS**
Plenty out of form and the pace was not strong for this modest amateur riders' handicap. The winner was taking a sizeable step up.

## 5601 32RED H'CAP (TAPETA) 5f 20y
**6:50** (6:52) (Class 5) (0-75,75) 3-Y-0+ **£2,911** (£866; £432; £216) **Stalls** Low

Form RPR

-543 **1** **Emjayem**[23] 4752 4-9-5 73 RobertTart(3) 5 84
(Ed McMahon) *s.i.s: sn pushed along in rr: rdn and r.o wl ins fnl f to ld towards fin* **4/1**[2]

5333 **2** *1* **Storm Lightning**[13] 5124 5-9-6 71 TomQueally 10 78
(Mark Brisbourne) *a.p: rdn to ld ins fnl f: hdd towards fin* **4/1**[2]

1542 **3** *nk* **The Dandy Yank (IRE)**[20] 4847 3-9-6 73 (p) LukeMorris 4 79
(Jamie Osborne) *chsd ldrs: swtchd rt over 1f out: rdn and ev ch ins fnl f: unable qck towards fin* **8/1**

530 **4** *1 ¼* **Dynamo Walt (IRE)**[16] 5012 3-9-1 68 DaleSwift 3 69
(Derek Shaw) *hld up: hdwy over 1f out: running on whn nt clr run ins fnl f: swtchd rt: r.o: nvr able to chal* **20/1**

0011 **5** *1* **Seamster**[44] 4050 7-9-5 75 (bt) CamHardie(5) 6 73
(Richard Ford) *sn led: rdn over 1f out: edgd lft and hdd ins fnl f: no ex* **11/2**[3]

3440 **6** *nk* **Colourbearer (IRE)**[50] 3848 7-9-4 69 (t) RichardKingscote 11 66
(Milton Bradley) *prom: rdn over 1f out: styd on same pce ins fnl f* **12/1**

4623 **7** *2 ¾* **Distant Past**[14] 5087 3-9-1 73 KevinStott(5) 2 60
(Kevin Ryan) *prom: rdn over 1f out: wknd ins fnl f* **7/2**[1]

6012 **8** *½* **Climaxfortackle (IRE)**[70] 3149 6-8-8 66 AdamMcLean(7) 7 51
(Derek Shaw) *s.i.s: outpcd* **14/1**

006 **9** *1* **Gottcher**[30] 4521 6-9-4 69 (b[1]) TomEaves 13 53
(Ian Semple) *prom: chsd ldr over 3f out: rdn whn hmpd 1f out: sn edgd lft and wknd* **20/1**

2130 **10** *10* **Amenable (IRE)**[31] 4494 7-9-4 69 (p) HayleyTurner 1 14
(Conor Dore) *sn outpcd* **12/1**

1m 1.72s (-0.18) **Going Correction** +0.10s/f (Slow)
**WFA** 3 from 4yo+ 2lb **10** Ran SP% **120.3**
Speed ratings (Par 103): **105,103,102,100,99 98,94,93,92,76**
CSF £21.18 CT £121.59 TOTE £2.70: £1.10, £2.10, £2.70; EX 24.10 Trifecta £161.70.
**Owner** Mrs J McMahon **Bred** Mrs J McMahon **Trained** Lichfield, Staffs

**FOCUS**
They were in the stalls a while waiting for the winner to load for this fair sprint handicap, but it did not appear to hamper any of them.

## 5602 32RED CASINO H'CAP (TAPETA) 5f 216y
**7:20** (7:20) (Class 6) (0-65,65) 3-Y-0+ **£2,264** (£673; £336; £168) **Stalls** Low

Form RPR

0646 **1** **Dream Catcher (FR)**[10] 5247 6-9-0 63 AmyScott(5) 13 72
(Henry Candy) *mde all: shkn up over 1f out: styd on* **14/1**

2021 **2** *½* **Chapellerie (IRE)**[13] 5136 5-8-13 62 (b) JennyPowell(5) 12 69
(Brendan Powell) *s.i.s: hld up: hdwy over 1f out: swtchd lft ins fnl f: continued to edgd lft: r.o* **6/1**[2]

1003 **3** *½* **Decent Fella (IRE)**[4] 5470 8-9-3 64 (t) MichaelJMMurphy(3) 7 69
(Ann Stokell) *hld up: hdwy on outer over 2f out: rdn and ev ch ins fnl f: styd on same pce* **9/2**[1]

0023 **4** *nk* **Divine Call**[19] 4908 7-9-3 61 (v) RichardKingscote 10 65
(Milton Bradley) *chsd ldrs: rdn: edgd rt and ev ch ins fnl f: styd on same pce* **9/1**

201 **5** *2* **Logans Lad (IRE)**[36] 4314 4-9-4 62 (vt) FrankieMcDonald 5 62
(Daniel Mark Loughnane) *hld up: hdwy over 2f out: rdn over 1f out: hmpd ins fnl f: kpt on* **8/1**

0-00 **6** *½* **Going French (IRE)**[63] 3393 7-8-11 60 DanielMuscutt(5) 9 57
(Grace Harris) *chsd wnr: rdn and ev ch over 1f out: edgd rt: no ex ins fnl f* **25/1**

6314 **7** *½* **Borough Boy (IRE)**[9] 5287 4-9-2 60 DaleSwift 3 55
(Derek Shaw) *s.i.s: hld up: rdn over 1f out: r.o ins fnl f: nvr nrr* **7/1**[3]

-000 **8** *¾* **Dennis**[14] 5088 4-9-2 60 (p) SilvestreDeSousa 6 56
(Tim Easterby) *mid-div: hdwy 1/2-way: rdn over 1f out: hamperted and no ex ins fnl f* **6/1**[2]

-006 **9** *¾* **Someone's Darling**[23] 4766 4-9-3 64 SimonPearce(3) 8 54
(Lydia Pearce) *prom: rdn over 1f out: no ex fnl f* **25/1**

0035 **10** *2 ¼* **Bilash**[21] 4833 7-9-2 60 (p) TomQueally 2 43
(Andrew Hollinshead) *prom: rdn over 1f out: sn wknd* **10/1**

5-40 **11** *½* **Avonvalley**[13] 5130 7-9-2 60 TomEaves 11 41
(Peter Grayson) *hld up: rdn over 1f out: nvr on terms* **33/1**

-003 **12** *nk* **Aye Aye Skipper (IRE)**[15] 5059 4-9-7 65 SebSanders 4 45
(Dean Ivory) *prom and sn pushed along: lost pl 5f out: rdn over 2f out: wknd over 1f out* **6/1**[2]

1300 **13** *2* **Avonmore Star**[28] 4571 6-9-3 64 BillyCray(3) 1 38
(Alan McCabe) *s.i.s: outpcd* **25/1**

1m 14.89s (0.39) **Going Correction** +0.10s/f (Slow) **13** Ran SP% **124.9**
Speed ratings (Par 101): **101,100,99,99,96 95,95,94,93,90 89,89,86**
CSF £96.29 CT £468.94 TOTE £20.10: £4.50, £3.50, £2.70; EX 127.80 Trifecta £414.00.
**Owner** Miss N M Haine **Bred** Daniel Cherdo **Trained** Kingston Warren, Oxon
■ Stewards' Enquiry : Amy Scott one-day ban: failed to ride to draw (Sep 4)
Jenny Powell three-day ban: careless riding (Sep 4,5,7)

**FOCUS**
A competitive if modest sprint and the two female riders, each claiming 5lb, filled the first two places with horses drawn wide.

## 5603 NEAL WOOD FIFTH ANNIVERSARY MEMORIAL H'CAP (BOBIS RACE) (TAPETA) 7f 32y
**7:50** (7:51) (Class 4) (0-80,80) 3-Y-0 **£5,175** (£1,540; £769; £384) **Stalls** High

Form RPR

16 **1** **Mr Bossy Boots (IRE)**[19] 4912 3-9-4 77 SilvestreDeSousa 6 86+
(Ralph Beckett) *n.m.r sn after s: hld up: hdwy over 1f out: sn rdn: r.o to ld towards fin: readily* **15/8**[1]

0301 **2** *¾* **Can't Change It (IRE)**[80] 2833 3-9-6 79 RichardKingscote 4 86
(David Simcock) *a.p: rdn to ld wl ins fnl f: hdd towards fin* **8/1**

4404 **3** *1 ¼* **Exceeder**[23] 4766 3-8-10 74 (p) DanielMuscutt(5) 8 78
(Marco Botti) *led: rdn and hdd wl ins fnl f: styd on same pce* **10/1**

3043 **4** *½* **Spreadable (IRE)**[27] 4612 3-8-13 72 SebSanders 3 75
(Nick Littmoden) *a.p: rdn over 1f out: styd on same pce ins fnl f* **10/1**

0540 **5** *nk* **Westminster (IRE)**[28] 4572 3-9-7 80 (b) RobertHavlin 7 82
(John Gosden) *chsd ldrs: rdn over 1f out: no ex wl ins fnl f* **12/1**

5216 **6** *1 ½* **Maraayill (IRE)**[28] 4572 3-9-6 79 (tp) MartinHarley 2 77
(Marco Botti) *hld up: hdwy and nt clr run over 1f out: shkn up and hung lft ins fnl f: one pce* **7/2**[2]

5250 **7** *3 ¾* **Constantine**[14] 5081 3-9-1 79 CamHardie(5) 1 67
(Richard Hannon) *hld up: rdn over 2f out: wknd fnl f* **16/1**

1101 **8** *3* **Red Primo (IRE)**[63] 3405 3-9-7 80 TomQueally 5 60
(Alan McCabe) *prom: chsd ldr over 5f out tl rdn over 1f out: wknd ins fnl f* **5/1**[3]

1m 28.64s (-0.16) **Going Correction** +0.10s/f (Slow) **8** Ran SP% **116.5**
Speed ratings (Par 102): **104,103,101,100,100 99,94,91**
CSF £18.29 CT £121.81 TOTE £2.80: £1.20, £2.30, £3.00; EX 19.20 Trifecta £139.10.
**Owner** Merriebelle Irish Farm Limited **Bred** Kilfrush Stud **Trained** Kimpton, Hants

**FOCUS**
The pace was true for this fair 3yo handicap in which a gamble was landed.

## 5604 £10 FREE BET AT 32REDSPORT.COM MAIDEN AUCTION STKS (TAPETA) 7f 32y
8:20 (8:24) (Class 6) 2-Y-O £2,264 (£673; £336; £168) Stalls High

Form RPR
023 1 **Runner Runner (IRE)**[21] 4825 2-8-10 76........................ KierenFallon 11 76
(George Baker) *hld up in tch: chsd ldr over 2f out: led over 1f out: rdn and edgd rt ins fnl f: r.o* **5/4**[1]
2 2 2 3/4 **Edge Of Heaven**[29] 4541 2-8-6 0........................ LukeMorris 10 65
(Jonathan Portman) *a.p: rdn over 1f out: chsd wnr ins fnl f: styd on same pce* **4/1**[2]
4 3 2 1/2 **Everyday (IRE)**[15] 5056 2-8-11 0........................ PatCosgrave 9 64
(George Baker) *hld up: hdwy over 2f out: rdn over 1f out: styd on same pce fnl f* **12/1**
44 4 1 1/2 **Lear's Rock (IRE)**[14] 5072 2-9-1 0........................ SilvestreDeSousa 8 64
(Ralph Beckett) *hld up: hdwy over 2f out: rdn over 1f out: nt trble ldrs* **4/1**[2]
3024 5 2 **York Express**[28] 4589 2-8-13 72........................(v[1]) MartinHarley 2 58
(Ismail Mohammed) *led: rdn and hdd over 1f out: wknd ins fnl f* **13/2**[3]
6 3/4 **Multistar** 2-8-7 0........................ AshleyMorgan(3) 6 53+
(Chris Wall) *s.i.s: hld up: hdwy on outer over 2f out: nt trble ldrs* **14/1**
0 7 3 1/2 **Laura B**[40] 4202 2-8-6 0........................ HarryBentley 7 40
(Chris Wall) *mid-div: pushed along over 2f out: sn wknd* **25/1**
05 8 3 3/4 **Dark Symphony (IRE)**[29] 4542 2-8-6 0........................ HayleyTurner 5 31
(Mark Usher) *chsd ldr tl rdn over 2f out: wknd over 1f out* **66/1**
9 3 3/4 **Kerrymerry (IRE)** 2-8-8 0........................ AhmadAlSubousi(7) 3 31+
(Ismail Mohammed) *s.i.s: nvr on terms* **33/1**
10 8 **Monsieur Rouge (IRE)** 2-9-1 0........................ BillyCray(3) 4 14
(Alan McCabe) *mid-div: n.m.r 6f out: plld hrd: pushed along whn hmpd 3f out: sn wknd* **33/1**
0 11 47 **Double Bronze**[17] 4965 2-8-11 0........................(t) RichardKingscote 1
(Milton Bradley) *chsd ldrs: pushed along 1/2-way: sn wknd* **100/1**
1m 30.75s (1.95) **Going Correction** +0.10s/f (Slow) **11** Ran SP% **124.3**
Speed ratings (Par 92): **92,88,86,84,82 81,77,72,68,59 5**
CSF £6.59 TOTE £1.80: £1.10, £1.80, £5.40; EX 7.90 Trifecta £53.60.
**Owner** PJL Racing 1 **Bred** Celtic Goose Syndicate **Trained** Manton, Wilts

**FOCUS**
They finished well strung out in what looked an ordinary maiden auction.

## 5605 WILLIAM BEARDSHAW "NOT FORGOTTEN" MEMORIAL H'CAP (TAPETA) 7f 32y
8:50 (8:50) (Class 6) (0-65,71) 3-Y-O+ £2,264 (£673; £336; £168) Stalls High

Form RPR
1054 1 **Zed Candy Girl**[15] 5041 4-8-13 57........................(p) AmyScott(5) 4 71
(Dai Burchell) *chsd ldr tl led over 1f out: rdn clr fnl f* **9/2**[2]
0561 2 2 1/2 **Madame Mirasol (IRE)**[10] 5257 3-9-8 71 6ex........................(p) KevinStott(5) 8 76
(Kevin Ryan) *hld up: hdwy over 1f out: wnt 2nd ins fnl f: no ch w wnr* **9/4**[1]
0060 3 1 3/4 **Elite Freedom (IRE)**[19] 4891 3-8-5 49........................ RoystonFfrench 7 49
(Brian Baugh) *prom: rdn and swtchd lft over 1f out: styd on same pce ins fnl f* **66/1**
100 4 3/4 **Welliesinthewater (IRE)**[27] 4613 4-9-9 62........................(v) DaleSwift 5 63
(Derek Shaw) *hld up: drvn along 1/2-way: r.o ins fnl f: nvr nrr* **14/1**
4401 5 1/2 **Bertie Blu Boy**[13] 5138 6-9-9 62........................(b) RichardKingscote 6 61
(Lisa Williamson) *led: rdn and hdd over 1f out: no ex ins fnl f* **9/2**[2]
4560 6 1/2 **Indian Affair**[9] 5287 4-9-2 60........................ TimClark(5) 9 58
(Milton Bradley) *chsd ldrs: pushed along 1/2-way: styd on same pce fr over 1f out* **14/1**
/0-0 7 hd **Forzarzi (IRE)**[73] 3056 10-8-5 49........................ JoeDoyle(5) 10 46
(John David Riches) *mid-div: hdwy over 2f out: rdn over 1f out: styd on same pce* **33/1**
2060 8 nk **Mercers Row**[17] 4961 7-9-7 65........................ GemmaTutty(5) 11 62
(Karen Tutty) *s.i.s: hld up: plld hrd: rdn over 1f out: n.d* **12/1**
0400 9 3/4 **Majestic Dream (IRE)**[27] 4632 6-9-12 65........................(v) PatCosgrave 2 60
(Michael Easterby) *prom: rdn over 2f out: wknd ins fnl f* **9/2**[2]
0500 10 3 **Spoken Words**[3] 5510 5-8-6 48........................(b) BillyCray(3) 1 35
(John David Riches) *s.i.s: a in rr* **33/1**
0615 11 1/2 **Indus Valley (IRE)**[43] 4072 7-9-9 62........................(b) BenCurtis 12 48
(Des Donovan) *hld up: rdn over 2f out: a in rr* **10/1**[3]
1m 30.06s (1.26) **Going Correction** +0.10s/f (Slow)
**WFA** 3 from 4yo+ 5lb **11** Ran SP% **122.8**
Speed ratings (Par 101): **96,93,91,90,89 89,88,88,87,84 83**
CSF £15.59 CT £612.25 TOTE £7.80: £1.60, £1.10, £14.60; EX 20.10 Trifecta £937.10.
**Owner** Robert Emmanuel **Bred** H H L Bloodstock **Trained** Briery Hill, Blaenau Gwent

**FOCUS**
The gallop was honest and few got into this modest handicap.

## 5606 BET NOW AT 32REDSPORT.COM MAIDEN STKS (TAPETA) 1m 1f 103y
9:20 (9:21) (Class 5) 3-Y-O+ £2,911 (£866; £432; £216) Stalls Low

Form RPR
2242 1 **Toast Of The Town (IRE)**[49] 3877 4-9-7 94........................(p) WilliamBuick 9 81+
(John Gosden) *a.p: chsd ldr over 6f out tl led over 2f out: sn clr: easily* **30/100**[1]
50 2 6 **Lord Empire (IRE)**[15] 5039 3-9-5 0........................ RichardKingscote 10 73+
(David Simcock) *prom: rdn over 2f out: wnt 2nd ins fnl f: no ch w wnr* **16/1**
003 3 1 1/4 **Tinga (IRE)**[20] 4845 3-9-0 77........................(t) SilvestreDeSousa 8 65
(Ralph Beckett) *s.i.s: hld up: hdwy over 1f out: nt rch ldrs* **7/2**[2]
4 2 **Two Jabs**[132] 4-9-12 0........................ PatCosgrave 5 66
(Mark Brisbourne) *s.s: hld up: r.o ins fnl f: nvr nrr* **14/1**
06 5 3/4 **Shaf (IRE)**[17] 4978 3-9-5 0........................ RobertHavlin 2 65
(Ed Dunlop) *prom: rdn over 2f out: wknd fnl f* **25/1**
0 6 3/4 **Heinrich (USA)**[15] 5044 3-9-5 0........................ LukeMorris 1 63
(Sylvester Kirk) *chsd ldrs: rdn over 2f out: wnt 2nd over 1f out tl wknd ins fnl f* **28/1**
36 7 5 **Lady Bingo (IRE)**[16] 5007 3-9-0 0........................ HarryBentley 11 48+
(Sir Mark Prescott Bt) *hld up: pushed along over 3f out: n.d* **12/1**[3]
00 8 shd **Moojaned (IRE)**[15] 5039 3-9-0 0........................ TimClark(5) 3 52
(Dai Burchell) *trckd ldrs: plld hrd: rdn over 2f out: wknd over 1f out* **100/1**
0- 9 1 1/2 **Sweet Charlie**[258] 8175 3-8-11 0........................ SladeO'Hara(3) 4 44
(Mike Murphy) *led: rdn and hdd over 2f out: wknd over 1f out* **50/1**
10 58 **My Sonny Boy** 3-9-5 0........................ RoystonFfrench 7
(Lisa Williamson) *hld up: pushed along 1/2-way: wknd over 3f out* **100/1**
2m 2.93s (2.13) **Going Correction** +0.10s/f (Slow)
**WFA** 3 from 4yo 7lb **10** Ran SP% **130.6**
Speed ratings (Par 103): **94,88,87,85,85 84,80,79,78,27**
CSF £10.05 TOTE £1.20: £1.02, £3.10, £1.60; EX 10.30 Trifecta £36.40.
**Owner** Lord Lloyd-Webber & Rachel Hood **Bred** N Cable & M Smith **Trained** Newmarket, Suffolk

**FOCUS**
A maiden lacking in depth.
T/Plt: £20.20 to a £1 stake. Pool of £77035.24 - 2773.44 winning tickets. T/Qpdt: £7.30 to a £1 stake. Pool of £6761.15, 685.10 winning tickets CR

# 5575 YORK (L-H)
Thursday, August 21

**OFFICIAL GOING: Good**
Wind: moderate 1/2 behind Weather: changeable, breezy with showers Rails: Races on traditional line and all distances as advertised

## 5607 DBS PREMIER YEARLING STKS 6f
1:55 (1:58) (Class 2) 2-Y-O
£159,884 (£63,979; £31,989; £15,962; £7,997; £7,997) Stalls High

Form RPR
2130 1 **Mubtaghaa (IRE)**[42] 4123 2-8-11 95........................ SilvestreDeSousa 13 101+
(William Haggas) *lw: w ldrs stands' side: led 2f out: kpt on wl ins fnl f* **12/1**
113 2 1 1/2 **New Providence**[19] 4913 2-8-7 87 ow1........................ WilliamBuick 3 93+
(Hugo Palmer) *hld up in rr far side: hdwy over 2f out: w ldrs over 1f out: styd on same pce last 100yds* **8/1**[3]
1 3 1 1/4 **Valley Of Fire**[26] 4684 2-8-11 80........................ AndreaAtzeni 8 93
(William Haggas) *lengthy: lw: mid-div centre: hdwy over 2f out: chsng ldrs over 1f out: keeping on same pce whn hmpd ins fnl f* **7/1**[2]
4341 4 nk **Gaudy (IRE)**[26] 4659 2-8-11 83........................(v[1]) JamieSpencer 10 92
(Kevin Ryan) *chsd ldrs centre: upsides over 1f out: edgd lft then rt ins fnl f: no ex* **33/1**
45 5 hd **Kasbah (IRE)**[11] 5218 2-8-11 0........................ PatSmullen 1 91
(J P Murtagh, Ire) *chsd ldrs far side: keeping on same pce whn hmpd ins fnl f* **16/1**
0112 6 1/2 **Kool Kompany (IRE)**[11] 5218 2-9-4 111........................ RichardHughes 19 97+
(Richard Hannon) *lw: trckd ldrs stands' side: swtchd lft over 2f out: kpt on same pce fnl f* **5/2**[1]
3410 7 2 3/4 **Vimy Ridge**[20] 4853 2-8-11 93........................ TonyHamilton 5 82
(Richard Fahey) *chsd ldrs far side: kpt on same pce over 1f out* **33/1**
21 8 1/2 **Gerry The Glover (IRE)**[37] 4286 2-8-11 84........................ TomEaves 7 80
(Brian Ellison) *mid-div centre: hdwy over 2f out: kpt on: nvr a threat* **40/1**
1624 9 nk **Mukhmal (IRE)**[23] 4757 2-9-2 101........................ JoeFanning 14 84
(Mark Johnston) *lw: t.k.h: w ldrs stands' side: fdd appr fnl f* **20/1**
3004 10 1 1/4 **Roudee**[18] 4936 2-8-11 88........................ RichardKingscote 11 76
(Tom Dascombe) *chsd ldrs stands' side: wknd wl over 1f out* **66/1**
1 11 1/2 **Sawaahel**[20] 4864 2-8-11 0........................ DaneO'Neill 6 74
(Richard Hannon) *str: s.s: in rr centre: kpt on fnl 2f* **25/1**
5132 12 3/4 **Fast Act (IRE)**[23] 4757 2-8-11 106........................ NeilCallan 17 72+
(Kevin Ryan) *t.k.h: overall ldr stands' side: hdd 2f out: sn wknd* **8/1**[3]
321 13 3/4 **Arthur MartinLeake (IRE)**[14] 5104 2-8-11 79........................ BenCurtis 15 70
(K R Burke) *racd stands' side: hld up in mid-div: effrt over 2f out: nvr a factor* **25/1**
3140 14 nk **Flyball**[65] 3322 2-8-11 78........................ PatDobbs 12 69
(Richard Hannon) *s.i.s: in rr centre: kpt on fnl 2f: nvr on terms* **100/1**
3220 15 1/2 **Winstanley (IRE)**[23] 4760 2-8-11 81........................ GrahamLee 2 67
(Richard Fahey) *chsd ldrs far side: wknd over 1f out* **66/1**
6310 16 2 **Tachophobia**[33] 4439 2-8-11 81........................ RyanMoore 4 61
(Richard Fahey) *chsd ldrs far side: lost pl wl over 1f out* **40/1**
413 17 nk **Ticks The Boxes (IRE)**[18] 4936 2-8-11 86........................ MartinHarley 16 60
(Clive Cox) *chsd ldrs stands' side: lost pl 2f out* **40/1**
31 18 1 1/4 **Marcano (IRE)**[53] 3748 2-8-11 84........................ RobertHavlin 9 56
(Rod Millman) *in rr centre: bhd fnl 2f* **22/1**
3245 19 1 **Union Rose**[23] 4757 2-8-11 97........................(p) WilliamTwiston-Davies 18 53
(Ronald Harris) *in rr stands' side: bhd fnl 2f* **28/1**
1m 10.97s (-0.93) **Going Correction** -0.20s/f (Firm) **19** Ran SP% **114.3**
Speed ratings (Par 100): **98,96,94,93,93 93,89,88,88,86 85,84,83,83,82 80,79,78,76**
CSF £74.43 TOTE £11.60: £3.50, £2.90, £2.30; EX 103.90 Trifecta £988.30.
**Owner** Hamdan Al Maktoum **Bred** Minch & Fullbury Bloodstock **Trained** Newmarket, Suffolk
■ Markaz withdrawn. Price at time of withdrawal 8/1. Rule 4 applies to all bets - deduct 10p in the pound.

**FOCUS**
After rain in the morning the going was changed to Good. The jockeys confirmed the official description. This valuable sales race attracted a big field of mixed ability and, the winner apart, the principals were drawn centre-to-far side. The time was 2.07secs slower than the following record-breaking Lowther Stakes. As last year William Haggas trained the winner and third. Mubtaghaa has the scope to do better but Kool Kompany was around a stone below form.

## 5608 PINSENT MASONS LOWTHER STKS (GROUP 2) (FILLIES) 6f
2:30 (2:31) (Class 1) 2-Y-O
£85,065 (£32,250; £16,140; £8,040; £4,035; £2,025) Stalls High

Form RPR
2121 1 **Tiggy Wiggy (IRE)**[33] 4439 2-9-0 117........................ RichardHughes 2 117
(Richard Hannon) *mde all: shkn up over 1f out: styd on wl last 150yds* **15/8**[1]
11 2 1 1/2 **Cursory Glance (USA)**[62] 3415 2-9-0 0........................ AndreaAtzeni 1 113
(Roger Varian) *lw: towards rr: hdwy over 2f out: w ldrs over 1f out: edgd lft and kpt on same pce last 100yds* **11/4**[3]
1 3 1/2 **Anthem Alexander (IRE)**[64] 3353 2-9-3 0........................ PatSmullen 5 114
(Edward Lynam, Ire) *lw: trckd ldrs: kpt on same pce last 150yds* **5/2**[2]
2125 4 5 **Realtra (IRE)**[33] 4439 2-9-0 90........................ TonyHamilton 4 96
(Richard Fahey) *in rr and sn pushed along: hdwy over 1f out: kpt on to take modest 4th in clsng stages* **33/1**
21 5 1/2 **Sulaalaat**[21] 4828 2-9-0 0........................ PaulHanagan 6 95
(Brian Meehan) *leggy: athletic: sn outpcd in rr: hdwy over 1f out: tk modest 5th in clsng stages* **11/1**
1134 6 1/2 **Patience Alexander (IRE)**[12] 5173 2-9-0 101........................ RyanMoore 3 93
(David Evans) *in rr: kpt on over 1f out: nvr on terms* **14/1**
313 7 1/2 **She's A Worldie (IRE)**[19] 4920 2-9-0 81........................ PaulMulrennan 8 92
(Bryan Smart) *leggy: chsd ldrs: lost pl over 1f out: wknd in clsng stages* **50/1**
13 8 4 **Bimbo**[44] 4057 2-9-0 79........................ GeorgeChaloner 10 80
(Richard Fahey) *w'like: s.i.s: drvn and hdwy 3f out: lost pl 2f out* **50/1**
0325 9 5 **Lady Gemini**[19] 4913 2-9-0 79........................ ThomasHenderson 7 65
(Jo Hughes) *chsd ldrs: lost pl over 1f out: sn eased* **66/1**
1m 8.9s (-3.00) **Going Correction** -0.20s/f (Firm) 2y crse rec **9** Ran SP% **113.4**
Speed ratings (Par 103): **112,110,109,102,102 101,100,95,88**
CSF £6.96 TOTE £2.60: £1.10, £1.20, £1.30; EX 7.50 Trifecta £12.80.
**Owner** Potensis Ltd C Giles Merriebelle Stables **Bred** Cbs Bloodstock **Trained** East Everleigh, Wilts


The Form Book, Raceform Ltd, Newbury, RG14 5SJ

**FOCUS**
A very strong edition of this event and the race didn't disappoint, with the three form fillies drawing clear. Tiggy Wiggy broke the juvenile course record and backed up her Newbury form. The second and third both took notable steps forward.

## 5609 CLIPPER LOGISTICS STKS (H'CAP) 1m
**3:05** (3:06) (Class 2) 3-Y-0+
**£49,800** (£14,912; £7,456; £3,728; £1,864; £936) **Stalls** Low

Form RPR
-054 **1** **Short Squeeze (IRE)**[26] 4681 4-9-4 **102**......................(tp) PatSmullen 18 112+
(Hugo Palmer) *lw: stdd and swtchd lft s: hld up in rr: stdy hdwy 2f out: nt clr run and repeatedly swtchd: r.o wl ins fnl f: pushed along to ld last strides* **8/1**[2]
4636 **2** *hd* **Top Notch Tonto (IRE)**[54] 3723 4-9-3 **108**.................... MikeyEnnis(7) 9 117
(Brian Ellison) *prom: stdy hdwy to ld jst ins fnl f: r.o: ct post* **16/1**
1310 **3** *3/4* **Balducci**[33] 4442 7-8-13 **97**.......................................(v) DanielTudhope 5 105
(David O'Meara) *led: hdd jst ins fnl f: no ex* **20/1**
4100 **4** *3/4* **Bronze Angel (IRE)**[20] 4851 5-9-1 **99**............................(b) MartinDwyer 12 105
(Marcus Tregoning) *hld up in rr: hdwy over 2f out: styd on same pce last 75yds* **15/2**[1]
2403 **5** *1/2* **Gabrial's Kaka (IRE)**[47] 3982 4-9-2 **103**................ GeorgeChaloner(3) 6 108
(Richard Fahey) *s.i.s: sn drvn into mid-div: hdwy over 3f out: kpt on fnl f* **10/1**
3001 **6** *hd* **Red Avenger (USA)**[20] 4851 4-9-1 **99**..........................(b) JamesDoyle 1 103
(Ed Dunlop) *prom: chsng ldrs over 2f out: kpt on same pce last 150yds* **12/1**
2104 **7** *1* **Russian Realm**[47] 3982 4-8-12 **96**.............................. RyanMoore 14 98
(Sir Michael Stoute) *lw: trckd ldrs: kpt on one pce appr fnl f* **9/1**[3]
1110 **8** *3/4* **Kosika (USA)**[26] 4668 4-8-12 **96**.............................. FrannyNorton 16 96
(Mark Johnston) *w ldr: one pce appr fnl f* **20/1**
-305 **9** *shd* **Prince Of Johanne (IRE)**[47] 3982 8-9-2 **100**................(p) GrahamLee 4 100
(Tom Tate) *prom: nt clr run over 1f out: kpt on* **14/1**
3203 **10** *nse* **Parbold (IRE)**[42] 4127 3-9-1 **105**.............................. PaulHanagan 8 104
(Richard Fahey) *s.i.s: in rr: styd on fnl 2f: nvr nr ldrs* **8/1**[2]
6406 **11** *1/2* **Fort Bastion (IRE)**[20] 4851 5-8-12 **96**........................ JamesSullivan 13 95
(Ruth Carr) *lw: in rr: kpt on fnl 2f: nvr a factor* **11/1**
060 **12** *nk* **Boom And Bust (IRE)**[23] 4758 7-9-0 **103**........................ JoeDoyle(5) 2 101
(Marcus Tregoning) *chsd ldrs: one pce fnl 2f* **25/1**
/656 **13** *1 3/4* **Energizer (GER)**[62] 3416 5-9-2 **100**........................ RichardHughes 19 94
(Charlie Appleby) *chsd ldrs: wknd over 1f out* **20/1**
5651 **14** *1/2* **Laffan (IRE)**[26] 4661 5-8-13 **97**.............................. RobertWinston 17 90
(Tim Easterby) *mid-div: effrt over 3f out: hung lft and lost pl over 1f out* **28/1**
3200 **15** *1 1/4* **My Freedom (IRE)**[26] 4648 6-9-2 **100**.................. SilvestreDeSousa 3 90
(Saeed bin Suroor) *hld up in rr: nvr on terms* **25/1**
1000 **16** *1 1/2* **Two For Two (IRE)**[12] 5163 6-8-13 **100**........................ SamJames(3) 10 87
(David O'Meara) *mid-div: sme hdwy over 3f out: nvr a factor* **20/1**
1205 **17** *1* **Passing Star**[21] 4826 3-8-13 **103**.............................. WilliamBuick 20 86
(Charles Hills) *a towards rr* **12/1**
-100 **18** *13* **Navajo Chief**[12] 5163 7-9-1 **99**.............................. KierenFallon 7 54
(Timothy Jarvis) *in rr: hdwy 4f out: lost pl over 2f out: eased whn bhd ins fnl f* **20/1**
0600 **19** *9* **Santefisio**[26] 4648 8-9-1 **99**..........................(b) JoeFanning 15 33
(Keith Dalgleish) *s.i.s: hdwy into midfield over 4f out: lost pl 2f out: eased whn bhd* **40/1**

1m 36.48s (-2.52) **Going Correction** -0.025s/f (Good)
**WFA** 3 from 4yo+ 6lb **19** Ran SP% **126.7**
Speed ratings (Par 109): **111,110,110,109,108 108,107,106,106,106 106,105,104,103,102 100,99,86,77**
CSF £110.93 CT £2564.71 TOTE £8.50: £2.60, £4.20, £5.10, £2.60; EX 188.50 Trifecta £6232.50 Part won. Pool of £8310.09 - 0.11 winning units..
**Owner** W Duff Gordon, R Smith, B Mathieson **Bred** Des Swan **Trained** Newmarket, Suffolk
■ Stewards' Enquiry : Martin Dwyer two-day ban: used whip above permitted level (Sep 4-5)

**FOCUS**
A classy and competitive mile handicap run below standard time and a terrific riding display by Pat Smullen on the winner. The first two two came from the year and this is solid form.

## 5610 DARLEY YORKSHIRE OAKS (BRITISH CHAMPIONS SERIES) (GROUP 1) (F&M) 1m 4f
**3:40** (3:41) (Class 1) 3-Y-0+
**£187,143** (£70,950; £35,508; £17,688; £8,877; £4,455) **Stalls** Centre

Form RPR
-062 **1** **Tapestry (IRE)**[33] 4461 3-8-11 112.............................. RyanMoore 6 121
(A P O'Brien, Ire) *hld up in rr: effrt 3f out: 3rd over 1f out: chsd wnr jst ins fnl f: r.o to ld nr fin* **8/1**[2]
-111 **2** *1/2* **Taghrooda**[26] 4649 3-8-11 125.............................. PaulHanagan 7 120
(John Gosden) *hld up in rr: hdwy 9f out: sn trcking ldrs: led over 2f out: hdd and no ex towards fin* **1/5**[1]
0101 **3** *7* **Tasaday (USA)**[27] 4634 4-9-7 113...................... SilvestreDeSousa 4 109
(Saeed bin Suroor) *str: hld up in rr: hdwy 4f out: upsides 2f out: kpt on same pce* **22/1**
205 **4** *2 1/2* **Lustrous**[19] 4894 3-8-11 104.............................. PatDobbs 2 105
(Richard Hannon) *mid-div: hdwy 7f out: chsng ldrs 3f out: one pce over 1f out* **66/1**
-534 **5** *8* **Talent**[21] 4824 4-9-7 103.............................. AndreaAtzeni 1 92
(Ralph Beckett) *trckd ldrs: t.k.h: wknd 2f out* **28/1**
3133 **6** *1* **Volume**[33] 4461 3-8-11 109.............................. RichardHughes 5 91
(Luca Cumani) *led: drvn over 3f out: hdd over 2f out: wknd over 1f out* **14/1**[3]
-123 **7** *38* **Venus De Milo (IRE)**[19] 4894 4-9-7 111........................[1] JosephO'Brien 3 30
(A P O'Brien, Ire) *trckd ldrs: drvn upsides 3f out: lost pl and heavily eased 2f out: virtually p.u: t.o* **16/1**

2m 28.59s (-4.61) **Going Correction** -0.025s/f (Good)
**WFA** 3 from 4yo 10lb **7** Ran SP% **116.3**
Speed ratings (Par 117): **114,113,109,107,102 101,76**
CSF £10.34 TOTE £11.00: £2.60, £1.10; EX 15.40 Trifecta £107.00.
**Owner** Mrs Magnier/Tabor/Smith/Flaxman Stables **Bred** Orpendale And The Niarchos Family **Trained** Cashel, Co Tipperary
■ Stewards' Enquiry : Ryan Moore four-day ban: used whip above permitted level (Sep 4-5,7-8)

**FOCUS**
This looked at the mercy of the unbeaten Taghrooda, but the Knavesmire has not proved a happy hunting ground for Oaks winners, with only Alexandrova in 2006 and Ramruma in 1999 completing the double of the last 11 to try in the same season. The pace was sound and the principals came from the rear, with the first two drawing well clear. There wasn't a great deal of depth, and Taghrooda is rated 7lb off her best, but Tapestry posted a clear personal best.

## 5611 SIR HENRY CECIL & EBF GALTRES STKS (LISTED RACE) (F&M) 1m 4f
**4:20** (4:20) (Class 1) 3-Y-0+
**£34,026** (£12,900; £6,456; £3,216; £1,614; £810) **Stalls** Centre

Form RPR
1534 **1** **Queen Of Ice**[33] 4443 3-8-11 93.............................. AndreaAtzeni 8 106
(William Haggas) *lw: led: qcknd pce 4f out: edgd lft ins fnl f: jst hld on* **20/1**
1312 **2** *nse* **Arabian Comet (IRE)**[21] 4824 3-8-11 99.................... JoeFanning 4 105
(William Haggas) *hld up towards rr: drvn and hdwy over 2f out: styd on to take 2nd last 50yds: jst hld* **9/2**[3]
5121 **3** *1 3/4* **Noble Protector**[33] 4443 4-9-11 105.......................... JamieSpencer 2 107
(Stuart Kittow) *lw: trckd ldrs: upsides over 2f out: carried lft ins fnl f: hld whn hung lft and sddle slipped in clsng stages* **7/2**[2]
3-50 **4** *2 1/4* **Island Remede**[76] 2960 3-8-11 89.............................. PaulHanagan 9 98
(Ed Dunlop) *in rr: outpcd over 3f out: hdwy over 2f out: kpt on one pce* **66/1**
-301 **5** *3/4* **Momentus (IRE)**[34] 4413 3-8-11 99.............................. JimCrowley 1 97
(David Simcock) *lw: chsd wnr: one pce fnl 2f* **12/1**
4223 **6** *2* **Waila**[21] 4824 4-9-7 99.............................. RyanMoore 10 94
(Sir Michael Stoute) *hld up in mid-div: effrt over 2f out: sn outpcd: kpt on fnl f* **13/2**
0455 **7** *3/4* **Quiz Mistress**[18] 4945 6-9-7 99..........................(b[1]) RichardHughes 6 93
(Hughie Morrison) *hld up in mid-div: t.k.h: hdwy over 3f out: sn chsng ldrs: wknd fnl 150yds* **16/1**
16 **8** *1 3/4* **Stella Bellissima (IRE)**[21] 4824 3-8-11 91...................... WilliamBuick 5 90
(John Gosden) *dwlt: hdwy to chse ldrs after 3f: outpcd over 3f out: lost pl over 2f out: eased in clsng stages* **10/1**
6-02 **9** *2 1/4* **Dark Crusader (IRE)**[16] 5024 4-9-7 102........................[1] KierenFallon 3 86
(A J Martin, Ire) *t.k.h: swtchd outside to trck ldrs after 2f: lost pl over 2f out: eased in clsng stages* **12/1**
**10** *4* **Starlet (IRE)**[42] 4141 3-8-11 0.............................. PatSmullen 7 80
(D K Weld, Ire) *athletic: lw: hld up in rr: hdwy over 4f out: outpcd over 3f out: lost pl over 2f out: eased in clsng stages* **5/2**[1]

2m 32.42s (-0.78) **Going Correction** -0.025s/f (Good)
**WFA** 3 from 4yo+ 10lb **10** Ran SP% **118.9**
Speed ratings: **101,100,99,98,97 96,95,94,93,90**
CSF £110.03 TOTE £25.70: £4.80, £1.90, £1.80; EX 148.30 Trifecta £1068.50.
**Owner** Cheveley Park Stud **Bred** Cheveley Park Stud Ltd **Trained** Newmarket, Suffolk

**FOCUS**
This Listed fillies' race has provided a stepping stone to Group company for such as Irish St Leger winner Kastoria and local heroine Anna Pavlova in recent years. The pace was steady until the straight and the time was 3.83secs slower than the Group 1 Yorkshire Oaks that preceded it. William Haggas had the one-two, the winner reversing Newmarket form with the third.

## 5612 EVENTMASTERS.CO.UK EBF STALLIONS FILLIES' STKS (H'CAP) 7f
**4:55** (4:55) (Class 2) (0-100,100) 3-Y-0+
**£24,900** (£7,456; £3,728; £1,864; £932; £468) **Stalls** Low

Form RPR
3121 **1** **Bragging (USA)**[26] 4668 3-9-4 **97**.............................. JamesDoyle 17 113+
(Sir Michael Stoute) *str: lw: towards rr: pushed along over 3f out: hdwy 2f out: led 1f out: forged clr: readily* **10/3**[1]
1600 **2** *3* **Little Shambles**[5] 5410 3-8-6 **85**.............................. FrannyNorton 11 91
(Mark Johnston) *chsd ldrs: upsides over 1f out: styd on same pce* **50/1**
0312 **3** *nk* **Ticking Katie (IRE)**[19] 4912 3-8-8 **90**......................(p) JoeyHaynes(3) 16 95
(K R Burke) *mid-div: hdwy over 2f out: hung lft and styd on to take 3rd in clsng stages* **11/1**
1303 **4** *3/4* **Dusky Queen (IRE)**[28] 4573 4-9-1 **89**.......................... TonyHamilton 6 94+
(Richard Fahey) *in rr: hdwy over 2f out: styd on to take 4th nr fin* **20/1**
1626 **5** *3/4* **Dutch Rose (IRE)**[26] 4681 5-9-12 **100**........................ DanielTudhope 9 103
(David O'Meara) *chsd ldrs: upsides over 2f out: kpt on same pce appr fnl f* **10/1**
4211 **6** *nk* **Jamesbo's Girl**[19] 4902 4-8-7 **81** oh1........................ GrahamGibbons 4 84
(David Barron) *led: hdd 1f out: kpt on same pce* **16/1**
21-4 **7** *1/2* **Enraptured (IRE)**[33] 4436 3-8-7 **86**.............................. WilliamBuick 10 85
(John Gosden) *chsd ldrs: drvn over 2f out: one pce over 1f out* **8/1**
400 **8** *3/4* **Askaud (IRE)**[5] 5418 6-9-3 **91**..............................(p) FrederikTylicki 13 90
(Scott Dixon) *lw: chsd ldrs: upsides over 2f out: one pce over 1f out* **50/1**
3634 **9** *1 1/4* **Azagal (IRE)**[26] 4661 3-8-13 **92**.............................. DavidAllan 15 86
(Tim Easterby) *in rr: kpt on fnl 2f: nvr a factor* **33/1**
1010 **10** *1 1/4* **Lady Frances**[5] 5438 3-8-10 **89**.............................. JoeFanning 18 80
(Mark Johnston) *lw: mid-div: hdwy over 2f out: lost pl over 1f out* **33/1**
5433 **11** *1 1/2* **Misplaced Fortune**[44] 4061 9-8-11 **85**..........................(v) JasonHart 14 74
(Nigel Tinkler) *mid-div: effrt over 2f out: wknd over 1f out* **33/1**
6406 **12** *1 1/4* **Dutch Courage**[54] 3724 3-9-1 **94**.............................. RyanMoore 5 78
(Richard Fahey) *hld up in rr: hmpd over 4f out: hdwy 3f out: lost pl over 1f out* **15/2**[3]
0520 **13** *5* **The Gold Cheongsam (IRE)**[20] 4854 4-9-11 **99**.......(vt) KierenFallon 12 72
(Jeremy Noseda) *mid-div: hdwy over 2f out: sn chsng ldrs: lost pl and eased jst ins fnl f* **20/1**
5 **14** *5* **Sparkle Factor (IRE)**[38] 4276 3-9-1 **94**..........................(t) PatSmullen 3 52
(D K Weld, Ire) *chsd ldrs: lost pl over 1f out: eased whn bhd in clsng stages* **4/1**[2]
6200 **15** *1 1/4* **Royal Rascal**[26] 4681 4-9-5 **93**..........................(tp) RobertWinston 1 49
(Tim Easterby) *in rr-div: sltly hmpd over 4f out: chsng ldrs 3f out: lost pl over 1f out: eased in clsng stages* **25/1**
6433 **F** **Wedding Ring (IRE)**[26] 4668 3-9-3 **96**........................ RichardHughes 7
(Charlie Appleby) *chsd ldrs: fell over 4f out: fatally injured* **16/1**
62 **U** **Artistic Charm**[33] 4445 3-8-6 **85**.............................. AndreaAtzeni 19
(David Simcock) *s.i.s: swtchd lft after s: last whn bdly hmpd and uns rdr over 4f out* **20/1**

1m 22.2s (-3.10) **Going Correction** -0.20s/f (Firm)
**WFA** 3 from 4yo+ 5lb **17** Ran SP% **126.0**
Speed ratings (Par 96): **109,105,105,104,103 103,102,101,100,98 97,95,90,84,82 ,**
CSF £200.40 CT £1709.65 TOTE £4.70: £1.40, £10.50, £2.60, £4.30; EX 343.90 Trifecta £6672.30 Part won. Pool of £8896.40 - 0.33 winning units..
**Owner** K Abdullah **Bred** Juddmonte Farms Inc **Trained** Newmarket, Suffolk

**FOCUS**
The fourth running of this event was rather lacking in progressive performers, but Bragging was an obvious exception. She's a Group filly, with more to offer. There was a nasty incident on the approach to the home turn where Wedding Ring broke a leg and fell, bringing down trailer Artistic Charm.
T/Jkpt: Not won. T/Plt: £61.50 to a £1 stake. Pool of £328462.20 - 3894.70 winning tickets. T/Qpdt: £14.60 to a £1 stake. Pool of £20771.75 - 1049.75 winning tickets. WG

5613 - 5615a (Foreign Racing) - See Raceform Interactive

## 5543 DEAUVILLE (R-H)
Thursday, August 21

**OFFICIAL GOING: Turf: very soft; polytrack: standard**

### 5616a PRIX D'EXMES (MAIDEN) (2YO COLTS & GELDINGS) (TURF) 6f
11:15 (12:00) 2-Y-O £10,416 (£4,166; £3,125; £2,083; £1,041)

RPR
1 **Kerman (FR)**[26] 2-9-2 0 ChristopheSoumillon 6 75
(J-C Rouget, France) **9/10**[1]
2 3/4 **Snow And Ice (FR)**[21] 2-9-2 0 Christophe-PatriceLemaire 3 73
(T Castanheira, France) **37/10**[2]
3 1 1/2 **Smaug (FR)** 2-8-13 0 ThomasMessina 5 66
(X Nakkachdji, France) **22/1**
4 1 3/4 **Serpentin (FR)** 2-9-2 0 Pierre-CharlesBoudot 7 63
(D Prod'Homme, France) **22/5**[3]
5 shd **Super Nothing (IRE)**[75] 2-9-2 0 CristianDemuro 8 63
(G Botti, France) **232/10**
6 3/4 **Jimmy's Hall**[14] 5118 2-9-2 0 IoritzMendizabal 1 61
(J S Moore) *w.w towards rr: rdn and effrt 1 1/2f out: 4th and styng on ins fnl f: run petered out last 100yds and dropped to 6th* **29/1**
7 6 **Sombre Heros (FR)**[19] 4932 2-9-2 0 (b[1]) MickaelBarzalona 2 43
(Mlle H Mennessier, France) **10/1**
8 nk **Mimulus (FR)**[35] 2-9-2 0 GregoryBenoist 9 42
(J E Pease, France) **35/1**
9 15 **Stylish Sky (FR)** 2-8-13 0 StephanePasquier 4
(Y Gourraud, France) **269/10**

1m 13.6s (2.60) 9 Ran SP% **119.7**
WIN (incl. 1 euro stake): 1.90. PLACES: 1.10, 1.30, 2.80. DF: 4.30. SF: 5.60.
**Owner** H H Aga Khan **Bred** S.A. Aga Khan **Trained** Pau, France

### 5617a PRIX DE PRETREVILLE (MAIDEN (2YO FILLIES) (TURF) 6f
11:45 (12:00) 2-Y-O £10,416 (£4,166; £3,125; £2,083; £1,041)

RPR
1 **Enough Paint (IRE)**[26] 2-9-0 0 IoritzMendizabal 7 84
(J Heloury, France) **68/10**[3]
2 1/2 **Lady Sybil (FR)**[34] 2-9-0 0 MickaelBarzalona 11 82
(Y Barberot, France) **21/10**[2]
3 3/4 **South Bank (USA)**[32] 4482 2-9-0 0 ThierryThulliez 3 80
(Mme C Head-Maarek, France) **6/5**[1]
4 hd **Pretty Picture**[14] 5119 2-9-0 0 Pierre-CharlesBoudot 4 79
(Gay Kelleway) *broke wl: a.p: pushed along and chsd ldr 1 1/2f out: one pce fnl f: dropped to 4th cl home* **30/1**
5 hd **Rose Doloise (FR)**[83] 2755 2-9-0 0 UmbertoRispoli 10 79
(A Bonin, France) **142/10**
6 2 **Maui (FR)**[23] 2-9-0 0 CristianDemuro 8 73
(Mlle V Dissaux, France) **47/1**
7 2 **Arystyn Gouli (FR)** 2-9-0 0 MaximeGuyon 1 67
(X Thomas-Demeaulte, France) **138/10**
8 hd **Road To Damascus (FR)**[21] 4839 2-9-0 0 AlexisBadel 6 66
(F Sanchez, France) **74/1**
9 1 3/4 **Elusive Lily**[46] 2-9-0 0 EddyHardouin 2 61
(Robert Collet, France) **62/1**
10 snk **Freaky Girl (FR)**[14] 5119 2-9-0 0 Christophe-PatriceLemaire 5 60
(Robert Collet, France) **45/1**
11 1 1/4 **Lydie Chope (FR)** 2-9-0 0 (p) JulienAuge 9 57
(A De Watrigant, France) **168/10**

1m 13.6s (2.60) 11 Ran SP% **119.9**
WIN (incl. 1 euro stake): 7.80. PLACES: 1.40, 1.20, 1.10. DF: 7.60. SF: 23.00.
**Owner** Aleyrion Bloodstock Ltd **Bred** Aleyrion Bloodstock Ltd **Trained** France

### 5618a PRIX DU MONT CANISY (CLAIMER) (2YO COLTS & GELDINGS) (POLYTRACK) 7f 110y
12:15 (12:00) 2-Y-O £9,583 (£3,833; £2,875; £1,916; £958)

RPR
1 **Chester Deal**[17] 4967 2-8-13 0 MickaelBarzalona 4 71
(Jo Hughes) *mde all: rdn whn pressed over 2f out and lened: edgd lft appr fnl f: r.o gamely u.p* **7/2**[2]
2 hd **Well Fleeced**[16] 2-9-2 0 PaulineProd'homme 3 74
(D Prod'Homme, France) **19/10**[1]
3 2 **Cat Bere (FR)**[16] 2-8-4 0 MllePaulineDominois(5) 2 62
(C Lerner, France) **114/10**
4 3/4 **Mystic Driver (FR)** 2-8-13 0 (p) CesarPasserat 9 64
(F-X De Chevigny, France) **83/1**
5 1 **Atilla (FR)**[42] 2-8-9 0 Christophe-PatriceLemaire 1 58
(M Boutin, France) **157/10**
6 snk **Rivolochop (FR)**[16] 2-8-13 0 AnthonyCrastus 8 62
(C Boutin, France) **153/10**
6 dht **Alandil (FR)** 2-8-9 0 GeraldMosse 6 58
(M Boutin, France) **115/10**
8 1/2 **Chiquito (FR)**[16] 2-9-2 0 (p) Pierre-CharlesBoudot 10 63
(J-L Pelletan, France) **73/10**
9 2 **Firefoot (ITY)** 2-8-9 0 CristianDemuro 7 52
(G Botti, France) **37/1**
10 3 1/2 **Atlas Royal (FR)**[20] 4881 2-8-13 0 UmbertoRispoli 11 47
(Mario Hofer, Germany) **13/2**[3]
11 12 **The Rebel (FR)**[21] 2-8-13 0 AntoineHamelin 5 18
(Matthieu Palussiere, France) **159/10**

1m 31.8s (91.80) 11 Ran SP% **120.0**
WIN (incl. 1 euro stake): 4.50. PLACES: 1.80, 1.30, 2.70. DF: 5.30. SF: 10.80.
**Owner** Chester Racing & Jo Hughes **Bred** Chester Racing Club Ltd **Trained** Lambourn, Berks

### 5619a PRIX DE LA CROIX D'HEULAND (CLAIMER) (2YO FILLIES) (POLYTRACK) 7f 110y
1:20 (12:00) 2-Y-O £9,583 (£3,833; £2,875; £1,916; £958)

RPR
1 **Eastern Promise (FR)** 2-8-9 0 AnthonyCrastus 6 63
(D Sepulchre, France) **191/10**
2 snk **Dame Des Lys (FR)**[28] 4603 2-9-0 0 ThierryJarnet 5 68
(J Heloury, France) **17/5**[1]
3 shd **Really Tonic (FR)**[35] 2-9-2 0 GregoryBenoist 15 69
(F Doumen, France) **14/1**
4 3/4 **Who Knows (IRE)**[16] 5026 2-8-4 0 MllePaulineDominois(5) 12 61
(C Lerner, France) **94/10**
5 snk **Areion (IRE)**[14] 5119 2-9-0 0 (b) IoritzMendizabal 1 65
(J S Moore) *trckd ldrs on inner: rdn to chse ldrs over 1f out: styd on u.p fnl f: nt pce to chal* **171/10**
6 1 **Beauty Traou Land (FR)**[16] 5026 2-8-13 0 (p) FabriceVeron 8 62
(B De Montzey, France) **14/1**
7 nse **Qoosine (FR)**[20] 4882 2-8-9 0 StephanePasquier 9 58
(Rod Collet, France) **117/10**
8 1 1/4 **A Ma Reine (FR)**[20] 4883 2-8-9 0 TheoBachelot 14 55
(S Wattel, France) **33/1**
9 hd **Whole Lotta Love (FR)**[16] 5026 2-8-9 0 MickaelBarzalona 2 54
(Y Barberot, France) **13/2**[3]
10 snk **Trust The Captain (FR)**[26] 2-9-2 0 EddyHardouin 13 61
(Robert Collet, France) **35/1**
11 snk **Against Rules (FR)**[34] 2-9-2 0 (b[1]) Christophe-PatriceLemaire 3 61
(Robert Collet, France) **54/1**
12 8 **Qwhipper (FR)** 2-8-13 0 MaximeGuyon 4 38
(C Boutin, France) **59/10**[2]
13 shd **Sulphur (FR)**[20] 4882 2-8-9 0 UmbertoRispoli 10 34
(Mario Hofer, Germany) **205/10**
14 1 1/2 **Fly Grazer (IRE)**[14] 5119 2-8-9 0 GeraldMosse 11 30
(J S Moore) *trckd ldrs on outer: cl 3rd and ev ch 2 1/2f out: sn rdn and nt qckn: wknd appr fnl f* **26/1**
15 1/2 **My Pupite (FR)**[42] 2-9-3 0 CristianDemuro 7 37
(G Botti, France) **78/10**

1m 30.6s (90.60) **15** Ran SP% **119.1**
WIN (incl. 1 euro stake): 20.10. PLACES: 5.50, 2.20, 4.20. DF: 56.40. SF: 162.30.
**Owner** D Sepulchre **Bred** Mme D Sepulchre **Trained** France

## 5271 FFOS LAS (L-H)
Friday, August 22

**OFFICIAL GOING: Flat course - good (7.9); jumps courses - good (good to firm in places; 7.6)**
Wind: light, half against Weather: dry, bright spells

### 5620 TOTEPOOL BET ON ALL UK RACING NURSERY H'CAP (BOBIS RACE) 6f
1:45 (1:47) (Class 4) (0-85,84) 2-Y-O £3,752 (£1,116; £557; £278) **Stalls** Centre

Form RPR
021 1 **Heartbreak Hero**[39] 4270 2-9-7 84 SebSanders 6 91+
(William Haggas) *broke fast: chsd ldr tl led 1/2-way: rdn hands and heels and wnt clr over 1f out: r.o wl: comf* **8/13**[1]
5502 2 1 1/2 **Lightning Stride**[34] 4430 2-9-5 82 HarryBentley 5 83+
(Brian Meehan) *hld up in tch: effrt over 2f out: chsd wnr and rdn over 1f out: edgd lft and no imp fnl f* **9/2**[2]
2101 3 3 1/4 **L'Etacq**[16] 5028 2-8-6 76 JoshQuinn(7) 3 67
(Richard Hannon) *s.i.s and bustled along early: in rr: hdwy and drvn ent fnl 2f: no ch w wnr but kpt on to go 3rd nr fin* **6/1**[3]
3504 4 1/2 **Charlie's Star**[19] 4939 2-8-9 72 JFEgan 1 61
(David Evans) *sn led: hdd 1/2-way: rdn and no ex over 1f out: wknd ins fnl f: lost 3rd nr fin* **14/1**
2322 5 7 **Amber Crystal**[16] 5028 2-8-7 70 HayleyTurner 4 38
(John Gallagher) *t.k.h: in tch in midfield: dropped to rr and rdn over 2f out: wknd over 1f out* **10/1**
3455 6 3/4 **Mylaporyours (IRE)**[16] 5043 2-8-5 68 WilliamCarson 2 34
(Rod Millman) *chsd ldrs tl rdn and lost pl ent fnl 2f: wknd over 1f out* **14/1**

1m 10.14s (0.14) **Going Correction** -0.025s/f (Good) 6 Ran SP% **116.8**
Speed ratings (Par 96): **98,96,91,91,81 80**
CSF £4.12 TOTE £1.50: £1.10, £2.90; EX 4.90 Trifecta £14.00.
**Owner** J C Smith **Bred** Mrs Johnny Eddis **Trained** Newmarket, Suffolk

**FOCUS**
Good ground for the four Flat races on this mixed card. The winner left his maiden form behind in this nursery.

### 5621 TOTESWINGER THREE WAYS TO WIN H'CAP 1m 2f (R)
2:20 (2:22) (Class 5) (0-70,68) 3-Y-O+ £2,587 (£770; £384; £192) **Stalls** Low

Form RPR
3241 1 **Greyemkay**[10] 5273 6-8-8 53 6ex DanielMuscutt(5) 8 63
(Richard Price) *in tch in midfield: hdwy to trck ldr and gng wl over 2f out: rdn to ld over 1f out: edgd lft u.p and r.o wl fnl f* **6/1**
6021 2 1 1/4 **Golden Jubilee (USA)**[17] 5002 5-9-13 67 (v) StevieDonohoe 5 74
(Nigel Twiston-Davies) *dwlt: bustled along early: hdwy to ld after 2f: rdn over 2f out: drvn and hdd over 1f out: swtchd rt and styd on same pce ins fnl f* **4/1**[2]
4032 3 6 **Canova (IRE)**[9] 5313 3-9-5 67 (bt) GeorgeBaker 2 63
(Roger Charlton) *led for 2f: chsd ldr tl 6f out: 3rd and rdn whn short of room and swtchd rt over 2f out: no ex: wl hld over 1f out: plugged on* **9/4**[1]
43-5 4 2 **Society Pearl (IRE)**[8] 5340 4-10-0 68 JFEgan 6 60
(David Evans) *in tch in midfield: rdn 3f out: no ex and btn 2f out: n.d but plugged on ins fnl f to snatch 4th last stride* **14/1**
5522 5 shd **Urban Space**[8] 5338 8-8-13 53 (t) WilliamCarson 3 45
(John Flint) *chsd ldrs: wnt 2nd 6f out tl over 2f out: losing pl whn sltly hmpd sn after: wknd over 1f out: lost 4th last stride* **5/1**[3]
2052 6 27 **Juvenal (IRE)**[17] 4996 5-9-9 66 (p) ThomasBrown(3) 1 6
(Paul Morgan) *s.i.s: a detached fr main ldng sextet: lost tch 3f out: t.o* **10/1**
0063 7 16 **Template (IRE)**[9] 5313 3-9-3 65 SebSanders 4
(Amanda Perrett) *in tch in rr of ldng sextet: rdn 3f out: sn btn: eased fnl 2f: t.o* **4/1**[2]

0/0- 8 8 **Hamilton Hill**[329] 6490 7-9-7 68 JoshQuinn(7) 7
(Bernard Llewellyn) *v.s.a and lost many l s: nvr on terms: t.o* **33/1**
2m 7.54s (-1.86) **Going Correction** -0.025s/f (Good)
**WFA** 3 from 4yo+ 8lb 8 Ran SP% **120.4**
Speed ratings (Par 103): **106,105,100,98,98 76,64,57**
CSF £31.94 CT £71.70 TOTE £5.70: £2.30, £1.70, £1.10; EX 26.70 Trifecta £36.50.
**Owner** Richard Price & Maria Slade **Bred** Shade Oak Stud **Trained** Ullingswick, H'fords
**FOCUS**
An ordinary handicap in which all of the runners had questions to answer. The only two course winners in the race came clear of the rest and the winner looks better than ever.

## 5622 TOTEPOOL HOME OF POOL BETTING MAIDEN FILLIES' STKS 1m (R)
2:55 (2:58) (Class 4) 3-Y-0+ **£4,690** (£1,395; £697; £348) **Stalls** Low

Form RPR
32 1 **Zora Seas (IRE)**[10] 5272 3-8-12 0 HarryBentley 2 72
(Brian Meehan) *hld up in tch in midfield: clsd and nt clr run 2f out: swtchd rt and effrt u.p 1f out: chal fnl 75yds: r.o to ld last stride* **3/1**[3]
3-54 2 shd **Water Queen**[68] 3277 3-8-13 73 ow1 (p) SebSanders 7 72
(William Haggas) *in tch in midfield: clsd to chal 2f out: rdn to ld and edgd lft 1f out: drvn ins fnl f: kpt on: hdd last stride* **11/4**[2]
5 3 ¾ **Ramshackle**[127] 1534 3-8-12 0 HayleyTurner 6 69
(Sir Michael Stoute) *t.k.h: chsd ldr after 1f: ev ch 2f out: rdn to ld over 1f out: hdd 1f out: one pce fnl 100yds* **11/10**[1]
4 hd **Brisk**[97] 3-8-12 0 JFEgan 4 68
(David Evans) *led for 1f: chsd ldrs: n.m.r jst over 2f out: kpt on same pce u.p ins fnl f* **12/1**
6-55 5 4 ½ **Tipsy Star**[30] 4540 3-8-12 60 [1] WilliamCarson 5 58
(Jonathan Geake) *dwlt: rdn and hdwy to ld after 1f: drvn and hdd over 1f out: wknd ins fnl f* **12/1**
-0 6 27 **Euroquip Susie**[16] 5039 6-9-4 0 StevieDonohoe 1
(Michael Scudamore) *a in last pair: lost tch 3f out: t.o* **66/1**
0 7 15 **Touig**[17] 5007 3-8-12 0 SamHitchcott 3
(Stuart Howe) *a in last pair: rdn 1/2-way: lost tch 3f out: t.o* **100/1**
1m 39.89s (-1.11) **Going Correction** -0.025s/f (Good)
**WFA** 3 from 6yo 6lb 7 Ran SP% **117.2**
Speed ratings (Par 102): **104,103,103,102,98 71,56**
CSF £12.23 TOTE £3.60: £1.40, £1.20; EX 9.60 Trifecta £19.30.
**Owner** Mrs B V Sangster **Bred** Rockfield Farm **Trained** Manton, Wilts
■ Stewards' Enquiry : Seb Sanders £290.00 fine; tried to weight out without a girth.
**FOCUS**
Quite a competitive little maiden but the front four finished in a bit of a heap suggesting the form isn't anything to get too excited about.

## 5623 TOTEPOOL SUPPORTING THE SPORT YOU LOVE H'CAP 6f
3:30 (3:33) (Class 2) (0-100,98) 3-Y-O+ £11,971 (£3,583; £1,791; £896; £446) **Stalls** Centre

Form RPR
1301 1 **Forest Edge (IRE)**[14] 5152 5-9-4 92 (b) JFEgan 1 101
(David Evans) *chsd ldr: rdn and effrt 2f out: drvn to ld 1f out: hrd pressed fnl 75yds: hld on gamely: all out* **12/1**
6410 2 nse **Liberty Jack (IRE)**[23] 4783 4-8-9 83 (p) HarryBentley 10 92
(Jim Boyle) *stdd s: t.k.h: hld up in tch in rr: hdwy over 1f out: rdn: edgd lft but str run to chal fnl 75yds: r.o: jst hld* **6/1**
-000 3 1 ½ **Secondo (FR)**[20] 4892 4-9-1 89 (p) GeorgeBaker 5 93
(Roger Charlton) *stdd s: hld up in tch in rr: hdwy over 1f out: drvn and chsd ldrs ins fnl f: no imp fnl 75yds* **4/1**[2]
1423 4 nk **Peace Seeker**[24] 4765 6-9-2 90 (t) WilliamCarson 2 93
(Anthony Carson) *led: rdn over 1f out: hdd 1f out: no ex and styd on same pce ins fnl f* **16/1**
2010 5 ½ **Joey's Destiny (IRE)**[20] 4895 4-9-2 95 DanielMuscutt(5) 8 96
(George Baker) *wl in tch and travelled strly in midfield: effrt and hung lft u.p over 1f out: styd on same pce ins fnl f* **3/1**[1]
0060 6 hd **Annunciation**[13] 5160 4-9-10 98 SebSanders 4 99
(Richard Hannon) *in tch in midfield: effrt u.p over 1f out: drvn and styd on same pce ins fnl f* **16/1**
6654 7 ½ **Gabbiano**[28] 4609 5-8-10 84 HayleyTurner 3 83
(Jeremy Gask) *stdd s: hld up in tch in rr: hdwy to chse ldrs 2f out: unable qck u.p over 1f out: wknd ins fnl f* **7/1**
3404 8 1 ¼ **Gramercy (IRE)**[13] 5189 7-8-11 85 StevieDonohoe 6 80
(David Simcock) *in tch towards rr: rdn 2f out: kpt on same pce u.p fr over 1f out* **7/1**
30-5 9 2 ½ **Cheveton**[19] 4946 10-8-1 80 PhilipPrince(5) 9 67
(Richard Price) *stdd and shifted rt s: in tch towards rr: hdwy 1/2-way: wknd u.p ent fnl f* **33/1**
0100 10 ½ **Deeds Not Words (IRE)**[13] 5165 3-9-4 95 SamHitchcott 7 81
(Mick Channon) *chsd ldrs: rdn 2f out: sn struggling and lost pl: wknd 1f out* **14/1**
1150 11 ¾ **Daylight**[20] 4892 4-8-8 85 (t) ThomasBrown(3) 11 68
(Andrew Balding) *in tch in midfield: rdn 2f out: no rspnse and sn lost pl: bhd 1f out* **5/1**[3]
1m 8.5s (-1.50) **Going Correction** -0.025s/f (Good)
**WFA** 3 from 4yo+ 3lb 11 Ran SP% **130.0**
Speed ratings (Par 109): **109,108,106,106,105 105,104,103,99,99 98**
CSF £91.15 CT £360.86 TOTE £11.50: £4.10, £3.10, £1.60; EX 66.60 Trifecta £1724.70.
**Owner** P & K Swinnerton **Bred** Alberto Panetta **Trained** Pandy, Monmouths
**FOCUS**
A competitive sprint handicap run at a sound clip and no reason why this form shouldn't stand up.

# 4892 GOODWOOD (R-H)
Friday, August 22

**OFFICIAL GOING: Good (7.3)**
Wind: Moderate, half against Weather: Fine but cloudy Rails: Rail on Lower bend moved out 6yds and distances increased by 10yds

## 5624 DOOM BAR APPRENTICE STKS (H'CAP) 6f
5:10 (5:12) (Class 5) (0-70,70) 3-Y-0+ **£3,234** (£962; £481; £240) **Stalls** High

Form RPR
0623 1 **Lindart (ITY)**[11] 5247 3-9-1 67 (b) GaryMahon(7) 7 78+
(Richard Hannon) *racd against nr side rail: prom: rdn over 2f out: led over 1f out: styd on wl: eased last 50yds* **14/1**
3243 2 1 ¼ **Lucky Di**[8] 5355 4-9-13 69 CharlesBishop 8 75
(Peter Hedger) *trckd ldrs: prog to ld 2f out: hdd and one pce over 1f out* **3/1**[1]
0302 3 1 ¾ **Freddy With A Y (IRE)**[27] 4674 4-9-7 70 (p) HectorCrouch(7) 5 70
(Gary Moore) *led: rdn and hdd 2f out: edgd rt and wl hld after: one pce* **3/1**[1]
5452 4 ½ **Diamond Vine (IRE)**[17] 5000 6-8-9 51 oh6 (p) RyanTate 6 50
(Ronald Harris) *in tch in rr: struggling sn after 1/2-way: kpt on fr over 1f out: nrst fin* **16/1**
3554 5 1 ¼ **Fair Ranger**[9] 5314 3-9-8 70 CamHardie(3) 1 65
(Richard Hannon) *in tch and racd wdst of all: outpcd fr 2f out: plugged on u.p fnl f* **6/1**[3]
5012 6 nse **Chevise (IRE)**[35] 4401 6-9-0 61 (b) KieranShoemark(5) 9 56
(Steve Woodman) *in tch in rr: rdn and struggling 1/2-way: nvr on terms after: plugged on* **5/1**[2]
660 7 nse **Valmina**[24] 4762 7-9-10 69 (t) GeorgeDowning(3) 4 63
(Tony Carroll) *v reluctant to enter stalls: sed awkwardly: in tch in rr: prog over 2f out: rdn to chal wl over 1f out: fnd little and wknd fnl f* **10/1**
2104 8 1 **Douneedahand**[9] 5307 3-8-13 63 ChrisMeehan(5) 3 54
(Seamus Mullins) *pressed ldrs tl steadily wknd fr 2f out* **25/1**
0536 9 3 ¾ **Night Trade (IRE)**[8] 5355 7-8-5 52 (p) DavidParkes(5) 2 31
(Ronald Harris) *trckd ldrs tl wknd qckly 2f out* **16/1**
1m 12.66s (0.46) **Going Correction** +0.175s/f (Good)
**WFA** 3 from 4yo+ 3lb 9 Ran SP% **112.3**
Speed ratings (Par 103): **103,101,99,98,96 96,96,95,90**
CSF £54.09 CT £162.03 TOTE £14.50: £4.20, £1.80, £1.20; EX 58.90 Trifecta £286.30.
**Owner** Richard Hannon **Bred** Giacinto Guglielmi Az Ag Sant'Agostino E **Trained** East Everleigh, Wilts
**FOCUS**
A modest apprentice handicap in which those racing nearest the rail came off best. The winner may yet to a bit better.

## 5625 DOCKER HUGHES MAIDEN STKS (BOBIS RACE) 1m
5:40 (5:44) (Class 4) 2-Y-O **£5,175** (£1,540; £769; £384) **Stalls** Low

Form RPR
6 1 **Best Of Times**[42] 4167 2-9-5 0 FrederikTylicki 6 88+
(Saeed bin Suroor) *t.k.h early: trckd ldrs: prog to ld wl over 1f out: clr fnl f: pushed out* **6/5**[1]
0 2 3 **Marma's Boy**[35] 4395 2-9-5 0 RichardKingscote 7 78
(Ralph Beckett) *trckd ldr: rdn to chal 2f out: wnr sn wnt by: chsd after and kpt on but no imp* **16/1**
6222 3 1 ½ **Silver Ranger**[22] 4809 2-9-0 82 CamHardie(5) 2 75
(Richard Hannon) *sltly awkward s: hld up in 8th: prog over 2f out: rdn and styd on to take 3rd ins fnl f: no ch* **2/1**[2]
02 4 3 ½ **Dutch Portrait**[17] 5009 2-9-5 0 LukeMorris 1 67
(Paul Cole) *mde most to wl over 1f out: steadily wknd* **12/1**
0 5 1 ½ **Explain**[43] 4109 2-9-5 0 SteveDrowne 4 63
(Martyn Meade) *cl up: nt clr run briefly on inner over 2f out: fdd fr over 1f out* **50/1**
6 ¾ **Dartmouth** 2-9-5 0 TedDurcan 5 61
(Sir Michael Stoute) *dwlt: in tch in midfield: shkn up and no prog wl over 2f out: sn outpcd and btn* **7/1**[3]
040 7 1 ½ **Silver Quay (IRE)**[20] 4896 2-9-5 67 JimCrowley 10 58
(Richard Hannon) *trckd ldng pair on outer: hanging and wknd 2f out* **20/1**
5 8 ¾ **Le Torrent**[12] 5212 2-9-5 0 FrankieMcDonald 9 56
(Henry Candy) *in tch: shkn up over 3f out: sn outpcd and btn* **33/1**
9 12 **Brigand Chief** 2-8-12 0 KieranShoemark(7) 8 29
(Luke Dace) *dwlt: rn green and a in last pair: struggling over 3f out: t.o* **100/1**
10 28 **St Lawrence Gap (IRE)** 2-9-5 0 TomQueally 3
(Robert Mills) *s.s: rn green in last pair: wl t.o* **33/1**
1m 39.52s (-0.38) **Going Correction** +0.075s/f (Good) 10 Ran SP% **118.5**
Speed ratings (Par 96): **104,101,99,96,94 93,92,91,79,51**
CSF £22.42 TOTE £2.30: £1.10, £4.30, £1.10; EX 28.40 Trifecta £100.20.
**Owner** Godolphin **Bred** Darley **Trained** Newmarket, Suffolk
**FOCUS**
A fair juvenile maiden, but only three mattered in the betting beforehand and the winner was value for extra.

## 5626 DOOM BAR FILLIES' NURSERY STKS (H'CAP) (BOBIS RACE) 7f
6:15 (6:16) (Class 4) (0-85,79) 2-Y-O **£5,453** (£1,610; £805) **Stalls** Low

Form RPR
21 1 **Arethusa**[34] 4444 2-9-4 76 JimCrowley 2 82
(Ed Dunlop) *trckd ldng pair after 1f: shkn up over 2f out: rdn to go 2nd over 1f out: styd on to ld last 120yds* **3/1**[2]
2522 2 ½ **Persun**[6] 5436 2-9-3 78 CharlesBishop(3) 3 83
(Mick Channon) *led: shkn up 2f out: rdn and pressed 1f out: hdd and nt qckn last 120yds* **2/1**[1]
221 3 1 ½ **Gleneely Girl (IRE)**[26] 4701 2-8-6 71 KieranShoemark(7) 7 72+
(Rae Guest) *trckd ldr 1f: sn in midfield: shkn up over 2f out: styd on u.p over 1f out to take 3rd last 100yds: nvr able to threaten* **6/1**[3]
551 4 ¾ **Sallabeh**[18] 4980 2-8-13 71 TomQueally 1 70
(George Margarson) *hld up towards rr: rdn over 2f out: styd on fr over 1f out to take 4th nr fin* **7/1**
005 5 ½ **Lady Mascot (IRE)**[34] 4444 2-8-2 65 CamHardie(5) 6 62
(Richard Hannon) *trckd ldr after 1f: rdn 2f out: edgd rt and nt qckn: lost 2nd over 1f out: lost 2 more pls last 100yds* **10/1**
540 6 3 ¾ **Rosie Royale (IRE)**[28] 4604 2-8-11 69 FrederikTylicki 4 56
(Roger Teal) *hld up towards rr: pushed along over 2f out: no prog and steadily fdd wl over 1f out* **33/1**
0020 7 hd **Cajoling (IRE)**[20] 4913 2-9-7 79 RichardKingscote 5 66
(Jonathan Portman) *sn trckd ldrs on outer: shkn up over 2f out: wknd tamely wl over 1f out* **14/1**
5100 8 ½ **Showcard**[21] 4853 2-9-3 75 [1] LiamKeniry 8 60
(Gary Moore) *late on to the crse: dwlt: hld up in last: shkn up and no prog 1/2-way: nvr a factor* **16/1**
1m 28.61s (1.61) **Going Correction** +0.075s/f (Good) 8 Ran SP% **109.7**
Speed ratings (Par 93): **93,92,90,89,89 85,84,84**
CSF £8.57 CT £28.72 TOTE £4.30: £1.70, £1.10, £2.00; EX 9.40 Trifecta £35.50.
**Owner** The Serendipity Partnership **Bred** Highbury Stud & John Troy **Trained** Newmarket, Suffolk
**FOCUS**
A competitive nursery that went more or less to market expectations.

## 5627 BREEDERS BACKING RACING EBF FILLIES' STKS (H'CAP) 1m
6:45 (6:45) (Class 3) (0-95,90) 3-Y-O+ **£9,703** (£2,887; £1,443; £721) **Stalls** Low

Form RPR
1330 1 **Saucy Minx (IRE)**[22] 4827 4-9-4 82 (b) JimCrowley 1 91
(Amanda Perrett) *trckd ldng pair: waiting for a gap 2f out: wnt 2nd over 1f out: drvn and styd on wl to ld last 75yds* **10/1**

-010 2 nk **Hiking (USA)**[23] 4782 3-9-0 **84** RichardKingscote 2 91
(Roger Charlton) *led at ordinary pce but untrbld: kicked on over 2f out: drvn over 1f out: hdd last 75yds: styd on* **3/1**[2]

1204 3 1 **Stereo Love (FR)**[41] 4211 3-8-9 **79** LukeMorris 7 84
(Clive Cox) *trckd ldr: rdn 2f out: edgd lft and nt qckn over 1f out: sn lost 2nd and one pce after* **14/1**

021 4 4 **Rekdhat (IRE)**[39] 4271 3-9-2 **86** FrederikTylicki 5 82
(Roger Varian) *t.k.h: trckd ldng trio: shkn up and nt qckn jst over 2f out: steadily lft bhd after* **4/1**[3]

21 5 1 1/4 **Momayyaz (IRE)**[17] 5007 3-8-11 **88** AhmadAlSubousi(7) 4 81
(Saeed bin Suroor) *t.k.h early: hld up in 6th in modly run event: hung lft whn asked to make prog over 2f out: sn btn* **8/1**

2250 6 1 1/2 **Musicora**[27] 4668 3-9-1 **90** CamHardie(5) 3 79
(Richard Hannon) *t.k.h early: hld up in 5th in modly run event: shkn up 2f out: no prog and sn btn* **7/1**

4305 7 2 **Psychometry (FR)**[13] 5176 3-9-6 **90** TedDurcan 6 75
(Sir Michael Stoute) *hld up in last in modly run event: tried to make prog jst over 2f out but ldrs nt stopping: sn btn: eased ins fnl f* **11/4**[1]

1m 40.26s (0.36) **Going Correction** +0.075s/f (Good)
**WFA** 3 from 4yo 6lb **7 Ran SP% 111.0**
Speed ratings (Par 104): **101,100,99,95,94 92,90**
CSF £37.73 TOTE £7.20: £2.40, £2.50; EX 49.90 Trifecta £516.40.
**Owner** Mr & Mrs F Cotton, Mr & Mrs P Conway **Bred** Summerhill & J Osborne **Trained** Pulborough, W Sussex

**FOCUS**
The feature race and a decent fillies' handicap run 0.74secs slower than the earlier maiden.

## 5628 CHICHESTER CITY STKS (H'CAP) 2m
**7:20** (7:20) (Class 5) (0-70,70) 3-Y-O **£3,234** (£962; £481; £240) **Stalls** Low

Form RPR

1526 1 **Frederic Chopin**[23] 4803 3-9-1 64 (t) RichardHughes 3 68
(Stuart Williams) *hld up in last pair: gd prog over 2f out: shkn up to ld jst over 1f out: rdn out* **7/1**

0-51 2 1 1/4 **Moscato**[22] 4834 3-9-5 68 LukeMorris 5 71
(Sir Mark Prescott Bt) *trckd ldr: shkn up 4f out: drvn to ld 2f out and edgd lft: hdd jst over 1f out: kpt on one pce u.p* **1/1**[1]

5304 3 1/2 **Arcamante (ITY)**[23] 4803 3-9-7 70 (e) JimCrowley 1 72
(K R Burke) *stdd s: hld up in last pair: prog on outer over 2f out: drvn over 1f out: kpt on to take 3rd ins fnl f* **7/2**[2]

0664 4 1 **Nelson Of The Nile**[17] 5011 3-8-13 62 RichardKingscote 8 63
(Jonathan Portman) *trckd ldng pair: rdn over 2f out: sn chalng: nt qckn over 1f out: one pce after* **6/1**[3]

0443 5 1 1/2 **Oakbank (USA)**[2] 5556 3-7-11 51 oh4 CamHardie(5) 6 50
(Brett Johnson) *trckd ldng pair: rdn over 3f out: sn lost pl: tried to rally over 1f out: no imp fnl f* **10/1**

0-00 6 1 **Hopeigetlucky**[30] 4543 3-8-2 51 oh6 KieranO'Neill 4 49
(Stuart Kittow) *w.w towards rr: rdn over 3f out: last whn nt clr run jst over 2f out: plugged on* **40/1**

-055 7 1 1/2 **Mr Wickfield**[16] 5062 3-8-9 58 TedDurcan 7 54
(John Best) *hld up in midfield: shkn up 3f out: no prog over 2f out: one pce after* **33/1**

0063 8 26 **Rookery (IRE)**[20] 4910 3-9-2 65 SteveDrowne 2 30
(Roger Ingram) *led: rdn and hdd 2f out: wknd qckly over 1f out: virtually p.u nr fin* **25/1**

3m 36.22s (7.22) **Going Correction** +0.075s/f (Good) **8 Ran SP% 117.3**
Speed ratings (Par 100): **84,83,83,82,81 81,80,67**
CSF £14.71 CT £30.06 TOTE £5.00: £1.80, £1.10, £1.50; EX 13.00 Trifecta £54.10.
**Owner** Mrs A Shone **Bred** Brook Stud **Trained** Newmarket, Suffolk

**FOCUS**
A modest staying handicap for 3yos run at an ordinary gallop, but the first and third came from the back.

## 5629 DOOM BAR STKS (H'CAP) 7f
**7:50** (7:52) (Class 5) (0-75,75) 3-Y-O+ **£3,234** (£962; £481; £240) **Stalls** Low

Form RPR

031 1 **Aqua Ardens (GER)**[36] 4352 6-9-10 74 (t) TedDurcan 6 87
(George Baker) *hld up in 10th: gd prog on outer fr 2f out: swept into the ld last 150yds: styd on strly* **8/1**

-211 2 2 **Wordismybond**[7] 5383 5-9-6 70 RichardHughes 10 78
(Peter Makin) *hld up in midfield: plld out and prog over 1f out: brought to chal fnl f as wnr swept past: styd on but outpcd* **3/1**[1]

1500 3 3/4 **Realize**[16] 5031 4-9-2 73 (p) CharlieBennett(7) 5 79
(Hughie Morrison) *hld up in midfield: cl enough and shkn up 2f out: styd on same pce fnl f to take 3rd nr fin* **9/1**

0003 4 nk **Al Manaal**[18] 4982 4-9-7 74 CharlesBishop(3) 3 79
(Mick Channon) *led: hrd rdn over 2f out: hdd and one pce last 150yds* **12/1**

254 5 1 **Alnoomaas (IRE)**[93] 2471 5-9-2 66 LukeMorris 1 68
(Luke Dace) *trckd ldrs: tried to chal on inner wl over 1f out: outpcd and edgd lft u.p fnl f* **12/1**

0200 6 shd **Snow Bay**[13] 5197 8-9-8 72 JimCrowley 11 74
(Paul Midgley) *w.w in rr: pushed along 3f out: no prog tl kpt on u.p fnl f* **25/1**

3306 7 1 1/2 **Dana's Present**[18] 4968 5-9-5 69 LiamKeniry 4 67
(George Baker) *trckd ldr: poised to chal gng strly over 2f out: rdn wl over 1f out: fnd nil and sn lost pl* **12/1**

0-54 8 hd **Lunette (IRE)**[35] 4408 4-9-5 69 RichardKingscote 2 67
(Ralph Beckett) *hld up towards rr on inner: tried to make prog 2f out: no hdwy over 1f out* **5/1**[3]

2516 9 1 **Supersta**[15] 5081 3-9-4 73 (p) SteveDrowne 8 66
(Ronald Harris) *rel to r: virtually t.o tl styd on fr over 1f out* **20/1**

5251 10 hd **Half Way**[16] 5044 3-9-0 74 AmyScott(5) 9 67
(Henry Candy) *trckd ldng pair: shkn up to chal 2f out: wknd jst over 1f out* **4/1**[2]

1046 11 2 1/2 **After The Goldrush**[18] 4982 3-9-1 75 (b) CamHardie(5) 7 61
(Richard Hannon) *chsd ldrs: pushed along bef 1/2-way: in tch 2f out: sn wknd* **25/1**

1m 26.74s (-0.26) **Going Correction** +0.075s/f (Good)
**WFA** 3 from 4yo+ 5lb **11 Ran SP% 118.3**
Speed ratings (Par 103): **104,101,100,100,99 99,97,97,96,95 93**
CSF £31.57 CT £225.77 TOTE £8.90: £2.30, £1.60, £3.80; EX 30.20 Trifecta £289.10.
**Owner** C.E.S Baker **Bred** Gestut Karlshof **Trained** Manton, Wilts

**FOCUS**
A competitive handicap run 1.87sec faster than the earlier nursery.
T/Plt: £15.80 to a £1 stake. Pool: £51,999.25 - 2390.07 winning units. T/Qpdt: £11.50 to a £1 stake. Pool: £4630.51 - 296.47 winning units. JN

# [4899]HAMILTON (R-H)
Friday, August 22

**OFFICIAL GOING: Good to soft (soft in places; 6.8)**
Wind: Virtually Nil Weather: Overcast Rails: Rail movement around the loop reduced distances on Round course by about 25yds

## 5630 LADBROKES NURSERY H'CAP 6f 5y
**5:30** (5:33) (Class 5) (0-70,67) 2-Y-O **£3,234** (£962; £481; £240) **Stalls** High

Form RPR

6411 1 **White Vin Jan**[3] 5525 2-8-8 59 6ex LouisSteward(5) 5 67+
(Michael Bell) *trckd ldng pair: led gng wl over 1f out: sn asserted: rdn and edgd rt appr fnl f: diminishing advantage nr fin but a holding on* **11/10**[1]

455 2 hd **Saltarello (IRE)**[15] 5078 2-9-7 67 PhillipMakin 9 74
(John Quinn) *midfield: rdn over 2f out: stl only 5th 1f out: styd on wl* **11/2**[2]

3442 3 3 **Indian Champ**[10] 5285 2-9-2 67 ShaneGray(5) 1 65
(Kevin Ryan) *led: rdn whn hdd over 1f out: one pce* **6/1**[3]

630 4 1/2 **Spirit Of The Sea (IRE)**[18] 4973 2-8-10 56 FergalLynch 2 53
(Jim Goldie) *sltly hmpd s: hld up: pushed along 1/2-way: kpt on ins fnl f* **10/1**

4344 5 1 1/2 **Bahango (IRE)**[10] 5266 2-9-5 65 (p) JamesSullivan 8 57
(Kristin Stubbs) *chsd ldng pair: rdn 1/2-way: wknd ins fnl f* **14/1**

5324 6 3/4 **Penalty Scorer**[7] 5384 2-8-7 53 (e) JoeFanning 6 43
(Richard Guest) *in tch on outer: rdn over 2f out: wknd fnl f* **16/1**

035 7 nk **Call Me Crockett (IRE)**[15] 5099 2-9-2 62 DuranFentiman 3 51
(Richard Guest) *hld up: rdn over 2f out: nvr threatened* **28/1**

051 8 3 1/2 **Smart Stepper (IRE)**[13] 5194 2-8-11 60 ConnorBeasley(3) 4 39
(Michael Dods) *w ldr: rdn 1/2-way: wknd over 1f out* **10/1**

2156 9 2 3/4 **Cabbies Lou**[37] 4313 2-9-7 67 PJMcDonald 7 38
(Noel Wilson) *dwlt: hld up: drvn 1/2-way: a bhd* **66/1**

1m 15.0s (2.80) **Going Correction** +0.40s/f (Good) **9 Ran SP% 113.0**
Speed ratings (Par 94): **97,96,92,92,90 89,88,84,80**
CSF £7.04 CT £24.67 TOTE £2.00: £1.10, £1.40, £1.90; EX 9.90 Trifecta £33.80.
**Owner** Middleham Park Racing XXIII & Partner **Bred** Redmyre Bloodstock Ltd **Trained** Newmarket, Suffolk

**FOCUS**
Plenty of unexposed types in this nursery which was run at a fair pace. The winner looks ahead of the game.

## 5631 TOUGH CONSTRUCTION 40TH ANNIVERSARY H'CAP 6f 5y
**6:05** (6:05) (Class 6) (0-65,64) 3-Y-O **£2,045** (£603; £302) **Stalls** Centre

Form RPR

4316 1 **Bearskin (IRE)**[15] 5089 3-9-4 61 (b) PJMcDonald 3 68
(Ann Duffield) *chsd ldrs: rdn over 2f out: kpt on: led 25yds out* **9/4**[1]

500 2 3/4 **Sketch Map (IRE)**[15] 5084 3-8-7 50 (b[1]) JamesSullivan 7 54
(Jedd O'Keeffe) *prom: rdn over 2f out: wandered appr fnl f: kpt on* **17/2**

0200 3 hd **Chookie's Lass**[21] 4861 3-9-7 64 TomEaves 4 67
(Keith Dalgleish) *prom: rdn to ld narrowly over 2f out: hdd 25yds out: wknd and lost anther pl nr fin* **16/1**

6620 4 2 1/4 **Secret Applause**[23] 4796 3-8-13 59 ConnorBeasley(3) 9 55
(Michael Dods) *hld up in rr: rdn 1/2-way: kpt on fnl f: nvr threatened* **6/1**[2]

3035 5 1/2 **Raise A Billion**[31] 4512 3-8-5 53 ow1 KevinStott(5) 5 47
(Alan Berry) *sn outpcd in rr: kpt on fnl f* **9/1**

6-10 6 2 3/4 **Autumn Tide (IRE)**[11] 5237 3-8-12 55 (t) BenCurtis 10 40
(Adrian Paul Keatley, Ire) *racd alone towards stands' rail: rdn over 2f out: wknd fnl f* **7/1**

45-0 7 1 3/4 **Captain Gee**[7] 5389 3-8-12 55 PhillipMakin 1 35
(John Quinn) *midfield: rdn over 2f out: wknd fnl f* **20/1**

435 8 1 **Sleeper Class**[13] 5169 3-9-7 64 FergalLynch 2 41
(Jim Goldie) *midfield: rdn and outpcd 1/2-way: wknd fnl f* **13/2**[3]

4330 9 3 1/2 **Soul Instinct**[18] 4974 3-8-9 57 ShaneGray(5) 6 22
(Kevin Ryan) *led narrowly: rdn whn hdd over 2f out: sn wknd* **12/1**

4030 10 18 **Starlite Jewel**[11] 5233 3-8-5 51 DuranFentiman(3) 8
(Stuart Coltherd) *virtually ref to r: a wl bhd* **25/1**

1m 14.62s (2.42) **Going Correction** +0.40s/f (Good) **10 Ran SP% 113.6**
Speed ratings (Par 98): **99,98,97,94,94 90,88,86,82,58**
CSF £21.19 CT £243.39 TOTE £2.20: £1.10, £3.20, £5.90; EX 30.20 Trifecta £233.50.
**Owner** Evelyn Duchess Of Sutherland **Bred** T Kenny & P Byrne **Trained** Constable Burton, N Yorks

**FOCUS**
The pace was honest for this modest handicap. The field raced mainly up the centre.

## 5632 DOWNLOAD THE LADBROKES APP H'CAP 6f 5y
**6:35** (6:39) (Class 4) (0-85,84) 3-Y-O+ **£5,175** (£1,540; £769; £192; £192) **Stalls** Centre

Form RPR

135 1 **Red Pike (IRE)**[14] 5143 3-9-7 84 PhillipMakin 9 95+
(Bryan Smart) *mde all: pushed along over 2f out: rdn over 1f out: edgd lft ent fnl f: kpt on wl* **11/4**[1]

6451 2 2 **Klynch**[11] 5236 8-9-5 79 6ex (b) JamesSullivan 8 84
(Ruth Carr) *hld up: rdn and hdwy to chse wnr over 1f out: sn hung rt: kpt on same pce* **7/1**[3]

0500 3 nse **Rasaman (IRE)**[15] 5081 10-9-7 81 FergalLynch 5 86
(Jim Goldie) *in tch: rdn over 2f out: kpt on ins fnl f* **22/1**

4630 4 1 1/4 **Sunraider (IRE)**[13] 5199 7-9-5 79 PJMcDonald 11 80
(Paul Midgley) *hld up: rdn 1/2-way: kpt on fnl f* **12/1**

5304 4 dht **Lothair (IRE)**[5] 5470 5-8-9 69 BenCurtis 2 70
(Alan Swinbank) *prom: rdn over 2f out: one pce and hld in 4th whn bmpd ins fnl f* **7/2**[2]

255 6 1 1/2 **Bunce (IRE)**[2] 5563 6-9-4 78 TomEaves 1 74
(Linda Perratt) *hld up in tch: rdn 2f out: one pce* **14/1**

6532 7 nse **Ralphy Boy (IRE)**[14] 5143 5-8-13 78 GarryWhillans(5) 4 74
(Alistair Whillans) *prom: rdn over 2f out: lost pl and already hld whn sltly short of room ins fnl f* **10/1**

/000 8 3 1/2 **Gabrial's Bounty (IRE)**[42] 4161 5-8-7 70 GeorgeChaloner(3) 10 55
(Richard Fahey) *chsd ldrs: rdn 1/2-way: wknd fnl f* **11/1**

0500 9 2 1/4 **Unsinkable (IRE)**[11] 5238 4-9-3 77 DuranFentiman 3 54
(Ian Semple) *slowly away: hld up: rdn over 2f out: sn wknd* **40/1**

1m 13.66s (1.46) **Going Correction** +0.40s/f (Good)
**WFA** 3 from 4yo+ 3lb **9 Ran SP% 100.0**
Speed ratings (Par 105): **106,103,103,101,101 99,99,94,91**
CSF £16.46 CT £206.22 TOTE £2.90: £1.30, £2.00, £5.60; EX 14.90 Trifecta £383.30.
**Owner** Sir A Ferguson, P Deal & G Lowe **Bred** Mrs M Marnane **Trained** Hambleton, N Yorks
■ Beautiful Stranger and Half A Billion were withdrawn. Prices at time of withdrawal 12-1 and 8-1. Rule 4 applies to all bets - deduction 15p in the pound.

**FOCUS**
A competitive sprint handicap run at a decent pace.

## 5633 LADBROKES LANARK SILVER BELL H'CAP 1m 4f 17y
7:05 (7:11) (Class 3) (0-90,90) 3-Y-O+
£16,185 (£4,846; £2,423; £1,211; £605; £304) Stalls Low

Form RPR
0464 1 **Swivel**[13] 5164 3-8-8 87 KevinStott(5) 11 97
(Mark Johnston) *hld up: rdn and stl in rr over 2f out: rdr dropped whip 2f out: r.o strly fr over 1f out: led 25yds out* 9/2[2]
-602 2 1 1/4 **Satanic Beat (IRE)**[23] 4454 5-9-1 79 RussKennemore 4 87
(Jedd O'Keeffe) *trckd ldrs: rdn to ld over 2f out: kpt on: hdd 25yds out* 16/1
6103 3 1 1/2 **Linguine (FR)**[28] 4622 4-9-10 88 PJMcDonald 5 94
(Paul Midgley) *midfield: rdn and hdwy to chse ldr over 2f out: kpt on* 25/1
4152 4 1 **Mister Fizz**[7] 5379 6-9-2 85 EoinWalsh(5) 2 90
(Miss Imogen Pickard) *trckd ldrs: rdn and lost pl over 2f out: swtchd lft on: kpt on fnl f* 8/1
11 5 1/2 **Wee Frankie (IRE)**[49] 3923 3-8-13 87 PhillipMakin 1 90
(Keith Dalgleish) *in tch: pushed along over 3f out: rdn 2f out: one pce* 3/1[1]
1410 6 1/2 **Corton Lad**[22] 4827 4-9-7 85 (tp) TomEaves 3 87
(Keith Dalgleish) *led: rdn whn hdd over 2f out: no ex fnl f* 28/1
32 7 1/2 **Dark Ruler (IRE)**[14] 5144 5-9-7 85 BenCurtis 12 87
(Alan Swinbank) *midfield: rdn over 2f out: one pce* 13/2
1051 8 1/2 **Dance King**[26] 4710 4-9-4 82 DavidAllan 6 83
(Tim Easterby) *midfield: rdn and hdwy to chse ldr wl over 1f out: wknd ins fnl f* 12/1
3455 9 2 1/2 **Local Hero (GER)**[17] 4995 7-8-10 77 (p) GeorgeChaloner(3) 9 74
(Steve Gollings) *slowly away: hld up in rr: a bhd* 14/1
5000 10 nk **Beaumont's Party (IRE)**[11] 5238 7-9-6 87 ConnorBeasley(3) 7 83
(Brian Ellison) *midfield: rdn over 2f out: sn btn* 25/1
1424 11 3 1/4 **Memory Cloth**[58] 3574 7-8-11 82 MeganCarberry(7) 8 73
(Brian Ellison) *hld up: sme hdwy on outer 4f out: rdn over 2f out: wknd appr fnl f* 16/1
6115 12 14 **Special Fighter (IRE)**[14] 5132 3-9-2 90 JoeFanning 10 59
(Mark Johnston) *prom: rdn over 3f out: wknd over 2f out: eased* 11/2[3]

2m 37.08s (-1.52) **Going Correction** +0.05s/f (Good)
**WFA** 3 from 4yo+ 10lb 12 Ran SP% 120.3
Speed ratings (Par 107): **107,106,105,104,104 103,103,103,101,101 99,89**
CSF £73.63 CT £1638.16 TOTE £6.30: £2.80, £7.00, £7.00; EX 119.80 Trifecta £1309.90.
**Owner** Sheikh Hamdan bin Mohammed Al Maktoum **Bred** Stratford Place Stud And Watership Down **Trained** Middleham Moor, N Yorks

**FOCUS**
A typically competitive renewal of the Silver Bell which was run at an honest pace. The form looks sound.

## 5634 AWARD WINNING SCULLION LAW OPEN MAIDEN STKS 1m 1f 36y
7:40 (7:40) (Class 5) 3-Y-O+ £3,234 (£962; £481; £240) Stalls Low

Form RPR
5 1 **Mistiroc**[20] 4886 3-9-5 0 FergalLynch 4 87
(Jim Goldie) *hld up in 4th: rdn and gd hdwy over 2f out: led 2f out: drvn fnl f: kpt on* 33/1[3]
6222 2 1 1/2 **Almashooqa (USA)**[41] 4211 3-9-0 87 JackMitchell 1 79
(Roger Varian) *in tch in 3rd: pushed along to chse ldr over 2f out: drvn over 1f out: one pce* 2/7[1]
0254 3 1 1/2 **Potent Embrace (USA)**[13] 5196 3-9-0 72 JoeFanning 2 76
(Mark Johnston) *led: rdn whn hdd 2f out: lost 2nd 110yds out: wknd* 3/1[2]
4530 4 33 **Haidees Reflection**[13] 5166 4-9-0 48 MeganCarberry(7) 3
(Lucy Normile) *trckd ldr: briefly pressed ldr over 3f out: sn rdn: wknd over 2f out* 100/1

2m 0.05s (0.35) **Going Correction** +0.05s/f (Good)
**WFA** 3 from 4yo 7lb 4 Ran SP% 106.7
Speed ratings (Par 103): **100,98,97,68**
CSF £45.25 TOTE £26.60; EX 61.00 Trifecta £84.20.
**Owner** Drew & Ailsa Russell **Bred** Jethro Bloodstock **Trained** Uplawmoor, E Renfrews

**FOCUS**
An uncompetitive maiden run at a steady pace and the form is tricky to pin down.

## 5635 JORDAN ELECTRICS H'CAP 5f 4y
8:10 (8:11) (Class 6) (0-65,68) 3-Y-O+ £1,940 (£577; £288; £72; £72) Stalls Centre

Form RPR
5440 1 **Live Dangerously**[15] 5089 4-9-11 63 TomEaves 9 71
(Keith Dalgleish) *mde all: pressed thrght: rdn 1/2-way: drvn over 1f out: hld on wl: asserted fnl 50yds* 8/1
3011 2 3/4 **Perfect Words (IRE)**[7] 5375 4-9-11 68 6ex (p) JordanNason(5) 5 73
(Marjorie Fife) *pressed ldr: rdn 2f out: kpt on: hld fnl 50yds* 9/4[1]
3645 3 shd **Sewn Up**[10] 5265 4-8-11 49 (p) JoeFanning 8 54
(Keith Dalgleish) *dwlt: hld up: rdn 1/2-way: kpt on fnl f* 5/1[3]
6506 4 hd **Ingenti**[7] 5375 6-9-5 62 KevinStott(5) 3 66
(Christopher Wilson) *trckd ldng pair: rdn to chal ins fnl f: one pce* 16/1
502 4 dht **Rock Canyon (IRE)**[11] 5237 5-8-12 50 (p) PJMcDonald 7 54
(Linda Perratt) *hld up: rdn 1/2-way: kpt on fnl f: sltly short of room nr fin* 8/1
0015 6 1 1/4 **Lord Buffhead**[7] 5375 5-9-0 52 6ex (v) DuranFentiman 4 52
(Richard Guest) *hld up: rdn 1/2-way: one pce and nvr threatened* 14/1
440 7 2 1/4 **Dartrix**[7] 5390 5-9-9 64 (b[1]) ConnorBeasley(3) 1 56
(Michael Dods) *slowly away: hld up: rdn 1/2-way: wknd ins fnl f* 7/1
6/03 8 3/4 **Elusive Gent (IRE)**[3] 5539 7-8-9 47 (be[1]) BenCurtis 2 36
(Adrian Paul Keatley, Ire) *in tch on outer: rdn and lost pl 1/2-way: wknd over 1f out* 9/2[2]
6003 9 4 **Wicked Wilma (IRE)**[11] 5237 10-8-5 46 ow1 GeorgeChaloner(3) 10 21
(Alan Berry) *chsd ldng pair: rdn 1/2-way: wknd over 1f out* 20/1

1m 1.52s (1.52) **Going Correction** +0.40s/f (Good) 9 Ran SP% 117.7
Speed ratings (Par 101): **103,101,101,101,101 99,95,94,88**
CSF £26.89 CT £102.32 TOTE £10.80: £2.60, £1.40, £1.80; EX 50.30 Trifecta £174.10.
**Owner** Lamont Racing **Bred** Manor Farm Stud & Mrs A J Ralli **Trained** Carluke, S Lanarks

**FOCUS**
An open sprint handicap run at a fair pace. The form is straightforward.
T/Plt: £4,433.40 to a £1 stake. Pool: £44,638.64 - 7.35 winning units. T/Qpdt: £1,786.30 to a £1 stake. Pool: £4345.21 - 1.80 winning units. AS

# 5384 NEWCASTLE (L-H)
Friday, August 22

**OFFICIAL GOING: Good to firm (good in places; 7.7)**
Wind: light 1/2 against Weather: fine Rails: Bend after Winning Post and into home straight moved to fresh ground

## 5636 SPEEDFLEX RDA "HANDS & HEELS" APPRENTICE SERIES H'CAP (PART OF THE RACING EXCELLENCE INITIATIVE) 6f
4:50 (4:57) (Class 6) (0-65,65) 3-Y-O+ £1,940 (£577; £288; £144) Stalls Centre

Form RPR
0446 1 **Black Douglas**[2] 5565 5-8-8 51 RachaelGrant(5) 3 61
(Jim Goldie) *in rr: hdwy over 2f out: edgd lft and led over 1f out: styd on wl* 6/1
0220 2 3 1/2 **Tadalavil**[11] 5236 9-9-0 55 JoshDoyle(3) 8 54
(Linda Perratt) *t.k.h: trckd ldr: led over 2f out: hdd over 1f out: kpt on same pce* 16/1
1353 3 1 3/4 **Exotic Guest**[7] 5390 4-9-10 65 RowanScott(3) 9 58
(Ruth Carr) *hld up in rr: hdwy over 2f out: kpt on same pce fnl f* 15/8[1]
550 4 3/4 **De Lesseps (USA)**[18] 4961 6-9-0 52 RachelRichardson 7 43
(James Moffatt) *mid-div: outpcd over 2f out: styd on over 1f out* 10/1
4200 5 2 **Novalist**[38] 4288 6-8-9 47 (b) LukeLeadbitter 10 31
(Robin Bastiman) *led: drvn and hdd over 2f out: rdr sat stl and kpt on same pce last 100yds* 20/1
0446 6 3/4 **Angels Calling**[17] 5000 4-8-10 51 (p) PeterSword(3) 6 33
(K R Burke) *chsd ldrs: kpt on one pce over 1f out* 5/1[3]
0065 7 1 1/4 **Rosie Hall (IRE)**[21] 4875 4-8-5 46 oh1 ClaireMurray(3) 2 24
(Les Eyre) *racd wd: in rr-div: hdwy over 2f out: one pce* 33/1
0040 8 3 3/4 **Sunrise Dance**[15] 5089 5-9-1 56 PaddyBradley(3) 5 22
(Robert Johnson) *in rr: drvn along 3f out: nvr on terms* 16/1
666U R **Bonnie Charlie**[23] 4796 8-9-11 63 AnnaHesketh 4
(David Nicholls) *unruly and led rdrless to post: ref to r* 9/2[2]

1m 14.91s (0.31) **Going Correction** -0.075s/f (Good) 9 Ran SP% 112.5
Speed ratings (Par 101): **94,89,87,86,83 82,80,75,**
CSF £92.25 CT £246.24 TOTE £6.40: £2.20, £3.30, £1.10; EX 50.50 Trifecta £157.40.
**Owner** Johnnie Delta Racing **Bred** D P And Mrs J A Martin **Trained** Uplawmoor, E Renfrews

**FOCUS**
A low-grade apprentice event won in decent style by the winner.

## 5637 NEWLINE POLYMERS RDA NURSERY H'CAP 5f
5:25 (5:25) (Class 5) (0-75,78) 2-Y-O £2,587 (£770; £384; £192) Stalls Centre

Form RPR
3221 1 **Primrose Valley**[11] 5253 2-9-13 78 6ex (p) RoystonFfrench 10 86
(Ed Vaughan) *hld up: hdwy over 2f out: sn drvn: led 1f out: styd on* 2/1[1]
433 2 1 3/4 **Flicka's Boy**[17] 5013 2-8-13 71 MikeyEnnis(7) 7 73
(Tony Coyle) *trckd ldrs: led wl over 1f out: hdd 1f out: styd on same pce* 6/1[3]
343 3 1/2 **Scarlet Bounty (IRE)**[25] 4723 2-9-0 65 TonyHamilton 6 65
(Richard Fahey) *hld up in rr: hdwy over 1f out: kpt on to take 3rd last 50yds* 6/1[3]
1533 4 1 1/2 **Olivia Fallow (IRE)**[21] 4869 2-9-7 72 DavidNolan 9 67
(Paul Midgley) *trckd ldrs: led briefly over 2f out: kpt on same pce* 5/1[2]
0462 5 shd **Pickle Lilly Pearl**[7] 5384 2-7-12 54 SammyJoBell(5) 4 48
(David C Griffiths) *hood removed late and s.s: hld up in rr: hdwy and n.m.r 2f out: one pce* 10/1
0452 6 1 1/4 **Classic Flyer**[17] 5014 2-8-9 63 SamJames(3) 3 53
(David O'Meara) *chsd ldrs: one pce over 1f out* 7/1
650 7 1 **Shortmile Lady (IRE)**[18] 4973 2-8-9 60 AndrewMullen 5 46
(Michael Dods) *stdd s: t.k.h in rr: hdwy over 2f out: wknd last 100yds* 25/1
1034 8 5 **Lazy Days In Loule (IRE)**[49] 3909 2-8-10 61 JasonHart 1 29
(Noel Wilson) *led: hdd over 2f out: lost pl over 1f out* 20/1
0202 9 3 1/4 **Elizabeth Flynn (IRE)**[11] 5254 2-8-9 63 [1] JoeyHaynes(3) 2 19
(K R Burke) *sn chsng ldrs: lost pl over 2f out: bhd whn eased clsng stages* 20/1

1m 0.62s (-0.48) **Going Correction** -0.075s/f (Good) 9 Ran SP% 113.5
Speed ratings (Par 94): **100,97,96,94,93 91,90,82,77**
CSF £13.32 CT £60.28 TOTE £2.20: £1.20, £2.50, £1.40; EX 14.20 Trifecta £78.10.
**Owner** A M Pickering **Bred** Alan Pickering CBE **Trained** Newmarket, Suffolk

**FOCUS**
This was just a fair nursery, but the winner may have a bit more to offer.

## 5638 NORTH SEA LOGISTICS RDA H'CAP 7f
5:55 (5:55) (Class 5) (0-75,75) 3-Y-O+ £2,587 (£770; £384; £192) Stalls Centre

Form RPR
6052 1 **Kyllachy Star**[13] 5168 8-9-4 67 (v) TonyHamilton 7 75
(Richard Fahey) *in rr: sn pushed along: hdwy stands' side over 1f out: styd on wl to ld last stride* 9/1
1650 2 nse **Ted's Brother (IRE)**[9] 5320 6-9-6 74 DuilioDaSilva(5) 1 82
(Richard Guest) *s.s: hdwy over 3f out: led over 1f out: hdd post* 20/1
2323 3 hd **Invoke (IRE)**[16] 5046 3-8-11 72 MikeyEnnis(7) 3 77
(Michael Bell) *w ldrs: led over 2f out: edgd rt and hdd over 1f out: kpt on: no ex clsng stages* 11/2
3533 4 1 1/2 **Real Tigress (IRE)**[15] 5079 5-9-9 72 DavidNolan 2 75
(Les Eyre) *trckd ldrs: nt clr run over 2f out: rdn over 1f out: kpt on same pce* 3/1[1]
2524 5 shd **Whispered Times (USA)**[14] 5142 7-8-11 60 (p) RoystonFfrench 8 63
(Tracy Waggott) *t.k.h in rr: effrt over 2f out: chsng ldrs over 1f out: kpt on same pce* 8/1
0065 6 5 **Footstepsintherain (IRE)**[30] 4537 4-9-9 75 JoeyHaynes(3) 6 65
(David Dennis) *chsd ldrs: drvn 3f out: wknd fnl f* 9/1
1225 7 1 1/2 **Native Falls (IRE)**[38] 4297 3-9-0 71 NeilFarley(3) 5 55
(Alan Swinbank) *t.k.h: led: hdd over 2f out: wknd appr fnl f* 7/2[2]
10-0 8 1 **Hulcolt (IRE)**[13] 5197 3-9-3 71 JasonHart 4 53
(Garry Moss) *led: hdd over 2f out: wknd over 1f out* 5/1[3]

1m 27.85s (0.05) **Going Correction** -0.075s/f (Good)
**WFA** 3 from 4yo+ 5lb 8 Ran SP% 115.1
Speed ratings (Par 103): **96,95,95,94,93 88,86,85**
CSF £163.66 CT £1091.84 TOTE £7.00: £2.40, £4.90, £2.10; EX 74.20 Trifecta £203.60.
**Owner** Dr Marwan Koukash **Bred** John James **Trained** Musley Bank, N Yorks

**FOCUS**
A close call at the end of this 7f handicap.

## 5639 NEWCASTLE FALCONS RDA H'CAP 1m 4f 93y
6:25 (6:25) (Class 4) (0-80,79) 4-Y-0+ £4,690 (£1,395; £697; £348) Stalls Centre

Form RPR
0303 1 **A Star In My Eye (IRE)**[27] 4663 4-9-4 76 BarryMcHugh 1 85
(Kevin Ryan) *mde all: qcknd pce 7f out: clr 3f out: pushed out: unchal* **5/1**[1]
3350 2 2 **Cloud Monkey (IRE)**[20] 4921 4-8-10 68 GrahamLee 11 74
(Martin Todhunter) *hld up in last: hdwy over 2f out: styd on to take 2nd last 75yds* **7/1**
6142 3 3/4 **Testa Rossa (IRE)**[13] 5172 4-8-2 60 oh1 RoystonFfrench 6 65
(Jim Goldie) *chsd ldrs: drvn 3f out: kpt on to take 3rd last 50yds* **7/1**
-600 4 3/4 **It's A Mans World**[11] 5235 8-8-7 65 PaulPickard 8 68
(Brian Ellison) *trckd ldrs: chsd wnr over 2f out: kpt on same pce* **18/1**
3504 5 nk **Ex Oriente (IRE)**[6] 5442 5-9-4 76 AndrewMullen 5 79
(Stuart Williams) *hld up in mid-div: t.k.h: effrt 3f out: kpt on ins fnl f* **7/1**
-156 6 2 **Arthurs Secret**[70] 3205 4-8-13 71 (b) IanBrennan 3 71
(John Quinn) *drvn to chse ldrs: reminders over 5f out: one pce fnl 3f* **7/1**
6463 7 2 **Art Scholar (IRE)**[11] 5238 7-9-2 79 AlistairRawlinson(5) 9 76
(Michael Appleby) *hld up in rr: drvn over 3f out: nvr a factor* **11/2**[2]
0364 8 2 **Royal Straight**[14] 5145 9-8-1 64 (t) SammyJoBell(5) 10 57
(Linda Perratt) *s.s: hld up in rr: hdwy on ins over 3f out: n.m.r 2f out: one pce* **16/1**
036 8 dht **Love Marmalade (IRE)**[14] 5144 4-9-5 77 DavidNolan 12 70
(Alistair Whillans) *chsd wnr: wknd fnl f* **13/2**[3]
4144 10 2 3/4 **Madrasa (IRE)**[15] 5090 6-8-8 66 AndrewElliott 7 55
(Keith Reveley) *mid-div: drvn over 3f out: wknd over 1f out* **12/1**
2m 41.59s (-4.01) **Going Correction** -0.20s/f (Firm) **10 Ran SP% 114.2**
Speed ratings (Par 105): **105,103,103,102,102 101,99,98,98,96**
CSF £38.85 CT £244.01 TOTE £6.00: £4.50, £2.80, £2.70; EX 44.70 Trifecta £534.20.
**Owner** Sultan Ali **Bred** Mrs Joan Murphy **Trained** Hambleton, N Yorks
**FOCUS**
A rather muddling race for they went a moderate gallop for the first half of the race.

## 5640 STRAIGHTLINE CONSTRUCTION RDA H'CAP 1m 3y(S)
6:55 (6:57) (Class 5) (0-70,68) 3-Y-0+ £2,587 (£770; £384; £192) Stalls Centre

Form RPR
5400 1 **Broctune Papa Gio**[15] 5088 7-9-8 64 DavidNolan 13 73
(Keith Reveley) *mid-div: hdwy stands' side over 2f out: led last 50yds: jst hld on* **20/1**
4512 2 hd **Dansili Dutch (IRE)**[13] 5166 5-9-4 67 JoshDoyle(7) 5 75
(David O'Meara) *in rr: drvn over 3f out: hdwy stands' side over 1f out: styd on wl to take 2nd nr fin* **9/1**[3]
0001 3 3/4 **Sky Crossing**[23] 4797 5-8-10 52 AndrewElliott 7 58
(Tom Tate) *led: hdd wl ins fnl f: no ex* **14/1**
0004 4 1 1/4 **Outlaw Torn (IRE)**[20] 4903 5-9-2 63 (e) DuilioDaSilva(5) 9 66
(Richard Guest) *chsd ldrs: drvn 3f out: one pce fnl f* **16/1**
5212 5 1 1/2 **Grace Hull**[38] 4294 4-9-12 68 (p) JasonHart 12 67
(Garry Moss) *in rr: hdwy over 2f out: sn chsng ldrs: kpt on same pce last 150yds* **12/1**
-662 6 1 **Berbice (IRE)**[25] 4727 9-8-2 49 oh3 SammyJoBell(5) 6 46
(Linda Perratt) *s.s: t.k.h in rr: hdwy over 2f out: kpt on one pce fnl f* **50/1**
1563 7 2 1/4 **Tanawar (IRE)**[8] 5337 4-9-6 62 (b) GrahamLee 14 54
(Ruth Carr) *trckd ldr: t.k.h: wknd fnl 150yds* **11/1**
5550 8 2 3/4 **Shearian**[14] 5142 4-9-0 56 RoystonFfrench 2 42
(Tracy Waggott) *chsd ldrs: lost pl over 2f out* **25/1**
-331 9 1 1/2 **Joyful Sound (IRE)**[25] 4730 6-9-6 62 (p) DaleSwift 11 44
(Brian Ellison) *chsd ldrs: drvn over 2f out: hung rt over 1f out: sn wknd: eased clsng stages* **8/1**[2]
0126 10 1/2 **Gabrial's Hope (FR)**[33] 4470 5-9-8 64 TonyHamilton 1 45
(Tracy Waggott) *hld up in mid-div: effrt over 2f out: sn wknd* **12/1**
30-0 11 2 1/4 **Blue Maisey**[136] 1356 6-9-8 64 PaulMulrennan 10 40
(Edwin Tuer) *bhd and drvn along: sme hdwy over 2f out: wknd over 1f out: eased ins fnl f* **25/1**
-311 12 8 **Jay Kay**[3] 5530 5-8-12 57 12ex JoeyHaynes(3) 3 15
(K R Burke) *chsd ldrs on outer: drvn over 3f out: lost pl over 2f out* **5/4**[1]
3600 13 7 **Bajan Rebel**[4] 5497 3-8-10 58 (p) BarryMcHugh 4
(Michael Easterby) *chsd ldrs: lost pl over 4f out: sn bhd* **33/1**
1m 42.12s (-1.28) **Going Correction** -0.075s/f (Good)
**WFA** 3 from 4yo+ 6lb **13 Ran SP% 119.2**
Speed ratings (Par 103): **103,102,102,100,99 98,96,93,91,91 89,81,74**
CSF £180.70 CT £2689.24 TOTE £34.50: £7.60, £2.30, £4.10; EX 346.80 Trifecta £1200.50.
**Owner** D Renton C Alessi D Young Reveley Farms **Bred** Lesley Winn And Reveley Farms **Trained** Lingdale, Redcar & Cleveland
■ Stewards' Enquiry : Josh Doyle two-day ban; used whip above permitted level (5th,7th Sept)
**FOCUS**
Exposed sorts in this 1m handicap which was run at a decent gallop.

## 5641 METNOR RDA FILLIES' H'CAP 6f
7:30 (7:33) (Class 5) (0-75,76) 3-Y-0+ £2,587 (£770; £384; £192) Stalls Centre

Form RPR
3536 1 **Meandmyshadow**[7] 5398 6-9-3 68 DaleSwift 6 77
(Alan Brown) *chsd ldr: drvn 3f out: led 1f out: kpt on gamely* **11/2**[3]
2334 2 1 1/4 **Percy's Gal**[16] 5055 3-8-12 71 GemmaTutty(5) 3 76
(Karen Tutty) *t.k.h: sn led: hdd 1f out: styd on same pce* **7/2**[2]
2252 3 2 1/4 **Diamond Blue**[20] 4891 6-9-2 67 (p) TonyHamilton 8 65
(Richard Fahey) *hld up in rr: effrt over 2f out: styd on to take 3rd last 50yds* **11/4**[1]
5201 4 1 1/2 **Midnight Dynamo**[2] 5563 7-9-8 76 6ex GaryBartley(3) 1 69
(Jim Goldie) *t.k.h: swtchd rt after 100yds: hld up towards rr: hdwy over 2f out: kpt on to take 4th nr fin* **13/2**
2254 5 hd **Traditionelle**[15] 5087 3-8-6 60 AndrewElliott 2 52
(Tim Easterby) *t.k.h: led early: w ldr: edgd lft over 1f out: wknd fnl 100yds* **12/1**
10 6 1 3/4 **Ella's Delight (IRE)**[20] 4925 4-9-10 75 GrahamLee 4 62
(Martin Todhunter) *trckd ldrs: effrt 2f out: sn btn* **8/1**
3462 7 3/4 **Thornaby Princess**[8] 5333 3-8-12 66 IanBrennan 5 50
(Marjorie Fife) *dwlt: hld up in rr: effrt over 2f out: btn over 1f out* **6/1**
1m 14.05s (-0.55) **Going Correction** -0.075s/f (Good)
**WFA** 3 from 4yo+ 3lb **7 Ran SP% 110.7**
Speed ratings (Par 100): **100,98,95,93,93 90,89**
CSF £23.34 CT £60.20 TOTE £6.60: £3.60, £2.20; EX 19.40 Trifecta £83.00.
**Owner** G Morrill **Bred** M J Dawson **Trained** Yedingham, N Yorks

**FOCUS**
A muddling race as they went no gallop, plenty raced keenly enough and the first two were in the first two virtually throughout.

## 5642 BROOK TAVERNER RDA MAIDEN STKS 7f
8:00 (8:01) (Class 5) 3-4-Y-0 £2,587 (£770; £384; £192) Stalls Centre

Form RPR
6-03 1 **Abbotsfield (IRE)**[23] 4791 4-9-5 65 AndrewElliott 3 64
(Ben Haslam) *chsd ldrs: drvn over 3f out: rallied over 1f out: led last 75yds: drvn out* **10/11**[1]
3-36 2 3/4 **Cash Is King**[93] 2469 4-9-3 62 MikeyEnnis(7) 1 67
(Robert Johnson) *led: hdd and no ex last 75yds* **4/1**[3]
0-04 3 5 **Llandanwg**[20] 4900 3-9-0 46 PaulMulrennan 8 47
(Bryan Smart) *hld up in rr: effrt over 2f out: one pce over 1f out* **10/1**
052 4 5 **Aphrilis (IRE)**[11] 5246 3-9-0 0 DaleSwift 4 34
(Brian Ellison) *mid-div: drvn 4f out: hdwy over 2f out: one pce: eased towards fin* **3/1**[2]
0460 5 2 3/4 **Patron Of Explores (USA)**[23] 4795 3-9-0 48 JackGarritty(5) 2 32
(Patrick Holmes) *hld up in rr: hdwy 3f out: sn chsng ldrs: wknd over 1f out* **22/1**
0 6 7 **Katies Joy (IRE)**[20] 4900 3-8-11 0 SamJames(3) 7 9
(Ian Semple) *t.k.h: sn w ldr: wknd 2f out* **18/1**
1m 27.18s (-0.62) **Going Correction** -0.075s/f (Good)
**WFA** 3 from 4yo 5lb **6 Ran SP% 116.1**
Speed ratings (Par 103): **100,99,93,87,84 76**
CSF £5.28 TOTE £1.80: £1.10, £2.30; EX 4.70 Trifecta £26.10.
**Owner** Middleham Park Racing I **Bred** Pier House Stud & Martinstown **Trained** Middleham Moor, N Yorks
**FOCUS**
A weak maiden.
T/Plt: £201.20 to a £1 stake. Pool: £50,954.06 - 184.87 winning units. T/Qpdt: £93.10 to a £1 stake. Pool: £4999.55 - 39.70 winning units. WG

# 5436 NEWMARKET (R-H)
Friday, August 22

**OFFICIAL GOING: Good (good to firm in places; 7.3)**
Wind: Fresh half-behind Weather: Cloudy Rails: Bend into the home straight repositioned and 10f races increased by 20m

## 5643 TRM CELEBRATING 25 YEARS IN EQUINE NUTRITION EBF MAIDEN FILLIES' STKS (BOBIS RACE) (DIV I) 7f
1:35 (1:36) (Class 4) 2-Y-O £4,528 (£1,347; £673; £336) Stalls High

Form RPR
1 **Mehronissa** 2-9-0 0 FrederikTylicki 6 80+
(Ed Vaughan) *s.i.s: hld up: hdwy over 1f out: shkn up to ld wl ins fnl f: readily* **14/1**
2 1 1/4 **Housemaker** 2-9-0 0 JimCrowley 5 76+
(K R Burke) *a.p: chsd ldr over 2f out: rdn over 1f out: styd on* **10/1**
4 3 1/2 **Stay Silent (IRE)**[20] 4914 2-9-0 0 ChrisCatlin 4 75
(Saeed bin Suroor) *led: rdn over 1f out: hdd and unable qck wl ins fnl f* **10/11**[1]
4 3/4 **Illogical** 2-9-0 0 RobertHavlin 2 73+
(Ed Dunlop) *hld up: hdwy over 1f out: r.o* **20/1**
5 3 **Graceland (FR)** 2-9-0 0 WilliamTwiston-Davies 1 65
(Michael Bell) *dwlt: hld up: pushed along over 1f out: effrt and nt clr run ins fnl f: nvr trbld ldrs* **12/1**
0 6 3/4 **Bling Ring (USA)**[20] 4914 2-9-0 0 RobertWinston 10 63
(Charles Hills) *trckd ldrs: racd keenly: shkn up over 1f out: wknd ins fnl f* **9/2**[2]
7 3 1/2 **Lipstickandpowder (IRE)** 2-9-0 0 DaneO'Neill 9 53
(William Jarvis) *trckd ldr tl rdn over 2f out: wknd fnl f* **25/1**
8 2 **Ballet Of Doha (IRE)** 2-9-0 0 PatDobbs 8 48
(Richard Hannon) *prom: pushed along over 2f out: wknd over 1f out* **8/1**[3]
9 1 **Fridge Kid** 2-8-11 0 RobertTart(3) 3 45
(Dr Jon Scargill) *prom: pushed along 1/2-way: wknd 2f out* **100/1**
1m 27.4s (1.70) **Going Correction** +0.075s/f (Good) **9 Ran SP% 114.7**
Speed ratings (Par 93): **93,91,91,90,86 85,81,79,78**
CSF £139.53 TOTE £25.30: £4.00, £2.60, £1.10; EX 206.40 Trifecta £569.00.
**Owner** Salem Rashid **Bred** Carmel Stud **Trained** Newmarket, Suffolk
**FOCUS**
Despite a shower before racing, the going remained Good, good to firm in places and the jockeys in the opener generally agreed. This maiden (or a division of it) has been won by some decent fillies' over the years, including the Group 1 winner Lyric Of Light three years ago. The stalls were placed against the far rail and the field mainly stayed there. The pace looked ordinary.

## 5644 TRM CELEBRATING 25 YEARS IN EQUINE NUTRITION EBF MAIDEN FILLIES' STKS (BOBIS RACE) (DIV II) 7f
2:10 (2:12) (Class 4) 2-Y-O £4,528 (£1,347; £673; £336) Stalls High

Form RPR
4 1 **What Say You (IRE)**[28] 4604 2-9-0 0 JimCrowley 10 86+
(K R Burke) *mde all: shkn up and c clr fnl f: comf* **11/8**[1]
3 2 3 1/4 **Ceaseless (IRE)**[22] 4828 2-9-0 0 MartinLane 9 76
(James Tate) *s.i.s: sn trcking ldrs: wnt 2nd 3f out: rdn over 1f out: styd on same pce fnl f* **6/1**[3]
0 3 nk **Lady Of Dubai**[43] 4126 2-9-0 0 DaneO'Neill 2 75+
(Luca Cumani) *s.i.s: hld up: hdwy over 1f out: r.o* **7/2**[2]
6 4 3 1/4 **Camagueyana**[32] 4499 2-9-0 0 SilvestreDeSousa 1 67+
(Ralph Beckett) *hld up: pushed along 1/2-way: hdwy u.p and hung lft over 1f out: nt trble ldrs* **7/2**[2]
5 1 3/4 **Starring Guest (IRE)** 2-9-0 0 ChrisCatlin 8 62
(Mick Channon) *chsd wnr 4f: rdn over 2f out: wknd fnl f* **16/1**
6 hd **Midas Haze** 2-9-0 0 WilliamTwiston-Davies 4 61
(Michael Bell) *hld up: hdwy over 2f out: rdn and edgd lft over 1f out: wknd fnl f* **50/1**
7 2 1/2 **Haalan** 2-8-11 0 DannyBrock(3) 3 55
(Clive Brittain) *prom: pushed along and lost pl 1/2-way: wknd over 1f out* **40/1**
00 8 10 **Katniss (IRE)**[7] 5391 2-8-7 0 AaronJones(7) 6 28
(Stuart Williams) *prom 5f* **150/1**
9 1 3/4 **Percy's Dream** 2-9-0 0 PatCosgrave 7 23
(William Jarvis) *hld up: hdwy 1/2-way: hung lft and wknd over 2f out* **66/1**
1m 24.96s (-0.74) **Going Correction** +0.075s/f (Good) **9 Ran SP% 113.3**
Speed ratings (Par 93): **107,103,102,99,97 97,94,82,80**
CSF £10.11 TOTE £1.90: £1.10, £1.90, £1.60; EX 10.10 Trifecta £25.60.


The Form Book, Raceform Ltd, Newbury, RG14 5SJ

**Owner** Hubert John Strecker **Bred** M V Magnier & Lynch-Bages Ltd **Trained** Middleham Moor, N Yorks

**FOCUS**

They looked to go a much more generous pace in this and the winning time was significantly faster than the first division. Possibly in view of how the first leg panned out, the jockeys soon made for the centre of the track.

## 5645 TRM GNF (GUT NUTRITION FORMULA) NURSERY H'CAP (BOBIS RACE) 1m

**2:45** (2:46) (Class 4) (0-80,79) 2-Y-O **£5,175** (£1,540; £769; £384) **Stalls** High

Form RPR

641 **1** **Crafty Choice**[16] 5029 2-8-13 **71**........................ PatCosgrave 4 78
(Richard Hannon) *hld up: hdwy over 2f out: rdn to chse ldr and edgd lft fnl f: r.o to ld post* **10/1**

432 **2** *nse* **Tom Hark (FR)**[23] 4800 2-9-7 **79**........................ SilvestreDeSousa 7 86
(Richard Hannon) *led: rdn over 1f out: r.o: hdd post* **2/1**[1]

015 **3** *3 ¾* **Shaakis (IRE)**[20] 4897 2-9-4 **76**........................ DaneO'Neill 8 76
(Marcus Tregoning) *trckd ldrs: nt clr run fr over 2f out tl ins fnl f: r.o: nvr able to chal* **5/1**[3]

5322 **4** *½* **Popeswood (IRE)**[11] 5250 2-9-3 **75**........................ WilliamTwiston-Davies 2 72
(Mick Channon) *hld up: hdwy and edgd lft over 1f out: styd on* **5/1**[3]

01 **5** *nk* **Pasticcio**[34] 4429 2-9-6 **78**........................ MartinLane 6 74
(Charlie Appleby) *prom: chsd ldr over 5f out tl rdn over 2f out: no ex fnl f* **10/3**[2]

0145 **6** *2 ¼* **Scutum (IRE)**[19] 4944 2-8-13 **74**........................ RyanClark(3) 3 65
(Brian Meehan) *chsd ldr tl over 5f out: wnt 2nd again over 2f out tl rdn over 1f out: wknd ins fnl f* **16/1**

0443 **7** *9* **Lord Of Words (IRE)**[11] 5241 2-8-1 **59**........................ RaulDaSilva 1 30
(Brian Ellison) *prom: pushed along 3f out: edgd lft and wknd over 1f out* **16/1**

1455 **8** *2 ½* **Magical Roundabout (IRE)**[49] 3922 2-9-6 **78**........................ PatDobbs 5 43
(Richard Hannon) *hld up: rdn and wknd over 2f out* **20/1**

1m 39.9s (-0.10) **Going Correction** +0.075s/f (Good) **8** Ran SP% **115.4**

Speed ratings (Par 96): **103,102,99,98,98 96,87,84**

CSF £30.74 CT £116.07 TOTE £7.70: £2.40, £1.10, £1.60; EX 29.90 Trifecta £127.20.

**Owner** Middleham Park Racing CIII **Bred** Pevens Racing **Trained** East Everleigh, Wilts

**FOCUS**

They went no pace early in this nursery and the runners reverted to sticking closer to the far rail. It resulted in a 1-2 for trainer Richard Hannon and the front pair pulled right away.

## 5646 TRM EXCELLENCE IN EQUINE NUTRITION EBF STALLIONS MAIDEN STKS (BOBIS RACE) 7f

**3:20** (3:22) (Class 4) 2-Y-O **£4,528** (£1,347; £673; £336) **Stalls** High

Form RPR

**1** **Tannaaf (IRE)** 2-9-0 0........................ PatCosgrave 14 85+
(M F De Kock, South Africa) *a.p: rdn to ld 1f out: r.o* **7/1**[3]

0 **2** *2* **Shadow Rock (IRE)**[27] 4666 2-9-0 0........................ RobertHavlin 11 80
(Richard Hannon) *disp ld tl wnt on 3f out: rdn and hdd over 1f out: styd on same pce ins fnl f* **66/1**

U **3** *nk* **Wentworth Falls**[10] 5278 2-9-0 0........................ MartinLane 4 79
(Charlie Appleby) *chsd ldrs: rdn to ld and hung rt over 1f out: sn hdd: styd on same pce* **5/1**[2]

**4** *2 ¼* **Stoked (IRE)** 2-9-0 0........................ NickyMackay 5 73+
(Ed Walker) *prom: rdn over 2f out: styd on* **25/1**

**5** *nk* **Dancetrack (USA)** 2-8-11 0........................ RobertTart(3) 7 74+
(Charles Hills) *s.i.s: hld up: nt clr run over 1f out: r.o ins fnl f: nvr nrr* **12/1**

**6** *1* **Recently Acquired** 2-9-0 0........................ ChrisCatlin 1 69+
(Lady Cecil) *hld up: shkn up over 1f out: nt trble ldrs* **14/1**

**7** *hd* **Stake Acclaim (IRE)** 2-9-0 0........................ RobertWinston 13 69+
(Dean Ivory) *mid-div: hdwy over 2f out: rdn over 1f out: wknd ins fnl f* **50/1**

**8** *2* **Capel Path (USA)** 2-9-0 0........................ ShaneKelly 6 63+
(Sir Michael Stoute) *hld up: rdn over 2f out: styd on ins fnl f: nvr nrr* **14/1**

**9** *½* **Sydney Ruffdiamond** 2-9-0 0........................ PatDobbs 8 62
(Richard Hannon) *hld up: hdwy 1/2-way: rdn over 2f out: wknd fnl f* **25/1**

**10** *2* **Keep Up (GER)** 2-8-11 0........................ MatthewLawson(3) 10 57
(Saeed bin Suroor) *disp ld 4f: wknd over 1f out* **7/1**[3]

**11** *½* **Flying Fantasy** 2-9-0 0........................ LiamJones 3 55
(William Haggas) *hld up: hdwy over 2f out: wknd over 1f out* **8/1**

**12** *1* **Alkhayyam (IRE)** 2-9-0 0........................ DaneO'Neill 2 53+
(Brian Meehan) *s.i.s: hld up: hdwy over 2f out: rdn and wknd over 1f out* **11/4**[1]

**13** *½* **Mr Morocco** 2-8-9 0........................ TobyAtkinson(5) 16 51
(Noel Quinlan) *chsd ldrs: rdn over 2f out: wknd over 1f out* **100/1**

**14** *hd* **Prayer Time** 2-9-0 0........................ JimmyQuinn 15 51
(Mark H Tompkins) *hld up: wknd over 2f out* **100/1**

**15** *3 ¾* **Polydus** 2-9-0 0........................ SilvestreDeSousa 9 41
(Ed Dunlop) *mid-div: hdwy 1/2-way: wknd over 1f out* **40/1**

1m 27.13s (1.43) **Going Correction** +0.075s/f (Good) **15** Ran SP% **116.0**

Speed ratings (Par 96): **94,91,91,88,88 87,87,84,84,81 81,80,79,79,75**

CSF £416.07 TOTE £9.80: £3.00, £8.50, £1.90; EX 421.60 Trifecta £2749.00.

**Owner** Sheikh Mohammed Bin Khalifa Al Maktoum **Bred** Churchtown House Stud **Trained** South Africa

**FOCUS**

An interesting maiden for colts and geldings and they came up the centre this time, but the pace was ordinary (the winning time was only just faster than the first division of the fillies' maiden and much slower than the second), and it suited those who raced handily. Only two of these had raced before and they made the places, which makes the successful debut of the well-backed einner all the more encouraging.

## 5647 TRM SUPPORTING CHAMPIONS GLOBALLY H'CAP (BOBIS RACE) 1m 2f

**3:55** (3:57) (Class 4) (0-80,77) 3-Y-O **£5,175** (£1,540; £769; £384) **Stalls** Centre

Form RPR

4130 **1** **Carnevale**[27] 4680 3-9-7 **77**........................ SilvestreDeSousa 3 89
(Ralph Beckett) *led 1f: chsd ldr: wnt upsides 3f out: shkn up to ld 2f out: rdn and r.o wl fnl f: comf* **11/4**[1]

0111 **2** *3 ½* **Hostile Fire (IRE)**[25] 4742 3-9-4 **74**........................ PatCosgrave 2 79
(Ed de Giles) *a.p: racd keenly: nt clr run fr over 2f out tl rdn to chse wnr ins fnl f: styd on same pce* **9/2**[3]

3441 **3** *1* **Charlie Wells (IRE)**[7] 5395 3-9-3 **73** 6ex........................(b) JohnFahy 6 76
(Eve Johnson Houghton) *hld up: rdn over 2f out: nt clr run over 1f out: swtchd lft and styd on to go 3rd nr fin: nt trble ldrs* **5/1**

3133 **4** *hd* **Watersmeet**[23] 4786 3-9-5 **75**........................ DaneO'Neill 5 78
(Mark Johnston) *chsd ldrs: wnt upsides 3f out tl rdn and edgd lft over 1f out: no ex ins fnl f* **7/2**[2]

054 **5** *3* **Crowded**[18] 4984 3-9-4 **74**........................ MartinLane 1 71
(Charlie Appleby) *hld up: hdwy u.p over 2f out: wknd ins fnl f* **12/1**

4561 **6** *½* **Guaracha**[15] 5096 3-8-12 **71**........................(b[1]) DannyBrock(3) 8 67
(Clive Brittain) *plld hrd: led 9f out: rdn and hdd 2f out: wknd ins fnl f* **14/1**

44-0 **7** *12* **Ian's Memory (USA)**[116] 1795 3-9-7 **77**........................ ShaneKelly 7 50
(Jeremy Noseda) *hld up: hdwy over 3f out: rdn and wknd over 1f out* **6/1**

2m 6.52s (1.02) **Going Correction** +0.175s/f (Good) **7** Ran SP% **112.4**

Speed ratings (Par 102): **102,99,98,98,95 95,85**

CSF £14.80 CT £56.71 TOTE £3.70: £1.40, £2.70; EX 16.80 Trifecta £67.80.

**Owner** Prince A A Faisal **Bred** Nawara Stud Co Ltd **Trained** Kimpton, Hants

**FOCUS**

A fair handicap run at a decent pace.

## 5648 HORSE REQUISITES NEWMARKET STOCKIST OF TRM MAIDEN STKS 1m

**4:30** (4:32) (Class 5) 3-Y-O+ **£3,881** (£1,155; £577; £288) **Stalls** High

Form RPR

2 **1** **Batrana**[21] 4867 3-9-0 0........................ PatCosgrave 4 86
(M F De Kock, South Africa) *chsd ldrs: led over 2f out: shkn up and edgd rt over 1f out: rdn and hung rt ins fnl f: r.o* **9/4**[2]

3-2 **2** *3 ¾* **Royal Flag**[16] 5039 4-9-11 0........................ SilvestreDeSousa 1 83
(Saeed bin Suroor) *chsd ldr tl rdn over 2f out: chsd wnr over 1f out: no ex ins fnl f* **4/9**[1]

0 **3** *6* **Frederic**[35] 4407 3-9-5 0........................ LemosdeSouza 5 68
(Luca Cumani) *prom: rdn over 1f out: edgd rt and wknd fnl f* **14/1**[3]

6-0 **4** *11* **Grey Odyssey**[18] 4984 3-9-5 0........................ RobertWinston 2 43
(Dean Ivory) *led: rdn and hdd over 2f out: wknd over 1f out* **66/1**

00 **5** *15* **Beaver Creek**[69] 3248 3-9-5 0........................ MartinLane 6 8
(Ralph J Smith) *racd alone: up w the pce tl rdn over 3f out: wknd 2f out* **100/1**

**6** *99* **Invisible Touch**[283] 4-9-1 0........................ RyanWhile(5) 3
(Martin Smith) *s.i.s: outpcd* **66/1**

1m 37.94s (-2.06) **Going Correction** +0.075s/f (Good)

**WFA** 3 from 4yo 6lb **6** Ran SP% **110.7**

Speed ratings (Par 103): **113,109,103,92,77**

CSF £3.48 TOTE £2.60: £1.30, £1.10; EX 3.90 Trifecta £7.40.

**Owner** Sheikh Mohammed Bin Khalifa Al Maktoum **Bred** Az Agr Francesca **Trained** South Africa

**FOCUS**

An uncompetitive maiden and effectively a two-horse race. Five of the runners came up the middle, while Beaver Creek raced alone more towards the far side.

## 5649 TRM INVEST IN CALPHORMIN H'CAP (BOBIS RACE) 7f

**5:05** (5:05) (Class 3) (0-90,89) 3-Y-O **£7,762** (£2,310; £1,154; £577) **Stalls** High

Form RPR

3214 **1** **Marmoom**[20] 4912 3-9-0 **82**........................ DaneO'Neill 6 92
(Charles Hills) *trckd ldrs: rdn to ld ins fnl f: r.o* **5/2**[1]

3022 **2** *1* **Crowdmania**[8] 5348 3-9-2 **84**........................ MartinLane 3 91
(Mark Johnston) *chsd ldr tl led over 2f out: rdn over 1f out: hdd and unable qck ins fnl f* **7/2**[3]

1210 **3** *1* **Baltic Brave (IRE)**[27] 4647 3-9-5 **87**........................(t) JohnFahy 1 91
(Hughie Morrison) *hld up: hdwy over 1f out: sn rdn: r.o* **5/1**

0-14 **4** *¾* **Amood (IRE)**[55] 3719 3-8-11 **79**........................ WilliamTwiston-Davies 8 81
(Simon West) *hld up: rdn over 2f out: r.o ins fnl f: nvr nrr* **16/1**

0000 **5** *3 ½* **Nezar (IRE)**[24] 4765 3-9-7 **89**........................(b) LiamJones 2 82
(George Margarson) *plld hrd and prom: rdn over 1f out: no ex ins fnl f* **18/1**

1054 **6** *6* **Provident Spirit**[13] 5177 3-9-3 **85**........................(b[1]) RobertHavlin 5 63
(John Gosden) *plld hrd: led at stdy pce tl qcknd over 3f out: hdd over 2f out: rdn and wknd over 1f out* **3/1**[2]

-210 **7** *14* **Jacquotte Delahaye**[48] 3957 3-9-1 **83**........................(b) SilvestreDeSousa 4 24
(David Brown) *hld up: racd keenly: hmpd after 1f: rdn and wknd wl over 1f out* **16/1**

1m 25.38s (-0.32) **Going Correction** +0.075s/f (Good) **7** Ran SP% **109.5**

Speed ratings (Par 104): **104,102,101,100,96 90,74**

CSF £10.45 CT £34.97 TOTE £2.80: £1.60, £2.10; EX 10.10 Trifecta £44.60.

**Owner** Hamdan Al Maktoum **Bred** Hellwood Stud Farm **Trained** Lambourn, Berks

**FOCUS**

A decent 3yo handicap and again they raced up the centre.

## 5650 TRM-IRELAND.COM H'CAP (JOCKEY CLUB GRASSROOTS FLAT SPRINT SERIES QUALIFIER) 6f

**5:35** (5:39) (Class 4) (0-85,85) 3-Y-O+ **£5,175** (£1,540; £769; £384) **Stalls** High

Form RPR

4401 **1** **Triple Chocolate**[18] 4983 4-9-1 **76**........................ JimmyQuinn 7 86+
(Roger Ingram) *a.p: chsd ldr over 1f out: r.o u.p to ld nr fin* **7/1**[2]

0000 **2** *nk* **Best Trip (IRE)**[6] 5444 7-9-1 **83**........................ KevinLundie(7) 5 92
(Brian Ellison) *led: rdn over 1f out: edgd lft ins fnl f: hdd nr fin* **8/1**[3]

3400 **3** *2 ¾* **Regal Dan (IRE)**[8] 5346 4-9-8 **83**........................ RobertWinston 3 83
(Charles Hills) *hld up in tch: rdn and hung lft over 1f out: styd on same pce ins fnl f* **8/1**[3]

0400 **4** *nse* **Front Page News**[21] 4866 4-9-1 **76**........................(v[1]) DaneO'Neill 9 76
(Robert Eddery) *chsd ldr tl rdn over 1f out: styd on same pce ins fnl f* **14/1**

5304 **5** *1 ½* **Olney Lass**[45] 4047 7-8-2 **66**........................ SimonPearce(3) 4 61+
(Lydia Pearce) *hld up: rdn over 2f out: r.o ins fnl f: nvr nrr* **25/1**

2344 **6** *1* **Atlantis Crossing (IRE)**[6] 5422 5-8-9 **70**........................ PatCosgrave 13 62
(Jim Boyle) *hld up: hdwy and hung lft over 1f out: sn rdn: styd on same pce fnl f* **7/1**[2]

0560 **7** *shd* **Amadeus Wolfe Tone (IRE)**[18] 4983 5-9-8 **83**........................(p) PatDobbs 10 75
(Jamie Osborne) *hld up in tch: rdn over 1f out: no ex fnl f* **8/1**[3]

0246 **8** *1* **Mon Brav**[6] 5444 7-9-5 **80**........................ DougieCostello 1 69
(Brian Ellison) *hld up: rdn over 2f out: r.o towards fin: nvr nrr* **8/1**[3]

102 **9** *1* **Vallarta (IRE)**[18] 4983 4-9-2 **77**........................(v) WilliamTwiston-Davies 2 62
(Mick Channon) *hld up: rdn over 2f out: nvr on terms* **8/1**[3]

0350 **10** *1 ¼* **Midnight Rider (IRE)**[42] 4146 6-9-2 **80**........................ AshleyMorgan(3) 11 61
(Chris Wall) *rrd s: hld up: shkn up over 1f out: a in rr* **12/1**

1010 **11** *2 ½* **Dinneratmidnight**[12] 5204 3-9-7 **85**........................ SilvestreDeSousa 12 58
(Ralph Beckett) *chsd ldrs: rdn over 2f out: wknd fnl f* **9/2**[1]

6514 **12** *2* **Majestic Song**[18] 4971 3-8-7 **71**........................ ChrisCatlin 8 38
(James Toller) *mid-div: pushed along over 2f out: wknd over 1f out* **22/1**

1m 12.02s (-0.48) **Going Correction** +0.075s/f (Good)

**WFA** 3 from 4yo+ 3lb **12** Ran SP% **116.8**

Speed ratings (Par 105): **106,105,101,101,99 98,98,97,95,94 90,88**

CSF £99.48 CT £803.45 TOTE £7.40: £2.80, £4.60, £3.40; EX 151.90 Trifecta £975.40.

**Owner** Fahed Al Dabbous **Bred** Lael Stables **Trained** Epsom, Surrey

**FOCUS**

A fair sprint handicap in which the they all came up the middle and few got into it.

T/Plt: £20.20 to a £1 stake. Pool: £48781.34 - 1755.11 winning tickets T/Qpdt: £10.00 to a £1 stake. Pool: £3270.5 - 240.15 winning tickets CR

## 5607 YORK (L-H)

Friday, August 22

**OFFICIAL GOING: Good (overall 6.9; home straight: far side 6.9; centre 7.0; stands' side 6.9)**

Wind: Moderate against Weather: Cloudy with sunny periods Rails: Rail realignment around home bend and back straight increased distances of races of 1m and further by 7yds

### 5651 SKY BET TRANSFER FUND STKS (H'CAP) 1m 4f

1:55 (1:55) (Class 2) (0-100,100) 3-Y-O+

£31,125 (£9,320; £4,660; £2,330; £1,165; £585) **Stalls** Centre

Form / RPR

0033 1 **Glenard**[26] 4696 4-9-4 90 ..... WilliamBuick 6 99
(Charles Hills) *swtg: led: pushed clr over 3f out: jnd and rdn jst over 2f out: sn hdd and cl up: drvn and rallied ins fnl f: led last 100yds: gamely* **12/1**

30 2 *nk* **Salutation (IRE)**[13] 5174 4-9-11 100 ..... MichaelJMMurphy(3) 18 108
(Mark Johnston) *lw: trckd wnr: hdwy 3f out: cl up 2f out: sn led and rdn: drvn ent fnl f: hdd and no ex last 100yds* **20/1**

11 3 *1 1/4* **Dolphin Village (IRE)**[30] 4538 4-8-11 86 ..... GeorgeChaloner(3) 4 92
(Richard Fahey) *t.k.h: trckd ldrs on inner: hdwy over 3f out: effrt and cl up over 2f out: sn rdn to chal and ev ch tl drvn and no ex last 100yds* **16/1**

0-14 4 *1/2* **Pearl Castle (IRE)**[22] 4173 4-9-1 92 ..... JoeDoyle(5) 5 97
(John Quinn) *trckd ldrs: hdwy 3f out: cl up and rdn wl over 1f out: drvn and kpt on same pce fnl f* **10/1**

4120 5 *1/2* **Stomachion (IRE)**[24] 4756 4-9-6 92 ..... RyanMoore 10 97
(Sir Michael Stoute) *trckd ldrs: hdwy over 4f out: rdn along 3f out: drvn over 1f out: kpt on ins fnl f: nrst fin* **15/2**[1]

122 6 *1/2* **Xinbama (IRE)**[28] 4622 5-8-12 84 ..... KierenFallon 20 87+
(Charles Hills) *lw: in rr: pushed along and hdwy wl over 2f out: rdn wl over 1f out: kpt on u.p fnl f: nrst fin* **16/1**

0006 7 *hd* **Lahaag**[13] 5174 5-9-6 92 ..... PaulHanagan 11 95
(John Gosden) *lw: midfield: effrt 3f out and sn rdn along: kpt on u.p fnl 2f: nrst fin* **8/1**[2]

3500 8 *nk* **Chancery (USA)**[13] 5174 6-9-8 94 ..... DanielTudhope 9 96
(David O'Meara) *stmbld s and hld up towards rr: hdwy 3f out: rdn along to chse ldrs 2f out: drvn over 1f out and kpt on same pce* **8/1**[2]

0002 9 *3/4* **Wigmore Hall (IRE)**[6] 5440 7-9-1 94 ..... MikeyEnnis(7) 2 95
(Michael Bell) *dwlt and in rr: hdwy 3f out: rdn wl over 1f out: styd on to chse ldrs ent fnl f: sn drvn and no imp* **8/1**[2]

1420 10 *1 1/2* **Satellite (IRE)**[13] 5179 3-8-13 95 ..... GrahamLee 1 94
(William Haggas) *t.k.h: hld up towards rr: hdwy wl over 2f out: rdn over 1f out: no imp fnl f* **9/1**[3]

0-0 11 *nk* **Zaidiyn (FR)**[34] 4437 4-9-8 94 ..... [1] DaleSwift 7 92
(Brian Ellison) *dwlt and in rr: rdn along over 3f out: kpt on u.p fnl 2f: n.d* **40/1**

0352 12 *1/2* **Proud Chieftain**[13] 5162 6-9-6 92 ..... (p) JamesDoyle 3 89
(Clifford Lines) *in tch: rdn along 3f out: drvn over 2f out: one pce* **20/1**

0/11 13 *3 3/4* **Gabrial The Hero (USA)**[20] 4917 5-9-0 86 ..... JamieSpencer 14 77
(David Simcock) *lw: s.i.s and lost many l s: jnd field after 3f: hdwy 3f out: rdn to chse ldrs wl over 1f out: eased ins fnl f* **12/1**

-401 14 *3* **Semeen**[13] 5162 5-9-6 92 ..... RichardHughes 13 79
(Luca Cumani) *lw: midfield: effrt on outer over 3f out: sn rdn along and no hdwy fnl 2f* **8/1**[2]

3006 15 *7* **Modernism**[42] 4160 5-9-0 86 ..... NeilCallan 15 61
(David Simcock) *swtg: chsd ldrs: rdn along 3f out: sn wknd* **40/1**

4333 16 *7* **Communicator**[13] 5162 6-9-8 94 ..... OisinMurphy 12 58
(Andrew Balding) *sn trcking ldrs on outer: rdn along 3f out: sn wknd* **12/1**

2m 33.64s (0.44) **Going Correction** +0.20s/f (Good)
**WFA** 3 from 4yo+ 10lb **16 Ran SP% 124.5**
Speed ratings (Par 109): **106,105,104,104,104 103,103,103,103,102 101,101,99,97,92 87**
CSF £242.97 CT £3827.53 TOTE £18.40: £3.10, £5.50, £3.90, £2.80; EX 359.10 Trifecta £4012.50.
**Owner** Highclere T'Bred Racing & John C Grant **Bred** Denford Stud Ltd **Trained** Lambourn, Berks

**FOCUS**
An overcast morning led into the third day of the meeting. Most jockeys after the opener declared the ground still to be riding near good yet definitely faster than the previous day. This was a highly competitive handicap. The first four were always prominent and the winner posted a minor personal best.

### 5652 WEATHERBYS HAMILTON INSURANCE LONSDALE CUP (BRITISH CHAMPIONS SERIES) (GROUP 2) 2m 88y

2:30 (2:30) (Class 1) 3-Y-O+

£85,065 (£32,250; £16,140; £8,040; £4,035; £2,025) **Stalls** Low

Form / RPR

04-3 1 **Pale Mimosa (IRE)**[36] 4380 5-9-0 109 ..... PatSmullen 5 112
(D K Weld, Ire) *trckd ldrs: hdwy 3f out: sn cl up: chal over 2f out: led wl over 1f out: rdn ent fnl f: drvn and kpt on wl towards fin* **2/1**[1]

0-20 2 *1/2* **Estimate (IRE)**[22] 4823 5-9-0 112 ..... RyanMoore 7 111
(Sir Michael Stoute) *hld up: hdwy over 2f out: rdn over 1f out: drvn to chse wnr ins fnl f: kpt on* **9/2**[3]

0-00 3 *2 1/4* **Times Up**[89] 2588 8-9-3 108 ..... WilliamBuick 4 112
(Ed Dunlop) *trckd ldr: hdwy 3f out: sn cl up: rdn 2f out and ev ch tl drvn and kpt on same pce ins fnl f* **10/1**

1211 4 *nse* **Cavalryman**[22] 4823 8-9-3 115 ..... KierenFallon 2 112
(Saeed bin Suroor) *trckd ldrs: hdwy 3f out: pushed along 2f out: rdn over 1f out: drvn and kpt on same pce fnl f* **9/4**[2]

1215 5 *3/4* **Angel Gabrial (IRE)**[22] 4823 5-9-3 106 ..... DavidNolan 8 111
(Richard Fahey) *hld up in rr: hdwy wl over 2f out: rdn to chse ldrs over 1f out: drvn and kpt on same pce fnl f* **14/1**

-240 6 *shd* **Forgotten Voice (IRE)**[22] 4823 9-9-3 109 ..... RichardHughes 6 111
(Nicky Henderson) *lw: sn led: pushed along 3f out: rdn 2f out: hdd wl over 1f out: sn drvn and wknd ins fnl f* **20/1**

3312 7 *6* **Certerach (IRE)**[36] 4380 6-9-3 111 ..... JamieSpencer 1 103
(M Halford, Ire) *hld up in rr: hdwy on outer 4f out: rdn along wl over 2f out: sn drvn and outpcd* **14/1**

3m 31.52s (-2.98) **Going Correction** +0.20s/f (Good) **7 Ran SP% 109.5**
Speed ratings: **115,114,113,113,113 113,110**
CSF £10.35 TOTE £3.30: £2.30, £2.60; EX 11.40 Trifecta £70.80.
**Owner** Dr R Lambe/Merriebelle Irish Farm Ltd **Bred** Irish National Stud **Trained** Curragh, Co Kildare

**FOCUS**
Actual race distance 2m 95yds. A decent renewal of this Group 2 prize, but it was run at an uneven gallop and it resulted in something of a dash for home, the runners taking the mid-track route in the home straight. The form is a little muddling and has to rate as ordinary for the grade. Estimate was 4lb off her Gold Cup figure.

### 5653 SKY BET CITY OF YORK STKS (LISTED RACE) 7f

3:05 (3:06) (Class 1) 3-Y-O+

£56,710 (£21,500; £10,760; £5,360; £2,690; £1,350) **Stalls** Low

Form / RPR

2102 1 **Absolutely So (IRE)**[41] 4200 4-9-0 103 ..... OisinMurphy 6 113
(Andrew Balding) *lw: trckd ldrs: hdwy 3f out: chsd ldr 2f out: rdn to ld ent fnl f: kpt on wl towards fin* **6/1**[1]

016 2 *1 1/2* **Glory Awaits (IRE)**[24] 4758 4-9-0 108 ..... (v[1]) NeilCallan 7 109
(Kevin Ryan) *lw: led: qcknd over 2f out: rdn over 1f out: edgd lft and hdd ent fnl f: sn drvn and kpt on* **14/1**

1200 3 *1* **Glen Moss (IRE)**[41] 4200 5-9-0 103 ..... SeanLevey 2 107
(David Brown) *trckd ldrs: hdwy over 2f out: rdn to chse ldng pair over 1f out: drvn and kpt on fnl f* **14/1**

5100 4 *nse* **Gabriel's Lad (IRE)**[27] 4648 5-9-0 109 ..... JamesDoyle 8 106
(Denis Coakley) *hld up in rr: hdwy wl over 2f out: rdn wl over 1f out: styd on fnl f: nrst fin* **15/2**[3]

406 5 *1* **Highland Colori (IRE)**[8] 5354 6-9-0 106 ..... DavidProbert 1 104
(Andrew Balding) *chsd ldrs on inner: rdn along over 2f out: one pce appr fnl f* **25/1**

1105 6 *3/4* **That Is The Spirit**[34] 4438 3-8-9 106 ..... RichardHughes 10 100
(David O'Meara) *lw: chsd ldr: pushed along over 3f out: rdn wl over 1f out: grad wknd* **6/1**[1]

5542 7 *1/2* **Alfred Hutchinson**[27] 4681 6-9-0 92 ..... BarryMcHugh 15 101
(Geoffrey Oldroyd) *towards rr: effrt over 2f out: sn rdn: drvn and no imp fnl f* **40/1**

1053 8 *1/2* **Ertijaal (IRE)**[19] 4937 3-8-9 104 ..... (p) PaulHanagan 14 97
(William Haggas) *plld hrd: chsd ldrs on outer: rdn along over 2f out: drvn over 1f out: sn wknd* **6/1**[1]

0140 9 *3/4* **Heaven's Guest (IRE)**[21] 4851 4-9-0 105 ..... RyanMoore 13 99+
(Richard Fahey) *towards rr whn hung rt and rn wd bnd over 4f out: n.d* **7/1**[2]

322- 10 *2 3/4* **Cable Bay (IRE)**[314] 7192 3-8-9 114 ..... JamieSpencer 12 88+
(Charles Hills) *dwlt and in rr whn carried wd bnd over 4f out: nvr a factor* **9/1**

-033 11 *1 1/2* **Rerouted (USA)**[8] 5354 6-9-0 112 ..... ChristopheSoumillon 11 86
(M F De Kock, South Africa) *midfield: rdn along wl over 2f out: sn btn* **9/1**

1005 12 *1 3/4* **Penitent**[41] 4187 8-9-5 110 ..... DanielTudhope 4 87
(David O'Meara) *midfield: rdn along 3f out: sn outpcd* **25/1**

2631 13 *hd* **Mushir**[21] 4872 3-8-9 102 ..... GrahamLee 3 79
(Roger Varian) *t.k.h: chsd ldrs: rdn along 3f out: sn wknd* **12/1**

1m 22.43s (-2.87) **Going Correction** -0.075s/f (Good)
**WFA** 3 from 4yo+ 5lb **13 Ran SP% 118.3**
Speed ratings: **113,111,110,110,108 108,107,106,106,102 101,99,99**
CSF £87.60 TOTE £5.90: £2.50, £4.50, £4.30; EX 124.90 Trifecta £2907.90.
**Owner** Jackie & George Smith **Bred** L Mulryan **Trained** Kingsclere, Hants

**FOCUS**
A wide-open Listed race. There was a fair early pace yet those handily placed 2f out were at an advantage. The winner progressed again.

### 5654 COOLMORE NUNTHORPE STKS (BRITISH CHAMPIONS SERIES) (GROUP 1) 5f

3:40 (3:42) (Class 1) 2-Y-O+

£150,281 (£56,975; £28,514; £14,204; £7,128; £3,577) **Stalls** High

Form / RPR

011 1 **Sole Power**[66] 3319 7-9-11 119 ..... RichardHughes 10 119+
(Edward Lynam, Ire) *hld up in rr: hdwy and swtchd rt over 1f out: sn nt clr run and swtchd lft ins fnl f: squeezed through and qcknd wl to ld last 40yds* **11/4**[1]

4264 2 *1/2* **Stepper Point**[21] 4852 5-9-11 112 ..... (p) MartinDwyer 2 115
(William Muir) *lw: chsd ldrs on outer: hdwy 2f out: sn cl up: rdn to ld ent fnl f: sn drvn: hdd and nt qckn last 40yds* **20/1**

1212 3 *shd* **Extortionist (IRE)**[21] 4852 3-9-9 113 ..... RyanMoore 7 115
(Olly Stevens) *trckd ldrs whn n.m.r after 1f: swtchd lft to outer and rdn wl over 1f out: styd on strly fnl f* **14/1**

5003 4 *1/2* **Moviesta (USA)**[21] 4852 4-9-11 112 ..... PaulMulrennan 4 113
(Bryan Smart) *lw: sltly hmpd s: trckd ldrs: hdwy 1/2-way: rdn to chal ent fnl f: ev ch tl drvn and nt qckn last 50yds* **11/1**

3130 5 *hd* **Hot Streak (IRE)**[41] 4201 3-9-9 115 ..... JamieSpencer 15 112
(Kevin Ryan) *lw: trckd ldrs: hdwy 2f out: rdn ent fnl f: drvn and nt qckn last 100yds* **8/1**[2]

1325 6 *nk* **G Force (IRE)**[21] 4852 3-9-9 106 ..... DanielTudhope 12 112+
(David O'Meara) *hld up in rr: pushed along and sltly outpcd over 2f out: n.m.r and swtchd lft ent fnl f: rdn and styng on whn nt clr run and hmpd 100yds out: swtchd rt and kpt on towards fin* **12/1**

2-11 7 *nk* **Rangali**[82] 2820 3-9-9 118 ..... FabriceVeron 11 110
(H-A Pantall, France) *leggy: athletic: prom: rdn along over 1f out: drvn ent fnl f: kpt on same pce* **8/1**[2]

-011 8 *nse* **Take Cover**[21] 4852 7-9-11 113 ..... JamesDoyle 9 110
(David C Griffiths) *led to 1/2-way: cl up: rdn along over 2f out: drvn and one pce ins fnl f* **8/1**[2]

5 9 *nse* **Cougar Mountain (IRE)**[41] 4201 3-9-9 0 ..... JosephO'Brien 8 110
(A P O'Brien, Ire) *lw: in rr and rdn along after 1f: hdwy u.p over 1f out: styd on fnl f: nrst fin* **8/1**[2]

5260 10 *1* **Astaire (IRE)**[41] 4201 3-9-9 112 ..... NeilCallan 6 106
(Kevin Ryan) *lw: cl up: led 1/2-way: rdn over 1f out: hdd and drvn ent fnl f: sn wknd* **12/1**

3300 11 *1 3/4* **Monsieur Joe (IRE)**[21] 4852 7-9-11 103 ..... GrahamLee 3 100
(Paul Midgley) *a towards rr* **66/1**

-130 12 *nse* **Shea Shea (SAF)**[66] 3319 7-9-11 116 ..... ChristopheSoumillon 13 100
(M F De Kock, South Africa) *in tch: rdn along over 2f out: sn wknd* **9/1**[3]

1465 13 *3 1/2* **Steps (IRE)**[48] 3981 6-9-11 110 ..... (b) KierenFallon 1 87
(Roger Varian) *in tch: on outer: rdn along 1/2-way: sn wknd* **20/1**

57.92s (-1.38) **Going Correction** +0.15s/f (Good)
**WFA** 3 from 4yo+ 2lb **13 Ran SP% 122.5**
Speed ratings: **117,116,116,115,114 114,113,113,113,112 109,109,103**
CSF £68.99 TOTE £3.50: £1.40, £7.20, £4.40; EX 75.40 Trifecta £1066.80.
**Owner** Mrs S Power **Bred** G Russell **Trained** Dunshaughlin, Co Meath

**FOCUS**
A solid edition of this Group 1 speed test. Perhaps the most notable absentee from the line-up was Tiggy Wiggy, who went for the Lowther instead, meaning fillies, successful for the past three years, were unrepresented. Sole Power confirmed himself the best around and the form makes a lot of sense.

## 5655 SKY BET ARE YOU IN? CONVIVIAL MAIDEN STKS (BOBIS RACE) 7f
4:20 (4:23) (Class 2) 2-Y-O
£24,900 (£7,456; £3,728; £1,864; £932; £468) Stalls Low

Form RPR
1 **White Lake** 2-9-5 0 RyanMoore 10 94+
(Luca Cumani) *gd sort: tall: str: hmpd s and towards rr: hdwy on wd outside 3f out: rdn over 1f out: sataed on wl to ld ins fnl f* **25/1**
36 2 2 **Secret Brief (IRE)**[20] 4896 2-9-5 0 FrannyNorton 7 88
(Mark Johnston) *lw: led: rdn along wl over 1f out: hdd ins fnl f: kpt on* **16/1**
3 3 1/4 **Foreign Diplomat** 2-9-5 0 FrankieDettori 12 80+
(William Haggas) *leggy: athletic: towards rr: hdwy over 2f out: rdn to chse ldrs over 1f out: styd on fnl f: nrst fin* **7/1**[3]
4 4 nse **Bright Flash**[23] 4781 2-9-0 0 SeanLevey 3 74
(David Brown) *leggy: t.k.h: chsd ldrs: effrt over 2f out: rdn wl over 1f out: kpt on same pce* **20/1**
5 5 1 1/4 **Dissolution**[35] 4395 2-9-5 0 JamesDoyle 5 76
(Sir Michael Stoute) *w'like: str: midfield: pushed along 3f out: rdn along 2f out: kpt on fnl f: nrst fin* **15/8**[1]
6 hd **Mount Tahan (IRE)** 2-9-5 0 NeilCallan 14 75+
(Kevin Ryan) *str: lw: in tch: hdwy on outer 3f out: rdn along to chse ldrs 2f out: hung lft over 1f out: sn one pce* **33/1**
7 nk **Erik The Red (FR)** 2-9-5 0 JamieSpencer 1 75+
(Kevin Ryan) *w'like: dwlt and in rr: hdwy on inner over 2f out: rdn over 1f out: kpt on fnl f: nrst fin* **25/1**
8 1/2 **All About Time** 2-9-0 0 DanielTudhope 8 68+
(David O'Meara) *w'like: sltly hmpd s: towards rr: hdwy over 2f out: rdn: edgd lft and green whn n.m.r over 1f out: n.d* **20/1**
9 nk **Muffarreh (USA)** 2-9-5 0 PaulHanagan 15 72+
(B W Hills) *w'like: t.k.h: midfield: pushed along 3f out: rdn over 2f out: no hdwy* **25/1**
4 10 2 **Brando**[85] 2698 2-9-5 0 MartinHarley 13 67+
(Kevin Ryan) *w'like: str: prom: rdn along over 2f out: sn wknd* **50/1**
2 11 1 **Acaster Malbis (FR)**[14] 5149 2-9-5 0 RichardHughes 11 64
(Richard Hannon) *str: trckd ldrs: effrt over 2f out: sn rdn and wknd* **4/1**[2]
2 12 shd **Swot**[21] 4864 2-9-5 0 WilliamBuick 4 64
(John Gosden) *w'like: t.k.h: chsd ldrs: rdn along over 2f out: sn wknd* **8/1**
4 13 shd **Beach Samba (IRE)**[14] 5149 2-9-5 0 PatSmullen 2 68
(Ed Dunlop) *leggy: chsd ldrs: rdn along over 3f out: sn wknd* **14/1**
4 14 1 1/4 **Able Spirit**[23] 4800 2-9-5 0 KierenFallon 6 60
(Brian Meehan) *w'like: t.k.h: chsd ldr: rdn along over 2f out: sn wknd* **33/1**
4 15 3 **Golden Spun (USA)**[52] 3827 2-9-5 0 PaulMulrennan 16 52
(Bryan Smart) *str: t.k.h: a in rr* **66/1**
16 hd **Bionic Indian** 2-9-5 0 GrahamGibbons 9 52
(Michael Easterby) *leggy: hmpd s: a in rr* **100/1**

1m 25.22s (-0.08) **Going Correction** -0.075s/f (Good) **16 Ran SP% 122.3**
Speed ratings (Par 100): **97,94,91,90,89 89,88,88,88,85 84,84,84,82,79 79**
CSF £350.83 TOTE £23.90: £6.10, £4.90, £2.60; EX 488.80 Trifecta £2129.30.
**Owner** Sheikh Mohammed Obaid Al Maktoum **Bred** Cheveley Park Stud Ltd **Trained** Newmarket, Suffolk

**FOCUS**
This usually works out to be an above-average maiden and the winner was impressive, but the second's proximity puts the form into some perspective.

## 5656 NATIONWIDE ACCIDENT REPAIR SERVICES STKS (H'CAP) (BOBIS RACE) 1m
4:55 (4:59) (Class 2) (0-100,100) 3-Y-O
£24,900 (£7,456; £3,728; £1,864; £932; £468) Stalls Low

Form RPR
0363 1 **Master The World (IRE)**[23] 4801 3-8-8 87 (v) KierenFallon 3 98
(David Elsworth) *dwlt: sn in midfield: hdwy 2f out: nt clr run over 1f out: rdn to chal jst ins fnl f: led last 100yds: r.o* **16/1**
1231 2 1 1/4 **Extremity (IRE)**[24] 4761 3-8-12 91 (p) RyanMoore 11 99
(Hugo Palmer) *lw: midfield: hdwy 3f out: trckd ldrs 2f out: rdn to take slt ld ent fnl f: hdd and no ex last 100yds* **7/2**[2]
5663 3 nk **Almuheet**[7] 5385 3-7-13 83 JoeDoyle(5) 1 90
(Brian Ellison) *trckd ldng pair: hdwy 2f out and sn chal: rdn and ev ch ent fnl f: sn drvn and kpt on same pce* **14/1**
-320 4 1 **Perfect Persuasion**[27] 4668 3-7-12 82 NathanAlison(5) 6 87
(William Haggas) *lw: hld up in rr: hdwy wl over 2f out: rdn along wl over 1f out: styd on fnl f: nrst fin* **14/1**
1301 5 1/2 **Munaaser**[27] 4671 3-9-1 94 PaulHanagan 10 98
(Sir Michael Stoute) *lw: towards rr: rdn along 3f out: drvn wl over 1f out: kpt on fnl f: nrst fin* **11/4**[1]
6 3/4 **Pit Stop (IRE)**[56] 3687 3-8-13 95 ConorHoban(3) 14 97
(M Halford, Ire) *str: lw: hld up in rr: hdwy over 2f out: rdn over 1f out: styd on fnl f: nrst fin* **16/1**
1550 7 nk **Regiment**[6] 5410 3-8-6 85 MartinDwyer 2 86
(Richard Fahey) *lw: cl up: led after 1f: rdn along over 2f out: drvn and edgd rt over 1f out: hdd ent fnl f: wknd* **50/1**
1211 8 3/4 **Halation (IRE)**[23] 4801 3-8-11 90 JamieSpencer 9 89
(David Simcock) *towards rr: hdwy on inner over 2f out: rdn wl over 1f out: one pce appr fnl f* **10/1**
6113 9 hd **Moohaarib (IRE)**[27] 4647 3-9-0 93 MartinHarley 5 92
(Marco Botti) *hld up: hdwy 3f out: rdn to chse ldrs wl over 1f out: drvn and one pce appr fnl f* **5/1**[3]
5152 10 nse **Lockhart (IRE)**[5] 5468 3-8-2 81 FrannyNorton 7 80
(Mark Johnston) *trckd ldrs: hdwy 3f out: rdn along wl over 1f out: grad wknd* **25/1**
4-45 11 1/2 **God Willing**[43] 4127 3-9-2 100 JackGarritty(5) 13 98
(Ed Dunlop) *hld up in rr: hdwy 3f out: rdn to chse ldrs whn n.m.r over 1f out: sn one pce* **33/1**
1402 12 3 **Lesha (IRE)**[13] 5177 3-8-10 89 JamesDoyle 15 80
(Kevin Ryan) *s.i.s: a in rr* **20/1**
1200 13 7 **Sir Guy Porteous (IRE)**[19] 4938 3-9-0 93 NeilCallan 12 68
(Mark Johnston) *led 1f: cl up: rdn along 2f out: drvn and wkng whn n.m.r over 1f out* **50/1**
4030 14 1 1/2 **Tiger Twenty Two**[28] 4635 3-8-2 81 PatrickMathers 4 52
(Richard Fahey) *trckd ldrs: effrt on inner 3f out: rdn along over 2f out: sn wknd* **20/1**

1m 39.27s (0.27) **Going Correction** +0.20s/f (Good) **14 Ran SP% 120.0**
Speed ratings (Par 106): **106,104,104,103,102 102,101,101,100,100 100,97,90,88**
CSF £65.96 CT £851.08 TOTE £15.50: £4.60, £1.90, £3.90; EX 81.40 Trifecta £1120.00.
**Owner** K Quinn/ C Benham/ I Saunders **Bred** A Hanahoe **Trained** Newmarket, Suffolk

**FOCUS**
This was run over seven yards further than advertised. A good handicap, but the form may not prove entirely reliable as the pace didn't look strong and things were a bit messy early. The winner's improved effort was no fluke, though. They came over to the stands' side in the home straight.
T/Jkpt: Not won. T/Plt: £3,065.20 to a £1 stake. Pool: £336,577.50 - 80.15 winning tickets
T/Qpdt: £235.30 to a £1 stake. Pool: £23822.51 - 74.90 winning tickets JR

5657 - 5660a (Foreign Racing) - See Raceform Interactive

# 5588 CLAIREFONTAINE (R-H)
Friday, August 22

**OFFICIAL GOING: Turf: very soft**

## 5661a PRIX DES FUSCHIAS (CLAIMER) (3YO) (TURF) 1m
11:35 (12:00) 3-Y-O £11,250 (£4,500; £3,375; £2,250; £1,125)

RPR
1 **Sainte Croix (FR)**[356] 3-8-11 0 GregoryBenoist 1 80
(J-C Rouget, France) **2/1**[2]
2 1 1/2 **Skaters Waltz (IRE)**[22] 4838 3-9-8 0 (b) OlivierPeslier 4 88
(Paul Cole) *in tch: pushed along 3f out: rdn in rr 2f out: styd on steadily against rail and wnt 2nd towards fin: nt pce of wnr* **4/5**[1]
3 2 **Skiperia (FR)**[10] 3-8-11 0 MickaelBarzalona 3 72
(Y Barberot, France) **9/2**[3]
4 2 **Eyasi (IRE)**[150] 3-8-11 0 (p) MaximeGuyon 2 67
(P Harley, Germany) **97/10**
5 3 **Pretty Luna (GER)**[31] 4526 3-9-3 0 CristianDemuro 5 67
(Henk Grewe, Germany) **169/10**

1m 43.8s (103.80) **5 Ran SP% 122.0**
WIN (incl. 1 euro stake): 3.00. PLACES: 1.10, 1.10. SF: 6.10.
**Owner** Gerard Augustin-Normand **Bred** Franklin Finance S A **Trained** Pau, France

# 4883 SAINT-MALO (L-H)
Friday, August 22

**OFFICIAL GOING: Turf: good**

## 5662a PRIX DE LA CHALOTAIS (CLAIMER) (2YO) (TURF) 5f 110y
3:50 (12:00) 2-Y-O £5,416 (£2,166; £1,625; £1,083; £541)

RPR
1 **Evasion Des Mottes (FR)**[21] 4883 2-8-9 0 ow1 (b) AdrienFouassier 4 58
(Mme A-M Poirier, France) **32/5**
2 3/4 **Princesse Rebelle (FR)**[21] 4882 2-9-1 0 AurelienLemaitre 8 62
(M Nigge, France) **7/1**
3 hd **Road Warrior (ITY)** 2-8-11 0 DavidBreux 10 57
(G Botti, France) **11/1**
4 hd **Maya Desnuda (IRE)**[43] 2-8-8 0 EddyHardouin 2 54
(J Heloury, France) **26/5**[3]
5 1 **Key Code**[15] 5118 2-8-11 0 (p) LouisBeuzelin 5 53
(E J O'Neill, France) **30/1**
6 nk **Dauphine De France (FR)** 2-9-1 0 MorganDelalande 6 56
(Y Barberot, France) **31/10**[1]
7 2 **Boann (IRE)**[3] 5544 2-8-5 0 (b) ValentinSeguy(3) 3 43
(J S Moore) *dwlt and a towards rr: rdn into st: sn outpcd: kpt on but nvr on terms* **9/2**[2]
8 3/4 **Stocksandshares (IRE)**[15] 5118 2-8-11 0 (b) TonyPiccone 9 43
(Matthieu Palussiere, France) **43/5**
9 2 **Charme Du Reverdy (FR)** 2-8-8 0 (b[1]) WilliamsSaraiva 7 34
(Alex Fracas, France) **27/1**
10 3 **Decisive Rebel**[44] 4065 2-8-11 0 AntoineCoutier 1 27
(Jo Hughes) *dwlt and a in rr: bhd and drvn fr bef 1/2-way: no imp and wl btn in st: eased fnl f: nvr a factor* **99/10**

1m 5.34s (65.34) **10 Ran SP% 119.4**
WIN (incl. 1 euro stake): 7.40. PLACES: 2.70, 2.60, 3.50. DF: 31.60. SF: 61.90.
**Owner** Earl Ecurie Des Mottes **Bred** Earl Ecurie Des Mottes & Earl Du Raynal **Trained** France

5663 - (Foreign Racing) - See Raceform Interactive

# 5624 GOODWOOD (R-H)
Saturday, August 23

**OFFICIAL GOING: Good (good to firm in places on round course; 7.7)**
Wind: Moderatre, against Weather: Fine Rails: Rail realignment around home bend and back straight increased distances of races of 1m and further by 7yds.

## 5664 WHITELEY CLINIC PRESTIGE STKS (GROUP 3) (FILLIES) 7f
2:20 (2:20) (Class 1) 2-Y-O
£22,684 (£8,600; £4,304; £2,144; £1,076; £540) Stalls Low

Form RPR
241 1 **Malabar**[29] 4604 2-9-0 101 RichardHughes 8 103+
(Mick Channon) *hld up towards rr: smooth prog fr 2f out: clsd to ld last 100yds: jst pushed out* **13/8**[1]
463 2 1 **Bonnie Grey**[30] 4585 2-9-0 84 OisinMurphy 5 98
(Rod Millman) *mde most: rdn over 2f out: jnd over 1f out: battled on wl fnl f but hdd and outpcd last 100yds* **20/1**
6321 3 3/4 **Zifena**[21] 4913 2-9-0 85 JohnFahy 9 96
(Eve Johnson Houghton) *blind off sltly late and dwlt: hld up in rr: prog on inner 3f out: jnd ldr over 1f out: stl upsides jst ins fnl f: nt qckn after* **11/1**
3211 4 1 **Astrelle (IRE)**[7] 5436 2-9-0 81 ShaneKelly 1 94
(Marco Botti) *pressed ldr: chal over 2f out: lost 2nd and one pce over 1f out* **14/1**
231 5 1/2 **Publilia**[36] 4382 2-9-0 87 JoeFanning 2 92
(Mark Johnston) *rrd s: in tch: shkn up over 2f out: nvr gng pce to threaten but kpt on ins fnl f* **11/2**[3]

1 **6** *9* **Efflorescence (USA)**[36] 4403 2-9-0 0 WilliamBuick 3 68
(Charlie Appleby) *t.k.h: trckd ldng pair: shkn up over 2f out: wknd qckly over 1f out: eased* 5/2[2]
311 **7** *2 3/4* **What A Party (IRE)**[11] 5279 2-9-0 76 HarryBentley 6 61
(Gay Kelleway) *trckd ldrs: rdn over 2f out: wknd wl over 1f out* 66/1
421 **8** *5* **Mystic And Artist**[12] 5232 2-9-0 76 JamesDoyle 4 47
(K R Burke) *a last: rdn 3f out: sn wknd: eased over 1f out* 12/1
1m 26.98s (-0.02) **Going Correction** 0.0s/f (Good) 8 Ran SP% **111.0**
Speed ratings: **100,98,98,96,96 86,82,77**
CSF £34.55 TOTE £2.40: £1.50, £3.60, £2.80; EX 28.90 Trifecta £338.90.
**Owner** Jon and Julia Aisbitt **Bred** Woodcote Stud Ltd **Trained** West Ilsley, Berks
**FOCUS**
Quite a few of these had marks in the 70's and 80's, so this probably won't be the strongest Group 3 run this season.

## 5665 32RED STKS (H'CAP) 7f
**2:55** (2:57) (Class 2) 3-Y-0+
**£62,250** (£18,640; £9,320; £4,660; £2,330; £1,170) **Stalls** Low

Form RPR
103 **1** **Almargo (IRE)**[23] 4826 3-8-11 **96** RoystonFfrench 7 106
(Mark Johnston) *mde all: rdn over 1f out: clr fnl f: styd on wl* 16/1
1031 **2** *2* **Rene Mathis (GER)**[14] 5189 4-9-5 **99** DavidNolan 1 105
(Richard Fahey) *mounted on crse and taken down early: dwlt: sn trckd ldrs on inner: rdn and cl up fr 2f out: styd on to take 2nd ins fnl f: no threat to wnr* 8/1
4233 **3** *nk* **Magic City (IRE)**[14] 5163 5-9-6 **100** RichardHughes 15 105+
(Richard Hannon) *hld up in last trio: stl wl in rr jst over 2f out: gd prog on outer wl over 1f out: r.o to take 3rd last strides: too much to do* 6/1[2]
4001 **4** *nk* **Safety Check (IRE)**[23] 4826 3-9-2 **101** WilliamBuick 18 103+
(Charlie Appleby) *hld up in last trio: stl last over 2f out: taken to wd outside and rapid prog over 1f out: r.o to take 4th nr fin: too much to do* 16/1
3100 **5** *1/2* **Majestic Moon (IRE)**[7] 5445 4-9-0 **94** SteveDrowne 2 97
(Richard Fahey) *chsd wnr: rdn 2f out: no imp over 1f out: lost 2nd and one pce ins fnl f* 12/1
400 **6** *3/4* **Redvers (IRE)**[28] 4648 6-9-1 **95** (b) GeorgeBaker 8 96
(Ed Vaughan) *wl in tch: trckd ldrs gng easily 2f out and wating for room: shkn up over 1f out: limited rspnse and kpt on same pce* 9/1
3124 **7** *1/2* **Dark Emerald (IRE)**[14] 5163 4-9-4 **98** JamesDoyle 13 98
(Brendan Powell) *wl plcd towards outer: rdn and prog over 2f out: disp 2nd over 1f out u.p: no ex* 20/1
3041 **8** *1 1/2* **Intransigent**[20] 4937 5-9-10 **104** LiamKeniry 4 100
(Andrew Balding) *sn trckd ldrs: prog over 2f out: rdn to dispute 2nd over 1f out: fdd fnl f* 10/1
0112 **9** *6* **Heavy Metal**[22] 4851 4-9-6 **100** JoeFanning 3 80+
(Mark Johnston) *hld up: hmpd on inner after 2f: swtchd towards outer and sme prog over 2f out: no hdwy over 1f out: wknd* 5/1[1]
0-02 **10** *nk* **Jammy Guest (IRE)**[37] 4347 4-8-8 **88** HarryBentley 17 67
(George Margarson) *s.v.s: mostly in last trio: rdn over 2f out: nvr a real factor* 25/1
2351 **11** *hd* **Related**[24] 4783 4-8-10 **90** (b) StevieDonohoe 9 69
(David Simcock) *taken down early: hld up in midfield: rdn over 2f out: no prog over 1f out: wknd* 25/1
3462 **12** *1 1/2* **American Hope (USA)**[28] 4647 3-9-5 **104** ShaneKelly 12 77+
(Mike Murphy) *t.k.h: hld up in midfield: impeded after 2f and dropped to rr: no prog on wd outside over 2f out: wknd over 1f out* 13/2[3]
2401 **13** *1 1/2* **Lexi's Hero (IRE)**[7] 5411 6-8-5 **92** (v) KieranShoemark(7) 5 63
(Richard Fahey) *t.k.h: hld up in midfield: rdn over 2f out: no prog over 1f out: wknd* 20/1
0000 **14** *hd* **Clockmaker (IRE)**[20] 4938 8-8-10 **90** HayleyTurner 6 61
(Conor Dore) *taken to post early and v steadily: disp 2nd pl to 3f out: lost pl qckly over 2f out: sn in rr* 33/1
-006 **15** *1 3/4* **Common Touch (IRE)**[14] 5189 6-8-10 **90** (b) ChrisCatlin 16 56
(Willie Musson) *racd v wd bnd after 2f: tried to make prog 3f out: wknd wl over 1f out* 40/1
-253 **16** *13* **Silent Bullet (IRE)**[28] 4681 3-9-1 **100** (p) NeilCallan 10 30
(Saeed bin Suroor) *nvr bttr than midfield: wknd and hung rt over 2f out: t.o* 16/1
1m 25.33s (-1.67) **Going Correction** 0.0s/f (Good)
**WFA** 3 from 4yo+ 5lb 16 Ran SP% **122.4**
Speed ratings (Par 109): **104,101,101,101,100 99,99,97,90,90 89,88,86,86,84 69**
CSF £126.94 CT £907.27 TOTE £29.80: £4.40, £2.50, £1.60, £3.90; EX 177.30 Trifecta £944.80.

**Owner** Sheikh Hamdan bin Mohammed Al Maktoum **Bred** Mountarmstrong Stud **Trained** Middleham Moor, N Yorks
**FOCUS**
With so many in-form horses taking part, this looked an impossible puzzle to work out prior to the off and, almost inevitably, there was trouble in running for some.

## 5666 DOOM BAR CELEBRATION MILE (GROUP 2) 1m
**3:30** (3:30) (Class 1) 3-Y-0+
**£56,710** (£21,500; £10,760; £5,360; £2,690; £1,350) **Stalls** Low

Form RPR
5223 **1** **Bow Creek (IRE)**[22] 4850 3-8-12 108 JoeFanning 1 111+
(Mark Johnston) *mde all: qcknd clr fr 2f out: in command whn hung bdly lft fnl f and careered across trck: stl hld on* 9/2[3]
-560 **2** *1 1/2* **Emell**[56] 3731 4-9-4 98 HarryBentley 6 109
(Richard Hannon) *chsd wnr: rdn and outpcd 2f out: no real imp after but kpt on to hold on for 2nd* 66/1
211 **3** *nk* **Captain Cat (IRE)**[9] 5354 5-9-4 115 JamesDoyle 8 108+
(Roger Charlton) *hld up in 7th: stl gng easily 2f out: asked for effrt over 1f out: hd at awkward angle but r.o to take 3rd nr fin: far too much to do* 9/4[1]
4426 **4** *1* **Producer**[7] 5434 5-9-4 112 RichardHughes 2 106
(Richard Hannon) *trckd ldng pair: rdn and outpcd 2f out: kpt on same pce after: lost 3rd nr fin* 14/1
5132 **5** *1 1/2* **Hors De Combat**[22] 4850 3-8-12 108 FrederikTylicki 9 101+
(James Fanshawe) *hld up in last: shkn up 2f out: styd on fnl f to take 5th nr fin: given no ch* 3/1[2]
0125 **6** *3/4* **Chil The Kite**[7] 5434 5-9-4 112 WilliamBuick 4 100
(Hughie Morrison) *hld up in 6th: shkn up and tried to cl 2f out: nt qckn over 1f out: fdd* 9/2[3]
3005 **7** *nse* **Belgian Bill**[22] 4851 6-9-4 103 (tp) MartinDwyer 5 100
(George Baker) *trckd ldrs: in 5th: shkn up over 2f out: sn outpcd and btn: fdd fnl f* 12/1

1014 **8** *3* **What About Carlo (FR)**[44] 4125 3-8-12 101 NeilCallan 7 92
(Eve Johnson Houghton) *chsd ldng trio: rdn over 2f out: wknd over 1f out* 16/1
1m 37.76s (-2.14) **Going Correction** 0.0s/f (Good)
**WFA** 3 from 4yo+ 6lb 8 Ran SP% **113.9**
Speed ratings (Par 115): **110,108,108,107,105 104,104,101**
CSF £202.81 TOTE £4.70: £1.60, £8.30, £1.50; EX 250.90 Trifecta £506.70.
**Owner** Sheikh Hamdan bin Mohammed Al Maktoum **Bred** Roundhill Stud **Trained** Middleham Moor, N Yorks
**FOCUS**
There aren't many jockeys currently riding better at getting the fractions right in front than Joe Fanning, and he again illustrated that with a fine ride on the winner.

## 5667 DOOM BAR MAIDEN FILLIES' STKS (BOBIS RACE) 6f
**4:05** (4:06) (Class 5) 2-Y-0
**£5,175** (£1,540; £769; £384) **Stalls** High

Form RPR
03 **1** **Flashy Diva**[13] 5210 2-9-0 0 JamesDoyle 3 75
(Henry Candy) *trckd ldrs: clsd fr 2f out: rdn to ld jst over 1f out: hrd pressed last 100yds: hld on wl* 4/1[3]
2 **2** *nk* **Penny Pepper (IRE)**[19] 4980 2-9-0 0 JohnFahy 2 74
(Eve Johnson Houghton) *w.w in midfield: prog jst over 2f out: shkn up over 1f out: chsd wnr fnl f: drvn to chal last 100yds: styd on but a jst hld* 3/1[2]
**3** *nk* **Mystic Jade** 2-9-0 0 RichardHughes 7 73+
(Richard Hannon) *wl in rr: swtchd rt over 2f out: prog on outer wl over 1f out: rdn to chse ldng pair ins fnl f: styd on and clsd at fin* 6/1
26 **4** *2 1/4* **Exceedingly**[44] 4126 2-9-0 0 WilliamBuick 12 66
(John Gosden) *led against nr side rail: drvn and hdd jst over 1f out: one pce* 11/4[1]
0 **5** *2 1/4* **Beauty Of The Sea**[51] 3888 2-9-0 0 HarryBentley 11 60
(Roger Varian) *trckd ldrs: shkn up 2f out: one pce after but kpt on* 16/1
5 **6** *1* **Medicean Bliss (IRE)**[17] 5042 2-9-0 0 ShaneKelly 8 57
(Jeremy Gask) *pressed ldr to over 1f out: wknd* 25/1
3 **7** *2 1/4* **Lolita**[19] 4980 2-9-0 0 AdamBeschizza 10 50
(J R Jenkins) *chsd ldng pair: rdn over 2f out: lost pl and wknd wl over 1f out* 12/1
0 **8** *nk* **Follow The Faith**[24] 4781 2-8-11 0 CharlesBishop(3) 5 49
(Mick Channon) *trckd ldrs: lost pl 2f out: pushed along and fdd* 28/1
0 **9** *2* **La Favorita (IRE)**[44] 4126 2-9-0 0 ChrisCatlin 6 43
(Charles Hills) *a towards rr: shkn up and no prog 2f out: no ch after* 33/1
00 **10** *10* **Epic Find (USA)**[44] 4129 2-9-0 0 WilliamTwiston-Davies 9 13
(Charles Hills) *dwlt: a in rr: wknd u.p 2f out: t.o* 28/1
**11** *4* **Razaan** 2-9-0 0 JoeFanning 1 1
(Mick Channon) *dwlt: a in rr: wknd over 2f out: t.o* 10/1
1m 13.19s (0.99) **Going Correction** 0.0s/f (Good) 11 Ran SP% **122.3**
Speed ratings (Par 91): **93,92,92,89,86 84,81,81,78,65 60**
CSF £16.48 TOTE £5.80: £2.10, £1.70, £2.10; EX 23.60 Trifecta £220.90.
**Owner** The Flashy Diva Partnership **Bred** D R Botterill **Trained** Kingston Warren, Oxon
**FOCUS**
This looked a fair maiden.

## 5668 ABSOLUTE AESTHETICS MARCH STKS (LISTED RACE) 1m 6f
**4:40** (4:40) (Class 1) 3-Y-0+
**£22,684** (£8,600; £4,304; £2,144; £1,076; £540) **Stalls** Low

Form RPR
-213 **1** **Forever Now**[44] 4122 3-8-9 102 WilliamBuick 3 110
(John Gosden) *mde virtually all: rdn 2f out: hrd pressed fr over 1f out: hld on wl fnl f: jst lasted* 4/1[3]
0011 **2** *shd* **Alex My Boy (IRE)**[15] 5144 3-8-9 105 JoeFanning 2 110+
(Mark Johnston) *pushed along early: trckd ldrs: waiting for gap on inner 2f out: appeared over 1f out and sn chsd wnr: persistent chal fnl f: kpt on wl nr fin: jst failed* 15/8[1]
4112 **3** *1* **Kings Fete**[21] 4893 3-8-9 99 JamesDoyle 4 108
(Sir Michael Stoute) *free to post: t.k.h: hld up in 6th: prog over 2f out: rdn and cl 3rd jst over 1f out: nt qckn last 150yds* 9/4[2]
1206 **4** *1 3/4* **Songcraft (IRE)**[22] 4849 6-9-7 109 (p) RichardHughes 6 106
(Saeed bin Suroor) *broke first but sn stdd into 4th: cl up bhd ldrs 2f out gng wl: gap clsd over 1f out and swtchd lft: rdn and one pce after* 10/1
6-00 **5** *nk* **Biographer**[86] 2704 5-9-7 105 (b) ShaneKelly 5 105
(David Lanigan) *hld up in last pair: covered up bhd ldrs over 2f out: shkn up over 1f out: nt qckn and outpcd: drvn and styd on fnl f: no ch* 20/1
4306 **6** *2 3/4* **Blue Surf**[25] 4756 5-9-7 97 HarryBentley 8 101
(Amanda Perrett) *hld up in last pair: shkn up over 2f out: no prog and btn over 1f out* 20/1
4-21 **7** *nk* **Miss Marjurie (IRE)**[77] 2991 4-9-2 93 OisinMurphy 1 96
(Denis Coakley) *trckd wnr 2f and again over 3f out: drvn over 2f out: lost 2nd over 1f out: wknd* 10/1
0-16 **8** *3/4* **Alwilda**[20] 4945 4-9-2 92 ChrisCatlin 7 95
(Sir Mark Prescott Bt) *prog to trck wnr after 2f to over 3f out: sn lost pl and btn* 33/1
3m 2.43s (-1.17) **Going Correction** 0.0s/f (Good)
**WFA** 3 from 4yo+ 12lb 8 Ran SP% **116.2**
Speed ratings: **103,102,102,101,101 99,99,99**
CSF £11.85 TOTE £5.20: £1.90, £1.10, £1.30; EX 14.00 Trifecta £23.20.
**Owner** Lady Bamford **Bred** Lady Bamford **Trained** Newmarket, Suffolk
**FOCUS**
This looked a quality event, but the early pace appeared ordinary and, with the field finishing mainly close up, one got the impression this developed into a speed test. The 3yos dominated.

## 5669 OLDHAM SEALS 50TH ANNIVERSARY STKS (H'CAP) 1m 1f
**5:15** (5:16) (Class 3) (0-90,89) 3-Y-0+
**£9,337** (£2,796; £1,398; £699; £349; £175) **Stalls** Low

Form RPR
1211 **1** **Balmoral Castle**[33] 4501 5-9-0 80 NedCurtis(5) 2 88
(Jonathan Portman) *trckd ldrs: taken wd and clsd fr 2f out: led jst over 1f out: rdn and hung lft sn after: pushed along and hld on nr fin* 11/2
3031 **2** *nk* **Angelic Upstart (IRE)**[23] 4827 6-9-3 85 KieranShoemark(7) 10 92
(Andrew Balding) *in tch towards rr: shkn up over 3f out: no prog 2f out: rallied jst over 1f out: styd on wl to take 2nd last strides* 7/2[2]
4100 **3** *shd* **Rapid Advance**[17] 5031 3-8-12 80 ShaneKelly 9 87
(Sir Michael Stoute) *hld up in last pair: prog over 2f out: cajoled along and clsd to chal ins fnl f: drvn and nt qckn last 100yds: lost 2nd nr fin* 12/1

3005 **4** *1* **Moonday Sun (USA)**[25] 4761 5-10-0 89........................ JamesDoyle 7 94
(Amanda Perrett) *trckd ldr: rdn over 2f out: nt qckn and lost 2nd over 1f out: kpt on same pce* **5/1**[3]
2610 **5** *½* **Sheila's Buddy**[25] 4761 5-9-4 79........................ JohnFahy 3 83
(J S Moore) *s.v.s: racd in last: stl there and shkn up 2f out: styd on fnl f: nrst fin* **20/1**
5165 **6** *1¾* **Insaany**[23] 4821 3-9-3 85........................ JoeFanning 4 85
(Mark Johnston) *led: rdn 2f out: hdd jst over 1f out: wknd fnl f* **5/2**[1]
265- **7** *2½* **Cruck Realta**[302] 7497 4-10-0 89........................ WilliamTwiston-Davies 1 84
(Mick Channon) *trckd ldng pair: drvn 3f out: wknd over 1f out* **12/1**
1510 **8** *3* **Ogbourne Downs**[25] 4761 4-9-10 85........................ HarryBentley 6 73
(Charles Hills) *trckd ldrs: shkn up 2f out: wknd qckly over 1f out* **8/1**

1m 54.58s (-1.72) **Going Correction** 0.0s/f (Good)
**WFA** 3 from 4yo+ 7lb **8** Ran SP% **114.1**
Speed ratings (Par 107): **107,106,106,105,105 103,101,98**
CSF £24.96 CT £222.54 TOTE £5.10: £1.60, £1.60, £3.50; EX 11.00 Trifecta £97.70.
**Owner** J G B Portman **Bred** Springcombe Park Stud **Trained** Upper Lambourn, Berks

**FOCUS**
There wasn't a lot of pace on in the early stages and the field spread out heading into the final 2f. The winner was recording a personal best.

## 5670 CHICHESTER OBSERVER STKS (H'CAP) (BOBIS RACE) 1m 4f
**5:50** (5:51) (Class 4) (0-80,80) 3-Y-O **£6,469** (£1,925; £962; £481) **Stalls** High

Form RPR
4521 **1** **Tall Ship (IRE)**[22] 4855 3-9-6 79........................ ShaneKelly 9 100
(Gary Moore) *trckd ldrs: clsd to ld wl over 2f out: sn powered clr: drvn over 1f out: styd on strly* **3/1**[2]
5223 **2** *7* **Artful Rogue (IRE)**[15] 5135 3-9-4 77........................ HarryBentley 3 87
(Amanda Perrett) *trckd ldng pair: led briefly 3f out: unavailing chse of wnr after but drew clr of rest* **8/1**[3]
5436 **3** *8* **Shadows Ofthenight (IRE)**[36] 4392 3-8-13 72........................ SamHitchcott 6 69
(Mick Channon) *hld up in last: pushed along 5f out: prog over 3f out: tk modest 3rd 1f out: kpt on* **25/1**
1-03 **4** *1* **Hooded (USA)**[28] 4651 3-9-7 80........................ JamesDoyle 4 76
(Roger Charlton) *led: shkn up and hdd 3f out: short of room briefly and sn outpcd: wknd and lost 3rd fnl f* **7/4**[1]
5413 **5** *1* **Opera Fan (FR)**[9] 5353 3-9-4 77........................ JoeFanning 5 71
(Mark Johnston) *pressed ldr to 3f out: sn btn: wknd over 1f out* **10/1**
-061 **6** *2* **Mustamir (IRE)**[23] 4812 3-9-0 80........................(b) KieranShoemark[(7)] 8 71
(James Tate) *slowly away and shoved along early: prog to trck ldrs after 4f: rdn and dropped to rr again over 3f out: plugged on u.p fnl 2f* **10/1**
0212 **7** *6* **Secure Cloud (IRE)**[14] 5185 3-9-4 77........................ RoystonFfrench 7 58
(Charles Hills) *in tch: rdn 3f out: sn wknd* **10/1**
1004 **8** *4½* **Gannicus**[57] 3655 3-8-13 72........................(t) WilliamTwiston-Davies 2 46
(Brendan Powell) *towards rr: rdn 5f out: struggling over 3f out: sn bhd* **25/1**
0245 **9** *35* **Mymatechris (IRE)**[12] 5259 3-8-12 71........................(t) OisinMurphy 1
(Andrew Balding) *wl in tch: rdn and wknd over 3f out: virtually p.u fnl f* **12/1**

2m 35.32s (-3.08) **Going Correction** 0.0s/f (Good) **9** Ran SP% **115.1**
Speed ratings (Par 102): **110,105,100,99,98 97,93,90,67**
CSF £27.23 CT £491.78 TOTE £3.10: £1.30, £2.00, £5.40; EX 25.90 Trifecta £792.80.
**Owner** R A Green **Bred** Kincorth Investments Inc **Trained** Lower Beeding, W Sussex

**FOCUS**
A fair handicap, in which the already respectable pace appeared to increase noticeably when the field got to the home straight. The winner is improving.
T/Plt: £47.60 to a £1 stake. Pool: £111,325.82 - 1704.39 winning tickets. T/Qpdt: £7.20 to a £1 stake. Pool: £6,727.59 - 688.34 winning tickets. JN

# 5643 NEWMARKET (R-H)
### Saturday, August 23

**OFFICIAL GOING: Good to firm**
Wind: Light half-behind Weather: Overcast with the odd shower Rails: Bend into the home straight repositioned and races of 10f & 13f increased by 20m

## 5671 STAY AT SOUTHEND AIRPORT HOLIDAY INN EBF MAIDEN STKS (BOBIS RACE) 6f
**2:10** (2:10) (Class 4) 2-Y-O **£4,528** (£1,347; £673; £336) **Stalls** High

Form RPR
42 **1** **Astrophysics**[16] 5091 2-9-2 0........................ JoeyHaynes[(3)] 5 80+
(David Elsworth) *mde all: rdn over 1f out: r.o* **7/2**[2]
**2** *1¼* **Encore D'Or** 2-9-5 0........................ MartinLane 1 76+
(Ralph Beckett) *chsd wnr: shkn up over 1f out: styd on* **4/1**[3]
3 **3** *½* **Rahmah (IRE)**[24] 4790 2-9-5 0........................ GrahamGibbons 7 75
(Robert Cowell) *s.i.s: sn rcvrd to join wnr tl pushed along over 2f out: rdn over 1f out: styd on* **20/1**
32 **4** *hd* **Wonder Of Qatar (IRE)**[13] 5201 2-9-5 0........................ SeanLevey 8 74
(Richard Hannon) *chsd ldrs: rdn over 1f out: styd on* **3/1**[1]
**5** *2½* **Waady (IRE)** 2-9-5 0........................ DaneO'Neill 3 67
(John Gosden) *s.i.s: hld up: plld hrd: hdwy over 2f out: rdn over 1f out: no ex ins fnl f* **7/2**[2]
6 **6** *1¾* **Zamperini (IRE)**[29] 4618 2-9-5 0........................ TedDurcan 4 61+
(Mike Murphy) *hld up: rdn over 2f out: styd on same pce fr over 1f out* **25/1**
532 **7** *3¾* **Henley**[26] 4739 2-9-5 79........................ MartinHarley 9 50
(William Jarvis) *hld up: rdn over 2f out: wknd fnl f* **11/2**

1m 11.62s (-0.88) **Going Correction** -0.15s/f (Firm) **7** Ran SP% **113.4**
Speed ratings (Par 96): **99,97,96,96,93 90,85**
CSF £17.55 TOTE £5.20: £2.90, £2.30; EX 16.90 Trifecta £133.50.
**Owner** D R C Elsworth **Bred** Sarah Stoneham **Trained** Newmarket, Suffolk

**FOCUS**
Probably no more than an average maiden for this track and the fact they finished in a bit of a heap suggests the form isn't anything to get too excited about, but the winner is progressing.

## 5672 FLY FLYBE FROM LONDON SOUTHEND AIRPORT NURSERY H'CAP (BOBIS RACE) 7f
**2:45** (2:47) (Class 3) (0-95,90) 2-Y-O **£7,762** (£2,310; £1,154; £577) **Stalls** High

Form RPR
120 **1** **Kasb (IRE)**[67] 3318 2-9-4 87........................ DaneO'Neill 6 94+
(John Gosden) *s.i.s: hld up: hdwy over 2f out: led over 1f out: rdn and edgd rt ins fnl f: r.o* **9/2**[1]
2251 **2** *½* **Flying Machine (IRE)**[43] 4157 2-8-11 83........................ GeorgeChaloner[(3)] 1 87
(Richard Fahey) *trckd ldrs: pushed along over 2f out: rdn and ev ch over 1f out: r.o* **11/2**[3]
1423 **3** *1¼* **Assault On Rome (IRE)**[32] 4524 2-8-12 81........................ FrannyNorton 8 81
(Mark Johnston) *w ldr tl pushed along 1/2-way: rdn and ev ch over 1f out: styd on same pce ins fnl f* **9/1**
2132 **4** *½* **Sunset Sail (IRE)**[15] 5134 2-9-7 90........................ SeanLevey 2 89
(Richard Hannon) *hld up: swtchd rt and hdwy over 1f out: sn rdn and hung lft: styd on same pce ins fnl f* **6/1**
514 **5** *1¼* **Inniscastle Lad**[22] 4853 2-9-1 84........................ TomQueally 7 80
(William Muir) *prom: lost pl 1/2-way: rallied over 1f out: no ex ins fnl f* **5/1**[2]
1100 **6** *nse* **Midterm Break (IRE)**[35] 4439 2-9-6 89........................ GrahamGibbons 5 84
(David Barron) *s.i.s: hld up: hdwy over 2f out: rdn and nt clr run over 1f out: no ex ins fnl f* **5/1**[2]
41 **7** *¾* **Spring Loaded (IRE)**[19] 4965 2-8-6 75........................ MartinLane 3 68
(Paul D'Arcy) *chsd ldrs: wnt 2nd 1/2-way: led 2f out: rdn and hdd over 1f out: wknd wl ins fnl f* **10/1**
5641 **8** *6* **Honcho (IRE)**[15] 5128 2-8-6 78........................ JoeyHaynes[(3)] 4 55
(David Elsworth) *led 5f: wknd fnl f* **7/1**

1m 24.86s (-0.84) **Going Correction** -0.15s/f (Firm) **8** Ran SP% **112.8**
Speed ratings (Par 98): **98,97,96,95,94 93,93,86**
CSF £28.34 CT £212.11 TOTE £4.80: £2.30, £1.70, £2.30; EX 32.90 Trifecta £435.40.
**Owner** Hamdan Al Maktoum **Bred** J O'Connor **Trained** Newmarket, Suffolk

**FOCUS**
A competitive-looking nursery and the winner looks sure to do better.

## 5673 FLY EASYJET FROM LONDON SOUTHEND AIRPORT H'CAP 1m 5f
**3:20** (3:20) (Class 2) (0-100,98) 3-Y-O+ **£25,876** (£7,700; £3,848; £1,924) **Stalls** High

Form RPR
5-20 **1** **Nautilus**[154] 1071 4-9-11 95........................(p) NickyMackay 9 104
(John Gosden) *racd keenly: led 11f out: clr over 9f out tl rdn over 1f out: jst hld on* **14/1**
0560 **2** *½* **Buthelezi (USA)**[10] 5299 6-8-9 79........................(p) BenCurtis 4 87
(Brian Ellison) *a.p: rdn over 3f out: chsd wnr ins fnl f: sn ev ch: styd on* **15/2**[3]
1550 **3** *¾* **Special Meaning**[35] 4443 4-9-9 93........................ FrannyNorton 3 100
(Mark Johnston) *sn led: hdd 11f out: chsd wnr: rdn over 1f out: styd on* **17/2**
2554 **4** *1* **Debdebdeb**[14] 5161 4-9-3 90........................ ThomasBrown[(3)] 1 96
(Andrew Balding) *hld up: rdn over 3f out: hdwy over 1f out: styd on* **11/2**[2]
562 **5** *1* **Esteaming**[73] 3111 4-9-10 94........................ GrahamGibbons 10 98
(David Barron) *hld up: hdwy over 1f out: sn rdn: styd on* **14/1**
3050 **6** *1½* **Kelinni (IRE)**[25] 4759 6-9-12 96........................ MartinHarley 2 98
(Marco Botti) *hld up: swtchd lft and hdwy over 2f out: rdn over 1f out: no ex ins fnl f* **14/1**
2130 **7** *7* **Sirvino**[84] 2785 9-9-10 94........................ PaddyAspell 5 85
(David Barron) *hld up: hdwy over 2f out: wknd over 1f out* **33/1**
2521 **8** *1¾* **Warrior Of Light (IRE)**[23] 4819 3-9-3 98........................ TedDurcan 11 87
(David Lanigan) *hld up: rdn over 2f out: sn edgd rt and wknd* **15/8**[1]
-005 **9** *7* **Boite (IRE)**[25] 4759 4-9-4 93........................ JordanNason[(5)] 8 71
(Peter Chapple-Hyam) *s.i.s: sn prom: rdn over 3f out: wknd over 1f out* **10/1**
113 **10** *22* **Nullarbor Sky (IRE)**[21] 4917 4-9-0 84........................(p) SeanLevey 6 56
(Lucy Wadham) *chsd ldrs: rdn over 3f out: wknd over 1f out: eased ins fnl f* **25/1**
0-04 **11** *¾* **Highland Castle**[98] 2342 6-9-3 90........................ JoeyHaynes[(3)] 7 34
(David Elsworth) *hld up: rdn and wknd over 2f out* **9/1**

2m 42.72s (-1.28) **Going Correction** +0.15s/f (Good)
**WFA** 3 from 4yo+ 11lb **11** Ran SP% **118.3**
Speed ratings (Par 109): **109,108,108,107,107 106,101,100,96,82 82**
CSF £115.87 CT £960.84 TOTE £16.50: £4.90, £3.10, £3.40; EX 155.70 Trifecta £1421.50 Part won..
**Owner** Abdulla Al Khalifa **Bred** Sheikh Abdulla Bin Isa Al Khalifa **Trained** Newmarket, Suffolk
■ Stewards' Enquiry : Martin Harley caution: careless riding.

**FOCUS**
This looked wide open on paper, but those that raced handily were at an advantage.

## 5674 STOBART MEMBERS CLUB HOPEFUL STKS (LISTED RACE) 6f
**3:55** (3:59) (Class 1) 3-Y-O+
**£22,684** (£8,600; £4,304; £2,144; £1,076; £540) **Stalls** High

Form RPR
5002 **1** **Tropics (USA)**[42] 4201 6-9-1 115........................ RobertWinston 4 117+
(Dean Ivory) *stdd s: hld up: plld hrd: hdwy and nt clr run over 1f out: qcknd up to ld and hmpd towards fin: readily* **11/4**[1]
0443 **2** *½* **Alben Star (IRE)**[21] 4895 6-9-1 107........................ GeorgeChaloner 1 113
(Richard Fahey) *chsd ldrs: rdn to ld ins fnl f: hdd towards fin* **11/2**[3]
355- **3** *nse* **Reckless Abandon**[321] 7054 4-9-1 113........................ MartinLane 2 113
(Charlie Appleby) *w ldrs: rdn to ld over 1f out: hdd ins fnl f: r.o* **6/1**
3224 **4** *½* **Naadirr (IRE)**[35] 4438 3-8-12 108........................(p) MartinHarley 8 111
(Marco Botti) *led to 1/2-way: rdn and ev ch whn hung rt ins fnl f: kpt on* **9/1**
4010 **5** *½* **Justice Day (IRE)**[42] 4201 3-8-12 108........................ BenCurtis 3 110
(David Elsworth) *w ldr tl led 1/2-way: rdn and hdd over 1f out: ev ch whn hmpd wl ins fnl f: no ex* **20/1**
10-0 **6** *2¾* **Brown Sugar (IRE)**[22] 4852 3-8-12 109........................ SeanLevey 11 101
(Richard Hannon) *hld up: swtchd rt over 1f out: styd on ins fnl f: nt trble ldrs* **25/1**
20-0 **7** *½* **Caspar Netscher**[13] 5223 5-9-1 108........................ GrahamGibbons 7 99
(David Simcock) *trckd ldrs: racd keenly: rdn over 1f out: no ex ins fnl f* **16/1**
-111 **8** *1* **Intrinsic**[21] 4895 4-9-1 101........................ TomQueally 10 96
(Robert Cowell) *prom: rdn and edgd lft over 1f out: no ex fnl f* **3/1**[2]
600- **9** *2¼* **Khubala (IRE)**[315] 7208 5-9-1 97........................(b) NickyMackay 12 89
(Hugo Palmer) *hld up: rdn over 2f out: wknd fnl f* **50/1**
0224 **10** *½* **Ruwaiyan (USA)**[21] 4895 5-9-1 103........................(p) FrannyNorton 13 87
(James Tate) *prom: rdn over 2f out: wknd fnl f* **8/1**

1m 9.84s (-2.66) **Going Correction** -0.15s/f (Firm)
**WFA** 3 from 4yo+ 3lb **10** Ran SP% **118.9**
Speed ratings: **111,110,110,109,108 105,104,103,100,99**
CSF £18.30 TOTE £3.80: £1.60, £2.00, £1.90; EX 18.70 Trifecta £122.90.
**Owner** Dean Ivory **Bred** D Konecny, S Branch & A Branch **Trained** Radlett, Herts

**FOCUS**
A classy Listed sprint in which the first and third were proven at Group 1 level, so the form is strong for the grade. Most of the runners ended up towards the stands' rail.

## 5675 FLY THOMSON FROM LONDON SOUTHEND AIRPORT H'CAP (BOBIS RACE) 6f
4:30 (4:31) (Class 3) (0-90,90) 3-Y-O £9,056 (£2,695; £1,346; £673) Stalls High

Form RPR
3612 1 **Mr Win (IRE)**25 4766 3-9-0 83 TedDurcan 2 97
(Chris Wall) *hld up: hdwy over 1f out: rdn to ld wl ins fnl f: r.o* 7/2[1]
-610 2 2 **Angel Flores (IRE)**21 4898 3-8-0 72 JoeyHaynes(3) 1 80
(Richard Fahey) *chsd ldrs: led over 1f out: sn rdn: hdd and unable qck wl ins fnl f* 10/1
5221 3 3 **Basil Berry**13 5204 3-9-4 90 ConnorBeasley(3) 8 88
(Chris Dwyer) *a.p: rdn over 1f out: styd on same pce ins fnl f* 8/1
10 4 ¾ **Greeb**28 4669 3-9-6 89 DaneO'Neill 7 85
(Charles Hills) *hld up: rdn over 1f out: nt clr run and r.o ins fnl f: nvr nrr* 9/2[2]
4214 5 ½ **Iseemist (IRE)**37 4339 3-9-2 85 TomQueally 3 79
(John Gallagher) *hld up: hdwy and edgd rt over 2f out: rdn over 1f out: styd on same pce fnl f* 16/1
6213 6 1 **Dont Have It Then**50 3936 3-8-6 75 JimmyQuinn 12 66
(Willie Musson) *hld up: hmpd over 2f out: hdwy over 1f out: sn rdn: no ex fnl f* 16/1
3445 7 2 **Our Queenie (IRE)**15 5152 3-9-5 88 SeanLevey 6 73
(Richard Hannon) *chsd ldrs: rdn 1/2-way: wknd ins fnl f* 10/1
5006 8 ½ **Charles Molson**13 5204 3-9-4 87 (b[1]) BenCurtis 5 70
(Henry Candy) *hld up: hmpd over 2f out: sn rdn: nvr on terms* 8/1
0050 9 1 ¾ **Ben Hall (IRE)**27 4712 3-9-1 84 (b[1]) GrahamGibbons 9 62
(Mike Murphy) *led and sn clr: wknd and hdd over 1f out* 33/1
-211 10 8 **Fyrecracker (IRE)**27 4697 3-8-11 80 MartinLane 4 32
(Marcus Tregoning) *chsd ldrs: pushed along and lost pl whn hmpd over 2f out: sn wknd* 5/1[3]
-640 11 1 ¾ **Bahamian Heights**28 4669 3-9-4 90 (b) DannyBrock(3) 10 36
(Clive Brittain) *chsd ldrs tl rdn and wknd over 1f out* 25/1
152 12 1 **Diamond Lady**21 4918 3-8-11 80 PaddyAspell 11 23
(William Stone) *s.i.s: hdwy over 4f out: rdn and wknd over 1f out* 16/1
1m 10.85s (-1.65) **Going Correction** -0.15s/f (Firm) 12 Ran SP% 121.9
Speed ratings (Par 104): **105,102,98,97,96 95,92,92,89,79 76,75**
CSF £40.65 CT £274.41 TOTE £4.40: £2.30, £3.50, £2.10; EX 53.90 Trifecta £452.70.
**Owner** Des Thurlby **Bred** Kevin Blake **Trained** Newmarket, Suffolk

**FOCUS**
They went a good clip and that set things up nicely for the hold-up horses who dominated the finish.

## 5676 FLY SKYWORK AIRLINES LONDON SOUTHEND AIRPORT H'CAP 1m 2f
5:05 (5:05) (Class 3) (0-95,95) 3-Y-O+ £9,056 (£2,695; £1,346; £673) Stalls Centre

Form RPR
-063 1 **Elhaame (IRE)**14 5174 4-9-12 93 MartinLane 7 102
(Luca Cumani) *hld up: hdwy over 2f out: rdn to ld over 1f out: styd on* 9/4[1]
3414 2 1 ¼ **Border Legend**21 4888 5-10-0 95 TedDurcan 10 101
(Roger Charlton) *s.i.s: hdwy over 8f out: rdn and ev ch over 1f out: styd on same pce ins fnl f* 11/2[3]
2651 3 1 **Saab Almanal**35 4435 3-9-6 95 TomQueally 9 99
(James Fanshawe) *hld up: hdwy over 2f out: rdn over 1f out: hung rt ins fnl f: styd on same pce* 7/2[2]
2131 4 nk **No Win No Fee**23 4832 4-8-5 77 ow1 AlistairRawlinson(5) 8 80
(Michael Appleby) *chsd ldr: chal over 3f out: rdn over 2f out: styng on same pce whn carried rt ins fnl f* 6/1
311- 5 ½ **Ghaawy**340 6501 3-9-0 89 DaneO'Neill 2 91
(Sir Michael Stoute) *hld up in tch: rdn and nt clr run over 1f out: styd on same pce ins fnl f* 7/2[2]
610 6 4 ½ **Tabreek (USA)**71 3200 3-9-1 90 SeanLevey 4 84
(Richard Hannon) *led: rdn: edgd rt and hdd over 1f out: sn wnt lft: hld whn hmpd ins fnl f* 12/1
2m 5.89s (0.39) **Going Correction** +0.15s/f (Good)
**WFA** 3 from 4yo+ 8lb 6 Ran SP% 112.6
Speed ratings (Par 107): **104,103,102,101,101 97**
CSF £15.05 CT £40.76 TOTE £2.80: £2.20, £2.30; EX 19.50 Trifecta £41.30.
**Owner** Sheikh Mohammed Obaid Al Maktoum **Bred** W Maxwell Ervine **Trained** Newmarket, Suffolk

**FOCUS**
A competitive heat despite the reduced field and all six were in with a chance two out. The winner was back to his best.

## 5677 FLY LONDON SOUTHEND AIRPORT TO BARCELONA H'CAP 5f
5:40 (5:40) (Class 4) (0-85,85) 3-Y-O+ £5,175 (£1,540; £769; £384) Stalls High

Form RPR
6206 1 **Holley Shiftwell**15 5152 4-9-4 79 GrahamGibbons 14 89
(Stuart Williams) *a.p: swtchd rt over 1f out: rdn to ld wl ins fnl f: hung lft: r.o* 10/1
24 2 1 **Angelito**49 3948 5-9-2 77 RobertWinston 11 83
(Ed McMahon) *hld up: hdwy 2f out: rdn to ld ins fnl f: sn hdd: styd on* 5/1[2]
0000 3 hd **Taajub (IRE)**27 4700 7-9-10 85 TedDurcan 12 90
(Peter Crate) *hld up: shkn up over 1f out: edgd rt and r.o ins fnl f* 16/1
5015 4 nk **Avon Breeze**7 5444 5-9-7 85 (p) ConnorBeasley(3) 9 89
(Richard Whitaker) *sn pushed along in rr: hdwy over 1f out: r.o: nt rch ldrs* 5/2[1]
3002 5 1 ¾ **Touch The Clouds**9 5350 3-8-9 72 PaddyAspell 4 70
(William Stone) *prom: pushed along 1/2-way: running on whn hmpd ins fnl f: kpt on but nt trble ldrs* 16/1
5320 6 ½ **Monumental Man**25 4762 5-9-6 81 (p) MartinLane 13 77
(James Unett) *led: rdn and hdd over 1f out: styd on same pce ins fnl f* 12/1
2326 7 ¾ **Whitecrest**11 5275 6-8-8 74 PhilipPrince(5) 7 67
(John Spearing) *prom: lost pl 3f out: r.o wl ins fnl f* 25/1
0230 8 2 **Vincentti (IRE)**29 4632 4-9-4 79 BenCurtis 2 76
(Ronald Harris) *s.i.s: in rr and pushed along 1/2-way: running on whn hmpd ins fnl f: nt rcvr* 12/1
150 9 nk **Powerful Wind (IRE)**25 4762 5-8-13 81 DavidParkes(7) 10 66
(Ronald Harris) *w ldrs: rdn to ld briefly ins fnl f: sn hdd & wknd* 20/1
3310 10 1 **Al Senad**38 4328 3-9-8 85 FrannyNorton 8 67
(Peter Chapple-Hyam) *chsd ldrs: pushed along 1/2-way: wknd fnl f* 12/1
1-20 11 hd **Agerzam**69 3275 4-9-5 80 (b) DaneO'Neill 5 61
(Roger Varian) *prom: rdn over 1f out: wknd fnl f* 10/1
064 12 3 ½ **Breccbennach**19 4983 4-9-4 79 (tp) SeanLevey 1 47
(Seamus Durack) *w ldrs: rdn to ld over 1f out: edghed rt: hdd & wknd ins fnl f* 6/1[3]
58.22s (-0.88) **Going Correction** -0.15s/f (Firm)
**WFA** 3 from 4yo+ 2lb 12 Ran SP% 121.2
Speed ratings (Par 105): **101,99,99,98,95 95,93,90,90,88 88,82**
CSF £60.73 CT £597.14 TOTE £9.70: £2.50, £2.30, £6.50; EX 62.90 Trifecta £650.80.
**Owner** J W Parry **Bred** Mr & Mrs K W Grundy, Mr & Mrs P Hopper **Trained** Newmarket, Suffolk

**FOCUS**
The final race of the season on the July course. A wide-open sprint with a contested pace.
T/Plt: £393.40 to a £1 stake. Pool: £56819.16 - 105.43 winning tickets T/Qpdt: £58.60 to a £1 stake. Pool: £4810.17 - 60.68 winning tickets CR

# 5194 REDCAR (L-H)
## Saturday, August 23

**OFFICIAL GOING: Good to firm (7.4)**
Wind: Virtually nil Weather: Mixture of sunshine and cloud, rain after race 5

## 5678 RACINGUK.COM/ANYWHERE: 3 DEVICES, 1 PRICE LADY AMATEUR RIDERS' H'CAP 1m 2f
5:30 (5:31) (Class 5) (0-75,75) 3-Y-O+ £3,119 (£967; £483; £242) Stalls Low

Form RPR
0414 1 **Nanton (USA)**7 5421 12-10-11 75 MrsCBartley 12 85
(Jim Goldie) *stdd s: hld up in rr: stl plenty to do whn n.m.r on inner 2f out: angled rt towards outer fr over 1f out: nt in clr tl ins fnl f: qcknd up wl: led 50yds out* 6/1[3]
1052 2 2 ½ **Run Fat Lass Run**13 5206 4-10-1 68 (p) MissJRRichards(3) 5 73
(Philip Kirby) *midfield: rdn and hdwy over 1f out: led ins fnl f: kpt on: hdd 50yds out* 10/1
0544 3 1 ½ **Al Furat (USA)**24 4797 6-9-6 56 oh5 MissADeniel 7 58
(Ron Barr) *trckd ldrs: led wl over 2f out: rdn 2f out: hdd ins fnl f: no ex* 20/1
3202 4 ½ **Merchant Of Medici**8 5371 7-9-13 63 (p) MissCWalton 3 64
(Micky Hammond) *in tch: rdn to chse ldr 2f out: no ex fnl f* 7/1
/302 5 ½ **Kudu Country (IRE)**17 5049 8-10-2 66 MissSBrotherton 9 66
(Tom Tate) *prom: rdn over 2f out: grad wknd fnl f* 4/1[1]
5-00 6 1 ¼ **On The Hoof**7 5421 5-9-12 65 MissJoannaMason(3) 2 63
(Michael Easterby) *in tch: rdn over 2f out: wknd fnl f* 20/1
1635 7 shd **Elizabeth Coffee (IRE)**28 4663 6-9-8 61 MissMeganNicholls(3) 6 59
(John Weymes) *trckd ldrs: rdn over 2f out: wknd fnl f* 9/1
6400 8 2 ¼ **Fujin Dancer (FR)**77 2981 9-10-8 72 MissHBethell 4 65
(Brian Ellison) *hld up: sme hdwy over 2f out: sn rdn: wknd fnl f* 9/2[2]
1500 9 ½ **Pertuis (IRE)**8 5371 8-10-5 69 MissAliceMills 10 61
(Micky Hammond) *hld up towards outer: rdn over 2f out: nvr threatened* 25/1
0000 10 ½ **Valentine's Gift**39 4293 6-9-1 56 oh1 MissLWilson(5) 11 48
(Neville Bycroft) *hld up in rr: rdn over 2f out: nvr threatened* 20/1
1533 11 2 ½ **Aldwick Bay (IRE)**8 5371 6-10-6 75 MissCAGreenway(5) 8 62
(Tom Dascombe) *sn led: rdn whn hdd wl over 2f out: wknd* 6/1[3]
2m 7.95s (0.85) **Going Correction** +0.20s/f (Good) 11 Ran SP% 116.5
Speed ratings (Par 103): **104,102,100,100,100 99,98,97,96,96 94**
CSF £59.42 CT £1128.30 TOTE £5.20: £1.80, £3.00, £5.10; EX 45.30 Trifecta £548.50 Part won..
**Owner** Johnnie Delta Racing **Bred** Samuel H And Mrs Rogers, Jr **Trained** Uplawmoor, E Renfrews

**FOCUS**
The ground was officially good to firm, but Carol Bartley said it was 'good, a bit loose on top'. This was a strongly run race for lady amateur riders and it favoured the hold-up horses. It's been rated through the runner-up to form.

## 5679 JAYNE PRESTON BIG BIRTHDAY CELEBRATIONS MAIDEN AUCTION STKS 6f
6:00 (6:01) (Class 5) 2-Y-O £3,234 (£962; £481; £240) Stalls Centre

Form RPR
32 1 **Mythmaker**16 5086 2-9-1 0 PaulMulrennan 11 76
(Bryan Smart) *prom: rdn to ld over 1f out: kpt on: edgd lft ins fnl f* 5/2[2]
U 2 ½ **Get Knotted (IRE)**16 5086 2-9-3 0 PhillipMakin 1 77
(Michael Dods) *in tch: rdn over 1f out: kpt on wl fnl f: wnt 2nd nr fin* 20/1
0223 3 hd **Bahamian Sunrise**42 4218 2-8-13 75 TonyHamilton 2 72
(Richard Fahey) *prom: rdn 2f out: ev ch ent fnl f: one pce: lost 2nd nr fin* 4/6[1]
4 6 **Hidden Rebel** 2-8-7 0 ow2 GarryWhillans(5) 10 53
(Alistair Whillans) *s.i.s: hld up: rdn 1/2-way: kpt on ins fnl f* 20/1
06 5 nk **Oricano**24 4790 2-8-3 0 GemmaTutty(5) 3 48
(Karen Tutty) *dwlt: hld up: rdn 1/2-way: kpt on ins fnl f* 25/1
00 6 1 ¼ **Bushranger Bay (IRE)**7 5443 2-9-3 0 DuranFentiman 7 53
(Tim Easterby) *in tch: rdn 1/2-way: wknd over 1f out* 50/1
7 ½ **Show Boat** 2-9-3 0 GrahamLee 6 52
(Ann Duffield) *hld up in tch: rdn 1/2-way: wknd over 1f out* 13/2[3]
8 2 ¾ **Euro Mac** 2-8-8 0 AndrewElliott 9 35
(Neville Bycroft) *in tch: rdn 1/2-way: hung lft and wknd appr fnl f* 33/1
00 9 ¾ **Pancake Day**10 5297 2-8-13 0 JamesSullivan 8 37
(Jason Ward) *led: rdn whn hdd over 1f out: wknd* 66/1
10 34 **Dancruise (IRE)** 2-9-3 0 TomEaves 5
(Kristin Stubbs) *prom: lost pl qckly over 3f out: sn t.o* 33/1
1m 11.76s (-0.04) **Going Correction** -0.125s/f (Firm) 10 Ran SP% 124.6
Speed ratings (Par 94): **95,94,94,86,85 84,83,79,78,33**
CSF £53.57 TOTE £3.10: £1.10, £6.80, £1.02; EX 87.60 Trifecta £169.10.
**Owner** Crossfields Racing **Bred** Crossfields Bloodstock Ltd **Trained** Hambleton, N Yorks

**FOCUS**
A fair maiden in which the first three drew clear in the final furlong. The winner has been rated as matching his Newcastle form.

## 5680 MARKET CROSS JEWELLERS NOVICE MEDIAN AUCTION STKS 7f
6:30 (6:30) (Class 5) 2-Y-O £3,234 (£962; £481; £240) Stalls Centre

Form RPR
124 1 **Russian Punch**30 4585 2-8-10 83 GrahamLee 2 89+
(James Given) *trckd ldr: led 2f out: pushed clr fr over 1f out: easily* 9/2[3]
116 2 5 **Lieutenant Kaffee (USA)**42 4199 2-9-6 93 TonyHamilton 3 86
(Richard Fahey) *hld up: tk str hold for 2f: rdn over 2f out: wnt 2nd jst ins fnl f: one pce and no ch w wnr* 4/6[1]
1323 3 2 ¾ **Buccaneers Vault (IRE)**16 5085 2-9-1 85 PaulMulrennan 5 72
(Michael Dods) *hld up in tch: rdn to chse wnr over 1f out: wknd ins fnl f* 7/2[2]

4 4 1/2 **Maureb (IRE)**[12] 5241 2-8-8 0 BarryMcHugh 4 64
(Tony Coyle) *trckd ldr: rdn over 2f out: wknd ins fnl f* **16/1**
5 5 1 1/4 **Bread**[34] 4467 2-8-13 0 PhillipMakin 1 65
(Garry Moss) *led: rdn whn hdd 2f out: sn wknd* **40/1**
1m 24.39s (-0.11) **Going Correction** -0.125s/f (Firm) **5** Ran SP% **108.7**
Speed ratings (Par 94): **95,89,86,85,84**
CSF £7.84 TOTE £4.80: £1.50, £1.10; EX 8.50 Trifecta £10.20.
**Owner** Lovely Bubbly Racing **Bred** Mrs Deborah O'Brien **Trained** Willoughton, Lincs

**FOCUS**
An interesting novice contest but it wouldn't be the best of form guides as the early gallop was ordinary.

## 5681 DOWNLOAD THE RACINGUK IPAD APP STRAIGHT-MILE CHAMPIONSHIP STKS (QUALIFIER) (H'CAP) 1m
**7:00** (7:00) (Class 4) (0-85,85) 3-Y-O+ **£6,469** (£1,925; £962; £481) **Stalls** Centre

Form RPR
6443 1 **Karaka Jack**[12] 5235 7-9-2 75 GrahamLee 7 83
(Jim Goldie) *prom: rdn over 2f out: kpt on: led towards fin* **11/2**[3]
11U6 2 1/2 **Border Bandit (USA)**[7] 5446 6-9-9 82 (p) DavidAllan 12 89
(Tracy Waggott) *prom: rdn over 2f out: led 1f out: kpt on: hdd towards fin* **8/1**
2310 3 3/4 **Anderiego (IRE)**[21] 4922 6-9-12 85 (v) DanielTudhope 11 90
(David O'Meara) *hld up in rr: rdn and hdwy over 2f out: chsd ldrs over 1f out: kpt on* **9/2**[2]
-056 4 nse **Favourite Treat (USA)**[183] 689 4-9-6 79 JamesSullivan 10 84
(Ruth Carr) *led: rdn over 2f out: hdd 1f out: one pce* **20/1**
4221 5 3/4 **Kiwi Bay**[17] 5054 9-9-11 84 PaulMulrennan 3 87
(Michael Dods) *t.k.h in midfield: rdn over 2f out: kpt on same pce* **4/1**[1]
2245 6 1/2 **Oddysey (IRE)**[23] 4832 5-9-8 81 TomEaves 9 83
(Michael Dods) *midfield: rdn over 2f out: kpt on same pce* **14/1**
3660 7 4 1/2 **Kalk Bay (IRE)**[63] 3483 7-9-9 82 (t) BarryMcHugh 6 74
(Michael Easterby) *hld up in rr: rdn over 2f out: sn btn* **10/1**
2420 8 2 3/4 **Who's Shirl**[59] 3572 8-9-3 76 MichaelStainton 13 62
(Chris Fairhurst) *in tch: rdn over 3f out: wknd over 1f out* **25/1**
6050 9 1/2 **Lazarus Bell**[14] 5197 4-9-3 76 (p) PhillipMakin 4 63
(Alan Brown) *dwlt: sn in midfield: rdn over 2f out: wknd ins fnl f: eased* **10/1**
2512 10 1 3/4 **Maiden Approach**[16] 5079 3-8-12 77 TonyHamilton 5 56
(Richard Fahey) *trckd ldrs: rdn over 2f out: sn wknd* **4/1**[1]
1m 36.74s (0.14) **Going Correction** -0.125s/f (Firm)
**WFA** 3 from 4yo+ 6lb **10** Ran SP% **118.1**
Speed ratings (Par 105): **94,93,92,92,91 91,86,84,83,81**
CSF £49.71 CT £216.91 TOTE £6.70: £2.40, £2.30, £1.40; EX 64.80 Trifecta £165.20.
**Owner** M Mackay & J Fyffe **Bred** Tarworth Bloodstock Investments Ltd **Trained** Uplawmoor, E Renfrews

**FOCUS**
A medium gallop to this handicap which was competitive enough for the grade though most of the runners were exposed. The runner-up has been rated as running a small pb in defeat.

## 5682 100% RACINGUK PROFITS RETURNED TO RACING H'CAP 1m 6f 19y
**7:30** (7:30) (Class 6) (0-65,60) 3-Y-O **£2,264** (£673; £336; £168) **Stalls** Low

Form RPR
033 1 **Modify**[8] 5402 3-8-8 50 SamJames(3) 3 57+
(David O'Meara) *hld up: hdwy fr over 2f out: nudged along to ld 1f out: pushed out: cosily* **9/2**[3]
0-00 2 1 **Crakehall Lad (IRE)**[68] 3303 3-9-7 60 DavidAllan 5 64
(Alan Swinbank) *in tch: rdn to ld narrowly over 2f out: hdd 1f out: kpt on but no ch w wnr* **10/3**[1]
5402 3 hd **Bentons Lad**[33] 4497 3-8-11 50 AndrewMullen 6 53
(George Moore) *midfield: rdn and hdwy 3f out: ev ch 2f out: kpt on* **11/2**
0040 4 1 1/4 **Two B'S**[19] 4979 3-9-7 60 GrahamLee 1 62
(Tim Easterby) *racd keenly: led for 2f: trckd ldr: rdn and n.m.r over 2f out: kpt on same pce fr over 1f out* **12/1**
0630 5 9 **Little Bruv**[16] 5102 3-8-6 45 JamesSullivan 8 34
(Tim Easterby) *racd keenly: trckd ldr: led after 2f: hdd 10f out: rdn to ld again over 3f out: hdd over 2f out: wknd* **11/2**
-044 6 2 1/4 **Major Rowan**[33] 4497 3-8-8 47 (b) DuranFentiman 7 33
(Bryan Smart) *t.k.h in midfield: plld way into ld 10f out: hdd over 3f out: wknd over 2f out* **11/1**
-034 7 4 1/2 **Soiree D'Ete**[15] 5122 3-8-9 48 (p) LukeMorris 2 28
(Sir Mark Prescott Bt) *hld up: drvn over 3f out: wknd over 2f out* **7/2**[2]
-400 8 nk **Petite Madame (IRE)**[14] 5200 3-8-9 53 (b) NoelGarbutt(5) 4 32
(David Thompson) *midfield: rdn over 3f out: wknd over 2f out* **33/1**
3m 8.06s (3.36) **Going Correction** +0.20s/f (Good) **8** Ran SP% **113.2**
Speed ratings (Par 98): **98,97,97,96,91 90,87,87**
CSF £19.48 CT £82.63 TOTE £4.70: £1.50, £1.80, £1.10; EX 20.30 Trifecta £60.40.
**Owner** Mrs F Denniff **Bred** A S Denniff **Trained** Nawton, N Yorks

**FOCUS**
A modest staying handicap for 3yos with few coming into it in much form. The first four were clear. The runner-up has been rated close to his 2yo form.

## 5683 FOLLOW REDCARRACING ON FACEBOOK & TWITTER H'CAP 6f
**8:00** (8:01) (Class 6) (0-55,55) 3-Y-O+ **£2,385** (£704; £352) **Stalls** Centre

Form RPR
5031 1 **Armelle (FR)**[8] 5390 3-8-11 53 MatthewHopkins(5) 5 67+
(Scott Dixon) *mde all: rdn clr 1/2-way: reduced advantage nr fin but a holding on* **9/4**[1]
5040 2 1 1/2 **Ad Vitam (IRE)**[8] 5376 6-9-4 52 (bt) RaulDaSilva 13 61
(Suzzanne France) *hld up: sn pushed along: hdwy over 1f out: wnt 2nd jst ins fnl f: kpt on* **28/1**
3006 3 2 1/2 **Abraham Monro**[11] 5287 4-9-0 48 JamesSullivan 7 49
(Ruth Carr) *chsd clr ldr: rdn over 2f out: one pce* **14/1**
0025 4 shd **Monsieur Royale**[30] 4571 4-9-6 54 (b) BarryMcHugh 8 55
(Geoffrey Oldroyd) *hld up in midfield: rdn over 2f out: kpt on* **10/1**
0036 5 nk **A J Cook (IRE)**[5] 5499 4-9-4 52 (v) GrahamLee 12 52
(Ron Barr) *in tch: rdn 1/2-way: kpt on same pce* **9/1**
0-60 6 nk **Natalia**[16] 5079 5-8-9 48 JackDuern(5) 1 47
(Andrew Hollinshead) *hld up in midfield: rdn 1/2-way: kpt on same pce* **14/1**
0202 7 4 **Knockamany Bends (IRE)**[16] 5105 4-9-5 53 TomEaves 15 39
(John Wainwright) *chsd clr ldr: rdn 1/2-way: wknd over 1f out* **8/1**[3]
0301 8 4 1/2 **Wimboldsley**[24] 4796 3-9-2 53 IanBrennan 11 25
(Scott Dixon) *hld up: rdn over 2f out: nvr threatened* **6/1**[2]
0025 9 3 **Tuibama (IRE)**[28] 4664 5-9-5 53 (p) DaleSwift 10 15
(Tracy Waggott) *dwlt: hld up: rdn 1/2-way: sn wknd* **16/1**
0606 10 1 1/4 **Shikari**[31] 4532 3-8-8 48 NeilFarley(3) 6 6
(Robin Bastiman) *chsd clr ldr: rdn 1/2-way: sn wknd* **16/1**
466 11 1 **Tell Me When**[24] 4796 3-9-0 51 PaulMulrennan 9 6
(Brian Rothwell) *midfield: rdn over 2f out: wknd over 1f out* **16/1**
0-63 12 nk **Redalani (IRE)**[53] 3832 4-9-4 52 (tp) PaulPickard 14 6
(Alan Brown) *midfield: rdn 1/2-way: sn wknd* **11/1**
5-00 13 1 **Noble Reach**[37] 4370 3-9-0 51 [1] PaulQuinn 3
(Lawrence Mullaney) *hld up: a towards rr* **66/1**
0000 14 6 **Rise To Glory (IRE)**[12] 5236 6-9-4 52 DuranFentiman 16
(Shaun Harris) *chsd clr ldr: rdn 1/2-way: wknd over 2f out* **33/1**
0-00 15 40 **Liberal Lady**[16] 5089 6-8-11 52 MikeyEnnis(7) 19
(Robert Johnson) *dwlt: a bhd: eased over 1f out* **50/1**
1m 10.93s (-0.87) **Going Correction** -0.125s/f (Firm)
**WFA** 3 from 4yo+ 3lb **15** Ran SP% **124.4**
Speed ratings (Par 101): **100,98,94,94,94 93,88,82,78,76 75,75,73,65,12**
CSF £83.06 CT £785.11 TOTE £3.60: £1.60, £5.30, £4.10; EX 104.80 Trifecta £981.10.
**Owner** The Friday Follies **Bred** J Vittori & Mme Y Dixon **Trained** Babworth, Notts

**FOCUS**
A 46-55 sprint handicap featuring mainly disappointing and hard-to-win with sorts. The runner-up runs well here and has been rated a shade off his 7f selling win in April.
T/Plt: £66.90 to a £1 stake. Pool: £43,424 - 473.71 winning tickets T/Qpdt: £16.70 to a £1 stake. Pool: £6,356 - 281.50 winning tickets AS

# 5500 WINDSOR (R-H)
Saturday, August 23

**OFFICIAL GOING: Good (good to firm in places; 8.6)**
Wind: light, half behind Weather: overcast Rails: Top bend dolled out 3yds from normal inner configuration adding 11yds to races of one mile and beyond. All Inner rails moved onto fresh ground. Inner of Straight dolled out 2yds at 6f and 2yds at Winning Post

## 5684 UNIBET 90 INSURANCE MONEY BACK MAIDEN STKS 6f
**5:10** (5:12) (Class 5) 2-Y-O **£3,234** (£962; £481; £240) **Stalls** Low

Form RPR
1 **Salt Island** 2-9-5 0 SteveDrowne 3 85+
(Charles Hills) *w ldr tl led 1/2-way: rdn and wnt clr ent fnl f: r.o strly: easily* **3/1**[2]
06 2 3 1/4 **Best Endeavour**[13] 5201 2-9-5 67 StevieDonohoe 8 72
(William Muir) *led tl 1/2-way: chsd wnr after: rdn over 1f out: outpcd by wnr and btn 1f out: kpt on for clr 2nd fnl f* **16/1**
3 2 3/4 **Russian Reward (IRE)** 2-9-5 0 LiamKeniry 6 64+
(Paul Cole) *chsd ldrs: rdn 2f out: outpcd over 1f out: no threat to ldrs but kpt on ins fnl f: wnt 3rd fnl 50yds* **16/1**
4 4 3/4 **Burauq**[12] 5248 2-9-5 0 DougieCostello 7 62
(William Muir) *in tch in rr of main gp: rdn and outpcd over 2f out: ralllied u.p and hung lft 1f out: styd on steadily to go 4th towards fin: nvr trbld ldrs* **16/1**
04 5 1 1/2 **Oriental Splendour (IRE)**[10] 5309 2-9-5 0 GeorgeBaker 12 57
(Roger Charlton) *pressed ldrs: rdn and fnd little over 1f out: 3rd and btn 1f out: wknd and lost 2 pls fnl 50yds* **7/4**[1]
6 6 nk **Finton Friend (IRE)**[20] 4943 2-8-12 0 TylerSaunders(7) 5 56
(Charles Hills) *s.i.s: sn wl outpcd and detached in rr: hdwy over 1f out: styd on strly ins fnl f: nvr a threat* **20/1**
7 1 3/4 **Treaty Of York (IRE)** 2-9-5 0 HayleyTurner 2 51
(Henry Candy) *in tch in midfield: effrt u.p 2f out: no imp: wl hld whn pushed lft 1f out: wknd* **15/2**
60 8 nk **Q Twenty Girl (IRE)**[13] 5210 2-8-7 0 CharlotteJenner(7) 11 45
(Mark Usher) *s.i.s: outpcd in last trio: sme hdwy ins fnl f: n.d* **33/1**
32 9 1/2 **State Of The Union (IRE)**[19] 4965 2-9-5 0 KieranO'Neill 9 49
(Richard Hannon) *stdd s: t.k.h: hld up in tch in midfield: rdn and no rspnse 2f out: btn whn pushed lft 1f out: wknd* **7/1**[3]
65 10 nk **Pipe Bomb**[53] 3827 2-9-0 0 ShaneGray(5) 10 48
(Kevin Ryan) *in tch in midfield: rdn over 2f out: sn btn and wknd wl over 1f out* **8/1**
11 12 **Mullion Cove** 2-9-0 0 WilliamCarson 1
(John Best) *s.i.s: a wl outpcd and detached in rr* **50/1**
1m 11.53s (-1.47) **Going Correction** -0.275s/f (Firm) **11** Ran SP% **124.1**
Speed ratings (Par 94): **98,93,90,89,87 86,84,83,83,82 66**
CSF £52.51 TOTE £4.40: £1.60, £5.10, £5.50; EX 87.40 Trifecta £1754.40 Part won..
**Owner** Julie Martin & David R Martin & Partner **Bred** A S Denniff **Trained** Lambourn, Berks

**FOCUS**
The opening contest on a good quality six-race card was a fair juvenile maiden in which they went a contested gallop. The winner picked up in style, the runner-up showed improved form and this was also a fair start from the third. The form could be rated higher.

## 5685 BLACKMORE FILLIES' H'CAP 1m 67y
**5:45** (5:45) (Class 5) (0-75,75) 3-Y-O+ **£3,234** (£962; £481; £240) **Stalls** Low

Form RPR
6043 1 **Ligeia**[8] 5398 3-9-5 74 KieranO'Neill 5 81
(Richard Hannon) *hld up in tch in last trio: rdn and hdwy over 1f out: str run ins fnl f to ld towards fin* **12/1**
6143 2 hd **Rayoumti (IRE)**[25] 4767 3-9-6 75 NeilCallan 9 81
(George Margarson) *chsd ldrs: effrt u.p to chse ldr 2f out: drvn and ev ch over 1f out: led ins fnl f: hdd and no ex towards fin* **6/1**[3]
4202 3 1/2 **Cornish Path**[29] 4623 3-9-6 75 HayleyTurner 1 80
(Henry Candy) *dwlt: sn bustled along and rcvrd to ld after 1f: rdn over 1f out: hdd ins fnl f: kpt on same pce fnl 100yds* **3/1**[1]
3610 4 1 **Baynunah (USA)**[36] 4397 3-9-6 75 FrederikTylicki 3 78
(James Fanshawe) *in tch in midfield: rdn and effrt over 2f out: pressed ldrs and drvn over 1f out: no ex and one-pce ins fnl f* **6/1**[3]
6202 5 4 **Lady Sylvia**[24] 4798 5-8-11 65 JennyPowell(5) 6 59
(Joseph Tuite) *t.k.h: hld up in tch in rr: hdwy on outer over 3f out: no ex u.p over 1f out: wknd ins fnl f* **7/2**[2]
4201 6 1/2 **Swiss Kiss**[17] 5046 3-9-6 75 SteveDrowne 2 67
(John Gosden) *stdd s: t.k.h: sn chsng ldrs: shuffled bk on inner over 3f out: rdn and no hdwy over 1f out: wl hld fnl f* **6/1**[3]
2434 7 hd **Welsh Inlet (IRE)**[12] 5252 6-8-12 61 WilliamCarson 7 54
(John Bridger) *led for 1f: chsd ldr tl 2f out: sn lost pl u.p: wknd fnl f* **20/1**
2664 8 2 **Distant High**[18] 5004 3-8-1 61 ShaneGray(5) 4 48
(Richard Price) *hld up in tch in last trio: rdn and effrt wl over 1f out: no prog: n.d* **16/1**

5104 **9** ½ **Betty Bere (FR)**[29] 4623 3-8-12 67............................(v[1]) DougieCostello 8 53
(K R Burke) *dwlt: in tch in midfield: hdwy 4f out: chsd ldrs and drvn 2f out: hung lft and btn ent fnl f: sn wknd* **10/1**

1m 41.59s (-3.11) **Going Correction** -0.275s/f (Firm)
**WFA** 3 from 5yo+ 6lb **9** Ran SP% **117.5**
Speed ratings (Par 100): **104,103,103,102,98 97,97,95,95**
CSF £83.43 CT £277.71 TOTE £12.80: £3.10, £2.00, £1.90; EX 100.80 Trifecta £1030.70 Part won..
**Owner** Pineapple Stud **Bred** Plantation Stud **Trained** East Everleigh, Wilts

**FOCUS**
A fair fillies' handicap in which they went a proper gallop. The form could be rated a length better through the third and fourth.

## 5686 SQUIRE FURNEAUX VOLVO H'CAP 1m 67y
**6:15** (6:15) (Class 4) (0-85,85) 3-Y-O+ **£4,851** (£1,443; £721; £360) **Stalls** Low

Form RPR

0212 **1** **Jailawi (IRE)**[24] 4794 3-9-6 85............................ MartinHarley 2 93+
(Ismail Mohammed) *sn led: awkward bnd 6f out and kicked rival: sn hdd: chsd ldr tl led again 2f out: drvn 1f out: kpt on wl ins fnl f: rdn out* **3/1**[2]

0-31 **2** 1¼ **Certificate**[61] 3537 3-9-4 83............................ FrederikTylicki 1 88+
(Roger Varian) *chsd ldrs: rdn over 2f out: stuck bhd ldrs and nowhere to go over 1f out tl gap opened fnl 75yds: styd on u.p to go 2nd nr fin: no threat to wnr* **15/8**[1]

4424 **3** nk **Nassau Storm**[109] 2062 5-9-11 84............................ NeilCallan 6 89
(William Knight) *broke wl: stdd and hld up in midfield: effrt u.p to chse wnr over 1f out: bmpd ent fnl f: kpt on same pce fnl 100yds: lost 2nd nr fin* **10/1**

044 **4** shd **Miss Atomic Bomb**[58] 3615 3-9-4 83............................ GeorgeBaker 7 87+
(Jeremy Noseda) *stdd s: hld up off the pce in last trio: clsd and wl in tch but nt clr run over 1f out: swtchd lft and forced way through fnl 100yds: r.o wl towards fin: no threat to wnr* **8/1**

2200 **5** ½ **Lord Ofthe Shadows (IRE)**[25] 4761 5-9-7 80............... MartinDwyer 10 84
(Richard Hannon) *stdd and dropped in bhd after s: wl off the pce in rr: rdn over 3f out: hdwy and swtchd lft 1f out: r.o strly ins fnl f: no threat to wnr* **6/1**[3]

40-5 **6** hd **Lizzie Tudor**[16] 5092 4-9-10 83............................ LiamKeniry 5 86
(Andrew Balding) *hmpd sn after s: hld up in tch: effrt u.p 2f out: chsd ldrs 1f out: kpt on same pce fnl 100yds* **12/1**

0023 **7** ½ **Set The Trend**[11] 5274 8-9-4 82............................ GeorgeDowning(5) 3 84
(David Dennis) *chsd ldrs: rdn ent fnl 2f: keeping on same pce and hld whn pushed lft fnl 100yds: no ex* **16/1**

1260 **8** ½ **Shifting Star (IRE)**[10] 5308 9-8-10 69............................(vt) WilliamCarson 4 70
(John Bridger) *pressed ldr: kicked by wnr 6f out: sn led: rdn and hdd 2f out: drvn and no ex over 1f out: wknd wl on ins fnl f* **16/1**

0-05 **9** 6 **Game Mascot**[22] 4868 4-8-11 77............................ JordanVaughan(7) 9 64
(Peter Hiatt) *hld up off the pce in last pair: rdn and no hdwy 2f out: bhd fnl f* **50/1**

1m 41.23s (-3.47) **Going Correction** -0.275s/f (Firm)
**WFA** 3 from 4yo+ 6lb **9** Ran SP% **115.7**
Speed ratings (Par 105): **106,104,104,104,103 103,103,102,96**
CSF £9.03 CT £48.13 TOTE £4.00: £1.50, £1.30, £3.00; EX 10.70 Trifecta £58.00.
**Owner** Saeed H Al Tayer **Bred** Stock Vale Ltd **Trained** Newmarket, Suffolk
■ Stewards' Enquiry : George Baker one-day ban: careless riding (Sep 7)

**FOCUS**
A decent handicap in which they went a good gallop. The first two are probably better than the bare form.

## 5687 188BET WINTER HILL STKS (GROUP 3) 1m 2f 7y
**6:45** (6:46) (Class 1) 3-Y-O+
**£34,026** (£12,900; £6,456; £3,216; £1,614; £810) **Stalls** Centre

Form RPR

26-4 **1** **Al Kazeem**[35] 4437 6-9-1 123............................ GeorgeBaker 1 115
(Roger Charlton) *chsd ldr tl 5f out: styd handy: effrt to chse ldr 2f out: upsides over 1f out: shkn up to ld 1f out: rdn and kpt on wl ins fnl f* **8/11**[1]

3053 **2** ½ **True Story**[14] 5175 3-8-7 112............................(v) SilvestreDeSousa 4 114
(Saeed bin Suroor) *dwlt: sn rcvrd to chse ldrs and t.k.h: wnt 2nd 5f out: rdn to ld 2f out: hrd drvn and hdd 1f out: kpt on but a hld ins fnl f* **2/1**[2]

0503 **3** 7 **Complicit (IRE)**[21] 4930 3-8-7 97............................ ChrisCatlin 2 101
(Paul Cole) *racd keenly: led: stdd gallop 5f out: rdn and hdd 2f out: outpcd and btn over 1f out: wl hld but kpt on for clr 3rd fnl f* **33/1**

5135 **4** 2¾ **Presburg (IRE)**[14] 5162 5-9-1 90............................ SteveDrowne 9 95
(Joseph Tuite) *stdd s: hld up in rr: effrt 2f out: sme hdwy and swtchd rt ent fnl f: styd on past btn horses ins fnl f: nvr trbld ldrs* **50/1**

206/ **5** nk **Bayrir (FR)**[161] 5-9-1 109............................ MartinHarley 5 95
(Marco Botti) *in tch in midfield: effrt u.p ent fnl 2f: sn btn and wknd over 1f out* **16/1**

0055 **6** ¾ **Zambucca (SAF)**[28] 4682 6-9-1 102............................(v[1]) StevieDonohoe 3 93
(Gay Kelleway) *in tch in midfield: rdn jst over 2f out: sn struggling: wknd over 1f out* **25/1**

0042 **7** 1½ **Gifted Girl (IRE)**[10] 5312 5-8-12 102............................(t) NeilCallan 6 88
(Paul Cole) *in tch in midfield: rdn and unable qck 3f out: btn 2f out: sn wknd* **8/1**[3]

2m 1.62s (-7.08) **Going Correction** -0.275s/f (Firm) course record
**WFA** 3 from 5yo+ 8lb **7** Ran SP% **117.0**
Speed ratings: **117,116,111,108,108 107,106**
CSF £2.46 TOTE £1.70: £1.10, £1.90; EX 2.30 Trifecta £29.30.
**Owner** D J Deer **Bred** D J And Mrs Deer **Trained** Beckhampton, Wilts

**FOCUS**
A fascinating renewal of this well-established Group 3 contest in which they went a proper gallop, and the two horses at the head of the betting fought out an engaging, if slightly one-sided, tussle from over 1f out. The runner-up, third and fourth have been rated to their marks.

## 5688 188BET AUGUST STKS (LISTED RACE) 1m 3f 135y
**7:15** (7:16) (Class 1) 3-Y-O+
**£20,982** (£7,955; £3,981; £1,983; £995; £499) **Stalls** Centre

Form RPR

-301 **1** **Glorious Protector (IRE)**[42] 4204 4-9-3 98.................. GeorgeBaker 4 109+
(Ed Walker) *stdd s: hld up in rr: clsd 4f out: smooth hdwy on outer to chal over 1f out: reminder to ld jst ins fnl f: sn qcknd clr: pushed out: comf* **4/1**[3]

3100 **2** 2¼ **Pinzolo**[48] 4007 3-8-12 102............................ WilliamBuick 2 109
(Charlie Appleby) *stdd s: hld up towards rr: hdwy to chse ldr 8f out: rdn to ld wl over 1f out: hdd ins fnl f: sn brushed aside by wnr but kpt on for clr 2nd* **6/1**

3 **3** 1¼ **Energia Fox (BRZ)**[160] 4-8-9 107............................ DanielMuscutt 3 94
(Marco Botti) *t.k.h: hld up in tch in midfield: effrt ent fnl 2f: squeezed through on inner over 1f out: kpt on ins fnl f: no threat to ldng pair* **20/1**

4061 **4** ½ **Sennockian Star**[25] 4756 4-9-3 106............................(v) SilvestreDeSousa 5 101
(Mark Johnston) *chsd ldr tl 8f out: chsd ldrs after: rdn ent fnl 2f: 3rd and no ex 1f out: kpt on same pce: lost 3rd towards fin* **3/1**[2]

00-5 **5** 3 **Quest For Peace (IRE)**[22] 4849 6-9-3 107.................. RichardHughes 1 96
(Luca Cumani) *stdd s: hld up in tch: hdwy into midfield on outer: rdn 2f out: no ex and btn 1f out: wknd 1f out* **11/4**[1]

040 **6** nk **Renew (IRE)**[84] 2785 4-9-3 105............................ MartinHarley 7 96
(Marco Botti) *chsd ldrs: lost pl but stl in tch whn rdn over 2f out: btn over 1f out: wknd 1f out* **7/1**

6-60 **7** ½ **Cameron Highland (IRE)**[25] 4756 5-9-3 102............(p) FrederikTylicki 6 95
(Roger Varian) *led: rdn and qcknd 3f out: hdd wl over 1f out: btn whn short of room ent fnl f: wknd* **8/1**

2m 23.17s (-6.33) **Going Correction** -0.275s/f (Firm)
**WFA** 3 from 4yo+ 10lb **7** Ran SP% **114.3**
Speed ratings: **110,108,107,107,105 105,104**
CSF £27.79 TOTE £5.10: £2.90, £3.00; EX 22.90 Trifecta £248.10.
**Owner** Ms A A Yap **Bred** T Boylan **Trained** Newmarket, Suffolk

**FOCUS**
A Listed race which proved the stepping-stone to Group 1 glory abroad for Sir Michael Stoute's Spanish Moon the season after winning this contest in 2008, and this seemingly competitive renewal had a thoroughly dominant winner. The runner-up, who has faced stiff tasks the last twice, has been rated to the more positive view of his Newmarket defeat of Master Carpenter.

## 5689 COPPAFEEL! H'CAP 1m 3f 135y
**7:45** (7:47) (Class 5) (0-70,69) 3-Y-O+ **£3,234** (£962; £481; £240) **Stalls** Centre

Form RPR

0103 **1** **Storm Rider (IRE)**[8] 5395 3-9-3 68............................(b[1]) RichardHughes 3 77+
(Richard Hannon) *chsd ldrs: rdn and effrt 2f out: drvn to ld 1f out: edgd rt and styd on ins fnl f: rdn out* **3/1**[2]

222 **2** 1¾ **Rowlestone Lass**[18] 5001 4-8-13 54............................ MartinHarley 4 60
(Richard Price) *in tch in midfield: travelling strly but nt clr run over 2f out: gap opened 1f out and sn chsng wnr: carried rt and hmpd ins fnl f: swtchd lft and kpt on same pce towards fin* **8/1**

0505 **3** nk **Do Wah Diddy Diddy**[10] 5313 3-9-4 69............................ NeilCallan 6 75
(Clive Cox) *in tch in midfield: effrt 2f out: swtchd lft and drvn jst over 1f out: styd on ins fnl f: wnt 3rd nr fin* **4/1**[3]

4532 **4** nk **Scoppio Del Carro**[18] 5002 3-9-4 69............................(t) WilliamBuick 7 74
(Andrew Balding) *in tch in midfield: swtchd lft and hdwy on outer 3f out: drvn and chsd ldrs over 1f out: kpt on same pce fnl f: lost 3rd nr fin* **11/8**[1]

00-2 **5** 2½ **Shot In The Dark (IRE)**[26] 4744 5-8-5 51............................ PhilipPrince(5) 8 52
(Jonathan Geake) *led tl 5f out: rdn to ld again ent fnl 2f: drvn and hdd 1f out: wknd ins fnl f* **20/1**

4011 **6** 9 **Honourable Knight (IRE)**[26] 4744 6-9-10 65............(v) LiamKeniry 2 51
(Mark Usher) *chsd ldr tl led on inner 5f out: rdn and hdd ent fnl 2f: sn btn: no ch whn hung lft over 1f out* **12/1**

055 **7** 2 **In Seine**[171] 839 3-8-11 62............................ SteveDrowne 1 45
(John Best) *s.i.s: hld up in last pair: rdn over 2f out: sn btn: wknd over 1f out* **33/1**

6600 **8** ½ **Remix (IRE)**[19] 4958 5-8-12 53............................(p) StevieDonohoe 5 35
(Ian Williams) *hld up in last pair: rdn and btn over 2f out: wknd over 1f out* **25/1**

2m 27.83s (-1.67) **Going Correction** -0.275s/f (Firm)
**WFA** 3 from 4yo+ 10lb **8** Ran SP% **117.5**
Speed ratings (Par 103): **94,92,92,92,90 84,83,83**
CSF £26.87 CT £98.10 TOTE £3.60: £1.60, £2.10, £1.60; EX 29.60 Trifecta £145.20.
**Owner** Carmichael Humber **Bred** Barronstown Stud **Trained** East Everleigh, Wilts
■ Stewards' Enquiry : Richard Hughes caution: careless riding.

**FOCUS**
A modest middle-distance handicap in which they went a muddling gallop. The third has been rated as improving for the step up in trip and the fourth as running to form.
T/Plt: £86.70 to a £1 stake. Pool: £57,010.24 - 479.61 winning tickets T/Qpdt: £10.10 to a £1 stake. Pool: £8,514.02 - 620.20 winning tickets SP

# 5651 YORK (L-H)
### Saturday, August 23

**OFFICIAL GOING: Good (good to firm in places; overall 7.2; home straight: stands' side 7.2, centre 7.3, far side 7.3)**
Wind: Moderate against Weather: Cloudy Rails: Rail realignment around home bend and back straight increased distances of races of 1m and further by 7yds

## 5690 BETFRED PLAY TODAY'S £2MILLION+ SCOOP6 STRENSALL STKS (GROUP 3) 1m 208y
**2:05** (2:06) (Class 1) 3-Y-O+
**£45,368** (£17,200; £8,608; £4,288; £2,152; £1,080) **Stalls** Low

Form RPR

3111 **1** **Custom Cut (IRE)**[9] 5361 5-9-9 112............................ DanielTudhope 3 117
(David O'Meara) *lw: set stdy pce: pushed along and qcknd over 3f out: rdn and jnd over 2f out: hdd 1f out: drvn and rallied wl to ld again last 75yds* **11/2**[3]

2402 **2** nk **Trade Storm**[35] 4425 6-9-5 112............................ JamieSpencer 1 112
(David Simcock) *lw: trckd ldng pair on inner: smooth hdwy 3f out and sn cl up: chal wl over 1f out: rdn to ld 1f out: sn drvn: hdd and no ex last 75yds* **13/2**

0352 **3** nk **Lady Lara (IRE)**[14] 5176 3-8-9 100............................ PaulHanagan 5 108
(Timothy Jarvis) *hld up in rr: hdwy on outer wl over 2f out: rdn over 1f out: drvn to chal and edgd lft ins fnl f: ev ch tl no ex towards fin* **16/1**

5511 **4** 1 **Farraaj (IRE)**[42] 4214 5-9-5 116............................ AndreaAtzeni 7 109
(Roger Varian) *t.k.h: trckd ldng pair: effrt on outer over 2f out: rdn along wl over 1f out: drvn and n.m.r ent fnl f: kpt on same pce* **5/4**[1]

601- **5** nk **Flying The Flag (IRE)**[421] 3798 4-9-5 110............................(t) PatCosgrave 4 108
(M F De Kock, South Africa) *tall: lengthy: trckd ldrs: pushed along 3f out: rdn 2f out: drvn and kpt on same pce fnl f* **16/1**

0045 **6** shd **Elleval (IRE)**[27] 4711 4-9-5 106............................ WayneLordan 2 108
(David Marnane, Ire) *hld up in rr: hdwy on inner over 2f out: rdn along wl over 1f out: drvn and kpt on same pce fnl f* **16/1**

1221 **7** 23 **Graphic (IRE)**[48] 4008 5-9-9 114 (p) RyanMoore 6 64
(William Haggas) *lw: trckd ldr: pushed along 3f out: rdn over 2f out: sn wknd and eased fnl f* **7/2**[2]
1m 50.83s (-1.17) **Going Correction** +0.10s/f (Good)
**WFA** 3 from 4yo+ 7lb 7 Ran SP% **113.0**
Speed ratings: **109,108,108,107,107 107,86**
CSF £39.22 TOTE £6.20: £2.60, £3.20; EX 40.20 Trifecta £220.00.
**Owner** Gary Douglas & Pat Breslin **Bred** Moyglare Stud Farm Ltd **Trained** Nawton, N Yorks

**FOCUS**
Several jockeys riding in the opener reckoned the ground was definitely on the firm side. This was not a strong edition of this race, which was switched from the September meeting in 2009. It was run at a fairly steady gallop and they finished in a heap, the first six separated by under 2l. They came up the middle of the track in the straight.

## 5691 BETFRED MELROSE STKS (H'CAP) (BOBIS RACE) 1m 6f
2:40 (2:43) (Class 2) (0-105,99) 3-Y-O
**£49,800** (£14,912; £7,456; £3,728; £1,864; £936) **Stalls** Low

Form RPR
5116 **1** **Vent De Force**[44] 4122 3-8-7 85 RichardKingscote 7 98
(Hughie Morrison) *hld up: nudged along and hdwy fr 3f out: rdn to chse ldr over 1f out: styd on wl: led 110yds out* **16/1**
-516 **2** ¾ **Adventure Seeker (IRE)**[21] 4893 3-8-11 89 JimCrowley 17 101
(Ed Vaughan) *lw: dwlt and swtchd lft s: hld up in rr: hdwy fr 3f out: briefly n.m.r over 2f out and swtchd rt: styd on wl: wnt 2nd towards fin* **8/1**
3111 **3** ½ **Connecticut**[29] 4622 3-9-7 99 AndreaAtzeni 8 110
(Luca Cumani) *lw: hld up in midfield: stdy hdwy fr 3f out: rdn to ld 1f out: hdd 110yds out: one pce: lost 2nd towards fin* **4/1**[1]
122 **4** 3 ¼ **Kashmiri Sunset**[11] 5276 3-7-10 79 NoelGarbutt(5) 3 85
(Ed de Giles) *hld up in rr: rdn over 4f out: styd on: lft 4th towards fin: nvr threatened ldrs* **20/1**
6- **5** 3 ¼ **Uradel (GER)**[83] 3-8-6 84 PaulHanagan 11 86
(W P Mullins, Ire) *w'like: medium-sized: prom: rdn over 2f out: grad wknd fnl f* **11/2**[2]
2411 **6** nk **Penhill**[35] 4452 3-8-11 89 PJMcDonald 5 90
(James Bethell) *lw: hld up in midfield: smooth hdwy 3f out to trck ldrs 2f out: sn rdn: wknd fnl f* **9/1**
3513 **7** ¾ **Sebastian Beach (IRE)**[9] 5356 3-8-1 84 CamHardie(5) 4 84
(Richard Hannon) *led: rdn whn hdd over 1f out: grad wknd* **25/1**
1221 **8** ½ **Our Gabrial (IRE)**[14] 5164 3-8-8 91 JackGarritty(5) 15 91
(Richard Fahey) *hld up: rdn over 3f out: one pce and nvr threatened* **16/1**
1213 **9** 1 ¼ **Captain Morley**[65] 3379 3-8-13 91 JamieSpencer 6 89
(David Simcock) *lw: hld up: rdn and sme hdwy 3f out: drvn and no further imp fr over 1f out: eased whn hld fnl 110yds* **7/1**[3]
3122 **10** 6 **Innocent Touch (IRE)**[21] 4887 3-8-4 82 PatrickMathers 1 72
(Richard Fahey) *lw: midfield: rdn over 3f out: wknd over 1f out* **20/1**
2211 **11** 3 **Rocket Ship**[17] 5052 3-8-13 91 RyanMoore 13 76
(Sir Michael Stoute) *midfield: rdn over 3f out: wknd over 1f out* **8/1**
5241 **12** ¾ **Fiery Sunset**[31] 4543 3-8-2 85 DanielMuscutt(5) 9 69
(Michael Bell) *trckd ldrs: tk str hold early: rdn over 3f out: wknd 2f out* **25/1**
6 **13** ½ **Urban Moon (IRE)**[63] 3491 3-9-0 95 ConnorKing(3) 16 79
(J P Murtagh, Ire) *swtg: midfield on outer: rdn over 3f out: wknd over 1f out* **20/1**
1106 **14** 2 ½ **From Frost**[14] 5164 3-8-6 84 (vt[1]) DavidProbert 19 64
(Andrew Balding) *midfield: rdn over 3f out: wknd over 2f out* **33/1**
5242 **15** 9 **Notarised**[7] 5414 3-8-7 85 SilvestreDeSousa 10 53
(Mark Johnston) *lw: racd keenly in tch: rdn over 3f out: sn wknd* **20/1**
505 **16** 1 **Fun Mac (GER)**[21] 4893 3-8-2 80 (b[1]) LukeMorris 14 46
(Hughie Morrison) *lw: trckd ldrs: rdn over 3f out: sn wknd* **20/1**
6361 **U** **Mantou (IRE)**[8] 5387 3-7-10 79 JoeDoyle(5) 2 88
(Michael Bell) *lw: in tch on inner: rdn to ld over 1f out: hdd 1f out: hld in 4th whn sddle slipped 50yds out: uns rdr nr fin* **33/1**
2m 56.54s (-3.66) **Going Correction** +0.10s/f (Good) 17 Ran SP% **129.3**
Speed ratings (Par 106): **114,113,113,111,109 109,108,108,107,104 102,102,102,100,95 94,**
CSF £124.69 CT £629.48 TOTE £29.80: £5.20, £2.50, £1.80, £5.50; EX 285.50 Trifecta £1388.00.
**Owner** The Fairy Story Partnership **Bred** Deepwood Farm Stud **Trained** East Ilsley, Berks

**FOCUS**
Always a devilishly competitive 3yo handicap, though none of the previous nine winners of the Melrose had started longer than 9-1. The winner this year, however, was sent off at rather more generous odds. They appeared to go a fair pace without being breakneck and, as is usually the case here, they came up the middle in the straight. There won't have been as many dramatic finishes to this event as this year, though. The runner-up has been rated as stepping up on his 1m4f win here in May that worked out well on the whole.

## 5692 IRISH THOROUGHBRED MARKETING GIMCRACK STKS (GROUP 2) (C&G) 6f
3:15 (3:16) (Class 1) 2-Y-O
**£113,420** (£43,000; £21,520; £10,720; £5,380; £2,700) **Stalls** High

Form RPR
133 **1** **Muhaarar**[28] 4645 2-9-0 104 PaulHanagan 5 109
(Charles Hills) *lw: sn trcking ldrs: hdwy over 2f out and sn pushed along: rdn to chal ins fnl f: drvn and kpt on wl to ld nr fin* **7/1**
1323 **2** nse **Jungle Cat (IRE)**[23] 4822 2-9-0 105 SilvestreDeSousa 6 109
(Mark Johnston) *led: jnd 2f out and sn rdn: drvn ent fnl f: hdd and no ex towards fin* **9/2**[2]
1324 **3** ½ **Ahlan Emarati (IRE)**[24] 4780 2-9-0 106 JamieSpencer 9 107
(Peter Chapple-Hyam) *lw: cl up: effrt to chal 2f out: rdn to dispute ld and ev ch ent fnl f: sn drvn and no ex last 50yds* **14/1**
1 **4** ½ **Glenalmond (IRE)**[33] 4486 2-9-0 75 DanielTudhope 7 107+
(K R Burke) *athletic: lw: trckd ldrs: hdwy 2f out: rdn over 1f out: n.m.r and swtchd rt ins fnl f: styd on wl towards fin* **16/1**
**5** 2 ¼ **Accepted (IRE)**[42] 4229 2-9-0 0 WayneLordan 8 99
(T Stack, Ire) *w'like: lengthy: lw: plld hrd: hld up: hdwy 2f out: sn rdn and kpt on fnl f: nrst fin* **13/2**[3]
1113 **6** shd **Beacon**[25] 4757 2-9-0 108 RyanMoore 4 99
(Richard Hannon) *lw: towards rr: pushed along and sltly outpcd over 2f out: swtchd lft and rdn wl over 1f out: kpt on to chse ldrs ent fnl f: sn no imp* **9/2**[2]
11 **7** 7 **Fendale**[15] 5140 2-9-0 0 PaulMulrennan 1 78
(Bryan Smart) *unf: scope: in tch: hdwy on outer 1/2-way: rdn to chse ldrs wl over 1f out: drvn and wknd ent fnl f* **10/1**
212 **8** 3 ¼ **Teruntum Star (FR)**[15] 5140 2-9-0 85 AndreaAtzeni 11 68
(Kevin Ryan) *chsd ldrs on outer: rdn along 2f out: sn drvn and wknd* **25/1**

2111 **9** 9 **Baitha Alga (IRE)**[65] 3374 2-9-3 108 FrankieDettori 3 44
(Richard Hannon) *trckd ldrs: rdn along over 2f out: sn wknd: bhd and eased fnl f* **11/4**[1]
1m 10.52s (-1.38) **Going Correction** -0.075s/f (Good) 9 Ran SP% **114.3**
Speed ratings (Par 106): **106,105,105,104,101 101,92,87,75**
CSF £38.11 TOTE £8.90: £2.30, £1.50, £4.90; EX 47.10 Trifecta £344.80.
**Owner** Hamdan Al Maktoum **Bred** Shadwell Estate Company Limited **Trained** Lambourn, Berks

**FOCUS**
The second running of this historic event since the prize money received a sizeable injection. It was a decent edition, but notable absentees were Kool Kompany, who ran in the DBS race on Thursday, The Great War, who rerouted to the Curragh and Limato, ruled out by a bad scope. Rock Of Gibraltar in 2001 was the last genuine star to take this race. Only a length covered the first four but the form seems sound and the race pays a compliment to Ivawood, who was too good for the first two home at Newmarket. It's been rated a fraction off the race average.

## 5693 BETFRED EBOR (HERITAGE H'CAP) 1m 6f
3:50 (3:55) (Class 2) 3-Y-O+
**£164,962** (£49,396; £24,698; £12,349; £6,174; £3,100) **Stalls** Low

Form RPR
222- **1** **Mutual Regard (IRE)**[37] 4380 5-9-4 106 (p) LouisSteward(5) 16 116
(J P Murtagh, Ire) *trckd ldng pair: hdwy 3f out: led jst over 2f out: sn rdn and edgd lft over 1f out: drvn and edgd lft ins fnl f: kpt on wl towards fin* **20/1**
5101 **2** 1 ¼ **Lord Van Percy**[25] 4759 4-9-2 99 4ex DavidProbert 14 107
(Andrew Balding) *midfield: hdwy 3f out: trckd ldrs 2f out: effrt to chse wnr jst ins fnl f: sn drvn and ev ch tl kpt on same pce towards fin* **14/1**
1344 **3** 1 **Elidor**[29] 4606 4-9-2 99 PaulHanagan 19 106
(Mick Channon) *in tch: hdwy 3f out: effrt whn n.m.r jst over 2f out: sn swtchd rt and rdn: styd on wl fnl f* **20/1**
5-21 **4** 1 **Pallasator**[27] 4696 5-9-10 107 4ex LukeMorris 22 112+
(Sir Mark Prescott Bt) *swtg: hld up in rr: pushed along over 3f out: rdn along and hdwy 3f out: rdn to chse ldrs wl over 1f out: sn drvn and kpt on same pce fnl f* **9/2**[1]
-041 **5** 1 **Retirement Plan**[14] 5161 4-9-2 99 4ex PaulMulrennan 1 103
(Lady Cecil) *chsd ldr: hdwy 3f out: cl up over 2f out: sn rdn and ev ch: drvn and hld whn n.m.r jst ins fnl f: one pce after* **16/1**
1110 **6** 1 **Clever Cookie**[42] 4214 6-9-9 106 GrahamLee 9 108
(Peter Niven) *hld up in tch: hdwy 3f out: chsd ldrs whn n.m.r wl over 1f out: sn swtchd rt and rdn: kpt on fnl f: nrst fin* **10/1**
6 **7** 1 ¼ **Sir Walter Scott (IRE)**[35] 4437 4-9-3 100 DanielTudhope 18 101
(Luca Cumani) *in tch on outer: hdwy over 3f out: rdn along 2f out: kpt on appr fnl f: nrst fin* **11/1**
02 **8** shd **Nearly Caught (IRE)**[91] 2561 4-9-3 100 JimCrowley 13 101
(Hughie Morrison) *lw: midfield: hdwy 3f out: rdn along over 2f out: kpt on appr fnl f: nrst fin* **33/1**
-312 **9** hd **Suegioo (FR)**[56] 3717 5-9-5 102 (p) PaoloSirigu 10 102
(Marco Botti) *hld up: hdwy 3f out: rdn over 2f out: styd on fnl f: nrst fin* **33/1**
0-10 **10** 3 ½ **Dare To Achieve**[77] 2991 4-9-2 99 SebSanders 15 94
(William Haggas) *lw: led: rdn along over 3f out: drvn and hdd jst over 2f out: grad wknd* **20/1**
6320 **11** hd **Repeater**[25] 4759 5-9-2 102 SamJames(3) 21 97
(David O'Meara) *swtchd lft s and hld up in rr: hdwy over 3f out: rdn along over 2f out: sn no imp* **50/1**
504 **12** nk **Aussie Reigns (IRE)**[22] 4849 4-9-2 99 RichardKingscote 2 94
(William Knight) *trckd ldrs: effrt over 3f out: rdn along wl over 2f out: sn drvn and wknd* **33/1**
0102 **13** 1 ¼ **Mighty Yar (IRE)**[43] 4173 4-9-1 98 FrankieDettori 8 91
(Lady Cecil) *lw: awkward s: sn trcking ldrs: pushed along over 4f out: rdn along 3f out: sn drvn and grad wknd* **6/1**[2]
4- **14** shd **Ted Veale (IRE)**[20] 5766 7-8-10 98 SeanCorby(5) 5 91
(A J Martin, Ire) *a towards rr* **14/1**
0-10 **15** 1 ¼ **Wadi Al Hattawi (IRE)**[63] 3449 4-9-2 99 (p) SilvestreDeSousa 12 90
(Saeed bin Suroor) *trckd ldrs: hdwy 5f out: rdn along over 3f out: wknd over 2f out* **9/1**[3]
0011 **16** ½ **De Rigueur**[49] 3962 6-9-4 101 (tp) AndreaAtzeni 6 91
(Marco Botti) *lw: nvr bttr than midfield* **10/1**
-323 **17** 2 ½ **Bold Sniper**[42] 4214 4-9-7 104 RyanMoore 17 91
(Sir Michael Stoute) *stdd and swtchd lft s: hld up: a towards rr* **14/1**
4500 **18** 7 **Gabrial (IRE)**[147] 1176 5-9-9 106 TomEaves 3 83
(Richard Fahey) *s.i.s: a bhd* **66/1**
-053 **19** 2 ¾ **Great Hall**[42] 4213 4-9-2 99 PhillipMakin 20 72
(John Quinn) *swtchd lft s: hld up: a towards rr* **20/1**
2m 56.48s (-3.72) **Going Correction** +0.10s/f (Good) 19 Ran SP% **126.2**
Speed ratings (Par 109): **114,113,112,112,111 111,110,110,110,108 108,107,107,107,106 106,104,100,99**
CSF £256.59 CT £5610.26 TOTE £26.00: £4.40, £3.30, £6.80, £2.10; EX 346.10 Trifecta £13835.70.
**Owner** Andrew Tinkler **Bred** Moyglare Stud Farm Ltd **Trained** Coolaghknock Glebe,Co Kildare

**FOCUS**
The previous nine winners of the Ebor had all been rated 101 or lower and seven of the remaining 19 runners this year were rated higher than that, including today's winner and fourth, suggesting this was a classy renewal. The last winner to start from a single-figure draw was Mephisto in 2004 and high draws again came to the fore, with the front four coming from stalls 16, 14, 19 and 22. The early pace was generous, but the final time was only marginally quicker than the Melrose. A clear personal best from the winner, with the second and third running as well as ever.

## 5694 JULIA GRAVES ROSES STKS (LISTED RACE) 5f
4:25 (4:27) (Class 1) 2-Y-O
**£28,355** (£10,750; £5,380; £2,680; £1,345; £675) **Stalls** High

Form RPR
2020 **1** **Mind Of Madness (IRE)**[44] 4123 2-9-0 103 JamieSpencer 1 103
(David Brown) *hld up in rr: hdwy 2f out: swtchd lft over 1f out: rdn to chal ins fnl f: drvn and led nr fin* **4/1**[3]
10 **2** nse **Moonraker**[23] 4822 2-9-0 0 RyanMoore 6 103
(Mick Channon) *lw: hld up in tch: hdwy whn n.m.r over 1f out: rdn and squeezed through to challnge ins fnl f: drvn to ld last 75yds: edgd lft: hdd and no ex nr fin* **2/1**[1]
2012 **3** nk **Al Fareej (IRE)**[8] 5380 2-8-9 98 JimCrowley 4 97
(James Tate) *sn prom: effrt 2f out: rdn to take slt ld and edgd rt ent fnl f: sn drvn: hdd and no ex last 75yds* **14/1**
14 **4** 1 ¾ **Lightscameraction (IRE)**[8] 5405 2-9-0 0 DavidProbert 5 95+
(Gay Kelleway) *w'like: led: rdn along over 2f out: drvn and edgd rt ent fnl f: hdd and no ex last 75yds* **20/1**

321 **5** ¾ **Cool Strutter (IRE)**[16] 5091 2-9-0 87 AndreaAtzeni 3 93
(Richard Hannon) *unf: lw: hld up towards rr: effrt over 2f out: sn rdn: kpt on fnl f: nrst fin* **15/2**

1255 **6** *nk* **Rosie's Premiere (IRE)**[8] 5380 2-8-9 90 PaulHanagan 7 87
(Dean Ivory) *chsd ldrs: rdn along 2f out: wknd over 1f out* **20/1**

150 **7** 1¾ **Littlemissblakeney**[56] 3721 2-8-9 95 WayneLordan 2 80
(Hugo Palmer) *chsd ldrs: rdn along over 2f out: grad wknd* **12/1**

2351 **8** *nk* **Horsforth**[25] 4751 2-8-9 69 BarryMcHugh 8 79
(Tony Coyle) *hld up in rr: sme hdwy 2f out: sn rdn and n.d* **80/1**

0154 **9** 4 **Commander Patten (IRE)**[7] 5409 2-9-0 82 RobertTart 10 70
(Alan Bailey) *a towards rr* **50/1**

11 **10** ½ **Showing Character**[43] 4159 2-9-0 0 RichardKingscote 9 68
(Tom Dascombe) *athletic: lw: cl up nr: rdn along 2f out: drvn and wkng whn n.m.r ent fnl f* **10/3**[2]

58.58s (-0.72) **Going Correction** -0.075s/f (Good) **10** Ran SP% **115.3**
Speed ratings: **102,101,101,98,97 96,94,93,87,86**
CSF £11.77 TOTE £4.30: £1.70, £1.30, £3.10; EX 16.80 Trifecta £164.20.
**Owner** Qatar Racing Limited **Bred** Mrs Jacqueline Norris **Trained** Averham Park, Notts

**FOCUS**
Fair form for the grade, and the pace was quick. The form has been rated around the average for the race, with the third close to form as well.

## 5695 BETFRED SUPPORTS JACK BERRY HOUSE STKS (H'CAP) 1m 2f 88y
5:00 (5:02) (Class 2) (0-105,102) 3-Y-O+
**£24,900** (£7,456; £3,728; £1,864; £932; £468) **Stalls** Low

Form RPR

-000 **1** **Queensberry Rules (IRE)**[14] 5174 4-9-8 96 (p) PaulHanagan 9 105
(William Haggas) *trckd ldng trio: hdwy on outer wl over 2f out: cl up wl over 1f out: rdn to chal ent fnl f: kpt on to ld last 100yds* **8/1**

0142 **2** 1¼ **Spirit Of The Law (IRE)**[21] 4888 5-8-10 89 JackGarritty(5) 16 96
(Richard Fahey) *led: rdn over 2f out: jnd wl over 1f out: drvn ent fnl f: hdd and no ex last 100yds* **16/1**

11-0 **3** *nk* **I'm Fraam Govan**[25] 4756 6-9-5 93 PatCosgrave 5 99
(George Baker) *trckd ldrs on inner: hdwy 3f out: rdn to chal wl over 1f out: ev ch tl drvn and kpt on same pce wl ins fnl f* **25/1**

4526 **4** 1½ **Hit The Jackpot (IRE)**[14] 5163 5-9-8 96 DanielTudhope 8 99
(David O'Meara) *lw: trckd ldr: hdwy 3f out: cl up 2f out: rdn and ev ch over 1f out tl drvn and one pce ins fnl f* **12/1**

6022 **5** 2¼ **Ajman Bridge**[25] 4756 4-9-7 95 AndreaAtzeni 3 94
(Luca Cumani) *lw: in tch: hdwy 3f out: rdn along over 2f out: drvn to chse ldrs over 1f out: no imp fnl f* **7/2**[1]

2264 **6** ¾ **Braidley (IRE)**[23] 4821 3-8-8 90 PJMcDonald 11 88
(James Bethell) *hld up in midfield: hdwy 3f out: rdn along 2f out: sn drvn and no imp* **15/2**[3]

2132 **7** 1¼ **Llanarmon Lad (IRE)**[14] 5174 5-9-10 98 RyanMoore 6 93
(Brian Ellison) *hld up towards rr: hdwy over 2f out: sn rdn and no imp* **9/2**[2]

4505 **8** ½ **Bancnuanaheireann (IRE)**[14] 5163 7-9-8 96 AndrewMullen 18 90
(Michael Appleby) *midfield: effrt 3f out: sn rdn along and n.d* **20/1**

53 **9** *hd* **Double Discount (IRE)**[42] 4184 4-8-12 86 RichardKingscote 17 80
(Tom Dascombe) *a towards rr* **20/1**

2043 **10** 1¼ **Maven**[28] 4680 6-8-12 86 DavidAllan 4 77
(Tim Easterby) *chsd ldng pair: rdn along 3f out: drvn over 2f out: sn wknd* **20/1**

0040 **11** 1 **Busatto (USA)**[14] 5174 4-9-0 91 MichaelJMMurphy(3) 12 81
(Mark Johnston) *a towards rr* **20/1**

-060 **12** ½ **Butterfly McQueen (USA)**[46] 4060 4-9-7 95 DavidProbert 14 84
(Andrew Balding) *lw: chsd ldrs: rdn along 3f out: sn drvn and grad wknd* **33/1**

1301 **13** ½ **Silver Rime (FR)**[19] 4963 9-8-10 89 SammyJoBell(5) 19 77
(Linda Perratt) *dwlt: a in rr* **50/1**

6631 **14** 4 **Whispering Warrior (IRE)**[21] 4888 5-9-7 95 JimCrowley 15 75
(David Simcock) *awkward s: a towards rr* **8/1**

0001 **15** 2 **Lyn Valley**[23] 4821 3-8-9 96 CamHardie(5) 13 72
(Mark Johnston) *dwlt: a in rr* **12/1**

2m 11.25s (-1.25) **Going Correction** +0.10s/f (Good)
**WFA** 3 from 4yo+ 8lb **15** Ran SP% **123.5**
Speed ratings (Par 109): **109,108,107,106,104 104,103,102,102,101 100,100,100,96,95**
CSF £118.05 CT £3072.47 TOTE £10.40: £3.20, £4.60, £5.40; EX 181.90 Trifecta £3148.00 Part won..
**Owner** Liam Sheridan **Bred** Gerard Kerin **Trained** Newmarket, Suffolk

**FOCUS**
It started to rain rain before this race. For a decent and competitive handicap (even with the five absentees), remarkably few ever got into it with the front four always either on or near the pace. This had gone to a 4yo in six of the previous nine runnings and that trend continued, with the winner one of only five from that age-group remaining in the contest. The winner has been rated back to his best.

## 5696 QIPCO FUTURE STARS APPRENTICE STKS (H'CAP) 5f
5:35 (5:36) (Class 2) (0-100,98) 3-Y-O
**£24,900** (£7,456; £3,728; £1,864; £932; £468) **Stalls** High

Form RPR

-421 **1** **Online Alexander (IRE)**[21] 4898 3-8-13 93 KevinStott(3) 19 107
(Kevin Ryan) *hld up: hdwy over 2f out: swtchd lft and rdn over 1f out: chal ins fnl f: led last 100yds: kpt on strly* **5/1**[1]

0142 **2** 1¼ **Lexington Abbey**[19] 4977 3-8-8 85 IanBrennan 8 94
(Kevin Ryan) *chsd ldrs: rdn along 2f out: drvn ent fnl f: kpt on same pce* **20/1**

1110 **3** *nk* **High On Life**[43] 4166 3-9-4 95 RossAtkinson 10 103
(Jamie Osborne) *lw: led: rdn 2f out: hung bdly rt over 1f out: drvn ent fnl f: hdd and one pce last 100yds* **11/1**

-110 **4** *shd* **Money Team (IRE)**[21] 4898 3-8-7 87 CamHardie(3) 4 95
(David Barron) *swtchd rt s: in tch and rdn along 1/2-way: hdwy wl over 1f out: kpt on u.p fnl f: nrst fin* **12/1**

5142 **5** ½ **Scarborough (IRE)**[70] 3219 3-8-5 82 MichaelJMMurphy 3 88
(Michael Appleby) *lw: racd far side: prom: rdn along over 1f out: drvn ins fnl f: kpt on same pce* **12/1**

**6** 1 **Full Steam Ahead (IRE)**[18] 5020 3-8-8 85 ConnorKing 11 87+
(David Marnane, Ire) *prom: rdn along 2f out: bdly hmpd over 1f out: kpt on u.p fnl f* **7/1**[2]

2110 **7** ½ **Rural Celebration**[70] 3253 3-8-10 87 SamJames 13 87
(David O'Meara) *chsd ldrs: rdn along 2f out: sn drvn and grad wknd* **20/1**

6201 **8** ¾ **Speed Hawk (USA)**[39] 4281 3-9-7 98 RobertTart 14 96+
(Robert Cowell) *towards rr: effrt and sme hdwy on stands' rail whn n.m.r over 1f out: n.d* **8/1**[3]

3161 **9** 1½ **Innocently (IRE)**[19] 4977 3-8-3 87 JoshDoyle(7) 6 79
(David O'Meara) *chsd ldrs: rdn along 2f out: drvn over 1f out and grad wknd* **18/1**

10-0 **10** ½ **Royal Mezyan (IRE)**[70] 3253 3-8-12 92 NathanAlison(3) 9 83
(William Haggas) *in tch whn n.m.r after 1f: sn rdn along and in rr after* **5/1**[1]

1004 **11** *shd* **Blithe Spirit**[43] 4158 3-9-3 94 JasonHart 1 84
(Eric Alston) *racd far rail: spd to 1/2-way: sn rdn along and wknd* **33/1**

0511 **12** *nk* **Searchlight**[22] 4847 3-8-6 86 JoeDoyle(3) 15 75
(Kevin Ryan) *prom on stands' rail: effrt 2f out: sn rdn and hld whn bdly hmpd over 1f out: nt rcvr* **16/1**

0551 **13** ¾ **Skye's The Limit**[12] 5243 3-8-0 80 JackGarritty(3) 12 66
(Richard Fahey) *dwlt: a towards rr* **12/1**

0116 **14** 3½ **Desert Ace (IRE)**[21] 4898 3-9-0 91 (tp) RyanTate 16 65
(Clive Cox) *lw: chsd ldrs: rdn along over 2f out: sn wknd* **20/1**

000 **15** *shd* **Sleeper King (IRE)**[28] 4669 3-9-0 94 (v[1]) MarcMonaghan(3) 17 67
(Kevin Ryan) *a towards rr* **16/1**

1334 **16** 3½ **Dutch Breeze**[19] 4977 3-7-12 80 (p) RachelRichardson(5) 18 41
(Tim Easterby) *s.i.s: a in rr* **20/1**

57.96s (-1.34) **Going Correction** -0.075s/f (Good) **16** Ran SP% **127.4**
Speed ratings (Par 106): **107,105,104,104,103 101,101,99,97,96 96,96,94,89,89 83**
CSF £115.56 CT £1128.76 TOTE £6.10: £2.20, £4.20, £2.90, £2.90; EX 159.60 Trifecta £1884.70.
**Owner** Noel O'Callaghan **Bred** Deer Forest Stud **Trained** Hambleton, N Yorks
■ Stewards' Enquiry : Ross Atkinson five-day ban: careless riding (Sep 6-10)

**FOCUS**
A competitive and classy handicap which has been confined to apprentices since 2012. Many of the runners had met before. The field raced down the stands' side with the exception of two, including the fifth, who stayed on the far flank. The winner looks progressive and the third has been rated to form.
T/Jkpt: Not won. T/Plt: £1,757.00 to a £1 stake. Pool: £291,797.88 - 121.23 winning tickets. T/Qpdt: £185.00 to a £1 stake. Pool: £18,501.96 - 74.0 winning tickets. JR

# 5215 CURRAGH (R-H)
Saturday, August 23

**OFFICIAL GOING: Straight course - good; round course - good to firm**

## 5699a RENAISSANCE STKS (GROUP 3) 6f
3:10 (3:11) 3-Y-O+ **£32,500** (£9,500; £4,500; £1,500)

RPR

**1** **Jamesie (IRE)**[13] 5219 6-9-6 105 ColmO'Donoghue 3 109
(David Marnane, Ire) *trckd ldrs in 4th: rdn to press ldr in 2nd over 1f out: disp fnl 150yds: all out cl home* **8/1**

**2** *nse* **Gordon Lord Byron (IRE)**[63] 3451 6-9-13 117 JosephO'Brien 6 116
(T Hogan, Ire) *hld up: 8th 2f out: chal between horses 1f out to dispute fnl 100yds: kpt on wl: jst hld* **7/2**[2]

**3** 1 **Hamza (IRE)**[13] 5219 5-9-9 108 (v) FMBerry 5 109
(Kevin Ryan) *trckd ldr in 2nd tl led over 2f out: strly pressed ent fnl f and hdd fnl 100yds: no ex* **3/1**[1]

**4** ¾ **Majestic Queen (IRE)**[52] 3864 4-9-6 102 PatSmullen 8 103
(Tracey Collins, Ire) *chsd ldrs in 5th: short of room appr fnl f and swtchd rt: kpt on wl cl home: nt rch principals* **7/1**

**5** 1 **Gathering Power (IRE)**[31] 4557 4-9-3 100 FergalLynch 1 97
(Edward Lynam, Ire) *hld up towards outer: prog under 2f out into 5th: no imp fnl 150yds: kpt on same pce* **16/1**

**6** *nk* **Russian Soul (IRE)**[15] 5154 6-9-9 110 (p) ShaneFoley 4 102
(M Halford, Ire) *trckd ldrs in 3rd tl nt qckn ent fnl f: kpt on one pce* **9/2**[3]

**7** 1¼ **An Saighdiur (IRE)**[13] 5219 7-9-6 105 BillyLee 9 95
(Andrew Slattery, Ire) *led tl hdd over 2f out: sn no ex* **25/1**

**8** *nk* **Maarek**[13] 5219 7-9-11 114 DeclanMcDonogh 7 99
(Miss Evanna McCutcheon, Ire) *slowly away and a in rr: kpt on fnl f but nvr on terms* **6/1**

**9** *shd* **Leitir Mor (IRE)**[9] 5361 4-9-6 107 (t) KevinManning 2 94
(J S Bolger, Ire) *sn towards rr: sme prog 2f out: sn no imp and wknd fnl f* **25/1**

1m 10.2s (-5.30) **Going Correction** -0.825s/f (Hard) **9** Ran SP% **116.9**
Speed ratings: **102,101,100,99,98 97,96,95,95**
CSF £36.63 TOTE £10.20: £2.60, £1.40, £2.00; DF 52.30 Trifecta £191.70.
**Owner** Damian Lavelle **Bred** John R Jeffers **Trained** Bansha, Co Tipperary
■ Stewards' Enquiry : F M Berry caution: used whip without giving gelding time to respond.

**FOCUS**
Surprisingly, there wasn't much pace on early. The winner was never too far away and 3l covered the first six home.

5700 - 5704a (Foreign Racing) - See Raceform Interactive

# 5616 DEAUVILLE (R-H)
Saturday, August 23

**OFFICIAL GOING: Turf: very soft; polytrack: standard**

## 5705a PRIX D'ISIGNY (PRIX PARIS-TURF) (MAIDEN) (3YO COLTS & GELDINGS) (POLYTRACK) 1m 1f 110y
11:30 (12:00) 3-Y-O **£10,416** (£4,166; £3,125; £2,083; £1,041)

RPR

**1** **Monoceros (USA)**[40] 3-9-2 0 StephanePasquier 2 87
(P Bary, France) **2/5**[1]

**2** 5 **Prometheus (IRE)**[18] 5027 3-9-2 0 Christophe-PatriceLemaire 1 77
(A De Royer-Dupre, France) **27/10**[2]

**3** *snk* **Medaillon (FR)**[52] 3869 3-9-2 0 TheoBachelot 3 76
(Mario Hofer, Germany) **249/10**

**4** *hd* **Sealed (USA)**[182] 720 3-9-2 0 Pierre-CharlesBoudot 4 76
(Gay Kelleway) *hld up in tch: pushed along 3f out: rdn and nt qckn fnl 2f: kpt on towards fin but no match for easy wnr* **161/10**

**5** ½ **Diyoudar (FR)**[18] 5027 3-8-10 0 Georges-AntoineAnselin(6) 5 75
(Rod Collet, France) **57/10**[3]

2m 0.45s (120.45) **5** Ran SP% **123.1**
WIN (incl. 1 euro stake): 1.40. PLACES: 1.10, 1.10. SF: 2.80.
**Owner** Niarchos Family **Bred** Flaxman Holdings Limited **Trained** Chantilly, France



The Form Book, Raceform Ltd, Newbury, RG14 5SJ

## 5706a PRIX DE CREVECOEUR (PRIX ARQANA) (MAIDEN) (UNRACED 2YO COLTS & GELDINGS) (TURF) 1m (R)
12:30 (12:00) 2-Y-O £10,416 (£4,166; £3,125; £2,083; £1,041)

RPR

1 **Mostaneer (IRE)** 2-9-2 0 ThierryThulliez 8 81
(N Clement, France) 66/10[3]

2 3/4 **Almanaar** 2-9-2 0 (b[1]) AurelienLemaitre 3 79
(F Head, France) 103/10

3 snk **Capo Maximo** 2-9-2 0 Pierre-CharlesBoudot 2 79
(Yves de Nicolay, France) 83/10

4 1 **King Of Normandy (FR)** 2-9-2 0 GeraldMosse 1 77
(Richard Hannon) *prom on inner: cl 2nd 3f out: pushed along and ev ch 2f out: rdn and nt qckn fnl f: kpt on same pce and hld* 11/5[2]

5 snk **All The News (USA)** 2-9-2 0 ChristopheSoumillon 5 76
(J-C Rouget, France) 21/10[1]

6 nk **Bornonville** 2-9-2 0 StephanePasquier 9 76
(J E Pease, France) 144/10

7 2 1/2 **Adechop (FR)** 2-9-2 0 JulienAuge 4 70
(A De Watrigant, France) 94/10

8 7 **Hey Joe (FR)** 2-8-10 0 Georges-AntoineAnselin[(6)] 6 55
(Mario Hofer, Germany) 217/10

9 dist **Qatar Breeze** 2-9-2 0 MaximeGuyon 7
(G E Mikhalides, France) 34/1

1m 50.05s (9.25) 9 Ran SP% 119.6
WIN (incl. 1 euro stake): 7.60. PLACES: 2.30, 2.90, 3.00. DF: 44.50. SF: 69.00.
**Owner** Muteb Bin Abdullah **Bred** Castlemartin Stud & Skymarc Farm **Trained** Chantilly, France

## 5707a LONGINES PRIX DU CALVADOS (GROUP 3) (2YO FILLIES) (STRAIGHT) (TURF) 7f
1:30 (12:00) 2-Y-O £33,333 (£13,333; £10,000; £5,000; £5,000)

RPR

1 **Queen Bee (FR)**[21] 4931 2-8-11 0 GregoryBenoist 2 104+
(E Lellouche, France) *trckd ldr: swtchd rt and rdn to chal over 1f out: led jst ins fnl f: r.o wl and a doing enough: shade cosily* 152/10

2 1/2 **Calypso Beat (USA)**[14] 5190 2-8-11 0 ChristopheSoumillon 1 103
(Kevin Ryan) *led: rdn 2f out: strly pressed fr over 1f out and hdd jst ins fnl f: kpt on wl but a being hld after* 13/10[1]

3 1 1/4 **Sivoliere (IRE)**[17] 2-8-11 0 Jean-BernardEyquem 6 100
(J-C Rouget, France) *dwlt sltly and hld up in last: pushed along to cl and swtchd lft to rail 2f out: rdn over 1f out: r.o and wnt 3rd ins fnl f: nt pce of front pair and nvr able to chal* 17/10[2]

4 3/4 **Kindly Dismiss (FR)**[17] 2-8-11 0 FabriceVeron 4 98
(H-A Pantall, France) *midfield in tch: rdn 2f out: nt qckn: kpt on same pce and hld fnl f: dead-heated for 4th* 114/10

4 dht **La Khaleesi (FR)**[41] 4248 2-8-11 0 ThierryThulliez 5 98
(Y Gourraud, France) *hld up in last pair: rdn to cl over 1f out: kpt on same pce and hld fnl f: dead-heated for 4th* 53/10[3]

6 10 **Santa Helena (FR)**[33] 2-8-11 0 MaximeGuyon 3 72
(Ana Imaz Ceca, Spain) *pressed ldr: rdn and brief effrt 2f out: wknd qckly over 1f out: sn in rr and btn: eased fnl f* 108/10

1m 29.21s (0.91) 6 Ran SP% 119.1
WIN (incl. 1 euro stake): 16.20. PLACES: 3.90, 1.60. SF: 42.10.
**Owner** G Augustin-Normand & Ecurie La Boetie **Bred** Earl Haras Du Logis & J Ince **Trained** Lamorlaye, France

5708 - 5710a (Foreign Racing) - See Raceform Interactive

# 5331 BEVERLEY (R-H)
Sunday, August 24

**OFFICIAL GOING: Good**
Wind: moderate 1/2 against Weather: changeable

## 5711 JOHN JENKINS MEMORIAL CLAIMING STKS 7f 100y
2:20 (2:21) (Class 5) 3-Y-O+ £3,234 (£962; £481; £240) Stalls Low

Form RPR

0000 1 **Doc Hay (USA)**[8] 5444 7-9-10 87 IanBrennan 4 87
(Brian Ellison) *wnt rt s: t.k.h: trckd ldrs: led over 4f out: clr over 3f out: hung rt and drvn out* 7/1[3]

0130 2 6 **Gaelic Wizard (IRE)**[9] 5376 6-8-11 56 GemmaTutty[(5)] 6 65
(Karen Tutty) *chsd ldrs: 2nd over 1f out: kpt on same pce* 33/1

0036 3 nk **Eeny Mac (IRE)**[11] 5299 7-8-11 73 (b[1]) MeganCarberry[(7)] 5 66
(Neville Bycroft) *chsd ldrs: kpt on fnl 2f: tk 3rd last 50yds* 7/2[2]

-424 4 2 **Dialogue**[51] 3908 8-9-0 63 DavidAllan 1 57
(Geoffrey Harker) *hmpd s: in rr: hdwy and swtchd rt over 1f out: nvr nr ldrs* 7/1[3]

2003 5 1 1/4 **Conry (IRE)**[20] 4959 8-9-2 77 GeorgeDowning[(5)] 9 61
(Ian Williams) *swvd bdly lft s: in rr: sme hdwy over 2f out: nvr a factor* 8/1

0026 6 3/4 **Thrust Control (IRE)**[9] 5376 7-8-12 50 (p) JoeFanning 7 51
(Tracy Waggott) *led tl over 4f out: chsd wnr: wknd fnl f* 28/1

6016 7 nk **Rasselas (IRE)**[12] 5267 7-8-6 65 (b) AnnaHesketh[(7)] 3 51
(David Nicholls) *hmpd s: in rr: kpt on fnl 2f: nvr on terms* 10/1

4000 8 13 **Best Of Order (IRE)**[15] 5178 7-9-10 93 (b) DanielTudhope 8 31
(David O'Meara) *wnt rt s: mid-div: effrt over 3f out: lost pl and hung rt over 2f out: sn bhd whn eased clsng stages* 9/4[1]

0056 P **Duke Of Grazeon (IRE)**[30] 4613 4-9-0 62 RaulDaSilva 2
(Mrs Ilka Gansera-Leveque) *bmpd s: in rr: injured and eased over 3f out: sn p.u: fatally injured* 8/1

1m 32.67s (-1.13) **Going Correction** -0.20s/f (Firm) 9 Ran SP% 115.7
Speed ratings (Par 103): **98,91,90,88,87 86,85,71,**
CSF £198.70 TOTE £9.80: £3.30, £5.20, £1.40; EX 257.00 Trifecta £1839.20 Part won..The winner was claimed by David O'Meara for £15,000.
**Owner** S Laffan **Bred** Colts Neck Stables Llc **Trained** Norton, N Yorks

**FOCUS**
This looked an interesting claimer, but the winner dominated and was never in any danger. The runner-up is the key to the level.

## 5712 EBF OLD CROSSLEYANS RUGBY CLUB'S 90TH BIRTHDAY MEDIAN AUCTION MAIDEN STKS 1m 100y
2:50 (2:51) (Class 5) 2-Y-O £3,881 (£1,155; £577; £288) Stalls Low

Form RPR

6324 1 **Rotherwick (IRE)**[11] 5306 2-9-5 80 LukeMorris 7 80
(Paul Cole) *t.k.h: trckd ldr: drvn over 2f out: led appr fnl f: styd on* 10/11[1]

65 2 2 1/4 **Classic Villager**[56] 3748 2-9-5 0 RobertWinston 4 75
(Philip Hide) *chsd ldrs: hmpd 7f out: styd on over 1f out: tk 2nd post* 10/3[3]

35 3 hd **Water Thief (USA)**[30] 4633 2-9-5 0 JoeFanning 2 75
(Mark Johnston) *led: drvn and hung rt over 2f out: hdd appr fnl f: kpt on same pce* 11/4[2]

0 4 5 **Arracourt**[13] 5241 2-9-5 0 DavidAllan 3 64+
(Tim Easterby) *rr-div and sn pushed along: styd on fnl 2f: nrst fin* 33/1

040 5 2 1/2 **Mistral**[39] 4330 2-8-9 55 JackDuern[(5)] 1 54
(Steph Hollinshead) *in rr and sn pushed along: sme hdwy over 4f out: nvr a factor* 33/1

0 6 1/2 **La Vien Zen (IRE)**[6] 5494 2-9-0 0 PJMcDonald 8 53
(Ann Duffield) *chsd ldrs: drvn over 4f out: outpcd and lost pl over 3f out: kpt on fnl f* 33/1

7 4 **Notnowdear** 2-8-12 0 RowanScott[(7)] 6 50
(Ann Duffield) *t.k.h: trckd ldrs: swtchd righ 7f out: wknd over 2f out* 25/1

8 15 **Danzing Girl (IRE)** 2-9-0 0 DanielTudhope 5 13
(David O'Meara) *s.s and wnt lft s: a last: wl bhd whn eased clsng stages* 12/1

1m 48.32s (0.72) **Going Correction** -0.20s/f (Firm) 8 Ran SP% 122.5
Speed ratings (Par 94): **88,85,85,80,78 77,73,58**
CSF £4.59 TOTE £2.20: £1.10, £1.30, £1.20; EX 4.40 Trifecta £11.00.
**Owner** H R H Sultan Ahmad Shah **Bred** Brian O'Neill **Trained** Whatcombe, Oxon
■ Stewards' Enquiry : Rowan Scott one-day ban: careless riding (Sep 7)

**FOCUS**
They went a decent pace in this maiden and the hot favourite scored in good style. The winner didn't need to improve to win.

## 5713 CONSTANT SECURITY H'CAP (BOBIS RACE) 1m 100y
3:25 (3:25) (Class 4) (0-80,80) 3-Y-O £5,175 (£1,540; £769; £384) Stalls Low

Form RPR

651 1 **Perfect Light (IRE)**[65] 3434 3-9-7 80 GrahamGibbons 6 93+
(William Haggas) *dwlt: chsd ldr after 1f: effrt over 2f out: rdn to ld appr fnl f: edgd lft: hld on wl* 11/4[1]

1031 2 nk **Arrowzone**[14] 5206 3-9-6 79 JasonHart 2 91+
(Garry Moss) *trckd ldng pair: effrt over 2f out: 2nd 1f out: no ex clsng stages* 5/1

0052 3 4 1/2 **Emef Diamond**[18] 5051 3-9-2 75 TomEaves 1 78
(Mick Channon) *led: qckn pce 7f out: drvn over 2f out: hdd appr fnl f: kpt on one pce* 7/1

1653 4 3 1/2 **Spiceupyourlife (IRE)**[30] 4631 3-9-2 75 TonyHamilton 4 71
(Richard Fahey) *trckd ldrs: t.k.h: dropped to rr 7f out: hdwy over 1f out: chsng ldrs over 1f out: sn fdd* 7/2[3]

2-14 5 6 **Bold Captain (IRE)**[19] 5015 3-8-12 76 JoeDoyle[(5)] 3 59
(John Quinn) *t.k.h off the pce: drvn over 3f out: wknd over 1f out* 7/1

2534 6 20 **King Of Macedon (IRE)**[10] 5349 3-9-6 79 (b) JoeFanning 5 20
(Mark Johnston) *t.k.h in rr: effrt on outer over 2f out: hung rt and nt run on: bhd whn eased ins fnl f: t.o* 3/1[2]

1m 45.49s (-2.11) **Going Correction** -0.20s/f (Firm) 6 Ran SP% 115.6
Speed ratings (Par 102): **102,101,97,93,87 67**
CSF £17.37 TOTE £3.20: £1.60, £2.40; EX 16.20 Trifecta £75.50.
**Owner** Liam Sheridan **Bred** Beauty Bright Syndicate **Trained** Newmarket, Suffolk

**FOCUS**
This looked a competitive handicap, but the first two pulled clear and the rest finished well strung out. The runner-up is going the right way and the winner is well bred and can rate higher.

## 5714 R & R COUNTRY NURSERY H'CAP (BOBIS RACE) 5f
4:00 (4:00) (Class 4) (0-85,82) 2-Y-O £6,469 (£1,925; £962; £481) Stalls Low

Form RPR

1040 1 **Clouds Rest**[29] 4686 2-8-13 79 JackGarritty[(5)] 1 88
(Richard Fahey) *mde all: qcknd clr over 1f out: rdn out* 9/2[2]

454 2 4 **Intruder**[13] 5253 2-8-9 70 TonyHamilton 3 65+
(Richard Fahey) *chsd ldrs: outpcd and lost pl over 3f out: swtchd lft over 1f out: styd on to take 2nd last 50yds* 10/1

0042 3 2 **Penny Royale**[12] 5266 2-8-6 67 DavidAllan 5 54
(Tim Easterby) *chsd ldrs: drvn over 2f out: 2nd 1f out: kpt on one pce* 7/1

330 4 4 **Eastern Racer (IRE)**[36] 4439 2-9-0 75 PaulMulrennan 8 48
(Brian Ellison) *wnt lft s: hdwy on outside over 3f out: outpcd and hung rt over 1f out: kpt on to take modest 4th nr fin* 7/1

5543 5 1/2 **Poolstock**[34] 4493 2-8-6 67 JoeFanning 2 38
(Les Eyre) *w wnr: wknd fnl f* 14/1

402 6 3/4 **Crosse Fire**[13] 5242 2-8-10 71 LukeMorris 4 40
(Scott Dixon) *chsd ldrs: drvn over 2f out: wknd over 1f out* 6/1[3]

411 7 1 3/4 **Indaria**[24] 4815 2-9-0 82 PatMillman[(7)] 7 44
(Rod Millman) *wnt lft s: hdwy to chse ldrs over 3f out: lost pl over 1f out* 9/2[2]

21 8 1 **Chances Are (IRE)**[22] 4919 2-9-0 75 TomEaves 6 34
(Keith Dalgleish) *chsd ldrs: drvn over 2f out: wknd over 1f out* 5/2[1]

1m 3.79s (0.29) **Going Correction** -0.025s/f (Good) 8 Ran SP% 120.0
Speed ratings (Par 96): **96,89,86,80,79 78,75,73**
CSF £50.50 CT £318.73 TOTE £5.30: £1.60, £3.50, £2.50; EX 51.00 Trifecta £402.80.
**Owner** Racegoers Club Owners Group **Bred** Whitsbury Manor Stud **Trained** Musley Bank, N Yorks

**FOCUS**
The market leaders were disappointing, but the winner was impressive and Richard Fahey trained the first and second in this nursery. The runner-up has been rated as recording a minor pb.

## 5715 BEVERLEY LIONS H'CAP 5f
4:35 (4:38) (Class 6) (0-60,64) 3-Y-O £2,726 (£805; £402) Stalls Low

Form RPR

2016 1 **Bashiba (IRE)**[15] 5169 3-9-7 60 (t) RobertWinston 4 72
(Nigel Tinkler) *chsd ldrs: led jst ins fnl f: drvn out* 8/1

3242 2 1 **Another Royal**[17] 5089 3-9-4 57 (b) TonyHamilton 7 65
(Tim Easterby) *in rr: hdwy 2f out: styd on wl fnl f: tk 2nd last 50yds* 5/1[2]

6020 3 2 **Dream Sika (IRE)**[97] 2388 3-8-11 50 JamesSullivan 6 51
(Ruth Carr) *led: hung lft and hdd jst ins fnl f: kpt on same pce* 25/1

6352 4 1 1/4 **Kiss From A Rose**[12] 5287 3-9-6 59 (b[1]) GrahamGibbons 8 56
(Rae Guest) *wnt lft s: chsd ldrs: kpt on same pce over 1f out* 7/2[1]

546 5 3/4 **Slick Indian**[8] 5417 3-8-10 56 (b[1]) AnnaHesketh[(7)] 1 50
(Michael Easterby) *n.m.r on inner and lost pl sn after s: hdwy on ins over 1f out: nt clr run: swtchd lft: styd on down outside ins fnl f* 12/1

2301 6 1 1/4 **Lucky Times**[9] 5389 3-9-11 64 DavidAllan 9 54
(Mel Brittain) *mid-div: hdwy 2f out: n.m.r over 1f out: kpt on same pce* 13/2

2550 7 3 **Under Approval**[19] 4998 3-8-8 52 GemmaTutty[(5)] 3 31
(Karen Tutty) *chsd ldrs: fdd fnl f* 25/1

40P0 **8** *3 1/2* **Spinner Lane**[25] 4795 3-8-4 46 oh1 ........................(p) ConnorBeasley(3) 2 12
(Richard Whitaker) *mid-div: outpcd 3f out: hdwy 2f out: wknd appr fnl f* **33/1**

-406 **9** *1* **Best Tamayuz**[9] 5390 3-8-11 50 ........................ LukeMorris 12 13
(Scott Dixon) *hmpd s: a towards rr* **12/1**

0011 **10** *1* **Lunarian**[11] 5316 3-9-8 64 ........................ CharlesBishop(3) 10 23
(Mick Channon) *mid-div: drvn over 2f out: nvr a factor* **11/2**[3]

3004 **11** *5* **Fujin**[9] 5389 3-9-5 58 ........................(p) JasonHart 11
(Noel Wilson) *hmpd s: in rr: bhd whn eased clsng stages* **20/1**

0005 **12** *15* **Chuckamental**[20] 4974 3-8-7 46 ........................(p) JoeFanning 13
(Bryan Smart) *chsd ldrs on wd outside: wknd 2f out: bhd whn heavily eased ins fnl f* **20/1**

1m 4.65s (1.15) **Going Correction** -0.025s/f (Good) **12** Ran SP% **114.3**
Speed ratings (Par 98): **89,87,84,82,81 79,74,68,67,65 57,33**
CSF £38.42 CT £721.95 TOTE £8.90: £2.70, £1.50, £5.50; EX 52.70 Trifecta £1178.10.
**Owner** Y T Szeto **Bred** John T Heffernan & Grainne Dooley **Trained** Langton, N Yorks
■ Lady Mai was withdrawn. Price at the time of withdrawal 13-2. Rule 4 applies to all bets. Deduction 10p in the pound.

**FOCUS**
The pace was not very strong in this minor sprint handicap, but the winner scored with something in hand. Lady Mai gave trouble at the start and was withdrawn. The runner-up and third help set the standard.

## 5716 BEVERLY MIDDLE DISTANCE SERIES FINAL ROUND H'CAP 1m 4f 16y
**5:05** (5:05) (Class 5) (0-75,74) 3-Y-0+ **£5,175** (£1,540; £769; £384) **Stalls** Low

Form RPR

050 **1** **Zeus Magic**[86] 2728 4-10-0 74 ........................ RobertWinston 2 82
(Brian Ellison) *in rr: hdwy on ins 7f out: effrt on inner over 2f out: led jst ins fnl f: drvn out* **8/1**

022 **2** *1* **Chant (IRE)**[28] 4704 4-9-13 73 ........................(p) PJMcDonald 6 79
(Ann Duffield) *trckd ldrs: effrt over 2f out: upsides over 1f out: kpt on same pce to take 2nd last 50yds* **10/3**[1]

0234 **3** *1 1/2* **Flying Cape (IRE)**[5] 5527 3-9-0 70 ........................(p) DanielTudhope 3 74
(Andrew Hollinshead) *trckd ldrs: upsides over 1f out: kpt on same pce: tk 3rd last 25yds* **4/1**[2]

5525 **4** *3/4* **Rex Whistler (IRE)**[17] 5077 4-9-8 68 ........................ PaulMulrennan 5 70
(Julie Camacho) *hld up in rr: hdwy 4f out: chsng ldrs over 1f out: styng on at fin* **6/1**

3060 **5** *hd* **Right Of Appeal**[13] 5259 3-8-11 67 ........................ JoeFanning 1 69
(Mark Johnston) *led: hdd jst ins fnl f: wknd nr fin* **11/2**

16-4 **6** *8* **Aryizad (IRE)**[17] 5101 5-9-9 69 ........................ BenCurtis 8 58
(Alan Swinbank) *hld up in mid-div: hdwy on outer 7f out: chsng ldrs over 3f out: edgd rt and wknd over 1f out* **10/1**

110 **7** *hd* **El Bravo**[17] 5073 8-9-13 73 ........................ JasonHart 4 62
(Shaun Harris) *chsd ldr: wknd qckly fnl f* **18/1**

1364 **8** *1 3/4* **Maybeme**[8] 5448 8-9-5 72 ........................(p) MeganCarberry(7) 7 58
(Neville Bycroft) *rn in snatches in rr: sme hdwy over 2f out: carried rt: wknd over 1f out* **5/1**[3]

6106 **9** *30* **Dabuki (FR)**[20] 4979 4-9-6 66 ........................(p) DavidAllan 9 4
(Geoffrey Harker) *trckd ldrs on outer: t.k.h: edgd rt and lost pl over 2f out: bhd whn eased fnl f: t.o* **25/1**

2m 38.38s (-1.42) **Going Correction** -0.20s/f (Firm)
**WFA** 3 from 4yo+ 10lb **9** Ran SP% **118.7**
Speed ratings (Par 103): **96,95,94,93,93 88,88,87,67**
CSF £35.91 CT £125.80 TOTE £13.40: £2.50, £1.40, £2.60; EX 40.00 Trifecta £388.20.
**Owner** Koo's Racing Club **Bred** The Kingwood Partnership **Trained** Norton, N Yorks

**FOCUS**
The pace was not very strong in this middle-distance handicap and there was not much separating the first five. Ordinary and straightforward form to rate.

## 5717 MALTON MARQUEES SUPPORTING JACK BERRY HOUSE H'CAP 1m 1f 207y
**5:35** (5:37) (Class 6) (0-65,66) 3-Y-0 **£2,587** (£770; £384; £192) **Stalls** Low

Form RPR

0534 **1** **Paddy's Rock (IRE)**[15] 5166 3-8-11 55 ........................ PJMcDonald 9 62
(Ann Duffield) *hmpd s: in rr: hdwy on outer over 2f out: styd on wl to ld clsng stages* **11/2**[3]

6531 **2** *1/2* **Where's Tiger**[11] 5300 3-9-5 63 ........................ PhillipMakin 1 69
(Jedd O'Keeffe) *s.i.s: in rr: hdwy on outer over 2f out: led last 50yds: hdd towards fin* **9/4**[1]

-306 **3** *1* **Jimmy Crackle (IRE)**[13] 5239 3-8-8 55 ........................(p) ConnorBeasley(3) 6 59
(Brian Ellison) *trckd ldrs: t.k.h: hung rt over 1f out: led briefly ins fnl f: hdd last 50yds: kpt on same pce* **16/1**

6324 **4** *nk* **Trinity Star (IRE)**[9] 5387 3-9-7 65 ........................(p) PaulMulrennan 12 68
(Michael Dods) *swtchd rt after s: sn trcking ldrs: led over 2f out: hung rt and hdd ins fnl f: no ex* **7/2**[2]

2660 **5** *2* **Les Gar Gan (IRE)**[16] 5142 3-9-7 65 ........................ TomEaves 3 65
(Keith Dalgleish) *trckd ldrs: edgd lft 2f out: n.m.r over 1f out: kpt on one pce* **16/1**

0400 **6** *1* **Acquaint (IRE)**[34] 4497 3-8-2 51 ........................(p) JoeDoyle(5) 5 49
(John Wainwright) *mid-div: chsng ldrs over 3f out: swtchd rt over 1f out: styd on ins fnl f* **11/1**

6554 **7** *nk* **Scrutiny**[11] 5295 3-9-8 66 ........................ DanielTudhope 10 63
(David O'Meara) *wnt rt s: in rr: hdwy over 2f out: nvr rchd ldrs* **7/1**

3503 **8** *7* **White Rose Runner**[10] 5336 3-9-2 60 ........................ DavidAllan 7 44
(Mel Brittain) *led tl 7f out: led 4f out: hdd over 2f out: wknd appr fnl f: eased last 100yds* **16/1**

0-44 **9** *6* **Lady Bubbles**[17] 5084 3-8-4 48 ........................ JamesSullivan 8 20
(Michael Easterby) *t.k.h: w ldr: led 7f out: hdd 4f out: wkng whn sltly hmpd 2f out* **12/1**

0555 **10** *1 3/4* **Edward Elgar**[40] 4300 3-8-5 52 ........................(p) GeorgeChaloner(3) 2 21
(Richard Whitaker) *sn drvn along in midfield: lost pl over 1f out* **10/1**

-000 **11** *2 1/4* **Sweet Summer**[90] 2621 3-7-11 46 oh1 ........................ JackGarritty(5) 4 11
(John Holt) *in rr: sme hdwy and drvn over 3f out: wknd 2f out* **33/1**

0000 **12** *49* **Moxey**[9] 5402 3-8-2 46 oh1 ........................(bt[1]) PatrickMathers 14
(John Davies) *chsd ldrs: lost pl over 2f out: sn bhd and eased: virtually p.u: hopelessly t.o* **50/1**

2m 6.75s (-0.25) **Going Correction** -0.20s/f (Firm) **12** Ran SP% **128.5**
Speed ratings (Par 98): **93,92,91,91,89 89,88,83,78,77 75,36**
CSF £19.85 CT £202.47 TOTE £6.30: £2.50, £1.70, £4.40; EX 23.90 Trifecta £328.60.
**Owner** Jimmy Kay **Bred** J O'Connor **Trained** Constable Burton, N Yorks
■ Stewards' Enquiry : Tom Eaves one-day ban: careless riding (Sep 7)

**FOCUS**
The first two came from some way back in this ordinary handicap. The fourth helps set the level.
T/Plt: £152.80 to a £1 stake. Pool: £65,108.92 - 310.89 winning tickets. T/Qpdt: £73.40 to a £1 stake. Pool: £4,855.80 - 48.95 winning tickets. WG

# 5664 GOODWOOD (R-H)
Sunday, August 24

**OFFICIAL GOING: Good (good to firm in places on round course; 7.2)**
Wind: Moderate, half against Weather: Fine but cloudy Rails: Back straight and Bottom bend dolled out 3m and races on Round course increased by 18yds

## 5718 FAIRGROUND MAIDEN AUCTION STKS 1m
**2:00** (2:00) (Class 5) 2-Y-O **£3,234** (£962; £481; £240) **Stalls** Low

Form RPR

4 **1** **Shalimah (IRE)**[10] 5351 2-8-11 0 ........................ RyanTate(3) 1 82+
(Clive Cox) *chsd clr ldng quartet: shkn up and clsd over 3f out: prog to ld over 1f out: drvn and styd on* **9/2**[2]

3 **2** *1 3/4* **The Lampo Genie**[17] 5078 2-8-12 0 ........................ JamesDoyle 3 76+
(K R Burke) *chsd ldng trio: clsd over 2f out: led briefly wl over 1f out: kpt on but no imp on wnr fnl f* **8/11**[1]

3 **3** *1* **Spring Dixie (IRE)**[18] 5056 2-8-0 0 ........................ NoelGarbutt(5) 2 67
(Rae Guest) *chsd ldng pair: rdn wl over 2f out: cl enough on inner wl over 1f out: one pce* **12/1**[3]

6435 **4** *2* **Hawkmeister (IRE)**[17] 5072 2-8-12 73 ........................(b) SeanLevey 4 69
(Richard Hannon) *chsd ldr: rdn over 3f out: drvn to ld jst over 2f out to wl over 1f out: wknd fnl f* **14/1**

**5** *1 1/2* **Ventura Castle** 2-8-13 0 ........................ KieranO'Neill 6 67+
(Richard Hannon) *dwlt: rn green and pushed along in rr: detached in last pair over 3f out: kpt on fr over 1f out: nrst fin* **16/1**

0 **6** *shd* **Jolie De Vivre (IRE)**[22] 4896 2-8-13 0 ........................ LiamKeniry 8 66
(Sylvester Kirk) *sn wl in rr: detached in last pair and rdn 3f out: kpt on fr over 1f out: nrst fin* **50/1**

2602 **7** *4 1/2* **Playboy Bay**[10] 5335 2-8-10 67 ........................ SamHitchcott 9 53
(Mick Channon) *wnt lft s: wl in rr: rdn 1/2-way: prog on outer over 2f out: hanging and wknd over 1f out* **16/1**

0 **8** *1/2* **Sonar (IRE)**[22] 4884 2-9-0 0 ........................ WilliamTwiston-Davies 7 56
(Michael Bell) *dwlt: wl in rr: reminders over 3f out: clsd and in tch 2f out: pushed along and wknd over 1f out* **20/1**

0 **9** *1* **Cassandane (IRE)**[24] 4825 2-8-7 0 ........................ FrannyNorton 5 47
(Mark Johnston) *led at gd pce to jst over 2f out: sn wknd* **12/1**[3]

1m 40.97s (1.07) **Going Correction** -0.05s/f (Good) **9** Ran SP% **116.6**
Speed ratings (Par 94): **92,90,89,87,85 85,81,80,79**
CSF £8.15 TOTE £4.60: £2.10, £1.10, £2.50; EX 10.70 Trifecta £55.00.
**Owner** Mrs Christine Craddock **Bred** Yeomanstown Stud **Trained** Lambourn, Berks

**FOCUS**
This is usually a competitive maiden, won in the past by the likes of subsequent of Group 1 winner Youmzain and Listed scorer Chil The Kite, and while this renewal lacked a little depth, the front three looked up to standard. The third helps set the level.

## 5719 REVIVAL (S) STKS 1m 3f
**2:30** (2:31) (Class 4) 3-Y-O **£6,469** (£1,925; £962; £481) **Stalls** High

Form RPR

0444 **1** **Sparkling Ice (IRE)**[6] 5491 3-8-2 55 ........................(b) AmyScott(5) 5 56
(Eve Johnson Houghton) *trckd ldr: shkn up to ld jst over 2f out: more than a l clr and coaxed along ins fnl f: ld dwindled qckly nr fin* **10/3**[2]

1304 **2** *nk* **Bishop Wulstan (IRE)**[5] 5520 3-8-12 62 ........................(b[1]) CamHardie(5) 1 65
(Richard Hannon) *shoved along vigorously early: chsd ldng pair to 5f out: rdn 3f out: no prog 2f out: styd on again fnl f: tk 2nd and clsd on wnr fin* **11/4**[1]

53-5 **3** *nk* **Ding Ding**[17] 5071 3-8-7 54 ........................ SamHitchcott 3 54
(Mick Channon) *in tch: trckd ldng pair 5f out: rdn 3f out: wnt 2nd over 1f out: nt qckn and hld fnl f: lost 2nd nr fin* **6/1**

056 **4** *1 1/4* **Classic Mission**[19] 5006 3-8-12 59 ........................(p) OisinMurphy 6 57
(Jonathan Portman) *led: rdn and hdd jst over 2f out: chsd wnr to over 1f out: one pce* **5/1**

5-00 **5** *2 1/4* **Edge (IRE)**[83] 2833 3-8-12 75 ........................(b[1]) MartinLane 2 54
(Bernard Llewellyn) *in tch: rdn 3f out: cl up whn swtchd lft 2f out: nt qckn over 1f out: fdd* **4/1**[3]

50 **6** *4 1/2* **Archiebeau**[163] 951 3-8-7 0 ........................ NedCurtis(5) 4 46
(Jonathan Portman) *dwlt: mostly in last pair: rdn over 3f out: no prog over 2f out: sn wknd* **8/1**

2m 29.92s (3.42) **Going Correction** -0.05s/f (Good) **6** Ran SP% **111.8**
Speed ratings (Par 102): **85,84,84,83,82 78**
CSF £12.79 TOTE £4.60: £2.10, £1.90; EX 14.40 Trifecta £42.20.There was no bid for the winner.
**Owner** Mrs E Rice & Mrs R F Johnson Houghton **Bred** Gerrardstown House Stud **Trained** Blewbury, Oxon
■ Stewards' Enquiry : Amy Scott two-day ban: used whip above permitted level (Sep 7-8)

**FOCUS**
An uncompetitive seller considering the prize fund. A race to be negative about with the future in mind.

## 5720 HARWOODS GROUP STKS (H'CAP) (BOBIS RACE) 1m 1f 192y
**3:05** (3:05) (Class 2) (0-100,100) 3-Y-O
**£12,450** (£3,728; £1,864; £932; £466; £234) **Stalls** Low

Form RPR

315 **1** **The Corsican (IRE)**[45] 4122 3-8-7 86 ow1 ........................ JimCrowley 8 95+
(David Simcock) *sn in midfield: cl up bhd ldrs 2f out but waiting for a gap: prog over 1f out: drvn and r.o to ld last 150yds: sn in command* **8/1**[3]

-603 **2** *1 1/2* **Madeed**[24] 4821 3-9-0 93 ........................(t) PaulHanagan 9 99+
(Brian Meehan) *w.w in midfield: wd bnd 5f out and dropped to last trio: in tch but only 9th 2f out: nt clr run briefly over 1f out: gd prog after: r.o to take 2nd nr fin: no ch to threaten* **5/2**[1]

4430 **3** *nse* **Examiner (IRE)**[24] 4821 3-8-7 86 ........................ LiamJones 3 92+
(William Haggas) *in tch: waiting for a gap on inner 3f out: nt clr run 2f out: prog over 1f out: r.o fnl f: tk 3rd nr fin and nrly snatched 2nd* **14/1**

2120 **4** *1 1/4* **Black Shadow**[22] 4893 3-9-1 94 ........................ JamesDoyle 6 98
(Amanda Perrett) *led: rdn over 2f out: jnd over 1f out: hdd and one pce last 150yds* **10/1**

3301 **5** *2* **First Flight (IRE)**[29] 4667 3-9-3 96 ........................ HarryBentley 10 96
(Saeed bin Suroor) *trckd ldng pair: wnt 2nd 3f out: jnd ldr over 1f out and pushed along: stl upsides jst ins fnl f: shkn up and fizzled out qckly* **3/1**[2]

020 **6** *2* **Pupil (IRE)**[24] 4821 3-8-6 90 ........................ CamHardie(5) 2 86
(Richard Hannon) *in tch: pushed along 4f out: prog on outer over 2f out: no hdwy u.p over 1f out: fdd* **16/1**

3135 **7** *3 1/4* **Raise Your Gaze**[15] 5164 3-8-4 86 ........................ RyanTate(3) 5 76
(Clive Cox) *t.k.h: trckd ldrs: shkn up to go 3rd over 2f out to over 1f out: wknd fnl f* **10/1**

2264 **8** *6* **Good Value**[28] 4698 3-8-4 **83**....................(v[1]) DavidProbert 1 61
(Sir Michael Stoute) *trckd ldrs: cl up on inner over 2f out: rdn and wknd qckly over 1f out* **12/1**

1033 **9** *2* **Bureau (IRE)**[9] 5401 3-8-7 **86**.................... FrannyNorton 4 61
(Mark Johnston) *chsd ldr to 3f out: sn lost pl: wknd over 1f out* **14/1**

1200 **10** *17* **Personal Opinion**[15] 5179 3-8-12 **91**.................... MartinLane 7 33
(Charlie Appleby) *mostly in last: bhd fr 4f out: t.o* **20/1**

0063 **11** *2* **Sir Jack Layden**[38] 4366 3-9-7 **100**.................... SeanLevey 11 38
(David Brown) *a in rr: wknd 3f out: eased and t.o* **50/1**

2m 5.86s (-2.24) **Going Correction** -0.05s/f (Good) **11** Ran SP% **116.5**
Speed ratings (Par 106): **106,104,104,103,102 100,97,93,91,77 76**
CSF £27.94 CT £281.56 TOTE £9.60: £2.90, £1.50, £3.80; EX 30.20 Trifecta £941.20.
**Owner** Mrs Fitri Hay **Bred** Mrs Fitriani Hay **Trained** Newmarket, Suffolk

**FOCUS**
They went no pace early on in this valuable handicap, but the form looks solid. The fourth has been rated to form after enjoying the run of the race.

## 5721 GOODWOOD AMATEUR RIDER CHALLENGE H'CAP (IN MEMORY OF THE LATE GAY KINDERSLEY) 1m 1f
**3:40** (3:40) (Class 5) (0-75,75) 4-Y-0+ **£6,239** (£1,935; £967; £484) **Stalls** Low

Form RPR

401 **1** **Victor's Bet (SPA)**[21] 4942 5-11-5 75.................... MissEllaSmith(5) 5 84+
(Ralph J Smith) *dwlt and s.i.s: virtually t.o after 2f: jst in tch 1/2-way: prog to go 5th over 1f out but stl plenty to do: clsd dramatically on flagging ldrs and swept into ld last 75yds* **8/1**

1300 **2** *1 3/4* **Automotive**[21] 4942 6-10-11 62.................... MrRBirkett 6 67
(Julia Feilden) *hld up in midfield: stdy prog to go 4th over 2f out: urged along and clsd over 1f out: brought to chal as wnr swept past ins fnl f: kpt on to take 2nd post* **11/2**[3]

2410 **3** *shd* **Living Leader**[25] 4798 5-11-4 69....................(p) MrMichaelJMurphy 2 74
(Grace Harris) *trckd ldr: led 3f out and asked to go for home: treading water fr 2f out: hdd last 75yds: lost 2nd post* **7/2**[1]

4110 **4** *hd* **Edgware Road**[26] 4755 6-10-5 61....................(b) MissBHampson(5) 3 65
(Andy Turnell) *chsd ldng pair: urged along fr 3f out: tried to cl fr 2f out: kpt on same pce over 1f out* **7/1**

100 **5** *2* **Le Deluge (FR)**[8] 5421 4-10-10 68.................... MrRobertHooper(7) 10 68+
(Ann Stokell) *won battle for ld and set str pce: hdd 3f out: chsd ldr and in tch tl jst ins fnl f: fdd* **10/1**

4554 **6** *1/2* **Peak Storm**[18] 5058 5-10-12 66.................... MissSMDoolan(3) 7 65
(John O'Shea) *towards rr and off the pce: urged along and no prog 3f out: no ch after: kpt on fnl f* **14/1**

145 **7** *2 1/2* **Angus Glens**[21] 4942 4-10-7 65....................(p) MissGFriswell(7) 1 59
(David Dennis) *chsd clr ldrs: pushed along and no prog 3f out: struggling after* **14/1**

0414 **8** *2* **Play Street**[6] 5503 5-11-5 73.................... MrJHarding(3) 8 63
(Jonathan Portman) *chsd ldng trio: urged along and struggling 3f out: wl btn fnl 2f* **6/1**

5312 **9** *11* **Estibdaad (IRE)**[8] 5428 4-10-1 57....................(t) MissMBryant(5) 9 25
(Paddy Butler) *chsd clr ldrs: pushed along and btn 3f out: wknd* **12/1**

3011 **10** *70* **Ancient Greece**[91] 2592 7-11-2 72....................(t) MrORJSangster(5) 4
(George Baker) *sn wl bhd: t.o after 3f: no prog 3f out: virtually p.u fnl f* **5/1**[2]

1m 58.11s (1.81) **Going Correction** -0.05s/f (Good) **10** Ran SP% **122.3**
Speed ratings (Par 103): **89,87,87,87,85 84,82,80,71,8**
CSF £54.24 CT £187.35 TOTE £9.20: £2.80, £2.60, £1.70; EX 66.90 Trifecta £722.50.
**Owner** Homecroft Wealth & Clear Racing **Bred** Jose Simo Vazquez **Trained** Epsom, Surrey
■ Hector's Chance was withdrawn. Price at the time of withdrawal 9-1. Rule 4 applies to board prices prior to withdrawal but not to SP bets. Deduction 10p in the pound. New market formed.
■ Stewards' Enquiry : Miss B Hampson four-day ban: used whip above permitted level (tbn)

**FOCUS**
This was run to suit the closers. The winner was impressive, while the third has been rated to his recent best.

## 5722 DOOM BAR SUPREME STKS (GROUP 3) 7f
**4:15** (4:17) (Class 1) 3-Y-0+
**£34,026** (£12,900; £6,456; £3,216; £1,614; £810) **Stalls** Low

Form RPR

-010 **1** **Ansgar (IRE)**[10] 5361 6-9-4 110....................(t) JamesDoyle 10 117
(Sabrina J Harty, Ire) *trckd ldr: led jst over 2f out: rdn over 1f out: hung lft fnl f but styd on wl* **14/1**

1112 **2** *1 3/4* **Muteela**[23] 4854 3-8-6 104.................... PaulHanagan 1 104
(Mark Johnston) *reluctant to go to post: stmbld s: chsd ldng pair: rdn 2f out: wnt 2nd jst over 1f out: styd on but no imp last 100yds* **2/1**[1]

2014 **3** *1* **Professor**[8] 5434 4-9-0 113.................... SeanLevey 2 105
(Richard Hannon) *t.k.h early: hld up in 5th: pushed along 3f out: prog u.p to dispute 2nd 1f out: one pce after* **9/2**[3]

133 **4** *2* **Indignant**[23] 4854 4-8-11 102.................... FrannyNorton 6 97
(Richard Hannon) *led: shkn up and hdd jst over 2f out: lost 2nd jst over 1f out: fdd* **12/1**

1200 **5** *1 1/4* **Horsted Keynes (FR)**[23] 4851 4-9-0 103....................[1] JimCrowley 5 97
(Roger Varian) *dwlt: hld up in last: pushed along 3f out: no prog whn rdn 2f out: n.d after* **6/1**

5034 **6** *1/2* **Steeler (IRE)**[23] 4851 4-9-0 107.................... MartinLane 9 95
(Charlie Appleby) *chsd ldrs: drvn over 2f out: steadily wknd over 1f out* **9/4**[2]

1m 26.2s (-0.80) **Going Correction** -0.05s/f (Good)
**WFA** 3 from 4yo+ 5lb **6** Ran SP% **110.9**
Speed ratings: **102,100,98,96,95 94**
CSF £41.42 TOTE £12.00: £4.30, £1.80; EX 37.70 Trifecta £254.20.
**Owner** Ms Chynel Phelan & Shane Fox **Bred** Miss Chynel Phelan **Trained** Newbridge, Co Kildare

**FOCUS**
A fair Group 3, run at a sound pace. Some of the winner's Irish form could be rated higher, but this looks like a pb from him.

## 5723 DOOM BAR FILLIES STKS (H'CAP) 1m 4f
**4:45** (4:47) (Class 3) (0-90,90) 3-Y-0+
**£9,337** (£2,796; £1,398; £699; £349; £175) **Stalls** High

Form RPR

2005 **1** **Jordan Princess**[36] 4436 3-9-1 87.................... JamesDoyle 3 96+
(Luca Cumani) *trckd ldrs: gng wl 3f out: cl up whn hmpd wl over 1f out: swtchd wd and plenty to do fnl f: str run to ld last strides* **11/4**[2]

3116 **2** *nk* **Tioga Pass**[44] 4145 3-9-4 90....................(b[1]) JimCrowley 8 96
(Paul Cole) *hld up in last pair: gng wl 3f out: prog over 2f out: led wl over 1f out and edgd rt: idled in front: drvn fnl f: hdd last strides* **12/1**

4021 **3** *hd* **Artistic Muse (IRE)**[19] 5003 3-8-4 76.................... RoystonFfrench 6 81
(Charles Hills) *hld up in last pair: rdn 3f out: prog on outer 2f out: lft in 2nd over 1f out: clsd on ldr fnl f but lost 2nd last strides* **8/1**

04 **4** *5* **Phaenomena (IRE)**[43] 4204 4-9-6 87.................... CamHardie(5) 7 84
(Lady Cecil) *pushed along early to chse ldrs: rdn 3f out: clsd to ld jst over 2f out: sn hung rt and caused carnage: hdd wl over 1f out: wknd fnl f* **13/2**[3]

0101 **5** *8* **Wilhana (IRE)**[29] 4663 4-9-7 83.................... LiamKeniry 1 71+
(Pam Sly) *led: jnd and shkn up 3f out: hdd jst over 2f out: bdly hmpd wl over 1f out: no ch after* **8/1**

0-21 **6** *16* **Spiritoftheunion**[20] 4978 3-8-10 82.................... MartinLane 2 57+
(Michael Bell) *trckd ldng pair: pushed along 3f out: lost pl and last whn hmpd wl over 1f out: eased* **9/4**[1]

4113 **7** *7* **Thurayaat**[63] 3502 3-8-13 85.................... PaulHanagan 5 67+
(Roger Varian) *trckd ldr: chal and upsides 3f out: hdd jst over 2f out: bdly hmpd wl over 1f out: eased* **7/1**

2m 38.46s (0.06) **Going Correction** -0.05s/f (Good)
**WFA** 3 from 4yo+ 10lb **7** Ran SP% **113.2**
Speed ratings (Par 107): **97,96,96,93,88 77,72**
CSF £33.48 CT £233.38 TOTE £4.40: £2.50, £3.80; EX 34.40 Trifecta £215.00.
**Owner** Sheikh Mohammed Obaid Al Maktoum **Bred** Darley **Trained** Newmarket, Suffolk
■ Stewards' Enquiry : Cam Hardie seven-day ban: careless riding (Sep 7-13)

**FOCUS**
The early pace was slow for this useful handicap and there was carnage just after the 2f marker when a concertina effect changed the complexion of the race as Phaenomena lugged right, hampering a trio. The first-time blinkered runner-up has been rated as building on her course win.

## 5724 AUGUST BANK HOLIDAY STKS (H'CAP) 5f
**5:15** (5:17) (Class 5) (0-70,70) 3-Y-0+ **£3,234** (£962; £481; £240) **Stalls** High

Form RPR

5110 **1** **Two Turtle Doves (IRE)**[6] 5499 8-9-2 60.................... HarryBentley 4 67
(Michael Mullineaux) *hld up in tch: rdn and prog over 1f out: drvn to ld last 100yds: styd on* **8/1**

4502 **2** *1/2* **Shilla (IRE)**[10] 5355 3-9-5 70.................... AmyScott(5) 7 75
(Henry Candy) *hld up in last: rdn over 1f out: styd on fnl f against nr side rail to take 2nd nr fin: nt rch wnr* **15/8**[1]

0455 **3** *nk* **Dreams Of Glory**[3] 5595 6-9-12 70....................(b) OisinMurphy 2 74
(Ron Hodges) *trckd ldrs: pushed along and nt hold pl 2f out: rallied jst over 1f out on wd outside: chal fnl f: one pce last 100yds* **5/1**[3]

-460 **4** *nk* **Go Glamorous (IRE)**[22] 4891 3-9-8 68.................... DavidProbert 1 71
(Ronald Harris) *trckd ldrs: clsd over 2f out: rdn to ld over 1f out: hung lft and hdd last 100yds: nt qckn* **6/1**

0431 **5** *1/2* **Only Ten Per Cent (IRE)**[14] 5207 6-9-11 69....................(v) JimCrowley 6 70
(J R Jenkins) *pressed ldr: led 2f out to over 1f out: nt qckn u.p: kpt on* **9/2**[2]

3025 **6** *1 3/4* **Monarch Maid**[22] 4890 3-9-5 65.................... ChrisCatlin 9 60
(Peter Hiatt) *hanging rt thrght: led to 2f out: sn lost pl: wl hld whn short of room briefly ins fnl f* **5/1**[3]

58.95s (-1.25) **Going Correction** -0.175s/f (Firm)
**WFA** 3 from 6yo+ 2lb **6** Ran SP% **111.7**
Speed ratings (Par 103): **103,102,101,101,100 97**
CSF £23.26 CT £81.67 TOTE £5.80: £2.20, £2.00; EX 18.90 Trifecta £81.60.
**Owner** G Cornes **Bred** M Sharkey **Trained** Alpraham, Cheshire
■ Stewards' Enquiry : David Probert caution: careless riding.

**FOCUS**
A modest sprint handicap in which nothing looked well treated.
T/Jkpt: £94,268.50 to a £1 stake. Pool: £199,158.90 - 1.5 winning tickets. T/Plt: £66.20 to a £1 stake. Pool: £94,344.15 - 1039.93 winning tickets. T/Qpdt: £34.00 to a £1 stake. Pool: £6,349.28 - 137.85 winning tickets. JN

# [5531]YARMOUTH (L-H)
Sunday, August 24

**OFFICIAL GOING: Good (good to firm in places; 7.3)**
Wind: light, half against Weather: light cloud, brighter spells

## 5725 BRITISH STALLION STUDS EBF TOTEJACKPOT MAIDEN FILLIES' STKS (BOBIS RACE) 6f 3y
**2:10** (2:12) (Class 5) 2-Y-O **£4,204** (£1,251; £625; £312) **Stalls** Centre

Form RPR

0 **1** **Touchline**[25] 4781 2-9-0 0.................... FrederikTylicki 3 81+
(Michael Bell) *chsd ldrs: wnt 2nd over 2f out: rdn to ld over 1f out: pushed along and styd on strly fnl f: readily* **8/1**

2 **2** *1 1/4* **Cockney Island**[10] 5344 2-9-0 0.................... MartinHarley 10 77
(Philip McBride) *led: rdn and hdd over 1f out: kpt on but no imp on wnr fnl f* **9/2**[3]

**3** *4* **Deep Blue Sea** 2-9-0 0.................... WilliamCarson 8 67+
(Anthony Carson) *s.i.s: in tch in rr: hdwy into modest 5th over 1f out: pushed along and kpt on wl to go 3rd wl ins fnl f: no threat to ldrs* **16/1**

22 **4** *1 1/2* **Russian Heroine**[94] 2493 2-9-0 0.................... RyanMoore 6 61
(Sir Michael Stoute) *in tch in midfield: effrt in 4th over 1f out: sn outpcd and btn 1f out: plugged on* **3/1**[2]

2 **5** *1/2* **March On (USA)**[24] 4828 2-9-0 0.................... ShaneKelly 7 59
(William Haggas) *wl in tch in midfield: hdwy to go 3rd 2f out: sn rdn and unable qck: btn 1f out: plugged on same pce and lost 2 pls ins fnl f* **5/4**[1]

3 **6** *7* **Pencil**[17] 5104 2-9-0 0.................... PaddyAspell 11 38
(James Eustace) *chsd ldrs: rdn ent fnl 2f: btn whn hung lft over 1f out: sn wknd* **20/1**

05 **7** *1 1/4* **Lady Atlas**[7] 5464 2-9-0 0.................... MichaelStainton 2 35
(David Brown) *in tch in midfield: rdn and outpcd ent fnl 2f: wknd wl over 1f out* **50/1**

00 **8** *4* **Pudding (IRE)**[10] 5344 2-8-11 0.................... AshleyMorgan(3) 5 23
(Lady Cecil) *w ldr tl lost pl u.p over 2f out: wknd wl over 1f out* **50/1**

0 **9** *3 1/2* **Shamiya (IRE)**[13] 5248 2-9-0 0.................... TedDurcan 9 12
(J S Moore) *in tch in rr: rdn over 2f out: sn struggling: bhd over 1f out* **66/1**

00 **10** *7* **With Charm (USA)**[22] 4914 2-9-0 0.................... AhmedAjtebi 4
(Charlie Appleby) *s.i.s: in tch in rr: rdn jst over 2f out: sn btn: bhd over 1f out* **50/1**

**11** *6* **Dancethenightaway (IRE)** 2-9-0 0....................(b[1]) DaneO'Neill 1
(William Jarvis) *s.i.s: v green and a wl in rr: t.o 1/2-way* **40/1**

1m 13.07s (-1.33) **Going Correction** -0.175s/f (Firm) **11** Ran SP% **119.2**
Speed ratings (Par 91): **101,99,94,92,91 82,80,75,70,61 53**
CSF £42.42 TOTE £10.80: £2.60, £1.80, £3.80; EX 47.60 Trifecta £861.20.
**Owner** The Queen **Bred** The Queen **Trained** Newmarket, Suffolk

**FOCUS**
This looked just an ordinary race of its type. The third could have finished closer, the fourth looked unhappy on the track and the fifth was well below form.

## 5726 TOTEPLACEPOT H'CAP 6f 3y
**2:40** (2:41) (Class 5) (0-75,75) 3-Y-O+ **£3,881** (£1,155; £577; £288) **Stalls** Centre

Form RPR
4-06 1 **Red Aggressor (IRE)**[12] 5281 5-8-13 68 (b) DannyBrock(3) 1 83+
(Clive Brittain) *chsd ldrs: clsd to chal over 1f out: shkn up to ld jst ins fnl f: edgd rt but r.o strly: comf* **14/1**
5004 2 3½ **Commanche**[18] 5060 5-9-1 72 ShelleyBirkett(5) 4 77
(Chris Dwyer) *chsd ldr tl 1/2-way: rdn over 1f out: no threat to wnr but kpt on u.p fnl 100yds: wnt 2nd last strides* **6/1**
1114 3 *nk* **Refuse Colette (IRE)**[9] 5398 5-9-8 74 PaoloSirigu 6 78
(Mick Quinn) *t.k.h: chsd ldrs: wnt 2nd 1/2-way: rdn to ld wl over 1f out: hdd jst ins fnl f: sn outpcd by wnr: kpt on same pce: lost 2nd last strides* **15/8**[1]
1 4 ½ **Artistic Queen**[15] 5181 3-9-6 75 RyanMoore 2 77
(James Tate) *s.i.s: hld up in tch in rr: rdn and effrt 2f out: sme hdwy over 1f out: kpt on same pce ins fnl f* **9/2**[3]
3311 5 ½ **Parisian Pyramid (IRE)**[8] 5422 8-9-1 72 (p) JennyPowell(5) 3 73
(Lee Carter) *led: rdn and hdd wl over 1f out: no ch w wnr and styd on same pce fnl f* **7/2**[2]
2600 6 7 **Welsh Sunrise**[22] 4918 4-9-6 72 MartinHarley 5 52
(Stuart Williams) *t.k.h: wl in tch: rdn ent fnl 2f: sn struggling and btn over 1f out: wknd 1f out* **6/1**

1m 12.65s (-1.75) **Going Correction** -0.175s/f (Firm)
**WFA** 3 from 4yo+ 3lb 6 Ran SP% 110.4
Speed ratings (Par 103): **104,99,98,98,97 88**
CSF £87.93 TOTE £15.20: £7.40, £3.80; EX 91.50 Trifecta £429.30.
**Owner** C E Brittain **Bred** John Foley & Miss A Foley **Trained** Newmarket, Suffolk

**FOCUS**
Only a reasonable race for the class. Straightforward form to rate.

## 5727 TOTEPOOLBETTING ON ALL UK RACES H'CAP 1m 3y
**3:15** (3:15) (Class 4) (0-80,80) 3-Y-O+ **£5,822** (£1,732; £865; £432) **Stalls** Centre

Form RPR
0614 1 **Desert Ranger (IRE)**[30] 4628 3-9-1 75 RyanMoore 2 83
(James Tate) *stdd s: hld up in last pair: rdn and effrt jst over 2f out: drvn to chal over 1f out: sustained duel w runner-up fnl f: led fnl 50yds: styd on: all out* **5/2**[1]
-030 2 *nk* **Pleasure Bent**[69] 3314 4-9-10 78 ShaneKelly 4 86
(Luca Cumani) *hld up in tch in midfield: clsd to press ldrs 2f out: rdn to ld over 1f out: sn hrd pressed: sustained duel w wnr fnl f: hdd fnl 50yds: kpt on but hld cl home* **9/2**[3]
2211 3 1 **Specialty (IRE)**[30] 4620 4-9-5 73 StephenCraine 1 79
(Pam Sly) *w ldr: rdn to ld wl over 1f out: sn hdd and hung rt: kpt on same pce ins fnl f* **7/2**[2]
1353 4 3½ **Pactolus (IRE)**[37] 4404 3-8-13 73 MartinHarley 7 70
(Stuart Williams) *racd nr stands' rail thrght: hld up in tch: clsd to trck ldrs 1/2-way: rdn and unable qck whn carried rt over 1f out: wknd ins fnl f* **7/2**[2]
5200 5 2¾ **Afkar (IRE)**[10] 5346 6-8-11 68 (b) DannyBrock(3) 3 59
(Clive Brittain) *led: rdn and hdd wl over 1f out: unable qck whn carried rt and sltly hmpd over 1f out: wknd ins fnl f* **12/1**
2156 6 7 **Jonnie Skull (IRE)**[5] 5537 8-8-10 64 (vt) WilliamCarson 5 39
(Phil McEntee) *chsd ldrs and swtchd to r nr stands' rail sn after s: rdn 1/2-way: wknd 2f out* **14/1**
-005 7 2½ **Mezmaar**[20] 4982 5-9-5 80 MikeyEnnis(7) 6 49
(Kevin Morgan) *hld up in tch in midfield: swtchd rt sn after s and then bk to centre over 6f out: rdn 3f out: wknd 2f out* **20/1**
06-0 8 3 **Sabre Rock**[146] 1209 4-9-0 68 SteveDrowne 8 31
(John Best) *a bhd: rdn 1/2-way: lost tch 2f out* **50/1**

1m 39.03s (-1.57) **Going Correction** -0.175s/f (Firm)
**WFA** 3 from 4yo+ 6lb 8 Ran SP% 112.3
Speed ratings (Par 105): **100,99,98,95,92 85,82,79**
CSF £13.49 CT £37.69 TOTE £2.90: £1.70, £2.10, £1.30; EX 13.70 Trifecta £56.80.
**Owner** Sheikh Juma Dalmook Al Maktoum **Bred** Tally-Ho Stud **Trained** Newmarket, Suffolk

**FOCUS**
The two horses who fought out the finish to this fair handicap made their bids towards the middle of the track, away from the remainder. The winner has been rated as running a small pb.

## 5728 TOTEEXACTA H'CAP 7f 3y
**3:50** (3:50) (Class 3) (0-95,95) 3-Y-O+ **£9,056** (£2,695; £1,346; £673) **Stalls** Centre

Form RPR
310- 1 **Prince's Trust**[407] 4295 4-9-5 88 ShaneKelly 8 105+
(William Haggas) *hld up in tch in midfield: hdwy to ld and travelling strly 2f out: barely nudged along and drew wl clr fnl f: v easily* **7/1**
-144 2 3¾ **Flow (USA)**[71] 3251 4-9-9 92 (t) TedDurcan 3 97+
(Lady Cecil) *stdd s: hld up in tch in midfield: rdn and effrt over 1f out: styd on u.p to snatch 2nd last strides: no ch w wnr* **7/2**[2]
2151 3 *nk* **Outback Traveller (IRE)**[22] 4912 3-9-5 93 RyanMoore 4 95
(Jeremy Noseda) *led: rdn 2f out and sn hdd: outpcd by wnr ins fnl f: kpt on same pce: lost 2nd last strides* **13/8**[1]
4206 4 1½ **Zacynthus (IRE)**[8] 5433 6-8-7 81 LouisSteward(5) 2 81
(Michael Bell) *chsd ldrs: effrt 2f out: unable qck and n.m.r over 1f out: no ch w wnr and one pce fnl f* **10/1**
1502 5 ¾ **Born To Surprise**[29] 4650 5-9-11 94 AmirQuinn 1 92
(Lee Carter) *in tch in midfield: effrt u.p to chse ldrs over 1f out: outpcd 1f out: wknd wl ins fnl f* **8/1**
0054 6 ½ **Mezzotint (IRE)**[8] 5418 5-9-2 85 DaneO'Neill 7 82
(Stuart Williams) *dwlt: in tch in last pair: shkn up and effrt 2f out: no imp u.p over 1f out* **9/2**[3]
7 1¾ **Counter Ridge (SAF)**[267] 5-9-5 88 MartinHarley 5 80
(Marco Botti) *t.k.h: chsd ldr tl lost pl u.p jst over 2f out: wknd over 1f out* **33/1**

1m 25.58s (-1.02) **Going Correction** -0.175s/f (Firm)
**WFA** 3 from 4yo+ 5lb 7 Ran SP% 114.1
Speed ratings (Par 107): **98,93,93,91,90 90,88**
CSF £31.46 CT £58.55 TOTE £11.50: £3.90, £2.30; EX 40.20 Trifecta £127.00.
**Owner** The Queen **Bred** The Queen **Trained** Newmarket, Suffolk

**FOCUS**
A decent handicap. The winner is lightly raced and has an excellent pedigree, and has been rated as a big improver off a break for his in-form yard.

## 5729 TOTEPOOL SUPPORTING THE SPORT YOU LOVE H'CAP 7f 3y
**4:25** (4:25) (Class 5) (0-70,71) 3-Y-O+ **£3,881** (£1,155; £577; £288) **Stalls** Centre

Form RPR
2450 1 **Sakash**[22] 4907 4-9-10 68 (p) FrederikTylicki 8 76
(J R Jenkins) *stdd s: hld up in tch in last trio: hdwy 2f out: rdn and qcknd to ld jst over 1f out: r.o wl fnl f: readily* **7/2**[2]
2465 2 2¼ **Tubeanie (IRE)**[17] 5105 3-8-5 59 (p) DanielMuscutt(5) 5 59
(Amy Weaver) *chsd ldr tl rdn to ld 2f out: hdd jst over 1f out: kpt on same pce and hld on for 2nd fnl f* **10/1**
0415 3 *nk* **Bishan Bedi (IRE)**[24] 4813 3-9-4 67 DaneO'Neill 7 66
(William Jarvis) *in tch in midfield: effrt and hdwy over 1f out: battling for 2nd and flashed tail ins fnl f: kpt on same pce* **13/2**
0505 4 3¼ **Toymaker**[109] 2079 7-9-12 70 PaddyAspell 6 62
(Phil McEntee) *in tch in midfield: effrt and shkn up over 1f out: no hdwy u.p 1f out: wknd ins fnl f* **25/1**
3000 5 *nk* **Silver Mirage**[17] 5079 3-9-5 68 RyanMoore 1 58
(Michael Bell) *t.k.h: chsd ldrs: hdwy 1/2-way: ev ch and rdn 2f out: btn ent fnl f: wknd fnl 150yds* **11/4**[1]
211 6 2¼ **Darnathean**[11] 5303 5-9-13 71 (p) MartinHarley 3 57
(Paul D'Arcy) *chsd ldrs: rdn and lost pl ent fnl 2f: wknd u.p jst over 1f out* **4/1**[3]
0425 7 1 **True Spirit**[17] 5103 4-8-12 56 ShaneKelly 2 39
(Paul D'Arcy) *led tl 2f out: sn lost pl and btn: bhd fnl f* **8/1**
1030 8 1½ **Sheikh The Reins (IRE)**[29] 4650 5-9-10 68 (v) SteveDrowne 4 47
(John Best) *restless in stalls: s.i.s: hld up in rr: rdn over 2f out: sn struggling: wknd over 1f out* **12/1**

1m 26.52s (-0.08) **Going Correction** -0.175s/f (Firm)
**WFA** 3 from 4yo+ 5lb 8 Ran SP% 114.0
Speed ratings (Par 103): **93,90,90,86,86 83,82,80**
CSF £37.50 CT £216.58 TOTE £4.20: £1.30, £3.70, £1.70; EX 45.50 Trifecta £316.80.
**Owner** Mr & Mrs C Schwick **Bred** Mr & Mrs C Schwick **Trained** Royston, Herts

**FOCUS**
A modest event and limited form.

## 5730 TOTETRIFECTA H'CAP 1m 2f 21y
**4:55** (4:55) (Class 4) (0-85,85) 3-Y-O+ **£5,822** (£1,732; £865; £432) **Stalls** Low

Form RPR
5520 1 **Erroneous (IRE)**[24] 4821 3-9-6 85 ShaneKelly 4 91
(David Simcock) *mde all: hung rt and slowed bnd over 4f out: rdn over 2f out: kpt finding ex and forged ahd over 1f out: hrd pressed again and hrd drvn fnl 100yds: hld on: drvn out* **11/4**[1]
-002 2 *shd* **Blighty (IRE)**[11] 5319 4-9-6 77 MartinHarley 6 83
(Lady Cecil) *stdd s: hld up in last pair: clsd and nt clr run wl over 1f out: swtchd lft and gd hdwy 1f out: hrd drvn and str chal fnl 100yds: r.o: hld towards fin* **8/1**[3]
-202 3 ½ **Miguel Grau (USA)**[20] 4975 4-9-7 78 (b) FrederikTylicki 2 83
(Roger Varian) *chsd ldrs: nt clr run on inner and swtchd lft over 2f out: drvn and chsd wnr 1f out: pressing ldrs fnl 100yds: kpt on same pce after* **9/2**[2]
11/3 4 ¾ **Daaree (IRE)**[16] 5150 4-8-12 69 DaneO'Neill 5 72
(Saeed bin Suroor) *t.k.h: in tch in midfield: rdn 2f out: styd on same pce u.p ins fnl f* **11/4**[1]
-210 5 4½ **Placidia (IRE)**[72] 3183 3-9-3 82 TedDurcan 1 77
(David Lanigan) *chsd wnr: clsd to press wnr over 4f out: ev ch and rdn 2f out: no ex and btn 1f out: wknd ins fnl f* **9/2**[2]
1631 6 7 **Silver Alliance**[18] 5049 6-9-1 77 (p) ShelleyBirkett(5) 3 59
(Julia Feilden) *in tch in last pair: rdn 2f out: no prog and wknd over 1f out* **10/1**

2m 9.54s (-0.96) **Going Correction** 0.0s/f (Good)
**WFA** 3 from 4yo+ 8lb 6 Ran SP% 109.9
Speed ratings (Par 105): **103,102,102,101,98 92**
CSF £23.72 TOTE £4.70: £2.00, £3.50; EX 25.40 Trifecta £61.00.
**Owner** Mrs Fitri Hay **Bred** Raffaele Nardi **Trained** Newmarket, Suffolk

**FOCUS**
Four of these finished fairly close up, so this may not be strong form. The winner has been rated as running a fractional pb.

## 5731 COLLECT TOTEPOOL WINNINGS AT BETFRED SHOPS APPRENTICE H'CAP 1m 2f 21y
**5:25** (5:25) (Class 6) (0-60,59) 4-Y-O+ **£3,234** (£962; £481; £240) **Stalls** Low

Form RPR
232 1 **Ela Goog La Mou**[5] 5533 5-9-2 59 BradleyBosley(5) 6 71
(Peter Charalambous) *taken down early: chsd ldr tl led over 2f out: clr and rdn over 1f out: in n.d fnl f: pushed out* **5/4**[1]
3456 2 5 **Pink Lips**[12] 5291 6-9-3 58 (v[1]) LukeLeadbitter(3) 7 60
(J R Jenkins) *s.i.s and rdn along early: in tch in midfield: rdn over 3f out: drifted rt u.p over 1f out: plugged on to chse clr wnr 1f out: no imp* **9/2**[2]
2226 3 3 **General Tufto**[55] 3798 9-8-4 47 (b) PaddyPilley(5) 3 43
(Charles Smith) *stdd s: hld up in rr: rdn but stl plenty to do 3f out: styd on steadily to go 3rd ins fnl f: nvr nr wnr* **16/1**
0630 4 2¾ **Sawwala**[27] 4737 4-8-13 54 CharlieBennett(3) 4 45
(J R Jenkins) *chsd ldrs: rdn 4f out: sn struggling: 4th and wl btn over 1f out: wknd ins fnl f* **10/1**
1015 5 2¼ **Nifty Kier**[5] 5533 5-8-12 55 PatrickO'Donnell(5) 2 41
(Phil McEntee) *led tl hdd and rdn over 2f out: sn outpcd and btn: lost 2nd 1f out: wknd fnl f* **6/1**[3]
6036 6 7 **Avidly**[65] 3427 4-9-1 58 (b) HectorCrouch(5) 1 31
(Julia Feilden) *hld up towards rr: hdwy over 4f out: 3rd and rdn 3f out: no prog: wl btn and wandered over 1f out: wknd* **9/2**[2]
400- 7 48 **Ottavino (IRE)**[245] 8390 5-8-4 45 KieranShoemark(3) 8
(Jane Chapple-Hyam) *chsd ldrs for 3f: dropped to rr 6f out: lost tch 4f out: t.o* **25/1**

2m 10.06s (-0.44) **Going Correction** 0.0s/f (Good) 7 Ran SP% 113.9
Speed ratings (Par 101): **101,97,94,92,90 85,46**
CSF £7.10 CT £57.75 TOTE £2.00: £1.20, £2.90; EX 7.20 Trifecta £28.00.
**Owner** pcracing.co.uk **Bred** Peter Charles **Trained** Newmarket, Suffolk

**FOCUS**
This is almost certainly weak form for the level. The runner-up is the guide to the level, although the race could be rated 4lb higher or lower.
T/Plt: £2,176.60 to a £1 stake. Pool: £88,258.13 - 29.6 winning tickets. T/Qpdt: £34.50 to a £1 stake. Pool: £8,567.75 - 183.55 winning tickets. SP

## [5697] CURRAGH (R-H)

Sunday, August 24

**OFFICIAL GOING: Good to firm**

### 5733a KILFRUSH STUD ROYAL WHIP STKS (GROUP 3) 1m 2f

2:55 (2:56) 3-Y-0+ £35,208 (£10,291; £4,875; £1,625)

RPR

1 **Hall Of Mirrors (IRE)**[65] 3416 4-9-9 105................ SeamieHeffernan 3 112
(A P O'Brien, Ire) *sn led: field wl strung out: pce slackened fr 5f out: gng wl and 2 l clr 3f out: pushed along whn chal over 1f out and sn hdd narrowly: kpt on wl again under hands and heels to ld 100yds out: comf* **13/2**

2 ½ **Kingsbarns (IRE)**[144] 1252 4-9-9 116................ JosephO'Brien 4 111
(A P O'Brien, Ire) *sn trckd ldr in 2nd: pushed along to chal under 2f out: sn rdn and led narrowly u.p 1f out: kpt on wl but hdd 100yds out and no ex cl home* **9/4**[2]

3 1½ **Parish Hall (IRE)**[35] 4477 5-9-12 112................(t) KevinManning 2 111
(J S Bolger, Ire) *hld up in rr of quartet: gng wl and prog fr 5f out on outer: rdr tk a pull over 2f out: sn disp 3rd: pushed along to chal under 2f out: rdn ent fnl f and nt qckn: sn no ex and one pce* **11/8**[1]

4 5½ **Magnolia Beach (IRE)**[38] 4379 3-9-1 100................(b¹) ColinKeane 5 98
(G M Lyons, Ire) *slowly away: sn rcvrd and settled in 3rd: clsd up on ldr fr 5f out and disp 3rd 2f out: rdn over 1f out and sn no ex: dropped to 4th ent fnl f* **7/2**[3]

2m 11.46s (2.16) **Going Correction** +0.125s/f (Good)
**WFA** 3 from 4yo+ 8lb 4 Ran SP% **108.4**
Speed ratings: **96,95,94,90**
CSF £20.55 TOTE £7.00; DF 21.40 Trifecta £47.30.
**Owner** Derrick Smith & Mrs John Magnier & Michael Tabor **Bred** Apache Dream Syndicate **Trained** Cashel, Co Tipperary

**FOCUS**
Questionable form with the winner afforded a lot of rope.

### 5734a DEBUTANTE STKS (GROUP 2) (FILLIES) 7f

3:30 (3:31) 2-Y-O £54,166 (£15,833; £7,500; £2,500)

RPR

1 **Raydara (IRE)**[31] 4598 2-9-0 98................ ShaneFoley 5 109+
(M Halford, Ire) *hld up in rr: 9th 1/2-way: gng wl and tk clsr order on outer fr 2f out: pushed along in 3rd ent fnl f: qcknd wl to ld 125yds out: r.o strly* **11/1**

2 ½ **Lucida (IRE)**[20] 4986 2-9-0 ................ KevinManning 1 108+
(J S Bolger, Ire) *chsd ldrs: cl 5th 1/2-way: pushed along under 2f out and rdn to ld narrowly 1f out: kpt on wl u.p but hdd 125yds out and sn no ex* **3/1**[1]

3 1¾ **Toogoodtobetrue (IRE)**[14] 5216 2-9-0 ................ SeamieHeffernan 8 103
(A P O'Brien, Ire) *chsd ldrs: 3rd 1/2-way: rdn 2f out and nt qckn immediately: dropped to 4th ent fnl f: kpt on wl again u.p to go 3rd cl home but no threat to wnr* **11/1**

4 1 **Jeanne Girl (IRE)**[56] 3763 2-9-0 99................ NGMcCullagh 7 100
(Mrs John Harrington, Ire) *mid-div: 6th on outer 1/2-way: rdn 2f out and kpt on wl u.p: readily outpcd by wnr ins fnl f but kpt on same pce to go 4th cl home* **9/1**[3]

5 ½ **Qualify (IRE)**[7] 5474 2-9-0 ................ JosephO'Brien 2 99
(A P O'Brien, Ire) *led: hdd after 1f and settled in 2nd: pushed along to ld again 2f out: rdn ent fnl f and hdd 1f out: sn no ex: wknd and lost several pls cl home* **5/1**[2]

6 nk **Beach Belle**[14] 5218 2-9-0 104................ ChrisHayes 3 98
(Kevin Prendergast, Ire) *hld up towards rr: pushed along under 2f out and sme prog but n.m.r bhd horses ent fnl f: swtchd ins but path blocked again and snatched up 150yds out: sn no ch* **3/1**[1]

7 shd **I Am Beautiful (IRE)**[14] 5218 2-9-0 100................ ColmO'Donoghue 6 98
(A P O'Brien, Ire) *towards rr: 8th 1/2-way: pushed along under 2f out: rdn ent fnl f and sme prog but sn one pce and no ex* **16/1**

8 6 **Tigrilla (IRE)**[22] 4931 2-9-0 101................ PatSmullen 4 82
(Roger Varian) *chsd ldrs: cl 4th 1/2-way: rdn over 2f out and sn no ex: wknd ent fnl f and eased cl home* **5/1**[2]

9 6½ **Run The Red Light (IRE)**[14] 5216 2-9-0 ................ FMBerry 9 64
(A Oliver, Ire) *rapid hdwy to ld after 1f: pushed along under 3f out and hdd 2f out: sn no ex and grad wknd* **20/1**

1m 25.68s (-5.12) **Going Correction** -0.575s/f (Hard) 9 Ran SP% **120.6**
Speed ratings: **106,105,103,102,101 101,101,94,86**
CSF £46.16 TOTE £17.60: £3.60, £1.80, £3.20; DF 55.60 Trifecta £356.80.
**Owner** H H Aga Khan **Bred** His Highness The Aga Khan's Studs S C **Trained** Doneany, Co Kildare

**FOCUS**
The winner improved and the runner-up is a good prospect.

### 5735a GALILEO EUROPEAN BREEDERS FUND FUTURITY STKS (GROUP 2) 7f

4:05 (4:05) 2-Y-O £50,000 (£15,833; £7,500; £2,500; £1,666)

RPR

1 **Gleneagles (IRE)**[31] 4599 2-9-3 107................ JosephO'Brien 1 115
(A P O'Brien, Ire) *chsd ldrs in cl 4th: pushed along 2f out and smooth hdwy on inner to ld 1 1/2f out: qcknd 2 l clr ent fnl f: kpt up to work ins fnl f and r.o wl: reduced advantage cl home* **8/13**[1]

2 ¾ **Vert De Grece (IRE)**[17] 5111 2-9-3 ................ ShaneFoley 5 111
(Joseph G Murphy, Ire) *hld up in rr: cl 5th 1/2-way: pushed along 3f out: rdn over 2f out and responded to press to chse wnr on outer ent fnl f: kpt on wl to cl gap on wnr nr fin* **8/1**

3 3½ **Hall Of Fame (IRE)**[31] 4596 2-9-3 ................(t) KevinManning 6 102
(J S Bolger, Ire) *chsd ldrs in cl 3rd: pushed along 2f out: rdn and outpcd by wnr ent fnl f: kpt on same pce* **7/1**[3]

4 3¼ **Itorio (IRE)**[36] 4460 2-9-3 99................ PatSmullen 4 93
(Ms Sheila Lavery, Ire) *sn trckd ldr in 2nd: pushed along 2f out: rdn over 1f out and sn outpcd by wnr: no ex and wknd ins fnl f* **16/1**

5 ¾ **Convergence (IRE)**[16] 5156 2-9-3 105................ ColinKeane 3 91
(G M Lyons, Ire) *led: pushed along over 2f out: rdn and hdd 1 1/2f out: sn no ex and wknd ins fnl f* **4/1**[2]

1m 26.32s (-4.48) **Going Correction** -0.575s/f (Hard) 5 Ran SP% **111.4**
Speed ratings: **102,101,97,93,92**
CSF £6.43 TOTE £1.60: £1.02, £3.00; DF 7.00 Trifecta £20.90.
**Owner** Michael Tabor & Mrs John Magnier & Derrick Smith **Bred** You'resothrilling Syndicate **Trained** Cashel, Co Tipperary

**FOCUS**
The winner was impressive and looks an up-to-scratch winner of this.

### 5736a PALMERSTOWN HOUSE ESTATE IRISH ST LEGER TRIAL STKS (GROUP 3) 1m 6f

4:40 (4:40) 3-Y-O+ £32,500 (£9,500; £4,500; £1,500)

RPR

1 **Leading Light (IRE)**[66] 3377 4-10-0 118................(p) JosephO'Brien 2 114+
(A P O'Brien, Ire) *hld up in 3rd: pushed along to chal over 2f out: rdn to ld 1 1/2f out: r.o wl and grad asserted: shifted sltly rt ins fnl f: kpt on strly: comf* **2/5**[1]

2 1¼ **Royal Diamond (IRE)**[66] 3377 8-9-9 112................ NGMcCullagh 1 107+
(J P Murtagh, Ire) *hld up in rr: 5th 1/2-way: pushed along over 2f out and sn 4th: rdn under 2f out and r.o wl u.p to cl up on wnr ins fnl f but nvr a threat: wnt 2nd on line* **5/1**[2]

3 shd **Shu Lewis (IRE)**[23] 4880 8-9-6 100................ SeamieHeffernan 3 104
(Ms M Dowdall Blake, Ire) *sn led: pushed along 3f out: rdn whn pressed for ld over 2f out: hdd 1 1/2f out: kpt on wl u.p but wl hld by wnr ins fnl f: lost 2nd on line* **33/1**

4 hd **Streetcar To Stars**[17] 5115 3-8-11 104................ DeclanMcDonogh 5 107
(John M Oxx, Ire) *sn trckd ldr in 2nd: pushed along over 3f out: rdn to chal over 2f out: almost upsides 2f out: sn no imp on wnr but kpt on wl u.p: no ex ins fnl f and dropped to 4th cl home* **7/1**[3]

5 32 **Dabadiyan (IRE)**[48] 4036 4-9-9 104................ ShaneFoley 4 65
(M Halford, Ire) *towards rr: 4th 1/2-way: rdn over 2f out and sn no imp: wknd and bhd fnl f* **14/1**

2m 59.85s (-9.55) **Going Correction** -0.275s/f (Firm)
**WFA** 3 from 4yo+ 12lb 5 Ran SP% **110.2**
Speed ratings: **116,115,115,115,96**
CSF £2.84 TOTE £1.40: £1.02, £1.80; DF 2.50 Trifecta £12.60.
**Owner** Derrick Smith & Mrs John Magnier & Michael Tabor **Bred** Lynch-Bages Ltd **Trained** Cashel, Co Tipperary
■ Stewards' Enquiry : Seamie Heffernan two-day ban: excessive use of the whip (tbn)

**FOCUS**
The third anchors the form.

## [5705] DEAUVILLE (R-H)

Sunday, August 24

**OFFICIAL GOING: Turf: very soft; polytrack: standard**

### 5739a PRIX DE VALMONT (CLAIMER) (2YO COLTS & GELDINGS) (POLYTRACK) 6f 110y

1:00 (12:00) 2-Y-O £11,250 (£4,500; £3,375; £2,250; £1,125)

RPR

1 **First Company (FR)**[59] 3640 2-8-2 0................ JeffersonSmith(7) 1 84
(J-C Rouget, France) **7/10**[1]

2 10 **Mister Arden (FR)**[78] 2993 2-8-9 0................(b¹) IoritzMendizabal 5 56
(Harry Dunlop) *last leaving stalls: chsd ldng pair after 1f: pressed ldr 2f out: sn rdn and readily outpcd by eventual wnr appr fnl f: kpt on at same pce* **31/5**[3]

3 nk **Its My Story (FR)**[44] 2-9-2 0................ UmbertoRispoli 7 62
(J Reynier, France) **27/10**[2]

4 3 **Jimmy's Hall**[3] 5616 2-8-9 0................ MickaelBarzalona 4 47
(J S Moore) *w.w in rr: tk clsr order to dispute 3rd 2 1/2f out: hrd rdn 1 1/2f out and no imp: one pce tl fdd fnl 150yds* **17/2**

5 1¾ **The Iron Man (FR)**[23] 4883 2-8-9 0................(b) LouisBeuzelin 3 42
(H-F Devin, France) **91/10**

1m 18.01s (78.01) 5 Ran SP% **120.2**
WIN (incl. 1 euro stake): 1.70. PLACES: 1.20, 2.00. DF: 9.20.
**Owner** Gerard Ben Lassin **Bred** Oceanic Bloodstock Inc **Trained** Pau, France

### 5740a CRITERIUM DU FONDS EUROPEEN DE L'ELEVAGE (LISTED RESTRICTED RACE) (2YO) (TURF) 1m (R)

1:30 (12:00) 2-Y-O £50,833 (£20,333; £15,250; £10,166; £5,083)

RPR

1 **Medley Chic (IRE)**[22] 4932 2-8-11 0................ MickaelBarzalona 2 103
(F Head, France) **68/10**[3]

2 1¼ **Faithful Creek (IRE)**[25] 4780 2-8-11 0................ FrankieDettori 3 100
(Brian Meehan) *t.k.h: hld up in midfield on inner: rdn and swtchd outside over 1 1/2f out: chsd ldr ent fnl f: r.o but nvr quite on terms* **11/1**

3 1¼ **Light In Paris (IRE)**[21] 2-8-8 0................ IoritzMendizabal 6 94
(J-C Rouget, France) **7/10**[1]

4 1¾ **Zeppelin (FR)**[22] 4932 2-8-11 0................ Pierre-CharlesBoudot 1 93
(H-F Devin, France) **87/10**

5 1 **Caprior Bere (FR)**[11] 5329 2-8-11 0................ JamieSpencer 4 91
(K R Burke) *w.w in rr: hdwy over 1 1/2f out: kpt on at same pce u.p fnl f: nvr threatened ldrs* **164/10**

6 1¼ **Kloud Gate (FR)**[22] 4933 2-8-11 0................ CristianDemuro 9 88
(J Heloury, France) **33/1**

7 2½ **Mindsomer (FR)**[21] 4953 2-8-11 0................ Christophe-PatriceLemaire 5 83
(F Chappet, France) **61/10**[2]

8 ½ **Filly Green (FR)**[49] 2-8-8 0................ UmbertoRispoli 8 79
(F Chappet, France) **243/10**

9 nk **Gomati**[18] 2-8-11 0................ AntoineHamelin 7 81
(Matthieu Palussiere, France) **25/1**

1m 45.79s (4.99) 9 Ran SP% **120.9**
WIN (incl. 1 euro stake): 7.80. PLACES: 1.70, 1.80, 1.10. DF: 31.90. SF: 76.60.
**Owner** Olivier Thomas **Bred** Petra Bloodstock Agency Ltd **Trained** France

### 5741a DARLEY PRIX MORNY (GROUP 1) (2YO COLTS & FILLIES) (TURF) 6f

2:40 (12:00) 2-Y-O £166,658 (£66,675; £33,337; £16,654; £8,341)

RPR

1 **The Wow Signal (IRE)**[68] 3318 2-9-0 0................ FrankieDettori 3 118
(John Quinn) *midfield: pushed along 1/2-way: clsd on outer and rdn to chal over 1f out: edgd lft and jnd ldr ent fnl f: r.o and led towards fin: pushed out firmly and asserted* **9/4**[1]

2 ½ **Hootenanny (USA)**[68] 3322 2-9-0 0................(b) LRGoncalves 6 116
(Wesley A Ward, U.S.A) *w ldr: rdn to ld 2f out: jnd ent fnl f: edgd rt u.p: kpt on but hdd towards fin and hld* **3/1**[2]

3 *1* **Ervedya (FR)**[21] 4953 2-8-10 0........................ ChristopheSoumillon 4 109
(J-C Rouget, France) *hld up in rr: pushed along and hdwy 2f out: wnt 3rd ent fnl f and sn swtchd lft for clr run: kpt on same pce and hld by front pair after* **9/4**[1]

4 *1 3/4* **Goken (FR)**[35] 4482 2-9-0 0........................ FabriceVeron 1 108
(H-A Pantall, France) *t.k.h early: sn chsng ldrs: rdn and effrt 2f out: sn outpcd by ldrs: kpt on for clr 4th fnl f* **12/1**

5 *3* **Power Of The Moon (IRE)**[9] 5405 2-8-10 0........................ TheoBachelot 2 95
(M Nigge, France) *midfield: rdn over 2f out: kpt on same pce and wl hld fnl f* **66/1**

6 *2 1/2* **Ride Like The Wind (IRE)**[21] 4953 2-9-0 0........................ MickaelBarzalona 9 92
(F Head, France) *led: rdn and hdd 2f out: sn no ex and btn: wknd fnl f* **10/1**[3]

7 *1 1/4* **Lehaim (FR)**[35] 4482 2-9-0 0........................ GeraldMosse 7 88
(M Nigge, France) *chsd ldrs: rdn and effrt 2f out: sn outpcd: wknd fnl f and eased nring fin* **22/1**

8 *4 1/2* **Malicieuse (IRE)**[22] 4931 2-8-10 0........................ StephanePasquier 5 70
(J E Pease, France) *hld up towards rr: rdn over 2f out: no imp and btn ent fnl f: eased: nvr a factor* **20/1**

9 *6* **Quevedo (SPA)**[42] 4248 2-9-0 0........................ MaximeGuyon 8 56
(Ana Imaz Ceca, Spain) *dwlt sltly and a towards rr: rdn in last 2f out: sn btn and eased: nvr a factor* **25/1**

1m 11.93s (0.93) **Going Correction** +0.425s/f (Yiel) **9 Ran SP% 117.8**
Speed ratings: **110,109,108,105,101 98,96,90,82**
WIN (incl. 1 euro stake): 3.60. PLACES: 1.30, 1.40, 1.20. DF: 4.90. SF: 12.00.
**Owner** Al Shaqab Racing **Bred** Mrs T Stack **Trained** Settrington, N Yorks

**FOCUS**
The Morny has very much an international roll of honour these days with winners from Britain (5), Ireland (2) and the US (1) in the previous nine runnings, while the host nation had only produced one winner during that period. It was an up-to-scratch renewal, run on testing ground.

## 5742a DARLEY PRIX JEAN ROMANET (GROUP 1) (4YO+ FILLIES & MARES) (TURF) 1m 2f
**3:10** (12:00) 4-Y-0+ **£119,041** (£47,625; £23,812; £11,895; £5,958)

RPR

1 **Ribbons**[106] 2144 4-9-0 0........................ FrankieDettori 10 114
(James Fanshawe) *hld up in rr: last 3f out: fanned wd and pushed along to cl into st: rdn to chal ent fnl f and sn qcknd to ld: styd on strly and asserted under hand ride fnl 100yds: impressive* **11/1**

2 *2* **Princess Loulou (IRE)**[67] 3355 4-9-0 0........................ OlivierPeslier 2 110
(Roger Varian) *prom on inner: rdn over 2f out: chal and ev ch ent fnl f: styd on wl for 2nd but nt pce of wnr* **20/1**

3 *1 1/2* **Secret Gesture**[29] 4682 4-9-0 0........................ JamieSpencer 6 107
(Ralph Beckett) *trckd ldr on outer: w ldr 3f out: rdn 2f out: stl disputing ld and ev ch ent fnl f: sn hdd and outpcd: styd on for wl hld 3rd* **9/2**[2]

4 *1 1/4* **Narniyn (IRE)**[22] 4894 4-9-0 0........................ ChristopheSoumillon 7 105
(A De Royer-Dupre, France) *midfield in tch: clsd 3f out: rdn and effrt 2f out: outpcd by ldrs fnl f: styd on and tk wl hld 4th post* **2/1**[1]

5 *nse* **Euphrasia (IRE)**[91] 2580 5-9-0 0........................ GaryCarroll 1 105
(Joseph G Murphy, Ire) *pushed along to go forward and sn led: jnd 3f out: rdn 2f out: stl disputing ld and ev ch ent fnl f: sn hdd and outpcd: fdd and dropped to 5th post* **16/1**

6 *snk* **Red Lips (GER)**[35] 4-9-0 0........................ FabriceVeron 3 104
(Andreas Lowe, Germany) *hld up and sn in rr: rdn over 1f out: styd on fnl f and tk n.d 6th post* **14/1**

7 *nse* **Calyxa**[28] 4720 4-9-0 0........................ ThierryThulliez 9 104
(Ferdinand J Leve, Germany) *sn midfield: rdn over 2f out: styd on same pce in st and nvr able to chal: dropped to 7th post* **10/1**

8 *1 1/2* **Hippy (FR)**[32] 4561 6-9-0 0........................ Pierre-CharlesBoudot 4 101
(E Libaud, France) *hld up in midfield: rdn 2f out: sn outpcd: plugged on but nvr threatened* **16/1**

9 *nk* **Gaga A (URU)**[10] 5369 5-9-0 0........................ GregoryBenoist 11 101
(D Smaga, France) *hld up: rdn and effrt to cl on outer into st: sn outpcd: plugged on but nvr threatened* **25/1**

10 *nk* **Ipswich (IRE)**[32] 4561 4-9-0 0........................ GeraldMosse 5 100+
(A De Royer-Dupre, France) *midfield on inner: rdn over 2f out: outpcd and wl hld fnl f: eased nring fin* **16/1**

11 *12* **Pollyana (IRE)**[91] 2587 5-9-0 0........................ FabienLefebvre 8 77+
(J E Hammond, France) *t.k.h: sn prom on outer: rdn and lost pl over 2f out: sn btn and dropped to last: eased* **5/1**[3]

2m 9.98s (-0.22) **Going Correction** +0.425s/f (Yiel) **11 Ran SP% 118.5**
Speed ratings: **117,115,114,113,113 113,113,111,111,111 101**
WIN (incl. 1 euro stake): 25.50. PLACES: 7.20, 8.10, 2.60. DF: 235.90. SF: 421.90.
**Owner** Elite Racing Club **Bred** Elite Racing Club **Trained** Newmarket, Suffolk

**FOCUS**
The 11th running of the Prix Jean Romanet and the sixth time as a Group 1, but the result will have many scratching their heads. They went just a fair pace and it resulted in a 1-2-3 for British stables. The winner is progressive and the form makes sense through those close up, and is in line with the eight-year average for the race.

## 5743a DARLEY PRIX KERGORLAY (GROUP 2) (3YO+) (TURF) 1m 7f
**3:40** (12:00) 3-Y-0+ **£61,750** (£23,833; £11,375; £7,583)

RPR

1 **Protectionist (GER)**[56] 3770 4-9-6 0........................ EPedroza 4 118+
(A Wohler, Germany) *w.w in 3rd: rdn to chal under 1 1/2f out: led appr fnl f: drvn out: readily* **6/4**[1]

2 *1 1/2* **Fly With Me (FR)**[42] 4250 4-9-6 0........................(b) MaximeGuyon 1 116
(E Libaud, France) *trckd ldr: chal 2f out: chsd wnr over 1f out: one pce fnl f* **3/1**[3]

3 *1 1/2* **Altano (GER)**[66] 3377 8-9-8 0........................ ChristopheSoumillon 3 116
(A Wohler, Germany) *led field in single file: brought field towards stands' side st: pushed along 2f out: hdd and outpcd appr 1 1/2f out: styd on again ins fnl f* **7/4**[2]

4 *1/2* **Bathyrhon (GER)**[38] 4-9-4 0........................ GregoryBenoist 2 112
(Mme Pia Brandt, France) *hld up in 4th: hdwy over 2 1/2f out: chal on inner 2f out: led appr 1 1/2f out: hdd appr fnl f: fdd* **12/1**

3m 30.08s (10.98) **Going Correction** +0.425s/f (Yiel) **4 Ran SP% 109.1**
Speed ratings: **87,86,85,85**
WIN (incl. 1 euro stake): 2.20. PLACES: 1.10, 1.30. SF: 4.10.
**Owner** Dr Christoph Berglar **Bred** Dr Christoph Berglar **Trained** Germany

**FOCUS**
The race has been rated around the eight-year average for the race.

# 4956 OVREVOLL (R-H)
Sunday, August 24

**OFFICIAL GOING: Turf: heavy**

## 5744a MARIT SVEAAS MINNELOP (GROUP 3) (3YO+) (TURF) 1m 1f
**4:00** (12:00) 3-Y-0+ **£79,601** (£25,870; £11,940; £7,164; £4,776)

RPR

1 **Bank Of Burden (USA)**[24] 4956 7-9-6 0........................ Per-AndersGraberg 13 105
(Niels Petersen, Norway) *w.w towards rr: gd hdwy over 3f out: led under 2f out: drvn clr fnl f: won a shade cosily* **42/10**[3]

2 *2 1/2* **Without Fear (FR)**[24] 4956 6-9-6 0........................ RafaelSchistl 6 100
(Niels Petersen, Norway) *chsd ldng trio: rdn to chal 2f out: chsd eventual wnr appr 1f out: sn outpcd by wnr and kpt on at same pce u.p* **5/2**[1]

3 *1* **Coprah**[21] 6-9-4 0........................ ElioneChaves 7 96
(Cathrine Erichsen, Norway) *midfield on inner: swtchd outside and hdwy 2 1/2f out: styd on wl fnl f to go 3rd 100yds out: nvr on terms w ldrs* **35/1**

4 *1* **Jubilance (IRE)**[21] 5-9-4 0........................ NikolajStott 15 94
(Bent Olsen, Denmark) *towards rr: hdwy 2f out: styd on fnl f: nrest at fin* **44/1**

5 *nk* **Fearless Hunter (GER)**[24] 4956 4-9-4 0........................ PatCosgrave 14 93
(Rune Haugen, Norway) *midfield: chsd ldrs 2 1/2f out: 3rd and hrd rdn ins fnl f: edgd rt and fdd fnl 100yds* **48/1**

6 *1/2* **Old Pal (FR)**[21] 5-9-4 0........................ WilliamBuick 10 92
(Niels Petersen, Norway) *midfield on inner: rdn to chse ldrs 2f out: plugged on at one pce fnl f* **127/10**

7 *1/2* **Falconet (DEN)**[21] 4-9-4 0........................ JacobJohansen 3 91
(Bent Olsen, Denmark) *settled in 5th: rdn and effrt 2f out: sn no further imp: one pce fnl f* **25/1**

8 *1* **Energia El Gigante (BRZ)**[24] 4956 5-9-4 0........................ RafaeldeOliveira 2 89
(Fabricio Borges, Sweden) *led on rail: scrubbed along 2 1/2f out: hdd 2f out: wknd appr fnl f* **98/10**

9 *6* **Giftorm (USA)**[24] 4957 4-9-4 0........................ GeorgeBaker 5 77
(Fredrik Reuterskiold, Sweden) *towards rr: sme prog 2f out: kpt on at same pce fnl f: nvr in contention* **127/10**

10 *nk* **Plantagenet (SPA)**[36] 7-9-4 0........................ ManuelSantos 11 77
(Niels Petersen, Norway) *detached in rr: sme mod late prog: nvr a factor* **34/1**

11 *3/4* **Weald**[474] 2146 9-9-4 0........................ AaseMarieBrown 12 75
(Hans-Inge Larsen, Sweden) *midfield: rdn and no hdwy over 2f out: sn btn* **34/1**

12 *3* **Wentworth (IRE)**[21] 4-9-4 0........................ OliverWilson 4 69
(Bettina Andersen, Denmark) *pressed ldr: cl 2nd whn scrubbed along over 2 1/2f out: sn rdn and wknd fr over 1 1/2f out* **16/5**[2]

13 *1 1/2* **Berling (IRE)**[56] 3772 7-9-4 0........................ CarlosLopez 9 66
(Jessica Long, Sweden) *prom early but sn dropped into midfield on outer: rdn and no imp 2f out: wknd fnl f* **37/1**

14 *2 1/2* **Manchester (FR)**[178] 773 6-9-4 0........................ ShaneKarlsson 1 61
(Niels Petersen, Norway) *hld up towards rr: rdn and no imp 2 1/2f out: sn wknd* **30/1**

15 *15 3/4* **Probably (IRE)**[75] 3090 4-9-4 0........................ SilvestreDeSousa 8 30
(Rune Haugen, Norway) *pressed ldr: rdn and nt qckn 2 1/2f out: wknd fnl 2f* **13/1**

1m 51.9s (2.00) **15 Ran SP% 125.1**
PARI-MUTUEL (including 1 unit stake): WIN 5.16 PLACE 2.05, 1.90, 5.87 SF 17.39.
**Owner** Stall Trick Or Treat **Bred** Bjarne Minde **Trained** Norway

# 5338 CHEPSTOW (L-H)
Monday, August 25

**OFFICIAL GOING: Round course - good to soft; straight course - soft changing to heavy all over after race 4 (4:30)**
Wind: almost nil Weather: rain

## 5745 BATH ALES / EBF MAIDEN STKS 1m 14y
**2:35** (2:37) (Class 5) 2-Y-0 **£2,911** (£866; £432; £216) **Stalls Centre**

Form RPR

244 1 **Paddys Motorbike (IRE)**[23] 4906 2-9-0 70........................ JFEgan 4 78
(David Evans) *wnt stands' side over 5f out: mde virtually all: rdn 3f out: drew clr over 1f out: styd on wl* **6/1**[3]

2 *3 1/4* **Grand Canyon (IRE)** 2-9-0 0........................ SteveDrowne 2 71+
(Ralph Beckett) *hld up in centre: pushed along and hdwy 3f out: chsd wnr wl over 1f out: one pce and no real imp* **9/2**[2]

03 3 *1 1/2* **Cahill (IRE)**[33] 4550 2-9-0 0........................ WilliamTwiston-Davies 1 68
(Alan King) *hld up in centre: rdn 3f out: styd on to go 3rd ins fnl f: nvr trbld ldng pair* **6/4**[1]

5 4 *4* **Dubawi Diamond**[12] 5296 2-9-0 0........................ JimCrowley 3 60
(James Tate) *chsd ldrs in centre: rdn over 2f out: one pce* **6/1**[3]

3 5 *6* **Stealing Thunder (IRE)**[37] 4440 2-9-0 0........................ JamieSpencer 5 47
(Eve Johnson Houghton) *chsd ldrs in centre: rdn 3f out: wnt 2nd over 2f out tl wl over 1f out: wknd ent fnl f: sn eased* **7/1**

3 6 *6* **Blues Dancer**[15] 5212 2-9-0 0........................ LiamKeniry 6 34
(Sylvester Kirk) *w wnr: wnt stands' side over 5f out: rdn over 2f out: sn wknd* **7/1**

1m 41.65s (5.45) **Going Correction** +0.55s/f (Yiel) **6 Ran SP% 111.8**
Speed ratings (Par 94): **94,90,89,85,79 73**
CSF £32.01 TOTE £5.20: £2.20, £3.30; EX 30.80 Trifecta £62.40.
**Owner** Walters Plant Hire Ltd Egan Waste Ltd **Bred** Peter And Jackie Grimes **Trained** Pandy, Monmouths

**FOCUS**
A wet, miserable day meant soft conditions. The winner seemed to relish the stiffer test.

## 5746 BATHWICK TYRES CARDIFF EBF MEDIAN AUCTION MAIDEN FILLIES' STKS (BOBIS RACE) 1m 14y
**3:15** (3:16) (Class 5) 2-Y-0 **£2,911** (£866; £432; £216) **Stalls Centre**

Form RPR

34 1 **Encore L'Amour**[31] 4626 2-9-0 0........................ JimCrowley 7 76+
(David Simcock) *hld up in last of quartet in centre: pushed along and hdwy over 2f out: led over 1f out: r.o wl* **7/4**[2]



The Form Book, Raceform Ltd, Newbury, RG14 5SJ

| | | | |
|---|---|---|---|
| 2 | 2¾ | **Jersey Jewel (FR)** 2-8-9 0 ... CamHardie(5) 1<br>(Richard Hannon) *trckd ldr in centre quartet: lost pl and shkn up over 2f out: rdn and r.o ins fnl f: wnt 2nd fnl 50yds* 7/1[3] | 70+ |
| 23 | 3 | 2 | **Shahah**[26] 4781 2-9-0 0 ... JamieSpencer 5<br>(Richard Hannon) *hld up in 3rd in centre quartet and racd keenly: hdwy 3f out: led 2f out tl over 1f out: wknd early ins fnl f and lost 2nd fnl 50yds* 10/11[1] | 68+ |
| 60 | 4 | 1 | **Nelsons Trick**[25] 4825 2-9-0 0 ... LiamKeniry 4<br>(Rod Millman) *racd stands' side and narrow ldr overall: hdd 2f out: kpt on same pce* 12/1 | 64 |
| 006 | 5 | 11 | **Powerfulstorm**[55] 3813 2-9-0 45 ... WilliamTwiston-Davies 3<br>(Ronald Harris) *led quartet in centre and cl up overall: rdn over 2f out: wknd over 1f out* 50/1 | 41 |
| 600 | 6 | 10 | **Emilys Girl (IRE)**[20] 4999 2-9-0 45 ... SteveDrowne 6<br>(Ronald Harris) *chsd ldr stands' side but a towards rr overall: rdn over 3f out: wknd qckly* 50/1 | 20 |

1m 43.21s (7.01) **Going Correction** +0.55s/f (Yiel) **6** Ran SP% **112.9**
Speed ratings (Par 91): **86,83,81,80,69 59**
CSF £14.37 TOTE £1.90: £1.20, £2.70; EX 10.40 Trifecta £23.90.
**Owner** Car Colston Hall Stud **Bred** Car Colston Hall Stud **Trained** Newmarket, Suffolk

**FOCUS**
The main action unfolded up the middle and the time was 1.56secs slower than the opening juvenile maiden for colts and geldings. The form looks modest.

## 5747 BATHWICK TYRES BRIDGEND APPRENTICE (S) STKS 1m 2f 36y
**3:55** (3:55) (Class 6) 3-4-Y-O **£1,940** (£577; £288; £144) **Stalls** Low

| Form | | | | RPR |
|---|---|---|---|---|
| 2445 | 1 | | **Yul Finegold (IRE)**[78] 3032 4-9-1 68 ... ChrisMeehan(5) 6<br>(George Baker) *hld up: hdwy 6f out: wnt cl 2nd gng wl 3f out: led over 1f out: shkn up and drew clr* 5/4[1] | 74 |
| 4455 | 2 | 6 | **Maid Of Tuscany (IRE)**[19] 5048 3-8-4 57 ... CharlotteJenner(3) 2<br>(Mark Usher) *trckd ldr 3f: wnt 2nd again 4f out: sn led and drvn along: jnd 3f out: hdd over 1f out: unable qck and no ch w wnr* 4/1[3] | 58 |
| 0-00 | 3 | 17 | **Enfys Hud**[33] 4536 3-8-2 54 ... HollieDoyle(5) 3<br>(David Evans) *hld up: pushed along 4f out: sn outpcd by ldrs and no ch: plugged on to take mod 3rd 75yds out* 8/1 | 25 |
| 0350 | 4 | 5 | **Beauchamp Melba**[13] 5283 3-8-5 49 ow1 ... (p) JennyPowell(3) 5<br>(Paul Fitzsimons) *led at stdy gallop: hdd over 3f out and qckly outpcd by ldng pair: wknd 2f out: hld mod 3rd tl 75yds out* 16/1 | 17 |
| 40-0 | 5 | 17 | **Sakuramachi**[207] 378 3-8-2 55 ... MichaelKenneally(5) 4<br>(Nikki Evans) *t.k.h in 3rd: chsd ldr after 3f to 4f out: wknd over 2f out: t.o* 33/1 | |
| 3246 | 6 | 5 | **Jazri**[44] 4209 3-8-12 62 ... LouisSteward 1<br>(Milton Bradley) *racd in 4th tl relegated to last 6f out: rdn 4f out: wknd 3f out: t.o* 5/2[2] | |

2m 18.84s (8.24) **Going Correction** +0.875s/f (Soft)
**WFA** 3 from 4yo 8lb **6** Ran SP% **113.0**
Speed ratings (Par 101): **102,97,83,79,66 62**
CSF £6.80 TOTE £2.10: £1.30, £1.90; EX 8.30 Trifecta £41.60.The winner was bought in for 12,500gns.
**Owner** Mrs Virginia Finegold **Bred** Mascara Partnership **Trained** Manton, Wilts

**FOCUS**
They were strung out like staying chasers in this weak seller.

## 5748 WESSEX GARAGE HYUNDAI H'CAP 1m 4f 23y
**4:30** (4:31) (Class 6) (0-60,58) 3-Y-O+ **£1,940** (£577; £288; £144) **Stalls** Low

| Form | | | | RPR |
|---|---|---|---|---|
| 316- | 1 | | **Gaelic Ice**[321] 7090 5-9-3 54 ... PatMillman(7) 7<br>(Martin Hill) *hld up in last: hdwy 3f out: rdn to ld 2f out: edgd lft and styd on wl to draw clr fnl 100yds* 9/1 | 64 |
| 2 | 2 | 4½ | **Zarosa (IRE)**[21] 4962 5-9-7 56 ... ShelleyBirkett(5) 2<br>(John Berry) *trckd ldrs: chsd wnr 2f out: kpt on u.p tl no ex fnl 100yds* 3/1[1] | 60 |
| 040- | 3 | 5 | **Iguacu**[22] 6895 10-8-11 46 ... LouisSteward(5) 3<br>(Richard Price) *s.i.s: hld up towards rr: rdn 3f out and no real imp: styd on fnl f to go 3rd post* 11/2 | 41 |
| 0/13 | 4 | nse | **Lady Percy (IRE)**[56] 3778 5-9-4 55 ... CharlotteJenner(3) 1<br>(Mark Usher) *led: rdn 3f out: hdd 2f out: sn outpcd by 1st 2: wknd ins fnl f and ct for 3rd post* 7/2[2] | 50 |
| 1660 | 5 | 9 | **Graphene**[22] 4948 3-9-4 58 ... LiamKeniry 6<br>(Rod Millman) *racd in 4th: rdn 3f out: sn outpcd by ldrs: wknd fnl f* 7/2[2] | 38 |
| 5523 | 6 | 6 | **Impeccability**[11] 5331 4-9-6 50 ... (p) JimCrowley 5<br>(John Mackie) *trckd ldr tl rdn and lost pl qckly 3f out: bhd fnl 2f* 4/1[3] | 21 |

2m 49.34s (10.34) **Going Correction** +0.875s/f (Soft)
**WFA** 3 from 4yo+ 10lb **6** Ran SP% **114.8**
Speed ratings (Par 101): **100,97,93,93,87 83**
CSF £36.95 CT £164.92 TOTE £10.00: £4.20, £1.30; EX 35.90 Trifecta £208.10.
**Owner** The Jack High Racing Partnership **Bred** Berry Racing **Trained** Littlehempston, Devon

**FOCUS**
It continued to pour down and the ground was changed to heavy following this moderate contest.

## 5749 BATHWICK TYRES H'CAP 1m 14y
**5:05** (5:09) (Class 2) (0-105,96) 3-Y-O+ **£12,938** (£3,850; £1,924; £962) **Stalls** Centre

| Form | | | | RPR |
|---|---|---|---|---|
| 0404 | 1 | | **Fury**[37] 4442 6-9-7 **91** ... (tp) SebSanders 9<br>(William Haggas) *racd stands' side and solo 2f: mde all: 4 l clr whn rdn 2f out: r.o strly: unchal* 3/1[2] | 103 |
| 6600 | 2 | 5 | **Starboard**[44] 4214 5-9-9 **93** ... JimCrowley 3<br>(David Simcock) *wnt to post early: trckd ldrs in centre: rdn and hdwy 3f out: sn chsng wnr: kpt on but no imp* 10/1 | 94 |
| -203 | 3 | 6 | **End Of Line**[88] 2706 3-9-4 **94** ... JamieSpencer 1<br>(Andrew Balding) *hld up in centre: c stands' side over 3f out and sn rdn: no real imp on ldrs: styd on ins fnl f: tk 3rd 50yds out* 9/2[3] | 80 |
| 2552 | 4 | ¾ | **Jack's Revenge (IRE)**[22] 4949 6-9-12 **96** ... (bt) LiamKeniry 8<br>(George Baker) *t.k.h: c stands' side after 2f and hld up 3rd in gp: hdwy on bit 3f out: let down wl over 1f out and nt qckn: lost modest 3rd 50yds out* 5/2[1] | 81 |
| 6305 | 5 | 5 | **Verse Of Love**[22] 4938 5-8-13 **83** ... JFEgan 6<br>(David Evans) *s.i.s: c stands' side after 2f and chsd wnr: rdn 3f out: wknd wl over 1f out* 12/1 | 56 |
| 040 | 6 | 4½ | **Gworn**[27] 4756 4-9-1 **85** ... WilliamTwiston-Davies 5<br>(Ed Dunlop) *chsd ldr in centre and in tch overall: rdn over 2f out: wknd over 1f out* 7/1 | 48 |
| 1110 | 7 | 17 | **Genius Boy**[11] 5354 4-9-10 **94** ... SteveDrowne 2<br>(James Tate) *c stands' side after 2f and hld up last in gp: pushed along 3f out: wknd over 1f out: t.o* 8/1 | 18 |
| 64-0 | 8 | 35 | **I'm Back (IRE)**[219] 240 4-9-12 **96** ... AhmedAjtebi 7<br>(Saeed bin Suroor) *trckd centre: ld gp and prom overall: rdn 3f out and qckly lost pl: bhd whn eased wl over 1f out: t.o* 20/1 | |

1m 40.83s (4.63) **Going Correction** +0.80s/f (Soft)
**WFA** 3 from 4yo+ 6lb **8** Ran SP% **116.9**
Speed ratings (Par 109): **108,103,97,96,91 86,69,34**
CSF £33.54 CT £135.39 TOTE £3.60: £1.10, £2.50, £2.10; EX 44.10 Trifecta £277.30.
**Owner** Cheveley Park Stud **Bred** Cheveley Park Stud Ltd **Trained** Newmarket, Suffolk

**FOCUS**
The winner made all up the stands' rail alone.

## 5750 BATHWICK TYRES NEWPORT H'CAP 6f 16y
**5:35** (5:38) (Class 4) (0-85,85) 3-Y-O+ **£4,690** (£1,395; £697; £348) **Stalls** Centre

| Form | | | | RPR |
|---|---|---|---|---|
| 564 | 1 | | **Dominate**[5] 5559 4-8-13 79 ... (b) CamHardie(5) 1<br>(Richard Hannon) *chsd ldrs tl led after 2f: rdn and edgd rt over 1f out: 3 l clr ent fnl f: sn began to flag: hld on* 9/2[3] | 88 |
| 4040 | 2 | ¾ | **Gramercy (IRE)**[3] 5623 7-9-10 85 ... JamieSpencer 7<br>(David Simcock) *hld up in last and sn rdn along: swtchd rt wl over 1f out: r.o wl u.p ins fnl f to cl on flagging wnr: no ex cl home* 11/4[1] | 92 |
| 600- | 3 | 1 | **Watts Up Son**[267] 7275 6-8-0 68 ow1 ... (t) KieranShoemark(7) 10<br>(Richard Price) *wnt to post early: chsd ldrs tl began to hang lft: hmpd and dropped in rr over 4f out: rdn 3f out: styd on to go 3rd ins fnl f: clsng at fin* 16/1 | 71 |
| 0060 | 4 | 2½ | **Corporal Maddox**[18] 5081 7-9-1 83 ... (p) MikeyEnnis(7) 6<br>(Ronald Harris) *prom: rdn 3f out: kpt on same pce* 14/1 | 78 |
| 2504 | 5 | nse | **Pashan Garh**[9] 5412 5-8-3 67 ... RyanPowell(3) 5<br>(Pat Eddery) *led 2f: sn rdn along bhd ldrs: one pce and hld whn n.m.r over 1f out: kpt on* 10/1 | 62 |
| 006R | 6 | 3¼ | **Steel Rain**[13] 5275 6-8-6 72 ... NoelGarbutt(5) 2<br>(Nikki Evans) *t.k.h early: trckd ldrs: rdn to chse wnr 2f out: wknd ins fnl f* 25/1 | 57 |
| 3620 | 7 | nk | **Rigolleto (IRE)**[32] 4581 6-8-6 72 ... LouisSteward(5) 4<br>(Anabel K Murphy) *chsd ldrs: rdn 3f out: unable qck: wknd appr fnl f* 12/1 | 56 |
| 0552 | 8 | 1¼ | **Joe Packet**[10] 5392 7-9-4 82 ... DannyBrock(3) 9<br>(Jonathan Portman) *towards rr: bmpd over 4f out: hdwy to chse ldrs 3f out: sn rdn: wknd fnl f* 3/1[2] | 62 |
| 0230 | 9 | 3½ | **Al's Memory (IRE)**[13] 5281 5-8-13 74 ... JFEgan 3<br>(David Evans) *sn pushed along and taken to r in tch towards stands' side: drvn 3f out: wknd 2f out* 10/1 | 43 |
| 424R | R | | **Caramack**[21] 4961 4-9-0 75 ... (b[1]) JimCrowley 8<br>(Richard Lee) *ref to r* 14/1 | |

1m 17.88s (5.88) **Going Correction** +1.05s/f (Soft) **10** Ran SP% **118.8**
Speed ratings (Par 105): **102,101,99,96,96 91,91,89,85,**
CSF £17.64 CT £188.27 TOTE £2.60: £1.40, £1.80, £4.60; EX 23.80 Trifecta £267.00.
**Owner** Godfrey Wilson **Bred** Mrs C R D Wilson **Trained** East Everleigh, Wilts

**FOCUS**
A fair sprint handicap. The winner was clear in final furlong and idled a little late on.

## 5751 BATHWICK TYRES BRISTOL H'CAP 7f 16y
**6:10** (6:10) (Class 6) (0-65,65) 3-Y-O+ **£1,940** (£577; £288; £144) **Stalls** Centre

| Form | | | | RPR |
|---|---|---|---|---|
| 06-6 | 1 | | **Marengo**[12] 5303 3-8-13 64 ... MeganCarberry(7) 9<br>(Ed de Giles) *in rr: rdn 3f out: hdwy over 1f out: stl 4th ent fnl f: r.o u.p to ld nr fin* 4/1[2] | 71 |
| 0015 | 2 | 1 | **Euroquip Boy (IRE)**[26] 4788 7-9-3 61 ... NoelGarbutt(5) 5<br>(Michael Scudamore) *hld up in mid-div: rdn and hdwy 3f out: led over 1f out tl hdd and no ex nr fin* 7/1[3] | 67 |
| 0-00 | 3 | 2 | **Actonetaketwo**[18] 5071 4-8-0 46 oh1 ... KieranShoemark(7) 2<br>(Ron Hodges) *mid-div: rdn 3f out: sn chsng ldrs: kpt on one pce u.p fnl f* 25/1 | 47 |
| 1336 | 4 | ½ | **Tenbridge**[13] 5274 5-9-3 61 ... (v) TimClark(5) 6<br>(Derek Haydn Jones) *chsd ldrs: rdn to ld over 3f out: hdd over 1f out: kpt on tl no ex fnl 100yds* 9/4[1] | 61 |
| 6/33 | 5 | 8 | **Avertor**[13] 5275 8-9-5 63 ... LouisSteward(5) 3<br>(Robert Stephens) *chsd ldrs: rdn 3f out: wknd 1f out* 8/1 | 42 |
| 1300 | 6 | 1¾ | **Bajan Story**[20] 5000 5-8-10 49 ... LiamKeniry 8<br>(Michael Blanshard) *mid-div: rdn and no imp whn n.m.r over 1f out* 20/1 | 23 |
| 0040 | 7 | 4 | **See No Ships**[17] 5138 3-8-4 48 ... HayleyTurner 10<br>(Mark Usher) *mid-div: rdn 3f out: no imp whn hmpd over 1f out* 12/1 | 10 |
| 4003 | 8 | ¾ | **Delightful Sleep**[13] 5273 6-9-1 54 ... JFEgan 1<br>(David Evans) *hld up towards rr: rdn and sme hdwy over 2f out: nvr trbld ldrs* 10/1 | 16 |
| 0060 | 9 | ¾ | **Echologic**[26] 4797 4-8-4 46 oh1 ... (p) RyanPowell(3) 14<br>(Brian Baugh) *cl up 2f: sn rdn: wkng whn sltly hmpd over 1f out* 33/1 | 6 |
| 0500 | 10 | 1½ | **It's Taboo**[14] 5252 4-9-4 57 ... SteveDrowne 7<br>(Mark Usher) *chsd ldrs: rdn 3f out: wknd over 1f out* 20/1 | 13 |
| 6554 | 11 | ½ | **Djinni (IRE)**[18] 5096 3-9-2 65 ... (b) CamHardie(5) 13<br>(Richard Hannon) *s.s and sn chsd along: swtchd lft 2f out: a towards rr* 7/1[3] | 18 |
| 6006 | 12 | nk | **Ficelle (IRE)**[13] 5273 5-8-7 46 oh1 ... (b) DannyBrock 12<br>(Nikki Evans) *led 3f: edgd rt over 2f out: wknd over 1f out* 33/1 | |

1m 30.47s (7.27) **Going Correction** +1.05s/f (Soft)
**WFA** 3 from 4yo+ 5lb **12** Ran SP% **122.9**
Speed ratings (Par 101): **100,98,96,96,86 84,80,79,78,76 76,75**
CSF £30.95 CT £640.50 TOTE £7.80: £2.50, £2.70, £6.10; EX 35.90 Trifecta £1181.40.
**Owner** Mrs Samantha Smith **Bred** Lilly Hall Farm **Trained** Ledbury, H'fords

**FOCUS**
A moderate but competitive handicap. The field finished strung out.
T/Plt: £182.20 to a £1 stake. Pool: £53428.96 - 214.02 winning tickets T/Qpdt: £10.40 to a £1 stake. Pool: £4882.59 - 344.50 winning tickets RL

# 4808 EPSOM (L-H)
Monday, August 25

**OFFICIAL GOING: Good to soft changing to soft after race 1 (2.05) changing to heavy after race 4 (3.45)**
Wind: Moderate, across Weather: Raining

## 5752 BRITISH STALLION STUDS EBF MEDIAN AUCTION MAIDEN STKS 7f
**2:05** (2:06) (Class 5) 2-Y-O **£3,881** (£1,155; £577; £288) **Stalls** Low

| Form | | | | RPR |
|---|---|---|---|---|
| 223 | 1 | | **Marshall Jennings (IRE)**[17] 5128 2-9-5 85 ... JamesDoyle 2<br>(Richard Hannon) *trckd ldr: pushed into ld wl over 1f out: rdn out and wl in command fnl f* 6/4[1] | 80 |

03 **2** 3 **Zigayani (IRE)**[19] 5050 2-9-5 0 RyanMoore 1 72
(Sir Michael Stoute) *led: tk field to nr side in st: sn pushed along: rdn and hdd wl over 1f out: styd on but no ch w wnr fnl f* **2/1**[2]

0 **3** 7 **Dark Wave**[25] 4829 2-9-5 0 NickyMackay 3 54
(Ed Walker) *dwlt: in tch: pushed along and racd wdst of all in st: rdn and lft bhd fr 2f out* **25/1**

**4** 2¾ **Enville (IRE)** 2-9-5 0 PatCosgrave 5 47
(William Haggas) *dwlt: in tch: pushed along over 2f out: sn lft bhd by ldng pair* **5/1**[3]

0 **5** 5 **Steevo (IRE)**[18] 5091 2-9-5 0 GeorgeBaker 6 34
(Gary Moore) *racd wd early: in tch: dropped to last and nudged along over 2f out: reminder 1f out: nvr involved* **16/1**

0 **6** 1¼ **Awjab (IRE)**[12] 5309 2-9-5 0 PaulHanagan 4 31
(Brian Meehan) *chsd ldng pair to 3f out: sn wknd* **6/1**

1m 26.91s (3.61) **Going Correction** +0.475s/f (Yiel) **6** Ran SP% **114.0**
Speed ratings (Par 94): **98,94,86,83,77 76**
CSF £4.89 TOTE £2.10: £1.40, £1.10; EX 4.40 Trifecta £34.60.
**Owner** Carmichael Jennings **Bred** J F Tuthill **Trained** East Everleigh, Wilts

**FOCUS**
Approximately 10mm of rain had fallen before the first race, and the going had eased considerably from the overnight description. After the jockeys offered their opinions the going was changed to soft. They came stands' side in this opening maiden and the winner was always in command late on.

## 5753 CAROLINE & BLOSSOM H'CAP 6f
**2:40** (2:40) (Class 5) (0-75,75) 3-Y-O **£5,175** (£1,540; £769; £384) **Stalls** High

Form RPR

4001 **1** **Inciting Incident (IRE)**[38] 4411 3-9-5 73 (p) RyanMoore 4 86
(Ed McMahon) *mde virtually all: tk field to nr side in st and grabbed rail: jnd 3f out to 2f out: urged along and drew clr fnl f* **2/1**[2]

2314 **2** 3¾ **Miss Brazil (IRE)**[16] 5182 3-9-6 74 KieranO'Neill 6 76
(Richard Hannon) *awkward s and then impeded: off the pce in last: clsd over 2f out: rdn to chse wnr ins fnl f: edgd lft and sn no imp* **7/1**

6016 **3** ¾ **Double Czech (IRE)**[10] 5381 3-9-4 72 (v) DavidProbert 2 72
(Patrick Chamings) *chsd ldng pair: nt qckn 2f out: sn lost pl: kpt on again fnl f to take 3rd nr fin* **5/1**[3]

4221 **4** 1¼ **Castorienta**[15] 5205 3-9-7 75 PatCosgrave 3 71
(George Baker) *hld up in 4th: clsd over 2f out: shkn up to chse wnr wl over 1f out tl ins fnl f: wknd* **6/4**[1]

5556 **5** 2 **Intense Feeling (IRE)**[9] 5427 3-8-5 59 ow2 (v) AdamBeschizza 7 49
(Lee Carter) *pressed wnr: upsides 3f out to 2f out but u.p and racd on outer: lost 2nd wl over 1f out: wknd and eased* **8/1**

1m 14.05s (4.65) **Going Correction** +0.575s/f (Yiel) **5** Ran SP% **113.6**
Speed ratings (Par 100): **92,87,86,84,81**
CSF £15.86 TOTE £3.40: £1.60, £2.60; EX 17.10 Trifecta £48.80.
**Owner** The W H O Society **Bred** Yeomanstown Stud **Trained** Lichfield, Staffs

**FOCUS**
The winner has improved for headgear the last twice, and made all on the stands' side.

## 5754 TOTEPOOL SUPPORTING THE SPORT YOU LOVE H'CAP 5f
**3:10** (3:13) (Class 2) (0-100,100) 3-Y-O+
**£15,562** (£4,660; £2,330; £1,165; £582; £292) **Stalls** High

Form RPR

040 **V** 3 **Bondesire**[9] 5445 4-9-3 96 SamJames(3) 5
(David O'Meara) *chsd ldrs: rdn and wknd over 1f out* **5/1**[3]

3414 **V** 2 **Taurus Twins**[35] 4488 8-8-9 85 (b) KieranO'Neill 6
(Richard Price) *stall opened sltly ahd of rest: led and crossed to nr side rail: hdd wl over 1f out: sn lost 2nd: fdd* **16/1**

6005 **V** 1¼ **Lady Gibraltar**[15] 5211 5-8-5 81 (v) MartinLane 10
(Timothy Jarvis) *chsd ldrs: rdn and wknd over 1f out* **14/1**

5311 **V** 1¼ **Come On Dave (IRE)**[19] 5045 5-8-2 83 DanielMuscutt(5) 3
(John Butler) *pressed ldr: led wl over 1f out: hdd last 150yds: styd on same pce* **5/1**[3]

2 **V** 1 **Long Awaited (IRE)**[9] 5419 6-8-13 89 (b) RyanMoore 7
(David Barron) *dwlt: mostly detached in last pair and sn pushed along: nvr a factor* **9/4**[1]

0211 **V** ¾ **Silvanus (IRE)**[20] 5016 9-9-4 94 PaulHanagan 2
(Paul Midgley) *racd wdst of all: chsd ldrs: lost pl 1/2-way: sn no ch* **12/1**

2120 **V** hd **Swiss Cross**[27] 4762 7-8-12 88 (bt) DavidProbert 12
(Phil McEntee) *dwlt: sn rdn and detached in last pair: nvr a factor* **10/1**

0655 **V** **Humidor (IRE)**[9] 5419 7-9-3 93 JamesDoyle 11
(George Baker) *trckd ldng pair against rail: plld out and wnt 2nd over 1f out: clsd to ld last 150yds: styd on wl* **11/4**[2]

**FOCUS**
This race was voided after none of the jockeys responded to a recall flag. The starter had called a false start in the belief that Taurus Twins' stall had opened early. The jockeys escaped punishment as visibility was poor and the flagman did not blow his whistle.

## 5755 STANLEY WOOTTON CONDITIONS STKS 1m 2f 18y
**3:45** (3:50) (Class 3) 3-Y-O+
**£9,337** (£2,796; £1,398; £699; £349; £175) **Stalls** Low

Form RPR

1600 **1** **Beacon Lady**[25] 4824 5-8-6 91 JackDuern(5) 7 102
(William Knight) *hld up in last: wnt 5th st: prog down centre of crse over 2f out: 2nd wl over 1f out: rdn to ld ins fnl f: styd on wl* **7/1**

10 **2** 2¼ **Ayrad (IRE)**[85] 2818 3-8-8 96 JamesDoyle 3 103
(Roger Varian) *trckd ldr after 2f: led over 3f out and grabbed nr side rail: drvn over 1f out: hdd and one pce last 150yds* **5/1**[3]

041 **3** 4½ **Fattsota**[9] 5440 6-9-2 103 PaulHanagan 6 97
(David O'Meara) *led: hdd over 3f out: lost 2nd and btn wl over 1f out: fdd* **2/1**[2]

1-22 **4** 12 **Haafaguinea**[207] 398 4-9-2 105 RyanMoore 2 71
(Saeed bin Suroor) *in tch: chsd ldng pair over 4f out to over 2f out: wknd* **6/4**[1]

-162 **5** 1¼ **Spark Plug (IRE)**[39] 4366 3-8-8 102 (b[1]) MartinLane 1 69
(Brian Meehan) *chsd ldr 2f: 4th and struggling st: styd centre of crse and sn btn* **10/1**

-600 **6** 12 **Global Thrill**[78] 5-8-11 99 DanielMuscutt(5) 5 46
(Bernard Llewellyn) *hld up: dropped to last st and sn toiling: t.o* **33/1**

2m 15.26s (5.56) **Going Correction** +0.675s/f (Yiel)
**WFA** 3 from 4yo+ 8lb **6** Ran SP% **114.5**
Speed ratings (Par 107): **104,102,98,89,88 78**
CSF £41.63 TOTE £5.70: £2.30, £2.50; EX 46.80 Trifecta £103.30.
**Owner** The Pro-Claimers **Bred** Ashley House Stud **Trained** Patching, W Sussex

**FOCUS**
Despite the small field this looked quite a competitive conditions race.

## 5756 INVESTEC AMATEUR DERBY (IN CELEBRATION OF CAROLINE BEAUMONT) (GENTLEMAN AMATEUR RIDERS' H'CAP) 1m 4f 10y
**4:20** (4:21) (Class 4) (0-85,83) 4-Y-O+ **£6,862** (£2,128; £1,063; £532) **Stalls** Centre

Form RPR

3231 **1** **Barwick**[18] 5073 6-11-5 81 MrRBirkett 10 90
(Lady Herries) *hld up and last to 1/2-way: prog and 4th st: clsd to ld jst over 2f out gng easily: drvn over 1f out: kpt on* **7/2**[2]

0032 **2** 2 **Sky Khan**[29] 4710 5-11-2 83 (p) MrKWood(5) 5 89
(John Wainwright) *hld up: prog 1/2-way: trckd ldr 4f out: clsd to ld briefly over 2f out: sn rdn: chsd wnr after: kpt on but a hld fnl f* **4/1**[3]

-412 **3** 5 **Jebril (FR)**[63] 3515 4-10-10 75 MrJHarding(3) 9 73
(Jonathan Portman) *prom: trckd ldr 6f out to 4f out: rt on terms w ldrs over 2f out: wknd over 1f out* **5/2**[1]

4522 **4** 8 **Taste The Wine (IRE)**[10] 5403 8-9-11 64 oh1 (t) MrJPWilliams(5) 1 49
(Bernard Llewellyn) *prom: lost pl sn after 1/2-way: 6th and struggling st: tk modest 4th u.p over 1f out* **12/1**

1040 **5** 2½ **Lady Of Yue**[31] 4622 4-10-6 68 MrPCollington 8 49
(Eugene Stanford) *hld up in last pair: 5th and struggling st: no prog after* **5/1**

1124 **6** 25 **Glennten**[5] 5560 5-9-11 64 oh4 (b) MrWillPettis(5) 6 5
(Jose Santos) *led and bounded clr: stl wl clr st: wknd rapidly and hdd over 2f out: t.o* **25/1**

0-01 **7** 4½ **Hyperlink (IRE)**[40] 4319 5-10-7 72 MrAlexFerguson(3) 2 6
(Michael Bell) *chsd ldr to 1/2-way: wknd over 4f out: t.o* **5/1**

2m 54.36s (15.46) **Going Correction** +0.775s/f (Yiel) **7** Ran SP% **115.7**
Speed ratings (Par 105): **79,77,74,69,67 50,47**
CSF £18.31 CT £40.39 TOTE £3.60: £1.30, £3.30; EX 18.50 Trifecta £74.60.
**Owner** Seymour Bloodstock (uk) Ltd **Bred** Dullingham Park **Trained** Patching, W Sussex
■ Stewards' Enquiry : Mr R Birkett caution: careless riding.

**FOCUS**
The going was changed to heavy before this race. This was run at a good gallop thanks to Glennten, who quickly built up a healthy advantage before inevitably hitting the wall early in the straight.

## 5757 EBBISHAM H'CAP 1m 2f 18y
**4:55** (4:58) (Class 3) (0-90,87) 3-Y-O+
**£9,337** (£2,796; £1,398; £699; £349; £175) **Stalls** Low

Form RPR

5222 **1** **One Pekan (IRE)**[47] 4091 4-9-10 83 RyanMoore 4 90
(Roger Varian) *racd wd in bk st: prom: 3rd st: rdn to ld 2f out: narrowly hdd ins fnl f: drvn ahd again nr fin* **9/2**[3]

4044 **2** nk **Pasaka Boy**[23] 4917 4-9-5 83 (p) NedCurtis(5) 6 89
(Jonathan Portman) *pushed along early: racd wd in bk st: in tch: 6th st: rdn and prog 3f out: clsd to chal 1f out: narrow ld ins fnl f: hdd nr fin* **3/1**[2]

1200 **3** ¾ **Pack Leader (IRE)**[16] 5164 3-9-6 87 GeorgeBaker 7 92
(Amanda Perrett) *trckd ldr: led 4f out: tk field down centre in home st: hdd 2f out: rt on terms 1f out: kpt on* **7/1**

-442 **4** ¾ **Raven Ridge (IRE)**[11] 5345 3-9-4 85 JamesDoyle 1 89
(Michael Bell) *chsd ldrs: 4th st: rdn over 2f out: cl up bhd ldrs after: nt qckn and a hld* **9/4**[1]

1140 **5** 1½ **Dandy (GER)**[9] 5413 5-8-13 79 (v) RobHornby(7) 2 80
(Andrew Balding) *hld up in last and racd wd in bk st: pushed along and tried to cl fr over 2f out: kpt on but nvr able to threaten* **25/1**

5552 **6** 19 **Cosmic Halo**[30] 4680 5-9-1 74 PaulHanagan 5 39
(Richard Fahey) *hld up: 5th st: wknd over 2f out: t.o* **8/1**

133- **7** 8 **Zumurudah (FR)**[311] 7336 3-8-10 80 MichaelJMMurphy(3) 8 29
(Mark Johnston) *led to 4f out: wknd rapidly 3f out: t.o* **6/1**

2m 18.25s (8.55) **Going Correction** +0.875s/f (Soft)
**WFA** 3 from 4yo+ 8lb **7** Ran SP% **115.7**
Speed ratings (Par 107): **100,99,99,98,97 82,75**
CSF £18.86 CT £92.95 TOTE £4.30: £1.60, £3.60; EX 20.60 Trifecta £91.60.
**Owner** H R H Sultan Ahmad Shah **Bred** Chris & James McHale **Trained** Newmarket, Suffolk

**FOCUS**
They went steadier in this race and the result was that there were several in with a chance at the finish. This time they shunned the stands' rail, which was probably the wrong decision, and opted to try and find better ground up the centre of the track.

## 5758 EWELL H'CAP 1m 114y
**5:30** (5:32) (Class 4) (0-80,79) 3-Y-O+ **£6,469** (£1,925; £962; £481) **Stalls** Low

Form RPR

6341 **1** **Starwatch**[15] 5213 7-10-0 79 (v) WilliamCarson 7 91
(John Bridger) *pressed ldr: c nr side st: led 2f out: rdn and drew clr fr over 1f out* **4/1**[2]

0535 **2** 3¼ **Whitby Jet (IRE)**[39] 4340 6-8-12 70 HectorCrouch(7) 3 75
(Ed Vaughan) *pushed along early in last: shkn up 4f out: stl last 2f out: r.o over 1f out: tk 2nd nr fin* **16/1**

0500 **3** ¾ **Lunar Deity**[11] 5346 5-9-10 75 GeorgeBaker 9 78
(Stuart Williams) *hld up in rr: 7th and pushed along st: styd centre after: sme prog 2f out: kpt on fnl f to take 3rd last strides* **9/2**[3]

3362 **4** hd **Bayleyf (IRE)**[14] 5252 5-9-1 66 (p) StevieDonohoe 12 68
(Lee Carter) *prom: 3rd st: styd centre and clr of that gp: on terms w wnr 2f out: no ex over 1f out: wknd and lost 2 pls nr fin* **10/1**

1422 **5** 3 **Alpine Storm (IRE)**[5] 5566 3-9-0 75 MichaelJMMurphy(3) 2 70
(Mark Johnston) *led at str pce: c nr side in st: hdd 2f out: wknd jst over 1f out* **3/1**[1]

6553 **6** ¾ **Exclusive Waters (IRE)**[14] 5252 4-8-11 62 (b) MartinLane 10 56
(Charles Hills) *towards rr: sme prog and 5th st: no hdwy 2f out: wl hld after* **10/1**

2030 **7** 7 **Tatting**[14] 5258 5-9-7 77 DanielMuscutt(5) 8 55
(Chris Dwyer) *chsd clr ldrs: 6th st: styd centre after: no prog 2f out: wknd over 1f out* **14/1**

-505 **8** 3¾ **Killing Time (IRE)**[19] 5040 3-9-5 77 DavidProbert 4 46
(Ralph Beckett) *chsd ldng pair tl 4th and rdn st: styd in centre: struggling 2f out: sn wknd* **3/1**[1]

1m 53.53s (7.43) **Going Correction** +0.975s/f (Soft)
**WFA** 3 from 4yo+ 7lb **8** Ran SP% **118.9**
Speed ratings (Par 105): **105,102,101,101,98 97,91,88**
CSF £66.12 CT £305.70 TOTE £4.00: £1.30, £4.70, £1.40; EX 68.70 Trifecta £356.60.
**Owner** J J Bridger **Bred** Mrs J A Chapman **Trained** Liphook, Hants

**FOCUS**
There was a difference of opinion here but, not for the first time, the one who grabbed the stands' rail was the one who came out on top.

T/Plt: £92.90 to a £1 stake. Pool of £62777.30 - 492.96 winning tickets. T/Qpdt: £40.40 to a £1 stake. Pool of £4022.16 - 73.56 winning tickets JN

# 5636 NEWCASTLE (L-H)

Monday, August 25

**OFFICIAL GOING: Good (good to firm in places; 7.3)**

Wind: Fresh, half behind Weather: Cloudy, dry

## 5759 EQUINE PRODUCTS UK SELENAVITE E/EBF MAIDEN STKS (BOBIS RACE) (DIV I) 7f

**1:45** (1:45) (Class 4) 2-Y-O **£4,075** (£1,212; £606; £303) **Stalls** Centre

Form RPR

03 **1** **Grey Sensation (IRE)**[20] 4993 2-9-2 0 JoeyHaynes(3) 10 79+
(K R Burke) *prom: led over 2f out: pushed clr fnl f: eased nr fin* 4/1[1]

64 **2** 3 1/4 **Sir Chauvelin**[16] 5167 2-9-5 0 FergalLynch 2 69+
(Jim Goldie) *hld up in tch: pushed along and outpcd 1/2-way: rallied 2f out: wnt 2nd wl ins fnl f: kpt on: nt rch wnr* 6/1[3]

0 **3** 1 1/2 **Yorkie Talkie (IRE)**[93] 2541 2-9-5 0 JoeFanning 4 65
(Mark Johnston) *trckd ldr: ev ch and rdn over 1f out: outpcd fnl f: lost 2nd last 50yds* 9/1

**4** 1 1/4 **Yeenaan (FR)** 2-9-5 0 MartinHarley 3 62+
(Marco Botti) *noisy and colty in paddock: slowly away: bhd tl hdwy over 1f out: kpt on fnl f: nvr able to chal* 4/1[1]

05 **5** 2 3/4 **A Lovable Rogue**[20] 5013 2-9-0 0 GarryWhillans(5) 8 54
(Ian Semple) *prom: shkn up and outpcd over 2f out: edgd rt and no imp over 1f out* 50/1

000 **6** 2 3/4 **Red Flute**[7] 5488 2-9-5 0 (v) IanBrennan 5 47
(Alan McCabe) *led to over 2f out: rdn and wknd over 1f out* 50/1

**7** 2 3/4 **Ciao Cielo (GER)** 2-9-5 0 RobertWinston 9 40
(David Barron) *green in paddock: missed break: bhd: pushed along and green over 2f out: sn n.d* 4/1[1]

**8** 7 **Silver Tycoon (IRE)** 2-9-5 0 PhillipMakin 6 21
(John Quinn) *dwlt: hld up towards rr: outpcd over 2f out: sn n.d* 5/1[2]

66 **9** nse **Aprovado (IRE)**[20] 5013 2-9-5 0 PaulMulrennan 1 20
(Michael Dods) *hld up: shkn up over 2f out: wknd over 1f out* 10/1

1m 25.36s (-2.44) **Going Correction** -0.50s/f (Hard) 9 Ran SP% 114.0
Speed ratings (Par 96): **93,89,87,86,83 79,76,68,68**
CSF £27.86 TOTE £4.70: £1.80, £1.90, £2.70; EX 25.90 Trifecta £244.70.
**Owner** M Nelmes-Crocker **Bred** Theo Waddington **Trained** Middleham Moor, N Yorks

**FOCUS**
Not a bad 2yo maiden. The winner was soon in command and is improving with racing.

## 5760 EQUINE PRODUCTS UK SELENAVITE E/EBF MAIDEN STKS (BOBIS RACE) (DIV II) 7f

**2:15** (2:15) (Class 4) 2-Y-O **£4,075** (£1,212; £606; £303) **Stalls** Centre

Form RPR

2332 **1** **Intiwin (IRE)**[31] 4633 2-9-2 0 GeorgeChaloner(3) 7 83
(Richard Fahey) *cl up: led over 2f out: sn hrd pressed: rdn and hung lft ins fnl f: all out* 7/2[2]

3 **2** nse **Bartel (IRE)**[17] 5149 2-9-5 0 JackMitchell 1 83
(Ed Vaughan) *t.k.h: cl up: chal over 2f out: bmpd ins fnl f: kpt on wl: jst hld* 9/4[1]

6 **3** 2 **Lostock Hall (IRE)**[30] 4659 2-9-5 0 JoeFanning 2 77
(K R Burke) *trckd ldrs: effrt over 2f out: kpt on ins fnl f: nt rch first two* 16/1

**4** 3/4 **Bravo Zolo (IRE)** 2-9-5 0 MartinHarley 6 75
(Marco Botti) *dwlt: hld up in tch: stdy hdwy to chse ldrs over 2f out: shkn up and one pce over 1f out: bttr for r* 13/2

3 **5** 6 **Swaheen**[37] 4429 2-9-5 0 ShaneKelly 4 59
(Sir Michael Stoute) *towards rr: pushed along 3f out: no imp fr 2f out* 5/1

3222 **6** 7 **Ythan Waters**[30] 4659 2-9-5 0 PaulMulrennan 8 40
(Bryan Smart) *led to over 2f out: rdn and wknd over 1f out* 9/2[3]

06 **7** 1 1/4 **Heading Home (FR)**[7] 5493 2-9-5 0 IanBrennan 5 37
(John Quinn) *t.k.h early: hld up towards rr: struggling over 2f out: sn btn* 66/1

**8** 8 **Tonto's Spirit** 2-9-5 0 TomEaves 9 15
(Michael Dods) *t.k.h in rr: struggling over 3f out: sn drifted to far rail: nvr on terms* 28/1

**9** 5 **Secrets Safe (IRE)** 2-9-5 0 PhillipMakin 3
(David Brown) *s.i.s: bhd and green: struggling fr over 3f out: btn whn hung lft 2f out* 33/1

1m 25.06s (-2.74) **Going Correction** -0.50s/f (Hard) 9 Ran SP% 114.9
Speed ratings (Par 96): **95,94,92,91,84 76,75,66,60**
CSF £11.58 TOTE £2.60: £1.10, £2.10, £5.00; EX 13.40 Trifecta £73.80.
**Owner** Mrs H Steel **Bred** Hugh O'Brien & Michael McCallan **Trained** Musley Bank, N Yorks

**FOCUS**
The second division of the 2yo maiden, which saw a great battle between the first two.

## 5761 EQUINE PRODUCTS UK RESTORELYTE CLAIMING STKS 1m 3y(S)

**2:50** (2:50) (Class 6) 3-Y-O+ **£1,940** (£577; £288; £144) **Stalls** Centre

Form RPR

2401 **1** **The Osteopath (IRE)**[13] 5267 11-9-5 72 PhillipMakin 7 68
(John Davies) *hld up and bhd: stdy hdwy over 2f out: led ins fnl f: rdn and r.o wl* 7/2[2]

4000 **2** 1/2 **Majestic Dream (IRE)**[4] 5605 6-9-9 65 (v) BarryMcHugh 13 71
(Michael Easterby) *hld up: hdwy over 2f out: ev ch ins fnl f: kpt on: hld nr fin* 9/1

0430 **3** 1 1/4 **King Pin**[16] 5197 9-8-13 61 (p) RoystonFfrench 9 58
(Tracy Waggott) *hld up: hdwy over 2f out: ev ch briefly ins fnl f: kpt on same pce last 100yds* 7/1

0045 **4** 3 3/4 **Jebel Tara**[5] 5571 9-9-1 56 (tp) PaulPickard 12 52
(Alan Brown) *led at decent gallop: rdn 2f out: hdd ins fnl f: sn outpcd* 33/1

0035 **5** 1 3/4 **Conry (IRE)**[1] 5711 8-9-13 77 DavidNolan 8 59
(Ian Williams) *hld up in tch: rdn over 3f out: effrt over 1f out: one pce fnl f* 11/2[3]

5245 **6** 1 3/4 **Whispered Times (USA)**[3] 5638 7-8-13 60 (p) RobertWinston 10 41
(Tracy Waggott) *hld up: stdy hdwy whn edgd rt over 2f out: rdn over 1f out: no ex ins fnl f* 11/4[1]

0500 **7** 1 1/4 **The Blue Banana (IRE)**[10] 5376 5-9-1 56 (p) PaulMulrennan 6 41
(Edwin Tuer) *towards rr: drvn along whn short of room briefly over 2f out: sn n.d* 8/1

2600 **8** 3/4 **Petergate**[13] 5269 3-8-8 56 (b[1]) JoeDoyle(5) 5 42
(Brian Rothwell) *prom: smooth hdwy over 2f out: effrt over 1f out: wknd ins fnl f* 25/1

60 **9** 6 **Lady Jamesway (IRE)**[52] 3908 3-7-11 0 JackGarritty(5) 4 17
(Ann Duffield) *cl up: rdn over 2f out: wknd over 1f out* 50/1

51-0 **10** 1 1/2 **Megamunch (IRE)**[14] 5235 4-9-9 72 (p) TomEaves 1 30
(Kristin Stubbs) *prom: drvn wl over 2f out: wknd over 1f out* 14/1

6000 **11** 3 3/4 **Flying Applause**[13] 5291 9-8-13 45 (b) RussKennemore 3 11
(Roy Bowring) *dwlt: sn prom: rdn 1/2-way: sn struggling* 40/1

6600 **12** 41 **Some Boy Lukey**[52] 3914 3-8-4 45 DuilioDaSilva(5) 11
(David Thompson) *bhd: struggling over 3f out: btn and eased fr 2f out* 100/1

1m 38.21s (-5.19) **Going Correction** -0.50s/f (Hard)
**WFA** 3 from 4yo+ 6lb 12 Ran SP% 116.7
Speed ratings (Par 101): **105,104,103,99,97 96,94,94,88,86 82,41**
CSF £33.00 TOTE £3.20: £1.40, £2.00, £2.70; EX 49.90 Trifecta £361.90.
**Owner** Kevin Kirkup **Bred** Joe Rogers **Trained** Piercebridge, Durham

**FOCUS**
A modest but competitive handicap. The first, second and fourth all came from the rear, and the winner didn't need to match his best of this year.

## 5762 EQUINE PRODUCTS UK TRANSVITE BLAYDON RACE (NURSERY H'CAP) (BOBIS RACE) 1m 3y(S)

**3:25** (3:26) (Class 2) 2-Y-O **£9,703** (£2,887; £1,443; £721) **Stalls** Centre

Form RPR

4321 **1** **Azraff (IRE)**[17] 5147 2-9-7 85 MartinHarley 1 94+
(Marco Botti) *cl up gng wl: led over 2f out: qcknd clr wl over 1f out: pushed out towards fin* 7/2[2]

51 **2** 1 1/2 **Moonlightnavigator (USA)**[34] 4518 2-9-4 82 PhillipMakin 4 88+
(John Quinn) *t.k.h: in tch: rdn over 2f out: rallied to chse (clr) wnr ins fnl f: r.o* 9/2[3]

544 **3** 1 1/4 **Multi Grain**[14] 5232 2-7-11 66 JoeDoyle(5) 5 69
(Brian Ellison) *chsd ldrs: drvn and outpcd over 2f out: kpt on strly fnl f: nrst fin* 14/1

21 **4** 1 **Berland (IRE)**[20] 4993 2-9-2 80 PaulMulrennan 9 80
(Michael Bell) *hld up: stdy hdwy 1/2-way: effrt and rdn 2f out: kpt on same pce ins fnl f* 9/4[1]

061 **5** 1/2 **Stardrifter**[33] 4528 2-8-5 72 GeorgeChaloner(3) 6 71
(Richard Fahey) *t.k.h: in tch: rdn and outpcd over 2f out: r.o ins fnl f: no imp* 7/1

0335 **6** 2 3/4 **Twin Turbo (IRE)**[11] 5335 2-8-4 68 JoeFanning 3 61
(Mark Johnston) *cl up: rdn over 2f out: wknd ins fnl f* 9/1

431 **7** 3 1/2 **Al Rayyan (IRE)**[18] 5078 2-8-13 77 TomEaves 7 62
(Kevin Ryan) *led: rdn and hdd over 2f out: wknd ent fnl f* 13/2

1m 38.75s (-4.65) **Going Correction** -0.50s/f (Hard) 7 Ran SP% 113.7
Speed ratings (Par 100): **103,101,100,99,98 96,92**
CSF £19.29 CT £192.39 TOTE £2.70: £1.30, £3.10; EX 17.60 Trifecta £253.50.
**Owner** Saleh Al Homaizi & Imad Al Sagar **Bred** Lodge Park Stud **Trained** Newmarket, Suffolk

**FOCUS**
The feature race was a decent nursery handicap in which they went an, at best, even gallop. The winner travelled all over these but got a bit tired late on.

## 5763 EQUINE PRODUCTS UK PREMIER E FILLIES' H'CAP 7f

**4:00** (4:00) (Class 5) (0-75,75) 3-Y-O+ **£2,587** (£770; £384; £192) **Stalls** Centre

Form RPR

3020 **1** **Simply Shining (IRE)**[31] 4635 4-9-5 73 JackGarritty(5) 5 82
(Richard Fahey) *chsd ldr: led 2f out: drvn out fnl f* 10/3[2]

3032 **2** nk **Hala Hala (IRE)**[18] 5107 3-8-12 73 AhmadAlSubousi(7) 6 79
(Michael Bell) *in tch: rdn and swtchd rt over 1f out: chsd wnr ins fnl f: kpt on: hld nr fin* 9/2[3]

424 **3** 2 **Inflection (IRE)**[20] 5007 3-9-4 72 (t) RobertWinston 4 73
(Hugo Palmer) *pressed ldrs: effrt and ev ch over 1f out: kpt on same pce ins fnl f* 11/4[1]

0120 **4** 1 1/2 **Medam**[9] 5415 5-8-10 59 JasonHart 2 58
(Shaun Harris) *hld up: rdn over 2f out: kpt on fnl f: nvr able to chal* 9/1

0345 **5** 1 **Milly's Secret (IRE)**[8] 5470 3-9-7 75 (p) PaulMulrennan 1 69
(Ann Duffield) *hld up in tch: rdn over 2f out: no imp fnl f* 5/1

0054 **6** 1 1/2 **Clever Miss**[15] 5205 3-8-10 64 (v) MartinHarley 3 54
(Alan McCabe) *t.k.h: led: rdn and hdd 2f out: wknd fnl f* 10/1

4200 **7** 4 **Thorntoun Lady (USA)**[35] 4487 4-9-5 68 FergalLynch 7 50
(Jim Goldie) *hld up in tch: rdn over 2f out: sn wknd* 11/1

1m 24.75s (-3.05) **Going Correction** -0.50s/f (Hard)
**WFA** 3 from 4yo+ 5lb 7 Ran SP% 112.0
Speed ratings (Par 100): **97,96,94,92,91 89,85**
CSF £17.83 TOTE £4.40: £1.80, £4.30; EX 21.10 Trifecta £55.10.
**Owner** Mrs H Steel **Bred** Ennistown Stud **Trained** Musley Bank, N Yorks

**FOCUS**
A modest fillies' handicap in which the winner recorded the best comparative time on the card.

## 5764 EQUINE PRODUCTS UK FEEDING TO WIN H'CAP 1m 6f 97y

**4:35** (4:35) (Class 5) (0-75,77) 4-Y-O+ **£2,587** (£770; £384; £192) **Stalls** Low

Form RPR

2123 **1** **Underwritten**[16] 5171 5-8-11 65 JasonHart 5 72
(Shaun Harris) *pressed ldr: rdn to ld over 1f out: drvn out fnl f* 7/1

1101 **2** 1 1/2 **Hot Spice**[24] 4874 6-9-7 75 BarryMcHugh 4 80
(Michael Easterby) *t.k.h: led: qcknd over 3f out: hdd over 1f out: kpt on same pce ins fnl f* 3/1[2]

21 **3** nk **Maoi Chinn Tire (IRE)**[5] 5564 7-9-4 77 6ex (t) JoeDoyle(5) 6 82
(Jennie Candlish) *prom: effrt and rdn 2f out: kpt on same pce ins fnl f* 11/4[1]

230 **4** 1/2 **Northside Prince (IRE)**[10] 5371 8-9-6 74 RobertWinston 7 78
(Alan Swinbank) *t.k.h: hld up: effrt over 2f out: kpt on same pce fnl f* 7/1

263 **5** 3/4 **Mason Hindmarsh**[20] 5017 7-8-9 66 GeorgeChaloner(3) 8 69
(Karen McLintock) *led rdrs: rdn over 2f out: one pce over 1f out* 11/2[3]

46-4 **6** 1 3/4 **Mojolika**[27] 4754 6-8-8 67 JackGarritty(5) 1 68
(Patrick Holmes) *hld up in last pl: stdy hdwy over 2f out: effrt and swtchd rt over 1f out: no imp* 11/1

1243 **7** 3 3/4 **Hallstatt (IRE)**[24] 4874 8-9-3 71 (t) PaulMulrennan 3 71
(John Mackie) *s.i.s: hld up in tch: rdn over 3f out: no imp whn hmpd over 1f out* 7/1

3m 8.83s (-2.47) **Going Correction** -0.15s/f (Firm) 7 Ran SP% 112.9
Speed ratings (Par 103): **101,100,99,99,99 98,96**
CSF £27.51 CT £71.25 TOTE £9.00: £6.70, £2.80; EX 34.20 Trifecta £191.20.
**Owner** W A Robinson **Bred** W And R Barnett Ltd **Trained** Carburton, Notts

**FOCUS**
An ordinary staying handicap. The winner chased the front-running runner-up.

## 5765 EQUINE PRODUCTS UK SUPPORTING GLOBAL CHAMPIONS H'CAP — 1m 4f 93y

5:10 (5:10) (Class 6) (0-65,63) 3-Y-O+ £1,940 (£577; £288; £144) Stalls Low

Form RPR

0U02 1 **Slunovrat (FR)**[22] 4948 3-8-13 58 RaulDaSilva 4 66+
(David Menuisier) *plld hrd early: cl up: effrt and rdn 2f out: led ins fnl f: styd on wl* 11/4[1]

256 2 ¾ **Ronald Gee (IRE)**[16] 5171 7-10-0 63 FergalLynch 10 69
(Jim Goldie) *pressed ldr: drvn over 2f out: led over 1f out to ins fnl f: kpt on* 15/2

5603 3 *nk* **Gioia Di Vita**[18] 5090 4-9-12 61 DavidNolan 9 67
(David Thompson) *hld up in midfield: effrt over 2f out: swtchd rt and styd on ins fnl f: nrst fin* 15/2

4214 4 *hd* **Wor Lass**[16] 5171 6-8-11 53 LukeLeadbitter(7) 7 58
(Iain Jardine) *hld up: stdy hdwy and in tch at 1/2-way: effrt and ev ch over 1f out: no ex wl ins fnl f* 3/1[2]

5300 5 2 **Stamp Duty (IRE)**[63] 3535 6-8-10 45 TomEaves 2 47
(Suzzanne France) *dwlt: hld up: shkn up over 2f out: kpt on fnl f: nvr able to chal* 28/1

4554 6 2 **Amazing Blue Sky**[7] 5495 8-9-2 51 PaulMulrennan 8 50
(Ruth Carr) *t.k.h: hld up: rdn over 2f out: kpt on fnl f: nvr able to chal* 9/2[3]

60-5 7 *hd* **Network Perfection**[10] 5402 3-8-5 50 BarryMcHugh 5 48
(Michael Easterby) *midfield: rdn over 2f out: effrt over 1f out: no imp fnl f* 22/1

2535 8 1 ½ **Troy Boy**[18] 5084 4-8-11 46 JasonHart 3 42
(Robin Bastiman) *led: rdn and hdd over 1f out: wknd ins fnl f* 10/1

-000 9 1 **Yorkshireman (IRE)**[54] 3843 4-9-3 52 PaddyAspell 11 46
(Lynn Siddall) *midfield: drvn and outpcd over 2f out: n.d after* 50/1

0006 10 3 ¾ **Magic Shoes (IRE)**[10] 5388 3-8-9 54 RoystonFfrench 6 42
(Susan Corbett) *cl up: rdn over 3f out: wknd over 1f out* 25/1

2m 43.05s (-2.55) **Going Correction** -0.15s/f (Firm)
**WFA** 3 from 4yo+ 10lb 10 Ran SP% **116.1**
Speed ratings (Par 101): **102,101,101,101,99 98,98,97,96,94**
CSF £22.67 CT £139.53 TOTE £3.80: £1.80, £2.50, £1.90; EX 31.30 Trifecta £471.90.
**Owner** Shinco Racing Limited **Bred** Jaques & Marie-Francoise Menuisier **Trained** Pulborough, W Sussex

**FOCUS**
A moderate affair. There was a muddling pace and the form could rate higher.

## 5766 HAEMAVITE B PLUS H'CAP — 6f

5:40 (5:40) (Class 4) (0-80,80) 3-Y-O+ £4,981 (£1,482; £740; £370) Stalls Centre

Form RPR

0054 1 **Bop It**[18] 5081 5-9-10 80 DavidNolan 7 89
(David O'Meara) *prom: hdwy to ld over 1f out: kpt on wl fnl f: jst hld on* 8/1[3]

0-06 2 *nse* **Barney McGrew (IRE)**[18] 5088 11-9-3 73 PaulMulrennan 3 82
(Michael Dods) *hld up in tch: effrt and rdn over 1f out: kpt on wl fnl f: jst failed* 16/1

6521 3 2 **Clubland (IRE)**[24] 4875 5-9-1 76 AlistairRawlinson(5) 5 79
(Roy Bowring) *led tl rdn and hdd over 1f out: edgd rt ins fnl f: kpt on same pce* 8/1[3]

-441 4 *nk* **Tiger Jim**[9] 5415 4-8-12 71 GaryBartley(3) 12 73
(Jim Goldie) *hld up: stdy hdwy over 2f out: rdn over 1f out: kpt on same pce ins fnl f* 7/4[1]

0053 5 *nse* **Head Space (IRE)**[7] 5498 6-9-9 79 (v) JasonHart 4 80
(Ruth Carr) *hld up: rdn over 1f out: kpt on fnl f: nvr able to chal* 7/1[2]

2433 6 1 **Available (IRE)**[33] 4537 5-9-8 78 (tp) StephenCraine 1 76
(John Mackie) *prom: rdn along over 2f out: kpt on same pce fnl f* 12/1

2004 7 2 ¾ **Eland Ally**[31] 4632 6-8-13 69 BarryMcHugh 9 58
(Tom Tate) *t.k.h: hld up: rdn over 2f out: kpt on fnl f: no imp* 8/1[3]

5141 8 *nk* **Gold Beau (FR)**[28] 4724 4-9-5 80 (p) JacobButterfield(5) 13 69
(Kristin Stubbs) *cl up: rdn over 2f out: wknd appr fnl f* 14/1

640 9 1 ¾ **Fitz Flyer (IRE)**[27] 4762 8-9-10 80 (v) RoystonFfrench 11 63
(David Nicholls) *t.k.h: w ldr: rdn over 2f out: wknd over 1f out* 10/1

5000 10 1 ¼ **Unsinkable (IRE)**[3] 5632 4-9-2 77 GarryWhillans(5) 10 56
(Ian Semple) *in tch: outpcd over 3f out: n.d after* 25/1

0406 11 ¾ **L'Ami Louis (IRE)**[28] 4724 6-8-11 67 TomEaves 6 44
(Ian Semple) *t.k.h in rr: rdn over 2f out: sn btn* 50/1

3000 12 3 ¼ **Avonmore Star**[4] 5602 6-8-8 64 IanBrennan 8 30
(Alan McCabe) *dwlt: bhd and sn rdn along: no ch fr 1/2-way* 66/1

1m 11.04s (-3.56) **Going Correction** -0.50s/f (Hard) 12 Ran SP% **118.8**
Speed ratings (Par 105): **103,102,100,99,99 98,94,94,92,90 89,85**
CSF £127.18 CT £1064.57 TOTE £10.20: £2.80, £3.50, £2.40; EX 94.10 Trifecta £955.30.
**Owner** A Turton, J Blackburn & R Bond **Bred** Bond Thoroughbred Corporation **Trained** Nawton, N Yorks

**FOCUS**
The concluding contest was a fair sprint handicap which produced a rousing finale, and the winner recorded the best comparative time on the card.
T/Jkpt: Part won. £7,100.00 to a £1 stake - 0.50 winning units. T/Plt: £47.10 to a £1 stake. Pool: £69102.31 - 1069.66 winning tickets T/Qpdt: £12.30 to a £1 stake. Pool: £4041.36 - 242.85 winning tickets RY

# 5443 RIPON (R-H)

Monday, August 25

**OFFICIAL GOING: Good (good to firm in places; 8.2)**
Wind: moderate 1/2 behind Weather: light rain

## 5767 SALLIE LINDLEY MEMORIAL (S) STKS — 6f

2:25 (2:26) (Class 6) 2-Y-O £3,408 (£1,006; £503) Stalls High

Form RPR

4653 1 **Black Pudding (IRE)**[16] 5194 2-9-2 57 (p[1]) PJMcDonald 5 58
(Ann Duffield) *chsd ldrs: drvn over 2f out: led ins fnl f: all out* 7/2[2]

5406 2 *shd* **Ripon Rose**[10] 5384 2-8-11 55 GrahamLee 4 53
(Paul Midgley) *trckd ldrs: plld wd over 2f out: upsides fnl f: hung lft: jst failed* 8/1

3041 3 2 ¼ **Studio Star**[10] 5384 2-9-2 65 (p) JacobButterfield(5) 7 56
(Ollie Pears) *w ldr: led over 2f out: hdd ins fnl f: kpt on same pce* 5/1[3]

5540 4 1 ¾ **Sunhill Lodge Lady**[16] 5194 2-8-4 38 (b[1]) RowanScott(7) 9 41
(Ann Duffield) *trckd ldrs: one pce over 1f out* 66/1

4003 5 5 **Lucilla Aurelius (IRE)**[10] 5372 2-8-11 48 (p) JamesSullivan 8 26
(Tony Coyle) *led: hdd 2f out: wknd over 1f out* 7/1

00 6 1 **Caties Do Dah**[13] 5264 2-8-8 0 ConnorBeasley(3) 6 23
(Alan Berry) *in rr and sn drvn along: nvr on terms* 100/1

0020 7 ½ **Lady Jade**[6] 5525 2-8-11 49 (v[1]) AndrewMullen 1 22
(Nigel Tinkler) *chsd ldrs: wknd 2f out* 16/1

8 28 **Champagne Royale** 2-8-11 0 PaddyAspell 2
(Sharon Watt) *s.i.s: sn bhd and drvn along: t.o* 33/1

05 P **Invisible Eye**[22] 4943 2-8-13 0 CharlesBishop(3) 3
(Mick Channon) *dwlt: in rr whn heavily eased over 4f out: sn p.u* 11/8[1]

1m 13.6s (0.60) **Going Correction** -0.05s/f (Good) 9 Ran SP% **115.9**
Speed ratings (Par 92): **94,93,90,88,81 80,79,42,**
CSF £31.34 TOTE £2.50: £1.10, £4.00, £2.80; EX 30.20 Trifecta £95.00.The winner was sold to Andrew Caygill for 3,000gns. Ripon Rose subject of friendly claim.
**Owner** Lee Bond **Bred** Tally-Ho Stud **Trained** Constable Burton, N Yorks

■ Stewards' Enquiry : P J McDonald two-day ban: used whip down the shoulder in the forehand (Sep 8-9)

**FOCUS**
A moderate juvenile seller, weakened when the favourite hit problems early.

## 5768 SIS VIRTUAL BETTING CHANNEL H'CAP — 1m 1f 170y

3:00 (3:15) (Class 5) (0-75,74) 3-Y-O £3,234 (£962; £481; £240) Stalls Low

Form RPR

4153 1 **Go Sakhee**[18] 5108 3-9-4 71 FrederikTylicki 3 84
(Roger Varian) *mde all: qckнd pce over 4f out: drvn out: unchal* 3/1[2]

5322 2 6 **An Chulainn (IRE)**[19] 5046 3-9-3 70 (b) FrannyNorton 2 73
(Mark Johnston) *trckd ldng pair: t.k.h: 2nd over 2f out: carried hd high and looked reluctant* 4/1[3]

3-21 3 3 ½ **Lunar Spirit**[94] 2523 3-9-5 72 GrahamGibbons 5 66
(Ralph Beckett) *dwlt: sn chsng ldr: drvn 3f out: wknd over 1f out* 2/1[1]

0-30 4 2 ½ **Maggie's Diamond**[26] 4791 3-8-11 64 TonyHamilton 6 52
(Richard Fahey) *stdd and swtchd rt s: t.k.h in rr: drvn over 3f out: lost pl over 2f out: tk modest 4th nr fin* 5/1

0432 5 *hd* **Mariners Moon (IRE)**[27] 4754 3-9-5 72 DanielTudhope 4 60
(David O'Meara) *hld up in rr: effrt over 3f out: wknd over 1f out* 9/2

2m 1.87s (-3.53) **Going Correction** -0.20s/f (Firm) 5 Ran SP% **113.2**
Speed ratings (Par 100): **106,101,98,96,96**
Moonlight Venture was withdrawn. Price at time of withdrawal 11-2. Rule 4 applies to bets placed prior to withdrawal but not to SP bets - deduction 15p in the pound. New market formed. CSF £15.35 TOTE £3.40: £1.90, £1.70; EX 10.60 Trifecta £23.20.
**Owner** K Allen G Moss R & S Marchant & G Jarvis **Bred** Whitsbury Manor Stud And Mrs M E Slade **Trained** Newmarket, Suffolk

**FOCUS**
A fair 3yo handicap, but there was a delay of nearly 15 minutes after Moonlight Venture broke out of the stalls. The winner made all.

## 5769 BILLY NEVETT MEMORIAL H'CAP (BOBIS RACE) — 6f

3:35 (3:37) (Class 4) (0-80,77) 3-Y-O £5,175 (£1,540; £769; £384) Stalls High

Form RPR

2562 1 **Pennine Warrior**[16] 5199 3-9-1 71 (p) FrederikTylicki 4 78+
(Scott Dixon) *mde all: drvn over 2f out: hld on towards fin* 85/40[1]

3316 2 ½ **Kommander Kirkup**[14] 5243 3-9-4 77 (p) ConnorBeasley(3) 6 82
(Michael Dods) *s.i.s: in rr: outpcd and lost pl over 3f out: swtchd wd and hdwy over 2f out: chsd wnr 1f out: rdr dropped whip last 50yds: keeping on at fin* 10/3[2]

0262 3 6 **Jamboree Girl**[23] 4890 3-9-3 73 DuranFentiman 1 59
(Tim Easterby) *chsd ldrs: effrt over 2f out: fdd fnl f* 6/1

2364 4 2 ¼ **Heroique (IRE)**[7] 5497 3-9-1 71 (e) DanielTudhope 3 50
(Tim Easterby) *w ldr: drvn over 2f out: wknd fnl f* 7/2[3]

6415 5 1 **Centre Haafhd**[19] 5055 3-9-5 75 GrahamGibbons 5 51
(David Barron) *sn chsng ldrs: effrt over 2f out: wknd over 1f out: eased ins fnl f* 5/1

1m 12.31s (-0.69) **Going Correction** -0.05s/f (Good) 5 Ran SP% **108.3**
Speed ratings (Par 102): **102,101,93,90,89**
CSF £9.03 TOTE £3.70: £1.10, £1.50; EX 8.40 Trifecta £30.10.
**Owner** Yorkshire Exiles **Bred** Mrs Yvette Dixon **Trained** Babworth, Notts

**FOCUS**
A pretty tight 3yo sprint on paper but two came clear. It was an ordinary time compared to the seller.

## 5770 IRISH STALLION FARMS EBF RIPON CHAMPION TWO YRS OLD TROPHY, 2014 (LISTED RACE) — 6f

4:10 (4:10) (Class 1) 2-Y-O
£17,013 (£6,450; £3,228; £1,608; £807; £405) Stalls High

Form RPR

2121 1 **Izzthatright (IRE)**[10] 5373 2-9-3 97 TonyHamilton 1 98
(Richard Fahey) *led: swtchd lft to stands' side rail after 100yds: drvn over 1f out: hld on wl clsng stages* 9/2[2]

1001 2 ½ **Bossy Guest (IRE)**[30] 4670 2-9-3 97 CharlesBishop 6 97
(Mick Channon) *trckd ldrs: effrt over 1f out: chsd wnr ins fnl f: edgd rt: no ex clsng stages* 9/4[1]

13 3 *nk* **Explosive Lady (IRE)**[30] 4646 2-8-12 0 BenCurtis 2 91
(K R Burke) *trckd ldrs: upsides over 1f out: kpt on same pce clsng stages* 9/4[1]

4002 4 2 ¾ **Prince Bonnaire**[9] 5447 2-9-3 92 GrahamLee 4 87
(David Brown) *trckd wnr: t.k.h: outpcd over 1f out: kpt on to take 4th nr fin* 11/1

4311 5 1 ½ **Dark Reckoning**[9] 5447 2-8-12 90 HarryBentley 7 78
(Ann Duffield) *hld up towards rr: hdwy over 2f out: chsng ldrs on outer over 1f out: wknd last 100yds* 13/2[3]

3015 6 2 **Adulation (IRE)**[32] 4603 2-8-12 88 GrahamGibbons 3 76
(William Haggas) *half rrd s: in rr: hdwy outer over 2f out: chsng ldrs on outer over 1f out: wknd last 100yds* 17/2

0112 7 *nse* **Shamrock Sheila (IRE)**[23] 4920 2-8-12 66 JoeyHaynes 5 72
(J S Moore) *trckd ldrs: upsides over 1f out: sn fdd* 100/1

1m 12.57s (-0.43) **Going Correction** -0.05s/f (Good) 7 Ran SP% **112.9**
Speed ratings: **100,99,98,95,93 90,90**
CSF £14.67 TOTE £3.70: £2.50, £3.20; EX 14.50 Trifecta £52.10.
**Owner** The Go 90 Partnership **Bred** Patrick Cummins **Trained** Musley Bank, N Yorks

**FOCUS**
This Listed race has produced its share of decent performers including last year's winner Supplicant, who next time out took the Group 2 Mill Reef Stakes. The time was 0.26secs slower than the preceding 3yo handicap.

## 5771 RIPON ROWELS H'CAP — 1m
4:45 (4:46) (Class 2) (0-100,97) 3-Y-£12,602 (£3,772; £1,886; £944; £470) **Stalls** Low

Form — RPR
2541 **1** **Bartack (IRE)**[9] 5446 4-9-6 91 ..........(v) DanielTudhope 4 100
(David O'Meara) *w ldr: led over 2f out: hld on gamely* **3/1**[1]
2225 **2** *1* **Bold Prediction (IRE)**[60] 3621 4-9-1 89 .......... JoeyHaynes(3) 9 96
(K R Burke) *anticipated s: racd wd: chsd ldng pair: 2nd over 1f out: styd on same pce* **12/1**
0601 **3** *nk* **Osteopathic Remedy (IRE)**[23] 4922 10-9-2 90 ..(t) ConnorBeasley(3) 10 96
(Michael Dods) *mid-div: effrt over 3f out: styd on same pce* **10/1**
1165 **4** *1* **King Torus (IRE)**[9] 5418 6-9-8 93 .......... JamesSullivan 2 97
(Ruth Carr) *mid-div: effrt over 3f out: kpt on same pce to take 4th jst ins fnl f* **8/1**
0020 **5** *1* **Ingleby Angel (IRE)**[16] 5163 5-9-12 97 .......... GrahamLee 7 99
(David O'Meara) *hld up in rr: effrt over 3f out: kpt on over 1f out: tk 5th clsng stages* **16/1**
223 **6** *1 1/2* **Multi Bene**[16] 5178 5-9-2 92 .......... KevinStott(5) 8 90
(Ed McMahon) *dwlt: swtchd rt after s: in rr: effrt over 3f out: kpt on same pce appr fnl f* **8/1**
3344 **7** *1/2* **Dubai Dynamo**[9] 5446 9-9-3 88 .......... PJMcDonald 11 85
(Ruth Carr) *dwlt: in rr: effrt over 3f out: kpt on fnl 2f: nvr a threat* **14/1**
2040 **8** *2 1/2* **Ifwecan**[9] 5410 3-9-3 94 .......... FrannyNorton 1 84
(Mark Johnston) *t.k.h: set str pce: hdd over 2f out: wknd fnl f* **6/1**[3]
0040 **9** *nk* **Norse Blues**[60] 3621 6-9-2 87 .......... GrahamGibbons 6 78
(David Barron) *hld up towards rr: effrt over 3f out: wknd fnl f* **20/1**
3-00 **10** *10* **Altharoos (IRE)**[9] 5446 4-9-1 86 .......... TonyHamilton 5 54
(Sally Hall) *chsd ldng trio: wknd over 2f out: bhd whn eased losing stages* **25/1**
6043 **P** **Mujazif (IRE)**[44] 4212 4-9-0 85 ..........(t) AdrianNicholls 3
(David Nicholls) *sn bhd: t.o 5f out: heavily eased over 3f out: p.u and dismntd ins fnl f* **5/1**[2]

1m 37.94s (-3.46) **Going Correction** -0.20s/f (Firm)
**WFA** 3 from 4yo+ 6lb — 11 Ran SP% **116.1**
Speed ratings (Par 109): **109,108,107,106,105 104,103,101,100,90**
CSF £40.24 CT £326.45 TOTE £3.10: £2.60, £4.00, £3.20; EX 33.10 Trifecta £297.80.
**Owner** Ebor Racing Club III **Bred** Alberto Panetta **Trained** Nawton, N Yorks

**FOCUS**
A typical renewal of this long established handicap, run at a strong pace.

## 5772 SIS LIVE MAIDEN STKS — 1m
5:20 (5:20) (Class 5) 3-4-Y-O £3,234 (£962; £481; £240) **Stalls** Low

Form — RPR
33U3 **1** **Lilly Junior**[16] 5198 3-9-0 70 .......... BenCurtis 3 74
(Brian Ellison) *mde all: drvn 3 l clr over 1f out: kpt on* **5/1**[3]
2322 **2** *1 1/2* **Hanno (USA)**[9] 5412 3-9-5 77 ..........(p) GrahamLee 6 76
(Ed Dunlop) *drvn to chse wnr: effrt over 3f out: hung rt: kpt on same pce fnl f* **2/1**[1]
4 **3** *1 3/4* **Kiss Of Spring (IRE)**[191] 626 3-9-0 0 .......... DanielTudhope 2 67
(David O'Meara) *trckd ldrs: effrt over 2f out: kpt on same pce* **7/1**
4 **4** *nse* **Tasmanian**[8] 5469 3-9-5 0 .......... FrannyNorton 1 73
(Mark Johnston) *dwlt: drvn along in rr: hdwy over 3f out: hmpd over 1f out: ducked rt ins fnl f: kpt on towards fin* **3/1**[2]
0 **5** *4* **Crysdal**[37] 4446 3-9-0 0 .......... TedDurcan 5 57
(David Lanigan) *dwlt: in rr: swtchd to outside and sme hdwy over 3f out: hmpd over 1f out: sn wknd* **5/1**[3]
5-24 **6** *1/2* **Iftikaar (IRE)**[23] 4924 4-9-11 67 .......... PJMcDonald 7 62
(Philip Kirby) *trckd ldrs: one pce whn edgd rt over 1f out: hmpd ins fnl f* **14/1**
**7** *35* **Royal Flush** 3-9-0 0 .......... JordanNason(5) 4
(Simon Waugh) *s.i.s: in rr: drvn over 4f out: bhd fnl 3f: t.o* **50/1**

1m 39.0s (-2.40) **Going Correction** -0.20s/f (Firm)
**WFA** 3 from 4yo 6lb — 7 Ran SP% **112.8**
Speed ratings (Par 103): **104,102,100,100,96 96,61**
CSF £15.02 TOTE £8.30: £3.10, £1.10; EX 12.10 Trifecta £67.20.
**Owner** Brian Ellison **Bred** Rabbah Bloodstock Limited **Trained** Norton, N Yorks

**FOCUS**
The experienced runners in this maiden set just a fair standard, but proved too good for the rest. The winner was making her debut for Brian Ellison having left William Haggas.

## 5773 BETFAIR NOVICE FLAT AMATEUR RIDERS' H'CAP (NOVICE AMATEUR RIDERS) — 1m 1f 170y
5:55 (5:56) (Class 6) (0-60,60) 4-Y-O+ £3,119 (£967; £483; £242) **Stalls** Low

Form — RPR
6000 **1** **Graceful Act**[11] 5337 6-10-11 50 .......... PhillipDennis 6 58
(Ron Barr) *hld up in mid-div: hdwy to chse ldrs over 3f out: led 1f out: drvn out* **14/1**
0055 **2** *3/4* **Rosy Ryan (IRE)**[11] 5337 4-10-7 46 oh1 .......... MissJWalton 1 52
(Tina Jackson) *trckd ldrs: led narrowly on inner 3f out: edgd lft and hdd 1f out: styd on same pce last 100yds* **11/1**
2044 **3** *2 1/2* **Flag Of Glory**[11] 5338 7-11-5 58 .......... MissMEdden 11 59
(Peter Hiatt) *sn chsng ldrs on outer: upsides over 3f out: styd on same pce fnl f* **9/1**
5406 **4** *nk* **Zainda (IRE)**[11] 5337 4-10-6 48 .......... MrAFrench(3) 7 48
(Paul Midgley) *led: hdd narrowly 3f out: kpt on same pce fnl f* **14/1**
0604 **5** *1* **Primary Route (IRE)**[10] 5374 4-11-4 60 .......... DylanMcDonagh(3) 4 58
(Jason Ward) *chsd ldrs: outpcd over 3f out: styd on same pce fnl 150yds* **22/1**
4533 **6** *shd* **Lil Sophella (IRE)**[13] 5291 5-11-1 57 .......... MrHMorshead(3) 9 55
(Patrick Holmes) *hld up in rr: hdwy on outer over 3f out: chsng ldrs 2f out: one pce* **4/1**[1]
66 **7** *4* **Kay Gee Be (IRE)**[21] 4958 10-10-8 50 ..........(p) MissGCochrane(3) 5 40
(Alan Berry) *in rr: kpt on fnl f: nvr on terms* **12/1**
-131 **8** *1 1/4* **Royal Caper**[39] 4341 4-11-5 58 .......... MissJoeyEllis 2 45
(Miss Joey Ellis) *in rr: hdwy on outer to chse ldrs over 2f out: wknd over 1f out* **4/1**[1]
0000 **9** *7* **Jewelled Dagger (IRE)**[10] 5371 10-10-4 46 oh1 .....(t) MissCWatling(3) 3 19
(Sharon Watt) *s.i.s: hdwy to chse ldrs after 2f: lost pl 4f out: sn bhd* **28/1**
-536 **10** *11* **Skyfire**[15] 5206 7-11-0 56 ..........(p) MrTPBroughton(3) 8 6
(Nick Kent) *sn chsng ldrs: lost pl over 2f out: sn bhd* **11/2**[2]
0016 **11** *1/2* **Silver Tigress**[18] 5084 6-10-9 51 .......... MissKMabon(3) 10
(Iain Jardine) *hdwy on outside to chse ldrs 7f out: lost pl over 2f out: sn bhd* **15/2**[3]

2m 6.75s (1.35) **Going Correction** -0.20s/f (Firm) — 11 Ran SP% **114.3**
Speed ratings (Par 101): **86,85,83,83,82 82,79,78,72,63 63**
CSF £154.59 CT £1462.96 TOTE £18.60: £3.90, £4.50, £3.00; EX 143.60 Trifecta £1028.10.
**Owner** D Thomson **Bred** Mayden Stud, J A And D S Dewhurst **Trained** Seamer, N Yorks

**FOCUS**
A moderate handicap, confined to novice amateur riders, run in a muddling/slow time.
T/Plt: £95.60 to a £1 stake. Pool: £56049.28 - 427.72 winning tickets T/Qpdt: £8.80 to a £1 stake. Pool: £3603.73 - 300.40 winning tickets WG

# 3933 WARWICK (L-H)
Monday, August 25

**OFFICIAL GOING: Good to soft changing to soft after race 1 (1.25)**
Wind: Light across Weather: Raining

## 5774 IRISH STALLION FARMS EBF FILLIES' MAIDEN STKS (BOBIS RACE) — 6f
1:25 (1:26) (Class 5) 2-Y-O £2,911 (£866; £432; £216) **Stalls** Low

Form — RPR
**1** **Terror (IRE)** 2-9-0 0 .......... SeanLevey 2 93+
(David Simcock) *chsd ldrs: led over 1f out: shkn up and c clr fnl f: easily* **5/1**[2]
23 **2** *10* **Robin Park**[8] 5464 2-9-0 0 .......... LukeMorris 9 62
(Clive Cox) *prom: chsd ldr over 4f out tl rdn over 1f out: sn outpcd* **6/1**[3]
2 **3** *1* **Quite Smart (IRE)**[18] 5104 2-9-0 0 .......... TedDurcan 6 59
(Robert Cowell) *chsd ldrs: rdn over 2f out: outpcd fr over 1f out* **3/1**[1]
**4** *1 1/4* **Shaw Ting** 2-9-0 0 .......... RichardKingscote 1 55+
(Tom Dascombe) *s.i.s: outpcd: r.o ins fnl f: nvr nrr* **16/1**
5 **5** *shd* **Torridonian**[32] 4583 2-9-0 0 .......... DaneO'Neill 4 55
(James Tate) *led: rdn and hdd over 1f out: wknd ins fnl f* **20/1**
6 **6** *2 3/4* **Mandria (IRE)**[20] 4999 2-8-11 0 .......... ThomasBrown(3) 10 47
(Daniel Kubler) *hld up: hdwy 2f out: rdn and wknd over 1f out* **50/1**
**7** *1* **Pilgrim** 2-9-0 0 .......... JohnFahy 5 44
(Eve Johnson Houghton) *in rr: pushed along 1/2-way: n.d* **12/1**
**8** *1/2* **Vixen Hill** 2-9-0 0 .......... JimmyQuinn 8 42
(Charles Hills) *s.i.s: hdwy over 4f out: wknd over 1f out* **9/1**
**9** *8* **Cherry Empress (IRE)** 2-9-0 0 .......... MartinDwyer 3 18
(Jo Hughes) *mid-div: sn pushed along: lost pl 1/2-way: sn bhd* **66/1**
**10** *1/2* **Classic Image** 2-9-0 0 .......... ChrisCatlin 7 17
(Rae Guest) *prom: pushed along 1/2-way: wknd over 1f out* **3/1**[1]
**11** *4* **Chester Bound** 2-9-0 0 .......... SamHitchcott 11 5
(Jo Hughes) *s.i.s: outpcd* **80/1**

1m 12.24s (0.44) **Going Correction** +0.25s/f (Good) — 11 Ran SP% **114.0**
Speed ratings (Par 91): **107,93,92,90,90 86,85,84,74,73 68**
CSF £33.06 TOTE £5.10: £2.00, £2.30, £1.30; EX 45.30 Trifecta £105.90.
**Owner** Qatar Racing Limited **Bred** Tally-Ho Stud **Trained** Newmarket, Suffolk

**FOCUS**
It was wet day for Warwick's final meeting on the Flat after around 300 years of racing. The course will be jumps-only now. The going was good to soft for an all sprint card and a realigned rail added 2.5 yards to official distances. A newcomer powered a long way clear in this maiden and the main form contenders finished placed.

## 5775 BREEDERS BACKING RACING EBF MAIDEN STKS — 6f
1:55 (1:58) (Class 5) 3-Y-O+ £3,881 (£1,155; £577; £288) **Stalls** Low

Form — RPR
**1** **Caffeine** 3-9-5 0 .......... SamHitchcott 4 86+
(William Muir) *chsd ldrs: led over 1f out: shkn up and r.o wl* **9/1**
25 **2** *4 1/2* **Debit**[76] 3083 3-9-5 0 .......... LukeMorris 10 72
(Clive Cox) *chsd ldrs: rdn over 1f out: styd on same pce fnl f* **5/2**[1]
6252 **3** *1 1/2* **Persian Bolt (USA)**[11] 5352 3-8-9 70 ..........(v[1]) GeorgeDowning(5) 5 62
(Eve Johnson Houghton) *led: rdn and hdd over 1f out: no ex ins fnl f* **7/2**[3]
**4** *1 3/4* **So Noble** 3-9-5 0 .......... MartinDwyer 2 62+
(William Muir) *sn pushed along in rr: r.o ins fnl f: nvr nrr* **10/3**[2]
55 **5** *nse* **Mon Cigar (IRE)**[14] 5249 3-9-5 0 .......... LiamJones 8 61
(Denis Coakley) *sed fr the wrong stall: mid-div: hdwy over 2f out: rdn and hung lft over 1f out: no ex fnl f* **16/1**
**6** *2 1/2* **Kings Chapel (USA)** 3-9-5 0 .......... RichardKingscote 1 53
(Jeremy Gask) *prom: rdn over 2f out: wknd over 1f out* **20/1**
2 **7** *4* **Our Grey Lady**[24] 4873 3-8-9 0 .......... RyanWhile(5) 7 36
(Bill Turner) *chsd ldrs: rdn: edgd rt and wknd over 1f out* **6/1**
6 **8** *3 1/2* **Kitty Bequick**[11] 5352 3-9-0 0 .......... JohnFahy 12 24
(Peter Hedger) *wnt rt s: sn pushed along in rr: wknd over 1f out* **100/1**
0 **9** *nse* **Picnic In The Glen**[16] 5181 3-9-0 0 .......... DaneO'Neill 9 24
(Sylvester Kirk) *a in rr: bhd fr 1/2-way* **66/1**
6 **10** *8* **Desperado Dancer**[13] 5272 3-9-5 0 .......... IrineuGoncalves 3 4
(Natalie Lloyd-Beavis) *prom: lost pl over 3f out: sn bhd* **100/1**

1m 13.27s (1.47) **Going Correction** +0.30s/f (Good) — 10 Ran SP% **112.3**
Speed ratings (Par 103): **102,96,94,91,91 88,82,78,78,67**
Flaming Star was withdrawn. Price at time of withdrawal 50/1. Rule 4 does not apply. CSF £30.20 TOTE £8.30: £2.80, £1.10, £2.60; EX 40.40 Trifecta £210.70.
**Owner** Muir Racing Partnership - Windsor **Bred** A J Coleing **Trained** Lambourn, Berks
■ Stewards' Enquiry : Liam Jones one-day ban: started from wrong stall (Sep 8)

**FOCUS**
A well-backed newcomer scored in good style in this maiden and the placed horses add substance for the form.

## 5776 HAPPY BIRTHDAY PENNY BLACKIE FILLIES' H'CAP — 6f
2:30 (2:30) (Class 4) (0-80,78) 3-Y-O+ £4,690 (£1,395; £697; £348) **Stalls** Low

Form — RPR
1640 **1** **Serenity Spa**[9] 5437 4-9-8 76 .......... SeanLevey 2 85
(Tony Carroll) *hld up in tch: shkn up to ld over 1f out: rdr dropped whip ins fnl f: pushed out* **5/1**
410 **2** *1 1/4* **Free Rein**[45] 4163 3-9-4 75 .......... RichardKingscote 3 80
(Ralph Beckett) *hld up: hdwy over 1f out: r.o to go 2nd wl ins fnl f: nt rch wnr* **9/2**[3]
1222 **3** *1 1/4* **Ginzan**[9] 5411 6-9-6 74 .......... DaneO'Neill 5 76
(Malcolm Saunders) *chsd ldrs: led wl over 1f out: sn rdn and hdd: styd on same pce ins fnl f* **3/1**[2]
0120 **4** *1 3/4* **Climaxfortackle (IRE)**[4] 5601 6-8-12 66 .......... DaleSwift 4 62
(Derek Shaw) *s.i.s: sn pushed along in rr: r.o ins fnl f: nt rch ldrs* **8/1**
4151 **5** *1 1/4* **Fever Few**[23] 4891 5-9-5 76 .......... AshleyMorgan(3) 6 69
(Chris Wall) *chsd ldrs: rdn over 2f out: wknd ins fnl f* **5/2**[1]

3566 **6** ½ **Queen Aggie (IRE)**[13] 5290 4-8-9 68 GeorgeDowning(5) 8 59
(Tony Carroll) *sn led: rdn and hdd wl over 1f out: wknd ins fnl f* **25/1**
4150 **7** 3 **Hannahs Turn**[28] 4741 4-9-5 78 MarcMonaghan(5) 1 60
(Chris Dwyer) *w ldr tl pushed along over 3f out: rdn over 1f out: wknd fnl f* **10/1**
1m 13.14s (1.34) **Going Correction** +0.35s/f (Good)
**WFA** 3 from 4yo+ 3lb **7** Ran SP% **112.5**
Speed ratings (Par 102): **105,103,101,99,97 97,93**
CSF £26.57 CT £77.58 TOTE £5.10: £2.40, £3.50; EX 28.10 Trifecta £97.30.
**Owner** Seasons Holidays **Bred** Barry Hurley **Trained** Cropthorne, Worcs
**FOCUS**
The pace was fair in this handicap and runners came over towards the stands' side. Sound form.

## 5777 CATHIE MATECKI'S DIAMOND JUBILEE H'CAP 6f
**3:05** (3:05) (Class 5) (0-70,69) 3-Y-O+ **£2,587** (£770; £384; £192) **Stalls** Low

Form RPR
2215 **1** **Mrs Warren**[34] 4515 4-9-10 69 MartinDwyer 1 78
(George Baker) *hld up: hdwy over 1f out: rdn to ld ins fnl f: r.o* **9/2**[2]
3140 **2** ¾ **Borough Boy (IRE)**[4] 5602 4-9-4 63 DaleSwift 7 70
(Derek Shaw) *hld up: hdwy 2f out: led over 1f out: rdn: edgd lft and hdd ins fnl f: styd on* **11/2**[3]
0461 **3** 2¼ **Divertimenti (IRE)**[13] 5287 10-8-5 53 (b) BillyCray(3) 10 53
(Roy Bowring) *s.i.s: sn rcvrd to chse ldr: rdn and ev ch over 1f out: styd on same pce fnl f* **12/1**
354 **4** 2¾ **Italian Tom (IRE)**[18] 5082 7-9-9 68 LukeMorris 5 59
(Ronald Harris) *prom: pushed along and lost pl over 3f out: rallied over 1f out: styd on same pce fnl f* **8/1**
2005 **5** 2 **Powerful Pierre**[10] 5392 7-9-3 67 (b) TobyAtkinson(5) 2 52
(Noel Quinlan) *sn pushed along in rr: r.o ins fnl f: nvr nrr* **33/1**
012 **6** 3 **Gracie's Games**[14] 5247 8-8-8 53 (v) LiamJones 4 28
(John Spearing) *sn pushed along in rr: hdwy 1/2-way: rdn and ev ch over 1f out: wknd fnl f* **3/1**[1]
5504 **7** ½ **Finflash (IRE)**[10] 5381 3-8-13 68 DanielCremin(7) 9 41
(Mick Channon) *prom: rdn over 1f out: wknd fnl f* **7/1**
000 **8** 1½ **Salvado (IRE)**[38] 4401 4-9-7 66 JimmyQuinn 3 35
(Tony Carroll) *prom tl rdn and wknd over 1f out* **10/1**
4216 **9** 1¼ **Goadby**[23] 4891 3-9-0 62 ChrisCatlin 6 27
(John Holt) *led: rdn and hdd over 1f out: wknd fnl f* **8/1**
1m 13.88s (2.08) **Going Correction** +0.40s/f (Good)
**WFA** 3 from 4yo+ 3lb **9** Ran SP% **113.0**
Speed ratings (Par 103): **102,101,98,94,91 87,87,85,83**
CSF £28.75 CT £275.89 TOTE £6.50: £2.00, £2.10, £3.30; EX 48.40 Trifecta £1109.50 Part won..
**Owner** Peter Russell **Bred** Freedom Farm Stud **Trained** Manton, Wilts
**FOCUS**
They finished fairly strung out in this handicap. The winner was back from a lesser effort to resume progress.

## 5778 PAULINE'S QUIRKY PERFORMING ARTS CUP CONDITIONS STKS 6f
**3:40** (3:40) (Class 3) 3-Y-O+ **£7,439** (£2,213; £1,106; £553) **Stalls** Low

Form RPR
3040 **1** **Complicate (AUS)**[37] 4438 5-9-0 105 DaneO'Neill 1 108
(Saeed bin Suroor) *trckd ldrs: rdn to ld ins fnl f: r.o* **11/4**[2]
1000 **2** 1¼ **Clear Spring (IRE)**[9] 5445 6-8-11 97 LiamJones 5 101
(John Spearing) *w ldr tl rdn to ld 2f out: edgd rt over 1f out: hdd and unable qck ins fnl f* **9/4**[1]
2000 **3** 4 **Rex Imperator**[23] 4895 5-8-11 105 JohnFahy 4 88
(William Haggas) *trckd ldrs: racd keenly: shkn up over 1f out: no ex fnl f* **9/4**[1]
0350 **4** 1 **Arnold Lane (IRE)**[23] 4895 5-9-5 98 SamHitchcott 7 93
(Mick Channon) *led: rdn and hdd 2f out: hmpd over 1f out: no ex fnl f* **7/2**[3]
1m 12.96s (1.16) **Going Correction** +0.45s/f (Yiel) **4** Ran SP% **110.4**
Speed ratings (Par 107): **110,108,103,101**
CSF £9.27 TOTE £3.90; EX 6.80 Trifecta £14.80.
**Owner** Godolphin **Bred** Darley **Trained** Newmarket, Suffolk
■ Stewards' Enquiry : Liam Jones caution: careless riding.
**FOCUS**
This conditions event was severely weakened by a few withdrawals but the winner is a smart performer when on song and scored in decent style from off the pace.

## 5779 CAROLINE'S VISION FOR CANCER NURSERY H'CAP 5f 110y
**4:15** (4:16) (Class 5) (0-75,74) 2-Y-O **£2,587** (£770; £384; £192) **Stalls** Low

Form RPR
3225 **1** **Amber Crystal**[3] 5620 2-9-3 70 (b[1]) MartinDwyer 4 73
(John Gallagher) *led: rdn over 1f out: hdd ins fnl f: rallied to ld again sn after: r.o* **7/1**
066 **2** ½ **Muzarkash**[17] 5128 2-9-0 67 DaneO'Neill 1 68
(B W Hills) *trckd ldrs: rdn over 1f out: led ins fnl f: sn hdd and unable qck* **9/4**[1]
2033 **3** 1¼ **Ar Colleen Aine**[17] 5129 2-8-7 67 DanielCremin(7) 6 64
(Mick Channon) *hld up in tch: rdn and ev ch over 1f out: styd on same pce ins fnl f* **5/1**[3]
001 **4** 1 **Pixeleen**[35] 4499 2-9-0 67 SeanLevey 2 61
(Malcolm Saunders) *hld up: rdn over 2f out: hdwy over 1f out: no ex ins fnl f* **3/1**[2]
6323 **5** 2¼ **Midnight Destiny (IRE)**[10] 5384 2-7-13 59 ow1 (v[1]) AdamMcLean(7) 8 45
(Derek Shaw) *s.i.s: hld up: effrt over 1f out: no ex ins fnl f* **11/1**
166 **6** 13 **Zebs Lad (IRE)**[25] 4815 2-9-7 74 LukeMorris 5 17
(Ronald Harris) *chsd wnr: rdn 1/2-way: wknd over 1f out* **5/1**[3]
1m 9.82s (3.92) **Going Correction** +0.50s/f (Yiel) **6** Ran SP% **109.9**
Speed ratings (Par 94): **93,92,90,89,86 69**
CSF £22.17 CT £79.28 TOTE £7.20: £3.60, £2.10; EX 23.50 Trifecta £120.40.
**Owner** R Biggs **Bred** R Biggs **Trained** Chastleton, Oxon
**FOCUS**
They went a decent pace in this nursery and the winner battled bravely to score under a positive ride.

## 5780 LEAMINGTON FOOD & DRINK FESTIVAL H'CAP 5f
**4:50** (4:51) (Class 6) (0-60,58) 3-Y-O+ **£1,940** (£577; £288; £144) **Stalls** Low

Form RPR
006 **1** **Louis Vee (IRE)**[52] 3939 6-9-2 53 (t) LukeMorris 8 60
(Roy Brotherton) *chsd ldrs: rdn to ld and hung lft fr over 1f out: all out* **7/2**[2]
1045 **2** shd **College Doll**[10] 5399 5-8-13 50 (t) JimmyQuinn 4 56
(Christine Dunnett) *chsd ldrs: rdn and ev ch fnl f: r.o* **4/1**[3]

6544 **3** 3 **Baby Queen (IRE)**[10] 5399 8-9-2 56 NeilFarley(3) 5 51
(Brian Baugh) *w ldr: rdn and ev ch over 1f out: no ex ins fnl f* **10/3**[1]
05 **4** 2¼ **Little Briar Rose**[52] 3939 3-8-12 51 LiamJones 7 38
(John Spearing) *led: rdn and hdd over 1f out: wknd ins fnl f* **7/2**[2]
6050 **5** 10 **Give Us A Belle (IRE)**[12] 5316 5-8-8 50 (vt) EoinWalsh(5) 6
(Christine Dunnett) *s.i.s: rdn 1/2-way: sn wknd* **4/1**[3]
1m 1.94s (2.34) **Going Correction** +0.55s/f (Yiel)
**WFA** 3 from 4yo+ 2lb **5** Ran SP% **107.5**
Speed ratings (Par 101): **103,102,98,94,78**
CSF £16.37 TOTE £3.20: £1.40, £2.90; EX 9.20 Trifecta £32.50.
**Owner** Mrs P A Wallis & M A Geobey **Bred** Rev James Browne **Trained** Elmley Castle, Worcs
**FOCUS**
This was the final Flat race at this track and there was an exciting finish between two runners who pulled clear. The first two's previous best figures came on the AW, so weak form.
T/Plt: £137.70 to a £1 stake. Pool of £42862.35 - 227.22 winning tickets. T/Qpdt: £101.20 to a £1 stake. Pool of £1792.19 - 13.10 winning tickets. CR

# 5483 DEL MAR (L-H)
Monday, August 25

**OFFICIAL GOING: Polytrack: fast**

## 5781a TVG PACIFIC CLASSIC STKS (GRADE 1) (3YO+) (POLYTRACK) 1m 2f
**1:46** (12:00) 3-Y-O+
**£361,445** (£120,481; £72,289; £36,144; £12,048; £150)

RPR
**1** **Shared Belief (USA)**[50] 3-8-6 0 MESmith 10 123+
(Jerry Hollendorfer, U.S.A) *settled in midfield on outer: gd hdwy 3f out: cl 3rd on outer 2f out: led 1 1/2f out: cut ins and sltly hmpd runner-up under 1 1/2f out: drvn clr fnl f: readily* **6/5**[1]
**2** 2¾ **Toast Of New York (USA)**[51] 3994 3-8-6 0 VictorEspinoza 7 116
(Jamie Osborne) *prom in main gp bhd two clr ldrs: pushed along to chse clr ldr over 3f out: rdn 2f out and sltly hmpd whn wnr cut ins under 1 1/2f out: r.o fnl f: no ch w wnr* **8/1**
**3** 2¼ **Imperative (USA)**[29] 4-8-12 0 (b) KDesormeaux 2 109
(George Papaprodromou, U.S.A) *in rr and wl off the pce: gd heaxdway over 2f out: styd on wl fnl f: nrest at fin* **38/1**
**4** nk **Game On Dude (USA)**[57] 3777 7-8-12 0 (b) MartinAGarcia 4 108+
(Bob Baffert, U.S.A) *led narrowly on rail: kicked 5 l clr 4f out: pressed appr 2f out: hdd over 1 1/2f out: briefly rallied: wknd fnl f* **5/2**[2]
**5** ½ **Irish Surf (USA)**[30] 4-8-12 0 (b) ElvisTrujillo 1 107
(Dan L Hendricks, U.S.A) *hdd main gp bhd two clr ldrs: outpcd over 3f out: kpt on at one pce fr 1 1/2f out* **153/10**
**6** 3¾ **Majestic Harbor (USA)**[57] 3777 6-8-12 0 TBaze 6 100
(Sean McCarthy, U.S.A) *midfield on inner: rdn and nt qckn 2f out: kpt on at same pce fnl f* **67/10**[3]
**7** 5½ **Ice Cream Truck (USA)**[30] 4-8-12 0 (b) TJPereira 3 89
(A C Avila, U.S.A) *hld up towards rr: rdn and effrt over 1 1/2f out: sn btn: nvr in contention* **88/1**
**8** 4¼ **You Know I Know (USA)**[29] 5-8-12 0 (b) EMaldonado 5 80
(John W Sadler, U.S.A) *towards rr: rdn and brief effrt 2f out: sn wknd* **29/1**
**9** 23 **Mystery Train (ARG)**[86] 4-8-12 0 FHPerez 9 34
(Darrell Vienna, U.S.A) *pressed ldr on outer: outpcd over 4f out: wknd qckly: t.o* **25/1**
**10** 9½ **Clubhouse Ride (USA)**[57] 3777 6-8-12 0 (b) JTalamo 8 15
(Craig A Lewis, U.S.A) *a towards rr: rdn and no imp fr 3f out: eased fnl f: t.o* **20/1**
2m 0.28s (120.28)
**WFA** 3 from 4yo+ 8lb **10** Ran SP% **119.9**
PARI-MUTUEL (all including 2 usd stake): WIN 4.40; PLACE (1-2) 3.20, 5.20; SHOW (1-2-3) 2.80, 4.60, 8.40; DF 21.60; SF 27.40.
**Owner** Jungle Racing Llc, KMN Racing Llc Et Al **Bred** Pam & Martin Wygod **Trained** USA
**FOCUS**
3yos finished first and second for the first time in the race's history.

# 5752 EPSOM (L-H)
Tuesday, August 26

**OFFICIAL GOING: Soft (heavy in places; 6.3)**
Wind: light, behind Weather: morning rain slowly clearing

## 5782 ROSEBERY MANOR NURSERY H'CAP 7f
**2:15** (2:15) (Class 5) (0-75,75) 2-Y-O **£4,528** (£1,347; £673; £336) **Stalls** Low

Form RPR
14 **1** **Jumeirah Glory (IRE)**[60] 3649 2-9-3 74 GeorgeChaloner(3) 2 78
(Richard Fahey) *chsd ldrs: rdn to ld ent fnl 2f: clr 1f out: tiring cl home but a holding on* **7/2**[2]
0353 **2** ½ **Outback Ruler (IRE)**[23] 4944 2-9-0 71 RyanTate(3) 7 74
(Clive Cox) *stdd after s: hld up in rr and struggling to handle downhill run: hdwy over 2f out: rdn to chse wnr over 1f out: no imp tl clsd on wnr fnl 50yds: nvr quite getting to wnr* **9/2**[3]
503 **3** 2¼ **Kifaaya**[17] 5167 2-9-3 71 DaneO'Neill 8 69
(Mark Johnston) *dwlt: in tch: dropped to rr and rdn over 3f out: detached and looked wl hld 3f out: rallied u.p over 1f out: wnt 3rd fnl 150yds: styd on* **11/4**[1]
51 **4** 2¾ **Mecado (IRE)**[18] 5120 2-9-2 70 SeanLevey 4 60
(Richard Hannon) *in tch: swtchd lft and effrt ent fnl 2f: wnt 3rd briefly 1f out: no ex: 4th and wl hld fnl 150yds* **7/1**
010 **5** 1½ **Guiding Light (IRE)**[24] 4897 2-9-7 75 JimmyFortune 3 63
(Andrew Balding) *broke fast: led: rdn over 2f out: sn hdd: no ex and btn over 1f out: wknd ins fnl f* **9/2**[3]
603 **6** ¾ **Digital Rebellion (IRE)**[13] 5315 2-9-7 75 MartinLane 5 60
(Charlie Appleby) *chsd ldr: effrt and ev ch over 2f out tl ent fnl 2f: drvn and btn over 1f out: wknd ins fnl f* **6/1**
1m 29.49s (6.19) **Going Correction** +0.625s/f (Yiel) **6** Ran SP% **112.0**
Speed ratings (Par 94): **89,88,85,82,81 80**
CSF £19.19 CT £47.57 TOTE £4.60: £2.30, £2.30; EX 19.90 Trifecta £55.50.
**Owner** Sheikh Rashid Dalmook Al Maktoum **Bred** Robert Norton **Trained** Musley Bank, N Yorks

**FOCUS**
The card was decimated by non-runners as the ground turned soft with heavy places, but a fresh strip of ground had been opened up for the last mile, meaning the course was almost full width in the straight. A tight nursery to kick-off the card with only 5lb separating the six runners and the jockeys on the two leaders, Guiding Light and Digital Rebellion, were both keen to bag the stands rail in the straight. That looked a strange manoeuvre given that part of the track was heavily chewed up after yesterday's racing and the pair paid the price by finishing last and second-last respectively.

## 5783 BRITISH STALLION STUDS/TOTEPOOL EBF MAIDEN STKS — 1m 114y
**2:50** (2:50) (Class 5) 2-Y-O — **£3,881** (£1,155) **Stalls** Low

Form — RPR
54 **1** **Dance Of Fire**[24] 4896 2-9-5 0 ........ DavidProbert 1 78+
(Andrew Balding) *led: jnd and rdn over 2f out: hdd wl over 1f out: styd upsides ldrs: led again fnl 50yds: r.o* **1/2**[1]
35 **2** ½ **Here Now**[38] 4424 2-9-5 0 ........ MartinLane 3 77
(Charlie Appleby) *stdd in bhd rival after s: rdn and effrt to chal over 2f out: led wl over 1f out: hdd and no ex fnl 50yds* **6/4**[2]
1m 56.81s (10.71) **Going Correction** +0.625s/f (Yiel) — 2 Ran SP% **106.7**
Speed ratings (Par 94): **77,76**
TOTE £1.50.
**Owner** J C Smith **Bred** Littleton Stud **Trained** Kingsclere, Hants
**FOCUS**
Just a match, but they were racing from at least 2f out down the middle of the track and there was just half a length between them at the line. The winner is rated to have made minor improvement.

## 5784 JOHN AKEHURST H'CAP — 6f
**3:25** (3:25) (Class 3) (0-90,90) 3-Y-O+ — **£9,337** (£2,796; £1,398; £699; £349; £175) **Stalls** High

Form — RPR
4612 **1** **Arctic Feeling (IRE)**[19] 5081 6-8-11 82 ........ SammyJoBell(5) 6 92
(Richard Fahey) *stdd after s: hld up in last pair: gd hdwy to ld ent fnl 2f: r.o strly: readily* **5/2**[2]
6036 **2** 3¾ **Huntsmans Close**[24] 4892 4-9-7 87 ........ GeorgeBaker 11 86
(Roger Charlton) *chsd ldrs: hdwy to press wnr 2f out: rdn and no ex over 1f out: btn 1f out: wknd ins fnl f* **9/4**[1]
1000 **3** 2¼ **Hopes N Dreams (IRE)**[10] 5444 6-9-9 89 ........ (t) JimmyFortune 4 81
(Kevin Ryan) *in tch in midfield: effrt over 2f out: 3rd and outpcd over 1f out: no imp after* **7/1**
1602 **4** 4½ **Links Drive Lady**[18] 5152 6-9-8 88 ........ SebSanders 10 67
(Dean Ivory) *stdd s: hld up in last pair: effrt over 2f out: modest 4th and no prog over 1f out* **5/1**[3]
0000 **5** 1 **Prince Regal**[39] 4401 4-8-6 72 ........ MartinLane 9 48
(Timothy Jarvis) *led tl ent fnl 2f: sn lost pl and hmpd 2f out: wl btn over 1f out* **8/1**
1005 **6** 16 **Firmdecisions (IRE)**[25] 4866 4-9-1 81 ........ (v) WilliamTwiston-Davies 12 9
(Brett Johnson) *pressed ldr tl rdn and lost pl over 2f out: wl bhd fnl f: t.o* **8/1**
1m 12.02s (2.62) **Going Correction** +0.625s/f (Yiel)
**WFA** 3 from 4yo+ 3lb — 6 Ran SP% **110.7**
Speed ratings (Par 107): **107,102,99,93,91 70**
CSF £8.30 CT £30.28 TOTE £3.70: £1.60, £2.20; EX 8.80 Trifecta £43.40.
**Owner** Percy / Green Racing 2 **Bred** John McEnery **Trained** Musley Bank, N Yorks
**FOCUS**
Only six runners, but this looks very strong form for the grade with the second, third and fourth all bringing good quality recent handicap form into the race. On top of that, the winner posted a time around 2sec faster than the winner of the previous day's Class 5 6f contest, which was run before the worst of the afternoon's weather.

## 5785 TERRY MILLS H'CAP — 7f
**3:55** (3:55) (Class 4) (0-80,77) 3-Y-O+ — **£7,762** (£2,310; £1,154; £577) **Stalls** Low

Form — RPR
5433 **1** **Ixelles Diamond (IRE)**[24] 4912 3-8-9 68 ........ GeorgeChaloner(3) 2 80
(Richard Fahey) *chsd ldrs: clsd to ld and travelling strly wl over 1f out: rdn and qcknd clr over 1f out: r.o wl: readily* **3/1**[2]
1235 **2** 7 **Intomist (IRE)**[33] 4588 5-9-7 77 ........ (p) StephenCraine 8 68
(Jim Boyle) *w ldr: rdn and ev ch over 2f out: outpcd by wnr and btn over 1f out: hld on for 2nd fnl f* **10/1**
6035 **3** nse **Fiftyshadesofgrey (IRE)**[13] 5311 3-9-5 75 ........ PatCosgrave 5 69
(George Baker) *hld up in tch: rdn and hdwy 2f out: battling for 2nd but no ch w wnr fnl f: kpt on* **11/4**[1]
2463 **4** 1¾ **Great Expectations**[12] 5346 6-9-10 75 ........ (t) PaddyAspell 4 66
(J R Jenkins) *stdd s: hld up in last pair: clsd and n.m.r ent fnl 2f: rdn and no hdwy over 1f out* **6/1**[3]
0613 **5** ½ **Mister Musicmaster**[33] 4580 5-9-7 77 ........ CamHardie(5) 9 67
(Ron Hodges) *in tch in midfield: rdn over 2f out: no ch w wnr and kpt on same pce fr over 1f out* **7/1**
4122 **6** hd **Royal Connection**[26] 4813 3-9-2 72 ........ JimmyFortune 7 59
(Richard Hannon) *led: rdn ent fnl 2f: hdd wl over 1f out: sn outpcd and btn: wknd ins fnl f* **6/1**[3]
0000 **7** 2 **Brocklebank (IRE)**[40] 4355 5-9-10 75 ........ JimCrowley 6 59
(Simon Dow) *stdd s: hld up in rr: rdn over 2f out: no hdwy: wl bhd over 1f out* **6/1**[3]
1m 27.72s (4.42) **Going Correction** +0.80s/f (Soft)
**WFA** 3 from 4yo+ 5lb — 7 Ran SP% **116.1**
Speed ratings (Par 105): **106,98,97,95,95 95,92**
CSF £32.98 CT £91.44 TOTE £3.40: £2.60, £8.50; EX 38.00 Trifecta £206.10.
**Owner** Miss Louise Tillett **Bred** Lynn Lodge Stud **Trained** Musley Bank, N Yorks
**FOCUS**
An open-looking handicap on paper. The winner seemed much improved for first try on soft ground.

## 5786 CHANTILLY H'CAP (JOCKEY CLUB GRASSROOTS FLAT MIDDLE DISTANCE SERIES QUALIFIER) — 1m 4f 10y
**4:30** (4:31) (Class 5) (0-70,65) 3-Y-O+ — **£4,528** (£1,347; £673; £336) **Stalls** Centre

Form — RPR
0041 **1** **Last Echo (IRE)**[12] 5343 3-9-4 65 ........ SilvestreDeSousa 5 79+
(Ralph Beckett) *chsd ldr: effrt over 3f out: led over 2f out: sn clr and in n.d: heavily eased ins fnl f* **4/9**[1]
0232 **2** 7 **Corn Maiden**[33] 4591 5-9-11 62 ........ WilliamTwiston-Davies 7 55
(Phil McEntee) *racd in 3rd tl dropped to last and rdn over 3f out: no ch w wnr but plugged on to go 2nd ins fnl f* **7/1**[3]
-350 **3** 1½ **Tingo In The Tale (IRE)**[58] 3761 5-9-12 63 ........ HayleyTurner 3 54
(David Arbuthnot) *hld up in last: wnt 3rd and rdn over 3f out: no ch w wnr but plugged on to go 2nd 1f out tl ins fnl f* **5/1**[2]
0053 **4** 6 **Power Up**[13] 5300 3-8-11 58 ........ (b) DaneO'Neill 2 40
(Mark Johnston) *s.i.s: sn rcvrd to ld and clr after 2f: hdd and rdn over 2f out: sn btn: lost 2 pls fnl f* **7/1**[3]
2m 52.51s (13.61) **Going Correction** +0.80s/f (Soft)
**WFA** 3 from 4yo+ 10lb — 4 Ran SP% **110.9**
Speed ratings (Par 103): **86,81,80,76**
CSF £4.29 TOTE £1.50; EX 4.10 Trifecta £8.90.
**Owner** R A Farmiloe & Partner **Bred** Ballylinch Stud **Trained** Kimpton, Hants
**FOCUS**
A very uncompetitive event, in which the well-backed favourite bolted up.

## 5787 JRA H'CAP — 1m 2f 18y
**5:05** (5:06) (Class 5) (0-75,73) 3-Y-O+ — **£4,528** (£1,347; £673; £336) **Stalls** Low

Form — RPR
0422 **1** **Coincidently**[10] 5413 4-10-0 73 ........ SilvestreDeSousa 2 86
(Alan Bailey) *chsd ldr: clsd 3f out: led over 1f out: sn pushed wl clr: eased towards fin* **11/8**[1]
434 **2** 12 **Megalala (IRE)**[11] 5383 13-9-4 63 ........ (v[1]) WilliamCarson 4 53
(John Bridger) *led: sn clr: rdn over 2f out: hdd over 1f out and sn btn* **9/2**
-033 **3** 21 **Pigeon Pie**[61] 3608 3-9-0 67 ........ DaneO'Neill 3 17
(Mark Johnston) *hld up in last: rdn over 5f out: no ch fnl 3f: wnt modest 3rd over 1f out: eased ins fnl f: t.o* **4/1**[3]
4312 **4** 24 **Cherry Princess**[19] 5096 4-8-12 57 ........ SeanLevey 7
(Stuart Williams) *racd in 3rd: rdn over 3f out: sn wl: dropped to last over 1f out: eased fnl f: t.o* **2/1**[2]
2m 16.65s (6.95) **Going Correction** +0.80s/f (Soft)
**WFA** 3 from 4yo+ 8lb — 4 Ran SP% **113.6**
Speed ratings (Par 103): **104,94,77,58**
CSF £8.03 TOTE £2.40; EX 6.80 Trifecta £16.20.
**Owner** Tom Mohan & Allan McNamee **Bred** Langton Stud **Trained** Newmarket, Suffolk
**FOCUS**
Just four runners and they finished strung out like 3m chasers, with the last two not handling the ground, so not form to pay too much attention to.
T/Plt: £85.10 to a £1 stake. Pool of £57011.25 - 488.77 winning tickets. T/Qpdt: £18.00 to a £1 stake. Pool of £4560.45 - 187.47 winning tickets. SP

# 5767 RIPON (R-H)
### Tuesday, August 26
**OFFICIAL GOING: Good to firm (good in places; 8.2)**
Wind: light 1/2 against Weather: fine

## 5788 AT THE RACES ON FACEBOOK (S) STKS — 1m 1f 170y
**2:00** (2:00) (Class 6) 3-4-Y-O — **£2,726** (£805; £402) **Stalls** Low

Form — RPR
5021 **1** **Mixed Message (IRE)**[27] 4792 4-9-7 67 ........ DaleSwift 3 69
(Brian Ellison) *chsd ldrs: styd on to ld ins fnl f: forged clr* **9/4**[2]
-600 **2** 1 **Aneedh**[10] 4710 4-9-12 68 ........ (b[1]) RussKennemore 6 72
(Jedd O'Keeffe) *hld up in rr: t.k.h: hdwy on ins over 2f out: nt clr run and swtchd ins fnl f: tk 2nd in clsng stages* **8/1**
1305 **3** 1¼ **Zaitsev (IRE)**[13] 5295 4-9-12 74 ........ [1] RobertWinston 7 69
(Ollie Pears) *led: t.k.h: hung lft and wknd ins fnl f* **15/8**[1]
/010 **4** 1¾ **Aseela (IRE)**[10] 5448 4-9-0 57 ........ KieranSchofield(7) 2 61
(George Moore) *s.i.s: hld up in rr: hdwy over 2f out: kpt on fnl f* **20/1**
-005 **5** 1¼ **Greeleys Love (USA)**[14] 5267 4-9-12 72 ........ (v) JoeFanning 4 63
(Mark Johnston) *trckd ldrs: 2nd 4f out: fnd little and wknd ins fnl f* **7/2**[3]
0004 **6** 6 **Hello Sweetness**[17] 5198 3-8-4 45 ........ JoeyHaynes(3) 5 40
(Jason Ward) *s.i.s: hdwy over 3f out: wknd over 1f out* **50/1**
0-60 **7** 20 **Rocked The Boat**[8] 5495 3-8-9 63 ........ SamJames(3) 8 4
(David O'Meara) *chsd ldrs: lost pl over 3f out: sn bhd: eased fnl f: t.o* **25/1**
2m 3.25s (-2.15) **Going Correction** -0.225s/f (Firm)
**WFA** 3 from 4yo 8lb — 7 Ran SP% **109.5**
Speed ratings (Par 101): **99,98,97,95,94 90,74**
CSF £17.89 TOTE £3.50: £1.40, £4.80; EX 20.80 Trifecta £48.20.There was no bid for the winner.
**Owner** W I Bloomfield **Bred** J Costello **Trained** Norton, N Yorks
**FOCUS**
A modest seller. The favourite disappointed having set the pace.

## 5789 AT THE RACES SKY 415 MAIDEN FILLIES' STKS (BOBIS RACE) — 5f
**2:30** (2:35) (Class 5) 2-Y-O — **£3,234** (£962; £481; £240) **Stalls** High

Form — RPR
**1** **Zebelini (IRE)** 2-9-0 0 ........ LemosdeSouza 13 68+
(Mrs Ilka Gansera-Leveque) *mde virtually all: kpt on wl in clsng stages* **40/1**
4250 **2** nk **Zuzinia (IRE)**[19] 5091 2-9-0 67 ........ JoeFanning 4 67
(Mick Channon) *in tch: hdwy over 2f out: chsd wnr over 1f out: no ex in clsng stages* **9/1**[3]
43 **3** 2 **Pacngo**[24] 4919 2-9-0 0 ........ DuranFentiman 1 60
(Tim Easterby) *wnt rt s: chsd ldrs: kpt on same pce fnl f* **10/1**
204 **4** 1¼ **Stinky Socks (IRE)**[22] 4965 2-9-0 68 ........ TomQueally 12 55
(Charles Hills) *wnt lft s: w wnr: nt qckn fnl f* **5/1**[1]
**5** ½ **Granola** 2-9-0 0 ........ GrahamLee 8 54+
(David Brown) *s.i.s: hdwy 2f out: kpt on* **10/1**
60 **6** nk **Ya Halla (IRE)**[24] 4919 2-8-7 0 ........ AhmadAlSubousi(7) 10 52
(Robert Cowell) *chsd ldrs: wknd over 1f out* **66/1**
0 **7** 1½ **Lydiate Lady**[22] 4973 2-9-0 0 ........ RaulDaSilva 9 47+
(Paul Green) *in rr: hdwy over 2f out: nvr nr ldrs* **200/1**
**8** hd **U Think Ur Funny (IRE)** 2-9-0 0 ........ [1] BarryMcHugh 5 46+
(Tony Coyle) *s.i.s: hdwy over 2f out: wknd over 1f out* **66/1**
**9** 1¾ **Mary's Secret** 2-9-0 0 ........ RichardKingscote 11 40
(Tom Dascombe) *chsd ldrs: lost pl over 1f out* **8/1**[2]
05 **10** 2 **My Girl Jo (FR)**[22] 4973 2-9-0 0 ........ DanielTudhope 3 33
(David O'Meara) *a in rr* **20/1**
6 **11** nk **Rubheira**[20] 5042 2-8-9 0 ........ RyanWhile(5) 7 32
(Hugo Froud) *chsd ldrs: hmpd over 2f out: sn wknd* **100/1**
1m 0.5s (0.50) **Going Correction** +0.075s/f (Good) — 11 Ran SP% **67.6**
Speed ratings (Par 91): **99,98,95,93,92 92,89,89,86,83 82**
CSF £104.64 TOTE £42.30: £10.70, £1.30, £1.90; EX 199.60 Trifecta £1114.00 Part won. Pool of £1485.34 - 0.41 winning units..
**Owner** Lamont Racing **Bred** John McEnery **Trained** Newmarket, Suffolk
■ Grand Beauty was withdrawn. Price at time of withdrawal 5/6F. Rule 4 applies to all bets - deduct 50p in the pound.

**FOCUS**
A maiden that lost much of its interest when the odds-on favourite Grand Beauty refused to go into the stalls. The winner took this with a bit in hand, overcoming a lack of experience.

## 5790 AT THE RACES VIRGIN 534 NURSERY H'CAP (BOBIS RACE) 6f
**3:05** (3:05) (Class 4) (0-85,78) 2-Y-O **£3,881** (£1,155; £577; £288) **Stalls** High

Form RPR
065 **1** **Pumaflor (IRE)**[18] 5128 2-8-6 63 JasonHart 6 64
(Richard Guest) *trckd ldrs: carried rt over 1f out: styd on to ld in clsng stages* **9/1**
2260 **2** ¾ **Midlander (IRE)**[34] 4529 2-9-7 78 JoeFanning 1 77
(Mark Johnston) *carried rt s: chsd ldrs: led over 1f out: hdd and no ex in clsng stages* **9/2[3]**
1530 **3** *nk* **Firgrove Bridge (IRE)**[45] 4218 2-9-1 77 KevinStott(5) 5 75
(Kevin Ryan) *chsd ldrs: nt clr run and swtchd rt over 1f out: kpt on same pce last 100yds* **14/1**
404 **4** 3 ½ **Little Belter (IRE)**[54] 3881 2-9-1 72 RichardKingscote 7 60
(Tom Dascombe) *hld up in rr: hdwy whn nt clr run over 2f out: kpt on fnl f* **11/4[1]**
6114 **5** ½ **Rise Up Lotus (IRE)**[25] 4869 2-9-6 77 PaulHanagan 3 63
(Charles Hills) *chsd ldrs: led 2f out: hung lft and sn hdd: kpt on same pce* **7/2[2]**
5214 **6** 2 ¼ **Ventura Shadow**[31] 4686 2-9-1 72 TonyHamilton 2 51
(Richard Fahey) *wnt rt s: hld up: hdwy over 2f out: carried rt over 1f out: wknd fnl f* **7/1**
1 **7** 2 ½ **Youcouldntmakeitup (IRE)**[12] 5332 2-9-5 76 DuranFentiman 4 48
(Tim Easterby) *led: hdd 2f out: wknd over 1f out* **5/1**

1m 13.93s (0.93) **Going Correction** +0.075s/f (Good) **7 Ran SP% 112.9**
Speed ratings (Par 96): **96,95,94,89,89 86,82**
CSF £47.42 TOTE £14.00: £7.00, £2.80; EX 62.10 Trifecta £697.50.
**Owner** Resdev **Bred** Kevin Hannon **Trained** Ingmanthorpe, W Yorks
■ Stewards' Enquiry : Kevin Stott two-day ban: careless riding (Sep 9-10)

**FOCUS**
A small field, but an interesting nursery nonetheless. The pace seemed solid enough and the winner came from the rear.

## 5791 21 ENGINEER REGIMENT SAPPER CONDITIONS STKS (BOBIS RACE) 5f
**3:40** (3:40) (Class 3) 2-Y-O **£6,301** (£1,886; £943; £472; £235) **Stalls** High

Form RPR
0221 **1** **Miss Mullberry**[24] 4920 2-8-6 77 SamJames(3) 2 85+
(David O'Meara) *wnt rt s: sn chsng ldrs: led over 1f out: styd on wl* **3/1[3]**
1431 **2** 1 ¾ **Snap Shots (IRE)**[33] 4566 2-9-3 95 JennyPowell(5) 5 90
(Tom Dascombe) *s.i.s: sn chsng ldrs: effrt over 2f out: n.m.r over 1f out: tk 2nd ins fnl f: no imp* **5/2[2]**
5142 **3** 1 **Zeb Un Nisa**[33] 4566 2-8-10 88 JoeyHaynes(3) 1 77
(Roger Charlton) *carried rt s: trckd ldrs: t.k.h: kpt on same pce fnl f* **6/4[1]**
1505 **4** *nk* **Diamond Creek (IRE)**[24] 4920 2-8-12 80 JackGarritty(5) 3 80
(Richard Fahey) *wnt rt s: chsd ldrs: kpt on same pce fnl f* **8/1**
0210 **5** 1 ¼ **Magic Florence (IRE)**[11] 5380 2-8-10 68 ConnorBeasley(3) 4 72
(James Given) *led: hdd over 1f out: sn wknd* **25/1**

1m 0.4s (0.40) **Going Correction** +0.075s/f (Good) **5 Ran SP% 108.5**
Speed ratings (Par 98): **99,96,94,94,92**
CSF £10.50 TOTE £2.40: £1.20, £1.10; EX 8.70 Trifecta £12.40.
**Owner** MiddlehamParkRacingXXXVII,CTasker&P'tner **Bred** Dachel Stud **Trained** Nawton, N Yorks

**FOCUS**
Some sharp juveniles on show in a race run at a good pace. The winner is thriving and her latest run had already worked out nicely.

## 5792 ATTHERACES.COM CITY OF RIPON STKS (H'CAP) 1m 1f 170y
**4:15** (4:15) (Class 3) (0-90,88) 3-Y-O+ **£7,561** (£2,263; £1,131; £566; £282) **Stalls** Low

Form RPR
360 **1** **Stormardal (IRE)**[25] 4855 3-9-4 86 DanielTudhope 6 96
(Ismail Mohammed) *trckd ldrs: led over 2f out: drvn out* **7/1[3]**
4112 **2** ½ **Woodacre**[13] 5299 7-9-1 78 ConnorBeasley(3) 5 87
(Richard Whitaker) *trckd ldrs: 2nd 2f out: kpt on wl ins fnl f* **11/4[2]**
1656 **3** 2 **San Cassiano (IRE)**[15] 5238 7-10-0 88 JamesSullivan 3 93
(Ruth Carr) *led: hdd over 2f out: rallied and kpt on same pce* **15/2**
5602 **4** ¾ **Las Verglas Star (IRE)**[15] 5238 6-9-4 83 JackGarritty(5) 7 86
(Richard Fahey) *s.i.s: hdwy over 3f out: chsng ldrs over 2f out: kpt on one pce* **7/1[3]**
102- **5** 2 **Ambleside**[363] 5888 4-9-6 80 PaulMulrennan 4 79
(Michael Easterby) *in rr-div: hdwy 4f out: kpt on steadily fnl 2f: carried hd high: swtchd lft ins fnl f* **12/1**
2336 **6** 4 **Artful Prince**[16] 5203 4-9-2 76 (b) GrahamLee 11 67
(James Given) *mid-div: drvn over 6f out: kpt on over 1f out: nvr a threat* **10/1**
2302 **7** 4 **Master Of Finance (IRE)**[17] 5188 3-9-6 88 JoeFanning 9 71
(Mark Johnston) *sn chsng ldrs on outer: lost pl over 1f out* **9/4[1]**
14-0 **8** 16 **Northern Star (IRE)**[136] 1439 4-9-8 82 BenCurtis 8 32
(John Mackie) *hld up in rr: drvn 4f out: sn lost pl and bhd: t.o* **40/1**

2m 1.35s (-4.05) **Going Correction** -0.225s/f (Firm)
**WFA** 3 from 4yo+ 8lb **8 Ran SP% 113.4**
Speed ratings (Par 107): **107,106,105,104,102 99,96,83**
CSF £26.16 CT £148.48 TOTE £7.10: £2.80, £1.30, £2.60; EX 30.50 Trifecta £194.80.
**Owner** Sheikh Juma Dalmook Al Maktoum **Bred** Kevin & Meta Cullen **Trained** Newmarket, Suffolk

**FOCUS**
The feature handicap on the card, but five non-runners made for a less-competitive renewal than expected. The winner had been given a chance by the handicapper.

## 5793 MICHAEL RABY MEMORIAL H'CAP 1m
**4:50** (4:50) (Class 5) (0-75,74) 3-Y-O+ **£4,204** (£1,251; £625; £312) **Stalls** Low

Form RPR
3240 **1** **Janaab (IRE)**[19] 5077 4-9-0 62 (t) PhillipMakin 9 71
(Tim Easterby) *led after 1f: mde rest: edgd lft over 1f out: hld on towards fin* **9/1**
6025 **2** 1 ½ **Charles De Mille**[18] 5127 6-8-10 58 AndrewMullen 6 64
(George Moore) *chsd ldrs: hung rt over 2f out: swtchd rt and styd on same pce ins fnl f* **20/1**
6166 **3** ¾ **Thankyou Very Much**[19] 5079 4-9-5 67 (p) JoeFanning 5 71
(James Bethell) *prom: effrt over 2f out: styd on same pce fnl f* **7/2[1]**
0305 **4** ½ **Fazza**[20] 5054 7-9-7 74 KevinStott(5) 8 77
(Edwin Tuer) *in rr: hdwy over 2f out: kpt on fnl f* **5/1[3]**
3256 **5** ½ **Running Reef (IRE)**[14] 5269 5-8-13 61 RobertWinston 1 63
(Tracy Waggott) *hld up in rr: hdwy over 2f out: styd on wl fnl f* **11/2**
1600 **6** ½ **Space War**[18] 5142 7-8-10 65 AnnaHesketh(7) 2 65
(Michael Easterby) *hld up in mid-div: effrt over 2f out: kpt on one pce* **20/1**
3301 **7** *nk* **Ewell Place (IRE)**[17] 5166 5-9-1 68 (p) JackGarritty(5) 7 68
(Richard Fahey) *chsd ldrs: edgd lft over 1f out: one pce* **9/2[2]**
6443 **8** 7 **Al Muheer (IRE)**[13] 5295 9-9-9 71 (e) JamesSullivan 3 55
(Ruth Carr) *chsd ldrs: rdn over 3f out: lost pl 2f out* **7/2[1]**
0306 **9** 5 **Lady Liz**[17] 5195 3-7-12 55 oh6 RosieJessop(3) 11 26
(George Moore) *in rr: bhd fnl 4f* **50/1**

1m 38.6s (-2.80) **Going Correction** -0.225s/f (Firm)
**WFA** 3 from 4yo+ 6lb **9 Ran SP% 116.2**
Speed ratings (Par 103): **105,103,102,102,101 101,100,93,88**
CSF £168.23 CT £756.64 TOTE £12.40: £2.40, £6.90, £1.10; EX 143.80 Trifecta £1396.90.
**Owner** Numac Engineering Ltd **Bred** Ballylinch Stud **Trained** Great Habton, N Yorks

**FOCUS**
Another handicap weakened by non-runners, but a good effort from the winner who pretty much made all and broke his Flat duck at the 15th attempt.

## 5794 VISIT ATTHERACES.COM/MOBILE STAYERS H'CAP 2m
**5:20** (5:20) (Class 6) (0-65,65) 3-Y-O+ **£3,234** (£962; £481; £240) **Stalls** High

Form RPR
0-44 **1** **Kodicil (IRE)**[9] 5466 6-10-0 65 (p) JasonHart 8 74
(Mark Walford) *trckd ldr: led over 2f out: hld on towards fin* **4/1[2]**
262 **2** ½ **Mighty Missile (IRE)**[10] 5449 3-8-11 62 JamesSullivan 7 70
(Tom Tate) *in rr-div: hung bdly lft over 10f out: drvn 6f out: chsng ldrs over 3f out: ev ch over 1f out: no ex in clsng stages* **5/4[1]**
5035 **3** 14 **Rokeby**[8] 5495 3-8-0 51 oh3 AndrewMullen 1 43
(George Moore) *in rr: hdwy 9f out: drvn 4f out: one pce fnl 2f* **7/1**
5030 **4** 11 **Cowslip**[17] 5200 5-8-7 51 KieranSchofield(7) 5 29
(George Moore) *hld up in rr: drvn over 6f out: tk poor 4th 1f out* **8/1**
4006 **5** 27 **Dubara Reef (IRE)**[37] 4474 7-8-4 46 JordanNason(5) 6
(Paul Green) *drvn to ld: hdd over 2f out: bhd and eased fnl f* **12/1**
2532 **6** 1 ½ **Anne's Valentino**[15] 5240 4-9-4 55 TomEaves 2
(Malcolm Jefferson) *chsd ldrs: hung lft and lost pl over 3f out: sn bhd* **11/2[3]**

3m 30.85s (-0.95) **Going Correction** -0.225s/f (Firm)
**WFA** 3 from 4yo+ 14lb **6 Ran SP% 111.1**
Speed ratings (Par 101): **93,92,85,80,66 66**
CSF £9.26 CT £30.29 TOTE £8.20: £3.00, £1.30; EX 12.00 Trifecta £61.90.
**Owner** The Elephant Group **Bred** Tally-Ho Stud **Trained** Sherriff Hutton, N Yorks
■ Stewards' Enquiry : James Sullivan two-day ban: used whip above permitted level (Sep 9-10)

**FOCUS**
A low-grade staying event to conclude the card with the winner taking the race for the second year in succession. The runner-up may not be straightforward.
T/Plt: £1,199.10 to a £1 stake. Pool of £70635.84 - 43.00 winning tickets. T/Qpdt: £91.40 to a £1 stake. Pool of £8317.75 - 67.32 winning tickets. WG

# 5600 WOLVERHAMPTON (A.W) (L-H)
Tuesday, August 26

**OFFICIAL GOING: Tapeta: standard**
No speed figures will be produced until revised median times for the new Tapeta surface can be calculated.
Wind: Fresh against Weather: Overcast

## 5795 32RED CASINO APPRENTICE H'CAP (TAPETA) 1m 141y
**6:20** (6:20) (Class 5) (0-75,75) 3-Y-O **£3,234** (£962; £481; £240) **Stalls** Low

Form RPR
1-64 **1** **Dutch Rifle**[19] 5100 3-9-7 75 KieranShoemark(5) 2 85
(James Tate) *chsd ldrs: rdn over 2f out: styd on to ld wl ins fnl f: hung rt nr fin* **7/2[2]**
2006 **2** 1 ¼ **Solo Hunter**[11] 5378 3-9-8 71 (v) NoelGarbutt 4 78
(David Evans) *chsd ldr: rdn over 2f out: led over 1f out: hdd and unable qck wl ins fnl f* **14/1**
1344 **3** *shd* **Allergic Reaction (IRE)**[23] 4942 3-8-8 62 CallumShepherd(5) 5 69
(William Knight) *a.p: rdn over 1f out: styd on* **5/1[3]**
01 **4** 1 **Hannington**[26] 4830 3-9-6 74 RobHornby(5) 8 78+
(Andrew Balding) *hld up: hdwy over 2f out: rdn and ev ch ins fnl f: styd on same pce* **8/1**
1245 **5** 1 ¾ **Derbyshire (IRE)**[10] 5420 3-9-5 68 (v[1]) ShaneGray 3 68
(Kevin Ryan) *led: clr 6f out: rdn and hdd over 1f out: no ex ins fnl f* **8/1**
-41F **6** ½ **Heska (IRE)**[19] 5108 3-9-2 68 (tp) AlistairRawlinson(3) 9 67
(Michael Appleby) *hld up: hdwy over 2f out: rdn over 1f out: edgd lft ins fnl f: styd on same pce* **5/2[1]**
-060 **7** 11 **Tancred (IRE)**[88] 2737 3-9-3 66 LouisSteward 10 40
(Michael Wigham) *hld up and bhd: pushed along over 3f out: nvr nr to chal* **6/1**
2306 **8** 15 **Dynamic Ranger (USA)**[40] 4356 3-9-4 72 HectorCrouch(5) 6 11
(Gary Moore) *mid-div: pushed along 1/2-way: wknd over 2f out* **16/1**
6000 **9** 4 **Quantum Dot (IRE)**[17] 5183 3-8-7 56 TimClark 1
(Lisa Williamson) *s.i.s: plld hrd and in tch: rdn over 3f out: sn wknd* **18/1**
0600 **10** 5 **Its Not Me Its You**[59] 3711 3-8-10 62 (v[1]) NedCurtis(3) 7
(Brendan Powell) *sn pushed along in rr: wknd 1/2-way* **33/1**

1m 49.61s (-0.49) **Going Correction** 0.0s/f (Stan) **10 Ran SP% 124.7**
Speed ratings (Par 100): **102,100,100,99,98 97,88,74,71,66**
CSF £55.78 CT £255.49 TOTE £5.80: £1.60, £3.20, £1.90; EX 64.60 Trifecta £358.40.
**Owner** Saeed Manana **Bred** Mr And Mrs R Newman **Trained** Newmarket, Suffolk

**FOCUS**
The fourth meeting on Tapeta with the going standard. They went a decent pace for this modest apprentice riders' handicap.

## 5796 STAY AT THE WOLVERHAMPTON HOLIDAY INN MAIDEN STKS (TAPETA) 1m 141y
**6:50** (6:53) (Class 5) 3-Y-O **£3,234** (£962; £481; £240) **Stalls** Low

Form RPR
6343 **1** **Venturous Spirit (IRE)**[21] 5008 3-9-0 71 WilliamBuick 1 77
(John Gosden) *led: rdn and hdd over 1f out: rallied and edgd rt ins fnl f: styd on to ld post* **3/1[2]**
4-3 **2** *nse* **Freemason**[12] 5347 3-9-5 0 RyanMoore 2 82
(Sir Michael Stoute) *trckd ldr: plld hrd: led over 1f out: rdn and edgd rt ins fnl f: hdd post* **6/5[1]**

0 **3** ¾ **Holiday Magic (IRE)**[47] 4130 3-9-5 0 PaulHanagan 6 80
(Charlie Appleby) *prom: pushed along: edgd lft and bmpd over 1f out: r.o* **22/1**

**4** 1¼ **New Year's Night (IRE)** 3-9-5 0 JamesDoyle 8 77
(Charlie Appleby) *s.i.s: hld up: hdwy over 1f out: r.o: nt rch ldrs* **11/2**[3]

**5** nse **Santa Teresa (IRE)** 3-9-0 0 MartinHarley 5 72
(William Haggas) *chsd ldrs: shkn up: edgd rt and bmpd over 1f out: styd on same pce ins fnl f* **16/1**

003- **6** 7 **Broughtons Secret**[305] 7493 3-9-0 79 ChrisCatlin 4 56
(Willie Musson) *chsd ldrs: rdn over 2f out: wknd ins fnl f* **16/1**

242 **7** nse **Flawless Pink**[9] 5469 3-9-0 0 TomQueally 11 56
(Jeremy Noseda) *hld up: pushed along over 3f out: nvr on terms* **8/1**

-5 **8** ¾ **Mississippi Queen (USA)**[30] 4699 3-8-9 0 LouisSteward(5) 9 54
(Michael Bell) *hld up: hdwy over 3f out: rdn and wknd over 1f out* **33/1**

40 **9** 6 **Dutch Lady Roseane**[53] 3925 3-9-0 0 AdamBeschizza 7 40
(James Unett) *mid-div: rdn over 3f out: sn wknd* **100/1**

**10** 5 **New Stream (IRE)** 3-9-5 0 FrederikTylicki 12 34
(Clive Brittain) *s.i.s: a in rr* **16/1**

**11** 1¼ **Resonated (USA)** 3-9-5 0 DaleSwift 3 31
(Brian Ellison) *prom: rdn 1/2-way: wknd over 2f out* **66/1**

5 **12** 4½ **Brian The Lion**[16] 5202 3-9-5 0 DuranFentiman 10 21
(Shaun Harris) *in rr 6f out: wknd over 3f out* **200/1**

1m 50.08s (-0.02) **Going Correction** 0.0s/f (Stan) **12** Ran SP% **124.9**
Speed ratings (Par 100): **100,99,99,98,98 91,91,91,85,81 80,76**
CSF £7.20 TOTE £3.40: £1.30, £1.10, £8.60; EX 8.60 Trifecta £136.30.
**Owner** George Strawbridge **Bred** J Hanly, T Stewart & A Stroud **Trained** Newmarket, Suffolk

**FOCUS**
Some fair stables in opposition for this maiden, but time was ordinary. The front two dominated from the off.

## 5797 ALL NEW 32REDSPORT.COM H'CAP (TAPETA) 7f 32y
**7:20** (7:22) (Class 6) (0-55,55) 3-Y-O+ **£2,102** (£625; £312; £156) **Stalls** High

Form RPR
**1** **Peace Accord**[340] 6613 4-9-6 55 RyanMoore 4 70
(Michael Wigham) *trckd ldr: led over 1f out: rdn and hung lft ins fnl f: r.o wl* **7/2**[2]

5066 **2** 3½ **Baltic Prince (IRE)**[30] 4707 4-9-4 53 RaulDaSilva 10 59
(Paul Green) *led 6f out: rdn and hdd over 1f out: styd on same pce ins fnl f* **14/1**

0036 **3** nk **Carrera**[10] 5425 4-8-13 55 KieranShoemark(7) 6 60
(Michael Blanshard) *hld up: hdwy over 1f out: r.o: nt rch ldrs* **9/1**

-004 **4** 1½ **Squirrel Wood (IRE)**[43] 4266 6-9-4 53 FergusSweeney 1 54
(Mary Hambro) *prom: rdn over 1f out: styd on* **14/1**

0066 **5** 1¼ **Declamation (IRE)**[17] 5172 4-9-1 55 GarryWhillans(5) 12 53
(Alistair Whillans) *hld up: hung lft and styd on ins fnl f: nvr nrr* **10/1**

0160 **6** nse **Blue Clumber**[6] 5573 4-9-3 52 JimmyQuinn 3 50
(Shaun Harris) *led 1f: chsd ldrs: rdn 1/2-way: hung lft and wknd ins fnl f* **25/1**

646 **7** ¾ **Heidi's Delight (IRE)**[6] 5573 5-9-3 52 (b) PJMcDonald 7 48
(Ann Duffield) *s.i.s: hld up: nt clr run over 1f out: n.d* **22/1**

032 **8** nk **Very First Blade**[8] 5510 5-8-13 51 (b) RobertTart(3) 5 46
(Michael Mullineaux) *plld hrd and prom: rdn over 1f out: wknd ins fnl f* **9/2**[3]

0000 **9** nk **Queen Hermione (IRE)**[14] 5287 6-9-3 52 (t) DaleSwift 8 46
(Derek Shaw) *sn pushed along in rr: rdn 1/2-way: nvr on terms* **33/1**

5050 **10** 1 **Severiano (USA)**[10] 5421 4-9-3 52 (be) MartinHarley 11 44
(Alan McCabe) *hld up: hdwy over 2f out: rdn and hung lft over 1f out: sn wknd* **9/2**[3]

160 **11** 4½ **Overrider**[27] 4798 4-9-6 55 (t) JamesDoyle 9 35
(Paul Cole) *hood removed late and s slowly: hld up: shkn up over 1f out: hmpd ins fnl f: eased* **11/4**[1]

1m 29.39s (0.59) **Going Correction** 0.0s/f (Stan) **11** Ran SP% **128.8**
Speed ratings (Par 101): **96,92,91,89,88 88,87,87,86,85 80**
CSF £56.06 CT £437.30 TOTE £3.50: £1.10, £4.40, £3.60; EX 48.40 Trifecta £657.30.
**Owner** D Hassan **Bred** Darley **Trained** Newmarket, Suffolk

**FOCUS**
Only 4lb covered the field for this modest handicap, which was run at a fair pace. Again the prominent runners dominated.

## 5798 £10 FREE BET AT 32REDSPORT.COM NURSERY H'CAP (TAPETA) 7f 32y
**7:50** (7:51) (Class 6) (0-65,65) 2-Y-O **£1,940** (£577; £288; £144) **Stalls** High

Form RPR
333 **1** **Faraajh (IRE)**[22] 4973 2-9-7 65 MartinHarley 2 76+
(James Tate) *led 1f: chsd ldrs: wnt 2nd over 2f out: led over 1f out: r.o wl* **9/2**[3]

604 **2** 5 **Charlotte's Secret**[19] 5086 2-9-5 63 TonyHamilton 7 61
(Richard Fahey) *a.p: rdn over 2f out: styd on same pce fnl f: wnt 2nd nr fin* **7/1**

003 **3** shd **Horsetracker**[23] 4935 2-9-2 65 GeorgeDowning(5) 8 62
(Ian Williams) *led 6f out: rdn and hdd over 1f out: no ex ins fnl f* **16/1**

060 **4** 1¼ **Mikandy (IRE)**[13] 5305 2-9-1 62 RyanTate(3) 10 56
(Clive Cox) *s.i.s: hld up: rdn over 1f out: r.o ins fnl f: nvr nrr* **11/1**

3344 **5** 1¼ **Diatomic (IRE)**[14] 5285 2-9-7 65 RichardKingscote 12 55
(Tom Dascombe) *prom: chsd ldr over 5f out tl over 2f out: sn rdn: wknd ins fnl f* **15/2**

6023 **6** 1½ **Western Playboy (IRE)**[13] 5306 2-9-7 65 JamesDoyle 4 51
(Sylvester Kirk) *mid-div: pushed along over 2f out: wknd fnl f* **7/2**[1]

0562 **7** shd **Old Fashion**[14] 5279 2-9-7 65 PaulHanagan 6 51
(Ed Dunlop) *prom: rdn over 2f out: edgd lft over 1f out: wknd fnl f* **4/1**[2]

0003 **8** nk **Auld Fyffee (IRE)**[14] 5279 2-9-6 64 GrahamLee 5 49
(John Ryan) *mid-div: rdn over 2f out: wknd fnl f* **12/1**

3046 **9** nk **Agadoo**[23] 4944 2-9-7 65 JimmyQuinn 9 50
(Shaun Harris) *hld up: hdwy over 1f out: sn rdn: wknd fnl f* **28/1**

0464 **10** nse **Piccadillo**[7] 5525 2-8-13 60 ThomasBrown(3) 3 44
(Daniel Kubler) *hld up: rdn over 2f out: nvr on terms* **10/1**

030 **11** 1¾ **Prince Rofan (IRE)**[15] 5253 2-8-3 47 FrannyNorton 1 27
(Derek Shaw) *mid-div: rdn over 2f out: wknd over 1f out* **66/1**

21P3 **12** 6 **Just Marion (IRE)**[7] 5525 2-9-1 64 NoelGarbutt(5) 11 27
(David Evans) *sn pushed along in rr: wknd 2f out* **33/1**

1m 29.98s (1.18) **Going Correction** 0.0s/f (Stan) **12** Ran SP% **123.5**
Speed ratings (Par 92): **93,87,87,85,84 82,82,82,81,81 79,72**
CSF £37.38 CT £485.13 TOTE £3.80: £1.50, £2.50, £8.00; EX 33.70 Trifecta £1236.30.
**Owner** Saeed Manana **Bred** Rabbah Bloodstock Limited **Trained** Newmarket, Suffolk

**FOCUS**
A fair contest for the grade and run at a sound pace. The winner left her previous turf form behind on Tapeta debut.

## 5799 DOWNLOAD OUR IPHONE APP MEDIAN AUCTION MAIDEN STKS (TAPETA) 5f 216y
**8:20** (8:20) (Class 6) 2-Y-O **£1,940** (£577; £288; £144) **Stalls** Low

Form RPR
45 **1** **Heaven's Secret (IRE)**[61] 3613 2-9-5 0 TonyHamilton 11 76+
(Richard Fahey) *chsd ldrs: shkn up over 1f out: r.o to ld and edgd lft wl ins fnl f* **8/1**[3]

02 **2** ½ **Captain Revelation**[19] 5099 2-9-5 0 RichardKingscote 2 74
(Tom Dascombe) *sn led: rdn over 1f out: hdd wl ins fnl f* **13/8**[1]

3243 **3** ¾ **Anonymous John (IRE)**[23] 4939 2-9-0 72 NoelGarbutt(5) 8 72
(David Evans) *led early: chsd ldrs: rdn and ev ch fr over 1f out tl unable qck towards fin* **9/1**

6222 **4** ½ **Vegas Rebel (IRE)**[45] 4203 2-9-5 77 MartinHarley 5 70
(Peter Chapple-Hyam) *hld up: hdwy over 1f out: sn rdn: r.o* **4/1**[2]

5 **5** hd **Solstalla**[27] 4784 2-9-0 0 GrahamLee 12 65
(William Jarvis) *hld up in tch: lost pl over 3f out: hdwy over 1f out: nt clr run ins fnl f: r.o* **4/1**[2]

4 **6** ¾ **Shar Shar (IRE)**[71] 3312 2-9-0 0 PJMcDonald 7 62+
(Brian Ellison) *hld up: hdwy over 1f out: r.o: nt rch ldrs* **25/1**

50 **7** shd **Alakhtal (IRE)**[70] 3330 2-9-5 0 PaulHanagan 6 68
(Charles Hills) *plld hrd: w ldrs: ev ch over 1f out: no ex wl ins fnl f* **8/1**[3]

50 **8** 7 **Gideon Jukes**[21] 5013 2-9-5 0 DavidNolan 10 46
(Richard Fahey) *prom: rdn over 2f out: wknd over 1f out* **40/1**

60 **9** 1¾ **Indian Joe**[28] 4760 2-9-5 0 LiamJones 4 41
(J S Moore) *chsd ldrs tl rdn and wknd over 1f out* **25/1**

00 **10** hd **Devilution (IRE)**[13] 5296 2-9-5 0 DaleSwift 9 40
(Derek Shaw) *broke wl: sn lost pl: wknd over 2f out* **100/1**

**11** 2 **Out Of Aces** 2-9-0 0 ShaneGray(5) 1 34
(Kevin Ryan) *dwlt: a in rr: wknd 2f out* **50/1**

1m 15.1s (0.60) **Going Correction** 0.0s/f (Stan) **11** Ran SP% **123.4**
Speed ratings (Par 92): **96,95,94,93,93 92,92,82,80,80 77**
CSF £21.86 TOTE £14.30: £3.60, £1.70, £1.80; EX 29.00 Trifecta £246.50.
**Owner** J K Shannon & M A Scaife **Bred** Rathasker Stud **Trained** Musley Bank, N Yorks

**FOCUS**
They went a steady pace in this fair maiden. The third helps to set the level.

## 5800 32RED H'CAP (TAPETA) 1m 5f 194y
**8:50** (8:50) (Class 4) (0-80,80) 3-Y-O+ **£5,175** (£1,540; £769; £384) **Stalls** Low

Form RPR
223 **1** **Echo Brava**[19] 5073 4-9-9 78 MichaelJMMurphy(3) 2 85
(Luke Dace) *hld up: hdwy over 2f out: rdn to ld over 1f out: styd on wl* **5/2**[1]

6230 **2** 2¼ **Lineman**[38] 4423 4-9-6 72 (p) TomQueally 7 76
(Andrew Hollinshead) *hld up: hdwy over 1f out: rdn to chse wnr ins fnl f: no imp* **15/2**

1231 **3** 2¼ **Underwritten**[1] 5764 5-9-5 71 6ex JimmyQuinn 3 72
(Shaun Harris) *chsd ldr tl led 2f out: rdn and hdd over 1f out: styd on same pce ins fnl f* **5/1**[3]

1140 **4** ½ **Manomine**[11] 5379 5-9-3 74 (b) LouisSteward(5) 1 74
(Clive Brittain) *chsd ldrs: nt clr run over 2f out: rdn over 1f out: styd on same pce fnl f* **11/1**

6424 **5** 1½ **Admirable Duque (IRE)**[20] 5047 8-9-3 69 (b) FrederikTylicki 8 68
(Dominic Ffrench Davis) *hld up: hdwy and nt clr run over 1f out: swtchd rt: kpt on: nt trble ldrs* **6/1**

00 **6** 4 **Guising**[30] 4710 5-9-10 76 (p) GrahamLee 5 68
(David Brown) *led: rdn and hdd 2f out: wknd fnl f* **15/2**

015 **7** 13 **Dino Mite**[14] 5288 3-9-2 80 ShaneKelly 4 54
(Peter Chapple-Hyam) *prom: rdn over 2f out: wknd over 1f out: eased* **7/2**[2]

3m 2.9s (-1.90) **Going Correction** 0.0s/f (Stan)
**WFA** 3 from 4yo+ 12lb **7** Ran SP% **113.6**
Speed ratings (Par 105): **105,103,102,102,101 99,91**
CSF £21.43 CT £86.15 TOTE £2.10: £1.10, £5.60; EX 22.00 Trifecta £120.10.
**Owner** Mark Benton **Bred** Adweb Ltd **Trained** Okehurst Lane, W Sussex
■ Stewards' Enquiry : Louis Steward one-day ban: careless riding (Sep 9)

**FOCUS**
The pace was steady in this fair staying handicap, and the first two home raced in the last three.

## 5801 RACING SPECIALS AT 32REDSPORT.COM H'CAP (TAPETA) 5f 20y
**9:20** (9:20) (Class 6) (0-55,55) 3-Y-O+ **£2,102** (£625; £312; £156) **Stalls** Low

Form RPR
0000 **1** **Rise To Glory (IRE)**[3] 5683 6-9-4 52 (tp) DuranFentiman 12 62
(Shaun Harris) *led 4f out: rdn over 1f out: styd on* **7/1**[3]

4565 **2** ¾ **China Excels**[118] 1887 7-8-10 47 RossAtkinson(3) 6 54
(Mandy Rowland) *s.i.s: hdwy 1/2-way: rdn over 1f out: r.o* **8/1**

4536 **3** 1¼ **Your Gifted (IRE)**[11] 5399 7-9-0 53 (v) JackGarritty(5) 10 56
(Lisa Williamson) *hld up: hdwy over 1f out: edgd lft: r.o* **8/1**

0300 **4** 1½ **Aaranyow (IRE)**[10] 5423 6-9-1 49 (t[1]) JimmyQuinn 3 46
(Clifford Lines) *mid-div: hdwy and nt clr run over 1f out: r.o: nt rch ldrs* **10/1**

500 **5** hd **Smart Dj**[25] 4873 3-8-6 47 JackDuern(5) 7 43
(Andrew Hollinshead) *hmpd s: chsd ldr 4f out: rdn over 1f out: no ex ins fnl f* **7/2**[2]

4306 **6** nse **Aussie Sky (IRE)**[119] 1855 3-8-10 46 FrankieMcDonald 9 42
(Daniel Mark Loughnane) *prom: rdn over 1f out: no ex fnl f* **25/1**

0056 **7** 1 **Sandsman's Girl (IRE)**[15] 5257 3-8-9 48 (b) ConnorBeasley(3) 8 41
(James Given) *wnt lft s: hld up: rdn over 1f out: nt trble ldrs* **8/1**

2344 **8** nse **Bubbly Bailey**[13] 5316 4-9-7 55 (v) FrederikTylicki 4 47
(J R Jenkins) *led 1f: chsd ldrs: rdn over 1f out: no ex fnl f* **3/1**[1]

-003 **9** ¾ **Compton Albion (IRE)**[18] 5126 4-8-8 49 (p) DavidParkes(7) 5 39
(Jeremy Gask) *sn pushed along in rr: nvr on terms* **8/1**

3005 **10** 2 **Ecliptic Sunrise**[16] 5205 3-9-1 54 (t) MichaelJMMurphy(3) 2 37
(Des Donovan) *s.i.s: a in rr* **16/1**

1m 2.15s (0.25) **Going Correction** 0.0s/f (Stan)
**WFA** 3 from 4yo+ 2lb **10** Ran SP% **123.0**
Speed ratings (Par 101): **98,96,94,92,92 92,90,90,89,85**
CSF £65.42 CT £480.55 TOTE £10.20: £3.00, £4.10, £2.90; EX 103.90 Trifecta £392.40.
**Owner** N Blencowe,J Sunderland,M Lenton,CHarris **Bred** Bryan Ryan **Trained** Carburton, Notts

**FOCUS**
A moderate sprint handicap run at a sound pace. The winner hadn't shown any form since February.
T/Jkpt: Not won. T/Plt: £245.30 to a £1 stake. Pool of £90804.39 - 270.22 winning tickets.
T/Qpdt: £77.80 to a £1 stake. Pool of £6515.61 - 61.97 winning tickets. CR

5802 - 5805a (Foreign Racing) - See Raceform Interactive

# 5264 CARLISLE (R-H)

Wednesday, August 27

**OFFICIAL GOING: Good to firm (7.2)**

Wind: Breezy, half against Weather: Fine, dry Rails: Rail out on home bend and distances on Round course increased by 3yds

## 5806 BETFAIR NOVICE FLAT AMATEUR RIDERS' H'CAP (FOR NOVICE AMATEUR RIDERS) 5f 193y

**2:00** (2:02) (Class 6) (0-65,64) 4-Y-0+ **£2,495** (£774; £386; £193) **Stalls Low**

Form RPR

6000 1 **Thewestwalian (USA)**[9] 5499 6-9-13 45 MissMollyKing(3) 4 51
(Peter Hiatt) *hld up: hdwy on outside to ld over 1f out: edgd rt ins fnl f: kpt on strly* **18/1**

3364 2 *nk* **Slim Chance (IRE)**[13] 5333 5-11-7 64 PhillipDennis 8 69
(Simon West) *taken early to post: t.k.h: trckd ldrs: effrt and ev ch ins fnl f: kpt on: hld towards fin* **2/1**[1]

0000 3 *1 1/4* **One Kool Dude**[12] 5390 5-9-13 45 (b) DylanMcDonagh(3) 3 46
(Micky Hammond) *taken early to post: trckd ldrs: effrt and ev ch over 1f out: kpt on same pce ins fnl f* **20/1**

4000 4 *3/4* **The Strig**[9] 5499 7-10-6 52 (v) MrOJPimlott(3) 6 51
(Nigel Tinkler) *hld up on ins: stdy hdwy over 2f out: effrt over 1f out: one pce ins fnl f* **16/1**

2462 5 *1/2* **Shillito**[26] 4875 4-11-3 60 MrKWood 5 58
(Tony Coyle) *s.i.s: hld up: stdy hdwy 2f out: rdn and no imp fnl f* **11/4**[2]

1450 6 *1* **Hab Reeh**[20] 5082 6-11-7 64 MissLWilson 2 59
(Ruth Carr) *t.k.h: led: rdn and hdd over 1f out: sn no ex* **6/1**

1201 7 *2 3/4* **Choc'A'Moca (IRE)**[28] 4795 7-11-0 60 (v) MrAFrench(3) 7 46
(Paul Midgley) *pressed ldr: rdn and outpcd wl over 1f out: btn fnl f* **9/2**[3]

566 8 *2 3/4* **Bix (IRE)**[41] 4358 4-9-13 45 MissGCochrane(3) 1 23
(Alan Berry) *dwlt: bhd: struggling 1/2-way: nvr on terms* **33/1**

1m 17.27s (3.57) **Going Correction** +0.375s/f (Good) **8 Ran SP% 111.3**
Speed ratings (Par 101): **91,90,88,87,87 85,82,78**
CSF £51.58 CT £735.98 TOTE £32.80: £10.40, £1.50, £7.10; EX 73.70 Trifecta £435.20.
**Owner** P W Hiatt **Bred** Liberation Farm & Oratis **Trained** Hook Norton, Oxon

**FOCUS**
A modest handicap, confined to novice amateur riders, run at a steady pace. The first and third limit the form.

## 5807 BRITISH STALLION STUDS EBF MAIDEN STKS 5f 193y

**2:30** (2:32) (Class 5) 2-Y-0 **£2,911** (£866; £432; £216) **Stalls Low**

Form RPR

2 1 **Charlie Croker (IRE)**[31] 4708 2-9-5 0 BarryMcHugh 4 85+
(Kevin Ryan) *mde all: rdn clr over 1f out: kpt on strly fnl f* **2/1**[1]

45 2 *3 3/4* **Shootingsta (IRE)**[55] 3881 2-9-5 0 PhillipMakin 2 72+
(Bryan Smart) *sn pushed along towards rr: hdwy over 1f out: chsd (clr) wnr ins fnl f: kpt on: no imp* **9/2**

5 3 *3 3/4* **Named Asset**[16] 5242 2-9-5 0 RussKennemore 12 61
(Jedd O'Keeffe) *t.k.h: in tch: hdwy 2f out: kpt on same pce fnl f* **10/1**

4 *shd* **Midnite Ride (IRE)** 2-9-0 0 IanBrennan 13 55+
(Richard Fahey) *s.i.s: bhd tl stdy hdwy over 1f out: kpt on fnl f: nvr nrr* **66/1**

3 5 *1/2* **Signoret (IRE)**[36] 4510 2-8-11 0 GeorgeChaloner(3) 5 54
(Richard Fahey) *trckd ldrs: hdwy and ev ch wl over 1f out: sn rdn and edgd rt: wknd ins fnl f* **7/2**[3]

4 6 *hd* **Codger's Gift (IRE)**[16] 5255 2-8-9 0 SammyJoBell(5) 10 53+
(Richard Fahey) *s.i.s: bhd: hdwy over 1f out: nvr able to chal* **20/1**

0 7 *7* **Bahamian Desert**[18] 5167 2-9-2 0 SamJames(3) 1 37+
(David O'Meara) *cl up: rdn over 2f out: edgd lft and wknd over 1f out* **25/1**

2325 8 *2 1/2* **Summer Times**[12] 5386 2-9-5 78 JoeFanning 6 30
(Mark Johnston) *trckd ldrs: rdn over 2f out: wknd wl over 1f out* **11/4**[2]

0 9 *hd* **Phoenix Storm (IRE)**[32] 4684 2-9-5 0 TonyHamilton 3 29
(Richard Fahey) *in tch: outpcd after 2f: n.d after* **33/1**

10 *1 1/4* **Spiritual Acclaim (IRE)** 2-8-9 0 JoeDoyle(5) 8 21
(John Weymes) *s.i.s: bhd: rdn over 2f out: nvr on terms* **100/1**

0 11 *6* **Hey Bob (IRE)**[31] 4701 2-9-5 0 PJMcDonald 7 8
(Keith Dalgleish) *towards rr on outside: struggling over 2f out: sn btn* **100/1**

0 12 *19* **Anneani (IRE)**[23] 4973 2-9-0 0 RaulDaSilva 11
(Paul Green) *prom on outside: rdn and hung lft 2f out: sn wknd* **125/1**

1m 15.88s (2.18) **Going Correction** +0.375s/f (Good) **12 Ran SP% 125.3**
Speed ratings (Par 94): **100,95,90,89,89 88,79,76,76,74 66,41**
CSF £11.88 TOTE £6.00: £1.50, £2.00, £4.00; EX 25.60 Trifecta £153.20.
**Owner** Malih Lahej Al Basti **Bred** R S Solomon **Trained** Hambleton, N Yorks

**FOCUS**
They went a decent pace in this fair maiden, and the winner made all. He might have a good bit more to offer.

## 5808 CHRISTMAS PARTIES AT CARLISLE RACECOURSE H'CAP (JOCKEY CLUB GRASSROOTS FLAT SPRINT QUALIFIER) 5f 193y

**3:00** (3:01) (Class 5) (0-70,68) 3-Y-0 **£2,587** (£770; £384) **Stalls Low**

Form RPR

2003 1 **Chookie's Lass**[5] 5631 3-9-2 64 PhillipMakin 1 71
(Keith Dalgleish) *t.k.h: mde all: rdn and qcknd over 1f out: kpt on strly fnl f: unchal* **3/1**[3]

3161 2 *2 1/2* **Bearskin (IRE)**[5] 5631 3-9-5 67 6ex (b) PJMcDonald 4 66
(Ann Duffield) *chsd wnr: rdn along and outpcd over 1f out: kpt on ins fnl f: no imp* **13/8**[2]

2236 3 *1 1/2* **Kirtling Belle**[36] 4511 3-9-6 68 JoeFanning 2 62
(Keith Dalgleish) *t.k.h: trckd ldrs: effrt and edgd lft wl over 1f out: kpt on same pce* **11/8**[1]

1m 15.86s (2.16) **Going Correction** +0.375s/f (Good) **3 Ran SP% 105.2**
Speed ratings (Par 100): **100,96,94**
CSF £7.49 TOTE £3.80; EX 5.90 Trifecta £6.70.
**Owner** Raeburn Brick Limited **Bred** D And J Raeburn **Trained** Carluke, S Lanarks

**FOCUS**
A tight handicap but the winner was gifted a lead and wasn't in danger.

## 5809 RACING HERE TUESDAY 2ND SEPTEMBER FILLIES' H'CAP 7f 200y

**3:30** (3:31) (Class 5) (0-75,68) 3-Y-0+ **£2,587** (£770; £384; £192) **Stalls Low**

Form RPR

0020 1 **Suni Dancer**[20] 5077 3-8-6 54 RaulDaSilva 3 61
(Paul Green) *in tch: hdwy 2f out: led ins fnl f: pushed out* **13/2**[3]

2132 2 *2* **Her Red Devil (IRE)**[16] 5239 3-8-9 60 GeorgeChaloner(3) 1 62
(Richard Fahey) *wnt rt s: t.k.h and sn disputing ld: led 3f out: edgd lft over 1f out: hdd and no ex ins fnl f* **7/4**[1]

1433 3 *1 1/4* **Indian Giver**[9] 5512 6-8-9 56 AlistairRawlinson(5) 4 57
(John David Riches) *slt ld to 3f out: rdn along and hung rt over 1f out: one pce ins fnl f* **7/2**[2]

6313 4 *nk* **La Havrese (FR)**[12] 5376 3-9-6 68 PJMcDonald 5 67
(Ann Duffield) *trckd ldrs: effrt and rdn 2f out: kpt on same pce over 1f out* **7/4**[1]

1m 43.13s (3.13) **Going Correction** +0.225s/f (Good)
**WFA** 3 from 6yo 6lb **4 Ran SP% 108.3**
Speed ratings (Par 100): **93,91,89,89**
CSF £17.92 TOTE £9.90; EX 19.60 Trifecta £43.90.
**Owner** Ian Furlong **Bred** Mickley Stud And G A Greaves **Trained** Lydiate, Merseyside

**FOCUS**
They went a steady pace for this modest fillies' handicap.

## 5810 WATCH RACINGUK SKY 432 H'CAP (LONDON MILE SERIES QUALIFIER) 7f 200y

**4:00** (4:01) (Class 4) (0-85,85) 3-Y-0+ **£5,175** (£1,540; £769; £384) **Stalls Low**

Form RPR

4-42 1 **Chinese Jade**[26] 4845 3-8-12 77 ChrisCatlin 4 84
(Sir Mark Prescott Bt) *prom: rdn over 2f out: styd on wl fnl f: led last stride* **6/1**

6600 2 *shd* **Argaki (IRE)**[27] 4827 4-9-1 74 PhillipMakin 8 82
(Keith Dalgleish) *stdd bhd ldng gp: hdwy on outside to ld over 1f out: edgd rt ins fnl f: kpt on: hdd last stride* **16/1**

316 3 *1 3/4* **Al Khan (IRE)**[19] 5143 5-9-1 79 (p) JacobButterfield(5) 1 83
(Ollie Pears) *t.k.h early: trckd ldrs: hdwy to chal over 1f out: kpt on same pce ins fnl f* **5/1**[2]

5112 4 *nk* **Bahamian C**[9] 5496 3-8-7 75 GeorgeChaloner(3) 6 79
(Richard Fahey) *in tch: rdn over 3f out: rallied over 1f out: edgd rt and kpt on ins fnl f* **7/2**[1]

0360 5 *1 3/4* **Red Charmer (IRE)**[11] 5446 4-8-13 72 PJMcDonald 7 71
(Ann Duffield) *prom: rdn over 2f out: kpt on same pce fnl f* **13/2**

0005 6 *nk* **Lord Of The Dance (IRE)**[23] 4963 8-8-4 70 (p) AnnaHesketh(7) 5 69
(Michael Mullineaux) *s.i.s: bhd and sn pushed along: stdy hdwy over 2f out: no imp fr over 1f out* **15/2**

0120 7 *1 1/2* **Talent Scout (IRE)**[12] 5385 8-9-7 85 GemmaTutty(5) 3 80
(Karen Tutty) *t.k.h: led to over 1f out: sn btn* **7/1**

0063 8 *9* **Henry The Aviator (USA)**[8] 5528 4-9-10 83 JoeFanning 2 57
(Mark Johnston) *trckd ldr: rdn and lost pl qckly 2f out: sn btn* **11/2**[3]

1m 40.97s (0.97) **Going Correction** +0.225s/f (Good)
**WFA** 3 from 4yo+ 6lb **8 Ran SP% 112.0**
Speed ratings (Par 105): **104,103,102,101,100 99,98,89**
CSF £89.19 CT £513.57 TOTE £5.00: £1.60, £4.50, £1.60; EX 65.20 Trifecta £521.90.
**Owner** Lady O'Reilly **Bred** Castlemartin Sky & Skymarc Farm **Trained** Newmarket, Suffolk

**FOCUS**
They went a sound pace for this competitive handicap. The winner just got past the strong-travelling runner-up in the final strides.

## 5811 JOIN NOW AT REWARDS4RACING.COM H'CAP 1m 1f 61y

**4:30** (4:30) (Class 5) (0-70,68) 3-Y-0+ **£2,587** (£770; £384; £192) **Stalls Low**

Form RPR

1133 1 **Remember Rocky**[20] 5084 5-8-8 55 (p) MeganCarberry(7) 3 63
(Lucy Normile) *prom: rdn over 2f out: swtchd lft over 1f out: kpt on wl fnl f: styd on to ld nr fin* **15/2**

2366 2 *nk* **Ferdy (IRE)**[19] 5127 5-9-0 54 RaulDaSilva 5 61
(Paul Green) *dwlt: hld up: hdwy over 2f out: led ins fnl f: kpt on: hdd cl home* **9/1**

0446 3 *2* **Life And Times (USA)**[23] 4975 6-9-10 64 JoeFanning 1 68
(Mark Johnston) *t.k.h: hld up: hdwy to ld over 1f out: sn rdn: hdd ins fnl f: kpt on same pce* **6/1**[3]

13 4 *1 1/2* **Senor George (IRE)**[19] 5142 7-9-12 66 BrianHughes 10 67
(Brian Ellison) *in tch: smooth hdwy to ld over 2f out: rdn and hdd over 1f out: no ex ins fnl f* **5/2**[1]

P124 5 *7* **Incurs Four Faults**[11] 5414 3-9-5 66 PhillipMakin 7 53+
(Keith Dalgleish) *t.k.h: trckd ldrs: rdn whn n.m.r briefly 2f out: outpcd appr fnl f* **5/1**[2]

1605 6 *11* **Roxy Lane**[12] 5383 5-8-12 52 ChrisCatlin 11 19+
(Peter Hiatt) *led to over 2f out: rdn and wknd over 1f out* **18/1**

0342 7 *3 1/2* **Mount Cheiron (USA)**[22] 4998 3-8-5 57 (p) EmmaSayer(5) 9 17
(Dianne Sayer) *t.k.h: chsd ldrs: lost pl after 2f: rdn over 2f out: hung rt and wknd over 1f out* **10/1**

0002 8 *76* **Nelson's Bay**[7] 5562 5-9-2 56 IanBrennan 8
(Wilf Storey) *pressed ldr: rdn over 3f out: wknd over 2f out: eased whn no ch over 1f out* **6/1**[3]

1m 58.95s (1.35) **Going Correction** +0.225s/f (Good)
**WFA** 3 from 4yo+ 7lb **8 Ran SP% 109.9**
Speed ratings (Par 103): **103,102,100,99,93 83,80,12**
CSF £66.22 CT £402.30 TOTE £4.30: £1.50, £3.20, £1.80; EX 62.80 Trifecta £823.80.
**Owner** Byrne Racing **Bred** Cherry Park Stud **Trained** Duncrievie, Perth & Kinross

■ Stewards' Enquiry : Megan Carberry two-day ban: use of whip (10-11 Sept)

**FOCUS**
Plenty of pace for this open handicap which suited the closers.

## 5812 CFM CASH FOR KIDS DAY H'CAP 1m 6f 32y

**5:00** (5:00) (Class 4) (0-85,82) 3-Y-0+ **£5,822** (£1,732; £865; £432) **Stalls Low**

Form RPR

5160 1 **Laughing Jack**[15] 5276 6-9-4 77 GeorgeDowning(5) 7 85
(George Baker) *prom: hdwy to chse ldr over 3f out: rdn and hung rt fr 2f out: led last 50yds: styd on* **11/2**

6613 2 *nk* **Late Shipment**[15] 5288 3-9-2 82 (p) JoeFanning 5 89
(Mark Johnston) *pressed ldr: led gng wl over 3f out: rdn 2f out: kpt on fnl f: hdd last 50yds: one pce* **7/4**[1]

1316 3 *3 3/4* **La Bacouetteuse (FR)**[7] 5564 9-9-3 71 (b) PJMcDonald 8 72
(Iain Jardine) *wnt lft s: hld up: rdn and outpcd over 3f out: rallied fnl f: kpt on: nt rch first two* **16/1**

663 4 *1/2* **Arantes**[14] 5302 3-8-12 78 SamHitchcott 6 79
(Mick Channon) *t.k.h early: hld up: hdwy and prom 3f out: rdn along 2f out: sn one pce* **3/1**[2]

3544 5 *6* **A Southside Boy (GER)**[23] 4962 6-8-4 63 oh1 JoeDoyle(5) 1 55
(Jim Goldie) *t.k.h: cl up: drvn and outpcd over 4f out: rallied 3f out: hung rt and outpcd fr 2f out* **9/2**[3]

4-05 **6** *10* **Australia Day (IRE)**[52] 3274 11-9-10 78........................ PhillipMakin 4 56
(Paul Webber) *led tl rdn and hdd over 3f out: wknd over 2f out* **7/1**
3m 8.33s (0.83) **Going Correction** +0.225s/f (Good)
**WFA** 3 from 5yo+ 12lb **6** Ran SP% **113.3**
Speed ratings (Par 105): **106,105,103,103,99 94**
CSF £15.90 CT £142.63 TOTE £5.80: £5.30, £1.70; EX 16.80 Trifecta £177.20.
**Owner** Paul Downing **Bred** Sir Thomas Pilkington **Trained** Manton, Wilts

**FOCUS**
A decent pace for this ordinary staying handicap.
T/Plt: £1,870.50 to a £1 stake. Pool: £50,685.26 - 19.78 winning tickets T/Qpdt: £295.10 to a £1 stake. Pool: £3,390.29 - 8.50 winning tickets RY

5371 **CATTERICK** (L-H)
Wednesday, August 27

**OFFICIAL GOING: Good to firm (8.5)**
Wind: Light behind Weather: Cloudy with sunny periods

## 5813 YORKSHIRE-OUTDOORS.CO.UK MEDIAN AUCTION MAIDEN STKS 5f
**2:10** (2:12) (Class 6) 2-Y-O **£2,385** (£704; £352) **Stalls** Low

Form RPR
3222 **1** **You're My Cracker**[16] 5253 2-9-0 74........................ GrahamLee 8 75
(Donald McCain) *slt ld: rdn clr over 1f out: kpt on strly* **7/4**[1]
630 **2** *3 3/4* **Compton River**[86] 2824 2-9-5 67........................ PaulMulrennan 4 65
(Bryan Smart) *trckd ldrs: hdwy 2f out: rdn to chse wnr ent fnl f: sn no imp* **7/1**
04 **3** *2 1/4* **Charlie Lad**[10] 5464 2-9-5 0........................ RobertWinston 9 56
(Ollie Pears) *cl up: rdn along 2f out: wknd fnl f* **5/1**[3]
02 **4** *3 1/2* **Wiseton (IRE)**[33] 4624 2-9-5 0........................ GrahamGibbons 6 46
(David Barron) *trckd ldrs: pushed along over 2f out: rdn wl over 1f out: sn btn* **15/8**[2]
**5** *4* **Captain Future** 2-9-5 0........................ DuranFentiman 3 29
(Bryan Smart) *towards rr: pushed along 1/2-way: modest hdwy fnl f* **16/1**
0 **6** *hd* **Bushtiger (IRE)**[14] 5297 2-9-5 0........................ TomEaves 5 29
(David Barron) *dwlt and in rr tl sme late hdwy* **25/1**
**7** *3/4* **Good Move (IRE)** 2-9-0 0........................ JamesSullivan 2 21
(Brian Rothwell) *chsd ldrs: rdn along 2f out: wknd over 1f out* **125/1**
**8** *8* **Little Polyanna** 2-9-0 0........................ PatrickMathers 7
(Alan Berry) *s.i.s: a bhd* **125/1**
58.95s (-0.85) **Going Correction** -0.175s/f (Firm) **8** Ran SP% **111.6**
Speed ratings (Par 92): **99,93,89,83,77 77,75,63**
CSF £13.84 TOTE £1.80: £1.10, £2.40, £1.30; EX 10.50 Trifecta £25.20.
**Owner** Paul & Clare Rooney **Bred** Richard Kent **Trained** Cholmondeley, Cheshire

**FOCUS**
A first ever juvenile winner for Donald McCain. His filly had the run of the race.

## 5814 RACING WELFARE FAMILY DAY MAIDEN STKS 7f
**2:40** (2:41) (Class 5) 3-Y-O+ **£2,911** (£866; £432; £216) **Stalls** Low

Form RPR
6232 **1** **Conquerant**[12] 5400 3-9-5 79........................(p) PaulMulrennan 6 84
(Charlie Appleby) *sn led: clr bef 1/2-way: shkn up 2f out: rdn and kpt on fnl f* **3/1**[2]
2002 **2** *3* **Two Smart (IRE)**[21] 5055 3-9-0 77........................ DanielTudhope 5 71
(K R Burke) *chsd wnr: effrt over 2f out: rdn wl over 1f out: no imp fnl f* **6/4**[1]
2 **3** *2 3/4* **Foxcover (IRE)**[116] 1962 3-9-5 0........................ DavidNolan 2 68
(Richard Fahey) *trckd ldrs: hdwy wl over 2f out: rdn to chse ldng pair and edgd lft wl over 1f out: sn one pce* **6/4**[1]
55 **4** *11* **Say Something**[25] 4900 3-8-7 0........................ RowanScott(7) 7 34
(Ann Duffield) *hld up: hdwy and in tch over 2f out: sn rdn and no imp* **66/1**[3]
66-5 **5** *6* **Only For You**[11] 5412 4-9-5 48........................ DaleSwift 1 20
(Alan Brown) *chsd ldng pair on inner: rdn along 1/2-way: outpcd fr wl over 2f out* **66/1**[3]
/6-0 **6** *59* **Smirfys Blackcat (IRE)**[123] 1722 5-9-5 0........................ TomEaves 3
(Michael Mullineaux) *green and sn pushed along in rr: rdn bef 1/2-way and bhd whn hung rt and rn v wd home turn: t.o* **150/1**
1m 25.19s (-1.81) **Going Correction** -0.175s/f (Firm)
**WFA** 3 from 4yo+ 5lb **6** Ran SP% **108.6**
Speed ratings (Par 103): **103,99,96,83,77 9**
CSF £7.42 TOTE £2.60: £1.60, £1.10; EX 8.50 Trifecta £10.10.
**Owner** Godolphin **Bred** Darley **Trained** Newmarket, Suffolk

**FOCUS**
The previously disappointing winner made all and comfortably held on.

## 5815 BARRIES ICES AND REFRESHMENTS H'CAP 1m 7f 177y
**3:10** (3:12) (Class 5) (0-70,70) 3-Y-O+ **£3,067** (£905; £453) **Stalls** Low

Form RPR
3356 **1** **Miss Macnamara (IRE)**[23] 4964 5-9-8 69........................ KevinStott(5) 2 76
(Martin Todhunter) *hld up in rr: hdwy on outer over 2f out: rdn over 1f out: styd on wl to ld last 100yds* **7/2**[3]
2250 **2** *1* **Dhaular Dhar (IRE)**[11] 5421 12-8-13 58........................ GaryBartley(3) 6 64
(Jim Goldie) *trckd ldr: led 4f out: pushed clr over 2f out: rdn wl over 1f out: hdd and no ex last 100yds* **28/1**
3043 **3** *2 1/4* **Arcamante (ITY)**[5] 5628 3-9-0 70........................(e) DanielTudhope 3 74
(K R Burke) *trckd ldng pair on inner: hdwy over 2f out: rdn along and sltly outpcd wl over 1f out: keeping on whn n.m.r on inner ins fnl f: one pce* **7/4**[1]
3141 **4** *1 1/4* **Giovanni Jack**[7] 5567 4-9-10 66 6ex........................ RobertWinston 1 68
(Alan Swinbank) *trckd ldng pair: hdwy to chse ldr over 3f out: rdn 2f out: drvn and edgd lft ent fnl f: kpt on same pce* **9/4**[2]
1623 **5** *3 3/4* **Jan Smuts (IRE)**[23] 4962 6-9-10 66........................(tp) GrahamLee 4 63
(Wilf Storey) *hld up in rr: pushed along 4f out: rdn wl over 2f out: sn one pce* **8/1**
-340 **6** *2 3/4* **Danceintothelight**[23] 4962 7-8-7 52........................ NeilFarley(3) 5 46
(Micky Hammond) *set stdy pce: qcknd over 5f out: rdn along and hdd 4f out: drvn and wknd over 2f out* **16/1**
3m 31.2s (-0.80) **Going Correction** -0.175s/f (Firm)
**WFA** 3 from 4yo+ 14lb **6** Ran SP% **109.8**
Speed ratings (Par 103): **95,94,93,92,90 89**
CSF £70.82 TOTE £4.60: £2.20, £10.20; EX 79.50 Trifecta £261.70.
**Owner** Javas Charvers **Bred** Airlie Stud **Trained** Orton, Cumbria

**FOCUS**
This was steadily run. The exposed runner-up was well ridden and only worn down late on.

## 5816 EAT SLEEP DRINK NAGS HEAD PICKHILL H'CAP (BOBIS RACE) 7f
**3:40** (3:42) (Class 4) (0-85,83) 3-Y-O **£5,822** (£1,732; £865; £432) **Stalls** Low

Form RPR
6002 **1** **Little Shambles**[6] 5612 3-9-7 83........................ FrannyNorton 6 94
(Mark Johnston) *trckd ldr: hdwy to ld 2f out: rdn clr over 1f out: styd on wl towards fin* **7/4**[1]
2310 **2** *2* **Mr McLaren**[12] 5385 3-9-5 81........................(p) DanielTudhope 2 87
(David O'Meara) *hld up: in rr whn n.m.r on inner bnd after 3f: swtchd rt to outer over 2f out: rdn wl over 1f out: styd on to chse wnr ent fnl f: sn drvn: edgd lft and no imp* **7/2**[2]
5021 **3** *3* **Smart Alec (IRE)**[12] 5376 3-8-2 64........................ DuranFentiman 4 62
(Alan Swinbank) *trckd ldrs: hdwy 1/2-way: rdn to chse wnr wl over 1f out: drvn and one pce fnl f* **5/1**[3]
0-11 **4** *2 3/4* **Jacob Black**[36] 4514 3-9-4 80........................ TomEaves 3 70
(Keith Dalgleish) *led: rdn along and hdd 2f out: sn drvn and grad wknd* **7/2**[2]
5355 **5** *4 1/2* **Spirit Of Alsace (IRE)**[20] 5080 3-8-2 64........................ RoystonFfrench 1 42
(Jim Goldie) *t.k.h: trckd ldng pair on inner: rdn along wl over 2f out: sn wknd* **16/1**
1m 25.38s (-1.62) **Going Correction** -0.175s/f (Firm) **5** Ran SP% **103.4**
Speed ratings (Par 102): **102,99,96,93,88**
CSF £6.99 TOTE £3.40: £2.20, £1.80; EX 5.80 Trifecta £23.70.
**Owner** Sheikh Hamdan bin Mohammed Al Maktoum **Bred** Darley **Trained** Middleham Moor, N Yorks
■ Woodland Girl was withdrawn. Price at time of withdrawal 12-1. Rule 4 applies to all bets - deduction 5p in the pound.

**FOCUS**
The winner was confirming her good York run and remains unbeaten at Catterick.

## 5817 RACING WELFARE CHARITY CAMEL RACING TODAY H'CAP 5f 212y
**4:15** (4:15) (Class 5) (0-75,74) 3-Y-O+ **£2,911** (£866; £432; £216) **Stalls** Low

Form RPR
0213 **1** **Layla's Hero (IRE)**[34] 4571 7-9-7 71........................(v) PaulMulrennan 5 79+
(David Nicholls) *trckd ldng pair: hdwy over 2f out: rdn over 1f out: drvn to ld ins fnl f: kpt on wl towards fin* **9/4**[2]
5245 **2** *3/4* **Pettochside**[40] 4401 5-9-10 74........................ KierenFallon 4 80
(Chris Gordon) *hld up in tch: hdwy on outer 2f out: rdn over 1f out: ev ch ins fnl f: drvn and kpt on same pce towards fin* **15/8**[1]
5361 **3** *3/4* **Meandmyshadow**[5] 5641 6-9-10 74 6ex........................ DaleSwift 6 78
(Alan Brown) *dwlt and sn rdn along to take slt ld after 200yds: rdn 2f out: drvn over 1f out: hdd ins fnl f whn rdr dropped whip: no ex last 75yds* **4/1**[3]
6233 **4** *2* **Red Cape (FR)**[22] 4997 11-8-5 55........................(b) JamesSullivan 9 53
(Ruth Carr) *led early: cl up: rdn wl over 1f out and ev ch tl drvn and wknd appr fnl f* **8/1**
2030 **5** *1 1/2* **Niceonemyson**[34] 4571 5-8-5 60........................ KevinStott(5) 3 53
(Christopher Wilson) *trckd ldng pair on inner: effrt over 2f out: sn rdn and wknd over 1f out* **17/2**
04 **6** *nk* **Perfect Blossom**[36] 4521 7-9-8 72........................ TomEaves 2 64
(Alan Berry) *hld up: effrt over 2f out: sn rdn and no imp* **25/1**
1m 12.81s (-0.79) **Going Correction** -0.175s/f (Firm)
**WFA** 3 from 4yo+ 3lb **6** Ran SP% **111.0**
Speed ratings (Par 103): **98,97,96,93,91 90**
CSF £6.72 CT £13.48 TOTE £1.80: £1.80, £1.70; EX 7.70 Trifecta £23.20.
**Owner** Hart Inn I **Bred** Epona Bloodstock Ltd **Trained** Sessay, N Yorks

**FOCUS**
No shortage of early pace here, but this is ordinary form.

## 5818 2014 CATTERICK TWELVE FURLONG SERIES H'CAP (BOBIS RACE) 1m 3f 214y
**4:45** (4:45) (Class 4) (0-85,84) 3-Y-O **£6,817** (£2,013; £1,007) **Stalls** Centre

Form RPR
2002 **1** **Galizzi (USA)**[11] 5442 3-9-7 84........................ KierenFallon 4 91
(Michael Bell) *hld up in rr: gd hdwy wl over 1f out: swtchd rt and rdn ent fnl f: styd on strly to ld nr fin* **9/4**[1]
0121 **2** *nk* **Indira**[11] 5449 3-8-12 75........................ RobertWinston 2 81
(John Berry) *trckd ldng pair: hdwy 3f out: chal 2f out: rdn to ld jst over 1f out: drvn and edgd lft ins fnl f: hdd and no ex nr fin* **7/2**[3]
4501 **3** *2 1/4* **Mendelita**[15] 5270 3-7-11 65 oh3........................ JackGarritty(5) 5 67
(Richard Fahey) *led: rdn along 2f out: drvn and hdd jst over 1f out: hld whn n.m.r on inner ins fnl f* **12/1**
4322 **4** *7* **Stanarley Pic**[12] 5387 3-8-7 70........................ DuranFentiman 1 61
(Alan Swinbank) *trckd ldrs: hdwy over 2f out: rdn along wl over 1f out: sn drvn and wknd appr fnl f* **7/1**
0140 **5** *4* **Rising Breeze (FR)**[32] 4651 3-8-11 77........................ JoeyHaynes(3) 6 61
(K R Burke) *hld up in rr: hdwy on outer wl over 2f out: sn rdn and wknd over 1f out* **8/1**
-213 **6** *1 1/2* **Sir Charlie Kunz**[14] 5299 3-9-3 80........................ FrannyNorton 7 62
(Mark Johnston) *t.k.h: trckd ldr: cl up over 4f out: rdn along wl over 2f out: sn wknd* **11/4**[2]
2m 35.8s (-3.10) **Going Correction** -0.175s/f (Firm) **6** Ran SP% **111.0**
Speed ratings (Par 102): **103,102,101,96,93 92**
CSF £10.15 TOTE £2.20: £1.50, £2.40; EX 9.30 Trifecta £101.90.
**Owner** Sheikh Marwan Al Maktoum **Bred** Darley **Trained** Newmarket, Suffolk

**FOCUS**
The winner looked to have a bit more to offer if it had been needed.

## 5819 RACING AGAIN SATURDAY 20TH SEPTEMBER H'CAP 5f
**5:15** (5:18) (Class 6) (0-65,65) 3-Y-O+ **£2,385** (£704; £352) **Stalls** Low

Form RPR
2001 **1** **Pastureyes**[41] 4344 4-9-4 64........................(p) MatthewHopkins(5) 6 74
(Scott Dixon) *cl up: rdn to chal over 1f out: drvn ins fnl f: kpt on wl to ld last 50yds* **6/1**[2]
042 **2** *1/2* **Irish Girls Spirit (IRE)**[22] 4994 5-9-0 55........................ GrahamLee 4 63
(Paul Midgley) *cl up on inner: slt ld 1/2-way: rdn over 1f out: drvn and edgd lft ins fnl f: hdd and no ex last 50yds* **9/2**[1]
0023 **3** *nk* **Pavers Star**[26] 4860 5-8-8 48 ow1........................(p) TonyHamilton 5 56
(Noel Wilson) *slt ld to 1/2-way: cl up: rdn wl over 1f out: drvn ent fnl f: ev ch tl no ex last 50yds* **16/1**
5064 **4** *hd* **Ingenti**[5] 5635 6-9-0 60........................ KevinStott(5) 13 66+
(Christopher Wilson) *towards rr: hdwy 2f out: rdn to chal on outer ent fnl f: sn drvn: edgd lft and kpt on towards fin* **9/1**

1662 **5** ½ **Windforpower (IRE)**[12] 5375 4-9-4 64....................(p) JordanNason(5) 9 69
(Tracy Waggott) *trckd ldrs: hdwy over 1f out: sn rdn: kpt on fnl f* **8/1**[3]

1060 **6** 1½ **Chosen One (IRE)**[12] 5375 9-9-4 59.......................... JamesSullivan 7 58
(Ruth Carr) *prom: rdn along wl over 1f out: drvn ent fnl f: hld whn n.m.r towards fin* **25/1**

0142 **7** 3 **Spring Bird**[7] 5565 5-9-6 61.......................................... AdrianNicholls 2 49
(David Nicholls) *chsd ldrs: rdn along wl over 1f out: sn drvn and one pce* **9/2**[1]

000 **8** ¾ **Lost In Paris (IRE)**[29] 4752 8-9-8 63........................(b) BarryMcHugh 14 49
(Tony Coyle) *dwlt and swtchd lft after s: in rr tl styd on fnl f: nrst fin* **20/1**

03-0 **9** ¾ **Gauchita**[120] 1855 3-8-8 54...........................................[1] JoeyHaynes(3) 8 37
(K R Burke) *chsd ldrs: rdn wl over 1f out: sn drvn and wknd appr fnl f* **12/1**

1000 **10** 4½ **Mr Mo Jo**[14] 5298 6-9-3 65..........................................(b) KevinLundie(7) 10 32
(Les Eyre) *in tch: rdn along 1/2-way: sn wknd* **22/1**

0300 **11** 3½ **Biscuiteer**[25] 4890 3-8-12 55...........................................(b) TomEaves 15 9
(Scott Dixon) *in tch on wd outside: rdn along 1/2-way: sn outpcd* **50/1**

1066 **12** 1 **Lady Poppy**[19] 5130 4-9-8 63............................................ KierenFallon 12 14
(George Moore) *in tch: rdn along 1/2-way: sn wknd* **12/1**

4400 **13** 2 **Lunesdale Buddy**[23] 4974 3-8-3 46 oh1..........................(p) PatrickMathers 1
(Alan Berry) *chsd ldrs on inner: rdn along 1/2-way: sn outpcd* **125/1**

58.79s (-1.01) **Going Correction** -0.175s/f (Firm)
**WFA** 3 from 4yo+ 2lb **13** Ran SP% **108.7**
Speed ratings (Par 101): **101,100,99,99,98 96,91,90,89,81 76,74,71**
CSF £25.65 CT £250.94 TOTE £10.00: £3.10, £1.70, £5.30; EX 51.80 Trifecta £291.60.
**Owner** Paul J Dixon & Mrs Jayne Jackson **Bred** Mrs Yvette Dixon **Trained** Babworth, Notts
■ Dancing Juice was withdrawn. Price at time of withdrawal 8/1. Rule 4 applies to all bets - deduction 10p in the pound.

**FOCUS**
A typically competitive race for the grade. The winner built on her previous win.
T/Plt: £40.00 to a £1 stake. Pool: £48,266.79 - 879.35 winning tickets T/Qpdt: £20.30 to a £1 stake. Pool: £2,691.60 - 98.10 winning tickets JR

## 5547 KEMPTON (A.W) (R-H)
### Wednesday, August 27

**OFFICIAL GOING: Standard**
Wind: Moderate, across (away from stands) Weather: Cloudy

## 5820 KEMPTON LIVE WITH DIZZEE RASCAL 06.09.14 H'CAP (JOCKEY CLUB GRASSROOTS FLAT SERIES' QUALIFIER) 6f (P)
**5:55** (5:55) (Class 6) (0-60,60) 3-Y-O **£1,940** (£577; £288; £144) **Stalls** Low

Form RPR

-465 **1** **Maymyo (IRE)**[35] 4535 3-9-4 57........................................ JamesDoyle 3 69+
(Sylvester Kirk) *trckd ldng pair: gng best over 2f out: led over 1f out: shkn up and sn in command* **7/1**[2]

0055 **2** 1¼ **La Napoule**[28] 4789 3-9-3 56........................................ RichardHughes 8 64
(Richard Hannon) *mounted on crse: stdd s: hld up in rr: shkn up over 2f out: prog over 1f out: styd on to take 2nd last strides* **8/1**[3]

0004 **3** ¾ **Stapleford Lad**[21] 5034 3-9-0 53......................................(v[1]) KierenFox 9 59
(Stuart Williams) *chsd ldr to over 2f out: drvn to chse wnr fnl f: no imp: lost 2nd last strides* **8/1**[3]

-400 **4** 3¼ **Shaft Of Light**[9] 5492 3-9-6 59......................................(b[1]) LukeMorris 10 55
(Sir Mark Prescott Bt) *taken down early and mounted on crse: awkward s but rousted along to ld: drvn over 2f out: hdd over 1f out: fdd* **9/1**

3566 **5** ½ **Baars Causeway (IRE)**[23] 4972 3-9-2 60........................(v) CamHardie(5) 5 55
(Timothy Jarvis) *chsd ldrs: drvn and nt qckn over 2f out: one pce and no imp after* **8/1**[3]

555 **6** nk **It's A Yes From Me**[18] 5195 3-9-6 59..........................(v[1]) FrederikTylicki 4 53
(James Fanshawe) *w.w in midfield: rdn over 2f out: no imp on ldrs over 1f out* **4/1**[1]

4U6 **7** hd **Dylan's Centenary**[23] 4969 3-8-9 55........................ SophieKilloran(7) 12 48+
(Rod Millman) *v.s.a: wl detached in last: shkn up over 2f out: styd on takingly fr over 1f out: nreast fin* **12/1**

1-55 **8** 1 **Bonnie Fairy**[6] 5598 3-8-11 50........................................ AndrewMullen 2 40
(Michael Appleby) *chsd ldrs: hrd rdn and no imp 2f out: wknd fnl f* **25/1**

405 **9** ½ **Dandys Perier (IRE)**[28] 4785 3-9-2 55............ WilliamTwiston-Davies 7 44
(Ronald Harris) *rdn in rr bef 1/2-way: nvr a factor* **7/1**[2]

6006 **10** ½ **Monashka Bay (IRE)**[42] 4324 3-9-1 54......................(b[1]) DavidProbert 1 41
(Michael Blanshard) *towards rr: tried to make prog over 2f out: wknd over 1f out* **8/1**[3]

3065 **11** 5 **Zafraaj**[8] 5518 3-8-12 58........................................(be) MikeyEnnis(7) 6 30
(Ronald Harris) *nvr bttr than midfield: wknd over 2f out* **25/1**

0000 **12** 7 **Song Of Rowland (IRE)**[27] 4820 3-8-11 53...................... SimonPearce(3) 11
(John Spearing) *chsd ldrs on outer: rdn 1/2-way: sn wknd: t.o* **20/1**

1m 12.3s (-0.80) **Going Correction** 0.0s/f (Stan) **12** Ran SP% **119.6**
Speed ratings (Par 98): **105,103,102,98,97 96,96,95,94,94 87,78**
CSF £60.92 CT £465.34 TOTE £11.80: £4.20, £5.00, £6.80; EX 79.00 Trifecta £1179.90.
**Owner** H Balasuriya **Bred** Barouche Stud Ireland Ltd **Trained** Upper Lambourn, Berks
■ Stewards' Enquiry : Kieren Fox two-day ban: use of whip ( 10-11 Sep)

**FOCUS**
None of the runners was in particularly good form beforehand, and a routine pace made it hard to come from behind. The winner was well on top late on.

## 5821 BRITISH STALLION STUDS EBF MAIDEN FILLIES' STKS (BOBIS RACE) 7f (P)
**6:25** (6:27) (Class 5) 2-Y-O **£2,911** (£866; £432; £216) **Stalls** Low

Form RPR

3 **1** **Light Fantastic**[18] 5187 2-9-0 0........................................ WilliamBuick 8 78
(Ed Dunlop) *trckd ldr: shkn up to chal 2f out: upsides after: drvn fnl f: led nr fin* **5/2**[2]

3 **2** nk **Commandaria (USA)**[78] 3076 2-9-0 0.......................... RichardHughes 5 77
(Jeremy Noseda) *led: shkn up whn pressed 2f out: drvn fnl f: styd on but worn down nr fin* **6/4**[1]

**3** 3¾ **Forte** 2-9-0 0.................................................... SilvestreDeSousa 9 67+
(Ralph Beckett) *dwlt: tk fierce hold early: hld up in rr: pushed along and prog fr 2f out: styd on to take 3rd nr fin* **4/1**[3]

0 **4** hd **Bobbie's Girl (IRE)**[28] 4784 2-9-0 0.................................. LiamJones 6 67
(William Haggas) *t.k.h early: prom: chsd ldng pair 2f out but outpcd: no imp after: lost 3rd nr fin* **16/1**

0 **5** ¾ **Gleaming Girl**[13] 5344 2-9-0 0........................................ PatCosgrave 1 65
(David Simcock) *wl in tch but rn green: pushed along over 2f out: one pce but kpt on steadily* **33/1**

**6** ¾ **Saint Honore** 2-9-0 0................................................ HarryBentley 2 62
(Pat Phelan) *chsd ldng pair to 2f out: steadily outpcd* **100/1**

**7** nk **Acquittal** 2-9-0 0.................................................. HayleyTurner 12 62+
(James Fanshawe) *dwlt: rn green in rr: pushed along and sme prog on inner over 2f out: no imp over 1f out: one pce after nt disgracd* **25/1**

0 **8** 1¼ **Cascades (IRE)**[18] 5187 2-9-0 0........................................ LiamKeniry 10 58
(David Elsworth) *t.k.h early: hld up in midfield on outer: pushed along 3f out: no prog 2f out: wl hld after* **9/1**

**9** 1½ **You Be Lucky (IRE)** 2-9-0 0........................................ FergusSweeney 3 54
(Jo Crowley) *chsd ldrs to over 2f out: steadily wknd* **33/1**

**10** 3¼ **Vivi's Charis (IRE)** 2-9-0 0........................................ RyanMoore 11 45
(Sir Michael Stoute) *sn in last and nt gng wl: nvr a factor* **12/1**

**11** 1¾ **Medicean Melody** 2-9-0 0.............................................. MartinLane 4 41
(David Simcock) *a in rr: struggling fr over 2f out* **33/1**

1m 27.58s (1.58) **Going Correction** 0.0s/f (Stan) **11** Ran SP% **125.8**
Speed ratings (Par 91): **90,89,85,85,84 83,83,81,79,76 74**
CSF £6.90 TOTE £3.60: £1.40, £1.10, £1.90; EX 8.60 Trifecta £41.20.
**Owner** Racing Fillies **Bred** Whitwell Bloodstock **Trained** Newmarket, Suffolk

**FOCUS**
The pace was ordinary until they quickened early in the straight, with the first two home both in an ideal position to cash in, but that shouldn't detract from their potential.

## 5822 KEMPTON LIVE WITH DIZZEE RASCAL 06.09.14 MEDIAN AUCTION MAIDEN STKS 1m 4f (P)
**6:55** (6:56) (Class 5) 3-5-Y-O **£2,587** (£770; £384; £192) **Stalls** Centre

Form RPR

042 **1** **Limousine**[18] 5186 3-8-12 79........................................ JamesDoyle 4 71
(Charles Hills) *mde all: rdn over 2f out: hung lft over 1f out: drvn and clung on nr fin* **13/8**[2]

**2** nk **Seamour (IRE)** 3-9-3 0.............................................. FergusSweeney 2 75+
(Jo Crowley) *cl up in 3rd: pushed along 5f out: drvn over 2f out and looked in trble: rallied to go 2nd fnl f: clsd on wnr at fin* **20/1**

3 **3** 1¼ **Graffiti Art**[32] 4653 5-9-8 0........................................ FrederikTylicki 6 68+
(Brendan Powell) *taken down early: hld up in last pair: urged along and prog fr 2f out: styd on to take 3rd ins fnl f: nrst fin* **16/1**

0 **4** 1½ **Golden Bird (IRE)**[22] 5010 3-9-3 0.................................. SteveDrowne 3 70
(Dean Ivory) *chsd ldrs: drvn over 2f out: nvr gng pce to threaten but kpt on fr over 1f out* **33/1**

0-22 **5** ½ **Allegation (FR)**[23] 4966 3-8-12 80..................................(b[1]) TedDurcan 8 64
(David Lanigan) *trckd wnr: rdn and fnd nil over 2f out: lost 2nd and fdd fnl f* **8/11**[1]

0/6 **6** 6 **Musical Moon**[19] 5135 4-9-8 0........................................ CamHardie(5) 7 60
(Lady Herries) *mostly in last: pushed along 1/2-way: lft bhd fr 3f out* **25/1**

0 **7** 3¾ **Perfect Legend**[18] 5186 3-9-3 0........................................ DavidProbert 1 54
(Andrew Balding) *in tch tl wknd qckly over 2f out* **12/1**[3]

**R** **Garvie Bay**[81] 4-9-13 0................................................ LiamKeniry 5
(Michael Blanshard) *c out of the stalls and stopped* **25/1**

2m 34.43s (-0.07) **Going Correction** 0.0s/f (Stan)
**WFA** 3 from 4yo+ 10lb **8** Ran SP% **125.0**
Speed ratings (Par 103): **100,99,98,97,97 93,91,**
CSF £39.11 TOTE £3.10: £1.10, £5.60, £3.00; EX 50.00 Trifecta £122.20.
**Owner** K Abdullah **Bred** Juddmonte Farms Ltd **Trained** Lambourn, Berks

**FOCUS**
This attracted a mixed bunch, with the winner making all at a medium pace. The favourite looked below-par, but those ahead of her should all win races.

## 5823 BETDAQ 3% COMMISSION NURSERY H'CAP 1m (P)
**7:25** (7:26) (Class 6) (0-60,60) 2-Y-O **£1,940** (£577; £288; £144) **Stalls** Low

Form RPR

4002 **1** **Winter Queen**[9] 5489 2-8-12 **56**........................................ CamHardie(5) 6 65+
(Charlie Appleby) *trckd ldng trio: prog to ld 2f out: sn looked in command: drvn and pressed ins fnl f: kpt on wl* **15/8**[1]

0005 **2** ¾ **Father Stone**[19] 5148 2-9-2 **55**........................................ LiamKeniry 8 62+
(David Elsworth) *dropped in fr s and hld up in last trio: gd prog on inner fr 3f out: drvn to chse wnr 1f out: styd on but nvr quite got there* **8/1**

6443 **3** 3¼ **Framley Garth (IRE)**[19] 5148 2-9-7 **60**.................... SilvestreDeSousa 10 60
(David Elsworth) *led after 2f and set str pce: rdn over 2f out: hd high: wandered and sn hdd: lost 2nd u.str.p 1f out: outpcd after but hld on for 3rd* **7/1**[3]

006 **4** 1 **Hold Firm**[20] 5098 2-8-6 **45**............................................ JimmyQuinn 2 43
(Mark H Tompkins) *hld up in rr: rdn and prog over 2f out: kpt on fnl f to take 4th nr fin* **66/1**

0504 **5** shd **Jet Mate (IRE)**[23] 4967 2-9-2 **55**.................................. MartinDwyer 4 52
(William Muir) *racd in ldng trio: rdn over 2f out: outpcd wl over 1f out: one pce after* **6/1**[2]

0060 **6** hd **El Campeon**[7] 5554 2-9-2 **55**........................................ HarryBentley 1 52
(Simon Dow) *disp 6th but pushed along bef 1/2-way: effrt u.p over 2f out: kpt on one pce* **20/1**

0465 **7** hd **Goolagong Girl (IRE)**[9] 5489 2-9-2 **55**.......................... MartinHarley 13 51
(Jane Chapple-Hyam) *trckd ldng trio: rdn whn sltly intimidated over 2f out: nt qckn after: kpt on same pce fnl f* **16/1**

600 **8** ¾ **Akavit (IRE)**[17] 5201 2-8-7 **46**........................................ LiamJones 3 41
(Ed de Giles) *slowly away and vigorously rdn to get in tch: drvn over 2f out: kpt on but nvr a threat* **16/1**

0000 **9** 1½ **Hidden Agenda**[9] 5489 2-8-10 **49**.................................. DavidProbert 9 40
(Michael Blanshard) *led 2f: chsd ldr: rdn and edgd lft over 2f out: sn fdd* **66/1**

506 **10** 1½ **Orobas (IRE)**[16] 5248 2-8-12 **56**.................................. LouisSteward(5) 11 44
(Harry Whittington) *in tch disputing 6th: rdn 3f out: no imp on ldrs over 1f out: wknd fnl f* **20/1**

003 **11** ¾ **Gipsy Doll**[19] 5120 2-8-9 **48**........................................ LukeMorris 7 34
(Paul Cole) *nvr beyond midfield: rdn and no prog over 2f out: sn wknd* **12/1**

0000 **12** 1 **Ocean Crystal**[11] 5436 2-9-2 **58**.................................. RyanPowell(3) 12 42
(John Ryan) *hld up in last trio: rdn and no prog wl over 2f out* **14/1**

6502 **13** 2¼ **Chilworth Bells**[12] 5372 2-8-12 **54**.......................... CharlesBishop(3) 14 33
(Mick Channon) *a in rr: drvn and no prog wl over 2f out* **16/1**

0004 **14** 1¾ **Sarah Catherine**[43] 4302 2-8-6 **45**.................................. AndrewMullen 5 20
(Mark Usher) *nvr gng wl: a wl in rr* **66/1**

1m 39.97s (0.17) **Going Correction** 0.0s/f (Stan) **14** Ran SP% **118.7**
Speed ratings (Par 92): **99,98,95,94,93 93,93,92,91,89 89,88,85,84**
CSF £15.43 CT £87.33 TOTE £3.20: £1.40, £3.70, £2.30; EX 32.00 Trifecta £127.00.
**Owner** Godolphin **Bred** S Boucheron **Trained** Newmarket, Suffolk

**FOCUS**
In a moderate race run at a decent pace, the winner was well-in and well placed after her previous outing.

## 5824 BETDAQ £50 FREE BET H'CAP (LONDON MILE SERIES QUALIFIER) 1m (P)
7:55 (7:56) (Class 3) (0-95,94) 3-Y-0+
£7,158 (£2,143; £1,071; £535; £267; £134) Stalls Low

Form RPR
15 1 **Sloane Avenue (USA)**[102] 2345 3-9-4 **92** JamesDoyle 3 104+
(Jeremy Noseda) *dwlt settled in 10th and wl off the pce: gd prog over 2f out: sustained effrt to ld ins fnl f: drvn and asserted nr fin* 6/1[3]
3116 2 ¾ **Billingsgate (IRE)**[32] 4647 3-9-4 **92** WilliamBuick 12 102
(Charlie Appleby) *trckd ldr after 2f: rdn over 2f out: hd at awkward angle but led over 1f out: hdd ins fnl f: tried to rally but hld last 75yds* 8/1
2212 3 1 ¼ **Musaddas**[21] 5040 4-9-4 **86** AndreaAtzeni 4 94
(Saeed bin Suroor) *off the pce disputing 5th: rdn wl over 2f out: prog on outer over 1f out: styd on to take 3rd ins fnl f* 5/1[2]
1500 4 2 ¼ **Zampa Manos (USA)**[69] 3378 3-9-2 **90** DavidProbert 1 92
(Andrew Balding) *chsd ldng trio: drvn and outpcd over 2f out: rallied over 1f out and edgd rt: 3rd briefly ins fnl f: wknd last 100yds* 12/1
6524 5 nk **Silverheels (IRE)**[17] 5222 5-9-6 **88** (b) LukeMorris 2 90
(Paul Cole) *off the pce disputing 6th: drvn 2f out: clsd over 1f out: kpt on same pce fnl f* 25/1
00-1 6 1 ½ **Homage (IRE)**[59] 3759 4-9-12 **94** RyanMoore 9 92
(William Haggas) *off the pce disputing 8th: rdn wl over 2f out: kpt on fr over 1f out: nvr gng pce to threaten* 15/8[1]
4103 7 nse **Bravo Echo**[20] 5092 8-9-11 **93** RobertHavlin 13 91
(Michael Attwater) *led at str pce and stretched field: drvn over 2f out: hdd & wknd over 1f out* 50/1
15-4 8 hd **Mystical Sapphire**[17] 5213 4-9-8 **90** FergusSweeney 8 88
(Jo Crowley) *off the pce disputing 8th: rdn over 2f out: tried to cl over 1f out but sn no imp* 14/1
0442 9 2 **Monsieur Chevalier (IRE)**[42] 4323 7-9-3 **88** RobertTart(3) 7 81
(P J O'Gorman) *slowly away: mostly in last trio: effrt on inner 2f out: n.d* 14/1
6064 10 1 ¾ **Secret Art (IRE)**[29] 4761 4-9-11 **93** (p) GeorgeBaker 5 82
(William Knight) *chsd ldr 2f: styd prom tl wknd wl over 1f out* 8/1
22/3 11 8 **Jamhoori**[160] 6-9-7 **89** TomQueally 10 59
(Jeremy Gask) *s.i.s: a in last trio: wknd 3f out: t.o* 50/1
316- 12 3 ½ **Talksalot (IRE)**[308] 7570 3-9-0 **88** StevieDonohoe 6 48
(J S Moore) *chsd ldrs tl wknd 3f out: t.o* 100/1
1m 37.06s (-2.74) **Going Correction** 0.0s/f (Stan)
**WFA** 3 from 4yo+ 6lb 12 Ran SP% 117.7
Speed ratings (Par 107): **113,112,111,108,108 106,106,106,104,102 94,91**
CSF £51.94 CT £263.19 TOTE £5.90: £2.60, £2.60, £3.00; EX 66.80 Trifecta £411.10.
**Owner** Mrs Susan Roy **Bred** Claiborne Farm & Adele B Dilschneider **Trained** Newmarket, Suffolk
**FOCUS**
This was a quality field of 1m handicappers, and the pace was good. The winner is held in some regard, but may have been aided by being able to come off a strong gallop.

## 5825 BETDAQ NO PREMIUM CHARGE H'CAP 2m (P)
8:25 (8:25) (Class 4) (0-85,85) 4-Y-0+ £4,690 (£1,395; £697; £348) Stalls Low

Form RPR
22-0 1 **Deficit (IRE)**[15] 5288 4-9-1 79 WilliamBuick 7 87
(Steve Gollings) *trckd ldr 6f: styd cl up: shkn up over 2f out: clsd to ld over 1f out: rdn out* 6/1[3]
0205 2 1 ¼ **Sir Frank Morgan (IRE)**[7] 5579 4-9-5 83 SilvestreDeSousa 2 90
(Mark Johnston) *hld up tl prog to trck ldr after 6f: drvn to ld over 2f out: hdd and one pce over 1f out* 3/1[1]
0606 3 1 ¼ **Tappanappa (IRE)**[22] 4995 7-8-9 73 AndrewMullen 1 78
(Michael Appleby) *dwlt: hld up in last trio: urged along 4f out: kpt on u.p fr over 2f out to take 3rd ins fnl f* 16/1
2103 4 nk **Perfect Summer (IRE)**[39] 4423 4-8-11 80 LouisSteward(5) 6 85
(Lady Cecil) *hld up in last: pushed along 3f out as pce lifting: no prog tl styd on fr over 1f out: nrly tk 3rd* 3/1[1]
3610 5 ¾ **Lion Beacon**[28] 4777 4-9-7 85 SebSanders 4 89
(Amanda Perrett) *led at mod pce: stepped it up fr 5f out: drvn and hdd over 2f out: fdd fnl f: stmbld after fin and qckly dismntd* 5/1[2]
3426 6 1 ¼ **Opera Buff**[20] 5083 5-8-9 78 (p) CamHardie(5) 5 80
(Jose Santos) *hld up in last trio: pushed along 3f out: nvr able to bridge the gap w those in front nt stopping* 8/1
1412 7 ¾ **See And Be Seen**[32] 4685 4-8-11 75 (p) JamesDoyle 3 76
(Sylvester Kirk) *prom: drvn over 2f out: tried to cl on inner wl over 1f out: wknd fnl f* 3/1[1]
3m 31.23s (1.13) **Going Correction** 0.0s/f (Stan) 7 Ran SP% 122.9
Speed ratings (Par 105): **97,96,95,95,95 94,94**
CSF £26.63 TOTE £6.70: £3.00, £2.90; EX 32.40 Trifecta £394.40.
**Owner** Irvin S Naylor **Bred** J Hanly, T Stewart & A Stroud **Trained** Scamblesby, Lincs
**FOCUS**
The pace was ordinary and the field finished in a bit of a heap.

## 5826 WIN £10,000,000 ON THE BETDAQ COLOSSUS FILLIES' H'CAP 7f (P)
8:55 (8:55) (Class 4) (0-85,85) 3-Y-0+ £4,690 (£1,395; £697; £348) Stalls Low

Form RPR
1110 1 **Ishiamber**[58] 3788 4-9-12 **85** PatCosgrave 3 92
(George Baker) *trckd ldng trio: rdn jst over 2f out: clsd to chal over 1f out: narrow ld ins fnl f: drvn and hld on* 8/1[3]
-220 2 nk **Gown (IRE)**[39] 4436 3-9-1 **79** SteveDrowne 4 83
(Charles Hills) *sn trckd ldr: rdn to chal over 1f out: upsides ins fnl f: jst hld* 8/1[3]
1-12 3 nse **Maria Bella (IRE)**[62] 3615 3-9-6 **84** WilliamBuick 5 88
(Charlie Appleby) *sn led at mod pce: sent for home jst over 2f out: drvn and pressed over 1f out: hdd ins fnl f: kpt on wl but lost 2nd last stride* 7/2[2]
-532 4 nk **Interception (IRE)**[85] 2861 4-9-10 **83** TedDurcan 8 88+
(David Lanigan) *hld up in last in modly run r: prog wl over 1f out: tk 4th ins fnl f: cajoled along and clsd nr fin: a too much to do* 9/4[1]
-005 5 1 ½ **Trucanini**[50] 4053 4-9-11 **84** GeorgeBaker 2 85
(Chris Wall) *trckd ldng pair: drvn over 2f out: nt qckn on inner over 1f out: one pce fnl f* 7/2[2]
0460 6 ½ **Miss Lillie**[39] 4436 3-8-12 **76** (p) JamesDoyle 6 74
(Roger Teal) *t.k.h: hld up: rdn and outpcd over 2f out: kpt on ins fnl f: n.d* 12/1
2464 7 ¾ **Subtle Knife**[20] 5092 5-9-5 **78** WilliamCarson 7 76
(Giles Bravery) *hld up towards rr: rdn and nt qckn over 2f out: nvr on terms after: kpt on fnl f* 12/1
1030 8 2 **Relation Alexander (IRE)**[10] 5467 3-8-11 **75** SeanLevey 9 65
(Paul D'Arcy) *hld up in rr: rdn over 2f out: no prog and sn btn* 20/1
0460 9 1 ¾ **Saffire Song**[15] 5281 3-8-6 **70** LiamJones 1 56
(Alan Bailey) *t.k.h: hld up in tch: rdn over 2f out: sn btn* 66/1
1m 26.1s (0.10) **Going Correction** 0.0s/f (Stan)
**WFA** 3 from 4yo+ 5lb 9 Ran SP% 119.1
Speed ratings (Par 102): **99,98,98,98,96 95,95,92,90**
CSF £72.23 CT £268.54 TOTE £8.90: £1.90, £2.50, £1.30; EX 99.60 Trifecta £181.30.
**Owner** Mrs P Scott-Dunn **Bred** Patricia Ann Scott-Dunn **Trained** Manton, Wilts
**FOCUS**
The early pace was weak and it didn't really test these decent 7f handicappers. A few finished with more to give.
T/Jkpt: Not won. T/Plt: £116.30 to a £1 stake. Pool: £65027.88 - 407.84 winning tickets T/Qpdt: £30.50 to a £1 stake. Pool: £6604.79 - 159.80 winning tickets JN

# 5554 LINGFIELD (L-H)
Wednesday, August 27

**OFFICIAL GOING: Polytrack: standard**
Wind: light, across Weather: overcast, dry

## 5827 £10 FREE BET AT 32REDSPORT.COM MAIDEN FILLIES' STKS (BOBIS RACE) 1m 1y(P)
2:20 (2:20) (Class 5) 2-Y-O £2,587 (£770; £384; £192) Stalls High

Form RPR
22 1 **Turning Times (IRE)**[21] 5037 2-9-0 0 WilliamBuick 1 76
(Charlie Appleby) *mde all: rdn and qcknd 3f out: kpt on wl fr over 1f out: rdn out* 1/1[1]
05 2 2 **Lexi's Red Devil (IRE)**[11] 5416 2-9-0 0 MartinHarley 5 71
(Marco Botti) *chsd wnr: rdn 3f out: drvn and kpt on same pce fr over 1f out* 7/1[3]
3 ¾ **Madam Midnight** 2-9-0 0 JimCrowley 2 69
(David Simcock) *dwlt: chsd ldrs: rdn and effrt on inner over 1f out: rdn and kpt on same pce fnl f* 8/1
4 4 ½ **Galileano (IRE)** 2-9-0 0 RyanMoore 3 59+
(Marco Botti) *s.i.s: hld up in tch in rr: rdn over 3f out: wknd wl over 1f out* 5/2[2]
5 8 **Tepeleni** 2-9-0 0 RichardHughes 4 39
(Clive Brittain) *in tch in last pair: rdn 3f out: btn 2f out: sn dropped to last and eased ins fnl f* 14/1
1m 38.39s (0.19) **Going Correction** -0.05s/f (Stan) 5 Ran SP% 108.8
Speed ratings (Par 91): **97,95,94,89,81**
CSF £8.32 TOTE £2.60: £1.20, £2.80; EX 4.80 Trifecta £16.70.
**Owner** Godolphin **Bred** Darley **Trained** Newmarket, Suffolk
**FOCUS**
Despite the small field this had the look of an okay fillies' maiden.

## 5828 32RED CASINO NURSERY H'CAP 6f 1y(P)
2:50 (2:51) (Class 6) (0-65,64) 2-Y-O £2,199 (£654; £327; £163) Stalls Low

Form RPR
050 1 **Barchan (USA)**[77] 3119 2-9-1 **63** CamHardie(5) 7 67+
(Charlie Appleby) *chsd ldrs: rdn and effrt 2f out: styd on ins fnl f to ld fnl 50yds: gng away at fin* 9/4[1]
0065 2 1 **Magic Mac**[15] 5279 2-8-3 **46** (p) LukeMorris 5 47
(Hughie Morrison) *chsd ldr: rdn and ev ch 2f out: drvn to ld 1f out: hdd and no ex fnl 50yds* 16/1
4646 3 ½ **Sportlobster (IRE)**[24] 4939 2-9-7 **64** (p) RichardKingscote 1 64
(Tom Dascombe) *broke fast: led: rdn 2f out: drvn and hdd 1f out: styd on same pce ins fnl f* 9/2[3]
400U 4 4 ½ **Piping Dream (IRE)**[8] 5517 2-8-12 **55** RichardHughes 2 43
(Richard Hannon) *hld up in tch in midfield: rdn and unable qck over 1f out: swtchd rt ent fnl f: wknd fnl 100yds* 10/1
554 5 shd **Mazoula (IRE)**[17] 5210 2-8-9 **57** NoelGarbutt(5) 3 43
(Hugo Palmer) *hld up in last pair: rdn and effrt on inner wl over 1f out: sn outpcd and btn 1f out* 6/1
4222 6 2 **Lady Zodiac (IRE)**[8] 5517 2-8-13 **56** DavidProbert 4 36
(Andrew Balding) *in tch in midfield: rdn and struggling ent fnl 2f: wknd over 1f out* 3/1[2]
060 7 2 ½ **Bakht A Rawan (IRE)**[60] 3728 2-9-5 **62** LiamKeniry 6 34
(Mark Usher) *s.i.s: in tch in rr: rdn and struggling over 2f out: wknd over 1f out* 8/1
1m 12.36s (0.46) **Going Correction** -0.05s/f (Stan) 7 Ran SP% 114.3
Speed ratings (Par 92): **94,92,92,86,85 83,79**
CSF £38.30 TOTE £4.40: £1.50, £7.20; EX 46.30 Trifecta £192.70.
**Owner** Godolphin **Bred** Upson Downs Farm **Trained** Newmarket, Suffolk
**FOCUS**
All seven of these were maidens coming into this race and it looks like modest nursery form.

## 5829 32RED H'CAP 1m 5f (P)
3:20 (3:20) (Class 6) (0-65,63) 3-Y-O £2,199 (£654; £327; £163) Stalls Low

Form RPR
3-03 1 **Ohio (IRE)**[9] 5491 3-8-8 50 LukeMorris 6 59+
(Nick Littmoden) *hld up in tch in last pair: hdwy to join ldrs over 2f out: drvn to ld over 1f out: hld on wl ins fnl f: all out* 6/1
0006 2 hd **Dire Straits (IRE)**[22] 5011 3-9-5 61 (p) TedDurcan 2 70+
(Chris Wall) *reminder sn after s: chsd ldrs: swtchd rt and reminder over 2f out: drvn and hdwy over 1f out: c clr w wnr but flashed tail u.p fnl f: jst hld* 9/4[1]
610 3 6 **Roman Riches**[48] 4106 3-9-6 62 (v) RyanMoore 1 62
(Gary Moore) *s.i.s: bhd: hdwy to chse ldrs over 2f out: drvn and no ex over 1f out: no ch w ldrs but kpt on to go 3rd ins fnl f* 4/1[3]
4434 4 ¾ **Passionate Affair (IRE)**[7] 5556 3-9-7 63 (tp) RichardHughes 5 62
(Jamie Osborne) *in tch in midfield: hdwy on outer to join ldrs over 3f out: drvn and ev ch 2f out: outpcd and btn 1f out: lost 3rd ins fnl f* 5/2[2]
055 5 2 ¼ **Perfect Outcome**[22] 5010 3-8-12 57 RyanTate(3) 4 53
(Patrick Chamings) *mde most: rdn over 2f out: hdd over 1f out: sn btn: wknd 1f out* 8/1
504 6 5 **Opus Too (IRE)**[15] 5282 3-8-7 54 (b[1]) ShelleyBirkett(5) 3 43
(Julia Feilden) *in tch: effrt and rdn over 2f out: wknd over 1f out* 20/1
00-0 7 28 **Desert Island Dusk**[9] 5491 3-8-3 45 WilliamCarson 8
(John Bridger) *chsd ldrs: rdn 5f out: sn lost pl: t.o fnl 2f* 100/1

6500 **8** *2 ¼* **Hiorne Tower (FR)**[22] 5011 3-9-4 60 ............................ GeorgeBaker 7
(John Best) *chsd ldr tl rdn and lost pl qckly 3f out: t.o and eased over 1f out: lame* **14/1**

2m 45.12s (-0.88) **Going Correction** -0.05s/f (Stan) **8** Ran SP% **117.2**
Speed ratings (Par 98): **100,99,96,95,94 91,74,72**
CSF £20.48 CT £61.46 TOTE £7.20: £1.60, £1.50, £1.10; EX 29.80 Trifecta £172.20.
**Owner** Franconson Partners, Maze Rattan Ltd **Bred** T J Monaghan **Trained** Newmarket, Suffolk

**FOCUS**
A moderate contest with question marks over plenty of these. The winner has been an improver since going up in trip.

## 5830 RACING SPECIALS AT 32REDSPORT.COM H'CAP — 5f 6y(P)

**3:50** (3:51) (Class 4) (0-80,80) 3-Y-O+ **£5,304** (£1,578; £788; £394) **Stalls** High

Form RPR

1-02 **1** **Brother Tiger**[34] 4581 5-9-4 75 ............................ OisinMurphy 5 84+
(David C Griffiths) *taken down early: chsd ldrs: effrt to chse ldr wl over 1f out: chal 1f out: rdn to ld fnl 75yds: r.o* **9/4**[1]

230 **2** *½* **Angel Way (IRE)**[49] 4078 5-9-2 73 ............................ ShaneKelly 9 80
(Mike Murphy) *led: drvn over 1f out: hdd fnl 75yds: kpt on* **16/1**

040 **3** *1 ½* **Arctic Lynx (IRE)**[15] 5281 7-9-4 75 ............................ (p) AndreaAtzeni 7 77
(Robert Cowell) *in tch in midfield: effrt u.p 2f out: no imp tl styd on 1f out: wnt 3rd fnl 100yds: kpt on* **10/1**

4161 **4** *2* **Dissent (IRE)**[15] 5281 5-9-7 78 ............................ (b) TomQueally 8 72
(James Given) *taken down early: nt best away: rcvrd to chse ldrs over 3f out: wnt 2nd briefly 2f out: 3rd and no imp over 1f out: wknd ins fnl f* **5/2**[2]

1030 **5** *½* **Expose**[102] 2332 6-9-1 77 ............................ CamHardie(5) 4 70
(Shaun Harris) *bustled along leaving stalls: hmpd after 1f: in tch in last trio: kpt on u.p ins fnl f: nvr trbld ldrs* **8/1**

0200 **6** *½* **Rebecca Romero**[24] 4946 7-9-4 75 ............................ RichardHughes 3 66
(Denis Coakley) *dwlt: n.m.r sn after s: hdwy on outer over 2f out: no imp and one pce over 1f out* **7/1**[3]

00 **7** *1* **Stone Of Folca**[29] 4762 6-9-9 80 ............................ GeorgeBaker 10 67
(John Best) *taken down early: chsd ldr tl 2f out: sn rdn and btn over 1f out: wknd ins fnl f* **8/1**

330 **8** *1 ¼* **O'Gorman**[15] 5281 5-9-8 79 ............................ LiamKeniry 1 62
(Gary Brown) *taken down early: in tch in midfield: effrt on inner 2f out: no imp* **16/1**

2005 **9** *4* **Royal Acquisition**[29] 4768 4-9-3 74 ............................ AdamBeschizza 2 42
(Robert Cowell) *s.i.s: a in rr: rdn and no hdwy over 2f out* **33/1**

58.44s (-0.36) **Going Correction** -0.05s/f (Stan) **9** Ran SP% **117.9**
Speed ratings (Par 105): **100,99,96,93,92 92,90,88,82**
CSF £40.55 CT £309.09 TOTE £3.10: £1.10, £7.00, £1.60; EX 46.20 Trifecta £525.80.
**Owner** Norcroft Park Stud **Bred** Norcroft Park Stud **Trained** Bawtry, S Yorks

**FOCUS**
Just a fair sprint handicap, but only 7lb covered the runners and it was competitive enough. The runner-up helps to set the level.

## 5831 GREYHOUND MAIDEN STKS — 1m 2f (P)

**4:25** (4:28) (Class 5) 3-4-Y-O **£2,587** (£770; £384; £192) **Stalls** Low

Form RPR

**1** **Spacelab** 3-9-0 0 ............................ JamesDoyle 6 80+
(Amanda Perrett) *chsd ldng trio: rdn and effrt over 1f out: str run to ld fnl 100yds: r.o wl: rdn out* **25/1**

0 **2** *½* **Rembrandt Van Rijn (IRE)**[102] 2334 3-9-5 0 ............................ TedDurcan 2 84
(David Lanigan) *chsd ldng pair: rdn and effrt 2f out: rn green 1f out: ev ch fnl 100yds: r.o but a hld by wnr* **7/4**[1]

5422 **3** *1* **Red Velour**[19] 5150 3-9-0 77 ............................ RyanMoore 7 77
(Jeremy Noseda) *chsd ldr tl led 2f out: drvn over 1f out: hdd fnl 100yds: no ex* **9/4**[2]

42 **4** *4 ½* **Past Forgetting (IRE)**[23] 4984 3-9-0 0 ............................ AndreaAtzeni 5 69
(Luca Cumani) *in tch in midfield: effrt jst over 2f out: 5th and outpcd wl over 1f out: no threat to ldrs but kpt on to go 4th nr fin* **5/1**[3]

32 **5** *½* **Glorious Sun**[18] 5195 3-9-5 0 ............................ RichardHughes 4 73
(Ed Walker) *led: rdn and hdd 2f out: 4th and btn 1f out: wknd ins fnl f: lost 4th nr fin* **10/1**

**6** *2 ¼* **Cerutty (IRE)** 3-9-5 0 ............................ MartinHarley 8 68+
(Marco Botti) *hld up in midfield: rdn and sme hdwy over 2f out: modest 6th and no imp over 1f out* **25/1**

00 **7** *1* **Zarliman (IRE)**[44] 4262 4-9-13 70 ............................ JackMitchell 9 66
(Martyn Meade) *t.k.h: hld up towards rr: rdn outpcd over 2f out: plugged on but wl hld after* **66/1**

4-6 **8** *6* **Sagua La Grande (IRE)**[42] 4325 4-9-10 0 ............(t) AshleyMorgan(3) 11 55
(Lady Cecil) *s.i.s: bhd: hdwy into midfield 5f out: rdn and btn over 2f out: no ch over 1f out* **25/1**

**9** *½* **Sea Vision (IRE)** 4-9-13 0 ............................ FergusSweeney 1 54
(Jo Crowley) *s.i.s: pushed along in rr early: rdn and lost tch over 2f out* **100/1**

3/0 **10** *1 ½* **Precinct**[22] 5007 4-9-8 0 ............................ [1] LukeMorris 13 46
(James Eustace) *in tch in midfield: rdn over 2f out: sn lost pl and wl btn 2f out* **50/1**

5- **11** *nk* **Cry Joy (USA)**[308] 7460 3-9-5 0 ............................ WilliamBuick 3 51
(Charlie Appleby) *chsd ldrs: rdn and btn ent fnl 2f: fdd over 1f out* **6/1**

54 **12** *2* **Roxy Hart**[22] 5010 3-9-0 0 ............................ JimmyQuinn 12 42
(Ed Vaughan) *s.i.s: a towards rr* **66/1**

0-0 **13** *23* **Graceful Willow**[78] 3074 4-9-5 0 ............................ NataliaGemelova(3) 10
(John E Long) *s.i.s: a in rr: lost tch 3f out: t.o: b.b.v* **100/1**

2m 3.45s (-3.15) **Going Correction** -0.05s/f (Stan)
**WFA** 3 from 4yo 8lb **13** Ran SP% **125.6**
Speed ratings (Par 103): **110,109,108,105,104 103,102,97,97,95 95,93,75**
CSF £70.68 TOTE £27.30: £6.60, £1.70, £1.10; EX 167.00 Trifecta £922.10.
**Owner** K Abdullah **Bred** Juddmonte Farms Ltd **Trained** Pulborough, W Sussex

**FOCUS**
Some top yards were represented here and most probably an above-average maiden for this time of the season.

## 5832 INDUS CATERING H'CAP (DIV I) — 1m 1y(P)

**4:55** (4:56) (Class 6) (0-60,60) 3-Y-O+ **£2,199** (£654; £327; £163) **Stalls** High

Form RPR

6045 **1** **Fiducia**[41] 4352 4-9-10 60 ............................ HarryBentley 8 67
(Simon Dow) *stdd after s: hld up in rr: n.m.r and jostling w rival 2f out: hdwy on outer 1f out: str run to ld fnl 75yds: sn in command: r.o wl* **16/1**

0602 **2** *1 ¼* **Celestial Knight**[23] 4970 3-9-4 60 ............................ (v) ShaneKelly 6 64
(James Fanshawe) *hld up in last in rr: n.m.r and jostling w wnr 2f out: rdn and hdwy between horses 1f out: styd on u.p to go 2nd towards fin: no threat to wnr* **1/1**[1]

5260 **3** *½* **Golly Miss Molly**[23] 4969 3-8-6 48 ............................ (p) AndreaAtzeni 2 50
(Jeremy Gask) *led: rdn and fnd ex 2f out: hdd and no ex fnl 75yds: lost 2nd towards fin* **16/1**

4450 **4** *nk* **Dancing Sal (IRE)**[39] 4428 3-9-0 56 ............................ (b) JimmyFortune 7 57
(Gary Moore) *chsd ldrs early: grad stdd bk into last pair: hdwy over 2f out: drvn and chsd ldrs over 1f out: one pce fnl f* **10/1**[3]

6343 **5** *nk* **Anginola (IRE)**[15] 5280 5-9-1 51 ............................ (p) LiamJones 3 54
(Laura Mongan) *in tch in midfield: nt clr run ent fnl 2f: hdwy on inner over 1f out: chsd ldrs and one pce fnl f* **6/1**[2]

000- **6** *2* **Bryant Park (USA)**[258] 8258 5-8-11 47 ............................ PatCosgrave 9 44
(Jane Chapple-Hyam) *chsd ldrs: wnt 2nd and hung lft bnd 2f out: no ex and btn over 1f out: wknd ins fnl f* **12/1**

0565 **7** *5* **Super Cookie**[20] 5109 4-9-4 57 ............................ RobertTart(3) 5 42
(Anthony Carson) *t.k.h: chsd ldr tl 2f out: sn no ex: wknd 1f out* **6/1**[2]

055 **8** *1 ¾* **Focail Mear**[12] 5400 3-8-1 46 oh1 ............................ RyanPowell(3) 1 26
(John Ryan) *in tch in midfield: effrt whn n.m.r 2f out: no ex over 1f out: wknd 1f out* **50/1**

0660 **9** *8* **Booktheband (IRE)**[57] 3824 4-8-6 47 ............................ (b) LouisSteward(5) 10 10
(Clive Brittain) *s.i.s: towards rr: hdwy on outer into midfield 1/2-way: rdn and struggling 2f out: sn wknd* **14/1**

1m 37.85s (-0.35) **Going Correction** -0.05s/f (Stan)
**WFA** 3 from 4yo+ 6lb **9** Ran SP% **115.7**
Speed ratings (Par 101): **99,97,97,96,96 94,89,87,79**
CSF £32.64 CT £286.51 TOTE £20.50: £3.70, £1.10, £4.60; EX 35.60 Trifecta £288.20.
**Owner** Paul G Jacobs **Bred** Aldridge Racing Partnership **Trained** Epsom, Surrey

**FOCUS**
A dearth of recent form in evidence and this looks to be very moderate form. The winner was fully entitled to take this on last year's form.

## 5833 INDUS CATERING H'CAP (DIV II) — 1m 1y(P)

**5:25** (5:25) (Class 6) (0-60,60) 3-Y-O+ **£2,199** (£654; £327; £163) **Stalls** High

Form RPR

4035 **1** **Lifejacket (IRE)**[29] 4763 3-8-13 55 ............................ (b[1]) AndreaAtzeni 5 62
(Ed Dunlop) *hld up in tch in midfield: rdn and effrt 1f out: r.o wl ins fnl to ld fnl 50yds* **3/1**[2]

2165 **2** *½* **Cyflymder (IRE)**[19] 5139 8-9-3 53 ............................ OisinMurphy 9 60
(David C Griffiths) *led: rdn and drifted rt over 1f out: kpt on wl u.p tl hdd and no ex fnl 50yds* **9/2**[3]

-604 **3** *1 ½* **Vied (USA)**[16] 5257 3-8-11 53 ............................ (p) AdamBeschizza 7 56
(Robert Cowell) *chsd ldr tl 1/2-way: styd chsng ldrs: drvn wl over 1f out: chsd wnr again 1f out tl fnl 100yds: no ex* **10/1**

0042 **4** *1* **Patronella (IRE)**[8] 5522 3-8-10 52 ............................ RichardKingscote 3 53
(David Simcock) *chsd ldrs: wnt 2nd 1/2-way: rdn and sltly hmpd over 1f out: lost 2nd and no ex ins fnl f* **11/4**[1]

4364 **5** *¾* **Dark Phantom (IRE)**[18] 5183 3-8-4 46 ............................ (t) MartinDwyer 8 45
(Peter Makin) *stdd s: t.k.h: hld up in rr: effrt but wdst bnd 2f out: kpt on ins fnl f: nt rch ldrs* **14/1**

4600 **6** *1* **Midnight Feast**[14] 5303 6-9-6 56 ............................ (p) StevieDonohoe 4 54
(Lee Carter) *s.i.s: in tch in last trio: hdwy over 1f out: no imp ins fnl f* **10/1**

6032 **7** *½* **El Mirage (IRE)**[11] 5425 4-9-10 60 ............................ JimCrowley 6 57
(Dean Ivory) *in tch in midfield but stuck wd: rdn and no rspnse over 1f out: hld and nt pushed ins fnl f* **5/1**

4-00 **8** *1 ½* **Mack's Sister**[19] 5138 7-8-7 50 ............................ KieranShoemark(7) 2 44
(Michael Madgwick) *in tch in midfield: lost pl u.p over 2f out: n.d over 1f out: plugged on* **33/1**

0500 **9** *4 ½* **Basingstoke (IRE)**[84] 2884 5-9-8 58 ............................ SteveDrowne 1 42
(Simon Hodgson) *hld up in last trio: rdn over 2f out: sn struggling: wknd over 1f out* **33/1**

1m 38.56s (0.36) **Going Correction** -0.05s/f (Stan)
**WFA** 3 from 4yo+ 6lb **9** Ran SP% **117.2**
Speed ratings (Par 101): **96,95,94,93,92 91,90,89,84**
CSF £17.32 CT £118.45 TOTE £4.70: £2.10, £2.30, £5.40; EX 16.00 Trifecta £242.40.
**Owner** Miltil Consortium **Bred** Mesnil, Mount Coote, New England Stud **Trained** Newmarket, Suffolk

**FOCUS**
This looked a bit stronger than the first division, but was still essentially moderate form. It was 0.7sec slower than that preceding race.

## 5834 ALL NEW 32REDSPORT.COM H'CAP — 7f 1y(P)

**6:00** (6:00) (Class 5) (0-75,75) 4-Y-O+ **£2,587** (£770; £384; £192) **Stalls** Low

Form RPR

0120 **1** **Secret Success**[14] 5308 4-9-7 75 ............................ (t) GeorgeBaker 1 83
(Paul Cole) *mde all: rdn and flashed tail u.p ins fnl f: kpt on and a doing enough* **11/4**[1]

0211 **2** *¾* **Exceedexpectations (IRE)**[35] 4544 5-9-7 75 ............(v) StevieDonohoe 2 81
(Lee Carter) *chsd wnr thrght: rdn and pressed wnr 2f out: kpt on but a hld ins fnl f* **4/1**[2]

32-4 **3** *1 ¾* **Charter (IRE)**[14] 5308 4-9-7 75 ............................ PaddyAspell 8 76
(Michael Wigham) *plld v hrd: hld up in tch: rdn and effrt over 1f out: kpt on same pce ins fnl f* **9/2**[3]

023 **4** *1* **Marjong**[15] 5281 4-9-7 75 ............................ SebSanders 6 74
(Simon Dow) *stdd s: hld up in tch in midfield: sme hdwy on inner over 1f out: no imp ins fnl f* **5/1**

66 **5** *2 ¾* **Evident (IRE)**[13] 5346 4-9-5 73 ............................ (p) JimmyFortune 3 64
(Jeremy Noseda) *in tch in midfield: effrt 2f out: unable qck and btn 1f out: wknd fnl 100yds* **5/1**

636 **6** *¾* **Harry Bosch**[12] 5394 4-9-5 73 ............................ TomQueally 5 62
(Gay Kelleway) *hld up in last trio: rdn but stl plenty to do whn hmpd wl over 1f out: no prog* **12/1**

0-45 **7** *1 ¼* **Boboli Gardens**[49] 4090 4-9-2 70 ............................ (t[1]) LemosdeSouza 10 56
(Mrs Ilka Gansera-Leveque) *stdd s: hld up in last pair: effrt but stl plenty to do whn hmpd wl over 1f out: no hdwy after* **25/1**

0300 **8** *nk* **Multitask**[34] 4581 4-9-6 74 ............................ WilliamCarson 4 59
(Michael Madgwick) *stdd after s: hld up off the pce in rr: clsd but stl plenty to do whn hmpd wl over 1f out: no ch after* **16/1**

1m 23.77s (-1.03) **Going Correction** -0.05s/f (Stan) **8** Ran SP% **115.6**
Speed ratings (Par 103): **103,102,100,99,95 95,93,93**
CSF £14.02 CT £47.52 TOTE £4.50: £3.00, £1.02, £1.50; EX 14.80 Trifecta £54.00.
**Owner** P F I Cole Ltd **Bred** Ray Bailey **Trained** Whatcombe, Oxon

**FOCUS**
A fair handicap to close the card and it paid to race close to the pace.

T/Plt: £25.10 to a £1 stake. Pool: £58042.95 - 1687.22 winning tickets T/Qpdt: £7.80 to a £1 stake. Pool: £5545.77 - 521.80 winning tickets SP

5835 - 5842a (Foreign Racing) - See Raceform Interactive

# 5739 DEAUVILLE (R-H)

## Wednesday, August 27

**OFFICIAL GOING: Turf: heavy; polytrack: standard**

### 5843a PRIX DE MONTREUIL-EN-AUGE (CONDITIONS) (3YO FILLIES) (POLYTRACK) 7f 110y

**1:20** (12:00) 3-Y-O **£14,166** (£5,666; £4,250; £2,833; £1,416)

RPR

1 **Summer Moon (FR)**[26] 3-9-0 0 ChristopheSoumillon 5 90
(J-C Rouget, France) **13/5**[1]

2 ¾ **Divina Comedia (FR)**[281] 7967 3-9-0 0 ThierryThulliez 11 88
(N Clement, France) **7/1**[3]

3 snk **Stosur (IRE)**[26] 4842 3-9-0 0 (b[1]) Pierre-CharlesBoudot 10 88
(Gay Kelleway) *w ldrs: led after 1 1/2f: scrubbed along and responded whn chal over 1 1/2f out: kpt on gamely u.p: hdd 100yds out: no ex* **231/10**

4 nk **Hestia (FR)**[53] 3-9-0 0 MaximeGuyon 4 87
(A Fabre, France) **89/10**

5 shd **Cosima (FR)**[25] 3-9-0 0 StephanePasquier 12 87
(G Doleuze, France) **115/10**

6 ½ **Raphinae**[39] 3-9-0 0 MickaelBarzalona 8 86
(H-A Pantall, France) *w.w towards rr: hdwy on outer 2f out: kpt on ins fnl f: nvr on terms w ldrs* **126/10**

7 ½ **Violet Symphony (FR)**[38] 3-9-0 0 UmbertoRispoli 2 85
(M Delzangles, France) **9/2**[2]

8 hd **Waikika (FR)**[16] 3-8-6 0 LukasDelozier(8) 7 84
(Y Barberot, France) **87/10**

9 hd **Tarnag (FR)**[24] 4952 3-8-6 0 MllePaulineDominois(8) 1 84
(E Lellouche, France) **10/1**

10 1 **Pam Pam (FR)**[15] 3-9-0 0 TheoBachelot 9 81
(S Wattel, France) **229/10**

11 snk **Blarney Stone (IRE)**[40] 3-9-0 0 GeraldMosse 6 81
(A De Royer-Dupre, France) **121/10**

1m 29.23s (89.23) **11** Ran **SP% 119.3**

WIN (incl. 1 euro stake): 3.60. PLACES: 1.70, 2.60, 5.60. DF: 14.10. SF: 20.00.

**Owner** M Zerolo, E Puerari & Scea Haras De Saint Pair **Bred** E Puerari, Oceanic Bloodstock Inc & Scea Haras De **Trained** Pau, France

### 5844a PRIX DE VALSEME (CLAIMER) (2YO FILLIES) (POLYTRACK) 6f 110y

**2:20** (12:00) 2-Y-O **£11,250** (£4,500; £3,375; £2,250; £1,125)

RPR

1 **La Mezcla (FR)**[20] 5119 2-8-13 0 ValentinSeguy(3) 4 77
(S Wattel, France) **27/10**[1]

2 1¼ **Lifeisforliving (FR)**[81] 3027 2-8-13 0 AntoineHamelin 2 71
(Matthieu Palussiere, France) **121/10**

3 ¾ **Lisnavagh (FR)**[41] 2-8-8 0 JeffersonSmith(6) 14 69
(H-F Devin, France) **87/10**

4 ¾ **Zinger (IRE)**[62] 3641 2-8-9 0 CristianDemuro 7 62
(E J O'Neill, France) **59/1**

5 hd **Areion (IRE)**[6] 5619 2-9-0 0 (b) MickaelBarzalona 9 67
(J S Moore) *w.w in midfield: pushed along and hdwy between horses 1 1/2f out: 7th and swtchd ins ent fnl f: styd on u.p: nvr on terms w ldrs* **164/10**

6 nk **Kunst Basel (FR)**[22] 5026 2-8-4 0 SebastienMartino(5) 8 61
(H-A Pantall, France) **31/5**[3]

7 2 **Ma Ptite Sarah (FR)**[14] 5329 2-8-9 0 SebastienMaillot 15 55
(E Caroux, France) **36/1**

8 snk **Claudia Eria (FR)**[8] 5543 2-9-2 0 UmbertoRispoli 12 62
(P Van De Poele, France) **53/10**[2]

9 nk **Loose Cannon (FR)**[12] 5405 2-9-2 0 (b) LukasDelozier(5) 3 66
(D Windrif, France) **197/10**

10 shd **Hesat (FR)**[38] 2-8-9 0 Christophe-PatriceLemaire 1 54
(M Boutin, France) **148/10**

11 1¼ **Palma Sola (FR)** 2-8-9 0 IoritzMendizabal 5 50
(D Guillemin, France) **115/10**

12 1½ **Freaky Girl (FR)**[6] 5617 2-9-2 0 GregoryBenoist 10 53
(Robert Collet, France) **37/1**

13 2½ **Machica (FR)**[19] 2-8-9 0 ThierryJarnet 6 39
(D Guillemin, France) **131/10**

14 3 **Boann (IRE)**[5] 5662 2-8-6 0 (b) SoufyaneMoulin(3) 11 31
(J S Moore) *hld up towards rr: rdn 2f out and no imp fr 1 1/2f out: wknd ins fnl f* **89/1**

15 1½ **Retouched (IRE)**[40] 2-8-13 0 TheoBachelot 16 30
(V Luka Jr, Czech Republic) **44/1**

16 3 **Elusive Lily**[6] 5617 2-9-2 0 EddyHardouin 13 25
(Robert Collet, France) **48/1**

1m 18.87s (78.87) **16** Ran **SP% 119.1**

WIN (incl. 1 euro stake): 3.70. PLACES: 1.70, 3.50, 3.00. DF: 31.50. SF: 44.70.

**Owner** L Haegel **Bred** J-P Larrieu & S Hillou-Lespes **Trained** France

# 5620 FFOS LAS (L-H)

## Thursday, August 28

**OFFICIAL GOING: Soft (6.5)**

Wind: fresh half behind Weather: sunny spells

### 5845 WALTERS LAND ROGERSTONE NURSERY H'CAP 5f

**2:00** (2:00) (Class 5) (0-75,73) 2-Y-O **£2,587** (£770; £384; £192) **Stalls** Centre

Form RPR

61 1 **Park Glen (IRE)**[21] 5086 2-9-3 72 SamJames(3) 5 80+
(Noel Quinlan) *trckd ldrs: wnt 2nd 1/2-way: led gng wl over 1f out: sn shkn up and in control: pushed out* **11/4**[2]

544 2 1¾ **The Wispe**[22] 5042 2-8-10 62 RichardHughes 2 64
(Robert Cowell) *led: rdn and hdd over 1f out: kpt on but a being hld by wnr* **4/1**[3]

303 3 3½ **Tansfeeq**[15] 5309 2-9-7 73 PaulHanagan 3 62
(B W Hills) *wnt to post early: chsd ldr tl relegated to 3rd 1/2-way: sn rdn and outpcd by ldng pair: kpt on ins fnl f* **2/1**[1]

5044 4 3½ **Charlie's Star**[6] 5620 2-9-6 72 AdamKirby 1 49
(David Evans) *chsd ldrs: rdn 1/2-way: wknd 1f out* **4/1**[3]

300 5 ½ **Dancing Moon (IRE)**[34] 4626 2-8-6 61 ow2 [1] CharlesBishop(3) 4 36+
(Mick Channon) *wnt to post early: dwlt: a bhd and pushed along fr 1/2-way: modest prog fnl f* **8/1**

1m 1.02s (2.72) **Going Correction** +0.425s/f (Yiel) **5** Ran **SP% 111.1**

Speed ratings (Par 94): **95,92,86,81,80**

CSF £13.86 TOTE £2.70: £2.90, £1.90; EX 12.70 Trifecta £26.50.

**Owner** Mrs C Cashman **Bred** Rathbarry Stud **Trained** Newmarket, Suffolk

**FOCUS**

An interesting opener but with many of these appearing not to handle the rain-softened ground. The winner was in total command.

### 5846 WALTERS UK H'CAP 1m (R)

**2:30** (2:31) (Class 6) (0-60,60) 3-Y-O **£1,940** (£577; £288; £144) **Stalls** Low

Form RPR

5506 1 **Improvized**[16] 5277 3-8-13 52 (p) MartinDwyer 2 61
(William Muir) *s.i.s and sn pushed along in rr: gd hdwy u.p over 2f out: led over 1f out: edgd rt ins fnl f but r.o wl* **8/1**[3]

0000 2 2 **Sarlat**[21] 5075 3-8-4 46 oh1 AmyScott(3) 3 50
(Mark Brisbourne) *chsd ldrs: rdn and wnt 2nd over 1f out: kpt on wl but a being hld by wnr* **50/1**

0450 3 8 **Heartstrings**[9] 5522 3-9-2 58 (v) CharlesBishop(3) 7 44
(Mick Channon) *chsd ldr: rdn 3f out: sn lost 2nd and no ch but kpt on to hold 3rd* **6/1**[2]

4661 4 1½ **Why Not Now**[9] 5522 3-9-4 57 6ex JamesDoyle 6 40
(Roger Charlton) *in rr: rdn and sme hdwy over 3f out: styd on fnl f: nvr trbld ldrs* **5/4**[1]

6065 5 nk **Mystical Maze**[20] 5122 3-8-7 46 oh1 DavidProbert 10 28
(Mark Brisbourne) *a abt same pl: rdn over 2f out: one pce* **33/1**

0055 6 1¾ **Purple Spot**[31] 4742 3-9-0 60 PatMillman(7) 9 38
(Rod Millman) *towards rr: rdn over 4f out: sme hdwy over 2f out: wknd fnl f* **8/1**[3]

6401 7 3½ **Honiton Lace**[21] 5106 3-9-3 56 (tp) AdamKirby 4 26
(Phil McEntee) *led: brought field to stands' side ent st 4f out: wnt 8 l clr 3f out: rdn over 2f out: hdd: wandered and wknd qckly over 1f out* **8/1**[3]

-003 8 ½ **Enfys Hud**[3] 5747 3-8-12 54 DeclanBates(3) 8 23
(David Evans) *chsd ldrs: drvn 3f out: sn wknd* **16/1**

-035 9 1 **Forest Glen (IRE)**[22] 5034 3-9-4 57 RichardHughes 5 23
(Sylvester Kirk) *mid-div: rdn over 3f out: wknd over 1f out* **8/1**[3]

0-00 10 ¾ **Wannabe Magic**[7] 5596 3-8-11 50 JohnFahy 1 15
(Geoffrey Deacon) *a towards rr: rdn and wknd wl over 2f out* **25/1**

1m 45.47s (4.47) **Going Correction** +0.525s/f (Yiel) **10** Ran **SP% 117.8**

Speed ratings (Par 98): **98,96,88,86,86 84,80,80,79,78**

CSF £349.72 CT £2641.51 TOTE £5.70: £2.80, £8.10, £2.70; EX 575.90 Trifecta £2274.20 Part won. Pool: £3,032.27 - 0.18 winning tickets..

**Owner** Foursome Thoroughbreds **Bred** Foursome Thoroughbreds **Trained** Lambourn, Berks

**FOCUS**

Low-grade fare but it was run at a blistering early pace in the taxing conditions.

### 5847 PT CIVIL ENGINEERING MAIDEN STKS (BOBIS RACE) 1m (R)

**3:00** (3:00) (Class 4) 2-Y-O **£3,752** (£1,116; £557; £278) **Stalls** Low

Form RPR

1 **Restorer** 2-9-5 0 MartinDwyer 4 78+
(William Muir) *hld up in 4th: clsd over 2f out: led over 1f out: edgd lft and pushed clr ins fnl f: readily* **8/1**

2 3 **Bold** 2-9-5 0 JamesDoyle 3 69+
(Roger Charlton) *dwlt: sn rcvrd and trckd ldr after 2f: rdn 2f out: sn outpcd by wnr but kpt on in duel for 2nd* **11/10**[1]

2432 3 hd **Split The Atom (IRE)**[19] 5167 2-9-5 74 RichardHughes 2 69
(John Patrick Shanahan, Ire) *led at stdy pce: drvn over 2f out: hdd over 1f out: hld after but kpt on in duel for 2nd ins fnl f* **2/1**[2]

4 4 ¾ **Gold Prince (IRE)**[21] 5093 2-9-5 0 LiamKeniry 1 67
(Sylvester Kirk) *cl up 2f: trckd ldng pair: rdn 2f out and unable qck: styd on ins fnl f* **5/1**[3]

05 5 7 **Dylan's Storm (IRE)**[16] 5271 2-9-0 0 GeorgeDowning(5) 5 52
(David Dennis) *in rr: pushed along and effrt over 3f out: outpcd and lft bhd over 1f out* **33/1**

1m 50.1s (9.10) **Going Correction** +0.525s/f (Yiel) **5** Ran **SP% 111.7**

Speed ratings (Par 96): **75,72,71,71,64**

CSF £17.82 TOTE £10.00: £4.10, £1.50; EX 26.80 Trifecta £34.80.

**Owner** C L A Edginton **Bred** Foursome Thoroughbreds **Trained** Lambourn, Berks

**FOCUS**

An ordinary maiden, run in testing conditions. The winner, however, was impressive.

### 5848 ARUP FILLIES' H'CAP 1m 2f (R)

**3:35** (3:35) (Class 5) (0-70,67) 3-Y-O+ **£2,587** (£770; £384; £192) **Stalls** Low

Form RPR

3435 1 **Fair Comment**[14] 5343 4-9-3 56 DavidProbert 5 65
(Michael Blanshard) *trckd ldr: rdn over 2f out: led over 1f out: styd on wl* **6/1**[3]

0-20 2 3½ **Princess Icicle**[175] 853 6-9-13 66 FergusSweeney 2 68
(Jo Crowley) *hld up towards rr: rdn and n.m.r over 2f out: hdwy to chse wnr early ins fnl f: no real imp* **10/1**

-246 3 ¾ **Lady Guinevere**[76] 3176 4-10-0 67 JamesDoyle 1 68
(Stuart Williams) *chsd ldrs: rdn over 1f out and briefly in 2nd: kpt on same pce* **3/1**[2]

3-54 4 ¾ **Society Pearl (IRE)**[6] 5621 4-9-11 64 [1] AdamKirby 4 64
(David Evans) *led: rdn over 2f out: hdd over 1f out: one pce* **8/1**

3236 5 ¾ **On Demand**[23] 5004 3-9-6 67 JimCrowley 3 65
(Andrew Balding) *s.i.s: hld up last: rdn 3f out and nt qckn: hld after but keeping on cl home* **11/4**[1]

564 6 1¾ **Helen's Armada (IRE)**[17] 5235 3-9-1 62 (t) RichardHughes 6 57
(John Patrick Shanahan, Ire) *chsd ldrs: rdn 3f out: ev ch 2f out: wknd appr fnl f* **11/4**[1]

2m 16.2s (6.80) **Going Correction** +0.525s/f (Yiel)

**WFA** 3 from 4yo+ 8lb **6** Ran **SP% 112.8**

Speed ratings (Par 100): **93,90,89,89,88 87**

CSF £59.26 TOTE £4.10: £2.20, £5.60; EX 57.40 Trifecta £128.60.

**Owner** Fair Comment Partnership **Bred** J & Mrs S Davis **Trained** Upper Lambourn, Berks

**FOCUS**
This sextet had managed just one win between them from 70 career starts prior to this and it's hard to get overly excited about the form. Ideally positioned in a tactically run affair.

## 5849 WALTERS LAND ROGERSTONE H'CAP 1m (R)
**4:05** (4:06) (Class 4) (0-80,80) 3-Y-0+ **£4,690** (£1,395; £697; £348) **Stalls** Low

| Form | | | | RPR |
|---|---|---|---|---|
| 2-41 | **1** | | **Merry Me (IRE)**[108] 2210 3-9-3 77 ........ JimCrowley 4<br>(Andrew Balding) *trckd ldrs tl led 2f out: rdn and styd on wl: drew clr fnl 100yds* **20/1** | 89+ |
| 3050 | **2** | 2 1/2 | **Big Baz (IRE)**[89] 2772 4-9-12 80 ........ MartinDwyer 6<br>(William Muir) *hld up in last: hdwy over 2f out: sn rdn: ev ch 1f out tl no ex fnl 100yds* **5/1**[2] | 87+ |
| 6014 | **3** | 1/2 | **Golden Spear**[83] 2968 3-9-1 78 ........ (p) SamJames(3) 8<br>(Noel Quinlan) *mid-div: hdwy 3f out: rdn 2f out: styd on to go 3rd fnl 50yds* **5/1**[2] | 83 |
| 250 | **4** | 3/4 | **Black Dave (IRE)**[24] 4968 4-8-9 66 ........ DeclanBates(3) 2<br>(David Evans) *led: rdn over 2f out: sn hdd: kpt on same pce: lost 3rd fnl 50yds* **50/1** | 70 |
| 4205 | **5** | 1 1/4 | **Swift Cedar (IRE)**[16] 5274 4-9-7 75 ........ DavidProbert 3<br>(David Evans) *hld up: rdn and hdwy over 2f out: edgd lft over 1f out: kpt on same pce fnl f* **14/1** | 76 |
| 4 | **6** | 1/2 | **Sweet Martoni**[18] 5206 4-9-7 75 ........ AdamKirby 10<br>(William Knight) *hdwy to chse ldr after 2f: ev ch 3f out: sn rdn: one pce appr fnl f* **8/1** | 75 |
| 21 | **7** | 4 | **Unison (IRE)**[16] 5274 4-9-9 77 ........ SteveDrowne 9<br>(Peter Makin) *chsd ldrs: rdn and n.m.r over 2f out: sn one pce* **7/2**[1] | 68 |
| 5/1- | **8** | 2 1/2 | **Prince Jock (USA)**[15] 5326 7-9-9 77 ........ RichardHughes 5<br>(John Patrick Shanahan, Ire) *in rr: rdn and hdwy over 3f out: wknd over 1f out* **7/1**[3] | 62 |
| 0315 | **9** | 4 1/2 | **Tides Reach (IRE)**[21] 5096 3-9-1 75 ........ JamesDoyle 1<br>(Roger Charlton) *mid-div: rdn over 2f out: wknd over 1f out* **10/1** | 49 |
| 2221 | **10** | 4 | **Taqneen (IRE)**[26] 4924 3-9-5 79 ........ (b) PaulHanagan 7<br>(Ed Dunlop) *hld up towards rr: rdn and nt qckn 3f out: wknd over 1f out* **5/1**[2] | 44 |

1m 44.16s (3.16) **Going Correction** +0.525s/f (Yiel)
**WFA** 3 from 4yo+ 6lb **10** Ran SP% **118.3**
Speed ratings (Par 105): **105,102,102,101,100 99,95,93,88,84**
CSF £118.88 CT £592.75 TOTE £15.20: £3.50, £3.70, £3.80; EX 217.90 Trifecta £3251.00 Part won. Pool: £4,334.75 - 0.98 winning units..
**Owner** Mrs Fitri Hay **Bred** Mrs Fitriani Hay **Trained** Kingsclere, Hants

**FOCUS**
A competitive feature. The time was the pick of the three races over C&D.

## 5850 NEAL SOIL SUPPLIERS H'CAP 1m 4f (R)
**4:35** (4:39) (Class 6) (0-55,50) 3-Y-0+ **£1,940** (£577; £288; £144) **Stalls** Low

| Form | | | | RPR |
|---|---|---|---|---|
| 4532 | **1** | | **Reach The Beach**[16] 5277 5-9-7 50 ........ (t) AdamKirby 1<br>(Brendan Powell) *mde all: rdn and increased pce 2f out: styd on wl and sn drew clr* **7/2**[2] | 60 |
| 5405 | **2** | 5 | **Just Duchess**[23] 5001 4-9-2 45 ........ DavidProbert 5<br>(Michael Blanshard) *chsd wnr virtually thrght: rdn over 2f out: no ch w wnr appr fnl f but a holding 2nd* **6/1** | 47 |
| 6-32 | **3** | 1 1/4 | **William Hogarth**[14] 5337 9-9-2 45 ........ RichardHughes 3<br>(Brian Ellison) *hld up: hdwy 1/2-way: rdn 3f out and outpcd: stl last appr fnl f: styd on to go 3rd 75yds out* **10/11**[1] | 45 |
| 00P4 | **4** | 1/2 | **Pindora (GER)**[19] 5200 3-8-7 49 ........ (t) SamJames(3) 4<br>(Noel Quinlan) *trckd ldng pair tl lost pl 1/2-way: styd wl in tch and effrt 3f out: one pce after: lost 3rd 75yds out* **9/2**[3] | 48 |
| 0-46 | **5** | 5 | **Richo**[16] 5283 8-8-13 45 ........ (b) CharlesBishop(3) 2<br>(Shaun Harris) *s.i.s: hld up: rdn and hdwy 3f out: sn chal for 2nd: wknd over 1f out* **20/1** | 36 |

2m 46.23s (8.83) **Going Correction** +0.525s/f (Yiel)
**WFA** 3 from 4yo+ 10lb **5** Ran SP% **111.8**
Speed ratings (Par 101): **91,87,86,86,83**
CSF £23.22 TOTE £3.30: £1.30, £4.30; EX 15.70 Trifecta £27.60.
**Owner** Winterbeck Manor Stud **Bred** Winterbeck Manor Stud **Trained** Upper Lambourn, Berks

**FOCUS**
This was weak and it proved a straightforward for the winner.

## 5851 WALTERS UK MAIDEN STKS 1m 4f (R)
**5:05** (5:05) (Class 5) 3-Y-0+ **£2,587** (£770; £384; £192) **Stalls** Low

| Form | | | | RPR |
|---|---|---|---|---|
| 35 | **1** | | **Le Maitre Chat (USA)**[24] 4984 3-9-2 0 ........ AdamKirby 1<br>(Clive Cox) *in tch in 4th: rdn along over 4f out: bk on bridle and hdwy 3f out: sn led: narrowly hdd 1f out: r.o u.p to ld again nr fin* **4/1**[3] | 84 |
| 0033 | **2** | 3/4 | **Dolce N Karama (IRE)**[42] 4360 3-9-2 84 ........ RichardHughes 3<br>(John Patrick Shanahan, Ire) *hld up last: stdy hdwy 3f out: rdn to take narrow ld 1f out: hdd and no ex nr fin* **2/1**[2] | 82 |
| 6362 | **3** | 14 | **Race To Glory (FR)**[33] 4672 3-9-2 78 ........ JamesDoyle 4<br>(Roger Charlton) *trckd ldrs: clsd 3f out: sn ev ch: drvn 2f out: grad wknd* **1/1**[1] | 59 |
| 05 | **4** | 10 | **Guard of Honour (IRE)**[20] 5135 3-9-2 0 ........ LiamKeniry 5<br>(Rebecca Curtis) *w ldr tl rdn ond outpcd over 3f out: wknd over 1f out: t.o* **12/1** | 43 |
| 0 | **5** | 23 | **Exton**[77] 3153 5-9-5 0 ........ MrAidenBlakemore(7) 2<br>(Shaun Harris) *t.k.h: led tl over 2f out: wknd qckly: t.o* **66/1** | 7 |

2m 44.4s (7.00) **Going Correction** +0.525s/f (Yiel)
**WFA** 3 from 5yo 10lb **5** Ran SP% **112.5**
Speed ratings (Par 103): **97,96,87,80,65**
CSF £12.71 TOTE £4.50: £1.40, £1.40; EX 8.80 Trifecta £17.00.
**Owner** Michael H Watt **Bred** Grundy Bloodstock **Trained** Lambourn, Berks

**FOCUS**
This was poorly contested. The winner returned to his debut form.
T/Plt: £1,747.40 to a £1 stake. Pool: £44,164.16 - 18.45 winning tickets. T/Qpdt: £203.20 to a £1 stake. Pool: £4,377.79 - 15.94 winning tickets. RL

# 5630 HAMILTON (R-H)
Thursday, August 28

**OFFICIAL GOING: Good to soft (7.3)**
Wind: Light, across Weather: Overcast, dry Rails: Rail movement around the loop reduced distances on Round course by about 25yds

## 5852 EBF STALLIONS DEBUTANTS MAIDEN STKS 6f 5y
**4:45** (4:45) (Class 5) 2-Y-0 **£3,234** (£962; £481; £240) **Stalls** High

| Form | | | | RPR |
|---|---|---|---|---|
| | **1** | | **Risen Sun** 2-9-0 0 ........ JoeFanning 3<br>(Mark Johnston) *a gng best: mde all against stands' rail: shkn up and qcknd clr over 1f out: promising* **2/1**[1] | 80+ |
| | **2** | 4 1/2 | **Hard N Sharp (IRE)** 2-9-5 0 ........ TonyHamilton 8<br>(Kevin Ryan) *pressed wnr: rdn over 2f out: one pce fr over 1f out* **7/1** | 70 |
| | **3** | 3 3/4 | **Go Dan Go (IRE)** 2-9-5 0 ........ TomEaves 2<br>(Keith Dalgleish) *dwlt: sn prom on outside: rdn over 2f out: outpcd fr over 1f out* **9/1** | 59 |
| | **4** | 6 | **Tommy Docc (IRE)** 2-9-5 0 ........ PhillipMakin 7<br>(Keith Dalgleish) *missed break: rn green in rr: sme late hdwy: nvr on terms* **12/1** | 41 |
| | **5** | 2 | **Mr Cool Cash** 2-9-5 0 ........ GrahamLee 5<br>(Ann Duffield) *dwlt: rn green towards rr: rdn over 2f out: nvr a factor* **4/1**[2] | 35 |
| | **6** | shd | **Bapak Asmara (IRE)** 2-9-0 0 ........ ShaneGray(5) 6<br>(Kevin Ryan) *s.i.s: rn green in rr: no ch fr 1/2-way* **10/1** | 34 |
| | **7** | 1 | **Fortuna Glas (IRE)** 2-9-5 0 ........ DavidNolan 4<br>(Donald McCain) *prom: rdn over 2f out: sn btn* **20/1** | 31 |
| | **8** | 4 | **Arms Around Me (IRE)** 2-9-5 0 ........ PaulMulrennan 1<br>(Bryan Smart) *prom: drvn along 1/2-way: wknd fr 2f out* **6/1**[3] | 19 |

1m 11.3s (-0.90) **Going Correction** -0.075s/f (Good) **8** Ran SP% **111.7**
Speed ratings (Par 94): **103,97,92,84,81 81,79,74**
CSF £15.65 TOTE £3.40: £1.70, £1.80, £1.50; EX 22.90 Trifecta £125.60.
**Owner** Sheikh Hamdan bin Mohammed Al Maktoum **Bred** Darley **Trained** Middleham Moor, N Yorks

**FOCUS**
The opening contest was a 6f juvenile maiden for newcomers won by subsequent 1m juvenile Listed winner/Group 1-placed Willie The Whipper in 2012 and 2012 Irish 2,000 Guineas runner-up Foxtrot Romeo in 2011. The winning time was nearly two seconds above standard on officially good to soft ground.

## 5853 AVIA SIGNS H'CAP 6f 5y
**5:20** (5:21) (Class 6) (0-60,60) 3-Y-0 **£2,385** (£704; £352) **Stalls** High

| Form | | | | RPR |
|---|---|---|---|---|
| -004 | **1** | | **Red Tide (IRE)**[17] 5244 3-9-0 58 ........ (p) JordanNason(5) 10<br>(Marjorie Fife) *mde all: rdn over 2f out: edgd lft over 1f out: styd on strly* **11/1** | 64 |
| 2651 | **2** | nk | **White Flag**[24] 4974 3-8-11 57 ........ RachelRichardson(7) 2<br>(Tim Easterby) *racd towards far rail: prom: effrt and chsd wnr over 1f out: kpt on fnl f* **10/1** | 62 |
| 0044 | **3** | 3/4 | **Skinny Latte**[23] 4998 3-8-7 46 oh1 ........ (p) PatrickMathers 8<br>(Micky Hammond) *bhd: rdn along 1/2-way: hdwy over 1f out: kpt on fnl f: nrst fin* **25/1** | 49 |
| -000 | **4** | nk | **Toboggan Star**[38] 4489 3-9-7 60 ........ GrahamLee 7<br>(Ann Duffield) *prom: drvn and edgd lft over 2f out: rallied over 1f out: kpt on ins fnl f* **12/1** | 62 |
| 4236 | **5** | 3/4 | **Nelson's Pride**[14] 5333 3-9-4 57 ........ (b) AmyRyan 5<br>(Kevin Ryan) *hld up: rdn and hdwy over 2f out: rdn and edgd lft over 1f out: one pce fnl f* **5/1**[3] | 57 |
| 4052 | **6** | 3/4 | **Cahal (IRE)**[10] 5499 3-9-2 55 ........ AdrianNicholls 12<br>(David Nicholls) *prom: rdn over 2f out: one pce fr over 1f out* **10/3**[1] | 52 |
| 0355 | **7** | 1 1/2 | **Raise A Billion**[6] 5631 3-8-8 52 ........ JoeDoyle(5) 9<br>(Alan Berry) *hld up: rdn and hdwy 2f out: no imp fnl f* **10/1** | 44 |
| 0646 | **8** | 1 3/4 | **Princess Rose**[37] 4512 3-9-1 54 ........ (be) PhillipMakin 11<br>(John Weymes) *hld up: rdn over 2f out: nvr able to chal* **20/1** | 41 |
| 002 | **9** | 1/2 | **Sketch Map (IRE)**[6] 5631 3-8-11 50 ........ (v[1]) RussKennemore 6<br>(Jedd O'Keeffe) *disp ld to over 2f out: rdn and wknd over 1f out* **4/1**[2] | 35 |
| -056 | **10** | 3/4 | **Tinchy Ryder**[182] 765 3-8-8 47 ........ JoeFanning 1<br>(Bryan Smart) *racd towards far rail: cl up tl wknd over 1f out* **14/1** | 30 |
| 3665 | **11** | 29 | **Countess Lupus (IRE)**[160] 1047 3-8-2 46 oh1 ........ (b) JackGarritty(5) 4<br>(Lisa Williamson) *bhd: drvn and struggling over 2f out: sn lost tch* **80/1** | |
| 0300 | **R** | | **Starlite Jewel**[6] 5631 3-8-6 50 ........ JacobButterfield(5) 3<br>(Stuart Coltherd) *dwlt: bhd: drvn and struggling over 2f out: no ch whn hung bdly rt and crashed through far rail 1f out* **25/1** | |

1m 12.22s (0.02) **Going Correction** -0.075s/f (Good) **12** Ran SP% **114.3**
Speed ratings (Par 98): **96,95,94,94,93 92,90,87,87,86 47,**
CSF £107.11 CT £2705.35 TOTE £11.50: £3.30, £2.80, £6.30; EX 138.60 Trifecta £1485.40.
**Owner** Mrs Jo McHugh **Bred** Rathasker Stud **Trained** Stillington, N Yorks

**FOCUS**
A moderate 3yo handicap in which they went a contested gallop across the track with the vast majority racing middle to nearside.

## 5854 BILL AND DAVID MCHARG "HANDS AND HEELS" APPRENTICE SERIES H'CAP (ROUND 4 OF APPRENTICE SERIES) 1m 65y
**5:50** (5:50) (Class 6) (0-55,61) 3-Y-0+ **£2,045** (£603; £302) **Stalls** Low

| Form | | | | RPR |
|---|---|---|---|---|
| 5341 | **1** | | **Paddy's Rock (IRE)**[4] 5717 3-9-3 61 6ex ........ (p) RowanScott(5) 7<br>(Ann Duffield) *hld up on outside: stdy hdwy over 3f out: rdn to ld over 1f out: pushed out fnl f* **9/4**[1] | 70+ |
| -033 | **2** | 3/4 | **Rock Band**[31] 4730 5-8-13 49 ........ (bt) GaryMahon(3) 2<br>(Emmet Michael Butterly, Ire) *t.k.h: led at ordinary gallop: rdn and qcknd over 3f out: hdd over 1f out: rallied: hld towards fin* **13/2**[3] | 57 |
| 3424 | **3** | 2 1/4 | **Benidorm**[13] 5376 6-8-12 48 ........ (e) AnnaHesketh(3) 4<br>(Richard Guest) *t.k.h: chsd ldr: effrt over 1f out: sn no ex* **11/1** | 51 |
| 4400 | **4** | 2 1/4 | **Spokesperson (USA)**[14] 5337 6-8-10 46 oh1 ........ (p) LukeLeadbitter(3) 10<br>(Frederick Watson) *hld up: pushed along 3f out: effrt and swtchd rt over 1f out: kpt on fnl f: nrst fin* **50/1** | 44 |
| 0006 | **5** | 3 | **Rio Cobolo (IRE)**[26] 4905 8-9-3 55 ........ (v) KevinLundie(5) 1<br>(Philip Kirby) *prom: drvn over 2f out: outpcd fr over 1f out* **12/1** | 46 |
| 0203 | **6** | 2 1/4 | **Torridon**[17] 5257 3-8-5 47 ........ (b) DavidParkes(3) 9<br>(Mark Johnston) *chsd ldrs: effrt and rdn over 2f out: wknd ins fnl f* **8/1** | 32 |
| 6626 | **7** | 2 | **Berbice (IRE)**[6] 5640 9-8-8 46 ........ JoshDoyle(5) 6<br>(Linda Perratt) *s.i.s: hld up: stdy hdwy 3f out: rdn and wknd over 1f out* **17/2** | 27 |



The Form Book, Raceform Ltd, Newbury, RG14 5SJ

0206 **8** 3/4 **Last Destination (IRE)**[15] 5295 6-9-2 52 ChrisMeehan(3) 8 31
(Nigel Tinkler) *t.k.h early: stdd towards rr: struggling over 4f out: nvr on terms* **12/1**

1050 **9** 1 1/2 **Hayek**[8] 5571 7-8-13 46 oh1 (b) RachelRichardson 3 22
(Tim Easterby) *hld up: struggling over 4f out: nvr on terms* **20/1**

U050 **10** *hd* **Mitchell**[13] 5376 4-9-3 55 PeterSword(5) 5 30
(K R Burke) *in tch: rdn over 3f out: sn struggling: n.d after* **9/2**[2]

1m 47.73s (-0.67) **Going Correction** -0.30s/f (Firm)
**WFA** 3 from 4yo+ 6lb **10** Ran SP% **114.4**
Speed ratings (Par 101): **91,90,88,85,82 80,78,77,76,76**
CSF £16.52 CT £134.59 TOTE £2.90: £1.10, £1.80, £3.90; EX 11.10 Trifecta £63.90.
**Owner** Jimmy Kay **Bred** J O'Connor **Trained** Constable Burton, N Yorks

**FOCUS**
A moderate handicap restricted to apprentice riders, and a respectable comparative winning time, despite an ordinary gallop, suggests the ground was a shade better on the round course.

## 5855 TAGGARTS JAGUAR LANARKSHIRE SCOTTISH TROPHY H'CAP 1m 1f 36y
6:20 (6:20) (Class 4) (0-80,79) 3-Y-O+ **£6,469** (£1,925; £962; £481) **Stalls** Low

Form RPR

-236 **1** **Jalingo (IRE)**[175] 854 3-9-5 76 JoeFanning 5 88+
(Mark Johnston) *trckd ldrs: led over 2f out: sn rdn and edgd rt: drew clr fr over 1f out* **8/1**[3]

442S **2** 4 1/2 **Lord Franklin**[29] 4793 5-9-7 71 JasonHart 10 74
(Eric Alston) *led: rdn and hdd over 2f out: rallied: kpt on fnl f: nt rch wnr* **8/1**[3]

010 **3** 1/2 **Henpecked**[80] 3052 4-8-7 60 ConnorBeasley(3) 4 62
(Alistair Whillans) *hld up in tch: rdn and outpcd over 3f out: rallied over 1f out: kpt on ins fnl f: nrst fin* **17/2**

3640 **4** *hd* **Royal Straight**[6] 5639 9-8-9 64 (t) SammyJoBell(5) 6 66
(Linda Perratt) *s.i.s: hld up: rdn 3f out: hdwy over 1f out: kpt on ins fnl f: no imp* **33/1**

4221 **5** 1 1/2 **Coincidently**[2] 5787 4-9-8 79 6ex MikeyEnnis(7) 11 77
(Alan Bailey) *t.k.h and sn chsng ldr: rdn over 2f out: no ex ins fnl f* **7/4**[1]

6502 **6** 4 1/2 **Ted's Brother (IRE)**[6] 5638 6-9-6 73 (e) PhilipPrince(3) 7 62
(Richard Guest) *in tch: rdn and hung rt over 2f out: btn over 1f out* **12/1**

2045 **7** 5 **I'm Super Too (IRE)**[19] 5172 7-9-6 70 BenCurtis 9 48
(Alan Swinbank) *hld up: hdwy on outside over 3f out: rdn and wknd fr 2f out* **14/1**

1024 **8** 5 **Dark Ocean (IRE)**[19] 5172 4-9-8 72 GrahamLee 8 40
(Jedd O'Keeffe) *hld up: rdn over 3f out: nvr able to chal* **9/1**

0-1 **9** 26 **Scottish Strand**[16] 5272 3-9-7 78 KierenFallon 12
(James Tate) *t.k.h in midfield: struggling 4f out: lost tch over 2f out: t.o* **4/1**[2]

1m 55.74s (-3.96) **Going Correction** -0.30s/f (Firm)
**WFA** 3 from 4yo+ 7lb **9** Ran SP% **116.4**
Speed ratings (Par 105): **105,101,100,100,99 95,90,86,63**
CSF £70.57 CT £561.86 TOTE £7.90: £2.20, £3.00, £3.60; EX 35.70 Trifecta £345.90.
**Owner** Sheikh Hamdan bin Mohammed Al Maktoum **Bred** Gerrardstown House Stud **Trained** Middleham Moor, N Yorks

■ Silver Duke (9-1) was withdrawn. Rule 4 applies to bets struck at board prices prior to withdrawal but not to SP bets - deduction - 10p in the pound. New market formed.

**FOCUS**
The feature race was a fairly decent handicap in which they went a solid gallop resulting in a good comparative winning time.

## 5856 RACING UK ON SKY 432 H'CAP (QUALIFIER FOR THE £15000 BETFAIR SCOTTISH STAYERS SERIES FINAL) 1m 4f 17y
6:50 (6:50) (Class 5) (0-70,65) 3-Y-O+ **£3,234** (£962; £481; £240) **Stalls** High

Form RPR

3222 **1** **Geanie Mac (IRE)**[8] 5567 5-8-13 55 (p) SammyJoBell(5) 5 62
(Linda Perratt) *prom: hdwy to ld and followed loose horse to stands' side over 3f out: hld on wl fnl f* **7/1**

4663 **2** 3/4 **In Vino Veritas (IRE)**[10] 5495 3-9-2 63 (v) PaulMulrennan 6 69
(Ann Duffield) *chsd ldr: chsd wnr over 2f out: edgd lft and kpt on wl ins fnl f: hld towards fin* **5/1**[3]

2653 **3** 6 **Harrison's Cave**[20] 5146 6-9-8 59 TomEaves 4 55
(Keith Dalgleish) *prom: rdn towards far side over 4f out: rallied over 2f out: no ch w stands' side ldrs* **7/1**

0425 **4** 3/4 **Latin Rebel (IRE)**[24] 4964 7-9-2 56 GaryBartley(3) 7 51
(Jim Goldie) *hld up: rdn towards far side over 3f out: no imp over 2f out* **4/1**[2]

-000 **5** 10 **Hero's Story**[10] 5495 4-9-3 54 (p) GrahamLee 1 33
(Jim Goldie) *hld up: rdn towards far side over 4f out: btn over 2f out* **12/1**

4000 **6** 1/2 **King Of Paradise (IRE)**[21] 5077 5-10-0 65 (p) JasonHart 8 43
(Eric Alston) *led: rdn and hdd far side over 3f out: wknd over 2f out* **7/2**[1]

0454 **U** **Triple Eight (IRE)**[13] 5371 6-9-7 65 (b) MikeyEnnis(7) 9
(Philip Kirby) *stmbld and uns rdr s* **4/1**[2]

2m 37.19s (-1.41) **Going Correction** -0.30s/f (Firm)
**WFA** 3 from 4yo+ 10lb **7** Ran SP% **111.6**
Speed ratings (Par 103): **92,91,87,87,80 80,**
CSF £39.29 CT £248.82 TOTE £5.80: £4.00, £3.70; EX 14.20 Trifecta £153.80.
**Owner** Ken McGarrity **Bred** J Mulligan **Trained** East Kilbride, S Lanarks

**FOCUS**
A modest middle-distance handicap run at an initially decent gallop until the leader attempted to stack up his pursuers turning in.

## 5857 OVERTON FARM MAIDEN STKS 6f 5y
7:20 (7:25) (Class 5) 3-Y-O+ **£3,408** (£1,006; £503) **Stalls** High

Form RPR

2420 **1** **Showtime Star**[13] 5375 4-9-8 64 KierenFallon 6 69
(Alan Swinbank) *cl up: led over 2f out: rdn clr fr over 1f out* **4/6**[1]

00 **2** 6 **Clabare**[52] 4022 3-9-5 0 TomEaves 5 50
(Ian Semple) *t.k.h: in tch: hdwy to chse wnr over 1f out: edgd rt: sn no imp* **12/1**[3]

0606 **3** 12 **Bannock Town**[8] 5566 3-9-2 45 (p) ConnorBeasley(3) 3 11
(Linda Perratt) *cl up: ev ch and rdn over 2f out: wknd over 1f out* **100/1**

05 **4** 11 **Oriental Heights**[12] 5417 3-9-0 0 GrahamLee 4
(Jim Goldie) *sddle sn slipped forward: led to over 2f out: eased* **11/2**[2]

406- **5** 12 **Lady Calantha**[308] 7484 4-9-3 45 PatrickMathers 1
(Alan Berry) *prom: drvn and struggling 1/2-way: sn btn: t.o* **33/1**

1m 12.57s (0.37) **Going Correction** -0.075s/f (Good)
**WFA** 3 from 4yo 3lb **5** Ran SP% **87.0**
Speed ratings (Par 103): **94,86,70,55,39**
CSF £4.38 TOTE £1.10: £1.10, £5.40; EX 4.10 Trifecta £41.10.
**Owner** Countrywide Classics Limited **Bred** Countrywide Classics Ltd **Trained** Melsonby, N Yorks
■ Biofocal (3-1) was withdrawn. Rule 4 applies to all bets. Deduction - 25p in the pound.

**FOCUS**
A weak 6f maiden in which they went an even gallop.

## 5858 DIGBY BROWN RACEDAY ON TUESDAY H'CAP 5f 4y
7:50 (7:58) (Class 6) (0-60,55) 3-Y-O+ **£2,385** (£704; £352) **Stalls** Centre

Form RPR

0553 **1** **New Lease Of Life**[10] 5499 5-9-0 51 (p) GaryBartley(3) 5 65
(Jim Goldie) *hld up: effrt and hdwy to ld over 1f out: pushed clr ins fnl f* **6/1**

3332 **2** 3 3/4 **Pull The Pin (IRE)**[10] 5486 5-9-7 55 (bt) JoeFanning 8 56
(Ann Stokell) *led at gd gallop: hrd pressed thrght: hung rt and hdd over 1f out: kpt on same pce ins fnl f* **9/4**[1]

2202 **3** *nk* **Tadalavil**[6] 5636 9-9-1 54 SammyJoBell(5) 4 53
(Linda Perratt) *in tch: rdn over 2f out: kpt on ins fnl f: nt pce of first two* **9/1**

33 **4** 1 **Captain Scooby**[15] 5316 8-8-12 49 (b[1]) PhilipPrince(3) 10 45
(Richard Guest) *s.i.s: hld up: rdn and hdwy over 1f out: kpt on fnl f: nvr able to chal* **5/1**[3]

024 **5** 1/2 **Rock Canyon (IRE)**[6] 5635 5-9-3 51 GrahamLee 6 45
(Linda Perratt) *prom: drvn and outpcd over 2f out: kpt on ins fnl f* **9/2**[2]

-040 **6** *nse* **Sherry For Nanny (IRE)**[34] 4627 3-8-4 45 (p) JordanNason(5) 3 39
(Marjorie Fife) *dwlt: hld up: stdy hdwy 1/2-way: rdn and no imp over 1f out* **33/1**

0000 **7** 1 **Fol Hollow (IRE)**[17] 5237 9-9-4 52 JasonHart 1 42
(Stuart Coltherd) *prom tl rdn and no ex fr over 1f out* **25/1**

4004 **8** 8 **Chloe's Dream (IRE)**[8] 5565 4-9-0 51 ConnorBeasley(3) 11 21
(Linda Perratt) *t.k.h: hung rt thrght: w wnr to over 2f out: wknd over 1f out* **5/1**[3]

59.61s (-0.39) **Going Correction** -0.075s/f (Good)
**WFA** 3 from 4yo+ 2lb **8** Ran SP% **113.4**
Speed ratings (Par 101): **100,94,93,91,91 91,89,76**
CSF £19.56 CT £119.76 TOTE £9.60: £2.60, £1.10, £3.20; EX 22.00 Trifecta £234.50.
**Owner** David McKenzie **Bred** Jim Goldie **Trained** Uplawmoor, E Renfrews

**FOCUS**
The concluding contest was a moderate sprint handicap, but quite an impressive winner for the grade clocked a good comparative winning time off a contested gallop right across the track, with the majority racing middle to nearside.
T/Plt: £253.20 to a £1 stake. Pool: £44,101.82 - 127.12 winning tickets. T/Qpdt: £25.00 to a £1 stake. Pool: £5,579.53 - 164.98 winning tickets. RY

# 5827 LINGFIELD (L-H)
Thursday, August 28

**OFFICIAL GOING: Turf: soft changing to good to soft after race 1 (4.40); polytrack: standard**
Wind: Fresh, half behind Weather: Fine

## 5859 INDUS CATERING MEDIAN AUCTION MAIDEN FILLIES' STKS 5f
4:40 (4:45) (Class 6) 2-Y-O **£2,458** (£731; £365; £182) **Stalls** Centre

Form RPR

023 **1** **Escrick (IRE)**[14] 5332 2-9-0 66 PatDobbs 6 70+
(David Simcock) *hld up in tch: prog to trck ldr 2f out: rdn to ld ins fnl f: in command last 75yds* **5/4**[1]

2205 **2** 3/4 **One Moment**[35] 4576 2-9-0 68 AdamBeschizza 1 67
(Robert Cowell) *reluctant to enter stalls: pressed ldr: led 1/2-way: drvn over 1f out: hdd and one pce ins fnl f* **11/4**[2]

2403 **3** 2 3/4 **Robin Hill**[10] 5506 2-9-0 67 SamHitchcott 4 57
(William Muir) *fast away: led against rail: hdd 1/2-way: sn rdn: fdd over 1f out* **11/4**[2]

02 **4** *hd* **Margot Rose**[27] 4846 2-9-0 0 LukeMorris 2 57
(Harry Dunlop) *pushed along to stay in tch after 2f: nvr on terms plugged on to press for 3rd nr fin* **7/1**[3]

0 **5** 3 3/4 **Kylies Wild Card**[9] 5519 2-9-0 0 WilliamCarson 5 43
(Simon Hodgson) *outpcd and bhd: nvr a factor* **50/1**

00 **6** 5 **Swift Susie**[21] 5091 2-8-7 0 AaronJones(7) 3 25
(Stuart Williams) *taken to post early and steadily: t.k.h: trckd ldng pair to 1/2-way: wknd qckly* **66/1**

59.96s (1.76) **Going Correction** +0.175s/f (Good) **6** Ran SP% **113.7**
Speed ratings (Par 89): **92,90,86,86,80 72**
CSF £5.14 TOTE £2.70: £1.30, £1.50; EX 5.50 Trifecta £12.00.
**Owner** Malih Lahej Al Basti **Bred** Malih L Al Basti **Trained** Newmarket, Suffolk

**FOCUS**
Overcast with a strong breeze blowing half behind them up the straight which helped them get through the soft ground. All participants in this fillies' maiden had previous experience and had recorded moderate form.

## 5860 HEART FM 97.5FM H'CAP 5f
5:10 (5:11) (Class 6) (0-65,64) 3-Y-O+ **£2,587** (£770; £384; £192) **Stalls** Centre

Form RPR

556 **1** **Pharoh Jake**[70] 3392 6-8-13 53 MartinHarley 3 65
(John Bridger) *prom in centre: chal 2f out: drvn to ld 1f out: styd on wl* **8/1**

3120 **2** *nk* **Birdie Queen**[35] 4564 4-9-7 61 GeorgeBaker 4 72
(Gary Moore) *racd centre: prom: overall ldr 2f out: hdd 1f out: styd on but hld nr fin* **5/1**[3]

1232 **3** 2 3/4 **Johnny Splash (IRE)**[20] 5126 5-9-2 56 (v) OisinMurphy 8 57
(Roger Teal) *led nr side gp: drvn 2f out: nt on terms w ldng pair fr over 1f out* **5/1**[3]

4543 **4** 1 3/4 **Oscars Journey**[16] 5290 4-9-10 64 (p) FrederikTylicki 9 59
(J R Jenkins) *racd nr side: nvr on terms w ldrs: rdn over 2f out: plugged on fnl f* **3/1**[1]

-061 **5** *nse* **Pieman's Girl**[22] 5061 3-9-7 63 WilliamCarson 5 58
(Anthony Carson) *racd towards centre: prom: rdn over 2f out: wknd fnl f* **8/1**

0505 **6** 1 **Give Us A Belle (IRE)**[3] 5780 5-8-10 50 (tp[1]) JimmyQuinn 6 41
(Christine Dunnett) *racd centre: outpcd and pushed along after 2f: nvr on terms: kpt on fnl f* **20/1**

6440 **7** 1 1/4 **Mossgo (IRE)**[36] 4546 4-8-13 53 (t) LukeMorris 1 40
(John Best) *racd alone against far rail: overall ldr to 2f out: wknd qckly* **20/1**

1025 **8** 1 **Picc Of Burgau**[24] 4981 4-9-9 63 AndreaAtzeni 10 46
(Geoffrey Deacon) *racd nr side: a struggling to go the pce in rr: no prog over 1f out* **4/1**[2]

4551 **9** 1 1/2 **Danzoe (IRE)**[8] 5574 7-8-10 55 6ex (v) EoinWalsh(5) 2 33
(Christine Dunnett) *sn drvn and struggling in rr: nvr a a factor* **14/1**

0-45 **10** *8* **Anytimeatall (IRE)**[22] 5061 3-8-10 57.......................... ShelleyBirkett(5) 7 6
(Alan Bailey) *fractious stalls: n.m.r after s: in tch to 1/2-way: wknd rapidly: t.o* **25/1**

58.73s (0.53) **Going Correction** +0.175s/f (Good)
**WFA** 3 from 4yo+ 2lb **10** Ran SP% **118.8**
Speed ratings (Par 101): **102,101,97,94,94 92,90,89,86,73**
CSF £47.54 CT £229.05 TOTE £7.80: £2.00, £1.90, £3.90; EX 89.60 Trifecta £702.20.
**Owner** The Hair & Haberdasher Partnership **Bred** J J Bridger **Trained** Liphook, Hants

**FOCUS**
A modest sprint handicap run at a fair pace for the soft ground. The first two were drawn towards the far rail and they drew clear.

## 5861 BUTTERFLIES & BOWS VENUE DECORATION H'CAP 6f
**5:40** (5:42) (Class 5) (0-70,70) 3-Y-O+ **£3,234** (£962; £481; £240) **Stalls** Centre

Form RPR
3654 **1** **Lady Phill**[14] 5355 4-9-6 64.......................... KierenFox 1 71
(Michael Attwater) *mde all and racd towards far side: rdn wl over 2f out: hrd pressed on both sides fnl f: hld on gamely* **20/1**

-243 **2** *nk* **Bint Malyana (IRE)**[17] 5256 3-9-6 67..........................[1] LukeMorris 7 73
(Paul D'Arcy) *w.w in midfield: prog over 2f out: chsd wnr jst over 1f out: chal fnl f: jst hld nr fin* **10/1**

063 **3** *hd* **House Captain**[13] 5378 3-9-4 70.......................... CamHardie(5) 4 75
(Richard Hannon) *towards rr: prog over 2f out: chsd wnr u.p jst over 1f out: chal fnl f: nt qckn nr fin* **8/1**

1000 **4** *1 ¼* **Another Try (IRE)**[48] 4156 9-9-5 70.......................... KieranShoemark(7) 12 71
(Timothy Jarvis) *racd towards nr side: led gp and in 2nd pl overall to jst over 1f out: one pce* **8/1**

4011 **5** *1 ¼* **Strike A Light**[15] 5320 3-9-9 70.......................... ChrisCatlin 5 67
(Rae Guest) *towards rr: pushed along bef 1/2-way: kpt on u.p fnl 2f: no threat* **9/4**[1]

3104 **6** *hd* **Welease Bwian (IRE)**[21] 5070 5-9-4 69.......................... AaronJones(7) 3 66
(Stuart Williams) *dwlt: hld up in last pair: stl there over 2f out: rdn and prog wl over 1f out: one pce fnl f* **25/1**

2624 **7** *4* **Ray Of Joy**[17] 5247 8-9-11 69..........................(v) FrederikTylicki 8 53
(J R Jenkins) *dwlt: a towards rr: rdn wl over 2f out: no real prog* **6/1**[3]

1034 **8** *2 ¼* **Uprise**[22] 5059 5-9-5 66..........................[1] RyanPowell(3) 2 43
(George Margarson) *dwlt: mostly in last pair: drvn and no prog over 2f out: no ch after* **14/1**

5 **9** *5* **Cardinal**[22] 5060 9-9-8 66..........................(p) AndreaAtzeni 6 27
(Robert Cowell) *nvr bttr than midfield: rdn wl over 2f out: no prog* **5/1**[2]

1-36 **10** *3 ½* **Dazza**[197] 573 3-9-9 70.......................... TomQueally 9 20
(Gary Moore) *chsd ldrs to 1/2-way: sn wknd* **12/1**

1322 **11** *1* **Billy Red**[22] 5045 10-9-7 68..........................(b) DannyBrock(3) 11 14
(J R Jenkins) *awkward s: sn prom: wknd qckly over 2f out* **16/1**

1m 12.02s (0.82) **Going Correction** +0.175s/f (Good)
**WFA** 3 from 4yo+ 3lb **11** Ran SP% **121.9**
Speed ratings (Par 103): **101,100,100,98,97 96,91,88,81,77 75**
CSF £213.70 CT £1794.19 TOTE £26.10: £6.30, £4.30, £2.30; EX 262.70 Trifecta £2383.90.
**Owner** Mrs M S Teversham **Bred** Mrs Monica Teversham **Trained** Epsom, Surrey
■ Stewards' Enquiry : Andrea Atzeni vet said horse lost a front shoe
Kieren Fox seven-day ban: used whip above permitted level (Sep 12-18)

**FOCUS**
There was a very modest pace and a difference of opinion on where the best ground was in a relatively competitive but modest sprint handicap. The winner made all.

## 5862 TBA NEXT GENERATION CLUB MAIDEN STKS 7f
**6:10** (6:10) (Class 5) 3-Y-O **£2,587** (£770; £384; £192) **Stalls** Centre

Form RPR
3423 **1** **Moonvoy**[14] 5352 3-9-0 82.......................... MartinHarley 2 81
(Jeremy Noseda) *w ldrs: led 4f out: rdn 2f out: pressed over 1f out: drvn out and styd on* **7/4**[2]

33 **2** *2 ½* **New Identity (IRE)**[66] 3517 3-9-5 0.......................... PatCosgrave 1 82
(Denis Coakley) *dwlt: hld up in tch: prog to chse wnr 2f out and rdn: tried to chal over 1f out: one pce fnl f* **5/4**[1]

0 **3** *2 ½* **Lostintheclouds**[23] 5007 3-9-0 0.......................... ShaneKelly 3 68
(Mike Murphy) *trckd ldrs: rdn over 2f out: lft bhd by ldng pair fr wl over 1f out: kpt on* **20/1**

-4 **4** *8* **Virile (IRE)**[19] 5181 3-9-5 0.......................... SeanLevey 8 52
(Richard Hannon) *tk kene hold: pressed ldrs: chsd wnr wl over 3f out to 2f out: wknd* **7/2**[3]

5-03 **5** *1 ¼* **Thrtypointstothree (IRE)**[95] 2591 3-9-5 58.......................... OisinMurphy 7 49
(Nikki Evans) *led to 4f out: sn rdn: wknd 3f out* **33/1**

0-5 **6** *¾* **Canary Lad (IRE)**[14] 5352 3-9-5 0.......................... TomQueally 4 47
(Timothy Jarvis) *lost tch and struggling after 3f: no ch after* **16/1**

00 **7** *3 ¼* **Tsarglas**[10] 5504 3-8-12 0.......................... AaronJones(7) 5 39
(Stuart Williams) *lost tch and struggling after 3f: no ch after* **50/1**

**8** *12* **Satchville Flyer** 3-9-5 0.......................... WilliamCarson 6 7
(Brett Johnson) *dwlt: t.k.h: cl up to 1/2-way: sn wknd* **33/1**

1m 25.04s (1.74) **Going Correction** +0.175s/f (Good) **8** Ran SP% **121.5**
Speed ratings (Par 100): **97,94,91,82,80 79,76,62**
CSF £4.50 TOTE £2.10: £1.10, £1.10, £8.20; EX 4.70 Trifecta £57.30.
**Owner** S E Construction (Kent) Ltd **Bred** D G Hardisty Bloodstock **Trained** Newmarket, Suffolk

**FOCUS**
An ordinary 3yo maiden which few got in to. The two market leaders raced towards the centre of the track and drew clear.

## 5863 OWAIN WITHERS 21ST BIRTHDAY H'CAP 1m 7f 169y(P)
**6:40** (6:40) (Class 5) (0-75,75) 4-Y-O+ **£3,234** (£962; £481; £240) **Stalls** Low

Form RPR
5002 **1** **Saborido (USA)**[20] 5137 8-9-7 75..........................(b) PatDobbs 7 83
(Amanda Perrett) *trckd ldr 6f and again over 4f out: rdn to chal 3f out: narrow ld over 1f out: steadily asserted fnl f* **3/1**[2]

5045 **2** *1 ¼* **Ex Oriente (IRE)**[6] 5639 5-9-7 75..........................[1] AndreaAtzeni 2 82
(Stuart Williams) *led: rdn and pressed over 2f out: hdd over 1f out: one pce fnl f* **11/4**[1]

2434 **3** *¾* **Wall Street Boss (USA)**[22] 5062 4-9-3 71.......................... FrederikTylicki 6 77
(James Fanshawe) *hld up and in last pair after 6f: prog 3f out: chsd ldng pair 2f out: hrd rdn on inner over 1f out: kpt on but nvr able to chal* **4/1**[3]

1420 **4** *4* **Men Don't Cry (IRE)**[21] 5073 5-9-7 75.......................... OisinMurphy 3 76
(Ed de Giles) *trckd ldrs: rdn over 5f out: wnt 3rd 3f out to 2f out: wl btn and hanging over 1f out* **5/1**

4242 **5** *hd* **No Such Number**[6] 5547 6-8-3 62.......................... ShelleyBirkett(5) 4 63
(Julia Feilden) *hld up: in last pair after 6f: pushed along 3f out: outpcd and no ch 2f out: r.o ins fnl f* **8/1**

5231 **6** *1* **Soundbyte**[13] 5403 9-7-11 56 oh3..........................(v) CamHardie(5) 5 56
(John Gallagher) *rousted along leaving stalls: rapid prog fr last to chse ldr after 6f: rdn and lost 2nd over 4f out: steadily wknd over 2f out* **12/1**

0505 **7** *4 ½* **Azrag (USA)**[7] 5600 6-9-2 70..........................(t) RobertHavlin 1 64
(Michael Attwater) *walked to post early: chsd ldrs: rdn and dropped to last 7f out: struggling after* **8/1**

3m 21.59s (-4.11) **Going Correction** -0.125s/f (Stan) **7** Ran SP% **118.2**
Speed ratings (Par 103): **105,104,104,102,101 101,99**
CSF £12.37 TOTE £3.10: £2.70, £1.50; EX 10.60 Trifecta £52.00.
**Owner** Mrs Amanda Perrett **Bred** R D Hubbard And R Masterson **Trained** Pulborough, W Sussex

**FOCUS**
A competitive and truly run stayers' handicap, with the pace increasing from 6f out and the spoils went to the proven stayer.

## 5864 HICKSTEAD INTERNATIONAL HORSESHOW H'CAP 1m 4f (P)
**7:10** (7:10) (Class 6) (0-60,60) 3-Y-O+ **£2,587** (£577; £577; £192) **Stalls** Low

Form RPR
0531 **1** **Zinnobar**[16] 5283 4-9-2 51..........................(p) DannyBrock(3) 4 60
(Jonathan Portman) *mde virtually all: skipped clr on inner wl over 1f out: drvn out and in n.d fnl f* **4/1**[2]

4041 **2** *2 ¼* **Giant Sequoia (USA)**[8] 5558 10-9-3 54 6ex..........(t) LouisSteward(5) 11 59+
(Des Donovan) *hld up in rr: prog on wd outside over 3f out: rdn over 2f out: disp 2nd fnl f but no imp on wnr* **9/4**[1]

-622 **2** *dht* **Rajeh (IRE)**[8] 5558 11-9-0 46.......................... TomQueally 8 51
(Peter Grayson) *pressed wnr after 2f tl drvn and nt qckn 2f out: disp 2nd fnl f: kpt on* **10/1**

500- **4** *½* **Awesome Rock (IRE)**[310] 7440 5-9-0 46.......................... RobertHavlin 7 50
(Roger Ingram) *plld hrd early: trckd wnr 2f: styd prom: rdn over 2f out: disp 2nd jst over 1f out: one pce* **33/1**

-030 **5** *½* **Alba Verde**[23] 5005 3-8-4 46 oh1.......................... LukeMorris 10 49
(Sir Mark Prescott Bt) *hld up in last trio: rdn and prog on inner wl over 1f out: kpt on but nvr rchd ldrs* **5/1**[3]

0000 **6** *1* **Chantecler**[20] 5139 3-9-4 60.......................... JimmyFortune 2 63
(Hughie Morrison) *t.k.h: trckd ldrs: rdn over 2f out: disp 2nd jst over 1f out: losing pl whn short of room nr fin* **6/1**

054 **7** *1 ¾* **Hamble**[18] 5208 5-9-10 56.......................... WilliamCarson 6 55
(Giles Bravery) *hld up in rr: rchd midfield and shkn up 2f out: sn outpcd: rdn and kpt on fnl f: no ch* **8/1**

2500 **8** *nk* **Illegale (IRE)**[16] 5283 8-9-1 47..........................(bt) OisinMurphy 9 46
(Nikki Evans) *stdd s: t.k.h: hld up in last trio: shkn up over 2f out: no ch whn rdn over 1f out: styd on fnl f* **25/1**

00-3 **9** *2 ¼* **Ghufa (IRE)**[16] 5283 10-9-0 49.......................... SimonPearce(3) 5 44
(Lydia Pearce) *wl in tch: rdn 3f out: lost pl and btn 2f out* **16/1**

0404 **10** *11* **Lingfield Lupus (IRE)**[22] 5048 3-8-4 46.......................... JimmyQuinn 3 23
(John Best) *wl in tch: rdn over 2f out: wknd rapidly wl over 1f out: t.o* **12/1**

6050 **11** *½* **Fire In Babylon (IRE)**[17] 5259 6-9-3 54..........................(p) TobyAtkinson(5) 1 31
(Noel Quinlan) *s.v.s: a in last: rdn 4f out: no prog: t.o* **33/1**

2m 34.41s (1.41) **Going Correction** -0.125s/f (Stan)
**WFA** 3 from 4yo+ 10lb **11** Ran SP% **125.2**
Speed ratings (Par 101): **90,88,88,88,87 87,86,85,84,76 76**
Place: Giant Sequoia, 2.70 Rajeh; EX: 6.00, 10.00; CSF: 7.07, 23.06; TC: 43.71, 56.95; TF: 35.90, 28.30; TOTE £4.10: £1.60.
**Owner** Prof C D Green **Bred** Llety Farms **Trained** Upper Lambourn, Berks

**FOCUS**
The pace was indifferent for this moderate handicap. The winner made all.

## 5865 BHEST RACING TO SCHOOL H'CAP 1m 2f (P)
**7:40** (7:42) (Class 6) (0-60,60) 3-Y-O **£2,587** (£770; £384; £192) **Stalls** Low

Form RPR
6103 **1** **Benoordenhout (IRE)**[12] 5428 3-9-2 55..........................(p) OisinMurphy 2 63+
(Jonathan Portman) *awkward s and rousted along to get gng: in tch: moving strly whn prog over 2f out: swept into ld over 1f out: idled in front and drvn fnl f: a holding on* **7/4**[1]

005 **2** *¾* **Saturation Point**[19] 5186 3-9-5 58.......................... AndreaAtzeni 3 64
(James Toller) *trckd ldrs: wnt 2nd over 2f out: drvn to ld v briefly over 1f out: chsd wnr after: styd on but a hld* **9/2**[3]

0004 **3** *2 ½* **Silken Waters**[13] 5402 3-9-2 55.......................... JimmyFortune 1 56+
(Eve Johnson Houghton) *trckd ldrs: rdn and waiting for room 2f out: outpcd over 1f out: styd on to take 3rd ins fnl f* **10/1**

3500 **4** *3* **Division Belle**[16] 5284 3-9-5 58.......................... DougieCostello 7 54
(William Muir) *dwlt but rushed up to ld: hdd after 3f: led over 4f out: hdd & wknd u.p over 1f out* **14/1**

3622 **5** *2* **Choral Clan (IRE)**[24] 4969 3-9-6 59..........................(t) JackMitchell 5 51
(Philip Mitchell) *detached in last early: in tch after 3f: outpcd 2f out: plugged on* **4/1**[2]

5306 **6** *1* **Harboured (USA)**[21] 5109 3-9-7 60..........................[1] PatCosgrave 4 50
(Jim Boyle) *in tch: rdn over 3f out: prog on outer over 2f out: wd bnd sn after and lost grnd: n.d after* **20/1**

0062 **7** *¾* **Sexy Secret**[22] 5030 3-9-2 55.......................... RobertHavlin 6 43
(Lydia Pearce) *hld up in last pair: nt gng wl fr 1/2-way: same pl whn impeded 2f out: no ch after* **8/1**

3-04 **8** *22* **Star Anise (FR)**[16] 5284 3-9-7 60.......................... SamHitchcott 8 7
(Harry Dunlop) *wd bnd after 1f: prog to ld after 3f: hdd over 4f out: losing pl whn hmpd jst over 2f out: t.o* **7/1**

2m 5.8s (-0.80) **Going Correction** -0.125s/f (Stan) **8** Ran SP% **118.7**
Speed ratings (Par 98): **98,97,95,93,91 90,90,72**
CSF £10.27 CT £62.35 TOTE £2.30: £1.10, £2.20, £3.50; EX 14.00 Trifecta £82.10.
**Owner** Prof C D Green **Bred** Prof C Green **Trained** Upper Lambourn, Berks

**FOCUS**
A modest 3yo handicap with a few unexposed sorts and the pace was solid. The winner returned to his best and may do a bit better.

T/Jkpt: Not won. T/Plt: £43.20 to a £1 stake. Pool: £56,751.63 - 957.90 winning units. T/Qpdt: £11.30 to a £1 stake. Pool: £6,762.28 - 439.80 winning units. JN

5866 - 5868a (Foreign Racing) - See Raceform Interactive

5153

## TIPPERARY (L-H)

Thursday, August 28

**OFFICIAL GOING: Good to firm**

### 5869a COOLMORE STUD FAIRY BRIDGE STKS (GROUP 3) (F&M) 7f 100y

6:30 (6:31) 3-Y-O+ £35,208 (£10,291; £4,875; £1,625)

RPR

1 **Tested**[28] [4836] 3-9-0 104 PatSmullen 9 109+
(D K Weld, Ire) *trckd ldr: clsr in 2nd 1/2-way: travelling wl into st and led fr 2f out: drvn clr ent fnl f and styd on wl: easily* 2/1[1]

2 4 **Some Spirit (IRE)**[42] [4376] 3-9-0 90 ColinKeane 5 98
(G M Lyons, Ire) *trckd ldrs tl sn led: over 1 l clr 1/2-way: rdn into st and hdd fr 2f out: no ch w easy wnr: kpt on same pce ins fnl f* 10/1

3 3 1/2 **Wannabe Better (IRE)**[39] [4478] 4-9-8 106 WayneLordan 10 94
(T Stack, Ire) *in tch: clsr in 3rd 1/2-way: rdn fr 2f out and no imp on easy wnr in 4th ent fnl f: kpt on one pce into mod 3rd clsng stages* 11/1

4 nk **Tobann (IRE)**[28] [4836] 4-9-8 102 (t) RoryCleary 3 93
(J S Bolger, Ire) *broke wl to ld narrowly tl sn settled bhd ldrs: dropped to 4th 1/2-way: rdn 2f out and no imp on easy wnr in 3rd ent fnl f: kpt on one pce and dropped to 4th clsng stages* 17/2[3]

5 1 3/4 **Witches Brew (IRE)**[23] [5022] 3-9-0 99 (t) SeamieHeffernan 6 84
(Edward Lynam, Ire) *bhd: pushed along in rr 1/2-way and no imp into st: clsd u.p into mod 5th ent fnl f: kpt on one pce* 6/1[2]

6 3 1/2 **Purr Along**[48] [4165] 4-9-8 109 JamieSpencer 4 80
(J P Murtagh, Ire) *dwlt sltly and settled towards rr: clsr in 6th 1/2-way: rdn 2f out and no imp on ldrs: kpt on one pce* 2/1[1]

7 3 3/4 **Harry's Princess (IRE)**[61] [3742] 3-9-0 98 DeclanMcDonogh 7 66
(John M Oxx, Ire) *chsd ldrs: 5th 1/2-way: pushed along in 6th under 3f out and sn dropped to rr: one pce fnl 2f* 33/1

1m 34.28s (94.28)
**WFA** 3 from 4yo+ 5lb **7 Ran SP% 111.8**
CSF £22.89 TOTE £2.30: £1.50, £5.00; DF 20.90 Trifecta £110.40.
**Owner** K Abdullah **Bred** Juddmonte Farms Ltd **Trained** Curragh, Co Kildare

**FOCUS**
The first two are rated having run personal bests.

5870 - 5872a (Foreign Racing) - See Raceform Interactive

5351

## SALISBURY (R-H)

Friday, August 29

**OFFICIAL GOING: Good (good to soft in places & good to soft in last 2.5f; 7.7)**
Wind: quite strong across Weather: overcast with showers

### 5873 LANGDOWNS DFK LADY RIDERS' H'CAP (FOR LADY AMATEUR RIDERS) 1m

5:10 (5:11) (Class 5) (0-70,68) 3-Y-O+ £2,807 (£870; £435; £217) Stalls Low

Form RPR

4604 1 **Pendo**[36] [4579] 3-9-8 61 MissAliceMills 5 74
(Paul Cole) *taken to s early: mde all: jnd 2f out: kpt on gamely to assert fnl 120yds: pushed out* 5/1[3]

4215 2 1 **Lady Crossmar (IRE)**[16] [5308] 3-9-12 68 MissMeganNicholls(3) 2 78
(Richard Hannon) *trckd ldrs: chal 2f out: sn rdn: stl upsides ent fnl f: no ex fnl 120yds* 2/1[1]

33-0 3 6 **Takitwo**[65] [3589] 11-8-12 52 MissLWest(7) 1 47
(Geoffrey Deacon) *trckd ldrs: rdn 2f out: kpt on same pce* 14/1

4463 4 9 **Beep**[14] [5383] 4-9-13 60 MissEJJones 3 32
(Lydia Richards) *hld up in tch: rdn over 2f out: nt pce to get on terms: wknd fnl f* 7/1

0563 5 6 **George Baker (IRE)**[33] [4717] 7-10-6 67 MissSBrotherton 4 23
(George Baker) *racd keenly: trckd ldrs: rdn over 2f out: sn btn: wknd over 1f out* 3/1[2]

0453 6 hd **Tamujin (IRE)**[10] [5529] 6-8-9 49 oh4 MissDHannaford(7) 6 5
(Ken Cunningham-Brown) *racd keenly: hld up: swtchd lft to centre 4f out: sn rdn: no imp: wknd over 1f out* 7/1

0-05 7 6 **Having A Ball**[15] [5338] 10-8-11 49 oh4 MissPFuller(5) 7
(Geoffrey Deacon) *cl up: rdn 3f out: sn btn* 20/1

0460 8 11 **Red Invader (IRE)**[11] [5499] 4-9-4 56 MrsRWilson(5) 8
(Paul D'Arcy) *hld up: hdwy over 3f out: wknd 2f out* 16/1

1m 43.81s (0.31) **Going Correction** +0.025s/f (Good)
**WFA** 3 from 4yo+ 6lb **8 Ran SP% 117.3**
Speed ratings (Par 103): **99,98,92,83,77 76,70,59**
CSF £15.89 CT £134.12 TOTE £7.80: £2.60, £1.10, £4.60; EX 30.40 Trifecta £223.30.
**Owner** Brett Hopson **Bred** Miss Sue Parkinson **Trained** Whatcombe, Oxon

**FOCUS**
A weak handicap for lady amateurs, in which few became involved. The runner-up sets the standard.

### 5874 BATHWICK TYRES MAIDEN AUCTION STKS 6f

5:40 (5:43) (Class 5) 2-Y-O £2,911 (£866; £432; £216) Stalls Low

Form RPR

03 1 **Wet Sail (USA)**[18] [5248] 2-9-2 0 FrederikTylicki 5 90+
(Charlie Fellowes) *trckd ldrs: led 2f out: r.o strly fnl f: easily* 7/1[3]

02 2 2 **Fast Dancer (IRE)**[13] [5443] 2-9-2 0 OisinMurphy 1 83+
(Joseph Tuite) *trckd ldrs: swtchd lft whn rdn over 1f out: chsd wnr ins fnl f but nvr gng pce to get on terms* 15/8[1]

4 3 4 1/2 **King Jerry (IRE)**[32] [4740] 2-9-2 0 AndreaAtzeni 4 70
(Ralph Beckett) *s.i.s: towards rr: pushed along and hdwy over 3f out: chsd ldrs 2f out: sn outpcd: styd on into 3rd nr fin* 4/1[2]

023 4 1 **Grenade**[13] [5408] 2-8-11 74 MartinHarley 6 62
(Richard Hannon) *racd keenly: led tl rdn 2f out: chsd wnr tl no ex ins fnl f: lost 3rd nr fin* 8/1

5 1 1/4 **Hard To Handel** 2-8-9 0 OscarPereira 10 56+
(Ralph Beckett) *towards rr: hdwy over 2f out: styd on fnl f but nvr gng pce to get involved* 33/1

02 6 3/4 **Ickymasho**[19] [5210] 2-8-1 0 CamHardie(5) 14 51
(Jonathan Portman) *sn trcking ldrs: rdn over 2f out: one pce after* 15/2

03 7 1 3/4 **Cartmell Cleave**[46] [4260] 2-8-8 0 MichaelJMMurphy(3) 8 50
(Stuart Kittow) *s.i.s: sn mid-div: edgd lft whn rdn over 2f out: nvr any imp* 50/1

5 8 nk **Master Zephyr**[30] [4800] 2-9-2 0 GeorgeBaker 11 54
(Roger Charlton) *racd keenly early: sme late prog but mainly towards rr* 16/1

023 9 3 1/4 **Lackaday**[11] [5500] 2-8-10 0 CharlesBishop(3) 12 42
(Mick Channon) *swtchd lft and rdn 2f out: nvr bttr than mid-div* 10/1

0 10 2 3/4 **Almoqatel (IRE)**[11] [5488] 2-8-11 0 TomQueally 13 31
(James Fanshawe) *a towards rr* 66/1

11 2 1/2 **Constant Applause** 2-8-9 0 (b[1]) LemosdeSouza 9 22+
(Mrs Ilka Gansera-Leveque) *s.i.s: mid-div after 2f: rdn to chse ldrs 2f out: sn wknd* 16/1

04 12 3 1/4 **Overlord**[20] [5184] 2-9-2 0 ChrisCatlin 16 19
(Sir Mark Prescott Bt) *s.i.s: a towards rr* 40/1

55 13 6 **Entente**[15] [5351] 2-8-8 0 LouisSteward(5) 7
(Peter Makin) *trckd ldr tl wknd over 2f out* 25/1

1m 15.34s (0.54) **Going Correction** +0.025s/f (Good) **13 Ran SP% 123.7**
Speed ratings (Par 94): **97,94,88,87,85 84,82,81,77,73 70,65,57**
CSF £20.50 TOTE £7.40: £2.60, £1.70, £1.60; EX 29.20 Trifecta £122.30.
**Owner** Saffron House Stables Partnership **Bred** Galleria Bloodstock **Trained** Newmarket, Suffolk

**FOCUS**
Conflicting views from the riders in the second, with George Baker saying "Good to Soft, lovely ground", Oisin Murphy agrreing it was good to soft but Tom Queally calling it "soft". An ordinary maiden auction but useful form from the front two.

### 5875 BATHWICK TYRES NURSERY H'CAP 1m

6:10 (6:13) (Class 5) (0-75,73) 2-Y-O £2,911 (£866; £432; £216) Stalls Low

Form RPR

0400 1 **Silver Quay (IRE)**[7] [5625] 2-9-1 67 MartinHarley 3 76+
(Richard Hannon) *trckd ldrs: chalng whn bmpd 2f out: rdn: edgd lft and led over 1f out: r.o wl fnl f: pushed out* 9/4[1]

0040 2 2 3/4 **My Mate (IRE)**[27] [4897] 2-8-10 67 LouisSteward(5) 6 73
(Clive Brittain) *towards rr: hdwy over 2f out: sn rdn: short of room whn trying to mount chal over 1f out: swtchd lft: sn chsng wnr but a being hld* 7/1

2303 3 1 3/4 **Euthenia**[18] [5250] 2-8-12 67 CharlesBishop(3) 7 66
(Mick Channon) *led after 1f: rdn over 2f out: hdd over 1f out: no ex whn lost 2nd ins fnl f* 16/1

000 4 3 3/4 **Pink Ribbon (IRE)**[48] [4207] 2-8-8 60 OisinMurphy 2 50
(Sylvester Kirk) *hld up towards rr: hdwy over 3f out: rdn over 2f out: wnt 4th ent fnl f: styd on wout threatening* 16/1

0031 5 2 **Seebeedee**[11] [5489] 2-9-0 66 6ex SamHitchcott 1 52
(Harry Dunlop) *led for 1f: trckd ldr: wandered u.p over 2f out: sn one pce* 12/1

6000 6 1/2 **All My Love (IRE)**[17] [5279] 2-8-5 62 CamHardie(5) 4 47
(Richard Hannon) *towards rr: struggling 1/2-way: styd on steadily fnl 2f: nvr a factor* 25/1

003 7 2 **Wolf Of Windlesham (IRE)**[17] [5278] 2-8-13 65 SteveDrowne 14 45
(Charles Hills) *s.i.s: bhd: outpcd over 3f out: styd on steadily past btn horses fnl 2f: nvr a danger* 16/1

565 8 1/2 **Star Of Spring (IRE)**[16] [5305] 2-9-2 68 GeorgeBaker 10 47+
(Charles Hills) *in tch: effrt over 2f out: wknd over 1f out* 5/1[2]

066 9 5 **Hillgrove Angel (IRE)**[15] [5351] 2-9-4 70 HayleyTurner 9 37
(Brian Meehan) *towards rr: swtchd lft over 2f out: wknd over 1f out* 20/1

2066 10 3 1/2 **Secret Lightning (FR)**[25] [4967] 2-9-1 67 DaneO'Neill 8 26
(Sylvester Kirk) *mid-div tl wknd 2f out* 25/1

402 11 2 **Stolen Story (IRE)**[19] [5212] 2-9-7 73 TomQueally 13 28
(George Margarson) *mid-div: effrt over 2f out: wknd over 1f out* 6/1[3]

6644 12 1 1/4 **Jersey Belle**[20] [5180] 2-7-13 58 PaddyPilley(7) 12 10
(Mick Channon) *bmpd leaving stalls: sn chsng ldrs: wknd over 2f out* 20/1

0063 13 41 **Arthur's Way (IRE)**[22] [5072] 2-8-13 65 (b[1]) AndreaAtzeni 11
(Paul Cole) *wnt lft s: midiv tl wknd over 2f out* 12/1

1m 44.11s (0.61) **Going Correction** +0.025s/f (Good) **13 Ran SP% 124.5**
Speed ratings (Par 94): **97,94,92,88,86 86,84,83,78,75 73,72,31**
CSF £17.45 CT £210.99 TOTE £2.90: £1.80, £2.60, £4.80; EX 17.70 Trifecta £364.10.
**Owner** H Robin Heffer **Bred** Michael Joyce **Trained** East Everleigh, Wilts

**FOCUS**
Just an ordinary nursery, but it could pay to follow the first two home. Low stalls dominated and the third helps the level.

### 5876 EBF STALLIONS STONEHENGE STKS (LISTED RACE) 1m

6:40 (6:41) (Class 1) 2-Y-O £17,013 (£6,450; £3,228; £1,608; £807) Stalls Low

Form RPR

31 1 **Elm Park**[14] [5377] 2-9-1 0 DavidProbert 1 100+
(Andrew Balding) *mde all: shkn up to assert over 1f out: kpt on wl: readily* 15/8[1]

0213 2 3 **Groor**[16] [5310] 2-9-1 79 MartinHarley 4 93
(James Tate) *hld up in cl 5th: sltly outpcd 3f out: styd on u.str.p fnl f: wnt 2nd towards fin: no ch w wnr* 33/1

215 3 nk **Mister Universe**[48] [4199] 2-9-1 94 DaneO'Neill 3 92
(Mark Johnston) *pressed wnr: wandered u.p fr over 2f out: hld in 2nd over 1f out: kpt on tl no ex and lost 2nd nring fin* 7/1

13 4 2 **Winters Moon (IRE)**[20] [5190] 2-8-10 0 AndreaAtzeni 5 82
(Saeed bin Suroor) *trckd ldrs: rdn wl over 2f out: edgd lft: kpt on same pce* 11/4[3]

123 5 2 3/4 **Tupi (IRE)**[12] [5478] 2-9-1 0 TomQueally 2 81
(Richard Hannon) *trckd ldrs: rdn over 2f out: nt pce to chal: fdd fnl 120yds* 2/1[2]

1m 44.37s (0.87) **Going Correction** +0.025s/f (Good) **5 Ran SP% 110.2**
Speed ratings: **96,93,92,90,87**
CSF £41.13 TOTE £2.30: £1.30, £4.50; EX 43.80 Trifecta £188.10.
**Owner** Kingsclere Racing Club **Bred** Kingsclere Stud **Trained** Kingsclere, Hants

**FOCUS**
A fair line-up for this Listed event, but there are doubts over the form with a couple of the likely ones below par. The time was marginally slower than the preceding nursery.

### 5877 BREEZE FM & JACK FM H'CAP (BOBIS RACE) 1m 4f

7:10 (7:10) (Class 4) (0-85,84) 3-Y-O £4,851 (£1,443; £721; £360) Stalls Low

Form RPR

1345 1 **Cape Caster (IRE)**[28] [4855] 3-9-3 80 RichardHughes 7 89
(Ralph Beckett) *mid-div: hdwy over 3f out: swtchd lft whn briefly short of room over 2f out: sn rdn: chal ent fnl f: styd on wl to ld fnl 120yds* 7/1[3]

4440 2 1/2 **Cotton Club (IRE)**[22] [5094] 3-8-6 74 LouisSteward(5) 4 82
(Rod Millman) *trckd ldr: rdn for str chal fr 2f out: ev ch ent fnl f: kpt on* 14/1

012 3 hd **Koliakhova (FR)**[15] [5340] 3-8-8 74 MichaelJMMurphy(3) 12 81
(John Flint) *led: rdn and hrd pressed fr over 2f out: battled on gamely: hdd fnl 120yds: no ex* 25/1

302 **4** *2 ¾* **Latin Charm (IRE)**[21] 5132 3-9-3 80..........(p) MartinHarley 11 82
(Marco Botti) *trckd ldr: rdn and edgd lft over 2f out: kpt on same pce fnl f* **3/1**[1]

5613 **5** *2* **Gavlar**[34] 4657 3-8-10 73..........(v) TomQueally 1 72
(William Knight) *s.i.s: in last pair: hdwy over 3f out: sn rdn: styd on but nt pce to get on terms* **16/1**

0431 **6** *1 ½* **High Church (IRE)**[44] 4332 3-9-5 82.......... GeorgeBaker 6 79+
(Roger Charlton) *hld up wl off pce: pushed along whn nt clr run and carried wd over 2f out: styd on fr over 1f out but nvr any ch* **4/1**[2]

11 **7** *1 ½* **Der Meister (IRE)**[109] 2225 3-9-0 77.......... OisinMurphy 5 71+
(Andrew Balding) *s.i.s: bhd: making hdwy whn nt clr run and tried to barge way through 3 times over 2f out: styd on but nvr any ch after* **7/1**[3]

0314 **8** *6* **Classical Art (IRE)**[17] 5276 3-8-13 76.......... AndreaAtzeni 8 61
(Roger Varian) *mid-div: hdwy over 3f out: sn rdn: wknd over 1f out* **7/1**[3]

541 **9** *nse* **Pennine Panther**[20] 5191 3-9-5 82.......... DaneO'Neill 2 67
(Henry Candy) *hld up towards rr: making hdwy and rdn whn bdly blkd 3 times over 2f out: sn btn: nt rcvr* **14/1**

6-06 **10** *5* **Laugharne**[115] 2060 3-9-7 84..........(b[1]) DavidProbert 10 61
(Roger Charlton) *trckd ldrs: rdn 3f out: wknd 2f out* **16/1**

4440 **11** *8* **Cameo Tiara (IRE)**[28] 4855 3-8-11 79.......... CamHardie(5) 9 43
(Richard Hannon) *mid-div: struggling 4f out: wknd over 2f out* **16/1**

2m 38.65s (0.65) **Going Correction** +0.025s/f (Good) **11** Ran SP% **117.3**
Speed ratings (Par 102): **98,97,97,95,94 93,92,88,88,85 79**
CSF £100.28 CT £2306.84 TOTE £7.10: £2.50, £4.50, £7.10; EX 125.00 Trifecta £1120.00.
**Owner** D P Barrie & D Redhead **Bred** Eimear Mulhern **Trained** Kimpton, Hants
■ Stewards' Enquiry : Oisin Murphy four-day ban; careless riding (12th,14th-16th Sept)

**FOCUS**
A decent handicap run at a good gallop. The principals were always prominent, avoiding some trouble further back in the field, and the first five all raced close to the rail. The form is rated a little cautiously.

## 5878 WESTOVER GROUP H'CAP — 1m 6f 21y
**7:40** (7:41) (Class 5) (0-75,74) 3-Y-0+ **£2,911** (£866; £432; £216)

Form RPR

3553 **1** **Cinnilla**[26] 4948 3-8-9 67.......... RichardKingscote 12 86
(Ralph Beckett) *led for 1f: trckd ldrs: led over 2f out: rdn clr over 1f out: in command after: easily* **7/2**[2]

0231 **2** *9* **Taws**[15] 5356 3-9-1 73.......... AndreaAtzeni 11 79
(Rod Millman) *mid-div: rdn and hdwy over 3f out: styd on to go 2nd ent fnl f: nvr any ch w easy wnr* **9/4**[1]

/043 **3** *2 ½* **Benbecula**[34] 4678 5-9-11 71.......... HayleyTurner 2 74
(Richard Mitchell) *trckd ldrs: led after 3f: pushed along wl over 4f out: rdn 3f out: hdd over 2f out: sn hld by wnr: no ex whn lost 2nd ent fnl f* **25/1**

-426 **4** *nk* **Aiyana**[44] 4322 4-9-6 66.......... RichardHughes 3 68+
(Hughie Morrison) *mid-div: rdn 3f out: styd on fnl 2f: nvr trbld ldrs* **16/1**

4235 **5** *2 ¾* **Dark Amber**[15] 5353 4-9-1 66.......... JennyPowell(5) 7 64+
(Brendan Powell) *mid-div: rdn over 3f out: styd on in centre fr over 1f out: nvr threatened to rch ldrs* **10/1**

5226 **6** *6* **Samtu (IRE)**[36] 4584 3-8-8 71.......... LouisSteward(5) 13 61
(Clive Brittain) *hld up up towards rr: hdwy 3f out: sn rdn: nvr threatened ldrs: wknd ent fnl f* **10/1**

6335 **7** *6* **Poitin**[9] 5551 4-9-10 70.......... OisinMurphy 1 51
(Harry Dunlop) *chsd ldrs: rdn 3f out: wknd over 1f out* **25/1**

205 **8** *½* **Shades Of Grey**[26] 4948 7-9-3 66.......... RyanTate(3) 9 47
(Clive Cox) *a towards rr* **20/1**

235 **9** *¾* **Ivanhoe**[15] 5341 4-9-9 69.......... DavidProbert 4 49
(Michael Blanshard) *a towards rr* **20/1**

4652 **10** *2 ¾* **Fighting Back**[10] 5527 3-9-0 72..........(b) TomQueally 6 48+
(Amanda Perrett) *chsd ldrs tl lost pl 5f out: sn rdn: wknd over 2f out* **10/1**

-536 **11** *1 ¼* **Norab (GER)**[99] 2494 3-9-2 74..........(p) MartinHarley 8 48+
(Marco Botti) *mid-div tl wknd over 2f out* **10/1**

0-02 **12** *2* **Laser Blazer**[22] 5073 6-9-12 72..........(p) FergusSweeney 10 43+
(Alan King) *hld up wl off pce: rdn 3f out: nvr any imp* **7/1**[3]

0023 **13** *2 ¼* **Significant Move**[8] 5597 7-9-2 65..........(b) MichaelJMMurphy(3) 5 33
(Stuart Kittow) *prom: led after 1f tl after 3f: chsd ldr: rdn over 3f out: wknd over 2f out* **20/1**

3m 4.44s (-2.96) **Going Correction** +0.025s/f (Good)
**WFA** 3 from 4yo+ 12lb **13** Ran SP% **129.7**
Speed ratings (Par 103): **109,103,102,102,100 97,93,93,93,91 90,89,88**
CSF £11.81 CT £181.18 TOTE £7.60: £2.80, £1.70, £7.10; EX 23.00 Trifecta £644.10.
**Owner** J L Rowsell **Bred** Ashbrittle Stud **Trained** Kimpton, Hants

**FOCUS**
They went a decent clip in this fair staying handicap. Few showed their form, with the third the best guide.
T/Plt: £136.90 to a £1 stake. Pool: £56,402.21 - 300.71 winning tickets T/Qpdt: £93.00 to a £1 stake. Pool: £6,071.61 - 48.26 winning tickets TM

# 5091 SANDOWN (R-H)
Friday, August 29

**OFFICIAL GOING: Sprint course - soft; round course - good to soft (soft in back straight) changing to good to soft after race 3**
Wind: Fresh, against Weather: Cloudy Rails: Rail out 4yyds from 9f to 2.5f where there was a 'drop in' and races on Round course increased by 5yds. Sprint track at full width

## 5879 ORLEANS NURSERY H'CAP (BOBIS RACE) — 5f 6y
**2:00** (2:00) (Class 4) (0-85,84) 2-Y-0 **£3,881** (£1,155; £577; £288) **Stalls** Low

Form RPR

4106 **1** **Majestic Hero (IRE)**[9] 5580 2-9-2 79.......... DavidProbert 4 82
(Ronald Harris) *disp ld: def advantage fr 2f out: drvn and styd on wl fnl f* **9/4**[1]

1331 **2** *1 ¼* **Perardua**[24] 5014 2-9-3 79.......... RyanMoore 6 79
(Richard Fahey) *wnt lft s: chsd ldng pair: shkn up over 2f out: drvn to take 2nd fnl f: kpt on but no imp on wnr* **3/1**[2]

435 **3** *1 ¼* **Tarando**[43] 4345 2-7-10 64.......... CamHardie(5) 1 58
(Michael Bell) *chsd ldng pair: pushed along fr 1/2-way: struggling in 4th over 1f out: kpt on to take 3rd nr fin* **8/1**

010 **4** *1* **Goldcrest**[34] 4646 2-9-4 81.......... DaneO'Neill 2 71
(Henry Candy) *racd against far rail: disp ld to 2f out: sn rdn: lost 2nd and wknd fnl f* **3/1**[2]

1103 **5** *7* **Dittander**[13] 5409 2-9-3 80.......... RichardHughes 3 45
(Richard Hannon) *a in last: pushed along after 2f: taken wd 2f out: wl btn whn eased fnl f* **9/2**[3]

1m 5.6s (4.00) **Going Correction** +0.675s/f (Yiel) **5** Ran SP% **110.1**
Speed ratings (Par 96): **95,93,91,89,78**
CSF £9.22 TOTE £3.30: £1.50, £1.50; EX 9.70 Trifecta £45.30.
**Owner** Mrs Jackie Jarrett & Ridge House Stables **Bred** Mrs Diane Williams **Trained** Earlswood, Monmouths

**FOCUS**
The going on the sprint course was given as soft, and as good to soft, soft in the home straight on the round course. GoingStick readings suggested the ground on the stands' side was marginally quicker up the home straight (6.8 stands, 6.4 centre, 6.3 far side). A competitive little heat.

## 5880 SPORTS TASTER DAY H'CAP — 5f 6y
**2:30** (2:31) (Class 5) (0-75,74) 3-Y-0+ **£3,234** (£962; £481; £240) **Stalls** Low

Form RPR

334- **1** **Macdillon**[338] 6745 8-9-3 67.......... RichardHughes 6 78
(Stuart Kittow) *hld up and racd towards far rail: gng easily whn plld out and prog wl over 1f out: clsd to ld last 150yds: sn clr: comf* **10/1**

241 **2** *2 ½* **Indian Tinker**[23] 5060 5-9-8 72.......... LiamJones 1 74
(Robert Cowell) *led against far rail: drvn 2 l clr wl over 1f out: hdd and readily outpcd last 150yds: styd on* **9/4**[1]

1042 **3** *1 ½* **Tychaios**[31] 4768 4-9-0 64.......... RyanMoore 4 61
(Stuart Williams) *hld up and racd against far rail: prog 2f out: wnt 2nd briefly over 1f out: one pce* **9/2**[3]

0000 **4** *1 ½* **Threes Grand**[31] 4762 4-9-6 70.......... DavidProbert 3 61
(Scott Dixon) *pressed ldrs but racd three off far rail: drvn to dispute 2nd 2f out to over 1f out: fdd* **7/2**[2]

2130 **5** *1 ¼* **Pucon**[50] 4121 5-9-8 72.......... JamesDoyle 5 59
(Roger Teal) *pressed ldrs but racd four off far rail: drvn to dispute 2nd 2f out to over 1f out: fdd* **14/1**

3530 **6** *3 ¾* **Monsieur Jamie**[111] 2159 6-9-10 74..........(v) JimCrowley 8 47
(J R Jenkins) *slowly away: racd on outer and a in rr: shkn up and struggling fr 2f out: wknd* **16/1**

-101 **7** *hd* **Beach Rhythm (USA)**[56] 3939 7-9-2 69.......... DeclanBates(3) 7 41
(Jim Allen) *rrd s and slowly away: racd on outer: a in rr: struggling wl over 1f out* **10/1**

6605 **8** *7* **Waseem Faris (IRE)**[17] 5275 5-9-9 73.......... WilliamTwiston-Davies 2 20
(Mick Channon) *chsd ldr to 2f out: wknd rapidly: fin tired* **8/1**

1m 4.46s (2.86) **Going Correction** +0.675s/f (Yiel) **8** Ran SP% **113.0**
Speed ratings (Par 103): **104,100,97,95,93 87,86,75**
CSF £32.12 CT £117.90 TOTE £9.60: £3.10, £1.10, £1.70; EX 35.50 Trifecta £127.10.
**Owner** Boswell,Pillans,Harris,Urquhart & Kittow **Bred** Hopkins, Kittow & Mrs Perry **Trained** Blackborough, Devon

**FOCUS**
The pace and time were good. The winner is rated to his turf best of the last two years.

## 5881 BRITISH STALLION STUDS EBF MAIDEN STKS — 7f 16y
**3:00** (3:02) (Class 5) 2-Y-0 **£3,881** (£1,155; £577; £288) **Stalls** Low

Form RPR

2 **1** **Time Test**[41] 4440 2-9-5 0.......... JamesDoyle 9 85+
(Roger Charlton) *trckd ldr: pushed into ld jst over 2f out: shkn up and clr 1f out: comf* **5/6**[1]

**2** *2 ¾* **Sweet Dream** 2-9-0 0.......... RichardKingscote 2 71+
(Ralph Beckett) *led: rdn and hdd jst over 2f out: no ch w wnr over 1f out: kpt on* **14/1**

**3** *nk* **Master Apprentice (IRE)** 2-9-5 0.......... DavidProbert 11 75+
(Andrew Balding) *chsd ldrs in 5th: pushed along over 2f out: green and edgd rt over 1f out: styd on to take 3rd last strides* **16/1**

**4** *¾* **Commemorative** 2-9-5 0.......... SteveDrowne 5 73+
(Charles Hills) *chsd ldrs in 7th: shkn up over 2f out: kpt on fr over 1f out: tk 4th last strides* **25/1**

**5** *shd* **Navigate (IRE)** 2-9-5 0.......... FergusSweeney 6 72+
(Martyn Meade) *sn chsd ldng pair: shkn up and clr of rest over 1f out: one pce fnl f* **20/1**

**6** *2* **Felix De Vega (IRE)** 2-9-5 0.......... RichardHughes 14 67+
(Richard Hannon) *dwlt: sn off the pce in 8th: shkn up over 2f out: kpt on one pce fr over 1f out: nt disgracd* **6/1**[2]

**7** *1 ¾* **Town Council (IRE)** 2-9-5 0.......... TonyHamilton 7 62
(Richard Fahey) *dwlt: towards rr and off the pce: sme prog and reminders over 1f out: kpt on* **20/1**

60 **8** *½* **Prince Of Paris**[29] 4809 2-9-5 0.......... RobertHavlin 8 61
(Roger Ingram) *chsd ldng trio: pushed along and outpcd 2f out: no imp after* **100/1**

0 **9** *hd* **Artesana**[52] 4054 2-9-0 0.......... JimCrowley 1 55
(William Knight) *chsd ldrs in 6th: shkn up over 2f out: sn outpcd: steadily fdd* **100/1**

**10** *1* **Stravagante (IRE)** 2-9-5 0.......... RyanMoore 12 58
(Sir Michael Stoute) *slowly away: mostly in last trio: pushed along over 2f out: no hdwy but kpt on* **7/1**[3]

**11** *nk* **International Name** 2-9-5 0.......... DaneO'Neill 15 57
(Saeed bin Suroor) *slowly away: a in last trio: pushed along and rn green over 2f out: no prog* **12/1**

**12** *shd* **Wind Place And Sho** 2-9-2 0.......... RyanTate(3) 3 57
(James Eustace) *dwlt: sn in last trio: jst pushed along fr over 2f out: no hdwy but nt totally disgracd* **66/1**

**13** *14* **Marlot** 2-9-5 0.......... PatCosgrave 13 19
(Jim Boyle) *a towards rr: wknd 2f out: t.o* **100/1**

1m 31.19s (1.69) **Going Correction** -0.025s/f (Good) **13** Ran SP% **119.4**
Speed ratings (Par 94): **89,85,85,84,84 82,80,79,79,78 77,77,61**
CSF £13.60 TOTE £1.90: £1.10, £2.60, £3.60; EX 15.10 Trifecta £166.80.
**Owner** K Abdullah **Bred** Juddmonte Farms Ltd **Trained** Beckhampton, Wilts

**FOCUS**
Despite several big stables being represented, none of the newcomers came in for much support.

## 5882 ROA OWNERS JACKPOT H'CAP (BOBIS RACE) — 1m 14y
**3:35** (3:35) (Class 3) (0-90,90) 3-Y-0
**£9,337** (£2,796; £1,398; £699; £349; £175) **Stalls** Low

Form RPR

12 **1** **Basem**[97] 2544 3-9-6 **89**.......... RichardHughes 5 98
(Saeed bin Suroor) *trckd ldng pair: clsd to ld wl over 2f out: rdn over 1f out: styd on wl* **7/2**[2]

4443 **2** *1 ½* **Grevillea (IRE)**[16] 5311 3-8-9 **78** ow1.......... WilliamTwiston-Davies 1 84
(Mick Channon) *hld up in 6th: prog 2f out: rdn to chse wnr jst over 1f out: styd on but no imp last 100yds* **12/1**

2-13 **3** 1 1/4 **Man Of Harlech**104 2330 3-9-3 86 DavidProbert 3 89
(Andrew Balding) trckd ldng trio: clsd to chal wl over 2f out: chsd wnr after: nt qckn over 1f out: sn lost 2nd: one pce **4/1**3
231- **4** 3/4 **Torrid**324 7128 3-9-7 90 JamesDoyle 2 91
(Amanda Perrett) hld up in 5th: pushed along over 2f out: no prog whn shkn up over 1f out and hanging rt: tk 4th last strides **5/1**
3464 **5** 1/2 **Hatsaway (IRE)**27 4886 3-9-2 85 WilliamBuick 7 85
(Clive Brittain) trckd ldr: styd out wd in st: lost 2nd 3f out but stl wl on terms: one pce fnl 2f **10/1**
1-21 **6** 1 1/2 **Beach Bar (IRE)**79 3108 3-9-6 89 RyanMoore 4 86
(William Knight) stdd s: hld up in last and sn tk fierce hold: urged along and no prog over 2f out: wl btn after **11/4**1
2111 **7** 1 1/2 **Imshivalla (IRE)**12 5468 3-8-12 81 6ex TonyHamilton 6 74
(Richard Fahey) led to wl over 2f out: steadily wknd **8/1**

1m 45.0s (1.70) **Going Correction** -0.025s/f (Good) 7 Ran SP% **113.4**
Speed ratings (Par 104): **90,88,87,86,86 84,83**
CSF £42.09 CT £173.09 TOTE £5.30: £2.80, £5.00; EX 42.80 Trifecta £225.40.
**Owner** Godolphin **Bred** Darley **Trained** Newmarket, Suffolk

**FOCUS**
The going on the round course was changed to good to soft prior to this race. They went a muddling pace. The winner has obvious potential to do better.

## 5883 SQUIRE FURNEAUX VOLVO MAIDEN FILLIES' STKS (BOBIS RACE) 7f 16y
**4:10** (4:10) (Class 5) 3-Y-O **£3,234** (£962; £481) **Stalls** Low

Form RPR
-304 **1** **Brown Diamond (IRE)**33 4699 3-9-0 75 RyanMoore 4 78
(Charles Hills) mde all: led field to nr side in st: rdn and racd awkwardly wl over 1f out: drvn clr fnl f: styd on wl **5/2**2
**2** 5 **Semblance** 3-9-0 0 WilliamBuick 2 65
(John Gosden) rn green and pushed along at times in last: shkn up and struggling over 2f out: styd on to take 2nd ins fnl f **7/4**2
22 **3** 3 1/2 **Childesplay**23 5044 3-8-11 0 RyanTate(3) 3 56
(Heather Main) trckd wnr: rdn 2f out: nt qckn over 1f out: wknd and lost 2nd ins fnl f **11/8**1

1m 32.25s (2.75) **Going Correction** -0.025s/f (Good) 3 Ran SP% **107.0**
Speed ratings (Par 97): **83,77,73**
CSF £6.67 TOTE £3.30; EX 5.00 Trifecta £6.50.
**Owner** Triermore Stud **Bred** Adjalisa Syndicate **Trained** Lambourn, Berks

**FOCUS**
For the first time the stands' side, which was noted as quicker judged on GoingStick readings prior to racing, was explored, and it was Ryan Moore, aboard the winner, who took the decision to lead his two rivals over. The form is essentially weak but the winner deserves a bit of credit.

## 5884 HWFA WILLIAMS H'CAP (BOBIS RACE) 1m 2f 7y
**4:45** (4:46) (Class 4) (0-80,80) 3-Y-O **£5,175** (£1,540; £769; £384) **Stalls** Low

Form RPR
4041 **1** **Ski Lift**16 5319 3-9-5 78 JamesDoyle 6 90
(John Gosden) prom: lost pl sltly and pushed along 4f out: looked in trble over 2f out: responded wl and r.o over 1f out: led jst ins fnl f: styd on wl **9/2**2
2540 **2** nk **Green Light**17 5276 3-9-2 75 SeanLevey 8 86
(Ralph Beckett) hld up wl in rr: nt clr run briefly over 2f out: prog after: rdn to chal and w wnr jst ins fnl f: styd on but a hld nr fin **16/1**
03-1 **3** 2 1/4 **Dance Of Heroes**179 827 3-9-7 80 WilliamBuick 10 87
(Jeremy Noseda) sn trckd ldng pair: gng strly over 2f out: produced to ld over 1f out: sn drvn: hdd and nt qckn jst ins fnl f **4/1**1
3-63 **4** 1 1/2 **Tucson Arizona**42 4402 3-8-13 75 RyanTate(3) 3 79
(Anthony Carson) hld up in detached last: stl last 3f out: prog fr 2f out but hanging rt: r.o to take 4th fnl f: unable to threaten **12/1**
500 **5** 1 1/4 **Collaboration**29 4821 3-9-7 80 (t) JimmyFortune 1 82
(Andrew Balding) trckd ldrs: rdn and cl up in 4th 2f out: nt qckn sn after: one pce **5/1**3
4130 **6** hd **Beakers N Num Nums (IRE)**34 4651 3-9-1 74 MartinDwyer 7 75
(William Jarvis) hld up towards rr: sme prog over 2f out: nt clr run briefly over 1f out: kpt on same pce **25/1**
5333 **7** 3 **The Character (IRE)**13 5413 3-9-4 77 RichardKingscote 9 73
(Tom Dascombe) wl in rr and nt gng wl: struggling bdly 3f out: kpt on fr over 1f out **6/1**
0535 **8** hd **Triple Chief (IRE)**16 5302 3-9-2 75 RobertHavlin 12 70
(Rod Millman) trckd ldr: drvn to chal jst over 2f out: wknd over 1f out **33/1**
6054 **9** 1 **Laurelita (IRE)**21 5123 3-9-4 77 PatCosgrave 11 73
(George Baker) in tch in midfield: pushed along 4f out: keeping on u.p whn nt clr run over 1f out and lost momentum: fdd **20/1**
3 **10** 1 **All Talk N No Do (IRE)**19 5203 3-9-4 77 FergusSweeney 5 68
(Seamus Durack) led: rdn over 2f out: hdd & wknd over 1f out: eased ins fnl f **11/1**
500 **11** 3 1/4 **Cabin Fever**41 4435 3-9-0 73 PatDobbs 4 58
(Ralph Beckett) wl in tch in midfield: no prog over 2f out: wknd qckly over 1f out **16/1**
455 **12** 36 **Savant (IRE)**23 5039 3-9-5 78 RyanMoore 2
(Sir Michael Stoute) hld up wl in rr: wknd u.p over 2f out: t.o: lame **7/1**

2m 9.65s (-0.85) **Going Correction** -0.025s/f (Good) 12 Ran SP% **121.0**
Speed ratings (Par 102): **102,101,99,98,97 97,95,95,94,93 90,62**
CSF £74.01 CT £317.83 TOTE £5.00: £1.90, £6.90, £1.90; EX 95.00 Trifecta £499.90.
**Owner** K Abdullah **Bred** Juddmonte Farms Ltd **Trained** Newmarket, Suffolk

**FOCUS**
An interesting handicap run at a good pace. The winner looks to have more to offer.
T/Plt: £64.30 to a £1 stake. Pool: £67392.06 - 764.96 winning tickets T/Qpdt: £33.80 to a £1 stake. Pool: £4761.68 - 104.00 winning tickets JN

# 5493 THIRSK (L-H)
Friday, August 29

**OFFICIAL GOING: Good (8.9)**
Wind: fresh 1/2 behind Weather: changeable, breezy, light showers Rails: Rail dolled out further from last meeting to provide fresh ground on back straight and around home bend. Away bend on previous dolled out line. Races of 7f & 8f increased by 35yds and 2m race by 410

Form RPR
4402 **1** **Designate (IRE)**11 5506 2-9-2 68 (bt) GrahamGibbons 3 68+
(Ralph Beckett) w ldr: led over 2f out: drvn out **3/1**2
0423 **2** 2 1/2 **Westhoughton**17 5266 2-9-12 63 DanielTudhope 10 71
(David O'Meara) chsd ldrs: 3rd over 2f out: chsd wnr last 150yds: no imp **11/2**3
4455 **3** 1 1/4 **Strategic Order (IRE)**13 5447 2-9-0 67 GrahamLee 6 55
(Paul Midgley) mid-div: hdwy over 2f out: kpt on same pce over 1f out **11/1**
0 **4** 1 **Star Pursuits**92 2692 2-9-0 0 TobyAtkinson(5) 4 57
(Noel Quinlan) s.s: in rr: kpt on fnl 2f: nrst fin **25/1**
4405 **5** 3 **Snoway**14 5384 2-8-7 50 BarryMcHugh 2 36
(Tony Coyle) in rr-div: sme hdwy over 2f out: nvr a factor **25/1**
5330 **6** 1 **Kidmeforever**20 5180 2-8-6 58 (b1) LukeMorris 11 32
(J S Moore) dwlt: in rr and sn drvn along: kpt on fnl 2f: nvr on terms **8/1**
0343 **7** 10 **Astrea**41 4449 2-8-7 51 AndrewMullen 8 9
(Nigel Tinkler) chsd ldrs on outer: hung lft and lost pl over 1f out: eased clsng stages **33/1**
3220 **8** 6 **Indian Keys**27 4913 2-9-2 71 JamieSpencer 9
(Kevin Ryan) led: hung lft and hdd over 2f out: lost pl over 1f out: sn heavily eased **13/8**1
500 **9** 3 1/2 **Aneto Peak**16 5297 2-8-13 55 AdrianNicholls 5
(Nigel Tinkler) sn chsng ldrs on outer: lost pl over 1f out: eased ins fnl f **66/1**
06 **10** 24 **Equiaire**48 4192 2-8-11 0 PhillipMakin 1
(John Weymes) dwlt: sn mid-div: lost pl over 2f out: eased over 1f out: virtually p.u: t.o **100/1**

1m 11.92s (-0.78) **Going Correction** -0.475s/f (Firm) 10 Ran SP% **111.0**
Speed ratings (Par 96): **86,82,81,79,75 74,61,53,48,16**
CSF £17.75 TOTE £4.60: £1.60, £1.60, £2.60; EX 20.30 Trifecta £123.20.
**Owner** Highclere Thoroughbred Racing - Approve **Bred** Rihana Partnership **Trained** Kimpton, Hants

**FOCUS**
A modest heat which was won in clear-cut fashion.

## 5886 BRITISH STALLION STUDS EBF MAIDEN STKS (BOBIS RACE) 1m
**2:40** (2:41) (Class 4) 2-Y-O **£4,204** (£1,251; £625; £312) **Stalls** Low

Form RPR
02 **1** **Deerfield**20 5184 2-9-5 0 PhillipMakin 1 79
(Charlie Appleby) trckd ldrs: effrt 2f out: styd on u.p to ld clsng stages **15/8**1
46 **2** 3/4 **Landwade Lad**37 4550 2-9-5 0 ShaneKelly 4 77
(James Fanshawe) doon chsng ldrs: effrt 3f out: led 1f out: hdd and no ex clsng stages **7/2**2
04 **3** 2 1/4 **Referendum (IRE)**16 5315 2-9-5 0 PaulMulrennan 5 72
(Sir Michael Stoute) trckd ldrs: led over 2f out: hdd 1f out: kpt on one pce **8/1**
0 **4** 4 1/2 **Game Show**11 5494 2-9-5 0 AhmedAjtebi 10 62+
(Charlie Appleby) in rr: hdwy and edgd rt over 2f out: styd on fnl f **11/2**3
0 **5** 2 3/4 **Red Majesty**30 4787 2-9-5 0 (v1) JamieSpencer 11 55
(Kevin Ryan) mid-div: effrt and chsng ldrs 3f out: wknd over 1f out **20/1**
40 **6** 1 1/4 **Loom Of Life (IRE)**41 4424 2-9-5 0 DavidNolan 7 53
(Richard Fahey) chsd ldrs: drvn 3f out: wknd over 1f out **6/1**
**7** 1 3/4 **Newgate Princess** 2-9-0 0 BarryMcHugh 8 44
(Tony Coyle) s.i.s: sme hdwy 3f out: hmpd 2f out: nvr nr ldrs **125/1**
46 **8** hd **Sweet Talker**16 5296 2-9-0 0 DavidAllan 3 43
(Tim Easterby) mid-div: chsd ldrs over 3f out: outpcd over 2f out: fdd over 1f out **40/1**
0 **9** 7 **Egmont**22 5078 2-9-5 0 DanielTudhope 14 32
(George Moore) s.i.s: bhd and drvn 3f out **100/1**
00 **10** 1 **Warapito**56 3934 2-9-2 0 NeilFarley(3) 6 30
(Richard Guest) t.k.h towards rr: bhd fnl 2f **200/1**
**11** 2 3/4 **Thowar (USA)** 2-9-5 0 1 TomEaves 12 23
(Kevin Ryan) racd wd: mid-div: lost pl over 2f out **18/1**
00 **12** 26 **Ted Larkin (IRE)**18 5242 2-9-5 0 RobertWinston 2
(Richard Guest) led: t.k.h: hdd over 2f out: lost pl over 1f out: heavily eased: t.o **100/1**

1m 42.18s (2.08) **Going Correction** -0.025s/f (Good) 12 Ran SP% **113.5**
Speed ratings (Par 96): **88,87,85,80,77 76,74,74,67,66 63,37**
CSF £7.56 TOTE £2.70: £1.30, £1.70, £2.30; EX 8.20 Trifecta £32.30.
**Owner** Godolphin **Bred** Biddestone Stud **Trained** Newmarket, Suffolk
■ Stewards' Enquiry : Ahmed Ajtebi one-day ban; careless riding (12th Sept)

**FOCUS**
A modest 2yo maiden.

## 5887 JW 4X4 NORTHALLERTON H'CAP 7f
**3:15** (3:15) (Class 4) (0-80,80) 3-Y-O+ **£4,851** (£1,443; £721; £360) **Stalls** Low

Form RPR
5025 **1** **Green Howard**20 5196 6-9-12 80 DanielTudhope 8 96
(Robin Bastiman) mid-div: smooth hdwy over 2f out: led appr fnl f: styd on strly: v readily **9/2**1
1042 **2** 4 **Almanack**10 5536 4-8-11 65 JamieSpencer 6 71
(Ian Williams) hld up in rr: hdwy on outer over 2f out: styd on fnl f: tk 2nd post **7/1**2
2006 **3** nse **Snow Bay**7 5629 8-9-4 72 GrahamLee 10 77
(Paul Midgley) led early: w ldr: t.k.h: led over 4f out: hdd 1f out: kpt on same pce **10/1**
4260 **4** nk **Cara's Request (AUS)**14 5385 9-9-2 73 ConnorBeasley(3) 1 78
(Michael Dods) sn led: hdd over 4f out: kpt on one pce over 1f out **12/1**
6302 **5** 1/2 **Millkwood**27 4924 4-9-7 75 PhillipMakin 2 78
(John Davies) chsd ldrs: one pce fnl 2f **8/1**3
6153 **6** 1 1/2 **Orpsie Boy (IRE)**20 5168 11-9-1 69 LukeMorris 3 68
(Ruth Carr) chsd ldrs: effrt over 2f out: one pce over 1f out **9/1**
1026 **7** 1 3/4 **True Pleasure (IRE)**23 5054 7-9-11 79 PJMcDonald 13 74
(James Bethell) wnt rt s: in rr: hdwy over 2f out: nvr a threat **12/1**
5630 **8** 3 1/4 **Lilac Lace (IRE)**20 5197 4-8-11 72 RachelRichardson(7) 7 58
(Tim Easterby) s.i.s: in rr: sme hdwy and edgd lft over 2f out: nvr a factor **11/1**
0-40 **9** 3/4 **Destination Aim**63 3668 7-8-12 66 JasonHart 4 51
(Frederick Watson) trckd ldrs: effrt over 2f out: wknd over 1f out **25/1**
0164 **10** 3 **Iceblast**15 5337 6-8-10 64 GrahamGibbons 9 41
(Michael Easterby) in rr: effrt and n.m.r 2f out: nvr on terms **17/2**
06-5 **11** 2 3/4 **Reposer (IRE)**14 5385 6-9-12 80 TomEaves 12 50
(Keith Dalgleish) trckd ldrs: drvn over 3f out: lost pl over 1f out **9/1**

0000 **12** *16* **Lewisham**[20] 5199 4-9-7 75 AdrianNicholls 11 3
(David Nicholls) *chsd ldrs: drvn over 3f out: lost pl 2f out: sn eased: virtually p.u: t.o* **16/1**

1m 26.43s (-0.77) **Going Correction** -0.025s/f (Good)
**WFA** 3 from 4yo+ 5lb **12** Ran SP% **114.9**
Speed ratings (Par 105): **103,98,98,98,97 95,93,90,89,85 82,64**
CSF £33.29 CT £298.22 TOTE £5.00: £1.80, £2.50, £4.30; EX 35.50 Trifecta £377.70.
**Owner** Ms M Austerfield **Bred** Miss A J Rawding & P M Crane **Trained** Cowthorpe, N Yorks

**FOCUS**
What looked quite a competitive handicap ended up being anything but, the winner bolting up. He rates a small personal best. It was run at a sound pace.

## 5888 THEAKSTON LIGHTFOOT H'CAP 6f
**3:50** (3:51) (Class 3) (0-90,90) 3-Y-O+ **£7,762** (£2,310; £1,154; £577) **Stalls** High

Form RPR

0110 **1** **Compton Park**[13] 5444 7-9-12 90 (t) DavidAllan 14 103+
(Les Eyre) *mid-div stands' side: hdwy over 2f out: led 1f out: styd on wl* **11/2**[1]

1261 **2** *1 ¼* **Bajan Bear**[25] 4961 6-9-1 79 AdrianNicholls 7 87+
(David Nicholls) *slowly away and swtchd rt s: racd stands' side: hdwy to chse ldrs over 2f out: 2nd 1f out: styd on same pce* **16/1**

2544 **3** *¾* **Cruise Tothelimit (IRE)**[13] 5411 6-8-13 77 LukeMorris 8 83
(Ian Williams) *chsd ldrs stands' side: led that gp and overall over 2f out: hdd 1f out: styd on same pce* **16/1**

4102 **4** *nk* **Liberty Jack (IRE)**[7] 5623 4-9-5 83 (p) StephenCraine 12 88
(Jim Boyle) *racd stands' side: mid-div: hdwy to chse ldrs over 2f out: styd on same pce fnl f* **6/1**[2]

220- **5** *nk* **Mehdi (IRE)**[349] 6384 5-9-4 87 (t) JackGarritty(5) 15 91
(Richard Fahey) *chsd ldrs stands' side: kpt on same pce fnl f* **8/1**

0535 **6** *nk* **Head Space (IRE)**[4] 5766 6-9-1 79 (b[1]) JamesSullivan 18 82
(Ruth Carr) *mid-div stands' side: hdwy and nt clr run over 1f out: kpt on* **12/1**

1014 **7** *1 ¾* **My Name Is Rio (IRE)**[25] 4976 4-9-6 84 PaulMulrennan 6 82
(Michael Dods) *led 5 others far side: kpt on same pce fnl f: 1st of 6 that gp* **7/1**[3]

0000 **8** *½* **Can You Conga**[13] 5419 4-9-5 83 PhillipMakin 3 79
(Michael Easterby) *chsd ldrs far side: upsides that gp fnl f: kpt on same pce: 2nd of 6 that gp* **25/1**

2430 **9** *nk* **Dark Castle**[33] 4712 5-9-4 82 PJMcDonald 16 77
(Micky Hammond) *racd stands' side: mid-div: hdwy over 2f out: sn chsng ldrs: one pce* **14/1**

5430 **10** *nse* **Mississippi**[20] 5199 5-9-6 84 GrahamGibbons 10 79
(David Barron) *towards rr stands' side: kpt on fnl 2f: nvr a factor* **14/1**

1062 **11** *1 ¼* **Adam's Ale**[24] 5016 5-9-3 81 RobertWinston 1 72
(Paul Midgley) *in rr far side: nvr a factor: 3rd of 6 that gp* **22/1**

1400 **12** *¾* **Rothesay Chancer**[20] 5170 6-9-1 79 GrahamLee 17 67
(Jim Goldie) *in rr stands' side: sme hdwy over 1f out: nvr on terms* **33/1**

000 **13** *½* **Rocksilla**[52] 4061 4-9-4 82 SebSanders 9 69
(Chris Wall) *in rr stands' side: sme hdwy over 2f out: wknd over 1f out* **25/1**

0003 **14** *hd* **Chooseday (IRE)**[13] 5444 5-9-5 83 (t) JamieSpencer 4 69
(Kevin Ryan) *stmbld s: sn w ldr far side: wknd fnl f: 4th of 6 that gp* **12/1**

1004 **15** *hd* **Tumblewind**[60] 3788 4-9-6 87 GeorgeChaloner(3) 2 73
(Richard Whitaker) *chsd ldrs far side: wknd fnl f: 5th of 6 that gp* **16/1**

3040 **16** *nk* **Hadaj**[34] 4650 5-9-3 84 (b) ConnorBeasley(3) 5 69
(Ruth Carr) *in rr far side: nvr a factor: last of 6 that gp* **22/1**

-000 **17** *½* **Sacrosanctus**[50] 4121 6-8-8 77 (p) MatthewHopkins(5) 11 60
(Scott Dixon) *overall ldr stands' side: hdd over 2f out: wknd over 1f out* **40/1**

00-0 **18** *12* **Rodrigo De Torres**[13] 5444 7-9-9 87 JasonHart 20 32
(John Murray) *chsd ldr stands' side: hung lft and lost pl over 2f out: bhd over 1f out: eased* **33/1**

1m 9.94s (-2.76) **Going Correction** -0.475s/f (Firm) **18** Ran SP% **124.4**
Speed ratings (Par 107): **99,97,96,95,95 95,92,92,91,91 90,89,88,88,87 87,86,70**
CSF £84.93 CT £1355.60 TOTE £5.90: £2.30, £3.10, £3.10, £1.30; EX 91.90 Trifecta £1409.20.
**Owner** Billy Parker **Bred** David Jamison Bloodstock **Trained** Catton, North Yorkshire

**FOCUS**
A pretty useful sprint. The field split from the stalls, the bigger stands' side group always holding sway. Sound form, the winner rated in line with his penultimate Haydock form.

## 5889 DOWNLOAD NEW RACING UK IPAD APP CLASSIFIED (S) STKS 6f
**4:25** (4:26) (Class 6) 3-4-Y-O **£2,576** (£770; £384; £192) **Stalls** High

Form RPR

2250 **1** **Native Falls (IRE)**[7] 5638 3-9-2 71 DavidAllan 7 70
(Alan Swinbank) *mde all: shkn up and styd on wl fnl f: readily* **13/8**[1]

4401 **2** *1 ¼* **Live Dangerously**[7] 5635 4-9-5 63 TomEaves 2 65
(Keith Dalgleish) *trckd wnr: effrt over 2f out: rdn and styd on same pce over 1f out: no imp* **15/8**[2]

630 **3** *2* **Emily Davison (IRE)**[14] 5375 3-8-11 63 (p) GemmaTutty(5) 4 59
(Karen Tutty) *trckd ldrs: effrt over 2f out: hung lft and kpt on same pce* **15/2**[3]

0614 **4** *shd* **Henke (IRE)**[19] 5202 3-9-2 55 (p) JasonHart 3 58
(Nigel Tinkler) *sn outpcd in rr and drvn along: hdwy over 2f out: kpt on one pce* **9/1**

4466 **5** *5* **Angels Calling**[7] 5636 4-8-8 51 (b[1]) RobJFitzpatrick(5) 6 36
(K R Burke) *s.i.s: hdwy to chse ldrs over 4f out: wknd appr fnl f* **8/1**

0540 **6** *15* **Fizzolo**[14] 5375 3-8-10 46 BarryMcHugh 5
(Karen Tutty) *in rr: brief effrt over 2f out: sn wknd and bhd: eased ins fnl f: t.o* **66/1**

1m 10.93s (-1.77) **Going Correction** -0.475s/f (Firm)
**WFA** 3 from 4yo 3lb **6** Ran SP% **107.2**
Speed ratings (Par 101): **92,90,87,87,80 60**
CSF £4.42 TOTE £2.80: £1.60, £1.10; EX 4.70 Trifecta £15.80.The winner was bought in for 8,000gns.
**Owner** Anthea Findlay & The Twopin Partnership **Bred** John Foley **Trained** Melsonby, N Yorks

**FOCUS**
A fair effort from the winner in this classified seller but the form is rated a bit cautiously.

## 5890 A FOR AGENCY H'CAP 2m
**4:55** (4:59) (Class 4) (0-80,80) 3-Y-O+ **£4,851** (£1,443; £721; £360) **Stalls** Centre

Form RPR

4311 **1** **Deauville Dancer (IRE)**[15] 5341 3-9-0 80 LukeMorris 13 88+
(Sir Mark Prescott Bt) *trckd ldrs: drvn over 2f out: led 1f out: hld on clsng stages* **2/1**[1]

4133 **2** *¾* **Longshadow**[9] 5564 4-9-10 76 (v) PJMcDonald 12 83
(Jason Ward) *hmpd s: drvn to sn chse ldrs: styd on same pce to take 2nd towards fin* **7/1**[2]

40-3 **3** *hd* **Big Time Billy (IRE)**[15] 5341 8-9-0 73 (v) SeanBowen(7) 15 80
(Alan Phillips) *hld up in rr: effrt over 3f out: chsng ldrs over 2f out: styd on ins fnl f: tk 3rd post* **11/1**

6225 **4** *nse* **Dr Irv**[24] 5017 5-9-0 73 MeganCarberry(7) 2 80
(Philip Kirby) *mid-div: hdwy 3f out: swtchd ins 2f out: led briefly over 1f out: kpt on same pce last 75yds* **11/1**

6033 **5** *4* **Ebony Express**[24] 4995 5-9-11 77 JamieSpencer 6 79
(Alan Swinbank) *in rr-div: hdwy over 2f out: kpt on fnl f* **18/1**

6112 **6** *1 ¼* **Precision Strike**[12] 5466 4-9-6 72 (v) RobertWinston 4 73
(Richard Guest) *hld up in rr: hdwy 9f out: chsng ldrs over 3f out: fdd over 1f out* **16/1**

4-06 **7** *nse* **Chevalgris**[12] 5465 4-9-12 78 DavidAllan 16 79
(Alan Swinbank) *in rr and sn drvn along: hdwy over 2f out: styd on fnl f* **40/1**

3225 **8** *1 ¼* **Beat The Tide**[15] 5334 4-9-10 76 PaulMulrennan 8 75
(Michael Dods) *mid-div: effrt over 2f out: one pce* **16/1**

2213 **9** *nk* **Kirkman (IRE)**[15] 5334 3-8-4 70 JamesSullivan 10 69
(James Bethell) *wnt rt s: sn led: drvn 3 l clr 3f out: hdd over 1f out: sn wknd* **10/1**[3]

6613 **10** *1* **Albonny (IRE)**[22] 5083 5-9-6 72 DanielTudhope 11 70
(Timothy Jarvis) *hmpd s: sn chsng ldrs: wknd over 1f out* **12/1**

01 **11** *hd* **Caledonia**[76] 3240 7-9-7 73 GrahamLee 14 70
(Jim Goldie) *hld up in mid-div: effrt over 3f out: nvr on terms* **7/1**[2]

0000 **12** *2 ¼* **Agreement (IRE)**[15] 5334 4-10-0 80 IanBrennan 1 75
(John Quinn) *led early: chsd ldrs: shkn up over 7f out: drvn over 4f out: wknd 2f out* **50/1**

3266 **13** *4 ½* **Rosairlie (IRE)**[24] 5017 6-9-12 78 TomEaves 3 67
(Micky Hammond) *hld up in rr: drvn 4f out: sn bhd* **40/1**

4634 **14** *4 ½* **Bowdler's Magic**[15] 5334 7-9-5 71 (t) RaulDaSilva 7 55
(David Thompson) *in rr: hdwy over 6f out: sn drvn: chsng ldrs over 3f out: lost pl 2f out: bhd whn eased clsng stages* **22/1**

3m 29.91s (1.61) **Going Correction** -0.025s/f (Good)
**WFA** 3 from 4yo+ 14lb **14** Ran SP% **120.0**
Speed ratings (Par 105): **94,93,93,93,91 90,90,90,90,89 89,88,86,83**
CSF £14.53 CT £128.50 TOTE £3.00: £1.70, £2.30, £4.40; EX 19.50 Trifecta £117.00.
**Owner** Suffolk Bloodstock **Bred** Ruskerne Ltd **Trained** Newmarket, Suffolk

**FOCUS**
This appeals as solid form for the level, the progressive winner outstaying some in-form rivals. It was sound run.

## 5891 RACING UK ANDROID APP RACINGUK.COM/MOBILE H'CAP (DIV I) 1m
**5:25** (5:26) (Class 5) (0-70,69) 3-Y-O **£3,408** (£1,006; £503) **Stalls** Low

Form RPR

4435 **1** **Rangi Chase (IRE)**[26] 4941 3-9-1 68 JackGarritty(5) 2 78
(Richard Fahey) *sn trcking ldrs: hung lft and led wl over 1f out: edgd rt and drvn out fnl f* **6/1**

063 **2** *2* **It's All A Game**[18] 5233 3-8-9 57 (b) JasonHart 7 62
(Richard Guest) *t.k.h: w ldr: led over 6f out: hdd 3f out: 2nd over 1f out: styd on same pce* **11/1**

4333 **3** *nse* **Baltic Fire (IRE)**[10] 5522 3-8-10 61 (p) JoeyHaynes(3) 5 66
(K R Burke) *rr-div: drvn and hdwy over 2f out: 3rd over 1f out: styd on same pce* **7/2**[1]

503 **4** *1 ½* **Norfolk Sound**[14] 5400 3-8-8 59 AshleyMorgan(3) 6 60
(Chris Wall) *in rr: effrt 3f out: hdwy on outside 2f out: 4th 1f out: kpt on* **5/1**[2]

5340 **5** *4* **Vale Mentor (IRE)**[22] 5084 3-8-2 50 oh2 (p) IanBrennan 9 42
(Tim Easterby) *chsd ldrs: drvn over 3f out: wknd over 1f out* **15/2**

3245 **6** *hd* **Beautiful Stranger (IRE)**[83] 3002 3-9-7 69 (p) TomEaves 1 61
(Keith Dalgleish) *dwlt: drvn to sn chse ldrs: wknd over 1f out* **12/1**

4130 **7** *nk* **Sooqaan**[55] 3946 3-8-12 60 PJMcDonald 3 51
(Mel Brittain) *s.i.s: in rr: kpt on fnl 2f: nvr a factor* **10/1**

0323 **8** *hd* **Bertha Burnett (IRE)**[18] 5245 3-8-6 57 ConnorBeasley(3) 11 48
(Brian Rothwell) *led tl over 6f out: w ldr: led 3f out: hdd wl over 1f out: sn wknd* **11/2**[3]

0000 **9** *¾* **Kraka Gym (IRE)**[45] 4300 3-8-6 54 (b) BarryMcHugh 10 43
(Michael Easterby) *chsd ldrs: lost pl 2f out* **33/1**

4506 **10** *7* **Playtothewhistle**[11] 5497 3-9-1 63 PaulMulrennan 4 36
(Bryan Smart) *in rr-div: hdwy over 4f out: sn chsng ldrs: drvn and lost pl 2f out: eased whn bhd clsng stages* **16/1**

1m 41.12s (1.02) **Going Correction** -0.025s/f (Good) **10** Ran SP% **114.3**
Speed ratings (Par 100): **93,91,90,89,85 85,84,84,84,77**
CSF £68.47 CT £272.59 TOTE £7.70: £1.60, £4.40, £1.70; EX 75.00 Trifecta £530.50.
**Owner** Dr Marwan Koukash **Bred** Tinnakill Bloodstock **Trained** Musley Bank, N Yorks

**FOCUS**
An ordinary contest which was soundly run, but slightly the slower division. A small personal best from the winner.

## 5892 RACING UK ANDROID APP RACINGUK.COM/MOBILE H'CAP (DIV II) 1m
**5:55** (5:56) (Class 5) (0-70,68) 3-Y-O **£3,408** (£1,006; £503) **Stalls** Low

Form RPR

0360 **1** **Disclosure**[12] 5470 3-9-5 66 GrahamLee 3 76
(Les Eyre) *t.k.h in rr: hdwy on ins over 2f out: led ins fnl f: wnt clr* **7/1**[3]

3035 **2** *3 ¼* **Dutch Lady**[28] 4871 3-8-12 59 PatrickMathers 10 61
(John Holt) *chsd ldrs: led wl over 1f out: hdd and no ex ins fnl f* **5/1**[2]

3226 **3** *1* **Sicilian Bay (IRE)**[20] 5198 3-8-6 53 PJMcDonald 5 52
(Paul Midgley) *hld up in rr: hdwy over 3f out: chsng ldrs over 1f out: kpt on same pce* **5/1**[2]

024 **4** *3 ¼* **Tortoise**[18] 5239 3-8-8 55 (b) JasonHart 1 46
(Richard Guest) *dwlt: sn chsng ldrs: lost pl 5f out: hdwy to chse ldrs over 2f out: one pce* **7/1**[3]

3140 **5** *nk* **Tamayuz Magic (IRE)**[22] 5088 3-8-13 60 (b) GrahamGibbons 9 50
(Michael Easterby) *w ldr: drvn over 3f out: wknd fnl f* **7/2**[1]

00-0 **6** *11* **Savanna Spring (IRE)**[61] 3755 3-9-0 61 PaulMulrennan 7 22
(Timothy Jarvis) *stdd s: hld up in rr: hdwy 4f out: lost pl 2f out* **14/1**

4600 **7** *½* **Quasqazah**[13] 5415 3-9-1 62 JamesSullivan 2 22
(Ruth Carr) *led: hdd wl over 1f out: sn wknd* **25/1**

0-66 **8** *2 ¾* **Presidente**[37] 4544 3-9-7 68 LukeMorris 8 38
(Ed Walker) *trckd ldrs: drvn over 3f out: sddle slipped and heavily eased over 1f out* **5/1**[2]

1m 40.38s (0.28) **Going Correction** -0.025s/f (Good) **8** Ran SP% **107.7**
Speed ratings (Par 100): **97,93,92,89,89 78,77,74**
CSF £36.88 CT £166.43 TOTE £8.30: £2.00, £1.80, £1.80; EX 51.70 Trifecta £328.70.

**Owner** Les Eyre Racing Partnership I **Bred** Bearstone Stud **Trained** Catton, North Yorkshire
**FOCUS**
The second division of the ordinary 3yo handicap and a quicker time than the preceding race. The winner is rated to his best.
T/Jkpt: £1,771.00 to a £1 stake. Pool: £34923.00 - 14.00 winning tickets T/Plt: £12.50 to a £1 stake. Pool: £76885.72 - 4482.54 winning tickets T/Qpdt: £4.70 to a £1 stake. Pool: £6414.72 - 1004.34 winning tickets WG

# [5795]WOLVERHAMPTON (A.W) (L-H)
Friday, August 29

**OFFICIAL GOING: Tapeta: standard**
Wind: Fresh behind Weather: Overcast

## 5893 BET TOTEJACKPOT APPRENTICE H'CAP (TAPETA) 1m 141y
**6:00** (6:00) (Class 6) (0-55,55) 3-Y-O+ **£2,264** (£673; £336; £168) **Stalls** Low

Form RPR
6544 **1** **Jumbo Prado (USA)**[11] 5512 5-9-7 55....................(p) EoinWalsh(3) 8 65
(John Stimpson) *a.p: chsd ldr over 3f out: rdn to ld over 1f out: edgd lft: styd on* **13/2**
0-05 **2** *1 3/4* **Key To Your Heart**[71] 3401 3-8-9 52.................... CharlieBennett(5) 5 58
(Hughie Morrison) *a.p: led 2f out: rdn and hdd over 1f out: styd on same pce ins fnl f* **11/1**
602 **3** *1/2* **City Of Angkor Wat (IRE)**[11] 5512 4-9-5 53..............(t) PhilipPrince(3) 9 58
(Jo Hughes) *hld up: pushed along over 3f out: hdwy over 2f out: sn rdn: styd on same pce ins fnl f* **10/3[1]**
0500 **4** *hd* **Eastward Ho**[53] 4014 6-9-5 53.................... KevinStott(3) 7 57
(Michael Herrington) *led 1f: chsd ldrs: rdn over 2f out: edgd lft and styd on same pce ins fnl f* **5/1[2]**
-306 **5** *2 1/4* **Jayeff Herring (IRE)**[71] 3407 3-8-8 53.............. MichaelKenneally(7) 13 52
(Michael Bell) *hld up: hdwy on outer over 2f out: rdn over 1f out: nt rch ldrs* **18/1**
654 **6** *1 1/2* **Adimendis (IRE)**[13] 5427 3-8-10 55.................... JosephineGordon(7) 4 51
(J S Moore) *plld hrd and prom: wnt 2nd over 6f out: led over 4f out: hdd 2f out: wknd ins fnl f* **9/1**
4000 **7** *nk* **Katmai River (IRE)**[11] 5512 7-9-2 52.................... CharlotteJenner(5) 1 47
(Mark Usher) *hld up: pushed along over 2f out: styd on ins fnl f: nvr nrr* **20/1**
4243 **8** *4 1/2* **Benidorm**[1] 5854 6-8-12 48....................(e) LukeLeadbitter(5) 2 33
(Richard Guest) *s.i.s: hdwy over 6f out: rdn over 2f out: wknd fnl f* **11/2[3]**
1030 **9** *nk* **Just Five (IRE)**[60] 3798 8-8-11 47....................(v) JordanNason(5) 10 31
(John Weymes) *hld up: rdn over 3f out: a in rr* **16/1**
0630 **10** *1 1/2* **Mcmonagle (USA)**[10] 5529 6-9-7 55....................(bt) JoeDoyle(3) 12 36
(Alan Brown) *led over 7f out: hdd over 4f out: wknd over 1f out* **15/2**

1m 50.96s (0.86) **Going Correction** +0.075s/f (Slow)
**WFA** 3 from 4yo+ 7lb **10 Ran SP% 114.5**
Speed ratings (Par 101): **99,97,97,96,94 93,93,89,88,87**
CSF £74.10 CT £279.08 TOTE £5.80: £2.40, £4.20, £1.10; EX 124.20 Trifecta £432.00.
**Owner** J T Stimpson **Bred** Mr & Mrs Foreman Hardy **Trained** Butterton, Staffs
**FOCUS**
A fresh breeze behind the runners up the home straight, and it paid to race prominently in this modest but competitive handicap.

## 5894 TOTEPOOL BET ON ALL UK RACING MEDIAN AUCTION MAIDEN STKS (TAPETA) 1m 141y
**6:30** (6:30) (Class 5) 3-4-Y-O **£2,911** (£866; £432; £216) **Stalls** Low

Form RPR
4 **1** **Seldom Seen**[14] 5382 3-9-0 0.................... ShaneKelly 3 82+
(Sir Michael Stoute) *trckd ldrs: wnt 2nd over 4f out: shkn up to ld ins fnl f: r.o wl* **5/4[2]**
323 **2** *2 3/4* **Tabjeel**[20] 5186 3-9-5 80....................(v[1]) PaulHanagan 1 81
(Saeed bin Suroor) *led: rdn and edgd lft over 1f out: hdd and no ex ins fnl f* **4/5[1]**
**3** *8* **I Do Know (IRE)** 4-9-7 0.................... BenCurtis 4 58
(S Donohoe, Ire) *s.s: hld up: hdwy over 3f out: sn rdn: wknd over 1f out* **16/1[3]**
5-0 **4** *10* **Cassie Jem**[94] 2655 4-9-7 0.................... StevieDonohoe 2 35
(David C Griffiths) *chsd ldr tl pushed along over 4f out: wknd over 2f out* **50/1**

1m 51.93s (1.83) **Going Correction** +0.075s/f (Slow)
**WFA** 3 from 4yo 7lb **4 Ran SP% 107.8**
Speed ratings (Par 103): **94,91,84,75**
CSF £2.56 TOTE £2.30; EX 3.20 Trifecta £3.90.
**Owner** K Abdullah **Bred** Millsec Limited **Trained** Newmarket, Suffolk
**FOCUS**
A small field, but no lack of quality in the two market leaders.

## 5895 BET TOTEQUADPOT H'CAP (TAPETA) 1m 141y
**7:00** (7:00) (Class 4) (0-85,91) 3-Y-O+ **£4,851** (£1,443; £721; £360) **Stalls** Low

Form RPR
2442 **1** **Postscript (IRE)**[10] 5528 6-9-10 81.................... DavidNolan 10 91
(David Simcock) *hld up: hdwy over 1f out: r.o u.p to ld post* **5/2[1]**
0001 **2** *shd* **The Great Gabrial**[71] 3402 5-9-8 84....................(p) KevinStott(5) 6 94
(Michael Appleby) *a.p: led over 2f out: rdn clr over 1f out: hdd post* **13/2[2]**
-041 **3** *nk* **Mazaaher**[18] 5258 4-9-3 74.................... PaulHanagan 5 83
(B W Hills) *s.i.s: hld up: hdwy over 2f out: rdn to chse clr ldr over 1f out: r.o* **5/2[1]**
-501 **4** *8* **Maverik**[10] 5528 6-10-1 91 6ex.................... JackDuern(5) 8 82
(William Knight) *sn led: rdn and hdd over 2f out: wknd fnl f* **8/1[3]**
0436 **5** *nk* **Ghosting (IRE)**[13] 5430 3-8-8 72....................(t) WilliamCarson 1 62
(Tom Dascombe) *hld up: rdn over 2f out: styd on ins fnl f: nt rch ldrs* **14/1**
2045 **6** *nse* **Order Of Service**[9] 5562 4-9-3 77.................... GaryBartley(3) 7 67
(Jim Goldie) *chsd ldrs: rdn over 2f out: wknd fnl f* **33/1**
1-20 **7** *1/2* **Mubtadi**[139] 1439 6-9-6 84.................... KieranShoemark(7) 3 73
(Ismail Mohammed) *hld up: hdwy and edgd lft over 2f out: sn rdn: wknd fnl f* **14/1**
312- **8** *1 1/2* **Ty Gwr**[308] 7498 5-9-7 85.................... MikeyEnnis(7) 11 70
(Brian Ellison) *s.s: hld up: rdn over 2f out: n.d* **12/1**
066- **9** *1 1/4* **An Cat Dubh (IRE)**[413] 4250 5-9-4 75.................... StevieDonohoe 9 57
(Tim Pitt) *sn chsng ldr: rdn and ev ch over 2f out: wknd over 1f out* **50/1**
4300 **10** *shd* **Skytrain**[13] 5446 4-9-13 84....................(v[1]) RoystonFfrench 2 66
(Mark Johnston) *mid-div: sn pushed along: wknd over 2f out* **8/1[3]**
0065 **11** *10* **Rio Cobolo (IRE)**[1] 5854 8-8-9 66....................(v) BenCurtis 4 25
(Philip Kirby) *chsd ldrs: rdn over 3f out: wkng whn hmpd over 2f out* **50/1**

1m 49.24s (-0.86) **Going Correction** +0.075s/f (Slow)
**WFA** 3 from 4yo+ 7lb **11 Ran SP% 120.6**
Speed ratings (Par 105): **106,105,105,98,98 98,97,96,95,95 86**
CSF £19.78 CT £45.99 TOTE £3.90: £1.80, £2.40, £1.30; EX 27.50 Trifecta £71.80.
**Owner** Dr Marwan Koukash **Bred** Darley **Trained** Newmarket, Suffolk
**FOCUS**
A decent contest for the grade, and a good gallop set throughout.

## 5896 BET TOTEEXACTA FILLIES' (S) STKS (TAPETA) 5f 20y
**7:30** (7:32) (Class 6) 2-Y-O **£2,264** (£673; £336; £168) **Stalls** Low

Form RPR
06 **1** **Ruby Rose (IRE)**[18] 5253 2-8-12 0.................... FrannyNorton 12 60
(Kevin Ryan) *chsd ldr: pushed along 1/2-way: r.o to ld wl ins fnl f* **14/1**
2020 **2** *1 1/2* **Elizabeth Flynn (IRE)**[7] 5637 2-9-4 66.................... MartinLane 11 61
(K R Burke) *led: rdn over 1f out: hdd and unable qck wl ins fnl f* **7/2[2]**
5060 **3** *1/2* **Strategise (IRE)**[14] 5384 2-8-12 55....................(p) LiamKeniry 7 53
(Tom Dascombe) *a.p: rdn over 1f out: styd on* **9/1**
0444 **4** *1 3/4* **Poppy In The Wind**[9] 5569 2-8-12 60.................... DaleSwift 6 47+
(Alan Brown) *sn pushed along in rr: r.o u.p ins fnl f: nt rch ldrs* **16/1**
3035 **5** *4* **Magic Time (IRE)**[28] 4869 2-8-12 67.................... PaulHanagan 3 32
(Ann Duffield) *chsd ldrs: rdn over 1f out: wknd ins fnl f* **8/11[1]**
045 **6** *2 1/4* **Macarthurs Park (IRE)**[10] 5517 2-8-12 54..............(b[1]) WilliamCarson 5 24
(Tom Dascombe) *mid-div: rdn 1/2-way: wknd fnl f* **7/1[3]**
**7** *5* **Gleaming Princess** 2-8-9 0.................... DeclanBates(3) 2 6
(Milton Bradley) *mid-div: drvn along 1/2-way: wknd 2f out* **25/1**
004 **8** *7* **Cap la Nna**[11] 5507 2-8-12 0....................(p) StevieDonohoe 10
(David C Griffiths) *sn pushed along in rr: wknd 1/2-way* **50/1**

1m 3.71s (1.81) **Going Correction** +0.075s/f (Slow) **8 Ran SP% 121.0**
Speed ratings (Par 89): **88,85,84,82,75 72,64,52**
CSF £66.24 TOTE £11.20: £2.70, £1.60, £2.60; EX 60.70 Trifecta £1023.90.There was no bid for the winner.
**Owner** Mrs Margaret Forsyth **Bred** Equine Associates Fr **Trained** Hambleton, N Yorks
**FOCUS**
A modest contest and, with the favourite disappointing, it produced a big-priced winner.

## 5897 BET TOTESWINGER H'CAP (TAPETA) 5f 216y
**8:00** (8:01) (Class 6) (0-65,65) 3-Y-O+ **£2,264** (£673; £336; £168) **Stalls** Low

Form RPR
015 **1** **Logans Lad (IRE)**[8] 5602 4-9-7 62....................(vt) FrankieMcDonald 7 70+
(Daniel Mark Loughnane) *trckd ldrs: rdn to ld ins fnl f: r.o* **15/2**
0234 **2** *1* **Divine Call**[8] 5602 7-9-6 61....................(v) DavidNolan 10 66
(Milton Bradley) *mid-div: hdwy over 1f out: rdn and nt clr run ins fnl f: r.o* **6/1**
22 **3** *shd* **Calling You (IRE)**[32] 4724 5-9-5 60....................(b) BenCurtis 8 65
(S Donohoe, Ire) *prom: hmpd over 4f out: rdn over 1f out: r.o* **5/2[1]**
-006 **4** *3/4* **Going French (IRE)**[8] 5602 7-9-0 60.................... DanielMuscutt(5) 6 62
(Grace Harris) *led early: chsd ldr: led again over 2f out: rdn: edgd rt and hdd ins fnl f: styd on same pce* **16/1**
6404 **5** *1/2* **Honey Meadow**[25] 4972 3-9-5 63.................... LiamKeniry 5 64
(Robert Eddery) *mid-div: rdn over 2f out: hdwy over 1f out: styd on* **11/2[3]**
2005 **6** *nk* **Lutine Charlie (IRE)**[59] 3825 7-8-9 50.................... StevieDonohoe 9 50
(Pat Eddery) *chsd ldrs: rdn over 1f out: n.m.r ins fnl f: styd on same pce* **18/1**
4461 **7** *2 1/4* **Black Douglas**[7] 5636 5-8-3 51.................... RachaelGrant(7) 12 44+
(Jim Goldie) *dwlt: hld up: nt clr run 2f out: hdwy over 1f out: nt rch ldrs* **8/1**
2331 **8** *1 3/4* **Consistant**[43] 4370 6-9-0 60.................... JoeDoyle(5) 1 47+
(Brian Baugh) *s.i.s: hld up: hdwy over 1f out: sn hung lft: styd on same pce fnl f* **5/1[2]**
5030 **9** *3/4* **Interchoice Star**[101] 2435 9-9-5 60....................(p) MartinLane 11 45
(Ray Peacock) *sn led: hdd over 2f out: sn rdn: wknd ins fnl f* **25/1**
2350 **10** *1 3/4* **Rose Buck**[16] 5307 3-9-4 62.................... WilliamCarson 4 41
(Giles Bravery) *sn pushed along and a in rr* **20/1**
/400 **11** *2 1/2* **Under Review (IRE)**[11] 5499 8-9-7 65..............(tp) PhilipPrince(3) 3 36
(Liam Corcoran) *hld up: rdn 1/2-way: a in rr* **50/1**
05-0 **12** *1 1/2* **Time For Crabbies (IRE)**[19] 5207 4-8-10 51.........(v[1]) RoystonFfrench 2 17
(Lisa Williamson) *s.i.s: sn mid-div: drvn along over 3f out: wknd over 2f out* **50/1**

1m 15.0s (0.50) **Going Correction** +0.075s/f (Slow)
**WFA** 3 from 4yo+ 3lb **12 Ran SP% 121.5**
Speed ratings (Par 101): **99,97,97,96,95 95,92,90,89,86 83,81**
CSF £51.59 CT £146.75 TOTE £9.20: £2.60, £2.20, £1.60; EX 61.80 Trifecta £181.60.
**Owner** Ian O'Connor **Bred** Tally-Ho Stud **Trained** Baldwin's Gate, Staffs
■ Stewards' Enquiry : Frankie McDonald four-day ban; used whip in incorrect place (12th,14th-16th Sept)
**FOCUS**
A typically competitive low-grade sprint handicap and the track was worked before this race.

## 5898 BET TOTETRIFECTA H'CAP (TAPETA) 1m 4f 50y
**8:30** (8:31) (Class 5) (0-70,70) 3-Y-O+ **£3,234** (£962; £481; £240) **Stalls** Low

Form RPR
-011 **1** **Ragged Robbin (FR)**[21] 5139 3-9-4 70....................(t) TedDurcan 7 83+
(David Lanigan) *chsd ldrs: led over 2f out: rdn out* **5/4[1]**
2140 **2** *4* **Nolecce**[11] 5508 7-8-11 60.................... AdamMcLean(7) 6 66
(Tony Forbes) *a.p: ev ch over 2f out: sn rdn: edgd lft and no ex fnl f* **25/1**
2553 **3** *1* **Elpida (USA)**[23] 5036 3-9-3 69.................... ShaneKelly 8 73+
(David Simcock) *hld up: hdwy over 3f out: rdn over 1f out: styd on same pce fnl f* **9/4[2]**
4326 **4** *7* **The Firm (IRE)**[13] 5421 5-9-12 68.................... FrankieMcDonald 1 61
(Daniel Mark Loughnane) *hld up: rdn over 2f out: nvr trbld ldrs* **8/1**
6-60 **5** *5* **Forward March**[86] 2904 4-9-13 69....................(t[1]) DougieCostello 2 54
(Johnny Farrelly) *chsd ldr tl pushed along over 3f out: wknd over 1f out* **40/1**
3223 **6** *7* **Dalgig**[18] 5259 4-10-0 70.................... MartinLane 4 44
(Jamie Osborne) *led: rdn and hdd over 2f out: wknd over 1f out* **7/2[3]**
000 **7** *6* **Pahente**[32] 4737 6-9-1 57.................... WilliamCarson 3 21
(Tony Carroll) *hld up: rdn over 3f out: sn wknd* **40/1**
**8** *56* **Sakhra**[90] 2791 3-9-0 66.................... FrannyNorton 9
(Mark Brisbourne) *mid-div: sn pushed along: rdn and wknd over 4f out* **25/1**

-100 **P** **Markami (FR)**[51] 4076 4-9-13 69........................................(t) LiamKeniry 5
(Johnny Farrelly) *hld up: bhd whn p.u over 6f out* **20/1**
2m 39.35s (-1.45) **Going Correction** +0.075s/f (Slow)
**WFA** 3 from 4yo+ 10lb **9** Ran SP% **125.9**
Speed ratings (Par 103): **107,104,103,99,95 91,87,49,**
CSF £44.95 CT £74.06 TOTE £2.50: £1.20, £4.20, £1.10; EX 32.50 Trifecta £115.80.
**Owner** Niarchos Family **Bred** Famille Niarchos **Trained** Upper Lambourn, Berks
**FOCUS**
The gallop was solid enough in this decent handicap.

## 5899 COLLECT TOTEPOOL WINNINGS AT BETFRED SHOPS H'CAP (TAPETA) 1m 1f 103y
**9:00** (9:00) (Class 6) (0-65,65) 3-Y-O+ **£2,264** (£673; £336; £168) **Stalls** Low

Form RPR
6334 **1** **Fiftyshadesfreed (IRE)**[21] 5139 3-9-5 65........................(p) TedDurcan 13 80
(George Baker) *hld up: hdwy over 2f out: rdn to ld over 1f out: styd on* **9/4**[1]
0541 **2** *1 ¼* **Rouge Nuage (IRE)**[10] 5537 4-9-4 62....................(b) JordanNason(5) 12 74
(Conrad Allen) *s.i.s: pushed along early in rr: hdwy over 2f out: rdn over 1f out: hung lft ins fnl f: kpt on* **11/2**[3]
301 **3** *hd* **Fresh Kingdom (IRE)**[27] 4911 3-9-5 65..........................(p) ShaneKelly 8 77
(James Fanshawe) *hld up: hdwy 3f out: led wl over 1f out: sn rdn and hdd: styd on same pce ins fnl f* **11/4**[2]
062 **4** *7* **Gabrial The Thug (FR)**[10] 5529 4-9-7 60......................(t) DavidNolan 11 57
(Richard Fahey) *chsd ldrs: led over 2f out: rdn and hdd wl over 1f out: wknd ins fnl f* **10/1**
1453 **5** *1 ¾* **Obboorr**[23] 5049 5-9-12 65................................................(p) PaddyAspell 2 59
(John Wainwright) *hld up: hdwy over 4f out: rdn and wknd over 1f out* **9/1**
3465 **6** *¾* **Arlecchino (IRE)**[10] 5521 4-9-9 62.....................................(p[1]) DaleSwift 7 54
(Ed McMahon) *pushed along in rr early: rdn over 2f out: nvr nrr* **8/1**
00 **7** *¾* **Settle For Red (IRE)**[79] 3112 4-9-9 62.......................... LiamKeniry 4 52
(Jeremy Gask) *prom: rdn over 2f out: wknd over 1f out* **33/1**
3000 **8** *2 ¾* **Hurricane Harry**[34] 4658 3-8-11 62...........................(p) JackDuern(5) 9 47
(William Knight) *hld up: nt clr run over 2f out: n.d* **12/1**
0000 **9** *1 ¾* **Enzaal (USA)**[13] 5421 4-9-5 65...............................(bt) MikeyEnnis(7) 6 46
(Philip Kirby) *chsd ldr: rdn and ev ch over 2f out: wknd over 1f out* **28/1**
1160 **10** *1* **Pipers Piping (IRE)**[51] 4073 8-9-4 60...................... RossAtkinson(3) 10 39
(Mandy Rowland) *hld up: pushed along over 2f out: nvr on terms* **25/1**
042 **11** *2* **Polar Forest**[10] 5537 4-9-5 65..................................(e) LukeLeadbitter(7) 3 40
(Richard Guest) *chsd ldrs: rdn over 2f out: wknd over 1f out* **25/1**
3451 **12** *3 ¼* **Highlife Dancer**[8] 5599 6-9-2 62................................(v) DanielCremin(7) 5 30
(Mick Channon) *led: rdn and hdd over 2f out: wknd over 1f out* **20/1**
414 **13** *1 ¾* **Dandarrell**[40] 4468 7-9-10 63.......................................... DougieCostello 1 27
(Julie Camacho) *mid-div: drvn along over 3f out: wknd over 2f out* **25/1**
2m 0.33s (-0.47) **Going Correction** +0.075s/f (Slow)
**WFA** 3 from 4yo+ 7lb **13** Ran SP% **133.4**
Speed ratings (Par 101): **105,103,103,97,95 95,94,92,90,89 87,85,83**
CSF £15.61 CT £39.86 TOTE £3.90: £1.60, £2.10, £2.50; EX 21.00 Trifecta £81.20.
**Owner** Team Fifty **Bred** Bernard Cloney **Trained** Manton, Wilts
**FOCUS**
A competitive handicap, and the runners with the best recent form came to the fore.
T/Plt: £111.70 to a £1 stake. Pool: £73667.79 - 481.27 winning tickets T/Qpdt: £19.30 to a £1 stake. Pool: £9000.85 - 344.60 winning tickets CR

# 5843 DEAUVILLE (R-H)
Friday, August 29
**OFFICIAL GOING: Turf: heavy: polytrack: standard (meeting transferred from clairefontaine)**

## 5900a PRIX DES LOBELIAS (CLAIMER) (2YO COLTS & GELDINGS) (YOUNG JOCKEYS & APPRENTICES) (POLYTRACK) 7f 110y
**11:15** (12:00) 2-Y-O **£7,916** (£3,166; £2,375; £1,583; £791)

RPR
**1** **Chester Deal**[8] 5618 2-9-1 0....................... Georges-AntoineAnselin(5) 5 82+
(Jo Hughes) *mde all: kicked 4 l clr over 1 1/2f out: wl clr ins fnl f: won easing down* **4/5**[1]
**2** *8* **Chiquito (FR)**[8] 5618 2-8-10 0...................................(p) JeffersonSmith(6) 1 59
(J-L Pelletan, France) **41/5**
**3** *¾* **Rivolochop (FR)**[8] 5618 2-8-10 0.................... MllePaulineDominois(6) 2 57
(C Boutin, France) **51/10**[2]
**4** *1* **Atilla (FR)**[8] 5618 2-8-8 0....................................(p) ValentinGambart(8) 3 55
(M Boutin, France) **53/10**[3]
**5** *hd* **Prince D'Aumone (FR)**[43] 2-8-8 0........................ NathanKasztelan(8) 8 55
(S Jesus, France) **147/10**
**6** *3* **Hilton Jelois (FR)**[28] 4881 2-8-7 0..........................(b) MathieuPelletan(6) 4 45
(J-L Pelletan, France) **241/10**
**7** *nk* **Le Bouscot (FR)** 2-8-7 0.............................................. MlleZoePfeil(6) 7 44
(Mme P Butel, France) **185/10**
**8** *snk* **Kingkevi (FR)** 2-8-10 0............................................. YoannBarille(6) 9 47
(N Leenders, France) **50/1**
**9** *5* **Mocky Glaz (FR)**[24] 2-8-13 0.................................(p) SoufyaneMoulin(3) 6 35
(D Windrif, France) **237/10**
1m 30.08s (90.08) **9** Ran SP% **120.2**
WIN (incl. 1 euro stake): 1.80. PLACES: 1.10, 1.40, 1.20. DF: 5.90. SF: 8.50.
**Owner** Chester Racing & Jo Hughes **Bred** Chester Racing Club Ltd **Trained** Lambourn. Berks
**FOCUS**
The meeting was switched when Clairefontaine earlier in the week was cancelled.

## 5901a PRIX DES GARDENIAS (CLAIMER) (2YO FILLIES) (YOUNG JOCKEYS & APPRENTICES) (POLYTRACK) 7f 110y
**12:45** (12:00) 2-Y-O **£7,916** (£3,166; £2,375; £1,583; £791)

RPR
**1** **Wild Wild West (FR)**[34] 2-8-4 0..............................(p) JeffersonSmith(5) 9 63
(H-F Devin, France) **78/10**
**2** *1* **Style D'Ouilly (FR)**[105] 2-8-7 0.............................. LukasDelozier(6) 6 65
(H De Nicolay, France) **29/1**
**3** *snk* **Trust The Captain (FR)**[8] 5619 2-8-10 0.......... NicolasLarenaudie(6) 5 68
(Robert Collet, France) **67/10**[3]
**4** *1 ¾* **Snow Guest (FR)**[10] 5544 2-8-10 0..............................(b[1]) MlleZoePfeil(6) 7 64
(D Windrif, France) **4/1**[2]
**5** *1 ¼* **Why Whipping (FR)**[9] 5590 2-8-7 0...............................(b) PierreBazire(6) 8 58
(Robert Collet, France) **11/1**

**6** *3* **Fly Grazer (IRE)**[8] 5619 2-8-4 0............................... RichardOliver(5) 12 47
(J S Moore) *towards rr on outer: gd hdwy 2 1/2f out to dispute 3rd 1 1/2f out: sn rdn and no ex: fdd ins fnl f* **19/1**
**7** *½* **Salut Lilly (FR)**[28] 4882 2-8-8 0..........................(p) NathanKasztelan(8) 1 52
(S Jesus, France) **57/1**
**8** *2 ½* **Qwhipper (FR)**[8] 5619 2-8-10 0.................... MllePaulineDominois(6) 3 46
(C Boutin, France) **7/1**
**9** *2 ½* **Attique (FR)** 2-8-5 0..................................................(p) FlorentMalbran(8) 4 38
(F-X De Chevigny, France) **71/1**
**10** *1 ¾* **Nordican Sea (FR)** 2-8-7 0.......................................... YoannBarille(6) 10 34
(N Leenders, France) **7/1**
**11** *1 ¾* **Komtess Ka (FR)**[28] 4882 2-8-4 0..................(p) MlleAngelaLeCorre(5) 11 25
(A Junk, France) **62/1**
**12** *10* **Chefchaouen (IRE)**[10] 5544 2-8-13 0...................... SoufyaneMoulin(3) 2 9
(J S Moore) *t.k.h: chsd ldrs on inner: pushed along over 2f out: wknd 1 1/2f out: eased fnl f* **5/2**[1]
1m 31.51s (91.51) **12** Ran SP% **119.3**
WIN (incl. 1 euro stake): 8.80. PLACES: 3.10, 6.40, 2.70. DF: 114.90. SF: 290.10.
**Owner** Benoit Jeffroy **Bred** Janus Bloodstock Inc. & G Lugon **Trained** France

5902 - (Foreign Racing) - See Raceform Interactive

# 5593 BATH (L-H)
Saturday, August 30
**OFFICIAL GOING: Good to soft (soft in places; 7.6)**
Weather: Overcast Rails: Races utilising bottom bend increased by 12yds

## 5903 FRAMING WORKSHOP H'CAP 1m 5y
**4:45** (4:45) (Class 5) (0-75,75) 3-Y-O+ **£2,911** (£866; £432; £216) **Stalls** Low

Form RPR
2-30 **1** **Rolling Dice**[10] 5557 3-9-1 70.......................................... LiamKeniry 7 78
(Dominic Ffrench Davis) *mde all: rdn over 2f out: strly pressed over 1f out: edgd lft: kpt on* **25/1**
3230 **2** *½* **Al Mukhdam**[14] 5413 4-9-5 75.................................. MeganCarberry(7) 2 83
(Ed de Giles) *trckd ldr: rdn to chal strly over 1f out: kpt on: hld nr fin* **4/1**[3]
4233 **3** *1 ½* **Faure Island**[11] 5526 3-8-12 70........................................ AmyScott(3) 6 74
(Henry Candy) *trcaked ldr: rdn over 2f out: kpt on same pce* **5/2**[1]
4-40 **4** *1* **Be Seeing You**[52] 4074 3-9-1 70..................................... GeorgeBaker 4 71
(Roger Charlton) *hld up in tch: rdn and outpcd over 2f out: kpt on ins fnl f: nvr threatened* **3/1**[2]
0-P0 **5** *4* **Rizal Park (IRE)**[17] 5308 3-9-2 74.............................. ThomasBrown(3) 8 66
(Andrew Balding) *dwlt: hld up in tch: racd keenly: rdn over 2f out: sn btn* **7/1**
1306 **6** *1* **Know Your Name**[42] 4426 3-9-3 72..............................(v) RichardHughes 3 62
(David Evans) *hld up in rr: rdn and sme hdwy 2f out: wknd ins fnl f: eased* **9/2**
1m 43.37s (2.57) **Going Correction** +0.225s/f (Good)
**WFA** 3 from 4yo+ 6lb **6** Ran SP% **108.1**
Speed ratings (Par 103): **96,95,94,93,89 88**
CSF £110.90 CT £307.24 TOTE £22.30: £6.00, £3.50; EX 62.20 Trifecta £329.00.
**Owner** Miss A Jones **Bred** Miss Alison Jones **Trained** Lambourn, Berks
■ Stewards' Enquiry : Megan Carberry two-day ban: used whip above permitted level (Sep 14-15)
**FOCUS**
A fair contest.

## 5904 MERLIN WOODBURNING STOVES H'CAP 1m 5f 22y
**5:15** (5:15) (Class 6) (0-55,55) 3-Y-O+ **£1,940** (£577; £288; £144) **Stalls** High

Form RPR
5-24 **1** **Halling's Wish**[16] 3780 4-9-9 54..................................... GeorgeBaker 5 62+
(Gary Moore) *hld up: pushed along and hdwy on outer over 2f out: led over 1f out: sn rdn: kpt on* **9/4**[1]
3045 **2** *1 ¼* **Well Owd Mon**[12] 5508 4-8-13 49.................................. JackDuern(5) 6 55
(Andrew Hollinshead) *hld up: rdn and hdwy on outer over 2f out: chsd wnr over 1f out: kpt on but a hld* **13/2**
5421 **3** *3 ½* **Sir Tyto (IRE)**[24] 5033 6-9-7 52.................................(p) RichardHughes 8 53
(Peter Makin) *in tch: drvn and outpcd over 2f out: plugged on fr over 1f out: no threat to ldng pair* **3/1**[2]
000 **4** *1 ¼* **En Reve**[42] 4435 3-8-13 55.......................................... FergusSweeney 1 54
(Seamus Durack) *in tch: effrt and briefly ev ch over 1f out: wknd fnl f* **16/1**
6-00 **5** *3 ¾* **Party Palace**[9] 2084 10-9-1 46 oh1.................................. MartinLane 7 40
(Stuart Howe) *trckd ldng pair: pressed ldr over 6f out: rdn 4f out: wknd over 2f out* **20/1**
0551 **6** *2 ¾* **Glens Wobbly**[9] 5597 6-9-4 52..................................... PhilipPrince(3) 4 41
(Jonathan Geake) *pressed ldr: led 9f out: rdn over 3f out: hdd over 1f out: wknd* **6/1**[3]
1-43 **7** *nse* **Vertueux (FR)**[45] 1150 9-9-10 55..................................(p) LiamKeniry 2 44
(Tony Carroll) *led: hdd 9f out: chsd ldr: rdn over 3f out: wknd over 2f out* **18/1**
**8** *3 ¼* **Paple Blessing (IRE)**[16] 5365 4-8-13 49............................ RyanWhile(5) 9 33
(David Bridgwater) *midfield: rdn over 3f out: sn wknd* **7/1**
665- **R** **Red Current**[380] 5433 10-9-1 46 oh1...............(t) WilliamTwiston-Davies 3
(Michael Scudamore) *ref to r* **20/1**
2m 55.69s (3.69) **Going Correction** +0.225s/f (Good)
**WFA** 3 from 4yo+ 11lb **9** Ran SP% **116.6**
Speed ratings (Par 101): **97,96,94,93,91 89,89,87,**
CSF £17.67 CT £42.86 TOTE £2.90: £1.10, £3.10, £1.70; EX 26.30 Trifecta £191.10.
**Owner** WBC Partnership **Bred** B R Marsden **Trained** Lower Beeding, W Sussex
**FOCUS**
It paid to be held up.

## 5905 BATHWICK CAR AND VAN HIRE H'CAP 5f 161y
**5:45** (5:46) (Class 6) (0-60,63) 3-Y-O **£1,940** (£577; £288; £144) **Stalls** Centre

Form RPR
5332 **1** **Captain Ryan**[11] 5518 3-9-2 54................................... RichardHughes 2 61
(Peter Makin) *stdd s: hld up: smooth hdwy over 2f out: led on bit 1f out: pushed clr ins fnl f* **6/4**[1]
0305 **2** *1 ¼* **Astral Rose**[22] 5136 3-8-8 46..............................................(b) JohnFahy 4 49
(Jonathan Portman) *chsd ldr: rdn to chal 2f out: kpt on but no ch w wnr ins fnl f* **10/1**
0144 **3** *3 ¼* **Connaught Water (IRE)**[30] 4820 3-9-2 59....................(p) NedCurtis(5) 9 51
(Jonathan Portman) *dwlt: hld up in tch: rdn over 2f out: one pce and nvr threatened ldrs* **11/4**[2]
-020 **4** *1 ¼* **Ignight**[15] 5399 3-8-8 46...........................................(p) KieranO'Neill 7 34
(Mark Usher) *chsd ldr: rdn and outpcd over 2f out: no threat after* **14/1**


The Form Book, Raceform Ltd, Newbury, RG14 5SJ

2423 **5** *1 ¾* **Go Charlie**[24] 5034 3-9-0 52............................ SteveDrowne 5 34
(Ronald Harris) *led: rdn over 2f out: hdd 1f out: wknd* **8/1**

0-52 **6** *2* **Plauseabella**[38] 4539 3-9-1 56.......................... MichaelJMMurphy(3) 6 31
(Stuart Kittow) *in tch: rdn over 2f out: sn wknd* **5/1**[3]

1m 14.0s (2.80) **Going Correction** +0.35s/f (Good) **6** Ran SP% **110.2**
Speed ratings (Par 98): **95,93,89,87,85 82**
CSF £16.51 CT £34.70 TOTE £2.00: £1.10, £4.10; EX 18.60 Trifecta £61.10.
**Owner** Og Partnership **Bred** Mrs C Lloyd **Trained** Ogbourne Maisey, Wilts

**FOCUS**
A riding master class from Richard Hughes.

## 5906 CLARKS VILLAGE DESIGNER OUTLET / EBF NOVICE STKS (BOBIS RACE) 5f 161y

**6:15** (6:19) (Class 4) 2-Y-O **£6,469** (£1,925; £962; £481) **Stalls** Centre

Form RPR

1 **1** **Elysian Flyer (IRE)**[18] 5271 2-9-4 0.......................... RichardHughes 3 90+
(Richard Hannon) *in tch: hdwy over 2f out: pushed along to ld over 1f out: rdn ent fnl f: in command whn edgd lft 110yds out: kpt on* **1/2**[1]

1 **2** *2 ¼* **Plymouth Sound**[35] 4676 2-9-7 78.......................... JohnFahy 6 85
(Eve Johnson Houghton) *dwlt: hld up: rdn over 2f out: kpt on: wnt 2nd 75yds out: no ch w wnr* **6/1**[3]

1013 **3** *½* **Expensive Date**[22] 5134 2-9-6 85.......................... MartinLane 4 82
(Paul Cole) *chsd ldr: rdn over 2f out: chal over 1f out: one pce fnl f: lost 2nd 75yds out* **14/1**

613 **4** *5* **Ivors Rebel**[20] 5209 2-9-4 72.......................... LiamKeniry 1 64
(David Elsworth) *led: rdn whn hdd over 1f out: wknd* **16/1**

**5** *1 ¼* **Major Attitude** 2-9-0 0.......................... AdamKirby 2 56
(Clive Cox) *dwlt: hld up: rdn over 2f out: nvr threatened* **5/1**[2]

1m 12.2s (1.00) **Going Correction** +0.35s/f (Good) **5** Ran SP% **110.2**
Speed ratings (Par 96): **107,104,103,96,95**
CSF £4.03 TOTE £1.40: £1.30, £1.40; EX 4.50 Trifecta £17.00.
**Owner** The Low Flyers **Bred** Tom Shirley **Trained** East Everleigh, Wilts

**FOCUS**
Comfortably the best race on the card and a visibly taking performance from the powerfully built winner.

## 5907 ARCRACINGSYNDICATES.CO.UK H'CAP 5f 11y

**6:45** (6:46) (Class 6) (0-55,57) 3-Y-O+ **£1,940** (£577; £288; £144) **Stalls** Centre

Form RPR

5350 **1** **Catalinas Diamond (IRE)**[16] 5355 6-9-7 55..............(t) SebSanders 12 64
(Pat Murphy) *dwlt: hld up: pushed along 1/2-way: swtchd rt towards stands' rail wl over 1f out: sn hdwy to chse ldr: led 110yds out: kpt on* **3/1**[2]

3322 **2** *1 ¼* **Pull The Pin (IRE)**[2] 5858 5-9-8 56........................(bt) RichardHughes 11 60
(Ann Stokell) *pressed ldr: swtchd towards stands' rail 1/2-way: sn led: rdn over 1f out: hdd 110yds out: no ex* **1/1**[1]

000 **3** *4 ½* **Petite Fille**[10] 5548 3-8-7 50.......................... DavidParkes(7) 7 38
(Jeremy Gask) *chsd clr ldng pair: rdn 1/2-way: one pce and nvr threatened* **25/1**

0006 **4** *nk* **Lucky Surprise**[37] 4564 3-9-2 52.......................... SteveDrowne 5 39
(Jeremy Gask) *chsd clr ldng pair: rdn 1/2-way: one pce and nvr threatened* **12/1**

054 **5** *4 ½* **Spic 'n Span**[9] 5594 9-8-12 46 oh1................(b) WilliamTwiston-Davies 1 17
(Ronald Harris) *led narrowly: hdd over 2f out: sn wknd* **12/1**

0405 **6** *3 ¼* **Studfarmer**[9] 5594 4-8-7 46..........................(p) NoelGarbutt(5) 4 5
(John Panvert) *sn outpcd in rr: a bhd* **8/1**[3]

460/ **7** *27* **Shake Baby Shake**[884] 1090 5-8-8 47 oh1 ow1.......... RyanWhile(5) 10
(Bill Turner) *slowly away and wnt rt s: a bhd* **33/1**

-540 **8** *2 ½* **Perrydot (IRE)**[85] 2946 3-9-2 52.......................... FergusSweeney 2
(Jo Crowley) *chsd clr ldng pair: rdn 3f out: sn struggling: eased and t.o* **12/1**

1m 4.24s (1.74) **Going Correction** +0.35s/f (Good)
**WFA** 3 from 4yo+ 2lb **8** Ran SP% **116.0**
Speed ratings (Par 101): **100,98,90,90,83 77,34,30**
CSF £6.44 CT £57.64 TOTE £4.50: £1.40, £1.20, £4.10; EX 8.40 Trifecta £83.90.
**Owner** Briton International **Bred** Sean Gorman **Trained** East Garston, Berks

**FOCUS**
This was run furiously and it was hard viewing for the many backers of the favourite.

## 5908 ARC RACING SYNDICATES H'CAP 1m 2f 46y

**7:15** (7:15) (Class 6) (0-65,63) 3-Y-O+ **£2,264** (£673; £336; £168) **Stalls** Low

Form RPR

1060 **1** **Zambeasy**[52] 4074 3-9-6 63.......................... GeorgeBaker 7 71
(Philip Hide) *mde all: a at least 2 l clr: rdn over 1f out: kpt on* **11/4**[1]

5513 **2** *2* **Cameley Dawn**[11] 5520 3-9-2 59.......................... FergusSweeney 2 63
(Malcolm Saunders) *midfield: rdn over 2f out: chsd ldr over 1f out: one pce fnl f* **6/1**

6002 **3** *nk* **Simma (IRE)**[19] 5257 3-9-4 61.......................... RichardHughes 1 64
(Sylvester Kirk) *hld up: rdn over 2f out: hdwy over 1f out: kpt on fnl f* **6/1**

2514 **4** *3 ¼* **Appyjack**[18] 5291 6-9-2 56.......................... GeorgeDowning(5) 5 53
(Tony Carroll) *hld up: rdn over 2f out: one pce and no imp* **5/1**[3]

-040 **5** *1 ¼* **Danglydontask**[35] 4658 3-9-1 58..........................(b) SebSanders 6 53
(David Arbuthnot) *hld up: rdn and sme hdwy over 3f out: wknd over 1f out* **20/1**

-555 **6** *½* **Tipsy Star**[8] 5622 3-9-0 60.......................... PhilipPrince(3) 3 54
(Jonathan Geake) *chsd ldr: rdn over 2f out: wknd over 1f out* **8/1**

0000 **7** *½* **Exceed Policy**[11] 5530 3-8-2 45.......................... KieranO'Neill 8 38
(David Dennis) *chsd ldr: rdn over 2f out* **33/1**

53-4 **8** *8* **Loraine**[18] 5280 4-10-0 63.......................... AdamKirby 4 41
(Jamie Osborne) *stdd s: hld up in rr: rdn over 3f out: a bhd* **3/1**[2]

2m 12.62s (1.62) **Going Correction** +0.225s/f (Good)
**WFA** 3 from 4yo+ 8lb **8** Ran SP% **115.7**
Speed ratings (Par 101): **102,100,100,97,96 96,95,89**
CSF £20.02 CT £91.34 TOTE £2.90: £1.20, £2.00, £2.00; EX 25.50 Trifecta £111.30.
**Owner** Heart Of The South Racing **Bred** Frank Brady **Trained** Findon, W Sussex

**FOCUS**
The winner was left alone in front and held on.

## 5909 SHARES AVAILABLE IN AN ARC SYNDICATE H'CAP 2m 1f 34y

**7:45** (7:45) (Class 6) (0-60,60) 4-Y-O+ **£1,940** (£577; £288; £144) **Stalls** Low

Form RPR

0-32 **1** **Noor Al Haya (IRE)**[108] 2252 4-8-12 58.......................... CharlotteJenner(7) 1 65
(Mark Usher) *hld up in rr: smooth hdwy over 2f out: upsides on bit appr fnl f: rdn ins fnl f: led post* **11/4**[1]

-415 **2** *nse* **Eastern Magic**[52] 4082 7-8-10 54.......................... JackDuern(5) 5 61
(Andrew Hollinshead) *in tch: hdwy to ld narrrowly over 2f out: sn rdn: kpt on: hdd post* **11/4**[1]

44 **3** *1* **Graylyn Ruby (FR)**[19] 5240 9-8-8 54.......................... KieranShoemark(7) 7 60
(Robert Eddery) *hld up: pushed along and hdwy over 2f out: rdn and ev ch jst ins fnl f: no ex and hld in 3rd nr fin* **9/1**[3]

3352 **4** *8* **Fuzzy Logic (IRE)**[16] 5342 5-8-8 47.......................... MartinLane 4 43
(Bernard Llewellyn) *trckd ldr: rdn over 4f out: wknd over 1f out* **9/2**[2]

0/35 **5** *1 ¾* **Safe Investment (USA)**[12] 5502 10-8-8 46 ow1(tp)
WilliamTwiston-Davies 6 41
(Lawney Hill) *led: rdn whn hdd over 2f out: sn wknd* **16/1**

6122 **6** *nk* **Lucky Diva**[32] 4769 7-9-2 60..........................(v) RyanWhile(5) 2 54
(Bill Turner) *trckd ldr: rdn 3f out: wknd over 1f out* **11/4**[1]

3m 58.46s (6.56) **Going Correction** +0.225s/f (Good) **6** Ran SP% **114.1**
Speed ratings (Par 101): **93,92,92,88,87 87**
CSF £10.75 CT £57.36 TOTE £4.50: £1.80, £1.40; EX 9.70 Trifecta £53.80.
**Owner** Imran Butt & High Five Racing **Bred** Victor Stud Bloodstock Ltd **Trained** Upper Lambourn, Berks

■ Stewards' Enquiry : Jack Duern two-day ban: used whip above permitted level (Sep 14-15)

**FOCUS**
A thrilling finish to this steadily run staying contest.
T/Plt: £30.40 to a £1 stake. Pool of £51667.95 - 1240.62 winning tickets. T/Qpdt: £4.40 to a £1 stake. Pool of £6656.28 - 1116.24 winning tickets. AS

5711

# BEVERLEY (R-H)

Saturday, August 30

**OFFICIAL GOING: Good to firm (good in places)**
Wind: Strong against Weather: Cloudy with sunny periods

## 5910 EUROPEAN BREEDERS' FUND GEORGE KILBURN MEMORIAL MAIDEN FILLIES' STKS (BOBIS RACE) 7f 100y

**1:55** (1:57) (Class 4) 2-Y-O **£5,175** (£1,540; £769; £384) **Stalls** Low

Form RPR

63 **1** **Natural Charm (IRE)**[24] 5029 2-9-0 0.......................... MartinDwyer 3 77
(Roger Varian) *trckd ldng pair: pushed along over 1f out: rdn ins fnl f: swtchd lft and styd on wl last 100yds to ld nr fin* **7/1**[3]

563 **2** *nk* **Hollie Point**[36] 4626 2-9-0 79.......................... SilvestreDeSousa 8 76
(Charlie Appleby) *trckd ldr: hdwy to chal over 2f out: rdn to take slt ld wl over 1f out: drvn ins fnl f: hdd and no ex nr fin* **11/8**[1]

6 **3** *¾* **Kelly's Finest (IRE)**[14] 5443 2-9-0 0.......................... PhillipMakin 2 74
(James Bethell) *led: pushed along and jnd over 2f out: hdd narrowly wl over 1f out and sn rdn: drvn and kpt on ins fnl f tl no ex last 75yds* **16/1**

04 **4** *2 ¼* **Roxie Lot**[20] 5201 2-9-0 0.......................... StephenCraine 7 69
(Pam Sly) *chsd ldrs: rdn along over 2f out: drvn and kpt on one pce appr fnl f* **10/1**

2 **5** *3 ¼* **Adele (GER)**[12] 5494 2-9-0 0.......................... GrahamLee 6 63+
(Mark Johnston) *towards rr: pushed along and sme hdwy wl over 2f out: rdn wl over 1f out and n.d* **6/4**[2]

0 **6** *4 ½* **The Wee Barra (IRE)**[26] 4973 2-9-0 0.......................... JamieSpencer 1 51+
(Kevin Ryan) *dwlt and in rr: sme hdwy 3f out: rdn along over 2f out and n.d* **20/1**

04 **7** *4 ½* **Arcossi**[15] 5372 2-8-7 0.......................... RowanScott(7) 4 40
(Ann Duffield) *in tch on inner: rdn along wl over 2f out: sn wknd* **100/1**

0 **8** *5* **Rose Acclaim (IRE)**[31] 4790 2-8-11 0.......................... SamJames(3) 9 28
(David O'Meara) *a towards rr* **50/1**

**9** *½* **May Hill Rebel** 2-8-7 0.......................... MelissaThompson(7) 10 27
(Richard Guest) *s.i.s: a in rr* **100/1**

0 **10** *21* **Cirtee**[16] 5332 2-9-0 0.......................... JamesSullivan 5
(Tim Etherington) *dwlt: a in rr: bhd fr 1/2-way* **100/1**

1m 35.12s (1.32) **Going Correction** -0.075s/f (Good) **10** Ran SP% **119.3**
Speed ratings (Par 93): **89,88,87,85,81 76,71,65,64,40**
CSF £17.33 TOTE £8.90: £2.10, £1.10, £3.40; EX 24.60 Trifecta £202.20.
**Owner** M Al-Qatami & K M Al-Mudhaf **Bred** M Al-Qatami & K M Al-Mudhaf **Trained** Newmarket, Suffolk

**FOCUS**
Few got into this modest fillies' maiden as the leaders went a solid pace. The fourth sets the level.

## 5911 BETFRED BEVERLEY BULLET SPRINT STKS (LISTED RACE) 5f

**2:25** (2:25) (Class 1) 3-Y-O+ **£23,680** (£8,956; £4,476; £2,236) **Stalls** Low

Form RPR

1020 **1** **Pearl Secret**[74] 3319 5-9-0 113.......................... JamieSpencer 1 107
(David Barron) *mde all: qcknd jst over 1f out: rdn ins fnl f: kpt on wl* **2/1**[1]

5021 **2** *nk* **Mirza**[30] 4841 7-9-4 108..........................(p) MartinDwyer 9 110
(Rae Guest) *hld up towards rr: pushed along wl over 1f out: swtchd lft to outer and rdn ent fnl f: fin strly: jst failed* **8/1**

1100 **3** *hd* **Line Of Reason (IRE)**[10] 5575 4-9-0 98.......................... GrahamLee 3 105
(Paul Midgley) *trckd wnr: n.m.r on inner and nt clr run over 1f out: swtchd lft and rdn ins fnl f: kpt on wl towards fin* **6/1**

3240 **4** *nk* **Kingsgate Native (IRE)**[29] 4852 9-9-0 110.......................... TonyHamilton 8 104
(Robert Cowell) *trckd ldrs: effrt wl over 1f out: sn rdn and ev ch ins fnl f: drvn and kpt on towards fin* **4/1**[3]

5114 **5** *1 ¾* **Willbeme**[50] 4171 6-8-9 97.......................... SilvestreDeSousa 4 93
(Neville Bycroft) *t.k.h: trckd ldrs on inner: effrt and n.m.r over 1f out: sn rdn and kpt on* **7/1**

1660 **6** *1 ½* **Rocky Ground (IRE)**[20] 5219 4-9-4 111.......................... RobertWinston 6 96
(Roger Varian) *cl up: rdn along wl over 1f out: drvn and wknd fnl f* **7/2**[2]

2014 **7** *7* **Midnight Dynamo**[8] 5641 7-8-9 75.......................... PaulPickard 10 62
(Jim Goldie) *in rr: pushed along over 2f out: rdn wl over 1f out and sn outpcd* **50/1**

1m 3.99s (0.49) **Going Correction** +0.275s/f (Good)
**WFA** 3 from 4yo+ 2lb **7** Ran SP% **115.4**
Speed ratings: **107,106,106,105,102 100,89**
CSF £19.41 TOTE £2.20: £1.90, £3.20; EX 19.40 Trifecta £79.20.
**Owner** Qatar Racing Limited **Bred** Whitsbury Manor Stud & Pigeon House Stud **Trained** Maunby, N Yorks

**FOCUS**
Not the most competitive running of the Beverley Bullet and there was a blanket finish. The time was ordinary and the winner is rated 10lb off his best.

## 5912 BETFRED RACING "LIKE US ON FACEBOOK" H'CAP (DIV I) 5f
**3:05** (3:05) (Class 5) (0-75,75) 3-Y-O+ **£3,881** (£1,155; £577; £288) **Stalls** Low

Form RPR

2000 **1** **Oldjoesaid**[12] 5498 10-9-8 73 ........ GrahamLee 10 81
(Paul Midgley) *n.m.r and swtchd rt s: hld up towards rr: hdwy 2f out: swtchd rt over 1f out: rdn ent fnl f: kpt on strly to ld nr fin* **14/1**

0-00 **2** *nse* **Pea Shooter**[14] 5444 5-9-10 75 ........ PaddyAspell 9 83
(David Nicholls) *trckd ldrs: hdwy whn nt clr run over 1f out: squeezed through and rdn to take narrow ld ins fnl f: sn drvn: hdd and no ex nr fin* **8/1**

0013 **3** *3/4* **Tinsill**[15] 5389 3-9-5 72 ........ SilvestreDeSousa 11 77
(Nigel Tinkler) *swtchd rt s and hld up towards rr: hdwy 2f out: swtchd lft and rdn on outer over 1f out: str run ins fnl f: nrst fin* **14/1**

6625 **4** *nk* **Windforpower (IRE)**[3] 5819 4-8-10 64 ........(p) JoeyHaynes(3) 6 68
(Tracy Waggott) *trckd ldrs: hdwy 2f out: rdn to chal over 1f out: ev ch tl drvn and no ex last 100yds* **9/1**

4160 **5** *1 1/4* **Rich Again (IRE)**[18] 5265 5-9-0 65 ........(b) JamieSpencer 3 65
(James Bethell) *hld up towards rr: hdwy on inner wl over 1f out: n.m.r and swtchd lft ent fnl f: sn rdn and kpt on: nrst fin* **10/3**[1]

51-0 **6** *shd* **Boris Grigoriev (IRE)**[40] 4494 5-9-6 71 ........ JamesSullivan 7 70
(Michael Easterby) *in tch: effrt 2f out and sn rdn: styd on u.p fnl f: nrst fin* **11/1**

0644 **7** *1/2* **Ingenti**[3] 5819 6-8-6 62 ........ KevinStott(5) 8 59
(Christopher Wilson) *trckd ldrs: hdwy over 1f out: swtchd lft and rdn to ld ent fnl f: sn drvn and hdd: wknd last 75yds* **15/2**[3]

0033 **8** *3/4* **Boxing Shadows**[24] 5053 4-9-4 69 ........ RobertWinston 12 64
(Les Eyre) *towards rr: hdwy 2f out: rdn along wl over 1f out: n.m.r ins fnl f: kpt on: nrst fin* **9/1**

660 **9** *2 3/4* **Thatcherite (IRE)**[13] 5470 6-9-8 73 ........(t) TonyHamilton 1 58
(Tony Coyle) *towards rr: sme hdwy 2f out: sn rdn and n.d* **6/1**[2]

0260 **10** *3* **Corncockle**[26] 4977 3-9-5 75 ........(v[1]) SamJames(3) 4 49
(David O'Meara) *slt ld: rdn along wl over 1f out: drvn and hdd ent fnl f: wknd qckly* **16/1**

5560 **11** *6* **Bronze Beau**[12] 5498 7-8-12 68 ........(tp) JacobButterfield(5) 13 20
(Kristin Stubbs) *qckly away and swtchd rt sn after s: cl up disp ld 2f out: sn rdn: wknd qckly over 1f out* **8/1**

060- **12** *1 1/2* **Fama Mac**[319] 7281 7-8-8 59 ........ PaulPickard 5 6
(Neville Bycroft) *chsd ldng pair: rdn along 2f out: sn wknd* **66/1**

1m 5.32s (1.82) **Going Correction** +0.275s/f (Good)
**WFA** 3 from 4yo+ 2lb **12 Ran SP% 120.4**
Speed ratings (Par 103): **96,95,94,94,92 92,91,90,85,80 71,68**
CSF £123.59 CT £1617.75 TOTE £15.90: £3.70, £3.40, £3.10; EX 81.10 Trifecta £1638.20.
**Owner** Pee Dee Tee Syndicate & T W Midgley **Bred** Mrs R D Peacock **Trained** Westow, N Yorks

**FOCUS**
The first division of a wide-open sprint handicap. It was run at a frantic pace and suited the closers. The tome was 0.96sec slower than division I. The winner is rated close to his best form for the past year.

## 5913 BETFRED RACING "LIKE US ON FACEBOOK" H'CAP (DIV II) 5f
**3:40** (3:45) (Class 5) (0-75,75) 3-Y-O+ **£3,881** (£1,155; £577; £288) **Stalls** Low

Form RPR

2003 **1** **Tom Sawyer**[10] 5563 6-9-5 73 ........(b) ConnorBeasley(3) 2 82
(Julie Camacho) *mde most: rdn over 1f out: drvn ins fnl f: hld on wl towards fin* **4/1**[2]

0026 **2** *nk* **Captain Royale (IRE)**[12] 5498 9-9-3 73 ........(p) JacobButterfield(5) 4 81
(Tracy Waggott) *trckd ldrs: hdwy 2f out: rdn to chse wnr ent fnl f: sn drvn and ev ch tl no ex nr fin* **14/1**

4240 **3** *3/4* **Medici Time**[14] 5437 9-9-0 65 ........(v) PhillipMakin 13 70
(Tim Easterby) *sltly hmpd s and in rr: hdwy on wd outside wl over 1f out: rdn and styd on fnl f: nrst fin* **16/1**

422- **4** *hd* **Ortac Rock (IRE)**[313] 7427 5-9-5 75 ........(t) SammyJoBell(5) 6 79+
(Richard Fahey) *hld up towards rr: hdwy 2f out: effrt whn nt clr run and bmpd over 1f out: rdn and kpt on fnl f* **10/3**[1]

344 **5** *3/4* **Mey Blossom**[32] 4752 9-8-2 56 ........(b) JoeyHaynes(3) 5 58+
(Richard Whitaker) *towards rr: hdwy 2f out: nt clr run and swtchd lft over 1f out: sn rdn and kpt on fnl f: nrst fin* **7/1**[3]

4662 **6** *1 1/2* **Haajes**[12] 5498 10-9-5 70 ........(v) GrahamLee 1 66+
(Paul Midgley) *trckd ldrs on inner: effrt wl over 1f out: sn rdn: kpt on fnl f: nrst fin* **10/3**[1]

3320 **7** *1/2* **Noble Asset**[26] 4977 3-9-6 73 ........ IanBrennan 7 67
(John Quinn) *chsd ldng pair: rdn along wl over 1f out: sn drvn and one pce* **9/1**

02 **8** *3* **Ambitious Icarus**[17] 5298 5-9-8 73 ........(e) JasonHart 10 57
(Richard Guest) *chsd ldrs: hdwy 2f out: sn rdn and edgd rt over 1f out: drvn and no imp ent fnl f* **12/1**

40-6 **9** *4* **Hello Beautiful (IRE)**[14] 5411 3-8-5 65 ........[1] RowanScott(7) 3 34
(Ann Duffield) *chsd ldrs: rdn along 2f out: sn drvn and wknd* **12/1**

0651 **10** *7* **Majestic Manannan (IRE)**[34] 4714 5-9-3 68 ........ PaddyAspell 11 12
(David Nicholls) *wnt lft s: sn cl up: disp ld 1/2-way: rdn along wl over 1f out: sn wknd* **11/1**

1m 4.36s (0.86) **Going Correction** +0.275s/f (Good)
**WFA** 3 from 5yo+ 2lb **10 Ran SP% 124.9**
Speed ratings (Par 103): **104,103,102,102,100 98,97,92,86,75**
CSF £63.25 CT £859.02 TOTE £5.90: £2.10, £3.80, £5.00; EX 98.50 Trifecta £2547.30.
**Owner** Bolingbroke J Howard FAO Mersey R & Ptns **Bred** Newsells Park Stud **Trained** Norton, N Yorks

■ Where The Boys Are was withdrawn. Price at time of withdrawal 15/2. Rule 4 applies to bets struck prior to withdrawal but not to SP bets. Deduct 10p in the pound. New market formed.

**FOCUS**
This second division of the modest sprint handicap was also run at a strong pace, but it proved a rough race out the back and there were a few eyecatchers. It was a quicker time than the first and the winner rates a small personal best.

## 5914 BETFRED "RACING'S BIGGEST SUPPORTER" H'CAP (BOBIS RACE) 1m 1f 207y
**4:15** (4:16) (Class 2) (0-105,92) 3-Y-O **£12,938** (£3,850; £1,924; £962) **Stalls** Low

Form RPR

4111 **1** **Truancy (IRE)**[25] 5015 3-8-6 80 ........(p) JoeyHaynes(3) 2 93
(K R Burke) *mde all: rdn clr wl over 1f out: styd on strly* **6/1**[3]

3123 **2** *1 1/4* **Fire Fighting (IRE)**[10] 5552 3-9-2 87 ........(b) SilvestreDeSousa 5 97
(Mark Johnston) *hld up in rr: hdwy whn nt clr run wl over 1f out: sn swtchd lft to outer and rdn: styd on wl fnl f: nt rch wnr* **6/1**[3]

4213 **3** *1* **Yenhaab (IRE)**[28] 4888 3-9-7 92 ........(p) JamieSpencer 3 100
(William Haggas) *trckd ldrs: hdwy to chse wnr 2f out: rdn over 1f out: drvn and edgd lft ins fnl f: sn no imp* **5/2**[1]

211 **4** *2 1/4* **Scallop**[15] 5401 3-9-2 87 ........ GrahamLee 7 91
(Sir Michael Stoute) *hld up towards rr: hdwy over 3f out: chsd ldrs 2f out: rdn over 1f out: sn no imp* **4/1**[2]

2520 **5** *3 1/4* **Ventura Quest (USA)**[30] 4821 3-8-13 84 ........ TonyHamilton 4 82
(Richard Fahey) *chsd wnr: rdn along wl over 2f out: sn drvn and grad wknd* **8/1**

10 **6** *1/2* **Got To Dream**[10] 5552 3-8-12 83 ........ RobertWinston 6 80
(Mark Johnston) *chsd ldrs on outer: rdn along wl over 2f out: drvn wl over 1f out and sn wknd* **16/1**

2646 **7** *17* **Braidley (IRE)**[7] 5695 3-9-3 88 ........ PhillipMakin 1 52
(James Bethell) *dwlt and in rr: hdwy and pushed along on inner over 3f out: rdn over 2f out: sn drvn and wknd* **4/1**[2]

2m 4.25s (-2.75) **Going Correction** -0.075s/f (Good) **7 Ran SP% 114.1**
Speed ratings (Par 106): **108,107,106,104,101 101,87**
CSF £40.85 TOTE £5.40: £2.90, £3.10; EX 44.10 Trifecta £173.80.
**Owner** Market Avenue Racing Club Ltd **Bred** Keogh Family **Trained** Middleham Moor, N Yorks

**FOCUS**
This appeared to be a fair and competitive 3yo handicap but few managed to land a blow and the form is worth treating with a little caution. The winner continues to progress.

## 5915 BETFRED "GOALS GALORE" H'CAP 7f 100y
**4:50** (4:50) (Class 4) (0-85,85) 3-Y-O+ **£5,175** (£1,540; £769; £384) **Stalls** Low

Form RPR

0506 **1** **Storm King**[14] 5418 5-9-12 85 ........(p) AndrewElliott 4 94
(David C Griffiths) *mde all: rdn wl over 1f out: drvn ins fnl f: hld on wl towards fin* **9/2**[1]

2215 **2** *1/2* **Kiwi Bay**[7] 5681 9-9-8 84 ........ ConnorBeasley(3) 3 92
(Michael Dods) *trckd ldng pair: hdwy 2f out: rdn over 1f out: chal ent fnl f: sn drvn and ev ch tl no ex towards fin* **8/1**

00 **3** *hd* **Earth Drummer (IRE)**[28] 4923 4-9-7 83 ........ SamJames(3) 1 91
(David O'Meara) *trckd ldrs on inner: hdwy over 2f out: effrt and nt clr run over 1f out: swtchd lft and rdn ent fnl f: kpt on wl towards fin* **8/1**

1301 **4** *4 1/2* **Big Storm Coming**[23] 5088 4-9-5 78 ........ JamesSullivan 5 74
(Ruth Carr) *midfield: hdwy over 2f out: swtchd lft to outer over 1f out: sn rdn and styd on to chse ldrs ent fnl f: sn edgd rt and no imp* **7/1**[3]

5064 **5** *1/2* **Just Paul (IRE)**[22] 5143 4-9-4 77 ........ GrahamLee 12 72
(Philip Kirby) *towards rr: hdwy over 2f out: effrt and n.m.r over 1f out: rdn and kpt on fnl f: nrst fin* **9/1**

0P02 **6** *1/2* **Our Boy Jack (IRE)**[28] 4923 5-9-9 82 ........ TonyHamilton 6 76
(Richard Fahey) *midfield: hdwy over 2f out: rdn to chse ldrs whn n.m.r over 1f out: one pce after* **8/1**

5334 **7** *nk* **Real Tigress (IRE)**[8] 5638 5-8-13 72 ........ RobertWinston 2 65
(Les Eyre) *in tch: hdwy on inner over 2f out: rdn to chse ldrs and n.m.r over 1f out: swtchd lft and drvn ent fnl f: sn one pce* **11/2**[2]

2613 **8** *4* **Jacbequick**[31] 4794 3-8-12 81 ........(p) JacobButterfield(5) 9 62
(Ollie Pears) *towards rr whn n.m.r and hmpd over 4f out: n.d* **9/1**

-042 **9** *1/2* **Ready (IRE)**[21] 5196 4-9-9 82 ........ JasonHart 8 64
(Garry Moss) *towards rr: hdwy on outer and in tch 1/2-way: rdn along over 2f out: sn wknd* **10/1**

2504 **10** *1 3/4* **Sakhalin Star (IRE)**[14] 5441 3-8-8 72 ........ DuranFentiman 13 47
(Richard Guest) *dwlt and swtchd rt s: a in rr* **50/1**

6166 **11** *1/2* **Relight My Fire**[28] 4923 4-9-0 73 ........(b) PhillipMakin 7 49
(Tim Easterby) *cl up: rdn along over 2f out: drvn wl over 1f out: wknd appr fnl f* **16/1**

1012 **12** *1 3/4* **Shadowtime**[24] 5054 9-9-10 83 ........ SilvestreDeSousa 10 55
(Tracy Waggott) *in tch: hdwy 3f out: rdn over 2f out: sn drvn and hld whn hmpd over 1f out* **11/1**

1m 32.21s (-1.59) **Going Correction** -0.075s/f (Good)
**WFA** 3 from 4yo+ 5lb **12 Ran SP% 124.7**
Speed ratings (Par 105): **106,105,105,100,99 98,98,94,93,91 90,88**
CSF £42.67 CT £237.20 TOTE £4.60: £2.00, £3.50, £4.70; EX 53.00 Trifecta £517.80.
**Owner** Norcroft Park Stud **Bred** Norcroft Park Stud And D Laidlaw **Trained** Bawtry, S Yorks

■ Stewards' Enquiry : Connor Beasley two-day ban: used whip above permitted level (Sep 14-15)

**FOCUS**
This looked wide-open. The principals came clear inside the final furlong. The winner was off his lowest mark since he was a 3yo.

## 5916 BETFRED MOBILE MAIDEN STKS 5f
**5:20** (5:22) (Class 5) 3-Y-O+ **£3,881** (£1,155; £577; £288) **Stalls** Low

Form RPR

-430 **1** **Master Of Suspense**[105] 2344 3-9-5 77 ........ GrahamLee 5 75
(Peter Chapple-Hyam) *trckd ldr: cl up 1/2-way: rdn to ld over 1f out: drvn out* **8/11**[1]

34 **2** *1 1/4* **Quick Touch**[10] 5568 3-9-5 0 ........ TonyHamilton 4 70
(Robert Cowell) *led: jnd 2f out: rdn and hdd over 1f out: sn hung lft and kpt on same pce* **7/1**[3]

3-22 **3** *3* **Cagoule**[10] 5568 3-9-2 75 ........ SamJames(3) 3 59
(David O'Meara) *trckd ldrs: hdwy 2f out: sn rdn and no imp fnl f* **9/5**[2]

06 **4** *1* **Byronaissance**[10] 5568 5-9-7 0 ........ AndrewElliott 2 55
(Neville Bycroft) *chsd ldng pair: rdn along over 2f out: sn drvn and one pce appr fnl f* **25/1**

6005 **5** *3 1/2* **Island Express (IRE)**[10] 5568 7-9-2 47 ........(tp) AnnStokell(5) 1 43
(Ann Stokell) *dwlt: a in rr* **33/1**

1m 4.26s (0.76) **Going Correction** +0.275s/f (Good)
**WFA** 3 from 5yo+ 2lb **5 Ran SP% 112.9**
Speed ratings (Par 103): **104,102,97,95,90**
CSF £6.97 TOTE £1.60: £1.10, £5.70; EX 5.10 Trifecta £9.00.
**Owner** Mrs Fitri Hay **Bred** Panda Bloodstock **Trained** Newmarket, Suffolk

**FOCUS**
A weak sprint maiden but the time was good. The winner is rated close to form.

## 5917 STARS OF THE FUTURE APPRENTICE H'CAP 1m 1f 207y
**5:50** (5:51) (Class 6) (0-65,63) 3-Y-O **£3,234** (£962; £481; £240) **Stalls** Low

Form RPR

4-22 **1** **Real Jazz (IRE)**[40] 4490 3-9-8 61 ........ RobHornby 5 73
(Sir Mark Prescott Bt) *mde all: rdn along wl over 1f out: drvn and edgd lft ins fnl f: kpt on wl* **6/4**[1]

3063 **2** *5* **Jimmy Crackle (IRE)**[6] 5717 3-8-13 55 ........(p) KevinLundie(3) 4 57
(Brian Ellison) *trckd wnr: hdwy over 2f out: chal wl over 1f out and sn rdn: drvn ins fnl f: sn edgd rt and one pce* **11/4**[2]

-440 **3** *3/4* **Lady Bubbles**[6] 5717 3-8-6 48 ........ DanielleMooney(3) 1 51
(Michael Easterby) *hld up in rr: hdwy over 2f out: rdn wl over 1f out: swtchd to inner and styd on fnl f: nrst fin* **9/1**

4006 **4** *nk* **Acquaint (IRE)**[6] 5717 3-8-12 51..............................(p) LukeLeadbitter 3 51
(John Wainwright) *hld up towards rr: hdwy 1/2-way: chsd ldrs wl over 2f out: rdn along wl over 1f out: sn drvn and one pce* **7/1**

3334 **5** *4 1/2* **Nam Ma Prow**[43] 4420 3-8-10 52..............................(p) RowanScott(3) 6 44
(Simon West) *trckd ldng pair: pushed along over 3f out: rdn wl over 2f out: sn btn* **7/2**[3]

2m 8.45s (1.45) **Going Correction** -0.075s/f (Good) **5** Ran SP% **111.4**
Speed ratings (Par 98): **91,87,86,86,82**
CSF £5.97 TOTE £2.10: £1.40, £1.70; EX 4.50 Trifecta £19.20.
**Owner** Timothy J Rooney **Bred** Alan Dargan **Trained** Newmarket, Suffolk
■ Stewards' Enquiry : Kevin Lundie five-day ban: careless riding (Sep 13-17)

**FOCUS**
This moderate handicap went pretty much to script. Another winner on the card to make all. The form is rated around the second and fourth.
T/Plt: £1,563.60 to a £1 stake. Pool: £81825.61 - 38.20 winning tickets T/Qpdt: £271.80 to a £1 stake. Pool: £4959.56 - 13.50 winning tickets JR

5408

# CHESTER (L-H)

## Saturday, August 30

**OFFICIAL GOING: Good to soft (6.6)**
Wind: Light, against Weather: Cloudy Rails: Rail out 3yd from 6f to 'drop in' at 1.5f . Races 1 &5 increased by 11yds, races 2, 4, 5 by 13yds, race 3 by 23yds and race 7 by 26yds

### 5918 SPORTINGBET H'CAP 5f 110y

2:20 (2:21) (Class 2) (0-100,98) 3-Y-0+ **£12,938** (£3,850; £1,924; £962) **Stalls** Low

Form RPR

2103 **1** **B Fifty Two (IRE)**[10] 5575 5-9-8 96..............................(bt) FrannyNorton 2 109
(Charles Hills) *mde all: rdn clr over 1f out: r.o wl and in command after: eased towards fin* **7/2**[1]

0004 **2** *3 3/4* **Dungannon**[18] 5289 7-8-11 92..............................(b) KieranShoemark(7) 1 93
(Andrew Balding) *midfield: impr to trck ldrs over 2f out: rdn to take 2nd 1f out: no ch w wnr ins fnl f* **5/1**[2]

003 **3** *2 3/4* **Ballesteros**[21] 5160 5-9-4 97.............................. JackGarritty(5) 6 89+
(Richard Fahey) *a.p: rdn over 1f out: nt qckn: kpt on same pce ins fnl f* **6/1**[3]

1330 **4** *2 1/2* **Love Island**[64] 3666 5-9-3 94.............................. GeorgeChaloner(3) 3 77
(Richard Whitaker) *trckd ldrs: wnt 2nd over 2f out: rdn over 1f out: sn lost 2nd: no ex ins fnl f: wl btn fnl 100yds* **8/1**

3011 **5** *1 1/4* **Forest Edge (IRE)**[8] 5623 5-9-9 97..............................(b) JFEgan 7 76
(David Evans) *s.i.s: towards rr: pushed along thrght: sme hdwy 2f out: nvr able to trble ldrs* **12/1**

2410 **6** *1 1/4* **Inxile (IRE)**[25] 5016 9-9-3 91..............................(p) TomQueally 12 66
(David Nicholls) *carried rt s: hld up in midfield: rdn and hdwy over 1f out: no imp on ldrs: one pce fnl f* **50/1**

4010 **7** *1 3/4* **Lexi's Hero (IRE)**[7] 5665 6-9-4 92..............................(v) DavidNolan 4 61
(Richard Fahey) *trckd ldrs: rdn over 2f out: wknd over 1f out* **7/1**

00 **8** *1 1/2* **Magical Macey (USA)**[77] 3241 7-9-9 97..............(b) GrahamGibbons 11 61
(David Barron) *bmpd s: in tch: rdn and wknd over 2f out* **25/1**

4310 **9** *1/2* **Top Boy**[49] 4179 4-9-2 90..............................(v) DaleSwift 5 53
(Derek Shaw) *bhd: struggling 3f out: nvr a threat* **8/1**

304- **10** *7* **Poole Harbour (IRE)**[427] 3840 5-9-7 95.............................. PaulMulrennan 10 35
(David Nicholls) *bmpd s: midfield: pushed along and outpcd 3f out: bhd after* **25/1**

5-02 **11** *9* **Pearl Acclaim (IRE)**[105] 2353 4-9-5 93.............................. AdrianNicholls 8 3
(David Nicholls) *dwlt: in rr: hung rt wl over 2f out: lost tch over 1f out* **20/1**

3604 **P** **Ballista (IRE)**[27] 4937 6-9-10 98.............................. RichardKingscote 9
(Tom Dascombe) *wnt rt s: chsd wnr tl wnt wd whn smething amiss over 2f out: lost pl qckly: sn bhd: t.o whn p.u ins fnl f: dismntd* **16/1**

1m 7.96s (1.76) **Going Correction** +0.525s/f (Yiel) **12** Ran SP% **115.9**
Speed ratings (Par 109): **109,104,100,97,95 93,91,89,88,79 67,**
CSF £18.73 CT £102.86 TOTE £4.50: £2.10, £2.40, £2.10; EX 24.00 Trifecta £136.70.
**Owner** Gary And Linnet Woodward **Bred** Mull Enterprises Ltd **Trained** Lambourn, Berks

**FOCUS**
There was 2.5mm of rain overnight and the going was given as good to soft (GoingStick 6.6). A decent quality sprint, but few got into it. The winner is rated back to his best.

### 5919 CRABBIE'S ALCOHOLIC GINGER BEER H'CAP 7f 122y

2:55 (2:55) (Class 2) 3-Y-0+

**£28,012** (£8,388; £4,194; £2,097; £1,048; £526) **Stalls** Low

Form RPR

1000 **1** **Ocean Tempest**[63] 3731 5-9-10 115.............................. JoeDoyle(5) 3 121
(John Ryan) *hld up: nt clr run 2f out: rdn and hdwy over 1f out: r.o to ld fnl 75yds: edgd rt whn on top cl home* **10/1**

0546 **2** *1/2* **Mezzotint (IRE)**[6] 5728 5-8-0 86 oh1.............................. RoystonFfrench 4 91
(Stuart Williams) *chsd ldrs: wnt 2nd 2f out: led 1f out: hdd fnl 75yds: jst hld cl home* **25/1**

3230 **3** *nk* **Beau Nash (IRE)**[72] 3378 3-8-0 92.............................. JimmyQuinn 1 95
(Richard Hannon) *midfield: rdn and hdwy over 1f out: swtchd rt ins fnl f: pressed ldrs fnl 75yds: r.o: jst hld cl home* **9/1**

331 **4** *1 1/4* **Apostle (IRE)**[27] 4938 5-8-7 93.............................. RichardKingscote 5 94
(David Simcock) *in tch: rdn over 1f out: styd on to chse ldrs ins fnl f: ch fnl 100yds: carried slty rt and kpt on same pce nr fin* **11/2**[2]

4131 **5** *1 3/4* **Alejandro (IRE)**[35] 4681 5-8-12 98.............................. PaulMulrennan 9 95
(David O'Meara) *led: rdn and hdd 1f out: no ex and fdd fnl 100yds* **11/1**

1040 **6** *1 1/4* **Russian Realm**[9] 5609 4-8-9 95.............................. DavidProbert 8 88+
(Sir Michael Stoute) *hld up: nt clr run over 2f out: nt clr run jst over 1f out: styd on ins fnl f: nt rch ldrs* **13/2**[3]

2302 **7** *3/4* **Foxtrot Romeo (IRE)**[14] 5433 5-8-8 94..............................(tp) PaulHanagan 2 86
(Marco Botti) *midfield: waited for run over 2f out: rdn and hdwy 1f out: kpt on ins fnl f: one pce fnl 75yds* **9/2**[1]

1300 **8** *2* **Chosen Character (IRE)**[27] 4938 6-8-6 92..............(vt) WilliamCarson 12 79
(Tom Dascombe) *chsd ldr: pushed along 3f out: rdn and lost 2nd 2f out: wknd fnl f* **66/1**

6510 **9** *shd* **Laffan (IRE)**[9] 5609 5-8-11 97.............................. DavidAllan 6 83
(Tim Easterby) *chsd ldrs: rdn over 1f out: sn wknd* **16/1**

1120 **10** *3/4* **Heavy Metal**[7] 5665 4-9-0 100.............................. FrannyNorton 10 84
(Mark Johnston) *chsd ldrs: pushed along over 4f out: plld out to rt over 1f out whn outpcd: wknd fnl 100yds* **8/1**

0013 **11** *3/4* **Big Johnny D (IRE)**[29] 4872 5-8-7 93.............................. GrahamGibbons 7 76
(David Barron) *midfield: rdn and carried wd ent st wl over 1f out: nt pick-up: wl btn ins fnl f* **14/1**

3440 **12** *3/4* **Dubai Dynamo**[5] 5771 9-8-2 88.............................. AndrewMullen 13 69
(Ruth Carr) *hld up: rdn over 1f out: no imp* **25/1**

1654 **13** *2 1/2* **King Torus (IRE)**[5] 5771 6-8-2 93.............................. JackGarritty(5) 11 67
(Ruth Carr) *hld up: carried rt ent st wl over 1f out: nvr on terms* **16/1**

3122 **14** *18* **Johnno**[42] 4442 5-8-7 93..............................(b) AdrianNicholls 14 22
(David Nicholls) *bhd: rdn over 4f out: nvr on terms* **12/1**

1m 35.75s (1.95) **Going Correction** +0.525s/f (Yiel)
**WFA** 3 from 4yo+ 6lb **14** Ran SP% **120.7**
Speed ratings (Par 109): **111,110,110,108,107 105,105,103,103,102 101,100,98,80**
CSF £243.13 CT £1486.47 TOTE £8.80: £2.00, £8.30, £3.70; EX 248.40 Trifecta £2276.60 Part won..
**Owner** W McLuskey & C Little **Bred** Old Mill Stud Ltd And Oomswell Ltd **Trained** Newmarket, Suffolk

**FOCUS**
A competitive handicap run at a good pace. The first five all benefited from a rails run. The winner rates a personal best.

### 5920 WIN £10,000,000 ON BETDAQ COLOSSUS CHESTER STKS (LISTED H'CAP) 1m 5f 89y

3:30 (3:31) (Class 1) (0-110,107) 3-Y-0+

**£20,982** (£7,955; £3,981; £1,983; £995; £499) **Stalls** Low

Form RPR

-214 **1** **Big Orange**[71] 3419 3-8-8 101 ow1.............................. TomQueally 1 109
(Michael Bell) *mde all: rdn over 2f out: kicked nrly 3 l clr wl over 1f out: kpt up to work wl ins fnl f* **5/1**

3 **2** *1 1/4* **Whiplash Willie**[93] 2704 6-9-11 107..............................(p) DavidProbert 2 113
(Andrew Balding) *hld up: hdwy 3f out: gng wl trcking ldrs over 2f out: wnt 2nd over 1f out: sn rdn: styd on ins fnl f: nt rch wnr* **11/4**[1]

0110 **3** *5* **De Rigueur**[7] 5693 6-9-5 101..............................(tp) PaulHanagan 3 100
(Marco Botti) *dwlt: in rr: pushed along 3f out: nt clr run 2f out: swtchd rt and hdwy over 1f out: rdn and edgd lft 1f out: chsd front two after: no imp and one pce ins fnl f* **4/1**[3]

5503 **4** *2 3/4* **Special Meaning**[7] 5673 4-8-12 94.............................. FrannyNorton 7 88
(Mark Johnston) *chsd wnr: lost 2nd over 3f out: sn edgd lft: outpcd over 2f out: wknd over 1f out* **7/2**[2]

4143 **5** *hd* **Noble Silk**[32] 4759 5-8-13 95..............................(p) PaulMulrennan 6 89
(Lucy Wadham) *trckd ldrs: effrt and ev ch 3f out: outpcd by wnr over 1f out: sn lost 2nd: hld whn checked 1f out: n.d after* **6/1**

5000 **6** *1 1/2* **Gabrial (IRE)**[7] 5693 5-9-8 104.............................. DavidNolan 4 96
(Richard Fahey) *hld up: effrt on outer 3f out: sn chsd ldrs: wknd over 1f out* **12/1**

25-6 **7** *5* **Livia's Dream (IRE)**[119] 1942 5-8-11 93 oh1.............. RichardKingscote 5 77
(Ed Walker) *chsd ldrs: shkn up whn nt clr run and hmpd over 3f out: sn pushed along and lost pl: n.d after* **22/1**

2m 57.31s (4.61) **Going Correction** +0.525s/f (Yiel)
**WFA** 3 from 4yo+ 11lb **7** Ran SP% **111.9**
Speed ratings: **106,105,102,100,100 99,96**
CSF £18.29 TOTE £6.00: £3.30, £2.10; EX 19.20 Trifecta £66.60.
**Owner** W J Gredley **Bred** Stetchworth & Middle Park Studs **Trained** Newmarket, Suffolk

**FOCUS**
This looked a tight race, but the early gallop was steady and the winner certainly had the run of things out in front. He backed up his Queen's Vase run.

### 5921 BETDAQ 3% COMMISSION / EBF STALLIONS FILLIES' CONDITIONS STKS (BOBIS RACE) 6f 18y

4:05 (4:05) (Class 2) 2-Y-0 **£12,602** (£3,772; £1,886; £944; £470) **Stalls** Low

Form RPR

4660 **1** **Spirit Of Xian (IRE)**[15] 5380 2-9-1 89.............................. SeanLevey 3 93
(Richard Hannon) *hld up in rr: impr to trck ldrs over 4f out: led jst over 1f out: r.o wl to draw clr wl ins fnl f: sn edgd lft whn in command* **9/1**

42 **2** *4 1/2* **Evening Rain (USA)**[14] 5429 2-8-12 0.............................. HarryBentley 5 77
(Saeed bin Suroor) *in tch: pushed along 4f out: effrt on outer over 2f out: rdn and nt qckn over 1f out: styd on ins fnl f: tk 2nd post: no ch w wnr* **2/1**[2]

1030 **3** *shd* **London Life (IRE)**[15] 5405 2-9-1 82.............................. RichardKingscote 1 79
(Tom Dascombe) *led: rdn over 1f out: sn hdd: outpcd and no ch w wnr fnl 100yds: no ex and lost 2nd post* **11/1**

123 **4** *6* **Enlace**[18] 5286 2-9-1 87.............................. FrannyNorton 6 64+
(Mark Johnston) *forced wd early on: swtchd lft and bhd over 4f out: nvr gng wl after: plugged on to take 4th 1f out: nvr a thrteat* **15/8**[1]

21 **5** *9* **Marigot Bay**[11] 5524 2-8-12 80.............................. DavidProbert 4 31
(Gay Kelleway) *in tch: lost pl 2f out: sn rdn: wknd over 1f out* **10/1**

3106 **6** *1 1/4* **Blue Aegean**[15] 5380 2-9-1 87.............................. PaulMulrennan 2 30
(Charlie Appleby) *chsd ldr: ev ch 2f out: sn lost 2nd: rdn and wknd over 1f out* **5/1**[3]

1m 17.86s (4.06) **Going Correction** +0.525s/f (Yiel) **6** Ran SP% **112.2**
Speed ratings (Par 97): **93,87,86,78,66 65**
CSF £27.44 TOTE £10.10: £4.50, £1.80; EX 39.00 Trifecta £347.60.
**Owner** Rockcliffe Stud **Bred** B Kennedy **Trained** East Everleigh, Wilts

**FOCUS**
Leaving the stalls it looked like five of the six runners wanted to lead, the exception being the winner.

### 5922 BETDAQ £50 FREE BET / IRISH STALLION FARMS EBF MAIDEN STKS 7f 2y

4:40 (4:42) (Class 4) 2-Y-0 **£6,469** (£1,925; £962; £481) **Stalls** Low

Form RPR

202 **1** **Azmaam (IRE)**[23] 5078 2-9-5 77.............................. PaulHanagan 1 80
(Richard Hannon) *awkward s: racd keenly: midfield: hdwy to trck ldrs over 4f out: wnt 2nd 2f out: led 1f out: r.o wl to draw clr fnl 100yds* **4/6**[1]

03 **2** *2 1/2* **Fast Charlie (IRE)**[17] 5296 2-9-5 0.............................. PJMcDonald 3 73
(Ann Duffield) *w ldr: led 5f out: rdn over 1f out: sn hdd: unable to go w wnr fnl 100yds* **7/1**[3]

**3** *1 1/4* **Gabrial The Viking (IRE)** 2-9-5 0.............................. DavidNolan 4 70+
(Richard Fahey) *trckd ldrs: rdn and nt qckn over 1f out: styd on same pce ins fnl f* **11/1**

0 **4** *5* **Philba**[36] 4633 2-9-5 0.............................. AndrewMullen 5 56
(Michael Appleby) *midfield: lost pl 4f out: u.p 2f out: styd on ins fnl f: nvr able to trble ldrs* **40/1**

5 **5** *1* **Crikey (IRE)**[31] 4790 2-9-5 0.............................. HarryBentley 11 54
(Kevin Ryan) *led: hdd 5f out: remained w ldr: rdn over 2f out: sn lost 2nd: wknd ins fnl f* **14/1**

35 **6** *6* **Best Dressed**[24] 5050 2-9-5 0.............................. GrahamGibbons 9 37
(David Brown) *chsd ldrs: rdn over 2f out: sn wknd* **9/1**

64 **7** *3/4* **Rocky Desert (IRE)**[30] 4809 2-9-0 0 ..................... MarcMonaghan(5) 12 35
(Marco Botti) *in rr: struggling 2f out: nvr on terms* **28/1**

0400 **8** *11* **Shamkhani**[15] 5384 2-9-5 45 ........................................ PatrickMathers 8 6
(Alan Berry) *racd on outer towards rr: hdwy over 4f out: wknd over 2f out* **150/1**

4 **9** *nk* **Le Rouquin (FR)**[15] 5391 2-9-5 0 ..................................... TomQueally 6 5
(Michael Bell) *dwlt: hld up: pushed along 3f out: struggling 2f out: nvr a threat* **6/1**[2]

1m 31.84s (5.34) **Going Correction** +0.525s/f (Yiel) **9** Ran SP% **118.3**
Speed ratings (Par 96): **90,87,85,80,78 72,71,58,58**
CSF £6.19 TOTE £1.20: £1.02, £2.60, £3.10; EX 6.10 Trifecta £28.40.
**Owner** Hamdan Al Maktoum **Bred** Yeomanstown Stud **Trained** East Everleigh, Wilts

**FOCUS**
No more than a fair maiden.

## 5923 STELLA ARTOIS H'CAP (BOBIS RACE) 5f 110y

**5:10** (5:12) (Class 4) (0-85,84) 3-Y-O **£6,469** (£1,925; £962; £481) **Stalls** Low

Form RPR

2- **1** **By Rights**[18] 5290 3-8-2 65 oh1 ........................................ RaulDaSilva 8 76
(Tony Carroll) *a.p: racd on outer: led over 1f out: r.o wl and in command fnl 100yds* **16/1**

6231 **2** *2 1/2* **Royal Connoisseur (IRE)**[19] 5246 3-8-8 74 ......... GeorgeChaloner(3) 5 77
(Richard Fahey) *in tch: effrt to chse ldrs 2f out: wnt 2nd ins fnl f: styd on: no imp on wnr fnl 100yds* **6/1**

526 **3** *1 3/4* **Red Forever**[15] 5389 3-8-2 65 oh2 ................................ PatrickMathers 7 62
(Alan Berry) *dwlt: in tch: effrt over 1f out: on inner and chsd ldrs over 1f out: kpt on ins fnl f: no imp on front two* **33/1**

5314 **4** *1* **Meadway**[19] 5243 3-9-6 83 .............................................. PaulMulrennan 3 77
(Bryan Smart) *sn led: rdn and hdd over 1f out: no ex fnl 100yds* **6/1**

314 **5** *2* **Captain Myles (IRE)**[28] 4898 3-9-7 84 ........................(p) StevieDonohoe 9 74
(Tim Pitt) *dwlt: in tch: effrt over 1f out: nt qckning whn n.m.r and snatched up ins fnl f: sn lost pl and wl btn* **5/1**[3]

1425 **6** *nk* **Scarborough (IRE)**[7] 5696 3-9-5 82 ................................ AndrewMullen 6 68
(Michael Appleby) *prom: chalng 2f out: rdn over 1f out: wknd fnl 100yds* **5/2**[1]

133 **7** *7* **Pushkin Museum (IRE)**[26] 4977 3-8-10 78 ..................... JackGarritty(5) 1 41
(Richard Fahey) *prom: lost pl over 2f out: wknd over 1f out* **4/1**[2]

1051 **8** *17* **Jolly Red Jeanz (IRE)**[49] 4186 3-8-3 66 .................(b) RoystonFfrench 4
(Tom Dascombe) *n.m.r and hmpd early: sn lost pl: bhd fnl 3f* **12/1**

12 **9** *51* **Ridge Ranger (IRE)**[11] 5526 3-9-1 78 ........................ GrahamGibbons 10
(Eric Alston) *hmpd early: a wl bhd: sn lost tch: t.o* **12/1**

1m 10.32s (4.12) **Going Correction** +0.525s/f (Yiel) **9** Ran SP% **118.0**
Speed ratings (Par 102): **93,89,87,86,83 82,73,50,**
CSF £110.89 CT £3139.88 TOTE £22.50: £6.50, £2.30, £4.80; EX 111.70 Trifecta £1166.00 Part won..
**Owner** Last Day Racing Partnership **Bred** Grove Farm Stud **Trained** Cropthorne, Worcs

**FOCUS**
A strange race in the context of the other races on the card, with the first four racing wide. The pace was strong but the time modest. The form is rated around the second.

## 5924 MARLEN AND JEAN ROBERTS CELEBRATION H'CAP 1m 7f 195y

**5:40** (5:41) (Class 4) (0-85,84) 3-Y-O+ **£6,469** (£1,925; £962; £481) **Stalls** Low

Form RPR

1323 **1** **Annaluna (IRE)**[29] 4843 5-8-10 66 ......................................(v) JFEgan 4 74
(David Evans) *midfield: niggled along: lost pl 4f out: sn outpcd: hdwy on outer over 1f out: styd on ins fnl f: led towards fin* **25/1**

0542 **2** *1/2* **Nafaath (IRE)**[16] 5341 8-9-5 75 .................................... PJMcDonald 5 82
(Donald McCain) *led: rdn abt 3 l clr over 2f out: reduced advantge ins fnl f: no ex and hdd towards fin* **12/1**

253 **3** *shd* **Nashville (IRE)**[21] 5193 5-9-6 76 .................................... DavidNolan 9 83
(Richard Fahey) *trckd ldrs: rdn over 3f out: wnt 2nd 2f out: lost 2nd ins fnl f but styd on to chal towards fin: jst hld* **11/2**[3]

536 **4** *6* **Kleitomachos (IRE)**[42] 4423 6-9-6 76 .............................. PaulHanagan 2 76
(Stuart Kittow) *hld up: hdwy over 5f out: rdn to chse ldrs over 3f out: sn outpcd: nt clr run over 1f out: kpt on ins fnl f but n.d* **17/2**

2313 **5** *1* **Underwritten**[4] 5800 5-8-10 71 6ex .................................. JoeDoyle(5) 7 70
(Shaun Harris) *trckd ldrs: rdn over 4f out: outpcd 3f out: plugged on fnl f wout threatening* **16/1**

1321 **6** *1/2* **English Summer**[27] 4940 7-9-7 82 ..........................(t) JackGarritty(5) 8 80
(Richard Fahey) *in tch: rdn and outpcd over 3f out: one pce fnl f* **10/3**[1]

2513 **7** *nk* **Rosslyn Castle**[14] 5442 5-9-8 81 .......................... GeorgeChaloner(3) 1 79
(Philip McBride) *hld up: hdwy over 3f out: rdn whn chalng for pls over 2f out: nt qckn over 1f out: wknd fnl 100yds* **6/1**

0-30 **8** *2* **Albert Bridge**[107] 2289 6-10-0 84 ........................... RichardKingscote 10 79
(Ralph Beckett) *chsd ldr: rdn over 4f out: lost 2nd 2f out: wknd over 1f out* **5/1**[2]

6063 **9** *21* **Tappanappa (IRE)**[3] 5825 7-8-12 68 ............................ AndrewMullen 11 38
(Michael Appleby) *missed break: a bhd: lost tch over 2f out* **16/1**

2302 **10** *48* **Ridgeway Storm (IRE)**[59] 3860 4-9-9 79 ........................... TomQueally 3
(Alan King) *trckd ldrs: rdn and wknd wl over 3f out: lost tch 3f out: t.o* **15/2**

3m 36.71s (8.71) **Going Correction** +0.525s/f (Yiel) **10** Ran SP% **115.0**
Speed ratings (Par 105): **99,98,98,95,95 94,94,93,83,59**
CSF £291.20 CT £1894.54 TOTE £39.10: £7.30, £3.30, £1.60; EX 134.40 Trifecta £818.20 Part won..
**Owner** Nick Shutts **Bred** Michael Dalton **Trained** Pandy, Monmouths

**FOCUS**
A fair staying handicap run at a sound pace. The form looks solid.
T/Plt: £750.00 to a £1 stake. Pool: £91653.88 - 89.20 winning tickets T/Qpdt: £32.30 to a £1 stake. Pool: £5528.13 - 126.40 winning tickets DO

# 5879 SANDOWN (R-H)

Saturday, August 30

**OFFICIAL GOING: Sprint course - soft (good to soft in places); round course - good to soft (good in back straight) (sprint 5.7, round 6.8; home straight: stands' side 6.8, centre 6.4, far side 6.3)**
Wind: medium, against Weather: dry, light cloud, bright spells Rails: Course at inner configuration and all distances as advertised. Sprint track at full width

## 5925 NATIONAL YOUTH MUSIC THEATRE CHARITY H'CAP 5f 6y

**2:05** (2:08) (Class 3) (0-95,95) 3-Y-O+
**£12,450** (£3,728; £1,864; £932; £466; £117) **Stalls** Low

Form RPR

4065 **1** **Chilworth Icon**[14] 5433 4-9-2 87 ................................. SamHitchcott 8 99
(Mick Channon) *pushed along towards rr: hdwy against far rail over 1f out: str run to ld fnl 75yds: sn clr* **20/1**

140 **2** *2 1/2* **Ladweb**[28] 4892 4-8-8 84 ............................................ CamHardie(5) 5 87
(John Gallagher) *wl in tch in midfield: effrt u.p over 1f out: styd on ins fnl f to snatch 2nd last strides: no threat to wnr* **20/1**

0230 **3** *hd* **Normal Equilibrium**[14] 5419 4-9-5 90 ..................(p) AndreaAtzeni 14 92
(Robert Cowell) *chsd ldr tl led 1/2-way: rdn over 1f out: hdd fnl 75yds: sn outpcd by wnr: lost 2nd last strides* **14/1**

230 **4** *1* **Eccleston**[77] 3253 3-9-8 95 ........................................ DanielTudhope 10 94
(David O'Meara) *hld up in midfield: short of room and shuffled bk towards rr 3f out: switching lft to find a run fr 1f out: styd on wl fnl 75yds: nvr trbld ldrs* **7/1**[2]

0563 **5** *shd* **Jamaican Bolt (IRE)**[14] 5419 6-9-3 88 ........................ BarryMcHugh 17 86
(Geoffrey Oldroyd) *towards rr: rdn 1/2-way: styd on wl u.p ins fnl f: nvr trbld ldrs* **9/1**[3]

0010 **6** *nk* **Judge 'n Jury**[10] 5575 10-9-1 93 ...............................(t) DavidParkes(7) 7 90
(Ronald Harris) *dwlt: rcvrd and hdwy to chse ldrs over 3f out: 3rd and no ex ins fnl f: wknd wl ins fnl f* **20/1**

3110 **6** *dht* **Iffranesia (FR)**[14] 5419 4-9-2 87 ................................ AdamBeschizza 11 84
(Robert Cowell) *in tch towards rr: hdwy u.p and swtchd lft ins fnl f: styd on wl fnl 75yds: nvr trbld ldrs* **16/1**

2020 **8** *shd* **Elusivity (IRE)**[84] 2989 6-9-4 89 ....................................... ShaneKelly 6 86
(Peter Crate) *in tch in midfield: hdwy jst over 1f out: chsng ldrs whn nt enough room and hmpd ins fnl f: styd on same pce u.p fnl 100yds* **10/1**

4651 **9** *1/2* **Pearl Blue (IRE)**[51] 4128 6-9-6 94 ........................ AshleyMorgan(3) 16 89
(Chris Wall) *in tch in midfield: effrt u.p over 1f out: kpt on same pce ins fnl f: hmpd nr fin* **10/1**

-010 **10** *1 1/4* **Asian Trader**[64] 3666 5-8-9 87 ....................................(t) GeorgiaCox(7) 9 78+
(William Haggas) *s.i.s: bhd: hdwy ins fnl f: styd on: n.d* **16/1**

0610 **11** *hd* **Keep It Dark**[92] 2727 5-8-11 82 ....................................... JoeFanning 4 72
(Tony Coyle) *chsd ldrs: wnt 2nd 2f out: drvn over 1f out: lost 2nd lost 2nd ins fnl f: fdd fnl 75yds* **20/1**

3023 **12** *hd* **Ziggy Lee**[27] 4946 8-8-7 83 ........................................ JordanNason(5) 12 72
(Peter Hedger) *taken down early: in tch in midfield: rdn 2f out: no imp over 1f out: one pce after* **33/1**

245 **13** *shd* **One Chance (IRE)**[22] 5154 3-9-7 94 ............................... WilliamBuick 1 83
(John Butler) *chsd ldrs: rdn over 1f out: keeping on same pce whn hmpd ins fnl f: n.d after* **7/1**[2]

04 **14** *1 1/4* **Tagula Night (IRE)**[40] 4502 8-8-11 82 ...........................(bt) RyanMoore 2 66+
(Dean Ivory) *hld up in tch in midfield: hdwy on far rail over 1f out: keeping on whn nt clr run ins fnl f: nowhere to go and eased after* **13/2**[1]

6020 **15** *nk* **Ajjaadd (USA)**[34] 4700 8-9-8 93 ...................... WilliamTwiston-Davies 3 76+
(Ted Powell) *s.i.s: hld up in tch in rr: stuck bhd a wall of horses and switching lft 1f out: nvr fnd a gap and unable to cl: n.d* **9/1**[3]

000 **16** *2 1/2* **Even Stevens**[14] 5419 6-9-0 85 ..............................(v) FrederikTylicki 15 59
(Scott Dixon) *racd in centre: overall ldr tl 1/2-way: rdn and btn ent fnl f: fdd fnl 150yds* **25/1**

003 **17** *6* **Free Zone**[18] 5289 5-9-8 93 .............................................. JimCrowley 13 46
(Robert Cowell) *a towards rr: struggling 2f out: bhd fnl f* **16/1**

1m 2.33s (0.73) **Going Correction** +0.35s/f (Good)
**WFA** 3 from 4yo+ 2lb **17** Ran SP% **126.7**
Speed ratings (Par 107): **108,104,103,102,101 101,101,101,100,98 98,97,97,95,95 91,81**
CSF £357.23 CT £5878.45 TOTE £30.60: £5.10, £5.40, £3.00, £2.60; EX 797.50 Trifecta £3003.30 Part won..
**Owner** Billy Parish **Bred** Norman Court Stud **Trained** West Ilsley, Berks

**FOCUS**
Course at inner configuration and all distances as advertised. Sprint track at full width. Several of the runners met trouble in what had looked an open sprint.

## 5926 EUROPEAN WEALTH SOLARIO STKS (GROUP 3) 7f 16y

**2:40** (2:41) (Class 1) 2-Y-O **£25,519** (£9,675; £4,842; £2,412; £1,210) **Stalls** Low

Form RPR

2212 **1** **Aktabantay**[49] 4199 2-9-1 104 .........................................(p) RyanMoore 3 104
(Hugo Palmer) *hld up in tch in rr: hdwy to chse ldrs over 2f out: sn rdn: no imp and drvn 1f out: hrd drvn and styd on fnl 100yds to ld last stride* **9/4**[2]

1 **2** *shd* **Future Empire**[35] 4666 2-9-1 0 ........................................ JamesDoyle 2 104
(Saeed bin Suroor) *chsd ldng pair: rdn over 2f out: no prog tl swtchd lft and hrd drvn 1f out: styd on fnl 100yds: wnt 2nd wl ins fnl f: led nr fin: hdd last stride* **5/4**[1]

2133 **3** *nk* **Lexington Times (IRE)**[14] 5447 2-9-1 91 ............................. PatDobbs 6 103
(Richard Hannon) *sn chsd ldr: upsides and gng best 2f out: rdn to ld over 1f out: stl 1 l clr but drvn fnl 100yds: worn down and hdd last strides* **16/1**

1203 **4** *hd* **Cock Of The North**[49] 4199 2-9-1 100 ........................ FrederikTylicki 4 102
(Scott Dixon) *t.k.h: hld up in tch: rdn over 2f out: no imp: rallied uder press ent fnl f: chsd ldr briefly fnl 75yds: styd on* **6/1**[3]

3115 **5** *3* **Pallister**[31] 4780 2-9-1 97 ............................................... JoeFanning 5 95
(Mark Johnston) *led: rdn ent fnl 2f: hdd over 1f out: no ex u.p: lost 2nd and wknd fnl 75yds* **7/1**

1m 29.84s (0.34) **Going Correction** -0.075s/f (Good) **5** Ran SP% **107.9**
Speed ratings: **95,94,94,94,90**
CSF £5.22 TOTE £2.70: £1.40, £1.30; EX 5.10 Trifecta £22.20.
**Owner** V I Araci **Bred** Fittocks Stud Ltd **Trained** Newmarket, Suffolk

■ Stewards' Enquiry : James Doyle two-day ban: used whip above permitted level (Sep 14-15)

**FOCUS**
Modest form for a Group 3 and there was little to separate the first four home, so an unsatisfactory renewal.

## 5927 THOROUGHBRED BREEDERS' ASSOCIATION ATALANTA STKS (GROUP 3) (F&M) 1m 14y
3:15 (3:15) (Class 1) 3-Y-0+
£36,861 (£13,975; £6,994; £3,484; £1,748; £877) Stalls Low

Form RPR
1 **1** **Fintry (IRE)**[90] 2817 3-9-2 114 MaximeGuyon 4 114+
(A Fabre, France) *chsd ldng trio: rdn and hdwy to ld 1f out: in command fnl 100yds: pushed out towards fin* **6/4**[1]
5324 **2** 1 ¼ **Odeliz (IRE)**[41] 4478 4-9-1 106 DanielTudhope 1 105
(K R Burke) *t.k.h: hld up towards rr: swtchd lft 2f out: hdwy ent fnl f: styd on u.p to chse wnr fnl 75yds: no imp* **6/1**[3]
1-11 **3** nk **Water Hole (IRE)**[22] 5151 3-8-9 92 WilliamBuick 6 103+
(John Gosden) *t.k.h: chsd ldrs: wnt 2nd 6f out tl unable qck over 1f out: rallied and kpt on again fnl 100yds* **9/2**[2]
1003 **4** ¾ **Zurigha (IRE)**[36] 4607 4-9-1 105 PatDobbs 5 103
(Richard Hannon) *t.k.h: hld up in midfield: rdn and effrt over 1f out: styd on steadily ins fnl f: nvr a threat to wnr* **14/1**
-601 **5** hd **Audacia (IRE)**[53] 4060 4-9-1 99 RyanMoore 9 102
(Hugo Palmer) *led: rdn 2f out: hdd and drvn 1f out: lost 2nd fnl 75yds: kpt on same pce after* **12/1**
-322 **6** nk **Diamond Dove (GER)**[27] 4955 3-8-9 108 FrederikTylicki 7 100
(Andreas Lowe, Germany) *t.k.h: chsd ldr for 2f: styd chsng ldrs: rdn 2f out: keeping on same pce and nt clr run ins fnl f: swtchd lft and one pce towards fin* **7/1**
14-3 **7** 1 ½ **Zibelina (IRE)**[119] 1945 4-9-1 109 AdamKirby 3 98
(Charlie Appleby) *in tch in midfield: rdn over 2f out: unable qck u.p over 1f out: swtchd lft and one pce ins fnl f* **8/1**
6206 **8** 1 ¼ **Lily Rules (IRE)**[64] 3665 3-8-9 96 BarryMcHugh 8 94
(Tony Coyle) *hld up in last pair: effrt and edging rt 2f out: no real imp but kpt on steadily ins fnl f* **33/1**
35-1 **9** 10 **Nur Jahan (IRE)**[10] 5570 4-9-1 69 TedDurcan 2 72
(David Lanigan) *taken down early: dwlt: a in rr: rdn over 2f out: sn btn: bhd over 1f out* **66/1**

1m 43.01s (-0.29) **Going Correction** -0.075s/f (Good)
**WFA** 3 from 4yo 6lb 9 Ran SP% **114.9**
Speed ratings: **98,96,96,95,95 95,93,92,82**
CSF £10.74 TOTE £2.30: £1.10, £1.90, £1.90; EX 10.90 Trifecta £48.20.
**Owner** Godolphin SNC **Bred** Darley **Trained** Chantilly, France

**FOCUS**
Run at a steady gallop.

## 5928 ST JAMES THEATRE H'CAP 1m 2f 7y
3:50 (3:51) (Class 2) 3-Y-0+
£37,350 (£11,184; £5,592; £2,796; £1,398; £702) Stalls Low

Form RPR
0111 **1** **Treasure The Ridge (IRE)**[24] 5035 5-7-12 **82** oh1 ow1(b) DannyBrock(3) 10 92
(Andrew Reid) *hld up in rr: stl plenty to do whn nt clr run over 1f out: gd hdwy u.p between horses ins fnl f: led fnl 75yds: r.o strly: rdn out* **25/1**
-142 **2** 1 ¼ **Calm Attitude (IRE)**[42] 4453 4-7-9 **81** oh1 NoelGarbutt(5) 16 89
(Rae Guest) *t.k.h: hld up in last trio: hdwy on outer u.p over 1f out: chsd wnr wl ins fnl f: kpt on* **16/1**
4431 **3** ½ **Clon Brulee (IRE)**[21] 5188 5-9-3 **105** MikeyEnnis(7) 14 112
(Saeed bin Suroor) *in tch in midfield: effrt to chse ldr 2f out: rdn to ld over 1f out: edgd rt 1f out: hdd fnl 75yds: no ex* **8/1**[3]
2020 **4** ¾ **Spa's Dancer (IRE)**[77] 3251 7-9-5 **100** RyanMoore 13 106
(James Eustace) *hld up towards rr: hdwy u.p over 1f out: chsd ldrs ins fnl f: no ex and outpcd fnl 75yds* **9/1**
3154 **5** ¾ **Running Deer (IRE)**[31] 4782 5-8-9 **90** KierenFallon 9 94
(Eve Johnson Houghton) *t.k.h: hld up in midfield: rdn and effrt to chse ldrs 2f out: chsd wnr over 1f out tl ins fnl f: wknd towards fin* **14/1**
0-01 **6** 2 **Forgotten Hero (IRE)**[36] 4608 5-8-12 **93** WilliamBuick 8 93
(Charles Hills) *chsd ldng trio: effrt to chse ldr 2f out tl over 1f out: no ex 1f out: wknd ins fnl f* **5/1**[1]
5010 **7** ½ **Balty Boys (IRE)**[32] 4771 5-9-6 **101** (b) DaneO'Neill 6 100
(Brian Ellison) *led: rdn 2f out: drvn and hdd over 1f out: no ex u.p 1f out: wknd ins fnl f* **33/1**
202 **8** 1 ¼ **Ajmany (IRE)**[35] 4667 4-9-2 **97** (b) AndreaAtzeni 3 94
(Luca Cumani) *dwlt: sn bustled along and rcvrd to r in midfield: rdn and unable qck 2f out: wknd 1f out* **10/1**
200 **9** shd **Tres Coronas (IRE)**[21] 5174 7-9-7 **102** ShaneKelly 5 99
(David Barron) *rrd as stalls opened: hld up towards rr: effrt and nt clr run over 1f out: swtchd lft and kpt on ins fnl f: nvr threatened ldrs* **16/1**
-053 **10** hd **Tinghir (IRE)**[21] 5188 4-8-10 **91** (b[1]) TedDurcan 7 88
(David Lanigan) *in tch in midfield: rdn and effrt 2f out: drvn and no imp over 1f out: plugged on same pce after* **12/1**
4134 **11** 1 ¼ **Rydan (IRE)**[29] 4855 3-7-9 **91** oh3 ow2 HectorCrouch(7) 4 89
(Robert Mills) *hld up in rr: swtchd ins over 2f out: switching lft but continually denied a clr run fr over 1f out tl ins fnl f: kpt on but no ch* **12/1**
0140 **12** ½ **What About Carlo (FR)**[7] 5666 3-8-11 **100** JimmyFortune 1 93
(Eve Johnson Houghton) *in tch in midfield: effrt u.p ent fnl 2f: no prog and btn over 1f out: wknd 1f out* **7/1**[2]
0054 **13** 3 **Moonday Sun (USA)**[7] 5669 5-8-7 **88** JimCrowley 15 75
(Amanda Perrett) *in tch in midfield but stuck wd: rdn over 2f out: wknd over 1f out* **20/1**
1 **14** ¾ **Mount Shamsan**[25] 5018 4-8-2 **83** HayleyTurner 12 69
(William Haggas) *chsd ldr tl ent fnl 2f: sn struggling: wknd over 1f out* **8/1**[3]
0606 **15** nk **Viewpoint (IRE)**[21] 5162 5-8-3 **89** CamHardie(5) 11 74
(Richard Hannon) *in tch in midfield: shkn up 7f out: nvr gng wl after and on and off the bridle after: lost pl u.p and bhd 2f out: no ch after* **12/1**
0400 **16** 10 **Busatto (USA)**[7] 5695 4-8-8 **89** JoeFanning 2 55
(Mark Johnston) *chsd ldrs tl rdn and lost pl ent fnl 2f: wknd over 1f out: bhd ins fnl f* **14/1**

2m 7.15s (-3.35) **Going Correction** -0.075s/f (Good)
**WFA** 3 from 4yo+ 8lb 16 Ran SP% **130.2**
Speed ratings (Par 109): **110,109,108,108,107 105,105,104,104,104 103,102,100,99,99 91**
CSF £398.75 CT £3503.61 TOTE £42.30: £8.10, £3.90, £2.50, £2.40; EX 815.40 Trifecta £11278.00.
**Owner** A S Reid **Bred** S Coughlan **Trained** Mill Hill, London NW7

**FOCUS**
Run at a fair gallop, several held a chance over 1f out in what was an open handicap, with those held up early coming to the fore late on.

## 5929 NYMT STUDENT FUND NURSERY H'CAP (BOBIS RACE) 7f 16y
4:25 (4:26) (Class 4) (0-85,83) 2-Y-0 £5,175 (£1,540; £769; £384) Stalls Low

Form RPR
3224 **1** **Popeswood (IRE)**[8] 5645 2-8-13 75 WilliamBuick 5 81
(Mick Channon) *hld up in tch: effrt and hanging rt wl over 1f out: swtchd lft over 1f out: str run 1f out: led ins fnl f: sn clr: readily* **5/1**[3]
305 **2** 2 ¼ **Laidback Romeo (IRE)**[28] 4884 2-8-9 74 RyanTate(3) 4 76+
(Clive Cox) *chsd ldrs: clsd and pressing ldng pair whn carried lft and hmpd 1f out: swtchd rt: flashed tail u.p: kpt on to go 2nd last strides: no threat to wnr* **9/2**[2]
4233 **3** nk **Assault On Rome (IRE)**[7] 5672 2-9-5 81 JoeFanning 2 80
(Mark Johnston) *led and set stdy gallop: hdd 3f out: rdn to ld again 2f out: hung lft 1f out: hdd and outpcd ins fnl f: lost 2nd last strides* **5/1**[3]
534 **4** 2 ½ **Looking Good**[12] 5493 2-8-9 71 AndreaAtzeni 6 67
(David Brown) *t.k.h: chsd ldr tl 4f out: rdn to chse ldr again over 1f out: pushed lft and bdly hmpd 1f out: nt rcvr and one pce after* **11/1**
10 **5** 1 ½ **Great Park (IRE)**[29] 4853 2-8-10 77 CamHardie(5) 1 65
(Martyn Meade) *hld up in tch in midfield: rdn and effrt 2f out: styd on same pce u.p fr over 1f out* **16/1**
4105 **6** 1 ¼ **Among Angels**[62] 3751 2-9-7 83 RyanMoore 8 68
(Richard Hannon) *stdd and dropped in bhd after s: hld up in last pair: rdn 2f out: no real imp: nvr trbld ldrs: lame* **4/1**[1]
51 **7** ¾ **Honey Required**[22] 5148 2-8-3 65 HayleyTurner 9 51
(Alan Bailey) *t.k.h: chsd ldrs: rdn and struggling to qckn whn short of room and bmpd 2f out: lost pl and n.d over 1f out* **12/1**
031 **8** nk **Sister Of Mercy (IRE)**[16] 5351 2-9-6 82 JamesDoyle 7 80
(Roger Charlton) *hld up towards rr: rdn and effrt whn bmpd 2f out: keeping on whn bdly hmpd 1f out: nt rcvr and n.d after* **4/1**[1]
440 **9** 7 **Essaka (IRE)**[49] 4216 2-8-5 67 SamHitchcott 3 30+
(Mick Channon) *stdd s: plld v hrd in rr: swtchd lft to outer and hdwy over 4f out: led 3f out tl 2f out: wknd over 1f out: bhd fnl f* **25/1**

1m 31.52s (2.02) **Going Correction** -0.075s/f (Good) 9 Ran SP% **117.3**
Speed ratings (Par 96): **85,82,82,79,77 76,75,74,66**
CSF £28.26 CT £119.34 TOTE £5.70: £1.90, £1.70, £2.00; EX 34.30 Trifecta £299.80.
**Owner** N J Hitchins **Bred** Mr & Mrs Nick Hitchins **Trained** West Ilsley, Berks
■ Stewards' Enquiry : Andrea Atzeni one-day ban: careless riding (Sep 14)
Joe Fanning three-day ban: careless riding (Sep 14-16)

**FOCUS**
Quite a few took a keen grip in this nursery, with the pace being a steady one.

## 5930 THANK YOU CHRISSY MORUM H'CAP (BOBIS RACE) 1m 14y
5:00 (5:02) (Class 4) (0-80,80) 3-Y-0 £5,175 (£1,540; £769; £384) Stalls Low

Form RPR
0314 **1** **Special Miss**[23] 5095 3-8-8 67 JimCrowley 3 78
(Ali Stronge) *in tch: clsd to join ldrs and gng best 2f out: rdn and forged ahd over 1f out: in command and kpt on fnl f: rdn out* **14/1**
3316 **2** 2 **Weekendatbernies (IRE)**[10] 5550 3-9-4 77 OisinMurphy 4 83
(Ed de Giles) *chsd ldrs: short of room and lost pl ent fnl 2f: rallied u.p and wnt between horses ins fnl f: chsd wnr fnl 75yds: no imp* **8/1**
010 **3** 1 ½ **Tercel (IRE)**[17] 5311 3-9-4 77[1] RyanMoore 1 80
(Sir Michael Stoute) *dwlt and bustled along early: hdwy to ld over 6f out: clr 1/2-way: jnd and drvn 2f out: hdd over 1f out: kpt on same pce after: lost 2nd fnl 75yds* **5/1**[2]
32 **4** shd **Zain Empire**[16] 5349 3-9-7 80 JamesDoyle 2 82
(Robert Cowell) *led tl over 6f out: chsd ldr: clsd and rdn to chal 2f out: 3rd and outpcd over 1f out: plugged on same pce fnl f* **9/4**[1]
23 **5** 1 ½ **Blue Bounty**[40] 4495 3-8-5 64 AndreaAtzeni 7 63
(Mark H Tompkins) *stdd and dropped in bhd after s: t.k.h: hld up in rr: hdwy over 2f out: drvn and styd on same pce fr over 1f out* **7/1**
0014 **6** 3 **Orion's Bow**[19] 5258 3-9-6 79 (bt) WilliamBuick 6 71
(John Gosden) *t.k.h: hld up in tch in last trio: clsd over 2f out: drvn and no hdwy wl over 1f out: wknd ins fnl f* **11/2**[3]
1101 **7** ¾ **Green Zone (IRE)**[16] 5349 3-9-3 76 (p) HayleyTurner 5 66
(Nigel Tinkler) *t.k.h: hld up in tch in last trio: effrt on inner over 2f out: no rspnse and sn struggling: wknd over 1f out* **5/1**[2]

1m 43.35s (0.05) **Going Correction** -0.075s/f (Good) 7 Ran SP% **109.8**
Speed ratings (Par 102): **96,94,92,92,90 87,87**
CSF £107.64 TOTE £12.40: £4.00, £4.00; EX 148.30 Trifecta £751.40.
**Owner** Tim Dykes **Bred** Team Valor **Trained** Eastbury, Berks

**FOCUS**
Although run at a decent gallop, there was a bit of a turn up in this handicap.

## 5931 DANIELLE WREN WILL YOU MARRY ME? H'CAP 1m 2f 7y
5:30 (5:34) (Class 4) (0-85,82) 3-Y-0+ £5,175 (£1,540; £769; £384) Stalls Low

Form RPR
0-00 **1** **War Singer (USA)**[42] 4441 7-9-5 75 (bt[1]) JimCrowley 9 85
(Johnny Farrelly) *hld up in last pair: swtchd lft and hdwy on outer after 2f: led 6f out and sn clr: 3 l clr and rdn 2f out: kpt on and a jst holding on cl home* **25/1**
4426 **2** nk **Little Buxted (USA)**[14] 5442 4-9-2 72 JoeFanning 5 81
(Robert Mills) *in midfield early: grad stdd into last trio: c wd of rivals and hdwy in centre over 2f out: styd on to chse clr wnr ins fnl f: grad clsd fnl 100yds: nvr quite getting to wnr* **14/1**
1-26 **3** 2 ½ **Norway Cross**[93] 2700 4-9-11 81 AndreaAtzeni 12 85
(Luca Cumani) *pressed ldr tl led after 2f: hdd and chsd clr ldr 6f out: rdn over 2f out: 3 l down and drvn 2f out: 3rd and plugged on same pce ins fnl f* **5/2**[2]
221 **4** 2 ¼ **Telefono**[68] 3525 3-9-4 82 JamesDoyle 4 82
(Amanda Perrett) *led for 2f: grad stdd bk and in tch in midfield: rdn over 2f out: drvn over 1f out: plugged on same pce fnl f* **9/4**[1]
0-00 **5** 3 ½ **Topamichi**[17] 5299 4-9-4 74[1] KierenFallon 2 67
(Mark H Tompkins) *t.k.h: hld up in midfield: rdn over 2f out: no prog: wl hld and plugged on same pce fnl 2f* **17/2**
3 **6** 3 **First Post (IRE)**[19] 5251 7-9-4 74 DaneO'Neill 6 62
(Derek Haydn Jones) *t.k.h: chsd ldrs early: plenty to do and rdn over 2f out: drvn and no prog over 1f out: wknd ins fnl f* **8/1**
0623 **7** 7 **Tight Lipped (IRE)**[88] 2876 5-9-0 73 RyanTate(3) 1 47
(James Eustace) *pressed ldr for 3f: lost pl and rdn over 2f out: sn wl btn* **11/2**[3]
3420 **8** 7 **Jack Of Diamonds (IRE)**[24] 5040 5-8-13 74 CamHardie(5) 3 35
(Roger Teal) *hld up in last pair: rdn and no hdwy over 2f out: sn wl btn* **11/1**

0-0 **9** *32* **Ruggero**[15] 5379 4-9-9 79 TedDurcan 11
(Roy Brotherton) *in tch towards rr: rdn and lost tch 3f out: wl t.o and eased fnl f* **33/1**

2m 9.33s (-1.17) **Going Correction** -0.075s/f (Good)
**WFA** 3 from 4yo+ 8lb 9 Ran SP% **118.2**
Speed ratings (Par 105): **101,100,98,96,94 91,86,80,54**
CSF £335.44 CT £1197.37 TOTE £33.30: £7.20, £3.80, £1.60; EX 248.90 Trifecta £2149.70 Part won..
**Owner** The War Cabinet **Bred** Hertrich-McCarthy Livestock **Trained** Enmore, Somerset

**FOCUS**
The field was tightly grouped early on, with little seemingly wanting to lead, and an enterprising piece of riding by Jim Crowley made the difference.
T/Jkpt: Not won. T/Plt: £1,193.70 to a £1 stake. Pool: £174,580.66 - 106.76 winning tickets
T/Qpdt: £198.30 to a £1 stake. Pool: £10,746.88 - 40.10 winning tickets SP

## 2814 BADEN-BADEN (L-H)
Saturday, August 30

**OFFICIAL GOING: Turf: soft**

### 5938a PREIS DER SPARKASSEN FINANZGRUPPE (GROUP 3) (4YO+) (TURF) 1m 2f
3:50 (12:00) 4-Y-0+
**£26,666** (£9,166; £4,583; £2,500; £1,666; £1,250)

RPR

**1** **Nausica Time (GER)**[34] 4720 4-8-10 0 AHelfenbein 4 111+
(S Smrczek, Germany) *a.p: rdn to chal into st: led over 1f out: styd on strly against rail and asserted ins fnl f: readily* **93/10**

**2** *2 ½* **Nuntius (GER)**[48] 4-8-11 0 EPedroza 2 107
(A Wohler, Germany) *t.k.h: trckd ldr: chal bef st and sn led: rdn and hdd over 1f out: styd on but nt pce of wnr fnl f* **18/5**[1]

**3** *2 ½* **Zazou (GER)**[34] 4720 7-9-2 0 APietsch 1 107
(Waldemar Hickst, Germany) *dwlt and hld up in last: smooth hdwy into st: rdn and wnt 3rd over 1f out: effrt ent fnl f: sn outpcd by front pair: styd on* **92/10**

**4** *1 ¼* **Polish Vulcano (GER)**[34] 4720 6-9-2 0 JBojko 12 105
(H-J Groschel, Germany) *dropped in fr wdst draw and hld up in midfield: clsd bef st: rdn 3f out: styd on and wnt 4th ins fnl f: nt pce to chal* **104/10**

**5** *1 ¼* **Ever Strong (GER)**[77] 6-9-0 0 FilipMinarik 13 100
(Dr A Bolte, Germany) *dropped in fr wdst draw and hld up towards rr: rdn and clsd 2f out: outpcd by ldrs fnl f: kpt on for wl hld 5th* **223/10**

**6** *½* **Quinzieme Monarque (USA)**[20] 4-8-11 0 MrVinzenzSchiergen 3 96
(P Schiergen, Germany) *dwlt and hld up in rr: rdn and clsd over 2f out: racd alone towards far side rail early in st: angled across to join remainder ent fnl f: kpt on same pce and wl hld after* **29/1**

**7** *3* **Bermuda Reef (IRE)**[34] 4720 4-9-2 0 AdriedeVries 7 95
(P Schiergen, Germany) *prom: rdn and effrt to chal into st: outpcd by ldrs over 1f out: plugged on but wl hld fnl f* **23/5**[2]

**8** *3* **Messi (GER)**[41] 4-9-0 0 RobertHavlin 10 87
(P Harley, Germany) *t.k.h: hld up towards rr: rdn 3f out: no imp and wl btn fnl f: nvr threatened* **236/10**

**9** *½* **Vanishing Cupid (SWI)**[55] 4006 4-9-0 0 (b) FabriceVeron 6 86
(H-A Pantall, France) *midfield: rdn 3f out: brief effrt early in st: sn outpcd: wknd fnl f* **47/10**[3]

**10** *nse* **Nicolosio (IRE)**[14] 5461 4-9-0 0 SHellyn 5 86
(Waldemar Hickst, Germany) *bobbled s: t.k.h: midfield: clsd and prom bef st: rdn and brief effrt 2f out: outpcd whn briefly squeezed for room over 1f out: sn btn: wknd and eased fnl f* **48/10**

**11** *3* **Emily Of Tinsdal (GER)**[20] 5231 5-8-10 0 DanielePorcu 8 76
(P Harley, Germany) *t.k.h: midfield: rdn 3f out: effrt to cl whn short of room briefly over 1f out: so no imp and btn: wknd and eased fnl f* **11/1**

**12** *29* **S Arancha (USA)**[41] 5-8-8 0 MichaelCadeddu 11 16
(J Hirschberger, Germany) *led: strly pressed bef st and sn hdd: rdn and qckly btn: wknd: eased and t.o* **248/10**

**13** *8* **Ideal (GER)**[6] 4-8-11 0 NRichter 9 3
(Ferdinand J Leve, Germany) *midfield on outer: rdn and lost pl bef st: sn last and btn: eased and t.o* **36/1**

2m 7.06s (2.07) 13 Ran SP% **129.3**
PARI-MUTUEL (all including 10 euro stake): WIN 103; PLACES 28, 18, 31; SF 484.
**Owner** Ulrich Zerrath **Bred** Stall No Doubt **Trained** Germany

5939 - (Foreign Racing) - See Raceform Interactive

## 5900 DEAUVILLE (R-H)
Saturday, August 30

**OFFICIAL GOING: Turf: very soft, polytrack: standard**

### 5940a PRIX DE SAINT-PIERRE AZIF (MAIDEN) (2YO COLTS & GELDINGS) (TURF) 1m (R)
11:45 (12:00) 2-Y-0 **£10,416** (£4,166; £3,125; £2,083; £1,041)

RPR

**1** **Cherek (FR)**[22] 2-9-2 0 ChristopheSoumillon 5 82
(J-C Rouget, France) **2/5**[1]

**2** *¾* **Detmann (FR)**[53] 2-9-2 0 JohanVictoire 3 80
(Y Durepaire, France) **124/10**[3]

**3** *1 ¾* **Green Sweet (USA)**[22] 2-9-2 0 OlivierPeslier 1 77
(F Head, France) **18/5**[2]

**4** *1* **Zariyano (FR)** 2-9-2 0 ThierryJarnet 2 74
(H-A Pantall, France) **126/10**

**5** *¾* **Badet (FR)** 2-9-2 0 CristianDemuro 4 73
(L A Urbano-Grajales, France) **163/10**

**6** *8* **I See You (FR)**[43] 2-9-2 0 StephanePasquier 7 55
(Mlle A Voraz, France) **42/1**

**7** *1* **Clever Love (FR)**[10] 5588 2-9-2 0 MickaelBarzalona 6 53
(Jo Hughes) *led: rdn and hdd over 1f out: wknd and dropped to last fnl f* **31/1**

1m 49.35s (8.55) 7 Ran SP% **119.2**
WIN (incl. 1 euro stake): 1.40. PLACES: 1.10, 2.00. SF: 8.50.
**Owner** H H Aga Khan **Bred** His Highness The Aga Khan's Studs S C **Trained** Pau, France

### 5941a PRIX DE PUTOT-EN-AUGE (MAIDEN) (2YO FILLIES) (TURF) 1m (R)
12:45 (12:00) 2-Y-0 **£10,416** (£4,166; £3,125; £2,083; £1,041)

RPR

**1** **Daramakfi (FR)**[27] 2-9-0 0 OlivierPeslier 3 79
(F Head, France) **4/5**[1]

**2** *¾* **Strelkita (FR)**[22] 2-9-0 0 GregoryBenoist 8 77
(D Smaga, France) **84/10**

**3** *1 ½* **Elegante (FR)**[22] 2-9-0 0 AnthonyCrastus 5 74
(E Lellouche, France) **106/10**

**4** *4* **Sculptured (FR)**[10] 5590 2-9-0 0 ThomasHenderson 6 65
(Jo Hughes) *led early: sn hdd and trckd ldr: cl 2nd 3f out: rdn and effrt 2f out: stl ev ch ent fnl f: no ex sn after: fdd* **58/10**[3]

**5** *½* **Shanawest (FR)** 2-9-0 0 UmbertoRispoli 1 64
(C Scandella, France) **201/10**

**6** *½* **Entree Parfaite (FR)**[18] 5293 2-9-0 0 StephanePasquier 7 63
(Yannick Fouin, France) **193/10**

**7** *7* **Fleur De Printemps**[18] 5293 2-9-0 0 CristianDemuro 9 48
(F Vermeulen, France) **53/10**[2]

**8** *2 ½* **Caritas (GER)**[76] 2-9-0 0 Christophe-PatriceLemaire 4 42
(M Nigge, France) **54/1**

**9** *2 ½* **La Giovanella (FR)**[10] 5590 2-9-0 0 WilliamsSaraiva 2 37
(Alex Fracas, France) **237/10**

1m 49.31s (8.51) 9 Ran SP% **120.9**
WIN (incl. 1 euro stake): 1.80. Places: 1.10, 1.80, 1.90. DF: 7.20. SF: 9.10..
**Owner** H H Sheikh Abdulla Bin Khalifa Al Thani **Bred** Razza Pallorsi Snc **Trained** France

## 5517 BRIGHTON (L-H)
Sunday, August 31

**OFFICIAL GOING: Good (7.5)**
Wind: Moderate, across away from stands Weather: Sunny spells Rails: Rail dolled out from 7f to 2f, 4f bend at minimum width and distances increased by about 20yds

### 5945 GATWICKAIRPORT.COM H'CAP 5f 59y
2:00 (2:00) (Class 4) (0-85,84) 3-Y-0+ **£5,175** (£1,540; £769; £384) **Stalls Centre**

Form RPR

5221 **1** **Secret Missile**[17] 5350 4-9-10 84 (b) MartinDwyer 1 92
(William Muir) *mde all: drvn to hold on fnl f* **7/2**[1]

1305 **2** *¾* **Secret Millionaire (IRE)**[23] 5124 7-8-10 77 KieranShoemark(7) 6 83
(Luke Dace) *cl up in 4th: drvn to chse wnr 1f out: r.o: jst hld* **17/2**

3260 **3** *hd* **Whitecrest**[8] 5677 6-8-12 72 WilliamTwiston-Davies 8 77
(John Spearing) *towards rr: rdn over 2f out: hdwy over 1f out: r.o u.p fnl f: clsng at fin* **12/1**

3332 **4** *1 ¾* **Storm Lightning**[10] 5601 5-8-7 72 CamHardie(5) 10 71
(Mark Brisbourne) *outpcd and sn detached in last pl: gd hdwy fnl f* **5/1**[2]

0056 **5** *½* **Lady Gibraltar**[6] 5754 5-9-7 81 (b[1]) AdamKirby 3 78
(Timothy Jarvis) *prom: chsd wnr 2f out tl 1f out: hrd rdn: no ex* **8/1**[3]

0330 **6** *nk* **Dutch Interior**[35] 4697 3-9-2 78 GeorgeBaker 7 74
(Gary Moore) *chsd ldrs: outpcd 2f out: kpt on again fnl f* **5/1**[2]

0003 **7** *½* **Jiroft (ITY)**[39] 4553 7-8-13 80 (t[1]) GaryMahon(7) 5 74
(Ann Stokell) *chsd wnr tl 2f out: wknd over 1f out* **16/1**

0033 **8** *2* **Sacha Park (IRE)**[11] 5553 3-9-1 77 (b[1]) RichardHughes 9 64
(Richard Hannon) *towards rr: sme hdwy 2f out: wknd over 1f out* **5/1**[2]

2431 **9** *½* **Vodka Chaser (IRE)**[12] 5535 3-8-9 74 PhilipPrince(3) 4 60
(Alison Hutchinson) *mid-div on rail: effrt 2f out: wknd 1f out* **9/1**

1m 3.1s (0.80) **Going Correction** +0.10s/f (Good)
**WFA** 3 from 4yo+ 2lb 9 Ran SP% **117.4**
Speed ratings (Par 105): **97,95,95,92,91 91,90,87,86**
CSF £34.60 CT £326.09 TOTE £4.00: £1.70, £3.20, £4.00; EX 28.00 Trifecta £214.30.
**Owner** Muir Racing Partnership - Manchester **Bred** Whitsbury Manor Stud **Trained** Lambourn, Berks

**FOCUS**
A fair sprint for the level.

### 5946 LGWOBVIOUSLY MAIDEN AUCTION STKS 5f 59y
2:30 (2:30) (Class 6) 2-Y-0 **£2,587** (£770; £384) **Stalls Centre**

Form RPR

2362 **1** **Tongue Twista**[13] 5509 2-8-8 88 JimCrowley 2 78
(Nick Littmoden) *mde all: rdn 2f out: hld on wl fnl f* **4/7**[1]

054 **2** *½* **Pretty Picture**[10] 5617 2-8-8 0 DavidProbert 1 76
(Gay Kelleway) *trckd ldng pair: drvn to press wnr 1f out: r.o: jst hld* **6/1**[3]

23 **3** *4 ½* **Rock Follies**[18] 5297 2-8-9 0 ow1 RichardHughes 4 64
(Lady Cecil) *pressed ldr tl rdn and btn 1f out: eased fnl 50yds* **5/2**[2]

1m 4.31s (2.01) **Going Correction** +0.10s/f (Good) 3 Ran SP% **106.5**
Speed ratings (Par 92): **87,86,79**
CSF £3.93 TOTE £1.70; EX 3.80 Trifecta £3.50.
**Owner** Franconson Partners & Nick Littmoden **Bred** Llety Farms **Trained** Newmarket, Suffolk

**FOCUS**
Little depth to this small-field maiden.

### 5947 TEMPTED BEFORE TAKEOFF MAIDEN STKS (BOBIS RACE) 6f 209y
3:00 (3:01) (Class 4) 2-Y-0 **£4,204** (£1,251; £625; £312) **Stalls Centre**

Form RPR

02 **1** **Grand Spirit (IRE)**[25] 5029 2-9-5 0 AdamKirby 7 86+
(Luca Cumani) *hld up in 6th: hdwy 2f out: led over 1f out: edgd lft: rdn clr* **6/4**[1]

0 **2** *3 ¾* **River Dart (IRE)**[16] 5377 2-9-5 0 GeorgeBaker 1 73
(Marcus Tregoning) *t.k.h: led tl over 1f out: one pce: hld whn crossed by wnr sn after* **10/1**

642 **3** *1 ¾* **Nufooth (IRE)**[29] 4906 2-9-0 70 DaneO'Neill 6 63
(Richard Hannon) *a.p: one pce appr fnl f* **7/2**[2]

**4** *3* **Consortium (IRE)** 2-9-5 0 JimCrowley 2 60+
(David Simcock) *hld up towards rr: promising hdwy over 1f out: shkn up and no ex fnl f* **11/2**[3]

**5** *2 ½* **Greatest Journey** 2-9-5 0 HarryBentley 5 53+
(Saeed bin Suroor) *s.s: hld: rdn 3f out: sme late hdwy* **7/2**[2]

00 **6** *1 ¼* **Noble Master**[63] 3748 2-9-5 0 DavidProbert 4 50
(Sylvester Kirk) *chsd ldrs: stmbld on road after 1f: wknd over 1f out* **66/1**

0 **7** *4* **Polydus**[9] 5646 2-9-5 0 WilliamTwiston-Davies 8 39
(Ed Dunlop) *in tch tl wknd over 1f out* **25/1**

5 8 1 1/2 **King's Concerto (IRE)**[12] 5519 2-9-5 0 HayleyTurner 3 35
(Dean Ivory) *chsd ldr tl wknd over 1f out* 33/1
1m 25.76s (2.66) **Going Correction** +0.10s/f (Good) **8** Ran SP% **117.2**
Speed ratings (Par 96): **88,83,81,78,75 74,69,67**
CSF £18.72 TOTE £2.70: £1.10, £2.50, £1.40; EX 13.60 Trifecta £78.40.
**Owner** Bruce Corman **Bred** Maurice Regan **Trained** Newmarket, Suffolk

## 5948 EBF / FAMILY FRIENDLY GATWICK AIRPORT FILLIES H'CAP 1m 1f 209y
3:30 (3:31) (Class 4) (0-85,83) 3-Y-O+ £8,086 (£2,406; £1,202; £601) Stalls High

Form RPR
-641 1 **Arabian Beauty (IRE)**[16] 5371 3-9-0 77 (p) KierenFallon 8 86
(Saeed bin Suroor) *dwlt: hld up towards rr: hdwy 2f out: slt ld over 1f out: hrd rdn and hung lft: all out* 3/1[1]
2044 2 shd **Yojojo (IRE)**[24] 5074 5-10-0 83 DavidProbert 6 91
(Gay Kelleway) *stdd s: t.k.h in rr: hdwy on stands' rail over 2f out: jnd wnr over 1f out: hung lft: kpt on wl* 7/1
0-33 3 4 1/2 **Russian Royale**[37] 4617 4-9-2 71 (p) RichardHughes 1 70
(Stuart Kittow) *chsd ldrs: one pce appr fnl f* 5/1[3]
6321 4 shd **Choral Festival**[21] 5214 8-9-1 70 WilliamCarson 3 69
(John Bridger) *towards rr: rdn 3f out: hdwy to ld briefly wl over 1f out: no ex fnl f* 14/1
2214 5 4 1/2 **Thatchereen (IRE)**[16] 5401 3-8-7 75 DanielMuscutt(5) 5 66
(Michael Bell) *chsd ldrs: hrd rdn 2f out: wknd over 1f out* 3/1[1]
1303 6 5 **Martinas Delight (USA)**[13] 5503 4-9-6 75 AdamKirby 4 56
(Timothy Jarvis) *led tl hrd rdn and wknd wl over 1f out* 20/1
3331 7 1 1/2 **Loch Ma Naire (IRE)**[17] 5340 3-9-1 78 (b) GeorgeBaker 7 56
(Ed Dunlop) *t.k.h: sn prom on outer: jnd ldr 7f out tl 3f out: wknd 2f out* 4/1[2]
5332 8 1 **Taro Tywod (IRE)**[19] 5284 5-8-13 73 CamHardie(5) 2 49
(Mark Brisbourne) *chsd ldrs tl wknd 2f out* 16/1
2m 4.15s (0.55) **Going Correction** +0.10s/f (Good)
**WFA** 3 from 4yo+ 8lb **8** Ran SP% **116.5**
Speed ratings (Par 105): **101,100,97,97,93 89,88,87**
CSF £25.23 CT £102.21 TOTE £4.80: £1.50, £2.20, £2.00; EX 30.90 Trifecta £124.00.
**Owner** Godolphin **Bred** Darley **Trained** Newmarket, Suffolk

**FOCUS**
The front pair pulled clear.

## 5949 GATWICK AIRPORT SUPPORTS CANCER RESEARCH UK H'CAP 1m 3f 196y
4:00 (4:01) (Class 6) (0-65,65) 3-Y-O £2,587 (£770; £384; £192) Stalls High

Form RPR
0445 1 **Hallbeck**[25] 5036 3-9-6 64 DaneO'Neill 2 75
(Henry Candy) *mde all: drvn clr ins fnl 2f: r.o wl: readily* 7/2[2]
0560 2 3 3/4 **Dark Days**[52] 4134 3-8-9 53 MartinLane 1 58
(Paul Cole) *in tch: rdn to dispute 2nd 2f out: one pce* 7/1
5325 3 1 **Tunnel Tiger (IRE)**[12] 5529 3-8-11 60 JackDuern(5) 6 63
(William Knight) *chsd ldrs: disp 2nd 2f out tl no ex ins fnl f* 9/2[3]
103 4 5 **Roman Riches**[4] 5829 3-9-4 62 (v) GeorgeBaker 4 57
(Gary Moore) *hld up in rr: rdn over 2f out: hung lft: no imp* 6/1
5000 5 32 **I Am Not Here (IRE)**[18] 5313 3-9-0 58 KierenFallon 3
(Timothy Jarvis) *chsd ldrs tl wknd over 2f out: wl btn and eased over 1f out* 25/1
3051 6 22 **Lochalsh (IRE)**[19] 5277 3-9-7 65 RichardHughes 5
(William Knight) *pressed wnr tl 3f out: 4th and hld whn eased over 1f out* 5/4[1]
2m 36.33s (3.63) **Going Correction** +0.10s/f (Good) **6** Ran SP% **115.5**
Speed ratings (Par 98): **91,88,87,84,63 48**
CSF £27.97 TOTE £4.20: £1.70, £3.40; EX 27.20 Trifecta £89.20.
**Owner** Major M G Wyatt **Bred** Dunchurch Lodge Stud Co **Trained** Kingston Warren, Oxon

**FOCUS**
Modest form.

## 5950 GATWICK AIRPORT SUPPORTS CHESTNUT TREE HOUSE APPRENTICE H'CAP 7f 214y
4:30 (4:30) (Class 5) (0-70,69) 4-Y-O+ £3,234 (£962; £481; £240) Stalls Centre

Form RPR
0315 1 **Emman Bee (IRE)**[15] 5425 5-9-7 67 DanielMuscutt(3) 5 80
(Luke Dace) *hld up in tch: smooth hdwy and squeezed through on inner to ld over 1f out: sn clr: easily* 5/1
2121 2 7 **Hawk Moth (IRE)**[12] 5523 6-8-13 61 (p) KieranShoemark(5) 4 58
(John Spearing) *bhd: rdn and hdwy 2f out: styd on to take 2nd nr fin* 7/2[1]
5412 3 3/4 **Rouge Nuage (IRE)**[2] 5899 4-9-7 69 (b) JordanNason(5) 9 64
(Conrad Allen) *pressed ldr: led 2f out: hung lft and hdd over 1f out: sn outpcd* 4/1[2]
143 4 1 1/4 **Elle Rebelle**[24] 5075 4-8-6 52 CamHardie(3) 7 44
(Mark Brisbourne) *dwlt: hld up in rr: hdwy 3f out: sn drvn along: styd on same pce* 5/1
2563 5 nk **Enriching (USA)**[12] 5537 6-8-11 61 (b[1]) JackOsborn(7) 3 53
(Nick Littmoden) *chsd ldrs for 3f: lost pl: n.d fnl 3f* 14/1
005 6 5 **Le Deluge (FR)**[7] 5721 4-9-3 65 (t) GaryMahon(5) 8 45
(Ann Stokell) *led at str pce tl 2f out: wknd over 1f out* 9/2[3]
2643 7 3/4 **Byrd In Hand (IRE)**[15] 5425 7-9-1 58 CharlesBishop 2 36
(John Bridger) *prom tl wknd over 2f out* 8/1
4024 8 1 1/4 **Hierarch (IRE)**[12] 5523 7-9-5 69 (p) SophieKilloran(7) 1 45
(David Simcock) *hld up in 6th: n.m.r on rail 5f out: bhd fnl 2f* 14/1
1m 36.09s (0.09) **Going Correction** +0.10s/f (Good) **8** Ran SP% **118.2**
Speed ratings (Par 103): **103,96,95,94,93 88,87,86**
CSF £23.72 CT £78.47 TOTE £6.50: £2.60, £1.70, £1.70; EX 22.00 Trifecta £109.90.
**Owner** Mark Benton **Bred** O Bourke **Trained** Okehurst Lane, W Sussex

**FOCUS**
A moderate handicap, run at a good gallop.

## 5951 GATWICK AIRPORT SUPPORTS GATWICK TRAVELCARE H'CAP 5f 213y
5:00 (5:00) (Class 5) (0-75,75) 3-Y-O+ £3,234 (£962; £481; £240) Stalls Centre

Form RPR
545 1 **Alnoomaas (IRE)**[9] 5629 5-9-1 66 (v[1]) RichardHughes 6 75
(Luke Dace) *in tch: effrt over 2f out: led ins fnl f: rdn out* 5/1[2]
3115 2 1/2 **Parisian Pyramid (IRE)**[7] 5726 8-9-4 72 (p) ThomasBrown(3) 3 79
(Lee Carter) *sluggish s: towards rr: hdwy 2f out: led 1f out tl ins fnl f: kpt on* 13/2[3]
0451 3 1 3/4 **Perfect Pastime**[12] 5518 6-8-11 62 (p) PatCosgrave 1 64
(Jim Boyle) *in tch: effrt and swtchd rt over 1f out: kpt on fnl f* 3/1[1]
0052 4 2 **Jontleman (IRE)**[12] 5523 4-9-3 71 CharlesBishop(3) 5 66
(Mick Channon) *chsd ldrs: hung lft and chal over 1f out: one pce* 3/1[1]
0005 5 1/2 **Prince Regal**[5] 5784 4-9-7 72 KierenFallon 7 66
(Timothy Jarvis) *sn w ldr: led after 2f tl over 2f out: wknd jst over 1f out* 7/1
5551 6 2 **Aye Aye Digby (IRE)**[22] 5182 9-9-10 75 GeorgeBaker 4 62
(Patrick Chamings) *led tl 4f out: led over 2f out tl 1f out: wknd ins fnl f* 5/1[2]
1300 7 2 1/4 **Amenable (IRE)**[10] 5601 7-9-8 73 (p) HayleyTurner 2 53
(Conor Dore) *prom tl wknd 2f out* 25/1
0100 8 3 **Meridius (IRE)**[15] 5422 4-9-0 65 (p) JimCrowley 8 36
(Nick Littmoden) *bhd: effrt in centre over 2f out: sn wknd* 14/1
1m 11.65s (1.45) **Going Correction** +0.10s/f (Good) **8** Ran SP% **119.7**
Speed ratings (Par 103): **94,93,91,88,87 85,82,78**
CSF £39.07 CT £117.10 TOTE £6.00: £1.60, £1.70, £1.50; EX 36.60 Trifecta £126.40.
**Owner** Mark Benton **Bred** Old Carhue & Graeng Bloodstock **Trained** Okehurst Lane, W Sussex

**FOCUS**
A modest sprint.
T/Jkpt: £3,108.70 to a £1 stake. Pool: £19,703.10 - 4.50 winning units T/Plt: £80.00 to a £1 stake. Pool: £106,019.47 - 966.67 winning units T/Qpdt: £21.60 to a £1 stake. Pool: £8,646.69 - 295.23 winning units LM

# 5732 CURRAGH (R-H)
Sunday, August 31

**OFFICIAL GOING: Round course - good - straight course - good to yielding**

## 5954a NESTLE SUPPORTING IRISH AUTISM ACTION ROUND TOWER STKS (GROUP 3) 6f
3:05 (3:05) 2-Y-O £32,500 (£9,500; £4,500; £1,500)

RPR
1 **Cappella Sansevero**[21] 5218 2-9-3 113 AndreaAtzeni 4 109+
(G M Lyons, Ire) *hld up bhd ldrs: 5th 1/2-way: gng wl 2f out and sn swtchd rt: qcknd between horses in 3rd ent fnl f to sn ld: rdn out towards fin* 6/4[1]
2 3/4 **Rapid Applause**[43] 4460 2-9-3 103 FergalLynch 5 107
(M D O'Callaghan, Ire) *trckd ldrs: clsr in 2nd bef 1/2-way: rdn to ld narrowly briefly over 1f out: sn hdd and no imp on wnr ins fnl 100yds: kpt on wl* 9/2[3]
3 3/4 **War Envoy (USA)**[64] 3738 2-9-3 104 JosephO'Brien 2 105
(A P O'Brien, Ire) *hld up bhd ldrs: 6th 1/2-way: impr into 3rd over 1f out and ev ch almost on terms: no ex u.p ins fnl 150yds* 5/2[2]
4 nk **Shepherd's Purse**[8] 5698 2-9-3 GaryCarroll 6 105
(Joseph G Murphy, Ire) *chsd ldrs: 4th 1/2-way: nt clr run gng wl nr side fr 2f out: swtchd rt over 1f out and sn rdn: kpt on towards fin: nvr trbld ldrs* 11/2
5 2 1/2 **Approbare (IRE)**[53] 4097 2-9-3 FMBerry 3 96
(T M Walsh, Ire) *w.w in rr: last 1/2-way: clsr bhd ldrs in 6th 1 1/2f out: rdn and no imp on ldrs ins fnl f: kpt on same pce into 5th clsng stages: nvr trbld ldrs* 50/1
6 1/2 **Blackbriar**[26] 5019 2-9-0 93 (p) WayneLordan 7 92
(T Stack, Ire) *led nr side: 1 l clr 1/2-way: rdn and hdd over 1f out: sn no ex u.p: wknd* 14/1
7 6 **Invincible Diamond (IRE)**[12] 5538 2-9-3 AdrianO'Shea 1 77
(Mrs A M O'Shea, Ire) *sn trckd ldrs: racd keenly early: 3rd 1/2-way: rdn and wknd 2f out* 25/1
1m 13.49s (-2.01) **Going Correction** -0.35s/f (Firm) **7** Ran SP% **114.6**
Speed ratings: **99,98,97,96,93 92,84**
CSF £8.84 TOTE £2.20: £1.40, £2.50; DF 9.50 Trifecta £13.70.
**Owner** Qatar Racing Limited **Bred** Genesis Green Stud Ltd **Trained** Dunsany, Co Meath

**FOCUS**
The winner was the clear pick and did this quite well. He may yet build on his Phoenix Stakes form.

## 5955a XTRAVISION & HMV SUPPORTING IRISH AUTISM ACTION DANCE DESIGN FILLIES STKS (GROUP 3) 1m 1f
3:35 (3:36) 3-Y-O+ £32,500 (£9,500; £4,500; £1,500)

RPR
1 **Carla Bianca (IRE)**[18] 5324 3-9-0 105 PatSmullen 3 108
(D K Weld, Ire) *chsd ldrs: 5th 1/2-way: impr on outer fr under 3f out: rdn into 2nd 1 1/2f out: and kpt on wl u.p to ld ins fnl 100yds* 5/4[1]
2 1 **Pearl Of Africa (IRE)**[63] 3766 4-9-7 107 AndreaAtzeni 9 106
(Edward Lynam, Ire) *s.i.s and racd in rr: clsr in 8th bef 1/2-way: prog fr over 2f out to chse ldrs in 3rd ins fnl f: r.o wl towards fin into 2nd cl home: a hld* 9/2[2]
3 1/2 **Alive Alive Oh**[18] 5324 4-9-7 99 FMBerry 7 105
(T Stack, Ire) *chsd ldrs: clsr in 3rd 1/2-way: prog gng wl to ld under 2f out: sn strly pressed and hdd u.p ins fnl 100yds: no ex in 3rd clsng stages* 7/1
4 3/4 **Waltzing Matilda (IRE)**[43] 4459 3-9-0 104 (p) WayneLordan 6 103+
(T Stack, Ire) *in tch: 7th 1/2-way: outpcd and dropped to rr over 2f out: kpt on again u.p ins fnl f into nvr threatening 4th fnl stride: nt trble principals* 6/1[3]
5 shd **Akira (IRE)**[11] 5584 4-9-7 94 NGMcCullagh 2 103
(J R Barry, Ire) *hld up towards rr: clsr in 6th bef 1/2-way: impr bhd horses 2f out: sn rdn disputing 3rd and no imp on ldrs in 4th ins fnl f: denied 4th on line* 33/1
6 1 **Beyond Brilliance (IRE)**[18] 5324 3-9-0 101 AnaO'Brien 5 101
(A P O'Brien, Ire) *chsd ldrs early tl sn dropped to rr: last 1/2-way: sme hdwy far side fr over 2f out to chse ldrs in 6th: no ex u.p ins fnl f: kpt on one pce* 20/1
7 1 1/4 **Mizzava (IRE)**[11] 5584 4-9-7 97 ColmO'Donoghue 1 98
(M Halford, Ire) *chsd ldrs: 4th 1/2-way: rdn into st and sn no ex u.p: one pce fnl 2f* 25/1
8 3 1/2 **Palace (IRE)**[17] 5361 3-9-0 102 (p) JosephO'Brien 8 91
(A P O'Brien, Ire) *chsd ldrs: clsr in 2nd after 1f: cl 2nd 1/2-way: rdn to ld over 2f out: sn hdd and no ex whn short of room between horses and checked: wknd* 9/2[2]
9 7 **Shanooan (USA)**[26] 5022 3-9-0 95 ConnorKing 4 76
(George Kent, Ire) *led: narrow advantage 1/2-way: rdn and hdd over 2f out: sn wknd* 66/1
1m 56.9s (2.00) **Going Correction** +0.325s/f (Good)
**WFA** 3 from 4yo 7lb **9** Ran SP% **120.6**
Speed ratings: **104,103,102,102,101 101,99,96,90**
CSF £7.27 TOTE £2.10: £1.50, £1.50, £2.10; DF 6.20 Trifecta £26.20.
**Owner** Moyglare Stud Farm **Bred** Moyglare Stud Farm Ltd **Trained** Curragh, Co Kildare

**FOCUS**
The performance of the fifth is the only question mark against the form.

## 5957a IRISH STALLION FARMS EUROPEAN BREEDERS FUND IRISH CAMBRIDGESHIRE (PREMIER H'CAP) 1m

**4:35** (4:38) 3-Y-0+

**£50,000** (£15,833; £7,500; £2,500; £1,666; £833)

RPR

1 **Sretaw (IRE)**[31] 4835 5-8-8 **84**.....(bt) WayneLordan 16 89
(Gavin Cromwell, Ire) *w.w in rr of mid-div: hdwy fr 2f out nr side and clsd u.p ins fnl f to ld clsng stages* **11/1**

2 ½ **Vastonea (IRE)**[14] 5477 6-8-13 **96**..... GaryHalpin(7) 19 100
(Kevin Prendergast, Ire) *in rr of mid-div: hdwy u.p fr 2f out to chse ldrs whn n.m.r between horses ent fnl f: kpt on wl in 3rd wl ins fnl f into 2nd cl home: hld* **16/1**

3 hd **Hasanour (USA)**[8] 5700 4-8-7 **83** 5ex..... ShaneFoley 11 87
(M Halford, Ire) *racd in mid-div: 10th 1/2-way: hdwy fr under 2f out and n.m.r between horses over 1f out: rdn and clsd u.p to dispute whn edgd lft fnl 150yds: sn led briefly tl hdd clsng stages* **4/1**[1]

4 ¾ **Maggie Dalton (IRE)**[43] 4458 5-9-4 **94**..... RonanWhelan 15 96
(J S Bolger, Ire) *w.w towards rr: n.m.r bhd horses over 1f out: rdn and r.o wl: nrst fin* **25/1**

5 hd **Canary Row (IRE)**[99] 2574 4-9-7 **97**.....(b) DeclanMcDonogh 5 98
(P J Prendergast, Ire) *trckd ldrs: 2nd 1/2-way: disp fr 2f out: hdd u.p ent fnl f and kpt on one pce in 4th: denied 4th fnl stride* **20/1**

6 ½ **No Dominion (IRE)**[8] 5700 5-8-7 **86**..... ConnorKing(3) 6 86
(A Oliver, Ire) *disp early tl sn led: jnd fr 2f out: rdn w narrow advantage ent fnl f tl hdd ins fnl 150yds whn edgd rt briefly: no ex and wknd towards fin* **12/1**

7 nk **Burn The Boats (IRE)**[51] 4246 5-9-7 **97**..... ColinKeane 10 97
(G M Lyons, Ire) *in rr of mid-div: tk clsr order gng wl over 1f out: rdn ins fnl f and sn n.m.r bhd horses: swtchd rt and kpt on wl towards fin* **14/1**

8 nk **Captain Joy (IRE)**[64] 3741 5-9-11 **101**..... JosephO'Brien 18 100
(Tracey Collins, Ire) *chsd ldrs: 6th 1/2-way: rdn 2f out and sn one pce* **16/1**

9 ½ **Warbird**[70] 3510 3-8-8 **95**..... SeanCorby(5) 13 92
(M Halford, Ire) *chsd ldrs: 5th 1/2-way: rdn in 3rd over 1f out and sn squeezed for room between horses and bdly hmpd: no imp after* **20/1**

10 hd **Sophie's World (IRE)**[32] 4806 3-8-2 **91**.....(p) TomMadden(7) 9 87
(Kevin F O'Donnell, Ire) *towards rr: rdn in rr: 1 1/2f out and sme late hdwy ins fnl f: nvr nrr* **14/1**

11 nk **Muharrer**[29] 4922 5-9-1 **91**..... FergalLynch 7 88
(Michael Dods) *on toes befhand: hld up towards rr: prog fr 2f out: swtchd rt far side over 1f out and sn no ex u.p: one pce towards fin* **12/1**

12 ¾ **Move To Strike (IRE)**[504] 1555 4-9-4 **94**..... RoryCleary 21 89
(J S Bolger, Ire) *racd in mid-div: pushed along 2f out and sn no imp towards rr: kpt on again towards fin* **33/1**

13 shd **Billyford (IRE)**[13] 5514 9-8-4 **80**..... LeighRoche 20 75
(Liam Roche, Ire) *chsd ldrs: 3rd 1/2-way: rdn and wknd 2f out* **66/1**

14 shd **Strait Of Zanzibar (USA)**[27] 4989 5-8-11 **87**.....(t) NGMcCullagh 17 81
(K J Condon, Ire) *disp early: sn settled bhd ldrs: 7th 1/2-way: rdn and no imp fr 2f out: wknd and eased fnl f* **20/1**

15 nk **Won Diamond**[65] 3687 4-9-0 **93**..... ConorHoban(3) 8 87
(M Halford, Ire) *in rr of mid-div for most: rdn and no ex 2f out: kpt on one pce* **16/1**

16 hd **Maskoon**[33] 4771 3-8-12 **94**..... ChrisHayes 14 86
(Kevin Prendergast, Ire) *in rr of mid-div: rdn towards rr 2f out and no imp: one pce fnl f* **8/1**[2]

17 ½ **Hint Of A Tint (IRE)**[33] 4771 4-9-10 **100**.....(p) FMBerry 3 92
(David Wachman, Ire) *in rr of mid-div: sme hdwy 2f out far side gng wl: rdn over 1f out and no imp on ldrs: eased towards fin* **9/1**[3]

18 1¾ **Prime Exhibit**[28] 4950 9-8-4 **80** oh7.....(t) AndreaAtzeni 12 68
(Daniel Mark Loughnane) *racd in mid-div: rdn and wknd fr under 2f out* **20/1**

19 ¾ **Intensical (IRE)**[33] 4771 3-9-9 **105**..... KevinManning 1 90
(J S Bolger, Ire) *in tch: 8th 1/2-way: rdn and no ex fr 2f out: wknd and eased ins fnl f* **25/1**

20 2¼ **Bold Thady Quill (IRE)**[33] 4771 7-9-7 **102**.....(p) RobbieDowney(5) 2 83
(K J Condon, Ire) *towards rr: rdn and no imp fr 2f out* **25/1**

21 9 **Defining Year (IRE)**[33] 4771 6-9-5 **95**.....(b) PatSmullen 4 55
(D K Weld, Ire) *chsd ldrs: 4th 1/2-way: rdn under 2f out and eased qckly over 1f out* **8/1**[2]

1m 39.2s (-6.80) **Going Correction** -0.60s/f (Hard)
**WFA** 3 from 4yo+ 6lb **21** Ran SP% **141.9**
Speed ratings: **110,109,109,108,108 107,107,107,106,106 106,105,105,105,105 104,104,102,101,99 90**
CSF £174.24 CT £874.19 TOTE £10.50: £2.50, £4.70, £2.10, £5.00; DF 250.60 Trifecta £1114.00.
**Owner** Eamon Waters **Bred** Alymer Stud **Trained** Navan, Co. Meath

**FOCUS**
A good race as one would expect for a big handicap.

## 5958a NEWSTALK SUPPORTING IRISH AUTISM ACTION H'CAP 6f

**5:05** (5:12) 3-Y-0+ **£5,750** (£1,333; £583; £333)

RPR

1 **Captain Cullen (IRE)**[14] 5477 5-10-0 **85**..... FergalLynch 2 93
(Gerard Keane, Ire) *hld up towards rr: 17th 1/2-way: hdwy fr 2f out and sn swtchd rt to far side: r.o wl to ld ins fnl f to ld ins fnl 150yds and drvn clr* **20/1**

2 2 **Hatton Cross (IRE)**[12] 5539 5-8-4 **61** oh1.....(bt[1]) WayneLordan 10 63
(T J O'Mara, Ire) *in rr of mid-div: prog bhd horses 1 1/2f out: rdn into 4th wl ins fnl f and kpt on u.p into 2nd towards fin: nt trble wnr* **16/1**

3 ½ **Oor Jock (IRE)**[7] 5732 6-9-10 **81**.....(b) BillyLee 8 81
(Adrian McGuinness, Ire) *hld up in mid-div: hdwy far side gng wl fr 2f out to ld ins fnl f: sn strly pressed and hdd u.p ins fnl 150yds: no ch w wnr and dropped to 3rd cl home* **10/1**[3]

4 1 **Verus Delicia (IRE)**[29] 4891 5-9-4 **75**..... FMBerry 5 72+
(Daniel Mark Loughnane) *w.w: last 1/2-way: rdn and hdwy fr 2f out: kpt on wl into nvr nrr 4th wl ins fnl f: nvr trbld ldrs* **11/1**

5 1 **Pencil Hill (IRE)**[7] 5732 9-9-5 **76**..... PatSmullen 3 70
(Tracey Collins, Ire) *in tch: hdwy to chal 2f out: no ex u.p ins fnl f in 4th and dropped to 5th nr fin* **7/2**[1]

6 1 **Invincible Ridge (IRE)**[17] 5358 6-9-5 **76**.....(t) LeighRoche 9 67
(D J Bunyan, Ire) *chsd ldrs: rdn to chal 1 1/2f out and sn no ex u.p: one pce fnl f* **8/1**[2]

7 nk **Chillie Billie**[8] 5702 5-8-4 **66**.....(p) RobbieDowney(5) 14 56
(J Larkin, Ire) *chsd ldrs: 3rd 1/2-way: impr to dispute 2f out: sn rdn and no ex u.p: wknd ins fnl f* **14/1**

8 1 **Red All Star (IRE)**[13] 5514 4-9-3 **77**.....(t) ConorHoban(3) 11 64
(Patrick Martin, Ire) *cl up: 2nd 1/2-way: effrt under 2f out: no ex ent fnl f and wknd* **14/1**

9 1 **Lake George (IRE)**[8] 5702 6-9-0 **71**..... RoryCleary 1 54
(James M Barrett, Ire) *towards rr: pushed along 1/2-way and no imp on ldrs u.p in 10th ins fnl f: kpt on one pce* **16/1**

10 ½ **Ramone (IRE)**[43] 4458 4-9-6 **77**..... SeamieHeffernan 18 59
(W T Farrell, Ire) *chsd ldrs: 4th 1/2-way: rdn and no ex fr under 2f out: wknd fnl f* **8/1**[2]

11 ½ **Expensive Taste (IRE)**[24] 5114 3-9-3 **77**.....(t) ChrisHayes 15 57
(A Oliver, Ire) *mid-div: tk clsr order under 2f out: rdn and no imp on ldrs ent fnl f: one pce fnl f* **12/1**

12 nk **Battleroftheboyne (IRE)**[7] 5732 5-9-1 **72**..... GaryCarroll 19 51
(Michael Mulvany, Ire) *broke wl to ld nr side early tl sn settled bhd ldrs: 5th 1/2-way: rdn and wknd fr 2f out* **20/1**

13 shd **Apache Gold (IRE)**[11] 5583 6-8-5 **62**.....(v) NGMcCullagh 20 41
(John J Walsh, Ire) *racd in mid-div: rdn and no ex 2f out: wknd* **16/1**

14 ¾ **Whaileyy (IRE)**[222] 271 6-9-13 **87**..... ShaneBKelly(3) 13 64
(M Halford, Ire) *in tch: pushed along in 8th fr 1/2-way and sn no ex u.p: wknd* **33/1**

15 1¼ **Angel Of Joy (IRE)**[25] 5065 3-9-8 **82**..... ColinKeane 7 55
(G M Lyons, Ire) *hld up: rdn and no imp 2f out* **16/1**

16 1¼ **Dynamite Dixie (IRE)**[8] 5700 5-9-9 **80**..... KevinManning 6 49
(J S Bolger, Ire) *towards rr: rdn and no imp 2f out* **14/1**

17 1¼ **Allegra Tak (ITY)**[105] 2369 8-9-3 **77**.....(tp) ConnorKing(3) 4 42
(H Rogers, Ire) *cl up and led after 1f: 1 l clr 1/2-way: rdn and hdd 2f out: sn wknd* **33/1**

18 6 **Wind Inher Sleeves (USA)**[21] 5221 3-9-8 **82**..... ShaneFoley 12 27
(M Halford, Ire) *in tch: pushed along in 11th and no ex u.p fr after 1/2-way: wknd* **25/1**

R **She's Not Simple (IRE)**[27] 4987 4-8-10 **72**.....(t) SeanCorby(5) 16
(Patrick Martin, Ire) *ref to r* **10/1**[3]

1m 12.26s (-3.24) **Going Correction** -0.35s/f (Firm)
**WFA** 3 from 4yo+ 3lb **19** Ran SP% **141.4**
Speed ratings: **107,104,103,102,101 99,99,97,96,95 95,94,94,93,92 90,88,80,**
Pick Six: @2,058.80. Pool: @36,427.30 - 8.50 winning units. Tote Aggregate: 2014 - @237,042.00 - 2013: @297,108.00 CSF £332.43 CT £3498.67 TOTE £31.50: £6.20, £3.60, £2.90, £2.10; DF 585.40.
**Owner** Ms Lisa Sheridan **Bred** Pollards Stables **Trained** Trim, Co Meath

**FOCUS**
A competitive contest.
T/Jkpt: @175.60. Pool: @5,520.39 - 22 winning tickets. T/Plt: @14.00. Pool: @38,705.27 - 1933.65 winning tickets. BF

# 5940 DEAUVILLE (R-H)

Sunday, August 31

**OFFICIAL GOING: Turf: very soft; polytrack: standard**

## 5959a PRIX DES NYMPHEAS (CLAIMER) (3YO) (POLYTRACK) 1m 4f 110y

**12:00** (12:00) 3-Y-0 **£9,583** (£3,833; £2,875; £1,916; £958)

RPR

1 **Ar Poulgwenn (IRE)**[12] 3-8-4 0.....(p) JeffersonSmith(7) 3 73
(J-C Rouget, France) **11/10**[1]

2 1¾ **T Kers (FR)**[163] 3-9-4 0..... TonyPiccone 5 77
(H Hesse, Germany) **53/10**

3 hd **Wadirum (IRE)**[16] 5404 3-8-9 0..... MllePaulineDominois(6) 4 74
(C Lotoux, France) **22/5**[2]

4 3 **Castlebay (FR)**[89] 3-8-8 0..... Christophe-PatriceLemaire 2 62
(N Bertran De Balanda, France) **113/10**

5 2½ **Danza Classica (GER)**[15] 3-8-8 0.....(p) TheoBachelot 7 58
(M Nigge, France) **27/1**

6 ¾ **Sweet Alibi (IRE)**[11] 5592 3-8-13 0.....(b) GeraldMosse 6 62
(J S Moore) *t.k.h: hld up: rdn and effrt to cl into st: sn outpcd by ldrs: plugged on for wl hld 6th* **188/10**

7 ½ **Crack The Whip (IRE)**[61] 3-8-8 0..... JeromeClaudic 9 56
(J-V Toux, France) **44/1**

8 hd **Such Fun (IRE)**[17] 5368 3-8-11 0.....(b[1]) RonanThomas 10 59
(F-H Graffard, France) **48/10**[3]

9 18 **Ptit Beaumont (FR)** 3-8-11 0..... AlexandreRoussel 1 30
(P Bourgoin, France) **79/1**

10 10 **Reminem Basc (FR)** 3-8-11 0..... YohannBourgois 8 14
(Mlle J Legatte, France) **85/1**

2m 41.8s (161.80) **10** Ran SP% **120.6**
WIN (incl. 1 euro stake): 2.10. PLACES: 1.20, 1.40, 1.40. DF: 5.10. SF: 6.20.
**Owner** J Seche & J-P Vallee-Lambert **Bred** Ecurie Des Monceaux **Trained** Pau, France

## 5960a PRIX QUINCEY LUCIEN BARRIERE (GROUP 3) (3YO+) (STRAIGHT) (TURF) 1m (R)

**1:30** (12:00) 3-Y-0+ **£33,333** (£13,333; £10,000; £6,666; £3,333)

RPR

1 **Solow**[20] 5263 4-9-0 0..... OlivierPeslier 4 119+
(F Head, France) *qckly crossed to nr side rail and mde all: shkn up and qcknd clr over 1f out: r.o strly and extended advantage further under hand ride fnl f: coasted home towards fin: impressive* **2/1**[1]

2 5 **Spoil The Fun (FR)**[37] 4644 5-9-2 0..... JulienAuge 5 109
(C Ferland, France) *t.k.h: hld up in tch: swtchd rt and rdn to cl over 1f out: kpt on and wnt 2nd ins fnl f: no ch w wnr* **5/1**[3]

3 1 **Fire Ship**[64] 3731 5-9-2 0..... ChristopheSoumillon 9 107
(William Knight) *prom thrght: rdn and effrt to chal 2f out: readily outpcd by wnr over 1f out: kpt on but dropped to 3rd fnl f and wl hld* **8/1**

4 ¾ **Redbrook (IRE)**[29] 4930 3-8-8 0..... FrankieDettori 2 102
(A De Royer-Dupre, France) *dwlt and hld up in rr: angled off rail and rdn to improve 2f out: kpt on and tk n.d 4th ins fnl f* **7/1**

5 1¼ **Roero (FR)**[16] 5-9-0 0..... Francois-XavierBertras 6 100
(F Rohaut, France) *t.k.h: midfield in tch: rdn and effrt to chal 2f out: readily outpcd by wnr over 1f out: no ex and fdd fnl f* **7/2**[2]

6 ¾ **Dastarhon (IRE)**[53] 4-9-2 0..... MaximeGuyon 7 100
(Mme Pia Brandt, France) *hld up in rr: rdn over 2f out: outpcd and btn fnl f: nvr threatened* **25/1**

7 *nk* **My Stone (FR)**[16] 6-9-0 0..............................(b) FredericSpanu 3 98
(Mme C Barande-Barbe, France) *trckd wnr: lost pl 3f out: rdn and outpcd in rr 2f out: plugged on fnl f but wl btn* **7/1**

8 *1 1/4* **Stormyra (FR)**[35] 4721 3-8-7 0..............................(p) ThierryJarnet 1 93
(J-P Gallorini, France) *trckd wnr on rail: rdn and outpcd over 1f out: sn btn and wknd* **25/1**

9 *shd* **Calvin Williams (FR)**[80] 3171 4-9-0 0.............................. TheoBachelot 8 95
(M Nigge, France) *midfield: rdn and effrt 2f out: sn outpcd by wnr: wknd fnl f: eased and dropped to last fnl strides* **25/1**

1m 42.75s (1.95)
**WFA** 3 from 4yo+ 6lb **9** Ran SP% **119.9**
WIN (incl. 1 euro stake): 2.50. PLACES: 1.30, 1.70, 2.30. DF: 7.80. SF: 12.00.
**Owner** Wertheimer & Frere **Bred** Wertheimer Et Frere **Trained** France

## 5961a PRIX CASINO BARRIERE DEAUVILLE (H'CAP) (4YO+) (POLYTRACK) 1m 4f 110y

**2:08** (12:00) 4-Y-O+ **£20,366** (£8,233; £6,066; £3,900; £2,383; £1,516)

RPR

1 **Special Request (FR)**[19] 7-8-10 **0**.............................. AntoineHamelin 12 89
(N Caullery, France) **5/1**[1]

2 *1 1/4* **Gris Noir (FR)**[83] 5-8-10 **0**.............................. JohanVictoire 1 87
(Y Durepaire, France) **98/10**

3 *1 1/2* **Impatiente (FR)**[31] 4-8-11 **0**.............................. FlavienPrat 11 86
(A Lyon, France) **143/10**

4 *snk* **Satanicjim (IRE)**[39] 4561 5-9-4 **0**.............................. AdrienFouassier 10 93
(Alain Couetil, France) **7/1**[3]

5 *3/4* **Solmen (FR)**[26] 6-9-1 **0**.............................. EddyHardouin 15 89
(K Demme, Germany) **33/1**

6 *snk* **Chene Boppe (FR)**[29] 4-8-6 **0**.............................. RaphaelMarchelli 7 79
(F-X De Chevigny, France) **94/10**

7 *1 1/2* **Varadero (IRE)**[35] 6-8-11 **0**.............................. AlexandreRoussel 3 82
(L Baudron, France) **184/10**

8 *1 1/2* **Balaythous (FR)**[83] 8-9-7 **0**.............................. StephaneLaurent 13 90
(Mlle B Renk, France) **59/1**

9 *nk* **Lando Blue (IRE)**[19] 4-8-10 **0**..............................(b) MarcLerner 14 78
(C Lerner, France) **138/10**

10 *4* **Tolka (IRE)**[14] 5-9-8 **0**..............................(p) GregoryBenoist 4 84
(S Wattel, France) **17/2**

11 *1 1/4* **Santillana (GER)**[19] 5-9-5 **0**.............................. MaximeGuyon 9 79
(Markus Klug, Germany) **59/10**[2]

12 *2* **Cellalando (FR)**[12] 5546 4-8-6 **0**.............................. MickaelBarzalona 5 62
(S Cerulis, France) **26/1**

13 *1/2* **Astrologo (SPA)**[73] 4-8-7 **0**.............................. UmbertoRispoli 16 63
(M Delzangles, France) **46/1**

14 *1/2* **Ucandri (IRE)**[62] 7-8-13 **0**.............................. Francois-XavierBertras 2 68
(C Ferland, France) **77/10**

15 *3* **Paris Snow**[83] 4-8-11 **0**..............................(p) GeraldMosse 6 61
(Ian Williams) *a.p on inner: cl 4th and scrubbed along to hold pl fr 3f out: rdn and wknd over 1 1/2f out: heavily eased fnl f* **30/1**

16 *20* **Moonyr (FR)**[21] 5225 6-8-13 **0**.............................. RonanThomas 8 31
(Mlle H Mennessier, France) **38/1**

2m 39.17s (159.17) **16** Ran SP% **119.2**
WIN (incl. 1 euro stake): 6.00. PLACES: 2.40, 3.70, 4.20. DF: 45.30. SF: 106.20.
**Owner** P Lorain & P Drioton **Bred** Mme H Devin **Trained** France

## 5962a LUCIEN BARRIERE GRAND PRIX DE DEAUVILLE (GROUP 2) (3YO+) (TURF) 1m 4f 110y

**2:40** (12:00) 3-Y-O+ **£95,000** (£36,666; £17,500; £11,666; £5,833)

RPR

1 **Cocktail Queen (IRE)**[15] 5461 4-9-0 0.............................. AlexisBadel 4 108
(Mme M Bollack-Badel, France) *mde all: rdn and strly pressed thrght fnl 2f: styd on strly and kpt finding u.p: drvn and hld on wl cl home* **5/1**[2]

2 *hd* **Gatewood**[21] 5224 6-9-3 0.............................. WilliamBuick 3 111+
(John Gosden) *trckd wnr on outer: rdn and effrt into st: sltly outpcd ent fnl f: styd on u.p and chal strly towards fin: jst hld* **1/1**[1]

3 *1* **Going Somewhere (BRZ)**[21] 5224 5-9-3 0.............................. GregoryBenoist 1 109+
(D Smaga, France) *hld up in tch on inner: rdn to chal and racd alone against far side rail into st: ev ch fnl f: styd on wl but dropped to 3rd and jst hld towards fin* **10/1**[3]

4 *5* **Rio Tigre (IRE)**[21] 5224 3-8-6 0.............................. MickaelBarzalona 5 101
(A Fabre, France) *stdd and hld up in tch: rdn over 2f out: plugged on same pce in st and nvr able to chal: no ex fnl f* **5/1**[2]

5 *8* **Empoli (GER)**[63] 3774 4-9-3 0.............................. AdriedeVries 2 89
(P Schiergen, Germany) *trckd wnr on inner: rdn and lost pl into st: last and btn ent fnl f: eased* **5/1**[2]

2m 51.84s (5.44)
**WFA** 3 from 4yo+ 10lb **5** Ran SP% **109.1**
WIN (incl. 1 euro stake): 7.40. PLACES: 2.00, 1.20. SF: 12.70.
**Owner** J C Smith **Bred** Littleton Stud **Trained** Lamorlaye, France

**FOCUS**
The time was very slow.

## 5963a PRIX DE MEAUTRY LUCIEN BARRIERE (GROUP 3) (3YO+) (TURF) 6f

**3:10** (12:00) 3-Y-O+ **£33,333** (£13,333; £10,000; £6,666; £3,333)

RPR

1 **Coulsty (IRE)**[15] 5410 3-8-11 0.............................. OlivierPeslier 5 110
(Richard Hannon) *trckd ldr: rdn to chal over 1f out and led ent fnl f: r.o strly and asserted: readily* **5/1**[3]

2 *1 1/4* **Gammarth (FR)**[21] 5223 6-9-1 0..............................(b) MickaelBarzalona 2 107
(H-A Pantall, France) *midfield in tch on rail: rdn 2f out: angled out ent fnl f: r.o and wnt 2nd towards fin: nt pce of wnr* **11/1**

3 *1 1/4* **Robert Le Diable (FR)**[8] 5-9-1 0.............................. FlavienPrat 4 103
(D Prod'Homme, France) *led and sn crossed to rail: rdn and strly pressed over 1f out: hdd ent fnl f: kpt on but sn outpcd by wnr and hld: dropped to 3rd towards fin* **4/1**[2]

4 *nk* **Aeolus**[74] 3352 3-8-13 0 ow2.............................. ChristopheSoumillon 6 103
(Ed McMahon) *midfield: rdn and effrt to chal over 1f out: nt qckn fnl f: kpt on for wl hld 4th* **6/1**

5 *snk* **Aksil (FR)**[8] 4-8-11 0.............................. Christophe-PatriceLemaire 7 98
(M Boutin, France) *hld up in rr: rdn to cl ent fnl f: kpt on but nvr able to chal* **25/1**

6 *2 1/2* **Myasun (FR)**[31] 4841 7-9-1 0.............................. MaximeGuyon 10 94
(C Baillet, France) *hld up in tch on outer: rdn 2f out: no ex and fdd fnl f* **10/1**

7 *2* **Ice Love (FR)**[51] 4171 3-8-8 0.............................. ThierryThulliez 3 83
(T Castanheira, France) *midfield: rdn 2f out: no ex and wknd fnl f* **25/1**

8 *nk* **Zejel**[21] 5223 4-8-11 0.............................. JulienAuge 8 82
(C Ferland, France) *hld up and a towards rr: rdn over 1f out: no imp and sn btn: eased fnl 150yds* **7/4**[1]

9 *3 1/2* **Fresles (IRE)**[31] 3-8-8 0.............................. GregoryBenoist 1 71
(Mme Pia Brandt, France) *prom on outer: ev ch 2f out: rdn and wknd qckly over 1f out: dropped to last fnl f: eased whn btn* **9/1**

1m 13.86s (2.86)
**WFA** 3 from 4yo+ 3lb **9** Ran SP% **122.4**
WIN (incl. 1 euro stake): 7.50. PLACES: 2.40, 4.00, 2.10. DF: 59.40. SF: 114.60.
**Owner** Lord Vestey **Bred** Peter & Sarah Fortune **Trained** East Everleigh, Wilts

## 5964a PRIX HOTEL NORMANDY BARRIERE DEAUVILLE (CLAIMER) (4YO+) (POLYTRACK) 1m 1f 110y

**3:40** (12:00) 4-Y-O+ **£7,916** (£3,166; £2,375; £1,583; £791)

RPR

1 **High Star (FR)**[21] 5222 7-8-11 0.............................. JeffersonSmith[(8)] 10 90
(J-C Rouget, France) **2/1**[1]

2 *2 1/2* **Lower East Side**[19] 4-9-1 0.............................. TheoBachelot 11 81
(S Wattel, France) **34/1**

3 *3/4* **Royal Talisman**[12] 5546 6-8-11 0.............................. MickaelBarzalona 13 75
(Jo Hughes) *towards rr on outer: hdwy into midfield 1/2-way: 5th and styng on fr 2f out: chsd ldr into fnl f: kpt on at same pce u.p: lost 2nd cl home* **53/10**[2]

4 *1 1/4* **Cashpoint**[22] 5162 9-9-6 0.............................. MaximeGuyon 6 82
(Ian Williams) *w.w in midfield: pushed along 2 1/2f out and no imp: rdn 1 1/2f out: styd on u.p fnl f: tk 4th fnl strides* **44/5**[3]

5 *nse* **Toni Fortebracci (FR)**[29] 4-8-11 0.............................. DavidBreux 9 73
(G Botti, France) **29/1**

6 *1 1/2* **Pepito Grillo**[21] 6-9-1 0..............................(b) FredericSpanu 3 74
(L A Urbano-Grajales, France) **37/1**

7 *snk* **Dragonnade (FR)**[143] 7-9-1 0.............................. AntoineHamelin 5 73
(P Hern, France) **26/1**

8 *1/2* **Falcolina (IRE)**[29] 4-9-2 0.............................. OlivierPeslier 1 73
(Yannick Fouin, France) **31/1**

9 *2 1/2* **La Regence (FR)**[26] 5-8-11 0..............................(p) GregoryBenoist 15 63
(S Wattel, France) **106/10**

10 *snk* **Anaxis (FR)**[31] 7-9-4 0.............................. RaphaelMarchelli 8 70
(Rod Collet, France) **119/10**

11 *3 1/2* **Russian Khan (GER)**[31] 6-8-11 0.............................. EddyHardouin 12 56
(Yasmin Almenrader, Germany) **97/10**

12 *nse* **Welcome Sir (FR)**[21] 5225 4-8-4 0.............................. MllePaulineDominois[(7)] 14 56
(E Lellouche, France) **197/10**

13 *1 3/4* **Catushaba (IRE)**[29] 4-8-13 0 ow2..............................(p) ChristopheSoumillon 2 54
(C Lerner, France) **121/10**

14 *1 3/4* **Nam June Paik (FR)**[52] 4-8-11 0..............................(p) TonyPiccone 4 49
(J Parize, France) **49/1**

15 *hd* **Caroz (FR)**[31] 7-8-11 0.............................. Christophe-PatriceLemaire 7 48
(M Boutin, France) **205/10**

1m 56.21s (116.21) **15** Ran SP% **119.9**
WIN (incl. 1 euro stake): 3.00. PLACES: 1.60, 5.10, 2.00. DF: 35.10. SF: 45.70.
**Owner** Simone Brogi **Bred** Scea De L'Aubay & S Bouvier **Trained** Pau, France

# 5938 BADEN-BADEN (L-H)

Sunday, August 31

**OFFICIAL GOING: Turf: soft**

## 5965a COOLMORE STUD BADEN-BADEN CUP (LISTED RACE) (3YO+ FILLIES & MARES) (TURF) 7f

**2:05** (12:00) 3-Y-O+ **£11,666** (£5,416; £2,500; £1,250)

RPR

1 **Athenian (IRE)**[14] 5467 5-9-1 0..............................(p) LukeMorris 2 100
(Sir Mark Prescott Bt) *settled in midfield on inner: tk clsr order fr 2 1/2f out: 4th and rdn 1 1/2f out: r.o to ld appr fnl f: drvn out* **187/10**

2 *nk* **Cape Factor (IRE)**[112] 2195 3-8-13 0.............................. ChrisCatlin 6 100
(Rae Guest) *chsd ldrs: rdn and lost pl over 2 1/2f out: scrubbed along 2f out: styd on appr fnl f: r.o u.p and gaining on wnr all the way to line: nvr quite getting there* **47/10**[2]

3 *1 1/2* **Al Quintana (GER)**[35] 5-9-3 0.............................. SHellyn 5 97
(S Richter, Germany) **143/10**

4 *3* **Ajaxana (GER)**[28] 4955 3-9-1 0.............................. APietsch 4 90
(Waldemar Hickst, Germany) **6/4**[1]

5 *nk* **Emerald Star**[51] 4171 3-9-1 0.............................. DanielePorcu 9 89
(P Schiergen, Germany) **53/10**[3]

6 *6* **Rock Of Ridd (IRE)**[57] 4-9-5 0.............................. ElioneChaves 14 74
(Lennart Reuterskiold Jr, Sweden) **143/10**

7 *hd* **Sugar Love (GER)**[25] 3-8-10 0.............................. RobertHavlin 10 67
(P Schiergen, Germany) **31/1**

8 *3* **Linarda (DEN)**[39] 4-9-1 0..............................(p) PierantonioConvertino 7 61
(Carmen Bocskai, Switzerland) **195/10**

9 *4* **Alice's Dancer (IRE)**[72] 3425 5-9-1 0.............................. AntoineWerle 11 51
(Mme G Rarick, France) **229/10**

10 *3/4* **Sharin (GER)**[25] 3-8-10 0.............................. AHelfenbein 8 47
(Markus Klug, Germany) **87/10**

11 *25* **Bluefire**[28] 4-9-1 0.............................. FabriceVeron 13
(H-A Pantall, France) *bmpd rival leaving stalls: sn outpcd in rr adrift of main gp: rdn and brief effrt 2 1/2f out: sn btn in last pl: eased ins fnl f: t.o* **53/10**[3]

1m 30.26s (6.36)
**WFA** 3 from 4yo+ 5lb **11** Ran SP% **129.9**
WIN (incl. 10 euro stake): 197. PLACES: 64, 28, 39. SF: 948.
**Owner** Axom (XXXI) **Bred** Keatly Overseas Ltd **Trained** Newmarket, Suffolk

## 5966a 144TH GOLDENE PEITSCHE POWERED BY BURDA@TURF (GROUP 3) (3YO+) (TURF) 6f
4:05 (12:00) 3-Y-0+

£26,666 (£9,166; £4,583; £2,500; £1,666; £1,250)

RPR
1 **Signs Of Blessing (IRE)**64 3746 3-9-1 0 StephanePasquier 5 112
(F Rohaut, France) *led stands' side gp of 9: rdn and hdd narrowly appr fnl f: rallied to regain ld ld 100yds out: sn asserted* **9/5**1
2 1 1/4 **Son Cesio (FR)**31 4841 3-9-1 0 FabriceVeron 7 108
(H-A Pantall, France) *chsd ldrs in stands' side gp: shkn up 2 1/2f out and r.o to ld narrowly appr fnl f: hdd 100yds out: no ex* **49/10**3
3 4 **Alcohuaz (CHI)**21 9-9-4 0 ElioneChaves 6 95
(Lennart Reuterskiold Jr, Sweden) *chsd ldrs in stands' side gp: nt qckn u.p fr 1 1/2f out and lft bhd by front two: kpt on at same pce fnl f* **152/10**
4 1 1/4 **Daring Match (GER)**31 3-9-1 0 SHellyn 4 91
(J Hirschberger, Germany) *towards rr in stands' side gp: tk clsr order 1/2-way: hrd rdn to go 4th ins fnl f: kpt on at one pce* **24/1**
5 2 1/2 **Birthday Prince (GER)**21 6-9-4 0 (p) APietsch 11 83+
(Christian Sprengel, Germany) *adrift of three ldrs in gp of 4 towards ins rail and probably last overall: rdn and styd on fr 1 1/2f out: nvr on terms* **36/1**
6 shd **Guinnevre (IRE)**35 4-9-1 0 EPedroza 12 80
(A Wohler, Germany) *in rr: rdn and prog over 2f out: 5th and hrd rdn 300yds out: run petered out ins fnl f* **165/10**
7 1 **Amarillo (IRE)**33 4758 5-9-4 0 DennisSchiergen 1 80
(P Schiergen, Germany) *prom in stands' side gp: sltly outpcd and rdn over 1 1/2f out: grad lft bhd appr fnl f* **74/10**
8 4 **Nocturnal Affair (SAF)**49 4235 8-9-4 0 MircoDemuro 10 67
(Frau Erika Mader, Germany) *chsd ldr towards ins rail: rdn and effrt 1 1/2f out: one pce fnl f* **45/1**
9 1/2 **Kolonel (GER)**288 7941 5-9-4 0 FrederikTylicki 13 65
(Mario Hofer, Germany) *chsd ldr far side gp: rdn and no imp over 1 1/2f out: fdd ins fnl f* **116/10**
10 3/4 **Alpha (GER)**21 5-9-1 0 (b) PJWerning 9 60
(R Werning, Germany) *sn led small gp towards ins rail: rdn and wknd fr 1 1/2f out* **32/1**
11 1/2 **Namera (GER)**21 5-9-1 0 (p) RobertHavlin 3 58
(P Harley, Germany) *a towards rr of stands' side gp: rdn and no imp fr 2 1/2f out: wl btn fnl f* **56/1**
12 3 **Donnerschlag**61 4-9-4 0 AHelfenbein 8 52
(Andreas Lowe, Germany) *chsd ldrs stands' side gp: outpcd 1/2-way: wknd ins fnl 1 1/2f* **6/1**
13 2 **Big Time (IRE)**74 3352 3-9-1 0 (b1) FilipMinarik 2 45
(John Joseph Murphy, Ire) *towards rr of stands' side gp: hrd rdn and no imp fr 2 1/2f out: nvr figured* **48/10**2

1m 13.91s (3.62)
**WFA** 3 from 4yo+ 3lb **13** Ran SP% **129.6**
WIN (incl. 10 euro stake): 28. PLACES: 15, 20, 33. SF: 85.
**Owner** Ecurie Pandora Racing **Bred** S Boucheron **Trained** Sauvagnon, France

5967 - 5968a (Foreign Racing) - See Raceform Interactive

# 5228 LES LANDES
Monday, August 25
**OFFICIAL GOING: Hurdle course - soft; flat course - heavy**

## 5969a VANTAGE CLARENDON 1m 4f
3:40 (3:40) 3-Y-0+ £1,905 (£685; £410)

RPR
1 **Midnight Sequel**15 5230 5-10-12 (tp) MarkQuinlan 5 60
(Neil Mulholland) **1/1**1
2 2 1/4 **King Kenny**15 5230 9-9-11 (p) NoraLooby 2 41
(Mrs A Corson, Jersey) **5/2**2
3 3 **River Du Nord (FR)**29 4718 7-9-3 JemmaMarshall 6 28
(Sue Gardner) **7/2**3
4 hd **Lady Petrus**15 5229 9-8-9 PhilipPrince 1 20
(K Kukk, Jersey) **7/2**3
5 15 **Sworn Mammy (GER)**29 4716 7-9-10 JoshuaBrowning 4 11
(R Storp, Germany) **5/1**

(10.00) **5** Ran SP% **139.7**

**Owner** Dajam Ltd **Bred** M Burbidge **Trained** Limpley Stoke, Wilts

## 5970a PENULTIMATE H'CAP 1m 2f
4:15 (4:17) 3-Y-0+ £1,270 (£455; £275)

RPR
1 **The Bay Bandit**36 2596 7-10-3 (p) MarkQuinlan 4 56
(Neil Mulholland) **10/11**1
2 12 **Herbalist**15 5230 4-10-12 PhilipPrince 2 41
(K Kukk, Jersey) **7/2**3
3 5 1/2 **Beck's Bolero (IRE)**29 4717 8-10-0 (b) CraigWalker 5 18
(Mrs A Corson, Jersey) **4/1**
4 10 **Up In Flames (IRE)**15 4718 5-9-11 (p) MattieBatchelor 3
(Mrs A Malzard, Jersey) **8/1**
5 2 **Rebel Woman**15 5229 8-9-4 NoraLooby 6
(Mrs A Corson, Jersey) **10/3**2
6 dist **Informality (IRE)** 3-10-4 MrHJFCruickshank 1
(J Moon, Jersey) **7/1**

2m 2.0s (-11.00)
**WFA** 3 from 4yo+ 8lb **6** Ran SP% **141.3**

**Owner** Neil Mulholland Racing Club **Bred** Darley **Trained** Limpley Stoke, Wilts

## 5971a GLORY BEE H'CAP 1m 100y
4:50 (4:50) 3-Y-0+ £1,460 (£525; £315)

RPR
1 **Kristal Hart**4 5596 5-11-5 7ex (p) MarkQuinlan 2 58
(Neil Mulholland) **1/2**1
2 1 1/2 **Lucifers Shadow (IRE)**29 4717 5-10-7 (v) MrFTett 5 43
(Mrs C Gilbert, Jersey) **5/2**2
3 12 **Jackpot**15 5229 4-9-11 (p) JemmaMarshall 4 7
(Mrs A Malzard, Jersey) **11/4**3
4 4 1/2 **Fast Freddie**15 10-10-8 (p) CraigWalker 1 8
(Mrs A Corson, Jersey) **10/3**
5 5 **Lively Little Lady**15 4-8-12 NoraLooby 3
(Mrs A Corson, Jersey) **5/1**

1m 55.0s (115.00) **5** Ran SP% **161.7**

**Owner** The White Hart Racing Syndicate **Bred** Carmel Stud **Trained** Limpley Stoke, Wilts

# 5945 BRIGHTON (L-H)
Monday, September 1
**OFFICIAL GOING: Good to firm (good in places) changing to good (good to firm in places) after race 1 (2:30)**
Wind: Moderate, half against Weather: Overcast Rails: Rail dolled out from 7f to 2f, 4f bend at minimum width and distances increased by about 20yds

## 5972 IAN CARNABY (S) H'CAP 5f 213y
2:30 (2:30) (Class 6) (0-60,57) 3-Y-0+ £2,045 (£603; £302) Stalls Centre

Form RPR
5-50 1 **Bookmaker**14 5504 4-9-5 55 (b1) LiamJones 3 64
(Olly Stevens) *prom: rdn 3f out: led over 1f out: hld on wl nr fin* **12/1**
4425 2 hd **Just Isla**19 5314 4-9-6 56 (p) RichardHughes 1 64
(Peter Makin) *in tch: effrt and swtchd rt over 1f out: pressed wnr ins fnl f: jst hld* **6/4**1
0446 3 2 1/2 **Swiss Lait**28 4970 3-9-5 57 AndreaAtzeni 2 57
(David Elsworth) *dwlt: towards rr: rdn 3f out: hdwy over 1f out: styd on same pce fnl f* **4/1**2
0604 4 2 1/2 **Commandingpresence (USA)**16 5423 8-9-4 54 WilliamCarson 7 46
(John Bridger) *chsd ldr tl over 1f out: no ex fnl f* **8/1**
-666 5 1 **Stonecrabstomorrow (IRE)**13 5518 11-8-12 53 (v) CamHardie(5) 5 42
(Michael Attwater) *bhd: shkn up over 1f out: n.d* **14/1**
5565 6 4 **Intense Feeling (IRE)**7 5753 3-9-5 57 (p) AmirQuinn 8 33
(Lee Carter) *chsd ldrs tl rdn and btn 2f out* **5/1**3
-454 7 1 1/2 **Play The Blues (IRE)**203 556 7-9-0 50 (t) AdamKirby 6 21
(Dominic Ffrench Davis) *led at gd pce: rdn and hung lft 2f out: hdd & wknd over 1f out* **8/1**

1m 11.36s (1.16) **Going Correction** +0.175s/f (Good)
**WFA** 3 from 4yo+ 2lb **7** Ran SP% **113.2**
Speed ratings (Par 101): **99,98,95,92,90 85,83**
CSF £30.02 CT £87.66 TOTE £13.30: £7.00, £1.90; EX 49.10 Trifecta £223.60.The winner was bought by John Bridger for 4,000gns.
**Owner** Giles, McCarthy & Newton **Bred** Benjamin Newton And Graycroft Farm **Trained** Chiddingfold, Surrey

**FOCUS**
The rail was dolled out from 7f to approx 2f to provide fresh ground. The 4f bend was at minimum width. The time has been rated up 7lb from last year's debut, and the runner-up rated to last year's form.

## 5973 GOOD LAW SOLICITORS MAIDEN FILLIES' STKS (BOBIS RACE) 5f 213y
3:00 (3:01) (Class 5) 2-Y-0 £2,587 (£770; £384; £192) Stalls Centre

Form RPR
5326 1 **Renaissant**16 5436 2-9-0 70 RichardHughes 13 74
(Richard Hannon) *mde all at gd pce: drvn out* **5/2**1
5 2 1/2 **Queen's Pearl (IRE)**32 4828 2-9-0 0 AndreaAtzeni 7 73
(Roger Varian) *hld up in 6th: hdwy 2f out: pressed wnr ins fnl f: jst hld* **11/4**2
33 3 3 3/4 **Siren's Cove**67 3626 2-9-0 0 KierenFallon 4 64
(James Tate) *mid-div: n.m.r on inner after 1f: hdwy over 2f out: drvn to chal over 1f out: one pce* **9/2**
005 4 2 3/4 **Stone Roses (IRE)**18 5344 2-9-0 73 RyanMoore 5 53
(Michael Bell) *chsd ldrs: briefly wnt 2nd 2f out: no ex over 1f out* **10/3**3
05 5 1 **Vinamar (IRE)**53 4117 2-9-0 0 StevieDonohoe 12 50
(Roger Teal) *prom tl hung lft and wknd over 1f out* **100/1**
50 6 3/4 **Candle Of The Sea (IRE)**26 5037 2-9-0 0 RobertHavlin 9 48+
(Ed Vaughan) *mid-div: rdn over 2f out: styd on fnl f* **25/1**
7 nse **Miss Minuty** 2-9-0 0 ChrisCatlin 10 48
(Sir Mark Prescott Bt) *chsd ldrs tl outpcd fnl 2f* **40/1**
8 3/4 **Elis Eliz (IRE)** 2-9-0 0 TomQueally 6 45+
(Michael Wigham) *dwlt: bhd: rdn and sme hdwy over 2f out: n.d* **33/1**
00 9 1 1/4 **World Fair (IRE)**19 5305 2-9-0 0 AdamKirby 8 42
(Charlie Appleby) *chsd wnr tl 2f out: sn wknd* **25/1**
0 10 4 **Razaan**9 5667 2-9-0 0 MartinDwyer 11 30
(Mick Channon) *dwlt: mid-div: rdn 3f out: n.d fnl 2f* **50/1**
11 nk **Beauchamp Ruby** 2-9-0 0 1 LiamJones 2 29
(Paul Fitzsimons) *dwlt: outpcd: a bhd* **66/1**
12 10 **Mythical Maid (IRE)** 2-9-0 0 SteveDrowne 1
(Seamus Mullins) *s.s: a trailing* **100/1**

1m 11.83s (1.63) **Going Correction** +0.175s/f (Good) **12** Ran SP% **115.0**
Speed ratings (Par 92): **96,95,90,86,85 84,84,83,81,76 75,62**
CSF £8.66 TOTE £2.80: £1.10, £1.30, £2.20; EX 11.00 Trifecta £39.40.
**Owner** Cheveley Park Stud **Bred** Natton House Thoroughbreds **Trained** East Everleigh, Wilts

**FOCUS**
An ordinary race with the third rated to her pre-race level.

## 5974 SHAWBROOK BANK NURSERY H'CAP 5f 213y
3:30 (3:31) (Class 5) (0-75,73) 2-Y-0 £2,587 (£770; £384; £192) Stalls Centre

Form RPR
5336 1 **Emef Rock (IRE)**45 4410 2-9-1 67 MartinDwyer 9 69
(Mick Channon) *hld up in rr: hdwy over 2f out: led 1f out: drvn out* **20/1**
0163 2 hd **Dream Approval (IRE)**12 5554 2-8-13 68 ThomasBrown(3) 6 69
(Daniel Kubler) *chsd ldrs on outer: jnd wnr and str chal ins fnl f: jst hld* **9/1**
2324 3 1 **Khawaater**27 4999 2-9-2 68 (t) PaulHanagan 8 67
(Roger Varian) *towards rr: nt clr run over 2f out tl swtchd lft and hdwy over 1f out: kpt on fnl f* **6/1**3
4155 4 1/2 **The Dapper Tapper (IRE)**12 5554 2-9-2 68 (v) AdamKirby 4 65
(Eve Johnson Houghton) *prom: led 2f out tl ins fnl f: kpt on* **5/1**2
16 5 1/2 **L'Addition**30 4913 2-9-4 70 1 RyanMoore 5 65
(William Jarvis) *in tch: drvn to chse ldrs over 1f out: styd on ins fnl f* **7/4**1

0015 **6** ½ **Classic Seniority**[19] 5306 2-9-5 71 ........ RichardHughes 1 65
(Richard Hannon) *led tl 2f out: ev ch tl one pce ins fnl f* **10/1**

2035 **7** ¾ **Artfilly (IRE)**[21] 5253 2-9-2 68 ........ AndreaAtzeni 7 66+
(Ed Walker) *hld up towards rr: nt clr run over 2f out and again over 1f out: nvr able to chal* **16/1**

14 **8** ½ **Sunny York (IRE)**[52] 4150 2-9-7 73 ........ KierenFallon 3 63
(James Tate) *dwlt: sn in tch: rdn to press ldrs over 1f out: no ex fnl f* **7/1**

6050 **9** 1 ¾ **Francis Scott Key (IRE)**[12] 5554 2-9-1 67 ........ StevieDonohoe 2 52
(Brian Meehan) *chsd ldr tl 2f out: sn wknd* **25/1**

1m 12.74s (2.54) **Going Correction** +0.175s/f (Good) **9** Ran SP% **113.4**
Speed ratings (Par 95): **90,89,88,87,87 86,85,84,82**
CSF £183.78 CT £1218.65 TOTE £20.20: £5.90, £2.60, £2.10; EX 191.60 Trifecta £3612.00.
**Owner** Mrs Margaret Forsyth & MF Logistic **Bred** Denis & David McDonnell **Trained** West Ilsley, Berks

**FOCUS**
A competitive nursery, but rated as ordinary and those challenging nearer the stands' side came to the fore late on. The winner and runner-up have been rated near their respective pre-race marks.

## 5975 NFU MUTUAL BRIGHTON & HOVE H'CAP 1m 1f 209y
**4:00** (4:00) (Class 5) (0-70,70) 3-Y-0+ **£2,587** (£770; £384; £192) **Stalls** High

Form RPR
4350 **1** **Ana Shababiya (IRE)**[26] 5036 4-9-6 66 ........ TomQueally 3 74
(Ismail Mohammed) *mde all: hrd rdn over 1f out: hld on wl fnl f: in control nr fin* **8/1**[2]

5352 **2** *nk* **Whitby Jet (IRE)**[7] 5758 6-9-3 70 ........ HectorCrouch(7) 2 77
(Ed Vaughan) *s.i.s: hld up in rr: hdwy 2f out: chal ins fnl f: jst hld* **8/1**[2]

5314 **3** 6 **Bennelong**[16] 5428 8-9-4 64 ........(b) AmirQuinn 7 60
(Lee Carter) *s.i.s: hld up in rr: hdwy on outer 4f out: chsd wnr over 2f out tl over 1f out: no ex* **10/1**[3]

4404 **4** 1 ½ **Darting**[58] 3978 3-9-1 68 ........[1] RichardHughes 6 61
(Andrew Balding) *in tch: dropped to last and rdn 3f out: sme hdwy over 1f out: no imp* **9/4**[1]

4646 **5** 6 **Alphabetique**[31] 4863 3-8-13 66 ........ RobertHavlin 8 48
(Peter Chapple-Hyam) *chsd ldrs: drvn along over 2f out: wknd over 1f out* **12/1**

4223 **6** 1 ½ **Light Of Asia (IRE)**[27] 5002 3-9-3 70 ........(b[1]) RyanMoore 1 49
(Ed Dunlop) *prom: chsd wnr 4f out tl over 2f out: wknd over 1f out* **9/4**[1]

0604 **7** ½ **Minstrel Lad**[17] 5395 6-9-1 64 ........ SimonPearce(3) 5 42
(Lydia Pearce) *in tch: rdn over 2f out: wknd over 1f out* **8/1**[2]

246- **8** 8 **Lexington Blue**[116] 5835 4-9-0 60 ........ SteveDrowne 4 23
(Seamus Mullins) *chsd wnr tl 4f out: wknd over 2f out: sn bhd* **40/1**

2m 5.25s (1.65) **Going Correction** +0.175s/f (Good) **8** Ran SP% **114.1**
**WFA** 3 from 4yo+ 7lb
Speed ratings (Par 103): **100,99,94,93,88 87,87,80**
CSF £68.97 CT £645.86 TOTE £12.00: £3.50, £2.00, £1.90; EX 59.20 Trifecta £425.90.
**Owner** Ahmad Abdulla Al Shaikh **Bred** Thomas Hassett **Trained** Newmarket, Suffolk
■ Stewards' Enquiry : Hector Crouch seven-day ban: used whip above permitted level (Sep 15-21)

**FOCUS**
The front pair pulled clear but were not obvious improvers and have been rated to form.

## 5976 KSD GROUP SUPPORT SERVICES MAIDEN STKS 1m 1f 209y
**4:30** (4:32) (Class 5) 3-Y-0+ **£2,587** (£770; £384; £192) **Stalls** High

Form RPR
33 **1** **Long View (IRE)**[28] 4966 3-9-0 0 ........ RyanMoore 8 86
(Sir Michael Stoute) *chsd ldr after 1f: led 2f out: rdn clr fnl f: comf* **11/8**[1]

4-36 **2** 5 **Steppe Daughter (IRE)**[42] 4500 3-8-9 73 ........ CamHardie(5) 5 76
(Denis Coakley) *in tch: chsd wnr 2f out: hung lft: no ex fnl f* **8/1**

**3** 7 **Viceroyalty** 3-9-5 0 ........ AdamKirby 1 67
(Charlie Appleby) *in tch tl outpcd and btn 2f out* **7/2**[2]

334 **4** 2 ½ **Kicking The Can (IRE)**[23] 5186 3-9-5 80 ........ RichardHughes 6 62
(Peter Chapple-Hyam) *led: hrd rdn and hdd 2f out: sn wknd* **9/2**[3]

42 **5** 6 **Haydn's Lass**[28] 4978 3-9-0 0 ........ MartinDwyer 2 45
(Marcus Tregoning) *prom tl hrd rdn and wknd 3f out* **6/1**

6 **6** 18 **Too Bend**[70] 3525 3-9-2 0 ........ ThomasBrown(3) 3 21
(Patrick Chamings) *hld up in rr: hrd rdn and no ch over 2f out: eased 1f out* **50/1**

**7** 22 **The Gay Cavalier** 3-9-2 0 ........(t) DannyBrock(3) 4
(John Ryan) *s.s: towards rr: pushed along 6f out: wl bhd fnl 3f: eased* **66/1**

2m 4.32s (0.72) **Going Correction** +0.175s/f (Good) **7** Ran SP% **111.4**
Speed ratings (Par 103): **104,100,94,92,87 73,55**
CSF £12.79 TOTE £2.10: £1.30, £4.40; EX 13.80 Trifecta £51.60.
**Owner** Ballymacoll Stud **Bred** Ballymacoll Stud Farm Ltd **Trained** Newmarket, Suffolk

**FOCUS**
There'd been some rain prior to this contest and the runners came stands' side. Little depth to this maiden. This has been rated around the runner-up.

## 5977 HARRINGTONS LETTINGS H'CAP (DIV I) 7f 214y
**5:00** (5:00) (Class 6) (0-55,55) 3-Y-0+ **£1,940** (£577; £288; £144) **Stalls** Centre

Form RPR
4423 **1** **Chanceuse**[25] 5106 3-9-1 54 ........ RyanMoore 10 62
(Gary Moore) *hld up in rr: hdwy and nt clr run over 1f out: swtchd rt and led ins fnl f: rdn out* **8/1**

434 **2** 1 ¾ **Elle Rebelle**[1] 5950 4-8-13 52 ........ CamHardie(5) 3 57
(Mark Brisbourne) *dwlt: bhd: rdn 3f out: hdwy and hung lft over 1f out: styd on to take 2nd fnl 100yds* **4/1**[1]

03 **3** 1 **Big City Boy (IRE)**[25] 5105 6-8-10 47 ........ DannyBrock(3) 1 50
(Phil McEntee) *led: hrd rdn and hdd ins fnl f: one pce* **7/1**

4044 **4** 1 ¾ **Bold Ring**[16] 5425 8-8-10 51 ........ RobertPWalsh(7) 5 50
(Edward Creighton) *hld up in midfield: hdwy over 2f out: one pce fnl f* **12/1**

0-56 **5** *hd* **Dansante**[226] 231 3-8-7 46 ........ AndreaAtzeni 4 44
(Amanda Perrett) *a.p: one pce appr fnl f* **5/1**[2]

600- **6** 1 **Wunderkind (USA)**[292] 7859 3-8-7 46 oh1 ........ ChrisCatlin 11 41
(Sir Mark Prescott Bt) *prom: outpcd 2f out: kpt on ins fnl f* **5/1**[2]

66-0 **7** 4 ½ **Thomas Blossom (IRE)**[242] 17 4-8-9 46 oh1...(v[1]) ThomasBrown(3) 7 32
(Patrick Chamings) *t.k.h towards rr: rdn and hdwy over 2f out: chsng ldrs but hld whn n.m.r over 1f out: wknd* **6/1**[3]

0054 **8** 3 ½ **Encapsulated**[13] 5518 4-9-3 51 ........(p) RobertHavlin 9 29
(Roger Ingram) *plld hrd in midfield: effrt and n.m.r on stands' rail over 2f out: n.d after* **16/1**

1600 **9** 5 **Overrider**[6] 5797 4-9-7 55 ........(t) AdamKirby 2 21
(Paul Cole) *prom: rdn over 2f out: hung lft and wknd over 1f out: eased* **10/1**

4-10 **10** 40 **Wicked Tara**[16] 5428 4-8-9 46 oh1 ........ PhilipPrince(3) 6
(Natalie Lloyd-Beavis) *chsd ldrs: drvn along and lost pl over 4f out: bhd and eased fnl 2f* **66/1**

1m 38.19s (2.19) **Going Correction** +0.175s/f (Good)
**WFA** 3 from 4yo+ 5lb **10** Ran SP% **115.4**
Speed ratings (Par 101): **96,94,93,91,91 90,85,82,77,37**
CSF £39.60 CT £241.73 TOTE £4.50: £1.60, £2.20, £1.80; EX 11.50 Trifecta £54.60.
**Owner** Ben Parish **Bred** Gracelands Stud **Trained** Lower Beeding, W Sussex

**FOCUS**
A personal best from the winner rated in line to best view of AW form.

## 5978 HARRINGTONS LETTINGS H'CAP (DIV II) 7f 214y
**5:30** (5:30) (Class 6) (0-55,52) 3-Y-0+ **£1,940** (£577; £288; £144) **Stalls** Centre

Form RPR
055 **1** **Claude Greenwood**[20] 5291 4-8-11 45 ........(b) CharlesBishop(3) 6 54
(Linda Jewell) *mde all at gd pce: hld on wl whn chal fr over 1f out: gamely* **14/1**

0234 **2** *hd* **Abigails Angel**[35] 4738 7-9-2 47 ........ WilliamCarson 9 55
(Brett Johnson) *prom: rdn 3f out: drew level 50yds out: unable qck fnl strides* **4/1**[1]

3435 **3** 1 ¼ **Anginola (IRE)**[5] 5832 5-9-6 51 ........ LiamJones 4 56
(Laura Mongan) *chsd ldrs: rdn 3f out: chal over 1f out: kpt on same pce* **11/2**[3]

-600 **4** ½ **Urban Sanctuary**[26] 5033 3-8-9 45 ........(b) AndreaAtzeni 3 48
(Ed Walker) *chsd ldrs: hrd rdn over 2f out: styd on same pce* **5/1**[2]

5626 **5** ½ **Libra Romana (IRE)**[23] 5183 3-8-13 49 ........ ChrisCatlin 11 51+
(Sir Mark Prescott Bt) *t.k.h towards rr: rdn and r.o fnl 2f: nrest at fin* **9/1**

3446 **6** 3 ¾ **Greek Islands (IRE)**[38] 4616 6-9-0 52 ........ RobertPWalsh(7) 8 46
(Edward Creighton) *t.k.h: prom: rdn 3f out: wknd over 1f out* **20/1**

5645 **7** 1 ¼ **Viking Warrior (IRE)**[17] 5376 7-9-6 51 ........ RichardHughes 10 42
(Shaun Harris) *mid-div: effrt 2f out: wknd 1f out* **5/1**[2]

0640 **8** *shd* **Jersey Cream (IRE)**[20] 5280 3-9-1 51 ........ RyanMoore 2 41
(Gary Moore) *stdd s and s.i.s: bhd: rdn 2f out: nvr rchd ldrs* **6/1**

5605 **9** *hd* **Gypsy Rider**[14] 5510 5-9-0 50 ........ NedCurtis(5) 5 41
(Henry Tett) *hld up in midfield: sme hdwy 2f out: wknd 1f out* **10/1**

6050 **10** 8 **Alberto**[40] 4534 4-9-0 45 ........ StevieDonohoe 7 17
(Jo Hughes) *plld hrd: a bhd* **66/1**

60-0 **11** 9 **Little Miss Becky**[17] 5400 3-8-4 45 ........ CamHardie(5) 1
(Giles Bravery) *s.i.s: towards rr: rdn 5f out: sn bhd* **33/1**

1m 36.73s (0.73) **Going Correction** +0.175s/f (Good)
**WFA** 3 from 4yo+ 5lb **11** Ran SP% **118.0**
Speed ratings (Par 101): **103,102,101,101,100 96,95,95,95,87 78**
CSF £68.53 CT £360.37 TOTE £15.80: £4.60, £1.60, £2.50; EX 81.20 Trifecta £352.60.
**Owner** Richard Dean **Bred** Mrs J A Rawding **Trained** Sutton Valence, Kent
■ Stewards' Enquiry : Charles Bishop four-day ban: used whip above permitted level (Sep 15-18)

**FOCUS**
A competitive handicap, run at a decent pace. 1-2-5-4; The winner is up slightly on this year's form, rated around the second and third.

## 5979 D.E.H. ELECTRICAL CONTRACTORS LTD H'CAP 6f 209y
**6:00** (6:00) (Class 5) (0-70,70) 3-Y-0+ **£2,587** (£770; £384; £192) **Stalls** Centre

Form RPR
3624 **1** **Bayleyf (IRE)**[7] 5758 5-9-6 66 ........(p) StevieDonohoe 3 78
(Lee Carter) *mde all: sn 3 l clr: rdn and r.o wl fnl 2f: a in control* **10/3**[2]

3023 **2** 3 ¼ **Freddy With A Y (IRE)**[10] 5624 4-9-9 69 ........(p) RyanMoore 4 73
(Gary Moore) *chsd wnr: rdn over 2f out: a hld* **6/4**[1]

3045 **3** 4 ½ **Olney Lass**[10] 5650 7-9-2 65 ........ SimonPearce(3) 5 57
(Lydia Pearce) *in tch: effrt over 2f out: wknd 1f out* **8/1**

1540 **4** *shd* **Perfect Mission**[13] 5523 6-8-12 65 ........(v) KieranShoemark(7) 2 57
(Andrew Balding) *s.s: bhd: hdwy 2f out: wknd 1f out* **10/1**

4340 **5** 1 ¾ **Welsh Inlet (IRE)**[9] 5685 6-9-0 60 ........ WilliamCarson 6 47
(John Bridger) *in tch tl rdn and btn 2f out* **8/1**

0033 **6** 5 **Decent Fella (IRE)**[11] 5602 8-9-10 70 ........(t) AdamKirby 1 44
(Ann Stokell) *in tch: disp 2nd over 2f out: wknd over 1f out* **9/2**[3]

1m 23.74s (0.64) **Going Correction** +0.175s/f (Good) **6** Ran SP% **112.6**
Speed ratings (Par 103): **103,99,94,94,92 86**
CSF £8.83 TOTE £5.00: £2.30, £1.30; EX 9.70 Trifecta £57.60.
**Owner** John Joseph Smith **Bred** Marchwood Aggregates **Trained** Epsom, Surrey

**FOCUS**
Another all-the-way winner.
T/Plt: £94.20 to a £1 stake. Pool: £76,375.70 - 591.86 winning tickets T/Qpdt: £25.10 to a £1 stake. Pool: £6,006.40 - 176.75 winning tickets LM

# 5524 LEICESTER (R-H)
## Monday, September 1

**OFFICIAL GOING: Good (good to firm in places; 7.7)**
Wind: Light against Weather: Overcast

## 5980 WIDMERPOOL H'CAP 1m 1f 218y
**2:10** (2:10) (Class 5) (0-70,73) 3-Y-0 **£2,587** (£770; £384; £192) **Stalls** Low

Form RPR
5324 **1** **Scoppio Del Carro**[9] 5689 3-9-7 70 ........(t) DavidProbert 1 80+
(Andrew Balding) *hld up in tch: nt clr run over 2f out: swtchd lft over 1f out: r.o to ld wl ins fnl f* **5/2**[1]

3215 **2** 1 ¼ **Ajig**[14] 5492 3-9-5 68 ........ JohnFahy 7 73
(Eve Johnson Houghton) *hld up: hdwy over 2f out: led over 1f out: rdn and hdd wl ins fnl f* **9/2**[2]

6044 **3** *nk* **Elite Force (IRE)**[22] 5214 3-9-6 69 ........(b[1]) JimmyFortune 4 73
(Roger Charlton) *trckd ldrs: wnt 2nd 4f out: rdn to ld 2f out: hdd over 1f out: styd on* **8/1**

1045 **4** *nk* **Sellingallthetime (IRE)**[38] 4631 3-9-6 69 ........(p) AndrewMullen 8 72
(Michael Appleby) *plld hrd and prom: ev ch whn hung rt over 1f out: sn rdn: nt run on* **7/1**

6640 **5** 2 ½ **Distant High**[9] 5685 3-8-6 60 ........(p) ShaneGray(5) 2 59
(Richard Price) *chsd ldr 6f: rdn over 1f out: styd on same pce fnl f* **20/1**

0320 **6** 7 **Chess Valley**[27] 5008 3-9-3 66 ........ JimmyQuinn 6 51
(Willie Musson) *s.s: hld up: nt clr run over 2f out: wknd over 1f out* **33/1**

3236 **7** 4 ½ **Keep To The Beat**[13] 5534 3-8-13 62 ........(p) JamieSpencer 3 39
(Kevin Ryan) *led: rdn and hdd 2f out: wknd fnl f* **5/1**[3]

556 **8** 14 **Dalasi (IRE)**[28] 4984 3-9-6 69 ........ DaneO'Neill 9 19
(Henry Candy) *hld up in tch: rdn over 3f out: wknd over 2f out* **9/2**[2]

2m 7.97s (0.07) **Going Correction** 0.0s/f (Good) **8** Ran SP% **112.9**
Speed ratings (Par 101): **99,98,97,97,95 89,86,75**
CSF £13.41 CT £75.81 TOTE £3.10: £1.10, £2.00, £1.40; EX 11.10 Trifecta £39.00.
**Owner** Martin & Valerie Slade & Partner **Bred** Sir Eric Parker **Trained** Kingsclere, Hants

**FOCUS**
A little messy, but the well-backed second is rated to form, and the third to his maiden form, with with the fourth running his best turf race.

## 5981 GILMORTON MAIDEN AUCTION STKS (DIV I) 7f 9y
**2:40** (2:41) (Class 5) 2-Y-O **£2,587** (£770; £384; £192) **Stalls** High

Form RPR
2222 **1** **Fingal's Cave (IRE)**[16] 5408 2-8-11 79 WilliamTwiston-Davies 2 76
(Mick Channon) *trckd ldrs: rdn to ld over 1f out: styd on* **1/1**[1]
025 **2** ½ **Thorkhill Star (IRE)**[16] 5443 2-8-12 75 TonyHamilton 10 76
(Richard Fahey) *hld up: hdwy over 1f out: sn rdn: r.o: nt quite rch wnr* **6/1**[3]
224 **3** ½ **Little Palaver**[20] 5271 2-8-6 74 RyanTate(3) 5 71
(Clive Cox) *racd keenly: w ldr tl shkn up to ld over 2f out: rdn and hdd over 1f out: edgd rt ins fnl f: styd on* **7/1**
22 **4** *hd* **Edge Of Heaven**[11] 5604 2-8-4 0 HarryBentley 4 66
(Jonathan Portman) *mid-div: pushed along and hdwy over 1f out: styd on* **9/1**
0 **5** 2 **Perceived**[18] 5351 2-8-5 0 DavidProbert 9 61
(Henry Candy) *chsd ldrs: rdn over 2f out: edgd rt over 1f out: styng on same pce whn nt clr run wl ins fnl f* **5/1**[2]
00 **6** 6 **Cassandane (IRE)**[8] 5718 2-8-8 0 JoeFanning 1 48+
(Mark Johnston) *mid-div: hdwy over 2f out: sn rdn: wknd fnl f* **33/1**
5333 **7** 2¼ **Rockaroundtheclock (IRE)**[25] 5118 2-9-0 74 (b[1]) JimCrowley 3 48
(Paul Cole) *led over 4f: sn rdn: wknd fnl f* **12/1**
0 **8** ½ **Je T'Aime Encore**[16] 5439 2-8-10 0 JimmyQuinn 8 45+
(Conrad Allen) *hld up: rdn over 2f out: wknd over 1f out* **50/1**
00 **9** 39 **Sonar (IRE)**[8] 5718 2-9-1 0 JamieSpencer 6
(Michael Bell) *dwlt: sn pushed along in rr: wknd and eased 1/2-way* **50/1**

1m 25.95s (-0.25) **Going Correction** 0.0s/f (Good) 9 Ran SP% **118.0**
Speed ratings (Par 95): **101,100,99,99,97 90,87,87,42**
CSF £7.65 TOTE £1.80: £1.10, £3.00, £2.20; EX 7.80 Trifecta £27.70.
**Owner** The Motley Cru I **Bred** Rathasker Stud **Trained** West Ilsley, Berks

**FOCUS**
The stronger of two ordinary 7f juvenile maidens in terms of prior form, and they went an honest gallop. Rated as straightforward form around the front trio, possibly a fraction better.

## 5982 GILMORTON MAIDEN AUCTION STKS (DIV II) 7f 9y
**3:10** (3:11) (Class 5) 2-Y-O **£2,587** (£770; £384; £192) **Stalls** High

Form RPR
3 **1** **Cape Xenia**[18] 5351 2-8-8 0 FergusSweeney 4 65+
(Henry Candy) *a.p: shkn up to ld over 2f out: rdn over 1f out: jst hld on* **4/5**[1]
6 **2** *nse* **Multistar**[11] 5604 2-8-8 0 TedDurcan 7 65
(Chris Wall) *s.i.s: hld up: hdwy over 1f out: r.o: jst failed* **7/1**[3]
05 **3** 1¼ **Colours Of Glory (IRE)**[32] 4809 2-8-8 0 JoeFanning 2 61+
(Charles Hills) *hld up: hdwy over 2f out: chsd wnr over 1f out: styd on same pce wl ins fnl f* **20/1**
6 **4** 2¼ **Comanche Chieftain (CAN)**[30] 4884 2-9-0 0 AndrewMullen 11 61
(Michael Appleby) *hld up: pushed along over 4f out: styd on u.p fr over 1f out: nt rch ldrs* **8/1**
0 **5** 2¾ **Dynamite Inventor (IRE)**[21] 5241 2-8-12 0 JamieSpencer 8 54
(Kevin Ryan) *led: hdd over 4f out: remained handy: rdn over 2f out: wknd ins fnl f* **25/1**
**6** 1¼ **Three Gracez** 2-8-0 0 JoeDoyle(5) 9 42
(Noel Quinlan) *prom: racd keenly: rdn over 1f out: wknd ins fnl f* **20/1**
43 **7** 2 **Miss Inga Sock (IRE)**[12] 5555 2-8-4 0 HarryBentley 10 35
(Eve Johnson Houghton) *hld up: rdn over 2f out: n.d* **5/1**[2]
0 **8** *hd* **Anniversarie**[46] 4346 2-8-3 0 ow2 ConnorBeasley(3) 1 37
(John Norton) *w ldr tl led over 4f out: rdn and hdd over 2f out: wknd over 1f out* **100/1**
06 **9** ½ **My Mo (FR)**[11] 5593 2-8-10 0 GeorgeDowning(5) 3 44
(David Dennis) *prom: rdn and ev ch over 2f out: wknd over 1f out* **100/1**
4 **10** 6 **Picture Postcard**[13] 5524 2-8-7 0 SilvestreDeSousa 6 20
(William Haggas) *prom: rdn 1/2-way: edgd lft and wknd over 1f out* **8/1**
6 **11** 9 **Excelling Oscar (IRE)**[14] 5507 2-8-10 0 HayleyTurner 5
(Conor Dore) *s.i.s: sn pushed along into mid-div: rdn 1/2-way: wknd over 2f out* **100/1**

1m 27.48s (1.28) **Going Correction** 0.0s/f (Good) 11 Ran SP% **123.3**
Speed ratings (Par 95): **92,91,90,87,84 83,81,80,80,73 63**
CSF £7.08 TOTE £1.90: £1.10, £2.20, £4.90; EX 7.80 Trifecta £83.90.
**Owner** Simms, Blackburn & Candy **Bred** Horizon Bloodstock Limited **Trained** Kingston Warren, Oxon

**FOCUS**
The weaker of the two 7f juvenile maidens in terms of prior form, and they went a muddling gallop with the action developing right across the track. This has to rate ordinary form with those clsoe up all rated as improvers.

## 5983 SHEPSHED FILLIES' NURSERY H'CAP (BOBIS RACE) 5f 218y
**3:40** (3:40) (Class 4) (0-85,79) 2-Y-O **£4,528** (£1,347; £673; £336) **Stalls** High

Form RPR
0110 **1** **Feeling Easy (IRE)**[30] 4913 2-9-7 79 JimmyQuinn 3 86
(Robert Eddery) *hld up: rdn over 1f out: hung rt and r.o ins fnl f to ld nr fin* **12/1**
031 **2** *nk* **Some Show**[22] 5210 2-8-10 68 DaneO'Neill 4 74
(Henry Candy) *led: rdn and hung rt fr over 1f out: hdd nr fin* **2/1**[2]
4111 **3** 1¼ **White Vin Jan**[10] 5630 2-8-1 66 MichaelKenneally(7) 2 68
(Michael Bell) *w ldr tl pushed along over 2f out: rdn and ev ch over 1f out: unable qck towards fin* **6/1**[3]
31 **4** 3½ **War Alert (USA)**[49] 4269 2-9-7 79 JamieSpencer 5 71
(David Brown) *trckd ldrs: rdn over 1f out: sn edgd rt: eased whn btn wl ins fnl f* **10/11**[1]

1m 13.41s (0.41) **Going Correction** 0.0s/f (Good) 4 Ran SP% **107.7**
Speed ratings (Par 94): **97,96,94,90**
CSF £34.71 TOTE £9.30; EX 33.30 Trifecta £41.50.
**Owner** Edwin Phillips & Mrs Pamela Aitken **Bred** Hyde Park Stud & Lisglen **Trained** Newmarket, Suffolk

**FOCUS**
A decent little fillies' nursery in which they went a proper gallop.

## 5984 IAN PILLINGER "AVE IT" MEMORIAL H'CAP 1m 3f 183y
**4:10** (4:11) (Class 5) (0-75,75) 3-Y-O+ **£2,587** (£770; £384; £192) **Stalls** Low

Form RPR
00-1 **1** **Fractal**[240] 51 3-9-3 75 MartinLane 9 87+
(David Simcock) *hld up: hdwy and hung rt fr over 2f out: rdn to ld over 1f out: styd on* **11/4**[2]
-206 **2** 2 **Moshe (IRE)**[12] 5557 3-9-3 75 JimmyFortune 2 83
(Hughie Morrison) *trckd ldrs: rdn over 2f out: nt clr run over 1f out: styd on u.p to go 2nd wl ins fnl f* **9/4**[1]
/3-4 **3** 2¼ **Favorite Girl (GER)**[128] 1729 6-8-13 62 AndrewMullen 5 66
(Michael Appleby) *trckd ldr: racd keenly: led 4f out: rdn over 2f out: hdd over 1f out: no ex ins fnl f* **12/1**
3205 **4** 1½ **Syncopate**[29] 3335 5-9-11 74 StephenCraine 3 76
(Pam Sly) *prom: rdn over 3f out: outpcd over 2f out: styd on fnl f* **16/1**
3132 **5** *nk* **Royal Marskell**[12] 5572 5-9-9 72 TomEaves 1 74
(Alison Hutchinson) *s.s: hld up: rdn over 3f out: nvr trbld ldrs* **7/1**
1026 **6** 7 **All The Winds (GER)**[21] 5259 9-9-4 67 (t) WilliamTwiston-Davies 6 57
(Shaun Lycett) *s.s: hld up: rdn over 3f out: n.d* **20/1**
1031 **7** ¾ **Storm Rider (IRE)**[9] 5689 3-9-1 73 (b) PatDobbs 4 62
(Richard Hannon) *led 8f: rdn and wknd over 1f out* **5/1**[3]
6235 **8** 4 **Di's Gift**[13] 5527 5-9-6 74 DuilioDaSilva(5) 7 57
(Richard Guest) *prom tl rdn and wknd over 2f out* **16/1**

2m 35.08s (1.18) **Going Correction** 0.0s/f (Good)
**WFA** 3 from 5yo+ 9lb 8 Ran SP% **110.8**
Speed ratings (Par 103): **96,94,93,92,91 87,86,84**
CSF £8.72 CT £56.14 TOTE £4.80: £1.80, £1.20, £2.40; EX 12.50 Trifecta £149.90.
**Owner** The Black Gold Partnership **Bred** Jeremy Green And Sons **Trained** Newmarket, Suffolk

**FOCUS**
A fair middle-distance handicap in which they went an honest gallop. The one-two were the least exposed and have improved.

## 5985 CROPSTON NURSERY H'CAP 5f 2y
**4:40** (4:41) (Class 6) (0-65,64) 2-Y-O **£2,587** (£770; £384; £192) **Stalls** High

Form RPR
062 **1** **Zipedeedodah (IRE)**[30] 4909 2-9-2 **64** ShaneGray(5) 6 69
(Joseph Tuite) *chsd ldrs: led wl over 1f out: sn rdn: jst hld on* **7/1**
6404 **2** *shd* **Fujiano**[32] 4815 2-9-5 **62** [1] DavidProbert 2 67
(Derek Haydn Jones) *hld up: swtchd lft 1/2-way: hdwy over 1f out: rdn and hung lft ins fnl f: r.o wl* **25/1**
3235 **3** 2¼ **Midnight Destiny (IRE)**[7] 5779 2-9-1 **58** (v) DaleSwift 11 55
(Derek Shaw) *s.i.s: hdwy over 1f out: rdn and hung lft ins fnl f: styd on same pce* **33/1**
006 **4** 1 **True Course**[68] 3583 2-9-5 **62** SilvestreDeSousa 13 55
(Charlie Appleby) *mid-div: hdwy 1/2-way: rdn over 1f out: styd on same pce ins fnl f* **7/2**[2]
4526 **5** *nk* **Classic Flyer**[10] 5637 2-9-5 **62** DanielTudhope 8 54
(David O'Meara) *a.p: rdn and ev ch wl over 1f out: no ex ins fnl f* **3/1**[1]
023 **6** ¾ **Candlelight (IRE)**[26] 5042 2-9-7 **64** JamieSpencer 3 53
(Charles Hills) *prom: lost pl over 3f out: sn pushed along: r.o ins fnl f* **5/1**[3]
3246 **7** 1 **Penalty Scorer**[10] 5630 2-8-4 **52** ow1 DuilioDaSilva(5) 10 38
(Richard Guest) *prom: rdn over 1f out: styd on same pce fnl f* **25/1**
6264 **8** *hd* **Frank The Barber (IRE)**[27] 5014 2-9-3 **60** (b[1]) GrahamGibbons 9 45
(Steph Hollinshead) *sn led: rdn and hdd wl over 1f out: nt clr run and no ex ins fnl f* **16/1**
4625 **9** ¾ **Pickle Lilly Pearl**[10] 5637 2-9-2 **59** RobertWinston 4 42
(David C Griffiths) *prom: rdn over 1f out: wknd fnl f* **12/1**
3324 **10** 8 **River Spirit**[26] 5028 2-9-6 **63** SamHitchcott 12 16
(Mick Channon) *sn pushed along in rr: bhd fr 1/2-way* **16/1**
063 **11** ½ **Fine Judgment**[30] 4909 2-8-13 **56** DougieCostello 7 8
(William Muir) *racd keenly: w ldr tl pushed along 1/2-way: wknd over 1f out* **12/1**
0663 **12** 1¾ **Rosie Crowe (IRE)**[12] 5569 2-8-13 **56** FrederikTylicki 5
(David C Griffiths) *prom: rdn 1/2-way: sn wknd* **33/1**

1m 1.55s (1.55) **Going Correction** 0.0s/f (Good) 12 Ran SP% **117.1**
Speed ratings (Par 93): **87,86,83,81,81 79,78,78,76,64 63,60**
CSF £174.05 CT £5344.36 TOTE £9.70: £2.80, £7.50, £5.20; EX 164.60 Trifecta £1505.80.
**Owner** M Wellbelove & J Tuite **Bred** Tally-Ho Stud **Trained** Great Shefford, Berks

**FOCUS**
A modest nursery, rated around the principals, in which they went a contested gallop.

## 5986 KINOULTON H'CAP 7f 9y
**5:10** (5:12) (Class 4) (0-80,80) 3-Y-O+ **£4,851** (£1,443; £721; £360) **Stalls** High

Form RPR
3163 **1** **Al Khan (IRE)**[5] 5810 5-9-4 79 (p) JacobButterfield(5) 7 88
(Ollie Pears) *chsd ldr: rdn to ld and edgd lft ins fnl f: r.o* **6/1**
3124 **2** 1¼ **Red Paladin (IRE)**[13] 5536 4-9-2 72 JamieSpencer 3 78
(Kevin Ryan) *s.i.s: sn pushed along in rr: rdn over 1f out: r.o to go 2nd wl ins fnl f* **5/1**[3]
4336 **3** ¾ **Available (IRE)**[7] 5766 5-9-8 78 (tp) FrannyNorton 8 82
(John Mackie) *led: rdn over 1f out: hdd ins fnl f: styd on same pce* **5/1**[3]
0656 **4** *shd* **Footstepsintherain (IRE)**[10] 5638 4-9-2 72 SilvestreDeSousa 5 76
(David Dennis) *hld up: plld hrd: rdn over 1f out: r.o ins fnl f: nt rch ldrs* **20/1**
0030 **5** ½ **Tidal's Baby**[34] 4762 5-9-6 76 [1] AndrewMullen 2 78
(Michael Appleby) *s.i.s: in rr and pushed along 1/2-way: hdwy u.p over 1f out: styd on same pce ins fnl f* **8/1**
3214 **6** *hd* **Biotic**[33] 4801 3-8-8 68 TedDurcan 4 68
(Rod Millman) *prom: rdn over 1f out: no ex ins fnl f* **9/2**[2]
0454 **7** *nk* **Good Luck Charm**[26] 5031 5-9-6 76 (v[1]) ShaneKelly 9 77
(Gary Moore) *trckd ldrs: rdn over 1f out: no ex ins fnl f* **7/1**
221 **8** 1½ **Elizona**[37] 4653 3-9-6 80 FrederikTylicki 6 75
(James Fanshawe) *plld hrd and prom: rdn over 1f out: no ex ins fnl f* **4/1**[1]
24RR **9** 1 **Caramack**[7] 5750 4-8-12 75 MikeyEnnis(7) 1 70
(Richard Lee) *s.i.s: sn prom: rdn and lost pl over 2f out: edgd lft over 1f out: styd on towards fin* **16/1**

1m 25.76s (-0.44) **Going Correction** 0.0s/f (Good)
**WFA** 3 from 4yo+ 4lb 9 Ran SP% **120.1**
Speed ratings (Par 105): **102,100,99,99,99 98,98,96,95**
CSF £37.59 CT £165.63 TOTE £6.70: £2.40, £2.10, £1.90; EX 38.60 Trifecta £283.00.
**Owner** Richard Walker **Bred** Galadari Sons Stud Company Limited **Trained** Norton, N Yorks

**FOCUS**
A fair handicap in which they went a sound gallop. The winner is rated close to last's year peak, with the second to form.

## 5987 SIX HILLS H'CAP 5f 218y
**5:40** (5:40) (Class 5) (0-70,70) 3-Y-O+ **£2,587** (£770; £384; £192) **Stalls** High

Form RPR
0353 **1** **Generalyse**[11] 5595 5-9-4 70 (b) RyanTate(3) 3 81
(Ben De Haan) *mde virtually all: rdn over 1f out: styd on* **6/1**
0602 **2** ¾ **Smokethatthunders (IRE)**[16] 5411 4-8-11 65 DanielMuscutt(5) 6 73
(James Unett) *a.p: chsd wnr over 1f out: sn rdn: r.o* **10/1**

6051 **3** 3 **Top Offer**[44] 4431 5-9-4 67 ShaneKelly 8 65+
(Peter Crate) *hld up: hdwy over 2f out: r.o: nt rch ldrs* **7/2**[1]
4613 **4** 2 3/4 **Divertimenti (IRE)**[7] 5777 10-8-4 56 oh3 (b) BillyCray(3) 10 45
(Roy Bowring) *racd alone: w ldrs over 2f: remained handy: rdn over 2f out: edgd rt fr over 1f out: styd on same pce* **12/1**
4205 **5** 1 1/2 **Three Pips**[13] 5526 3-9-2 67 [1] RobertWinston 7 51
(Ed McMahon) *w wnr over 3f: sn rdn: wknd fnl f* **33/1**
1402 **6** 1/2 **Borough Boy (IRE)**[7] 5777 4-9-0 63 DaleSwift 1 46
(Derek Shaw) *dwlt: rdn over 1f out: nvr on terms* **5/1**[3]
3434 **7** 3 1/2 **Coiste Bodhar (IRE)**[40] 4535 3-8-5 63 (p) NoraLooby(7) 2 35
(Joseph Tuite) *chsd wnr: rdn over 2f out: wknd over 1f out* **16/1**
0030 **8** 6 **Aye Aye Skipper (IRE)**[11] 5602 4-8-13 62 TedDurcan 5 14
(Dean Ivory) *prom: rdn 1/2-way: wknd over 1f out* **10/1**
0002 **9** 3 1/2 **Majestic Dream (IRE)**[7] 5761 6-9-0 63 (v) GrahamGibbons 4 4
(Michael Easterby) *prom: lost pl over 4f out: bhd and rdn 1/2-way: eased ins fnl f* **9/2**[2]
2235 **10** 11 **Bonjour Steve**[59] 3936 3-8-5 61 (p) ShaneGray(5) 9
(Richard Price) *w ldrs tl rdn over 2f out: sn wknd* **8/1**
1m 12.54s (-0.46) **Going Correction** 0.0s/f (Good)
**WFA** 3 from 4yo+ 2lb **10** Ran SP% **117.2**
Speed ratings (Par 103): **103,102,98,94,92 91,87,79,74,59**
CSF £64.80 CT £248.35 TOTE £9.10: £2.30, £3.30, £1.40; EX 77.00 Trifecta £365.30.
**Owner** Mrs D Vaughan **Bred** Mrs D Vaughan **Trained** Lambourn, Berks
**FOCUS**
The concluding contest was a modest sprint handicap in which they went a contested gallop across the track. The winner is rated to his best since a C&D win off the same mark last October.
T/Jkpt: Not won. T/Plt: £472.60 to a £1 stake. Pool: £76988.28 - 118.90 winning tickets T/Qpdt: £216.00 to a £1 stake. Pool: £4290.91 - 14.70 winning tickets CR

5988 - 5993a (Foreign Racing) - See Raceform Interactive

5806
# CARLISLE (R-H)
Tuesday, September 2

**OFFICIAL GOING: Good to firm (good in places) changing to good (good to firm in places) after race 2 (2.30)**
Wind: Virtually Nil Weather: Sunny Rails: Inside rail moved out from 1m and around Old Stable bend to 3f marker and distances on Round course increased by about 7yds

## 5994 KINGMOOR PARK SUPPORTS CARLISLE YOUTH ZONE APPRENTICE H'CAP 5f 193y
**2:00** (2:00) (Class 6) (0-65,71) 3-Y-O **£2,264** (£673; £336; £168) **Stalls** Low

Form RPR
4220 **1** **Shades Of Silk**[18] 5389 3-9-7 65 MeganCarberry 3 71
(James Given) *hld up in tch: rdn and hdwy over 1f out: kpt on: led 75yds out* **11/4**[2]
6003 **2** 3/4 **Madagascar Moll (IRE)**[19] 5333 3-8-12 61 JoshDoyle(5) 1 64
(David O'Meara) *dwlt: sn chsd ldr: rdn to ld over 1f out: one pce: hdd 75yds out* **9/2**[3]
5465 **3** shd **Slick Indian**[9] 5715 3-8-9 56 (b) AnnaHesketh(3) 4 58
(Michael Easterby) *hld up in tch: rdn over 2f out: kpt on fr over 1f out* **10/1**
0031 **4** 1 **Chookie's Lass**[6] 5808 3-9-8 71 6ex PeterSword(5) 2 70
(Keith Dalgleish) *s.i.s: hld up in tch: rdn and hdwy over 1f out: ev ch ins fnl f: no ex fnl 50yds* **9/4**[1]
3300 **5** 6 **Soul Instinct**[11] 5631 3-8-7 54 (b) GaryMahon(3) 6 34
(Kevin Ryan) *led: rdn whn hdd over 1f out: wknd* **16/1**
6303 **6** 2 3/4 **Emily Davison (IRE)**[4] 5889 3-9-5 63 (b[1]) GemmaTutty 7 34
(Karen Tutty) *chsd ldr: rdn over 2f out: wknd over 1f out* **9/2**[3]
1m 15.3s (1.60) **Going Correction** +0.325s/f (Good) **6** Ran SP% **108.8**
Speed ratings (Par 99): **102,101,100,99,91 87**
CSF £14.30 CT £92.17 TOTE £3.90: £2.00, £2.70; EX 12.70 Trifecta £65.00.
**Owner** The Cool Silk Partnership **Bred** Mrs F S Williams **Trained** Willoughton, Lincs
**FOCUS**
This was a competitive little sprint handicap, confined to apprentice riders. There was a solid pace on and it produced a tight four-way finish down the centre of the home straight. The second filly is rated to this year's form and there was a personal best from the third.

## 5995 NORTH ASSOCIATES LAND & PROPERTY SPECIALISTS MAIDEN STKS 5f 193y
**2:30** (2:30) (Class 5) 2-Y-O **£2,911** (£866; £432; £216) **Stalls** Low

Form RPR
40 **1** **Golden Spun (USA)**[11] 5655 2-9-5 0 DavidNolan 9 73
(Bryan Smart) *chsd ldrs towards outer: rdn to ld wl over 1f out: wandered but kpt on* **7/1**
33 **2** 1 **Doppler Effect**[13] 5561 2-9-5 0 PJMcDonald 4 70
(Ann Duffield) *chsd ldrs: rdn over 2f out: kpt on fnl f: wnt 2nd 75yds out* **10/3**[2]
64 **3** 1/2 **Dark Wonder (IRE)**[33] 4829 2-9-5 0 DaleSwift 2 68
(James Given) *dwlt: sn pushed along to chse ldrs: rdn over 2f out: kpt on* **11/2**[3]
2602 **4** 2 **Midlander (IRE)**[7] 5790 2-9-5 78 FrannyNorton 1 62
(Mark Johnston) *sn led: rdn whn hdd wl over 1f out: wknd ins fnl f: lost 2 pls fnl 75yds* **10/11**[1]
0 **5** nk **Splash Of Verve (IRE)**[17] 5443 2-9-5 0 GrahamGibbons 6 61
(Philip Kirby) *hld up: pushed along over 2f out: kpt on ins fnl f* **50/1**
0 **6** 12 **Notnowdear**[9] 5712 2-8-12 0 RowanScott(7) 10 24
(Ann Duffield) *hld up: rdn 1/2-way: sn wknd* **33/1**
06 **7** 1 1/2 **Sir Acclam (IRE)**[46] 4382 2-9-5 0 TomEaves 3 19
(Keith Dalgleish) *w ldr: rdn over 2f out: wknd over 1f out* **16/1**
0 **8** 1 1/4 **Xander (IRE)**[15] 5494 2-9-5 0 IanBrennan 11 16
(Tim Easterby) *slowly away: a towards rr* **50/1**
1m 16.24s (2.54) **Going Correction** +0.325s/f (Good) **8** Ran SP% **116.1**
Speed ratings (Par 95): **96,94,94,91,90 74,72,71**
CSF £30.79 TOTE £9.50: £1.70, £1.90, £1.90; EX 39.00 Trifecta £143.40.
**Owner** Fiddes, Chappell & Unique Sports **Bred** Carl Schexnayder & Harold Babineaux **Trained** Hambleton, N Yorks
**FOCUS**
An ordinary 2yo maiden, run at a fair pace and again the riders shunned the far rail.

## 5996 CARR'S MILLING INDUSTRIES PLC (S) STKS 5f 193y
**3:05** (3:06) (Class 6) 3-Y-O+ **£2,264** (£673; £336; £168) **Stalls** Low

Form RPR
1302 **1** **Gaelic Wizard (IRE)**[9] 5711 6-8-8 56 GemmaTutty(5) 3 65
(Karen Tutty) *in tch in 3rd: rdn and hdwy to chse ldr over 1f out: led ins fnl f: kpt on* **11/2**[3]
4012 **2** 1 1/4 **Live Dangerously**[4] 5889 4-9-5 66 TomEaves 4 67
(Keith Dalgleish) *led narrowly: rdn over 1f out: hdd ins fnl f: one pce* **9/4**[2]
0200 **3** 3 3/4 **Waffle (IRE)**[17] 5444 8-8-13 78 (p) GrahamGibbons 2 49
(David Barron) *dwlt: sn rdn along to press ldr: drvn 2f out: hld in poor 3rd fr over 1f out* **6/5**[1]
2210 **4** 4 **Mission Impossible**[21] 5265 9-9-5 66 (p) DaleSwift 5 42
(Tracy Waggott) *hld up in rr: rdn over 2f out: nvr threatened* **7/1**
00 **5** 2 1/4 **Plunder**[60] 3908 4-8-13 50 (b) PatrickMathers 1 29
(Alan Berry) *hld up: rdn 1/2-way: sn btn* **66/1**
1m 15.72s (2.02) **Going Correction** +0.325s/f (Good) **5** Ran SP% **105.6**
Speed ratings (Par 101): **99,97,92,87,84**
CSF £16.66 TOTE £5.20: £2.20, £2.20; EX 17.90 Trifecta £37.90.No bid for the winner.
**Owner** Grange Park Racing **Bred** Mrs Mary Gallagher **Trained** Osmotherley, N Yorks
**FOCUS**
The going was changed slightly to good, good to firm in places after the second race. The winner is rated to a bit better view of recent form in this grade.

## 5997 EXPLOSIVE PRODUCTIONS LTD 10TH ANNIVERSARY MAIDEN FILLIES' STKS 5f 193y
**3:40** (3:40) (Class 5) 3-4-Y-O **£3,234** (£962; £481; £240) **Stalls** Low

Form RPR
3342 **1** **Percy's Gal**[11] 5641 3-8-9 72 GemmaTutty(5) 1 71
(Karen Tutty) *racd keenly: trckd ldr: led on bit over 1f out: rdn and kpt on* **5/2**[2]
003 **2** 2 1/2 **Asha**[17] 5417 3-9-0 60 AndrewElliott 2 63
(David C Griffiths) *dwlt: hld up: rdn 1/2-way: kpt on fr over 1f out despite edging rt: wnt 2nd ins fnl f* **25/1**
0022 **3** 3/4 **Two Smart (IRE)**[6] 5814 3-9-0 77 PJMcDonald 4 61
(K R Burke) *led: rdn whn hdd over 1f out: no ex* **11/10**[1]
6-02 **4** 4 1/2 **Great Wave (IRE)**[14] 5532 3-9-0 70 GrahamGibbons 6 46
(David Simcock) *chsd ldr: rdn over 2f out: wknd fnl f* **3/1**[3]
5554 **5** 2 3/4 **Puppet Theatre (IRE)**[13] 5570 4-8-13 45 SamJames(3) 5 37
(David O'Meara) *chsd ldrs: rdn 1/2-way: wknd over 1f out* **33/1**
1m 15.43s (1.73) **Going Correction** +0.325s/f (Good)
**WFA** 3 from 4yo 2lb **5** Ran SP% **108.0**
Speed ratings (Par 100): **101,97,96,90,87**
CSF £41.62 TOTE £3.80: £1.30, £4.20; EX 20.90 Trifecta £72.80.
**Owner** Arrand & Tutty **Bred** R W Huggins **Trained** Osmotherley, N Yorks
**FOCUS**
A modest fillies' maiden with the form trio less than robust. The winner is rated to form, with the second improving again.

## 5998 CUBBY CONSTRUCTION LTD NURSERY H'CAP (BOBIS RACE) 5f
**4:15** (4:15) (Class 4) (0-85,85) 2-Y-O **£4,204** (£1,251; £625; £312) **Stalls** Low

Form RPR
2201 **1** **King Crimson**[12] 5593 2-9-0 78 CharlesBishop(3) 1 81
(Mick Channon) *mde all: rdn over 1f out: drvn and reduced advantage ins fnl f: jst hld on* **4/1**[3]
5511 **2** hd **Bowson Fred**[17] 5409 2-9-1 76 GrahamGibbons 2 78
(Michael Easterby) *chsd ldr: rdn over 1f out: kpt on fnl f: jst hld* **4/1**[3]
0401 **3** 5 **Clouds Rest**[9] 5714 2-9-5 85 6ex JackGarritty(5) 5 69
(Richard Fahey) *trckd ldr: rdn 2f out: sn one pce and hld in 3rd* **6/4**[1]
2615 **4** 4 1/2 **Danot (IRE)**[21] 5266 2-8-11 72 TomEaves 3 40
(Keith Dalgleish) *hld up: rdn 1/2-way: nvr threatened* **16/1**
3410 **5** hd **Indescribable (IRE)**[31] 4920 2-9-7 82 FrannyNorton 4 49
(Mark Johnston) *hld up: rdn 1/2-way: nvr threatened* **7/2**[2]
1m 2.43s (1.63) **Going Correction** +0.325s/f (Good) **5** Ran SP% **108.1**
Speed ratings (Par 97): **99,98,90,83,83**
CSF £18.81 TOTE £4.70: £2.20, £2.50; EX 26.90 Trifecta £34.30.
**Owner** Wilde & Webster **Bred** Mickley Stud **Trained** West Ilsley, Berks
**FOCUS**
Competitive stuff but the favourite faoled to back up his Beverley effort. It was predictably run at a decent pace.

## 5999 YESSS ELECTRICAL WHOLESALER OF THE YEAR H'CAP 7f 200y
**4:50** (4:51) (Class 4) (0-85,80) 3-Y-O+ **£5,175** (£1,540; £769; £384) **Stalls** Low

Form RPR
-114 **1** **Jacob Black**[6] 5816 3-9-5 80 TomEaves 5 91
(Keith Dalgleish) *mde all: rdn 2f out: wandered ins fnl f: kpt on wl* **10/3**[2]
0340 **2** 3 **Party Royal**[59] 3955 4-9-8 78 PJMcDonald 3 83
(Ruth Carr) *trckd ldr: rdn over 2f out: kpt on same pce and no ch w wnr* **13/2**
3222 **3** hd **An Chulainn (IRE)**[8] 5768 3-8-9 70 (b) FrannyNorton 2 74
(Mark Johnston) *hld up: racd keenly: pushed along and hdwy to dispute 2nd over 1f out: rdn ins fnl f: carried hd high and no further imp* **9/2**[3]
3200 **4** 4 1/2 **Alquimia (IRE)**[17] 5446 3-9-0 75 TonyHamilton 4 68
(Richard Fahey) *trckd ldr: rdn over 2f out: wknd fnl f* **5/2**[1]
5555 **5** nk **Correggio**[20] 5299 4-8-13 74 (p) JackGarritty(5) 1 68
(Micky Hammond) *hld up: rdn over 2f out: sn btn* **5/2**[1]
1m 41.48s (1.48) **Going Correction** +0.325s/f (Good)
**WFA** 3 from 4yo 5lb **5** Ran SP% **111.7**
Speed ratings (Par 105): **105,102,101,97,97**
CSF £23.46 TOTE £3.50: £2.40, £3.50; EX 22.10 Trifecta £47.00.
**Owner** Redgate Bloodstock **Bred** Miss Emma Foley **Trained** Carluke, S Lanarks
**FOCUS**
Another tight handicap. The winner resumed his progress under a more efficient front-running ride than last time, and this was easier too, particularly with the joint-favourites disappointing.

## 6000 BAINES WILSON LAWYERS FOR BUSINESS H'CAP 1m 3f 107y
**5:20** (5:20) (Class 6) (0-65,65) 3-Y-O+ **£2,264** (£673; £336; £168) **Stalls** High

Form RPR
522 **1** **Saint Thomas (IRE)**[20] 5301 7-9-9 62 FrannyNorton 2 71
(John Mackie) *in tch: rdn over 2f out: led over 1f out: edgd lft: styd on wl* **11/4**[1]
2324 **2** 2 **Call Of Duty (IRE)**[10] 5268 9-9-0 58 EmmaSayer(5) 8 64
(Dianne Sayer) *hld up in rr: rdn and hdwy fr over 2f out: wnt 2nd ins fnl f: edgd rt: kpt on* **10/1**
0-01 **3** 5 **Moon Over Rio (IRE)**[19] 5331 3-8-13 60 AndrewElliott 3 58
(Ben Haslam) *trckd ldr: rdn over 3f out: led over 2f out: hdd over 1f out: wknd* **9/2**[2]
553 **4** 2 **Chilly Miss**[18] 5388 5-9-9 62 BrianHughes 4 56
(Malcolm Jefferson) *midfield: rdn over 3f out: one pce and nvr threatened* **9/2**[2]
5244 **5** 4 **Vicky Valentine**[21] 5270 4-9-7 65 GarryWhillans(5) 6 53
(Alistair Whillans) *in tch: rdn to chal over 2f out: wknd over 1f out* **6/1**[3]

6533 **6** 4 1/2 **Harrison's Cave**[5] 5856 6-9-6 59........................(b[1]) TomEaves 1 39
(Keith Dalgleish) *sn led: rdn whn hdd over 2f out: sn wknd* **8/1**
0026 **7** 3 1/2 **Taxiformissbyron**[36] 4730 4-8-5 51 oh2........................ RowanScott(7) 5 26
(Iain Jardine) *midfield: rdn over 4f out: sn struggling* **22/1**
-055 **8** 6 **Mitcd (IRE)**[68] 3603 3-8-0 52........................ JoeDoyle(5) 7 17
(Martin Todhunter) *midfield: rdn over 3f out: sn wknd* **8/1**
2m 26.94s (3.84) **Going Correction** +0.325s/f (Good)
**WFA** 3 from 4yo+ 8lb **8 Ran SP% 113.0**
Speed ratings (Par 101): **99,97,93,92,89 86,83,79**
CSF £30.57 CT £118.43 TOTE £3.20: £1.60, £2.70, £1.80; EX 22.20 Trifecta £88.50.
**Owner** P Riley **Bred** S Coughlan **Trained** Church Broughton , Derbys
**FOCUS**
A moderate handicap, run at a strong early pace. The winner built on recent runs, but is still rated 7lb off last year's best.
T/Plt: £184.50 to a £1 stake. Pool: £41,708.03 - 165.01 winning tickets. T/Qpdt: £39.20 to a £1 stake. Pool: £3,547.07 - 66.90 winning tickets. AS

# 5718 GOODWOOD (R-H)

Tuesday, September 2

**OFFICIAL GOING: Straight course - good to soft; round course - good**
Wind: Almost nil Weather: Fine

## 6001 EBF STALLIONS MAIDEN FILLIES' STKS (BOBIS RACE) 1m
2:20 (2:21) (Class 5) 2-Y-O £3,234 (£962; £481; £240) Stalls Low

Form RPR
**1** **Timba** 2-9-0........................ WilliamBuick 4 84+
(John Gosden) *dwlt: hld up in last: clsd over 2f out: plld out and shkn up over 1f out: rn green but chsd ldr fnl f: r.o to ld last 100yds: readily* **8/1**[3]
3 **2** 1 1/4 **Mystic Jade**[10] 5667 2-9-0........................ RichardHughes 1 80
(Richard Hannon) *t.k.h: led after 2f to 4f out: led wl over 2f out: kicked for home wl over 1f out: rdn and hdd last 100yds: styd on but outpcd* **9/4**[2]
3 **3** 4 **Cartier (IRE)**[17] 5416 2-9-0........................ TedDurcan 3 71
(David Simcock) *dwlt: hld up in 4th: clsd over 2f out: chsd ldr wl over 1f out: sn shkn up and nt qckn: lost 2nd and wl outpcd fnl f* **10/11**[1]
5 **4** 7 **Starring Guest (IRE)**[11] 5644 2-9-0........................ JamesDoyle 5 55
(Mick Channon) *led 2f: led 4f out to wl over 2f out: wknd qckly over 1f out* **8/1**[3]
0 **5** 2 3/4 **Kipuka**[46] 4396 2-9-0........................ JimCrowley 2 48
(Paul Cole) *plld hrd early: chsd ldng pair to over 2f out: racd awkwardly after: wknd qckly and hung lft fnl f* **14/1**
1m 41.44s (1.54) **Going Correction** +0.075s/f (Good) **5 Ran SP% 112.0**
Speed ratings (Par 92): **95,93,89,82,80**
CSF £26.59 TOTE £7.00: £3.20, £1.30; EX 15.10 Trifecta £34.40.
**Owner** George Strawbridge **Bred** George Strawbridge **Trained** Newmarket, Suffolk
**FOCUS**
It was dry overnight and the going was good to soft on the straight course and good on the round course. This looked quite an interesting maiden. The third was a bit disappointing, just to the bare form of her debut.

## 6002 GOODWOOD RACEHORSE OWNERS GROUP MAIDEN STKS 1m 1f 192y
2:55 (2:56) (Class 5) 3-Y-O £3,234 (£962; £481; £240) Stalls Low

Form RPR
2-42 **1** **Soviet Courage (IRE)**[19] 5347 3-9-5 80........................ RyanMoore 4 93
(William Haggas) *trckd clr ldr: led over 3f out: shkn up over 2f out: drew rt away over 1f out* **1/3**[1]
03 **2** 13 **Too The Stars (IRE)**[18] 5382 3-9-0........................ WilliamBuick 7 68
(John Gosden) *trckd ldng pair: wnt 2nd jst over 3f out: shkn up over 2f out: easily lft bhd over 1f out* **7/2**[2]
3356 **3** 13 **Turnbury**[122] 1947 3-8-12 62........................(t) SophieRalston(7) 6 44
(Robert Mills) *t.k.h: led: clr after 3f: 10 l up whn hung lft bnd 1/2-way and lost most of the advantage: hdd over 3f out: wknd rapidly 2f out* **100/1**
00 **4** 5 **Jack Bear**[27] 5039 3-9-0........................ NedCurtis(5) 1 34
(Jonathan Portman) *s.s: a detached in last: t.o* **66/1**
0-5 **P** **Rosarina**[18] 5382 3-9-0........................ FergusSweeney 3
(Jo Crowley) *hld up: 4th whn lost action and p.u 6f out* **14/1**[3]
**P** **Ferayha (IRE)** 3-9-0........................ AndreaAtzeni 5
(Roger Varian) *slowly away: lost action and p.u after 2f* **16/1**
2m 8.12s (0.02) **Going Correction** +0.075s/f (Good) **6 Ran SP% 112.3**
Speed ratings (Par 101): **102,91,81,77,**
CSF £1.85 TOTE £1.50: £1.10, £1.10; EX 2.00 Trifecta £21.80.
**Owner** Somerville Lodge Limited **Bred** Michael Downey & Roalso Ltd **Trained** Newmarket, Suffolk
**FOCUS**
A modest maiden for the track, rendered even less competitive when Ferayha (reported lame in front) and Rosarina (reported to have hung badly right) were pulled up early in the race. The level is a bit fluid.

## 6003 FINANCIAL SERVICES EXPO NURSERY STKS (H'CAP) (BOBIS RACE) 6f
3:30 (3:30) (Class 2) 2-Y-O £9,703 (£2,887; £1,443; £721) Stalls High

Form RPR
0421 **1** **Johnny B Goode (IRE)**[22] 5242 2-8-2 76........................ AndreaAtzeni 3 79+
(Richard Fahey) *mde all against nr side rail: sent for wl over 1f out: drvn and pressed fnl f: styd on* **9/2**
321 **2** 3/4 **Flash Fire (IRE)**[18] 5397 2-8-11 85........................ WilliamBuick 4 86
(Mark Johnston) *trckd wnr after 2f: chal over 1f out: drvn and nt qckn fnl f* **15/8**[1]
1324 **3** 3/4 **Sunset Sail (IRE)**[10] 5672 2-9-1 89........................ RichardHughes 5 88
(Richard Hannon) *trckd wnr 2f: cl up after: rdn and nt qckn 1f out: one pce after* **4/1**[3]
0403 **4** nk **Billyoakes (IRE)**[18] 5373 2-7-7 74 oh2........................ PaddyPilley(7) 2 72
(Mick Channon) *awkward s: t.k.h early: sn in 4th: shkn up and nt qckn over 1f out: one pce after* **16/1**
105 **5** 1 1/2 **George Bowen (IRE)**[32] 4853 2-8-10 84........................ RyanMoore 7 77
(Richard Fahey) *hld up and sn in last: pushed along 2f out: no imp on ldrs after: one pce* **9/4**[2]
1m 13.04s (0.84) **Going Correction** +0.075s/f (Good) **5 Ran SP% 109.6**
Speed ratings (Par 101): **97,96,95,94,92**
CSF £13.25 TOTE £4.60: £2.50, £1.80; EX 13.10 Trifecta £27.90.
**Owner** Jonathan Gill **Bred** Noel Brosnan **Trained** Musley Bank, N Yorks
**FOCUS**
The positions changed little in this sprint, with the leader dictating a sensible pace.

## 6004 EBFSTALLIONS.COM PETER WILLETT CONDITIONS STKS (BOBIS RACE) 7f
4:05 (4:05) (Class 2) 2-Y-O £15,562 (£4,660; £2,330; £1,165) Stalls Low

Form RPR
12 **1** **Make It Up**[17] 5424 2-9-2........................ DavidProbert 1 97
(Andrew Balding) *mde all: shkn up and wl in command over 1f out: rdn out* **11/4**[3]
21 **2** 1 3/4 **Good Contact (USA)**[23] 5201 2-9-2........................ JamesDoyle 2 93
(Saeed bin Suroor) *trckd ldng pair: wnt 2nd over 2f out: sn rdn: no imp on wnr over 1f out: kpt on* **13/8**[1]
1 **3** 3 1/2 **Johnny Barnes (IRE)**[20] 5315 2-9-2........................ WilliamBuick 4 84
(John Gosden) *wl in tch in last: effrt whn nudged by rival jst over 2f out: rdn to dispute 2nd over 1f out: sn btn: wknd fnl f* **15/8**[2]
3114 **4** 7 **Step To The Shears**[46] 4398 2-9-8 96........................ PatDobbs 3 72
(Richard Hannon) *chsd wnr: rdn wl over 2f out: edgd lft and sn lost 2nd: wknd* **10/1**
1m 27.38s (0.38) **Going Correction** +0.075s/f (Good) **4 Ran SP% 108.6**
Speed ratings (Par 101): **100,98,94,86**
CSF £7.60 TOTE £3.70; EX 7.50 Trifecta £13.80.
**Owner** George Strawbridge **Bred** George Strawbridge **Trained** Kingsclere, Hants
**FOCUS**
Some promising types lined up for this conditions race and it has been rated on the positive side. The winner is rated a minor improver, with the standard pretty much to Listed level. The second improved and the third is rated near his debut win.

## 6005 ROYAL SUSSEX REGIMENT STKS (H'CAP) 2m
4:40 (4:40) (Class 2) (0-105,99) 3-Y-O+ £12,938 (£3,850; £1,924; £962) Stalls Low

Form RPR
2130 **1** **Kashgar**[24] 5161 5-8-6 82........................ DanielMuscutt(5) 5 89
(Bernard Llewellyn) *hld up in 6th: clsd 3f out: rdn to chal on inner 2f out: led over 1f out but sn jnd: hld on wl fnl f* **4/1**[2]
3066 **2** hd **Blue Surf**[10] 5668 5-9-12 97........................ PatDobbs 3 103
(Amanda Perrett) *trckd ldr after 2f: covered up after: gng strly over 2f out: clsd to chal over 1f out: w wnr fnl f: drvn and nt qckn last 100yds* **8/1**
/2-0 **3** 1 1/4 **Triumphant (IRE)**[17] 5432 5-9-7 99........................ HectorCrouch(7) 1 103
(Gary Moore) *cl up: rdn to ld over 2f out: hdd over 1f out: kpt on same pce* **25/1**
5064 **4** 3 **Statutory (IRE)**[13] 5579 4-9-12 97........................ AndreaAtzeni 4 98
(Saeed bin Suroor) *cl up: rdn and nt qckn over 2f out: sn outpcd: n.d fnl f* **11/4**[1]
1551 **5** 1 1/2 **Spice Fair**[19] 5334 7-9-3 88........................ RichardHughes 2 87
(Mark Usher) *hld up in last: plld out and rdn 2f out: hung lft and no real prog after: eased last 50yds* **7/1**
13 **6** 3 **Dolphin Village (IRE)**[11] 5651 4-9-2 87........................ RyanMoore 7 82
(Richard Fahey) *wnt 2nd after 2f: w ldr 1/2-way to over 2f out: sn rdn and wknd* **4/1**[2]
1150 **7** 1 1/2 **Special Fighter (IRE)**[11] 5633 3-8-0 89........................ CamHardie(5) 6 82
(Mark Johnston) *led: rdn and hdd over 2f out: wknd wl over 1f out* **9/2**[3]
3m 34.01s (5.01) **Going Correction** +0.075s/f (Good)
**WFA** 3 from 4yo+ 13lb **7 Ran SP% 112.3**
Speed ratings (Par 109): **90,89,89,87,87 85,84**
CSF £33.68 TOTE £5.70: £2.10, £4.90; EX 33.70 Trifecta £450.30.
**Owner** Alex James **Bred** J L C Pearce **Trained** Fochriw, Caerphilly
**FOCUS**
A bit muddling. The winner is rated to form, but the race might not prove solid.

## 6006 GOLF AT GOODWOOD STKS (H'CAP) 6f
5:10 (5:10) (Class 4) (0-80,80) 3-Y-O+ £6,469 (£1,925; £962; £481) Stalls High

Form RPR
0011 **1** **Inciting Incident (IRE)**[8] 5753 3-9-4 79 6ex........................(p) RyanMoore 1 88
(Ed McMahon) *racd centre: mde virtually all: rdn over 1f out: kpt on wl fnl f: drvn out* **4/1**[2]
4614 **2** 1/2 **Langley Vale**[25] 5124 5-9-4 77........................(p) SebSanders 5 84
(Roger Teal) *racd centre: pressed wnr: rdn to chal over 1f out: styd on but a jst hld* **10/1**
5-64 **3** 3/4 **Shamahan**[12] 5595 5-9-0 73........................ RobertHavlin 3 78
(Luke Dace) *chsd ldng pair in centre: drvn over 1f out: nt qckn but kpt on fnl f* **12/1**
3-10 **4** hd **Secret Hint**[33] 4826 3-9-5 80........................ DavidProbert 10 84+
(Andrew Balding) *racd alone against nr side rail: nt on terms w main gp ldrs: rdn and hung rt fr 2f out but had mde prog: chsd ldrs fnl f: kpt on one pce: rn wl* **3/1**[1]
131 **5** shd **Spiraea**[19] 5355 4-9-2 75........................ RichardHughes 7 79
(Mark Rimell) *chsd ldrs in centre: rdn over 1f out: tried to cl fnl f: one pce last 100yds* **6/1**[3]
2432 **6** nk **Lucky Di**[11] 5624 4-8-11 70........................ JimCrowley 6 73
(Peter Hedger) *chsd ldrs in centre: rdn over 2f out: nvr able to cl but kpt on fnl f* **6/1**[3]
-064 **7** 3/4 **Rocket Rob (IRE)**[18] 5392 8-8-11 70........................ ChrisCatlin 4 70
(Willie Musson) *dwlt: prom in centre: shkn up wl over 1f out: nt qckn after: fdd ins fnl f* **12/1**
020 **8** 2 1/4 **Vallarta (IRE)**[11] 5650 4-9-4 77........................ WilliamBuick 12 70
(Mick Channon) *racd in nr side quartet tl jnd main gp in centre 1/2-way: wl in rr after: no real hdwy fnl f* **8/1**
0050 **9** 2 **Harwoods Volante (IRE)**[31] 4912 3-9-5 80........................ PatDobbs 9 67
(Amanda Perrett) *t.k.h: hld up in nr side quartet: jnd centre gp 1/2-way and in rr: rdn and no prog over 1f out* **25/1**
2300 **10** 2 **Vincentti (IRE)**[10] 5677 4-8-12 78........................ MikeyEnnis(7) 8 58
(Ronald Harris) *led quartet towards nr side: jnd main gp 1/2-way and prom: rdn and wknd qckly wl over 1f out* **16/1**
1m 11.89s (-0.31) **Going Correction** +0.075s/f (Good)
**WFA** 3 from 4yo+ 2lb **10 Ran SP% 118.9**
Speed ratings (Par 105): **105,104,103,103,102 102,101,98,95,93**
CSF £44.71 CT £354.68 TOTE £4.60: £1.50, £3.90, £4.60; EX 59.70 Trifecta £573.50.
**Owner** The W H O Society **Bred** Yeomanstown Stud **Trained** Lichfield, Staffs

**FOCUS**
There was a difference of opinion here as Ryan Moore from stall one led a group of six up the centre of the track, while the four highest-drawn runners started racing stands' side. Three of those four abandoned that project in favour of tacking over to join the centre group, and they finished in the last three places. The winner earned a small personal-best rating, with the second to form and the third at his best since winning at Bath in August.

## 6007 GOODWOOD AVIATION & FLYING SCHOOL H'CAP — 1m 3f
**5:40** (5:40) (Class 5) (0-70,69) 4-Y-O+ — **£3,234** (£962; £481; £240) **Stalls** High

Form — RPR

333 **1** **Last Minute Lisa (IRE)**[17] 5435 4-9-1 63 .................... RichardHughes 9 — 75+
(Sylvester Kirk) *taken down early: hld up in last pair: stdy prog to trck ldrs 2f out: plld out over 1f out: r.o to ld last 150yds: sn clr* **15/8**[1]

4655 **2** *2 ¼* **Red Dragon (IRE)**[38] 4656 4-9-1 63 .................... DavidProbert 6 — 68
(Michael Blanshard) *hld up in tch: trckd ldrs over 2f out gng wl: waiting for a gap tl got through over 1f out: chal fnl f: outpcd last 150yds* **8/1**[3]

4-05 **3** *1* **Foxhaven**[88] 2947 12-9-3 68 ....................(v) ThomasBrown(3) 2 — 71
(Patrick Chamings) *led after 2f: sn jnd: rdn 2f out: kpt on wl but hdd and outpcd last 150yds* **12/1**

4634 **4** *½* **Beep**[4] 5873 4-8-12 60 .................... RobertHavlin 4 — 62
(Lydia Richards) *cl up: gng strly and poised to chal over 2f out: rdn over 1f out: nt qckn and outpcd fnl f* **25/1**

4-22 **5** *4 ½* **Comedy House**[134] 1100 6-8-4 59 .................... KieranShoemark(7) 11 — 53
(Michael Madgwick) *hld up in last pair: pushed along on outer over 3f out: prog but hung rt and ended against rail on inner 2f out: cl up over 1f out: wknd fnl f* **16/1**

4564 **6** *1 ½* **Tilstarr (IRE)**[13] 5551 4-9-2 69 .................... MarcMonaghan(5) 10 — 61
(Roger Teal) *taken down early: wl in tch: rdn on outer 3f out: no prog over 2f out: steadily wknd* **12/1**

11-2 **7** *1 ¾* **Brave Decision**[228] 210 7-8-12 60 .................... MartinLane 3 — 48
(Suzy Smith) *jnd ldr after 2f: drvn and wknd wl over 1f out* **12/1**

-320 **8** *nk* **Hector's Chance**[70] 3556 5-9-3 68 .................... RyanTate(3) 8 — 56
(Heather Main) *taken down early: trckd ldrs: rdn wl over 2f out: no prog over 1f out: wknd* **8/1**[3]

6412 **9** *4* **Hallingham**[25] 5139 4-8-12 65 ....................(b) CamHardie(5) 7 — 46
(Jonathan Portman) *in tch in rr: shoved along fr 1/2-way: no prog 3f out: steadily wknd* **7/2**[2]

0045 **10** *13* **Double Dealites**[38] 4678 4-8-4 57 .................... DanielMuscutt(5) 1 — 14
(Jamie Poulton) *led 2f: lost pl after 4f: rdn and struggling 5f out: sn btn: t.o* **20/1**

0100 **11** *nk* **April Ciel**[30] 4948 5-8-11 66 ....................(p) MikeyEnnis(7) 5 — 23
(Ronald Harris) *chsd ldrs: rdn and wknd over 4f out: t.o* **25/1**

2m 30.33s (3.83) **Going Correction** +0.075s/f (Good) — **11** Ran SP% **120.6**
Speed ratings (Par 103): **89,87,86,86,83 81,80,80,77,68 67**
CSF £17.61 CT £143.32 TOTE £2.90: £1.50, £2.50, £3.30; EX 21.60 Trifecta £182.90.
**Owner** Gerry Dolan **Bred** Geoffrey Croke **Trained** Upper Lambourn, Berks

**FOCUS**
They didn't go much of a gallop early on, they bunched up in the straight and a turn of foot won the day. A personal-best performance from the winner.
T/Plt: £438.50 to a £1 stake. Pool: £66,648.07 - 110.93 winning tickets. T/Qpdt: £132.50 to a £1 stake. Pool: £4,370.96 - 24.40 winning tickets. JN

# 5852 HAMILTON (R-H)
## Tuesday, September 2

**OFFICIAL GOING: Good to soft (good in places; 7.2)**
Wind: Almost nil Weather: Overcast Rails: Rail movement around the loop reduced distances on Round course by about 25yds

## 6008 ST ANDREWS AMBULANCE NURSERY H'CAP — 6f 5y
**2:10** (2:10) (Class 5) (0-75,75) 2-Y-O — **£3,881** (£1,155; £577; £288) **Stalls** High

Form — RPR

450 **1** **Secret Friend (IRE)**[45] 4450 2-8-3 57 ....................(b[1]) DuranFentiman 8 — 62
(Tim Easterby) *t.k.h: chsd ldrs against stands' rail: rdn and outpcd 2f out: rallied to ld wl ins fnl f: r.o* **33/1**

4552 **2** *1 ¼* **Saltarello (IRE)**[11] 5630 2-9-3 71 .................... PhillipMakin 2 — 72
(John Quinn) *led: rdn and jnd over 1f out: hdd wl ins fnl f: kpt on same pce* **15/8**[1]

3354 **3** *shd* **Atreus**[18] 5373 2-8-8 62 .................... JamesSullivan 7 — 63
(Michael Easterby) *cl up: chal and hung rt over 1f out: kpt on same pce wl ins fnl f* **7/1**[3]

4520 **4** *1 ¼* **Anastazia**[21] 5285 2-9-4 72 .................... KierenFallon 4 — 69
(Paul D'Arcy) *dwlt: hld up: hdwy on outside over 2f out: chal over 1f out to ins fnl f: one pce towards fin* **3/1**[2]

2364 **5** *¾* **Straightothepoint**[13] 5561 2-9-4 72 ....................(v[1]) GrahamLee 6 — 67
(Bryan Smart) *t.k.h: hld up in tch: effrt and rdn wl over 1f out: no imp fnl f* **8/1**

004 **6** *1 ¼* **Moon Arc (IRE)**[22] 5242 2-7-12 55 ow1 .................... JoeyHaynes(3) 1 — 46
(Keith Dalgleish) *t.k.h: cl up tl rdn and wknd over 1f out* **7/1**[3]

626 **7** *¾* **Muhaarib Al Emarat (IRE)**[21] 5264 2-9-1 72 ........ GeorgeChaloner(3) 9 — 61
(Richard Fahey) *dwlt: t.k.h and sn cl up: rdn over 2f out: wknd over 1f out* **15/2**

1m 13.44s (1.24) **Going Correction** +0.025s/f (Good) — **7** Ran SP% **110.6**
Speed ratings (Par 95): **92,90,90,88,87 85,84**
CSF £89.16 CT £482.28 TOTE £24.50: £8.10, £1.40; EX 72.40 Trifecta £632.20.
**Owner** Mrs Jennifer E Pallister **Bred** Old Carhue & Graeng Bloodstock **Trained** Great Habton, N Yorks

**FOCUS**
A fair nursery in which they went a decent gallop on ground officially described as good to soft, good in places. Improved form from the winner, and the second and third help opening level.

## 6009 DIGBY BROWN H'CAP — 1m 65y
**2:40** (2:42) (Class 5) (0-75,74) 3-Y-O+ — **£3,234** (£962; £481; £240) **Stalls** Low

Form — RPR

1316 **1** **Hanalei Bay (IRE)**[17] 5413 4-9-10 74 .................... PhillipMakin 5 — 85
(Keith Dalgleish) *mde all at ordinary gallop: qcknd clr wl over 1f out: pushed along whn edgd rt and flashed tail ins fnl f: unchal* **3/1**[1]

0042 **2** *2 ¼* **Royal Holiday (IRE)**[13] 5571 7-9-1 65 ....................(b) DanielTudhope 2 — 70
(Marjorie Fife) *trckd ldrs: rdn and outpcd over 2f out: rallied over 1f out: kpt on to take 2nd towards fin: nt pce of wnr* **10/3**[2]

0306 **3** *hd* **Tectonic (IRE)**[22] 5235 5-9-1 65 ....................(p) KierenFallon 8 — 69
(Keith Dalgleish) *hld up: stdy hdwy over 2f out: effrt and chsd wnr whn hung bdly rt over 1f out: one pce fnl f: lost 2nd towards fin* **17/2**

1100 **4** *2 ¼* **Lady Artiste (IRE)**[18] 5385 4-9-8 72 .................... BenCurtis 3 — 71
(Alan Swinbank) *hld up bhd ldng gp: rdn over 3f out: rallied over 1f out: kpt on fnl f: nvr able to chal* **8/1**

2605 **5** *2 ¼* **Zain Zone (IRE)**[15] 5497 3-9-5 74 ....................(p) JamesSullivan 9 — 67
(Ruth Carr) *t.k.h: sn cl up on outside: rdn over 2f out: wknd over 1f out* **17/2**

6505 **6** *3 ¾* **Spavento (IRE)**[50] 4255 8-8-10 60 .................... JasonHart 1 — 45
(Eric Alston) *dwlt: hld up: rdn over 3f out: no imp fr 2f out* **9/1**

600 **7** *2* **Rioja Day (IRE)**[42] 4523 4-8-10 60 oh1 .................... GrahamLee 6 — 41
(Jim Goldie) *cl up tl rdn: edgd rt and wknd fr 2f out* **16/1**

-613 **8** *2 ¼* **Cosquillas (IRE)**[200] 613 3-8-11 66 .................... JoeFanning 7 — 40
(Mark Johnston) *s.i.s: hld up: outpcd over 3f out: n.d after* **6/1**[3]

30-0 **9** *3 ¾* **Chamberlain**[15] 5497 3-8-10 65 ....................(p) DavidAllan 4 — 31
(John Murray) *t.k.h: prom: rdn over 2f out: wknd wl over 1f out* **80/1**

1m 46.63s (-1.77) **Going Correction** -0.25s/f (Firm)
**WFA** 3 from 4yo+ 5lb — **9** Ran SP% **111.6**
Speed ratings (Par 103): **98,95,95,93,91 87,85,83,79**
CSF £12.38 CT £72.45 TOTE £3.80: £2.00, £1.70, £3.10; EX 13.80 Trifecta £64.20.
**Owner** Mrs Francesca Mitchell **Bred** Holborn Trust Co **Trained** Carluke, S Lanarks

**FOCUS**
A fair handicap in which a notably quicker winning time than the first race, off an even gallop, does suggests the round course was riding slightly better than on the straight track. This is rated around the runner-up to his recent efforts.

## 6010 "BECAUSE IT MATTERS" H'CAP — 1m 1f 36y
**3:15** (3:15) (Class 6) (0-60,59) 3-Y-O — **£1,940** (£577; £288; £144) **Stalls** Low

Form — RPR

0-41 **1** **Quest Of Colour (IRE)**[34] 4793 3-9-4 59 .................... GeorgeChaloner(3) 1 — 70
(Richard Fahey) *t.k.h early: trckd ldrs: rdn over 3f out: rallied to ld over 2f out: drifted lft over 1f out: rdn out* **7/4**[1]

-600 **2** *2 ¼* **Neuf Des Coeurs**[67] 3662 3-9-7 59 .................... JoeFanning 4 — 65
(Keith Dalgleish) *hld up towards rr: effrt and hdwy to chse wnr over 1f out: kpt on same pce ins fnl f* **14/1**

**3** *4 ½* **Ed Led Jed (IRE)**[7] 5805 3-8-7 45 ....................(p) JamesSullivan 8 — 42
(John C McConnell, Ire) *missed break: bhd and sn pushed along: hdwy over 2f out: effrt and rdn over 1f out: no imp* **6/1**

42 **4** *2 ¾* **Shiftin Bobbins**[22] 5234 3-8-12 50 .................... PaulMulrennan 6 — 41
(Michael Dods) *t.k.h: chsd ldr: ev ch over 3f out to over 2f out: rdn and lost 2nd over 1f out: wknd ins fnl f* **9/2**[2]

4551 **5** *1 ¼* **Notts So Blue**[22] 5239 3-9-0 52 .................... JasonHart 7 — 40
(Shaun Harris) *led: rdn and hdd over 2f out: wknd over 1f out* **9/2**[2]

0244 **6** *12* **Tortoise**[4] 5892 3-8-12 55 ....................(b) DuilioDaSilva(5) 2 — 18
(Richard Guest) *prom: drvn over 2f out: wknd wl over 1f out* **11/2**[3]

506- **7** *2 ¾* **The Bunny Catcher**[280] 8044 3-8-4 45 .................... JoeyHaynes(3) 5 — 2
(Sharon Watt) *hld up: rdn and struggling over 3f out: btn fnl 2f* **66/1**

0060 **8** *5* **Magic Shoes (IRE)**[8] 5765 3-9-2 54 .................... RoystonFfrench 3 — 1
(Susan Corbett) *in tch: struggling wl over 3f out: sn btn* **50/1**

1m 57.19s (-2.51) **Going Correction** -0.25s/f (Firm) — **8** Ran SP% **112.5**
Speed ratings (Par 99): **101,99,95,92,91 80,78,73**
CSF £28.66 CT £120.65 TOTE £2.70: £1.40, £3.20, £3.20; EX 29.50 Trifecta £150.10.
**Owner** Havelock Racing 2 **Bred** Awbeg Stud **Trained** Musley Bank, N Yorks

**FOCUS**
An unconvincing field, but it was soundly run and the second filly is rated to her 2yo form.

## 6011 ALWAYS TRYING OPEN MAIDEN STKS — 1m 1f 36y
**3:50** (3:51) (Class 5) 3-Y-O+ — **£3,408** (£1,006; £503) **Stalls** Low

Form — RPR

2223 **1** **Legal Waves (IRE)**[27] 5052 4-9-11 78 .................... KierenFallon 1 — 88
(Alan Swinbank) *in tch: stdy hdwy over 2f out: shkn up to ld over 1f out: sn clr: eased nr fin* **13/8**[1]

2543 **2** *8* **Potent Embrace (USA)**[11] 5634 3-9-0 71 .................... JoeFanning 2 — 66
(Mark Johnston) *t.k.h: w ldr: led over 3f out to over 2f out: kpt on: no ch w wnr* **5/2**[2]

**3** *1 ¼* **L'Inganno Felice (FR)**[710] 4-9-11 0 .................... DavidAllan 9 — 69
(Iain Jardine) *hld up: stdy hdwy over 3f out: effrt and chsd first two over 1f out: no imp* **40/1**

**4** *2 ¼* **Never Up (GER)**[71] 3-9-5 0 .................... DanielTudhope 5 — 64
(David O'Meara) *chsd ldrs: effrt and wnt 2nd briefly over 2f out: outpcd over 1f out* **3/1**[3]

444 **5** *1 ¼* **Braes Of Lochalsh**[18] 5388 3-9-5 0 .................... GrahamLee 3 — 61
(Jim Goldie) *hld up: pushed along and effrt over 3f out: edgd rt and no imp fr over 2f out* **12/1**

**6** *½* **So It's War (FR)** 3-9-5 0 .................... PhillipMakin 4 — 60
(Keith Dalgleish) *hld up in tch: effrt and pushed along over 2f out: wknd appr fnl f* **16/1**

50 **7** *23* **Justcallhimbilly**[18] 5374 4-9-11 0 .................... DuranFentiman 7 — 12
(Shaun Harris) *in tch tl lost pl 1/2-way: struggling fr 4f out: t.o* **100/1**

0 **8** *1 ¼* **Silver Lightening (IRE)**[34] 4796 4-9-11 62 .................... JasonHart 8 — 9
(Eric Alston) *led to over 3f out: rdn and wknd over 2f out: t.o* **66/1**

5 **9** *13* **Ballyhurst (IRE)**[126] 1841 3-9-2 0 .................... GeorgeChaloner(3) 6
(Richard Fahey) *hld up: struggling over 4f out: sn btn: t.o* **28/1**

1m 56.19s (-3.51) **Going Correction** -0.25s/f (Firm)
**WFA** 3 from 4yo 6lb — **9** Ran SP% **113.6**
Speed ratings (Par 103): **105,97,96,94,93 93,72,71,60**
CSF £5.60 TOTE £2.70: £1.10, £1.50, £7.10; EX 5.40 Trifecta £130.40.
**Owner** Mrs B V Sangster **Bred** Airlie Stud **Trained** Melsonby, N Yorks

**FOCUS**
This is rated around the winner with doubts over the rest of the field.

## 6012 NEILSLAND AND EARNOCK H'CAP — 1m 3f 16y
**4:25** (4:25) (Class 5) (0-75,71) 3-Y-O+ — **£3,234** (£962; £481; £240) **Stalls** Low

Form — RPR

413 **1** **Nakeeta**[30] 4941 3-9-4 71 .................... DavidNolan 2 — 80+
(Iain Jardine) *t.k.h: hld up: hdwy on outside to ld over 2f out: rdn and edgd rt wl over 1f out: kpt on fnl f* **9/4**[1]

/6-6 **2** *1 ¾* **Rockawango (FR)**[110] 1485 8-9-2 61 ....................(tp) PaulMulrennan 6 — 65
(James Ewart) *t.k.h: hld up: rdn 3f out: gd hdwy on outside fnl f: tk 2nd towards fin: no ch w wnr* **22/1**

4613 **3** *nk* **Clear Spell (IRE)**[18] 5387 3-9-1 71 .................... ConnorBeasley(3) 3 — 76+
(Alistair Whillans) *hld up in tch: stdy hdwy whn n.m.r briefly over 2f out: effrt and chsng ldrs whn hmpd wl over 1f out: kpt on fnl f: nt pce to chal* **11/4**[2]

6404 **4** *1* **Royal Straight**[5] 5855 9-8-13 63 ....................(t) SammyJoBell(5) 8 — 65
(Linda Perratt) *taken early to post: hld up: stdy hdwy on ins over 3f out: effrt and chsng ldrs whn n.m.r briefly over 1f out: one pce fnl f* **9/1**

5 ½ **Stynes (IRE)**[11] 5366 4-9-2 64..............................(t) GeorgeChaloner(3) 1 65
(John C McConnell, Ire) *led: rdn and hdd over 2f out: edgd rt wl over 1f out: one pce fnl f* 9/2[3]
562 6 nk **Ronald Gee (IRE)**[8] 5765 7-9-4 63.................................. GrahamLee 5 63
(Jim Goldie) *t.k.h: pressed ldr: rdn 3f out: kpt on same pce fnl f* 11/2
1100 7 2 ½ **El Bravo**[9] 5716 8-9-12 71.......................................... BenCurtis 7 67
(Shaun Harris) *chsd ldrs: drvn over 2f out: no ex over 1f out* 22/1
230- 8 2 **Roc De Prince**[17] 2118 5-9-10 69.............................(tp) LucyAlexander 4 61
(James Ewart) *dwlt: sn prom: rdn over 3f out: wknd 2f out* 33/1

2m 24.32s (-1.28) **Going Correction** -0.25s/f (Firm)
**WFA** 3 from 4yo+ 8lb 8 Ran SP% **112.6**
Speed ratings (Par 103): **94,92,92,91,91 91,89,87**
CSF £53.24 CT £140.17 TOTE £4.20: £1.10, £5.00, £1.20; EX 50.00 Trifecta £273.90.
**Owner** Alex and Janet Card **Bred** Mike Channon Bloodstock Ltd **Trained** Bonchester Bridge, Roxburgh

**FOCUS**
The pace looked ordinary yet the first four home raced in the last four positions.

## 6013 BETFAIR SCOTTISH SPRINT SERIES FINAL H'CAP 6f 5y
**5:00** (5:04) (Class 3) 3-Y-0+ **£9,703** (£2,887; £1,443; £721) **Stalls** High

Form RPR
310 1 **Baron Run**[22] 5236 4-8-10 71.......................................... JoeyHaynes(3) 9 81
(K R Burke) *mde all: rdn over 2f out: hld on gamely fnl f* 5/1[1]
2131 2 ¾ **Layla's Hero (IRE)**[6] 5817 7-9-5 77 6ex..................(v) PaulMulrennan 11 85
(David Nicholls) *prom on nr side of gp: effrt and wnt 2nd over 2f out: sn pushed along: kpt on ins fnl f: nt rch wnr* 13/2[2]
1230 3 ½ **Gran Canaria Queen**[17] 5444 5-9-7 79........................... DavidAllan 13 85
(Tim Easterby) *midfield: rdn over 2f out: kpt on wl fnl f: nvr able to chal* 10/1
2216 4 ½ **Classy Anne**[24] 5170 4-8-12 70.......................................... GrahamLee 6 75
(Jim Goldie) *chsd wnr to over 2f out: kpt on same pce ins fnl f* 14/1
6122 5 ¾ **Alexandrakollontai (IRE)**[18] 5396 4-9-1 76..............(b) JulieBurke(3) 12 78
(Alistair Whillans) *hld up in tch: drvn and outpcd 1/2-way: kpt on fnl f: nvr able to chal* 10/1
3436 6 nk **Jinky**[22] 5236 6-8-12 70.......................................................... JoeFanning 7 71
(Linda Perratt) *prom: effrt and rdn over 2f out: one pce fr over 1f out* 14/1
4512 7 nk **Klynch**[11] 5632 8-9-8 80.......................................(b) JamesSullivan 2 80
(Ruth Carr) *prom: rdn over 2f out: hung rt over 1f out: no ex* 12/1
3300 8 1 **Tango Sky (IRE)**[22] 5236 5-9-0 72 ow1............................ DavidNolan 14 69
(Richard Fahey) *bhd: rdn over 2f out: hdwy over 1f out: kpt on: nrst fin* 15/2[3]
2556 9 3 ¾ **Bunce (IRE)**[11] 5632 6-9-2 77..................................... ConnorBeasley(3) 1 62
(Linda Perratt) *hld up on far side of gp: rdn over 2f out: no imp fr over 1f out* 22/1
-100 10 ½ **Mandalay King (IRE)**[46] 4383 9-8-6 69...................(b) JordanNason(5) 8 53
(Marjorie Fife) *bhd: rdn along 1/2-way: nvr on terms* 20/1
5431 11 ¾ **Go Go Green (IRE)**[15] 5498 8-8-12 73.......................... GaryBartley(3) 5 54
(Jim Goldie) *bhd: pushed along 1/2-way: no imp fr 2f out* 20/1
1050 12 1 ½ **Foxy Clarets (IRE)**[17] 5444 3-9-7 84..................(b) GeorgeChaloner(3) 4 60
(Richard Fahey) *wnt lft s: bhd: drvn along 1/2-way: nvr on terms* 8/1
33 13 nk **Salvatore Fury (IRE)**[35] 4762 4-9-0 72........................(p) PhillipMakin 10 48
(Keith Dalgleish) *dwlt: hld up: pushed along over 2f out: sn btn* 10/1
4230 14 1 **Opt Out**[24] 5168 4-8-8 66.......................................................... JasonHart 3 38
(Alistair Whillans) *midfield: struggling over 2f out: sn btn* 22/1

1m 11.32s (-0.88) **Going Correction** +0.025s/f (Good)
**WFA** 3 from 4yo+ 2lb 14 Ran SP% **119.4**
Speed ratings (Par 107): **106,105,104,103,102 102,101,100,95,94 93,91,91,90**
CSF £33.12 CT £312.54 TOTE £5.60: £1.80, £2.20, £3.60; EX 39.80 Trifecta £547.10.
**Owner** Mrs Elaine M Burke **Bred** Mrs D Hughes **Trained** Middleham Moor, N Yorks

**FOCUS**
The feature contest was a decent sprint handicap in which the winner recorded by far the best comparative time of the day on the straight track. This was a small personal-best performance from the winner, with the runner-up edging closer to his old form. The third is rated a shade off her best.

## 6014 COMPENSATE PERSONAL INJURY NETWORK AMATEUR RIDERS' H'CAP 6f 5y
**5:30** (5:32) (Class 6) (0-65,64) 4-Y-0+ **£1,975** (£607; £303) **Stalls** High

Form RPR
0001 1 **Rise To Glory (IRE)**[7] 5801 6-10-5 55 6ex..................(tp) MrsCBartley 8 66
(Shaun Harris) *mde all: rdn and edgd to stands' rail over 1f out: hld on wl fnl f* 16/1
156 2 ¾ **Lord Buffhead**[11] 5635 5-9-9 52.........................(v) DylanMcDonagh(7) 12 61
(Richard Guest) *chsd wnr: effrt and rdn 2f out: kpt on ins fnl f: hld towards fin* 12/1
3642 3 nk **Slim Chance (IRE)**[6] 5806 5-11-0 64.................................. MrWHogg 4 72
(Simon West) *trckd ldrs: effrt and pushed along 2f out: kpt on ins fnl f* 10/1
1640 4 1 ¼ **Iceblast**[4] 5887 6-10-11 64.................................(b) MissJoannaMason(3) 7 68
(Michael Easterby) *prom: rdn and edgd lft over 1f out: kpt on same pce ins fnl f* 9/1
334 5 1 **Captain Scooby**[5] 5858 8-9-13 49..................................(b) MissCWalton 10 50
(Richard Guest) *hld up: smooth hdwy and prom over 1f out: sn rdn: one pce ins fnl f* 8/1[3]
4600 6 1 ¼ **Red Invader (IRE)**[4] 5873 4-9-13 54................................ MrsRWilson(5) 1 51
(Paul D'Arcy) *bhd and outpcd: hdwy over 1f out: kpt on fnl f: nvr able to chal* 40/1
7 nk **Rockview Emperor (IRE)**[6] 5838 4-9-10 51..........(b) MrJohnWilley(5) 6 47
(John C McConnell, Ire) *missed break: bhd and pushed along: rdn 1/2-way: hdwy over 1f out: no imp fnl f* 16/1
4506 8 1 ½ **Hab Reeh**[6] 5806 6-11-0 64.................................................. MissSBrotherton 9 55
(Ruth Carr) *hld up in midfield: stdy hdwy over 2f out: pushed along and no imp over 1f out* 13/2[2]
6453 9 nk **Sewn Up**[11] 5635 4-10-0 50.......................................(p) MrSWalker 13 40
(Keith Dalgleish) *hld up nr side: rdn over 2f out: no imp fr over 1f out* 7/2[1]
0245 10 2 ¾ **Rock Canyon (IRE)**[5] 5858 5-9-10 51...........................(p) MrHStock(5) 3 32
(Linda Perratt) *towards rr on far side of gp: rdn over 2f out: wknd over 1f out* 12/1
565- 11 1 ¼ **Opus Dei**[488] 1964 7-9-13 56..................................................(p) MrLHall(7) 11 33
(John Murray) *s.i.s: bhd: rdn 1/2-way: nvr on terms* 100/1
4625 12 nse **Shillito**[6] 5806 4-10-5 60.......................................................... MrKWood(5) 5 37
(Tony Coyle) *cl up tl rdn and wknd over 1f out* 12/1
3046 13 2 ¾ **Mysterious Wonder**[55] 4069 4-10-0 55..................(b) PhillipDennis(5) 2 23
(Philip Kirby) *cl up tl rdn and wknd wl over 1f out* 13/2[2]

1m 13.18s (0.98) **Going Correction** +0.025s/f (Good) 13 Ran SP% **117.4**
Speed ratings (Par 101): **94,93,92,90,89 87,87,85,85,81 79,79,76**
CSF £192.38 CT £2084.56 TOTE £15.20: £5.10, £3.40, £2.60; EX 256.40 Trifecta £1748.20.
**Owner** N Blencowe,J Sunderland,M Lenton,CHarris **Bred** Bryan Ryan **Trained** Carburton, Notts

**FOCUS**
The concluding contest was a modest sprint handicap restricted to amateur riders. The winner is rated a bit off last autumn/winter peak, and the second and third help set the level in a race where few got involved.
T/Plt: £11.40 to a £1 stake. Pool: £61,256.99 - 3,913.71 winning tickets. T/Qpdt: £6.40 to a £1 stake. Pool: £5,255.15 - 599.86 winning tickets. RY

# 5820 KEMPTON (A.W) (R-H)
### Tuesday, September 2

**OFFICIAL GOING: Polytrack: standard**
Wind: virtually nil Weather: dry

## 6015 BOOK NOW FOR JUMP SUNDAY 19.10.14 CLASSIFIED STKS 1m 2f (P)
**5:50** (5:54) (Class 6) 3-Y-0+ **£1,940** (£577; £288; £144) **Stalls** Low

Form RPR
0620 1 **Sexy Secret**[5] 5865 3-8-8 55..............................(v1) SimonPearce(3) 11 66
(Lydia Pearce) *pressed ldrs tl led over 8f out: mde rest: rdn and clr wl over 1f out: styd on: rdn out* 10/1
0646 2 4 ½ **Sheer Poetry (IRE)**[14] 5529 3-8-11 52.................................. LukeMorris 8 57
(Mike Murphy) *chsd ldrs: wnt 2nd over 3f out: hrd drvn and no imp over 1f out* 5/1[3]
0044 3 2 ¾ **Lola Montez (IRE)**[21] 5283 3-8-11 55..............................(b) TedDurcan 6 52
(David Lanigan) *hld up in midfield: switching lft 3f out: outpcd and racing awkwardly over 2f out: cajoled along and wnt 3rd 1f out: kpt on but no ch w wnr* 9/4[2]
052 4 3 **Smile For Me (IRE)**[38] 4653 3-8-11 47.............................. SamHitchcott 10 47
(Harry Dunlop) *plld v hrd: hld up towards rr: hdwy into midfield 3f out: no ch w wnr but plugged on u.p fnl f* 8/1
060 5 1 **Byronegetonefree**[24] 5186 3-8-11 55.............................. JimmyQuinn 13 45
(John E Long) *chsd ldrs: 4th and drvn 3f out: sn outpcd and wl btn fnl 2f: plugged on* 20/1
0-00 6 nk **Miss Rebero**[18] 5376 4-9-4 45.......................................... TomQueally 3 44
(Tim Fitzgerald) *led tl over 8f out: chsd wnr tl over 3f out: 3rd and btn 2f out: sn wknd* 33/1
0032 7 10 **First Sargeant**[12] 5599 4-9-4 55.................................. AndrewMullen 5 25
(Michael Appleby) *sn dropped towards and rdn: nvr gng wl: n.d* 7/4[1]
0-50 8 ¾ **Percys Princess**[15] 5504 3-8-11 50................................ SteveDrowne 14 24
(Pat Murphy) *in toouch in midfield: effrt and hdwy 4f out: drvn and btn 3f out: sn wknd* 33/1
000 9 8 **Mountain River (IRE)**[17] 5427 3-8-11 45................(b1) StevieDonohoe 2 8
(J S Moore) *chsd ldrs: u.p 5f out: wknd over 3f out: t.o* 33/1
0500 10 18 **Arryzona**[20] 5321 3-8-6 45.......................................... EoinWalsh(5) 4
(Christine Dunnett) *sn bhd and rdn: t.o fnl 4f* 66/1
00R0 11 9 **My Gigi**[20] 5303 4-9-4 54.......................................................... AmirQuinn 1
(Laura Mongan) *taken down early: v.s.a: a bhd: t.o fnl 3f* 25/1
060- P **Commanding Force**[315] 7442 3-8-11 45.......................... WilliamCarson 9
(John Bridger) *chsd ldrs tl dropped out rapidly 4f out: t.o and p.u 2f out* 66/1

2m 6.38s (-1.62) **Going Correction** -0.10s/f (Stan)
**WFA** 3 from 4yo 7lb 12 Ran SP% **124.4**
Speed ratings (Par 101): **102,98,96,93,93 92,84,84,77,63 56,**
CSF £58.79 TOTE £6.90: £3.10, £1.80, £1.80; EX 51.80 Trifecta £235.90.
**Owner** Oceana racing **Bred** W G H Barrons **Trained** Newmarket, Suffolk
■ Kirkstall Abbey (25-1) was withdrawn. Rule 4 does not apply.

**FOCUS**
They finished well strung out in this weak classified and the favourite was disappointing. Kirkstall Abbey refused to go into the stalls and was withdrawn. The winner is rated as having run a personal best, but with little confidence in the level.

## 6016 DOWNLOAD THE BETVICTOR APP NOW NURSERY H'CAP 5f (P)
**6:20** (6:25) (Class 5) (0-75,69) 2-Y-0 **£2,587** (£770; £384; £192) **Stalls** Low

Form RPR
413 1 **Loumarin (IRE)**[40] 4576 2-9-4 66................................ FergusSweeney 8 71
(Martyn Meade) *broke fast to ld and cross to inner rail: clr 2f out: drvn over 1f out: a jst lasting home: all out* 10/1
5525 2 nk **Lyfka**[33] 4815 2-8-13 61.......................................................... LukeMorris 6 65
(Paul Cole) *dwlt: sn bustled along and rcvrd to r in midfield: drvn and hdwy over 1f out: chsd wnr 1f out: steadily clsd: nvr quite getting up* 12/1
6214 3 1 ½ **Somedaysrdiamonds**[31] 4920 2-8-12 60................................ LiamJones 4 59
(J S Moore) *chsd wnr: rdn over 1f out: 3rd and styd on same pce ins fnl f* 6/1
004 4 2 ½ **Presto Boy**[15] 5488 2-9-7 69........................................(t) HayleyTurner 9 59
(James Fanshawe) *chsd ldrs: rdn and unable qck over 1f out: no imp fnl f* 5/1[3]
5551 5 nk **Arlecchino's Leap**[15] 5506 2-8-13 66....................(v) RachealKneller(5) 1 55
(Mark Usher) *stdd s: hld up in detached last: effrt and swtchd lft over 1f out: nt clr run and swtchd lft again ins fnl f: r.o wl: nvr trbld ldrs* 9/2[2]
2105 6 ½ **Magic Florence (IRE)**[7] 5791 2-9-6 68............................ TomQueally 3 55
(James Given) *a towards rr of main gp: effrt u.p over 2f out: kpt on but nvr threatened ldrs* 11/4[1]
4460 7 ¾ **Alpha Spirit**[21] 5285 2-9-3 65..........................................[1] SamHitchcott 2 49
(Mick Channon) *a towards rr of main gp: drvn 2f out: kpt on but nvr a threat* 7/1
2226 8 1 **Lady Zodiac (IRE)**[6] 5828 2-8-11 59................................ SteveDrowne 5 40
(Andrew Balding) *chsd ldrs: rdn and uable to qckn 2f out: btn over 1f out: wknd fnl f* 12/1
005 9 nk **Mullionheir**[23] 5210 2-8-12 60.................................. WilliamCarson 7 40
(John Best) *a towards rr of main gp: wd bnd 3f out: n.d* 20/1

59.92s (-0.58) **Going Correction** -0.10s/f (Stan) 9 Ran SP% **117.5**
Speed ratings (Par 95): **100,99,97,93,92 91,90,89,88**
CSF £123.81 CT £792.43 TOTE £7.90: £2.70, £3.00, £1.80; EX 80.10 Trifecta £169.40.
**Owner** Barry O'Connor **Bred** Oliver Donlon **Trained** Newmarket, Suffolk

**FOCUS**
The lightly raced winner dominated this sprint nursery and produced improved form.

## 6017 KEMPTON LIVE WITH DIZZEE RASCAL 06.09.14 CLAIMING STKS 6f (P)
**6:50** (6:50) (Class 6) 2-Y-0 **£1,940** (£577; £288; £144) **Stalls** Low

Form RPR
03 1 **Tinkers Kiss (IRE)**[17] 5443 2-8-4 0................................ DannyBrock(3) 2 62+
(Philip McBride) *stdd after s: hld up in last pair: clsd 3f out: rdn to ld but edgd rt over 1f out: in command and r.o wl fnl f: rdn out* 1/1[1]

0000 **2** *2* **Sparbrook (IRE)**[21] 5279 2-8-5 50.................................. HarryBentley 3 54
(Simon Dow) *chsd ldr: rdn and ev ch 2f out: carried rt and unable qck w wnr over 1f out: styd on same pce after* **14/1**

45 **3** *½* **Paris Carver (FR)**[25] 5133 2-8-8 0.................................. JohnFahy 6 56
(Jonathan Portman) *dwlt: dropped in bhd after s: rdn and effrt ent fnl 2f: hdwy to go 3rd fnl 150yds: kpt on but no threat to wnr* **8/1**

5260 **4** *3 ¼* **Diminutive (IRE)**[14] 5525 2-8-7 62..............................(p) LiamJones 1 45
(Grace Harris) *chsd ldrs: rdn and unable qck jst over 2f out: wknd u.p over 1f out* **5/1**[3]

2016 **5** *7* **Jimmy's Girl (IRE)**[15] 5506 2-8-8 65.............................. LukeMorris 5 25
(Chris Dwyer) *led: rdn ent fnl 2f: hdd over 1f out: sn btn: wknd fnl f* **11/4**[2]

1m 13.0s (-0.10) **Going Correction** -0.10s/f (Stan) 5 Ran SP% **111.1**
Speed ratings (Par 93): **96,93,92,88,79**
CSF £15.60 TOTE £2.50: £1.50, £6.90; EX 14.90 Trifecta £72.70.
**Owner** Peter Charter **Bred** Gerry Flannery Developments **Trained** Newmarket, Suffolk

**FOCUS**
The unexposed favourite scored with plenty in hand in this weak claimer.

## 6018 FOLLOW @BETVICTORRACING ON TWITTER MAIDEN STKS 1m (P)
7:20 (7:22) (Class 5) 3-Y-O+ **£2,587** (£770; £384; £192) **Stalls** Low

Form RPR

03 **1** **Holiday Magic (IRE)**[7] 5796 3-9-5 0.............................. WilliamBuick 12 74+
(Charlie Appleby) *chsd ldrs tl prog to ld 5f out: mde rest: kpt on wl u.p fnl f* **5/2**[1]

-362 **2** *¾* **Swordbearer**[28] 5008 3-9-5 70.............................. FrederikTylicki 5 72+
(James Fanshawe) *in tch in midfield: nt clr run and shuffled bk over 2f out: rdn and gd hdwy ent fnl f: chsd wnr wl ins fnl f: r.o* **5/2**[1]

03 **3** *½* **Frederic**[11] 5648 3-9-5 0.............................. LemosdeSouza 9 71+
(Luca Cumani) *t.k.h: hld up in tch in midfield: nt clr run over 2f out tl ent fnl f: r.o strly ins fnl f: nt rch ldrs* **8/1**[3]

03 **4** *¾* **Kubeba (IRE)**[17] 5427 3-9-5 0.............................. JimCrowley 14 69
(Paul Cole) *w ldr tl 5f out: styd chsng ldrs: effrt u.p to chse wnr again 1f out: no ex and lost 2 pls fnl 75yds* **16/1**

55 **5** *¾* **Guesshowmuchiloveu (IRE)**[15] 5504 3-9-5 0.............................. AdamKirby 10 67
(Charlie Fellowes) *t.k.h: hld up in tch in midfield: rdn ent fnl 2f: styd on same pce u.p ins fnl f* **9/2**[2]

66 **6** *½* **John Caesar (IRE)**[24] 5181 3-9-5 0..............................(t) JamesDoyle 11 66+
(Jeremy Noseda) *stdd s: hld up towards rr early: hdwy into midfield after 3f: kpt on same pce fr over 1f out* **25/1**

**7** *¾* **The Steward (USA)** 3-9-5 0.............................. LukeMorris 8 64+
(Sir Mark Prescott Bt) *bustled along in midfield: rdn ent fnl 2f: kpt on ins fnl f* **12/1**

55 **8** *1* **Oskar Denarius (IRE)**[27] 5044 3-9-5 0.............................. PatDobbs 2 62+
(Marcus Tregoning) *stdd s: hld up in tch towards rr: pushed along and effrt over 1f out: kpt on steadily ins fnl f* **33/1**

0 **9** *½* **Kirtling**[19] 5347 3-9-2 0.............................. RobertTart[(3)] 4 61
(Andi Brown) *s.i.s: in tch in last trio: swtchd lft and effrt wl over 2f out: kpt on but nvr enough pce to rch ldrs* **100/1**

06 **10** *½* **Heinrich (USA)**[12] 5606 3-9-5 0.............................. RenatoSouza 13 59
(Sylvester Kirk) *stdd after s: t.k.h: hld up towards rr: rdn wl over 2f out: kpt on but nvr able to chal* **50/1**

4 **11** *1* **Tayma (IRE)**[13] 5548 3-9-0 0.............................. HarryBentley 6 52
(Saeed bin Suroor) *led tl 5f out: chsd ldr tl 1f out: wknd ins fnl f* **8/1**[3]

**12** *½* **Geordan Murphy** 3-9-5 0.............................. HayleyTurner 1 56
(Andrew Balding) *s.i.s: bustled along and hdwy into midfield after 2f: hdwy on inner 2f out: wknd ins fnl f* **16/1**

00 **13** *2* **Frankie**[27] 5039 3-9-5 0.............................. SteveDrowne 7 51
(Jimmy Fox) *in tch towards rr: rdn wl over 2f out: no imp: bhd ins fnl f* **66/1**

1m 40.03s (0.23) **Going Correction** -0.10s/f (Stan)
**WFA** 3 from 4yo 5lb 13 Ran SP% **128.2**
Speed ratings (Par 103): **94,93,92,92,91 90,90,89,88,88 87,86,84**
CSF £8.55 TOTE £4.10: £1.80, £1.10, £3.20; EX 13.20 Trifecta £87.60.
**Owner** Godolphin **Bred** Mrs Ann Fortune **Trained** Newmarket, Suffolk

**FOCUS**
A bit muddling, compressed field and rated around the fourth initially. The winner found enough without matching his latest form.

## 6019 PLAY ROULETTE & BLACKJACK AT BETVICTOR.COM H'CAP 1m 4f (P)
7:50 (7:51) (Class 5) (0-70,76) 3-Y-O+ **£2,587** (£770; £384; £192) **Stalls** Centre

Form RPR

0111 **1** **Ragged Robbin (FR)**[4] 5898 3-9-11 76 6ex..............................(t) TedDurcan 9 89+
(David Lanigan) *chsd ldrs: rdn and effrt on inner 2f out: gd hdwy to ld 1f out: r.o strly: readily* **4/5**[1]

26-0 **2** *3 ¼* **Ze King**[147] 1362 5-9-9 65.............................. GeorgeBaker 2 73
(Chris Wall) *chsd ldrs: rdn and chsd ldr briefly ent fnl 2f: kpt on to chse wnr ins fnl f: no imp* **5/1**[2]

0316 **3** *¾* **Censorius**[27] 5038 3-9-3 68..............................(v) AdamKirby 4 75
(Ed Walker) *led: rdn ent fnl 2f: hdd 1f out: no ex and plugged on same pce: lost 2nd ins fnl f* **5/1**[2]

1203 **4** *8* **Shalambar (IRE)**[152] 1262 8-9-8 64.............................. LukeMorris 6 58
(Tony Carroll) *in tch in midfield: effrt over 2f out: no ch w ldrs but plugged on to go modest 4th towards fin* **25/1**

1002 **5** *¾* **The Ginger Berry**[28] 5011 4-9-5 64.............................. RobertTart[(3)] 8 57
(Dr Jon Scargill) *in tch in midfield: hdwy 5f out: clr in ldng quintet and rdn 3f out: outpcd and btn 2f out: wknd and lost 4th nr fin* **5/1**[2]

4551 **6** *4 ½* **Lily Edge**[17] 5428 5-9-7 63..............................(v) WilliamCarson 1 49
(John Bridger) *in tch in midfield: rdn and struggling over 3f out: no ch fnl 2f* **16/1**

6001 **7** *¾* **Menelik (IRE)**[13] 5560 5-9-12 68..............................(v) AmirQuinn 10 52
(Lee Carter) *hld up in last qurtet: rdn and no prog over 2f out: no ch fnl 2f* **14/1**[3]

-000 **8** *1* **Calrissian (IRE)**[28] 5006 3-8-11 62..............................(v[1]) JimCrowley 5 45
(Timothy Jarvis) *chsd ldr tl over 2f out: sn btn: fdd over 1f out* **14/1**[3]

-560 **9** *2 ¾* **Top Set (IRE)**[83] 3112 4-9-12 68..............................(b) SebSanders 3 46
(Simon Dow) *hld up in last pair: effrt and no real prog over 2f out: no ch fnl 2f* **33/1**

0005 **10** *¾* **Munsarim (IRE)**[13] 5560 7-9-6 62..............................(p) StevieDonohoe 7 39
(Lee Carter) *stdd s: hld up in rr: lost tch 3f out* **25/1**

0-40 **11** *hd* **Boston Blue**[150] 657 7-8-7 56 oh1.............................. RussellHarris[(7)] 12 33
(Tony Carroll) *a in rr: lost tch 3f out* **33/1**

2m 34.51s (0.01) **Going Correction** -0.10s/f (Stan)
**WFA** 3 from 4yo+ 9lb 11 Ran SP% **138.3**
Speed ratings (Par 103): **95,92,92,87,86 83,83,82,80,80 79**
CSF £6.52 CT £17.83 TOTE £1.80: £1.10, £3.80, £2.30; EX 10.40 Trifecta £55.10.
**Owner** Niarchos Family **Bred** Famille Niarchos **Trained** Upper Lambourn, Berks

**FOCUS**
Again, a bit muddling, but the front three finished clear and none of them are fully exposed, so this might prove better than it has been rated. For now, it's set around the front-running third.

## 6020 BETVICTOR.COM H'CAP (DIV I) 6f (P)
8:20 (8:20) (Class 4) (0-85,84) 3-Y-O+ **£4,690** (£1,395; £697; £348) **Stalls** Low

Form RPR

2153 **1** **Major Jack**[23] 5204 3-9-6 82.............................. JamesDoyle 6 91
(Roger Charlton) *chsd ldr tl 4f out: trckd ldng pair after: clsd and jnd ldrs on bit 2f out: rdn to ld jst ins fnl f: a jst doing enough after: rdn out* **5/2**[1]

4062 **2** *nk* **Sweet Talking Guy (IRE)**[21] 5281 4-8-6 69..............(t) SimonPearce[(3)] 7 77
(Lydia Pearce) *ducked lft s: sn chsng ldrs: wnt 2nd 4f out: rdn and ev ch 2f out: led 1f out: sn hdd: battled on wl but a jst hld* **6/1**

1 **3** *1 ½* **Crazy Chic (IRE)**[17] 5417 3-8-13 80.............................. MarcMonaghan[(5)] 5 83+
(Marco Botti) *hld up in tch towards rr: rdn and effrt over 1f out: kpt on ins fnl f* **4/1**[3]

1102 **4** *¾* **Desert Strike**[89] 2919 8-9-7 81..............................(p) HayleyTurner 9 82
(Conor Dore) *taken down early: led: rdn and hrd pressed 2f out: hdd 1f out: no ex and wknd fnl 100yds* **20/1**

2313 **5** *¾* **Light From Mars**[17] 5437 9-9-3 84..............................(p) MikeyEnnis[(7)] 3 82
(Ronald Harris) *in tch in midfield: rdn and effrt 2f out: styd on same pce fr over 1f out* **8/1**

6120 **6** *½* **Flying Bear (IRE)**[17] 5438 3-8-11 78..............................(b) CamHardie[(5)] 1 75
(Jeremy Gask) *chsd ldrs: 4th and unable qck ent fnl 2f: outpcd and btn over 1f out: one pce fnl f* **7/1**

-110 **7** *1* **Gone With The Wind (GER)**[148] 1350 3-9-0 76.........(p) WilliamBuick 2 70
(Jeremy Noseda) *in tch towards rr: rdn and effrt jst over 2f out: no imp: kpt on ins fnl f: no threat to ldrs* **7/2**[2]

0040 **8** *6* **Novellen Lad (IRE)**[55] 4078 9-9-3 77.............................. TomQueally 4 51
(Willie Musson) *stdd after s: hld up towards rr: effrt on inner 2f out: wknd ent fnl f* **16/1**

662- **9** *2 ¾* **Blue Jack**[442] 3415 9-9-4 78.............................. LukeMorris 8 44
(Zoe Davison) *hld up in rr: rdn and no hdwy over 2f out: bhd over 1f out* **33/1**

1m 11.85s (-1.25) **Going Correction** -0.10s/f (Stan)
**WFA** 3 from 4yo+ 2lb 9 Ran SP% **122.3**
Speed ratings (Par 105): **104,103,101,100,99 98,97,89,85**
CSF £19.39 CT £60.96 TOTE £2.10: £1.10, £2.20, £2.20; EX 24.30 Trifecta £121.20.
**Owner** D J Deer **Bred** D J And Mrs Deer **Trained** Beckhampton, Wilts

**FOCUS**
The winner has been rated as improving on his turf form, with the second running at least as well as ever.

## 6021 BETVICTOR.COM H'CAP (DIV II) 6f (P)
8:50 (8:50) (Class 4) (0-85,83) 3-Y-O+ **£4,690** (£1,395; £697; £348) **Stalls** Low

Form RPR

4004 **1** **Front Page News**[11] 5650 4-9-2 75.............................. AndreaAtzeni 2 83
(Robert Eddery) *stdd and wnt lft leaving stalls: racd off the pce in last trio: rdn 2f out: hdwy and edging lft ins fnl f: r.o strly to ld towards fin* **6/1**[3]

4034 **2** *1* **Meritocracy (IRE)**[16] 5482 3-9-7 82.............................. JimCrowley 8 87+
(Paul Cole) *led: rdn 2f out: fnd ex and 2 l clr over 1f out: drvn 1f out: hdd towards fin: sn btn* **6/4**[1]

0503 **3** *½* **New Leyf (IRE)**[20] 5308 8-8-10 69..............................(b) SteveDrowne 5 72
(Jeremy Gask) *hld up off the pce in last trio: rdn wl over 1f out: hdwy 1f out: r.o wl ins fnl f* **8/1**

1050 **4** *¾* **Green Monkey**[15] 5498 4-9-6 79..............................(v[1]) HayleyTurner 9 80
(James Fanshawe) *bmpd s: sn rcvrd to chse ldr: rdn over 2f out: drvn and over 1f out: kpt on same pce ins fnl f* **12/1**

0014 **5** *½* **Taquka (IRE)**[13] 5553 3-8-12 80.............................. JaneElliott[(7)] 6 79
(Ralph Beckett) *chsd ldrs: pushed along and effrt over 2f out: kpt on same pce fr over 1f out* **7/1**

0000 **6** *nk* **Lupo D'Oro (IRE)**[39] 4609 5-8-12 71.............................. LiamJones 4 69
(John Best) *short of room sn after s: in rr: rdn over 2f out: hdwy 1f out: styd on wl ins fnl f* **20/1**

523 **7** *1* **Jungle Bay**[14] 5536 7-9-3 76..............................(b) LukeMorris 1 71
(Jane Chapple-Hyam) *chsd ldrs: drvn and unable qck 2f out: wknd ins fnl f* **5/1**[2]

34 **8** *2 ½* **Amygdala (USA)**[23] 5211 3-9-5 80.............................. JamesDoyle 3 67
(Stuart Williams) *in tch in midfield: effrt u.p 2f out: no imp: wknd ins fnl f* **8/1**

1m 11.84s (-1.26) **Going Correction** -0.10s/f (Stan)
**WFA** 3 from 4yo+ 2lb 8 Ran SP% **118.1**
Speed ratings (Par 105): **104,102,102,101,100 99,98,95**
CSF £16.01 CT £75.10 TOTE £10.00: £2.70, £1.10, £3.00; EX 20.00 Trifecta £152.40.
**Owner** Gurnett, Rayment & Anderson **Bred** Helen Plumbly And Wendy Balding **Trained** Newmarket, Suffolk

**FOCUS**
The winner is rated to her best, with the third close to recent form.

## 6022 DOWNLOAD THE BETVICTOR INSTABET APP H'CAP 7f (P)
9:20 (9:21) (Class 6) (0-65,65) 3-Y-O **£1,940** (£577; £288; £144) **Stalls** Low

Form RPR

5006 **1** **Ganymede**[14] 5521 3-9-7 65..............................(b[1]) GeorgeBaker 2 73
(Eve Johnson Houghton) *mde all: rdn clr wl over 1f out: clr and in command 1f out: rdn out* **6/1**[3]

5255 **2** *1 ¼* **Aristocratic Duty**[38] 4654 3-9-3 61.............................. LukeMorris 6 65
(Sylvester Kirk) *in tch in midfield: hdwy u.p over 1f out: wnt 2nd fnl 100yds: r.o: nvr gng to rch wnr* **12/1**

050 **3** *2* **Scarlet Plum**[105] 2432 3-9-3 61.............................. JamesDoyle 10 60+
(Roger Charlton) *hld up off the pce towards rr: effrt but stl plenty to do on inner 2f out: styd on wl ins fnl f: nt rch ldrs* **9/2**[2]

00-4 **4** *nk* **Berkeley Vale**[38] 4654 3-9-7 65.............................. SebSanders 12 63
(Roger Teal) *chsd ldrs: rdn and unable qck over 2f out: rallied and kpt on ins fnl f* **14/1**

0000 **5** *shd* **Crafty Business (IRE)**[41] 4545 3-9-2 60..............................(v) SeanLevey 4 58
(Gary Moore) *in tch in midfield: rdn and effrt 2f out: kpt on same pce u.p fnl f* **20/1**

503 **6** *½* **Unbridled Joy (IRE)**[13] 5548 3-9-4 62.............................. AdamKirby 13 58
(Clive Cox) *chsd ldrs: wnt 2nd over 2f out: rdn and outpcd wl over 1f out: btn 1f out: wknd ins fnl f* **7/2**[1]

0541 **7** *1 ¾* **Venus Marina**[20] 5321 3-8-9 56.............................. AshleyMorgan[(3)] 7 48
(Chris Wall) *hld up in tch in midfield: rdn and little rspnse 2f out: kpt on same pce after* **7/2**[1]

0000 **8** *nk* **Berrahri (IRE)**[20] 5304 3-9-5 63.............................. SteveDrowne 11 54
(John Best) *hld up in tch towards rr: rdn and hdwy ent fnl f: styd on: nvr trbld ldrs* **20/1**

-062 **9** *nk* **Sweet Lily Pea (USA)**[24] 5183 3-8-10 54.................... LemosdeSouza 9 44
(Mrs Ilka Gansera-Leveque) *in tch in midfield: rdn and no hdwy over 2f out: sn outpcd and btn over 1f out* **14/1**

0506 **10** *1½* **Triple Star**[25] 5136 3-9-2 60.................................. RichardKingscote 3 46
(Hughie Morrison) *chsd wnr tl over 2f out: wknd u.p over 1f out* **20/1**

1002 **11** *3¾* **Born To Fly (IRE)**[17] 5427 3-9-4 62.........................(b) JimCrowley 5 39
(Nick Littmoden) *hld up towards rr: rdn and no imp 2f out: n.d* **8/1**

4000 **12** *48* **Gaelic O'Reagan**[33] 4830 3-8-13 57.............................. AndreaAtzeni 14
(Robert Eddery) *a in rr: lost tch over 2f out: t.o* **25/1**

1m 24.91s (-1.09) **Going Correction** -0.10s/f (Stan) **12** Ran SP% **127.2**
Speed ratings (Par 99): **102,100,98,97,97 97,95,94,94,92 88,33**
CSF £76.69 CT £372.31 TOTE £5.40: £3.00, £3.70, £1.80; EX 91.00 Trifecta £398.00.
**Owner** Ganymede Partnership **Bred** The Kingwood Partnership **Trained** Blewbury, Oxon

**FOCUS**
A modest 3yo handicap, lacking improvers. The second, rated to her handicap best, helps set the level.
T/Jkpt: Part won. £8,699.70 to a £1 stake. Pool: £12,253.00 - 0.50 winning tickets. T/Plt: £32.70 to a £1 stake. Pool: £84,315.00 - 1,878.98 winning tickets. T/Qpdt: £4.10 to a £1 stake. Pool: £8,943.00 - 1,607.24 winning tickets. SP

## 5903 BATH (L-H)
### Wednesday, September 3

**OFFICIAL GOING: Good (8.2)**
Wind: virtually nil Weather: sunny Rails: Races utilising bottom bend increased by 12yds

## 6023 BATH RUH FOREVER FRIENDS APPEAL APPRENTICE TRAINING SERIES H'CAP (RACING EXCELLENCE) (DIV I) 5f 161y
**2:20** (2:20) (Class 6) (0-55,55) 3-Y-O+ **£2,264** (£673; £336; £168) **Stalls** Centre

Form RPR

0002 **1** **Methaaly (IRE)**[27] 5082 11-9-1 52.............................(b) AnnaHesketh(3) 1 62
(Michael Mullineaux) *hood removed by stall handler: mid-div: rdn and hdwy fr over 2f out: led over 1f out: r.o wl: pushed out* **10/1**

6605 **2** *2¼* **Tregereth (IRE)**[20] 5355 4-8-12 53.................................. JackBudge(7) 8 56
(Jonathan Portman) *towards rr: pushed along and stdy prog fr over 2f out: r.o to go 2nd ins fnl f: nvr threatening wnr* **9/2**[2]

004 **3** *3¾* **Red Explorer (USA)**[26] 5125 4-9-4 55.......................... DavidParkes(3) 2 46
(Ann Stokell) *chsd ldrs: rdn over 2f out: swtchd lft over 1f out: sn short of room: kpt on same pce fnl f* **11/2**[3]

0505 **4** *1¼* **Chester Deelyte (IRE)**[18] 5422 6-8-12 46 oh1...............(v) CamHardie 9 33
(Lisa Williamson) *chsd ldrs: rdn over 2f out: ev ch briefly over 1f out: kpt on same pce* **20/1**

0623 **5** *1* **Arch Walker (IRE)**[13] 5594 7-9-0 48...........................(b) JordanNason 5 31
(John Weymes) *wnt lft s: disp ld tl over 1f out: no ex fnl f* **12/1**

1253 **6** *1* **Clear Focus (IRE)**[15] 5518 3-9-2 52.............................(v) JennyPowell 4 32
(Brendan Powell) *squeezed out s: rdn over 2f out: a mid-div* **3/1**[1]

000 **7** *1* **Rat Catcher (IRE)**[19] 5399 4-8-13 50..........................(b) RobHornby(3) 3 29
(Lisa Williamson) *blkd s: disp ld tl over 1f out: wknd fnl f* **18/1**

4524 **8** *1* **Diamond Vine (IRE)**[12] 5624 6-8-7 46.......................(p) HectorCrouch(5) 6 19
(Ronald Harris) *sn outpcd: a towards rr* **3/1**[1]

0000 **9** *12* **Phantom Spirit**[37] 4733 3-8-7 46 oh1.........................(p) ChrisMeehan(3) 7
(George Baker) *dwlt bdly: a in bhd* **66/1**

1m 10.95s (-0.25) **Going Correction** -0.15s/f (Firm)
**WFA** 3 from 4yo+ 2lb **9** Ran SP% **111.9**
Speed ratings (Par 101): **95,92,87,85,84 82,81,80,64**
CSF £52.30 CT £274.41 TOTE £8.50: £3.20, £2.80, £2.30; EX 61.80 Trifecta £357.50.
**Owner** S A Pritchard **Bred** Scuderia Golden Horse S R L **Trained** Alpraham, Cheshire

**FOCUS**
This took little winning and with many of the market principals failing to run their races.

## 6024 EXCALIBUR COMMUNICATIONS MAIDEN AUCTION STKS 5f 161y
**2:50** (2:52) (Class 5) 2-Y-O **£2,911** (£866; £432; £216) **Stalls** Centre

Form RPR

03 **1** **Conjuring (IRE)**[16] 5509 2-8-6 0.................................. RoystonFfrench 1 70
(Mike Murphy) *racd keenly: trckd ldrs: swtchd rt and rdn over 1f out: r.o wl to ld fnl 120yds: rdn out* **5/1**[3]

4 **2** *¾* **Clergyman**[14] 5555 2-9-1 0.......................................... JackMitchell 10 77
(Martyn Meade) *trckd ldr: led 2f out: sn rdn: kpt on but no ex whn hdd fnl 120yds* **7/2**[2]

2 **3** *2¼* **Little**[15] 5524 2-8-1 0............................................... CamHardie(5) 9 60
(Jamie Osborne) *mid-div: swtchd rt and rdn 2f out: sn chsng ldrs: edgd lft fnl f: kpt on same pce* **5/1**[3]

4 **4** *3½* **John Joiner**[33] 4846 2-8-7 0 ow1..........................(b) ChrisMeehan(7) 2 57
(Peter Makin) *led tl rdn 2f out: kpt chsng ldr tl no ex ins fnl f* **16/1**

03 **5** *1½* **Galago (IRE)**[31] 4943 2-9-1 0....................................... JimmyFortune 3 53
(Sylvester Kirk) *trckd ldr: effrt over 2f out: hld over 1f out: wknd ins fnl f* **7/4**[1]

0403 **6** *9* **Spirit In Time (IRE)**[15] 5517 2-8-8 54.............................. MartinDwyer 6 16
(Malcolm Saunders) *mid-div: rdn over 2f out: wknd jst over 1f out* **20/1**

04 **7** *2½* **Wesie's Dream**[16] 5509 2-8-1 0..................................... DannyBrock(3) 7
(Mark Usher) *a towards rr* **14/1**

0 **8** *1½* **Simone On Time (IRE)**[18] 5429 2-8-10 0............................ ShaneKelly 4
(Sylvester Kirk) *towards rr: sme hdwy on inner 3f out: sn outpcd and btn* **25/1**

00 **9** *3½* **Red Renee**[39] 4676 2-8-4 0 ow3.................................... DeclanBates(3) 8
(Mark Gillard) *squeezed out s: sn outpcd: a towards rr* **200/1**

**10** *14* **Dancing Springs (IRE)** 2-7-13 0.................................... NoelGarbutt(5) 5
(Bill Turner) *towards rr: struggling 3f out: sn wknd* **50/1**

1m 11.29s (0.09) **Going Correction** -0.15s/f (Firm) **10** Ran SP% **115.5**
Speed ratings (Par 95): **93,92,89,84,82 70,67,65,60,41**
CSF £21.97 CT £11.20: £3.10, £1.20, £2.30; EX 22.90 Trifecta £111.80.
**Owner** The Hocus-Pocus Partnership **Bred** The Kathryn Stud Ltd **Trained** Westoning, Beds

**FOCUS**
The favourite set a fair standard but it's dubious that he ran up to his best. The winner's previous run could be rated this good, but it's harder to rate this race any higher given the time and overall balance of principals.

## 6025 XPERIA SMART PHONE H'CAP 5f 161y
**3:20** (3:21) (Class 5) (0-75,75) 3-Y-O+ **£2,911** (£866; £432; £216) **Stalls** Centre

Form RPR

114 **1** **Sleep Walk**[29] 5012 3-9-4 74........................................... JamesDoyle 7 90+
(Roger Charlton) *trckd ldrs: rdn 2f out: led jst over 1f out: edgd lft: r.o wl: readily* **7/4**[1]

5423 **2** *3¼* **The Dandy Yank (IRE)**[13] 5601 3-9-3 73.................(p) WilliamCarson 10 77
(Jamie Osborne) *mid-div: rdn over 2f out: hdwy over 1f out: kpt on to go 2nd fnl 120yds but no ch w wnr* **16/1**

36 **3** *shd* **Hamoody (USA)**[81] 3213 10-9-2 75.............................. DanielMuscutt(5) 12 79
(Joseph Tuite) *towards rr: rdn and hdwy fr 2f out: kpt on to chal for 2nd fnl 120yds but no ch w wnr* **16/1**

1060 **4** *½* **Ashkari (IRE)**[61] 3936 3-9-5 75................................(p) AdamKirby 3 77
(Clive Cox) *mid-div: hdwy over 2f out: sn rdn: kpt on to chal for 2nd fnl 120yds: no ex nring fin* **12/1**

1404 **5** *1¾* **Edged Out**[22] 5275 4-8-12 71........................................ JennyPowell(5) 8 67
(Christopher Mason) *w ldr: rdn and ev ch 2f out tl ent fnl f: fdd fnl 120yds* **20/1**

6600 **6** *¾* **Valmina**[12] 5624 7-8-8 67................................................(t) CamHardie(5) 1 64
(Tony Carroll) *towards rr: hdwy fr 2f out: nt clr run ent fnl f: kpt on but nvr any ch* **12/1**

0411 **7** *2¾* **My Meteor**[13] 5594 7-8-6 65........................................ NoelGarbutt(5) 11 50
(Tony Newcombe) *towards rr: rdn and sme prog wl over 1f out: no further imp fnl f* **14/1**

4410 **8** *2¼* **Ada Lovelace**[20] 5355 4-9-4 72.......................................... BenCurtis 5 55
(John Gallagher) *led: rdn over 2f out: hdd jst over 1f out: wknd ins fnl f* **10/1**[3]

3021 **9** *½* **Silverrica (IRE)**[13] 5595 4-9-2 75............................... MarcMonaghan(5) 2 51
(Malcolm Saunders) *trckd ldrs: rdn over 2f out: wknd ent fnl f* **4/1**[2]

2041 **10** *2* **Fantasy Justifier (IRE)**[27] 5080 3-9-1 71............................ ChrisCatlin 6 40
(Ronald Harris) *s.i.s: sn outpcd: a towards rr* **12/1**

5000 **11** *1¼* **Time Medicean**[79] 3313 8-8-12 66................................. RobertWinston 4 31
(Tony Carroll) *s.i.s: a towards rr* **25/1**

/606 **12** *nse* **Living It Large (FR)**[27] 5070 7-9-0 71......................... DeclanBates(3) 9 36
(Ed de Giles) *trckd ldrs: rdn over 2f out: wknd over 1f out* **28/1**

1m 10.23s (-0.97) **Going Correction** -0.15s/f (Firm)
**WFA** 3 from 4yo+ 2lb **12** Ran SP% **119.0**
Speed ratings (Par 103): **100,95,95,94,92 91,87,84,84,81 79,79**
CSF £32.73 CT £361.48 TOTE £2.60: £1.40, £3.70, £2.90; EX 23.60 Trifecta £269.80.
**Owner** K Abdullah **Bred** Juddmonte Farms Ltd **Trained** Beckhampton, Wilts

**FOCUS**
The winner looks a good bit better than the grade, and the runner-up and third set a solid basis for the level.

## 6026 DRIBUILD LTD FILLIES' H'CAP 1m 2f 46y
**3:50** (3:50) (Class 5) (0-75,75) 3-Y-O+ **£3,234** (£962; £481; £240) **Stalls** Low

Form RPR

4345 **1** **Micras**[16] 5490 3-9-5 75...............................................(v[1]) JimmyFortune 3 85+
(Andrew Balding) *trckd ldr: led over 2f out: sn rdn: in command fnl f: comf* **7/1**

652 **2** *2¾* **Bright Cecily (IRE)**[31] 4947 3-9-3 73.............................(p) AdamKirby 1 78
(Clive Cox) *s.i.s: sn trcking ldrs: rdn 2f out: chsd wnr over 1f out but a being hld* **11/2**

0551 **3** *2* **Dubai Hadeia**[40] 4617 3-8-12 73...................................... CamHardie(5) 7 74
(Charlie Appleby) *nvr really travelling after 2f and niggled along: in tch: effrt to cl on outer over 3f out: sn rdn: styd on same pce fnl 2f* **15/8**[1]

-641 **4** *1¼* **Dutch Rifle**[8] 5795 3-9-5 75............................................... JohnFahy 4 74
(James Tate) *hld up: pushed along over 3f out: rdn wl over 2f out: styd on to go 4th ins fnl f but nvr finding pce to get involved* **4/1**[2]

333 **5** *1* **Miss Crystal (IRE)**[19] 5374 3-9-1 71.................................[1] RobertWinston 2 68
(Charles Hills) *taken to s early: led: rdn and hdd over 2f out: sn hanging lft: wknd fnl f* **5/1**[3]

5556 **6** *2* **Tipsy Star**[4] 5908 3-8-5 61 oh1...................................... WilliamCarson 5 54
(Jonathan Geake) *in tch: rdn over 2f out: wknd ent fnl f* **14/1**

0460 **7** *7* **Upper Street (IRE)**[28] 5036 3-8-10 66.............................(v) ShaneKelly 6 46
(Sir Michael Stoute) *trckd ldrs: effrt over 2f out: wknd jst over 1f out* **16/1**

2m 10.2s (-0.80) **Going Correction** -0.025s/f (Good) **7** Ran SP% **111.9**
Speed ratings (Par 100): **102,99,98,97,96 94,89**
CSF £42.54 TOTE £8.90: £3.10, £3.30; EX 36.80 Trifecta £166.40.
**Owner** The Queen **Bred** The Queen **Trained** Kingsclere, Hants

**FOCUS**
A clear personal best from the winner.

## 6027 UNIVERSITY AND LITERARY CLUB H'CAP 1m 5f 22y
**4:25** (4:26) (Class 6) (0-60,60) 4-Y-O+ **£2,328** (£693; £346; £173) **Stalls** High

Form RPR

5516 **1** **Glens Wobbly**[4] 5904 6-8-6 52.................................... ChrisMeehan(7) 6 61
(Jonathan Geake) *sn led: 5 l clr over 5f out: rdn over 1f out: styd on wl* **7/2**[3]

222 **2** *3¼* **Rowlestone Lass**[11] 5689 4-8-13 55............................... DeclanBates(3) 2 58
(Richard Price) *trckd ldrs: rdn in 3rd over 2f out: styd on same pce: wnt 2nd fnl 75yds: nvr threatened wnr* **5/2**[2]

0134 **3** *nk* **Sweeping Rock (IRE)**[13] 5597 4-9-7 60.......................(tp) MartinDwyer 7 63
(Marcus Tregoning) *little s.i.s: trckd wnr after 2f: rdn 3f out: nvr able to get on terms w wnr: no ex whn lost 2nd fnl 75yds* **13/8**[1]

3424 **4** *1½* **Evergreen Forest (IRE)**[26] 5121 6-8-9 55..................(b) DavidParkes(7) 3 56
(Natalie Lloyd-Beavis) *hld up bhd ldrs: rdn over 4f out: no real imp tl styd on ins fnl f* **20/1**

1604 **5** *13* **Samoset**[100] 2607 4-9-2 55........................................... StephenCraine 10 38
(Pam Sly) *trckd ldrs: rdn 3f out: wknd over 1f out* **7/1**

0/0- **6** *57* **Shakespeare Dancer**[17] 2714 5-8-7 46 oh1.....................(p) ChrisCatlin 4
(James Evans) *w wnr for 1st f: chsd ldrs after 2f: lost tch 6f out: t.o* **66/1**

2m 51.96s (-0.04) **Going Correction** -0.025s/f (Good) **6** Ran SP% **107.6**
Speed ratings (Par 101): **99,97,96,95,87 52**
CSF £11.56 CT £15.38 TOTE £3.70: £1.10, £1.90; EX 8.70 Trifecta £20.30.
**Owner** Glen Symes **Bred** H J Manners **Trained** East Kennett, Wilts

**FOCUS**
The winner and second help set a straightforward level to a modest race.

## 6028 BATHWICK CAR AND VAN HIRE H'CAP 1m 2f 46y
**4:55** (4:55) (Class 6) (0-55,54) 4-Y-O+ **£2,328** (£693; £346; £173) **Stalls** Low

Form RPR

0205 **1** **Medal Of Valour (JPN)**[13] 5596 6-9-4 54.............(bt) DeclanBates(3) 12 67+
(Mark Gillard) *mid-div: hdwy over 3f out: led wl over 2f out: sn rdn clr: styd on strly* **12/1**

0042 **2** *6* **Royal Mizar (SPA)**[13] 5596 4-9-2 49............ WilliamTwiston-Davies 14 51
(Ralph J Smith) *mid-div: rdn and hdwy over 2f out: styd on to chse wnr ent fnl f but a being comf hld* **7/2**[1]

534 **3** *nk* **Polydamos**[28] 5033 5-8-11 51....................................... JordanVaughan(7) 5 52
(Tony Carroll) *in tch: hdwy 3f out: rdn to chse wnr over 2f out tl ent fnl f: styd on same pce* **7/1**[3]

0044 **4** 3/4 **Squirrel Wood (IRE)**[8] 5797 6-9-6 53 JimmyFortune 9 53
(Mary Hambro) *hld up towards rr: hdwy 3f out: sn rdn: styd on fnl 2f wout threatening to rch ldrs* **17/2**

0000 **5** *shd* **Berwin (IRE)**[14] 5547 5-9-4 51 RenatoSouza 6 50
(Sylvester Kirk) *s.i.s and rousted along early: bhd: hdwy 3f out: sn rdn: hung lft over 1f out: styd on same pce* **25/1**

4000 **6** *2* **Bold Cross (IRE)**[13] 5596 11-8-12 50 EoinWalsh(5) 10 46
(Edward Bevan) *hld up towards rr: rdn over 2f out: hdwy over 1f out: styd on but nvr threatening to rch ldrs* **16/1**

6053 **7** *4 1/2* **My New Angel (IRE)**[13] 5596 5-9-3 50 (e) FrankieMcDonald 13 37
(Daniel Mark Loughnane) *a in mid-div* **5/1**[2]

0514 **8** *9* **Mazij**[20] 5331 6-8-13 46 ChrisCatlin 8 16
(Peter Hiatt) *trckd ldr: rdn wl over 2f out: wknd over 1f out* **7/1**[3]

04-5 **9** *1 1/2* **Zeteah**[119] 2066 4-9-0 47 StevieDonohoe 4 14
(David Lanigan) *trckd ldr: rdn and ev ch briefly wl over 2f out: wknd over 1f out* **15/2**

0306 **10** *1 1/4* **Rezwaan**[18] 5428 7-8-13 53 (b) HectorCrouch(7) 2 18
(Murty McGrath) *trckd ldrs: rdn over 2f out: wknd over 1f out* **12/1**

0002 **11** 3/4 **Market Puzzle (IRE)**[28] 5033 7-8-7 45 CamHardie(5) 11 8
(Mark Brisbourne) *mid-div: rdn on outer 3f out: wknd over 1f out* **20/1**

000- **12** *9* **Smirfy's Silver**[288] 7963 10-8-12 45 LiamJones 1
(Michael Mullineaux) *racd keenly: led tl rdn over 2f out: sn wknd* **80/1**

0400 **13** *5* **Hammered Silver (IRE)**[37] 4737 4-9-5 52 ShaneKelly 3
(Mike Murphy) *a towards rr* **20/1**

2m 10.87s (-0.13) **Going Correction** -0.025s/f (Good) **13** Ran SP% **122.1**
Speed ratings (Par 101): **99,94,93,93,93 91,88,80,79,78 78,70,66**
CSF £52.68 CT £330.59 TOTE £17.10: £5.00, £2.20, £1.50; EX 45.80 Trifecta £257.00.
**Owner** S Garnett **Bred** Runnymeade Farm, Inc & Peter Callahan **Trained** Holwell, Dorset

**FOCUS**
The winner has improved with each start this year and thrashed this motley crew in good style. This could been rated a bit higher but it looks a race to have some reservations about.

## 6029 EXCALIBUR COMMUNICATIONS CHARITY H'CAP 5f 11y
**5:25** (5:26) (Class 5) (0-70,68) 3-Y-O £2,911 (£866; £432; £216) **Stalls** Centre

Form RPR
0161 **1** **Bashiba (IRE)**[10] 5715 3-9-5 66 6ex (t) RobertWinston 5 76
(Nigel Tinkler) *chsd ldr: led 2f out: kpt on wl fnl f: rdn out* **5/1**[3]

0256 **2** *2* **Monarch Maid**[10] 5724 3-9-4 65 ChrisCatlin 7 67
(Peter Hiatt) *chsd ldr: rdn over 2f out: kpt on ins fnl f but a being hld by wnr* **9/2**[2]

223 **3** *nse* **Narborough**[19] 5399 3-8-13 60 SamHitchcott 8 62
(Mick Channon) *sn pushed along towards rr: rdn and hdwy over 2f out: disp 2nd over 1f out: kpt on but a being hld by wnr* **8/1**

5043 **4** 1/2 **Gold Club**[41] 4565 3-9-2 63 (p) FrannyNorton 6 63
(Ed McMahon) *trckd ldrs: rdn over 2f out: nt pce to mount chal: no ex fnl 75yds* **7/2**[1]

0-50 **5** *4 1/2* **Gower Princess**[70] 3588 3-9-1 62 BenCurtis 9 46
(Ronald Harris) *in last trio: rdn 2f out: hung bdly lft over 1f out: kpt on but nt pce to get on terms* **33/1**

2233 **6** 1/2 **Gulland Rock**[16] 5486 3-9-5 66 MartinDwyer 10 48
(William Muir) *chsd ldrs: rdn over 2f out: nt quite pce to chal: no ex ins fnl f* **7/2**[1]

4604 **7** *2 1/2* **Go Glamorous (IRE)**[10] 5724 3-9-7 68 (p) WilliamTwiston-Davies 2 41
(Ronald Harris) *led after 1f: rdn and hdd 2f out: wknd fnl f* **11/1**

0-00 **8** *1 1/2* **Tableforten**[137] 1570 3-9-4 65 (b) LiamJones 4 32
(J S Moore) *hmpd s: a struggling in rr* **16/1**

3524 **9** *1 1/2* **Kiss From A Rose**[10] 5715 3-8-12 59 (b) JimmyFortune 3 24
(Rae Guest) *in tch: effrt over 2f out where sn hmpd: wknd over 1f out* **7/1**

1m 1.29s (-1.21) **Going Correction** -0.15s/f (Firm) **9** Ran SP% **120.1**
Speed ratings (Par 101): **103,99,99,98,91 90,86,84,82**
CSF £29.01 CT £181.41 TOTE £3.90: £2.50, £2.50, £2.90; EX 35.70 Trifecta £254.20.
**Owner** Y T Szeto **Bred** John T Heffernan & Grainne Dooley **Trained** Langton, N Yorks

**FOCUS**
The runner-up and those in behind set a straightforward level.

## 6030 BATH RUH FOREVER FRIENDS APPEAL APPRENTICE TRAINING SERIES H'CAP (RACING EXCELLENCE) (DIV II) 5f 161y
**5:55** (5:55) (Class 6) (0-55,55) 3-Y-O+ £2,264 (£673; £336; £168) **Stalls** Centre

Form RPR
5622 **1** **See Vermont**[48] 4337 6-8-13 47 (p) CamHardie 8 52
(Robin Bastiman) *chsd ldrs: rdn over 2f out: kpt on wl ins fnl f: led cl home* **9/4**[1]

U60 **2** *nk* **Dylan's Centenary**[7] 5820 3-8-12 55 SophieKilloran(7) 6 59
(Rod Millman) *slowly away: bhd: rdn over 2f out: hdwy whn nt clr run and swtchd lft over 1f out: r.o fnl f: snatched 2nd fnl stride* **4/1**[3]

5360 **3** *hd* **Night Trade (IRE)**[12] 5624 7-8-13 50 (p) DavidParkes(3) 4 53
(Ronald Harris) *chsd ldr: rdn to ld over 2f out: no ex whn hdd fnl strides* **7/2**[2]

0004 **4** *1 3/4* **The Strig**[7] 5806 7-9-1 52 (v) AnnaHesketh(3) 2 50
(Nigel Tinkler) *hld up in last pair: rdn and stdy prog fr 2f out: kpt on but nt pce to get on terms* **4/1**[3]

5006 **5** *3* **Ishi Honest**[16] 5510 4-9-2 55 MichaelKenneally(5) 1 43
(Mark Usher) *chsd ldrs: rdn over 2f out: nt pce to chal: fdd fnl 120yds* **6/1**

6650 **6** *12* **Countess Lupus (IRE)**[6] 5853 3-8-10 46 oh1 (b) JennyPowell 7
(Lisa Williamson) *led: rdn and hdd over 2f out: wknd over 1f out* **33/1**

0046 **7** *1 1/4* **Rosie Prospects**[28] 5034 3-8-4 47 (b[1]) RhiainIngram(7) 5
(Roger Ingram) *chsd ldr: rdn over 2f out: wknd over 1f out* **20/1**

1m 11.65s (0.45) **Going Correction** -0.15s/f (Firm)
**WFA** 3 from 4yo+ 2lb **7** Ran SP% **115.0**
Speed ratings (Par 101): **91,90,90,88,84 68,66**
CSF £11.73 CT £29.91 TOTE £2.70: £2.00, £2.80; EX 11.90 Trifecta £44.30.
**Owner** John Smith **Bred** Oakhill Stud **Trained** Cowthorpe, N Yorks

**FOCUS**
Not really a race to be taking many positives from.

T/Jkpt: Not won. T/Plt: £250.00 to a £1 stake. Pool: £68,950.00 - 201.26 winning units. T/Qpdt: £39.00 to a £1 stake. Pool: £5952.16 - 112.75 winning units. TM

# 6015 KEMPTON (A.W) (R-H)
## Wednesday, September 3

**OFFICIAL GOING: Polytrack: standard**
Wind: Fresh, half behind Weather: Fine, warm

## 6031 BETBRIGHT MOBILE APPRENTICE H'CAP 1m 3f (P)
**5:40** (5:40) (Class 6) (0-60,60) 4-Y-O+ £1,940 (£577; £288; £144) **Stalls** Low

Form RPR
4550 **1** **Thane Of Cawdor (IRE)**[74] 3473 5-9-2 60 MeganCarberry(5) 10 66
(Joseph Tuite) *stdd s: hld up in last: no move tl swift prog 2f out: swept into the ld jst over 1f out: idled in front and drvn out* **11/4**[1]

335 **2** 3/4 **Ferryview Place**[18] 5428 5-8-8 50 (p) GeorgeDowning(3) 7 55
(Ian Williams) *hld up in last trio: smooth prog to chal 2f out: rdn to chse wnr ins fnl f: styd on but a hld* **3/1**[2]

3120 **3** 3/4 **Estibdaad (IRE)**[10] 5721 4-8-11 57 (t) CallumShepherd(7) 1 61
(Paddy Butler) *trckd ldng pair: pushed along and clsd to ld 2f out: hdd jst over 1f out: kpt on same pce* **11/2**

/134 **4** *6* **Lady Percy (IRE)**[9] 5748 5-8-11 55 CharlotteJenner(5) 3 49
(Mark Usher) *chsd ldng trio: pushed along 4f out: clsd on ldrs 2f out: outpcd over 1f out* **7/1**

4005 **5** *3 1/4* **Highly Likely (IRE)**[14] 5558 5-8-12 51 RyanTate 4 40
(Steve Woodman) *led: stretched on over 3f out: rdn and no rspnse over 2f out: sn hdd and btn* **4/1**[3]

100 **6** *1* **Addikt (IRE)**[160] 1138 9-8-10 52 LouisSteward(3) 5 39
(John Spearing) *hld up in last trio: pushed along and clsd over 2f out: wknd qckly over 1f out* **14/1**

0006 **7** *2 1/4* **Mists Of Time (IRE)**[49] 4326 4-8-4 46 oh1[1] ShelleyBirkett(3) 9 30
(Pat Eddery) *chsd ldr: rdn over 3f out: lost 2nd over 2f out: losing pl qckly whn hmpd sn after* **25/1**

2m 21.56s (-0.34) **Going Correction** -0.075s/f (Stan) **7** Ran SP% **110.1**
Speed ratings (Par 101): **98,97,96,92,90 89,87**
CSF £10.35 CT £37.20 TOTE £3.10: £2.60, £2.40; EX 12.40 Trifecta £49.50.
**Owner** Alan & Christine Bright **Bred** Balmerino Bldstock & Newsells Park Stud **Trained** Great Shefford, Berks

**FOCUS**
The runner-up helps set an ordinary level.

## 6032 DIGIPOS PARTNER / BRITISH STALLION STUDS EBF MAIDEN FILLIES' STKS (BOBIS RACE) 6f (P)
**6:10** (6:11) (Class 5) 2-Y-O £2,911 (£866; £432; £216) **Stalls** Low

Form RPR
0 **1** **Tendu**[18] 5429 2-9-0 0 JamesDoyle 6 93+
(John Gosden) *trckd ldr: swept into the ld over 1f out: sn clr: pushed out: impressive* **7/4**[2]

32 **2** *5* **Commandaria (USA)**[7] 5821 2-9-0 0 SilvestreDeSousa 3 75
(Jeremy Noseda) *led: drvn 2f out: hdd and brushed aside over 1f out: kpt on and jst hld on for 2nd* **6/4**[1]

**3** *nk* **Luna Mission (IRE)** 2-9-0 0 MartinHarley 4 74+
(Marco Botti) *trckd ldrs in 5th: shkn up over 2f out: tk 3rd fnl f: styd on steadily and nrly snatched 2nd* **16/1**

0 **4** *4 1/2* **Inauguration (IRE)**[35] 4781 2-9-0 0 SteveDrowne 2 61
(Charles Hills) *chsd ldng pair: outpcd fr 2f out: no ch after: lost 3rd fnl f* **16/1**

6 **5** *3 1/2* **Most Tempting**[16] 5509 2-9-0 0 AdamBeschizza 7 50
(Robert Cowell) *chsd ldng trio: rdn over 2f out: steadily wknd fnl 2f* **66/1**

4 **6** *1* **Poyle Jessica**[20] 5344 2-9-0 0 RichardKingscote 8 47
(Ralph Beckett) *in tch in 7th: outpcd whn tk 6th 2f out: lost further grnd after* **4/1**[3]

**7** *3* **Perfect Bounty** 2-8-11 0 RyanTate(3) 9 38
(Clive Cox) *awkward s: chsd ldrs in 6th: wd bnd 3f out: struggling after: no ch fnl 2f* **50/1**

60 **8** *nk* **Fleetwood Poppy**[18] 5429 2-9-0 0 KierenFox 12 37
(Michael Attwater) *a wl in rr: shkn up wl over 2f out: no prog* **100/1**

00 **9** *nk* **Follow The Faith**[11] 5667 2-8-11 0 CharlesBishop(3) 1 36+
(Mick Channon) *hld up in last trio: pushed along and modest prog over 2f out: nvr a factor* **50/1**

00 **10** *2* **Shamiya (IRE)**[10] 5725 2-9-0 0 (b[1]) LukeMorris 10 30
(J S Moore) *nvr bttr than 8th: rdn bef 1/2-way: wknd 2f out* **100/1**

**11** 1/2 **Sea Fantasy** 2-9-0 0 FergusSweeney 5 29
(Jo Crowley) *dwlt: a in rr: struggling fr 1/2-way* **50/1**

**12** *5* **Perdurable** 2-9-0 0 MartinLane 11 14
(Charlie Fellowes) *slowly away: a last and wl bhd* **33/1**

1m 11.36s (-1.74) **Going Correction** -0.075s/f (Stan) 2y crse rec **12** Ran SP% **120.4**
Speed ratings (Par 92): **108,101,100,94,90 88,84,84,84,81 80,74**
CSF £4.70 TOTE £3.90: £1.20, £1.10, £5.10; EX 4.30 Trifecta £48.10.
**Owner** K Abdullah **Bred** Juddmonte Farms Ltd **Trained** Newmarket, Suffolk

**FOCUS**
They'd watered the track beforehand, so that probably had a bearing on the final time, but the winner lowered the juvenile course record by 0.08sec. The winner was hugely impressive, routing a fairly good field in the style of one who will rate 100+ next time. The runner-up helps the level.

## 6033 BETBRIGHT.COM MAIDEN FILLIES' STKS 1m (P)
**6:40** (6:45) (Class 5) 3-Y-O+ £2,587 (£770; £384; £192) **Stalls** Low

Form RPR
4364 **1** **She's Gorgeous (IRE)**[26] 5150 3-9-0 70 (v[1]) AndreaAtzeni 8 75
(James Fanshawe) *trckd ldng pair: chal 2f out: rdn over 1f out: styd on fnl f to ld last 100yds* **4/1**[2]

3 **2** *1* **Emirates Joy (USA)**[29] 5007 3-9-0 0 WilliamBuick 6 73
(Charlie Appleby) *trckd ldrs: pushed along to ld 2f out: sn pressed: rdn fnl f: hdd and nt qckn last 100yds* **1/2**[1]

06 **3** *1* **Noble Descent**[14] 5548 3-9-0 0 RyanMoore 7 70
(Sir Michael Stoute) *racd wd: in tch: shkn up over 2f out: styd on fr over 1f out: tk 3rd last 100yds* **14/1**

4- **4** 3/4 **Jacqueline Jouliac**[427] 3958 3-9-0 0[1] NickyMackay 5 69
(John Gosden) *t.k.h: hld up in rr: prog on inner over 2f out: shkn up over 1f out: one pce fnl f* **6/1**[3]

-330 **5** *1 1/4* **Spellbind**[14] 5548 3-9-0 75 AdamKirby 2 66
(Charlie Appleby) *led: shkn up and hdd 2f out: steadily fdd* **8/1**

00- **6** *3 3/4* **Rochelle (IRE)**[301] 7764 3-9-0 0 SteveDrowne 4 57
(William Muir) *w ldr to over 2f out: lost pl qckly: wknd fnl f* **100/1**

0 **7** *2 3/4* **Perfect Rhythm**[29] 5007 3-8-11 0 RyanTate(3) 3 51
(Patrick Chamings) *trckd ldrs: rdn and wknd fr 2f out* **25/1**

0 **8** *6* **Sea Whisper**85 3083 3-9-0 0 FergusSweeney 9 37
(Jo Crowley) *sn pushed along in last: nvr a factor: bhd fnl 2f* **50/1**

-06 **9** *1 1/4* **Euroquip Susie**12 5622 6-9-0 0 NoelGarbutt(5) 1 35
(Michael Scudamore) *dwlt: in tch: shkn up over 3f out: sn struggling: bhd fnl 2f* **100/1**

1m 39.66s (-0.14) **Going Correction** -0.075s/f (Stan)
**WFA** 3 from 6yo 5lb **9** Ran SP% **126.5**
Speed ratings (Par 100): **97,96,95,94,93 89,86,80,79**
CSF £7.00 TOTE £4.90: £1.10, £1.10, £4.10; EX 8.80 Trifecta £64.20.
**Owner** Johnstone Partnership **Bred** Stephanie Von Schilcher & David Powell **Trained** Newmarket, Suffolk

**FOCUS**
With the favourite eclipsed this was no more than a fair maiden. The opening level is perhaps not as solid as first impressions might suggest.

## 6034 BETBRIGHT - LIVE THE MOMENT H'CAP 1m (P)
**7:10** (7:12) (Class 5) (0-75,75) 3-Y-0 **£2,587** (£770; £384; £192) **Stalls** Low

Form RPR

6015 **1** **Matravers**42 4549 3-9-4 72 RyanMoore 4 82+
(Sir Michael Stoute) *settled in rr: rdn over 2f out: sustained prog on outer after: clsd to ld last 150yds: drvn out* **10/1**

5652 **2** *1* **Cape Summit**21 5304 3-9-3 71 JamesDoyle 5 79
(Ed Dunlop) *w.w in midfield: prog 3f out: drvn to ld wl over 1f out: hdd last 150yds: styd on same pce* **11/2**3

4611 **3** *3 1/2* **Windy Citi**21 5304 3-9-7 75 GeorgeBaker 8 75
(Chris Wall) *trckd ldr 3f: settled into 4th: moved up to chal 2f out: rdn and nt qckn over 1f out: one pce after* **3/1**1

4230 **4** *2 3/4* **Plucky Dip**14 5557 3-8-2 61 JoeDoyle(5) 9 55
(John Ryan) *trckd ldr after 3f: led 3f out: drvn and hdd wl over 1f out: fdd* **12/1**

1165 **5** *1 1/4* **Like A Prayer**93 2847 3-9-0 68 SilvestreDeSousa 10 59
(Ralph Beckett) *settled in last trio: long way off the pce whn rdn over 2f out: kpt on fr over 1f out: no ch* **9/2**2

1452 **6** *1 1/2* **Dalaki (IRE)**15 5521 3-9-4 72 (b) KierenFallon 11 60
(Clive Brittain) *racd wd: prog to press ldng pair 1/2-way: drvn to chal wl over 2f out: nt qckn sn after: wknd over 1f out* **20/1**

-064 **7** *1/2* **Redinha**23 5256 3-9-4 72 AdamKirby 1 58
(Clive Cox) *chsd ldrs: rdn 3f out: no prog and btn 2f out* **25/1**

6-61 **8** *1 1/4* **Marengo**9 5751 3-8-9 70 6ex MeganCarberry(7) 7 53
(Ed de Giles) *dwlt: mostly in last: rdn 1/2-way: wl bhd whn impeded over 2f out: v modest late hdwy* **10/1**

2314 **9** *4 1/2* **Fruit Pastille**15 5521 3-9-1 69 JimCrowley 2 42
(Hughie Morrison) *rdn in midfield sn after 1/2-way: wknd wl over 2f out* **12/1**

2500 **10** *3 1/2* **Gay Marriage (IRE)**14 5557 3-9-5 73 (b1) WilliamBuick 3 38
(John Gosden) *nvr on terms: drvn towards rr 1/2-way: bhd fnl 2f* **7/1**

5-43 **11** *37* **Punk**21 5320 3-9-5 73 LukeMorris 6
(George Peckham) *racd freely: led to 3f out: wknd rapidly: t.o* **25/1**

1m 37.85s (-1.95) **Going Correction** -0.075s/f (Stan) **11** Ran SP% **117.1**
Speed ratings (Par 101): **106,105,101,98,97 96,95,94,89,86 49**
CSF £62.20 CT £206.05 TOTE £13.00: £2.90, £3.30, £1.90; EX 80.50 Trifecta £313.60.
**Owner** Mr & Mrs James Wigan **Bred** Mrs James Wigan & London TB Services Ltd **Trained** Newmarket, Suffolk

**FOCUS**
The early pace was fairly steady. The second helps opening level and the form has a sound feel, with every chance it could be worth 2lb-4lb more.

## 6035 BETBRIGHT MONEYBACK OFFERS H'CAP 1m (P)
**7:40** (7:40) (Class 5) (0-75,75) 4-Y-0+ **£2,587** (£770; £384; £192) **Stalls** Low

Form RPR

1545 **1** **Barnmore**16 5487 6-9-2 73 CharlesBishop(3) 2 82
(Peter Hedger) *trckd ldrs in 5th: rdn and plld out over 2f out: prog to ld jst over 1f out: drvn out* **9/2**1

3240 **2** *1 1/2* **St Paul De Vence (IRE)**30 4968 4-8-13 67 (t) LukeMorris 5 73
(Paul Cole) *trckd ldng trio: drvn over 2f out: styd on fr over 1f out to take 2nd last strides* **12/1**

-400 **3** *1/2* **Captain Starlight (IRE)**30 4968 4-9-1 69 FergusSweeney 8 73
(Jo Crowley) *pressed ldr in modly run event: chal 3f out: led briefly over 1f out: one pce fnl f* **50/1**

0410 **4** *1* **Aomen Rock**28 5040 4-9-5 73 (v) DaneO'Neill 6 75
(James Fanshawe) *chsd ldrs: rdn and nt qckn over 2f out: kpt on fr over 1f out: unable to chal* **6/1**3

0415 **5** *shd* **Tommy's Secret**28 5058 4-9-7 75 PatDobbs 9 77
(Jane Chapple-Hyam) *racd wd: hld up in midfield in modly run r: rdn and outpcd over 2f out: styd on fr over 1f out: nrst fin* **10/1**

0021 **6** *1 1/2* **Blazeofenchantment (USA)**14 5571 4-9-0 73 JacobButterfield(5) 11 71
(John Wainwright) *dwlt: rchd midfield after 2f: rdn wl over 2f out: no imp on ldrs over 1f out* **14/1**

0504 **7** *hd* **Anton Chigurh**21 5320 5-9-4 75 DannyBrock(3) 13 73+
(Philip McBride) *stdd s: t.k.h: hld up in last in modly run event: drvn over 2f out: stl last wl over 1f out: styd on quite wl fnl f: no ch* **5/1**2

2112 **8** *1* **Exceedexpectations (IRE)**7 5834 5-9-7 75 (v) StevieDonohoe 4 71
(Lee Carter) *mde most: set mod pce tl kicked on jst over 3f out: sn jnd: hdd & wknd over 1f out* **6/1**3

6350 **9** *hd* **Fantasy Gladiator**21 5320 8-9-5 73 WilliamBuick 1 68
(John Quinn) *trckd ldng pair: drvn over 2f out: nt qckn over 1f out: wknd fnl f* **16/1**

3060 **10** *2 3/4* **Dana's Present**12 5629 5-9-0 68 PatCosgrave 3 57+
(George Baker) *hld up in midfield: pushed along fr over 2f out: no real prog but one to nte* **8/1**

0000 **11** *nk* **Persepolis (IRE)**62 3878 4-9-7 75 AmirQuinn 10 63+
(Lee Carter) *stdd after s: hld up in last trio in modly run event: rdn and no prog over 2f out* **20/1**

0605 **12** *3 1/4* **Flamborough Breeze**32 4905 5-8-9 68 LouisSteward(5) 7 49+
(Ed Vaughan) *dwlt: hld up in rr in modly run event: rdn over 2f out: no prog* **10/1**

6150 **13** *6* **Indus Valley (IRE)**13 5605 7-8-7 61 (b) AdamBeschizza 12 28+
(Des Donovan) *stdd s: t.k.h: hld up in last trio: rdn and no prog 3f out: wknd* **50/1**

1m 39.49s (-0.31) **Going Correction** -0.075s/f (Stan) **13** Ran SP% **121.6**
Speed ratings (Par 103): **98,96,96,95,94 93,93,92,92,89 88,85,79**
CSF £59.29 CT £2470.28 TOTE £5.90: £2.40, £3.80, £14.00; EX 74.60 Trifecta £1230.70 Part won..
**Owner** P C F Racing Ltd **Bred** J J Whelan **Trained** Eastergate, W Sussex

**FOCUS**
Those held up looked at a bit of a disadvantage.

## 6036 BETBRIGHT.COM H'CAP 1m 4f (P)
**8:10** (8:10) (Class 4) (0-85,85) 3-Y-0+ **£4,690** (£1,395; £697; £348) **Stalls** Centre

Form RPR

0041 **1** **Anglo Irish**14 5552 3-9-1 83 WilliamBuick 6 92+
(John Gosden) *trckd ldr: styd w her whn pce qcknd 4f out: led jst over 2f out and poached decisive ld over 1f out: dwindling advantage fin but a holding on* **11/4**1

0111 **2** *1/2* **Sleeper**20 5353 3-8-9 77 AndreaAtzeni 3 85+
(Ralph Beckett) *prom early: steadily lost pl: shoved along in rr 4f out: outpcd over 2f out: rallied over 1f out: tk 2nd ins fnl f: clsng on wnr fin* **9/2**3

3552 **3** *1 3/4* **Noble Gift**24 5203 4-9-12 85 GeorgeBaker 7 90
(William Knight) *stdd s: hld up in detached last in slowly run event: rdn wl over 2f out: styd on fr over 1f out to take 3rd last strides: far too much to do* **12/1**

3435 **4** *1/2* **Don't Stare**24 5203 4-9-9 82 (t) ShaneKelly 9 87
(James Fanshawe) *hld up towards rr in slowly run event: outpcd and rdn over 2f out: n.d after but styd on wl again fnl f* **12/1**

-400 **5** *shd* **Festival Theatre (IRE)**33 4855 3-9-0 82 RyanMoore 8 86
(Sir Michael Stoute) *trckd ldng trio: bdly outpcd and drvn wl over 2f out: no ch after but styd on wl fnl f* **6/1**

0122 **6** *hd* **Grasped**16 5487 4-9-9 82 JamesDoyle 1 86
(Lady Cecil) *led at modest pce: kicked on fr 4f out: hdd jst over 2f out: wl hld by wnr over 1f out: lost 2nd and fdd ins fnl f* **10/1**

2153 **7** *2 1/4* **Mythical Madness**18 5430 3-9-2 84 AdamKirby 5 85
(Charlie Appleby) *racd on outer: prog to trck ldrs 1/2-way: drvn over 2f out: nt qckn after: wknd fnl f* **3/1**2

0650 **8** *2 1/2* **Thecornishcowboy**16 5487 5-8-10 74 (t) JoeDoyle(5) 4 71
(John Ryan) *in tch: outpcd and drvn over 2f out: no prog after* **33/1**

35 **9** *1 1/4* **Odin (IRE)**32 4917 6-9-8 81 DaneO'Neill 2 76
(Don Cantillon) *trckd ldng pair: rdn and outpcd over 2f out: no prog over 1f out: wknd and eased ins fnl f* **25/1**

2m 35.61s (1.11) **Going Correction** -0.075s/f (Stan)
**WFA** 3 from 4yo+ 9lb **9** Ran SP% **115.4**
Speed ratings (Par 105): **93,92,91,91,91 90,89,87,86**
CSF £15.43 CT £125.99 TOTE £2.90: £2.00, £2.30, £2.40; EX 13.00 Trifecta £44.70.
**Owner** George Strawbridge **Bred** George Strawbridge **Trained** Newmarket, Suffolk

**FOCUS**
This looked fairly competitive and the form has a solid look. The third helps set the opening level.

## 6037 DIZZEE RASCAL LIVE HERE ON SATURDAY H'CAP 1m 3f (P)
**8:40** (8:40) (Class 6) (0-65,65) 3-Y-0 **£1,940** (£577; £288; £144) **Stalls** Low

Form RPR

1221 **1** **King Calypso**16 5491 3-8-8 57 CamHardie(5) 9 69+
(Denis Coakley) *trckd ldrs disputing 5th: prog over 2f out: rdn over 1f out: r.o wl fnl f: readily* **11/4**1

0564 **2** *2 1/2* **Classic Mission**10 5719 3-8-10 59 (b1) NedCurtis(5) 11 67
(Jonathan Portman) *sn w ldr: led after 3f: kicked on wl over 2f out: hdd over 1f out: styd on but readily outpcd* **50/1**

600 **3** *2 1/4* **May Queen**57 4052 3-8-13 57 TedDurcan 3 62
(Chris Wall) *trckd ldrs disputing 5th: rdn over 2f out: kpt on one pce fr over 1f out to take 3rd ins fnl f* **12/1**

4034 **4** *1* **Anjin (IRE)**8 5426 3-9-4 62 LukeMorris 2 65
(Sir Mark Prescott Bt) *trckd ldng pair: drvn to go 2nd briefly over 2f out: outpcd fr over 1f out* **10/3**2

2332 **5** *1 1/4* **Sandy Cove**15 5520 3-9-1 62 RyanTate(3) 8 63
(James Eustace) *hld up disputing 7th: tried to creep clsr over 2f out: rchd 5th over 1f out: rdn and one pce after* **9/2**3

4552 **6** *3* **Maid Of Tuscany (IRE)**9 5747 3-8-6 57 CharlotteJenner(7) 4 53
(Mark Usher) *wl off the pce early: rdn and prog fr last quartet over 2f out: kpt on one pce: no ch* **25/1**

5035 **7** *4* **Citizen Kaine (IRE)**14 5556 3-9-4 62 (b1) MartinDwyer 14 52
(Jo Hughes) *c out of the stalls slowly: wl off the pce in last quartet early: shkn up in last trio over 2f out: passed a few late on: nvr involved* **14/1**

3066 **8** *2* **Harboured (USA)**6 5865 3-9-2 60 (p1) PatCosgrave 6 47
(Jim Boyle) *hld up disputing 7th: drvn over 2f out: no prog wl over 1f out: wknd* **50/1**

2420 **9** *2 1/2* **Flawless Pink**8 5796 3-9-7 65 (p) RyanMoore 13 48
(Jeremy Noseda) *pushed up to chse ldng pair: rdn and lost pl wl over 2f out: sn wknd* **11/2**

6005 **10** *2 1/2* **Sebs Sensei (IRE)**18 5427 3-9-7 65 RobertHavlin 5 44
(Mark Hoad) *wl off the pce in last quartet early: rdn in last trio 3f out: no prog* **66/1**

006 **11** *10* **Tribulina**30 4966 3-8-10 59 (b1) DanielMuscutt(5) 1 22
(Marco Botti) *led 3f: w ldr to 3f out: wknd qckly over 2f out* **16/1**

4240 **12** *21* **Mercury Magic**15 5529 3-8-11 58 RobertTart(3) 7
(David Menuisier) *a wl in rr: wknd u.p over 2f out: t.o* **16/1**

2m 19.58s (-2.32) **Going Correction** -0.075s/f (Stan) **12** Ran SP% **118.7**
Speed ratings (Par 99): **105,103,101,100,99 97,94,93,91,89 82,67**
CSF £162.33 CT £1453.98 TOTE £2.50: £1.30, £10.40, £3.60; EX 155.40 Trifecta £2121.70 Part won..
**Owner** Count Calypso Racing **Bred** Miss K Rausing **Trained** West Ilsley, Berks

**FOCUS**
There was a bit of a rush for the lead early on but things soon slowed down in the back straight and they sprinted up the straight. The winner is on the up and the shock runner-up has one bit of form that fits. This could be shade better.
T/Plt: £15.60 to a £1 stake. Pool: £54,235.65 - 2,524.40 winning units. T/Qpdt: £8.00 to a £1 stake. Pool: £8,319.17 - 761.85 winning units. JN

# 5859 LINGFIELD (L-H)
Wednesday, September 3

**OFFICIAL GOING: Turf course: good (6.9); polytrack: standard**
Wind: Light, across Weather: Fine

## 6038 188BET CASINO MAIDEN STKS (DIV I) 6f
**2:00** (2:01) (Class 5) 2-Y-0 **£3,234** (£962; £481; £240) **Stalls** Centre

Form RPR

2 **1** **Charming Thought**19 5397 2-9-5 0 WilliamBuick 9 88+
(Charlie Appleby) *chsd ldng pair: smooth hdwy to chal over 1f out: led 1f out: pushed clr: readily* **4/11**1

023 **2** 2 **Kinematic**[82] 3193 2-9-0 77 RyanMoore 5 77
(Andrew Balding) *led: rdn over 1f out: hdd 1f out: sn outpcd but kpt on* **9/2**[2]
0 **3** 2 1/4 **Harbour Patrol (IRE)**[36] 4760 2-9-5 0 RichardHughes 4 75+
(Richard Hannon) *in tch in midfield: effrt u.p 2f out: one pce fnl f* **8/1**[3]
2323 **4** 1 1/4 **Aussie Ruler (IRE)**[23] 5242 2-9-5 77 LukeMorris 10 72
(Ronald Harris) *chsd ldrs: rdn 2f out: styd on same pce fnl f* **8/1**[3]
66 **5** 4 1/2 **Finton Friend (IRE)**[11] 5684 2-9-5 0 SteveDrowne 7 58
(Charles Hills) *outpcd and detached last: hdwy over 1f out: styd on: nvr trbld ldrs* **33/1**
0 **6** 1/2 **Treaty Of York (IRE)**[11] 5684 2-9-5 0 DaneO'Neill 11 57+
(Henry Candy) *chsd ldr tl over 1f out: wknd fnl f* **14/1**
35 **7** 1 3/4 **Stealing Thunder (IRE)**[9] 5745 2-9-5 0 HarryBentley 6 51+
(Eve Johnson Houghton) *a towards rr: drifted lft 1/2-way: wknd over 1f out* **50/1**
**8** 2 1/4 **Toot Your Flute (IRE)** 2-9-5 0 AndreaAtzeni 2 45
(William Haggas) *s.i.s: hld up towards rr: rdn 2f out: sn wknd* **16/1**
**9** 7 **Autumn Tonic (IRE)** 2-9-5 0 SebSanders 8 24
(Simon Dow) *s.i.s: a outpcd towards rr: lost tch 2f out* **66/1**

1m 11.56s (0.36) **Going Correction** +0.15s/f (Good) **9** Ran SP% **132.7**
Speed ratings (Par 95): **103,100,97,95,89 89,86,83,74**
CSF £3.37 TOTE £1.40: £1.10, £1.10, £2.80; EX 4.60 Trifecta £26.20.
**Owner** Godolphin **Bred** Merry Fox Stud Limited **Trained** Newmarket, Suffolk

**FOCUS**
The ground had dried out slightly and was now officially good all over on the turf course. The stands' rail was in its true position, meaning that the turf track was at its widest for the first time this year, and although the stalls were in the centre on the straight track, the jockeys wasted no time in making a beeline for the nearside rail in the opener. Punters only wanted to know about one horse in the first division of this maiden and it proved plain sailing for the red-hot favourite. Straightforward form, rated around the runner-up.

## 6039 188BET CASINO MAIDEN STKS (DIV II) 6f
**2:30** (2:32) (Class 5) 2-Y-O **£3,234** (£962; £481; £240) **Stalls** Centre

Form RPR
5 **1** **Qatar Road (FR)**[18] 5439 2-9-5 0 MartinHarley 5 76
(Marco Botti) *chsd ldng pair: rdn and ev ch over 1f out: led ins fnl f: r.o wl* **11/4**[2]
642 **2** nk **Chevallier**[18] 5439 2-9-5 76 RichardHughes 2 75
(Richard Hannon) *w ldr: rdn to ld over 1f out: hdd ins fnl f: kpt on but hld towards fin* **1/1**[1]
0 **3** 3 1/4 **Sydney Ruffdiamond**[12] 5646 2-9-5 0 RyanMoore 8 65
(Richard Hannon) *wl in tch in midfield: effrt over 1f out: 3rd and outpcd fnl 100yds* **6/1**[3]
**4** nk **Winning Hunter** 2-9-5 0 TomEaves 10 64
(Philip Hide) *hld up wl in tch in midfield: swtchd lft over 1f out: battling for 3rd and one pce fnl f* **16/1**
0 **5** 1/2 **Its Gonna Be Me (IRE)**[18] 5439 2-9-5 0 PaulHanagan 3 63+
(William Haggas) *in tch in midfield: rdn 2f out: styd on same pce fnl f* **8/1**
64 **6** 4 **Beauchamp Ace**[28] 5029 2-9-5 0 RichardKingscote 9 51
(Paul Fitzsimons) *led: rdn and hdd over 1f out: fdd ins fnl f* **16/1**
0 **7** 3/4 **Kyllarney**[30] 4980 2-9-0 0 SteveDrowne 4 44
(Charles Hills) *hld up in tch towards rr: rdn 2f out: sn outpcd and wknd* **20/1**
05 **8** 1/2 **Steevo (IRE)**[9] 5752 2-9-5 0 GeorgeBaker 1 47+
(Gary Moore) *stdd s: hld up towards rr: pushed along over 1f out: sn outpcd and btn* **33/1**
00 **9** 9 **Bounty Bah**[14] 5555 2-9-5 0 PatDobbs 7 20
(Mark Usher) *hld up wl in tch towards rr: rdn over 1f out: sn btn: fdd* **100/1**
**10** 13 **Delysdream** 2-9-5 0 JimmyQuinn 6
(Christine Dunnett) *s.i.s: a in rr: lost tch 2f out* **50/1**

1m 12.39s (1.19) **Going Correction** +0.15s/f (Good) **10** Ran SP% **124.5**
Speed ratings (Par 95): **98,97,93,92,92 86,85,85,73,55**
CSF £6.15 TOTE £6.00: £1.40, £1.10, £3.50; EX 6.70 Trifecta £28.20.
**Owner** Mubarak Al Naemi **Bred** Scea De L'Aubay & Serge Bouvier **Trained** Newmarket, Suffolk

**FOCUS**
The winning time was 0.83sec slower than the first division. The winner improved from his debut and the runner-up helps the opening level.

## 6040 188BET NURSERY H'CAP 6f
**3:00** (3:00) (Class 6) (0-60,60) 2-Y-O **£2,587** (£770; £384; £192) **Stalls** Centre

Form RPR
00U4 **1** **Piping Dream (IRE)**[7] 5828 2-9-2 55 RichardHughes 5 58
(Richard Hannon) *mde all: hrd pressed ent fnl f: hld on wl u.p: all out* **8/1**[3]
060 **2** hd **Jubilee Spirit**[55] 4110 2-9-5 58 [1] BarryMcHugh 12 60+
(Geoffrey Oldroyd) *in tch in midfield: swtchd lft and squeezed through to chal over 1f out: r.o: jst hld* **5/1**[2]
0630 **3** 3/4 **Diracan (IRE)**[18] 5436 2-9-7 60 (b) GeorgeBaker 10 60+
(Nick Littmoden) *hld up in rr: stuck bhd horses 2f out: rdn and hdwy 1f out: styd on wl* **2/1**[1]
600 **4** 3/4 **Q Twenty Girl (IRE)**[11] 5684 2-8-9 55 CharlotteJenner(7) 11 53
(Mark Usher) *chsd ldrs: ev ch 1f out: no ex fnl 100yds* **10/1**
350 **5** hd **Scent Of Power**[26] 5133 2-8-13 52 LukeMorris 9 53+
(Anthony Carson) *in tch towards rr: lost pl and bhd whn swtchd rt over 1f out: rallied u.p fnl f: styd on wl* **10/1**
4313 **6** 1/2 **Baileys Pursuit**[47] 4410 2-9-7 60 JimmyQuinn 8 56
(Christine Dunnett) *hld up in rr: swtchd lft and hdwy over 1f out: no ex fnl 100yds* **12/1**
020 **7** 1 3/4 **Lady Charlie**[48] 4338 2-8-11 53 PhilipPrince(3) 2 44
(Jo Hughes) *chsd ldr: ev ch u.p over 1f out: wknd ins fnl f* **16/1**
3605 **8** 2 **Chetan**[30] 4967 2-9-5 58 RichardKingscote 6 42
(Milton Bradley) *in tch in midfield: rdn 2f out: sn lost pl: one pce after* **8/1**[3]
652 **9** 1/2 **Cupulation**[16] 5507 2-9-2 55 MartinHarley 4 40+
(Amy Weaver) *in tch towards rr: nt clr run and hmpd over 1f out: kpt on but nt rcvr* **20/1**
4444 **10** shd **Surrey Pink (FR)**[15] 5517 2-8-11 50 (p) JimCrowley 7 33
(William Muir) *stdd s: hld up in rr: effrt u.p 2f out: wknd fnl f* **8/1**[3]
0050 **11** 1/2 **Activation**[16] 5489 2-9-6 59 (p) PatDobbs 1 40
(Hughie Morrison) *chsd ldrs: lost pl qckly over 1f out: wknd fnl f* **20/1**
5065 **12** 4 1/2 **Paco's Dream**[25] 5180 2-8-13 52 PatCosgrave 3 20
(Harry Dunlop) *s.i.s and wnt lft s: hdwy into midfield 1/2-way: wknd u.p over 1f out* **12/1**

1m 13.13s (1.93) **Going Correction** +0.15s/f (Good) **12** Ran SP% **132.3**
Speed ratings (Par 93): **93,92,91,90,90 89,87,84,84,84 83,77**
CSF £53.59 CT £116.97 TOTE £11.90: £4.30, £3.60, £1.10; EX 85.60 Trifecta £263.00.
**Owner** Pall Mall Partners **Bred** L White & D McGregor **Trained** East Everleigh, Wilts
■ Stewards' Enquiry : Barry McHugh caution: careless riding.

**FOCUS**
Only one of these had been successful before and that was in a seller, which underlines the weakness of this nursery, and the winning time was significantly slower than both divisions of the maiden. Those who raced closest to the stands' rail were very much favoured.

## 6041 BRITISH STALLION STUDS EBF MAIDEN FILLIES' STKS (BOBIS RACE) 7f
**3:30** (3:32) (Class 5) 2-Y-O **£2,911** (£866; £432; £216) **Stalls** Centre

Form RPR
3 **1** **Majestic Manner**[44] 4499 2-9-0 0 RichardHughes 11 75
(William Haggas) *mde all: rdn over 1f out: asserted fnl f: r.o* **5/2**[1]
24 **2** 1 1/4 **Ajaadat**[28] 5037 2-9-0 0 AndreaAtzeni 4 72
(Roger Varian) *chsd wnr thrght: rdn and ev ch over 1f out: no ex and one pce fnl f* **11/4**[2]
**3** 1/2 **Moonlight Sonata** 2-9-0 0 RyanMoore 5 71+
(Sir Michael Stoute) *s.i.s: in tch in midfield: rdn and hdwy over 1f out: wnt 3rd ins fnl f: kpt on* **6/1**[3]
04 **4** 3/4 **Heart Of Africa**[14] 5549 2-9-0 0 MartinLane 7 69
(Charlie Appleby) *chsd ldng pair: rdn and outpcd over 1f out: keeping on again whn swtchd lft nr fin* **20/1**
**5** 3 1/4 **Journey** 2-9-0 0 WilliamBuick 12 60+
(John Gosden) *s.i.s: hld up in last pair: wnt lft and hdwy 2f out: swtchd lft and rdn over 1f out: outpcd fnl f* **11/4**[2]
**6** nk **Music And Dance** 2-9-0 0 PatDobbs 10 59+
(Sir Michael Stoute) *s.i.s: in tch towards rr: pushed along whn nt clr run over 1f out: styd on wl fnl f* **25/1**
**7** 2 1/2 **Dominike (ITY)** 2-9-0 0 MartinHarley 9 52
(Marco Botti) *stdd s: hld up in midfield: shkn up 2f out: outpcd and btn 1f out* **33/1**
**8** 1 1/4 **Lamsa (IRE)** 2-9-0 0 PaulHanagan 2 49+
(Ed Dunlop) *s.i.s: hld up in last pair: sme hdwy whn pushed lft over 1f out: wknd fnl f* **16/1**
**9** shd **Taqweem (USA)** 2-9-0 0 DaneO'Neill 1 49
(Saeed bin Suroor) *s.i.s: rcvrd to chse ldrs after 2f: rdn and wknd over 1f out* **14/1**
0 **10** 2 3/4 **Dancethenightaway (IRE)**[10] 5725 2-9-0 0 (b) SteveDrowne 3 41
(William Jarvis) *in tch in midfield: rdn and struggling 2f out: bhd fnl f* **100/1**

1m 25.28s (1.98) **Going Correction** +0.15s/f (Good) **10** Ran SP% **121.3**
Speed ratings (Par 92): **94,92,92,91,87 87,84,82,82,79**
CSF £9.72 TOTE £2.80: £1.30, £1.10, £2.70; EX 11.50 Trifecta £32.80.
**Owner** Jaber Abdullah **Bred** Rabbah Bloodstock Limited **Trained** Newmarket, Suffolk

**FOCUS**
Some nicely bred newcomers, but it was dominated by a pair that had already shown ability who were on the pace throughout. Again racing close to the stands' rail was an advantage. Just fair form.

## 6042 BRITISH ASSESSMENT BUREAU MEDIAN AUCTION MAIDEN STKS 7f
**4:05** (4:06) (Class 6) 3-5-Y-O **£2,587** (£770; £384; £192) **Stalls** Centre

Form RPR
5362 **1** **Whaleweigh Station**[15] 5531 3-9-5 79 RichardHughes 6 89+
(J R Jenkins) *led tl 1 1/2-way: led again ent fnl 2f: rdn and drew wl clr wl over 1f out: rdn out* **3/1**[2]
6 **2** 9 **Quaintrelle (IRE)**[46] 4446 3-9-0 0 AndreaAtzeni 2 60+
(Ed Vaughan) *hld up in last trio: pushed along and sme hdwy over 1f out: wnt 2nd ins fnl f: no ch w wnr* **8/1**
2033 **3** 1 1/2 **Rome**[16] 5504 4-9-9 78 (p) RyanMoore 5 63
(Gary Moore) *chsd ldrs: rdn to chse wnr 2f out: btn over 1f out: wknd and lost 2nd ins fnl f* **11/10**[1]
3654 **4** 1 3/4 **Song Of Norway**[20] 5352 3-9-0 70 (p) SteveDrowne 3 51
(Peter Makin) *in tch in midfield: effrt u.p 2f out: wl btn whn hung rt 1f out* **7/2**[3]
044 **5** 4 1/2 **Bond Empire**[25] 5195 4-9-9 64 BarryMcHugh 1 46
(Geoffrey Oldroyd) *stdd and dropped in bhd after s: rdn and struggling 3f out: no ch fnl 2f* **33/1**
40 **6** 2 3/4 **Rectitude**[16] 5504 3-9-0 0 WilliamBuick 4 31
(John Gosden) *midfield: rdn 1/2-way: struggling and btn 2f out* **14/1**
0-05 **7** 1 1/2 **Aster's Approval**[68] 3677 4-9-9 50 (bt) PaddyAspell 8 34
(Mrs Ilka Gansera-Leveque) *taken down early: racd keenly: w wnr: led 1/2-way tl ent fnl 2f: fdd over 1f out* **80/1**
5 **8** 3 **Tilsworth Annalisa**[15] 5531 3-8-7 0 VictorSantos(7) 7 19
(J R Jenkins) *s.i.s: hld up in rr: rdn 2f out: sn lost tch* **100/1**

1m 24.31s (1.01) **Going Correction** +0.15s/f (Good)
**WFA** 3 from 4yo 4lb **8** Ran SP% **117.8**
Speed ratings (Par 101): **100,89,88,86,80 77,76,72**
CSF £27.55 TOTE £4.30: £1.10, £2.40, £1.10; EX 35.20 Trifecta £61.50.
**Owner** B Silkman **Bred** A Black **Trained** Royston, Herts

**FOCUS**
An ordinary older-horse maiden and more of the same with Richard Hughes soon managing to grab the stands' rail in front, but his mount turned this into a procession. It's perhaps worth not taking the form too literally, with the time not supporting.

## 6043 188BET CLAIMING STKS 1m 4f (P)
**4:35** (4:35) (Class 6) 3-4-Y-O **£2,134** (£635; £317; £158) **Stalls** Low

Form RPR
4441 **1** **Sparkling Ice (IRE)**[10] 5719 3-8-3 59 (b) AmyScott(3) 4 61
(Eve Johnson Houghton) *mde all: drvn 2f out: asserted over 1f out: styd on* **7/1**
1602 **2** 2 **Conquestadim**[39] 4656 4-9-12 69 RichardHughes 2 69
(Hughie Morrison) *chsd ldrs: effrt between horses to chse wnr 3f out: drvn and fnd little over 1f out: one pce* **5/4**[1]
06 **3** 8 **Bally Broadwell**[16] 5490 4-8-8 0 KieranShoemark(7) 5 45
(Michael Madgwick) *hld up in tch: rdn and outpcd 3f out: plugged on to go modest 3rd ins fnl f* **33/1**
645 **4** 3 **Kagami**[80] 3270 3-9-4 73 DaneO'Neill 3 52
(Simon Dow) *dwlt: t.k.h in midfield: hdwy to join ldr over 4f out tl 3f out: sn outpcd: wknd over 1f out* **9/4**[2]
4344 **5** 2 3/4 **Passionate Affair (IRE)**[7] 5829 3-8-12 64 (tp) WilliamBuick 1 42
(Jamie Osborne) *hld up in last pair: rdn over 3f out: immediately btn* **7/2**[3]

6000 **P** **Its Not Me Its You**[8] 5795 3-8-4 62 .......................... JemmaMarshall(3) 6
(Brendan Powell) *dwlt: hdwy to chse wnr 10f out tl over 4f out: lost tch 3f out: p.u 1f out: dismntd* **50/1**

2m 31.18s (-1.82) **Going Correction** -0.15s/f (Stan)
**WFA** 3 from 4yo 9lb **6** Ran SP% **114.8**
Speed ratings (Par 101): **100,98,93,91,89**
CSF £16.86 TOTE £4.50: £3.10, £1.10; EX 14.80 Trifecta £185.10.Sparkling Ice was claimed by Miss Z C Davison for £6000
**Owner** Mrs E Rice & Mrs R F Johnson Houghton **Bred** Gerrardstown House Stud **Trained** Blewbury, Oxon

**FOCUS**
A moderate Polytrack claimer. The form is rated towards the negative end of the possibilities.

## 6044 188BET GREAT IN PLAY H'CAP (BOBIS RACE) 1m 2f (P)
5:05 (5:07) (Class 4) (0-85,85) 3-Y-O **£5,336** (£1,588; £793; £396) **Stalls** Low

Form RPR

-414 **1** **Alex Vino (IRE)**[17] 5465 3-9-7 **85** .......................... RyanMoore 10 97
(Sir Michael Stoute) *chsd ldrs: wnt 2nd 7f out: rdn to ld 1f out: hld on: all out* **2/1**[1]

-051 **2** *hd* **Zugzwang (IRE)**[14] 5557 3-8-11 **75** .......................... PatCosgrave 7 87
(Ed de Giles) *in tch in midfield: effrt to chse ldrs 2f out: drvn and ev ch fnl f: kpt on: jst hld* **12/1**

221 **3** *nk* **Wrood (USA)**[25] 5186 3-9-1 **79** .......................... TomQueally 13 90
(James Fanshawe) *dwlt: hld up towards rr: rdn and hdwy over 1f out: styng on whn swtchd lft ins fnl f: nt quite rch ldrs* **6/1**[2]

2105 **4** *3/4* **Placidia (IRE)**[10] 5730 3-9-4 **82** .......................... TedDurcan 9 92
(David Lanigan) *hld up towards rr: hdwy into midfield 1/2-way: drvn and effrt 2f out: chsd ldrs fnl f: kpt on* **8/1**

4635 **5** *7* **Master Dancer**[14] 5550 3-8-8 **72** .......................... TomEaves 6 68
(Philip Hide) *chsd ldrs: wnt 2nd 8f out tl 7f out: drvn 2f out: wknd fnl f* **16/1**

-210 **6** *1/2* **Fast Delivery**[104] 2481 3-9-6 **84** .......................... AndreaAtzeni 5 80
(Saeed bin Suroor) *hld up towards rr: nt clr run 2f out: effrt whn hmpd over 1f out: kpt on fnl f: nvr trbld ldrs* **8/1**

4235 **7** *hd* **Gilbey's Mate**[56] 4074 3-9-1 **79** .......................... (b[1]) WilliamBuick 4 74
(John Gosden) *sn led: rdn and qcknd 2f out: hdd 1f out: sn btn and wknd* **7/1**[3]

0324 **8** *1* **Barye**[28] 5038 3-8-10 **74** .......................... JimCrowley 2 70+
(David Simcock) *hld up towards rr: effrt whn short of room and sltly hmpd 1f out: nvr trbld ldrs* **8/1**

-215 **9** *2* **Bishop Of Ruscombe**[28] 5038 3-8-6 **77** .......................... KieranShoemark(7) 12 66
(Andrew Balding) *in tch in midfield on outer: rdn and struggling 2f out: hung lft and wknd over 1f out* **10/1**

4346 **10** *5* **Castle Combe (IRE)**[17] 5468 3-8-13 **77** .......................... PatDobbs 8 59
(Marcus Tregoning) *dwlt: in rr: effrt and plenty to do on inner over 1f out: hmpd 1f out: no ch after* **50/1**

-156 **11** *5* **Rasameel (USA)**[20] 5345 3-9-7 **85** .......................... PaulHanagan 1 59
(B W Hills) *broke wl to ld early: stdd bk into midfield: rdn and no hdwy over 2f out: btn whn bdly hmpd 1f out* **33/1**

5025 **12** *3 1/2* **Champagne Sydney (IRE)**[18] 5410 3-9-6 **84** .......................... RichardHughes 3 50
(Richard Hannon) *prom early: stdd bk into midfield after 2f: rdn and struggling over 2f out: wkng and btn whn hmpd 1f out* **14/1**

2m 3.51s (-3.09) **Going Correction** -0.15s/f (Stan) **12** Ran SP% **127.7**
Speed ratings (Par 103): **106,105,105,105,99 99,98,98,96,92 88,85**
CSF £31.41 CT £136.85 TOTE £3.50: £1.50, £3.40, £2.70; EX 28.80 Trifecta £183.20.
**Owner** Nurlan Bizakov **Bred** Hesmonds Stud Ltd **Trained** Newmarket, Suffolk
■ Stewards' Enquiry : Kieran Shoemark two-day ban: careless riding (Sep 17-18)

**FOCUS**
A competitive handicap in which they went a good pace and the front four pulled clear. The form makes plenty of sense.

## 6045 SAVILLS MEDIAN AUCTION MAIDEN STKS 1m 4f (P)
5:35 (5:36) (Class 6) 3-4-Y-O **£2,587** (£770; £384; £192) **Stalls** Low

Form RPR

0220 **1** **Invasor Luck (USA)**[14] 5552 3-9-5 79 .......................... TomQueally 4 81
(James Fanshawe) *mde all: rdn 2f out: sn drew clr: comf* **10/11**[1]

2 **2** *6* **Shuriken (IRE)**[25] 5191 3-9-0 0 .......................... RobertHavlin 2 64
(Peter Chapple-Hyam) *dwlt: hld up in tch: effrt to chse wnr over 2f out: btn over 1f out: wknd fnl f* **5/2**[2]

3026 **3** *hd* **Black Label**[42] 4540 3-9-5 70 .......................... RichardHughes 5 69
(Harry Dunlop) *chsd wnr tl over 2f out: sn outpcd and no ch w wnr: kpt on again u.p fnl f* **4/1**[3]

**4** *8* **Jeremy's Jet (IRE)** 3-9-2 0 .......................... ThomasBrown(3) 1 56
(Andrew Balding) *chsd ldrs: rdn and sltly outpcd over 3f out: rallied 2f out: fdd fnl f* **8/1**

**5** *1/2* **Tiger Stone** 3-9-0 0 .......................... HayleyTurner 3 50
(Michael Blanshard) *a in rr: rdn over 3f out: lost tch 2f out* **33/1**

2m 32.32s (-0.68) **Going Correction** -0.15s/f (Stan) **5** Ran SP% **115.0**
Speed ratings (Par 101): **96,92,91,86,86**
CSF £3.71 TOTE £2.50: £1.10, £1.50; EX 4.00 Trifecta £6.40.
**Owner** Mohamed Obaida **Bred** Rabbah Bloodstock Llc **Trained** Newmarket, Suffolk

**FOCUS**
A very one-sided 3yo maiden. The dominant winner is rated to his recent level.
T/Plt: £3.90 to a £1 stake. Pool: £49,030.20 - 9175.31 winning units. T/Qpdt: £2.90 to a £1 stake. Pool: £3449.53 - 871.21 winning units.

6046 - 6052a (Foreign Racing) - See Raceform Interactive

# 5965 BADEN-BADEN (L-H)
Wednesday, September 3

**OFFICIAL GOING: Turf: soft**

## 6053a KRONIMUS-RENNEN (LISTED RACE) (2YO) (TURF) 6f
4:10 (12:00) 2-Y-O **£11,666** (£5,416; £2,500; £1,250)

RPR

**1** **Peace Society (USA)** 2-8-9 0 .......................... EPedroza 2 87
(A Wohler, Germany) **57/10**

**2** *1/2* **Copleys Walk (IRE)**[17] 5472 2-8-13 0 .......................... SHellyn 3 90
(John Joseph Murphy, Ire) *midfield: rdn into st: chal fnl f: kpt on wl but nt quite pce of wnr and jst hld* **214/10**

**3** *1* **Disprove (IRE)**[14] 5555 2-8-11 0 .......................... DavidProbert 8 85
(Hugo Palmer) *a.p: rdn to chal into st and sn led: kpt on but strly pressed and hdd towards fin: no ex and dropped to 3rd* **7/2**[2]

**4** *1 1/2* **Banana Split**[43] 4524 2-9-2 0 .......................... FabriceVeron 9 85
(P Harley, Germany) **17/2**

**5** *nse* **Neve (GER)** 2-8-11 0 .......................... StefanieHofer 5 80
(Mario Hofer, Germany) **147/10**

**6** *nk* **Laleh (GER)**[43] 4524 2-8-11 0 .......................... FilipMinarik 4 79
(Mario Hofer, Germany) **96/10**

**7** *3* **Showstoppa**[22] 5266 2-9-2 0 .......................... JoeFanning 10 75
(Mark Johnston) *midfield: rdn into st: chal over 1f out and ev ch ent fnl f: sn no ex and btn: wknd: eased towards fin* **16/5**[1]

**8** *3/4* **Drummer (GER)** 2-9-1 0 .......................... AdriedeVries 6 72
(P Schiergen, Germany) **53/10**

**9** *1* **Seaforth (IRE)**[37] 4745 2-8-13 0 .......................... MircoDemuro 7 67
(John Joseph Murphy, Ire) *dwlt sltly and hld up towards rr: rdn and effrt to cl into st: no ex and btn fnl f: wknd and eased* **9/2**[3]

**10** *34* **Felitsia (BUL)** 2-8-9 0 .......................... MaximPecheur 1
(Gerald Geisler, Germany) **27/1**

1m 11.97s (1.68) **10** Ran SP% **129.4**
WIN (incl. 10 euro stake): 67. PLACES: 22, 43, 20. SF: 1,118.
**Owner** Dr Christoph Berglar **Bred** Dr Christoph Berglar **Trained** Germany

## 6054a DARLEY OETTINGEN-RENNEN (GROUP 2) (3YO+) (TURF) 1m
5:45 (12:00) 3-Y-O+
**£33,333** (£9,166; £9,166; £3,333; £2,083; £1,250)

RPR

**1** **Here Comes When (IRE)**[77] 3356 4-9-0 0 .......................... DavidProbert 6 112+
(Andrew Balding) *t.k.h: hld up: clsd into st: rdn to chal 2f out: led over 1f out: r.o strly and asserted fnl f: readily* **66/10**

**2** *1 1/2* **Amaron**[52] 4247 5-9-0 0 .......................... MircoDemuro 3 109
(Andreas Lowe, Germany) *trckd ldr: led 1/2-way: rdn and hdd over 1f out: kpt on wl fnl f but nt pce of wnr: dead-heated for 2nd post* **12/5**[1]

**2** *dht* **Magic Artist (IRE)**[38] 4720 3-8-9 0 .......................... FrederikTylicki 2 108
(W Figge, Germany) *midfield: clsd 3f out: rdn to chal and ev ch 2f out: kpt on wl fnl f but nt pce of wnr: dead-heated for 2nd post* **51/10**[3]

**4** *2 1/2* **Felician (GER)**[52] 4247 6-9-0 0 .......................... SHellyn 8 103
(Ferdinand J Leve, Germany) *hld up: clsd gng strly into st: rdn to chal 2f out: outpcd and fdd fnl f* **123/10**

**5** *2* **Neatico (GER)**[18] 5461 7-9-0 0 .......................... AdriedeVries 4 98
(P Schiergen, Germany) *midfield: rdn into st: sn outpcd: tk mod 5th fnl f: nvr able to chal* **78/10**

**6** *nk* **Red Dubawi (IRE)**[17] 5480 6-9-3 0 .......................... EddyHardouin 9 101
(Frau Erika Mader, Germany) *dwlt and hld up in rr: rdn into st: sn outpcd by ldrs and no imp: n.d* **14/5**[2]

**7** *shd* **Peace At Last (IRE)**[52] 4247 4-9-0 0 .......................... FabriceVeron 1 97
(H-A Pantall, France) *t.k.h: prom: rdn and brief effrt to chal into st: sn outpcd by ldrs: wknd fnl f* **68/10**

**8** *1 3/4* **Gereon (GER)**[18] 6-9-3 0 .......................... FilipMinarik 5 96
(C Zschache, Germany) *led: hdd 1/2-way: racd alone but continued to press new ldr: rdn and moved across to join remainder into st: no ex appr fnl f: wknd* **12/1**

**9** *2 1/2* **Avon Pearl**[34] 4957 5-9-0 0 .......................... (b) EPedroza 7 88
(Rune Haugen, Norway) *t.k.h: midfield: towards rr 3f out: rdn in last 2f out: no imp and wl btn fnl f* **188/10**

1m 42.48s (3.37)
**WFA** 3 from 4yo+ 5lb **9** Ran SP% **129.7**
WIN (incl. 10 euro stake): 76. PLACES: 31, 17, 19. SF: 172.
**Owner** Mrs Fitri Hay **Bred** Old Carhue & Graeng Bloodstock **Trained** Kingsclere, Hants

6055 - (Foreign Racing) - See Raceform Interactive

# 5173 HAYDOCK (L-H)
Thursday, September 4

**OFFICIAL GOING: Good to soft (good in places; 7.5)**
Wind: Light, half behind Weather: Sunny Rails: All races on inside home straight and distances on Round course reduced by about 8yds

## 6056 BETFRED JACK BERRY MBE EBF MAIDEN STKS 1m
2:00 (2:02) (Class 5) 2-Y-O **£2,911** (£866; £432; £216) **Stalls** Low

Form RPR

4 **1** **Lord Ben Stack (IRE)**[47] 4424 2-9-5 0 .......................... DanielTudhope 12 86+
(K R Burke) *led after: 1f: mde rest: abt 3 l clr 2f out: sn rdn: kpt on wl fnl f* **6/1**[3]

55 **2** *1 1/2* **Dissolution**[13] 5655 2-9-5 0 .......................... JamesDoyle 11 83+
(Sir Michael Stoute) *towards rr: rdn after 2f: hdwy over 2f out: sn wnt 2nd: styd on ins fnl f: nt rch wnr* **1/1**[1]

4 **3** *5* **Darrington**[20] 5386 2-9-5 0 .......................... TonyHamilton 4 72
(Richard Fahey) *trckd ldrs: rdn over 2f out: sn sltly outpcd: styd on same pce ins fnl f: no imp on front two* **14/1**

**4** *hd* **Rocky Rider** 2-9-5 0 .......................... AndreaAtzeni 7 71+
(Andrew Balding) *midfield: nt clr run over 2f out: hdwy over 1f out: styd on ins fnl f: nvr trbld front two: promising* **8/1**

**5** *4 1/2* **Rosenbaum** 2-9-5 0 .......................... MartinLane 8 61
(Charlie Appleby) *s.i.s: sn rdn along in rr: rdn and hdwy over 1f out: styd on ins fnl f: no further prog fnl 100yds* **33/1**

**6** *hd* **Taraz** 2-9-5 0 .......................... SeanLevey 10 61
(Richard Hannon) *midfield: rdn and hdwy over 2f out: chsd ldrs u.p over 1f out: nvr able to chal: kpt on same pce ins fnl f* **33/1**

2 **7** *1 1/4* **Arabian Oasis**[20] 5393 2-9-5 0 .......................... AdamKirby 2 58
(Charlie Appleby) *led for 1f: chsd ldr: rdn and lost 2nd 2f out: wknd fnl f* **3/1**[2]

6 **8** *2 1/2* **Newera**[28] 5078 2-9-5 0 .......................... RichardKingscote 9 53
(Tom Dascombe) *prom tl rdn and wknd 2f out* **40/1**

**9** *3 1/4* **Mister Rockandroll** 2-9-5 0 .......................... JoeFanning 6 46
(Mark Johnston) *chsd ldrs: rdn over 3f out: wknd 2f out* **33/1**

06 **10** *1* **Blythe Star (IRE)**[19] 5408 2-9-5 0 .......................... HayleyTurner 13 43
(Danielle McCormick) *nvr bttr than midfield: sn pushed along: nvr on terms* **150/1**

0 **11** *2 1/4* **Secrets Safe (IRE)**[10] 5760 2-9-5 0 .......................... GrahamGibbons 1 38
(David Brown) *s.i.s: sn trckd ldrs: rdn and lost pl over 3f out: wknd over 2f out* **150/1**

50 **12** *3/4* **Stormin Tom (IRE)**[22] 5296 2-9-5 0 .......................... DavidAllan 3 37
(Tim Easterby) *midfield: pushed along and wknd over 3f out* **150/1**

**13** *1/2* **Art Charter (FR)** 2-8-11 0 .......................... JoeyHaynes(3) 14 31
(K R Burke) *bhd: sn rdn along: nvr on terms* **66/1**

14 3/4 **Royal Altitude** 2-9-5 0 TedDurcan 5 34
(Chris Wall) *towards rr: rdn and lost pl over 3f out: nvr on terms* 100/1

1m 40.97s (-2.73) **Going Correction** -0.225s/f (Firm) 14 Ran SP% 122.8
Speed ratings (Par 95): **104,102,97,97,92 92,91,88,85,84 82,81,81,80**
CSF £12.33 TOTE £8.60: £1.80, £1.10, £3.60; EX 19.40 Trifecta £144.30.
**Owner** Owners For Owners: Lord Ben Stack **Bred** G Rollain **Trained** Middleham Moor, N Yorks

**FOCUS**
The winner looks a decent horse who can rate a good bit higher for a trainer who has done tremendously well with 2yos in meaningful races this year, possibly 90+ next time.

## 6057 BETFRED SUPPORTS JACK BERRY HOUSE H'CAP 1m
**2:30** (2:31) (Class 4) (0-80,80) 3-Y-O+ **£5,175** (£1,540; £769; £384) **Stalls** Low

Form RPR
5360 1 **Berlusca (IRE)**19 5446 5-9-9 79 DanielTudhope 9 89
(David O'Meara) *towards rr: swtchd rt over 2f out: hdwy sn after: led jst over 1f out: asserted ins fnl f: r.o and in command after* 9/1

0513 2 1 3/4 **No Poppy (IRE)**26 5196 6-9-7 77 DavidAllan 8 82
(Tim Easterby) *midfield: rdn and hdwy 2f out: styd on ins fnl f: tk 2nd nr fin: nt trble wnr* 8/1

0000 3 nk **Woody Bay**61 3979 4-8-12 68 JasonHart 11 72
(Mark Walford) *hld up: hdwy over 3f out: chalng over 1f out: unable to go w wnr ins fnl f: lost 2nd nr fin* 20/1

4322 4 1 1/4 **Starlight Serenade**20 5394 3-8-12 73 GrahamGibbons 7 73
(Ralph Beckett) *trckd ldrs: led over 2f out: sn rdn: hdd jst over 1f out: no ex fnl 75yds* 7/2[1]

0521 5 3/4 **Kyllachy Star**13 5638 8-9-0 70 (v) TonyHamilton 5 70
(Richard Fahey) *in rr: rdn and nt clr run briefly over 2f out: hdwy over 1f out: styd on ins fnl f: nvr able to rch ldrs* 20/1

0322 6 shd **Hala Hala (IRE)**10 5763 3-8-5 73 AhmadAlSubousi(7) 2 71
(Michael Bell) *w ldr: led over 3f out: hdd over 2f out: no ex fnl 100yds* 9/1

1112 7 3/4 **Hostile Fire (IRE)**13 5647 3-9-0 75 (p) AndreaAtzeni 12 75
(Ed de Giles) *hld up: rdn over 2f out: hdwy whn nt clr run over 1f out: nt clr run again ins fnl f: kpt on but nvr trbld ldrs* 9/2[2]

2456 8 1/2 **Oddysey (IRE)**12 5681 5-9-10 80 TomEaves 10 77
(Michael Dods) *prom: rdn and nt qckn over 1f out: wknd fnl 150yds* 14/1

0230 9 1/2 **Set The Trend**12 5686 8-9-10 80 JoeFanning 4 75
(David Dennis) *midfield: rdn over 2f out: no imp over 1f out: one pce ins fnl f* 10/1

2301 10 1/2 **Imaginary World (IRE)**24 5256 6-9-0 75 (e) ShaneGray(5) 1 69
(John Balding) *in tch: rdn over 2f out: n.m.r ins fnl f: wknd fnl 100yds* 20/1

0000 11 6 **Goldstorm**16 5528 6-9-3 73 (p) PaddyAspell 6 54
(Brian Baugh) *trckd ldrs: rdn over 2f out: wknd over 1f out* 50/1

142 12 6 **We'll Shake Hands (FR)**17 5497 3-8-8 72 JoeyHaynes(3) 3 38
(K R Burke) *sn led: rdn and hdd over 3f out: wknd over 2f out* 13/2[3]

1m 40.78s (-2.92) **Going Correction** -0.225s/f (Firm)
**WFA** 3 from 4yo+ 5lb 12 Ran SP% 116.9
Speed ratings (Par 105): **105,103,102,101,100 100,100,99,99,98 92,86**
CSF £73.73 CT £1406.96 TOTE £12.90: £3.80, £2.60, £7.30; EX 84.90 Trifecta £1498.10.
**Owner** Peter R Ball **Bred** Value Bloodstock **Trained** Nawton, N Yorks

**FOCUS**
The second, rated to her recent form, helps set the level.

## 6058 BETFRED SUPPORTS JACK BERRY EBF MAIDEN STKS (C&G) (DIV I) 6f
**3:00** (3:02) (Class 5) 2-Y-O **£2,911** (£866; £432; £216) **Stalls** High

Form RPR
1 **Use Your Filbert (IRE)** 2-9-0 0 SeanLevey 4 76+
(Robert Cowell) *chsd ldrs: rdn over 2f out: r.o to chal ins fnl f: nosed ahd nr fin* 33/1

54 2 hd **Subversive (IRE)**19 5439 2-9-0 0 JoeFanning 7 75
(Mark Johnston) *rrd s: led: rdn over 1f out: strly pressed ins fnl f: narrowly hdd nr fin* 4/1[2]

3 1/2 **Especial** 2-9-0 0 PhillipMakin 6 74+
(Bryan Smart) *midfield: hdwy over 1f out: rdr sn dropped whip: r.o to chal wl ins fnl f: jst hld nr fin* 50/1

4 shd **American Artist (IRE)** 2-9-0 0 AndreaAtzeni 9 73+
(Roger Varian) *chsd ldrs: rdn to chal over 1f out: r.o and ev ch wl ins fnl f: jst hld nr fin* 10/11[1]

40 5 3 1/4 **Able Spirit**13 5655 2-9-0 0 MartinLane 5 63
(Brian Meehan) *racd keenly: w ldr: rdn and nt qckn over 1f out: one pce and unable to go w front quartet fnl 150yds* 6/1[3]

6 7 **Normandy Barriere (IRE)** 2-9-0 0 JasonHart 10 42
(Nigel Tinkler) *dwlt: hld up: impr into midfield over 3f out: one pce and no imp fr over 1f out* 33/1

7 3 1/4 **Frosty Flyer (FR)** 2-9-0 0 TonyHamilton 2 33
(Richard Fahey) *hld up: rdn over 2f out: sn outpcd: nvr a danger* 11/1

0 8 7 **Ponty Grigio (IRE)**33 4884 2-9-0 0 DuranFentiman 3 12
(Tim Easterby) *prom tl rdn and wknd over 2f out* 80/1

9 3 1/4 **Beatabout (IRE)** 2-9-0 0 RaulDaSilva 1
(Paul Green) *bhd: wl outpcd 4f out: nvr on terms* 50/1

10 1 **Rise To Power** 2-9-0 0 PaulMulrennan 8
(Kevin Ryan) *dwlt: hld up: rdn over 2f out: lost tch over 1f out* 10/1

1m 14.42s (0.62) **Going Correction** +0.05s/f (Good) 10 Ran SP% 115.1
Speed ratings (Par 95): **97,96,96,95,91 82,77,68,64,62**
CSF £156.47 TOTE £43.70: £8.90, £1.50, £12.30; EX 175.90 Trifecta £3476.10.
**Owner** G Johnson **Bred** Pier House Stud **Trained** Six Mile Bottom, Cambs

**FOCUS**
A modest maiden and a bunched finish.

## 6059 BETFRED SUPPORTS JACK BERRY EBF MAIDEN STKS (C&G) (DIV II) 6f
**3:35** (3:37) (Class 5) 2-Y-O **£2,911** (£866; £432; £216) **Stalls** High

Form RPR
422 1 **Skate**17 5500 2-9-0 82 JamesDoyle 9 77
(Roger Charlton) *trckd ldrs: rdn 2f out: hung lft over 1f out: r.o to ld fnl 110yds: kpt on and a doing enough cl home* 4/5[1]

54 2 1/2 **Red Harry (IRE)**20 5397 2-9-0 0 AndrewElliott 2 76+
(Tom Tate) *midfield: pushed along 1/2-way: hdwy 1f out: styd on ins fnl f: clsd to take 2nd at fin: nt quite pce to get to wnr* 10/1[3]

3 shd **Yazan (IRE)** 2-9-0 0 RichardKingscote 4 75
(Tom Dascombe) *in tch: effrt over 1f out: styd on to chal ins fnl f: hld nr fin* 7/2[2]

5 4 1 3/4 **Shipwright (IRE)**17 5488 2-9-0 0 JoeFanning 1 70
(Mark Johnston) *racd keenly: prom: led 2f out: rdn and pressed 1f out: hdd fnl 110yds: no ex towards fin* 12/1

0 5 3 **Rainbow Orse**17 5488 2-9-0 0 SeanLevey 3 61
(Robert Cowell) *w ldr: led 1/2-way: hdd over 2f out: rdn and stl ev ch 1f out: no ex fnl 75yds* 50/1

0 6 1/2 **Juncart**30 5013 2-9-0 0 PaulMulrennan 7 59
(Kevin Ryan) *led: hdd 1/2-way: stl there and rdn over 1f out: no ex fnl 150yds* 22/1

7 2 3/4 **Storytale** 2-9-0 0 WilliamTwiston-Davies 6 51
(Michael Bell) *dwlt: bhd: pushed along and outpcd over 2f out: nvr a threat* 14/1

8 6 **Citisonsmith (IRE)** 2-9-0 0[1] RaulDaSilva 8 33
(Paul Green) *bhd: outpcd 4f out: nvr on terms* 66/1

04 9 3/4 **Mercury**23 5264 2-9-0 0 GrahamLee 5 31
(Kevin Ryan) *restless in stalls: dwlt: towards rr: outpcd over 2f out: nvr a threat* 12/1

1m 14.36s (0.56) **Going Correction** +0.05s/f (Good) 9 Ran SP% 116.7
Speed ratings (Par 95): **98,97,97,94,90 90,86,78,77**
CSF £10.27 TOTE £2.00: £1.10, £2.40, £1.20; EX 11.60 Trifecta £46.20.
**Owner** Lady Rothschild **Bred** The Rt Hon Lord Rothschild **Trained** Beckhampton, Wilts

**FOCUS**
The form looks worth taking at face value for now.

## 6060 BETFRED INJURED JOCKEYS FUND EBF CONDITIONS STKS 7f
**4:05** (4:06) (Class 3) 3-Y-O+ **£11,320** (£3,368; £1,683; £841) **Stalls** Low

Form RPR
20 1 **Baltic Knight (IRE)**47 4437 4-8-12 107 SeanLevey 2 113
(Richard Hannon) *disp ld: def advantage and qcknd away over 1f out: r.o wl and in command fnl f* 11/4[2]

6265 2 1 3/4 **Dutch Rose (IRE)**14 5612 5-8-4 100 SamJames(3) 4 103
(David O'Meara) *disp ld: rdn 2f out: nt qckn w wnr over 1f out: kpt on u.p ins fnl f: a hld* 9/4[1]

0241 3 nse **Morache Music**19 5418 6-8-12 106 TedDurcan 3 108
(Peter Makin) *hld up in tch: effrt 2f out: styd on for press ins fnl f: unable to pass runner-up: no threat to wnr* 9/4[1]

6000 4 6 **Krypton Factor**159 1180 6-8-12 104 LukeMorris 5 93
(George Peckham) *trckd ldrs: rdn over 2f out: one pce over 1f out* 10/1

1 5 8 **Unforgiving Minute**29 5039 3-8-11 83 JamesDoyle 6 81
(Clive Cox) *restless in stalls: hld up in rr: rdn over 2f out: no imp: wl btn fnl f: eased* 15/2[3]

1m 26.87s (-3.83) **Going Correction** -0.225s/f (Firm)
**WFA** 3 from 4yo+ 4lb 5 Ran SP% 109.1
Speed ratings (Par 107): **112,110,109,103,93**
CSF £9.13 TOTE £3.80: £1.30, £3.90; EX 10.70 Trifecta £20.00.
**Owner** Thurloe Thoroughbreds XXX **Bred** Henry O'Callaghan **Trained** East Everleigh, Wilts

**FOCUS**
A decent small-field conditions contest and the winner is rated to his best.

## 6061 BETFRED DUKE OF LANCASTER'S REGIMENT CUP H'CAP 1m 3f 200y
**4:40** (4:43) (Class 2) (0-100,96) 3-Y-O+ **£14,231** (£4,235; £2,116; £1,058) **Stalls** Centre

Form RPR
3160 1 **Latenightrequest**84 3143 3-8-1 85 JackGarritty(5) 5 95
(Richard Fahey) *chsd ldrs: effrt over 2f out: led over 1f out: strly pressed ins fnl f: r.o u.p: hld on gamely* 11/1

-404 2 shd **Headline News (IRE)**25 5203 5-8-12 82 oh1 ChrisCatlin 1 91
(Rae Guest) *midfield: hdwy 3f out: rdn to chal strly ins fnl f: r.o: jst hld* 9/1

-040 3 1 1/2 **Highland Castle**12 5673 6-9-4 88 GrahamLee 11 95+
(David Elsworth) *hld up towards rr: rdn and hdwy over 2f out: n.m.r briefly 1f out: styd on ins fnl f: gng on at fin* 20/1

1510 4 nk **Kings Bayonet**37 4759 7-9-3 87 HayleyTurner 15 93
(Alan King) *hld up: hdwy on inner whn nt clr run over 2f out: nt clr run again over 1f out: styd on ins fnl f: nt rch ldrs* 22/1

20 5 shd **Dark Ruler (IRE)**13 5633 5-9-0 84 BenCurtis 4 90
(Alan Swinbank) *chsd ldrs: rdn over 2f out: nt qckn over 1f out: styd on same pce fnl 100yds* 8/1

226 6 hd **Xinbama (IRE)**13 5651 5-9-0 84 RichardKingscote 12 90+
(Charles Hills) *hld up: hdwy 2f out: styd on u.p ins fnl f: nt quite able to chal* 6/1[2]

6-52 7 3/4 **Kikonga**55 4145 4-9-7 91 AndreaAtzeni 14 95
(Luca Cumani) *in tch: effrt 3f out: chsd ldrs over 2f out: no imp over 1f out: one pce ins fnl f* 5/1[1]

2200 8 nk **Pilgrims Rest (IRE)**82 3217 5-9-3 87 PatCosgrave 8 91
(George Baker) *led: rdn and hdd over 1f out: no ex fnl 75yds* 20/1

1524 9 3 3/4 **Mister Fizz**13 5633 6-8-13 88 GeorgeDowning(5) 6 86
(Miss Imogen Pickard) *chsd ldr: rdn and ev ch over 2f out: sn lost 2nd: wknd ins fnl f* 16/1

1300 10 4 1/2 **Sirvino**12 5673 9-9-9 93 PhillipMakin 2 84
(David Barron) *hld up: pushed along over 2f out: nvr on terms* 33/1

-040 11 shd **Bantam (IRE)**15 5579 4-9-4 88 PaulMulrennan 9 79
(Ed Dunlop) *hld up: struggling over 2f out: nvr on terms* 16/1

2641 12 2 3/4 **Nicholascopernicus (IRE)**24 5251 5-9-11 95 AdamKirby 3 81
(Ed Walker) *midfield: pushed along over 3f out: rdn and no imp 2f out: wknd fnl f* 12/1

5210 13 nk **Warrior Of Light (IRE)**12 5673 3-9-3 96 TedDurcan 13 82
(David Lanigan) *hld up: rdn and hung lft 2f out: no imp over 1f out: wl btn* 7/1[3]

1-00 14 12 **Lady Tyne**32 4945 3-8-7 86 LiamJones 7 53
(Roger Charlton) *prom: pushed along over 5f out: wknd over 3f out* 15/2

2m 28.43s (-5.37) **Going Correction** -0.225s/f (Firm)
**WFA** 3 from 4yo+ 9lb 14 Ran SP% 120.9
Speed ratings (Par 109): **108,107,106,106,106 106,106,105,103,100 100,98,98,90**
CSF £101.37 CT £1971.44 TOTE £16.40: £4.10, £4.10, £6.80; EX 120.10 Trifecta £3931.30 Part won..
**Owner** Middleham Park Racing XVI & Partner **Bred** Mrs S J Walker **Trained** Musley Bank, N Yorks

**FOCUS**
A good, competitive handicap. The winner looks to have improved, with the second rated close to her best.

## 6062 BETFRED PLEASE DONATE ON YOUR WAY OUT H'CAP (FOR GENTLEMAN AMATEUR RIDERS) 1m 3f 200y
**5:10** (5:10) (Class 5) (0-70,70) 4-Y-O+ **£2,495** (£774; £386; £193) **Stalls** Centre

Form RPR
2232 1 **Gift Of Silence**17 5502 5-10-10 64 MrJPWilliams(5) 7 72
(Bernard Llewellyn) *trckd ldrs: sn dropped to midfield: effrt whn edgd lft over 2f out: hdwy whn swtchd rt over 1f out: r.o ins fnl f: led towards fin* 12/1

1332 **2** ½ **The Ducking Stool**[22] 5317 7-11-5 68........ MrRBirkett 11 75
(Julia Feilden) *rdr lost iron briefly s: trckd ldrs: led wl over 2f out: edgd lft over 1f out: hdd towards fin* **9/1**

6-46 **3** ¾ **Aryizad (IRE)**[11] 5716 5-11-6 69........ MrSWalker 1 75
(Alan Swinbank) *hld up: hdwy 5f out: rdn to chal over 1f out: nt qckn ins fnl f: kpt on: hld towards fin* **5/1**[1]

6601 **4** 2¼ **A Little Bit Dusty**[17] 5495 6-11-4 70........(p) MrMLegg(3) 9 72
(Conor Dore) *missed break: midfield: hdwy over 4f out: rdn over 3f out: tried to chal over 2f out: hung lft over 1f out: styd on same pce ins fnl f* **13/2**[2]

2450 **5** 10 **Magnolia Ridge (IRE)**[31] 4964 4-10-8 62........(p) MrAaronJames(5) 13 48
(Kristin Stubbs) *bhd: u.p over 2f out: styd on ins fnl f: nt trble ldrs* **18/1**

5000 **6** nse **Pertuis (IRE)**[12] 5678 8-11-2 65........(p) MrWHogg 3 51
(Micky Hammond) *hld up: hdwy 5f out: sn chsd ldrs: wknd over 1f out* **25/1**

2024 **7** 3¾ **Merchant Of Medici**[12] 5678 7-10-7 63........(p) DylanMcDonagh(7) 2 43
(Micky Hammond) *missed break: sn trckd ldrs: led 4f out: hdd wl over 2f out: wknd over 1f out* **15/2**

004 **8** 1½ **Good Speech (IRE)**[31] 4979 4-10-13 67........ MrHStock(5) 6 45
(Tom Tate) *led: hdd 4f out: wkng whn bmpd over 2f out* **7/1**[3]

42 **9** 3¾ **Frosty Berry**[32] 4942 5-10-9 65........ MrAFrench(7) 10 37
(Paul Midgley) *racd keenly: prom after 2f: wnt wd on bnd 5f out: rdn and wknd over 2f out* **5/1**[1]

4055 **10** 1¾ **Candelita**[20] 5403 7-10-0 56 oh4........ MrStanSheppard(7) 4 25
(Matt Sheppard) *trckd ldrs early: sn lost pl: in rr and struggling 4f out: n.d after* **25/1**

2003 **11** 8 **Missy Wells**[19] 5421 4-10-6 60........ MrKWood(5) 5 16
(Mark Walford) *midfield: pushed along and wknd over 4f out* **13/2**[2]

5-00 **12** 17 **Anton Dolin (IRE)**[14] 5600 6-10-4 60........(v[1]) MrHFNugent(7) 12
(Michael Mullineaux) *prom tl rdn and wknd 4f out* **100/1**

00/0 **13** 1½ **Business Bay (USA)**[16] 5529 7-10-0 56 oh11........ MrTEley(7) 8
(Patrick Clinton) *midfield: lost pl over 5f out: bhd after* **100/1**

2m 33.21s (-0.59) **Going Correction** -0.225s/f (Firm) 13 Ran SP% **116.9**
Speed ratings (Par 103): **92,91,91,89,83 82,80,79,76,75 70,59,58**
CSF £110.73 CT £615.52 TOTE £9.70: £2.80, £2.60, £1.90; EX 50.60 Trifecta £2107.70.
**Owner** Mrs E A Llewellyn **Bred** Henry And Mrs Rosemary Moszkowicz **Trained** Fochriw, Caerphilly
■ Stewards' Enquiry : Mr R Birkett two-day ban: used whip above permitted level (Sep 23,Oct 6)

**FOCUS**
A modest handicap restricted to amateur riders in which they went a muddling gallop. The runner-up was not an obvious improver on profile and the form is rated around him.
T/Jkpt: Not won. T/Plt: £305.30 to a £1 stake. Pool: £60,124.53 - 143.72 winning units. T/Qpdt: £87.50 to a £1 stake. Pool: £5676.06 - 47.95 winning units. DO

# 5873 SALISBURY (R-H)
## Thursday, September 4

**OFFICIAL GOING: Good (8.3)**
Wind: virtually nil Weather: cloudy with sunny periods Rails: Rail erected up last 6.5f of home straight 20ft off permanent far side rail

## 6063 WHITSBURY MANOR STUD EBF STALLIONS NOVICE STKS (BOBIS RACE) 1m
**2:10** (2:11) (Class 4) 2-Y-O **£6,792** (£2,021; £1,010) **Stalls** Low

Form RPR

4322 **1** **Tom Hark (FR)**[13] 5645 2-8-12 84........ RichardHughes 4 88+
(Richard Hannon) *unf: scope: mde all: set stdy pce for 3f: jnd over 3f out: rdn over 2f out: kpt on strly to assert ent fnl f: won gng away* **4/6**[1]

4 **2** 2¼ **Equitanus (IRE)**[30] 5009 2-8-12 0........ JimCrowley 2 83+
(Andrew Balding) *athletic: lw: dwlt: trckd ldng pair: effrt to chal over 3f out: sltly outpcd over 2f out: styd on ins fnl f: snatched 2nd fnl strides* **4/1**[3]

123 **3** shd **Zephuros (IRE)**[19] 5424 2-9-5 92........ WilliamBuick 1 90
(Charlie Appleby) *trckd wnr: chal wl over 3f out: sn rdn: ev ch tl no ex ent fnl f: lost 2nd fnl strides* **3/1**[2]

1m 47.78s (4.28) **Going Correction** -0.025s/f (Good) 3 Ran SP% **105.0**
Speed ratings (Par 97): **77,74,74**
CSF £3.32 TOTE £1.60; EX 3.20 Trifecta £3.50.
**Owner** John Manley **Bred** S A R L Ecurie Des Monceaux Et Al **Trained** East Everleigh, Wilts

**FOCUS**
A disappointing turnout for this novice stakes which was run at a steady pace. The level is fluid.

## 6064 QUALITY & VALUE AT IRISH YEARLING SALES NURSERY H'CAP 6f 212y
**2:40** (2:41) (Class 5) (0-75,75) 2-Y-O **£3,234** (£962; £481; £240) **Stalls** Centre

Form RPR

1 **1** **Rosalie Bonheur**[59] 4018 2-8-11 **68**........ RyanTate(3) 10 76+
(Clive Cox) *unf: lengthy: trckd ldrs: rdn 2f out: str run ent fnl f: led fnl 75yds: won gng away* **8/1**

444 **2** ½ **Lear's Rock (IRE)**[14] 5604 2-9-0 **68**........ SilvestreDeSousa 8 75
(Ralph Beckett) *a.p: rdn over 2f out: drifted lft: led over 1f out: kpt on tl no ex whn hdd fnl 75yds* **14/1**

0100 **3** ¾ **Kingsbridge**[15] 5580 2-9-7 **75**........ GeorgeBaker 12 80
(Rod Millman) *led: rdn over 2f out: hdd over 1f out: kpt on but no ex fnl f* **8/1**

024 **4** 1¼ **Dutch Portrait**[13] 5625 2-9-4 **72**........ JimCrowley 2 73+
(Paul Cole) *mid-div: making hdwy whn nt clr run briefly 2f out: sn rdn: kpt on fnl f* **7/1**[3]

435 **5** 1 **Maftoon (IRE)**[33] 4896 2-9-7 **75**........(b[1]) PaulHanagan 4 74
(Richard Hannon) *trckd ldrs: rdn 2f out: fdd fnl 120yds* **4/1**[1]

2514 **6** ½ **Buckleberry**[32] 4944 2-9-1 **72**........ DannyBrock(3) 13 69
(Jonathan Portman) *trckd ldrs: rdn over 2f out: kpt on but nt pce to get on terms* **20/1**

3331 **7** ¾ **Faraajh (IRE)**[9] 5798 2-9-3 **71** 6ex........ MartinHarley 14 66
(James Tate) *trckd ldrs: rdn and ch 2f out: fdd ins fnl f* **5/1**[2]

0051 **8** 1¾ **Pinter**[15] 5554 2-9-2 **75**........ CamHardie(5) 3 65+
(Charlie Appleby) *lw: s.i.s: towards rr: rdn and sme hdwy into midfield over 2f out: no further imp fr over 1f out* **5/1**[2]

354 **9** ½ **Golden Wedding (IRE)**[38] 4731 2-9-4 **72**........ JohnFahy 1 61
(Eve Johnson Houghton) *rdn over 2f out: nvr bttr than mid-div* **33/1**

1013 **10** hd **L'Etacq**[13] 5620 2-9-7 **75**........ RichardHughes 6 64
(Richard Hannon) *stdd s: bhd: rdn over 2f out: little imp: nvr a factor* **12/1**

400 **11** 4 **Gilded Lace**[58] 4054 2-8-9 **70**........ JosephineGordon(7) 5 48
(J S Moore) *mid-div tl outpcd over 2f out: wknd over 1f out* **100/1**

5514 **12** 7 **Sallabeh**[13] 5626 2-9-3 **71**........ TomQueally 9 30
(George Margarson) *a towards rr* **14/1**

6460 **13** 2 **Invincible Zeb (IRE)**[31] 4967 2-9-0 **68**........ SteveDrowne 11 21
(Ronald Harris) *mid-div tl rdn 3f out: sn btn* **66/1**

1m 28.67s (0.07) **Going Correction** -0.025s/f (Good) 13 Ran SP% **119.3**
Speed ratings (Par 95): **98,97,96,95,94 93,92,90,90,89 85,77,74**
CSF £111.36 CT £933.62 TOTE £8.00: £2.80, £3.70, £5.10; EX 79.20 Trifecta £1146.90.
**Owner** Mrs Hugh Maitland-Jones **Bred** Mrs Hugh Maitland-Jones **Trained** Lambourn, Berks

**FOCUS**
A good nursery for the grade run at a steady pace. It paid to race handy. The winner built on her debut and the third helps set the level.

## 6065 VIRGINIA WALWYN MEMORIAL EBF QUIDHAMPTON MAIDEN FILLIES' STKS (BOBIS RACE) (DIV I) 6f 212y
**3:15** (3:15) (Class 3) 2-Y-O **£7,115** (£2,117; £1,058; £529) **Stalls** Centre

Form RPR

**1** **Jelly Monger (IRE)** 2-9-0 0........ JimCrowley 3 74+
(Dominic Ffrench Davis) *tall: str: trckd ldrs: rdn over 2f out: r.o wl to ld fnl 120yds: rdn out* **66/1**

**2** ¾ **Banzari** 2-9-0 0........ FrankieDettori 9 72+
(Michael Bell) *athletic: hld up bhd: rdn whn swtchd to centre and hdwy wl over 1f out: r.o strly ins fnl f: snatched 2nd fnl stride* **16/1**

**3** nse **Wiener Valkyrie** 2-9-0 0........ WilliamBuick 12 72+
(Ed Walker) *lengthy: mid-div: pushed along and hdwy but nt best of runs fr over 2f out: swtchd lft over 1f out: rdn and r.o ent fnl f: wnt 2nd briefly nring fin* **8/1**

04 **4** 1¼ **Hawkin (IRE)**[68] 3728 2-9-0 0........ SilvestreDeSousa 6 68
(Ralph Beckett) *w'like: trckd ldr: rdn to ld 2f out: hdd fnl 120yds: no ex whn lost 2 pls towards fin* **7/1**

**5** shd **Atab (IRE)** 2-9-0 0........ PaulHanagan 1 68
(Charles Hills) *str: tall: trckd ldrs: rdn 2f out: swtchd lft ent fnl f: nt pce to chal: no ex whn lost 2 pls towards fin* **9/2**[2]

5 **6** 2¼ **I'm A Butterfly (IRE)**[26] 5187 2-9-0 0........ JohnFahy 11 62
(Eve Johnson Houghton) *athletic: mid-div: hdwy over 3f out: rdn over 2f out: kpt on same pce fnl f* **7/1**

2 **7** 2¼ **Dutch Party**[111] 2306 2-9-0 0........ JimmyFortune 7 56
(Richard Fahey) *unf: sn led: rdn and hdd 2f out: wknd ins fnl f* **4/1**[1]

**8** 3 **Ninepins (IRE)** 2-9-0 0........ RichardHughes 8 48
(Richard Hannon) *athletic: bit bkwd: racd keenly: mid-div: rdn over 2f out: wknd fnl f* **9/2**[2]

0 **9** 6 **Forbidden Love**[19] 5429 2-9-0 0........ PatDobbs 2 32
(Richard Hannon) *w'like: bit bkwd: in tch: rdn 3f out: wknd over 1f out* **25/1**

**10** 6 **Chain Of Daisies** 2-9-0 0........ FergusSweeney 10 16
(Henry Candy) *unf: scope: tall: s.i.s: a towards rr* **6/1**[3]

1m 28.91s (0.31) **Going Correction** -0.025s/f (Good) 10 Ran SP% **118.0**
Speed ratings (Par 96): **97,96,96,94,94 91,89,85,79,72**
CSF £891.75 TOTE £62.00: £11.80, £5.10, £3.20; EX 470.60 Trifecta £3706.20 Part won..
**Owner** Gary Black & Mark Duthie **Bred** Stephanie Hanley **Trained** Lambourn, Berks

**FOCUS**
The pace was steady for this fillies' maiden. The action unfolded mainly up the centre. This looked ordinary by the track's standards, but the big-priced winner did not appear flattered.

## 6066 VIRGINIA WALWYN MEMORIAL EBF QUIDHAMPTON MAIDEN FILLIES' STKS (BOBIS RACE) (DIV II) 6f 212y
**3:45** (3:47) (Class 3) 2-Y-O **£7,115** (£2,117; £1,058; £529) **Stalls** Centre

Form RPR

2 **1** **Fadhayyil (IRE)**[26] 5187 2-9-0 0........ PaulHanagan 11 81+
(B W Hills) *lengthy: str: lw: bmpd leaving stalls: racd freely: trcking ldrs tl settled mid-div after 1f: hdwy 3f out: shkn up to go through gap to ld over 1f out: kpt on wl: pushed out* **11/8**[1]

53 **2** 1¼ **Black Cherry**[48] 4396 2-9-0 0........ RichardHughes 8 76
(Richard Hannon) *str: trckd ldr: led over 2f out: sn rdn whn chal: hdd over 1f out: kpt on but a being hld by wnr* **5/2**[2]

05 **3** 1 **Raspberry Ripple**[19] 5429 2-9-0 0........ KieranO'Neill 12 73
(Richard Hannon) *athletic: mid-div: hdwy 3f out: rdn to chal 2f out: kpt on same pce fnl f* **16/1**

**4** 3½ **Angel Vision (IRE)** 2-9-0 0........ ShaneKelly 7 63+
(Sir Michael Stoute) *str: mid-div: pushed along over 2f out: wnt 4th over 1f out: styd on but nt pce to get involved* **9/1**[3]

**5** ¾ **Lulani (IRE)** 2-9-0 0........ TomQueally 2 61+
(Harry Dunlop) *athletic: towards rr: stdy prog but nt best of runs fr over 2f out: styd on nicely fnl f* **50/1**

**6** ½ **Gentlemusic (FR)** 2-9-0 0........ MartinHarley 1 60
(Marco Botti) *a mid-div* **14/1**

**7** 2½ **Sampera (IRE)** 2-9-0 0........ FrederikTylicki 10 53
(Michael Bell) *lengthy: lean: hld up towards rr: midfield 3f out: sn rdn: no further imp* **33/1**

**8** 1¾ **Uele River** 2-9-0 0........ OisinMurphy 3 49
(Henry Candy) *tall: lengthy: bit bkwd: led tl rdn over 2f out: wknd ent fnl f* **9/1**[3]

66 **9** 1½ **Zubaidah**[47] 4444 2-9-0 0........ FergusSweeney 5 45
(George Baker) *leggy: trckd ldrs: rdn over 2f out: wknd jst over 1f out* **25/1**

**10** 2¾ **Beach Walker** 2-9-0 0........ JimmyFortune 4 37+
(Brian Meehan) *lengthy: str: s.i.s: towards rr: hdwy into midfield 2f out: wknd fnl f* **20/1**

**11** 1 **Luv U** 2-9-0 0........ WilliamBuick 9 34
(Ed Dunlop) *lengthy: a towards rr* **10/1**

60 **12** 4 **Tatiani**[15] 5549 2-9-0 0........ IrineuGoncalves 6 24
(Jose Santos) *unf: weak: chsd ldrs tl wknd over 2f out* **100/1**

1m 29.08s (0.48) **Going Correction** -0.025s/f (Good) 12 Ran SP% **126.8**
Speed ratings (Par 96): **96,94,93,89,88 88,85,83,81,78 77,72**
CSF £4.84 TOTE £2.70: £1.10, £1.20, £5.80; EX 5.10 Trifecta £42.40.
**Owner** Hamdan Al Maktoum **Bred** Keatly Overseas Ltd **Trained** Upper Lambourn, Berks

**FOCUS**
This fillies' maiden looked stronger than the first division. It was run at a steady pace with the front three, who all had experience, pulling clear.

## 6067 COUNTRY GENTLEMEN'S ASSOCIATION DICK POOLE FILLIES' STKS (GROUP 3) 6f
**4:20** (4:20) (Class 1) 2-Y-O
**£24,101** (£9,137; £4,573; £2,278; £1,143; £573) **Stalls** Low

Form RPR

1132 **1** **New Providence**[14] 5607 2-9-0 94........ JimCrowley 1 102+
(Hugo Palmer) *in tch: rdn wl over 1f out: r.o to chal ins fnl f: led fnl stride* **4/1**[2]

1 **2** *shd* **Marsh Hawk**[26] 5187 2-9-0 0 ........ RichardHughes 3 102+
(Richard Hannon) *lengthy: trckd ldr: pushed along 2f out: rdn to ld ins fnl f: kpt on: hdd fnl stride* **11/8**[1]

316 **3** *1 1/4* **Stroll Patrol**[26] 5190 2-9-0 91 ........ OisinMurphy 14 98
(Philip McBride) *str: hld up towards rr: making hdwy whn carried lft over 1f out: swtchd rt ent fnl f: r.o wl to go 3rd fnl 100yds but a being hld* **9/1**

361 **4** *2 1/2* **Vesnina**[19] 5429 2-9-0 83 ........ SteveDrowne 11 90
(Richard Hannon) *s.i.s: towards rr: hdwy over 2f out: sn rdn: r.o: wnt 4th fnl stride* **50/1**

021 **5** *nse* **Royal Razalma (IRE)**[36] 4781 2-9-0 87 ........ SilvestreDeSousa 10 90
(Jonathan Portman) *wnt lft s: trckd ldrs: rdn over 2f out: sn lost ch by drifting bdly lft: fin on stands' side rails: keeping on in hld 4th whn looking short of room briefly fnl 75yds* **33/1**

2141 **6** *shd* **Prize Exhibit**[23] 5286 2-9-0 98 ........ GeorgeBaker 6 90
(Jamie Osborne) *lengthy: hld up last: swtchd lft over 2f out: making hdwy whn carried lft over 1f out: swtchd rt and r.o strly fnl f: nt rch ldrs* **7/1**[3]

16 **7** *3/4* **Efflorescence (USA)**[12] 5664 2-9-0 0 ........ WilliamBuick 9 88
(Charlie Appleby) *racd freely: led: rdn 2f out: hdd ins fnl f: wknd* **20/1**

2211 **8** *hd* **Primrose Valley**[13] 5637 2-9-0 86 ........ (p) FrederikTylicki 7 88
(Ed Vaughan) *in tch: rdn over 2f out: kpt on but nt pce to threaten* **25/1**

01 **9** *2 1/2* **Touchline**[11] 5725 2-9-0 0 ........ FrankieDettori 12 82
(Michael Bell) *athletic: lw: mid-div: hdwy 3f out: carried lft briefly over 1f out: keeping on at same pce whn appeared to lose action ins fnl f* **16/1**

3213 **10** *2 1/2* **Zifena**[12] 5664 2-9-0 90 ........ JohnFahy 8 72
(Eve Johnson Houghton) *hld up towards rr: rdn over 1f out: nt pce to get involved* **14/1**

022 **11** *3/4* **Pastoral Girl**[40] 4646 2-9-0 98 ........ TomQueally 4 70
(James Given) *wnt lft s: in tch: rdn 3f out: wknd jst over 1f out* **25/1**

1010 **12** *2 3/4* **Dangerous Moonlite (IRE)**[20] 5380 2-9-0 95 ........ PatDobbs 2 62
(Richard Hannon) *mid-div: rdn over 2f out: wknd over 1f out* **33/1**

4 **13** *2* **Amaze Me**[19] 5429 2-9-0 0 ........ SebSanders 5 56
(Nick Littmoden) *cmpt: s.i.s and hmpd: a towards rr* **33/1**

1m 13.43s (-1.37) **Going Correction** -0.025s/f (Good) **13 Ran SP% 120.4**
Speed ratings: **108,107,106,102,102 102,101,101,98,94 93,90,87**
CSF £9.07 TOTE £5.40: £2.50, £1.10, £3.20; EX 12.20 Trifecta £108.20.
**Owner** Chris Humber **Bred** James Ortega Bloodstock **Trained** Newmarket, Suffolk

**FOCUS**
The day's feature was upgraded from Listed to Group 3 level for the first time. It had been won by some smart types such as Winning Express and Joyeuse in the recent past and this renewal looked well up to scratch. This could be rated higher on recent race average.

## 6068 EBF STALLIONS BREEDING WINNERS "LOCHSONG" FILLIES' STKS (H'CAP) 6f 212y

**4:50** (4:50) (Class 2) (0-100,96) 3-Y-O+
**£14,161** (£4,240; £2,120; £1,060; £530; £266) **Stalls** Centre

Form RPR

1121 **1** **Felwah**[20] 5396 3-8-12 88 ........ PaulHanagan 3 99+
(William Haggas) *lw: led for 3f: led 2f out: sn rdn: r.o strly ins fnl f: readily* **11/4**[2]

3301 **2** *2 1/2* **Saucy Minx (IRE)**[13] 5627 4-8-13 85 ........ (b) JimCrowley 4 91
(Amanda Perrett) *trckd ldrs: rdn whn swtchd lft over 1f out: disputing 2nd ent fnl f: kpt on but a being readily hld* **10/1**

6100 **3** *3/4* **Royal Seal**[35] 4826 3-9-0 90 ........ ShaneKelly 2 92
(Sir Michael Stoute) *s.i.s: in last trio: hdwy 2f out: sn rdn: disp hld 2nd ent fnl f: kpt on* **17/2**

1243 **4** *1* **Remember**[26] 5165 3-9-6 96 ........ RichardHughes 8 95
(Richard Hannon) *lw: hld up in last pair: rdn 2f out: wnt 4th ins fnl f: kpt on same pce* **9/4**[1]

4060 **5** *1 3/4* **Dutch Courage**[14] 5612 3-9-2 92 ........ JimmyFortune 1 87
(Richard Fahey) *trckd ldrs: rdn over 2f out: one pce fnl f* **8/1**[3]

6200 **6** *hd* **Jillnextdoor (IRE)**[37] 4762 4-8-12 84 ........ WilliamBuick 7 80
(Mick Channon) *hld up last: rdn over 2f out: nvr gng pce to get involved* **14/1**

2506 **7** *3* **Musicora**[13] 5627 3-8-12 88 ........[1] PatDobbs 5 75
(Richard Hannon) *trckd ldrs: rdn 2f out: wknd fnl f* **14/1**

2062 **8** *1/2* **Tight Fit**[42] 4573 4-9-0 86 ........ FergusSweeney 6 73
(Henry Candy) *trckd ldr: led after 3f tl 2f out: sn rdn: wknd ent fnl f* **8/1**[3]

1m 27.68s (-0.92) **Going Correction** -0.025s/f (Good)
**WFA** 3 from 4yo 4lb **8 Ran SP% 112.6**
Speed ratings (Par 96): **104,101,100,99,97 96,93,92**
CSF £29.11 CT £203.97 TOTE £2.20: £1.20, £2.30, £1.90; EX 25.80 Trifecta £146.30.
**Owner** Khalil Alsayegh **Bred** Khalil Al Sayegh **Trained** Newmarket, Suffolk

**FOCUS**
A competitive fillies' handicap, rated around the runner-up, run at a steady pace.

## 6069 CGA "PERSIAN PUNCH" CONDITIONS STKS 1m 6f 21y

**5:20** (5:21) (Class 2) 3-Y-O+ **£12,450** (£3,728; £1,864; £932)

Form RPR

2446 **1** **Rawaki (IRE)**[19] 5432 6-9-2 107 ........ ThomasBrown 1 107
(Andrew Balding) *lw: trckd ldrs: jnd ldrs gng best 2f out: shkn up to ld over 1f out: edgd rt: rdn clr* **15/8**[2]

5040 **2** *2 3/4* **Aussie Reigns (IRE)**[12] 5693 4-9-5 101 ........ (v) RichardHughes 2 106
(William Knight) *hld up in 4th: tk clsr order 5f out: rdn over 2f out: swtchd lft over 1f out: styd on to go 2nd ins fnl f but no ch w wnr* **6/1**[3]

406 **3** *2 3/4* **Renew (IRE)**[12] 5688 4-9-5 105 ........ (p) MartinHarley 3 102
(Marco Botti) *led: rdn and hdd over 2f out: kpt on w ev ch tl ent fnl f: no ex whn lost 2nd fnl 75yds* **7/1**

1100 **4** *12* **Maid In Rio (IRE)**[18] 5481 3-8-0 103 ........ SilvestreDeSousa 4 77
(Mark Johnston) *lw: trckd ldr: led over 2f out: sn rdn: hdd over 1f out: sn squeezed up and wknd* **6/5**[1]

3m 6.1s (-1.30) **Going Correction** -0.025s/f (Good)
**WFA** 3 from 4yo+ 11lb **4 Ran SP% 107.0**
Speed ratings (Par 109): **102,100,98,92**
CSF £11.56 TOTE £2.70; EX 9.90 Trifecta £22.30.
**Owner** Kingsclere Racing Club **Bred** Kingsclere Stud **Trained** Kingsclere, Hants

**FOCUS**
The favourite was again below her standout Ascot win, and the second has been rated to his turf best.

## 6070 CGA RACING EXCELLENCE APPRENTICE H'CAP (WHIPS SHALL BE CARRIED BUT NOT USED) 1m

**5:50** (5:50) (Class 5) (0-70,70) 3-Y-O+ **£2,911** (£866; £432; £216) **Stalls** Low

Form RPR

2025 **1** **Lady Sylvia**[12] 5685 5-9-7 65 ........ AlistairRawlinson 11 77
(Joseph Tuite) *hld up: hdwy 3f out: r.o to ld ins fnl f: drew clr fnl 120yds: comf* **10/3**[2]

040 **2** *4 1/2* **Jersey Brown (IRE)**[21] 5355 3-9-0 63 ........ DanielCremin 8 64
(Mick Channon) *hld up: smooth hdwy fr 3f out: swtchd rt ent fnl f: ev ch sn after: outpcd by wnr fnl 120yds* **16/1**

5635 **3** *3/4* **George Baker (IRE)**[6] 5873 7-9-2 67 ........ AlfieDavies[(7)] 12 67
(George Baker) *trckd ldrs: kpt on to hold ev ch ins fnl f: no ex fnl 120yds* **20/1**

4103 **4** *3 1/4* **Living Leader**[11] 5721 5-9-11 69 ........ (p) DavidPrichard 6 61
(Grace Harris) *trckd ldr: led over 3f out: hdd ins fnl f: fdd fnl 120yds* **3/1**[1]

4445 **5** *hd* **Lady Bayside**[17] 5503 6-9-7 68 ........ RobHornby[(3)] 9 60
(Malcolm Saunders) *racd centre: in tch: one pce fnl 2f: nvr threatened* **11/1**

0502 **6** *2 3/4* **Cadmium**[22] 5314 3-8-0 56 oh5 ........ Leah-AnneAvery[(7)] 1 41
(Harry Dunlop) *hld up: sme late prog: nvr a threat* **33/1**

1620 **7** *nk* **Eugenic**[35] 4817 3-8-10 59 ........ JordanVaughan 3 43
(Rod Millman) *chsd ldrs: edgd lft and one pce fnl 2f: nvr threatened* **16/1**

0430 **8** *3/4* **Suitsus**[28] 5080 3-9-2 68 ........ (p) ChrisMeehan[(3)] 7 50
(Peter Makin) *racd keenly: trckd ldrs: wknd fnl f* **10/1**

035 **9** *3/4* **Southern Cross**[118] 2126 3-8-10 62 ........ CharlieBennett[(3)] 2 43
(Hughie Morrison) *a towards rr* **12/1**

3030 **10** *7* **Harwoods Star (IRE)**[29] 5041 4-8-13 60 ........ (t) KieranShoemark[(3)] 10 25
(Amanda Perrett) *awkward leaving stalls: racd centre: mid-div tl 2f out* **12/1**

4233 **11** *8* **Go For Broke**[22] 5314 3-9-4 70 ........ (b) GaryMahon[(3)] 5 16
(Richard Hannon) *chsd ldrs tl 2f out* **8/1**[3]

0010 **12** *6* **Rapunzal**[16] 5522 3-8-11 60 ........ CharlotteJenner 4
(Henry Candy) *led tl over 3f out: wknd over 2f out* **10/1**

1m 42.58s (-0.92) **Going Correction** -0.025s/f (Good)
**WFA** 3 from 4yo+ 5lb **12 Ran SP% 120.6**
Speed ratings (Par 103): **103,98,97,94,94 91,91,90,89,82 74,68**
CSF £57.35 CT £946.49 TOTE £4.20: £2.00, £3.70, £4.30; EX 75.70 Trifecta £1352.10.
**Owner** David J Keast **Bred** Highclere Stud **Trained** Great Shefford, Berks

**FOCUS**
This open handicap, confined to apprentice riders, was run at an honest pace. The winner is rated to her AW best, and there's a chance this is worth a bit more.
T/Plt: £295.80 to a £1 stake. Pool: £55,197.84 - 136.20 winning units. T/Qpdt: £47.30 to a £1 stake. Pool: £5029.53 - 78.65 winning units. TM

# 5893 WOLVERHAMPTON (A.W) (L-H)

Thursday, September 4

**OFFICIAL GOING: Tapeta: standard**
Wind: Light against Weather: Fine

## 6071 FREE BETS AT MONSTERBET NOVICE AUCTION STKS (TAPETA) 7f 32y

**5:40** (5:41) (Class 5) 2-Y-O **£2,749** (£818; £408; £204) **Stalls** Low

Form RPR

2 **1** **Fidelma Moon (IRE)**[29] 5056 2-8-3 0 ........ JoeyHaynes[(3)] 4 76+
(K R Burke) *s.s: hdwy to ld and edgd lft over 5f out: rdn over 1f out: edgd rt ins fnl f: styd on* **7/1**

2215 **2** *1/2* **Lady Moscou (IRE)**[42] 4585 2-8-11 84 ........ KierenFallon 5 80
(James Tate) *trckd ldrs: racd keenly: hmpd over 5f out: wnt 2nd over 4f out: rdn over 1f out: r.o* **5/2**[2]

1 **3** *1* **Marsh Pride**[19] 5443 2-8-10 0 ........ PJMcDonald 1 76
(Ann Duffield) *trckd ldrs: plld hrd: lost pl 5f out: hdwy over 1f out: sn rdn: styd on* **1/1**[1]

4 **4** *1 1/4* **Willow Creek**[52] 4260 2-8-9 0 ........ AndrewMullen 3 72
(William Haggas) *hld up: hdwy over 2f out: sn rdn: styd on same pce ins fnl f* **11/2**[3]

00 **5** *6* **Laura B**[14] 5604 2-8-6 0 ........ HarryBentley 2 55
(Chris Wall) *sn led: hdd over 5f out: remained handy: rdn over 1f out: wknd fnl f* **100/1**

1m 30.92s (2.12) **Going Correction** +0.10s/f (Slow) **5 Ran SP% 107.4**
Speed ratings (Par 95): **91,90,89,87,81**
CSF £23.33 TOTE £5.70: £1.70, £1.10; EX 20.90 Trifecta £25.90.
**Owner** The Mount Racing Club & Mrs E Burke **Bred** Jan H Stulen **Trained** Middleham Moor, N Yorks

**FOCUS**
This was slowly run, the fifth's improvement is a concern and the race has been rated on the negative side.

## 6072 ENHANCED ODDS AT MONSTERBET CLAIMING STKS (TAPETA) 7f 32y

**6:10** (6:11) (Class 6) 2-Y-O **£1,940** (£577; £288; £144) **Stalls** Low

Form RPR

1P30 **1** **Just Marion (IRE)**[9] 5798 2-8-5 63 ........ RoystonFfrench 4 50
(David Evans) *chsd ldrs: pushed along 1/2-way: nt clr run wl over 1f out: sn swtchd lft: rdn to ld ins fnl f: r.o* **13/2**[3]

5045 **2** *1* **Jet Mate (IRE)**[8] 5823 2-9-2 55 ........ (p) SamHitchcott 2 59
(William Muir) *sn led: rdn and hdd ins fnl f: styd on same pce* **7/2**[2]

000 **3** *nk* **Sky Steps (IRE)**[42] 4589 2-8-7 45 ........ (v[1]) AndrewMullen 3 49
(Philip McBride) *hld up: hdwy and nt clr run over 1f out: swtchd rt: r.o* **8/1**

3205 **4** *1 1/2* **Reet Petite (IRE)**[20] 5372 2-7-11 48 ........ JoeDoyle[(3)] 6 40
(James Evans) *hld up: hdwy over 1f out: styd on same pce ins fnl f* **16/1**

2005 **5** *1 1/2* **Blue Burmese (IRE)**[15] 5569 2-8-2 65 ........ JoeFanning 5 36
(Mark Usher) *trckd ldr: rdn and ev ch over 1f out: wknd ins fnl f* **12/1**

0531 **6** *3* **Frosty Times (FR)**[20] 5372 2-8-8 57 ........ GeorgeChaloner[(3)] 9 38
(Richard Fahey) *s.i.s: sn pushed along and prom: rdn over 2f out: wknd fnl f* **5/4**[1]

050 **7** *9* **Dark Symphony (IRE)**[14] 5604 2-7-11 45 ........ JoeyHaynes[(3)] 8 5
(Mark Usher) *hld up: wknd over 2f out* **25/1**

1m 30.44s (1.64) **Going Correction** +0.10s/f (Slow) **7 Ran SP% 108.5**
Speed ratings (Par 93): **94,92,92,90,89 85,75**
CSF £26.37 TOTE £10.10: £3.70, £1.80; EX 29.20 Trifecta £253.90.
**Owner** Exors of the late Mrs Sally Edwards **Bred** M A Doyle **Trained** Pandy, Monmouths

**FOCUS**
A low-grade claimer and the winner did not need to improve unless those in behind have progressed. Time will tell.

## 6073 MONSTERBET MAIDEN STKS (TAPETA) 7f 32y
6:40 (6:40) (Class 5) 3-Y-0+ £2,587 (£770; £384; £192) Stalls Low

Form RPR
53 1 **Ramshackle**[13] 5622 3-9-0 0 JamesDoyle 9 75+
(Sir Michael Stoute) *w ldr tl led 5f out: rdn and r.o to assert wl ins fnl f* **8/13**[1]
-043 2 1 ½ **Nathr (USA)**[19] 5412 3-9-5 74 DaneO'Neill 2 76
(Charles Hills) *led: hdd 5f out: remained w wnr: rdn over 1f out: unable qck wl ins fnl f* **5/2**[2]
3 2 ½ **Mr Frankie** 3-9-2 0 DeclanBates(3) 11 70+
(Ed de Giles) *hld up: hdwy over 2f out: edgd lft fr over 1f out: nt rch ldrs* **25/1**
0 4 7 **Resonated (USA)**[9] 5796 3-9-5 0 DaleSwift 6 51
(Brian Ellison) *in rr: drvn along 1/2-way: mod late prog* **50/1**
5 6 **Hard Run (USA)** 4-9-9 0 AndreaAtzeni 10 38+
(Robert Cowell) *chsd ldrs: rdn over 2f out: sn wknd* **10/1**[3]
3463 6 2 ¼ **Templar Boy**[22] 5321 3-9-0 52 JoeDoyle(5) 4 30
(J R Jenkins) *trckd ldrs: plld hrd: wknd over 2f out* **20/1**
00-6 7 10 **My Stroppy Poppy**[117] 2177 5-9-4 33 [1] AndrewMullen 3
(Alan Phillips) *chsd ldrs: edgd lft 1/2-way: sn wknd* **66/1**
8 1 **Aduvee** 4-8-11 0 MikeyEnnis(7) 5
(Ronald Harris) *hld up: wknd 3f out* **50/1**
9 6 **Gabrial's Lady (IRE)** 3-8-11 0 GeorgeChaloner(3) 1
(Richard Fahey) *sn pushed along and prom: hmpd and wknd 1/2-way* **12/1**
10 11 **Grey Star** 3-9-0 0 FrankieMcDonald 8
(Daniel Mark Loughnane) *a in rr: wknd 3f out* **50/1**

1m 28.5s (-0.30) **Going Correction** +0.10s/f (Slow)
**WFA** 3 from 4yo+ 4lb 10 Ran SP% **123.3**
Speed ratings (Par 103): **105,103,100,92,85 83,71,70,63,51**
CSF £2.34 TOTE £1.70: £1.10, £1.10, £8.00; EX 2.60 Trifecta £27.90.
**Owner** K Abdullah **Bred** Juddmonte Farms Ltd **Trained** Newmarket, Suffolk

**FOCUS**
This weak maiden only concerned two from the top of the home straight. The winner was unimpressive and did not need to match her best.

## 6074 EXCLUSIVE OFFERS AT MONSTERBET H'CAP (TAPETA) 7f 32y
7:10 (7:11) (Class 5) (0-70,69) 3-Y-0+ £2,749 (£818; £408; £204) Stalls Low

Form RPR
215 1 **For Shia And Lula (IRE)**[16] 5523 5-9-5 69 EoinWalsh(5) 6 77
(Daniel Mark Loughnane) *a.p: rdn to ld 1f out: styd on* **15/2**
6050 2 ¾ **Malaysian Boleh**[57] 4072 4-9-6 65 HarryBentley 1 71
(Simon Dow) *s.i.s: hld up: hdwy over 1f out: rdn and hung lft ins fnl f: r.o to go 2nd post: nt rch wnr* **6/1**[3]
4401 3 hd **Wotalad**[17] 5510 4-8-7 55 (p) GeorgeChaloner(3) 10 60
(Richard Whitaker) *led: rdn over 2f out: hdd 1f out: styd on u.p* **15/2**
0541 4 nk **Zed Candy Girl**[14] 5605 4-9-3 65 (p) AmyScott(3) 3 69
(Dai Burchell) *mid-div: hdwy over 2f out: nt clr run wl over 1f out: sn rdn: r.o* **6/1**[3]
3232 5 shd **Schottische**[23] 5273 4-9-0 59 (v) DaneO'Neill 4 63
(Derek Haydn Jones) *sn pushed along in rr: rdn over 1f out: edgd lft and r.o ins fnl f: nrst fin* **9/2**[1]
0655 6 3 **Saranta**[21] 5336 3-8-6 60 JackGarritty(5) 2 54
(Richard Fahey) *prom: lost pl 1/2-way: hdwy over 1f out: styd on same pce fnl f* **25/1**
10-5 7 shd **Summer Dancer (IRE)**[19] 5415 10-9-6 65 KierenFallon 5 61
(Eugene Stanford) *hld up: hdwy over 1f out: sn rdn: styd on same pce ins fnl f* **20/1**
1204 8 ½ **Medam**[10] 5763 5-9-8 67 JasonHart 8 62
(Shaun Harris) *chsd ldrs: rdn over 1f out: no ex ins fnl f* **9/1**
3010 9 ¾ **Ewell Place (IRE)**[9] 5793 5-9-4 63 (v[1]) DavidNolan 9 56
(Richard Fahey) *s.i.s: sn pushed along into mid-div: hdwy over 2f out: rdn over 1f out: wknd ins fnl f* **11/2**[2]
6000 10 ¾ **Bogsnog (IRE)**[69] 3668 4-9-8 67 TomEaves 7 58
(Kristin Stubbs) *chsd ldr tl rdn over 2f out: wknd ins fnl f* **7/1**
5003 11 3 **Wild Hill Boy**[15] 5570 4-8-5 55 oh3 JacobButterfield(5) 11 38
(David C Griffiths) *s.i.s: hld up: rdn over 2f out: sn wknd* **25/1**

1m 29.28s (0.48) **Going Correction** +0.10s/f (Slow)
**WFA** 3 from 4yo+ 4lb 11 Ran SP% **120.6**
Speed ratings (Par 103): **101,100,99,99,99 96,95,95,94,93 90**
CSF £52.07 CT £358.45 TOTE £12.00: £1.90, £3.50, £2.60; EX 76.70 Trifecta £448.90.
**Owner** Over The Moon Racing IV **Bred** A M F Persse **Trained** Baldwin's Gate, Staffs

**FOCUS**
A small personal best from the winner whose Lingfield win in July worked out well and could be this good.

## 6075 MONSTERBET FOR MONSTER DEALS H'CAP (BOBIS RACE) (TAPETA) 1m 4f 50y
7:40 (7:40) (Class 4) (0-80,80) 3-Y-O £4,851 (£1,443; £721; £360) Stalls Low

Form RPR
423- 1 **Charlotte's Day**[355] 6378 3-9-3 76 LukeMorris 6 87+
(Sir Mark Prescott Bt) *chsd ldr tl led over 2f out: rdn and edgd lft over 1f out: c clr fnl f* **8/1**[3]
6526 2 4 **Master Dan**[21] 5343 3-9-0 73 DaleSwift 5 78
(James Given) *led: rdn and hdd over 2f out: nt clr run over 1f out: styng on same pce whn hung rt ins fnl f* **12/1**
41F6 3 nse **Heska (IRE)**[9] 5795 3-8-9 68 (tp) AndrewMullen 4 73
(Michael Appleby) *s.s: hld up: hdwy 5f out: rdn and hung lft over 1f out: styd on same pce* **12/1**
3-31 4 6 **Authorized Too**[22] 5318 3-9-7 80 AndreaAtzeni 1 75
(William Haggas) *hld up: rdn over 3f out: wknd over 2f out* **1/2**[1]
0503 5 16 **Sir Rosco**[30] 5010 3-9-1 74 KierenFallon 2 60
(Sir Michael Stoute) *chsd ldrs: rdn over 3f out: wknd over 2f out* **5/1**[2]

2m 41.46s (0.66) **Going Correction** +0.10s/f (Slow) 5 Ran SP% **109.8**
Speed ratings (Par 103): **101,98,98,94,83**
CSF £78.39 TOTE £3.00: £3.00, £3.60; EX 44.60 Trifecta £106.80.
**Owner** Lord Derby **Bred** Stanley House Stud **Trained** Newmarket, Suffolk

**FOCUS**
The winner is progressive and the runner-up seemed to confirm his Southwell form.

## 6076 FREEBETS.ORG.UK DOWNLOAD OUR APP H'CAP (TAPETA) 1m 1f 103y
8:10 (8:10) (Class 6) (0-60,60) 3-Y-0+ £2,264 (£673; £336; £168) Stalls Low

Form RPR
0-04 1 **Hidden Asset**[16] 5529 4-8-11 47 AndrewMullen 4 57+
(Michael Appleby) *hmpd sn after s: hld up: hdwy over 1f out: r.o u.p to ld wl ins fnl f* **7/1**[3]
4213 2 1 ½ **Lynngale**[28] 5109 3-9-4 60 TomEaves 3 67
(Kristin Stubbs) *sn led: hdd over 4f out: led again 3f out: rdn over 1f out: hdd and unable qck wl ins fnl f* **10/1**
0265 3 2 ¼ **Yorksters Prince (IRE)**[21] 5331 7-9-1 56 (b) JordanNason(5) 6 58
(Marjorie Fife) *pushed along and edgd lft sn after s: mid-div: hdwy 6f out: edgd lft and chsd ldr over 5f out: led over 4f out tl hdd 3f out: rdn over 1f out: styd on same pce ins fnl f* **20/1**
5004 4 ½ **Eastward Ho**[6] 5893 6-9-3 53 PaulMulrennan 13 54
(Michael Herrington) *chsd ldrs: rdn over 2f out: styd on same pce fnl f* **5/1**[2]
4304 5 1 ¾ **Stanlow**[14] 5596 4-9-0 55 (v) EoinWalsh(5) 5 52
(Daniel Mark Loughnane) *hmpd sn after s: hld up: hdwy over 1f out: nt rch ldrs* **5/2**[1]
5000 6 ½ **Spoken Words**[14] 5605 5-8-5 46 [1] JoeDoyle(5) 12 42
(John David Riches) *s.i.s: hld up: hdwy u.p over 1f out: nt trble ldrs* **40/1**
4203 7 nk **Excellent News (IRE)**[91] 2937 5-8-3 46 oh1 (p) AdamMcLean(7) 10 42
(Tony Forbes) *chsd ldrs: rdn and rn wd wl over 1f out: styd on same pce fnl f* **40/1**
306/ 8 2 ½ **Godwit**[16] 5212 6-8-7 46 oh1 RobertTart(3) 2 36
(Eugene Stanford) *mid-div: lost pl over 5f out: n.d after* **33/1**
2321 9 1 **Ela Goog La Mou**[11] 5731 5-9-9 59 ChrisCatlin 8 47
(Peter Charalambous) *s.i.s: sn prom: hmpd over 5f out: rdn over 2f out: sn wknd* **5/2**[1]
03-0 10 hd **Miss Ella Jade**[207] 546 5-8-10 46 oh1 (p) PaulQuinn 1 34
(Richard Whitaker) *chsd ldrs: rdn over 2f out: wknd fnl f* **66/1**
5050 11 ¾ **Mary's Prayer**[46] 4473 3-8-8 50 PatrickMathers 7 36
(John Holt) *mid-div: rdn over 3f out: wknd over 2f out* **66/1**
0056 12 11 **Poor Duke (IRE)**[17] 5512 4-9-0 57 (b) LewisStones(7) 11 20
(Michael Mullineaux) *rdr unbalanced and lost iron leaving stalls: rode wout both irons fr over 6f out: a in rr: wknd and eased over 2f out* **14/1**

2m 1.91s (1.11) **Going Correction** +0.10s/f (Slow)
**WFA** 3 from 4yo+ 6lb 12 Ran SP% **117.6**
Speed ratings (Par 101): **99,97,95,95,93 93,92,90,89,89 89,79**
CSF £69.17 CT £1334.49 TOTE £7.90: £2.40, £2.00, £3.60; EX 59.50 Trifecta £1904.10.
**Owner** Terry Pryke **Bred** R J Cornelius **Trained** Danethorpe, Notts

**FOCUS**
The pace looked good and the form seems solid.

## 6077 MONSTERBET - YOUR BOOKMAKER COMPARISON SITE H'CAP (TAPETA) 5f 216y
8:40 (8:40) (Class 6) (0-65,65) 3-Y-0+ £2,264 (£673; £336; £168) Stalls Low

Form RPR
0212 1 **Chapellerie (IRE)**[14] 5602 5-9-5 63 (b) LiamKeniry 7 72
(Brendan Powell) *hld up: hdwy over 1f out: sn rdn: hung lft and r.o to ld nr fin* **2/1**[1]
445 2 ¾ **Mey Blossom**[5] 5913 9-8-9 56 (b) GeorgeChaloner(3) 2 63
(Richard Whitaker) *chsd ldrs: rdn over 2f out: led wl ins fnl f: hdd nr fin* **9/1**
2334 3 ½ **Red Cape (FR)**[8] 5817 11-9-5 63 (b) JamesSullivan 9 68
(Ruth Carr) *chsd ldr: rdn to ld over 1f out: hdd wl ins fnl f* **11/1**
3661 4 3 ¼ **Silvala Dance**[28] 5105 4-8-12 56 TedDurcan 8 51
(Chris Wall) *hld up: hdwy over 2f out: rdn over 1f out: no ex ins fnl f* **5/2**[2]
400 5 1 ¾ **Avonvalley**[14] 5602 7-8-13 57 TomEaves 6 46
(Peter Grayson) *mid-div: rdn over 2f out: wknd ins fnl f* **40/1**
004 6 ¾ **Hit The Lights (IRE)**[33] 4908 4-9-1 59 (p) LukeMorris 1 46
(Patrick Chamings) *chsd ldrs: rdn over 1f out: wknd ins fnl f* **10/1**
0-00 7 ½ **Forzarzi (IRE)**[14] 5605 10-8-2 51 oh4 JoeDoyle(5) 4 36
(John David Riches) *hld up: rdn over 1f out: sme hdwy whn hmpd ins fnl f: n.d* **50/1**
2000 8 ¾ **Lyrical**[16] 5530 3-9-0 60 DaneO'Neill 11 43
(Derek Haydn Jones) *hld up: rdn over 2f out: wknd over 1f out* **33/1**
0000 9 1 **Gabrial's Bounty (IRE)**[13] 5632 5-9-2 65 JackGarritty(5) 3 44
(Richard Fahey) *led: rdn and hdd over 1f out: wknd ins fnl f* **11/2**[3]
0430 P **Hazard Warning (IRE)**[43] 4532 4-9-4 62 (b) GrahamLee 10
(James Given) *s.s: bhd whn p.u 5f out* **7/1**

1m 14.79s (0.29) **Going Correction** +0.10s/f (Slow)
**WFA** 3 from 4yo+ 2lb 10 Ran SP% **124.6**
Speed ratings (Par 101): **102,101,100,96,93 92,92,91,89,**
CSF £22.93 CT £175.95 TOTE £3.20: £1.60, £2.50, £3.00; EX 29.40 Trifecta £111.10.
**Owner** T M Clarke **Bred** Castellane Partnership **Trained** Upper Lambourn, Berks

**FOCUS**
The winner is rated to a length personal best, with the well-placed second helping set the level.
T/Plt: £481.90 to a £1 stake. Pool: £65,273.50 - 98.86 winning units. T/Qpdt: £77.50 to a £1 stake. Pool: £11,041.38 - 105.40 winning units. CR

# LAYTOWN
Thursday, September 4

**OFFICIAL GOING: Standard**

## 6078a TOTE MOBILE BETTING H'CAP 6f
2:35 (2:36) (50-70,70) 4-Y-0+ £4,887 (£1,133; £495; £283)

RPR
1 **Seamster**[14] 5601 7-10-9 **65** (t) ColinKeane 73+
(Richard Ford) *sweated up befhand: sn led: rdn 2f out and extended advantage ent fnl f: kpt on wl u.p towards fin where reduced advantage* **3/1**[1]
2 1 ¾ **Doonard Prince (IRE)**[12] 5702 5-10-12 **68** PatSmullen 70+
(Ross O'Sullivan, Ire) *w.w in rr: last 1/2-way: pushed along in 9th 2f out and prog on outer into mod 2nd wl ins fnl f: kpt on wl u.p towards fin: nvr on terms* **6/1**[3]
3 ¾ **City Of Culture (IRE)**[30] 5021 6-11-0 **70** BillyLee 70
(W McCreery, Ire) *hld up in tch: 7th 1/2-way: n.m.r bhd horses 2f out and sn swtchd rt: kpt on u.p ins fnl f and no imp on wnr in 3rd towards fin* **9/1**

4 2 1/2 **Connacht Council (IRE)**[36] 4805 4-10-8 **67**.................(t) ConnorKing(3) 59
(W McCreery, Ire) *w.w: 9th 1/2-way: hdwy whn nt clr run bhd horses 1f out: kpt on u.p ins fnl f to snatch mod 4th fnl stride* **7/1**

5 shd **Shabra Emperor (IRE)**[18] 5476 5-9-8 **53**.................. MarkEnright(3) 45
(Patrick O Brady, Ire) *chsd ldrs: pushed along in 5th 1/2-way and clsd u.p into mod 2nd briefly ins fnl f: no ex and wknd towards fin: denied mod 4th fnl stride* **12/1**

6 3 1/4 **Above The Law (IRE)**[18] 5471 5-10-7 **68**.................. SeanCorby(5) 49
(A Oliver, Ire) *sweated up befhand: trckd ldrs: clsr in 2nd bef 1/2-way: sn rdn and no ex u.p 2f out: wknd* **11/2**[2]

7 nk **Ask Dad**[33] 4234 4-10-8 **67**..................................(t) IanMcCarthy(3) 47
(Damian Joseph English, Ire) *trckd ldrs early tl dropped to 6th bef 1/2-way: n.m.r bhd horses over 1f out: sn rdn and wknd* **20/1**

8 1 1/4 **Decision By One**[8] 5840 5-10-5 **61**...................(t) SeamieHeffernan 37
(S J Mahon, Ire) *chsd ldrs: clsr in 3rd 1/2-way: rdn and wknd 2f out* **12/1**

9 1 3/4 **Elusive In Paris (IRE)**[69] 3687 5-11-0 **70**.......................... PaulTownend 41
(M C Grassick, Ire) *prom: sn settled bhd ldr in 2nd tl dropped to 3rd bef 1/2-way: sn pushed along and no ex u.p fr 2f out: wknd* **11/1**

10 19 **Scatty Cat (IRE)**[316] 7474 4-10-9 **65**.......................................... FMBerry
(John James Feane, Ire) *hld up: 8th 1/2-way: dropped to rr 2f out and no imp: wknd and eased* **7/1**

1m 13.4s (73.40) **10 Ran SP% 118.2**
CSF £21.03 TOTE £3.00: £1.40, £1.40, £3.00; DF 14.90.
**Owner** P Bamford **Bred** D G Hardisty Bloodstock **Trained** Garstang, Lancs

**FOCUS**
All six races had tape starts. They got away at the first time of asking in the opener and the winning time was 1.2secs quicker than the same race last year. The winner made all and had everything in trouble 2f out, and he's rated in line with his recent form.

## 6082a BARRY MATTHEWS APPRECIATION SOCIETY (Q.R.) H'CAP 7f
4:45 (4:45) (50-80,79) 4-Y-0+ £6,037 (£1,400; £612; £350)

RPR

1 **Prince Jock (USA)**[7] 5849 7-11-13 **77**...................... MrRPQuinlan(3) 81
(John Patrick Shanahan, Ire) *mde all: 1 l clr 1/2-way: rdn fr under 2f out and strly pressed u.p wl ins fnl f: all out towards fin: kpt on wl* **12/1**

2 nk **Korbous (IRE)**[7] 5871 5-11-11 **75**...................... MissJMMangan(3) 78
(Richard Brabazon, Ire) *chsd ldrs: 5th bef 1/2-way: rdn into 2nd 1 1/2f out and ev ch almost on terms wl ins fnl f: kpt on wl towards fin: hld* **6/1**

3 1 1/2 **Beat The Ballot (IRE)**[12] 5702 5-11-1 **67**.......................... MrRJKiely(5) 66
(Tracey Collins, Ire) *in tch: 6th bef 1/2-way: rdn into 4th ins fnl f and kpt on wl towards fin wout ever threatening principals* **6/1**

4 3/4 **My Son Max**[22] 5295 6-11-10 **71**.......................................... MsKWalsh 68
(Richard Ford) *chsd ldrs: 3rd 1/2-way: rdn 2f out and no imp on wnr in 3rd ent fnl f: kpt on one pce and dropped to 4th clsng stages* **5/1**[3]

5 1 1/4 **Six Of Hearts**[17] 5514 10-12-4 **79**.......................................... MrJJCodd 73
(Cecil Ross, Ire) *hld up: 8th bef 1/2-way: rdn 1 1/2f out on outer and kpt on u.p ins fnl f: nvr nrr* **16/1**

6 1 1/4 **Six Silver Lane**[15] 5583 6-11-6 **72**.......................... MrDGLavery(5) 62
(John James Feane, Ire) *trckd ldr in 2nd: rdn 2f out and no imp on wnr in 4th ent fnl f: wknd towards fin* **7/2**[1]

7 2 1/4 **Arbitrageur (IRE)**[68] 3737 5-11-12 **78**.......................... MrJJKing(5) 62
(Donal Kinsella, Ire) *chsd ldrs: 4th bef 1/2-way: rdn in 5th 1 1/2f out and sn no imp on ldrs: wknd ins fnl f* **14/1**

8 hd **Landau (IRE)**[10] 4951 4-12-0 **75**..................................(t) MsNCarberry 59
(Gordon Elliott, Ire) *in tch: 7th bef 1/2-way: rdn fr after 1/2-way and sn no imp on ldrs: one pce* **4/1**[2]

9 1 1/2 **He's Got Rhythm (IRE)**[17] 5514 9-11-12 **73**.......................... RobbieMcNamara 53
(David Marnane, Ire) *chsd ldrs early far side tl dropped to rr bef 1/2-way: sme modest hdwy 2f out: sn rdn and no ex in rr ent fnl f* **7/1**

1m 23.4s (83.40) **9 Ran SP% 120.2**
CSF £85.34 TOTE £16.20: £4.50, £2.70, £3.00; DF 128.00.
**Owner** Thistle Bloodstock Limited **Bred** Clover Leaf Farms II Inc **Trained** Kells, Co Kilkenny

**FOCUS**
This only concerned two when it mattered. The winner made all and was really brave in the closing stages. The runner-up helps set the level.

6083 - 6084a (Foreign Racing) - See Raceform Interactive

# 5745 CHEPSTOW (L-H)
Friday, September 5

**OFFICIAL GOING: Good to soft**
Wind: almost nil Weather: sunny spells

## 6085 SIS MAIDEN AUCTION STKS 1m 14y
2:10 (2:11) (Class 6) 2-Y-0 £1,940 (£577; £288; £144) Stalls Centre

Form RPR

3 1 **Jen Jos Enigma (IRE)**[38] 4764 2-8-8 0.......................... OisinMurphy 7 73+
(Noel Quinlan) *trckd ldrs: chal over 2f out: rdn to ld appr fnl f: r.o wl* **9/4**[1]

2 2 **Storm Rock** 2-8-13 0.............................................. SamHitchcott 1 73+
(Harry Dunlop) *s.s: in rr and chsd along early: gd hdwy 1/2-way: led over 2f out: sn chal: hdd appr fnl f: kpt on* **14/1**

0 3 7 **Magical Thomas**[22] 5351 2-8-8 0.......................... LouisSteward(5) 3 58
(Marcus Tregoning) *mid-div: hdwy 1/2-way: rdn 3f out: outpcd by ldng pair 2f out but kpt on to hold modest 3rd* **9/2**[3]

4 3/4 **Bold Appeal** 2-8-13 0.............................................. JamesRogers(5) 2 61
(Ralph Beckett) *dwlt: sn in mid-div: rdn over 3f out: qckly outpcd by ldrs and no ch after: styd on fnl f* **12/1**

003 5 4 1/2 **Emperors Warrior (IRE)**[17] 5519 2-9-1 64.......................... PatDobbs 4 48
(Richard Hannon) *prom: rdn 3f out: outpcd by ldng pair 2f out: no ch after* **8/1**

6 hd **Celestial Magic** 2-8-11 0.......................... WilliamTwiston-Davies 5 44
(Jonathan Portman) *s.s: in rr: rdn over 3f out: no imp tl r.o ins fnl f* **33/1**

06 7 1/2 **Theydon Bois**[22] 5344 2-8-6 0.......................... HarryBentley 9 38
(Peter Charalambous) *hld up towards rr: rdn over 3f out: one pce and no real imp* **7/2**[2]

8 1 3/4 **Mysterious Star (FR)** 2-8-13 0.......................... FergusSweeney 10 41
(Martyn Meade) *chsd ldrs: rdn 3f out: wknd over 1f out* **7/1**

00 9 nk **Harps Of Bretagne**[29] 5078 2-8-1 0.......................... TimClark(5) 6 33
(Lisa Williamson) *led: drvn and hdd over 2f out: grad wknd* **100/1**

0 10 1 **Deeper Magic (IRE)**[28] 5148 2-8-6 0.......................... JosephineGordon(7) 8 38
(J S Moore) *t.k.h in mid-div: dropped to rr over 4f out: struggling and no ch after* **100/1**

1m 38.18s (1.98) **Going Correction** +0.175s/f (Good) **10 Ran SP% 114.1**
Speed ratings (Par 93): **97,95,88,87,82 82,82,80,80,79**
CSF £35.54 TOTE £2.70: £1.20, £4.00, £2.30; EX 36.10 Trifecta £231.70.
**Owner** Burns Farm Racing **Bred** Miss Tamaria Butler **Trained** Newmarket, Suffolk

**FOCUS**
This looked hard work for these 2yos and the front pair pulled clear. The bare form is only ordinary.

## 6086 32RED.COM H'CAP 1m 14y
2:40 (2:42) (Class 6) (0-65,64) 3-Y-0+ £1,940 (£577; £288; £144) Stalls Centre

Form RPR

1353 1 **Belle Park**[22] 5338 7-8-13 60.......................... KieranShoemark(7) 2 70
(Victor Dartnall) *s.i.s: sn in mid-div: hdwy over 2f out: sn rdn: r.o ins fnl f to ld post* **10/1**

0056 2 nse **Hill Fort**[33] 4942 4-9-7 61.......................(p) WilliamTwiston-Davies 7 70
(Ronald Harris) *cl up: racd detached in centre fr 1/2-way: sn led: rdn over 2f out: hdd post* **25/1**

2312 3 1 1/2 **Pour La Victoire (IRE)**[128] 1877 4-9-5 59.......................... AdamKirby 8 65
(Tony Carroll) *mid-div: rdn and hdwy over 2f out: sn chsd ldr: nt quite get on terms and no ex fnl 75yds* **10/1**

6042 4 8 **Celestial Bay**[21] 5383 5-9-10 64.......................... PatDobbs 1 52
(Sylvester Kirk) *in rr: hdwy 3f out: sn rdn: one pce and no further imp on ldrs* **12/1**

2506 5 4 **Botanist**[17] 5530 7-9-3 57.......................... OisinMurphy 9 35
(Shaun Harris) *mid-div: rdn over 2f out: one pce* **12/1**

4351 6 1 **Fair Comment**[8] 5848 4-9-8 62 6ex.......................... DavidProbert 10 38
(Michael Blanshard) *mid-div: rdn 1/2-way: wknd over 2f out: passed btn rivals ins fnl f* **8/1**[3]

0520 7 hd **Acton Gold**[18] 5512 5-8-7 50 oh4.......................(p) RyanPowell(3) 6 26
(Brian Baugh) *chsd ldrs: rdn 3f out: edgd lft and wknd over 1f out* **66/1**

5050 8 3/4 **Guilded Spirit**[23] 5313 4-9-8 62.......................(p) LiamKeniry 3 36
(Stuart Kittow) *towards rr: sn swtchd rt to r stands' side: rdn 1/2-way: nvr trbld ldrs* **8/1**[3]

3364 9 1 **Tenbridge**[11] 5751 5-9-2 61.......................(v) TimClark(5) 12 33
(Derek Haydn Jones) *racd keenly: cl up: led after 2f tl over 3f out: wknd over 1f out* **9/2**[1]

0/45 10 nk **Mini's Destination**[71] 3614 6-9-1 55.......................... StevieDonohoe 5 26
(John Holt) *towards rr: sme hdwy 1/2-way: rdn 3f out: grad wknd* **33/1**

2411 11 1 3/4 **Greyemkay**[14] 5621 6-9-1 60.......................... EoinWalsh(5) 14 27
(Richard Price) *prom: rdn 3f out: wknd over 1f out* **6/1**[2]

2420 12 nk **Hot Mustard**[21] 5394 4-9-4 63.......................... LouisSteward(5) 13 29
(Michael Bell) *led 2f: styd cl up: rdn 3f out: sn wknd* **8/1**[3]

6600 13 6 **Strong Conviction**[38] 1717 4-9-10 64.......................(v) SamHitchcott 11 16
(Simon Hodgson) *chsd ldrs: pushed along 1/2-way: wkng whn n.m.r over 3f out* **16/1**

4-00 14 26 **Dark Reality (IRE)**[32] 4969 3-8-12 57.......................... HarryBentley 4
(Ralph Beckett) *dwlt: in rr: sn swtchd rt to r stands' side: rdr looked down after 3f: sn rdn along and no rspnse: wl bhd whn eased 2f out: t.o* **10/1**

1m 37.06s (0.86) **Going Correction** +0.175s/f (Good)
**WFA** 3 from 4yo+ 5lb **14 Ran SP% 122.6**
Speed ratings (Par 101): **102,101,100,92,88 87,87,86,85,85 83,83,77,51**
CSF £245.11 CT £2628.74 TOTE £13.50: £4.40, £11.00, £2.00; EX 485.60 Trifecta £1524.60 Part won..
**Owner** V R A Dartnall **Bred** C A Green **Trained** Brayford, Devon

**FOCUS**
An open if moderate handicap and again the conditions seemed to find out a few, with the first three pulling right away. The field raced centre-to-stands' side, but those who came down the middle seemed to be at an advantage. A small personal best from the winner.

## 6087 32RED ON THE APP STORE APPRENTICE (S) STKS 1m 14y
3:10 (3:12) (Class 6) 3-4-Y-0 £1,940 (£577; £288; £144) Stalls Centre

Form RPR

525 1 **Admirable Art (IRE)**[83] 3242 4-9-4 60.........(p) WilliamTwiston-Davies 6 59
(Tony Carroll) *hld up towards rr: hdwy 3f out: rdn over 1f out: led fnl 100yds: drvn out* **5/1**[3]

-003 2 1 **Actonetaketwo**[11] 5751 4-8-10 44.......................... PhilipPrince(3) 1 52
(Ron Hodges) *chsd ldrs: rdn to ld over 2f out: hdd fnl 100yds: no ex* **25/1**

6252 3 3/4 **Inkerman (IRE)**[26] 5202 4-9-4 70.......................(tp) DannyBrock 4 55
(Jamie Osborne) *in tch: hdwy over 3f out: rdn and nt qckn 2f out: kpt on same pce ins fnl f* **3/1**[1]

5024 4 3 3/4 **Mary Le Bow**[23] 5302 3-8-3 60.......................(v[1]) KieranShoemark(5) 7 41
(Karen George) *awkward s: mid-div: rdn and sme hdwy 3f out: kpt on one pce fnl 2f* **5/1**[3]

0406 5 3 1/4 **Encore Encore (FR)**[25] 5256 3-8-1 61.............(b[1]) Leah-AnneAvery(7) 3 33
(Harry Dunlop) *prom: led after 2f tl over 2f out: sn wknd* **8/1**

5-50 6 5 **Pink Mirage (IRE)**[116] 2224 3-8-5 62.......................... LouisSteward(3) 11 22
(Jonathan Portman) *towards rr: rdn and sme hdwy 3f out: wknd over 1f out* **7/2**[2]

0606 7 1 1/2 **Pacific Trip**[31] 5005 3-8-13 50.......................(vt) OisinMurphy 10 23
(Andrew Balding) *racd keenly: in tch: rdn and nt qckn 3f out: wknd 2f out* **8/1**

0460 8 1/2 **Up Hill Battle's**[16] 5558 3-8-5 44.......................(p) EoinWalsh(3) 9 17
(Daniel Mark Loughnane) *chsd ldrs: rdn 3f out: sn wknd* **20/1**

0-05 9 6 **Sakuramachi**[11] 5747 3-8-1 55.......................... MichaelKenneally(7) 12 3
(Nikki Evans) *towards rr: rdn over 3f out: no ch fnl 2f* **100/1**

0 10 1/2 **Out Of Orbit**[41] 4677 3-8-5 0.......................... TimClark(3) 5 2
(Mark Gillard) *t.k.h: led 2f: styd prom tl drifted lft and wknd u.p over 2f out* **100/1**

0 11 37 **Alzarica (IRE)**[18] 5504 3-8-8 0.......................... RyanWhile(5) 8
(Malcolm Saunders) *mid-div tl dropped to rr after 2f: wl bhd fr 1/2-way: t.o* **66/1**

1m 39.41s (3.21) **Going Correction** +0.175s/f (Good)
**WFA** 3 from 4yo 5lb **11 Ran SP% 114.9**
Speed ratings (Par 101): **90,89,88,84,81 76,74,74,68,67 30**
CSF £124.52 TOTE £8.70: £2.80, £4.80, £1.40; EX 115.80 Trifecta £199.60.There was no bid for the winner.
**Owner** D Morgan **Bred** Longview Stud & Bloodstock Ltd **Trained** Cropthorne, Worcs

**FOCUS**
This was a poor seller and not form to dwell on. The time was slow.

## 6088 £10 FREE BET AT 32REDSPORT.COM H'CAP 7f 16y
3:45 (3:47) (Class 6) (0-65,65) 3-Y-0+ £1,940 (£577; £288; £144) Stalls Centre

Form RPR

6510 1 **Belle Bayardo (IRE)**[34] 4905 6-9-8 63.......................... WilliamCarson 5 76
(Tony Carroll) *tk v t.k.h: trckd ldrs tl led after 3f: rdn over 1f out: sn 3 l clr: r.o wl* **7/1**[3]

004 2 3 1/2 **Emperor Julius (IRE)**[41] 4655 4-9-7 62.......................... FergusSweeney 3 66
(Jo Crowley) *trckd ldr: rdn to chse wnr 2f out: kpt on same pce and no further imp* **7/1**[3]

2201 **3** *3¾* **Mister Mayday (IRE)**[25] 5252 3-9-6 65..............(b) AdamKirby 1 57+
(George Baker) *walked to post early: in rr: rdn and hdwy over 2f out: wnt 3rd 1f out: kpt on but no further prog* **5/2**[1]

-004 **4** *2¾* **Almax**[31] 5000 3-8-4 54..............(v[1]) LouisSteward(5) 10 39
(Michael Bell) *trckd ldrs: chsd wnr briefly over 2f out: edgd rt over 1f out: one pce after* **8/1**

4400 **5** *3* **Trigger Park (IRE)**[17] 5530 3-8-8 53.............. DavidProbert 7 30
(Ronald Harris) *led 3f: chsd ldrs: once pce fnl 2f* **20/1**

654 **6** *½* **Avon Scent**[24] 5272 4-8-3 51.............. KieranShoemark(7) 12 29
(Christopher Mason) *mid-div: rdn and outpcd over 3f out: styd on u.p fnl 2f* **25/1**

0152 **7** *3½* **Euroquip Boy (IRE)**[11] 5751 7-9-1 61.............. NoelGarbutt(5) 13 30+
(Michael Scudamore) *racd keenly: chsd ldrs: rdn over 2f out: wknd over 1f out* **3/1**[2]

4303 **8** *1* **Jessy Mae**[24] 5272 3-8-3 53.............. TimClark(5) 4 17
(Derek Haydn Jones) *mid-div: rdn over 3f out: one pce* **25/1**

0004 **9** *nk* **Reflection**[23] 5321 3-8-6 51.............. SamHitchcott 6 14
(Brian Baugh) *chsd ldrs: rdn over 3f out: sn one pce* **100/1**

56 **10** *1* **Monty Fay (IRE)**[20] 5423 5-8-7 51..............(t) RosieJessop(3) 11 14
(Derek Haydn Jones) *prom: rdn over 3f out: wknd over 2f out* **33/1**

000 **11** *nk* **Dimitar (USA)**[58] 4073 5-9-8 63.............. LiamKeniry 8 25
(Johnny Farrelly) *pushed along over 2f out: a towards rr* **8/1**

0600 **12** *5* **Echologic**[11] 5751 4-8-7 51.............. RyanPowell(3) 2
(Brian Baugh) *rdn along after 2f: a towards rr* **100/1**

0-00 **13** *11* **Basle**[65] 3848 7-8-10 51..............(tp) OisinMurphy 9
(Roy Brotherton) *rdn over 2f out: a towards rr* **50/1**

1m 23.94s (0.74) **Going Correction** +0.175s/f (Good)
**WFA** 3 from 4yo+ 4lb 13 Ran SP% **120.1**
Speed ratings (Par 101): **102,98,93,90,87 86,82,81,81,79 79,,67**
CSF £52.29 CT £148.57 TOTE £8.60: £1.20, £3.90, £1.40; EX 55.80 Trifecta £219.90.
**Owner** Richard Ward **Bred** L Mulryan **Trained** Cropthorne, Worcs

**FOCUS**
A moderate handicap and further confirmation the centre of the track was the place to be. The winner's best form since he was a 2yo.

## 6089 FESTIVAL RACING H'CAP — 6f 16y
**4:20** (4:20) (Class 4) (0-85,84) 3-Y-O+ **£4,690** (£1,395; £697; £348) **Stalls** Centre

Form RPR

5600 **1** **Amadeus Wolfe Tone (IRE)**[14] 5650 5-9-5 82..............(p) AdamKirby 8 90
(Jamie Osborne) *chsd ldrs: rdn over 2f out: nt clr run wl over 1f out: r.o to ld fnl 100yds: edgd rt towards fin* **8/1**

641 **2** *¾* **Dominate**[11] 5750 4-9-6 83 6ex..............(b) PatDobbs 11 89
(Richard Hannon) *chsd ldrs: rdn 2f out: ev ch ins fnl f: r.o* **5/1**[3]

0604 **3** *shd* **Corporal Maddox**[11] 5750 7-9-6 83..............(p) DavidProbert 10 88
(Ronald Harris) *in tch: rdn and hdwy over 1f out: ev ch ins fnl f: jst hld* **16/1**

0402 **4** *¾* **Gramercy (IRE)**[11] 5750 7-9-1 83..............(p) LouisSteward(5) 9 86
(David Simcock) *hld up in last: rdn and hdwy over 2f out: hung lft over 1f out: ch ins fnl f: unable qck last 100yds* **7/2**[1]

1663 **5** *nk* **Sarangoo**[26] 5211 6-8-13 76.............. FergusSweeney 7 78
(Malcolm Saunders) *led: jnd after 2f: hdd over 2f out: led again 1f out tl fnl 100yds: no ex* **16/1**

40 **6** *1* **Pandar**[20] 5444 5-9-4 81.............. StevieDonohoe 4 80
(Milton Bradley) *bmpd s: trckd ldrs: rdn 2f out: one pce fnl f* **33/1**

1500 **7** *nk* **Daylight**[14] 5623 4-9-7 84..............(t) OisinMurphy 5 82
(Andrew Balding) *taken to post early: hld up: rdn 2f out and unable qck: edgd rt and sme hdwy ins fnl f* **4/1**[2]

00-1 **8** *2* **Seal Rock**[24] 5265 6-8-9 72..............(b) LiamKeniry 1 63
(John Quinn) *broke wl: sn hld up towards rr: rdn 2f out: wknd fnl f* **7/2**[1]

-650 **9** *¾* **Threetimesalady**[50] 4367 3-8-9 77..............(p) RosieJessop(3) 2 66
(Sir Mark Prescott Bt) *bmpd s: t.k.h: hdwy to dispute ld after 2f: led over 2f out to 1f out: edgd lft and wknd* **12/1**

1m 12.05s (0.05) **Going Correction** +0.175s/f (Good)
**WFA** 3 from 4yo+ 2lb 9 Ran SP% **114.6**
Speed ratings (Par 105): **106,105,104,103,103 102,101,99,98**
CSF £47.31 CT £626.51 TOTE £8.80: £3.10, £1.70, £4.40; EX 57.70 Trifecta £573.00.
**Owner** B T McDonald **Bred** Brian Williamson **Trained** Upper Lambourn, Berks

**FOCUS**
A fair sprint handicap in which the field raced as one unit up the centre, and competitive with seven of the nine runners still within a length or so of each other inside the last furlong. The form is rated a bit cautiously.

## 6090 D & M LANDSCAPING H'CAP — 5f 16y
**4:55** (4:55) (Class 6) (0-55,61) 3-Y-O+ **£1,940** (£577; £288; £144) **Stalls** Centre

Form RPR

0011 **1** **Rise To Glory (IRE)**[3] 6014 6-9-10 61 12ex..........(tp) LouisSteward(5) 5 72+
(Shaun Harris) *mde all: rdn over 1f out: sn clr and r.o strly: eased cl home* **11/8**[1]

0-02 **2** *2½* **Posh Bounty**[30] 5034 3-8-12 45.............. OisinMurphy 2 45
(Joseph Tuite) *wnt to post early: chsd ldrs: rdn 2f out: sn wnt 2nd: no imp tl wnr eased cl home* **9/4**[2]

0430 **3** *4½* **Lucky Clover**[31] 5000 3-9-0 47.............. FergusSweeney 1 31
(Malcolm Saunders) *chsd wnr: pushed along 1/2-way: lost 2nd over 1f out: one pce* **8/1**[3]

4235 **4** *3¾* **Go Charlie**[6] 5905 3-9-5 52.............. AdamKirby 4 22
(Ronald Harris) *half-rrd s: hld up and racd keenly: rdn 2f out: no imp on ldrs* **8/1**[3]

0466 **5** *2½* **Silken Poppy**[23] 5307 3-9-6 53.............. LiamKeniry 6 14
(Patrick Chamings) *s.i.s: chsd ldrs: pushed along 1/2-way: sn edgd rt and outpcd* **10/1**

545 **6** *7* **Spic 'n Span**[6] 5907 9-8-13 45..............(b) WilliamTwiston-Davies 8
(Ronald Harris) *wnt to post early: wl in tch 2f: sn rdn along: bhd fnl 2f* **14/1**

1m 0.11s (0.81) **Going Correction** +0.175s/f (Good)
**WFA** 3 from 5yo+ 1lb 6 Ran SP% **110.9**
Speed ratings (Par 101): **100,96,88,82,78 67**
CSF £4.50 CT £14.31 TOTE £1.80: £1.10, £2.10; EX 5.20 Trifecta £26.70.
**Owner** N Blencowe,J Sunderland,M Lenton,CHarris **Bred** Bryan Ryan **Trained** Carburton, Notts

**FOCUS**
Effectively a two-horse race according to the market in this moderate sprint handicap and that is how it played out. Most of the runners raced centre-to-far side. The winner is in cracking form but there was no depth to this.

## 6091 32RED CASINO H'CAP — 1m 4f 23y
**5:25** (5:26) (Class 5) (0-70,73) 3-Y-O+ **£2,587** (£770; £384; £192) **Stalls** Low

Form RPR

5531 **1** **Cinnilla**[7] 5878 3-9-6 73 6ex.............. PatDobbs 2 93
(Ralph Beckett) *hld up in tch: smooth hdwy 3f out: led over 2f out: styd on wl* **7/4**[1]

-221 **2** *3½* **Real Jazz (IRE)**[6] 5917 3-8-5 61.............. RosieJessop(3) 8 76
(Sir Mark Prescott Bt) *chsd ldrs: rdn over 2f out: wnt 2nd over 1f out: hung lft and one pce after* **7/4**[1]

0611 **3** *6* **Shades Of Silver**[17] 5529 4-9-2 60.............. WilliamTwiston-Davies 5 65
(Michael Scudamore) *chsd ldrs: rdn in 2nd over 2f out tl over 1f out: one pce* **10/1**[3]

5053 **4** *8* **Do Wah Diddy Diddy**[13] 5689 3-9-3 70.............. AdamKirby 9 62
(Clive Cox) *in rr and chsd along at times: rdn 4f out and no imp on ldrs: styd on u.p fnl 2f: wnt modest 4th post* **6/1**[2]

3104 **5** *shd* **Loving Your Work**[43] 4591 3-9-1 68.............. LiamKeniry 7 60
(George Baker) *hld up towards rr: sme hdwy 3f out: nt run on u.p fnl 2f: ct for modest 4th post* **16/1**

3323 **6** *4½* **Interconnection**[17] 5534 3-9-0 67..............(b) FergusSweeney 6 52
(Ed Vaughan) *chsd along leaving stalls: sn w ldr: led 4f out: rdn and hdd over 2f out: wknd over 1f out* **14/1**

0-20 **7** *30* **Laura Secord (CAN)**[112] 2305 4-9-7 70.............. NoelGarbutt(5) 10 7
(Heather Main) *towards rr: rdn over 4f out: wknd over 3f out: t.o* **33/1**

1000 **8** *20* **April Ciel**[3] 6007 5-9-8 66..............(p) OisinMurphy 3
(Ronald Harris) *led tl rdn and hdd 4f out: wknd qckly: t.o* **25/1**

2m 36.71s (-2.29) **Going Correction** -0.05s/f (Good)
**WFA** 3 from 4yo+ 9lb 8 Ran SP% **115.4**
Speed ratings (Par 103): **105,102,98,93,93 90,70,56**
CSF £4.64 CT £21.08 TOTE £2.90: £1.30, £1.20, £3.20; EX 5.00 Trifecta £19.80.
**Owner** J L Rowsell **Bred** Ashbrittle Stud **Trained** Kimpton, Hants

**FOCUS**
With the first two home both well-in compared to their revised marks and the third bidding for a hat-trick, this was an above-average contest of its type. It was run at a fair pace too, with April Ciel and Interconnection soon taking each other on up front.
T/Plt: £93.00 to a £1 stake. Pool: £63,910.46 - 501.27 winning tickets T/Qpdt: £18.50 to a £1 stake. Pool: £5,102.36 - 203.86 winning tickets RL

# 6056 HAYDOCK (L-H)
### Friday, September 5

**OFFICIAL GOING: Good (7.8)**
Wind: Light across Weather: Cloudy Rails: All races on inside home straight and distances on Round course reduced by about 8yds

## 6092 BETFRED J W LEES MAIDEN STKS — 1m 3f 200y
**2:00** (2:01) (Class 5) 3-Y-O+ **£3,234** (£962; £481; £240) **Stalls** Centre

Form RPR

0332 **1** **Saarrem (USA)**[28] 5135 3-9-5 79..............(b[1]) PaulHanagan 5 84
(John Gosden) *set stdy pce: qcknd over 4f out: pushed along and qcknd again over 2f out: rdn clr wl over 1f out: styd on* **7/1**[2]

**2** *2¼* **Karezak (IRE)**[70] 3688 3-9-5 0.............. RichardHughes 10 82
(Alan King) *towards rr: stdy hdwy on outer to trck ldrs after 5f: cl up over 4f out: chsd wnr 3f out: effrt 2f out: sn rdn and edgd lft: drvn and edgd lft again ins fnl f: no imp* **11/10**[1]

5-66 **3** *2¼* **Lovelocks (IRE)**[121] 2077 3-9-0 71.............. WilliamBuick 14 72
(Charles Hills) *trckd ldrs: hdwy 4f out: rdn along to chse ldng pair over 2f out: drvn appr fnl f and sn no imp* **12/1**

0 **4** *1¾* **Panatella**[21] 5382 3-9-0 0.............. RobertHavlin 3 69
(James Fanshawe) *midfield: hdwy 4f out: rdn along over 2f out: chsd ldrs over 1f out: kpt on one pce* **50/1**

3-46 **5** *1* **Skilled**[48] 4435 3-9-5 75.............. JamesDoyle 8 72
(Roger Charlton) *midfield: hdwy on outer 5f out: pushed along 3f out: rdn to chse ldrs 2f out: kpt on same pce appr fnl f* **10/1**[3]

4 **6** *1* **Two Jabs**[15] 5606 4-10-0 0.............. GrahamGibbons 2 71
(Mark Brisbourne) *hld up in midfield: pushed along and sltly outpcd 3f out: kpt on appr fnl f: nrst fin* **25/1**

32 **7** *1* **Will**[18] 5490 3-9-5 0.............. LukeMorris 13 69
(Nick Littmoden) *cl up: pushed along over 3f out: rdn over 2f out: sn drvn and wknd over 1f out* **25/1**

4- **8** *¾* **Trendsetter (IRE)**[355] 6430 3-9-5 0.............. TomQueally 9 68
(John Butler) *hld up in rr: hdwy 4f out: swtchd lft to inner wl over 2f out: n.m.r and swtchd rt to outer wl over 1f out: sn rdn and kpt on fnl f: nrst fin* **100/1**

6 **9** *2¾* **Taweyla (IRE)**[21] 5382 3-9-0 0.............. FrederikTylicki 6 59
(Roger Varian) *t.k.h: trckd ldrs on inner: hdwy to chse ldng pair 1/2-way: rdn along 3f out: wknd 2f out and hld whn n.m.r over 1f out* **14/1**

0-32 **10** *nk* **Magic Music Man**[21] 5374 3-9-5 75.............. DanielTudhope 7 63
(K R Burke) *in tch: hdwy to chse ldrs over 3f out: rdn along wl over 2f out: sn btn* **7/1**[2]

**11** *¾* **The New Pharaoh (IRE)** 3-9-5 0.............. GeorgeBaker 1 62
(Chris Wall) *hld up: a towards rr* **12/1**

-6 **12** *1¼* **Georgian Firebird**[21] 5374 4-9-9 0.............. DavidAllan 4 55
(Alan Swinbank) *a in rr* **80/1**

-0 **13** *½* **Rock On Bollinski**[21] 5374 4-10-0 0.............. BrianHughes 11 59
(Tim Fitzgerald) *s.i.s: a in rr* **100/1**

0 **14** *54* **Lady Sorento**[31] 5010 3-9-0 0.............. AndrewMullen 12
(Tim Pitt) *midfield: pushed along 1/2-way: rdn along over 4f out: sn lost pl and bhd* **125/1**

2m 31.31s (-2.49) **Going Correction** -0.30s/f (Firm)
**WFA** 3 from 4yo 9lb 14 Ran SP% **117.4**
Speed ratings (Par 103): **96,94,93,91,91 90,89,89,87,87 86,85,85,49**
CSF £14.16 TOTE £5.60: £2.20, £1.10, £3.80; EX 16.50 Trifecta £195.10.
**Owner** Hamdan Al Maktoum **Bred** Stonestreet Throughbred Holdings Llc **Trained** Newmarket, Suffolk

**FOCUS**
This was a typically modest older maiden for the time of year, featuring mainly late-maturing performers. It was run at an uneven pace and suited those racing handy. A minor bset from the winner, with the second 10lb off his best Irish form.

## 6093 BETFRED THWAITES EBF MAIDEN FILLIES' STKS (BOBIS RACE) 6f
2:30 (2:32) (Class 5) 2-Y-O £2,911 (£866; £432; £216) Stalls High

Form RPR
2 **1** **Mistrusting (IRE)**[42] 4604 2-9-0 0 RichardHughes 11 80+
(Charlie Appleby) *trckd ldrs: smooth hdwy to ld wl over 1f out: pushed out* 1/3[1]
4 **2** ¾ **Tropicana Bay**[23] 5305 2-9-0 0 FrederikTylicki 9 77+
(Roger Varian) *t.k.h: hld up in tch: hdwy wl over 1f out: rdn to chse wnr ins fnl f: kpt on* 10/1[3]
5 **3** ¾ **Mallymkun**[22] 5332 2-9-0 0 DanielTudhope 5 74
(K R Burke) *in tch: hdwy over 2f out: n.m.r and swtchd lft ent fnl f: sn rdn and kpt on* 20/1
**4** *hd* **Goodnightsuzy (IRE)** 2-9-0 0 RichardKingscote 7 74
(Ed Walker) *cl up: rdn and ev ch 2f out tl drvn and kpt on same pce ins fnl f* 33/1
**5** 2 ¼ **The Fairy (IRE)** 2-9-0 0 WilliamBuick 6 67+
(John Gosden) *hld up in rr: hdwy over 2f out: rdn ent fnl f: kpt on wl: nrst fin* 8/1[2]
0 **6** *nk* **Kizingo (IRE)**[32] 4980 2-9-0 0 JamesDoyle 4 66
(Charles Hills) *cl up: rdn along 2f out: drvn over 1f out: wknd fnl f* 14/1
0 **7** *nk* **Jellwa (IRE)**[48] 4444 2-8-11 0 CharlesBishop[(3)] 1 65
(Mick Channon) *trckd ldrs: hdwy on outer over 2f out: cl up and rdn over 1f out: drvn and wknd ins fnl f* 28/1
**8** *hd* **Rose Abella** 2-9-0 0 RobertHavlin 8 65+
(Andrew Hollinshead) *dwlt and in rr: hdwy over 2f out: rdn over 1f out: kpt on fnl f: nrst fin* 50/1
44 **9** 2 ¾ **Brindle**[22] 5332 2-9-0 0 PaulHanagan 2 56
(Richard Fahey) *slt ld: rdn along over 2f out: hdd wl over 1f out: sn wknd* 14/1
00 **10** 7 **Lydiate Lady**[10] 5789 2-9-0 0 JamesSullivan 12 35
(Paul Green) *a towards rr* 100/1
0 **11** 3 ½ **Italian Beauty (IRE)**[26] 5210 2-9-0 0 LukeMorris 3 25
(Timothy Jarvis) *chsd ldrs: rdn along 1/2-way: sn wknd* 66/1
**12** 2 ¾ **Mrs Eve (IRE)** 2-9-0 0 FrannyNorton 14 17
(Alan Bailey) *a towards rr: outpcd and bhd fnl 2f* 33/1
**13** 14 **Signorina Roseina** 2-9-0 0 JasonHart 10
(Eric Alston) *t.k.h: chsd ldrs: rdn along and lost pl bef 1/2-way: sn bhd* 66/1

1m 14.65s (0.85) **Going Correction** +0.15s/f (Good) **13** Ran SP% **128.6**
Speed ratings (Par 92): **100,99,98,97,94 94,93,93,90,80 76,72,53**
CSF £4.94 TOTE £1.50: £1.10, £2.80, £4.30; EX 6.40 Trifecta £53.10.
**Owner** Godolphin **Bred** Rabbah Bloodstock Limited **Trained** Newmarket, Suffolk
**FOCUS**
A fair 2yo fillies' maiden with some nice types on show. A race that should produce winners.

## 6094 BETFRED BOLTON LADS & GIRLS CLUB H'CAP (DIV I) 6f
3:00 (3:02) (Class 4) (0-85,85) 3-Y-O+ £5,175 (£1,540; £769; £384) Stalls High

Form RPR
5443 **1** **Cruise Tothelimit (IRE)**[7] 5888 6-8-13 77 PaulHanagan 8 86
(Ian Williams) *led: rdn along and hdd ent fnl f: drvn and rallied wl last 100yds to ld nr fin* 7/2[1]
6400 **2** *nk* **Bahamian Heights**[13] 5675 3-9-5 85 (b) JamesDoyle 7 93+
(Clive Brittain) *hld up in tch: hdwy over 2f out: led ent fnl f: one l advantage whn rdn: edgd lft and fnd little last 100yds: hdd nr fin* 16/1
0060 **3** ¾ **Tamayuz Star (IRE)**[41] 4650 4-9-6 84 TomQueally 1 90
(George Margarson) *trckd ldrs: hdwy 2f out: rdn over 1f out: drvn and kpt on fnl f* 9/1
0320 **4** 1 **Powerful Presence (IRE)**[28] 5143 8-9-4 82 DanielTudhope 5 84
(David O'Meara) *trckd ldrs: hdwy 2f out: sn rdn: kpt on fnl f: nrst fin* 7/1[3]
5003 **5** *nk* **Rasaman (IRE)**[14] 5632 10-9-3 81 (p) FergalLynch 6 82
(Jim Goldie) *hld up in rr: hdwy whn n.m.r and swtchd lft over 1f out: sn rdn and kpt on fnl f: nrst fin* 16/1
002 **6** *nk* **Baby Strange**[20] 5437 10-9-2 80 RobertWinston 4 81
(Derek Shaw) *dwlt and in rr: hdwy 2f out: sn rdn and kpt on fnl f: nrst fin* 8/1
0000 **7** 7 **Can You Conga**[7] 5888 4-9-5 83 (p) GrahamGibbons 2 61
(Michael Easterby) *prom: hdwy and cl up over 2f out: rdn wl over 1f out: sn wknd* 5/1[2]
0005 **8** 1 **Bachotheque (IRE)**[20] 5411 4-8-8 72 (p) DavidAllan 9 47
(Tim Easterby) *cl up: rdn along 1/2-way: sn drvn and wknd over 2f out* 10/1
3162 **9** ¾ **Kommander Kirkup**[11] 5769 3-8-11 77 (p) RichardHughes 3 50
(Michael Dods) *hld up in rr: sme hdwy on outer wl over 1f out: sn rdn and btn* 7/2[1]

1m 14.16s (0.36) **Going Correction** +0.15s/f (Good)
**WFA** 3 from 4yo+ 2lb **9** Ran SP% **115.6**
Speed ratings (Par 105): **103,102,101,100,99 99,90,88,87**
CSF £61.87 CT £468.96 TOTE £3.00: £1.10, £5.20, £3.20; EX 72.30 Trifecta £395.20.
**Owner** Odysian Ltd T/A Cruise Nightspot **Bred** D And Mrs D Veitch **Trained** Portway, Worcs
**FOCUS**
Not a bad sprint handicap in which the middle of the track was the place to be. A similar time yo division II.

## 6095 BETFRED CLIFTON H'CAP (DIV II) 6f
3:35 (3:35) (Class 4) (0-85,84) 3-Y-O+ £5,175 (£1,540; £769; £384) Stalls High

Form RPR
4011 **1** **Triple Chocolate**[14] 5650 4-9-3 80 JimmyQuinn 1 91
(Roger Ingram) *trckd ldrs: hdwy 2f out: rdn to chal ent fnl f: drvn to ld last 75yds: kpt on wl* 6/1[3]
3311 **2** ¾ **Poyle Vinnie**[19] 5470 4-9-6 83 AndrewMullen 2 92
(Michael Appleby) *trckd ldng pair: hdwy and cl up over 2f out: rdn to ld wl over 1f out: jnd and drvn ins fnl f: hdd and no ex last 75yds* 9/2[2]
2122 **3** ¾ **Mishaal (IRE)**[27] 5197 4-9-4 81 DanielTudhope 3 88
(Michael Herrington) *led: rdn along over 2f out: hdd wl over 1f out: drvn and kpt on same pce fnl f* 7/2[1]
62-0 **4** 1 ½ **Ambitious Boy**[29] 5081 5-8-13 76 TomQueally 4 78
(Andrew Hollinshead) *in tch: hdwy on outer over 2f out: rdn to chse ldrs over 1f out: drvn and kpt on same pce fnl f* 8/1
4102 **5** 1 **Free Rein**[11] 5776 3-8-10 75 RichardHughes 9 74
(Ralph Beckett) *trckd ldrs: hdwy over 2f out: rdn along wl over 1f out: drvn appr fnl f and sn no imp* 9/2[2]
4330 **6** 1 ¼ **Misplaced Fortune**[15] 5612 9-9-2 84 (v) ShelleyBirkett[(5)] 7 79
(Nigel Tinkler) *hld up towards rr: hdwy 2f out: sn rdn and n.d* 9/1
2131 **7** 4 ½ **Cape Of Hope (IRE)**[26] 5202 4-8-8 71 (v) RichardKingscote 5 51
(Tom Dascombe) *chsd ldr: rdn along wl over 2f out: sn wknd* 7/1
000- **8** 2 ¼ **Chester Aristocrat**[324] 7314 5-9-4 81 JasonHart 8 54
(Eric Alston) *hld up: a in rr* 25/1
U-00 **9** 6 **Hoofalong**[111] 2350 4-9-6 83 JamesSullivan 6 37
(Michael Easterby) *blind removed sltly late: awkward and dwlt s: a in rr: outpcd and bhd fnl 2f* 28/1

1m 14.02s (0.22) **Going Correction** +0.15s/f (Good)
**WFA** 3 from 4yo+ 2lb **9** Ran SP% **113.8**
Speed ratings (Par 105): **104,103,102,100,98 97,91,88,80**
CSF £32.61 CT £103.17 TOTE £6.80: £2.30, £1.70, £1.30; EX 25.80 Trifecta £124.40.
**Owner** Fahed Al Dabbous **Bred** Lael Stables **Trained** Epsom, Surrey
■ Stewards' Enquiry : Jimmy Quinn two-day ban; used whip above permitted level (19th-20th Sept)
**FOCUS**
Although few landed a serious blow in this second division of the 6f handicap, the finish was fought out by progressive sprinters and the form is decent. The time was similar to division I.

## 6096 BETFRED JOBWISE H'CAP 5f
4:10 (4:11) (Class 4) (0-85,84) 3-Y-O+ £5,175 (£1,540; £769; £384) Stalls High

Form RPR
0003 **1** **Apricot Sky**[22] 5350 4-9-3 80 WilliamBuick 10 92
(Henry Candy) *in tch: hdwy to trck ldrs 2f out: rdn to chal ent fnl f: sn led: drvn and kpt on wl* 11/2[2]
5112 **2** ¾ **Master Bond**[16] 5563 5-9-6 83 DanielTudhope 3 92
(David O'Meara) *hld up: hdwy 2f out: rdn to chse ldrs over 1f out: ev ch ins fnl f: drvn and no ex towards fin* 5/1[1]
3-0 **3** ¾ **Smart Daisy K**[20] 5419 4-9-7 84 TomQueally 11 90
(Andrew Hollinshead) *a.p: rdn to ld briefly over 1f out: drvn and hdd ins fnl f: kpt on* 9/1
3321 **4** ¾ **Newton's Law (IRE)**[18] 5501 3-9-0 78 (t) RichardHughes 1 82
(Brian Meehan) *hld up in rr: hdwy wl over 1f out: rdn and styd on wl fnl f: nrst fin* 11/2[2]
42 **5** ½ **Angelito**[13] 5677 5-9-1 78 SeanLevey 14 80
(Ed McMahon) *swtchd lft s and hld up towards rr: hdwy wl over 1f out: sn rdn: kpt on fnl f: nrst fin* 9/1
0-30 **6** ¾ **Lexington Place**[83] 3239 4-9-5 82 JamesSullivan 12 81
(Ruth Carr) *midfield: hdwy over 2f out: sn rdn: kpt on fnl f: nrst fin* 28/1
5024 **7** 1 **Sleepy Blue Ocean**[17] 5535 8-8-11 74 (p) RobertWinston 6 70
(John Balding) *trckd ldrs: hdwy wl over 1f out: rdn and ch ent fnl f: sn drvn and one pce* 20/1
3112 **8** 1 **Come On Dave (IRE)**[11] 5754 5-9-1 83 DanielMuscutt[(5)] 2 75
(John Butler) *sn chsng ldrs: cl up 1/2-way: rdn along wl over 1f out: grad wknd* 15/2[3]
0205 **9** ¾ **Red Baron (IRE)**[44] 4531 5-9-4 84 NeilFarley[(3)] 8 73
(Eric Alston) *led: rdn along wl over 1f out: drvn and hdd jst over 1f out: wknd* 25/1
6162 **10** *hd* **Cheworee**[38] 4762 5-9-7 84 (tp) RichardKingscote 4 72
(Tom Dascombe) *chsd ldrs: effrt and cl up 2f out: sn rdn and wknd appr fnl f* 9/1
0100 **11** ¾ **Captain Dunne (IRE)**[18] 5498 9-9-1 78 DavidAllan 15 64
(Tim Easterby) *racd alone nr stands' rail: in tch: rdn along 2f out: grad wknd* 25/1
2031 **12** ½ **First In Command (IRE)**[24] 5275 9-9-0 77 (t) FrankieMcDonald 17 61
(Daniel Mark Loughnane) *swtchd lft s: a towards rr* 25/1
6010 **13** ¾ **Space Artist (IRE)**[16] 5563 4-9-4 81 PaulHanagan 9 62
(Bryan Smart) *a towards rr* 22/1
3206 **14** *nk* **Monumental Man**[13] 5677 5-9-3 80 (p) LukeMorris 13 60
(James Unett) *a towards rr* 20/1
1255 **15** 2 ¾ **Tyfos**[18] 5498 9-9-1 78 JasonHart 5 48
(Brian Baugh) *chsd ldrs: rdn along 2f out: sn wknd* 33/1
3115 **16** 2 ¼ **Mister Manannan (IRE)**[30] 5053 7-9-5 82 AdrianNicholls 7 44
(David Nicholls) *dwlt: a in rr* 20/1

1m 0.79s (-0.01) **Going Correction** +0.15s/f (Good)
**WFA** 3 from 4yo+ 1lb **16** Ran SP% **125.8**
Speed ratings (Par 105): **106,104,103,102,101 100,98,97,96,95 94,93,92,92,87 84**
CSF £28.66 CT £264.28 TOTE £8.50: £1.80, £2.00, £2.70, £1.60; EX 35.60 Trifecta £218.80.
**Owner** Simon Broke & Partners III **Bred** Mrs James Bethell **Trained** Kingston Warren, Oxon
**FOCUS**
There was no more than a fair pace on in this competitive sprint handicap and the main action was on the far side late on. The winner was back to his reappearance form.

## 6097 BETFRED G-CASINO H'CAP 7f
4:45 (4:46) (Class 3) (0-90,90) 3-Y-O+ £8,086 (£2,406; £1,202; £601) Stalls Low

Form RPR
0141 **1** **Pearl Nation (USA)**[29] 5100 5-9-3 85 AndrewMullen 3 95
(Michael Appleby) *midfield: hdwy and in tch 3f out: nt clr run jst over 2f out: swtchd rt and effrt wl over 1f out: sn rdn: drvn and styd on wl fnl f to ld on line* 13/2[3]
6000 **2** *nse* **Deauville Prince (FR)**[33] 4938 4-9-7 89 RichardKingscote 2 99
(Tom Dascombe) *led: stdd pce after 2f: pushed along and qcknd wl over 2f out: rdn wl over 1f out: drvn ins fnl f: hdd on line* 9/2[2]
1602 **3** ¾ **Yourartisonfire**[27] 5178 4-9-1 86 (v) JoeyHaynes[(3)] 7 94
(K R Burke) *towards rr and sn pushed along: hdwy on wd outside over 2f out: rdn to chse ldrs wl over 1f out: drvn and kpt on fnl f* 7/2[1]
55-4 **4** ½ **Democretes**[89] 3036 5-9-8 90 RichardHughes 4 97+
(Seamus Durack) *trckd ldrs on inner: effrt over 2f out whn nt clr run: swtchd markedly rt to outer ins fnl f: rdn and styd on strly towards fin* 8/1
-026 **5** ½ **Secret Look**[32] 4976 4-9-7 89 GrahamGibbons 6 94
(Ed McMahon) *in tch: hdwy to trck ldrs 1/2-way: effrt over 2f out: rdn to chse ldrs over 1f out: hld whn n.m.r wl ins fnl f* 14/1
0130 **6** 2 **Escape To Glory (USA)**[21] 5385 6-9-2 84 PaulHanagan 11 84
(Michael Dods) *chsd ldrs: pushed along 3f out: rdn over 2f out and grad wknd* 16/1
0060 **7** 1 ¾ **Common Touch (IRE)**[13] 5665 6-9-6 88 (b) RobertWinston 5 84
(Willie Musson) *midfield: gd hdwy 1/2-way: effrt on outer over 2f out and sn chal: rdn wl over 1f out: ev ch tl drvn and wknd appr fnl f* 20/1
3000 **8** 1 **Trail Blaze (IRE)**[27] 5174 5-9-4 86 FergalLynch 1 79
(Kevin Ryan) *chsd ldng pair on inner: rdn along over 2f out: wknd wl over 1f out* 9/1
3040 **9** ½ **Marcret (ITY)**[55] 4212 7-9-8 90 JamesSullivan 12 82
(Ruth Carr) *in tch: hdwy over 3f out and sn cl up: rdn to chal over 2f out: drvn and wknd over 1f out* 12/1

0066 **10** *3* **Smarty Socks (IRE)**[50] 4347 10-9-5 87 DanielTudhope 10 71
(David O'Meara) *hld up in rr: sme hdwy on outer over 2f out: sn rdn and wknd over 1f out* **14/1**

-020 **11** *½* **Jammy Guest (IRE)**[13] 5665 4-9-6 88 TomQueally 8 71
(George Margarson) *dwlt: a in rr* **14/1**

00 **12** *nse* **Tellovoi (IRE)**[40] 4712 6-9-4 86 (p) SeanLevey 9 69
(Ann Stokell) *chsd ldr: rdn along 3f out: drvn over 2f out and sn wknd* **25/1**

1m 27.37s (-3.33) **Going Correction** -0.30s/f (Firm) **12** Ran SP% **117.0**
Speed ratings (Par 107): **107,106,106,105,104 102,100,99,98,95 94,94**
CSF £35.30 CT £121.82 TOTE £5.10: £1.80, £2.10, £2.10; EX 37.70 Trifecta £153.40.
**Owner** Iddon, M&C Dixon, Taylor, Finn, O'Brien **Bred** William A Carl Estate **Trained** Danethorpe, Notts

**FOCUS**
They went hard up front in this fair and competitive handicap. Sound form, with a turf best from the winner.

## 6098 BETFRED BRUNTWOOD H'CAP 1m 2f 95y
5:20 (5:20) (Class 3) (0-95,95) 3-Y-O+ £8,086 (£2,406; £1,202; £300; £300) Stalls Centre

Form RPR

51 **1** **Mistiroc**[14] 5634 3-8-7 83 ow1 FergalLynch 1 93+
(Jim Goldie) *hld up towards rr: hdwy wl over 2f out: chsd ldrs over 1f out: rdn ent fnl f: sn n.m.r: swtchd rt and drvn last 50yds: kpt on wl to ld on line* **20/1**

0435 **2** *nse* **Enobled**[27] 5188 4-9-0 83 RichardKingscote 14 93
(Sir Michael Stoute) *trckd ldng pair: hdwy 3f out: led wl over 1f out and sn rdn: drvn ins fnl f: hdd on line* **8/1**[2]

6032 **3** *2* **Madeed**[12] 5720 3-9-3 93 (t) PaulHanagan 13 99
(Brian Meehan) *trckd ldrs: hdwy over 3f out: rdn to chse ldr wl over 1f out: drvn ins fnl f: kpt on same pce towards fin* **5/4**[1]

12-0 **4** *¾* **Docs Legacy (IRE)**[27] 5174 5-8-12 81 LukeMorris 3 86
(Richard Fahey) *hld up towards rr: hdwy over 2f out: rdn wl over 1f out: chsd ldrs ent fnl f: sn drvn and kpt on same pce* **25/1**

6066 **4** *dht* **Flemish School**[48] 4443 4-9-2 88 (p) JoeyHaynes(3) 11 93+
(David Elsworth) *hld up towards rr: hdwy over 2f out: rdn along on outer and chsd ldrs over 1f out: drvn and kpt on fnl f: nrst fin* **16/1**

0510 **6** *¾* **Dance King**[14] 5633 4-8-13 82 DavidAllan 4 85
(Tim Easterby) *hld up in rr: hdwy wl over 2f out: rdn to chse ldrs over 1f out: styng on wl whn nt clr run ins fnl f and no imp after* **16/1**

65-0 **7** *2 ½* **Cruck Realta**[13] 5669 4-9-2 88 CharlesBishop(3) 5 87
(Mick Channon) *sltly hmpd s: hld up towards rr: hdwy over 2f out: sn rdn along and no imp* **20/1**

54 **8** *1 ½* **Stepping Ahead (FR)**[20] 5440 4-9-12 95 DanielTudhope 6 91
(K R Burke) *sltly hmpd s: in tch: hdwy on outer 4f out: rdn along wl over 2f out: sn no imp* **10/1**[3]

0431 **9** *1* **Croquembouche (IRE)**[29] 5095 5-8-10 82 DeclanBates(3) 12 76
(Ed de Giles) *cl up: led wl over 2f out: sn rdn and hdd wl over 1f out: grad wknd* **12/1**

5653 **10** *hd* **Automated**[29] 5094 3-8-10 86 (p) FrannyNorton 9 79
(Clive Brittain) *led: rdn along 3f out: sn hdd & wknd* **14/1**

4240 **11** *2 ¾* **Memory Cloth**[14] 5633 7-8-12 81 oh1 RobertWinston 15 69
(Brian Ellison) *hld up towards rr: hdwy over 2f out: rdn to chse ldrs wl over 1f out: sn drvn and btn* **18/1**

0000 **12** *nk* **Beaumont's Party (IRE)**[14] 5633 7-9-1 84 (p) JasonHart 10 72
(Brian Ellison) *chsd ldrs on inner: rdn along wl 3f out: sn wknd* **33/1**

6563 **13** *4* **San Cassiano (IRE)**[10] 5792 7-9-5 88 JamesSullivan 2 68
(Ruth Carr) *midfield: rdn along 4f out: sn wknd* **33/1**

-063 **14** *8* **Silvery Moon (IRE)**[102] 2618 7-9-6 89 GrahamGibbons 8 54
(Tim Easterby) *wnt lft s: chsd ldrs: rdn along over 3f out: sn wknd* **16/1**

2m 10.27s (-5.23) **Going Correction** -0.30s/f (Firm)
**WFA** 3 from 4yo+ 7lb **14** Ran SP% **121.2**
Speed ratings (Par 107): **108,107,106,105,105 105,103,101,101,101 98,98,95,88**
CSF £164.24 CT £352.97 TOTE £31.00: £7.20, £2.90, £1.20; EX 358.20 Trifecta £2644.30 Part won..
**Owner** Drew & Ailsa Russell **Bred** Jethro Bloodstock **Trained** Uplawmoor, E Renfrews
■ Stewards' Enquiry : Fergal Lynch two-day ban; used whip above permitted level (19th-20th Sept)

**FOCUS**
There was no hanging about in this good-quality handicap and the second and third set the level.

## 6099 BETFRED JOSEPH HOLTS H'CAP 1m 6f
5:55 (5:55) (Class 4) (0-80,79) 3-Y-O+ £5,175 (£1,540; £769; £384) Stalls Low

Form RPR

0002 **1** **William Of Orange**[22] 5339 3-9-0 76 LukeMorris 4 89+
(Sir Mark Prescott Bt) *trckd ldrs: pushed along 6f out: rdn along and hdwy 3f out: led 2f out: drvn clr ent fnl f and kpt on strly* **8/1**

5224 **2** *2 ½* **Cosette (IRE)**[22] 5353 3-9-1 77 RichardKingscote 3 86
(Henry Candy) *trckd ldng pair on inner: hdwy 3f out: rdn to chse wnr ent fnl f: sn drvn and no imp towards fin* **3/1**[1]

2501 **3** *2 ¼* **Bayan Kasirga (IRE)**[20] 5414 4-9-6 71 PaulHanagan 10 77
(Richard Fahey) *hld up: hdwy 3f out: rdn along to chse ldrs wl over 1f out: drvn and kpt on same pce fnl f* **9/2**[3]

3524 **4** *1 ¾* **Deepsand (IRE)**[31] 5017 5-9-11 76 (p) DavidAllan 5 79
(Tim Easterby) *hld up in rr: hdwy 3f out: rdn wl over 1f out: kpt on fnl f: nrst fin* **8/1**

-302 **5** *nk* **Highway Code (USA)**[28] 5127 8-9-0 72 (t) MikeyEnnis(7) 2 75
(Richard Lee) *trckd ldrs: smooth hdwy 3f out: effrt wl over 1f out: rdn ent fnl f and sn one pce* **12/1**

51-0 **6** *nk* **Bradbury (IRE)**[43] 4575 6-9-4 69 JasonHart 9 72
(Eric Alston) *cl up: rdn to ld 3f out: drvn and hdd 2f out: grad wknd* **33/1**

-630 **7** *½* **Perennial**[31] 5017 5-10-0 79 DanielTudhope 12 81
(Philip Kirby) *hld up in rr: effrt and sme hdwy 4f out: rdn along 3f out: sn btn* **9/1**

-421 **8** *19* **Thorntoun Care**[39] 4726 3-8-13 75 FergalLynch 6 50
(Jim Goldie) *slt ld: rdn along over 3f out: sn hdd & wknd* **4/1**[2]

2302 **9** *1 ¼* **Lineman**[10] 5800 4-9-4 69 (v[1]) TomQueally 11 43
(Andrew Hollinshead) *in tch: pushed along and lost pl 6f out: rdn and hdwy to chse ldrs 3f out: sn drvn and wknd* **11/1**

2m 59.96s (-2.04) **Going Correction** -0.30s/f (Firm)
**WFA** 3 from 4yo+ 11lb **9** Ran SP% **114.4**
Speed ratings (Par 105): **93,91,90,89,89 88,88,77,77**
CSF £31.93 CT £122.28 TOTE £6.10: £2.00, £1.20, £2.40; EX 29.50 Trifecta £104.70.
**Owner** Nicholas Jones **Bred** Coln Valley Stud **Trained** Newmarket, Suffolk

**FOCUS**
A competitive staying handicap for the class. There was a fair enough pace on and the form is sound.

T/Jkpt: Part won. £27,043.00 to a £1 stake. T/Plt: £9.70 to a £1 stake. Pool: £99,074.47 - 7,445.53 winning tickets T/Qpdt: £8.10 to a £1 stake. Pool: £6,163.23 - 557.70 winning tickets JR

# 6031 KEMPTON (A.W) (R-H)
Friday, September 5

**OFFICIAL GOING: Polytrack: standard**
Wind: virtually nil Weather: dry

## 6100 JOCKEY CLUB CATERING APPRENTICE H'CAP 1m (P)
5:50 (5:50) (Class 4) (0-85,84) 3-Y-O+ £4,690 (£1,395; £697; £348) Stalls Low

Form RPR

0540 **1** **Spiritual Star (IRE)**[22] 5346 5-9-9 83 (t) RobertTart 10 92
(Anthony Carson) *stdd s and hld up in rr: clsd over 2f out: drvn to chse ldrs over 1f out: styd on u.p to ld fnl 100yds: gng away at fin: rdn out* **9/4**[1]

1-21 **2** *1 ½* **Stormbound (IRE)**[72] 3562 5-8-11 71 AshleyMorgan 5 77
(Paul Cole) *chsd ldr tl led over 2f out: drvn and hrd pressed over 1f out: hdd ins fnl f: kpt on same pce fnl 100yds* **5/1**[3]

6003 **3** *nk* **Whipper Snapper (IRE)**[26] 5213 4-8-12 79 CallumShepherd(7) 8 84
(William Knight) *stdd s: hld up in last pair: hdwy into midfield 5f out: rdn and hdwy to chal over 1f out: no ex and one pce fnl 100yds* **7/1**

4243 **4** *hd* **Nassau Storm**[13] 5686 5-9-7 84 JackDuern(3) 3 89
(William Knight) *chsd ldrs: sltly outpcd 1/2-way: rallied u.p to chal over 1f out: led ins fnl f: hdd and no ex fnl 100yds: lost 2 pls nr fin* **7/1**

014 **5** *4 ½* **Hannington**[10] 5795 3-8-4 74 RobHornby(5) 7 68
(Andrew Balding) *stdd s: hld up towards rr: clsd over 2f out: drvn and no ex over 1f out: wknd fnl f* **9/2**[2]

0300 **6** *7* **Tatting**[11] 5758 5-9-2 79 MarcMonaghan(3) 6 57
(Chris Dwyer) *midfield: rdn over 3f out: drvn and btn 2f out: sn wknd* **25/1**

10-3 **7** *28* **Wandsworth (IRE)**[83] 3212 4-9-4 78 RossAtkinson 1
(Roger Varian) *led and set stdy gallop: qcknd 4f out: rdn and hdd over 2f out: sn dropped out: t.o fnl f* **5/1**[3]

1m 38.19s (-1.61) **Going Correction** -0.05s/f (Stan)
**WFA** 3 from 4yo+ 5lb **7** Ran SP% **111.1**
Speed ratings (Par 105): **106,104,104,104,99 92,64**
CSF £12.88 CT £63.15 TOTE £4.10: £2.90, £3.80; EX 17.60 Trifecta £89.90.
**Owner** Hugh and Mindi Byrne & Macattack **Bred** John Quigley **Trained** Newmarket, Suffolk
■ Stewards' Enquiry : Jack Duern two-day ban; used whip above shoulder height (19th-20th Sep)

**FOCUS**
This useful handicap for apprentice riders was as competitive as the market suggested. The steady pace suited closers and the form stacks up.

## 6101 IRISH STALLION FARMS EBF MAIDEN STKS (DIV I) 1m (P)
6:20 (6:21) (Class 5) 2-Y-O £2,911 (£866; £432; £216) Stalls Low

Form RPR

4 **1** **Nona Blu**[100] 2666 2-9-5 0 JimCrowley 2 75
(Harry Dunlop) *dwlt: in tch in last pair: rdn and forced to switch lft arnd many rivals 2f out: hdwy over 1f out: str run u.p fnl f: led last strides* **20/1**

6 **2** *nk* **Voice Control (IRE)**[28] 5149 2-9-5 0 ShaneKelly 5 75
(Sir Michael Stoute) *dwlt: pushed along towards rr: hdwy u.p over 1f out: chsd ldrs and swtchd rt ins fnl f: edgd lft and styd on strly fnl 100yds: snatched 2nd last strides* **2/1**[2]

523 **3** *hd* **Ventriloquist**[29] 5093 2-9-5 90 WilliamBuick 9 74
(Charlie Appleby) *t.k.h: chsd ldrs: wnt 2nd after 2f out tl rdn to ld 2f out: hrd pressed and drvn 1f out: edgd lft fnl 100yds: hdd last strides* **5/4**[1]

0 **4** *1* **Forza Blacky**[28] 5149 2-9-2 0 DannyBrock(3) 1 72
(Philip McBride) *dwlt and stdd after s: hld up in tch in rr: effrt on outer over 2f out: hdwy to press ldrs over 1f out: chsd wnr ins fnl f: one pce and lost 2 pls towards fin* **20/1**

**5** *¾* **Ali Bin Nayef** 2-9-5 0 DaneO'Neill 3 70
(Charles Hills) *in tch in midfield: effrt on inner and rdr dropped whip over 1f out: styd on same pce ins fnl f* **16/1**

033 **6** *nk* **Cahill (IRE)**[11] 5745 2-9-5 0 MartinHarley 10 70
(Alan King) *chsd ldrs: rdn 2f out: drvn and pressing ldrs over 1f out: keeping on same pce whn squeezed out and bdly hmpd towards fin* **7/1**[3]

0 **7** *5* **Indomitable Spirit**[30] 5056 2-8-12 0 NatalieHambling-Yates(7) 7 58
(Martin Smith) *chsd ldr for 2f: styd wl in tch in midfield: rdn 2f out: wknd ins fnl f* **100/1**

**8** *¾* **Envisioning (IRE)** 2-9-5 0 JamesDoyle 4 56
(Richard Hannon) *t.k.h: hld up in tch towards rr: effrt on inner over 2f out: no ex over 1f out: wknd ins fnl f* **12/1**

**9** *6* **Alfie The Pug** 2-9-2 0 JemmaMarshall(3) 8 43
(Pat Phelan) *led tl rdn and hdd 2f out: wknd ent fnl f* **100/1**

0 **10** *14* **Destiny's Shadow (IRE)**[22] 5351 2-9-5 0 MartinLane 6 10
(George Baker) *chsd ldrs: drvn 1/2-way: lost pl over 2f out: bhd over 1f out* **66/1**

1m 40.09s (0.29) **Going Correction** -0.05s/f (Stan) **10** Ran SP% **116.8**
Speed ratings (Par 95): **96,95,95,94,93 93,88,87,81,67**
CSF £59.14 TOTE £32.00: £7.00, £1.10, £1.10; EX 88.20 Trifecta £301.80.
**Owner** Mrs Susan Roy **Bred** Yeguada De Milagro Sa **Trained** Lambourn, Berks

**FOCUS**
The pace was modest early for what looked a useful juvenile maiden. Although the first two came from well off the pace and they finished in something of a heap, the form may well hold up. The sixth and seventh limit the ratings.

## 6102 IRISH STALLION FARMS EBF MAIDEN STKS (DIV II) 1m (P)
6:50 (6:50) (Class 5) 2-Y-O £2,911 (£866; £432; £216) Stalls Low

Form RPR

62 **1** **Who'Sthedude (IRE)**[22] 5351 2-9-5 0 SilvestreDeSousa 8 80+
(Ralph Beckett) *led for 1f: chsd ldr after tl led again over 2f out: rdn and qcknd clr over 1f out: kpt on: rdn out* **15/8**[1]

0 **2** *1 ½* **Belgrade**[41] 4666 2-9-5 0 RichardHughes 5 77+
(Richard Hannon) *chsd ldr tl led after 1f and set stdy gallop: hdd over 2f out and outpcd whn wnr qcknd over 1f out: rallied and kpt on again ins fnl f* **3/1**[2]

**3** *3 ¾* **Mustard** 2-9-5 0 ShaneKelly 6 68
(Sir Michael Stoute) *t.k.h: in tch in outer: 3rd and rdn 2f out: outpcd and rn green over 1f out: kpt on same pce fnl f* **9/2**[3]

0 **4** *1 ¾* **Thanksgiving Day (IRE)**[17] 5519 2-9-5 0 JimCrowley 3 64
(Jamie Osborne) *t.k.h: chsd ldrs: 4th and outpcd u.p 2f out: plugged on but no threat to ldrs after* **20/1**

0 **5** *2* **The Twisler**[49] 4395 2-9-5 0 SteveDrowne 1 59
(Charles Hills) *dwlt: in tch towards rr: rdn over 2f out: outpcd ent fnl 2f: n.d after* **9/1**

6 ½ **Londonia** 2-9-5 0 MartinLane 4 58
(Paul Cole) *t.k.h: wl in tch in midfield: rdn over 2f out: sn struggling and outpcd 2f out: n.d after* **25/1**

7 1¾ **London Mayor (IRE)** 2-9-5 0 AndreaAtzeni 7 54
(Roger Varian) *dwlt: in tch towards rr: rdn over 2f out: sn struggling and btn 2f out* **10/1**

0 8 4½ **Directional**[31] 5009 2-9-5 0 WilliamBuick 2 44
(Charlie Appleby) *a in rr: rdn 3f out: sn struggling: bhd fnl 2f* **9/1**

06 9 3 **Avenue Des Champs**[29] 5104 2-9-5 0 (p) FrederikTylicki 9 37
(Jane Chapple-Hyam) *hld up towards rr: sme hdwy on outer 1/2-way: rdn and btn over 2f out: sn wknd* **100/1**

1m 40.57s (0.77) **Going Correction** -0.05s/f (Stan) 9 Ran SP% **116.7**
Speed ratings (Par 95): **94,92,88,87,85 84,82,78,75**
CSF £7.43 TOTE £2.60: £1.10, £1.60, £1.60; EX 9.30 Trifecta £25.10.
**Owner** Robert Ng **Bred** Island Dreams Syndicate **Trained** Kimpton, Hants

**FOCUS**
Very few got into this interesting juvenile maiden, with the first three turning for home, the first three home. They finished well strung out and while the first three look decent, this looked the weaker of the two divisions.

## 6103 IRISH EBF MAIDEN STKS 6f (P)
7:20 (7:20) (Class 5) 2-Y-O £2,911 (£866; £432; £216) Stalls Low

Form RPR

3 1 **Acolyte (IRE)**[21] 5377 2-9-5 0 WilliamBuick 1 77+
(Roger Charlton) *mde all: pressed and rdn ent fnl f: r.o wl under hands and heels: asserted fnl 75yds: readily* **8/13**[1]

2 1¼ **Frognal Bear (IRE)** 2-9-5 0 RichardHughes 6 73+
(Richard Hannon) *t.k.h: chsd wnr for 2f: effrt on inner to chse wnr over 1f out: drvn and pressed wnr 1f out: no ex and outpcd fnl 75yds* **7/2**[2]

3 2 **Al** 2-9-5 0 LemosdeSouza 2 67+
(Luca Cumani) *in tch in midfield: pushed along and effrt 2f: battling for 3rd and kpt on fnl f: wnt 3rd nr fin* **12/1**

64 4 nk **Haarib**[17] 5519 2-9-5 0 HayleyTurner 9 66
(Ed Walker) *chsd ldrs: wnt 2nd 4f out tl over 1f out: styd on same pce u.p fnl f: lost 3rd nr fin* **20/1**

00 5 1 **Andretti**[52] 4301 2-9-5 0 AndreaAtzeni 7 63
(Roger Varian) *in tch in midfield: rdn jst over 2f out: kpt on same pce fr over 1f out* **25/1**

6 ½ **Capsize** 2-9-5 0 JamesDoyle 4 62+
(Sir Michael Stoute) *dwlt: in tch in midfield: rdn over 2f out: edging rt and unable qck over 1f out: one pce fnl f* **7/1**[3]

7 1¼ **Kill Or Cure (IRE)** 2-9-5 0 JimCrowley 8 58
(Charles Hills) *dwlt: in tch in last pair: rdn over 2f out: no imp* **12/1**

6 8 2½ **Tangramm**[32] 4965 2-9-5 0 SebSanders 5 51
(Simon Dow) *awkward leaving stalls: in tch in last pair: rdn 3f out: outpcd and btn 2f out* **25/1**

1m 13.7s (0.60) **Going Correction** -0.05s/f (Stan) 8 Ran SP% **124.5**
Speed ratings (Par 95): **94,92,89,89,87 87,85,82**
CSF £3.40 TOTE £1.50: £1.10, £1.30, £5.40; EX 4.30 Trifecta £23.10.
**Owner** HighclereThoroughbredRacing(Coronation) **Bred** Drumlin Bloodstock **Trained** Beckhampton, Wilts

**FOCUS**
Some fairly decent newcomers on show, but after setting no more than a sensible pace the more experienced favourite got off the mark in good style. It's hard to rate the form any higher.

## 6104 ASHES IS TYING THE KNOT NURSERY H'CAP 6f (P)
7:50 (7:51) (Class 5) (0-75,75) 2-Y-O £2,587 (£770; £384; £192) Stalls Low

Form RPR

320 1 **State Of The Union (IRE)**[13] 5684 2-9-4 72 RichardHughes 12 75+
(Richard Hannon) *mde all: broke fast and crossed to inner rail: t.k.h: stdd gallop 4f out: rdn and qcknd clr 2f out: drvn fnl f: a jst holding on: all out* **6/1**[3]

1061 2 ½ **Gold Waltz**[30] 5043 2-9-1 69 SilvestreDeSousa 4 71
(Ralph Beckett) *hld up in midfield: nt clr run ent fnl 2f: hdwy u.p over 1f out: r.o wl ins fnl f: wnt 2nd nr fin* **9/2**[2]

410 3 nk **Spring Loaded (IRE)**[13] 5672 2-9-5 73 MartinHarley 5 74
(Paul D'Arcy) *wl in tch in midfield: rdn and effrt 2f out: drvn and chsd clr wnr 1f out: kpt on wl: lost 2nd nr fin* **10/3**[1]

520 4 1¼ **British Embassy (IRE)**[50] 4364 2-9-0 68 JohnFahy 11 65
(Eve Johnson Houghton) *dwlt and dropped in bhd: detached in last: hdwy u.p and squeezed between rivals 1f out: styd on strly: nvr trbld ldrs* **12/1**

4202 5 nk **Madamoiselle Bond**[21] 5373 2-8-13 72 CamHardie(5) 9 68
(William Jarvis) *in tch towards rr: rdn and over 2f out: hdwy u.p 1f out: kpt on wl ins fnl f: nvr trbld ldrs* **8/1**

2163 6 1¼ **Brown Velvet**[30] 5028 2-9-3 71 (v) JamesDoyle 10 63
(Hugo Palmer) *chsd ldrs: rdn and unable qck jst over 2f out: plugged on same pce after* **16/1**

240 7 1½ **Shahralasal (IRE)**[49] 4403 2-9-7 75 (p) DaneO'Neill 2 63
(Roger Varian) *pushed along towards rr: styd on ins fnl f: nvr trbld ldrs* **12/1**

0333 8 1¾ **Ar Colleen Aine**[11] 5779 2-8-13 67 SamHitchcott 1 49
(Mick Channon) *chsd ldrs: effrt u.p to chse clr wnr over 1f out tl 1f out: wknd ins fnl f* **20/1**

045 9 1¼ **Red Tycoon (IRE)**[25] 5248 2-9-7 75 (b[1]) ShaneKelly 8 54
(Ed Dunlop) *dwlt: hld up in tch in last trio: effrt on inner 2f out: stl plenty to do whn nt clr run and hmpd over 1f out: n.d after* **13/2**

650 10 nk **Pipe Bomb**[13] 5684 2-9-4 72 (b[1]) AndreaAtzeni 7 50
(Kevin Ryan) *chsd wnr tl 2f out: sn btn: wknd over 1f out* **10/1**

3616 11 4 **Rocking The Boat (IRE)**[20] 5409 2-9-6 74 JimCrowley 3 40
(Charles Hills) *chsd ldrs: rdn and chsd clr wnr 2f out tl over 1f out: sn wknd* **12/1**

1m 12.59s (-0.51) **Going Correction** -0.05s/f (Stan) 11 Ran SP% **122.8**
Speed ratings (Par 95): **101,100,99,98,97 96,94,91,90,89 84**
CSF £34.77 CT £110.49 TOTE £5.30: £2.50, £1.90, £1.30; EX 41.10 Trifecta £200.00.
**Owner** Mrs J Wood **Bred** Yeomanstown Stud **Trained** East Everleigh, Wilts

**FOCUS**
At best this was a fair nursery and few got into it. The winner possibly had a bit in hand.

## 6105 IRISH CHAMPIONS WEEKEND EBF FILLIES' CONDITIONS STKS (BOBIS RACE) 7f (P)
8:20 (8:21) (Class 3) 2-Y-O £9,570 (£3,029; £1,631) Stalls Low

Form RPR

1 **Yodelling (USA)** 2-8-12 0 WilliamBuick 4 88+
(Charlie Appleby) *trckd ldrs: plld out and clsd to join ldrs on bit 2f out: shkn up to ld ins fnl f: readily qcknd clr: impressive* **9/4**[2]

2 2 2½ **Jersey Jewel (FR)**[11] 5746 2-8-12 0 RichardHughes 1 78
(Richard Hannon) *w ldr on inner: rdn ent fnl 2f: brushed aside by wnr ins fnl f: battled on to go 2nd again towards fin* **3/1**[3]

31 3 hd **Light Fantastic**[9] 5821 2-9-2 0 JamesDoyle 2 81
(Ed Dunlop) *led: rdn ent fnl 2f: kpt on tl hdd and brushed aside by wnr ins fnl f: lost 2nd towards fin* **11/10**[1]

P **Lady Spangles (IRE)** 2-8-12 0 StevieDonohoe 3
(J S Moore) *ponied to s and taken down early: s.i.s: in tch in rr tl lost action and p.u 5f out: dismntd* **16/1**

1m 25.97s (-0.03) **Going Correction** -0.05s/f (Stan) 4 Ran SP% **109.3**
Speed ratings (Par 96): **98,95,94,**
CSF £9.04 TOTE £2.80; EX 8.50 Trifecta £10.50.
**Owner** Godolphin **Bred** Darley **Trained** Newmarket, Suffolk

**FOCUS**
An interesting fillies' conditions event won in the past by the likes of subsequent Oaks winner Talent and American Grade 2 winner Quiet Oasis. The winner did it well and the form is rated on the positive side.

## 6106 JOCKEY CLUB CATERING H'CAP (LONDON MIDDLE DISTANCE SERIES QUALIFIER) 1m 3f (P)
8:50 (8:50) (Class 3) (0-95,91) 3-Y-O+ £7,158 (£2,143; £1,071; £535; £267; £134) Stalls Low

Form RPR

416 1 **Famous Kid (USA)**[98] 2748 3-9-1 88 RichardHughes 5 97+
(Saeed bin Suroor) *s.i.s: grad rcvrd and in midfield after 2f: hdwy to join ldr 6f out: led over 2f out: styd on wl u.p fnl f* **11/4**[1]

0016 2 1½ **Gone Dutch**[20] 5440 4-9-9 88 FrederikTylicki 9 94
(James Fanshawe) *hld up in tch in midfield: nt clr run ent fnl 2f: hdwy u.p over 1f out: chsd wnr ins fnl f: kpt on* **7/2**[2]

530 3 nk **Double Discount (IRE)**[13] 5695 4-9-6 85 JimCrowley 8 90
(Tom Dascombe) *stdd s: hld up in tch towards rr: rdn and hdwy over 1f out: kpt on wl ins fnl f* **12/1**

4-04 4 nk **Opera Box**[123] 2010 6-9-5 84 JamesDoyle 6 89
(Marcus Tregoning) *stdd after s: hld up towards rr: nt clr run 2f out: hdwy u.p 1f out: styd on wl ins fnl f* **25/1**

3322 5 nk **Hedge End (IRE)**[29] 5094 3-8-2 80 CamHardie(5) 7 84
(Richard Hannon) *stdd after s: hld up in rr: rdn and effrt on outer over 2f out: kpt on u.p ins fnl f* **12/1**

2421 6 ½ **Solidarity**[53] 4272 3-9-3 90 WilliamBuick 2 93
(Charlie Appleby) *in tch in midfield: effrt on inner 2f out: no ex jst ins fnl f: one pce fnl 100yds* **11/2**

-223 7 1 **Jazz Master**[86] 3111 4-9-8 87 AndreaAtzeni 3 89
(Luca Cumani) *chsd ldrs: wnt 2nd over 8f out tl sltly outpcd ent fnl 2f: kpt on same pce ins fnl f* **4/1**[3]

3530 8 hd **God's Speed (IRE)**[77] 3419 3-9-3 90 SilvestreDeSousa 1 91
(Rae Guest) *t.k.h: chsd ldr tl over 8f out: styd chsng ldrs: rdn and unable qckn 2f out: wknd ins fnl f* **20/1**

3520 9 8 **Proud Chieftain**[14] 5651 6-9-12 91 (p) DaneO'Neill 4 78
(Clifford Lines) *led tl over 2f out: sn struggling u.p: bhd ins fnl f* **12/1**

2m 18.88s (-3.02) **Going Correction** -0.05s/f (Stan)
**WFA** 3 from 4yo+ 8lb 9 Ran SP% **116.0**
Speed ratings (Par 107): **108,106,106,106,106 105,105,105,99**
CSF £12.42 CT £97.68 TOTE £4.00: £2.00, £1.50, £3.00; EX 16.30 Trifecta £172.30.
**Owner** Godolphin **Bred** Darley **Trained** Newmarket, Suffolk

**FOCUS**
The tempo was pedestrian and a muddling race ensured they finished in a heap. The form may not be rock solid.

## 6107 JCC H'CAP 2m (P)
9:20 (9:20) (Class 5) (0-75,81) 4-Y-O+ £2,587 (£770; £384; £192) Stalls Low

Form RPR

0021 1 **Saborido (USA)**[8] 5863 8-9-6 81 6ex (b) KieranShoemark(7) 2 90
(Amanda Perrett) *hld up in tch: effrt on inner ent fnl 2f: led ins fnl f: styd on wl: rdn out* **3/1**[2]

0200 2 2¼ **Java Rose**[29] 5083 5-9-5 73 (p) JimCrowley 1 79
(Charlie Longsdon) *led for 2f: chsd ldrs after: drvn and ev ch over 1f out: hdd ins fnl f: one pce after* **6/1**

413 3 3 **Air Squadron**[19] 5466 4-8-12 66 SilvestreDeSousa 4 69
(Ralph Beckett) *s.i.s: t.k.h: led after 2f: rdn 3f out: hdd 1f out: kpt on same pce after* **11/10**[1]

4653 4 2 **Carraig Rock**[20] 5426 4-9-0 68 RichardHughes 6 68
(Hughie Morrison) *stdd and dropped in bhd after s: hld up in rr: hdwy to chse ldr 6f out: rdn 3f out: ev ch 2f out: wknd ins fnl f* **7/2**[3]

1110 5 7 **Kingscombe (USA)**[129] 1848 5-9-7 75 RobertHavlin 5 67
(Linda Jewell) *chsd ldr after 3f out tl 6f out: styd handy: rdn 3f out: wknd 2f out* **20/1**

0-00 6 5 **Superciliary**[114] 2252 5-8-2 56 HayleyTurner 3 42
(Chris Gordon) *in tch: dropped to rr and rdn over 3f out: wknd 2f out* **25/1**

3m 28.79s (-1.31) **Going Correction** -0.05s/f (Stan) 6 Ran SP% **117.7**
Speed ratings (Par 103): **101,99,98,97,93 91**
CSF £22.01 TOTE £6.50: £3.00, £2.90; EX 21.20 Trifecta £68.90.
**Owner** Mrs Amanda Perrett **Bred** R D Hubbard And R Masterson **Trained** Pulborough, W Sussex

**FOCUS**
A modest staying handicap bereft of a solid pace.
T/Plt: £15.00 to a £1 stake. Pool: £88,470.60 - 4295.16 winning tickets T/Qpdt: £13.90 to a £1 stake. Pool: £4,885.14 - 258.81 winning tickets SP

# 5561 MUSSELBURGH (R-H)
Friday, September 5

**OFFICIAL GOING: Good to firm changing to good (good to soft in places) after race 1 (4:30)**
Wind: fresh half behind Weather: overcast with drizzle

## 6108 WATERMANS ACCIDENT CLAIMS AND CARE MEDIAN AUCTION MAIDEN STKS 7f 30y
4:30 (4:30) (Class 5) 2-Y-O £2,587 (£770; £384; £192) Stalls Low

Form RPR

46 1 **Swift Approval (IRE)**[27] 5167 2-9-5 0 PaulMulrennan 6 81+
(Kevin Ryan) *mde all: rdn 2f out: drvn ins fnl f: kpt on wl* **9/2**[3]

352 2 1¼ **Third Time Lucky (IRE)**[18] 5493 2-9-0 78 JackGarritty(5) 5 78
(Richard Fahey) *in tch towards outer: pushed along and hdwy 2f out: sn chsd wnr: rdn and hung rt appr fnl f: kpt on but a jst hld* **15/8**[1]

4 **3** *7* **Enville (IRE)**[11] 5752 2-9-5 0 ........ GrahamLee 2 64+
(William Haggas) *hld up: rdn and outpcd over 2f out: kpt on ins fnl f: wnt 3rd post* **9/2**[3]

353 **4** *nse* **Water Thief (USA)**[12] 5712 2-9-5 0 ........ JoeFanning 4 59
(Mark Johnston) *trckd ldr: rdn over 2f out: wknd ins fnl f* **10/3**[2]

045 **5** *½* **Gea And Tea**[35] 4864 2-9-5 74 ........ ChrisCatlin 1 58
(Robert Eddery) *in tch: racd keenly: rdn over 2f out: wknd ins fnl f* **13/2**

5 **6** *28* **Disushe Star**[46] 4486 2-9-5 0 ........ TomEaves 3
(Keith Dalgleish) *dwlt: hld up: rdn over 2f out: sn wknd* **66/1**

1m 30.3s (1.30) **Going Correction** +0.075s/f (Good) **6** Ran SP% **109.1**
Speed ratings (Par 95): **95,93,85,85,84 52**
CSF £12.60 TOTE £7.70: £2.50, £1.10; EX 14.30 Trifecta £58.60.
**Owner** Middleham Park Racing XLIX **Bred** Mrs Jean Brennan **Trained** Hambleton, N Yorks
■ Stewards' Enquiry : Jack Garritty two-day ban; careless riding (19th-20th Sep)

**FOCUS**
This was run in steady, persistent rain and it's possible the deteriorating conditions found out a few of these. The winner has the scope to do a good bit better.

## 6109 CALA HOMES STRAIGHT H'CAP 5f
**5:05** (5:05) (Class 5) (0-75,75) 3-Y-0+ **£3,324** (£962; £481; £240) **Stalls** High

Form RPR

3200 **1** **Noble Asset**[6] 5913 3-9-4 73 ........ PhillipMakin 8 81
(John Quinn) *mde all: pressed thrght: rdn over 1f out: edgd rt ins fnl f: hld on wl* **6/1**[3]

3215 **2** *nk* **Royal Brave (IRE)**[34] 4898 3-9-5 74 ........ MartinDwyer 7 81
(William Muir) *dwlt: hld up: rdn and outpcd 1/2-way: hdwy over 1f out: r.o wl fnl 110yds* **15/8**[1]

46 **3** *½* **Perfect Blossom**[9] 5817 7-8-13 72 ........ JackGarritty(5) 9 77
(Alan Berry) *dwlt: sn chsd ldng pair: swtchd rt appr fnl f: sn ev ch: kpt on same pce* **18/1**

3221 **4** *¾* **Flash City (ITY)**[36] 4833 6-9-4 72 ........ PJMcDonald 4 74
(Ruth Carr) *chsd ldng pair: rdn 1/2-way: kpt on* **4/1**[2]

1406 **5** *¾* **Storyline (IRE)**[47] 4469 3-8-9 64 ........ DuranFentiman 2 64
(Tim Easterby) *pressed ldr: rdn 2f out: no ex fnl 110yds* **14/1**

142 **6** *3¾* **Scoreline**[21] 5389 3-8-13 71 ........ (p) SamJames(3) 6 57
(David O'Meara) *chsd ldng pair: rdn 1/2-way: wknd ins fnl f* **6/1**[3]

0140 **7** *1* **Midnight Dynamo**[6] 5911 7-9-7 75 ........ GrahamLee 3 58
(Jim Goldie) *hld up: rdn 2f out: nvr threatened* **8/1**

0165 **8** *nk* **Lexington Rose**[29] 5087 3-9-3 72 ........ PaulMulrennan 1 53
(Bryan Smart) *hld up: rdn 1/2-way: nvr threatened* **16/1**

060 **9** *8* **Gottcher**[15] 5601 6-8-13 67 ........ (b) TomEaves 5 20
(Ian Semple) *hld up: a bhd* **40/1**

1m 0.29s (-0.11) **Going Correction** +0.075s/f (Good)
**WFA** 3 from 6yo+ 1lb **9** Ran SP% **114.7**
Speed ratings (Par 103): **103,102,101,100,99 93,91,91,78**
CSF £17.51 CT £181.91 TOTE £10.90: £2.00, £1.30, £5.20; EX 25.40 Trifecta £319.20.
**Owner** Caron & Paul Chapman **Bred** Horizon Bloodstock Limited **Trained** Settrington, N Yorks

**FOCUS**
The official going was changed to good, good to soft in places following the running of the opening juvenile maiden. This was a fair race for the grade. The first three raced nearest to the rail.

## 6110 VISITEASTLOTHIAN.ORG H'CAP 1m 4f 100y
**5:40** (5:40) (Class 5) (0-70,68) 3-Y-0 **£5,175** (£1,540; £769; £384) **Stalls** Centre

Form RPR

5526 **1** **Mambo Rhythm**[17] 5520 3-9-5 66 ........ (v[1]) JoeFanning 2 79
(Mark Johnston) *hld up in tch: smooth hdwy 3f out: led 2f out: rdn clr* **6/1**

1004 **2** *8* **Westerly**[16] 5557 3-9-7 68 ........ (p) PaulMulrennan 4 69
(William Haggas) *led: rdn 3f out: hdd 2f out: kpt on but no ch w wnr* **9/4**[1]

6605 **3** *2¼* **Les Gar Gan (IRE)**[12] 5717 3-9-4 65 ........ TomEaves 7 63
(Keith Dalgleish) *hld up in tch: rdn over 2f out: plugged on: wnt 3rd ins fnl f* **14/1**

2125 **4** *½* **Mister Uno (IRE)**[20] 5449 3-9-5 66 ........ (p) PJMcDonald 1 63
(Ann Duffield) *trckd ldng pair: rdn over 2f out: plugged on* **5/1**[3]

4400 **5** *2½* **Olymnia**[31] 5011 3-8-6 60 ........ MeganCarberry(7) 3 53
(Robert Eddery) *trckd ldng pair on outer: rdn to chal over 3f out: hung rt fnl 2f: wknd over 1f out* **16/1**

6062 **6** *1½* **Silver Duke (IRE)**[20] 5420 3-9-5 66 ........ GrahamLee 6 57
(Jim Goldie) *hld up: wnt a little in snatches: rdn over 2f out: nvr threatened* **3/1**[2]

2534 **7** *13* **Avocadeau (IRE)**[23] 5318 3-9-6 67 ........ (p) MartinDwyer 5 37
(William Muir) *prom: rdn and lost pl over 2f out: wknd over 1f out: eased* **8/1**

2m 45.8s (3.80) **Going Correction** +0.075s/f (Good) **7** Ran SP% **110.4**
Speed ratings (Par 101): **90,84,83,82,81 80,71**
CSF £18.51 TOTE £7.30: £3.50, £1.60; EX 25.70 Trifecta £125.20.
**Owner** Around The World Partnership **Bred** Gordon Phillips **Trained** Middleham Moor, N Yorks

**FOCUS**
It's hard to pin down the form, with the second and third the key.

## 6111 ST ANDREWS TIMBER AND BUILDING SUPPLIES H'CAP 1m
**6:10** (6:10) (Class 4) (0-85,86) 3-Y-0+ **£6,469** (£1,925; £962; £481) **Stalls** Low

Form RPR

0251 **1** **Green Howard**[7] 5887 6-10-1 86 6ex ........ GrahamLee 4 96+
(Robin Bastiman) *hld up: pushed along and hdwy on inner over 1f out: squeezed through gap to ld 110yds out: pushed out* **15/8**[1]

-421 **2** *¾* **Chinese Jade**[9] 5810 3-9-7 83 6ex ........ (p) ChrisCatlin 6 90
(Sir Mark Prescott Bt) *s.i.s: rdn along to sn r promly: rdn to press ldr fr over 3f out: led ins fnl f: sn hdd: kpt on but a hld* **11/2**[3]

5320 **3** *1¾* **Ralphy Boy (IRE)**[14] 5632 5-9-7 78 ........ PJMcDonald 1 82
(Alistair Whillans) *led: rdn and pressed fr over 3f out: hdd ins fnl f: no ex* **6/1**

2134 **4** *¾* **Ellaal**[18] 5496 5-9-3 74 ........ PaulMulrennan 7 76
(Ruth Carr) *trckd ldng pair: rdn over 2f out: kpt on same pce* **4/1**[2]

1520 **5** *5* **Lockhart (IRE)**[14] 5656 3-9-5 81 ........ JoeFanning 3 71
(Mark Johnston) *trckd ldng pair: rdn over 2f out: wknd fnl f* **4/1**[2]

1401 **6** *2¾* **Porthos Du Vallon**[46] 4490 3-8-9 71 ........ (p) TomEaves 5 54
(Keith Dalgleish) *hld up: rdn over 2f out: sn wknd* **14/1**

1m 40.51s (-0.69) **Going Correction** +0.075s/f (Good)
**WFA** 3 from 4yo+ 5lb **6** Ran SP% **111.1**
Speed ratings (Par 105): **106,105,103,102,97 95**
CSF £12.29 TOTE £2.80: £2.00, £2.00; EX 10.80 Trifecta £63.30.
**Owner** Ms M Austerfield **Bred** Miss A J Rawding & P M Crane **Trained** Cowthorpe, N Yorks

**FOCUS**
The winner rates better than ever, with the third the best guide.

## 6112 EBF STALLIONS BREEDING WINNERS FILLIES' H'CAP 7f 30y
**6:40** (6:41) (Class 3) (0-90,92) 3-Y-0+ **£10,997** (£3,272; £1,635; £817) **Stalls** Low

Form RPR

222 **1** **Meeting Waters**[30] 5032 3-9-3 87 ........ GrahamLee 2 93
(William Haggas) *chsd ldng pair: rdn over 2f out: led narrowly jst ins fnl f: kpt on* **10/3**[2]

0100 **2** *hd* **Lady Frances**[15] 5612 3-9-4 88 ........ JoeFanning 1 93
(Mark Johnston) *led: rdn 2f out: hdd jst ins fnl f: kpt on: jst hld* **13/2**

2335 **3** *1¾* **Lady Horatia**[20] 5437 3-9-0 84 ........ MartinDwyer 7 85
(William Muir) *hld up: rdn over 2f out: hdwy on outer over 1f out: kpt on* **7/2**[3]

6122 **4** *1¼* **First Experience**[21] 5398 3-8-6 76 ........ ChrisCatlin 8 74
(Rae Guest) *hld up in rr: rdn over 2f out: kpt on ins fnl f* **9/1**

4331 **5** *1¼* **Ixelles Diamond (IRE)**[10] 5785 3-8-1 76 6ex ........ JackGarritty(5) 3 70
(Richard Fahey) *s.i.s: midfield: rdn over 2f out: one pce and nvr threatened* **9/4**[1]

6340 **6** *2¼* **Azagal (IRE)**[15] 5612 3-9-6 90 ........ DuranFentiman 6 79
(Tim Easterby) *midfield: rdn and hdwy over 2f out: wknd over 1f out* **8/1**

1200 **7** *8* **Sandra's Diamond (IRE)**[18] 5496 3-8-10 80 ........ TomEaves 5 48
(Keith Dalgleish) *prom: rdn 3f out: wknd over 1f out* **28/1**

1m 28.88s (-0.12) **Going Correction** +0.075s/f (Good) **7** Ran SP% **114.0**
Speed ratings (Par 104): **103,102,100,99,97 95,86**
CSF £24.74 CT £79.35 TOTE £3.50: £2.00, £3.90; EX 28.40 Trifecta £71.20.
**Owner** Liam Sheridan **Bred** T R G Vestey **Trained** Newmarket, Suffolk

**FOCUS**
They appeared to go a good clip but the time was ordinary. The winner turned around Brighton form with the runner-up.

## 6113 WILLIAM HILL H'CAP (QUALIFIER FOR £15000 BETFAIR SCOTTISH STAYERS SERIES FINAL) 1m 4f 100y
**7:10** (7:10) (Class 5) (0-70,70) 4-Y-0+ **£5,175** (£1,540; £769; £384) **Stalls** Centre

Form RPR

-046 **1** **Pressure Point**[16] 5562 4-9-4 67 ........ PhillipMakin 5 76
(Keith Dalgleish) *midfield: rdn over 2f out: r.o wl fr over 1f out: led 110yds out* **10/1**

1423 **2** *2* **Testa Rossa (IRE)**[14] 5639 4-8-11 60 ........ (p) JoeFanning 8 66
(Jim Goldie) *trckd ldr: rdn 3f out: led 2f out: hdd 110yds out: one pce and sn no ch w wnr* **11/4**[1]

-016 **3** *1¼* **Titus Bolt (IRE)**[16] 5567 5-8-11 60 ........ GrahamLee 2 64
(Jim Goldie) *led: rdn 3f out: hdd 2f out: remained w ev ch tl tl no ex ins fnl f* **11/4**[1]

4654 **4** *2* **Eilean Mor**[16] 5567 6-8-2 51 ........ DuranFentiman 7 52
(R Mike Smith) *in tch: rdn 3f out: one pce* **16/1**

3323 **5** *2½* **Grand Diamond (IRE)**[16] 5567 10-7-11 53 ........ RachaelGrant(7) 1 50
(Jim Goldie) *hld up: rdn over 2f out: nvr threatened* **12/1**

1414 **6** *nse* **Giovanni Jack**[9] 5815 4-9-7 70 ........ BenCurtis 6 67
(Alan Swinbank) *trckd ldr: rdn over 2f out: wknd fnl f* **3/1**[2]

6165 **7** *1¼* **Gold Chain (IRE)**[13] 4962 4-8-10 64 ........ EmmaSayer(5) 4 59
(Dianne Sayer) *hld up in rr: a bhd* **7/1**[3]

2m 44.55s (2.55) **Going Correction** +0.075s/f (Good) **7** Ran SP% **113.5**
Speed ratings (Par 103): **94,92,91,90,88 88,87**
CSF £37.11 CT £97.44 TOTE £9.70: £4.20, £1.70; EX 44.70 Trifecta £197.60.
**Owner** Mrs Janis Macpherson **Bred** Juddmonte Farms Ltd **Trained** Carluke, S Lanarks

**FOCUS**
The winner is rated back to his 3yo form and could do better still.

## 6114 EASTERN ELECTRIC (SCOTLAND) LTD H'CAP 5f
**7:40** (7:41) (Class 6) (0-60,60) 3-Y-0+ **£2,587** (£770; £384; £192) **Stalls** High

Form RPR

0233 **1** **Pavers Star**[9] 5819 5-8-9 48 ........ (p) JoeFanning 14 57
(Noel Wilson) *mde all: rdn 2f out: kpt on* **4/1**[2]

2010 **2** *¾* **Choc'A'Moca (IRE)**[9] 5806 7-9-7 60 ........ (v) GrahamLee 9 66
(Paul Midgley) *chsd ldng pair: rdn 1/2-way: kpt on: wnt 2nd nr fin* **14/1**

0203 **3** *¾* **Dream Sika (IRE)**[12] 5715 3-8-10 50 ........ PJMcDonald 5 54
(Ruth Carr) *pressed ldr: rdn 2f out: no ex and lost 2nd nr fin* **9/1**

0050 **4** *1¾* **Here Now And Why (IRE)**[16] 5565 7-8-9 48 ........ (p) TomEaves 10 45
(Ian Semple) *chsd ldng pair: rdn 1/2-way: one pce* **18/1**

5531 **5** *1* **New Lease Of Life**[8] 5858 5-9-1 57 6ex ........ (p) GaryBartley(3) 3 51+
(Jim Goldie) *hld up: rdn 1/2-way: sme hdwy on wd outside over 1f out: kpt on* **3/1**[1]

2023 **6** *1* **Tadalavil**[8] 5858 9-8-10 54 ........ SammyJoBell(5) 6 44+
(Linda Perratt) *in tch on outer: rdn 1/2-way: wknd ins fnl f* **9/1**

3351 **7** *½* **Saxonette**[16] 5565 6-8-13 55 ........ SamJames(3) 12 43
(Linda Perratt) *in tch: rdn 1/2-way: wknd ins fnl f* **6/1**[3]

0553 **8** *1½* **The Nifty Fox**[16] 5565 10-9-3 56 ........ (p) PhillipMakin 8 39
(Tim Easterby) *hld up: rdn 1/2-way: nvr threatened* **7/1**

6260 **9** *shd* **Berbice (IRE)**[8] 5854 9-8-2 46 ........ (b) JackGarritty(5) 2 29
(Linda Perratt) *slowly away: hld up in rr: rdn 1/2-way: nvr threatened* **20/1**

0066 **10** *hd* **Kalani's Diamond**[35] 4873 4-8-4 50 ........ JoshDoyle(7) 4 32
(David O'Meara) *hld up: nvr threatened* **20/1**

04- **11** *8* **Pitt Rivers**[330] 7148 5-8-8 54 ........ MeganCarberry(7) 13 7
(Linda Perratt) *dwlt: a outpcd in rr* **25/1**

1m 0.4s **Going Correction** +0.075s/f (Good)
**WFA** 3 from 4yo+ 1lb **11** Ran SP% **117.1**
Speed ratings (Par 101): **103,101,100,97,96 94,93,91,91,90 78**
CSF £56.45 CT £487.34 TOTE £5.30: £2.00, £3.00, £3.00; EX 62.80 Trifecta £926.70.
**Owner** Mrs Michael John Paver **Bred** Mrs C K Paver **Trained** Middleham, N Yorks

**FOCUS**
The first three all raced close to the rail again. The winner was up slightly on his C&D latest.
T/Plt: £153.10 to a £1 stake. Pool: £42,127.99 - 200.86 winning tickets T/Qpdt: £18.90 to a £1 stake. Pool: £4,739.96 - 185.45 winning tickets AS

# 5759 NEWCASTLE (L-H)

Friday, September 5

**OFFICIAL GOING: Good to firm (good in places; 7.5)**

Wind: almost nil Weather: fine

## 6115 STONBURY/BRITISH STALLION STUDS EBF MAIDEN STKS 6f

1:50 (1:51) (Class 5) 2-Y-O £2,911 (£866; £432; £216) Stalls High

| Form | | | | RPR |
|---|---|---|---|---|
| 64 | 1 | | **Honeysuckle Lil (IRE)**[32] 4973 2-8-7 0 RachelRichardson(7) 12 (Tim Easterby) *mid-div: hdwy to chse ldrs over 3f out: r.o wl to ld last 100yds* **12/1** | 76 |
| 4332 | 2 | 2 1/2 | **Flicka's Boy**[14] 5637 2-9-5 73 BarryMcHugh 13 (Tony Coyle) *led: t.k.h: edgd lft over 1f out: hdd and no ex ins fnl f* **4/1**[2] | 73 |
| 062 | 3 | 1 | **Best Endeavour**[13] 5684 2-9-5 77 DougieCostello 5 (William Muir) *dwlt: sn chsng ldrs: upsides over 1f out: styd on same pce last 150yds* **5/1**[3] | 70 |
| 40 | 4 | nse | **Beach Samba (IRE)**[14] 5655 2-9-5 0 GrahamLee 6 (Ed Dunlop) *chsd ldrs: kpt on same pce fnl f* **6/4**[1] | 70 |
| 0 | 5 | 2 1/2 | **My Specialbru**[44] 4527 2-9-5 0 RoystonFfrench 3 (Tracy Waggott) *chsd ldrs: one pce over 1f out* **200/1** | 62 |
| 0 | 6 | 3 1/4 | **Choppy Water (IRE)**[24] 5264 2-9-5 0 DuranFentiman 9 (Tim Easterby) *mid-div: outpcd over 2f out: kpt on fnl f* **66/1** | 53 |
| | 7 | 3/4 | **Cadeau Magnifique** 2-9-5 0 TonyHamilton 2 (Richard Fahey) *mid-div: effrt over 2f out: nvr a factor* **8/1** | 50+ |
| 20 | 8 | 1 3/4 | **Blackfoot Brave (IRE)**[21] 5386 2-9-5 0 PaulMulrennan 7 (Michael Dods) *hld up in rr: kpt on over 1f out: nvr on terms* **16/1** | 45 |
| | 9 | 1 1/4 | **Dark War (IRE)** 2-9-5 0 DaleSwift 4 (James Given) *dwlt: in rr: hdwy over 2f out: wknd fnl 150yds* **50/1** | 41 |
| | 10 | 1 | **Fair Venture (IRE)** 2-9-2 0 ConnorBeasley(3) 8 (Michael Dods) *a towards rr* **40/1** | 38 |
| 0 | 11 | nk | **Cloak And Degas (IRE)**[23] 5297 2-9-5 0 TomEaves 10 (Scott Dixon) *w ldr: lost pl over 2f out* **40/1** | 37 |
| | 12 | 1 3/4 | **Twinkle Twinkle** 2-9-0 0 IanBrennan 11 (Julie Camacho) *dwlt: a in rr* **25/1** | 27 |
| | 13 | 1 | **Crown Green** 2-9-0 0 RussKennemore 1 (Karen Tutty) *mid-div: lost pl over 1f out* **66/1** | 24 |

1m 14.0s (-0.60) **Going Correction** -0.225s/f (Firm) 13 Ran SP% **115.5**

Speed ratings (Par 95): **95,91,90,90,86 82,81,79,77,76 75,73,72**

CSF £55.98 TOTE £16.90: £3.60, £1.70, £2.00; EX 67.40 Trifecta £236.60.

**Owner** Ambrose Turnbull **Bred** Mrs C A Moore **Trained** Great Habton, N Yorks

**FOCUS**

The going was good to firm, good in places on a watered track. Barry McHugh reported that the ground was on the fast side.They went a fair pace in this maiden and raced centre to stands' side. The favourite was a bit disappointing and there was a surprise result. Improvement from the winner with the runner-up key to the level.

## 6116 J N BENTLEY MAIDEN STKS 5f

2:20 (2:24) (Class 5) 3-Y-O+ £3,234 (£962; £481; £240) Stalls High

| Form | | | | RPR |
|---|---|---|---|---|
| 5-00 | 1 | | **Simply Black (IRE)**[21] 5375 3-8-11 60 (p) SamJames(3) 3 (David O'Meara) *w ldr: led over 1f out: briefly hdd 100yds out: hld on towards fin* **8/1** | 54 |
| 2 | 2 | nk | **Jan Van Hoof (IRE)**[172] 994 3-9-5 0 TonyHamilton 5 (Richard Fahey) *dwlt: sn trckd ldrs: 2nd over 1f out: led briefly ins fnl f: fnd little and worried out of it: no ex clsng stages* **11/8**[1] | 58+ |
| 0055 | 3 | 1 1/2 | **Island Express (IRE)**[6] 5916 7-9-1 47 (bt) AnnStokell(5) 9 (Ann Stokell) *chsd ldrs: outpcd over 2f out: hdwy over 1f out: kpt on to take 3rd clsng stages* **100/1** | 53 |
| 0-33 | 4 | 1 | **Resist**[35] 4873 3-8-11 57 ConnorBeasley(3) 6 (James Given) *led tl over 1f out: kpt on one pce* **3/1**[2] | 44 |
| 054 | 5 | 1 3/4 | **Oriental Heights**[8] 5857 3-8-11 0 GaryBartley(3) 7 (Jim Goldie) *sn outpcd and bhd: hdwy over 1f out: kpt on* **12/1** | 38 |
| 6460 | 6 | 3/4 | **Princess Rose**[8] 5853 3-9-0 54 (b) PhillipMakin 8 (John Weymes) *chsd ldrs: outpcd over 2f out: hdwy over 1f out: one pce* **12/1** | 35 |
| 3-3 | 7 | 1 | **Normanna (IRE)**[17] 5531 3-9-0 0 PaddyAspell 4 (Marco Botti) *chsd ldrs: wknd over 1f out* **15/2**[3] | 32 |
| 660 | 8 | 3/4 | **Tell Me When**[13] 5683 3-8-7 49 (p) KevinLundie(7) 2 (Brian Rothwell) *s.i.s: outpcd in rr: reminders over 3f out: sn bhd* **20/1** | 29 |
| 06 | 9 | 3 3/4 | **Katies Joy (IRE)**[14] 5642 3-8-11 0 GeorgeChaloner(3) 1 (Ian Semple) *uns rdr at s and rn 3f rdrless: dwlt: sn chsng ldrs on outer: lost pl over 1f out: eased whn bhd clsng stages* **50/1** | 16 |

1m 0.65s (-0.45) **Going Correction** -0.225s/f (Firm)

**WFA** 3 from 7yo 1lb 9 Ran SP% **113.1**

Speed ratings (Par 103): **94,93,91,89,86 85,83,82,76**

CSF £18.81 TOTE £10.30: £3.00, £1.10, £4.00; EX 23.70 Trifecta £1034.80.

**Owner** Sterling Racing **Bred** Liam Ormsby **Trained** Nawton, N Yorks

**FOCUS**

An exposed type denied the inexperienced favourite in this weak maiden. The third anchors the form and the winner was still a fair way off her 2yo best.

## 6117 FASTFLOW H'CAP 2m 19y

2:50 (2:50) (Class 6) (0-60,59) 3-Y-O+ £2,911 (£866; £432; £216) Stalls Low

| Form | | | | RPR |
|---|---|---|---|---|
| 00-0 | 1 | | **Scrafton**[21] 5388 3-8-9 53 TonyHamilton 11 (James Bethell) *hld up in rr: t.k.h: hdwy 6f out: chal over 1f out: hrd rdn and styd on to ld last 75yds: all out* **15/2** | 62 |
| 2144 | 2 | 1/2 | **Wor Lass**[11] 5765 6-9-8 53 DavidNolan 4 (Iain Jardine) *prom: lost pl after 5f: hdwy over 5f out: n.m.r over 2f out: led narrowly over 1f out: hdd wl ins fnl f: no ex* **3/1**[1] | 61 |
| -323 | 3 | 5 | **William Hogarth**[8] 5850 9-9-0 45 DaleSwift 5 (Brian Ellison) *hld up in mid-div: t.k.h: effrt over 2f out: kpt on fnl f: tk 3rd clsng stages* **7/2**[2] | 47 |
| 4666 | 4 | nk | **My Escapade (IRE)**[46] 4497 3-8-6 50 RoystonFfrench 2 (Simon Waugh) *chsd ldrs: led briefly 2f out: one pce* **16/1** | 52 |
| 0-60 | 5 | 4 | **Weybridge Light**[13] 4319 9-9-2 47 (b) PaddyAspell 10 (David Thompson) *trckd ldrs: 2nd after 5f: led over 3f out: hdd 2f out: grad wknd fnl f* **16/1** | 44 |
| 6036 | 6 | 3 1/4 | **Claude Carter**[10] 5146 10-8-9 45 (p) GarryWhillans(5) 8 (Alistair Whillans) *s.i.s: hdwy to chse ldrs after 6f: drvn over 5f out: wknd last 150yds* **28/1** | 38 |
| 6444 | 7 | 1 1/2 | **Blue Top**[47] 4474 5-9-6 58 (p) AnnaHesketh(7) 3 (Mark Walford) *hld up in rr: effrt on outer over 2f out: nvr a factor* **7/1** | 49 |
| 0404 | 8 | 2 1/4 | **Two B'S**[13] 5682 3-9-1 59 DougieCostello 12 (Tim Easterby) *wnt rt s: hld up in rr: hdwy to trck ldrs after 5f: wknd over 1f out* **9/2**[3] | 47 |
| 4-65 | 9 | 3/4 | **I Am Who I Am**[216] 434 4-8-11 45 (t) ConnorBeasley(3) 9 (Iain Jardine) *mid-div: drvn over 3f out: wknd fnl 2f* **20/1** | 33 |
| 6040 | 10 | 2 1/4 | **Golden Future**[10] 5146 11-9-0 48 GeorgeChaloner(3) 6 (Peter Niven) *chsd ldrs: drvn over 3f out: lost pl over 1f out* **25/1** | 33 |
| 6000 | 11 | 7 | **Jebulani**[22] 5331 4-9-0 45 (tp) BarryMcHugh 1 (Barry Murtagh) *hld up in rr: hdwy on ins 3f out: hung rt and wknd 2f out: bhd whn eased nr fin* **50/1** | 21 |
| 0600 | 12 | 7 | **Secret Kode (IRE)**[29] 5084 3-8-2 46 ow1 PatrickMathers 7 (Simon Waugh) *led: t.k.h: hdd over 3f out: wknd 2f out: bhd whn eased clsng stages* **50/1** | 14 |

3m 34.13s (-5.27) **Going Correction** -0.30s/f (Firm)

**WFA** 3 from 4yo+ 13lb 12 Ran SP% **117.4**

Speed ratings (Par 101): **101,100,98,98,96 94,93,92,92,91 87,84**

CSF £28.31 CT £93.63 TOTE £10.70: £2.80, £1.90, £2.20; EX 54.20 Trifecta £189.50.

**Owner** Clarendon Thoroughbred Racing **Bred** Bearstone Stud **Trained** Middleham Moor, N Yorks

**FOCUS**

They went a stop-start gallop but the first two pulled clear from off the pace and the form looks fairly sound.

## 6118 GOWLAND & DAWSON MAIDEN STKS 1m 3y(S)

3:25 (3:25) (Class 5) 3-Y-O+ £3,234 (£962; £481; £240) Stalls High

| Form | | | | RPR |
|---|---|---|---|---|
| 44 | 1 | | **Tasmanian**[11] 5772 3-9-5 0 RoystonFfrench 2 (Mark Johnston) *s.i.s: chsng ldrs after 3f: drvn to ld over 2f out: wnt lft ins fnl f: rdn out* **15/8**[1] | 76+ |
| 43 | 2 | 1 1/4 | **Kiss Of Spring (IRE)**[11] 5772 3-9-0 0 DavidNolan 1 (David O'Meara) *hld up in rr: hdwy over 4f out: sn trcking ldrs: upsides over 1f out: styd on same pce ins fnl f* **2/1**[2] | 67 |
| 02 | 3 | shd | **Gleese The Devil (IRE)**[40] 4705 3-9-2 0 GeorgeChaloner(3) 3 (Richard Fahey) *chsd ldrs: styd on same pce fnl f* **9/4**[3] | 72 |
| 00 | 4 | 1 1/2 | **Mr Gatsby**[19] 5469 3-9-5 0 (b[1]) PaddyAspell 6 (Mark Walford) *w ldr: kpt on same pce appr fnl f* **66/1** | 68 |
| 0 | 5 | 12 | **Bulas Belle**[21] 5374 4-9-0 0 KevinStott(5) 4 (Edwin Tuer) *s.i.s: in rr and sn drvn along: hdwy to chse ldrs over 2f out: edgd lft and lost pl over 1f out* **16/1** | 37 |
| 05 | 6 | 3 1/4 | **Im Dapper Too**[19] 5469 3-9-0 0 JoeDoyle(5) 5 (John Davies) *led: hdd over 2f out: lost pl over 1f out: sn bhd* **20/1** | 33 |
| 4- | 7 | 17 | **Nonagon**[496] 1833 3-9-0 0 EmmaSayer(5) 7 (Wilf Storey) *mid-div: lost pl over 3f out: wl bhd whn eased* **25/1** | |
| 00 | 8 | 44 | **Red Legacy**[52] 4299 6-9-5 0 MichaelStainton 8 (Sean Regan) *trckd ldrs: t.k.h: drvn 4f out: sn lost pl and wl bhd: t.o over 1f out: virtually p.u* **100/1** | |

1m 39.76s (-3.64) **Going Correction** -0.225s/f (Firm)

**WFA** 3 from 4yo+ 5lb 8 Ran SP% **115.9**

Speed ratings (Par 103): **109,107,107,106,94 90,73,29**

CSF £5.89 TOTE £3.30: £1.30, £1.20, £1.10; EX 5.90 Trifecta £12.80.

**Owner** Sheikh Hamdan bin Mohammed Al Maktoum **Bred** Darley **Trained** Middleham Moor, N Yorks

**FOCUS**

The market leaders filled the first three places in this maiden and the fourth was a long way clear of the rest. The form makes sense.

## 6119 NWG H'CAP 1m 4f 93y

4:00 (4:00) (Class 6) (0-65,63) 3-Y-O+ £2,264 (£673; £336; £168) Stalls Low

| Form | | | | RPR |
|---|---|---|---|---|
| 6033 | 1 | | **Gioia Di Vita**[11] 5765 4-9-10 61 DavidNolan 1 (David Thompson) *hld up towards rr: effrt 3f out: chsng ldng pair and swtchd rt appr fnl f: sn led: hld on towards fin* **4/1**[2] | 69 |
| 1260 | 2 | 1/2 | **Gabrial's Hope (FR)**[14] 5640 5-9-12 63 TonyHamilton 7 (Tracy Waggott) *swtchd lft s: hld up in rr: hdwy on ins over 2f out: styd on to take 2nd last 100yds: no ex* **11/2** | 70 |
| 6412 | 3 | 1 | **Midnight Warrior**[18] 5495 4-8-11 53 JoeDoyle(5) 2 (Ron Barr) *trckd ldrs: led over 1f out: hdd jst ins fnl f: kpt on same pce* **7/2**[1] | 58 |
| 5016 | 4 | 5 | **Oracle Boy**[15] 5596 3-9-2 62 (p) DougieCostello 5 (William Muir) *led: t.k.h: drvn 3f out: hdd over 1f out: fdd* **5/1**[3] | 59 |
| 0160 | 5 | 2 1/4 | **Silver Tigress**[11] 5773 6-8-11 51 ConnorBeasley(3) 12 (Iain Jardine) *t.k.h in mid-div: hdwy over 5f out: one pce fnl 2f* **8/1** | 45 |
| 0000 | 6 | 2 1/4 | **Yorkshireman (IRE)**[11] 5765 4-9-1 52 PaddyAspell 10 (Lynn Siddall) *sn prom: drvn 4f out: wknd over 1f out* **50/1** | 42 |
| 3005 | 7 | 3/4 | **Stamp Duty (IRE)**[11] 5765 6-8-12 49 oh4 RaulDaSilva 9 (Suzzanne France) *swtchd lft s: hld up in rr: effrt over 2f out: nvr a factor* **20/1** | 38 |
| 6045 | 8 | shd | **Primary Route (IRE)**[11] 5773 4-9-9 60 AndrewElliott 3 (Jason Ward) *chsd ldrs: drvn 3f out: fdd appr fnl f* **12/1** | 49 |
| 0104 | 9 | 1 1/2 | **Aseela (IRE)**[10] 5788 4-8-13 57 KieranSchofield(7) 11 (George Moore) *in rr: sn pushed along: sme hdwy over 5f out: wknd 2f out* **8/1** | 43 |
| -000 | 10 | 45 | **Arabian Sunset (IRE)**[46] 4495 3-8-3 49 oh4 RoystonFfrench 4 (Simon Waugh) *chsd ldr: t.k.h: lost pl over 3f out: bhd whn eased 2f out: virtually p.u: hopelessly t.o* **66/1** | |
| -005 | R | | **Thundering Cloud (IRE)**[29] 5090 3-8-5 56 JordanNason(5) 6 (Simon Waugh) *ref to r: lft in stalls* **25/1** | |

2m 41.96s (-3.64) **Going Correction** -0.30s/f (Firm)

**WFA** 3 from 4yo+ 9lb 11 Ran SP% **116.2**

Speed ratings (Par 101): **100,99,99,95,94 92,92,92,91,61**

CSF £25.02 CT £84.21 TOTE £4.50: £1.80, £1.60, £1.50; EX 29.70 Trifecta £136.50.

**Owner** Seneca Racing **Bred** Hyphen Bloodstock **Trained** Bolam, Co Durham

**FOCUS**

They went a good pace and the first three finished clear. The form is rated around the second.

## 6120 ESH CONSTRUCTION H'CAP 6f

4:35 (4:36) (Class 6) (0-55,61) 3-Y-O+ £2,264 (£673; £336; £168) Stalls High

| Form | | | | RPR |
|---|---|---|---|---|
| 1 | 1 | | **Peace Accord**[10] 5797 4-9-13 61 6ex JackMitchell 9 (Michael Wigham) *trckd ldrs: led over 1f out: edgd lft: pushed out* **7/2**[1] | 76+ |
| 0402 | 2 | 2 1/4 | **Ad Vitam (IRE)**[13] 5683 6-9-6 54 (bt) RaulDaSilva 4 (Suzzanne France) *mid-div: hdwy far side over 2f out: chsng wnr 1f out: styd on same pce* **14/1** | 62 |
| 6221 | 3 | 2 3/4 | **See Vermont**[2] 6030 6-8-13 47 (p) TonyHamilton 11 (Robin Bastiman) *mid-div: effrt over 2f out: kpt on same pce to take 3rd last 100yds* **7/2**[1] | 46 |

0000 4 1 **Yankee Red**17 5532 3-9-2 52 (b) DavidNolan 2 48
(John Best) *chsd ldrs: kpt on same pce appr fnl f* **28/1**

6134 5 3/4 **Divertimenti (IRE)**4 5987 10-9-2 53 (b) BillyCray(3) 15 47
(Roy Bowring) *w ldrs: lft to r alone stands' side over 4f out: kpt on same pce over 1f out* **9/1**

0422 6 1 1/2 **Red Shadow**21 5390 5-9-4 52 (p) PaulPickard 5 41
(Alan Brown) *chsd ldrs: one pce fnl 2f* **13/2**3

0063 7 1/2 **Abraham Monro**13 5683 4-9-0 48 IanBrennan 14 35
(Ruth Carr) *awkward s: sn chsng ldrs stands' side: edgd lft over 4f out: one pce fnl 2f* **7/1**

000- 8 1 **On The High Tops (IRE)**332 7101 6-9-0 48 (t) RoystonFfrench 13 32
(Colin Teague) *t.k.h in rr: effrt over 2f out: nvr a factor* **66/1**

2020 9 1/2 **Knockamany Bends (IRE)**13 5683 4-9-5 53 PaddyAspell 3 35
(John Wainwright) *led: hdd over 1f out: sn wknd* **14/1**

1562 10 nk **Lord Buffhead**3 6014 5-8-13 52 (v) DuilioDaSilva(5) 12 33
(Richard Guest) *dwlt: hdwy to chse ldrs over 3f out: wknd over 1f out* **11/2**2

6-55 11 5 **Only For You**9 5814 4-9-0 48 (t) DaleSwift 8 13
(Alan Brown) *in rr: bhd fnl 2f* **40/1**

0003 12 2 **One Kool Dude**9 5806 5-8-12 46 oh1 (b) PatrickMathers 7 5
(Micky Hammond) *dwlt: in rr: sme hdwy over 2f out: sn wknd* **25/1**

1m 12.99s (-1.61) **Going Correction** -0.225s/f (Firm)
**WFA** 3 from 4yo+ 2lb **12 Ran SP% 120.2**
Speed ratings (Par 101): **101,98,94,93,92 90,89,88,87,86 80,77**
CSF £55.65 CT £190.84 TOTE £4.20: £1.60, £4.10, £1.80; EX 69.80 Trifecta £449.20.
**Owner** D Hassan **Bred** Darley **Trained** Newmarket, Suffolk
■ Stewards' Enquiry : Billy Cray four-day ban; used whip above permitted level (19th-22nd Sept)

**FOCUS**
Most of the runners raced towards the far side and the favourite scored with plenty in hand from the clear second. The runner-up is the best guide.

## 6121 WATERAID H'CAP (DIV I) 7f
5:10 (5:10) (Class 6) (0-60,60) 3-Y-O+ £2,264 (£673; £336; £168) Stalls High

Form RPR

-064 1 **Old Man Clegg**18 5499 4-9-8 58 BarryMcHugh 8 68
(Michael Easterby) *trckd ldrs: effrt over 2f out: led last 100yds: drvn out* **13/2**2

6013 2 1 **See Clearly**16 5573 5-9-7 57 (p) DavidNolan 16 64
(Tim Easterby) *rr-div stands' side: hdwy over 2f out: chsng ldrs jst ins fnl f: kpt on same pce last 75yds* **8/1**3

0100 3 nk **Street Boss (IRE)**21 5376 3-9-4 58 (b) RussKennemore 10 62
(Jedd O'Keeffe) *dwlt: t.k.h: stdy hdwy to ld over 4f out: hdd ins fnl f: no ex* **20/1**

5400 4 3/4 **Funding Deficit (IRE)**16 5565 4-9-7 60 GaryBartley(3) 7 64
(Jim Goldie) *hld up in mid-div: effrt over 2f out: styd on same pce last 150yds* **16/1**

0632 5 1 1/4 **It's All A Game**7 5891 3-8-12 57 (b) DuilioDaSilva(5) 2 56
(Richard Guest) *chsd ldrs: hung rt over 1f out: kpt on one pce* **8/1**3

0454 6 1 3/4 **Jebel Tara**11 5761 9-9-4 54 (tp) PaulPickard 11 50
(Alan Brown) *mid-div stands' side: hdwy whn hmpd over 2f out: kpt on same pce over 1f out* **11/1**

0020 7 nk **Nelson's Bay**9 5811 5-9-10 60 IanBrennan 5 56
(Wilf Storey) *in rr: hdwy over 2f out: hmpd over 1f out: kpt on fnl f* **16/1**

5500 8 nk **Shearian**14 5640 4-9-3 53 (p) RoystonFfrench 13 48
(Tracy Waggott) *mid-div: effrt and nt clr run over 2f out: kpt on fnl f* **10/1**

1504 9 1/2 **Romantic Bliss (IRE)**37 4785 3-8-10 55 (v) RobJFitzpatrick(5) 4 47
(K R Burke) *mid-div: edgd rt and n.m.r over 1f out: sn fdd* **14/1**

0126 10 2 1/2 **Sugar Town**28 5142 4-9-2 55 ConnorBeasley(3) 12 42
(Peter Niven) *w ldrs stands' side: edgd lft over 2f out: fdd over 1f out* **3/1**1

030 11 6 **Genax (IRE)**29 5103 3-8-6 51 JoeDoyle(5) 9 21
(John Wainwright) *led: hdd over 4f out: wknd over 1f out* **9/1**

060 12 hd **Habeshia**17 5532 4-8-10 46 (bt) DaleSwift 6 17
(John Best) *chsd ldrs: lost pl over 2f out* **28/1**

-004 13 nk **Seraphima**18 5510 4-8-12 48 (v) AndrewElliott 15 18
(Lisa Williamson) *dwlt: in rr stands' side: nvr on terms* **66/1**

5550 14 17 **Edward Elgar**12 5717 3-8-9 52 (v1) GeorgeChaloner(3) 3
(Richard Whitaker) *sn drvn along in rr: bhd fnl 5f: t.o* **25/1**

5-00 15 16 **Time For Crabbies (IRE)**7 5897 4-8-10 51 (v) KevinStott(5) 1
(Lisa Williamson) *rr-div: hdwy 3f out: sn lost pl and bhd: eased ins fnl f: t.o* **50/1**

1m 27.09s (-0.71) **Going Correction** -0.225s/f (Firm)
**WFA** 3 from 4yo+ 4lb **15 Ran SP% 121.9**
Speed ratings (Par 101): **95,93,93,92,91 89,88,88,87,85 78,78,77,58,39**
CSF £55.02 CT £1024.84 TOTE £6.70: £3.10, £3.40, £3.80; EX 39.30 Trifecta £526.20.
**Owner** Irkroy Racing & Steve Hull **Bred** R S Cockerill (farms) Ltd **Trained** Sheriff Hutton, N Yorks

**FOCUS**
The pace was not very strong in this handicap but one of the market leaders battled well to score. The form is rated around the runner-up.

## 6122 WATERAID H'CAP (DIV II) 7f
5:45 (5:46) (Class 6) (0-60,60) 3-Y-O+ £2,264 (£673; £336; £168) Stalls High

Form RPR

0020 1 **Rocky's Pride (IRE)**18 5512 8-8-8 47 GeorgeChaloner(3) 3 57
(Richard Whitaker) *w ldrs: led over 2f out: jnd ins fnl f: hld on towards fin* **6/1**3

4256 2 nk **Blue Sonic**25 5234 4-9-3 53 DavidNolan 4 62
(Jim Goldie) *in rr-div: hdwy over 3f out: sn drvn: chsng ldrs over 1f out: 2nd last 100yds: no ex clsng stages* **16/1**

0305 3 2 1/4 **Niceonemyson**9 5817 5-9-5 60 1 KevinStott(5) 5 64
(Christopher Wilson) *in rr: hdwy over 2f out: chsng ldrs 1f out: wknd towards fin* **12/1**

0310 4 1 **Secret City (IRE)**21 5376 8-9-9 59 (p) AdamBeschizza 7 60
(Robin Bastiman) *rr-div: hdwy over 2f out: kpt on same pce appr fnl f* **16/1**

0013 5 2 1/4 **Sky Crossing**14 5640 5-9-3 53 DougieCostello 11 48
(Tom Tate) *led: hdd over 2f out: one pce over 1f out* **7/2**1

6254 6 hd **Lewamy (IRE)**17 5537 4-8-9 48 BillyCray(3) 16 43
(John Best) *in rr: styd on over 1f out: nvr nr ldrs* **28/1**

0000 7 1 1/4 **Dennis**15 5602 4-9-8 58 (b1) AndrewElliott 10 49
(Tim Easterby) *chsd ldrs: one pce fnl 2f* **8/1**

6204 8 1 1/2 **Secret Applause**14 5631 3-9-1 58 ConnorBeasley(3) 6 43
(Michael Dods) *s.s: in rr: sme hdwy over 2f out: nvr a factor* **11/1**

03-4 9 3/4 **Crossley**95 2843 5-9-5 55 BarryMcHugh 2 41
(Geoffrey Oldroyd) *hld up in mid-div: effrt over 2f out: nvr a factor* **14/1**

-000 10 1 **Noble Reach**13 5683 3-8-3 48 JordanNason(5) 15 29
(Lawrence Mullaney) *in rr: drvn and sme hdwy 3f out: nvr nr ldrs* **66/1**

3 11 nk **Hazza The Jazza**39 4727 4-8-10 51 (b) DuilioDaSilva(5) 8 33
(Richard Guest) *dwlt: in rr: hdwy over 2f out: nvr on terms* **11/2**2

6400 12 1/2 **Bold And Free**37 4792 4-8-11 47 PaddyAspell 9 28
(David Thompson) *chsd ldrs: wknd over 1f out* **25/1**

0005 13 7 **Card High (IRE)**24 5269 4-8-12 48 (t) IanBrennan 12 11
(Wilf Storey) *a towards rr: bhd whn eased clsng stages* **20/1**

00-0 14 1 3/4 **Last Supper**24 5269 5-9-1 51 (p) TonyHamilton 1 9
(James Bethell) *chsd ldrs: lost pl 2f out: bhd whn eased clsng stages* **28/1**

4015 15 2 1/2 **Bertie Blu Boy**15 5605 6-9-6 56 (b) RoystonFfrench 13 8
(Lisa Williamson) *chsd ldr: wknd qckly over 1f out: bhd whn eased clsng stages* **16/1**

020 16 2 1/4 **Mitchum**21 5376 5-9-4 54 (v) DaleSwift 14
(Ron Barr) *swtchd lft after s: in rr: sme hdwy over 2f out: sn wknd: bhd whn eased clsng stages* **16/1**

1m 27.01s (-0.79) **Going Correction** -0.225s/f (Firm)
**WFA** 3 from 4yo+ 4lb **16 Ran SP% 126.2**
Speed ratings (Par 101): **95,94,92,90,88 88,86,85,84,83 82,82,74,72,69 66**
CSF £95.95 CT £770.45 TOTE £8.70: £2.10, £2.90, £3.90, £2.70; EX 155.10 Trifecta £1006.90.
**Owner** R M Whitaker **Bred** London Thoroughbred Services Ltd **Trained** Scarcroft, W Yorks
■ Stewards' Enquiry : David Nolan two-day ban; careless riding (19th-20th Sept)

**FOCUS**
They were spread across the track in this handicap and there was a tight finish. The time was similar to division I.
T/Plt: £10.20 to a £1 stake. Pool: £71,032.04 - 5,077.94 winning tickets T/Qpdt: £2.40 to a £1 stake. Pool: £4,792.51 - 1,469.26 winning tickets WG

# 6053 BADEN-BADEN (L-H)
Friday, September 5

**OFFICIAL GOING: Turf: good**

## 6123a BADEN-BADENER ZUKUNFTSRENNEN (GROUP 3) (2YO) (TURF) 7f
4:25 (12:00) 2-Y-O
£26,666 (£9,166; £4,583; £2,500; £1,666; £1,250)

RPR

1 **Citron Spirit (IRE)**25 2-9-0 0 AntoineHamelin 1 104+
(Matthieu Palussiere, France) *mde all: rdn 2f out: r.o strly and forged clr: in full control fnl f: easily* **3/1**3

2 4 **Niyama (GER)**54 2-8-10 0 SHellyn 5 89
(Mario Hofer, Germany) *t.k.h: hld up and towards rr early: midfield 1/2-way: rdn into st: kpt on and wnt 2nd nring fin: no ch w wnr* **113/10**

3 nk **Le Tiger Still (GER)** 2-9-0 0 FilipMinarik 8 92
(P Vovcenko, Germany) *trckd wnr: rdn and effrt to chal into st: sn outpcd: kpt on but wl hld and dropped to 3rd nring fin* **249/10**

4 1 1/4 **Majestic Hope (GER)** 2-8-10 0 EPedroza 3 85
(A Wohler, Germany) *t.k.h: prom on inner: rdn 2f out: sn outpcd by wnr: no ex and dropped to 4th fnl f* **11/2**

5 1 **Starwood (GER)** 2-9-0 0 AdriedeVries 6 86
(P Schiergen, Germany) *niggled along and sn towards rr: rdn over 3f out: plugged on u.p in st but n.d* **13/5**1

6 1 **Dashing Home (GER)** 2-9-0 0 APietsch 10 84
(Waldemar Hickst, Germany) *midfield in tch on outer: rdn over 2f out: outpcd whn short of room on rail over 1f out: kpt on but n.d after and wl hld* **57/10**

7 nk **Tamakh (FR)**36 2-9-0 0 DanielePorcu 7 83
(M Rulec, Germany) *a towards rr: rdn over 2f out: plugged on u.p in st but nvr a factor* **189/10**

8 1 1/2 **Palace Prince (GER)**45 4524 2-9-2 0 AHelfenbein 4 81
(Andreas Lowe, Germany) *midfield in tch: rdn and brief effrt into st: sn outpcd by wnr: no ex and wknd fnl f: eased toward fin* **27/10**2

9 10 **Meqlaam (GER)**45 4524 2-9-0 0 (p) BGanbat 9 52
(K Demme, Germany) *niggled along and a in rr: rdn and no imp in st: sn btn: wknd and bhd fnl f: nvr a factor* **44/1**

1m 26.58s (2.68) **9 Ran SP% 129.4**
WIN (incl. 10 euro stake): 40. PLACES: 18, 27, 47. SF: 389.
**Owner** Zalim Bifov **Bred** Mrs E Bifova **Trained** France

# 5160 ASCOT (R-H)
Saturday, September 6

**OFFICIAL GOING: Good to firm (good in places; straight 8.4, round 8.0)**
Wind: Almost nil Weather: Becoming brighter

## 6124 FLY LONDON SOUTHEND AIRPORT H'CAP (QUALIFIER FOR BALMORAL HCAP ON QIPCO BRITISH CHAMPIONS DAY) 7f
1:55 (1:57) (Class 2) 3-Y-O+ £51,752 (£15,400; £7,696; £3,848) Stalls High

Form RPR

0014 1 **Safety Check (IRE)**14 5665 3-8-12 101 CamHardie(5) 12 108
(Charlie Appleby) *trckd ldng pair nr side: chal fr 2f out: upsides 1f out: chsd ldr after and looked hld: styd on to ld fnl stride* **8/1**3

06 2 hd **Redvers (IRE)**14 5665 6-9-1 95 (b) TedDurcan 13 104+
(Ed Vaughan) *hld up in midfield nr side: smooth prog 2f out: rdn to ld 1f out: looked sure to win tl idled last 75yds: hdd fnl stride* **7/1**2

11-1 3 shd **Cornrow**28 5178 4-9-0 94 WilliamBuick 6 102+
(John Gosden) *overall ldr in centre: shkn up 2f out: hdd 1f out: styd on wl nr fin: jst failed* **4/1**1

4060 4 shd **Fort Bastion (IRE)**16 5609 5-9-1 95 (b1) JamesSullivan 7 103
(Ruth Carr) *hld up in centre: shkn up and prog 2f out: tried to chal fnl f: styd on wl but a jst hld* **20/1**

3311 5 hd **Highland Acclaim (IRE)**28 5165 3-8-11 98 SamJames(3) 2 103
(David O'Meara) *stdd s and swtchd to r nr side: hld up: prog 2f out against nr side rail: styd on wl fnl f: gaining at fin* **16/1**

0000 6 3/4 **Hawkeyethenoo (IRE)**42 4648 8-9-6 100 GrahamLee 18 106
(Jim Goldie) *hld up in last pair of nr side gp: stl there 2f out: waiting for room over 1f out: gd prog after: r.o wl nr fin* **20/1**

0100 7 1 **Louis The Pious**42 4648 6-9-10 104 FMBerry 4 107
(David O'Meara) *hld up in last of centre gp: rdn 2f out: prog on outer over 1f out: styd on fnl f: nrst fin* **16/1**

3-24 **8** *nk* **Day Of Conquest**[28] 5192 3-9-4 **102**.......... RyanMoore 14 102
(Richard Hannon) *w.w in last trio nr side: rdn over 2f out: sme prog over 1f out: kpt on but n.d* **10/1**

6102 **9** *1* **Free Wheeling (AUS)**[36] 4872 6-9-10 **104**..........(t) HarryBentley 17 104
(Saeed bin Suroor) *trckd nr side ldrs: rdn 2f out: one pce and no real imp after* **25/1**

5420 **10** *hd* **Alfred Hutchinson**[15] 5653 6-9-3 **97**.......... BarryMcHugh 3 96
(Geoffrey Oldroyd) *chsd ldrs in centre: rdn over 2f out: sn outpcd: one pce over 1f out* **25/1**

0003 **11** *3* **Pacific Heights (IRE)**[34] 4949 5-8-12 **99**.......... MikeyEnnis(7) 1 90
(Brian Ellison) *chsd ldrs in centre: rdn over 2f out: outpcd sn after: no prog fnl f* **14/1**

0051 **12** *3 1/4* **Don't Call Me (IRE)**[28] 5163 7-9-3 **97**..........(t) PaulHanagan 15 80
(David Nicholls) *chsd nr side ldrs: rdn over 2f out: wknd over 1f out* **7/1**[2]

5060 **13** *shd* **Captain Ramius (IRE)**[21] 5445 8-9-4 **98**.......... PJMcDonald 8 81
(Kevin Ryan) *chsd ldr in centre to 2f out: steadily wknd* **50/1**

1200 **14** *1 3/4* **Heavy Metal**[7] 5919 4-9-5 **99**.......... JoeFanning 5 77
(Mark Johnston) *chsd ldrs in centre: lost pl 2f out: sn btn* **14/1**

031 **15** *5* **Almargo (IRE)**[14] 5665 3-9-4 **102**.......... RoystonFfrench 16 65
(Mark Johnston) *led nr side gp: rdn over 2f out: hdd & wknd qckly over 1f out* **14/1**

0016 **16** *6* **Red Avenger (USA)**[16] 5609 4-9-5 **99**..........(b) JimmyFortune 11 48
(Ed Dunlop) *hld up in rr nr side: no prog 2f out: sn wknd* **20/1**

1100 **17** *3 3/4* **Purcell (IRE)**[98] 2758 4-9-1 **95**..........(v[1]) DavidProbert 10 35
(Andrew Balding) *w nr side ldr to over 2f out: wknd rapidly* **25/1**

1m 26.44s (-1.16) **Going Correction** +0.05s/f (Good)
**WFA** 3 from 4yo+ 4lb **17 Ran SP% 124.8**
Speed ratings (Par 109): **108,107,107,107,107 106,105,104,103,103 100,96,96,94,88 81,77**
CSF £57.59 CT £265.58 TOTE £8.30: £2.10, £2.40, £1.60, £5.50; EX 61.60 Trifecta £196.30.
**Owner** Godolphin **Bred** Malih Al Basti **Trained** Newmarket, Suffolk

**FOCUS**
Straight course stands' rail was 7yds inside normal position. Round course rail positioned 4yds inside from 1m2f, increased to 9yds at bend into straight and continued at 9yds along far side of straight to winning post. Old Mile increased by 10yds and 1m4f by 16yds. A cracking handicap. There was a solid enough pace, with the main action developing stands-to-middle side and, although there was a bunch finish, the form is solid, set around the fourth.

## 6125 MCGEE GROUP EBF STALLIONS MAIDEN STKS (BOBIS RACE) 7f
**2:25** (2:30) (Class 4) 2-Y-O **£5,175** (£1,540; £769; £384) **Stalls** High

Form RPR

3 **1** **Mutasayyid**[27] 5201 2-9-5 0.......... FrankieDettori 9 86+
(Richard Hannon) *trckd ldng pair: clsd to ld over 1f out: rdn and styd on wl fnl f* **9/2**[2]

**2** *1/2* **Akeed Champion** 2-9-5 0.......... JamesDoyle 10 85+
(Michael Bell) *w.w towards rr: prog jst over 2f out: chsd wnr jst over 1f out: chal fnl f: r.o but jst hld* **12/1**

**3** *1 3/4* **Intilaaq (USA)** 2-9-5 0.......... PaulHanagan 8 79+
(Roger Varian) *trckd ldrs: pushed along over 2f out: prog to take 3rd fnl f: shkn up and styd on same pce* **8/1**

**4** *1/2* **Muqtaser (USA)** 2-9-5 0.......... JackMitchell 4 78+
(Roger Varian) *rrd s: wl in rr: pushed along over 2f out: prog over 1f out: styd on to press for 3rd nr fin* **25/1**

**5** *2 1/4* **Ashridge Lad** 2-9-5 0.......... JimmyFortune 2 72+
(Brian Meehan) *dwlt: hld up in rr: pushed along over 2f out: nvr on terms but styd on steadily fnl f* **33/1**

2 **6** *nse* **Auspicion**[41] 4695 2-9-5 0.......... RyanMoore 5 71
(William Haggas) *led: rdn 2f out: hdd over 1f out: sn wknd* **6/5**[1]

**7** *3/4* **Wally's Wisdom** 2-9-5 0.......... JoeFanning 7 69+
(William Haggas) *chsd ldrs: shkn up and no prog 2f out: steadily fdd* **20/1**

**8** *1 1/4* **Dagher** 2-9-5 0.......... GrahamLee 1 66
(Peter Chapple-Hyam) *dwlt: wl in rr: pushed along over 2f out: kpt on one pce fr over 1f out* **20/1**

**9** *1/2* **Sugar Boy (GER)** 2-9-5 0.......... WilliamBuick 12 65
(John Gosden) *dwlt: mostly detached in last: pushed along 3f out: nvr a factor but kpt on fnl f* **7/1**[3]

**10** *nk* **Spirited Acclaim (IRE)** 2-9-0 0.......... TedDurcan 6 59
(David Elsworth) *chsd ldrs tl wknd fr 2f out* **33/1**

4 **11** *7* **Azzir (IRE)**[29] 5131 2-9-5 0.......... FMBerry 3 45
(Timothy Jarvis) *pressed ldr: rdn and racd awkwardly over 2f out: wknd rapidly wl over 1f out* **50/1**

1m 29.44s (1.84) **Going Correction** +0.05s/f (Good) **11 Ran SP% 116.2**
Speed ratings (Par 97): **91,90,88,87,85 85,84,82,82,82 74**
CSF £49.03 TOTE £5.50: £1.90, £3.10, £2.50; EX 54.40 Trifecta £342.80.
**Owner** Hamdan Al Maktoum **Bred** Jeremy Green & Sons & P Bickmore **Trained** East Everleigh, Wilts

**FOCUS**
A good 2yo maiden that will produce winners. They kept towards the centre of the track and two came right away near the finish.

## 6126 ACTIVIA HYPERION FILLIES' CONDITIONS STKS (10K FIELD SIZE BONUS RACE) (BOBIS RACE) 1m (R)
**3:00** (3:01) (Class 2) 2-Y-O **£9,056** (£2,695; £1,346; £673) **Stalls** Low

Form RPR

21 **1** **Good Place (USA)**[21] 5424 2-8-12 0.......... RyanMoore 1 94+
(Saeed bin Suroor) *sn hld up in 3rd: shkn up over 2f out: clsd to ld 1f out: pushed out firmly last 100yds* **10/11**[1]

01 **2** *nk* **Montalcino (IRE)**[21] 5416 2-8-12 **85**.......... JimmyFortune 2 93
(Brian Meehan) *led: shkn up 2f out: hdd and edgd lft 1f out: styd on to press wnr after but a hld* **6/1**

421 **3** *2 1/4* **Shagah (IRE)**[37] 4825 2-8-12 **84**.......... FrankieDettori 5 88
(Richard Hannon) *hld up in last: shkn up over 1f out: rdn and nt qckn over 1f out: kpt on fnl f to take 3rd nr fin* **10/3**[2]

1241 **4** *1/2* **Russian Punch**[14] 5680 2-8-12 **95**.......... GrahamLee 3 87
(James Given) *trckd ldr: rdn 2f out: tried to chal over 1f out: fdd fnl f* **5/1**[3]

1m 41.89s (1.19) **Going Correction** +0.05s/f (Good) **4 Ran SP% 106.4**
Speed ratings (Par 98): **96,95,93,92**
CSF £6.30 TOTE £1.70; EX 6.40 Trifecta £19.10.
**Owner** Godolphin **Bred** Darley **Trained** Newmarket, Suffolk

**FOCUS**
They went a fair tempo. This good-quality fillies' conditions event proved a decent test and the form ought to work out.

## 6127 WINNING POST BOOKMAKERS BRISTOL H'CAP (HERITAGE HANDICAP) (BOBIS RACE) 1m 4f
**3:30** (3:31) (Class 2) 3-Y-O **£97,035** (£28,875; £14,430; £7,215) **Stalls** Low

Form RPR

521 **1** **Battersea**[56] 4183 3-9-0 **90**.......... GrahamLee 16 103+
(Roger Varian) *hld up in midfield: pushed along and prog over 2f out: led 1f out: sn in command: pushed out: comf* **8/1**[1]

5212 **2** *1 1/2* **Gwafa (IRE)**[28] 5179 3-8-11 **87**.......... ColmO'Donoghue 10 97
(Marco Botti) *trckd ldng trio: clsd gng wl to ld 2f out: rdn and hdd 1f out: styd on but no match for wnr* **8/1**[1]

112 **3** *1 1/4* **Agent Murphy**[41] 4698 3-9-5 **95**.......... JimmyFortune 7 103
(Brian Meehan) *t.k.h early: trckd ldrs and sn in 7th: rdn and nt qckn 2f out: styd on fr over 1f out to take 3rd nr fin* **12/1**[3]

2102 **4** *1/2* **Astronereus (IRE)**[28] 5164 3-9-1 **91**.......... PatDobbs 8 98
(Amanda Perrett) *trckd ldrs in 6th: rdn to cl over 2f out: chsd ldng pair over 1f out: no imp: lost 3rd nr fin* **8/1**[1]

2041 **5** *1 1/2* **Gothic**[27] 5203 3-9-0 **90**.......... RyanMoore 17 95
(Sir Michael Stoute) *nt that wl away: wl in rr: 14th 4f out: drvn on outer over 2f out: styd on fr over 1f out: nrst fin* **16/1**

0021 **6** *1/2* **Galizzi (USA)**[10] 5818 3-8-9 **90**.......... DanielMuscutt(5) 6 94
(Michael Bell) *hld up in last quartet: nt clrest of runs but stdy prog fr over 2f out: chsd ldrs 1f out: effrt flattened out last 100yds* **25/1**

-113 **7** *nk* **Second Step (IRE)**[35] 4893 3-9-3 **93**.......... ShaneKelly 18 96+
(Luca Cumani) *hld up in rr: 12th 4f out: pushed along and weaved way through fr 2f out: nvr on terms w ldrs but kpt on* **10/1**[2]

2251 **8** *shd* **Montaly**[28] 5179 3-9-7 **97**.......... DavidProbert 5 100
(Andrew Balding) *hld up wl in rr: pushed along in last 3f out: brought wd in st: drvn and styd on fr over 1f out: nrst fin* **12/1**[3]

1012 **9** *1 1/4* **Hidden Gold (IRE)**[31] 5052 3-8-10 **86**.......... HarryBentley 11 87
(Saeed bin Suroor) *trckd ldrs in 5th: shkn up over 2f out: no imp over 1f out: fdd* **20/1**

4641 **10** *2 1/4* **Swivel**[15] 5633 3-9-4 **94**.......... JoeFanning 2 92
(Mark Johnston) *hld up in midfield: disputing 10th 4f out: trying to make prog but no real ch whn short of room over 1f out: no hdwy after* **16/1**

4116 **11** *hd* **Penhill**[14] 5691 3-8-13 **89**.......... PJMcDonald 9 86
(James Bethell) *a in midfield: shkn up and no prog over 2f out* **10/1**[2]

2210 **12** *1 1/2* **Our Gabrial (IRE)**[14] 5691 3-8-10 **91**.......... JackGarritty(5) 1 86
(Richard Fahey) *hld up wl in rr on inner: pushed along 4f out: prog over 2f out: swtchd lft jst over 1f out: no hdwy fnl f: nvr involved* **20/1**

2420 **13** *1/2* **Notarised**[14] 5691 3-8-8 **84**.......... RoystonFfrench 15 78
(Mark Johnston) *sn led: hdd 2f out: wknd over 1f out* **33/1**

0610 **14** *nse* **Trip To Paris (IRE)**[28] 5164 3-9-0 **90**..........(b) FMBerry 4 84
(Ed Dunlop) *hld up in last quartet: shkn up and no prog over 2f out: nvr a factor* **16/1**

4061 **15** *1 1/4* **Nancy From Nairobi**[33] 4984 3-9-1 **94**.......... CharlesBishop(3) 13 86
(Mick Channon) *t.k.h: trckd ldr to over 2f out: wknd qckly* **33/1**

4200 **16** *2 1/2* **Satellite (IRE)**[15] 5651 3-9-3 **93**.......... FrankieDettori 12 81
(William Haggas) *slowest away and in last early: sme prog on outer fr 1/2-way: disp 10th 4f out: sn rdn: wknd 2f out* **14/1**

2312 **17** *3/4* **Rainbow Rock (IRE)**[37] 4821 3-8-5 **86**.......... CamHardie(5) 14 73
(Mark Johnston) *sn wl in rr: rdn 4f out: no prog* **8/1**[1]

0330 **18** *22* **Bureau (IRE)**[13] 5720 3-8-9 **85**.......... WilliamBuick 3 37
(Mark Johnston) *trckd ldng trio to over 2f out: wknd qckly over 1f out: virtually p.u nr fin* **40/1**

2m 30.31s (-2.19) **Going Correction** +0.05s/f (Good) **18 Ran SP% 124.0**
Speed ratings (Par 107): **109,108,107,106,105 105,105,105,104,102 102,101,101,101,100 98,98,83**
CSF £62.19 CT £783.97 TOTE £6.30: £1.60, £2.40, £3.60, £2.60; EX 58.90 Trifecta £2199.20.
**Owner** H R H Sultan Ahmad Shah **Bred** Newsells Park Stud **Trained** Newmarket, Suffolk

**FOCUS**
Another tremendously competitive edition of this valuable 3yo handicap. It was run at a strong pace and should prove to be top form.

## 6128 WONDERING WINE COMPANY NURSERY H'CAP (10K FIELD SIZE BONUS RACE) (BOBIS RACE) 5f
**4:05** (4:06) (Class 2) 2-Y-O **£15,525** (£4,620; £2,308; £1,154) **Stalls** High

Form RPR

4131 **1** **Squats (IRE)**[28] 5173 2-9-1 **89**.......... RyanMoore 5 96+
(William Haggas) *hld up in last pair: stl there 2f out: swtchd sharply lft over 1f out: hrd rdn and r.o strly fnl f to ld post* **9/4**[1]

312 **2** *nse* **Profitable (IRE)**[28] 5173 2-8-10 **84**.......... WilliamBuick 3 91+
(Clive Cox) *hld up in last pair: prog 2f out: rdn to ld jst ins fnl f: styd on wl but hdd post* **3/1**[2]

2450 **3** *1 3/4* **Union Rose**[16] 5607 2-9-7 **95**..........(p) WilliamTwiston-Davies 11 96
(Ronald Harris) *led: rdn over 1f out: hdd jst ins fnl f: one pce after and lost 2nd nr fin* **14/1**

3243 **4** *3/4* **Sunset Sail (IRE)**[4] 6003 2-9-1 **89**.......... PatDobbs 1 87
(Richard Hannon) *pressed ldrs: nt pce to hold pl fr 2f out: styd on again fnl f to take 4th nr fin* **8/1**[3]

5112 **5** *1/2* **Bowson Fred**[4] 5998 2-8-2 **76**.......... JamesSullivan 10 72
(Michael Easterby) *trckd ldrs: shkn up and prog 2f out: chsd ldng pair briefly fnl f: one pce after* **8/1**[3]

4162 **6** *hd* **Geological (IRE)**[21] 5409 2-8-3 **82**.......... CamHardie(5) 4 77
(Richard Hannon) *pressed ldr: shkn up 1/2-way: lost 2nd over 1f out: steadily fdd* **16/1**

4110 **7** *1 1/2* **Indaria**[13] 5714 2-8-8 **82**.......... TedDurcan 6 72
(Rod Millman) *hld up bhd ldrs: nt qckn 2f out: steadily fdd over 1f out* **33/1**

1061 **8** *1 1/4* **Majestic Hero (IRE)**[8] 5879 2-8-10 **84**.......... DavidProbert 9 69
(Ronald Harris) *hld up bhd ldrs: shkn up 2f out: nt qckn and wl hld after: fdd* **11/1**

0240 **9** *3/4* **Denzille Lane (IRE)**[17] 5580 2-8-11 **85**.......... JoeFanning 7 68
(Mark Johnston) *pressed ldrs to 1/2-way: steadily fdd fnl 2f* **20/1**

3145 **10** *1 1/4* **Epithet (IRE)**[56] 4218 2-9-1 **89**.......... GrahamLee 8 67
(Charlie Appleby) *trckd ldrs: nt qckn 2f out: wl in rr whn short of room 1f out* **11/1**

1m 0.21s (-0.29) **Going Correction** +0.05s/f (Good) **10 Ran SP% 114.9**
Speed ratings (Par 101): **104,103,101,99,99 98,96,94,93,91**
CSF £8.63 CT £74.85 TOTE £2.90: £1.60, £1.50, £3.10; EX 7.00 Trifecta £53.90.
**Owner** Sheikh Rashid Dalmook Al Maktoum **Bred** Paul McEnery **Trained** Newmarket, Suffolk

**FOCUS**
A decent nursery and pretty straightforward form.

## 6129 RITZ CLUB FILLIES' H'CAP 1m (S)
4:40 (4:42) (Class 3) (0-95,90) 3-Y-O+ £9,703 (£2,887; £1,443; £721) Stalls High

Form RPR
2012 1 **Bold Lass (IRE)**[19] 5505 3-9-3 86 WilliamBuick 7 97+
(David Lanigan) *hld up in midfield: clsd on ldrs fr 2f out gng wl: drvn to ld jst ins fnl f: hrd pressed after: hld on wl* 7/2[1]
6213 2 nk **Joys Of Spring (IRE)**[30] 5107 3-9-1 84 RyanMoore 6 94
(Luca Cumani) *hld up in rr: prog wl over 1f out: drvn to chal ins fnl f: nt qckn last 75yds* 6/1[3]
1211 3 1 ¼ **Who's That Chick (IRE)**[30] 5074 5-8-9 76 RyanTate(3) 3 84
(Ralph J Smith) *prom: rdn to ld over 1f out: hdd and one pce jst ins fnl f* 16/1
0450 4 nk **Auction (IRE)**[23] 5369 4-9-7 90 CamHardie(5) 2 97
(Ed Dunlop) *hld up and sn in last: prog jst over 2f out: shkn up over 1f out: styd on to take 4th nr fin: nvr nr enough to chal* 8/1
4225 5 1 ¾ **Alpine Storm (IRE)**[12] 5758 3-8-6 75 JoeFanning 4 77
(Mark Johnston) *led: rdn and hdd over 1f out: kpt on tl one pce last 100yds* 20/1
4640 6 2 ¼ **Subtle Knife**[10] 5826 5-8-12 76 WilliamCarson 11 74
(Giles Bravery) *in tch: rdn and nt qckn over 2f out: sn btn: plugged on again fnl f* 50/1
2122 7 shd **Lulu The Zulu (IRE)**[38] 4783 6-9-7 85 AndrewMullen 8 83
(Michael Appleby) *dwlt: hld up towards rr: rdn and no prog jst over 2f out: nvr on terms after* 7/1
3041 8 shd **Brown Diamond (IRE)**[8] 5883 3-8-9 78 DavidProbert 10 75
(Charles Hills) *settled towards rr: tried to make prog fr 2f out: rdn and no hdwy over 1f out* 33/1
1-16 9 2 ¼ **Alzanti (USA)**[42] 4679 3-9-1 84 PatDobbs 13 75
(Amanda Perrett) *wl in tch: rdn over 2f out: no prog and btn over 1f out: fdd fnl f* 14/1
0201 10 2 ¼ **Simply Shining (IRE)**[12] 5763 4-8-7 76 JackGarritty(5) 5 63
(Richard Fahey) *mostly chsd ldr to 2f out: sn wknd* 25/1
2115 11 1 ½ **Laftah (IRE)**[42] 4668 3-9-0 83 GrahamLee 9 66
(Roger Varian) *trckd ldrs: shkn up over 2f out: wknd over 1f out* 16/1
1161 12 8 **Buredyma**[30] 5107 3-9-0 83 (p) FrankieDettori 1 47
(William Haggas) *racd away fr rest: prom: rdn over 2f out: wknd rapidly wl over 1f out* 14/1
1-12 13 13 **Fray**[29] 5151 3-8-13 82 JimmyFortune 12 17
(Roger Charlton) *awkward s: in tch in midfield: shkn up over 2f out: wknd qckly and heavily eased* 4/1[2]

1m 39.36s (-1.44) **Going Correction** +0.05s/f (Good)
**WFA** 3 from 4yo+ 5lb 13 Ran SP% 118.7
Speed ratings (Par 104): **109,108,107,107,105 103,103,102,100,98 96,88,75**
CSF £23.06 CT £301.08 TOTE £4.00: £1.70, £2.40, £3.90; EX 23.60 Trifecta £284.20.
**Owner** B E Nielsen **Bred** Bjorn E Nielsen **Trained** Upper Lambourn, Berks

**FOCUS**
A highly competitive fillies' handicap where again the centre of the track was favoured, but the main action developed more towards the far side. The winner progressed again. It was run at just an average pace.

## 6130 RARC IN AID OF THE IJF H'CAP 5f
5:15 (5:17) (Class 3) (0-90,90) 3-Y-O+ £8,409 (£2,502; £1,250; £625) Stalls High

Form RPR
5331 1 **Algar Lad**[36] 4859 4-9-4 90 SamJames(3) 6 104
(David O'Meara) *trckd ldng pair far side: gng strly over 1f out: produced to ld jst ins fnl f but immediately jnd: drvn and r.o wl* 20/1
3353 2 hd **Marmalady (IRE)**[17] 5559 4-8-10 79 WilliamBuick 4 92
(Gary Moore) *trckd ldng pair far side: rdn to chal and w wnr jst ins fnl f: r.o but jst hld last strides* 12/1
0003 3 2 ½ **Taajub (IRE)**[14] 5677 7-9-3 86 ShaneKelly 10 90
(Peter Crate) *pressed ldr nr side: led grpoup 2f out: kpt on but nvr on terms w ldng pair fnl f* 20/1
1100 4 ½ **Rural Celebration**[14] 5696 3-9-2 86 GrahamLee 9 88
(David O'Meara) *prom nr side: chal fr 2f out: rdn and styd on same pce fr over 1f out* 20/1
3052 5 hd **Secret Millionaire (IRE)**[6] 5945 7-8-3 77 CamHardie(5) 16 78
(Luke Dace) *w nr side ldrs: chal 2f out: styd pressing fnl f but nt on terms w ldng pair far side* 14/1
0000 6 nk **Zero Money (IRE)**[35] 4895 8-9-7 90 (b) JoeFanning 1 90
(Hugo Palmer) *w ldr far side: upsides 1f out: fdd last 150yds* 20/1
0600 7 nse **Riskit Fora Biskit (IRE)**[21] 5419 4-9-1 89 LouisSteward(5) 3 89
(Michael Bell) *overall ldr far side: hdd and fdd jst ins fnl f* 20/1
6540 8 nse **Gabbiano**[15] 5623 5-8-7 83 DavidParkes(7) 2 83
(Jeremy Gask) *dwlt: hld up in rr far side: gng bttr than many whn prog wl over 1f out: rdn and styd on same pce fnl f* 14/1
2004 9 hd **Slip Sliding Away (IRE)**[35] 4892 7-8-13 85 ThomasBrown(3) 13 84
(Peter Hedger) *in tch nr side: rdn and outpcd fr 2f out: styd on again ins fnl f* 10/1
3300 10 hd **Secret Witness**[17] 5575 8-9-6 89 (b) DavidProbert 5 88
(Ronald Harris) *in rr of far side gp: rdn and struggling wl over 1f out: styd on ins fnl f* 16/1
211 11 ½ **Perfect Muse**[45] 4553 4-8-7 79 RyanTate(3) 18 81+
(Clive Cox) *last of nr side gp and last overall: detached 2f out: picked up over 1f out: running on wl and ch of a pl whn impeded and lost momentum 100yds out* 5/1[2]
2061 12 ½ **Holley Shiftwell**[14] 5677 4-9-0 83 HarryBentley 17 78
(Stuart Williams) *trckd nr side ldrs: swtchd rt over 1f out: styd on same pce and no imp on ldrs fnl f* 10/1
0151 13 1 ¼ **Extrasolar**[53] 4284 4-9-5 88 (t) PatDobbs 7 79
(Amanda Perrett) *in rr of far side gp: no prog over 1f out: fdd fnl f* 20/1
1-35 14 hd **Foxy Forever (IRE)**[87] 3122 4-9-4 87 RyanMoore 8 77
(Michael Wigham) *hld up in rr of far side gp: rdn and no prog over 1f out: eased whn no ch last 100yds* 4/1[1]
0050 15 shd **Burning Thread (IRE)**[21] 5419 7-9-7 90 (v[1]) JamesSullivan 12 79
(Tim Etherington) *chsd nr side ldrs: rdn over 1f out: no imp after: fdd* 33/1
2104 16 2 ¼ **Oh So Sassy**[21] 5419 4-9-7 90 TedDurcan 11 77
(Chris Wall) *dwlt: in tch nr side: no prog over 1f out: wl hld whn hmpd 50yds out and eased* 8/1[3]
4143 17 ¾ **Taurus Twins**[12] 5754 8-8-11 85 (b) DanielMuscutt(5) 15 64
(Richard Price) *led nr side gp to 2f out: sn btn* 33/1
0600 18 7 **New Fforest**[41] 4700 4-9-4 87 JimmyFortune 14 40
(Andrew Balding) *in tch nr side: wknd rapidly wl over 1f out: t.o* 20/1

59.8s (-0.70) **Going Correction** +0.05s/f (Good)
**WFA** 3 from 4yo+ 1lb 18 Ran SP% 132.1
Speed ratings (Par 107): **107,106,102,101,101 101,101,100,100,100 99,98,96,96,96 92,91,80**
CSF £227.48 CT £4853.60 TOTE £20.50: £5.30, £2.60, £7.30, £4.90; EX 214.70 Trifecta £2703.40 Part won..
**Owner** Great Northern Partnership **Bred** Highclere Stud **Trained** Nawton, N Yorks

**FOCUS**
A fair and competitive sprint handicap. The field split into two groups before merging and, while the first pair kept to the far side, there appeared no real bias. Another personal best from the winner.
T/Plt: £68.60 to a £1 stake. Pool: £120,366.61 - 1,279.22 winning tickets T/Qpdt: £8.20 to a £1 stake. Pool: £7,238.11 - 647.94 winning tickets JN

# 6092 HAYDOCK (L-H)
Saturday, September 6

**OFFICIAL GOING: Good (8.2)**
Wind: Moderate to strong, half against Weather: Cloudy, turning fine. Rails: All races on Stands side home straight. 1m races increased by 50yds and 1m 6f by 100yds

## 6131 BETFRED MOBILE BE FRIENDLY H'CAP 5f
2:05 (2:06) (Class 2) (0-100,96) 3-Y-O+ £17,789 (£5,293; £2,645; £1,322) Stalls Centre

Form RPR
1406 1 **Kickboxer (IRE)**[21] 5438 3-9-3 93 LukeMorris 4 105
(Mick Channon) *in tch: rdn 2f out: chalng over 1f out: led fnl 150yds: r.o wl: in command after* 10/1
25 2 2 **Long Awaited (IRE)**[12] 5754 6-9-0 89 GrahamGibbons 6 94
(David Barron) *hld up in midfield: hdwy 2f out: r.o ins fnl f: tk 2nd towards fin: nt rch wnr* 15/2[3]
2303 3 hd **Normal Equilibrium**[7] 5925 4-9-1 90 (p) OisinMurphy 5 94
(Robert Cowell) *a.p: led wl over 1f out: sn rdn: hdd fnl 150yds: rdr sn dropped reins: kpt on u.p but hld towards fin* 8/1
0050 4 2 ¼ **Borderlescott**[35] 4895 12-9-3 92 DanielTudhope 3 88
(Robin Bastiman) *prom: lost pl over 3f out: pushed along and outpcd 1/2-way: hdwy to chse ldrs over 1f out: one pce fnl 50yds* 14/1
621 5 1 **Barnet Fair**[35] 4892 6-9-7 96 RichardHughes 1 89
(David Nicholls) *stdd s: hld up in rr: rdn over 1f out: kpt on ins fnl f: nvr able to trble ldrs* 9/2[2]
4106 6 ½ **Inxile (IRE)**[7] 5918 9-9-1 90 (p) FrannyNorton 9 81
(David Nicholls) *prom: rdn 2f out: nt qckn over 1f out: styd on same pce ins fnl f* 16/1
0100 7 hd **Sleepy Sioux**[21] 5419 3-8-7 86 (p) JoeyHaynes(3) 10 76
(David Elsworth) *led: rdn 2f out: sn hdd: wkng whn hanging lft ins fnl f* 14/1
4203 8 1 **Confessional**[21] 5445 7-9-3 92 (e) PaulMulrennan 11 78
(Tim Easterby) *hld up in mdfield: pushed along over 2f out: no imp over 1f out: one pce* 7/2[1]
65 9 1 ¾ **Doctor Parkes**[50] 4412 8-8-9 84 DeclanMcDonogh 8 64
(Stuart Williams) *midfield: rdn over 2f out: no imp over 1f out: wknd ins fnl f* 14/1
0000 10 1 ¾ **Valbchek (IRE)**[70] 3732 5-9-7 96 (p) GeorgeBaker 7 70
(Jane Chapple-Hyam) *in rr: outpcd 1/2-way: nvr on terms* 12/1
2200 11 6 **Bear Behind (IRE)**[35] 4895 5-9-5 94 HayleyTurner 12 46
(Tom Dascombe) *chsd ldr to 1/2-way: rdn and wknd 2f out* 9/1

1m 0.15s (-0.65) **Going Correction** +0.075s/f (Good)
**WFA** 3 from 4yo+ 1lb 11 Ran SP% 115.9
Speed ratings (Par 109): **108,104,104,100,99 98,98,96,93,90 81**
CSF £81.81 CT £634.33 TOTE £10.80: £2.10, £2.60, £3.30; EX 88.50 Trifecta £1869.80.
**Owner** Living Legend Racing Partnership 1 **Bred** Rathasker Stud **Trained** West Ilsley, Berks

**FOCUS**
All races were run on the Stands' Side Straight. Actual race distances: 5f, 6f, 1m 50yds, 1m 6f 100yds. Stalls: Centre: 5f and 6f Inside: 1m and 1m6f. Following 2.5mm of rain leading up to racing, the ground was officially given as good. They raced middle to stands' side, and the four horses closest to the far rail filled the first four placings. A clear personal best from the winner.

## 6132 BETFRED.COM SUPERIOR MILE (GROUP 3) 1m
2:40 (2:40) (Class 1) 3-Y-O+
£35,727 (£13,545; £6,778; £3,376; £1,694; £850) Stalls Low

Form RPR
113 1 **Captain Cat (IRE)**[14] 5666 5-9-7 115 GeorgeBaker 6 117+
(Roger Charlton) *hld up: hdwy travelling wl over 2f out: led on bit wl over 1f out: sn rdn: edgd lft ins fnl f: r.o wl and in command: comf* 15/8[1]
0100 2 1 ½ **Balty Boys (IRE)**[7] 5928 5-9-3 100 (b) PaulPickard 1 108
(Brian Ellison) *trckd ldrs: rdn and outpcd whn n.m.r briefly over 2f out: n.m.r and swtchd rt over 1f out: styd on ins fnl f: fin wl: tk 2nd fnl stride: no ch w wnr* 18/1
0001 3 hd **Ocean Tempest**[7] 5919 5-9-3 117 AdamKirby 7 108
(John Ryan) *chsd ldr: rdn to chal over 2f out: styd on same pce u.p ins fnl f* 11/4[3]
5602 4 nk **Emell**[14] 5666 4-9-3 107 RichardHughes 4 107
(Richard Hannon) *racd keenly: trckd ldrs: led over 2f out: sn rdn: hdd wl over 1f out: kpt on same pce u.p ins fnl f* 10/1
0050 5 1 ¼ **Penitent**[15] 5653 8-9-7 108 DanielTudhope 3 109
(David O'Meara) *led: rdn and hdd over 2f out: nt qckn over 1f out: kpt on ins fnl f: n.m.r towards fin and eased* 18/1
0541 6 1 **Short Squeeze (IRE)**[16] 5609 4-9-3 107 (tp) PatSmullen 5 102
(Hugo Palmer) *hld up in rr: hdwy on outer over 2f out: rdn over 1f out: one pce ins fnl f: nvr able to chal* 5/2[2]

1m 44.1s (0.40) **Going Correction** +0.225s/f (Good) 6 Ran SP% 109.6
Speed ratings: **107,105,105,105,103 102**
CSF £32.08 TOTE £2.10: £1.60, £4.70; EX 30.90 Trifecta £142.30.
**Owner** Seasons Holidays **Bred** Azienda Agricola Mediterranea **Trained** Beckhampton, Wilts

**FOCUS**
An ordinary Group 3 overall but the winner's effort was well up to scratch.

## 6133 BETFRED TV OLD BOROUGH CUP (H'CAP) 1m 6f
3:15 (3:15) (Class 2) (0-105,101) 3-Y-O£38,814 (£11,550; £5,772; £2,886) Stalls Low

Form RPR
-201 1 **Nautilus**[14] 5673 4-9-7 98 (p) NickyMackay 7 108
(John Gosden) *in rr: pushed along over 3f out: rdn over 2f out: hdwy over 1f out: r.o ins fnl f: lft fnl 75yds: in command nr fin* 10/1

6211 **2** *1* **Epsom Hill (SWE)**[22] 5379 3-8-8 96........................(p) PaulMulrennan 11 104
(Charlie Fellowes) *chsd ldrs: wnt 2nd over 3f out: led 2f out: hrd pressed fr over 1f out: hdd fnl 75yds: kpt on but hld nr fin* **13/2**[2]

3330 **3** *1 3/4* **Communicator**[15] 5651 6-9-2 93........................ OisinMurphy 1 99
(Andrew Balding) *hld up: rdn 3f out: hdwy over 2f out: styd on to chal u.p ins fnl f: styd on same pce fnl 50yds* **20/1**

23-3 **4** *nse* **Novirak (IRE)**[22] 5379 6-8-12 89........................ GrahamGibbons 2 95
(James Fanshawe) *midfield: hdwy over 2f out: rdn to chse ldrs ins fnl f: styd on: gng on at fin* **14/1**

0331 **5** *nse* **Glenard**[15] 5651 4-9-3 94........................ GeorgeBaker 13 100
(Charles Hills) *led: rdn and hdd 2f out: stl chalng u.p ins fnl f: styd on same pce fnl 50yds* **12/1**

6123 **6** *hd* **Hassle (IRE)**[28] 5161 5-9-4 95........................(p) AdamKirby 14 101
(Clive Cox) *midfield: hdwy over 3f out: rdn to chse ldrs over 2f out: chalng fr 1f out: kpt on same pce u.p fnl 50yds* **7/1**[3]

-030 **7** *2 1/4* **Lady Kashaan (IRE)**[17] 5579 5-8-11 88........................ RobertWinston 9 90
(Alan Swinbank) *in tch: effrt 3f out: rdn over 2f out: chsd ldrs ins fnl f: one pce fnl 75yds* **18/1**

040- **8** *1/2* **Shrewd**[67] 7823 4-8-12 89........................ DeclanMcDonogh 5 91
(Keith Dalgleish) *hld up: pushed along over 3f out: rdn and swtchd lft over 2f out: one pce ins fnl f: nvr able to chal* **33/1**

1501 **9** *nk* **Aramist (IRE)**[20] 5465 4-8-12 89........................ BenCurtis 6 93
(Alan Swinbank) *hld up: rdn over 3f out: hdwy whn n.m.r and hmpd over 1f out: snatched up twice: swtchd lft ins fnl f: styd on: nt rch ldrs* **20/1**

2160 **10** *shd* **Eagle Rock (IRE)**[17] 5579 6-8-8 85........................(p) WayneLordan 15 86
(Tom Tate) *chsd ldr after 3f: rdn and lost 2nd 4f out: outpcd over 2f out: kpt on u.p fnl f but no imp* **20/1**

6200 **11** *1 1/4* **Saptapadi (IRE)**[17] 5579 8-8-11 88........................(t) PaulPickard 10 87
(Brian Ellison) *hld up: rdn 2f out: kpt on ins fnl f: no imp* **20/1**

3122 **12** *2 1/4* **Quest For More (IRE)**[17] 5579 4-8-11 88........................(b) PatSmullen 3 84
(Roger Charlton) *prom: rdn over 2f out: wknd over 1f out* **7/1**[3]

0642 **13** *5* **Be Perfect (USA)**[23] 5334 5-8-10 87........................ FrannyNorton 4 76
(David Nicholls) *chsd ldrs: rdn over 3f out: wknd over 1f out* **33/1**

5000 **14** *1/2* **Chancery (USA)**[15] 5651 6-9-2 93........................ DanielTudhope 8 82
(David O'Meara) *midfield: rdn and lost pl over 2f out: n.d after* **11/1**

024- **15** *18* **Goodwood Mirage (IRE)**[178] 6991 4-9-8 99........................ JamieSpencer 12 62
(Jonjo O'Neill) *missed break: hld up in rr: rdn over 3f out: nvr on terms: eased whn wl btn ins fnl f* **20/1**

-362 **U** **Havana Cooler (IRE)**[39] 4759 4-9-10 101........................ RichardHughes 16
(Luca Cumani) *lft stalls awkwardly and uns rdr s* **4/1**[1]

3m 1.92s (-0.08) **Going Correction** +0.225s/f (Good)
**WFA** 3 from 4yo+ 11lb **16** Ran SP% **125.1**
Speed ratings (Par 109): **109,108,107,107,107 107,105,105,105,105 104,103,100,100,90**
CSF £67.47 CT £1301.03 TOTE £11.80: £3.00, £2.30, £5.10, £3.90; EX 101.00 Trifecta £2686.10.
**Owner** Abdulla Al Khalifa **Bred** Sheikh Abdulla Bin Isa Al Khalifa **Trained** Newmarket, Suffolk

**FOCUS**
A typically competitive running of the Old Borough Cup, but favourite Havana Cooler unseated his rider after making an awkward start. They raced middle to far side in the straight. Strong form, which reads sound.

## 6134 BETFRED SPRINT CUP (BRITISH CHAMPIONS SERIES) (GROUP 1) 6f
**3:50** (3:51) (Class 1) 3-Y-O+
**£154,818** (£58,695; £29,374; £14,632; £7,343; £3,685) **Stalls** Centre

Form RPR

3256 **1** **G Force (IRE)**[15] 5654 3-9-1 111........................ DanielTudhope 10 121
(David O'Meara) *hld up: hdwy whn nt clr run under 2f out: burst through gap over 1f out: r.o and edgd rt ins fnl f: led fnl 50yds and in control* **11/1**

6002 **2** *3/4* **Gordon Lord Byron (IRE)**[14] 5699 6-9-3 117........................ WayneLordan 18 119
(T Hogan, Ire) *trckd ldrs: led 2f out: sn rdn: hdd fnl 50yds: kpt on but hld fnl strides* **6/1**[2]

1641 **3** *1 1/2* **Music Master**[49] 4438 4-9-3 112........................ DaneO'Neill 13 114
(Henry Candy) *trckd ldrs: rdn to chal over 1f out: styd on same pce and unable to go w front pair fnl 50yds* **15/2**[3]

111 **4** *1/2* **Sole Power**[15] 5654 7-9-3 118........................ RichardHughes 9 112
(Edward Lynam, Ire) *hld up in rr: last 1/2-way: hdwy whn nt clr run over 1f out: styd on ins fnl f: nt rch ldrs: one pce fnl strides* **5/2**[1]

0201 **5** *1 3/4* **Pearl Secret**[7] 5911 5-9-3 113........................ OisinMurphy 16 107
(David Barron) *midfield: rdn and hdwy over 1f out: chsd ldrs: styd on same pce fnl 75yds* **33/1**

0031 **6** *1/2* **Es Que Love (IRE)**[39] 4758 5-9-3 113........................ AdamKirby 8 105
(Clive Cox) *hld up in midfield: rdn and hdwy over 1f out: kpt on ins fnl f: nvr able to chal* **20/1**

0-00 **7** *1/2* **Caspar Netscher**[14] 5674 5-9-3 106........................ GrahamGibbons 2 104
(David Simcock) *midfield towards centre of trck: hdwy 2f out: effrt and ch over 1f out: kpt on same pce fnl 100yds* **100/1**

-221 **8** *3/4* **Baccarat (IRE)**[77] 3452 5-9-3 112........................ GeorgeBaker 4 101
(Richard Fahey) *midfield towards centre of trck: rdn and hdwy over 1f out: no imp and one pce ins fnl f* **9/1**

6335 **9** *nk* **Dinkum Diamond (IRE)**[34] 4937 6-9-3 106........................ BenCurtis 1 100
(Henry Candy) *prom: rdn and ev ch over 1f out: nt qckn: wknd fnl 150yds* **100/1**

1250 **10** *hd* **Maarek**[14] 5699 7-9-3 113........................ DeclanMcDonogh 3 100
(Miss Evanna McCutcheon, Ire) *rrd bef s: awkwardly away: towards rr: nvr travelling wl: swtchd arnd field towards centre of trck 2f out: nvr able to trble ldrs* **25/1**

2600 **11** *nk* **Astaire (IRE)**[15] 5654 3-9-1 111........................ AmyRyan 14 99
(Kevin Ryan) *prom: rdn 2f out: lost pl over 1f out: wknd ins fnl f* **50/1**

50 **12** *3/4* **Cougar Mountain (IRE)**[15] 5654 3-9-1 112........................ JosephO'Brien 6 96
(A P O'Brien, Ire) *midfield: rdn 2f out: no imp over 1f out and outpcd: one pce ins fnl f* **9/1**

0143 **13** *1 1/4* **Professor**[13] 5722 4-9-3 111........................ ChrisHayes 15 92
(Richard Hannon) *trckd ldrs: rdn over 2f out: wknd over 1f out* **33/1**

0021 **14** *3/4* **Tropics (USA)**[14] 5674 6-9-3 115........................ RobertWinston 12 90
(Dean Ivory) *racd keenly in midfield: hdwy 2f out: rdn and chsd ldrs over 1f out: wknd fnl 150yds: eased whn btn towards fin* **9/1**

2123 **15** *2 1/4* **Extortionist (IRE)**[15] 5654 3-9-1 113........................ PatSmullen 7 83
(Olly Stevens) *stdd s: hld up: nvr on terms: eased whn no ch fnl 100yds* **20/1**

1305 **16** *nk* **Hot Streak (IRE)**[15] 5654 3-9-1 114........................ JamieSpencer 17 82
(Kevin Ryan) *led: hdd 2f out: rdn and wknd over 1f out* **20/1**

0034 **17** *1 1/4* **Moviesta (USA)**[15] 5654 4-9-3 112........................ PaulMulrennan 11 78
(Bryan Smart) *hld up: pushed along over 2f out: rdn and nt clr run over 1f out: nvr on terms: dropped away ins fnl f: eased* **25/1**

1m 12.95s (-0.85) **Going Correction** +0.225s/f (Good)
**WFA** 3 from 4yo+ 2lb **17** Ran SP% **124.8**
Speed ratings (Par 117): **114,113,111,110,108 107,106,105,105,105 104,103,101,100,97 97,95**
CSF £68.77 TOTE £12.80: £4.20, £2.40, £3.20; EX 94.90 Trifecta £634.70.
**Owner** Middleham Park Racing XVIII & Partner **Bred** Kildaragh Stud & Twelve Oaks Stud Est **Trained** Nawton, N Yorks

**FOCUS**
Owner Sabena Power and trainer Eddie Lynam had won all four previous Group 1 sprints in Britain this season, but their 6f horse Slade Power (Diamond Jubilee and July Cup) was absent so they relied on Sole Power (King's Stand and Nunthorpe), who has never won beyond the minimum trip. The main action unfolded towards the stands' side. A clear personal best from G Force, with Gordon Lord Byron close to last year's figure in this.

## 6135 BETFRED GOALS GALORE NURSERY H'CAP (BOBIS RACE) 6f
**4:25** (4:26) (Class 2) 2-Y-O **£11,320** (£3,368; £1,683; £841) **Stalls** Centre

Form RPR

2120 **1** **Teruntum Star (FR)**[14] 5692 2-9-4 85........................ JamieSpencer 9 97+
(Kevin Ryan) *sltly awkward s: in rr: hdwy gng wl over 1f out: led ins fnl f: drew clr fnl 100yds: readily* **10/1**

5145 **2** *3 1/4* **Inniscastle Lad**[14] 5672 2-9-2 83........................ RichardHughes 8 83
(William Muir) *a.p: rdn over 1f out: wnt 2nd fnl 150yds: no ch w wnr* **8/1**

6214 **3** *1/2* **Roossey (IRE)**[17] 5580 2-9-3 84........................ PatSmullen 4 83
(William Haggas) *racd keenly: trckd ldrs: pushed along over 2f out: rdn to ld over 1f out: hdd ins fnl f: kpt on same pce fnl 150yds* **2/1**[1]

0135 **4** *1* **Alpine Affair**[29] 5129 2-8-10 77........................(b) DaneO'Neill 6 73
(Brian Meehan) *racd keenly: hld up in rr: rdn over 1f out: styd on u.p ins fnl f: nvr able to trble ldrs* **33/1**

1235 **5** *1 3/4* **Steve Prescott**[34] 4936 2-9-2 86........................ GeorgeChaloner(3) 3 76
(Richard Fahey) *trckd ldrs: rdn and lost pl over 2f out: outpcd: kpt on ins fnl f: no imp* **16/1**

1 **6** *nk* **Gun Case**[21] 5439 2-8-13 80........................ NickyMackay 1 69
(Ed Walker) *prom: rdn 2f out: wknd fnl 100yds* **11/2**[3]

2111 **7** *1 1/4* **Felix Leiter**[17] 5580 2-9-7 88........................ BenCurtis 2 74
(K R Burke) *led: rdn and hdd over 1f out: wknd ins fnl f* **3/1**[2]

221 **8** *2* **Don Sigfredo (IRE)**[34] 4939 2-9-4 85........................(p) HayleyTurner 7 65
(Tom Dascombe) *racd keenly: hld up: hdwy over 3f out: sn chsd ldrs: rdn over 1f out: sn wknd* **12/1**

6410 **9** *3/4* **Honcho (IRE)**[14] 5672 2-8-8 78........................ JoeyHaynes(3) 5 55
(David Elsworth) *racd keenly: hld up: hdwy 3f out: rdn 2f out: wknd over 1f out* **20/1**

1m 15.15s (1.35) **Going Correction** +0.225s/f (Good) **9** Ran SP% **115.2**
Speed ratings (Par 101): **100,95,95,93,91 90,89,86,85**
CSF £86.67 CT £226.83 TOTE £12.20: £2.90, £2.50, £1.10; EX 104.90 Trifecta £284.50.
**Owner** T A Rahman **Bred** Petra Bloodstock Agency **Trained** Hambleton, N Yorks

**FOCUS**
They raced up the middle in this nursery. The winner would not be out in place back in stakes company.

## 6136 BETFRED FUN AND FRIENDLY STKS (REGISTERED AS ASCENDANT STAKES) (LISTED RACE) 1m
**5:00** (5:01) (Class 1) 2-Y-O **£14,461** (£5,482; £2,743; £1,366; £685) **Stalls** Low

Form RPR

1 **1** **Celestial Path (IRE)**[43] 4633 2-9-2 0........................ LukeMorris 6 106+
(Sir Mark Prescott Bt) *s.i.s: in rr: u.p over 1f out: hdwy 3f out: wnt 2nd over 2f out: rdn to ld ins fnl f: r.o to draw clr fnl 100yds: comf* **11/8**[1]

021 **2** *4* **Medrano**[49] 4424 2-9-2 83........................ RobertWinston 2 97
(David Brown) *s.i.s: sn chsd ldr: led after 2f: rdn over 1f out: hdd ins fnl f: no ch w wnr fnl 100yds* **5/1**[3]

1031 **3** *3 1/2* **Smaih (GER)**[18] 5543 2-9-2 92........................ RichardHughes 5 89
(Richard Hannon) *chsd ldrs: pushed along and outpcd over 2f out: rdn and hdwy to take 3rd over 1f out: one pce fnl 100yds* **11/4**[2]

2160 **4** *5* **Chadic**[17] 5576 2-9-2 95........................ FrannyNorton 3 78
(Mark Johnston) *led: hdd after 2f: chsd ldr tl over 2f out: rdn and wknd over 1f out* **6/1**

0215 **5** *4* **Caprior Bere (FR)**[13] 5740 2-9-2 87........................ DanielTudhope 1 68
(K R Burke) *hld up: rdn over 1f out: no imp: wl btn ins fnl f* **8/1**

1m 45.02s (1.32) **Going Correction** +0.225s/f (Good) **5** Ran SP% **110.8**
Speed ratings: **102,98,94,89,85**
CSF £8.67 TOTE £2.20: £1.40, £2.30; EX 8.50 Trifecta £25.10.
**Owner** G C Woodall **Bred** Miss Catherine Monaghan **Trained** Newmarket, Suffolk

**FOCUS**
This Listed race saw an impressive performance from Celestial Path. The form could be rated higher.

## 6137 BETFRED SUPPORTS JACK BERRY HOUSE H'CAP (BOBIS RACE) 1m 6f
**5:30** (5:32) (Class 2) (0-100,90) 3-Y-O **£16,172** (£4,812; £2,405; £1,202) **Stalls** Low

Form RPR

411 **1** **Mizzou (IRE)**[35] 4887 3-9-6 89........................ AdamKirby 9 101+
(Luca Cumani) *hld up: rdn along 6f out: rdn and hdwy 2f out: led jst ins fnl f: styd on wl towards fin* **5/2**[1]

0641 **2** *1 3/4* **Intense Tango**[29] 5132 3-8-5 77........................ JoeyHaynes(3) 10 85
(K R Burke) *in tch: hdwy to chal 3f out: led 2f out: hdd jst ins fnl f: one pce towards fin* **8/1**

1315 **3** *3/4* **Spectator**[38] 4803 3-8-7 76........................(p) OisinMurphy 3 83
(Andrew Balding) *hld up: hdwy 3f out: rdn 2f out: chsd ldrs over 1f out: styd on u.p: nt quite pce to get to ldrs* **20/1**

224 **4** *1/2* **Kashmiri Sunset**[14] 5691 3-8-6 80........................ NoelGarbutt(5) 4 86
(Ed de Giles) *hld up in rr: pushed along over 4f out: hdwy over 2f out: chsd ldrs over 1f out but nt qckn: styd on towards fin* **8/1**

0411 **5** *2 1/2* **Yaakooum (IRE)**[18] 5527 3-9-2 85........................ RichardHughes 7 89
(Richard Hannon) *midfield: hdwy 7f out: sn chsd ldrs: rdn to chal 3f out: hung lft 2f out: wknd ins fnl f* **8/1**

1222 **6** *nse* **Reesha**[32] 5003 3-9-3 86........................ DaneO'Neill 6 88
(Roger Varian) *in tch: effrt over 2f out: sn chalng: wknd ins fnl f: eased whn btn fnl 75yds* **16/1**

1441 **7** *2* **Tiger Lilly (IRE)**[25] 5288 3-8-9 81........................ GeorgeChaloner(3) 8 81
(Richard Fahey) *chsd ldr early: handy: rdn over 3f out: lost pl over 2f out: one pce fnl f* **13/2**[3]

0612 **8** *1 1/2* **Purple Spectrum**[28] 5193 3-9-3 86........................ PatSmullen 5 84
(William Haggas) *upset in stalls: led: jinked rt 6f out: rdn and hdd over 2f out: wknd jst over 1f out* **5/1**[2]

621 **9** *5* **Classical Duet (USA)**[19] 5490 3-9-3 86 ........................ FrannyNorton 2 77
(Mark Johnston) *racd keenly: trckd ldrs: lost pl over 3f out: wknd over 2f out* **20/1**

0213 **10** *8* **Artistic Muse (IRE)**[13] 5723 3-8-9 78 ........................ RobertWinston 1 57
(Charles Hills) *racd keenly: hld up: struggling over 3f out: nvr on terms* **20/1**

361U **11** *3* **Mantou (IRE)**[14] 5691 3-9-0 83 ........................ JamieSpencer 11 58
(Michael Bell) *chsd ldr after 1f: rdn to ld over 2f out: sn hdd: wknd over 1f out: sn eased* **10/1**

3m 4.94s (2.94) **Going Correction** +0.225s/f (Good) **11 Ran SP% 121.2**
Speed ratings (Par 107): **100,99,98,98,96 96,95,94,91,87 85**
CSF £22.96 CT £317.82 TOTE £3.10: £1.50, £2.70, £5.30; EX 32.30 Trifecta £617.00.
**Owner** Jon S Kelly **Bred** Matrix Bloodstock **Trained** Newmarket, Suffolk

**FOCUS**
A couple of improvers finished one-two in this interesting handicap. The winner is progressing well.

T/Jkpt: Not won. T/Plt: £188.30 to a £1 stake. Pool: £168,960.06 - 654.78 winning tickets T/Qpdt: £24.80 to a £1 stake. Pool: £10,673.45 - 317.80 winning tickets DO

# 6100 KEMPTON (A.W) (R-H)

## Saturday, September 6

**OFFICIAL GOING: Polytrack: standard**
Wind: virtually nil Weather: dry, overcast

## 6138 TOTEPOOL PLAY TODAY'S £3.5 MILLION SCOOP6 CONDITIONS STKS (BOBIS RACE) (C&G) 7f (P)

**1:45** (1:46) (Class 4) 2-Y-O **£3,881** (£1,155; £577; £288) **Stalls Low**

Form RPR

4 **1** **Bravo Zolo (IRE)**[12] 5760 2-8-12 0 ........................ MartinHarley 3 87+
(Marco Botti) *mde all: rdn over 2f out: kpt on wl u.p fnl f: drvn out* **2/1**[2]

**2** *1* **Strong Chemistry** 2-8-12 0 ........................ SilvestreDeSousa 1 84+
(Charlie Appleby) *dwlt: hld up in tch in rr: rdn and effrt over 2f out: hdwy u.p to chse wnr over 1f out: kpt on but no imp fnl 100yds* **6/1**[3]

3 **3** *2 ½* **Russian Reward (IRE)**[14] 5684 2-8-12 0 ........................ JimCrowley 2 78
(Paul Cole) *chsd ldr tl over 4f out: rdn over 3f out: outpcd 2f out: pushed along after and kpt on to go 3rd again ins fnl f* **10/1**

2 **4** *2* **Power Game**[19] 5488 2-8-12 0 ........................ FrederikTylicki 4 72
(Saeed bin Suroor) *t.k.h: chsd ldrs: wnt 2nd over 4f out: rdn and unable qck ent fnl 2f: 3rd and btn 1f out: wknd ins fnl f* **10/11**[1]

1m 25.63s (-0.37) **Going Correction** -0.125s/f (Stan) **4 Ran SP% 109.1**
Speed ratings (Par 97): **97,95,93,90**
CSF £12.48 TOTE £5.20; EX 11.20 Trifecta £26.10.
**Owner** Mohamed Albousi Alghufli **Bred** Tipper House Stud **Trained** Newmarket, Suffolk

**FOCUS**
An interesting conditions event, even if no previous winners took their chance, but with the odds-on favourite running poorly it remains to be seen what the form adds up to. The winner looks the type to go on from here.

## 6139 TOTESCOOP6 SEPTEMBER STKS (GROUP 3) 1m 4f (P)

**2:20** (2:20) (Class 1) 3-Y-O+
**£35,160** (£13,330; £6,671; £3,323; £1,667; £837) **Stalls Centre**

Form RPR

-110 **1** **Prince Bishop (IRE)**[161] 1183 7-9-12 116 ........................ (v) FrederikTylicki 2 121
(Saeed bin Suroor) *t.k.h: chsd ldr for 2f: hld up in tch: rdn and hdwy 2f out: lft in ld over 1f out: r.o wl: rdn out* **15/2**

361- **2** *2* **Secret Number**[336] 7012 4-9-5 114 ........................ SilvestreDeSousa 7 111
(Saeed bin Suroor) *stuck wd: in tch in midfield: effrt u.p over 2f out: chsd wnr over 1f out: one pce fnl f* **5/2**[1]

-105 **3** *1 ¼* **Battalion (IRE)**[70] 3722 4-9-5 108 ........................ TomQueally 5 109
(William Haggas) *led and set stdy gallop: rdn and qcknd over 2f out: hung bdly lft 2f out: hdd and racing against stands' rail over 1f out: 3rd and one pce fnl f* **12/1**

-662 **4** *3 ½* **Dandino**[21] 5457 7-9-5 108 ........................ MartinHarley 6 103
(Marco Botti) *stdd s: hld up in tch: effrt u.p over 2f out: outpcd and btn over 1f out: plugged on* **6/1**

1043 **5** *1 ¾* **Cat O'Mountain (USA)**[161] 1183 4-9-5 113 ........................ JimCrowley 3 100
(Charlie Appleby) *chsd ldr 9f out tl 2f out: sn outpcd u.p: wknd ins fnl f* **3/1**[2]

1413 **6** *8* **Robin Hoods Bay**[141] 1559 6-9-8 107 ........................ SeanLevey 4 91
(Ed Vaughan) *stdd s: hld up in tch: rdn and effrt over 2f out: wknd over 1f out* **12/1**

-604 **7** *7* **Red Cadeaux**[21] 5432 8-9-5 112 ........................ GeraldMosse 1 82
(Ed Dunlop) *t.k.h: chsd ldr 8f out tl 9f out: styd chsng ldrs: rdn over 3f out: wknd 2f out: bhd fnl f* **9/2**[3]

2m 29.77s (-4.73) **Going Correction** -0.125s/f (Stan) **7 Ran SP% 113.2**
Speed ratings: **110,108,107,105,104 99,94**
CSF £26.06 TOTE £8.10: £2.80, £1.70; EX 27.10 Trifecta £172.80.
**Owner** Godolphin **Bred** Thurso Ltd **Trained** Newmarket, Suffolk

**FOCUS**
A fascinating renewal of the September Stakes featuring a couple of well-known globetrotters, while a few (including all three Godolphin representatives) were returning from absences. The last two winners of the race were back for another go, but the race was spoilt slightly when nothing wanted to go on early and the contest developed into something of a sprint from the home bend. It resulted in a 1-2 for trainer Saeed Bin Suroor. Prince Bishop put up a high-class polytrack performance and rates a 3lb best.

## 6140 TOTEPOOL LONDON MILE H'CAP (SERIES FINAL) 1m (P)

**2:55** (2:55) (Class 2) 3-Y-O+
**£37,350** (£11,184; £5,592; £2,796; £1,398; £702) **Stalls Low**

Form RPR

2034 **1** **Tigers Tale (IRE)**[37] 4827 5-8-5 **87** ........................ (v) DannyBrock(3) 16 100
(Roger Teal) *chsd ldrs: wnt 2nd over 4f out: rdn to ld wl over 1f out: clr and edging rt ent fnl f: styd on: drvn out* **20/1**

0640 **2** *1 ¼* **Secret Art (IRE)**[10] 5824 4-8-13 **92** ........................ MartinHarley 11 102
(William Knight) *hld up in midfield on outer: rdn over 2f out: hdwy u.p to chse wnr fnl 150yds: kpt on* **16/1**

0212 **3** *3* **Buckstay (IRE)**[39] 4761 4-8-13 **92** ........................ JimCrowley 5 95
(Peter Chapple-Hyam) *hld up in midfield: rdn and effrt ent fnl 2f: kpt on u.p ins fnl f: snatched 3rd last stride: no threat to wnr* **5/1**[2]

6000 **4** *nse* **Santefisio**[16] 5609 8-9-2 **95** ........................ (b) SeanLevey 12 98
(Keith Dalgleish) *hld up in last quartet: hdwy u.p over 1f out: styd on strly ins fnl f: no threat to wnr* **14/1**

311 **5** *nse* **Si Senor (IRE)**[17] 5550 3-8-4 **88** ........................ JimmyQuinn 6 90
(Ed Vaughan) *wl in tch in midfield: effrt u.p in 3rd 2f out: edgd rt and no imp fnl f: lost 2 pls last stride* **4/1**[1]

4123 **6** *hd* **George Cinq**[37] 4827 4-8-4 **88** ........................ LouisSteward(5) 10 91
(Michael Bell) *stdd s: hld up in last quartet: shifting rt and hdwy 2f out: no imp u.p ins fnl f* **9/1**

5000 **7** *nk* **Loving Spirit**[56] 4200 6-9-1 **97** ........................[1] RobertTart(3) 14 99
(James Toller) *hld up towards rr: effrt u.p over 2f out: kpt on ins fnl f: nvr trbld ldrs* **16/1**

4420 **8** *¾* **Monsieur Chevalier (IRE)**[10] 5824 7-8-10 **89** ow2 ........................ GeraldMosse 13 90
(P J O'Gorman) *dwlt and bustled along early: towards rr: effrt u.p over 2f out: no imp tl plugged on fnl f: nvr threatened ldrs* **25/1**

5245 **9** *¾* **Silverheels (IRE)**[10] 5824 5-8-5 **87** ........................ (b) AshleyMorgan(3) 15 85
(Paul Cole) *chsd ldr tl led after 2f: rdn and hdd wl over 1f out: unable qck over 1f out: lost 2nd fnl 150yds: wknd* **25/1**

1122 **10** *1 ¾* **Tenor (IRE)**[28] 5163 4-9-5 **103** ........................ (t) JoeDoyle(5) 9 97+
(John Ryan) *chsd ldrs: rdn ent fnl 2f: unable qck over 1f out: wknd ins fnl f: b.b.v* **8/1**[3]

030 **11** *2 ¾* **Bravo Echo**[10] 5824 8-8-12 **91** ........................ RobertHavlin 4 79
(Michael Attwater) *hld up in midfield: rdn and no hdwy over 2f out: wknd over 1f out* **66/1**

1110 **12** *1 ½* **Lawmans Thunder**[77] 3456 4-9-2 **95** ........................ TomQueally 3 80+
(Ismail Mohammed) *in tch in midfield tl hmpd and lost pl after 1f: effrt u.p 2f out: wknd ins fnl f* **10/1**

2215 **13** *hd* **Sound Advice**[47] 4491 5-8-13 **92** ........................ TomEaves 7 76
(Keith Dalgleish) *broke fast: led for 2f: chsd ldr tl over 4f out: rdn and no ex ent fnl 2f: wknd u.p over 1f out* **20/1**

2123 **14** *3 ¼* **Musaddas**[10] 5824 4-8-7 **86** ........................ SilvestreDeSousa 1 63+
(Saeed bin Suroor) *in tch in midfield tl bdly hmpd and dropped to last after 1f: nvr able to rcvr: effrt on inner 2f out: nt clr run and btn over 1f out* **8/1**[3]

2054 **15** *¾* **High Time Too (IRE)**[31] 5040 4-8-5 **84** ........................ KieranO'Neill 2 59
(Hugo Palmer) *in tch in midfield: rdn and no hdwy over 2f out: wknd u.p over 1f out* **20/1**

0-15 **16** *4* **Suehail**[73] 3577 5-8-0 **86** ow3 ........................ KieranShoemark(7) 8 52
(Robert Cowell) *a in rr: n.d: lost tch over 1f out* **20/1**

1m 36.28s (-3.52) **Going Correction** -0.125s/f (Stan)
**WFA** 3 from 4yo+ 5lb **16 Ran SP% 124.6**
Speed ratings (Par 109): **112,110,107,107,107 107,107,106,105,103 101,99,99,96,95 91**
CSF £292.98 CT £1938.40 TOTE £27.30: £5.20, £5.30, £2.10, £3.60; EX 563.00 Trifecta £2124.40 Part won..
**Owner** B Kitcherside & Big Cat Partnership **Bred** Butlersgrove Stud **Trained** Ashtead, Surrey

■ Stewards' Enquiry : Tom Eaves four-day ban: careless riding (Sep 20-23)
Tom Queally one-day ban: careless riding (Sep 20)

**FOCUS**
A typically competitive London Mile Final with several of these taking each other on here throughout the year. On only one previous occasion since the race was first run in 2006 had it not gone to a 4yo, but this was another one for the older brigade. With a field of this size there was always likely to be some trouble early as the runners jostled for position and that was the case after a furlong when Lawmans Thunder and, to a greater degree, Musaddas suffered serious interference. Both can have their efforts ignored. The first four all came down the centre.

## 6141 TOTEPOOL BETTING ON ALL UK RACING H'CAP (JOCKEY CLUB GRASSROOTS FLAT MIDDLE DISTANCE QUALIFIER) 1m 3f (P)

**3:35** (3:35) (Class 4) (0-80,80) 3-Y-O+ **£4,690** (£1,395; £697; £348) **Stalls Low**

Form RPR

0315 **1** **Red Runaway**[21] 5442 4-9-12 80 ........................ GeraldMosse 7 90
(Ed Dunlop) *dwlt: hld up in midfield: nt clr run over 2f out: qcknd and gd hdwy u.p over 1f out: led ins fnl f: r.o wl* **7/2**[1]

1255 **2** *1* **Jacob Cats**[37] 4827 5-9-9 77 ........................ (v) JimCrowley 9 85+
(William Knight) *s.i.s in rr: hdwy u.p on inner over 1f out: swtchd lft and then rt 1f out: chsd wnr fnl 100yds: r.o: a hld* **8/1**

-105 **3** *1 ¾* **Morning Watch (IRE)**[42] 4672 3-9-2 78 ........................ (p) FrederikTylicki 13 83
(Lady Cecil) *in tch in last trio: effrt u.p on outer over 2f out: styd on wl to go 3rd ins fnl f: kpt on but no threat to ldng pair* **7/1**[3]

1460 **4** *¾* **Ocean Applause**[19] 5487 4-9-4 77 ........................ (t) JoeDoyle(5) 10 81
(John Ryan) *hld up in midfield: effrt u.p over 2f out: hdwy over 1f out: styd on wl to go 4th ins fnl f: nvr gng to rch ldrs* **12/1**

3642 **5** *1* **Mystery Drama**[23] 5353 4-9-10 78 ........................ FergusSweeney 8 80
(Alan King) *broke wl stdd bk and hld up in midfield: hdwy and rdn to chse ldrs 2f out: no ex u.p 1f out: wknd ins fnl f* **10/1**

2136 **6** *1 ½* **Sir Charlie Kunz**[10] 5818 3-9-4 80 ........................ SilvestreDeSousa 3 80
(Mark Johnston) *chsd ldr tl over 2f out: wnt 2nde again 6f out tl rdn to ld over 2f out: drvn and hdd ins fnl f: wknd fnl 100yds* **11/2**[2]

4424 **7** *1* **Silver Dixie (USA)**[19] 5487 4-9-8 76 ........................ (p) SeanLevey 1 74
(Peter Hedger) *led tl over 2f out: sn drvn: styd pressing ldrs tl no ex 1f out: wknd ins fnl f* **10/1**

020 **8** *nk* **Indian Trifone (IRE)**[29] 5150 4-9-3 71 ........................ RobertHavlin 4 69
(Ed Walker) *squeezed for room leaving stalls: in tch in midfield: effrt u.p 2f out: keeping on same pce and hld whn hmpd ins fnl f* **14/1**

600/ **9** *2 ½* **Cherry Street**[688] 7195 5-9-6 74 ........................ AntonioFresu 5 67
(Denis Quinn) *in tch in midfield: effrt u.p 2f out: drvn and btn over 1f out: wknd ins fnl f* **66/1**

0603 **10** *2 ¼* **Aviator (GER)**[31] 5035 6-9-5 73 ........................ (v[1]) TomQueally 2 63
(James Eustace) *in tch in midfield: rdn and unable qck 2f out: btn whn hmpd ins fnl f: wknd* **16/1**

6410 **11** *3* **Compton Bird**[30] 5073 5-9-6 79 ........................ LouisSteward(5) 6 63
(Paul Fitzsimons) *stdd s: hld up in rr: swtchd rt and effrt on inner 2f out: sme hdwy over 1f out: no ex and btn whn nt clr run 1f out: wknd* **10/1**

0050 **12** *2 ¾* **Mallory Heights (IRE)**[40] 4736 4-9-8 76 ........................ (b[1]) MartinHarley 11 56
(Luca Cumani) *dwlt: rcvrd to chse ldr over 8f out tl 6f out: lost pl u.p over 2f out: wknd over 1f out* **10/1**

2m 19.12s (-2.78) **Going Correction** -0.125s/f (Stan)
**WFA** 3 from 4yo+ 8lb **12 Ran SP% 119.3**
Speed ratings (Par 105): **105,104,103,102,101 100,99,99,97,96 94,92**
CSF £31.51 CT £189.87 TOTE £5.10: £2.00, £3.80, £1.40; EX 36.00 Trifecta £700.80.
**Owner** The Hon R J Arculli **Bred** Lofts Hall, M Philipson & Cheveley Park **Trained** Newmarket, Suffolk

**FOCUS**
A fair middle-distance handicap in which the principals came from well off the pace. The winner seemed to confirm he's better on Polytrack now.

## 6142 TOTESCOOP6 "THE MILLIONAIRE MAKER" SIRENIA STKS (GROUP 3) 6f (P)
**4:10** (4:11) (Class 1) 2-Y-O

**£23,818** (£9,030; £4,519; £2,251; £1,129; £567) **Stalls** Low

Form RPR

2215 **1** **Burnt Sugar (IRE)**[17] 5580 2-9-1 85........................ GeraldMosse 10 110
(Richard Hannon) *hld up in tch in last trio: rdn and gd hdwy over 1f out: qcknd to ld ins fnl f: sn drew clr: readily* **12/1**[3]

21 **2** 2 ¼ **Maftool (USA)**[31] 5050 2-9-1 0........................ PaulHanagan 2 103+
(Saeed bin Suroor) *chsd ldrs on inner: effrt u.p 2f out: kpt on to go 2nd fnl 100yds: no ch w wnr* **5/2**[2]

21 **3** ¾ **Home Of The Brave (IRE)**[43] 4618 2-9-1 0........................ KevinManning 3 101
(Hugo Palmer) *t.k.h: chsd ldrs: rdn and ev ch 2f out: drvn to ld 1f out: sn hdd and brushed aside by wnr: r.o same pce and lost 2nd fnl 100yds* **11/10**[1]

315 **4** nk **Fanciful Angel (IRE)**[42] 4670 2-9-1 89........................ MartinHarley 7 100
(Marco Botti) *hld up in midfield: effrt and n.m.r 2f out: sltly hmpd and swtchd lft 1f out: styd on wl fnl 100yds: nvr trbld ldrs* **20/1**

5104 **5** 1 **Accipiter**[22] 5380 2-8-12 88........................ AshleyMorgan 4 94
(Chris Wall) *wl in tch in midfield: rdn and effrt 2f out: ev ch over 1f out: no ex and wknd ins fnl f* **25/1**

1003 **6** nk **Dr No**[29] 5131 2-9-1 98........................(b[1]) SeanLevey 9 96
(Richard Hannon) *chsd ldrs on outer: rdn 2f out: pressing ldrs whn hung rt u.p over 1f out: outpcd ins fnl f* **12/1**[3]

1254 **7** 2 ½ **Surewecan**[21] 5447 2-9-1 99........................ SilvestreDeSousa 5 89
(Mark Johnston) *dwlt: hld up in tch in last trio: effrt u.p 2f out: styng on but stl plenty to do whn nt clr run and hmpd 1f out: nvr trbld ldrs* **14/1**

1 **8** 2 ¾ **Misleading**[39] 4760 2-9-1 0........................ JimCrowley 11 80
(Peter Chapple-Hyam) *dropped in bhd after s: effrt over 2f out: no hdwy: nvr trbld ldrs* **14/1**

0116 **9** ¾ **Escalating**[100] 2703 2-9-1 90........................ JamesDoyle 1 78
(Pat Eddery) *t.k.h: led: rdn 2f out: hdd 1f out: wkng whn short of room and hmpd jst ins fnl f: eased towards fin* **20/1**

0311 **10** nse **Speedy Move (IRE)**[24] 5306 2-9-1 83........................ TomQueally 6 78
(Ismail Mohammed) *in tch in midfield: rdn and effrt on inner 2f out: btn over 1f out: wknd ins fnl f* **33/1**

1m 11.79s (-1.31) **Going Correction** -0.125s/f (Stan) **10 Ran SP% 121.2**
Speed ratings: **103,100,99,98,97 96,93,89,88,88**
CSF £42.01 TOTE £16.90: £3.70, £1.80, £1.10; EX 63.40 Trifecta £241.90.
**Owner** De La Warr Racing **Bred** Ballylinch Stud **Trained** East Everleigh, Wilts

**FOCUS**
This hasn't always looked the strongest Group 3 in the world and this year's field didn't look that high on quality, not that any of that will bother the connections of the winner. Burnt Sugar has more to offer on this surface.

## 6143 TOTEEXACTA "PICK THE 1, 2" H'CAP (BOBIS RACE) 2m (P)
**4:45** (4:46) (Class 4) (0-80,80) 3-Y-O+ **£4,690** (£1,395; £697; £348) **Stalls** Low

Form RPR

-041 **1** **Jelly Fish**[56] 4209 3-9-7 80........................(t) JamesDoyle 4 90
(Amanda Perrett) *mounted on crse: chsd ldr: rdn 3f out: drvn to ld over 1f out: forged ahd ins fnl f: drvn out* **2/1**[1]

603 **2** 2 **Belfilo (IRE)**[44] 4584 3-9-3 76........................(p) JimCrowley 3 84
(Andrew Balding) *led: rdn over 2f out: hdd and drvn over 1f out: no ex and btn ins fnl f: kpt on* **11/4**[2]

1625 **3** 2 ¼ **Bold Runner**[25] 5276 3-9-3 76........................ SilvestreDeSousa 2 81
(Jose Santos) *a 3rd: rdn 3f out: edgd lft u.p and plugged on same pce fr over 1f out* **3/1**[3]

0304 **4** 13 **Pas De Cheval (IRE)**[19] 5490 3-9-0 73........................(v) SeanLevey 1 65
(Sir Michael Stoute) *hld up in tch in last pair: rdn 4f out: drvn and btn 2f out: sn wknd* **11/2**

3416 **5** 1 **Mabdhool (IRE)**[61] 4020 3-9-2 75........................ FergusSweeney 6 63
(Ali Stronge) *stdd and dropped in bhd after s: hld up in tch in rr: clsd and travelling wl 3f out: rdn and fnd nil over 2f out: wknd over 1f out* **10/1**

3m 30.96s (0.86) **Going Correction** -0.125s/f (Stan) **5 Ran SP% 109.5**
Speed ratings (Par 105): **92,91,89,83,82**
CSF £7.65 TOTE £1.60: £1.10, £1.70; EX 6.10 Trifecta £12.90.
**Owner** K Abdullah **Bred** Millsec Limited **Trained** Pulborough, W Sussex

**FOCUS**
With such a small field this was always likely to be run at an ordinary gallop, so not the test of stamina it might have been. However the first two were not exposed as stayers.

## 6144 TRY A TOTETRIFECTA H'CAP (DIV I) 7f (P)
**5:20** (5:20) (Class 4) (0-85,85) 3-Y-O+ **£4,690** (£1,395; £697; £348) **Stalls** Low

Form RPR

0243 **1** **Compton**[49] 4447 5-9-9 84........................(t) SeanLevey 5 93
(Stuart Williams) *hld up in tch in midfield: nt clr run and shuffled bk 2f out: swtchd lft and rallied over 1f out: str chal ins fnl f: r.o wl to ld towards fin* **7/1**

6200 **2** nk **Rogue Wave (IRE)**[24] 5311 3-8-13 78........................ JimCrowley 8 84
(Timothy Jarvis) *chsd ldrs: effrt u.p 2f out: drvn to ld over 1f out: hrd pressed and battled on wl ins fnl f: hdd and no ex towards fin* **14/1**

3462 **3** 1 ¼ **Good Authority (IRE)**[24] 5308 7-8-5 73........................ KieranShoemark[(7)] 2 78+
(Karen George) *stdd s: t.k.h: hld up in rr: gd hdwy on inner 2f out: drvn and ev ch over 1f out: no ex and outpcd fnl 100yds* **9/2**[1]

0060 **4** hd **Charles Molson**[14] 5675 3-9-6 85........................ FergusSweeney 10 87
(Henry Candy) *dropped in bhd after s: hld up in last pair: clsd and nt clr run 2f out: squeezed between rivals 1f out: chsd ldrs and kpt on same pce ins fnl f* **10/1**

0656 **5** ½ **Kung Hei Fat Choy (USA)**[26] 5258 5-9-5 80........................(b) PaulHanagan 9 83
(James Given) *hld up in tch in last quartet: rdn and hdwy on outer over 1f out: kpt on same pce ins fnl f* **18/1**

0005 **6** 2 **Twenty One Choice (IRE)**[41] 4712 5-9-3 81........................ DeclanBates[(3)] 4 79
(Ed de Giles) *chsd ldrs: rdn over 2f out: shkn up and n.m.r 2f out: drvn and r.o same pce fnl f* **6/1**[3]

5300 **7** 1 ¼ **Kinglami**[21] 5433 5-9-3 78........................(p) SilvestreDeSousa 1 72
(Brian Gubby) *in tch in midfield: effrt u.p and ev ch over 1f out: btn 1f out: wknd ins fnl f* **7/1**

450 **8** 1 ½ **Willy Brennan (IRE)**[32] 5012 3-9-2 81........................ JamesDoyle 3 70
(Andrew Balding) *bustled along early: in tch in last quartet: effrt on inner 2f out: keeping on same pce whn nvr enough room fnl f* **5/1**[2]

0000 **9** ¾ **Clockmaker (IRE)**[14] 5665 8-9-10 85........................ FrederikTylicki 6 74
(Conor Dore) *led: rdn 2f out: hdd 2f out: unable qck over 1f out: wkng whn hmpd jst ins fnl f* **7/1**

0055 **10** hd **Trucanini**[10] 5826 4-9-7 82........................ SebSanders 7 70
(Chris Wall) *chsd ldr: rdn to ld 2f out: hdd over 1f out: wkng whn n.m.r jst ins fnl f* **8/1**

1m 24.74s (-1.26) **Going Correction** -0.125s/f (Stan)
**WFA** 3 from 4yo+ 4lb **10 Ran SP% 118.8**
Speed ratings (Par 105): **102,101,100,100,99 97,95,94,93,92**
CSF £101.65 CT £505.29 TOTE £7.50: £2.30, £3.80, £2.20; EX 153.10 Trifecta £529.40.
**Owner** The Morley Family **Bred** Lawn Stud **Trained** Newmarket, Suffolk

**FOCUS**
The two leaders, Clockmaker and Trucanini, may have gone off too quick in the first division of this fair handicap and set it up for the closers, even though the field were still in a bunch coming to the last furlong. The winner's best form since he was a 3yo.

## 6145 TRY A TOTETRIFECTA H'CAP (DIV II) 7f (P)
**5:55** (5:55) (Class 4) (0-85,85) 3-Y-O+ **£4,690** (£1,395; £697; £348) **Stalls** Low

Form RPR

5322 **1** **Dutch Art Dealer**[21] 5441 3-9-1 80........................(p) SilvestreDeSousa 3 95
(Paul Cole) *led briefly: stdd to chse ldrs: rdn and effrt to ld wl over 1f out: clr 1f out: r.o strly: readily* **11/4**[1]

4-16 **2** 3 **Pageant Belle**[45] 4551 3-8-13 78........................ JamesDoyle 6 85
(Roger Charlton) *hld up in tch in last trio: rdn and hdwy 2f out: chsd clr wnr 1f out: kpt on but no imp* **16/1**

4123 **3** 1 **Athletic**[36] 4866 5-9-1 79........................(v) DannyBrock[(3)] 4 86
(Andrew Reid) *stdd s: t.k.h: hld up in rr: swtchd wd and effrt over 2f out: hdwy over 1f out: 3rd and no imp fnl f* **6/1**

3165 **4** ½ **Gravitational (IRE)**[38] 4783 4-9-3 81........................ AshleyMorgan[(3)] 8 86
(Chris Wall) *t.k.h: hld up in midfield: effrt 2f out: 4th and plugged on same pce fnl f* **6/1**

3000 **5** 2 ¼ **Multitask**[10] 5834 4-8-4 72........................ KieranShoemark[(7)] 2 71
(Michael Madgwick) *hld up in tch in last trio: hdwy on inner 2f out: pressed ldrs over 1f out: no ex and wknd 1f out* **25/1**

5005 **6** 5 **Dubawi Fun**[32] 5012 3-8-12 84........................ AhmadAlSubousi[(7)] 9 68
(Ismail Mohammed) *taken down early: chsd ldrs: rdn over 2f out: outpcd and btn over 1f out: sn wknd* **25/1**

0222 **7** 4 **Crowdmania**[15] 5649 3-9-6 85........................ PaulHanagan 1 59
(Mark Johnston) *chsd ldr: drvn and ev ch ent fnl 2f: no ex and btn wl over 1f out: sn wknd* **7/2**[2]

1005 **8** 4 **Tasrih (USA)**[44] 4580 5-9-7 82........................ SeanLevey 7 48
(Alan McCabe) *taken down early: sn led: rdn and hdd wl over 1f out: sn btn and wknd: wl bhd fnl f* **12/1**

6002 **9** 9 **Obliterefight (IRE)**[23] 5346 5-9-9 84........................ JimCrowley 5 26
(William Knight) *in tch in last trio: rdn 3f out: sn struggling: wknd 2f out: wl bhd fnl f: t.o* **9/2**[3]

1m 23.9s (-2.10) **Going Correction** -0.125s/f (Stan)
**WFA** 3 from 4yo+ 4lb **9 Ran SP% 116.9**
Speed ratings (Par 105): **107,103,102,101,99 93,89,84,74**
CSF £49.45 CT £242.64 TOTE £3.20: £1.10, £4.60, £3.10; EX 49.80 Trifecta £315.00.
**Owner** R A Green **Bred** Raymond Clive Tooth **Trained** Whatcombe, Oxon

**FOCUS**
The winning time was 0.84sec quicker than the first division and, as in the first leg, the pair that helped force the early pace, Tasrih and Crowdmania, ended up dropping right out. Useful form from the winner, who chased the pace.
T/Plt: £119.60 to a £1 stake. Pool: £54,058.50 - 329.81 winning tickets T/Qpdt: £12.40 to a £1 stake. Pool: £4,636.74 - 274.95 winning tickets SP

# 5885 THIRSK (L-H)
### Saturday, September 6

**OFFICIAL GOING: Good changing to good to soft (good in places) after race 1 (2.00) changing to good to soft (soft in places) after race 3**
Wind: Light half behind Weather: Overcast Rails: All previous dolling removed to provide fresh ground on inside and distances as advertised

## 6146 BRITISH STALLION STUDS EBF MAIDEN STKS (BOBIS RACE) (DIV I) 7f
**2:00** (2:01) (Class 4) 2-Y-O **£4,528** (£1,347; £673; £336) **Stalls** Low

Form RPR

362 **1** **Secret Brief (IRE)**[15] 5655 2-9-5 88........................ AdrianNicholls 2 88
(Mark Johnston) *mde all: rdn clr wl over 1f out: kpt on strly* **2/5**[1]

**2** 3 ½ **Bleu Astral (FR)** 2-9-5 0........................ TonyHamilton 8 80+
(Richard Fahey) *trckd ldrs: hdwy on outer 1/2-way: effrt over 2f out: rdn to chse wnr wl over 1f out: edgd lft ins fnl f: no imp* **7/1**[3]

3 **3** 6 **Sands Chorus**[70] 3701 2-9-5 0........................ PhillipMakin 9 65
(James Given) *trckd ldng pair: hdwy to chse wnr over 3f out: rdn along 2f out: drvn and one pce fr wl over 1f out* **5/1**[2]

04 **4** 3 **Arracourt**[13] 5712 2-9-5 0........................ DavidAllan 6 57
(Tim Easterby) *chsd ldrs on inner: rdn along 3f out: outpcd fnl 2f* **16/1**

55 **5** ½ **Cosmic Statesman**[28] 5167 2-9-0 0........................ SammyJoBell[(5)] 5 59+
(Richard Fahey) *dwlt and towards rr: hdwy 3f out: pushed along over 2f out: kpt on appr fnl f: n.d* **10/1**

04 **6** 7 **Boldbob (IRE)**[19] 5494 2-9-5 0........................ MichaelStainton 1 38
(Micky Hammond) *dwlt: a in rr* **20/1**

**7** 5 **Parliament (IRE)** 2-8-12 0........................ RowanScott[(7)] 7 26
(Ann Duffield) *a in rr: bhd fnl 3f* **33/1**

00 **8** 1 **The Fulwell End**[21] 5443 2-9-5 0........................ JasonHart 3 23
(Noel Wilson) *chsd wnr: rdn along over 3f out: drvn and wknd over 2f out* **100/1**

0 **9** 4 ½ **Colours Of Victory**[22] 5386 2-9-5 0........................ FergalLynch 4 12
(Kevin Ryan) *in tch: rdn along bef 1/2-way: sn outpcd* **25/1**

1m 29.39s (2.19) **Going Correction** +0.30s/f (Good) **9 Ran SP% 128.1**
Speed ratings (Par 97): **99,95,88,84,84 76,70,69,64**
CSF £4.78 TOTE £1.50: £1.02, £2.40, £1.90; EX 6.10 Trifecta £18.70.
**Owner** Sheikh Hamdan bin Mohammed Al Maktoum **Bred** Airlie Stud **Trained** Middleham Moor, N Yorks

**FOCUS**
An uncompetitive maiden run at a fair pace.

## 6147 BRITISH STALLION STUDS EBF MAIDEN STKS (BOBIS RACE) (DIV II) 7f
**2:30** (2:37) (Class 4) 2-Y-O **£4,528** (£1,347; £673; £336) **Stalls** Low

Form RPR
60 **1** **Cape Hideaway**[19] 5493 2-9-5 0 JasonHart 5 73
(Mark Walford) *cl up: led over 2f out: rdn wl over 1f out: hdd ins fnl f: rallied gamely last 100yds to ld again towards fin* **22/1**
5 **2** *nk* **Tadqeeq**[30] 5104 2-9-5 0 LiamJones 3 72
(William Haggas) *chsd ldrs: rdn along 1/2-way: hdwy over 2f out and sn cl up: rdn to ld wl over 1f out: drvn ins fnl f: hdd and no ex towards fin* **7/4**[1]
0 **3** *4 ½* **Multellie**[19] 5494 2-9-5 0 DavidAllan 8 61+
(Tim Easterby) *towards rr: hdwy over 3f out: rdn over 2f out: chsd ldng pair over 1f out: kpt on same pce* **25/1**
3 **4** *1 ½* **Sekuras Girl (IRE)**[77] 3481 2-8-11 0 [1] ConnorBeasley(3) 2 52
(Michael Dods) *pushed along s and sn led: clr over 3f out: rdn along over 2f out: sn hdd and grad wknd* **5/1**[2]
0 **5** *2 ½* **Fit The Bill (IRE)**[125] 1977 2-9-5 0 SteveDrowne 7 51
(James Tate) *chsd ldrs: effrt on outer 3f out: sn rdn along and wknd* **11/2**[3]
**6** *1 ½* **Passionate Appeal** 2-9-5 0 DaleSwift 4 47+
(Ann Duffield) *s.i.s: green and outpcd in rr tl sme late hdwy* **11/1**
06 **7** *3 ½* **Milady Eileen (IRE)**[44] 4570 2-9-0 0 TonyHamilton 9 34
(Richard Fahey) *hld up in rr: effrt and sme hdwy on outer 3f out: rdn along over 2f out: sn wknd* **5/1**[2]
**8** *3 ½* **Play Nicely** 2-9-5 0 PhillipMakin 1 30
(James Given) *t.k.h: chsd ldng pair on inner: rdn along over 3f out: sn wknd* **9/1**
000 **9** *1 ½* **Ted Larkin (IRE)**[8] 5886 2-9-0 0 DuilioDaSilva(5) 6 26
(Richard Guest) *dwlt: midfield tl rdn along: outpcd and bhd fnl 3f* **100/1**

1m 31.6s (4.40) **Going Correction** +0.425s/f (Yiel) **9** Ran SP% **112.6**
Speed ratings (Par 97): **91,90,85,83,80 79,75,71,69**
CSF £58.68 TOTE £19.20: £4.90, £1.50, £6.00; EX 100.10 Trifecta £663.40 Part won..
**Owner** Cornborough Racing Club **Bred** Minster Stud **Trained** Sherriff Hutton, N Yorks

**FOCUS**
The pace was honest for this weak second division of the 2yo maiden.

## 6148 BREEDERS BACKING RACING EBF MAIDEN FILLIES STKS (BOBIS RACE) 1m
**3:05** (3:05) (Class 4) 2-Y-O **£6,469** (£1,925; £962; £481) **Stalls** Low

Form RPR
3 **1** *nse* **Tadpole**[22] 5391 2-9-0 0 LiamJones 9 74+
(William Haggas) *trckd ldr: cl up 3f out: rdn to ld over 1f out: edgd lft appr fnl f: drvn and narrowly hdd whn bmpd ins fnl f: styng on whn edgd lft and bmpd nr fin: jst failed: fin 2nd: awrdd the r* **9/4**[2]
0 **2** **All About Time**[15] 5655 2-9-0 0 DavidNolan 6 74+
(David O'Meara) *trckd ldrs: hdwy on inner to chal 2f out: rdn over 1f out: sn edgd rt: slt ld whn green: edgd rt and slipped ins fnl f: edgd rt again last 50yds: jst hld on: fin 1st: disqualified and plcd 2nd* **13/8**[1]
3 **3** *3 ¾* **Justify**[17] 5549 2-9-0 0 MartinDwyer 3 68
(Roger Varian) *led: jnd and pushed along 3f out: rdn 2f out: hdd over 1f out: n.m.r and squeezed out appr fnl f: one pce after* **7/2**[3]
**4** *nk* **Yorkidding** 2-9-0 0 AdrianNicholls 8 65
(Mark Johnston) *in tch: hdwy 1/2-way: chsd ldng trio over 2f out: sn rdn and no imp appr fnl f* **8/1**
0 **5** *4 ½* **Newgate Princess**[8] 5886 2-9-0 0 PatrickMathers 5 55
(Tony Coyle) *in rr: hdwy wl over 2f out: kpt on appr fnl f: n.d* **66/1**
005 **6** *3 ¼* **Sparkle Girl**[74] 3542 2-9-0 48 (b[1]) DavidAllan 7 48
(Tim Easterby) *in tch: rdn along 3f out: sn outpcd* **33/1**
0 **7** *1* **May Hill Rebel**[7] 5910 2-8-7 0 MelissaThompson(7) 2 46
(Richard Guest) *a in rr* **100/1**
0 **8** *12* **Mustique Dancer (IRE)**[21] 5416 2-9-0 0 TonyHamilton 1 20
(Richard Fahey) *trckd ldng pair on inner: pushed along over 3f out: sn rdn and wknd* **12/1**

1m 45.61s (5.51) **Going Correction** +0.55s/f (Yiel) **8** Ran SP% **115.3**
Speed ratings (Par 97): **93,94,90,89,85 82,81,69**
CSF £6.34 TOTE £2.90: £1.20, £1.10, £1.70; EX 8.10 Trifecta £20.20.
**Owner** B Haggas **Bred** J B Haggas **Trained** Newmarket, Suffolk

**FOCUS**
They went a steady pace for this fillies' maiden. The front two were involved in a barging match inside the final furlong which led to an amended result.

## 6149 PERSONAL TOUCHES H'CAP (BOBIS RACE) 1m
**3:40** (3:40) (Class 3) (0-95,94) 3-Y-O **£9,703** (£2,887; £1,443; £721) **Stalls** Low

Form RPR
2312 **1** **Extremity (IRE)**[15] 5656 3-9-7 94 (p) SteveDrowne 6 106
(Hugo Palmer) *trckd ldr: cl up 3f out: rdn to ld wl over 1f out: drvn out* **5/2**[1]
4020 **2** *1 ¼* **Lesha (IRE)**[15] 5656 3-9-2 89 FergalLynch 4 98
(Kevin Ryan) *hld up in rr: swtchd wd and hdwy 3f out: rdn to chal 2f out and ev ch tl drvn and no ex last 100yds* **8/1**
3631 **3** *1* **Master The World (IRE)**[15] 5656 3-9-6 93 (v) LiamKeniry 8 100
(David Elsworth) *dwlt: sn trcking ldrs: cl up over 2f out: sn rdn and ev ch tl drvn ent fnl f and kpt on same pce* **11/4**[2]
3123 **4** *1* **Ticking Katie (IRE)**[16] 5612 3-8-12 90 (p) RobJFitzpatrick(5) 5 94
(K R Burke) *hld up: hdwy 3f out: rdn to chse ldrs 2f out: sn drvn and no imp fnl f* **3/1**[3]
5231 **5** *¾* **Above The Rest (IRE)**[22] 5400 3-8-3 81 ShaneGray(5) 3 84
(Timothy Jarvis) *trckd ldng pair: hdwy over 3f out: rdn along over 2f out: drvn over 1f out and sn one pce* **6/1**
0042 **6** *12* **Langavat (IRE)**[22] 5378 3-8-9 87 ShelleyBirkett(5) 2 62
(Nigel Tinkler) *led: rdn along 3f out: drvn 2f out: sn hdd & wknd* **28/1**

1m 42.79s (2.69) **Going Correction** +0.55s/f (Yiel) **6** Ran SP% **109.1**
Speed ratings (Par 105): **108,106,105,104,104 92**
CSF £20.88 CT £51.24 TOTE £3.00: £1.50, £3.10; EX 14.10 Trifecta £25.00.
**Owner** Kremlin Cottage II **Bred** B Holland, S Hillen & J Cullinan **Trained** Newmarket, Suffolk

**FOCUS**
A fair handicap.

## 6150 BARKERS OF NORTHALLERTON H'CAP 6f
**4:20** (4:21) (Class 4) (0-80,84) 4-Y-O+ **£6,469** (£1,925; £962; £481) **Stalls** High

Form RPR
4431 **1** **Cruise Tothelimit (IRE)**[1] 6094 6-9-6 84 6ex GeorgeDowning(5) 12 92
(Ian Williams) *mde all: rdn over 1f out: drvn ins fnl f: hld on wl* **7/2**[1]
6000 **2** *½* **Teetotal (IRE)**[20] 5470 4-8-7 71 ShelleyBirkett(5) 10 77
(Nigel Tinkler) *trckd ldrs: hdwy to chal whn rdr dropped whip ent fnl f: kpt on* **9/1**
4610 **3** *½* **Solar Spirit (IRE)**[20] 5470 9-9-0 76 ConnorBeasley(3) 5 81
(Tracy Waggott) *hld up in rr: hdwy 2f out: rdn ent fnl f: drvn and kpt on wl towards fin* **22/1**
0012 **4** *nk* **We'll Deal Again**[20] 5470 7-9-2 75 PhillipMakin 9 79
(Michael Easterby) *trckd ldrs on inner: cl up 1/2-way: rdn and sltly outpcd wl over 1f out: kpt on u.p fnl f* **7/2**[1]
0541 **5** *1 ¼* **Bop It**[12] 5766 5-9-10 83 DavidNolan 3 83
(David O'Meara) *hld up in rr: hdwy 2f out: rdn to chse ldrs appr fnl f: sn drvn and no imp towards fin* **4/1**[2]
5066 **6** *¾* **Penny Garcia**[58] 4132 4-8-10 69 DuranFentiman 11 66
(Tim Easterby) *in tch on inner: hdwy 2f out: sn rdn and kpt on same pce fnl f* **20/1**
5356 **7** *¾* **Head Space (IRE)**[8] 5888 6-9-5 78 (b) JasonHart 8 73
(Ruth Carr) *dwlt and in rr tl styd on fnl f: n.d* **11/2**[3]
6400 **8** *2 ¼* **Fitz Flyer (IRE)**[12] 5766 8-9-5 78 AdrianNicholls 2 66
(David Nicholls) *cl up: rdn 2f out: drvn and wknd appr fnl f* **16/1**
5004 **9** *¾* **Hazelrigg (IRE)**[19] 5498 9-8-12 71 DavidAllan 7 56
(Tim Easterby) *trckd ldrs: pushed along over 2f out: sn rdn and wknd wl over 1f out* **14/1**
0205 **10** *1 ¼* **Bosham**[24] 5298 4-8-10 69 FergalLynch 1 50
(Michael Easterby) *chsd ldrs on outer: rdn along wl over 1f out: sn wknd* **20/1**

1m 14.38s (1.68) **Going Correction** +0.30s/f (Good) **10** Ran SP% **116.2**
Speed ratings (Par 105): **100,99,98,98,96 95,94,91,90,88**
CSF £34.27 CT £617.06 TOTE £3.80: £1.20, £3.50, £6.40; EX 40.00 Trifecta £289.00.
**Owner** Odysian Ltd T/A Cruise Nightspot **Bred** D And Mrs D Veitch **Trained** Portway, Worcs

**FOCUS**
A fair sprint handicap run at a sound pace.

## 6151 JENNY ROBERTS ORIGINAL BRITISH MILLINERY NURSERY H'CAP (BOBIS RACE) 1m
**4:55** (4:55) (Class 3) (0-95,85) 2-Y-O **£8,409** (£2,502; £1,250; £625) **Stalls** Low

Form RPR
61 **1** **Mukhayyam**[22] 5386 2-9-0 78 PhillipMakin 6 90+
(Sir Michael Stoute) *trckd ldng pair: chsd ldr fr 1/2-way: led 2f out: sn rdn clr: hung lft ent fnl f: kpt on strly* **5/4**[1]
5421 **2** *2 ¾* **Abbey Angel (IRE)**[23] 5335 2-9-3 81 TonyHamilton 5 87
(Richard Fahey) *hld up: hdwy wl over 2f out: rdn to chse wnr over 1f out: drvn ins fnl f: no imp* **7/2**[2]
211 **3** *3* **Alans Pride (IRE)**[29] 5141 2-8-12 79 ConnorBeasley(3) 3 78
(Michael Dods) *trckd ldrs: effrt 3f out and sn rdn along: drvn and kpt on same pce fr wl over 1f out* **6/1**
412 **4** *1 ½* **Special Venture (IRE)**[35] 4897 2-9-0 78 DavidAllan 7 74
(Tim Easterby) *led: rdn along 3f out: hdd 2f out and sn drvn: wknd over 1f out* **8/1**
0011 **5** *1 ¾* **Grigolo**[24] 5310 2-9-7 85 AdrianNicholls 4 77+
(Mark Johnston) *trckd ldr on inner: pushed along over 3f out: rdn over 2f out: sn drvn and btn* **9/2**[3]

1m 44.96s (4.86) **Going Correction** +0.55s/f (Yiel) **5** Ran SP% **110.2**
Speed ratings (Par 99): **97,94,91,89,88**
CSF £5.86 TOTE £1.80: £1.10, £2.40; EX 5.80 Trifecta £13.80.
**Owner** Hamdan Al Maktoum **Bred** Mrs James Wigan **Trained** Newmarket, Suffolk

**FOCUS**
A fair nursery and a progressive winner.

## 6152 HAMBLETON CUP (H'CAP) 1m 4f
**5:25** (5:25) (Class 4) (0-85,82) 3-Y-O+ **£6,469** (£1,925; £962; £481) **Stalls** Low

Form RPR
250- **1** **Pintrada**[420] 4301 6-9-4 74 TonyHamilton 2 86
(James Bethell) *trckd ldrs: smooth hdwy 3f out: cl up over 2f out: rdn to ld wl over 1f out: drvn out* **10/1**
01 **2** *1 ¾* **Knife Point (GER)**[22] 5374 3-8-12 77 (p) SteveDrowne 6 86
(Hugo Palmer) *trckd ldr: cl up 4f out: effrt to chal over 2f out: sn rdn and ev ch: drvn ins fnl f and kpt on same pce* **9/2**
6120 **3** *6* **Galactic Heroine**[35] 4893 3-9-3 82 PhillipMakin 5 82
(James Given) *led: pushed along over 3f out: jnd and rdn over 2f out: hdd wl over 1f out: sn drvn and kpt on same pce* **3/1**[1]
060 **4** *shd* **Chevalgris**[8] 5890 4-9-5 75 DavidAllan 8 74
(Alan Swinbank) *trckd ldrs: hdwy on outer over 4f out: rdn along 3f out: drvn and one pce fnl 2f* **7/2**[3]
3342 **5** *2 ½* **Lexington Bay (IRE)**[21] 5421 6-9-1 76 SammyJoBell(5) 1 71
(Richard Fahey) *trckd ldng pair on inner: pushed along over 3f out: rdn wl over 2f out: sn wknd* **10/3**[2]
6124 **6** *17* **Next Stop**[47] 4490 3-8-5 70 AdrianNicholls 7 38
(David Nicholls) *a in rr: rdn along 3f out: drvn 2f out: sn bhd and eased fnl f* **7/1**

2m 41.52s (5.32) **Going Correction** +0.55s/f (Yiel)
**WFA** 3 from 4yo+ 9lb **6** Ran SP% **110.1**
Speed ratings (Par 105): **104,102,98,98,97 85**
CSF £51.01 CT £158.45 TOTE £12.20: £4.00, £2.10; EX 61.10 Trifecta £205.40.
**Owner** Scotyork Partnership I **Bred** Carmel Stud **Trained** Middleham Moor, N Yorks

**FOCUS**
Not much pace for this competitive handicap.

## 6153 CHRISTMAS PARTY NIGHTS AT THIRSK RACECOURSE H'CAP (BOBIS RACE) 5f
**6:00** (6:00) (Class 4) (0-85,82) 3-Y-O **£6,469** (£1,925; £962; £481) **Stalls** High

Form RPR
6230 **1** **Distant Past**[16] 5601 3-8-6 72 ShaneGray(5) 8 82
(Kevin Ryan) *qckly away: mde all: rdn over 1f out: kpt on strly towards fin* **4/1**[3]
5142 **2** *1 ¼* **Cordial**[19] 5501 3-9-2 77 SteveDrowne 4 83
(Stuart Williams) *trckd wnr: effrt and nt clr run wl over 1f out: swtchd lft and rdn to chse wnr ins fnl f: kpt on* **7/2**[2]

2623 **3** 2 1/2 **Jamboree Girl**[12] 5769 3-8-11 72 DuranFentiman 2 69
(Tim Easterby) *cl up: rdn 2f out and ev ch: drvn and edgd lft ent fnl f: wknd* **8/1**

6622 **4** 1 1/4 **One Boy (IRE)**[26] 5243 3-9-4 82 ConnorBeasley(3) 5 74
(Michael Dods) *chsd ldrs: rdn wl over 1f out: drvn and no imp fnl f* **11/4**[1]

5403 **5** nk **Oriental Relation (IRE)**[26] 5243 3-8-13 74 (v) PhillipMakin 1 65
(James Given) *chsd ldrs on outer: rdn along wl over 1f out: sn drvn and btn* **9/2**

0025 **6** 3/4 **Touch The Clouds**[14] 5677 3-8-10 71 TonyHamilton 3 59
(William Stone) *in rr and sn rdn along: nvr a factor* **11/2**

1m 0.55s (0.95) **Going Correction** +0.30s/f (Good) **6** Ran SP% **113.6**
Speed ratings (Par 103): **104,102,98,96,95 94**
CSF £18.58 CT £104.78 TOTE £5.60: £2.50, £2.30; EX 24.60 Trifecta £81.70.
**Owner** M Wynne **Bred** J E Rose **Trained** Hambleton, N Yorks

**FOCUS**
An open sprint handicap, run at a fair pace.
T/Plt: £14.30 to a £1 stake. Pool: £47,883.02 - 2,440.77 winning tickets T/Qpdt: £10.10 to a £1 stake. Pool: £3,061.31 - 222.50 winning tickets JR

## 6071 WOLVERHAMPTON (A.W) (L-H)
Saturday, September 6

**OFFICIAL GOING: Tapeta: standard**
Wind: Light half-against Weather: Cloudy

### 6154 TILE CHOICE BILSTON CANNOCK & WALSALL H'CAP (TAPETA) 7f 32y
5:45 (5:47) (Class 5) (0-70,70) 3-Y-O **£2,911** (£866; £432; £216) **Stalls High**

Form RPR

2455 **1** **Derbyshire (IRE)**[11] 5795 3-8-12 66 (v) KevinStott(5) 4 79
(Kevin Ryan) *a.p: led wl over 1f out: sn rdn and hung lft: styd on* **9/2**

6022 **2** 2 1/2 **Slingsby**[22] 5376 3-8-7 56 oh1 (b) BarryMcHugh 7 63
(Michael Easterby) *chsd ldrs: rdn over 1f out: hung lft and styd on ins fnl f* **25/1**

6-35 **3** 1 1/2 **Purple Lane (IRE)**[32] 5004 3-9-5 68 MartinLane 6 71
(David Simcock) *in rr: pushed along 1/2-way: hdwy over 1f out: sn rdn and hung lft: styd on same pce ins fnl f* **5/2**[1]

0422 **4** 5 **Mendacious Harpy (IRE)**[16] 5598 3-9-1 64 (b) PatCosgrave 8 54
(George Baker) *hld up: rdn over 2f out: nt clr run over 1f out: nt trble ldrs* **9/1**

2432 **5** 2 1/2 **Bint Malyana (IRE)**[9] 5861 3-9-6 69 (e[1]) PatrickDonaghy 5 52
(Paul D'Arcy) *prom: chsd ldr 4f out: led over 2f out: rdn and hdd wl over 1f out: sn hung lft: wknd fnl f* **18/1**

3-66 **6** 6 **Cockney Belle**[24] 5304 3-8-12 66 MarcMonaghan(5) 2 34
(Marco Botti) *led: hdd over 5f out: rdn and wknd 2f out* **28/1**

31 **7** 2 1/4 **Hardy Black (IRE)**[232] 218 3-9-7 70 GrahamGibbons 3 44
(Jamie Osborne) *hmpd s: sn w ldr: led over 5f out: pushed along and hdd over 2f out: wknd and almost p.u fnl f* **4/1**[3]

4054 **R** **Scruffy Tramp (IRE)**[19] 5492 3-8-13 69 ChrisMeehan(7) 1
(John Butler) *ref to r* **7/2**[2]

1m 28.98s (0.18) **Going Correction** +0.075s/f (Slow) **8** Ran SP% **111.5**
Speed ratings (Par 101): **101,98,96,90,87 81,78,**
CSF £96.78 CT £331.65 TOTE £7.70: £2.50, £3.20, £1.80; EX 148.90 Trifecta £682.80.
**Owner** Matt & Lauren Morgan **Bred** Sas Haras De La Huderie **Trained** Hambleton, N Yorks

**FOCUS**
Just an ordinary 0-70 but they looked to go a strong gallop and the two who were front rank turning for home dropped out as the closers took over. They finished quite well strung out.

### 6155 IN MEMORY OF CAROLE RUDKIN CLAIMING STKS (TAPETA) 7f 32y
6:20 (6:20) (Class 5) 3-Y-O+ **£2,911** (£866; £432; £216) **Stalls High**

Form RPR

0355 **1** **Conry (IRE)**[12] 5761 8-9-4 70 StevieDonohoe 1 77
(Ian Williams) *sn pushed along and prom: lost pl 1/2-way: hdwy over 1f out: r.o to ld nr fin* **20/1**

0055 **2** 1 **Greeleys Love (USA)**[11] 5788 4-8-11 68 (v) RobertHavlin 10 67
(Mark Johnston) *sn chsng ldrs: rdn to ld and edgd lft ins fnl f: hdd nr fin* **8/1**

0400 **3** 1/2 **Hadaj**[8] 5888 5-9-1 82 (b) KevinStott(5) 9 75
(Ruth Carr) *led: hdd over 5f out: led again 3f out: rdn and edgd rt over 1f out: hdd wl ins fnl f* **6/1**[3]

5414 **4** 1/2 **Zed Candy Girl**[2] 6074 4-8-10 65 (p) TimClark(5) 5 69
(Dai Burchell) *hld up: hdwy 1/2-way: rdn and nt clr run fr over 1f out tl swtchd rt ins fnl f: styd on* **9/1**

0002 **5** 2 1/2 **Best Trip (IRE)**[15] 5650 7-9-7 85 MeganCarberry(5) 11 73
(Brian Ellison) *chsd ldrs: rdn and nt clr run over 1f out: btn whn hit over hd by rivals whip ins fnl f* **5/2**[1]

0066 **6** 8 **Buaiteoir (FR)**[62] 4039 8-8-9 47 PhilipPrince(3) 2 39
(Nikki Evans) *sn pushed along in rr: nvr on terms* **200/1**

2133 **7** 1/2 **Ain't No Surprise (IRE)**[12] 541 3-8-0 69 (p) JoeDoyle(5) 6 32
(Jennie Candlish) *hld up: rdn 1/2-way: a in rr* **25/1**

2510 **8** 3/4 **Half Way**[15] 5629 3-9-2 72 AmyScott(5) 8 44
(Henry Candy) *hmpd s: sn prom: led over 5f out: hdd 3f out: wknd over 1f out* **7/2**[2]

1m 29.79s (0.99) **Going Correction** +0.075s/f (Slow)
**WFA** 3 from 4yo+ 4lb **8** Ran SP% **95.3**
Speed ratings (Par 103): **97,95,95,94,91 82,82,81**
CSF £114.12 TOTE £17.20: £4.20, £2.40, £2.30; EX 143.10 Trifecta £306.20.Greeleys Love was claimed by Mr Luke Dace for £3,000.
**Owner** Mr & Mrs H Parmar **Bred** Shay White **Trained** Portway, Worcs
■ Mac's Superstar was withdrawn. Price at time of withdrawal 5-1. Rule 4 applies to all bets - deduction 15p in the pound.

**FOCUS**
An open claimer run at a strong pace.

### 6156 CARVERS RETAIL VILLAGE H'CAP (TAPETA) 1m 4f 50y
6:50 (6:51) (Class 3) (0-95,91) 3-Y-O+ **£7,246** (£2,168; £1,084; £542; £270) **Stalls Low**

Form RPR

0003 **1** **Hunting Ground (USA)**[46] 4520 4-9-11 **90** RobertHavlin 6 100
(Mark Johnston) *a.p: rdn over 1f out: styd on to ld nr fin* **16/1**

425 **2** hd **Devilment**[28] 5179 3-9-3 **91** MartinLane 7 102+
(Charlie Appleby) *hld up: racd keenly: hdwy over 5f out: hung rt: bit slipped through mouth and led over 2f out: rdn and edgd lft over 1f out: hdd nr fin* **6/5**[1]

0021 **3** 3/4 **Cousin Khee**[17] 5572 7-9-2 **81** DanielTudhope 1 89
(Hughie Morrison) *chsd ldrs: rdn over 2f out: edgd lft over 1f out: styd on* **3/1**[2]

0462 **4** 7 **Magic Art (IRE)**[42] 4663 4-9-2 **81** MartinHarley 3 78
(Marco Botti) *chsd ldr 4f: remained handy: rdn and ev ch over 2f out: wknd fnl f* **8/1**[3]

0060 **5** 1 1/4 **Modernism**[15] 5651 5-9-3 **82** PatCosgrave 4 77
(David Simcock) *hld up: hdwy over 2f out: sn rdn: wknd over 1f out* **9/1**

1001 **6** 10 **Flying Power**[29] 5127 6-9-4 **83** PaddyAspell 5 62
(John Norton) *led 4f: chsd ldr tl led again wl over 2f out: sn hdd: wknd wl over 1f out* **16/1**

0103 **7** 12 **Epic Battle (IRE)**[44] 4586 4-9-5 **84** JimmyQuinn 8 44
(George Margarson) *mid-div: drvn along over 3f out: wknd 2f out* **16/1**

3304 **8** 2 **Back Burner (IRE)**[31] 5035 6-8-9 **77** oh5 (p) AmyScott(3) 2 34
(Dai Burchell) *hld up: hdwy to ld 8f out: clr 7f out: hdd & wknd wl over 2f out* **40/1**

2244 **9** 52 **Tepmokea (IRE)**[45] 4538 8-9-8 **87** (p) HayleyTurner 9
(Conor Dore) *mid-div: lost pl over 6f out: bhd fnl 5f* **33/1**

2m 37.98s (-2.82) **Going Correction** +0.075s/f (Slow)
**WFA** 3 from 4yo+ 9lb **9** Ran SP% **114.6**
Speed ratings (Par 107): **112,111,111,106,105 99,91,89,55**
CSF £35.46 CT £78.33 TOTE £10.70: £4.40, £1.10, £2.00; EX 44.10 Trifecta £184.60.
**Owner** Sheikh Hamdan bin Mohammed Al Maktoum **Bred** Darley **Trained** Middleham Moor, N Yorks

**FOCUS**
A good-quality handicap, although the topweight was 5lb below the ceiling rating for the grade. The pace was very steady early but picked up when Back Burner took over around a mile from the finish. The front three came a long way clear.

### 6157 YOUR CHOICE BATHROOMS H'CAP (TAPETA) 1m 4f 50y
7:20 (7:20) (Class 6) (0-60,60) 3-Y-O+ **£2,264** (£673; £336; £168) **Stalls Low**

Form RPR

-602 **1** **Kelamita (IRE)**[19] 5491 3-8-12 55 RichardHughes 9 68+
(Hughie Morrison) *led at stdy pce tl pushed along and hdd over 2f out: rallied u.p to ld ins fnl f: edgd rt: styd on wl* **1/1**[1]

0055 **2** 3 **Royal Trooper (IRE)**[31] 5030 8-9-1 56 ow3 BeckyBrisbourne(7) 1 64
(Mark Brisbourne) *s.i.s: hld up: hdwy on outer over 3f out: led over 2f out: sn rdn: hdd and no ex ins fnl f* **66/1**

0323 **3** 3 1/4 **Give Us A Reason**[19] 5508 4-9-11 59 LukeMorris 11 62
(James Toller) *hld up: hdwy over 4f out: rdn and edgd lft over 1f out: no ex ins fnl f* **9/2**[2]

3404 **4** nk **Snow Dancer (IRE)**[16] 5600 10-9-0 53 AlistairRawlinson(5) 6 55
(John David Riches) *prom: rdn over 2f out: styd on same pce fr over 1f out* **25/1**

1402 **5** 1 **Nolecce**[8] 5898 7-9-5 60 AdamMcLean(7) 10 61
(Tony Forbes) *chsd ldrs: wnt 2nd over 3f out tl rdn over 2f out: wknd ins fnl f* **10/1**

2000 **6** 1 1/2 **My Renaissance**[18] 5529 4-8-13 52 RobJFitzpatrick(5) 12 50
(Ben Case) *hld up: hdwy over 1f out: sn rdn: wknd ins fnl f* **40/1**

0-50 **7** 2 1/2 **Network Perfection**[12] 5765 3-8-6 49 GrahamGibbons 3 43
(Michael Easterby) *hld up: shkn up over 1f out: nvr on terms* **8/1**[3]

6222 **8** 1 1/4 **Rajeh (IRE)**[9] 5864 11-8-13 47 TomQueally 4 39
(Peter Grayson) *prom: chsd ldr 10f out tl rdn over 3f out: wknd over 1f out* **20/1**

**9** 1 1/2 **Bane (IRE)**[17] 5585 3-9-2 59 TomEaves 2 49
(Ronald O'Leary, Ire) *chsd wnr 2f: remained handy: tl rdn over 3f out: wknd over 2f out* **18/1**

5236 **10** nse **Impeccability**[12] 5748 4-9-0 48 (p) FrannyNorton 5 38
(John Mackie) *prom over 8f* **28/1**

3002 **11** 1 1/2 **Essanar**[22] 5402 3-8-6 54 JackDuern(5) 7 41
(Andrew Hollinshead) *hld up: rdn and wknd over 3f out* **14/1**

2m 43.62s (2.82) **Going Correction** +0.075s/f (Slow)
**WFA** 3 from 4yo+ 9lb **11** Ran SP% **116.3**
Speed ratings (Par 101): **93,91,88,88,87 86,85,84,83,83 82**
CSF £118.91 CT £234.00 TOTE £2.00: £1.10, £7.60, £1.70; EX 72.50 Trifecta £230.50.
**Owner** M E Wates **Bred** M E Wates **Trained** East Ilsley, Berks

**FOCUS**
A weak race run at a crawl so not form to get excited about.

### 6158 EBF STALLIONS BILSTON BATHROOMS MAIDEN STKS (TAPETA) 5f 20y
7:50 (7:52) (Class 5) 2-Y-O **£3,234** (£962; £481; £240) **Stalls Low**

Form RPR

52 **1** **Equally Fast**[44] 4583 2-9-5 0 DougieCostello 3 80
(William Muir) *w ldr tl led 4f out: rdn out* **5/1**[3]

42 **2** 3/4 **Field Game**[17] 5569 2-9-5 0 RichardHughes 7 77
(Hughie Morrison) *chsd ldrs: wnt 2nd over 1f out: sn rdn: r.o* **6/4**[1]

3530 **3** 1 **Burning The Clocks (IRE)**[39] 4757 2-9-0 79 JordanNason(5) 4 74
(Peter Chapple-Hyam) *trckd ldrs: nt clr run over 1f out: styd on* **7/2**[2]

2200 **4** 1/2 **Winstanley (IRE)**[16] 5607 2-9-2 79 GeorgeChaloner(3) 11 72
(Richard Fahey) *chsd ldrs: pushed along 1/2-way: styd on same pce ins fnl f* **7/2**[2]

0245 **5** 3 1/4 **York Express**[16] 5604 2-9-0 70 TomQueally 5 55
(Ismail Mohammed) *mid-div: hdwy 2f out: sn rdn: styd on same pce fnl f* **10/1**

40 **6** 3 **Alaskan Wing (IRE)**[123] 2051 2-9-5 0 BarryMcHugh 2 49
(Tony Coyle) *led 1f: chsd wnr to 1/2-way: rdn and wknd over 1f out* **80/1**

**7** 1/2 **Glenbuck Lass (IRE)** 2-8-11 0 RobertTart(3) 12 43
(Alan Bailey) *prom over 3f* **40/1**

**8** nk **Compton Viking (IRE)** 2-9-5 0 (t) LukeMorris 1 47
(Paul Fitzsimons) *mid-div: sn pushed along: wknd 2f out* **33/1**

4 **9** 1/2 **Grumpy Angel**[19] 5511 2-9-0 0 TomEaves 10 40
(Richard Fahey) *hld up: a in rr* **25/1**

6 **10** 3/4 **Junior Ben**[73] 3580 2-9-5 0 DaleSwift 13 42
(Derek Shaw) *sn pushed along in rr: wknd 1/2-way* **150/1**

06 **11** 3 1/4 **Auntie Dif**[17] 5569 2-8-7 0 AdamMcLean(7) 6 25
(Derek Shaw) *hld up: plld hrd: bhd fr 1/2-way* **100/1**

1m 2.44s (0.54) **Going Correction** +0.075s/f (Slow) **11** Ran SP% **122.3**
Speed ratings (Par 95): **98,96,95,94,89 84,83,83,82,81 75**
CSF £13.23 TOTE £7.60: £1.30, £1.40, £2.20; EX 17.50 Trifecta £74.60.
**Owner** Muir Racing Partnership - Haydock **Bred** Newsells Park Stud **Trained** Lambourn, Berks

**FOCUS**
Probably not a bad maiden for the track with a couple of 79-rated runners finishing third and fourth, and judging by his post-race comments, William Muir appears to think quite a bit of the winner. The order changed little and the form could be worth up to 9lb higher.

## 6159 SUSAN BEASLEY 25TH ANNIVERSARY H'CAP (TAPETA) 5f 216y
**8:20** (8:22) (Class 2) (0-100,100) 3-Y-O+ **£11,971** (£3,583; £1,791; £896; £446) Stalls Low

Form RPR

4211 **1** **Go Far**[21] 5419 4-9-1 **94** ....(v) FergalLynch 10 106
(Alan Bailey) *hld up: hdwy over 1f out: rdn to ld ins fnl f: r.o* **11/2**[3]

3020 **2** ¾ **Foxtrot Romeo (IRE)**[7] 5919 5-9-0 **93** ....(tp) MartinHarley 3 103+
(Marco Botti) *hld up: hdwy and nt clr run over 1f out: shkn up and edgd lft ins fnl f: r.o* **11/4**[1]

2010 **3** 3 ½ **Speed Hawk (USA)**[14] 5696 3-9-3 **98** .... GrahamGibbons 9 97
(Robert Cowell) *chsd ldr tl led over 1f out: sn rdn: hdd and no ex ins fnl f* **5/1**[2]

2-04 **4** *nk* **Invincible Strike (IRE)**[36] 4872 3-9-2 **97** ....(b[1]) RobertHavlin 12 95
(James Tate) *chsd ldrs: rdn over 1f out: styd on same pce fnl f* **20/1**

200 **5** 3 ½ **Swiss Cross**[12] 5754 7-9-4 **97** ....(bt) StevieDonohoe 2 84
(Phil McEntee) *sn pushed along in rr: edgd lft and styd on u.p ins fnl f: nvr nrr* **25/1**

3404 **6** ½ **Desert Law (IRE)**[70] 3732 6-9-4 **97** .... RichardHughes 6 82
(Saeed bin Suroor) *hld up in tch: plld hrd: rdn over 1f out: hmpd and wknd ins fnl f* **11/2**[3]

-404 **7** 1 **Muir Lodge**[65] 3876 3-8-9 **90** .... PatCosgrave 11 72
(George Baker) *hld up: nvr trbld ldrs* **22/1**

0100 **8** *hd* **Racy**[17] 5575 7-9-2 **100** .... MeganCarberry(5) 7 81
(Brian Ellison) *hld up: rdn over 2f out: wknd fnl f* **14/1**

0040 **9** 3 ½ **Blithe Spirit**[14] 5696 3-8-11 **92** .... JasonHart 5 62
(Eric Alston) *led: rdn and hdd over 1f out: wknd ins fnl f* **50/1**

02-0 **10** ½ **Blockade (IRE)**[143] 1515 3-9-4 **99** .... DanielTudhope 8 67
(James Tate) *prom: rdn over 2f out: wknd fnl f* **20/1**

1124 **11** 2 ¾ **Trojan Rocket (IRE)**[173] 991 6-8-9 **88** .... LukeMorris 1 48
(Michael Wigham) *chsd ldrs: rdn 1/2-way: wknd fnl f* **14/1**

000 **12** 3 ½ **Barracuda Boy (IRE)**[35] 4895 4-9-0 **98** ....(v) JennyPowell(5) 13 46
(Tom Dascombe) *s.i.s: outpcd* **9/1**

1m 13.15s (-1.35) **Going Correction** +0.075s/f (Slow)
**WFA** 3 from 4yo+ 2lb **12 Ran SP% 117.1**
Speed ratings (Par 109): **112,111,106,105,101 100,99,99,94,93 90,85**
CSF £19.04 CT £82.58 TOTE £6.70: £1.90, £1.80, £1.90; EX 25.20 Trifecta £120.50.
**Owner** R West **Bred** Michael Turner **Trained** Newmarket, Suffolk

**FOCUS**
A cracking sprint run at a hot tempo and this looks strong form.

## 6160 TILE CHOICE QUALITY TILES LOW PRICES H'CAP (TAPETA) (DIV I) 1m 141y
**8:50** (8:50) (Class 6) (0-65,73) 3-Y-O+ **£2,264** (£673; £336; £168) Stalls Low

Form RPR

3341 **1** **Fiftyshadesfreed (IRE)**[8] 5899 3-9-12 73 ....(p) PatCosgrave 8 94
(George Baker) *hld up: hdwy over 3f out: led over 2f out: rdn clr and edgd lft fr over 1f out* **9/4**[2]

-521 **2** 7 **Flipping**[19] 5512 7-9-3 58 .... RichardHughes 6 63
(Stuart Kittow) *chsd ldrs: rdn over 2f out: no ex fnl f* **11/8**[1]

0000 **3** ½ **Spirit Of Gondree (IRE)**[31] 5041 6-9-6 61 ....(b) LukeMorris 2 65
(Milton Bradley) *hld up: plld hrd: hdwy over 2f out: sn rdn: styd on same pce fr over 1f out* **25/1**

0044 **4** 2 **Outlaw Torn (IRE)**[15] 5640 5-9-2 62 ....(e) DuilioDaSilva(5) 10 61
(Richard Guest) *led: rdn and hdd over 2f out: wknd fnl f* **9/1**

4156 **5** 3 **Be Royale**[58] 4108 4-9-10 65 .... AndrewMullen 1 58
(Michael Appleby) *mid-div: hdwy over 2f out: rdn over 1f out: sn wknd* **6/1**[3]

6043 **6** 1 ¼ **Vied (USA)**[10] 5833 3-8-6 53 ....(p) AdamBeschizza 4 43
(Robert Cowell) *prom: n.m.r and lost pl after 1f: rdn over 2f out: sn wknd* **22/1**

2400 **7** 3 ¾ **Aureolin Gulf**[50] 4415 5-8-5 51 oh6 .... JackDuern(5) 5 32
(Andrew Hollinshead) *hld up: rdn over 3f out: wknd wl over 1f out* **66/1**

0600 **8** 5 **Officer In Command (USA)**[44] 4578 8-9-0 60 ....(p) DanielMuscutt(5) 7 30
(John Butler) *s.s: outpcd* **25/1**

0603 **9** 1 **Elite Freedom (IRE)**[16] 5605 3-8-4 51 oh3 .... RoystonFfrench 3 18
(Brian Baugh) *chsd ldrs 5f* **50/1**

16-5 **10** 1 ¾ **Larghetto (USA)**[216] 445 6-9-7 62 .... StevieDonohoe 9 25
(Ian Williams) *s.i.s: hdwy to chse ldr over 7f out: rdn and ev ch over 2f out: wknd over 1f out* **25/1**

1m 50.7s (0.60) **Going Correction** +0.075s/f (Slow)
**WFA** 3 from 4yo+ 6lb **10 Ran SP% 116.5**
Speed ratings (Par 101): **100,93,93,91,88 87,84,80,79,77**
CSF £5.22 CT £56.92 TOTE £3.40: £1.70, £1.10, £5.00; EX 6.70 Trifecta £112.30.
**Owner** Team Fifty **Bred** Bernard Cloney **Trained** Manton, Wilts

**FOCUS**
Most of these had something to prove on one count or another and two dominated the market for this weak handicap, but it became a one-horse contest from some way out.

## 6161 TILE CHOICE QUALITY TILES LOW PRICES H'CAP (TAPETA) (DIV II) 1m 141y
**9:20** (9:20) (Class 6) (0-65,65) 3-Y-O+ **£2,264** (£673; £336; £168) Stalls Low

Form RPR

1246 **1** **Glennten**[12] 5756 5-9-10 65 .... IrineuGoncalves 9 74
(Jose Santos) *a.p: chsd ldr over 5f out: led over 1f out: r.o* **14/1**

444 **2** 1 **Eddiemaurice (IRE)**[17] 5566 3-8-13 65 ....(v) DuilioDaSilva(5) 8 71
(Richard Guest) *hld up: hdwy over 3f out: rdn over 1f out: r.o* **7/2**[2]

5441 **3** 1 ¼ **Jumbo Prado (USA)**[8] 5893 5-9-0 60 ....(p) EoinWalsh(5) 3 63
(John Stimpson) *hld up: edgd lft and bmpd over 6f out: rdn over 3f out: hdwy over 2f out: nt rch ldrs* **7/2**[2]

6006 **4** 1 **Space War**[11] 5793 7-9-9 64 .... GrahamGibbons 7 65
(Michael Easterby) *sn led: clr 6f out: hdd over 1f out: no ex ins fnl f* **15/8**[1]

1606 **5** 8 **Blue Clumber**[11] 5797 4-8-10 51 .... JimmyQuinn 5 33
(Shaun Harris) *sn pushed along in rr: hung lft and kpt on ins fnl f: nt trble ldrs* **20/1**

-306 **6** 3 ¼ **Kingswinford (IRE)**[31] 5041 8-9-7 62 ....(p) PaddyAspell 6 37
(John Norton) *chsd ldrs: rdn over 2f out: wknd over 1f out* **12/1**

4-40 **7** ¾ **Meydan Style (USA)**[25] 5291 8-8-3 51 oh6 .... JordanSwarbrick(7) 1 24
(Brian Baugh) *led early: chsd ldr tl over 5f out: rdn over 3f out: wknd over 2f out* **50/1**

00 **8** 4 ½ **Silver Lightening (IRE)**[4] 6011 4-9-7 62 .... JasonHart 4 25
(Eric Alston) *s.s: a in rr* **9/1**[3]

-640 **9** 99 **Speedy Rio (IRE)**[31] 5044 3-8-4 51 oh3 .... LukeMorris 2
(Luke Dace) *prom: lost pl whn hmpd over 6f out: sn eased* **12/1**

1m 51.14s (1.04) **Going Correction** +0.075s/f (Slow)
**WFA** 3 from 4yo+ 6lb **9 Ran SP% 118.0**
Speed ratings (Par 101): **98,97,96,95,88 85,84,80,**
CSF £64.05 CT £217.09 TOTE £5.80: £2.20, £2.30, £1.20; EX 71.90 Trifecta £55.90.
**Owner** R Cooper Racing Ltd **Bred** The Hon Mrs R Pease **Trained** Upper Lambourn, Berks
■ The first winner in Britain for Brazilian Irineu Goncalves, who has ridden more than 750 winners in South America.
■ Stewards' Enquiry : Irineu Goncalves five-day ban: careless riding (Sep 20-24)

**FOCUS**
A slightly slower overall time than the first division but the pace looked sound and the front four finished clear.
T/Plt: £24.20 to a £1 stake. Pool: £81,374.33 - 2446.90 winning units. T/Qpdt: £2.40 to a £1 stake. Pool: £13,816.77 - 4199.05 winning units. CR

# 6123 BADEN-BADEN (L-H)
Saturday, September 6
**OFFICIAL GOING: Turf: good**

## 6162a T VON ZASTROW STUTENPREIS (GROUP 3) (3YO+ FILLIES & MARES) (TURF) 1m 3f
**3:50** (12:00) 3-Y-O+
**£26,666** (£9,166; £4,583; £2,500; £1,666; £1,250)

RPR

**1** **Lacy (GER)**[34] 4955 3-8-10 0 .... AdriedeVries 2 105
(Waldemar Hickst, Germany) *hld up towards rr on inner: hdwy 2f out: chal between horses ins fnl f: rdn and r.o to ld post* **11/5**[2]

**2** *shd* **Heartily (IRE)**[42] 4694 3-8-10 0 .... AnthonyCrastus 4 105
(H-A Pantall, France) *trckd ldr on inner: rdn to press ldr under 2f out: led over 1f out: r.o u.p: hdd post* **48/10**[3]

**3** 1 ¾ **Virginia Sun (GER)**[34] 3-8-10 0 .... SHellyn 9 102
(J Hirschberger, Germany) *led on outer: rdn and hdd over 1f out: one pce fnl f* **8/5**[1]

**4** 2 **Abilene**[23] 5369 4-9-4 0 .... CristianDemuro 3 98
(F-H Graffard, France) *trckd ldng trio on inner: dropped towards rr 1/2-way but wl in tch: shkn up to chse ldrs 2f out: rdn and nt qckn fnl f: fdd last 75yds* **43/5**

**5** 2 **Lady Liberty (IRE)**[101] 4-9-4 0 .... AHelfenbein 6 95
(Andreas Lowe, Germany) *w.w in midfield: rdn and nt qckn over 2f out: one pce u.p fnl f* **44/5**

**6** ¾ **Lutindi (GER)**[28] 3-8-10 0 .... DanielePorcu 5 93
(P Schiergen, Germany) *settled in 3rd on outer: shkn up to chse ldr 2 1/2f out: sn rdn and outpcd: wknd fnl f* **211/10**

**7** 1 **Oriental Magic (GER)**[34] 4955 3-8-10 0 .... MichaelCadeddu 7 92
(J Hirschberger, Germany) *w.w in rr: rdn and no imp fnl 2f: nvr in contention* **116/10**

**8** *hd* **Glee (GER)**[34] 4-9-4 0 .... FilipMinarik 8 91
(Jean-Pierre Carvalho, Germany) *hld up towards rr on outer: gd hdwy to go 4th bef 1/2-way: rdn and outpcd over 1 1/2f out: fdd ins fnl f* **91/10**

2m 27.53s (8.26)
**WFA** 3 from 4yo 8lb **8 Ran SP% 129.9**
WIN (incl. 10 euro stake): 32. PLACES: 12, 15, 13. SF: 183.
**Owner** Stiftung Gestut Fahrhof **Bred** Gestut Fahrhof **Trained** Germany

# VELIEFENDI
Saturday, September 6
**OFFICIAL GOING: Polytrack: standard; turf: good**

## 6163a INTERNATIONAL FRANCE GALOP - FRBC ANATOLIA TROPHY (LOCAL GROUP 2) (3YO+) (POLYTRACK) 1m 2f (P)
**6:30** (12:00) 3-Y-O+ **£95,833** (£38,333; £19,166; £9,583)

RPR

**1** **Windhoek**[42] 4682 4-9-6 0 .... MickaelBarzalona 3 108
(Saeed bin Suroor) *t.k.h: hld up in tch: clsd on rail 1/2-way: pushed along and swtchd out over 1f out: r.o and reeled in ldr fnl f: rdn to ld towards fin: shade cosily* **30/100**[1]

**2** ½ **Hakeem (USA)**[35] 3-9-0 0 ow3 .... SelimKaya 1 108
(En B Ogullari, Turkey) *led: set stdy pce: rdn and kicked on 2f out: 1 l in front ent fnl f: kpt on but worn down and hdd towards fin: no ex and hld* **37/20**[3]

**3** *hd* **Danadana (IRE)**[28] 5175 6-9-6 0 .... AndreaAtzeni 2 107
(Luca Cumani) *midfield in tch: clsd after 2f and trckd ldr on outer: rdn and effrt to chal over 2f out: outpcd by ldrs over 1f out: kpt on wl fnl f but hld* **13/10**[2]

**4** 2 ½ **Assez Clair (USA)**[78] 4-9-6 0 .... ThierryThulliez 4 102
(Mme C Head-Maarek, France) *trckd ldr early: stdd off heels and midfield in tch after 3f: rdn over 2f out: kpt on same pce fr over 1f out and nvr able to chal* **4/1**

**5** 3 **Maximus Dream (TUR)**[22] 5-9-6 0 .... GokhanKocakaya 5 96
(C Turan, Turkey) *hld up and a in rr: rdn and fanned wd into st: sn outpcd and no imp: nvr threatened* **14/5**

2m 6.96s (1.96)
**WFA** 3 from 4yo+ 7lb **5 Ran SP% 201.8**
DIVIDENDS (INCLUDING 1 UNIT STAKE): WIN 1.30; SF 3.55.
**Owner** Godolphin **Bred** Horizon Bloodstock Limited **Trained** Newmarket, Suffolk

## 6164a INTERNATIONAL ISTANBUL TROPHY (GROUP 3) (3YO+ FILLIES & MARES) (TURF) 1m
**7:00** (12:00) 3-Y-O+ **£95,833** (£38,333; £19,166; £9,583)

RPR

**1** **Shuruq (USA)**[161] 1176 4-9-6 0 ....(p) MickaelBarzalona 6 113
(Saeed bin Suroor) *stdd and settled in midfield: pushed along and clsd over 1f out: rdn to chal jst ins fnl f and sn led: qcknd clr towards fin: readily* **7/20**[1]



The Form Book, Raceform Ltd, Newbury, RG14 5SJ

**2** 2 1/2 **Crowley's Law**[24] 5312 3-8-13 0 RichardKingscote 3 104
(Tom Dascombe) *w ldr early: sn restrained but remained prom: pushed along to chal 2f out: rdn to ld over 1f out: strly pressed jst ins fnl f and sn hdd: no ex and readily outpcd by wnr* **15/2**

**3** 2 1/2 **Dancing Sands (IRE)**[41] 4721 3-8-13 0 FabriceVeron 5 99
(H-A Pantall, France) *hld up in last: rdn and stl in rr ent fnl f: str run fnl 120yds and wnt 3rd cl home: nvr nrr* **7/20**[1]

**4** 1/2 **Suzi Gold (TUR)**[17] 3-8-13 0 HalisKaratas 7 97
(C Turan, Turkey) *hld up towards rr: rdn over 2f out: kpt on steadily but nt pce to chal: wnt 3rd briefly towards fin: dropped to 4th again cl home* **27/20**[2]

**5** 1/2 **Kosika (USA)**[16] 5609 4-9-6 0 KierenFallon 8 99
(Mark Johnston) *sn trcking ldr on outer: pushed along 1/2-way: led over 2f out: rdn and hdd over 1f out: no ex and wknd fnl f: lost 2 pls and dropped to 5th towards fin* **9/5**[3]

**6** 3 **Chachkova (USA)**[20] 4-9-6 0 AndreaAtzeni 1 92
(D B Bagceci, Turkey) *prom on inner: rdn and brief effrt to chal on rail over 2f out: swtchd lft and outpcd over 1f out: sn btn and wknd* **66/10**

**7** 2 1/2 **Elevato (TUR)**[17] 4-9-6 0 GokhanKocakaya 4 87
(Z Guneli, Turkey) *stdd and hld up towards rr on inner: rdn into st: outpcd and no imp over 1f out: eased whn btn fnl f* **94/10**

**8** 4 1/2 **Hard Baby (TUR)**[17] 3-8-13 0 (b) AhmetCelik 2 73
(En B Ogullari, Turkey) *led: set even pce: rdn and hdd over 2f out: sn no ex and btn: wknd: eased and dropped to last fnl f* **13/2**

1m 35.53s (0.20)
**WFA** 3 from 4yo 5lb **8** Ran SP% **274.3**
DIVIDENDS (INCLUDING 1 UNIT STAKE): WIN 1.35 (coupled with Dancing Sands); DF 7.00; SF 8.75.
**Owner** Godolphin **Bred** Darley **Trained** Newmarket, Suffolk

# 5690 YORK (L-H)

## Sunday, September 7

**OFFICIAL GOING: Good to firm (good in places; 6.8)**
Wind: Moderate; half against Weather: Fine Rails: Rail at innermost position provide fresh ground from 9f to entrance to home straight and races of 1m and beyond reduced in distance by 24yds

## 6165 JUDITH MARSHALL MEMORIAL STKS (NURSERY H'CAP) (BOBIS RACE) 7f

**2:00** (2:02) (Class 4) (0-85,84) 2-Y-O **£6,469** (£1,925; £962; £481) **Stalls** Low

Form RPR

621 **1** **Invincible Gold (IRE)**[20] 5488 2-9-7 84 GeorgeBaker 7 90
(Ed Walker) *led 1f: chsd ldr: led 1f out: jst hld on* **15/2**[3]

31 **2** *shd* **Spring Offensive (IRE)**[49] 4467 2-9-0 77 TonyHamilton 11 82
(Richard Fahey) *mid-div: effrt over 2f out: styd on strly fnl f: jst failed* **9/2**[2]

4012 **3** *shd* **Binky Blue (IRE)**[30] 5141 2-7-10 64 JoeDoyle(5) 2 69
(Brian Ellison) *chsd ldrs: led briefly over 1f out: kpt on wl ins fnl f: jst hld* **33/1**

11 **4** *nse* **Supreme Occasion (IRE)**[31] 5085 2-9-5 82 DanielTudhope 9 88
(David O'Meara) *prom: effrt on inner over 2f out: chsng ldrs over 1f out: styd on wl ins fnl f* **7/2**[1]

512 **5** 1 1/4 **Moonlightnavigator (USA)**[13] 5762 2-9-6 83 PhillipMakin 15 84
(John Quinn) *chsd ldrs: kpt on same pce over 1f out* **8/1**

3315 **6** 3 **Kylach Me If U Can**[31] 5085 2-8-12 75 JamieSpencer 4 68
(Kevin Ryan) *wnt rt s: in rr: nt clr run over 2f out: swtchd rt over 1f out: styd on: nt rch ldrs* **20/1**

4334 **7** *nk* **Grand Proposal**[24] 5335 2-8-4 72 ShaneGray(5) 3 65
(Kevin Ryan) *in rr: kpt on fnl 2f: nrst fin* **33/1**

4450 **8** 3 1/4 **Burtonwood**[18] 5580 2-9-3 80 (v[1]) AdamKirby 12 64
(Richard Fahey) *led after 1f: hdd over 1f out: wknd fnl 150yds* **25/1**

2241 **9** 3/4 **Popeswood (IRE)**[8] 5929 2-9-4 81 WilliamBuick 14 63
(Mick Channon) *hld up in rr: hdwy over 2f out: wknd fnl f* **11/1**

645 **10** 1 **Upward Trend (IRE)**[76] 3529 2-8-1 65 DuranFentiman 13 43
(Tim Easterby) *mid-div: effrt over 2f out: nvr a factor* **25/1**

0651 **11** *hd* **Pumaflor (IRE)**[12] 5790 2-8-4 66 ow1 JasonHart 6 46
(Richard Guest) *hld up in rr: effrt and nt clr run over 1f out: nvr a factor* **25/1**

036 **12** *nk* **Lysander The Greek**[25] 5309 2-8-7 70 SilvestreDeSousa 8 48
(Ralph Beckett) *in rr: drvn and sme hdwy 4f out: n.m.r whn sltly hmpd over 1f out* **9/1**

2152 **13** *hd* **Arabian Bride (IRE)**[31] 5085 2-9-6 83 FrannyNorton 10 60
(Mark Johnston) *chsd ldrs: lost pl over 1f out* **16/1**

0402 **14** 2 1/2 **My Mate (IRE)**[9] 5875 2-8-8 71 RobertWinston 5 41
(Clive Brittain) *hmpd s: hld up in rr: drvn over 3f out: lost pl over 1f out: eased nr fin* **18/1**

136 **15** 5 **Muqaawel (USA)**[36] 4897 2-9-1 78 PaulHanagan 1 35
(Mark Johnston) *chsd ldrs: lost pl over 4f out: sme hdwy over 3f out: wknd 2f out: eased whn bhd clsng stages* **20/1**

1m 25.98s (0.68) **Going Correction** +0.05s/f (Good) **15** Ran SP% **119.7**
Speed ratings (Par 97): **98,97,97,97,96 92,92,88,87,86 86,86,86,83,77**
CSF £36.50 CT £1082.70 TOTE £9.70: £1.90, £2.50, £6.40; EX 48.70 Trifecta £2250.10 Part won..
**Owner** John Coleman & Clarence Cheng **Bred** Rockfield Farm **Trained** Newmarket, Suffolk
■ Stewards' Enquiry : Jamie Spencer caution: careless riding.

**FOCUS**
A competitive nursery to start with and run at a decent gallop. It paid to be handy and barely a head separated the front four at the line. They stayed against the inside rail in the straight. The form has been positively rated despite the tight finish.

## 6166 BARKERS GARAGE STKS (H'CAP) 1m 2f 88y

**2:30** (2:31) (Class 4) (0-80,83) 3-Y-O+ **£6,469** (£1,925; £962; £481) **Stalls** Low

Form RPR

5526 **1** **Cosmic Halo**[13] 5757 5-9-5 73 PaulHanagan 13 82
(Richard Fahey) *in rr: hdwy on outer over 1f out: styd on wl to ld last 100yds* **5/1**[2]

5202 **2** 1/2 **Duke Of Yorkshire**[25] 5300 4-8-13 67 DuranFentiman 12 75
(Tim Easterby) *rr-div: hdwy 3f out: chsng ldrs over 1f out: styd on to take 2nd last 50yds* **12/1**

13 **3** 1 1/4 **Ribblehead (USA)**[22] 5420 3-9-2 77 DavidAllan 1 83
(Tim Easterby) *s.i.s: hdwy on inner 4f out: chsng ldrs over 3f out: no ex last 75yds* **9/1**

2361 **4** 3/4 **Jalingo (IRE)**[10] 5855 3-9-8 83 FrannyNorton 5 87
(Mark Johnston) *s.i.s: hdwy on ins over 3f out: chsng ldrs over 1f out: kpt on same pce* **7/2**[1]

3640 **5** *hd* **Maybeme**[14] 5716 8-9-3 71 (p) AndrewElliott 14 75
(Neville Bycroft) *hld up in rr: hdwy on outside over 2f out: styd on ins fnl f* **40/1**

3366 **6** 1/2 **Artful Prince**[12] 5792 4-9-7 75 (b) GrahamLee 2 78
(James Given) *led early: chsd ldrs: led over 2f out: wnt rt over 1f out: hdd and one pce last 100yds* **14/1**

4325 **7** 1/2 **Mariners Moon (IRE)**[13] 5768 3-8-7 71 (p) SamJames(3) 10 73
(David O'Meara) *mid-div: hdwy over 3f out: sn chsng ldrs: kpt on same pce fnl f* **20/1**

1126 **8** 2 **Sheriff Of Nawton (IRE)**[27] 5245 3-8-12 73 DanielTudhope 3 71
(David O'Meara) *in tch: drvn to chse ldrs over 3f out: kpt on same pce over 1f out* **12/1**

4554 **9** 1/2 **Dolphin Rock**[22] 5413 7-9-0 68 (p) DaleSwift 15 65
(Brian Ellison) *prom: drvn to chse ldrs over 3f out: wknd fnl 150yds* **20/1**

5310 **10** *nk* **Unex Michelangelo (IRE)**[23] 5371 5-9-2 70 GrahamGibbons 6 67
(Michael Easterby) *mid-div: hdwy to chse ldrs over 2f out: wknd over 1f out* **25/1**

42S2 **11** 6 **Lord Franklin**[10] 5855 5-9-2 70 JasonHart 11 55
(Eric Alston) *sn led: hdd after 1f: led over 3f out: hdd over 2f out: sn wknd* **12/1**

0601 **12** 2 **Chapter And Verse (IRE)**[39] 4786 8-8-13 67 ShaneKelly 4 48
(Mike Murphy) *chsd ldrs: wknd over 1f out: eased clsng stages* **16/1**

1010 **13** 2 **Tower Power**[22] 5420 3-9-5 80 (t) MartinHarley 7 58
(Ismail Mohammed) *chsd ldrs: wknd over 1f out: eased clsng stages* **17/2**[3]

3025 **14** *nk* **Millkwood**[9] 5887 4-9-6 74 PhillipMakin 9 51
(John Davies) *in rr: drvn 5f out: n.m.r over 2f out: sn wknd: eased clsng stages* **25/1**

0363 **15** 13 **Eeny Mac (IRE)**[14] 5711 7-9-5 73 (p) SilvestreDeSousa 8 25
(Neville Bycroft) *led after 1f: hdd over 2f out: sn wknd and eased* **20/1**

2m 9.06s (-3.44) **Going Correction** -0.175s/f (Firm)
**WFA** 3 from 4yo+ 7lb **15** Ran SP% **117.6**
Speed ratings (Par 105): **106,105,104,104,103 103,103,101,101,100 96,94,92,92,82**
CSF £70.17 CT £705.57 TOTE £5.40: £2.40, £4.10, £2.70; EX 69.30 Trifecta £959.90.
**Owner** The Cosmic Cases **Bred** The Cosmic Cases **Trained** Musley Bank, N Yorks

**FOCUS**
A competitive handicap, but unlike in the opener those held up were at an advantage and they came up the middle once into the straight.

## 6167 BETFRED GARROWBY STKS (LISTED RACE) 6f

**3:00** (3:00) (Class 1) 3-Y-O+
**£20,982** (£7,955; £3,981; £1,983; £995; £499) **Stalls** Low

Form RPR

2244 **1** **Naadirr (IRE)**[15] 5674 3-8-12 108 (p) MartinHarley 5 112
(Marco Botti) *trckd ldrs: led over 1f out: hung rt ins fnl f: drvn out* **2/1**[1]

0104 **2** 1 **Ladies Are Forever**[21] 5467 6-9-2 107 (b) BarryMcHugh 6 111
(Geoffrey Oldroyd) *trckd ldrs: t.k.h: rdn over 1f out: styd on to take 2nd towards fin* **11/2**[3]

6661 **3** *nk* **Justineo**[36] 4889 5-9-0 107 WilliamBuick 8 108
(Roger Varian) *led: hdd over 1f out: styd on same pce last 100yds* **4/1**[2]

650 **4** 1 1/2 **Artistic Jewel (IRE)**[58] 4171 5-8-9 100 GrahamGibbons 7 98
(Ed McMahon) *w ldr: drvn over 1f out: hmpd ins fnl f: fdd last 50yds* **20/1**

1003 **5** 3 1/2 **Line Of Reason (IRE)**[8] 5911 4-9-0 104 GrahamLee 4 92
(Paul Midgley) *sn trcking ldrs: t.k.h: rdn 2f out: fdd fnl f* **12/1**

-500 **6** *nk* **Hallelujah**[36] 4895 6-8-9 100 (t) HayleyTurner 3 86
(James Fanshawe) *in rr: drvn over 2f out: kpt on fnl f: nvr a factor* **11/2**[3]

640 **7** 9 **Mass Rally (IRE)**[18] 5575 7-9-0 105 (b) PaulMulrennan 2 70
(Michael Dods) *hood removed v late: s.i.s: hld up in rr: effrt 2f out: sn wknd: eased ins fnl f* **13/2**

1m 11.51s (-0.39) **Going Correction** +0.175s/f (Good)
**WFA** 3 from 4yo+ 2lb **7** Ran SP% **109.9**
Speed ratings: **109,107,107,105,100 100,88**
CSF £12.18 TOTE £2.60: £1.50, £2.70; EX 13.40 Trifecta £32.60.
**Owner** Sheikh Mohammed Bin Khalifa Al Maktoum **Bred** Castlemartin Sky & Skymarc Farm **Trained** Newmarket, Suffolk
■ Stewards' Enquiry : Martin Harley two-day ban: careless riding (Sep 21-22)

**FOCUS**
A decent Listed sprint with the pair who fought out a close finish last year back again. Despite the stalls being placed next to the far rail, the runners gradually migrated across and ended up racing towards the nearside.

## 6168 MINSTER ALARMS IRISH CHAMPIONS WEEKEND EBF MAIDEN STKS (BOBIS RACE) 5f 89y

**3:35** (3:36) (Class 3) 2-Y-O **£7,439** (£2,213; £1,106; £553) **Stalls** Low

Form RPR

5 **1** **Bamboccianti**[23] 5397 2-9-5 0 PaulHanagan 1 83+
(Richard Fahey) *uns rdr and rn loose for over 2f on way to s: dwlt: in rr: hdwy over 2f out: edgd rt and led last 75yds: drvn out* **4/1**[2]

2 **2** 3/4 **Beau Eile (IRE)**[24] 5332 2-9-0 0 GrahamGibbons 3 75
(David Barron) *led: hdd over 1f out: kpt on wl: hung lft and no ex clsng stages* **5/1**[3]

40 **3** *nk* **Brando**[16] 5655 2-9-5 0 JamieSpencer 9 79
(Kevin Ryan) *trckd ldrs: upsides ins fnl f: kpt on same pce* **8/1**

20 **4** 2 3/4 **La Cuesta (IRE)**[81] 3353 2-9-0 0 AdamKirby 2 68
(Jamie Osborne) *trckd ldr: led over 1f out: hdd last 100yds: hmpd and eased clsng stages* **15/8**[1]

4 **5** 1 3/4 **Cabelo (IRE)**[25] 5297 2-9-0 0 BenCurtis 11 58+
(Brian Ellison) *drvn along in rr: hdwy 3f out: edgd lft and one pce over 1f out* **33/1**

502 **6** 1/2 **Zuzinia (IRE)**[12] 5789 2-9-0 69 WilliamBuick 4 56
(Mick Channon) *led: hdd over 1f out: sn edgd rt and wknd* **12/1**

3 **7** 2 **Excellent George**[31] 5091 2-9-5 0 MartinHarley 6 54
(Stuart Williams) *trckd ldrs: drvn and outpcd 3f out: chsng ldrs over 1f out: sn fdd* **8/1**

**8** *nk* **You're Cool** 2-9-5 0 GrahamLee 5 61+
(James Given) *hld up towards rr: hdwy 3f out: no imp whn hmpd 1f out* **22/1**

03 **9** 3 1/4 **Normandy Knight**[22] 5439 2-9-5 0 TonyHamilton 8 41
(Richard Fahey) *chsd ldrs: drvn over 2f out: wknd over 1f out* **14/1**

**10** 3 **Kinloch Pride** 2-9-0 0 DuranFentiman 10 25
(Noel Wilson) *s.s: a outpcd and in rr* **66/1**

1m 4.95s (0.85) **Going Correction** +0.175s/f (Good) **10** Ran SP% **116.8**
Speed ratings (Par 99): **100,98,98,93,91 90,87,86,81,76**
CSF £24.01 TOTE £6.40: £1.30, £1.90, £2.50; EX 28.70 Trifecta £262.60.

**Owner** Al Shira'aa Stable **Bred** Bumble Bloodstock And Catridge Farm Stud **Trained** Musley Bank, N Yorks
■ Stewards' Enquiry : Graham Gibbons jockey said filly hung right final 2f

**FOCUS**
A decent 2yo maiden in which the runners came up the centre. Improved efforts from the winner and third, with the runner-up rated to his debut mark.

## 6169 CASTLES UK EDUCATIONAL AND RESIDENTIAL FURNITURE STKS (H'CAP) 2m 88y
**4:05** (4:06) (Class 4) (0-85,85) 3-Y-0+ **£6,469** (£1,925; £962; £481) **Stalls** Low

Form RPR
6262 **1** **Entihaa**[18] 5564 6-9-9 80 RobertWinston 9 89
(Alan Swinbank) *in rr: drvn and hdwy over 3f out: styd on appr fnl f: led last 100yds: styd on wl towards fin* **5/1**[3]
2254 **2** 2 1/2 **Dr Irv**[9] 5890 5-8-13 75 MeganCarberry(5) 5 81
(Philip Kirby) *rr-div: hdwy 9f out: trcking ldrs over 2f out: shkn up to chal ins fnl f: kpt on same pce* **12/1**
0120 **3** 3/4 **Knightly Escapade**[18] 5579 6-9-6 77 BenCurtis 12 82
(Brian Ellison) *swtchd lft s: hld up in rr: hdwy over 2f out: styd on ins fnl f: tk 3rd post* **12/1**
222 **4** shd **Chant (IRE)**[14] 5716 4-9-4 75 (p) PJMcDonald 8 80+
(Ann Duffield) *trckd ldrs: led over 2f out: hdd last 100yds: wknd towards fin* **11/1**
0001 **5** hd **Riptide**[38] 4818 8-9-5 76 (v) WilliamTwiston-Davies 11 81
(Michael Scudamore) *sn chsng ldrs: drvn over 4f out: one pce fnl 2f* **14/1**
-304 **6** 1 1/2 **Kiwayu**[33] 4995 5-9-12 83 (p) PhillipMakin 2 86
(Philip Kirby) *rr-div: effrt over 3f out: one pce whn n.m.r over 1f out* **16/1**
0510 **7** 5 **Itlaaq**[18] 5579 8-10-0 85 (t) GrahamGibbons 6 82
(Michael Easterby) *sn chsng ldrs: edgd lft and wknd fnl f* **9/1**
1531 **8** 2 **Chivers (IRE)**[29] 5200 3-8-0 70 SilvestreDeSousa 4 65
(Tim Easterby) *mid-div: drvn to chse ldrs over 3f out: edgd rt 1f out: sn wknd* **4/1**[1]
0452 **9** 8 **Ex Oriente (IRE)**[10] 5863 5-9-5 76 SeanLevey 1 61
(Stuart Williams) *chsd ldrs: drvn 4f out: wknd over 1f out* **25/1**
0-33 **10** 2 1/4 **Big Time Billy (IRE)**[9] 5890 8-9-4 75 (v) DougieCostello 10 57
(Alan Phillips) *rr-div: hdwy 7f out: drvn over 4f out: sn outpcd and in rr* **9/1**
1140 **11** 6 **Masterful Act (USA)**[142] 1556 7-9-9 83 BillyCray(3) 7 58
(Alan McCabe) *mid-div: hdwy 9f out: chsng ldrs over 4f out: lost pl 3f out* **33/1**
1226 **12** 7 **Gambol (FR)**[18] 5579 4-9-11 82 PaulHanagan 3 49
(B W Hills) *led: t.k.h: qcknd pce 4f out: hdd over 2f out: sn wknd and eased* **9/2**[2]

3m 32.0s (-2.50) **Going Correction** -0.175s/f (Firm)
**WFA** 3 from 4yo+ 13lb 12 Ran SP% **117.9**
Speed ratings (Par 105): **99,97,97,97,97 96,93,92,88,87 84,81**
CSF £63.53 CT £688.74 TOTE £8.00: £2.20, £4.60, £4.60; EX 74.40 Trifecta £1451.10.
**Owner** Elsa Crankshaw & G Allan **Bred** Wardall Bloodstock **Trained** Melsonby, N Yorks

**FOCUS**
The leaders set a decent pace in this staying handicap, but probably went off too quick and ended up setting it up for the closers.

## 6170 HANSON SPRINGS STKS (H'CAP) (BOBIS RACE) 6f
**4:40** (4:41) (Class 3) (0-95,95) 3-Y-0 **£9,703** (£2,887; £1,443; £721) **Stalls** Low

Form RPR
1 **1** **Caffeine**[13] 5775 3-8-11 85 MartinDwyer 1 98+
(William Muir) *dwlt: hld up in rr: hdwy and edgd rt over 2f out: styd on wl to ld last 75yds* **8/1**[3]
1422 **2** 1 1/4 **Lexington Abbey**[15] 5696 3-8-13 87 JamieSpencer 10 95
(Kevin Ryan) *hld up in rr: hdwy over 2f out: led briefly ins fnl f: styd on same pce* **17/2**
1104 **3** 1 **Money Team (IRE)**[15] 5696 3-9-0 88 PhillipMakin 11 93+
(David Barron) *chsd ldrs stands' side: styd on same pce last 150yds* **11/1**
0241 **4** shd **Elusive George (IRE)**[45] 4572 3-8-7 81 oh1 IanBrennan 12 85
(John Quinn) *w ldr stands' side: kpt on same pce fnl f* **20/1**
4400 **5** 1 **The Hooded Claw (IRE)**[22] 5410 3-8-11 85 PaulMulrennan 5 86
(Tim Easterby) *in rr: hdwy over 1f out: styng on wl at fin* **16/1**
6002 **6** 1 1/4 **Ventura Mist**[22] 5438 3-9-7 95 (p) DuranFentiman 3 92
(Tim Easterby) *chsd ldrs: led over 1f out: hdd ins fnl f: no ex* **12/1**
3000 **7** 1 1/4 **Major Crispies**[29] 5165 3-9-7 95 GrahamLee 15 88
(James Eustace) *hld up in rr stands' side: hdwy to chse ldrs over 2f out: one pce over 1f out* **25/1**
5500 **8** 1 **Regiment**[16] 5656 3-8-9 83 PaulHanagan 7 73
(Richard Fahey) *mid-div: effrt over 2f out: one pce* **16/1**
-124 **9** shd **Jacob's Pillow**[20] 5501 3-8-6 85 (p) NathanAlison(5) 14 75
(William Haggas) *chsd ldrs stands' side: wknd over 1f out* **12/1**
0-00 **10** nse **Royal Mezyan (IRE)**[15] 5696 3-9-2 90 SilvestreDeSousa 2 80
(William Haggas) *mid-div: chsd ldrs over 2f out: wknd over 1f out* **9/2**[2]
1000 **11** 1/2 **Deeds Not Words (IRE)**[16] 5623 3-9-3 94 CharlesBishop(3) 8 82
(Mick Channon) *chsd ldrs: wknd over 1f out* **20/1**
100 **12** 1/2 **Soul Brother (IRE)**[22] 5444 3-8-10 84 (t) DavidAllan 4 70
(Tim Easterby) *mid-div far side: effrt over 2f out: wknd fnl f* **20/1**
0500 **13** 2 1/4 **Ben Hall (IRE)**[15] 5675 3-8-7 81 oh1 OisinMurphy 13 60
(Mike Murphy) *overall ldr stands' side: hdd over 2f out: sn wknd* **33/1**
-421 **14** 1 3/4 **Fast Track**[43] 4669 3-9-5 93 GrahamGibbons 9 67
(David Barron) *w ldrs: led over 2f out: hdd over 1f out: sn wknd and eased* **3/1**[1]

1m 11.99s (0.09) **Going Correction** +0.175s/f (Good) 14 Ran SP% **121.4**
Speed ratings (Par 105): **106,104,103,102,101 99,98,96,96,96 96,95,92,90**
CSF £68.84 CT £784.46 TOTE £8.10: £2.50, £2.10, £4.30; EX 60.20 Trifecta £580.60.
**Owner** Muir Racing Partnership - Windsor **Bred** A J Coleing **Trained** Lambourn, Berks

**FOCUS**
A hot 3yo sprint handicap run at a decent pace in which the runners raced centre-to-stands' side. The form should stand up.

## 6171 COOPERS MARQUEES APPRENTICE STKS (H'CAP) (A LEG OF THE GO RACING IN YORKSHIRE FUTURE STARS) 1m 4f
**5:10** (5:10) (Class 4) (0-80,80) 4-Y-0+ **£6,469** (£1,925; £962; £481) **Stalls** Centre

Form RPR
501 **1** **Zeus Magic**[14] 5716 4-9-5 78 OisinMurphy 9 87
(Brian Ellison) *trckd ldrs: effrt and hung lft 3f out: led 2f out: hdd ins fnl f: tightened up: rallied to ld again nr fin* **9/4**[1]
0-02 **2** shd **Next Edition (IRE)**[36] 4921 6-9-3 76 JoeyHaynes 5 84
(Philip Kirby) *mid-div: hdwy 3f out: upsides appr fnl f: led narrowly last 100yds: edgd lft and hdd nr fin* **13/2**[3]
2304 **3** 4 1/2 **Northside Prince (IRE)**[13] 5764 8-8-9 73 GemmaTutty(5) 6 74
(Alan Swinbank) *trckd ldrs: t.k.h: rdn and outpcd over 2f out: kpt on fnl f: tk 3rd nr fin* **10/1**
1351 **4** 1/2 **Ssafa**[18] 5551 6-9-3 79 (p) LouisSteward(3) 2 79
(Paul Cole) *hld up in rr: effrt 3f out: kpt on same pce to take 3rd ins fnl f* **8/1**
0200 **5** 2 1/4 **Streets Of Newyork**[18] 5579 7-9-1 79 MeganCarberry(5) 4 75
(Brian Ellison) *mid-div: effrt over 3f out: one pce fnl 2f* **9/2**[2]
4505 **6** 1 **Warlu Way**[30] 5150 7-8-6 70 AnnaHesketh(5) 3 65
(Michael Easterby) *awkward s and sn stdd: t.k.h in rr: hdwy over 3f out: one pce fnl 2f* **7/1**
0453 **7** 5 **Choisan (IRE)**[25] 5301 5-8-6 70 (tp) RachelRichardson(5) 1 57
(Tim Easterby) *w ldrs: led after 2f: hdd over 2f out: wknd over 1f out* **16/1**
1500 **8** 2 1/4 **Royal Alcor (IRE)**[31] 5073 7-8-11 73 (t) ShelleyBirkett(3) 7 56
(Gay Kelleway) *led 2f: chsd ldr: led over 2f out: sn hdd: wknd over 1f out* **25/1**
02-5 **9** 8 **Ambleside**[12] 5792 4-9-0 80 DanielleMooney(7) 8 50
(Michael Easterby) *hld up in rr: drvn and bhd over 3f out* **17/2**

2m 34.61s (1.41) **Going Correction** -0.175s/f (Firm) 9 Ran SP% **115.2**
Speed ratings (Par 105): **88,87,84,84,83 82,79,77,72**
CSF £17.09 CT £121.28 TOTE £3.10: £1.50, £2.50, £3.10; EX 19.30 Trifecta £151.90.
**Owner** Koo's Racing Club **Bred** The Kingwood Partnership **Trained** Norton, N Yorks
■ Stewards' Enquiry : Joey Haynes caution: careless riding

**FOCUS**
A fair apprentice handicap in which they didn't go much of a pace, but it produced a thrilling finish.
T/Jkpt: Not won. T/Plt: £680.00 to a £1 stake. Pool: £155,240.89 - 166.65 winning units T/Qpdt: £77.00 to a £1 stake. Pool: £11,280.27 - 108.30 winning units WG

# 5471 DUNDALK (A.W) (L-H)
Sunday, September 7

**OFFICIAL GOING: Polytrack: standard**

## 6172a DUNDALK STADIUM RACE 5f (P)
**1:50** (1:50) 3-Y-0+ **£8,625** (£2,000; £875; £500)

RPR
**1** **Caspian Prince (IRE)**[37] 4852 5-9-11 105 (t) LukeMorris 3 87+
(Tony Carroll) *mde all: narrow advantage 1/2-way: rdn and pressed clly fr under 2f out: kpt on wl u.p to assert ins fnl f* **1/1**[1]
**2** 1 1/4 **Flight Risk (IRE)**[28] 5219 3-9-5 (t) KevinManning 1 78
(J S Bolger, Ire) *dwlt and outpcd and in rr early: rdn and no imp 2f out: r.o wl ins fnl f into nvr threatening 2nd fnl stride: nrst fin* **5/2**[2]
**3** shd **My Good Brother (IRE)**[30] 5154 5-9-11 102 (v) ColinKeane 5 82
(T G McCourt, Ire) *cl up in 2nd: stl gng wl 2f out: sn rdn and no imp on wnr u.p ins fnl f: denied 2nd fnl stride* **13/2**
**4** 2 1/2 **Yulong Baoju (IRE)**[21] 5473 4-9-6 94 (vt) PatSmullen 4 68
(Edward Lynam, Ire) *dwlt and towards rr: tk clsr order disputing 3rd 1/2-way: sn no imp on ldrs u.p: one pce fnl f* **11/2**[3]
**5** 1 3/4 **Autumn Tide (IRE)**[16] 5631 3-9-5 (t) MichaelHussey 2 62
(Adrian Paul Keatley, Ire) *chsd ldrs in 3rd: pushed along over 2f out and sn no imp on ldrs u.p: one pce fnl 2f* **100/1**

58.5s (58.50)
**WFA** 3 from 4yo+ 1lb 5 Ran SP% **108.3**
CSF £3.58 TOTE £1.70: £1.02, £1.02; DF 3.10 Trifecta £10.10.
**Owner** Stephen Louch **Bred** Ballygallon Stud Limited **Trained** Cropthorne, Worcs
■ Stewards' Enquiry : Luke Morris caution: used whip above shoulder height

**FOCUS**
Only five runners but they went a blistering gallop and put up a fast time.

# 6162 BADEN-BADEN (L-H)
Sunday, September 7

**OFFICIAL GOING: Turf: good**

## 6180a LONGINES - GROSSER PREIS VON BADEN (GROUP 1) (3YO+) (TURF) 1m 4f
**3:50** (12:00) 3-Y-0+ **£125,000** (£50,000; £20,833; £12,500)

RPR
**1** **Ivanhowe (GER)**[98] 2819 4-9-6 0 FilipMinarik 8 117+
(Jean-Pierre Carvalho, Germany) *w.w towards rr on inner: hdwy 3f out: chsd ldrs into st over 2f out: 3rd and rdn whn c to stands' rail 1 1/2f out: r.o to ld ins fnl f: drvn clr: readily* **106/10**
**2** 3 **Sea The Moon (GER)**[63] 4007 3-8-11 0 CristianDemuro 2 112+
(Markus Klug, Germany) *t.k.h: led after 1f: pushed along and c towards stands' side st: 2 l clr 1 1/2f out: rdn appr fnl f: hdd ins fnl f: no ex* **1/2**[1]
**3** 2 **Night Wish (GER)**[42] 4720 4-9-6 0 APietsch 4 109
(W Figge, Germany) *w.w towards rr: 9th and shkn up turning for home: rdn and styng on fr 1 1/2f out: wnt 3rd ins fnl f: nt pce to trble first two* **34/1**
**4** 1 1/2 **Giant's Cauldron (GER)**[21] 3-8-11 0 (b) AHelfenbein 3 107
(P Schiergen, Germany) *in rr: last and scrubbed along 2 1/2f out: styng on whn rdn 1 1/2f out: kpt on u.p fnl f: nvr on terms w ldrs* **39/1**
**5** 1/2 **Sirius (GER)**[28] 5231 3-8-11 0 (b) SHellyn 5 106
(Andreas Lowe, Germany) *trckd ldng gp: rdn to chse ldr 2f out: hrd rdn and nt qckn appr 1f out: one pce ins fnl f* **41/5**[3]
**6** 1 **Berlin Berlin**[28] 5231 5-9-3 0 FrederikTylicki 1 101
(Markus Klug, Germany) *midfield: scrubbed along to hold pl over 3f out: kpt on again fr 1 1/2f out: nvr in contention* **231/10**
**7** 3 1/2 **Lucky Lion**[42] 4720 3-8-11 0 IoritzMendizabal 9 99
(Andreas Lowe, Germany) *cl up in midfield: rdn and lost pl 2 1/2f out: bhd fnl 1 1/2f* **26/5**[2]
**8** 3/4 **Iniciar (GER)**[28] 5231 4-9-6 0 GeraldPardon 11 97
(Jean-Pierre Carvalho, Germany) *pressed ldr on outer: hrd rdn over 2f out: sn wknd* **48/1**
**9** 3 **Lucky Speed (IRE)**[28] 5231 4-9-6 0 AdriedeVries 10 93
(P Schiergen, Germany) *led tl hdd after 1f: hld up bhd ldng gp: cl 3rd and ev ch 2 1/2f out: rdn over 2f out and no imp: sn btn and eased fnl f* **135/10**
**10** 3 1/2 **Amonit (FR)**[22] 5461 4-9-6 0 AnthonyCrastus 7 87
(J Hirschberger, Germany) *midfield: clsd up on outer 4f out: 5th and rdn over 2 1/2f out: no further imp: wknd fnl 1 1/2f* **46/1**

11 6 **Terrubi (IRE)**56 4250 4-9-6 0 EPedroza 6 87
(A Wohler, Germany) *midfield on outer: rdn and outpcd over 3 1/2f out: wknd and bhd fnl 2f* **104/10**

2m 36.3s (2.84)
**WFA** 3 from 4yo+ 9lb **11 Ran SP% 131.6**
WIN (incl. 10 euro stake): 116. PLACES: 25, 16, 45. SF: 353.
**Owner** Gestut Schlenderhan **Bred** Gestut Schlenderhan **Trained** Germany

## 6084 LONGCHAMP (R-H)
Sunday, September 7

**OFFICIAL GOING: Turf: good**

### 6181a PRIX LA ROCHETTE (GROUP 3) (2YO) (TURF) 7f
**2:40** (12:00) 2-Y-O **£33,333** (£13,333; £10,000; £6,666; £3,333)

RPR

1 **Full Mast (USA)**22 2-8-11 0 ThierryThulliez 1 108+
(Mme C Head-Maarek, France) *mde all: set stdy pce: qcknd 2f out: pushed along ent fnl f: r.o wl under hand ride and a doing enough: cosily: gd ride* **9/1**

2 3/4 **Nucifera (USA)**21 5478 2-8-11 0 StephanePasquier 3 106
(J E Pease, France) *t.k.h: prom early: sn midfield in tch: pushed along 2f out: rdn and wnt 2nd over 1f out: r.o and chsd wnr fnl f: clsd towards fin but a hld* **11/4**2

3 1/2 **Territories (IRE)**40 2-8-11 0 MaximeGuyon 4 105
(A Fabre, France) *t.k.h: hld up in tch on outer: pushed along 2f out: rdn in clsng 5th ent fnl f: r.o wl and wnt 3rd towards fin: nvr nrr* **11/2**3

4 3/4 **Romeo Lima (USA)**38 2-8-11 0 ChristopheSoumillon 2 103
(J-C Rouget, France) *midfield in tch on inner: pushed along 2f out: nt qckn: kpt on under hand ride fnl f but nvr able to chal: dropped to 4th towards fin* **1/1**1

5 1 1/2 **Kenfreeze (FR)**56 4248 2-8-11 0 MickaelBarzalona 6 99
(H-A Pantall, France) *sn trcking wnr on outer: rdn in 2nd and brief effrt 2f out: outpcd and lost pl over 1f out: kpt on but dropped to 5th and wl hld fnl f* **11/1**

6 2 **Max La Fripouille (FR)**43 2-8-11 0 RonanThomas 5 93
(Rod Collet, France) *plld hrd: hld up in tch but a in rr: rdn and outpcd fnl 2f: eased whn hld towards fin: nvr threatened* **16/1**

1m 25.38s (4.68) **Going Correction** +0.25s/f (Good) **6 Ran SP% 116.3**
Speed ratings: **83,82,81,80,79 76**
WIN (incl. 1 euro stake): 8.30. PLACES: 3.10, 2.10. SF: 33.20.
**Owner** K Abdullah **Bred** Juddmonte Farms Inc **Trained** Chantilly, France

### 6182a PRIX DU PIN (GROUP 3) (3YO+) (TURF) 7f
**3:10** (12:00) 3-Y-O+ **£33,333** (£13,333; £10,000; £6,666; £3,333)

RPR

1 **Bamiyan (FR)**64 3997 4-9-1 0 ThierryJarnet 5 109
(T Lemer, France) *hld up towards rr: pushed along and hdwy over 1 1/2f out: r.o wl fnl f: led fnl strides* **20/1**

2 1/2 **Another Party (FR)**28 5223 3-8-11 0 AntoineHamelin 1 106
(Matthieu Palussiere, France) *chsd ldng pair on inner: 5 l 3rd and rdn over 1f out: styd on u.p fnl f: led cl home and almost immediately hdd fnl strides* **11/1**3

3 shd **American Devil (FR)**64 3997 5-9-5 0 Pierre-CharlesBoudot 7 112
(E Libaud, France) *w.w in midfield: shkn up and hdwy 1 1/2f out: r.o u.p to ld 70yds out: hdd clsd home: no ex* **9/4**2

4 1 1/2 **Blue Soave (FR)**40 6-9-1 0 TonyPiccone 8 104+
(F Chappet, France) *led: 4 l clr 3f out: stl clr and rdn appr 1f out: sed tying up ins fnl f and hdd 70yds out: no ex* **12/1**

5 snk **Sir Oscar (GER)**42 7-9-1 0 StephanePasquier 9 103
(T Potters, Germany) *w.w in rr: pushed along 2f out: rdn 1 1/2f out and hdwy: styd on wl fnl f: nrest at fin* **16/1**

6 3/4 **Desert Blanc**64 3997 6-9-1 0 GregoryBenoist 4 101
(C Baillet, France) *chsd ldng pair on outer: rdn and nt qckn 2f out: kpt on at same pce u.p fnl f* **16/1**

7 nk **This Time (FR)**37 4854 3-8-8 0 MickaelBarzalona 3 95
(H-A Pantall, France) *midfield on inner: 5th and rdn 2f out: kpt on at one pce fr over 1f out: nvr on terms* **14/1**

8 shd **Noozhoh Canarias (SPA)**57 4201 3-8-11 0 ChristopheSoumillon 2 98
(C Laffon-Parias, France) *tk a t.k.h: trckd ldr: 4 l 2nd and shkn up over 2f out but no imp: wknd wl ins fnl f* **13/8**1

9 3/4 **Amy Eria (IRE)**23 5407 3-8-8 0 ThierryThulliez 6 93
(F Rohaut, France) *hld up towards rr: pushed along 2f out: sme hdwy 1 1/2f out but sn rdn and no further imp: one pce fnl f* **12/1**

10 nse **So Long Malpic (FR)**28 5223 7-8-11 0 OlivierPeslier 10 94
(T Lemer, France) *hld up towards rr: rdn and effrt on outer over 1 1/2f out: no further imp fnl f* **12/1**

11 7 **My Catch (IRE)**162 1180 3-8-11 0 PatDobbs 11 77
(A Savujev, Czech Republic) *midfield on outer: lost pl 2f out: wl bhd whn eased ins fnl f* **25/1**

1m 20.09s (-0.61) **Going Correction** +0.25s/f (Good)
**WFA** 3 from 4yo+ 4lb **11 Ran SP% 127.3**
Speed ratings: **113,112,112,110,110 109,109,109,108,108 100**
WIN (incl. 1 euro stake): 19.30. PLACES: 3.50, 2.30, 1.40. DF: 84.20. SF: 213.50.
**Owner** Henri De La Chauvelais **Bred** Comtesse Marie-France De La Chauvelais **Trained** France

### 6183a PRIX DE LUTECE (GROUP 3) (3YO) (TURF) 1m 7f
**3:40** (12:00) 3-Y-O **£33,333** (£13,333; £10,000; £6,666; £3,333)

RPR

1 **Auvray (FR)**21 5481 3-8-9 0 GregoryBenoist 4 107+
(E Lellouche, France) *midfield: rdn over 2f out: styd on strly to chal fnl f: drvn to ld towards fin* **5/1**3

2 1/2 **Glaring**84 3290 3-8-9 0 MaximeGuyon 1 106
(A Fabre, France) *hld up in midfield: clsd on outer and prom 5f out: rdn to chal 2f out: led narrowly over 1f out: styd on but strly pressed fnl f and hdd towards fin: no ex and hld* **11/8**1

3 1 1/4 **Theme Astral (FR)**33 3-8-9 0 ThierryJarnet 6 104
(P Bary, France) *hld up in last: clsd on outer 4f out and prom into st: rdn to chal and led 2f out: hdd narrowly over 1f out: styd on but fnl f but dropped to 3rd and hld* **16/1**

4 1 1/2 **Doumaran (FR)**21 5481 3-8-9 0 ChristopheSoumillon 2 102
(A De Royer-Dupre, France) *trckd ldr: led 1/2-way: hdd 5f out and shuffled bk on rail but stl wl in tch: gng best whn swtchd lft 2f out: rdn and over 1f out: keeping on whn squeezed out fnl f: nt rcvr and hld in 4th after* **7/4**2

5 2 1/2 **Sarina (GER)**33 3-8-6 0 AntoineHamelin 3 96
(J Hirschberger, Germany) *led: hdd 1/2-way and trckd ldr on inner: shuffled bk to rr over 4f out: rdn in last 3f out: outpcd in st: plugged on but wl hld fnl f: eased nring fin* **22/1**

6 5 **Noble Raven (FR)**21 5481 3-8-6 0 SylvainRuis 5 90
(Mme A-M Poirier, France) *midfield: clsd to trck new ldr 1/2-way: led 5f out: rdn and hdd 2f out: sn btn and wknd: dropped to last and eased fnl f* **18/1**

3m 16.7s (0.70) **Going Correction** +0.25s/f (Good) **6 Ran SP% 110.6**
Speed ratings: **108,107,107,106,104 102**
WIN (incl. 1 euro stake): 4.60. PLACES: 2.10, 1.60. SF: 17.40.
**Owner** G Augustin-Normand & Mme E Vidal **Bred** Franklin Finance S.A. & Mme E Vidal **Trained** Lamorlaye, France

## 6163 VELIEFENDI
Sunday, September 7

**OFFICIAL GOING: Turf: very soft**

### 6184a INTERNATIONAL BOSPHORUS CUP (GROUP 2) (3YO+) (TURF) 1m 4f
**2:30** (12:00) 3-Y-O+ **£150,000** (£60,000; £30,000; £15,000)

RPR

1 **Pether's Moon (IRE)**22 5432 4-9-6 0 RichardHughes 2 115
(Richard Hannon) *w.w in rr: pushed along and clsd 2 1/2f out: drvn to chse ldng pair 2 1/2f out: bk on bridle to trck ldr 2f out: shkn up to ld appr 1f out: sn clr and idled: kpt up to work cl home* **2/5**1

2 1 **Village Wind (TUR)**35 4-9-6 0 NurettinSen 3 113
(R Tasdemir, Turkey) *w.w towards rr: pushed along and hdwy to trck ldrs after 1/2-way: hrd rdn and outpcd 2 1/2f out: swtchd outside and styd on over 1f out: tk 2nd 150yds out: clsd on idling wnr but nvr on terms* **3/1**3

3 4 1/2 **Vif Monsieur (GER)**46 4561 4-9-6 0 KClijmans 5 106
(S Smrczek, Germany) *chsd ldr: rdn to ld over 2f out: hrd rdn 1 1/2f out: hdd appr fnl f: kpt on at one pce fnl f* **26/5**

4 6 **Nymphea (IRE)**38 4824 5-9-2 0 DennisSchiergen 4 92
(P Schiergen, Germany) *led: rdn and hdd over 2f out: grad lft bhd fr 1 1/2f out* **71/20**

5 2 1/2 **Excellent Result (IRE)**38 4823 4-9-6 0 AndreaAtzeni 1 92
(Saeed bin Suroor) *settled in 3rd: shuffled bk to 5th 4f out but wl in tch: pushed along and outpcd 2 1/2f out: swtchd outside and rdn 2 1/2f out: no imp and sn btn* **7/10**2

6 26 **Sanzatu (TUR)**23 5-9-6 0 (t) AhmetCelik 6 51
(H Harmanbasi, Turkey) *towards rr: 4th and wl in tch 3 1/2f out: rdn and lost pl 2 1/2f out: sn wl bhd: t.o* **885/100**

2m 36.6s (7.80) **6 Ran SP% 203.5**
DIVIDENDS (INCLUDING 1 UNIT STAKE): WIN 1.40; SF 6.60.
**Owner** John Manley **Bred** Michael G Daly **Trained** East Everleigh, Wilts

### 6185a INTERNATIONAL TOPKAPI TROPHY (GROUP 2) (3YO+) (TURF) 1m
**3:30** (12:00) 3-Y-O+ **£225,000** (£90,000; £45,000; £22,500)

RPR

1 **Glory Awaits (IRE)**16 5653 4-9-6 0 (b) NeilCallan 1 111
(Kevin Ryan) *sn led and mde rest: rdn 2f out: qcknd over 1f out: r.o wl u.p fnl f: reduced advantage cl home but a doing enough* **29/10**

2 1/2 **Our Channel (USA)**37 4851 3-8-13 0 AndreaAtzeni 7 107
(William Haggas) *trckd wnr on outer: rdn and effrt into st: sn outpcd by wnr: kpt on wl u.p fnl 2f and clsng again at fin but a hld* **107/10**

3 1/2 **Toormore (IRE)**40 4758 3-9-0 0 ow1 RichardHughes 6 107
(Richard Hannon) *t.k.h: stdd and hld up in midfield: travelled strly into st: rdn and nt qckn 2f out: 3rd ent fnl f: kpt on but no real imp on wnr and hld* **1/5**1

4 1/2 **El Conquerador (TUR)**21 4-9-6 0 HalisKaratas 5 108
(Onur Dogan, Turkey) *hld up in rr: pushed along in last 1/2-way: rdn into st: kpt on steadily u.p and wnt 4th ent fnl f: clsng on ldng trio at fin but nvr able to chal* **5/2**3

5 5 1/2 **Ayaar (IRE)**43 4648 4-9-6 0 FrankieDettori 3 95
(Luca Cumani) *midfield in tch: rdn over 2f out: kpt on same pce tl no ex and btn ins fnl f: wknd* **19/10**2

6 6 **Belgian Bill**15 5666 6-9-6 0 (bt1) JamesDoyle 2 81
(George Baker) *dwlt sltly and hld up towards rr: rdn over 2f out: sn outpcd and btn: wknd: eased fnl f: n.d* **112/10**

7 14 **Astorya (TUR)**35 5-9-6 0 SelimKaya 4 49
(U Bilik, Turkey) *broke wl and led early stages: sn hdd and trckd ldrs: swtchd ins to rail after 3f: rdn and effrt into st: no ex and wknd qckly 2f out: eased and sn dropped to last* **66/10**

1m 39.76s (4.43)
**WFA** 3 from 4yo+ 5lb **7 Ran SP% 201.9**
DIVIDENDS (INCLUDING 1 UNIT STAKE): WIN 3.90; DF 36.95; SF 112.25.
**Owner** Ahmad Abdulla Al Shaikh & Co **Bred** J Fisher **Trained** Hambleton, N Yorks

## 5969 LES LANDES
Sunday, September 7

**OFFICIAL GOING: Good**

### 6186a BILL SHOEMAKER RECORD H'CAP 5f 100y
**3:05** (3:05) 3-Y-O+ **£1,200** (£435; £265)

RPR

1 **Spanish Bounty**13 9-10-3 CraigWalker 4 51
(Mrs A Malzard, Jersey) **9/1**

2 hd **Chester'slittlegem (IRE)**13 5-9-9 (p) PhilipPrince 2 42
(Mrs A Corson, Jersey) **2/1**2

3 1 **Country Blue (FR)**28 5228 5-9-7 (p) NoraLooby 5 37
(Mrs A Malzard, Jersey) **7/1**

4 hd **Purley Queen (IRE)**13 5-10-9 MattieBatchelor 6 52
(Mrs C Gilbert, Jersey) **3/1**3

5 1 **Novabridge**[28] 5228 6-10-12 ....(b) MarkQuinlan 3 52
(Neil Mulholland) 5/4[1]
6 5 1/2 **Kersivay**[28] 5228 8-8-13 ....(p) JemmaMarshall 1 7
(Mrs A Malzard, Jersey) 3/1[3]
1m 9.0s 6 Ran SP% 150.3

**Owner** Mr & Mrs J Cunningham **Bred** Farleigh Court Racing Partnership **Trained** St Ouen, Jersey

## 6187a ANIMAL HEALTH TRUST CELEBRATION MILE (H'CAP) 1m 100y
3:40 (3:40) 3-Y-0+ £1,760 (£650; £390)

RPR
1 **City Ground (USA)**[31] 5076 7-10-12 .... MissSBrotherton 4 74
(Michael Easterby) 10/11[1]
2 3 1/2 **Lucifers Shadow (IRE)**[13] 5971 5-8-12 ....(v) MatthewCosham 9 38
(Mrs C Gilbert, Jersey) 6/1
3 1 1/2 **Kristal Hart**[13] 5971 5-9-13 ....(p) MarkQuinlan 8 50
(Neil Mulholland) 2/1[2]
4 2 **Hawaiian Freeze**[13] 5-8-10 .... HarryBurns 3 28
(J Moon, Jersey) 18/1
5 1 **Pas D'Action**[13] 6-10-1 ....(p) JemmaMarshall 6 45
(Mrs A Malzard, Jersey) 5/1
6 1 1/2 **First Cat**[13] 7-10-3 .... PhilipPrince 2 44
(K Kukk, Jersey) 9/2[3]
7 2 **Beck's Bolero (IRE)**[13] 5970 8-9-3 ....(b) CraigWalker 1 25
(Mrs A Corson, Jersey) 11/1
8 1/2 **Fast Freddie**[13] 5971 10-8-11 ....(p) JoshuaBrowning 7 18
(Mrs A Corson, Jersey) 10/1
9 15 **Lively Little Lady**[13] 5971 4-8-5 .... NoraLooby 5
(Mrs A Corson, Jersey) 13/2
1m 50.0s (110.00) 9 Ran SP% 170.9

**Owner** Steve Hull **Bred** Mrs E Scott Jr & Mrs L Macelree **Trained** Sheriff Hutton, N Yorks

## 6188a "IT DOESN'T MATTER ANY MORE" H'CAP 1m 4f
4:50 (4:50) 3-Y-0+ £1,200 (£435; £265)

RPR
1 **River Du Nord (FR)**[13] 5969 7-8-13 .... JemmaMarshall 6 35
(Sue Gardner) 10/3[2]
2 2 **Midnight Sequel**[13] 5969 5-10-12 ....(tp) MarkQuinlan 4 59
(Neil Mulholland) 8/13[1]
3 5 **Jackpot**[13] 5971 4-8-5 ....(p) MatthewCosham 5 16
(Mrs A Malzard, Jersey) 7/1[3]
4 4 **King Kenny**[13] 5969 9-9-8 ....(p) NoraLooby 1 26
(Mrs A Corson, Jersey) 10/3[2]
5 1 1/2 **Lady Petrus**[13] 5969 9-8-5 .... PhilipPrince 2 7
(K Kukk, Jersey) 10/1
6 7 **Sweet Liberta (IRE)**[28] 5230 5-9-13 .... MrRHodson 3 18
(T Le Brocq, Jersey) 7/1[3]
P **Informality (IRE)**[13] 5970 3-10-3 ....(p) MrHJFCruickshank 8
(J Moon, Jersey) 25/1
2m 5.0s (-45.00)
**WFA** 3 from 4yo+ 9lb 7 Ran SP% 146.0

**Owner** J Mercier & Miss J Edgar **Bred** Mrs Jane Edgar & John Mercier **Trained** Longdown, Devon

# 5972 BRIGHTON (L-H)
Monday, September 8

**OFFICIAL GOING: Good (good to firm in places; 7.3)**
Wind: Light, half against towards stand Weather: Sunny and warm

## 6189 JADEY'S DREAM FILLIES' H'CAP 5f 213y
2:30 (2:30) (Class 5) (0-75,75) 3-Y-0+ £2,587 (£770; £384; £192) Stalls Low

Form RPR
1202 1 **Birdie Queen**[11] 5860 4-8-3 64 .... HectorCrouch(7) 1 76
(Gary Moore) *mde all: clr tl 2f out: hrd drvn over 1f out: hld on wl: rdn out fnl 100yds* 6/1
0123 2 2 1/4 **Poetic Choice**[21] 5501 3-9-5 75 .... GeorgeBaker 2 81
(Nick Littmoden) *prom: angling out for run whn gap clsd and boxed in on inner fr over 1f out: r.o to snatch 2nd on line* 4/1[2]
2223 3 nse **Ginzan**[14] 5776 6-9-6 74 .... FergusSweeney 4 79
(Malcolm Saunders) *chsd ldrs: drvn to press wnr over 1f out: one pce fnl f* 9/2[3]
3142 4 5 **Miss Brazil (IRE)**[14] 5753 3-9-4 74 .... RichardHughes 3 63
(Richard Hannon) *chsd ldr tl 2f out: no ex and eased fnl f* 9/2[3]
-216 5 nk **Byron's Gold**[42] 4741 3-9-0 73 .... RyanTate(3) 6 61
(Ben De Haan) *dwlt: outpcd and detached last tl styd on fnl f: gng on at fin* 12/1
0453 6 3/4 **Olney Lass**[7] 5979 7-8-8 65 .... SimonPearce(3) 5 50
(Lydia Pearce) *sn outpcd and bhd* 12/1
2214 7 1 1/4 **Castorienta**[14] 5753 3-9-5 75 .... AdamKirby 8 56
(George Baker) *hld up: hdwy in centre 2f out: wknd 1f out: eased* 7/2[1]
-016 8 30 **Maria Montez**[30] 5182 5-9-4 72 .... SebSanders 7
(Charles Hills) *in tch tl outpcd 2f out: wl btn whn virtually p.u 1f out* 16/1
1m 9.82s (-0.38) **Going Correction** 0.0s/f (Good)
**WFA** 3 from 4yo+ 2lb 8 Ran SP% 114.1
Speed ratings (Par 100): **102,99,98,92,91 90,89,49**
CSF £30.07 CT £117.78 TOTE £6.80: £2.40, £1.40, £1.90; EX 32.30 Trifecta £149.00.
**Owner** The Golf Partnership **Bred** D R Tucker **Trained** Lower Beeding, W Sussex

**FOCUS**
Rail on inner line and all distances as advertised. A modest fillies' sprint handicap.

## 6190 EBF/SEAGULLSTICKETS.COM MAIDEN STKS 6f 209y
3:00 (3:00) (Class 5) 2-Y-0 £2,911 (£866; £432; £216) Stalls Low

Form RPR
632 1 **Fieldsman (USA)**[24] 5391 2-9-5 79 .... GeorgeBaker 5 85+
(Ed Dunlop) *mde all: qcknd 2 l ahd 2f out: sn rdn: a in control* 11/8[1]
2 1 3/4 **Shakopee** 2-9-5 0 .... LemosdeSouza 7 80+
(Luca Cumani) *hld up in 5th: hdwy into 2nd over 2f out: hung lft into rail bhd wnr: kpt on fnl f: a hld* 25/1
0 3 7 **Pleiades**[29] 5201 2-9-5 0 .... ShaneKelly 6 61
(Sir Michael Stoute) *dwlt: in rr: hdwy 2f out: rdn to take fair 3rd wl over 1f out: no imp* 8/1[3]
44 4 6 **Buraug**[16] 5684 2-9-5 0 .... MartinDwyer 1 45
(William Muir) *chsd wnr tl over 2f out: sn hrd rdn and wknd* 11/1
4 5 6 **Best Example (USA)**[58] 4216 2-9-5 0 .... FrederikTylicki 2 29
(Saeed bin Suroor) *chsd ldrs: rdn and nt handling downhill run fr over 4f out: wknd 2f out* 7/4[2]
2 6 22 **Glorious Magic (IRE)**[27] 5278 2-9-5 0 .... HarryBentley 4
(Olly Stevens) *in tch: rdn 3f out: wknd 2f out: eased whn wl btn* 14/1
1m 22.38s (-0.72) **Going Correction** 0.0s/f (Good) 6 Ran SP% 108.4
Speed ratings (Par 95): **104,102,94,87,80 55**
CSF £30.79 TOTE £2.10: £1.10, £10.00; EX 27.70 Trifecta £121.80.
**Owner** Highclere Thoroughbred Racing- Hard Spun **Bred** H Sexton, S Sexton & Silver Fern Farm **Trained** Newmarket, Suffolk

**FOCUS**
An uncompetitive 2yo maiden in which the winner was in total control from some way out.

## 6191 MAYO WYNNE BAXTER H'CAP 6f 209y
3:30 (3:30) (Class 5) (0-75,75) 3-Y-0+ £2,587 (£770; £384; £192) Stalls Low

Form RPR
6241 1 **Bayleyf (IRE)**[7] 5979 5-9-6 72 6ex....(p) StevieDonohoe 7 84
(Lee Carter) *mde all and sn crossed to ins rail fr wdst stall: rdn and r.o wl fnl 2f: readily* 3/1[2]
6050 2 4 1/2 **Waseem Faris (IRE)**[10] 5880 5-9-6 72....(v) GeorgeBaker 5 72
(Mick Channon) *bhd: rdn and hdwy 2f out: styd on to take 2nd ins fnl f: unable to trble wnr* 11/1
2600 3 1 3/4 **Shifting Star (IRE)**[16] 5686 9-9-2 68....(vt) WilliamCarson 1 64
(John Bridger) *prom: drvn to chse wnr wl over 1f out: no imp: lost 2nd ins fnl f* 10/1
6564 4 1 **Footstepsintherain (IRE)**[7] 5986 4-9-6 72.... LukeMorris 6 65
(David Dennis) *s.s: rcvrd into 5th: effrt over 2f out: sn drvn along and one pce* 6/1
1110 5 4 1/2 **Siouxperhero (IRE)**[20] 5528 5-9-9 75....(b) DougieCostello 3 56
(William Muir) *chsd ldrs: lost pl and struggling in rr over 2f out: n.d after* 12/1
0353 6 1/2 **Fiftyshadesofgrey (IRE)**[13] 5785 3-9-4 74....(p) AdamKirby 2 52
(George Baker) *chsd wnr tl wknd wl over 1f out* 9/4[1]
1226 7 1 1/4 **Royal Connection**[13] 5785 3-9-2 72.... RichardHughes 4 47
(Richard Hannon) *t.k.h early: hld up in rr: effrt over 2f out: wknd wl over 1f out* 11/2[3]
1m 22.34s (-0.76) **Going Correction** 0.0s/f (Good)
**WFA** 3 from 4yo+ 4lb 7 Ran SP% 110.6
Speed ratings (Par 103): **104,98,96,95,90 90,88**
CSF £32.16 TOTE £4.50: £2.10, £3.90; EX 42.40 Trifecta £263.10.
**Owner** John Joseph Smith **Bred** Marchwood Aggregates **Trained** Epsom, Surrey
■ Stewards' Enquiry : Stevie Donohoe one-day ban: use of whip (22 Sep)

**FOCUS**
An ordinary handicap and another winner to make all.

## 6192 LIFESTYLE MOTORGROUP H'CAP 1m 1f 209y
4:00 (4:01) (Class 5) (0-75,75) 3-Y-0+ £2,587 (£770; £384; £192) Stalls High

Form RPR
023 1 **This Is The Day**[20] 5521 3-9-3 73.... FrederikTylicki 2 90
(Charlie Fellowes) *prom: hrd rdn wl over 1f out: styd on to ld ins fnl f: wl on top at fin* 7/1
2221 2 3 3/4 **Hesbaan (IRE)**[22] 5469 3-9-5 75.... PaulHanagan 7 85
(Marcus Tregoning) *chsd ldr: led over 1f out tl ins fnl f: one pce* 9/4[1]
0426 3 3 **Dianora**[23] 5448 3-9-4 74.... ShaneKelly 8 78
(Sir Michael Stoute) *chsd ldrs: one pce fnl 2f* 12/1
213 4 1/2 **Law Keeper (IRE)**[20] 5527 3-9-5 75.... RichardHughes 4 78
(James Tate) *led tl over 1f out: no ex fnl f* 3/1[2]
0425 5 1 **Captain George (IRE)**[19] 5557 3-9-2 72....(v[1]) GeorgeBaker 5 73
(James Fanshawe) *hld up in rr: effrt over 2f out: no imp* 13/2[3]
3416 6 2 1/4 **Penny's Boy**[31] 5123 3-9-3 73....(t) LiamKeniry 1 70
(Sylvester Kirk) *hld up in 6th: rdn 2f out: sn btn* 10/1
131 7 2 1/2 **Diletta Tommasa (IRE)**[41] 4763 4-9-3 71....(p) EoinWalsh(5) 6 63
(John Stimpson) *t.k.h in rr: rdn over 2f out: sn wknd* 16/1
3522 8 13 **Whitby Jet (IRE)**[7] 5975 6-9-0 70.... HectorCrouch(7) 3 38
(Ed Vaughan) *s.s: bhd and rdn along early: sme hdwy towards centre 4f out: wknd over 2f out: eased whn wl btn over 1f out* 9/1
2m 2.47s (-1.13) **Going Correction** 0.0s/f (Good)
**WFA** 3 from 4yo+ 7lb 8 Ran SP% 114.3
Speed ratings (Par 103): **104,101,98,98,97 95,93,83**
CSF £23.14 CT £186.93 TOTE £8.50: £2.30, £1.40, £3.40; EX 24.50 Trifecta £242.20.
**Owner** A E Oppenheimer **Bred** Hascombe And Valiant Studs **Trained** Newmarket, Suffolk

**FOCUS**
A modest handicap in hwich the winner progressed again.

## 6193 DONATELLO ITALIAN RESTAURANT H'CAP 1m 3f 196y
4:30 (4:31) (Class 6) (0-60,60) 3-Y-O £1,940 (£577; £288; £144) Stalls High

Form RPR
2405 1 **Snow Conditions**[58] 4210 3-9-3 56.... GeorgeBaker 10 64+
(Philip Hide) *led after 1f and crossed to ins rail: easily qcknd 4 l clr and had clr rest of field in trble over 2f out: shkn up over 1f out: drvn to hold on nr fin* 7/1[2]
3353 2 1 **Hallouella**[70] 3796 3-9-4 57....(p) LiamKeniry 1 63
(David Elsworth) *prom: rdn over 3f out: chsd wnr over 2f out: clsd fnl f but a hld* 17/2[3]
3253 3 3 1/2 **Tunnel Tiger (IRE)**[8] 5949 3-9-2 60.... JackDuern(5) 3 61
(William Knight) *hld up in rr: rdn and hdwy in centre over 2f out: styd on u.p: nrest at fin* 7/2[1]
135 4 3 1/4 **Assoluta (IRE)**[21] 5491 3-9-4 57.... RenatoSouza 5 53
(Sylvester Kirk) *towards rr: hrd rdn and hdwy over 2f out: styd on same pce* 22/1
0044 5 2 1/4 **Little Flo**[38] 4844 3-9-0 53.... SebSanders 4 45
(Brendan Powell) *chsd ldrs: hrd rdn and btn over 2f out* 12/1
5132 6 7 **Cameley Dawn**[9] 5908 3-9-6 59.... FergusSweeney 11 40
(Malcolm Saunders) *sn chsng wnr: rdn 4f out: wknd over 2f out* 17/2[3]
5060 7 1 3/4 **Born To Reign**[24] 5402 3-8-6 50....(b[1]) LouisSteward(5) 9 28
(Michael Bell) *towards rr: rdn over 3f out: nvr nr ldrs* 33/1
-031 8 nse **Ohio (IRE)**[12] 5829 3-9-5 58.... LukeMorris 12 36
(Nick Littmoden) *mid-div: rdn 5f out: drvn along and wknd 3f out* 10/1
3665 9 2 **Armourer (IRE)**[20] 5520 3-9-7 60....(p) MartinDwyer 7 35
(William Muir) *mid-div: rdn and lost pl over 3f out: sn bhd* 7/1[2]

0405 **10** 1 1/4 **Danglydontask**[9] 5908 3-9-2 55 ....(b) PaddyAspell 6 28
(David Arbuthnot) *chsd ldrs on outer: rdn 4f out: wknd over 2f out* 33/1
3042 **11** 3 3/4 **Bishop Wulstan (IRE)**[15] 5719 3-9-7 60 ....(b) RichardHughes 2 27
(Richard Hannon) *led for 1f: prom tl wknd 4f out* 7/2[1]
0000 **12** 2 3/4 **Exceed Policy**[9] 5908 3-8-7 46 oh1 ....(t) KieranO'Neill 8 8
(David Dennis) *a bhd* 66/1
2m 32.48s (-0.22) **Going Correction** 0.0s/f (Good) **12** Ran SP% **121.0**
Speed ratings (Par 99): **100,99,97,94,93 88,87,87,86,85 82,80**
CSF £64.52 CT £248.06 TOTE £8.50: £2.80, £3.00, £1.70; EX 100.60 Trifecta £357.80.
**Owner** P Turner, J Davies & The Hides **Bred** Tondoro Srl **Trained** Findon, W Sussex
**FOCUS**
Another front-running winner, the fourth from five races on the card to this point.

## 6194 1901CLUB.CO.UK H'CAP 7f 214y
**5:00** (5:00) (Class 6) (0-60,58) 3-Y-O £1,940 (£577; £288; £144) **Stalls** Low

Form RPR
-463 **1** **Pelagian (USA)**[30] 5183 3-8-13 50 .... SteveDrowne 4 58
(Michael Attwater) *hld up: hdwy to ld 2f out: edgd rt fnl f: rdn out* 8/1
3-53 **2** 1 3/4 **Ding Ding**[15] 5719 3-8-8 52 .... DanielCremin(7) 5 56
(Mick Channon) *hld up in rr: hdwy and hrd rdn 2f out: kpt on to take 2nd ins fnl f* 9/2[2]
500 **3** 1 1/2 **Mr Soprano**[77] 3537 3-9-7 58 .... GeorgeBaker 2 59
(Stuart Williams) *chsd ldrs: n.m.r and lost pl 5f out: rallied to chse wnr wl over 1f out: lost 2nd and one pce ins fnl f* 3/1[1]
0000 **4** 1 1/2 **Cueca (FR)**[35] 4970 3-8-9 49 ....(b[1]) DannyBrock(3) 10 46
(Jonathan Portman) *chsd ldrs: led 3f out tl 2f out: one pce* 12/1
4005 **5** 1 3/4 **Previous Acclaim (IRE)**[32] 5106 3-8-3 45 ....(b) ShelleyBirkett(5) 7 38
(Julia Feilden) *t.k.h in midfield: n.m.r and lost pl 5f out: effrt and hung lft fr 2f out: styd on same pce* 40/1
0-56 **6** 1 1/2 **Stilla Afton**[26] 5313 3-8-11 55 ....(p) CharlotteJenner(7) 11 45
(Marcus Tregoning) *bhd: pushed along 4f out: flashed tail whn hrd rdn over 1f out: cajoled along and styd on wl fnl f* 7/1
-005 **7** 1 **Monte Viso**[20] 5522 3-9-3 54 ....(t) RichardHughes 6 41
(Stuart Kittow) *dwlt: sn prom: wknd 2f out* 6/1[3]
0400 **8** 1 3/4 **See No Ships**[14] 5751 3-8-11 48 ....(p) HayleyTurner 8 31
(Mark Usher) *prom: squeezed by loose horse over 4f out: hrd rdn and wknd 2f out* 14/1
-045 **9** 4 1/2 **Tidal Beauty**[157] 1285 3-8-8 45 .... AndrewMullen 9 18
(Michael Appleby) *plld hrd: mid-div tl drvn along and wknd over 2f out* 7/1
0-00 **10** 3/4 **Desert Island Dusk**[12] 5829 3-8-8 45 .... WilliamCarson 1 16
(John Bridger) *led: hrd rdn and hdd 3f out: sn wknd* 100/1
0000 **U** **Water For Life**[26] 5321 3-8-3 45 ....(p) NathanAlison(5) 3
(Dave Morris) *uns rdr leaving stalls* 50/1
1m 37.26s (1.26) **Going Correction** 0.0s/f (Good) **11** Ran SP% **113.3**
Speed ratings (Par 99): **93,91,89,88,86 85,84,82,77,77**
CSF £42.00 CT £132.37 TOTE £8.70: £3.30, £1.50, £1.50; EX 26.30 Trifecta £189.30.
**Owner** John Khan **Bred** Anthem Bloodstock **Trained** Epsom, Surrey
■ Stewards' Enquiry : Danny Brock three-day ban: careless riding (23-25 Sep)
**FOCUS**
A really moderate contest for 3yos.

## 6195 SEAGULLSDIRECT.CO.UK APPRENTICE H'CAP 7f 214y
**5:30** (5:30) (Class 6) (0-60,60) 4-Y-O+ £1,940 (£577; £288; £144) **Stalls** Low

Form RPR
6-00 **1** **Thomas Blossom (IRE)**[7] 5977 4-8-4 46 oh1 ....(v) RobHornby(3) 7 51
(Patrick Chamings) *in tch in 4th: effrt over 2f out: styd on to ld ins fnl f* 7/1
6560 **2** 3/4 **Tax Reform (IRE)**[46] 4579 4-9-2 60 ....(b) HectorCrouch(5) 2 63
(Gary Moore) *trckd ldng pair: drvn to ld over 1f out: carried hd awkwardly: hdd ins fnl f: kpt on* 7/2[1]
0005 **3** 1/2 **Berwin (IRE)**[5] 6028 5-8-9 51 .... KieranShoemark(3) 6 53
(Sylvester Kirk) *outpcd and bhd: hdwy and squeezed through to chal on inner ins fnl f: kpt on* 6/1[3]
4353 **4** nk **Anginola (IRE)**[7] 5978 5-8-11 50 ....(b) CharlotteJenner 4 51
(Laura Mongan) *outpcd and bhd: hrd rdn over 2f out: hdwy over 1f out: styd on fnl f* 7/2[1]
6665 **5** 1 1/4 **Stonecrabstomorrow (IRE)**[7] 5972 11-9-0 53 .... DanielCremin 1 51
(Michael Attwater) *outpcd in 6th: hdwy in centre 2f out: pressed ldrs over 1f out: one pce ins fnl f* 16/1
0/3- **6** 7 **Flumps**[608] 105 5-8-7 46 oh1 .... AdamMcLean 3 28
(John Stimpson) *s.i.s: off the pce in 5th: effrt u.p and nt clr run over 1f out: wknd fnl f* 20/1
6360 **7** 1 3/4 **Arabian Flight**[19] 5573 5-8-10 49 .... GeorgeBuckell 8 27
(Michael Appleby) *led for 2f: prom tl wknd over 1f out* 7/1
033 **8** 4 **Big City Boy (IRE)**[7] 5977 6-8-8 47 .... JordanVaughan 5 16
(Phil McEntee) *led after 2f and travelled wl in front at str pce: rdn and hdd over 1f out: wknd qckly ins fnl f* 5/1[2]
1m 36.18s (0.18) **Going Correction** 0.0s/f (Good) **8** Ran SP% **111.0**
Speed ratings (Par 101): **99,98,97,97,96 89,87,83**
CSF £29.84 CT £151.26 TOTE £7.90: £2.40, £1.70, £2.00; EX 34.40 Trifecta £246.00.
**Owner** www.Select-Racing-Club.co.uk **Bred** Ecurie Des Monceaux **Trained** Baughurst, Hants
**FOCUS**
A very weak handicap, confined to apprentice riders, and a strong pace suited the closers.
T/Jkpt: Not won. T/Plt: £82.80 to a £1 stake. Pool: £92,471.87 - 815.10 winning tickets T/Qpdt: £26.40 to a £1 stake. Pool: £6,745.30 - 188.71 winning tickets LM

# 5980 LEICESTER (R-H)
### Tuesday, September 9

**OFFICIAL GOING: Good (good to firm in places)**
Wind: Light behind Weather: Fine

## 6203 BRITISH STALLION STUDS EBF APOLLO MAIDEN STKS (BOBIS RACE) (DIV I) 7f 9y
**2:20** (2:20) (Class 4) 2-Y-O £5,175 (£1,540; £769; £384) **Stalls** High

Form RPR
3 **1** **Outlaw Country (IRE)**[116] 2308 2-9-5 0 .... WilliamBuick 4 81+
(Charlie Appleby) *trckd ldrs: plld hrd: shkn up to ld over 1f out: r.o: comf* 8/11[1]
**2** 3 3/4 **Kisumu** 2-9-5 0 .... JamesDoyle 5 71+
(Sir Michael Stoute) *hld up: hdwy over 2f out: r.o to go 2nd wl ins fnl f: no ch w wnr* 7/1[3]
5 **3** 3/4 **Manolito**[25] 5377 2-9-5 0 .... JimmyFortune 11 69
(Hughie Morrison) *led: rdn and hdd over 1f out: styd on same pce ins fnl f* 8/1
50 **4** 1 **Little Riggs**[27] 5309 2-8-12 0 .... CliffordLee(7) 6 66
(Ed Walker) *chsd ldrs: pushed along over 2f out: styd on same pce fnl f* 50/1
**5** 1 1/2 **Alnashama** 2-9-5 0 .... PaulHanagan 7 62
(Charles Hills) *prom and sn pushed along: rdn over 2f out: styd on same pce fr over 1f out* 7/2[2]
0 **6** 9 **Prayer Time**[18] 5646 2-9-5 0 .... JimmyQuinn 1 38
(Mark H Tompkins) *hld up: shkn up over 2f out: wknd over 1f out* 100/1
**7** 2 **Master Choice (IRE)** 2-9-5 0 .... TomQueally 9 32
(William Haggas) *s.i.s: sn pushed along and a in rr* 16/1
**8** 2 **The Olympus Man** 2-9-5 0 .... JamieSpencer 2 27
(Eve Johnson Houghton) *s.i.s: hdwy to chse ldr over 5f out tl wknd and eased over 1f out* 20/1
**9** 21 **Basoco** 2-9-5 0 .... JimCrowley 10
(Harry Dunlop) *s.i.s: sn pushed along in rr: bhd fr 1/2-way* 33/1
1m 25.96s (-0.24) **Going Correction** -0.025s/f (Good) **9** Ran SP% **120.3**
Speed ratings (Par 97): **100,95,94,93,92 81,79,77,53**
CSF £6.92 TOTE £2.00: £1.10, £1.70, £2.80; EX 6.90 Trifecta £28.40.
**Owner** Godolphin **Bred** T Stewart **Trained** Newmarket, Suffolk
**FOCUS**
Ground on the fast side of good and stalls positioned on the stands' side in the straight. An interesting maiden, although it's hard to gauge how strong this form will turn out to be.

## 6204 BRITISH STALLION STUDS EBF APOLLO MAIDEN STKS (BOBIS RACE) (DIV II) 7f 9y
**2:50** (2:52) (Class 4) 2-Y-O £5,175 (£1,540; £769; £384) **Stalls** High

Form RPR
5 **1** **Dancetrack (USA)**[18] 5646 2-9-5 0 .... JamesDoyle 6 83+
(Charles Hills) *chsd ldr: led over 1f out: pushed out* 8/11[1]
0 **2** 2 3/4 **Hills And Dales (IRE)**[32] 5149 2-9-5 0 .... WilliamBuick 11 76+
(Charlie Appleby) *led: rdn and hdd over 1f out: styd on same pce ins fnl f* 11/2[2]
**3** 1 1/4 **Natural Nine (IRE)** 2-9-5 0 .... FrederikTylicki 5 72
(Roger Varian) *a.p: pushed along 1/2-way: styd on same pce fnl f* 50/1
**4** 1 3/4 **Mezajy (IRE)** 2-9-5 0 .... TomQueally 8 67
(Michael Bell) *chsd ldrs: rdn over 2f out: styd on same pce fr over 1f out* 14/1
**5** 1 1/2 **Quick Defence (USA)** 2-9-5 0 .... RyanMoore 2 63+
(Sir Michael Stoute) *s.s: in rr tl styd on fr over 1f out: nvr nrr* 8/1[3]
**6** 1/2 **King Bolete (IRE)** 2-9-5 0 .... AndreaAtzeni 1 62+
(Luca Cumani) *sn pushed along in rr: r.o ins fnl f: nrst fin* 20/1
**7** 3 **Sporting Prince** 2-9-5 0 .... JimCrowley 10 54
(Ed Dunlop) *s.i.s: hld up: nvr trbld ldrs* 66/1
03 **8** 2 1/4 **Dark Wave**[15] 5752 2-9-5 0 .... GeorgeBaker 7 48
(Ed Walker) *hld up: shkn up over 2f out: sn outpcd* 20/1
6 **9** 4 **Albecq**[25] 5377 2-9-5 0 .... JFEgan 9 37
(David Evans) *plld hrd and prom: stdd and lost pl over 5f out: wknd over 2f out* 20/1
1m 25.1s (-1.10) **Going Correction** -0.025s/f (Good) **9** Ran SP% **108.8**
Speed ratings (Par 97): **105,101,100,98,96 96,92,90,85**
CSF £3.70 TOTE £1.90: £1.30, £1.20, £3.70; EX 5.60 Trifecta £61.90.
**Owner** K Abdullah **Bred** Millsec Limited **Trained** Lambourn, Berks
■ Glorious Dubai (14-1) and Awjab (33-1) were withdrawn. Rule 4 applies to all bets. Deduction - 5p in the pound.
**FOCUS**
This division appeared to lack a bit of strength in depth, but it was run in a faster time than the first division.

## 6205 RANCLIFFE (S) STKS 7f 9y
**3:20** (3:20) (Class 6) 2-Y-O £1,940 (£577; £288; £144) **Stalls** High

Form RPR
0660 **1** **Secret Lightning (FR)**[11] 5875 2-8-7 63 .... LiamKeniry 4 60
(Sylvester Kirk) *chsd ldr: rdn over 1f out: led ins fnl f: styd on* 7/2[2]
0660 **2** 3/4 **Hillgrove Angel (IRE)**[11] 5875 2-8-12 67 ....(b[1]) JimmyFortune 7 63
(Brian Meehan) *hld up in tch: swtchd rt over 2f out: rdn over 1f out: styd on to go 2nd wl ins fnl f* 4/1[3]
2140 **3** 1 1/4 **Ciaras Cookie (IRE)**[20] 5554 2-8-12 64 .... JFEgan 1 60
(David Evans) *led: rdn over 2f out: hdd and unable qck ins fnl f* 11/4[1]
0500 **4** 2 1/2 **Activation**[6] 6040 2-8-12 59 .... RichardHughes 5 53
(Hughie Morrison) *hld up: hdwy over 1f out: styd on: nt rch ldrs* 8/1
5020 **5** nk **Chilworth Bells**[13] 5823 2-8-5 52 .... DanielCremin(7) 2 52
(Mick Channon) *chsd ldrs: rdn 1/2-way: no ex ins fnl f* 15/2
6000 **6** 1 1/4 **Pyrocumulus (IRE)**[35] 5009 2-8-12 45 .... JoeFanning 9 49
(Jo Hughes) *dwlt: hdwy over 4f out: rdn over 2f out: wknd ins fnl f* 16/1
0 **7** nk **Lexi Grady Alice**[31] 5187 2-8-7 0 .... JimmyQuinn 10 43
(Mark H Tompkins) *sn pushed along in rr: hdwy over 1f out: no ex ins fnl f* 20/1
064 **8** 7 **Tilly Range (IRE)**[32] 5133 2-8-7 54 .... RoystonFfrench 3 24
(David Evans) *chsd ldrs: rdn 1/2-way: wknd over 2f out* 20/1
**9** shd **Kicking Leaves (IRE)**[94] 3015 2-8-12 0 .... LiamJones 12 29
(J S Moore) *sn pushed along in rr: swtchd rt 1/2-way: n.d* 66/1
040 **10** 5 **Arcossi**[10] 5910 2-8-0 45 .... RowanScott(7) 8 10
(Ann Duffield) *chsd ldrs tl wknd over 2f out* 25/1
0 **11** 55 **Dancing Springs (IRE)**[6] 6024 2-8-3 0 ow1 .... RyanWhile(5) 6
(Bill Turner) *prom: lost pl over 5f out: bhd fnl 4f* 100/1
00 **U** **Bonita Brown Eyes (IRE)**[62] 4079 2-8-8 0 ow1 .... StevieDonohoe 11
(J S Moore) *prom whn uns rdr over 5f out* 100/1
1m 26.57s (0.37) **Going Correction** -0.025s/f (Good) **12** Ran SP% **114.5**
Speed ratings (Par 93): **96,95,93,90,90 89,88,80,80,74 12,**
CSF £15.98 TOTE £4.70: £2.50, £2.00, £1.90; EX 21.10 Trifecta £70.60.The winner was bought by M Appleby for 7,200gns. Hillgrove Angel claimed by David Evans for £7,000.
**Owner** J C Smith **Bred** Jeffrey Colin Smith **Trained** Upper Lambourn, Berks
**FOCUS**
A desperate contest in truth.

## 6206 MARKFIELD H'CAP 1m 3f 183y
**3:50** (3:50) (Class 4) (0-85,83) 3-Y-O+ £4,690 (£1,395; £697; £348) **Stalls** Low

Form RPR
4316 **1** **High Church (IRE)**[11] 5877 3-9-2 82 .... JamesDoyle 4 95+
(Roger Charlton) *s.i.s: hld up: hdwy 2f out: shkn up to ld and edgd rt 1f out: r.o wl: comf* 11/8[1]
4135 **2** 2 3/4 **Opera Fan (FR)**[17] 5670 3-8-10 76 .... JoeFanning 3 83
(Mark Johnston) *led: hdd over 10f out: chsd ldr tl 5f out: remained handy: shkn up over 2f out: n.m.r 1f out: styd on same pce* 12/1

3031 **3** *4* **A Star In My Eye (IRE)**[18] 5639 4-9-11 82 ..................... RyanMoore 6 83
(Kevin Ryan) *w ldr tl led over 10f out: rdn and hdd 1f out: wknd ins fnl f* **5/1**[3]

231 **4** *¾* **Mustadaam (IRE)**[54] 4368 3-9-3 83 ..................... PaulHanagan 2 82
(Brian Meehan) *prom: chsd ldr 5f out: rdn over 2f out: wknd ins fnl f* **7/4**[2]

4 **5** *8* **Arizona John (IRE)**[84] 3341 9-9-9 80 ..................... StephenCraine 5 67
(John Mackie) *prom: rdn over 2f out: wknd over 1f out* **16/1**

2m 31.75s (-2.15) **Going Correction** -0.025s/f (Good)
**WFA** 3 from 4yo+ 9lb **5** Ran SP% **108.7**
Speed ratings (Par 105): **106,104,101,101,95**
CSF £16.53 TOTE £2.80: £1.80, £5.60; EX 15.60 Trifecta £48.60.
**Owner** Lady Rothschild **Bred** The Rt Hon Lord Rothschild **Trained** Beckhampton, Wilts

**FOCUS**
Competitive enough despite the small field. The winner was back on track with the form rated around the third.

## 6207 WEATHERBYS HAMILTON INSURANCE H'CAP 7f 9y
**4:20** (4:20) (Class 3) (0-95,94) 3-Y-0+ **£7,762** (£2,310; £1,154; £577) **Stalls** High

Form RPR

4011 **1** **Take A Note**[33] 5092 5-9-3 87 ..................... (v) JimCrowley 1 96
(Patrick Chamings) *a.p: chsd ldr over 5f out: rdn to ld over 1f out: jst hld on* **8/1**

6003 **2** *hd* **Secretintheapark**[24] 5418 4-9-8 92 ..................... RichardHughes 6 100
(Ed McMahon) *chsd ldr tl over 5f out: remained handy: rdn to chse wnr over 1f out: r.o* **3/1**[1]

3055 **3** *hd* **Verse Of Love**[15] 5749 5-8-12 82 ..................... JFEgan 4 89
(David Evans) *s.i.s: hdwy over 4f out: lost pl over 2f out: rallied over 1f out: r.o* **25/1**

1442 **4** *1 ¼* **Flow (USA)**[16] 5728 4-9-8 92 ..................... (t) JamesDoyle 9 96
(Lady Cecil) *hld up: hdwy over 2f out: rdn over 1f out: r.o* **5/1**[2]

1513 **5** *¾* **Outback Traveller (IRE)**[16] 5728 3-9-5 93 ..................... WilliamBuick 8 93+
(Jeremy Noseda) *hld up: swtchd rt and hdwy over 1f out: r.o: nt rch ldrs* **6/1**[3]

51 **6** *1* **Fieldgunner Kirkup (GER)**[31] 5197 6-8-12 82 ..................... GrahamGibbons 5 82
(David Barron) *led: rdn and hdd over 1f out: no ex ins fnl f* **25/1**

4301 **7** *1* **Kakatosi**[26] 5346 7-9-1 85 ..................... TomQueally 10 82
(Mike Murphy) *hld up: swtchd rt and hdwy over 1f out: styd on same pce ins fnl f* **20/1**

0-00 **8** *1* **One Word More (IRE)**[81] 3420 4-9-10 94 ..................... GeorgeBaker 12 88
(Charles Hills) *hld up: hmpd 3f out: rdn over 1f out: nvr trbld ldrs* **14/1**

000 **9** *¾* **Askaud (IRE)**[19] 5612 6-9-5 89 ..................... (p) FrederikTylicki 11 82
(Scott Dixon) *hld up: hmpd 3f out: n.d* **12/1**

0003 **10** *2 ¼* **Pastoral Player**[24] 5433 7-9-2 93 ..................... CharlieBennett(7) 3 80
(Hughie Morrison) *s.i.s: plld hrd and hdwy over 5f out: rdn over 1f out: wknd fnl f* **13/2**

5-40 **11** *11* **Mystical Sapphire**[13] 5824 4-9-5 89 ..................... FergusSweeney 7 47
(Jo Crowley) *mid-div: hdwy over 2f out: wknd over 1f out* **20/1**

0020 **12** *7* **Victoire De Lyphar (IRE)**[24] 5418 7-9-6 90 ..................... (e) PaulHanagan 2 30
(Ruth Carr) *s.i.s: hdwy over 4f out: wknd over 2f out* **25/1**

1m 24.6s (-1.60) **Going Correction** -0.025s/f (Good)
**WFA** 3 from 4yo+ 4lb **12** Ran SP% **115.8**
Speed ratings (Par 107): **108,107,107,106,105 104,102,101,100,98 85,77**
CSF £28.76 CT £578.93 TOTE £6.40: £2.40, £1.30, £9.70; EX 36.80 Trifecta £644.70.
**Owner** The Foxford House Partnership **Bred** P J L Wright **Trained** Baughurst, Hants
■ Stewards' Enquiry : J F Egan two-day ban: used whip above permitted level (Sep 23-24)

**FOCUS**
A really competitive handicap run at a sound gallop and no reason why this form shouldn't work out well. A length best from the winner, with the second rated to form.

## 6208 BRITISH STALLION STUDS EBF FILBERT MAIDEN FILLIES' STKS (BOBIS RACE) 1m 60y
**4:50** (4:51) (Class 4) 2-Y-0 **£5,175** (£1,540; £769; £384) **Stalls** Low

Form RPR

**1** **Sagaciously (IRE)** 2-9-0 0 ..................... JamesDoyle 8 78+
(Ed Dunlop) *a.p: chsd ldr 2f out: edgd rt and r.o to ld wl ins fnl f* **50/1**

2 **2** *1* **Housemaker**[18] 5643 2-9-0 0 ..................... JimCrowley 6 76
(K R Burke) *led 1f: chsd ldr tl led again over 2f out: rdn and hdd wl ins fnl f* **9/4**[1]

**3** *shd* **Martlet** 2-9-0 0 ..................... WilliamBuick 3 76+
(John Gosden) *s.s: hld up: hdwy over 1f out: r.o* **5/1**[3]

4 **4** *½* **Shaw Ting**[15] 5774 2-9-0 0 ..................... RichardKingscote 4 75+
(Tom Dascombe) *hld up: r.o ins fnl f: nt rch ldrs* **12/1**

**5** *6* **Tingleo** 2-9-0 0 ..................... RyanMoore 5 61
(Sir Michael Stoute) *chsd ldrs: pushed along over 3f out: wknd fnl f* **3/1**[2]

**6** *nk* **Phantasmagoric (IRE)** 2-9-0 0 ..................... JimmyFortune 2 60
(Sir Michael Stoute) *prom: nt clr run fr over 2f out tl lost pl over 1f out: nt rcvr* **16/1**

**7** *3* **Amber Mile** 2-9-0 0 ..................... AndreaAtzeni 1 53
(Ralph Beckett) *led after 1f: rdn and hdd over 2f out: wknd over 1f out* **7/1**

**8** *28* **Flamme Fantastique (GER)** 2-9-0 0 ..................... PaulHanagan 7
(William Haggas) *s.s: rn green and a in rr: bhd fr 1/2-way* **13/2**

1m 46.48s (1.38) **Going Correction** -0.025s/f (Good) **8** Ran SP% **113.8**
Speed ratings (Par 94): **92,91,90,90,84 84,81,53**
CSF £159.99 TOTE £28.10: £6.80, £1.10, £1.30; EX 215.40 Trifecta £1433.40.
**Owner** The Sagacious Lot **Bred** Keatly Overseas Ltd **Trained** Newmarket, Suffolk

**FOCUS**
Hard to know what to make of this form as most of the newcomers looked green, the pace was steady and the outsider of the field got the better of the market leader in the closing stages.

## 6209 PRESTWOLD CONDITIONS STKS 5f 2y
**5:25** (5:27) (Class 3) 3-Y-0+ **£7,561** (£2,263; £1,131; £566; £282) **Stalls** High

Form RPR

0200 **1** **Ajjaadd (USA)**[10] 5925 8-8-9 93 ..................... WilliamTwiston-Davies 3 104
(Ted Powell) *hld up: hdwy 1/2-way: rdn and hung rt ins fnl f: r.o wl to ld towards fin* **7/2**[2]

0202 **2** *1 ¼* **Green Door (IRE)**[28] 5289 3-8-13 104 ..................... (p) JamieSpencer 5 105
(Olly Stevens) *trckd ldr: rdn to ld and edgd lft wl ins fnl f: sn hdd and unable qck* **9/4**[1]

00-0 **3** *1 ¾* **Duke Of Firenze**[28] 5289 5-8-9 97 ..................... (p) RichardHughes 4 93
(Robert Cowell) *sn led: shkn up over 1f out: hdd: bmpd and no ex wl ins fnl f* **11/2**[3]

2110 **4** *3 ½* **Silvanus (IRE)**[15] 5754 9-8-12 94 ..................... PaulHanagan 6 84
(Paul Midgley) *chsd ldrs: pushed along 1/2-way: outpcd fr over 2f out* **6/1**

345- **5** *5* **Boston Rocker (IRE)**[310] 7719 4-8-4 0 ..................... (v) AndreaAtzeni 2 58
(Hughie Morrison) *s.i.s: outpcd* **9/4**[1]

58.84s (-1.16) **Going Correction** -0.025s/f (Good)
**WFA** 3 from 4yo+ 1lb **5** Ran SP% **113.4**
Speed ratings (Par 107): **108,106,103,97,89**
CSF £12.14 TOTE £6.30: £2.00, £3.40; EX 14.80 Trifecta £47.30.
**Owner** Katy & Lol Pratt **Bred** Darley **Trained** Reigate, Surrey

**FOCUS**
A good quality conditions event run at a very strong gallop thanks to Duke Of Firenze, who probably went off too fast. There is a slight doubt over the form with the second and third both below their bests in a similar race latest.

## 6210 SWAN APPRENTICE H'CAP 1m 1f 218y
**5:55** (5:55) (Class 6) (0-65,64) 4-Y-0+ **£1,940** (£577; £288; £144) **Stalls** Low

Form RPR

0443 **1** **Flag Of Glory**[15] 5773 7-9-0 57 ..................... PatMillman 5 65
(Peter Hiatt) *chsd ldr who wnt clr 6f out: rdn to cl over 2f out: led over 1f out: r.o* **6/1**

0006 **2** *2 ¾* **Bold Cross (IRE)**[6] 6028 11-8-7 50 ..................... DanielCremin 2 53
(Edward Bevan) *hld up: hdwy over 2f out: rdn and ev ch over 1f out: styd on same pce ins fnl f* **20/1**

4505 **3** *1 ½* **Magnolia Ridge (IRE)**[5] 6062 4-9-2 62 ..................... (p) KieranShoemark(3) 6 62
(Kristin Stubbs) *chsd ldrs: rdn over 2f out: styd on same pce fnl f* **11/2**[3]

3210 **4** *3 ¼* **Ela Goog La Mou**[5] 6076 5-9-2 64 ..................... BradleyBosley(5) 1 58
(Peter Charalambous) *led after 1f: clr 6f out: rdn and hdd over 1f out: no ex fnl f* **2/1**[1]

4463 **5** *½* **Life And Times (USA)**[13] 5811 6-9-1 63 ..................... AhmadAlSubousi(5) 8 56
(Mark Johnston) *prom: lost pl over 6f out: rdn and edgd rt fr over 2f out: no imp* **5/2**[2]

2564 **6** *hd* **Cabuchon (GER)**[19] 5599 7-8-9 57 ..................... (vt) HollieDoyle(5) 3 49
(David Evans) *hld up: hdwy over 3f out: wknd fnl f* **14/1**

0540 **7** *1 ¾* **Maillot Jaune (IRE)**[10] 5084 4-8-2 50 oh5 ..................... RowanScott(5) 4 39
(Patrick Holmes) *led 1f: chsd ldrs: rdn over 2f out: wknd fnl f* **50/1**

-360 **8** *14* **Stun Gun**[164] 1168 4-9-0 57 ..................... AdamMcLean 9 19
(Derek Shaw) *hld up: rdn 1/2-way: sn wknd* **14/1**

0060 **9** *13* **Slip Of A Girl (IRE)**[15] 4066 4-8-2 50 oh5 ..................... JoshDoyle(5) 7
(Patrick Holmes) *hld up in tch: n.m.r and lost pl over 5f out: wknd 1/2-way* **100/1**

2m 7.15s (-0.75) **Going Correction** -0.025s/f (Good) **9** Ran SP% **112.6**
Speed ratings (Par 101): **102,99,98,96,95 95,94,82,72**
CSF £108.74 CT £691.32 TOTE £5.30: £1.10, £5.50, £1.80; EX 95.30 Trifecta £509.80.
**Owner** N D Edden **Bred** Follow The Flag Partnership **Trained** Hook Norton, Oxon
■ Stewards' Enquiry : Hollie Doyle two-day ban: failed to ride out gelding that could have finished 4th (Sep 23-24)

**FOCUS**
A weak apprentice riders' race in which the fourth set a strong gallop. The form is rated a bit cautiously.
T/Plt: £7.00 to a £1 stake. Pool: £62,792.10 - 6,489.07 winning tickets. T/Qpdt: £4.80 to a £1 stake. Pool: £4,229.10 - 650.05 winning tickets. CR

# 5678 REDCAR (L-H)
Tuesday, September 9

**OFFICIAL GOING: Good to firm (watered; 9.0)**
Wind: Light across Weather: Cloudy with sunny periods

## 6211 RACINGUK 100% PROFITS RETURNED TO RACING NURSERY H'CAP 7f
**2:30** (2:30) (Class 5) (0-75,75) 2-Y-0 **£2,587** (£770; £384; £192) **Stalls** Centre

Form RPR

0130 **1** **Mr Shekells**[26] 5335 2-8-7 64 ..................... GeorgeChaloner(3) 13 67
(Philip McBride) *hld up towards rr: stdy hdwy 3f out: chsd ldrs wl over 1f out: sn rdn: styd on strly ins fnl f to ld last 50yds* **8/1**

4605 **2** *½* **Dominic Cork**[22] 5506 2-8-7 61 ..................... FergalLynch 10 63
(Kevin Ryan) *t.k.h: mde most: rdn over 1f out: drvn and edgd rt wl ins fnl f: hdd and no ex last 50yds* **14/1**

3316 **3** *1* **Summer Stroll (IRE)**[26] 5335 2-8-13 67 ..................... DanielTudhope 9 66
(David O'Meara) *in rr: pushed along 1/2-way: rdn 3f out: hdwy u.p wl over 1f out: styd on wl fnl f* **6/1**[3]

6042 **4** *½* **Charlotte's Secret**[14] 5798 2-8-11 65 ..................... TonyHamilton 2 63
(Richard Fahey) *in tch: rdn along and sltly outpcd wl over 2f out: styd on u.p fnl f: nrst fin* **6/1**[3]

1 **5** *¾* **Dragon King (IRE)**[102] 2736 2-9-7 75 ..................... PaulMulrennan 15 71
(Michael Dods) *wnt rt s: keen towards rr: hdwy to trck ldrs after 2f: smooth effrt to chal over 2f out and ev ch: rdn appr fnl f and kpt on same pce* **4/1**[1]

0000 **6** *¾* **Chollima**[26] 5335 2-8-0 54 oh9 ..................... (b) DuranFentiman 6 48
(Tim Easterby) *cl up: disp ld 3f out: rdn along 2f out and ev ch tl drvn ent fnl f and grad wknd* **100/1**

6050 **7** *2 ½* **Secret Of Dubai**[26] 5335 2-7-9 54 oh4 ..................... JackGarritty(5) 7 41
(Brian Ellison) *in tch: hdwy to chse ldrs over 2f out: rdn wl over 1f out: wknd ent fnl f* **33/1**

5522 **8** *1* **Saltarello (IRE)**[7] 6008 2-9-3 71 ..................... PhillipMakin 11 55
(John Quinn) *trckd ldrs: pushed along over 3f out: rdn over 2f out: sn one pce* **9/2**[2]

006 **9** *6* **North Bay Lady (IRE)**[42] 4750 2-7-11 56 oh5 ow2 ..................... JoeDoyle(5) 12 24
(John Wainwright) *chsd ldrs: rdn along 3f out: sn wknd* **20/1**

0560 **10** *2* **Mutafarrej**[25] 5373 2-9-6 74 ..................... DaneO'Neill 14 37
(Mark Johnston) *towards rr: hdwy 3f out: rdn along over 2f out: sn btn* **15/2**

0340 **11** *nk* **Lazy Days In Loule (IRE)**[18] 5637 2-8-3 60 ..................... [1] JoeyHaynes(3) 5 22
(Noel Wilson) *a towards rr* **33/1**

5343 **12** *1* **Fazenda's Girl**[26] 5335 2-8-0 54 oh1 ..................... (v[1]) JamesSullivan 1 13
(Michael Easterby) *t.k.h: prom: rdn along 3f out: sn wknd* **18/1**

4000 **13** *6* **Shamkhani**[10] 5922 2-8-0 54 oh9 ..................... PatrickMathers 4
(Alan Berry) *dwlt: pushed along and hdwy to join ldrs after 1f: cl up on outer tl rdn along 3f out and sn wknd* **100/1**

0000 **14** *½* **Esk Valley Lady**[48] 4528 2-7-9 54 oh9 ..................... NoelGarbutt(5) 8
(Philip Kirby) *dwlt: a in rr* **100/1**

1m 25.94s (1.44) **Going Correction** 0.0s/f (Good) **14** Ran SP% **115.2**
Speed ratings (Par 95): **91,90,89,88,87 87,84,83,76,73 73,72,65,64**
CSF £104.06 CT £716.30 TOTE £10.70: £3.60, £5.20, £2.40; EX 133.80 Trifecta £1671.90 Part won. Pool: £2,229.31 - 0.66 winning tickets..
**Owner** Nigel Davies & P J McBride **Bred** Warwick Stud **Trained** Newmarket, Suffolk

**FOCUS**
A hotly contested opener, albeit an ordinary nursery.

## 6212 MARKET CROSS JEWELLERS MAIDEN AUCTION STKS 5f
**3:00** (3:01) (Class 6) 2-Y-O **£2,045** (£603; £302) **Stalls** Centre

Form RPR
4 **1** **Snow Cloud (IRE)**[123] 2134 2-8-5 0 SamJames(3) 5 69+
(David O'Meara) *dwlt: sn in tch: hdwy to trck ldrs 2f out: rdn to chal ent fnl f: led last 100yds: kpt on* **9/2**[3]
6302 **2** *1 1/4* **Compton River**[13] 5813 2-9-1 68 PaulMulrennan 7 68
(Bryan Smart) *led: rdn wl over 1f out: drvn ins fnl f: hdd and no ex last 100yds* **11/4**[1]
00 **3** *hd* **Zaza Zest (IRE)**[27] 5297 2-8-5 0 JackGarritty(5) 8 62
(Richard Fahey) *cl up: chal 2f out: sn rdn and ev ch: drvn and kpt on same pce ins fnl f* **33/1**
3664 **4** *1 1/4* **Jimmy's Hall**[16] 5739 2-8-6 0 JosephineGordon(7) 13 61
(J S Moore) *towards rr: hdwy 1/2-way: rdn along to chse ldrs over 1f out: kpt on ins fnl f: nrst fin* **20/1**
6230 **5** *1/2* **Stanghow**[45] 4686 2-8-11 70 PJMcDonald 1 57
(Mel Brittain) *chsd ldrs on outer: effrt 2f out and ev ch tl rdn appr fnl f and kpt on same pce* **3/1**[2]
0 **6** *1 1/2* **U Think Ur Funny (IRE)**[14] 5789 2-8-10 0 BarryMcHugh 2 51+
(Tony Coyle) *in rr: hdwy 2f out: sn rdn and kpt on fnl f: nrst fin* **7/1**
0 **7** *5* **Constant Applause**[11] 5874 2-8-13 0 LemosdeSouza 9 36
(Mrs Ilka Gansera-Leveque) *awkward and wnt lft s: sn chsng ldrs: rdn along wl over 1f out: grad wknd* **9/1**
2640 **8** *3/4* **Frank The Barber (IRE)**[8] 5985 2-8-10 60 JackDuern(5) 4 35
(Steph Hollinshead) *chsd ldrs: rdn along over 2f out: sn edgd lft and wknd* **16/1**
000 **9** *hd* **Pancake Day**[17] 5679 2-8-11 55 JamesSullivan 11 30
(Jason Ward) *a towards rr* **100/1**
**10** *hd* **Lilac Vale (IRE)** 2-8-6 0 DuranFentiman 10 24
(Tim Easterby) *dwlt: a towards rr* **40/1**
060 **11** *1/2* **Ryedale Mist**[42] 4751 2-8-10 45 DavidAllan 3 27
(Tim Easterby) *a in rr* **25/1**
0600 **12** *1/2* **Cheeky Chapman**[27] 5297 2-9-0 56 GeorgeChaloner(3) 12 32
(Clive Mulhall) *dwlt: sn in tch: rdn along over 2f out: sn wknd* **50/1**
0 **13** *26* **Little Polyanna**[13] 5813 2-8-6 0 PatrickMathers 6
(Alan Berry) *dwlt: sn chsng ldrs: rdn along 1/2-way: sn lost pl and bhd whn eased fnl f* **200/1**

59.7s (1.10) **Going Correction** 0.0s/f (Good) 13 Ran SP% **115.7**
Speed ratings (Par 93): **91,89,88,86,85 83,75,74,73,73 72,72,30**
CSF £15.73 TOTE £8.10: £3.10, £1.30, £10.60; EX 18.50 Trifecta £301.60.
**Owner** Middleham Park Racing L & Partner **Bred** Vincent Kelly **Trained** Nawton, N Yorks

**FOCUS**
This looked a good opportunity for the winner on paper and she duly delivered.

## 6213 WEATHERBYS BANK H'CAP 6f
**3:30** (3:30) (Class 5) (0-75,75) 3-Y-O+ **£2,587** (£770; £384; £192) **Stalls** Centre

Form RPR
3035 **1** **Manatee Bay**[20] 5565 4-8-7 61 (v1) FrannyNorton 3 74
(David Nicholls) *midfield: hdwy over 2f out: swtchd lft over 1f out: rdn ent fnl f: led last 100yds: kpt on* **20/1**
002 **2** *2* **Enderby Spirit (GR)**[28] 5265 8-9-1 69 PhillipMakin 14 76
(Bryan Smart) *trckd ldrs: hdwy and cl up wl over 2f out: rdn to ld appr fnl f: sn drvn: hdd and no ex last 100yds* **12/1**
3533 **3** *nk* **Exotic Guest**[18] 5636 4-8-11 65 (p) JamesSullivan 2 71
(Ruth Carr) *towards rr: hdwy over 2f out: rdn over 1f out: styd on fnl f: nrst fin* **14/1**
2501 **4** *shd* **Native Falls (IRE)**[11] 5889 3-9-0 70 DavidAllan 5 76
(Alan Swinbank) *cl up: led over 3f out: rdn along 2f out: hdd and drvn over 1f out: kpt on same pce fnl f* **7/1**[3]
5324 **5** *1* **Vodka Time (IRE)**[45] 4674 3-8-6 62 BenCurtis 6 66
(Shaun Harris) *towards rr: hdwy over 2f out: effrt whn n.m.r over 1f out and again appr fnl f: sn swtchd lft and rdn: kpt on nrst fin* **40/1**
0412 **6** *nk* **He's My Boy (IRE)**[22] 5492 3-8-10 66 (v) HayleyTurner 1 68
(James Fanshawe) *dwlt and in rr: hdwy 2f out: sn rdn: kpt on fnl f: nrst fin* **4/1**[1]
1605 **7** *1* **Rich Again (IRE)**[10] 5912 5-8-11 65 TonyHamilton 11 63
(James Bethell) *towards rr: pushed along 1/2-way: rdn over 2f out: hdwy whn n.m.r and swtchd lft over 1f out: kpt on: nrst fin* **12/1**
4610 **8** *nk* **Black Douglas**[11] 5897 5-8-0 61 oh3 RachaelGrant(7) 13 58
(Jim Goldie) *dwlt and in rr: sn swtchd lft: hdwy on wd outside 2f out: sn rdn and edgd lft to far rail over 1f out: n.d* **28/1**
1660 **9** *1 1/4* **Relight My Fire**[10] 5915 4-9-4 72 (b) JasonHart 10 65
(Tim Easterby) *led: hdd over 3f out and cl up tl rdn along and wknd over 1f out* **20/1**
3403 **10** *nk* **Lucky Lodge**[33] 5089 4-8-8 62 (b) AndrewElliott 9 54
(Mel Brittain) *a towards rr* **10/1**
0040 **11** *3/4* **Eland Ally**[15] 5766 6-9-0 68 (p) BarryMcHugh 15 58
(Tom Tate) *in tch on wd outside: rdn along over 2f out: sn wknd* **6/1**[2]
0060 **12** *1/2* **Dream Ally (IRE)**[23] 5470 4-8-8 62 PJMcDonald 12 50
(Micky Hammond) *a towards rr* **40/1**
5440 **13** *1 1/2* **Ruby's Day**[36] 4976 5-9-7 75 (v1) GrahamLee 7 59
(David Brown) *trckd ldrs: pushed along wl over 2f out: rdn and wknd wl over 1f out: btn whn hmpd appr fnl f* **17/2**
6440 **14** *1/2* **Ingenti**[10] 5912 6-8-8 62 TomEaves 8 44
(Christopher Wilson) *trckd ldrs: rdn along over 2f out: sn wknd* **33/1**
-062 **15** *nse* **Barney McGrew (IRE)**[15] 5766 11-9-7 75 PaulMulrennan 4 57
(Michael Dods) *trckd ldng pair: effrt over 2f out: sn rdn along and wknd over 1f out* **8/1**

1m 11.17s (-0.63) **Going Correction** 0.0s/f (Good)
**WFA** 3 from 4yo+ 2lb 15 Ran SP% **120.4**
Speed ratings (Par 103): **104,101,100,100,99 99,97,97,95,95 94,93,91,90,90**
CSF £226.64 CT £3520.34 TOTE £27.70: £6.00, £3.40, £3.30; EX 255.60 Trifecta £3149.00 Part won. Pool: £4,198.70 - 0.25 winning tickets..
**Owner** Pinnacle Royal Applause Partnership **Bred** Miss A J Rawding & P M Crane **Trained** Sessay, N Yorks

**FOCUS**
This was landed in good style by the winner.

## 6214 WEATHERBYS STALLION BOOK H'CAP (STRAIGHT MILE CHAMPIONSHIP QUALIFIER) 1m
**4:00** (4:03) (Class 4) (0-85,85) 3-Y-O+ **£6,469** (£1,925; £962; £481) **Stalls** Centre

Form RPR
1405 **1** **Knight Owl**[21] 5528 4-9-9 84 DaneO'Neill 12 94
(James Fanshawe) *hld up: hdwy over 2f out: swtchd lft and rdn over 1f out: led jst ins fnl f: sn drvn and jst hld on* **5/1**[1]
6633 **2** *shd* **Almuheet**[18] 5656 3-9-5 85 DaleSwift 13 94
(Brian Ellison) *trckd ldrs: hdwy and cl up 3f out: led over 1f out: rdn: edgd lft and hdd jst ins fnl f: sn drvn and hung lft: kpt on wl towards fin: jst failed* **6/1**[2]
3103 **3** *3/4* **Anderiego (IRE)**[17] 5681 6-9-10 85 (v) DanielTudhope 2 93
(David O'Meara) *hld up towards rr: hdwy over 3f out: chsd ldrs 2f out: rdn to chal and ev ch ent fnl f: sn drvn and kpt on same pce towards fin* **5/1**[1]
4300 **4** *3 1/4* **Hakuna Matata**[22] 5496 7-9-0 78 (b) ConnorBeasley(3) 5 79
(Michael Dods) *hld up towards rr: hdwy over 2f out: sn rdn: styd on fnl f: nrst fin* **16/1**
3014 **5** *nk* **Big Storm Coming**[10] 5915 4-9-3 78 JamesSullivan 1 78
(Ruth Carr) *in tch: hdwy to chse ldrs over 2f out: rdn wl over 1f out: drvn and one pce fnl f* **9/1**
0630 **6** *nk* **Henry The Aviator (USA)**[13] 5810 4-9-8 83 FrannyNorton 4 82
(Mark Johnston) *chsd ldrs: rdn along over 2f out: sn drvn and grad wknd appr fnl f* **22/1**
0564 **7** *2 1/2* **Favourite Treat (USA)**[17] 5681 4-9-4 79 PaulMulrennan 3 72
(Ruth Carr) *prom: led 1/2-way: rdn along 2f out: hdd and drvn over 1f out: wknd ent fnl f* **8/1**
4124 **8** *hd* **Express Himself (IRE)**[21] 5528 3-9-1 81 (p) SteveDrowne 11 73
(Ed McMahon) *s.i.s: a in rr* **13/2**[3]
3605 **9** *1/2* **Red Charmer (IRE)**[13] 5810 4-8-10 71 oh1 PJMcDonald 10 63
(Ann Duffield) *a towards rr* **20/1**
0420 **10** *1/2* **Ready (IRE)**[10] 5915 4-9-7 82 (p) AndrewMullen 9 73
(Garry Moss) *trckd ldrs: effrt wl over 2f out: sn rdn and wknd* **18/1**
0313 **11** *12* **Cameroonеy**[20] 5562 11-8-13 74 (p) PhillipMakin 7 37
(Marjorie Fife) *led: hdd 1/2-way and sn pushed along: rdn 3f out and sn wknd* **25/1**
0155 **U** **Lawyer (IRE)**[29] 5258 3-9-3 83 LukeMorris 6
(Luca Cumani) *hld up in tch whn stmbld and uns rdr after 1f* **9/1**

1m 36.95s (0.35) **Going Correction** 0.0s/f (Good)
**WFA** 3 from 4yo+ 5lb 12 Ran SP% **116.2**
Speed ratings (Par 105): **98,97,97,93,93 93,90,90,90,89 77,**
CSF £32.38 CT £160.07 TOTE £8.00: £2.10, £2.50, £1.60; EX 44.70 Trifecta £164.30.
**Owner** Miss Annabelle Condon **Bred** Car Colston Hall Stud **Trained** Newmarket, Suffolk

**FOCUS**
A dramatic feature, run at a searching pace and a hard-fought success for the winner.

## 6215 RACING UK ANYWHERE AVAILABLE NOW MAIDEN STKS 6f
**4:35** (4:37) (Class 5) 3-Y-O+ **£2,587** (£770; £384; £192) **Stalls** Centre

Form RPR
-460 **1** **Foxtrot Pearl (IRE)**[41] 4795 3-9-0 65 FrannyNorton 3 68
(John Holt) *mde all: rdn 2f out: drvn ent fnl f: edgd lft and kpt on wl* **12/1**
0 **2** *1* **Rememberance Day**[23] 5469 3-9-0 0 DavidAllan 4 65
(Les Eyre) *a.p: chal wl over 1f out: sn rdn: drvn and kpt on fnl f* **40/1**
2422 **3** *1* **Another Royal**[16] 5715 3-9-0 60 (b) TonyHamilton 9 62
(Tim Easterby) *hld up in rr: hdwy 2f out: sn rdn: kpt on fnl f: nrst fin* **3/1**[2]
46- **4** *2 1/4* **Random**[290] 8017 3-9-0 0 FrankieMcDonald 2 55
(Daniel Mark Loughnane) *hld up: hdwy over 2f out: rdn to chse ldrs wl over 1f out: sn edgd lft and one pce* **25/1**
6022 **5** *1/2* **Tap Your Toes (IRE)**[24] 5417 3-9-5 74 ShaneKelly 1 58
(Luca Cumani) *trckd ldrs: hdwy over 2f out: sn niggled along: rdn to chse wnr over 1f out: drvn and wknd ent fnl f* **5/6**[1]
23/5 **6** *3* **Pearl Bell (IRE)**[31] 5181 4-9-2 75 DanielTudhope 10 44
(Olly Stevens) *racd wd: prom: effrt and cl up wl 2f out: sn rdn and wknd appr fnl f* **5/1**[3]
0P00 **7** *10* **Spinner Lane**[16] 5715 3-8-11 45 (b) GeorgeChaloner(3) 8 12
(Richard Whitaker) *cl up: rdn along bef 1/2-way: sn outpcd and bhd fnl 2f* **100/1**

1m 12.44s (0.64) **Going Correction** 0.0s/f (Good)
**WFA** 3 from 4yo+ 2lb 7 Ran SP% **111.2**
Speed ratings (Par 103): **95,93,92,89,88 84,71**
CSF £303.28 TOTE £15.40: £6.20, £9.80; EX 457.80 Trifecta £1346.30.
**Owner** J R Holt **Bred** E Mulryan **Trained** Peckleton, Leics

**FOCUS**
Not a race that will live long in the memory and uncomfortable viewing throughout for the backers of the odds-on favourite, who trailed in a well-beaten fifth.

## 6216 REDCAR RACECOURSE WEDDING FAYRE 21ST SEPTEMBER H'CAP 1m 6f 19y
**5:05** (5:05) (Class 6) (0-65,65) 3-Y-O+ **£2,045** (£603; £302) **Stalls** Low

Form RPR
-002 **1** **Crakehall Lad (IRE)**[17] 5682 3-8-13 61 DavidAllan 7 69
(Alan Swinbank) *trckd ldng pair: hdwy to trck ldr 1/2-way: cl up over 4f out: led briefly 3f out: rdn and led again over 1f out: drvn ins fnl f: edgd lft last 100yds: kpt on wl* **11/4**[1]
1440 **2** *nk* **Madrasa (IRE)**[18] 5639 6-9-7 65 (bt) MikeyEnnis(7) 1 72
(Keith Reveley) *hld up in tch: hdwy on inner wl over 2f out: rdn to chse ldrs wl over 1f out: drvn and styd on wl fnl f: jst hld* **5/1**[3]
5062 **3** *1 1/4* **District Attorney (IRE)**[14] 5200 5-9-0 51 MichaelStainton 9 56
(Chris Fairhurst) *hld up in rr: hdwy 3f out: rdn to chse ldrs wl over 1f out: swtchd rt and drvn ent fnl f: kpt on wl towards fin* **12/1**
2030 **4** *nk* **Rocky Two (IRE)**[20] 5567 4-9-2 53 (p) TonyHamilton 6 58
(Philip Kirby) *led: pushed along over 4f out: rdn and hdd briefly 3f out: sn led again: drvn and hdd over 1f out: hld whn n.m.r last 100yds* **16/1**
3100 **5** *1* **That Be Grand**[45] 4657 3-8-12 60 JasonHart 10 63
(Shaun Harris) *hld up in rr: hdwy over 3f out: rdn over 2f out: kpt on same pce appr fnl f* **16/1**
3053 **6** *1/2* **Dr Finley (IRE)**[20] 5547 7-8-13 53 (v) SimonPearce(3) 2 55
(Lydia Pearce) *hld up in tch: hdwy on outer over 4f out: chsd ldrs 3f out: rdn over 2f out: drvn and no imp appr fnl f* **12/1**
331 **7** *5* **Modify**[17] 5682 3-8-6 57 SamJames(3) 4 52
(David O'Meara) *hld up towards rr: hdwy over 3f out: rdn along over 2f out: sn no imp* **3/1**[2]

0/00 **8** *7* **Takaatuf (IRE)**[14] 5371 8-9-8 62 .................................... JoeyHaynes(3) 3 48
(Tina Jackson) *trckd ldrs: effrt over 3f out: sn rdn along and wknd 2f out* **66/1**

-202 **9** *hd* **Waltz Darling (IRE)**[120] 2213 6-9-9 60 .................................... TomEaves 8 45
(Keith Reveley) *trckd ldrs: hdwy to chse ldng pair over 3f out: rdn along over 2f out: sn wknd* **14/1**

5140 **10** *1 ¼* **Blue Talisman (IRE)**[61] 4134 3-8-12 60 ..................(b) DuranFentiman 5 44
(Tim Easterby) *trckd ldr: pushed along over 4f out: rdn over 3f out: wknd fnl 2f* **8/1**

3m 7.33s (2.63) **Going Correction** +0.25s/f (Good)
**WFA** 3 from 4yo+ 11lb **10** Ran SP% **114.8**
Speed ratings (Par 101): **102,101,101,100,100 100,97,93,93,92**
CSF £16.46 CT £139.68 TOTE £4.20: £1.70, £1.40, £4.70; EX 16.40 Trifecta £171.80.
**Owner** G Brogan **Bred** Albert Conneally **Trained** Melsonby, N Yorks
■ Stewards' Enquiry : David Allan two-day ban: careless riding (Sep 23-24)

**FOCUS**
This looked hard work for all of these, including the winner.

## 6217 RACING REPLAY, ALL TODAY'S RACING SKY 432 APPRENTICE H'CAP 7f

**5:40** (5:40) (Class 5) (0-75,75) 3-Y-O+ **£2,587** (£770; £384; £192) **Stalls** Centre

Form RPR

4001 **1** **Broctune Papa Gio**[18] 5640 7-9-0 67 .................................... JoeDoyle(3) 6 76
(Keith Reveley) *hld up: stdy hdwy over 2f out: swtchd rt and rdn to chse ldrs over 1f out: chal and n.m.r ins fnl f: kpt on wl to ld nr fin* **5/1**[1]

0-00 **2** *½* **Blue Maisey**[18] 5640 6-8-13 63 .................................... ConnorBeasley 5 71
(Edwin Tuer) *hld up towards rr: hdwy over 2f out: swtchd rt and rdn over 1f out: styd on to chal ins fnl f: ev ch whn drvn and edgd lft last 75yds: no ex towards fin* **12/1**

4414 **3** *nk* **Shamaheart (IRE)**[20] 5562 4-9-4 71 ..........................(p) KevinStott(3) 13 78
(Geoffrey Harker) *dwlt and in rr: hdwy 1/2-way: trckd ldrs over 2f out: swtchd lft and effrt to chal wl over 1f out: led appr fnl f and sn rdn: drvn last 100yds: hdd and no ex towards fin* **9/1**

4200 **4** *2 ½* **Patrona Ciana (FR)**[20] 5562 4-9-6 70 ..........................(p) SamJames 7 71
(David O'Meara) *hld up towards rr: hdwy over 2f out: n.m.r and swtchd rt wl over 1f out: sn rdn to chse ldrs: drvn and kpt on fnl f: nrst fin* **20/1**

5630 **5** *nk* **Tanawar (IRE)**[18] 5640 4-8-12 62 ..........................(b) JasonHart 12 62
(Ruth Carr) *led: pushed along wl over 2f out: rdn and wandered wl over 1f out: hdd and drvn appr fnl f: wknd* **14/1**

1210 **6** *¾* **The Dukkerer (IRE)**[24] 5415 3-9-1 69 .................................... IanBrennan 8 65
(Garry Moss) *chsd ldrs: rdn along over 2f out: drvn over 1f out: sn one pce* **10/1**

1130 **7** *1* **Kimbali (IRE)**[38] 4922 5-9-6 75 .................................... LukeLeadbitter(5) 9 70
(Declan Carroll) *trckd ldrs: effrt over 2f out: sn rdn and no imp appr fnl f* **15/2**

0132 **8** *1 ½* **See Clearly**[4] 6121 5-8-6 61 oh4 ......................(p) RachelRichardson(5) 2 52
(Tim Easterby) *prom: cl up 2f out: sn rdn and wknd appr fnl f* **12/1**

200 **9** *2 ¾* **Mitchum**[4] 6122 5-8-8 61 oh7 .................................... ShelleyBirkett(3) 4 45
(Ron Barr) *a towards rr* **66/1**

5060 **10** *1 ¾* **Hab Reeh**[7] 6014 6-8-7 62 .................................... GemmaTutty(5) 14 42
(Ruth Carr) *a towards rr* **33/1**

4016 **11** *hd* **Porthos Du Vallon**[4] 6111 3-8-13 74 ......................(p) JamieGormley(7) 1 51
(Keith Dalgleish) *dwlt: a towards rr* **20/1**

5431 **12** *1* **No Quarter (IRE)**[29] 5244 7-8-9 64 .................................... JordanNason(5) 3 41
(Tracy Waggott) *midfield: rdn along over 2f out: sn wknd* **7/1**[3]

0500 **13** *3 ½* **Circuitous**[24] 5444 6-9-10 74 ..........................(v) JoeyHaynes 10 42
(Keith Dalgleish) *prom: rdn along 3f out: drvn and edgd rt wl over 1f out: sn wknd* **16/1**

3645 **P** **Icy Blue**[22] 5496 6-8-11 61 oh1 ..........................(p) GeorgeChaloner 11
(Richard Whitaker) *chsd ldrs: pushed along 3f out: rdn over 2f out: hld whn hmpd and squeezed out over 1f out: sn p.u and dismntd* **6/1**[2]

1m 24.68s (0.18) **Going Correction** 0.0s/f (Good)
**WFA** 3 from 4yo+ 4lb **14** Ran SP% **116.2**
Speed ratings (Par 103): **98,97,97,94,93 93,91,90,87,85 84,83,79,**
CSF £59.66 CT £541.72 TOTE £4.60: £2.40, £5.20, £3.60; EX 60.70 Trifecta £923.80.
**Owner** D Renton C Alessi D Young Reveley Farms **Bred** Lesley Winn And Reveley Farms **Trained** Lingdale, Redcar & Cleveland

**FOCUS**
A commendable effort by the winner in a race where those held up were favoured.
T/Jkpt: Not won. T/Plt: £9,925.20 to a £1 stake. Pool: £69,068.92 - 5.08 winning tickets. T/Qpdt: £741.70 to a £1 stake. Pool: £6,315.26 - 6.30 winning tickets. JR

# 6055 CHANTILLY (R-H)

Tuesday, September 9

**OFFICIAL GOING: Turf: good to soft; polytrack: standard**

## 6218a PRIX DES TOURELLES (LISTED RACE) (3YO+ FILLIES & MARES) (TURF) 1m 4f

**12:30** (12:00) 3-Y-O+ **£21,666** (£8,666; £6,500; £4,333; £2,166)

RPR

**1** **Quiz Mistress**[19] 5611 6-9-3 0 .................................... IoritzMendizabal 4 106
(Hughie Morrison) *dwlt sltly and hld up towards rr: pushed along 3f out: nt clr run fr over 2f out tl rdn and swtchd lft over 1f out: styd on strly and chal fnl f: led towards fin and asserted: shade cosily* **11/2**[3]

**2** *¾* **Valdiyana (FR)**[44] 3-8-8 0 .................................... ThierryJarnet 2 104
(A De Royer-Dupre, France) **17/5**[2]

**3** *hd* **Shared Account**[24] 5462 4-9-3 0 .................................... ChristopheSoumillon 3 104
(P Bary, France) **6/5**[1]

**4** *6* **Commute**[51] 4484 4-9-3 0 .................................... AlexisBadel 7 94
(D Smaga, France) **127/10**

**5** *¾* **Kyurem (IRE)**[28] 4-9-3 0 .................................... FlavienPrat 5 93
(T Clout, France) **41/1**

**6** *1 ¾* **Rawoof (IRE)**[21] 5534 3-8-8 0 .................................... ChrisCatlin 1 90
(Rae Guest) *sn led: rdn 2f out: strly pressed and hdd over 1f out: no ex and wknd fnl f* **129/10**

**7** *4* **Discrete (FR)**[58] 4249 3-8-9 0 ow1 .................................... Pierre-CharlesBoudot 6 85
(H-F Devin, France) **77/10**

**8** *10* **West Of Venus (USA)**[44] 4722 4-9-3 0 .................................... StephanePasquier 8 68
(J E Pease, France) **115/10**

2m 29.56s (-1.44)
**WFA** 3 from 4yo+ 9lb **8** Ran SP% **119.9**
WIN (incl. 1 euro stake): 6.50. PLACES: 1.40, 1.30, 1.10. DF: 14.30. SF: 35.90.
**Owner** The Fairy Story Partnership **Bred** Deepwood Farm Stud **Trained** East Ilsley, Berks

## 6219a PRIX D'AUMALE (GROUP 3) (2YO FILLIES) (TURF) 1m

**1:05** (12:00) 2-Y-O **£33,333** (£13,333; £10,000; £6,666; £3,333)

RPR

**1** **Shahah**[15] 5746 2-8-9 0 .................................... Pierre-CharlesBoudot 2 105
(A Fabre, France) *dwlt: pushed along to rcvr and sn led: mde rest: kicked on into st: rdn 2f out: 2 l clr ent fnl f: r.o: sltly reduced advantage at fin but in control: readily* **13/2**

**2** *1 ¼* **Night Of Light (IRE)**[32] 2-8-9 0 .................................... StephanePasquier 4 102
(P Bary, France) *restrained and trckd wnr on outer: rdn to try and cl over 2f out: kpt on same pce fr over 1f out: no real imp fnl f and a hld* **17/5**[2]

**3** *1 ¼* **Thank You Bye Bye (FR)**[30] 2-8-9 0 .................................... AntoineHamelin 3 100
(J-P Gauvin, France) *midfield in tch on inner: rdn and swtchd lft 2f out: kpt on and wnt 3rd ins fnl f: nt pce to chal* **152/10**

**4** *½* **Moonee Valley (FR)**[17] 2-8-9 0 .................................... MickaelBarzalona 7 98
(Mario Hofer, Germany) *s.i.s and pushed along in rr: rdn 2f out: kpt on steadily u.p and wnt 4th post: nvr nrr* **124/10**

**5** *shd* **Colonialiste (IRE)**[18] 2-8-9 0 .................................... OlivierPeslier 1 98
(F Head, France) *led early: restrained once hdd and trckd wnr on inner: shuffled bk on rail into st: sn rdn: kpt on same pce and hld fnl 2f: dropped to 5th post* **49/10**[3]

**6** *3* **Al Naamah (IRE)**[78] 2-8-9 0 .................................... FrankieDettori 6 92
(A Fabre, France) *midfield in tch on outer: rdn and nt qckn 2f out: no ex and btn ent fnl f: fdd: eased nring fin* **6/5**[1]

**7** *dist* **Kindly Dismiss (FR)**[17] 5707 2-8-9 0 .................................... FabriceVeron 5
(H-A Pantall, France) *hld up and a towards rr: rdn over 3f out: outpcd in last 2f out: sn btn: wknd and eased: t.o* **126/10**

1m 37.96s (-0.04) **7** Ran SP% **119.5**
WIN (incl. 1 euro stake): 1.70 (Shahah coupled with Al Naamah). PLACES: 9.70, 3.20. SF: 36.30.
**Owner** Al Shaqab Racing **Bred** The Kathryn Stud **Trained** Chantilly, France

## 6220a PRIX D'ARENBERG (GROUP 3) (2YO) (TURF) 5f 110y

**1:35** (12:00) 2-Y-O **£33,333** (£13,333; £10,000; £6,666; £3,333)

RPR

**1** **High Celebrity (FR)**[60] 4164 2-8-8 0 .................................... MaximeGuyon 4 108+
(A Fabre, France) *midfield in tch: rdn and hdwy to chal over 1f out: led jst ins fnl f: r.o strly and asserted: comf* **7/10**[1]

**2** *1 ¾* **City Money (IRE)**[37] 4953 2-8-11 0 .................................... StephanePasquier 2 105
(M Delcher Sanchez, France) *trckd ldr: rdn to chal 2f out: led briefly ent fnl f: sn hdd and outpcd by wnr: kpt on for wl hld 2nd* **37/10**[2]

**3** *shd* **Souvenir Delondres (FR)**[25] 5405 2-8-8 0 Christophe-PatriceLemaire 1 102
(J E Pease, France) *midfield in tch: racd alone against rail fnl 2f: rdn over 1f out: kpt on and wnt 3rd fnl f: nt pce of wnr* **67/10**

**4** *2 ½* **Dikta Del Mar (SPA)**[47] 4603 2-8-8 0 .................................... J-LMartinez 6 94
(T Martins, Spain) *got across fr wdst draw and led: rdn and strly pressed fr 2f out: hdd ent fnl f: sn no ex and btn: wknd* **31/1**

**5** *3* **Kenouska (FR)**[37] 4953 2-8-8 0 .................................... FabriceVeron 5 84
(H-A Pantall, France) *trckd ldr: rdn and brief effrt 2f out: outpcd over 1f out: wknd: eased nring fin* **66/10**[3]

**6** *dist* **Mocklershill (FR)**[37] 4953 2-8-13 0 ow2 .................................... ChristopheSoumillon 3
(F Chappet, France) *hld up and a in rr: rdn and outpcd 2f out: sn lost tch and btn: eased: t.o* **81/10**

1m 3.1s (-1.40) **6** Ran SP% **120.4**
WIN (incl. 1 euro stake): 1.70. PLACES: 1.20, 1.60. SF: 4.70.
**Owner** Ecurie Victoria Dreams **Bred** J P H Dubois **Trained** Chantilly, France

## 6221a PRIX DU BOIS DU TRIANGLE (CLAIMER) (3YO) (POLYTRACK) 1m

**2:05** (12:00) 3-Y-O **£9,583** (£3,833; £2,875; £1,916; £958)

RPR

**1** **Skaters Waltz (IRE)**[18] 5661 3-9-8 0 ..........................(b) CesarPasserat 3 92
(Paul Cole) *bmpd early stages: midfield in tch: swtchd lft and rdn over 2f out: r.o and chal ent fnl f: sn led: asserted under hand ride towards fin: readily* **6/4**[1]

**2** *2* **Darselect**[16] 3-8-11 0 .................................... GaetanFaucon 6 76
(F Vermeulen, France) **18/5**[2]

**3** *3 ½* **Zamuja**[275] 3-9-2 0 .................................... SoufyaneMoulin 1 73
(G Botti, France) **79/10**[3]

**4** *snk* **Bombelli (USA)**[30] 3-9-4 0 .................................... TonyFarina 11 75
(Mme A Fabre, France) **123/10**

**5** *½* **Espoir En Tete (FR)**[16] 3-9-5 0 ..........................(p) NicolasLarenaudie 12 74
(P Adda, France) **182/10**

**6** *1 ½* **Mukaynis (IRE)**[24] 3-8-11 0 .................................... AnthonyCaramanolis 10 63
(G E Mikhalides, France) **29/1**

**7** *1 ¼* **Captain Sun (FR)**[504] 3-8-11 0 .................................... LouisBeuzelin 7 60
(Y-M Porzier, France) **40/1**

**8** *2* **Vehemence D'Amour (FR)**[44] 3-9-2 0 .................................... FabriceNicoleau 13 61
(H-A Pantall, France) **83/10**

**9** *hd* **Get Lucky (FR)**[23] 5482 3-9-1 0 .................................... FreddyDiFede 2 59
(C Lerner, France) **151/10**

**10** *3 ½* **San Benedetto (USA)** 3-9-6 0 .................................... YohannBourgois 9 56
(Gianluca Bietolini, Italy) **201/10**

**11** *3 ½* **Pretty Luna (GER)**[18] 5661 3-9-3 0 .................................... CyrilleStefan 5 45
(Henk Grewe, Germany) **224/10**

**12** *¾* **Green Paradise**[111] 3-8-11 0 ..........................(b[1]) NJeanpierre 4 37
(G E Mikhalides, France) **45/1**

1m 39.1s (99.10) **12** Ran SP% **119.6**
WIN (incl. 1 euro stake): 2.50. PLACES: 1.30, 1.40, 1.70. DF: 5.20. SF: 7.40.
**Owner** Sir George Meyrick **Bred** Patrick A Cluskey **Trained** Whatcombe, Oxon

## 5994 CARLISLE (R-H)

Wednesday, September 10

**OFFICIAL GOING: Good to firm (good in places; 7.4)**

Wind: Almost nil Weather: Sunny

### 6222 BOOK YOUR XMAS PARTY AT CARLISLE RACECOURSE NURSERY H'CAP — 5f 193y

2:20 (2:21) (Class 5) (0-75,71) 2-Y-O — £2,587 (£770; £384; £192) Stalls Low

Form — RPR

1632 **1** **Dream Approval (IRE)**[9] 5974 2-9-4 68 ........ RobertWinston 2 — 74
(Daniel Kubler) *dwlt: hld up: smooth hdwy over 2f out: rdn to ld over 1f out: edgd rt ins fnl f: kpt on wl* 5/2[2]

4542 **2** *2* **Intruder**[17] 5714 2-9-7 71 ........ TonyHamilton 1 — 71
(Richard Fahey) *t.k.h early: cl up: rdn and effrt whn n.m.r and swtchd rt over 1f out: chsd wnr ins fnl f: kpt on: no imp* 2/1[1]

565 **3** *3 ½* **Reassert**[121] 2214 2-8-5 55 ........ DuranFentiman 6 — 44
(Tim Easterby) *hld up: rdn over 2f out: hdwy over 1f out: kpt on ins fnl f: nt gng pce to chal* 10/1

360 **4** *1 ½* **Sweet Missi (IRE)**[27] 5332 2-8-9 59 ........ BenCurtis 7 — 44
(Brian Ellison) *in tch on outside: rdn and outpcd over 2f out: kpt on ins fnl f: no imp* 9/1

554 **5** *nk* **Monksford Lady**[34] 5099 2-8-7 57 ........ PJMcDonald 3 — 41
(Donald McCain) *led: rdn: edgd lft and hdd over 1f out: wknd ins fnl f* 8/1

004 **6** *6* **Maid In Rome (IRE)**[57] 4286 2-8-11 61 ........ AndrewElliott 4 — 30
(Tim Easterby) *prom: drvn and outpcd over 2f out: btn fnl f* 6/1[3]

1560 **7** *6* **Cabbies Lou**[19] 5630 2-8-9 62 ........(v[1]) JoeyHaynes(3) 5 — 9
(Noel Wilson) *pressed ldr: drvn over 2f out: wknd wl over 1f out* 25/1

1m 15.59s (1.89) **Going Correction** +0.20s/f (Good) — **7** Ran SP% **110.2**

Speed ratings (Par 95): **95,92,87,85,85 77,69**

CSF £7.30 TOTE £2.70: £1.20, £2.10; EX 5.50 Trifecta £32.30.

**Owner** Denarius Consulting Ltd **Bred** Myles Sunderland **Trained** Whitsbury, Hants

**FOCUS**

Rail at innermost position and all distances as advertised. After winning this race Robert Winston described the ground as 'good to firm with no jar'. This looked a modest nursery.

### 6223 HAPPY BIRTHDAY JOHN HOUGHTON 80 TODAY H'CAP — 1m 1f 61y

2:50 (2:50) (Class 5) (0-70,70) 3-Y-O+ — £2,587 (£770; £384; £192) Stalls Low

Form — RPR

1331 **1** **Remember Rocky**[14] 5811 5-8-7 58 ........(p) MeganCarberry(5) 10 — 68
(Lucy Normile) *led to over 1f out: rallied to ld ins fnl f: kpt on strly: eased nr fin* 4/1[2]

2505 **2** *2 ½* **Outbacker (IRE)**[36] 4997 3-8-10 62 ........ FrannyNorton 2 — 67
(Mark Johnston) *cl up: lft 2nd after 4f: led over 1f out: sn rdn: hdd ins fnl f: one pce towards fin* 9/1

2411 **3** *½* **Frontline Phantom (IRE)**[22] 5533 7-9-3 70 ........ PeterSword(7) 3 — 74
(K R Burke) *prom: rdn over 2f out: kpt on ins fnl f: nt gng pce to chal* 10/3[1]

3662 **4** *1* **Ferdy (IRE)**[14] 5811 5-8-10 56 ........ RaulDaSilva 1 — 58
(Paul Green) *t.k.h: hld up: hdwy and prom 3f out: effrt and rdn over 1f out: one pce ins fnl f* 5/1[3]

3242 **5** *1 ¼* **Call Of Duty (IRE)**[8] 6000 9-8-7 58 ........ EmmaSayer(5) 4 — 58
(Dianne Sayer) *dwlt: hld up: rdn over 2f out: hdwy and edgd rt over 1f out: no imp ins fnl f* 10/1

4044 **6** *hd* **Royal Straight**[8] 6012 9-8-11 62 ........(t) SammyJoBell(5) 7 — 61
(Linda Perratt) *hld up: hdwy on outside over 2f out: no imp fnl f* 14/1

3502 **7** *2 ¼* **Cloud Monkey (IRE)**[19] 5639 4-9-9 69 ........ PhillipMakin 9 — 64
(Martin Todhunter) *hld up: drvn and outpcd 3f out: n.d after* 11/2

40 **8** *1* **Painted Tail (IRE)**[29] 5270 7-9-0 60 ........ DuranFentiman 6 — 53
(Andrew Crook) *midfield: drvn and outpcd over 4f out: btn fnl 2f* 100/1

5336 **9** *3 ¾* **Lil Sophella (IRE)**[16] 5773 5-8-5 56 ........ JackGarritty(5) 5 — 42+
(Patrick Holmes) *cl up: j. path and lost grnd after 4f: sn rcvrd: rdn and wknd wl over 1f out* 9/1

4004 **10** *2 ¼* **Spokesperson (USA)**[13] 5854 6-8-6 56 oh11 ow3(v) LukeLeadbitter(7) 8 — 41
(Frederick Watson) *hld up: stdy hdwy 3f out: rdn and wknd wl over 1f out* 125/1

1m 58.22s (0.62) **Going Correction** +0.15s/f (Good)

**WFA** 3 from 4yo+ 6lb — **10** Ran SP% **112.7**

Speed ratings (Par 103): **103,100,100,99,98 98,96,95,91,89**

CSF £38.39 CT £130.71 TOTE £5.30: £1.50, £2.60, £1.80; EX 39.50 Trifecta £207.90.

**Owner** Byrne Racing **Bred** Cherry Park Stud **Trained** Duncrievie, Perth & Kinross

**FOCUS**

A modest handicap run at an ordinary gallop and a race in which it proved difficult to make ground from off the pace.

### 6224 BOOKMAKERS.CO.UK MAIDEN FILLIES' STKS (BOBIS RACE) — 6f 192y

3:25 (3:25) (Class 5) 2-Y-O — £2,587 (£770; £384; £192) Stalls Low

Form — RPR

44 **1** **Bright Flash**[19] 5655 2-9-0 0 ........ PJMcDonald 7 — 76+
(David Brown) *in tch on outside: hdwy over 3f out: led and edgd rt over 1f out: drvn clr fnl f* 8/13[1]

4 **2** *3 ¾* **Midnite Ride (IRE)**[14] 5807 2-9-0 0 ........ TonyHamilton 4 — 66+
(Richard Fahey) *t.k.h: trckd ldrs: effrt and rdn 2f out: chsd wnr ins fnl f: kpt on* 7/2[2]

04 **3** *¾* **Bobbie's Girl (IRE)**[14] 5821 2-9-0 0 ........ GrahamGibbons 3 — 64
(William Haggas) *led: rdn and hdd over 1f out: one pce ins fnl f* 11/2[3]

**4** *½* **Triple Dip (IRE)** 2-9-0 0 ........ FrannyNorton 5 — 63
(Mark Johnston) *cl up: drvn along 3f out: rallied: kpt on same pce ins fnl f* 14/1

065 **5** *14* **Oricano**[18] 5679 2-8-9 53 ........ GemmaTutty(5) 6 — 25
(Karen Tutty) *dwlt: t.k.h: in tch: struggling over 3f out: sn btn* 33/1

1m 28.93s (1.83) **Going Correction** +0.15s/f (Good) — **5** Ran SP% **109.1**

Speed ratings (Par 92): **95,90,89,89,73**

CSF £2.98 TOTE £1.40: £1.10, £1.50; EX 3.20 Trifecta £4.70.

**Owner** J C Fretwell **Bred** Lady Legard **Trained** Averham Park, Notts

**FOCUS**

A race lacking depth with the four non-runners.

### 6225 BRITISH STALLION STUDS EBF MAIDEN STKS — 7f 200y

4:00 (4:01) (Class 5) 2-Y-O — £3,067 (£905; £453) Stalls Low

Form — RPR

62 **1** **Jolievitesse (FR)**[26] 5386 2-9-5 0 ........ DanielTudhope 2 — 92+
(K R Burke) *trckd ldrs: pushed along over 3f out: led 2f out: sn qcknd clr: eased ins fnl f* 13/8[2]

536 **2** *5* **Dominada (IRE)**[21] 5576 2-9-5 85 ........ PJMcDonald 5 — 73
(Brian Ellison) *chsd ldrs: drvn along 3f out: wnt 2nd over 1f out: kpt on: nt rch eased-down wnr* 1/1[1]

5033 **3** *2 ½* **Kifaaya**[15] 5782 2-9-5 70 ........ JoeFanning 3 — 67
(Mark Johnston) *dwlt: hdwy to chse ldr after 3f: rdn along over 2f out: one pce fr over 1f out* 9/2[3]

0 **4** *4* **Sir Lancelott**[32] 5167 2-9-5 0 ........ TomEaves 1 — 57
(Keith Dalgleish) *unruly in preliminaries: led to 2f out: sn rdn and outpcd* 50/1

**5** *31* **Mister Archie** 2-9-0 0 ........ GarryWhillans(5) 6
(Alistair Whillans) *s.i.s: rn green in rr: lost tch after 2f: t.o* 66/1

1m 41.67s (1.67) **Going Correction** +0.15s/f (Good) — **5** Ran SP% **109.7**

Speed ratings (Par 95): **97,92,89,85,54**

CSF £3.56 TOTE £2.30: £1.10, £1.10; EX 3.90 Trifecta £5.50.

**Owner** Owners For Owners: Jolievitesse **Bred** Pontchartrain Stud **Trained** Middleham Moor, N Yorks

**FOCUS**

A race short on numbers, but nevertheless a very useful display from the progressive winner who scored with plenty in hand. The gallop was only fair.

### 6226 COMLONGON CASTLE H'CAP — 7f 200y

4:35 (4:35) (Class 3) (0-95,95) 3-Y-O+ — £8,086 (£2,406; £1,202; £601) Stalls Low

Form — RPR

0130 **1** **Big Johnny D (IRE)**[11] 5919 5-9-7 92 ........ GrahamGibbons 1 — 102
(David Barron) *trckd ldrs: effrt and edgd lft over 1f out: led wl ins fnl f: kpt on* 8/1

2252 **2** *¾* **Bold Prediction (IRE)**[16] 5771 4-9-2 90 ........ JoeyHaynes(3) 4 — 98
(K R Burke) *led: rdn over 2f out: faltered and hdd wl ins fnl f: kpt on same pce nr fin* 9/2[3]

5411 **3** *1 ¾* **Bartack (IRE)**[16] 5771 4-9-10 95 ........(v) DanielTudhope 5 — 99
(David O'Meara) *t.k.h: pressed ldr: drvn over 2f out: edgd lft over 1f out: kpt on ins fnl f* 5/2[1]

0005 **4** *¾* **Burano (IRE)**[54] 4400 5-9-6 91 ........(p) StevieDonohoe 8 — 93
(Brian Meehan) *sn prom on outside: drvn along over 2f out: kpt on ins fnl f* 7/2[2]

6540 **5** *2* **King Torus (IRE)**[11] 5919 6-9-2 92 ........ JackGarritty(5) 6 — 89
(Ruth Carr) *in tch: hdwy on outside over 2f out: edgd rt over 1f out: kpt on same pce* 11/2

1U62 **6** *1 ¼* **Border Bandit (USA)**[18] 5681 6-8-13 84 ........(p) RobertWinston 7 — 78
(Tracy Waggott) *hld up: rdn over 2f out: no imp fr over 1f out* 9/1

3100 **7** *2 ¾* **Shahdaroba (IRE)**[46] 4681 4-9-1 86 ........(p) PJMcDonald 3 — 74
(Micky Hammond) *hld up in tch: rdn over 4f out: outpcd fnl 2f* 50/1

3010 **8** *3 ¼* **Silver Rime (FR)**[18] 5695 9-9-1 89 ........ ConnorBeasley(3) 2 — 69
(Linda Perratt) *s.i.s: hld up: rdn along over 2f out: sn btn* 25/1

1m 39.85s (-0.15) **Going Correction** +0.15s/f (Good) — **8** Ran SP% **111.3**

Speed ratings (Par 107): **106,105,103,102,100 99,96,93**

CSF £41.37 CT £114.00 TOTE £11.90: £4.90, £2.50, £1.10; EX 41.10 Trifecta £123.70.

**Owner** Clive Washbourn **Bred** David McGuinness **Trained** Maunby, N Yorks

**FOCUS**

A competitive handicap run at a fair gallop and the form should prove sound.

### 6227 BET & WATCH WITH RACING UK'S APP H'CAP — 7f 200y

5:05 (5:05) (Class 5) (0-70,69) 3-Y-O+ — £2,726 (£805; £402) Stalls Low

Form — RPR

3063 **1** **Tectonic (IRE)**[8] 6009 5-9-6 65 ........(p) PhillipMakin 1 — 74
(Keith Dalgleish) *hld up on ins: hdwy and prom whn nt clr run appr fnl f: kpt on wl to ld nr fin* 11/2[3]

050- **2** *shd* **Venutius**[296] 7950 7-9-8 67 ........ GrahamGibbons 7 — 75
(Ed McMahon) *led: rdn over 2f out: edgd lft over 1f out: kpt on fnl f: hdd nr fin* 14/1

420 **3** *1* **Mount Cheiron (USA)**[14] 5811 3-8-6 56 ........ PJMcDonald 4 — 61
(Dianne Sayer) *midfield: drvn over 3f out: rallied 2f out: ev ch ins fnl f: hld nr fin* 14/1

3103 **4** *2* **Staffhoss**[29] 5267 4-9-3 62 ........ FrannyNorton 2 — 63
(Mark Johnston) *prom: drvn along over 2f out: effrt over 1f out: kpt on same pce ins fnl f* 6/1

0201 **5** *2 ½* **Suni Dancer**[14] 5809 3-8-8 58 ........ JoeFanning 10 — 52
(Paul Green) *t.k.h: hld up: rdn and hdwy wl over 1f out: no imp fnl f* 5/1[2]

0645 **6** *1 ½* **Prophesy (IRE)**[25] 5421 5-9-7 66 ........(p) DuranFentiman 6 — 57
(Tim Easterby) *midfield: drvn along over 2f out: sn no imp* 9/2[1]

2565 **7** *¾* **Running Reef (IRE)**[15] 5793 5-9-0 59 ........ RobertWinston 5 — 48
(Tracy Waggott) *hld up: rdn over 2f out: hdwy over 1f out: nvr able to chal* 11/2[3]

0600 **8** *5* **Mercers Row**[20] 5605 7-9-5 69 ........ GemmaTutty(5) 3 — 46
(Karen Tutty) *hld up: rdn along over 2f out: btn over 1f out* 12/1

0662 **9** *½* **Baltic Prince (IRE)**[15] 5797 4-8-10 55 oh2 ........ RaulDaSilva 9 — 31
(Paul Green) *cl up tl rdn and wknd over 1f out* 9/1

4-00 **10** *12* **Conjuror's Bluff**[44] 4730 6-8-6 58 oh10 ow3 ........(p) LukeLeadbitter(7) 8 — 5
(Frederick Watson) *chsd ldrs tl rdn and wknd fr 2f out* 100/1

1m 41.12s (1.12) **Going Correction** +0.15s/f (Good)

**WFA** 3 from 4yo+ 5lb — **10** Ran SP% **111.9**

Speed ratings (Par 103): **100,99,98,96,94 92,92,87,86,74**

CSF £75.89 CT £1034.23 TOTE £6.10: £1.90, £4.50, £5.30; EX 75.30 Trifecta £743.60.

**Owner** Mrs L A Ogilvie **Bred** W Maxwell Ervine **Trained** Carluke, S Lanarks

**FOCUS**

A modest handicap in which the gallop was sound throughout.

### 6228 RACINGUK.COM H'CAP — 1m 6f 32y

5:35 (5:35) (Class 3) (0-90,83) 3-Y-O+ — £8,086 (£2,406; £1,202; £601) Stalls Low

Form — RPR

0335 **1** **Ebony Express**[12] 5890 5-9-7 76 ........ BenCurtis 5 — 84
(Alan Swinbank) *in tch: hdwy to ld over 1f out: drvn out fnl f* 11/4[1]

6040 **2** *1 ½* **Number One London (IRE)**[21] 5579 4-9-11 80 ........(p) StevieDonohoe 3 — 86
(Brian Meehan) *sn led: rdn over 2f out: hdd over 1f out: rallied: kpt on same pce ins fnl f* 13/2[3]

2052 **3** *3 ½* **Sir Frank Morgan (IRE)**[14] 5825 4-10-0 83 ........ JoeFanning 7 — 84
(Mark Johnston) *early ldr: pressed ldr: drvn 3f out: kpt on same pce fr over 1f out* 11/4[1]

4 **4** *nse* **Bell Weir**[16] 5456 6-9-1 75 ........ EmmaSayer(5) 1 — 76
(Dianne Sayer) *dwlt: bhd and outpcd: hdwy on ins 2f out: kpt on fnl f: no imp* 12/1

2052 **5** *1 ½* **O Ma Lad (IRE)**[34] 5083 6-9-7 81 ........ JoeDoyle(5) 6 — 80
(John Quinn) *hld up in tch: effrt and rdn over 2f out: no imp over 1f out* 7/2[2]

3561 **6** *2 1/4* **Miss Macnamara (IRE)**[14] 5815 5-9-3 72........................ PhillipMakin 2 69
(Martin Todhunter) *t.k.h: chsd ldrs tl rdn and wknd over 1f out* **7/1**

3m 6.96s (-0.54) **Going Correction** +0.15s/f (Good)
**WFA** 3 from 4yo+ 11lb **6** Ran SP% **109.1**
Speed ratings (Par 107): **107,106,104,104,103 101**
CSF £19.41 TOTE £3.90: £3.10, £2.70; EX 15.60 Trifecta £73.10.
**Owner** Mrs T Blackett **Bred** Miss E J Wright **Trained** Melsonby, N Yorks

**FOCUS**
A strongly run staying handicap.
T/Plt: £26.40 to a £1 stake. Pool: £46,933.87 - 1,295.55 winning tickets T/Qpdt: £12.10 to a £1 stake. Pool: £3,123.00 - 189.61 winning tickets RY

# 5415 DONCASTER (L-H)
Wednesday, September 10

**OFFICIAL GOING: Round course - good to soft (good in places); straight course - good (good to soft in places; 6.9)**
Wind: Virtually nil Weather: Cloudy with sunny periods

## 6229 1STSECURITYSOLUTIONS.CO.UK NURSERY H'CAP (BOBIS RACE) 7f
**2:00** (2:00) (Class 2) 2-Y-O **£9,703** (£2,887; £1,443; £721) **Stalls** High

Form RPR
3215 **1** **Salateen**[21] 5576 2-9-7 92........................ JamieSpencer 2 98+
(Kevin Ryan) *overall ldr centre: shkn up and qcknd over 1f out: rdn clr ent fnl f: kpt on strly* **9/4**[1]
6303 **2** *1 1/4* **Goring (GER)**[29] 5271 2-8-4 75........................ PaulHanagan 3 75
(Eve Johnson Houghton) *trckd wnr centre: rdn along wl over 1f out: drvn and kpt on same pce fnl f: 2nd of 3 in gp* **12/1**
1142 **3** *shd* **When Will It End (IRE)**[28] 5310 2-9-0 85........................ RyanMoore 1 85
(Richard Hannon) *trckd ldng pair centre: hdwy wl over 1f out: rdn ent fnl f: kpt on same pce: 3rd of 3 in gp* **5/1**[3]
031 **4** *3 3/4* **Grey Sensation (IRE)**[16] 5759 2-8-7 78........................ SeanLevey 7 68+
(K R Burke) *hld up nr stands' rail: hdwy wl over 1f out: rdn appr fnl f: sn no imp: 1st of 4 in gp* **17/2**
1434 **5** *hd* **Percy Alleline**[46] 4670 2-9-5 90........................(p) SilvestreDeSousa 6 79+
(Ralph Beckett) *trckd ldrs stands' side: pushed along 1/2-way: rdn and outpcd over 2f out: kpt on u.p appr fnl f: n.d: 2nd of 4 in gp* **9/1**
0615 **6** *1 3/4* **Stardrifter**[16] 5762 2-8-0 71 oh1........................ PatrickMathers 4 55+
(Richard Fahey) *trckd ldr stands' side: pushed along 2f out: sn rdn and wknd: 3rd of 4 in gp* **16/1**
351 **7** *1* **Only Joking**[30] 5241 2-8-7 78........................ WilliamBuick 5 60+
(Hugo Palmer) *led stands' side gp: rdn along over 2f out: sn wknd: 4th of 4 in gp* **5/2**[2]

1m 25.34s (-0.96) **Going Correction** -0.225s/f (Firm) **7** Ran SP% **110.1**
Speed ratings (Par 101): **96,94,94,90,89 87,86**
CSF £26.90 TOTE £2.20: £1.10, £5.30; EX 25.60 Trifecta £125.80.
**Owner** Sheikh Abdullah Almalek Alsabah **Bred** Mrs Janis Macpherson **Trained** Hambleton, N Yorks

**FOCUS**
A decent nursery to start with, but the field split early with the larger group of four staying towards the nearside rail, while three came up the centre, and that trio filled the first three places.

## 6230 IRISH STALLION FARMS EBF CONDITIONS STKS (BOBIS RACE) 6f
**2:30** (2:30) (Class 2) 2-Y-O **£12,450** (£3,728; £1,864; £932) **Stalls** High

Form RPR
165 **1** **Angelic Lord (IRE)**[62] 4123 2-8-13 106........................ RichardKingscote 2 101+
(Tom Dascombe) *trckd ldr on outer: hdwy 2f out: rdn to ld and hung bdly rt over 1f out and again ent fnl f: styd on* **4/6**[1]
6412 **2** *1 3/4* **Markaz (IRE)**[40] 4853 2-8-13 89........................ PaulHanagan 5 97
(B W Hills) *trckd ldr: hdwy and cl up whn hmpd over 1f out: rdn whn sltly hmpd again and swtchd lft ent fnl f: kpt on same pce* **5/2**[2]
0213 **3** *1 1/2* **Fuwairt (IRE)**[32] 5173 2-8-11 90........................ FrankieDettori 4 90
(Richard Hannon) *hld up: hdwy 2f out: cl up whn hmpd over 1f out: rdn and one pce after* **9/1**[3]
0024 **4** *2 1/4* **Prince Bonnaire**[16] 5770 2-8-11 92........................ GrahamLee 1 85
(David Brown) *led: rdn along over 2f out: hdd wl over 1f out: sn hmpd and wknd after* **11/1**

1m 11.87s (-1.73) **Going Correction** -0.225s/f (Firm) **4** Ran SP% **106.9**
Speed ratings (Par 101): **102,99,97,94**
CSF £2.49 TOTE £1.50; EX 2.30 Trifecta £5.30.
**Owner** The Mad March Hares **Bred** Joe Fogarty **Trained** Malpas, Cheshire

**FOCUS**
A small-field conditions event in which the four runners raced up the middle and were in a line coming to the last furlong. There was no shortage of drama.

## 6231 JOHN SMITH'S ORIGINAL SCARBROUGH STKS (LISTED RACE) 5f
**3:00** (3:00) (Class 1) 2-Y-O+ **£23,680** (£8,956; £4,476; £2,236) **Stalls** High

Form RPR
115 **1** **Mecca's Angel (IRE)**[121] 2226 3-9-5 106........................ PaulMulrennan 2 113
(Michael Dods) *cl up: led wl over 1f out: rdn and qcknd clr ent fnl f: kpt on strly* **7/1**
55-3 **2** *2 1/4* **Reckless Abandon**[18] 5674 4-9-11 113........................ AdamKirby 4 110
(Charlie Appleby) *trckd ldrs: hdwy over 2f out: rdn whn n.m.r and edgd lft 1f out: sn drvn to chse wnr: no imp* **15/8**[1]
4650 **3** *hd* **Steps (IRE)**[19] 5654 6-10-0 110........................(b) AndreaAtzeni 5 112
(Roger Varian) *in tch: hdwy 2f out: swtchd rt and rdn over 1f out: styd on wl fnl f* **6/1**[2]
-140 **4** *hd* **Demora**[40] 4852 5-9-6 102........................ AndrewMullen 8 104
(Michael Appleby) *cl up: rdn along 2f out: drvn and edgd lft 1f out: kpt on same pce* **9/1**
1055 **5** *1 1/4* **Swan Song**[32] 5160 5-9-6 99........................ DavidProbert 6 99
(Andrew Balding) *qckly away: led: rdn along 2f out: hdd wl over 1f out: sn drvn and wknd fnl f* **25/1**
4211 **6** *shd* **Online Alexander (IRE)**[18] 5696 3-9-5 99........................ JamieSpencer 3 99
(Kevin Ryan) *dwlt: hdwy 1/2-way: rdn to chse ldrs over 1f out: drvn ent fnl f: grad wknd* **13/2**[3]
3000 **7** *hd* **Monsieur Joe (IRE)**[19] 5654 7-9-11 103........................ GrahamLee 11 103
(Paul Midgley) *towards rr: effrt and sme hdwy over 2f out: sn rdn and n.d* **20/1**
0100 **8** *1 1/2* **Gladiatrix**[25] 5419 5-9-6 89........................ RobertHavlin 1 93
(Rod Millman) *chsd ldrs on outer: rdn along 1/2-way: sn wknd* **100/1**
2404 **9** *2 3/4* **Kingsgate Native (IRE)**[11] 5911 9-9-11 107........................ RyanMoore 9 88
(Robert Cowell) *tardy s: sn rdn along: a in rr* **9/1**
1031 **10** *1* **B Fifty Two (IRE)**[11] 5918 5-9-11 103........................(bt) FrankieDettori 7 84
(Charles Hills) *chsd ldrs: rdn along 2f out: grad wknd* **17/2**
-010 **11** *1 3/4* **Noble Storm (USA)**[102] 2766 8-9-11 105........................ JasonHart 10 78
(Ed McMahon) *a towards rr* **50/1**

57.73s (-2.77) **Going Correction** -0.225s/f (Firm)
**WFA** 3 from 4yo+ 1lb **11** Ran SP% **117.0**
Speed ratings: **113,109,109,108,106 106,106,103,99,97 95**
CSF £19.77 TOTE £6.50: £2.10, £1.40, £2.20; EX 24.70 Trifecta £141.70.
**Owner** David T J Metcalfe **Bred** Yeomanstown Stud & Doc Bloodstock **Trained** Denton, Co Durham

**FOCUS**
A decent Listed sprint, won by the likes of Majestic Missile and Sole Power in the previous ten runnings. The field raced up the centre and, with there being no hanging about, the form looks solid. The 3yo generation had a poor record in this race in recent years, but the winner put that right this time.

## 6232 CLIPPER LOGISTICS LEGER LEGENDS CLASSIFIED STKS 1m (S)
**3:35** (3:36) (Class 5) 3-Y-O+ **£6,469** (£1,925; £962; £481) **Stalls** High

Form RPR
0035 **1** **Bob**[91] 3094 4-11-0 70........................ DaleGibson 2 77
(Les Eyre) *midfield: hdwy 3f out: chsd ldrs 2f out: rdn to chal ent fnl f: styd on to ld last 100yds* **8/1**[3]
2401 **2** *nk* **Janaab (IRE)**[15] 5793 4-11-0 66........................(t) KellyHarrison 16 76
(Tim Easterby) *cl up: led over 3f out: rdn wl over 1f out: jnd an drvn ent fnl f: hdd and no ex last 100yds* **22/1**
5122 **3** *1 1/2* **Dansili Dutch (IRE)**[19] 5640 5-11-0 69........................ MichaelHills 17 73
(David O'Meara) *hld up in midfield: hdwy over 2f out: swtchd rt and rdn over 1f out: styd on wl fnl f: nrst fin* **7/1**[2]
4414 **4** *3/4* **Tiger Jim**[16] 5766 4-11-0 70........................ GeorgeDuffield 7 71
(Jim Goldie) *trckd ldrs: hdwy 3f out: rdn wl over 1f out: drvn ent fnl f: kpt on same pce* **11/4**[1]
5332 **5** *1 1/2* **Cliff (IRE)**[25] 5415 4-11-0 70........................(v) WNewnes 1 68
(Nigel Tinkler) *t.k.h: swtchd rt s and hld up towards rr: hdwy over 3f out: chsd ldrs 2f out: sn rdn and one pce appr fnl f* **12/1**
0211 **6** *1 1/4* **Mixed Message (IRE)**[15] 5788 4-11-0 67........................ WillieSupple 3 65
(Brian Ellison) *chsd ldrs on outer: rdn along over 2f out: kpt on same pce* **11/1**
4113 **7** *1* **Kuwait Star**[37] 4963 5-11-0 70........................ JimmyMcCarthy 14 63
(Michael Herrington) *chsd ldrs: rdn along over 2f out: drvn and one pce fr over 1f out* **12/1**
0466 **8** *1/2* **Patriotic (IRE)**[22] 5533 6-11-0 69........................(p) JCulloty 13 64+
(Chris Dwyer) *in rr: swtchd lft and hdwy over 3f out: rdn over 2f out: styng on whn n.m.r and swtchd rt ent fnl f: kpt on: nrst fin* **22/1**
1423 **9** *3/4* **Comanchero (IRE)**[31] 5206 3-10-9 69........................ KevinDarley 11 59
(Andrew Balding) *towards rr: hdwy over 2f out: sn rdn and kpt on fnl f: nrst fin* **10/1**
3114 **10** *6* **Clumber Place**[25] 5415 8-11-0 67........................ WillieRyan 18 46
(Shaun Harris) *led: pushed along and hdd over 3f out: rdn over 2f out: wknd* **40/1**
/320 **11** *1 1/2* **Naoise (IRE)**[35] 5054 6-11-0 70........................(t) OlliePears 15 43
(Ollie Pears) *dwlt and hld up in rr: hdwy 3f out: swtchd rt to stands' rail 2f out: sn rdn to chse ldrs over 1f out: sn drvn and wknd* **16/1**
1221 **12** *1/2* **Gambino (IRE)**[21] 5562 4-11-0 68........................(p) LukeHarvey 8 41
(John David Riches) *t.k.h: prom: cl up 1/2-way: rdn along over 2f out: grad wknd* **14/1**
60-0 **13** *1/2* **Chiswick Bey (IRE)**[32] 5197 6-11-0 68........................(t) GaryBardwell 4 40
(Richard Fahey) *towards rr: swtchd rt to stands' rail 1/2-way: rdn along 3f out: n.d* **33/1**
5040 **14** *1 1/4* **Sakhalin Star (IRE)**[11] 5915 3-10-9 70........................ RodneyLappin 9 36
(Richard Guest) *midfield: hdwy over 3f out: rdn to chse ldrs over 2f out: sn wknd* **33/1**
6366 **15** *12* **Harry Bosch**[14] 5834 4-11-0 70........................(p) GayKelleway 5 10
(Gay Kelleway) *chsd ldrs: rdn along wl over 2f out: sn wknd* **25/1**
2125 **16** *6* **Grace Hull**[19] 5640 4-11-0 68........................(p) CarlLlewellyn 12
(Garry Moss) *a towards rr* **20/1**

1m 39.17s (-0.13) **Going Correction** -0.225s/f (Firm)
**WFA** 3 from 4yo+ 5lb **16** Ran SP% **121.3**
Speed ratings (Par 103): **91,90,89,88,86 85,84,84,83,77 75,75,74,73,61 55**
CSF £177.71 TOTE £10.00: £3.00, £6.40, £2.60; EX 259.90 Trifecta £4410.20 Part won..
**Owner** GIB Bloodstock Limited **Bred** Lady Green **Trained** Catton, North Yorkshire

**FOCUS**
The fifth running of this unique event and a chance to admire some individual riding styles from yesteryear. The runners came centre to nearside.

## 6233 PARK HILL HOSPITAL CONDITIONS STKS 1m 2f 60y
**4:10** (4:10) (Class 2) 3-5-Y-O
**£12,450** (£3,728; £1,864; £932; £466; £234) **Stalls** Low

Form RPR
4313 **1** **Clon Brulee (IRE)**[11] 5928 5-9-2 107........................ RyanMoore 2 108+
(Saeed bin Suroor) *trckd ldrs: hdwy over 2f out: rdn to ld over 1f out: drvn ins fnl f: jst hld on* **6/5**[1]
6500 **2** *nk* **Red Galileo**[21] 5577 3-8-9 106........................ AndreaAtzeni 4 107
(Ed Dunlop) *hld up in rr: hdwy 2f out: rdn along on outer over 1f out: styd on strly ins fnl f: jst failed* **10/1**
06/5 **3** *1* **Bayrir (FR)**[18] 5687 5-9-8 107........................ MartinHarley 6 112
(Marco Botti) *hld up: smooth hdwy 3f out: swtchd rt and effrt wl over 1f out: rdn to chse wnr ins fnl f: sn drvn and kpt on same pce towards fin* **28/1**
3364 **4** *nk* **Nabucco**[25] 5461 5-9-2 109........................ WilliamBuick 1 105
(John Gosden) *trckd ldng pair: hdwy over 2f out: chsd wnr appr fnl f: sn rdn and kpt on same pce ins fnl f* **2/1**[2]
1130 **5** *3* **Magic Hurricane (IRE)**[43] 4756 4-9-2 96........................ FrederikTylicki 3 99
(James Fanshawe) *trckd ldng pair on inner: pushed along over 2f out: rdn wl over 1f out: sn drvn and one pce* **8/1**[3]
0-50 **6** *1 1/2* **Cap O'Rushes**[102] 2785 4-9-2 104........................ SilvestreDeSousa 5 96
(Charlie Appleby) *led: rdn along over 2f out: hdd over 1f out: wknd* **14/1**

2m 12.06s (2.66) **Going Correction** +0.25s/f (Good)
**WFA** 3 from 4yo+ 7lb **6** Ran SP% **109.1**
Speed ratings (Par 109): **99,98,97,97,95 94**
CSF £13.21 TOTE £1.80: £1.10, £3.50; EX 11.00 Trifecta £62.70.
**Owner** Godolphin **Bred** Collette Twomey **Trained** Newmarket, Suffolk


The Form Book, Raceform Ltd, Newbury, RG14 5SJ

**FOCUS**
A good-quality conditions event, but they went no pace and it developed into a 3f sprint.

## 6234 ROMERO INSURANCE BROKERS LTD H'CAP (BOBIS RACE) 7f
4:45 (4:47) (Class 2) (0-100,98) 3-Y-O
£12,450 (£3,728; £1,864; £932; £466; £234) Stalls High

Form RPR
3224 1 **Lincoln (IRE)**[25] 5410 3-8-11 88 GrahamLee 2 96
(Mick Channon) *trckd ldrs: hdwy over 2f out: rdn to chse ldr jst over 1f out: drvn to ld last 100yds: hld on wl towards fin* 13/2[3]
4505 2 ½ **Sir Robert Cheval**[32] 5165 3-9-1 92 MartinHarley 7 99+
(Marco Botti) *in tch: effrt over 2f out and sn rdn: styd on strly ins fnl f: jst failed* 12/1
0005 3 ½ **Nezar (IRE)**[19] 5649 3-8-8 85 (v[1]) AndreaAtzeni 5 90
(George Margarson) *sn led: rdn clr over 1f out: drvn and egded lft ins fnl f: hdd and no ex last 100yds* 28/1
5604 4 *nk* **Expert (IRE)**[27] 5348 3-9-6 97 RyanMoore 11 101
(Richard Hannon) *hld up towards rr: hdwy over 2f out: rdn wl over 1f out: styd on wl fnl f: nrst fin* 15/2
1213 5 *nk* **Wilde Inspiration (IRE)**[25] 5410 3-8-8 85 PaulMulrennan 6 89
(Julie Camacho) *chsd ldng pair: rdn along 2f out: drvn over 1f out: kpt on same pce fnl f* 11/2[2]
3406 6 ½ **Azagal (IRE)**[5] 6112 3-8-13 90 DavidAllan 4 92
(Tim Easterby) *hld up: hdwy on outer wl over 2f out: sn rdn and kpt on fnl f: nrst fin* 12/1
010 7 ½ **Nakuti (IRE)**[41] 4826 3-8-11 88 JimmyFortune 8 89
(Sylvester Kirk) *towards rr: hdwy over 2f out: rdn wl over 1f out: kpt on fnl f: nrst fin* 20/1
0535 8 ½ **Suzi's Connoisseur**[25] 5438 3-9-7 98 (p) WilliamBuick 10 98
(Hugo Palmer) *towards rr: pushed along over 2f out: rdn wl over 1f out: kpt on fnl f: nrst fin* 9/2[1]
2213 9 1¼ **Basil Berry**[18] 5675 3-8-13 90 SilvestreDeSousa 3 86
(Chris Dwyer) *chsd ldr: rdn along over 2f out: drvn wl over 1f out: wknd fnl f* 8/1
2141 10 1¾ **Marmoom**[19] 5649 3-8-9 86 PaulHanagan 9 78
(Charles Hills) *chsd ldrs: rdn along 2f out: drvn and wknd apprh fnl f* 9/2[1]
11- 11 12 **Evening Attire**[368] 6197 3-9-1 92 SeanLevey 12 51+
(William Stone) *a towards rr* 33/1
1m 24.56s (-1.74) **Going Correction** -0.225s/f (Firm) 11 Ran SP% 114.5
Speed ratings (Par 107): **100,99,98,98,98 97,97,96,95,93 79**
CSF £77.30 CT £2055.27 TOTE £7.50: £2.60, £3.70, £6.80; EX 94.30 Trifecta £4119.00 Part won..
**Owner** Billy Parish **Bred** Tipper House Stud **Trained** West Ilsley, Berks

**FOCUS**
A decent 3yo handicap in which they all raced up the middle. The early pace was steady, but soon quickened up after a couple of furlongs thanks to the third horse.

## 6235 MAGICAL MOMENTS ON CANVAS H'CAP 5f
5:15 (5:19) (Class 4) (0-85,84) 3-Y-O+ £6,469 (£1,925; £962; £481) Stalls High

Form RPR
0305 1 **Expose**[14] 5830 6-8-8 76 JordanNason(5) 4 88
(Shaun Harris) *hld up: hdwy on outer wl over 1f out: rdn ent fnl f: led last 100yds: hld on wl towards fin* 25/1
-002 2 ½ **Pea Shooter**[11] 5912 5-9-0 77 AdrianNicholls 10 87
(David Nicholls) *in tch: hdwy 2f out: effrt and nt clr run ent fnl f: sn rdn and squeezed through last 100yds: fin strly: jst hld* 9/1
0504 3 *shd* **Singeur (IRE)**[21] 5563 7-9-4 81 PaulMulrennan 2 90
(Robin Bastiman) *racd wd: a.p: effrt wl over 1f out: rdn and ev ch ins fnl f: drvn and nt qckn towards fin* 8/1[3]
0620 4 *shd* **Adam's Ale**[12] 5888 5-9-4 81 PaulHanagan 21 92
(Paul Midgley) *racd nr stands' rail: hld up in rr: gd hdwy wl over 1f out: chsd ldrs and nt clr run 1f out: swtchd rt and rdn ins fnl f: fin wl* 7/1[2]
0240 5 1 **Sleepy Blue Ocean**[5] 6096 8-8-6 74 (p) ShaneGray(5) 19 79
(John Balding) *racd nr stands' rail: trckd ldrs: hdwy over 1f out: rdn ent fnl f and ev ch tl drvn and nt qckn towards fin* 16/1
4050 6 *nse* **Imperial Legend (IRE)**[21] 5563 5-9-3 80 (p) AndrewMullen 3 85
(David Nicholls) *racd wd: trckd ldrs: effrt wl over 1f out: rdn to ld jst ins fnl f: hdd and no ex last 100yds* 16/1
0040 7 1 **Hazelrigg (IRE)**[4] 6150 9-8-8 71 DavidAllan 15 73
(Tim Easterby) *racd towards stands' rail: in tch: hdwy to chse ldrs wl over 1f out: rdn and n.m.r jst ins fnl f: kpt on towards fin* 14/1
020 8 *hd* **Ambitious Icarus**[11] 5913 5-8-9 72 (e) PatrickMathers 6 73
(Richard Guest) *towards rr: hdwy on outer wl over 1f out: rdn and styd on fnl f: nrst fin* 33/1
1350 9 *nk* **Mutafaakir (IRE)**[21] 5563 5-9-3 80 (b) DaleSwift 17 80
(Ruth Carr) *racd towards stands' rail: cl up: rdn wl over 1f out: drvn appr fnl f: one pce* 20/1
2050 10 *nk* **Red Baron (IRE)**[5] 6096 5-9-4 84 NeilFarley(3) 20 83
(Eric Alston) *cl up nr stands' rail: rdn to ld briefly jst over 1f out: drvn and hdd jst ins fnl f: wknd* 25/1
0042 11 *hd* **Commanche**[17] 5726 5-8-10 73 SilvestreDeSousa 11 71
(Chris Dwyer) *towards rr: hdwy in centre 2f out: rdn over 1f out: no imp fnl f* 10/1
3460 12 ¾ **Bondi Beach Boy**[61] 4174 5-8-9 75 GeorgeChaloner(3) 16 70
(James Turner) *racd towards stands' rail: chsd ldrs: rdn over 1f out: wknd ins fnl f* 14/1
0001 13 *nk* **Oldjoesaid**[11] 5912 10-8-13 76 GrahamLee 8 70
(Paul Midgley) *dwlt: a in rr* 20/1
0005 14 1 **Go Nani Go**[27] 5350 8-9-2 82 DeclanBates(3) 14 73
(Ed de Giles) *chsd ldrs: rdn along over 2f out: sn drvn and wknd over 1f out* 25/1
-004 15 *nk* **Pull The Plug (IRE)**[67] 3957 3-8-13 77 JimmyFortune 1 67
(Declan Carroll) *in tch on wd outside: rdn along over 2f out: grad wknd* 33/1
0004 16 ¾ **Lastchancelucas**[39] 4925 4-9-0 77 JasonHart 13 64
(Declan Carroll) *chsd ldrs: rdn along over 2f out: drvn wl over 1f out: grad wknd* 20/1
22 17 *hd* **Dangerous Age**[20] 5595 4-9-1 78 RyanMoore 5 64
(Charles Hills) *a towards rr* 13/2[1]
0216 18 ½ **Noodles Blue Boy**[21] 5563 8-8-11 77 (p) JacobButterfield(3) 12 61
(Ollie Pears) *a towards rr* 25/1
000 19 ¾ **Even Stevens**[11] 5925 6-9-5 82 (v) FrederikTylicki 22 64
(Scott Dixon) *racd nr stands' rail: led: rdn along 2f out: drvn and hdd over 1f out: wknd* 11/1
0000 20 3¼ **Sacrosanctus**[12] 5888 6-8-10 73 (b[1]) AndreaAtzeni 18 43
(Scott Dixon) *racd nr stands' rail: chsd ldrs: rdn along over 2f out: sn wknd* 28/1
58.62s (-1.88) **Going Correction** -0.225s/f (Firm)
**WFA** 3 from 4yo+ 1lb 20 Ran SP% 128.5
Speed ratings (Par 105): **106,105,105,104,103 103,101,101,100,100 100,98,98,96,96 95,94,93,92,87**
CSF £216.02 CT £1997.82 TOTE £43.80: £5.50, £2.40, £2.40, £2.40; EX 486.30 Trifecta £3449.90.
**Owner** The Giggle Factor Partnership **Bred** John And Susan Davis **Trained** Carburton, Notts

**FOCUS**
A real cavalry charge in which they again raced centre-to-stands' side. There was a complete pace burn-up towards the nearside involving Even Stevens, Red Baron and Mutaafakir, but they ended up setting it up for the closers.
T/Plt: £166.50 to a £1 stake. Pool: £106,162.81 - 465.41 winning tickets T/Qpdt: £47.30 to a £1 stake. Pool: £9321.19 - 145.60 winning tickets JR

# 6138 KEMPTON (A.W) (R-H)
Wednesday, September 10

**OFFICIAL GOING: Polytrack: standard**
Wind: virtually nil Weather: dry

## 6236 BETDAQ NO PREMIUM CHARGE CLASSIFIED CLAIMING STKS 6f (P)
5:45 (5:45) (Class 5) 3-Y-O+ £2,587 (£770; £384; £192) Stalls Low

Form RPR
4232 1 **The Dandy Yank (IRE)**[7] 6025 3-8-13 73 (p) WilliamCarson 4 80
(Jamie Osborne) *t.k.h: chsd ldrs: effrt u.p 1f out: led fnl 75yds: hld on wl towards fin: rdn out* 5/1[3]
2265 2 *shd* **Noverre To Go (IRE)**[21] 5559 8-8-11 75 (p) JamesDoyle 12 76
(Ronald Harris) *stdd s: t.k.h: hld up in midfield on outer: rdn and effrt over 1f out: ev ch and drvn fnl 100yds: r.o but hld towards fin* 4/1[1]
0403 3 ¾ **Arctic Lynx (IRE)**[14] 5830 7-9-1 75 (p) AdamBeschizza 9 77
(Robert Cowell) *hld up in tch towards rr of main gp: rdn and gd hdwy over 1f out: ev ch fnl 100yds: no ex towards fin* 15/2
363 4 *hd* **Hamoody (USA)**[7] 6025 10-8-12 75 DanielMuscutt(5) 8 79
(Joseph Tuite) *taken down early: chsd ldr and travelled wl: rdn to ld over 1f out: drvn and hdd fnl 75yds: no ex and wknd towards fin* 7/1
2515 5 2¾ **My Inspiration (IRE)**[23] 5501 3-9-7 75 PatCosgrave 5 77
(Jim Boyle) *led: rdn and hdd over 1f out: btn 1f out: wknd fnl 100yds* 20/1
5602 6 1½ **Lujeanie**[25] 5423 8-8-5 72 (p) JimmyQuinn 1 54
(Peter Crate) *stdd s: t.k.h: hld up in tch: effrt on inner to chse ldrs over 1f out: no ex 1f out: wknd ins fnl f* 8/1
-045 7 ¾ **Chelwood Gate (IRE)**[26] 5378 4-9-1 72 (v[1]) LiamKeniry 11 62
(Patrick Chamings) *chsd ldrs: rdn and unable qck ent fnl 2f: wknd fnl f* 10/1
464 8 2¼ **Profile Star (IRE)**[106] 2637 5-8-6 74 CharlesBishop(3) 7 49
(Ann Stokell) *stdd s: t.k.h: hld up towards rr of main gp: rdn and effrt 2f out: sn struggling: wknd ent fnl f* 33/1
0633 9 5 **House Captain**[13] 5861 3-8-13 72 RichardHughes 2 40
(Richard Hannon) *chsd ldrs: rdn over 3f out: lost pl and btn over 2f out: bhd over 1f out* 9/2[2]
6231 10 1¼ **Lindart (ITY)**[19] 5624 3-8-6 72 (b) GaryMahon(7) 3 36
(Richard Hannon) *sn outpcd in detached last: nvr on terms* 12/1
1m 12.37s (-0.73) **Going Correction** -0.075s/f (Stan)
**WFA** 3 from 4yo+ 2lb 10 Ran SP% 114.7
Speed ratings (Par 103): **101,100,99,99,95 93,92,89,83,81**
CSF £24.87 TOTE £4.00: £1.80, £1.90, £2.90; EX 22.40 Trifecta £298.00.My Inspiration was claimed by Miss A. Weaver £14,000. The Dandy Yank was subject to a friendly claim of £10,000.
**Owner** Chris Watkins And David N Reynolds **Bred** Martyn J McEnery **Trained** Upper Lambourn, Berks

**FOCUS**
The opening contest was a fair claimer in which they went an honest gallop. The form looks straightforward.

## 6237 KEMPTON.CO.UK NURSERY H'CAP 7f (P)
6:15 (6:16) (Class 6) (0-65,64) 2-Y-O £1,940 (£577; £288; £144) Stalls Low

Form RPR
0052 1 **Father Stone**[14] 5823 2-9-2 59 LiamKeniry 2 65+
(David Elsworth) *hld up in tch in last quartet: rdn and gd hdwy on inner 2f out: chal ins fnl f: led fnl 75yds: sn hung lft but r.o wl* 9/4[1]
4433 2 1½ **Framley Garth (IRE)**[14] 5823 2-9-3 60 JamesDoyle 9 60
(David Elsworth) *chsd ldrs: rdn and effrt 2f out: drvn and ev ch ins fnl f: wnt 2nd and sltly hmpd fnl 50yds* 7/2[3]
4600 3 *shd* **Tommys Geal**[23] 5489 2-7-11 47 ow2 HectorCrouch(7) 8 45
(Michael Madgwick) *chsd ldrs: rdn and ev ch over 1f out: led ins fnl f: sn hdd and kpt on same pce: lost 2nd fnl 50yds* 100/1
050 4 1¼ **Lady Atlas**[17] 5725 2-9-1 58 MichaelStainton 5 54
(David Brown) *in tch in midfield: rdn and effrt over 1f out: chsd ldrs and r.o same pce fnl f* 15/2
006 5 ½ **Decibelle**[21] 5549 2-8-10 53 PatCosgrave 12 48
(Jane Chapple-Hyam) *chsd ldr tl led over 2f out: drvn and hrd pressed over 1f out: hdd ins fnl f: struggling whn squeezed for room and hmpd ins fnl f: wknd towards fin* 50/1
006 6 1 **More Drama (IRE)**[23] 5488 2-8-8 51 MartinDwyer 7 46+
(Sylvester Kirk) *bmpd s: t.k.h: hld up in tch towards rr: rdn and effrt 2f out: no imp fnl f* 14/1
050 7 3½ **Arousal**[123] 2173 2-8-7 50 HayleyTurner 11 33
(Michael Bell) *stdd s: t.k.h: hld up in tch in last quartet: effrt u.p 2f out: no prog: nvr trbld ldrs* 16/1
0042 8 *nk* **Gen I Am**[22] 5525 2-9-7 64 RichardHughes 3 46
(Richard Hannon) *chsd ldrs tl shuffled bk into midfield over 3f out: effrt u.p 2f out: no prog: wl hld fnl f* 11/4[2]
000 9 ¾ **Senor Firecracker (IRE)**[21] 5555 2-8-10 53 WilliamCarson 4 33
(Brett Johnson) *hld up in tch in last quartet: rdn and effoer 2f out: sn outpcd and btn over 1f out* 25/1
600 10 4½ **Elevator Action (IRE)**[37] 4973 2-8-8 51 ChrisCatlin 6 19
(Richard Fahey) *wnt lft s: led tl rdn and hdd over 2f out: wknd u.p over 1f out* 33/1
6541 11 8 **Arizona Snow**[22] 5517 2-9-6 63 WilliamTwiston-Davies 10 9
(Ronald Harris) *t.k.h: hld up towards rr: hdwy on outer into midfield 4f out: rdn and dropped out over 2f out: bhd and hung bdly lft after* 16/1
1m 26.1s (0.10) **Going Correction** -0.075s/f (Stan) 11 Ran SP% 119.6
Speed ratings (Par 93): **96,94,94,92,92 91,87,86,85,80 71**
CSF £10.24 CT £617.45 TOTE £5.00: £2.00, £1.60, £11.30; EX 13.00 Trifecta £531.60.
**Owner** The Pro-Claimers **Bred** Chasemore Farm **Trained** Newmarket, Suffolk

■ Stewards' Enquiry : Hector Crouch three-day ban: weighed in 2lb heavy (Sep 24-25)
Liam Keniry caution: careless riding.

**FOCUS**
A modest nursery in which they went an even gallop, but the winner looks a bit better than the facts.

## 6238 BETDAQ 50 FREE BET MAIDEN FILLIES' STKS — 1m 4f (P)
**6:45** (6:46) (Class 5) 3-4-Y-O — **£2,587** (£770; £384; £192) **Stalls** Centre

Form — RPR

3-24 **1** **Sweeping Up**[97] 2925 3-9-0 74........(t) PatDobbs 10 — 77+
(Hughie Morrison) *chsd ldr tl rdn to ld over 1f out: styd on strly and clr 1f out: comf* **10/1**

0042 **2** *3 ¼* **Shining Glitter (IRE)**[35] 5036 3-9-0 72........ TomQueally 4 — 72+
(James Fanshawe) *in tch in midfield: chsd wnr over 1f out: no imp but clr 2nd fnl f: kpt on* **10/3[2]**

-226 **3** *3 ¼* **Dalmatia (IRE)**[53] 4434 3-9-0 74........ ShaneKelly 5 — 67
(Sir Michael Stoute) *led: rdn ent fnl 2f: drvn and hdd over 1f out: 3rd and wl hld fnl f* **5/2[1]**

0-5 **4** *½* **Heavens Eyes (IRE)**[21] 5548 3-9-0 0........ PatCosgrave 3 — 66
(Jo Hughes) *chsd ldrs: rdn and unable qck ent fnl 2f: wl hld and plugged on fr over 1f out* **66/1**

42 **5** *2 ¾* **Bright Beacon**[26] 5382 3-9-0 0........ AdamKirby 2 — 61
(Charlie Appleby) *hld up in tch in midfield: rdn and little rspnse 2f out: wl btn and drifted rt over 1f out* **7/2[3]**

05 **6** *1 ½* **Curved**[37] 4966 3-9-0 0........ JamesDoyle 8 — 59+
(Lady Cecil) *stdd s: hld up off the pce in last trio: swtchd lft and pushed along to make sme hdwy 2f out: no imp after* **9/1**

0 **7** *1 ¼* **Havana Girl (IRE)**[128] 2025 3-9-0 0........ DaneO'Neill 1 — 57+
(Harry Dunlop) *hld up in midfield: rdn 3f out: drvn and no hdwy over 2f out: sn wknd* **40/1**

033 **8** *¾* **Tinga (IRE)**[20] 5606 3-9-0 77........(t) RichardHughes 9 — 56+
(Ralph Beckett) *stdd s: hld up off the pce in rr: c wd and effrt over 2f out: no hdwy: n.d* **7/1**

5 **9** *nk* **Well Finished**[27] 5347 3-9-0 0........ OisinMurphy 6 — 55
(Ralph Beckett) *chsd ldrs: rdn and struggling wl over 2f out: sn lost pl: wknd 2f out* **10/1**

0 **10** *6* **Willshebetrying**[32] 5186 3-9-0 0........ WilliamTwiston-Davies 7 — 46+
(Robert Mills) *hld up off the pce in last pair: no hdwy u.p over 2f out: bhd fnl 2f* **100/1**

2m 33.3s (-1.20) **Going Correction** -0.075s/f (Stan) — **10** Ran SP% **119.5**
Speed ratings (Par 100): **101,98,96,96,94 93,92,92,91,87**
CSF £44.44 TOTE £8.60: £2.00, £2.30, £1.60; EX 40.70 Trifecta £100.80.
**Owner** Ben & Sir Martyn Arbib **Bred** Arbib Bloodstock Partnership **Trained** East Ilsley, Berks

**FOCUS**
A fair middle-distance fillies' maiden in which they went an even gallop and it was hard to make up ground.

## 6239 BETDAQ 50% COMMISSION REFUND H'CAP — 1m 4f (P)
**7:15** (7:15) (Class 5) (0-75,75) 3-Y-O — **£2,587** (£770; £384; £192) **Stalls** Centre

Form — RPR

3013 **1** **Fresh Kingdom (IRE)**[12] 5899 3-9-2 70........(p) ShaneKelly 6 — 81+
(James Fanshawe) *hld up in tch: rdn and hdwy to ld 2f out: in command and wnt lft wl ins fnl f: r.o wl* **5/2[1]**

220 **2** *2 ½* **Perspicace**[56] 4325 3-9-7 75........ JamesDoyle 12 — 82
(Roger Charlton) *s.i.s: rdn along in rr: hdwy u.p over 1f out: chsd wnr 1f out: kpt on* **6/1[2]**

3-21 **3** *¾* **Royal Warranty**[113] 2418 3-9-4 72........ LiamKeniry 3 — 78
(Andrew Balding) *hld up towards rr: rdn and hdwy over 1f out: wnt 3rd 1f out: kpt on* **6/1[2]**

5166 **4** *¾* **Yeah Baby (IRE)**[32] 5185 3-9-2 70........ TomQueally 2 — 75+
(Charles Hills) *hld up in last trio: hdwy u.p but stl plenty to do over 1f out: styd on wl fnl f: nt rch ldrs* **50/1**

0164 **5** *2 ½* **Golden Journey (IRE)**[21] 5552 3-9-7 75........ AdamKirby 1 — 76
(Clive Cox) *hld up in tch in midfield: effrt u.p over 2f out: hdwy over 1f out: no imp fnl f* **10/1**

0225 **6** *nk* **Billy Blue (IRE)**[25] 5430 3-9-7 75........(b[1]) RobertHavlin 5 — 75
(John Gosden) *t.k.h: chsd ldrs: effrt to press ldrs and drvn 2f out: wknd 1f out* **7/1[3]**

6520 **7** *nk* **Fighting Back**[12] 5878 3-9-4 72........ RichardHughes 7 — 72
(Amanda Perrett) *led tl 7f out: chsd ldr: rdn over 2f out: outpcd and btn over 1f out: wknd 1f out* **8/1**

4523 **8** *5* **By Jupiter**[36] 5003 3-9-4 72........ JamieSpencer 8 — 64
(Michael Bell) *dwlt: hdwy to chse ldr after 2f out: led 7f out tl 2f out: sn drvn and btn over 1f out: wknd 1f out* **14/1**

-044 **9** *4* **Crystal Pearl**[64] 4051 3-9-3 71........ TedDurcan 10 — 56
(Mark H Tompkins) *chsd ldrs: rdn and effrt 2f out: sn struggling and wknd over 1f out* **20/1**

-443 **10** *8* **Mishko (IRE)**[40] 4863 3-9-6 74........ OisinMurphy 9 — 46
(Steve Gollings) *dwlt: t.k.h and sn in tch in midfield: hdwy to chse ldrs 1/2-way: wknd u.p 2f out* **16/1**

4242 **11** *2* **Kinema (IRE)**[22] 5534 3-9-2 70........(p) GeorgeBaker 4 — 39
(Ed Walker) *t.k.h: wl in tch in midfield: lost pl and bhd 4f out: rdr unable to offer any assistance and n.d after* **14/1**

4506 **12** *6* **Norse Star (IRE)**[27] 5356 3-9-6 74........ DaneO'Neill 11 — 34
(Sylvester Kirk) *dwlt: in tch towards rr: rdn 3f out: sn btn: t.o* **33/1**

2m 32.94s (-1.56) **Going Correction** -0.075s/f (Stan) — **12** Ran SP% **118.7**
Speed ratings (Par 101): **102,100,99,99,97 97,97,93,91,85 84,80**
CSF £16.38 CT £83.20 TOTE £3.90: £1.90, £3.10, £2.30; EX 22.60 Trifecta £188.10.
**Owner** Cheng Wai Tao **Bred** Graiguelin Stud **Trained** Newmarket, Suffolk

**FOCUS**
A fair middle-distance 3yo handicap in which the pace was adequate to halfway and no more.

## 6240 JUMP RACING STARTS HERE 19.10.14 H'CAP — 7f (P)
**7:45** (7:46) (Class 5) (0-70,70) 3-Y-O+ — **£2,587** (£770; £384; £192) **Stalls** Low

Form — RPR

11 **1** **Peace Accord**[5] 6120 4-9-9 69 6ex........ RichardHughes 9 — 84+
(Michael Wigham) *wl in tch in midfield: pushed along and effrt to chal over 1f out: led ins fnl f: r.o and gng away at fin* **10/11[1]**

35 **2** *1 ¾* **Blue Bounty**[11] 5930 3-9-1 65........ TedDurcan 2 — 71
(Mark H Tompkins) *trckd ldrs: rdn to chal over 1f out: led and edgd lft 1f out: hdd and outpcd by wnr ins fnl f: kpt on* **8/1[3]**

00-0 **3** *1 ¾* **Ertikaan**[46] 4650 7-9-10 70........ GeorgeBaker 3 — 74
(Miss Joey Ellis) *hld up in rr of main gp: shkn up and hdwy on outer over 1f out: rdn and kpt on wl fnl f: wnt 3rd towards fin* **20/1**

2152 **4** *¾* **Lady Crossmar (IRE)**[12] 5873 3-8-13 70........ JoshQuinn(7) 8 — 70
(Richard Hannon) *pressed ldr: rdn to ld over 1f out: hdd 1f out: wknd ins fnl f* **16/1**

0265 **5** *1 ¼* **Loud**[33] 5125 4-9-8 68........(b) MartinLane 1 — 66
(Amy Weaver) *in tch in midfield: rdn over 2f out: hdwy u.p to press ldrs over 1f out: wknd ins fnl f* **25/1**

5033 **6** *nk* **New Leyf (IRE)**[8] 6021 8-9-9 69........(b) SteveDrowne 11 — 66
(Jeremy Gask) *in tch in midfield: rdn and effrt 2f out: styd on same pce fr over 1f out* **16/1**

0261 **7** *2 ¼* **Galatian**[28] 5308 7-9-3 70........ PatMillman(7) 7 — 61
(Rod Millman) *led: rdn ent fnl 2f: hdd over 1f out: outpcd whn sltly hmpd 1f out: wknd ins fnl f* **7/1[2]**

-00 **8** *nk* **Greek Spirit (IRE)**[39] 4891 4-9-5 65........ TomQueally 6 — 55
(Alan McCabe) *s.i.s: in rr of main gp: rdn over 2f out: sme hdwy fnl f: nvr trbld ldrs* **66/1**

5054 **9** *1 ½* **Toymaker**[17] 5729 7-9-8 68........ PaddyAspell 12 — 54
(Phil McEntee) *in tch in midfield on outer: rdn and no hdwy over 2f out: wl hld and one pce over 1f out* **33/1**

-660 **10** *½* **Presidente**[12] 5892 3-9-4 68........ AdamKirby 10 — 51
(Ed Walker) *dropped in bhd after s: hld up in rr of main gp: effrt u.p 2f out: no hdwy: nvr trbld ldrs* **8/1[3]**

0444 **11** *7* **Putin (IRE)**[23] 5486 6-9-2 67........(tp) RachealKneller(5) 13 — 33
(Phil McEntee) *pressed ldrs on outer tl 3f out: sn struggling u.p: wknd 2f out* **33/1**

440 **12** *8* **Captain Kendall (IRE)**[34] 5082 5-9-7 67........ OisinMurphy 4 — 12
(Harry Chisman) *in tch towards rr of main gp: rdn and no hdwy over 2f out: bhd over 1f out* **33/1**

0300 **13** *26* **Sheikh The Reins (IRE)**[17] 5729 5-9-10 70........(v) RobertHavlin 5
(John Best) *restless in stalls: v.s.a: t.o thrght* **25/1**

1m 24.52s (-1.48) **Going Correction** -0.075s/f (Stan)
**WFA** 3 from 4yo+ 4lb — **13** Ran SP% **121.6**
Speed ratings (Par 103): **105,103,101,100,98 98,95,95,93,93 85,76,46**
CSF £7.75 CT £101.13 TOTE £1.50: £1.10, £3.20, £7.50; EX 11.20 Trifecta £152.30.
**Owner** D Hassan **Bred** Darley **Trained** Newmarket, Suffolk

**FOCUS**
A modest handicap in which the winner recorded the best comparative time on the card so far.

## 6241 WIN 10,000,000 ON THE BETDAQ COLOSSUS CONDITIONS STKS (BOBIS RACE) — 1m (P)
**8:15** (8:15) (Class 4) 2-Y-O — **£3,881** (£1,155; £577; £288) **Stalls** Low

Form — RPR

41 **1** **Local Time**[35] 5037 2-8-9 0........ JamesDoyle 3 — 92+
(Saeed bin Suroor) *chsd ldrs: wnt 2nd 2f out: rdn hands and heels and qcknd to ld ins fnl f: r.o wl: comf* **11/10[1]**

51 **2** *1 ½* **Sharp Sailor (USA)**[32] 5184 2-9-0 85........ MartinHarley 2 — 90
(Marco Botti) *led: rdn over 1f out: hdd ins fnl f: r.o same pce fnl 100yds* **13/8[2]**

1 **3** *4* **Restorer**[13] 5847 2-9-0 0........ MartinDwyer 1 — 81
(William Muir) *hld up in tch in last pair: effrt in 3rd and edgd lft wl over 1f out: wknd ins fnl f* **7/1[3]**

0 **4** *10* **St Lawrence Gap (IRE)**[19] 5625 2-9-0 0........ TedDurcan 5 — 57
(Robert Mills) *chsd ldr: drvn over 2f out: lost 2nd 2f out and sn wknd* **66/1**

**5** *2 ¼* **Mr Quicksilver** 2-9-0 0........ OisinMurphy 4 — 51+
(Andrew Balding) *dwlt: in tch in last pair: rdn and rn green ent fnl 2f: sn btn and bhd over 1f out* **10/1**

1m 40.35s (0.55) **Going Correction** -0.075s/f (Stan) — **5** Ran SP% **108.8**
Speed ratings (Par 97): **94,92,88,78,76**
CSF £3.04 TOTE £1.60: £1.10, £1.10; EX 2.80 Trifecta £4.80.
**Owner** Godolphin **Bred** Darley **Trained** Newmarket, Suffolk

**FOCUS**
A decent small-field juvenile conditions contest in which they went a steady gallop.

## 6242 BARN DANCE CHRISTMAS PARTIES AT KEMPTON H'CAP (DIV I) — 1m (P)
**8:45** (8:45) (Class 6) (0-65,65) 3-Y-O+ — **£1,940** (£577; £288; £144) **Stalls** Low

Form — RPR

0251 **1** **Lady Sylvia**[6] 6070 5-9-5 65........ JennyPowell(5) 6 — 76
(Joseph Tuite) *hld up in tch in midfield: rdn and hdwy to chal 2f out: led 1f out: kpt on wl: rdn out* **2/1[1]**

6041 **2** *hd* **Pendo**[12] 5873 3-9-5 65........ MartinLane 9 — 74
(Paul Cole) *led: rdn ent fnl 2f: hdd 1f out: ev ch after and kpt on wl: u.p: a jst hld* **5/1[2]**

5002 **3** *1 ½* **Princess Spirit**[35] 5041 5-9-3 58........(p) ShaneKelly 8 — 64
(Edward Creighton) *hld up towards rr: rdn and hdwy towards inner 2f out: ev ch and drvn 1f out: wknd fnl 100yds* **7/1**

0351 **4** *1* **Lifejacket (IRE)**[14] 5833 3-8-13 59........(b) JamesDoyle 2 — 62
(Ed Dunlop) *hld up in midfield: swtchd rt and effrt u.p 2f out: styd on u.p fnl f* **8/1**

2364 **5** *nse* **Stybba**[36] 5006 3-9-1 61........(p) JamieSpencer 10 — 64
(Andrew Balding) *stdd after s: hld up in last pair: hdwy u.p over 1f out: kpt on u.p fnl f* **11/2[3]**

3550 **6** *3* **Warbond**[58] 4266 6-8-12 53........(v) LiamKeniry 4 — 50
(Michael Madgwick) *s.i.s: hld up towards rr: rdn and hdwy 2f out: drvn and no prog over 1f out* **12/1**

0303 **7** *2* **Executrix**[20] 5598 3-9-2 62........ RichardHughes 11 — 53
(Sir Michael Stoute) *chsd ldrs: rdn and unable qck 2f out: 4th and btn over 1f out: wknd fnl f* **9/1**

3330 **8** *hd* **My Manekineko**[35] 5041 5-9-6 61........ DougieCostello 7 — 53
(J R Jenkins) *t.k.h: chsd ldrs: rdn and unable qck 2f out: 5th and btn over 1f out: wknd fnl f* **25/1**

3233 **9** *1 ¾* **Two In The Pink (IRE)**[21] 5560 4-9-8 63........(b[1]) MartinHarley 3 — 51
(Ralph J Smith) *t.k.h: chsd ldrs: shuffled bk and in last quartet 4f out: rdn and effrt 2f out: sn wknd* **10/1**

0-00 **10** *27* **Triple O Seven (IRE)**[88] 3228 3-8-5 51 oh3........ MartinDwyer 1
(John Best) *chsd ldrs tl lost pl qckly u.p over 3f out: t.o over 1f out* **66/1**

1m 38.99s (-0.81) **Going Correction** -0.075s/f (Stan)
**WFA** 3 from 4yo+ 5lb — **10** Ran SP% **121.1**
Speed ratings (Par 101): **101,100,99,98,98 95,93,93,91,64**
CSF £12.36 CT £61.27 TOTE £3.70: £1.70, £2.50, £2.10; EX 16.00 Trifecta £78.10.
**Owner** David J Keast **Bred** Highclere Stud **Trained** Great Shefford, Berks



The Form Book, Raceform Ltd, Newbury, RG14 5SJ

**FOCUS**
The first division of a modest handicap in which they went a respectable gallop.

## 6243 BARN DANCE CHRISTMAS PARTIES AT KEMPTON H'CAP (DIV II) 1m (P)
9:15 (9:15) (Class 6) (0-65,64) 3-Y-O+ £1,940 (£433; £433; £144) Stalls Low

Form RPR
6022 1 **Celestial Knight**[14] 5832 3-9-2 61....(v) ShaneKelly 4 67
(James Fanshawe) *dwlt and bustled along early: racd in last trio: swtchd lft and effrt over 2f out: hdwy over 1f out: styd on wl u.p to ld last strides* 5/2[1]
2304 2 hd **Plucky Dip**[7] 6034 3-9-2 61.... AdamKirby 3 66
(John Ryan) *chsd ldrs: rdn and hdwy on inner to ld over 1f out: hrd pressed but kpt on wl ins fnl f: hdd last strides* 17/5[2]
0000 2 dht **Fiftyshadesdarker (IRE)**[36] 5006 3-8-12 57.... PatCosgrave 1 62
(George Baker) *hld up in tch in midfield: hdwy u.p over 1f out: ev ch ins fnl f: kpt on* 33/1
3-40 4 nk **Loraine**[11] 5908 4-9-7 61.... GeorgeBaker 7 66
(Jamie Osborne) *stdd s: hld up in last pair: rdn and hdwy over 1f out: ev ch ins fnl f: kpt on* 5/1
000 5 1 1/4 **Barbary (IRE)**[67] 3971 3-8-13 58.... DaneO'Neill 6 60
(Charlie Fellowes) *chsd ldrs: rdn to chal 2f out: ev ch after tl no ex and btn whn short of room towards fin* 6/1
3143 6 2 3/4 **Bennelong**[9] 5975 8-9-10 64....(b) RichardHughes 10 60
(Lee Carter) *stdd after s: hld up in last pair: rdn and effrt 2f out: kpt on ins fnl f: nvr trbld ldrs* 4/1[3]
000 7 1 1/4 **Settle For Red (IRE)**[12] 5899 4-9-5 59....(v[1]) MartinLane 5 52
(Jeremy Gask) *w ldr tl led 5f out: rdn ent fnl 2f: hdd over 1f out: wknd ins fnl f* 10/1
0-02 8 1 1/2 **Gracefilly**[21] 5548 3-9-3 62.... RichardKingscote 2 51
(Ed Walker) *led tl 5f out: styd w ldr tl unable qck wl over 1f out: wknd fnl f* 12/1
6400 9 13 **Speedy Rio (IRE)**[4] 6161 3-7-12 50.... HectorCrouch[(7)] 8 9
(Luke Dace) *in tch in midfield: u.p and struggling over 3f out: wknd over 2f out: bhd fnl f* 33/1

1m 39.26s (-0.54) **Going Correction** -0.075s/f (Stan)
**WFA** 3 from 4yo+ 5lb 9 Ran SP% 124.9
Speed ratings (Par 101): **99,98,98,98,97 94,93,91,78**
WIN: 6.90 Celestial Knight; PL: 1.60 Celestial Knight, 1.30 Plucky Dip, 8.60 Fiftyshadesdarker; EX: CK&PD 10.20, CK&FSD 54.30; CSF: CK&PD 6.11, CK&FSD 48.07; TC: CK&PD&FSD 116.07, CK&FSD&PD 148.53; TF: CK&PD&FSD 191.50, CK&FSD&PD383.10;.
**Owner** Carivalis, Eady, Papworth & Swinburn **Bred** G B Balding & Whitsbury Manor Stud **Trained** Newmarket, Suffolk

**FOCUS**
The second division of a modest handicap in which the winner recorded a marginally slower comparative time.
T/Jkpt: £7,228.40 to a £1 stake. Pool: £478,501.62 - 47.00 winning tickets T/Plt: £11.90 to a £1 stake. Pool: £66,453.84 - 4,061.73 winning tickets T/Qpdt: £2.70 to a £1 stake. Pool: £8,989.88 - 2,391.3 winning tickets SP

# 6181 LONGCHAMP (R-H)
## Wednesday, September 10

**OFFICIAL GOING: Turf: good**

## 6244a PRIX DU ROUVRAY (CLAIMER) (2YO) (TURF) 1m
3:40 (12:00) 2-Y-O £11,250 (£4,500; £3,375; £2,250; £1,125)

RPR
1 **Dulciadargent (FR)**[41] 4839 2-8-11 0.... ThierryThulliez 10 74
(N Clement, France) 47/10[2]
2 1 3/4 **Sculptured (FR)**[11] 5941 2-8-11 0.... ThomasHenderson 4 70
(Jo Hughes) *trckd ldr on outer: rdn and nt qckn 1 1/2f out: chsd eventual wnr into fnl f: kpt on u.p but nt pce of wnr: jst hld on for 2nd* 2/1[1]
3 shd **Ever One (FR)**[22] 5544 2-8-11 0.... ValentinSeguy[(4)] 9 74
(A Bonin, France) 59/10
4 2 **Alasdair (FR)**[55] 2-8-11 0.... AntoineCoutier 1 65
(Matthieu Palussiere, France) 61/1
5 1 1/2 **Portenio (FR)**[22] 5544 2-9-2 0.... MarcLerner 7 66
(C Lerner, France) 83/10
6 1 1/2 **Racy Rules (IRE)** 2-8-8 0.... TheoBachelot 5 55
(Mario Hofer, Germany) 177/10
7 3/4 **Zinger (IRE)**[14] 5844 2-8-8 0.... CristianDemuro 3 53
(E J O'Neill, France) 28/1
8 1 1/4 **Really Tonic (FR)**[20] 5619 2-8-11 0.... GregoryBenoist 2 53
(F Doumen, France) 44/5
9 2 1/2 **Take A Guess (FR)**[22] 5544 2-9-2 0....(b) Jean-BernardEyquem 8 52
(Matthieu Palussiere, France) 58/10[3]
10 2 **Dayaday (FR)**[22] 5543 2-8-8 0.... AnthonyCrastus 6 39
(C Boutin, France) 11/1

1m 42.75s (4.35) 10 Ran SP% 119.8
WIN (incl. 1 euro stake): 5.70. PLACES: 1.80, 1.40, 1.90. DF: 9.30. SF: 19.30.
**Owner** Guy Pariente **Bred** Guy Pariente Holding **Trained** Chantilly, France

## 6245a PRIX DES MELEZES (CONDITIONS) (2YO) (TURF) 7f
5:40 (12:00) 2-Y-O £14,166 (£5,666; £4,250; £2,833; £1,416)

RPR
1 **Inordinate (USA)**[33] 2-9-0 0.... Christophe-PatriceLemaire 6 98
(P Bary, France) 8/5[2]
2 2 **Ride Like The Wind (IRE)**[17] 5741 2-9-0 0.... MickaelBarzalona 3 93
(F Head, France) 4/5[1]
3 2 1/2 **Royal Dolois (FR)**[34] 5118 2-8-5 0.... NicolasLarenaudie[(5)] 2 82
(J-M Lefebvre, France) 26/1
4 1/2 **Chester Deal**[12] 5900 2-9-0 0.... MaximeGuyon 1 85
(Jo Hughes) *led: niggled along 2f out: rdn over 1 1/2f out: hdd appr fnl f: kpt on at same pce* 48/10[3]
5 1 1/4 **Vianella (FR)**[55] 2-8-4 0.... ValentinSeguy[(3)] 4 75
(S Wattel, France) 225/10
6 2 1/2 **Maui (FR)**[20] 5617 2-8-7 0.... CristianDemuro 5 68
(Mlle V Dissaux, France) 38/1

1m 23.67s (2.97) 6 Ran SP% 121.8
WIN (incl. 1 euro stake): 2.60. PLACES: 1.20, 1.20. SF: 3.80.
**Owner** K Abdullah **Bred** Juddmonte Farms Llc **Trained** Chantilly, France

# 6085 CHEPSTOW (L-H)
## Thursday, September 11

**OFFICIAL GOING: Good (6.5)**
Wind: slight half behind Weather: cloudy

## 6246 IRISH STALLION FARMS EBF MAIDEN FILLIES' STKS (BOBIS RACE) 7f 16y
1:50 (1:51) (Class 5) 2-Y-O £2,911 (£866; £432; £216) Stalls Centre

Form RPR
46 1 **Finial**[55] 4396 2-9-0 0.... AdamKirby 6 78
(Clive Cox) *mid-div: rdn and hdwy over 2f out: led over 1f out: sn jnd: edgd lft early ins fnl f: asserted fnl 25yds* 5/1[3]
0 2 1/2 **Taqneyya (IRE)**[63] 4126 2-9-0 0.... ChrisCatlin 2 77
(Charles Hills) *t.k.h: hld up towards rr: hdwy 1/2-way: rdn and ev ch 2f out tl hld fnl 25yds* 5/1[3]
44 3 2 **Ya Latif (IRE)**[26] 5416 2-9-0 0.... FrederikTylicki 4 71
(Roger Varian) *trckd ldrs: led over 2f out tl over 1f out: hld in 3rd whn carried lft and n.m.r early ins fnl f: unable qck after* 7/4[1]
065 4 4 1/2 **Powerfulstorm**[17] 5746 2-9-0 45.... WilliamTwiston-Davies 12 59
(Ronald Harris) *cl up: led after 1f tl rdn and hdd over 2f out: one pce after: edgd lft fnl f* 100/1
0 5 1/2 **Belle Dormant (IRE)**[55] 4396 2-9-0 0.... FergusSweeney 3 58
(Seamus Durack) *s.s: in rr: rdn and hdwy over 2f out: sn outpcd by ldrs: styd on fnl f* 4/1[2]
5 6 1 1/2 **Tepeleni**[15] 5827 2-9-0 0.... SeanLevey 1 54
(Clive Brittain) *prom: rdn over 3f out: one pce fnl 2f* 100/1
54 7 2 1/2 **Starring Guest (IRE)**[9] 6001 2-9-0 0.... SamHitchcott 10 47
(Mick Channon) *chsd ldrs: rdn over 3f out: one pce* 10/1
5 8 1 **Cascading Stars (IRE)**[38] 4980 2-9-0 0.... StevieDonohoe 9 44
(J S Moore) *mid-div: rdn 1/2-way: styd on fnl f* 25/1
9 1 1/2 **Skylight (IRE)** 2-9-0 0.... SebSanders 13 40
(William Haggas) *s.i.s: towards rr: rdn and sme hdwy 1/2-way: wknd over 1f out* 8/1
0 10 3/4 **Cherry Empress (IRE)**[17] 5774 2-9-0 0.... JFEgan 7 38
(Jo Hughes) *led 1f: styd prom tl rdn and wknd over 1f out* 100/1
0 11 1 3/4 **Beauchamp Ruby**[10] 5973 2-9-0 0.... LukeMorris 8 33
(Paul Fitzsimons) *s.i.s: rdn over 3f out: a towards rr* 100/1
12 56 **Riba Roja** 2-9-0 0.... BenCurtis 5
(John Gallagher) *s.s: rn green and sn hung lft: a wl bhd: t.o* 100/1

1m 25.59s (2.39) **Going Correction** +0.175s/f (Good) 12 Ran SP% 118.7
Speed ratings (Par 92): **93,92,90,85,84 82,79,78,77,76 74,10**
CSF £29.94 TOTE £6.20: £2.10, £2.10, £1.10; EX 57.30 Trifecta £192.50.
**Owner** Cheveley Park Stud **Bred** Cheveley Park Stud Ltd **Trained** Lambourn, Berks

**FOCUS**
Th3 45-rated fourth holds down this maiden form.

## 6247 ENTERPRISE LTD MAIDEN FILLIES' STKS (BOBIS RACE) 7f 16y
2:20 (2:21) (Class 5) 3-Y-O £3,234 (£962; £481; £240) Stalls Centre

Form RPR
-542 1 **Water Queen**[20] 5622 3-9-0 75....(p) SebSanders 2 72
(William Haggas) *chsd ldrs: wnt 2nd after 3f: rdn over 2f out: chal over 1f out: led 100yds out: r.o u.p* 30/100[1]
2523 2 nk **Persian Bolt (USA)**[17] 5775 3-8-11 70....(b) AmyScott[(3)] 1 71
(Eve Johnson Houghton) *led: rdn over 2f out: jnd 1f out: hdd 100yds out: jst hld* 9/2[2]
60 3 14 **The Reel Way (GR)**[66] 4029 3-9-0 0.... LiamKeniry 4 35
(Patrick Chamings) *chsd ldr tl relegated to 3rd after 3f: sn rdn: grad outpcd by ldng pair* 50/1
4 6 **Cape Good Hope** 3-9-0 0.... LukeMorris 6 19
(Clive Brittain) *dwlt: sn pushed along and outpcd: wnt mod 4th 2f out: nvr nr ldrs* 12/1[3]
5 8 **Sail With Sultana** 3-9-0 0.... FergusSweeney 5
(Mark Rimell) *s.s: sn wl in rr: t.o 1/2-way: modest late hdwy past one rival* 66/1
66 6 12 **Daisy's Secret**[66] 4029 3-9-0 0.... AdamKirby 3
(George Baker) *chsd ldng trio tl rdn and wknd over 2f out* 16/1

1m 25.15s (1.95) **Going Correction** +0.175s/f (Good) 6 Ran SP% 112.1
Speed ratings (Par 98): **95,94,78,71,62 48**
CSF £2.07 TOTE £1.20: £1.02, £2.40; EX 2.40 Trifecta £21.60.
**Owner** Mohammed Jaber **Bred** Rabbah Bloodstock Limited **Trained** Newmarket, Suffolk
■ Stewards' Enquiry : Seb Sanders two-day ban: used whip above permitted level (Sep 25-26)

**FOCUS**
A moderate maiden.

## 6248 32RED NURSERY H'CAP 5f 16y
2:50 (2:50) (Class 6) (0-60,59) 2-Y-O £1,940 (£577; £288; £144) Stalls Centre

Form RPR
0652 1 **Magic Mac**[15] 5828 2-8-10 48....(p) JohnFahy 8 58
(Hughie Morrison) *chsd ldr in stands' side trio and prom overall: rdn over 2f out: led appr fnl f: pushed out towards fin* 7/2[1]
064 2 2 **Go Gently (IRE)**[30] 5278 2-8-12 50....(b[1]) LiamKeniry 4 53
(George Baker) *mid-div in centre: rdn over 3f out: hdwy 2f out: chsd wnr appr fnl f: kpt on same pce* 4/1[2]
400 3 6 **Air Of York (IRE)**[23] 5525 2-8-10 48....(b[1]) WilliamTwiston-Davies 10 29
(Ronald Harris) *led stands' side trio and overall ldr: rdn and hdd appr fnl f: one pce* 14/1
606 4 1/2 **Ya Halla (IRE)**[16] 5789 2-8-11 56....(p) AhmadAlSubousi[(7)] 6 35
(Robert Cowell) *squeezed out sn after s: racd centre: towards rr: pushed along 1/2-way: edgd rt over 1f out: r.o ins fnl f* 9/2[3]
4036 5 1/2 **Spirit In Time (IRE)**[8] 6024 2-9-2 54.... FergusSweeney 11 32
(Malcolm Saunders) *chsd other pair stands' side: pushed along and hung rt over 2f out: rdn whn hmpd 1f out: one pce after* 16/1
050 6 hd **Noble Cause**[36] 5042 2-8-2 45.... DanielMuscutt[(5)] 1 22
(Luke Dace) *s.s: towards rr in centre: rdn 1/2-way: hdwy over 1f out: nt rch ldrs* 25/1
6006 7 1/2 **Emilys Girl (IRE)**[17] 5746 2-8-7 45.... BenCurtis 2 20
(Ronald Harris) *s.s: sn bhd and rdn along in centre: stl last ent fnl f: r.o* 66/1
0U41 8 1 1/4 **Piping Dream (IRE)**[8] 6040 2-9-7 59 6ex.... SeanLevey 3 30
(Richard Hannon) *led main gp in centre and prom overall: rdn 2f out: wknd fnl f* 9/2[3]
024 9 7 **Margot Rose**[14] 5859 2-9-7 59....(b[1]) LukeMorris 5 4
(Harry Dunlop) *chsd ldrs in centre: rdn over 2f out: wknd over 1f out* 5/1

5030 **10** *12* **Johnny Sorrento**[24] 5506 2-9-6 58..........................(tp) StevieDonohoe 7
(Tim Pitt) *prom main gp in centre: rdn over 2f out: sn wknd* **66/1**
1m 2.03s (2.73) **Going Correction** +0.175s/f (Good) **10** Ran SP% **114.6**
Speed ratings (Par 93): **85,81,72,71,70 70,69,67,56,37**
CSF £17.04 CT £174.51 TOTE £5.40: £2.30, £1.60, £2.60; EX 20.10 Trifecta £175.70.
**Owner** Adrian N R Mcalpine & Partners **Bred** H Morrison **Trained** East Ilsley, Berks
**FOCUS**
A weak nursery.

## 6249 CHARLES STANLEY PERSONAL INVESTMENT SERVICE H'CAP 6f 16y
**3:25** (3:26) (Class 4) (0-80,79) 3-Y-0+ **£4,690** (£1,395; £697; £348) **Stalls** Centre

Form RPR
0524 **1** **Jontleman (IRE)**[11] 5951 4-8-13 71.............................. SamHitchcott 11 80
(Mick Channon) *hld up: last and outpcd whn swtchd rt to r on stands' rail 3f out: hdwy 2f out: r.o to ld 100yds out: hld on* **14/1**
6135 **2** *nk* **Mister Musicmaster**[16] 5785 5-9-5 77.......................... AdamKirby 13 85
(Ron Hodges) *led 2f: styd prom: rdn over 2f out: chsd wnr ins fnl f: r.o* **7/2**[1]
252 **3** *½* **Debit**[17] 5775 3-8-13 73.......................................(p) LukeMorris 8 79
(Clive Cox) *chsd ldrs: rdn over 2f out: styd on same pce fnl f* **7/2**[1]
0330 **4** *1¼* **Sacha Park (IRE)**[11] 5945 3-9-3 77.......................... SeanLevey 4 79
(Richard Hannon) *prom: rdn to ld over 2f out: hdd 100yds out: no ex* **16/1**
2504 **5** *¾* **Black Dave (IRE)**[14] 5849 4-8-7 65.................................. JFEgan 1 65
(David Evans) *towards rr: pushed along 3f out: swtchd 1f out: r.o* **7/1**[3]
0240 **6** *shd* **Top Cop**[21] 5595 5-8-13 71.............................(p) WilliamTwiston-Davies 10 71
(Ronald Harris) *hld up towards rr: rdn and hdwy 2f out: nt qckn fnl f* **16/1**
1534 **7** *½* **Eastern Dragon (IRE)**[49] 4588 4-8-12 75.................. JackDuern(5) 6 73
(Michael Scudamore) *towards rr: rdn and clsd over 3f out: n.m.r over 1f out: styd on ins fnl f* **6/1**[2]
6635 **8** *¾* **Sarangoo**[6] 6089 6-9-4 76.................................... FergusSweeney 9 72
(Malcolm Saunders) *cl up: led after 2f tl over 2f out: sn rdn: grad wknd fnl f* **10/1**
6200 **9** *2½* **Rigolleto (IRE)**[17] 5750 6-8-12 70.......................... StevieDonohoe 3 58
(Anabel K Murphy) *prom: rdn over 2f out: wknd ins fnl f* **33/1**
0-06 **10** *3* **Storm Trooper (IRE)**[26] 5441 3-9-3 77...................... KieranO'Neill 12 55
(Richard Hannon) *t.k.h: mid-div: rdn over 3f out: wknd over 1f out* **33/1**
14 **11** *2* **Shingle**[23] 5526 3-9-4 78...................................... FrederikTylicki 5 50
(Ed de Giles) *hld up: hdwy to chse ldrs over 3f out: rdn over 2f out: wknd rapidly fnl f* **7/1**[3]
1m 12.85s (0.85) **Going Correction** +0.175s/f (Good)
**WFA** 3 from 4yo+ 2lb **11** Ran SP% **117.1**
Speed ratings (Par 105): **101,100,99,98,97 97,96,95,92,88 85**
CSF £62.36 CT £217.90 TOTE £13.70: £3.20, £2.30, £2.80; EX 68.00 Trifecta £106.60.
**Owner** Paul Corbett **Bred** Old Carhue & Graeng Bloodstock **Trained** West Ilsley, Berks
**FOCUS**
A modest sprint handicap and a tight finish. The winner was back to something like his best.

## 6250 32RED.COM ON THE APP STORE NURSERY H'CAP 1m 14y
**4:00** (4:00) (Class 6) (0-65,65) 2-Y-O **£1,940** (£577; £288; £144) **Stalls** Centre

Form RPR
4605 **1** **Vita Mina**[31] 5250 2-8-13 **60**..............................(v[1]) DeclanBates(3) 2 64
(David Evans) *taken to post early: mde all: rdn over 2f out: hung lft fnl f: r.o wl* **33/1**
455 **2** *1¾* **Romance Story (IRE)**[24] 5500 2-9-6 **64**.................. FrederikTylicki 10 64+
(Saeed bin Suroor) *hld up: rdn over 3f out: hdwy over 1f out: r.o to go 2nd cl home* **7/4**[1]
01 **3** *hd* **Percy Veer**[35] 5072 2-9-7 **65**.................................... SeanLevey 9 65
(Sylvester Kirk) *s.i.s: sn chsng ldrs: wnt 2nd 1f out: one pce after and ct for 2nd cl home* **7/1**
0604 **4** *½* **Mikandy (IRE)**[16] 5798 2-9-3 **61**.............................. AdamKirby 7 60
(Clive Cox) *chsd ldrs: rdn 3f out: one pce fnl f* **5/1**[2]
545 **5** *½* **Offshore**[78] 3584 2-9-5 **63**..........................................(p) LukeMorris 11 61
(James Tate) *mid-div: pushed along 4f out: styd on u.p fnl 2f: nt quite rch ldrs* **6/1**[3]
0000 **6** *6* **Hidden Agenda**[15] 5823 2-8-1 **45**.............................. KieranO'Neill 6 29
(Michael Blanshard) *t.k.h: chsd wnr: rdn over 3f out: wknd fnl f* **100/1**
0030 **7** *½* **Auld Fyffee (IRE)**[16] 5798 2-9-1 **62**........................ RyanPowell(3) 4 45
(John Ryan) *towards rr: rdn and outpcd over 3f out: styd on fnl f* **20/1**
0650 **8** *hd* **Paco's Dream**[8] 6040 2-8-8 **52**............................(v[1]) StevieDonohoe 1 34
(Harry Dunlop) *chsd ldrs: rdn 3f out: wknd fnl f* **33/1**
050 **9** *1* **Retro Valley (IRE)**[24] 5500 2-8-11 **55**.................... FergusSweeney 13 35
(David Dennis) *taken to post early: in rr: rdn over 3f out: sme hdwy fnl f* **33/1**
5666 **10** *½* **Smugglers Lane (IRE)**[24] 5489 2-8-10 **54**........................ JFEgan 3 33
(David Evans) *mid-div: rdn over 3f out: wknd over 1f out* **16/1**
665 **11** *2½* **Tumut (IRE)**[56] 4353 2-9-7 **65**.................. WilliamTwiston-Davies 8 38
(Mick Channon) *hld up towards rr: rdn 3f out: wknd 2f out* **8/1**
6550 **12** *19* **First Class Mail**[23] 5525 2-9-4 **62**.............................. SamHitchcott 12
(Mick Channon) *in rr: rdn over 3f out: wknd 2f out: t.o* **20/1**
505 **13** *7* **King's Bond**[21] 5593 2-8-6 **50**...................................... ChrisCatlin 5
(Ronald Harris) *hld up on outer: dropped to last 4f out: lost tch 3f out: t.o* **33/1**
1m 39.06s (2.86) **Going Correction** +0.175s/f (Good) **13** Ran SP% **119.1**
Speed ratings (Par 93): **92,90,90,89,89 83,82,82,81,80 78,59,52**
CSF £86.42 CT £503.75 TOTE £30.50: £10.00, £1.20, £2.10; EX 180.70 Trifecta £2113.30 Part won..
**Owner** Lowther Racing & Richard Kent **Bred** Richard Kent & Lady Lonsdale **Trained** Pandy, Monmouths
■ Stewards' Enquiry : Declan Bates one-day ban: failed to ride to draw (Sep 25)
**FOCUS**
An ordinary staying nursery.

## 6251 £10 FREE BET AT 32REDSPORT.COM H'CAP 1m 14y
**4:35** (4:37) (Class 5) (0-75,73) 3-Y-0+ **£2,587** (£770; £384; £192) **Stalls** Centre

Form RPR
0110 **1** **Ancient Greece**[18] 5721 7-9-8 71..............................(t) AdamKirby 4 79
(George Baker) *rdn along leaving stalls: led after 1f: mde rest: rdn over 1f out: styd on wl u.p* **8/1**
4455 **2** *¾* **Lady Bayside**[7] 6070 6-9-5 68.............................. FergusSweeney 7 74
(Malcolm Saunders) *hld up: rdn over 2f out: chsd wnr appr fnl f: r.o u.p: jst hld* **5/1**
5413 **3** *1* **Evervescent (IRE)**[34] 5127 5-9-4 72.............................. JoeDoyle(5) 2 76
(Graeme McPherson) *half-rrd s: sn cl up racing keenly: rdn to chse wnr over 2f out: lost 2nd appr fnl f: one pce* **7/2**[3]
2055 **4** *½* **Swift Cedar (IRE)**[14] 5849 4-9-10 73................................ JFEgan 5 76
(David Evans) *led 1f: cl up: rdn over 2f out: sn outpcd by ldrs: styd on fnl 100yds* **5/2**[1]
4041 **5** *9* **Concrete Mac**[47] 4674 3-8-9 70.............................. CharlieBennett(7) 6 51
(Hughie Morrison) *hld up in tch: rdn over 3f out: wknd over 1f out* **11/4**[2]
-050 **6** *27* **Game Mascot**[19] 5686 4-9-9 72.......................................... ChrisCatlin 3
(Peter Hiatt) *sn in rr: rdn over 3f out: qckly lost tch: t.o* **25/1**
1m 36.63s (0.43) **Going Correction** +0.175s/f (Good)
**WFA** 3 from 4yo+ 5lb **6** Ran SP% **109.1**
Speed ratings (Par 103): **104,103,102,101,92 65**
CSF £43.57 TOTE £6.40: £3.30, £2.80; EX 31.30 Trifecta £87.70.
**Owner** George Baker & Partners **Bred** Darley **Trained** Manton, Wilts
**FOCUS**
A decent pace for this competitive handicap.

## 6252 32RED CASINO H'CAP 1m 4f 23y
**5:10** (5:10) (Class 6) (0-65,70) 3-Y-0+ **£1,940** (£577; £288; £144) **Stalls** Low

Form RPR
4-01 **1** **Now What**[62] 4149 7-9-2 61........................................ JackBudge(7) 5 67
(Jonathan Portman) *trckd ldrs tl lost pl after 4f: rdn and clsd 3f out: nt clr run over 2f out tl over 1f out: r.o wl to ld fnl 100yds* **7/1**
5321 **2** *nk* **Reach The Beach**[14] 5850 5-9-4 56..............................(t) AdamKirby 4 62
(Brendan Powell) *led tl rdn and hdd over 3f out: led again early ins fnl f tl 100yds out: no ex* **6/1**[3]
-205 **3** *½* **Walter De La Mare (IRE)**[13] 4279 7-8-12 50 oh5...........(t) JohnFahy 3 55?
(Anabel K Murphy) *s.s: in rr: hdwy over 3f out: rdn 2f out: r.o fnl f* **14/1**
4245 **4** *2¼* **Admirable Duque (IRE)**[16] 5800 8-9-8 60......................(b) LiamKeniry 6 61
(Dominic Ffrench Davis) *hld up: hdwy after 5f: rdn to ld over 3f out: hdd early ins fnl f: wknd* **7/1**
450 **5** *1¼* **Angus Glens**[18] 5721 4-9-11 63......................................(p) LukeMorris 7 62
(David Dennis) *wnt rt s: sn trcking ldr: ev ch 3f out to 2f out: cl 3rd whn n.m.r over 1f out: grad wknd* **5/1**[2]
4451 **6** *nse* **Hallbeck**[11] 5949 3-9-9 70 6ex.......................................... FergusSweeney 1 75+
(Henry Candy) *trckd ldrs: rdn over 3f out: n.m.r 2f out tl appr fnl f: styd on same pce after* **7/4**[1]
63-3 **7** *2¼* **Cherry Tiger**[17] 4473 4-9-0 57.......................................... JoeDoyle(5) 2 52
(Graeme McPherson) *t.k.h: bhd ldrs: rdn over 3f out: wknd over 1f out* **8/1**
2m 40.39s (1.39) **Going Correction** +0.175s/f (Good)
**WFA** 3 from 4yo+ 9lb **7** Ran SP% **110.1**
Speed ratings (Par 101): **102,101,101,99,99 99,97**
CSF £44.07 TOTE £6.40: £2.80, £2.30; EX 20.70 Trifecta £231.20.
**Owner** Mrs S J Portman **Bred** Mrs D O Joly **Trained** Upper Lambourn, Berks
**FOCUS**
A moderate handicap.
T/Plt: £53.60 to a £1 stake. Pool: £52,189.20 - 709.84 winning units. T/Qpdt: £39.10 to a £1 stake. Pool: £3644.66 - 68.90 winning units. RL

# [6229] DONCASTER (L-H)
Thursday, September 11

**OFFICIAL GOING: Round course - good to soft (good in places); straight course - good (good to soft in places; 7.0)**
Wind: Virtually nil Weather: Fine & dry

## 6253 EBF STALLIONS BREEDING WINNERS CARRIE RED FILLIES' NURSERY STKS (H'CAP) (BOBIS RACE) 6f 110y
**1:40** (1:41) (Class 2) 2-Y-O **£25,204** (£7,544; £3,772; £1,888; £940) **Stalls** High

Form RPR
214 **1** **Home Cummins (IRE)**[26] 5436 2-9-2 85.................. JackGarritty(5) 11 91
(Richard Fahey) *w ldrs: led over 1f out: jst hld on* **12/1**
310 **2** *nse* **East Coast Lady (IRE)**[40] 4913 2-9-0 83.................. NoelGarbutt(5) 3 89
(Robert Eddery) *prom: hdwy and nt clr run over 1f out: edgd rt and styd on strly fnl f: jst failed* **14/1**
015 **3** *½* **Little Lady Katie (IRE)**[26] 5436 2-8-5 72.................. JoeyHaynes(3) 13 76
(K R Burke) *prom: effrt over 2f out: kpt on wl ins fnl f* **10/1**
1101 **4** *1¼* **Feeling Easy (IRE)**[10] 5983 2-9-7 85 6ex.................. JimmyQuinn 12 86
(Robert Eddery) *chsd ldrs: effrt over 2f out: styd on same pce fnl f* **25/1**
6313 **5** *nk* **Gregoria (IRE)**[26] 5436 2-8-13 77.................................. RyanMoore 7 77
(William Haggas) *led: hdd over 1f out: kpt on one pce* **6/1**[2]
0231 **6** *nk* **Escrick (IRE)**[14] 5859 2-8-6 70.................................. DavidProbert 5 69
(David Simcock) *mid-div: hdwy over 2f out: chsng ldrs and edgd lft over 1f out: kpt on same pce* **20/1**
5222 **7** *¾* **Persun**[20] 5626 2-9-3 81.................................................. WilliamBuick 15 78
(Mick Channon) *in rr: hdwy over 1f out: styng on at fin* **17/2**[3]
3203 **8** *hd* **Secret Spirit**[30] 5285 2-8-7 74.................................. RyanTate(3) 16 71
(Clive Cox) *in rr: hdwy 2f out: kpt on fnl f* **18/1**
026 **9** *hd* **Stocking**[26] 5429 2-8-7 71........................................(p) AndreaAtzeni 17 67
(Roger Varian) *hld up in rr: hdwy over 2f out: nvr rchd ldrs* **14/1**
130 **10** *¾* **Bimbo**[21] 5608 2-9-1 79.................................................. PaulHanagan 10 73
(Richard Fahey) *t.k.h in rr: hdwy over 2f out: nvr rchd ldrs* **12/1**
0423 **11** *1½* **Penny Royale**[18] 5714 2-8-2 66.................................. JamesSullivan 8 56
(Tim Easterby) *in rr: hdwy over 2f out: kpt on ins fnl f* **33/1**
051 **12** *nse* **Angels Wings (IRE)**[31] 5255 2-9-0 78.......................... JamesDoyle 14 68
(Charles Hills) *in rr: hdwy over 1f out: nvr a factor* **17/2**[3]
0200 **13** *hd* **Cajoling (IRE)**[20] 5626 2-8-13 77.............................. HarryBentley 6 66
(Jonathan Portman) *in tch: drvn over 2f out: lost pl over 1f out* **50/1**
3614 **14** *1¾* **Vesnina**[7] 6067 2-9-5 83.............................................. RichardHughes 4 68
(Richard Hannon) *w ldrs: wknd appr fnl f* **4/1**[1]
2333 **15** *2* **Assault On Rome (IRE)**[12] 5929 2-9-3 81.......................... JoeFanning 1 60
(Mark Johnston) *w ldrs: wknd over 1f out* **20/1**
0210 **16** *2½* **Mary McPhee**[49] 4585 2-8-13 77..................................[1] JamieSpencer 18 49
(Charles Hills) *stdd and swtchd lft s: in rr: swtchd lft and hdwy over 2f out: wknd over 1f out* **20/1**
4501 **17** *23* **Secret Friend (IRE)**[9] 6008 2-8-0 64 6ex..................(b) DuranFentiman 9
(Tim Easterby) *in rr: bhd whn eased over 1f out: t.o* **33/1**
1m 18.1s (-1.80) **Going Correction** -0.30s/f (Firm) **17** Ran SP% **124.4**
Speed ratings (Par 98): **98,97,97,95,95 95,94,94,93,93 91,91,91,89,86 83,57**
CSF £157.18 CT £1816.36 TOTE £15.70: £2.70, £3.60, £3.10, £7.30; EX 205.60 Trifecta £1752.80 Part won..
**Owner** Mrs H Steel **Bred** Yeguada De Milagro Sa **Trained** Musley Bank, N Yorks


The Form Book, Raceform Ltd, Newbury, RG14 5SJ

**FOCUS**
A few of the previous nine winners of this have gone on to run well at a higher level, so it was probably a good race of its type. The early gallop seemed only modest and the field stayed mainly towards the middle-to-inside of the track.

## 6254 JAPAN RACING ASSOCIATION SCEPTRE STKS (GROUP 3) (F&M) 7f
**2:10** (2:13) (Class 1) 3-Y-O+ **£35,520** (£13,434; £6,714; £3,354) **Stalls** High

Form RPR

0624 **1** **Kiyoshi**[27] 5407 3-8-12 106 (p) JamieSpencer 9 111+
(Charles Hills) *hld up towards rr: smooth hdwy over 2f out: trckd ldrs over 1f out: rdn and qcknd wl to ld ins fnl f: styd on strly* **11/1**

1211 **2** 1 ¼ **Bragging (USA)**[21] 5612 3-8-12 107 JamesDoyle 4 108
(Sir Michael Stoute) *trckd ldrs: effrt 2f out: sn rdn along and sltly outpcd: styd on strly ins fnl f* **15/8[1]**

-200 **3** *shd* **Al Thakhira**[109] 2581 3-8-12 103 FrankieDettori 16 107
(Marco Botti) *hld up: hdwy 2f out: effrt on outer over 1f out: sn rdn and ev ch ent fnl f: drvn: edgd lft and no ex last 100yds* **14/1**

3541 **4** *nse* **Valonia**[25] 5467 3-8-12 104 AndreaAtzeni 15 107
(Henry Candy) *in tch: hdwy over 2f out: chsd ldrs over 1f out: rdn to chal jst ins fnl f and ev ch: sn drvn: edgd lft and no ex last 100yds* **20/1**

2416 **5** ¾ **Evita Peron**[27] 5407 3-8-12 103 RichardKingscote 2 105
(Ralph Beckett) *in tch: hdwy over 2f out: rdn to ld briefly ent fnl f: sn drvn and hdd: no ex last 100yds* **16/1**

1122 **6** ¾ **Muteela**[18] 5722 3-8-12 104 PaulHanagan 1 103
(Mark Johnston) *slt ld: rdn along wl over 1f out: drvn end hdd ent fnl f: grad wknd* **9/1**

1001 **7** *shd* **J Wonder (USA)**[41] 4854 3-9-1 109 JimmyFortune 6 106
(Brian Meehan) *t.k.h early: hld up towards rr: stdy hdwy over 2f out: trckd ldrs over 1f out: rdn to chal ent fnl f and ev ch: sn drvn and kpt on same pce* **7/1[2]**

1-00 **8** ¾ **Lucky Kristale**[83] 3418 3-8-12 105 TomQueally 3 101
(George Margarson) *hld up in tch: hdwy on outer 2f out: rdn to chal ent fnl f and ev ch: sn drvn and wknd last 100yds* **25/1**

1220 **9** 1 ½ **Joyeuse**[32] 5223 3-8-12 106 RyanMoore 13 97
(Lady Cecil) *hld up in rr: hdwy 2f out: kpt on fnl f: nvr nr ldrs* **17/2[3]**

1-00 **10** 1 ¾ **Amazing Maria (IRE)**[27] 5407 3-8-12 101 WilliamBuick 8 93
(Ed Dunlop) *chsd ldrs: rdn along 2f out: sn wknd* **25/1**

3121 **11** 1 ½ **Token Of Love**[33] 5176 3-8-12 103 JoeFanning 5 89
(William Haggas) *dwlt and sltly hmpd s: towards rr: hdwy over 2f out: rdn over 1f out: sn no imp* **9/1**

1334 **12** 1 ¾ **Indignant**[18] 5722 4-9-2 102 RichardHughes 7 86
(Richard Hannon) *cl up: disp ld 1/2-way: rdn along wl over 2f out: grad wknd* **33/1**

1320 **13** 1 ½ **Inyordreams**[62] 4171 3-8-12 96 DaleSwift 11 80
(James Given) *chsd ldng pair: rdn along 2f out: grad wknd* **100/1**

2652 **14** *shd* **Dutch Rose (IRE)**[7] 6060 5-9-2 100 DanielTudhope 14 82
(David O'Meara) *racd wd: chsd ldrs: rdn wl over 1f out: grad wknd* **33/1**

0010 **15** 4 **Dancealot**[38] 4971 3-8-12 82 SilvestreDeSousa 10 70
(Clive Brittain) *in tch: rdn along wl over 2f out: sn wknd* **100/1**

1m 22.74s (-3.56) **Going Correction** -0.30s/f (Firm)
**WFA** 3 from 4yo+ 4lb **15** Ran **SP%** **119.0**
Speed ratings: **108,106,106,106,105 104,104,103,102,100 98,96,94,94,89**
CSF £29.24 TOTE £14.30: £3.90, £1.50, £4.10; EX 49.40 Trifecta £636.90.
**Owner** Qatar Racing Limited **Bred** Lowther Racing **Trained** Lambourn, Berks

**FOCUS**
A really competitive Group 3, far more so than the betting indicated, with all but three runners within 6lb of each other on adjusted official ratings. There were a few in the line-up who like to get on with it, and a good pace resulted in those held up being favoured. Well up to race stanadrd, with Kiyoshi rated back to her 2yo best.

## 6255 DFS PARK HILL STKS (GROUP 2) (F&M) 1m 6f 132y
**2:40** (2:42) (Class 1) 3-Y-O+
**£51,039** (£19,350; £9,684; £4,824; £2,421; £1,215) **Stalls** Low

Form RPR

1351 **1** **Silk Sari**[39] 4945 4-9-5 99 AndreaAtzeni 4 111+
(Luca Cumani) *mid-div: hdwy over 3f out: styd on wl to ld over 1f out: forged clr: v readily* **8/1**

0535 **2** 5 **Groovejet**[42] 4824 3-8-7 96 FrannyNorton 6 103
(Peter Chapple-Hyam) *in rr-div: pushed along 9f out: hdwy over 2f out: edgd lft and 2nd 1f out: styd on: no ch w wnr* **40/1**

2324 **3** 1 ¾ **Criteria (IRE)**[25] 5479 3-8-7 104 WilliamBuick 11 101
(John Gosden) *trckd ldr: led over 2f out: hdd over 1f out: styd on same pce* **7/1**

-403 **4** ¾ **Seal Of Approval**[26] 5432 5-9-5 109 GeorgeBaker 9 100
(James Fanshawe) *in rr: effrt and n.m.r over 3f out: nt clr run and swtchd rt over 1f out: styd on: nrst fin* **7/2[1]**

3122 **5** ¾ **Arabian Comet (IRE)**[21] 5611 3-8-7 104 JoeFanning 3 99
(William Haggas) *trckd ldrs: effrt 3f out: one pce over 1f out* **9/2[2]**

6424 **6** 1 ½ **Moment In Time (IRE)**[26] 5457 5-9-5 98 JamieSpencer 12 97
(David Simcock) *dwlt: in rr: styd on fnl 2f: nvr a factor* **20/1**

324 **7** 2 ¼ **Sohar**[86] 3321 6-9-5 90 TomQueally 13 94
(James Toller) *in rr: sn pushed along: styd on fnl 2f: nvr nr ldrs* **80/1**

4513 **8** ½ **Cascading**[39] 4945 3-8-7 97 RobertHavlin 14 94
(Hughie Morrison) *led: qcknd clr over 7f out: hdd over 2f out: wknd over 1f out* **33/1**

-121 **9** 6 **Melrose Abbey (IRE)**[75] 3725 3-8-7 89 SilvestreDeSousa 1 86
(Ralph Beckett) *trckd ldrs: drvn over 3f out: lost pl over 1f out* **25/1**

1230 **10** 14 **Venus De Milo (IRE)**[21] 5610 4-9-5 111 JosephO'Brien 8 68
(A P O'Brien, Ire) *hld up towards rr: hdwy on ins over 3f out: chsng ldrs over 2f out: wknd and eased over 1f out* **6/1[3]**

-020 **11** 1 **Dark Crusader (IRE)**[21] 5611 4-9-5 102 FMBerry 2 66
(A J Martin, Ire) *mid-div: hdwy on ins over 3f out: wknd 2f out: eased whn bhd clsng stages* **33/1**

5544 **12** 2 ¼ **Debdebdeb**[19] 5673 4-9-5 90 DavidProbert 10 63
(Andrew Balding) *chsd ldrs: drvn over 3f out: lost pl over 2f out: eased whn bhd clsng stages* **33/1**

3 **13** ½ **Energia Fox (BRZ)**[19] 5688 4-9-1 105 MartinHarley 7 59
(Marco Botti) *t.k.h in mid-div: effrt over 3f out: lost pl over 2f out: eased whn bhd clsng stages* **14/1**

3m 5.11s (-2.29) **Going Correction** +0.175s/f (Good)
**WFA** 3 from 4yo+ 12lb **13** Ran **SP%** **113.3**
Speed ratings: **113,110,109,109,108 107,106,106,103,95 95,93,93**
CSF £300.08 TOTE £7.80: £2.90, £10.00, £2.30; EX 233.40 Trifecta £3245.50 Part won..
**Owner** Fittocks Stud & Andrew Bengough **Bred** Fittocks Stud Ltd & Arrow Farm Stud **Trained** Newmarket, Suffolk

**FOCUS**
This looked up to the standard of previous renewals, and the gallop appeared to be decent considering how strung out they were rounding the final bend. Silk Sari impressed and the runner-up is the key to the form.

## 6256 WEATHERBYS HAMILTON INSURANCE £300,000 2-Y-O STKS (BOBIS RACE) 6f 110y
**3:15** (3:18) (Class 2) 2-Y-O
**£274,621** (£109,893; £54,946; £27,417; £13,736; £13,736) **Stalls** High

Form RPR

1104 **1** **Bond's Girl**[54] 4439 2-8-1 82 PatrickMathers 20 95
(Richard Fahey) *racd wd: in tch: hdwy 2f out: rdn to chal jst ins fnl f: led last 100yds: styd on* **14/1**

0211 **2** 2 **Heartbreak Hero**[20] 5620 2-9-2 91 RyanMoore 11 105
(William Haggas) *led: rdn along wl over 1f out: drvn ent fnl f: hdd and no ex last 100yds* **12/1**

211 **3** *hd* **Mattmu**[39] 4936 2-8-6 95 DavidAllan 6 94
(Tim Easterby) *in tch: hdwy over 2f out: rdn to chse ldrs over 1f out: drvn and ev ch jst ins fnl f: one pce last 100yds* **10/1**

22 **4** ¾ **Cockney Island**[16] 5725 2-8-1 0 SilvestreDeSousa 10 87
(Philip McBride) *in tch: hdwy 2f out: chsd ldrs over 1f out: rdn to chal and ev ch ent fnl f: sn drvn and kpt on same pce* **25/1**

1100 **5** 1 ¾ **Dougal (IRE)**[44] 4757 2-8-12 94 JimmyFortune 7 93
(Richard Hannon) *hld up towards rr: hdwy 2f out: sn rdn: drvn and styd on strly fnl f: nrst fin* **40/1**

1201 **6** *shd* **Kasb (IRE)**[19] 5672 2-8-12 93 DaneO'Neill 13 94
(John Gosden) *hmpd s and in rr: hdwy over 2f out: n.m.r over 1f out: sn swtchd rt and rdn: styd on: nrst fin* **11/1**

20 **7** ¾ **Acaster Malbis (FR)**[20] 5655 2-8-12 0 JamesDoyle 4 91+
(Richard Hannon) *in rr: pushed along 1/2-way: rdn over 2f out: kpt on appr fnl f: nrst fin* **40/1**

1333 **8** ½ **Lexington Times (IRE)**[12] 5926 2-8-12 102 RichardHughes 18 89
(Richard Hannon) *chsd ldrs on outer: rdn along 2f out: drvn and kpt on same pce fnl f* **17/2[3]**

1 **9** ¾ **Grandad's World (IRE)**[25] 5464 2-8-12 0 TonyHamilton 17 87
(Richard Fahey) *chsd ldrs: rdn along wl over 1f out: wknd appr fnl f* **16/1**

1324 **10** ½ **Natural Order (USA)**[61] 4199 2-8-12 95 WilliamBuick 21 86+
(K R Burke) *chsd ldrs towards outer: rdn along 2f out: no imp whn edgd lft ent fnl f* **16/1**

56 **11** *nse* **The Great War (USA)**[19] 5701 2-9-2 0 JosephO'Brien 2 90
(A P O'Brien, Ire) *hld up towards rr: gd hdwy over 2f out: rdn to chse ldrs over 1f out: wknd ins fnl f* **6/1[2]**

4100 **12** ¾ **Vimy Ridge**[21] 5607 2-8-9 92 JasonHart 8 81
(Richard Fahey) *hld up: hdwy over 2f out: effrt whn n.m.r over 1f out: one pce after* **40/1**

1122 **13** ½ **Kibaar**[22] 5580 2-8-9 96 PaulHanagan 1 79
(B W Hills) *towards rr: effrt and sme hdwy over 2f out: sn rdn along and n.d* **10/1**

3414 **14** 1 ¼ **Gaudy (IRE)**[21] 5607 2-9-0 94 (v) JamieSpencer 15 81
(Kevin Ryan) *sltly hmpd s: sn swtchd lft and midfield: effrt over 2f out: sn rdn and n.d* **25/1**

3321 **15** 1 **Intiwin (IRE)**[17] 5760 2-8-12 82 FMBerry 14 76
(Richard Fahey) *wnt lft s: chsd ldrs: rdn along 2f out: sn wknd* **40/1**

210 **16** *nse* **Gerry The Glover (IRE)**[21] 5607 2-8-9 84 TomEaves 22 73+
(Brian Ellison) *racd wd: chsd ldrs: rdn along wl over 2f out: sn wknd* **40/1**

14 **17** 1 ½ **Fox Trotter (IRE)**[42] 4822 2-8-6 0 MartinLane 5 66
(Brian Meehan) *dwlt: a towards rr* **7/2[1]**

5054 **18** ½ **Diamond Creek (IRE)**[16] 5791 2-8-7 80 FrannyNorton 12 66
(Richard Fahey) *chsd ldrs: rdn along wl over 2f out: sn wknd* **100/1**

12 **19** *nk* **Plymouth Sound**[12] 5906 2-9-2 0 TomQueally 3 74
(Eve Johnson Houghton) *a towards rr* **50/1**

415 **20** *hd* **Al Gomry**[30] 5286 2-9-2 87 FrankieDettori 19 73
(Richard Fahey) *prom towards outer: rdn along over 2f out: sn wknd* **50/1**

4500 **21** 3 ¼ **Burtonwood**[4] 6165 2-9-2 80 (v) DavidNolan 16 64
(Richard Fahey) *wnt lft s: racd wd: chsd ldrs: rdn along wl over 2f out: sn wknd* **100/1**

1m 17.27s (-2.63) **Going Correction** -0.30s/f (Firm) **21** Ran **SP%** **125.5**
Speed ratings (Par 101): **103,100,100,99,97 97,96,96,95,94 94,93,93,91,90 90,88,88,87,87 83**
CSF £159.85 TOTE £15.80: £4.70, £4.10, £4.70; EX 223.90 Trifecta £3643.70 Part won..
**Owner** Crown Select **Bred** David Holgate **Trained** Musley Bank, N Yorks

**FOCUS**
As usual for this type of race, more quantity than quality, and it was one of the joint bottom-weights that came out on top.

## 6257 CROWNHOTEL-BAWTRY.COM H'CAP 1m 2f 60y
**3:45** (3:46) (Class 2) (0-110,103) 3-Y-O+ **£16,172** (£4,812; £2,405; £1,202) **Stalls** Low

Form RPR

151 **1** **The Corsican (IRE)**[18] 5720 3-8-9 **93** JimCrowley 5 105+
(David Simcock) *in rr-div: hdwy 3f out: styd on to ld last 75yds: drvn out* **11/2[2]**

3151 **2** 1 **Mange All**[47] 4647 3-8-8 **92** LiamJones 7 102
(William Haggas) *chsd ldrs: led appr fnl f: hdd and no ex ins fnl f* **7/1[3]**

1115 **3** 2 ½ **Arab Dawn**[84] 3379 3-8-6 **90** DavidProbert 3 95
(Hughie Morrison) *sn mid-div: smooth hdwy over 3f out: chsng ldrs over 1f out: kpt on same pce last 150yds* **17/2**

0506 **4** *hd* **Kelinni (IRE)**[19] 5673 6-9-4 **95** MartinHarley 11 100
(Marco Botti) *led after 1f: hdd over 1f out: styd on same pce* **18/1**

0-55 **5** 3 ¼ **Out Of Bounds (USA)**[54] 4437 5-9-12 **103** SilvestreDeSousa 6 102
(Saeed bin Suroor) *sn chsng ldrs: one pce fnl 2f* **16/1**

0631 **6** ¾ **Elhaame (IRE)**[19] 5676 4-9-6 **97** AndreaAtzeni 8 94
(Luca Cumani) *in rr-div: hdwy over 2f out: kpt on one pce* **9/1**

0312 **7** 1 ½ **Angelic Upstart (IRE)**[19] 5669 6-8-12 **89** oh3 OisinMurphy 10 84
(Andrew Balding) *in rr: drvn over 3f out: kpt on fnl 2f: nvr a factor* **25/1**

41 **8** 1 **Long Cross**[28] 5347 3-8-7 **91** ow1 WilliamBuick 12 84
(John Gosden) *mid-div: hdwy on outside 7f out: hung rt: rn wd and lost pl bnd over 4f out: kpt on fnl 2f* **9/4[1]**

1300 **9** ½ **Saxo Jack (FR)**[61] 4214 4-9-10 **101** JamesDoyle 2 93
(Saeed bin Suroor) *mid-div: t.k.h: hdwy over 3f out: sn chsng ldrs: hung lft and wknd over 1f out* **20/1**

1210 **10** 3 ¼ **Cosseted**[39] 4945 4-9-0 **91** RyanMoore 9 77
(James Fanshawe) *hld up towards rr: effrt over 2f out: nvr nr ldrs: eased clsng stages* **8/1**

305 **11** 12 **Truth Or Dare**[69] 3930 3-8-11 **95** MartinDwyer 1 58
(Richard Hannon) *mid-div: effrt over 3f out: lost pl over 1f out: eased whn bhd clsng stages* **40/1**

0010 **12** *1 ½* **Lyn Valley**[19] 5695 3-8-12 **96**.......................................... JoeFanning 13 56
(Mark Johnston) *restless in stalls: dwlt: sn mid-div: drvn 3f out: lost pl 2f out: eased whn bhd clsng stages* **33/1**

1140 **13** *3 ¾* **Sea Shanty (USA)**[44] 4756 4-9-7 **98**.......................................... RichardHughes 4 51
(Richard Hannon) *led 1f: chsd ldrs: wknd over 1f out: bhd whn eased clsng stages* **25/1**

2m 8.49s (-0.91) **Going Correction** +0.175s/f (Good)
**WFA** 3 from 4yo+ 7lb 13 Ran SP% **119.3**
Speed ratings (Par 109): **110,109,107,107,104 103,102,101,101,98 89,88,85**
CSF £40.70 CT £329.25 TOTE £6.70: £1.90, £2.80, £3.00; EX 45.00 Trifecta £292.80.
**Owner** Mrs Fitri Hay **Bred** Mrs Fitriani Hay **Trained** Newmarket, Suffolk

**FOCUS**
A decent handicap run at just an ordinary gallop early and 3yos dominated the finish. The form is rated around the fourth.

## 6258 ONE CALL INSURANCE THOROUGHBRED BREEDERS ASSOCIATION FILLIES' H'CAP 1m 2f 60y

**4:25** (4:25) (Class 3) (0-90,88) 3-Y-0+ **£10,350** (£3,080; £1,539; £769) **Stalls** Low

Form RPR

221 **1** **Blue Waltz**[27] 5382 3-9-0 83.......................................... AndreaAtzeni 6 99+
(Luca Cumani) *hld up in tch: smooth hdwy on outer over 2f out: led wl over 1f out: sn rdn clr: readily* **7/2**[2]

2102 **2** *5* **Principle Equation (IRE)**[26] 5448 3-8-13 82.......................................... FrankieDettori 2 88
(Ralph Beckett) *hld up in tch: hdwy 3f out: rdn to chse wnr over 1f out: sn drvn and kpt on: no ch w wnr* **7/2**[2]

0430 **3** *1* **Maven**[19] 5695 6-9-8 84.......................................... DavidAllan 7 88
(Tim Easterby) *set stdy pce: pushed along and qcknd over 3f out: rdn over 2f out: hdd wl over 1f out: sn drvn and kpt on same pce* **11/1**

4056 **4** *1 ¾* **Hot Coffee (IRE)**[43] 4782 3-9-4 87.......................................... RichardKingscote 1 88
(Tom Dascombe) *trckd ldng pair on inner: hdwy over 2f out: rdn along wl over 1f out: sn drvn and one pce* **5/1**[3]

01 **5** *shd* **Flippant (IRE)**[26] 5430 3-9-0 88.......................................... NathanAlison(5) 3 89
(William Haggas) *hld up in rr: hdwy on inner 3f out: rdn to chse ldrs 2f out: sn drvn and one pce* **3/1**[1]

0442 **6** *4* **Yojojo (IRE)**[11] 5948 5-9-7 83.......................................... RichardHughes 4 76
(Gay Kelleway) *t.k.h early: hld up in rr: swtchd lft over 3f out: hdwy over 2f out: sn rdn and btn* **7/1**

0421 **7** *4* **Limousine**[15] 5822 3-8-11 80.......................................... JamesDoyle 5 65
(Charles Hills) *trckd ldr: effrt 3f out: rdn over 2f out: sn wknd* **16/1**

2m 9.29s (-0.11) **Going Correction** +0.175s/f (Good)
**WFA** 3 from 5yo+ 7lb 7 Ran SP% **112.8**
Speed ratings (Par 104): **107,103,102,100,100 97,94**
CSF £15.69 TOTE £4.20: £2.20, £2.30; EX 17.10 Trifecta £102.90.
**Owner** Fittocks Stud & Andrew Bengough **Bred** Fittocks Stud **Trained** Newmarket, Suffolk

**FOCUS**
This fillies' handicap was taken apart by handicap debutante Blue Waltz, who took a big step forward.

## 6259 DFS BRITISH STALLION STUDS EBF MAIDEN STKS (BOBIS RACE) 1m (S)

**5:00** (5:03) (Class 3) 2-Y-0 **£7,762** (£2,310; £1,154; £577) **Stalls** High

Form RPR

4 **1** **Commemorative**[13] 5881 2-9-5 0.......................................... JamesDoyle 2 85
(Charles Hills) *w ldrs: led over 1f out: drvn out* **4/1**[2]

**2** *1* **Decorated Knight** 2-9-5 0.......................................... AndreaAtzeni 14 82+
(Roger Varian) *in rr-div: hdwy over 2f out: chsng ldrs over 1f out: styd on ins fnl f* **11/2**[3]

**3** *½* **Archery Peak** 2-9-5 0.......................................... DanielTudhope 16 81+
(Luca Cumani) *chsd ldrs: effrt over 2f out: styd on same pce last 150yds* **20/1**

**4** *¾* **Game Pie (IRE)** 2-9-5 0.......................................... JoeFanning 6 79
(Hugo Palmer) *led: hdd over 1f out: kpt on same pce* **25/1**

**5** *½* **Mohatem (USA)** 2-9-5 0.......................................... PaulHanagan 12 78+
(B W Hills) *in rr: hdwy over 1f out: kpt on wl ins fnl f: will do bttr* **9/1**

0 **6** *1 ¼* **Erik The Red (FR)**[20] 5655 2-9-5 0.......................................... JamieSpencer 9 75
(Kevin Ryan) *chsd ldrs: effrt over 2f out: hung rt and one pce fnl f* **7/2**[1]

**7** *1 ½* **Dannyday** 2-9-5 0.......................................... RyanMoore 10 71+
(Sir Michael Stoute) *in rr: hdwy over 1f out: styd on wl ins fnl f: will improve* **16/1**

**8** *hd* **Secateur** 2-9-5 0.......................................... WilliamBuick 11 71+
(John Gosden) *in rr: hdwy over 1f out: gng on at fin: will do bttr* **10/1**

4 **9** *nk* **King Of Normandy (FR)**[19] 5706 2-9-5 0.......................................... RichardHughes 17 70
(Richard Hannon) *chsd ldrs: one pce over 1f out* **9/1**

**10** *¾* **Brutus (FR)** 2-9-5 0.......................................... OisinMurphy 15 68
(Richard Hannon) *dwlt: hdwy to chse ldrs over 2f out: fdd fnl 75yds* **33/1**

0 **11** *3 ¾* **Proposed**[27] 5377 2-9-5 0.......................................... JimmyFortune 13 59
(Richard Hannon) *mid-div: effrt over 2f out: wknd over 1f out* **25/1**

**12** *1* **Alshaahraman (USA)** 2-9-5 0.......................................... DaneO'Neill 8 57
(Brian Meehan) *in rr: hdwy over 1f out: kpt on: nvr on terms* **50/1**

**13** *3 ¼* **Sociopath (IRE)** 2-9-5 0.......................................... JimCrowley 5 49
(Peter Chapple-Hyam) *mid-div: rdn 3f out: lost pl 2f out* **16/1**

**14** *1* **Kitten's Red (USA)** 2-9-5 0.......................................... GeorgeBaker 4 47
(Ed Dunlop) *chsd ldrs: wknd over 1f out* **40/1**

**15** *5* **Magic Circle (IRE)** 2-9-5 0.......................................... SilvestreDeSousa 3 35
(Ralph Beckett) *s.i.s: in rr: bhd fnl 2f* **40/1**

**16** *2 ½* **Illya Kuryakin** 2-9-5 0.......................................... MartinHarley 7 29
(Peter Chapple-Hyam) *mid-div: effrt over 3f out: rdn and lost pl over 2f out* **80/1**

**17** *20* **Chatty Man (IRE)** 2-9-5 0.......................................... MartinDwyer 1
(David C Griffiths) *dwlt: sn chsng ldrs: lost pl over 2f out: bhd whn eased ins fnl f: t.o* **100/1**

1m 37.78s (-1.52) **Going Correction** -0.30s/f (Firm) 2y crse rec 17 Ran SP% **122.9**
Speed ratings (Par 99): **95,94,93,92,92 91,89,89,89,88 84,83,80,79,74 71,51**
CSF £23.79 TOTE £5.10: £2.20, £2.50, £6.00; EX 36.60 Trifecta £706.70.
**Owner** K Abdullah **Bred** Juddmonte Farms Ltd **Trained** Lambourn, Berks

**FOCUS**
This maiden has produced some nice types down the years, and not always the one that wins is the horse to follow. Both Nathaniel (2010) and Encke (2011) finished second to horses they easily surpassed in the future.

## 6260 DOWNLOAD THE LADBROKES BINGO APP H'CAP 6f

**5:35** (5:38) (Class 3) (0-90,89) 3-Y-0+ **£9,703** (£2,887; £1,443; £721) **Stalls** High

Form RPR

0231 **1** **Shore Step (IRE)**[62] 4146 4-9-7 89.......................................... RichardHughes 3 99
(Mick Channon) *led: pushed along 2f out: rdn over 1f out: hdd narrowly ent fnl f: rallied to ld last 100yds: hld on gamely nr fin* **11/1**

0 **2** *nk* **Counter Ridge (SAF)**[18] 5728 5-9-4 86.......................................... MartinHarley 8 95
(Marco Botti) *midfield: hdwy 2f out: rdn over 1f out: styd on to chal ins fnl f: drvn and ev ch: nt qckn towards fin* **66/1**

20 **3** *hd* **Run With Pride (IRE)**[33] 5199 4-9-0 82.......................................... DaleSwift 14 90+
(Derek Shaw) *trckd ldrs: hdwy 2f out: rdn to chal ent fnl f: ev ch tl drvn and no ex towards fin* **14/1**

4002 **4** *nk* **Bahamian Heights**[6] 6094 3-9-1 85..........................................(b) JamesDoyle 2 92+
(Clive Brittain) *dwlt and in rr: hdwy wl over 1f out: rdn and str run ins fnl f: nrst fin* **14/1**

2332 **5** *1 ¼* **Mission Approved**[40] 4892 4-9-7 89.......................................... FrankieDettori 9 92
(Luca Cumani) *hld up towards rr: hdwy 2f out: n.m.r and swtchd lft appr fnl f: sn rdn and styd on wl: nrst fin* **9/2**[1]

4300 **6** *nse* **Mississippi**[13] 5888 5-9-0 82.......................................... GrahamGibbons 4 85
(David Barron) *midfield: hdwy over 2f out: chsd ldrs over 1f out: sn rdn and kpt on fnl f: nrst fin* **10/1**

1510 **7** *nk* **Extrasolar**[5] 6130 4-9-6 88..........................................(t) WilliamBuick 13 90
(Amanda Perrett) *prom: cl up 2f out: rdn to ld narrowly ent fnl f: sn drvn: hdd & wknd last 100yds* **25/1**

4300 **8** *1 ¼* **Dark Castle**[13] 5888 5-8-12 80.......................................... PJMcDonald 17 78
(Micky Hammond) *hld up in tch: hdwy 2f out: rdn over 1f out: n.m.r ent fnl f: kpt on: nrst fin* **20/1**

3000 **9** *½* **Secret Witness**[5] 6130 8-9-7 89..........................................(b) JoeFanning 6 85
(Ronald Harris) *hld up towards rr: hdwy 2f out: rdn over 1f out: kpt on fnl f: nrst fin* **20/1**

2162 **10** *1* **Souville**[22] 5553 3-9-3 87.......................................... GeorgeBaker 19 80
(Chris Wall) *racd towards stands' rail: chsd ldrs: hdwy and cl up 2f out: sn rdn and wknd appr fnl f* **12/1**

10U4 **11** *hd* **Johnny Cavagin**[27] 5385 5-9-2 84..........................................(t) TomEaves 12 76
(Richard Guest) *plld hrd early: chsd ldrs: rdn along 2f out: sn wknd* **16/1**

2612 **12** *1* **Bajan Bear**[13] 5888 6-9-0 82.......................................... AdrianNicholls 16 71
(David Nicholls) *nvr bttr than midfield* **9/1**[3]

5621 **13** *2* **Pennine Warrior**[17] 5769 3-8-5 75..........................................(p) SilvestreDeSousa 20 58
(Scott Dixon) *gd spd stands' rail and cl up: rdn along over 2f out: drvn wl over 1f out and grad wknd* **16/1**

0001 **14** *nk* **Doc Hay (USA)**[18] 5711 7-9-5 87.......................................... DanielTudhope 18 69
(David O'Meara) *racd nr stands' rail: chsd ldrs: rdn along 1/2-way: sn wknd* **10/1**

3-00 **15** *shd* **Wahaab (IRE)**[40] 4918 3-9-2 86..........................................(b[1]) PaulHanagan 5 68
(Richard Hannon) *a towards rr* **25/1**

40 **16** *¾* **Tagula Night (IRE)**[12] 5925 8-9-0 82..........................................(bt) RobertWinston 21 61
(Dean Ivory) *racd towards stands' rail: in rr fr 1/2-way* **25/1**

0416 **17** *1 ½* **Angus Og**[99] 2898 4-9-2 87.......................................... JoeyHaynes(3) 10 61
(K R Burke) *chsd ldrs: rdn along 2f out: sn wknd* **25/1**

0650 **18** *6* **El Viento (FR)**[40] 4892 6-9-5 87..........................................(b) RyanMoore 11 42
(Richard Fahey) *chsd ldrs: rdn along 2f out: sn wknd* **8/1**[2]

1m 10.7s (-2.90) **Going Correction** -0.30s/f (Firm)
**WFA** 3 from 4yo+ 2lb 18 Ran SP% **125.0**
Speed ratings (Par 107): **107,106,106,105,104 104,103,102,101,100 99,98,95,95,95 94,92,84**
CSF £624.08 CT £10096.72 TOTE £10.90: £3.30, £9.50, £3.80, £3.80; EX 863.60 Trifecta £2598.50 Part won..
**Owner** Jon and Julia Aisbitt **Bred** Lynn Lodge Stud **Trained** West Ilsley, Berks

**FOCUS**
A wide-open sprint handicap.
T/Jkpt: Not won. T/Plt: £1269.80 to a £1 stake. Pool: £181,784.28 - 104.50 winning units.
T/Qpdt: £74.90 to a £1 stake. Pool: £13,367.71 - 131.90 winning units. JR

# 5782 EPSOM (L-H)

### Thursday, September 11

**OFFICIAL GOING: Good (good to firm in places; overall 8.3; home straight: stands' side 8.0; far side 7.7)**
Wind: virtually nil Weather: dry, overcast

## 6261 EBF STALLIONS MEDIAN AUCTION MAIDEN STKS 7f

**2:30** (2:33) (Class 5) 2-Y-0 **£3,881** (£1,155; £577; £288) **Stalls** Low

Form RPR

2320 **1** **Harlequin Striker (IRE)**[29] 5309 2-9-2 75.......................................... CharlesBishop(3) 11 75
(Mick Channon) *mde all: rdn 2f out: kpt on wl u.p fnl f: rdn out* **3/1**[2]

0252 **2** *¾* **Thorkhill Star (IRE)**[10] 5981 2-9-2 75.......................................... GeorgeChaloner(3) 10 73
(Richard Fahey) *chsd wnr thrght: rdn ent fnl 2f: styd pressing wnr but one pce ins fnl f* **5/4**[1]

**3** *½* **Delaire** 2-9-5 0.......................................... JackMitchell 2 74+
(Roger Varian) *hld up in last quartet: swtchd rt and nt clr run wl over 1f out: hdwy 1f out: styd on strly to go 3rd wl ins fnl f: nt rch ldrs* **20/1**

**4** *1 ¼* **Inke (IRE)** 2-9-0 0.......................................... WilliamCarson 9 63
(Jim Boyle) *hld up in last quartet: rdn and hdwy ent fnl 2f: chsd ldng pair 1f out: kpt on but nvr threatening ldrs: lost 3rd wl ins fnl f* **50/1**

0 **5** *1* **Fridge Kid**[20] 5643 2-8-11 0.......................................... RobertTart(3) 1 61
(Dr Jon Scargill) *in tch in midfield: rdn and effrt over 2f out: wnt 3rd over 1f out tl 1f out: kpt on same pce fnl f* **66/1**

0 **6** *¾* **Herecomestheband**[24] 5500 2-9-5 0.......................................... PatCosgrave 6 64
(George Baker) *chsd ldrs: rdn and unable qck ent fnl 2f: lost 3rd over 1f out: plugged on same pce fnl f* **33/1**

053 **7** *3* **Colours Of Glory (IRE)**[10] 5982 2-9-0 0.......................................... GrahamLee 7 50
(Charles Hills) *chsd ldng trio: rdn and unable qck over 2f out: lost pl and btn over 1f out: wknd ins fnl f* **8/1**

30 **8** *1 ½* **Bridgekeeper**[24] 5500 2-9-5 0.......................................... PaddyAspell 5 51
(James Eustace) *dwlt: hld up in last quartet: effrt on outer over 2f out: sme hdwy but no threat to ldrs over 1f out: wknd 1f out* **25/1**

**9** *1* **Blackadder** 2-8-12 0..........................................[1] PaddyBradley(7) 4 49
(Pat Phelan) *short of room and stdd sn after s: hld up in detached last: pushed along 2f out: hdwy ent fnl f: styd on: n.d* **66/1**

6 **10** *3 ½* **Kingston Sassafras**[24] 5500 2-9-5 0.......................................... KierenFallon 3 39
(Ed Walker) *in tch in midfield: rdn and no rspnse over 2f out: lost pl 2f out: sn wknd: bhd 1f out* **9/2**[3]

00 **11** *4* **Polydus**[11] 5947 2-9-5 0.......................................... PhillipMakin 8 28
(Ed Dunlop) *t.k.h: hld up in midfield: shkn up and fnd nil 2f out: wknd qckly and bhd 1f out* **33/1**

1m 25.49s (2.19) **Going Correction** +0.125s/f (Good) 11 Ran SP% **118.2**
Speed ratings (Par 95): **92,91,90,89,88 87,83,82,80,76 72**
CSF £6.71 TOTE £3.30: £1.10, £1.30, £3.60; EX 8.80 Trifecta £96.20.
**Owner** Harlequin Direct Ltd **Bred** John Doyle **Trained** West Ilsley, Berks

**FOCUS**
Rail dolled out 3yds from 10f to bottom of Tattenham Corner and 6f races increased by 3yds, 7f by 4yds and 1m and beyond races by 6yds. A steadily-run but relatively weak median auction maiden for juveniles. The front two in the market had it to themselves throughout and the rest finished in a heap.

## 6262 MERLAND RISE H'CAP 1m 114y
3:00 (3:05) (Class 5) (0-75,74) 3-Y-O £5,175 (£1,540; £769; £384) Stalls Low

Form RPR
4151 1 **Gratzie**[21] 5598 3-9-3 73 CharlesBishop(3) 8 84
(Mick Channon) *in tch in midfield: hdwy to chse ldrs 5f out: rdn to ld over 1f out: kpt on and a holding on towards fin: rdn out* 6/1[3]

0166 2 ½ **Inspector Norse**[29] 5311 3-9-3 70 PatDobbs 1 80
(Sylvester Kirk) *chsd ldr tl 3f out: 3rd and outpcd u.p over 1f out: chsd clr wnr 1f out: kpt on steadily ins fnl f: nvr quite getting to wnr* 7/2[1]

455 3 3 ½ **Sixties Love**[83] 3423 3-9-0 67 SteveDrowne 2 69+
(Simon Dow) *stdd s: hld up off the pce in last trio: rdn 3f out: hdwy over 1f out: styd on wl ins fnl f: wnt 3rd towards fin: nvr trbld ldrs* 25/1

-P05 4 hd **Rizal Park (IRE)**[12] 5903 3-9-0 70 ThomasBrown(3) 4 71
(Andrew Balding) *chsd ldrs: rdn and outpcd 2f out: kpt on same pce and no threat to ldrs after: wnt 3rd fnl 75yds tl towards fin* 8/1

0434 5 3 **Spreadable (IRE)**[21] 5603 3-9-0 67 JackMitchell 7 62
(Nick Littmoden) *led: rdn over 2f out: hdd over 1f out: sn no ex and btn 3rd 1f out: wknd ins fnl f* 12/1

0215 6 2 ½ **Tete Orange**[27] 5395 3-8-11 64 PatCosgrave 6 55+
(Stuart Williams) *in tch in midfield: effrt but unbalanced and nt handling trck 2f out: no prog and hung lft to inner rail over 1f out: wl hld after* 6/1[3]

0 7 ½ **Victory Rich (IRE)**[29] 5313 3-8-12 65 GrahamLee 3 53
(Henry Tett) *hld up off the pce in last pair: rdn 3f out: modest hdwy ins fnl f: n.d* 66/1

-331 8 2 ¼ **Lady Sparkler (IRE)**[47] 4654 3-9-2 74 LouisSteward(5) 9 57+
(Roger Varian) *hld up in last trio: effrt u.p in 6th over 2f out: no imp: wknd over 1f out* 4/1[2]

41-0 9 2 ½ **Approach The West (IRE)**[138] 1723 3-9-6 73 (p) KierenFallon 5 50
(James Tate) *hld up off the pce in last trio: rdn 3f out: no hdwy: n.d* 7/1

1m 45.2s (-0.90) **Going Correction** +0.125s/f (Good) 9 Ran SP% 107.4
Speed ratings (Par 101): **109,108,105,105,102 100,99,97,95**
CSF £23.19 CT £359.61 TOTE £5.90: £1.70, £1.10, £6.90; EX 24.20 Trifecta £481.70.
**Owner** C Corbett, David Hudd, Chris Wright **Bred** John Troy & Robert Levitt **Trained** West Ilsley, Berks

■ Rolling Dice was withdrawn. Price at time of withdrawal 8-1. Rule 4 applies to all bets - deduction 10p in the pound.

**FOCUS**
The gallop was solid for this fair 3yo handicap which few got into.

## 6263 PINSENT MASONS H'CAP 7f
3:35 (3:37) (Class 4) (0-80,80) 3-Y-O+ £8,086 (£2,406; £1,202; £601) Stalls Low

Form RPR
311 1 **Aqua Ardens (GER)**[20] 5629 6-9-10 80 (t) PatCosgrave 12 89
(George Baker) *hld up in last quartet: rdn and hdwy 2f out: edgd lft down camber but styd on to chal 1f out: led fnl 100yds: hld on wl: all out* 9/2[2]

1152 2 nk **Parisian Pyramid (IRE)**[11] 5951 8-8-13 72 (p) ThomasBrown(3) 4 80
(Lee Carter) *hld up in midfield: nt clr run 2f out: swtchd rt over 1f out: styd on strly ins fnl f: wnt 2nd last strides* 14/1

3162 3 hd **Weekendatbernies (IRE)**[12] 5930 3-9-0 79 LouisSteward(5) 11 84
(Ed de Giles) *dwlt and bustled along early: in tch in midfield: hdwy u.p to chal and edging lft down camber 1f out: led ins fnl f: sn hdd and unable qck towards fin: lost 2nd last strides* 6/1[3]

3534 4 ½ **Pactolus (IRE)**[18] 5727 3-8-11 71 RoystonFfrench 7 75
(Stuart Williams) *in tch in midfield: effrt 2f out: carried lft and sltly hmpd 1f out: rallied and hdwy ins fnl f: kpt on fnl 100yds* 10/1

0000 5 1 ½ **Brocklebank (IRE)**[16] 5785 5-9-2 72 PhillipMakin 6 74
(Simon Dow) *hld up in rr of main gp: c wdst over 2f out: hdwy ent fnl f: styd on strly fnl 150yds: nvr trbld ldrs* 16/1

021 6 1 **Enliven**[26] 5412 3-9-0 74 [1] SteveDrowne 1 72+
(Andrew Balding) *hld up towards rr: hdwy and nt clr run 2f out: switching lft and clsng on ldrs over 1f out: chsng ldrs whn nt clr run on inner and forced to ease 1f out: swtchd rt ins fnl f: kpt on: unable to chal* 3/1[1]

2352 7 ½ **Intomist (IRE)**[16] 5785 5-9-1 71 (p) StephenCraine 3 69
(Jim Boyle) *chsd ldrs: effrt and ev ch over 2f out: rdn to ld 2f out: hdd ins fnl f: sn btn and wknd fnl 75yds* 12/1

1120 8 2 ¼ **Exceedexpectations (IRE)**[8] 6035 5-9-7 77 (v) AmirQuinn 14 69
(Lee Carter) *chsd ldrs: effrt and ev ch over 2f out: sltly outpcd whn short of room and hmpd 1f out: wknd ins fnl f* 33/1

5346 9 2 **King Of Macedon (IRE)**[18] 5713 3-9-4 78 (b) KierenFallon 9 63
(Mark Johnston) *chsd ldrs: rdn and ev ch over 2f out tl ent fnl f: hmpd 1f out: outpcd and btn whn hmpd again ins fnl f: wknd* 9/1

0063 10 shd **Snow Bay**[13] 5887 8-9-2 72 GrahamLee 5 59
(Paul Midgley) *led tl hdd and rdn 2f out: drvn and btn over 1f out: wknd fnl f* 7/1

000 11 ¾ **Rakaan (IRE)**[44] 4761 7-8-12 73 JennyPowell(5) 8 58
(Brendan Powell) *v.s.a: a in rr* 20/1

1410 12 7 **Gold Beau (FR)**[17] 5766 4-9-10 80 (p) DougieCostello 2 47
(Kristin Stubbs) *in tch in midfield: struggling u.p over 2f out: wknd over 1f out* 50/1

3160 13 10 **Spellmaker**[30] 5281 5-8-9 70 EoinWalsh(5) 10 11
(Tony Newcombe) *t.k.h: chsd ldr tl ent fnl 2f: sn lost pl: bhd fnl f* 33/1

1m 23.23s (-0.07) **Going Correction** +0.125s/f (Good)
**WFA** 3 from 4yo+ 4lb 13 Ran SP% 121.9
Speed ratings (Par 105): **105,104,104,103,102 101,100,97,95,95 94,86,75**
CSF £64.99 CT £401.81 TOTE £4.40: £1.60, £4.70, £2.50; EX 47.80 Trifecta £109.10.
**Owner** C.E.S Baker **Bred** Gestut Karlshof **Trained** Manton, Wilts

**FOCUS**
The pace was genuine for this fair and competitive handicap, with the time well over 2sec faster than the 2yos managed earlier. A tight finish ensued.

## 6264 HCC INTERNATIONAL JUMP JOCKEYS DERBY H'CAP (TO BE RIDDEN BY PROFESSIONAL JUMP JOCKEYS) 1m 4f 10y
4:10 (4:11) (Class 4) (0-80,77) 4-Y-O+ £8,086 (£2,406; £1,202; £601) Stalls Centre

Form RPR
3223 1 **Eton Rambler (USA)**[61] 4209 4-11-3 70 AndrewTinkler 7 76
(George Baker) *hld up in midfield: clsd to trck ldrs and gng wl 2f out: swtchd rt and upsides ldrs over 1f out: shkn up to ld 1f out: drvn and kpt on fnl 100yds* 6/1[3]

1661 2 ½ **Whinging Willie (IRE)**[23] 5521 5-11-5 72 JamieMoore 8 77
(Gary Moore) *t.k.h: hld up in tch in last pair: swtchd rt and effrt over 1f out: str run u.p fnl f: wnt 2nd towards fin: nvr quite getting to wnr* 10/1

0212 3 ½ **Golden Jubilee (USA)**[20] 5621 5-11-3 70 (v) SamTwiston-Davies 5 74
(Nigel Twiston-Davies) *chsd ldrs for 2f: settled bk in midfield after: effrt to chal 2f out: drvn over 1f out: no ex and one pce fnl 100yds* 8/1

331 4 1 ½ **Last Minute Lisa (IRE)**[9] 6007 4-11-2 69 6ex BrendanPowell 9 71
(Sylvester Kirk) *stdd s: hld up in tch in last trio: clsd and nt clr run 2f out tl over 1f out: effrt u.p ent fnl f: styd on same pce fnl 150yds* 7/2[2]

5 ½ **Stephen Hero (IRE)**[29] 7289 4-11-0 67 HarrySkelton 1 68
(Dan Skelton) *led: rdn over 2f out: drvn and hdd 1f out: no ex and one pce ins fnl f* 9/4[1]

1325 6 1 ½ **Royal Marskell**[10] 5984 5-11-5 72 DougieCostello 3 71
(Alison Hutchinson) *t.k.h: chsd ldrs: wnt 2nd ent fnl 2f: rdn and ev ch 2f out tl no ex 1f out: wknd ins fnl f* 25/1

0041 7 2 ¾ **Medburn Cutler**[28] 5342 4-10-10 63 oh12 (p) NickScholfield 10 57?
(Paul Henderson) *in tch in midfield: rdn and effrt over 2f out: styng on same pce whn squeezed for room and hmpd 1f out: plugged on same pce after* 33/1

4604 8 3 ½ **Ocean Applause**[5] 6141 4-11-10 77 RichieMcLernon 6 66
(John Ryan) *stdd s: hld up in tch in last pair: hdwy on inner over 2f out: rdn 2f out: sn btn and wknd over 1f out* 10/1

1110 9 nk **King's Request (IRE)**[146] 1556 4-11-9 76 TomCannon 2 64
(Laura Mongan) *chsd ldrs tl lost pl over 2f out: sn rdn: wknd over 1f out* 33/1

1126 10 6 **Ifan (IRE)**[45] 4736 6-11-8 75 MichaelByrne 4 54
(Tim Vaughan) *t.k.h: chsd wnr tl lost pl ent fnl 2f: sn dropped out: bhd 1f out* 7/1

2m 44.46s (5.56) **Going Correction** +0.125s/f (Good) 10 Ran SP% 118.8
Speed ratings (Par 105): **86,85,85,84,84 83,81,78,78,74**
CSF £64.12 CT £484.01 TOTE £8.20: £2.30, £2.20, £2.30; EX 58.90 Trifecta £390.40.
**Owner** The Eton Ramblers **Bred** Darley, Bengal B'Stock Llc, J D Vice,Dvm **Trained** Manton, Wilts

**FOCUS**
A fair middle-distance handicap and a unique test for professional jump jockeys. Even with the horses carrying more weight than is usual, the winning time was below standard.

## 6265 TAFFY MAIDEN STKS 1m 2f 18y
4:45 (4:47) (Class 5) 3-4-Y-O £3,881 (£1,155; £577; £288) Stalls Low

Form RPR
332 1 **Labise (IRE)**[24] 5504 3-9-0 76 (t) PatDobbs 1 77
(Ralph Beckett) *chsd ldrs: rdn and effrt to chal on inner over 2f out: led ins fnl f: clr fnl 75yds: a holding on* 11/8[1]

3 2 nk **Viceroyalty**[10] 5976 3-9-5 0 AhmedAjtebi 6 81
(Charlie Appleby) *hld up in last pair: modest 4th 4f out: shkn up over 1f out: swtchd rt and hdwy 1f out: rdn and styd on strly ins fnl f: wnt 2nd wl ins fnl f: nvr quite getting to wnr* 8/1

34 3 1 ¾ **Park Place**[29] 5299 4-9-12 77 PhillipMakin 2 78
(John Quinn) *chsd ldr: upsides and gng best over 2f out: rdn and ld narrowly over 1f out: edgd lft 1f out: hdd ins fnl f: lost 2nd wl ins fnl f: wknd towards fin* 11/4[2]

262 4 ½ **Dreaming Beauty**[27] 5388 3-9-0 72 (p) GrahamLee 4 72
(Jeremy Noseda) *led: rdn and hrd pressed over 2f out: drvn and hdd over 1f out: outpcd whn short of room and swtchd rt 1f out: kpt on same pce after* 7/2[3]

5 53 **Debutante Blues (USA)** 3-9-0 0 KierenFallon 3
(Mark Johnston) *stdd s: hld up in last pair: dropped to last 4f out: sn lost tch: t.o* 12/1

2m 10.78s (1.08) **Going Correction** +0.125s/f (Good)
**WFA** 3 from 4yo 7lb 5 Ran SP% 109.8
Speed ratings (Par 103): **100,99,98,97,55**
CSF £12.56 TOTE £2.40: £1.50, £4.10; EX 12.20 Trifecta £41.70.
**Owner** Mrs Emma Kennedy **Bred** Kenilworth House Stud **Trained** Kimpton, Hants

**FOCUS**
A small field for this weak maiden. There was not much pace, but it still collapsed and that suited those coming from off the pace.

## 6266 BENNETT CONSTRUCTION H'CAP 6f
5:20 (5:21) (Class 5) (0-70,70) 3-Y-O+ £5,175 (£1,540; £769; £384) Stalls High

Form RPR
0423 1 **Tychaios**[13] 5880 4-9-3 63 PatDobbs 12 71
(Stuart Williams) *in tch in midfield: rdn and effrt over 1f out: hdwy u.p 1f out: led fnl 50yds: r.o wl* 5/1[2]

3500 2 ¾ **Rose Buck**[13] 5897 3-8-12 60 JackMitchell 15 66
(Giles Bravery) *hld up towards rr and stuck on outer: rdn 2f out: styd on strly ins fnl f: snatched 2nd last strides: nt rch wnr* 33/1

561 3 hd **Pharoh Jake**[14] 5860 6-8-11 57 WilliamCarson 10 62
(John Bridger) *t.k.h: chsd ldrs: rdn and ev ch 2f out: led ins fnl f: hdd and no ex fnl 50yds: lost 2nd last strides* 8/1

3232 4 hd **Hipz (IRE)**[29] 5307 3-9-4 66 KierenFallon 1 70
(Laura Mongan) *chsd ldr: rdn and ev ch 2f out: led over 1f out: hdd ins fnl f: no ex and one pce fnl 75yds* 6/1[3]

0025 5 nse **Koharu**[35] 5082 4-9-0 60 (p) SteveDrowne 9 64
(Peter Makin) *in tch in midfield: lost pl bnd over 3f out: hdwy u.p over 1f out: chsd ldrs and kpt on same pce fnl 100yds* 12/1

4052 6 1 ½ **Sakhee's Rose**[29] 5303 4-9-2 62 (b) GrahamLee 2 61
(Ed McMahon) *towards rr tl hdwy into midfield on inner 4f out: n.m.r and trying to switch rt 2f out: rdn and effrt over 1f out: styd on same pce fnl f* 9/2[1]

6423 7 shd **Slim Chance (IRE)**[9] 6014 5-9-5 65 DougieCostello 6 64
(Simon West) *stdd s: hld up in touch in rr: n.m.r 2f out: swtchd rt over 1f out: styd on ins fnl f: nvr trbld ldrs* 10/1

6461 8 nk **Dream Catcher (FR)**[21] 5602 6-9-3 66 AmyScott(3) 13 64
(Henry Candy) *led and crossed over to inner: rdn and hrd pressed 2f out: hdd over 1f out: wknd ins fnl f* 8/1

310 9 nse **Mambo Spirit (IRE)**[38] 4961 10-9-1 66 EoinWalsh(5) 4 64
(Tony Newcombe) *t.k.h: hld up towards rr: hdwy into midfield and swtchd lft over 2f out: drvn and no imp over 1f out: one pce fnl f* 16/1

0050 10 1 ¾ **Lionheart**[47] 4673 4-8-11 64 (e[1]) HectorCrouch(7) 7 56
(Peter Crate) *hld up in tch towards rr: effrt on inner 2f out: no prog: nvr trbld ldrs* 16/1

4513 11 nk **Perfect Pastime**[11] 5951 6-9-2 62 (p) PatCosgrave 5 53
(Jim Boyle) *in tch in midfield: rdn and effrt 2f out: no imp over 1f out: kpt on same pce fnl f* 6/1[3]

1046 **12** *1 3/4* **Welease Bwian (IRE)**[14] 5861 5-9-1 68........................ AaronJones(7) 3 54
(Stuart Williams) *rring in stalls: t.k.h: in tch in midfield: rdn and unable qck 2f out: wknd fnl f* **20/1**

1m 10.55s (1.15) **Going Correction** +0.125s/f (Good)
**WFA** 3 from 4yo+ 2lb 12 Ran SP% **121.9**
Speed ratings (Par 103): **97,96,95,95,95 93,93,92,92,90 90,87**
CSF £160.47 CT £958.12 TOTE £3.70: £2.00, £11.70, £3.00; EX 206.90 Trifecta £1688.60 Part won..
**Owner** Panny Ellinas **Bred** L Ellinas & Old Mill Stud **Trained** Newmarket, Suffolk

**FOCUS**
The pace held up for this competitive, if modest handicap and they finished in a bunch. The form looks viable, however.
T/Plt: £175.30 to a £1 stake. Pool: £58,575.47 - 243.90 winning units. T/Qpdt: £42.30 to a £1 stake. Pool: £4305.11 - 75.21 winning units. SP

# 6154 WOLVERHAMPTON (A.W) (L-H)
## Thursday, September 11

**OFFICIAL GOING: Tapeta: standard**
Wind: Light half-against Weather: Fine

## 6267 HOTEL & CONFERENCING AT WOLVERHAMPTON APPRENTICE H'CAP (TAPETA) 1m 1f 103y
**5:30** (5:31) (Class 6) (0-60,60) 3-Y-O+ **£1,940** (£577; £288; £144) **Stalls** Low

Form RPR
6150 **1** **Pim Street (USA)**[24] 5495 4-9-7 59........................ JoshDoyle(5) 10 68
(David O'Meara) *hld up: rdn over 3f out: str run ins fnl f: led post* **12/1**
5642 **2** *shd* **Classic Mission**[8] 6037 3-9-2 55........................(b) NedCurtis 5 63
(Jonathan Portman) *sn pushed along to chse ldr: rdn to ld over 1f out: hdd post* **9/2**[2]
0552 **3** *1* **Royal Trooper (IRE)**[5] 6157 8-9-3 53.................. BeckyBrisbourne(3) 11 59
(Mark Brisbourne) *s.i.s: hld up: hdwy on outer over 3f out: rdn over 1f out: edgd lft ins fnl f: r.o* **14/1**
1322 **4** *nse* **Her Red Devil (IRE)**[15] 5809 3-9-2 60........................ RowanScott(5) 8 67
(Richard Fahey) *a.p: nt clr run fr over 1f out tl wl ins fnl f: r.o: nvr able to chal* **7/1**[3]
2132 **5** *2 1/4* **Lynngale**[7] 6076 3-9-4 60........................ KieranShoemark(3) 6 61
(Kristin Stubbs) *sn led: rdn and hdd over 1f out: no ex ins fnl f* **7/4**[1]
0560 **6** *nk* **Poor Duke (IRE)**[7] 6076 4-9-3 57........................(be) LewisStones(7) 12 57
(Michael Mullineaux) *hld up: r.o ins fnl f: nvr nrr* **22/1**
2603 **7** *nse* **Golly Miss Molly**[15] 5832 3-8-6 48........................(p) DavidParkes(3) 9 48
(Jeremy Gask) *prom: n.m.r over 3f out: lost pl wl over 2f out: r.o ins fnl f* **33/1**
2036 **8** *nk* **Torridon**[14] 5854 3-8-8 47........................(v[1]) DanielCremin 7 46
(Mark Johnston) *pushed along in rr early: hmpd after 1f out: hdwy over 2f out: sn rdn: styd on same pce fnl f* **25/1**
406 **9** *1* **Youm Jamil (USA)**[45] 4738 7-8-13 46........................[1] JordanVaughan 4 43
(Tony Carroll) *chsd ldrs: hmpd sn after s: rdn and ev ch over 1f out: no ex ins fnl f* **22/1**
/420 **10** *1 1/2* **Lord Of The Storm**[22] 5558 6-9-4 51........................ RyanWhile 1 45
(Bill Turner) *prom: rdn over 2f out: wknd ins fnl f* **22/1**
0-50 **11** *2* **Rex Romanorum (IRE)**[68] 3958 6-9-7 59........................ PeterSword(5) 13 49
(Patrick Holmes) *hld up: pushed along over 2f out: n.d* **12/1**
1600 **12** *2* **Pipers Piping (IRE)**[13] 5899 8-9-9 59........................ RobHornby(3) 3 45
(Mandy Rowland) *hld up: pushed along over 2f out: nvr on terms* **40/1**
0530 **13** *5* **My New Angel (IRE)**[8] 6028 5-8-8 48........................ LouiseDay(7) 2 23
(Daniel Mark Loughnane) *mid=div: lost pl over 3f out: wknd over 2f out* **28/1**

2m 2.7s (1.90) **Going Correction** +0.10s/f (Slow)
**WFA** 3 from 4yo+ 6lb 13 Ran SP% **114.8**
Speed ratings (Par 101): **95,94,94,93,91 91,91,91,90,89 87,85,81**
CSF £56.94 CT £772.68 TOTE £13.10: £3.00, £2.60, £4.10; EX 100.60 Trifecta £1862.90.
**Owner** Dundalk Racing Club **Bred** Mr & Mrs D Probert, R Cowley & Darley **Trained** Nawton, N Yorks
■ Stewards' Enquiry : Lewis Stones caution: careless riding.
Kieran Shoemark three-day ban: careless riding (Sep 26,28,29)

**FOCUS**
The market got this spectacularly wrong as the winner was seemingly friendless.

## 6268 BRITISH STALLION STUDS EBF MAIDEN STKS (TAPETA) 7f 32y
**6:00** (6:03) (Class 5) 2-Y-O **£2,911** (£866; £432; £216) **Stalls** High

Form RPR
0 **1** **Todegica**[55] 4403 2-9-0 0........................ SebSanders 7 72+
(Ralph Beckett) *a.p: chsd ldr over 2f out: sn rdn: hung lft fr over 1f out: styd on to ld wl ins fnl f* **25/1**
U3 **2** *nk* **Wentworth Falls**[20] 5646 2-9-5 0........................ RobertHavlin 5 76
(Charlie Appleby) *led: rdn and hung lft ins fnl f: hung rt and hdd wl ins fnl f: nt qckn* **11/4**[3]
04 **3** *2 1/2* **Thanksgiving Day (IRE)**[6] 6102 2-9-5 0........................ ShaneKelly 1 70
(Jamie Osborne) *chsd ldrs: rdn over 2f out: styd on* **14/1**
6 **4** *1/2* **Doubly Clever (IRE)**[47] 4666 2-9-5 0........................ TomQueally 9 69
(Charles Hills) *mid-div: drvn along over 1/2-way: hdwy over 2f out: styd on: nt trble ldrs* **2/1**[1]
**5** *hd* **Cyril** 2-9-5 0........................ FergalLynch 8 70+
(Kevin Ryan) *sn pushed along in rr: r.o ins fnl f: nvr nrr* **33/1**
**6** *1/2* **Sammy's Warrior** 2-9-0 0........................ DanielMuscutt(5) 4 67
(Marco Botti) *hld up: hdwy over 2f out: rdn over 1f out: styd on* **40/1**
50 **7** *hd* **River Of Dreams (IRE)**[63] 4129 2-9-0 0........................[1] ShaneGray(5) 10 67
(Kevin Ryan) *hld up: rdn over 2f out: r.o ins fnl f: nrst fin* **100/1**
3 **8** *1 3/4* **Carnival King (IRE)**[59] 4270 2-9-5 0........................ MartinLane 12 62
(Brian Meehan) *mid-div: rdn 1/2-way: hdwy over 2f out: styd on same pce fr over 1f out* **9/4**[2]
0 **9** *10* **Percy's Dream**[20] 5644 2-9-0 0........................ PaulMulrennan 3 33
(William Jarvis) *s.i.s: nvr on terms* **200/1**
55 **10** *3/4* **The Paco Kid**[54] 4430 2-9-5 78........................ HayleyTurner 2 36
(Olly Stevens) *chsd ldr tl over 5f out: remained handy: rdn over 2f out: wknd over 1f out* **22/1**
26 **11** *11* **Glorious Magic (IRE)**[3] 6190 2-9-5 0........................ NickyMackay 6 9
(Olly Stevens) *prom: chsd ldr over 5f out tl rdn over 2f out: wknd wl over 1f out* **33/1**
0 **12** *13* **Sir Veillance**[27] 5397 2-9-0 0........................ AlistairRawlinson(5) 11
(Michael Appleby) *mid-div: pushed along over 4f out: sn wknd* **250/1**

1m 29.64s (0.84) **Going Correction** +0.10s/f (Slow) 12 Ran SP% **115.8**
Speed ratings (Par 95): **99,98,95,95,95 94,94,92,80,79 67,52**
CSF £88.79 TOTE £25.50: £8.30, £1.10, £2.90; EX 127.20 Trifecta £2939.40.
**Owner** Nurlan Bizakov **Bred** Hesmonds Stud Ltd **Trained** Kimpton, Hants

**FOCUS**
With many of the market principals failing to give their running, it was the once-raced winner who sprang a surprise.

## 6269 WOLVERHAMPTON-RACECOURSE.CO.UK FILLIES' H'CAP (TAPETA) 7f 32y
**6:30** (6:31) (Class 4) (0-80,75) 3-Y-O+ **£4,690** (£1,395; £697; £348) **Stalls** High

Form RPR
0034 **1** **Al Manaal**[20] 5629 4-9-5 74........................ CharlesBishop(3) 6 83
(Mick Channon) *chsd ldrs: rdn to go 2nd over 1f out: led and edgd lft ins fnl f: jst hld on* **8/1**
3-31 **2** *nse* **Aragosta**[22] 5548 4-9-6 72........................ HayleyTurner 5 81+
(James Fanshawe) *s.i.s: hld up: shkn up over 2f out: hdwy 1f out: rdn to chse wnr wl ins fnl f: r.o: jst failed* **6/4**[1]
0645 **3** *2 1/4* **Valen (IRE)**[29] 5320 3-9-3 73........................ WilliamTwiston-Davies 8 74
(Michael Bell) *hld up: hdwy and hmpd over 1f out: styd on same pce ins fnl f* **10/1**
2016 **4** *1 1/2* **Swiss Kiss**[19] 5685 3-9-5 75........................ RobertHavlin 3 72
(John Gosden) *chsd ldr tl led 3f out: rdn over 1f out: hdd and no ex ins fnl f* **13/2**[2]
5612 **5** *3/4* **Madame Mirasol (IRE)**[21] 5605 3-9-3 73........................(p) FergalLynch 4 68
(Kevin Ryan) *prom: rdn over 1f out: styd on same pce fnl f* **7/1**[3]
3010 **6** *5* **Imaginary World (IRE)**[7] 6057 6-9-4 75........................(e) ShaneGray(5) 2 59
(John Balding) *hld up: pushed along 4f out: nvr on terms* **11/1**
**7** *1 1/2* **Bint Dandy (IRE)**[71] 3866 3-9-2 72........................ JimmyQuinn 1 50
(Chris Dwyer) *prom: rdn 1/2-way: wknd fnl f* **50/1**
3U31 **8** *2 1/2* **Lilly Junior**[17] 5772 3-9-3 73........................ BenCurtis 7 45
(Brian Ellison) *led 4f: rdn and edgd rt over 1f out: sn wknd* **13/2**[2]

1m 28.63s (-0.17) **Going Correction** +0.10s/f (Slow)
**WFA** 3 from 4yo+ 4lb 8 Ran SP% **109.7**
Speed ratings (Par 102): **104,103,101,99,98 93,91,88**
CSF £18.76 CT £111.45 TOTE £10.00: £2.80, £1.10, £3.70; EX 23.50 Trifecta £283.60.
**Owner** M Channon **Bred** Darley **Trained** West Ilsley, Berks

**FOCUS**
They went no pace early.

## 6270 WOLVERHAMPTON HOLIDAY INN MAIDEN STKS (TAPETA) (DIV I) 5f 216y
**7:00** (7:02) (Class 5) 2-Y-O **£2,587** (£770; £384; £192) **Stalls** Low

Form RPR
53 **1** **Rio Ronaldo (IRE)**[43] 4787 2-9-5 0........................ ShaneKelly 4 76
(Mike Murphy) *hld up in tch: swtchd rt over 2f out: shkn up to ld over 1f out: edgd lft ins fnl f: drvn out* **2/1**[2]
03 **2** *3/4* **Amazour (IRE)**[24] 5488 2-9-5 0........................ MartinLane 11 74
(Ismail Mohammed) *led: rdn and hdd over 1f out: styd on* **7/4**[1]
020 **3** *nk* **Biting Bullets (USA)**[49] 4570 2-9-5 76........................ StevieDonohoe 7 73
(Jo Hughes) *a.p: chsd ldr over 3f out tl rdn over 1f out: r.o* **13/2**[3]
**4** *hd* **Slovak (IRE)** 2-9-0 0........................ JimmyQuinn 10 67+
(James Tate) *hld up: hdwy over 2f out: r.o* **16/1**
0 **5** *5* **Matron**[28] 5344 2-9-0 0........................ HayleyTurner 1 52
(James Fanshawe) *chsd ldr tl over 3f out: remained handy: rdn over 1f out: no ex fnl f* **12/1**
6 **6** *2 1/2* **Gin Trap (USA)**[35] 5091 2-9-5 0........................ HarryBentley 5 50
(Olly Stevens) *chsd ldrs: rdn over 2f out: styd on same pce fr over 1f out* **14/1**
**7** *3 1/4* **First Summer** 2-9-5 0........................ PaulMulrennan 3 40
(Ed McMahon) *dwlt: outpcd: styd on ins fnl f: nvr nrr* **28/1**
55 **8** *2 3/4* **Shimmering Silver (IRE)**[24] 5509 2-9-0 0........................ FrankieMcDonald 8 27
(Daniel Mark Loughnane) *sn pushed along in rr: hmpd over 2f out: n.d* **40/1**
00 **9** *1 1/4* **Bahamian Desert**[15] 5807 2-9-2 0........................ SamJames(3) 9 28
(David O'Meara) *chsd ldrs: lost pl 5f out: wknd over 2f out* **40/1**
0 **10** *1 1/2* **Lonely Ranger (USA)**[22] 5555 2-9-5 0........................ RobertHavlin 2 24
(Amy Weaver) *hld up: nt clr run over 2f out: rdn and wknd wl over 1f out* **150/1**

1m 15.35s (0.85) **Going Correction** +0.10s/f (Slow) 10 Ran SP% **112.3**
Speed ratings (Par 95): **98,97,96,96,89 86,82,78,76,74**
CSF £5.43 TOTE £2.90: £1.20, £1.30, £1.90; EX 6.70 Trifecta £25.10.
**Owner** The Castaways **Bred** Knocktoran Stud & Kildaragh Stud **Trained** Westoning, Beds

**FOCUS**
An ordinary juvenile event was fought out by those with experience.

## 6271 WOLVERHAMPTON HOLIDAY INN MAIDEN STKS (TAPETA) (DIV II) 5f 216y
**7:30** (7:30) (Class 5) 2-Y-O **£2,587** (£770; £384; £192) **Stalls** Low

Form RPR
542 **1** **Subversive (IRE)**[7] 6058 2-9-5 0........................ FrannyNorton 3 74+
(Mark Johnston) *sn led: hdd over 3f out: led again over 2f out: rdn and edgd rt over 1f out: hung lft ins fnl f: styd on* **5/6**[1]
46 **2** *3/4* **Shar Shar (IRE)**[16] 5799 2-9-0 0........................ PaulPickard 7 66
(Brian Ellison) *plld hrd: trckd ldr 1f: remained handy: rdn over 1f out: hung lft ins fnl f: r.o* **6/1**[3]
0 **3** *nk* **Elis Eliz (IRE)**[10] 5973 2-9-0 0........................ TomQueally 6 65
(Michael Wigham) *hld up in tch: rdn over 1f out: r.o* **66/1**
03 **4** *3/4* **Dark Side Dream**[35] 5099 2-9-5 0........................ JimmyQuinn 4 68
(Chris Dwyer) *plld hrd: trckd wnr 5f out tl led over 3f out: hdd over 2f out: sn rdn: edgd lft and styd on same pce ins fnl f* **25/1**
**5** *3/4* **Bonfire Heart** 2-9-0 0........................ FrankieMcDonald 8 60
(Daniel Mark Loughnane) *s.i.s: hld up: hdwy over 2f out: hung lft fnl f: styd on* **22/1**
5 **6** *nk* **Hard To Handel**[13] 5874 2-9-5 0........................ SebSanders 9 64
(Ralph Beckett) *prom: rdn and hung lft over 1f out: styd on* **3/1**[2]
5 **7** *8* **Granola**[16] 5789 2-9-0 0........................ HarryBentley 2 35
(David Brown) *chsd ldrs: rdn over 3f out: wknd 2f out* **12/1**
6 **8** *1/2* **Don Ricardo (IRE)**[108] 2601 2-9-2 0........................ GeorgeChaloner(3) 1 39
(Richard Fahey) *sn pushed along in rr: wknd over 2f out* **10/1**

1m 16.07s (1.57) **Going Correction** +0.10s/f (Slow) 8 Ran SP% **120.3**
Speed ratings (Par 95): **93,92,91,90,89 86,78,77**
CSF £6.98 TOTE £1.40: £1.02, £2.70, £6.70; EX 8.40 Trifecta £192.80.
**Owner** Sheikh Hamdan bin Mohammed Al Maktoum **Bred** Darley **Trained** Middleham Moor, N Yorks



The Form Book, Raceform Ltd, Newbury, RG14 5SJ

**FOCUS**
A race littered with potential improvers.

## 6272 MCCLAREN CHARTERED LOSS ADJUSTERS H'CAP (TAPETA) 5f 216y
**8:00** (8:01) (Class 6) (0-60,68) 3-Y-O+ **£1,940** (£577; £288; £144) **Stalls** Low

Form RPR
464 **1** **Reaffirmed (IRE)**$^{36}$ 5061 3-9-2 57 LukeMorris 1 66+
(Ed Vaughan) *hld up: nt clr run over 2f out: hdwy over 1f out: swtchd lft and r.o to ld wl ins fnl f* **5/1$^{2}$**
5020 **2** ¾ **High Tone**$^{35}$ 5105 4-8-10 49 HarryBentley 11 56
(Dean Ivory) *a.p: rdn over 1f out: r.o to go 2nd towards fin* **8/1$^{3}$**
0111 **3** *nk* **Rise To Glory (IRE)**$^{6}$ 6090 6-9-8 68 12ex.....(tp) MrAidenBlakemore$^{(7)}$ 9 74
(Shaun Harris) *led: rdn over 1f out: hdd and unable qck wl ins fnl f* **4/1$^{1}$**
2050 **4** ½ **Hamis Al Bin (IRE)**$^{71}$ 3848 5-9-3 56 (t) DavidNolan 4 60
(Milton Bradley) *a.p: rdn over 1f out: r.o* **14/1**
126 **5** *1* **Gracie's Games**$^{17}$ 5777 8-8-9 48 (v) WilliamTwiston-Davies 12 49
(John Spearing) *chsd ldr 5f out: rdn and ev ch ins fnl f: styd on same pce* **25/1**
3501 **6** ¾ **Catalinas Diamond (IRE)**$^{12}$ 5907 6-9-5 58 (t) SebSanders 8 57
(Pat Murphy) *hld up: hdwy over 1f out: sn rdn: styd on: nt rch ldrs* **9/1**
-050 **7** ¾ **Aster's Approval**$^{8}$ 6042 4-8-11 50 (bt) LemosdeSouza 7 46
(Mrs Ilka Gansera-Leveque) *chsd ldr 1f: remained handy: rdn over 1f out: styng on same pce whn hmpd ins fnl f* **9/1**
0021 **8** *hd* **Methaaly (IRE)**$^{8}$ 6023 11-8-6 52 (b) AnnaHesketh$^{(7)}$ 5 48
(Michael Mullineaux) *hld up: r.o ins fnl f: nt trble ldrs* **8/1$^{3}$**
6650 **9** *shd* **Prigsnov Dancer (IRE)**$^{30}$ 5287 9-8-12 56 ShaneGray$^{(5)}$ 3 51
(Deborah Sanderson) *prom: rdn and nt clr run over 1f out: no ex ins fnl f* **22/1**
0 **10** *6* **Hazza The Jazza**$^{6}$ 6122 4-8-12 51 (b) JasonHart 6 27
(Richard Guest) *s.s: sn drvn along and a in rr* **4/1$^{1}$**
436- **11** *3* **Bountiful Forest**$^{347}$ 6872 3-9-3 58 StevieDonohoe 10 25
(Kevin Frost) *hld up: racd keenly: rdn and wknd over 1f out* **50/1**
0000 **12** *10* **Saga Lout**$^{65}$ 4049 4-8-10 54 (p) JackDuern$^{(5)}$ 2
(Andrew Hollinshead) *hld up: wknd over 1f out* **20/1**

1m 15.55s (1.05) **Going Correction** +0.10s/f (Slow)
**WFA** 3 from 4yo+ 2lb **12** Ran SP% **120.5**
Speed ratings (Par 101): **97,96,95,94,93 92,91,91,83 79,65**
CSF £43.34 CT £181.61 TOTE £7.00: £2.50, £3.20, £1.80; EX 63.70 Trifecta £611.00.
**Owner** Ballymore Downunder Syndicate **Bred** Floors Farming, S Roy & Admington Hall **Trained** Newmarket, Suffolk
■ Stewards' Enquiry : Luke Morris two-day ban: careless riding (Sep 25-26); two-day ban: used whip above shoulder height (Sep 28-29)

**FOCUS**
This was competitive for the grade and there was plenty to like about the performance of the winner.

## 6273 BOOK NOW FOR CHRISTMAS H'CAP (TAPETA) 5f 20y
**8:30** (8:31) (Class 6) (0-60,60) 3-Y-O+ **£1,940** (£577; £288; £144) **Stalls** Low

Form RPR
0350 **1** **Bilash**$^{21}$ 5602 7-9-1 59 JackDuern$^{(5)}$ 13 68
(Andrew Hollinshead) *mid-div: hdwy over 1f out: edgd lft and r.o to ld wl ins fnl f* **15/2$^{3}$**
5056 **2** ¾ **Give Us A Belle (IRE)**$^{14}$ 5860 5-9-4 57 (vt) AdamBeschizza 5 63
(Christine Dunnett) *chsd ldr tl led over 3f out: rdn and hung rt fr over 1f out: hdd wl ins fnl f* **16/1**
6233 **3** *shd* **Lucky Mark (IRE)**$^{22}$ 5574 5-8-11 55 (p) ShaneGray$^{(5)}$ 8 61
(John Balding) *chsd ldrs: rdn over 1f out: r.o* **11/4$^{1}$**
5330 **4** *1* **Passionada**$^{27}$ 5375 5-9-7 60 $^{1}$ PaulMulrennan 3 62
(Ed McMahon) *chsd ldrs: rdn over 1f out: styd on same pce ins fnl f* **7/2$^{2}$**
5363 **5** *1* **Your Gifted (IRE)**$^{16}$ 5801 7-8-9 53 (v) JackGarritty$^{(5)}$ 10 52
(Lisa Williamson) *hld up: hdwy over 1f out: nt clr run ins fnl f: styd on same pce* **11/1**
0061 **6** *5* **Louis Vee (IRE)**$^{17}$ 5780 6-9-7 60 (t) LukeMorris 9 41
(Roy Brotherton) *chsd ldrs: hung rt 1/2-way: nt clr run over 1f out: wknd ins fnl f* **11/4$^{1}$**
005 **7** *1* **Avonvalley**$^{7}$ 6077 7-9-4 57 TomQueally 1 34
(Peter Grayson) *s.i.s: nvr on terms* **33/1**
5443 **8** 3½ **Baby Queen (IRE)**$^{17}$ 5780 8-8-13 55 NeilFarley$^{(3)}$ 4 20
(Brian Baugh) *led: hdd over 3f out: rdn over 1f out: wknd fnl f* **22/1**
0666 **9** 1½ **Irish Boy (IRE)**$^{41}$ 4848 6-8-6 50 (t) DanielMuscutt$^{(5)}$ 11 9
(Christine Dunnett) *sn drvn along and outpcd* **80/1**
0600 **10** ½ **Hejaz (IRE)**$^{35}$ 5075 4-8-11 50 (p) StevieDonohoe 6 7
(John Butler) *sn pushed along in rr: bhd fr 1/2-way* **33/1**

1m 2.41s (0.51) **Going Correction** +0.10s/f (Slow) **10** Ran SP% **113.0**
Speed ratings (Par 101): **99,97,97,96,94 86,84,79,76,76**
CSF £108.38 CT £419.65 TOTE £11.50: £2.30, £4.50, £1.60; EX 126.80 Trifecta £1406.40.
**Owner** Pyle & Hollinshead **Bred** M Pyle & Mrs T Pyle **Trained** Upper Longdon, Staffs

**FOCUS**
This was strongly run and it played into the hands of the winner, who was off a career-low mark.

## 6274 SPONSOR A RACE BY CALLING 01902 390000 H'CAP (TAPETA) 1m 4f 50y
**9:00** (9:01) (Class 5) (0-75,75) 3-Y-O+ **£2,587** (£770; £384; £192) **Stalls** Low

Form RPR
1/34 **1** **Daaree (IRE)**$^{18}$ 5730 4-9-6 69 AhmedAjtebi 4 78+
(Saeed bin Suroor) *s.i.s: hld up: hdwy over 3f out: rdn and edgd lft over 1f out: r.o to ld nr fin* **15/8$^{1}$**
4204 **2** ¾ **Men Don't Cry (IRE)**$^{14}$ 5863 5-9-8 74 (b) DeclanBates$^{(3)}$ 6 82
(Ed de Giles) *hld up: hdwy over 3f out: rdn to ld wl ins fnl f: hdd nr fin* **22/1**
1404 **3** 1¼ **Manomine**$^{16}$ 5800 5-9-3 71 (b) LouisSteward$^{(5)}$ 10 77
(Clive Brittain) *led: 1f: chsd ldrs: led over 2f out: rdn and hdd wl ins fnl f* **12/1**
3240 **4** 2¼ **Norse Light**$^{38}$ 4985 3-9-1 73 (p) RichardKingscote 7 75
(Ralph Beckett) *a.p: rdn over 2f out: no ex ins fnl f* **6/1$^{3}$**
103 **5** 4½ **Spanish Plume**$^{39}$ 4940 6-9-7 75 (p) JackDuern$^{(5)}$ 5 70
(Andrew Hollinshead) *hld up: hdwy 4f out: rdn over 1f out: wknd fnl f* **25/1**
0344 **6** ½ **Strawberry Martini**$^{52}$ 4504 3-9-0 72 MartinDwyer 12 66
(William Muir) *chsd ldrs: led over 8f out: rdn and hdd over 2f out: wknd over 1f out* **15/2**
621/ **7** *9* **Artisan**$^{592}$ 6478 6-9-4 67 PaulPickard 2 47
(Brian Ellison) *hld up: hung rt fnl 6f: n.d* **33/1**
100P **8** 2¾ **Markami (FR)**$^{13}$ 5898 4-9-6 69 (t) StevieDonohoe 11 45
(Johnny Farrelly) *prom: sn pushed along: lost pl 8f out: n.d after* **33/1**
246/ **9** 4½ **Crafty Roberto**$^{306}$ 2447 6-9-9 72 (t) WilliamTwiston-Davies 8 40
(Alex Hales) *hld up: a in rr* **66/1**
4513 **10** ½ **Incendo**$^{24}$ 5502 8-9-9 72 (v) HayleyTurner 9 40
(Conor Dore) *hld up: rdn over 3f out: a in rr* **22/1**
0/66 **11** *12* **Musical Moon**$^{15}$ 5822 4-9-7 70 SebSanders 1 18
(Lady Herries) *chsd ldrs tl rdn and wknd over 3f out* **66/1**
2220 **12** *72* **Mountain Kingdom (IRE)**$^{28}$ 5356 3-9-3 75 (p) LukeMorris 3
(Sir Mark Prescott Bt) *led after 1f tl over 8f out: remained w ldr tl rdn 5f out: sn lost pl: wknd over 3f out* **9/4$^{2}$**

2m 39.68s (-1.12) **Going Correction** +0.10s/f (Slow)
**WFA** 3 from 4yo+ 9lb **12** Ran SP% **120.7**
Speed ratings (Par 103): **107,106,105,104,101 100,94,93,90,89 81,33**
CSF £51.50 CT £408.37 TOTE £3.00: £1.10, £3.60, £3.60; EX 40.30 Trifecta £380.40.
**Owner** Godolphin **Bred** Shadwell Estate Company Limited **Trained** Newmarket, Suffolk

**FOCUS**
A fair finale and a good ending for most punters.
T/Plt: £42.70 to a £1 stake. Pool: £77,662.56 - 1327.67 winning units. T/Qpdt: £2.70 to a £1 stake. Pool: £12,263.84 - 3257.26 winning units. CR

6275 - 6278a (Foreign Racing) - See Raceform Interactive

# 5918 CHESTER (L-H)
Friday, September 12

**OFFICIAL GOING: Good (good to firm in places) changing to good after race 1 (2:30)**
Wind: almost nil Weather: fine, overcast

## 6279 BETFAIR HOME OF THE PRICE RUSH / EBF MAIDEN STKS (BOBIS RACE) (C&G) 7f 122y
**2:00** (2:01) (Class 4) 2-Y-O **£6,469** (£1,925; £962; £481) **Stalls** Low

Form RPR
3 **1** **Gabrial The Viking (IRE)**$^{13}$ 5922 2-9-0 0 DavidNolan 3 77
(Richard Fahey) *chsd ldr: drvn over 3f out: styd on to ld clsng stages* **7/2$^{3}$**
24 **2** ½ **Manshaa (IRE)**$^{28}$ 5393 2-9-0 0 JoeFanning 1 76
(Mark Johnston) *led: hdd and no ex towards fin* **2/1$^{1}$**
52 **3** ¾ **Cosmic Ray**$^{24}$ 5519 2-9-0 0 LiamKeniry 6 74+
(Andrew Balding) *hld up in rr: t.k.h: hdwy on outside over 2f out: kpt on to take 3rd nr fin* **10/1**
2224 **4** ¾ **Vegas Rebel (IRE)**$^{17}$ 5799 2-9-0 77 ChrisCatlin 7 72
(Peter Chapple-Hyam) *in rr: hdwy over 3f out: chsng ldrs over 1f out: kpt on same pce* **7/1**
6 **5** 2¼ **Felix De Vega (IRE)**$^{14}$ 5881 2-9-0 0 SeanLevey 8 67
(Richard Hannon) *chsd ldr: drvn over 3f out: hung lft ins fnl f: wknd nr fin* **5/2$^{2}$**
**6** 4½ **Doesyourdogbite (IRE)** 2-9-0 0 RoystonFfrench 2 56
(Andrew Hollinshead) *s.s: sn chsng ldrs: wknd over 1f out* **33/1**
0 **7** 1¾ **Pafiya**$^{31}$ 5264 2-9-0 0 JamesSullivan 4 52
(Kristin Stubbs) *trckd ldrs: wknd over 1f out* **100/1**
0 **8** ½ **Silver Tycoon (IRE)**$^{18}$ 5759 2-9-0 0 IanBrennan 5 50
(John Quinn) *t.k.h: trckd ldrs: lost pl over 4f out* **50/1**

1m 36.86s (3.06) **Going Correction** +0.35s/f (Good) **8** Ran SP% **111.6**
Speed ratings (Par 97): **98,97,96,96,93 89,87,87**
CSF £10.35 TOTE £3.50: £1.70, £1.20, £2.50; EX 9.80 Trifecta £51.50.
**Owner** Dr Marwan Koukash **Bred** Patrick A Cluskey **Trained** Musley Bank, N Yorks

**FOCUS**
The entire length of rail moved out by between 3yds and 6yds. Consequently races 1, 2, 3 and 7 increased by 24yds, race 4 and 6 by 26yds, and race 5 by 46yds. After a dry night the going remained as the official good, good to firm in places. A fair maiden in which it paid to race handily off an ordinary pace.

## 6280 RIPPLEFFECT NURSERY H'CAP (BOBIS RACE) 7f 2y
**2:30** (2:30) (Class 3) (0-95,80) 2-Y-O **£7,115** (£2,117; £1,058) **Stalls** Low

Form RPR
3313 **1** **Guilty (IRE)**$^{35}$ 5147 2-9-2 78 SeanLevey 1 81
(Richard Hannon) *mde all: qcknd pce over 3f out: drvn and kpt on wl fnl f* **2/1$^{2}$**
321 **2** *1* **Mythmaker**$^{20}$ 5679 2-9-3 79 TomEaves 3 79
(Bryan Smart) *hld up in last: effrt over 2f out: chsd wnr over 1f out: styd on ins fnl f* **7/1$^{3}$**
341 **3** *9* **Bizzario**$^{27}$ 5408 2-9-4 80 JoeFanning 2 56
(Mark Johnston) *chsd wnr: drvn over 2f out: wknd fnl f: eased clsng stages* **4/6$^{1}$**

1m 30.57s (4.07) **Going Correction** +0.35s/f (Good) **3** Ran SP% **105.8**
Speed ratings (Par 99): **90,88,78**
CSF £9.91 TOTE £2.20; EX 7.80 Trifecta £8.60.
**Owner** Mrs J K Powell **Bred** John Doyle **Trained** East Everleigh, Wilts

**FOCUS**
Only three runners, but a fair nursery and the winner controlled the race from the off. The winner's previous win could be rated this high.

## 6281 FEEL THE RUSH AT BETFAIR H'CAP 7f 2y
**3:05** (3:05) (Class 3) (0-95,94) 3-Y-O+ **£7,762** (£2,310; £1,154; £577) **Stalls** Low

Form RPR
1233 **1** **Athletic**$^{6}$ 6145 5-8-7 79 (v) JennyPowell$^{(5)}$ 5 92
(Andrew Reid) *in rr: hdwy on outer 3f out: edgd lft and led 1f out: drew clr* **11/2**
3402 **2** *4* **Gatepost (IRE)**$^{28}$ 5385 5-9-1 82 DavidNolan 6 85
(Richard Fahey) *mid-div: hdwy 3f out: 2nd and hmpd over 1f out: kpt on same pce* **9/1**
3314 **3** 1¼ **Apostle (IRE)**$^{13}$ 5919 5-9-7 93 DanielMuscutt$^{(5)}$ 3 93
(David Simcock) *in rr: nt clr run on inner over 2f out: effrt and n.m.r over 1f out: swtchd rt and styd on to take 3rd last 100yds* **3/1$^{1}$**
160 **4** *2* **Dr Red Eye**$^{27}$ 5444 6-9-2 83 (p) TomEaves 2 78
(Scott Dixon) *led: hdd 1f out: grad wknd* **15/2**
1002 **5** ½ **Lady Frances**$^{7}$ 6112 3-9-3 88 JoeFanning 7 79
(Mark Johnston) *sn chsng ldrs: wkng whn hmpd jst ins fnl f* **12/1**
2303 **6** *nse* **Beau Nash (IRE)**$^{13}$ 5919 3-9-7 92 SeanLevey 4 83
(Richard Hannon) *chsd ldrs: lost pl over 5f out: drvn and outpcd over 2f out: hdwy on outside 1f out: styng on at fin: lame* **7/2$^{2}$**
3000 **7** 1¾ **Chosen Character (IRE)**$^{13}$ 5919 6-9-10 91 (vt) RichardKingscote 8 80
(Tom Dascombe) *sn chsng ldrs on outer: wknd appr fnl f* **28/1**
1000 **8** 1¾ **Kimberella**$^{23}$ 5575 4-9-13 94 AdrianNicholls 1 78
(David Nicholls) *trckd ldrs on inner: t.k.h: effrt over 1f out: sn wknd: eased clsng stages* **9/2$^{3}$**

1m 27.49s (0.99) **Going Correction** +0.35s/f (Good)
**WFA** 3 from 4yo+ 4lb **8** Ran SP% **113.7**
Speed ratings (Par 107): **108,103,102,99,99 99,97,95**
CSF £52.58 CT £174.53 TOTE £5.20: £2.20, £3.20, £1.10; EX 55.40 Trifecta £168.10.

**Owner** A S Reid **Bred** A S Reid **Trained** Mill Hill, London NW7
■ Stewards' Enquiry : Jenny Powell one-day ban: careless riding (26 Sep)
**FOCUS**
A useful handicap run at a solid, if not overly strong pace. The winner put it all together.

## 6282 STELLA CIDRE MAIDEN FILLIES' STKS — 1m 2f 75y
3:40 (3:40) (Class 4) 3-Y-0+ £6,469 (£1,925; £962; £481) Stalls High

Form RPR
2222 **1** **Almashooqa (USA)**[21] 5634 3-9-0 87........ JackMitchell 4 85
(Roger Varian) *mde all: pushed along over 2f out: styd on over 1f out: drew clr* **4/5**[1]
2425 **2** *3 3/4* **Shama's Song (IRE)**[53] 4504 3-9-0 73........ TedDurcan 1 78
(Sir Michael Stoute) *trckd wnr: upsides over 2f out: kpt on same pce over 1f out* **5/2**[2]
0 **3** *3/4* **Bikini Island (USA)**[75] 3750 3-9-0 0........ LiamKeniry 5 77
(Andrew Balding) *t.k.h: pushed wd bnd over 7f out: sn trcking ldrs: effrt over 2f out: hung lft and one pce fnl f* **7/1**[3]
0-0 **4** *15* **Sr Swing**[67] 4022 3-9-0 0........ JoeFanning 2 48
(Philip Kirby) *mid-div: wd bnd over 7f out: drvn over 4f out: lost pl over 2f out: sn bhd* **40/1**
0 **5** *3 1/4* **Gabrial's Lady (IRE)**[8] 6073 3-9-0 0........ DavidNolan 3 42
(Richard Fahey) *chsd ldrs: drvn over 4f out: hung rt and lost pl over 2f out: sn bhd* **12/1**
**6** *1 1/2* **Magic Maisie** 3-9-0 0........ RichardKingscote 6 39
(Alistair Whillans) *dwlt: bhd and drvn along: hdwy over 5f out: lost pl over 2f out: sn bhd* **25/1**

2m 16.12s (4.92) **Going Correction** +0.35s/f (Good) 6 Ran SP% **110.6**
Speed ratings (Par 102): **94,91,90,78,75 74**
CSF £2.85 TOTE £1.20: £1.10, £1.40; EX 3.30 Trifecta £10.30.
**Owner** Hamdan Al Maktoum **Bred** Shadwell Farm LLC **Trained** Newmarket, Suffolk
**FOCUS**
No depth to this maiden and the class runner took advantage. She did not need to be at her best.

## 6283 BOODLES DIAMOND H'CAP — 1m 7f 195y
4:15 (4:16) (Class 3) (0-95,91) 3-Y-0+ £7,762 (£2,310; £1,154; £577) Stalls Low

Form RPR
0446 **1** **Snowy Dawn**[50] 4575 4-8-6 74........ JackDuern(5) 4 80+
(Ben Case) *trckd ldrs: led over 4f out: edgd rt ins fnl f: drvn out* **6/1**[3]
1301 **2** *1* **Kashgar**[10] 6005 5-9-6 88 6ex........ DanielMuscutt(5) 3 93
(Bernard Llewellyn) *mid-div: trckd ldrs after 5f: drvn to chse wnr over 2f out: styd on same pce last 100yds* **3/1**[2]
0406 **3** *3/4* **Arty Campbell (IRE)**[29] 5341 4-8-10 73........ MartinLane 2 77
(Bernard Llewellyn) *hld up in rr: effrt over 3f out: 3rd over 1f out: kpt on same pce* **16/1**
4100 **4** *3 1/2* **Gabrial's Star**[104] 2760 5-9-8 85........(b) DavidNolan 7 85
(Richard Fahey) *hld up towards rr: effrt over 3f out: outpcd over 2f out: kpt on to take modest 4th last 150yds* **7/1**
0050 **5** *6* **Boite (IRE)**[20] 5673 4-10-0 91........ JoeFanning 6 84
(Peter Chapple-Hyam) *led: hdd over 4f out: lost pl over 1f out* **13/2**
23-1 **6** *23* **Charlotte's Day**[8] 6075 3-8-6 82 6ex........ ChrisCatlin 1 47
(Sir Mark Prescott Bt) *trckd ldrs: t.k.h: drvn over 4f out: lost pl over 2f out: bhd whn eased ins fnl f: t.o* **6/4**[1]

3m 34.63s (6.63) **Going Correction** +0.35s/f (Good)
**WFA** 3 from 4yo+ 13lb 6 Ran SP% **111.0**
Speed ratings (Par 107): **97,96,96,94,91 79**
CSF £23.60 TOTE £11.50: £5.50, £1.40; EX 23.70 Trifecta £140.10.
**Owner** Mrs Christine Stevenson **Bred** Southcourt Stud **Trained** Edgcote, Northants
■ Stewards' Enquiry : Jack Duern nine-day ban: use of whip (26-30 Sep, 1-4 Oct)
**FOCUS**
Not the strongest staying handicap for the class. The winner was up slightly on this year's form.

## 6284 BETTER ODDS WITH BETFAIR PRICE RUSH H'CAP — 1m 2f 75y
4:50 (4:50) (Class 3) (0-90,88) 3-Y-0 £7,762 (£2,310; £1,154; £557) Stalls High

Form RPR
5261 **1** **Mambo Rhythm**[7] 6110 3-8-5 72 6ex........(v) JoeFanning 1 78
(Mark Johnston) *trckd ldrs: swtchd lft over 1f out: narrow ld last 100yds: hld on wl* **3/1**[3]
512 **2** *1/2* **Potentate (IRE)**[30] 5311 3-9-0 81........ SeanLevey 2 86
(Richard Hannon) *trckd ldr: pushed along over 3f out: cl 2nd over 2f out: pushed wd over 1f out: no ex clsng stages* **5/2**[1]
333 **3** *shd* **El Beau (IRE)**[37] 5051 3-8-9 76........ IanBrennan 3 81
(John Quinn) *hld up in rr: effrt on ins over 1f out: cl up ins fnl f: n.m.r: kpt on nr fin* **6/1**
5201 **4** *1/2* **Erroneous (IRE)**[19] 5730 3-9-7 88........ RichardKingscote 5 92
(David Simcock) *led: edgd rt over 1f out: hdd last 100yds: no ex* **11/4**[2]
3016 **5** *2* **Roskilly (IRE)**[30] 5302 3-9-1 82........ LiamKeniry 4 82
(Andrew Balding) *hld up in rr: effrt over 3f out: sn chsng ldrs: one pce appr fnl f* **7/1**
-005 **6** *20* **Edge (IRE)**[19] 5719 3-8-3 70........(b) MartinLane 6 32
(Bernard Llewellyn) *sn trcking ldrs: drvn over 3f out: lost pl 2f out: sn bhd: eased clsng stages: t.o* **33/1**

2m 14.83s (3.63) **Going Correction** +0.35s/f (Good) 6 Ran SP% **110.0**
Speed ratings (Par 105): **99,98,98,98,96 80**
CSF £10.44 TOTE £3.60: £2.00, £1.50; EX 11.80 Trifecta £38.40.
**Owner** Around The World Partnership **Bred** Gordon Phillips **Trained** Middleham Moor, N Yorks
**FOCUS**
Again not the strongest 3yo handicap for the grade and the form looks ordinary, with a bunch finish.

## 6285 EMILY FFION TRUST H'CAP (FOR GENTLEMAN AMATEUR RIDERS) — 7f 122y
5:20 (5:21) (Class 4) (0-80,85) 3-Y-0+ £6,239 (£1,935; £967; £484) Stalls Low

Form RPR
2321 **1** **Gift Of Silence**[8] 6062 5-10-7 70 6ex........ MrJPWilliams(5) 10 79
(Bernard Llewellyn) *rr-div: hdwy 2f out: 4th 1f out: edgd rt and styd on wl to ld last stride* **14/1**
2013 **2** *shd* **My Single Malt (IRE)**[40] 4938 6-11-1 78........(p) MrHStock(5) 9 86
(Julie Camacho) *trckd ldrs: 2nd over 1f out: led last 50yds: hdd post* **8/1**
3203 **3** *1 3/4* **Ralphy Boy (IRE)**[7] 6111 5-11-6 78........ MrWHogg 2 82
(Alistair Whillans) *led: drvn clr over 1f out: hdd and no ex last 50yds* **7/1**[3]
4012 **4** *3/4* **Janaab (IRE)**[2] 6232 4-10-5 66........(t) MrWEasterby(3) 7 68
(Tim Easterby) *mid-div: effrt over 2f out: kpt on same pce over 1f out* **4/1**[2]
2320 **5** *1 1/2* **Celtic Sixpence (IRE)**[25] 5496 6-10-13 74........ MrJHarding(3) 11 72
(Nick Kent) *chsd ldrs: kpt on same pce over 1f out: fdd towards fin* **22/1**
4416 **6** *shd* **Mime Dance**[27] 5410 3-10-12 80........(p) MrHHunt(5) 1 77
(Andrew Balding) *dwlt: in rr: effrt whn nt clr run and swtchd ins over 1f out: styd on: nt rch ldrs* **11/4**[1]
5003 **7** *3* **Lunar Deity**[18] 5758 5-11-2 74........ MrPCollington 3 64
(Stuart Williams) *mid-div: lost pl over 4f out: effrt and edgd rt over 1f out: kpt on: nvr a factor* **8/1**
1656 **8** *2* **Luhaif**[30] 5319 4-11-7 79........(b) MrRBirkett 5 64
(Julia Feilden) *mid-div: effrt on outside over 2f out: nvr a factor* **16/1**
3320 **9** *3/4* **Prime Exhibit**[12] 5957 9-11-1 73........(t) MrJJCodd 8 56
(Daniel Mark Loughnane) *hld up in rr: sme hdwy 2f out: nvr on terms* **12/1**
2016 **10** *7* **Le Laitier (FR)**[26] 5470 3-10-4 72........ MrKLocking(5) 14 37
(Scott Dixon) *chsd ldrs on outside: lost pl over 2f out* **33/1**
1631 **11** *8* **Al Khan (IRE)**[11] 5986 5-11-8 85 6ex........(p) MrKWood(5) 12 31
(Ollie Pears) *sn trcking ldrs: t.k.h: drvn over 3f out: lost pl 2f out: sn bhd* **14/1**

1m 36.55s (2.75) **Going Correction** +0.35s/f (Good)
**WFA** 3 from 4yo+ 5lb 11 Ran SP% **115.6**
Speed ratings (Par 105): **100,99,98,97,95 95,92,90,90,83 75**
CSF £119.47 CT £874.59 TOTE £12.00: £2.90, £1.90, £2.50; EX 53.60 Trifecta £242.40.
**Owner** Mrs E A Llewellyn **Bred** Henry And Mrs Rosemary Moszkowicz **Trained** Fochriw, Caerphilly
**FOCUS**
A competitive handicap for amateur riders, run at a decent pace. A clear personal best from the winner.
T/Plt: £47.80 to a £1 stake. Pool: £47993.21 - 732.40 winning tickets T/Qpdt: £8.80 to a £1 stake. Pool: £3210.28 - 269.50 winning tickets WG

# 6253 DONCASTER (L-H)
### Friday, September 12

**OFFICIAL GOING: Round course - good to soft (good in places); straight course - good (good to firm in places; good to firm from 1m to 6f 110yds; 7.0)**
Wind: Virtually nil Weather: Cloudy with sunny periods

## 6286 POLYPIPE FLYING CHILDERS STKS (GROUP 2) — 5f
1:40 (1:42) (Class 1) 2-Y-0
£39,697 (£15,050; £7,532; £3,752; £1,883; £945) Stalls High

Form RPR
1136 **1** **Beacon**[20] 5692 2-9-1 107........ WilliamBuick 3 107
(Richard Hannon) *in rr: pushed along and detached wl over 1f out: sn swtchd lft to outer and rdn: str run ins fnl f: lft cl 3rd last 40yds: kpt on to ld nr fin* **8/1**
421 **2** *hd* **Astrophysics**[20] 5671 2-9-1 83........ GrahamLee 14 106
(David Elsworth) *in tch: hdwy over 2f out: rdn to chse ldr ins fnl f: lft in ld briefly last 40yds: hdd nr fin* **50/1**
5 **3** *1/2* **Accepted (IRE)**[20] 5692 2-9-1 0........ WayneLordan 1 104
(T Stack, Ire) *chsd ldrs on outer: hdwy wl over 1f out: sn rdn and kpt on fnl f* **15/2**
1320 **4** *1* **Fast Act (IRE)**[22] 5607 2-9-1 105........ JamesDoyle 15 102
(Kevin Ryan) *racd wd: chsd ldrs: cl up over 2f out: rdn wl over 1f out: drvn and kpt on same pce fnl f* **16/1**
**5** *nk* **Ainippe (IRE)**[20] 5701 2-8-12 0........ AndreaAtzeni 4 97
(G M Lyons, Ire) *chsd ldrs: rdn along 2f out: drvn over 1f out: kpt on same pce fnl f* **7/2**[1]
12 **6** *1/2* **George Dryden (IRE)**[31] 5286 2-9-1 0........ PJMcDonald 10 98
(Ann Duffield) *towards rr: pushed along over 2f out: rdn and hdwy over 1f out: swtchd lft ent fnl f: kpt on: nrst fin* **20/1**
102 **7** *1 1/4* **Moonraker**[20] 5694 2-9-1 102........ RyanMoore 11 94
(Mick Channon) *in tch: hdwy 2f out: sn rdn and no imp fnl f* **11/2**[2]
3130 **8** *shd* **She's A Worldie (IRE)**[22] 5608 2-8-12 87........ PaulMulrennan 5 90
(Bryan Smart) *chsd ldrs: rdn along 2f out: sn drvn and grad wknd appr fnl f* **50/1**
0201 **9** *1/2* **Mind Of Madness (IRE)**[20] 5694 2-9-1 103........ JamieSpencer 7 91
(David Brown) *dwlt and towards rr: rdn and sme hdwy wl over 1f out: no imp appr fnl f* **11/1**
3621 **10** *1 1/4* **Tongue Twista**[12] 5946 2-8-12 88........(b[1]) LukeMorris 9 84
(Nick Littmoden) *in tch: rdn along 1/2-way: sn wknd* **100/1**
6240 **11** *shd* **Mukhmal (IRE)**[22] 5607 2-9-1 100........ PaulHanagan 2 86
(Mark Johnston) *prom: rdn along 2f out: wknd over 1f out* **25/1**
3211 **12** *1/2* **Bronze Maquette (IRE)**[28] 5380 2-8-12 104........ MartinHarley 13 82
(Gary Moore) *racd wd: towards rr: hdwy 2f out: rdn along wl over 1f out: sn btn* **16/1**
3243 **13** *nk* **Ahlan Emarati (IRE)**[20] 5692 2-9-1 109........ JimmyFortune 8 84
(Peter Chapple-Hyam) *chsd ldrs: rdn along 2f out: sn drvn and wknd over 1f out* **8/1**
6121 **U** **Cotai Glory**[45] 4757 2-9-1 107........ GeorgeBaker 6 111
(Charles Hills) *qckly away and led: rdn clr over 1f out: edgd rt jst ins fnl f: two l clr whn swvd bdly rt last 50yds: sddle slipped and uns rdr* **6/1**[3]

58.36s (-2.14) **Going Correction** -0.20s/f (Firm) 14 Ran SP% **119.5**
Speed ratings: **109,108,107,106,105 105,103,102,102,100 99,99,98,**
CSF £376.19 TOTE £8.90: £3.00, £10.90, £2.80; EX 369.40 Trifecta £4126.10.
**Owner** Highclere Thoroughbred Racing (Albany) **Bred** J M Cole **Trained** East Everleigh, Wilts
**FOCUS**
This was a most competitive Group 2 Flying Childers. There was a frantic early pace on, with runners fanning across the track, and high drama late on as Cotai Glory hung badly right with the race at his mercy, causing his saddle to slip and giving George Baker no chance of staying aboard. He's rated a 1.75l winner.

## 6287 LADBROKES MALLARD STKS (H'CAP) — 1m 6f 132y
2:10 (2:11) (Class 2) (0-110,105) 3-Y-0+ £25,876 (£7,700; £3,848; £1,924) Stalls Low

Form RPR
1205 **1** **Stomachion (IRE)**[21] 5651 4-9-1 92........ RyanMoore 4 103
(Sir Michael Stoute) *hld up in tch: hdwy 4f out: effrt to chse ldrs over 2f out: rdn to ld appr fnl f: sn clr: styd on wl* **15/2**[3]
0415 **2** *2 3/4* **Retirement Plan**[20] 5693 4-9-9 100........ JamesDoyle 6 107
(Lady Cecil) *led 2f: trckd ldng pair: hdwy over 3f out: rdn to ld briefly 1 1/2f out: sn hdd and drvn: kpt on u.p fnl f* **8/1**
3120 **3** *1 3/4* **Suegioo (FR)**[20] 5693 5-9-11 102........(p) MartinHarley 12 107
(Marco Botti) *midfield: hdwy over 3f out: rdn along and n.m.r over 2f out: swtchd lft and drvn over 1f out: kpt on fnl f: nrst fin* **16/1**
3443 **4** *nse* **Elidor**[20] 5693 4-9-11 102........ GrahamLee 9 106
(Mick Channon) *trckd ldrs: hdwy on outer over 3f out: rdn along 2f out: drvn over 1f out: kpt on same pce* **11/1**

0530 **5** *2 1/4* **Great Hall**[20] 5693 4-9-6 **97**.......... PhillipMakin 14 98
(John Quinn) *hld up in rr: hdwy on wd outside 3f out: rdn to chse ldrs whn edgd lft wl over 1f out: sn one pce* **33/1**
5162 **6** *1* **Adventure Seeker (IRE)**[20] 5691 3-8-6 **95**.......... DavidProbert 7 95
(Ed Vaughan) *hld up in rr: hdwy on outer over 3f out: rdn along to chse ldrs 2f out: sn drvn and one pce* **4/1**[1]
-144 **7** *3/4* **Pearl Castle (IRE)**[21] 5651 4-9-1 **92**.......... PaulMulrennan 3 91
(John Quinn) *hld up in midfield: hdwy 3f out: rdn along to chse ldrs wl over 1f out: drvn and one pce appr fnl f* **14/1**
0060 **8** *3/4* **Big Thunder**[23] 5579 4-9-3 **94**.......... LukeMorris 10 92
(Sir Mark Prescott Bt) *dwlt and reminders s: pushed along and hdwy to trck ldr after 2f: chal 3f out: rdn along over 2f out: drvn wl over 1f out and grad wknd* **18/1**
60 **9** *4 1/2* **Sir Walter Scott (IRE)**[20] 5693 4-9-8 **99**.......... AndreaAtzeni 2 91
(Luca Cumani) *hld up on inner in midfield: effrt over 3f out: rdn along wl over 2f out: n.d* **7/1**[2]
6410 **10** *1* **Swivel**[6] 6127 3-8-5 **94**.......... FrannyNorton 15 84
(Mark Johnston) *trckd ldrs: pushed along over 3f out: rdn along wl over 2f out: sn wknd* **9/1**
0060 **11** *nk* **Lahaag**[21] 5651 5-9-1 **92**.......... PaulHanagan 1 82
(John Gosden) *trckd ldrs on inner: effrt 3f out: rdn along over 2f out: sn wknd* **11/1**
4 **12** *4 1/2* **Farquhar (IRE)**[34] 5179 3-7-10 **90**.......... JackGarritty(5) 13 73
(Peter Chapple-Hyam) *hld up: a bhd* **8/1**
5302 **13** *11* **Buckland (IRE)**[34] 5161 6-8-10 **87** oh2.......... NickyMackay 11 55
(Charlie Fellowes) *prom: led after 2f: rdn along 3f out: drvn over 2f out: hdd 1 1/2f out and wknd qckly* **33/1**

3m 9.0s (1.60) **Going Correction** +0.10s/f (Good)
**WFA** 3 from 4yo+ 12lb **13** Ran SP% **116.8**
Speed ratings (Par 109): **99,97,96,96,95 94,94,94,91,91 90,88,82**
CSF £64.84 CT £928.29 TOTE £8.00: £2.60, £2.50, £4.10; EX 54.90 Trifecta £247.40.
**Owner** Niarchos Family **Bred** Niarchos Family **Trained** Newmarket, Suffolk

**FOCUS**
A good-quality handicap, run at no more than a fair gallop and it produced quite a clear-cut winner. The form is rated around the third and fourth.

## 6288 SOCIALITES ELECTRIC CIGARETTES DONCASTER CUP (BRITISH CHAMPIONS SERIES) (GROUP 2) 2m 2f

**2:40** (2:40) (Class 1) 3-Y-O+
**£56,710** (£21,500; £10,760; £5,360; £2,690; £1,350) **Stalls Low**

Form RPR
-202 **1** **Estimate (IRE)**[21] 5652 5-9-0 112.......... RyanMoore 10 108
(Sir Michael Stoute) *trckd ldrs: hdwy 3f out: chal wl over 1f out: rdn to take slt ld appr fnl f: sn drvn and kpt on wl towards fin* **11/8**[1]
2 **2** *1 1/4* **Whiplash Willie**[13] 5920 6-9-3 108..........(p) DavidProbert 5 110
(Andrew Balding) *hld up in midfield: hdwy 3f out: rdn to chse ldrs over 1f out: sn swtchd lft and drvn ent fnl f: kpt on* **13/2**[3]
6/-0 **3** *nk* **Kalann (IRE)**[19] 5737 7-9-3 80.......... LeighRoche 12 109
(Sabrina J Harty, Ire) *hld up towards rr: stdy hdwy on outer over 3f out: chsd ldrs 2f out: rdn to chal over 1f out and ev ch tl drvn ins fnl f and no ex last 100yds* **80/1**
1106 **4** *1/2* **Clever Cookie**[20] 5693 6-9-3 106.......... GrahamLee 4 109
(Peter Niven) *hld up towards rr: hdwy 3f out: swtchd rt and effrt 2f out: rdn over 1f out: styd on wl fnl f: nrst fin* **17/2**
005 **5** *3/4* **Biographer**[20] 5668 5-9-3 102..........(b) GeorgeBaker 9 108
(David Lanigan) *hld up towards rr: hdwy on outer over 3f out: rdn to chse ldrs 2f out: drvn over 1f out: kpt on same pce fnl f* **20/1**
5534 **6** *shd* **Brass Ring**[43] 4823 4-9-3 103.......... JamesDoyle 6 108
(John Gosden) *chsd clr ldr: tk clsr order over 3f out: led wl over 2f out: jnd and rdn wl over 1f out: drvn and hdd appr fnl f: one pce fnl f* **12/1**
2155 **7** *3 1/4* **Angel Gabrial (IRE)**[21] 5652 5-9-3 109.......... PaulHanagan 7 105
(Richard Fahey) *trckd ldrs on inner: hdwy over 3f out: rdn along over 2f out: sn drvn and grad wknd* **10/1**
-003 **8** *6* **Times Up**[21] 5652 8-9-3 110.......... WilliamBuick 11 98
(Ed Dunlop) *trckd ldrs: hdwy 3f out: rdn wl over 1f out: sn drvn and btn* **9/2**[2]
-160 **9** *4 1/2* **Alwilda**[20] 5668 4-9-0 91.......... LukeMorris 3 90
(Sir Mark Prescott Bt) *trckd ldng pair: hdwy over 3f out: rdn 2f out: sn drvn and wknd* **100/1**
3200 **10** *6* **Repeater**[20] 5693 5-9-3 100.......... DanielTudhope 1 86
(David O'Meara) *hld up: a in rr* **25/1**
0000 **11** *7* **Battle Of Marengo (IRE)**[42] 4849 4-9-3 106.......... JamieSpencer 8 79
(David Simcock) *hld up: a in rr* **50/1**
0/0- **12** *8* **Very Good Day (FR)**[492] 2149 7-9-3 90.......... TonyHamilton 2 70
(Richard Fahey) *led and sn clr: rdn along over 3f out: hdd wl over 2f out and wknd qckly* **100/1**

3m 55.91s (0.91) **Going Correction** +0.10s/f (Good) **12** Ran SP% **114.7**
Speed ratings: **101,100,100,100,99 99,98,95,93,90 87,84**
CSF £9.49 TOTE £2.50: £1.10, £2.10, £11.10; EX 12.00 Trifecta £397.90.
**Owner** The Queen **Bred** His Highness The Aga Khan's Studs S C **Trained** Newmarket, Suffolk

**FOCUS**
Although this year's Doncaster Cup was run at a fair early pace thanks to front-running Very Good Day, it did develop into something of a dash in the home straight and there was a muddling finish. Estimate did not need to be at her best.

## 6289 JOHN SMITH'S EXTRA SMOOTH MAY HILL STKS (GROUP 2) (FILLIES) 1m (S)

**3:15** (3:15) (Class 1) 2-Y-O
**£39,697** (£15,050; £7,532; £3,752; £1,883; £945) **Stalls High**

Form RPR
2 **1** **Agnes Stewart (IRE)**[50] 4598 2-9-0 0.......... BillyLee 1 107+
(Edward Lynam, Ire) *hld up: stdy hdwy on outer 3f out: sn cl up: rdn to ld over 1f out: kpt on strly* **11/4**[2]
141 **2** *1 1/4* **Muraaqaba**[34] 5190 2-9-0 103.......... PaulHanagan 2 104
(Mark Johnston) *trckd ldrs: pushed along 3f out: hdwy to ld wl over 1f out and sn rdn: hdd jst over 1f out: kpt on same pce* **13/8**[1]
4213 **3** *nk* **Shagah (IRE)**[6] 6126 2-9-0 84.......... FrankieDettori 8 103
(Richard Hannon) *hld up in tch: hdwy on outer wl over 1f out: sn rdn: kpt on same pce fnl f* **12/1**
114 **4** *1 1/4* **Supreme Occasion (IRE)**[5] 6165 2-9-0 82.......... DanielTudhope 7 100
(David O'Meara) *trckd ldrs: hdwy and cl up over 2f out: ev ch: rdn over 1f out: kpt on same pce fnl f* **8/1**
2 **5** *2 3/4* **Banzari**[8] 6065 2-9-0 0.......... JamieSpencer 5 94
(Michael Bell) *hld up in rr: rdn along over 2f out: styd on appr fnl f: nrst fin* **28/1**
4632 **6** *1 1/4* **Bonnie Grey**[20] 5664 2-9-0 92.......... AndreaAtzeni 6 91
(Rod Millman) *cl up: rdn along over 2f out: drvn wl over 1f out and sn wknd* **12/1**
2114 **7** *2 1/4* **Astrelle (IRE)**[20] 5664 2-9-0 88.......... MartinHarley 3 86
(Marco Botti) *trckd ldrs: effrt over 2f out: sn rdn and wknd wl over 1f out* **25/1**
114 **8** *3 1/2* **Alonsoa (IRE)**[34] 5190 2-9-0 96.......... FergusSweeney 4 78
(Henry Candy) *led: qcknd 3f out: rdn along 2f out: drvn and hdd wl over 1f out: sn wknd* **13/2**[3]

1m 37.2s (-2.10) **Going Correction** -0.20s/f (Firm) 2y crse rec **8** Ran SP% **111.9**
Speed ratings: **102,100,100,99,96 95,92,89**
CSF £7.23 TOTE £3.50: £1.30, £1.10, £2.50; EX 7.30 Trifecta £82.20.
**Owner** Clipper Logistics Group Ltd **Bred** John O'Connor & Ballyhane Stud **Trained** Dunshaughlin, Co Meath

**FOCUS**
Not a strong race for the level, with the close-up third/fourth rated in the 80s, but a handy winner in Agnes Stewart, who built on her Irish form. The runner-up is rated to her mark.

## 6290 COOPERS MARQUEES H'CAP 6f 110y

**3:45** (3:45) (Class 2) (0-105,105) 3-Y-O+ **£12,938** (£3,850; £1,924; £962) **Stalls High**

Form RPR
4-42 **1** **Badr Al Badoor (IRE)**[27] 5418 4-8-10 91 oh1.......... TomQueally 4 103
(James Fanshawe) *hmpd s and hld up in rr: smooth hdwy on outer wl over 2f out: chal over 1f out: rdn and carried sltly lft ins fnl f: kpt on gamely to ld last 75yds* **5/1**[2]
-101 **2** *hd* **Danzeno**[76] 3715 3-9-6 105.......... AndrewMullen 9 115
(Michael Appleby) *dwlt: t.k.h: hdwy 3f out: rdn to ld and hung lft jst over 1f out: drvn and edgd lft ins fnl f: hdd and nt qckn last 75yds* **9/4**[1]
0362 **3** *3 3/4* **Huntsmans Close**[17] 5784 4-8-5 91 oh4.......... JackGarritty(5) 2 92
(Roger Charlton) *wnt rt s: trckd ldrs: hdwy to ld 2f out: sn rdn: hdd and hmpd jst over 1f out: kpt on same pce after* **12/1**
0500 **4** *1/2* **Hitchens (IRE)**[27] 5445 9-8-12 93.......... GrahamGibbons 11 93
(David Barron) *in tch: hdwy 2f out: rdn over 1f out: kpt on fnl f* **18/1**
1315 **5** *1/2* **Alejandro (IRE)**[13] 5919 5-9-3 98.......... DanielTudhope 1 96
(David O'Meara) *led: rdn along over 2f out: sn hdd and grad wknd* **11/2**[3]
3060 **6** *1 1/2* **Yeeoow (IRE)**[48] 4681 5-8-7 91.......... JoeyHaynes(3) 10 85
(K R Burke) *chsd ldrs: rdn along wl over 1f out: drvn appr fnl f and sn one pce* **13/2**
04-0 **7** *1 1/2* **Shropshire (IRE)**[27] 5445 6-9-6 101.......... WilliamBuick 13 91
(Charles Hills) *hld up: effrt and sme hdwy over 2f out: sn rdn and no imp* **10/1**
0000 **8** *1 3/4* **Whozthecat (IRE)**[48] 4683 7-8-8 92..........(v) NeilFarley(3) 8 77
(Declan Carroll) *prom: rdn along over 2f out: sn wknd* **33/1**
2045 **9** *4 1/2* **Sir Reginald**[48] 4681 6-8-11 92.......... PaulHanagan 5 64
(Richard Fahey) *wnt rt s: midfield: rdn along over 2f out: outpcd wl over 1f out* **13/2**
04-0 **10** *3/4* **Poole Harbour (IRE)**[13] 5918 5-8-12 93.......... FrannyNorton 6 63
(David Nicholls) *prom: rdn along wl over 2f out: sn wknd* **25/1**

1m 16.62s (-3.28) **Going Correction** -0.20s/f (Firm)
**WFA** 3 from 4yo+ 2lb **10** Ran SP% **118.3**
Speed ratings (Par 109): **110,109,105,104,104 102,100,98,93,92**
CSF £16.89 CT £132.56 TOTE £7.10: £2.10, £1.20, £4.30; EX 20.90 Trifecta £122.90.
**Owner** Mohamed Obaida **Bred** Con Harrington **Trained** Newmarket, Suffolk
■ Stewards' Enquiry : Paul Hanagan trainer's representative could not offer any explanation for the geldings performance
Andrew Mullen one-day ban: careless riding (26 Sep)

**FOCUS**
While two came well clear in this good-quality sprint handicap, it was a messy race run at just a modest early tempo. A step up on last year's form from the winner.

## 6291 WEATHERBYS STALLION BOOK FLYING SCOTSMAN STKS (LISTED RACE) 7f

**4:25** (4:25) (Class 1) 2-Y-O
**£15,311** (£5,805; £2,905; £1,447; £726; £364) **Stalls High**

Form RPR
41 **1** **Nafaqa (IRE)**[56] 4395 2-9-0 0.......... PaulHanagan 5 103+
(B W Hills) *trckd ldrs: hdwy on outer over 2f out: rdn to take slt ld jst over 1f out: edgd lft ins fnl f: green: jinked rt and hesitated nr fin* **8/1**[3]
312 **2** *1/2* **Toocoolforschool (IRE)**[23] 5576 2-9-0 101.......... BenCurtis 4 102
(K R Burke) *cl up: chal 2f out: rdn to ld briefly 1 1/2f: hdd appr fnl f: sn drvn: edgd lft and kpt on* **11/4**[2]
15 **3** *nk* **Peacock**[48] 4645 2-9-0 0.......... RyanMoore 6 101
(Richard Hannon) *in rr: pushed along and outpcd over 2f out: rdn wl over 1f out: styd on wl fnl f: nrst fin* **20/1**
1 **4** *3/4* **White Lake**[21] 5655 2-9-0 0.......... AndreaAtzeni 7 99
(Luca Cumani) *trckd ldrs: swtchd lft and effrt 2f out: rdn along over 1f out: no imp fnl f* **8/11**[1]
1 **5** *2* **Risen Sun**[15] 5852 2-8-9 0.......... FrannyNorton 3 89
(Mark Johnston) *led: rdn along and jnd 2f out: hdd 1 1/2f out: hld whn n.m.r and edgd rt ent fnl f: one pce* **12/1**
14 **6** *hd* **Carry On Deryck**[27] 5431 2-9-0 0.......... JamesDoyle 1 93
(Sylvester Kirk) *dwlt: sn chsng ldrs: rdn along wl over 2f out: drvn and wknd over 1f out* **50/1**
3341 **7** *8* **Sea Wolf (IRE)**[35] 5131 2-9-0 94.......... PaulMulrennan 2 72
(Michael Dods) *trckd ldng pair: effrt over 2f out: sn rdn and wknd wl over 1f out* **40/1**

1m 23.38s (-2.92) **Going Correction** -0.20s/f (Firm) **7** Ran SP% **112.5**
Speed ratings: **108,107,107,106,103 103,94**
CSF £29.15 TOTE £7.70: £2.80, £1.30; EX 20.50 Trifecta £173.90.
**Owner** Hamdan Al Maktoum **Bred** Shadwell Estate Company Limited **Trained** Upper Lambourn, Berks

**FOCUS**
The form looks up to scratch for a Listed event. The winner bounced back towards his debut form.

## 6292 FRANK WHITTLE PARTNERSHIP CLASSIFIED STKS 1m 2f 60y

**5:00** (5:01) (Class 3) 3-Y-O+
**£8,092** (£2,423; £1,211; £605; £302; £152) **Stalls Low**

Form RPR
4354 **1** **Don't Stare**[9] 6036 4-9-4 80..........(t) AndreaAtzeni 5 97
(James Fanshawe) *trckd ldrs: smooth hdwy over 2f out: led wl over 1f out: sn rdn clr: readily* **11/1**
4352 **2** *6* **Enobled**[7] 6098 4-9-4 83.......... RyanMoore 9 86
(Sir Michael Stoute) *hld up in tch: hdwy over 3f out: rdn 2f out: styd on fnl f: no ch w wnr* **2/1**[1]

3221 **3** 3/4 **Loving Home**$^{31}$ 5282 3-8-11 85 ........ WilliamBuick 3 85
(John Gosden) *led: pushed along 3f out: rdn 2f out: drvn and hdd wl over 1f out: kpt on same pce fnl f* **2/1**$^{1}$

5416 **4** *nk* **Eurystheus (IRE)**$^{62}$ 4184 5-9-4 80 ........ (p) AndrewMullen 10 84
(Michael Appleby) *hld up in rr: hdwy over 3f out: swtchd rt to outer and rdn wl over 1f out: kpt on u.p fnl f* **25/1**

0-56 **5** 1/2 **Lizzie Tudor**$^{20}$ 5686 4-9-1 82 ........ DavidProbert 2 80
(Andrew Balding) *in tch: hdwy over 3f out: rdn along over 2f out: kpt on u.p fnl f* **18/1**

2111 **6** 2 3/4 **Puzzle Time**$^{27}$ 5448 4-9-1 85 ........ TonyHamilton 6 75
(Giles Bravery) *trckd ldr: cl up 3f out: rdn along 2f out: sn drvn and wknd over 1f out* **7/1**$^{2}$

6310 **7** 1 **Arable**$^{43}$ 4821 3-8-11 84 ........ JamesDoyle 11 76
(Charles Hills) *hld up in rr: effrt and sme hdwy on outer over 3f out: rdn along over 2f out and sn wknd* **9/1**$^{3}$

3442 **8** 3 1/2 **Innsbruck**$^{63}$ 4175 4-9-4 83 ........ (b) PhillipMakin 4 69
(John Quinn) *trckd ldng pair on inner: pushed along 3f out: rdn 2f out: sn wknd* **16/1**

2m 8.81s (-0.59) **Going Correction** +0.10s/f (Good)
**WFA** 3 from 4yo+ 7lb **8** Ran SP% **112.5**
Speed ratings (Par 107): **106,101,100,100,99 97,96,94**
CSF £32.35 TOTE £11.40: £2.80, £1.10, £1.30; EX 36.70 Trifecta £145.60.
**Owner** Guy A A C Gredley **Bred** Denford Stud Ltd **Trained** Newmarket, Suffolk

**FOCUS**
A fair classified event. It was run at something of an uneven pace and the form looks best rated around the fourth.
T/Jkpt: Not won. T/Plt: £156.50 to a £1 stake. Pool: £222,187.78 - 1,035.91 winning tickets
T/Qpdt: £5.40 to a £1 stake. Pool: £16,193.99 - 2,179.45 winning tickets JR

## 6063 SALISBURY (R-H)

Friday, September 12

**OFFICIAL GOING: Good to firm (good in the last furlong, in the dip at 3f, and between 6f and 5f) changing to good after race 1 (4:40)**
Wind: mild breeze half against Weather: cloudy

### 6293 SERVE ON INTERNATIONAL RESPONSE MEDIAN AUCTION MAIDEN STKS — 1m
**4:40** (4:44) (Class 5) 2-Y-O **£2,911** (£866; £432; £216) **Stalls** Low

Form RPR

44 **1** **Gold Prince (IRE)**$^{15}$ 5847 2-9-5 0 ........ DaneO'Neill 9 81
(Sylvester Kirk) *led 1f: mde rest: rdn clr 2f out: edgd lft but wl in command fnl f: comf* **25/1**

02 **2** 3 1/2 **Marma's Boy**$^{21}$ 5625 2-9-5 0 ........ SilvestreDeSousa 12 73
(Ralph Beckett) *sn trcking wnr: rdn over 2f out: nt pce to get on terms but kpt on fnl f* **11/8**$^{1}$

**3** 1 3/4 **Sunday Royal (FR)** 2-9-5 0 ........ SamHitchcott 7 69+
(Harry Dunlop) *mid-div: pushed along over 3f out: rdn over 2f out: no imp tl r.o ent fnl f: wnt 3rd towards fin* **66/1**

02 **4** 3/4 **Shadow Rock (IRE)**$^{21}$ 5646 2-9-5 0 ........ RichardHughes 8 67
(Richard Hannon) *sn nudged along to chse ldrs: rdn over 3f out: nvr gng pce to get on terms: drifted rt ins fnl f: lost 3rd nring fin* **10/3**$^{3}$

**5** 1/2 **Marmot** 2-9-5 0 ........ WilliamTwiston-Davies 6 66
(Roger Charlton) *s.i.s: towards rr: styd on nicely fnl f: nvr threatened ldrs* **16/1**

0 **6** 1/2 **Wind Place And Sho**$^{14}$ 5881 2-9-5 0 ........ StevieDonohoe 3 65
(James Eustace) *s.i.s: mid-div: rdn over 2f out: styd on same pce fnl f* **66/1**

**7** 1/2 **Maxwell (IRE)** 2-9-5 0 ........ OscarPereira 10 63+
(Ralph Beckett) *s.i.s: towards rr: styd on fnl f: nvr trbld ldrs* **33/1**

**8** *nk* **Step On It (IRE)** 2-9-5 0 ........ JFEgan 1 65
(Eve Johnson Houghton) *towards rrdn 2f out: styng on ins fnl f whn hmpd fnl 120yds: no further imp* **25/1**

6 **9** 1/2 **Recently Acquired**$^{21}$ 5646 2-9-5 0 ........ JimCrowley 11 61
(Lady Cecil) *trckd ldrs: wandered u.p fr over 2f out: nt gng pce to chal: wknd fnl f* **11/4**$^{2}$

0 **10** 5 **Reflation**$^{25}$ 5500 2-9-5 0 ........ KieranO'Neill 5 49
(Richard Hannon) *racd keenly: broke wl: led for 1f: trckd ldrs: rdn over 2f out: wknd over 1f out* **40/1**

**11** 2 3/4 **Major Mac** 2-8-12 0 ........ CharlieBennett$^{(7)}$ 4 43
(Hughie Morrison) *a towards rr* **40/1**

**12** 60 **Top Pocket** 2-9-0 0 ........ RyanWhile$^{(5)}$ 2
(Michael Madgwick) *mid-div tl wknd over 3f out: t.o* **150/1**

1m 42.72s (-0.78) **Going Correction** -0.05s/f (Good) **12** Ran SP% **116.9**
Speed ratings (Par 95): **101,97,95,95,94 94,93,93,92,87 84,24**
CSF £57.60 TOTE £22.70: £5.70, £1.10, £16.90; EX 78.00 Trifecta £3557.70 Part won..
**Owner** J C Smith **Bred** Littleton Stud **Trained** Upper Lambourn, Berks

**FOCUS**
Rail erected 15ft off permanent far-side rail between 6.5f and 4f. The ground was changed to good after the clerk of the course canvassed jockeys' opinions after this opener, while the time backed that up.

### 6294 BATHWICK TYRES NURSERY H'CAP — 6f 212y
**5:10** (5:11) (Class 5) (0-70,68) 2-Y-O **£2,587** (£770; £384; £192) **Stalls** Centre

Form RPR

666 **1** **Black Granite (IRE)**$^{56}$ 4409 2-9-6 67 ........ (v$^{1}$) RobertHavlin 6 72+
(Jeremy Noseda) *mid-div: hdwy over 3f out: rdn to chal over 2f out: led wl over 1f out: styd on: rdn out* **7/2**$^{1}$

656 **2** 2 **On High**$^{30}$ 5305 2-9-7 68 ........ RichardHughes 9 68
(Richard Hannon) *wnt lft s: led: rdn and hdd wl over 1f out: kpt pressing wnr tl no ex fnl f: jst hld on for 2nd* **7/2**$^{1}$

5004 **3** *hd* **Mywayalways (IRE)**$^{35}$ 5147 2-9-5 66 ........ JFEgan 4 65
(David Evans) *trckd ldrs: rdn whn swtchd lft 2f out: r.o wl fnl f: nrly snatched 2nd fnl stride* **6/1**

0004 **4** 1 1/4 **Pink Ribbon (IRE)**$^{14}$ 5875 2-8-10 57 ........ ShaneKelly 10 53
(Sylvester Kirk) *hmpd s: sn trcking ldr: rdn and ev ch 2f out: hld over 1f out: no ex fnl f* **10/1**

0600 **5** 1 **Bakht A Rawan (IRE)**$^{16}$ 5828 2-8-10 57 ........ StevieDonohoe 11 50
(Mark Usher) *trckd ldrs: rdn 3f out: hmpd 2f out: kpt on same pce fnl f* **25/1**

604 **6** 2 1/4 **Nelsons Trick**$^{18}$ 5746 2-9-6 67 ........ SilvestreDeSousa 5 54
(Rod Millman) *mid-div: rdn over 2f out: swtchd lft over 1f out: nvr gng pce to get on terms* **14/1**

204 **7** 1 1/4 **British Embassy (IRE)**$^{7}$ 6104 2-9-7 68 ........ DaneO'Neill 8 51
(Eve Johnson Houghton) *racd keenly: mid-div: rdn 2f out: nt pce to get on terms: fdd ins fnl f* **5/1**$^{3}$

523 **8** 1 3/4 **Giannizzero (IRE)**$^{28}$ 5397 2-9-1 67 ........ MarcMonaghan$^{(5)}$ 7 46
(Marco Botti) *rdn wl over 2f out: a towards rr* **4/1**$^{2}$

000 **9** 3 3/4 **Birdie Must Fly**$^{72}$ 3858 2-8-4 51 ........ KieranO'Neill 3 20
(Jimmy Fox) *a towards rr* **50/1**

005 **10** *hd* **Prima Pagina**$^{30}$ 5315 2-7-12 50 ........ NoelGarbutt$^{(5)}$ 1 18
(Dr Jon Scargill) *a towards rr* **25/1**

1m 28.1s (-0.50) **Going Correction** -0.05s/f (Good) **10** Ran SP% **120.8**
Speed ratings (Par 95): **100,97,97,96,94 92,90,88,84,84**
CSF £16.14 CT £75.11 TOTE £6.30: £2.30, £1.40, £2.30; EX 21.30 Trifecta £208.70.
**Owner** The ABC Partnership **Bred** Yeomanstown Stud **Trained** Newmarket, Suffolk
■ Stewards' Enquiry : Stevie Donohoe three-day ban: careless riding (26, 28, 29 Sep)

**FOCUS**
A modest nursery, but the pace looked even (overall time not bad for the grade) and it was dominated by those towards the head of the market, so the form looks sound enough for the level.

### 6295 EBF STALLIONS LIN WHITE MEMORIAL FILLIES' CONDITIONS STKS (BOBIS RACE) — 6f 212y
**5:45** (5:45) (Class 3) 2-Y-O **£9,056** (£2,695; £1,346; £673) **Stalls** Centre

Form RPR

10 **1** **Elite Gardens (USA)**$^{84}$ 3415 2-8-12 0 ........ RichardHughes 2 103
(Saeed bin Suroor) *mde all: pushed along whn chal 2f out: kpt on strly to assert ins fnl f: pushed out* **3/1**$^{2}$

215 **2** 3 1/4 **Sulaalaat**$^{22}$ 5608 2-8-12 96 ........ DaneO'Neill 4 94
(Brian Meehan) *racd keenly: trckd wnr: rdn and ev ch 2f out tl jst ins fnl f: no ex* **8/11**$^{1}$

**3** 1 1/2 **Sympathy (USA)** 2-8-9 0 ........ ShaneKelly 3 87+
(Sir Michael Stoute) *trckd ldrs: pushed along for effrt 2f out: kpt on wl enough but nt pce to chal front pair* **10/1**

31 **4** *hd* **Taaqah (USA)**$^{56}$ 4396 2-8-12 0 ........ JimCrowley 1 89
(James Tate) *trckd ldrs: rdn wl over 1f out: kpt on but nt pce to chal* **11/2**$^{3}$

1m 27.3s (-1.30) **Going Correction** -0.05s/f (Good) **4** Ran SP% **107.4**
Speed ratings (Par 96): **105,101,99,99**
CSF £5.64 TOTE £3.40; EX 8.50 Trifecta £18.80.
**Owner** Godolphin **Bred** Dr Catherine Wills **Trained** Newmarket, Suffolk

**FOCUS**
Just the four runners, but quite a hot little fillies' conditions event with Group-race form being represented.

### 6296 MICHAEL STEINBACH BIRTHDAY H'CAP — 5f
**6:15** (6:16) (Class 4) (0-85,82) 3-Y-O+ **£4,851** (£1,443; £721; £360) **Stalls** Low

Form RPR

2110 **1** **Perfect Muse**$^{6}$ 6130 4-9-4 79 ........ AdamKirby 2 92+
(Clive Cox) *trckd ldrs: gng best but nt clr run fr over 1f out tl ins fnl f: qcknd up wl to ld fnl 50yds: readily* **13/8**$^{1}$

1305 **2** 1/2 **Pucon**$^{14}$ 5880 5-8-11 72 ........ StevieDonohoe 6 78
(Roger Teal) *led: rdn over 1f out: kpt on but nt pce of wnr whn hdd fnl 50yds* **16/1**

0502 **3** 1 1/4 **Waseem Faris (IRE)**$^{4}$ 6191 5-8-4 72 ........ (v) DanielCremin$^{(7)}$ 1 74
(Mick Channon) *blkd s: in last pair: rdn and hdwy fr over 1f out: swtchd lft ent fnl f: kpt on to go 3rd fnl 150yds* **11/2**$^{3}$

0342 **4** 1 1/2 **Meritocracy (IRE)**$^{10}$ 6021 3-9-6 82 ........ JimCrowley 5 78
(Paul Cole) *trckd ldr: rdn 2f out: no ex whn lost 2 pls ins fnl f* **11/4**$^{2}$

206 **5** 1/2 **Swendab (IRE)**$^{37}$ 5060 6-9-1 76 ........ (b) DaneO'Neill 4 70
(John O'Shea) *wnt bdly rt s and barged into rival: in last pair: rdn over 2f out: nvr finding pce to get on terms* **16/1**

2603 **6** 1/2 **Whitecrest**$^{12}$ 5945 6-8-11 72 ........ WilliamTwiston-Davies 7 65
(John Spearing) *in tch: rdn 3f out: nvr gng pce to get involved* **7/1**

356 **7** 5 **Mr Dandy Man (IRE)**$^{25}$ 5501 3-8-10 72 ........ (p) RobertHavlin 3 47
(Ronald Harris) *bdly hmpd s: racd keenly in tch: rdn wl over 2f out: hld whn hmpd 1f out: wknd* **14/1**

59.98s (-1.02) **Going Correction** -0.05s/f (Good)
**WFA** 3 from 4yo+ 1lb **7** Ran SP% **111.1**
Speed ratings (Par 105): **106,105,103,100,100 99,91**
CSF £27.37 CT £112.27 TOTE £2.80: £1.70, £5.40; EX 30.60 Trifecta £86.30.
**Owner** R J Vines **Bred** R J Vines **Trained** Lambourn, Berks
■ Stewards' Enquiry : Daniel Cremin one-day ban: careless riding (26 Sep)

**FOCUS**
A strongly run sprint and the winner is value for more.

### 6297 HARRIET HODGKINSON 18TH BIRTHDAY H'CAP — 6f
**6:45** (6:46) (Class 6) (0-65,66) 3-Y-O **£2,587** (£770; £384; £192) **Stalls** Low

Form RPR

0061 **1** **Ganymede**$^{10}$ 6022 3-9-8 66 6ex ........ (b) JimCrowley 7 77
(Eve Johnson Houghton) *trckd ldrs: led 2f out: sn rdn: kpt on wl to draw clr fnl f: rdn out* **4/1**$^{1}$

443 **2** 2 1/4 **Lead A Merry Dance**$^{39}$ 4972 3-9-5 63 ........ RichardHughes 6 67
(Sylvester Kirk) *mid-div: rdn over 2f out: stdy prog over 1f out: chsd wnr ins fnl f but a being hld* **15/2**$^{2}$

6160 **3** 1 3/4 **Caminel (IRE)**$^{41}$ 4908 3-9-4 62 ........ (v$^{1}$) DaneO'Neill 13 60
(Jeremy Gask) *towards rr: rdn over 2f out: hdwy over 1f out: r.o fnl f: wnt 3rd nring fin* **16/1**

0050 **4** 1/2 **Ecliptic Sunrise**$^{17}$ 5801 3-8-3 52 ........ NoelGarbutt$^{(5)}$ 2 49
(Des Donovan) *mid-div: rdn 2f out: kpt on to go 3rd briefly towards fin: nvr trbld ldrs* **50/1**

01 **5** 1 1/2 **Razin' Hell**$^{43}$ 4820 3-9-7 65 ........ (v) SilvestreDeSousa 9 57
(Alan McCabe) *trckd ldr: rdn and ev ch 2f out: sn hld by wnr: no ex whn lost 3 pls ins fnl f* **11/1**

-505 **6** 1 1/4 **Gower Princess**$^{9}$ 6029 3-9-4 62 ........ WilliamTwiston-Davies 10 50
(Ronald Harris) *led: rdn and hdd 2f out: fdd ins fnl f* **25/1**

003 **7** 1 1/4 **What A Dandy (IRE)**$^{24}$ 5532 3-9-2 60 ........ AdamKirby 5 44
(Jim Boyle) *rdn 2f out: a mid-div* **8/1**$^{3}$

040 **8** 3 1/2 **Finflash (IRE)**$^{18}$ 5777 3-9-7 65 ........ (v$^{1}$) SamHitchcott 8 38
(Mick Channon) *mid-div: hdwy 3f out: sn rdn: wknd fnl f* **10/1**

0000 **9** 1 **Phantom Spirit**$^{9}$ 6023 3-8-7 51 oh6 ........ $^{1}$ KieranO'Neill 1 21
(George Baker) *short of room sn after leaving stalls: mid-div: rdn over 2f out: wknd fnl f* **66/1**

3010 **10** 3 1/4 **Wimboldsley**$^{20}$ 5683 3-8-4 53 ........ MatthewHopkins$^{(5)}$ 14 12
(Scott Dixon) *a towards rr* **8/1**$^{3}$

2536 **10** *dht* **Clear Focus (IRE)**$^{9}$ 6023 3-8-8 52 ........ (v) StevieDonohoe 4 11
(Brendan Powell) *trckd ldr: rdn 3f out: grad fdd* **10/1**

0335 **12** 5 **Roring Samson (IRE)**$^{35}$ 5138 3-9-1 59 ........ (p) PatCosgrave 3
(George Baker) *stmbld leaving stalls: sn trcking ldr: rdn over 2f out: wknd over 1f out* **8/1**$^{3}$

1443 **13** 1 1/4 **Connaught Water (IRE)**[13] 5905 3-8-9 58..................(p) NedCurtis(5) 11
(Jonathan Portman) *s.i.s: sn swtchd rt: nvr bttr than mid-div: wknd 2f out* **10/1**

5234 **14** 2 **Kodafine (IRE)**[42] 4847 3-9-6 64.......................................... JFEgan 12
(David Evans) *dwlt: a bhd* **10/1**

1m 14.54s (-0.26) **Going Correction** -0.05s/f (Good) **14** Ran SP% **123.0**
Speed ratings (Par 99): **99,96,93,93,91 89,87,83,81,77 77,70,69,66**
CSF £33.00 CT £460.46 TOTE £5.20: £2.20, £1.80, £7.50; EX 23.40 Trifecta £485.60.
**Owner** Ganymede Partnership **Bred** The Kingwood Partnership **Trained** Blewbury, Oxon

**FOCUS**
A low-grade handicap.

## 6298 BREEDERS BACKING RACING EBF MAIDEN STKS 1m 1f 198y
7:15 (7:15) (Class 5) 3-Y-O £3,881 (£1,155; £577; £288) Stalls Low

Form RPR

**1** **Tamasha** 3-9-0 0............................................... SilvestreDeSousa 8 87+
(Ralph Beckett) *sn trcking ldrs: chal over 4f out: led over 2f out: sn clr: comf* **11/4**[1]

0-2 **2** 6 **Almuhalab**[49] 4621 3-9-5 0............................................ DaneO'Neill 5 78
(Charles Hills) *led after 1f: rdn and hdd over 2f out: sn hld by wnr: kpt on same pce* **4/1**[2]

4 **3** 2 1/4 **Brisk**[21] 5622 3-9-0 72.................................................. JFEgan 7 69
(David Evans) *led for 1f: trckd ldr: rdn over 3f out: kpt on same pce fnl 2f* **4/1**[2]

**4** 2 1/4 **Western Bella** 3-9-0 0............................................... AdamKirby 2 65+
(Clive Cox) *hld up towards rr: struggling in last over 5f out: stl plenty to do over 3f out: styd on wl fr over 2f out but no ch* **16/1**

6 **5** 10 **Cerutty (IRE)**[16] 5831 3-9-0 0................................ MarcMonaghan(5) 6 51
(Marco Botti) *hld up towards rr: rdn over 3f out: plugged on but nvr any imp on ldrs* **11/4**[1]

6 **6** 15 **Hidden Power**[28] 5400 3-9-5 0.................................. StevieDonohoe 9 22
(Jo Hughes) *rdn over 4f out: a towards rr: t.o* **16/1**

005 **7** 9 **Beaver Creek**[21] 5648 3-9-5 0.................................... OscarPereira 4 5
(Ralph J Smith) *mid-div: hdwy to join ldrs 5f out: wknd over 3f out: t.o* **66/1**

0 **8** 2 3/4 **Bright Acclaim**[213] 564 3-9-5 0.................................... PatCosgrave 1
(Jo Hughes) *mid-div: hdwy 4f out: sn rdn: drifted lft over 3f out: wknd 2f out: t.o* **50/1**

**9** 8 **Mateka** 3-9-0 0...................................................... WilliamTwiston-Davies 3
(Roger Charlton) *a towards rr: wknd over 3f out: t.o* **12/1**[3]

2m 8.9s (-1.00) **Going Correction** -0.05s/f (Good) **9** Ran SP% **116.2**
Speed ratings (Par 101): **102,97,95,93,85 73,66,64,57**
CSF £14.05 TOTE £5.00: £2.20, £1.80, £1.40; EX 13.60 Trifecta £50.00.
**Owner** Nurlan Bizakov **Bred** Hesmonds Stud Ltd **Trained** Kimpton, Hants

**FOCUS**
Not much depth to this ordinary maiden and they were strung out like 3m chasers up the straight, but the front two look useful and are the ones to concentrate on.
T/Plt: £98.00 to a £1 stake. Pool: £50989.29 - 379.58 winning tickets T/Qpdt: £22.00 to a £1 stake. Pool: £6879.72 - 231.19 winning tickets TM

# 5925 SANDOWN (R-H)
Friday, September 12

**OFFICIAL GOING: Good (good to firm in places; sprint 7.9, round 8.1)**
Wind: Light, behind Weather: Fine, warm

## 6299 EBFSTALLIONS.COM MAIDEN STKS 5f 6y
1:50 (1:50) (Class 5) 2-Y-O £3,881 (£1,155; £577; £288) Stalls Low

Form RPR

5 **1** **Waady (IRE)**[20] 5671 2-9-5 0............................................[1] DaneO'Neill 1 80
(John Gosden) *dwlt: detached in last pair: plld out wd and rapid prog jst over 1f out: shkn up to ld last 50yds: readily* **3/1**[3]

5 **2** 1 **Just Us Two (IRE)**[36] 5091 2-9-5 0.............................. FrederikTylicki 3 76
(Robert Cowell) *trckd ldr: rdn 2f out: led jst over 1f out: kpt on but hdd and outpcd last 50yds* **25/1**

4 **3** 1/2 **Manofmanytalents**[36] 5091 2-9-5 0.......................... AdamBeschizza 2 75
(Michael Squance) *chsd ldr: pushed along fr 1/2-way: effrt u.p over 1f out: kpt on one pce* **14/1**

3250 **4** 3/4 **Lady Gemini**[22] 5608 2-9-0 79.................................... MartinDwyer 6 67
(Jo Hughes) *led: drvn over 1f out: sn hdd: one pce fnl f* **5/2**[2]

2 **5** 1/2 **Frognal Bear (IRE)**[7] 6103 2-9-5 0............................. RichardHughes 4 70
(Richard Hannon) *racd wd: chsd ldrs: pushed along 1/2-way: drvn and one pce fr over 1f out* **7/4**[1]

0 **6** 2 3/4 **El Fenix (IRE)**[25] 5500 2-9-5 0..................................... AdamKirby 7 60
(Gary Moore) *dwlt: sn in tch: rdn 2f out: no imp on ldrs 1f out* **25/1**

**7** 6 **Beach Action (FR)** 2-9-5 0........................................... SteveDrowne 5 39
(Charles Hills) *taken down early: dwlt: a detached in last pair: no prog over 1f out* **16/1**

1m 1.13s (-0.47) **Going Correction** -0.05s/f (Good) **7** Ran SP% **110.2**
Speed ratings (Par 95): **101,99,98,97,96 92,82**
CSF £61.39 TOTE £4.50: £1.70, £7.40; EX 53.20 Trifecta £454.00.
**Owner** Hamdan Al Maktoum **Bred** Knocklong House Stud **Trained** Newmarket, Suffolk

**FOCUS**
Sprint track at full width. Rail on Round course dolled out 3yds from 7f to Winning Post and distances on Round course increased by 6yds. An ordinary maiden to start with, but an extraordinary performance from the winner.

## 6300 BRITISH STALLION STUDS EBF MAIDEN STKS 1m 14y
2:20 (2:21) (Class 5) 2-Y-O £3,881 (£1,155; £577; £288) Stalls Low

Form RPR

**1** **Christophermarlowe (USA)** 2-9-5 0............................ RobertHavlin 5 88+
(John Gosden) *s.i.s and green early: sn disputyed 5th: stdy prog over 2f out: led 1f out: shkn up and styd on wl: promising* **12/1**

3 **2** 3 1/2 **Master Apprentice (IRE)**[14] 5881 2-9-2 0................ ThomasBrown(3) 6 80
(Andrew Balding) *trckd ldng pair: clsd 2f out: jnd ldr jst over 1f out but wnr sn swept by: styd on but no match* **11/10**[1]

0 **3** 5 **Capel Path (USA)**[21] 5646 2-9-5 0.............................. ShaneKelly 7 68
(Sir Michael Stoute) *disp ld tl led 3f out: drvn over 1f out: sn hdd: wknd fnl f* **8/1**[3]

**4** 1 1/2 **Oceanographer** 2-9-5 0................................................ AdamKirby 4 64
(Charlie Appleby) *trckd ldng pair: shkn up and rn green 2f out: sn outpcd: fdd fnl f* **8/1**[3]

**5** shd **Sleep Easy** 2-9-5 0................................................... HayleyTurner 2 64+
(Hughie Morrison) *s.i.s: rn green and detached in 7th early: shkn up 3f out: nvr a factor but kpt on fr over 1f out* **50/1**

52 **6** 14 **Deluxe**[36] 5093 2-9-5 0............................................... RichardHughes 3 30
(Richard Hannon) *disp ld to 3f out: sn btn: eased over 1f out and ended up t.o* **11/4**[2]

**7** 8 **Searching (IRE)** 2-9-5 0............................................ FrederikTylicki 8 11
(Roger Varian) *s.i.s: sn wl detached in last: a t.o* **20/1**

**8** 5 **First Dream (IRE)** 2-9-5 0........................................... PatDobbs 1
(Richard Hannon) *in tch disputing 5th: wknd rapidly over 2f out: t.o* **25/1**

1m 43.12s (-0.18) **Going Correction** +0.025s/f (Good) **8** Ran SP% **114.8**
Speed ratings (Par 95): **101,97,92,91,90 76,68,63**
CSF £25.54 TOTE £9.30: £3.10, £1.10, £1.90; EX 40.90 Trifecta £279.10.
**Owner** Michael Tabor **Bred** Dress Rehearsal Syndicate **Trained** Newmarket, Suffolk

**FOCUS**
Not a particularly competitive maiden according to the market and they finished well spread out.

## 6301 SUNGARD H'CAP (BOBIS RACE) 1m 14y
2:50 (2:52) (Class 3) (0-90,90) 3-Y-O £9,337 (£2,796; £1,398; £699; £349; £175) Stalls Low

Form RPR

40-1 **1** **Gm Hopkins**[156] 1395 3-9-4 87...................................... RobertHavlin 1 97+
(John Gosden) *trckd ldng trio: prog 2f out: rdn over 1f out: clsd to ld jst ins fnl f: styd on wl* **8/1**

444 **2** 3/4 **Miss Atomic Bomb**[20] 5686 3-9-0 83............................... AdamKirby 5 91
(Jeremy Noseda) *hld up in last trio: rdn over 2f out: prog jst over 1f out: disp 2nd ins fnl f and looked a threat: kpt on same pce after* **7/1**

-411 **3** hd **Merry Me (IRE)**[15] 5849 3-8-11 83............................ ThomasBrown(3) 6 91
(Andrew Balding) *t.k.h: hld up in last trio: prog on outer 2f out: sn rdn: chsd wnr ins fnl f: nt qckn and hld after: lost 2nd nr fin* **5/1**[3]

2101 **4** 1 1/4 **Between Wickets**[30] 5311 3-9-3 86................................ MartinDwyer 4 91
(Marcus Tregoning) *stdd s: hld up in last: prog on outer 2f out: rdn and tried to cl fnl f: one pce* **3/1**[1]

31-4 **5** 1 1/4 **Torrid**[14] 5882 3-9-7 90................................................ PatDobbs 7 92+
(Amanda Perrett) *trckd ldr after 1f: led gng strly over 2f out: rdn over 1f out: hdd jst ins fnl f: wknd tamely* **5/1**[3]

4645 **6** 7 **Hatsaway (IRE)**[14] 5882 3-9-0 83................................... KierenFallon 3 69
(Clive Brittain) *trckd ldr 1f: lost pl and rdn over 2f out: sn wknd* **10/1**

4363 **7** 2 3/4 **Cricklewood Green (USA)**[64] 4104 3-8-13 82............. RichardHughes 2 62
(Richard Hannon) *led: rdn and hdd over 2f out: wknd wl over 1f out: eased last 75yds* **4/1**[2]

1m 42.77s (-0.53) **Going Correction** +0.025s/f (Good) **7** Ran SP% **111.0**
Speed ratings (Par 105): **103,102,102,100,99 92,89**
CSF £57.62 TOTE £6.70: £3.00, £3.20; EX 56.00 Trifecta £310.80.
**Owner** R J H Geffen **Bred** Cadran-Earl Blot-Scea Des Bissons **Trained** Newmarket, Suffolk

**FOCUS**
A decent 3yo handicap, run at an even pace, and it provided trainer John Gosden with a treble.

## 6302 21 DEGREES HEATING 10TH ANNIVERSARY FILLIES' H'CAP 7f 16y
3:25 (3:25) (Class 4) (0-85,85) 3-Y-O+ £5,175 (£1,540; £769; £384) Stalls Low

Form RPR

3012 **1** **Saucy Minx (IRE)**[8] 6068 4-9-0 85..............(b) KieranShoemark(7) 7 94
(Amanda Perrett) *hld up in last: smooth prog on outer jst over 2f out: pushed into ld over 1f out: sn clr: rdn out nr fin* **4/1**[2]

4233 **2** 3 **Khatiba (IRE)**[37] 5032 3-8-12 80..........................(b[1]) FrederikTylicki 5 79
(Roger Varian) *led: rdn 2f out: hdd over 1f out: outpcd by wnr but kpt on* **6/1**[3]

4621 **3** 1/2 **Pretty Bubbles**[23] 5573 5-9-4 82................................... PaddyAspell 3 82
(J R Jenkins) *hld up in 5th: prog 2f out but nt as rapid as wnr who was bhd her: rdn to chse ldng pair fnl f: styd on but no threat* **8/1**

2202 **4** 7 **Gown (IRE)**[16] 5826 3-8-12 80..................................... SteveDrowne 4 60
(Charles Hills) *hld up in 4th: clsd on ldrs over 2f out: wnt 2nd briefly wl over 1f out: sn wknd* **6/1**[3]

3233 **5** 1 1/4 **Invoke (IRE)**[21] 5638 3-8-6 74..............................(v[1]) HayleyTurner 6 51
(Michael Bell) *t.k.h: sn trckd ldr: rdn over 2f out: lost 2nd and wknd wl over 1f out: hung rt fnl f* **12/1**

0213 **6** 5 **White Russian**[27] 5441 3-8-3 71..................................... HarryBentley 1 35
(Henry Candy) *trckd ldng pair: rdn over 2f out: no prog and wknd over 1f out: eased whn btn* **5/4**[1]

1m 28.46s (-1.04) **Going Correction** +0.025s/f (Good)
**WFA** 3 from 4yo+ 4lb **6** Ran SP% **111.8**
Speed ratings (Par 102): **106,102,102,94,92 86**
CSF £26.95 TOTE £4.10: £2.40, £2.60; EX 21.30 Trifecta £33.90.
**Owner** Mr & Mrs F Cotton, Mr & Mrs P Conway **Bred** Summerhill & J Osborne **Trained** Pulborough, W Sussex

**FOCUS**
A fair fillies' handicap and, despite the pace looking ordinary and a couple taking a tug, they finished well spread out.

## 6303 INKERMAN LONDON H'CAP 1m 2f 7y
4:00 (4:00) (Class 4) (0-80,79) 3-Y-O+ £4,851 (£1,443; £721; £360) Stalls Low

Form RPR

5004 **1** **Karam Albaari (IRE)**[32] 5251 6-9-4 71........................(p) PaddyAspell 10 79
(J R Jenkins) *wl in rr: pushed along over 4f out: no prog u.p 3f out: hdwy 2f out: c between rivals fnl f: styd on wl to ld last strides* **16/1**

1531 **2** hd **Go Sakhee**[18] 5768 3-9-4 78.......................................... FrederikTylicki 2 86+
(Roger Varian) *led 4f: trckd ldr: led jst over 2f out: rdn 2 l clr 1f out but nt doing much in front: hrd pressed last 100yds: hdd fnl strides* **2/1**[1]

5033 **3** nk **Gracious George (IRE)**[36] 5096 4-9-2 69......................(p) PatDobbs 5 76
(Jimmy Fox) *hld up in last pair: rdn and prog on outer over 2f out: tk 2nd jst ins fnl f: clsd to chal 100yds out: nt qckn and lost 2nd last strides* **16/1**

4413 **4** 1 3/4 **Charlie Wells (IRE)**[21] 5647 3-8-12 72........................(b) JohnFahy 11 76
(Eve Johnson Houghton) *settled wl in rr: in last pair over 3f out: rdn and prog on outer 2f out: racd awkwardly after: hrd drvn and styd on to take 4th ins fnl f* **13/2**[2]

-001 **5** 2 3/4 **War Singer (USA)**[13] 5931 7-9-12 79........................(bt) KierenFallon 12 78
(Johnny Farrelly) *sn prom on outer: rdn over 2f out: chsd ldr wl over 1f out tl jst ins fnl f: wknd* **7/1**[3]

0302 **6** 1 3/4 **Tinshu (IRE)**[36] 5095 8-9-9 76..................................(p) HayleyTurner 6 71
(Derek Haydn Jones) *restrained into midfield: shkn up 2f out: sme prog and swtchd lft over 1f out: no hdwy after* **12/1**

6230 **7** 3/4 **Tight Lipped (IRE)**[13] 5931 5-9-1 71........................... RosieJessop(3) 9 65
(James Eustace) *pressed ldr: led after 4f to jst over 2f out: wknd over 1f out* **8/1**

0040 **8** 1 **Gannicus**[20] 5670 3-8-12 72........................................(p) DougieCostello 7 64
(Brendan Powell) *hld up in rr: shkn up wl over 2f out: no real prog over 1f out* **25/1**

3214 **9** 2 **Choral Festival**[12] 5948 8-9-3 70 WilliamCarson 1 58
(John Bridger) *trckd ldrs: shkn up over 2f out: no prog and wl btn whn short of room 1f out* **20/1**

2113 **10** 9 **Specialty (IRE)**[19] 5727 4-9-6 73 StephenCraine 8 44
(Pam Sly) *chsd ldrs: rdn 4f out: lost pl 3f out: sn btn* **8/1**

6610 **11** hd **Secular Society**[37] 5031 4-9-6 73 (p) PatCosgrave 4 44
(George Baker) *rousted along to chse ldrs: wknd qckly over 2f out* **9/1**

6-00 **12** 33 **Sabre Rock**[19] 5727 4-8-12 65 oh2 SteveDrowne 3
(John Best) *a in rr: wknd over 3f out: t.o and eased* **66/1**

2m 9.85s (-0.65) **Going Correction** +0.025s/f (Good)
**WFA** 3 from 4yo+ 7lb **12** Ran SP% **120.9**
Speed ratings (Par 105): **103,102,102,101,99 97,97,96,94,87 87,60**
CSF £48.27 CT £556.21 TOTE £22.30: £6.10, £1.10, £4.30; EX 84.20 Trifecta £1105.30.
**Owner** Mark Goldstein **Bred** Morecool Stud **Trained** Royston, Herts
■ Stewards' Enquiry : Pat Dobbs two-day ban: use of whip (26 and 28 Sept)

**FOCUS**
A competitive handicap run at a fair pace with a disputed lead and little covering the first three at the line.

## 6304 TWICKENHAM H'CAP 1m 14y
4:30 (4:33) (Class 4) (0-80,80) 3-Y-O+ £4,851 (£1,443; £721; £360) Stalls Low

Form RPR

36 **1** **First Post (IRE)**[13] 5931 7-9-2 72 HayleyTurner 5 82
(Derek Haydn Jones) *trckd ldng trio: clsng whn short of room 2f out: rdn over 1f out: short of room briefly ins fnl f: drvn and r.o gamely to ld last strides* **8/1**

0502 **2** hd **Big Baz (IRE)**[15] 5849 4-9-10 80 MartinDwyer 6 89+
(William Muir) *hld up off the pce in 6th: stdy prog 3f out: gng wl 2f out: pushed into ld over 1f out: rdn ins fnl f: hdd last strides* **13/8**[1]

2152 **3** ½ **Ajig**[11] 5980 3-8-7 68 (p) JohnFahy 7 75
(Eve Johnson Houghton) *hld up in 5th and off the pce: clsd fr 3f out: swtchd lft 2f out: drvn and r.o to chal ins fnl f: nt qckn last 50yds* **6/1**[3]

2302 **4** 4½ **Al Mukhdam**[13] 5903 4-9-6 76 (p) KierenFallon 3 74
(Ed de Giles) *pressed ldng pair: rdn to ld wl over 2f out: hdd over 1f out: sn wknd* **6/1**[3]

4431 **5** 5 **Marydale**[25] 5492 3-8-12 73 HarryBentley 2 58
(Henry Candy) *led 1f: trckd ldr: led briefly 3f out: sn wknd* **5/1**[2]

00 **6** ¾ **Malicho**[137] 1796 5-9-5 75 SebSanders 1 59
(Dean Ivory) *heavily restrained into last after s and wl off the pce: pushed along over 2f out: no prog and nvr remotely involved* **33/1**

2005 **7** nk **Lord Ofthe Shadows (IRE)**[20] 5686 5-9-9 79 PatDobbs 4 63
(Richard Hannon) *hld up in 7th and wl off the pce: nt clr run briefly over 2f out: sn shkn up and no prog* **6/1**[3]

026- **8** 21 **Eton Dorney (USA)**[301] 7894 5-9-9 79 IrineuGoncalves 8 14
(Kevin Tork) *led after 1f to 3f out: wknd rapidly: t.o* **66/1**

1m 43.51s (0.21) **Going Correction** +0.025s/f (Good)
**WFA** 3 from 4yo+ 5lb **8** Ran SP% **113.2**
Speed ratings (Par 105): **99,98,98,93,88 88,87,66**
CSF £21.00 CT £84.27 TOTE £8.10: £2.70, £1.10, £2.00; EX 31.30 Trifecta £163.00.
**Owner** Llewelyn, Runeckles **Bred** D Llewelyn & J Runeckles **Trained** Efail Isaf, Rhondda C Taff

**FOCUS**
They went a good pace in this thanks to Eton Dorney carting himself into the lead early and a couple of his rivals going with him.
T/Plt: £300.60 to a £1 stake. Pool: £53,639.96 - 130.22 winning tickets T/Qpdt: £63.30 to a £1 stake. Pool: £4,819.95 - 56.30 winning tickets JN

6305 - 6311a (Foreign Racing) - See Raceform Interactive

# 6023 BATH (L-H)

Saturday, September 13

**OFFICIAL GOING: Firm (9.9)**
Wind: Moderate, behind Weather: Fine but cloudy

## 6312 FESTIVAL RACING NURSERY H'CAP (BOBIS RACE) 5f 161y
2:15 (2:15) (Class 4) (0-85,81) 2-Y-O £3,752 (£1,116; £577; £278) Stalls Centre

Form RPR

314 **1** **War Alert (USA)**[12] 5983 2-9-5 79 GeorgeBaker 12 83+
(David Brown) *hld up in 6th: prog on outer over 2f out: rdn over 1f out: led ins fnl f: pushed out nr fin* **4/1**[2]

4105 **2** ¾ **Indescribable (IRE)**[11] 5998 2-9-7 81 AdrianNicholls 9 83
(Mark Johnston) *trckd ldr: rdn to ld over 2f out: drvn wl over 1f out: hdd ins fnl f: styd on* **10/1**

1626 **3** 1¼ **Geological (IRE)**[7] 6128 2-9-7 81 PatDobbs 11 78
(Richard Hannon) *s.i.s: hld up in last pair: prog on outer over 2f out: rdn wl over 1f out: styd on to take 3rd nr fin* **7/2**[1]

0014 **4** nk **Pixeleen**[19] 5779 2-8-7 67 MartinDwyer 4 63
(Malcolm Saunders) *led to over 2f out: pressed ldr tl jst ins fnl f: fdd last 100yds* **10/1**

5650 **5** 1¾ **Star Of Spring (IRE)**[15] 5875 2-8-6 66 [1] WilliamCarson 1 57
(Charles Hills) *chsd ldrs: rdn over 2f out: lost pl over 1f out: kpt on same pce after* **9/1**

4200 **6** 2¾ **Brazen Spirit**[43] 4853 2-9-3 77 (b[1]) SteveDrowne 8 59
(Clive Cox) *chsd ldng pair: rdn over 2f out: lost 3rd over 1f out: fdd* **16/1**

031 **7** 1¼ **Flashy Diva**[21] 5667 2-9-4 78 FergusSweeney 7 55
(Henry Candy) *in tch in rr: pushed along 1/2-way: no prog 2f out: nvr a factor* **4/1**[2]

4034 **8** ¾ **Billyoakes (IRE)**[11] 6003 2-8-9 72 CharlesBishop(3) 5 51
(Mick Channon) *chsd ldrs: rdn over 2f out: losing pl whn short of room over 1f out: fdd* **7/1**[3]

0662 **9** 5 **Muzarkash**[19] 5779 2-8-9 69 (p) ChrisCatlin 2 27
(B W Hills) *fractious in preliminaries: a in last pair and nvr gng wl: bhd fnl 2f* **16/1**

1m 9.75s (-1.45) **Going Correction** -0.30s/f (Firm) **9** Ran SP% **114.7**
Speed ratings (Par 97): **97,96,94,93,91 87,86,85,78**
CSF £43.06 CT £140.77 TOTE £4.00: £1.30, £2.60, £1.20; EX 48.00 Trifecta £63.00.
**Owner** Qatar Bloodstock Partnership **Bred** Highfield Farm **Trained** Averham Park, Notts

**FOCUS**
This didn't look an overly strong race of its type but the winner ought to rate a bit higher.

## 6313 DISTINCTION PROPERTY SERVICES APPRENTICE H'CAP 5f 161y
2:50 (2:50) (Class 4) (0-85,85) 3-Y-O+ £4,690 (£1,395; £697; £348) Stalls Centre

Form RPR

3532 **1** **Marmalady (IRE)**[7] 6130 4-9-2 85 HectorCrouch(7) 3 95
(Gary Moore) *mde all: pressed and pushed along 1f out: kpt on wl fnl f* **3/1**[1]

330 **2** 1¼ **Salvatore Fury (IRE)**[11] 6013 4-8-4 71 (p) KieranShoemark(5) 2 76
(Keith Dalgleish) *chsd ldrs: wnt 2nd 2f out: rdn to chal jst over 1f out: nt qckn and a hld* **10/1**

2-04 **3** 1½ **Ambitious Boy**[8] 6095 5-8-10 75 JackDuern(3) 1 75
(Andrew Hollinshead) *in tch: shkn up over 2f out: no imp over 1f out: kpt on to take 3rd wl ins fnl f* **4/1**[2]

2233 **4** 1¾ **Ginzan**[5] 6189 6-8-7 74 (p) RyanWhile(5) 6 68
(Malcolm Saunders) *chsd wnr to 2f out: steadily wknd fnl f* **8/1**

-643 **5** ½ **Shamahan**[11] 6006 5-8-6 73 DanielCremin(5) 10 66
(Luke Dace) *chsd ldng pair: rdn and nt qckn 2f out: steadily fdd* **8/1**

266 **6** ¾ **Tidentime (USA)**[51] 4594 5-9-6 82 (v[1]) CharlesBishop 4 72
(Mick Channon) *in tch: rdn and struggling over 2f out: no ch over 1f out: plugged on* **8/1**

065 **7** ¾ **Swendab (IRE)**[1] 6296 6-9-0 76 (b) ThomasBrown 7 64
(John O'Shea) *w.w in rr: nt clr run briefly 2f out: rdn and sme prog over 1f out: no hdwy fnl f* **25/1**

634 **8** 7 **Hamoody (USA)**[3] 6236 10-8-8 75 JennyPowell(5) 9 54
(Joseph Tuite) *in tch: rdn whn stmbld bdly over 2f out: sn wknd: eased w rdr looking down fnl f* **7/1**[3]

0200 **9** 16 **Trader Jack**[28] 5433 5-9-3 82 PhilipPrince(3) 5
(David Flood) *sn outpcd: wl bhd 1/2-way: t.o* **14/1**

500 **10** 5 **Powerful Wind (IRE)**[21] 5677 5-9-0 79 ShaneGray(3) 8
(Ronald Harris) *chsd ldrs to jst over 2f out: wknd rapidly: t.o* **20/1**

1m 8.82s (-2.38) **Going Correction** -0.30s/f (Firm) **10** Ran SP% **115.2**
Speed ratings (Par 105): **103,101,99,97,96 95,94,85,63,57**
CSF £33.48 CT £114.79 TOTE £3.10: £1.60, £3.20, £1.70; EX 24.70 Trifecta £171.90.
**Owner** Heart Of The South Racing **Bred** Tribes Man Syndicate **Trained** Lower Beeding, W Sussex

**FOCUS**
A fair handicap. Another personal best from the winner.

## 6314 PROFAB WINDOWS FILLIES' H'CAP 5f 11y
3:25 (3:25) (Class 4) (0-85,86) 3-Y-O+ £4,690 (£1,395; £697; £348) Stalls Centre

Form RPR

-03 **1** **Smart Daisy K**[8] 6096 4-9-3 86 JackDuern(5) 6 95
(Andrew Hollinshead) *taken down early: trckd ldr: rdn to ld over 1f out: styd on wl* **3/1**[2]

2006 **2** 1¼ **Jillnextdoor (IRE)**[9] 6068 4-9-1 82 CharlesBishop(3) 2 87
(Mick Channon) *settled in last: rdn and prog over 1f out: r.o to take 2nd nr fin: no ch of chalng* **15/2**

2016 **3** ¾ **Random Success (IRE)**[30] 5350 4-9-2 80 GeorgeBaker 8 82
(Roger Charlton) *dwlt: hld up in 7th: effrt gng wl on outer 2f out: rdn and fnd little over 1f out: kpt on to take 3rd last strides* **9/4**[1]

44 **4** shd **Autumns Blush (IRE)**[43] 4862 3-8-7 72 (v[1]) ChrisCatlin 1 73
(Jeremy Noseda) *taken down early: chsd ldng pair: rdn over 1f out: wnt 2nd jst ins fnl f: one pce and lost 2 pls nr fin* **11/1**

0210 **5** ¾ **Silverrica (IRE)**[10] 6025 4-8-6 75 JennyPowell(5) 5 74
(Malcolm Saunders) *led to over 1f out: steadily fdd fnl f* **8/1**

5022 **6** 1½ **Shilla (IRE)**[20] 5724 3-8-3 71 oh1 AmyScott(3) 3 66
(Henry Candy) *in tch: pushed along 2f out: trying to stay on but no ch whn hmpd ins fnl f* **6/1**[3]

4045 **7** hd **Edged Out**[10] 6025 4-8-1 72 oh1 ow1 KieranShoemark(7) 9 65
(Christopher Mason) *in tch: rdn over 2f out: no prog over 1f out: edgd lft fnl f* **14/1**

1500 **8** 1 **Hannahs Turn**[19] 5776 4-8-13 77 MartinDwyer 7 66
(Chris Dwyer) *taken down early: chsd ldng pair to over 1f out: steadily wknd u.p* **20/1**

1m 0.14s (-2.36) **Going Correction** -0.30s/f (Firm)
**WFA** 3 from 4yo 1lb **8** Ran SP% **112.7**
Speed ratings (Par 102): **106,104,102,102,101 99,98,97**
CSF £24.86 CT £58.47 TOTE £4.80: £1.50, £2.10, £1.10; EX 30.00 Trifecta £92.20.
**Owner** Mr & Mrs D J Smart **Bred** D J And Mrs K D Smart **Trained** Upper Longdon, Staffs
■ Stewards' Enquiry : Kieran Shoemark three-day ban: careless riding (Sep 30,Oct 1-2)

**FOCUS**
A decent sprint. A personal best from the winner.

## 6315 MALCOLM SAUNDERS TRAINER H'CAP (BOBIS RACE) 1m 3f 144y
4:00 (4:04) (Class 3) (0-90,90) 3-Y-O £7,439 (£2,213; £1,106; £553) Stalls Low

Form RPR

1232 **1** **Fire Fighting (IRE)**[14] 5914 3-9-7 90 (b) AdrianNicholls 3 105+
(Mark Johnston) *t.k.h: trckd ldr: led over 2f out: rdn clr over 1f out: eased nr fin* **5/2**[1]

3115 **2** 2½ **Serena Grae**[36] 5123 3-8-9 78 MartinDwyer 2 87
(Marcus Tregoning) *led: shkn up and hdd over 2f out: no ch w wnr over 1f out: kpt on* **5/2**[1]

6411 **3** 3¼ **Arabian Beauty (IRE)**[13] 5948 3-8-10 82 (p) MatthewLawson(3) 5 86
(Saeed bin Suroor) *hld up in last pair: pushed along over 2f out: rdn and nt qckn over 1f out: one pce after* **5/2**[1]

3225 **4** hd **Hedge End (IRE)**[8] 6106 3-8-10 79 PatDobbs 4 82
(Richard Hannon) *hld up in last pair: shkn up over 2f out: one pce and no prog* **7/2**[2]

2m 30.66s (0.06) **Going Correction** -0.15s/f (Firm) **4** Ran SP% **107.9**
Speed ratings (Par 105): **93,91,89,89**
CSF £8.77 TOTE £2.90; EX 8.30 Trifecta £16.20.
**Owner** A D Spence **Bred** P Bellaiche **Trained** Middleham Moor, N Yorks

**FOCUS**
An easy success for the winner, continuing his fine run since being blinkered.

## 6316 PROFAB WINDOWS H'CAP (BOBIS RACE) 1m 5y
4:35 (4:35) (Class 4) (0-80,79) 3-Y-O £4,690 (£1,395; £679; £348) Stalls Low

Form RPR

2043 **1** **Stereo Love (FR)**[22] 5627 3-9-7 79 GeorgeBaker 4 88
(Clive Cox) *hld up bhd ldng pair: smooth prog over 2f out: led over 1f out: pushed out: comf* **9/4**[1]

2023 **2** 1½ **Cornish Path**[21] 5685 3-9-4 76 FergusSweeney 6 80
(Henry Candy) *trckd ldr: led briefly wl over 1f out: kpt on u.p but readily hld by wnr* **7/2**[3]

0402 **3** nk **Jersey Brown (IRE)**[9] 6070 3-8-1 66 oh3 ow1 DanielCremin(7) 1 69
(Mick Channon) *hld up in last and detached early: pushed along and prog over 1f out: disp 2nd ins fnl f: effrt flattened out nr fin* **9/1**

2255 **4** 4 **Alpine Storm (IRE)**[7] 6129 3-9-2 74 AdrianNicholls 5 68
(Mark Johnston) *led: rdn over 2f out: hdd wl over 1f out: steadily wknd* **3/1**[2]

1222 **5** *5* **Picks Pinta**[58] 4342 3-9-3 75 SteveDrowne 2 57
(Jo Hughes) *trckd ldng pair: pushed along over 3f out: struggling over 2f out: wknd fnl f* **7/2**[3]

1m 38.65s (-2.15) **Going Correction** -0.15s/f (Firm) 5 Ran SP% **110.2**
Speed ratings (Par 103): **104,102,102,98,93**
CSF £10.34 TOTE £2.10: £1.10, £3.20; EX 7.60 Trifecta £42.10.
**Owner** Al Asayl Bloodstock Ltd **Bred** Sheik Khalifa Bin Zayed Al Nahyan **Trained** Lambourn, Berks

**FOCUS**
Not much separated the first four in the betting. The form is rated around the runner-up.

## 6317 P K BUILDING MAIDEN STKS (BOBIS RACE) 1m 5y
**5:05** (5:05) (Class 4) 2-Y-O **£3,752** (£1,116; £557; £278) **Stalls Low**

Form RPR

3 **1** **Khusoosy (USA)**[29] 5393 2-9-2 0 MatthewLawson(3) 5 78+
(Saeed bin Suroor) *nt that wl away: sn chsd ldng pair: shkn up 3f out: rdn to go 2nd 2f out: clsd to ld ins fnl f: pushed out firmly to assert* **4/6**[1]

33 **2** *1* **Spring Dixie (IRE)**[20] 5718 2-9-0 0 ChrisCatlin 1 69
(Rae Guest) *led: rdn over 1f out: hdd and one pce ins fnl f* **7/1**[2]

**3** *3/4* **Brandon Castle** 2-9-2 0 ThomasBrown(3) 2 72+
(Andrew Balding) *dwlt: t.k.h in last pair: pushed along over 2f out: sme prog and rdn over 1f out: sn tk 3rd: r.o last 100yds and gaining at fin* **9/1**[3]

0 **4** *2 1/2* **Mister Rockandroll**[9] 6056 2-9-5 0 AdrianNicholls 3 66
(Mark Johnston) *t.k.h: trckd ldrs: rdn and outpcd over 2f out: kpt on same pce fnl f* **10/1**

0 **5** *3 3/4* **Envisioning (IRE)**[8] 6101 2-9-5 0 PatDobbs 6 57
(Richard Hannon) *chsd ldr to 2f out: wknd over 1f out* **10/1**

**6** *6* **Imperial War (IRE)** 2-9-5 0 KieranO'Neill 4 42
(Richard Hannon) *rn green and sn in last pair: shkn up 3f out: wknd and hanging rt 2f out* **7/1**[2]

1m 40.81s (0.01) **Going Correction** -0.15s/f (Firm) 6 Ran SP% **113.2**
Speed ratings (Par 97): **93,92,91,88,85 79**
CSF £6.12 TOTE £1.70: £1.10, £2.10; EX 4.50 Trifecta £22.20.
**Owner** Godolphin **Bred** Shadwell Farm LLC **Trained** Newmarket, Suffolk

**FOCUS**
The winner needed to be really pushed out to land the odds. He did not need to match his debut figure.

## 6318 EXPRESS GLAZING H'CAP 1m 5f 22y
**5:40** (5:40) (Class 4) (0-80,80) 3-Y-O+ **£4,690** (£1,395; £697; £348) **Stalls High**

Form RPR

1406 **1** **Sunny Future (IRE)**[28] 5414 8-8-9 74 MartinDwyer 3 81
(Malcolm Saunders) *hld up in last: rdn over 3f out: prog on outer 2f out: sustained effrt to ld last 100yds: drvn out* **8/1**

-333 **2** *nk* **Russian Royale**[13] 5948 4-9-4 70 (p) PatDobbs 6 76
(Stuart Kittow) *hld up: clsd on ldrs gng best over 2f out: led wl over 1f out: sn rdn: hdd last 100yds: kpt on but hld nr fin* **6/1**

423 **3** *1 3/4* **Winter Spice (IRE)**[65] 4134 3-8-8 70 (b) SteveDrowne 1 73
(Clive Cox) *trckd ldrs: nt clr run and dropped to last 2f out: plld arnd rivals and prog to go 3rd 1f out: styd on but unable to chal* **5/1**[3]

3112 **4** *3* **Statsminister**[30] 5356 3-9-2 78 FergusSweeney 4 77
(Luke Dace) *pushed up to ld but hdd after 3f: rdn over 4f out: stl on terms 2f out: wknd jst over 1f out* **2/1**[2]

-034 **5** *3 1/2* **Hooded (USA)**[21] 5670 3-9-4 80 (p) GeorgeBaker 5 74
(Roger Charlton) *t.k.h: w ldr: led after 3f: rdn over 4f out: hdd wl over 1f out: sn wknd* **7/4**[1]

2m 48.36s (-3.64) **Going Correction** -0.15s/f (Firm)
**WFA** 3 from 4yo+ 10lb 5 Ran SP% **111.8**
Speed ratings (Par 105): **105,104,103,101,99**
CSF £50.65 TOTE £12.70: £7.60, £5.60; EX 46.00 Trifecta £137.30.
**Owner** M S Saunders **Bred** Mrs G Stanga **Trained** Green Ore, Somerset
■ Stewards' Enquiry : Pat Dobbs one-day ban: careless riding (Sep 29)

**FOCUS**
A fair staying contest, run at a respectable gallop. The winner had been given a chance by the handicapper.
T/Plt: £12.00 to a £1 stake. Pool: £57,646.39 - 3479.74 winning units. T/Qpdt: £4.80 to a £1 stake. Pool: £2809.28 - 430.21 winning units. JN

# 6279 CHESTER (L-H)
Saturday, September 13

**OFFICIAL GOING: Good (7.0)**
Wind: light 1/2 behind Weather: fine

## 6319 BETFAIR PRICE RUSH / EBF STALLIONS MAIDEN STKS (BOBIS RACE) 6f 18y
**1:50** (1:50) (Class 4) 2-Y-O **£6,469** (£1,925; £962; £481) **Stalls Low**

Form RPR

**1** **Gabrial The Tiger (IRE)** 2-9-5 0 DavidNolan 5 71
(Richard Fahey) *dwlt: sn mid-div: hdwy over 2f out: styd on wl fnl f: led post* **4/1**[3]

**2** *hd* **Landing Night (IRE)** 2-9-5 0 PJMcDonald 10 70
(Ann Duffield) *chsd ldr: led appr fnl f: hdd last strides* **33/1**

**3** *1 1/4* **Character Onesie (IRE)** 2-9-5 0 TonyHamilton 11 67
(Richard Fahey) *s.i.s: in rr: hdwy over 1f out: styd on to take 3rd nr fin* **8/1**

55 **4** *1/2* **Crikey (IRE)**[14] 5922 2-9-5 0 PaulMulrennan 2 65
(Kevin Ryan) *led: hdd appr fnl f: kpt on same pce* **11/4**[2]

**5** *nk* **Tortilla Jackson** 2-9-5 0 RichardKingscote 1 64
(Tom Dascombe) *drvn to chse ldrs: one pce over 1f out* **2/1**[1]

40 **6** *1* **Racing Knight (IRE)**[26] 5493 2-9-5 0 IanBrennan 4 61
(John Quinn) *in rr: swtchd lft over 1f out: styd on ins fnl f* **16/1**

40 **7** *3/4* **Doctor Kehoe**[77] 3728 2-9-0 0 JackGarritty(5) 7 59
(Richard Fahey) *chsd ldrs: drvn over 2f out: outpcd over 1f out* **20/1**

05 **8** *3/4* **Splash Of Verve (IRE)**[11] 5995 2-9-5 0 TomEaves 3 57
(Philip Kirby) *hld up in mid-div: sme hdwy over 1f out: sn wknd* **14/1**

1m 18.02s (4.22) **Going Correction** +0.45s/f (Yiel) 8 Ran SP% **111.4**
Speed ratings (Par 97): **89,88,87,86,86 84,83,82**
CSF £107.59 TOTE £4.20: £1.10, £8.10, £2.90; EX 59.10 Trifecta £203.40.
**Owner** Dr Marwan Koukash **Bred** Kenneth Heelan **Trained** Musley Bank, N Yorks

**FOCUS**
The entire length of rail moved out a further 3yds from Friday (6yds in total). Consequently races 1 and 2 increased by 37yds, race 3 by 58yds, race 4 by 33yds, race 5 by 39yds, race 6 by 30yds and race 7 by 70yds. The going was given as good, but after riding in the first Paul Mulrennan said it was "loose" and Tony Hamilton said it was "good to soft". This didn't look a strong maiden, with those that had racing experience not setting a great standard, but the first three are entitled to improve. Half the field were sired by Kodiac, including the first two.

## 6320 BETFAIR HOME OF THE PRICE RUSH H'CAP 7f 122y
**2:20** (2:22) (Class 3) (0-90,89) 3-Y-O+ **£14,231** (£4,235; £2,116; £1,058) **Stalls Low**

Form RPR

0400 **1** **Marcret (ITY)**[8] 6097 7-9-8 88 JamesSullivan 11 98
(Ruth Carr) *t.k.h in rr: hdwy over 1f out: styd on wl to ld last 50yds* **16/1**

5014 **2** *1 1/4* **Maverik**[15] 5895 6-9-6 86 TomQueally 12 93
(William Knight) *led after 1f: hdd and no ex wl ins fnl f* **25/1**

3034 **3** *1/2* **Dusky Queen (IRE)**[23] 5612 4-9-4 89 JackGarritty(5) 5 95
(Richard Fahey) *hld up in rr: hdwy on ins over 1f out: styd on same pce last 75yds* **7/1**[3]

5061 **4** *3/4* **Storm King**[14] 5915 5-9-9 89 (p) AndrewElliott 2 93
(David C Griffiths) *mid-div: effrt over 2f out: swtchd outside over 1f out: styd on ins fnl f* **6/1**[1]

0400 **5** *1/2* **Norse Blues**[19] 5771 6-9-4 84 GrahamGibbons 1 87
(David Barron) *trckd ldrs on inner: effrt over 2f out: kpt on same pce appr fnl f* **13/2**[2]

4141 **6** *3/4* **Accession (IRE)**[28] 5433 5-9-6 86 TedDurcan 13 87
(Charlie Fellowes) *stmbld s: in rr: hdwy on outside over 1f out: styd on ins fnl f* **7/1**[3]

0021 **7** *1/2* **Little Shambles**[17] 5816 3-9-4 89 RoystonFfrench 7 88
(Mark Johnston) *led 1f: chsd ldrs: drvn over 2f out: one pce over 1f out* **8/1**

20-5 **8** *1/2* **Mehdi (IRE)**[15] 5888 5-9-7 87 (t) DavidNolan 8 85
(Richard Fahey) *chsd ldrs: one pce over 1f out* **7/1**[3]

5462 **9** *1* **Mezzotint (IRE)**[14] 5919 5-9-7 87 PaulMulrennan 6 83
(Stuart Williams) *chsd ldrs on outer: effrt over 1f out: one pce* **13/2**[2]

0006 **10** *1* **Mabait**[44] 4827 8-9-7 87 DavidProbert 14 80
(David Simcock) *mid-div: effrt on wd outside over 1f out: kpt on: nvr nr ldrs* **18/1**

0000 **11** *3 1/4* **Clockmaker (IRE)**[7] 6144 8-9-8 88 HayleyTurner 4 73
(Conor Dore) *trckd ldrs: t.k.h: wknd appr fnl f* **14/1**

00 **12** *7* **Tellovoi (IRE)**[8] 6097 6-9-4 84 (p) BenCurtis 3 52
(Ann Stokell) *t.k.h in rr: lost pl 2f out: sn bhd and eased* **16/1**

1m 35.95s (2.15) **Going Correction** +0.45s/f (Yiel)
**WFA** 3 from 4yo+ 5lb 12 Ran SP% **117.1**
Speed ratings (Par 107): **107,105,105,104,104 103,102,102,101,100 97,90**
CSF £357.23 CT £3082.09 TOTE £22.00: £7.60, £9.00, £2.10; EX 563.60 Trifecta £2386.70 Part won..
**Owner** Northern Line Racing Ltd **Bred** Az Ag Antezzate Srl **Trained** Huby, N Yorks

**FOCUS**
A fiercely competitive handicap, but the gallop wasn't strong. The runner-up sets the standard.

## 6321 FEEL THE RUSH AT BETFAIR STAND CUP (LISTED RACE) 1m 4f 66y
**2:55** (2:55) (Class 1) 3-Y-O+ **£23,680** (£8,956; £4,476; £2,236) **Stalls Low**

Form RPR

**1** **Energia Fribby (BRZ)**[181] 4-8-9 112 TedDurcan 1 98
(Marco Botti) *hld up in mid-div: hdwy and cl 3rd over 3f out: chal over 1f out: led jst ins fnl f: fnd ex nr fin* **10/3**[2]

5-60 **2** *nk* **Livia's Dream (IRE)**[14] 5920 5-8-11 90 HayleyTurner 4 99
(Ed Walker) *hld up in rr: effrt over 2f out: hdwy over 1f out: styd on to take 2nd last 50yds: no ex* **20/1**

1002 **3** *1 1/2* **Pinzolo**[21] 5688 3-8-12 103 PaulMulrennan 2 107
(Charlie Appleby) *trckd ldrs: cl 2nd over 3f out: led 2f out: hdd jst ins fnl f: no ex* **2/1**[1]

0006 **4** *3/4* **Gabrial (IRE)**[14] 5920 5-9-2 102 DavidNolan 7 100
(Richard Fahey) *hld up in mid-div: effrt 3f out: chsng ldrs 2f out: kpt on same pce last 150yds* **8/1**

0614 **5** *4 1/2* **Sennockian Star**[21] 5688 4-9-2 106 (v) RoystonFfrench 3 93
(Mark Johnston) *chsd ldr: drvn over 4f out: wknd over 1f out* **4/1**[3]

6310 **6** *1 1/4* **Whispering Warrior (IRE)**[21] 5695 5-9-2 95 TomQueally 6 91
(David Simcock) *hld up in rr: hdwy over 2f out: drvn over 1f out: sn wknd* **9/1**

106 **7** *5* **Got To Dream**[14] 5914 3-8-2 83 DavidProbert 5 78
(Mark Johnston) *led: hdd 2f out: sn wknd: eased ins fnl f* **12/1**

2m 41.41s (2.91) **Going Correction** +0.45s/f (Yiel)
**WFA** 3 from 4yo+ 9lb 7 Ran SP% **110.0**
Speed ratings: **108,107,106,106,103 102,99**
CSF £56.68 TOTE £5.70: £2.50, £4.70; EX 43.70 Trifecta £141.80.
**Owner** Stefan Friborg **Bred** Haras Estrela Energia **Trained** Newmarket, Suffolk

**FOCUS**
This was a proper test at the trip, thanks to front-runner Got To Dream setting a good gallop. It's hard to equate the winner's Brazilian form.

## 6322 GET BETTER ODDS WITH BETFAIR PRICE RUSH NURSERY H'CAP (BOBIS RACE) 5f 110y
**3:30** (3:30) (Class 3) (0-95,84) 2-Y-O **£11,341** (£3,394; £1,697; £849; £423) **Stalls Low**

Form RPR

140 **1** **Captain Colby (USA)**[56] 4439 2-9-3 80 (b[1]) TomEaves 2 87
(Kevin Ryan) *led tl over 1f out: edgd lft and styd on to regain ld last 100yds* **6/1**[3]

2355 **2** *2* **Steve Prescott**[7] 6135 2-9-7 84 (b[1]) DavidNolan 5 84
(Richard Fahey) *swtchd lft after s: hdwy into mid-div over 4f out: chsng ldrs over 2f out: kpt on to take 2nd nr fin* **7/1**

3510 **3** *1* **Horsforth**[21] 5694 2-8-13 76 BarryMcHugh 1 73
(Tony Coyle) *chsd ldrs: led over 1f out: hdd ins fnl f: no ex* **8/1**

1310 **4** *3/4* **Showstoppa**[10] 6053 2-9-0 77 RoystonFfrench 7 71
(Mark Johnston) *in rr: hdwy on inner to chse ldrs over 1f out: kpt on one pce* **16/1**

3210 **5** *1 1/2* **Arthur MartinLeake (IRE)**[23] 5607 2-9-2 79 BenCurtis 8 68
(K R Burke) *in rr: hdwy over 1f out: kpt on same pce fnl f* **7/2**[1]

3322 **6** *1 1/2* **Flicka's Boy**[8] 6115 2-8-7 75 JoeDoyle(5) 9 59
(Tony Coyle) *in rr: hdwy on outer to chse ldrs over 2f out: one pce over 1f out* **11/1**

2251 **7** *7* **Amber Crystal**[19] 5779 2-8-11 74 (b) RichardKingscote 3 35
(John Gallagher) *chsd ldrs: wknd wl over 1f out: eased towards fin* **11/1**

2221 **8** *2* **You're My Cracker**[17] 5813 2-8-13 76 PJMcDonald 6 31
(Donald McCain) *chsd ldrs: lost pl 2f out* **7/1**

3312 **9** 1 ¼ **Perardua**[15] 5879 2-8-12 80 ........ JackGarritty[(5)] 4 31
(Richard Fahey) *sn chsng ldrs on outer: lost pl 2f out* **9/2**[2]
1m 9.45s (3.25) **Going Correction** +0.45s/f (Yiel) **9 Ran SP% 113.3**
Speed ratings (Par 99): **96,93,92,91,89 87,77,75,73**
CSF £46.48 CT £338.23 TOTE £5.70: £1.30, £3.40, £6.00; EX 39.40 Trifecta £805.40.
**Owner** Mrs R G Hillen **Bred** Castleton Lyons & Kilboy Estate **Trained** Hambleton, N Yorks
**FOCUS**
This was 0-95 in name only as the top-weight was rated just 84, 11lb below the ceiling. They went a strong pace with a slow-motion finish. The winner showed improved form.

## 6323 BETFAIR SUPPORTS PRIDE OF RACING AWARDS H'CAP 1m 2f 75y
**4:10** (4:10) (Class 4) (0-80,79) 3-Y-0+ **£7,762** (£2,310; £1,154; £577) **Stalls High**

Form RPR
5432 **1** **Potent Embrace (USA)**[11] 6011 3-8-11 71 ........ RoystonFfrench 1 82
(Mark Johnston) *chsd ldrs: cl 2nd over 1f out: styd on to ld fnl strides* **8/1**
0512 **2** *hd* **Zugzwang (IRE)**[10] 6044 3-9-5 79 ........ RichardKingscote 2 89
(Ed de Giles) *chsd ldrs: chal over 2f out: sn led and edgd lft: hung rt ins fnl f: hdd nr fin* **10/3**[1]
4313 **3** ½ **Excellent Puck (IRE)**[30] 5345 4-9-7 74 ........ TedDurcan 3 83+
(Shaun Lycett) *hld up in mid-div: hdwy to trck ldrs 3f out: hmpd 2f out: hung lft over 1f out: upsides ins fnl f: no ex towards fin* **9/2**[3]
3241 **4** 3 ¾ **Scoppio Del Carro**[12] 5980 3-9-1 75 ........ (t) DavidProbert 9 77+
(Andrew Balding) *in rr: drvn 3f out: hdwy over 1f out: kpt on: nvr a threat* **9/2**[3]
5215 **5** ½ **Kyllachy Star**[9] 6057 8-9-3 70 ........ (v) DavidNolan 8 71
(Richard Fahey) *in rr: hmpd bnd 7f out: hdwy and nt clr run 2f out: sn hmpd and swtchd rt: kpt on same pce* **16/1**
2022 **6** 5 **Duke Of Yorkshire**[6] 6166 4-9-0 67 ........ GrahamGibbons 7 58
(Tim Easterby) *in rr: drvn and hdwy over 4f out: chsng ldrs over 2f out: wknd over 1f out* **4/1**[2]
5034 **7** 4 ½ **Hydrant**[31] 5319 8-9-5 72 ........ JasonHart 4 55
(Richard Guest) *led: hdd over 4f out: sn hrd drvn: lost pl over 1f out* **16/1**
3320 **8** 12 **Taro Tywod (IRE)**[13] 5948 5-9-4 71 ........ TomQueally 5 31
(Mark Brisbourne) *in rr: hmpd bnd 7f out: drvn after 3f: bhd and eased over 1f out* **25/1**
1344 **9** 9 **Ellaal**[8] 6111 5-9-6 73 ........ PaulMulrennan 6 16
(Ruth Carr) *trckd ldr: led over 4f out: hdd 2f out: n.m.r and sn lost pl: bhd whn eased in clsng stages* **12/1**
2m 14.09s (2.89) **Going Correction** +0.45s/f (Yiel)
**WFA** 3 from 4yo+ 7lb **9 Ran SP% 113.9**
Speed ratings (Par 105): **106,105,105,102,102 98,94,84,77**
CSF £34.34 CT £135.39 TOTE £8.20: £2.30, £1.60, £1.70; EX 42.40 Trifecta £177.50.
**Owner** Sheikh Hamdan bin Mohammed Al Maktoum **Bred** Darley **Trained** Middleham Moor, N Yorks
**FOCUS**
A fair handicap run at a good pace. The winner is rated back to her best.

## 6324 BETFAIR SUPPORTS RACING WELFARE H'CAP 5f 16y
**4:45** (4:48) (Class 4) (0-80,80) 3-Y-0+ **£7,762** (£2,310; £1,154; £577) **Stalls Low**

Form RPR
2550 **1** **Tyfos**[8] 6096 9-9-3 76 ........ JasonHart 1 86
(Brian Baugh) *mde all: wnt clr over 2f out: hld on towards fin* **9/1**
2060 **2** ¾ **Monumental Man**[8] 6096 5-9-0 78 ........ (p) DanielMuscutt[(5)] 9 85
(James Unett) *mid-div: hdwy over 2f out: styd on to take 2nd last 100yds* **16/1**
-021 **3** 1 ¼ **Brother Tiger**[17] 5830 5-9-7 80 ........ DavidProbert 8 83
(David C Griffiths) *chsd ldrs: kpt on fnl f: tk 3rd nr fin* **6/1**[3]
5431 **4** *hd* **Emjayem**[23] 5601 4-9-4 77 ........ GrahamGibbons 4 79
(Ed McMahon) *restless in stalls: mid-div: hdwy to chse ldrs over 2f out: kpt on same pce fnl f* **3/1**[1]
425 **5** ½ **Angelito**[8] 6096 5-9-5 78 ........ DaleSwift 11 78
(Ed McMahon) *s.i.s: in rr: hdwy 2f out: kpt on same pce fnl f* **9/1**
2/21 **6** 2 ¾ **Strategic Heights (IRE)**[27] 5473 5-8-13 77 ........ JackGarritty[(5)] 5 67
(John James Feane, Ire) *chsd ldrs: wknd fnl 150yds* **8/1**
0030 **7** 1 ¾ **Jiroft (ITY)**[13] 5945 7-9-5 78 ........ (t) BenCurtis 3 62
(Ann Stokell) *dwlt in rr: hdwy on inner over 1f out: wknd last 100yds* **16/1**
1000 **8** 6 **Captain Dunne (IRE)**[8] 6096 9-8-11 77 ........ RachelRichardson[(7)] 10 39
(Tim Easterby) *chsd ldrs on outer: lost pl 2f out* **25/1**
330 **9** 3 ¾ **Pushkin Museum (IRE)**[14] 5923 3-9-3 77 ........ DavidNolan 2 26
(Richard Fahey) *chsd ldrs: lost pl over 1f out* **9/2**[2]
1m 3.06s (2.06) **Going Correction** +0.45s/f (Yiel)
**WFA** 3 from 4yo+ 1lb **9 Ran SP% 104.2**
Speed ratings (Par 105): **101,99,97,97,96 92,89,79,73**
CSF £114.28 CT £689.68 TOTE £17.10: £6.60, £9.70, £3.00; EX 163.50 Trifecta £933.40.
**Owner** Magnate Racing **Bred** J Tomlinson And G Williams **Trained** Audley, Staffs
■ Head Space was withdrawn. Price at time of withdrawal 7/1. Rule 4 applies to all bets - deduct 10p in the pound.
**FOCUS**
A fine example of front-running round here. The winner was not an obvious improver.

## 6325 BETFAIR COMMITS £40MILLION TO BRITISH RACING H'CAP (BOBIS RACE) 1m 7f 195y
**5:20** (5:20) (Class 3) (0-90,85) 3-Y-O **£14,231** (£4,235; £2,116; £1,058) **Stalls Low**

Form RPR
3321 **1** **Chesil Beach**[25] 5520 3-8-7 71 ........ DavidProbert 7 79
(Andrew Balding) *s.i.s: hld up in rr: hdwy over 3f out: n.m.r over 1f out: styd on to ld last 75yds* **7/2**[2]
6112 **2** 1 ¼ **Needless Shouting (IRE)**[31] 5318 3-8-12 76 ........ SamHitchcott 4 82
(Mick Channon) *led at stdy pce: qcknd pce over 5f out: hdd and no ex ins fnl f* **13/2**[3]
6132 **3** 1 ¼ **Late Shipment**[17] 5812 3-9-7 85 ........ (p) RoystonFfrench 3 89
(Mark Johnston) *trckd ldr: drvn over 2f out: kpt on one pce fnl f* **7/2**[2]
2312 **4** ¾ **Taws**[15] 5878 3-8-6 75 ........ JackGarritty[(5)] 6 78
(Rod Millman) *trckd ldrs: effrt 3f out: kpt on one pce appr fnl f* **3/1**[1]
2343 **5** 1 ¼ **Flying Cape (IRE)**[20] 5716 3-8-6 70 ........ (p) PaulQuinn 2 72
(Andrew Hollinshead) *t.k.h in rr: hdwy and swtchd outside over 1f out: kpt on ins fnl f* **11/1**
-046 **6** 2 ½ **Layla's Red Devil (IRE)**[63] 4189 3-8-2 66 oh3 ........ PatrickMathers 1 65
(Richard Fahey) *trckd ldrs: pushed along over 5f out: wknd over 1f out* **7/1**
2211 **7** 1 ¼ **Sweetheart Abbey**[23] 5600 3-9-6 84 ........ (p) TomQueally 5 81
(William Knight) *hld up in rr: effrt 3f out: chsng ldrs on outer over 1f out: wknd last 150yds: eased nr fin* **8/1**
3m 36.6s (8.60) **Going Correction** +0.45s/f (Yiel) **7 Ran SP% 114.7**
Speed ratings (Par 105): **96,95,94,94,93 92,91**
CSF £26.28 TOTE £2.90: £1.40, £2.10; EX 23.70 Trifecta £129.20.
**Owner** Kingsclere Racing Club **Bred** Kingsclere Stud **Trained** Kingsclere, Hants
**FOCUS**
Not a bad little handicap. The winner continues to progress.
T/Plt: £4,495.50 to a £1 stake. Pool of £73899.70 - 12.0 winning tickets. T/Qpdt: £104.60 to a £1 stake. Pool of £5913.75 - 41.80 winning tickets. WG

# 6286 DONCASTER (L-H)
Saturday, September 13
**OFFICIAL GOING: Good (good to soft in places n round course; good to firm in places on straight course; 7.6)**
Wind: Virtually nil Weather: Cloudy

## 6326 AT THE RACES CHAMPAGNE STKS (GROUP 2) (C&G) 7f
**2:05** (2:05) (Class 1) 2-Y-O
**£42,532** (£16,125; £8,070; £4,020; £2,017; £1,012) **Stalls High**

Form RPR
211 **1** **Estidhkaar (IRE)**[63] 4199 2-9-3 113 ........ PaulHanagan 5 116
(Richard Hannon) *trckd ldr: rdn over 1f out: led ent fnl f: kpt on strly* **10/11**[1]
3033 **2** 1 ¼ **War Envoy (USA)**[13] 5954 2-9-0 0 ........ RyanMoore 4 110
(A P O'Brien, Ire) *hld up in rr: hdwy over 2f out: rdn over 1f out: styd on fnl f* **11/1**
1 **3** *nk* **Aces (IRE)**[26] 5500 2-9-0 0 ........ OisinMurphy 2 109
(Charles Hills) *led: rdn along and jnd wl over 1f out: hdd ent fnl f: sn drvn and kpt on same pce* **18/1**
141 **4** 1 **Belardo (IRE)**[28] 5431 2-9-0 106 ........ AndreaAtzeni 1 106
(Roger Varian) *trckd ldr: hdwy and cl up wl over 1f out: rdn and ev ch ent fnl f: sn drvn and kpt on same pce* **3/1**[2]
123 **5** 1 ½ **Room Key**[45] 4780 2-9-0 102 ........ DaneO'Neill 3 102
(Eve Johnson Houghton) *t.k.h early: trckd ldrs: effrt over 2f out: sn rdn along and wknd wl over 1f out* **20/1**
14 **6** 2 ¼ **Glenalmond (IRE)**[21] 5692 2-9-0 0 ........ DanielTudhope 6 96
(K R Burke) *chsd ldrs on outer: rdn along 2f out: sn wknd* **6/1**[3]
1m 24.18s (-2.12) **Going Correction** -0.175s/f (Firm) **6 Ran SP% 110.0**
Speed ratings (Par 107): **105,103,103,102,100 97**
CSF £11.69 TOTE £2.00: £1.10, £4.50; EX 9.70 Trifecta £48.30.
**Owner** Hamdan Al Maktoum **Bred** BEC Bloodstock **Trained** East Everleigh, Wilts
**FOCUS**
The general consensus among riders was that the ground was good, although Andrea Atzeni felt it was good to firm. The time of the the opener, in which they didn't go overly fast, seemed to confirm the going was on the quick side in the straight. Not the deepest edition of this race, but Estidhkaar looks on a par with most recent winners of the race, Toronado being the exception. There's every chance the winner can improve again.

## 6327 LADBROKES PORTLAND H'CAP 5f 140y
**2:40** (2:41) (Class 2) 3-Y-0+
**£37,350** (£11,184; £5,592; £2,796; £1,389; £702) **Stalls High**

Form RPR
215 **1** **Muthmir (IRE)**[42] 4895 4-9-7 100 ........ PaulHanagan 15 115+
(William Haggas) *stmbld shortly after s and in rr: gd hdwy 2f out: nt clr run and swtchd lft jst over 1f out: rdn and qcknd to ld ins fnl f: kpt on strly* **3/1**[1]
0006 **2** 2 **Bogart**[24] 5575 5-9-0 93 ........ AmyRyan 9 100
(Kevin Ryan) *prom: led 2f out: rdn and edgd rt over 1f out and again ins fnl f: kpt on towards fin* **25/1**
6551 **3** *nse* **Humidor (IRE)**[19] 5754 7-9-0 93 ........ JamesDoyle 21 100
(George Baker) *racd towards stands' rail: hld up towards rr: hdwy wl over 1f out: rdn and styd on strly fnl f* **14/1**
321 **4** ½ **Goldream**[35] 5160 5-9-9 102 ........ (p) AndreaAtzeni 11 107
(Robert Cowell) *slt ld: pushed along and hdd 2f out: rdn over 1f out: n.m.r ent fnl f: kpt on u.p towards fin* **14/1**
0651 **5** ¾ **Chilworth Icon**[14] 5925 4-9-1 94 ........ SamHitchcott 22 97
(Mick Channon) *hld up towards rr: hdwy wl over 1f out: rdn and nt clr run ent fnl f: swtchd lft and styd on wl towards fin* **22/1**
2111 **6** *nk* **Go Far**[7] 6159 4-9-8 101 ........ (v) MartinHarley 14 103
(Alan Bailey) *hld up towards rr: hdwy 2f out: nt clr run and swtchd lft over 1f out: sn rdn and kpt on fnl f: nrst fin* **16/1**
103 **7** 1 ½ **High On Life**[21] 5696 3-9-1 96 ........ AdamKirby 19 93
(Jamie Osborne) *racd nr stands' rail: in tch: hdwy to chse ldrs over 2f out: rdn and cl up over 1f out: drvn and edgd lft ent fnl f: one pce* **12/1**
200 **8** ½ **Seeking Magic**[42] 4895 6-9-4 100 ........ (t) RyanTate[(3)] 5 95
(Clive Cox) *in tch: hdwy over 2f out: rdn wl over 1f out: no imp appr fnl f* **16/1**
3531 **9** 1 ½ **Out Do**[28] 5445 5-9-4 97 ........ (v) DanielTudhope 10 87
(David O'Meara) *in tch: effrt whn n.m.r over 1f out: no imp* **10/1**[3]
0002 **10** *nse* **Clear Spring (IRE)**[19] 5778 6-9-4 97 ........ LiamJones 3 87
(John Spearing) *chsd ldrs: rdn along 2f out: wknd over 1f out* **50/1**
3304 **11** ¾ **Love Island**[14] 5918 5-8-11 93 ........ (p) GeorgeChaloner[(3)] 17 80
(Richard Whitaker) *racd towards stands' rail: chsd ldrs: rdn along over 2f out: sn wknd* **40/1**
3311 **12** 1 **Algar Lad**[7] 6130 4-9-1 97 ........ SamJames[(3)] 7 81
(David O'Meara) *a towards rr* **25/1**
1660 **13** *hd* **See The Sun**[24] 5575 3-9-0 95 ........ DuranFentiman 16 78
(Tim Easterby) *chsd ldrs: rdn along 2f out: drvn and wkng whn n.m.r jst over 1f out* **25/1**
4306 **14** *nk* **Addictive Dream (IRE)**[35] 5160 7-9-9 102 ........ RobertWinston 8 84
(John Murray) *cl up on outer: rdn along 2f out: drvn over 1f out: wknd ent fnl f* **40/1**
1101 **15** 1 ¾ **Compton Park**[15] 5888 7-9-4 97 ........ (t) DavidAllan 4 74
(Les Eyre) *towards rr: hdwy 2f out: sn rdn along: n.m.r over 1f out: n.d* **12/1**
00 **16** 1 ½ **Magical Macey (USA)**[14] 5918 7-9-2 95 ........ (b) PhillipMakin 13 67
(David Barron) *cl up: rdn along over 2f out: sn wknd* **40/1**
1000 **17** *shd* **Smoothtalkinrascal (IRE)**[98] 2989 4-9-10 103 ........ SilvestreDeSousa 20 74
(David O'Meara) *dwlt: and swtchd lft s: a in rr* **28/1**
1110 **18** ½ **Intrinsic**[21] 5674 4-9-8 101 ........ RichardHughes 6 71
(Robert Cowell) *trckd ldrs: rdn 2f out: wkng whn n.m.r wl over 1f out* **9/2**[2]
-020 **19** 1 ¼ **Pearl Acclaim (IRE)**[14] 5918 4-9-0 93 ........ JoeFanning 2 59
(David Nicholls) *wnt sltly lft s: in tch on outer: rdn along 2f out: sn wknd* **50/1**

0000 **20** ½ **York Glory (USA)**[24] 5575 6-9-7 100..............................(b) RyanMoore 1 64
(Kevin Ryan) *a in rr* **16/1**
1m 5.38s (-3.42) **Going Correction** -0.175s/f (Firm) course record
**WFA** 3 from 4yo+ 2lb **20** Ran SP% **129.2**
Speed ratings (Par 109): **115,112,112,111,110 110,108,107,105,105 104,103,102,102,100 98,98,97,95,95**
CSF £90.43 CT £984.18 TOTE £4.10: £1.70, £6.40, £5.10, £3.20; EX 110.50 Trifecta £1533.80.
**Owner** Hamdan Al Maktoum **Bred** Sunderland Holdings Ltd **Trained** Newmarket, Suffolk

**FOCUS**
Solid handicap form. Muthmir showed himself a contender for Group races, with the runner-up rated to his best form since last August.

## 6328 OLBG PARK STKS (GROUP 2) 7f
**3:15** (3:15) (Class 1) 3-Y-O+
**£56,710** (£21,500; £10,760; £5,360; £2,690; £1,350) **Stalls** High

Form RPR
0101 **1** **Ansgar (IRE)**[20] 5722 6-9-4 111..............................(t) JamesDoyle 1 117
(Sabrina J Harty, Ire) *mde all: rdn and qcknd wl over 1f out: drvn ins fnl f: kpt on wl towards fin* **7/2**[3]
-330 **2** ½ **Aljamaaheer (IRE)**[63] 4201 5-9-4 115..............................(p) PaulHanagan 6 116
(Roger Varian) *towards rr: niggled along 2f out: rdn and hdwy over 1f out: styd on wl to chal last 100yds: no ex towards fin* **2/1**[1]
1302 **3** ½ **Gregorian (IRE)**[28] 5434 5-9-4 116.............................. WilliamBuick 2 114
(John Gosden) *trckd ldng pair: hdwy 2f out: rdn to chal and edgd lft jst over 1f out: sn drvn and ev ch tl no ex last 100yds* **5/2**[2]
0316 **4** 1 **Es Que Love (IRE)**[7] 6134 5-9-8 113.............................. AdamKirby 8 116
(Clive Cox) *hld up in tch hdwy over 2f out: rdn to chse ldng pair over 1f out: drvn ins fnl f: kpt on same pce* **15/2**
1430 **5** 1¾ **Professor**[7] 6134 4-9-4 110.............................. KierenFallon 7 107
(Richard Hannon) *bhd: rdn along and outpcd wl over 1f out: hdwy ent fnl f: kpt on: nrst fin* **14/1**
22-0 **6** 1¾ **Cable Bay (IRE)**[22] 5653 3-9-0 114.............................. FrankieDettori 4 101
(Charles Hills) *trckd ldrs: hdwy 2f out: rdn over 1f out: hld whn sltly hmpd ent fnl f* **12/1**
0505 **7** nk **Penitent**[7] 6132 8-9-4 108.............................. DanielTudhope 3 102
(David O'Meara) *trckd wnr: pushed along wl over 2f out: sn rdn and outpcd wl over 1f out: kpt on fnl f* **25/1**
1m 22.41s (-3.89) **Going Correction** -0.175s/f (Firm)
**WFA** 3 from 4yo+ 4lb **7** Ran SP% **114.1**
Speed ratings (Par 115): **115,114,113,112,110 108,108**
CSF £10.90 TOTE £5.00: £2.50, £1.70; EX 14.20 Trifecta £47.20.
**Owner** Ms Chynel Phelan & Shane Fox **Bred** Miss Chynel Phelan **Trained** Newbridge, Co Kildare

**FOCUS**
Under a nicely judged front-running ride, the winner got away from them. He confirmed he's better than ever, with the next two a shade off their bests.

## 6329 LADBROKES ST LEGER STKS (BRITISH CHAMPIONS SERIES) (GROUP 1) (ENTIRE COLTS & FILLIES) 1m 6f 132y
**3:50** (3:55) (Class 1) 3-Y-O
**£368,615** (£139,750; £69,940; £34,840; £17,485; £8,775) **Stalls** Low

Form RPR
024 **1** **Kingston Hill**[70] 3984 3-9-1 120.............................. AndreaAtzeni 4 119+
(Roger Varian) *hld up in rr: hdwy on wd outside wl over 2f out: chal over 1f out: rdn to ld and hung lft jst ins fnl f: drvn: kpt on wl* **9/4**[1]
1230 **2** 1¼ **Romsdal**[49] 4649 3-9-1 115.............................. WilliamBuick 14 117
(John Gosden) *trckd ldrs: hdwy over 3f out: rdn to ld wl over 1f out: drvn and hdd jst ins fnl f: sn carried lft: kpt on same pce last 100yds* **13/2**[3]
1412 **3** 2 **Snow Sky**[24] 5577 3-9-1 111.............................. JamesDoyle 7 115
(Sir Michael Stoute) *hld up towards rr: hdwy on outer 3f out: pushed along and rdr dropped rein 2f out: rdn and ev ch over 1f out: hld in cl 3rd whn hmpd jst ins fnl f: kpt on same pce* **11/2**[2]
2222 **4** nk **Windshear**[45] 4778 3-9-1 110.............................. RichardHughes 3 113
(Richard Hannon) *trckd ldrs on inner: hdwy 3f out: rdn along 2f out: drvn on inner over 1f out: kpt on same pce fnl f* **13/2**[3]
2354 **5** 1¼ **Marzocco (USA)**[24] 5577 3-9-1 107..............................(b) RobertHavlin 2 112
(John Gosden) *midfield on inner: swtchd rt and hdwy over 3f out: rdn to chse ldrs over 2f out: drvn over 1f out: kpt on same pce* **50/1**
2131 **6** hd **Forever Now**[21] 5668 3-9-1 106.............................. FrankieDettori 13 111
(John Gosden) *trckd ldng pair: hdwy 4f out: rdn to ld wl over 2f out: hdd wl over 1f out: sn drvn and grad wknd* **14/1**
2116 **7** 1½ **Hartnell**[24] 5577 3-9-1 110.............................. JoeFanning 6 109
(Mark Johnston) *led 2f: prom: effrt 3f out and cl up: rdn over 2f out: drvn wl over 1f out: kpt on one pce appr fnl f* **12/1**
0112 **8** 3¾ **Alex My Boy (IRE)**[21] 5668 3-9-1 105.............................. SilvestreDeSousa 5 104
(Mark Johnston) *hld up in rr: effrt and sme hdwy on inner over 2f out: sn rdn and n.d* **14/1**
1123 **9** 1¼ **Kings Fete**[21] 5668 3-9-1 104.............................. RyanMoore 12 102
(Sir Michael Stoute) *hld up and bhd: hdwy wl over 3f out: rdn along wl over 2f out: n.d* **12/1**
0335 **10** ¾ **Somewhat (USA)**[28] 5432 3-9-1 109.............................. FrannyNorton 11 101
(Mark Johnston) *chsd ldrs: rdn along over 3f out: wknd wl over 2f out* **33/1**
5 **11** 1½ **Granddukeoftuscany (IRE)**[24] 5577 3-9-1 105.............................. ColmO'Donoghue 10 99
(A P O'Brien, Ire) *prom: led after 2f: clr 5f out: rdn along over 3f out: hdd wl over 2f out and sn wknd* **20/1**
4335 **12** 1 **Scotland (GER)**[45] 4778 3-9-1 109.............................. JimCrowley 9 98
(Andrew Balding) *a in rr* **16/1**
3m 5.42s (-1.98) **Going Correction** -0.025s/f (Good) **12** Ran SP% **117.1**
Speed ratings (Par 115): **104,103,102,102,101 101,100,98,97,97 96,96**
CSF £15.69 CT £72.79 TOTE £3.20: £1.60, £3.00, £2.10; EX 21.40 Trifecta £136.40.
**Owner** Paul Smith **Bred** Ridgecourt Stud **Trained** Newmarket, Suffolk

**FOCUS**
Run at a fair gallop, there's every reason to believe this was a strong edition of the race, with the Derby second and third coming through late to dominate the finish, and the right horses finishing in behind. Although there was a bunch finish, the form has a sound look to it.

## 6330 NAPOLEANS CASINOS AND RESTAURANTS H'CAP 1m 4f
**4:25** (4:28) (Class 2) (0-105,103) 3-Y-O+**£16,172** (£4,812; £2,405; £1,202) **Stalls** Low

Form RPR
-133 **1** **Mount Logan (IRE)**[35] 5179 3-8-10 **96**.............................. AndreaAtzeni 7 108
(Luca Cumani) *hld up: hdwy to trck ldrs 7f out: cl up over 2f out: rdn to ld wl over 1f out: kpt on strly towards fin* **7/4**[1]
-016 **2** 2¼ **Forgotten Hero (IRE)**[14] 5928 5-9-2 **93**.............................. MartinHarley 3 101
(Charles Hills) *hld up in rr: hdwy wl over 2f out: rdn over 1f out: styd on to chse wnr ins fnl f: no imp towards fin* **8/1**
3230 **3** 1½ **Bold Sniper**[21] 5693 4-9-12 **103**.............................. RichardHughes 1 109
(Sir Michael Stoute) *plld hrd: trckd ldrs on inner: hdwy 2f out and ev ch: rdn over 1f out: carried hd high and one pce fnl f* **7/1**
1-03 **4** 2 **I'm Fraam Govan**[21] 5695 6-9-4 **95**.............................. PatCosgrave 5 97
(George Baker) *trckd ldrs: hdwy 3f out: rdn to chse ldng pair over 1f out: drvn and one pce fnl f* **10/1**
5130 **5** nk **Tha'ir (IRE)**[46] 4756 4-9-5 **103**.............................. MikeyEnnis(7) 8 105
(Saeed bin Suroor) *t.k.h early: prom: trckd ldr after 2f: hdwy and cl up 3f out: led briefly jst over 2f out: sn rdn and hdd wl over 1f out: sn drvn: wknd appr fnl f* **14/1**
1020 **6** 4½ **Mighty Yar (IRE)**[21] 5693 4-9-7 **98**.............................. GrahamLee 6 93
(Lady Cecil) *t.k.h: trckd ldrs on outer: effrt over 2f out and sn pushed along: rdn wl over 1f out and sn wknd* **13/2**[3]
0403 **7** 1½ **Highland Castle**[9] 6061 6-8-12 **89**.............................. KierenFallon 4 81
(David Elsworth) *t.k.h: in tch on inner: hdwy wl over 2f out: effrt wl over 1f out: sn rdn and btn* **6/1**[2]
1033 **8** 1½ **Linguine (FR)**[22] 5633 4-8-13 **90**.............................. PhillipMakin 2 80
(Paul Midgley) *led: rdn along 3f out: hdd jst over 2f out: sn wknd* **22/1**
0020 **F** **Wigmore Hall (IRE)**[22] 5651 7-9-8 **99**.............................. AdamKirby 9
(Michael Bell) *hld up in rr: effrt 3f out: sn lost action and fell wl over 2f out; fatally injured* **16/1**
2m 31.4s (-3.50) **Going Correction** -0.025s/f (Good)
**WFA** 3 from 4yo+ 9lb **9** Ran SP% **113.6**
Speed ratings (Par 109): **110,108,107,106,105 102,101,100,**
CSF £15.98 CT £78.33 TOTE £2.90: £1.10, £2.40, £2.20; EX 18.00 Trifecta £84.20.
**Owner** Sheikh Mohammed Obaid Al Maktoum **Bred** Ladyswood Stud & Canning Downs Stud Aus **Trained** Newmarket, Suffolk

**FOCUS**
This looked a decent enough handicap, if lacking improvers. The winner was the exception.

## 6331 AGRIARGO UK TRACTOR CHALLENGE NURSERY H'CAP (BOBIS RACE) 1m (S)
**5:00** (5:01) (Class 2) 2-Y-O **£9,703** (£2,887; £1,443; £721) **Stalls** High

Form RPR
541 **1** **Dance Of Fire**[18] 5783 2-8-12 76.............................. OisinMurphy 5 85+
(Andrew Balding) *cl up: led after 2f: rdn over 1f out: drvn ins fnl f: hld on wl towards fin* **7/2**[2]
2231 **2** ¾ **Marshall Jennings (IRE)**[19] 5752 2-9-7 85.............................. RichardHughes 1 88
(Richard Hannon) *dwlt and hld up in rr: hdwy over 2f out: chsd ldrs over 1f out: rdn and edgd rt jst ins fnl f: sn drvn and ev ch: hld whn edgd rt nr fin* **3/1**[1]
3241 **3** ½ **Rotherwick (IRE)**[20] 5712 2-9-2 80.............................. SilvestreDeSousa 9 82
(Paul Cole) *in rr: pushed along wl over 2f out: rdn to chse ldrs and edgd lft wl over 1f out: drvn to chal ent fnl f: kpt on u.p towards fin* **7/2**[2]
4001 **4** shd **Silver Quay (IRE)**[15] 5875 2-9-0 78.............................. KierenFallon 7 80
(Richard Hannon) *trckd ldrs: hdwy 3f out: rdn to chse ldrs over 1f out: drvn and ch ent fnl f: kpt on same pce* **13/2**[3]
0153 **5** 2 **Shaakis (IRE)**[22] 5645 2-8-13 77.............................. DaneO'Neill 4 75
(Marcus Tregoning) *led 2f: cl up: rdn wl over 1f out: hld whn n.m.r and squeezed out jst ins fnl f: one pce after* **7/1**
0144 **6** 8 **Sakhee's Return**[37] 5085 2-8-12 76.............................. DuranFentiman 6 55
(Tim Easterby) *in tch: hdwy 3f out: rdn 2f out and sn wknd* **20/1**
635 **7** hd **Servery**[29] 5393 2-9-1 79.............................. SeanLevey 2 57
(Richard Hannon) *trckd ldrs: hdwy on outer 3f out: cl up over 2f out: rdn and edgd rt over 1f out: sn wknd* **25/1**
511 **8** ½ **Jargon (FR)**[47] 4731 2-9-7 85.............................. AdamKirby 3 62
(Michael Bell) *prom: cl up over 2f out: sn rdn and wkng whn n.m.r over 1f out* **11/1**
3550 **9** 8 **Danny O'Ruairc (IRE)**[24] 5576 2-8-11 75.............................. GrahamLee 8 34
(James Moffatt) *in tch: rdn along 3f out: wknd over 2f out* **25/1**
1m 36.72s (-2.58) **Going Correction** -0.175s/f (Firm) 2y crse rec **9** Ran SP% **116.1**
Speed ratings (Par 101): **105,104,103,103,101 93,93,92,84**
CSF £14.11 CT £37.84 TOTE £3.60: £1.20, £1.20, £2.00; EX 13.90 Trifecta £42.80.
**Owner** J C Smith **Bred** Littleton Stud **Trained** Kingsclere, Hants

**FOCUS**
There wasn't much between several of these in what was a decent nursery, run in a 2yo track record time. The winner gave the impression there's more to come, and the form is straightforward in behind.

## 6332 HARRIET DE-VERE POWELL H'CAP 1m (S)
**6:05** (6:08) (Class 2) (0-110,100) 3-Y-O+**£16,172** (£4,812; £2,405; £1,202) **Stalls** High

Form RPR
3203 **1** **Championship (IRE)**[35] 5177 3-8-12 93.............................. RichardHughes 3 104+
(Richard Hannon) *cl up: led after 1f: hdd over 4f out: cl up: slt ld 2f out: sn pushed along and hdd ent fnl f: rdn and styd on to ld again last 75yds* **14/1**
1004 **2** ¾ **Bronze Angel (IRE)**[23] 5609 5-9-4 99..............................(b) LouisSteward(5) 6 109
(Marcus Tregoning) *hld up in tch: hdwy 3f out: trckd ldrs 2f out: swtchd lft and effrt over 1f out: rdn to ld ent fnl f: sn drvn and edgd lft: hdd and no ex last 75yds* **3/1**[2]
4010 **3** 1¼ **Velox**[43] 4851 4-9-7 97.............................. AndreaAtzeni 9 104
(Luca Cumani) *hld up in rr: hdwy 2f out: rdn over 1f out: styd on to chse ldng pair ins fnl f: sn edgd lft and no imp* **5/1**[3]
1-12 **4** 1½ **Maverick Wave (USA)**[35] 5192 3-9-3 98.............................. WilliamBuick 11 101
(John Gosden) *cl up: led over 4f out: pushed along and hdd 2f out: cl up tl drvn and one pce ent fnl f* **13/8**[1]
0000 **5** 2½ **Levitate**[87] 3356 6-9-8 98..............................(v) PhillipMakin 2 96
(John Quinn) *towards rr: pushed along 3f out: hdwy 2f out: sn rdn: kpt on fnl f* **28/1**
3050 **6** nk **Prince Of Johanne (IRE)**[23] 5609 8-9-8 98..............................(p) GrahamLee 5 95
(Tom Tate) *led 1f: prom: effrt 2f out: sn rdn and ev ch: drvn over 1f out: sn edgd lft and wknd* **10/1**
0205 **7** ½ **Ingleby Angel (IRE)**[19] 5771 5-9-6 96.............................. DanielTudhope 1 92
(David O'Meara) *chsd ldrs: rdn along 2f out: sn wknd* **18/1**
-600 **8** 3 **Consign**[140] 1719 4-9-2 92..............................(v) KierenFallon 8 81
(Jeremy Noseda) *hld up: hdwy over 2f out: sn rdn and n.d* **25/1**
2033 **9** nse **End Of Line**[19] 5749 3-8-12 93.............................. OisinMurphy 10 81
(Andrew Balding) *hld up in rr: hdwy on outer to chse ldrs 3f out: rdn along over 2f out: sn wknd* **12/1**
**10** 10 **Arc Lighter (USA)**[463] 5-9-9 99..............................(t) AdamKirby 7 65
(Seamus Durack) *trckd ldrs: pushed along over 3f out: sn rdn and wknd: bhd and eased ins fnl f* **28/1**
1m 36.06s (-3.24) **Going Correction** -0.175s/f (Firm)
**WFA** 3 from 4yo+ 5lb **10** Ran SP% **119.2**
Speed ratings (Par 109): **109,108,107,105,103 102,102,99,99,89**
CSF £56.18 CT £252.09 TOTE £14.00: £3.60, £1.70, £1.10; EX 57.30 Trifecta £380.80.
**Owner** Mrs J Wood **Bred** Ms Natalie Cleary **Trained** East Everleigh, Wilts

■ Stewards' Enquiry : Louis Steward two-day ban: used whip above permitted level (Sep 28-29)
**FOCUS**
A decent handicap.
T/Jkpt: £2010.40 to a £1 stake. Pool: £36,810.47 - 13.00 winning units. T/Plt: £14.20 to a £1 stake. Pool: £192,170.71 - 9878.37 winning units. T/Qpdt: £4.20 to a £1 stake. Pool: £11,723.49 - 2053.15 winning units. JR

# 6038 LINGFIELD (L-H)
Saturday, September 13
**OFFICIAL GOING: Turf course: good to firm (8.1); polytrack: standard**
Wind: light, across Weather: dry, bright spells

## 6333 BRITISH STALLION STUDS EBF MAIDEN FILLIES' STKS (BOBIS RACE) 7f 140y
**2:00** (2:01) (Class 5) 2-Y-O **£3,067** (£905; £453) **Stalls Centre**

Form RPR
5 **1** **Pulcinella (IRE)**[91] 3223 2-9-0 0 AhmedAjtebi 2 81+
(Charlie Appleby) *chsd ldrs and a travelling strly: led on bit ent fnl 2f: shkn up and readily wnt clr 1f out: r.o strly: easily* **5/2**[2]
5 **2** *3 ¾* **Graceland (FR)**[22] 5643 2-9-0 0 WilliamTwiston-Davies 6 69+
(Michael Bell) *in tch in midfield: effrt to chse wnr and rdn over 1f out: outpcd and btn 1f out: kpt on for clr 2nd* **1/1**[1]
05 **3** *5* **Vivo Per Lei (IRE)**[24] 5549 2-8-9 0 MarcMonaghan(5) 1 57
(Marco Botti) *stdd s: hld up in last trio: swtchd rt 4f out: rdn and effrt over 2f out: no ch w wnr but battling for 3rd 1f out: plugged on to go 3rd last strides* **25/1**
**4** *hd* **Precast** 2-9-0 0 MartinLane 7 57
(David Simcock) *chsd ldr tl ent fnl 2f: 3rd and outpcd over 1f out: wl btn and plugged on same pce fnl f: lost 3rd last strides* **14/1**
**5** *shd* **Pyla (IRE)** 2-9-0 0 HarryBentley 4 57
(Ed Dunlop) *hld up in tch: rdn and effrt 3f out: no ch w wnr but battling for 3rd 1f out: plugged on* **10/1**
600 **6** *4 ½* **Weardiditallgorong**[66] 4075 2-9-0 48 [1] ShaneKelly 8 46
(Des Donovan) *led tl ent fnl 2f: sn rdn and btn: wknd over 1f out* **66/1**
**7** *3* **Resolve** 2-9-0 0 LukeMorris 5 39
(David Simcock) *v.s.a and rdn along leaving stalls: in tch: rdn and struggling 4f out: lost tch 2f out* **6/1**[3]
**8** *11* **Reigning** 2-9-0 0 LiamKeniry 3 13
(Michael Blanshard) *s.i.s: a in rr: hmpd 4f out: lost tch 3f out* **50/1**
1m 32.4s (0.10) **Going Correction** -0.025s/f (Good) **8** Ran SP% **115.9**
Speed ratings (Par 92): **98,94,89,89,88 84,81,70**
CSF £5.37 TOTE £3.40: £1.10, £1.10, £5.90; EX 6.10 Trifecta £42.10.
**Owner** Godolphin **Bred** Darley **Trained** Newmarket, Suffolk
■ Stewards' Enquiry : Marc Monaghan one-day ban: careless riding (Sep 28)
**FOCUS**
An ordinary fillies' maiden, run at a steady pace, but a likeable performance from the winner. The first two have better to offer.

## 6334 HISCOX ASM H'CAP 7f
**2:30** (2:30) (Class 4) (0-85,84) 3-Y-O+ **£5,175** (£1,540; £769; £384) **Stalls Centre**

Form RPR
0404 **1** **Bluegrass Blues (IRE)**[30] 5346 4-9-10 84 LukeMorris 7 93
(Paul Cole) *in tch in midfield: effrt and switching lft 2f out: hrd drvn to ld 1f out: kpt on wl* **11/4**[1]
4413 **2** *1 ¼* **Scottish Glen**[38] 5031 8-9-3 77 LiamKeniry 3 83
(Patrick Chamings) *in tch in last pair: bustled along 4f out: wnt 4th and swtchd lft 1f out: styd on to go 2nd wl ins fnl f: no threat to wnr* **9/2**[2]
2064 **3** *1 ¼* **Zacynthus (IRE)**[20] 5728 6-9-5 79 WilliamTwiston-Davies 8 82
(Michael Bell) *dwlt: rcvrd to ld after 1f: hdd and rdn 2f out: styd on same pce ins fnl f* **7/1**
5003 **4** *1 ¼* **Realize**[22] 5629 4-8-6 73 (p) CharlieBennett(7) 6 72
(Hughie Morrison) *chsd ldrs tl wnt 2nd after 2f: led 2and rdn 2f out: hdd 1f out: wknd fnl 100yds* **5/1**[3]
005 **5** *2 ¾* **Mr Matthews (IRE)**[27] 5468 3-8-7 74 JoeyHaynes(3) 1 64
(K R Burke) *in tch in midfield: rdn and effrt jst over 2f out: fnd little for press and btn over 1f out: wknd* **16/1**
0422 **6** *nk* **Almanack**[15] 5887 4-8-7 72 oh5 ow2 GeorgeDowning(5) 4 63
(Ian Williams) *t.k.h: led for 1f: chsd ldrs after: rdn ent fnl 2f: wknd over 1f out* **8/1**
2434 **7** *1 ¾* **Nassau Storm**[8] 6100 5-9-10 84 (v[1]) AmirQuinn 2 71
(William Knight) *in tch in last pair: swtchd lft and effrt 2f out: sn btn: wknd over 1f out* **8/1**
0000 **8** *4 ½* **Birdman (IRE)**[38] 5040 4-9-8 82 (be) MartinLane 5 57
(David Simcock) *dwlt: bhd: swtchd lft and hdwy after 2f: jnd ldrs 4f out tl rdn and btn over 2f out: wknd wl over 1f out* **10/1**
1m 22.91s (-0.39) **Going Correction** -0.025s/f (Good)
**WFA** 3 from 4yo+ 4lb **8** Ran SP% **111.2**
Speed ratings (Par 105): **101,99,98,96,93 93,91,86**
CSF £14.10 CT £73.72 TOTE £3.20: £1.30, £1.40, £3.40; EX 12.10 Trifecta £56.00.
**Owner** Mrs Fitri Hay **Bred** Yeomanstown Stud **Trained** Whatcombe, Oxon
**FOCUS**
A fair handicap and the pace looked reasonable. The winner is rated to his AW form.

## 6335 DAVID CLIFFORD BRITISH STALLION STUDS EBF CONDITIONS STKS 7f
**3:05** (3:05) (Class 3) 3-Y-O+ **£9,703** (£2,887; £1,443; £721) **Stalls Centre**

Form RPR
1-45 **1** **Patentar (FR)**[107] 2706 3-8-12 99 LukeMorris 5 111
(Marco Botti) *hld up in tch: swtchd sharply lft and effrt 2f out: led over 1f out: drifting rt but gng clr 1f out: r.o strly: readily* **4/1**[3]
1240 **2** *5* **Dark Emerald (IRE)**[21] 5665 4-9-2 98 SebSanders 2 100
(Brendan Powell) *w ldr tl rdn to ld over 2f out: hdd and unable qck over 1f out: no ch w wnr but kpt on for clr 2nd ins fnl f* **7/2**[2]
0060 **3** *2 ½* **Georgian Bay (IRE)**[49] 4648 4-8-13 97 (v) JoeyHaynes(3) 4 94
(K R Burke) *chsd ldrs: ev ch and rdn 2f out: 3rd and btn 1f out: wknd ins fnl f* **7/4**[1]
2601 **4** *2 ¾* **Noble Citizen (USA)**[42] 4916 9-9-2 93 (b) MartinLane 1 86
(David Simcock) *s.i.s: niggled along in rr: rdn 1/2-way: swtchd lft and wnt 4th wl over 1f out: no imp: wknd ins fnl f* **12/1**
0402 **5** *11* **Miracle Of Medinah**[63] 4187 3-8-12 102 LiamKeniry 3 56
(Mark Usher) *led tl hdd and rdn over 2f out: sn btn and dropped out: wl bhd and eased wl ins fnl f* **7/2**[2]
1m 21.44s (-1.86) **Going Correction** -0.025s/f (Good)
**WFA** 3 from 4yo+ 4lb **5** Ran SP% **108.5**
Speed ratings (Par 107): **109,103,100,97,84**
CSF £17.29 TOTE £4.40: £2.50, £1.60; EX 18.10 Trifecta £39.40.
**Owner** Saleh Al Homaizi & Imad Al Sagar **Bred** Peter Dane Player **Trained** Newmarket, Suffolk
**FOCUS**
An interesting conditions event in which the winning time was 1.47sec quicker than the preceding handicap. The winner was impressive and the form is rated slightly positively.

## 6336 LAURIE GREEN MEMORIAL FILLIES' H'CAP 6f
**3:40** (3:42) (Class 4) (0-85,84) 3-Y-O+ **£5,175** (£1,540; £769; £384) **Stalls Centre**

Form RPR
5324 **1** **Interception (IRE)**[17] 5826 4-9-7 84 ShaneKelly 2 95+
(David Lanigan) *hld up in rr: smooth hdwy on outer over 2f out: led and drifted rt over 1f out: pushed along and a doing enough ins fnl f* **2/1**[1]
520 **2** *¾* **Diamond Lady**[21] 5675 3-8-12 80 RobertTart(3) 4 87
(William Stone) *hld up in tch: swtchd lft and effrt u.p 2f out: chsd wnr over 1f out: kpt on but a hld by wnr* **6/1**
0234 **3** *½* **Marjong**[17] 5834 4-8-12 75 HarryBentley 3 80
(Simon Dow) *stdd and dropped in bhd after s: t.k.h: hld up in tch: rdn and hdwy over 1f out: 3rd and one pce fnl f* **5/1**[3]
4606 **4** *6* **Miss Lillie**[17] 5826 3-8-9 74 (p) LiamKeniry 6 60
(Roger Teal) *taken down early: led: rdn 2f out: hdd over 1f out: 4th and btn 1f out: wknd fnl f* **10/1**
3353 **5** *1 ¼* **Lady Horatia**[8] 6112 3-9-5 84 DougieCostello 5 66
(William Muir) *t.k.h: w ldr: rdn and ev ch 2f out: btn ent fnl f: wknd* **9/4**[2]
223 **6** *4 ½* **Childesplay**[15] 5883 3-8-10 75 LukeMorris 1 43
(Heather Main) *chsd ldrs: rdn and pressing ldrs 2f out: no ex and btn over 1f out: wknd fnl f* **14/1**
1m 10.12s (-1.08) **Going Correction** -0.025s/f (Good)
**WFA** 3 from 4yo 2lb **6** Ran SP% **110.8**
Speed ratings (Par 102): **106,105,104,96,94 88**
CSF £13.91 TOTE £2.70: £1.40, £4.20; EX 12.60 Trifecta £41.30.
**Owner** B E Nielsen **Bred** Corduff Bloodstock Ltd & David Egan **Trained** Upper Lambourn, Berks
**FOCUS**
A fair fillies' handicap. Sound form.

## 6337 DR PETER MAGAURAN MEMORIAL H'CAP 1m 1y(P)
**4:15** (4:18) (Class 5) (0-70,70) 3-Y-O+ **£3,234** (£692; £481; £240) **Stalls High**

Form RPR
3140 **1** **Fruit Pastille**[10] 6034 3-8-10 68 (b[1]) CharlieBennett(7) 2 84
(Hughie Morrison) *chsd ldr: rdn to chal and clr 2f out: led wl over 1f out: clr ins fnl f: kpt on* **8/1**
2333 **2** *1 ½* **Faure Island**[14] 5903 3-9-4 69 JohnFahy 11 82+
(Henry Candy) *t.k.h: hld up towards rr: nt clr run 2f out: gd hdwy and swtchd lft ent fnl f: wnt 2nd fnl 100yds: r.o wl: no threat to wnr* **7/1**[3]
0521 **3** *2* **Plough Boy (IRE)**[40] 4970 3-9-0 65 SebSanders 9 73
(Willie Musson) *t.k.h: in tch in midfield but stuck wd: effrt and wdst bnd 2f out: hdwy 1f out: wnt 3rd fnl 100yds: no imp after* **5/2**[1]
0451 **4** *3* **Fiducia**[17] 5832 4-9-4 64 HarryBentley 8 66
(Simon Dow) *in tch in midfield: hdwy to chse clr ldng pair 2f out: drvn to chse wnr over 1f out: no imp: lost 2nd and wknd fnl 100yds* **10/1**
212 **5** *1* **Sonnetation (IRE)**[43] 4842 4-9-9 69 (p) LukeMorris 12 69
(Jim Boyle) *chsd ldrs: drvn and unable qck ent fnl 2f: wl hld and plugged on same pce after* **6/1**[2]
5265 **6** *nk* **Cape Mystery**[41] 4947 3-9-0 65 (b[1]) ShaneKelly 4 63
(Peter Chapple-Hyam) *led: rdn and clr w wnr 2f out: sn hdd: 3rd and btn over 1f out: wknd fnl f* **25/1**
0600 **7** *¾* **Dana's Present**[10] 6035 5-9-6 66 LiamKeniry 5 63
(George Baker) *taken down early: in tch in midfield: rdn and effrt 2f out: sme hdwy over 1f out: keeping on but no threat to wnr whn hmpd ins fnl f* **8/1**
3505 **8** *1 ¾* **The Happy Hammer (IRE)**[56] 4428 8-9-1 64 RobertTart(3) 10 57
(Eugene Stanford) *hld up in last pair: sme hdwy on outer over 2f out: no imp and btn 2f out: wknd over 1f out* **16/1**
3563 **9** *2* **Turnbury**[11] 6002 3-9-1 66 (t) WilliamTwiston-Davies 6 54
(Robert Mills) *s.i.s: hld up in rr: rdn over 2f out: no prog: n.d* **33/1**
6165 **10** *1* **Tyrsal (IRE)**[46] 4766 3-9-5 70 JimmyQuinn 7 55
(Robert Eddery) *chsd ldrs: rdn and struggling over 2f out: wknd over 1f out* **33/1**
0300 **11** *2 ¼* **Tiptree Lace**[32] 5284 3-8-8 66 (v[1]) CallumShepherd(7) 3 46
(William Knight) *s.i.s: sn pushed along and rcvrd: hdwy into midfield 5f out: rdn and lost pl over 2f out: bhd over 1f out* **8/1**
1m 35.99s (-2.21) **Going Correction** -0.05s/f (Stan)
**WFA** 3 from 4yo+ 5lb **11** Ran SP% **113.4**
Speed ratings (Par 103): **109,107,105,102,101 101,100,98,96,95 93**
CSF £59.42 CT £181.61 TOTE £9.50: £3.10, £2.50, £1.10; EX 78.20 Trifecta £222.90.
**Owner** The Caledonian Racing Society **Bred** M E Broughton **Trained** East Ilsley, Berks
**FOCUS**
Quite a competitive, if modest Polytrack handicap. A personal best from the winner.

## 6338 PATRICK AND ANNE TIERNAN GOLDEN ANNIVERSARY FILLIES' H'CAP 1m 4f (P)
**4:50** (4:53) (Class 5) (0-70,69) 3-Y-O+ **£3,234** (£962; £481; £240) **Stalls Low**

Form RPR
1443 **1** **Atalanta Bay (IRE)**[24] 5551 4-9-8 65 ShaneKelly 1 73
(Marcus Tregoning) *led tl 7f out: chsd ldrs after: 3rd and rdn 2f out: styd on u.p fnl 100yds: led last strides* **7/1**
5646 **2** *nk* **Tilstarr (IRE)**[11] 6007 4-9-5 67 (p) MarcMonaghan(5) 4 74
(Roger Teal) *t.k.h: hld up wl in tch in midfield: hdwy to join ldr 3f out: rdn and ld 2f out: forged in front 1f out: drvn ins fnl f: hdd last strides* **14/1**
360 **3** *1 ¼* **Lady Bingo (IRE)**[23] 5606 3-8-13 65 HarryBentley 6 70
(Sir Mark Prescott Bt) *t.k.h: chsd ldr tl led 3f out: rdn and hdd 2f out: styd on same pce after: lost 2nd ins fnl f* **4/1**[2]
416 **4** *1 ½* **Bella Varenna (IRE)**[38] 5036 3-9-3 69 LukeMorris 9 71
(Marco Botti) *hld up in tch in midfield: shuffled bk to rr 5f out: rdn and wnt between rivals 2f out: styd on same pce fnl f* **6/1**[3]
443 **5** *nk* **Social Riser (IRE)**[26] 5490 3-9-2 68 (b[1]) JimmyQuinn 7 70
(Charles Hills) *s.i.s and reminders sn after s: in rr tl swtchd to outer and hdwy to ld 7f out: rdn and hdd 3f out: kpt on same pce u.p fnl 2f* **12/1**
0052 **6** *3 ¾* **Saturation Point**[16] 5865 3-8-8 60 LiamKeniry 5 56
(James Toller) *t.k.h: hld up in tch towards rr: effrt and hung lft over 1f out: no imp and wl hld fnl f* **9/2**[2]


The Form Book, Raceform Ltd, Newbury, RG14 5SJ

542 **7** *1* **Happy Families**[23] 5597 4-9-9 66 WilliamTwiston-Davies 2 60
(Heather Main) *chsd ldrs: shuffled bach towards rr over 3f out: rdn and no hdwy over 2f out* **14/1**

1142 **8** *9* **Elegant Ophelia**[24] 5551 5-9-10 67 (t) SebSanders 3 47
(Dean Ivory) *t.k.h: hld up towards rr: effrt and rdn jst over 2f out: sn btn: wknd over 1f out* **10/1**

2m 31.42s (-1.58) **Going Correction** -0.05s/f (Stan)
**WFA** 3 from 4yo+ 9lb **8** Ran SP% **95.1**
Speed ratings (Par 100): **103,102,101,100,100 98,97,91**
CSF £65.20 CT £233.73 TOTE £7.30: £1.60, £5.40, £1.10; EX 71.90 Trifecta £586.80.
**Owner** Miss S Sharp **Bred** Manister House Stud **Trained** Whitsbury, Hants
■ Elpida was withdrawn. Price at time of withdrawal 4-1. Rule 4 applies to all bets - deduction 20p in the pound.

**FOCUS**
An ordinary fillies' handicap weakened by the withdrawal of the fancied Elpida, who refused to enter the stalls. The remaining eight fillies took part in a rather messy affair. A small step up from the winner.

## 6339 PAYNE & COMPANY H'CAP 1m 5f (P)
**5:25** (5:25) (Class 6) (0-60,60) 3-Y-O+ **£2,587** (£770; £384; £192) **Stalls** Low

Form RPR

0305 **1** **Alba Verde**[16] 5864 3-8-4 46 oh1 LukeMorris 6 62
(Sir Mark Prescott Bt) *chsd ldr tl 10f out: chsd ldrs after: rdn and effrt to ld on inner 2f out: flashed tail u.p: styd on under hands and heels fnl f: gng away at fin* **5/2[1]**

5311 **2** *2 1/4* **Zinnobar**[16] 5864 4-9-5 56 (p) NedCurtis(5) 9 69
(Jonathan Portman) *chsd ldrs: wnt 2nd 10f out tl led 3f out: rdn and hdd 2f out: hld and kpt on same pce fnl f* **3/1[2]**

0412 **3** *7* **Giant Sequoia (USA)**[16] 5864 10-9-13 59 (t) ShaneKelly 1 61
(Des Donovan) *hld up in last trio: effrt but stl plenty to do jst over 2f out: no ch w ldng pair: plugged on to go 3rd wl ins fnl f* **5/1[3]**

0050 **4** *1* **Rollin 'n Tumblin**[50] 4615 10-9-0 46 oh1 JimmyQuinn 7 47
(Michael Attwater) *t.k.h: hld up in tch in midfield: hdwy on outer to join ldrs 3f out: 3rd and outpcd 2f out: wl btn 1f out: lost 3rd wl ins fnl f* **33/1**

/023 **5** *1 1/2* **Black Iceman**[24] 5558 6-9-3 52 SimonPearce(3) 2 50
(Lydia Pearce) *stdd s: hld up in rr: plenty to do and effrt wl over 1f out: sme hdwy fnl f: n.d* **12/1**

0130 **6** *1 1/4* **Poste Restante**[39] 5001 4-9-6 52 MartinLane 3 48
(David Simcock) *s.i.s: hld up in last trio: effrt on outer over 3f out: outpcd and btn over 2f out: wknd 2f out* **12/1**

4005 **7** *hd* **Olymnia**[8] 6110 3-8-13 55 (p) NickyMackay 8 51
(Robert Eddery) *led tl rdn and hdd 3f out: outpcd and btn 2f out: wknd over 1f out* **10/1**

0550 **8** *1/2* **In Seine**[21] 5689 3-9-4 60 HarryBentley 10 55
(John Best) *chsd ldrs: rdn and struggling over 2f out: wknd 2f out* **33/1**

4040 **9** *shd* **Lingfield Lupus (IRE)**[16] 5864 3-8-1 46 oh1 (v) RyanPowell(3) 4 41
(John Best) *t.k.h: chsd ldrs: rdn and lost pl over 2f out: wknd 2f out* **25/1**

361 **10** *3/4* **Magicalmysterytour (IRE)**[104] 2801 11-9-11 57 SebSanders 5 51
(Willie Musson) *hld up in midfield: lost pl and bhd whn nt clr run 2f out: no ch after* **8/1**

2m 47.46s (1.46) **Going Correction** -0.05s/f (Stan)
**WFA** 3 from 4yo+ 10lb **10** Ran SP% **115.6**
Speed ratings (Par 101): **93,91,87,86,85 85,84,84,84,84**
CSF £9.64 CT £32.86 TOTE £2.50: £1.10, £1.30, £2.90; EX 12.80 Trifecta £27.20.
**Owner** Miss K Rausing **Bred** Miss K Rausing **Trained** Newmarket, Suffolk

**FOCUS**
A moderate staying handicap in which two grey fillies finished well clear of the others. Rather muddling form.
T/Plt: £17.60 to a £1 stake. Pool: £55,493.41 - 2291.89 winning units. T/Qpdt: £12.40 to a £1 stake. Pool: £2813.68 - 167.42 winning units. SP

# 6267 WOLVERHAMPTON (A.W) (L-H)
### Saturday, September 13

**OFFICIAL GOING: Tapeta: standard**
Wind: Light half-against Weather: Overcast

## 6340 FOLLOW US ON TWITTER @WOLVESRACES H'CAP (TAPETA) 5f 20y
**6:10** (6:11) (Class 6) (0-65,65) 3-Y-O **£2,264** (£673; £336; £168) **Stalls** Low

Form RPR

2545 **1** **Traditionelle**[22] 5641 3-9-0 58 DavidAllan 7 73
(Tim Easterby) *chsd ldrs: shkn up to ld over 1f out: hung lft ins fnl f: r.o wl* **11/4[1]**

-001 **2** *4 1/2* **Simply Black (IRE)**[8] 6116 3-9-2 63 (p) SamJames(3) 8 62
(David O'Meara) *hld up: hdwy over 1f out: r.o to go 2nd towards fin: no ch w wnr* **9/1[3]**

2033 **3** *3/4* **Dream Sika (IRE)**[8] 6114 3-8-7 51 oh1 JamesSullivan 3 47
(Ruth Carr) *led: rdn and hdd over 1f out: no ex ins fnl f* **9/2[2]**

2201 **4** *3/4* **Meebo (IRE)**[24] 5568 3-9-2 65 (vt) ShelleyBirkett(5) 4 58
(J R Jenkins) *prom: rdn over 1f out: styd on same pce fnl f* **9/2[2]**

0032 **5** *nk* **Madagascar Moll (IRE)**[11] 5994 3-8-10 61 (v) JoshDoyle(7) 6 53
(David O'Meara) *s.i.s: sn pushed along in rr: rdn over 1f out: hung lft ins fnl f: n.d* **11/4[1]**

3066 **6** *2 3/4* **Aussie Sky (IRE)**[18] 5801 3-8-7 51 oh5 FrankieMcDonald 1 33
(Daniel Mark Loughnane) *sn pushed along and prom: rdn over 1f out: wknd fnl f* **20/1**

4600 **7** *2* **Anfield**[78] 3679 3-8-7 51 oh4 (t) PaoloSirigu 5 26
(Mick Quinn) *chsd ldrs: rdn 1/2-way: wknd fnl f* **28/1**

1m 2.25s (0.35) **Going Correction** +0.10s/f (Slow) **7** Ran SP% **107.9**
Speed ratings (Par 99): **101,93,92,91,90 86,83**
CSF £25.06 CT £91.66 TOTE £3.90: £2.70, £5.10; EX 23.00 Trifecta £175.80.
**Owner** Lovely Bubbly Racing **Bred** Mrs D O'Brien **Trained** Great Habton, N Yorks

**FOCUS**
The opener was a modest 3yo sprint handicap in which they went a proper gallop. The winner is rated up a length on her turf form.

## 6341 BOOK HOSPITALITY AT WOLVERHAMPTON RACECOURSE H'CAP (TAPETA) 1m 1f 103y
**6:40** (6:40) (Class 5) (0-70,70) 3-Y-O+ **£2,911** (£866; £432; £216) **Stalls** Low

Form RPR

420 **1** **Polar Forest**[15] 5899 4-9-5 64 (e) JasonHart 4 71
(Richard Guest) *a.p: rdn over 1f out: r.o u.p to ld wl ins fnl f* **50/1**

4441 **2** *hd* **Sequester**[32] 5284 3-9-2 67 (p) DavidAllan 2 74
(David Lanigan) *chsd ldrs: pushed along over 3f out: rdn over 1f out: r.o* **11/2**

6236 **3** *3/4* **Cincinnati Girl (IRE)**[41] 4947 3-8-8 66 KieranShoemark(7) 13 71
(Denis Coakley) *led after 1f: rdn over 1f out: hdd and unable qck wl ins fnl f* **12/1**

3264 **4** *1/2* **The Firm (IRE)**[15] 5898 5-9-7 66 FrankieMcDonald 5 70
(Daniel Mark Loughnane) *prom: plld hrd: nt clr run and lost pl over 7f out: hdwy over 2f out: rdn over 1f out: r.o* **5/1[3]**

2461 **5** *1/2* **Glennten**[7] 6161 5-9-10 69 IrineuGoncalves 9 72
(Jose Santos) *chsd ldrs: wnt 2nd over 3f out: rdn and ev ch fr over 1f out tl no ex wl ins fnl f* **9/1**

4030 **6** *1 1/4* **Sofias Number One (USA)**[25] 5529 6-9-8 70 (b) BillyCray(3) 10 70
(Roy Bowring) *prom: rdn over 2f out: edgd rt wl over 1f out: styd on* **14/1**

-535 **7** *nse* **Super Moment (IRE)**[32] 5284 3-9-4 69 FrederikTylicki 1 69
(Saeed bin Suroor) *led 1f: chsd ldr tl over 3f out: remained handy: rdn over 1f out: no ex fnl f* **7/2[1]**

0006 **8** *3/4* **Apache Glory (USA)**[32] 5284 6-9-5 69 (p) EoinWalsh(5) 12 68
(John Stimpson) *s.i.s: hld up: rdn over 2f out: styd on ins fnl f: nt trble ldrs* **33/1**

0000 **9** *1/2* **Enzaal (USA)**[15] 5899 4-9-2 61 TomEaves 6 59
(Philip Kirby) *hld up: rdn over 2f out: styd on ins fnl f: nvr nrr* **33/1**

4123 **10** *1 1/2* **Rouge Nuage (IRE)**[13] 5950 4-9-4 68 (b) JordanNason(5) 8 62
(Conrad Allen) *hld up: plld hrd: hdwy over 3f out: rdn whn carried rt wl over 1f out: sn edgd lft and styd on same pce* **9/2[2]**

4430 **11** *1 1/4* **Al Muheer (IRE)**[18] 5793 9-9-11 70 (e) JamesSullivan 3 62
(Ruth Carr) *hld up: plld hrd: shkn up over 2f out: n.d* **25/1**

0-03 **12** *6* **Mountain Range (IRE)**[222] 458 6-9-6 65 StevieDonohoe 7 44
(Willie Musson) *s.i.s: hld up: rdn over 2f out: sn wknd* **14/1**

2m 2.32s (1.52) **Going Correction** +0.10s/f (Slow)
**WFA** 3 from 4yo+ 6lb **12** Ran SP% **115.2**
Speed ratings: **97,96,96,95,95 94,94,93,93,91 90,85**
CSF £294.50 CT £3540.73 TOTE £32.30: £7.00, £4.00, £5.30; EX 211.00 Trifecta £1545.70 Part won. Pool of £2061.04 - 0.07 winning units..
**Owner** Maze Rattan Limited **Bred** Worksop Manor Stud **Trained** Ingmanthorpe, W Yorks

**FOCUS**
An ordinary handicap in which they went an even gallop. A bunch finish with the surprise winner back to his best.

## 6342 BOOK HORIZONS RESTAURANT AT WOLVERHAMPTON RACECOURSE H'CAP (TAPETA) 1m 141y
**7:10** (7:13) (Class 6) (0-65,67) 3-Y-O+ **£2,264** (£673; £336; £168) **Stalls** Low

Form RPR

4413 **1** **Jumbo Prado (USA)**[7] 6161 5-9-0 60 (p) EoinWalsh(5) 4 69
(John Stimpson) *led 1f: chsd ldr: rdn over 2f out: led over 1f out: edgd lft ins fnl f: styd on gamely* **7/1**

0003 **2** *hd* **Spirit Of Gondree (IRE)**[7] 6160 6-9-5 60 (b) BenCurtis 5 68
(Milton Bradley) *hld up: hdwy over 2f out: rdn to chse wnr over 1f out: sn ev ch: styd on* **16/1**

000 **3** *1 3/4* **Dimitar (USA)**[8] 6088 5-8-12 60 (p) ChrisMeehan(7) 13 64
(Johnny Farrelly) *s.i.s: hld up: hdwy over 2f out: rdn over 1f out: edgd lft ins fnl f: styd on* **7/1**

0364 **4** *hd* **Choice Of Destiny**[25] 5522 3-9-2 63 MartinHarley 12 67
(Philip McBride) *hld up: rdn and hdwy over 1f out: styd on* **6/1[3]**

442 **5** *2 3/4* **Eddiemaurice (IRE)**[7] 6161 3-9-6 67 (v) JasonHart 6 64
(Richard Guest) *prom: nt clr run and lost pl over 2f out: swtchd rt and hdwy over 1f out: sn rdn: no imp ins fnl f* **3/1[1]**

2250 **6** *2 1/4* **Yourinthewill (USA)**[139] 1761 6-9-0 62 LouiseDay(7) 2 54
(Daniel Mark Loughnane) *hld up: r.o ins fnl f: nvr nrr* **25/1**

0000 **7** *1 1/4* **Berrahri (IRE)**[11] 6022 3-8-13 60 RobertHavlin 8 49
(John Best) *hld up: rdn over 1f out: nvr trbld ldrs* **18/1**

2-00 **8** *9* **Tarquin (IRE)**[37] 5105 5-9-6 61 JamesSullivan 1 29
(Kristin Stubbs) *led over 7f out: clr over 5f out tl rdn and hdd over 1f out: sn wknd* **28/1**

-652 **9** *3 1/2* **Hope For Glory**[32] 5267 5-9-10 65 TonyHamilton 7 25
(Jason Ward) *hld up: rdn over 2f out: sn wknd* **16/1**

030/ **10** *nk* **Mr Hichens**[1132] 4860 9-9-3 65 KieranShoemark(7) 10 25
(Karen George) *prom: rdn over 2f out: wknd over 1f out* **16/1**

000- **11** *9* **Vaguely Spanish**[323] 7502 3-8-8 55 StevieDonohoe 3
(Tony Carroll) *s.i.s: sn chsng ldrs: rdn over 2f out: wknd over 1f out* **16/1**

2325 **12** *3* **Schottische**[9] 6074 4-8-13 59 (v) TimClark(5) 11
(Derek Haydn Jones) *broke wl enough but sn pushed along and unruly: lost pl qckly and sn wl bhd* **9/2[2]**

1m 51.29s (1.19) **Going Correction** +0.10s/f (Slow)
**WFA** 3 from 4yo+ 6lb **12** Ran SP% **118.6**
Speed ratings (Par 101): **98,97,96,96,93 91,90,82,79,79 71,68**
CSF £113.55 CT £830.90 TOTE £7.30: £2.30, £3.90, £2.70; EX 64.90 Trifecta £530.20.
**Owner** J T Stimpson **Bred** Mr & Mrs Foreman Hardy **Trained** Butterton, Staffs

**FOCUS**
A modest handicap in which they went a respectable gallop. The winner is rated to last year's best.

## 6343 JULIA GAUTIER MEMORIAL H'CAP (TAPETA) 2m 119y
**7:40** (7:44) (Class 6) (0-65,65) 3-Y-O+ **£2,264** (£673; £336; £168) **Stalls** Low

Form RPR

6401 **1** **Uncle Bernie (IRE)**[26] 5508 4-9-3 57 (p) RobertTart(3) 2 70+
(Andrew Hollinshead) *hld up: plld hrd: hdwy over 4f out: led over 2f out: clr and hung rt fr over 1f out: comf* **7/2[2]**

0550 **2** *7* **Mr Wickfield**[22] 5628 3-8-12 62 RobertHavlin 8 64
(John Best) *a.p: chsd ldr 1/2-way tl led over 3f out: rdn and hdd over 2f out: styd on same pce fr over 1f out* **11/1**

-222 **3** *hd* **Wintour Leap**[24] 5556 3-8-9 64 DanielMuscutt(5) 11 66
(Robert Stephens) *chsd ldr to 1/2-way: remained handy: rdn over 2f out: styd on same pce fr over 1f out* **5/1[3]**

4025 **4** *4* **Nolecce**[7] 6157 7-9-2 60 AdamMcLean(7) 1 57
(Tony Forbes) *mid-div: hdwy over 2f out: sn rdn: wknd ins fnl f* **20/1**

5050 **5** *8* **Azrag (USA)**[16] 5863 6-9-13 64 (vt) FrederikTylicki 7 52
(Michael Attwater) *chsd ldrs: drvn along and lost pl 7f out: sn bhd: styd on ins fnl f* **11/4[1]**

0042 **6** *3/4* **Stormy Morning**[26] 5508 8-8-13 53 (p) JoeyHaynes(3) 4 40
(Philip Kirby) *hld up: hdwy 2f out: sn rdn: wknd fnl f* **6/1**

65-R **7** *3 1/4* **Red Current**[14] 5904 10-8-9 51 oh6 NoelGarbutt(5) 3 34
(Michael Scudamore) *s.i.s: hld up: effrt on outer over 2f out: wknd over 1f out* **33/1**

2364 **8** *1/2* **Jezza**[24] 5547 8-10-0 65 (bt) StevieDonohoe 10 47
(Karen George) *s.i.s: hld up: rdn over 2f out: sn wknd* **8/1**

0004 **9** *3 1/2* **Passion Play**[31] 5317 6-9-4 60 RyanWhile(5) 5 38
(Bill Turner) *led tl hdd over 3f out: wknd over 2f out* **33/1**

0 **10** *3 ¼* **Sakhra**[15] 5898 3-9-1 65 .......... PaulMulrennan 6 39
(Mark Brisbourne) *hld up: hdwy 10f out: rdn and wknd over 2f out* **28/1**

3m 44.18s (0.48) **Going Correction** +0.10s/f (Slow)
**WFA** 3 from 4yo+ 13lb 10 Ran SP% **113.4**
Speed ratings (Par 101): **102,98,98,96,92 92,91,90,89,87**
CSF £37.79 CT £188.74 TOTE £4.10: £2.10, £3.30, £2.00; EX 42.70 Trifecta £220.00.
**Owner** Graham Brothers Racing Partnership **Bred** Roundhill Stud & Gleadhill House Stud Ltd **Trained** Upper Longdon, Staffs

**FOCUS**
A modest staying handicap in which they went a steady gallop. A clear personal best from the winner.

## 6344 STAY AT THE HOLIDAY INN WOLVERHAMPTON MAIDEN STKS (TAPETA) 1m 4f 50y

**8:10** (8:13) (Class 5) 3-Y-O+ **£2,911** (£866; £432; £216) **Stalls** Low

Form RPR

62- **1** **Flag War (GER)**[360] 6528 3-9-5 0 .......... FrederikTylicki 10 94+
(Saeed bin Suroor) *chsd ldr tl shkn up to ld 2f out: pushed out* **13/8**[2]

0222 **2** *2* **Altaayil (IRE)**[72] 3884 3-9-5 89 .......... DaneO'Neill 3 91+
(Sir Michael Stoute) *sn pushed along to chse ldrs: rdn to chse wnr over 1f out: eased whn hld nr fin* **11/10**[1]

46 **3** *8* **Two Jabs**[8] 6092 4-10-0 0 .......... PatCosgrave 4 78
(Mark Brisbourne) *hld up: hdwy over 2f out: styd on same pce fr over 1f out: wnt 3rd post* **25/1**

2225 **4** *nse* **Button Down**[30] 5356 3-9-0 83 .......... (p) MartinHarley 1 73
(Lady Cecil) *led: rdn and hdd 2f out: wknd ins fnl f* **7/2**[3]

**5** *hd* **Everlasting Spring (IRE)**[10] 6052 6-9-11 0 .......... (t) MarkEnright(3) 8 78
(David Peter Nagle, Ire) *hld up: hmpd over 3f out: sn rdn: nt trble ldrs* **22/1**

33 **6** *3 ¼* **Graffiti Art**[17] 5822 5-9-9 0 .......... DougieCostello 7 67
(Brendan Powell) *hld up in tch: plld hrd: lost pl 3f out: wknd over 1f out* **25/1**

**7** *9* **Blue Valentino** 5-9-9 0 .......... JackDuern(5) 6 58
(Andrew Hollinshead) *s.i.s: hld up: hdwy on outer over 2f out: sn wknd* **66/1**

0 **8** *9* **Bahama Dancer**[39] 5018 3-8-11 0 .......... JoeyHaynes(3) 5 39
(Jason Ward) *prom: rdn over 3f out: wknd over 2f out* **100/1**

2m 42.89s (2.09) **Going Correction** +0.10s/f (Slow)
**WFA** 3 from 4yo+ 9lb 8 Ran SP% **122.5**
Speed ratings (Par 103): **97,95,90,90,90 88,82,76**
CSF £3.97 TOTE £2.60: £1.30, £1.10, £3.90; EX 4.40 Trifecta £37.80.
**Owner** Godolphin **Bred** Graf U Grafin V Stauffenberg **Trained** Newmarket, Suffolk

**FOCUS**
A fairly decent middle-distance maiden in which they went an ordinary gallop. The first two finished clear and are probably a bit better than the bare form.

## 6345 WOLVERHAMPTON-RACECOURSE.CO.UK H'CAP (TAPETA) (BOBIS RACE) 7f 32y

**8:40** (8:40) (Class 4) (0-85,82) 3-Y-O **£4,851** (£1,443; £721; £360) **Stalls** High

Form RPR

6033 **1** **Instant Attraction (IRE)**[26] 5496 3-9-0 **80** .......... JackGarritty(5) 6 89
(Jedd O'Keeffe) *chsd ldr: shkn up to ld over 1f out: r.o: comf* **13/2**

241- **2** *2* **Art Obsession (IRE)**[319] 7602 3-9-2 **77** .......... AndrewMullen 3 81
(David Barron) *hld up: rdn over 2f out: hdwy over 1f out: chsd wnr fnl f: r.o u.p* **9/2**[3]

2100 **3** *nk* **Jacquotte Delahaye**[22] 5649 3-9-7 **82** .......... MartinHarley 2 85
(David Brown) *hld up: rdn over 2f out: r.o ins fnl f* **22/1**

1161 **4** *6* **In Focus (IRE)**[24] 5566 3-9-0 **75** .......... DavidAllan 1 62
(Alan Swinbank) *chsd ldrs: rdn over 2f out: wknd ins fnl f* **7/2**[2]

6214 **5** *2 ¼* **Doctor Sardonicus**[49] 4671 3-9-4 **82** .......... JoeyHaynes(3) 5 64
(David Simcock) *hld up: rdn over 2f out: wknd over 1f out* **7/2**[2]

2321 **6** *½* **Conquerant**[17] 5814 3-9-0 **82** .......... (p) AhmadAlSubousi(7) 4 62
(Charlie Appleby) *sn led: clr over 4f out: rdn and hdd over 1f out: wknd fnl f* **15/8**[1]

1m 28.47s (-0.33) **Going Correction** +0.10s/f (Slow) 6 Ran SP% **115.1**
Speed ratings (Par 103): **105,102,102,95,92 92**
CSF £36.04 TOTE £7.50: £4.70, £4.70; EX 23.50 Trifecta £268.40.
**Owner** United We Stand **Bred** Mrs Julia Hayes **Trained** Middleham Moor, N Yorks

**FOCUS**
A fair 3yo handicap in which the pace was unsustainable. The winner had been consistent without looking an obvious improver.

## 6346 DINE IN HORIZONS H'CAP (TAPETA) 5f 216y

**9:10** (9:10) (Class 5) (0-75,75) 3-Y-O+ **£2,911** (£866; £432; £216) **Stalls** Low

Form RPR

5222 **1** **Dominium (USA)**[28] 5422 7-9-2 70 .......... (b) DaneO'Neill 4 79
(Jeremy Gask) *hld up: rdn over 1f out: str run and edgd lft ins fnl f: led post* **11/4**[1]

6022 **2** *shd* **Smokethatthunders (IRE)**[12] 5987 4-8-13 72 .......... DanielMuscutt(5) 8 80
(James Unett) *chsd ldrs: rdn to ld wl ins fnl f: hdd post* **15/2**

5213 **3** *shd* **Clubland (IRE)**[19] 5766 5-9-2 75 .......... AlistairRawlinson(5) 10 83
(Roy Bowring) *a.p: chsd ldr over 3f out: led 2f out: rdn and hdd wl ins fnl f: r.o* **7/2**[2]

5014 **4** *2 ½* **Native Falls (IRE)**[4] 6213 3-8-13 69 .......... DavidAllan 6 69
(Alan Swinbank) *chsd ldr tl led over 4f out: rdn and hdd 2f out: no ex ins fnl f* **9/1**

0-10 **5** *hd* **Seal Rock**[8] 6089 6-9-4 72 .......... (b) TomEaves 11 71
(John Quinn) *hld up in tch: rdn over 1f out: styd on same pce ins fnl f* **10/1**

66-0 **6** *½* **An Cat Dubh (IRE)**[15] 5895 5-9-5 73 .......... (p) StevieDonohoe 7 70
(Tim Pitt) *mid-div: rdn over 1f out: styd on same pce ins fnl f* **33/1**

4406 **7** *1 ½* **Colourbearer (IRE)**[23] 5601 7-9-0 68 .......... (t) KierenFallon 3 61
(Milton Bradley) *mid-div: rdn over 2f out: hdwy over 1f out: edgd lft and no ex ins fnl f* **6/1**[3]

3456 **8** *shd* **Thataboy (IRE)**[24] 5553 3-9-2 72 .......... RichardKingscote 12 64
(Tom Dascombe) *swtchd lft sn after s: hld up and bhd: r.o ins fnl f: nvr nrr* **14/1**

2423 **9** *½* **Whipphound**[71] 3939 6-9-2 70 .......... PaulMulrennan 9 61
(Mark Brisbourne) *hld up: hdwy on outer over 2f out: rdn over 1f out: wknd ins fnl f* **20/1**

4026 **10** *shd* **Borough Boy (IRE)**[12] 5987 4-8-11 65 .......... DaleSwift 1 55
(Derek Shaw) *hld up: rdn over 1f out: nt trble ldrs* **33/1**

3343 **11** *½* **Red Cape (FR)**[9] 6077 11-8-11 65 .......... (b) JamesSullivan 5 54
(Ruth Carr) *led: hdd over 4f out: rdn over 1f out: wknd ins fnl f* **20/1**

2151 **12** *3* **Mrs Warren**[19] 5777 4-9-6 74 .......... PatCosgrave 2 53
(George Baker) *prom: rdn over 1f out: wknd fnl f* **12/1**

1m 14.36s (-0.14) **Going Correction** +0.10s/f (Slow)
**WFA** 3 from 4yo+ 2lb 12 Ran SP% **123.8**
Speed ratings (Par 103): **104,103,103,100,100 99,97,97,96,96 95,91**
CSF £23.85 CT £77.06 TOTE £5.90: £2.20, £3.00, £2.10; EX 32.90 Trifecta £116.90.
**Owner** Horses First Racing Limited **Bred** Corbett Farm **Trained** Sutton Veny, Wilts

**FOCUS**
The concluding contest was a fair sprint handicap in which they went a decent gallop.
T/Plt: £329.20 to a £1 stake. Pool of £71898.58 - 159.39 winning tickets. T/Qpdt: £32.00 to a £1 stake. Pool of £9027.55 - 208.20 winning tickets. CR

6347 - (Foreign Racing) - See Raceform Interactive

5357

# LEOPARDSTOWN (L-H)

Saturday, September 13

**OFFICIAL GOING: Good to firm (good in places)**

## 6348a JOHN DEERE JUVENILE TURF STKS (GROUP 3) 1m

**4:05** (4:06) 2-Y-O

**£50,000** (£15,833; £7,500; £2,500; £1,666; £833)

RPR

**1** **John F Kennedy (IRE)**[34] 5215 2-9-3 .......... JosephO'Brien 3 113+
(A P O'Brien, Ire) *trckd ldrs: prog to press ldrs in 3rd 2f out: sn led and pushed clr ins fnl f: styd on wl* **4/7**[1]

**2** *3 ¼* **Tombelaine (USA)**[51] 4599 2-9-3 105 .......... PatSmullen 1 105
(D K Weld, Ire) *chsd ldrs: rdn along in 4th under 2f out: styd on wl into 2nd ins fnl f: nt trble wnr* **4/1**[2]

**3** *2 ¼* **Faithful Creek (IRE)**[20] 5740 2-9-3 98 .......... FMBerry 7 100
(Brian Meehan) *trckd ldrs: led briefly under 2f out: sn hdd and no match for wnr: sltly short of room and no imp whn dropped to 3rd ins fnl f* **20/1**

**4** *1 ¼* **Bertie Le Belge (IRE)**[72] 3901 2-9-3 101 .......... GaryCarroll 5 97
(G M Lyons, Ire) *chsd ldrs: rdn along in 4th appr fnl f and no imp: kpt on one pce* **9/1**[3]

**5** *3 ¼* **Vocaliser (IRE)**[12] 5988 2-9-3 85 .......... KevinManning 2 90
(J S Bolger, Ire) *hld up: rdn along over 2f out: sn no imp* **40/1**

**6** *1* **East India**[36] 5156 2-9-3 98 .......... SeamieHeffernan 4 87
(A P O'Brien, Ire) *led tl hdd under 2f out: sn wknd and eased ins fnl f* **11/1**

**7** *5 ½* **Approbare (IRE)**[13] 5954 2-9-3 97 .......... BillyLee 6 75
(T M Walsh, Ire) *a in rr: nvr a factor* **100/1**

1m 38.44s (-2.76) **Going Correction** -0.20s/f (Firm) 7 Ran SP% **110.2**
Speed ratings: **105,101,99,98,95 94,88**
CSF £2.76 TOTE £1.50: £1.30, £1.30; DF 2.10 Trifecta £17.70.
**Owner** Mrs John Magnier & Michael Tabor & Flaxman Stables **Bred** Orpendale And The Niarchos Family **Trained** Cashel, Co Tipperary

**FOCUS**
Australia won this last year. A clear win for a well-regarded colt in John F Kennedy, who was pretty impressive.

## 6349a IRISH STALLION FARMS EUROPEAN BREEDERS FUND "PETINGO" H'CAP (PREMIER HANDICAP) 1m 6f

**4:40** (4:41) 3-Y-O+

**£75,000** (£23,750; £11,250; £3,750; £2,500; £1,250)

RPR

**1** **Toe The Line (IRE)**[23] 5615 5-8-11 **86** .......... FMBerry 14 93
(John E Kiely, Ire) *hld up: prog into 11th 2f out: rapid hdwy to press ldrs 1f out: led fnl 100yds: all out cl home* **7/1**[3]

**2** *nk* **Cassells Rock (IRE)**[16] 5116 4-8-5 **85** .......... (t) SeanCorby(5) 6 92
(A J Martin, Ire) *hld up towards rr: hdwy over 1f out: styd on strly into 3rd ins fnl f: kpt on wl to press wnr in 2nd cl home* **10/1**

**3** *½* **Silwana (IRE)**[42] 4928 3-8-6 **92** .......... LeighRoche 8 98
(D K Weld, Ire) *chsd ldrs: rdn along in 4th 2f out: styd on wl to ld ins fnl f: hdd fnl 100yds: kpt on same pce and dropped to 3rd cl home* **10/1**

**4** *3* **Bayan (IRE)**[44] 4139 5-9-1 **90** .......... (tp) WayneLordan 15 92
(Gordon Elliott, Ire) *hld up: prog in mid-div 3f out: rdn along to chse ldrs in 5th ent fnl f: kpt on same pce into 4th cl home: nvr quite on terms* **8/1**

**5** *nk* **Winter Lion (IRE)**[22] 5660 4-8-6 **81** .......... (p) ChrisHayes 9 82
(Denis Gerard Hogan, Ire) *led after 2f: qckdn to extend advantage 3f out: hdd ent fnl f: sn one pce* **10/1**

**6** *nk* **Spacious Sky (USA)**[24] 5579 5-8-10 **85** .......... (t) ShaneFoley 2 86
(A J Martin, Ire) *hld up towards rr: stl plenty to do 2f out: swtchd rt over 1f out: styd on wl ins fnl f: nvr nrr* **8/1**

**7** *1* **Digeanta (IRE)**[21] 5704 7-8-12 **87** .......... (t) PatSmullen 11 86
(W P Mullins, Ire) *chsd ldrs: rdn along in 3rd over 2f out: sn chsd ldr in 2nd tl no imp ent fnl f and wknd* **6/1**[2]

**8** *1* **Blue Hussar (IRE)**[111] 2579 3-9-0 **100** .......... JosephO'Brien 5 98
(A P O'Brien, Ire) *hld up: rdn along in mid-div under 2f out: prog to chse ldrs ent fnl f: sn no imp and one pce* **11/2**[1]

**9** *2 ¼* **Pivot Bridge**[10] 6050 6-8-1 **79** oh3 .......... ConorHoban(3) 74
(Adrian McGuinness, Ire) *chsd ldrs towards inner tl rdn under 2f out and no imp appr fnl f: sn one pce* **33/1**

**10** *1 ¾* **Chamonix (IRE)**[363] 6441 5-9-2 **101** .......... (p) DonnachaO'Brien(10) 13 93
(A P O'Brien, Ire) *hld up in mid-div on outer: rdn fr 3f out: no imp 2f out* **20/1**

**11** *nse* **Egyptian Warrior (IRE)**[7] 5477 5-8-7 **89** .......... (b) AnaO'Brien(7) 16 81
(A P O'Brien, Ire) *racd in rr thrght tl kpt on at one pce on inner fr under 2f out: nvr on terms* **20/1**

**12** *½* **English Summer**[14] 5924 7-8-7 **82** .......... (t) MichaelHussey 10 74
(Richard Fahey) *chsd ldrs on inner in 4th tl nt qckn 2f out: sn wknd* **20/1**

**13** *nk* **Wexford Town (IRE)**[58] 4380 3-9-7 **107** .......... (t) KevinManning 4 98
(J S Bolger, Ire) *led for 2f: trckd ldr in 2nd tl nt qckn over 1f out: sn no imp and eased* **10/1**

**14** *6* **Erlkonig (GER)**[33] 3286 4-9-1 **90** .......... SeamieHeffernan 7 73
(Anthony Mullins, Ire) *chsd ldrs tl nt qckn 3f out: sn wknd* **33/1**

**15** *5 ½* **Dalasiri (IRE)**[47] 4746 5-8-3 **83** .......... RobbieDowney(5) 12 58
(Sabrina J Harty, Ire) *trckd ldrs in 3rd tl rdn and nt qckn under 3f out: sn no ex* **16/1**

2m 54.87s (-6.13) **Going Correction** -0.20s/f (Firm)
**WFA** 3 from 4yo+ 11lb 15 Ran SP% **126.8**
Speed ratings: **109,108,108,106,106 106,105,105,104,103 103,102,102,99,96**
CSF £73.08 CT £716.21 TOTE £7.80: £2.90, £2.50, £3.50; DF 85.50 Trifecta £1028.20.
**Owner** Exors of the Late A Lillingston **Bred** A Lillingston **Trained** Dungarvan, Co Waterford

**FOCUS**
A staying handicap worth a lot of money. The pace was reasonably generous but the tempo increased leaving the back straight. Both the winner and the second came from a long way back.

## 6350a KPMG ENTERPRISE STKS (GROUP 3) 1m 2f
5:15 (5:15) 3-Y-O+ £54,166 (£15,833; £7,500; £2,500)

RPR

1 **Free Eagle (IRE)**[371] 6223 3-9-0 105 PatSmullen 7 120+
(D K Weld, Ire) *hld up tl travelled wl to take clsr order over 2f out: sn led and qcknd clr appr fnl f: impressive* **9/10**[1]

2 7 **Elleval (IRE)**[21] 5690 4-9-7 106 (b[1]) WayneLordan 2 106
(David Marnane, Ire) *slowly away and racd in rr tl prog on outer 2f out: styd on wl into 2nd ins fnl f: nt trble wnr* **20/1**

3 ½ **Chance To Dance (IRE)**[37] 5115 4-9-7 106 (t) KevinManning 8 105
(J S Bolger, Ire) *chsd ldrs: nt qckn w wnr over 1f out: kpt on same pce into 3rd ins fnl f* **14/1**

4 ½ **Prince Of All**[88] 3320 3-9-0 110 ChrisHayes 6 104
(P D Deegan, Ire) *t.k.h early to trck ldr in 2nd: nt qckn under 2f out: kpt on one pce and dropped to 4th ins fnl f* **13/2**

5 3¾ **Qewy (IRE)**[30] 5361 4-9-7 104 DeclanMcDonogh 5 97
(John M Oxx, Ire) *racd towards rr: prog whn sltly short of room 2f out: kpt on wl into 5th ins fnl f: nvr on terms* **33/1**

6 1¼ **Hall Of Mirrors (IRE)**[20] 5733 4-9-10 113 JosephO'Brien 1 97
(A P O'Brien, Ire) *trckd ldrs in 3rd tl rdn over 2f out: no imp in 4th whn squeezed for room under 2f out: sn one pce* **6/1**[3]

7 3 **Maid Of The Glens (IRE)**[5] 6200 3-8-11 97 RonanWhelan 4 85
(John Patrick Shanahan, Ire) *chsd ldrs tl rdn along over 2f out and sn dropped towards rr: kpt on again at one pce in clsng stages* **50/1**

8 6 **Rock Critic (IRE)**[381] 5907 9-9-7 94 LeighRoche 10 76
(D K Weld, Ire) *led tl hdd under 2f out: sn no ex* **100/1**

9 5½ **Brendan Brackan (IRE)**[30] 5361 5-9-7 111 JamieSpencer 9 65
(G M Lyons, Ire) *chsd ldrs tl rdn under 3f out: wknd qckly over 1f out* **5/1**[2]

10 9 **Indian Maharaja (IRE)**[24] 5577 3-9-0 98 SeamieHeffernan 3 47
(A P O'Brien, Ire) *hld up on inner: nt qckn under 3f out: sn no ex* **25/1**

2m 3.12s (-5.08) **Going Correction** -0.20s/f (Firm)
**WFA** 3 from 4yo+ 7lb **10 Ran SP% 118.1**
Speed ratings: **112,106,106,105,102 101,99,94,90,82**
CSF £27.77 TOTE £1.80: £1.20, £4.50, £1.90; DF 29.80 Trifecta £268.50.
**Owner** Moyglare Stud Farm **Bred** Moyglare Stud Farm Ltd **Trained** Curragh, Co Kildare

**FOCUS**
A really taking performance by a horse returning from a lengthy break. The time was slightly quicker than the Irish Champion Stakes.

## 6351a COOLMORE FASTNET ROCK MATRON STKS (GROUP 1) (F&M) 1m
5:45 (5:47) 3-Y-O+
£150,000 (£47,500; £22,500; £7,500; £3,750; £3,750)

RPR

1 **Fiesolana (IRE)**[34] 5223 5-9-5 112 BillyLee 4 108+
(W McCreery, Ire) *hld up: travelled wl in rr appr fnl f: qcknd wl between horses to ld fnl 50yds* **5/1**[3]

2 ½ **Rizeena (IRE)**[27] 5480 3-9-0 112 RyanMoore 3 106
(Clive Brittain) *chsd ldrs in 4th tl nt qckn in 6th appr fnl f: kpt on wl to dispute ins fnl f: hdd fnl 50yds: kpt on wl* **7/4**[1]

3 ¾ **Tobann (IRE)**[16] 5869 4-9-5 102 (t) KevinManning 1 105
(J S Bolger, Ire) *hld up on inner: travelled wl to trck ldr in 2nd appr fnl f: kpt on same pce tl no ex in 3rd fnl 50yds* **40/1**

4 hd **Kenhope (FR)**[20] 4-9-5 109 Christophe-PatriceLemaire 2 105
(H-A Pantall, France) *trckd ldrs: rdn in 3rd appr fnl f: nt qckn fnl 100yds: kpt on same pce* **7/1**

5 ½ **Wannabe Better (IRE)**[16] 5869 4-9-5 105 WayneLordan 5 104
(T Stack, Ire) *hld up: pushed along towards rr over 2f out: kpt on wl on outer ins fnl f: nvr nrr* **33/1**

5 dht **Wee Jean**[35] 5176 3-9-0 103 JoeFanning 8 103
(Mick Channon) *led and sn jnd: advantage again 2f out tl hdd ins fnl f: kpt on one pce* **50/1**

7 1¼ **Purr Along**[16] 5869 4-9-5 108 JamieSpencer 7 101
(J P Murtagh, Ire) *hld up in rr: travelled wl to chse ldrs on inner appr fnl f: short of room ins fnl f and sn no ex* **16/1**

8 nk **Flying Jib**[39] 5022 3-9-0 105 PatSmullen 6 99
(D K Weld, Ire) *hld up: rdn along over 2f out: chsd ldrs appr fnl f tl no imp fnl 100yds* **25/1**

9 1 **Tapestry (IRE)**[23] 5610 3-9-0 122 JosephO'Brien 9 97
(A P O'Brien, Ire) *chsd ldrs: prog into 3rd 1/2-way: rdn and nt qckn appr fnl f: no ex whn hmpd ins fnl f* **9/4**[2]

10 7 **Palace (IRE)**[13] 5955 3-9-0 102 SeamieHeffernan 10 81
(A P O'Brien, Ire) *sn disp tl wknd over 1f out: eased* **33/1**

1m 38.16s (-3.04) **Going Correction** -0.20s/f (Firm)
**WFA** 3 from 4yo+ 5lb **10 Ran SP% 116.3**
Speed ratings: **107,106,105,105,105 105,103,103,102,95**
CSF £13.56 TOTE £9.10: £2.10, £1.02, £13.00; DF 21.40 Trifecta £643.60.
**Owner** Flaxman Stables Ireland Ltd **Bred** Robert De Vere Hunt **Trained** Rathbride, Co Kildare

**FOCUS**
There was a bunch finish to this Group race. The winner did not need to produce her best.

## 6352a CLIPPER BOOMERANG MILE (GROUP 2) 1m
6:15 (6:16) 3-Y-O+
£100,000 (£31,666; £15,000; £5,000; £3,333; £1,666)

RPR

1 **Bow Creek (IRE)**[21] 5666 3-9-3 111 JoeFanning 1 118
(Mark Johnston) *led for 1f: chsd clr ldr in 2nd tl led again appr fnl f: sn strly pressed: kpt on wl* **7/1**

2 ½ **Mustajeeb**[87] 3352 3-9-3 119 PatSmullen 5 117+
(D K Weld, Ire) *hld up towards rr: tk clsr order over 1f out: styd on wl to press ldr in 2nd ins fnl f: no imp on wnr fnl 50yds* **1/1**[1]

3 1½ **Gordon Lord Byron (IRE)**[7] 6134 6-9-11 116 WayneLordan 2 117+
(T Hogan, Ire) *hld up in 5th: rdn along over 1f out: kpt on same pce into 3rd ins fnl f: nt rch principals* **9/2**[2]

4 hd **Top Notch Tonto (IRE)**[23] 5609 4-9-8 111 ColmO'Donoghue 7 114+
(Brian Ellison) *racd in rr: c wd home turn: styd on wl on outer into 4th ins fnl f: nvr on terms* **10/1**

5 2¼ **Leitir Mor (IRE)**[21] 5699 4-9-8 106 (tp) RonanWhelan 8 109
(J S Bolger, Ire) *led after 1f and sn clr: hdd appr fnl f: sn one pce* **100/1**

6 nk **Parish Hall (IRE)**[20] 5733 5-9-8 112 (t) KevinManning 6 108
(J S Bolger, Ire) *chsd ldrs in 4th tl rdn over 2f out: nt qckn appr fnl f and sn no ex* **16/1**

7 ¾ **Darwin (USA)**[45] 4779 4-9-8 119 (t) JosephO'Brien 3 106
(A P O'Brien, Ire) *chsd ldrs in 3rd tl rdn along under 2f out: wknd fnl 1f out* **11/2**[3]

8 3 **Michaelmas (USA)**[52] 4560 3-9-3 104 RyanMoore 4 98
(A P O'Brien, Ire) *hld up: rdn along under 2f out: no imp over 1f out* **25/1**

1m 37.63s (-3.57) **Going Correction** -0.20s/f (Firm)
**WFA** 3 from 4yo+ 5lb **8 Ran SP% 115.9**
Speed ratings: **109,108,107,106,104 104,103,100**
CSF £14.65 TOTE £7.00: £2.10, £1.10, £1.40; DF 14.50 Trifecta £77.90.
**Owner** Sheikh Hamdan bin Mohammed Al Maktoum **Bred** Roundhill Stud **Trained** Middleham Moor, N Yorks
■ The first running of this.

**FOCUS**
This was probably a Group 1 in all but name with the winner heading in that direction and the runner-up not far off that level either. The fifth sets the standard.

## 6353a QIPCO IRISH CHAMPION STKS (GROUP 1) 1m 2f
6:50 (6:52) 3-Y-O+
£483,333 (£158,333; £75,000; £25,000; £16,666; £8,333)

RPR

1 **The Grey Gatsby (IRE)**[24] 5578 3-9-0 122 RyanMoore 2 126
(Kevin Ryan) *hld up in rr: pushed along in 6th 2f out: styd on wl to chse ldr in 2nd 1f out: kpt on strly to ld in clsng strides* **7/1**[2]

2 nk **Australia**[24] 5578 3-9-1 127 ow1 JosephO'Brien 5 125+
(A P O'Brien, Ire) *hld up in 6th tl gd hdwy on outer off home turn: led over 1f out: strly pressed ins fnl f and hdd in clsng strides* **30/100**[1]

3 4½ **Trading Leather (IRE)**[49] 4649 4-9-7 118 KevinManning 1 116
(J S Bolger, Ire) *racd in modest 4th tl nt qckn over 1f out in 5th: kpt on same pce into 3rd ins fnl f wout troubling principals* **20/1**

4 1¾ **Mukhadram**[24] 5578 5-9-7 122 PaulHanagan 4 113+
(William Haggas) *trckd early ldr in 2nd: sn settled in 3rd tl clsd under 3f out: led briefly under 2f out but sn hdd: no imp in 3rd 1f out: kpt on one pce and dropped to 4th ins fnl f* **12/1**

5 nk **Al Kazeem**[21] 5687 6-9-7 117 (p) JamesDoyle 3 112
(Roger Charlton) *racd in 5th tl tk clsr order in 3rd over 2f out: sn rdn and nt qckn over 1f out: kpt on one pce* **10/1**[3]

6 9½ **Kingfisher (IRE)**[24] 5578 3-9-0 111 SeamieHeffernan 6 93+
(A P O'Brien, Ire) *sn trckd ldr in 2nd: led 3f out tl hdd under 2f out: sn no ex* **100/1**

7 43 **Alkasser (IRE)**[77] 3737 3-9-0 104 PatSmullen 7 7+
(D K Weld, Ire) *led to 3f out: sn wknd* **150/1**

2m 3.18s (-5.02) **Going Correction** -0.20s/f (Firm)
**WFA** 3 from 4yo+ 7lb **7 Ran SP% 112.6**
Speed ratings: **112,111,108,106,106 98,64**
CSF £9.33 TOTE £6.80: £1.60, £1.02; DF 10.90 Trifecta £81.40.
**Owner** F Gillespie **Bred** M Parrish **Trained** Hambleton, N Yorks

**FOCUS**
The time was slightly slower than the Group 3 earlier on the card but the form is up to scratch for the race.

## 6354a IRISH STALLION FARMS EUROPEAN BREEDERS FUND "SOVEREIGN PATH" H'CAP (PREMIER HANDICAP) 7f
7:20 (7:23) 3-Y-O+
£75,000 (£23,750; £11,250; £3,750; £2,500; £1,250)

RPR

1 **Baraweez (IRE)**[41] 4949 4-9-3 **96** ColmO'Donoghue 18 103
(Brian Ellison) *racd in mid-div tl prog over 1f out to chse ldrs: styd on strly to ld cl home* **12/1**

2 ½ **Almargo (IRE)**[7] 6124 3-9-6 **103** JoeFanning 17 106
(Mark Johnston) *racd in mid-div: gd hdwy to chse ldrs over 1f out: led fnl 150yds: kpt on wl: strly pressed and hdd cl home* **14/1**

3 ½ **Bold Thady Quill (IRE)**[13] 5957 7-9-7 **100** (v) BillyLee 12 104+
(K J Condon, Ire) *hld up in rr: stl last 2f out: styd on strly on outer fr over 1f out into 3rd on line: nt rch principals* **33/1**

4 shd **Piri Wango (IRE)**[46] 4771 5-9-12 **105** (p) GaryCarroll 13 109
(G M Lyons, Ire) *chsd ldrs: rdn in 4th under 2f out: briefly wnt 2nd ins fnl f: no ex fnl 50yds and dropped to 4th on line* **12/1**

5 ½ **Maremmadiavola (IRE)**[27] 5473 3-8-5 **93** (t) RobbieDowney[(5)] 1 93
(Edward Lynam, Ire) *broke wl and led tl hdd fnl 150yds: kpt on same pce and dropped to 5th in clsng stages* **20/1**

6 nk **Stay De Night (IRE)**[60] 4309 3-9-5 **102** (t) PatSmullen 7 102
(D K Weld, Ire) *hld up towards rr: plenty to do under 2f out: wnt 9th 1f out: kpt on wl: nvr on terms* **10/1**

7 ¾ **Colour Blue (IRE)**[24] 5584 3-8-9 **95** ConnorKing[(3)] 11 93
(W McCreery, Ire) *racd in mid-div: prog into 6th appr fnl f: n.m.r ins fnl f: kpt on same pce* **16/1**

8 ½ **Elusive Time (IRE)**[27] 5473 6-9-1 **94** (p) DeclanMcDonogh 3 92
(Takashi Kodama, Ire) *trckd ldrs in 3rd on inner tl nt qckn ins fnl f: wknd ins fnl 100yds* **66/1**

9 shd **Dream Walker (FR)**[28] 5446 5-8-12 **91** ChrisHayes 9 89
(Brian Ellison) *racd in mid-div tl dropped towards rr under 2f out: kpt on again ins fnl f: nvr nrr* **16/1**

10 ½ **Sretaw (IRE)**[13] 5957 5-8-10 **89** (bt) WayneLordan 10 86
(Gavin Cromwell, Ire) *hld up towards rr: c wd home turn: kpt on wl fr over 1f out: nvr on terms* **12/1**

11 ¾ **Pit Stop (IRE)**[22] 5656 3-8-8 **94** ConorHoban[(3)] 14 87
(M Halford, Ire) *hld up towards rr: prog on inner whn short of room over 1f out: kpt on same pce ins fnl f* **6/1**[3]

12 1 **Intensical (IRE)**[13] 5957 3-9-7 **104** (p) KevinManning 16 94
(J S Bolger, Ire) *hld up: prog under 2f out: no imp appr fnl f* **33/1**

13 hd **Rene Mathis (GER)**[21] 5665 4-9-7 **100** FMBerry 4 91
(Richard Fahey) *trckd ldr in 2nd tl rdn and no imp in 5th whn bdly squeezed up ins fnl f: sn no ex* **5/1**[2]

14 1½ **Captain Joy (IRE)**[13] 5957 5-9-2 **100** MeganCarberry[(5)] 15 87
(Tracey Collins, Ire) *hld up: rdn fr 2f out: no imp appr fnl f* **33/1**

15 1 **Burn The Boats (IRE)**[13] 5957 5-9-4 **97** JosephO'Brien 6 82
(G M Lyons, Ire) *racd in mid-div: rdn and nt qckn under 2f out: sn no imp* **9/2**[1]

16 1¼ **Dalkova**[44] 4836 5-8-13 **97** (p) RossCoakley[(5)] 8 78
(J P Murtagh, Ire) *chsd ldrs on inner in 5th tl nt qckn appr fnl f: wknd* **7/1**

17 shd **Barkston Ash**[57] 4384 6-8-11 **97** (p) GaryHalpin[(7)] 5 78
(Eric Alston) *chsd ldrs in 3rd: pushed along in 4th 3f out: wknd under 2f out* **33/1**

18 2 ½ **Rummaging (IRE)**[27] 5473 6-9-4 97 ShaneFoley 2 71
(M Halford, Ire) *racd in mid-div on inner tl sltly hmpd home turn: sn rdn and wknd fr 1f out* **25/1**
1m 25.4s (-3.30) **Going Correction** -0.20s/f (Firm)
**WFA** 3 from 4yo+ 4lb 18 Ran SP% **135.9**
Speed ratings: **110,109,108,108,108 107,106,106,106,105 104,103,103,101,100 99,99,96**
Pick Six: 11,666.60. Pool of 100,000.00 – 6 winning units. Tote Aggregates: 2013 Total: 445,410.00; 2014 Total: 795,510.00. CSF £174.37 CT £5414.37 TOTE £13.50: £2.90, £2.90, £6.80, £5.30; DF 199.20 Trifecta £2283.80.
**Owner** A Barnes **Bred** Sunderland Holdings Inc **Trained** Norton, N Yorks
■ Stewards' Enquiry : Joe Fanning severe caution: careless riding
**FOCUS**
Solid handicap form.
T/Jkpt: @1,631.80. Pool of @11,656.36 - 5 winning units. T/Plt: @20.00. Pool of @37,544.00 - 1309.26 winning units. AH

# 6312 BATH (L-H)

## Sunday, September 14

**OFFICIAL GOING: Firm (9.9)**
Wind: mild breeze behind Weather: sunny

## 6355 BATHWICK TYRES H'CAP (BOBIS RACE) 5f 11y
**2:15** (2:15) (Class 4) (0-85,80) 3-Y-O £4,690 (£1,395; £697; £348) **Stalls** Centre

Form RPR
3163 1 **Red Lady (IRE)**[44] 4859 3-9-1 77 RyanClark(3) 3 83
(Brian Meehan) *mde all: rdn 2f out: kpt on gamely fnl f: hld on wl* **7/2**[3]
2152 2 *nk* **Royal Brave (IRE)**[9] 6109 3-9-3 76 SamHitchcott 7 81
(William Muir) *trckd wnr: rdn over 2f out: kpt on wl ins fnl f* **2/1**[1]
4310 3 *nk* **Vodka Chaser (IRE)**[14] 5945 3-8-12 74 PhilipPrince(3) 6 78
(Alison Hutchinson) *trckd ldrs: rdn over 2f out: ev ch thrght fnl f: kpt on* **6/1**
4620 4 1 ¼ **Drive On (IRE)**[30] 5381 3-9-7 80 (p) JohnFahy 4 79
(Eve Johnson Houghton) *chsd ldrs: rdn 2f out: kpt on same pce fnl f* **12/1**
1206 5 *nk* **Flying Bear (IRE)**[12] 6020 3-8-11 77 (v[1]) DavidParkes(7) 1 75
(Jeremy Gask) *hld up bhd ldrs: rdn 2f out: kpt on but nt gng pce to get on terms* **11/4**[2]
440 6 1 ¼ **National Service (USA)**[51] 4636 3-8-10 69 (p) DaneO'Neill 5 63
(Stuart Williams) *s.i.s: trckd ldrs: rdn wl over 1f out: kpt on but nt gng pce to involved* **11/1**
1m 0.31s (-2.19) **Going Correction** -0.35s/f (Firm) 6 Ran SP% **112.5**
Speed ratings (Par 103): **103,102,102,100,99 97**
CSF £11.01 TOTE £4.30: £2.70, £1.20; EX 11.40 Trifecta £43.40.
**Owner** D J Burke **Bred** Brook Stud Bloodstock Ltd **Trained** Manton, Wilts
■ Stewards' Enquiry : Ryan Clark four-day ban: used whip above permitted level (Sep 28-Oct 1)
**FOCUS**
With the top weight 5lb below the ceiling rating for the race, this is probably just ordinary form for the level.

## 6356 BATHWICK CAR AND VAN HIRE MAIDEN STKS (BOBIS RACE) 5f 11y
**2:45** (2:45) (Class 4) 3-Y-O £4,690 (£1,395; £697; £348) **Stalls** Centre

Form RPR
2333 1 **Eternitys Gate**[34] 5249 3-9-5 74 JimCrowley 3 74
(Peter Chapple-Hyam) *travelled wl: trckd ldr: led ent fnl f: pushed clr: easily* **11/8**[1]
342 2 3 **Quick Touch**[15] 5916 3-9-5 65 FrederikTylicki 5 63
(Robert Cowell) *led: rdn 2f out: hdd ent fnl f: kpt on but nt pce of easy wnr* **13/8**[2]
20 3 1 ¼ **Our Grey Lady**[20] 5775 3-8-9 0 RyanWhile(5) 2 54
(Bill Turner) *trckd ldr: rdn 2f out: kpt on same pce fnl f* **8/1**[3]
6 4 *nk* **Kings Chapel (USA)**[20] 5775 3-9-5 0 LiamJones 7 58
(Jeremy Gask) *s.i.s: chsd ldrs: rdn over 2f out: edgd rt over 1f out: kpt on same pce* **11/1**
00 5 2 ¾ **Picnic In The Glen**[20] 5775 3-9-0 0 RenatoSouza 6 43
(Sylvester Kirk) *little slowly away: chsd ldrs: rdn over 2f out: sn one pce* **50/1**
-526 6 5 **Plauseabella**[15] 5905 3-9-0 53 DaneO'Neill 4 36
(Stuart Kittow) *chsd ldrs: rdn over 2f out: nvr threatened: wknd fnl f* **14/1**
60 7 ½ **Kitty Bequick**[20] 5775 3-8-11 0 CharlesBishop(3) 1 23
(Peter Hedger) *in tch tl outpcd wl over 2f out: nvr bk on terms* **50/1**
1m 1.26s (-1.24) **Going Correction** -0.35s/f (Firm) 7 Ran SP% **110.2**
Speed ratings (Par 103): **95,90,88,87,83 75,74**
CSF £3.50 TOTE £2.30: £1.10, £1.90; EX 4.50 Trifecta £9.30.
**Owner** Mrs Fitri Hay **Bred** Cheveley Park Stud Ltd **Trained** Newmarket, Suffolk
**FOCUS**
Not many got into this.

## 6357 BATHWICK TYRES CHIPPENHAM H'CAP 1m 2f 46y
**3:15** (3:15) (Class 4) (0-85,83) 3-Y-O+ £4,690 (£1,395; £697; £348) **Stalls** Low

Form RPR
4310 1 **Croquembouche (IRE)**[9] 6098 5-9-9 82 FrederikTylicki 2 89
(Ed de Giles) *mde all: rdn 2f out: kpt on v gamely: rdn out* **11/4**[2]
1560 2 1 **Rasameel (USA)**[11] 6044 3-8-13 79 DaneO'Neill 5 84
(B W Hills) *trckd wnr thrght: rdn over 2f out: styd on but nt pce to mount chal* **16/1**
3614 3 *nk* **Jalingo (IRE)**[7] 6166 3-9-3 83 RoystonFfrench 1 88
(Mark Johnston) *little slowly away: trckd wnr after 1f: rdn over 3f out: unable to mount chal: kpt on same pce fnl f* **6/4**[1]
100 4 ¾ **Perfect Cracker**[27] 5487 6-9-2 78 RyanTate(3) 4 81
(Clive Cox) *trckd ldrs: rdn over 2f out: kpt on fnl f but nt pce to get on terms* **5/1**[3]
1405 5 1 ½ **Dandy (GER)**[20] 5757 5-8-12 78 (v) RobHornby(7) 3 78
(Andrew Balding) *trckd ldrs: rdn over 2f out: kpt on same pce tl no ex fnl 100yds* **6/1**
154- 6 3 **Ardingly (IRE)**[148] 4-9-1 74 JimCrowley 6 69
(Paul Cole) *trckd ldrs: rdn over 2f out: nt quite pce to get on terms: fdd fnl 120yds* **16/1**
2m 7.88s (-3.12) **Going Correction** -0.225s/f (Firm)
**WFA** 3 from 4yo+ 7lb 6 Ran SP% **109.4**
Speed ratings (Par 105): **103,102,101,101,100 97**
CSF £38.38 TOTE £4.40: £2.60, £3.60; EX 36.00 Trifecta £188.40.
**Owner** John Manser **Bred** Ballymacoll Stud Farm Ltd **Trained** Ledbury, H'fords

**FOCUS**
The early pace for this decent handicap didn't appear strong.

## 6358 BATHWICK TYRES CARDIFF SOMERSETSHIRE CONDITIONS STKS 1m 5y
**3:50** (3:50) (Class 3) 3-Y-O+ £7,762 (£2,310; £1,154; £577) **Stalls** Low

Form RPR
1220 1 **Tenor (IRE)**[8] 6140 4-9-0 103 (t) JoeDoyle(5) 2 110
(John Ryan) *trckd ldr: rdn 2f out: led ins fnl f: kpt on wl: rdn out* **3/1**[2]
0346 2 1 ½ **Steeler (IRE)**[21] 5722 4-9-2 107 JimCrowley 4 104
(Charlie Appleby) *little slowly away: trckd ldrs: rdn over 2f out: styd on but nt pce to threaten fnl f: wnt 2nd nring fin* **1/1**[1]
103 3 *nk* **The Rectifier (USA)**[49] 4711 7-9-7 106 (t) FergusSweeney 1 108
(Seamus Durack) *led: rdn 2f out: edgd rt over 1f out: hdd ins fnl f: no ex whn lost 2nd nring fin* **11/2**
0600 4 9 **Boom And Bust (IRE)**[24] 5609 7-8-11 100 LouisSteward(5) 3 82
(Marcus Tregoning) *trckd ldr: rdn over 2f out: wknd ent fnl f* **4/1**[3]
1m 37.39s (-3.41) **Going Correction** -0.225s/f (Firm) 4 Ran SP% **110.4**
Speed ratings (Par 107): **108,106,106,97**
CSF £6.63 TOTE £2.50; EX 8.20 Trifecta £10.20.
**Owner** Kilco (International) Ltd **Bred** Epona Bloodstock Ltd And P A Byrne **Trained** Newmarket, Suffolk
**FOCUS**
Not form to go overboard about considering the field size.

## 6359 BATHWICK CAR AND VAN HIRE FILLIES' NURSERY H'CAP (BOBIS RACE) 1m 5y
**4:25** (4:25) (Class 4) (0-80,79) 2-Y-O £3,752 (£1,116; £557; £278) **Stalls** Low

Form RPR
631 1 **Natural Charm (IRE)**[15] 5910 2-9-2 79 LouisSteward(5) 4 83+
(Roger Varian) *in tch: rdn and hdwy over 2f out: chal jst over 1f out: led fnl 120yds: kpt on: rdn out* **9/2**[3]
534 2 ½ **Hoorayforhollywood**[45] 4825 2-9-0 72 JimCrowley 3 75
(Sir Michael Stoute) *prom: rdn to ld briefly over 2f out: kpt pressing ldr: styd on to regain 2nd nring fin but a being hld by wnr* **5/2**[1]
3422 3 *nk* **Simply Magic (IRE)**[25] 5554 2-8-7 72 GaryMahon(7) 2 74
(Richard Hannon) *trckd ldr: rdn to ld over 2f out: hdd fnl 120yds: no ex whn lost 2nd nring fin* **8/1**
510 4 4 ½ **Mahsooba (USA)**[29] 5436 2-9-5 77 DaneO'Neill 7 68
(Ed Dunlop) *trckd ldrs: rdn over 2f out: styd on but nt pce to get involved* **10/3**[2]
000 5 2 ½ **Eileen Gray (IRE)**[39] 5037 2-8-0 58 oh9 (p) JimmyQuinn 5 43
(Charles Hills) *s.i.s: in last pair: rdn over 2f out: sn hung lft: nvr threatened* **33/1**
3033 6 8 **Euthenia**[16] 5875 2-8-6 67 CharlesBishop(3) 1 33
(Mick Channon) *led: rdn and hdd over 2f out: wknd over 1f out* **9/2**[3]
6051 7 ½ **Vita Mina**[3] 6250 2-8-3 66 6ex [1] NoelGarbutt(5) 6 31
(David Evans) *sn struggling in last: nvr a factor* **12/1**
1m 39.51s (-1.29) **Going Correction** -0.225s/f (Firm) 2y crse rec 7 Ran SP% **109.8**
Speed ratings (Par 94): **97,96,96,91,89 81,80**
CSF £14.82 TOTE £6.20: £2.40, £1.10; EX 19.50 Trifecta £63.10.
**Owner** M Al-Qatami & K M Al-Mudhaf **Bred** M Al-Qatami & K M Al-Mudhaf **Trained** Newmarket, Suffolk
■ Stewards' Enquiry : Louis Steward four-day ban: used whip above permitted level (Sep 30-Oct 3)
**FOCUS**
The early pace for this fair contest was strong thanks to the free-running Euthenia, which surely helped the race produce a new 2yo course record.

## 6360 BATHWICK TYRES NEWPORT H'CAP 2m 1f 34y
**4:55** (4:57) (Class 4) (0-80,80) 4-Y-O+ £4,690 (£1,395; £697; £348) **Stalls** Centre

Form RPR
301 1 **Teak (IRE)**[20] 4777 7-9-7 80 (p) JimCrowley 4 88
(Ian Williams) *trckd ldrs: led 2f out: in command fnl f: comf* **2/1**[1]
4120 2 3 ¾ **See And Be Seen**[18] 5825 4-9-2 75 (p) RenatoSouza 5 79
(Sylvester Kirk) *led: rdn and hdd 2f out: styd on but sn hld by wnr* **5/1**[3]
5234 3 *shd* **Our Folly**[31] 5341 6-8-13 72 (b[1]) DaneO'Neill 3 76
(Stuart Kittow) *s.i.s: in last pair but wl in tch: rdn 2f out: styd on fnl f: nrly snatched 2nd fnl stride* **5/1**[3]
-321 4 *nk* **Noor Al Haya (IRE)**[15] 5909 4-8-2 61 oh1 KieranO'Neill 2 65
(Mark Usher) *hld up last: rdn over 2f out: no imp tl styd on ins fnl f* **13/2**
3231 5 1 **Annaluna (IRE)**[15] 5924 5-8-9 68 (v) ChrisCatlin 1 70
(David Evans) *trckd ldrs: rdn over 2f out: styd on same pce fr over 1f out* **9/2**[2]
5350 6 1 ¾ **Hi Note**[17] 5073 6-8-12 74 CharlesBishop(3) 6 75
(Sheena West) *jockeys foot slipped out of iron briefly sn after s: sn prom: rdn over 2f out: wknd fnl f* **8/1**
3m 45.73s (-6.17) **Going Correction** -0.225s/f (Firm) 6 Ran SP% **109.3**
Speed ratings (Par 105): **105,103,103,103,102 101**
CSF £11.49 TOTE £2.30: £1.10, £2.80; EX 11.20 Trifecta £40.70.
**Owner** Farranamanagh **Bred** Michael Morrissey **Trained** Portway, Worcs
**FOCUS**
Nothing more than an ordinary gallop was set by the leader in what was a fair staying event. The pace seemed to increase about 3f out.

## 6361 BATHWICK TYRES BRIDGEND MEDIAN AUCTION MAIDEN FILLIES' STKS (BOBIS RACE) 5f 161y
**5:25** (5:29) (Class 4) 2-Y-O £3,752 (£1,116; £557; £278) **Stalls** Centre

Form RPR
1 **Air Of Mystery** 2-9-0 0 DaneO'Neill 1 83+
(Marcus Tregoning) *trckd ldrs: rdn to ld over 1f out: r.o wl to draw clr fnl f: readily* **9/1**[3]
5332 2 4 **Red Perdita (IRE)**[52] 4589 2-9-0 75 FergusSweeney 3 70
(George Baker) *prom: rdn 2f out: ev ch over 1f out: kpt on but nt pce of wnr fnl f* **10/11**[1]
3 *nk* **Dutch Robin (IRE)** 2-9-0 0 SamHitchcott 8 69
(Mick Channon) *prom: rdn over 2f out: kpt on same pce ins fnl f* **11/2**[2]
44 4 1 ½ **Dear Bruin (IRE)**[46] 4787 2-9-0 0 LiamJones 5 64
(John Spearing) *led: rdn and hdd over 1f out: no ex ins fnl f* **11/2**[2]
00 5 2 ½ **Cherry Empress (IRE)**[3] 6246 2-8-7 0 JoshuaBrowning(7) 6 56+
(Jo Hughes) *trckd ldrs: rdn over 2f out: nt pce to chal: no ex fnl 120yds* **40/1**
00 6 2 ¾ **Avenue Du Monde (FR)**[31] 5344 2-9-0 0 KieranO'Neill 2 47
(Richard Hannon) *trckd ldrs: rdn over 2f out: wknd fnl f* **11/1**

0 7 9 **Pilgrim**[20] 5774 2-9-0 0 JohnFahy 10 17
(Eve Johnson Houghton) *chsd ldrs: rdn over 2f out: wknd over 1f out* **14/1**
1m 10.22s (-0.98) **Going Correction** -0.35s/f (Firm) 7 Ran SP% **110.6**
Speed ratings (Par 94): **92,86,86,84,80 77,65**
CSF £16.56 TOTE £9.50: £2.50, £1.30; EX 20.30 Trifecta £60.10.
**Owner** Mrs M E Slade **Bred** Mrs M E Slade **Trained** Whitsbury, Hants
**FOCUS**
This probably wasn't an overly strong race, but the winner impressed. The second and fourth help shape the level.
T/Jkpt: £1,290.90 to a £1 stake. Pool: £10,000.00 - 5.50 winning tickets T/Plt: £53.50 to a £1 stake. Pool: £3925.760 - 54.30 winning tickets T/Qpdt: £53.50 to a £1 stake. Pool: £3925.76 - 54.30 winning tickets TM

## 5845 FFOS LAS (L-H)
Sunday, September 14

**OFFICIAL GOING: Good to firm (8.4)**
Wind: moderate half behind Weather: sunny spells

### 6362 BRITISH STALLION STUDS EBF MAIDEN STKS 1m (R)
**2:30** (2:30) (Class 5) 2-Y-O £2,911 (£866; £432; £216) **Stalls** Low

Form RPR
1 **My Reward** 2-9-5 0 JamesDoyle 1 82+
(Charles Hills) *dwlt: hld up in last tl shkn up and hdwy on outer over 2f out: rdn 1f out: r.o wl to ld last strides* **11/4**[2]
2 *nk* **Emirates Skywards (IRE)** 2-9-5 0 SilvestreDeSousa 3 81+
(Charlie Appleby) *s.i.s: racd in 4th tl hdwy to trck ldr after 2f: qcknd to ld 2f out: rdn and r.o wl: hdd last strides* **9/4**[1]
3 *3 ¼* **Resonant (IRE)** 2-9-5 0 FrannyNorton 4 71
(Mark Johnston) *led tl rdn and hdd 2f out: kpt on but nt gng pce of first 2* **5/1**
4 *½* **Subcontinent (IRE)** 2-9-0 0 CamHardie(5) 2 70
(Charlie Appleby) *trckd ldr 2f: styd cl up: rdn 3f out: sn outpcd by principals: styd on fnl f* **8/1**
6 5 *4 ½* **Taraz**[10] 6056 2-9-5 0 SeanLevey 5 59
(Richard Hannon) *t.k.h bhd ldrs: rdn 2f out and unable qck: fdd fnl f* **3/1**[3]
1m 44.14s (3.14) **Going Correction** -0.10s/f (Good) 5 Ran SP% **110.2**
Speed ratings (Par 95): **80,79,76,75,71**
CSF £9.34 TOTE £4.20: £1.50, £2.70; EX 9.90 Trifecta £31.60.
**Owner** K Abdullah **Bred** Millsec Limited **Trained** Lambourn, Berks
**FOCUS**
Three of the four previous winners of this maiden have gone on to record three-figure RPRs and, given the connections represented this time, there's a good chance that trend can continue. Nice starts from the front two.

### 6363 SAXTON DRILLING LTD MAIDEN STKS (BOBIS RACE) 6f
**3:00** (3:02) (Class 4) 2-Y-O £4,690 (£1,395; £697; £348) **Stalls** Centre

Form RPR
324 1 **Wonder Of Qatar (IRE)**[22] 5671 2-9-5 79 SeanLevey 4 78
(Richard Hannon) *mde all: rdn over 2f out: edgd rt appr fnl f: jnd 100yds out: fnd more nr fin* **5/2**[2]
022 2 *1 ¼* **Fast Dancer (IRE)**[16] 5874 2-9-5 85 JamesDoyle 5 74
(Joseph Tuite) *chsd ldrs: rdn 2f out: jinked lft over 1f out: r.o to chal ins fnl f: hld nr fin* **11/10**[1]
3234 3 *nk* **Aussie Ruler (IRE)**[11] 6038 2-9-5 75 RobertWinston 6 73
(Ronald Harris) *in rr: hdwy over 2f out: r.o u.p: nt quite rch ldrs* **7/1**[3]
63 4 *1 ¼* **Quintus Cerialis (IRE)**[78] 3728 2-9-5 0 SteveDrowne 7 70
(Clive Cox) *hld up: rdn 2f out: r.o* **8/1**
6 5 *½* **Code Red**[33] 5271 2-9-5 0 DougieCostello 3 68
(William Muir) *t.k.h early: trckd ldrs tl wnt 2nd 1/2-way: rdn 2f out: sn one pce* **20/1**
323 6 *3 ½* **Colour Catcher**[87] 3387 2-9-5 80 SilvestreDeSousa 2 58
(Charlie Appleby) *s.i.s: towards rr: rdn 2f out: unable qck and no imp* **11/1**
0 7 *17* **Gleaming Princess**[16] 5896 2-9-0 0 DavidProbert 1 2
(Milton Bradley) *t.k.h: prom tl rdn and wknd over 2f out: t.o* **100/1**
1m 9.0s (-1.00) **Going Correction** -0.10s/f (Good) 2y crse rec 7 Ran SP% **113.9**
Speed ratings (Par 97): **102,100,99,98,97 92,70**
CSF £5.55 TOTE £5.50: £3.60, £1.10; EX 7.20 Trifecta £26.50.
**Owner** H H Sheikh Mohammed Bin Khalifa Al Thani **Bred** Pier House Stud **Trained** East Everleigh, Wilts
**FOCUS**
A fair maiden, and straightforward form.

### 6364 DOUBLE DRAGON - NATIONAL ALE OF WALES NURSERY H'CAP 1m (R)
**3:30** (3:31) (Class 5) (0-75,75) 2-Y-O £2,587 (£770; £384; £192) **Stalls** Low

Form RPR
352 1 **Here Now**[19] 5783 2-9-7 75 SilvestreDeSousa 2 78
(Charlie Appleby) *t.k.h: hld up in tch: wnt 2nd 4f out: rdn to ld over 1f out: r.o wl ins fnl f* **1/1**[1]
3534 2 *¾* **Water Thief (USA)**[9] 6108 2-9-6 74 FrannyNorton 3 75
(Mark Johnston) *trckd ldr tl relegated to 3rd 4f out: rdn 2f out: r.o ins fnl f: tk 2nd fnl 25yds* **7/2**[3]
252 3 *½* **La Estatua**[40] 4993 2-9-0 68 JamesDoyle 1 68
(James Tate) *led tl rdn and hdd over 1f out: r.o: lost 2nd fnl 25yds* **9/4**[2]
033 4 *1 ½* **Horsetracker**[19] 5798 2-8-8 67 GeorgeDowning(5) 5 63
(Ian Williams) *hld up in tch: rdn over 2f out: hung lft over 1f out: one pce* **12/1**
1m 42.04s (1.04) **Going Correction** -0.10s/f (Good) 4 Ran SP% **110.7**
Speed ratings (Par 95): **90,89,88,87**
CSF £4.96 TOTE £1.60; EX 4.70 Trifecta £6.00.
**Owner** Godolphin **Bred** Darley **Trained** Newmarket, Suffolk
**FOCUS**
This nursery was run at a fairly steady pace. A cosy winner but not form to place too much faith in.

### 6365 O.J. WILLIAMS PREMIER FUEL DISRIBUTORS FILLIES H'CAP 1m 2f (R)
**4:05** (4:05) (Class 4) (0-80,77) 3-Y-O+ £4,851 (£1,443; £721; £360) **Stalls** Low

Form RPR
6522 1 **Bright Cecily (IRE)**[11] 6026 3-9-1 73 (p) SteveDrowne 4 83
(Clive Cox) *s.i.s: hld up in 4th: hdwy over 2f out: led over 1f out: rdn and r.o wl* **6/1**
2136 2 *¾* **Swan Lakes (IRE)**[40] 5003 3-9-5 77 JamesDoyle 1 85
(David Simcock) *trckd ldrs: rdn and unable qck 3f out: styd on wl ins fnl f: a being hld by wnr* **6/4**[1]
4140 3 *2* **Play Street**[21] 5721 5-9-2 72 NedCurtis(5) 3 76
(Jonathan Portman) *hld up in last: swtchd rt and hdwy over 2f out: disp 2nd 1f out: hung lft and one pce after* **10/1**
2223 4 *6* **An Chulainn (IRE)**[12] 5999 3-8-12 70 (v[1]) FrannyNorton 2 63
(Mark Johnston) *led after 1f: rdn 2f out: sn hdd: wknd appr fnl f* **7/2**[3]
5513 5 *2 ½* **Dubai Hadeia**[11] 6026 3-8-10 73 (p) CamHardie(5) 6 61
(Charlie Appleby) *led 1f: trckd ldr: rdn 3f out and sn lost 2nd: wknd over 1f out* **3/1**[2]
2m 7.14s (-2.26) **Going Correction** -0.10s/f (Good)
**WFA** 3 from 5yo 7lb 5 Ran SP% **110.6**
Speed ratings (Par 105): **105,104,102,98,96**
CSF £15.64 TOTE £5.90: £3.20, £2.90; EX 13.50 Trifecta £66.30.
**Owner** Old Peartree Stud **Bred** J Stan Cosgrove **Trained** Lambourn, Berks
**FOCUS**
Probably not strong form, but a personal best from the winner.

### 6366 MARUBENI KOMATSU H'CAP 1m 4f (R)
**4:40** (4:40) (Class 3) (0-95,89) 3-Y-O+ £7,762 (£2,310; £1,154; £577) **Stalls** Low

Form RPR
2-03 1 **Saoi (USA)**[45] 4832 7-9-8 85 JamesDoyle 4 92
(William Knight) *hld up in last: clsd 3f out: rdn 2f out: sn chal: led narrowly ins fnl f: hld on* **5/2**[2]
351 2 *hd* **Le Maitre Chat (USA)**[17] 5851 3-8-13 85 SteveDrowne 3 91
(Clive Cox) *trckd ldr: rdn to ld 2f out: sn jnd: hdd narrowly ins fnl f: r.o* **9/2**
4216 3 *1 ¼* **Solidarity**[9] 6106 3-9-3 89 SilvestreDeSousa 1 93
(Charlie Appleby) *t.k.h: racd in 3rd tl rdn: swtchd rt and dropped to last 2f out: styd on fnl f: nt rch ldng pair* **7/4**[1]
1500 4 *5* **Special Fighter (IRE)**[12] 6005 3-9-1 87 FrannyNorton 2 83
(Mark Johnston) *led: rdn and hdd 2f out: unable qck: eased whn btn ins fnl f* **3/1**[3]
2m 39.91s (2.51) **Going Correction** -0.10s/f (Good)
**WFA** 3 from 7yo 9lb 4 Ran SP% **108.1**
Speed ratings (Par 107): **87,86,86,82**
CSF £12.61 TOTE £3.80; EX 11.80 Trifecta £15.80.
**Owner** D A Docherty **Bred** Kilboy Estate Inc **Trained** Patching, W Sussex
**FOCUS**
Just the four runners, a steady early pace and a sprint to finish. It's hard to be positive about the form.

### 6367 OC DAVIES ROUNDABOUT CAR CENTRE NEYLAND H'CAP 1m 4f (R)
**5:10** (5:11) (Class 5) (0-70,70) 3-Y-O+ £2,587 (£770; £384; £192) **Stalls** Low

Form RPR
3-45 1 **Solaras Exhibition (IRE)**[32] 5317 6-9-11 69 DavidProbert 2 77
(Tim Vaughan) *s.i.s: hld up: nt clr run 3f out: rdn and hdwy over 2f out: edgd lft and led appr fnl f: styd on wl* **12/1**
2123 2 *1* **Golden Jubilee (USA)**[3] 6264 5-9-12 70 (v) WilliamTwiston-Davies 6 76
(Nigel Twiston-Davies) *led: rdn 2f out: hdd appr fnl f: kpt on* **7/4**[1]
053/ 3 *½* **Castlemorris King**[14] 5507 6-9-2 65 CamHardie(5) 3 70
(Brian Barr) *chsd ldrs: rdn over 2f out: kpt on same pce* **2/1**[2]
2355 4 *6* **Dark Amber**[16] 5878 4-9-7 65 RobertWinston 1 61
(Brendan Powell) *chsd ldrs: swtchd rt and rdn 3f out: ev ch 2f out: wknd 1f out* **7/2**[3]
0/00 5 *12* **Rockinit (IRE)**[24] 5005 8-8-7 56 oh6 DanielMuscutt(5) 4 32
(Peter Bowen) *t.k.h: trckd ldr tl rdn and lost pl 3f out: bhd fnl 2f* **33/1**
0-00 6 *8* **Dream And Search (GER)**[91] 3268 3-8-13 66 (t) SteveDrowne 5 30
(Anthony Honeyball) *s.s: hld up in rr: rdn over 3f out: sn wknd* **7/1**
2m 37.18s (-0.22) **Going Correction** -0.10s/f (Good)
**WFA** 3 from 4yo+ 9lb 6 Ran SP% **115.1**
Speed ratings (Par 103): **96,95,95,91,83 77**
CSF £34.67 TOTE £9.50: £4.00, £1.20; EX 37.00 Trifecta £69.10.
**Owner** C Davies **Bred** John Skehan **Trained** Aberthin, Vale of Glamorgan
**FOCUS**
Just a modest handicap. The runner-up sets the standard.

### 6368 BLUEBELL RECRUITMENT H'CAP 5f
**5:40** (5:40) (Class 6) (0-60,59) 3-Y-O+ £1,940 (£577; £288; £144) **Stalls** Centre

Form RPR
0511 1 **Spider Lily**[30] 5399 3-9-0 56 DeclanBates(3) 4 66+
(Peter Makin) *least wl away and chsd other 3: hdwy 1/2-way: led appr fnl f: comf* **4/6**[1]
456 2 *1 ½* **Spic 'n Span**[9] 6090 9-8-7 45 (p) WilliamTwiston-Davies 1 48
(Ronald Harris) *wnt to post early: cl up: led over 3f out: rdn 2f out: hdd appr fnl f: kpt on but no ch w wnr* **8/1**[3]
4400 3 *5* **Notnow Penny**[81] 3564 3-8-6 45 DavidProbert 3 30
(Milton Bradley) *led over 1f: styd prom tl rdn and outpcd by ldrs 2f out: tk modest 3rd ins fnl f* **16/1**
0064 4 *1* **Going French (IRE)**[16] 5897 7-9-2 59 DanielMuscutt(5) 5 40
(Grace Harris) *chsd ldng pair: rdn 1/2-way: one pce after: lost modest 3rd ins fnl f* **2/1**[2]
57.84s (-0.46) **Going Correction** -0.10s/f (Good)
**WFA** 3 from 7yo+ 1lb 4 Ran SP% **110.3**
Speed ratings (Par 101): **99,96,88,87**
CSF £6.63 TOTE £2.30; EX 6.30 Trifecta £28.50.
**Owner** Hoofbeats Racing Club 1 **Bred** Mrs P J Makin **Trained** Ogbourne Maisey, Wilts
**FOCUS**
Uncompetitive stuff, and shaky form, but a step up from the winner.
T/Plt: £59.20 to a £1 stake. Pool: £59,995.12 - 738.72 winning tickets T/Qpdt: £39.60 to a £1 stake. Pool: £4,120.22 - 76.83 winning tickets RL

## 5952 CURRAGH (R-H)
Sunday, September 14

**OFFICIAL GOING: Good to firm (watered)**

### 6369a IRISH STALLION FARMS EUROPEAN BREEDERS FUND "BOLD LAD" SPRINT H'CAP (PREMIER HANDICAP) 6f
**2:05** (2:06) 3-Y-O+
£75,000 (£23,750; £11,250; £3,750; £2,500; £1,250)

RPR
1 **Watchable**[50] 4648 4-9-6 98 (p) DanielTudhope 19 107
(David O'Meara) *a.p: cl up tl disp gng wl 1/2-way: led 2f out: sn rdn and wnt over 1 l clr ent fnl f: all out towards fin to jst hold on* **5/1**[1]

2 hd **Zalty (FR)**[28] 5473 4-9-1 93 (b) ColmO'Donoghue 16 101
(David Marnane, Ire) *hld up: clsr in 11th 1/2-way: hdwy fr over 2f out gng wl where nt clr run bhd horses: rdn and clsd u.p whn swtchd rt ins fnl f: sn wnt 2nd and kpt on wl towards fin: jst failed* 9/1

3 1 **Forest Edge (IRE)**[15] 5918 5-9-5 97 (b) JFEgan 15 102
(David Evans) *trckd ldrs: pushed along 1/2-way and no imp on wnr disputing 3rd ins fnl f: kpt on same pce* 22/1

4 1 **Arctic Feeling (IRE)**[19] 5784 6-8-6 89 SammyJoBell(5) 9 91
(Richard Fahey) *hld up towards rr: hdwy over 2f out to chse ldrs ins fnl f where swtchd lft: kpt on wl u.p towards fin: nvr nrr* 16/1

5 hd **Discussiontofollow (IRE)**[43] 4895 4-9-6 98 ShaneBKelly 20 99
(Mike Murphy) *chsd ldrs: effrt under 2f out: sn rdn in 2nd and no imp on wnr ent fnl f: kpt on one pce* 11/2[2]

6 ½ **Kernoff (IRE)**[28] 5473 3-9-0 94 (b1) ShaneFoley 4 94+
(M Halford, Ire) *bhd: last 1/2-way: rdn and hdwy far side under 2f out: kpt on wl towards fin: nvr nrr* 25/1

7 1 **Liberty Jack (IRE)**[16] 5888 4-8-8 86 (p) PatCosgrave 21 83
(Jim Boyle) *chsd ldrs: rdn and no imp on wnr over 1f out: kpt on one pce* 16/1

8 nk **Shipyard (USA)**[27] 5514 5-8-8 86 ChrisHayes 7 82
(A Oliver, Ire) *chsd ldrs: rdn over 2f out and no imp on wnr in 6th 1f out: one pce fnl f* 20/1

9 nk **Bubbly Bellini (IRE)**[21] 5732 7-9-1 93 (p) DeclanMcDonogh 17 88
(Adrian McGuinness, Ire) *hld up in tch: 12th 1/2-way: rdn 2f out and no imp on ldrs ins fnl f: kpt on one pce* 33/1

10 shd **Tatlisu (IRE)**[29] 5445 4-9-0 92 TonyHamilton 6 86
(Richard Fahey) *cl up: rdn in 2nd under 2f out and sn no imp on wnr: wknd ins fnl f* 10/1

11 1¾ **Tylery Wonder (IRE)**[21] 5732 4-8-9 87 (be) WayneLordan 18 76
(W McCreery, Ire) *cl up: 3rd 1/2-way: rdn and wknd fr under 2f out* 12/1

12 nse **Lady Mega (IRE)**[37] 5155 3-8-3 88 RobbieDowney(5) 5 77
(Edward Lynam, Ire) *towards rr: rdn over 2f out and tk clsr order far side over 1f out: no ex and one pce fnl f* 9/1

13 nk **Masai (IRE)**[21] 5732 3-8-4 91 (t) AnaO'Brien(7) 8 79
(A P O'Brien, Ire) *towards rr: no imp on ldrs over 1f out: kpt on one pce ins fnl f* 20/1

14 nk **Strait Of Zanzibar (USA)**[14] 5957 5-8-5 86 (tp) ConorHoban(3) 14 73
(K J Condon, Ire) *chsd ldrs: rdn over 2f out and sn no ex u.p: wknd fnl f* 33/1

15 nk **Majestic Queen (IRE)**[22] 5699 4-9-11 103 PatSmullen 12 89
(Tracey Collins, Ire) *in tch: sme hdwy 2f out: rdn and no ex over 1f out: wknd* 8/1[3]

16 1 **My Good Brother (IRE)**[7] 6172 5-9-3 102 (v) GaryHalpin(7) 11 84
(T G McCourt, Ire) *sn led narrowly: jnd 1/2-way and hdd 2f out: wknd* 25/1

17 1 **Oor Jock (IRE)**[14] 5958 6-8-4 82 oh1 (b) RoryCleary 3 61
(Adrian McGuinness, Ire) *dwlt sltly: towards rr tl tk clsr order 1/2-way: rdn and no ex under 2f out: wknd fnl f* 20/1

18 1½ **Sunraider (IRE)**[23] 5632 7-8-4 82 oh4 LeighRoche 2 56
(Paul Midgley) *a bhd: pushed along 1/2-way and no imp* 66/1

19 2¼ **Local Flier**[21] 5732 3-7-13 84 oh2 (v) SeanCorby(5) 10 51
(T G McCourt, Ire) *in tch: sltly hmpd between horses bef 1/2-way and lost few pls: pushed along over 2f out and no ex: wknd fnl f* 25/1

20 1¾ **Farmleigh House (IRE)**[213] 597 7-9-12 104 NGMcCullagh 1 66
(W J Martin, Ire) *chsd ldrs: pushed along fr 1/2-way and sn no ex u.p: wknd fnl 2f* 50/1

1m 11.87s (-3.63) **Going Correction** -0.35s/f (Firm)
**WFA** 3 from 4yo+ 2lb 20 Ran SP% 131.2
Speed ratings: **110,109,108,107,106 106,104,104,104,103 101,101,101,100,100 98,97,95,92,90**
CSF £43.52 CT £955.30 TOTE £6.60: £1.80, £3.00, £4.50, £4.70; DF 54.10 Trifecta £937.00.
**Owner** P Bamford **Bred** Cheveley Park Stud Ltd **Trained** Nawton, N Yorks
■ Day two of Irish Champions Weekend.
■ Stewards' Enquiry : Gary Halpin two-day ban: continued to use whip when chance had gone (tbn)

**FOCUS**
Those drawn low didn't really get into this. It certainly paid to be drawn middle to high as the winner came out of stall 19, the second out of stall 16 and the third came from stall 15. The winner made his move 2f out and always looked to be doing enough inside the final furlong.

## 6370a MOYGLARE "JEWELS" BLANDFORD STKS (GROUP 2) (F&M) 1m 2f
2:40 (2:41) 3-Y-0+

£100,000 (£31,666; £15,000; £5,000; £3,333; £1,666)

RPR

1 **Tarfasha (IRE)**[57] 4461 3-9-0 111 PatSmullen 1 112
(D K Weld, Ire) *chsd ldrs: 3rd 1/2-way: hdwy into st and wnt 2nd over 2f out: rdn to ld 1 1/2f out and kpt on wl ins fnl f* 11/10[1]

2 1¾ **Chicquita (IRE)**[421] 4550 4-9-7 115 JosephO'Brien 6 109+
(A P O'Brien, Ire) *w.w towards rr: 6th 1/2-way: hdwy fr 2f out into 2nd ent fnl f: kpt on wl u.p towards fin wout ever troubling wnr* 11/4[2]

3 2¾ **Roheryn (IRE)**[38] 5115 3-9-0 105 AndreaAtzeni 5 103
(G M Lyons, Ire) *sn settled bhd ldr: 2nd 1/2-way: rdn in 3rd 2f out and no imp on wnr u.p ent fnl f: kpt on one pce* 6/1[3]

4 nse **Cosmic Cannonball (IRE)**[25] 5587 4-9-7 98 KevinManning 3 103
(J S Bolger, Ire) *hld up in tch: 5th 1/2-way: rdn into st and no imp on ldrs in 6th over 1f out: r.o wl u.p ins fnl f to snatch nvr nrr 4th on line* 33/1

5 nk **Mango Diva**[43] 4894 4-9-7 108 DeclanMcDonogh 4 102
(Sir Michael Stoute) *hld up in tch: 4th 1/2-way: rdn in 4th 2f out and no imp on wnr ent fnl f: kpt on one pce and denied 4th on line* 7/1

6 3 **Shell House (IRE)**[6] 6200 3-9-0 98 SeamieHeffernan 2 96
(A P O'Brien, Ire) *sn led: over 1 l clr 1/2-way: extended advantage fr over 4f out: reduced advantage 2f out and sn strly pressed: hdd 1 1/2f out and no ex: wknd* 25/1

7 1½ **Beyond Brilliance (IRE)**[6] 6200 3-9-0 100 AnaO'Brien 7 93
(A P O'Brien, Ire) *s.i.s and in rr thrght: rdn and no imp 2f out* 25/1

2m 4.76s (-4.54) **Going Correction** -0.35s/f (Firm)
**WFA** 3 from 4yo 7lb 7 Ran SP% 111.7
Speed ratings: **104,102,100,100,100 97,96**
CSF £3.97 TOTE £2.00: £1.02, £1.70; DF 4.70 Trifecta £14.10.
**Owner** Hamdan Al Maktoum **Bred** Rockfield Farm **Trained** Curragh, Co Kildare

**FOCUS**
The was a small step up in form by the winner.

## 6371a DERRINSTOWN STUD FLYING FIVE STKS (GROUP 3) 5f
3:10 (3:11) 3-Y-0+ £54,166 (£15,833; £7,500; £2,500)

RPR

1 **Stepper Point**[23] 5654 5-9-4 113 (p) MartinDwyer 6 117+
(William Muir) *sn led: extended advantage travelling best over 1f out: styd on wl: easily* 9/4[1]

2 2¾ **Sir Maximilian (IRE)**[37] 5154 5-9-4 109 StevieDonohoe 7 107
(Tim Pitt) *hld up in mid-div: 5th 1/2-way: sme hdwy on outer fr 2f out to chse ldrs in 3rd ent fnl f: sn wnt 2nd and kpt on wl towards fin: nt trble easy wnr* 7/1

3 nk **Russian Soul (IRE)**[22] 5699 6-9-4 110 (p) ShaneFoley 3 106
(M Halford, Ire) *s.i.s and racd in rr: last gng wl 1 1/2f out: nt clr run ins fnl f and swtchd lft in 8th: r.o wl between horses into nvr nrr 3rd fnl stride: nt trble easy wnr* 12/1

4 nse **Robot Boy (IRE)**[25] 5575 4-9-4 102 GrahamGibbons 9 106
(David Barron) *chsd ldrs: 4th 1/2-way: rdn 1 1/2f out and no imp on easy wnr in 3rd ins fnl f: denied 3rd fnl stride* 7/1

5 ½ **Jamesie (IRE)**[22] 5699 6-9-4 108 ColmO'Donoghue 4 104
(David Marnane, Ire) *broke wl and sn settled bhd ldr: 3rd 1/2-way: sn rdn and no imp on easy wnr u.p in 4th ins fnl f: dropped to 5th clsng stages* 8/1

6 1 **Fountain Of Youth (IRE)**[78] 3736 3-9-3 107 (b) SeamieHeffernan 5 100
(A P O'Brien, Ire) *chsd ldrs: pushed along early and clsr in 2nd 1/2-way: sn rdn and no imp on easy wnr 1 1/2f out: wknd fnl f* 14/1

7 ½ **Extortionist (IRE)**[8] 6134 3-9-3 113 AndreaAtzeni 8 99
(Olly Stevens) *towards rr: 8th 1/2-way: rdn under 2f out and sme hdwy far side over 1f out: no ex and one pce ins fnl f* 7/2[2]

8 ½ **Guerre (USA)**[89] 3319 3-9-3 110 JosephO'Brien 10 97
(A P O'Brien, Ire) *chsd ldrs early tl settled towards rr: 7th 1/2-way: gng wl bhd horses 2f out: rdn over 1f and sn hmpd between horses and dropped to rr: no imp after* 13/2[3]

9 nse **Master Speaker (IRE)**[21] 5732 4-9-4 94 (t) SJHassett 2 97
(Martin Hassett, Ire) *hld up: clsr in 6th 1/2-way: rdn under 2f out and no imp on easy wnr: wknd* 80/1

59.04s (-3.86) **Going Correction** -0.35s/f (Firm)
**WFA** 3 from 4yo+ 1lb 9 Ran SP% 118.0
Speed ratings: **116,111,111,111,110 108,107,107,106**
CSF £19.23 TOTE £3.00: £1.40, £1.80, £2.50; DF 19.40 Trifecta £178.80.
**Owner** C L A Edginton **Bred** Whitsbury Manor Stud **Trained** Lambourn, Berks
■ Stewards' Enquiry : Colm O'Donoghue severe caution: failed to ride to draw
Martin Dwyer three-day ban: careless riding (tbn)

**FOCUS**
Take Sole Power and Slade Power out of the equation and the depth of talent in the Irish sprinting brigade is exposed as being short of the mark, and that was demonstrated by the manner of victory of the winner.

## 6372a MOYGLARE STUD STKS (GROUP 1) (FILLIES) 7f
3:40 (3:41) 2-Y-0

£145,000 (£47,500; £22,500; £7,500; £5,000; £2,500)

RPR

1 **Cursory Glance (USA)**[24] 5608 2-9-0 112 AndreaAtzeni 8 112
(Roger Varian) *chsd ldrs: 6th 3f out: hdwy to ld over 1f out and sn rdn over 1 l clr: pressed clly u.p wl ins fnl f: kpt on wl* 11/8[1]

2 nk **Lucida (IRE)**[21] 5734 2-9-0 106 KevinManning 2 111+
(J S Bolger, Ire) *hld up in tch: 8th 3f out: nt clr run under 2f out: rdn and prog into 4th ins fnl f: r.o wl to press wnr clsng stages: hld* 6/1

3 ½ **Found (IRE)**[22] 5697 2-9-0 JosephO'Brien 6 110
(A P O'Brien, Ire) *dwlt and hld up towards rr: 7th 3f out: prog fr 2f out to chse ldrs over 1f out where wandered u.p: clsr in 3rd wl ins fnl f: kpt on wl: a hld* 7/2[2]

4 ½ **Malabar**[22] 5664 2-9-0 101 MartinHarley 3 108
(Mick Channon) *towards rr: 9th 3f out: rdn under 2f out and clsd u.p to chse ldrs in 6th ins fnl f: kpt on wl towards fin to snatch nvr threatening 4th fnl stride* 5/1[3]

5 hd **Osaila (IRE)**[50] 4646 2-9-0 103 PatSmullen 4 108
(Richard Hannon) *cl up and sn settled bhd ldr: 3rd 1/2-way: effrt 1 1/2f out: sn no imp on wnr u.p in 2nd: one pce and dropped to 4th towards fin: denied 4th fnl stride* 11/1

6 2¼ **Qualify (IRE)**[21] 5734 2-9-0 100 MichaelHussey 10 102
(A P O'Brien, Ire) *cl up tl disp bef 1/2-way: sn led narrowly: extended advantage 2f out: sn rdn and hdd u.p over 1f out: wknd* 50/1

7 2¼ **Beach Belle**[21] 5734 2-9-0 106 ChrisHayes 9 96
(Kevin Prendergast, Ire) *dwlt and settled towards rr: last 3f out: rdn under 2f out and no imp on wnr in 9th ent fnl f: kpt on one pce towards fin* 16/1

8 hd **Jeanne Girl (IRE)**[21] 5734 2-9-0 100 NGMcCullagh 1 95
(Mrs John Harrington, Ire) *sn led tl jnd bef 1/2-way: sn hdd narrowly: rdn over 2f out and sn wknd* 33/1

9 5 **I Am Beautiful (IRE)**[21] 5734 2-9-0 100 ColmO'Donoghue 5 82
(A P O'Brien, Ire) *hld up: clsr in 4th 3f out: rdn 2f out and sn wknd* 50/1

10 2½ **Simply A Star (IRE)**[22] 5701 2-9-0 98 SeamieHeffernan 7 75
(A P O'Brien, Ire) *chsd ldrs: 4th 1/2-way: pushed along in 5th 3f out and sn wknd* 33/1

1m 24.8s (-6.00) **Going Correction** -0.60s/f (Hard) 10 Ran SP% 119.3
Speed ratings: **110,109,109,108,108 105,103,102,97,94**
CSF £10.30 CT £25.46 TOTE £2.10: £1.02, £1.90, £1.80; DF 11.00 Trifecta £40.40.
**Owner** Merry Fox Stud Limited **Bred** Merry Fox Stud Limited **Trained** Newmarket, Suffolk

**FOCUS**
The winner improved on her Lowther form to hold the possibly unlucky runner-up.

## 6373a GOFFS VINCENT O'BRIEN NATIONAL STKS (GROUP 1) (ENTIRE COLTS & FILLIES) 7f
4:15 (4:15) 2-Y-0 £145,000 (£47,500; £22,500; £7,500; £5,000)

RPR

1 **Gleneagles (IRE)**[21] 5735 2-9-3 113 JosephO'Brien 5 116+
(A P O'Brien, Ire) *w.w in rr: last 1/2-way: hdwy on outer fr over 2f out: rdn to ld ent fnl f and extended advantage towards fin: comf* 1/3[1]

2 1½ **Toscanini (IRE)**[28] 5472 2-9-3 105 ShaneFoley 2 111
(M Halford, Ire) *chsd ldrs: 4th 1/2-way: tk clsr order bhd ldrs 2f out: effrt in 2nd 1f out and sn no imp on wnr: kpt on same pce* 7/1[3]

3 1 **Dutch Connection**[25] 5576 2-9-3 102 GeorgeBaker 1 108
(Charles Hills) *led and disp early tl settled bhd ldr in 2nd after 1f: racd keenly: impr to ld 2f out: hdd ent fnl f and sn no imp on wnr u.p in 3rd: kpt on same pce* 9/2[2]
4 2 3/4 **Hall Of Fame (IRE)**[21] 5735 2-9-3 104 (t) KevinManning 4 101
(J S Bolger, Ire) *dwlt sltly: chsd ldrs in 3rd: tk clsr order and rdn over 2f out: sn no ex and dropped towards rr 1f out: kpt on one pce* 16/1
5 1 1/2 **Toscanelli (IRE)**[17] 5868 2-9-3 94 (b) SeamieHeffernan 3 97
(A P O'Brien, Ire) *cl up and led after 1f: 3 l clr 1/2-way: reduced advantage fr under 3f out and hdd 2f out: sn dropped to rr and no ex u.p over 1f out* 50/1

1m 25.29s (-5.51) **Going Correction** -0.60s/f (Hard) 5 Ran SP% 113.5
Speed ratings: **107,105,104,101,99**
CSF £3.68 TOTE £1.30: £1.02, £3.20; DF 3.30 Trifecta £8.50.
**Owner** Michael Tabor & Mrs John Magnier & Derrick Smith **Bred** You'resothrilling Syndicate **Trained** Cashel, Co Tipperary

**FOCUS**
Weakly contested for what can be a very strong Group 1.

## 6374a PALMERSTOWN HOUSE ESTATE IRISH ST LEGER (GROUP 1) 1m 6f
**4:50** (4:53) 3-Y-O+
**£145,000** (£47,500; £22,500; £7,500; £5,000; £2,500)

RPR
1 **Brown Panther**[45] 4823 6-9-11 113 RichardKingscote 5 119+
(Tom Dascombe) *chsd ldr in 2nd: led gng best wl over 2f out: sn clr and in command ent fnl f: styd on wl: easily* 14/1
2 6 1/2 **Leading Light (IRE)**[21] 5736 4-9-11 118 (p) JosephO'Brien 10 110+
(A P O'Brien, Ire) *hld up: 6th 1/2-way: pushed along and tk clsr order under 3f out: sn rdn and no imp on easy wnr in 3rd where edgd rt over 1f out: kpt on into mod 2nd wl ins fnl f: nt trble wnr* 9/10[1]
3 hd **Encke (USA)**[44] 4849 5-9-11 114 AdamKirby 7 110+
(Charlie Appleby) *hld up: 5th 1/2-way: tk clsr order under 3f out: sn rdn and wnt 3rd u.p between horses under 2f out: no imp on easy wnr in 2nd ent fnl f: dropped to mod 3rd clsng stages* 9/1
4 1 1/2 **Willing Foe (USA)**[29] 5432 7-9-11 111 FMBerry 1 108+
(Saeed bin Suroor) *prom early: hld up: 7th 1/2-way: hdwy to chse ldrs over 2f out: rdn in 5th over 1f out and no imp on easy wnr: kpt on same pce into mod 4th ins fnl f* 10/1
5 2 1/2 **Pale Mimosa (IRE)**[23] 5652 5-9-8 111 PatSmullen 4 101+
(D K Weld, Ire) *chsd ldrs: 3rd 1/2-way: rdn into 2nd under 2f out and no imp on easy wnr over 1f out: no ex and one pce ins fnl f* 9/2[2]
6 1 3/4 **Royal Diamond (IRE)**[21] 5736 8-9-11 112 NGMcCullagh 8 102+
(J P Murtagh, Ire) *in rr of mid-div: racd keenly: 8th 1/2-way: tk clsr order under 3f out: rdn and no imp on wnr 2f out: kpt on one pce ins fnl f* 16/1
7 hd **Pallasator**[22] 5693 5-9-11 111 AndreaAtzeni 6 101+
(Sir Mark Prescott Bt) *on toes and unruly befhand: chsd ldrs: 4th 1/2-way: racd keenly: rdn and no imp on easy wnr 2f out: hmpd between horses over 1f out and dropped to 6th: kpt on one pce* 6/1[3]
8 2 3/4 **Shu Lewis (IRE)**[21] 5736 8-9-8 103 SeamieHeffernan 9 95+
(Ms M Dowdall Blake, Ire) *in rr of mid-div: 9th 1/2-way: swtchd rt over 2f out and no imp on ldrs over 1f out: kpt on one pce* 66/1
9 13 **Certerach (IRE)**[23] 5652 6-9-11 110 ShaneFoley 2 79+
(M Halford, Ire) *dwlt and w.w: last 1/2-way: pushed along in 9th appr st and no imp over 2f out* 66/1
10 3/4 **Eye Of The Storm (IRE)**[29] 5457 4-9-11 110 ColmO'Donoghue 3 78+
(A P O'Brien, Ire) *sn led: hdd over 2f out and no ch w wnr: wknd and eased* 50/1
11 15 **Achtung**[15] 5936 4-9-11 50 GaryCarroll 11 57
(Luke Comer, Ire) *towards rr: 10th 1/2-way: pushed along in rr and no imp appr st: nvr a factor* 200/1

2m 57.15s (-12.25) **Going Correction** -0.35s/f (Firm) 11 Ran SP% 122.2
Speed ratings: **121,117,117,116,114 113,113,112,104,104 95**
CSF £28.25 CT £138.63 TOTE £10.30: £2.70, £1.02, £3.30; DF 37.80 Trifecta £265.10.
**Owner** A Black & Owen Promotions Limited **Bred** Owen Promotions Ltd **Trained** Malpas, Cheshire

**FOCUS**
A truly extraordinary race which you don't see too often at this level.

## 6375a TATTERSALLS IRELAND SUPER AUCTION SALE STKS 6f 63y
**5:20** (5:28) 2-Y-O
**£82,291** (£32,291; £19,791; £11,458; £5,208; £1,041)

RPR
1 **Midterm Break (IRE)**[22] 5672 2-9-3 86 GrahamGibbons 16 89
(David Barron) *chsd ldrs: 3rd 1/2-way: rdn to ld 1f out and kpt on wl towards fin: all out* 16/1
2 1/2 **Explosive Lady (IRE)**[20] 5770 2-8-10 95 BenCurtis 29 84+
(K R Burke) *in tch: rdn over 2f out and tk clsr order: swtchd rt in 6th ins fnl f and r.o wl towards fin into nvr nrr 2nd fnl strides: hld* 4/1[2]
3 shd **Realtra (IRE)**[24] 5608 2-8-8 95 TonyHamilton 14 78
(Richard Fahey) *chsd ldrs: 5th 1/2-way: effrt over 1f out: ev ch in cl 2nd wl ins fnl f: no ex and denied 2nd fnl strides* 7/2[1]
4 1/2 **Fruity (IRE)**[79] 3648 2-8-12 83 AndreaAtzeni 15 81
(Clive Cox) *chsd ldrs: 4th 1/2-way: rdn and tk clsr order over 1f out: cl 2nd ins fnl f and no ex clsng stages and dropped to 4th* 7/1
5 3/4 **Captain My Captain (IRE)**[22] 5698 2-8-13 ShaneFoley 3 80+
(John Joseph Murphy, Ire) *in tch far side: rdn under 2f out and no imp on ldrs ins fnl f: kpt on same pce towards fin into nvr threatening 5th on line* 25/1
6 nse **Intense Pride (IRE)**[26] 5538 2-8-11 RonanWhelan 26 77
(T Hogan, Ire) *chsd ldrs: rdn under 2f out and tk clsr order whn swtchd rt ins fnl f: no ex u.p in 5th clsng stages: denied 5th on line* 25/1
7 1/2 **Ivors Rebel**[15] 5906 2-8-13 72 LiamKeniry 23 78
(David Elsworth) *sn led: rdn and hdd 1f out: sn no ex u.p and one pce towards fin* 33/1
8 3/4 **Mattydillon**[11] 6046 2-8-13 ChrisHayes 27 76
(Kevin Prendergast, Ire) *in tch: rdn 2f out and sme hdwy u.p 1f out: no imp on ldrs ins fnl f: kpt on one pce* 50/1
9 shd **Outback Ruler (IRE)**[19] 5782 2-8-13 73 PatSmullen 10 75+
(Clive Cox) *in tch: rdn fr 2f out and no imp on ldrs ins fnl f: kpt on towards fin* 25/1
10 shd **Duca Valentinois (IRE)**[27] 5513 2-8-13 NGMcCullagh 18 75
(J P Murtagh, Ire) *in tch: rdn and no imp on ldrs over 1f out: kpt on one pce* 50/1
11 hd **Diaz (IRE)**[29] 5431 2-9-1 95 FMBerry 28 77
(Mark Johnston) *prom: cl 2nd 1/2-way: rdn 2f out and sn no ex u.p: wknd fnl f* 6/1[3]
12 nk **The Ice Meister (IRE)**[32] 5323 2-9-3 89 (p) GaryCarroll 17 78
(G M Lyons, Ire) *in tch: 11th 1/2-way: sme hdwy u.p over 1f out: no ex ins fnl f whn forced sltly rt: wknd clsng stages* 11/1
13 1/2 **Mzuri (IRE)**[6] 6198 2-8-8 MichaelHussey 11 67
(Ms Sheila Lavery, Ire) *racd in mid-div: 12th 1/2-way: rdn and no imp over 1f out: kpt on one pce* 33/1
14 1/2 **Come Uppence**[29] 5408 2-8-11 72 JFEgan 2 69
(David Evans) *in rr of mid-div: pushed along after 1/2-way and no imp u.p ins fnl f: kpt on towards fin* 33/1
15 shd **Just Marion (IRE)**[10] 6072 2-8-8 59 ConnorKing 25 65
(David Evans) *nvr bttr than mid-div: rdn and no imp over 1f out: nt clr run briefly bhd horses ins fnl f: kpt on one pce* 50/1
16 nk **Ventura Shadow**[19] 5790 2-8-12 72 DanielTudhope 22 69
(Richard Fahey) *in tch: rdn and no ex over 1f out: kpt on one pce* 33/1
17 nk **Buccaneers Vault (IRE)**[22] 5680 2-9-1 83 PaulMulrennan 1 71
(Michael Dods) *in tch: rdn and no imp under 2f out: kpt on one pce ins fnl f* 25/1
18 1 3/4 **Maureb (IRE)**[22] 5680 2-8-8 71 BarryMcHugh 12 60
(Tony Coyle) *in tch: rdn 2f out and no imp over 1f out: one pce fnl f* 66/1
19 1/2 **Devious Spirit (IRE)**[34] 5241 2-8-13 EmmetMcNamara 19 62
(Richard Fahey) *racd in mid-div: rdn 2f out and sn no ex u.p: kpt on one pce fnl f* 33/1
20 1 **No Fear (IRE)**[18] 5839 2-9-1 66 SeamieHeffernan 24 61
(W McCreery, Ire) *in tch: pushed along fr 1/2-way and no ex u.p 2f out: wknd fnl f* 40/1
21 1 1/4 **Spirit Of Wedza (IRE)**[37] 5153 2-9-1 80 WayneLordan 13 57
(David Wachman, Ire) *in tch: rdn and wknd over 1f out* 50/1
22 4 1/2 **Zebed (IRE)**[18] 5839 2-8-13 72 (p) DeclanMcDonogh 5 42
(John M Oxx, Ire) *in rr of mid-div: rdn and no imp under 2f out: one pce* 50/1
23 2 1/2 **Paco's Sunshine (IRE)**[47] 4751 2-8-6 [1] RoryCleary 7 28
(Brian Ellison) *in rr of mid-div: rdn and no ex fr 1/2-way: wknd* 33/1
24 2 1/4 **Make On Madam (IRE)**[87] 3403 2-8-8 71 ColmO'Donoghue 20 23
(Brian Ellison) *in rr: rdn and wknd fr 1/2-way* 20/1
25 2 1/4 **Dancing Bride (IRE)**[7] 6175 2-8-6 ConorHoban 6 14
(John C McConnell, Ire) *a bhd: rdn and no imp 1/2-way* 66/1
26 nk **Vocal Nation (IRE)**[35] 5216 2-8-10 [1] KevinManning 8 18
(J S Bolger, Ire) *towards rr thrght: rdn and no imp fr 1/2-way* 33/1
27 nse **Charava (IRE)**[18] 5835 2-8-11 72 BillyLee 9 18
(W McCreery, Ire) *towards rr: rdn and no imp fr after 1/2-way* 50/1
28 2 **Newton Bomb (IRE)**[26] 5538 2-8-8 66 LeighRoche 4 9+
(W McCreery, Ire) *chsd ldrs far side early: rdn and wknd 1/2-way: eased 1 1/2f out* 50/1
29 nk **Dandyleekie (IRE)**[7] 6174 2-9-3 93 (p) JosephO'Brien 30 18
(G M Lyons, Ire) *racd in mid-div: rdn and wknd 2f out: eased* 9/1

1m 16.49s (-2.61) **Going Correction** -0.35s/f (Firm) 29 Ran SP% 153.1
Speed ratings: **103,102,102,101,100 100,99,98,98,98 98,97,97,96,96 96,95,93,92,91 89,83,80,77,74 73,73,71,70**
CSF £77.43 TOTE £23.10: £6.40, £2.40, £2.10; DF 228.30 Trifecta £1409.10.
**Owner** Laurence O'Kane & Harrowgate B'stk Ltd **Bred** J O'Connor **Trained** Maunby, N Yorks

**FOCUS**
The value of a high draw or the ability to get across quickly from a low one was likely to be well-advertised in this race.

# 4955 DUSSELDORF (R-H)
Sunday, September 14

**OFFICIAL GOING: Turf: good**

## 6377a GROSSER PREIS VON ENGEL & VOLKERS DUSSELDORF - 90TH JUNIOREN-PREIS (LISTED RACE) (2YO) (TURF) 1m
**3:05** (12:00) 2-Y-O **£11,666** (£5,416; £2,500; £1,250)

RPR
1 **Molly Le Clou (GER)**[35] 2-9-0 0 SHellyn 5 95
(J Hirschberger, Germany) 9/5[2]
2 shd **Groor**[16] 5876 2-9-0 0 DavidAllan 2 95
(James Tate) *led tl hdd and chsd ldr on rail after 1f: rdn to chal 2f out: led 1 1/2f out and drvn 2 l clr appr fnl f: hdd 75yds out: rallied u.p: jst hld* 7/5[1]
3 2 **Nabhan**[54] 4524 2-9-0 0 JBojko 1 90
(A Wohler, Germany) 7/2[3]
4 1 **Ebeltoft (IRE)** 2-9-0 0 AHelfenbein 4 88
(P Schiergen, Germany) 7/2[3]
5 14 **Zazoulino (GER)** 2-9-2 0 StefanieHofer 3 56
(P Vovcenko, Germany) 83/10

1m 40.87s (-0.29) 5 Ran SP% 132.6
WIN (incl. 10 euro stake): 28. PLACES: 16, 15. SF: 105.
**Owner** Gestut Auenquelle **Bred** Gestut Auenquelle **Trained** Germany

# 6244 LONGCHAMP (R-H)
Sunday, September 14

**OFFICIAL GOING: Turf: good**

## 6378a QATAR PRIX DU PETIT COUVERT (GROUP 3) (3YO+) (TURF) 5f (S)
**12:30** (12:00) 3-Y-O+ **£33,333** (£13,333; £10,000; £6,666; £3,333)

RPR
1 **Mirza**[15] 5911 7-8-13 0 (p) FrankieDettori 4 113
(Rae Guest) *sn disputing ld on rail: rdn over 1f out: led ent fnl f: kpt on strly and asserted: readily* 7/1
2 1/2 **Move In Time**[25] 5575 6-8-13 0 RichardHughes 6 111
(David O'Meara) *midfield: rdn and hdwy on outer over 1f out: r.o and wnt 2nd fnl f: nt pce of wnr* 13/2[3]
3 1 **Caledonia Lady**[45] 4841 5-8-9 0 AlexisBadel 11 104+
(Mme M Bollack-Badel, France) *hld up: rdn 2f out: r.o down wd outside fnl f and wnt 3rd post: nrst fin* 14/1
4 1 1/2 **Wind Fire (USA)**[44] 4852 3-8-8 0 GeraldMosse 7 99
(David Brown) *w ldrs early: dropped bk 3f out: rdn in midfield 2f out: kpt on same pce and hld: wnt 5th post: fin 5th: plcd 4th* 10/1
5 shd **Caspian Prince (IRE)**[7] 6172 5-8-13 0 LukeMorris 9 103
(Tony Carroll) *disp ld in centre: rdn 2f out: hdd ent fnl f: no ex and fdd: dropped to 6th post: fin 6th: plcd 5th* 12/1

**6** ½ **Catcall (FR)**105 2820 5-9-2 0.......................................... OlivierPeslier 3 104
(P Sogorb, France) *hld up in rr on rail: rdn over 1f out: swtchd rt whn short of room fnl f: nvr able to chal: fin 7th: plcd 6th* **5/2**1

**7** *nk* **Penmaen (IRE)**66 4-8-9 0.......................................... FabienLefebvre 10 96
(J E Hammond, France) *a in rr: rdn in last over 1f out: no imp fnl f: nvr a factor: fin 8th: plcd 7th* **12/1**

**8** *2* **Cambio De Planes**22 5-8-13 0..................(p) Pierre-CharlesBoudot 5 93
(C Delcher-Sanchez, France) *in tch: rdn 2f out: keeping on same pce and hld whn short of room on rail towards fin: snatched up and lost all momentum: eased and dropped to last: fin 9th: plcd 8th* **16/1**

**D** *shd* **Rangali**23 5654 3-9-3 0.......................................... FabriceVeron 8 113
(H-A Pantall, France) *trckd ldrs: rdn and effrt to chal over 1f out: edgd lft and kpt on same pce fnl f: dropped to 4th post: fin 4th: disqualified and plcd last* **10/3**2

55.68s (-0.62)
**WFA** 3 from 4yo+ 1lb **9** Ran SP% **114.5**
WIN (incl. 1 euro stake): 4.00. PLACES: 2.10, 4.00, 4.40. DF: 20.10. SF: 34.30.
**Owner** C J Mills **Bred** C J Mills **Trained** Newmarket, Suffolk

## 6379a QATAR PRIX NIEL (GROUP 2) (3YO COLTS & FILLIES) (TURF) 1m 4f
**1:30** (12:00) 3-Y-O £61,750 (£23,833; £11,375; £7,583; £3,791)

RPR

**1** **Ectot**154 1481 3-9-2 0.......................................... GregoryBenoist 8 117+
(E Lellouche, France) *t.k.h: stdd and hld up in last: smooth hdwy on outer 2f out: qckned smartly to ld gng strly over 1f out: rdn fnl f: styd on: idling and reduced advantage at fin but a doing enough: shade cosily* **15/8**1

**2** *nk* **Teletext (USA)**63 4251 3-9-2 0.......................... Christophe-PatriceLemaire 6 116
(P Bary, France) *hld up towards rr: last 2f out: rdn and gd hdwy into 2nd over 1f out: styd on and clsd on wnr fnl f but a being hld* **9/2**3

**3** 1¼ **Adelaide (IRE)**29 5458 3-9-2 0.......................................... RyanMoore 1 114+
(A P O'Brien, Ire) *hld up towards rr: clsd on rail 5f out: shuffled bk whn nt clr run fr 2f out tl angled lft and rdn over 1f out: styd on v strly fnl f and wnt 3rd cl home: unlucky* **5/1**

**4** ½ **Elliptique (IRE)**126 2194 3-9-2 0.......................................... MaximeGuyon 5 113
(A Fabre, France) *t.k.h: restrained early and hld up in midfield: pushed along to cl 2f out: rdn and outpcd by wnr over 1f out: styd on fnl f but hld: dropped to 4th cl home* **14/1**

**5** *6* **Guardini (FR)**63 4251 3-9-2 0.......................................... ChristopheSoumillon 4 104
(Jean-Pierre Carvalho, Germany) *prom on inner: nt clr run on rail 2f out and shuffled bk to rr: sn lost all ch: kpt on under hand ride fnl f but nt rcvr* **14/1**

**6** ¾ **Gallante (IRE)**63 4251 3-9-2 0.......................................... Pierre-CharlesBoudot 7 102
(A Fabre, France) *trckd ldr early: sn midfield in tch: effrt gng strly 2f out: pushed along and readily outpcd by wnr over 1f out: fnd little under v considerate ride and wknd fnl f* **10/3**2

**7** *7* **Vadamos (FR)**50 4694 3-9-2 0.......................................... Francois-XavierBertras 3 91
(F Rohaut, France) *t.k.h under restraint whn hld up early and sn allowed to stride on: trckd ldr: chal and w ldr 2f out: rdn and hdd over 1f out: sn no ex and btn: wknd: eased towards fin* **14/1**

**8** *15* **Serans (FR)**154 1481 3-9-2 0.......................................... CyrilleStefan 2 67
(E Lellouche, France) *led: rdn and strly pressed 2f out: hdd over 1f out: qckly btn and wknd on rail: eased over 1f out: t.o* **200/1**

2m 26.36s (-4.04) **Going Correction** -0.025s/f (Good) **8** Ran SP% **113.2**
Speed ratings: **112,111,110,110,106 106,101,91**
WIN (incl. 1 euro stake): 2.90 (Ectot coupled with Serans). PLACES: 1.40, 1.50, 1.50. DF: 7.30. SF: 12.50.
**Owner** Al Shaqab Racing **Bred** Skymarc Farm Inc And Ecurie Des Monceaux **Trained** Lamorlaye, France

**FOCUS**
Traditionally a strong Arc trial, although you have to go back to Rail Link in 2006 to find the last winner to emerge from this race. This was run at a fair gallop and the time was the fastest of the three trials.

## 6380a QATAR PRIX VERMEILLE (GROUP 1) (3YO+ FILLIES & MARES) (TURF) 1m 4f
**2:45** (12:00) 3-Y-O+ £166,658 (£66,675; £33,337; £16,654; £8,341)

RPR

**1** **Baltic Baroness (GER)**56 4484 4-9-3 0.......................................... MaximeGuyon 2 113
(A Fabre, France) *a.p on inner: pushed along and effrt between rivals whn short of room briefly 2f out: rdn and swtchd bk to rail over 1f out: styd on and persistent chal fnl f: drvn and edgd ahd towards fin: jst prevailed* **22/1**

**2** *shd* **Pomology (USA)**71 3961 4-9-3 0.......................................... WilliamBuick 4 113
(John Gosden) *sn led: rdn 2f out: strly pressed fnl f: drvn and styd on gamely but hdd towards fin and jst hld* **9/2**2

**3** 1¼ **Dolniya (FR)**77 3773 3-8-9 0 ow1.......................................... ChristopheSoumillon 9 112+
(A De Royer-Dupre, France) *hld up towards rr: rdn and hdwy over 1f out: styd on steadily fnl f and wnt 3rd cl home: nvr able to chal* **7/1**3

**4** *hd* **Treve (FR)**88 3354 4-9-3 0.......................................... ThierryJarnet 8 113+
(Mme C Head-Maarek, France) *stdd and hld up in last: fanned wd into st: pushed along and hdwy fr 2f out: rdn and edgd rt over 1f out: styd on same pce fnl f and nt given hrd time once hld towards fin* **4/5**1

**5** *snk* **Sultanina**43 4894 4-9-3 0.......................................... RyanMoore 3 110
(John Gosden) *led early: sn hdd and trckd ldr: rdn and effrt to chal over 2f out: outpcd by front pair ent fnl f: styd on but hld after and lost 2 pls cl home* **7/1**3

**6** 1¾ **Madame Chiang**100 2960 3-8-8 0.......................................... MickaelBarzalona 7 108
(David Simcock) *midfield in tch: rdn 3f out: outpcd by ldrs over 1f out: plugged on fnl f but wl hld* **33/1**

**7** 1½ **Siljan's Saga (FR)**77 3774 4-9-3 0.......................................... Pierre-CharlesBoudot 1 105
(J-P Gauvin, France) *t.k.h: midfield in tch on inner: rdn over 1f out: outpcd and fdd fnl f* **20/1**

**8** *6* **Red Lips (GER)**21 5742 4-9-3 0.......................................... FabriceVeron 6 96
(Andreas Lowe, Germany) *t.k.h: midfield: rdn 3f out: outpcd and dropped to rr over 1f out: sn btn: eased towards fin* **50/1**

**9** 1¼ **Chalnetta (FR)**29 5462 4-9-3 0.......................................... JulienAuge 10 94
(C Ferland, France) *midfield in tch on outer: rdn to cl and brief effrt into st: outpcd and dropped to rr over 1f out: last and btn fnl f: eased* **40/1**

2m 28.22s (-2.18) **Going Correction** -0.025s/f (Good)
**WFA** 3 from 4yo+ 9lb **9** Ran SP% **115.2**
Speed ratings: **106,105,105,104,104 103,102,98,97**
WIN (incl. 1 euro stake): 21.30. PLACES: 3.60, 1.80, 1.80. DF: 40.40. SF: 121.60.
**Owner** Gestut Ammerland **Bred** Gestut Ammerland **Trained** Chantilly, France

**FOCUS**
Quite the turn up here.

## 6381a QATAR PRIX FOY (GROUP 2) (4YO+ NO GELDINGS) (TURF) 1m 4f
**3:25** (12:00) 4-Y-O+ £61,750 (£23,833; £11,375; £7,583; £3,791)

RPR

**1** **Ruler Of The World (IRE)**169 1183 4-9-2 0..................(p) FrankieDettori 4 121
(A P O'Brien, Ire) *mde all: rdn and kicked clr over 1f out: styd on strly fnl f: reduced advantage towards fin but and in full control: readily: gd ride* **3/1**3

**2** 1½ **Flintshire**77 3774 4-9-2 0.......................................... MaximeGuyon 6 119+
(A Fabre, France) *midfield: rdn and wnt 2nd over 1f out: styd on and chsd wnr fnl f: clsd towards fin but n.d* **6/4**1

**3** 1½ **Spiritjim (FR)**77 3774 4-9-2 0.......................................... Christophe-PatriceLemaire 1 117
(P Bary, France) *prom on inner: restrained off heels early stages: rdn and outpcd by wnr over 1f out: styd on for wl hld 3rd fnl f* **11/4**2

**4** *2* **Au Revoir (IRE)**129 2106 4-9-2 0.......................................... Pierre-CharlesBoudot 2 113
(A Fabre, France) *trckd wnr: rdn and outpcd over 1f out: no ex and fdd fnl f* **14/1**

**5** ¾ **Kingsbarns (IRE)**21 5733 4-9-2 0.......................................... RyanMoore 3 112
(A P O'Brien, Ire) *hld up towards rr: rdn over 1f out: outpcd and btn fnl f: n.d* **10/1**

**6** *snk* **Meleagros (IRE)**35 5224 5-9-2 0.......................................... AdrienFouassier 5 112
(Alain Couetil, France) *dwlt and hld up: last thrght: rdn 2f out: sn no imp and btn: nvr a factor* **33/1**

2m 26.93s (-3.47) **Going Correction** -0.025s/f (Good) **6** Ran SP% **110.4**
Speed ratings: **110,109,108,106,106 106**
WIN (incl. 1 euro stake): 4.50. PLACES: 1.90, 1.40. SF: 11.50.
**Owner** Al Shaqab Racing, Magnier, Tabor & Smith **Bred** Southern Bloodstock **Trained** Cashel, Co Tipperary

**FOCUS**
Traditionally the weakest of the three trials and the two with the strongest form dominated.

## 6382a QATAR PRIX DU MOULIN DE LONGCHAMP (GROUP 1) (3YO+ NO GELDINGS) (TURF) 1m
**3:55** (12:00) 3-Y-O+ £214,275 (£85,725; £42,862; £21,412; £10,725)

RPR

**1** **Charm Spirit (IRE)**62 4278 3-8-11 0.......................................... ThierryJarnet 1 121+
(F Head, France) *prom on inner: pushed along and chal on rail over 1f out: sn led: strly pressed thrght fnl f but r.o wl and a jst doing enough* **11/2**3

**2** *hd* **Toronado (IRE)**46 4779 4-9-2 0.......................................... RichardHughes 6 122+
(Richard Hannon) *trckd ldr: rdn to chal over 1f out: w wnr ent fnl f: kpt on wl and sustained battle to fin but a jst being hld* **11/10**1

**3** *nk* **Night Of Thunder (IRE)**71 3984 3-8-11 0.......................................... RyanMoore 2 120+
(Richard Hannon) *dwlt sltly and hld up towards rr on inner: rdn 2f out: r.o and wnt 3rd ins fnl f: clsd on front pair and nrst fin but nvr able to chal* **9/2**2

**4** *1* **Esoterique (IRE)**42 4954 4-8-13 0.......................................... MaximeGuyon 8 116+
(A Fabre, France) *hld up towards rr: rdn over 1f out: r.o strly fnl f and wnt 4th cl home: nvr nrr* **8/1**

**5** ¾ **Bawina (IRE)**30 5407 3-8-8 0.......................................... OlivierPeslier 7 113
(C Laffon-Parias, France) *midfield: pushed along 2f out: rdn and wnt 4th jst ins fnl f: kpt on same pce and sn hld: dropped to 5th cl home* **10/1**

**6** *nk* **Sommerabend**35 5223 7-9-2 0.......................................... TheoBachelot 4 116
(M Rulec, Germany) *t.k.h: midfield in tch: rdn over 1f out: kpt on same pce and hld fnl f* **25/1**

**7** 1¾ **Mogadishio (FR)**13 7-9-2 0.......................................... DelphineSantiago 5 112?
(S Smrczek, Germany) *led: rdn and strly pressed over 1f out: sn hdd: no ex and wknd fnl f* **100/1**

**8** *2* **Grand Vintage (FR)**13 5-9-2 0.......................................... StephanePasquier 10 108?
(W Mongil, Germany) *dwlt and hld up in rr: ct on heels and restrained after 2f: rdn 2f out: sn no imp and btn: nvr a factor* **100/1**

**9** *hd* **Decathlete (USA)**26 3-8-11 0.......................................... MickaelBarzalona 9 106
(A Fabre, France) *hld up in rr: pushed along in last 2f out: no imp and btn fnl f: nvr a factor* **16/1**

**10** 1¼ **Master Carpenter (IRE)**56 4483 3-8-11 0.......................................... ChristopheSoumillon 3 103
(Rod Millman) *midfield on inner: pushed along over 1f out: wknd on rail wout being given hrd time and eased fnl f: dropped to last towards fin* **40/1**

1m 35.9s (-2.50) **Going Correction** -0.025s/f (Good)
**WFA** 3 from 4yo+ 5lb **10** Ran SP% **115.5**
Speed ratings: **111,110,110,109,108 108,106,104,104,103**
Win (incl. 1 euro stake): 7.10. PLACES: 1.80, 1.30, 1.90. DF: 8.00. SF: 12.40.
**Owner** H H Sheikh Abdulla Bin Khalifa Al Thani **Bred** Ecurie Des Monceaux **Trained** France

**FOCUS**
Strong form, with the three market principals, all of whom boast some top-class form to their name, dominating the finish.

## 6383a QATAR PRIX GLADIATEUR (GROUP 3) (4YO+) (TURF) 1m 7f 110y
**4:25** (12:00) 4-Y-O+ £33,333 (£13,333; £10,000; £6,666; £3,333)

RPR

**1** **Bathyrhon (GER)**21 5743 4-8-11 0.......................................... MaximeGuyon 9 112
(Mme Pia Brandt, France) *wl in tch in midfield: rdn and effrt 2f out: str run to ld 1f out: in command ins fnl f: r.o wl* **14/1**

**2** *2* **Kicky Blue (GER)**29 5462 4-8-8 0.......................................... MickaelBarzalona 3 107
(T Clout, France) *in tch in midfield: nt clrest of runs and swtchd lft 2f out: hdwy u.p over 1f out: styd on wl to go 2nd wl ins fnl f: nvr gng to rch wnr* **16/1**

**3** ½ **High Jinx (IRE)**49 4722 6-9-0 0.......................................... RyanMoore 4 112
(James Fanshawe) *led: rdn and qcknd 3f out: hdd and no ex 1f out: kpt on same pce after and lost 2nd wl ins fnl f* **3/1**1

**4** 1½ **Hidden Cove (IRE)**33 4-8-8 0.......................................... GeraldMosse 10 104
(A De Royer-Dupre, France) *chsd ldrs: rdn over 2f out: kpt on same pce fnl 2f and no imp fnl 2f* **16/1**

**5** *nk* **Trip To Rhodos (FR)**49 4722 5-8-11 0.......................................... CristianDemuro 6 107
(Pavel Tuma, Czech Republic) *hld up in tch in last trio: rdn and effrt 2f out: styd on wl u.p ins fnl f: nvr threatened ldrs* **7/1**3

**6** *snk* **Ederan (IRE)**49 4722 4-8-11 0.......................................... Pierre-CharlesBoudot 1 107
(Rod Collet, France) *in tch in midfield: trapped on inner 4f out: effrt u.p 2f out: kpt on wl u.p ins fnl f: nvr able to chal* **12/1**

**7** *shd* **Going Somewhere (BRZ)**14 5962 5-9-0 0.......................................... GregoryBenoist 2 110
(D Smaga, France) *chsd ldr tl 6f out: chsd ldrs tl wnt 2nd again 3f out tl no ex u.p over 1f out: outpcd fnl f* **3/1**1

8 *7* **Domeside**[83] 8-9-2 0........ ChristopheSoumillon 8 103
(M Delcher Sanchez, France) *hld up in tch in rr: rdn and btn 2f out: bhd fnl f* **6/1**[2]

9 *½* **Goldtara (FR)**[63] 4250 6-8-10 0........ Christophe-PatriceLemaire 5 97
(A Lyon, France) *in tch in midfield: rdn and effrt over 2f out: wknd over 1f out: bhd fnl f* **11/1**

10 *10* **Biladi (FR)**[25] 5-8-11 0........ OlivierPeslier 11 86
(X Thomas-Demeaulte, France) *chsd ldrs: rdn and unable qck over 2f out: sn wknd: bhd fnl f* **16/1**

11 *2* **Les Beaufs (FR)**[83] 5-9-0 0........ JulienGuillochon 7 86
(Mme V Seignoux, France) *hld up in last trio: hdwy on outer 1/2-way: jnd ldr 6f out tl rdn and lost pl 3f out: bhd fnl f* **16/1**

3m 15.76s (-5.74) **Going Correction** -0.025s/f (Good) **11** Ran SP% **123.0**
Speed ratings: **113,112,111,111,110 110,110,107,106,101 100**
WIN (incl. 1 euro stake): 17.80. PLACES: 4.00, 4.50, 1.70. DF: 102.60. SF: 116.40.
**Owner** Avaz Ismoilov **Bred** Frau I Meinke & D Meinke **Trained** France

## 4720 MUNICH (L-H)

Sunday, September 14

**OFFICIAL GOING: Turf: soft**

### 6384a BAYERISCHE HAUSBAU - WERTE, DIE BLEIBEN-RENNEN - GROSSE EUROPA MEILE (GROUP 3) (3YO+) (TURF) 1m

3:50 (12:00) 3-Y-O+

**£26,666** (£9,166; £4,583; £2,500; £1,666; £1,250)

RPR

1 **Nordico (GER)**[28] 5484 3-8-11 0........ EddyHardouin 1 105+
(Mario Hofer, Germany) *chsd ldrs: rdn and effrt 2f out: str chal ent fnl f: sustained duel w ldr after: r.o wl to ld fnl stride* **39/10**[2]

2 *nse* **Longina (GER)**[42] 4955 3-8-13 0........ AdriedeVries 5 107
(P Schiergen, Germany) *t.k.h: chsd ldr: rdn and effrt to ld over 1f out: hrd pressed and sustained duel w wnr fnl f: r.o wl: hdd fnl stride* **7/5**[1]

3 *1½* **Felician (GER)**[11] 6054 6-9-2 0........ AnthonyCrastus 3 103
(Ferdinand J Leve, Germany) *stdd after s: hld up in rr: rdn and hdwy over 1f out: pressed ldrs 1f out: no ex and outpcd fnl 50yds* **63/10**[3]

4 *2* **Marcelli (GER)**[21] 5-9-2 0........ FrauASchneider 4 98
(W Figge, Germany) *stdd after s: hld up in tch in last pair: rdn and effrt to chse ldrs jst over 1f out: hung lft and no ex ins fnl f: outpcd fnl 100yds* **15/2**

5 *¾* **Point Blank (GER)**[53] 6-9-2 0........ APietsch 2 96
(Mario Hofer, Germany) *led: rdn and qcknd 2f out: hdd over 1f out: no ex u.p and wknd ins fnl f* **17/1**

6 *3* **Artwork Genie (IRE)**[21] 3-8-8 0........ FilipMinarik 6 85
(Jean-Pierre Carvalho, Germany) *chsd ldrs: rdn and effrt 2f out: struggling and dropped to last 1f out: wknd fnl f* **15/2**

1m 43.54s (103.54)
**WFA** 3 from 4yo+ 5lb **6** Ran SP% **104.9**
WIN (incl. 10 euro stake): 49. PLACES: 16, 15. SF: 123.
**Owner** Eckhard Sauren **Bred** Gestut Brummerhof **Trained** Germany

## STRASBOURG

Sunday, September 14

**OFFICIAL GOING: Turf: very soft**

### 6385a PRIX URBAN TV (MAIDEN) (2YO) (TURF) 7f

2:00 (12:00) 2-Y-O **£6,666** (£2,666; £2,000; £1,333; £666)

RPR

1 **Yat Ding Yau (FR)**[41] 4973 2-8-13 0........ RonanThomas 10 72
(William Jarvis) *sn trcking ldr on outer: shkn up over 2f out: rdn to ld 1 1/2f out: drvn fnl f: grad asserted fnl 110yds* **68/10**

2 *2* **Celestial House**[91] 2-9-2 0........ AnthonyCaramanolis 1 70
(N Clement, France) **14/5**[1]

3 *2* **Morera (IRE)**[33] 5293 2-8-13 0........(b[1]) PatrickGibson 2 62
(P Schiergen, Germany) **42/10**[3]

4 *4* **Pennyking (FR)** 2-8-11 0........ FranciscoDaSilva 5 50
(Frau Marion Rotering, Germany) **41/10**[2]

5 *nk* **Agnes Seice (IRE)**[129] 2-8-13 0........ VendulaKoreckova 6 51
(V Luka Jr, Czech Republic) **11/1**

6 *1* **Panthero (FR)** 2-8-11 0........ FranckForesi 9 47
(J Antoniello, France) **213/10**

7 *2* **Black Rose (GER)** 2-8-8 0........ BertrandFlandrin 4 39
(Frau Marion Rotering, Germany) **237/10**

8 *2* **Yagulin (IRE)** 2-8-11 0........ TonyPiccone 8 37
(W Hefter, Germany) **76/10**

9 *¾* **Rouge Desir (FR)** 2-8-11 0........ AlexisAchard 11 35
(Mlle Y Vollmer, France) **134/10**

10 *15* **Miisele (FR)** 2-8-8 0........ LudovicProietti 3
(P Munsch, France) **233/10**

F **Sun My Dance (FR)** 2-8-3 0........ ChristmyDerhoua(5) 7
(C Schiff, France) **58/1**

1m 32.06s (92.06) **11** Ran SP% **119.2**
WIN (incl. 1 euro stake): 7.80. PLACES: 2.10, 1.70, 3.70. DF: 8.30..
**Owner** Dr J Walker **Bred** Mme I M Queron **Trained** Newmarket, Suffolk

## 3090 TABY (R-H)

Sunday, September 14

**OFFICIAL GOING: Turf: good; dirt: standard**

### 6386a AMACITALOPNING (CONDITIONS) (2YO FILLIES) (TURF) 5f 165y

1:30 (12:00) 2-Y-O **£14,071** (£7,035; £3,377; £2,251; £1,407)

RPR

1 **Red Caviar (SWE)** 2-9-4 0........ CarlosLopez 5 88
(Patrick Wahl, Sweden) **31/5**[3]

2 *2½* **Victoria Prada (FR)** 2-9-4 0........ Per-AndersGraberg 13 80
(Niels Petersen, Norway) **43/10**[2]

3 *nk* **Pretty Picture**[14] 5946 2-9-4 0........ TomQueally 3 79
(Gay Kelleway) *broke wl: sn outpcd: rdn and hdwy 1 1/2f out: r.o fnl f: nrest at fin* **5/2**[1]

4 *nse* **Antigua (SWE)** 2-9-4 0........ JacobJohansen 9 79
(Tommy Gustafsson, Sweden) **135/10**

5 *1* **Bubbles In Paris** 2-9-4 0........ ElioneChaves 4 76
(Lennart Reuterskiold Jr, Sweden) **144/10**

6 *1½* **Allinornothing (IRE)** 2-9-4 0........ RafaelSchistl 2 71
(Cathrine Witso Slettemark, Norway) **26/1**

7 *hd* **Dancewithastranger (IRE)** 2-9-4 0........ RafaeldeOliveira 1 70
(Cathrine Witso Slettemark, Norway) **77/10**

8 *nk* **Miss Alicia (IRE)** 2-9-4 0........ OliverWilson 10 69
(Bodil Hallencreutz, Sweden) **28/1**

9 *2½* **Mumm Mumm De Mumm (SWE)** 2-9-4 0........ FannyOlsson 8 61
(Tommy Gustafsson, Sweden) **76/10**

10 *hd* **Red Glory (SWE)** 2-9-4 0........ PatDobbs 14 60
(Henrik Engblom, Sweden) **47/1**

11 *1½* **Cafe Cortado (IRE)**[44] 4870 2-9-4 0........ RebeccaColldin 7 55
(Claes Bjorling, Sweden) **176/10**

12 *2* **Lille Prinsesse** 2-9-4 0........ MRobaldo 12 48
(Bent Olsen, Denmark) **33/1**

13 *2½* **Sugarpie (SWE)** 2-9-4 0........ MadeleineSmith 11 40
(Madeleine Smith, Sweden) **44/1**

14 *dist* **Miss Phone Girl** 2-9-4 0........ ManuelSantos 6
(Bent Olsen, Denmark) **114/10**

1m 9.2s (2.50) **14** Ran SP% **125.7**
PARI-MUTUEL (all including 1sek stake): WIN 7.20; PLACE 3.04, 1.83, 1.67; SF 68.62.
**Owner** Claes Andersson **Bred** Ravdansens Stuteri **Trained** Sweden

### 6387a TABY OPEN SPRINT CHAMPIONSHIP (LISTED RACE) (3YO+) (TURF) 5f 165y

2:05 (12:00) 3-Y-O+ **£18,761** (£9,380; £4,502; £3,001; £1,876)

RPR

1 **Ragazzo (NOR)**[45] 4957 5-9-4 0........(b) JacobJohansen 3 102
(Annike Bye Hansen, Norway) **19/10**[1]

2 *½* **Liber**[45] 4957 4-9-4 0........ OliverWilson 4 100
(Bent Olsen, Denmark) **34/1**

3 *1* **Beat Baby (IRE)**[124] 2244 7-9-4 0........ Per-AndersGraberg 11 97
(Niels Petersen, Norway) **19/10**[1]

4 *1½* **Ambiance (IRE)**[85] 3478 3-9-2 0........ TomQueally 1 92
(Katharina Stenefeldt, Sweden) **41/1**

5 *nk* **Over The Ocean (USA)**[45] 4957 4-9-4 0........ RafaelSchistl 7 91
(Niels Petersen, Norway) **78/10**[3]

6 *½* **Hansinger (IRE)**[80] 9-9-4 0........(b) ElioneChaves 2 89
(Cathrine Erichsen, Norway) **208/10**

7 *hd* **Ruwaiyan (USA)**[22] 5674 5-9-4 0........(p) KierenFallon 9 89
(James Tate) *w.w toward rr: pushed along 2 1/2f out: sme hdwy fnl 1 1/2f: nvr plcd to trble ldrs* **91/10**

8 *1¼* **Mr David (USA)**[71] 3996 7-9-4 0........(b) RebeccaColldin 5 85
(Claes Bjorling, Sweden) **59/10**[2]

9 *nse* **Umneyati**[36] 5165 3-8-13 0........ RobertHavlin 10 82
(James Tate) *hld up in rr: prog on inner 2f out: sn rdn and nt qckn: no further imp appr fnl f* **56/1**

10 *nk* **Saving Kenny (IRE)**[435] 4-9-4 0........ PatDobbs 8 84
(Roy Arne Kvisla, Sweden) **133/10**

11 *7* **Raw Sugar (IRE)** 4-9-4 0........ ShaneKarlsson 6 60
(Francisco Castro, Sweden) **33/1**

1m 6.9s (0.20)
**WFA** 3 from 4yo+ 2lb **11** Ran SP% **126.2**
PARI-MUTUEL (all including 1sek stake): WIN 2.92; PLACE 1.52, 4.60, 1.50; SF 85.54.
**Owner** Stall Trotting **Bred** Johan C Loken **Trained** Norway

### 6388a LANWADES STUD STKS (LISTED RACE) (3YO+ FILLIES & MARES) (TURF) 1m

3:20 (12:00) 3-Y-O+ **£18,761** (£9,380; £4,502; £3,001; £1,876)

RPR

1 **Angel Light (SWE)**[52] 6-9-4 0........ JacobJohansen 12 94
(Tommy Gustafsson, Sweden) **4/1**[3]

2 *¾* **Forever Snow (USA)**[71] 5-9-4 0........ RafaeldeOliveira 1 92
(Fabricio Borges, Sweden) **18/1**

3 *½* **Liebling**[80] 3-9-0 0........ Per-AndersGraberg 2 90
(Niels Petersen, Norway) **7/2**[2]

4 *hd* **Stosur (IRE)**[18] 5843 3-9-0 0........(b) TomQueally 7 90
(Gay Kelleway) *chsd ldng gp: nudged along 2 1/2f out: short of room and swtchd outside over 1f out: styd on ins fnl f: jst missed 3rd* **12/1**

5 *1* **Rock Of Ridd (IRE)**[14] 5965 4-9-4 0........ ElioneChaves 4 86
(Lennart Reuterskiold Jr, Sweden) **16/5**[1]

6 *½* **Marmala (FR)**[52] 4-9-4 0........ RafaelSchistl 10 86
(Niels Petersen, Norway) **205/10**

7 *nk* **Annaboda (IRE)**[42] 4-9-4 0........(b) OliverWilson 11 85
(Soren Jensen, Denmark) **212/10**

8 *nk* **Windy Mandy (USA)**[71] 4-9-4 0........ RobertHavlin 13 83
(Fredrik Reuterskiold, Sweden) **182/10**

9 *½* **Indigo (FR)**[347] 6962 4-9-4 0........ CarlosLopez 8 82
(Hanne Bechmann, Denmark) **116/10**

10 *nk* **Paid (SWE)** 4-9-4 0........(b) PatDobbs 3 81
(Henrik Engblom, Sweden) **32/1**

11 *1¼* **Rock The Legend (IRE)**[52] 4-9-4 0........ Jan-ErikNeuroth 6 78
(Wido Neuroth, Norway) **47/1**

12 *1¾* **Hoku (IRE)**[42] 3-9-0 0........ ManuelSantos 9 72
(Bent Olsen, Denmark) **63/10**

13 *1* **Ashbina**[96] 5-9-4 0........ MadeleineSmith 5 70
(Madeleine Smith, Sweden) **70/1**

14 *hd* **Prinsessen**[42] 3-9-0 0........ MRobaldo 14 69
(Bent Olsen, Denmark) **205/10**

1m 37.1s (97.10)
**WFA** 3 from 4yo+ 5lb **14** Ran SP% **126.2**
PARI-MUTUEL (all including 1sek stake): WIN 4.99; PLACE 1.64, 6.02, 1.82; SF 80.51.
**Owner** Stall Skumpa **Bred** HBE Aktivitetssupport KB, Nittzell Cons **Trained** Sweden

## 6389a STOCKHOLM CUP INTERNATIONAL (GROUP 3) (3YO+) (TURF) 1m 4f
3:50 (12:00) 3-Y-O+ £37,523 (£18,761; £9,005; £6,003; £3,752)

RPR
1 Bank Of Burden (USA)21 5744 7-9-4 0............ Per-AndersGraberg 4 100
(Niels Petersen, Norway) hld up in tch towards rr: effrt and gd hdwy on outer 3f out: led over 1f out: clr and in control ins fnl f: r.o wl 154/100[1]
2 1 1/2 Energia El Gigante (BRZ)21 5744 5-9-4 0............ RafaeldeOliveira 6 98
(Fabricio Borges, Sweden) led: rdn over 2f out: hdd over 1f out: kpt on wl to hold 2nd ins fnl f but no imp on wnr 111/10
3 1 Regal Hawk51 4634 4-9-1 0............ KierenFallon 2 93
(James Tate) chsd ldrs: pushed along 4f out: 3rd and drvn over 1f out: kpt on same pce ins fnl f 269/10
4 shd Hurricane Red (IRE)35 5231 4-9-4 0............ ElioneChaves 8 96
(Lennart Reuterskiold Jr, Sweden) chsd ldrs: effrt and cl 3rd over 2f out: unable qck over 1f out: styd on same pce fnl f 13/5[2]
5 1/2 Without Fear (FR)21 5744 6-9-4 0............ RafaelSchistl 10 95
(Niels Petersen, Norway) chsd ldrs: rdn 3f out: lost pl over 1f out: plugged on same pce fnl f 27/10[3]
6 hd Free House77 3772 5-9-4 0............(b) DinaDanekilde 5 95
(Jessica Long, Sweden) sn dropped to rr and pushed along: nvr travelling in last tl hdwy u.p 1f out: styd on: nvr trbld ldrs 36/1
7 3/4 Zen Zansai Zaid (SWE)700 5-9-4 0............(b) CarlosLopez 1 94
(Tommy Gustafsson, Sweden) wl in tch in midfield: nt clr run on inner 4f out: effrt 2f out: outpcd over 1f out: rallied and kpt on again ins fnl f: no threat to wnr 116/10
8 nk Jubilance (IRE)21 5744 5-9-4 0............ JacobJohansen 7 93
(Bent Olsen, Denmark) in tch towards rr: effrt and hdwy on outer 2f out: hung lft and no imp over 1f out: wknd ins fnl f 32/1
9 3 1/2 Kalendar Girl (IRE)96 6-9-2 0 ow1............ ValmirDeAzeredo 9 85
(Maria Sandh, Sweden) v.s.a: t.k.h: hld up in tch in last pair: effrt over 2f out: sn struggling: wknd over 1f out 78/1
10 nk Probably (IRE)21 5744 4-9-4 0............ PatDobbs 3 87
(Rune Haugen, Norway) in tch in midfield: rdn and effrt over 2f out: no prog and wknd over 1f out 186/10

2m 28.5s (-0.70) **10** Ran SP% **126.1**
PARI-MUTUEL (all including 1sek stake): WIN 2.54; PLACE 1.37, 2.88, 4.84; SF 41.71.
**Owner** Stall Trick Or Treat **Bred** Bjarne Minde **Trained** Norway

# WOODBINE (R-H)
Sunday, September 14
**OFFICIAL GOING: Turf: good**

## 6390a NORTHERN DANCER TURF STKS (GRADE 1) (3YO+) (TURF) 1m 4f (T)
8:32 (12:00) 3-Y-O+
£102,272 (£40,909; £17,045; £8,522; £3,409; £2,045)

RPR
1 Sheikhzayedroad50 4682 5-8-11 0............ MartinLane 8 115
(David Simcock) dwlt sltly and hld up in rr: clsd 1/2-way: rdn into st: swtchd lft to rail and chal over 1f out: styd on strly and led ins fnl f: pushed out and a doing enough whn edgd rt cl home: shade cosily 63/20[2]
2 1/2 Dynamic Sky (CAN)29 4-8-7 0............ JRosario 6 110
(Mark Casse, Canada) hld up towards rr: rdn 2f out: styd on and wnt 2nd towards fin: nt quite pce of wnr 242/10
3 3/4 Reporting Star (USA)29 4-8-7 0............ JStein 2 109
(Pat Parente, Canada) led: jinked and lost ld briefly after 2f: sn bk in front: rdn 2f out: strly pressed and hdd ins fnl f: kpt on but dropped to 3rd and hld whn hmpd by wnr towards fin 114/10
4 4 1/2 Villandry (USA)43 5-8-7 0............ JJCastellano 5 102
(Charles LoPresti, U.S.A) midfield: rdn and clsd on outer into st: effrt over 1f out: outpcd by ldrs and fdd fnl f 103/10
5 1/2 The Pizza Man (USA)29 5457 5-8-9 0............ FGeroux 1 103
(Roger Brueggemann, U.S.A) prom: rdn and effrt to chal into st: outpcd by ldrs fnl f and fdd 6/5[1]
6 2 Aldous Snow (CAN)29 5-8-9 0............(b) ERosaDaSilva 7 100
(Malcolm Pierce, Canada) midfield: rdn and clsd on rail over 3f out: outpcd by ldrs fnl f and fdd 179/10
7 4 3/4 Perfect Timber (CAN)28 5485 5-8-7 0............ JRVelazquez 9 90
(Roger L Attfield, Canada) hld up and a towards rr: rdn in last 3f out: no imp and btn in st: nvr a factor 164/10
8 2 Karibu Gardens (USA)29 4-8-11 0............(b) LContreras 4 91
(Josie Carroll, Canada) prom early: sn midfield on outer: rdn and lost pl 3f out: no imp and btn over 1f out: eased fnl f 6/1[3]
9 6 1/2 Forte Dei Marmi29 8-8-11 0............ DJMoran 3 81
(Roger L Attfield, Canada) trckd ldr: led briefly after 2f: rdn to chal into st: no ex and lost pl qckly over 1f out: sn btn: eased and dropped to last fnl f 42/1

2m 32.37s (2.77) **9** Ran SP% **118.1**
PARI-MUTUEL (all including 2 cad stake): WIN 8.30; PLACE (1-2) 4.90, 17.00; SHOW (1-2-3) 4.10, 10.40, 7.20; SF 161.60.
**Owner** Rabbah Bloodstock Ltd **Bred** Rabbah Bloodstock Limited **Trained** Newmarket, Suffolk

## 6391a RICOH WOODBINE MILE STKS (GRADE 1) (3YO+) (TURF) 1m (T)
11:13 (12:00) 3-Y-O+
£340,909 (£136,363; £56,818; £34,090; £11,363; £5,681)

RPR
1 Trade Storm22 5690 6-8-7 0............ JamieSpencer 2 113
(David Simcock) 91/20
2 1/2 Kaigun (CAN)35 4-8-9 0............ PHusbands 5 114
(Mark Casse, Canada) 41/10[3]
3 1 3/4 Bobby's Kitten (USA)37 3-8-5 0 ow5............ JRosario 8 110
(Chad C Brown, U.S.A) 79/10
4 hd River Seven (CAN)29 4-8-6 0 ow1............ JesseMCampbell 1 107
(Nicholas Gonzalez, Canada) 28/1
5 3/4 Grand Arch (USA)36 5-8-9 0............ DJMoran 11 108
(Brian A Lynch, Canada) 18/5[2]
6 3 Lockout (USA)35 5-8-5 0............ GBoulanger 7 97
(Mark Casse, Canada) 173/10
7 2 1/4 Dorsett (USA)36 4-8-5 0............ LContreras 6 92
(Brian A Lynch, Canada) 185/10
8 nk His Race To Win (CAN)42 4-8-7 0............(b) ERosaDaSilva 10 93
(Malcolm Pierce, Canada) 41/1
9 1 Jack Milton (USA)36 4-8-7 0............ JJCastellano 9 91
(Todd Pletcher, U.S.A) 71/20[1]
10 7 Silver Freak (USA)39 5-8-5 0............ JRVelazquez 4 73
(Brian A Lynch, Canada) 114/10
11 15 Ancil (USA)89 3319 5-8-5 0............ JStein 3 38
(Mrs Joan Scott, U.S.A) 91/1

1m 36.87s (96.87)
**WFA** 3 from 4yo+ 5lb **11** Ran SP% **118.2**
PARI-MUTUEL (all including 2 cad stake): WIN 11.10; PLACE (1-2) 6.20, 4.80; SHOW (1-2-3) 4.40, 3.40, 6.10; SF 53.30.
**Owner** Qatar Racing Limited **Bred** G T Lucas **Trained** Newmarket, Suffolk

# SAN SEBASTIAN (R-H)
Friday, September 12
**OFFICIAL GOING: Turf: firm**

## 6392a GRAN PREMIO DE DONOSTIA - SAN SEBASTIAN - C. P. (CONDITIONS) (3YO+) (TURF) 1m 6f
6:35 (12:00) 3-Y-O+ £12,500 (£5,000; £2,500; £1,250)

RPR
1 Tindaro (FR)26 4917 7-9-2 0............ OscarUrbina 4 82
(Paul Webber) 9/5[1]
2 nk Andry Brusselles43 4-9-3 0............ J-LMartinez 3 83
(C Delcher-Sanchez, France) 16/5
3 2 1/4 Achtung (SPA)47 4722 6-9-2 0............ MGomes 6 79
(J Lopez Sanchez, Spain) 21/10[2]
4 nk Suspiron (IRE)28 5-9-2 0............ VJanacek 5 78
(G Arizkorreta Elosegui, Spain) 13/5[3]
5 4 Sentence (SPA) 5-8-13 0............ MSecci 2 70
(G Arizkorreta Elosegui, Spain) 17/2
6 7 1/4 Artesa 4-8-13 0............(p) JeremyCrocquevieille 1 60
(M Augelli, Spain) 193/10

2m 57.81s (177.81) **6** Ran SP% **135.0**
DIVIDENDS (all including 1 unit stake): WIN 2.80; PLACE 1.60, 1.60; SF 4.20.
**Owner** The Tindaro Partnership **Bred** J P Dubois **Trained** Mollington, Oxon

# 6189 BRIGHTON (L-H)
Monday, September 15
**OFFICIAL GOING: Good (good to firm in places; 7.4)**
Wind: light, half behind Weather: overcast, bright spells

## 6393 CHANDLERS BMW MAIDEN AUCTION STKS 6f 209y
2:20 (2:21) (Class 6) 2-Y-O £1,940 (£577; £288; £144) Stalls Centre

Form RPR
23 1 Little12 6024 2-8-2 0............ CamHardie(5) 5 67
(Jamie Osborne) chsd ldng pair: swtchd rt and effrt to chse ldr over 1f out: drvn and upsides 1f out: led fnl 75yds: styd on 7/2[2]
4225 2 1/2 Pivot Point (IRE)30 5408 2-9-0 74............ RichardHughes 6 73
(Brian Meehan) chsd ldr tl led over 4f out: rdn over 1f out: hrd pressed and drvn 1f out: hdd and no ex fnl 75yds 2/5[1]
04 3 8 Star Pursuits17 5885 2-8-9 0............ ShaneKelly 4 46
(Noel Quinlan) led tl over 3f out: rdn 3f out: lost 2nd and drvn over 1f out: sn btn: wknd fnl f 8/1[3]
0 4 1 1/4 Alexi (IRE)44 4906 2-8-8 0............ LukeMorris 2 42
(Harry Dunlop) a same pl: rdn and struggling 3f out: no ch after: plugged on fnl f 100/1
5 10 Lady Ampthill (IRE) 2-8-7 0............ WilliamCarson 1 14
(John Spearing) s.i.s: rn green and a pushed along in rr: lost tch 3f out 50/1
6 5 Kodiac Krossing 2-8-6 0............ DavidProbert 3
(Jamie Osborne) s.i.s: a in last pair: lost tch 3f out 33/1

1m 24.6s (1.50) **Going Correction** +0.025s/f (Good) **6** Ran SP% **110.7**
Speed ratings (Par 93): **92,91,82,80,69 63**
CSF £5.17 TOTE £4.70: £2.00, £1.10; EX 5.70 Trifecta £11.50.
**Owner** A F Tait **Bred** Highclere Stud Ltd **Trained** Upper Lambourn, Berks

**FOCUS**
The rail was dolled out by 3yds from 6f to 2.5f, adding 6yds to distances. There was a turn up in this opening maiden, in which the first two were clear.

## 6394 SIS APPRENTICE (S) H'CAP 1m 1f 209y
2:50 (2:51) (Class 6) (0-60,55) 3-Y-O+ £1,940 (£577; £288; £144) Stalls High

Form RPR
3534 1 Anginola (IRE)7 6195 5-9-9 50............(b) JennyPowell 9 62+
(Laura Mongan) hld up in tch in last trio: swtchd rt 3f out: hdwy u.p to ld ent fnl f: drifting lft but sn clr: eased towards fin 11/4[1]
5526 2 4 Maid Of Tuscany (IRE)12 6037 3-9-7 55............ CharlotteJenner 2 57
(Mark Usher) dwlt: sn rcvrd to chse ldrs: nt clr run over 2f out: swtchd rt 2f out: no ch w wnr but plugged on to go 2nd ins fnl f 4/1[2]
0055 3 1 3/4 Previous Acclaim (IRE)7 6194 3-8-11 45............(b) AdamMcLean 6 44
(Julia Feilden) t.k.h: hld up in midfield: hdwy to ld over 4f out: rdn 2f out: hdd ent fnl f: sn btn: lost 2nd ins fnl f and wknd towards fin 12/1
0422 4 nk Royal Mizar (SPA)12 6028 4-9-1 49............ RhiainIngram(7) 7 48
(Ralph J Smith) in tch in midfield: rdn and effrt 2f out: 3rd and btn 1f out: wknd wl ins fnl f 11/4[1]
0020 5 3/4 Market Puzzle (IRE)12 6028 7-9-4 45............ DanielCremin 8 42
(Mark Brisbourne) hld up in tch in rr: rdn and effrt wl over 2f out: no hdwy u.p over 1f out: plugged on 16/1
-050 6 6 Escarlata Rossa40 5048 3-8-6 45............(b) JosephineGordon(5) 4 31
(J S Moore) broke fast: sn stdd and hld up in last trio: effrt on inner over 2f out: wknd over 1f out 50/1
0530 7 7 Copperwood30 5425 9-9-11 55............(v) KieranShoemark(3) 10 27
(Lee Carter) chsd ldrs tl led after 1f: hdd 5f out: wknd u.p 2f out: wl bhd 1f out 6/1[3]

0060 **8** ¾ **Carrowbeg (IRE)**26 5567 6-9-9 50.....(vt) NedCurtis 5 21
(Lawney Hill) *led for 1f: chsd ldr tl led again 5f out: sn hdd: wknd u.p wl over 1f out: wl btn and heavily eased ins fnl f* **9/1**

2m 5.22s (1.62) **Going Correction** +0.025s/f (Good)
**WFA** 3 from 4yo+ 7lb **8** Ran SP% **113.2**
Speed ratings (Par 101): **94,90,89,89,88 83,78,77**
.Anginola was bought by David Dennis for 4,200gns.\n\x\x Maid Of Tuscany was bought by Neil Mulholland for £3,000
**Owner** Condover Racing **Bred** T C Clarke **Trained** Epsom, Surrey

**FOCUS**
Weak handicap form. The winner is rated close to last year's form.

## 6395 OVERLINE TELECOMS H'CAP 1m 3f 196y
**3:20** (3:21) (Class 6) (0-65,64) 3-Y-O+ **£1,940** (£577; £288; £144) **Stalls** High

Form RPR
4213 **1** **Sir Tyto (IRE)**16 5904 6-9-0 52.....(p) RichardHughes 2 61
(Peter Makin) *chsd ldrs: rdn and effrt 2f out: drvn to ld over 1f out: kpt on u.p ins fnl f: forged ahd fnl 75yds* **3/1**1

2533 **2** 1¼ **Tunnel Tiger (IRE)**7 6193 3-8-7 59..... JennyPowell(5) 1 66
(William Knight) *stdd s: hld up in tch in rr: swtchd rt and effrt 3f out: edging lft and chal jst over 2f out: led over 1f out: sn hdd: no ex and btn fnl 75yds* **3/1**1

1343 **3** 1¾ **Sweeping Rock (IRE)**12 6027 4-9-3 60.....(t) CamHardie(5) 4 64
(Marcus Tregoning) *stdd s: hld up in last pair: swtchd rt over 3f out: nt clr run and shuffled bk over 2f out: hdwy over 1f out: wnt 3rd ins fnl f: kpt on* **9/2**3

4051 **4** 6 **Snow Conditions**7 6193 3-8-10 62 6ex.....1 ShelleyBirkett(5) 5 57
(Philip Hide) *taken down early: chsd ldr tl led wl over 2f out: rdn and hdd over 1f out: wknd ins fnl f* **7/2**2

4510 **5** 5 **Highlife Dancer**17 5899 6-9-5 64.....(v) DanielCremin(7) 7 51
(Mick Channon) *in tch in midfield: rdn 4f out: sn swtchd rt and sme hdwy 3f out: wknd 2f out* **16/1**

505 **6** ½ **Angus Glens**4 6252 4-9-11 63.....(p) LukeMorris 3 49
(David Dennis) *chsd ldrs: effrt to press ldrs whn sltly hmpd over 2f out: sn btn: wknd over 1f out* **10/1**

4342 **7** 17 **Megalala (IRE)**20 5787 13-9-10 62..... WilliamCarson 6 21
(John Bridger) *led tl wl over 2f out: sn rdn and dropped out: bhd and heavily eased ins fnl f* **16/1**

2m 33.01s (0.31) **Going Correction** +0.025s/f (Good)
**WFA** 3 from 4yo+ 9lb **7** Ran SP% **111.3**
Speed ratings (Par 101): **99,98,97,93,89 89,78**
CSF £11.48 TOTE £3.50: £2.40, £2.10; EX 11.10 Trifecta £47.20.
**Owner** WH And Mrs Jennifer Simpson **Bred** Michael Conlon **Trained** Ogbourne Maisey, Wilts

**FOCUS**
A moderate handicap, but sound form.

## 6396 HARVEYS AWARD WINNING SUSSEX BEER RANGE H'CAP 7f 214y
**3:50** (3:50) (Class 6) (0-60,60) 3-Y-O+ **£1,940** (£577; £288; £144) **Stalls** Centre

Form RPR
0056 **1** **Lutine Charlie (IRE)**17 5897 7-8-9 49..... DanielMuscutt(5) 4 59
(Pat Eddery) *t.k.h: chsd ldrs: drvn to ld jst over 1f out: kpt on and a holding rivals ins fnl f: rdn out* **20/1**

0551 **2** ¾ **Claude Greenwood**14 5978 4-8-8 48.....(b) CamHardie(5) 8 56
(Linda Jewell) *t.k.h: chsd ldr tl led 4f out: shifted rt u.p 2f out: hdd jst over 1f out: kpt on same pce ins fnl f* **8/1**

6265 **3** hd **Libra Romana (IRE)**14 5978 3-8-9 49..... LukeMorris 6 56
(Sir Mark Prescott Bt) *hld up in tch in last trio: rdn and hdwy over 2f out: drvn to chse ldrs over 1f out: kpt on u.p fnl 100yds* **7/1**

2342 **4** 2½ **Abigails Angel**14 5978 7-9-0 49.....(p) StevieDonohoe 3 51
(Lee Carter) *chsd ldng trio: effrt on inner jst over 2f out: no ex u.p 1f out: wknd fnl 100yds* **5/1**

6614 **5** shd **Why Not Now**18 5846 3-9-2 56..... DavidProbert 9 57
(Roger Charlton) *hld up in tch in last trio: rdn over 2f out: hdwy u.p jst over 1f out: kpt on steadily ins fnl f: nvr threatened ldrs* **3/1**1

1310 **6** 7 **Royal Caper**21 5773 4-9-9 58..... SteveDrowne 1 43
(Miss Joey Ellis) *in tch in midfield: lost pl and rdn 3f out: wknd u.p over 1f out* **14/1**

3124 **7** 1½ **Cherry Princess**20 5787 4-9-8 57..... RichardHughes 7 39
(Stuart Williams) *in tch in midfield: hdwy u.p 2f out: drifting lft and no imp over 1f out: fdd ins fnl f* **9/2**3

6000 **8** 2 **Strong Conviction**10 6086 4-9-11 60..... WilliamCarson 2 37
(Simon Hodgson) *led: hdd 4f out: rdn and wknd qckly over 1f out: bhd and eased ins fnl f* **25/1**

4231 **9** 11 **Chanceuse**14 5977 3-9-5 59..... GeorgeBaker 5 10
(Gary Moore) *stdd s: hld up in rr: plenty to do and effrt 3f out: no hdwy: wl bhd and eased ins fnl f* **4/1**2

1m 35.94s (-0.06) **Going Correction** +0.025s/f (Good)
**WFA** 3 from 4yo+ 5lb **9** Ran SP% **118.7**
Speed ratings (Par 101): **101,100,100,97,97 90,88,86,75**
CSF £174.44 CT £1256.75 TOTE £20.60: £7.00, £3.00, £3.30; EX 185.90 Trifecta £2991.60 Part won..
**Owner** Miss Emma L Owen **Bred** Patrice O'Connell **Trained** Nether Winchendon, Bucks

**FOCUS**
The winner's best run since her C&D effort in June.

## 6397 HARVEYS BREWERY H'CAP 6f 209y
**4:20** (4:22) (Class 6) (0-65,65) 3-Y-O+ **£1,940** (£577; £288; £144) **Stalls** Centre

Form RPR
3123 **1** **Pour La Victoire (IRE)**10 6086 4-9-4 60...(b1) WilliamTwiston-Davies 12 71
(Tony Carroll) *wl in tch in midfield: hdwy to ld over 2f out: hung lft u.p and racing on far rail 1f out: clr ins fnl f: tiring fnl 50yds: rdn out* **5/1**1

4252 **2** ¾ **Just Isla**14 5972 4-9-3 59.....(p) RichardHughes 5 67
(Peter Makin) *chsd ldr: rdn ent fnl 2f: pressing wnr whn squeezed for room and snatched up 1f out: sn swtchd rt: rallied and styd on fnl 100yds: nvr getting bk to wnr* **6/1**2

0303 **3** 1½ **Burnhope**54 4534 5-8-6 53..... MatthewHopkins(5) 10 57
(Scott Dixon) *led: rdn and hdd over 2f out: 3rd and unable qck whn swtchd rt ent fnl f: styd on same pce after* **12/1**

0340 **4** 1 **Uprise**18 5861 5-9-5 64.....(t) RyanPowell(3) 14 66
(George Margarson) *chsd ldrs: rdn jst over 2f out: drvn and sltly outpcd over 1f out: rallied and styd on again ins fnl f* **25/1**

6655 **5** ½ **Stonecrabstomorrow (IRE)**7 6195 11-8-6 51..... DeclanBates(3) 8 51
(Michael Attwater) *in tch in midfield: drvn ent fnl 2f: sltly outpcd over 1f out: styd on again ins fnl f* **25/1**

0-50 **6** nk **Summer Dancer (IRE)**11 6074 10-9-4 63..... RobertTart(3) 1 62
(Eugene Stanford) *hld up towards rr: effrt on inner 2f out: hdwy u.p over 1f out: kpt on ins fnl f: nt rch ldrs* **16/1**

1212 **7** hd **Hawk Moth (IRE)**15 5950 6-9-5 61.....(p) LukeMorris 2 60
(John Spearing) *chsd ldrs: rdn over 2f out: drvn and unable qck over 1f out: plugged on same pce ins fnl f* **5/1**1

6044 **8** 1 **Commandingpresence (USA)**14 5972 8-8-10 52..... WilliamCarson 3 48
(John Bridger) *in tch in midfield: effrt u.p 2f out: kpt on but no real imp fr over 1f out* **33/1**

4652 **9** 3 **Tubeanie (IRE)**22 5729 3-8-8 59.....(p) DanielMuscutt(5) 6 46
(Amy Weaver) *in tch in midfield: rdn and effrt jst over 2f out: no imp: wknd 1f out* **14/1**

6020 **10** 1¼ **High On The Hog (IRE)**39 5071 6-8-4 51 oh5..... CamHardie(5) 4 36
(Mark Brisbourne) *stdd s: hld up in last quartet: rdn and effrt over 2f out: no real prog: wknd over 1f out* **50/1**

0500 **11** ½ **Lionheart**4 6266 4-9-8 64.....(e) ShaneKelly 13 48
(Peter Crate) *fly-jmpd as stalls opened and slowly away: bhd: c towards stands' rail 3f out: hung lft u.p and no hdwy over 1f out: wknd fnl f* **12/1**

2523 **12** 1¼ **Inkerman (IRE)**10 6087 4-9-9 65.....(tp) GeorgeBaker 9 46
(Jamie Osborne) *stdd s: hld up in rr: effrt 2f out: no hdwy u.p over 1f out: nvr trbld ldrs* **6/1**2

5000 **13** ½ **It's Taboo**21 5751 4-8-12 54..... SteveDrowne 11 33
(Mark Usher) *t.k.h: hld up towards rr: rdn and effrt 2f out: no prog: nvr trbld ldrs* **33/1**

0-44 **14** hd **Berkeley Vale**13 6022 3-9-4 64..... SebSanders 7 41
(Roger Teal) *in tch in midfield: rdn and lost pl 3f out: bhd 1f out* **7/1**3

1m 23.48s (0.38) **Going Correction** +0.025s/f (Good)
**WFA** 3 from 4yo+ 4lb **14** Ran SP% **117.9**
Speed ratings (Par 101): **98,97,95,94,93 93,93,92,88,87 86,85,84,84**
CSF £31.36 CT £354.41 TOTE £5.00: £1.90, £2.70, £4.30; EX 23.10 Trifecta £388.50.
**Owner** Curry House Corner **Bred** L Fox **Trained** Cropthorne, Worcs
■ Stewards' Enquiry : William Twiston-Davies two-day ban: careless riding (Sep 29-30)

**FOCUS**
Little got into this from off the pace. Sound form for the grade.

## 6398 WHY'S HARVEYS NEW BEER CALLED R H'CAP 5f 213y
**4:50** (4:50) (Class 4) (0-80,79) 3-Y-O+ **£4,690** (£1,395; £697; £348) **Stalls** Centre

Form RPR
5451 **1** **Alnoomaas (IRE)**15 5951 5-8-13 71.....(v) RichardHughes 1 82
(Luke Dace) *mde all: rdn and fnd ex 2f out: styd on wl and asserted ins fnl f: gng away at fin* **6/1**

111 **2** 2½ **Panther Patrol (IRE)**26 5559 4-9-7 79.....(v) JohnFahy 6 82
(Eve Johnson Houghton) *chsd wnr thrght: rdn 2f out: drvn over 1f out: no ex and btn ins fnl f: kpt on for clr 2nd* **11/4**1

2411 **3** 3¾ **Bayleyf (IRE)**7 6191 5-9-7 79 6ex.....(p) StevieDonohoe 3 70
(Lee Carter) *chsd ldrs: shuffled bk and swtchd rt 2f out: battling for 3rd over 1f out: wnt 3rd ins fnl f: no ch w ldrs* **4/1**2

6142 **4** 1¾ **Langley Vale**13 6006 5-9-7 79.....(p) SebSanders 2 64
(Roger Teal) *hld up in tch: short of room and dropped to rr over 4f out: hdwy u.p 2f out: chsd clr ldng pair over 1f out: no imp: lost 3rd ins fnl f* **9/2**3

0513 **5** ¾ **Top Offer**14 5987 5-8-9 67..... ShaneKelly 7 50
(Peter Crate) *dwlt: hld up in last pair: effrt on outer over 2f out: hung lft and btn over 1f out* **9/2**3

3324 **6** 4 **Storm Lightning**15 5945 5-8-9 72..... CamHardie(5) 4 42
(Mark Brisbourne) *chsd ldrs early: steadily lost pl: rdn over 2f out: wknd over 1f out* **8/1**

0000 **7** 1¾ **Sacrosanctus**5 6235 6-9-1 73.....(p) LukeMorris 5 38
(Scott Dixon) *in tch in midfield: rdn and sme hdwy over 2f out: wknd over 1f out* **25/1**

1m 9.55s (-0.65) **Going Correction** +0.025s/f (Good) **7** Ran SP% **112.3**
Speed ratings (Par 105): **105,101,96,94,93 88,85**
CSF £22.00 CT £72.75 TOTE £5.30: £2.70, £1.70; EX 20.70 Trifecta £32.00.
**Owner** Mark Benton **Bred** Old Carhue & Graeng Bloodstock **Trained** Okehurst Lane, W Sussex

**FOCUS**
A race in which it paid to race handily, Richard Hughes judging it nicely. The winner is rated to his best.

## 6399 DOWNLOAD THE HARVEYS BEER FINDER APP H'CAP 5f 59y
**5:20** (5:20) (Class 5) (0-70,69) 3-Y-O+ **£2,587** (£770; £384; £192) **Stalls** Centre

Form RPR
0550 **1** **Dusty Storm (IRE)**32 5333 4-9-5 67..... SebSanders 8 78
(Ed McMahon) *in tch in midfield and travelled strly: shkn up and qcknd to ld ins fnl f: sn clr: eased towards fin* **9/2**3

0064 **2** 2½ **Lucky Surprise**16 5907 3-8-1 55 oh5.....(b) CamHardie(5) 9 58
(Jeremy Gask) *dwlt: bustled along in rr: rdn 1/2-way: hdwy u.p 1f out: styd on to go 2nd wl ins fnl f: no threat to wnr* **20/1**

-006 **3** 1 **Howyadoingnotsobad (IRE)**86 3470 6-8-13 66..... RyanWhile(5) 7 65
(Bill Turner) *w ldr: rdn and ev ch over 1f out: led 1f out: hdd ins fnl f: sn btn and one pce: lost 2nd wl ins fnl f* **10/1**

3321 **4** 1¾ **Captain Ryan**16 5905 3-8-12 61..... RichardHughes 1 54
(Peter Makin) *in tch in midfield: clsd to trck ldrs and nt clr run 2f out: gap opened and rdn 1f out: fnd little and no hdwy after* **2/1**1

6010 **5** 1 **Pearl Noir**50 4714 4-8-8 56.....(b) LukeMorris 6 45
(Scott Dixon) *w ldrs: ev ch and drvn 2f out tl ins fnl f: wknd fnl 100yds* **8/1**

0011 **6** ½ **Pastureyes**19 5819 4-9-2 69.....(p) MatthewHopkins(5) 4 57
(Scott Dixon) *in tch in midfield: rdn and unable qck whn short of room and swtchd rt over 1f out: sn outpcd and btn 1f out* **3/1**2

3030 **7** ½ **Imaginary Diva**33 5316 8-8-0 55..... JordanVaughan(7) 2 41
(George Margarson) *in tch in last pair: effrt whn nt clr run and swtchd lft over 1f out: kpt on same pce fnl f* **16/1**

6060 **8** ½ **Living It Large (FR)**12 6025 7-9-3 68.....(p) DeclanBates(3) 5 52
(Ed de Giles) *sn bustled along to ld on inner: rdn over 1f out: hdd 1f out: sn wknd* **12/1**

1m 2.67s (0.37) **Going Correction** +0.025s/f (Good)
**WFA** 3 from 4yo+ 1lb **8** Ran SP% **115.1**
Speed ratings (Par 103): **98,94,92,89,88 87,86,85**
CSF £85.56 CT £648.13 TOTE £7.70: £2.20, £5.90, £2.60; EX 151.30 Trifecta £1681.60.
**Owner** Mrs R L Bedding **Bred** Yeomanstown Stud **Trained** Lichfield, Staffs
■ Stewards' Enquiry : Matthew Hopkins one-day ban: careless riding (Sep 29)

**FOCUS**
Modest sprint form. The winner was on a good mark compared with her 3yo efforts.
T/Plt: £157.60 to a £1 stake. Pool: £76,309.64 - 353.40 winning units. T/Qpdt: £66.80 to a £1 stake. Pool: £4979.67 - 55.15 winning units. SP

# 6108 MUSSELBURGH (R-H)

Monday, September 15

**OFFICIAL GOING: Good to soft (soft in places; 7.0)**
Wind: Light, half behind Weather: Misty, drizzle

## 6400 BATLEYS FOODSERVICE (S) STKS — 7f 30y
2:10 (2:11) (Class 6) 2-Y-O — £1,940 (£577; £288; £144) Stalls Low

Form — RPR
6154 1 **Danot (IRE)**[13] 5998 2-9-2 69 ... TomEaves 2 — 69
(Keith Dalgleish) *mde all: pushed along 2f out: kpt on strly fnl f* 11/4[2]
4000 2 3 **Gilded Lace**[11] 6064 2-8-3 64 ... JoeyHaynes(3) 3 — 51
(J S Moore) *pressed wnr thrght: rdn over 2f out: kpt on same pce fnl f* 6/4[1]
0460 3 6 **Agadoo**[20] 5798 2-8-6 62 ... JasonHart 4 — 35
(Shaun Harris) *t.k.h: in tch: effrt and drvn over 3f out: no imp fr 2f out* 6/4[1]
60 4 32 **Kepple's Best (IRE)**[37] 5167 2-8-11 0 ... (b[1]) PatrickMathers 1
(Alan Berry) *chsd ldrs: drvn over 3f out: sn btn: t.o* 50/1[3]
1m 33.63s (4.63) **Going Correction** +0.375s/f (Good) 4 Ran SP% **108.6**
Speed ratings (Par 93): **88,84,77,41**
CSF £7.29 TOTE £2.70; EX 5.00 Trifecta £7.10.There was no bid for the winner.
**Owner** Equus Syndicate **Bred** Tally-Ho Stud **Trained** Carluke, S Lanarks

**FOCUS**
A miserable day and the ground had turned good to soft after persistent morning rain. Visibility was desperate as this meeting got underway and the runners could only be seen briefly towards the end of the back straight before disappearing again. A weak 2yo seller, given a token rating.

## 6401 BEST ONE NURSERY H'CAP — 5f
2:40 (2:40) (Class 5) (0-75,75) 2-Y-O — £3,234 (£962; £481; £240) Stalls High

Form — RPR
003 1 **Tecumseh (IRE)**[49] 4739 2-8-10 67 ...[1] JoeyHaynes(3) 6 — 70+
(K R Burke) *in tch: effrt: swtchd rt and hdwy to ld ins fnl f: kpt on strly* 6/1
5435 2 1 1/4 **Poolstock**[22] 5714 2-8-8 65 ... ConnorBeasley(3) 2 — 64
(Les Eyre) *cl up: rdn to ld over 1f out: hdd ins fnl f: kpt on: nt rch wnr* 25/1
2143 3 nk **Somedaysrdiamonds**[13] 6016 2-8-9 63 ... RobertWinston 8 — 60
(J S Moore) *led to over 1f out: rallied: kpt on ins fnl f* 9/1
4232 4 nk **Westhoughton**[17] 5885 2-9-7 75 ... DanielTudhope 7 — 71
(David O'Meara) *prom: effrt and rdn 2f out: kpt on same pce ins fnl f* 7/2[2]
1 5 shd **Zebelini (IRE)**[20] 5789 2-9-2 70 ... LemosdeSouza 3 — 66
(Mrs Ilka Gansera-Leveque) *cl up: ev ch over 1f out to ins fnl f: one pce last 100yds* 8/1
10 6 2 **Youcouldntmakeitup (IRE)**[20] 5790 2-9-7 75 ... DavidAllan 10 — 64
(Tim Easterby) *trckd ldrs: drvn along over 2f out: one pce fr over 1f out* 11/2[3]
455 7 3 1/2 **Spend A Penny (IRE)**[66] 4170 2-9-0 68 ... PhillipMakin 1 — 47
(John Quinn) *in tch on outside: rdn over 2f out: wknd over 1f out* 2/1[1]
040 8 6 **Little Sista**[47] 4790 2-8-5 59 ... DuranFentiman 9 — 14+
(Bryan Smart) *missed break: bhd and outpcd: no ch fr 1/2-way* 14/1
1m 2.0s (1.60) **Going Correction** +0.375s/f (Good) 8 Ran SP% **116.8**
Speed ratings (Par 95): **102,100,99,99,98 95,90,80**
CSF £135.25 CT £1353.01 TOTE £8.20: £2.30, £5.40, £2.40; EX 142.10 Trifecta £355.10.
**Owner** S O'Sullivan & Mrs E Burke **Bred** Corrin Stud **Trained** Middleham Moor, N Yorks

**FOCUS**
An open nursery on paper and they posted a time 4sec slower than standard, suggesting the good to soft going description was about right. Most of this race was run out of view. The winner has more to offer in similar races.

## 6402 DRINKS EXPRESS CLAIMING STKS — 1m 1f
3:10 (3:10) (Class 6) 3-Y-O+ — £2,587 (£770; £384; £192) Stalls Low

Form — RPR
-205 1 **Stand My Ground (IRE)**[96] 3109 7-10-0 94 ... DanielTudhope 2 — 83
(David O'Meara) *hld up: hdwy over 2f out: led 1f out: hld on wl towards fin* 8/15[1]
1133 2 nk **Valantino Oyster (IRE)**[42] 4979 7-9-3 71 ... (p) ConnorBeasley(3) 4 — 74
(Tracy Waggott) *chsd ldrs: drvn over 4f out: rallied to ld over 2f out: hdd ent fnl f: rallied: hld nr fin* 7/2[2]
0160 3 7 **Rasselas (IRE)**[22] 5711 7-8-7 65 ... (b) AnnaHesketh(7) 6 — 53
(David Nicholls) *chsd ldrs: led over 3f out to over 2f out: outpcd by first two fr over 1f out* 10/1[3]
6544 4 1 1/4 **Eilean Mor**[10] 6113 6-8-13 50 ... JordanNason(5) 3 — 54
(R Mike Smith) *prom: rdn along 3f out: no imp fr 2f out* 40/1
0266 5 1 1/2 **Thrust Control (IRE)**[22] 5711 7-9-0 49 ... (p) RobertWinston 1 — 47
(Tracy Waggott) *led to over 3f out: rdn and outpcd over 2f out: n.d after* 33/1
4244 6 12 **Dialogue**[22] 5711 8-9-2 62 ... DavidAllan 5 — 22
(Geoffrey Harker) *hld up in tch: struggling wl over 2f out: sn btn* 12/1
1m 56.28s (2.38) **Going Correction** +0.375s/f (Good) 6 Ran SP% **109.6**
Speed ratings (Par 101): **104,103,97,96,95 84**
CSF £2.47 TOTE £1.50: £1.10, £2.00; EX 2.90 Trifecta £8.50.
**Owner** Middleham Park Racing XLVIII & Partners **Bred** N P Bloodstock Ltd **Trained** Nawton, N Yorks

**FOCUS**
An ordinary claimer. The runner-up is rated to form, with the winner below par.

## 6403 BEST IN H'CAP STKS (QUALIFIER FOR THE £15000 BETFAIR SCOTTISH STAYERS' SERIES FINAL) — 1m 4f 100y
3:40 (3:40) (Class 5) (0-70,70) 3-Y-O+ — £3,234 (£962; £481; £240) Stalls Centre

Form — RPR
2330 1 **Merchant Of Dubai**[26] 5564 9-10-0 70 ... GrahamLee 4 — 78
(Jim Goldie) *trckd ldrs: hdwy to ld over 2f out: edgd lft ins fnl f: pushed out* 6/5[1]
1000 2 1 1/4 **El Bravo**[13] 6012 8-9-7 70 ... MrAidenBlakemore(7) 7 — 75
(Shaun Harris) *in tch: hdwy and ev ch over 2f out to 1f out: kpt on same pce last 150yds* 10/1
0605 3 8 **Right Of Appeal**[22] 5716 3-9-2 67 ... FrannyNorton 8 — 59
(Mark Johnston) *prom: led after 2f: rdn over 3f out: hdd over 2f out: sn outpcd by first two* 6/4[2]
2445 4 46 **Vicky Valentine**[13] 6000 4-9-2 63 ... GarryWhillans(5) 1
(Alistair Whillans) *led 2f: w ldr: rdn over 4f out: wknd fr 3f out: t.o* 9/2[3]
2m 49.61s (7.61) **Going Correction** +0.375s/f (Good)
**WFA** 3 from 4yo+ 9lb 4 Ran SP% **112.7**
Speed ratings (Par 103): **89,88,82,52**
CSF £12.04 TOTE £1.60; EX 11.00 Trifecta £12.00.
**Owner** Highland Racing 2 **Bred** A Smith **Trained** Uplawmoor, E Renfrews

■ Royal Straight and Schmooze were withdrawn. Prices at time of withdrawal 5-1 and 10-1. Rule 4 applies to bets struck prior to withdrawal but not to SP bets - deduction 15p in the pound.

**FOCUS**
Nine morning runners were reduced to just four by race time, although Royal Straight would have run but he spread a plate on the way to post. They appeared to go quite a good gallop early (although it's impossible to know what happened to the tempo after that given they were out of view) and the pair that sat just behind the pace took over in the closing stages and drew clear. The winner is rated to form.

## 6404 BATLEYS CASH AND CARRY H'CAP — 2m
4:10 (4:10) (Class 4) (0-85,83) 3-Y-O+ — £6,225 (£1,864; £932; £466; £233) Stalls High

Form — RPR
5244 1 **Deepsand (IRE)**[10] 6099 5-9-5 74 ... (p) DavidAllan 7 — 82
(Tim Easterby) *trckd ldrs: effrt and wnt 2nd over 2f out: led ins fnl f: pushed out* 11/4[2]
3135 2 1/2 **Underwritten**[16] 5924 5-8-13 68 ... JasonHart 3 — 75
(Shaun Harris) *led: rdn over 3f out: edgd lft 2f out: hdd ins fnl f: kpt on: hld nr fin* 9/2
2/10 3 1 1/2 **Pass Muster**[93] 3240 7-9-7 78 ... PhillipMakin 6 — 83
(Philip Kirby) *dwlt: hld up in tch: stdy hdwy over 3f out: rdn over 2f out: kpt on ins fnl f* 7/2[3]
1344 4 4 1/2 **Aleksandar**[26] 5564 5-9-2 71 ... GrahamLee 5 — 71
(Jim Goldie) *pressed ldr: drvn and outpcd over 2f out: no imp fr over 1f out* 85/40[1]
6235 5 1/2 **Jan Smuts (IRE)**[19] 5815 6-8-5 65 ... (tp) EmmaSayer(5) 4 — 64
(Wilf Storey) *t.k.h: hld up in tch: struggling and hung lft over 2f out: sn n.d* 8/1
3m 40.05s (6.55) **Going Correction** +0.375s/f (Good) 5 Ran SP% **110.2**
Speed ratings (Par 105): **98,97,97,94,94**
CSF £14.91 TOTE £3.30: £2.20, £2.60; EX 14.80 Trifecta £52.00.
**Owner** Trevor Hemmings **Bred** Gleahill House Stud Ltd **Trained** Great Habton, N Yorks

**FOCUS**
Not a race deep in quality and the overall time was 15sec slower than standard, although that may partly be down to the ground getting opened up by the earlier races. The winner is rated to this year's form.

## 6405 XTRA LOCAL H'CAP — 7f 30y
4:40 (4:41) (Class 6) (0-65,65) 3-Y-O+ — £2,587 (£770; £384; £192) Stalls Low

Form — RPR
5650 1 **Running Reef (IRE)**[5] 6227 5-9-4 59 ... (p) RobertWinston 12 — 73
(Tracy Waggott) *disp ld: led and c to centre 3f out: rdn clr fnl f* 5/1[3]
4544 2 5 **Jumbo Steps (IRE)**[35] 5236 7-9-10 65 ... GrahamLee 1 — 66
(Jim Goldie) *led: rdn and hdd 3f out: rallied: kpt on same pce fr over 1f out* 9/2[2]
1324 3 3/4 **Orwellian**[50] 4707 5-9-10 65 ... PaulMulrennan 4 — 64
(Bryan Smart) *dwlt: bhd: rdn and hdwy over 2f out: kpt on fnl f: nrst fin* 7/2[1]
3053 4 1/2 **Niceonemyson**[10] 6122 5-9-0 60 ... KevinStott(5) 7 — 58
(Christopher Wilson) *hld up in midfield: hdwy over 2f out: rdn and edgd rt over 1f out: kpt on same pce* 9/1
002 5 1 3/4 **Clabare**[18] 5857 3-8-10 55 ... TomEaves 8 — 46
(Ian Semple) *rrd s: sn in tch: rdn and hung rt over 1f out: sn no ex* 20/1
0254 6 1 1/4 **Monsieur Royale**[23] 5683 4-8-12 53 ... (p[1]) JasonHart 10 — 43
(Geoffrey Oldroyd) *bhd: rdn and plenty to do 1/2-way: styd on wl fr over 1f out: nrst fin* 9/1
-246 7 2 1/2 **Iftikaar (IRE)**[21] 5772 4-9-9 64 ... DanielTudhope 2 — 47
(Philip Kirby) *in tch: rdn over 2f out: wknd over 1f out* 6/1
4530 8 1/2 **Sewn Up**[13] 6014 4-8-10 51 oh1 ... (p) PhillipMakin 11 — 33
(Keith Dalgleish) *bhd: drvn and struggling 1/2-way: sme late hdwy: nvr able to chal* 12/1
2600 9 3 **Berbice (IRE)**[10] 6114 9-8-5 51 oh6 ... SammyJoBell(5) 3 — 25
(Linda Perratt) *s.i.s: sn in tch: rdn over 2f out: wknd over 1f out* 40/1
4653 10 7 **Slick Indian**[13] 5994 3-8-4 56 ... AnnaHesketh(7) 6 — 10
(Michael Easterby) *bhd: struggling 1/2-way: nvr on terms* 12/1
0-00 11 2 1/2 **Chamberlain**[13] 6009 3-9-1 60 ... (p) DavidAllan 5 — 8
(John Murray) *midfield: hmpd after 3f: rdn and struggling fr 3f out* 50/1
1m 32.56s (3.56) **Going Correction** +0.375s/f (Good)
**WFA** 3 from 4yo+ 4lb 11 Ran SP% **115.9**
Speed ratings (Par 101): **94,88,87,86,84 83,80,80,76,68 65**
CSF £26.84 CT £90.21 TOTE £7.70: £2.60, £1.80, £1.80; EX 32.40 Trifecta £137.60.
**Owner** Elsa Crankshaw Gordon Allan **Bred** C O'Reilly & Co **Trained** Spennymoor, Co Durham

**FOCUS**
A weak handicap in which the field was well strung out from an early stage, but the pace held up. The winner is rated back to his best.

## 6406 PETRUSHKA VODKA H'CAP — 5f
5:10 (5:11) (Class 5) (0-70,70) 3-Y-O+ — £3,234 (£962; £481; £240) Stalls High

Form — RPR
1420 1 **Spring Bird**[19] 5819 5-8-9 62 ... AnnaHesketh(7) 10 — 71
(David Nicholls) *w ldrs: led 1/2-way: hld on wl fnl f* 16/1
0330 2 hd **Boxing Shadows**[16] 5912 4-9-8 68 ... DavidAllan 14 — 76
(Les Eyre) *in tch: effrt and hdwy over 1f out: kpt on fnl f: jst hld* 7/2[1]
2331 3 hd **Pavers Star**[10] 6114 5-8-3 52 ... (p) JoeyHaynes(3) 5 — 59
(Noel Wilson) *dwlt: effrt and swtchd towards stands' rail after 2f: effrt and rdn over 1f out: kpt on ins fnl f* 7/1[3]
0112 4 nk **Perfect Words (IRE)**[24] 5635 4-9-4 69 ... (p) JordanNason(5) 2 — 75
(Marjorie Fife) *cl up: ev ch over 1f out to wl ins fnl f: hld towards fin* 7/1[3]
4546 5 3 1/4 **Ypres**[33] 5298 5-9-5 70 ... KevinStott(5) 11 — 64
(Jason Ward) *towards rr: effrt whn n.m.r and swtchd lft over 1f out: kpt on fnl f: nrst fin* 7/1[3]
0236 6 2 1/4 **Tadalavil**[10] 6114 9-8-2 53 ... SammyJoBell(5) 3 — 39
(Linda Perratt) *bhd and sn outpcd: hdwy over 1f out: kpt on fnl f: nvr able to chal* 25/1
5600 7 3/4 **Bronze Beau**[16] 5912 7-9-3 66 ... (t) NataliaGemelova(3) 7 — 49
(Kristin Stubbs) *cl up tl rdn and wknd 1f out* 20/1
6254 8 nk **Windforpower (IRE)**[16] 5912 4-9-4 64 ... (p) RobertWinston 1 — 46
(Tracy Waggott) *towards rr and sn pushed along: rdn and hdwy wl over 1f out: edgd lft and sn no imp* 17/2
0644 9 3 1/2 **Economic Crisis (IRE)**[33] 5298 5-9-5 65 ... PaulMulrennan 12 — 35
(Alan Berry) *chsd ldrs tl rdn and wknd over 1f out* 12/1
0122 10 1 1/4 **Live Dangerously**[13] 5996 4-9-5 65 ... PhillipMakin 8 — 30
(Keith Dalgleish) *midfield: lost pl 1/2-way: n.d after* 9/2[2]
5530 11 3 **The Nifty Fox**[10] 6114 10-8-9 55 ... (p) TomEaves 4 — 9
(Tim Easterby) *in tch: effrt and pushed along whn nt clr run over 1f out: sn btn* 16/1

0040 **12** *12* **Chloe's Dream (IRE)**[18] 5858 4-8-5 51 oh1 DuranFentiman 13
(Linda Perratt) *rrd in stalls: led to 1/2-way: hung rt and wknd over 1f out* **40/1**
1m 1.83s (1.43) **Going Correction** +0.375s/f (Good) **12** Ran SP% **118.9**
Speed ratings (Par 103): **103,102,102,101,96 93,91,91,85,83 79,59**
CSF £70.18 CT £449.63 TOTE £16.90: £4.80, £2.10, £2.70; EX 110.90 Trifecta £2053.30.
**Owner** D G Clayton **Bred** D G Clayton **Trained** Sessay, N Yorks
■ Stewards' Enquiry : Jordan Nason four-day ban: used whip above permitted level (Sep 29-Oct 2)
**FOCUS**
A wide-open sprint in which a group of four drew clear and there was very little between them at the line. The form looks sound for the grade with a length best from the winner.
T/Plt: £251.20 to a £1 stake. Pool: £51,779.65 - 150.47 winning units. T/Qpdt: £8.70 to a £1 stake. Pool: £5207.57 - 439.56 winning units. RY

# 6340 WOLVERHAMPTON (A.W) (L-H)
## Monday, September 15

**OFFICIAL GOING: Tapeta: standard**
Wind: Light against Weather: Overcast

## 6407 DOWNLOAD OUR IPHONE APP APPRENTICE H'CAP (TAPETA) 1m 141y
2:30 (2:31) (Class 6) (0-55,55) 3-Y-0+ £1,940 (£577; £288; £144) Stalls Low

Form RPR
342 **1** **Elle Rebelle**[14] 5977 4-9-4 52 BeckyBrisbourne 5 63
(Mark Brisbourne) *s.i.s: hld up: plld hrd: nt clr run over 7f out: hdwy over 2f out: rdn to ld and edgd lft wl ins fnl f: r.o* **11/1**
0363 **2** *2* **Carrera**[20] 5797 4-9-6 54 ChrisMeehan 2 60
(Michael Blanshard) *mid-div: hdwy over 3f out: rdn and ev ch fr over 1f out tl no ex wl ins fnl f* **10/1**
0032 **3** *nk* **Actonetaketwo**[10] 6087 4-8-7 46 CallumShepherd(5) 11 51
(Ron Hodges) *s.i.s: hld up: hdwy 2f out: rdn over 1f out: styd on same pce ins fnl f* **11/1**
3034 **4** *1/2* **Evacusafe Lady**[27] 5534 3-8-10 53 (t) JoshDoyle(3) 9 57
(John Ryan) *mid-div: hdwy over 2f out: rdn and nt clr run over 1f out: styd on* **12/1**
-052 **5** *nk* **Key To Your Heart**[17] 5893 3-8-13 53 (t) CharlieBennett 10 56+
(Hughie Morrison) *prom: chsd ldr 5f out tl led over 1f out: hdd and no ex wl ins fnl f* **3/1**[1]
5343 **6** *3/4* **Polydamos**[12] 6028 5-9-3 51 DavidParkes 6 53
(Tony Carroll) *hld up: hdwy over 1f out: nt rch ldrs* **8/1**
3045 **7** *4* **Stanlow**[11] 6076 4-9-7 55 (v) RobHornby 3 48
(Daniel Mark Loughnane) *hld up: r.o ins fnl f: nvr nrr* **5/1**[2]
4603 **8** *3/4* **Supa Seeker (USA)**[40] 5033 8-8-9 50 RussellHarris(7) 8 41
(Tony Carroll) *hld up: nt clr run over 2f out: sme hdwy over 1f out: n.d* **16/1**
0332 **9** *1/2* **Rock Band**[18] 5854 5-9-4 52 (bt) GaryMahon 13 42
(Emmet Michael Butterly, Ire) *chsd ldr tl led 6f out: rdn over 2f out: hdd over 1f out: wknd fnl f* **7/1**[3]
1660 **10** *1 1/2* **Look On By**[49] 4730 4-9-3 54 DanielleMooney(3) 7 40
(Ruth Carr) *led: hdd 6f out: chsd ldrs tl wknd 2f out* **50/1**
2263 **11** *1/2* **General Tufto**[22] 5731 9-9-1 54 (b) PaddyPilley(5) 12 39
(Charles Smith) *s.i.s: outpcd* **20/1**
2446 **12** *2 1/2* **Tortoise**[13] 6010 3-8-13 53 (b) LukeLeadbitter 4 32
(Richard Guest) *chsd ldrs: rdn over 2f out: wknd over 1f out* **25/1**
6065 **13** *nk* **Blue Clumber**[9] 6161 4-8-11 48 JoshQuinn(3) 1 27
(Shaun Harris) *prom: rdn over 3f out: sn wknd* **33/1**
1m 51.91s (1.81) **Going Correction** +0.175s/f (Slow)
**WFA** 3 from 4yo+ 6lb **13** Ran SP% **118.1**
Speed ratings (Par 101): **98,96,95,95,95 94,91,90,89,88 88,85,85**
CSF £110.52 CT £1284.82 TOTE £7.30: £2.40, £4.50, £5.30; EX 139.40 Trifecta £2524.80 Part won..
**Owner** The Bourne Connection **Bred** Mette Campbell-Andenaes **Trained** Great Ness, Shropshire
**FOCUS**
This was run at a searching pace. The winner's best form since her early days.

## 6408 BRITISH STALLION STUDS EBF MAIDEN FILLIES' STKS (BOBIS RACE) (TAPETA) 5f 20y
3:00 (3:02) (Class 5) 2-Y-0 £2,911 (£866; £432; £216) Stalls Low

Form RPR
204 **1** **La Cuesta (IRE)**[8] 6168 2-9-0 0 AdamKirby 9 87+
(Jamie Osborne) *hld up in tch: a gng wl: led ins fnl f: shkn up and qcknd clr* **1/2**[1]
56 **2** *5* **Medicean Bliss (IRE)**[23] 5667 2-9-0 0 HarryBentley 13 69
(Jeremy Gask) *mid-div: pushed along 1/2-way: hdwy over 1f out: r.o to go 2nd nr fin: no ch w wnr* **25/1**
2052 **3** *1* **One Moment**[18] 5859 2-9-0 67 SamHitchcott 10 65
(Robert Cowell) *trckd ldr tl wnt upsides 1/2-way: rdn to ld over 1f out: edgd lft: hdd and no ex ins fnl f* **8/1**[2]
0 **4** *hd* **Mary's Secret**[20] 5789 2-9-0 0 RichardKingscote 5 64
(Tom Dascombe) *prom: rdn 1/2-way: outpcd 2f out: styd on ins fnl f* **16/1**
0236 **5** *1 1/2* **Candlelight (IRE)**[14] 5985 2-9-0 64 JimCrowley 1 59
(Charles Hills) *chsd ldrs: rdn and edgd lft over 1f out: no ex fnl f* **12/1**[3]
0 **6** *1* **Courier**[32] 5344 2-9-0 0 SilvestreDeSousa 12 55
(Jeremy Noseda) *s.i.s: sn pushed along in rr: r.o ins fnl f: nrst fin* **14/1**
0 **7** *shd* **Signorina Roseina**[10] 6093 2-8-11 0 NeilFarley(3) 8 55
(Eric Alston) *trckd ldrs: rdn 1/2-way: wknd ins fnl f* **200/1**
**8** *hd* **Vivre La Reve** 2-9-0 0 GrahamGibbons 6 54
(Ed McMahon) *sn pushed along in rr: r.o ins fnl f: nvr nrr* **20/1**
55 **9** *1/2* **Torridonian**[21] 5774 2-9-0 0 FergusSweeney 3 52
(James Tate) *led: rdn and hdd over 1f out: wknd ins fnl f* **16/1**
**10** *5* **Southview Lady** 2-9-0 0 LiamKeniry 4 34
(Mark Walford) *in rr whn hmpd over 3f out: nvr on terms* **100/1**
**11** *1 1/4* **Miss Laroc (IRE)** 2-9-0 0 RobertHavlin 7 30
(Jeremy Gask) *sn pushed along and a in rr* **66/1**
**12** *99* **Drastic Art** 2-9-0 0 MartinDwyer 2
(Michael Bell) *s.s: outpcd* **40/1**
1m 2.12s (0.22) **Going Correction** +0.175s/f (Slow) **12** Ran SP% **117.9**
Speed ratings (Par 92): **105,97,95,95,92 91,90,90,89,81 79,**
CSF £24.92 TOTE £1.50: £1.10, £5.70, £2.20; EX 18.60 Trifecta £124.00.
**Owner** Mr & Mrs R Kelvin-Hughes **Bred** Glenvale Stud **Trained** Upper Lambourn, Berks
**FOCUS**
They went hard up front and very few figured. The winner could be rated in the low 90s.

## 6409 SPONSOR A RACE BY CALLING 01902 390000 H'CAP (TAPETA) 5f 216y
3:30 (3:30) (Class 6) (0-55,55) 3-Y-0+ £1,940 (£577; £288; £144) Stalls Low

Form RPR
/0-6 **1** **Indastar**[39] 5103 4-9-2 50 DaleSwift 6 65
(Michael Herrington) *trckd ldrs: racd keenly: rdn to ld 1f out: r.o wl* **8/1**
5652 **2** *3 1/4* **China Excels**[20] 5801 7-9-1 49 HarryBentley 12 54
(Mandy Rowland) *trckd ldr tl led wl over 1f out: rdn and hdd 1f out: styd on same pce* **10/1**
4226 **3** *1 3/4* **Red Shadow**[10] 6120 5-9-4 52 (p) PaulPickard 8 51+
(Alan Brown) *hld up: hdwy over 2f out: rdn: edgd lft and r.o ins fnl f: nt rch ldrs* **9/1**
05 **4** *2 1/2* **First Rebellion**[41] 5000 5-9-3 51 AdamKirby 3 42
(Tony Carroll) *sn pushed along to ld: rdn and hdd wl over 1f out: wkng whn hmpd ins fnl f* **9/1**
4640 **5** *2* **Bondi Beach Babe**[68] 4070 4-9-7 55 TonyHamilton 10 40
(James Turner) *hld up: hdwy over 2f out: sn rdn: wknd fnl f* **16/1**
0030 **6** *1/2* **Major Muscari (IRE)**[62] 4287 6-9-4 52 (p) MartinHarley 4 35+
(Shaun Harris) *hld up: r.o towards fin: nvr nrr* **7/2**[1]
3-00 **7** *hd* **Gauchita**[19] 5819 3-8-9 52 PeterSword(7) 13 35
(K R Burke) *hld up: hdwy over 2f out: sn rdn: wknd fnl f* **33/1**
0065 **8** *1 3/4* **Ishi Honest**[12] 6030 4-9-7 55 SilvestreDeSousa 9 32
(Mark Usher) *chsd ldrs: rdn over 1f out: wknd fnl f* **14/1**
5620 **9** *1/2* **Lord Buffhead**[10] 6120 5-9-3 54 (v) BillyCray(3) 2 30
(Richard Guest) *sn pushed along in mid-div: hdwy over 3f out: drvn along over 2f out: wknd wl over 1f out* **20/1**
6512 **10** *hd* **White Flag**[18] 5853 3-8-12 55 RachelRichardson(7) 11 30
(Tim Easterby) *prom: lost pl 4f out: n.d after* **4/1**[2]
0632 **11** *1/2* **Reginald Claude**[38] 5136 6-9-6 54 LiamKeniry 5 27+
(Mark Usher) *hld up: nt clr run over 2f out: wknd wl over 1f out* **15/2**[3]
-004 **12** *2 1/2* **Port Lairge**[27] 5532 4-9-4 52 (b) MartinDwyer 1 17
(John Gallagher) *s.i.s: sn drvn along and a in rr* **16/1**
0000 **13** *3* **Saga Lout**[4] 6272 4-8-13 54 RobHornby(7) 7 10
(Andrew Hollinshead) *s.s: a in rr* **40/1**
1m 14.75s (0.25) **Going Correction** +0.175s/f (Slow)
**WFA** 3 from 4yo+ 2lb **13** Ran SP% **122.8**
Speed ratings (Par 101): **105,100,98,95,92 91,91,89,88,88 87,84,80**
CSF £86.42 CT £771.82 TOTE £10.90: £3.60, £3.00, £2.30; EX 143.60 Trifecta £2481.40.
**Owner** K Blackstone **Bred** Bearstone Stud **Trained** Cold Kirby, N Yorks
**FOCUS**
Another fiercely run affair, but the pace held up. The form is rated around the runner-up.

## 6410 LIKE US ON FACEBOOK WOLVERHAMPTON RACECOURSE H'CAP (TAPETA) 1m 4f 50y
4:00 (4:00) (Class 6) (0-60,60) 3-Y-0+ £1,940 (£577; £288; £144) Stalls Low

Form RPR
0006 **1** **Chantecler**[18] 5864 3-9-3 60 RobertHavlin 12 73
(Hughie Morrison) *hld up in tch: plld hrd: jnd ldrs over 2f out: rdn to ld ins fnl f: styd on* **11/2**
5523 **2** *1* **Royal Trooper (IRE)**[4] 6267 8-9-2 57 BeckyBrisbourne(7) 4 68
(Mark Brisbourne) *s.i.s: hld up: hdwy over 3f out: led 2f out: rdn and hdd ins fnl f: styd on same pce* **6/1**
0534 **3** *4 1/2* **Power Up**[20] 5786 3-9-1 58 (v[1]) AdamKirby 3 62
(Mark Johnston) *hld up: pushed along and hdwy over 2f out: rdn over 1f out: styd on same pce fnl f* **4/1**[2]
4044 **4** *4* **Snow Dancer (IRE)**[9] 6157 10-8-12 51 AlistairRawlinson(5) 8 48
(John David Riches) *prom: led wl over 2f out: rdn and hdd 2f out: wknd fnl f* **16/1**
0452 **5** *2 1/4* **Well Owd Mon**[16] 5904 4-8-10 51 RobHornby(7) 1 45
(Andrew Hollinshead) *hld up: hdwy u.p over 1f out: nvr on terms* **5/1**[3]
0500 **6** *1 1/4* **Fire In Babylon (IRE)**[18] 5864 6-8-12 51 (b) TobyAtkinson(5) 11 43
(Noel Quinlan) *s.i.s: hld up: hdwy 1/2-way: rdn and wknd over 1f out* **28/1**
2220 **7** *4 1/2* **Rajeh (IRE)**[9] 6157 11-8-12 46 FergusSweeney 6 31
(Peter Grayson) *mid-div: hdwy 1/2-way: pushed along over 4f out: wknd over 3f out* **28/1**
060- **8** *9* **Pink Mischief**[114] 7637 4-8-11 48 NeilFarley(3) 9 18
(Andrew Crook) *hld up: rdn and wknd over 2f out* **66/1**
200 **9** *3 1/2* **Innoko (FR)**[41] 5001 4-9-4 57 (t) GeorgeDowning(5) 10 22
(Tony Carroll) *chsd ldr tl led over 3f out: hdd wl over 2f out: sn wknd* **22/1**
4440 **10** *12* **Blue Top**[10] 6117 5-9-9 57 (p) LiamKeniry 2
(Mark Walford) *chsd ldrs tl rdn and wknd over 3f out* **16/1**
0350 **11** *3 1/4* **Citizen Kaine (IRE)**[12] 6037 3-9-3 60 (bt) SilvestreDeSousa 5
(Jo Hughes) *led: hdd over 3f out: wknd over 2f out* **10/3**[1]
44-4 **12** *52* **Moaning Butcher**[17] 430 4-9-7 55 (v) RussKennemore 7
(Dave Roberts) *chsd ldrs: pushed along 10f out: rdn and lost pl over 6f out: sn wl bhd* **100/1**
2m 40.82s (0.02) **Going Correction** +0.175s/f (Slow)
**WFA** 3 from 4yo+ 9lb **12** Ran SP% **114.9**
Speed ratings (Par 101): **106,105,102,99,98 97,94,88,86,78 75,41**
CSF £35.40 CT £146.09 TOTE £8.10: £2.50, £1.30, £2.20; EX 38.70 Trifecta £227.20.
**Owner** Sir Thomas Pilkington **Bred** Sir Thomas Pilkington **Trained** East Ilsley, Berks
**FOCUS**
This was weak, but the first two pulled nicely clear and it may prove fair form for the level. The winner rates a personal best.

## 6411 WOLVERHAMPTON-RACECOURSE.CO.UK H'CAP (TAPETA) 1m 141y
4:30 (4:30) (Class 3) (0-95,94) 3-Y-0 **+£7,246** (£2,168; £1,084; £542; £270) Stalls Low

Form RPR
215 **1** **Momayyaz (IRE)**[24] 5627 3-8-3 **86** AhmadAlSubousi(7) 6 99+
(Saeed bin Suroor) *s.i.s: sn prom: led and edgd lft 1f out: rdn out* **7/1**
600 **2** *2* **Capo Rosso (IRE)**[45] 4851 4-9-10 **94** RichardKingscote 8 102
(Tom Dascombe) *led at stdy pce tl qcknd over 2f out: rdn and hdd 1f out: styd on same pce ins fnl f* **2/1**[1]
2220 **3** *1 1/4* **Crowdmania**[9] 6145 3-8-9 **85** SilvestreDeSousa 5 90
(Mark Johnston) *chsd ldr: rdn and ev ch over 1f out: hmpd jst ins fnl f: edgd lft and styd on same pce ins fnl f* **10/3**[3]
014 **4** *shd* **Mindurownbusiness (IRE)**[44] 4915 3-9-0 **90** JimCrowley 1 95
(David Simcock) *trckd ldrs: shkn up whn n.m.r over 1f out: styd on same pce ins fnl f* **9/4**[2]
00 **5** *2 1/4* **Free Code (IRE)**[67] 4125 3-9-0 **90** (p) KierenFallon 2 90
(James Tate) *hld up: pushed along over 3f out: outpcd fnl 2f* **12/1**

3551 **6** *hd* **Conry (IRE)**[9] 6155 8-8-5 **80** oh8 ShaneGray(5) 3 79
(Ian Williams) *hld up: plld hrd: rdn over 2f out: nvr trbld ldrs* **28/1**
1m 50.47s (0.37) **Going Correction** +0.175s/f (Slow)
**WFA** 3 from 4yo+ 6lb **6** Ran SP% **110.8**
Speed ratings (Par 107): **105,103,102,102,100 99**
CSF £20.90 CT £52.41 TOTE £8.10: £2.00, £2.50; EX 24.70 Trifecta £77.30.
**Owner** Godolphin **Bred** Darley **Trained** Newmarket, Suffolk
**FOCUS**
A trappy feature on paper proved equally so in the race itself. The winner was unexposed but the form makes sense.

## 6412 HOLIDAY INN WOLVERHAMPTON NURSERY H'CAP (TAPETA) (DIV I) 7f 32y
**5:00** (5:00) (Class 6) (0-60,60) 2-Y-O **£1,940** (£577; £288; £144) **Stalls** High

Form RPR
5545 **1** **Mazoula (IRE)**[19] 5828 2-9-4 57 JimCrowley 7 60
(Hugo Palmer) *hld up in tch: rdn to ld 1f out: r.o: comf* **9/1**
453 **2** *1 1/4* **Paris Carver (FR)**[13] 6017 2-9-3 56 MartinHarley 3 56
(Jonathan Portman) *chsd ldrs: rdn over 2f out: led over 1f out: sn hdd: styd on same pce ins fnl f* **7/1**
506 **3** *1 3/4* **Candle Of The Sea (IRE)**[14] 5973 2-9-4 57 HarryBentley 8 53
(Ed Vaughan) *hld up: hdwy over 2f out: rdn over 1f out: edgd lft and styd on same pce ins fnl f* **3/1**[1]
3550 **4** *3 1/4* **Flatcapper (IRE)**[39] 5085 2-9-0 58 JackGarritty(5) 2 46
(Richard Fahey) *led 1f: chsd ldrs: wnt 2nd 3f out: sn rdn and ev ch tl no ex fnl f* **8/1**
006 **5** *2 1/2* **Noble Master**[15] 5947 2-9-7 60 SilvestreDeSousa 5 42
(Sylvester Kirk) *chsd ldrs: nt clr run over 2f out: rdn over 1f out: styd on same pce* **6/1**[3]
061 **6** *1 1/4* **Ruby Rose (IRE)**[17] 5896 2-9-2 60 ShaneGray(5) 12 39
(Kevin Ryan) *s.i.s: hld up: hdwy 2f out: sn rdn: wknd fnl f* **4/1**[2]
006 **7** *1/2* **Bushranger Bay (IRE)**[23] 5679 2-9-6 59 JamesSullivan 10 36
(Tim Easterby) *hld up: effrt over 2f out: wknd over 1f out* **20/1**
600 **8** *3/4* **Tatiani**[11] 6066 2-8-12 51 IrineuGoncalves 4 26
(Jose Santos) *chsd ldrs: led 5f out: rdn and hdd over 1f out: wknd fnl f* **33/1**
0004 **9** *6* **Saphira Silver (IRE)**[35] 5254 2-8-5 49 JoeDoyle(5) 1 10
(James Evans) *led 6f out tl 5f out: remained handy tl rdn and wknd over 1f out* **66/1**
4444 **10** *nse* **Poppy In The Wind**[17] 5896 2-9-1 54 DaleSwift 9 15
(Alan Brown) *hld up: nt clr run over 2f out: sn wknd* **33/1**
5050 **11** *1 1/2* **Verchild Lad (IRE)**[42] 4967 2-8-11 50 RoystonFfrench 6 7
(David Evans) *hld up: a in rr* **25/1**
0000 **12** *9* **Ocean Crystal**[19] 5823 2-9-2 55 KierenFallon 11
(John Ryan) *hld up: pushed along 1/2-way: sn wknd* **6/1**[3]
1m 31.63s (2.83) **Going Correction** +0.175s/f (Slow) **12** Ran SP% **123.2**
Speed ratings (Par 93): **90,88,86,82,80 78,78,77,70,70 68,58**
CSF £69.53 CT £243.71 TOTE £10.00: £3.10, £2.10, £1.60; EX 66.00 Trifecta £341.60.
**Owner** Anglia Bloodstock Syndicate IV **Bred** Johnston King **Trained** Newmarket, Suffolk
**FOCUS**
This first division looked the more competitive of the two, but the form is just modest.

## 6413 HOLIDAY INN WOLVERHAMPTON NURSERY H'CAP (TAPETA) (DIV II) 7f 32y
**5:30** (5:31) (Class 6) (0-60,60) 2-Y-O **£1,940** (£577; £288; £144) **Stalls** High

Form RPR
505 **1** **Invincible Wish (IRE)**[27] 5525 2-8-12 51 PaulPickard 12 54
(Brian Ellison) *chsd ldrs: rdn to ld ins fnl f: styd on* **9/1**
0003 **2** *1* **Sky Steps (IRE)**[11] 6072 2-8-10 49 (v) SilvestreDeSousa 4 51+
(Philip McBride) *mid-div: hdwy and nt clr run over 1f out: swtchd rt: rdn and r.o wl to go 2nd nr fin: nt rch wnr* **5/2**[1]
2223 **3** *nk* **Wink Oliver**[28] 5489 2-9-7 60 (p) AdamKirby 7 60
(Kristin Stubbs) *trckd ldr: racd keenly: led wl over 1f out: sn rdn: hdd and unable qck ins fnl f* **11/2**
0452 **4** *1 1/4* **Jet Mate (IRE)**[11] 6072 2-9-6 59 (p) JimCrowley 11 56
(William Muir) *hld up: r.o ins fnl f: nvr nrr* **4/1**[3]
3005 **5** *shd* **Dancing Moon (IRE)**[18] 5845 2-9-2 55 SamHitchcott 3 52
(Mick Channon) *a.p: rdn over 1f out: styd on same pce ins fnl f* **14/1**
5044 **6** *3/4* **Robben**[28] 5489 2-8-13 57 (b) ShaneGray(5) 6 52
(Kevin Ryan) *hld up: hdwy over 2f out: rdn over 1f out: styd on* **3/1**[2]
0305 **7** *3/4* **Lunar Knot**[103] 2903 2-9-5 58 MartinHarley 2 51
(Alan McCabe) *led: rdn over 2f out: hdd wl over 1f out: wknd ins fnl f* **66/1**
5060 **8** *2 1/4* **Orobas (IRE)**[19] 5823 2-9-0 53 (p) DougieCostello 1 41
(Harry Whittington) *chsd ldrs: rdn 1/2-way: wknd ins fnl f* **33/1**
4506 **9** *6* **Go White Lightning (IRE)**[60] 4364 2-9-2 55 MartinDwyer 9 28
(Malcolm Saunders) *hld up: rdn over 2f out: nvr on terms* **66/1**
0660 **10** *shd* **Yukos Flyer (IRE)**[32] 5335 2-8-3 47 JackGarritty(5) 10 20
(Richard Fahey) *hld up: rdn over 2f out: a in rr* **28/1**
5600 **11** *6* **Toytown (IRE)**[53] 4576 2-9-3 56 DaleSwift 5 14
(Derek Shaw) *hld up: hdwy over 2f out: sn rdn and wknd* **40/1**
1m 31.43s (2.63) **Going Correction** +0.175s/f (Slow) **11** Ran SP% **117.4**
Speed ratings (Par 93): **91,89,89,88,87 87,86,83,76,76 69**
CSF £30.92 CT £141.41 TOTE £8.80: £2.70, £1.80, £1.10; EX 37.90 Trifecta £190.00.
**Owner** Brian Ellison **Bred** Cyril Ryan **Trained** Norton, N Yorks
■ Stewards' Enquiry : Paul Pickard seven-day ban: used whip above permitted level and didn't give gelding time to respond (Sep 29-Oct 4,6)
**FOCUS**
A lively betting heat. It was run at a steady tempo and the runner-up was unlucky.

## 6414 HOTEL & CONFERENCEING AT WOLVERHAMPTON H'CAP (TAPETA) 7f 32y
**6:00** (6:01) (Class 5) (0-75,75) 3-Y-O+ **£2,587** (£770; £384; £192) **Stalls** High

Form RPR
151 **1** **For Shia And Lula (IRE)**[11] 6074 5-9-1 71 EoinWalsh(5) 7 80
(Daniel Mark Loughnane) *trckd ldr: pushed along over 2f out: led over 1f out: rdn and edgd lft ins fnl f: jst hld on* **3/1**[2]
00-0 **2** *hd* **Gigawatt**[33] 5308 4-9-6 71 PatCosgrave 2 79
(Jim Boyle) *hld up in tch: rdn over 1f out: r.o wl* **20/1**
-430 **3** *1 3/4* **Punk**[12] 6034 3-9-4 73 JimCrowley 5 74
(George Peckham) *trckd ldrs: rdn over 1f out: styd on* **20/1**
4501 **4** *hd* **Sakash**[22] 5729 4-9-9 74 (p) FrederikTylicki 4 77
(J R Jenkins) *hdled: rdn and hdd over 1f out: no ex ins fnl f* **7/4**[1]
6055 **5** *3* **Zain Zone (IRE)**[13] 6009 3-9-3 72 (p) JamesSullivan 8 65
(Ruth Carr) *hld up: rdn over 2f out: styd on ins fnl f: nvr nrr* **8/1**

0300 **6** *shd* **Relation Alexander (IRE)**[19] 5826 3-9-5 74 AdamKirby 9 67
(Paul D'Arcy) *hld up: rdn over 1f out: edgd lft and styd on ins fnl f: nt rch ldrs* **12/1**
0315 **7** *3 1/4* **Hill Of Dreams (IRE)**[167] 1215 5-9-6 71 HarryBentley 1 57
(Dean Ivory) *chsd ldrs: rdn over 2f out: wknd fnl f* **50/1**
0510 **8** *2* **Shaunas Spirit (IRE)**[167] 1217 6-9-3 75 PaulBooth(7) 6 56
(Dean Ivory) *s.i.s: hld up: a in rr* **50/1**
0056 **9** *2 3/4* **Lord Of The Dance (IRE)**[19] 5810 8-9-2 67 SilvestreDeSousa 11 41
(Michael Mullineaux) *prom: rdn over 2f out: wknd over 1f out* **7/2**[3]
4RR0 **R** **Caramack**[14] 5986 4-9-8 73 RobertHavlin 10
(Richard Lee) *ref to r* **16/1**
1m 30.0s (1.20) **Going Correction** +0.175s/f (Slow)
**WFA** 3 from 4yo+ 4lb **10** Ran SP% **121.7**
Speed ratings (Par 103): **100,99,97,97,94 94,90,88,84,**
CSF £67.07 CT £1044.21 TOTE £5.40: £2.00, £4.90, £4.10; EX 112.30 Trifecta £652.80.
**Owner** Over The Moon Racing IV **Bred** A M F Persse **Trained** Baldwin's Gate, Staffs
**FOCUS**
An interesting finale and one of the finishes of the day. The winner confirmed he's better than ever.
T/Jkpt: Not won. T/Plt: £131.40 to a £1 stake. Pool: £82,009.91 - 455.45 winning units. T/Qpdt: £20.10 to a £1 stake. Pool: £7213.79 - 265.00 winning units. CR

6415 - 6418a (Foreign Racing) - See Raceform Interactive

# 3773 SAINT-CLOUD (L-H)
Monday, September 15

**OFFICIAL GOING: Turf: good**

## 6419a PRIX JOUBERT (LISTED RACE) (3YO FILLIES) (TURF) 1m 4f
**4:40** (12:00) 3-Y-O **£22,916** (£9,166; £6,875; £4,583; £2,291)

RPR
**1** **Mayhem (IRE)**[25] 3-8-11 0 OlivierPeslier 3 108
(P Sogorb, France) **7/2**[3]
**2** *3 1/2* **My Spirit (IRE)**[33] 5312 3-8-11 0 GregoryBenoist 5 102
(William Haggas) *led: kicked 2 l clr 2 1/2f out: sn rdn: hdd appr fnl f: readily outpcd by wnr and kpt on at same pce to fin clr of remainder* **27/10**[2]
**3** *4 1/2* **Sahrawi (GER)**[14] 5992 3-8-11 0 Christophe-PatriceLemaire 7 95
(M Delzangles, France) **9/5**[1]
**4** *1/2* **Whim**[106] 2816 3-8-11 0 (b) ThierryJarnet 1 94
(F Head, France) **79/10**
**5** *3/4* **Hand Puppet (IRE)**[29] 5479 3-8-11 0 MaximeGuyon 6 93
(A Fabre, France) *w.w in tch: pushed along 2 1/2f out and no imp: sn rdn: plugged on at same pce fnl f: nvr trbld ldrs* **87/10**
**6** *shd* **Mayumi (IRE)**[16] 3-8-11 0 Pierre-CharlesBoudot 4 93
(A Fabre, France) **13/2**
2m 29.65s (-10.75) **6** Ran SP% **119.8**
WIN (incl. 1 euro stake): 4.50. PLACES: 2.30, 2.00. SF: 15.40.
**Owner** Mme Anne-Marie Hayes **Bred** Kilfrush Stud Farm **Trained** France

# 6246 CHEPSTOW (L-H)
Tuesday, September 16

**OFFICIAL GOING: Good (good to firm in places)**
Wind: light, half across Weather: hazy sunshine

## 6420 ANGEL HOTEL IN ABERGAVENNY/EBF MAIDEN STKS 7f 16y
**2:20** (2:46) (Class 5) 2-Y-O **£2,911** (£866; £432; £216) **Stalls** Centre

Form RPR
**1** **Dark Kingdom (IRE)** 2-9-5 0 GeorgeBaker 1 74+
(Ed Walker) *swtchd rt after 2f and dropped in rr: rdn over 1f out: stl 6th ent fnl f: r.o wl to ld nr fin* **10/1**
43 **2** *nk* **King Jerry (IRE)**[18] 5874 2-9-5 0 RichardHughes 8 73
(Ralph Beckett) *cl up: led 3f out: rdn 2f out and edgd lft: edgd rt ins fnl f: ct nr fin* **7/4**[2]
0 **3** *nk* **Chain Of Daisies**[12] 6065 2-9-0 0 DaneO'Neill 6 67
(Henry Candy) *s.s: towards rr: hdwy 3f out: sn rdn: styd on ins fnl f: jst hld* **33/1**
2 **4** *3 1/4* **Cymro (IRE)**[108] 2756 2-9-5 0 RichardKingscote 5 64
(Tom Dascombe) *chsd ldrs: rdn over 2f out: one pce whn edgd rt early ins fnl f: wknd last 100yds* **6/4**[1]
05 **5** *3/4* **Beauty Of The Sea**[24] 5667 2-9-0 0 JamieSpencer 2 57
(Roger Varian) *hld up towards rr: rdn and hdwy on outside over 1f out: wknd fnl 100yds* **7/1**[3]
000 **6** *8* **Follow The Faith**[13] 6032 2-9-0 0 SamHitchcott 4 35
(Mick Channon) *pushed along after 2f: a towards rr* **66/1**
**7** *hd* **Eagle Empire (IRE)** 2-9-0 0 CamHardie(5) 7 39
(Richard Hannon) *s.i.s: racd keenly: chsd ldrs: rdn over 2f out: wknd over 1f out* **16/1**
042 **8** *3/4* **Keen Move**[40] 5098 2-9-5 66 AdamKirby 3 47
(Ismail Mohammed) *led tl rdn and hdd 3f out: wkng whn sltly hmpd early ins fnl f: sn eased* **16/1**
1m 22.71s (-0.49) **Going Correction** +0.025s/f (Good) **8** Ran SP% **114.2**
Speed ratings: **103,102,102,98,97 88,88,87**
CSF £27.88 TOTE £11.20: £3.30, £1.30, £5.00; EX 33.60 Trifecta £643.90.
**Owner** F Ma **Bred** David Harrison **Trained** Newmarket, Suffolk
**FOCUS**
Racing was delayed due to an inspection of an area in the dip around a furlong and a half out. The track has a history of loose, unsafe ground due to problems with nematodes. Martin Dwyer, after riding the winner of the second race, described the ground as "bad and slippery". Those that had already run didn't set a great standard in this maiden, but the winner made a nice enough start.

## 6421 TRUELINEPRODUCTS.CO.UK MAIDEN STKS 7f 16y
**2:50** (3:20) (Class 5) 3-Y-O+ **£2,587** (£770; £384; £192) **Stalls** Centre

Form RPR
4 **1** **So Noble**[22] 5775 3-9-5 0 MartinDwyer 5 73+
(William Muir) *chsd ldrs: rdn and hdwy 1/2-way: led 2f out: edgd rt ins fnl f: pushed out* **10/11**[1]
**2** *1/2* **Wu Zetian** 3-9-0 0 DavidProbert 8 67
(Andrew Balding) *s.i.s: hdwy after 2f: rdn 2f out: styd on fnl f: wnt 2nd cl home* **6/1**[3]
5 **3** *3/4* **Copperbelt**[27] 5570 3-9-5 0 FrannyNorton 10 70
(Mark Johnston) *racd keenly: led narrowly tl rdn and hdd 2f out: kpt on same pce: lost 2nd cl home* **5/1**[2]

0306 **4** *3* **Mad Endeavour**[32] 5402 3-9-5 60 AdamKirby 4 62
(Stuart Kittow) *w ldr: rdn 2f out: kpt on tl no ex fnl 100yds* **7/1**
0605 **5** *4½* **Borough Belle**[85] 3527 3-8-11 49 AmyScott(3) 9 45
(Henry Candy) *chsd ldrs: rdn over 2f out: sn outpcd by principals* **12/1**
**6** *5* **Man Of Music** 3-9-5 0 LiamKeniry 11 37
(Tony Carroll) *wnt rt s and slowly away: towards rr tl r.o fnl f: nvr nr ldrs* **20/1**
**7** *½* **Road Map (IRE)** 3-9-0 0 EoinWalsh(5) 6 36
(Daniel Mark Loughnane) *dwlt: towards rr: no ch fnl 3f: uns rdr after fin* **66/1**
0-60 **8** *2* **My Stroppy Poppy**[12] 6073 5-9-3 45 RaulDaSilva 2 27
(Alan Phillips) *mid-div: rdn 1/2-way: sn no ch* **100/1**
**9** *½* **Farmshop Boy** 3-8-12 0 CharlieBennett(7) 1 30
(Natalie Lloyd-Beavis) *rdn after 3f: a towards rr: uns rdr after fin* **100/1**
0 **10** *9* **Aduvee**[12] 6073 4-9-3 0 WilliamTwiston-Davies 3 2
(Ronald Harris) *cl up tl rdn over 2f out: wknd over 1f out* **100/1**
0 **11** *13* **Zand Man**[85] 3517 4-9-5 0 RobertTart(3) 7
(Milton Bradley) *in tch tl grad lost pl after 2f: bhd fnl 3f: t.o* **100/1**

1m 23.13s (-0.07) **Going Correction** +0.025s/f (Good)
**WFA** 3 from 4yo+ 3lb **11** Ran SP% **113.7**
Speed ratings (Par 103): **101,100,99,96,91 85,84,82,81,71 56**
CSF £6.23 TOTE £2.60: £1.10, £2.30, £1.80; EX 8.50 Trifecta £25.10.
**Owner** Muir Racing Partnership - Windsor **Bred** Cheveley Park Stud Ltd **Trained** Lambourn, Berks
**FOCUS**
This didn't look a particularly strong maiden.

## 6422 DAVE EVANS RACING NURSERY H'CAP 6f 16y
**3:20** (3:50) (Class 5) (0-70,70) 2-Y-O **£2,587** (£770; £384; £192) **Stalls** Centre

Form RPR
514 **1** **Mecado (IRE)**[21] 5782 2-9-7 70 RichardHughes 9 73+
(Richard Hannon) *chsd ldrs: pushed along over 2f out: rdn appr fnl f: r.o to ld 75yds out: sn edgd rt: pushed out* **11/4**[1]
6050 **2** *nk* **Chetan**[13] 6040 2-8-6 55 FrannyNorton 1 57
(Milton Bradley) *cl up: rdn over 2f out: ev ch 1f out: r.o u.p* **33/1**
3243 **3** *nk* **Khawaater**[15] 5974 2-9-4 67 (t) DaneO'Neill 4 68
(Roger Varian) *in rr: pushed along and hdwy over 2f out: qcknd to ld appr fnl f: edgd rt: hdd 75yds out: no ex* **4/1**[2]
5034 **4** *1¾* **Lady Marita (IRE)**[54] 4576 2-9-0 63 JFEgan 8 59
(David Evans) *mid-div: hdwy 3f out: rdn 2f out: kpt on same pce* **10/1**
0621 **5** *nk* **Zipedeedodah (IRE)**[15] 5985 2-9-1 69 ShaneGray(5) 11 66
(Joseph Tuite) *hld up in tch: nt clr run over 3f out to 2f out: rdn and sme hdwy over 1f out: nt rch ldrs: eased nr fin* **9/2**[3]
026 **6** *2* **Ickymasho**[18] 5874 2-9-3 66 AdamKirby 5 55
(Jonathan Portman) *mid-div: hdwy on outer over 2f out: one pce fnl f* **6/1**
003 **7** *¾* **Air Of York (IRE)**[5] 6248 2-8-0 49 oh1 (b) RaulDaSilva 10 37
(Ronald Harris) *racd keenly: led: rdn over 1f out: sn hdd: grad wknd* **20/1**
4400 **8** *1* **Essaka (IRE)**[17] 5929 2-9-1 64 SamHitchcott 7 61
(Mick Channon) *sltly hmpd sn after s: in rr: nt clr run over 3f out tl over 1f out: shkn up whn sltly hmpd 1f out: no ch after* **6/1**
0253 **9** *1¾* **June's Moon**[28] 5524 2-9-3 66 RichardKingscote 6 45
(Jonathan Portman) *chsd ldrs: rdn over 1f out: wknd fnl f* **14/1**

1m 12.1s (0.10) **Going Correction** +0.025s/f (Good) **9** Ran SP% **116.9**
Speed ratings (Par 95): **100,99,99,96,96 93,92,91,89**
CSF £98.18 CT £368.60 TOTE £3.20: £1.30, £5.90, £1.60; EX 86.70 Trifecta £510.30.
**Owner** Potensis Ltd & J Palmer-Brown **Bred** J F Tuthill **Trained** East Everleigh, Wilts
**FOCUS**
Just a modest nursery, and a couple found trouble. The winner won with a shade in hand.

## 6423 GET FREE BETS AT THEBOOKIESOFFERS.CO.UK CLAIMING STKS 7f 16y
**3:50** (4:21) (Class 6) 3-Y-O+ **£1,940** (£577; £288; £144) **Stalls** Centre

Form RPR
6001 **1** **Amadeus Wolfe Tone (IRE)**[11] 6089 5-9-10 85 (p) AdamKirby 8 83
(Jamie Osborne) *hld up last on stands' side: smooth hdwy 2f out: sn rdn: chal wl ins fnl f: r.o: won on nod* **6/4**[1]
0062 **2** *nse* **Solo Hunter**[21] 5795 3-9-3 72 (v) JFEgan 4 78
(David Evans) *led stands' side gp and chsd overall ldr: rdn 3f out: led over 1f out: jnd wl ins fnl f: r.o: lost on nod* **7/1**
200 **3** *6* **Desert Society (IRE)**[41] 5031 3-8-13 79 (b) RichardHughes 2 58
(Richard Hannon) *racd alone centre and overall ldr: rdn over 2f out: sn edgd rt to join main gp: hdd over 1f out: wknd but hld 3rd* **2/1**[2]
5546 **4** *¾* **Peak Storm**[23] 5721 5-8-11 64 (p) CamHardie(5) 3 57
(John O'Shea) *s.i.s: towards rr stands' side: rdn 3f out: hdwy over 1f out: one pce fnl f* **9/2**[3]
**5** *½* **Springlike (IRE)**[80] 3-8-8 76 LouisSteward(5) 5 55
(Amy Weaver) *trckd ldrs stands' side: rdn over 2f out: wknd fnl f* **16/1**
0650 **6** *1¾* **Blue Clumber**[1] 6407 4-8-5 48 FrannyNorton 7 41
(Shaun Harris) *chsd ldrs stands' side: pushed along after 3f: dropped to last over 2f out: one pce and no ch after* **25/1**

1m 22.46s (-0.74) **Going Correction** +0.025s/f (Good)
**WFA** 3 from 4yo+ 3lb **6** Ran SP% **113.7**
Speed ratings (Par 101): **105,104,98,97,96 94**
CSF £12.98 TOTE £2.00: £1.10, £5.50; EX 8.40 Trifecta £30.10.Solo Hunter was claimed by M Meade for £14000.
**Owner** B T McDonald **Bred** Brian Williamson **Trained** Upper Lambourn, Berks
**FOCUS**
This looked a pretty good claimer and the first two finished nicely clear.

## 6424 THEBOOKIESOFFERS.CO.UK FOR THE BEST BOOKIES OFFERS H'CAP 7f 16y
**4:20** (4:52) (Class 4) (0-85,85) 3-Y-O+ **£4,690** (£1,395; £697; £348) **Stalls** Centre

Form RPR
553 **1** **Verse Of Love**[7] 6207 5-9-7 82 JFEgan 4 90
(David Evans) *chsd ldrs: led 3f out: rdn 2f out: jnd 1f out: r.o: asserted last strides* **5/2**[1]
4623 **2** *nk* **Good Authority (IRE)**[10] 6144 7-9-6 81 RichardHughes 1 88
(Karen George) *t.k.h in rr: hdwy to join ldrs after 3f: shkn up 1f out: ev ch tl hld last strides* **4/1**[3]
0604 **3** *2¾* **Charles Molson**[10] 6144 3-9-7 85 DaneO'Neill 3 84
(Henry Candy) *s.i.s: hld up in rr: rdn and hdwy over 2f out: nt clr run and swtchd lft 1f out: styd on same pce* **3/1**[2]
0056 **4** *1¼* **Dubawi Fun**[10] 6145 3-9-4 82 AdamKirby 6 78
(Ismail Mohammed) *led to 3f out: sn rdn: outpcd by ldrs fnl f* **8/1**
0400 **5** *1½* **Monsea (IRE)**[34] 5311 3-8-10 79 CamHardie(5) 7 71
(Richard Hannon) *chsd ldrs: rdn and sltly outpcd 3f out: kpt on same pce after* **16/1**

4634 **6** *2½* **Great Expectations**[21] 5785 6-8-13 74 (t) PaddyAspell 2 60
(J R Jenkins) *t.k.h early: hld up: rdn over 2f out: no imp* **14/1**
3000 **7** *3¼* **Skytrain**[18] 5895 4-9-2 77 (v) FrannyNorton 5 55
(Mark Johnston) *trckd ldr to 3f out: losing pl whn sltly hmpd over 2f out: last and one pce after* **6/1**

1m 22.32s (-0.88) **Going Correction** +0.025s/f (Good)
**WFA** 3 from 4yo+ 3lb **7** Ran SP% **111.5**
Speed ratings (Par 105): **106,105,102,101,99 96,92**
CSF £12.10 TOTE £3.40: £1.70, £1.50; EX 10.80 Trifecta £37.90.
**Owner** Wayne Clifford **Bred** Mrs S Clifford **Trained** Pandy, Monmouths
**FOCUS**
Recent winning form was thin on the ground here.

## 6425 FREE CASINO BONUSES AT THEBOOKIESOFFERS.CO.UK H'CAP 1m 4f 23y
**4:50** (5:20) (Class 4) (0-85,85) 3-Y-O+ **£4,690** (£1,395; £697; £348) **Stalls** Low

Form RPR
0-11 **1** **Fractal**[15] 5984 3-9-4 85 MartinLane 2 101
(David Simcock) *dwlt: hld up in last: hdwy to chse clr ldr over 4f out: rdn to ld over 2f out: sn drew clr: easily* **8/11**[1]
210 **2** *8* **Jupiter Storm**[99] 3065 5-9-12 85 (p) GeorgeBaker 5 88
(Gary Moore) *led: sn 4 l clr: 6 l advantage 5f out but grad reeled in: rdn and hdd over 2f out: one pce and no ch w wnr* **2/1**[2]
01 **3** *7* **Madame Rouge**[33] 5339 3-8-8 75 JFEgan 3 67
(David Evans) *t.k.h: chsd ldr: hung rt and awkward bnd 5f out: sn dropped to 3rd: one pce and no ch after* **9/2**[3]
0-00 **4** *97* **Ruggero**[17] 5931 4-8-13 75 (p) DeclanBates(3) 4
(Roy Brotherton) *racd in 3rd tl relegated to last over 4f out: wknd qckly: t.o fnl 3f* **33/1**

2m 35.13s (-3.87) **Going Correction** -0.15s/f (Firm)
**WFA** 3 from 4yo+ 8lb **4** Ran SP% **112.4**
Speed ratings (Par 105): **106,100,96,31**
CSF £2.63 TOTE £1.60; EX 2.20 Trifecta £3.20.
**Owner** The Black Gold Partnership **Bred** Jeremy Green And Sons **Trained** Newmarket, Suffolk
**FOCUS**
George Baker tried to put it up to the rest by poaching an early advantage and playing catch-me-if-you-can aboard Jupiter Storm, but the tactic didn't pay off.

## 6426 UNIBET CHAMPIONS LEAGUE INJURY TIME MONEYBACK H'CAP 1m 2f 36y
**5:20** (5:53) (Class 6) (0-65,65) 3-Y-O+ **£1,940** (£577; £288; £144) **Stalls** Low

Form RPR
5225 **1** **Urban Space**[25] 5621 8-9-0 55 (t) LiamKeniry 15 65
(John Flint) *chsd ldrs: led over 2f out: rdn and r.o wl* **6/1**[3]
0244 **2** *3½* **Mary Le Bow**[11] 6087 3-8-3 57 (p) KieranShoemark(7) 3 60
(Karen George) *hld up: hdwy 5f out: wnt 2nd 2f out: sn rdn and no imp on wnr* **12/1**
3143 **3** *1½* **Cataria Girl (USA)**[26] 5599 5-9-2 64 (t) JordanVaughan(7) 11 65
(Marcus Tregoning) *mid-div: hdwy over 2f out: sn rdn: styd on fnl f* **9/2**[2]
0062 **4** *2¼* **Bold Cross (IRE)**[7] 6210 11-8-7 51 oh3 DeclanBates(3) 9 47
(Edward Bevan) *hld up: stdy hdwy over 3f out: one pce fnl 2f* **8/1**
2400 **5** *1½* **Mercury Magic**[13] 6037 3-8-8 55 RaulDaSilva 13 48
(David Menuisier) *s.i.s: sn mid-div: rdn along 5f out: hdwy over 3f out: one pce fnl 2f* **12/1**
-465 **6** *2½* **Richo**[19] 5850 8-8-5 51 oh6 (b) CamHardie(5) 12 40
(Shaun Harris) *dwlt: in rr: rdn and hdwy 3f out: one pce fnl 2f* **66/1**
6405 **7** *½* **Distant High**[15] 5980 3-8-7 59 (p) RachealKneller(5) 10 47
(Richard Price) *chsd ldrs tl rdn and lost pl 4f out: styd on again fnl f* **8/1**
0300 **8** *½* **Harwoods Star (IRE)**[12] 6070 4-9-2 57 MartinLane 1 44
(Amanda Perrett) *chsd ldrs: rdn 2f out: sn wknd* **10/1**
-544 **9** *2½* **Society Pearl (IRE)**[19] 5848 4-9-8 63 (b) JFEgan 2 45
(David Evans) *cl up: led after 2f tl over 2f out: wknd over 1f out* **12/1**
0000 **10** *8* **April Ciel**[11] 6091 5-9-8 63 (p) WilliamTwiston-Davies 7 30
(Ronald Harris) *led 2f: styd cl up: rdn over 2f out: wkng whn hmpd over 1f out* **16/1**
0500 **11** *7* **Guilded Spirit**[11] 6086 4-9-5 60 (p) RichardHughes 5 13
(Stuart Kittow) *hld up towards rr: hmpd on ins 5f out: rdn and no imp 3f out: no ch whn eased ins fnl f* **4/1**[1]
260 **12** *12* **Amourita (IRE)**[113] 2613 3-9-1 62 RichardKingscote 8
(Jonathan Portman) *a towards rr: struggling 4f out: t.o* **16/1**
6000 **13** *40* **Byrae**[39] 5138 4-8-11 52 JohnFahy 14
(Polly Gundry) *mid-div tl wknd over 3f out: t.o* **33/1**

2m 7.94s (-2.66) **Going Correction** -0.15s/f (Firm)
**WFA** 3 from 4yo+ 6lb **13** Ran SP% **123.1**
Speed ratings (Par 101): **104,101,100,98,97 95,94,94,92,85 80,70,38**
CSF £78.69 CT £362.84 TOTE £7.50: £2.90, £3.90, £1.40; EX 84.50 Trifecta £429.00.
**Owner** Jason Tucker **Bred** Winterbeck Manor Stud **Trained** Kenfig Hill, Bridgend
**FOCUS**
An ordinary handicap.
T/Plt: £15.20 to a £1 stake. Pool of £44891.56 - 2153.14 winning tickets. T/Qpdt: £3.80 to a £1 stake. Pool of £3670.13 - 713.35 winning tickets. RL

# 6146 THIRSK (L-H)
Tuesday, September 16

**OFFICIAL GOING: Good (good to firm in places) changing to good after race 1 (2.10)**
Wind: virtually nil Weather: Mixture of sunshine and cloud

## 6427 THIRSKRACECOURSE.NET NURSERY H'CAP (BOBIS RACE) 6f
**2:10** (2:10) (Class 4) (0-85,79) 2-Y-O **£4,090** (£1,207; £604) **Stalls** High

Form RPR
1 **1** **Twilight Son**[34] 5309 2-9-5 77 FergusSweeney 5 86+
(Henry Candy) *s.i.s: hld up in rr: sltly hmpd over 2f out: gng wl whn n.m.r over 1f out: sn swtchd rt: r.o: led 75yds out* **4/7**[1]
3304 **2** *½* **Eastern Racer (IRE)**[23] 5714 2-9-1 73 (p) BenCurtis 3 76
(Brian Ellison) *chsd ldrs towards outer: rdn over 2f out: led jst ins fnl f: kpt on but hdd 75yds out* **20/1**
401 **3** *2¼* **Golden Spun (USA)**[14] 5995 2-9-5 77 PaulMulrennan 4 73
(Bryan Smart) *trckd ldr: rdn 2f out: led appr fnl f: sn hdd: no ex* **8/1**[3]
6153 **4** *1¼* **Just The Tip (IRE)**[39] 5140 2-9-7 79 TomEaves 6 71
(Keith Dalgleish) *led: rdn whn hdd appr fnl f: edgd lft and wknd* **16/1**
560 **5** *1¼* **Perfect Girl (IRE)**[63] 4286 2-8-2 60 JamesSullivan 1 48
(Tim Easterby) *hld up: rdn 2f out: kpt on same pce* **16/1**
5303 **6** *2* **Firgrove Bridge (IRE)**[21] 5790 2-9-5 77 (b1) JamesDoyle 8 59
(Kevin Ryan) *midfield: rdn over 2f out: wknd fnl f* **9/1**

433 7 1 **Pacngo**[21] 5789 2-8-4 62 DuranFentiman 7 41
(Tim Easterby) *trckd ldr: rdn over 1f out: sn wknd* 15/2[2]
01 8 ½ **Star Cracker (IRE)**[34] 5297 2-9-2 77 ConnorBeasley(3) 2 55
(Michael Dods) *midfield: rdn over 2f out: already struggling whn sltly short of room appr fnl f* 10/1
1m 12.25s (-0.45) **Going Correction** -0.15s/f (Firm) 8 Ran SP% **119.2**
Speed ratings (Par 97): **97,96,93,91,90 87,86,85**
CSF £16.79 CT £58.98 TOTE £1.50: £1.02, £5.10, £2.50; EX 15.40 Trifecta £107.70.
**Owner** Godfrey Wilson **Bred** Mrs C R D Wilson **Trained** Kingston Warren, Oxon
**FOCUS**
The rail into the home straight was dolled out adding approximately 18yds to all distances beyond 7f. A dry night and morning, but after James Sullivan said "It is good ground, probably just on the slow side" and Paul Mulrennan added "It is a fraction on the slow side of good", the ground was changed to good. Several in-form sorts in a fair nursery but the winner won in the manner of a horse that had plenty in hand of his opening mark. He looks sure to do better. The gallop was fair and the field raced against the stands' rail.

## 6428 CHRISTMAS PARTY NIGHTS AT THIRSK RACECOURSE (S) NURSERY H'CAP 7f
**2:40** (2:40) (Class 5) (0-75,59) 2-Y-O £2,726 (£805; £402) **Stalls** Low

Form RPR
0205 1 **Chilworth Bells**[7] 6205 2-9-0 52 GrahamGibbons 8 56
(Mick Channon) *trckd ldr: led 5f out: mde rest: rdn over 2f out: drvn over 1f out: pressed fnl 110yds: hld on wl* 7/2[2]
4055 2 nk **Snowy**[18] 5885 2-8-7 45 BarryMcHugh 2 48
(Tony Coyle) *in tch: rdn and hdwy over 2f out: chsd wnr ins fnl f: kpt on: jst hld* 13/2
0006 3 shd **Pyrocumulus (IRE)**[7] 6205 2-8-7 45 BenCurtis 4 48
(Jo Hughes) *s.i.s: hld up: rdn and gd hdwy on outside 2f out: edgd lft appr fnl f: chsd wnr ins fnl f: kpt on* 4/1[3]
6440 4 3¼ **Jersey Belle**[18] 5875 2-9-4 56 TomEaves 3 50
(Mick Channon) *in tch: rdn over 2f out: hdwy to chal over 1f out: wknd ins fnl f* 7/1
0056 5 3 **Sparkle Girl**[10] 6148 2-8-10 48 (b) DavidAllan 1 34
(Tim Easterby) *midfield: rdn and sme hdwy over 2f out: wknd fnl f* 12/1
0400 6 1¾ **Arcossi**[7] 6205 2-8-0 45 (b[1]) RowanScott(7) 9 26
(Ann Duffield) *trckd ldr: rdn over 2f out: sn wknd* 25/1
6531 7 4½ **Black Pudding (IRE)**[22] 5767 2-9-4 59 (p) JacobButterfield(3) 7 28
(Ollie Pears) *racd keenly: trckd ldr: rdn over 2f out: sn wknd* 3/1[1]
060 8 1¾ **Seraffimo**[32] 5386 2-8-4 45 JoeyHaynes(3) 10 9
(Sharon Watt) *sn pushed along in rr: a bhd* 33/1
3430 9 18 **Astrea**[18] 5885 2-8-11 49 (v) AndrewMullen 5
(Nigel Tinkler) *midfield: rdn 3f out: sn wknd* 16/1
0200 10 16 **Lady Jade**[22] 5767 2-8-7 45 AdrianNicholls 6
(Nigel Tinkler) *led: hdd 5f out: trckd ldr: rdn 3f out: sn wknd* 22/1
1m 29.42s (2.22) **Going Correction** +0.15s/f (Good) 10 Ran SP% **117.8**
Speed ratings (Par 95): **93,92,92,88,85 83,78,76,55,37**
CSF £26.23 CT £97.24 TOTE £4.80: £2.00, £2.10, £1.90; EX 30.90 Trifecta £148.70.There was no bid for the winner. Pyrocumulus was claimed J Babb for £6000.
**Owner** Living Legend Racing Partnership 1 **Bred** Norman Court Stud **Trained** West Ilsley, Berks
**FOCUS**
A weak, low-grade nursery in which the gallop was on the steady side to the home turn. The first three pulled clear of the rest.

## 6429 DAVID BOWIE JORDAN THIRSK COMPETITION WINNER MAIDEN STKS 1m
**3:10** (3:13) (Class 5) 3-Y-O+ £3,234 (£962; £481; £240) **Stalls** Low

Form RPR
0342 1 **Eye Contact**[27] 5550 3-9-5 75 JamesDoyle 9 81
(Sir Michael Stoute) *trckd ldr: rdn over 2f out: kpt on: led 50yds out* 5/4[1]
0250 2 ½ **Millkwood**[9] 6166 4-9-7 74 (b) PhillipMakin 4 80
(John Davies) *led: stl gng wl 2f out: rdn over 1f out: drvn and one pce ins fnl f: hdd 50yds out* 5/1[2]
50 3 6 **Tom Mann (IRE)**[90] 3362 3-9-5 0 GrahamGibbons 6 66
(David Barron) *trckd ldr: rdn and outpcd over 3f out: plugged on but no threat to ldng pair* 25/1
0- 4 2¼ **Betty The Thief (IRE)**[353] 6828 3-9-0 0 GrahamLee 12 56
(Tom Dascombe) *in tch on outer: pushed along over 3f out: one pce and nvr threatened* 9/1[3]
5 3½ **Sirdal**[142] 3-9-5 0 DanielTudhope 2 53
(David O'Meara) *midfield on inner: rdn over 3f out: sn no imp* 20/1
05 6 4 **Exton**[19] 5851 5-9-2 0 MrAidenBlakemore(7) 8 44
(Shaun Harris) *dwlt: sn in tch: rdn over 2f out: wknd over 1f out* 100/1
0- 7 1¼ **Van Mildert (IRE)**[476] 2754 5-8-13 0 EmmaSayer(5) 10 36
(Dianne Sayer) *hld up: rdn over 3f out: sn struggling* 100/1
0- 8 27 **Missfire**[271] 8348 4-9-1 0 NeilFarley(3) 3
(Brian Baugh) *hld up: a bhd* 100/1
9 1 **Moorsholm (IRE)** 3-9-5 0 BenCurtis 1
(Alan Swinbank) *s.i.s: hld up: rdn over 3f out: sn wknd: t.o* 33/1
1m 41.34s (1.24) **Going Correction** +0.15s/f (Good)
**WFA** 3 from 4yo+ 4lb 9 Ran SP% **85.6**
Speed ratings (Par 103): **99,98,92,90,86 82,81,54,53**
CSF £3.15 TOTE £1.50: £1.02, £1.90, £4.10; EX 3.80 Trifecta £24.20.
**Owner** K Abdullah **Bred** Juddmonte Farms Ltd **Trained** Newmarket, Suffolk
■ Golden Emerald was withdrawn. Price at time of withdrawal 2/1. Rule 4 applies to all bets - deduct 30p in the pound. Denala was withdrawn. Price at time of withdrawal 33/1. Rule 4 does not apply.
**FOCUS**
An uncompetitive maiden in which the second favourite refused to enter the stalls. The gallop was an ordinary one and the first two pulled clear. The form is rated around the runner-up.

## 6430 CONSTANT SECURITY SERVICES H'CAP 7f
**3:40** (3:44) (Class 4) (0-85,85) 3-Y-O+ £4,851 (£1,443; £721; £360) **Stalls** Low

Form RPR
0401 1 **Comino (IRE)**[29] 5497 3-8-9 76 TomEaves 9 85
(Kevin Ryan) *trckd ldr: rdn to ld 2f out: pressed ins fnl f: hld on wl* 8/1
0000 2 ½ **Nameitwhatyoulike**[45] 4923 5-9-1 79 PaulMulrennan 10 87
(Bryan Smart) *in tch: stmbld over 3f out: sn hdwy to chse ldr: pressed wnr ins fnl f: kpt on but a jst hld* 7/1[2]
0012 3 1 **The Great Gabrial**[18] 5895 5-9-0 78 (p) AndrewMullen 4 83+
(Michael Appleby) *racd keenly in tch: rdn over 2f out: swtchd rt over 1f out: kpt on* 7/1[2]
4335 4 shd **Kingscroft (IRE)**[31] 5413 6-9-1 79 (b) RobertWinston 8 84
(Michael Herrington) *midfield: rdn over 2f out: kpt on* 15/2[3]
516 5 nk **Fieldgunner Kirkup (GER)**[7] 6207 6-9-4 82 GrahamGibbons 2 86
(David Barron) *trckd ldr: rdn over 2f out: one pce* 8/1

1300 6 1 **Kimbali (IRE)**[7] 6217 5-8-8 75 NeilFarley(3) 6 76
(Declan Carroll) *hld up in midfield: rdn over 2f out: kpt on ins fnl f* 20/1
0660 7 2 **Smarty Socks (IRE)**[11] 6097 10-9-7 85 DanielTudhope 3 81
(David O'Meara) *hld up: rdn over 2f out: sme hdwy on outer over 1f out: no ex ins fnl f* 8/1
1200 8 hd **Talent Scout (IRE)**[20] 5810 8-9-1 84 GemmaTutty(5) 11 80
(Karen Tutty) *led: rdn whn hdd 2f out: grad wknd* 14/1
0645 9 1 **Just Paul (IRE)**[17] 5915 4-8-13 77 GrahamLee 5 70
(Philip Kirby) *midfield on inner: rdn over 2f out: no imp* 9/2[1]
0400 10 1¼ **Showboating (IRE)**[52] 4661 6-9-2 80 (tp) KierenFallon 1 70
(Alan McCabe) *slowly away: hld up in rr: a bhd* 10/1
4003 11 1 **Hadaj**[10] 6155 5-8-10 79 (b) KevinStott(5) 7 66
(Ruth Carr) *hld up in midfield: rdn over 2f out: sn btn* 8/1
1m 27.14s (-0.06) **Going Correction** +0.15s/f (Good)
**WFA** 3 from 4yo+ 3lb 11 Ran SP% **119.9**
Speed ratings (Par 105): **106,105,104,104,103 102,100,100,99,97 96**
CSF £64.35 CT £426.19 TOTE £8.70: £3.00, £2.80, £2.40; EX 88.50 Trifecta £752.80.
**Owner** Exors of the late D W Barker **Bred** Tom Twomey **Trained** Hambleton, N Yorks
**FOCUS**
Mainly exposed sorts in a fair handicap. The gallop was only routine and it was difficult to make ground from off the pace. The fourth and fifth help with the standard.

## 6431 FOLLOW US @THIRSKRACES H'CAP (BOBIS RACE) 1m
**4:15** (4:16) (Class 4) (0-85,83) 3-Y-O £4,851 (£1,443; £721; £360) **Stalls** Low

Form RPR
1120 1 **Hostile Fire (IRE)**[12] 6057 3-8-13 75 (p) JamesDoyle 2 83
(Ed de Giles) *midfield: rdn and hdwy 2f out: led ins fnl f: kpt on* 9/2[3]
0523 2 ¾ **Emef Diamond**[23] 5713 3-8-12 74 TomEaves 8 80
(Mick Channon) *led: rdn whn hdd 2f out: sn dropped to 3rd: rallied ins fnl f: wnt 2nd towards fin* 6/1
3102 3 nk **Mr McLaren**[20] 5816 3-9-6 82 DanielTudhope 7 87+
(David O'Meara) *in tch: hdwy to trck ldr 1/2-way: led 2f out: sn rdn: hdd ins fnl f: no ex: lost 2nd towards fin* 11/2
1003 4 ½ **Rapid Advance**[24] 5669 3-9-5 81 [1] ShaneKelly 9 85
(Sir Michael Stoute) *midfield on outer: rdn over 2f out: kpt on* 6/1
4425 5 ½ **Eddiemaurice (IRE)**[3] 6342 3-8-13 75 (v) JasonHart 6 78
(Richard Guest) *s.i.s: hld up: hdwy over 2f out: sn rdn: one pce* 20/1
6130 6 4 **Jacbequick**[17] 5915 3-9-1 80 JacobButterfield(3) 3 74
(Ollie Pears) *trckd ldr: pushed along and lost pl 1/2-way: wknd over 1f out* 16/1
-120 7 ½ **Mutawathea**[66] 4198 3-9-7 83 PaulHanagan 5 76
(Richard Hannon) *trckd ldr: rdn over 3f out: wknd over 1f out* 10/3[1]
3601 8 1 **Disclosure**[18] 5892 3-8-12 74 GrahamLee 4 65
(Les Eyre) *half-rrd s: racd keenly hld up: rdn over 2f out* 4/1[2]
-640 9 6 **Munjally**[31] 5417 3-8-12 74 [1] PaulMulrennan 1 51
(Patrick Holmes) *midfield: rdn over 2f out: sn wknd* 40/1
1m 40.71s (0.61) **Going Correction** +0.15s/f (Good) 9 Ran SP% **118.3**
Speed ratings (Par 103): **102,101,100,100,99 95,95,94,88**
CSF £32.51 CT £154.61 TOTE £4.20: £2.10, £2.00, £1.70; EX 34.50 Trifecta £277.30.
**Owner** Ali Mortazavi **Bred** Thomas Hassett **Trained** Ledbury, H'fords
**FOCUS**
A useful handicap but one that took less winning than seemed likely with a couple of the market leaders underperforming. The gallop was reasonable.

## 6432 THIRSK RACECOURSE FOR WEDDING RECEPTIONS MAIDEN STKS 1m 4f
**4:45** (4:45) (Class 5) 3-Y-O+ £3,408 (£1,006; £503) **Stalls** High

Form RPR
3360 1 **Karraar**[45] 4893 3-9-5 83 (p) PaulHanagan 2 82
(Richard Hannon) *mde all: rdn over 1f out: sn firmly in command: eased nr fin* 11/8[1]
3623 2 1¾ **Race To Glory (FR)**[19] 5851 3-9-5 78 JamesDoyle 5 78
(Roger Charlton) *trckd ldng pair: rdn over 2f out: wnt 2nd over 1f out: kpt on but no threat wnr* 4/1[2]
4 3 1½ **Never Up (GER)**[14] 6011 3-9-5 0 DanielTudhope 8 76
(David O'Meara) *prom: rdn over 2f out: edgd lft and lost 2nd over 1f out: one pce fnl f* 9/1
-00 4 2 **Rock On Bollinski**[11] 6092 4-9-13 0 BarryMcHugh 6 72
(Tim Fitzgerald) *dwlt: hld up in midfield: rdn over 2f out: kpt on fr over 1f out* 100/1
32 5 8 **Molly Cat**[135] 1969 4-9-8 0 RobertWinston 4 55
(Alan Swinbank) *trckd ldng pair: rdn over 2f out: hung lft and wknd over 1f out* 5/1
6 1¾ **Maison De Ville (GER)**[31] 6-9-8 0 TomEaves 3 52
(Brian Ellison) *hld up: rdn over 3f out: sn btn* 20/1
-60 7 7 **Georgian Firebird**[11] 6092 4-9-8 0 DavidAllan 7 41
(Alan Swinbank) *a towards rr* 40/1
2235 8 shd **New Tarabela**[63] 4289 3-9-5 79 KierenFallon 1 61
(James Tate) *midfield: rdn over 2f out: wknd over 1f out: eased* 9/2[3]
2m 40.22s (4.02) **Going Correction** +0.15s/f (Good)
**WFA** 3 from 4yo+ 8lb 8 Ran SP% **115.1**
Speed ratings (Par 103): **92,90,89,88,83 82,77,77**
CSF £7.04 TOTE £2.60: £1.10, £1.90, £2.40; EX 7.50 Trifecta £46.20.
**Owner** Hamdan Al Maktoum **Bred** Shadwell Estate Company Limited **Trained** East Everleigh, Wilts
**FOCUS**
An uncompetitive maiden but fair form from the principals, although the winner didn't need to be at his best. The gallop was an ordinary one.

## 6433 THIRSK RACES SATURDAY 18TH APRIL 2015 H'CAP 1m 4f
**5:15** (5:17) (Class 4) (0-85,85) 3-Y-O+ £4,851 (£1,443; £721; £360) **Stalls** High

Form RPR
-213 1 **Ruwasi**[78] 3787 3-8-13 80 DavidAllan 7 92
(James Tate) *trckd ldng pair: rdn to ld over 1f out: kpt on* 3/1[1]
3425 2 2¼ **Brigadoon**[41] 5052 7-9-8 81 AndrewMullen 6 88
(Michael Appleby) *midfield: rdn and hdwy to chse ldr over 1f out: kpt on* 16/1
-463 3 1 **Aryizad (IRE)**[12] 6062 5-8-12 71 oh1 RobertWinston 5 76
(Alan Swinbank) *prom: pressed ldr over 4f out: led over 2f out: rdn whn hdd over 1f out: one pce* 9/1
5415 4 ¾ **Noble Alan (GER)**[36] 5238 11-9-11 84 IanBrennan 3 88
(Nicky Richards) *hld up: sme hdwy over 2f out: rdn ovre 1f out: kpt on same pce* 6/1
0322 5 1¾ **Sky Khan**[22] 5756 5-9-7 85 (p) JoeDoyle(5) 2 86
(John Wainwright) *hld up in midfield: rdn 2f out: no imp* 7/2[2]
6210 6 8 **Classical Duet (USA)**[10] 6137 3-9-2 83 KierenFallon 9 72
(Mark Johnston) *led at stdy pce: rdn whn hdd over 2f out: sn wknd* 4/1[3]

50-1 **7** *nk* **Pintrada**[10] 6152 6-9-7 80 TonyHamilton 1 68
(James Bethell) *midfield: rdn over 2f out: wknd over 1f out* **6/1**

346- **8** *21* **Montaff**[395] 5520 8-9-1 74 JasonHart 4 29
(Richard Guest) *dwlt: hld up in rr: a bhd* **33/1**

2m 38.18s (1.98) **Going Correction** +0.15s/f (Good)
**WFA** 3 from 4yo+ 8lb **8** Ran SP% **114.6**
Speed ratings (Par 105): **99,97,96,96,95 89,89,75**
CSF £51.15 CT £387.87 TOTE £4.90: £1.70, £3.70, £2.20; EX 47.80 Trifecta £322.60.
**Owner** Saeed Manana **Bred** Highbury Terrace Owners Club **Trained** Newmarket, Suffolk

**FOCUS**
A useful handicap in which the gallop was on the steady side to the home straight. The winner built on his maiden form.
T/Jkpt: £2,131.20 to a £1 stake. Pool of £10506.19 - 3.50 winning tickets. T/Plt: £45.30 to a £1 stake. Pool of £49255.89 - 792.83 winning units. T/Qpdt: £11.80 to a £1 stake. Pool of £3847.66 - 240.61 winning tickets. AS

# 5725 YARMOUTH (L-H)
Tuesday, September 16

**OFFICIAL GOING: Good (good to firm in places; 7.2)**
Wind: virtually nil Weather: sunny and warm

## 6434 BRITISH STALLION STUDS/GREENE KING EBF MAIDEN FILLIES' STKS (BOBIS RACE) (DIV I) 6f 3y
**2:30** (2:32) (Class 5) 2-Y-O **£3,234** (£962; £481; £240) **Stalls** Centre

Form RPR

3 **1** **Deep Blue Sea**[23] 5725 2-9-0 0 WilliamCarson 9 71+
(Anthony Carson) *hld up in tch: effrt over 1f out: str run u.p ins fnl f to ld last strides* **4/1**[3]

05 **2** *hd* **Alhella**[36] 5232 2-9-0 0 PatCosgrave 2 70
(Kevin Ryan) *chsd ldr tl led ent fnl 2f: rdn over 1f out: kpt on but edgd rt u.p ins fnl f: hdd last strides* **25/1**

3 **3** *1* **Luna Mission (IRE)**[13] 6032 2-9-0 0 MartinHarley 3 67+
(Marco Botti) *trckd ldrs: chsd ldr wl over 1f out: drvn and pressing ldr over 1f out: kpt on same pce ins fnl f* **11/4**[1]

0 **4** *shd* **Imperial Link**[44] 4943 2-9-0 0 LukeMorris 5 67
(Paul Cole) *led tl hdd ent fnl 2f: sn drvn: kpt on and stl pressing ldrs but hld whn carried rt wl ins fnl f* **40/1**

35 **5** *shd* **Jillanar (IRE)**[53] 4604 2-9-0 0 TomQueally 8 67
(George Margarson) *wnt lft s: t.k.h: hld up in tch in last quartet: hdwy over 1f out: chsd ldrs and rdn 1f out: styd on fnl 100yds: nt rch ldrs* **8/1**

6 **6** *½* **Music And Dance**[13] 6041 2-9-0 0 RyanMoore 10 65
(Sir Michael Stoute) *wl in tch in midfield: rdn and chsd ldrs over 1f out: keeping on same pce and hld whn carried rt and hmpd wl ins fnl f* **4/1**[3]

**7** *nk* **Bipartisan (IRE)** 2-9-0 0 FrederikTylicki 4 64+
(Michael Bell) *in tch in midfield: rdn and hdwy 2f out: chsd ldrs 1f out: styd on same pce ins fnl f* **33/1**

**8** *¾* **Imtiyaaz (IRE)** 2-9-0 0 AndreaAtzeni 7 62
(Roger Varian) *pushed lft s and slowly away: in tch towards rr: hdwy 2f out: kpt on but no real imp fnl f* **7/2**[2]

**9** *10* **Machiavelian Storm (IRE)** 2-9-0 0 RobertHavlin 11 32
(Ed Dunlop) *s.i.s: in tch in last quartet: rdn 2f out: sn btn: bhd fnl f* **50/1**

0 **10** *½* **Mullion Cove**[24] 5684 2-9-0 0 HayleyTurner 1 31
(John Best) *chsd ldrs: rdn and lost pl ent fnl 2f: wknd over 1f out* **150/1**

**11** *2¾* **Exceedwell** 2-8-11 0 RyanPowell(3) 6 22
(John Ryan) *in tch in midfield: rdn and lost pl over 2f out: wknd over 1f out: sn bhd* **100/1**

**12** *3¾* **Nouveau Foret** 2-9-0 0 WilliamBuick 12 11
(Ed Walker) *awkward leaving stalls: rn green and a in rr: lost tch wl over 1f out* **40/1**

1m 13.25s (-1.15) **Going Correction** -0.25s/f (Firm) **12** Ran SP% **115.3**
Speed ratings (Par 92): **97,96,95,95,95 94,94,93,79,79 75,70**
CSF £99.97 TOTE £4.30: £1.50, £6.60, £1.60; EX 112.80 Trifecta £426.40.
**Owner** The Chriselliam Partnership **Bred** Moyns Park Estate And Stud Ltd **Trained** Newmarket, Suffolk

**FOCUS**
This had been won by some notable horses in recent years, but there was a compressed finish and this has to rate ordinary form.

## 6435 BRITISH STALLION STUDS/GREENE KING EBF MAIDEN FILLIES' STKS (BOBIS RACE) (DIV II) 6f 3y
**3:00** (3:02) (Class 5) 2-Y-O **£3,234** (£962; £481; £240) **Stalls** Centre

Form RPR

52 **1** **Queen's Pearl (IRE)**[15] 5973 2-9-0 0 AndreaAtzeni 3 78
(Roger Varian) *chsd ldr tl led wl over 1f out: rdn over 1f out: styd on wl ins fnl f: rdn out* **2/1**[1]

264 **2** *1* **Exceedingly**[24] 5667 2-9-0 75 WilliamBuick 9 75
(John Gosden) *chsd ldrs: rdn and effrt to chse wnr over 1f out: wnt clr wirth wnr 1f out: styd on same pce and hld fnl 150yds* **4/1**[3]

4 **3** *5* **Illogical**[25] 5643 2-9-0 0 RobertHavlin 5 60+
(Ed Dunlop) *t.k.h: hld up in tch in midfield: rdn and effrt over 1f out: wnt 3rd 1f out: kpt on but no threat to ldrs* **8/1**

**4** *½* **Edge Of Love** 2-9-0 0 LukeMorris 10 59
(Ed Walker) *s.i.s: in tch in rr: rdn and hdwy over 1f out: styd on and battling for 3rd ins fnl f: no threat to ldrs* **20/1**

**5** *1¼* **Muffri'Ha (IRE)** 2-9-0 0 RyanMoore 6 55
(William Haggas) *in tch in midfield: rdn ent fnl 2f: outpcd and btn over 1f out: wknd ins fnl f* **11/4**[2]

0 **6** *½* **Red Words (IRE)**[48] 4784 2-9-0 0 TomQueally 4 53+
(George Margarson) *flashed tail leaving stalls: in tch towards rr: effrt and flashed tail u.p over 1f out: no threat to ldrs and kpt on same pce ins fnl f* **100/1**

0 **7** *½* **Perfect Slipper**[29] 5509 2-8-9 0 TobyAtkinson(5) 7 52
(Noel Quinlan) *led tl rdn and hdd wl over 1f out: 3rd and btn over 1f out: wknd ins fnl f* **100/1**

**8** *2¼* **Lovely Memory (IRE)** 2-9-0 0 HarryBentley 2 45+
(Saeed bin Suroor) *in tch in midfield: rdn and effrt over 2f out: no ex and btn over 1f out: sn wknd* **10/1**

30 **9** *1½* **Lolita**[24] 5667 2-9-0 0 FrederikTylicki 1 41+
(J R Jenkins) *chsd ldrs: rdn and no ex ent fnl 2f: wknd over 1f out* **20/1**

65 **10** *3¾* **Most Tempting**[13] 6032 2-9-0 0 AdamBeschizza 8 29
(Robert Cowell) *a towards rr: rdn over 2f out: sn btn: bhd over 1f out* **50/1**

0 **11** *2* **Purple Surprise**[29] 5488 2-8-9 0 JennyPowell(5) 11 23
(Andrew Reid) *in tch towards rr: rdn over 3f out: bhd over 1f out* **100/1**

1m 12.82s (-1.58) **Going Correction** -0.25s/f (Firm) **11** Ran SP% **114.7**
Speed ratings (Par 92): **100,98,92,91,89 89,88,85,83,78 75**
CSF £9.37 TOTE £2.50: £1.90, £1.02, £3.20; EX 11.10 Trifecta £40.60.
**Owner** Ziad A Galadari **Bred** Galadari Sons Stud Company Limited **Trained** Newmarket, Suffolk

**FOCUS**
It's unlikely that this second division was as strong as the first but there was still plenty to like about the performances of the first two home, who came clear. The runner-up and the time offer a fair starting point.

## 6436 RACHAEL KEATLEY MEMORIAL NURSERY H'CAP (BOBIS RACE) (FOR THE JACK LEADER CHALLENGE TROPHY) 1m 3y
**3:30** (3:30) (Class 4) (0-85,82) 2-Y-O **£3,881** (£1,155; £577; £288) **Stalls** Centre

Form RPR

2413 **1** **Rotherwick (IRE)**[3] 6331 2-9-5 80 LukeMorris 5 87+
(Paul Cole) *dwlt: in tch in last pair: rdn 2f out: hdwy to ld over 1f out: edgd lft ins fnl f: asserting whn rdr dropped rein wl ins fnl f* **5/4**[1]

2152 **2** *1½* **Lady Moscou (IRE)**[12] 6071 2-9-7 82 RyanMoore 4 85
(James Tate) *chsd ldr: rdn 2f out: ev ch over 1f out: no ex and one pce fnl 100yds* **7/2**[2]

1301 **3** *2¾* **Mr Shekells**[7] 6211 2-8-9 70 6ex SilvestreDeSousa 1 66
(Philip McBride) *led: rdn ent fnl 2f: hdd over 1f out: wknd ins fnl f* **11/2**

2410 **4** *5* **Popeswood (IRE)**[9] 6165 2-9-6 81 WilliamBuick 3 65
(Mick Channon) *s.i.s: hld up in tch in last pair: rdn and effrt 2f out: no ex and wknd 1f out* **9/2**[3]

3110 **5** *17* **What A Party (IRE)**[24] 5664 2-8-10 76 ShelleyBirkett(5) 2 20
(Gay Kelleway) *chsd ldng pair: shkn up 2f out: dropped to last wl over 1f out and immediately lost tch* **14/1**

1m 39.61s (-0.99) **Going Correction** -0.25s/f (Firm) **5** Ran SP% **106.9**
Speed ratings (Par 97): **94,92,89,84,67**
CSF £5.42 TOTE £1.90: £1.10, £1.50; EX 5.30 Trifecta £11.00.
**Owner** H R H Sultan Ahmad Shah **Bred** Brian O'Neill **Trained** Whatcombe, Oxon

**FOCUS**
This was a fair contest and the market proved correct. The form is rated slightly positively.

## 6437 THOMAS PRIOR MEMORIAL MAIDEN STKS 6f 3y
**4:00** (4:00) (Class 5) 3-Y-O+ **£3,234** (£962; £481; £240) **Stalls** Centre

Form RPR

3023 **1** **Goodwood Storm**[38] 5181 3-9-0 72 AndreaAtzeni 5 74+
(William Knight) *stdd s: t.k.h: trckd ldrs tl led on bit over 1f out: sn cruised clr: v easily* **1/1**[1]

2605 **2** *4* **Stroll On (IRE)**[28] 5532 3-9-0 62 ChrisCatlin 4 61
(Rae Guest) *taken down early: led: rdn and hdd over 1f out: no ch w wnr to plugged on for clr 2nd fnl f* **13/2**[3]

456 **3** *3* **Swilken**[82] 3631 3-9-5 67 (e[1]) TedDurcan 9 57
(Mark H Tompkins) *stdd and dropped in bhd after s: racd off the pce in last pair: rdn over 2f out: hdwy past btn horses over 1f out: wnt 3rd ins fnl f: nvr trbld ldrs* **7/2**[2]

5 **4** *2¾* **Hard Run (USA)**[12] 6073 4-9-7 0 AdamBeschizza 2 48
(Robert Cowell) *t.k.h: chsd ldr tl 2f out: sn drvn: 3rd and btn over 1f out: wknd ins fnl f* **7/1**

50 **5** *1½* **Tilsworth Annalisa**[13] 6042 3-8-9 0 ShelleyBirkett(5) 6 38
(J R Jenkins) *in tch in midfield: rdn ent fnl 2f: outpcd and wl btn over 1f out* **100/1**

**6** *2¾* **Barwah (USA)** 3-9-0 0 (t) WilliamCarson 7 29
(Anthony Carson) *stdd and dropped in bhd after s: hdwy over 2f out: 4th and no ex u.p over 1f out: fdd fnl f* **12/1**

**7** *1* **Mareef (IRE)** 4-9-4 0 AshleyMorgan(3) 1 31
(Kevin Morgan) *s.i.s: outpcd in detached last: n.d* **28/1**

0553 **8** *2¼* **Island Express (IRE)**[11] 6116 7-9-2 50 (bt) AnnStokell(5) 3 24
(Ann Stokell) *t.k.h: chsd ldrs tl lost pl and rdn ent fnl 2f: wknd over 1f out* **22/1**

1m 12.76s (-1.64) **Going Correction** -0.25s/f (Firm)
**WFA** 3 from 4yo+ 2lb **8** Ran SP% **114.5**
Speed ratings: **100,94,90,87,85 81,80,77**
CSF £8.06 TOTE £1.80: £1.10, £2.20, £1.10; EX 7.40 Trifecta £17.50.
**Owner** Goodwood Racehorse Owners Group (20) Ltd **Bred** St Clare Hall Stud **Trained** Patching, W Sussex

**FOCUS**
This was a weak maiden run in a slow time. The easy winner was perhaps value for extra.

## 6438 EAST ANGLIAN AIR AMBULANCE H'CAP (BOBIS RACE) 1m 3f 101y
**4:30** (4:30) (Class 2) (0-100,90) 3-Y-**£12,602** (£3,772; £1,886; £944; £470) **Stalls** Low

Form RPR

4200 **1** **Notarised**[10] 6127 3-8-13 82 SilvestreDeSousa 5 90
(Mark Johnston) *chsd ldr: clsd and rdn to chal 2f out: drvn to ld 1f out: kpt on gamely: jst hld on: all out* **6/1**

4110 **2** *nse* **Kinshasa**[66] 4183 3-9-5 88 AndreaAtzeni 2 96
(Luca Cumani) *chsd ldng pair: clsd 2f out: rdn and effrt over 1f out: pressed wnr fnl 150yds: styd on u.p and steadily clsd after: jst hld* **15/8**[1]

4141 **3** *3¼* **Alex Vino (IRE)**[13] 6044 3-9-7 90 (v[1]) RyanMoore 3 93
(Sir Michael Stoute) *racd keenly: led and sn clr: jnd 2f out: rdn over 1f out: hdd 1f out: wknd fnl 100yds* **5/2**[2]

6100 **4** *1¼* **Trip To Paris (IRE)**[10] 6127 3-9-6 89 (p) WilliamBuick 1 90
(Ed Dunlop) *hld up in tch in last pair: rdn over 3f out: drvn ent fnl 2f: plugged on same pce after* **13/2**

024 **5** *1¼* **Latin Charm (IRE)**[18] 5877 3-8-11 80 (p) MartinHarley 4 79
(Marco Botti) *hld up in tch in rr: c wd of rivals and clsd 3f out: rdn and hld hd high 2f out: sn btn* **5/1**[3]

2m 25.49s (-3.21) **Going Correction** -0.15s/f (Firm) **5** Ran SP% **107.6**
Speed ratings (Par 107): **105,104,102,101,100**
CSF £16.88 TOTE £6.80: £2.50, £1.60; EX 16.90 Trifecta £57.50.
**Owner** Hugh Hart **Bred** Mrs P Hart **Trained** Middleham Moor, N Yorks

**FOCUS**
A tremendous finish to this feature handicap. The winner is rated to form.

## 6439 NICHOLSONS OF STALHAM JCB DEALERS H'CAP 1m 6f 17y
**5:00** (5:00) (Class 4) (0-85,85) 3-Y-O+ **£5,170** (£1,626; £875) **Stalls** High

Form RPR

3113 **1** **Meetings Man (IRE)**[41] 5047 7-9-8 81 (p) RyanMoore 3 87
(Ali Stronge) *mde all: hrd pressed and rdn ent fnl 2f: sustained duel w rivals after: hld on gamely: all out* **9/4**[1]

31 **2** *nk* **Echo Brava**[21] 5800 4-9-8 81 LukeMorris 5 86
(Luke Dace) *chsd ldrs: rdn and effrt over 2f out: ev ch 2f out: sustained duel w rivals after: styd on but hld cl home* **5/2**[2]

4122 **3** *shd* **Wannabe Your Man**[81] 3680 4-9-3 76 PatCosgrave 2 81
(George Baker) *chsd wnr: rdn and ev ch ent fnl 2f: sustained duel w rivals after: hung rt 1f out: styd on but hld cl home* **5/2**[2]
5130 **P** **Rosslyn Castle**[17] 5924 5-9-7 80 SilvestreDeSousa 1
(Philip McBride) *hld up in tch in last tl lost action and p.u 4f out: dismntd: fatally injured* **4/1**[3]
3m 8.06s (0.46) **Going Correction** -0.15s/f (Firm)
**WFA** 3 from 4yo+ 10lb **4** Ran SP% **107.9**
Speed ratings (Par 105): **92,91,91,**
CSF £7.96 TOTE £2.20; EX 5.40 Trifecta £9.30.
**Owner** Mrs Bettine Evans **Bred** Hakan Keles **Trained** Eastbury, Berks
■ The first winner under her married name for Ali Stronge, who previously traned as Ali Brewer.
**FOCUS**
Tactics played a big part in this staying event. The winner rates better than ever.

## 6440 AT THE RACES CONDITIONS STKS 6f 3y
**5:30** (5:31) (Class 3) 3-Y-0+ **£7,561** (£2,263; £1,131; £566; £282) **Stalls** Centre

Form RPR
-302 **1** **Royal Rock**[45] 4889 10-8-9 98 TedDurcan 1 103
(Chris Wall) *niggled along in rr: hdwy u.p to chse ldr 1f out: led ins fnl f: styd on wl and drew clr towards fin* **9/2**
0020 **2** *3* **Clear Spring (IRE)**[3] 6327 6-8-9 97 LiamJones 2 93
(John Spearing) *chsd ldr for 2f: styd chsng ldrs: rdn to ld wl over 1f out: edgd rt u.p over 1f out: hdd ins fnl f: sn outpcd and btn: kpt on* **11/4**[1]
0004 **3** *1 1/4* **Krypton Factor**[12] 6060 6-8-9 102 (b) LukeMorris 5 89
(George Peckham) *led for 2f: chsd ldr after: rdn and ev ch whn carried rt over 1f out: no ex and one pce ins fnl f* **6/1**
0000 **4** *hd* **Valbchek (IRE)**[10] 6131 5-8-9 94 (p) PatCosgrave 3 89
(Jane Chapple-Hyam) *in tch: rdn and effrt over 1f out: no ch w wnr but kpt on u.p ins fnl f* **16/1**
0003 **5** *3* **Rex Imperator**[22] 5778 5-8-9 102 AndreaAtzeni 6 79
(William Haggas) *chsd ldrs tl hdwy to ld 4f out: rdn and hdd whn hmpd over 1f out: wknd ins fnl f* **10/3**[3]
00-0 **6** *9* **Khubala (IRE)**[24] 5674 5-8-9 97 (b) WilliamBuick 4 50
(Hugo Palmer) *dwlt: in tch: rdn and no rspnse over 1f out: wknd fnl f* **3/1**[2]
1m 11.48s (-2.92) **Going Correction** -0.25s/f (Firm) **6** Ran SP% **113.1**
Speed ratings (Par 107): **109,105,103,103,99 87**
CSF £17.48 TOTE £3.50: £1.60, £2.30; EX 16.30 Trifecta £82.20.
**Owner** Ms Aida Fustoq **Bred** Deerfield Farm **Trained** Newmarket, Suffolk
**FOCUS**
There are doubts over the field but the winner is rated up a length on his latest form.

## 6441 MOULTON NURSERIES H'CAP 5f 43y
**6:00** (6:03) (Class 4) (0-85,84) 3-Y-0+ **£5,045** (£1,501; £750; £375) **Stalls** Centre

Form RPR
1000 **1** **Sleepy Sioux**[10] 6131 3-9-6 84 (p) SilvestreDeSousa 7 96
(David Elsworth) *racd keenly: chsd ldr tl rdn to ld 2f out: styd on strly and drew clr fnl f: rdn out* **10/3**[1]
0525 **2** *3* **Secret Millionaire (IRE)**[10] 6130 7-9-2 79 LukeMorris 8 80
(Luke Dace) *in tch in midfield: rdn and effrt to press ldrs 2f out: outpcd 1f out: chsd clr wnr fnl 100yds: kpt on* **5/1**
3103 **3** *1 1/2* **Vodka Chaser (IRE)**[2] 6355 3-8-5 74 JackDuern(5) 3 70
(Alison Hutchinson) *chsd ldrs: rdn and chsd wnr wl over 1f out: no ex and btn jst ins fnl f: lost 2nd fnl 100yds* **8/1**
0603 **4** *1/2* **Tamayuz Star (IRE)**[11] 6094 4-9-7 84 TomQueally 2 78
(George Margarson) *dwlt: sn rdn along in rr: sme hdwy u.p over 1f out: styd on same pce ins fnl f* **4/1**[2]
0031 **5** *2* **Tom Sawyer**[17] 5913 6-8-13 76 (b) FrederikTylicki 1 63
(Julie Camacho) *led tl 2f out: sn drvn and unable qck: wknd ins fnl f* **10/1**
0504 **6** *nk* **Green Monkey**[14] 6021 4-9-1 78 (v) HayleyTurner 6 64
(James Fanshawe) *in tch: rdn and no rspnse over 1f out: wknd ins fnl f* **9/2**[3]
4033 **7** *3 1/2* **Arctic Lynx (IRE)**[6] 6236 7-8-12 75 (p) AdamBeschizza 4 48
(Robert Cowell) *in tch in midfield: rdn 1/2-way: wknd over 1f out* **12/1**
1m 1.29s (-1.41) **Going Correction** -0.25s/f (Firm)
**WFA** 3 from 4yo+ 1lb **7** Ran SP% **105.8**
Speed ratings (Par 105): **101,96,93,93,89 89,83**
CSF £17.10 CT £88.41 TOTE £3.70: £2.90, £2.20; EX 17.00 Trifecta £79.00.
**Owner** Ten Green Bottles I **Bred** New Hall Stud **Trained** Newmarket, Suffolk
■ Doctor Parkes was withdrawn. Price at time of withdrawal 8/1. Rule 4 applies to all bets - deduct 10p in the pound.
**FOCUS**
The winner is rated back to her Windsor form.
T/Plt: £11.80 to a £1 stake. Pool of £50649.28 - 3132.35 winning units. T/Qpdt: £5.70 to a £1 stake. Pool of £2832.55 - 362.87 winning units. SP

6442 - 6445a (Foreign Racing) - See Raceform Interactive

# 4721 MAISONS-LAFFITTE (R-H)
Tuesday, September 16
**OFFICIAL GOING: Turf: good**

## 6446a PRIX CRYSTAL PALACE (CONDITIONS) (3YO) (TURF) 6f (S)
**1:20** (12:00) 3-Y-0 **£14,166** (£5,666; £4,250; £2,833; £1,416)

RPR
**1** **Helwan (FR)**[16] 3-9-0 0 FrankieDettori 2 109
(J-F Bernard, France) **9/2**[3]
**2** *nk* **Farmah (USA)**[60] 3-8-10 0 Francois-XavierBertras 3 104
(F Rohaut, France) **1/1**[1]
**3** *3* **Victorious Champ (FR)**[28] 3-9-0 0 GregoryBenoist 1 98
(D Smaga, France) **87/10**
**4** *1 1/2* **Laia Chope (FR)**[28] 3-8-10 0 ThomasMessina 4 89
(X Nakkachdji, France) **269/10**
**5** *1/2* **Passion Blanche**[47] 3-8-10 0 ChristopheSoumillon 6 88
(J-C Rouget, France) **33/10**[2]
**6** *shd* **Dani Wallon (FR)**[29] 3-9-0 0 J-LMartinez 7 91
(C Delcher-Sanchez, France) **122/10**
**7** *1 1/2* **Belletriste (FR)**[37] 5226 3-8-10 0 IoritzMendizabal 5 82
(Sylvester Kirk) *a last: hld up in rr: rdn and no imp fr 1 1/2f out: wl hld fnl f* **129/10**
1m 13.93s (0.53) **7** Ran SP% **120.1**
WIN (incl. 1 euro stake): 5.50. PLACES: 2.10, 1.30. SF: 16.50.
**Owner** Al Shaqab Racing **Bred** Mme G Forien & G Forien **Trained** France

# 5910 BEVERLEY (R-H)
Wednesday, September 17
**OFFICIAL GOING: Good to firm (8.5)**
Wind: Moderate across Weather: Heavy grey cloud

## 6447 BET TOTEJACKPOT CLAIMING STKS 5f
**2:10** (2:10) (Class 6) 2-Y-0 **£2,385** (£704; £352) **Stalls** Low

Form RPR
6034 **1** **Mecca's Mirage (IRE)**[30] 5506 2-8-7 67 ConnorBeasley(3) 3 68
(Michael Dods) *trckd ldrs: swtchd rt to inner and hdwy over 1f out: sn rdn: styd on wl to ld last 50yds* **5/1**[3]
3616 **2** *3/4* **Millar Rose (IRE)**[52] 4702 2-8-11 68 MichaelStainton 6 66
(K R Burke) *slt ld: rdn along wl over 1f out: drvn ent fnl f: hdd and no ex last 75yds* **16/1**
1662 **3** *nk* **Honest Bob'S**[30] 5511 2-9-2 85 JackGarritty(5) 14 75
(Brian Ellison) *cl up on outer: effrt wl over 1f out and ev ch: rdn ins fnl f: no ex last 75yds* **4/1**[2]
3240 **4** *1/2* **River Spirit**[16] 5985 2-8-6 60 JoeFanning 11 58
(Mick Channon) *in tch: hdwy on outer 2f out: rdn wl over 1f out: drvn and kpt on fnl f: nrst fin* **16/1**
0413 **5** *3/4* **Studio Star**[23] 5767 2-8-10 63 (p) JacobButterfield(3) 7 63
(Ollie Pears) *in tch: rdn along and hdwy over 1f out: drvn ins fnl f: kpt on: nrst fin* **12/1**
4021 **6** *1 1/4* **Designate (IRE)**[19] 5885 2-9-4 73 (bt) GrahamGibbons 10 63
(Ralph Beckett) *cl up: rdn wl over 1f out: sn drvn and wknd appr fnl f* **6/4**[1]
0P **7** *4* **Double K**[54] 4624 2-9-0 0 PaulMulrennan 1 45+
(Paul Midgley) *dwlt and bhd: rdn along 1/2-way: sme late hdwy* **100/1**
5404 **8** *3/4* **Sunhill Lodge Lady**[23] 5767 2-7-13 45 (v) JoeDoyle(5) 5 32
(Ann Duffield) *nvr bttr than midfield* **80/1**
0164 **9** *1/2* **Fairweather Trader (IRE)**[70] 4065 2-8-9 60 GrahamLee 9 35
(Paul Midgley) *a towards rr* **33/1**
**10** *1 3/4* **Scottish Isles** 2-9-2 0 BarryMcHugh 2 36
(Michael Easterby) *sn outpcd in rr: bhd fr 1/2-way* **66/1**
**11** *1* **Ilumination** 2-8-9 0 JamesSullivan 8 25
(Michael Easterby) *s.i.s: green and sn outpcd: bhd fr 1/2-way* **80/1**
0355 **12** *1 3/4* **Magic Time (IRE)**[19] 5896 2-7-12 61 (b[1]) RowanScott(7) 4 15+
(Ann Duffield) *cl up on inner: chal over 2f out: rdn whn edgd rt and hit rail 1 1/2f out: sn wknd* **9/1**
5000 **13** *nk* **Aneto Peak**[19] 5885 2-8-10 51 JasonHart 12 19
(Nigel Tinkler) *a in rr* **125/1**
1m 2.76s (-0.74) **Going Correction** -0.275s/f (Firm) **13** Ran SP% **114.8**
Speed ratings (Par 93): **94,92,92,91,90 88,81,80,79,77 75,72,72**
CSF £76.11 TOTE £7.00: £1.80, £4.90, £2.00; EX 73.50 Trifecta £344.60.Mecca's Mirage was subject to a friendly claim.
**Owner** David T J Metcalfe **Bred** Miss S Von Schilcher **Trained** Denton, Co Durham
**FOCUS**
The going was officially good to firm. A modest 2yo claimer to start with and, with a quartet battling for the early lead, not that many got into it. Straightforward form.

## 6448 BET TOTEPLACEPOT EBF MAIDEN FILLIES' STKS (BOBIS RACE) 7f 100y
**2:40** (2:41) (Class 5) 2-Y-0 **£3,557** (£1,058; £529; £264) **Stalls** Low

Form RPR
242 **1** **Ajaadat**[14] 6041 2-9-0 78 JackMitchell 4 77
(Roger Varian) *trckd ldng pair: hdwy on outer and cl up over 2f out: chal wl over 1f out: rdn to ld ent fnl f: styd on* **2/1**[1]
44 **2** *1 1/4* **Willow Creek**[13] 6071 2-9-0 0 GrahamGibbons 9 74
(William Haggas) *led: clr 1/2-way: jnd 3f out: pushed along 2f out: sn rdn: hdd and drvn ent fnl f: kpt on same pce* **6/1**
06 **3** *6* **The Wee Barra (IRE)**[18] 5910 2-9-0 0 PaulMulrennan 6 60+
(Kevin Ryan) *chsd ldrs: rdn along and edgd rt wl over 1f out: swtchd lft ent fnl f: kpt on u.p on outer to take modest 3rd nr fin* **33/1**
**4** *3/4* **Yorkindred Spirit** 2-9-0 0 JoeFanning 5 58
(Mark Johnston) *in tch: hdwy to trck ldrs 3f out: effrt to chse ldng pair wl over 1f out: sn rdn: green and edgd lft: one pce and lost modest 3rd nr fin* **11/4**[2]
63 **5** *hd* **Kelly's Finest (IRE)**[18] 5910 2-9-0 0 GrahamLee 1 58
(James Bethell) *chsd ldr: hdwy and cl up 3f out: chal over 2f out: sn rdn and wknd wl over 1f out* **10/3**[3]
044 **6** *1 1/2* **Heart Of Africa**[14] 6041 2-9-0 73 MartinLane 7 54
(Charlie Appleby) *in tch: effrt and sme hdwy 3f out: rdn along over 2f out: sn drvn and n.d* **8/1**
**7** *17* **Almost Nowhere (IRE)** 2-9-0 0 AndrewMullen 2 14
(Michael Appleby) *dwlt: green and rdn along in rr: bhd fr 1/2-way* **80/1**
05 **8** *11* **Newgate Princess**[11] 6148 2-9-0 0 BarryMcHugh 8
(Tony Coyle) *dwlt: flashed tail and sn detached: hung lft and rn wd bnd 4f out* **100/1**
1m 31.15s (-2.65) **Going Correction** -0.275s/f (Firm) **8** Ran SP% **113.6**
Speed ratings (Par 92): **104,102,95,94,94 92,73,60**
CSF £14.51 TOTE £3.50: £1.40, £3.20, £5.70; EX 14.20 Trifecta £169.30.
**Owner** Sheikh Ahmed Al Maktoum **Bred** Darley **Trained** Newmarket, Suffolk
**FOCUS**
An ordinary fillies' maiden and it only concerned the front pair throughout the latter stages.

## 6449 BET TOTEQUADPOT MAIDEN AUCTION STKS 7f 100y
**3:15** (3:15) (Class 5) 2-Y-0 **£3,234** (£962; £481; £240) **Stalls** Low

Form RPR
5443 **1** **Multi Grain**[23] 5762 2-8-12 65 JoeFanning 6 69
(Brian Ellison) *a trcking ldr: hdwy 2f out and sn cl up: rdn to chal over 1f out: ev ch whn carried bdly lft ins fnl f: kpt on gamely to ld nr fin* **2/1**[1]
05 **2** *hd* **Dynamite Inventor (IRE)**[16] 5982 2-8-10 0 KevinStott(5) 12 72
(Kevin Ryan) *led: jnd 2f out and sn rdn: drvn and hung bdly lft ins fnl f: hdd towards fin* **16/1**
3340 **3** *3/4* **Grand Proposal**[10] 6165 2-8-10 72 ShaneGray(5) 7 70
(Kevin Ryan) *in tch: hdwy wl over 2f out: rdn wl over 1f out: styd on wl fnl f* **9/4**[2]
445 **4** *2 1/4* **Star Ascending (IRE)**[86] 3529 2-8-11 58 DaleSwift 10 60+
(Brian Ellison) *hmpd s and towards rr: hdwy 3f out: rdn to chse ldrs over 1f out: swtchd rt and kpt on fnl f: nrst fin* **14/1**
00 **5** *3 1/2* **Ponty Grigio (IRE)**[13] 6058 2-9-3 0 DuranFentiman 3 58
(Tim Easterby) *towards rr: hdwy over 2f out: sn rdn and kpt on fnl f: nrst fin* **125/1**

6 **6** ½ **Passionate Appeal**[11] 6147 2-9-1 0 GrahamLee 1 55
(Ann Duffield) *trckd ldrs on inner: hdwy over 2f out: rdn along wl over 1f out: sn no imp* **13/2**[3]
000 **7** 1¾ **Pixey Punk**[54] 4626 2-8-10 54 DavidAllan 2 46
(Tim Easterby) *trckd ldng pair on inner: rdn along over 2f out: drvn over 1f out: grad wknd* **40/1**
**8** *hd* **Mclovin Riverdance** 2-8-8 0 RowanScott(7) 9 50
(Ann Duffield) *hmpd s: a in rr* **16/1**
00 **9** 2 **What Usain**[49] 4790 2-8-13 0 BarryMcHugh 11 44
(Geoffrey Oldroyd) *wnt rt s: trckd ldrs: hdwy to chse ldng pair wl over 2f out: rdn wl over 1f out: sn drvn and wknd* **125/1**
0 **10** *nk* **Parliament (IRE)**[11] 6146 2-9-3 0 TomEaves 8 47
(Ann Duffield) *hmpd s: a in rr* **33/1**
00 **11** 10 **May Hill Rebel**[11] 6148 2-7-13 0 MelissaThompson(7) 5 13
(Richard Guest) *chsd ldrs on outer: hung lft and rn wd bnd 4f out: rdn along 3f out: sn wknd* **150/1**
**12** 5 **Duchess Of Ripon (IRE)** 2-8-12 0 PaulMulrennan 4 7
(Bryan Smart) *a in rr: bhd fr 1/2-way* **7/1**
1m 32.8s (-1.00) **Going Correction** -0.275s/f (Firm) **12** Ran SP% **116.0**
Speed ratings (Par 95): **94,93,92,90,86 85,83,83,81,80 69,63**
CSF £34.65 TOTE £2.40: £1.30, £3.80, £1.10; EX 32.60 Trifecta £124.30.
**Owner** Mike And Eileen Newbould **Bred** Miss K Rausing **Trained** Norton, N Yorks
■ Stewards' Enquiry : Kevin Stott three-day ban: careless riding (Oct 1-3)
**FOCUS**
A moderate maiden auction event and very few ever got into it. Straightforward form, the winner pretty much to her mark.

## 6450 BET TOTEEXACTA H'CAP (BOBIS RACE) 1m 4f 16y
**3:50** (3:50) (Class 4) (0-85,80) 3-Y-O **£6,469** (£1,925; £962; £481) **Stalls** Low

Form RPR
1151 **1** **Leaderene**[39] 5185 3-8-13 72 JoeFanning 5 80+
(Mark Johnston) *mde all: pushed along and qckna over 2f out: rdn over 1f out: styd on strly fnl f* **7/4**[1]
1366 **2** 3 **Sir Charlie Kunz**[11] 6141 3-9-6 79 FrannyNorton 2 82
(Mark Johnston) *wnt rt s: trckd ldng pair: pushed along over 3f out: rdn to chse wnr jst over 2f out: drvn and no imp fnl f* **7/2**[3]
4131 **3** ¾ **Nakeeta**[15] 6012 3-9-7 80 DavidNolan 4 82
(Iain Jardine) *bmpd s: hld up in rr: hdwy on outer 3f out: effrt 2f out: sn rdn and kpt on same pce fnl f* **4/1**
6230 **4** ¾ **Mr Gallivanter (IRE)**[20] 5164 3-9-7 80 (p) PhillipMakin 6 81
(John Quinn) *trckd wnr: effrt over 2f out and sn rdn along: drvn over 1f out: sn btn* **5/2**[2]
2m 34.75s (-5.05) **Going Correction** -0.275s/f (Firm) course record **4** Ran SP% **107.2**
Speed ratings (Par 103): **105,103,102,102**
CSF £7.77 TOTE £2.00; EX 8.80 Trifecta £15.30.
**Owner** Miss K Rausing **Bred** Miss K Rausing **Trained** Middleham Moor, N Yorks
**FOCUS**
Just the four runners, but a decent pace under the circumstances. It resulted in a 1-2 for the Mark Johnston yard. The winner could go on from here.

## 6451 TOTEPOOL SUPPORTING THE ROA OWNERS JACKPOT H'CAP (DIV I) 5f
**4:20** (4:21) (Class 5) (0-75,75) 3-Y-O+ **£3,881** (£1,155; £577; £288) **Stalls** Low

Form RPR
4600 **1** **Bondi Beach Boy**[7] 6235 5-9-4 75 GeorgeChaloner(3) 8 83
(James Turner) *chsd ldr: cl up 1/2-way: rdn to chal over 1f out: led ins fnl f: drvn out* **4/1**[2]
5060 **2** ¾ **Sunny Side Up (IRE)**[42] 5053 5-8-3 62 GemmaTutty(5) 1 67
(Karen Tutty) *qckly away and led: jnd and rdn over 1f out: drvn: edgd lft and hdd ins fnl f: kpt on* **11/1**
2214 **3** *nk* **Flash City (ITY)**[12] 6109 6-9-4 72 JamesSullivan 2 76
(Ruth Carr) *trckd ldrs: hdwy 2f out: rdn to chal on inner ins fnl f: ev ch tl drvn and nt qckn towards fin* **4/1**[2]
0351 **4** 1¼ **Manatee Bay**[8] 6213 4-8-13 67 6ex (v) FrannyNorton 5 66+
(David Nicholls) *dwlt and in rr: hdwy wl over 1f out: swtchd lft and rdn ent fnl f: kpt on: nrst fin* **7/2**[1]
1611 **5** ½ **Bashiba (IRE)**[14] 6029 3-9-4 73 (t) RobertWinston 7 71
(Nigel Tinkler) *chsd ldrs: rdn 2f out: drvn and one pce ent fnl f* **5/1**[3]
0160 **6** 3 **Banovallum**[95] 3256 4-9-4 72 GrahamGibbons 4 59
(Michael Easterby) *hld up: a towards rr* **7/1**
6626 **7** *nk* **Haajes**[18] 5913 10-9-2 70 (v) GrahamLee 9 56
(Paul Midgley) *chsd ldrs on outer: rdn along over 2f out: sn wknd* **8/1**
1m 1.73s (-1.77) **Going Correction** -0.275s/f (Firm)
**WFA** 3 from 4yo+ 1lb **7** Ran SP% **110.8**
Speed ratings (Par 103): **103,101,101,99,98 93,93**
CSF £42.39 CT £177.25 TOTE £3.70: £2.40, £5.30; EX 51.50 Trifecta £359.40.
**Owner** G R Turner & H Turner **Bred** G R & H Turner **Trained** Norton-le-Clay, N Yorks
**FOCUS**
An ordinary sprint handicap and another race where it paid to be handy. The form fits around the second and third.

## 6452 TOTEPOOL SUPPORTING THE ROA OWNERS JACKPOT H'CAP (DIV II) 5f
**4:50** (4:51) (Class 5) (0-75,73) 3-Y-O+ **£3,881** (£1,155; £577; £288) **Stalls** Low

Form RPR
0200 **1** **Ambitious Icarus**[7] 6235 5-9-6 72 (e) JasonHart 7 78
(Richard Guest) *dwlt and in rr: pushed along 1/2-way: rdn wl over 1f out: styd on wl fnl f to ld nr line* **5/1**[2]
0420 **2** *nk* **Tweety Pie (IRE)**[46] 4891 3-8-13 69 NeilFarley(3) 8 74
(Declan Carroll) *trckd ldrs: hdwy 2f out: rdn whn rdr dropped whip jst over 1f out: styd on ins fnl f: led briefly last 20yds: hdd nr line* **17/2**
0102 **3** *shd* **Choc'A'Moca (IRE)**[12] 6114 7-8-10 62 (v) GrahamLee 9 67
(Paul Midgley) *towards rr: rdn along over 2f out: hdwy on outer over 1f out: drvn and styd on strly fnl f* **10/1**
0000 **4** *nk* **Mr Mo Jo**[21] 5819 6-8-11 63 (b) DavidAllan 1 67
(Les Eyre) *qckly away and led: rdn jst over 1f out: drvn ins fnl f: hdd and no ex last 20yds* **8/1**
00 **5** 1¼ **Thatcherite (IRE)**[18] 5912 6-9-6 72 (t) BarryMcHugh 10 71
(Tony Coyle) *dwlt and swtchd rt s: bhd: hdwy 2f out: sn rdn: styd on wl fnl f: nrst fin* **10/1**
0133 **6** ½ **Tinsill**[18] 5912 3-9-6 73 AdrianNicholls 2 71
(Nigel Tinkler) *trckd ldrs on inner: effrt 2f out: sn rdn and kpt on same pce fnl f* **13/2**[3]
2050 **7** ¾ **Bosham**[11] 6150 4-9-1 67 GrahamGibbons 6 62
(Michael Easterby) *cl up: rdn wl over 1f out: drvn and wknd ent fnl f* **3/1**[1]

426 **8** 2 **Scoreline**[12] 6109 3-9-4 71 (v[1]) DanielTudhope 4 59
(David O'Meara) *cl up: effrt 2f out: sn rdn and wknd ent fnl f* **5/1**[2]
1650 **9** 1¾ **Lexington Rose**[12] 6109 3-9-4 71 PaulMulrennan 5 52
(Bryan Smart) *trckd ldrs: rdn along wl over 1f out: sn wknd* **16/1**
1m 1.83s (-1.67) **Going Correction** -0.275s/f (Firm)
**WFA** 3 from 4yo+ 1lb **9** Ran SP% **117.4**
Speed ratings (Par 103): **102,101,101,100,98 98,96,93,90**
CSF £47.64 CT £412.63 TOTE £8.60: £2.40, £2.20, £1.60; EX 55.30 Trifecta £469.20.
**Owner** ABS Metals & Waste **Bred** L T Roberts **Trained** Ingmanthorpe, W Yorks
**FOCUS**
Despite the winning time being 0.1sec slower than the first division, they may have gone off too quick in this leg and the first three came from well off the pace. Ordinary form.

## 6453 COLLECT TOTEPOOL WINNINGS AT BETFRED SHOPS MAIDEN STKS 5f
**5:25** (5:27) (Class 5) 2-Y-O **£3,234** (£962; £481; £240) **Stalls** Low

Form RPR
02 **1** **Canny Kool**[31] 5464 2-9-5 0 TomEaves 9 84+
(Brian Ellison) *cl up: led 1/2-way: rdn clr appr fnl f: readily* **3/1**[2]
026 **2** 4½ **Zuzinia (IRE)**[10] 6168 2-9-0 69 JoeFanning 1 63
(Mick Channon) *midfield: hdwy 2f out: rdn to chse ldrs over 1f out: drvn and kpt on ins fnl f: no ch w wnr* **7/2**[3]
2324 **3** ½ **Westhoughton**[2] 6401 2-9-5 75 DanielTudhope 8 66
(David O'Meara) *trckd ldrs: hdwy 2f out: sn rdn to chse wnr over 1f out: drvn and one pce fnl f* **11/4**[1]
**4** *hd* **Apache Storm** 2-9-0 0 AndrewMullen 12 60+
(Michael Appleby) *dwlt: green and outpcd in rr: rdn along 1/2-way: edgd lft wl over 1f out: str run ent fnl f: nrst fin* **20/1**
53 **5** 2¼ **Named Asset**[21] 5807 2-9-5 0 RussKennemore 11 57
(Jedd O'Keeffe) *chsd ldrs: rdn wl over 1f out: kpt on one pce appr fnl f* **9/1**
5 **6** ¾ **Belle Nellie (IRE)**[75] 3909 2-9-0 0 JasonHart 2 50
(Nigel Tinkler) *midfield: hdwy over 2f out: rdn to chse ldrs wl over 1f out: sn drvn and wknd* **20/1**
40 **7** 3½ **Never Easy (IRE)**[30] 5493 2-9-5 0 TonyHamilton 7 42+
(Richard Fahey) *nvr bttr than midfield* **25/1**
000 **8** 1½ **Edie White**[32] 5443 2-8-9 48 (b[1]) JordanNason(5) 5 32
(Lawrence Mullaney) *wnt lft s: cl up: rdn along 1/2-way: sn wknd* **80/1**
0 **9** *hd* **Reckless Blue**[64] 4286 2-9-0 0 JamesSullivan 10 31
(Michael Easterby) *chsd ldrs: rdn along 1/2-way: sn wknd* **100/1**
06 **10** 5 **Bushtiger (IRE)**[21] 5813 2-9-5 0 PhillipMakin 15 18
(David Barron) *a towards rr* **100/1**
0 **11** ¾ **Unforgettable You (IRE)**[64] 4286 2-8-11 0 NeilFarley(3) 4 10
(Declan Carroll) *a towards rr* **66/1**
0 **12** ¾ **Classic Image**[23] 5774 2-9-0 0 ChrisCatlin 6 8
(Rae Guest) *slt ld: hdd 1/2-way: sn rdn and wknd wl over 1f out* **8/1**
**13** ¾ **Bracka Legend (IRE)** 2-9-5 0 GrahamGibbons 14 10
(David Barron) *dwlt and swtchd rt s: a bhd* **14/1**
**14** 5 **Perfect Peak** 2-8-7 0 DanielleMooney(7) 3
(Michael Easterby) *a towards rr* **100/1**
1m 1.85s (-1.65) **Going Correction** -0.275s/f (Firm) **14** Ran SP% **120.7**
Speed ratings (Par 95): **102,94,94,93,90 88,83,80,80,72 71,70,68,60**
CSF £13.11 TOTE £3.60: £1.60, £1.60, £2.10; EX 15.00 Trifecta £42.20.
**Owner** Market Avenue Racing Club Ltd **Bred** Old Mill Stud **Trained** Norton, N Yorks
**FOCUS**
A big field, but a modest maiden. The second and third set the level.

## 6454 BET TOTETRIFECTA APPRENTICE TRAINING SERIES CLASSIFIED STKS (PART OF RACING EXCELLENCE INITIATIVE) 1m 100y
**5:55** (5:55) (Class 6) 3-Y-O+ **£2,385** (£704; £352) **Stalls** Low

Form RPR
3335 **1** **Ice Mayden**[58] 4495 3-8-10 55 JoeDoyle 9 57
(Bryan Smart) *hld up towards rr: stdy hdwy over 3f out: effrt 2f out: sn chsng ldr: rdn over 1f out: led ent fnl f: sn edgd lft: kpt on wl towards fin* **9/4**[1]
0460 **2** 2 **Mysterious Wonder**[15] 6014 4-9-0 53 JordanVaughan 11 52
(Philip Kirby) *hld up in rr: hdwy wl over 2f out: swtchd lft to outer and rdn over 1f out: styd on strly ent fnl f: swtchd rt last 100yds and no imp tgowards fin* **10/1**
0526 **3** 1 **Belle Peinture (FR)**[64] 4292 3-8-10 46 RachelRichardson 1 50
(Alan Lockwood) *led: pushed clr 3f out: rdn wl over 1f out: hdd ent fnl f: kpt on same pce* **12/1**
0000 **4** ½ **Noble Reach**[12] 6122 3-8-10 45 JordanNason 12 49
(Lawrence Mullaney) *chsd ldng pair: rdn along over 2f out: swtchd rt to inner over 1f out: sn drvn and kpt on same pce* **66/1**
550 **5** ½ **Focail Mear**[21] 5832 3-8-5 45 JoshDoyle(5) 4 48
(John Ryan) *hld up: hdwy 3f out: rdn to chse ldrs wl over 1f out: drvn and no imp fnl f* **33/1**
3-40 **6** *nk* **Crossley**[12] 6122 5-8-9 52 (p) JoshQuinn(5) 2 47
(Geoffrey Oldroyd) *chsd ldr: rdn along over 2f out: drvn and wknd over 1f out* **9/1**
4503 **7** 1 **Heartstrings**[20] 5846 3-8-10 55 (v) DanielCremin 3 45
(Mick Channon) *chsd ldrs: rdn along over 2f out: edgd rt and one pce fr over 1f out* **6/1**[2]
5400 **8** 2¾ **Maillot Jaune (IRE)**[8] 6210 4-8-9 45 RowanScott(5) 16 38
(Patrick Holmes) *nvr bttr than midfield* **50/1**
6056 **9** 1¾ **Roxy Lane**[21] 5811 5-9-0 51 PatMillman 10 34
(Peter Hiatt) *hld up: hdwy and in tch 3f out: rdn along over 2f out: n.d* **9/1**
0500 **10** *nk* **Mary's Prayer**[13] 6076 3-8-10 45 (p) GemmaTutty 13 33
(John Holt) *nvr nr ldrs* **40/1**
4030 **11** 5 **Synonym (ITY)**[120] 2416 3-8-10 46 AlistairRawlinson 6 22
(Michael Appleby) *chsd ldrs: rdn along 3f out: sn wknd* **7/1**[3]
3006 **12** ½ **Rio Yuma (ITY)**[55] 4563 3-8-7 55 GaryMahon(3) 14 20
(Kristin Stubbs) *a in rr* **40/1**
006 **13** 1½ **Soviet Union (IRE)**[31] 5469 3-8-7 45 AnnaHesketh(3) 8 17
(Mark Walford) *a in rr* **33/1**
1050 **14** 4½ **Robbian**[28] 5574 3-8-5 48 PaddyPilley(5) 17 6
(Charles Smith) *a in rr* **50/1**
0/0- **15** *hd* **Beautifulwildthing**[477] 2742 4-9-0 55 JackGarritty 15 6
(Richard Fahey) *a bhd* **12/1**
0000 **16** ¾ **Classy Lassy (IRE)**[30] 5512 3-8-10 45 (b[1]) MeganCarberry 7 4
(Brian Ellison) *a towards rr* **16/1**
1m 46.21s (-1.39) **Going Correction** -0.275s/f (Firm)
**WFA** 3 from 4yo+ 4lb **16** Ran SP% **124.1**
Speed ratings (Par 101): **95,93,92,91,91 90,89,86,85,84 79,79,77,73,73 72**
CSF £24.77 TOTE £2.80: £1.40, £4.10, £3.80; EX 25.30 Trifecta £257.40.
**Owner** Julian Ball **Bred** Bearstone Stud **Trained** Hambleton, N Yorks

**FOCUS**
Another big field, but a moderate classified event. Not a race to take positives from.
T/Jkpt: £2,366.60 to a £1 stake. Pool of £10000.00 - 3.00 winning tickets. T/Plt: £289.10 to a £1 stake. Pool of £60453.34 - 152.60 winning tickets. T/Qpdt: £59.40 to a £1 stake. Pool of £4227.67 - 52.65 winning tickets. JR

## 6299 SANDOWN (R-H)
Wednesday, September 17

**OFFICIAL GOING: Good**
Wind: strong breeze across Weather: overcast

### 6455 RACEHORSE SANCTUARY REMEMBERS MOORCROFT BOY H'CAP (JOCKEY CLUB GRASSROOTS SPRINT SERIES QUALIF.) 5f 6y
**2:00** (2:01) (Class 5) (0-75,75) 3-Y-O+ **£3,234** (£962; £481; £240) **Stalls** Low

Form RPR
4315 **1** **Only Ten Per Cent (IRE)**[24] 5724 6-9-1 69....................(v) AdamKirby 1 78
(J R Jenkins) *trckd ldrs: r.o wl to ld fnl 120yds: rdn out* **9/1**[3]
4553 **2** *1* **Dreams Of Glory**[24] 5724 6-9-1 69....................(b) OisinMurphy 8 74
(Ron Hodges) *trckd ldrs: rdn 2f out: led ent fnl f: hdd fnl 120yds: kpt on but no ex* **12/1**
0640 **3** *½* **Rocket Rob (IRE)**[15] 6006 8-9-0 68.......................... JimmyFortune 14 71
(Willie Musson) *towards rr: swtchd lft and rdn over 1f out: r.o strly fnl f: clsng fast at fin: snatched 3rd fnl stride* **11/2**[2]
406 **4** *nse* **National Service (USA)**[3] 6355 3-9-0 69....................[1] DaneO'Neill 5 72
(Stuart Williams) *s.i.s: towards rr: swtchd lft and nt best of runs fr over 1f out: weaved through and r.o wl fnl f: nt quite rch ldrs: lost 3rd fnl stride* **10/1**
3015 **5** *¾* **Dishy Guru**[36] 5281 5-8-11 65....................(b) LiamKeniry 12 65
(Michael Blanshard) *hld up towards rr: stdy hdwy over 1f out but nt best of runs: r.o fnl f but nvr quite gng pce to get on terms* **50/1**
1461 **6** *1* **Where The Boys Are (IRE)**[46] 4890 3-8-13 68........... JamesDoyle 15 65
(Ed McMahon) *chsd ldrs: rdn over 2f out: kpt on same pce fnl f* **10/1**
2226 **7** *nk* **Burnt Cream**[27] 5594 7-8-8 62....................(t) RobertHavlin 11 61
(Martin Bosley) *s.i.s: towards rr: nt clr run fr over 2f out tl over 1f out: r.o but no ch after* **25/1**
1101 **8** *½* **Two Turtle Doves (IRE)**[24] 5724 8-8-8 62.............. HarryBentley 10 58
(Michael Mullineaux) *trckd ldrs: rdn over 2f out: hmpd jst over 1f out: fdd ins fnl f* **14/1**
560 **9** *nse* **Mr Dandy Man (IRE)**[5] 6296 3-9-3 72..........(p) WilliamTwiston-Davies 2 66
(Ronald Harris) *led: rdn 2f out: hdd ent fnl f: fdd fnl 120yds* **16/1**
-200 **10** *¾* **Shirley's Pride**[118] 2486 4-8-13 67....................(t) DavidProbert 7 58
(Michael Appleby) *taken to s early: mid-div: rdn 2f out: no imp whn bmpd jst over 1f out* **10/1**
3000 **11** *hd* **Amenable (IRE)**[17] 5951 7-9-3 71....................(p) HayleyTurner 3 62
(Conor Dore) *taken to s early: sn pushed along in tch: nvr gng pce to threaten: fdd ins fnl f* **20/1**
34-1 **12** *2* **Macdillon**[19] 5880 8-9-7 75.......................... RichardHughes 4 58+
(Stuart Kittow) *slowly away: towards rr: pushed along and sme hdwy whn nt clr run 1f out: no ch and eased after* **5/2**[1]
316- **13** *2* **Clement (IRE)**[307] 6488 4-9-1 74.......................... DanielMuscutt(5) 6 50
(John O'Shea) *s.i.s: sn mid-div: rdn 2f out: wknd over 1f out* **33/1**
5225 **14** *2* **Alpha Delta Whisky**[29] 5535 6-9-5 73....................(v) MartinDwyer 13 42
(John Gallagher) *led after 1f tl rdn over 2f out: wknd ent fnl f* **20/1**
1m 1.02s (-0.58) **Going Correction** 0.0s/f (Good)
**WFA** 3 from 4yo+ 1lb 14 Ran SP% **119.7**
Speed ratings (Par 103): **104,102,101,101,100 98,98,97,97,96 95,92,89,86**
CSF £104.07 CT £673.76 TOTE £8.00: £2.60, £3.90, £2.10; EX 105.10 Trifecta £740.40.
**Owner** B Silkman **Bred** Sandro Garavelli **Trained** Royston, Herts

**FOCUS**
The rail on the Round course was at its innermost configuration. Dane O'Neill described the ground on the sprint course as "a bit loose but good ground overall". A low draw is often advantageous in the 5f races at the track and so it proved again. The winner looks as good on turf as sand now.

### 6456 BRITISH STALLION STUDS / EXHIBITION NEWS EBF MAIDEN STKS 1m 14y
**2:30** (2:30) (Class 5) 2-Y-O **£3,881** (£1,155; £577; £288) **Stalls** Low

Form RPR
6 **1** **Dartmouth**[26] 5625 2-9-5 0.......................... RyanMoore 2 78+
(Sir Michael Stoute) *trckd ldr: rdn over 2f out: led over 1f out: styd on strly fnl f* **5/2**[1]
0 **2** *2* **Delusional**[68] 4142 2-9-5 0.......................... JamesDoyle 5 73
(Roger Charlton) *hld up bhd ldrs: shkn up and hdwy jst over 2f out: chsd wnr jst ins fnl f: styd on but a being hld* **15/2**
**3** *2* **Chicago Bere (FR)** 2-9-5 0.......................... RichardHughes 3 68
(Richard Hannon) *led: rdn whn pressed over 2f out: hdd over 1f out: no ex ins fnl f* **5/1**[3]
04 **4** *½* **Philba**[18] 5922 2-9-5 0.......................... DavidProbert 1 67
(Michael Appleby) *in tch: rdn whn outpcd over 2f out: styd on fnl f: wnt 4th towards fin* **20/1**
5 **5** *1* **Rosenbaum**[13] 6056 2-9-5 0.......................... AdamKirby 6 65
(Charlie Appleby) *trckd ldr: chal over 2f out: sn rdn: hld over 1f out: fdd fnl 120yds: lost 4th towards fin* **11/4**[2]
**6** *4 ½* **Nota Cambiata (USA)** 2-9-5 0.......................... RobertHavlin 7 54
(John Gosden) *s.i.s: sn pushed along in last pair: outpcd over 2f out* **5/1**[3]
**7** *1 ¼* **Port** 2-9-5 0.......................... PatDobbs 4 51
(Richard Hannon) *s.i.s: in last pair: outpcd over 2f out: wknd fnl f* **16/1**
1m 47.58s (4.28) **Going Correction** +0.125s/f (Good) 7 Ran SP% **111.0**
Speed ratings (Par 95): **83,81,79,78,77 73,71**
CSF £20.21 TOTE £3.00: £1.70, £3.40; EX 19.70 Trifecta £72.40.
**Owner** The Queen **Bred** Darley **Trained** Newmarket, Suffolk

**FOCUS**
Although run at a steady gallop, it's likely this was a decent maiden, although the bare form is ordinary by track standard.

### 6457 MAX PATEL WEALTH MANAGER OF CHOICE NOVICE STKS (BOBIS RACE) 7f 16y
**3:05** (3:07) (Class 3) 2-Y-O **£6,469** (£1,925; £962; £481) **Stalls** Low

Form RPR
41 **1** **Latharnach (USA)**[49] 4800 2-9-5 0.......................... AdamKirby 4 97+
(Charlie Appleby) *mde all: qcknd pce over 2f out: styd on strly and in command fnl f: readily* **4/6**[1]
21 **2** *2 ¾* **Time Test**[19] 5881 2-9-5 0.......................... JamesDoyle 2 90
(Roger Charlton) *trckd wnr: hanging rt whn asked for effrt 2f out: nvr threatened: styd on same pce* **6/4**[2]
**3** *1 ¾* **Mister Brightside (IRE)** 2-8-12 0.......................... RyanMoore 1 78+
(Jeremy Noseda) *plld hrd early: trckd wnr tl over 3f out: rdn over 2f out: kpt on same pce* **20/1**[3]
**4** *8* **Quality Song (USA)** 2-8-12 0.......................... DaneO'Neill 3 57
(Roger Varian) *little slowly away: trckd ldrs: rdn over 2f out: nt gng pce to threaten: wknd fnl f* **25/1**
1m 32.99s (3.49) **Going Correction** +0.125s/f (Good) 4 Ran SP% **108.6**
Speed ratings (Par 99): **85,81,79,70**
CSF £1.92 TOTE £1.90; EX 2.20 Trifecta £3.70.
**Owner** Godolphin **Bred** Darley **Trained** Newmarket, Suffolk

**FOCUS**
As in the previous contest, they went just a steady gallop. The winner impressed and the form is rated positively.

### 6458 NIGEL & CAROLYN ELWES FORTUNE STKS (LISTED RACE) 1m 14y
**3:40** (3:40) (Class 1) 3-Y-O+
**£20,982** (£7,955; £3,981; £1,983; £995; £499) **Stalls** Low

Form RPR
2201 **1** **Tenor (IRE)**[3] 6358 4-9-4 103.......................... (t) AdamKirby 7 110
(John Ryan) *prom: pushed along 3f out: rdn 2f out: led over 1f out: 2 l clr ent fnl f: kpt on: rdn out* **5/2**[1]
4264 **2** *1* **Producer**[25] 5666 5-9-4 110.......................... RichardHughes 8 108
(Richard Hannon) *hld up in tch: swtchd out for effrt over 2f out: no imp tl r.o ent fnl f: drifted rt: wnt 2nd fnl 120yds but a being hld* **5/2**[1]
6024 **3** *1 ½* **Emell**[11] 6132 4-9-4 105.......................... RyanMoore 2 104
(Richard Hannon) *wnt lft s: trckd ldrs: rdn over 2f out: kpt on but nt gng pce to chal: wnt 3rd fnl stride* **6/1**[2]
0046 **4** *nse* **Amulet**[54] 4607 4-8-13 89....................(b[1]) JimmyFortune 1 99
(Eve Johnson Houghton) *led: rdn over 2f out: hdd over 1f out: kpt on but no ex fnl f: lost 3rd fnl stride* **66/1**
0306 **5** *2* **Empire Storm (GER)**[37] 5263 7-9-4 104....................(t) RobertHavlin 5 100
(Michael Attwater) *trckd ldrs: rdn over 2f out: kpt on same pce fnl f* **25/1**
0003 **6** *2 ¼* **Bold Thady Quill (IRE)**[4] 6354 7-9-4 100....................(v) DaneO'Neill 4 94
(K J Condon, Ire) *s.i.s: in last pair: rdn over 2f out: nvr any imp* **10/1**
0204 **7** *1 ½* **Spa's Dancer (IRE)**[18] 5928 7-9-4 101.......................... JimCrowley 3 91
(James Eustace) *slowly away and short of room s: in last pair: rdn over 2f out: nvr any imp* **6/1**[2]
055 **8** *7* **Cordite (IRE)**[95] 3252 3-9-0 104.......................... JamesDoyle 6 75
(Michael Appleby) *taken to s early: racd keenly in tch: effrt over 2f out: wknd over 1f out* **7/1**[3]
1m 42.18s (-1.12) **Going Correction** +0.125s/f (Good)
**WFA** 3 from 4yo+ 4lb 8 Ran SP% **112.6**
Speed ratings: **110,109,107,107,105 103,101,94**
CSF £8.04 TOTE £3.80: £1.10, £1.30, £2.30; EX 9.40 Trifecta £26.50.
**Owner** Kilco (International) Ltd **Bred** Epona Bloodstock Ltd And P A Byrne **Trained** Newmarket, Suffolk

■ Stewards' Enquiry : Adam Kirby two-day ban: used whip above permitted level (Oct 1-4), + deffered days (OCT 6-9)

**FOCUS**
Solid form for the level, with the tiome and the fourth offering perspective.

### 6459 ST JAMES'S PLACE WEALTH MANAGEMENT FILLIES' H'CAP (BOBIS RACE) 1m 14y
**4:15** (4:18) (Class 4) (0-85,82) 3-Y-O **£5,175** (£1,540; £769; £384) **Stalls** Low

Form RPR
1523 **1** **Ajig**[5] 6304 3-8-7 68....................(p) JohnFahy 2 75
(Eve Johnson Houghton) *trckd ldrs: qcknd to ld jst over 1f out: kpt on: rdn out* **13/2**[3]
3105 **2** *½* **Palerma**[33] 5401 3-9-1 76.......................... DavidProbert 6 82
(Mick Channon) *trckd ldrs: rdn over 2f out: ev ch over 1f out: kpt on fnl 120yds* **9/1**
3204 **3** *½* **Perfect Persuasion**[26] 5656 3-9-7 82.......................... RyanMoore 3 87+
(William Haggas) *s.i.s: in last pair: rdn whn swtchd lft over 2f out: styd on fnl f* **7/4**[1]
531 **4** *1 ¼* **Ramshackle**[13] 6073 3-9-0 75.......................... JamesDoyle 7 77
(Sir Michael Stoute) *racd keenly: pressed ldr: led 3f out: sn rdn: hdd jst over 1f out: no ex ins fnl f* **9/2**[2]
0431 **5** *2 ¾* **Ligeia**[25] 5685 3-9-2 77.......................... RichardHughes 4 73
(Richard Hannon) *hld up in last pair: rdn over 2f out: nvr finding pce to get on terms* **8/1**
3141 **6** *4 ½* **Special Miss**[18] 5930 3-8-12 73.......................... JimCrowley 1 58
(Ali Stronge) *led tl 3f out: sn rdn: kpt on tl fdd fnl f* **9/2**[2]
6564 **7** *4* **Tea In Transvaal (IRE)**[35] 5304 3-8-8 69.......................... OisinMurphy 8 45
(John O'Shea) *in tch: rdn whn edgd rt over 2f out: wknd over 1f out* **33/1**
1m 43.1s (-0.20) **Going Correction** +0.125s/f (Good) 7 Ran SP% **110.1**
Speed ratings (Par 100): **106,105,105,103,101 96,92**
CSF £56.61 CT £135.72 TOTE £6.90: £2.20, £5.50; EX 47.40 Trifecta £148.80.
**Owner** Eden Racing Club **Bred** Southcourt Stud **Trained** Blewbury, Oxon

**FOCUS**
A fair fillies' handicap that went to the tough and progressive Ajig. Not the deepest race, but straightforward form.

### 6460 SUPPORT RACEHORSE SANCTUARY TEXT : 70070 "HORS20 £5" H'CAP (BOBIS) (JCG MIDDLE DISTANCE QUALIFIER) 1m 2f 7y
**4:45** (4:47) (Class 4) (0-85,85) 3-Y-O **£5,175** (£1,540; £769; £384) **Stalls** Low

Form RPR
1350 **1** **Raise Your Gaze**[24] 5720 3-9-4 85.......................... RyanTate(3) 4 95+
(Clive Cox) *trckd ldrs: nt clr run whn pushed along over 2f out tl jst over 1f out: led ins fnl f: styd on wl: comf* **7/2**[2]
1306 **2** *2* **Beakers N Num Nums (IRE)**[19] 5884 3-8-8 72............ MartinDwyer 3 78
(William Jarvis) *hld up: trckd ldrs after 4f: rdn over 2f out: ev ch over 1f out: kpt on but nt gng pce of wnr* **10/1**
21 **3** *½* **Shama's Crown (IRE)**[30] 5504 3-9-2 80.......................... RyanMoore 1 85
(Jeremy Noseda) *racd keenly: stdd to last after 2f: hdwy 2f out: sn rdn: ev ch ent fnl f: styd on but no ex* **15/8**[1]
30 **4** *1 ¼* **All Talk N No Do (IRE)**[19] 5884 3-8-13 77.......................... OisinMurphy 2 80
(Seamus Durack) *trckd ldrs tl lost pl after 4f: rdn wl over 2f out: tended to hang rt: kpt on same pce: regained 4th ins fnl f* **10/1**
1130 **5** *2 ¾* **Thurayaat**[24] 5723 3-9-6 84.......................... DaneO'Neill 7 82
(Roger Varian) *trckd ldrs: led after 4f: rdn whn strly pressed fr over 2f out: hdd jst ins fnl f: wknd* **14/1**

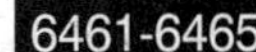


2214 **6** 3 1/4 **Telefono**18 5931 3-9-3 81 JamesDoyle 6 74
(Amanda Perrett) *led for 4f: trckd ldrs: nt clr run on rails over 2f out: rdn over 1f out: wknd fnl f* **9/2**3

6634 **7** hd **Arantes**21 5812 3-8-13 77 RichardHughes 5 68
(Mick Channon) *hld up: hdwy after 4f to trck ldrs: rdn over 2f out: wknd jst over 1f out* **8/1**

2m 9.73s (-0.77) **Going Correction** +0.125s/f (Good) 7 Ran SP% **111.1**
Speed ratings (Par 103): **108,106,106,105,102 100,100**
CSF £34.79 TOTE £3.50: £1.60, £4.30; EX 45.20 Trifecta £316.70.
**Owner** Miss J Deadman & S Barrow **Bred** James Ortega Bloodstock **Trained** Lambourn, Berks

**FOCUS**
The right horses came to the fore in this handicap. The form is rated around those in behind the winner.

## 6461 WILDWOOD GOLF AND COUNTRY CLUB H'CAP 1m 6f
5:20 (5:20) (Class 5) (0-75,74) 3-Y-O £2,587 (£770; £384; £192) Stalls Low

Form RPR

5360 **1** **Norab (GER)**19 5878 3-9-0 72 DanielMuscutt(5) 1 81
(Marco Botti) *mde all: edgd lft whn rdn clr wl over 1f out: in command after: readily* **13/2**

0433 **2** 3 **Arcamante (ITY)**21 5815 3-9-3 70 (e) JimCrowley 3 74
(K R Burke) *in tch: rdn and stdy prog over 2f out: chsd wnr over 1f out: styd on but nvr threatening to get to wnr* **7/2**2

4363 **3** 2 **Shadows Ofthenight (IRE)**25 5670 3-9-3 70 SamHitchcott 4 72
(Mick Channon) *hld up bhd: rdn wl over 2f out: styd on fr wl over 1f out: wnt 3rd ins fnl f: nvr threatened ldrs* **9/1**

6253 **4** 2 1/2 **Bold Runner**11 6143 3-9-6 73 IrineuGoncalves 8 71
(Jose Santos) *in tch: hdwy into 3rd 8f out: rdn over 3f out: kpt ldrs tl no ex ins fnl f* **8/1**

0062 **5** nk **Dire Straits (IRE)**21 5829 3-9-1 68 (p) SebSanders 2 66
(Chris Wall) *trckd ldrs: rdn over 2f out: nt pce to chal: no ex fnl f* **4/1**3

6640 **6** 5 **Cape Karli (IRE)**29 5534 3-8-12 65 RichardHughes 6 56
(Kevin Ryan) *hld up in last pair: rdn over 3f out: nvr any imp fdd ins fnl f* **20/1**

0530 **7** 6 **Peacemaker (IRE)**48 4834 3-8-8 61 (b1) JohnFahy 5 45
(Eve Johnson Houghton) *slowly away: sn chsng ldrs: rdn 3f out: wknd ent fnl f* **12/1**

-663 **8** 10 **Lovelocks (IRE)**12 6092 3-9-7 74 RyanMoore 7 45
(Charles Hills) *trckd ldr: effrt 3f out: sn btn* **3/1**1

3m 5.05s (0.55) **Going Correction** +0.125s/f (Good) 8 Ran SP% **114.1**
Speed ratings (Par 101): **103,101,100,98,98 95,92,86**
CSF £29.38 CT £205.06 TOTE £8.00: £2.10, £1.70, £2.50; EX 30.30 Trifecta £151.40.
**Owner** Marc Keller **Bred** Gestut Etzean **Trained** Newmarket, Suffolk

**FOCUS**
Little got into this, with the winner making all. Straightforward form.
T/Plt: £327.40 to a £1 stake. Pool of £57756.72 - 128.74 winning tickets. T/Qpdt: £106.20 to a £1 stake. Pool of £3432.33 - 23.90 winning tickets. TM

# 6434 YARMOUTH (L-H)
## Wednesday, September 17

**OFFICIAL GOING: Good (good to firm; 7.3)**
Wind: light, half behind Weather: dry, overcast and misty

## 6462 BRITISH STALLION STUDS/GREENE KING EBF MAIDEN STKS 7f 3y
2:20 (2:23) (Class 5) 2-Y-O £3,234 (£962; £481; £240) Stalls Centre

Form RPR

32 **1** **Bartel (IRE)**23 5760 2-9-5 0 FrederikTylicki 11 84
(Ed Vaughan) *hld up in tch in midfield: hdwy to chse ldrs 3f out: rdn and ev ch over 1f out: led fnl 100yds: rdn out* **11/8**1

0 **2** 1/2 **Spiriting (IRE)**40 5149 2-9-5 0 AndreaAtzeni 8 83
(Luca Cumani) *t.k.h: chsd ldrs: wnt 2nd 3f out: rdn to ld over 1f out: hdd and styd on same pce fnl 100yds* **15/8**2

05 **3** 5 **Explain**26 5625 2-9-5 0 FergusSweeney 10 69+
(Martyn Meade) *led: rdn and hdd over 1f out 3rd and btn 1f out: wknd ins fnl f* **33/1**

**4** 1 1/2 **Firmament** 2-9-5 0 WilliamBuick 6 65+
(Jeremy Noseda) *bmpd s: off the pce towards rr: rdn 1/2-way: hdwy past btn horses 2f out: modest 4th over 1f out: styd on: nvr trbld ldrs* **14/1**

0 **5** 6 **Kerrymerry (IRE)**27 5604 2-8-12 0 AhmadAlSubousi(7) 7 49+
(Ismail Mohammed) *t.k.h: hld up in tch in midfield: rdn and struggling over 2f out: wknd wl over 1f out* **100/1**

0 **6** 1 **Luv U**13 6066 2-9-0 0 PaulHanagan 3 41
(Ed Dunlop) *chsd ldrs: rdn and btn ent fnl 2f: wknd over 1f out* **33/1**

00 **7** 1/2 **Secrets Safe (IRE)**13 6056 2-9-5 0 ShaneKelly 13 45
(David Brown) *in tch in midfield: rdn and rn green over 2f out: sn struggling and btn 2f out: no ch whn wnt lft over 1f out* **150/1**

06 **8** 1 3/4 **Prayer Time**8 6203 2-9-5 0 JimmyQuinn 4 40
(Mark H Tompkins) *t.k.h: hld up in midfield: rdn and struggling over 2f out: sn wknd* **150/1**

0 **9** 2 1/4 **Snappy Guest**65 4270 2-9-5 0 TomQueally 1 34
(George Margarson) *s.i.s: sn rdn along in rr: n.d* **40/1**

**10** 6 **Baroot** 2-9-5 0 PatCosgrave 5 18
(M F De Kock, South Africa) *t.k.h and rn green: hld up in tch in midfield: rdn and outpcd ent fnl 2f: wknd over 1f out* **5/1**3

**11** 5 **Exact Science (IRE)** 2-9-5 0 MartinHarley 9 4+
(David Brown) *s.i.s: rn green and outpcd thrght: t.o over 1f out* **40/1**

00 **12** 2 3/4 **Colours Of Victory**11 6146 2-9-5 0 (b1) JamieSpencer 12
(Kevin Ryan) *chsd ldr tl 3f out: sn btn: bhd and eased over 1f out: t.o* **66/1**

0 **13** 8 **Delysdream**14 6039 2-9-5 0 RichardKingscote 2
(Christine Dunnett) *in tch in midfield: steadily lost pl fr 1/2-way: t.o over 1f out* **200/1**

1m 24.71s (-1.89) **Going Correction** -0.30s/f (Firm) 13 Ran SP% **115.3**
Speed ratings (Par 95): **98,97,91,90,83 82,81,79,76,70 64,61,52**
CSF £3.68 TOTE £2.40: £1.10, £1.10, £5.50; EX 4.50 Trifecta £32.50.
**Owner** Ballymore Sterling Syndicate **Bred** Kildaragh Stud **Trained** Newmarket, Suffolk

**FOCUS**
The opener was a fairly good juvenile maiden in which they went an even gallop across the track on ground officially described as good, good to firm in places.

## 6463 DANNY WRIGHT MEMORIAL FILLIES' H'CAP (FOR THE CHALLENGE TROPHY) 6f 3y
2:50 (2:51) (Class 5) (0-75,75) 3-Y-O+ £3,234 (£962; £481; £240) Stalls Centre

Form RPR

1143 **1** **Refuse Colette (IRE)**24 5726 5-9-6 74 PaoloSirigu 4 86
(Mick Quinn) *chsd ldrs: rdn over 2f out: led over 1f out: forged ahd u.p ins fnl f: styd on wl* **3/1**2

1515 **2** 2 3/4 **Fever Few**23 5776 5-9-4 75 AshleyMorgan(3) 3 81
(Chris Wall) *awkward as stalls opened: stdd s and hld up in tch in midfield: effrt to chse ldrs 2f out: rdn to chal ent fnl f: no ex and btn fnl 100yds: wknd towards fin* **9/4**1

6006 **3** 3/4 **Welsh Sunrise**24 5726 4-9-0 68 1 AndreaAtzeni 5 70+
(Stuart Williams) *hld up in tch in midfield: rdn 2f out: outpcd and looked wl hld 1f out: rallied and styd on u.p fnl 100yds: no threat to wnr* **10/1**

6240 **4** 3/4 **Ray Of Joy**20 5861 8-8-13 67 (v) FrederikTylicki 2 67+
(J R Jenkins) *stdd and dropped in bhd after s: rdn 1/2-way: outpcd u.p over 1f out: rallied and kpt on ins fnl f: no threat to wnr* **9/1**

3416 **5** hd **Joyous**44 4981 4-8-13 67 TomQueally 7 66
(Dean Ivory) *chsd ldr tl 2f out: 4th and outpcd over 1f out: swtchd lft and plugged on ins fnl f* **13/2**3

4536 **6** nk **Honeymoon Express (IRE)**50 4765 4-9-0 73 (p) ShelleyBirkett(5) 6 71
(Julia Feilden) *led: rdn and hrd pressed 2f out: hdd over 1f out: no ex: wknd ins fnl f* **7/1**

056 **7** 4 1/2 **Shushu Sugartown (IRE)**35 5314 3-8-10 66 1 SilvestreDeSousa 8 51
(Ian Williams) *in tch in last pair: rdn over 3f out: wknd over 1f out* **8/1**

1m 12.0s (-2.40) **Going Correction** -0.30s/f (Firm)
**WFA** 3 from 4yo+ 2lb 7 Ran SP% **111.8**
Speed ratings (Par 100): **104,100,99,98,98 97,91**
CSF £9.70 CT £55.35 TOTE £3.30: £2.20, £1.80; EX 10.70 Trifecta £94.30.
**Owner** YNWA Partnership **Bred** Patrick O'Reilly **Trained** Newmarket, Suffolk

**FOCUS**
A fair fillies' sprint handicap in which they went a contested gallop.

## 6464 EBF AT THE RACES JOHN MUSKER FILLIES' STKS (FOR THE JOHN MUSKER TROPHY) (LISTED RACE) 1m 2f 21y
3:25 (3:27) (Class 1) 3-Y-O+
£22,488 (£8,560; £4,284; £2,136; £1,072; £540) Stalls Low

Form RPR

13 **1** **Hadaatha (IRE)**124 2299 3-8-10 93 PaulHanagan 1 104+
(Roger Varian) *hld up in last trio: swtchd rt and hdwy 2f out: rdn to chse ldr over 1f out: led fnl 100yds: r.o wl: rdn out* **10/3**2

53U- **2** 3/4 **Albasharah (USA)**418 4732 5-9-2 108 FrederikTylicki 5 102
(Saeed bin Suroor) *chsd ldr: rdn over 2f out: sltly outpcd and shuffled bk 2f out: rallied u.p 1f out: styd on wl fnl 100yds: wnt 2nd last strides* **6/1**3

1024 **3** hd **Wall Of Sound**54 4634 4-9-2 96 RichardKingscote 6 101
(Tom Dascombe) *led: rdn ent fnl 2f: kpt on wl tl hdd and no ex fnl 100yds: lost 2nd last strides* **16/1**

2110 **4** 2 1/2 **Kleo (GR)**35 5312 3-8-10 90 ShaneKelly 9 96
(Luca Cumani) *chsd ldrs: rdn and effrt over 2f out: unable qck over 1f out: outpcd ins fnl f* **14/1**

3311 **5** 1 1/2 **Pleasant Valley (IRE)**32 5420 3-8-10 87 AndreaAtzeni 2 94
(Luca Cumani) *hld up in tch in midfield: effrt on inner 2f out: n.m.r over 1f out: no imp 1f out: kpt on* **7/1**

-000 **6** 3/4 **Agent Allison**49 4782 4-9-2 95 SilvestreDeSousa 13 92
(Peter Chapple-Hyam) *stdd and dropped in bhd after s: hld up in tch: swtchd rt and effrt 2f out: hdwy u.p over 1f out: styd on: nvr trbld ldrs* **50/1**

0420 **7** hd **Gifted Girl (IRE)**25 5687 5-9-2 102 (t) TomQueally 8 92
(Paul Cole) *hld up in tch in last trio: rdn and effrt 2f out: no real imp and kpt on same pce fr over 1f out* **11/1**

6511 **8** hd **Perfect Light (IRE)**24 5713 3-8-10 86 JamieSpencer 11 91
(William Haggas) *chsd ldr: rdn over 2f out: struggling to qckn whn short of room over 1f out: wknd 1f out* **18/1**

0122 **9** 3 1/2 **Raskova (USA)**54 4634 4-9-2 95 TedDurcan 10 85
(William Jarvis) *hld up in tch in midfield: rdn and effrt ent fnl 2f: no hdwy: wknd 1f out* **14/1**

-113 **10** 1 1/2 **Water Hole (IRE)**18 5927 3-8-10 103 WilliamBuick 3 82
(John Gosden) *chsd ldrs: rdn 3f out: styd pressing ldr tl struggling to qckn whn short of room and jostled over 1f out: sn wknd* **3/1**1

2454 **11** 1 1/2 **Veiled Intrigue**35 5312 3-8-10 98 FergusSweeney 4 79
(Henry Candy) *in tch in midfield: rdn 4f out: lost pl and bhd 2f out: n.d after* **20/1**

2m 7.48s (-3.02) **Going Correction** -0.125s/f (Firm)
**WFA** 3 from 4yo+ 6lb 11 Ran SP% **114.4**
Speed ratings: **107,106,106,104,103 102,102,102,99,98 96**
CSF £23.04 TOTE £4.30: £2.10, £1.80, £5.00; EX 24.90 Trifecta £294.00.
**Owner** Hamdan Al Maktoum **Bred** Shadwell Estate Company Limited **Trained** Newmarket, Suffolk

**FOCUS**
A good-quality Listed fillies' contest in which they went an even gallop.

## 6465 PARKLANDS LEISURE OF NORFOLK H'CAP (FOR THE GOLDEN JUBILEE TROPHY) 1m 2f 21y
4:00 (4:01) (Class 3) (0-90,85) 3-Y-O- £7,561 (£2,263; £1,131; £566; £282) Stalls Low

Form RPR

1223 **1** **Qanan**30 5487 5-9-9 **84** TedDurcan 1 95
(Chris Wall) *chsd ldrs: drvn to chse ldr and swtchd rt over 1f out: styd on wl u.p to ld last stride* **9/2**3

30 **2** shd **Nullarbor Sky (IRE)**25 5673 4-9-7 **82** (p) FrederikTylicki 4 92
(Lucy Wadham) *led: rdn 2f out: stl 2 l clr and drvn 1f out: kpt on wl but worn down and hdd last stride* **7/1**

0426 **3** 3 1/4 **Endless Credit (IRE)**29 5528 4-9-5 **80** AndreaAtzeni 6 84
(Luca Cumani) *hld up in tch in last trio: rdn and effrt over 2f out: no ex 1f out: plugged on to go 3rd fnl 75yds* **3/1**1

3300 **4** 1 3/4 **Bureau (IRE)**11 6127 3-9-4 **85** SilvestreDeSousa 5 85
(Mark Johnston) *chsd ldr: rdn over 2f out: drvn and dropped to 3rd over 1f out: wknd ins fnl f: lost 3rd fnl 75yds* **10/1**

5 **5** 5 **L'Orfeo**37 5251 4-9-10 **85** 1 KierenFallon 2 76
(Saeed bin Suroor) *in tch in midfield: effrt u.p over 2f out: 5th and btn 1f out: wknd ins fnl f* **14/1**

0022 **6** hd **Blighty (IRE)**24 5730 4-9-4 **79** MartinHarley 3 69
(Lady Cecil) *t.k.h: hld up in tch in last trio: rdn and effrt 2f out: no ex and btn jst over 1f out: wknd ins fnl f* **10/3**2

6530 **7** *22* **Automated**[12] 6098 3-8-13 85..................................(p) LouisSteward(5) 8 34
(Clive Brittain) *in tch in midfield: rdn 3f out: sn hung rt and btn: t.o and eased ins fnl f* **6/1**
6316 **8** *47* **Silver Alliance**[24] 5730 6-8-10 76..............................(p) ShelleyBirkett(5) 7
(Julia Feilden) *stdd s: hld up in rr: rdn over 3f out: sn lost tch: t.o over 1f out* **25/1**
2m 7.56s (-2.94) **Going Correction** -0.125s/f (Firm)
**WFA** 3 from 4yo+ 6lb **8** Ran SP% **112.6**
Speed ratings (Par 107): **106,105,103,101,97 97,80,42**
CSF £34.57 CT £107.36 TOTE £4.90: £2.10, £1.70, £1.90; EX 37.30 Trifecta £115.30.
**Owner** Alan & Jill Smith **Bred** Genesis Green Stud Ltd **Trained** Newmarket, Suffolk
**FOCUS**
A decent handicap in which they went a sensible gallop.

## 6466 SEA-DEER H'CAP 1m 3y
**4:30** (4:30) (Class 4) (0-85,85) 3-Y-0+ **£5,175** (£1,540; £769; £384) **Stalls** Centre

Form RPR
5205 **1** **Lockhart (IRE)**[12] 6111 3-9-0 79..........................(b1) SilvestreDeSousa 1 90
(Mark Johnston) *mde all: rdn ent fnl 2f: fnd ex and clr over 1f out: edgd rt u.p and pressed again ins fnl f: styd on and holding runner-up fnl 100yds* **12/1**
-312 **2** *1* **Certificate**[25] 5686 3-9-6 85........................................ AndreaAtzeni 6 94
(Roger Varian) *chsd wnr: rdn 2f out: no imp over 1f out: rallied u.p and pressing wnr ins fnl f: no ex and hld fnl 75yds* **2/1**[1]
0302 **3** *2* **Pleasure Bent**[24] 5727 4-9-5 80........................................ ShaneKelly 8 84
(Luca Cumani) *in tch in last trio: rdn over 2f out: hdwy u.p over 1f out: chsd ldng pair ins fnl f: kpt on but nvr enough pce to chal* **9/2**[2]
6406 **4** *1/2* **Subtle Knife**[11] 6129 5-8-13 74........................................ WilliamCarson 9 77
(Giles Bravery) *hld up in tch in rr: rdn 3f out: hdwy u.p jst over 1f out: styd on to go 4th ins fnl f: nvr trbld ldrs* **10/1**
12-2 **5** *2* **Never To Be (USA)**[195] 854 3-9-5 84..........................(t) WilliamBuick 4 82
(John Gosden) *t.k.h: chsd ldrs: rdn and unable qck ent fnl 2f: wknd u.p 1f out* **5/1**[3]
4155 **6** *hd* **Tommy's Secret**[14] 6035 4-8-9 75........................................ CamHardie(5) 2 73
(Jane Chapple-Hyam) *chsd ldrs: rdn and effrt ent fnl f: no ex and btn 1f out: wknd ins fnl f* **20/1**
2300 **7** *1 3/4* **Set The Trend**[13] 6057 8-9-3 78........................................ MartinHarley 5 72
(David Dennis) *travelled wl: trckd ldrs: rdn over 2f out: fnd nil and sn struggling: wknd over 1f out* **20/1**
6141 **8** *1 3/4* **Desert Ranger (IRE)**[24] 5727 3-8-13 78........................................ KierenFallon 7 68
(James Tate) *stdd s: t.k.h: hld up in tch in rr: shkn up over 2f out: rdn and no hdwy 2f out: sn wknd* **6/1**
2005 **9** *7* **Afkar (IRE)**[24] 5727 6-8-5 71 oh6........................................ LouisSteward(5) 3 45
(Clive Brittain) *chsd ldrs: lost pl u.p over 2f out: bhd overt 1f out* **40/1**
1m 37.17s (-3.43) **Going Correction** -0.30s/f (Firm)
**WFA** 3 from 4yo+ 4lb **9** Ran SP% **111.2**
Speed ratings (Par 105): **105,104,102,101,99 99,97,95,88**
CSF £34.20 CT £124.40 TOTE £14.20: £3.50, £1.10, £1.90; EX 44.90 Trifecta £181.60.
**Owner** Sheikh Hamdan bin Mohammed Al Maktoum **Bred** Old Carhue Stud **Trained** Middleham Moor, N Yorks
**FOCUS**
A fairly good handicap in which the winner recorded the best comparative time on the card so far.

## 6467 STANLEY THREADWELL MEMORIAL H'CAP 5f 43y
**5:00** (5:00) (Class 2) (0-100,97) 3-Y-**£12,602** (£3,772; £1,886; £944; £470) **Stalls** Centre

Form RPR
0103 **1** **Speed Hawk (USA)**[11] 6159 3-9-6 97........................................ AndreaAtzeni 10 105+
(Robert Cowell) *hld up in tch: rdn and hdwy to chse ldr jst over 1f out: hanging lft but r.o wl to ld fnl 50yds: gng away at fin* **3/1**[1]
3033 **2** *1/2* **Normal Equilibrium**[11] 6131 4-8-9 90..........................(p) LouisSteward(5) 5 96
(Robert Cowell) *chsd ldr tl led wl over 1f out: sn rdn: kpt on tl hdd and no ex fnl 50yds* **11/2**[3]
0000 **3** *1 1/4* **Barracuda Boy (IRE)**[11] 6159 4-8-13 89.................. RichardKingscote 9 91
(Tom Dascombe) *in tch in midfield: rdn 2f out: keeping on same pce whn sltly hmpd 1f out: rallied: edgd lft and styd on fnl 100yds: wnt 3rd towards fin* **20/1**
-061 **4** *1/2* **Red Aggressor (IRE)**[24] 5726 5-8-2 83 oh5................(b) CamHardie(5) 6 83
(Clive Brittain) *hld up in tch in rr: hdwy 1/2-way: chsd ldrs and rdn over 1f out: styd on same pce fnl f: lost 3rd fnl 50yds* **18/1**
0504 **5** *nk* **Borderlescott**[11] 6131 12-9-1 91........................................ FrederikTylicki 1 90
(Robin Bastiman) *chsd ldrs: rdn 1/2-way: no ex u.p over 1f out: kpt on same pce after* **12/1**
0003 **6** *2* **Hopes N Dreams (IRE)**[22] 5784 6-8-11 87.................. JamieSpencer 8 78
(Kevin Ryan) *taken down early: hld up in tch in rr: rdn 2f out: kpt on but nvr a threat to ldrs* **11/1**
1106 **7** *3/4* **Sandfrankskipsgo**[50] 4762 5-8-13 89........................................ ShaneKelly 7 78
(Peter Crate) *broke fast: sn stdd and t.k.h in midfield: rdn 2f out: no imp over 1f out: wknd ins fnl f* **16/1**
252 **8** *4 1/2* **Long Awaited (IRE)**[11] 6131 6-9-0 90........................................ PaulHanagan 3 63
(David Barron) *in tch in midfield: lost pl and struggling u.p 2f out: wknd over 1f out* **7/2**[2]
-044 **9** *nk* **Invincible Strike (IRE)**[11] 6159 3-8-13 90..........................(b) KierenFallon 2 61
(James Tate) *chsd ldrs: lost pl and rdn 1/2-way: wknd over 1f out* **10/1**
234 **10** *3/4* **Peace Seeker**[26] 5623 6-9-0 90..........................(t) WilliamCarson 4 59
(Anthony Carson) *led tl wl over 1f out: sn rdn and btn: bhd fnl f* **7/1**
1m 0.87s (-1.83) **Going Correction** -0.30s/f (Firm)
**WFA** 3 from 4yo+ 1lb **10** Ran SP% **116.1**
Speed ratings (Par 109): **102,101,99,98,97 94,93,86,85,84**
CSF £19.55 CT £285.26 TOTE £3.80: £1.10, £2.00, £4.90; EX 20.20 Trifecta £538.40.
**Owner** Khalifa Dasmal **Bred** Santa Rosa Partners **Trained** Six Mile Bottom, Cambs
**FOCUS**
A particularly good sprint handicap won in 2012 by subsequent Listed winner My Propeller, and they went a solid gallop right across the track.

## 6468 LA CONTINENTAL CAFE IN GREAT YARMOUTH H'CAP (BOBIS RACE) 6f 3y
**5:30** (5:30) (Class 4) (0-85,85) 3-Y-0 **£5,175** (£1,540; £769; £384) **Stalls** Centre

Form RPR
1422 **1** **Cordial**[11] 6153 3-8-13 77........................................ AndreaAtzeni 6 88
(Stuart Williams) *chsd ldr: gng best 2f out: rdn to chal over 1f out: led ins fnl f: sn in command: comf* **7/2**[2]
2136 **2** *1 1/2* **Dont Have It Then**[25] 5675 3-8-10 74........................................ StevieDonohoe 4 80
(Willie Musson) *hld up in tch in last pair: swtchd rt and effrt 1f out: styd on wl to go 2nd wl ins fnl f: no threat to wnr* **9/1**
2112 **3** *1* **Mia San Triple**[38] 5211 3-9-7 85........................................ WilliamBuick 8 88
(Jeremy Noseda) *taken down early: nt best away: t.k.h and sn rcvrd to ld: rdn 2f out: hdd ins fnl f: one pce after: lost 2nd wl ins fnl f* **5/2**[1]
321 **4** *1 1/2* **Eleusis**[29] 5531 3-9-2 80........................................ TedDurcan 5 78
(Chris Wall) *fly-jmpd as stalls opened: sn rcvrd and in tch in midfield: chsd ldrs and c towards stands' side 4f out: rdn 2f out: 3rd and btn 1f out: plugged on* **9/2**[3]
1232 **5** *nk* **Poetic Choice**[9] 6189 3-8-6 75........................................ CamHardie(5) 1 72
(Nick Littmoden) *in rr: rdn 2f out: sme hdwy u.p over 1f out: no imp fnl f* **9/2**[3]
1120 **6** *nk* **Syrian Pearl**[32] 5437 3-8-13 80........................................ AshleyMorgan(3) 2 76
(Chris Wall) *in tch in midfield: effrt wl over 1f out: no ex 1f out: plugged on same pce fnl f* **10/1**
0426 **7** *8* **Langavat (IRE)**[11] 6149 3-9-5 83..........................(v1) SilvestreDeSousa 3 59
(Nigel Tinkler) *chsd ldrs: rdn and lost pl 1/2-way: wknd over 1f out* **20/1**
1m 11.8s (-2.60) **Going Correction** -0.30s/f (Firm) **7** Ran SP% **111.0**
Speed ratings (Par 103): **105,103,101,99,99 98,88**
CSF £31.85 CT £87.04 TOTE £4.00: £3.20, £4.40; EX 25.40 Trifecta £160.90.
**Owner** D A Shekells **Bred** Juddmonte Farms Ltd **Trained** Newmarket, Suffolk
**FOCUS**
The concluding race was a fairly decent 3yo sprint handicap in which the comparative winning time was notably competitive with the previous contest.
T/Plt: £22.60 to a £1 stake. Pool of £88135.89 - 2842.91 winning tickets. T/Qpdt: £11.30 to a £1 stake. Pool of £6380.0 - 417.30 winning tickets. SP

6469 - 6472a (Foreign Racing) - See Raceform Interactive

# 5232 AYR (L-H)
### Thursday, September 18
**OFFICIAL GOING: Good (good to firm in places; 8.9; sprint course: stands' side 8.5, centre 8.7, far side 8.6)**
Wind: Light, half behind Weather: Overcast

## 6473 BRITISH STALLION STUDS EBF NOVICE STKS (BOBIS RACE) 1m
**1:40** (1:40) (Class 4) 2-Y-0 **£6,469** (£1,925; £962; £481) **Stalls** Low

Form RPR
5125 **1** **Moonlightnavigator (USA)**[11] 6165 2-9-7 83.................. PhillipMakin 1 88
(John Quinn) *trckd ldrs: effrt over 2f out: led ins fnl f: edgd rt: kpt on strly* **13/8**[1]
461 **2** *1 1/2* **Swift Approval (IRE)**[13] 6108 2-9-4 79........................................ GrahamLee 2 81
(Kevin Ryan) *led at modest gallop: rdn over 2f out: hdd ins fnl f: kpt on same pce* **2/1**[3]
2 **3** *1 1/2* **Farham (USA)**[57] 4550 2-9-0 0........................................ TonyHamilton 3 74
(Richard Fahey) *t.k.h early: trckd ldr: rdn over 2f out: one pce fr over 1f out* **15/8**[2]
0300 **4** *1* **Auld Fyffee (IRE)**[7] 6250 2-8-6 62........................................ RyanPowell(3) 4 66
(John Ryan) *s.i.s: in tch: effrt and rdn over 2f out: no imp fr over 1f out* **66/1**
1m 39.18s (-4.62) **Going Correction** -0.475s/f (Firm) 2y crse rec **4** Ran SP% **107.7**
Speed ratings (Par 97): **104,102,101,100**
CSF £5.16 TOTE £2.40; EX 4.60 Trifecta £5.90.
**Owner** Malcolm Walker **Bred** Highfield Farm **Trained** Settrington, N Yorks
**FOCUS**
Track at full width and distances as advertised. An interesting novice event to start, but despite a modest pace and these only being 2yos, the winning time was relatively fast, suggesting the ground was on the quick side. The winning rider said "It's lovely ground, good with no jar in it".

## 6474 SM SIGNS MAIDEN AUCTION STKS 6f
**2:10** (2:12) (Class 5) 2-Y-0 **£3,881** (£1,155; £577; £288) **Stalls** Centre

Form RPR
U2 **1** **Get Knotted (IRE)**[26] 5679 2-8-11 0........................................ PhillipMakin 4 78
(Michael Dods) *prom: smooth hdwy and ev ch over 1f out: sn rdn: led ins fnl f: kpt on wl* **2/1**[2]
24 **2** *nk* **Fullon Clarets**[44] 5013 2-8-13 0........................................ TonyHamilton 8 79
(Richard Fahey) *trckd ldrs: led and rdn over 1f out: edgd lft: hdd ins fnl f: kpt on: hld nr fin* **5/1**[3]
620 **3** *2 1/4* **Spirit Of Zeb (IRE)**[61] 4439 2-8-8 79........................................ JackGarritty(5) 3 72
(Richard Fahey) *t.k.h: cl up: effrt and ev ch over 1f out: one pce ins fnl f* **15/8**[1]
04 **4** *6* **Sir Lancelott**[8] 6225 2-8-11 0........................................ TomEaves 1 52
(Keith Dalgleish) *led: rdn and hdd over 1f out: edgd rt and sn wknd* **14/1**
**5** *8* **Regal Ways (IRE)** 2-8-8 0........................................ JoeFanning 5 25+
(Mark Johnston) *dwlt and wnt rt s: sn pushed along bhd ldng gp: rdn and outpcd over 2f out: n.d after* **8/1**
**6** *5* **It's Time For Bed** 2-8-3 0........................................ ConnorBeasley(3) 2 8
(Linda Perratt) *green in preliminaries: missed break and green in rr: hdwy 1/2-way: rdn and wknd over 1f out* **66/1**
0 **7** *13* **Out Of Aces**[23] 5799 2-8-11 0........................................ FergalLynch 6
(Kevin Ryan) *dwlt and blkd s: bhd: drvn along 1/2-way: edgd rt and sn wknd* **20/1**
1m 10.94s (-1.46) **Going Correction** -0.275s/f (Firm) **7** Ran SP% **108.8**
Speed ratings (Par 95): **98,97,94,86,75 69,51**
CSF £11.15 TOTE £2.70: £1.80, £2.60; EX 10.20 Trifecta £16.50.
**Owner** D Neale **Bred** Rossenarra Bloodstock Limited **Trained** Denton, Co Durham
**FOCUS**
The stalls were placed in the centre on the straight track and the jockeys in this contest decided to stay there throughout. This looked an ordinary and uncompetitive maiden, but it produced a stirring finish.

## 6475 WALLACE MCDOWALL H'CAP 5f
**2:40** (2:44) (Class 5) (0-70,70) 3-Y-0+ **£3,881** (£1,155; £577; £288) **Stalls** Centre

Form RPR
63 **1** **Orient Class**[60] 4469 3-9-4 68..........................(v) GrahamLee 18 79
(Paul Midgley) *racd alone stands' rail: cl up: overall ldr over 2f out: kpt on strly fnl f* **8/1**
5300 **2** *2 1/4* **Sewn Up**[3] 6405 4-8-4 56 oh6..........................(p) JoeyHaynes(3) 7 59
(Keith Dalgleish) *towards rr: rdn and hdwy over 1f out: kpt on to ld centre gp towards fin: nt rch stands' side wnr* **18/1**
1065 **3** *nk* **Autumn Tide (IRE)**[11] 6172 3-8-1 56 oh1..........................(tp) JackGarritty(5) 6 58
(Adrian Paul Keatley, Ire) *cl up: led centre gp over 1f out: kpt on fnl f: lost 2nd that gp towards fin* **14/1**
1113 **4** *nk* **Rise To Glory (IRE)**[7] 6272 6-9-5 68..........................(tp) DuranFentiman 3 69
(Shaun Harris) *in tch: rdn over 2f out: kpt on ins fnl f: nrst fin* **10/1**
2363 **5** *1* **Kirtling Belle**[22] 5808 3-9-3 67........................................ DeclanMcDonogh 2 64
(Keith Dalgleish) *s.i.s: bhd tl rdn and hdwy over 1f out: kpt on ins fnl f: nrst fin* **16/1**

4366 **6** *nse* **Jinky**[16] 6013 6-9-6 69 JoeFanning 10 66
(Linda Perratt) *bhd: pushed along over 2f out: gd hdwy fnl f: fin strly* **6/1**[1]
6510 **7** *shd* **Majestic Manannan (IRE)**[19] 5913 5-9-5 68 AdrianNicholls 4 65
(David Nicholls) *t.k.h: led centre and overall ldr to over 2f out: hdd and no ex centre gp over 1f out* **20/1**
2006 **8** *1 1/2* **Be Lucky**[84] 3612 4-9-7 70 GrahamGibbons 16 61
(Michael Easterby) *prom: rdn over 2f out: edgd lft over 1f out* **14/1**
0400 **9** *1/2* **Hazelrigg (IRE)**[8] 6235 9-9-7 70 (e) DavidAllan 9 60
(Tim Easterby) *in tch: rdn over 2f out: no imp over 1f out* **13/2**[2]
5315 **9** *dht* **New Lease Of Life**[13] 6114 5-8-7 59 (p) GaryBartley(3) 13 49
(Jim Goldie) *midfield: drvn over 2f out: no imp fr over 1f out* **14/1**
1220 **11** *1* **Live Dangerously**[3] 6406 4-9-2 65 PhillipMakin 11 51
(Keith Dalgleish) *midfield: rdn along over 2f out: nvr able to chal* **6/1**[1]
2366 **12** *1* **Tadalavil**[3] 6406 9-8-2 56 oh3 SammyJoBell(5) 14 38
(Linda Perratt) *towards rr: pushed along over 2f out: nt pce to chal* **28/1**
2523 **13** *1/2* **Diamond Blue**[27] 5641 6-9-3 66 (p) TonyHamilton 12 47
(Richard Fahey) *rrd s: bhd and sn pushed along: nvr able to chal* **15/2**[3]
3510 **14** *1/2* **Saxonette**[13] 6114 6-8-7 56 oh2 IanBrennan 17 35
(Linda Perratt) *in tch: rdn over 2f out: wknd over 1f out* **33/1**
0600 **15** *4 1/2* **Royal Bajan (USA)**[49] 4833 6-9-1 67 (v) ConnorBeasley(3) 8 30
(James Given) *dwlt: bhd and outpcd: nvr on terms* **20/1**
4-0 **16** *8* **Pitt Rivers**[13] 6114 5-8-7 56 oh4 BarryMcHugh 5
(Linda Perratt) *dwlt: bhd and sn struggling: drifted rt fr 1/2-way: nvr on terms* **66/1**

57.54s (-1.86) **Going Correction** -0.275s/f (Firm)
**WFA** 3 from 4yo+ 1lb **16** Ran SP% **122.4**
Speed ratings (Par 103): **103,99,98,98,96 96,96,94,93,93 91,90,89,88,81 68**
CSF £135.29 CT £2086.10 TOTE £9.10: £2.00, £5.40, £3.10, £2.70; EX 180.60 Trifecta £2388.80.
**Owner** Frank & Annette Brady **Bred** Frank Brady **Trained** Westow, N Yorks

**FOCUS**
A big field for this ordinary sprint handicap and competitive on paper. The bulk of the field, led by the trailblazing Majestic Manannan, raced up the centre, but the winner raced alone stands' side. It's hard to know how much of an advantage that was.

## 6476 HILLHOUSE QUARRY SUPPORTING THE AYRSHIRE HOSPICE H'CAP 1m

**3:10** (3:12) (Class 4) (0-85,85) 3-Y-O+ **£6,469** (£1,925; £962; £481) **Stalls** Low

Form RPR
1033 **1** **Anderiego (IRE)**[9] 6214 6-9-10 85 (v) DanielTudhope 4 96
(David O'Meara) *hld up and bhd: gd hdwy on outside over 1f out: led ins fnl f: kpt on wl* **11/2**[2]
2215 **2** *1 1/4* **Coincidently**[21] 5855 4-9-5 80 JoeFanning 7 88
(Alan Bailey) *trckd ldrs: rdn to ld over 1f out: hdd ins fnl f: nt pce of wnr* **14/1**
6332 **3** *1 1/2* **Almuheet**[9] 6214 3-9-1 85 MeganCarberry(5) 11 90
(Brian Ellison) *hld up: rdn and hdwy on outside over 2f out: kpt on ins fnl f: nrst fin* **4/1**[1]
4005 **4** *hd* **Norse Blues**[5] 6320 6-9-9 84 GrahamGibbons 5 88
(David Barron) *led: rdn over 2f out: hdd over 1f out: kpt on same pce ins fnl f* **15/2**[3]
1306 **5** *nk* **Escape To Glory (USA)**[13] 6097 6-9-5 83 ConnorBeasley(3) 8 87
(Michael Dods) *hld up in midfield: lost pl over 2f out: rallied over 1f out: r.o ins fnl f* **22/1**
0000 **6** *hd* **Trail Blaze (IRE)**[13] 6097 5-9-9 84 (p) AmyRyan 13 87
(Kevin Ryan) *cl up: rdn over 2f out: ev ch over 1f out: one pce fnl f* **12/1**
0460 **7** *1* **Shot In The Sun (IRE)**[49] 4826 3-8-13 83 JackGarritty(5) 2 84
(Richard Fahey) *midfield: pushed along over 2f out: kpt on ins fnl f: no imp* **8/1**
2140 **8** *hd* **Extraterrestrial**[40] 5178 10-9-3 78 TomEaves 12 78+
(Richard Fahey) *dwlt: hld up: hdwy over 1f out: no room and swtchd rt ins fnl f: kpt on: nvr able to chal* **40/1**
5046 **9** *shd* **Barren Brook**[40] 5196 7-9-3 78 BarryMcHugh 3 78
(Michael Easterby) *dwlt: hld up on ins: hdwy 2f out: no room ins fnl f: no imp* **16/1**
3161 **10** *nse* **Hanalei Bay (IRE)**[16] 6009 4-9-4 79 PhillipMakin 14 79
(Keith Dalgleish) *t.k.h: in tch: rdn over 2f out: no ex ins fnl f* **14/1**
1110 **11** *1 3/4* **Imshivalla (IRE)**[20] 5882 3-9-2 81 TonyHamilton 6 77
(Richard Fahey) *chsd ldrs: drvn over 3f out: rallied: wknd ins fnl f* **14/1**
043P **12** *3 1/2* **Mujazif (IRE)**[24] 5771 4-9-10 85 (t) AdrianNicholls 9 73
(David Nicholls) *midfield on outside: rdn and edgd lft over 2f out: wknd over 1f out* **11/1**
002 **13** *2 1/4* **Argaki (IRE)**[22] 5810 4-9-2 77 DeclanMcDonogh 1 60
(Keith Dalgleish) *midfield on ins: outpcd over 2f out: n.d after* **20/1**
1506 **14** *nse* **Another For Joe**[45] 4963 6-9-3 78 GrahamLee 10 61
(Jim Goldie) *chsd ldrs tl rdn and wknd fr 2f out* **25/1**

1m 38.26s (-5.54) **Going Correction** -0.475s/f (Firm)
**WFA** 3 from 4yo+ 4lb **14** Ran SP% **115.6**
Speed ratings (Par 105): **108,106,105,105,104 104,103,103,103,103 101,97,95,95**
CSF £72.66 CT £349.93 TOTE £5.20: £1.90, £5.80, £1.80; EX 97.60 Trifecta £500.00.
**Owner** Ebor Racing Club **Bred** Gerrardstown House Stud **Trained** Nawton, N Yorks

**FOCUS**
A competitive handicap in which several held a chance. The form looks pretty straightforward.

## 6477 QUALITY AND VALUE AT THE IRISH YEARLING SALES H'CAP (DIV I) 7f 50y

**3:40** (3:41) (Class 5) (0-75,75) 3-Y-O+ **£3,881** (£1,155; £577; £288) **Stalls** High

Form RPR
0050 **1** **Bachotheque (IRE)**[13] 6094 4-9-2 70 DavidAllan 4 81
(Tim Easterby) *hld up in midfield: hdwy over 2f out: led ins fnl f: keeping on wl whn edgd rt nr fin* **11/1**
0641 **2** *1 1/4* **Old Man Clegg**[13] 6121 4-8-8 62 (t) BarryMcHugh 5 70
(Michael Easterby) *t.k.h: sn cl up: led over 2f out: rdn over 1f out: hdd ins fnl f: kpt on same pce* **4/1**[1]
2456 **3** *3/4* **Beautiful Stranger (IRE)**[20] 5891 3-8-10 67 (p) JoeFanning 11 72
(Keith Dalgleish) *hld up: rdn over 2f out: gd hdwy on outside over 1f out: kpt on ins fnl f* **8/1**
2604 **4** *1 1/2* **Cara's Request (AUS)**[20] 5887 9-9-2 73 ConnorBeasley(3) 12 75
(Michael Dods) *led: hdd over 2f out: rallied: kpt on same pce fnl f* **8/1**
0-22 **5** *1 1/4* **Brooke's Bounty**[36] 5295 4-9-0 68 TonyHamilton 10 67
(Richard Fahey) *midfield: drvn and outpcd over 2f out: kpt on fnl f: nt pce to chal* **6/1**[2]
041- **6** *nk* **Haymarket**[359] 6722 5-9-0 68 DanielTudhope 2 66
(R Mike Smith) *hld up on ins: rdn and outpcd over 2f out: kpt on fnl f: no imp* **16/1**

4540 **7** *nse* **Injaz**[31] 5492 3-8-4 61 (v[1]) IanBrennan 13 58
(Kevin Ryan) *s.s: bhd tl hdwy on ins over 1f out: kpt on fnl f: nrst fin* **18/1**
0004 **8** *1* **Another Try (IRE)**[21] 5861 9-9-2 70 BenCurtis 3 65
(Timothy Jarvis) *in tch: drvn over 2f out: wknd appr fnl f* **25/1**
6565 **9** *nk* **Kung Hei Fat Choy (USA)**[12] 6144 5-8-10 69 (b) MeganCarberry(5) 8 63
(James Given) *hld up: rdn along over 2f out: nvr able to chal* **7/1**[3]
1450 **10** *1 1/4* **Mowhoob**[41] 5143 4-9-3 71 FergalLynch 6 62
(Jim Goldie) *bhd and sn outpcd: nvr on terms* **25/1**
6155 **11** *hd* **Goninodaethat**[38] 5236 6-8-12 66 GrahamLee 14 57
(Jim Goldie) *chsd ldrs tl rdn: edgd lft and wknd over 1f out* **10/1**
5000 **12** *11* **Circuitous**[9] 6217 6-9-6 74 (v) TomEaves 9 36
(Keith Dalgleish) *chsd ldrs tl rdn and wknd 2f out* **10/1**

1m 29.27s (-4.13) **Going Correction** -0.475s/f (Firm)
**WFA** 3 from 4yo+ 3lb **12** Ran SP% **114.4**
Speed ratings (Par 103): **104,102,101,100,98 98,98,97,96,95 95,82**
CSF £52.61 CT £378.22 TOTE £10.00: £3.10, £2.00, £3.10; EX 76.60 Trifecta £1144.00.
**Owner** Richard Taylor & Philip Hebdon **Bred** Tally-Ho Stud **Trained** Great Habton, N Yorks

**FOCUS**
A modest handicap and not that many got into it. The winner's best form since his 3yo reappearance.

## 6478 QUALITY AND VALUE AT THE IRISH YEARLING SALES H'CAP (DIV II) 7f 50y

**4:10** (4:11) (Class 5) (0-75,75) 3-Y-O+ **£3,881** (£1,155; £577; £288) **Stalls** High

Form RPR
0600 **1** **Evanescent (IRE)**[40] 5196 5-9-2 70 IanBrennan 5 86+
(John Quinn) *prom: smooth hdwy to ld over 1f out: shkn up and qcknd clr fnl f: readily* **5/1**[2]
0124 **2** *3* **We'll Deal Again**[12] 6150 7-9-7 75 BarryMcHugh 4 81
(Michael Easterby) *t.k.h in midfield: effrt over 2f out: hdwy to chse (clr) wnr wl ins fnl f: kpt on* **12/1**
4226 **3** *nk* **Almanack**[5] 6334 4-8-11 65 GrahamLee 10 70
(Ian Williams) *hld up: rdn over 2f out: hdwy over 1f out: kpt on fnl f: nrst fin* **9/2**[1]
4551 **4** *hd* **Derbyshire (IRE)**[12] 6154 3-9-1 72 (v) DeclanMcDonogh 1 76
(Kevin Ryan) *cl up: rdn over 2f out to over 1f out: kpt on same pce ins fnl f* **9/2**[1]
0456 **5** *1 3/4* **Order Of Service**[20] 5895 4-8-12 69 GaryBartley(3) 9 69
(Jim Goldie) *hld up towards rr: drvn over 2f out: kpt on fnl f: nvr able to chal* **12/1**
6600 **6** *1/2* **Relight My Fire**[9] 6213 4-9-4 72 (b) DavidAllan 8 71
(Tim Easterby) *trckd ldrs: drvn over 2f out: no ex over 1f out* **10/1**
6000 **7** *nse* **Berbice (IRE)**[3] 6405 9-8-2 61 oh16 SammyJoBell(5) 7 60?
(Linda Perratt) *dwlt: hld up: stdy hdwy whn n.m.r and swtchd rt ins fnl f: no imp* **100/1**
2004 **8** *1 1/2* **Patrona Ciana (FR)**[9] 6217 4-9-2 70 (v) DanielTudhope 6 65
(David O'Meara) *in tch: rdn over 2f out: edgd lft and wknd appr fnl f* **15/2**[3]
300 **9** *1/2* **Opt Out**[16] 6013 4-8-8 65 ConnorBeasley(3) 11 59
(Alistair Whillans) *bhd: rdn over 2f out: kpt on fnl f: nvr able to chal* **20/1**
0160 **10** *nk* **Porthos Du Vallon**[9] 6217 3-9-0 71 (p) PhillipMakin 3 63
(Keith Dalgleish) *hld up towards rr: drvn over 2f out: sn no imp* **18/1**
1436 **11** *1/2* **Monel**[33] 5415 6-8-11 65 FergalLynch 13 56
(Jim Goldie) *stdd in rr: rdn over 2f out: nvr on terms* **10/1**
0000 **12** *1 1/2* **Lewisham**[20] 5887 4-9-5 73 AdrianNicholls 2 61
(David Nicholls) *hld up on ins: struggling over 2f out: sn btn* **22/1**
0314 **13** *2 1/2* **Chookie's Lass**[16] 5994 3-8-12 69 TomEaves 12 49
(Keith Dalgleish) *led to over 2f out: rdn and wknd over 1f out* **25/1**

1m 28.93s (-4.47) **Going Correction** -0.475s/f (Firm)
**WFA** 3 from 4yo+ 3lb **13** Ran SP% **117.6**
Speed ratings (Par 103): **106,102,102,102,100 99,99,97,97,96 96,94,91**
CSF £59.77 CT £300.52 TOTE £10.00: £2.80, £3.20, £1.70; EX 67.40 Trifecta £608.80.
**Owner** Mrs S Quinn **Bred** Oliver Donlon **Trained** Settrington, N Yorks

**FOCUS**
A truly run race and the winning time was 0.34sec quicker than the first division. The winner's first form for nearly a year.

## 6479 WILLIAM HILL H'CAP (FOR THE KILKERRAN CUP) 1m 2f

**4:40** (4:41) (Class 2) (0-100,96) 3-Y-O+
**£15,562** (£4,660; £2,330; £1,165; £582; £292) **Stalls** Low

Form RPR
2321 **1** **Fire Fighting (IRE)**[5] 6315 3-9-7 96 6ex (b) JoeFanning 9 107
(Mark Johnston) *hld up towards rr: gd hdwy over 2f out: led over 1f out: edgd lft: rdn out fnl f* **9/2**[1]
4303 **2** *1 1/4* **Maven**[7] 6258 6-8-8 84 RachelRichardson(7) 4 92
(Tim Easterby) *t.k.h: early ldr: cl up: led over 2f out to over 1f out: edgd lft ins fnl f: kpt on* **12/1**
5106 **3** *1 1/4* **Dance King**[13] 6098 4-8-13 82 DavidAllan 3 88
(Tim Easterby) *in tch: stdy hdwy over 2f out: rdn over 1f out: kpt on same pce ins fnl f* **7/1**
4106 **4** *5* **Corton Lad**[27] 5633 4-9-2 85 (tp) TomEaves 1 81
(Keith Dalgleish) *chsd ldrs: drvn over 2f out: outpcd over 1f out* **25/1**
511 **5** *nse* **Mistiroc**[13] 6098 3-9-1 90 FergalLynch 8 86
(Jim Goldie) *hld up: rdn 3f out: kpt on fnl f: nvr able to chal* **9/2**[1]
1354 **6** *1 1/2* **Presburg (IRE)**[26] 5687 5-9-2 90 ShaneGray(5) 6 83
(Joseph Tuite) *s.i.s: hld up: rdn and hdwy over 2f out: no imp fr over 1f out* **13/2**[3]
115 **7** *2 1/2* **Wee Frankie (IRE)**[27] 5633 3-8-12 87 PhillipMakin 7 75
(Keith Dalgleish) *in tch: rdn over 2f out: wknd over 1f out* **5/1**[2]
5630 **8** *2 1/4* **San Cassiano (IRE)**[13] 6098 7-9-5 88 JamesSullivan 11 72
(Ruth Carr) *sn led: hdd after 4f: cl up tl rdn and wknd over 2f out* **50/1**
0211 **9** *3 3/4* **Ingleby Symphony (IRE)**[38] 5235 4-9-1 84 TonyHamilton 5 61
(Richard Fahey) *in tch: drvn 3f out: wknd 2f out* **12/1**
4060 **10** *shd* **Hi There (IRE)**[51] 4756 5-9-10 93 GrahamLee 10 70
(Richard Fahey) *s.i.s: bhd: drvn over 3f out: nvr on terms* **20/1**
1300 **11** *3/4* **St Moritz (IRE)**[40] 5178 8-9-8 91 (v) DanielTudhope 2 66
(David O'Meara) *midfield on outside: hdwy to ld after 4f: hdd over 2f out: wknd over 1f out* **10/1**

2m 5.08s (-6.92) **Going Correction** -0.475s/f (Firm)
**WFA** 3 from 4yo+ 6lb **11** Ran SP% **113.9**
Speed ratings (Par 109): **108,107,106,102,101 100,98,96,93,93 93**
CSF £55.42 CT £370.99 TOTE £5.50: £2.00, £5.10, £2.20; EX 60.00 Trifecta £352.40.
**Owner** A D Spence **Bred** P Bellaiche **Trained** Middleham Moor, N Yorks

**FOCUS**
A hot handicap and with a few in here that like to force it, a decent pace was always likely. They went a good tempo early until St Moritz circled the field to lead before halfway, at which point he dropped anchor. The first three home pulled clear, with another personal best from the winner.

## 6480 GRANTS FRUIT MERCHANTS PRESTWICK H'CAP — 1m 5f 13y
**5:10** (5:12) (Class 5) (0-70,70) 3-Y-O+ — **£3,881** (£1,155; £577; £288) **Stalls** Low

Form — RPR

5336 **1** **Harrison's Cave**[16] 6000 6-8-13 57.................... JoeFanning 8 65
(Keith Dalgleish) *hld up towards rr: hdwy over 2f out: kpt on wl fnl f to ld towards fin* **12/1**

4530 **2** *nk* **Choisan (IRE)**[11] 6171 5-9-12 70....................(tp) DavidAllan 1 77
(Tim Easterby) *midfield: rdn and hdwy over 2f out: led over 1f out: kpt on fnl f: hdd towards fin* **16/1**

5013 **3** *1* **Bayan Kasirga (IRE)**[13] 6099 4-9-7 70.................... JackGarritty(5) 12 75
(Richard Fahey) *midfield on outside: hdwy to ld over 2f out: edgd lft and hdd over 1f out: kpt on same pce ins fnl f* **7/2[1]**

5445 **4** *nk* **A Southside Boy (GER)**[22] 5812 6-9-3 61.................... FergalLynch 7 66
(Jim Goldie) *hld up: rdn over 2f out: hdwy over 1f out: kpt on fnl f: nrst fin* **17/2**

4254 **5** *hd* **Latin Rebel (IRE)**[21] 5856 7-8-9 56 oh1.................... GaryBartley(3) 3 61
(Jim Goldie) *prom: effrt and rdn 2f out: rdr dropped whip ins fnl f: kpt on same pce* **14/1**

6632 **6** *3 3/4* **In Vino Veritas (IRE)**[21] 5856 3-9-0 67..............(v) DeclanMcDonogh 10 66
(Ann Duffield) *led: rdn and hdd over 2f out: outpcd whn n.m.r appr fnl f* **12/1**

4232 **7** *hd* **Testa Rossa (IRE)**[13] 6113 4-9-4 62....................(p) GrahamLee 5 61
(Jim Goldie) *hld up in midfield: effrt and pushed along over 2f out: no imp fr over 1f out* **5/1[2]**

6053 **8** *3 1/4* **Les Gar Gan (IRE)**[13] 6110 3-8-10 63.................... TomEaves 6 57
(Keith Dalgleish) *midfield: drvn along over 2f out: wknd over 1f out* **12/1**

3235 **9** *1 1/4* **Grand Diamond (IRE)**[13] 6113 10-8-5 56 oh3.......... RachaelGrant(7) 15 48
(Jim Goldie) *s.i.s: hld up: shkn up over 2f out: n.m.r briefly over 1f out: nvr on terms* **25/1**

340/ **10** *1 3/4* **Nay Secret**[692] 6311 6-8-12 56 oh7.................... IanBrennan 9 45
(Jim Goldie) *hld up: rdn over 3f out: hdwy over 1f out: nvr able to chal* **100/1**

0 **11** *3 1/4* **Schmooze (IRE)**[40] 5172 5-8-12 59.................... ConnorBeasley(3) 14 43
(Linda Perratt) *missed break: bhd: drvn along over 4f out: btn fnl 2f* **16/1**

3113 **12** *2 1/4* **Sergeant Pink (IRE)**[10] 5270 8-8-13 62.................... EmmaSayer(5) 13 43
(Dianne Sayer) *bhd: struggling over 4f out: nvr on terms* **25/1**

-051 **13** *3/4* **Always Resolute**[42] 5077 3-8-9 65.................... JoeyHaynes(3) 16 45
(Timothy Jarvis) *prom tl rdn and wknd over 2f out* **7/1[3]**

1005 **14** *6* **That Be Grand**[9] 6216 3-8-7 60.................... JasonHart 2 31
(Shaun Harris) *chsd ldrs tl rdn and wknd qckly over 2f out* **18/1**

1400 **15** *2 1/2* **Blue Talisman (IRE)**[9] 6216 3-8-7 60....................(b) DuranFentiman 4 27
(Tim Easterby) *t.k.h early: cl up tl rdn and wknd over 2f out* **40/1**

2m 49.63s (-4.37) **Going Correction** -0.475s/f (Firm)
**WFA** 3 from 4yo+ 9lb — **15** Ran SP% **119.8**
Speed ratings (Par 103): **94,93,93,93,92 90,90,88,87,86 84,83,82,79,77**
CSF £183.33 CT £822.35 TOTE £10.70: £4.10, £5.90, £1.10; EX 178.50 Trifecta £2126.30.
**Owner** Keith Dalgleish **Bred** Carragh Bloodstock And T E Pocock **Trained** Carluke, S Lanarks
■ Stewards' Enquiry : David Allan two-day ban: used whip above permitted level (Oct 2-3)

**FOCUS**
The early pace looked solid enough in this competitive, if modest staying handicap, though there wasn't much covering the front five at the line. The form is rated around the winner's efforts this year.
T/Jkpt: Not won. T/Plt: £197.10 to a £1 stake. Pool: £65,874.44 - 243.89 winning units. T/Qpdt: £49.50 to a £1 stake. Pool: £8984.75 - 134.20 winning units. RY

# 6236 KEMPTON (A.W) (R-H)
### Thursday, September 18

**OFFICIAL GOING: Polytrack: standard**
Wind: Fresh, half behind Weather: Fine, warm

## 6481 BOOK CHRISTMAS PARTIES ON 01932 753518 H'CAP — 1m (P)
**5:40** (5:40) (Class 6) (0-55,56) 3-Y-O+ — **£1,940** (£577; £288; £144) **Stalls** Low

Form — RPR

00-6 **1** **Rochelle (IRE)**[15] 6033 3-9-2 55.................... MartinDwyer 9 64
(William Muir) *trckd ldr after 1f: shkn up over 2f out: chal over 1f out: kpt on to ld last 150yds: rdn out* **16/1**

4013 **2** *nk* **Wotalad**[14] 6074 4-9-6 55....................(p) SilvestreDeSousa 4 63
(Richard Whitaker) *led: rdn over 2f out: hdd last 140yds: kpt on but a jst hld* **5/1[2]**

3320 **3** *1 1/2* **Rock Band**[3] 6407 5-9-3 52....................(t[1]) MartinHarley 10 57
(Emmet Michael Butterly, Ire) *settled wl in rr: rdn on outer over 2f out: kpt on fr over 1f out to take 3rd last stride* **7/1**

2333 **4** *hd* **Bladewood Girl**[42] 5110 6-9-5 54.................... FrederikTylicki 13 58
(J R Jenkins) *in tch but forced to r wd: rdn over 2f out: kpt on fr over 1f out to chse ldng pair ins fnl f: one pce and lost 3rd last stride* **12/1**

4466 **5** *1/2* **Greek Islands (IRE)**[17] 5978 6-9-2 51.................... JimmyQuinn 3 54
(Edward Creighton) *dwlt: rushed up to go prom then t.k.h: rdn over 2f out: nt qckn over 1f out: one pce after* **14/1**

5506 **6** *hd* **Warbond**[8] 6242 6-9-4 53....................(b) WilliamTwiston-Davies 5 55
(Michael Madgwick) *s.i.s: wl in rr: rdn wl over 2f out: kpt on fr over 1f out: nrst fin* **9/2[1]**

652 **7** *1 1/2* **Cyflymder (IRE)**[22] 5833 8-9-6 55.................... OisinMurphy 8 54
(David C Griffiths) *trckd ldr 1f: settled in 4th after: rdn and nt qckn over 2f out: no imp over 1f out: fdd nr fin* **8/1**

0444 **8** *hd* **Squirrel Wood (IRE)**[15] 6028 6-9-3 52.................... JimCrowley 6 51
(Mary Hambro) *in tch in midfield: drvn and no prog over 2f out: n.d after* **6/1[3]**

5555 **9** *1 3/4* **Buzz Law (IRE)**[30] 5537 6-9-2 51.................... DavidProbert 7 46
(John Weymes) *hld up and sn in last: rdn and no real prog over 2f out* **25/1**

0053 **10** *1 1/4* **Berwin (IRE)**[10] 6195 5-9-2 51.................... LiamKeniry 12 43
(Sylvester Kirk) *s.i.s: a in last quartet: shkn up and no prog over 2f out* **20/1**

3405 **11** *1 1/2* **Welsh Inlet (IRE)**[17] 5979 6-9-3 52.................... WilliamCarson 11 40
(John Bridger) *dwlt: sn in tch in midfield: rdn over 2f out: wknd over 1f out* **14/1**

0606 **12** *nse* **Divine Rule (IRE)**[49] 4808 6-9-5 54....................(b) LiamJones 2 42
(Laura Mongan) *t.k.h: hld up in midfield: rdn over 2f out: wknd wl over 1f out* **12/1**

1m 39.83s (0.03) **Going Correction** +0.025s/f (Slow)
**WFA** 3 from 4yo+ 4lb — **12** Ran SP% **116.0**
Speed ratings (Par 101): **100,99,98,98,97 97,95,95,93,92 91,91**
CSF £92.13 CT £630.67 TOTE £18.10: £5.40, £1.30, £3.90; EX 126.50 Trifecta £992.50 Part won..
**Owner** Mr & Mrs G Middlebrook **Bred** Timmy & Michael Hillman **Trained** Lambourn, Berks

**FOCUS**
A typically tight low-grade handicap in which it paid to race handily. The winner was unexposed.

## 6482 £25 FREE BET AT BETVICTOR.COM MAIDEN STKS (DIV I) — 1m (P)
**6:10** (6:15) (Class 5) 3-Y-O+ — **£2,587** (£770; £384; £192) **Stalls** Low

Form — RPR

5 **1** **Santa Teresa (IRE)**[23] 5796 3-9-0 0.................... MartinHarley 6 83
(William Haggas) *led 1f: trckd ldr: shkn up over 2f out: rdn to ld jst ins fnl f: drvn out* **3/1[2]**

4 **2** *1/2* **New Year's Night (IRE)**[23] 5796 3-9-5 0.................... SilvestreDeSousa 9 87
(Charlie Appleby) *sweating profusely: led after 1f: rdn over 2f out: hdd jst ins fnl f: tried to rally but a hld* **6/5[1]**

**3** *8* **Nightlight** 3-9-0 0.................... JimmyFortune 5 63
(Jeremy Noseda) *in tch: pushed along over 3f out: tk modest 3rd jst over 1f out: no inroads into ldng pair* **7/1[3]**

**4** *1/2* **Priors Brook** 3-9-5 0.................... DavidProbert 8 67
(Andrew Balding) *s.s: jst in tch in 7th: pushed along firmly over 3f out: kpt on one pce to chal for 3rd fnl f* **33/1**

03 **5** *2 1/4* **Lostintheclouds**[21] 5862 3-9-0 0.................... ShaneKelly 2 57
(Mike Murphy) *trckd ldng pair: easily lft bhd fr over 2f out: lost 3rd jst over 1f out* **25/1**

**6** *7* **Otterbridge** 3-9-0 0.................... SteveDrowne 3 41
(Rod Millman) *s.s: rn v green in last pair: shoved along fr 1/2-way: nvr on terms* **50/1**

0 **7** *2 1/4* **Famous Tales**[29] 5548 4-8-11 0.................... RobertPWalsh(7) 1 36
(Edward Creighton) *t.k.h: hld up in midfield: wknd over 2f out* **100/1**

**8** *16* **Duke Of Dunton (IRE)** 3-9-5 0.................... WilliamTwiston-Davies 12 4
(Tony Carroll) *s.s: rn v green in last pair: wknd 3f out: t.o* **66/1**

26-0 **9** *14* **Eton Dorney (USA)**[6] 6304 5-9-4 79.................... NathanAlison(5) 10
(Kevin Tork) *stdd s: t.k.h and racd wd: in tch: wknd rapidly w rdr looking down fr 3f out: wl t.o* **33/1**

1m 38.48s (-1.32) **Going Correction** +0.025s/f (Slow)
**WFA** 3 from 4yo+ 4lb — **9** Ran SP% **97.1**
Speed ratings (Par 103): **107,106,98,98,95 88,86,70,56**
CSF £4.79 TOTE £3.00: £1.10, £1.10, £2.10; EX 5.30 Trifecta £15.00.
**Owner** Saeed Manana **Bred** Rabbah Bloodstock Limited **Trained** Newmarket, Suffolk
■ Dubai Star was withdrawn. Price at time of withdrawal 5-1. Rule 4 applies to all bets - deduction 15p in the pound.

**FOCUS**
Little depth to this maiden and the two market leaders pulled well clear, showing improved form. The time was 1.88sec, or 20lb, faster than the second division.

## 6483 £25 FREE BET AT BETVICTOR.COM MAIDEN STKS (DIV II) — 1m (P)
**6:40** (6:42) (Class 5) 3-Y-O+ — **£2,587** (£770; £384; £192) **Stalls** Low

Form — RPR

0 **1** **The Steward (USA)**[16] 6018 3-9-5 0.................... ChrisCatlin 11 81+
(Sir Mark Prescott Bt) *trckd ldr: rdn over 2f out: looked hld over 1f out: drvn and r.o fnl f to ld last 75yds* **6/1[3]**

6522 **2** *3/4* **Cape Summit**[15] 6034 3-9-5 75.................... JimmyFortune 7 79
(Ed Dunlop) *led: rdn 2f out: kpt on u.p fr over 1f out: hdd and outpcd last 75yds* **5/4[1]**

23- **3** *1 1/2* **Moonfaarid**[229] 438 3-9-5 0.................... PatCosgrave 4 76
(M F De Kock, South Africa) *t.k.h: trckd ldng pair: rdn to chal on inner over 1f out: nt qckn ins fnl f* **7/4[2]**

**4** *2 3/4* **Wowee** 3-9-5 0.................... DavidProbert 3 69
(Tony Carroll) *dwlt: sn in midfield: last of those w a ch 3f out: pushed into 4th wl over 1f out: kpt on but no imp* **66/1**

00 **5** *4 1/2* **Keeper's Ring (USA)**[31] 5504 3-9-0 0.................... FrederikTylicki 6 54
(Roger Varian) *chsd ldng trio: urged along over 3f out: wknd 2f out* **16/1**

0-0 **6** *2 1/4* **Sweet Charlie**[28] 5606 3-9-0 0.................... ShaneKelly 2 49
(Mike Murphy) *dwlt: sn chsd ldrs: rdn in 5th wl over 2f out: sn wknd* **66/1**

0 **7** *1* **Satchville Flyer**[21] 5862 3-9-5 0.................... WilliamTwiston-Davies 8 51
(Brett Johnson) *sn restrained into last pair and t.k.h: rdn over 2f out: sme modest prog over 1f out: nvr a factor* **66/1**

-50 **8** *1* **Mississippi Queen (USA)**[23] 5796 3-8-9 0.............. LouisSteward(5) 5 44
(Michael Bell) *heavily restrained into last pair after s: lost tch 3f out: passed wkng rivals under considerate riding fnl 2f: do bttr* **50/1**

**9** *7* **Dubai Skyline (USA)** 3-9-0 0.................... WilliamBuick 9 28
(Clive Brittain) *sn in rr: lost tch over 3f out: wl bhd over 2f out* **14/1**

060- **10** *1 1/2* **Majnon Fajer (IRE)**[338] 7265 4-9-4 47.................... CamHardie(5) 12 30
(Jane Chapple-Hyam) *chsd ldrs on outer to 1/2-way: sn dropped to rr u.p: wl bhd over 2f out* **100/1**

00 **11** *3 1/2* **Fine Tune (IRE)**[106] 2881 3-9-5 0.................... SteveDrowne 1 22
(Linda Jewell) *slowly away: a towards rr: lost tch 3f out: wl bhd after* **50/1**

1m 40.36s (0.56) **Going Correction** +0.025s/f (Slow)
**WFA** 3 from 4yo 4lb — **11** Ran SP% **117.0**
Speed ratings (Par 103): **98,97,95,93,88 86,85,84,77,75 72**
CSF £13.80 TOTE £9.50: £2.20, £1.10, £1.40; EX 16.90 Trifecta £29.00.
**Owner** Donald R Dizney **Bred** Fairway Thoroughbreds **Trained** Newmarket, Suffolk
■ Stewards' Enquiry : Louis Steward ten-day ban: failed to take all permissible measures to ensure filly ran on merits (4 Oct, 6-14 Oct)

**FOCUS**
As in the first division of this maiden, the three market leaders came to the fore. The time was relatively slow and the form is rated around the runner-up.

## 6484 DOWNLOAD THE BETVICTOR APP NOW H'CAP — 1m (P)
**7:10** (7:10) (Class 5) (0-75,75) 3-Y-0 — **£2,587** (£770; £384; £192) **Stalls** Low

Form — RPR

031 **1** **Holiday Magic (IRE)**[16] 6018 3-9-7 75.................... WilliamBuick 1 82
(Charlie Appleby) *pushed up to go prom and disp 2nd after 2f: led over 2f out and sent for home: drvn and maintained l ld fnl f* **7/2[2]**

4365 **2** *3/4* **Ghosting (IRE)**[20] 5895 3-9-3 71....................(t) RichardKingscote 11 76
(Tom Dascombe) *stdd s and hld up in last pair: prog jst over 2f out: drvn and r.o to take 2nd last 100yds: nvr able to chal* **8/1**

3325 **3** *1/2* **Surety (IRE)**[44] 5008 3-9-1 74.................... LouisSteward(5) 2 78
(Clive Brittain) *t.k.h early: trckd ldrs: shkn up over 2f out: prog to chse wnr fnl f: styd on but hld: lost 2nd last 100yds* **16/1**

034 **4** *nk* **Kubeba (IRE)**[16] 6018 3-9-2 **70** JimCrowley 10 73
(Paul Cole) *trckd ldrs on outer: rdn over 2f out: one of many chsng wnr 1f out: kpt on same pce* **16/1**

1655 **5** *½* **Like A Prayer**[15] 6034 3-9-0 **68** SilvestreDeSousa 6 70
(Ralph Beckett) *t.k.h: hld up in midfield: lost pl and rdn in rr over 2f out: rallied over 1f out: kpt on fnl f: nvr able to threaten* **4/1**[3]

6125 **6** *¾* **Madame Mirasol (IRE)**[7] 6269 3-9-5 **73** (p) MartinHarley 7 74
(Kevin Ryan) *in tch but wd: v wd bnd 3f out and lost grnd: renewed effrt 2f out and one of many chsng wnr fnl f: wknd last 100yds* **20/1**

0503 **7** *1* **Scarlet Plum**[16] 6022 3-8-7 **61** DavidProbert 8 59
(Roger Charlton) *hld up in last pair: rdn in detached last over 2f out: styd on fr over 1f out: nrst fin* **14/1**

45-1 **8** *3¼* **Lady Marl**[129] 2224 3-9-4 **72** JimmyFortune 4 63
(Gary Moore) *racd freely: led after 1f to over 2f out: wknd qckly fnl f* **8/1**

1U26 **9** *3¼* **Dream Impossible (IRE)**[38] 5252 3-8-9 **63** SteveDrowne 3 46
(Peter Makin) *led 1f: chsd ldr to over 2f out: sn wknd* **50/1**

033 **10** *¾* **Frederic**[16] 6018 3-9-5 **73** LemosdeSouza 5 55
(Luca Cumani) *dwlt: sn in tch towards rr: urged along on inner 2f out: wknd over 1f out* **9/4**[1]

1m 39.49s (-0.31) **Going Correction** +0.025s/f (Slow) **10** Ran SP% **120.4**
Speed ratings (Par 101): **102,101,100,100,99 99,98,94,91,90**
CSF £33.00 CT £417.62 TOTE £3.70: £1.70, £3.60, £6.40; EX 33.90 Trifecta £757.60.
**Owner** Godolphin **Bred** Mrs Ann Fortune **Trained** Newmarket, Suffolk

**FOCUS**
A fair handicap for 3yos, but the form is a bit muddling. The wuinner continues to progress.

## 6485 DOWNLOAD THE BETVICTOR INSTABET APP MEDIAN AUCTION MAIDEN STKS 1m 4f (P)
**7:40** (7:43) (Class 5) 3-4-Y-O £2,587 (£770; £384; £192) **Stalls** Centre

Form RPR

2232 **1** **Artful Rogue (IRE)**[26] 5670 3-9-5 80 JimCrowley 8 84
(Amanda Perrett) *mde virtually all: rdn over 2f out: edgd lft after but styd on strly fr over 1f out* **3/1**[2]

02 **2** *3¼* **Rembrandt Van Rijn (IRE)**[22] 5831 3-9-5 0 WilliamBuick 3 79
(David Lanigan) *trckd ldrs: rousted along to go 2nd wl over 2f out: edgd lft u.p fr wl over 1f out: no imp on wnr after* **1/2**[1]

0263 **3** *4½* **Black Label**[15] 6045 3-9-5 69 SilvestreDeSousa 11 72
(Harry Dunlop) *pressed wnr to wl over 2f out: steadily outpcd after* **14/1**

54 **4** *1½* **Gale Force**[45] 4966 3-9-0 0 HayleyTurner 4 65
(James Fanshawe) *trckd ldrs: gng bttr than most 3f out: outpcd and pushed along sn after: one pce after* **8/1**[3]

**5** *½* **Instant Karma (IRE)** 3-9-5 0 WilliamTwiston-Davies 7 69
(Michael Bell) *hld up in last pair: pushed along 4f out: struggling in last and drvn over 2f out: styd on fr wl over 1f out: nvr nrr* **25/1**

04 **6** *2¼* **Golden Bird (IRE)**[22] 5822 3-9-5 0 SteveDrowne 1 65
(Dean Ivory) *dwlt: hld up in tch: shkn up 3f out and sn wl outpcd: plugged on fnl 2f* **25/1**

**7** *4½* **Perdu** 4-9-13 0 OisinMurphy 9 58
(Marcus Tregoning) *hld up in last pair: rdn 4f out: struggling fr 3f out* **25/1**

00-0 **8** *3¼* **Mad About Harry (IRE)**[57] 4548 4-9-6 64 (v[1]) DanielCremin(7) 2 53
(Linda Jewell) *plld hrd early: hld up: rdn 4f out: wknd over 2f out* **66/1**

5 **9** *2¼* **Tiger Stone**[15] 6045 3-9-0 0 DavidProbert 10 44
(Michael Blanshard) *prog to go prom after 3f: wknd qckly fr 3f out* **100/1**

2m 35.03s (2.03) **Going Correction** +0.025s/f (Slow)
**WFA** 3 from 4yo 8lb **9** Ran SP% **123.5**
Speed ratings (Par 103): **99,96,93,92,92 91,88,85,84**
CSF £5.05 TOTE £5.10: £1.10, £1.10, £2.70; EX 5.70 Trifecta £15.80.
**Owner** Mr & Mrs F Cotton, Mr & Mrs P Conway **Bred** Michael Morrissey **Trained** Pulborough, W Sussex

**FOCUS**
An ordinary maiden and a muddling race. The winner was closed to his previous form.

## 6486 FOLLOW @BETVICTORRACING ON TWITTER H'CAP 2m (P)
**8:10** (8:14) (Class 6) (0-60,60) 3-Y-O+ £1,940 (£577; £288; £144) **Stalls** Low

Form RPR

43 **1** **Graylyn Ruby (FR)**[19] 5909 9-9-8 54 MartinHarley 4 62
(Robert Eddery) *hld up in rr: only 10th over 3f out but gng strly: prog over 2f out: rdn to ld over 1f out: styd on wl* **2/1**[1]

4435 **2** *1¼* **Oakbank (USA)**[27] 5628 3-8-5 49 KieranO'Neill 1 56
(Brett Johnson) *trckd ldr: led over 3f out and sent for home: drvn and hdd over 1f out: styd on but readily hld last 150yds* **7/1**[3]

0536 **3** *1½* **Dr Finley (IRE)**[9] 6216 7-9-4 53 (v) SimonPearce(3) 14 58
(Lydia Pearce) *trckd ldrs: drvn wl over 2f out: prog to take 3rd over 1f out: styd on but unable to chal* **14/1**

6304 **4** *4½* **Sawwala**[25] 5731 4-9-4 50 FrederikTylicki 10 49
(J R Jenkins) *sn crossed to inner to trck ldrs: lost pl over 3f out: outpcd in midfield 2f out: pushed along and kpt on steadily after* **10/1**

/55- **5** *½* **Flashy Star**[21] 4655 5-9-4 50 SilvestreDeSousa 5 49
(Paul Henderson) *hld up in last pair: hrd rdn on outer 3f out: kpt on passed toiling rivals fr 2f out: nrst fin* **25/1**

1226 **6** *4½* **Lucky Diva**[19] 5909 7-9-8 59 (v) RyanWhile(5) 3 52
(Bill Turner) *trckd ldng pair: wnt 2nd 3f out gng v easily: poised to chal over 2f out: sn rdn and wknd in an instant* **25/1**

0505 **7** *½* **Newtown Cross (IRE)**[41] 5137 4-9-10 56 (p) PatDobbs 12 49
(Jimmy Fox) *nvr bttr than midfield: rdn wl over 2f out: lft bhd fr over 1f out* **5/1**[2]

0 **8** *hd* **Paple Blessing (IRE)**[19] 5904 4-9-0 46 WilliamTwiston-Davies 11 38
(David Bridgwater) *nvr beyond midfield: rdn and no prog 3f out* **25/1**

006 **9** *hd* **Superciliary**[13] 6107 5-9-6 52 HayleyTurner 8 44
(Chris Gordon) *hmpd on inner after 1f: trckd ldrs: rdn wl over 2f out: stl cl enough wl over 1f out: wknd* **14/1**

6-00 **10** *1¾* **Vexillum (IRE)**[168] 747 5-9-8 54 (t) SteveDrowne 2 44
(Simon Hodgson) *hld up in last quartet: prog on wd outside to trck ldrs 5f out: shkn up and lost pl over 2f out: eased* **66/1**

506 **11** *½* **Archiebeau**[25] 5719 3-8-11 60 NedCurtis(5) 9 50
(Jonathan Portman) *nvr beyond midfield: rdn 3f out: no prog and sn btn* **8/1**

-400 **12** *11* **Boston Blue**[16] 6019 7-9-8 54 (p) JimCrowley 6 30
(Tony Carroll) *hld up in last pair: stl there but gng wl enough over 3f out: shkn up and no prog over 2f out: t.o* **8/1**

406/ **13** *3* **Spanish Fork (IRE)**[10] 7293 5-9-6 57 HarryPoulton(5) 7 30
(Sheena West) *rousted along early: wl in rr: prog into midfield after 6f: rdn and struggling sn after 1/2-way: t.o* **33/1**

0/05 **14** *16* **Bogey Hole (IRE)**[35] 5342 5-8-11 46 oh1 PhilipPrince(3) 13
(Nikki Evans) *led to over 3f out: wknd rapidly: wl t.o* **50/1**

3m 32.14s (2.04) **Going Correction** +0.025s/f (Slow)
**WFA** 3 from 4yo+ 12lb **14** Ran SP% **125.1**
Speed ratings (Par 101): **95,94,93,91,91 88,88,88,88,87 87,81,80,72**
CSF £15.45 CT £167.20 TOTE £3.80: £2.00, £2.10, £4.10; EX 23.80 Trifecta £148.80.
**Owner** Graham & Lynn Knight **Bred** Jonathan Jay **Trained** Newmarket, Suffolk

**FOCUS**
A modest staying handicap that was run at a steady pace. The third sets the standard.

## 6487 BETVICTOR.COM H'CAP (LONDON MIDDLE DISTANCE SERIES QUALIFIER) 1m 3f (P)
**8:40** (8:43) (Class 4) (0-80,79) 3-Y-O+ £4,690 (£1,395; £697; £348) **Stalls** Low

Form RPR

-550 **1** **Almerzem (USA)**[63] 4359 3-9-0 **74** DaneO'Neill 7 87+
(Saeed bin Suroor) *dwlt: t.k.h: hld up in rr: gd prog over 2f out to ld over 1f out: sn clr: won decisively* **13/2**[3]

3460 **2** *3* **Castle Combe (IRE)**[15] 6044 3-8-12 **72** PatDobbs 9 78
(Marcus Tregoning) *hld up in last pair: looking for room over 2f out: drvn and prog over 1f out: styd on wl to take 2nd last strides: no ch w wnr* **14/1**

4043 **3** *½* **Manomine**[7] 6274 5-8-13 **71** (b) LouisSteward(5) 2 76
(Clive Brittain) *prom: rdn to try to chal over 2f out: outpcd over 1f out: styd on same pce* **14/1**

-226 **4** *nk* **Itsnowcato**[54] 4651 3-8-13 **73** RichardKingscote 11 78
(Ed Walker) *trckd ldr: rdn to ld 2f out: hdd over 1f out and sn outpcd by wnr: lost 2 pls nr fin* **2/1**[2]

2005 **5** *½* **Kastini**[35] 5345 4-9-2 **74** (v) CamHardie(5) 10 78
(Denis Coakley) *t.k.h: trckd ldrs: cl up and rdn jst over 2f out: nt qckn and one pce after* **33/1**

4262 **6** *¾* **Little Buxted (USA)**[19] 5931 4-9-8 **75** DavidProbert 3 78
(Robert Mills) *hld up in tch: sme prog on inner to chse ldrs over 2f out: rdn and one pce fnl 2f* **7/1**

006 **7** *nk* **Guising**[23] 5800 5-9-5 **72** (p) MartinHarley 8 74
(David Brown) *led: drvn and hdd 2f out: wknd fnl f* **33/1**

31 **8** *10* **Elbereth**[44] 5010 3-9-5 **79** OisinMurphy 5 64
(Andrew Balding) *trckd ldrs: rdn over 3f out: wknd qckly 2f out: sn bhd* **7/4**[1]

2054 **9** *¾* **Syncopate**[17] 5984 5-9-6 **73** LiamKeniry 6 57
(Pam Sly) *t.k.h: hld up in tch: rdn over 3f out: lost pl over 2f out: wknd and bhd over 1f out* **20/1**

3200 **10** *8* **Hector's Chance**[16] 6007 5-9-4 **71** PatCosgrave 4 41
(Heather Main) *awkward s: checked after 1f whn in last pl: prog on outer 5f out: wknd rapidly over 2f out: t.o* **33/1**

2m 19.69s (-2.21) **Going Correction** +0.025s/f (Slow)
**WFA** 3 from 4yo+ 7lb **10** Ran SP% **122.4**
Speed ratings (Par 105): **109,106,106,106,105 105,105,97,97,91**
CSF £91.22 CT £1231.21 TOTE £8.10: £3.10, £6.30, £3.50; EX 95.70 Trifecta £1254.70.
**Owner** Godolphin **Bred** Shadwell Farm LLC **Trained** Newmarket, Suffolk

**FOCUS**
Not a particularly strong handicap for the grade. The first two came from the rear and the form looks sound.

## 6488 BARN DANCE CHRISTMAS PARTIES AT KEMPTON H'CAP 6f (P)
**9:10** (9:12) (Class 6) (0-65,65) 3-Y-O £1,940 (£577; £288; £144) **Stalls** Low

Form RPR

0-64 **1** **Findhorn Magic**[38] 5249 3-9-4 62 SteveDrowne 9 71
(Peter Makin) *mde all and sn 3 l clr: rdn and hung lft fr 2f out: hld on wl* **16/1**

3050 **2** *¾* **Wedgewood Estates**[45] 4972 3-8-8 52 DavidProbert 11 58
(Tony Carroll) *hld up in last trio: prog and threaded between rivals jst over 2f out: rdn and styd on to take 2nd ins fnl f: nvr quite able to chal* **66/1**

0043 **3** *½* **Stapleford Lad**[22] 5820 3-8-9 53 (v) SilvestreDeSousa 4 57
(Stuart Williams) *chsd ldng pair: rdn to dispute 2nd wl over 1f out: styd on same pce after and a hld* **9/2**[3]

352 **4** *hd* **Blue Bounty**[8] 6240 3-9-7 65 TedDurcan 2 69
(Mark H Tompkins) *trckd ldrs: disp 2nd wl over 1f out: sn rdn and nt qckn: edgd lft but styd on same pce after* **13/8**[1]

0204 **5** *3¾* **Ignight**[19] 5905 3-8-0 51 oh6 (p) CharlotteJenner(7) 8 43
(Mark Usher) *chsd wnr: rdn over 2f out: lost 2nd wl over 1f out and fdd* **66/1**

4045 **6** *shd* **Honey Meadow**[20] 5897 3-9-4 62 MartinHarley 10 53
(Robert Eddery) *hld up in last trio: pushed along 2f out: no ch whn impeded over 1f out: kpt on fnl f: nvr involved* **8/1**

602 **7** *½* **Dylan's Centenary**[15] 6030 3-8-5 56 SophieKilloran(7) 1 46
(Rod Millman) *s.s: detached in last: pushed along and threatened briefly to get involved over 1f out: no hdwy after* **20/1**

-005 **8** *¾* **Sir Percy Blakeney**[37] 5273 3-8-2 51 oh6 CamHardie(5) 6 38
(Marcus Tregoning) *chsd ldrs: rdn on outer over 3f out: struggling over 2f out* **25/1**

0615 **9** *½* **Pieman's Girl**[21] 5860 3-9-5 63 WilliamCarson 5 49
(Anthony Carson) *in tch in midfield: rdn over 2f out: lft bhd fr wl over 1f out* **25/1**

4651 **10** *½* **Maymyo (IRE)**[22] 5820 3-9-5 63 PatDobbs 7 47
(Sylvester Kirk) *hld up in tch: nt clr run on inner 1/2-way: shkn up and no prog over 2f out: n.d after* **11/4**[2]

1m 12.64s (-0.46) **Going Correction** +0.025s/f (Slow) **10** Ran SP% **115.4**
Speed ratings (Par 99): **104,103,102,102,97 96,96,95,94,93**
CSF £771.67 CT £5561.36 TOTE £12.60: £5.60, £9.00, £1.10; EX 344.60 Trifecta £1722.30 Part won..
**Owner** R P Marchant **Bred** Michael E Broughton **Trained** Ogbourne Maisey, Wilts

■ Stewards' Enquiry : Steve Drowne two-day ban: used whip in incorrect place (Oct 2-3)

**FOCUS**
A modest sprint handicap in which the winner was the least exposed. The form makes sense.

T/Plt: £10.60 to a £1 stake. Pool: £68,929.25 - 4704.42 winning units. T/Qpdt: £3.50 to a £1 stake. Pool: £9400.47 - 1939.39 winning units. JN

# 5464 PONTEFRACT (L-H)

Thursday, September 18

**OFFICIAL GOING: Good to firm (8.1)**
Wind: almost nil Weather: fine

## 6489 RACING UK ANYWHERE AVAILABLE NOW MEDIAN AUCTION MAIDEN STKS 5f
**2:30** (2:32) (Class 5) 2-Y-0 **£3,234** (£962; £481; £240) **Stalls** Low

Form RPR
222 1 **Free Entry (IRE)**28 5593 2-9-0 80 KierenFallon 1 75
(James Tate) *chsd ldrs: drvn over 2f out: styd on to ld jst ins fnl f: hld on towards fin* **11/8**1
4 2 ½ **Gold Pursuit**138 1955 2-9-5 0 RobertWinston 6 78
(Alan Swinbank) *led: hdd jst ins fnl f: no ex clsng stages* **12/1**
42 3 ½ **Clergyman**15 6024 2-9-5 0 JackMitchell 8 76
(Martyn Meade) *trckd ldrs: pushed wd over 3f out: styd on to take 3rd nr fin* **11/4**2
4 ½ **Secret Glance** 2-9-5 0 DaleSwift 9 75+
(Ed McMahon) *dwlt and wnt rt s: in rr: hdwy over 1f out: fin strly to take 4th fnl strides* **25/1**
35 5 *nse* **Signoret (IRE)**22 5807 2-8-11 0 GeorgeChaloner(3) 3 69
(Richard Fahey) *t.k.h in mid-div: hdwy over 2f out: chsng ldrs over 1f out: kpt on same pce* **7/1**3
23 6 13 **Cumbrianna**37 5264 2-9-0 0 PaulMulrennan 4 23
(Bryan Smart) *chsd ldrs: swtchd rt over 3f out: wknd over 1f out* **7/1**3
7 1 ¾ **Etienne Gerard** 2-9-5 0 HayleyTurner 5 21
(Nigel Tinkler) *mid-div: reminder and outpcd over 2f out: sn lost pl* **100/1**
8 13 **Smoke Ring (USA)** 2-9-5 0 DavidNolan 7
(Donald McCain) *s.i.s: in rr: wnt rt bnd over 2f out: sn bhd* **50/1**
9 8 **Charlie's Approval (IRE)** 2-9-0 0 AndrewElliott 2
(Ben Haslam) *dwlt: in rr: wl bhd fnl 2f* **16/1**

1m 3.1s (-0.20) **Going Correction** -0.15s/f (Firm) 9 Ran SP% **114.1**
Speed ratings (Par 95): **95,94,93,92,92 71,68,48,35**
CSF £19.57 TOTE £2.10: £1.20, £2.80, £1.10; EX 20.00 Trifecta £78.90.
**Owner** Sheikh Rashid Dalmook Al Maktoum **Bred** Yeomanstown Stud **Trained** Newmarket, Suffolk
**FOCUS**
A modest 2yo maiden.

## 6490 WATCH RACINGUK ANYWHERE USING OUR IPAD APP H'CAP 1m 4y
**3:00** (3:01) (Class 4) (0-80,78) 3-Y-0+ **£5,175** (£1,540; £769; £384) **Stalls** Low

Form RPR
4321 1 **Potent Embrace (USA)**5 6323 3-9-5 77 6ex FrannyNorton 7 89
(Mark Johnston) *trckd ldrs: led wl over 1f out: kpt on wl towards fin* **9/2**1
4560 2 1 ¼ **Oddysey (IRE)**14 6057 5-9-10 78 DavidNolan 9 87
(Michael Dods) *mid-div: hdwy over 3f out: upsides over 1f out: kpt on same pce last 50yds* **12/1**
3402 3 4 **Party Royal**16 5999 4-9-10 78 DaleSwift 10 78
(Ruth Carr) *swtchd lft after s: hld up in rr: gd hdwy on outside over 1f out: edgd lft and styd on to take 3rd last 75yds* **10/1**
0011 4 2 **Broctune Papa Gio**9 6217 7-8-8 67 JoeDoyle(5) 8 62
(Keith Reveley) *chsd ldrs: drvn and outpcd over 2f out: kpt on one pce over 1f out* **7/1**3
3004 5 3 ½ **Hakuna Matata**9 6214 7-9-10 78 (b) PaulMulrennan 2 65
(Michael Dods) *s.i.s: in rr: hdwy 3f out: one pce over 1f out* **8/1**
2400 6 1 **Wannabe King**31 5496 8-9-8 76 (v) AndrewMullen 6 61
(Geoffrey Harker) *drvn to ld: hdd wl over 1f out: wknd jst ins fnl f* **28/1**
3325 7 1 ½ **Cliff (IRE)**8 6232 4-9-2 70 (v) HayleyTurner 3 51
(Nigel Tinkler) *hld up towards rr: effrt over 1f out: nvr a factor* **7/1**3
3054 8 2 ¾ **Fazza**23 5793 7-9-0 73 KevinStott(5) 5 48
(Edwin Tuer) *mid-div: lost pl over 3f out: sme hdwy over 1f out: nvr a factor* **9/2**1
3053 9 2 ½ **Zaitsev (IRE)**23 5788 4-9-4 72 RobertWinston 1 41
(Ollie Pears) *t.k.h: trckd ldrs: wknd jst ins fnl f: eased clsng stages* **5/1**2
0546 10 1 ¾ **Destiny Blue (IRE)**15 5331 7-8-10 64 oh5 (t) RaulDaSilva 4 29
(Suzzanne France) *stdd s: in rr: drvn 4f out: nvr on terms* **66/1**
2646 11 ½ **Mayfield Boy**33 5420 3-9-0 72 KierenFallon 11 36
(Mel Brittain) *dwlt: hdwy on outer over 4f out: hung lft and lost pl over 1f out: bhd whn eased clsng stages* **20/1**

1m 43.57s (-2.33) **Going Correction** -0.15s/f (Firm)
**WFA** 3 from 4yo+ 4lb 11 Ran SP% **115.6**
Speed ratings (Par 105): **105,103,99,97,94 93,91,89,86,84 84**
CSF £56.63 CT £513.44 TOTE £3.80: £1.60, £4.30, £3.90; EX 62.20 Trifecta £556.90.
**Owner** Sheikh Hamdan bin Mohammed Al Maktoum **Bred** Darley **Trained** Middleham Moor, N Yorks
**FOCUS**
A modest handicap which was run at a strong pace. The form has been rated positively.

## 6491 BOOK YOUR CHRISTMAS PARTY HERE ON 0113 2876387 H'CAP 1m 2f 6y
**3:30** (3:30) (Class 4) (0-85,82) 3-Y-0+ **£6,469** (£1,925; £962; £481) **Stalls** Low

Form RPR
2231 1 **Legal Waves (IRE)**16 6011 4-9-9 81 KierenFallon 4 91
(Alan Swinbank) *hld up in mid-div: hdwy 2f out: edgd lft and led last 75yds: drvn out* **9/4**1
3330 2 ¾ **The Character (IRE)**20 5884 3-8-13 77 StephenCraine 2 85
(Tom Dascombe) *chsd ldr: led over 6f out: drvn over 2f out: hdd ins fnl f: no ex* **9/2**3
0454 3 3 ¾ **Sellingallthetime (IRE)**17 5980 3-8-5 69 (p) AndrewMullen 6 70
(Michael Appleby) *chsd ldrs: upsides over 5f out: styd on same pce fnl f* **9/1**
5261 4 *hd* **Cosmic Halo**11 6166 5-9-4 79 6ex GeorgeChaloner(3) 7 79
(Richard Fahey) *trckd ldrs: drvn over 2f out: kpt on same pce fnl f* **6/1**
21 5 3 **Sophisticated Heir (IRE)**36 5299 4-9-10 82 DavidNolan 1 77
(David O'Meara) *led tl over 6f out: drvn over 2f out: wknd fnl 150yds* **7/2**2
5555 6 15 **Correggio**16 5999 4-9-0 72 (p) PaulMulrennan 5 38
(Micky Hammond) *swtchd lft after s: t.k.h in rr: effrt over 2f out: lost pl over 1f out: eased whn bhd clsng stages* **8/1**
-000 7 26 **Altharoos (IRE)**24 5771 4-9-5 82 KevinStott(5) 3
(Sally Hall) *dwlt: hld up in rr: drvn over 2f out: sn lost pl: eased whn bhd: t.o* **14/1**

2m 10.65s (-3.05) **Going Correction** -0.15s/f (Firm)
**WFA** 3 from 4yo+ 6lb 7 Ran SP% **113.2**
Speed ratings (Par 105): **106,105,102,102,99 87,67**
CSF £12.36 TOTE £2.30: £1.40, £2.70; EX 14.50 Trifecta £129.70.
**Owner** Mrs B V Sangster **Bred** Airlie Stud **Trained** Melsonby, N Yorks
**FOCUS**
A fairly useful handicap. The gallop didn't appear overly strong. The winner backed up his maiden form.

## 6492 EBF STALLIONS BREEDING WINNERS FILLIES' H'CAP 6f
**4:00** (4:02) (Class 3) (0-90,87) 3-Y-0+
**£9,337** (£2,796; £1,398; £699; £349; £175) **Stalls** Low

Form RPR
4305 1 **Augusta Ada**47 4902 3-8-12 77 RobertWinston 4 89
(Ollie Pears) *hld up in rr: hdwy on ins and nt clr run 2f: squeezed through to chse ldr appr fnl f: led last 150yds: r.o wl* **16/1**
3306 2 2 ½ **Misplaced Fortune**13 6095 9-9-2 82 (v) GeorgeChaloner(3) 10 86
(Nigel Tinkler) *mid-div: hdwy over 1f out: kpt on to take 2nd nr fin* **6/1**3
2111 3 ½ **Guishan**34 5398 4-9-1 78 AndrewMullen 3 80
(Michael Appleby) *chsd ldr: led over 2f out: hdd and no ex ins fnl f* **9/2**2
1101 4 2 ½ **Ishiamber**22 5826 4-9-10 87 KierenFallon 7 81
(George Baker) *in rr: hdwy over 2f out: kpt on same pce over 1f out: nvr a threat* **8/1**
0223 5 1 ¼ **Two Smart (IRE)**16 5997 3-8-10 75 (p1) FrannyNorton 1 65
(K R Burke) *mid-div: effrt over 2f out: chsng ldrs over 1f out: fdd last 100yds* **9/1**
2116 6 1 **Jamesbo's Girl**28 5612 4-9-3 80 PaulMulrennan 6 67
(David Barron) *led: hdd over 2f out: fdd fnl f* **9/4**1
315 7 ½ **Spiraea**16 6006 4-8-12 75 RobertHavlin 5 61
(Mark Rimell) *chsd ldrs: one pce over 1f out* **10/1**
4400 8 2 ½ **Ruby's Day**9 6213 5-8-7 75 KevinStott(5) 8 53
(David Brown) *in rr: hdwy on ins 2f out: wknd appr fnl f* **25/1**
321 9 1 ¾ **Ziggy's Secret**30 5536 4-9-5 82 DougieCostello 9 54
(Lucy Wadham) *chsd ldrs: wknd appr fnl f* **10/1**

1m 15.41s (-1.49) **Going Correction** -0.15s/f (Firm)
**WFA** 3 from 4yo+ 2lb 9 Ran SP% **112.3**
Speed ratings (Par 104): **103,99,99,95,94 92,92,88,86**
CSF £104.94 CT £511.86 TOTE £16.00: £3.30, £1.70, £1.40; EX 141.40 Trifecta £542.00.
**Owner** Timothy O'Gram **Bred** L C And Mrs A E Sigsworth **Trained** Norton, N Yorks
**FOCUS**
A fair fillies' event which was soundly run. A clear personal best from the winner.

## 6493 BOOK YOUR 20TH OCTOBER TOTEPOOL PACKAGE H'CAP (ROUND 6 OF PONTEFRACT STAYERS CHAMPIONSHIP 2014) 2m 1f 22y
**4:30** (4:30) (Class 5) (0-75,72) 3-Y-0+ **£3,234** (£962; £481; £240) **Stalls** Low

Form RPR
-614 1 **Hell Hath No Fury**41 5137 5-8-9 53 AndrewMullen 4 64
(Michael Appleby) *chsd ldr: upsides over 5f out: led over 2f out: 3 l clr 100yds out: hld on nr fin* **5/1**3
4264 2 ½ **Aiyana**20 5878 4-9-7 65 RobertHavlin 3 75
(Hughie Morrison) *trckd ldrs: 2nd over 2f out: styd on wl ins fnl f: jst hld* **11/4**1
0604 3 10 **Chevalgris**12 6152 4-10-0 72 KierenFallon 2 72
(Alan Swinbank) *hld up in rr: hdwy over 5f out: drvn over 4f out: kpt on fnl 2f: tk modest 3rd nr fin* **11/4**1
3163 4 ½ **La Bacouetteuse (FR)**22 5812 9-9-13 71 (b) DavidNolan 6 71
(Iain Jardine) *sn chsng ldrs: drvn over 4f out: one pce fnl 2f* **5/1**3
1-60 5 1 ½ **Madam Lilibet (IRE)**150 1605 5-9-3 61 PaulQuinn 1 59
(Sharon Watt) *hld up in rr: effrt 4f out: disputing modest 3rd over 1f out: wknd nr fin* **16/1**
6340 6 13 **Bowdler's Magic**20 5890 7-9-11 69 (tp) PaulMulrennan 5 54
(David Thompson) *led: hdd over 2f out: wknd over 1f out: eased clsng stages* **9/2**2

3m 48.81s (4.21) **Going Correction** -0.15s/f (Firm) 6 Ran SP% **110.7**
Speed ratings (Par 103): **84,83,79,78,78 72**
CSF £18.53 TOTE £4.50: £2.80, £1.80; EX 27.20 Trifecta £47.30.
**Owner** C L Bacon **Bred** K F Fallon **Trained** Danethorpe, Notts
**FOCUS**
The first two came clear in this modest handicap.

## 6494 DON'T MISS ANY ACTION WITH RACINGUK ANYWHERE MAIDEN STKS 1m 2f 6y
**5:00** (5:00) (Class 5) 3-Y-0+ **£3,234** (£962; £481; £240) **Stalls** Low

Form RPR
1 **Sov (IRE)** 3-9-5 0 KierenFallon 6 71+
(Alan McCabe) *dwlt: sn chsng ldrs: 2nd over 7f out: reminders over 2f out: led over 1f out: hung bdly rt ins fnl f: drvn out* **5/6**1
05 2 3 ¾ **Bulas Belle**13 6118 4-9-1 0 KevinStott(5) 1 56
(Edwin Tuer) *hld up in rr: effrt over 2f out: hdwy over 1f out: styd on to take 2nd last 50yds* **9/2**3
3 ½ **Arsenale (GER)** 3-9-0 0 AndrewMullen 2 55
(Michael Appleby) *dwlt: green in mid-div: hdwy over 3f out: chsng ldrs 2f out: kpt on same pce fnl f* **7/2**2
04 4 3 **Highfield Lass**34 5400 3-9-0 0 MichaelStainton 4 49
(Chris Fairhurst) *t.k.h: led: hdd over 1f out: wknd towards fin* **11/1**
00 5 13 **Sea Whisper**15 6033 3-8-11 0 GeorgeChaloner(3) 3 25
(Ann Stokell) *dwlt: mid-div: hdwy 4f out: sn chsng ldrs: drvn over 2f out: wknd fnl f* **28/1**
0- 6 39 **Lucky North**373 6272 4-9-11 0 PaulMulrennan 5
(Mel Brittain) *chsd ldrs: reminders over 4f out: lost pl over 3f out: sn bhd: t.o 2f out: eased fnl f* **20/1**

2m 15.79s (2.09) **Going Correction** -0.15s/f (Firm)
**WFA** 3 from 4yo 6lb 6 Ran SP% **111.5**
Speed ratings (Par 103): **85,82,81,79,68 37**
CSF £4.91 TOTE £2.00: £1.10, £3.10; EX 5.00 Trifecta £13.00.
**Owner** A J McCabe **Bred** Colm McEvoy **Trained** Averham Park, Notts
**FOCUS**
A very weak maiden, run in a slow time, and shaky form. The winner is entitled to do better, though.

## 6495 RACINGUK ALL PROFITS RETURNED TO RACING APPRENTICE H'CAP 6f
**5:30** (5:31) (Class 5) (0-70,76) 3-Y-0+ **£3,234** (£962; £481; £240) **Stalls** Low

Form RPR
0022 1 **It Must Be Faith**30 5535 4-9-6 69 GaryMahon 1 78
(Michael Appleby) *chsd ldr: led over 2f out: edgd rt ins fnl f: hld on towards fin* **10/3**2
111 2 ½ **Peace Accord**8 6240 4-9-10 76 6ex JoshDoyle(3) 9 83
(Michael Wigham) *trckd ldrs: effrt and 3rd over 1f out: styd on and 2nd last 75yds: no ex clsng stages* **7/4**1

0001 **3** *1 ½* **Thewestwalian (USA)**[22] 5806 6-8-7 56 oh9................ DavidParkes 10 59
(Peter Hiatt) *hld up towards rr: hdwy over 1f out: kpt on wl to take 3rd nr fin* **50/1**

65-0 **4** *3* **Opus Dei**[16] 6014 7-8-4 56 oh1..............................(p) AaronJones(3) 8 49
(John Murray) *s.i.s: in rr: hdwy on outside over 1f out: styd on ins fnl f* **100/1**

1260 **5** *shd* **Sugar Town**[13] 6121 4-8-2 56 oh3..............................(p) PaddyPilley(5) 4 49
(Peter Niven) *led tl over 2f out: hung rt ins fnl f: one pce* **5/1**

1003 **6** *shd* **Street Boss (IRE)**[13] 6121 3-8-2 58..............................(v[1]) RowanScott(5) 2 50
(Jedd O'Keeffe) *mid-div: hdwy on ins over 2f out: one pce over 1f out* **4/1**[3]

0044 **7** *¾* **The Strig**[15] 6030 7-8-7 56 oh6..............................(v) AnnaHesketh 3 46
(Nigel Tinkler) *chsd ldrs: one pce fnl 2f* **25/1**

0230 **8** *1 ¼* **Amis Reunis**[31] 5499 5-8-2 56 oh3............................ JordanHibberd(5) 5 42
(Alan Berry) *in rr: sme hdwy over 1f out: nvr a factor* **20/1**

0000 **9** *2 ¾* **Avonmore Star**[24] 5766 6-8-8 62.............................. CallumShepherd(5) 6 39
(Alan McCabe) *rrd s and v.s.a: a in rr: rn wd bnd 2f out* **33/1**

1345 **10** *9* **Divertimenti (IRE)**[13] 6120 10-8-2 56 oh5..................(b) KevinLundie(5) 7 4
(Roy Bowring) *chsd ldrs on outer: drvn over 2f out: c wd: lost pl over 1f out: eased whn bhd ins fnl f* **20/1**

1m 16.27s (-0.63) **Going Correction** -0.15s/f (Firm)
**WFA** 3 from 4yo+ 2lb **10** Ran SP% **115.4**
Speed ratings (Par 103): **98,97,95,91,91 91,90,88,84,72**
CSF £8.73 CT £239.70 TOTE £3.70: £1.40, £1.60, £4.50; EX 9.90 Trifecta £167.50.
**Owner** Michael Appleby **Bred** Matthew Sharkey & Newsells Park Stud Ltd **Trained** Danethorpe, Notts

**FOCUS**
A modest apprentice event in which all bar four were out of the handicap. The winner is rated back to his best.
T/Plt: £48.90 to a £1 stake. Pool: £60,688.45 - 905.82 winning units. T/Qpdt: £18.50 to a £1 stake. Pool: £3210.47 - 127.80 winning units. WG

## 6462 YARMOUTH (L-H)
### Thursday, September 18

**OFFICIAL GOING: Good (good to firm in places) 7.4**
Yarmouth's last meeting before it shuts for remedial work on the track. It's scheduled to reopen in June 2915.
Wind: light, across Weather: sunny and warm

## 6496 GREENE KING BRITISH STALLION STUDS EBF SPRINT MAIDEN STKS 6f 3y
**2:20** (2:20) (Class 5) 2-Y-O £3,150 (£943; £471; £236; £117) **Stalls** Centre

Form RPR

**1** **Very Special (IRE)** 2-9-0 0..............................[1] JamesDoyle 5 87+
(Saeed bin Suroor) *stdd s: hld up in rr: clsd over 2f out: rdn to ld jst over 1f out: sn clr and r.o strly: readily* **6/1**[3]

**2** *5* **Temperance Society (IRE)** 2-9-5 0.............................. RyanMoore 4 75+
(Richard Fahey) *in tch in midfield: rdn 2f out: sn outpcd and lost pl: rallied and styd on wl ins fnl f: wnt 2nd fnl 75yds: no threat to wnr* **9/1**

53 **3** *1 ½* **Aledaid (IRE)**[104] 2964 2-9-5 0.............................. FrankieDettori 6 71
(Richard Hannon) *racd in last trio: niggled along 4f out: rdn and hdwy to chse ldr 2f out: led over 1f out: sn hdd and outpcd: lost 2nd fnl 75yds* **4/5**[1]

33 **4** *½* **Rahmah (IRE)**[26] 5671 2-8-12 0.............................. AhmadAlSubousi(7) 1 69
(Robert Cowell) *chsd ldrs: rdn and pressed ldrs over 1f out: wknd ins fnl f* **9/2**[2]

54 **5** *1 ½* **Shipwright (IRE)**[14] 6059 2-9-5 0.............................. RoystonFfrench 2 65
(Mark Johnston) *led tl 4f out: struggling whn sltly hmpd and swtchd rt 2f out: wknd over 1f out* **12/1**

**6** *¾* **Penny Dreadful** 2-9-0 0.............................. LukeMorris 3 57
(Scott Dixon) *dwlt: a towards rr: rdn over 2f out: no imp* **100/1**

0 **7** *2 ¼* **The Olympus Man**[9] 6203 2-9-5 0.............................. JamieSpencer 7 56
(Eve Johnson Houghton) *racd keenly and hung lft thrght: sn chsd ldr: led 4f out tl over 1f out: fdd ins fnl f* **50/1**

1m 11.7s (-2.70) **Going Correction** -0.225s/f (Firm) **7** Ran SP% **108.7**
Speed ratings (Par 95): **109,102,100,99,97 96,93**
CSF £51.03 TOTE £4.30: £3.30, £5.50; EX 23.00 Trifecta £79.70.
**Owner** Godolphin **Bred** Ballylinch Stud **Trained** Newmarket, Suffolk

**FOCUS**
A fair maiden that was won in quite taking style by the Godolphin newcomer.

## 6497 BRITISH STALLION STUDS EBF / KEN LINDSEY MEMORIAL MAIDEN STKS 1m 3y
**2:50** (2:51) (Class 5) 2-Y-O £3,234 (£962; £481; £240) **Stalls** Centre

Form RPR

2 **1** **Bartholomew Fair**[36] 5315 2-9-5 0.............................. AndreaAtzeni 9 83+
(Luca Cumani) *trckd ldrs: upsides ldr on bit over 2f out: nudged into ld 1f out: readily drew clr fnl 100yds: v easily* **4/7**[1]

0 **2** *3 ¼* **Royal Altitude**[14] 6056 2-9-5 0.............................. TedDurcan 3 72+
(Chris Wall) *led: rdn 2f out: hdd 1f out: brushed aside by wnr fnl 100yds: kpt on for clr 2nd* **50/1**

**3** *3 ¾* **Donna Graciosa (GER)** 2-9-0 0.............................. RoystonFfrench 7 58
(Mark Johnston) *chsd ldr tl over 2f out: 3rd and btn over 1f out: wl hld but plugged on to hold 3rd fnl f* **20/1**

**4** *1 ¼* **Rewritten** 2-9-5 0.............................. AdamKirby 5 60
(Charlie Appleby) *dwlt: in tch in last pair: rdn over 2f out: no ch w ldrs over 1f out: plugged on to go modest 4th ins fnl f* **8/1**[3]

00 **5** *1 ½* **Je T'Aime Encore**[17] 5981 2-9-5 0.............................. LukeMorris 6 57
(Gay Kelleway) *chsd ldrs: 4th and struggling whn wandered u.p wl over 1f out: no ch 1f out: lost 4th ins fnl f* **100/1**

**6** *¾* **Chief Spirit** 2-9-5 0.............................. StevieDonohoe 2 55
(James Eustace) *s.i.s: in rr: rdn over 2f out: no imp and outpcd 2f out: no ch over 1f out* **66/1**

**7** *2* **High Valley** 2-9-5 0.............................. MartinLane 4 50
(Charlie Appleby) *dwlt and rn green early: rdn over 2f out: sn btn: bhd over 1f out* **9/1**

**8** *2 ¾* **Jakodima (IRE)** 2-9-5 0.............................. RichardHughes 1 44
(Richard Hannon) *in tch in midfield: lost pl and rdn over 2f out: bhd and no ch 2f out* **6/1**[2]

0 **9** *6* **Keep Up (GER)**[27] 5646 2-9-5 0.............................. JamesDoyle 8 30
(Saeed bin Suroor) *t.k.h: in tch in midfield: rdn and btn over 2f out: bhd over 1f out* **8/1**[3]

1m 38.76s (-1.84) **Going Correction** -0.225s/f (Firm) **9** Ran SP% **119.4**
Speed ratings (Par 95): **100,96,93,91,90 89,87,84,78**
CSF £55.29 TOTE £1.50: £1.10, £10.00, £7.00; EX 37.10 Trifecta £385.40.
**Owner** Sheikh Mohammed Obaid Al Maktoum **Bred** Hascombe And Valiant Studs **Trained** Newmarket, Suffolk

**FOCUS**
Plenty of good yards were represented in this maiden and an impressive winner.

## 6498 SEAJACKS H'CAP 7f 3y
**3:20** (3:20) (Class 3) (0-90,90) 3-Y-O+ £7,439 (£2,213; £1,106; £553) **Stalls** Centre

Form RPR

6652 **1** **Red Refraction (IRE)**[33] 5444 4-9-6 89.............................. RyanMoore 7 101
(Richard Hannon) *hld up in tch in last pair: rdn and hdwy over 2f out: drvn to ld over 1f out: drew clr 1f out: styd on strly* **3/1**[2]

5-44 **2** *5* **Democretes**[13] 6097 5-9-7 90.............................. RichardHughes 6 89
(Seamus Durack) *hld up in tch in last trio: clsd 3f out: rdn: racd awkwardly and fnd little 2f out: no ch w wnr but kpt on ins fnl f to go 2nd towards fin* **4/1**[3]

-500 **3** *½* **The Confessor**[50] 4783 7-9-1 84.............................. DaneO'Neill 4 82
(Henry Candy) *chsd ldr: rdn over 2f out: ev ch tl unable qck w wnr 1f out: wl hld and one pce fnl f: lost 2nd towards fin* **10/1**

6560 **4** *¾* **Luhaif**[6] 6285 4-8-5 79..............................(b) ShelleyBirkett(5) 5 75
(Julia Feilden) *bustled along early: chsd ldrs tl led 4f out: rdn over 2f out: hdd over 1f out: no ch w wnr and plugged on same pce fnl f* **20/1**

0210 **5** *nk* **Little Shambles**[5] 6320 3-9-3 89.............................. RoystonFfrench 1 83
(Mark Johnston) *led tl 4f out: rdn over 2f out: drvn and styd on same pce fr over 1f out* **11/2**

-154 **6** *½* **Sir Mike**[90] 3431 5-9-6 89.............................. FrankieDettori 3 83
(Luca Cumani) *in tch: rdn and effrt jst over 2f out: no imp: wl hld and plugged on same pce fnl f* **5/2**[1]

3000 **7** *¾* **Set The Trend**[1] 6466 8-8-9 78.............................. LukeMorris 2 70
(David Dennis) *rdn along early: in tch in midfield: rdn 1/2-way: dropped to rr 2f out: plugged on same pce and wl hld after* **14/1**

1m 23.81s (-2.79) **Going Correction** -0.225s/f (Firm)
**WFA** 3 from 4yo+ 3lb **7** Ran SP% **109.5**
Speed ratings (Par 107): **106,100,99,98,98 97,97**
CSF £14.00 TOTE £3.00: £1.70, £3.10; EX 7.80 Trifecta £69.40.
**Owner** Middleham Park Racing IV & James Pak **Bred** Tally-Ho Stud **Trained** East Everleigh, Wilts

**FOCUS**
What had looked quite a tight handicap was won in dominant fashion by Red Refraction, who improved again.

## 6499 AT THE RACES NURSERY H'CAP (BOBIS RACE) 7f 3y
**3:50** (3:50) (Class 4) (0-85,81) 2-Y-O £4,010 (£1,193; £596; £298) **Stalls** Centre

Form RPR

2120 **1** **Panda Spirit (USA)**[47] 4913 2-9-7 81.............................. RyanMoore 4 85
(Sir Michael Stoute) *wl in tch in midfield: clsd to chse ldr 3f out: rdn to ld over 1f out: sustained battle w runner-up fnl f: jst prevailed* **4/1**[2]

3221 **2** *shd* **Al Bandar (IRE)**[30] 5519 2-9-3 77.............................. RichardHughes 2 81+
(Richard Hannon) *chsd ldr tl 3f: styd chsng ldrs: rdn over 2f out: drvn and ev ch over 1f out: sustained battled w wnr fnl f: jst hld* **6/4**[1]

105 **3** *2* **Great Park (IRE)**[19] 5929 2-8-11 74.............................. AshleyMorgan(3) 1 73
(Martyn Meade) *t.k.h: chsd ldrs: rdn and effrt wl over 1f out: kpt on same pce ins fnl f: snatched 3rd last stride* **11/1**

0455 **4** *shd* **Gea And Tea**[13] 6108 2-8-8 68.............................. AndreaAtzeni 3 66
(Robert Eddery) *hld up in tch: rdn and hdwy 2f out: ev ch over 1f out: no ex and outpcd fnl 100ydslost 3rd last stride* **8/1**

510 **5** *¾* **Honey Required**[19] 5929 2-8-4 64.............................. RoystonFfrench 6 60
(Alan Bailey) *led: rdn over 2f out: hdd over 1f out: unable qck 1f out: hld and one pce fnl f* **25/1**

3100 **6** *nk* **Tachophobia**[28] 5607 2-9-4 78.............................. JamesDoyle 7 73
(Richard Fahey) *in tch: rdn over 2f out: edging lft and no imp over 1f out: one pce fnl f* **13/2**

31 **7** *2* **Cape Xenia**[17] 5982 2-8-12 72.............................. DaneO'Neill 5 62
(Henry Candy) *s.i.s: in tch in rr: swtchd lft 5f out: no imp u.p over 1f out* **6/1**[3]

1m 25.18s (-1.42) **Going Correction** -0.225s/f (Firm) **7** Ran SP% **110.9**
Speed ratings (Par 97): **99,98,96,96,95 95,93**
CSF £9.76 TOTE £4.90: £2.30, £1.30; EX 11.50 Trifecta £100.50.
**Owner** Robert Ng **Bred** SF Bloodstock LLC **Trained** Newmarket, Suffolk
■ Stewards' Enquiry : Richard Hughes one-day ban: careless riding (Oct 2)

**FOCUS**
The right horses came to the fore in this nursery.

## 6500 HUNDRED HERRING CLUB FILLIES' H'CAP 1m 3f 101y
**4:20** (4:21) (Class 4) (0-80,80) 3-Y-O+ £5,045 (£1,501; £750; £375) **Stalls** Low

Form RPR

1054 **1** **Placidia (IRE)**[15] 6044 3-9-5 80.............................. GeorgeBaker 3 90+
(David Lanigan) *chsd ldrs: clsd to trck ldrs 4f out: led on bit 2f out: sn wnt clr: eased towards fin: nt extended* **9/4**[1]

3314 **2** *2* **Last Minute Lisa (IRE)**[7] 6264 4-9-5 73.............................. RichardHughes 4 76
(Sylvester Kirk) *stdd s: hld up in last: clsd and wl in tch over 3f out: rdn 2f out: no ch w wnr but kpt on to go 2nd wl ins fnl f* **3/1**[2]

3322 **3** *½* **The Ducking Stool**[14] 6062 7-8-11 70.............................. ShelleyBirkett(5) 6 72
(Julia Feilden) *led for 2f: chsd ldr after: rdn and ev ch 3f out tl 2f out: no ch w wnr and kpt on same pce after* **10/3**[3]

6414 **4** *nk* **Dutch Rifle**[15] 6026 3-8-13 74.............................. RyanMoore 2 76
(James Tate) *chsd ldr tl led after 2f out: rdn and hdd 2f out: outpcd by wnr and btn over 1f out: kpt on same pce and lost 2 pls wl ins fnl f* **7/2**

540 **5** *½* **Roxy Hart**[22] 5831 3-8-6 67.............................. LukeMorris 1 68
(Ed Vaughan) *hld up in 4th: dropped to last and rdn 3f out: no ch w wnr and kpt on same pce fnl f* **12/1**

2m 27.56s (-1.14) **Going Correction** -0.225s/f (Firm)
**WFA** 3 from 4yo+ 7lb **5** Ran SP% **108.8**
Speed ratings (Par 102): **95,93,93,92,92**
CSF £8.98 TOTE £2.90: £1.70, £2.00; EX 9.40 Trifecta £23.10.
**Owner** B E Nielsen **Bred** Bjorn Nielsen **Trained** Upper Lambourn, Berks

**FOCUS**
An ordinary handicap run at a steady pace. The winner was value for a bit extra.

## 6501 DAN HAGUE RAILS BOOKMAKER H'CAP 1m 6f 17y
**4:50** (4:50) (Class 2) (0-100,98) 3-Y-O£12,602 (£3,772; £1,886; £944; £470) **Stalls** High

Form RPR

4010 **1** **Semeen**[27] 5651 5-9-7 91.............................. AndreaAtzeni 3 97+
(Luca Cumani) *hld up in last pair: rdn 4f out: clsd on ldr over 2f out: drvn and ev ch over 1f out: drifting lft after: styd on to ld fnl 150yds: rdn out* **7/2**[2]

0300 **2** ½ **Lady Kashaan (IRE)**[12] 6133 5-9-3 87 JamieSpencer 1 92
(Alan Swinbank) *stdd s: hld up in rr: clsd on ldr over 2f out: drvn to ld over 1f out: hdd fnl 150yds: kpt on but a hld after* **9/2[3]**

4520 **3** ½ **Ex Oriente (IRE)**[11] 6169 5-8-9 79 oh3 AdamBeschizza 2 83
(Stuart Williams) *hld up in midfield: rdn and clsd on ldr 3f out: ev ch over 1f out: unable qck fnl 100yds* **25/1**

4100 **4** 3 **Swivel**[6] 6287 3-9-0 94 RoystonFfrench 4 94
(Mark Johnston) *chsd ldr: rdn 4f out: clsd u.p over 2f out: ev ch over 1f out tl ins fnl f: wknd fnl 100yds* **6/1**

0-11 **5** 7 **Mick Duggan**[41] 5137 4-8-10 80 JamesDoyle 6 70
(Ralph Beckett) *chsd ldrs: rdn and clsd on ldr 3f out: ev ch over 1f out: wknd 1f out* **5/1**

-100 **6** 1¾ **Dare To Achieve**[26] 5693 4-10-0 98 (p) RyanMoore 7 86
(William Haggas) *racd keenly: led and wnt wl clr 12f out: rdn over 2f out: drvn and hdd over 1f out: wknd 1f out* **15/8[1]**

3m 1.12s (-6.48) **Going Correction** -0.225s/f (Firm)
**WFA** 3 from 4yo+ 10lb **6** Ran SP% **110.0**
Speed ratings (Par 109): **109,108,108,106,102 101**
CSF £18.44 TOTE £4.40: £2.30, £2.90; EX 23.50 Trifecta £179.70.
**Owner** Sheikh Mohammed Obaid Al Maktoum **Bred** Darley **Trained** Newmarket, Suffolk
■ Stewards' Enquiry : Andrea Atzeni one-day ban: careless riding (Oct 2)

**FOCUS**
A good-quality handicap in which the first three came from the back. The third is a bit of doubt over the form.

## 6502 BARTHOLOMEWS JEWELLERS OF GREAT YARMOUTH H'CAP (BOBIS RACE) 2m
**5:20** (5:20) (Class 4) (0-85,85) 3-Y-O **£5,045** (£1,501; £750; £375) **Stalls** High

Form RPR

-512 **1** **Moscato**[27] 5628 3-8-5 69 LukeMorris 1 78+
(Sir Mark Prescott Bt) *mde all: sn clr: hung rt bnd and rdn 5f out: stl clr and u.p over 2f out: drvn: drifted rt but styd on wl fr over 1f out* **15/8[1]**

0411 **2** 2¼ **Jelly Fish**[12] 6143 3-9-7 85 (t) JamesDoyle 3 91
(Amanda Perrett) *chsd wnr thrght: rdn over 3f out: clsd and 2 l down whn drifted rt over 1f out: no imp fnl f* **5/2[2]**

61U0 **3** 2 **Mantou (IRE)**[12] 6137 3-9-4 82 JamieSpencer 2 86
(Michael Bell) *hld up in rr: rdn and effrt 3f out: hdwy u.p to go 3rd 1f out: no imp after* **5/1**

-631 **4** 4½ **Hoist The Colours (IRE)**[41] 5135 3-9-7 85 (b) GeorgeBaker 4 83
(David Lanigan) *hld up in 3rd: rdn and effrt over 3f out: sme hdwy over 2f out: dropped to 4th and btn 1f out: wknd* **11/4[3]**

3m 33.26s (0.86) **Going Correction** -0.225s/f (Firm) **4** Ran SP% **106.7**
Speed ratings (Par 103): **88,86,85,83**
CSF £6.58 TOTE £2.60; EX 5.80 Trifecta £20.00.
**Owner** The Green Door Partnership **Bred** Miss K Rausing **Trained** Newmarket, Suffolk

**FOCUS**
A fair staying handicap. The winner should do better.
T/Plt: £127.40 to a £1 stake. Pool: £60,253.88 - 345.05 winning units. T/Qpdt: £12.50 to a £1 stake. Pool: £5646.54 - 333.95 winning units. SP

6503 - 6508a (Foreign Racing) - See Raceform Interactive

# 6473 AYR (L-H)
### Friday, September 19

**OFFICIAL GOING: Good (good to firm in places; 8.7; sprint course: stands' side 8.5, centre 8.6, far side 8.7)**
Wind: Light, half behind Weather: Overcast

## 6509 BRITISH STALLION STUDS EBF MAIDEN STKS (BOBIS RACE) 7f 50y
**1:30** (1:32) (Class 4) 2-Y-O **£5,175** (£1,540; £769; £384) **Stalls** High

Form RPR

63 **1** **Lostock Hall (IRE)**[25] 5760 2-9-5 0 DanielTudhope 8 84+
(K R Burke) *prom: rdn and hdwy to ld appr fnl f: drvn out* **9/4[1]**

324 **2** 1 **Henrytheaeroplane (USA)**[47] 4935 2-9-5 81 TonyHamilton 1 81
(Richard Fahey) *t.k.h: cl up: led 3f out: rdn and hdd appr fnl f: kpt on* **7/2[2]**

**3** ¾ **Lord Of The Rock (IRE)** 2-9-5 0 PaulMulrennan 2 79+
(Michael Dods) *dwlt: sn prom: n.m.r fr over 2f out tl swtchd rt ins fnl f: kpt on: bttr for r* **9/2[3]**

4 **4** hd **Properus (IRE)**[44] 5050 2-9-5 0 GrahamLee 7 79
(Kevin Ryan) *cl up: ev ch over 2f out to over 1f out: kpt on same pce ins fnl f* **13/2**

**5** 4 **Mythical City (IRE)** 2-9-0 0 JoeFanning 3 64+
(Mark Johnston) *dwlt: hld up: hdwy to chse ldrs 2f out: pushed along and outpcd fnl f* **33/1**

**6** 1 **Count Montecristo (FR)** 2-9-5 0 JamieSpencer 4 68+
(Kevin Ryan) *missed break: hld up: hdwy on outside 2f out: shkn up and no imp fnl f: improve* **15/2**

2 **7** 6 **Jewelled Prince**[38] 5264 2-9-5 0 DavidNolan 9 53
(Richard Fahey) *midfield: effrt and drvn over 2f out: wknd over 1f out* **18/1**

3 **8** ½ **Go Dan Go (IRE)**[22] 5852 2-9-5 0 TomEaves 10 50
(Keith Dalgleish) *hld up: hdwy and in tch 2f out: sn rdn and wknd* **20/1**

0 **9** 8 **Mr Christopher (IRE)**[124] 2359 2-9-5 0 DuranFentiman 5 30
(Noel Wilson) *towards rr: rdn over 3f out: shortlived effrt over 2f out: sn btn* **100/1**

56 **10** 18 **Disushe Star**[14] 6108 2-9-5 0 PhillipMakin 6
(Keith Dalgleish) *led to 3f out: sn rdn and wknd: t.o* **200/1**

1m 31.43s (-1.97) **Going Correction** -0.25s/f (Firm) **10** Ran SP% **110.7**
Speed ratings (Par 97): **101,99,99,98,94 93,86,85,76,55**
CSF £9.16 TOTE £4.60: £1.10, £1.70, £2.60; EX 10.20 Trifecta £56.80.
**Owner** D W Armstrong & Mrs E Burke **Bred** Piercetown Stud **Trained** Middleham Moor, N Yorks

**FOCUS**
The home bend was in two metres, adding approximately six yards to distances between 7f-2m1f. An interesting enough maiden and it ought to produce a few winners.

## 6510 ENABLE SCOTLAND DIAMOND ANNIVERSARY NURSERY H'CAP (BOBIS RACE) 6f
**2:05** (2:06) (Class 2) 2-Y-O
**£15,562** (£4,660; £2,330; £1,165; £582; £292) **Stalls** Centre

Form RPR

2143 **1** **Roossey (IRE)**[13] 6135 2-8-13 84 GrahamLee 11 88
(William Haggas) *cl up against stands' rail: led over 2f out: rdn and r.o strly fnl f: 1st of 8 in gp* **3/1[1]**

1541 **2** 1¼ **Danot (IRE)**[4] 6400 2-8-1 75 6ex JoeyHaynes(3) 7 75
(Keith Dalgleish) *chsd stands' side ldrs: effrt and wnt 2nd 2f out: kpt on same pce ins fnl f: 2nd of 8 in gp* **33/1**

1055 **3** 2½ **George Bowen (IRE)**[17] 6003 2-8-12 83 TonyHamilton 3 78+
(Richard Fahey) *prom centre: effrt 2f out: led that gp ent fnl f: kpt on: nt rch stands' side ldrs: 1st of 4 in gp* **10/1**

1233 **4** ½ **Geordie George (IRE)**[30] 5580 2-9-2 92 JoeDoyle(5) 9 83
(John Quinn) *hld up bhd ldng gp stands' side: drvn and outpcd over 2f out: rallied fnl f: no imp: 3rd of 8 in gp* **5/1[3]**

210 **5** shd **Doc Charm**[50] 4822 2-8-13 84 TomEaves 8 75
(Keith Dalgleish) *dwlt: hld up in tch stands' side: rdn over 2f out: kpt on ins fnl f: nvr able to chal: 4th of 8 in gp* **16/1**

451 **6** 1 **Heaven's Secret (IRE)**[24] 5799 2-8-7 78 PatrickMathers 6 66
(Richard Fahey) *t.k.h: in tch stands' side gp: rdn and outpcd over 2f out: kpt on ins fnl f: 5th of 8 in gp* **16/1**

641 **7** ½ **Honeysuckle Lil (IRE)**[14] 6115 2-7-13 77 RachelRichardson(7) 4 65+
(Tim Easterby) *t.k.h: cl up centre: led that gp over 2f out to ent fnl f: kpt on same pce: 2nd of 4 in gp* **14/1**

4211 **8** 1¼ **Johnny B Goode (IRE)**[17] 6003 2-8-6 80 ow1 GeorgeChaloner(3) 12 63
(Richard Fahey) *hung lft thrght: led stands' side gp to 2f out: sn rdn and no ex: 6th of 8 in gp* **10/1**

2400 **9** 2 **Denzille Lane (IRE)**[13] 6128 2-8-11 82 (b[1]) FrannyNorton 2 61+
(Mark Johnston) *t.k.h: led centre gp to over 2f out: wknd over 1f out: 3rd of 4 in gp* **25/1**

161 **10** 1¾ **Son Of Africa**[49] 4853 2-9-4 89 DanielTudhope 1 62+
(Henry Candy) *chsd centre ldrs: ev ch whn drifted to far rail fr over 2f out: btn over 1f out: last of 4 in gp* **4/1[2]**

1234 **11** ½ **Enlace**[20] 5921 2-9-0 85 JoeFanning 5 55
(Mark Johnston) *chsd stands' side ldrs tl rdn and wknd fr 2f out: 7th of 8 in gp* **13/2**

5600 **12** 8 **Cabbies Lou**[9] 6222 2-8-1 72 oh9 ow1 DuranFentiman 10 18
(Noel Wilson) *dwlt: bhd and outpcd stands' side: no ch fr over 2f out: last of 8 in gp* **150/1**

1m 10.44s (-1.96) **Going Correction** -0.325s/f (Firm) **12** Ran SP% **119.1**
Speed ratings (Par 101): **100,98,95,94,94 92,92,90,87,85 84,74**
CSF £115.24 CT £911.61 TOTE £4.90: £1.80, £9.90, £3.60; EX 135.10 Trifecta £2471.90.
**Owner** Sheikh Ahmed Al Maktoum **Bred** Ballyreddin Stud **Trained** Newmarket, Suffolk

**FOCUS**
Not that many runners yet they were spread all over the place in what was an unsatisfactory contest.

## 6511 WILLIAM HILL AYR BRONZE CUP H'CAP 6f
**2:40** (2:42) (Class 2) 3-Y-O+
**£18,675** (£5,592; £2,796; £1,398; £699; £351) **Stalls** Centre

Form RPR

3051 **1** **Expose**[9] 6235 6-9-8 82 5ex DavidNolan 27 93
(Shaun Harris) *midfield on stands' side: stdy hdwy over 1f out: rdn to ld wl ins fnl f: kpt on wl: 1st of 16 in gp* **12/1**

2145 **2** 1¼ **Iseemist (IRE)**[27] 5675 3-9-3 84 ShaneGray(5) 19 91
(John Gallagher) *chsd stands' side ldr: rdn and led that gp over 1f out: hdd wl ins fnl f: kpt on: 2nd of 16 in gp* **25/1**

0140 **3** hd **My Name Is Rio (IRE)**[21] 5888 4-9-10 84 PaulMulrennan 11 90
(Michael Dods) *prom stands' side: rdn and ev ch ins fnl f: hung lft: kpt on same pce towards fin: 3rd of 16 in gp* **12/1**

1614 **4** ½ **Dissent (IRE)**[23] 5830 5-9-1 78 (b) ConnorBeasley(3) 15 82
(James Given) *taken early to post: led stands' side gp: rdn over 2f out: hdd over 1f out: kpt on same pce ins fnl f: 4th of 16 in gp* **33/1**

1223 **5** shd **Mishaal (IRE)**[14] 6095 4-9-7 81 DaleSwift 24 85
(Michael Herrington) *in tch stands' side: rdn over 2f out: rallied over 1f out: carried lft ins fnl f: kpt on: 5th of 16 in gp* **4/1[1]**

1400 **6** 1 **Midnight Dynamo**[14] 6109 7-9-1 75 PhillipMakin 25 76
(Jim Goldie) *midfield stands' side: rdn over 2f out: kpt on ins fnl f: nvr able to chal: 6th of 16 in gp* **33/1**

2033 **7** nk **Ralphy Boy (IRE)**[7] 6285 5-8-13 78 GarryWhillans(5) 18 78
(Alistair Whillans) *towards rr stands' side: drvn over 2f out: hdwy over 1f out: kpt on fnl f: no imp: 7th of 16 in gp* **33/1**

4000 **8** nse **Rothesay Chancer**[21] 5888 6-9-5 79 GrahamLee 26 79
(Jim Goldie) *hld up stands' side: rdn and hdwy over 1f out: kpt on fnl f: nrst fin: 8th of 16 in gp* **16/1**

2460 **9** ¾ **Mon Brav**[28] 5650 7-9-5 79 BarryMcHugh 23 80
(Brian Ellison) *bhd stands' side: rdn along 1/2-way: hdwy whn n.m.r ins fnl f: kpt on: 9th of 16 in gp* **14/1**

6120 **10** ½ **Bajan Bear**[8] 6260 6-9-5 79 AdrianNicholls 4 75+
(David Nicholls) *prom far side: rdn to ld that gp over 1f out: hung rt: kpt on fnl f: no ch w stands' side ldrs: 1st of 8 in gp* **20/1**

2303 **11** shd **Gran Canaria Queen**[17] 6013 5-9-5 79 DavidAllan 22 74
(Tim Easterby) *midfield stands' side: drvn along over 2f out: no imp fr over 1f out: 10th of 16 in gp* **9/1[3]**

5110 **12** ½ **Searchlight**[27] 5696 3-9-10 86 JamieSpencer 21 80
(Kevin Ryan) *chsd stands' side ldrs: drvn along over 2f out: no ex fr over 1f out: 11th of 16 in gp* **18/1**

1312 **13** nk **Layla's Hero (IRE)**[17] 6013 7-9-2 76 5ex (v) FrannyNorton 7 69+
(David Nicholls) *hld up bhd ldng gp far side: rdn and hdwy over 1f out: r.o ins fnl f: 2nd of 8 in gp* **16/1**

0035 **14** ½ **Rasaman (IRE)**[14] 6094 10-9-4 81 GaryBartley(3) 3 72+
(Jim Goldie) *in tch far side gp: effrt and hdwy over 1f out: kpt on ins fnl f: 3rd of 8 in gp* **25/1**

4022 **15** hd **Gatepost (IRE)**[7] 6281 5-9-5 82 GeorgeChaloner(3) 8 73+
(Richard Fahey) *chsd far side ldrs: effrt and rdn over 1f out: kpt on same pce ins fnl f: 4th of 8 in gp* **8/1[2]**

2001 **16** hd **Ambitious Icarus**[2] 6452 5-9-4 78 5ex (e) PatrickMathers 14 68
(Richard Guest) *taken early to post: hld up stands' side: rdn over 2f out: no imp fr over 1f out: 12th of 16 in gp* **40/1**

3006 **17** nk **Mississippi**[8] 6260 5-9-10 84 (b) GrahamGibbons 12 73
(David Barron) *bhd stands' side: drvn along 1/2-way: nvr able to chal: 13th of 16 in gp* **20/1**

6366 **18** ¾ **Jack Luey**[34] 5419 7-9-9 83 DanielTudhope 9 70+
(Lawrence Mullaney) *prom far side: effrt and edgd lft over 1f out: no ex ins fnl f: 5th of 8 in gp* **20/1**

4311 **19** hd **Cruise Tothelimit (IRE)**[13] 6150 6-9-6 85 8ex GeorgeDowning(5) 1 71+
(Ian Williams) *led far side to over 1f out: sn rdn and no ex: 6th of 8 in gp* **20/1**

00-0 **20** 3¼ **Chester Aristocrat**[14] 6095 5-9-7 81 JasonHart 20 57
(Eric Alston) *bhd stands' side: drvn along 1/2-way: nvr on terms: 14th of 16 in gp* **33/1**

4100 **21** shd **Gold Beau (FR)**[8] 6263 4-9-6 80 AmyRyan 10 55
(Kristin Stubbs) *bhd on outside of stands' side gp: pushed along 1/2-way: sn btn: 15th of 16 in gp* **40/1**

000 **22** 1¾ **Stonefield Flyer**[51] 4783 5-9-6 80......................... TomEaves 13 50
(Keith Dalgleish) *midfield stands' side: struggling over 2f out: sn btn: last of 16 in gp* **33/1**

3101 **23** ¾ **Baron Run**[17] 6013 4-8-13 76 5ex......................... JoeyHaynes(3) 5 43+
(K R Burke) *taken early to post: cl up far side tl rdn and wknd over 1f out: 7th of 8 in gp* **20/1**

4000 **24** 1½ **Fitz Flyer (IRE)**[13] 6150 8-9-6 80.........................(v) JoeFanning 6 42+
(David Nicholls) *hld up far side: rdn whn hmpd over 2f out: sn wknd: last of 8 in gp* **33/1**

1m 9.55s (-2.85) **Going Correction** -0.325s/f (Firm)
**WFA** 3 from 4yo+ 2lb **24** Ran SP% **133.7**
Speed ratings (Par 109): **106,104,104,103,103 101,101,101,100,99 99,99,98,97,97 97,97,96,95,91 91,88,87,85**
CSF £289.70 CT £3721.67 TOTE £17.00: £3.40, £7.00, £3.70, £10.00; EX 555.50 Trifecta £1985.20.
**Owner** The Giggle Factor Partnership **Bred** John And Susan Davis **Trained** Carburton, Notts
■ Polski Max and Galvanize were withdrawn. Prices at time of withdrawal 9/1 and 33/1 respectively. Rule 4 applies to all bets - deduction 10p in the pound.
■ Stewards' Enquiry : Daniel Tudhope one-day ban; careless riding (3rd Oct)

**FOCUS**
The sixth running of the minor consolation race for the main feature. The topweight was on a mark of 85 and there was a spread of only 10lb between the 24 runners. One of the market leaders Polski Max was withdrawn after arriving at the start with undeclared cheekpieces on. They split into two groups but there was a draw bias and the first nine all raced on the stands' side. The time was 0.45 seconds faster than standard and the winner is rated better than ever.

## 6512 VOKERA & GRAHAM THE PLUMBERS' MERCHANT H'CAP (FOR THE SOUTH AYRSHIRE CUP) 5f
**3:10** (3:20) (Class 4) (0-85,85) 3-Y-O+ **£6,469** (£1,925; £962; £481) **Stalls** Centre

Form RPR

2001 **1** **Noble Asset**[14] 6109 3-8-11 76......................... PhillipMakin 14 86
(John Quinn) *sn trcking ldrs stands' side: str run to ld last 75yds: readily* **16/1**

402 **2** 1¼ **Ladweb**[20] 5925 4-9-3 84......................... JoeyHaynes(3) 16 90
(John Gallagher) *w ldrs stands' side: led overall 1f out: hdd and no ex last 75yds* **12/1**

0500 **3** *shd* **Red Baron (IRE)**[9] 6235 5-9-2 83.........................(b) NeilFarley(3) 4 88
(Eric Alston) *sn clr of 4 others far side: led that gp and sn clr: kpt on wl fnl f: 1st of 5 that gp* **50/1**

6526 **4** *nse* **Jofranka**[49] 4859 4-8-11 75......................... GrahamGibbons 13 80
(David Barron) *overall ldr stands' side: hdd 1f out: styd on same pce* **25/1**

2164 **5** *hd* **Classy Anne**[17] 6013 4-8-0 71 oh1......................... RachaelGrant(7) 21 75+
(Jim Goldie) *wnt rt s: in rr stands' side: hdwy over 1f out: nt clr run and swtchd lft ins fnl f: fin strly* **9/1**

0506 **6** 1 **Imperial Legend (IRE)**[9] 6235 5-9-2 80.........................(p) AndrewMullen 20 81
(David Nicholls) *prom stands' side: effrt 2f out: kpt on same pce appr fnl f* **11/2**[1]

302 **7** ½ **Salvatore Fury (IRE)**[6] 6313 4-8-7 71.........................(p) JoeFanning 12 72
(Keith Dalgleish) *mid-div stands' side: hdwy and nt clr run over 1f out: styd on ins fnl f: nt rch ldrs* **8/1**[3]

4310 **8** 1 **Go Go Green (IRE)**[17] 6013 8-8-9 73......................... BenCurtis 23 68
(Jim Goldie) *in rr stands' side: hdwy over 1f out: styng on at fin* **14/1**

2301 **9** *hd* **Distant Past**[13] 6153 3-8-6 76......................... ShaneGray(5) 5 71
(Kevin Ryan) *swtchd lft s and racd slone centre: chsd ldrs: kpt on same pce over 1f out* **20/1**

5510 **10** *nse* **Skye's The Limit**[27] 5696 3-9-0 79......................... TonyHamilton 18 73
(Richard Fahey) *chsd ldrs on stands' side: one pce over 1f out* **14/1**

0022 **11** *nk* **Pea Shooter**[9] 6235 5-8-13 77......................... AdrianNicholls 3 70
(David Nicholls) *chsd clr ldr far side: fdd fnl f: 3rd of 5 that gp* **7/1**[2]

5560 **12** *nk* **Bunce (IRE)**[17] 6013 6-8-11 75......................... PJMcDonald 1 67
(Linda Perratt) *chsd two others far side: kpt on ins fnl f: tk 2nd of 5 in that gp nr fin* **50/1**

2000 **13** ½ **Sandra's Diamond (IRE)**[14] 6112 3-8-13 78.........................(b[1]) TomEaves 22 68
(Keith Dalgleish) *hmpd s: racd stands' side: in rr: kpt on fnl 2f: nvr a factor* **12/1**

1-06 **14** ½ **Boris Grigoriev (IRE)**[20] 5912 5-8-7 71.........................(b) BarryMcHugh 6 60
(Michael Easterby) *swtchd lft s and hld up in last of 5 far side gp: sme hdwy over 1f out: nvr on terms: 4th of 5 that gp* **22/1**

3000 **15** *nk* **Tango Sky (IRE)**[17] 6013 5-8-7 71 oh1.........................(p) PatrickMathers 9 59
(Richard Fahey) *rr-div stands' side: edgd lft over 1f out: nvr a factor* **25/1**

-306 **16** *shd* **Lexington Place**[14] 6096 4-9-4 82......................... JamesSullivan 11 69
(Ruth Carr) *prom stands' side: wknd over 1f out* **33/1**

0030 **17** 1¼ **Chooseday (IRE)**[21] 5888 5-9-5 83.........................(bt[1]) JamieSpencer 10 66
(Kevin Ryan) *mid-div stands': hdwy over 2f out: edgd lft and lost pl over 1f out* **8/1**[3]

0440 **18** 1¾ **Megaleka**[34] 5419 4-9-2 85......................... TimClark(5) 7 61
(Alan Bailey) *chsd ldrs stands' side: edgd lft and lost pl appr fnl f* **25/1**

1150 **19** 1¼ **Mister Manannan (IRE)**[14] 6096 7-9-4 82......................... DavidAllan 17 54
(David Nicholls) *mid-div stands' side: hdwy over 2f out: edgd lft and lost pl over 1f out* **25/1**

63 **20** 5 **Perfect Blossom**[14] 6109 7-8-3 72......................... JoeDoyle(5) 2 26
(Alan Berry) *outpcd 4th of 5 far side: bhd fnl 2f* **50/1**

57.4s (-2.00) **Going Correction** -0.325s/f (Firm)
**WFA** 3 from 4yo+ 1lb **20** Ran SP% **128.0**
Speed ratings (Par 105): **103,101,100,100,100 98,98,96,96,96 95,95,94,93,93 92,90,88,86,78**
CSF £179.27 CT £9262.30 TOTE £19.70: £4.10, £3.20, £9.10, £5.50; EX 264.90 Trifecta £4975.60.
**Owner** Caron & Paul Chapman **Bred** Horizon Bloodstock Limited **Trained** Settrington, N Yorks

**FOCUS**
A strong handicap for the grade and the rating/weight range was similar to the Bronze Cup. Seven of the first eight raced on the stands' side but the third was not beaten far after setting a fast pace in a small group on the far side. The winner built on his latest personal best.

## 6513 EBF STALLIONS HARRY ROSEBERY STKS (LISTED RACE) 5f
**3:45** (3:48) (Class 1) 2-Y-O
**£22,684** (£8,600; £4,304; £2,144; £1,076; £540) **Stalls** Centre

Form RPR

1045 **1** **Accipiter**[13] 6142 2-8-12 90......................... AshleyMorgan 5 94
(Chris Wall) *cl up: effrt and drvn over 1f out: led and hrd pressed ins fnl f: hld on wl towards fin* **25/1**

2010 **2** *hd* **Mind Of Madness (IRE)**[7] 6286 2-9-6 103......................... JamieSpencer 11 101
(David Brown) *hld up: hdwy and swtchd lft 1f out: kpt on wl towards fin: jst hld* **4/1**[2]

1311 **3** *shd* **Squats (IRE)**[13] 6128 2-9-3 96......................... JoeFanning 4 98
(William Haggas) *prom: hdwy over 1f out: ev ch and rdn ins fnl f: kpt on: hld cl home* **3/1**[1]

1020 **4** *nk* **Secret Liaison (IRE)**[55] 4686 2-8-12 75......................... AdrianNicholls 10 92
(James Tate) *led: rdn over 2f out: hdd ins fnl f: kpt on: hld nr fin* **80/1**

110 **5** 1 **Fendale**[27] 5692 2-9-3 92......................... PaulMulrennan 14 97+
(Bryan Smart) *trckd ldrs: effrt and rdn over 1f out: nt clr run ent fnl f: edgd lft and bmpd last 50yds: r.o* **9/2**[3]

2211 **6** *shd* **Miss Mullberry**[24] 5791 2-8-12 85......................... DanielTudhope 12 88
(David O'Meara) *t.k.h: hld up: hdwy whn nt clr run over 1f out: squeezed through wl ins fnl f: kpt on* **12/1**

011 **7** ½ **Al Ghuwariyah (IRE)**[49] 4869 2-8-12 78......................... TonyHamilton 8 86
(Kevin Ryan) *w ldr: drvn over 1f out: keeping on same pce whn bmpd last 50yds* **33/1**

144 **8** ½ **Lightscameraction (IRE)**[27] 5694 2-9-3 0......................... GrahamLee 6 89
(Gay Kelleway) *dwlt: hld up in tch: effrt and rdn over 1f out: kpt on same pce ins fnl f* **18/1**

2110 **9** *hd* **Primrose Valley**[15] 6067 2-8-12 90.........................(p) RoystonFfrench 7 84
(Ed Vaughan) *hld up: rdn over 2f out: effrt and swtchd lft over 1f out: nvr able to chal* **20/1**

0123 **10** 1½ **Al Fareej (IRE)**[27] 5694 2-8-12 97......................... DavidAllan 1 78
(James Tate) *prom: rdn over 2f out: wknd ins fnl f* **10/1**

3215 **11** ½ **Cool Strutter (IRE)**[27] 5694 2-9-3 95......................... PhillipMakin 9 81
(Richard Hannon) *hld up bhd ldng gp: n.m.r briefly wl over 1f out: sn outpcd: n.d after* **20/1**

122 **12** 1¾ **Jane's Memory (IRE)**[81] 3806 2-8-12 0......................... MartinDwyer 15 70
(Rae Guest) *s.i.s: bhd: drvn along 1/2-way: nvr able to chal* **9/2**[3]

1120 **13** 1¼ **Shamrock Sheila (IRE)**[25] 5770 2-8-12 71......................... GrahamGibbons 13 71
(J S Moore) *prom: drvn 2f out: outpcd whn hmpd ent fnl f* **100/1**

1534 **14** 5 **Just The Tip (IRE)**[3] 6427 2-8-12 79......................... TomEaves 2 48
(Keith Dalgleish) *prom on outside tl rdn and wknd over 2f out* **80/1**

58.28s (-1.12) **Going Correction** -0.325s/f (Firm) **14** Ran SP% **123.2**
Speed ratings: **95,94,94,94,92 92,91,90,90,87 87,84,82,74**
CSF £120.64 TOTE £33.40: £7.60, £1.90, £1.70; EX 283.50 Trifecta £2102.60.
**Owner** Follow The Flag Partnership **Bred** The Lavington Stud **Trained** Newmarket, Suffolk

**FOCUS**
A Listed contest but an ordinary, closely matched bunch whose jockeys all wanted to get as close to the stands' rail as possible, and if you ran the race ten times you'd probably get a different result on near enough each occasion.

## 6514 BAM PROPERTIES LTD H'CAP 2m 1f 105y
**4:20** (4:21) (Class 3) (0-95,88) 4-Y-O+ **£9,703** (£2,887; £1,443; £721) **Stalls** Low

Form RPR

533 **1** **Nashville (IRE)**[20] 5924 5-8-7 77......................... GeorgeChaloner(3) 1 86
(Richard Fahey) *chsd ldrs: drvn and outpcd 3f out: rallied to ld over 1f out: hung rt wl ins fnl f: styd on* **15/2**

5000 **2** ½ **Jonny Delta**[42] 5144 7-8-12 79......................... GrahamLee 5 87
(Jim Goldie) *hld up: smooth hdwy over 2f out: effrt and chsd wnr ins fnl f: kpt on: hld nr fin* **8/1**

0015 **3** 3½ **Moidore**[41] 5161 5-9-5 86......................... PhillipMakin 2 90
(John Quinn) *trckd ldrs: hdwy to ld over 2f out: sn rdn: hdd over 1f out: kpt on same pce ins fnl f* **6/1**[3]

40-0 **4** 2¼ **Shrewd**[13] 6133 4-9-7 88......................... JoeFanning 4 90
(Keith Dalgleish) *hld up: stdy hdwy over 2f out: n.m.r over 1f out: kpt on ins fnl f: no imp* **8/1**

5422 **5** ¾ **Nafaath (IRE)**[20] 5924 8-8-9 76......................... PJMcDonald 8 77
(Donald McCain) *chsd ldrs: led 4f out to over 2f out: rdn and wknd appr fnl f* **17/2**

6130 **6** 3 **Albonny (IRE)**[21] 5890 5-8-1 71......................... JoeyHaynes(3) 6 69
(Timothy Jarvis) *hld up in midfield: hdwy to chse ldrs 2f out: sn rdn: wknd appr fnl f* **33/1**

151 **7** 5 **Carraroe Flyer (IRE)**[12] 6179 4-8-1 71 6ex ow2...... ConnorBeasley(3) 7 63
(Adrian Paul Keatley, Ire) *plld hrd: in tch: hdwy and cl up over 3f out: wknd 2f out* **11/4**[1]

213 **8** ¾ **Maoi Chinn Tire (IRE)**[25] 5764 7-8-5 79.........................(t) JoeDoyle(5) 10 68
(Jennie Candlish) *t.k.h: hld up: rdn over 3f out: rallied to chse ldrs 2f out: wknd over 1f out* **18/1**

1332 **9** 13 **Longshadow**[21] 5890 4-8-11 78.........................(v) GrahamGibbons 3 55
(Jason Ward) *cl up: led 1/2-way to 4f out: rdn and wknd over 2f out* **5/1**[2]

6420 **10** 15 **Be Perfect (USA)**[13] 6133 5-9-5 86......................... AdrianNicholls 9 46
(David Nicholls) *t.k.h: led to 1/2-way: cl up tl rdn and wknd over 2f out* **14/1**

3m 47.72s (-7.28) **Going Correction** -0.25s/f (Firm) **10** Ran SP% **117.0**
Speed ratings (Par 107): **107,106,105,104,103 102,99,99,93,86**
CSF £66.37 CT £386.89 TOTE £5.20: £1.80, £3.00, £2.90; EX 83.60 Trifecta £701.80.
**Owner** Dr Marwan Koukash **Bred** B L Harvey & Balmerino Bloodstock **Trained** Musley Bank, N Yorks

**FOCUS**
A fair staying handicap, rated around the runner-up.

## 6515 ENTERPRISE SCREEN 10 YEARS OF VIDEO H'CAP (DIV I) 1m
**4:50** (4:50) (Class 5) (0-70,70) 3-Y-O **£3,881** (£1,155; £577; £288) **Stalls** Low

Form RPR

4563 **1** **Beautiful Stranger (IRE)**[1] 6477 3-9-4 67.........................(p) TomEaves 1 77
(Keith Dalgleish) *stdd s: hld up: stdy hdwy over 2f out: effrt over 1f out: led ins fnl f: pricked ears: pushed out* **11/2**[3]

4252 **2** 2 **Mfiftythreedotcom (IRE)**[43] 5088 3-9-3 69.......(p) GeorgeChaloner(3) 5 74
(Richard Fahey) *in tch: rdn over 2f out: rallied and ev ch over 1f out: chsd wnr ins fnl f: r.o* **15/8**[1]

603 **3** *hd* **Dark Crystal**[30] 5566 3-8-9 63......................... MeganCarberry(5) 6 68
(Linda Perratt) *chsd ldrs: led over 2f out to ins fnl f: kpt on same pce* **11/1**

3204 **4** *nk* **Aran Sky (IRE)**[93] 3360 3-9-1 67......................... JoeyHaynes(3) 9 71
(K R Burke) *prom on outside: rdn over 2f out: rallied over 1f out: kpt on ins fnl f* **4/1**[2]

0333 **5** 1 **Pigeon Pie**[24] 5787 3-9-2 65......................... JoeFanning 3 67
(Mark Johnston) *led to over 4f out: rallied and ev ch over 2f out: one pce fnl f* **7/1**

0632 **6** 1½ **Jimmy Crackle (IRE)**[20] 5917 3-8-7 56.........................(p) BenCurtis 2 55
(Brian Ellison) *prom: drvn along over 2f out: one pce appr fnl f* **15/2**

3555 **7** *hd* **Spirit Of Alsace (IRE)**[23] 5816 3-8-13 62......................... GrahamLee 7 61
(Jim Goldie) *plld hrd: cl up: led over 4f out to over 2f out: rallied: checked and wknd ins fnl f* **20/1**

6530 **8** 1¾ **Slick Indian**[4] 6405 3-8-1 57 ow1.........................(b) AnnaHesketh(7) 4 51
(Michael Easterby) *hld up: rdn over 2f out: hung lft and wknd wl over 1f out* **40/1**

465 **9** *7* **French Flirt**[45] 5007 3-9-7 70........................................ DanielTudhope 8 48
(Timothy Jarvis) *hld up: drvn along 3f out: sn struggling: btn fnl 2f* **20/1**
1m 41.93s (-1.87) **Going Correction** -0.25s/f (Firm) **9** Ran SP% **114.7**
Speed ratings (Par 101): **99,97,96,96,95 94,93,92,85**
CSF £15.70 CT £109.99 TOTE £6.20: £2.50, £1.10, £2.70; EX 13.70 Trifecta £70.60.
**Owner** Weldspec Glasgow Limited **Bred** D Veitch & B Douglas **Trained** Carluke, S Lanarks

**FOCUS**
The pace was not strong in this minor handicap but the winner forged clear turned out quickly. The form makes a fair bit of sense.

## 6516 ENTERPRISE SCREEN 10 YEARS OF VIDEO H'CAP (DIV II) 1m
**5:20** (5:20) (Class 5) (0-70,70) 3-Y-O **£3,881** (£1,155; £577; £288) **Stalls** Low

Form RPR
3244 **1** **Trinity Star (IRE)**[26] 5717 3-9-2 65..............................(p) PaulMulrennan 5 82
(Michael Dods) *prom: effrt over 2f out: drvn to ld ins fnl f: keeping on wl whn veered rt nr fin* **5/1**[3]
1662 **2** *1 ¾* **Inspector Norse**[8] 6262 3-9-7 70........................................ LiamKeniry 8 83
(Sylvester Kirk) *sn led: rdn along 2f out: hdd ins fnl f: kpt on same pce* **7/4**[1]
355- **3** *3 ¾* **Breakable**[333] 7418 3-9-4 67.................................................. DavidAllan 3 71
(Tim Easterby) *early ldr: pressed ldr: effrt and ev ch over 1f out: no ex ins fnl f* **16/1**
320 **4** *1 ¾* **Solid Justice (IRE)**[63] 4420 3-9-3 66........................... GrahamGibbons 4 66
(Jason Ward) *s.i.s: hld up in tch: rdn over 2f out: kpt on ins fnl f: nvr able to chal* **9/1**
1022 **5** *¾* **Musical Molly (IRE)**[30] 5573 3-9-2 65.................................. DaleSwift 7 64
(Brian Ellison) *hld up in tch: rdn along over 2f out: no imp fr over 1f out* **11/1**
6002 **6** *2 ¼* **Neuf Des Coeurs**[17] 6010 3-8-13 62................................ PhillipMakin 9 55
(Keith Dalgleish) *hld up: rdn along over 2f out: no imp fr over 1f out* **11/1**
3333 **7** *hd* **Baltic Fire (IRE)**[21] 5891 3-8-9 61..............................(p) JoeyHaynes(3) 2 54
(K R Burke) *t.k.h: cl up tl rdn and wknd over 1f out* **4/1**[2]
2344 **8** *6* **McCarthy Mor (IRE)**[45] 4997 3-8-8 57........................... TonyHamilton 1 36
(Richard Fahey) *t.k.h: trckd ldrs tl rdn and wknd fr 2f out* **10/1**
6063 **9** *14* **Bannock Town**[22] 5857 3-8-4 56 oh11..................(p) ConnorBeasley(3) 6
(Linda Perratt) *bhd: struggling over 2f out: sn btn: t.o* **100/1**
1m 40.6s (-3.20) **Going Correction** -0.25s/f (Firm) **9** Ran SP% **115.7**
Speed ratings (Par 101): **106,104,100,98,98 95,95,89,75**
CSF £14.16 CT £130.52 TOTE £6.50: £1.50, £1.60, £3.70; EX 18.20 Trifecta £147.30.
**Owner** Trinity Racing **Bred** Ms Natalie Cleary **Trained** Denton, Co Durham

**FOCUS**
They went a fair pace in the second division of this handicap and finished quite well strung out. It was the faster division. A clear best from the winner.
T/Jkpt: Not won. T/Plt: £1,149.30 to a £1 stake. Pool: £112,716.87 - 71.59 winning tickets
T/Qpdt: £368.90 to a £1 stake. Pool: £10,968.70 - 22.00 winning tickets RY

# 5429 NEWBURY (L-H)
Friday, September 19

**OFFICIAL GOING: Good to soft changing to good to soft (soft in places) after race 3 (3:00)**
Wind: Nil Weather: Muggy, thundery shower before racing

## 6517 AL BASTI EQUIWORLD EBF MAIDEN STKS (BOBIS RACE) 6f 8y
**1:50** (1:52) (Class 4) 2-Y-O **£6,469** (£1,925; £962; £481) **Stalls** Centre

Form RPR
42 **1** **Desert Force**[37] 5309 2-9-5 0........................................ RichardHughes 8 84
(Richard Hannon) *mde all: pushed along 2f out: a holding runner-up ins fnl f* **8/1**[3]
3 **2** *1* **Foreign Diplomat**[28] 5655 2-9-5 0.................................... RyanMoore 12 81
(William Haggas) *lw: chsd ldrs: rdn to chal wl over 1f out: kpt on fnl f: a hld* **4/5**[1]
**3** *1 ¼* **Lightning Charlie** 2-9-5 0.................................................. PatDobbs 11 77
(Amanda Perrett) *unf: chsd ldrs: rdn and kpt on fnl 2f* **100/1**
06 **4** *nk* **Awjab (IRE)**[25] 5752 2-9-5 0............................................. DaneO'Neill 14 76
(Brian Meehan) *prom: rdn and one pce appr fnl f* **100/1**
**5** *¾* **Beautiful Ending** 2-9-0 0.............................................. HarryBentley 7 69+
(Saeed bin Suroor) *dwlt: sn in midfield: shkn up and r.o fr over 1f out* **20/1**
0 **6** *2 ½* **Commodore (IRE)**[67] 4270 2-9-5 0................................... PatCosgrave 3 67
(George Baker) *athletic: in tch: effrt over 2f out: one pce appr fnl f* **100/1**
0 **7** *½* **Kill Or Cure (IRE)**[14] 6103 2-9-5 0.................................. JimCrowley 15 65
(Charles Hills) *leggy: chsd ldrs: rdn over 2f out: btn over 1f out* **100/1**
**8** *1 ¼* **Krazy Paving** 2-9-5 0.............................. WilliamTwiston-Davies 19 61+
(Mick Channon) *athletic: towards rr: rdn 3f out: sme late hdwy* **66/1**
**9** *½* **Takafol (IRE)** 2-9-5 0............................................................ PaulHanagan 13 60+
(Charles Hills) *cmpt: t.k.h in midfield: shkn up and no hdwy fnl 2f* **50/1**
**10** *hd* **Poppet Rocket (IRE)** 2-8-11 0................................... RyanClark(3) 16 54+
(Brian Meehan) *dwlt: bhd: shkn up and styd on fr over 1f out* **100/1**
2 **11** *nk* **Encore D'Or**[27] 5671 2-9-5 0...................................... SilvestreDeSousa 17 58
(Ralph Beckett) *tall: lengthy: attractive: lw: in tch: rdn over 2f out: sn btn* **3/1**[2]
60 **12** *½* **Albecq**[10] 6204 2-9-2 0............................................... DeclanBates(3) 5 57+
(David Evans) *towards rr: modest effrt and hrd rdn 2f out: n.d* **100/1**
**13** *½* **My Bubba** 2-9-5 0................................................................ JimmyFortune 18 55+
(Brian Meehan) *athletic: sn pushed along in last pl: styng on at fin* **33/1**
**14** *shd* **Lucy The Painter (IRE)** 2-9-0 0...................................... SteveDrowne 10 50+
(Peter Makin) *leggy: unf: s.s: a towards rr* **100/1**
00 **15** *¾* **Starlight June**[67] 4270 2-9-0 0....................................... LukeMorris 6 48
(Jonathan Portman) *pressed wnr tl over 2f out: sn wknd* **100/1**
**16** *2* **Priors Gate (IRE)** 2-9-5 0............................................... WilliamBuick 9 47+
(Marcus Tregoning) *athletic: sn towards rr* **50/1**
**17** *1* **Royal Silk** 2-9-0 0................................................................ JamesDoyle 20 39+
(Roger Charlton) *athletic: a bhd* **50/1**
**18** *3 ¼* **Beauty Prince** 2-9-5 0...................................................... AdamKirby 2 34
(Clive Cox) *strong: q lengthy: bit bkwd: in tch tl rdn and wknd 3f out* **20/1**
02 **19** *½* **River Dart (IRE)**[19] 5947 2-9-5 0..................................... GeorgeBaker 4 33
(Marcus Tregoning) *lw: prom tl wknd 2f out* **33/1**
1m 16.31s (3.31) **Going Correction** +0.525s/f (Yiel) **19** Ran SP% **122.4**
Speed ratings (Par 97): **98,96,95,94,93 90,89,87,87,87 86,85,85,85,84 81,80,75,75**
CSF £13.41 TOTE £9.50: £2.50, £1.10, £10.40; EX 19.70 Trifecta £535.00.
**Owner** Malih Lahej Al Basti **Bred** Newsells Park Stud **Trained** East Everleigh, Wilts

**FOCUS**
Rail realignment on Round between 5f and 7f increased distances by 4m on that course. They didn't go that quickly in this interesting 2yo maiden, with the field tightly bunched down the centre, and they began to get sorted out nearing the final furlong. Previous experience counted for plenty.

## 6518 DUBAI DUTY FREE FINEST SURPRISE H'CAP 1m 4f 5y
**2:25** (2:25) (Class 3) (0-95,94) 3-Y-O+ **£7,439** (£2,213; £1,106; £553) **Stalls** Low

Form RPR
3341 **1** **Rhombus (IRE)**[41] 5193 4-9-7 94.................................... CamHardie(5) 2 103
(Ismail Mohammed) *lw: lost 8 l s: hdwy into 4th after 2f: effrt over 2f out: led jst ins fnl f: in control whn edgd lft nr fin* **2/1**[1]
6513 **2** *½* **Saab Almanal**[27] 5676 3-9-4 94........................................... TomQueally 4 102
(James Fanshawe) *lw: chsd ldrs: rdn to chal over 2f out: kpt on fnl f: jst hld last 100yds* **9/4**[2]
4115 **3** *¾* **Yaakooum (IRE)**[13] 6137 3-8-8 84.............................. RichardHughes 7 91
(Richard Hannon) *chsd ldr: slt ld over 2f out tl ins fnl f: cl 3rd and jst hld whn n.m.r nr fin* **9/4**[2]
312- **4** *6* **Stock Hill Fair**[414] 4914 6-9-3 85........................................ PatDobbs 8 82
(Brendan Powell) *bit bkwd: led tl over 2f out: wknd over 1f out* **9/1**[3]
405/ **5** *17* **Stand To Reason (IRE)**[244] 7175 6-9-11 93..................... AdamKirby 5 63
(Tony Carroll) *last after 2f: lost tch 3f out* **14/1**
2m 42.07s (6.57) **Going Correction** +0.525s/f (Yiel)
**WFA** 3 from 4yo+ 8lb **5** Ran SP% **111.5**
Speed ratings (Par 107): **99,98,98,94,82**
CSF £6.96 TOTE £2.90: £1.50, £1.70; EX 6.20 Trifecta £15.90.
**Owner** Sheikh Rashid Dalmook Al Maktoum **Bred** Ruskerne Ltd **Trained** Newmarket, Suffolk
■ Stewards' Enquiry : Tom Queally one-day ban; careless riding (3rd Oct)

**FOCUS**
This fair handicap was decimated by non-runners. It was run at an steady pace, resulting in a pedestrian time. a small personal best from the winner.

## 6519 DUBAI DUTY FREE CONDITIONS STKS 1m 1f
**3:00** (3:00) (Class 3) 3-Y-O+ **£7,158** (£2,143; £1,071) **Stalls** Low

Form RPR
2-02 **1** **Code Of Honor**[218] 595 4-8-11 108.............................. RichardHughes 1 103+
(Saeed bin Suroor) *lw: trckd ldr: led over 1f out: in control fnl f: rdn out* **10/11**[1]
-450 **2** *1 ¾* **God Willing**[28] 5656 3-8-6 97............................................. AndreaAtzeni 2 99
(Ed Dunlop) *lw: hld up in 3rd: led and qcknd tempo 2f out: hdd over 1f out: one pce* **7/2**[3]
460 **3** *16* **Highland Knight (IRE)**[54] 4711 7-8-11 105...................(t) DavidProbert 3 63
(Andrew Balding) *led and set modest tempo: hdd 2f out: sn wknd* **2/1**[2]
1m 59.54s (4.04) **Going Correction** +0.525s/f (Yiel)
**WFA** 3 from 4yo+ 5lb **3** Ran SP% **107.9**
Speed ratings (Par 107): **103,101,87**
CSF £4.09 TOTE £1.50; EX 4.50 Trifecta £3.40.
**Owner** Godolphin **Bred** J Byrne And Partners **Trained** Newmarket, Suffolk

**FOCUS**
A good-quality condions event. The winner is rated 7lb off his best.

## 6520 HAYNES, HANSON & CLARK CONDITIONS STKS (BOBIS RACE) (C&G) 1m (S)
**3:35** (3:36) (Class 2) 2-Y-O **£9,960** (£2,982; £1,491; £745; £372) **Stalls** Centre

Form RPR
01 **1** **Snoano**[43] 5093 2-9-1 0....................................................... PaulHanagan 3 98
(John Gosden) *attractive: athletic: trckd ldr: led 3f out: hrd rdn over 1f out: hld on gamely whn chal ins fnl f: all out* **3/1**[3]
200 **2** *shd* **Acaster Malbis (FR)**[8] 6256 2-8-12 0................................. RyanMoore 2 95
(Richard Hannon) *lw: hld up in 4th: chsd wnr over 2f out: drvn level ins fnl f: r.o wl* **9/4**[2]
**3** *7* **Perceus** 2-8-12 0................................................................... WilliamBuick 1 80+
(Marcus Tregoning) *unf: scope: hld up in rr: wnt 3rd 2f out: no ch w ldng pair* **8/1**
2441 **4** *5* **Paddys Motorbike (IRE)**[25] 5745 2-9-1 82.......................... AdamKirby 4 71
(David Evans) *swtg: led tl 3f out: wknd 2f out* **25/1**
1 **5** *15* **Gibeon (IRE)**[42] 5149 2-9-1 0........................................ RichardHughes 5 38
(Richard Hannon) *lengthy: chsd ldrs tl wknd 2f out: eased whn btn* **7/4**[1]
1m 42.8s (3.10) **Going Correction** +0.525s/f (Yiel) **5** Ran SP% **107.1**
Speed ratings (Par 101): **105,104,97,92,77**
CSF £9.53 TOTE £4.10: £2.30, £1.90; EX 11.00 Trifecta £60.70.
**Owner** Hamdan Al Maktoum **Bred** Minster Stud **Trained** Newmarket, Suffolk

**FOCUS**
A contest with a strong tradition, but high-class winners have been thin on the ground in recent years. The first pair had it pretty much to themselves from 2f out and very little separated them at the finish.

## 6521 DUBAI DUTY FREE FULL OF SURPRISES EBF FILLIES' CONDITIONS STKS (BOBIS RACE) 7f (S)
**4:05** (4:06) (Class 2) 2-Y-O **£9,960** (£2,982; £1,491; £745; £372) **Stalls** Centre

Form RPR
12 **1** **Marsh Hawk**[15] 6067 2-9-1 0........................................ RichardHughes 4 96+
(Richard Hannon) *lw: mde all: shkn up over 1f out: edgd lft ins fnl f: comf* **4/7**[1]
1 **2** *3 ½* **Timba**[17] 6001 2-9-1 0....................................................... WilliamBuick 2 87+
(John Gosden) *ang: lw: t.k.h: trckd wnr: chal 2f out: one pce fnl f* **11/4**[2]
**3** *6* **Crystal Zvezda** 2-8-12 0.................................................. RyanMoore 3 69+
(Sir Michael Stoute) *str: gd sort: restless in stalls: dwlt: plld hrd and sn settled in rr: wnt 3rd 2f out: no ch w ldng pair over 1f out* **13/2**[3]
**4** *2 ½* **Just Silca** 2-8-12 0........................................................ SamHitchcott 1 63+
(Mick Channon) *leggy: unf: plld hrd: sn cl up in 3rd: rdn and wknd 2f out* **50/1**
0310 **5** *6* **Sister Of Mercy (IRE)**[20] 5929 2-8-12 82............................ JamesDoyle 5 48
(Roger Charlton) *chsd ldrs tl wknd wl over 1f out* **20/1**
1m 29.43s (3.73) **Going Correction** +0.525s/f (Yiel) **5** Ran SP% **110.4**
Speed ratings (Par 98): **99,95,88,85,78**
CSF £2.42 TOTE £1.60: £1.10, £1.40; EX 2.60 Trifecta £5.50.
**Owner** Rockcliffe Stud **Bred** Rockcliffe Stud **Trained** East Everleigh, Wilts

**FOCUS**
A compelling little 2yo fillies' event and form to be positive about.

## 6522 DUBAI DUTY FREE CUP (LISTED RACE) 7f (S)
**4:40** (4:41) (Class 1) 3-Y-O+
**£20,982** (£7,955; £3,981; £1,983; £995; £499) **Stalls** Centre

Form RPR
3523 **1** **Lady Lara (IRE)**[27] 5690 3-8-8 106 LukeMorris 8 104
(Timothy Jarvis) *in tch: led 2f out and sn qcknd 2 l clr: drvn to hold on fnl 100yds* **6/1**[3]
0200 **2** ½ **Jallota**[50] 4826 3-8-13 98 JimCrowley 3 107
(Charles Hills) *mid-div: hdwy 2f out: chsd wnr over 1f out: clsng at fin: a hld* **40/1**
0-06 **3** 1 ¼ **Brown Sugar (IRE)**[27] 5674 3-8-13 107 RyanMoore 4 104
(Richard Hannon) *lw: bhd: hdwy and edgd lft over 1f out: kpt on same pce fnl f* **16/1**
0620 **4** nk **Sirius Prospect (USA)**[90] 3452 6-9-2 106 RobertWinston 2 104
(Dean Ivory) *lw: towards rr: rdn 3f out: swtchd lft and hdwy over 1f out: nrest at fin* **11/1**
0000 **5** 5 **Loving Spirit**[13] 6140 6-9-2 95 RobertTart 10 91
(James Toller) *mid-div: hrd rdn and hdwy over 1f out: no imp* **20/1**
0141 **6** hd **Safety Check (IRE)**[13] 6124 3-8-13 105 WilliamBuick 5 90
(Charlie Appleby) *trckd ldrs: swtchd rt and lft over 2f out: wknd over 1f out* **4/1**[2]
2003 **7** 1 ¼ **Glen Moss (IRE)**[28] 5653 5-9-2 104 SeanLevey 6 87
(David Brown) *w ldrs tl wknd over 1f out* **7/1**
1021 **8** 1 **Absolutely So (IRE)**[28] 5653 4-9-2 109 OisinMurphy 9 85
(Andrew Balding) *chsd ldr: led over 3f out tl 2f out: sn wknd* **6/4**[1]
4025 **9** 11 **Miracle Of Medinah**[6] 6335 3-8-13 102 StevieDonohoe 1 55
(Mark Usher) *towards rr: rdn 3f out: n.d* **50/1**
0330 **10** 1 ¾ **Rerouted (USA)**[28] 5653 6-9-2 110 (p) PatCosgrave 11 52
(M F De Kock, South Africa) *sn w ldrs and wd of others on stands' rail: wknd wl over 1f out* **25/1**
-100 **11** 18 **Magnus Maximus**[50] 4826 3-8-13 98 RichardHughes 7 4
(Richard Hannon) *led tl over 3f out: wknd over 2f out* **25/1**

1m 29.52s (3.82) **Going Correction** +0.525s/f (Yiel)
**WFA** 3 from 4yo+ 3lb **11** Ran SP% **117.9**
Speed ratings: **99,98,97,96,90 90,89,88,75,73 53**
CSF £231.65 TOTE £7.80: £2.60, £7.30, £2.60; EX 355.30 Trifecta £1783.60.
**Owner** Mrs B V Sangster **Bred** Shanty Syndicate **Trained** Twyford, Bucks

**FOCUS**
Not a bad Listed event, run at a fair pace, although the taxing surface played its part. The principals were all 3yos and the winner confirmed her latest personal best.

## 6523 AL BASTI EQUIWORD H'CAP 1m 2f 6y
**5:10** (5:11) (Class 4) (0-85,85) 3-Y-O+ **£4,690** (£1,395; £697; £348) **Stalls** Low

Form RPR
3411 **1** **Starwatch**[25] 5758 7-9-10 85 (v) WilliamCarson 10 94
(John Bridger) *b.hind: t.k.h: led tl wl over 1f out: rallied ins fnl f: drvn to ld fnl 50yds: gamely* **14/1**
0103 **2** ¾ **Tercel (IRE)**[20] 5930 3-8-9 76 RyanMoore 12 84+
(Sir Michael Stoute) *t.k.h: trckd wnr: led wl over 1f out: gard rdn and hdd fnl 50yds: no ex* **7/2**[1]
6105 **3** 1 ¾ **Sheila's Buddy**[27] 5669 5-9-3 78 RichardHughes 11 82
(J S Moore) *stdd s: hld up in rr: hdwy into midfield and hrd rdn over 1f out: styd on wl fnl f* **8/1**
1-30 **4** 1 **The Alamo (IRE)**[125] 2347 3-8-10 77 PatDobbs 1 79
(Richard Hannon) *trckd ldrs: hrd rdn 2f out: kpt on same pce* **12/1**
2111 **5** ½ **Balmoral Castle**[27] 5669 5-9-3 83 NedCurtis(5) 5 84
(Jonathan Portman) *in tch: drvn to press ldrs 2f out: edgd lft 1f out: no ex* **7/1**
0333 **6** 2 ½ **Gracious George (IRE)**[7] 6303 4-8-4 71 oh2 ow1(p) KieranShoemark(7) 6 69
(Jimmy Fox) *prom tl wknd wl over 1f out* **14/1**
4100 **7** ¾ **Compton Bird**[13] 6141 5-9-2 77 FergusSweeney 2 72
(Paul Fitzsimons) *mid-div: hdwy 2f out: wknd over 1f out* **25/1**
2-0 **8** 3 ¼ **Ty Gwr**[21] 5895 5-9-8 83 DaneO'Neill 8 72
(Brian Ellison) *swtg: stdd s: t.k.h towards rr: rdn over 2f out: nvr able to chal* **13/2**[3]
2402 **9** 3 ¾ **St Paul De Vence (IRE)**[16] 6035 4-8-10 71 oh3 (t) LukeMorris 7 53
(Paul Cole) *bhd: rdn over 2f out: n.d* **20/1**
0413 **10** 2 ¼ **Mazaaher**[21] 5895 4-9-1 76 PaulHanagan 9 54
(B W Hills) *stdd s: hld up in rr: shkn up 2f out: no rspnse* **9/2**[2]
050 **11** 8 **Weapon Of Choice (IRE)**[50] 4827 6-9-10 85 AdamKirby 4 47
(Stuart Kittow) *mid-div: effrt 3f out: wknd 2f out* **9/1**
211 **12** 9 **If I Were A Boy (IRE)**[32] 5503 7-8-10 71 oh1 (p) JimCrowley 3 16
(Dominic Ffrench Davis) *chsd ldrs tl wknd 2f out* **16/1**

2m 12.38s (3.58) **Going Correction** +0.525s/f (Yiel)
**WFA** 3 from 4yo+ 6lb **12** Ran SP% **122.9**
Speed ratings (Par 105): **106,105,104,103,102 100,100,97,94,92 86,79**
CSF £64.84 CT £438.65 TOTE £17.20: £4.50, £2.10, £2.60; EX 84.70 Trifecta £1077.80.
**Owner** J J Bridger **Bred** Mrs J A Chapman **Trained** Liphook, Hants

**FOCUS**
Not a bad handicap. There was a fair enough pace on and the runners stuck to the centre in the home straight. The winner was back towards his old best.
T/Plt: £33.00 to a £1 stake. Pool: £58,241.98 - 1,284.82 winning tickets T/Qpdt: £17.30 to a £1 stake. Pool: £3,060.82 - 130.85 winning tickets LM

6524 - 6528a (Foreign Racing) - See Raceform Interactive

# 6509 AYR (L-H)
### Saturday, September 20

**OFFICIAL GOING: Good to firm (good in places; 8.9; sprint course: stands' side 8.8, centre 8.6, far side 8.8)**
Wind: Breezy, across Weather: Overcast

## 6529 QTS NURSERY H'CAP (BOBIS RACE) 1m
**1:30** (1:30) (Class 2) 2-Y-O
**£12,450** (£3,728; £1,864; £932; £466; £234) **Stalls** High

Form RPR
2131 **1** **Power Play (IRE)**[48] 4944 2-9-6 88 JamesDoyle 3 90
(Richard Hannon) *prom: effrt and drvn over 2f out: plld out over 1f out: led and edgd lft last 40yds: kpt on u.p* **6/1**[3]
642 **2** ½ **Sir Chauvelin**[26] 5759 2-8-0 68 oh1 JamesSullivan 1 69
(Jim Goldie) *s.i.s: hld up on ins: rdn and outpcd over 2f out: rallied over 1f out: ev ch wl ins fnl f: hld cl home* **6/1**[3]
2113 **3** nk **Alans Pride (IRE)**[14] 6151 2-8-8 79 ConnorBeasley(3) 4 79
(Michael Dods) *t.k.h: led: rdn and hdd over 1f out: rallied: kpt on ins fnl f* **7/1**
141 **4** shd **Jumeirah Glory (IRE)**[25] 5782 2-8-10 78 TonyHamilton 7 78
(Richard Fahey) *pressed ldr: rdn to ld over 1f out: hdd last 40yds: one pce whn n.m.r nr fin* **11/2**[2]
31 **5** 1 ¾ **Gabrial The Viking (IRE)**[8] 6279 2-8-5 78 JackGarritty(5) 5 74
(Richard Fahey) *hld up in tch on outside: rdn over 2f out: edgd lft and styd on ins fnl f: nvr able to chal* **4/1**[1]
2100 **6** nse **Gerry The Glover (IRE)**[9] 6256 2-9-2 84 PaulPickard 2 80
(Brian Ellison) *trckd ldrs: rdn over 2f out: kpt on same pce fnl f* **8/1**
3242 **7** 3 **Sculptured (FR)**[10] 6244 2-8-6 74 BenCurtis 6 62
(Jo Hughes) *hld up: effrt on outside over 2f out: no imp fnl f* **22/1**
124 **8** 3 ¼ **Special Venture (IRE)**[14] 6151 2-8-9 77 DavidAllan 9 58
(Tim Easterby) *hld up: rdn along over 2f out: no imp fr over 1f out* **10/1**
3314 **9** 2 ¼ **Divine Law**[40] 5250 2-8-5 78 CamHardie(5) 8 53
(Richard Hannon) *dwlt: bhd: drvn and outpcd over 2f out: sn btn* **25/1**
1604 **9** dht **Chadic**[14] 6136 2-9-7 89 FrannyNorton 10 64+
(Mark Johnston) *trckd ldrs on outside: stdy hdwy over 3f out: rdn whn hmpd and lost pl 2f out: sn n.m.r and btn* **8/1**

1m 41.97s (-1.83) **Going Correction** -0.30s/f (Firm) **10** Ran SP% **116.0**
Speed ratings (Par 101): **97,96,96,96,94 94,91,88,85,85**
CSF £41.64 CT £214.69 TOTE £4.70: £1.50, £2.20, £2.30; EX 48.00 Trifecta £252.50.
**Owner** Mohamed Saeed Al Shahi **Bred** Barnane Stud **Trained** East Everleigh, Wilts
■ Stewards' Enquiry : James Doyle one-day ban: careless riding (6 Oct)

**FOCUS**
Home bend moved 4m and distances on Round course increased by about 12yds. Winning jockey James Doyle said after the first that it was "on the quick side, but lovely ground", while runner-up James Sullivan said it hadn't quickened up much from Friday, "particularly in the back straight where it's good". The time was nearly four seconds outside standard. Top Notch Tonto won this nursery two years ago, while 2004 winner Comic Strip went on to win Grade 1 races in Hong Kong under the name Viva Pataca. They went no more than a fair gallop until the tempo increased in the home straight. Straightforward form.

## 6530 WILLIAM HILL FIRTH OF CLYDE STKS (GROUP 3) (FILLIES) 6f
**2:05** (2:06) (Class 1) 2-Y-O
**£34,026** (£12,900; £6,456; £3,216; £1,614; £810) **Stalls** Centre

Form RPR
3115 **1** **Dark Reckoning**[26] 5770 2-9-0 90 GrahamLee 12 100
(Ann Duffield) *hld up against stands' rail: hdwy whn n.m.r briefly over 1f out: styd on wl fnl f to ld nr fin* **25/1**
4613 **2** shd **Parsley (IRE)**[36] 5380 2-9-0 95 JamesDoyle 10 100
(Richard Hannon) *dwlt: hld up: weaved through fr 2f out: led ins fnl f: kpt on wl: hdd cl home* **9/1**
5 **3** 2 ¼ **Ainippe (IRE)**[8] 6286 2-9-0 0 ColinKeane 9 95
(G M Lyons, Ire) *hld up: hdwy whn nt clr run wl over 1f out: renewed effrt whn checked appr and ent fnl f: kpt on wl: nt rch first two* **3/1**[1]
0215 **4** ½ **Royal Razalma (IRE)**[16] 6067 2-9-0 95 RichardKingscote 13 91
(Jonathan Portman) *cl up: drvn to ld over 1f out: hdd ins fnl f: sn outpcd* **10/1**
3141 **5** 1 ¾ **War Alert (USA)**[7] 6312 2-9-0 85 MartinHarley 15 86
(David Brown) *trckd ldrs: effrt whn hung lft over 1f out: no ex ins fnl f* **12/1**
56 **6** ½ **Blackbriar**[20] 5954 2-9-0 0 (p) BillyLee 16 85
(T Stack, Ire) *led to over 1f out: rdn and wknd ins fnl f* **25/1**
416 **7** hd **Prize Exhibit**[16] 6067 2-9-0 95 DanielTudhope 6 84+
(Jamie Osborne) *dwlt: t.k.h: hld up: hdwy on outside over 1f out: wknd ins fnl f* **6/1**[2]
13 **8** 1 ½ **Marsh Pride**[16] 6071 2-9-0 81 PJMcDonald 4 80
(Ann Duffield) *midfield: drvn and outpcd over 2f out: rallied fnl f: nvr able to chal* **33/1**
4213 **9** 2 ½ **Disprove (IRE)**[17] 6053 2-9-0 83 ChrisHayes 14 72
(Hugo Palmer) *awkward s: plld hrd and sn cl up: rdn and outpcd whn hmpd over 1f out: sn btn* **14/1**
10 **10** ½ **Effusive**[92] 3415 2-9-0 85 PatSmullen 7 72
(William Haggas) *cl up: rdn over 2f out: outpcd whn hmpd appr fnl f* **8/1**[3]
6601 **11** 1 ½ **Spirit Of Xian (IRE)**[21] 5921 2-9-0 95 FMBerry 3 66
(Richard Hannon) *trckd ldrs: rdn over 2f out: wknd ins fnl f* **12/1**
411 **12** 2 **Lady Desire (IRE)**[43] 5129 2-9-0 86 PhillipMakin 8 60
(Keith Dalgleish) *in tch: drvn and outpcd over 2f out: sn btn* **9/1**
0220 **13** ½ **Pastoral Girl**[16] 6067 2-9-0 99 JamesSullivan 5 59
(James Given) *dwlt: hld up: rdn along over 2f out: sn struggling* **28/1**

1m 11.01s (-1.39) **Going Correction** -0.20s/f (Firm) **13** Ran SP% **119.5**
Speed ratings: **101,100,97,97,94 94,93,91,88,87 85,83,82**
CSF £232.28 TOTE £27.00: £5.40, £2.70, £1.70; EX 217.10 Trifecta £2384.90 Part won..
**Owner** Qatar Racing Limited **Bred** Newsells Park Stud **Trained** Constable Burton, N Yorks

**FOCUS**
Not the strongest Group 3 for 2yo fillies. Unsurprisingly the field made a bee-line for the stands' rail nearing the five-furlong marker and that proved the place to be again nearing the finish.

## 6531 WILLIAM HILL AYR SILVER CUP (H'CAP) 6f
**2:40** (2:42) (Class 2) 3-Y-O+
**£31,125** (£9,320; £4,660; £2,330; £1,165; £585) **Stalls** Centre

Form RPR
3623 **1** **Huntsmans Close**[8] 6290 4-9-2 87 JamesDoyle 27 98
(Roger Charlton) *t.k.h: trckd stands' side ldrs: smooth hdwy to ld appr fnl f: sn rdn and edgd rt: kpt on wl: 1st of 16 in gp* **9/1**[2]
0-50 **2** 1 **Mehdi (IRE)**[7] 6320 5-9-2 87 (t) PJMcDonald 26 95
(Richard Fahey) *in tch stands' side: rdn and hdwy over 1f out: chsd wnr ins fnl f: kpt on: 2nd of 16 in gp* **14/1**
0062 **3** 1 ¾ **Bogart**[7] 6327 5-9-8 93 AmyRyan 25 95
(Kevin Ryan) *led stands' side: rdn and hdd appr fnl f: kpt on: 3rd of 16 in gp* **8/1**[1]
0202 **4** hd **Foxtrot Romeo (IRE)**[14] 6159 5-9-9 94 (tp) MartinHarley 18 96
(Marco Botti) *hld up stands' side: rdn and hdwy over 1f out: kpt on ins fnl f: nvr able to chal: 4th of 16 in gp* **14/1**
4222 **5** 1 **Lexington Abbey**[13] 6170 3-9-0 87 PatSmullen 22 86
(Kevin Ryan) *midfield stands' side: rdn along over 2f out: hdwy over 1f out: kpt on fnl f: nrst fin: 5th of 16 in gp* **10/1**[3]
3325 **6** nk **Mission Approved**[9] 6260 4-9-4 89 FMBerry 8 87
(Luca Cumani) *dwlt: swtchd lft and hld up in tch far side: effrt over 1f out: led that gp ins fnl f: kpt on: nt rch stands' side ldrs: 1st of 10 in gp* **16/1**

1214 **7** *nk* **Arctic Feeling (IRE)**[6] 6369 6-8-11 87 5ex................ SammyJoBell(5) 1 84
(Richard Fahey) *prom far side: led that gp over 1f out to ins fnl f: kpt on: 2nd of 10 in gp* **20/1**

2330 **8** *hd* **Tatlisu (IRE)**[6] 6369 4-9-7 92.............................. GrahamLee 7 88
(Richard Fahey) *hld up far side: rdn and hdwy over 1f out: kpt on ins fnl f: 3rd of 10 in gp* **16/1**

0004 **9** *nse* **Santefisio**[14] 6140 8-9-10 95..............................(b) PhillipMakin 20 91
(Keith Dalgleish) *dwlt: hld up stands' side: n.m.r over 2f out: rdn and kpt on fnl f: nrst fin: 6th of 16 in gp* **20/1**

2511 **10** *nse* **Green Howard**[15] 6111 6-9-3 88 8ex.......................... DanielTudhope 10 84
(Robin Bastiman) *hld up far side: rdn and hdwy over 1f out: kpt on wl fnl f: nrst fin: 4th of 10 in gp* **16/1**

062 **11** *½* **Redvers (IRE)**[14] 6124 6-9-10 95........................(v[1]) RichardKingscote 13 89
(Ed Vaughan) *hld up stands' side: weaved through over 1f out: rdn and one pce ins fnl f: 7th of 16 in gp* **9/1**[2]

3220 **12** *2¼* **Ansaab**[35] 5418 6-9-4 89..............................(t) BillyLee 23 76
(Alan McCabe) *bhd stands' side: rdn along over 2f out: kpt on fnl f: nvr able to chal: 8th of 16 in gp* **25/1**

5404 **13** *nk* **Farlow (IRE)**[35] 5433 6-9-3 88.............................. TonyHamilton 12 74
(Richard Fahey) *hld up on outside of stands' side gp: rdn over 2f out: sn no imp: 9th of 16 in gp* **33/1**

1150 **14** *½* **Repetition**[49] 4923 4-8-9 85.............................. ShaneGray(5) 6 69
(Kristin Stubbs) *cl up far side: led that gp 1/2-way to over 1f out: outpcd ins fnl f: 5th of 10 in gp* **50/1**

4620 **15** *shd* **Mezzotint (IRE)**[7] 6320 5-9-0 85.............................. ColinKeane 9 69
(Stuart Williams) *dwlt: hld up far side: rdn and hdwy over 1f out: kpt on: no imp: 6th of 10 in gp* **33/1**

1005 **16** *nk* **Majestic Moon (IRE)**[28] 5665 4-9-4 94..............................(p) JackGarritty(5) 24 77
(Richard Fahey) *prom stands' side: rdn over 2f out: wknd over 1f out: 10th of 16 in gp* **9/1**[2]

0450 **17** *shd* **Sir Reginald**[8] 6290 6-9-4 92.............................. GeorgeChaloner(3) 15 75
(Richard Fahey) *dwlt: bhd stands' side: rdn over 2f out: sme late hdwy: nvr rchd ldrs: 11th of 16 in gp* **33/1**

3644 **18** *1½* **Newstead Abbey**[99] 3189 4-9-9 94.............................. JamesSullivan 21 72
(David Barron) *t.k.h: prom stands' side: rdn over 2f out: sn lost pl: 12th of 16 in gp* **28/1**

1066 **19** *nk* **Inxile (IRE)**[14] 6131 9-9-6 91..............................(p) FrannyNorton 16 68
(David Nicholls) *disp ld stands' side to 1/2-way: rdn and wknd over 1f out: 13th of 16 in gp* **66/1**

1240 **20** *1* **Trojan Rocket (IRE)**[14] 6159 6-9-0 88..............................(p) ConnorBeasley(3) 14 62
(Michael Wigham) *midfield stands' side: rdn and outpcd over 2f out: n.d after: 14th of 16 in gp* **66/1**

0100 **21** *¾* **Lexi's Hero (IRE)**[21] 5918 6-9-7 92..............................(v) DavidNolan 19 63
(Richard Fahey) *trckd stands' side ldrs: rdn over 2f out: wknd wl over 1f out: 15th of 16 in gp* **33/1**

0606 **22** *¾* **Yeeoow (IRE)**[8] 6290 5-9-6 91.............................. DeclanMcDonogh 5 60
(K R Burke) *in tch far side: drvn and outpcd over 2f out: btn fnl f: 7th of 10 in gp* **28/1**

1010 **23** *¾* **Compton Park**[7] 6327 7-9-10 95 5ex..............................(t) DavidAllan 17 62
(Les Eyre) *prom stands' side: effrt and rdn over 2f out: wknd over 1f out: last of 16 in gp* **16/1**

5004 **24** *2¼* **Hitchens (IRE)**[8] 6290 9-9-3 93.............................. CamHardie(5) 11 52
(David Barron) *in tch far side: struggling over 2f out: sn btn: 8th of 10 in gp* **33/1**

3000 **25** *4½* **Cosmic Chatter**[47] 4976 4-9-3 88.............................. JasonHart 2 33
(David Barron) *led far side to 1/2-way: wknd 2f out: 9th of 10 in gp* **40/1**

4160 **26** *2¼* **Angus Og**[9] 6260 4-9-2 87.............................. BenCurtis 4 25
(K R Burke) *prom far side tl rdn and wknd fr 2f out: last of 10 in gp* **66/1**

1m 10.01s (-2.39) **Going Correction** -0.20s/f (Firm)
**WFA** 3 from 4yo+ 2lb **26** Ran SP% **130.9**
Speed ratings (Par 109): **107,105,103,103,101 101,100,100,100,100 99,96,96,95,95 95,95,93,92,91 90,89,88,85,79 76**
CSF £109.59 CT £708.82 TOTE £10.20: £2.80, £5.00, £2.30, £2.60; EX 93.70 Trifecta £171.20.
**Owner** Brook House **Bred** Darley **Trained** Beckhampton, Wilts

**FOCUS**
With topweight Telmeyd (lame) taken out this was effectively an 85-95 handicap, and a highly competitive one, but the draw played a major part. The field split into two groups, with ten opting for the far-side route, and the first five came from the larger bunch on the stands' rail. Following on from Friday's Bronze Cup, won by Expose from stall 27, it was 27 that prevailed again here, with 26 and 25 next home. The far-side group could be worth 8lb higher.

## 6532 WILLIAM HILL 80TH ANNIVERSARY BOOK LAUNCH DOONSIDE CUP STKS (LISTED RACE) 1m 2f
**3:15** (3:15) (Class 1) 3-Y-O+
**£34,026** (£12,900; £6,456; £3,216; £1,614; £810) **Stalls** High

Form RPR

6145 **1** *2* **Sennockian Star**[7] 6321 4-9-0 106..............................(v) FrannyNorton 8 108
(Mark Johnston) *led early: w ldr: led 3f out: hdd over 1f out: rallied jst ins fnl f: styd on same pce* **10/3**[2]

4640 **2** *2½* **Mutatis Mutandis (IRE)**[38] 5312 3-8-3 92.............................. JamesSullivan 2 98
(Ed Walker) *sn trcking ldrs: effrt over 2f out: kpt on to take 3rd appr fnl f* **8/1**

0064 **3** *½* **Gabrial (IRE)**[7] 6321 5-9-0 98.............................. DavidNolan 3 102
(Richard Fahey) *sn chsng ldrs: drvn over 2f out: styd on same pce over 1f out* **5/1**

1000 **4** *1½* **Abseil (USA)**[56] 4648 4-9-0 95.............................. JamesDoyle 7 99
(Sir Michael Stoute) *stdd s and hld up in last: hdwy over 3f out: kpt on same pce over 1f out* **9/2**[3]

1111 **5** *2* **Treasure The Ridge (IRE)**[21] 5928 5-9-0 87..............................(b) JennyPowell 5 95
(Andrew Reid) *hld up in rr: hdwy 4f out: sn drvn and outpcd: kpt on fnl 2f* **12/1**

2040 **6** *2¼* **Mirsaale**[53] 4759 4-9-0 95..............................(p) PhillipMakin 1 91
(Keith Dalgleish) *sn led: hdd 3f out: lost pl over 1f out* **20/1**

3-46 **D** **Sky Hunter**[126] 2335 4-9-0 109..............................[1] GrahamLee 4 112
(Saeed bin Suroor) *trckd ldrs: led over 1f out: styd on wl ins fnl f: drvn out* **9/4**[1]

2m 6.31s (-5.69) **Going Correction** -0.30s/f (Firm)
**WFA** 3 from 4yo+ 6lb **7** Ran SP% **112.3**
Speed ratings: **108,106,106,104,103 101,110**
CSF £9.48 TOTE £2.50: £1.60, £2.00; EX 7.20 Trifecta £61.90.
**Owner** The Vine Accord **Bred** Cheveley Park Stud Ltd **Trained** Middleham Moor, N Yorks

**FOCUS**
A fair Listed event run at a modest gallop, and the form makes plenty of sense, around the first two at least.

## 6533 WILLIAM HILL AYR GOLD CUP (HERITAGE H'CAP) 6f
**3:50** (3:51) (Class 2) 3-Y-O+
**£99,600** (£29,824; £14,912; £7,456; £3,728; £1,872) **Stalls** Centre

Form RPR

1000 **1** **Louis The Pious**[14] 6124 6-9-4 104..............................(v[1]) JamesDoyle 19 114
(David O'Meara) *t.k.h early: midfield stands' side: hdwy to ld appr fnl f: drvn clr last 150yds: 1st of 17 in gp* **10/1**[3]

-041 **2** *2¾* **Minalisa**[59] 4557 5-9-1 101.............................. FMBerry 2 103+
(Rae Guest) *chsd far side ldrs: effrt and rdn over 1f out: led that gp ins fnl f: kpt on: nt rch stands' side wnr: 1st of 8 in gp* **33/1**

U101 **3** *hd* **Blaine**[31] 5575 4-9-4 104..............................(b) AmyRyan 26 105
(Kevin Ryan) *hld up stands' side: drvn along 1/2-way: hdwy over 1f out: kpt on fnl f: nrst fin: 2nd of 17 in gp* **7/1**[1]

1400 **4** *nk* **Heaven's Guest (IRE)**[29] 5653 4-9-0 105.............................. SammyJoBell(5) 24 105
(Richard Fahey) *cl up stands' side: led that gp over 2f out: hdd appr fnl f: kpt on same pce: 3rd of 17 in gp* **12/1**

1400 **5** *hd* **Fast Shot**[35] 5445 6-8-3 96.............................. RachelRichardson(7) 25 95
(Tim Easterby) *hld up stands' side: rdn and hdwy over 1f out: kpt on ins fnl f: nrst fin: 4th of 17 in gp* **20/1**

2400 **6** *hd* **Ruwaiyan (USA)**[6] 6387 5-9-3 103..............................(p) DavidAllan 1 102
(James Tate) *hld up far side: rdn and hdwy over 1f out: kpt on fnl f: 2nd of 8 in gp* **33/1**

3060 **7** *¾* **An Saighdiur (IRE)**[28] 5699 7-9-3 103..............................(p) BillyLee 23 99
(Andrew Slattery, Ire) *led stands' side to over 2f out: rdn and kpt on same pce fr over 1f out: 5th of 17 in gp* **20/1**

5000 **8** *shd* **Jack Dexter**[70] 4201 5-9-10 110.............................. GrahamLee 4 106
(Jim Goldie) *hld up far side: rdn and hdwy over 1f out: r.o fnl f: 3rd of 8 in gp* **20/1**

3115 **9** *nse* **Highland Acclaim (IRE)**[14] 6124 3-8-7 98.............................. SamJames(3) 18 94+
(David O'Meara) *hld up stands' side: rdn and hdwy over 1f out: kpt on fnl f: nvr able to chal: 6th of 17 in gp* **10/1**[3]

033 **10** *½* **Ballesteros**[21] 5918 5-8-11 97.............................. FrannyNorton 20 91
(Richard Fahey) *prom stands' side: rdn over 2f out: one pce over 1f out: 7th of 17 in gp* **25/1**

0006 **11** *1* **Hawkeyethenoo (IRE)**[14] 6124 8-8-11 100.............................. GaryBartley(3) 16 91
(Jim Goldie) *dwlt: hld up stands' side: rdn and kpt on fnl f: nvr rchd ldrs: 8th of 17 in gp* **16/1**

4331 **12** *½* **Watchable**[6] 6369 4-9-3 103 5ex..............................(p) DanielTudhope 5 92
(David O'Meara) *led far side: drvn over 2f out: hdd that gp ins fnl f: sn outpcd: 4th of 8 in gp* **9/1**[2]

1000 **13** *shd* **Racy**[14] 6159 7-9-0 100..............................(p) PaulPickard 27 89
(Brian Ellison) *taken early to post: t.k.h: trckd ldrs stands' side tl rdn and wknd over 1f out: 9th of 17 in gp* **20/1**

215 **14** *nse* **Barnet Fair**[14] 6131 6-8-5 96.............................. CamHardie(5) 17 85
(David Nicholls) *mounted on crse: rrd s: bhd stands' side: rdn and hdwy over 1f out: no imp fnl f: 10th of 17 in gp* **20/1**

6000 **15** *½* **Supplicant**[35] 5445 3-8-7 98.............................. GeorgeChaloner(3) 22 85
(Richard Fahey) *dwlt: hld up stands' side: rdn over 2f out: hdwy over 1f out: nvr rchd ldrs: 11th of 17 in gp* **12/1**

0600 **16** *nk* **Captain Ramius (IRE)**[14] 6124 8-8-12 98.............................. FergalLynch 8 84
(Kevin Ryan) *racd w one other in centre: in tch: outpcd 1/2-way: styd on fnl f: n.d* **50/1**

0633 **17** *hd* **Hamza (IRE)**[28] 5699 5-9-8 108..............................(v) PatSmullen 6 94
(Kevin Ryan) *racd w one other in centre: spd tl rdn and wknd over 1f out* **20/1**

1116 **18** *nk* **Go Far**[7] 6327 4-8-13 99 5ex..............................(v) MartinHarley 14 84
(Alan Bailey) *prom on outside of stands' side gp: rdn and edgd lft 2f out: sn btn: 12th of 17 in gp* **16/1**

3120 **19** *hd* **Rene Mathis (GER)**[7] 6354 4-9-0 100.............................. DavidNolan 13 84
(Richard Fahey) *taken early to post: midfield stands' side: drvn and outpcd over 2f out: btn over 1f out: 13th of 17 in gp* **25/1**

400 **20** *1½* **Mass Rally (IRE)**[13] 6167 7-9-5 105..............................(b) PJMcDonald 15 84
(Michael Dods) *hld up stands' side: drvn on outside of gp over 1f out: nvr on terms: 14th of 17 in gp* **25/1**

4200 **21** *nk* **Jimmy Styles**[91] 3452 10-8-12 101..............................(p) RyanTate(3) 12 79
(Clive Cox) *sn chsng ldrs stands' side: rdn over 2f out: wknd over 1f out: 15th of 17 in gp* **50/1**

0-03 **22** *nk* **Duke Of Firenze**[11] 6209 5-8-11 97..............................(p) RichardKingscote 10 74
(Robert Cowell) *swtchd to outside of stands' side gp sn after s: drvn over 2f out: wknd over 1f out: 16th of 17 in gp* **33/1**

1005 **23** *2½* **Ashpan Sam**[31] 5575 5-9-3 103.............................. PhillipMakin 9 72
(John Spearing) *t.k.h: sn chsng far side ldrs: drvn over 2f out: wknd wl over 1f out: 5th of 8 in gp* **33/1**

0000 **24** *½* **Burn The Boats (IRE)**[7] 6354 5-8-11 97.............................. ColinKeane 3 65
(G M Lyons, Ire) *hld up far side: stdy hdwy over 2f out: rdn and wknd over 1f out: 6th of 8 in gp* **28/1**

0000 **25** *¾* **York Glory (USA)**[7] 6327 6-9-0 100..............................(v) DeclanMcDonogh 21 65
(Kevin Ryan) *dwlt: hld up stands' side: rdn 2f out: sn btn: last of 17 in gp* **25/1**

4432 **26** *½* **Alben Star (IRE)**[28] 5674 6-9-4 109.............................. JackGarritty(5) 7 73
(Richard Fahey) *taken early to post: cl up far side tl rdn and wknd over 2f out: 7th of 8 in gp* **16/1**

1521 **27** *3½* **Eastern Impact (IRE)**[35] 5438 3-9-3 105.............................. TonyHamilton 11 58
(Richard Fahey) *swtchd to r far side over 4f out: prom: rdn and wknd over 2f out: last of 8 in gp* **20/1**

1m 9.53s (-2.87) **Going Correction** -0.20s/f (Firm)
**WFA** 3 from 4yo+ 2lb **27** Ran SP% **141.6**
Speed ratings (Par 109): **111,107,107,106,106 106,105,105,104,104 102,102,102,102,101 101,100,100,100,98 97,97,93,93,92**
CSF £313.34 CT £2536.46 TOTE £11.10: £3.40, £7.20, £4.70; EX 610.50 Trifecta £6580.60.
**Owner** F Gillespie **Bred** Ashbrittle Stud **Trained** Nawton, N Yorks

**FOCUS**
This was a cracking Ayr Gold Cup. However, the definite draw bias towards high numbers at the meeting dominated. Most elected to come near side, with just two sticking to the centre, and a select group kept to their low draws. Once again the near side proved the place to be. The far-side runners could be worth 6-7lb more.

## 6534 WILLIAM HILL AYRSHIRE H'CAP — 1m
4:25 (4:26) (Class 2) (0-105,99) 3-Y-O+
**£15,562** (£4,660; £2,330; £1,165; £582; £292) **Stalls** High

Form — RPR

1234 **1** **Ticking Katie (IRE)**[14] 6149 3-8-13 90 ....(p) MartinHarley 9 — 99
(K R Burke) *trckd ldrs: led 2f out: hld on towards fin* **10/1**

0510 **2** ¾ **Don't Call Me (IRE)**[14] 6124 7-10-10 97 ....(t) PhillipMakin 3 — 105
(David Nicholls) *awkward s and rdr briefly lost irons: in rr: hdwy on ins over 2f out: nt clr run over 1f out: chsd wnr ins fnl f: no ex clsng stages* **12/1**

0000 **3** nk **Two For Two (IRE)**[30] 5609 6-9-12 99 ....(p) DanielTudhope 11 — 106
(David O'Meara) *hld up in rr: hdwy over 2f out: styd on to take 3rd nr fin* **15/2**[3]

4160 **4** ½ **Muharrer**[20] 5957 5-9-3 90 .... GrahamLee 2 — 96
(Michael Dods) *mid-div: effrt over 2f out: kpt on same pce fnl f* **8/1**

2152 **5** 1½ **Kiwi Bay**[21] 5915 9-9-0 87 .... PJMcDonald 4 — 89
(Michael Dods) *prom: effrt over 2f out: kpt on one pce fnl f* **14/1**

1141 **6** 1 **Jacob Black**[18] 5999 3-8-9 86 .... DeclanMcDonogh 12 — 86
(Keith Dalgleish) *swtchd lft after s: led after 1f: hdd 2f out: fdd ins fnl f* **10/1**

0054 **7** nk **Norse Blues**[2] 6476 6-8-10 83 .... JasonHart 1 — 82
(David Barron) *led 1f: chsd ldrs: drvn 3f out: one pce over 1f out* **8/1**

2152 **8** ¾ **Coincidently**[2] 6476 4-8-7 80 .... FrannyNorton 5 — 78
(Alan Bailey) *mid-div: effrt and n.m.r over 2f out: one pce: eased nr fin* **7/1**[2]

5100 **9** nk **Laffan (IRE)**[21] 5919 5-9-9 96 .... DavidAllan 7 — 93
(Tim Easterby) *prom: drvn over 3f out: outpcd and lost pl 2f out: kpt on ins fnl f* **20/1**

21 **10** 1¾ **Top Of The Glas (IRE)**[35] 5410 3-8-5 87 .... CamHardie(5) 6 — 80
(Brian Ellison) *dwlt: in rr: effrt 3f out: nvr a factor* **3/1**[1]

6013 **11** ¾ **Osteopathic Remedy (IRE)**[26] 5771 10-9-0 90 ....(t) ConnorBeasley(3) 8 — 81
(Michael Dods) *hld up in mid-div: hdwy on outside 3f out: wknd over 1f out* **14/1**

0343 **12** 2 **Dusky Queen (IRE)**[7] 6320 4-8-11 89 .... JackGarritty(5) 10 — 76
(Richard Fahey) *trckd ldrs: hdwy to chal over 2f out: wknd over 1f out* **10/1**

1m 39.6s (-4.20) **Going Correction** -0.30s/f (Firm)
**WFA** 3 from 4yo+ 4lb — **12** Ran SP% **124.5**
Speed ratings (Par 109): **109,108,107,107,105 104,104,103,103,101 101,99**
CSF £130.60 CT £984.14 TOTE £11.50: £3.70, £3.10, £3.00; EX 136.30 Trifecta £710.70.
**Owner** Ontoawinner 6, M Hulin, E Burke **Bred** Tally-Ho Stud **Trained** Middleham Moor, N Yorks

**FOCUS**
A decent handicap run at a reasonable gallop. The form seems sound.

## 6535 MICROTECH SUPPORT H'CAP — 7f 50y
5:00 (5:00) (Class 3) (0-95,92) 3-Y-O+ **£9,703** (£2,887; £1,443; £721) **Stalls** High

Form — RPR

003 **1** **Earth Drummer (IRE)**[21] 5915 4-9-1 86 .... DanielTudhope 7 — 103
(David O'Meara) *prom: effrt and rdn over 2f out: led over 1f out: edgd lft: rdn clr fnl f* **7/2**[1]

2331 **2** 4½ **Athletic**[8] 6281 5-8-11 87 ....(v) JennyPowell(5) 4 — 92
(Andrew Reid) *t.k.h: chsd ldrs: led over 2f out: rdn and hdd over 1f out: kpt on same pce ins fnl f* **4/1**[2]

3335 **3** 1¾ **George Rooke (IRE)**[35] 5446 4-8-11 82 ow1 ....(p) PhillipMakin 10 — 82
(Keith Dalgleish) *hld up bhd ldng gp: styd alone far side ent st: effrt and rdn over 2f out: kpt on same pce fnl f* **8/1**

0202 **4** 3 **Lesha (IRE)**[14] 6149 3-9-2 90 .... FergalLynch 13 — 82+
(Kevin Ryan) *blkd s: bhd and sn rdn along: hdwy over 1f out: kpt on fnl f: nvr able to chal* **8/1**

0002 **5** 4 **Deauville Prince (FR)**[15] 6097 4-9-7 92 .... RichardKingscote 3 — 74
(Tom Dascombe) *led to over 2f out: sn drvn: wknd wl over 1f out* **5/1**[3]

0100 **6** nk **Silver Rime (FR)**[10] 6226 9-8-12 88 .... CamHardie(5) 2 — 69
(Linda Perratt) *s.i.s: bhd and sn pushed along: short-lived effrt over 3f out: wknd fr 2f out* **20/1**

24-0 **7** 1½ **Frog Hollow**[147] 1721 5-9-2 90 .... SamJames(3) 12 — 68
(David O'Meara) *hld up: rdn over 3f out: nvr able to chal* **7/1**

0000 **8** 1 **Stonefield Flyer**[1] 6511 5-8-9 80 .... DeclanMcDonogh 14 — 55
(Keith Dalgleish) *prom: rdn over 3f out: wknd over 2f out* **20/1**

5165 **9** 2 **Fieldgunner Kirkup (GER)**[4] 6430 6-8-11 82 .... JasonHart 9 — 52
(David Barron) *cl up tl rdn and wknd over 2f out* **16/1**

2101 **10** hd **Khelman (IRE)**[43] 5143 4-8-13 87 .... GeorgeChaloner(3) 6 — 56
(Richard Fahey) *chsd ldrs: struggling over 2f out: sn btn* **17/2**

1m 30.06s (-3.34) **Going Correction** -0.30s/f (Firm)
**WFA** 3 from 4yo+ 3lb — **10** Ran SP% **119.5**
Speed ratings (Par 107): **107,101,99,96,91 91,89,88,86,86**
CSF £17.91 CT £103.19 TOTE £4.60: £2.00, £1.40, £3.00; EX 15.90 Trifecta £214.40.
**Owner** Middleham Park Racing LXV & Partner **Bred** M Ryan **Trained** Nawton, N Yorks

**FOCUS**
This fair handicap rather fell apart from the top of the home straight but the placed horses give the form substance. The winner built on his latest promise.

## 6536 JORDAN ELECTRICS LTD H'CAP — 1m 5f 13y
5:35 (5:35) (Class 3) (0-90,88) 3-Y-O+ **£9,703** (£2,887; £1,443; £721) **Stalls** Low

Form — RPR

5602 **1** **Buthelezi (USA)**[28] 5673 6-9-7 81 ....(p) BenCurtis 2 — 90
(Brian Ellison) *cl up: rdn over 3f out: hung lft and led over 2f out: hld on wl fnl f* **11/4**[1]

4210 **2** ¾ **Thorntoun Care**[15] 6099 3-8-0 74 .... JackGarritty(5) 11 — 82
(Jim Goldie) *hld up on ins: rdn and hdwy over 2f out: swtchd rt and effrt over 1f out: chsd wnr ins fnl f: r.o* **7/1**

205 **3** 1¼ **Dark Ruler (IRE)**[16] 6061 5-9-10 84 .... DavidAllan 1 — 90
(Alan Swinbank) *trckd ldrs: effrt and ev ch over 2f out: checked over 1f out: kpt on same pce ins fnl f* **4/1**[2]

3425 **4** 2 **Lexington Bay (IRE)**[14] 6152 6-9-1 75 .... TonyHamilton 5 — 78
(Richard Fahey) *trckd ldrs: effrt and rdn over 2f out: one pce fr over 1f out* **12/1**

3301 **5** 2¼ **Merchant Of Dubai**[5] 6403 9-9-2 76 6ex .... GrahamLee 8 — 76
(Jim Goldie) *in tch: drvn and outpcd over 2f out: styd on fnl f: nvr able to chal* **8/1**

0461 **6** ¾ **Pressure Point**[15] 6113 4-8-12 72 .... PhillipMakin 3 — 71
(Keith Dalgleish) *hld up in tch: effrt over 2f out: rdn and outpcd over 1f out* **6/1**[3]

5240 **7** 1¼ **Mister Fizz**[16] 6061 6-9-7 86 .... GeorgeDowning(5) 4 — 83
(Miss Imogen Pickard) *led: rdn and hdd over 2f out: hmpd wl over 1f out: sn btn* **10/1**

0-04 **8** ½ **Shrewd**[1] 6514 4-10-0 88 .... JasonHart 10 — 84
(Keith Dalgleish) *hld up: rdn over 2f out: btn over 1f out* **9/1**

360 **9** 1¾ **Love Marmalade (IRE)**[29] 5639 4-9-2 76 .... PJMcDonald 9 — 69
(Alistair Whillans) *hld up towards rr: struggling over 2f out: sn btn* **16/1**

2m 51.02s (-2.98) **Going Correction** -0.30s/f (Firm)
**WFA** 3 from 4yo+ 9lb — **9** Ran SP% **117.2**
Speed ratings (Par 107): **97,96,95,94,93 92,91,91,90**
CSF £22.84 CT £77.15 TOTE £4.50: £1.40, £2.90, £1.70; EX 31.30 Trifecta £127.20.
**Owner** Westbourne Racing Club 1 & Brian Ellison **Bred** Dr John A Chandler **Trained** Norton, N Yorks

■ Stewards' Enquiry : Ben Curtis five-day ban: careless riding (6-10Oct)

**FOCUS**
A modest staying handicap, run at an average pace. Straightforward form.
T/Jkpt: Not won. T/Plt: £366.80 to a £1 stake. Pool: £144,670.48 - 287.88 winning tickets.
T/Qpdt: £84.90 to a £1 stake. Pool: £15,128.56 - 131.80 winning tickets. RY

5813

# CATTERICK (L-H)
### Saturday, September 20

**OFFICIAL GOING: Good (good to firm in places; 8.4)**
Wind: Light half against Weather: Heavy grey cloud

## 6537 BRITISH STALLIONS STUDS EBF MAIDEN STKS — 5f 212y
2:10 (2:10) (Class 5) 2-Y-O **£3,234** (£962; £481; £240) **Stalls** Low

Form — RPR

6024 **1** **Midlander (IRE)**[18] 5995 2-9-5 78 .... AdrianNicholls 6 — 78
(Mark Johnston) *mde all: rdn clr wl over 1f out: styd on strly* **6/4**[1]

06 **2** 1½ **Juncart**[16] 6059 2-9-0 0 .... KevinStott(5) 5 — 74
(Kevin Ryan) *chsd wnr: effrt over 2f out: rdn wl over 1f out: clsng whn rn green and edgd lft ins fnl f: sn no imp* **5/1**[3]

332 **3** 7 **Doppler Effect**[18] 5995 2-9-5 74 .... DaleSwift 1 — 53
(Ann Duffield) *chsd ldrs and sn pushed along: rdn 1/2-way: drvn wl over 1f out: one pce* **7/4**[2]

00 **4** 6 **Magic Empress (IRE)**[35] 5443 2-9-0 0 .... PatrickMathers 4 — 30
(Tony Coyle) *towards rr and sn pushed along: rdn wl over 2f out: plugged on appr fnl f: n.d* **100/1**

05 **5** nk **My Specialbru**[15] 6115 2-9-5 0 .... RoystonFfrench 2 — 34
(Tracy Waggott) *chsd ldrs: rdn along 1/2-way: wknd fnl 2f* **14/1**

**6** 21 **Kyllach Me (IRE)** 2-9-5 0 .... DuranFentiman 3
(Bryan Smart) *s.i.s: green: outpcd and a bhd* **10/1**

1m 14.58s (0.98) **Going Correction** +0.15s/f (Good) — **6** Ran SP% **109.8**
Speed ratings (Par 95): **99,97,87,79,79 51**
CSF £9.05 TOTE £1.60: £1.40, £3.30; EX 7.40 Trifecta £31.40.
**Owner** Sheikh Hamdan bin Mohammed Al Maktoum **Bred** Darley **Trained** Middleham Moor, N Yorks

**FOCUS**
A fair juvenile maiden in which they went a decent gallop on ground officially described as good, good to firm in places. The winning time suggested that the ground was riding no quicker than good.

## 6538 ETS (UK) LTD ANNIVERSARY NURSERY H'CAP (BOBIS RACE) — 7f
2:45 (2:47) (Class 4) (0-85,85) 2-Y-O **£4,657** (£1,386; £692; £346) **Stalls** Low

Form — RPR

3212 **1** **Flash Fire (IRE)**[18] 6003 2-9-7 85 .... AdrianNicholls 3 — 90
(Mark Johnston) *led 1f: chsd ldr: led again 2f out: sn rdn: edgd lft ent fnl f: drvn out* **1/1**[1]

6500 **2** 1½ **Pipe Bomb**[15] 6104 2-8-4 68 ....(p) IanBrennan 5 — 69
(Kevin Ryan) *cl up: led after 1f: rdn along and hdd 2f out: swtchd rt and drvn ent fnl f: kpt on* **16/1**

2025 **3** 3¼ **Madamoiselle Bond**[15] 6104 2-8-3 72 .... JoeDoyle(5) 4 — 64
(William Jarvis) *in rr: hdwy wl over 2f out: rdn to chse ldng pair wl over 1f out: drvn and no imp fnl f* **7/2**[2]

032 **4** 24 **Fast Charlie (IRE)**[21] 5922 2-8-4 75 .... RowanScott(7) 2 — 2
(Ann Duffield) *t.k.h: chsd ldng pair: rdn along 3f out: sn outpcd* **6/1**[3]

1m 28.34s (1.34) **Going Correction** +0.15s/f (Good) — **4** Ran SP% **92.4**
Speed ratings (Par 97): **98,96,92,65**
CSF £10.03 TOTE £1.30; EX 13.00 Trifecta £33.80.
**Owner** Sheikh Hamdan bin Mohammed Al Maktoum **Bred** Darley **Trained** Middleham Moor, N Yorks

■ Little Belter was withdrawn. Price at time of withdrawal 11-2. Rule 4 applies to all bets - deduction 15p in the pound.

**FOCUS**
A fair little nursery handicap in which they went a respectable gallop and no better.

## 6539 TONY GARGAN H'CAP (BOBIS RACE) — 1m 5f 175y
3:20 (3:21) (Class 4) (0-80,80) 3-Y-O **£6,135** (£1,811; £906) **Stalls** Low

Form — RPR

0-01 **1** **Scrafton**[15] 6117 3-7-13 61 oh1 .... JoeyHaynes(3) 5 — 69+
(James Bethell) *trckd ldrs: hdwy 3f out: rdn to ld wl over 1f out: drvn ins fnl f: kpt on wl towards fin* **4/1**[3]

1-00 **2** ½ **Istimraar (IRE)**[26] 2769 3-9-0 73 ....(p) PatCosgrave 2 — 78
(Philip Kirby) *trckd ldng pair on inner: effrt and n.m.r over 2f out: sn rdn along: swtchd rt and drvn ent fnl f: styd on wl towards fin* **12/1**

0021 **3** 1¼ **Crakehall Lad (IRE)**[11] 6216 3-8-6 65 .... DuranFentiman 4 — 68
(Alan Swinbank) *led: pushed along 3f out: rdn over 2f out: hdd and drvn wl over 1f out: kpt on u.p fnl f* **7/2**[2]

622 **4** 1½ **Mighty Missile (IRE)**[25] 5794 3-8-6 65 ....(p) AndrewElliott 1 — 66
(Tom Tate) *hld up towards rr: hdwy over 2f out: rdn wl over 1f out: drvn and edgd lft ent fnl f: sn no imp* **5/2**[1]

2611 **5** 6 **Mambo Rhythm**[8] 6284 3-9-7 80 ....(v) AdrianNicholls 6 — 73
(Mark Johnston) *trckd ldr: effrt and cl up 3f out: rdn over 2f out: sn drvn and wknd* **4/1**[3]

126 **6** 3¼ **Exclusive Contract (IRE)**[35] 5449 3-8-4 63 .... IanBrennan 3 — 51
(Ollie Pears) *hld up in rr: effrt 3f out: rdn along over 2f out: sn btn* **8/1**

3m 7.3s (3.70) **Going Correction** +0.325s/f (Good) — **6** Ran SP% **109.6**
Speed ratings (Par 103): **102,101,101,100,96 94**
CSF £43.84 TOTE £6.10: £4.70, £9.00; EX 63.90 Trifecta £232.70.
**Owner** Clarendon Thoroughbred Racing **Bred** Bearstone Stud **Trained** Middleham Moor, N Yorks

**FOCUS**
A fair staying 3yo handicap in which they went a steady gallop in the formative stages.

## 6540 PIN POINT RECRUITMENT MAIDEN STKS 7f
3:55 (3:56) (Class 5) 3-4-Y-O £3,234 (£962; £481; £240) Stalls Low

Form RPR
4224 1 **Mendacious Harpy (IRE)**[14] 6154 3-9-0 63 PatCosgrave 6 69
(George Baker) *chsd ldr: cl up after 2f: effrt to ld over 2f out: rdn wl over 1f out: drvn and edgd lft ins fnl f: flashed tail but kpt on towards fin* **9/2**[3]
432 2 ½ **Kiss Of Spring (IRE)**[15] 6118 3-9-0 66 RobertWinston 5 67
(David O'Meara) *led: jnd after 2f: rdn along and hdd over 2f out: cl up and ev ch: drvn and edgd lft ent fnl f: kpt on u.p towards fin* **11/8**[1]
3 3 2 **Muzaahim (IRE)**[120] 2630 3-9-0 0 KevinStott(5) 1 67
(Kevin Morgan) *trckd ldng pair: rdn along over 2f out: n.m.r and swtchd rt ent fnl f: sn drvn and kpt on same pce* **6/1**
0 4 ¾ **The Gay Cavalier**[19] 5976 3-9-0 0 (t) JoeDoyle(5) 4 65
(John Ryan) *dwlt and in rr: hdwy 1/2-way: rdn along wl over 2f out: kpt on u.p fr wl over 1f out: nrst fin* **50/1**
2333 5 1¼ **Irondale Express**[66] 4318 3-9-0 69 AdrianNicholls 3 56
(Tony Coyle) *chsd ldrs: rdn along 1/2-way: drvn 2f out: one pce* **5/2**[2]
30-4 6 15 **Retrofit**[51] 4816 3-9-5 69 DougieCostello 2 22
(William Muir) *in tch: effrt 3f out: sn rdn along and nvr nr ldrs* **14/1**
7 29 **High Meadow Jenny** 3-9-0 0 IanBrennan 7
(James Turner) *s.i.s: green: a outpcd and bhd* **100/1**
1m 29.25s (2.25) **Going Correction** +0.325s/f (Good) 7 Ran SP% **112.8**
Speed ratings (Par 103): **100,99,97,96,94 77,44**
CSF £10.80 TOTE £4.30: £2.20, £1.40; EX 13.60 Trifecta £82.70.
**Owner** R M F Curry **Bred** Val & Angela Leeson **Trained** Manton, Wilts
**FOCUS**
An ordinary maiden in which they went an honest gallop.

## 6541 BAPP GROUP OF COMPANIES H'CAP (THE FINAL OF 2014 CATTERICK TWELVE FURLONG SERIES) 1m 3f 214y
4:30 (4:30) (Class 2) 3-Y-O+ £12,938 (£3,850; £1,924; £962) Stalls Centre

Form RPR
5314 1 **Poetic Verse**[26] 5049 4-8-8 73 JoeDoyle(5) 8 85+
(John Quinn) *hld up towards rr: smooth hdwy over 3f out: cl up over 2f out: led on bit wl over 1f out: shkn up ins fnl f: readily* **8/1**
1212 2 1¾ **Indira**[24] 5818 3-8-10 78 RobertWinston 7 84
(John Berry) *hld up towards rr: hdwy over 3f out: chsd ldrs 2f out: sn cl up and rdn: drvn ent fnl f: kpt on: no ch w wnr* **3/1**[1]
0166 3 nk **Sherman McCoy**[75] 4015 8-8-3 68 (p) JordanNason(5) 5 73
(Marjorie Fife) *chsd ldrs: hdwy on outer and cl up 1/2-way: rdn to ld ld briefly 2f out: sn hdd and drvn: kpt on same pce fnl f* **14/1**
3435 4 10 **Flying Cape (IRE)**[7] 6325 3-8-1 69 (p) RoystonFfrench 3 58
(Andrew Hollinshead) *prom: cl up 1/2-way: led 5f out: rdn along 3f out: hdd 2f out: sn drvn and grad wknd* **13/2**
011 5 2 **Zeus Magic**[13] 6171 4-9-7 84 JacobButterfield(3) 2 70
(Brian Ellison) *chsd ldrs on inner: rdn along over 3f out: drvn over 2f out and sn outpcd* **4/1**[2]
0106 6 4 **Tinseltown**[36] 5371 8-8-7 67 IanBrennan 1 47
(Brian Rothwell) *led: rdn along 1/2-way: hdd 5f out: cl up tl drvn wl over 2f out and sn wknd* **14/1**
3662 7 4½ **Sir Charlie Kunz**[3] 6450 3-8-11 79 AdrianNicholls 4 51
(Mark Johnston) *towards rr: rdn along over 4f out: sn outpcd and bhd* **9/2**[3]
5013 8 2 **Mendelita**[24] 5818 3-7-11 68 oh3 JoeyHaynes(3) 9 37
(Richard Fahey) *chsd ldrs: rdn along over 4f out: sn wknd* **11/1**
5443 9 33 **Al Furat (USA)**[28] 5678 6-8-1 61 oh7 ow1 PatrickMathers 6
(Ron Barr) *chsd ldrs: rdn along over 4f out: sn wknd* **33/1**
2m 40.71s (1.81) **Going Correction** +0.325s/f (Good)
**WFA** 3 from 4yo+ 8lb 9 Ran SP% **112.2**
Speed ratings (Par 109): **106,104,104,97,96 93,90,89,67**
CSF £31.09 CT £329.62 TOTE £10.50: £2.90, £2.40, £3.80; EX 37.70 Trifecta £409.20.
**Owner** J N Blackburn **Bred** The Links Partnership **Trained** Settrington, N Yorks
**FOCUS**
A decent middle-distance handicap in which they went a respectable gallop.

## 6542 RACING UK ANYWHERE AVAILABLE NOW H'CAP 1m 5f 175y
5:05 (5:05) (Class 6) (0-65,65) 4-Y-O+ £2,726 (£805; £402) Stalls Low

Form RPR
4123 1 **Midnight Warrior**[15] 6119 4-8-4 53 JoeDoyle(5) 13 63+
(Ron Barr) *a cl up: slt ld on bit led wl over 2f out: shkn up ent fnl f: sn rdn: edgd sltly rt and bmpd last 75yds: styd on* **6/1**[2]
454U 2 ¾ **Triple Eight (IRE)**[23] 5856 6-9-2 65 (b) KevinStott(5) 4 73
(Philip Kirby) *hld up in midfield: hdwy on inner 3f out: chsd ldrs 2f out: sn swtchd rt to outer and rdn to chal ent fnl f: ev ch whn edgd lft and no ex last 75yds* **8/1**[3]
2360 3 1¾ **Impeccability**[14] 6157 4-8-2 46 (p) PatrickMathers 14 53+
(John Mackie) *trckd ldrs: hdwy 4f out: rdn to chal over 2f out and ev ch: drvn ent fnl f: hld whn hmpd last 75yds* **25/1**
555/ 4 2¾ **Stags Leap (IRE)**[618] 6137 7-8-8 55 JoeyHaynes(3) 9 57
(Philip Kirby) *in tch: hdwy to chse ldrs 4f out: rdn along over 2f out: swtchd lft and drvn appr fnl f: kpt on same pce* **12/1**
0220 5 1¼ **Cool Baranca (GER)**[28] 5171 8-8-3 52 ow3 EmmaSayer(5) 3 52+
(Dianne Sayer) *hld up towards rr: hdwy wl over 2f out: sn rdn: kpt on appr fnl f: nrst fin* **9/1**
3415 6 ¾ **Grayswood**[30] 5597 4-9-4 62 (p) DougieCostello 10 61
(William Muir) *hld up and bhd: hdwy over 2f out: rdn and styd on fnl f: nrst fin* **9/1**
0000 7 shd **Enzaal (USA)**[7] 6341 4-8-13 57 DuranFentiman 12 56
(Philip Kirby) *midfield: effrt over 3f out: rdn along 2f out: sn no imp* **16/1**
0304 8 1½ **Rocky Two (IRE)**[11] 6216 4-8-6 53 (p) JacobButterfield(3) 5 50
(Philip Kirby) *led: pushed along 4f out: rdn and hdd wl over 2f out: sn drvn and grad wknd* **6/1**[2]
2020 9 3¼ **Waltz Darling (IRE)**[11] 6216 6-8-10 59 JordanNason(5) 7 52
(Keith Reveley) *hld up towards rr: effrt on outer over 5f out: sn rdn along and n.d* **11/1**
2053 10 shd **Walter De La Mare (IRE)**[9] 6252 7-8-5 49 (t) PaulQuinn 6 41
(Anabel K Murphy) *a towards rr* **14/1**
0331 11 hd **Gioia Di Vita**[15] 6119 4-9-6 64 RobertWinston 11 56
(David Thompson) *hld up in rr: hdwy 5f out: rdn to chse ldrs wl over 2f out: wknd wl over 1f out* **9/2**[1]
0000 12 ½ **Jebulani**[15] 6117 4-8-4 48 oh1 ow2 (tp) IanBrennan 15 39
(Barry Murtagh) *a in rr* **80/1**
4664 13 3 **Wasabi (IRE)**[37] 5342 5-8-2 46 oh1 (tp) RoystonFfrench 2 33
(John Berry) *chsd ldrs: rdn along over 3f out: sn wknd* **28/1**
0036 14 2¾ **Rhinestone Rebel (IRE)**[57] 3976 8-8-4 48 oh1 ow2 AndrewElliott 1 31
(Peter Hiatt) *in tch on inner: rdn along over 4f out: sn wknd* **50/1**
3m 8.2s (4.60) **Going Correction** +0.325s/f (Good) 14 Ran SP% **116.9**
Speed ratings (Par 101): **99,98,97,96,95 94,94,93,92,92 91,91,89,88**
CSF £50.34 CT £1120.05 TOTE £5.10: £2.60, £2.70, £7.60; EX 51.70 Trifecta £1237.80 Part won..
**Owner** K Trimble **Bred** Tarworth Bloodstock Investments Ltd **Trained** Seamer, N Yorks
■ Stewards' Enquiry : Joe Doyle two-day ban: careless riding (6-7 October)
**FOCUS**
A modest staying handicap which provided a true test.

## 6543 BOOK NOW FOR SATURDAY 18TH OCTOBER H'CAP (DIV I) 7f
5:40 (5:43) (Class 6) (0-65,65) 3-Y-O+ £2,726 (£805; £402) Stalls Low

Form RPR
5000 1 **The Blue Banana (IRE)**[26] 5761 5-8-6 55 (b) KevinStott(5) 9 66
(Edwin Tuer) *hld up towards rr: hdwy wl over 2f out: effrt over 1f out: chal on outer ins fnl f: rdn to ld and hung bdly lft 100yds: kpt on* **9/1**
3243 2 2 **Orwellian**[5] 6405 5-9-2 65 JoeDoyle(5) 1 71
(Bryan Smart) *hld up in rr: hdwy 3f out: effrt and swtchd lft wl over 1f out: rdn and styng on whn nt clr run and hmpd last 100yds: swtchd rt and styd on wl towards fin* **15/8**[1]
1320 3 1 **See Clearly**[11] 6217 5-9-0 58 (p) DuranFentiman 11 62
(Tim Easterby) *chsd clr ldr: hdwy 2f out: rdn to ld jst ins fnl f: sn drvn and edgd lft: hdd and hmpd last 100yds* **9/1**
4606 4 ¾ **Princess Rose**[15] 6116 3-8-1 51 oh2 (v[1]) JoeyHaynes(3) 6 51
(John Weymes) *led and sn clr: rdn along 2f out: drvn over 1f out: hdd jst ins fnl f: sn wknd* **40/1**
6325 5 1½ **It's All A Game**[15] 6121 3-8-10 57 (b) RobertWinston 10 54
(Richard Guest) *chsd ldrs on outer: rdn along wl over 2f out: drvn and one pce fr over 1f out* **15/2**
4310 6 ½ **No Quarter (IRE)**[11] 6217 7-9-6 64 RoystonFfrench 7 60
(Tracy Waggott) *chsd ldng pair: rdn over 2f out: drvn and wknd over 1f out* **10/1**
0643 7 hd **Day Of The Eagle (IRE)**[32] 5530 8-9-6 64 (b[1]) IanBrennan 3 60
(Michael Easterby) *dwlt: a in rr* **5/1**[2]
2665 8 1¼ **Thrust Control (IRE)**[5] 6402 7-8-5 52 oh2 ow1 (p) JacobButterfield(3) 4 44
(Tracy Waggott) *midfield: rdn along 3f out: n.d* **7/1**[3]
6600 9 4½ **Look On By**[5] 6407 4-8-10 54 (b[1]) AndrewElliott 12 35
(Ruth Carr) *rrd s and s.i.s: a bhd* **22/1**
5003 10 ½ **La Danza**[33] 5510 4-8-7 51 oh2 (v) PatrickMathers 5 30
(Lisa Williamson) *chsd ldrs on inner: rdn along wl over 2f out: sn wknd* **22/1**
1m 29.23s (2.23) **Going Correction** +0.325s/f (Good)
**WFA** 3 from 4yo+ 3lb 10 Ran SP% **115.9**
Speed ratings (Par 101): **100,97,96,95,94 93,93,91,86,86**
CSF £25.53 CT £164.25 TOTE £10.30: £3.20, £1.80, £3.00; EX 34.90 Trifecta £265.40.
**Owner** E Tuer **Bred** Tally-Ho Stud **Trained** Birkby, N Yorks
**FOCUS**
The first division of a modest 7f handicap in which they went an honest gallop.

## 6544 BOOK NOW FOR SATURDAY 18TH OCTOBER H'CAP (DIV II) 7f
6:10 (6:11) (Class 6) (0-65,65) 3-Y-O+ £2,726 (£805; £402) Stalls Low

Form RPR
6305 1 **Tanawar (IRE)**[11] 6217 4-9-3 61 (b) IanBrennan 4 69
(Ruth Carr) *trckd ldrs: swtchd lft to outer and hdwy 2f out: rdn wl over 1f out: led ins fnl f: drvn out* **9/2**[3]
0200 2 ¾ **Nelson's Bay**[15] 6121 5-8-9 58 KevinStott(5) 1 64
(Wilf Storey) *hld up: hdwy on inner over 2f out: rdn wl over 1f out: styd on ent fnl f: drvn and no ex last 50yds* **8/1**
0000 3 shd **Bogsnog (IRE)**[16] 6074 4-9-7 65 RoystonFfrench 3 71
(Kristin Stubbs) *cl up: rdn 2f out: drvn over 1f out: ev ch tl nt qckn wl ins fnl f* **12/1**
6501 4 1 **Running Reef (IRE)**[5] 6405 5-9-5 63 6ex (p) RobertWinston 11 66
(Tracy Waggott) *racd wd: sn led: rdn wl over 1f out: drvn over 1f out: hdd jst ins fnl f: kpt on same pce* **13/8**[1]
203 5 ½ **Mount Cheiron (USA)**[10] 6227 3-8-4 56 (p) EmmaSayer(5) 2 57
(Dianne Sayer) *hld up: hdwy over 2f out: chsd ldrs over 1f out: rdn and styng on whn n.m.r ins fnl f: nrst fin* **4/1**[2]
056 6 ½ **Im Dapper Too**[15] 6118 3-8-5 52 AndrewElliott 5 52
(John Davies) *chsd ldrs on outer: rdn along wl over 2f out: drvn over 1f out: kpt on u.p fnl f* **40/1**
2430 7 10 **Benidorm**[3] 5893 6-8-4 51 oh4 (e) JoeyHaynes(3) 7 26
(Richard Guest) *chsd ldng pair: rdn along over 2f out: sn drvn and wknd* **12/1**
6250 8 3½ **Shillito**[18] 6014 4-9-0 58 DougieCostello 9 24
(Tony Coyle) *chsd ldrs on outer: rdn along over 3f out: sn wknd* **16/1**
1m 28.92s (1.92) **Going Correction** +0.325s/f (Good)
**WFA** 3 from 4yo+ 3lb 8 Ran SP% **111.1**
Speed ratings (Par 101): **102,101,101,99,99 98,87,83**
CSF £37.48 CT £386.18 TOTE £3.40: £1.10, £2.90, £2.60; EX 43.80 Trifecta £354.50.
**Owner** G Scruton, D Williamson & R Carr **Bred** J Hanly, Castlemartin Sky & Skymarc Far **Trained** Huby, N Yorks
**FOCUS**
The second division of a modest 7f handicap and the winning time was marginally quicker.
T/Plt: £104.50 to a £1 stake. Pool: £41,537.93 - 290.16 winning units. T/Qpdt: £46.60 to a 31 stake. Pool: £2528.37 - 40.10 winning units. JR

# 6517 NEWBURY (L-H)
Saturday, September 20

**OFFICIAL GOING: Soft (6.0)**
Wind: mild half across Weather: overcast

## 6545 WEDGEWOOD ESTATES EBF STALLIONS MAIDEN STKS (BOBIS RACE) (DIV I) 7f (S)
1:20 (1:24) (Class 4) 2-Y-O £5,175 (£1,540; £769; £384) Stalls Centre

Form RPR
4 1 **Yeenaan (FR)**[26] 5759 2-9-0 0 DanielMuscutt(5) 11 83+
(Marco Botti) *travelled wl: trckd ldrs: led 2f out: pushed along and in command fnl f: readily* **9/2**[2]
4 2 ¾ **Stoked (IRE)**[29] 5646 2-9-5 0 RyanMoore 7 79
(Ed Walker) *prom: rdn to chse wnr wl over 1f out: kpt on but a being hld fnl f* **10/3**[1]



The Form Book, Raceform Ltd, Newbury, RG14 5SJ

03 3 3/4 **Harbour Patrol (IRE)**[17] 6038 2-9-5 0 ........................ RichardHughes 9 77
(Richard Hannon) *led tl rdn 2f out: kpt on same pce fnl f* **9/2**[2]

4 3/4 **Compton Mill** 2-9-5 0 ........................................ JohnFahy 5 75+
(Hughie Morrison) *s.i.s: towards rr: pushed along wl over 2f out: hdwy over 1f out: styd on nicely fnl f: wnt 4th nring fin* **33/1**

5 5 3/4 **Ashridge Lad**[14] 6125 2-9-5 0 ........................ JimmyFortune 2 73
(Brian Meehan) *in tch: hdwy 2f out: sn rdn: kpt on same pce fnl f: lost 4th nring fin* **5/1**[3]

6 2 1/2 **Azilian** 2-9-5 0 ........................................ SilvestreDeSousa 1 67
(Paul Cole) *mid-div: rdn over 2f out: styd on fnl f wout ever threatening* **40/1**

7 1/2 **Victory Megastar** 2-9-5 0 ........................................ AdamKirby 16 66
(Clive Cox) *trckd ldrs: rdn 2f out: kpt on tl no ex fnl 120yds* **8/1**

8 2 3/4 **Prince Of Cardamom (IRE)** 2-9-5 0 ........................ OisinMurphy 6 59
(Andrew Balding) *mid-div: rdn 2f out: wknd fnl f* **16/1**

9 3 3/4 **Revision (FR)** 2-9-5 0 ........................................ SteveDrowne 8 50
(John Best) *mid-div: pushed along over 3f out: fdd ent fnl f* **100/1**

10 1/2 **Grass Roots** 2-9-5 0 ........................................ WilliamBuick 10 48
(Charles Hills) *s.i.s: sn mid-div: rdn over 2f out: wknd jst over 1f out* **22/1**

50 11 1/2 **Master Zephyr**[22] 5874 2-9-5 0 ........................ GeorgeBaker 3 47
(Roger Charlton) *a towards rr* **20/1**

12 shd **Officer Sydney (IRE)** 2-9-5 0 ........................ MartinLane 15 47
(Brian Meehan) *mid-div: pushed along over 3f out: wknd jst over 1f out* **40/1**

13 3 3/4 **Rosslare (IRE)** 2-9-0 0 ........................................ JamieSpencer 12 33
(Charles Hills) *a towards rr* **14/1**

14 1 1/2 **Burma Bridge** 2-9-5 0 ........................................ SeanLevey 13 34
(Richard Hannon) *s.i.s: a towards rr* **66/1**

1m 29.08s (3.38) **Going Correction** +0.40s/f (Good) **14** Ran SP% **119.2**
Speed ratings (Par 97): **96,95,94,93,92 89,89,86,81,81 80,80,76,74**
CSF £18.37 TOTE £6.50: £2.40, £1.60, £1.80; EX 25.00 Trifecta £110.20.

**Owner** Sheikh Mohammed Bin Khalifa Al Maktoum **Bred** Malcolm Parrish **Trained** Newmarket, Suffolk

**FOCUS**
The rails were moved out overnight from 5f-7f, and all races on the round course were eight metres longer than advertised. Subsequent Racing Post Trophy and St Leger hero Kingston Hill won a division of this last year. This one didn't strike as the strongest of Newbury maidens, but there was an awful lot to like about the winner, who was value for a bit extra.

## 6546 DUBAI DUTY FREE LEGACY CUP (REGISTERED AS THE ARC TRIAL) (GROUP 3) 1m 3f 5y

**1:50** (1:51) (Class 1) 3-Y-O+

**£34,026** (£12,900; £6,456; £3,216; £1,614; £810) **Stalls** Low

Form RPR

222 1 **Hillstar**[42] 5175 4-9-3 113 ........................ RyanMoore 7 117
(Sir Michael Stoute) *trckd ldrs: rdn to chse ldr 2f out: led jst over 1f out: styd on wl* **11/4**[1]

1013 2 1 1/2 **Tasaday (USA)**[30] 5610 4-9-0 113 ........................ SilvestreDeSousa 5 111
(Saeed bin Suroor) *trckd ldr: narrow ld 2f out: sn rdn: hdd jst over 1f out: styd on but sn hld by wnr* **7/2**[2]

-100 3 1 3/4 **Cubanita**[112] 2764 5-9-3 110 ........................ AndreaAtzeni 2 111
(Ralph Beckett) *trckd ldrs: rdn over 2f out: wnt 3rd ent fnl f: styd on* **5/1**

3011 4 1 3/4 **Glorious Protector (IRE)**[28] 5688 4-9-3 105 ........................ GeorgeBaker 3 109
(Ed Walker) *hld up in 5th: rdn over 2f out: styd on wout ever threatening: wnt 4th ins fnl f* **9/2**[3]

0-55 5 3/4 **Quest For Peace (IRE)**[28] 5688 6-9-3 101 ........................ AdamKirby 1 107
(Luca Cumani) *led tl rdn 2f out: kpt chsng ldng pair tl no ex ent fnl f* **12/1**

0000 6 1 1/2 **Camborne**[35] 5432 6-9-3 105 ........................(p) WilliamBuick 9 105
(John Gosden) *hld up in last pair but wl in tch: effrt wl over 2f out but nvr threatened: styd on same pce* **7/1**

6001 7 1/2 **Beacon Lady**[26] 5755 5-9-0 99 ........................ JackDuern 6 101
(William Knight) *hld up in last but in tch: rdn over 3f out: styd on but nt pce to get on terms* **20/1**

2m 30.83s (9.63) **Going Correction** +0.40s/f (Good) **7** Ran SP% **108.7**
Speed ratings: **80,78,77,76,75 74,74**
CSF £11.17 TOTE £3.00: £1.80, £2.10; EX 8.20 Trifecta £46.90.

**Owner** Sir Evelyn De Rothschild **Bred** Southcourt Stud **Trained** Newmarket, Suffolk

**FOCUS**
A decent enough Group 3. Hillstar is rated to his best batr last season's King George.

## 6547 DUBAI DUTY FREE MILL REEF STKS (GROUP 2) 6f 8y

**2:20** (2:21) (Class 1) 2-Y-O

**£42,532** (£16,125; £8,070; £4,020; £2,017; £1,012) **Stalls** Centre

Form RPR

3122 1 **Toocoolforschool (IRE)**[8] 6291 2-9-1 103 ..........(p) SilvestreDeSousa 6 116
(K R Burke) *mde all: qcknd clr over 1f out: r.o strly: rdn out* **4/1**[3]

10 2 7 **Growl**[31] 5576 2-9-1 0 ........................(t) JimmyFortune 1 95
(Brian Meehan) *in last pair: hdwy 2f out: sn rdn: wnt 2nd ent fnl f: nvr any ch w wnr* **11/1**

1220 3 1/2 **Kibaar**[9] 6256 2-9-1 96 ........................................ DaneO'Neill 4 94
(B W Hills) *trckd wnr: rdn 2f out: readily hld by wnr whn narrowly losing 2nd ent fnl f: kpt on same pce* **16/1**

12 4 3 **Strath Burn**[62] 4482 2-9-1 0 ........................ JamieSpencer 2 85
(Charles Hills) *s.i.s: last but in tch: snatched up after 1f: rdn wl over 2f out: nvr any real imp on ldrs: wnt btn 4th ins fnl f* **11/8**[1]

3232 5 2 1/2 **Jungle Cat (IRE)**[28] 5692 2-9-1 110 ........................ WilliamBuick 8 77
(Mark Johnston) *trckd wnr tl rdn 2f out: wknd ent fnl f* **10/3**[2]

1110 6 hd **Baitha Alga (IRE)**[28] 5692 2-9-4 108 ........................ FrankieDettori 7 79
(Richard Hannon) *racd keenly: trckd ldrs: rdn over 2f out: wknd fnl f* **15/2**

1m 14.35s (1.35) **Going Correction** +0.40s/f (Good) **6** Ran SP% **111.2**
Speed ratings (Par 107): **107,97,97,93,89 89**
CSF £42.24 TOTE £5.10: £2.40, £5.50; EX 39.40 Trifecta £420.00.

**Owner** Ontoawinner 6, M Hulin, E Burke **Bred** Mark Salmon **Trained** Middleham Moor, N Yorks

■ Stewards' Enquiry : Silvestre De Sousa 21-day ban (7-days deferred): excessive use of the whip (totting-up procedure) (Oct 3-19)

**FOCUS**
This race fell apart with Limato and Mubtaghaa both non-runners, and the fourth, fifth and sixth home failing to get anywhere near their best. Toocoolforschool rates up with the best recent winners of this and Growl improved on his Acomb Stakes figure.

## 6548 DUBAI DUTY FREE H'CAP 1m 2f 6y

**2:55** (2:55) (Class 2) (0-105,105) 3-Y-O+

**£46,687** (£13,980; £6,990; £3,495; £1,747; £877) **Stalls** Low

Form RPR

212 1 **Air Pilot**[106] 2957 5-8-6 87 ........................ OisinMurphy 2 107+
(Ralph Beckett) *trckd ldrs: shkn up to ld 2f out: drew wl clr: heavily eased fnl 100yds* **9/2**[1]

3015 2 3 3/4 **First Flight (IRE)**[27] 5720 3-8-9 96 ........................ RichardHughes 13 104
(Saeed bin Suroor) *hld up towards rr: making hdwy whn nt clr run over 2f out: hanging lft but styd on wl fr wl over 1f out: wnt 2nd ent fnl f but no ch w v easy wnr* **13/2**[3]

5205 3 2 3/4 **Ventura Quest (USA)**[21] 5914 3-8-0 87 oh3 ............ FrankieMcDonald 1 90
(Richard Fahey) *mid-div: hdwy 3f out: sn rdn: wnt 3rd ent fnl f: styd on wout threatening* **40/1**

1153 4 1 1/4 **Arab Dawn**[9] 6257 3-8-3 90 ........................ MartinDwyer 3 90
(Hughie Morrison) *mid-div: hdwy over 3f out: rdn to dispute 3rd over 2f out: styd on same pce* **6/1**[2]

6410 5 1 1/2 **Nicholascopernicus (IRE)**[16] 6061 5-9-0 95 ........................ JamieSpencer 18 93
(Ed Walker) *hld up towards rr: stdy prog fr over 2f out but nvr best of runs switching lft and rt: styd on to go 5th ins fnl f: nvr a threat* **16/1**

1422 6 1 **Spirit Of The Law (IRE)**[28] 5695 5-8-11 92 ........................ PaulMulrennan 7 88
(Richard Fahey) *trckd ldrs: led 4f out: rdn and hdd 2f out: no ex whn lost 2 pls ent fnl f: lost 5th towards fin* **25/1**

4142 7 1 1/2 **Border Legend**[28] 5676 5-9-0 95 ........................(p) WilliamBuick 5 88
(Roger Charlton) *trckd ldrs: rdn 3f out: fdd ent fnl f* **12/1**

1116 8 1 1/4 **Roseburg (IRE)**[51] 4821 3-9-1 102 ........................ AndreaAtzeni 11 92
(Luca Cumani) *s.i.s: sn mid-div: rdn 3f out: sme minor late prog: nvr a threat* **9/2**[1]

4000 9 4 1/2 **Busatto (USA)**[21] 5928 4-8-8 89 ........................ RobertHavlin 9 71
(Mark Johnston) *rdn over 3f out: a mid-div* **25/1**

4200 10 1/2 **Monsieur Chevalier (IRE)**[14] 6140 7-8-8 89 ow1 ........................ RobertTart 17 70
(P J O'Gorman) *hld up towards rr: sme prog u.p into midfield wl over 2f out: no further imp fr wl over 1f out* **40/1**

5641 11 3 1/4 **Energia Davos (BRZ)**[42] 5174 6-9-10 105 ........................ TedDurcan 8 80
(Marco Botti) *towards rr of mid-div: rdn over 3f out: nvr any imp* **11/1**

4005 12 1/2 **Regulation (IRE)**[84] 3726 5-9-1 96 ........................ JohnFahy 14 70
(Neil King) *s.i.s: towards rr of mid-div: rdn 3f out: nvr any imp* **50/1**

1545 13 3 1/2 **Running Deer (IRE)**[21] 5928 5-8-9 90 ........................ SilvestreDeSousa 12 57
(Eve Johnson Houghton) *rdn over 3f out: nvr bttr than mid-div: wknd jst over 1f out* **20/1**

1204 14 14 **Black Shadow**[27] 5720 3-8-7 94 ........................ MartinLane 10 35
(Amanda Perrett) *w ldr: rdn 4f out: wknd wl over 2f out* **8/1**

540 15 2 3/4 **Stepping Ahead (FR)**[15] 6098 4-9-0 95 ........................(b[1]) AdamKirby 6 30
(K R Burke) *led: rdn whn hdd 4f out: wknd 3f out* **20/1**

2m 9.79s (0.99) **Going Correction** +0.40s/f (Good)
**WFA** 3 from 4yo+ 6lb **15** Ran SP% **121.1**
Speed ratings (Par 109): **112,109,106,105,104 103,102,101,98,97 95,94,91,80,78**
CSF £29.91 CT £1058.18 TOTE £4.90: £2.10, £2.30, £13.70; EX 32.30 Trifecta £1784.50.

**Owner** Lady Cobham **Bred** Lady Cobham **Trained** Kimpton, Hants

**FOCUS**
What is usually a highly competitive handicap was turned into an absolute procession by the returning Air Pilot, who was value for further.

## 6549 DUBAI INTERNATIONAL AIRPORT WORLD TROPHY (GROUP 3) 5f 34y

**3:30** (3:31) (Class 1) 3-Y-O+

**£34,026** (£12,900; £6,456; £3,216; £1,614; £810) **Stalls** Centre

Form RPR

151 1 **Mecca's Angel (IRE)**[10] 6231 3-8-11 109 ........................ PaulMulrennan 12 115
(Michael Dods) *trckd ldr: led over 2f out: qcknd up wl to assert fnl 120yds: readily* **13/8**[1]

0105 2 2 1/2 **Justice Day (IRE)**[28] 5674 3-9-0 108 ........................ SilvestreDeSousa 13 109
(David Elsworth) *trckd ldrs: rdn for str chal jst over 1f out: kpt on but outpcd by wnr fnl 120yds* **6/1**[3]

2001 3 1 1/2 **Ajjaadd (USA)**[11] 6209 8-9-1 98 ........................ WilliamTwiston-Davies 5 104
(Ted Powell) *hld up bhd ldrs: rdn over 2f out: hdwy whn swtchd rt but hanging lft jst over 1f out: r.o to go 3rd ins fnl f* **33/1**

0110 4 3/4 **Take Cover**[29] 5654 7-9-6 113 ........................ RyanMoore 8 106
(David C Griffiths) *led tl over 2f out: sn rdn: kpt on same pce fnl f* **7/2**[2]

5661 5 1 1/4 **Scream Blue Murder (IRE)**[41] 5219 4-9-1 104 ........................ WayneLordan 7 97
(T Stack, Ire) *trckd ldrs: rdn over 2f out: one pce fnl f* **7/1**

50 6 1 1/4 **One Chance (IRE)**[21] 5925 3-8-11 94 ........................ WilliamBuick 2 90
(John Butler) *trckd ldrs: rdn 2f out: wknd fnl f* **33/1**

3350 7 1 1/2 **Dinkum Diamond (IRE)**[14] 6134 6-9-1 105 ........................ OisinMurphy 4 87
(Henry Candy) *trckd ldrs: rdn over 2f out: wknd ent fnl f* **7/1**

2100 8 2 1/4 **Hay Chewed (IRE)**[50] 4852 3-8-11 99 ........................ MartinDwyer 3 77
(Conrad Allen) *prom: rdn over 2f out: wknd ent fnl f* **25/1**

4 9 6 **Graphic Guest**[119] 2564 4-8-12 93 ........................ RichardHughes 1 56
(Robert Cowell) *s.i.s: hld up: effrt over 2f out: nvr threatened: eased whn btn fnl f* **16/1**

1m 1.71s (0.31) **Going Correction** +0.40s/f (Good)
**WFA** 3 from 4yo+ 1lb **9** Ran SP% **115.2**
Speed ratings: **113,109,106,105,103 101,99,95,85**
CSF £11.55 TOTE £2.60: £1.10, £2.00, £6.60; EX 12.30 Trifecta £198.70.

**Owner** David T J Metcalfe **Bred** Yeomanstown Stud & Doc Bloodstock **Trained** Denton, Co Durham

**FOCUS**
A weak Group 3 sprint. The form is rated around the runner-up.

## 6550 DUBAI DUTY FREE NURSERY H'CAP (BOBIS RACE) 7f (S)

**4:05** (4:06) (Class 3) (0-95,85) 2-Y-O

**£6,225** (£1,864; £932; £466; £233; £117) **Stalls** Centre

Form RPR

3201 1 **Harlequin Striker (IRE)**[9] 6261 2-8-11 78 ........................ CharlesBishop(3) 4 81
(Mick Channon) *mde all: rdn 2f out: kpt on gamely* **7/1**

5344 2 1 **Looking Good**[21] 5929 2-8-6 70 ........................ SilvestreDeSousa 3 70
(David Brown) *trckd wnr: rdn 2f out: kpt on but nt quite pce to chal: jst hld on for 2nd* **10/1**

2243 3 nse **Little Palaver**[19] 5981 2-8-10 74 ........................ AndreaAtzeni 7 74
(Clive Cox) *trckd ldrs: drifting lft over 1f out: sn rdn: kpt on towards fin: jst failed to snatch 2nd* **6/1**[3]

0130 **4** *hd* **L'Etacq**[16] 6064 2-8-11 75.................................. RyanMoore 2 74
(Richard Hannon) *last but in tch: hdwy 2f out: sn rdn: kpt on towards fin* **10/1**

0014 **5** *3 ¾* **Silver Quay (IRE)**[7] 6331 2-9-2 80.................................. RichardHughes 8 70
(Richard Hannon) *trckd wnr: rdn and edgd lft over 2f out: sn one pce* **11/8**[1]

2310 **6** *21* **Polarisation**[31] 5580 2-9-2 80.................................. WilliamBuick 1 18
(Mark Johnston) *in tch: niggled along 4f out: rdn wl over 2f out: sn btn: eased ins fnl f* **7/2**[2]

1m 29.14s (3.44) **Going Correction** +0.40s/f (Good) **6 Ran SP% 109.3**
Speed ratings (Par 99): **96,94,94,94,90 66**
CSF £64.56 CT £406.20 TOTE £8.30: £3.30, £3.40; EX 40.30 Trifecta £173.70.
**Owner** Harlequin Direct Ltd **Bred** John Doyle **Trained** West Ilsley, Berks

**FOCUS**
Not a bad nursery, and straightforward form.

## 6551 WEDGEWOOD ESTATES EBF STALLIONS MAIDEN STKS (BOBIS RACE) (DIV II) 7f (S)

**4:40** (4:40) (Class 4) 2-Y-O **£5,175** (£1,540; £769; £384) **Stalls** Centre

Form RPR

**1** **McCreery** 2-9-5 0.................................. GeorgeBaker 12 78+
(Roger Charlton) *mid-div: hdwy 2f out: str run ent fnl f: edgd lft: led fnl 75yds: pushed out* **14/1**

04 **2** *nk* **Maraakib (IRE)**[78] 3924 2-9-5 0.................................. MartinDwyer 7 76
(Brian Meehan) *led: rdn clr over 1f out: kpt on but no ex whn hdd fnl 75yds* **6/1**[2]

**3** *1 ¾* **Sarsted** 2-9-5 0.................................. RobertHavlin 16 72+
(Hughie Morrison) *mid-div: hdwy 2f out: sn rdn: wnt 3rd ent fnl f: styd on* **40/1**

**4** *nk* **Purple Rock (IRE)** 2-9-5 0.................................. WilliamBuick 8 71+
(Charles Hills) *trckd ldrs: rdn 2f out: edgd rt: kpt on ins fnl f* **12/1**

**5** *1 ¾* **Miracle Ninetynine (IRE)** 2-9-5 0.................................. JimmyFortune 6 67+
(Richard Hannon) *mid-div: rdn over 2f out: styd on fnl f: nvr trbld ldrs* **14/1**

**6** *nk* **Winterval** 2-9-5 0.................................. AndreaAtzeni 11 66+
(Luca Cumani) *in tch: rdn over 2f out: styd on same pce fnl f* **13/2**[3]

**7** *½* **Sonnolento (IRE)** 2-9-5 0.................................. OisinMurphy 13 65+
(Andrew Balding) *hld up towards rr: pushed along over 2f out: no imp tl styd on nicely fnl f* **16/1**

**8** *¾* **Puissant (IRE)** 2-9-5 0.................................. JamieSpencer 15 63+
(Marco Botti) *s.i.s: towards rr: rdn 2f out: styd on fnl f: nvr threatened ldrs* **7/2**[1]

**9** *1 ½* **Napoleon Solo** 2-9-5 0.................................. AdamKirby 9 59
(Peter Chapple-Hyam) *prom: rdn to chse ldr over 1f out: wknd ent fnl f* **6/1**[2]

00 **10** *nk* **Kyllarney**[17] 6039 2-9-0 0.................................. PaulMulrennan 5 53
(Charles Hills) *trckd ldrs: rdn over 2f out: wknd jst over 1f out* **66/1**

**11** *¾* **Coorg (IRE)** 2-9-5 0.................................. RyanMoore 1 56
(Sir Michael Stoute) *s.i.s: rn green in rr: nvr a factor* **10/1**

**12** *nk* **Boarding Party (USA)** 2-9-5 0.................................. MartinLane 10 56
(Charlie Fellowes) *in tch: rdn to chse ldrs over 2f out: wknd over 1f out* **25/1**

**13** *½* **Who Dares Wins (IRE)** 2-9-5 0.................................. SeanLevey 4 54
(Richard Hannon) *s.i.s: sn mid-div: rdn over 2f out: wknd over 1f out* **11/1**

**14** *1* **Georgia's Gamble (IRE)** 2-9-5 0.................................. SilvestreDeSousa 3 52
(Paul Cole) *in tch: rdn over 2f out: wknd over 1f out* **33/1**

**15** *29* **Zebella** 2-9-0 0.................................. TedDurcan 2
(Rod Millman) *a towards rr: lost tch 2f out* **25/1**

1m 30.11s (4.41) **Going Correction** +0.40s/f (Good) **15 Ran SP% 121.1**
Speed ratings (Par 97): **90,89,87,87,85 84,84,83,81,81 80,80,79,78,45**
CSF £92.52 TOTE £12.80: £4.40, £2.50, £9.20; EX 142.00 Trifecta £1852.80 Part won..
**Owner** Lady Rothschild **Bred** The Rt Hon Lord Rothschild **Trained** Beckhampton, Wilts

**FOCUS**
This was run about a second slower than the first division. It contained some well-bred newcomers and winners should come out of it, although the field was compressed and it's hard to rate the bare form higher.

## 6552 HEATHERWOLD STUD H'CAP (BOBIS RACE) 7f (S)

**5:15** (5:15) (Class 4) (0-80,82) 3-Y-O **£4,690** (£1,395; £697; £348) **Stalls** Centre

Form RPR

2315 **1** **Above The Rest (IRE)**[14] 6149 3-9-7 80.................................. WilliamBuick 15 91
(Timothy Jarvis) *mde all: rdn clr over 1f out: styd on strly* **3/1**[1]

0250 **2** *2 ½* **Champagne Sydney (IRE)**[17] 6044 3-9-6 79.................................. SeanLevey 10 83
(Richard Hannon) *cl up: rdn to chse wnr over 1f out: hung lft ent fnl f: a hld* **15/2**[2]

0240 **3** *3 ¼* **La Tinta Bay**[36] 5381 3-9-3 76.................................. KieranO'Neill 8 72
(Richard Hannon) *racd keenly: trckd wnr: rdn 2f out: kpt on same pce fnl f* **25/1**

6044 **4** *2 ¼* **Art Official (IRE)**[31] 5550 3-9-6 79.................................. JimmyFortune 16 69
(Richard Hannon) *cl up: rdn 2f out: sn one pce* **8/1**[3]

1623 **5** *7* **Weekendatbernies (IRE)**[9] 6263 3-9-9 82.................................. JamieSpencer 13 54
(Ed de Giles) *s.i.s: in last pair but in tch: rdn 2f out: nvr threatened: wknd fnl f* **3/1**[1]

55-6 **6** *½* **Conflicting**[248] 187 3-9-2 75..................................(t[1]) MartinLane 2 45
(Charlie Fellowes) *slowly away: last: swtchd rt over 3f out: effrt over 2f out: wknd jst over 1f out* **16/1**

5135 **7** *18* **Classic Pursuit**[36] 5381 3-8-11 70..................................(p) RobertHavlin 4
(Ronald Harris) *racd keenly: trckd ldrs: rdn over 2f out: wknd over 1f out* **16/1**

2523 **8** *12* **Debit**[9] 6249 3-9-1 74..................................(p) AdamKirby 11
(Clive Cox) *trckd wnr: rdn over 2f out: wknd ent fnl f* **3/1**[1]

1m 28.6s (2.90) **Going Correction** +0.40s/f (Good) **8 Ran SP% 113.5**
Speed ratings (Par 103): **99,96,92,89,81 81,60,47**
CSF £26.53 CT £469.62 TOTE £3.40: £1.10, £2.10, £5.20; EX 32.40 Trifecta £395.80.
**Owner** Cedars Two **Bred** J C Carr **Trained** Twyford, Bucks

**FOCUS**
There were no fewer than ten non-runners. A fair and straightforward 3yo handicap in which the winner made all. The form is rated around the second.
T/Plt: £357.00 to a £1 stake. Pool: £110,570.19 - 226.06 winning tickets T/Qpdt: £191.80 to a £1 stake. Pool: £5728.33 - 22.10 winning tickets TM

# 5671 NEWMARKET (R-H)

Saturday, September 20

**OFFICIAL GOING: Good to firm (good in places) changing to good after race 1 (1.55) changing to good to soft after race 3 (3.05)**
Wind: light, across Weather: dull, rain threatening

## 6553 FEDERATION OF BLOODSTOCK AGENTS "EBF STALLIONS" MAIDEN FILLIES' STKS (BOBIS RACE) (DIV I) 1m

**1:55** (1:56) (Class 4) 2-Y-O **£4,528** (£1,347; £673; £336) **Stalls** Centre

Form RPR

**1** **Toujours L'Amour** 2-9-0 0.................................. JoeFanning 10 74+
(William Haggas) *stdd and wnt lft s: hld up in tch in rr: pushed along and hdwy 2f out: rdn to go 3rd ins fnl f: styd on wl to ld on post* **25/1**

3 **2** *nse* **Moonlight Sonata**[17] 6041 2-9-0 0.................................. ShaneKelly 6 74+
(Sir Michael Stoute) *in tch in midfield: rdn and effrt to chse ldr over 1f out: led 1f out: looked in command fnl 100yds: kpt on but wnt down and hdd on post* **6/4**[1]

0 **3** *2 ½* **Spirited Acclaim (IRE)**[14] 6125 2-9-0 0.................................. LiamKeniry 3 68
(David Elsworth) *led: rdn wl over 1f out: hdd 1f out: lost 2nd fnl 100yds and wknd towards fin* **16/1**

**4** *1 ½* **Al Nofor (IRE)** 2-9-0 0.................................. PatDobbs 2 65
(Richard Hannon) *chsd ldng pair: rdn wl over 1f out: unable qck and outpcd 1f out: kpt on same pce after* **5/1**[3]

**5** *nk* **Eastern Romance** 2-9-0 0.................................. LiamJones 1 64
(William Haggas) *in tch in midfield: effrt 2f out: chsd ldrs but unable qck u.p 1f out: wknd fnl 100yds* **14/1**

**6** *1* **Dreamlike** 2-9-0 0.................................. TomQueally 8 62
(Luca Cumani) *stdd s: hld up in tch in last quartet: pushed along and outpcd 2f out: rallied and swtchd rt ins fnl f: styd on steadily after: no threat to ldrs* **25/1**

2 **7** *nk* **Sweet Dream**[22] 5881 2-9-0 0.................................. HarryBentley 9 61
(Ralph Beckett) *in tch in midfield: rdn ent fnl 2f: outpcd wl over 1f out: rallied and kpt on again ins fnl f: no threat to ldrs* **9/4**[2]

**7** *dht* **Asima (IRE)** 2-9-0 0.................................. LukeMorris 4 61
(Charles Hills) *t.k.h: chsd ldr: rdn 2f out: lost 2nd over 1f out: sn struggling: wknd ins fnl f* **33/1**

**9** *½* **Tocororo (IRE)** 2-9-0 0.................................. JimCrowley 5 60
(Ed Dunlop) *s.i.s: in tch in last quartet: rdn and struggling over 2f out: no threat to ldrs but plugged on steadily fnl f* **50/1**

**10** *nk* **Maybe Tomorrow** 2-9-0 0.................................. FergusSweeney 7 59
(David Simcock) *t.k.h: rn green and hld up towards rr: rdn and struggling ent fnl f: n.d after but kpt on steadily fnl f* **40/1**

1m 41.13s (2.53) **Going Correction** +0.30s/f (Good) **10 Ran SP% 115.0**
Speed ratings (Par 94): **99,98,96,94,94 93,93,93,92,92**
CSF £60.42 TOTE £23.80: £5.50, £1.10, £4.60; EX 81.30 Trifecta £951.70.
**Owner** Christopher Wright & Lordship Stud **Bred** Stratford Place Stud **Trained** Newmarket, Suffolk

**FOCUS**
Far side of Rowley Mile course used. Stalls: Centre. There were some interesting middle-distance types in this inexperienced field. The pace was solid, making it a decent test, but the time was slower than the second division. It's hard to rate the bare form higher.

## 6554 FEDERATION OF BLOODSTOCK AGENTS "EBF STALLIONS" MAIDEN FILLIES' STKS (BOBIS RACE) (DIV II) 1m

**2:30** (2:31) (Class 4) 2-Y-O **£4,528** (£1,347; £673; £336) **Stalls** Centre

Form RPR

03 **1** **Lady Of Dubai**[29] 5644 2-9-0 0.................................. TomQueally 6 84+
(Luca Cumani) *chsd ldr tl led 2f out: rdn over 1f out: styd on strly and drew clr fnl f: readily* **6/4**[1]

3 **2** *3 ¾* **Wiener Valkyrie**[16] 6065 2-9-0 0.................................. LukeMorris 3 73
(Ed Walker) *wnt lft s: in tch in midfield: rdn and effrt 2f out: chsd wnr over 1f out: no imp but kpt on fnl f* **9/2**[3]

**3** *½* **Teofilo's Princess (IRE)** 2-9-0 0.................................. HarryBentley 7 72
(Clive Brittain) *in tch in midfield: rdn and outpcd 2f out: rallied ent fnl f: styd on steadily: no threat to wnr* **40/1**

0 **4** *3 ½* **Beach Walker**[16] 6066 2-9-0 0.................................. HayleyTurner 5 64
(Brian Meehan) *led tl hdd and rdn 2f out: unable qck and lost 2nd over 1f out: wknd fnl f* **50/1**

00 **5** *nse* **Cascades (IRE)**[24] 5821 2-9-0 0.................................. JimCrowley 8 64
(David Elsworth) *in tch in midfield: effrt 2f out: wnt 3rd but no imp on wnr 1f out: wknd ins fnl f* **20/1**

**6** *shd* **Scots Fern** 2-9-0 0.................................. DavidProbert 9 64+
(Andrew Balding) *s.i.s: in tch in last pair: rdn over 2f out: sn outpcd and wl hld over 1f out: rallied and styd on past btn horses ins fnl f: nvr trbld ldrs* **25/1**

**7** *3 ¾* **Sylvette** 2-9-0 0.................................. FrederikTylicki 2 55
(Roger Varian) *chsd ldrs: rdn over 2f out: immediately outpcd and struggling: bhd 1f out* **16/1**

**8** *nk* **Sperry (IRE)** 2-9-0 0.................................. NickyMackay 4 55
(John Gosden) *s.i.s: hld up in tch in last pair: effrt into midfield and rdn 2f out: no imp: drifted lft and racing against stands' rail 1f out: wknd* **15/8**[2]

0 **9** *12* **Flamme Fantastique (GER)**[11] 6208 2-9-0 0.................................. PaulHanagan 1 27
(William Haggas) *chsd ldrs: rdn 3f out: lost pl and over 2f out: wl bhd fnl f* **25/1**

1m 40.1s (1.50) **Going Correction** +0.30s/f (Good) **9 Ran SP% 115.7**
Speed ratings (Par 94): **104,100,99,96,96 96,92,92,80**
CSF £8.12 TOTE £2.30: £1.10, £1.80, £9.80; EX 8.40 Trifecta £207.30.
**Owner** Sheikh Mohammed Obaid Al Maktoum **Bred** Fittocks Stud **Trained** Newmarket, Suffolk

**FOCUS**
The pace looked less testing than division one, but the time was faster and the winner impressed and was value for further.

## 6555 £100,000 TATTERSALLS MILLIONS FILLIES' MEDIAN AUCTION STKS (BOBIS RACE) 6f

**3:05** (3:05) (Class 2) 2-Y-O
**£56,055** (£25,478; £10,195; £5,087; £3,067; £2,041) **Stalls** Centre

Form RPR

0320 **1** **Lacing**[49] 4913 2-8-7 73.................................. PaulHanagan 6 84
(Richard Fahey) *chsd ldr tl led 2f out: styd on wl u.p fnl f: rdn out* **9/1**

023 **2** *1 ¾* **Hundi (IRE)**[35] 5429 2-8-13 79.................................. JimCrowley 8 85
(Charles Hills) *chsd ldrs: rdn and chsd wnr over 1f out: styd on same pce ins fnl f* **4/1**[3]

1144 **3** 5 **Supreme Occasion (IRE)**[8] 6289 2-8-13 99.............. PatDobbs 3 70
(David O'Meara) *wl in tch in midfield: rdn and effrt 2f out: 4th and no ex 1f out: wknd ins fnl f: wnt 3rd wl ins fnl f* **15/8**[1]

**4** 1 1/4 **Phoibe**[41] 2-8-7 0.............. JoeFanning 2 60
(P Schiergen, Germany) *stdd s: hld up in tch in midfield: rdn and effrt to chse ldrs 2f out: no ex 1f out: wknd ins fnl f* **9/4**[2]

6505 **5** 2 1/2 **Star Of Spring (IRE)**[7] 6312 2-8-13 64.............. DavidProbert 1 59
(Charles Hills) *hld up in tch in last trio: rdn 1/2-way: outpcd and btn 2f out: wl hld but plugged on ins fnl f* **50/1**

0260 **6** 1 1/4 **Stocking**[9] 6253 2-8-11 71..............(b[1]) FrederikTylicki 4 53
(Roger Varian) *led tl hdd and rdn 2f out: drvn and btn over 1f out: sn wknd* **14/1**

10 **7** 1 1/4 **Sleepy Dust (IRE)**[35] 5436 2-8-9 77.............. LiamKeniry 7 47
(Sylvester Kirk) *hld up in last pair: grad c across to stands' rail: effrt over 2f out: wknd u.p over 1f out* **25/1**

5204 **8** 1 1/2 **Anastazia**[18] 6008 2-8-9 71..............(b[1]) LukeMorris 5 43
(Paul D'Arcy) *dwlt: sn rcvrd and in tch in midfield: rdn over 2f out: sn struggling: bhd over 1f out* **33/1**

1m 13.79s (1.59) **Going Correction** +0.30s/f (Good) **8** Ran SP% **111.0**
Speed ratings (Par 98): **101,98,92,90,87 85,83,81**
CSF £41.89 TOTE £11.90: £2.30, £1.50, £1.30; EX 44.00 Trifecta £124.60.
**Owner** Cheveley Park Stud **Bred** Newsells Park Stud **Trained** Musley Bank, N Yorks

**FOCUS**
With the exception of the favourite, who was unsuited by the drop to 6f, most of these fillies had official ratings in the 70s, making the form the level of a mid-range handicap. The first two improved and the third ran as well as expected down in trip.

## 6556 £100,000 TATTERSALLS MILLIONS MEDIAN AUCTION TROPHY (BOBIS RACE) 6f

**3:40** (3:42) (Class 2) 2-Y-O
**£56,055** (£25,478; £10,195; £5,087; £3,067; £2,041) **Stalls** Centre

Form RPR

3621 **1** **Secret Brief (IRE)**[14] 6146 2-9-1 91.............. JoeFanning 2 101
(Mark Johnston) *chsd ldrs: rdn and chal 2f out: clr w rival and led over 1f out: hung lft but styd on wl fnl f* **7/2**[2]

0012 **2** 3/4 **Bossy Guest (IRE)**[26] 5770 2-8-13 101.............. LiamKeniry 1 97
(Mick Channon) *in tch in midfield: hdwy 3f out: rdn to chse ldrs wl over 1f out: wnt 2nd ins fnl f: styd on but a hld* **4/1**[3]

312 **3** 3 1/4 **Ballymore Castle (IRE)**[105] 2987 2-9-1 90.............. PaulHanagan 6 89
(Richard Fahey) *in tch in midfield: effrt 2f out: no imp whn lost action wl over 1f out: plenty to do after: edging rt and rallied 1f out: r.o strly fnl f: snatched 3rd last strides: no ch w ldng pair* **13/2**

2112 **4** nk **Heartbreak Hero**[9] 6256 2-8-13 106.............. SebSanders 5 86
(William Haggas) *led: rdn ent fnl 2f: clr w wnr and hdd over 1f out: wknd ins fnl f* **11/10**[1]

454 **5** 4 **Prince Of Time**[38] 5296 2-8-7 70.............. LiamJones 4 68
(Mark Johnston) *in tch in midfield: rdn and effrt ent fnl 2f: outpcd and btn over 1f out: wknd fnl f* **50/1**

30 **6** 2 **Excellent George**[13] 6168 2-8-11 0.............. HarryBentley 3 66
(Stuart Williams) *restless in stalls: in tch towards rr: effrt 2f out: sn outpcd and struggling: wknd over 1f out* **50/1**

03 **7** 5 **Yorkie Talkie (IRE)**[26] 5759 2-8-7 0.............. DavidProbert 7 47
(Mark Johnston) *pressed ldr tl over 2f out: sn rdn: outpcd and btn over 1f out: sn wknd* **33/1**

64 **8** 4 1/2 **Doubly Clever (IRE)**[9] 6268 2-8-13 0.............. JimCrowley 9 40
(Charles Hills) *in tch in midfield: rdn over 2f out: sn btn and bhd* **33/1**

**9** 2 **Silence In Court (IRE)** 2-8-13 0.............. TomQueally 8 34
(Eve Johnson Houghton) *s.i.s: a in rr: lost tch over 2f out* **33/1**

1m 13.73s (1.53) **Going Correction** +0.30s/f (Good) **9** Ran SP% **115.9**
Speed ratings (Par 101): **101,100,95,95,89 87,80,74,71**
CSF £17.15 TOTE £3.70: £1.30, £1.50, £1.80; EX 20.60 Trifecta £84.70.
**Owner** Sheikh Hamdan bin Mohammed Al Maktoum **Bred** Airlie Stud **Trained** Middleham Moor, N Yorks

**FOCUS**
This was a stronger contest than the the fillies' event, with the winner rated 91 and two of his rivals even higher.

## 6557 BETFRED SUPPORTING THE INJURED JOCKEYS FUND CESAREWITCH TRIAL STKS (H'CAP) 2m 2f

**4:15** (4:20) (Class 2) (0-105,98) 3-Y-O+
**£31,125** (£9,320; £4,660; £2,330; £1,165; £585) **Stalls** Centre

Form RPR

1202 **1** **See And Be Seen**[6] 6360 4-7-10 75..............(p) NoelGarbutt(5) 4 85
(Sylvester Kirk) *chsd ldrs: rdn and squeezed through 2f out: rdn to ld over 1f out: styd on wl: rdn out* **20/1**

00- **2** nk **Big Easy (GER)**[133] 7193 7-8-13 87.............. TomQueally 7 97
(Philip Hobbs) *hld up in tch: clsd and nt clr run over 2f out: rdn and hdwy between horses jst over 1f out: chsd wnr jst ins fnl f: styd on wl: nvr quite getting to wnr* **16/1**

0062 **3** 3 3/4 **Ray Ward (IRE)**[52] 4777 4-9-5 93.............. JimCrowley 2 99
(David Simcock) *stdd s: hld up in rr: clsd and nt clr run over 2f out: hdwy u.p over 1f out: wnt 3rd ins fnl f: no imp: wknd towards fin* **9/4**[1]

0500 **4** 2 1/2 **Argent Knight**[46] 5017 4-8-7 81.............. DavidProbert 10 84
(William Jarvis) *chsd ldrs: clsd 3f out: rdn and pressing ldrs 2f out: no ex 1f out: wknd ins fnl f* **16/1**

0523 **5** 3/4 **Sir Frank Morgan (IRE)**[10] 6228 4-8-8 82.............. JoeFanning 1 84
(Mark Johnston) *led tl 12f out: chsd ldr after: clsd 3f out: rdn to ld 2f out: hdd over 1f out: wknd ins fnl f* **9/1**[3]

2621 **6** nk **Entihaa**[13] 6169 6-8-9 83.............. JimmyQuinn 11 85
(Alan Swinbank) *hld up towards rr: clsd 3f out: pressing ldrs and rdn wl over 1f out: no ex 1f out: wknd ins fnl f* **10/1**

5203 **7** 1 3/4 **Ex Oriente (IRE)**[2] 6501 5-8-1 75.............. HarryBentley 5 75
(Stuart Williams) *stdd s: hld up in rr: clsd 3f out: rdn and effrt 2f out: sn outpcd and btn* **12/1**

2401 **8** 2 3/4 **Gabrial's King (IRE)**[70] 4217 5-9-4 92.............. FergusSweeney 3 89
(David Simcock) *t.k.h: hld up towards rr: stdy hdwy and chsd ldrs 8f out: rdn and unable qck 2f out: wknd over 1f out* **12/1**

2000 **9** 11 **Repeater**[8] 6288 5-9-10 98..............(p) ShaneKelly 9 83
(David O'Meara) *t.k.h: hld up in midfield: swtchd lft away fr rivals after 2f: hdwy to ld 12f out and moved bk to inner: hdd 2f out: sn squeezed for room and dropped out: bhd and eased ins fnl f* **12/1**

3-24 **10** 3 1/2 **Mubaraza (IRE)**[136] 2073 5-9-10 98.............. PaulHanagan 8 79
(Ed Dunlop) *hld up towards rr: clsd 3f out: n.m.r ent fnl 2f: sn rdn and btn: bhd and eased ins fnl f* **11/4**[2]

4m 2.2s (10.20) **Going Correction** +0.30s/f (Good) **10** Ran SP% **116.1**
Speed ratings (Par 109): **89,88,87,86,85 85,84,83,78,77**
CSF £300.75 CT £1006.89 TOTE £13.40: £4.70, £4.40, £1.30; EX 255.90 Trifecta £2260.10.
**Owner** Timothy Pearson **Bred** Exors Of The Late T E Pocock **Trained** Upper Lambourn, Berks

**FOCUS**
In a decent race of its type, the pace was routine for a stamina test until quickening in the last 3f. Quite muddling form.

## 6558 INJURED JOCKEYS FUND 50TH ANNIVERSARY H'CAP 6f

**4:50** (4:53) (Class 4) (0-85,83) 3-Y-O+ **£5,175** (£1,540; £769; £384) **Stalls** Centre

Form RPR

2-43 **1** **Charter (IRE)**[24] 5834 4-8-13 75..............[1] JimCrowley 5 85+
(Michael Wigham) *stdd s: hld up in rr: effrt 2f out: hdwy u.p over 1f out: drvn and str run ins fnl f to ld towards fin* **3/1**[1]

000 **2** 1/2 **Tellovoi (IRE)**[7] 6320 6-9-6 82..............(p) LiamKeniry 7 90
(Ann Stokell) *led main gp and chsd ldr: rdn 2f out: kpt on u.p to ld wl ins fnl f: sn hdd and no ex* **25/1**

0420 **3** 1/2 **Commanche**[10] 6235 5-8-11 73.............. JimmyQuinn 2 79
(Chris Dwyer) *chsd ldrs: rdn ent fnl 2f: drvn and kpt on to press ldrs wl ins fnl f: no ex towards fin* **12/1**

0100 **4** 3/4 **Nova Champ (IRE)**[46] 5012 3-9-2 80..............(p) HarryBentley 1 84
(Stuart Williams) *racd along on far rail: overall ldr: rdn over 1f out: hdd wl ins fnl f: wknd towards fin* **12/1**

5520 **5** 3 1/4 **Joe Packet**[26] 5750 7-9-5 81..............(p) JoeFanning 6 74
(Jonathan Portman) *t.k.h: hld up in midfield: effrt u.p wl over 1f out: wknd fnl 100yds* **7/1**[3]

5241 **6** 1/2 **Jontleman (IRE)**[9] 6249 4-8-12 74.............. SamHitchcott 3 66
(Mick Channon) *in tch in midfield: effrt u.p 2f out: no imp 1f out: wknd fnl 100yds* **12/1**

000 **7** 1 **Rocksilla**[22] 5888 4-9-3 79.............. SebSanders 8 67
(Chris Wall) *in tch in midfield: rdn and effrt 2f out: outpcd and btn over 1f out: wknd ins fnl f* **13/2**[2]

041 **8** nk **Front Page News**[18] 6021 4-8-11 78.............. LouisSteward(5) 11 65
(Robert Eddery) *hld up towards rr: rdn and hdwy over 1f out: no imp 1f out: wknd ins fnl f* **8/1**

5000 **9** 1 1/4 **Daylight**[15] 6089 4-9-7 83..............(t) DavidProbert 9 66
(Andrew Balding) *in tch in midfield: rdn and unable qck jst over 2f out: outpcd and btn wl over 1f out* **8/1**

6043 **10** 1 **Corporal Maddox**[15] 6089 7-9-7 83..............(p) TomQueally 10 63
(Ronald Harris) *s.i.s: hld up in rr: rdn and effrt 2f out: no imp: n.d* **14/1**

3135 **11** 2 1/4 **Light From Mars**[18] 6020 9-9-2 83..............(p) MarcMonaghan(5) 13 56
(Ronald Harris) *stdd s: hld up in tch: rdn ent fnl 2f: no rspnse: sn lost pl and btn* **12/1**

3613 **12** 5 **Meandmyshadow**[24] 5817 6-8-11 73.............. StevieDonohoe 14 30
(Alan Brown) *chsd ldrs: rdn over 2f out: sn struggling and lost pl: bhd fnl f* **16/1**

1m 13.18s (0.98) **Going Correction** +0.30s/f (Good)
**WFA** 3 from 4yo+ 2lb **12** Ran SP% **120.2**
Speed ratings (Par 105): **105,104,103,102,98 97,96,95,94,92 89,83**
CSF £92.09 CT £811.14 TOTE £4.20: £1.70, £9.50, £3.80; EX 134.40 Trifecta £2781.80 Part won..
**Owner** J Searchfield, D Hassan **Bred** Barouche Stud (IRE) Ltd **Trained** Newmarket, Suffolk

**FOCUS**
This competitive sprint was won by a relatively unexposed horse who has been well backed in all three races this season. The winner looks capable of a bit better.

## 6559 THOROUGHBRED BREEDERS' ASSOCIATION EBF STALLIONS FILLIES' H'CAP 1m 4f

**5:25** (5:26) (Class 3) (0-95,90) 3-Y-O+ **£9,703** (£2,887; £1,443; £721) **Stalls** Centre

Form RPR

41 **1** **Rewaaya (IRE)**[117] 2613 3-9-2 **86**.............. PaulHanagan 3 102
(John Gosden) *chsd ldr tl led 4f out: rdn 2f out: in command 1f out: styd on strly: readily* **5/1**[3]

2214 **2** 4 **Desert Snow**[63] 4452 3-9-0 **84**.............. FrederikTylicki 7 94
(Saeed bin Suroor) *chsd ldrs: effrt u.p over 2f out: chsd wnr over 1f out: no imp: kpt on to hold 2nd ins fnl f* **13/2**

4042 **3** 1 **Headline News (IRE)**[16] 6061 5-9-9 **85**.............. ChrisCatlin 9 93
(Rae Guest) *stdd s: hld up in tch in rr: rdn 3f out: hdwy u.p to chse ldrs over 1f out: styd on same pce ins fnl f* **10/1**

426 **4** 3 1/2 **Yojojo (IRE)**[9] 6258 5-9-5 **86**..............[1] DanielMuscutt(5) 8 88
(Gay Kelleway) *stdd s: hld up in rr: rdn and hdwy 3f out: no imp and btn over 1f out: plugged on to go modest 4th ins fnl f* **25/1**

-520 **5** 3/4 **Kikonga**[16] 6061 4-9-9 **90**.............. LouisSteward(5) 1 91
(Luca Cumani) *in tch in midfield: hdwy to chse ldrs 3f out: rdn 2f out: no ex and btn over 1f out: wknd ins fnl f* **9/2**[2]

1112 **6** 1 1/2 **Sleeper**[17] 6036 3-8-11 **81**.............. PatDobbs 4 80
(Ralph Beckett) *in tch in midfield: effrt u.p over 2f out: no imp and btn over 1f out: wknd fnl f* **7/1**

0411 **7** 2 1/2 **Ski Lift**[22] 5884 3-9-2 **86**.............. NickyMackay 2 81
(John Gosden) *hld up in last trio: effrt 3f out: drvn and no hdwy 2f out: wknd over 1f out* **7/1**

1-21 **8** 1 **Asyad (IRE)**[77] 3968 3-9-6 **90**.............. FrankieDettori 10 83
(Sir Michael Stoute) *led tl 4f out: chsd wnr tl over 1f out: sn btn and wknd fnl f* **4/1**[1]

100- **9** 26 **Princess Caetani (IRE)**[121] 7250 5-9-12 **88**.............. SebSanders 5 40
(David Dennis) *in tch towards rr: rdn over 3f out: sn struggling: lost tch 2f out: t.o* **66/1**

-216 **10** 8 **Spiritoftheunion**[27] 5723 3-8-11 **81**..............[1] JimCrowley 6 20
(Michael Bell) *chsd ldrs: rdn and lost pl 4f out: lost tch 2f out: t.o* **14/1**

2m 33.35s (1.35) **Going Correction** +0.30s/f (Good)
**WFA** 3 from 4yo+ 8lb **10** Ran SP% **114.3**
Speed ratings (Par 104): **107,104,103,101,100 99,98,97,80,74**
CSF £36.70 CT £311.45 TOTE £5.50: £1.90, £2.50, £2.90; EX 27.00 Trifecta £262.10.
**Owner** Hamdan Al Maktoum **Bred** Shadwell Estate Company Limited **Trained** Newmarket, Suffolk

**FOCUS**
In a race containing a number of useful fillies, some of them still lightly raced, an ordinary pace led to a notable increase in the tempo in the last 3f. A taking success from the winner.

## 6560 1STSECURITYSOLUTIONS.CO.UK H'CAP 1m
5:55 (5:57) (Class 2) (0-100,98) 3-Y-O+ £12,938 (£3,850; £1,924; £962) Stalls Centre

Form RPR
2402 1 **Dark Emerald (IRE)**[7] 6335 4-9-10 **98** SebSanders 2 106
(Brendan Powell) *racd against far rail thrght: mde all: rdn over 2f out: hld on u.p fnl f: all out: gamely* **10/1**
6313 2 *nk* **Master The World (IRE)**[14] 6149 3-9-1 **93** (p) LiamKeniry 1 100
(David Elsworth) *chsd wnr: rdn over 2f out: ev ch over 1f out: sustained duel w wnr fnl f: kpt on wl: a jst hld* **7/2**[2]
1236 3 *1 1/2* **George Cinq**[14] 6140 4-8-9 **88** LouisSteward(5) 5 92
(Michael Bell) *hld up in tch in midfield: effrt 2f out: swtchd rt and then bk lft over 1f out: chsd ldrs and one pce u.p ins fnl f* **6/1**[3]
0540 4 *1* **Moonday Sun (USA)**[21] 5928 5-8-13 **87** (p) PatDobbs 4 89
(Amanda Perrett) *chsd ldrs: rdn 2f out: drvn over 1f out: styd on same pce ins fnl f* **9/1**
11 5 *hd* **Dream Spirit (IRE)**[42] 5192 3-9-4 **96** LiamJones 6 97
(William Haggas) *stdd s: t.k.h: hld up in tch in rr: hdwy against far rail over 1f out: one pce and no imp ins fnl f* **2/1**[1]
6560 6 *1/2* **Energizer (GER)**[30] 5609 5-9-10 **98** JimCrowley 3 98
(Charlie Appleby) *taken down early: chsd ldrs: pushed along and edgd rt 2f out: styd on same pce u.p fnl f* **7/1**
060 7 *3 1/4* **Mabait**[7] 6320 8-8-3 **84** oh1 SophieKilloran(7) 8 76
(David Simcock) *hld up in last pair: effrt over 1f out: no imp* **14/1**
464- 8 *11* **Stormy Paradise (IRE)**[348] 7084 3-8-11 **92** RyanClark(3) 7 59
(Brian Meehan) *in tch in midfield: rdn and lost pl over 2f out: bhd and wknd over 1f out* **25/1**

1m 39.68s (1.08) **Going Correction** +0.30s/f (Good)
**WFA** 3 from 4yo+ 4lb **8** Ran SP% **111.9**
Speed ratings (Par 109): **106,105,104,103,103 102,99,88**
CSF £43.06 CT £230.39 TOTE £9.70: £2.90, £2.10, £2.50; EX 39.40 Trifecta £116.10.
**Owner** K Rhatigan **Bred** Olive O'Connor **Trained** Upper Lambourn, Berks
**FOCUS**
The winner was rated 98, so this was a high-class handicap despite the smallish field. The pace held up again and the winner rates a small personal best.
T/Plt: £37.70 to a £1 stake. Pool: £65,238.19 - 1263.16 winning units. T/Qpdt: £16.20 to a £1 stake. Pool: £4206.82 - 191.10 winning units. SP

# 6407 WOLVERHAMPTON (A.W) (L-H)
### Saturday, September 20

**OFFICIAL GOING: Tapeta: standard**
Wind: Light, against Weather: Overcast

## 6561 WIN BIG WITH THE TOTEJACKPOT H'CAP (TAPETA) 5f 20y
5:50 (5:51) (Class 6) (0-55,56) 3-Y-O+ £2,264 (£673; £336; £168) Stalls Low

Form RPR
0333 1 **Dream Sika (IRE)**[7] 6340 3-9-1 50 DaleSwift 12 59
(Ruth Carr) *mde all: hld on wl u.p fnl f* **8/1**[3]
2333 2 *1/2* **Lucky Mark (IRE)**[9] 6273 5-9-8 56 (p) LukeMorris 4 63
(John Balding) *chsd wnr thrght: rdn over 2f out: r.o fnl f: jst hld* **2/1**[1]
000 3 *3/4* **Rat Catcher (IRE)**[17] 6023 4-8-7 48 (b) RobHornby(7) 6 53
(Lisa Williamson) *in tch: rdn over 2f out: r.o fnl f* **33/1**
3635 4 *nk* **Your Gifted (IRE)**[9] 6273 7-8-13 52 (v) AlistairRawlinson(5) 11 55
(Lisa Williamson) *bmpd s: outpcd towards rr: gd late hdwy* **10/1**
054 5 *1/2* **First Rebellion**[5] 6409 5-9-3 51 (b) RaulDaSilva 8 53
(Tony Carroll) *prom: chal for 2nd 2f out: hrd rdn over 1f out: one pce* **7/2**[2]
3004 6 *1 3/4* **Aaranyow (IRE)**[25] 5801 6-9-0 48 (t) RobertTart 9 43
(Clifford Lines) *bmpd s: in tch on outer: rdn and styd on same pce fnl 2f* **11/1**
5510 7 *shd* **Danzoe (IRE)**[23] 5860 7-9-0 53 (p[1]) EoinWalsh(5) 5 48
(Christine Dunnett) *hld up in midfield: rdn and no imp fnl 2f* **10/1**
4206 8 *1* **Volcanic Dust (IRE)**[67] 4285 6-9-1 52 (t) DeclanBates(3) 2 43
(Milton Bradley) *bhd tl styd on fnl f* **22/1**
0050 9 *1/2* **Avonvalley**[9] 6273 7-9-6 54 StephenCraine 1 44
(Peter Grayson) *a abt same pl* **28/1**
0000 10 *1 3/4* **Saga Lout**[5] 6409 4-8-13 52 (p) JackDuern(5) 13 35
(Andrew Hollinshead) *towards rr: rdn over 2f out: n.d* **33/1**
054 11 *shd* **Little Briar Rose**[26] 5780 3-9-2 51 WilliamCarson 7 34
(John Spearing) *chsd ldrs tl wknd 2f out* **25/1**
0004 12 *4 1/2* **Yankee Red**[15] 6120 3-9-1 50 (b) SteveDrowne 3 17
(John Best) *outpcd: sn wl bhd* **25/1**

1m 1.88s (-0.02) **Going Correction** -0.025s/f (Stan)
**WFA** 3 from 4yo+ 1lb **12** Ran SP% **114.6**
Speed ratings (Par 101): **99,98,97,96,95 92,92,91,90,87 87,80**
CSF £21.41 CT £504.96 TOTE £9.80: £3.00, £1.10, £9.10; EX 18.80 Trifecta £1548.90 Part won..
**Owner** Michael Hill **Bred** Lady Janet Brookeborough **Trained** Huby, N Yorks
**FOCUS**
Overcast and muggy. The excellent Tapeta surface was harrowed on Tuesday to a depth of between three and four inches, before being rolled back to racing speed. Plenty out of form for a low-grade handicap and the front two, who had at least been relatively consistent of late, were prominent from the start.

## 6562 TOTEPOOL HOME OF POOL BETTING H'CAP (TAPETA) 5f 216y
6:20 (6:20) (Class 5) (0-75,76) 3-Y-O+ £2,911 (£866; £432; £216) Stalls Low

Form RPR
3304 1 **Sacha Park (IRE)**[9] 6249 3-8-12 75 KieranShoemark(7) 5 85
(Richard Hannon) *hld up in 4th: effrt and led 1f out: rdn out* **9/4**[1]
0604 2 *1 1/4* **Ashkari (IRE)**[17] 6025 3-9-4 74 (p) SteveDrowne 7 80
(Clive Cox) *prom: led briefly over 1f out: one pce fnl f* **13/2**
3100 3 *2 3/4* **Mambo Spirit (IRE)**[9] 6266 10-8-2 61 oh1 EoinWalsh(5) 4 58
(Tony Newcombe) *s.i.s: outpcd and bhd: r.o fr over 1f out: nrest at fin* **33/1**
5666 4 *nk* **Queen Aggie (IRE)**[26] 5776 4-8-12 66 RobertTart 6 62
(Tony Carroll) *hld up towards rr: shkn up and styd on fr over 1f out* **33/1**
2655 5 *shd* **Loud**[10] 6240 4-8-12 66 (b) BarryMcHugh 8 62
(Amy Weaver) *towards rr: rdn over 2f out: styd on fnl f* **12/1**
304 6 *hd* **Dynamo Walt (IRE)**[30] 5601 3-8-11 67 DaleSwift 3 62
(Derek Shaw) *mid-div: rdn over 2f out: styd on same pce* **11/1**
2121 7 *1 1/4* **Chapellerie (IRE)**[16] 6077 5-9-1 69 (b) DaneO'Neill 9 60
(Brendan Powell) *s.s: outpcd* **4/1**[2]
2321 8 *1* **The Dandy Yank (IRE)**[10] 6236 3-9-6 76 (p) WilliamCarson 2 64
(Jamie Osborne) *prom: rdn 2f out: wknd fnl f* **11/2**[3]
26 9 *5* **Point North (IRE)**[133] 2159 7-9-0 68 (b) LukeMorris 1 40
(John Balding) *sn led: hdd & wknd over 1f out* **9/1**

1m 13.63s (-0.87) **Going Correction** -0.025s/f (Stan)
**WFA** 3 from 4yo+ 2lb **9** Ran SP% **111.4**
Speed ratings (Par 103): **104,102,98,98,98 97,96,94,88**
CSF £16.24 CT £356.10 TOTE £2.90: £1.40, £2.50, £5.60; EX 15.80 Trifecta £577.10.
**Owner** Middleham Park Racing XLI **Bred** Kildaragh Stud **Trained** East Everleigh, Wilts
**FOCUS**
A fair sprint handicap, two drew clear of the remainder and the money spoke.

## 6563 TOTEQUADPOT FOUR PLACES IN FOUR RACES (S) STKS (TAPETA) 5f 216y
6:50 (6:50) (Class 6) 2-Y-O £2,264 (£673; £336; £168) Stalls Low

Form RPR
3330 1 **Ar Colleen Aine**[15] 6104 2-8-6 65 LukeMorris 4 61
(Mick Channon) *mde all: drvn clr over 1f out: readily* **5/4**[1]
4432 2 *2 3/4* **Itsindebag**[43] 5133 2-7-13 56 (p) JosephineGordon(7) 10 53
(J S Moore) *mid-div: rdn over 2f out: late hdwy to take 2nd fnl strides* **9/1**
0603 3 *nk* **Strategise (IRE)**[22] 5896 2-8-6 55 (p) WilliamCarson 1 52
(Tom Dascombe) *prom: rdn to chse wnr 2f out: one pce: lost 2nd fnl strides* **6/1**[2]
40 4 *nse* **Picture Postcard**[19] 5982 2-8-1 0 (p) NathanAlison(5) 7 52
(William Haggas) *chsd ldrs: kpt on same pce fnl 2f* **9/1**
2604 5 *nse* **Diminutive (IRE)**[18] 6017 2-8-5 57 (p) KieranShoemark(7) 5 58
(Grace Harris) *prom: rdn 2f out: one pce* **28/1**
6520 6 *3/4* **Cupulation**[17] 6040 2-8-6 55 EoinWalsh(5) 12 54
(Amy Weaver) *hld up in midfield: rdn and wnt wd bnd into st: styd on same pce* **8/1**[3]
3430 7 *3/4* **Fazenda's Girl**[11] 6211 2-8-6 51 (b) BarryMcHugh 3 47
(Michael Easterby) *chsd ldrs: drvn along 2f out: sn btn* **14/1**
0 8 *nk* **Ilumination**[3] 6447 2-7-13 0 DanielleMooney(7) 11 46+
(Michael Easterby) *s.s: outpcd and bhd tl styd on fnl f* **50/1**
60 9 *1 1/4* **Excelling Oscar (IRE)**[19] 5982 2-8-11 0 DaleSwift 8 47
(Conor Dore) *chsd ldrs: hrd rdn and outpcd 3f out: btn whn wnt wd into st* **100/1**
0055 10 *1/2* **Blue Burmese (IRE)**[16] 6072 2-8-1 53 NoelGarbutt(5) 2 41
(Mark Usher) *s.s: outpcd and bhd: styng on 1f out: eased whn n.d ins fnl f* **12/1**
00U 11 *14* **Bonita Brown Eyes (IRE)**[11] 6205 2-8-3 0 PhilipPrince(3) 6
(J S Moore) *s.i.s: outpcd: sn wl bhd* **66/1**

1m 15.52s (1.02) **Going Correction** -0.025s/f (Stan) **11** Ran SP% **112.1**
Speed ratings (Par 93): **92,88,87,87,87 86,85,85,83,83 64**
CSF £12.07 TOTE £2.40: £1.40, £2.50, £1.80; EX 11.10 Trifecta £26.10.
**Owner** Anne & Steve Fisher **Bred** Wansdyke Farms Ltd **Trained** West Ilsley, Berks
**FOCUS**
Modest form in a seller run at a reasonable pace. Few got into it.

## 6564 TRY A TOTETRIFECTA TODAY H'CAP 1m 4f 50y
7:20 (7:20) (Class 6) (0-65,65) 3-Y-O+ £2,264 (£673; £336; £168) Stalls Low

Form RPR
-045 1 **Lucky Jim**[108] 2893 3-9-4 65 GeorgeBaker 11 75+
(Chris Wall) *stdd in rr s: gd hdwy on outer 2f out: led over 1f out: drvn to hold on fnl f* **2/1**[1]
0426 2 *nk* **Majestic Sun (IRE)**[66] 4333 3-9-3 64 LukeMorris 10 73
(Peter Chapple-Hyam) *t.k.h in rr: rdn and hdwy over 2f out: sustained chal fr over 1f out: r.o wl* **7/2**[2]
0060 3 *4* **Red Pilgrim (IRE)**[44] 5101 4-9-9 62 RobertTart 6 65
(James Toller) *bhd: drvn along over 4f out: rapid hdwy on inner 2f out: one pce fnl f* **20/1**
6000 4 *1 1/4* **Gentlemax (FR)**[31] 5547 4-9-10 63 (b) PatCosgrave 3 64
(Jim Boyle) *in tch: wnt prom over 2f out: hrd rdn and wknd 1f out* **33/1**
5403 5 *3/4* **Tapis Libre**[30] 5600 6-9-11 64 BarryMcHugh 7 64
(Michael Easterby) *mid-div: effrt and hmpd over 1f out: styd on same pce* **11/2**[3]
5343 6 *nk* **Power Up**[5] 6410 3-8-11 58 (v) DaneO'Neill 2 57
(Mark Johnston) *hld up in midfield: promising hdwy and in tch 2f out: sn rdn and no imp* **11/2**[3]
2456 7 *5* **Medieval Bishop (IRE)**[42] 5200 5-9-9 62 (p) DaleSwift 9 53
(Mark Walford) *prom tl wknd wl over 1f out* **20/1**
0260 8 *3/4* **Taxiformissbyron**[18] 6000 4-8-7 53 RowanScott(7) 12 43
(Iain Jardine) *chsd ldrs: wnt 2nd after 4f: lft in ld 6f out: hdd & wknd wl over 1f out* **33/1**
2030 9 *13* **Excellent News (IRE)**[16] 6076 5-8-5 51 oh6 AdamMcLean(7) 8 20
(Tony Forbes) *chsd ldrs tl wknd 2f out* **50/1**
0350 10 *1/2* **Southern Cross**[16] 6070 3-8-13 60 RichardHughes 1 29
(Hughie Morrison) *prom tl wknd wl over 1f out* **12/1**
4403 11 *14* **Lady Bubbles**[21] 5917 3-7-13 51 oh3 NoelGarbutt(5) 5
(Michael Easterby) *t.k.h in rr: rdn 4f out: sn wl bhd* **33/1**
050 12 *20* **Pepperello**[42] 5195 3-7-13 53 oh5 ow2 DanielleMooney(7) 4
(Tim Etherington) *led: wl clr after 4f: rdr mistk winning post and hdd 6f out: wknd 4f out: sn t.o* **100/1**

2m 41.25s (0.45) **Going Correction** -0.025s/f (Stan)
**WFA** 3 from 4yo+ 8lb **12** Ran SP% **115.3**
Speed ratings (Par 101): **97,96,94,93,92 92,89,88,80,79 70,57**
CSF £7.67 CT £104.42 TOTE £3.20: £1.30, £1.50, £8.60; EX 12.90 Trifecta £136.20.
**Owner** Follow The Flag Partnership **Bred** Follow The Flag Partnership **Trained** Newmarket, Suffolk
■ Stewards' Enquiry : Danielle Mooney 12-day ban: appeared to ride a finish a circuit too soon 4, 7-10 October)
**FOCUS**
Another modest race and the pace was steady, save for an embarrassing faux pas by the rider of Pepperello. The steady gallop by the remainder helped those coming from off the pace and two drew clear. The form should hold up.

## 6565 TOTEEXACTA PICK THE 1,2 EBF MAIDEN STKS (TAPETA) 1m 141y
7:50 (7:51) (Class 5) 2-Y-O £2,911 (£866; £432; £216) Stalls Low

Form RPR
02 1 **Belgrade**[15] 6102 2-9-5 0 RichardHughes 8 77
(Richard Hannon) *hld up towards rr on outer: pushed along 4f out: hdwy 2f out: styd on to ld 1f out: drvn out* **5/4**[1]
62 2 *3/4* **Indelible Ink (IRE)**[62] 4467 2-9-5 0 ShaneKelly 5 75
(Sir Michael Stoute) *trckd ldr: led 2f out tl 1f out: kpt on* **3/1**[2]
0 3 *nk* **International Name**[22] 5881 2-9-5 0 FrederikTylicki 4 75
(Saeed bin Suroor) *dwlt: hld up: hdwy and eased outside over 1f out: rn green: gng on wl at fin* **7/2**[3]


The Form Book, Raceform Ltd, Newbury, RG14 5SJ

652 4 2 1/4 **Classic Villager**[27] 5712 2-9-5 75 GeorgeBaker 1 70
(Philip Hide) *led tl 2f out: wknd fnl f* **10/1**
5 5 3/4 **Ali Bin Nayef**[15] 6101 2-9-5 0 DaneO'Neill 7 68
(Charles Hills) *hld up in 5th: rdn to chse ldrs over 2f out: one pce* **15/2**
6 5 **Sea Of Heaven (IRE)** 2-9-5 0 LukeMorris 3 58
(Sir Mark Prescott Bt) *prom tl wknd 2f out* **28/1**
0 7 14 **Hier Encore (FR)**[70] 4207 2-9-5 0 RaulDaSilva 2 29
(David Menuisier) *s.s and early reminders: a bhd: no ch fnl 3f* **100/1**
8 1/2 **Funtime Barry (IRE)** 2-9-5 0 PatCosgrave 6 28
(Richard Hannon) *a towards rr: outpcd and wl bhd fnl 3f* **25/1**
1m 50.66s (0.56) **Going Correction** -0.025s/f (Stan) **8** Ran SP% **120.8**
Speed ratings (Par 95): **96,95,95,93,92 87,75,75**
CSF £5.54 TOTE £1.60: £1.10, £1.20, £1.80; EX 6.30 Trifecta £21.30.
**Owner** Mohamed Saeed Al Shahi **Bred** Cavendish Bloodstock **Trained** East Everleigh, Wilts
**FOCUS**
The pace was reasonable, although it would not do to get too carried away with the form of this juvenile maiden, despite it contested by representatives from some powerful yards.

## 6566 FOLLOW @TOTEPOOL ON TWITTER H'CAP 1m 1f 103y
**8:20** (8:22) (Class 3) (0-95,95) 3-Y-O **£7,246** (£2,168; £1,084; £542; £270) **Stalls** Low

Form RPR
0530 1 **Tinghir (IRE)**[21] 5928 4-9-4 **89** (b) GeorgeBaker 3 101
(David Lanigan) *dwlt: hld up in tch: smooth hdwy 3f out: led over 1f out: rdn clr: readily* **5/2**[1]
1301 2 2 1/4 **Wahgah (USA)**[33] 5487 3-9-5 **95** DaneO'Neill 1 103
(Saeed bin Suroor) *chsd ldrs: lost pl 5f out: rallied 2f out: kpt on to take 2nd ins fnl f* **9/2**[2]
5401 3 1 **Spiritual Star (IRE)**[15] 6100 5-9-2 **87** (t) RobertTart 7 92
(Anthony Carson) *t.k.h towards rr: rdn and hdwy 2f out: styd on* **12/1**
5300 4 1 3/4 **God's Speed (IRE)**[15] 6106 3-8-10 **86** ChrisCatlin 5 89
(Rae Guest) *prom: led 4f out tl over 1f out: no ex* **16/1**
2110 5 1 **Halation (IRE)**[29] 5656 3-9-0 **90** JamieSpencer 10 90
(David Simcock) *dwlt: hld up towards rr: rdn and sme hdwy over 1f out: nt rch ldrs* **9/2**[2]
24-1 6 3/4 **Night Party (IRE)**[149] 1662 3-8-11 **90** MatthewLawson(3) 9 89
(Saeed bin Suroor) *s.s: bhd: rdn 3f out: sme late hdwy* **11/1**
2-04 7 2 1/4 **Docs Legacy (IRE)**[15] 6098 5-8-10 **81** RichardHughes 4 74
(Richard Fahey) *chsd ldrs: led briefly over 4f out: wknd 2f out* **7/1**[3]
3040 8 3 **Back Burner (IRE)**[14] 6156 6-8-5 **81** oh9 (p) TimClark(5) 6 68
(Dai Burchell) *t.k.h in midfield: hdwy 4f out: wknd over 2f out* **100/1**
5004 9 12 **Zampa Manos (USA)**[24] 5824 3-8-13 **89** DavidProbert 2 52
(Andrew Balding) *led tl over 4f out: wknd 3f out* **11/1**
6306 10 1/2 **Henry The Aviator (USA)**[11] 6214 4-8-10 **81** AdrianNicholls 8 42
(Mark Johnston) *wd thrght: mid-div: effrt 4f out: wknd 3f out* **33/1**
1m 59.07s (-1.73) **Going Correction** -0.025s/f (Stan)
**WFA** 3 from 4yo+ 5lb **10** Ran SP% **111.6**
Speed ratings (Par 107): **106,104,103,101,100 100,98,95,84,84**
CSF £12.66 CT £107.03 TOTE £2.70: £1.30, £1.90, £3.80; EX 11.10 Trifecta £125.40.
**Owner** B E Nielsen **Bred** Bjorn Nielsen **Trained** Upper Lambourn, Berks
**FOCUS**
A true pace for this useful handicap and the form looks solid.

## 6567 COLLECT TOTEPOOL WINNINGS AT BETFRED SHOPS H'CAP (DIV I) 7f 32y
**8:50** (8:51) (Class 6) (0-65,65) 3-Y-O **£2,264** (£673; £336; £168) **Stalls** High

Form RPR
5125 1 **Marmarus**[38] 5303 3-9-7 65 AdamKirby 7 78
(Clive Cox) *chsd ldr: led 1f out: drvn clr* **9/2**[2]
0222 2 2 1/4 **Slingsby**[14] 6154 3-8-13 57 (b) BarryMcHugh 6 64
(Michael Easterby) *led: hrd rdn and hdd 1f out: one pce* **7/2**[1]
0406 3 3 1/2 **Applejack Lad**[33] 5492 3-9-1 62 (t) RyanPowell(3) 9 60
(John Ryan) *chsd ldrs: hrd rdn 2f out: one pce* **25/1**
0002 4 3/4 **Fiftyshadesdarker (IRE)**[10] 6243 3-9-0 58 PatCosgrave 10 54
(George Baker) *bhd: rdn and struggling 4f out: styd on fnl 2f: nrest at fin* **11/2**[3]
-022 5 1/2 **Posh Bounty**[15] 6090 3-8-7 51 oh6 LukeMorris 8 46
(Joseph Tuite) *towards rr: rdn over 3f out: styd on appr fnl f* **33/1**
0553 6 1 3/4 **Lacock**[41] 5214 3-9-7 65 DaneO'Neill 5 55
(Henry Candy) *prom: rdn over 3f out: wknd wl over 1f out* **7/2**[1]
2552 7 14 **Aristocratic Duty**[18] 6022 3-9-4 62 RichardHughes 4 16
(Sylvester Kirk) *in tch tl wknd over 2f out* **9/2**[2]
5050 8 2 1/4 **Miss Moppet**[74] 4063 3-9-6 64 GeorgeBaker 3 12
(Hughie Morrison) *mid-div: rdn over 3f out: n.d after* **16/1**
0044 9 47 **Almax**[15] 6088 3-8-7 51 (v) StevieDonohoe 2
(Michael Bell) *in tch on rail: wknd 4f out: sn bhd* **33/1**
1m 28.4s (-0.40) **Going Correction** -0.025s/f (Stan) **9** Ran SP% **111.8**
Speed ratings (Par 99): **101,98,94,93,93 91,75,72,18**
CSF £19.49 CT £341.92 TOTE £4.60: £1.10, £2.30, £7.80; EX 21.00 Trifecta £306.80.
**Owner** Ms Gillian Khosla **Bred** Vimal And Gillian Khosla **Trained** Lambourn, Berks
**FOCUS**
A seemingly competitive handicap for the lowly grade was anything but as very few got into it and they finished well strung out.

## 6568 COLLECT TOTEPOOL WINNINGS AT BETFRED SHOPS H'CAP (DIV II) 7f 32y
**9:20** (9:20) (Class 6) (0-65,65) 3-Y-O **£2,264** (£673; £336; £168) **Stalls** High

Form RPR
3042 1 **Plucky Dip**[10] 6243 3-9-4 62 AdamKirby 7 76
(John Ryan) *hld up in midfield: hdwy over 2f out: led wl over 1f out: drvn clr* **7/4**[1]
0000 2 3 **Kraka Gym (IRE)**[22] 5891 3-8-7 51 (b) BarryMcHugh 8 57
(Michael Easterby) *short of room early and sn towards rr: hdwy and wd on bnd over 2f out: wnt 2nd over 1f out: no ch w wnr* **14/1**
060 3 4 1/2 **Heinrich (USA)**[18] 6018 3-9-7 65 RichardHughes 5 59
(Sylvester Kirk) *hld up towards rr: rdn and hdwy over 1f out: no imp fnl f* **9/4**[2]
-000 4 1 1/2 **Tableforten**[17] 6029 3-9-5 63 (p) LiamJones 6 53
(J S Moore) *bhd: rdn and hdwy over 1f out: nt rch ldrs* **40/1**
-666 5 5 **Cockney Belle**[14] 6154 3-9-5 63 LukeMorris 1 40
(Marco Botti) *led tl 4f out: hrd rdn and wknd over 1f out* **14/1**
-565 6 hd **Dansante**[19] 5977 3-8-0 51 oh6 KieranShoemark(7) 3 28
(Amanda Perrett) *towards rr: modest effrt 2f out: sn wknd* **16/1**
4164 7 1 1/4 **Seven Lucky Seven**[77] 3946 3-9-7 65 DaleSwift 9 39
(Michael Herrington) *t.k.h: chsd ldrs tl wknd 2f out* **9/2**[3]
000 8 1 1/4 **Moojaned (IRE)**[30] 5606 3-8-9 58 TimClark(5) 4 28
(Dai Burchell) *prom tl wknd wl over 1f out* **33/1**

3350 9 2 1/2 **Caledonia Laird**[32] 5530 3-8-13 57 (p) ShaneKelly 2 21
(Jo Hughes) *prom: led 4f out tl wknd wl over 1f out* **25/1**
1m 28.45s (-0.35) **Going Correction** -0.025s/f (Stan) **9** Ran SP% **113.8**
Speed ratings (Par 99): **101,97,92,90,85 84,83,81,79**
CSF £26.96 CT £56.70 TOTE £2.20: £1.30, £2.30, £1.30; EX 27.20 Trifecta £80.90.
**Owner** Byron, Lavallin & Donnison **Bred** Cheveley Park Stud Ltd **Trained** Newmarket, Suffolk
**FOCUS**
The second division of the modest 3yo handicap was a more truly run affair but they still finished strung out.
T/Plt: £11.70 to a £1 stake. Pool: £87,719.89 - 5437.96 winning units. T/Qpdt: £3.00 to a £1 stake. Pool: £8734.05 - 2085.30 winning units. LM

# 6378 LONGCHAMP (R-H)
### Saturday, September 20
**OFFICIAL GOING: Turf: soft**

## 6569a PRIX DES AMAZONES (CLAIMER) (4YO+) (LADY AMATEUR RIDERS) (TURF) 1m 2f
**12:00** (12:00) 4-Y-O+ **£7,916** (£3,166; £2,375; £1,583; £791)

RPR
1 **Royal Talisman**[20] 5964 6-9-7 0 MissMPlat 6 82
(Jo Hughes) *broke wl and mde all: sn clr: reduced advantage 4f out: rdn 2f out: styd on wl and extended advantage again fr over 1f out: in full control fnl f: unchal* **6/4**[1]
2 4 **La Messalina (FR)**[49] 4-9-7 0 MlleMarieRollando(5) 5 79
(Alex Fracas, France) **5/1**[2]
3 hd **Alara (FR)**[218] 4-9-12 0 MlleAlisonMassin 2 79
(P Monfort, France) **38/1**
4 3/4 **Tianjin City (FR)**[32] 4-10-2 0 MmeCatherineRieb-Menard 3 81
(A Bonin, France) **43/5**
5 1 1/2 **Garlin Blues (FR)**[32] 6-9-7 0 MllePaulineBoisgontier 10 69
(J Phelippon, France) **15/2**[3]
6 4 **Monolite (FR)**[167] 5-9-1 0 KatjaMarkwalder 7 55
(J Hirschberger, Germany) **96/10**
7 1/2 **Moonyr (FR)**[20] 5961 6-9-4 0 MissMSlamanig 11 57
(Mlle H Mennessier, France) **245/10**
8 1/2 **Mister Romaldo (ITY)** 4-9-13 0 (p) MlleDianaLopezLeret 4 65
(Gianluca Bietolini, Italy) **26/1**
9 nk **Contesurmoi (FR)**[64] 4-9-4 0 MlleLaraLeGeay 8 56
(P Adda, France) **52/1**
10 3 1/2 **Prophets Pride**[204] 4-9-11 0 MlleSandrineHagenbach 1 56
(F Vermeulen, France) **83/10**
11 4 **Clara De Lune (FR)**[87] 3598 5-9-7 0 MlleDelphineGarcia-Dubois 9 44
(R Le Gal, France) **107/10**
2m 12.32s (8.32) **11** Ran SP% **119.7**
WIN (incl. 1 euro stake): 2.50. PLACES: 1.40, 1.80, 6.50. DF: 6.70. SF: 10.10.
**Owner** R P Phillips **Bred** The National Stud **Trained** Lambourn. Berks

## 6570a PRIX DES CHENES (GROUP 3) (2YO COLTS & GELDINGS) (TURF) 1m
**12:30** (12:00) 2-Y-O **£33,333** (£13,333; £10,000; £6,666; £3,333)

RPR
1 **Evasive's First (FR)**[49] 4933 2-9-2 0 FranckBlondel 3 107+
(F Rossi, France) *midfield: rdn 2f out: swtchd lft ent fnl f: r.o strly and led towards fin: qcknd clr: readily* **18/5**[3]
2 1 1/2 **De Treville**[65] 2-9-2 0 MaximeGuyon 6 104
(A Fabre, France) *prom bhd clr ldr: rdn 2f out: chal ent fnl f and sn disputing: hdd towards fin: kpt on wl for 2nd but nt pce of wnr and hld* **7/2**[2]
3 snk **Cherek (FR)**[21] 5940 2-9-2 0 ChristopheSoumillon 5 103
(J-C Rouget, France) *trckd clr ldr: clsd 3f out: hung lft whn shkn up to chal 2f out: rdn to ld ent fnl f: sn jnd: kpt on but hdd towards fin: dropped to 3rd and hld* **6/4**[1]
4 1 3/4 **Mindsomer (FR)**[27] 5740 2-9-2 0 Christophe-PatriceLemaire 1 100
(F Chappet, France) *led and sn clr: reduced advantage 3f out: rdn and hdd ent fnl f: sn no ex: fdd* **26/1**
5 2 **Kenfreeze (FR)**[13] 6181 2-9-2 0 FabriceVeron 7 95
(H-A Pantall, France) *hld up in last: pushed along 2f out: kpt on same pce under hand ride fnl f and nvr threatened* **158/10**
6 1 1/4 **Iceberg (FR)**[34] 5478 2-9-2 0 OlivierPeslier 4 92
(C Ferland, France) *hld up in last pair: pushed along over 3f out: rdn 2f out: sn outpcd by ldrs: edgd rt to rail and btn fnl f: nvr a factor* **5/1**
7 8 **Courtofversailles (USA)**[48] 4953 2-9-2 0 Pierre-CharlesBoudot 2 75
(A Fabre, France) *midfield: rdn 2f out: fnd little and sn btn: wknd and dropped to last: eased and bhd fnl f* **91/10**
1m 43.04s (4.64) **7** Ran SP% **120.2**
WIN (incl. 1 euro stake): 4.60. PLACES: 2.30, 2.20. SF: 19.20.
**Owner** Jean-Claude Seroul **Bred** Haras De Grandcamp Earl **Trained** France

## 6571a PRIX DU PRINCE D'ORANGE (GROUP 3) (3YO) (TURF) 1m 2f
**1:30** (12:00) 3-Y-O **£33,333** (£13,333; £10,000; £6,666; £3,333)

RPR
1 **Free Port Lux**[36] 5406 3-9-2 0 (b) MickaelBarzalona 2 114
(F Head, France) *midfield in tch: rdn to chal over 1f out: styd on and led ins fnl f: drvn out and jst hld on fr wayward runner-up* **4/5**[1]
2 hd **Bodhi (FR)**[82] 3807 3-9-2 0 Jean-BernardEyquem 5 114
(J-F Bernard, France) *hld up in last: rdn 2f out: hung lft and chal over 1f out: styd on and ev ch thrght fnl f: hung lft again towards fin: jst failed* **32/5**[3]
3 3/4 **Calling Out (FR)**[68] 4278 3-9-2 0 AntoineHamelin 1 112
(J-P Gauvin, France) *t.k.h: trckd ldr on inner: swtchd out to chal gng strly 2f out: rdn to ld over 1f out: styd on but hdd ins fnl f: sn dropped to 3rd and hld* **104/10**
4 3 **Mr Pommeroy (FR)**[55] 4720 3-9-2 0 FabriceVeron 6 106
(H-A Pantall, France) *led: rdn 2f out: hdd over 1f out: no ex and fdd fnl f* **91/10**
5 4 **Orienteer**[16] 3-9-2 0 MaximeGuyon 4 98
(A Fabre, France) *trckd ldr on outer: rdn to chal 2f out: fnd little and sn btn: dropped to last ent fnl f: sn eased* **21/10**[2]
2m 12.67s (8.67) **5** Ran SP% **120.0**
WIN (incl. 1 euro stake): 1.80. PLACES: 1.40, 2.00. SF: 6.40.
**Owner** Olivier Thomas **Bred** Ecurie Des Monceaux **Trained** France

6572 - 6573a (Foreign Racing) - See Raceform Interactive

6008 **HAMILTON** (R-H)

Sunday, September 21

**OFFICIAL GOING: Good (good to firm in places; 7.0)**

Wind: Almost nil Weather: Sunny

## 6574 BET TOTEJACKPOT NURSERY H'CAP 6f 5y
2:20 (2:22) (Class 5) (0-75,75) 2-Y-O £3,881 (£1,155; £577; £288) Stalls High

Form RPR

356 1 **Best Dressed**[22] 5922 2-9-2 70 SeanLevey 8 76+
(David Brown) *trckd ldrs: rdn and rn green over 2f out: rallied and squeezed through to ld ins fnl f: r.o* **9/2**

3645 2 2 1/2 **Straightothepoint**[19] 6008 2-9-1 69 (v) PaulMulrennan 4 68
(Bryan Smart) *led: rdn over 1f out: hdd ins fnl f: kpt on same pce* **12/1**

3361 3 1 3/4 **Emef Rock (IRE)**[20] 5974 2-9-2 70 RobertWinston 7 63
(Mick Channon) *t.k.h: in tch: rdn over 1f out: kpt on ins fnl f: tk 3rd cl home* **7/2**[2]

6052 4 shd **Dominic Cork**[12] 6211 2-8-10 64 FergalLynch 2 57
(Kevin Ryan) *pressed ldr: rdn over 2f out: kpt on same pce ins fnl f* **4/1**[3]

6321 5 1/2 **Dream Approval (IRE)**[11] 6222 2-9-7 75 JoeFanning 5 66
(Daniel Kubler) *trckd ldrs on outside: effrt and rdn 2f out: kpt on same pce ins fnl f* **3/1**[1]

210 6 3 1/4 **Chances Are (IRE)**[28] 5714 2-9-5 73 PhillipMakin 6 55
(Keith Dalgleish) *s.i.s: hld up bhd ldng gp: effrt and hung rt over 1f out: sn wknd* **9/2**

1m 13.13s (0.93) **Going Correction** +0.025s/f (Good) 6 Ran SP% **111.3**
Speed ratings (Par 95): **94,90,88,88,87 83**
CSF £50.42 CT £202.49 TOTE £7.30: £3.70, £5.40; EX 49.80 Trifecta £202.10.
**Owner** J C Fretwell **Bred** L T Roberts **Trained** Averham Park, Notts

**FOCUS**
Course at normal configuration and all distances as advertised. A modest nursery run at what appeared a sound enough gallop as the field congregated up the stands' rail. The runner-up guides the level.

## 6575 TOTEPOOL SUPPORTING THE SPORT YOU LOVE H'CAP 6f 5y
2:50 (2:50) (Class 5) (0-75,75) 3-Y-O £3,234 (£962; £481; £240) Stalls Centre

Form RPR

3413 1 **Munfallet (IRE)**[37] 5381 3-9-7 75 SeanLevey 2 83
(David Brown) *t.k.h early: mde virtually all: rdn and hung lft ins fnl f: kpt on wl* **15/8**[1]

2312 2 2 3/4 **Royal Connoisseur (IRE)**[22] 5923 3-9-3 74 GeorgeChaloner(3) 5 73
(Richard Fahey) *trckd ldrs: drvn over 2f out: rallied to chal over 1f out: bmpd ins fnl f: kpt on same pce* **2/1**[2]

3140 3 3 3/4 **Chookie's Lass**[3] 6478 3-9-1 69 PhillipMakin 4 56
(Keith Dalgleish) *pressed ldr: ev ch over 1f out: sn rdn and briefly short of room: outpcd fnl f* **7/1**

1612 4 1 1/2 **Bearskin (IRE)**[25] 5808 3-8-11 65 (b) PJMcDonald 3 47
(Ann Duffield) *s.i.s: bhd: outpcd over 3f out: sme hdwy and hung rt over 1f out: no imp* **9/2**[3]

3220 5 6 **Bereka**[41] 5257 3-8-11 65 TonyHamilton 1 28
(Richard Fahey) *prom tl rdn and wknd over 2f out* **9/1**

1m 11.54s (-0.66) **Going Correction** +0.025s/f (Good) 5 Ran SP% **108.8**
Speed ratings (Par 101): **105,101,96,94,86**
CSF £5.80 TOTE £2.60: £1.10, £2.10; EX 4.80 Trifecta £18.20.
**Owner** J C Fretwell **Bred** Miss Joann Lyons **Trained** Averham Park, Notts

**FOCUS**
A moderate sprint handicap.

## 6576 TOTEQUADPOT EBF STALLIONS CONDITIONS STKS 6f 5y
3:20 (3:20) (Class 2) 3-Y-O+ £14,940 (£4,473; £2,236; £1,118; £559) Stalls Centre

Form RPR

0043 1 **Krypton Factor**[5] 6440 6-9-1 102 (b) PaulMulrennan 4 106
(George Peckham) *mde all against stands' rail: rdn 2f out: kpt on strly fnl f* **10/1**[3]

0126 2 nk **Another Wise Kid (IRE)**[36] 5445 6-9-1 99 GrahamLee 2 105
(Paul Midgley) *racd alone centre: prom: effrt and chsd wnr over 1f out: clsd ins fnl f: kpt on: hld nr fin* **9/2**[2]

0036 3 7 **Hopes N Dreams (IRE)**[4] 6467 6-9-4 87 BarryMcHugh 5 86
(Kevin Ryan) *dwlt: sn prom: drvn and outpcd fr over 1f out* **14/1**

2210 4 3 3/4 **Baccarat (IRE)**[15] 6134 5-9-1 111 GeorgeChaloner 1 71
(Richard Fahey) *s.i.s: sn chsng wnr: drvn over 2f out: wknd over 1f out* **1/3**[1]

660 5 22 **Bix (IRE)**[25] 5806 4-9-1 45 PatrickMathers 3
(Alan Berry) *dwlt: sn in tch: struggling 1/2-way: sn btn: t.o* **200/1**

1m 11.08s (-1.12) **Going Correction** +0.025s/f (Good) 5 Ran SP% **109.5**
Speed ratings (Par 109): **108,107,98,93,63**
CSF £50.42 TOTE £9.40: £3.70, £2.00; EX 33.50 Trifecta £53.50.
**Owner** Fawzi Abdulla Nass **Bred** Lady Fairhaven **Trained** Newmarket, Suffolk
■ The first winner for George Peckham, a former assistant to Ed Dunlop.

**FOCUS**
A good-quality affair.

## 6577 BRITISH STALLION STUDS EBF MAIDEN STKS 1m 65y
3:50 (3:52) (Class 5) 2-Y-O £3,881 (£1,155; £577; £288) Stalls Low

Form RPR

4 1 **Yorkidding**[15] 6148 2-9-0 0 JoeFanning 7 76+
(Mark Johnston) *pressed ldr: led over 2f out: gng clr and pushed along whn hung lft over 1f out: kpt on fnl f: readily* **4/6**[1]

2 4 1/2 **Barbarous (IRE)** 2-9-5 0 PhillipMakin 1 67+
(David Barron) *dwlt: hld up: stdy hdwy over 3f out: rdn to chse (clr) wnr ins fnl f: kpt on: no imp* **11/4**[2]

0 3 2 **Fortuna Glas (IRE)**[24] 5852 2-9-5 0 GrahamLee 2 62
(Donald McCain) *chsd ldrs: drvn and outpcd over 3f out: hung rt over 2f out: rallied over 1f out: kpt on: no imp* **8/1**[3]

0 4 5 **Thowar (USA)**[23] 5886 2-9-5 0 FergalLynch 4 51
(Kevin Ryan) *led tl rdn: edgd lft and hdd over 2f out: wknd over 1f out* **16/1**

5 5 3 1/2 **Mister Archie**[11] 6225 2-9-0 0 GarryWhillans(5) 6 43
(Alistair Whillans) *s.i.s: hld up: drvn and outpcd over 3f out: n.d after* **66/1**

6 3/4 **Life Knowledge (IRE)** 2-9-2 0 JoeyHaynes(3) 5 41
(Patrick Holmes) *colty in preliminaries: bhd and green: sme hdwy on outside over 2f out: btn over 1f out* **100/1**

06 7 2 **Notnowdear**[19] 5995 2-9-5 0 PJMcDonald 3 36
(Ann Duffield) *prom: drvn and outpcd over 3f out: sn btn* **20/1**

1m 47.93s (-0.47) **Going Correction** +0.025s/f (Good) 7 Ran SP% **110.9**
Speed ratings (Par 95): **103,98,96,91,88 87,85**
CSF £2.44 TOTE £1.90: £1.10, £2.10; EX 3.00 Trifecta £6.60.
**Owner** Paul Robert York **Bred** Bluehills Racing Limited **Trained** Middleham Moor, N Yorks

**FOCUS**
No depth to this maiden.

## 6578 FOLLOW @TOTEPOOL ON TWITTER H'CAP 1m 1f 36y
4:20 (4:20) (Class 5) (0-70,70) 3-Y-O+ £3,234 (£962; £481; £240) Stalls Low

Form RPR

2S20 1 **Lord Franklin**[14] 6166 5-9-10 70 JasonHart 3 78
(Eric Alston) *mde virtually all: rdn over 3f out: hrd pressed fr over 1f out: hld on gamely fnl f* **4/1**[2]

210 2 hd **Raamz (IRE)**[49] 4942 7-8-10 61 CamHardie(5) 1 68
(Kevin Morgan) *t.k.h: cl up: effrt and disp ld over 1f out: kpt on u.p fnl f: jst hld* **7/1**

0631 3 nk **Tectonic (IRE)**[11] 6227 5-9-8 68 (p) PhillipMakin 6 74
(Keith Dalgleish) *s.i.s: t.k.h: hld up in tch: stdy hdwy whn n.m.r briefly over 1f out: effrt and ch ins fnl f: no ex nr fin* **5/1**[3]

201 4 1/2 **Polar Forest**[8] 6341 4-9-6 66 (e) RobertWinston 5 71
(Richard Guest) *hld up: pushed along over 2f out: hdwy on outside over 1f out: kpt on ins fnl f* **8/1**

5052 5 2 1/2 **Outbacker (IRE)**[11] 6223 3-8-12 63 JoeFanning 7 64
(Mark Johnston) *prom: stdy hdwy over 2f out: rdn and ev ch briefly over 1f out: wknd ins fnl f* **5/1**[3]

3311 6 3/4 **Remember Rocky**[11] 6223 5-9-0 65 (p) MeganCarberry(5) 4 63
(Lucy Normile) *pressed wnr: rdn over 3f out: edgd rt and wknd over 1f out* **85/40**[1]

1m 59.65s (-0.05) **Going Correction** +0.025s/f (Good)
**WFA** 3 from 4yo+ 5lb 6 Ran SP% **108.9**
Speed ratings (Par 103): **101,100,100,100,97 97**
CSF £28.73 TOTE £4.70: £1.80, £3.90; EX 36.80 Trifecta £189.10.
**Owner** Liam & Tony Ferguson **Bred** Tony Ferguson & Liam Ferguson **Trained** Longton, Lancs

**FOCUS**
An ordinary handicap.

## 6579 BET TOTETRIFECTA H'CAP 1m 5f 9y
4:50 (4:50) (Class 4) (0-80,78) 3-Y-O+ £5,822 (£1,732; £865; £432) Stalls Low

Form RPR

6053 1 **Right Of Appeal**[6] 6403 3-8-8 67 JoeFanning 5 76
(Mark Johnston) *t.k.h: trckd ldrs: nt clr run over 2f out: squeezed through and led over 1f out: drvn out fnl f* **7/2**[3]

45 2 2 1/4 **Arizona John (IRE)**[12] 6206 9-9-9 78 JoeDoyle(5) 6 84
(John Mackie) *t.k.h: in tch: smooth hdwy on outside to chal over 2f out to over 1f out: rdn and one pce ins fnl f* **11/2**

224 3 2 3/4 **Chant (IRE)**[14] 6169 4-9-10 74 (p) PJMcDonald 1 76
(Ann Duffield) *led at stdy pce: rdn over 2f out: hdd over 1f out: sn outpcd* **6/4**[1]

3444 4 1 1/2 **Aleksandar**[6] 6404 5-9-7 71 GrahamLee 3 70
(Jim Goldie) *pressed ldr: drvn and outpcd over 2f out: edgd rt and sn no imp* **5/2**[2]

2m 53.62s (-0.28) **Going Correction** +0.025s/f (Good)
**WFA** 3 from 4yo+ 9lb 4 Ran SP% **106.2**
Speed ratings (Par 105): **101,99,97,97**
CSF £18.80 TOTE £3.40; EX 12.40 Trifecta £23.60.
**Owner** Sheikh Hamdan bin Mohammed Al Maktoum **Bred** Lordship Stud **Trained** Middleham Moor, N Yorks

**FOCUS**
Not form to take at face value, because this was run at a very steady overall gallop and it turned into a dash from the two pole.

## 6580 COLLECT TOTEPOOL WINNINGS AT BETFRED SHOPS H'CAP 5f 4y
5:20 (5:20) (Class 6) (0-65,65) 4-Y-O+ £1,940 (£577; £288; £144) Stalls Centre

Form RPR

4230 1 **Slim Chance (IRE)**[10] 6266 5-9-7 65 AndrewElliott 2 82
(Simon West) *prom: effrt over 1f out: rdn to ld ins fnl f: kpt on strly* **5/1**[2]

46 2 2 1/2 **Rylee Mooch**[36] 5437 6-9-5 63 (e) JasonHart 6 71
(Richard Guest) *disp ld: led 1/2-way: rdn and hung lft over 1f out: hdd ins fnl f: kpt on same pce* **4/1**[1]

4400 3 2 3/4 **Ingenti**[12] 6213 6-8-11 60 KevinStott(5) 9 58
(Christopher Wilson) *hld up: rdn and hdwy over 1f out: kpt on fnl f: nt rch first two* **6/1**[3]

0504 4 2 1/4 **Here Now And Why (IRE)**[16] 6114 7-7-13 48 (p) CamHardie(5) 7 38
(Ian Semple) *hld up in tch: rdn and outpcd over 2f out: rallied fnl f: nvr able to chal* **7/1**

6440 5 3/4 **Economic Crisis (IRE)**[6] 6406 5-9-2 65 JoeDoyle(5) 10 52
(Alan Berry) *t.k.h: cl up: rdn whn checked briefly over 1f out: btn ins fnl f* **5/1**[2]

006 6 1 **Rutterkin (USA)**[45] 5082 6-7-11 46 oh1 JackGarritty(5) 5 30
(James Moffatt) *bhd: rdn 1/2-way: sme late hdwy: nvr rchd ldrs* **28/1**

3400 7 1/2 **Bosun Breese**[56] 4714 9-9-5 63 GrahamLee 1 45
(Paul Midgley) *racd away fr main gp towards far side: slt ld to 1/2-way: rdn and wknd over 1f out* **16/1**

000 8 2 1/4 **Lizzy's Dream**[68] 4287 6-8-9 53 AdamBeschizza 3 27
(Robin Bastiman) *missed break: bhd and rdn along: nvr on terms* **14/1**

-414 9 1 1/4 **Mandy Layla (IRE)**[51] 4860 4-9-3 61 PaulMulrennan 4 30
(Bryan Smart) *prom: drvn over 2f out: wknd over 1f out* **4/1**[1]

59.88s (-0.12) **Going Correction** +0.025s/f (Good) 9 Ran SP% **116.1**
Speed ratings: **101,97,92,89,87 86,85,81,79**
CSF £25.49 CT £123.80 TOTE £6.20: £2.50, £1.40, £3.00; EX 21.90 Trifecta £172.60.
**Owner** Mrs Barbara Hothersall **Bred** David Brickley **Trained** Middleham Moor, N Yorks

**FOCUS**
A weak sprint handicap.

T/Plt: £895.60 to a £1 stake. Pool: £49,038.81 - 39.97 winning units. T/Qpdt: £77.80 to a £1 stake. Pool: £3652.42 - 34.70 winning units. RY

6581 - 6584a (Foreign Racing) - See Raceform Interactive

# 6046 GOWRAN PARK (R-H)

Sunday, September 21

**OFFICIAL GOING: Good to firm (good in places)**

## 6585a DENNY CORDELL LAVARACK & LANWADES STUD FILLIES STKS (GROUP 3) 1m 1f 100y

**3:55** (3:56) 3-Y-O+ **£39,270** (£11,479; £5,437; £1,812)

RPR

1 **Brooch (USA)**[32] 5584 3-9-0 .......... PatSmullen 7 105+
(D K Weld, Ire) *trckd ldrs: wnt 2nd 1/2-way: rdn to press ldr 2f out: led fnl 100yds: kpt on wl* **11/8**[1]

2 1/2 **Regardez**[58] 4634 3-9-0 102 .......... (p) JosephO'Brien 3 104
(Ralph Beckett) *attempted to make all: strly pressed 2f out: rallied wl tl hdd fnl 100yds: kpt on wl* **4/1**[3]

3 1 3/4 **Odeliz (IRE)**[22] 5927 4-9-5 106 .......... DanielTudhope 4 99
(K R Burke) *hld up: rdn along to chse ldrs in 4th under 2f out: no imp ent fnl f: kpt on same pce into 3rd fnl 100yds* **11/4**[2]

4 3/4 **Akira (IRE)**[21] 5955 4-9-5 101 .......... NGMcCullagh 1 98
(J R Barry, Ire) *trckd ldrs on inner in 3rd: rallied wl appr fnl f tl no ex and dropped to 4th fnl 100yds* **20/1**

5 3/4 **Mizzava (IRE)**[21] 5955 4-9-5 96 .......... ConorHoban 2 96
(M Halford, Ire) *hld up: pushed along in 5th 2f out: no imp ins fnl f: kpt on same pce* **33/1**

6 4 1/2 **Adeste Fideles (USA)**[6] 6417 3-9-0 74 .......... SeamieHeffernan 5 88?
(A P O'Brien, Ire) *racd in rr: rdn and no imp under 2f out: kpt on one pce fnl f* **50/1**

7 1/2 **Maggie Dalton (IRE)**[21] 5957 5-9-5 94 .......... KevinManning 6 86
(J S Bolger, Ire) *hld up: rdn over 2f out on outer and sn no imp* **20/1**

8 7 **Alive Alive Oh**[21] 5955 4-9-5 103 .......... FMBerry 8 80
(T Stack, Ire) *chsd ldrs in 4th tl nt qckn under 2f out and dropped towards rr: eased fr 1f out* **11/2**

2m 0.62s (-6.38)
**WFA** 3 from 4yo+ 5lb **8 Ran SP% 118.6**
CSF £7.27 TOTE £2.00: £1.02, £1.70, £1.90; DF 8.00 Trifecta £15.60.
**Owner** K Abdullah **Bred** Juddmonte Farms Inc **Trained** Curragh, Co Kildare

**FOCUS**
With two very useful British challengers this was right up to Group 3 standard, and it produced a smart winner.

6586 - 6588a (Foreign Racing) - See Raceform Interactive

# 3511 DORTMUND (R-H)

Sunday, September 21

**OFFICIAL GOING: Turf: very soft**

## 6589a GROSSER PREIS VON DSW21 - 130TH DEUTSCHES ST.LEGER (GROUP 3) (3YO+) (TURF) 1m 6f

**4:15** (12:00) 3-Y-O+
**£26,666** (£9,166; £4,583; £2,500; £1,666; £1,250)

RPR

1 **Kaldera (GER)**[15] 3-8-7 0 .......... EddyHardouin 4 108+
(P Harley, Germany) *hld up and sn towards rr: last 1/2-way: hdwy on outer into st: styd on steadily fnl 2f: grad clsd on ldr fnl f and led towards fin* **14/5**[2]

2 3/4 **Virginia Sun (GER)**[15] 6162 3-8-7 0 .......... SHellyn 9 107
(J Hirschberger, Germany) *hld up towards rr: clsd on outer and prom 1/2-way: rdn to ld 2f out: clr ent fnl f: styd on but grad reeled in and hdd towards fin: no ex and hld* **27/10**[1]

3 4 1/2 **Rock Of Romance (IRE)**[32] 4-9-6 0 .......... EPedroza 2 104+
(A Wohler, Germany) *midfield in tch: rdn into st: styd on for wl hld 3rd: nt pce of front pair* **9/2**[3]

4 1 1/2 **Special Meaning**[22] 5920 4-9-3 0 .......... FrannyNorton 7 99
(Mark Johnston) *disp ld: led bef st: rdn and hdd 2f out: sn outpcd by ldr: styd on fnl f but dropped to 4th and wl hld* **32/5**

5 1 1/4 **Ostinato (GER)**[15] 6-9-6 0 .......... (b) DanielePorcu 3 100
(Andreas Lowe, Germany) *hld up in rr: rdn and hdwy into st: briefly short of room over 1f out: plugged on same pce and wl hld fnl f* **38/1**

6 14 **Firestorm (GER)**[14] 3-8-10 0 .......... AdriedeVries 10 80
(P Schiergen, Germany) *t.k.h: midfield: shuffled bk 1/2-way: rdn into st: sn outpcd and btn* **77/10**

7 1 1/2 **Best Fouad (FR)**[23] 5902 3-8-10 0 .......... MlleZoePfeil 1 78
(M Le Forestier, France) *midfield in tch: rdn into st: no ex and btn fnl 2f: wknd* **54/10**

8 2 **Macbeth (IRE)**[36] 5440 5-9-6 0 .......... AndrewMullen 8 75
(Michael Appleby) *trckd ldrs: lost pl fr 1/2-way: sn rdn: no imp and btn over 1f out: eased fnl f* **133/10**

9 17 **Pipita (GER)**[29] 4-9-3 0 .......... KClijmans 5 49
(Daniel Paulick, Germany) *midfield: rdn and dropped to rr into st: sn wl btn: eased and t.o* **34/1**

10 16 **Ephraim**[21] 3-8-10 0 .......... AHelfenbein 6 29
(Markus Klug, Germany) *disp ld: rdn and hdd bef st: qckly btn and wknd: dropped to last and eased: t.o* **136/10**

3m 11.88s (6.38)
**WFA** 3 from 4yo+ 10lb **10 Ran SP% 131.4**
WIN (incl. 10 euro stake): 38. PLACES: 14, 17, 15. SF: 112.
**Owner** Stall Torjager **Bred** Gestut Zoppenbroich **Trained** Germany

# 3775 SAN SIRO (R-H)

Sunday, September 21

**OFFICIAL GOING: Turf: good**

## 6590a PREMIO FEDERICO TESIO (4YO+) (GROUP 2) (TURF) 1m 3f

**3:30** (12:00) 3-Y-O+ **£39,583** (£17,416; £9,500; £4,750)

RPR

1 **Dylan Mouth (IRE)**[93] 3417 3-8-7 0 .......... FabioBranca 2 115+
(Stefano Botti, Italy) *t.k.h: trckd ldr on inner: rdn and briefly outpcd 3f out: chal over 2f out and sn led: styd on strly and asserted: eased towards fin: easily* **6/5**[1]

2 3 **Biz The Nurse (IRE)**[105] 3047 4-8-11 0 .......... DarioVargiu 3 105
(Stefano Botti, Italy) *wnt rt s: hld up in tch: rdn over 3f out: styd on steadily and wnt 2nd towards fin: no ch w easy wnr* **5/2**[3]

3 1 **Oil Of England (GER)**[57] 4694 3-8-5 0 .......... CristianDemuro 6 104
(M Figge, Germany) *t.k.h: trckd ldr on outer: rdn to chal 3f out: outpcd by wnr fnl 2f: styd on but wl hld: dropped to 3rd towards fin* **124/10**

4 1 **Orsino (GER)**[14] 7-8-11 0 .......... MircoDemuro 7 101
(R Rohne, Germany) *hld up and sn last: fanned wd and hdwy on outer into st: rdn and effrt over 2f out: sn outpcd by wnr: plugged on for wl hld 4th* **176/100**[2]

5 1 **Awake My Soul (IRE)**[41] 5238 5-8-11 0 .......... GBietolini 5 100
(David O'Meara) *midfield in tch on outer: rdn to chal over 2f out: outpcd by wnr over 1f out: no ex fnl f: fdd and dropped to 5th* **118/10**

6 dist **Victis Hill (FR)**[14] 3-8-5 0 .......... PierantonioConvertino 4
(A Marcialis, Italy) *t.k.h: midfield in tch on inner: rdn over 2f out: outpcd whn qckly eased over 1f out: bhd fnl f* **202/10**

7 dist **Orpello (IRE)**[105] 3047 5-8-11 0 .......... (b) NicolaPinna 1
(Stefano Botti, Italy) *led: rdn and strly pressed 3f out: hdd over 2f out: immediately btn and eased: sn dropped to last: t.o* **6/5**[1]

2m 15.3s (-3.30)
**WFA** 3 from 4yo+ 7lb **7 Ran SP% 175.7**
WIN (incl. 1 euro stake): 2.20 (Dylan Mouth coupled with Orpello). PLACES: 1.58, 1.76. SF: 3.87.
**Owner** Scuderia Effevi SRL **Bred** Azienda Agricola Mariano **Trained** Italy

# 6446 MAISONS-LAFFITTE (R-H)

Friday, September 19

**OFFICIAL GOING: Turf: good**

## 6591a PRIX DE PORT MARLY (CLAIMER) (2YO) (TURF) 6f (S)

**2:20** (2:20) 2-Y-O **£11,250** (£4,500; £3,375; £2,250; £1,125)

RPR

1 **Takara Girl (FR)** 2-8-3 0 .......... (b) MllePaulineDominois(5) 14 72
(P Sogorb, France) **83/10**

2 2 **Plume D'Outarde**[31] 5544 2-8-11 0 .......... (p) CristianDemuro 8 69
(F Doumen, France) **48/1**

3 1/2 **Laleh (GER)**[16] 6053 2-8-13 0 .......... ChristopheSoumillon 15 70
(Mario Hofer, Germany) **41/10**[1]

4 hd **Amandichope (FR)**[146] 2-8-11 0 .......... TheoBachelot 7 67
(S Wattel, France) **43/5**

5 1 3/4 **Something Lucky (IRE)**[10] 2-9-1 0 .......... AntoineHamelin 9 66
(Matthieu Palussiere, France) **6/1**[3]

6 hd **Princesse Rebelle (FR)**[28] 5662 2-8-8 0 .......... AurelienLemaitre 1 58
(M Nigge, France) **223/10**

7 2 **Stevalseba (FR)**[98] 2-9-1 0 .......... FabriceVeron 3 59
(P Monfort, France) **87/10**

8 1 **Pierre Precieuse (FR)**[10] 2-8-11 0 .......... SebastienMaillot 13 52
(E Caroux, France) **152/10**

9 nse **Aimee (IRE)**[52] 2-8-8 0 .......... StephaneLaurent 10 49
(Mlle B Renk, France) **30/1**

10 hd **Max Attack (FR)**[30] 5588 2-9-1 0 .......... ThierryJarnet 12 55
(A Junk, France) **207/10**

11 nk **Freaky Girl (FR)**[23] 5844 2-8-11 0 .......... JimmyTastayre 6 51
(Robert Collet, France) **102/1**

12 1 1/4 **Jimmy's Hall**[10] 6212 2-8-11 0 .......... IoritzMendizabal 5 47
(J S Moore) *midfield: rdn over 2f out: sn outpcd and no imp: eased whn btn towards fin* **113/10**

13 3/4 **Evasion Des Mottes (FR)**[28] 5662 2-8-8 0 .......... (b) TonyPiccone 2 42
(Mme A-M Poirier, France) **191/10**

14 2 **Diktari (FR)**[75] 2-8-11 0 .......... (p) Christophe-PatriceLemaire 11 39
(F Chappet, France) **197/10**

15 3 **Claudia Eria (FR)**[23] 5844 2-8-9 0 .......... NicolasLarenaudie(6) 4 34
(P Van De Poele, France) **59/10**[2]

1m 12.15s (-1.25) **15 Ran SP% 119.1**
WIN (incl. 1 euro stake): 9.30. PLACES: 3.80, 14.20, 2.50. DF: 197.70. SF: 465.90.
**Owner** Simon Springer **Bred** Comunidad Hereditaria Quereda Hurtado Cb **Trained** France

## 6592a LA COUPE DE MAISONS-LAFFITTE (GROUP 3) (3YO+) (STRAIGHT) (TURF) 1m 2f (S)

**2:50** (2:50) 3-Y-O+ **£33,333** (£13,333; £10,000; £6,666; £3,333)

RPR

1 **Fractional (IRE)**[18] 5-9-0 0 .......... MaximeGuyon 8 113
(A Fabre, France) *hld up in tch: rdn to cl on outer over 1f out: chal ins fnl f: styd on wl and led fnl 120yds: sn asserted: readily* **18/5**[3]

2 1 **Smoking Sun (USA)**[34] 5460 5-9-5 0 .......... (b) StephanePasquier 6 116
(P Bary, France) *midfield in tch: clsd on outer and rdn to chal 2f out: led narrowly over 1f out: strly pressed fnl f: kpt on but hdd fnl 120yds and hld* **19/10**[1]

3 nk **Planetaire**[30] 5591 3-8-8 0 .......... OlivierPeslier 4 110
(C Laffon-Parias, France) *trckd ldr on outer: rdn to chal 2f out: w ldr and ev ch ent fnl f: kpt on but dropped to 3rd fnl 120yds and hld* **13/5**[2]

4 1/2 **Feuerblitz (GER)**[68] 5-9-0 0 .......... ThierryThulliez 3 109
(M Figge, Germany) *t.k.h: led early stages: trckd ldr on inner once hdd: rdn and angled off rail over 1f out: kpt on same pce u.p fnl f and hld* **5/1**

5 1 **Calvin Williams (FR)**[19] 5960 4-9-0 0 .......... TheoBachelot 5 107
(M Nigge, France) *hld up: rdn 2f out: swtchd rt ent fnl f: kpt on same pce and nvr able to chal* **34/1**

6 ¾ **Gaga A (URU)**[26] 5742 5-8-10 0.................. Christophe-PatriceLemaire 7 102
(D Smaga, France) *sn led: rdn and hdd over 1f out: no ex and fdd fnl f*
**245/10**

7 1 ½ **Vally Jem (FR)**[58] 4561 5-8-10 0.............................(p) IoritzMendizabal 2 99
(D Sepulchre, France) *dwlt sltly and hld up in rr: rdn 2f out: sn outpcd: nvr a factor*
**207/10**

8 3 ½ **Line Drummer (FR)**[35] 4-9-0 0.............................. UmbertoRispoli 1 96
(J Reynier, France) *t.k.h: midfield in tch on inner: angled out and rdn 2f out: sn outpcd: dropped to last and btn fnl f: eased*
**133/10**

2m 6.35s (3.95)
**WFA** 3 from 4yo+ 6lb **8** Ran SP% **119.0**
WIN (incl. 1 euro stake): 4.60. PLACES: 1.30, 1.20, 1.40. DF: 5.60. SF: 13.10.
**Owner** Godolphin SNC **Bred** Darley Stud Management Co, Ltd **Trained** Chantilly, France

**FOCUS**
This was slowly run.

6593 - (Foreign Racing) - See Raceform Interactive

# [6574]HAMILTON (R-H)

## Monday, September 22

**OFFICIAL GOING: Good (good to firm in places; 7.1)**
Wind: Light, half behind Weather: Cloudy, bright

### 6594 BRITISH STALLION STUDS EBF MAIDEN STKS 6f 5y
**1:50** (1:50) (Class 5) 2-Y-O **£3,234** (£962; £481; £240) **Stalls** High

Form RPR

2 **1** **Hard N Sharp (IRE)**[25] 5852 2-9-5 0.................................. GrahamLee 2 81+
(Kevin Ryan) *dwlt: hung rt thrght: sn chsng ldrs: rdn to ld over 1f out: kpt on strly fnl f*
**15/8**[1]

452 **2** 2 ¼ **Shootingsta (IRE)**[26] 5807 2-9-5 77.............................. PaulMulrennan 3 75+
(Bryan Smart) *t.k.h: in tch: rdn 2f out: hdwy to chse (clr) wnr ins fnl f: kpt on*
**5/2**[2]

2004 **3** 2 ½ **Winstanley (IRE)**[16] 6158 2-9-5 76.............................. TonyHamilton 4 67
(Richard Fahey) *cl up: rdn 2f out: outpcd ins fnl f* **11/2**

2 **4** 1 ¾ **Landing Night (IRE)**[9] 6319 2-9-5 0.............................. PJMcDonald 5 61
(Ann Duffield) *t.k.h: led: rdn over 2f out: wknd ins fnl f* **3/1**[3]

**5** 5 **Missisipi Baileys (FR)** 2-9-0 0.................................. JoeFanning 1 41
(Mark Johnston) *s.i.s: hld up in tch: effrt on outside over 2f out: wknd over 1f out*
**20/1**

1m 12.93s (0.73) **Going Correction** -0.025s/f (Good) **5** Ran SP% **108.5**
Speed ratings (Par 95): **94,91,87,85,78**
CSF £6.62 TOTE £2.20: £1.70, £1.50; EX 7.90 Trifecta £20.60.
**Owner** Mrs J Ryan **Bred** Barbara Keller **Trained** Hambleton, N Yorks

**FOCUS**
Course at normal configuration and all distances as advertised. A fair 2yo maiden despite the small field. The runner-up can rate higher.

### 6595 TOTEPOOL SUPPORTING THE SPORT YOU LOVE H'CAP 6f 5y
**2:20** (2:21) (Class 6) (0-65,71) 3-Y-O+ **£2,264** (£673; £336; £168) **Stalls** High

Form RPR

2301 **1** **Slim Chance (IRE)**[1] 6580 5-9-11 71 6ex..................... RowanScott[(7)] 5 82
(Simon West) *walked to s: cl up centre: led gng wl over 1f out: drvn out fnl f*
**3/1**[1]

0000 **2** 2 **Berbice (IRE)**[4] 6478 9-8-2 46 oh1.............................. SammyJoBell[(5)] 8 51
(Linda Perratt) *s.i.s: hld up centre: hdwy to chse wnr over 1f out: kpt on fnl f: no imp*
**14/1**

45 **3** ¾ **Captain Scooby**[20] 6014 8-8-9 48..............................(b) TonyHamilton 12 51
(Richard Guest) *hld up centre: rdn and hdwy over 1f out: kpt on fnl f: nvr able to chal*
**8/1**

4-00 **4** 1 ¾ **Pitt Rivers**[4] 6475 5-8-13 52.................................. PaulMulrennan 7 49
(Linda Perratt) *hld up centre: hdwy on far side of bunch over 1f out: kpt on fnl f: no imp*
**50/1**

320 **5** ½ **Very First Blade**[27] 5797 5-8-12 51..............................(v[1]) RaulDaSilva 1 46
(Michael Mullineaux) *cl up on far side of centre gp: rdn over 2f out: one pce over 1f out*
**15/2**

2300 **6** nse **Amis Reunis**[4] 6495 5-9-0 53..............................(p) PatrickMathers 6 48
(Alan Berry) *prom centre: rdn over 2f out: one pce fr over 1f out* **12/1**

5100 **7** hd **Saxonette**[4] 6475 6-8-12 54.................................. ConnorBeasley[(3)] 9 49
(Linda Perratt) *chsd ldrs in centre: drvn over 2f out: no ex over 1f out* **20/1**

0600 **8** ½ **Dream Ally (IRE)**[13] 6213 4-9-7 60.............................. PJMcDonald 11 53
(Micky Hammond) *hld up in tch on nr side of centre gp: drvn over 2f out: no imp fr over 1f out*
**7/1**[3]

2450 **9** ½ **Rock Canyon (IRE)**[20] 6014 5-8-10 49.............................. JoeFanning 13 40
(Linda Perratt) *chsd stands' side ldrs: rdn and hung rt 2f out: rallied appr fnl f: no imp*
**12/1**

2213 **10** 3 ½ **See Vermont**[17] 6120 6-8-10 49..............................(p) AdamBeschizza 15 29
(Robin Bastiman) *led stands' side trio: drvn over 2f out: edgd rt and wknd fr over 1f out*
**13/2**[2]

4405 **11** nk **Economic Crisis (IRE)**[1] 6580 5-9-7 65.............................. KevinStott[(5)] 2 44
(Alan Berry) *led centre gp to over 1f out: sn rdn and btn* **12/1**

0-40 **12** 2 ¼ **Stoneacre Oskar**[38] 5390 5-8-8 47 ow1.............................. DavidAllan 10 19
(Peter Grayson) *hld up centre: drvn along over 2f out: sn btn* **12/1**

00-0 **13** 4 ½ **Rio Sands**[135] 2166 9-8-7 46 oh1.............................. PaulQuinn 14 4
(Richard Whitaker) *cl up stands' side: rdn over 3f out: wknd over 2f out*
**66/1**

0545 **14** nk **Oriental Heights**[17] 6116 3-8-9 50.............................. FergalLynch 3 7
(Jim Goldie) *hld up in tch centre: struggling over 2f out: sn btn* **22/1**

1m 11.87s (-0.33) **Going Correction** -0.025s/f (Good)
**WFA** 3 from 4yo+ 2lb **14** Ran SP% **123.7**
Speed ratings (Par 101): **101,98,97,95,94 94,94,93,92,88 87,84,78,78**
CSF £48.37 CT £327.11 TOTE £4.10: £1.60, £6.70, £2.40; EX 59.30 Trifecta £602.40.
**Owner** Mrs Barbara Hothersall **Bred** David Brickley **Trained** Middleham Moor, N Yorks

**FOCUS**
The pace was honest for this modest handicap. The action unfolded up the centre.The winner is rated back to the level of his early form. Solid form, with the third running to a similar level to here early this month.

### 6596 TOTEQUADPOT FOUR PLACES IN FOUR RACES H'CAP 1m 3f 16y
**2:50** (2:51) (Class 5) (0-70,70) 3-Y-O **£3,234** (£962; £481; £240) **Stalls** High

Form RPR

3224 **1** **Stanarley Pic**[26] 5818 3-9-7 70.................................. DavidAllan 6 80
(Alan Swinbank) *dwlt: sn cl up: led and hung rt over 2f out: sn rdn: edgd lft ins fnl f: kpt on strly*
**2/1**[1]

1254 **2** 2 ½ **Mister Uno (IRE)**[17] 6110 3-9-2 65..............................(p) PJMcDonald 4 70
(Ann Duffield) *chsd ldrs: rdn over 3f out: rallied over 1f out: styd on to take 2nd wl ins fnl f: nt rch wnr*
**13/2**

3250 **3** ½ **Mariners Moon (IRE)**[15] 6166 3-9-6 69..............................(p) DanielTudhope 5 73
(David O'Meara) *prom: rdn and effrt over 2f out: edgd lft over 1f out: kpt on same pce ins fnl f*
**3/1**[3]

2442 **4** nse **Zanouska (USA)**[40] 5302 3-9-3 66.............................. JoeFanning 2 70
(Mark Johnston) *t.k.h: led: rdn and hdd over 2f out: rallied: kpt on same pce and lost 2nd wl ins fnl f*
**85/40**[2]

6556 **5** 8 **Saranta**[18] 6074 3-8-9 58.................................. TonyHamilton 3 48
(Richard Fahey) *in tch: drvn and outpcd over 2f out: hung rt and wknd over 1f out*
**16/1**

2m 23.99s (-1.61) **Going Correction** -0.025s/f (Good) **5** Ran SP% **109.5**
Speed ratings (Par 101): **104,102,101,101,95**
CSF £14.48 TOTE £3.50: £1.80, £3.00; EX 17.50 Trifecta £38.40.
**Owner** The Twopin Partnership **Bred** J L Dunlop **Trained** Melsonby, N Yorks

**FOCUS**
A fair handicap for the grade run at an even pace. The second to fourth are rated close to their marks.

### 6597 TOTEEXACTA PICK THE 1, 2 H'CAP 1m 3f 16y
**3:20** (3:20) (Class 6) (0-65,65) 4-Y-O+ **£2,587** (£770; £384; £192) **Stalls** High

Form RPR

5444 **1** **Eilean Mor**[7] 6402 6-8-3 50.................................. ConnorBeasley[(3)] 12 61
(R Mike Smith) *prom: wnt 2nd 1/2-way: effrt and led over 1f out: drvn out fnl f*
**8/1**

0006 **2** 3 ¼ **King Of Paradise (IRE)**[25] 5856 5-9-2 60.............................. JasonHart 11 65
(Eric Alston) *led and sn clr: rdn over 3f out: hdd over 1f out: kpt on same pce ins fnl f*
**11/2**[2]

502 **3** shd **Dhaular Dhar (IRE)**[26] 5815 12-8-12 59.............................. GaryBartley[(3)] 4 64
(Jim Goldie) *hld up: rdn over 3f out: hdwy over 1f out: kpt on fnl f: nrst fin*
**11/1**

103 **4** 1 ¼ **Henpecked**[25] 5855 4-9-1 59.................................. PJMcDonald 8 62
(Alistair Whillans) *midfield: drvn over 3f out: effrt over 2f out: kpt on ins fnl f: no imp*
**4/1**[1]

00 **5** 4 **Schmooze (IRE)**[4] 6480 5-9-1 59.............................. PhillipMakin 14 55
(Linda Perratt) *bhd tl styd on fr 2f out: nrst fin* **28/1**

5626 **6** ¾ **Ronald Gee (IRE)**[20] 6012 7-9-5 63.............................. GrahamLee 5 58
(Jim Goldie) *s.i.s: bhd: rdn over 3f out: styd on fnl f: nvr able to chal* **8/1**

0444 **7** nk **Snow Dancer (IRE)**[7] 6410 10-8-4 51.............................. PhilipPrince[(3)] 15 46
(John David Riches) *in tch: rdn and outpcd over 3f out: no imp fr 2f out*
**28/1**

54U2 **8** 3 ¾ **Triple Eight (IRE)**[2] 6542 6-9-7 65..............................(b) JoeFanning 13 53
(Philip Kirby) *dwlt: hld up: stdy hdwy 1/2-way: rdn and hung rt over 3f out: wknd 2f out*
**6/1**[3]

0446 **9** 5 **Royal Straight**[12] 6223 9-8-13 62..............................(t) SammyJoBell[(5)] 6 42
(Linda Perratt) *hld up: rdn over 3f out: nvr on terms* **14/1**

0240 **10** 5 **Merchant Of Medici**[18] 6062 7-8-13 62..............................(p) JoeDoyle[(5)] 9 33
(Micky Hammond) *in tch: drvn and outpcd over 3f out: no imp fr 2f out*
**17/2**

330- **11** 1 **May's Boy**[28] 6598 6-8-3 52.................................. JackGarritty[(5)] 3 22
(James Moffatt) *hld up: pushed along whn hmpd and hit rail over 4f out: sn struggling*
**17/2**

1060 **12** 3 ¾ **Dabuki (FR)**[29] 5716 4-9-7 65..............................(b) DavidAllan 10 28
(Geoffrey Harker) *hld up in tch: rdn and outpcd over 3f out: btn fnl 2f* **28/1**

6-06 **13** dist **Smirfys Blackcat (IRE)**[26] 5814 5-8-2 46 oh1.............................. RaulDaSilva 2
(Michael Mullineaux) *sn chsng ldr: lost pl 1/2-way: struggling whn hmpd over 4f out: virtually p.u fr 2f out*
**100/1**

2m 23.28s (-2.32) **Going Correction** -0.025s/f (Good) **13** Ran SP% **119.3**
Speed ratings (Par 101): **107,104,104,103,100 100,99,97,93,89 89,86,**
CSF £49.99 CT £494.16 TOTE £11.40: £2.50, £2.80, £2.20; EX 74.50 Trifecta £1317.80.
**Owner** R Michael Smith **Bred** Triple H Stud Ltd **Trained** Galston, E Ayrshire

**FOCUS**
They went a sound pace for this open handicap. It paid to race handy. The winner is rated up a length on this year's form.

### 6598 TOTEPOOL EBF STALLIONS FLOWER OF SCOTLAND FILLIES' H'CAP 6f 5y
**3:50** (3:50) (Class 3) (0-95,94) 3-Y-O+ **£9,703** (£2,887; £1,443; £721) **Stalls** High

Form RPR

1225 **1** **Alexandrakollontai (IRE)**[20] 6013 4-8-3 76.........(b) ConnorBeasley[(3)] 2 89
(Alistair Whillans) *chsd ldrs: drvn over 3f out: rallied to ld over 1f out: pushed clr fnl f*
**11/4**[2]

0026 **2** 3 ½ **Ventura Mist**[15] 6170 3-9-1 94..............................(p) RachelRichardson[(7)] 5 96
(Tim Easterby) *in tch: effrt and pushed along 2f out: chsd (clr) wnr ins fnl f: kpt on: no imp*
**9/4**[1]

0025 **3** ¾ **Lady Frances**[10] 6281 3-9-4 90.................................. JoeFanning 1 89
(Mark Johnston) *led to over 4f out: cl up: rdn and edgd rt over 1f out: one pce ins fnl f*
**4/1**

120 **4** nk **Ridge Ranger (IRE)**[23] 5923 3-8-6 78.............................. JasonHart 3 76
(Eric Alston) *dwlt: t.k.h and led over 4f out: rdn: edgd lft and hdd over 1f out: kpt on same pce ins fnl f*
**10/1**

3040 **5** 3 ¼ **Love Island**[9] 6327 5-9-4 91..............................(p) GeorgeChaloner[(3)] 4 79
(Richard Whitaker) *chsd ldrs: drvn along over 2f out: checked and outpcd over 1f out: sn btn*
**10/3**[3]

1m 11.2s (-1.00) **Going Correction** -0.025s/f (Good)
**WFA** 3 from 4yo+ 2lb **5** Ran SP% **109.6**
Speed ratings (Par 104): **105,100,99,98,94**
CSF £9.23 TOTE £2.70: £1.80, £2.80; EX 7.60 Trifecta £23.40.
**Owner** Chris Spark & William Orr **Bred** Sean O'Sullivan **Trained** Newmill-On-Slitrig, Borders

**FOCUS**
Not a bad fillies' handicap, run at a fair pace. The winner has been rated as running a pb.

### 6599 TOTETRIFECTA PICK THE 1, 2, 3 MAIDEN STKS 1m 1f 36y
**4:20** (4:22) (Class 5) 3-4-Y-O **£3,234** (£962; £481; £240) **Stalls** Low

Form RPR

33- **1** **Stetchworth (IRE)**[325] 7655 3-9-5 0.................................. JoeFanning 7 69+
(Mark Johnston) *pressed ldr: led 2f out: sn rdn and edgd rt: kpt on strly fnl f*
**8/15**[1]

343 **2** 2 ¾ **Park Place**[11] 6265 4-9-10 76.................................. PhillipMakin 8 62+
(John Quinn) *prom: effrt over 2f out: chsd (clr) wnr ins fnl f: kpt on: nt pce to chal*
**5/2**[2]

3 **3** hd **L'Inganno Felice (FR)**[20] 6011 4-9-10 0.............................. DavidAllan 3 62
(Iain Jardine) *t.k.h: chsd ldrs: rdn and edgd rt 2f out: kpt on ins fnl f: no imp*
**10/1**[3]

0050 **4** ¾ **Miguela McGuire**[69] 4292 3-9-0 45.............................. PatrickMathers 1 56?
(Eric Alston) *led at stdy pce: rdn and hdd 2f out: kpt on same pce ins fnl f*
**100/1**

6 **5** ½ **So It's War (FR)**[20] 6011 3-9-5 0 GrahamLee 6 60
(Keith Dalgleish) *hld up in tch: drvn and outpcd over 3f out: rallied over 1f out: no imp fnl f* **16/1**

4 **6** ½ **Archipeligo**[53] 4830 3-9-5 0 DavidNolan 2 59
(Iain Jardine) *hld up: rdn over 3f out: kpt on same pce fr 2f out* **33/1**

**7** 26 **Hello Paris** 3-8-9 0 MeganCarberry(5) 4
(Lucy Normile) *s.s: bhd: struggling over 3f out: sn btn: t.o* **100/1**

1m 59.79s (0.09) **Going Correction** -0.025s/f (Good)
**WFA** 3 from 4yo 5lb 7 Ran SP% **113.7**
Speed ratings (Par 103): **98,95,95,94,94 93,70**
CSF £2.06 TOTE £1.60: £1.10, £1.50; EX 2.40 Trifecta £5.40.
**Owner** Sheikh Hamdan bin Mohammed Al Maktoum **Bred** Lodge Park Stud **Trained** Middleham Moor, N Yorks

**FOCUS**
An uncompetitive maiden run at a steady pace. Shaky form, with the fourth close enough.

## 6600 COLLECT TOTEPOOL WINNINGS AT BETFRED SHOPS H'CAP (DIV I) 1m 65y
**4:50** (4:50) (Class 6) (0-65,62) 3-Y-O+ **£2,726** (£805; £402) **Stalls** Low

Form RPR

4004 **1** **Funding Deficit (IRE)**[17] 6121 4-9-7 59 FergalLynch 6 67
(Jim Goldie) *hld up in tch: stdy hdwy and cl up over 3f out: rdn over 2f out: edgd rt: led ins fnl f: drvn out* **15/2**[3]

1034 **2** ¾ **Staffhoss**[12] 6227 4-9-10 62 JoeFanning 4 68
(Mark Johnston) *cl up: rdn and ev ch over 3f out: outpcd and edgd rt over 1f out: styd on to chse wnr wl ins fnl f: r.o* **4/1**[1]

0100 **3** nk **Rust (IRE)**[46] 5088 4-9-8 60 (b) PJMcDonald 8 66
(Ann Duffield) *trckd ldrs: effrt and rdn whn nt clr run wl over 1f out: kpt on ins fnl f* **20/1**

0201 **4** nk **Rocky's Pride (IRE)**[17] 6122 8-8-11 52 GeorgeChaloner(3) 9 57
(Richard Whitaker) *led: rdn along over 2f out: hdd ins fnl f: no ex and lost two pls towards fin* **4/1**[1]

3050 **5** 2 **Violent Velocity (IRE)**[39] 5337 11-9-0 57 JoeDoyle(5) 1 58
(John Quinn) *in tch: rdn over 2f out: one pce whn n.m.r wl over 1f out: one pce fnl f* **10/1**

2002 **6** 3¼ **Nelson's Bay**[2] 6544 5-9-1 58 EmmaSayer(5) 3 51
(Wilf Storey) *t.k.h: hld up in tch: effrt and pushed along over 2f out: edgd lft and no imp over 1f out* **4/1**[1]

4333 **7** nk **Indian Giver**[26] 5809 6-8-12 55 AlistairRawlinson(5) 2 47
(John David Riches) *hld up: effrt on outside over 3f out: outpcd fr 2f out* **9/2**[2]

0665 **8** 8 **Declamation (IRE)**[27] 5797 4-8-10 53 GarryWhillans(5) 5 26
(Alistair Whillans) *hld up: rdn along over 3f out: btn fnl 2f* **9/1**

1m 48.33s (-0.07) **Going Correction** -0.025s/f (Good) 8 Ran SP% **113.8**
Speed ratings (Par 101): **99,98,97,97,95 92,92,84**
CSF £37.15 CT £575.58 TOTE £6.70: £2.30, £1.60, £5.30; EX 43.10 Trifecta £394.50.
**Owner** D Pryde & J Callow **Bred** Rancho San Peasea S A **Trained** Uplawmoor, E Renfrews
■ Stewards' Enquiry : George Chaloner two-day ban: use of whip (6-7 Oct)

**FOCUS**
Not a strong handicap, run at a steady pace. The second is the best guide, the third has been rated as finishing second.

## 6601 COLLECT TOTEPOOL WINNINGS AT BETFRED SHOPS H'CAP (DIV II) 1m 65y
**5:20** (5:21) (Class 6) (0-65,63) 3-Y-O+ **£2,726** (£805; £402) **Stalls** Low

Form RPR

3360 **1** **Lil Sophella (IRE)**[12] 6223 5-9-2 55 DanielTudhope 2 64
(Patrick Holmes) *s.i.s: hld up and bhd: hdwy over 2f out: led ins fnl f: rdn and r.o strly* **3/1**[2]

0444 **2** 2¼ **Outlaw Torn (IRE)**[16] 6160 5-9-9 62 (e) JasonHart 6 66
(Richard Guest) *pressed ldr: drvn to ld over 2f out: hdd ins fnl f: kpt on same pce* **11/4**[1]

6033 **3** 2 **Dark Crystal**[3] 6515 3-9-1 63 MeganCarberry(5) 5 62
(Linda Perratt) *prom: effrt and rdn over 2f out: hung rt wl over 1f out: kpt on same pce fnl f* **9/2**[3]

000 **4** ½ **Rioja Day (IRE)**[20] 6009 4-9-1 57 GaryBartley(3) 3 55
(Jim Goldie) *trckd ldrs: drvn and outpcd over 2f out: rallied over 1f out: kpt on same pce ins fnl f* **10/1**

5056 **5** 4½ **Spavento (IRE)**[20] 6009 8-9-5 58 DavidAllan 4 46
(Eric Alston) *hld up: rdn over 3f out: hdwy over 2f out: no imp fr over 1f out* **8/1**

2060 **6** 3½ **Last Destination (IRE)**[25] 5854 6-8-13 52 JoeFanning 7 32
(Nigel Tinkler) *hld up: rdn and hdwy 3f out: wknd over 1f out* **14/1**

2562 **7** 1 **Blue Sonic**[17] 6122 4-9-4 57 GrahamLee 9 34
(Jim Goldie) *reluctant to enter stalls: bhd: rdn over 3f out: sn n.d* **13/2**

00-0 **8** nse **Smirfy's Silver**[19] 6028 10-8-10 49 oh4 RaulDaSilva 1 26
(Michael Mullineaux) *led at decent gallop: rdn and hdd over 2f out: wknd over 1f out* **100/1**

3550 **9** 5 **Raise A Billion**[25] 5853 3-8-2 50 JoeDoyle(5) 8 16
(Alan Berry) *hld up: rdn along 1/2-way: struggling fr over 2f out* **18/1**

1m 47.7s (-0.70) **Going Correction** -0.025s/f (Good)
**WFA** 3 from 4yo+ 4lb 9 Ran SP% **116.3**
Speed ratings (Par 101): **102,99,97,97,92 89,88,88,83**
CSF £11.80 CT £36.28 TOTE £4.30: £1.10, £1.80, £2.40; EX 10.90 Trifecta £47.90.
**Owner** Mrs S B Porteous **Bred** Waterford Hall Stud **Trained** Middleham, N Yorks

**FOCUS**
They went a sound pace for this modest handicap. This rates a small personal best from the winner.
T/Plt: £56.70 to a £1 stake. Pool: £49,388.91 - 635.41 winning tickets T/Qpdt: £12.30 to a £1 stake. Pool: £3,994.78 - 239.51 winning tickets RY

# 6481 KEMPTON (A.W) (R-H)
Monday, September 22

**OFFICIAL GOING: Polytrack: standard**
Wind: virtually nil Weather: fine

## 6602 BETVICTOR.COM/BRITISH STALLION STUD EBF MAIDEN STKS 1m 2f (P)
**2:10** (2:11) (Class 5) 2-Y-O **£2,911** (£866; £432; £216) **Stalls** Low

Form RPR

04 **1** **Game Show**[24] 5886 2-9-5 0 WilliamBuick 7 76+
(Charlie Appleby) *hld up in last quartet: hmpd after 1f: rdn and hdwy on outer 3f out: clsng whn hmpd and pushed wd bnd 2f out: led ent fnl f: styd on strly* **5/2**[1]

04 **2** 3 **Mister Rockandroll**[9] 6317 2-9-5 0 DaneO'Neill 3 70
(Mark Johnston) *chsd ldrs: effrt to chse ldr over 2f out: ev ch over 1f out: 2nd and outpcd by wnr after: kpt on for clr 2nd* **9/1**

6524 **3** 3¼ **Classic Villager**[2] 6565 2-9-5 75 RyanMoore 11 64
(Philip Hide) *hld up in midfield: hdwy to go 4th over 1f out: kpt on u.p to go 3rd wl ins fnl f: no ch w wnr* **11/4**[2]

4332 **4** 1 **Framley Garth (IRE)**[12] 6237 2-9-5 62 SilvestreDeSousa 8 62
(David Elsworth) *t.k.h: led: rdn wl over 1f out: hdd ent fnl f: wknd* **14/1**

06 **5** 2¼ **Jolie De Vivre (IRE)**[29] 5718 2-9-5 0 LiamKeniry 9 58
(Sylvester Kirk) *chsd ldrs: rdn after 2f: struggling and outpcd over 1f out: sn wknd* **14/1**

04 **6** 1 **Forza Blacky**[17] 6101 2-9-5 0 AndreaAtzeni 5 56
(Philip McBride) *hld up in last quartet: rdn and sme hdwy over 1f out: kpt on: nvr trbld ldrs* **3/1**[3]

00 **7** ¾ **Deeper Magic (IRE)**[17] 6085 2-9-5 0 RobertWinston 2 55
(J S Moore) *hld up in last quartet: effrt and hung rt over 1f out: n.d* **100/1**

00 **8** 4 **Directional**[17] 6102 2-9-5 0 JamesDoyle 4 47
(Charlie Appleby) *in tch in midfield: rdn 2f out: sn struggling and outpcd: wknd over 1f out* **33/1**

06 **9** 2½ **Who'Shedaddy**[43] 5212 2-9-2 0 ThomasBrown(3) 10 42
(Daniel Kubler) *dwlt and sltly hmpd s: sn rcvrd and chsd ldr after 1f tl just over 2f out: struggling whn veered lft bnd 2f out: sn wknd* **100/1**

4 **10** 5 **Sheila Belle (IRE)**[43] 5212 2-9-0 0 DavidProbert 6 28
(J S Moore) *in tch in midfield: rdn over 2f out: sn wknd* **66/1**

**11** 40 **Danegeld** 2-9-5 0 LukeMorris 1
(Paul Cole) *v.s.a and rdn along early: clsd and tagged on top bk of field 5f out: rdn 3f out: sn lost tch: t.o fnl 2f: lame* **25/1**

2m 7.36s (-0.64) **Going Correction** -0.075s/f (Stan) 11 Ran SP% **113.8**
Speed ratings (Par 95): **99,96,94,93,91 90,90,86,84,80 48**
CSF £24.14 TOTE £4.60: £2.10, £2.50, £1.20; EX 25.30 Trifecta £111.10.
**Owner** Godolphin **Bred** Darley **Trained** Newmarket, Suffolk

**FOCUS**
A thorough stamina test for juveniles to open proceedings and the winner proved well suited by the extra distance. Ordinary form.

## 6603 COMPETITIVE DAY DELEGATE RATES MAIDEN STKS (DIV I) 7f (P)
**2:40** (2:41) (Class 5) 2-Y-O **£2,587** (£770; £384; £192) **Stalls** Low

Form RPR

2 **1** **Strong Chemistry**[16] 6138 2-9-5 0 WilliamBuick 1 95+
(Charlie Appleby) *mde all: rdn and qcknd clr 2f out: r.o strly: eased towards fin: readily* **1/2**[1]

55 **2** 6 **Giantouch (USA)**[60] 4570 2-9-0 0 DanielMuscutt(5) 14 76
(Marco Botti) *hld up in tch in midfield: rdn and effrt 2f out: chsd clr wnr 1f out: no ch but kpt on wl for clr 2nd* **20/1**

**3** 3½ **Tuco (IRE)** 2-9-5 0 RyanMoore 6 66+
(Jamie Osborne) *hld up in tch towards rr: rdn and effrt over 2f out: hdwy over 1f out: styd on wl to go 3rd wl ins fnl f: no ch w wnr* **12/1**

4 **4** 2¼ **Winning Hunter**[19] 6039 2-9-5 0 RobertWinston 12 60
(Philip Hide) *chsd ldng pair: wnt 2nd over 3f out: rdn and outpcd by wnr 2f out: lost 2nd 1f out: wknd ins fnl f* **20/1**

5 **5** shd **Greatest Journey**[22] 5947 2-9-5 0 DaneO'Neill 5 60
(Saeed bin Suroor) *in tch in midfield: rdn and outpcd 2f out: 4th and wl hld whn hung rt 1f out* **4/1**[2]

**6** 3½ **Rock Lobster** 2-9-5 0 JimCrowley 8 50
(Ed Dunlop) *in tch in midfield: rdn 3f out: outpcd and wl btn 2f out* **50/1**

0 **7** ½ **Flying Fantasy**[31] 5646 2-9-5 0 SebSanders 11 49
(William Haggas) *t.k.h: hld up in last quartet: rdn and wnt rt over 2f out: no ch after: kpt on past btn rivals ins fnl f* **12/1**

0 **8** 1½ **Always Be Ready**[42] 5248 2-9-5 0 JamesDoyle 3 45
(Lady Cecil) *chsd ldrs: rdn over 2f out: outpcd and btn 2f out: sn wknd* **66/1**

60 **9** 1¼ **Red Stripes (USA)**[46] 5078 2-9-2 0 RyanClark(3) 13 42
(Brian Meehan) *t.k.h: hld up towards rr: hung lft bnd 3f out: no ch fnl 2f* **100/1**

**10** 1 **Vale Of Iron (IRE)** 2-9-5 0 PatCosgrave 7 39+
(Edward Creighton) *s.i.s: sn rcvrd and in tch in midfield: swtchd lft and rdn over 2f out: sn outpcd and wknd* **100/1**

**11** nk **Hambletts (IRE)** 2-9-5 0 TomQueally 9 38
(Robert Mills) *t.k.h: hld up in last quartet: rdn and effrt on inner jst over 2f out: sn wknd* **50/1**

0 **12** 2 **Diamond Sam**[164] 1417 2-9-5 0 (t) LiamKeniry 2 33
(Sylvester Kirk) *chsd wnr tl over 3f out: rdn and lost pl over 2f out: wknd 2f out* **50/1**

**13** ¾ **Rokbaan** 2-9-5 0 AndreaAtzeni 10 31
(Roger Varian) *in tch in midfield: rdn 1/2-way: lost pl u.p over 2f out: no ch after* **10/1**[3]

**14** 23 **Pact** 2-8-11 0 ThomasBrown(3) 4
(Lee Carter) *a towards rr: rdn and struggling wl over 2f out: sn lost tch and t.o fnl 2f* **25/1**

1m 25.33s (-0.67) **Going Correction** -0.075s/f (Stan) 14 Ran SP% **133.9**
Speed ratings (Par 95): **100,93,89,86,86 82,81,80,78,77 77,74,74,47**
CSF £22.26 TOTE £1.40: £1.02, £3.50, £3.90; EX 15.70 Trifecta £157.80.
**Owner** Godolphin **Bred** Rashit Shaykhutdinov **Trained** Newmarket, Suffolk

**FOCUS**
A one-sided betting market and the favourite's supporters never had a moment of concern. The fourth has been rated a bit below his best.

## 6604 COMPETITIVE DAY DELEGATE RATES MAIDEN STKS (DIV II) 7f (P)
**3:10** (3:11) (Class 5) 2-Y-O **£2,587** (£770; £384; £192) **Stalls** Low

Form RPR

2 **1** **Mulzamm (IRE)**[60] 4570 2-9-5 0 [1] WilliamBuick 6 77+
(Charlie Appleby) *hld up in wl in tch in midfield: swtchd lft and effrt 2f out: rdn hands and heels and hdwy to ld ins fnl f: r.o wl: comf* **11/10**[1]

**2** 1½ **Gold Will (IRE)** 2-9-5 0 SilvestreDeSousa 11 71
(Ralph Beckett) *pressed ldr: rdn and ev ch 2f out: drvn to ld over 1f out: hdd ins fnl f: styd on same pce after* **3/1**[2]

0 **3** 2 **Mutamid**[85] 3748 2-9-5 0 SeanLevey 9 65
(Ismail Mohammed) *chsd ldrs: effrt u.p 2f out: no ex and styd on same pce ins fnl f* **100/1**

**4** ½ **Wind In My Sails** 2-9-5 0 FrederikTylicki 10 64
(Ed de Giles) *led: rdn ent fnl 2f: hdd over 1f out: no ex and wknd fnl 100yds* **25/1**

06 **5** 3¼ **El Fenix (IRE)**[10] 6299 2-8-12 0 HectorCrouch(7) 12 55+
(Gary Moore) *stdd and dropped in bhd after s: hld up towards rr: rdn and effrt in centre 2f out: wnt modest 5th 1f out: kpt on but no threat to ldrs* **33/1**

6 2 3/4 **Scooner (USA)** 2-9-5 0 JamesDoyle 4 48+
(Roger Charlton) *hld up in tch towards rr: rdn and effrt on inner 2f out: no imp and kpt on same pce fr over 1f out* 5/1[3]

6 7 1 1/4 **Londonia**[17] 6102 2-9-5 0 LukeMorris 13 44
(Paul Cole) *sltly impeded leaving stalls: sn rcvrd and chsd ldrs after 1f: rdn over 2f out: outpcd wl over 1f out: wknd over 1f out* 16/1

8 3/4 **Dutch Law** 2-9-5 0 JimCrowley 3 42+
(Hughie Morrison) *s.i.s: hld up in last trio: rdn and over 2f out: no imp and kpt on same pce fnl 2f* 14/1

9 3 1/4 **Giovanni Di Bicci** 2-9-5 0 AndreaAtzeni 1 33
(Lady Cecil) *in tch in midfield: rdn and unable qck jst over 2f out: wknd u.p over 1f out* 14/1

0 10 2 1/4 **Master Choice (IRE)**[13] 6203 2-9-5 0 TomQueally 7 27
(William Haggas) *in tch in midfield: rdn over 2f out: sn struggling: wknd over 1f out* 25/1

11 3/4 **Admiral's Gold (IRE)** 2-9-5 0 LiamKeniry 2 25+
(Edward Creighton) *stdd s: t.k.h: hld up in tch in rr: rdn and effrt jst over 2f out: no hdwy: n.d* 100/1

12 4 **Lionel Joseph** 2-9-5 0 PatCosgrave 5 15+
(George Baker) *s.i.s: rn green and a in rr* 66/1

1m 27.15s (1.15) **Going Correction** -0.075s/f (Stan) 12 Ran SP% 122.6
Speed ratings (Par 95): **90,88,86,85,81 78,77,76,72,70 69,64**
CSF £4.26 TOTE £1.90: £1.10, £2.20, £15.00; EX 6.20 Trifecta £142.90.
**Owner** Godolphin **Bred** Darley **Trained** Newmarket, Suffolk

**FOCUS**
The cosy winner was completing a quick treble on the card for Charlie Appleby and William Buick. A steady early pace resulted in a time nearly two seconds slower than the first division.

## 6605 DOWNLOAD THE BETVICTOR APP/BRITISH STALLIONS EBF MAIDEN FILLIES' STKS (BOBIS RACE) (DIV I) 7f (P)
**3:40** (3:43) (Class 5) 2-Y-O £2,911 (£866; £432; £216) **Stalls** Low

Form RPR

1 **Forest Maiden (IRE)** 2-9-0 0 SilvestreDeSousa 4 76+
(Charlie Appleby) *hld up in tch in midfield: swtchd lft and rdn jst over 2f out: hdwy over 1f out: chsd wnr ins fnl f: styd on wl to ld last stride* 11/2[2]

32 2 shd **Mystic Jade**[20] 6001 2-9-0 0 SeanLevey 5 76
(Richard Hannon) *chsd ldrs: rdn to chse ldr 2f out: led over 1f out: drvn ins fnl f: kpt on: hdd last stride* 4/5[1]

3 3 1/2 **Light Of The World (IRE)** 2-8-9 0 RachealKneller(5) 8 67+
(Jamie Osborne) *s.i.s: outpcd in last quartet: pushed along and hdwy on inner 2f out: styd on wl to go 3rd wl ins fnl f: no threat to ldng pair* 66/1

4 hd **Lady Pinnacle** 2-9-0 0 DavidProbert 10 66+
(Andrew Balding) *hld up in tch in midfield: rdn ent fnl 2f: hdwy jst over 1f out: styd on to go 4th wl ins fnl f: no threat to ldrs* 40/1

05 5 2 **Gleaming Girl**[26] 5821 2-9-0 0 JimCrowley 9 61
(David Simcock) *chsd ldr tl 2f out: 3rd and outpcd u.p over 1f out: wknd and lost 2 pls wl ins fnl f* 12/1

6 nse **Vallemi (IRE)** 2-9-0 0 RyanMoore 6 60+
(Sir Michael Stoute) *t.k.h: chsd ldrs: rdn and unable qck 2f out: 4th and btn 1f out: wknd insidne fnl f* 7/1[3]

7 3/4 **Arrowtown** 2-9-0 0[1] JamesDoyle 11 58
(Roger Charlton) *s.i.s: rn green and outpcd in rr: hdwy and wandering arnd over 1f out: swtchd rt nr fin: nvr trbld ldrs* 16/1

0 8 4 **You Be Lucky (IRE)**[26] 5821 2-9-0 0 DaneO'Neill 3 48
(Jo Crowley) *led: rdn ent fnl 2f: drvn and hdd over 1f out: wknd fnl f* 66/1

0 9 2 **Skylight (IRE)**[11] 6246 2-9-0 0 LiamJones 1 42
(William Haggas) *in tch in midfield: rdn 1/2-way: outpcd u.p 2f out: wknd over 1f out* 25/1

0 10 6 **Stellar Jet (IRE)**[54] 4784 2-9-0 0 AndreaAtzeni 7 26
(Roger Varian) *in tch in midfield: rdn and no rspnse over 2f out: wknd wl over 1f out* 25/1

11 4 **Zamorano (IRE)** 2-8-7 0 AhmadAlSubousi(7) 12 15
(Ismail Mohammed) *sn wl outpcd in last pair: n.d* 50/1

12 4 1/2 **Politico** 2-9-0 0 WilliamBuick 2 3
(John Gosden) *s.i.s: rn green and a wl outpcd in rr* 10/1

1m 26.23s (0.23) **Going Correction** -0.075s/f (Stan) 12 Ran SP% 121.2
Speed ratings (Par 92): **95,94,90,90,88 88,87,82,80,73 69,64**
CSF £10.03 TOTE £10.50: £2.00, £1.10, £10.60; EX 14.20 Trifecta £307.20.
**Owner** Godolphin **Bred** Darley **Trained** Newmarket, Suffolk

**FOCUS**
Quite an interesting maiden on paper but the field were well strung out at halfway and plenty needed the experience. The fifth and eighth help set the early level.

## 6606 DOWNLOAD THE BETVICTOR APP/BRITISH STALLIONS EBF MAIDEN FILLIES' STKS (BOBIS RACE) (DIV II) 7f (P)
**4:10** (4:12) (Class 5) 2-Y-O £2,911 (£866; £432; £216) **Stalls** Low

Form RPR

1 **Comedy Queen (USA)** 2-9-0 0[1] SilvestreDeSousa 7 74
(Charlie Appleby) *hld up in midfield: rdn over 2f out: hdwy u.p in centre over 1f out: styd on wl to ld fnl 75yds: gng away at fin* 12/1

2 1 **Zari** 2-9-0 0 AndreaAtzeni 6 71+
(Roger Varian) *chsd ldr: rdn and effrt over 2f out: drvn and pressing ldr 2f out: kpt on same pce ins fnl f: snatched 2nd last stride* 10/1

52 3 shd **Simple Elegance (USA)**[75] 4075 2-9-0 0 JamesDoyle 1 71
(Charlie Appleby) *led: rdn over 1f out: kpt on u.p: hdd fnl 75yds: no ex and lost 2nd last stride* 11/4[2]

0 4 nk **Uele River**[18] 6066 2-9-0 0 DaneO'Neill 8 70
(Henry Candy) *t.k.h: rdn and effrt ent fnl 2f: drvn and pressing ldr 1f out: kpt on same pce ins fnl f* 11/2

40 5 1 1/2 **Rastanora (USA)**[51] 4914 2-9-0 0 WilliamBuick 2 66
(John Gosden) *chsd ldrs: rdn 3f out: unable qck u.p over 1f out: hld and kpt on same pce ins fnl f* 5/1[3]

0 6 5 **Acquittal**[26] 5821 2-9-0 0 HayleyTurner 10 53
(James Fanshawe) *in tch in midfield: rdn and effrt on inner 2f out: drvn and no imp 1f out: wknd ins fnl f* 12/1

7 1 1/4 **Entity** 2-9-0 0[1] RyanMoore 5 49
(Sir Michael Stoute) *in tch in midfield: rdn ent fnl 2f: sn outpcd and btn over 1f out: wknd fnl f* 5/2[1]

8 1 **Jo Bibidia** 2-9-0 0 LukeMorris 4 47
(Jonathan Portman) *s.i.s: rn green and pushed along in last pair: effrt on inner ent fnl 2f: sn wknd* 66/1

0 9 1 3/4 **Medicean Melody**[26] 5821 2-9-0 0 LiamKeniry 11 42
(David Simcock) *t.k.h: hld up in tch: rdn over 2f out: sn outpcd: and btn: wknd over 1f out* 100/1

10 5 **Hayed** 2-8-7 0 (b[1]) RobertPWalsh(7) 9 28
(Edward Creighton) *dwlt: hld up in rr: rdn over 2f out: sn lost tch* 100/1

1m 27.12s (1.12) **Going Correction** -0.075s/f (Stan) 10 Ran SP% 115.2
Speed ratings (Par 92): **90,88,88,88,86 80,79,78,76,70**
CSF £123.54 TOTE £12.00: £3.30, £3.20, £1.20; EX 118.80 Trifecta £274.70.
**Owner** Godolphin **Bred** Darley **Trained** Newmarket, Suffolk

**FOCUS**
5-5 on the card for Charlie Appleby, all of them juveniles, with the less-fancied of his pair completing the nap hand. The time was 0.89secs slower than division one. The standard is ordinary rated around the third and a few down the field.

## 6607 £25 FREE BET AT BETVICTOR.COM H'CAP (BOBIS RACE) 6f (P)
**4:40** (4:40) (Class 3) (0-95,94) 3-Y-O
£7,158 (£2,143; £1,071; £535; £267; £134) **Stalls** Low

Form RPR

1515 1 **Polybius**[57] 4697 3-9-7 94 TedDurcan 9 106
(David Lanigan) *stdd and dropped in bhd: hld up in tch: rdn and hdwy on inner 2f out: qckned to ld ent fnl f: r.o strly and drew clr fnl f: rdn out* 7/2[1]

-000 2 2 1/4 **Royal Mezyan (IRE)**[15] 6170 3-9-1 88 (p) SebSanders 6 93
(William Haggas) *t.k.h: chsd ldrs: drvn and ev ch over 1f out: styd on same pce ins fnl f* 12/1

0501 3 shd **Outer Space**[33] 5553 3-9-0 87 WilliamTwiston-Davies 2 92
(Jamie Osborne) *hld up in rr: rdn and hdwy 2f out: swtchd rt and squeezed between rivals 1f out: pressing for 2nd ins fnl f: kpt on* 11/2[3]

0500 4 1 **Harwoods Volante (IRE)**[20] 6006 3-9-2 89 AndreaAtzeni 8 90
(Amanda Perrett) *chsd ldrs: rdn to chal and c towards centre 2f out: no ex and outpcd fnl 150yds* 13/2

1620 5 1/2 **Souville**[11] 6260 3-9-0 87 WilliamBuick 5 87
(Chris Wall) *in tch in midfield: rdn and effrt 2f out: kpt on u.p ins fnl f* 6/1

1001 6 1 1/2 **Perfect Alchemy (IRE)**[43] 5211 3-8-9 82 ow1 JamesDoyle 7 77
(Ralph Beckett) *hld up in tch in midfield: rdn and effrt 2f out: drvn and styd on same pce fr over 1f out* 9/2[2]

3424 7 nk **Meritocracy (IRE)**[10] 6296 3-8-9 82 (t) LukeMorris 3 76
(Paul Cole) *chsd ldrs: drvn pressing ldrs 2f out: no ex 1f out: wknd ins fnl f* 7/1

4035 8 1 **Oriental Relation (IRE)**[16] 6153 3-8-13 86 (v) TomQueally 10 77
(James Given) *stdd and dropped in after s: hld up towards rr: rdn and effrt in centre 2f out: no real imp* 33/1

4450 9 shd **Our Queenie (IRE)**[30] 5675 3-9-0 87 RyanMoore 1 78
(Richard Hannon) *dropped to rr 5f out: sn detached and rdn: no ch but styd on ins fnl f* 20/1

1100 10 1 **Captain Secret**[135] 2161 3-9-2 94 DanielMuscutt(5) 4 81
(Marco Botti) *led: rdn and hrd pressed 2f out: hdd ent fnl f: sn btn and wknd ins fnl f* 16/1

1m 11.47s (-1.63) **Going Correction** -0.075s/f (Stan) 10 Ran SP% 117.2
Speed ratings (Par 105): **107,104,103,102,101 99,99,98,98,96**
CSF £47.27 CT £234.31 TOTE £5.30: £1.80, £4.20, £2.70; EX 56.30 Trifecta £388.80.
**Owner** Niarchos Family **Bred** Niarchos Family **Trained** Upper Lambourn, Berks

**FOCUS**
The first handicap on the card, run at a sound pace, and it threw up an impressive winner. The third has matched his latest C&D effort.

## 6608 DOWNLOAD THE BETVICTOR INSTABET APP H'CAP (BOBIS RACE) 1m 4f (P)
**5:10** (5:12) (Class 4) (0-80,80) 3-Y-O £4,690 (£1,395; £697; £348) **Stalls** Centre

Form RPR

-213 1 **Royal Warranty**[12] 6239 3-9-0 73 DavidProbert 3 81+
(Andrew Balding) *in tch in midfield: hdwy u.p to chal over 1f out: led fnl 100yds: styd on wl: rdn out* 12/1

050 2 3/4 **Fun Mac (GER)**[30] 5691 3-9-6 79 (t) JamesDoyle 7 86
(Hughie Morrison) *hld up in tch: rdn and hdwy ent fnl f: styd on wl to chse wnr wl ins fnl f: no imp towards fin* 6/1[3]

2201 3 3/4 **Invasor Luck (USA)**[19] 6045 3-9-7 80 TomQueally 8 86+
(James Fanshawe) *chsd ldr tl led 2f out: rdn over 1f out: drvn and hdd fnl 100yds: one pce after* 12/1

1F63 4 3/4 **Heska (IRE)**[18] 6075 3-8-9 68 (tp) SilvestreDeSousa 10 72
(Michael Appleby) *stdd and dropped in bhd after s: hld up in rr: swtchd lft over 1f out: hdwy u.p over 1f out: styd on same pce u.p ins fnl f* 66/1

6135 5 hd **Gavlar**[24] 5877 3-8-13 72 (b[1]) AndreaAtzeni 2 76
(William Knight) *in tch in midfield: effrt on inner 2f out: chsd ldrs and kpt on same pce ins fnl f* 8/1

-634 6 2 3/4 **Tucson Arizona**[24] 5884 3-9-2 75 (tp) WilliamCarson 9 75
(Anthony Carson) *stdd and dropped in bhd after s: hld up in tch: hdwy 2f out: chsd ldrs and rdn over 1f out: wknd ins fnl f* 12/1

1404 7 1 1/2 **Crystal Nymph (IRE)**[37] 5430 3-9-2 75 SeanLevey 5 72
(Richard Hannon) *chsd ldrs: rdn ent fnl 2f: unable qck over 1f out: wknd ins fnl f* 33/1

4402 8 1 **Cotton Club (IRE)**[24] 5877 3-8-12 78 PatMillman(7) 4 74
(Rod Millman) *in tch in midfield: rdn over 2f out: no ex over 1f out: hld and one pce fnl f* 25/1

1215 9 10 **Daydreamer**[52] 4863 3-9-7 80 SebSanders 6 60
(William Haggas) *led tl hdd and rdn 2f out: outpcd and btn over 1f out: sn wknd* 7/2[2]

4-32 10 81 **Freemason**[27] 5796 3-9-2 75 RyanMoore 1
(Sir Michael Stoute) *chsd ldrs: rdn over 3f out: lost action and eased ent fnl 2f: sn t.o and virtually p.u after* 11/10[1]

2m 32.89s (-1.61) **Going Correction** -0.075s/f (Stan) 10 Ran SP% 126.6
Speed ratings (Par 103): **102,101,101,100,100 98,97,96,90,36**
CSF £88.13 CT £914.15 TOTE £7.40: £2.50, £2.60, £3.50; EX 60.40 Trifecta £704.00.
**Owner** Sir Gordon Brunton **Bred** Sir Gordon Brunton **Trained** Kingsclere, Hants

**FOCUS**
An interesting handicap with one of the least-exposed runners coming out on top. The level is set by the fourth and fifth.

## 6609 FOLLOW @BETVICTORRACING ON TWITTER H'CAP 1m (P)
**5:40** (5:42) (Class 4) (0-85,85) 3-Y-O+ £4,690 (£1,395; £697; £348) **Stalls** Low

Form RPR

5050 1 **Killing Time (IRE)**[28] 5758 3-8-11 76 (b) JimCrowley 11 85
(Ralph Beckett) *chsd ldr: rdn and ev ch 2f out: led over 1f out: kpt on and forged ahd ins fnl f: a jst lasting home* 10/1

0151 2 nk **Matravers**[19] 6034 3-8-13 78 RyanMoore 5 86
(Sir Michael Stoute) *hld up in midfield: rdn over 2f out: hdwy u.p 1f out: str run ins fnl f: wnt 2nd wl ins fnl f: nvr quite getting to wnr* 2/1[1]

0033 3 ½ **Whipper Snapper (IRE)**[17] 6100 4-9-4 **79**.................... AndreaAtzeni 10 86
(William Knight) *hld up in tch in rr: rdn over 2f out: styd on strly u.p ins fnl f: wnt 3rd wl ins fnl f: nt rch ldrs* **12/1**

-300 4 1¼ **Big Whiskey (IRE)**[145] 1871 4-9-5 **80**............................(t) PatCosgrave 9 84
(Edward Creighton) *chsd ldrs: rdn and effrt jst over 2f out: ev ch over 1f out tl no ex ins fnl f: wknd towards fin* **33/1**

5100 5 1¼ **Ogbourne Downs**[30] 5669 4-9-9 **84**............................ SteveDrowne 12 85
(Charles Hills) *hld up in tch in rr: pushed along and hdwy whn nt clrest of run over 1f out: pushed along and kpt on ins fnl f: nvr threatened ldrs* **33/1**

-424 6 hd **Royal Preserve**[122] 2510 3-8-11 **76**................................ DavidProbert 4 77
(Andrew Balding) *in tch in midfield: rdn and effrt to chse ldrs wl over 1f out: no ex u.p 1f out: one pce ins fnl f* **10/1**

3150 7 ½ **Tides Reach (IRE)**[25] 5849 3-8-10 **75**........................... JamesDoyle 13 75
(Roger Charlton) *hld up in tch in rrt: hdwy u.p over 1f out: kpt on fnl f: nvr trbld ldrs* **33/1**

3113 8 1¾ **Bombardment (USA)**[39] 5349 3-9-2 **81**.................. SilvestreDeSousa 6 77
(Charlie Appleby) *led: rdn over 2f out: hdd over 1f out: wknd ins fnl f* **9/4**[2]

4321 9 ½ **Messila Star**[49] 4968 4-9-5 **80**.......................................(v) TomQueally 1 74
(Jeremy Noseda) *in tch in midfield: drvn and unable qck over 1f out: wknd ins fnl f* **8/1**[3]

0146 10 4 **Orion's Bow**[23] 5930 3-9-0 **79**......................................(bt) WilliamBuick 7 64
(John Gosden) *chsd ldrs: rdn 2f out: no ex and btn over 1f out: wknd fnl f* **14/1**

1000 11 ¾ **Myboyalfie (USA)**[43] 5213 7-9-10 **85**.........................(p) FrederikTylicki 8 69
(J R Jenkins) *in tch in midfield: rdn and lost pl over 1f out: bhd fnl f* **25/1**

1m 38.03s (-1.77) **Going Correction** -0.075s/f (Stan)
**WFA** 3 from 4yo+ 4lb **11** Ran SP% **120.4**
Speed ratings (Par 105): **105,104,104,102,101 101,101,99,98,94 94**
CSF £30.13 CT £252.07 TOTE £11.20: £2.60, £1.40, £3.80; EX 42.60 Trifecta £394.40.
**Owner** Kennet Valley Thoroughbreds VIII **Bred** Kilfrush Stud **Trained** Kimpton, Hants

**FOCUS**
A competitive 3yo handicap, run at a fair pace. The winner has been rated as running a pb, with the third close to form and the fourth close to his best.
T/Jkpt: £2,366.60 to a £1 stake. Pool: £10,000.00 - 3.00 winning tickets T/Plt: £14.50 to a £1 stake. Pool: £48,980.71 - 2,465.64 winning tickets T/Qpdt: £5.90 to a £1 stake. Pool: £5,035.03 - 625.85 winning tickets SP

# 6203 LEICESTER (R-H)
## Monday, September 22

**OFFICIAL GOING: Good to firm (good in places; 7.8)**
Wind: almost nil Weather: bright and sunny; 19 degrees

## 6610 ASTON FLAMVILLE FILLIES' NURSERY H'CAP 5f 218y
**2:00** (2:00) (Class 5) (0-75,75) 2-Y-O **£3,234** (£962; £481; £240) **Stalls** High

Form RPR

3433 1 **Scarlet Bounty (IRE)**[31] 5637 2-8-11 65........................ PaulHanagan 1 70
(Richard Fahey) *trckd ldrs and t.k.h: gng v wl 2f out: rdn to dispute ld 1f out: drvn and jst prevailed* **11/2**[2]

1113 2 nk **White Vin Jan**[21] 5983 2-8-7 66.............................. LouisSteward(5) 10 70
(Michael Bell) *midfield: effrt over 2f out: chal and w ldr wl over 1f out: edgd rt: ev ch tl no ex clsng strides* **7/1**[3]

405 3 hd **Hound Music**[40] 5309 2-8-13 67.................................. JimmyFortune 5 71
(Jonathan Portman) *effrt outside over 2f out: rdn and ev ch ins fnl f: nt qckn fnl 50yds* **10/1**

044 4 2¼ **Roxie Lot**[23] 5910 2-9-2 70.......................................... StephenCraine 2 67
(Pam Sly) *w ldr: drvn 2f out: hdd and one pce wl over 1f out* **8/1**

6521 5 nk **Magic Mac**[11] 6248 2-7-13 58.......................................(p) CamHardie(5) 6 54
(Hughie Morrison) *pushed along in rr: rdn and edgd rt 2f out: nt rch ldrs fnl f* **10/1**

1636 6 ½ **Brown Velvet**[17] 6104 2-9-1 69......................................(v) OisinMurphy 8 63
(Hugo Palmer) *cl up tl drvn and nt qckn over 1f out* **12/1**

3261 7 ½ **Renaissant**[21] 5973 2-9-7 75.................................... RichardHughes 11 68
(Richard Hannon) *towards rr: drvn and outpcd 1/2-way: styng on wl ins fnl f* **5/1**[1]

0262 8 1 **Zuzinia (IRE)**[5] 6453 2-8-9 66.................................... CharlesBishop(3) 4 56
(Mick Channon) *prom tl rdn and wknd over 1f out* **8/1**

0350 9 7 **Artfilly (IRE)**[21] 5974 2-8-13 67.................................. JamieSpencer 9 36
(Ed Walker) *dwlt: a outpcd in rr* **12/1**

1403 10 1¾ **Claras Cookie (IRE)**[13] 6205 2-8-7 64........................ DeclanBates(3) 7 28
(David Evans) *w ldr tl 1/2-way: rdn and sn lost pl* **33/1**

014 11 1½ **As A Dream (IRE)**[41] 5279 2-9-4 72.............................. AdamKirby 12 31
(David Evans) *sn struggling in rr* **100/1**

3204 12 ¾ **War Paint (IRE)**[45] 5129 2-8-11 65..................(p) RichardKingscote 3 22
(Tom Dascombe) *rdn and bhd fr 1/2-way* **16/1**

6303 13 3¾ **Diracan (IRE)**[19] 6040 2-8-8 62.................................(b) ChrisCatlin 14 8
(Nick Littmoden) *drvn in rr: reluctant and nvr travelling: t.o* **20/1**

1m 12.71s (-0.29) **Going Correction** -0.10s/f (Good) **13** Ran SP% **114.9**
Speed ratings (Par 92): **97,96,96,93,92 92,91,90,80,78 76,75,70**
CSF £41.28 CT £386.20 TOTE £7.10: £1.70, £2.70, £3.50; EX 45.40 Trifecta £542.40.
**Owner** Malih Lahej Al Basti **Bred** Malih L Al Basti **Trained** Musley Bank, N Yorks

**FOCUS**
A fair fillies' nursery in which they went a proper gallop towards the centre of the track. The form looks okay.

## 6611 BREEDERS BACKING RACING EBF MAIDEN STKS 1m 3f 183y
**2:30** (2:31) (Class 5) 3-Y-O+ **£3,881** (£1,155; £577; £288) **Stalls** Low

Form RPR

2062 1 **Moshe (IRE)**[21] 5984 3-9-5 79.................................... JimmyFortune 2 86
(Hughie Morrison) *mde all: drvn 2f out: hanging and wandering in both directions fr over 1f out: clr ins fnl f* **13/8**[2]

32 2 9 **Viceroyalty**[11] 6265 3-9-5 0.............................................. AdamKirby 5 76
(Charlie Appleby) *hld up in last pair: wnt 2nd over 2f out: sn hrd drvn: no imp in mod 2nd fr over 1f out* **11/8**[1]

0 3 3½ **Gold Run**[66] 4407 3-9-5 0............................................. HarryBentley 3 66
(Olly Stevens) *pushed along in 3rd pl: rdn 4f out: plugged on same pce wl btn 3f* **33/1**

3053 4 13 **Mawaseel**[44] 5191 3-9-5 71.......................................(t) PaulHanagan 4 45
(B W Hills) *t.k.h early: rdn over 3f out: 2nd tl over 2f out: sn fdd: t.o and eased nr fin* **10/1**

5 30 **Tweedswood (IRE)** 3-9-5 0.................................... RichardHughes 1
(Roger Varian) *last pair: outpcd after 4f: t.o and eased fnl 2f* **5/1**[3]

2m 30.52s (-3.38) **Going Correction** -0.075s/f (Good) **5** Ran SP% **108.9**
Speed ratings (Par 103): **108,102,99,91,71**
CSF £4.12 TOTE £3.00: £1.30, £1.10; EX 4.40 Trifecta £43.80.
**Owner** Capt J Macdonald-Buchanan **Bred** Lavington Stud **Trained** East Ilsley, Berks

**FOCUS**
A fair little maiden in which they went a decent gallop. No depth to the form.

## 6612 BRITISH STALLION STUDS EBF KEGWORTH NOVICE STKS (BOBIS RACE) 5f 218y
**3:00** (3:00) (Class 4) 2-Y-O **£6,469** (£1,925; £962; £481) **Stalls** High

Form RPR

21 1 **Charming Thought**[19] 6038 2-9-5 0................................... AdamKirby 2 100+
(Charlie Appleby) *hld up and plld hrd: rdn and effrt 2f out: led ins fnl f: holding rival after* **10/11**[1]

2540 2 ½ **Surewecan**[16] 6142 2-9-5 96.......................................... FrannyNorton 1 96
(Mark Johnston) *led after 1f: rdn over 1f out: hdd ins fnl f: kpt on gamely but a hld* **8/1**

21 3 2¾ **Charlie Croker (IRE)**[26] 5807 2-9-5 0........................... JamieSpencer 5 88
(Kevin Ryan) *led 1f: rdn 2f out: wknd over 1f out* **6/1**[3]

140 4 2½ **Fox Trotter (IRE)**[11] 6256 2-9-5 100.........................[1] JimmyFortune 3 80
(Brian Meehan) *t.k.h early: in last pair: pushed along 1/2-way: fdd tamely over 1f out: eased ins fnl f* **11/4**[2]

1m 12.56s (-0.44) **Going Correction** -0.10s/f (Good) **4** Ran SP% **104.4**
Speed ratings (Par 97): **98,97,93,90**
CSF £7.50 TOTE £1.60; EX 7.00 Trifecta £18.50.
**Owner** Godolphin **Bred** Merry Fox Stud Limited **Trained** Newmarket, Suffolk

**FOCUS**
A good quality small-field juvenile novice contest in which they went respectable gallop and no more. The runner-up helps set the level.

## 6613 GOLDEN HAND (S) STKS 7f 9y
**3:30** (3:31) (Class 6) 3-Y-O **£1,940** (£577; £288; £144) **Stalls** High

Form RPR

5100 1 **Half Way**[16] 6155 3-8-13 70.......................................... AmyScott(3) 11 72
(Henry Candy) *t.k.h: trckd ldrs: led over 2f out: sn rdn: hld on gamely ins fnl f* **7/2**[3]

4463 2 nk **Swiss Lait**[21] 5972 3-8-1 55...................................... CamHardie(5) 10 61
(David Elsworth) *cl up and t.k.h: drvn and outpcd 2f out: rallied 1f out: edgd rt: sn pressing wnr: outbattled fnl 100yds* **7/1**

0555 3 2¼ **Zain Zone (IRE)**[7] 6414 3-9-2 72............................(p) JamesSullivan 1 65
(Ruth Carr) *rrd s: plld hrd: hdwy after 3f: cl up over 2f out: sn hrd rdn: nt qckn fnl f* **11/4**[2]

0004 4 1½ **Cueca (FR)**[14] 6194 3-8-6 48....................................(b) FrannyNorton 9 51
(Jonathan Portman) *slt ld tl rdn and hdd over 2f out: kpt on same pce after* **33/1**

4065 5 3¾ **Encore Encore (FR)**[17] 6087 3-8-11 58..................(b) RichardHughes 2 47
(Harry Dunlop) *towards rr: rdn and effrt wl over 1f out: sn no further imp* **14/1**

-060 6 1½ **Crown Pleasure (IRE)**[38] 5394 3-8-6 65......................... ChrisCatlin 12 38
(Willie Musson) *chsd ldrs: rdn 3f out: btn wl over 1f out* **16/1**

3052 7 1¼ **Astral Rose**[23] 5905 3-8-7 48 ow1..................................(b) JohnFahy 6 36
(Jonathan Portman) *stdd s: plld hrd: a bhd* **33/1**

3455 8 hd **Milly's Secret (IRE)**[28] 5763 3-8-11 72.....................(p) PaulHanagan 5 39
(Ann Duffield) *prom and t.k.h: ev ch 2f out: sn drvn: btn 1f out: eased cl home* **9/4**[1]

00 9 1½ **The Pocket Dot**[130] 2281 3-7-13 0................................ PaddyPilley(7) 3 30
(Mick Channon) *sn drvn and a outpcd* **100/1**

00 10 24 **Lady Sorento**[17] 6092 3-8-7 0 ow1.............................. StevieDonohoe 4
(Tim Pitt) *sn cl up: rdn 3f out: lost pl qckly 2f out: sn t.o: eased fnl f* **100/1**

1m 25.52s (-0.68) **Going Correction** -0.10s/f (Good) **10** Ran SP% **112.6**
Speed ratings (Par 99): **99,98,96,94,90 88,86,86,85,57**
CSF £26.55 TOTE £5.40: £1.80, £2.50, £1.90; EX 21.40 Trifecta £81.40.The winner bought in 5,500gns. Milly's Secret was claimed by Mr K. Nicholson for £7,000.
**Owner** Henry Candy **Bred** Shadwell Estate Company Limited **Trained** Kingston Warren, Oxon

**FOCUS**
A modest 3yo seller, run at an ordinary pace. The runner-up and fourth have been rated to their marks.

## 6614 SIS LIVE H'CAP 5f 2y
**4:00** (4:00) (Class 3) (0-95,95) 3-Y-O- **£7,561** (£2,263; £1,131; £566; £282) **Stalls** High

Form RPR

0120 1 **Milly's Gift**[57] 4700 4-9-4 95........................................ RyanTate(3) 8 103+
(Clive Cox) *settled trcking ldrs: rdn 2f out: styd on to ld wl ins fnl f: jst hld on* **9/4**[1]

0033 2 nk **Taajub (IRE)**[16] 6130 7-8-12 86..................................... ShaneKelly 4 93
(Peter Crate) *hmpd s: last and rdn and wl off pce 1/2-way: rallied ins fnl f: jst failed* **8/1**

5100 3 hd **Extrasolar**[11] 6260 4-8-13 87....................................(t) RichardHughes 1 93
(Amanda Perrett) *pressed ldr: led over 1f out: sn drvn: hdd and no ex wl ins fnl f* **9/2**[3]

0000 4 1 **Major Crispies**[15] 6170 3-9-4 93.............................. StevieDonohoe 7 96
(James Eustace) *t.k.h: prom tl rdn 1/2-way: sn outpcd: rallied 1f out: no imp fnl 100yds* **20/1**

1104 5 ¾ **Silvanus (IRE)**[13] 6209 9-9-6 94.................................. PaulHanagan 9 94
(Paul Midgley) *led: rdn and hdd over 1f out: no ex fnl f* **16/1**

-031 6 1 **Smart Daisy K**[9] 6314 4-8-11 90................................... JackDuern(5) 2 86
(Andrew Hollinshead) *cl up tl rdn and wknd ins fnl f* **11/4**[2]

3100 7 1½ **Top Boy**[23] 5918 4-9-1 89.......................................(v) DaleSwift 3 80
(Derek Shaw) *in rr and drvn 1/2-way: nvr gng wl enough to chal* **11/1**

0610 U **Holley Shiftwell**[16] 6130 4-8-9 83................................ HarryBentley 6
(Stuart Williams) *lowered hd and uns rdr leaving stalls* **10/1**

59.63s (-0.37) **Going Correction** -0.10s/f (Good)
**WFA** 3 from 4yo+ 1lb **8** Ran SP% **114.8**
Speed ratings (Par 107): **98,97,97,95,94 92,90,**
CSF £21.14 CT £75.19 TOTE £3.10: £1.30, £2.40, £1.70; EX 22.30 Trifecta £77.50.
**Owner** Ken Lock Racing **Bred** Ken Lock Racing **Trained** Lambourn, Berks

**FOCUS**
The feature race was a fair sprint handicap in which they went a decent gallop. The runner-up built on his recent run, while the third also helps set the level.

## 6615 HENRY ALKEN CLASSIFIED CLAIMING STKS 1m 1f 218y
**4:30** (4:30) (Class 5) 3-4-Y-O **£2,587** (£770; £384; £192) **Stalls** Low

Form RPR

4255 1 **Eddiemaurice (IRE)**[6] 6431 3-9-0 75..........................(v) CamHardie(5) 3 78
(Richard Guest) *hld up in last pl: drvn and stdy prog fr over 2f out: led over 1f out: sn in command: rdn out* **9/2**[2]

4166 2 2 **Penny's Boy**[14] 6192 3-9-5 72..................................(t) RichardHughes 1 74
(Sylvester Kirk) *settled towards rr: effrt but drvn over 2f out: ev ch briefly 1f out: sn no match for wnr* **2/1**[1]

0522 **3** *5* **Run Fat Lass Run**[30] 5678 4-9-9 68................................(p) AdamKirby 4 63
(Conor Dore) *hld up: wnt 2nd 4f out: led wl over 2f out: drvn and hdd over 1f out: sn fdd* **9/2**[2]
152 **4** *2* **World Record (IRE)**[24] 5269 4-9-5 70.............................. IanBrennan 7 55
(John Quinn) *plld hrd: pressed ldrs tl drvn wl over 2f out: wknd wl over 1f out* **2/1**[1]
0056 **5** *12* **Edge (IRE)**[10] 6284 3-8-13 62.....................................(b) StevieDonohoe 6 32
(Bernard Llewellyn) *plld hrd on outside: cl up: led 4f out: rdn and hdd wl over 2f out: fdd tamely: t.o and eased* **25/1**[3]
1330 **6** *14* **Ain't No Surprise (IRE)**[16] 6155 3-8-7 65......................(t) PaulHanagan 2
(Jennie Candlish) *sweating: sn setting stdy pce: hdd 4f out: rdn and sn struggling: t.o over 1f out: heavily eased* **25/1**[3]

2m 8.26s (0.36) **Going Correction** -0.075s/f (Good)
**WFA** 3 from 4yo 6lb **6** Ran SP% **110.7**
Speed ratings (Par 103): **95,93,89,87,78 67**
CSF £13.56 TOTE £5.60: £2.40, £2.20; EX 18.10 Trifecta £36.80.Eddiemaurice was claimed by Mr J. L. Flint £12,000.
**Owner** Advance Group UK Ltd **Bred** Declan Murphy **Trained** Ingmanthorpe, W Yorks

**FOCUS**
This claimer was run at a modest gallop. The winner has been rated as running a small pb.

## 6616 HIGHFIELDS H'CAP 1m 60y
**5:00** (5:00) (Class 5) (0-75,74) 3-Y-O+ **£3,234** (£962; £481; £240) **Stalls** Low

Form RPR
3332 **1** **Faure Island**[9] 6337 3-9-4 72...................................... FergusSweeney 10 85+
(Henry Candy) *settled trcking ldrs and gng wl: effrt 3f out to ld over 2f out: edgd rt: rdn 4 l clr and wl in command 1f out* **7/2**[1]
0412 **2** *2* **Pendo**[12] 6242 3-9-0 68...................................... RichardHughes 9 75
(Paul Cole) *cl up: chsd wnr 2f out: sn rdn and outpcd by him: a hld after* **7/2**[1]
4230 **3** *½* **Comanchero (IRE)**[12] 6232 3-9-1 69...................................... OisinMurphy 2 76
(Andrew Balding) *pushed along in rr: drvn and outpcd over 2f out: swtchd lft: rallied 1f out: kpt on but no imp on ldrs* **8/1**
333 **4** *hd* **Vainglory (USA)**[34] 5533 10-9-3 74.............................. GeorgeBuckell(7) 6 79
(David Simcock) *bhd: hdwy 2f out: wnt rt but styd on stoutly ins fnl f: nrly snatched 3rd* **20/1**
413 **5** *3* **Cincuenta Pasos (IRE)**[35] 5492 3-9-3 71.............................. AdamKirby 1 69
(Joseph Tuite) *settled in midfield: effrt 3f out: swtchd lft 2f out: rdn and btn wl over 1f out* **9/2**[2]
5045 **6** *13* **Black Dave (IRE)**[11] 6249 4-8-10 63.............................. DeclanBates(3) 5 32
(David Evans) *sn led and set str pce: rdn and hdd over 2f out: dropped out qckly: t.o and eased* **16/1**
2554 **7** *shd* **Alpine Storm (IRE)**[9] 6316 3-9-4 72.............................. FrannyNorton 4 46
(Mark Johnston) *prom: shkn up 3f out: little rspnse: btn 2f out: t.o and eased* **6/1**[3]
4510 **8** *¾* **Trulee Scrumptious**[35] 5503 5-9-0 64.............................(v) JimmyQuinn 8 31
(Peter Charalambous) *drvn along early: prom: rdn 3f out: sn fdd: eased and t.o* **10/1**
1105 **9** *1 ¾* **Siouxperhero (IRE)**[14] 6191 5-9-5 74..............................(v[1]) CamHardie(5) 7 37
(William Muir) *drvn and labouring in 9th after 4f: t.o fnl 3f: eased* **20/1**
5600 **10** *3 ¼* **Top Set (IRE)**[20] 6019 4-8-9 66..............................(b) TomasHarrigan(7) 3 21
(Simon Dow) *poor last after 4f: t.o fnl 3f: eased* **50/1**

1m 43.28s (-1.82) **Going Correction** -0.10s/f (Good)
**WFA** 3 from 4yo+ 4lb **10** Ran SP% **114.5**
Speed ratings (Par 103): **105,103,102,102,99 86,86,85,83,80**
CSF £14.71 CT £91.53 TOTE £4.90: £2.10, £1.90, £2.10; EX 19.10 Trifecta £110.10.
**Owner** The Earl Cadogan **Bred** The Earl Cadogan **Trained** Kingston Warren, Oxon

**FOCUS**
An ordinary handicap in which the winner recorded the quickest comparative time on the card. The fourth has been rated to the best of his form over the last year.

## 6617 RACING EXCELLENCE "HANDS AND HEELS" APPRENTICE SERIES H'CAP 7f 9y
**5:30** (5:31) (Class 5) (0-70,70) 3-Y-O+ **£2,587** (£770; £384; £192) **Stalls** High

Form RPR
1524 **1** **Lady Crossmar (IRE)**[12] 6240 3-9-5 70.............................. CamHardie 8 82
(Richard Hannon) *trckd ldrs: pushed into ld over 1f out: sn clr: smoothly* **7/2**[1]
5232 **2** *5* **Persian Bolt (USA)**[11] 6247 3-9-5 70..............................(v) JennyPowell 5 69
(Eve Johnson Houghton) *prom: w ldr over 2f out tl over 1f out: urged along: nt qckn and wnr sn clr* **9/2**[3]
3660 **3** *1 ½* **Harry Bosch**[12] 6232 4-9-0 67.............................. Keely-JoPhillips(5) 6 63
(Gay Kelleway) *prom: slt ld over 2f out: hdd over 1f out: kpt on same pce* **25/1**
4606 **4** *¾* **Speedy Writer**[38] 5383 4-8-12 60.............................. CharlotteJenner 7 54+
(Henry Candy) *sn wl bhd: kpt on nicely fr over 2f out: too much to do and nvr able to chal* **7/1**
5404 **5** *1 ¼* **Perfect Mission**[21] 5979 6-9-1 63..............................(v) RobHornby 2 54
(Andrew Balding) *a abt same pl: rdn and lost tch w ldng quartet over 1f out* **8/1**
2013 **6** *1* **Mister Mayday (IRE)**[17] 6088 3-9-0 65..............................(b) ChrisMeehan 10 52
(George Baker) *towards rr: effrt over 2f out: trckd ldrs briefly: pushed along and wknd over 1f out* **4/1**[2]
0424 **7** *1 ¼* **Celestial Bay**[17] 6086 5-9-1 63.............................. DavidParkes 9 48
(Sylvester Kirk) *towards rr and nt travelling: labouring over 3f out* **16/1**
5002 **8** *1 ¾* **Rose Buck**[11] 6266 3-8-6 60.............................. MichaelKenneally(3) 4 40
(Giles Bravery) *chsd ldrs over 4f: sn btn* **16/1**
0502 **9** *12* **Malaysian Boleh**[18] 6074 4-8-5 56.............................. TomasHarrigan(3) 1 5
(Simon Dow) *s.s: swtchd lft fr outside to stands' rails but wl bhd: t.o fr 1/2-way* **12/1**
5255 **10** *25* **Ostralegus**[112] 2841 4-9-0 62.............................. GaryMahon 11
(John Gallagher) *led and almost alone on stands' rails: edgd rt after 1f: drvn and hdd over 2f out: dropped out rapidly: t.o and heavily eased* **16/1**

1m 25.43s (-0.77) **Going Correction** -0.10s/f (Good)
**WFA** 3 from 4yo+ 3lb **10** Ran SP% **113.2**
Speed ratings (Par 103): **100,94,92,91,90 89,87,85,72,43**
CSF £18.49 CT £332.20 TOTE £3.40: £1.30, £2.00, £5.80; EX 11.90 Trifecta £334.00.
**Owner** Middleham Park Racing Vi **Bred** Scuderia San Pancrazio **Trained** East Everleigh, Wilts

**FOCUS**
A moderate handicap of its type in which they went an even gallop. The runner-up has been rated a little off his mark.
T/Plt: £51.90 to a £1 stake. Pool: £69292.87 - 973.51 winning tickets T/Qpdt: £15.30 to a £1 stake. Pool: £5485.68 - 264.71 winning tickets IM

# 6218 CHANTILLY (R-H)
Monday, September 22
**OFFICIAL GOING: Turf: soft: polytrack: standard**

## 6618a PRIX DE LA MANIGUETTE (CONDITIONS) (2YO) (TURF) 1m
**11:30** (11:30) 2-Y-O **£14,166** (£5,666; £4,250; £2,833; £1,416)

RPR
**1** **Red Tornado (FR)**[33] 5588 2-9-0 0.............................. GeraldMosse 1 88
(Harry Dunlop) *racd in tch on inner: cl 3rd and n.m.r over 2f out: rdn and swtchd outside 1 1/2f out: r.o to ld ins fnl f: drvn out* **47/10**[3]
**2** *hd* **The Blue Eye**[43] 2-9-0 0.............................. JulienAuge 6 88
(C Ferland, France) **4/5**[1]
**3** *2* **Alto Adige (FR)**[31] 2-9-0 0.............................. GregoryBenoist 2 84
(F Chappet, France) **31/10**[2]
**4** *1 ¼* **Leader Writer (FR)**[78] 2-9-0 0.............................. ThierryJarnet 5 81
(H-A Pantall, France) **89/10**
**5** *5* **Majik Charly (FR)**[21] 2-8-10 0.............................. Christophe-PatriceLemaire 3 66
(T Castanheira, France) **269/10**
**6** *2* **Magic Frost (FR)**[41] 5292 2-8-10 0.............................. StephanePasquier 7 61
(Y Gourraud, France) **224/10**
**7** *8* **Nakkado (FR)**[13] 2-8-10 0.............................. ThierryThulliez 4 44
(R Chotard, France) **209/10**

1m 42.31s (4.31) **7** Ran SP% **120.0**
WIN (incl. 1 euro stake): 5.70. PLACES: 1.90, 1.30. SF: 10.70.
**Owner** Blockley,Cross,Johnson,Whitaker,Woodley **Bred** Jean-Francois Gribomont **Trained** Lambourn, Berks

## 6619a PRIX DES CLOSEAUX (MAIDEN) (2YO) (TURF) 6f
**12:00** (12:00) 2-Y-O **£10,416** (£4,166; £3,125; £2,083; £1,041)

RPR
**1** **Immediate**[21] 2-8-13 0.............................. GregoryBenoist 7 85
(D Smaga, France) **19/5**[3]
**2** *1 ¼* **Smaug (FR)**[32] 5616 2-9-2 0.............................. ThierryJarnet 4 84
(X Nakkachdji, France) **16/5**[2]
**3** *1 ¾* **Power Of The Moon (IRE)**[29] 5741 2-8-13 0.............................. TheoBachelot 1 76
(M Nigge, France) **11/10**[1]
**4** *1 ½* **Seradora (FR)**[19] 2-8-7 0.............................. Georges-AntoineAnselin(6) 3 71
(S Smrczek, Germany) **136/10**
**5** *snk* **Maui (FR)**[12] 6245 2-8-13 0.............................. RonanThomas 6 71
(Mlle V Dissaux, France) **53/1**
**6** *5* **Mamourg (FR)** 2-9-2 0.............................. StephanePasquier 5 59
(Mlle C Chenu, France) **161/10**
**7** *12* **Mister Arden (FR)**[29] 5739 2-9-2 0..............................(b) GeraldMosse 2 23
(Harry Dunlop) *led: sn racing along stands' rail: shkn up whn pressed and hdd over 2f out: wknd fr 1 1/2f out: eased whn bhd fnl f* **87/10**
**8** *5* **Chipie Royale (FR)** 2-8-13 0.............................. FredericSpanu 8 5
(Mme C Barande-Barbe, France) **38/1**

1m 12.9s (1.50) **8** Ran SP% **119.7**
WIN (incl. 1 euro stake): 4.80. PLACES: 1.20, 1.20, 1.10. DF: 9.20. SF: 21.40.
**Owner** K Abdullah **Bred** Juddmonte Farms Ltd **Trained** Lamorlaye, France

# CRAON (R-H)
Monday, September 22
**OFFICIAL GOING: Turf: good to soft**

## 6620a PRIX FOURRAGES THIERRY DUTERTRE (PRIX DU POINT DU JOUR) (LISTED RACE) (3YO+) (TURF) 1m 55y
**2:20** (2:20) 3-Y-O+ **£21,666** (£8,666; £6,500; £4,333; £2,166)

RPR
**1** **Maningrey (GER)**[42] 5263 5-9-1 0.............................. MickaelBarzalona 10 101
(Waldemar Hickst, Germany) **22/5**[2]
**2** *1* **More Than Sotka (FR)**[39] 5369 4-8-11 0.............................. AntoineHamelin 9 95
(Matthieu Palussiere, France) **26/1**
**3** *½* **Alice's Dancer (IRE)**[22] 5965 5-8-11 0.............................. MickaelForest 6 94
(Mme G Rarick, France) **75/1**
**4** *1* **Etalondes (FR)**[52] 4-9-1 0.............................. Jean-BernardEyquem 8 95
(J-C Rouget, France) **97/10**
**5** *½* **Frankyfourfingers (FR)**[42] 5263 4-9-1 0.............................. Pierre-CharlesBoudot 5 94
(C Delcher-Sanchez, France) **58/10**[3]
**6** *1* **Zayade (FR)**[18] 5-8-11 0..............................(p) AlexandreRoussel 2 88
(J Boisnard, France) **29/1**
**7** *nk* **Fire Ship**[22] 5960 5-9-1 0.............................. IoritzMendizabal 3 91
(William Knight) *outpcd early: racd towards rr on outer: rdn and effrt 1 1/2f out: kpt on at same pce fnl f but no real imp on ldrs* **22/5**[2]
**8** *½* **Guinnevre (IRE)**[22] 5966 4-9-2 0.............................. CristianDemuro 4 91
(A Wohler, Germany) **213/10**
**9** *2* **Tekneas (GR)**[16] 3-8-10 0.............................. ClementCadel 7 84
(F Sanchez, France) **34/1**
**10** *snk* **Silas Marner (FR)**[99] 3291 7-9-5 0.............................. ChristopheSoumillon 1 89
(J-C Rouget, France) **13/10**[1]

1m 45.74s (105.74)
**WFA** 3 from 4yo+ 4lb **10** Ran SP% **120.3**
WIN (incl. 1 euro stake): 5.40. PLACES: 2.50, 6.40, 15.50. DF: 46.50. SF: 94.40.
**Owner** Gestut Hony-Hof **Bred** Gestut Hony-Hof **Trained** Germany

# [6447]BEVERLEY (R-H)

## Tuesday, September 23

**OFFICIAL GOING: Good to firm (good in places; 8.2)**
Wind: light 1/2 against Weather: fine

### 6621 IRISH STALLION FARMS EBF MAIDEN STKS — 7f 100y
**2:10** (2:13) (Class 5) 2-Y-O — **£3,408** (£1,006; £503) **Stalls** Low

Form — RPR

03 **1** **Pleiades**[15] 6190 2-9-5 0 ... GrahamLee 3 — 83
(Sir Michael Stoute) *mde all: qcknd pce over 3f out: styd on strly: forged clr appr fnl f: unchal* — **7/1**

3 **2** 2 ½ **Natural Nine (IRE)**[14] 6204 2-9-5 0 ... AndreaAtzeni 2 — 77
(Roger Varian) *chsd ldrs: 2nd over 2f out: kpt on same pce: no imp* — **1/1**[1]

2522 **3** 2 ½ **Thorkhill Star (IRE)**[12] 6261 2-9-5 77 ... DavidNolan 6 — 71
(Richard Fahey) *chsd ldrs: kpt on one pce to take 3rd 1f out* — **3/1**[2]

3 **4** 3 ½ **Resonant (IRE)**[9] 6362 2-9-5 0 ... JoeFanning 5 — 63
(Mark Johnston) *dwlt: in rr: rn green: drvn over 3f out: sn outpcd and edgd lft: kpt on ins fnl f: tk modest 4th nr fin* — **6/1**[3]

5 **5** ½ **Toofeeg (IRE)**[96] 3381 2-9-5 0 ... LiamJones 1 — 62
(William Haggas) *dwlt: drvn along in rr: hdwy over 2f out: wknd last 150yds* — **10/1**

0 **6** 8 **Rise To Power**[19] 6058 2-9-5 0 ... PhillipMakin 4 — 43
(Kevin Ryan) *chsd wnr: drvn over 3f out: lost pl over 1f out: bhd whn eased nr fin* — **40/1**

1m 33.11s (-0.69) **Going Correction** -0.10s/f (Good) — **6** Ran SP% **113.3**
Speed ratings (Par 95): **99,96,93,89,88 79**
CSF £14.85 TOTE £7.40: £3.80, £1.10; EX 15.00 Trifecta £36.10.
**Owner** Lady Rothschild **Bred** Kincorth Investments Inc **Trained** Newmarket, Suffolk

**FOCUS**
An unseasonably warm day helped bring the curtain down on racing at Beverley for 2014. This looked a modest opening maiden, but the pace lifted after 2f and they finished fairly strung out so the form is worth being positive about. The third has been rated a bit below form.

### 6622 BEVERLEY ANNUAL BADGEHOLDERS (S) STKS — 1m 4f 16y
**2:40** (2:40) (Class 5) 3-4-Y-O — **£3,234** (£962; £481; £240) **Stalls** Low

Form — RPR

6002 **1** **Aneedh**[13] 5788 4-9-2 67 ...(b) PJMcDonald 5 — 71
(Jedd O'Keeffe) *mid-div: effrt 3f out: styd on fnl f: led last 50yds* — **5/1**[3]

034 **2** ½ **Jammy Moment**[77] 4052 3-8-3 67 ... AndreaAtzeni 6 — 65
(William Muir) *sn chsng ldr: chal over 2f out: led 1f out: hdd and no ex clsng stages* — **5/6**[1]

0000 **3** 2 ½ **Agreement (IRE)**[25] 5890 4-9-2 77 ...(b[1]) PhillipMakin 3 — 66
(John Quinn) *led: hdd 1f out: sn fdd* — **9/4**[2]

6005 **4** 7 **Barbara Elizabeth**[56] 4749 3-7-12 45 ... JoeDoyle(5) 2 — 50
(Tony Coyle) *hld up towards rr: effrt over 3f out: wknd appr fnl f* — **25/1**

00 **5** 3 **Paple Blessing (IRE)**[5] 6486 4-8-11 46 ...(p) AndrewMullen 1 — 45
(David Bridgwater) *in rr: hdwy to chse ldrs 8f out: hung rt 2f out: sn lost pl* — **20/1**

2m 37.84s (-1.96) **Going Correction** -0.10s/f (Good)
**WFA** 3 from 4yo 8lb — **5** Ran SP% **110.6**
Speed ratings (Par 103): **102,101,100,95,93**
CSF £9.81 TOTE £4.50: £1.70, £1.10; EX 8.10 Trifecta £18.00.The winner sold for £7,000 to Clive Mulhall & Carl Chapman. Agreement was claimed by Mrs Nikki Evans for £6,000. Jammy Moment was claimed by Mr Ken McGarrity for £6,000.
**Owner** Limegrove Racing **Bred** Rabbah Bloodstock Limited **Trained** Middleham Moor, N Yorks

**FOCUS**
This trappy seller was run at an uneven pace. The fourth and fifth shown this form is very limited.

### 6623 THANKS FOR YOUR SUPPORT IN 2014 MAIDEN AUCTION STKS — 5f
**3:10** (3:11) (Class 5) 2-Y-O — **£3,752** (£1,116; £557; £278) **Stalls** Low

Form — RPR

3226 **1** **Flicka's Boy**[10] 6322 2-9-0 75 ... BarryMcHugh 7 — 73
(Tony Coyle) *swtchd rt after s: mde all: kpt on wl* — **7/2**[2]

34 **2** 2 **Ocean Sheridan (IRE)**[38] 5443 2-9-2 67 ... AndrewMullen 10 — 68
(Michael Dods) *chsd wnr: styd on same pce fnl f* — **12/1**[3]

423 **3** nk **Clergyman**[5] 6489 2-9-0 0 ... AndreaAtzeni 3 — 65
(Martyn Meade) *chsd ldrs: outpcd over 1f out: styd on wl last 100yds* — **8/13**[1]

5 **4** hd **George Bailey (IRE)**[73] 4192 2-8-13 0 ... PhillipMakin 2 — 63+
(Bryan Smart) *mid-div: hdwy to chse ldrs over 2f out: styd on fnl 75yds* — **14/1**

**5** 2 ¾ **Spiritual Journey (IRE)** 2-8-11 0 ... PJMcDonald 12 — 51
(Ann Duffield) *swtchd rt after s: mid-div: hdwy 2f out: kpt on same pce fnl f* — **20/1**

0046 **6** 1 ½ **Maid In Rome (IRE)**[13] 6222 2-8-9 60 ... AndrewElliott 11 — 44
(Tim Easterby) *sn chsng ldrs: one pce over 1f out* — **20/1**

**7** ½ **Deep Blue Diamond** 2-8-6 0 ... JoeFanning 1 — 39
(Ollie Pears) *dwlt: in rr: hdwy over 3f out: one pce fnl 2f* — **20/1**

0 **8** 1 ½ **Lilac Vale (IRE)**[14] 6212 2-8-0 0 ... RachelRichardson(7) 9 — 35+
(Tim Easterby) *in rr-div: sme hdwy appr fnl f: nvr on terms* — **66/1**

003 **9** nk **Rocco's Delight**[111] 2903 2-8-10 62 ... JacobButterfield(3) 14 — 39
(John Wainwright) *dwlt: in rr: hdwy over 1f out: nvr a factor* — **66/1**

060 **10** 1 ½ **Right Madam (IRE)**[55] 4784 2-8-10 60 ... LiamJones 4 — 31
(Andrew Hollinshead) *chsd ldrs: lost pl over 1f out* — **20/1**

0 **11** 3 ½ **Billy Bond**[143] 1955 2-8-6 0 ... SammyJoBell(5) 6 — 19+
(Richard Fahey) *restless in stalls: rrd s: a bhd* — **25/1**

1m 3.67s (0.17) **Going Correction** -0.10s/f (Good) — **11** Ran SP% **124.4**
Speed ratings (Par 95): **94,90,90,90,85 83,82,80,79,77 71**
CSF £41.65 TOTE £3.70: £1.60, £1.90, £1.10; EX 26.70 Trifecta £47.20.
**Owner** Twenty Four Seven Recruitment **Bred** Mrs R D Peacock **Trained** Norton, N Yorks

**FOCUS**
A moderate 2yo maiden and straightforward form. The winner has been rated to his mark.

### 6624 EDDIE AND VIOLET SMITH CONDITIONS STKS — 5f
**3:45** (3:45) (Class 3) 3-Y-O+ — **£7,498** (£2,264; £1,146; £587; £307) **Stalls** Low

Form — RPR

4040 **1** **Kingsgate Native (IRE)**[13] 6231 9-8-10 107 ow1 ... JimCrowley 2 — 103
(Robert Cowell) *trckd ldrs: nt clr run over 1f out: squeezed through and r.o wl to ld last 75yds* — **13/8**[1]

2022 **2** 1 ¾ **Green Door (IRE)**[14] 6209 3-8-8 102 ...(p) AndreaAtzeni 6 — 96
(Olly Stevens) *hmpd and stmbld s: sn swtchd rt: t.k.h: hdwy on ins and nt clr run over 1f out: swtchd lft and styng on whn bdly hmpd ins fnl f: styd on to take 2nd nr fin* — **3/1**[2]

0500 **3** hd **Burning Thread (IRE)**[17] 6130 7-8-9 88 ...(b) AdamBeschizza 4 — 95?
(Tim Etherington) *in rr: drvn over 2f out: hdwy over 1f out: chsng ldrs whn edgd rt and hmpd ins fnl f: kpt on* — **33/1**

4002 **4** hd **Tangerine Trees**[84] 3830 9-8-10 95 ow1 ...(v) PhillipMakin 3 — 95
(Bryan Smart) *chsd ldr: edgd lft and hmpd ins fnl f: kpt on* — **9/2**[3]

0100 **5** 2 ¾ **Noble Storm (USA)**[13] 6231 8-8-9 104 ... GrahamGibbons 1 — 84
(Ed McMahon) *led: hdd & wknd last 75yds* — **7/1**

5420 **P** **Iptisam**[143] 1949 5-8-9 102 ...(p) JoeFanning 5
(James Tate) *wnt lft s: chsd ldrs: lost pl over 1f out: sn eased: p.u ins fnl f: b.b.v* — **11/2**

1m 2.15s (-1.35) **Going Correction** -0.10s/f (Good)
**WFA** 3 from 5yo+ 1lb — **6** Ran SP% **112.1**
Speed ratings (Par 107): **106,103,102,102,98**
CSF £6.69 TOTE £3.10: £1.40, £1.50; EX 5.90 Trifecta £77.00.
**Owner** Cheveley Park Stud **Bred** Peter McCutcheon **Trained** Six Mile Bottom, Cambs

**FOCUS**
Although all of these sprinters had something to prove, this was a fascinating affair and predictably there was no hanging about. The third has been rated back to his Ayr handicap win in June.

### 6625 LECONFIELD SEARCH & RESCUE SQUADRON 50TH ANNIVERSARY H'CAP — 7f 100y
**4:15** (4:15) (Class 5) (0-75,75) 3-Y-O+ — **£3,234** (£962; £481; £240) **Stalls** Low

Form — RPR

0-00 **1** **Hulcolt (IRE)**[32] 5638 3-8-11 68 ... AndrewMullen 1 — 77
(Garry Moss) *mde all: hld on wl clsng stages* — **11/1**

1230 **2** ¾ **Rouge Nuage (IRE)**[10] 6341 4-9-0 68 ...(b) LiamJones 2 — 76
(Conrad Allen) *chsd ldrs: 2nd over 2f out: keeping on whn hung bdly lft clsng stages* — **8/1**

0064 **3** 2 ¾ **Space War**[17] 6161 7-8-9 63 ... GrahamGibbons 8 — 64
(Michael Easterby) *trckd ldrs: effrt 2f out: kpt on fnl f: tk 3rd post* — **4/1**[2]

4351 **4** nse **Rangi Chase (IRE)**[25] 5891 3-9-1 72 ... DavidNolan 10 — 72
(Richard Fahey) *chsd ldrs: drvn 3f out: styd on same pce appr fnl f* — **11/2**

4143 **5** ½ **Shamaheart (IRE)**[14] 6217 4-8-13 72 ...(p) KevinStott(5) 6 — 72
(Geoffrey Harker) *mid-div: hdwy on outer over 2f out: kpt on fnl f* — **5/1**[3]

441 **6** shd **Tasmanian**[18] 6118 3-9-4 75 ... JoeFanning 7 — 74
(Mark Johnston) *drvn early: sn mid-div: sme hdwy over 2f out: kpt on: nvr a threat* — **5/2**[1]

3200 **7** ¾ **Naoise (IRE)**[13] 6232 6-8-11 68 ...(t) JacobButterfield(3) 5 — 66
(Ollie Pears) *s.s: swtchd lft after s: in rr: hdwy and nt clr run 2f: swtchd rt jst ins fnl f: kpt on same pce last 75yds* — **10/1**

-506 **8** 3 **Summer Dancer (IRE)**[8] 6397 10-8-11 65 ow2 ... PhillipMakin 4 — 55
(Eugene Stanford) *a in rr* — **22/1**

00-0 **9** ½ **Kerbaaj (USA)**[140] 2054 4-9-4 72 ... PJMcDonald 3 — 61
(Ruth Carr) *in rr: hdwy on ins over 2f out: sn chsng ldrs: wknd fnl f* — **66/1**

**10** 11 **Walk Right Back (IRE)**[37] 5475 3-8-9 66 ... AndreaAtzeni 11 — 27
(Micky Hammond) *chsd ldrs on outer: wknd over 1f out: bhd whn eased clsng stages* — **25/1**

1m 31.82s (-1.98) **Going Correction** -0.10s/f (Good)
**WFA** 3 from 4yo+ 3lb — **10** Ran SP% **119.3**
Speed ratings (Par 103): **107,106,103,102,102 102,101,97,97,84**
CSF £95.85 CT £429.28 TOTE £12.90: £3.70, £2.50, £1.90; EX 86.50 Trifecta £800.30.
**Owner** Ron Hull **Bred** Kilshannig Stud **Trained** Tickhill, S Yorks

**FOCUS**
This modest handicap was run at a strong early pace but still it paid to be handy. The runner-up has been rated pretty much to his best.

### 6626 CHRIS WALKER'S 60TH YEAR RACING HERE H'CAP — 1m 100y
**4:45** (4:47) (Class 5) (0-75,74) 3-Y-O+ — **£3,234** (£962; £481; £240) **Stalls** Low

Form — RPR

-002 **1** **Blue Maisey**[14] 6217 6-8-7 65 ... KevinStott(5) 11 — 75
(Edwin Tuer) *sn bhd: hdwy on outside over 2f out: styd on wl to ld last 50yds* — **14/1**

3006 **2** 2 ¼ **Kimbali (IRE)**[7] 6430 5-9-4 74 ... NeilFarley(3) 7 — 79
(Declan Carroll) *reluctant to go to post: in rr: hdwy 4f out: styd on down outside fnl 2f: tk 2nd nr fin* — **10/1**

3440 **3** ½ **Ellaal**[10] 6323 5-9-4 71 ... JoeFanning 12 — 75
(Ruth Carr) *chsd ldr: led 1f out: hdd and no ex last 50yds* — **8/1**

5540 **4** 1 **Dolphin Rock**[16] 6166 7-8-11 64 ...(p) JimCrowley 3 — 65
(Brian Ellison) *chsd ldrs: drvn over 2f out: kpt on same pce fnl f* — **9/2**[2]

020 **5** ¾ **Rocket Ronnie (IRE)**[36] 5496 4-9-7 74 ... AdrianNicholls 9 — 76
(David Nicholls) *mid-div: hdwy on ins over 2f out: nt clr run: chsng ldrs whn n.m.r on inner and swtchd lft jst ins fnl f: kpt on towards fin* — **7/1**[3]

3630 **6** ¾ **Eeny Mac (IRE)**[16] 6166 7-9-4 71 ... AndrewElliott 1 — 69
(Neville Bycroft) *led: hdd 1f out: wknd fnl 75yds* — **14/1**

6050 **7** hd **Red Charmer (IRE)**[14] 6214 4-9-2 69 ... PJMcDonald 4 — 68
(Ann Duffield) *in rr: hdwy over 3f out: styng on whn hmpd jst ins fnl f* — **17/2**

6534 **8** 2 **Spiceupyourlife (IRE)**[30] 5713 3-9-0 74 ... GeorgeChaloner(3) 10 — 67
(Richard Fahey) *chsd ldrs: wknd fnl f* — **10/1**

3340 **9** 2 ½ **Real Tigress (IRE)**[24] 5915 5-9-4 71 ...(t) PhillipMakin 2 — 58
(Les Eyre) *chsd ldrs: wknd fnl 150yds* — **4/1**[1]

2211 **10** 16 **City Ground (USA)**[16] 6187 7-9-3 70 ... BarryMcHugh 5 — 20
(Michael Easterby) *chsd ldrs: pushed along 4f out: lost pl over 1f out: bhd whn eased clsng stages* — **7/1**[3]

004 **11** 35 **Mr Gatsby**[18] 6118 3-8-10 67 ...(b) GrahamGibbons 6
(Mark Walford) *dwlt: dropped to rr 6f out: t.o whn eased over 2f out: virtually p.u* — **25/1**

1m 45.91s (-1.69) **Going Correction** -0.10s/f (Good)
**WFA** 3 from 4yo+ 4lb — **11** Ran SP% **120.2**
Speed ratings (Par 103): **104,101,101,100,99 98,98,96,94,78 43**
CSF £149.74 CT £1211.83 TOTE £16.10: £4.60, £3.30, £2.30; EX 227.10 Trifecta £1827.50.
**Owner** Ontoawinner **Bred** Worksop Manor Stud **Trained** Birkby, N Yorks
■ Stewards' Enquiry : Adrian Nicholls one-day ban: careless riding (7 Oct)

**FOCUS**
A run-of-the mill handicap, run at a solid pace. The runner-up has been rated to his summer form here.

### 6627 BRIAN AND JASON MERRINGTON MEMORIAL AMATEUR RIDERS' H'CAP (DIV I) — 1m 1f 207y
**5:15** (5:15) (Class 6) (0-60,60) 3-Y-O+ — **£2,183** (£677; £338; £169) **Stalls** Low

Form — RPR

1405 **1** **Tamayuz Magic (IRE)**[25] 5892 3-10-4 59 ....(b) MissJoannaMason(3) 11 — 68
(Michael Easterby) *mid-div: hdwy over 3f out: 2nd over 2f out: led over 1f out: styd on wl* — **7/1**

0/ **2** 2 ¼ **Engai (GER)**[26] 67 8-10-7 60 ... MissPBridgwater(7) 3 — 65
(David Bridgwater) *trckd ldrs: led over 3f out: hdd over 1f out: styd on same pce* — **14/1**

5546 **3** 2 1/2 **Amazing Blue Sky**[29] 5765 8-10-4 50 MissSBrotherton 13 50
(Ruth Carr) *in rr: hdwy over 4f out: chsng ldrs over 2f out: tk 3rd last 50yds* **4/1**[1]
2653 **4** 1 **Yorksters Prince (IRE)**[19] 6076 7-10-4 55 (p) MrKWood(5) 9 53
(Marjorie Fife) *chsd ldrs: kpt on one pce over 1f out* **5/1**[2]
2630 **5** 1 1/4 **General Tufto**[8] 6407 9-9-11 46 oh1 (b) MrTHamilton(3) 4 42
(Charles Smith) *in rr: sn pushed along: hdwy over 2f out: kpt on one pce* **20/1**
0064 **6** 5 **Acquaint (IRE)**[24] 5917 3-9-7 50 (p) MrDLevey(5) 5 36
(John Wainwright) *mid-div: hdwy over 4f out: wknd over 1f out* **12/1**
3430 **7** nk **Surround Sound**[38] 5415 4-10-10 59 MrWEasterby(3) 8 45
(Tim Easterby) *in rr: hdwy over 3f out: sn chsng ldrs: wknd over 1f out* **4/1**[1]
3401 **8** 6 **Think**[40] 5337 7-10-1 47 (p) MrHAABannister 12 21
(Clive Mulhall) *chsd ldrs: wd behnd 4f out: lost pl over 2f out* **13/2**[3]
0-00 **9** nk **Landesherr (GER)**[50] 4964 7-9-11 46 oh1 MissHCuthbert(3) 2 20
(Thomas Cuthbert) *hld up in mid-div: hdwy to chse ldrs over 3f out: wknd appr fnl f* **33/1**
5650 **10** 28 **Super Cookie**[27] 5832 4-10-4 55 MrGrahamCarson(5) 10
(Anthony Carson) *led early: w ldr: led briefly 4f out: lost pl over 2f out: sn bhd and eased: t.o* **15/2**
0006 **11** 8 **Connexion Francais**[33] 5598 3-9-3 46 oh1 MissLWilson(5) 1
(Tim Etherington) *mid-div: lost pl over 3f out: bhd whn eased over 1f out: t.o* **100/1**
60-0 **12** 22 **Fama Mac**[24] 5912 7-10-6 57 MrAaronJames(5) 6
(Neville Bycroft) *sn led: hdd 4f out: sn lost pl and bhd: eased over 1f out: tailed rt off* **25/1**

2m 6.6s (-0.40) **Going Correction** -0.10s/f (Good)
**WFA** 3 from 4yo+ 6lb **12 Ran SP% 121.2**
Speed ratings (Par 101): **97,95,93,92,91 87,87,82,82,59 53,35**
CSF £98.68 CT £452.14 TOTE £8.70: £2.70, £5.20, £1.70; EX 126.90 Trifecta £1535.20 Part won..
**Owner** W H & Mrs J A Tinning **Bred** Eimear Mulhern **Trained** Sheriff Hutton, N Yorks

**FOCUS**
The field bunched up at the top of the home straight in this amateur riders' handicap, but only the first pair mattered a furlong out. There are few solid in here to rate the form around.

## 6628 BRIAN AND JASON MERRINGTON MEMORIAL AMATEUR RIDERS' H'CAP (DIV II) 1m 1f 207y
**5:45** (5:45) (Class 6) (0-60,60) 3-Y-O+ **£2,183** (£677; £338; £169) **Stalls** Low

Form RPR
5504 **1** **Brockfield**[41] 5300 8-10-9 55 MissSBrotherton 13 67
(Mel Brittain) *fast away: led early: chsd ldrs: led 3f out: clr over 1f out: pushed out* **6/1**[2]
5065 **2** 3 **Botanist**[18] 6086 7-10-4 55 MrAidenBlakemore(5) 12 61+
(Shaun Harris) *hld up towards rr: hdwy over 2f out: swtchd outside over 1f out: 10th 1f out: 2nd last 100yds: fin strly* **9/1**[3]
4064 **3** 5 **Zainda (IRE)**[29] 5773 4-9-8 47 MrAFrench(7) 3 44
(Paul Midgley) *t.k.h: sn led: hdd 3f out: kpt on same pce fnl 2f* **10/1**
530 **4** 1/2 **Edas**[40] 5337 12-9-13 48 MissHCuthbert(3) 11 44
(Thomas Cuthbert) *sn chsng ldrs on outer: outpcd over 3f out: kpt on fnl 2f: tk 4th clsng stages* **33/1**
0300 **5** 1/2 **Kheskianto (IRE)**[35] 5529 8-10-0 46 oh1 (t) MissAliceMills 5 41
(Michael Chapman) *mid-div: hdwy to chse ldrs over 3f out: one pce* **10/1**
0001 **6** 1 3/4 **Graceful Act**[29] 5773 6-10-4 55 PhillipDennis(5) 2 47
(Ron Barr) *mid-div: hdwy over 3f out: chsng ldrs 2f out: one pce* **12/1**
-060 **7** 1 1/4 **Jan De Heem**[55] 4793 4-10-11 60 (b) MrTHamilton(3) 8 49
(Tina Jackson) *chsd ldrs: wknd appr fnl f* **16/1**
0000 **8** 1 **Valentine's Gift**[31] 5678 6-10-6 52 MissCWalton 4 39
(Neville Bycroft) *hld up in rr: kpt on fnl 2f: n.m.r on inner 1f out: nvr a factor* **18/1**
00-6 **9** 1 1/2 **Wunderkind (USA)**[22] 5977 3-9-8 46 oh1 MrSWalker 7 42
(Sir Mark Prescott Bt) *in tch: drvn over 3f out: wknd and eased ins fnl f* **15/8**[1]
5263 **10** 3/4 **Belle Peinture (FR)**[6] 6454 3-9-8 46 MissADeniel 1 29
(Alan Lockwood) *chsd ldrs: wknd over 1f out* **6/1**[2]
6-30 **11** nk **Stag Hill (IRE)**[185] 490 5-10-7 58 (p) MrJPWilliams(5) 6 40
(Bernard Llewellyn) *s.i.s: in rr: brief effrt on outer over 3f out: sn wknd* **25/1**
1605 **12** 10 **Silver Tigress**[18] 6119 6-9-11 50 MissKMabon(7) 10 13
(Iain Jardine) *s.i.s: brief effrt on outer 3f out: sn lost pl and bhd* **25/1**
0/00 **13** 13 **Business Bay (USA)**[19] 6062 7-9-7 46 oh1 (v[1]) MrTEley(7) 9
(Patrick Clinton) *sn chsng ldrs on outer: lost pl over 3f out: bhd fnl 2f* **100/1**

2m 7.15s (0.15) **Going Correction** -0.10s/f (Good)
**WFA** 3 from 4yo+ 6lb **13 Ran SP% 122.0**
Speed ratings (Par 101): **95,92,88,88,87 86,85,84,83,82 82,74,64**
CSF £58.58 CT £543.19 TOTE £6.80: £2.30, £2.10, £2.40; EX 81.50 Trifecta £738.50.
**Owner** Mel Brittain **Bred** Cheveley Park Stud Ltd **Trained** Warthill, N Yorks
■ Stewards' Enquiry : Mr T Eley five-day ban: use of whip (TBA)
Mr T Hamilton two-day ban: careless riding (TBA)

**FOCUS**
This second division of the amateur riders' handicap was turned into something of a procession. The winner has been rated back to the form he was showing this time last year.
T/Plt: £55.60 to a £1 stake. Pool: £44,111.76 - 579.01 winning tickets T/Qpdt: £22.70 to a £1 stake. Pool: £2,935.65 - 95.30 winning tickets WG

# 6333 LINGFIELD (L-H)
## Tuesday, September 23

**OFFICIAL GOING: Polytrack: standard**
Wind: light, across Weather: dry, bright spells

## 6629 188BET NURSERY H'CAP 5f 6y(P)
**2:20** (2:20) (Class 5) (0-75,74) 2-Y-O **£3,234** (£962; £481; £240) **Stalls** High

Form RPR
1340 **1** **Ivors Rebel**[9] 6375 2-9-5 72 LiamKeniry 2 82+
(David Elsworth) *bustled along in midfield: clsd to chse ldrs and travelling bttr 2f out: chse ldr wl over 1f out: drvn to ld ins fnl f: styd on wl* **7/2**[2]
6215 **2** 1 1/2 **Zipedeedodah (IRE)**[7] 6422 2-9-2 69 OisinMurphy 1 74+
(Joseph Tuite) *led: rdn and fnd ex wl over 2f out: drvn and hrd pressed over 1f out: hdd and one pce ins fnl f* **8/1**
045 **3** 2 1/2 **Oriental Splendour (IRE)**[31] 5684 2-9-4 71 JamesDoyle 5 67
(Roger Charlton) *in tch in midfield: u.p and outpcd by ldng pair over 1f out: wnt 3rd 1f out: kpt on* **11/4**[1]
2044 **4** hd **Stinky Socks (IRE)**[28] 5789 2-8-12 65 RyanMoore 10 61
(Charles Hills) *sn outpcd in rr: effrt and swtchd rt wl over 1f out: styd on strly fnl f: nvr threatened ldrs* **12/1**
065 **5** 4 1/2 **Just Because**[96] 3387 2-8-7 67 RobertPWalsh(7) 4 46
(Edward Creighton) *sn outpcd towards rr: rdn and sme hdwy over 1f out: kpt on: nvr trbld ldrs* **100/1**
554 **6** 1/2 **Crikey (IRE)**[10] 6319 2-9-1 68 (p) JamieSpencer 3 45
(Kevin Ryan) *pressed ldr: drvn 2f out: outpcd and btn over 1f out: wknd ins fnl f* **7/1**
5515 **7** 1/2 **Arlecchino's Leap**[21] 6016 2-8-8 66 (v) RachealKneller(5) 9 41
(Mark Usher) *v.s.a: hld up in detached last: stl last and urged along over 1f out: styd on ins fnl f: n.d* **20/1**
2510 **8** 1 1/4 **Amber Crystal**[10] 6322 2-9-7 74 (b) MartinDwyer 7 45
(John Gallagher) *w ldrs tl unable qck 2f out: wknd u.p over 1f out* **33/1**
363 **9** 3/4 **Dolorous**[43] 5253 2-9-2 69 WilliamBuick 6 37
(John Gosden) *a outpcd towards rr: n.d* **8/1**
405 **10** 1 3/4 **Able Spirit**[19] 6058 2-9-4 71 (b[1]) JimmyFortune 8 33
(Brian Meehan) *sn bustled along to press ldrs on outer: struggling u.p 2f out: sn wknd* **5/1**[3]

58.11s (-0.69) **Going Correction** -0.25s/f (Stan) 2y crse rec **10 Ran SP% 116.7**
Speed ratings (Par 95): **95,92,88,88,81 80,79,77,76,73**
CSF £31.13 CT £87.80 TOTE £3.90: £1.80, £2.60, £1.70; EX 39.60 Trifecta £136.40.
**Owner** Ivor Perry **Bred** Ghelardini Marco **Trained** Newmarket, Suffolk

**FOCUS**
There was money about in the morning for a few of these and it looked a fair race of its type, the field lowering the 2yo course record in the process. It's been rated on the positive side.

## 6630 EBFSTALLIONS.COM MAIDEN STKS 1m 1y(P)
**2:50** (2:53) (Class 5) 2-Y-O **£3,234** (£962; £481; £240) **Stalls** High

Form RPR
3 **1** **Bnedel (IRE)**[45] 5184 2-9-5 0 FrankieDettori 8 73+
(Richard Hannon) *stdd s: t.k.h: hld up in tch in midfield: edging lft and drvn to chse ldrs over 1f out: led wl ins fnl f: styd on wl* **9/2**
0 **2** 1/2 **Thawraat**[38] 5416 2-9-0 0 JamesDoyle 10 67
(Saeed bin Suroor) *restless in stalls: chsd ldrs: rdn and effrt 2f out: drvn to ld ins fnl f: sn hdd: kpt on wl but a hld after* **7/2**[3]
0 **3** 3 3/4 **Toot Your Flute (IRE)**[20] 6038 2-9-5 0 SilvestreDeSousa 11 63
(William Haggas) *led: rdn 2f out: edgd rt u.p over 1f out: hdd ins fnl f: sn btn: wknd wl ins fnl f* **20/1**
0 **4** nk **Sugar Boy (GER)**[17] 6125 2-9-5 0 WilliamBuick 1 64
(John Gosden) *hld up in tch: nt clr run and shuffled bk 2f out: swtchd lft and hdwy over 1f out: wnt 4th ins fnl f: kpt on but no imp* **5/1**
**5** 2 **Dark Swan (IRE)** 2-9-0 0 ChrisCatlin 9 52
(Sir Mark Prescott Bt) *restless in stalls: s.i.s: bustled along and rcvrd to chse ldr 6f out tl outpcd under pressre wl over 1f out: wl hld and plugged on same pce after* **25/1**
35 **6** 1 3/4 **Swaheen**[29] 5760 2-9-5 0 RyanMoore 4 53
(Sir Michael Stoute) *in tch in midfield: nt clr run and shuffled bk 2f: no hdwy u.p over 1f out: wl hld fnl f* **11/4**[1]
0 **7** 5 **Brigand Chief**[32] 5625 2-9-5 0 SebSanders 2 41
(Luke Dace) *chsd ldr for 2f: chsd ldr fr 2f out: rdn and lost pl ent fnl 2f: wknd over 1f out* **66/1**
00 **8** 1 3/4 **Beauchamp Ruby**[12] 6246 2-9-0 0 WilliamCarson 5 32
(Paul Fitzsimons) *s.i.s: t.k.h: hld up wl in tch in rr: rdn ent fnl 2f: wknd wl over 1f out* **100/1**
0 **9** 93 **Riba Roja**[12] 6246 2-9-0 0 MartinDwyer 7
(John Gallagher) *chsd ldrs for 3f: sn lost pl and bhd: t.o fnl 3f* **100/1**
**P** **Glorious Dubai (IRE)** 2-9-5 0 JamieSpencer 6
(Saeed bin Suroor) *s.i.s: in rr tl lost action 5f out: immediately p.u and dismntd* **3/1**[2]

1m 38.19s (-0.01) **Going Correction** -0.25s/f (Stan) **10 Ran SP% 120.8**
Speed ratings (Par 95): **90,89,85,85,83 81,76,74, ,**
CSF £20.81 TOTE £4.20: £1.90, £1.30, £6.00; EX 19.00 Trifecta £432.50.
**Owner** Al Shaqab Racing **Bred** Deer Forest Stud **Trained** East Everleigh, Wilts

**FOCUS**
Not a particularly strong-looking maiden but the front pair pulled well clear in the final furlong.

## 6631 188BET H'CAP 5f 6y(P)
**3:20** (3:21) (Class 6) (0-60,62) 3-Y-O+ **£2,264** (£673; £336; £168) **Stalls** High

Form RPR
2323 **1** **Johnny Splash (IRE)**[26] 5860 5-9-4 56 (v) GeorgeBaker 7 70
(Roger Teal) *broke fast: mde all: rdn and qcknd clr over 1f out: in n.d fnl f: easily* **11/10**[1]
0642 **2** 4 **Lucky Surprise**[8] 6399 3-8-11 50 (b) SteveDrowne 9 50
(Jeremy Gask) *chsd ldrs: rdn wl over 1f out: no ch w wnr fnl f: wnt 2nd fnl 150yds: kpt on* **7/1**[3]
-444 **3** 1 3/4 **Sylvan Spirit (IRE)**[110] 2931 3-8-12 51 LiamKeniry 3 44
(Roger Teal) *in tch in midfield: rdn and effrt over 1f out: no ch w wnr 1f out: kpt on to go 3rd wl ins fnl f* **20/1**
163/ **4** 1 **Lucky Royale**[774] 5033 6-8-10 55 DavidParkes(7) 1 45
(Jeremy Gask) *hld up in tch towards rr: rdn and hdwy on inner over 1f out: no ch w wnr but kpt on ins fnl f* **12/1**
0452 **5** hd **College Doll**[29] 5780 5-9-6 58 (t) JimmyQuinn 4 47
(Christine Dunnett) *rdr late removing hood: hld up in tch in last trio: effrt and nt clr run over 1f out: swtchd lft and styd on u.p ins fnl f: no ch w wnr* **10/1**
5111 **6** nk **Spider Lily**[9] 6368 3-9-6 62 6ex DeclanBates(3) 10 50
(Peter Makin) *in tch in midfield: rdn 2f out: outpcd u.p and btn over 1f out* **9/2**[2]
4000 **7** shd **Quality Art (USA)**[125] 2459 6-9-4 59 CharlesBishop(3) 6 47
(Simon Hodgson) *chsd wnr: rdn and outpcd over 1f out: no ch w wnr 1f out: lost 2nd and wknd ins fnl f* **33/1**
4400 **8** 3/4 **Mossgo (IRE)**[26] 5860 4-8-13 51 (t) MartinDwyer 2 36
(John Best) *t.k.h: chsd ldrs: drvn and outpcd over 1f out: wknd ins fnl f* **8/1**
0606 **9** 1 **Catalyze**[38] 5422 6-9-0 52 (t) WilliamCarson 5 33
(Paddy Butler) *in tch in rr: struggling and rdn 2f out: drvn and wknd over 1f out* **25/1**
5530 **10** nk **Island Express (IRE)**[7] 6437 7-8-7 50 (bt) AnnStokell(5) 8 30
(Ann Stokell) *taken down early: stuck wd: in tch in last trio: v wd bnd 2f out: wl hld after* **66/1**

58.36s (-0.44) **Going Correction** -0.25s/f (Stan)
**WFA** 3 from 4yo+ 1lb **10 Ran SP% 119.2**
Speed ratings (Par 101): **93,86,83,82,81 81,81,80,78,77**
CSF £9.22 CT £107.04 TOTE £2.40: £1.10, £2.40, £4.30; EX 9.80 Trifecta £103.90.
**Owner** Barry Kitcherside **Bred** J Connolly **Trained** Ashtead, Surrey

**FOCUS**
A one-horse betting market and the winner landed the gamble in emphatic fashion. He's been rated better than ever.

## 6632 QIC ACQUISITION OF ANTARES H'CAP 1m 7f 169y(P)
3:55 (3:58) (Class 6) (0-65,65) 3-Y-O+ £2,264 (£673; £336; £168) Stalls Low

Form RPR
2642 1 **Aiyana**[5] 6493 4-10-0 65 JimmyFortune 6 75
(Hughie Morrison) *led for 1f: chsd ldr after: clsd 4f out: rdn to ld 2f out: clr 1f out: styd on: rdn out* 9/2[2]

006 2 1 3/4 **Ermyn Lodge**[34] 5547 8-9-11 62 (t) JackMitchell 3 70
(Pat Phelan) *bustled along early: racd off the pce in midfield: rdn and clsng in 4th over 2f out: chsd wnr 1f out: kpt on but nvr a threat* 33/1

2123 3 2 3/4 **Ninfea (IRE)**[16] 5317 6-9-10 61 HayleyTurner 11 66
(Neil King) *led after 1f and sn clr: rdn and hdd 2f out: no ex and btn 1f out: plugged on same pce after: lame* 20/1

0235 4 1 1/2 **Black Iceman**[10] 6339 6-8-11 51 SimonPearce(3) 4 54
(Lydia Pearce) *hld up off the pce in last quartet: stdy hdwy 4f out: rdn and effrt over 2f out: chsd ldrs 1f out: no imp ins fnl f* 33/1

0344 5 nse **Anjin (IRE)**[20] 6037 3-8-12 61 ChrisCatlin 7 64
(Sir Mark Prescott Bt) *chsd ldrs: clsd 4f out: drvn and pressing ldrs 2f out: unable qck u.p over 1f out: one pce after* 11/4[1]

3211 6 3/4 **Mister Bob (GER)**[34] 5547 5-9-12 63 (p) TedDurcan 8 65
(James Bethell) *hld up off the pce in midfield: hdwy 5f out: 5th and drvn over 2f out: styd on same pce and no imp over 1f out* 11/4[1]

000 7 17 **Uncle Muf (USA)**[83] 3856 4-9-10 61 AdamKirby 1 42
(Ali Stronge) *racd off the pce in midfield: rdn over 3f out: wknd 2f out* 10/1[3]

5000 8 29 **Arryzona**[21] 6015 3-7-7 49 oh4 RobertPWalsh(7) 10
(Christine Dunnett) *hld up wl in rr: rdn 1/2-way: lost tch 4f out: t.o* 100/1

000/ 9 2 3/4 **First Battalion (IRE)**[850] 2502 6-9-4 55 JamesDoyle 12
(Ian Williams) *racd off the pce in midfield: rdn and lost tch 3f out: t.o and virtually p.u ins fnl f: lame* 16/1

0116 10 2 3/4 **Honourable Knight (IRE)**[31] 5689 6-9-13 64 (v) LiamKeniry 5 4
(Mark Usher) *racd in midfield: rdn over 5f out: lost tch 3f out: t.o and virtually p.u ins fnl f* 25/1

-360 11 2 3/4 **Rock Of Ages**[96] 3404 5-9-6 57 (b) GeorgeBaker 13
(Neil King) *dwlt: hld up off the pce in last quartet: rdn and lost tch over 3f out: t.o and virtually p.u ins fnl f* 14/1

0504 P **Rollin 'n Tumblin**[10] 6339 10-8-10 47 oh2 JimmyQuinn 2
(Michael Attwater) *t.k.h: hld up in rr tl p.u 1/2-way: lame* 100/1

3m 19.9s (-5.80) **Going Correction** -0.25s/f (Stan)
**WFA** 3 from 4yo+ 12lb 12 Ran SP% 109.6
Speed ratings (Par 101): **104,103,101,101,100 100,92,77,76,74 73,**
CSF £128.41 CT £1957.39 TOTE £5.10: £2.30, £10.50, £3.40; EX 98.50 Trifecta £2616.70 Part won..
**Owner** The End-R-Ways Partnership & Partners **Bred** The Lavington Stud **Trained** East Ilsley, Berks
■ Nelson Of The Nile was withdrawn. Price at time of withdrawal 6/1. Rule 4 applies to all bets - deduction 10p in the pound.

**FOCUS**
A low-grade staying handicap in which the field were well strung out from an early stage. The front-running third has been rated close to her recent turf form.

## 6633 188BET CASINO H'CAP 1m 1y(P)
4:30 (4:31) (Class 5) (0-75,74) 3-Y-O £3,363 (£1,001; £500; £250) Stalls High

Form RPR
4345 1 **Spreadable (IRE)**[12] 6262 3-9-4 71 JackMitchell 3 81
(Nick Littmoden) *led for over 1f out: settled bk and chsd ldrs after: rdn and qcknd to ld 1f out: r.o wl: readily* 10/1

1350 2 2 3/4 **Moonlight Venture**[34] 5550 3-9-7 74 SilvestreDeSousa 2 78
(Kevin Ryan) *t.k.h: chsd ldr: drvn and ev ch over 1f out: chsd wnr and one pce fnl f* 8/1[3]

4060 3 3/4 **Elysian Prince**[80] 3974 3-9-6 73 (t) MartinLane 11 76
(Paul Cole) *hld up in tch in rr: nt clr run and swtchd rt over 1f out: r.o strly ins fnl f: no threat to wnr* 9/2[1]

6064 4 nk **Miss Lillie**[10] 6336 3-9-5 72 [1] JamesDoyle 5 74
(Roger Teal) *dwlt and bustled along in rr: hdwy and swtchd rt over 1f out: wnt between rivals ins fnl f: r.o wl: no threat to wnr* 8/1[3]

310 5 1/2 **Hardy Black (IRE)**[17] 6154 3-8-10 68 RachealKneller(5) 10 68
(Jamie Osborne) *stdd s: hld up in midfield: short of room over 1f out tl 1f out: eventually c u.p fnl 100yds: r.o same pce* 16/1

0 6 nse **Bint Dandy (IRE)**[12] 6269 3-9-2 69 JimmyQuinn 4 69
(Chris Dwyer) *t.k.h: hld up in tch in midfield on inner: swtchd lft and effrt over 1f out: kpt on: no threat to wnr* 50/1

0040 7 hd **Boogangoo (IRE)**[50] 4968 3-9-2 69 DavidProbert 12 69
(Grace Harris) *in tch in midfield: effrt over 1f out: styd on ins fnl f: no threat to wnr* 16/1

0306 8 1/2 **Saltwater Creek (IRE)**[36] 5505 3-9-7 74 JamieSpencer 7 76
(Michael Bell) *hld up in tch in midfield: racd awkwardly and lost pl bnd 2f out: rallied and kpt on ins fnl f: no threat to wnr: lame* 6/1[2]

100 9 1 1/4 **Space Walker (IRE)**[42] 5274 3-9-7 74 (b[1]) AdamKirby 6 70
(Harry Dunlop) *sn busted along to chse ldrs: unable qck u.p over 1f out: wknd ins fnl f* 10/1

-450 10 nk **Market Storm (FR)**[73] 4191 3-9-1 68 (b) JimmyFortune 8 63
(Brian Meehan) *in tch in midfield but stuck wd: rdn and unable qck over 1f out: one pce and wl hld fnl f* 16/1

4255 11 3/4 **Captain George (IRE)**[15] 6192 3-9-4 71 (v) ShaneKelly 1 64
(James Fanshawe) *sn dropped to last pair and nvr travelling wl after: c wd and drvn wl over 1f out: no imp* 9/2[1]

2212 12 6 **Black Vale (IRE)**[92] 3523 3-9-3 70 OisinMurphy 9 50
(Ralph J Smith) *led: rdn ent fnl 2f: hdd 1f out: sn wknd* 8/1[3]

1m 36.13s (-2.07) **Going Correction** -0.25s/f (Stan) 12 Ran SP% 121.8
Speed ratings (Par 101): **100,97,96,96,95 95,95,94,93,93 92,86**
CSF £90.19 CT £425.06 TOTE £13.00: £3.80, £2.30, £1.50; EX 60.30 Trifecta £1727.50.
**Owner** G F Chesneaux **Bred** Patsy Myers & Edward Myers **Trained** Newmarket, Suffolk

**FOCUS**
This looked wide open beforehand but the winner produced an impressive display for the grade. The winner has been rated as running a small pb.

## 6634 188BET GREAT IN PLAY MAIDEN STKS 1m 2f (P)
5:00 (5:01) (Class 5) 3-Y-O+ £2,911 (£866; £432; £216) Stalls Low

Form RPR
3232 1 **Tabjeel**[25] 5894 3-9-5 80 (p) SilvestreDeSousa 1 84
(Saeed bin Suroor) *mde all: rdn wl over 1f out: drvn fnl f: c together w runner-up towards fin: jst hld on: all out* 6/1[3]

-362 2 shd **Steppe Daughter (IRE)**[22] 5976 3-9-0 76 OisinMurphy 4 78
(Denis Coakley) *chsd ldrs: rdn and effrt over 1f out: chsd wnr 1f out: steadily clsd and ev ch whn c together w wnr towards fin: jst hld* 12/1

65 3 1 1/2 **Cerutty (IRE)**[11] 6298 3-9-5 0 AdamKirby 5 80
(Marco Botti) *in tch in midfield: rdn 4f out: hdwy to chse ldrs 2f out: kpt on to go 3rd ins fnl f: gng on steadily at fin* 20/1

4223 4 1 **Red Velour**[27] 5831 3-9-0 77 RyanMoore 2 73
(Jeremy Noseda) *chsd wnr: rdn and pressing wnr 2f out: 3rd and no ex jst ins fnl f: styd on same pce after* 2/1[1]

04 5 3 **The Gay Cavalier**[3] 6540 3-9-2 0 (t) ThomasBrown(3) 3 73
(John Ryan) *hld up in tch in last trio: hdwy over 2f out: kpt on same pce and no imp over 1f out* 66/1

4 6 1/2 **Peril**[40] 5347 3-9-5 0 JamesDoyle 10 72
(Lady Cecil) *dwlt: stuck wd thrght: in tch towards rr: rdn over 3f out: outpcd in 6th 2f out: no prog after* 5/2[2]

- 7 13 **Shamal**[76] 4-9-11 0 WilliamBuick 8 47
(John Gosden) *in tch in midfield: rdn and effrt jst over 2f out: sn btn: wknd over 1f out* 8/1

00 8 1/2 **Perfect Legend**[27] 5822 3-9-5 0 DavidProbert 9 46
(Andrew Balding) *hld up in tch in last trio: rdn 4f out: lost tch 2f out* 100/1

0U 9 5 **Prince Ballygowen**[111] 2883 3-9-5 0 RobertTart 7 36
(Clifford Lines) *hld up in tch in rr: rdn over 3f out: lost tch 2f out* 100/1

-225 10 34 **Allegation (FR)**[27] 5822 3-9-0 80 (b) ShaneKelly 6
(David Lanigan) *wl in tch in midfield: rdn and no rspnse over 2f out: sn dropped to rr: bhd and eased over 1f out: t.o* 6/1[3]

2m 2.9s (-3.70) **Going Correction** -0.25s/f (Stan)
**WFA** 3 from 4yo 6lb 10 Ran SP% 117.5
Speed ratings (Par 103): **104,103,102,101,99 99,88,88,84,57**
CSF £73.06 TOTE £3.90: £1.30, £3.30, £4.00; EX 54.20 Trifecta £437.40.
**Owner** Godolphin **Bred** Shadwell Estate Company Limited **Trained** Newmarket, Suffolk

**FOCUS**
With some of the fancied runners failing to give their running this might not have taken a great deal of winning. The first two have been rated around the better view of their previous form.

## 6635 LINGFIELD PARK OWNERS GROUP 2014 H'CAP (DIV I) 1m 2f (P)
5:30 (5:30) (Class 6) (0-65,65) 3-Y-O+ £2,587 (£770; £384; £192) Stalls Low

Form RPR
3443 1 **Allergic Reaction (IRE)**[28] 5795 3-9-2 63 AdamKirby 2 73
(William Knight) *chsd ldrs: rdn to chal 2f out: led over 1f out: sn in command: r.o strly* 7/2[1]

-404 2 3 **Loraine**[13] 6243 4-9-6 61 GeorgeBaker 6 65+
(Jamie Osborne) *hld up in last quartet: sme hdwy but stl plenty to do 3f out: rdn and effrt over 1f out: styd on wl to go 2nd wl ins fnl f: no ch w wnr* 9/2[2]

6201 3 1 3/4 **Sexy Secret**[21] 6015 3-9-1 65 (v) SimonPearce(3) 5 66
(Lydia Pearce) *chsd ldr: rdn 3rd and unable qck over 1f out: styd on same pce fnl f* 16/1

3650 4 3/4 **Understory (USA)**[105] 3080 7-9-3 58 (b) HayleyTurner 4 58
(Tim McCarthy) *led: rdn ent 2f: hdd over 1f out: sn brushed aside by wnr: wknd and lost 2 pls wl ins fnl f* 7/1

3514 5 3 **Lifejacket (IRE)**[13] 6242 3-8-12 59 (b) JamesDoyle 8 53
(Ed Dunlop) *racd off the pce in midfield: effrt over 1f out: styd on ins fnl f: no ch* 5/1[3]

5516 6 3/4 **Lily Edge**[21] 6019 5-9-8 63 (v) WilliamCarson 1 55
(John Bridger) *racd off the pce in midfield: sme hdwy u.p on inner 2f out: no prog 1f out: wknd ins fnl f* 20/1

4000 7 3/4 **Zaeem**[35] 5521 5-9-5 60 (p) ChrisCatlin 7 51
(Dean Ivory) *t.k.h: hld up in midfield: rdn and effrt 3f out: no hdwy 2f out: wknd over 1f out* 50/1

-065 8 1 **Saxon Princess (IRE)**[126] 2416 3-8-6 53 DavidProbert 3 42
(Roger Charlton) *chsd ldrs: rdn and unable qck 2f out: sn outpcd and btn: wknd fnl f* 5/1[3]

-225 9 3/4 **Comedy House**[21] 6007 6-9-9 64 (p) LiamKeniry 12 52
(Michael Madgwick) *hld up off the pce in last quartet: effrt wl over 1f out: nvr trbld ldrs* 33/1

6000 10 3 1/2 **Remix (IRE)**[31] 5689 5-8-10 51 oh1 (p) SilvestreDeSousa 9 32
(Ian Williams) *chsd ldrs: rdn over 3f out: drvn and btn 2f out: wknd over 1f out* 25/1

6050 11 1 3/4 **Flamborough Breeze**[20] 6035 5-9-10 65 JimmyFortune 10 43
(Ed Vaughan) *hld up off the pce in last quartet: n.d* 25/1

-000 12 3/4 **Sabre Rock**[11] 6303 4-9-1 56 (t) SteveDrowne 13 32
(John Best) *stdd s: hld up in rr: n.d* 16/1

000 13 12 **Flight Fight**[131] 2271 3-9-1 62 TedDurcan 11 16
(Chris Wall) *dwlt: a in rr: lost tch 2f out: eased ins fnl f* 8/1

2m 3.3s (-3.30) **Going Correction** -0.25s/f (Stan)
**WFA** 3 from 4yo+ 6lb 13 Ran SP% 121.6
Speed ratings (Par 101): **103,100,99,98,96 95,95,94,93,90 89,88,79**
CSF £17.90 CT £229.38 TOTE £3.80: £1.50, £2.10, £3.40; EX 20.10 Trifecta £138.20.
**Owner** Four Men & A Dream Partnership **Bred** Worksop Manor Stud **Trained** Patching, W Sussex

**FOCUS**
A modest handicap run at a steady race, the runner-up deserving plenty of credit for coming from some way back. The runner-up has been rated close to form.

## 6636 LINGFIELD PARK OWNERS GROUP 2014 H'CAP (DIV II) 1m 2f (P)
6:00 (6:01) (Class 6) (0-65,64) 3-Y-O+ £2,587 (£770; £384; £192) Stalls Low

Form RPR
0-04 1 **Sweet P**[33] 5598 3-9-4 64 [1] WilliamBuick 4 73+
(Marcus Tregoning) *wl in tch in midfield: swtchd rt and effrt to chse ldrs over 1f out: pushed along to ld ins fnl f: kpt on* 8/1

2330 2 1 1/4 **Two In The Pink (IRE)**[13] 6242 4-9-8 62 GeorgeBaker 5 68
(Ralph J Smith) *chsd ldrs: rdn to chse ldr 2f out: drvn to ld 1f out: hdd and one pce ins fnl f* 10/1

0443 3 nk **Lola Montez (IRE)**[21] 6015 3-8-8 54 (b) TedDurcan 1 59
(David Lanigan) *hld up in tch towards rr: rdn and hdwy on inner over 1f out: kpt on ins fnl f* 10/1

2334 4 1 1/4 **Oyster (IRE)**[53] 4863 3-9-3 63 (b) SebSanders 3 66
(Nick Littmoden) *hld up in tch in rr: hdwy u.p ent fnl f: styd on wl: no threat to wnr* 6/1[3]

0366 5 1/2 **Avidly**[30] 5731 4-8-11 56 ShelleyBirkett(5) 2 58
(Julia Feilden) *s.i.s: hld up in rr: switching rt jst over 2f out: hdwy 1f out: styd on wl: nvr trbld ldrs* 33/1

1203 6 1 **Estibdaad (IRE)**[20] 6031 4-9-3 57 (t) MartinLane 13 57
(Paddy Butler) *led: rdn 2f out: drvn and hdd 1f out: wknd ins fnl f* 16/1

000 7 1/2 **Salient**[69] 4326 10-8-10 50 oh5 KierenFox 10 49
(Michael Attwater) *in tch in midfield: effrt u.p over 2f out: no ex and one pce fr over 1f out* 50/1

1436 **8** ¾ **Bennelong**[13] 6243 8-9-9 63 ....(b) AmirQuinn 6 61
(Lee Carter) *rdn along leaving stalls: hld up towards rr: sme hdwy over 2f out: nt clr run and shuffled bk 2f out: rallied and kpt on ins fnl f: no threat to wnr* **14/1**

4431 **9** ¾ **Flag Of Glory**[14] 6210 7-9-3 64 .... PatMillman(7) 12 60
(Peter Hiatt) *chsd ldr tl 2f out: sn no ex u.p: wknd ins fnl f* **14/1**

0000 **10** 1½ **Strong Conviction**[8] 6396 4-9-3 60 ....(p) CharlesBishop(3) 7 54
(Simon Hodgson) *hld up in tch towards rr: dropped to rr and swtchd rt 4f out: hdwy but v wd 3f out: lost pl bnd 2f out: wl hld and one pce after* **50/1**

0050 **11** 1¾ **Sebs Sensei (IRE)**[20] 6037 3-9-2 62 ....(b[1]) SteveDrowne 11 52
(Mark Hoad) *t.k.h: chsd ldrs: lost pl over 2f out: bhd over 1f out* **66/1**

1031 **12** 2½ **Benoordenhout (IRE)**[26] 5865 3-8-13 59 ....(p) OisinMurphy 9 44
(Jonathan Portman) *chsd ldrs: rdn and no rspnse over 1f out: sn btn: wknd ins fnl f* **5/2[1]**

5602 **13** 7 **Tax Reform (IRE)**[15] 6195 4-9-6 60 ....(be) RyanMoore 8 32
(Gary Moore) *hld up in tch towards rr: wd and short-lived effrt jst over 2f out: bhd over 1f out* **7/2[2]**

2m 3.98s (-2.62) **Going Correction** -0.25s/f (Stan)
**WFA** 3 from 4yo+ 6lb **13** Ran SP% **121.9**
Speed ratings (Par 101): **100,99,98,97,97 96,96,95,94,93 92,90,84**
CSF £85.96 CT £822.65 TOTE £8.90: £3.50, £2.60, £4.50; EX 81.00 Trifecta £1760.70.
**Owner** M P N Tregoning **Bred** W & T Barrons And Mr & Mrs A Pakenham **Trained** Whitsbury, Hants

**FOCUS**
The second division of the 1m2f handicap and although the gallop looked stronger, the winning time was 0.68s slower. The third and fourth have been rated close to their recent handicap form.
T/Plt: £224.80 to a £1 stake. Pool: £66,459.87 - 215.74 winning tickets T/Qpdt: £39.10 to a £1 stake. Pool: £5,309.57 - 100.40 winning tickets SP

## 6115 NEWCASTLE (L-H)
### Tuesday, September 23

**OFFICIAL GOING: Good (good to firm in places last 3f) changing to good after race 6 (5:50)**
Wind: Light, across Weather: Overcast

### 6637 PETTY WOOD H'CAP — 1m 4f 93y
**3:15** (3:16) (Class 4) (0-85,83) 3-Y-O **£4,690** (£1,395; £697; £348) **Stalls** Low

Form RPR

5435 **1** **Ryeolliean**[39] 5387 3-8-7 72 ....(p) SamJames(3) 3 80
(David O'Meara) *mde all at stdy pce: rdn and qcknd 2f out: hld on wl fnl f* **13/2**

6133 **2** 1 **Clear Spell (IRE)**[21] 6012 3-8-7 72 .... ConnorBeasley(3) 2 78
(Alistair Whillans) *trckd ldrs: rdn and wnt 2nd over 1f out: kpt on fnl f: hld last 50yds* **9/2[3]**

5310 **3** 1 **Chivers (IRE)**[16] 6169 3-8-7 69 .... DavidAllan 7 73
(Tim Easterby) *chsd wnr: rdn over 3f out: effrt over 2f out: kpt on same pce fnl f* **4/1[2]**

6412 **4** ¾ **Intense Tango**[17] 6137 3-9-3 79 .... DanielTudhope 5 82
(K R Burke) *hld up last but in tch in slowly run r: rdn and outpcd over 3f out: rallied 2f out: kpt on fnl f: nvr able to chal* **4/5[1]**

4046 **5** 17 **Tactical Strike**[111] 2893 3-8-2 64 .... DuranFentiman 6 40
(Shaun Harris) *dwlt: sn prom: drvn and outpcd 3f out: hung lft and sn btn: t.o* **28/1**

2m 47.7s (2.10) **Going Correction** 0.0s/f (Good) **5** Ran SP% **110.5**
Speed ratings (Par 103): **93,92,91,91,79**
CSF £33.79 TOTE £6.70: £2.30, £2.50; EX 27.60 Trifecta £87.20.
**Owner** James Munroe **Bred** Dale Ablitt **Trained** Nawton, N Yorks

**FOCUS**
A fair opener on a damp, drizzly day. The runner-up and third help set the standard.

### 6638 GROCERYAID.ORG.UK MAIDEN FILLIES' STKS — 7f
**3:50** (3:50) (Class 5) 3-Y-O+ **£2,587** (£770; £384; £192) **Stalls** Centre

Form RPR

43 **1** **Brisk**[11] 6298 3-8-13 72 .... RoystonFfrench 4 66
(David Evans) *trckd ldrs: rdn and outpcd over 2f out: rallied to ld ins fnl f: edgd rt: rdn out* **7/2[3]**

04 **2** 1¾ **Gharaaneej (IRE)**[48] 5044 3-8-13 0 .... DaneO'Neill 6 61
(John Gosden) *dwlt: hld up: hdwy to ld over 1f out: rdn and hdd ins fnl f: kpt on same pce* **9/4[2]**

0606 **3** nse **Magical Mischief**[55] 4797 4-9-2 45 .... MichaelStainton 5 62?
(Chris Fairhurst) *pressed ldr: led over 2f out to over 1f out: rallied: kpt on same pce ins fnl f* **100/1**

2235 **4** hd **Two Smart (IRE)**[5] 6492 3-8-13 75 .... MartinHarley 1 61
(K R Burke) *plld hrd: hld up: hdwy to chse wnr over 1f out to ins fnl f: sn one pce* **2/1[1]**

02 **5** 5 **Rememberance Day**[14] 6215 3-8-13 0 .... DavidAllan 8 48
(Les Eyre) *trckd ldrs: rdn over 2f out: wknd fnl f* **7/1**

-630 **6** 5 **Redalani (IRE)**[31] 5683 4-9-2 49 ....(tp) PaulPickard 3 36
(Alan Brown) *plld hrd: led to over 2f out: wknd over 1f out* **66/1**

0-0 **7** 3 **Van Mildert (IRE)**[7] 6429 5-8-11 0 .... EmmaSayer(5) 2 28
(Dianne Sayer) *hld up: struggling over 2f out: sn btn* **50/1**

5-03 **8** 23 **Wedding Wish (IRE)**[54] 4816 3-8-13 80 ....[1] KierenFallon 7
(George Margarson) *in tch: outpcd 1/2-way: lost tch fr over 2f out: t.o* **13/2**

1m 27.4s (-0.40) **Going Correction** -0.05s/f (Good)
**WFA** 3 from 4yo+ 3lb **8** Ran SP% **116.6**
Speed ratings (Par 100): **100,98,97,97,92 86,82,56**
CSF £12.11 TOTE £3.90: £1.10, £1.20, £10.90; EX 17.60 Trifecta £2174.80 Part won..
**Owner** Mrs I M Folkes **Bred** Juddmonte Farms **Trained** Pandy, Monmouths

**FOCUS**
This was weak and with those towards the head of the market floundering in the closing stages, it was the ex-French trained Brisk, who came out on top. The third is the doubt but the time was all right in comparison with the other races over the C&D.

### 6639 GROCERYAID CHARITY H'CAP — 7f
**4:20** (4:21) (Class 4) (0-85,84) 3-Y-O+ **£4,690** (£1,395; £697; £348) **Stalls** Centre

Form RPR

4144 **1** **Tiger Jim**[13] 6232 4-8-7 70 .... FergalLynch 2 82
(Jim Goldie) *hld up: hdwy over 2f out: rdn to ld ins fnl f: kpt on wl* **4/1[2]**

0351 **2** 1¼ **Bob**[13] 6232 4-8-8 71 .... DavidAllan 4 80
(Les Eyre) *prom: led over 2f out: sn rdn: hdd ins fnl f: kpt on: nt pce of wnr* **5/2[1]**

0145 **3** 1¼ **Big Storm Coming**[14] 6214 4-9-0 77 .... JamesSullivan 8 83
(Ruth Carr) *hld up bhd ldng gp: hdwy and ev ch over 1f out: sn rdn: kpt on same pce last 100yds* **11/2[3]**

1266 **4** 1¼ **Illustrious Prince (IRE)**[39] 5385 7-8-9 75 ....(p) ConnorBeasley(3) 9 78
(Julie Camacho) *rrd in stalls and dwlt: hld up: hdwy over 2f out: rdn and kpt on same pce fnl f* **12/1**

0643 **5** 4½ **Zacynthus (IRE)**[10] 6334 6-8-11 79 .... LouisSteward(5) 7 70
(Michael Bell) *cl up: rdn and outpcd over 2f out: n.d after* **13/2**

2300 **6** nk **Al's Memory (IRE)**[29] 5750 5-8-9 72 .... RoystonFfrench 11 62
(David Evans) *cl up: rdn over 2f out: wknd over 1f out* **28/1**

3204 **7** 7 **Powerful Presence (IRE)**[18] 6094 8-9-4 81 ....(p) DanielTudhope 12 53
(David O'Meara) *hld up in tch: drvn and outpcd over 2f out: sn btn* **11/1**

1000 **8** 4 **Shahdaroba (IRE)**[13] 6226 4-9-7 84 ....(p) LukeMorris 10 45
(Micky Hammond) *dwlt: sn in tch: drvn 3f out: sn wknd* **25/1**

6-50 **9** 11 **Reposer (IRE)**[25] 5887 6-9-0 77 ....(p) KierenFallon 5 10
(Keith Dalgleish) *led tl rdn and hdd over 2f out: sn btn* **16/1**

1242 **10** 3 **Red Paladin (IRE)**[22] 5986 4-8-10 73 .... MartinHarley 1
(Kevin Ryan) *hld up: rdn along wl over 2f out: sn wknd* **8/1**

1m 26.56s (-1.24) **Going Correction** -0.05s/f (Good)
**WFA** 3 from 4yo+ 3lb **10** Ran SP% **117.6**
Speed ratings (Par 105): **105,103,102,100,95 95,87,82,70,66**
CSF £14.54 CT £55.41 TOTE £6.50: £2.70, £1.30, £2.30; EX 13.10 Trifecta £41.20.
**Owner** J S Goldie **Bred** Dunchurch Lodge Stud Co **Trained** Uplawmoor, E Renfrews

**FOCUS**
They went plenty quick enough in the early stages. There are grounds for thinking the first three might be better than their marks.

### 6640 GROCERYAID.ORG.UK H'CAP — 2m 19y
**4:50** (4:50) (Class 4) (0-85,82) 3-Y-O+ **£4,690** (£1,395; £697; £348) **Stalls** Low

Form RPR

5121 **1** **Moscato**[5] 6502 3-8-9 75 6ex ....(p) LukeMorris 6 87+
(Sir Mark Prescott Bt) *trckd ldr: led over 2f out: drvn and edgd lft over 1f out: kpt on strly* **5/6[1]**

2542 **2** 2¾ **Dr Irv**[16] 6169 5-9-2 75 ....(p) MeganCarberry(5) 2 83
(Philip Kirby) *prom: smooth hdwy to chse wnr over 2f out: rdn and edgd lft over 1f out: kpt on same pce fnl f* **5/1[2]**

0616 **3** 2 **Mustamir (IRE)**[31] 5670 3-8-12 78 ....(b) MartinHarley 1 84
(James Tate) *t.k.h: trckd ldrs: drvn along 3f out: hung lft over 1f out: kpt on same pce* **7/1[3]**

000 **4** 4½ **Waterclock (IRE)**[40] 5334 5-10-0 82 ....(b) RussKennemore 5 83
(Jedd O'Keeffe) *hld up in tch on ins: rdn and hdwy over 2f out: wknd over 1f out* **16/1**

0 **5** ¾ **Caledonia**[25] 5890 7-9-4 72 .... FergalLynch 9 72
(Jim Goldie) *hld up: pushed along over 4f out: hdwy over 2f out: kpt on fr over 1f out: nvr rchd ldrs* **11/1**

2315 **6** 3 **Annaluna (IRE)**[9] 6360 5-9-0 68 ....(v) RoystonFfrench 4 64
(David Evans) *in tch: pushed along over 5f out: outpcd 3f out: n.d after* **12/1**

44 **7** 1¼ **Bell Weir**[13] 6228 6-9-1 74 .... EmmaSayer(5) 8 69
(Dianne Sayer) *dwlt: t.k.h: hld up: rdn and outpcd over 2f out: sn btn* **16/1**

312- **8** 7 **Attention Seaker**[412] 5137 4-9-4 72 .... DuranFentiman 3 58
(Tim Easterby) *rrd s: hld up: rdn and effrt on ins over 2f out: wknd wl over 1f out* **33/1**

2635 **9** ¾ **Mason Hindmarsh**[29] 5764 7-8-11 65 .... TonyHamilton 7 50
(Karen McLintock) *led to over 3f out: rdn and wknd fr 2f out* **16/1**

3m 35.02s (-4.38) **Going Correction** 0.0s/f (Good)
**WFA** 3 from 4yo+ 12lb **9** Ran SP% **120.3**
Speed ratings (Par 105): **110,108,107,105,105 103,102,99,99**
CSF £5.58 CT £19.64 TOTE £2.00: £1.10, £1.60, £4.00; EX 7.60 Trifecta £24.80.
**Owner** The Green Door Partnership **Bred** Miss K Rausing **Trained** Newmarket, Suffolk

**FOCUS**
This was more competitive than the lopsided market suggested and it was hard not to be impressed by the style in which Moscato followed up last week's Yarmouth win. The runner-up has been rated as running a small pb.

### 6641 FACTORY TO STORE WE'RE YOUR CHARITY/EBF MAIDEN FILLIES' STKS (BOBIS RACE) — 7f
**5:20** (5:22) (Class 5) 2-Y-O **£2,911** (£866; £432; £216) **Stalls** Centre

Form RPR

01 **1** dht **All About Time**[17] 6148 2-9-0 0 .... DanielTudhope 6 74
(David O'Meara) *led: rdn and hdd over 1f out: styd upsides: carried lft ins fnl f: keeping on wl whn bmpd nr fin: jnd ldr on post: dead-heated for 1st: awrdd r outrt* **11/10[1]**

5632 **2** **Hollie Point**[24] 5910 2-9-0 78 .... AhmedAjtebi 11 74
(Charlie Appleby) *t.k.h: w ldrs: led over 1f out: hung lft ins fnl f: bmpd rival nr fin: out: dead-heated for 1st: disqualified and plcd 2nd* **11/4[2]**

45 **3** ½ **Cabelo (IRE)**[16] 6168 2-9-0 0 .... BenCurtis 10 73
(Brian Ellison) *trckd ldrs: rdn over 2f out: rallied over 1f out: kpt on ins fnl f* **20/1**

**4** nse **Figment** 2-9-0 0 .... RobertHavlin 3 73+
(John Gosden) *dwlt: swtchd rt and hld up: effrt over 2f out: kpt on ins fnl f: bttr for r* **10/1**

6 **5** 4½ **Gentlemusic (FR)**[19] 6066 2-9-0 0 .... MartinHarley 14 60
(Marco Botti) *prom: rdn over 2f out: outpcd over 1f out* **7/1[3]**

**6** 2¾ **Twice Certain (IRE)** 2-9-0 0 .... DaneO'Neill 8 53
(Ed Walker) *prom: rdn over 2f out: wknd over 1f out* **25/1**

00 **7** nse **Rose Acclaim (IRE)**[24] 5910 2-8-11 0 .... SamJames(3) 1 53
(David O'Meara) *t.k.h: prom: rdn over 2f out: sn wknd* **100/1**

**8** 1½ **Beta Tauri (USA)** 2-8-7 0 .... AhmadAlSubousi(7) 15 49
(Charlie Appleby) *s.i.s: hld up: pushed along over 2f out: sn no imp* **20/1**

**9** 2¼ **La Hoofon** 2-8-11 0 .... ConnorBeasley(3) 4 43
(Michael Dods) *hld up: rdn and outpcd over 2f out: sn btn* **11/1**

00 **10** 4 **Strong Flame**[38] 5416 2-9-0 0 .... GrahamLee 12 32
(David Brown) *t.k.h: hld up: pushed along over 2f out: sn btn* **50/1**

**11** 1¾ **Artistic Flare** 2-9-0 0 .... IanBrennan 9 27
(John Quinn) *dwlt: sn midfield: rdn 1/2-way: wknd over 2f out* **50/1**

**12** ½ **Marsoomah** 2-9-0 0 .... TonyHamilton 7 26
(Richard Fahey) *slowly away: t.k.h in rr: struggling over 2f out: sn btn* **33/1**

1m 29.11s (1.31) **Going Correction** -0.05s/f (Good) **12** Ran SP% **125.4**
Speed ratings (Par 92): **90,90,89,89,84 81,81,79,76,72 70,69**
CSF £3.98 TOTE £2.60: £3.70, £1.10, £4.00; EX 4.00.
**Owner** P D Player **Bred** Whatton Manor Stud **Trained** Nawton, N Yorks

**FOCUS**
The placings were reversed in this fair maiden. A compressed finish and there's a chance the form could have been rated a little too high.

## 6642 HELPING PEOPLE ACROSS THE INDUSTRY NURSERY H'CAP (DIV I) 6f
5:50 (5:52) (Class 6) (0-65,65) 2-Y-O £1,940 (£577; £288; £144) Stalls Centre

Form RPR
240 1 **Mighty Warrior**[46] 5128 2-9-7 65..............................(b[1]) TonyHamilton 10 76
(Richard Fahey) *prom: effrt and chsd wnr over 2f out: rdn and hung lft over 1f out: rallied to ld ins fnl f: kpt on wl* **6/1**[3]
043 2 2 **Charlie Lad**[27] 5813 2-9-4 62.............................. RobertWinston 6 67
(Ollie Pears) *t.k.h: led: rdn and qcknd wl over 1f out: hdd ins fnl f: kpt on same pce* **9/2**[2]
0060 3 4½ **Sparkling Sapphire**[50] 4973 2-8-1 45..............................(p) PaulQuinn 13 37
(Richard Whitaker) *in tch: drvn along over 2f out: sn outpcd: rallied over 1f out: nvr able to chal* **50/1**
466 4 3½ **Little Houidini**[39] 5386 2-8-8 52.............................. JasonHart 12 33
(Keith Dalgleish) *midfield: effrt and drvn over 2f out: no imp wl over 1f out* **9/1**
6064 5 shd **Ya Halla (IRE)**[12] 6248 2-8-2 53..............................(p) AhmadAlSubousi(7) 7 34
(Robert Cowell) *prom: effrt over 2f out: hung lft and wknd over 1f out* **10/1**
3400 6 3¾ **Lazy Days In Loule (IRE)**[14] 6211 2-9-2 60.............................. FergalLynch 5 29+
(Noel Wilson) *hld up: struggling over 3f out: sme late hdwy: nvr rchd ldrs* **40/1**
0602 7 shd **Jubilee Spirit**[20] 6040 2-9-4 62.............................. GrahamLee 9 31
(Geoffrey Oldroyd) *missed break: hld up: stdy hdwy 1/2-way: rdn and no imp fr 2f out* **10/3**[1]
050 8 nse **Splash Of Verve (IRE)**[10] 6319 2-9-7 65.............................. RussKennemore 2 34
(Philip Kirby) *hld up bhd ldng gp: struggling over 2f out: sn btn* **10/1**
4205 9 3¼ **Bannister Bell (IRE)**[46] 5120 2-9-5 63..............................(v[1]) BenCurtis 3 22
(David Evans) *cl up tl rdn and wknd over 2f out* **20/1**
0000 10 4 **Edie White**[6] 6453 2-7-13 48..............................(p) JackGarritty(5) 1
(Lawrence Mullaney) *chsd ldrs to 1/2-way: sn rdn and wknd* **25/1**
000 11 ½ **Soldier Sam (IRE)**[39] 5377 2-8-12 56.............................. DaneO'Neill 14
(Brian Ellison) *awkward s: hld up: struggling over 2f out: sn btn* **9/2**[2]

1m 14.73s (0.13) **Going Correction** -0.05s/f (Good) **11 Ran SP% 114.9**
Speed ratings (Par 93): **97,94,88,83,83 78,78,78,74,68 68**
CSF £29.74 CT £1095.38 TOTE £6.00: £1.60, £1.80, £10.90; EX 18.80 Trifecta £1863.20 Part won..
**Owner** Sheikh Juma Dalmook Al Maktoum **Bred** The National Stud **Trained** Musley Bank, N Yorks
■ Chollima was withdrawn. Price at time of withdrawal 12-1. Rule 4 applies to all bets - deduction 5p in the pound.

**FOCUS**
This was fiercely run and few got involved.

## 6643 HELPING PEOPLE ACROSS THE INDUSTRY NURSERY H'CAP (DIV II) 6f
6:20 (6:22) (Class 6) (0-65,65) 2-Y-O £1,940 (£577; £288; £144) Stalls Centre

Form RPR
5265 1 **Classic Flyer**[22] 5985 2-9-2 60.............................. DanielTudhope 7 64
(David O'Meara) *t.k.h: mde all: rdn 2f out: sn hrd pressed: kpt on wl fnl f* **5/1**[3]
0504 2 1¼ **Lady Atlas**[13] 6237 2-8-13 57.............................. MichaelStainton 4 57+
(David Brown) *missed break: hld up: smooth hdwy over 2f out: rdn over 1f out: styd on wl to take 2nd towards fin* **8/1**
4440 3 nse **Poppy In The Wind**[8] 6412 2-8-10 54.............................. FergalLynch 2 54
(Alan Brown) *w ldrs: rdn over 2f out: kpt on ins fnl f: lost 2nd towards fin* **66/1**
6510 4 nk **Pumaflor (IRE)**[16] 6165 2-9-7 65.............................. JasonHart 5 64
(Richard Guest) *hld up: stdy hdwy 1/2-way: rdn and outpcd wl over 1f out: kpt on ins fnl f* **9/2**[2]
050 5 nse **Magh Meall**[40] 5332 2-8-8 52.............................. PaulQuinn 1 51
(David Nicholls) *in tch: effrt and ev ch over 1f out: sn rdn: no ex ins fnl f* **50/1**
640 6 5 **Rocky Desert (IRE)**[24] 5922 2-9-6 64.............................. MartinHarley 6 48
(Marco Botti) *t.k.h: hld up in tch: effrt and drvn 2f out: sn outpcd* **7/2**[1]
060 7 1½ **Milady Eileen (IRE)**[17] 6147 2-8-2 51.............................. JackGarritty(5) 11 30
(Richard Fahey) *t.k.h: cl up: rdn over 2f out: wknd over 1f out* **11/1**
3543 8 ¾ **Atreus**[21] 6008 2-9-5 63.............................. JamesSullivan 3 40
(Michael Easterby) *hld up in tch: outpcd over 2f out: n.d after* **9/1**
5326 9 1¼ **Clodovil Doll (IRE)**[61] 4576 2-9-7 65.............................. GrahamLee 12 38
(James Tate) *hld up: rdn along over 2f out: sn btn* **8/1**
0500 10 1¾ **Secret Of Dubai**[14] 6211 2-8-5 49.............................. PaulPickard 9 17
(Brian Ellison) *chsd ldrs tl rdn and wknd over 2f out* **20/1**
5605 11 8 **Perfect Girl (IRE)**[7] 6427 2-9-2 60.............................. DavidAllan 10 4
(Tim Easterby) *racd cl to stands' side away fr main gp: in tch tl wknd over 2f out* **10/1**
4603 12 7 **Agadoo**[8] 6400 2-9-4 62..............................(p[1]) BenCurtis 13
(Shaun Harris) *towards rr towards jst away fr main gp: drvn over 3f out: sn struggling* **25/1**
000 P **Polydus**[12] 6261 2-8-2 46.............................. LukeMorris 8
(Ed Dunlop) *hld up: rdn and shortlived effrt over 3f out: wknd over 2f out: sn eased: p.u ins fnl f* **25/1**

1m 15.13s (0.53) **Going Correction** -0.05s/f (Good) **13 Ran SP% 122.6**
Speed ratings (Par 93): **94,92,92,91,91 85,83,82,80,78 67,58,**
CSF £43.47 CT £2391.09 TOTE £5.10: £2.00, £3.50, £12.20; EX 62.10 Trifecta £1491.70.
**Owner** The Classic Strollers Partnership **Bred** Pippa Bloodstock **Trained** Nawton, N Yorks

**FOCUS**
The market got this badly wrong.

## 6644 FACTORY TO STORE WE'RE YOUR CHARITY H'CAP 1m 4f 93y
6:50 (6:50) (Class 6) (0-60,60) 3-Y-O+ £1,940 (£577; £288; £144) Stalls Low

Form RPR
000- 1 **High Secret (IRE)**[321] 7774 3-8-10 52.............................. LukeMorris 4 63+
(Sir Mark Prescott Bt) *t.k.h: prom: rdn over 2f out: edgd lft and hdwy to ld over 1f out: r.o strly fnl f* **13/8**[1]
0156 2 1½ **Voice From Above (IRE)**[51] 4522 5-9-1 49.............................. DuranFentiman 9 58
(Patrick Holmes) *led at stdy pce: rdn over 2f out: hdd over 1f out: kpt on ins fnl f: nt pce of wnr* **25/1**
1442 3 3½ **Wor Lass**[18] 6117 6-9-10 58.............................. KierenFallon 5 61
(Iain Jardine) *t.k.h in midfield: rdn and outpcd wl over 2f out: rallied over 1f out: kpt on fnl f: nrst fin* **11/4**[2]
0005 4 nk **Time Of My Life (IRE)**[65] 4474 5-9-3 51..............................(t) BenCurtis 3 54
(Patrick Holmes) *trckd ldrs: rdn along over 2f out: kpt on same pce over 1f out* **9/1**
0426 5 ½ **Stormy Morning**[10] 6343 8-9-4 52..............................(p) TonyHamilton 10 54
(Philip Kirby) *dwlt: hld up: drvn along and effrt over 2f out: kpt on fnl f: no imp* **20/1**
-225 6 ¾ **Thackeray**[42] 5270 7-9-11 59.............................. MichaelStainton 8 60
(Chris Fairhurst) *hld up: drvn along over 3f out: gd hdwy on outside over 1f out: nrst fin* **8/1**
1200 7 ¾ **Sirpertan**[36] 5495 3-8-8 55..............................(p) JordanNason(5) 1 55
(Marjorie Fife) *t.k.h: trckd ldrs: drvn over 2f out: no ex fnl f* **6/1**[3]
0006 8 ¾ **Yorkshireman (IRE)**[18] 6119 4-8-10 49..............................(b[1]) JackGarritty(5) 6 48
(Lynn Siddall) *hld up towards rr: pushed along 2f out: nvr able to chal* **40/1**
-600 9 ¾ **Spithead**[63] 4069 4-9-3 51.............................. JamesSullivan 2 48
(Mike Sowersby) *plld hrd in midfield: smooth hdwy over 2f out: sn rdn: wknd fnl f* **50/1**
6350 10 1 **Elizabeth Coffee (IRE)**[31] 5678 6-9-12 60.............................. MartinHarley 7 56
(John Weymes) *trckd ldrs: rdn over 2f out: wknd over 1f out* **20/1**
005/ 11 1¼ **Salford Dream**[837] 2895 5-9-5 53.............................. GrahamLee 11 47
(Pauline Robson) *t.k.h: hld up: pushed along over 2f out: sn btn* **25/1**
-22 12 2¼ **Ptolomeos**[114] 2806 11-8-5 46.............................. AnnaHesketh(7) 13 36
(Sean Regan) *hld up: stdy hdwy wl over 2f out: rdn and wknd over 1f out* **25/1**

2m 50.79s (5.19) **Going Correction** 0.0s/f (Good)
**WFA** 3 from 4yo+ 8lb **12 Ran SP% 125.6**
Speed ratings (Par 101): **82,81,78,78,78 77,77,76,76,75 74,73**
CSF £56.44 CT £118.75 TOTE £3.20: £2.20, £7.40, £1.50; EX 56.90 Trifecta £229.60.
**Owner** Charles C Walker - Osborne House **Bred** Norelands, Marston & A V Nicoll **Trained** Newmarket, Suffolk

**FOCUS**
Moderate stuff. The third and fourth help set the level.
T/Jkpt: Not won. T/Plt: £61.90 to a £1 stake. Pool: £63,661.74 - 750.07 winning tickets T/Qpdt: £4.10 to a £1 stake. Pool: £6,926.12 - 1,232.80 winning tickets RY

# 5397 NOTTINGHAM (L-H)
Tuesday, September 23

**OFFICIAL GOING: Good to firm (7.5)**
Wind: Light against Weather: Fine & dry

## 6645 RACING UK ANYWHERE AVAILABLE NOW (S) STKS 5f 13y
2:00 (2:01) (Class 6) 2-Y-O £2,045 (£603; £302) Stalls High

Form RPR
4000 1 **Essaka (IRE)**[7] 6422 2-8-11 64.............................. RichardHughes 7 56
(Mick Channon) *dwlt and t.k.h early: towards rr: hdwy to chse ldrs 2f out: rdn over 1f out: styd on wl fnl f: led nr line* **4/6**[1]
2460 2 shd **Penalty Scorer**[22] 5985 2-8-3 48.............................. NeilFarley(3) 8 51
(Richard Guest) *trckd ldng pair: hdwy to ld wl over 1f out: rdn ent fnl f: hdd nr line* **10/1**
0510 3 nk **Smart Stepper (IRE)**[32] 5630 2-9-2 60.............................. PaulMulrennan 6 60
(Michael Dods) *led: pushed along and hdd wl over 1f out: sn rdn: kpt on u.p fnl f* **7/1**[3]
0000 4 1 **Pancake Day**[14] 6212 2-8-8 48.............................. JoeyHaynes(3) 9 51
(Jason Ward) *chsd ldrs: rdn along 2f out: drvn over 1f out: kpt on* **50/1**
006 5 1 **Wiggle**[43] 5255 2-8-7 0 ow1..............................(b[1]) StevieDonohoe 2 44
(Tim Pitt) *dwlt and in rr: rdn along 1/2-way: styd on fr over 1f out: nrst fin* **50/1**
6033 6 nk **Strategise (IRE)**[3] 6563 2-8-6 55..............................(p) FrannyNorton 1 42
(Tom Dascombe) *chsd ldrs: rdn along wl over 1f out: drvn and one pce fnl f* **6/1**[2]
6000 7 2¾ **Toytown (IRE)**[8] 6413 2-8-11 56..............................(v[1]) DaleSwift 4 37
(Derek Shaw) *chsd ldrs: rdn along 2f out: sn drvn and wknd over 1f out* **25/1**
0060 8 1¼ **Emilys Girl (IRE)**[12] 6248 2-8-6 45.............................. RaulDaSilva 5 27
(Ronald Harris) *sn rdn along and outpcd: a in rr* **50/1**
0165 9 19 **Jimmy's Girl (IRE)**[21] 6017 2-8-6 60.............................. CamHardie(5) 3
(Chris Dwyer) *chsd ldr: rdn along over 2f out: sn wknd* **8/1**

1m 2.53s (1.03) **Going Correction** -0.175s/f (Firm) **9 Ran SP% 116.7**
Speed ratings (Par 93): **84,83,83,81,80 79,75,73,42**
CSF £8.44 TOTE £1.20: £1.10, £2.70, £5.10; EX 8.50 Trifecta £59.30.There was no bid for the winner.
**Owner** Box 41 **Bred** Dream Vision Partnership **Trained** West Ilsley, Berks

**FOCUS**
Outer track used and distances as advertised. Richard Hughes described the ground as "beautiful". They raced stands' side in what was a lowly seller.

## 6646 AWESOME AUTUMN 2FOR£10 AT NOTTINGHAM RACECOURSE MAIDEN AUCTION STKS 1m 75y
2:30 (2:32) (Class 5) 2-Y-O £2,726 (£805; £402) Stalls Centre

Form RPR
2 1 **Frantical**[34] 5555 2-8-11 0.............................. TomQueally 9 63
(Luke Dace) *hld up: hdwy to trck ldrs over 3f out: rdn to chse ldr jst over 1f out: styd on ins fnl f: led nr fin* **8/1**
00 2 hd **Simone On Time (IRE)**[20] 6024 2-8-9 0.............................. RenatoSouza 11 61
(Sylvester Kirk) *cl up: led wl over 3f out: rdn wl over 1f out: drvn ins fnl f: hdd and no ex towards fin* **100/1**
5 3 1¼ **Ventura Castle**[30] 5718 2-9-3 0.............................. RichardHughes 6 66
(Richard Hannon) *hld up towards rr: hdwy wl over 2f out: pushed along to chse ldrs wl over 1f out: rdn and kpt on fnl f* **7/4**[1]
05 4 ½ **Perceived**[22] 5981 2-8-4 0.............................. AmyScott(3) 1 55
(Henry Candy) *trckd ldrs: swtchd rt and hdwy 3f out: chsd ldrs 2f out: sn rdn: drvn and kpt on same pce fnl f* **7/2**[3]
6 5 3¼ **Three Gracez**[22] 5982 2-8-7 0.............................. PaulHanagan 8 48
(Noel Quinlan) *towards rr: hdwy wl over 2f out: rdn wl over 1f out: kpt on fnl f: nrst fin* **20/1**
62 6 nk **Multistar**[22] 5982 2-8-8 0.............................. AshleyMorgan(3) 4 51
(Chris Wall) *dwlt and in rr: hdwy and pushed along on inner wl over 2f out: rdn wl over 1f out: plugged on: n.d* **5/2**[2]
066 7 ¾ **New Abbey Dancer (IRE)**[48] 5056 2-8-3 45..........(p) DanielMuscutt(5) 2 46
(Gay Kelleway) *chsd ldrs: rdn along over 3f out: sn one pce* **100/1**
060 8 1 **Avenue Des Champs**[18] 6102 2-8-11 45..........(p) CamHardie(5) 3 52
(Jane Chapple-Hyam) *sn led: pushed along and hdd over 3f out: rdn over 2f out and sn wknd* **100/1**
6 9 1¾ **Celestial Magic**[18] 6085 2-8-11 0.............................. WilliamTwiston-Davies 7 43
(Jonathan Portman) *hld up in rr: sme hdwy on outer and in tch 3f out: rdn along over 2f out and sn wknd* **33/1**

0 **10** *hd* **Mysterious Star (FR)**[18] 6085 2-8-13 0 FergusSweeney 5 45
(Martyn Meade) *trckd ldrs: hdwy over 3f out: cl up and rdn along 2f out: sn drvn and wknd* 33/1

1m 48.12s (-0.88) **Going Correction** -0.175s/f (Firm) 10 Ran SP% **111.9**
Speed ratings (Par 95): **97,96,95,95,91 91,90,89,88,87**
CSF £577.65 TOTE £6.70: £2.00, £16.40, £1.10; EX 330.60 Trifecta £2155.90.
**Owner** Mrs Charles Cyzer **Bred** L J Vaessen **Trained** Okehurst Lane, W Sussex

**FOCUS**
Little got into what was just a modest maiden.

## 6647 DOWNLOAD NEW RACING UK IPAD APP H'CAP 1m 75y
**3:00** (3:03) (Class 6) (0-65,71) 3-Y-O £1,940 (£577; £288; £144) Stalls Centre

Form RPR
2441 **1** **Trinity Star (IRE)**[4] 6516 3-9-13 71 6ex (p) PaulMulrennan 10 79+
(Michael Dods) *in tch: hdwy to trck ldrs over 3f out: effrt over 1f out: sn ev ch: rdn to ld last 100yds: kpt on* 2/1[1]

4023 **2** *½* **Jersey Brown (IRE)**[10] 6316 3-8-13 64 DanielCremin(7) 1 71
(Mick Channon) *s.i.s and bhd: stdy hdwy over 3f out: swtchd rt wl over 1f out: rdn ent fnl f: styd on wl towards fin* 8/1

3062 **3** *1* **Royal Encounter**[35] 5530 3-9-5 63 RichardKingscote 14 68
(Ed Vaughan) *slt ld: pushed along over 2f out: rdn wl over 1f out: drvn ent fnl f: hdd and no ex last 100yds* 5/1[2]

2300 **4** *1 ¾* **Rockie Road (IRE)**[49] 4998 3-8-7 51 PaoloSirigu 11 52
(Mick Quinn) *hld up towards rr: hdwy on outer 3f out: rdn to chse ldrs over 1f out: drvn and one pce fnl f* 25/1

0620 **5** *nk* **Sweet Lily Pea (USA)**[21] 6022 3-8-10 54 LemosdeSouza 2 54
(Mrs Ilka Gansera-Leveque) *cl up: chal 3f out: rdn 2f out and ev ch tl drvn ent fnl f and grad wknd* 25/1

0352 **6** *hd* **Dutch Lady**[25] 5892 3-9-1 59 PatrickMathers 7 59
(John Holt) *in tch on inner: pushed along and outpcd over 3f out: rdn over 2f out: kpt on u.p appr fnl f: nrst fin* 10/1

5034 **7** *shd* **Norfolk Sound**[25] 5891 3-8-8 59 SamuelClarke(7) 5 59
(Chris Wall) *chsd ldrs: rdn along wl over 2f out: drvn over 1f out and sn one pce* 7/1[3]

5540 **8** *2 ¾* **Djinni (IRE)**[29] 5751 3-9-7 65 (b) RichardHughes 4 58
(Richard Hannon) *trckd ldrs: hdwy over 3f out: rdn along over 2f out: drvn wl over 1f out: sn btn* 14/1

5065 **9** *nk* **Aya's Gift**[38] 5423 3-8-11 55 (b) PatCosgrave 12 48
(Ed Walker) *a towards rr* 33/1

3206 **10** *nk* **Chess Valley**[22] 5980 3-9-7 65 StevieDonohoe 9 57
(Willie Musson) *a towards rr* 20/1

0002 **11** *¾* **Sarlat**[26] 5846 3-8-4 51 oh5 AmyScott(3) 3 41
(Mark Brisbourne) *trckd ldng pair: rdn along over 2f out: wknd over 1f out* 25/1

3645 **12** *1* **Dark Phantom (IRE)**[27] 5833 3-8-2 51 oh6 CamHardie(5) 6 39
(Peter Makin) *chsd ldrs: rdn along 3f out: sn wknd* 20/1

4200 **13** *11* **Flawless Pink**[20] 6037 3-9-7 65 (p) TomQueally 13 28
(Jeremy Noseda) *midfield: hdwy on outer over 3f out: rdn along over 2f out: sn drvn and wknd* 12/1

1m 45.85s (-3.15) **Going Correction** -0.175s/f (Firm) 13 Ran SP% **121.1**
Speed ratings (Par 99): **108,107,106,104,104 104,104,101,101,100 100,99,88**
CSF £16.18 CT £76.41 TOTE £2.90: £1.60, £2.70, £1.70; EX 18.40 Trifecta £138.90.
**Owner** Trinity Racing **Bred** Ms Natalie Cleary **Trained** Denton, Co Durham

**FOCUS**
A race that set up for the closers. The third helps set the standard.

## 6648 NOTTINGHAM RACECOURSE SHERWOODS RESTAURANT NURSERY H'CAP 1m 1f
**3:30** (3:30) (Class 5) (0-75,75) 2-Y-O £2,587 (£770; £384; £192) Stalls Low

Form RPR
4355 **1** **Maftoon (IRE)**[19] 6064 2-9-7 **75** PaulHanagan 2 79+
(Richard Hannon) *hld up: hdwy 3f out: n.m.r 2f out: swtchd rt and effrt over 1f out: sn rdn and styd on strly to ld last 100yds* 3/1[1]

6602 **2** *1 ¼* **Hillgrove Angel (IRE)**[14] 6205 2-8-13 **67** PaulMulrennan 1 69
(David Evans) *trckd ldrs: hdwy on inner over 2f out: rdn to ld appr fnl f: sn drvn: hdd and no ex last 100yds* 33/1

4554 **3** *nk* **Gea And Tea**[5] 6499 2-8-9 **68** (p) NoelGarbutt(5) 9 69
(Robert Eddery) *plld hrd: towards rr: hdwy on outer over 3f out: effrt 2f out: sn rdn and ev ch tl drvn ins fnl f and kpt on same pce* 12/1

043 **4** *1 ½* **Referendum (IRE)**[25] 5886 2-8-11 **70** CamHardie(5) 11 68
(Sir Michael Stoute) *prom: chsd ldr over 5f out: cl up 3f out: rdn to ld briefly wl over 1f out: hdd and drvn appr fnl f: sn one pce* 9/2[2]

555 **5** *nk* **Cosmic Statesman**[17] 6146 2-8-7 **61** PatrickMathers 12 58+
(Richard Fahey) *awkward s and bhd: hdwy on outer over 3f out: rdn over 2f out: drvn and kpt on appr fnl f: nrst fin* 16/1

3445 **6** *½* **Diatomic (IRE)**[28] 5798 2-8-9 **63** RichardKingscote 3 59
(Tom Dascombe) *hld up towards rr: hdwy over 2f out: rdn wl over 1f out: kpt on fnl f: nrst fin* 50/1

4552 **7** *½* **Romance Story (IRE)**[12] 6250 2-8-11 **65** FrannyNorton 6 60
(Saeed bin Suroor) *trckd ldrs: pushed along over 3f out: rdn over 2f out: sn btn* 3/1[1]

4020 **8** *nk* **Stolen Story (IRE)**[25] 5875 2-9-5 **73** TomQueally 4 68
(George Margarson) *t.k.h: hld up towards rr: hdwy on outer 1/2-way: chsd ldrs 3f out: rdn 2f out: sn edgd lft and wknd over 1f out* 20/1

0336 **9** *nse* **Cahill (IRE)**[18] 6101 2-9-6 **74** WilliamTwiston-Davies 10 69
(Alan King) *led: pushed along and jnd wl over 2f out: rdn and hdd wl over 1f out: grad wknd* 8/1[3]

334 **10** *3* **Horsetracker**[9] 6364 2-8-13 **67** StevieDonohoe 5 56
(Ian Williams) *chsd ldrs: rdn along wl over 2f out: sn wknd* 33/1

044 **11** *8* **Arracourt**[17] 6146 2-8-10 **64** RichardHughes 7 37
(Tim Easterby) *trckd ldrs: hdwy 3f out and sn cl up: rdn 2f out and sn wknd* 8/1[3]

1m 56.44s (-1.16) 11 Ran SP% **116.6**
CSF £117.93 CT £1071.63 TOTE £3.20: £1.30, £6.60, £4.30; EX 120.50 Trifecta £1812.30.
**Owner** Hamdan Al Maktoum **Bred** Glebe Farm Stud **Trained** East Everleigh, Wilts

**FOCUS**
A fair nursery that was run at just an ordinary gallop.

## 6649 JOIN US FOR CONSTRUCTION DAY 15TH OCTOBER H'CAP 1m 2f 50y
**4:05** (4:05) (Class 4) (0-80,79) 3-Y-O+ £5,175 (£1,540; £769; £384) Stalls Low

Form RPR
-212 **1** **Daisy Boy (IRE)**[40] 5336 3-8-0 66 CamHardie(5) 6 76+
(Stuart Williams) *cl up: led after 2f and sn wl clr: pushed along wl over 2f out: sn rdn: hdd jst over 1f out: drvn ins fnl f: rallied gamely to ld again nr fin* 7/2[2]

2212 **2** *nk* **Hesbaan (IRE)**[15] 6192 3-9-2 77 PaulHanagan 5 86
(Marcus Tregoning) *led 2f: styd 2nd bhd clr ldr: hdwy over 3f out: tk clsr order 2f out: led jst over 1f out: rdn ins fnl f: hdd and no ex towards fin* 15/8[1]

0041 **3** *3 ¾* **Karam Albaari (IRE)**[11] 6303 6-9-7 76 (p) PaddyAspell 1 78
(J R Jenkins) *hld up: hdwy over 3f out: rdn over 2f out: styd on appr fnl f: nrst fin* 8/1

1124 **4** *3 ¼* **Bahamian C**[27] 5810 3-9-2 77 PaulMulrennan 8 73
(Richard Fahey) *chsd ldrs: rdn along over 3f out: drvn over 2f out: one pce* 6/1

4-00 **5** *5* **Northern Star (IRE)**[28] 5792 4-9-10 79 FrannyNorton 4 65
(John Mackie) *chsd ldrs: rdn along 3f out: drvn 2f out and sn wknd* 33/1

4526 **6** *4 ½* **Dalaki (IRE)**[20] 6034 3-8-11 72 (b) RichardHughes 3 50
(Clive Brittain) *in tch: rdn along over 3f out: sn outpcd* 9/2[3]

0342 **7** *2 ½* **Zafranagar (IRE)**[113] 2834 9-8-7 67 GeorgeDowning(5) 2 40
(Ian Williams) *s.i.s: a bhd* 16/1

2m 9.76s (-4.54) **Going Correction** -0.175s/f (Firm)
**WFA** 3 from 4yo+ 6lb 7 Ran SP% **109.4**
Speed ratings (Par 105): **111,110,107,105,101 97,95**
CSF £9.53 CT £41.42 TOTE £6.40: £3.20, £1.10; EX 12.70 Trifecta £21.40.
**Owner** G Johnson **Bred** Shadwell Estate Company Limited **Trained** Newmarket, Suffolk

**FOCUS**
Bit of a strange race with the winner pulling his way into a clear lead before battling back having been headed. The third has been rated close to his Sandown form.

## 6650 VIP HOSPITALITY BOXES AT NOTTINGHAM RACECOURSE H'CAP 5f 13y
**4:35** (4:35) (Class 4) (0-80,80) 3-Y-O+ £4,851 (£1,443; £721; £360) Stalls High

Form RPR
3500 **1** **Mutafaakir (IRE)**[13] 6235 5-9-6 79 (b) DaleSwift 6 90
(Ruth Carr) *swtchd rt to stands' rail sn after s: mde most: rdn clr over 1f out: kpt on* 5/1[3]

0602 **2** *1 ¾* **Monumental Man**[10] 6324 5-9-1 79 (p) DanielMuscutt(5) 11 84
(James Unett) *racd towards stands' rail: trckd ldrs: hdwy 2f out: rdn to chse wnr ent fnl f: sn drvn and no imp towards fin* 7/2[2]

5501 **3** *nk* **Tyfos**[10] 6324 9-9-7 80 PaulHanagan 5 84
(Brian Baugh) *prom: rdn along wl over 1f out: drvn ent fnl f: kpt on same pce* 10/1

4043 **4** *½* **Ubetterbegood (ARG)**[35] 5535 6-8-5 69 (v) CamHardie(5) 4 71
(Robert Cowell) *hld up: hdwy on outer wl over 1f out: sn rdn: kpt on fnl f: nrst fin* 8/1

5110 **5** *1* **Dawn Catcher**[56] 4762 4-8-10 76 PaddyPilley(7) 1 74
(Geoffrey Deacon) *wnt lft s: racd towards centre: prom: rdn along wl over 1f out: drvn and wknd fnl f* 20/1

650 **6** *1* **Swendab (IRE)**[10] 6313 6-9-1 74 (p) StevieDonohoe 8 69
(John O'Shea) *dwlt and in rr: rdn along over 2f out: styd on fr wl over 1f out: nrst fin* 20/1

6036 **7** *hd* **Whitecrest**[11] 6296 6-9-0 73 WilliamTwiston-Davies 7 67
(John Spearing) *towards rr: rdn along 2f out: n.d* 20/1

4314 **8** *6* **Emjayem**[10] 6324 4-9-4 77 RichardHughes 9 49
(Ed McMahon) *trckd ldrs: effrt 2f out: sn rdn and btn* 5/2[1]

0100 **9** *1 ½* **Space Artist (IRE)**[18] 6096 4-9-7 80 (v[1]) PaulMulrennan 3 47
(Bryan Smart) *wnt lft s: prom: rdn along 2f out: sn drvn and wknd* 14/1

5000 **10** *12* **Powerful Wind (IRE)**[10] 6313 5-9-4 77 RaulDaSilva 10
(Ronald Harris) *racd towards stands' rail: chsd ldrs: rdn along 1/2-way: sn wknd* 20/1

1m 0.23s (-1.27) **Going Correction** -0.175s/f (Firm) 10 Ran SP% **113.4**
Speed ratings (Par 105): **103,100,99,98,97 95,95,85,83,64**
CSF £20.57 CT £168.73 TOTE £8.60: £1.20, £1.50, £2.20; EX 20.30 Trifecta £106.80.
**Owner** Ms Helen Barbour & Dario Neri **Bred** Shadwell Estate Company Limited **Trained** Huby, N Yorks

**FOCUS**
Little got into this. The runner-up has been rated close to form.

## 6651 WATCH RACINGUK ON SKY CHANNEL 432 H'CAP 1m 6f 15y
**5:05** (5:05) (Class 5) (0-75,75) 3-Y-O+ £2,726 (£805; £402) Stalls Low

Form RPR
4233 **1** **Winter Spice (IRE)**[10] 6318 3-8-10 70 (b) RyanTate(3) 9 83
(Clive Cox) *hld up in rr: stdy hdwy on inner wl over 2f out: rdn to chal ent fnl f: squeezed through to ld fnl 100yds: styd on* 7/2[2]

3446 **2** *1 ¼* **Strawberry Martini**[12] 6274 3-9-0 71 RichardHughes 6 82
(William Muir) *trckd ldr: hdwy and cl up over 3f out: rdn and slt ld wl over 1f out: drvn ent fnl f: hdd and no ex last 100yds* 5/1[3]

3415 **3** *3 ¼* **Hurry Home Poppa (IRE)**[61] 4575 4-9-1 62 FrannyNorton 2 68
(John Mackie) *trckd ldrs: hdwy 4f out: effrt and swtchd rt 2f out: sn rdn to chal and ev ch: drvn ins fnl f and kpt on same pce* 5/2[1]

222 **4** *1 ½* **Rowlestone Lass**[20] 6027 4-8-4 56 oh1 CamHardie(5) 8 60
(Richard Price) *trckd ldrs: hdwy on outer over 3f out: rdn wl over 1f out: drvn and no imp ent fnl f* 8/1

506 **5** *1 ¾* **Desert Recluse (IRE)**[38] 5435 7-9-6 67 (p) StevieDonohoe 5 68
(Ian Williams) *hld up: hdwy on inner over 4f out: swtchd rt to outer wl over 2f out: sn rdn and no imp* 12/1

4026 **6** *¾* **Grand Liaison**[36] 5495 5-9-0 61 PaulHanagan 1 61
(James Given) *t.k.h: trckd ldrs on inner: effrt over 3f out and sn pushed along: rdn 2f out and sn btn* 20/1

2250 **7** *½* **Beat The Tide**[25] 5890 4-10-0 75 (p) PaulMulrennan 4 75
(Michael Dods) *trckd ldrs: cl up 1/2-way: chal 3f out: sn rdn: drvn and wknd wl over 1f out* 7/1

2430 **8** *1 ¼* **Hallstatt (IRE)**[29] 5764 8-9-9 70 (t) DaleSwift 10 68
(John Mackie) *hld up in rr: effrt 3f out: sn rdn along and nvr a factor* 12/1

00P0 **9** *2* **Markami (FR)**[12] 6274 4-9-7 68 PatCosgrave 7 63
(Johnny Farrelly) *led: rdn along 3f out: drvn 2f out: sn hdd & wknd* 100/1

3m 6.3s (-0.70) **Going Correction** -0.175s/f (Firm)
**WFA** 3 from 4yo+ 10lb 9 Ran SP% **112.2**
Speed ratings (Par 103): **95,94,92,91,90 90,89,89,88**
CSF £20.57 CT £49.51 TOTE £3.20: £2.10, £2.30, £1.10; EX 18.10 Trifecta £105.40.
**Owner** Spice Traders **Bred** Irish National Stud **Trained** Lambourn, Berks

**FOCUS**
The right horses came to the fore. The third has been rated close to form.
T/Plt: £43.50 to a £1 stake. Pool: £46,798.94 - 783.82 winning tickets T/Qpdt: £14.50 to a £1 stake. Pool: £3,151.49 - 160.10 winning tickets JR

6001 **GOODWOOD** (R-H)
Wednesday, September 24

**OFFICIAL GOING: Good (good to firm in places on round course; 7.4)**
Wind: fresh against Weather: sunny with cloudy periods

## 6652 BRITISH STALLIONS STUD EBF MAIDEN STKS 7f
2:05 (2:09) (Class 5) 2-Y-O £3,234 (£962; £481; £240) Stalls Low

Form RPR
4 1 **American Artist (IRE)**[20] 6058 2-9-5 0 AndreaAtzeni 8 85+
(Roger Varian) *athletic; trckd ldr: led over 1f out: shkn up and r.o strly fnl f: readily* 15/8[1]
5 2 1 **Quick Defence (USA)**[15] 6204 2-9-5 0 JamesDoyle 5 82+
(Sir Michael Stoute) *str: tall: lw: little slowly away: hld up in last trio: hdwy over 2f out: rdn to chse wnr jst over 1f out: kpt on but a being readily hld* 9/4[2]
25 3 3 3/4 **Frognal Bear (IRE)**[12] 6299 2-9-5 0 RichardHughes 4 73
(Richard Hannon) *leggy: mid-div: hdwy 3f out: swtchd rt and briefly disp 2nd ent fnl f: no ex fnl 100yds* 6/1[3]
4 4 2 **Inke (IRE)**[13] 6261 2-9-0 0 WilliamCarson 3 62
(Jim Boyle) *unf: trckd ldrs: rdn in cl 3rd over 2f out tl ent fnl f: no ex fnl 120yds* 20/1
3 5 1 1/4 **Dutch Robin (IRE)**[10] 6361 2-9-0 0 SamHitchcott 1 58
(Mick Channon) *neat: led: rdn over 2f out: hdd over 1f out: no ex fnl f* 14/1
4 6 2 **Consortium (IRE)**[24] 5947 2-9-5 0 RyanMoore 2 58
(David Simcock) *str: lw: trckd ldrs: rdn over 2f out: wknd jst over 1f out* 13/2
00 7 hd **Quae Supra**[70] 4330 2-9-5 0 PatDobbs 10 57
(Richard Hannon) *leggy: unf: mid-div: rdn over 2f out: nvr any imp: fdd fnl f* 100/1
8 2 1/4 **Gentle Persuasion** 2-9-0 0 JimCrowley 11 46
(Amanda Perrett) *athletic: hld up bhd: rdn and no imp fr over 2f out: wknd fnl f* 25/1
9 1/2 **Hala Madrid** 2-9-0 0 DavidProbert 12 45
(Andrew Balding) *athletic: s.i.s: rcvrd into mid-div after 1f: effrt over 2f out: nvr threatened: wknd ent fnl f* 33/1
10 21 **Arcanman (IRE)** 2-9-5 0 BenCurtis 7
(Ronald Harris) *w'like: bit bkwd: s.i.s: rdn 3f out: a towards rr* 100/1

1m 28.37s (1.37) **Going Correction** +0.075s/f (Good) 10 Ran SP% 113.4
Speed ratings (Par 95): **95,93,89,87,85 83,83,80,80,56**
CSF £5.67 TOTE £2.40: £1.20, £1.40, £2.20; EX 6.60 Trifecta £22.80.
**Owner** Thurloe Thoroughbreds XXXV **Bred** Dayton Investments Ltd **Trained** Newmarket, Suffolk

**FOCUS**
Lower bend dolled out about 6yds from 6f to 2f and distances incorporating that bend increased by about 10yds. The official going was good, good to firm in places on the Round course, although Richard Hughes came back after the first and said "there's no good to firm out there", and the time of the first race was 4.37sec slower than standard. Derby winner Workforce took this maiden five years ago but there was nothing of his calibre in the race this time. The standard makes sense through the third and those in behind.

## 6653 WATERAID EBF STALLIONS MAIDEN STKS (BOBIS RACE) 1m 1f
2:40 (2:40) (Class 4) 2-Y-O £5,175 (£1,540; £769; £384) Stalls Low

Form RPR
552 1 **Dissolution**[20] 6056 2-9-5 80 (v[1]) JamesDoyle 6 80
(Sir Michael Stoute) *pushed along leaving stalls: trckd ldr: pushed into narrow ld over 1f out: rdn ins fnl f: hld on: all out* 4/6[1]
024 2 shd **Shadow Rock (IRE)**[12] 6293 2-9-5 77 RichardHughes 1 80
(Richard Hannon) *led: rdn and hdd over 1f out: kpt pressing wnr: rallied gamely fnl 120yds: jst hld* 14/1
3 3 1/4 **Ya Hade Ye Delil** 2-9-5 0 FrankieDettori 2 75+
(Richard Hannon) *lengthy: str: slowly away: sn trcking ldrs: pushed along over 2f out: kpt on but nt gng pce to chal front pair* 8/1[3]
2 4 3 1/2 **Constable Buckley**[40] 5377 2-9-5 0 SamHitchcott 4 67
(Mick Channon) *lw: trckd ldrs: rdn 3f out: tended to hang rt: nvr threatened: one pce fnl 2f* 7/2[2]
5 1/2 **Scarlet Minstrel** 2-9-5 0 DavidProbert 3 66
(Andrew Balding) *cl cpld: trckd ldrs: rdn over 2f out: nvr threatened: kpt on same pce* 33/1
6 4 1/2 **Atalan** 2-9-5 0 RyanMoore 5 57
(Hughie Morrison) *angular: lengthy: hld up in last but wl in tch: struggling over 3f out: outpcd over 2f out* 14/1

1m 58.27s (1.97) **Going Correction** +0.075s/f (Good) 6 Ran SP% 109.6
Speed ratings (Par 97): **94,93,91,87,87 83**
CSF £11.02 TOTE £1.70: £1.10, £3.20; EX 9.30 Trifecta £22.10.
**Owner** K Abdullah **Bred** Juddmonte Farms Ltd **Trained** Newmarket, Suffolk

**FOCUS**
This didn't look the strongest of maidens for the track, with the odds-on favourite officially rated 80. It's been rated at face value, with the runner-up helping to set the level.

## 6654 HILDON NATURAL MINERAL WATER STKS (H'CAP) (BOBIS RACE) 1m 3f
3:15 (3:15) (Class 4) (0-80,80) 3-Y-O £6,469 (£1,925; £962; £481) Stalls High

Form RPR
1152 1 **Serena Grae**[11] 6315 3-9-5 78 MartinDwyer 4 89
(Marcus Tregoning) *mde most: rdn whn chal over 1f out: hdd narrowly jst ins fnl f: edgd lft: kpt on gamely to regain ld cl home* 4/1[2]
1 2 nk **Spacelab**[28] 5831 3-9-7 80 JamesDoyle 1 91
(Amanda Perrett) *str: lw: trckd wnr: pushed along over 2f out: led narrowly jst ins fnl f: sn rdn: no ex whn hdd cl home* 15/8[1]
2211 3 nk **King Calypso**[21] 6037 3-8-2 66 CamHardie(5) 5 76
(Denis Coakley) *disp 4th: rdn into 3rd over 1f out: nt quite pce to chal but kpt on wl and clsng fnl 100yds* 4/1[2]
3032 4 5 **Starlit Cantata**[35] 5557 3-8-13 72 RyanMoore 3 74
(Eve Johnson Houghton) *disp 4th: rdn 2f out: disp 3rd briefly over 1f out: kpt on same pce fnl f* 6/1[3]
6400 5 5 **Strait Run (IRE)**[62] 4574 3-8-11 70 RichardHughes 6 64
(Richard Hannon) *hld up in last: effrt to cl over 3f out: nvr threatened: wnt btn 5th nring fin* 14/1
1645 6 hd **Golden Journey (IRE)**[14] 6239 3-8-13 75 RyanTate(3) 2 69
(Clive Cox) *lw: trckd ldng pair: rdn over 2f out: lost 3rd over 1f out: wknd fnl f* 15/2

2m 27.31s (0.81) **Going Correction** +0.075s/f (Good) 6 Ran SP% 107.5
Speed ratings (Par 103): **100,99,99,95,92 92**
CSF £10.89 TOTE £5.20: £2.00, £1.60; EX 12.00 Trifecta £33.10.
**Owner** Mrs Heather Raw **Bred** Heather Raw **Trained** Whitsbury, Hants

**FOCUS**
A fair handicap. The principals are generally progressive and have been rated a tad positively.

## 6655 R H HALL FOUNDATION STKS (LISTED RACE) 1m 1f 192y
3:50 (3:50) (Class 1) 3-Y-O+ £22,684 (£8,600; £4,304; £2,144; £1,076; £540) Stalls Low

Form RPR
342 1 **Grandeur (IRE)**[74] 4231 5-9-2 113 (p) RyanMoore 3 111+
(Jeremy Noseda) *hld up in last pair: tk clsr order 3f out: nudged along to ld ent fnl f: shkn up to assert fnl 150yds: comf* 4/5[1]
3653 2 2 **Danadana (IRE)**[18] 6163 6-9-2 109 AndreaAtzeni 1 107
(Luca Cumani) *lw: trckd ldrs: rdn over 2f out: wnt 3rd ent fnl f: kpt on into 2nd towards fin but no ch w wnr* 4/1[2]
1106 3 nk **Marsh Daisy**[38] 5479 3-8-5 104 SilvestreDeSousa 4 102
(Hughie Morrison) *trckd ldrs: rdn to dispute 2f out tl enteiring fnl f: sn hld by wnr: no ex whn lost 2nd towards fin* 8/1[3]
1310 4 3 1/2 **Be My Gal**[36] 5545 3-8-8 107 JamesDoyle 5 98
(Roger Charlton) *lw: led for 4f: trckd ldrs: rdn to dispute ld 2f out tl ent fnl f: fdd* 4/1[2]
0610 5 1 1/4 **Nancy From Nairobi**[18] 6127 3-8-5 89 JoeFanning 6 93
(Mick Channon) *lw: sn trcking ldr: led after 4f: rdn and hdd 2f out: wknd fnl f* 33/1
/00- 6 11 **Salam Alaykum (IRE)**[342] 6121 6-9-2 90 PatDobbs 2 77
(Gary Moore) *s.i.s: last but in tch: rdn over 3f out: sn hld* 80/1

2m 5.8s (-2.30) **Going Correction** +0.075s/f (Good)
**WFA** 3 from 5yo+ 6lb 6 Ran SP% 110.8
Speed ratings: **112,110,110,107,106 97**
CSF £4.23 TOTE £1.70: £1.30, £2.50; EX 3.80 Trifecta £14.80.
**Owner** Miss Yvonne Jacques **Bred** Mrs Cherry Faeste **Trained** Newmarket, Suffolk

**FOCUS**
This could be rated a few lengths higher but the winner always looked in control and the impression is that he did not need to be quite at his peak to prevail.

## 6656 GENTRACK VELOCITY STKS (H'CAP) 1m 4f
4:25 (4:25) (Class 2) (0-105,98) 3-Y-O+ £12,938 (£3,850; £1,924; £962) Stalls High

Form RPR
5523 1 **Noble Gift**[21] 6036 4-9-2 86 AndreaAtzeni 7 93
(William Knight) *taken to s early: stdd s: racd keenly: detached in last tl hdwy to ld 6f out: qcknd pce over 3f out: 3 l clr ent fnl f: a holding on: rdn out* 4/1[2]
2552 2 nk **Jacob Cats**[18] 6141 5-8-10 80 (v) JimCrowley 3 86
(William Knight) *hld up: hdwy 3f out: sn rdn: disp 2nd ent fnl f: kpt on wl fnl 120yds: nvr quite getting there* 8/1
0662 3 1 **Blue Surf**[22] 6005 5-10-0 98 PatDobbs 6 102
(Amanda Perrett) *lw: trckd ldrs: rdn 2f out: nvr quite gng pce to chal: kpt on ins fnl f* 9/2[3]
1060 4 nk **From Frost**[32] 5691 3-8-3 81 (vt) DavidProbert 5 85
(Andrew Balding) *hld up in tch: last over 5f out: swittched to centre over 3f out and hdwy: rdn and lost pl over 2f out: styd on wl fnl 160yds: snatched 4th fnl stride* 13/2
2003 5 shd **Pack Leader (IRE)**[30] 5757 3-8-10 88 SilvestreDeSousa 4 92
(Amanda Perrett) *trckd ldrs: rdn 3f out: wandered u.p thrght fnl f: keeping on at same pce and hld fnl 100yds: lost 4th fnl stride* 9/2[3]
3120 6 7 **Rainbow Rock (IRE)**[18] 6127 3-8-8 86 (v) JoeFanning 1 79
(Mark Johnston) *lw: trckd ldrs: rdn to chse wnr over 2f out: wknd ins fnl f* 11/4[1]
7 37 **Kingdom (IRE)**[402] 5572 4-9-10 94 GeorgeBaker 2 27
(Gary Moore) *str: led tl 6f out: trckd wnr tl rdn 3f out: sn wknd: eased fnl f* 20/1

2m 39.09s (0.69) **Going Correction** +0.075s/f (Good)
**WFA** 3 from 4yo+ 8lb 7 Ran SP% 112.2
Speed ratings (Par 109): **100,99,99,98,98 94,69**
CSF £33.64 TOTE £5.10: £2.70, £3.20; EX 35.90 Trifecta £114.90.
**Owner** Gail Brown Racing (V) **Bred** Theakston Stud **Trained** Patching, W Sussex
■ Stewards' Enquiry : Silvestre De Sousa two-day ban: use of whip (8-9 Oct)

**FOCUS**
This was always likely to be run at a steady gallop considering the lack of potential front-runners. Very ordinary form for the grade.

## 6657 BIDVEST 3663 STKS (H'CAP) 7f
4:55 (4:57) (Class 4) (0-80,80) 3-Y-O+ £6,469 (£1,925; £962; £481) Stalls Low

Form RPR
4540 1 **Good Luck Charm**[23] 5986 5-9-1 74 (b[1]) RyanMoore 1 85
(Gary Moore) *hld up towards rr: hdwy whn nt clr run fr 2f out: squeezed through gap jst over 1f out: qcknd up wl to ld jst ins fnl f: r.o* 4/1[1]
0611 2 1/2 **Ganymede**[12] 6297 3-8-10 72 (b) JimCrowley 10 81
(Eve Johnson Houghton) *mid-div: rdn and hdwy over 2f out: disp 2nd ent fnl f: kpt on wl clsng stages but a being hld* 9/1
300 3 2 1/4 **Bravo Echo**[18] 6140 8-9-6 79 RobertHavlin 2 83
(Michael Attwater) *lw: led: rdn over 2f out: kpt on tl hdd jst ins fnl f: no ex whn lost 2nd sn after* 6/1[2]
1034 4 2 1/2 **Living Leader**[20] 6070 5-8-9 68 (tp) OisinMurphy 14 65
(Grace Harris) *slowly away fr wd draw: bhd: carried wd ent st: sn rdn: stdy prog fr 2f out: r.o fnl f: wnt 4th fnl stride* 6/1[2]
0063 5 nse **Welsh Sunrise**[7] 6463 4-8-9 68 (v) SilvestreDeSousa 6 65
(Stuart Williams) *mid-div: hdwy over 3f out: rdn over 2f out: styd on same pce fnl f: lost 4th fnl stride* 14/1
1522 6 1 1/2 **Parisian Pyramid (IRE)**[13] 6263 8-8-13 75 (p) ThomasBrown(3) 5 68
(Lee Carter) *trckd ldr: rdn 3f out: kpt on but nt pce to chal: no ex fnl f* 6/1[2]
5160 7 1 1/4 **Supersta**[33] 5629 3-8-11 73 BenCurtis 11 61
(Ronald Harris) *s.i.s: towards rr: rdn over 3f out: hdwy fr over 2f out but nt best of runs: kpt on same pce fnl f* 33/1
6003 8 shd **Shifting Star (IRE)**[16] 6191 9-8-8 67 (vt) WilliamCarson 7 57
(John Bridger) *mid-div: hmpd whn rdn wl over 1f out: no imp after* 20/1
6435 9 1 3/4 **Shamahan**[11] 6313 5-9-0 73 SteveDrowne 3 57
(Luke Dace) *trckd ldrs: rdn over 2f out: wknd ent fnl f* 14/1
1231 10 2 1/2 **Pour La Victoire (IRE)**[9] 6397 4-8-2 66 6ex (b) CamHardie(5) 13 44
(Tony Carroll) *trckd ldrs: rdn wl over 2f out: wknd jst over 1f out* 8/1[3]
105 11 hd **Bountybeamadam**[37] 5505 4-9-4 77 (p) PatCosgrave 4 54
(George Baker) *mid-div: rdn 3f out: wknd over 1f out* 16/1
0410 12 3/4 **Fantasy Justifier (IRE)**[21] 6025 3-8-9 71 ChrisCatlin 9 45+
(Ronald Harris) *s.i.s: towards rr: carried wd ent st: nvr rcvrd* 50/1
101 13 3/4 **Belle Bayardo (IRE)**[19] 6088 6-8-12 71 JoeFanning 8 44+
(Tony Carroll) *taken to s early: hld up towards rr: smething amiss and plld wd ent st: immediately eased off* 12/1

0163 **14** *2 ½* **Double Czech (IRE)**[30] 5753 3-8-9 71..........................(v) LiamKeniry 12 36
(Patrick Chamings) *chsd ldrs: rdn over 2f out: wknd wl over 1f out* **50/1**

1m 26.12s (-0.88) **Going Correction** +0.075s/f (Good)
**WFA** 3 from 4yo+ 3lb **14** Ran SP% **122.5**
Speed ratings (Par 105): **108,107,104,102,101 100,98,98,96,93 93,92,91,89**
CSF £39.59 CT £223.90 TOTE £5.10: £2.10, £2.60, £2.10; EX 54.00 Trifecta £155.80.
**Owner** Heart Of The South Racing **Bred** John And Caroline Penny **Trained** Lower Beeding, W Sussex

**FOCUS**
There was a fair amount of pace on here. The third set his usual decent pace and ran well again. He looks the key to the level.

## 6658 CLANCY DOCWRA APPRENTICE STKS (H'CAP) 5f
**5:25** (5:25) (Class 5) (0-75,74) 3-Y-0+ **£3,234** (£962; £481; £240) **Stalls** High

Form RPR

0155 **1** **Dishy Guru**[7] 6455 5-8-12 65..........................(b) ThomasBrown 7 74
(Michael Blanshard) *chsd ldrs: rdn 2f out: led ins fnl f: pushed out fnl 120yds* **10/1**

6541 **2** *¾* **Lady Phill**[27] 5861 4-8-11 67.......................... LouisSteward(3) 3 71
(Michael Attwater) *racd alone in centre: chsd ldrs: rdn over 2f out: led over 1f out: kpt on whn hdd ins fnl f: hld nring fin* **7/1**

3052 **3** *2 ½* **Pucon**[12] 6296 5-9-4 74.......................... MarcMonaghan(3) 6 69+
(Roger Teal) *led: rdn and hdd over 1f out: kpt on same pce fnl f* **8/1**

5023 **4** *½* **Waseem Faris (IRE)**[12] 6296 5-9-0 72.......................... DanielCremin(5) 1 66
(Mick Channon) *hld up: rdn over 2f out: no imp tl r.o fnl f: nvr threatened* **7/2**[1]

006 **5** *1* **Valmina**[21] 6025 7-8-9 65..........................(t) CamHardie(3) 5 55
(Tony Carroll) *hld up: rdn over 2f out: hdwy over 1f out: kpt on same pce fnl f* **9/2**[3]

0063 **6** *1* **Howyadoingnotsobad (IRE)**[9] 6399 6-8-8 66.......... RyanWhile(5) 10 52
(Bill Turner) *chsd ldrs: rdn over 2f out: sn one pce* **16/1**

5532 **7** *1 ¾* **Dreams Of Glory**[7] 6455 6-9-2 69..........................(b) OisinMurphy 9 55
(Ron Hodges) *prom: rdn and hung rt fr 2f out: hld over 1f out: hanging quite bdly whn eased fnl 120yds* **4/1**[2]

2406 **8** *3 ¼* **Top Cop**[13] 6249 5-9-2 69..........................(p) WilliamTwiston-Davies 8 37
(Ronald Harris) *in tch: rdn over 2f out: wknd over 1f out* **12/1**

0450 **9** *nk* **Chelwood Gate (IRE)**[14] 6236 4-8-12 70..........................(v) RobHornby(5) 4 37
(Patrick Chamings) *in tch tl wknd 2f out* **9/1**

58.3s (-1.90) **Going Correction** +0.075s/f (Good) **9** Ran SP% **116.7**
Speed ratings (Par 103): **118,116,112,112,110 108,106,100,100**
CSF £78.65 CT £597.03 TOTE £10.70: £3.50, £2.10, £2.10; EX 88.60 Trifecta £501.40.
**Owner** Clifton Partners **Bred** J W Ford **Trained** Upper Lambourn, Berks

**FOCUS**
A modest sprint handicap. Strightforward form.
T/Plt: £23.00 to a £1 stake. Pool: £71,389.22 - 2,257.70 winning tickets T/Qpdt: £13.20 to a £1 stake. Pool: £4,978.68 - 277.22 winning tickets TM

# 6602 KEMPTON (A.W) (R-H)
## Wednesday, September 24

**OFFICIAL GOING: Polytrack: standard**
Wind: almost nil Weather: clear

## 6659 BETBRIGHT.COM MAIDEN STKS 5f (P)
**5:50** (5:55) (Class 5) 2-Y-0 **£2,587** (£770; £384; £192) **Stalls** Low

Form RPR

422 **1** **Field Game**[18] 6158 2-9-5 79..........................(t) RichardKingscote 8 87+
(Hughie Morrison) *mde all: rdn and qcknd over 1f out: r.o wl: comf* **9/4**[2]

6422 **2** *5* **Chevallier**[21] 6039 2-9-5 74.......................... RichardHughes 1 70
(Richard Hannon) *chsd ldrs: wnt 2nd 1/2-way: rdn and outpcd by wnr over 1f out: one pce* **1/1**[1]

**3** *2 ¼* **Fligaz (FR)** 2-9-0 0.......................... FergusSweeney 5 56
(Martyn Meade) *bhd: rdn 1/2-way: swtchd lft and hdwy over 1f out: styd on wl* **50/1**

B **4** *½* **Star Fire**[72] 4269 2-9-0 0.......................... JamesDoyle 3 54
(Roger Charlton) *hld up in rr: hdwy 1/2-way: 3rd and outpcd over 1f out: wl hld after* **8/1**

0 **5** *2* **You're Cool**[17] 6168 2-9-5 0.......................... TomQueally 7 52+
(James Given) *chsd ldrs tl pushed wd and lost pl after 1f: racd awkwardly bnd 2f out: rallied 1f out: styd on* **6/1**[3]

00 **6** *1 ¾* **Jellwa (IRE)**[19] 6093 2-8-11 0.......................... CharlesBishop(3) 6 41
(Mick Channon) *chsd wnr tl hung lft bnd after 1f: lost 2nd 1/2-way: midfield and btn over 1f out* **14/1**

44 **7** *¾* **John Joiner**[21] 6024 2-8-12 0..........................(be) ChrisMeehan(7) 4 43
(Peter Makin) *in tch: struggling 2f out: sn wknd* **25/1**

60 **8** *½* **Junior Ben**[18] 6158 2-8-12 0.......................... AdamMcLean(7) 2 41
(Derek Shaw) *hld up in tch: rdn 2f out: sn wknd* **100/1**

60 **9** *1* **Tangramm**[19] 6103 2-9-5 0.......................... SebSanders 10 38
(Simon Dow) *s.i.s: a outpcd* **100/1**

**10** *4 ½* **Equita** 2-9-0 0.......................... LiamJones 9 16
(Robert Stephens) *dwlt: hdwy into midfield after 1f: wknd 2f out: bhd fnl f* **66/1**

1m 0.28s (-0.22) **Going Correction** -0.075s/f (Stan) **10** Ran SP% **122.1**
Speed ratings (Par 95): **98,90,86,85,82 79,78,77,76,68**
CSF £5.05 TOTE £2.60: £1.10, £1.10, £20.80; EX 5.90 Trifecta £117.80.
**Owner** Lord Carnarvon **Bred** Earl Of Carnarvon **Trained** East Ilsley, Berks

**FOCUS**
A fair maiden with an easy winner. The runner-up has been rated a bit below form.

## 6660 BETBRIGHT MOBILE MAIDEN STKS 6f (P)
**6:20** (6:22) (Class 5) 2-Y-0 **£2,587** (£770; £384; £192) **Stalls** Low

Form RPR

43 **1** **Koptoon**[37] 5493 2-9-5 0..........................(t) RichardKingscote 10 80+
(Tom Dascombe) *mde all: rdn over 1f out: hung lft but in command ins fnl f: r.o* **9/4**[2]

**2** *2 ¾* **Silvery Blue** 2-9-0 0.......................... JamesDoyle 11 67
(Hugo Palmer) *hld up in midfield: rdn and effrt over 1f out: styd on wl to go 2nd fnl 75yds: no threat to wnr* **33/1**

3 **3** *1 ½* **Chicago Bere (FR)**[7] 6456 2-9-5 0.......................... RichardHughes 7 70+
(Richard Hannon) *in tch: racd awkwardly bnd 4f out: rdn over 2f out: no imp tl kpt on ins fnl f* **5/1**[3]

**4** *½* **Darma (IRE)** 2-9-0 0.......................... FergusSweeney 5 61
(Martyn Meade) *chsd ldrs: rdn over 1f out: styd on same pce fnl f* **50/1**

**5** *1* **Midnight Dance (IRE)** 2-9-0 0.......................... PatDobbs 6 58
(Ralph Beckett) *chsd ldrs: effrt on inner to chse wnr over 1f out: lost 2nd fnl 75yds: wknd towards fin* **5/1**[3]

**6** *1 ¾* **Absolute Champion (USA)** 2-9-5 0.......................... DaneO'Neill 2 58
(Jamie Osborne) *in tch in midfield: effrt 2f out: sn no imp* **50/1**

**7** *½* **Mystify Me** 2-9-5 0.......................... SeanLevey 8 56+
(Ed McMahon) *outpcd and wl bhd: styd on wl fnl f: nvr trbld ldrs* **20/1**

**8** *hd* **Loudly (USA)** 2-9-0 0.......................... KierenFallon 4 53
(Jeremy Noseda) *chsd ldrs: rdn and unable qck over 1f out: wknd fnl f* **7/4**[1]

**9** *nse* **Ainslie (IRE)** 2-9-5 0.......................... TomQueally 1 55+
(David Simcock) *rn green and outpcd in rr: styd on wl fnl f: n.d* **14/1**

**10** *6* **Come Up And See Me** 2-8-12 0.......................... VictorSantos(7) 3 37
(J R Jenkins) *s.i.s: a outpcd* **100/1**

**11** *15* **Any Given Time (IRE)** 2-9-5 0.......................... MartinLane 9
(David Simcock) *rn green and sn wl bhd* **50/1**

1m 13.02s (-0.08) **Going Correction** -0.075s/f (Stan) **11** Ran SP% **121.7**
Speed ratings (Par 95): **97,93,91,90,89 87,86,86,86,78 58**
CSF £85.60 TOTE £3.10: £1.30, £7.70, £1.80; EX 50.50 Trifecta £418.70.
**Owner** Lyn Rutherford, Mike O'Halloran & Mhs **Bred** Bearstone Stud **Trained** Malpas, Cheshire

**FOCUS**
The last two renewals of this maiden were taken by Invincible Warrior (2012) and Mushir (2013), who were both good enough to subsequently record a Listed win and, while nothing may prove up to that standard, it should pay to take a positive view of this form too. It's been rated around the averages for the race.

## 6661 BETBRIGHT MONEYBACK OFFERS MEDIAN AUCTION MAIDEN STKS 1m (P)
**6:50** (6:51) (Class 5) 3-5-Y-0 **£2,587** (£770; £384; £192) **Stalls** Low

Form RPR

325 **1** **Glorious Sun**[28] 5831 3-9-5 74.......................... GeorgeBaker 10 76+
(Ed Walker) *trckd ldrs: led 2f out: readily wnt clr over 1f out: easily* **8/11**[1]

0 **2** *2 ¼* **Geordan Murphy**[22] 6018 3-9-5 0.......................... DavidProbert 11 67+
(Andrew Balding) *in tch in midfield: hdwy u.p to chse wnr over 1f out: kpt on same pce* **8/1**[3]

62 **3** *2 ¼* **Quaintrelle (IRE)**[21] 6042 3-9-0 0.......................... AndreaAtzeni 8 57
(Ed Vaughan) *chsd ldrs: drvn to go 3rd over 1f out: no imp fnl f* **5/1**[2]

06 **4** *nk* **Jethou Island**[37] 5504 3-9-0 0.......................... DaneO'Neill 1 56+
(Henry Candy) *midfield: shuffled bk towards rr 1/2-way: hdwy u.p over 1f out: styd on* **5/1**[2]

**5** *1 ½* **Sunny Again** 3-9-0 0.......................... PatDobbs 12 53+
(Amanda Perrett) *hld up towards rr: rdn over 2f out: kpt on fr over 1f out* **16/1**

6000 **6** *1 ¼* **Nouvelle Ere**[58] 4742 3-9-5 53.......................... SebSanders 3 55
(Tony Carroll) *led tl 2f out: sn rdn and no ex: wknd 1f out* **50/1**

6 **7** *5* **Barwah (USA)**[8] 6437 3-9-0 0..........................(t) WilliamCarson 7 38
(Anthony Carson) *t.k.h: hld up towards rr: rdn over 2f out: hung lft and wknd over 1f out* **33/1**

-500 **8** *5* **Movie Magic**[118] 2688 3-9-0 45.......................... HayleyTurner 2 27
(John Bridger) *midfield: rdn and outpcd 2f out: sn wknd* **66/1**

6 **9** *9* **Sea Tiger**[191] 988 4-9-9 0.......................... SamHitchcott 9 11
(Chris Gordon) *s.i.s: a bhd* **33/1**

0050 **10** *2 ½* **Beaver Creek**[12] 6298 3-9-5 45.......................... RichardKingscote 5 5
(Ralph J Smith) *chsd ldr tl over 2f out: sn wknd* **50/1**

1m 39.94s (0.14) **Going Correction** -0.075s/f (Stan)
**WFA** 3 from 4yo 4lb **10** Ran SP% **119.5**
Speed ratings (Par 103): **96,93,91,91,89 88,83,78,69,66**
CSF £7.56 TOTE £1.70: £1.10, £2.30, £2.40; EX 7.90 Trifecta £26.60.
**Owner** Ms Judy Yap & Ms Salina Yang **Bred** Mrs Lucille Bone **Trained** Newmarket, Suffolk

**FOCUS**
A weak maiden, with little depth to it, which provided a good chance for the favourite to get off the mark. Solid enough form.

## 6662 SQUIRE FURNEAUX VOLVO NURSERY H'CAP (DIV I) 7f (P)
**7:20** (7:21) (Class 6) (0-65,65) 2-Y-0 **£1,940** (£577; £288; £144) **Stalls** Low

Form RPR

005 **1** **Andretti**[19] 6103 2-9-7 65.......................... AndreaAtzeni 9 70
(Roger Varian) *in tch in midfield: rdn 2f out: styd on to ld nr fin* **4/1**[2]

060 **2** *nk* **My Mo (FR)**[23] 5982 2-8-7 51.......................... MartinLane 12 55
(David Dennis) *led and grad crossed to inner: rdn 2f out: battled on gamely: hdd nr fin* **50/1**

6003 **3** *½* **Tommys Geal**[14] 6237 2-8-5 49.......................... WilliamCarson 6 52
(Michael Madgwick) *chsd ldrs: rdn to chal 2f out: no ex cl home* **20/1**

0521 **4** *hd* **Father Stone**[14] 6237 2-9-7 65.......................... LiamKeniry 4 67+
(David Elsworth) *hld up towards rr: hdwy 2f out: pressed ldrs fnl f: kpt on* **6/4**[1]

005 **5** *1 ¼* **Laura B**[20] 6071 2-8-11 55.......................... TedDurcan 7 54
(Chris Wall) *in tch in midfield: rdn and outpcd 2f out: rallied fnl f: kpt on* **25/1**

0006 **6** *1* **Hidden Agenda**[13] 6250 2-8-1 45.......................... KieranO'Neill 11 41
(Michael Blanshard) *chsd ldr tl 2f out: styd pressing ldrs tl wknd ins fnl f* **50/1**

350 **7** *½* **Stealing Thunder (IRE)**[21] 6038 2-8-12 56..........................(b[1]) HarryBentley 8 51
(Eve Johnson Houghton) *in tch in midfield: rdn 1/2-way: drvn and no ex 1f out* **6/1**

031 **8** *1 ¼* **Tinkers Kiss (IRE)**[22] 6017 2-9-4 62.......................... KierenFallon 1 53
(Philip McBride) *chsd ldrs: swtchd lft 2f out: unable qck over 1f out: wknd ins fnl f* **9/2**[3]

6650 **9** *2 ½* **Tumut (IRE)**[13] 6250 2-9-1 62.......................... CharlesBishop(3) 10 46+
(Mick Channon) *hld up in rr: rdn 3f out: wknd over 1f out* **20/1**

055 **10** *2 ½* **Vinamar (IRE)**[23] 5973 2-9-2 60.......................... StevieDonohoe 2 38+
(Roger Teal) *hld up in rr: n.d* **33/1**

3010 **11** *¾* **Just Marion (IRE)**[10] 6375 2-9-1 59..........................(p) RichardHughes 5 35+
(David Evans) *hld up in tch: effrt 2f out: wknd over 1f out* **12/1**

1m 26.95s (0.95) **Going Correction** -0.075s/f (Stan) **11** Ran SP% **120.4**
Speed ratings (Par 93): **91,90,90,89,88 87,86,85,82,79 78**
CSF £202.23 CT £3619.73 TOTE £5.40: £1.90, £11.40, £4.10; EX 250.00 Trifecta £1503.80 Part won..
**Owner** Nurlan Bizakov **Bred** Hesmonds Stud Ltd **Trained** Newmarket, Suffolk

**FOCUS**
Modest form. It looked to favour those who raced prominently and it resulted in a bunched finish. The fourth has been rated to form.

## 6663 SQUIRE FURNEAUX VOLVO NURSERY H'CAP (DIV II) 7f (P)
**7:50** (7:50) (Class 6) (0-65,65) 2-Y-O **£1,940** (£577; £288; £144) **Stalls** Low

Form RPR

004 **1** **Gavarnie Encore**$^{77}$ 4079 2-8-11 55.............................. DavidProbert 11 57
(Michael Blanshard) *in tch: rdn and wnt between rivals to ld 1f out: r.o wl: hung lft nr nr fin* **33/1**

600 **2** *1* **Prince Of Paris**$^{26}$ 5881 2-9-7 65........................................ RobertHavlin 2 64
(Roger Ingram) *in tch in midfield: rdn and swtchd lft over 1f out: styd on wl fnl f: wnt 2nd nr fin* **8/1$^{3}$**

3505 **3** *shd* **Scent Of Power**$^{21}$ 6040 2-8-8 52.............................. WilliamCarson 12 51
(Anthony Carson) *dropped in bhd after s: hdwy u.p over 1f out: styd on wl to go 3rd nr fin* **14/1**

0035 **4** *½* **Emperors Warrior (IRE)**$^{19}$ 6085 2-9-6 64.............. RichardHughes 4 62
(Richard Hannon) *led: rdn 2f out: hdd 1f out: one pce* **7/1$^{2}$**

3324 **5** *hd* **Framley Garth (IRE)**$^{2}$ 6602 2-9-4 62............................ KierenFallon 3 61
(David Elsworth) *chsd ldr: drvn and ev ch over 1f out: 3rd and hld whn hmpd and lost two pls nr fin* **9/4$^{1}$**

0032 **6** *4* **Sky Steps (IRE)**$^{9}$ 6413 2-8-5 49..........................(v) SilvestreDeSousa 1 35
(Philip McBride) *chsd ldrs: drvn over 1f out: wknd ins fnl f* **9/4$^{1}$**

540 **7** *¾* **Starring Guest (IRE)**$^{13}$ 6246 2-8-12 59.............. CharlesBishop$^{(3)}$ 10 43
(Mick Channon) *hld up in rr: rdn 2f out: sme hdwy fnl f: n.d* **8/1$^{3}$**

2054 **8** *nk* **Reet Petite (IRE)**$^{20}$ 6072 2-7-10 45.............................. NoelGarbutt$^{(5)}$ 7 29
(James Evans) *hld up towards rr: effrt 2f out: wknd fnl f* **33/1**

2233 **9** *4* **Wink Oliver**$^{9}$ 6413 2-9-2 60..................................................(p) AdamKirby 6 33
(Kristin Stubbs) *t.k.h: wknd u.p over 1f out* **8/1$^{3}$**

055 **10** *3* **Freedom Rose (IRE)**$^{44}$ 5255 2-7-10 45.......................... CamHardie$^{(5)}$ 5 10
(Derek Shaw) *midfield: rdn 1/2-way: lost pl over 2f out: n.d after* **50/1**

1m 27.11s (1.11) **Going Correction** -0.075s/f (Stan) **10** Ran SP% **121.9**
Speed ratings (Par 93): **90,88,88,88,87 83,82,82,77,74**
CSF £285.76 CT £3963.72 TOTE £47.00: £6.40, £2.80, £3.80; EX 427.30 Trifecta £1190.80 Part won..
**Owner** Hill, Price & Williams **Bred** Shinko Foods International Ltd **Trained** Upper Lambourn, Berks

**FOCUS**
The second division of the nursery looked even weaker and, with none of these previously successful, was a maiden handicap in all but name. The fourth and fifth help set the level.

## 6664 BETBRIGHT.COM H'CAP 1m 4f (P)
**8:20** (8:22) (Class 4) (0-85,91) 4-Y-O+ **£4,960** (£1,395; £697; £348) **Stalls** Centre

Form RPR

0241 **1** **Soul Intent (IRE)**$^{83}$ 3874 4-9-0 78.............................. WilliamBuick 2 86
(Charles Hills) *mde all: rdn and qcknd 2f out: r.o wl* **3/1$^{3}$**

303 **2** *1 ½* **Double Discount (IRE)**$^{19}$ 6106 4-9-7 85.............(p) RichardKingscote 5 91
(Tom Dascombe) *hld up in tch: effrt 2f out: chsd wnr 1f out: kpt on* **9/4$^{1}$**

0605 **3** *nk* **Modernism**$^{18}$ 6156 5-9-1 79.............................................. JimCrowley 7 84
(David Simcock) *hld up in rr: effrt u.p over 1f out: wnt 3rd ins fnl f: kpt on* **5/1**

4630 **4** *2 ½* **Art Scholar (IRE)**$^{33}$ 5639 7-8-13 77.................................(p) TomQueally 8 78
(Michael Appleby) *hld up in last pair: hdwy to chse ldrs 4f out: styd on same pce fr over 1f out* **16/1**

0213 **5** *¾* **Cousin Khee**$^{18}$ 6156 7-9-6 84...................................... RichardHughes 3 84
(Hughie Morrison) *chsd wnr: drvn 2f out: lost 2nd 1f out: wknd fnl 100yds* **5/2$^{2}$**

1-16 **6** *2 ¼* **Asia Minor (IRE)**$^{159}$ 1553 5-8-12 76..................................(t) RobertTart 4 72
(Dr Jon Scargill) *rn wout declared tongue-tie: chsd ldrs: rdn 2f out: wknd ins fnl f* **8/1**

312- **7** *15* **Bushel (USA)**$^{94}$ 5258 4-9-2 80.....................................(b$^{1}$) JamesDoyle 6 52
(James Given) *in tch in midfield: lost pl over 2f out: sn lost tch* **12/1**

2m 33.33s (-1.17) **Going Correction** -0.075s/f (Stan) **7** Ran SP% **125.7**
Speed ratings (Par 105): **100,99,98,97,96 95,85**
CSF £11.60 CT £34.76 TOTE £5.60: £2.90, £2.10; EX 17.50 Trifecta £90.50.
**Owner** Andy Weller & Gary Styles **Bred** Flamingo Guitar Syndicate **Trained** Lambourn, Berks

**FOCUS**
A fair, tight-knit handicap. It was unsatisfactory though with the field crawling through the first mile and the winner able to kick on from the front. The runner-up has been rated pretty much to his mark.

## 6665 BETBRIGHT - LIVE THE MOMENT H'CAP (BOBIS RACE) (LONDON MIDDLE DISTANCE SERIES QUALIFIER) 1m 3f (P)
**8:50** (8:51) (Class 3) (0-95,95) 3-Y-O
**£7,158** (£2,143; £1,071; £535; £267; £134) **Stalls** Low

Form RPR

1340 **1** **Rydan (IRE)**$^{25}$ 5928 3-8-12 **86**.......................................... TomQueally 3 99+
(Robert Mills) *hld up in rr: smooth hdwy 2f out: rdn to ld over 1f out: sn clr* **7/1$^{3}$**

1301 **2** *6* **Carnevale**$^{33}$ 5647 3-8-13 **87**.............................. SilvestreDeSousa 1 90
(Ralph Beckett) *chsd ldr: ev ch over 2f out tl over 1f out: kpt on same pce* **10/1**

4252 **3** *hd* **Devilment**$^{18}$ 6156 3-9-7 **95**................................................ WilliamBuick 5 97
(Charlie Appleby) *t.k.h: chsd ldrs: led over 2f out: drvn and hdd over 1f out: sn outpcd* **4/6$^{1}$**

1111 **4** *1 ½* **Ragged Robbin (FR)**$^{22}$ 6019 3-8-13 **87**.............................(t) TedDurcan 4 87
(David Lanigan) *in tch: rdn 3f out: outpcd over 2f out: n.d but plugged on fnl f* **7/2$^{2}$**

4016 **5** *½* **Grand Meister**$^{35}$ 5552 3-8-2 **81** oh1.............................. CamHardie$^{(5)}$ 2 80
(Michael Bell) *pushed along early: in tch: rdn and outpcd 2f out: n.d after* **25/1**

-000 **6** *16* **Lady Tyne**$^{20}$ 6061 3-8-11 **85**.........................................(b$^{1}$) JamesDoyle 6 57
(Roger Charlton) *led tl over 2f out: sn btn* **20/1**

2m 17.38s (-4.52) **Going Correction** -0.075s/f (Stan) **6** Ran SP% **112.4**
Speed ratings (Par 105): **113,108,108,107,107 95**
CSF £68.12 TOTE £9.80: £3.80, £3.50; EX 48.90 Trifecta £142.00.
**Owner** Jacobs Construction & Mrs B B Mills **Bred** R Coffey **Trained** Headley, Surrey

**FOCUS**
The inaugural running of this decent handicap. The winner was impressive and has been rated 7lb up on his previous best.

## 6666 COLIN MURRAY AND FRIENDS ON TALKSPORT H'CAP 6f (P)
**9:20** (9:21) (Class 6) (0-60,60) 3-Y-O+ **£1,940** (£577; £288; £144) **Stalls** Low

Form RPR

0000 **1** **Varsovian**$^{42}$ 5303 4-9-2 55.............................................. SebSanders 4 70+
(Dean Ivory) *chsd ldrs: swtchd lft over 2f out: rdn to ld over 1f out: r.o wl* **6/1$^{3}$**

0433 **2** *2* **Stapleford Lad**$^{6}$ 6488 3-8-12 53..........................(v) SilvestreDeSousa 3 62
(Stuart Williams) *led: rdn 2f out: hdd over 1f out: one pce* **5/2$^{1}$**

0000 **3** *nse* **New Rich**$^{53}$ 4908 4-9-3 56..............................................(b$^{1}$) JohnFahy 1 64
(Eve Johnson Houghton) *t.k.h: chsd ldrs: effrt 2f out: one pce* **9/2$^{2}$**

-501 **4** *1 ½* **Bookmaker**$^{23}$ 5972 4-9-6 59..........................................(b) WilliamCarson 9 63
(John Bridger) *hld up and bhd: hdwy over 1f out: kpt on u.p fnl f* **8/1**

5016 **5** *¾* **Catalinas Diamond (IRE)**$^{13}$ 6272 6-9-0 58..................(t) CamHardie$^{(5)}$ 6 59
(Pat Murphy) *hld up towards rr: hdwy over 1f out: kpt on fnl f* **12/1**

0504 **6** *nk* **Hamis Al Bin (IRE)**$^{13}$ 6272 5-9-3 56..................................(t) KierenFallon 8 56
(Milton Bradley) *in tch in midfield: rdn 2f out: styd on same pce after* **14/1**

1030 **7** *1 ½* **Black Truffle (FR)**$^{104}$ 3150 4-8-11 57..............(v) CharlotteJenner$^{(7)}$ 12 52
(Mark Usher) *hld up towards rr: hdwy 1f out: kpt on* **25/1**

0350 **8** *½* **Forest Glen (IRE)**$^{27}$ 5846 3-9-1 56.................................... LiamKeniry 10 50
(Sylvester Kirk) *hld up in rr: sme hdwy u.p over 1f out: nvr trbld ldrs* **33/1**

2322 **9** *1 ¾* **Assertive Agent**$^{53}$ 4908 4-9-7 60.................................... DavidProbert 7 48
(Tony Carroll) *chsd ldrs: rdn and unable qck 2f out: wknd 1f out* **8/1**

6050 **10** *hd* **Gypsy Rider**$^{23}$ 5978 5-8-9 48.........................................(v$^{1}$) LiamJones 11 36
(Henry Tett) *t.k.h: in tch: hdwy to chse ldrs 1/2-way: wknd over 1f out* **16/1**

0202 **11** *3 ¾* **High Tone**$^{13}$ 6272 4-8-11 50.......................................... RichardHughes 2 26
(Dean Ivory) *w ldr tl no ex u.p 1f out: wknd fnl f* **6/1$^{3}$**

4000 **12** *½* **Under Review (IRE)**$^{26}$ 5897 8-9-7 60..............................(tp) TomQueally 5 34
(Liam Corcoran) *t.k.h: midfield: rdn 2f out: sn wknd* **50/1**

1m 12.45s (-0.65) **Going Correction** -0.075s/f (Stan)
**WFA** 3 from 4yo+ 2lb **12** Ran SP% **126.5**
Speed ratings (Par 101): **101,98,98,96,95 94,92,92,89,89 84,83**
CSF £22.55 CT £79.03 TOTE £8.10: £2.30, £1.50, £1.60; EX 29.00 Trifecta £115.10.
**Owner** Geoff Copp & Radlett Racing **Bred** Darley **Trained** Radlett, Herts

**FOCUS**
A typically weak low-grade AW handicap. Ordinary form rated around those who finished close up.
T/Plt: £193.40 to a £1 stake. Pool: £87,811.24 - 331.42 winning tickets T/Qpdt: £72.50 to a £1 stake. Pool: £7,905.83 - 80.64 winning tickets SP

# 6211 REDCAR (L-H)
### Wednesday, September 24

**OFFICIAL GOING: Good to firm (good in places) changing to good after race 3 (2:50)**
Wind: fresh 1/2 against Weather: fine

## 6667 BRITISH STALLION STUDS EBF MAIDEN STKS (DIV I) 7f
**1:45** (1:46) (Class 5) 2-Y-O **£2,911** (£866; £432; £216) **Stalls** Centre

Form RPR

**1** **Swift Emperor (IRE)** 2-9-5 0.............................................. GrahamGibbons 3 78
(David Barron) *in tch: hdwy over 2f out: chsd ldng pair over 1f out: rdn to chal ins fnl f: kpt on wl to ld nr fin* **33/1**

2244 **2** *nk* **Vegas Rebel (IRE)**$^{12}$ 6279 2-9-5 75.................................. MartinHarley 2 77
(Peter Chapple-Hyam) *trckd ldrs: hdwy 3f out: cl up 2f out: sn carried lft: rdn to ld over 1f out: jnd and drvn ins fnl f: hdd and no ex nr fin* **7/1$^{3}$**

6 **3** *5* **Mount Tahan (IRE)**$^{33}$ 5655 2-9-5 0.................................. PaulMulrennan 8 64+
(Kevin Ryan) *wnt lft s: prom: led after 1f: pushed along and edgd lft over 2f out: rdn and hung lft wl over 1f out: sn hdd and one pce* **7/4$^{2}$**

0 **4** *7* **Cadeau Magnifique**$^{19}$ 6115 2-9-5 0.................................. TonyHamilton 7 45+
(Richard Fahey) *trckd ldrs: effrt over 2f out: sn rdn along and no imp* **33/1**

**5** *4 ½* **The Kurator (IRE)** 2-9-5 0.................................................. PJMcDonald 1 32
(Ann Duffield) *green and towards rr: pushed along 3f out: kpt on fnl 2f: nvr nr ldrs* **33/1**

00 **6** *½* **Molly Approve (IRE)**$^{40}$ 5386 2-9-0 0.............................. BarryMcHugh 4 26
(Tony Coyle) *towards rr: pushed along 3f out: rdn and sme hdwy 2f out: nvr nr ldrs* **100/1**

03 **7** *nk* **Multellie**$^{18}$ 6147 2-8-12 0.............................. RachelRichardson$^{(7)}$ 5 30
(Tim Easterby) *led 1f: cl up: rdn along over 2f out: sn wknd* **33/1**

33 **8** *3 ½* **Sands Chorus**$^{18}$ 6146 2-9-5 0.............................................. GrahamLee 12 21
(James Given) *in tch on wd outside: sme hdwy 3f out: rdn along over 2f out: sn outpcd* **10/1**

**9** *1 ¾* **The Name's Bond** 2-9-5 0...................................................... TomEaves 6 16
(Keith Reveley) *s.i.s: green and bhd tl sme late hdwy* **66/1**

**10** *3 ¼* **Happy As Harry** 2-9-5 0.................................................. PhillipMakin 11 7
(Bryan Smart) *dwlt: a in rr* **25/1**

5 **11** *1 ½* **Red Unico (IRE)**$^{56}$ 4787 2-9-5 0.................................. DanielTudhope 9 3
(Alan McCabe) *chsd ldrs: rdn along bef 1/2-way: sn lost pl and bhd* **40/1**

02 **12** *7* **Hills And Dales (IRE)**$^{15}$ 6204 2-9-5 0.............................. PaulHanagan 10
(Charlie Appleby) *t.k.h: trckd ldrs: hdwy to chse ldr wl over 2f out: rdn wl over 1f out: sn btn and heavily eased fnl f* **6/4$^{1}$**

1m 27.21s (2.71) **Going Correction** +0.375s/f (Good) **12** Ran SP% **118.5**
Speed ratings (Par 95): **99,98,92,84,79 79,78,74,72,69 67,59**
CSF £237.08 TOTE £22.30: £6.80, £1.50, £1.10; EX 210.20 Trifecta £294.40.
**Owner** DC Racing Partnership **Bred** John Davison **Trained** Maunby, N Yorks

**FOCUS**
After 2.5mm of overnight rain the ground eased to good to firm, good in places (from good to firm). A fair maiden run at an honest pace. The front two pulled clear. The form could be better than rated if the runner-up can back this up.

## 6668 BRITISH STALLION STUDS EBF MAIDEN STKS (DIV II) 7f
**2:15** (2:16) (Class 5) 2-Y-O **£2,911** (£866; £432; £216) **Stalls** Centre

Form RPR

**1** **Second Wave (IRE)** 2-9-5 0.............................................. PaulHanagan 8 73
(Charlie Appleby) *in rr: drvn and hdwy over 2f out: edgd lft ins fnl f: styd on wl to ld fnl strides* **9/4$^{1}$**

404 **2** *nk* **Beach Samba (IRE)**$^{19}$ 6115 2-9-5 72.................................. MartinHarley 4 72
(Ed Dunlop) *hld up in rr: hdwy over 2f out: styd on to ld last 50yds: hdd fnl strides* **11/4$^{2}$**

5 **3** *¾* **Cyril**$^{13}$ 6268 2-9-5 0...................................................... PaulMulrennan 1 70
(Kevin Ryan) *wnt lft s: led 1f: w ldr: led over 2f out: wnt lft over 1f out: hdd and no ex last 50yds* **7/2$^{3}$**

4 3/4 **Lewis Valentine (IRE)** 2-9-5 0 PhillipMakin 7 68
(Bryan Smart) *dwlt: hdwy to chse ldrs over 4f out: upsides over 1f out: kpt on same pce last 100yds* 12/1

5 nk **Unnoticed** 2-9-2 0 JacobButterfield(3) 10 67
(Ollie Pears) *chsd ldrs: styd on same pce fnl f* 40/1

6 6 1 3/4 **Montefalcon (IRE)**[147] 1879 2-9-5 0 TonyHamilton 11 62
(Richard Fahey) *hld up in rr: hdwy over 1f out: gng on at fin* 7/1

7 3 1/4 **Stoneboat Bill** 2-9-2 0 NeilFarley(3) 9 54
(Declan Carroll) *in rr: drvn over 3f out: kpt on fnl f: nvr a factor* 66/1

0 8 4 1/2 **Euro Mac**[32] 5679 2-9-0 0 AndrewElliott 2 36
(Neville Bycroft) *w ldr: led after 1f: edgd rt 4f out: hdd over 2f out: sn wknd* 50/1

9 1 **Let Right Be Done** 2-9-5 0 DaleSwift 6 39
(Ed McMahon) *mid-div: hdwy to chse ldrs over 2f out: lost pl over 1f out* 14/1

64 10 3 1/4 **Dew Pond**[48] 5098 2-9-5 0 DuranFentiman 5 30
(Tim Easterby) *chsd ldrs: drvn and outpcd over 3f out: sn lost pl* 33/1

0 11 2 1/4 **Fair Venture (IRE)**[19] 6115 2-9-2 0 ConnorBeasley(3) 3 24
(Michael Dods) *chsd ldrs: wknd 2f out* 50/1

0 12 3 1/4 **Play Nicely**[18] 6147 2-9-5 0 GrahamLee 12 15
(James Given) *in rr: bhd fnl 2f* 33/1

1m 27.97s (3.47) **Going Correction** +0.375s/f (Good) 12 Ran SP% **120.3**
Speed ratings (Par 95): **95,94,93,92,92 90,86,81,80,76 74,70**
CSF £8.25 TOTE £2.50: £1.10, £1.80, £1.80; EX 9.60 Trifecta £19.90.
**Owner** Godolphin **Bred** Darley **Trained** Newmarket, Suffolk

**FOCUS**
They went an even pace for this interesting maiden. The second and third have been rated close to their pre-race marks.

## 6669 HOLD YOUR CHRISTMAS PARTY HERE NURSERY H'CAP 1m
**2:50** (2:51) (Class 6) (0-65,65) 2-Y-O £2,587 (£770; £384; £192) **Stalls** Centre

Form RPR

030 1 **Dark Wave**[15] 6204 2-9-2 60 GrahamLee 6 65+
(Ed Walker) *hld up in rr: stdy hdwy 3f out: in tch 2f out: effrt and swtchd rt jst over 1f out: rdn ent fnl f: sn led and kpt on strly* 5/1[3]

6450 2 1 3/4 **Upward Trend (IRE)**[17] 6165 2-9-2 60 DuranFentiman 19 61
(Tim Easterby) *midfield: hdwy wl over 2f out: effrt and edgd lft over 1f out: rdn to chal ent fnl f and ev ch tl drvn and kpt on same pce last 100yds* 16/1

0060 3 nk **North Bay Lady (IRE)**[15] 6211 2-8-5 49 RaulDaSilva 7 49
(John Wainwright) *in rr: hdwy wl over 2f out: swtchd rt and rdn over 1f out: styd on wl fnl f: nrst fin* 33/1

0064 4 1 **Hold Firm**[28] 5823 2-8-1 45 JimmyQuinn 2 43
(Mark H Tompkins) *hld up towards rr: swtchd lft to outer and hdwy 3f out: rdn to ld jst over 1f out: drvn and hdd ins fnl f: one pce* 16/1

006 5 1 3/4 **Kopassus (IRE)**[42] 5315 2-9-2 60 MartinHarley 9 54+
(Peter Chapple-Hyam) *in tch: pushed along and outpcd over 3f out: rdn and hdwy 2f out: n.m.r over 1f out: sn swtchd lft and kpt on fnl f: nrst fin* 10/1

0350 6 3/4 **Call Me Crockett (IRE)**[33] 5630 2-9-2 60 JasonHart 3 52
(Richard Guest) *hld up in tch: hdwy to trck ldrs 3f out: effrt 2f out: rdn and edgd rt wl over 1f out: wknd appr fnl f* 9/2[2]

060 7 1/2 **Blythe Star (IRE)**[20] 6056 2-8-6 53 JoeyHaynes(3) 10 44
(Danielle McCormick) *prom: cl up 1/2-way: rdn to ld 2f out: drvn and hdd appr fnl f: sn one pce* 33/1

050 8 1/2 **Phantasmo (IRE)**[37] 5493 2-8-10 54 PaulMulrennan 18 44
(John Quinn) *chsd ldrs: rdn along wl over 2f out: kpt on same pce appr fnl f* 12/1

0424 9 1/2 **Charlotte's Secret**[15] 6211 2-9-2 65 JackGarritty(5) 17 53
(Richard Fahey) *cl up: rdn along wl over 2f out: grad wknd* 4/1[1]

0552 10 1 1/4 **Snoway**[8] 6428 2-8-1 45 PatrickMathers 15 30
(Tony Coyle) *prom: led after 3f: rdn along and hdd 3f out: grad wknd fnl 2f* 9/1

0446 11 3 1/2 **Robben**[9] 6413 2-8-13 57 (v[1]) TomEaves 4 34
(Kevin Ryan) *dwlt: sn in midfield: hdwy to join ldrs 1/2-way: led 3f out: rdn and hdd 2f out: drvn and wknd over 1f out* 12/1

5620 12 hd **Old Fashion**[29] 5798 2-9-5 63 PaulHanagan 5 40
(Ed Dunlop) *towards rr: sme hdwy over 3f out: rdn along wl over 2f out: sn outpcd* 7/1

000 13 1 3/4 **Just No Rules**[84] 3842 2-7-10 45 JoeDoyle(5) 14 17
(Tony Coyle) *led 3f: rdn along over 3f out: sn wknd* 50/1

300 14 1 **Cisco Boy**[41] 5335 2-9-7 65 PhillipMakin 1 35
(Tim Easterby) *chsd ldrs: rdn along wl over 2f out: hld whn n.m.r and hmpd over 1f out: wknd* 33/1

000 15 2 **Pencaitland**[81] 3945 2-8-1 48 ow3 NeilFarley(3) 12 13
(Noel Wilson) *in tch: pushed along over 3f out: sn lost pl and bhd* 50/1

400 16 16 **Tantric Lady**[82] 3933 2-8-6 53 (p) BillyCray(3) 13
(Alan McCabe) *s.i.s and in rr: hdwy on wd outside and in tch after 3f: rdn along 3f out: sn wknd* 25/1

1m 42.39s (5.79) **Going Correction** +0.375s/f (Good) 16 Ran SP% **130.2**
Speed ratings (Par 93): **86,84,83,82,81 80,79,79,78,77 74,74,72,71,69 53**
CSF £83.57 CT £2536.63 TOTE £5.90: £1.60, £4.50, £8.50, £5.10; EX 145.90 Trifecta £2041.00 Part won..
**Owner** F Ma **Bred** Lady Bland & Miss Anthea Gibson-Fleming **Trained** Newmarket, Suffolk

**FOCUS**
A modest if competitive nursery run at a decent pace. It suited the closers. The third has been rated as running a minor pb.

## 6670 RACING UK 100% PROFITS RETURNED TO RACING (S) STKS 1m
**3:25** (3:26) (Class 5) 3-Y-O+ £2,911 (£866; £432; £216) **Stalls** Centre

Form RPR

0450 1 **Toto Skyllachy**[49] 5054 9-8-11 78 JacobButterfield(3) 9 63+
(Marjorie Fife) *reluctant to go to post: sn w ldr: led 4f out: rdn and hung lft over 1f out: fnd ex nr fin* 7/2[2]

4011 2 1/2 **The Osteopath (IRE)**[30] 5761 11-9-5 72 PhillipMakin 6 67+
(John Davies) *mid-div: 2nd over 2f out: upsides fnl f: no ex clsng stages* 6/4[1]

2000 3 5 **Mitchum**[15] 6217 5-9-0 51 (v) GrahamLee 8 50
(Ron Barr) *trckd ldrs: kpt on one pce to take modest 3rd last 150yds* 20/1

0040 4 nk **Spokesperson (USA)**[14] 6223 6-8-11 45 NeilFarley(3) 4 49
(Frederick Watson) *mid-div: drvn 4f out: kpt on fnl 2f: tk modest 4th last 50yds* 66/1

5000 5 2 3/4 **Shearian**[19] 6121 4-9-0 50 (p) IanBrennan 1 42
(Tracy Waggott) *t.k.h: led 4f: wknd fnl f* 8/1

-006 6 3 3/4 **On The Hoof**[32] 5678 5-9-0 64 GrahamGibbons 5 33
(Michael Easterby) *s.i.s: in rr: drvn over 3f out: nvr a factor* 11/2

21/0 7 1/2 **Artisan**[13] 6274 6-9-0 67 PaulPickard 3 32
(Brian Ellison) *in rr: sn drvn along: hung rt and ended up alone on stands' side over 3f out: nvr a factor* 4/1[3]

P000 8 28 **Spinner Lane**[15] 6215 3-8-2 45 (p) ConnorBeasley(3) 7
(Richard Whitaker) *in rr: drvn 4f out: sn bhd: t.o whn eased fnl f* 100/1

-000 9 40 **Conjuror's Bluff**[14] 6227 6-9-0 45 (p) JasonHart 2
(Frederick Watson) *chsd ldrs: drvn over 3f out: sn lost pl: eased whn bhd over 1f out: tailed rt off* 66/1

1m 40.95s (4.35) **Going Correction** +0.375s/f (Good)
**WFA** 3 from 4yo+ 4lb 9 Ran SP% **117.5**
Speed ratings (Par 103): **93,92,87,87,84 80,80,52,12**
CSF £9.21 TOTE £4.30: £1.90, £1.10, £4.30; EX 10.00 Trifecta £66.00.There was no bid for winner.
**Owner** Richard Walker **Bred** Mrs G Slater **Trained** Stillington, N Yorks

**FOCUS**
They went a sound pace for this modest seller. The front two pulled clear. The form might be a bit better, but only if the fourth can prove that to be the case.

## 6671 RACING UK IPAD APP RACINGUK.COM/MOBILE H'CAP 5f
**4:00** (4:01) (Class 5) (0-70,74) 3-Y-O+ £2,911 (£866; £432; £216) **Stalls** Centre

Form RPR

0004 1 **Little Eli**[68] 4391 4-8-12 63 (p) NeilFarley(3) 8 71
(Eric Alston) *qckly away: mde all: rdn and hung rt ent fnl f: sn drvn and wandered: kpt on wl towards fin* 10/1

4065 2 nk **Storyline (IRE)**[19] 6109 3-9-0 63 DuranFentiman 14 70
(Tim Easterby) *in tch: hdwy to chse ldrs 2f out: rdn whn n.m.r and swtchd lft ent fnl f: sn drvn to chal and ev ch tl edgd lft and no ex nr fin* 16/1

0365 3 1/2 **A J Cook (IRE)**[32] 5683 4-8-2 55 oh4 (v) JoeDoyle(5) 9 60
(Ron Barr) *towards rr and sn rdn along: hdwy wl over 1f out: swtchd lft and drvn ent fnl f: kpt on wl towards fin* 12/1

6611 4 nk **Fredricka**[58] 4725 3-9-4 67 JasonHart 13 71
(Garry Moss) *towards rr: hdwy 2f out: rdn to chse ldrs whn edgd lft ent fnl f: sn drvn and kpt on same pce* 6/1[2]

6000 5 shd **Royal Bajan (USA)**[6] 6475 6-9-2 67 (v) ConnorBeasley(3) 16 71
(James Given) *racd wd: cl up: rdn to chal over 1f out: drvn and edgd lft ent fnl f: kpt on same pce* 33/1

631 6 1 **Orient Class**[6] 6475 3-9-11 74 6ex (v) GrahamLee 3 74
(Paul Midgley) *prom on outer: effrt 2f out sn rdn and ev ch tl drvn and one pce ent fnl f* 4/1[1]

3036 7 1 **Emily Davison (IRE)**[22] 5994 3-8-7 61 (p) GemmaTutty(5) 12 57
(Karen Tutty) *towards rr: pushed along over 2f out: rdn wl over 1f out: styd on fnl f: nrst fin* 33/1

4003 8 3/4 **Ingenti**[3] 6580 6-8-7 60 KevinStott(5) 7 54
(Christopher Wilson) *trckd ldrs: effrt wl over 1f out: sn rdn: edgd lft and wknd ent fnl f* 10/1

5030 9 1 1/4 **Foreign Rhythm (IRE)**[48] 5089 9-8-12 60 DaleSwift 18 49
(Ron Barr) *in rr tl sme late hdwy* 33/1

3635 10 1/2 **Kirtling Belle**[6] 6475 3-9-4 67 TomEaves 4 54
(Keith Dalgleish) *nvr bttr than midfield* 9/1[3]

0500 11 nk **Bosham**[7] 6452 4-9-5 67 GrahamGibbons 17 53
(Michael Easterby) *chsd ldrs: rdn over 2f out: sn wknd* 16/1

0000 12 1 **Lorimer's Lot (IRE)**[70] 4315 3-9-4 67 TonyHamilton 10 50
(Mark Walford) *prom: rdn along over 2f out: sn wknd* 25/1

0660 13 3/4 **Lady Poppy**[28] 5819 4-8-13 61 AndrewMullen 11 41
(George Moore) *chsd ldrs: rdn along over 2f out: sn wknd: lame* 33/1

0400 14 hd **Eland Ally**[15] 6213 6-9-4 66 (p) JamesSullivan 2 45+
(Tom Tate) *stmbld bdly s: a towards rr* 4/1[1]

620 15 1/2 **Thornaby Princess**[33] 5641 3-9-3 66 RussKennemore 5 44
(Marjorie Fife) *chsd ldrs: rdn along over 2f out: sn wknd* 12/1

000 16 3/4 **Lost In Paris (IRE)**[28] 5819 8-8-13 61 (b) BarryMcHugh 6 36
(Tony Coyle) *dwlt: a towards rr* 33/1

5451 17 1/2 **Traditionelle**[11] 6340 3-8-13 69 RachelRichardson(7) 1 42
(Tim Easterby) *in tch on wd outside: rdn along over 2f out: sn wknd* 12/1

1m 0.24s (1.64) **Going Correction** +0.375s/f (Good)
**WFA** 3 from 4yo+ 1lb 17 Ran SP% **137.7**
Speed ratings (Par 103): **101,100,99,99,99 97,95,94,92,91 91,89,88,88,87 86,85**
CSF £167.67 CT £1975.99 TOTE £12.10: £2.70, £3.90, £3.40, £2.30; EX 178.60 Trifecta £2245.60 Part won..
**Owner** Whittle Racing Partnership **Bred** J E Jackson **Trained** Longton, Lancs

**FOCUS**
A wide-open sprint handicap run at a fair pace. It paid to race handy. Ordinary form.

## 6672 VOLTIGEUR RESTAURANT 2 COURSE SPECIAL FOR £11.95 H'CAP 1m 2f
**4:35** (4:36) (Class 5) (0-75,75) 3-Y-O+ £2,911 (£866; £432; £216) **Stalls** Low

Form RPR

336- 1 **Beltor**[368] 6628 3-9-0 71 LukeMorris 6 80+
(Sir Mark Prescott Bt) *chsd ldrs: hdwy on outer over 3f out: chal over 1f out: edgd lft ins fnl f: styd on to ld last 50yds* 5/1[2]

1332 2 nk **Valantino Oyster (IRE)**[9] 6402 7-9-3 71 (p) ConnorBeasley(3) 2 79
(Tracy Waggott) *led: crowded and hdd ins fnl f: no ex wl ins fnl f* 9/1[3]

5536 3 1 **Exclusive Waters (IRE)**[30] 5758 4-8-7 61 JacobButterfield(3) 9 67
(Tracy Waggott) *mid-div: hdwy 4f out: chsng ldrs whn swtchd rt over 2f out: kpt on to take 3rd last 75yds* 50/1

5536 4 1 3/4 **Save The Bees**[53] 4921 6-9-7 75 NeilFarley(3) 7 78
(Declan Carroll) *chsd ldrs: slipped bnd over 4f out: kpt on same pce over 1f out* 20/1

1310 5 nk **Diletta Tommasa (IRE)**[16] 6192 4-9-1 71 (p) EoinWalsh(5) 4 73
(John Stimpson) *in rr-div: hdwy on outer over 2f out: kpt on fnl f* 20/1

2602 6 1 3/4 **Gabrial's Hope (FR)**[19] 6119 5-9-0 65 TonyHamilton 11 64
(Tracy Waggott) *s.s: in rr: hdwy on ins 3f out: nvr a threat* 16/1

424 7 1 **Past Forgetting (IRE)**[28] 5831 3-9-1 72 DanielTudhope 13 69
(Luca Cumani) *in rr-div: hdwy on outer over 2f out: kpt on: nvr a factor* 11/4[1]

0040 8 3/4 **Good Speech (IRE)**[20] 6062 4-9-0 65 JamesSullivan 8 61
(Tom Tate) *rr-div: drvn 5f out: sme hdwy over 2f out: kpt on fnl f: nvr a factor* 25/1

-542 9 1 1/4 **My Guardian Angel**[25] 5395 5-9-0 65 (p) JimmyQuinn 12 58
(Mark H Tompkins) *s.i.s: sme hdwy over 3f out: kpt on fnl f: nvr a factor* 12/1

2503 10 1 **Mariners Moon (IRE)**[2] 6596 3-8-9 69 (p) SamJames(3) 10 63
(David O'Meara) *mid-div: hdwy over 3f out: hmpd over 2f out: wknd over 1f out* 5/1[2]

2116 11 hd **Mixed Message (IRE)**[14] 6232 4-9-2 67 DaleSwift 3 58
(Brian Ellison) *mid-div: effrt and edgd lft over 2f out: wknd over 1f out* 16/1

0604 **12** *17* **King Of The Celts (IRE)**[51] 4975 6-8-13 64........................ TomEaves 1 23
(Tim Easterby) *chsd ldrs: hmpd over 2f out: lost pl over 1f out: bhd whn eased clsng stages: t.o* **20/1**

3666 **13** *2* **Artful Prince**[17] 6166 4-9-9 74........................................(b) GrahamLee 15 29
(James Given) *mid-div: lost pl over 6f out: sn bhd: eased clsng stages: t.o* **12/1**

0252 **14** *11* **Charles De Mille**[29] 5793 6-8-10 61 oh3........................ AndrewMullen 5
(George Moore) *chsd ldrs: lost pl over 2f out: bhd whn eased ins fnl f: tailed rt off* **25/1**

2-00 **15** *2 1/2* **Khelac**[137] 2164 4-8-10 61 oh4........................................(b) PJMcDonald 14
(Micky Hammond) *in rr: drvn over 4f out: sn bhd: eased clsng stages: tailed rt off* **66/1**

2m 6.07s (-1.03) **Going Correction** +0.175s/f (Good)
**WFA** 3 from 4yo+ 6lb **15** Ran SP% **122.6**
Speed ratings (Par 103): **111,110,109,108,108 106,106,105,104,103 103,89,88,79,77**
CSF £45.45 CT £2048.86 TOTE £4.80: £2.30, £2.30, £8.30; EX 49.10 Trifecta £2352.80 Part won..
**Owner** Miss Fiona Aitken **Bred** Stewart Aitken **Trained** Newmarket, Suffolk
■ Stewards' Enquiry : Neil Farley jockey said the gelding slipped on the final bend turning into the home straight
Jacob Butterfield one-day ban: use of whip (8 Oct)

**FOCUS**
Plenty of pace for this competitive handicap. The winner was quite impressive.

## 6673 RACING UK ANYWHERE AVAILABLE NOW (S) STKS 1m 2f
**5:05** (5:07) (Class 5) 3-5-Y-O **£2,726** (£805; £402) **Stalls Low**

Form RPR

5500 **1** **Edward Elgar**[19] 6121 3-8-6 49........................(p) GeorgeChaloner(3) 3 54
(Richard Whitaker) *cl up on inner: pushed along 4f out: rdn along and sltly outpcd over 2f out: hdwy over 1f out: drvn and styd on wl on inner ins fnl f to ld last 75yds* **13/2**

6520 **2** *nk* **Hope For Glory**[11] 6342 5-8-12 60........................ JoeyHaynes(3) 6 53
(Jason Ward) *led: rdn along 3f out: hdd 2f out: styd cl up and drvn to ld again ent fnl f: hdd and no ex last 75yds* **3/1**[3]

4000 **3** *nk* **Bold And Free**[19] 6122 4-9-1 45........................[1] JimmyQuinn 7 53
(David Thompson) *in rr: hdwy 3f out: rdn along 2f out: swtchd rt to outer and drvn wl over 1f out: drvn and styd on to chal ins fnl f: kpt on same pce* **10/1**

5 **4** *1 1/4* **Sirdal**[8] 6429 3-8-6 0........................(v[1]) SamJames(3) 5 50
(David O'Meara) *trckd ldng pair: hdwy 4f out: cl up over 3f out: rdn to ld narrowly 2f out: sn drvn and hdd ent fnl f: wknd last 100yds* **9/4**[2]

0100 **P** **Soul Of Motion**[42] 5304 3-8-10 65........................ DanielMuscutt(5) 4
(Gay Kelleway) *trckd ldrs: effrt whn lost action and p.u 3f out: fatally injured* **85/40**[1]

2m 10.27s (3.17) **Going Correction** +0.175s/f (Good)
**WFA** 3 from 4yo+ 6lb **5** Ran SP% **110.2**
Speed ratings (Par 103): **94,93,93,92,**
CSF £25.67 TOTE £12.40: £3.80, £3.20; EX 25.60 Trifecta £122.80.There was no bid for winner.
**Owner** Paul Davies & The Barflys **Bred** Hellwood Stud Farm & Paul Davies (h'Gate) **Trained** Scarcroft, W Yorks

**FOCUS**
A desperately weak seller run at a steady pace. Very weak form rated around the winner and third.

## 6674 RACING REPLAY, ALL TODAY'S RACING SKY432 H'CAP 6f
**5:35** (5:37) (Class 6) (0-65,65) 3-Y-O+ **£2,726** (£805; £402) **Stalls Centre**

Form RPR

0-00 **1** **Chiswick Bey (IRE)**[14] 6232 6-9-2 65........................ SammyJoBell(5) 2 74
(Richard Fahey) *mid-div: hdwy over 2f out: chsng ldrs over 1f out: styd on to ld nr fin* **20/1**

5333 **2** *1/2* **Exotic Guest**[15] 6213 4-9-7 65........................(p) JamesSullivan 1 72
(Ruth Carr) *hld up in rr: hdwy over 2f out: upsides and kpt on fnl f: tk 2nd nr fin* **9/1**[3]

4223 **3** *nk* **Another Royal**[15] 6215 3-9-0 60........................(b) PhillipMakin 12 66
(Tim Easterby) *chsd ldrs: led over 1f out: hdd and no ex clsng stages* **14/1**

4000 **4** *3/4* **Iggy**[100] 3298 4-8-13 57........................(t) GrahamGibbons 7 61
(Michael Easterby) *chsd ldrs: kpt on same pce fnl f* **33/1**

6050 **5** *1* **Rich Again (IRE)**[15] 6213 5-9-6 64........................(p) TonyHamilton 20 65
(James Bethell) *in rr: hdwy over 2f out: kpt on wl fnl f* **9/1**[3]

4022 **6** *3/4* **Ad Vitam (IRE)**[19] 6120 6-8-12 56........................(bt) RaulDaSilva 4 54
(Suzzanne France) *rr-div: hdwy over 2f out: swtchd lft over 1f out: sn chsng ldrs: wknd towards fin* **14/1**

0534 **7** *hd* **Niceonemyson**[9] 6405 5-8-11 60........................(b[1]) KevinStott(5) 16 58
(Christopher Wilson) *mid-div: hdwy over 2f out: styd on fnl f* **20/1**

5300 **8** *hd* **The Nifty Fox**[9] 6406 10-8-4 55........................(p) RachelRichardson(7) 17 52
(Tim Easterby) *led early: chsd ldrs: one pce over 1f out* **33/1**

3021 **9** *1/2* **Gaelic Wizard (IRE)**[22] 5996 6-8-13 62........................ GemmaTutty(5) 3 58
(Karen Tutty) *chsd ldrs: drvn over 2f out: one pce appr fnl f* **20/1**

0600 **10** *2 1/4* **Hab Reeh**[15] 6217 6-9-2 60........................ PaulMulrennan 6 48
(Ruth Carr) *in rr: swtchd lft over 1f out: nvr a factor* **33/1**

6100 **11** *1/2* **Black Douglas**[15] 6213 5-8-7 58........................ RachaelGrant(7) 15 45
(Jim Goldie) *s.i.s: in rr: sme hdwy 2f out: nvr a factor* **25/1**

3430 **12** *nk* **Red Cape (FR)**[11] 6346 11-8-11 55........................(b) PJMcDonald 8 41
(Ruth Carr) *w ldr: wknd appr fnl f* **20/1**

151 **13** *hd* **Logans Lad (IRE)**[26] 5897 4-9-7 65........................(bt) FrankieMcDonald 14 50
(Daniel Mark Loughnane) *mid-div: effrt over 2f out: sn chsng ldrs: wknd fnl f* **16/1**

-000 **14** *nk* **Chamberlain**[9] 6405 3-9-0 60........................(p) JasonHart 19 44
(John Murray) *sn led: hdd over 1f out: sn wknd* **50/1**

1023 **15** *1* **Choc'A'Moca (IRE)**[7] 6452 7-9-4 62........................(v) GrahamLee 5 43
(Paul Midgley) *mid-div: effrt over 2f out: wknd over 1f out* **11/1**

0526 **16** *5* **Sakhee's Rose**[13] 6266 4-9-4 62........................(b) DaleSwift 13 27
(Ed McMahon) *mid-div: hdwy over 2f out: sn chsng ldrs lost pl over 1f out* **8/1**[2]

2500 **17** *1* **Shillito**[4] 6544 4-9-0 58........................(v[1]) BarryMcHugh 10 20
(Tony Coyle) *chsd ldrs: edgd lft and wknd over 1f out* **25/1**

-362 **18** *nk* **Cash Is King**[33] 5642 4-9-1 62........................ ConnorBeasley(3) 11 23
(Robert Johnson) *a towards rr* **8/1**[2]

4601 **19** *3/4* **Foxtrot Pearl (IRE)**[15] 6215 3-9-5 65........................ FrannyNorton 18 23
(John Holt) *hit hd on stalls: mid-div: hdwy over 2f out: wknd over 1f out* **20/1**

3245 **20** *nse* **Vodka Time (IRE)**[15] 6213 3-8-11 62........................ EoinWalsh(5) 9 20+
(Shaun Harris) *v.s.a: swtchd stands' side over 2f out: nvr on terms* **9/2**[1]

1m 13.56s (1.76) **Going Correction** +0.375s/f (Good)
**WFA** 3 from 4yo+ 2lb **20** Ran SP% **130.2**
Speed ratings (Par 101): **103,102,101,100,99 98,98,98,97,94 93,93,93,92,91 84,83,82,81,81**
CSF £173.36 CT £2705.85 TOTE £33.90: £6.50, £2.70, £3.70, £7.90; EX 263.90 Trifecta £1730.10 Part won..
**Owner** M J Macleod **Bred** Mrs Kay Egan **Trained** Musley Bank, N Yorks

**FOCUS**
An open if modest handicap run at a sound pace. The action unfolded towards the far side. The second and third have been rated close to their recent form.
T/Jkpt: Not won. T/Plt: £191.20 to a £1 stake. Pool: £52,951.62 - 202.07 winning tickets T/Qpdt: £46.00 to a £1 stake. Pool: £7,207.67 - 115.90 winning tickets WG

# 6659 KEMPTON (A.W) (R-H)
### Thursday, September 25

**OFFICIAL GOING: Polytrack: standard**
Wind: Moderate, across (away from stands) Weather: Fine but cloudy

## 6675 VISIT AND DINE IN THE PANORAMIC MAIDEN AUCTION STKS 6f (P)
**5:40** (5:42) (Class 6) 2-Y-O **£1,940** (£577; £288; £144) **Stalls Low**

Form RPR

**1** **Mountain Rescue (IRE)** 2-9-0 0........................ OisinMurphy 4 73+
(Roger Charlton) *hld up in rr: stl only 10th jst over 2f out: gd prog on outer over 1f out: swept into the ld last 150yds: sn clr* **8/1**[3]

**2** *2 1/4* **Caught On The Bid (IRE)** 2-9-1 0........................ DeclanBates(3) 3 69
(Ed de Giles) *trckd ldrs: shkn up over 1f out: clsd fnl f: outpcd by wnr but styd on to take 2nd last stride* **25/1**

5 **3** *shd* **Closing**[82] 3975 2-8-3 0........................ RyanPowell(3) 6 57
(Nick Littmoden) *chsd ldr: rdn over 2f out: clsd to ld briefly jst ins fnl f: sn outpcd by wnr: lost 2nd last stride* **25/1**

03 **4** *hd* **Captain Marmalade (IRE)**[85] 3842 2-9-4 0........................ GeorgeBaker 12 68
(Roger Charlton) *hld up in midfield: stdy prog jst over 2f out: hanging as clsd 1f out: pushed along and styd on same pce* **4/5**[1]

**5** *1* **Pomme De Guerre (IRE)** 2-9-4 0........................ JohnFahy 2 65
(Eve Johnson Houghton) *rousted fr s to dispute 2nd: rdn over 2f out: one pce fr over 1f out* **5/1**[2]

0 **6** *2 1/4* **Blackadder**[14] 6261 2-8-11 0........................ FergusSweeney 5 51
(Pat Phelan) *led: rdn 2f out: hdd & wknd ins fnl f* **66/1**

6 **7** *nk* **Paloma Dancer**[36] 5555 2-8-6 0........................ SilvestreDeSousa 11 45
(Harry Dunlop) *chsd ldrs: rdn and lost pl over 1f out: one pce after* **12/1**

0 **8** *nse* **Machiavelian Storm (IRE)**[9] 6434 2-8-13 0........................ ShaneKelly 10 52
(Ed Dunlop) *dwlt: towards rr: sme prog 2f out: no imp on ldrs 1f out: fdd* **33/1**

**9** *shd* **Celtic Ava (IRE)** 2-8-6 0........................ JemmaMarshall(3) 1 48
(Pat Phelan) *dwlt: hld up in last pair: sme prog on inner 2f out: no imp on ldrs whn pushed along over 1f out: nt disgracd* **50/1**

**10** *2 1/4* **Viva Madiba (IRE)** 2-8-9 0........................ SteveDrowne 7 41
(Daniel Kubler) *dwlt: sn in midfield: prog to chse ldrs 2f out: wknd fnl f* **50/1**

6 **11** *7* **Saint Honore**[29] 5821 2-8-6 0........................ HarryBentley 9 17
(Pat Phelan) *a in rr: bhd over 2f out* **8/1**[3]

**12** *9* **Catakanta** 2-8-11 0........................ KieranO'Neill 8
(Denis Coakley) *rn green: hmpd after 1f and dropped to last pair: wknd sn after 1/2-way: t.o* **66/1**

1m 14.2s (1.10) **Going Correction** -0.05s/f (Stan) **12** Ran SP% **119.7**
Speed ratings (Par 93): **90,87,86,86,85 82,81,81,81,78 69,57**
CSF £188.74 TOTE £9.10: £2.30, £4.50, £4.80; EX 260.60 Trifecta £2189.20 Part won..
**Owner** Lady Richard Wellesley **Bred** Lady Richard Wellesley **Trained** Beckhampton, Wilts

**FOCUS**
A moderate 2yo maiden.

## 6676 COLIN MURRAY AND FRIENDS ON TALKSPORT CLAIMING STKS 7f (P)
**6:15** (6:16) (Class 6) 2-Y-O **£1,940** (£577; £288; £144) **Stalls Low**

Form RPR

00 **1** **Almoqatel (IRE)**[27] 5874 2-9-1 0........................ ShaneKelly 7 63
(James Fanshawe) *trckd ldng trio: rdn and clsd over 2f out: chal u.p fnl f: led last stride* **9/2**

6500 **2** *nse* **Tumut (IRE)**[1] 6662 2-8-10 62........................ CharlesBishop(3) 6 61
(Mick Channon) *trckd ldr: rdn to ld wl over 2f out: hrd pressed fnl f: hdd last stride* **4/1**[3]

0444 **3** *3/4* **Charlie's Star**[28] 5845 2-8-8 68........................ JFEgan 2 54
(David Evans) *chsd ldng pair: rdn 3f out: chal on inner over 1f out: kpt on but nt qckn ins fnl f* **2/1**[2]

4532 **4** *1 1/2* **Paris Carver (FR)**[10] 6412 2-8-6 56........................ JohnFahy 1 48
(Jonathan Portman) *sn in 7th: urged along over 2f out: sme prog wl over 1f out: tk 4th fnl f: rdn and no imp after* **6/4**[1]

0 **5** *1 3/4* **Kicking Leaves (IRE)**[16] 6205 2-8-10 0........................(b[1]) PhilipPrince(3) 5 50
(J S Moore) *rousted leaving stalls: rdn in 6th 1/2-way: nvr on terms: kpt on fr over 1f out* **33/1**

5060 **6** *1 1/2* **Go White Lightning (IRE)**[10] 6413 2-8-10 55........................(p) MartinDwyer 3 43
(Malcolm Saunders) *rousted leaving stalls: mostly in last: detached over 2f out: plugged on fnl f* **33/1**

0300 **7** *1 1/4* **Johnny Sorrento**[14] 6248 2-8-5 53........................(tp) SilvestreDeSousa 8 35
(Tim Pitt) *racd freely: led: hdd and nt qckn wl over 2f out: wknd qckly over 1f out* **16/1**

0500 **8** *2* **Dark Symphony (IRE)**[21] 6072 2-8-0 45........................(p) KieranO'Neill 4 24
(Mark Usher) *chsd ldrs in 5th: no prog 2f out: wknd qckly over 1f out* **50/1**

1m 27.78s (1.78) **Going Correction** -0.05s/f (Stan) **8** Ran SP% **125.2**
Speed ratings (Par 93): **87,86,86,84,82 80,79,76**
CSF £24.93 TOTE £8.00: £1.70, £2.30, £1.20; EX 29.20 Trifecta £84.90.Charlie's Star was claimed by Mr Andrew Bain for £7,000
**Owner** Mohamed Obaida **Bred** Mark Hanly **Trained** Newmarket, Suffolk

**FOCUS**
A very weak 2yo claimer.

## 6677 FOLLOW @BETVICTORRACING ON TWITTER MAIDEN STKS 1m 4f (P)
**6:45** (6:45) (Class 5) 3-Y-O+ **£2,587** (£770; £384; £192) **Stalls Centre**

Form RPR

2 **1** **Seamour (IRE)**[29] 5822 3-9-5 0........................ FergusSweeney 8 86
(Jo Crowley) *trckd ldr: led over 2f out and sent for home: rdn and hung rt over 1f out: styd on wl* **6/1**[2]

2 **2** 3¼ **Karezak (IRE)**[20] 6092 3-9-5 85....................................(p) JamesDoyle 5 81
(Alan King) *trckd ldng trio: rdn over 2f out: tk 2nd wl over 1f out: nt qckn and no imp on wnr* **4/9**[1]

04 **3** 2¾ **Panatella**[20] 6092 3-9-0 0.................................................. ShaneKelly 2 72+
(James Fanshawe) *hld up in 5th: outpcd and pushed along jst over 2f out: hanging rt after and stl green but styd on steadily to take 3rd ins fnl f* **8/1**

0 **4** 2 **Sea Vision (IRE)**[29] 5831 4-9-13 0.............................. AdamBeschizza 3 74
(Jo Crowley) *chsd ldng pair: rdn 3f out: disp 2nd briefly wl over 1f out: sn wknd* **50/1**

0 **5** 7 **Dukes Den**[117] 2773 3-9-0 0.......................................... JoshBaudains(5) 6 64
(Sylvester Kirk) *dwlt: in tch tl rdn and wknd over 2f out* **66/1**

5-0 **6** nse **Cry Joy (USA)**[29] 5831 3-9-5 0.......................................... MartinLane 9 63
(Charlie Appleby) *led: rdn and hdd over 2f out: wknd qckly over 1f out* **7/1**[3]

**7** 2 **Mobhirr** 3-9-5 0..............................................................(p) MartinHarley 1 60
(Marco Botti) *dwlt: in tch: shkn up wl over 2f out: sn wknd* **10/1**

6-00 **8** 20 **Eton Dorney (USA)**[7] 6482 5-9-13 75.............................. OisinMurphy 7 30
(Kevin Tork) *stdd s: t.k.h: hld up in last pair: shkn up and wknd 3f out: t.o* **66/1**

**9** 12 **Macs Scwar**[527] 7-9-8 0.............................................. DanielMuscutt(5) 4 12
(Paul Morgan) *dwlt: a in last pair: rdn and wknd over 3f out: wl t.o* **100/1**

2m 35.34s (0.84) **Going Correction** -0.05s/f (Stan)
**WFA** 3 from 4yo+ 8lb **9** Ran SP% **122.2**
Speed ratings (Par 103): **95,92,91,89,85 84,83,70,62**
CSF £9.67 TOTE £7.30: £1.80, £1.10, £2.10; EX 15.20 Trifecta £44.10.
**Owner** Mrs Jackie Cornwell **Bred** Barbara Prendergast **Trained** Whitcombe, Dorset

**FOCUS**
There was a turn up here. The third is the guide. Muddling form.

## 6678 £25 FREE BET AT BETVICTOR.COM NURSERY H'CAP (DIV I) 6f (P)
**7:15** (7:15) (Class 5) (0-75,75) 2-Y-O **£2,587** (£770; £384; £192) **Stalls** Low

Form RPR

0623 **1** **Best Endeavour**[20] 6115 2-9-6 74.................................... MartinDwyer 4 79
(William Muir) *trckd ldng pair: wnt 2nd sn after 1/2-way: rdn to ld 2f out: clr fnl f: styd on* **8/1**

0340 **2** 1¾ **Billyoakes (IRE)**[12] 6312 2-8-13 70......................... CharlesBishop(3) 10 70
(Mick Channon) *racd freely: led after 2f: rdn and hdd 2f out: one pce after* **16/1**

055 **3** ¾ **Dylan's Storm (IRE)**[28] 5847 2-8-12 66.......................... FergusSweeney 7 64
(David Dennis) *settled in last trio: shkn up over 2f out: prog over 1f out: styd on to take 3rd nr fin* **66/1**

0312 **4** ½ **Some Show**[24] 5983 2-9-3 71............................................. DaneO'Neill 9 67
(Henry Candy) *mostly in midfield: outpcd and racd awkwardly over 2f out: styd on again fr over 1f out: chal for 3rd nr fin* **4/1**[2]

31 **5** ½ **Steal The Scene (IRE)**[45] 5248 2-9-7 75................................. PatDobbs 2 72+
(Richard Hannon) *awkward s: hld up in last: pushed along whn nt clr run briefly 2f out: stl only 10th 1f out: styd on takingly fnl f: gng on at fin* **9/2**[3]

6463 **6** nk **Sportlobster (IRE)**[29] 5828 2-8-13 67............................(p) HayleyTurner 5 61
(Tom Dascombe) *wl away: led 2f: sn rdn: lost 2nd wl over 2f out and racd v awkwardly: one pce after* **8/1**

3330 **7** nk **Rockaroundtheclock (IRE)**[24] 5981 2-8-10 71............. PaulBooth(7) 1 64
(Paul Cole) *mostly in midfield: outpcd over 2f out: tried to make prog over 1f out: no hdwy fnl f* **20/1**

531 **8** shd **Lady Maesmor**[50] 5056 2-9-4 72...................................... JackMitchell 8 64
(Martyn Meade) *chsd ldrs: rdn to go 4th jst over 2f out but nt on terms: no imp after: wknd fnl f* **20/1**

5406 **9** 1¾ **Rosie Royale (IRE)**[34] 5626 2-9-1 69.............................. JamesDoyle 11 56
(Roger Teal) *chsd ldng trio: rdn bef 1/2-way: lost pl jst over 2f out: wknd* **14/1**

043 **10** ½ **Aqlette**[45] 5255 2-8-10 64................................................. MartinHarley 6 50
(Marco Botti) *towards rr: shkn up and tried to make prog 2f out: no hdwy 1f out: wknd* **5/2**[1]

0056 **11** 6 **Bombay Mix**[44] 5285 2-8-6 60........................................... MartinLane 3 28
(Charlie Fellowes) *a in last trio: wknd wl over 1f out* **33/1**

1m 12.93s (-0.17) **Going Correction** -0.05s/f (Stan) **11** Ran SP% **115.5**
Speed ratings (Par 95): **99,96,95,95,94 93,93,93,91,90 82**
CSF £118.13 CT £7761.01 TOTE £7.80: £2.20, £6.90, £12.40; EX 183.10 Trifecta £1485.10 Part won..
**Owner** C L A Edgington & D G Clarke **Bred** Cheveley Park Stud Ltd **Trained** Lambourn, Berks

**FOCUS**
An ordinary nursery.

## 6679 £25 FREE BET AT BETVICTOR.COM NURSERY H'CAP (DIV II) 6f (P)
**7:45** (7:45) (Class 5) (0-75,75) 2-Y-O **£2,587** (£770; £384; £192) **Stalls** Low

Form RPR

4103 **1** **Spring Loaded (IRE)**[20] 6104 2-9-7 **75**.............................. SeanLevey 6 78
(Paul D'Arcy) *trckd ldng pair: rdn to ld wl over 1f out: in command fnl f: styd on wl* **4/1**[3]

2103 **2** 1¼ **Jaganory (IRE)**[75] 4205 2-9-6 **74**...................................... JFEgan 3 73
(David Evans) *led 1f: pressed ldr: led wl over 2f out to wl over 1f out: chsd wnr after: styd on but no real imp* **16/1**

0360 **3** 2¾ **Lysander The Greek**[18] 6165 2-9-0 **68**...............(b[1]) SilvestreDeSousa 8 59
(Ralph Beckett) *chsd ldrs on outer: rdn 1/2-way: kpt on one pce u.p fnl 2f to take 3rd nr fin* **11/4**[2]

0144 **4** ½ **Pixeleen**[12] 6312 2-8-13 **67**.............................................. OisinMurphy 9 57
(Malcolm Saunders) *led after 1f to wl over 2f out: steadily outpcd u.p over 1f out* **20/1**

0044 **5** 1½ **Presto Boy**[23] 6016 2-8-12 **66**......................................... ShaneKelly 7 51
(James Fanshawe) *hld up in tch: gng bttr than many over 2f out: n.m.r after: no hdwy whn rdn fnl f* **6/1**

0501 **6** 1¾ **Barchan (USA)**[29] 5828 2-8-12 **71**...............................(p) CamHardie(5) 10 51+
(Charlie Appleby) *dwlt: hung bdly lft and ended against outside rail after 2f: continued to be impossible to steer and virtually t.o 1/2-way: r.o fnl f: did wl to fin so cl* **2/1**[1]

51 **7** ½ **Rictrude (FR)**[38] 5509 2-9-2 **70**...................................... HayleyTurner 5 48
(Tom Dascombe) *hld up in last of main gp: shkn up and no prog jst over 2f out: n.d after* **7/1**

3104 **8** shd **Jersey Bull (IRE)**[82] 3963 2-9-2 **70**.............................[1] SamHitchcott 1 48
(Michael Madgwick) *chsd ldrs: rdn bef 1/2-way: no prog 2f out: wknd over 1f out* **33/1**

1m 12.73s (-0.37) **Going Correction** -0.05s/f (Stan) **8** Ran SP% **120.4**
Speed ratings (Par 95): **100,98,94,94,92 89,89,88**
CSF £66.96 CT £210.22 TOTE £3.70: £1.20, £3.60, £1.90; EX 51.50 Trifecta £150.50.
**Owner** Rowley Racing **Bred** Swordlestown Little **Trained** Newmarket, Suffolk

**FOCUS**
The second division of the ordinary sprint nursery and a marginally quicker time.

## 6680 DOWNLOAD THE BETVICTOR APP NOW H'CAP 6f (P)
**8:15** (8:15) (Class 5) (0-75,77) 3-Y-O+ **£2,587** (£770; £384; £192) **Stalls** Low

Form RPR

3306 **1** **Dutch Interior**[25] 5945 3-9-5 75....................................... JamesDoyle 7 84+
(Gary Moore) *hld up in 6th and off the pce: prog over 2f out and gng best: tk 2nd 1f out: rdn and qckly clsd to ld last 120yds: styd on* **11/4**[1]

140 **2** ¾ **Shingle**[14] 6249 3-9-2 75............................................. DeclanBates(3) 8 81
(Ed de Giles) *chsd ldrs: rdn wl over 2f out: prog over 1f out: styd on to take 2nd last 50yds: no real threat to wnr but clsd at fin* **20/1**

1100 **3** 1¼ **Gone With The Wind (GER)**[23] 6020 3-9-5 75..(p) SilvestreDeSousa 10 77
(Jeremy Noseda) *hld up in last trio: wl off the pce and rdn 1/2-way: no prog u.p tl r.o wl fr jst over 1f out: tk 3rd last stride* **8/1**[3]

4511 **4** shd **Alnoomaas (IRE)**[10] 6398 5-9-4 77 6ex.......................(v) CamHardie(5) 6 79
(Luke Dace) *led at str pce: stretched field 1/2-way: more than 2 l clr 2f out and drvn: hdd & wknd last 120yds* **4/1**[2]

4326 **5** nk **Lucky Di**[23] 6006 4-8-13 70........................................ CharlesBishop(3) 9 71
(Peter Hedger) *towards rr and wl off the pce: u.p 1/2-way: prog 2f out: drvn and styd on to press for 3rd nr fin* **12/1**

0160 **6** 2 **Maria Montez**[17] 6189 5-9-4 72....................................... GeorgeBaker 3 67
(Charles Hills) *chsd clr ldng pair to 2f out: steadily wknd* **33/1**

0622 **7** 1½ **Sweet Talking Guy (IRE)**[23] 6020 4-9-1 72.............(t) SimonPearce(3) 5 62
(Lydia Pearce) *propped bdly s and rdr nrly off: sn swtchd to inner and rcvrd into midfield: prog to dispute 3rd 2f out: wknd fnl f* **4/1**[2]

4303 **8** ½ **Punk**[10] 6414 3-9-3 73..............................................(p) JimCrowley 11 61
(George Peckham) *chsd ldr: drvn and no imp 2f out whn stl clr of rest: lost 2nd and wknd 1f out* **20/1**

3051 **9** 3 **Moonspring (IRE)**[40] 5437 3-9-5 75..............................(e) OisinMurphy 4 54
(Robert Cowell) *s.s: nvr gng wl and mostly in last trio: brief effrt over 1f out: sn wknd* **10/1**

0400 **10** 2¼ **Novellen Lad (IRE)**[23] 6020 9-9-7 75................................ TedDurcan 1 46
(Willie Musson) *hmpd on inner after 100yds: a wl in rr after: no prog 2f out* **14/1**

1m 12.07s (-1.03) **Going Correction** -0.05s/f (Stan)
**WFA** 3 from 4yo+ 2lb **10** Ran SP% **113.7**
Speed ratings (Par 103): **104,103,101,101,100 98,96,95,91,88**
CSF £62.31 CT £392.00 TOTE £3.20: £1.20, £5.80, £2.80; EX 51.20 Trifecta £381.20.
**Owner** R A Green **Bred** Cheveley Park Stud Ltd **Trained** Lower Beeding, W Sussex
■ Stewards' Enquiry : Simon Pearce three-day ban; careless riding (9th-11th Oct)

**FOCUS**
A competitive sprint handicap, run at a strong pace. The winner has been rated as running a small pb.

## 6681 BETVICTOR.COM FILLIES' H'CAP 1m (P)
**8:45** (8:46) (Class 4) (0-85,82) 3-Y-O+ **£4,690** (£1,395; £697; £348) **Stalls** Low

Form RPR

0431 **1** **Stereo Love (FR)**[12] 6316 3-9-6 **82**.................................... GeorgeBaker 7 93
(Clive Cox) *w.w in midfield: stdy prog jst over 2f out: led 1f out: hrd pressed and edgd lft ins fnl f: jst hld on* **8/1**

3021 **2** shd **Anya**[38] 5505 5-9-5 **77**............................................... DaneO'Neill 6 87
(Henry Candy) *hld up in last pair: rdn and prog on outer 2f out: tk 2nd ins fnl f: str chal last 100yds: jst failed* **10/1**

3641 **3** 4½ **She's Gorgeous (IRE)**[22] 6033 3-8-10 **72**..................(v) FrederikTylicki 3 72
(James Fanshawe) *wl in tch: drvn to chse ldng pair over 2f out to over 1f out: kpt on same pce to take 3rd again ins fnl f* **7/1**[3]

41 **4** ¾ **Seldom Seen**[27] 5894 3-9-6 **82**...................................... JamesDoyle 10 80
(Sir Michael Stoute) *chsd ldr: shkn up and no imp 2f out: lost 2nd and fdd over 1f out* **9/2**[2]

5123 **5** nk **Maggie Pink**[160] 1554 5-9-5 **82**............................... AlistairRawlinson(5) 12 80
(Michael Appleby) *led: sent for home over 2f out: hdd & wknd 1f out* **16/1**

-162 **6** 2½ **Pageant Belle**[19] 6145 3-8-11 **78**................................... CamHardie(5) 2 70
(Roger Charlton) *hld up in last trio: tried to make prog fr 2f out: no hdwy 1f out: wknd* **10/1**

-423 **7** 4 **History Book (IRE)**[38] 5505 4-9-10 **82**......................... SilvestreDeSousa 5 65
(Charlie Appleby) *trapped out wd in midfield: u.p and struggling 3f out: no ch fnl 2f* **9/4**[1]

3224 **8** 1 **Starlight Serenade**[21] 6057 3-8-11 **73**............................. OisinMurphy 1 53
(Ralph Beckett) *awkward s: sn in midfield: rdn and no prog over 2f out: wknd over 1f out* **16/1**

54-6 **9** 1¼ **Ardingly (IRE)**[11] 6357 4-9-2 **74**....................................... JimCrowley 8 51
(Paul Cole) *chsd ldng pair to over 2f out: sn btn* **40/1**

-132 **10** nse **Sequined (USA)**[49] 5074 3-9-6 **82**.................................... MartinLane 4 59
(Charlie Appleby) *hld up in last pair: rdn and no prog on inner 2f out* **7/1**[3]

1m 37.7s (-2.10) **Going Correction** -0.05s/f (Stan)
**WFA** 3 from 4yo+ 4lb **10** Ran SP% **117.4**
Speed ratings (Par 102): **108,107,103,102,102 99,95,94,93,93**
CSF £85.67 CT £592.24 TOTE £10.40: £2.10, £3.00, £3.20; EX 105.10 Trifecta £592.00.
**Owner** Al Asayl Bloodstock Ltd **Bred** Sheik Khalifa Bin Zayed Al Nahyan **Trained** Lambourn, Berks
■ Stewards' Enquiry : Dane O'Neill 21 day ban: misuse of whip (10-23 Oct, 23-31 Dec)

**FOCUS**
A competitive-looking fillies' handicap, run at a fair enough pace and two came well clear. The winner has been rated as running a pb.

## 6682 DOWNLOAD THE BETVICTOR INSTABET APP H'CAP 1m 4f (P)
**9:15** (9:17) (Class 6) (0-60,60) 3-Y-O+ **£1,940** (£577; £288; £144) **Stalls** Centre

Form RPR

6113 **1** **Shades Of Silver**[20] 6091 4-9-12 60.................................... JimCrowley 5 74
(Michael Scudamore) *trckd ldrs: prog on wd outside to go 2nd 1/2-way: rdn over 2f out: led over 1f out: styd on* **5/1**

006- **2** 1½ **Thunder Pass (IRE)**[353] 7069 3-9-4 60................................ PatDobbs 14 72
(Hughie Morrison) *dwlt: quick rcvry to chse ldr over 10f out to 1/2-way: 4th 3f out: drvn to chse wnr jst over 1f out: kpt on but unable to chal* **2/1**[1]

6003 **3** 1 **May Queen**[22] 6037 3-9-1 57........................................... TedDurcan 12 67
(Chris Wall) *led 1f: styd prom: rdn over 2f out: tried to chal over 1f out: one pce fnl f* **4/1**[2]

500 **4** 1¼ **May Hay**[38] 5490 4-9-10 58....................................... WilliamCarson 2 66
(Anthony Carson) *in tch in midfield: outpcd whn making and effrt over 2f out: urged along and styd on to take 4th ins fnl f: nrst fin* **12/1**

0555 **5** 3 **Perfect Outcome**[29] 5829 3-8-11 56.................................. RyanTate(3) 11 59
(Patrick Chamings) *chsd ldrs: outpcd over 2f out: kpt on one pce fr over 1f out* **33/1**

5004 **6** 1 **Division Belle**[28] 5865 3-9-0 56...................................... MartinDwyer 13 58
(William Muir) *led: drvn over 2f out: hdd & wknd over 1f out* **14/1**



The Form Book, Raceform Ltd, Newbury, RG14 5SJ

2200 **7** *3* **Rajeh (IRE)**[10] 6410 11-8-9 46........................................ DeclanBates(3) 8 43
(Peter Grayson) *wl in rr: rdn and tried to make prog on outer 4f out: outpcd over 2f out: plugged on* **33/1**

000- **8** *8* **Gladstone (IRE)**[269] 7984 6-8-9 50........................................ DavidParkes(7) 9 34
(Jeremy Gask) *nvr bttr than midfield: rdn 3f out: sn wknd* **33/1**

004 **9** *4* **Deadline Day (IRE)**[115] 2842 3-9-1 57........................................ JackMitchell 10 35
(Roger Varian) *dwlt: a in rr and mostly nt gng wl: bhd fnl 2f* **9/2**[3]

0556 **10** *3 3/4* **Purple Spot**[28] 5846 3-8-8 55........................................ CamHardie(5) 6 27
(Rod Millman) *a wl in rr: no ch fnl 2f* **50/1**

**11** *9* **Fast Green (FR)**[43] 3-9-4 60........................................ SteveDrowne 1 17
(Rod Millman) *wl in tch tl wknd rapidly over 2f out: t.o* **66/1**

5500 **12** *60* **In Seine**[12] 6339 3-9-1 57........................................ FergusSweeney 4
(John Best) *rel to r: a detached in last: t.o sn after 1/2-way* **66/1**

2m 33.49s (-1.01) **Going Correction** -0.05s/f (Stan)
**WFA** 3 from 4yo+ 8lb **12** Ran SP% **116.3**
Speed ratings (Par 101): **101,100,99,98,96 95,93,88,85,83 77,37**
CSF £13.92 CT £38.74 TOTE £5.90: £2.30, £1.70, £1.50; EX 22.30 Trifecta £72.80.
**Owner** The Champion Family & Michael Scudamore **Bred** Newsells Park Stud **Trained** Bromsash, H'fords

■ Numrood was withdrawn. Price at time of withdrawal 14-1. Rule 4 applies to all bets - deduction 5p in the pound.

**FOCUS**
Not a bad handicap for the class. The third has been rated as running a small pb and the fourth as improving on her muddling maiden form.
T/Plt: £1,004.50 to a £1 stake. Pool: £82,425.02 - 59.90 winning units T/Qpdt: £86.10 to a £1 stake. Pool: £13,710.15 - 117.70 winning units JN

## 6553 NEWMARKET (R-H)
### Thursday, September 25

**OFFICIAL GOING: Good (7.2)**
Wind: Medium; across Weather: Dry; overcast

## 6683 NGK SPARK PLUGS EBF STALLIONS MAIDEN STKS (BOBIS RACE) (C&G) 1m
**2:00** (2:02) (Class 4) 2-Y-O **£4,528** (£1,347; £673; £336) **Stalls** High

Form RPR

5 **1** **Mohatem (USA)**[14] 6259 2-9-0 0........................................ PaulHanagan 12 83+
(B W Hills) *w'like: scope: str: lw: sn led and mde rest: rdn wl over 1f out: kpt on wl and forged ahd fnl 100yds: rdn out* **11/8**[1]

4 **2** *1* **Game Pie (IRE)**[14] 6259 2-9-0 0........................................ RyanMoore 3 81
(Hugo Palmer) *str: chsd ldrs: wnt 2nd over 3f out: rdn and ev ch 2f out: no ex and one pce fnl 100yds* **4/1**[3]

**3** *1 1/4* **Tawaasheeh (IRE)** 2-9-0 0........................................ DaneO'Neill 1 78+
(Roger Varian) *unf: in tch in midfield: effrt u.p over 2f out: chsd ldng pair over 1f out: kpt on* **14/1**

0 **4** *1 3/4* **Secateur**[14] 6259 2-9-0 0........................................ WilliamBuick 6 74
(John Gosden) *unf: scope: in tch in midfield: rdn over 3f out: outpcd over 2f out: rallied u.p to go 4th over 1f out: styd on same pce after* **7/2**[2]

**5** *2 3/4* **Captain Navarre** 2-8-11 0........................................ SimonPearce(3) 10 68
(Lydia Pearce) *tall: s.i.s: hld up in rr: shkn up and hdwy against stands' rail over 2f out: kpt on steadily but no imp fr over 1f out* **100/1**

0 **6** *1/2* **Kitten's Red (USA)**[14] 6259 2-9-0 0........................................ JamesDoyle 11 67
(Ed Dunlop) *unf: stdd bk after s: hld up off the pce in last quartet: rdn over 3f out: no threat to ldrs but kpt on steadily ins fnl f* **50/1**

**7** *nse* **Tempus Temporis (USA)** 2-9-0 0........................................ RobertHavlin 4 67
(John Gosden) *str: bit bkwd: s.i.s: rdn and effrt over 2f out: 6th and no imp over 1f out: plugged on* **20/1**

**8** *3* **My Strategy (IRE)** 2-9-0 0........................................ TomQueally 5 60
(Michael Bell) *w'like: chsd wnr tl over 3f out: lost pl u.p over 2f out: wknd over 1f out* **66/1**

0 **9** *9* **Baroot**[8] 6462 2-9-0 0........................................ PatCosgrave 2 39
(M F De Kock, South Africa) *w'like: t.k.h: chsd ldrs: rdn 2f out: sn struggling and btn over 1f out: fdd* **20/1**

**10** *7* **Chorus of Lies** 2-9-0 0........................................ RichardHughes 8 23
(Charlie Appleby) *w'like: s.i.s: a bhd: rdn 1/2-way: lost tch 2f out* **11/1**

00 **11** *1 1/2* **Indomitable Spirit**[20] 6101 2-8-10 0 ow3...... NatalieHambling-Yates(7) 9 22
(Martin Smith) *str: lengthy: chsd ldrs tl lost pl u.p over 2f out: wl bhd and eased wl ins fnl f* **100/1**

1m 38.44s (-0.16) **Going Correction** -0.025s/f (Good) **11** Ran SP% **114.3**
Speed ratings (Par 97): **99,98,96,95,92 91,91,88,79,72 71**
CSF £6.20 TOTE £2.40: £1.10, £1.50, £3.10; EX 7.20 Trifecta £49.80.
**Owner** Hamdan Al Maktoum **Bred** W S Farish & Kilroy Thoroughbred Partnership **Trained** Upper Lambourn, Berks

**FOCUS**
Far side track used. Stalls Stands Side except 12f &16f: Centre. A fair maiden that went the way the market suggested it would.

## 6684 EBM-PAPST NURSERY H'CAP (BOBIS RACE) 1m
**2:35** (2:35) (Class 2) 2-Y-O **£9,056** (£2,695; £1,346; £673) **Stalls** High

Form RPR

6661 **1** **Black Granite (IRE)**[13] 6294 2-8-0 74........................................(v) CamHardie(5) 5 86+
(Jeremy Noseda) *unf: chsd ldr: led 2f out: rdn and fnd ex over 1f out: in command 1f out: r.o wl: comf* **5/1**[3]

310 **2** *2 3/4* **Prince Gagarin (IRE)**[36] 5576 2-9-7 90........................................ RyanMoore 2 96
(Ed Dunlop) *dwlt and pushed along early: in tch in last pair: hdwy u.p over 1f out: chsd wnr 1f out: kpt on but no imp* **4/1**[2]

462 **3** *3/4* **Landwade Lad**[27] 5886 2-8-6 75........................................ AndreaAtzeni 6 79
(James Fanshawe) *athletic: lw: in tch in midfield: clsd to trck ldrs 3f out: rdn and outpcd 2f out: rallied u.p over 1f out: wnt 3rd ins fnl f: styd on wl but no threat to wnr* **7/2**[1]

4310 **4** *2 1/2* **Al Rayyan (IRE)**[31] 5762 2-8-8 77........................................ JamieSpencer 3 76
(Kevin Ryan) *led: hdd and rdn 2f out: unable qck over 1f out: wknd ins fnl f* **9/1**

4345 **5** *1* **Percy Alleline**[15] 6229 2-8-13 87........................................(b[1]) JamesRogers(5) 7 83
(Ralph Beckett) *wnt rt s: t.k.h: in tch: hdwy to chse ldr over 5f out: rdn 2f out: lost pl and hung rt over 1f out: wknd ins fnl f* **14/1**

2021 **6** *nk* **Azmaam (IRE)**[26] 5922 2-8-12 81........................................ PaulHanagan 8 77
(Richard Hannon) *stdd and dropped in bhd after s: hld up in tch in rr: effrt u.p 2f out: wknd ins fnl f* **4/1**[2]

041 **7** *2 3/4* **Orlando Rogue (IRE)**[72] 4301 2-8-9 78........................................ PatCosgrave 1 67
(George Baker) *lengthy: lw: t.k.h: chsd ldrs: rdn and ev ch over 2f out: btn and lost pl over 1f out: wknd fnl f* **5/1**[3]

1m 38.3s (-0.30) **Going Correction** -0.025s/f (Good) **7** Ran SP% **112.2**
Speed ratings (Par 101): **100,97,96,94,93 92,89**
CSF £24.19 CT £77.38 TOTE £6.30: £3.10, £1.90; EX 29.60 Trifecta £146.60.
**Owner** The ABC Partnership **Bred** Yeomanstown Stud **Trained** Newmarket, Suffolk

**FOCUS**
Most of these held a chance in the final 3f, with the early pace having been steady.

## 6685 TURFTRAX.CO.UK SECTIONAL TIMING AT NEWMARKET H'CAP 1m 4f
**3:10** (3:13) (Class 3) (0-90,89) 3-Y-O+ **£9,056** (£2,695; £1,346; £673) **Stalls** Centre

Form RPR

110 **1** **Der Meister (IRE)**[27] 5877 3-8-5 76........................................ DavidProbert 10 89
(Andrew Balding) *lw: chsd ldrs: wnt 2nd and travelling strly 3f out: rdn to chal and clr w ldr over 1f out: led and edgd rt ins fnl f: styd on* **12/1**

012 **2** *shd* **Knife Point (GER)**[19] 6152 3-8-9 80........................................(p) JamesDoyle 2 92
(Hugo Palmer) *led: rdn ent fnl 2f: clr w wnr over 1f out: hdd ins fnl f: battled on gamely: jst hld* **12/1**

3451 **3** *2 1/4* **Cape Caster (IRE)**[27] 5877 3-9-1 86........................................ PatDobbs 6 94
(Ralph Beckett) *stdd s: in tch in midfield: hdwy u.p over 2f out: chsd ldng pair over 1f out: kpt on* **12/1**

24 **4** *4 1/2* **Missed Call (IRE)**[62] 4622 4-9-8 85........................................ TomQueally 8 86
(James Fanshawe) *hld up in midfield: rdn and effrt over 2f out: plugged on to go 4th 1f out: no threat to ldrs* **20/1**

3-13 **5** *1* **Dance Of Heroes**[27] 5884 3-8-10 81........................................ WilliamBuick 3 81
(Jeremy Noseda) *lw: t.k.h: in tch in midfield: effrt u.p over 2f out: no ex and btn over 1f out: wknd ins fnl f* **4/1**[2]

2124 **6** *hd* **Oasis Fantasy (IRE)**[54] 4893 3-9-2 87........................................ RyanMoore 4 86
(Ed Dunlop) *chsd ldrs: rdn over 2f out: outpcd and btn over 1f out: wl hld fnl f* **3/1**[1]

2-50 **7** *nk* **Toptempo**[117] 2782 5-8-12 75........................................ TedDurcan 12 74
(Mark H Tompkins) *hld up in last trio: effrt and rdn over 2f out: no imp whn edgd rt over 1f out* **50/1**

5200 **8** *3 1/2* **Proud Chieftain**[20] 6106 6-9-12 89........................................ RobertTart 7 82
(Clifford Lines) *hld up in midfield: lost pl and rdn 3f out: bhd and swtchd rt 2f out: no ch but styd on past btn horses fnl f* **25/1**

5501 **9** *3/4* **Almerzem (USA)**[7] 6487 3-8-9 80 6ex........................................ PaulHanagan 11 72
(Saeed bin Suroor) *t.k.h: hld up towards rr: effrt but no imp ent fnl 2f: wknd over 1f out* **15/2**

2311 **10** *3 1/2* **Barwick**[31] 5756 6-9-4 86........................................ CamHardie(5) 9 72
(Lady Herries) *hld up in last trio: effrt u.p over 2f out: sn no imp: wknd wl over 1f out* **14/1**

1012 **11** *16* **Old Town Boy**[117] 2761 3-9-4 89........................................ RichardHughes 5 50
(Philip McBride) *lw: chsd ldr tl 3f out: lost pl over 2f out: wl bhd fnl f: t.o* **11/2**[3]

4310 **12** *42* **Isabella Liberty (FR)**[42] 5368 3-8-8 79........................................ AndreaAtzeni 1
(Robert Eddery) *a towards rr: dropped to last 4f out: sn lost tch and t.o* **25/1**

2m 30.41s (-1.59) **Going Correction** +0.025s/f (Good)
**WFA** 3 from 4yo+ 8lb **12** Ran SP% **116.3**
Speed ratings (Par 107): **106,105,104,101,100 100,100,98,97,95 84,56**
CSF £138.07 CT £1765.66 TOTE £12.30: £2.80, £4.20, £4.20; EX 153.10 Trifecta £1857.20.
**Owner** James/Michaelson/Greenwood 1 **Bred** Mrs C L Weld **Trained** Kingsclere, Hants

**FOCUS**
A good-quality handicap, in which the 3yos dominated, and the front pair drew clear. They went a fair gallop. The first two are unexposed and have been rated as improving, while the fourth has been rated 3lb off this year's form on her debut for her new yard.

## 6686 SOMERVILLE TATTERSALL STKS (GROUP 3) (C&G) 7f
**3:40** (3:46) (Class 1) 2-Y-O
**£28,355** (£10,750; £5,380; £2,680; £1,345; £675) **Stalls** High

Form RPR

212 **1** **Maftool (USA)**[19] 6142 2-9-0 99........................................ RichardHughes 7 110
(Saeed bin Suroor) *tall: lengthy: stdd s: hld up in tch in rr: swtchd rt and hdwy jst over 2f out: rdn to chal over 1f out: led ins fnl f: r.o wl and gng away at fin* **7/2**[2]

4122 **2** *2 1/2* **Markaz (IRE)**[15] 6230 2-9-0 98........................................ DaneO'Neill 1 103
(B W Hills) *dwlt and pushed along early: pressed ldr after 1f: led 1/2-way: rdn and fnd ex wl over 1f out: hdd and one pce ins fnl f* **16/1**

1301 **3** *2 1/2* **Mubtaghaa (IRE)**[35] 5607 2-9-0 102........................................ PaulHanagan 3 96
(William Haggas) *hld up in tch in last trio: rdn and hdwy 2f out: chsd ldng pair over 1f out: no imp* **3/1**[1]

3211 **4** *4 1/2* **Azraff (IRE)**[31] 5762 2-9-0 93........................................ MartinHarley 5 84
(Marco Botti) *str: in tch in midfield: effrt u.p over 2f out: outpcd and no ch w ldrs over 1f out: wnt modest 4th ins fnl f* **8/1**

51 **5** *shd* **Dancetrack (USA)**[16] 6204 2-9-0 0........................................ JamesDoyle 4 84
(Charles Hills) *str: lengthy: lw: chsd ldrs tl lost pl u.p ent fnl f: no ch w ldrs over 1f out: battling for modest 4th ins fnl f* **12/1**

3240 **6** *1 3/4* **Natural Order (USA)**[14] 6256 2-9-0 95........................................[1] JimCrowley 8 79
(K R Burke) *in tch in last trio: rdn and effrt over 2f out: no ex and wknd over 1f out: no ch whn short of room ins fnl f* **25/1**

121 **7** *nk* **Make It Up**[23] 6004 2-9-0 99........................................ DavidProbert 6 78
(Andrew Balding) *leggy: athletic: led tl 1/2-way: rdn ent fnl 2f: 4th and btn over 1f out: wknd fnl f* **5/1**

13 **8** *3 3/4* **Valley Of Fire**[35] 5607 2-9-0 0........................................ AndreaAtzeni 2 68
(William Haggas) *lw: hld up in tch: effrt u.p and hdwy jst over 2f out: no prog wl over 1f out: sn wknd* **4/1**[3]

1m 23.34s (-2.06) **Going Correction** -0.025s/f (Good) **8** Ran SP% **112.4**
Speed ratings: **110,107,104,99,99 97,96,92**
CSF £54.04 TOTE £4.70: £1.80, £3.30, £1.60; EX 55.20 Trifecta £215.30.
**Owner** Godolphin **Bred** C Kidder & J K & Linda Griggs **Trained** Newmarket, Suffolk

**FOCUS**
Not a terribly strong race for the grade. They raced under the stands' rail and the first three drew clear.

## 6687 JOCKEY CLUB ROSE BOWL (FORMERLY THE FENWOLF STKS) (LISTED RACE) 2m
**4:15** (4:24) (Class 1) 3-Y-O+ **£22,684** (£8,600; £4,304; £2,144; £1,076) **Stalls** Centre

Form RPR

2140 **1** **Pallasator**[11] 6374 5-9-3 111........................................ AndreaAtzeni 5 110
(Sir Mark Prescott Bt) *swtg: taken down early and ponied to s: led: rdn and hdd over 2f out: styd w ldr: led again over 1f out: hung lft but forged ahd ins fnl f: styd on* **11/8**[1]

/1-1 **2** *1 1/2* **Flying Officer (USA)**[169] 1398 4-9-6 106........................................ WilliamBuick 3 111
(John Gosden) *lw: chsd wnr: rdn to ld over 2f out: drvn and hdd over 1f out: no ex and btn ins fnl f* **13/8**[2]

3-34 **3** *9* **Novirak (IRE)**[19] 6133 6-9-3 89........................................ FrederikTylicki 1 97
(James Fanshawe) *a 3rd: rdn 3f out: sn btn and no ch whn hung lft 1f out* **12/1**

3000 **4** *11* **Shwaiman (IRE)**[58] 4759 4-9-3 100 TomQueally 2 84
(James Fanshawe) *stdd s: hld up in rr: rdn 4f out: sn lost tch* **20/1**

0030 **5** *23* **Times Up**[13] 6288 8-9-3 108 RyanMoore 4 56
(Ed Dunlop) *hld up in 4th: rdn 4f out: sn lost tch: dropped to last and eased over 2f out: t.o* **11/2**[3]

3m 26.27s (-4.23) **Going Correction** +0.025s/f (Good) **5** Ran SP% **108.0**
Speed ratings: **111,110,105,100,88**
CSF £3.71 TOTE £2.50: £1.60, £1.30; EX 4.00 Trifecta £16.70.
**Owner** Qatar Racing Limited **Bred** Newsells Park Stud **Trained** Newmarket, Suffolk
■ Stewards' Enquiry : Andrea Atzeni caution; entered wrong stall

**FOCUS**
Two highly progressive stayers put distance between themselves and the remainder in a race run at a steady early gallop, with the first three more or less holding their positions throughout. The winner didn't need to be at his best to score.

## 6688 ARKLE FINANCE H'CAP — 1m
**4:50** (4:54) (Class 3) (0-95,95) 3-Y-O+

**£8,715** (£2,609; £1,304; £652; £326; £163) **Stalls** High

Form RPR

6000 **1** **Consign**[12] 6332 4-9-3 **88** (v) RyanMoore 2 99
(Jeremy Noseda) *dwlt: in tch in last pair: rdn and hdwy over 1f out: drvn and r.o wl fnl 100yds to ld last strides* **8/1**

2-10 **2** *hd* **Exchequer (IRE)**[167] 1420 3-8-2 **82** CamHardie(5) 10 92
(Richard Hannon) *short of room leaving stalls: in tch: clsd to trck ldrs and nt clr run over 1f out: rdn and chal 1f out: drvn to ld fnl 100yds: r.o: hdd last strides* **12/1**

155U **3** *1* **Lawyer (IRE)**[16] 6214 3-8-8 **83** AndreaAtzeni 1 91
(Luca Cumani) *lw: chsd ldrs: rdn and ev ch over 1f out: led and edgd rt 1f out: hdd fnl 100yds: no ex* **12/1**

4400 **4** *¾* **Dubai Dynamo**[26] 5919 9-9-1 **86** PJMcDonald 11 92
(Ruth Carr) *wl in tch in midfield: nt clr run and shuffled bk over 1f out: swtchd rt 1f out: styd on u.p fnl f* **20/1**

1162 **5** *hd* **Billingsgate (IRE)**[29] 5824 3-9-6 **95** WilliamBuick 3 101
(Charlie Appleby) *hld up wl in tch: rdn and effrt to chal over 1f out: ev ch after tl no ex wl ins fnl f: wknd towards fin* **7/2**[2]

0054 **6** *1¼* **Burano (IRE)**[15] 6226 5-9-4 **89** (p[1]) RichardHughes 5 92
(Brian Meehan) *hld up in rr: rdn and effrt over 1f out: swtchd rt ins fnl f: styd on fnl 100yds: nvr trbld ldrs* **9/2**[3]

3132 **7** *½* **Master The World (IRE)**[5] 6560 3-9-4 **93** (p) LiamKeniry 9 95
(David Elsworth) *t.k.h: in tch in midfield: switching rt wl over 1f out: effrt u.p to chse ldrs 1f out: no ex fnl 100yds* **3/1**[1]

1100 **8** *1* **Lawmans Thunder**[19] 6140 4-9-5 **95** LouisSteward(5) 4 94
(Ismail Mohammed) *in tch in midfield: hdwy u.p over 1f out: no ex 1f out: wknd ins fnl f* **20/1**

-130 **9** *1¾* **Shafrah (IRE)**[40] 5430 3-8-10 **85** PaulHanagan 8 80
(Richard Hannon) *led: rdn ent fnl 2f: drvn and hdd 1f out: wknd ins fnl f* **10/1**

0000 **10** *1½* **Askaud (IRE)**[16] 6207 6-9-2 **87** (p) FrederikTylicki 7 79
(Scott Dixon) *chsd ldr tl over 1f out: sn no ex u.p: wknd ins fnl f* **33/1**

3260 **11** *¾* **George Guru**[55] 4851 7-9-10 **95** RobertHavlin 6 79
(John Bridger) *in tch in midfield: rdn ent fnl 2f: lost pl over 1f out: bhd fnl f* **33/1**

1m 37.43s (-1.17) **Going Correction** -0.025s/f (Good)
**WFA** 3 from 4yo+ 4lb **11** Ran SP% **116.4**
Speed ratings (Par 107): **104,103,102,102,101 100,100,99,97,95 92**
CSF £92.85 CT £1156.86 TOTE £9.60: £2.60, £4.00, £2.50; EX 121.20 Trifecta £809.20.
**Owner** Miss Yvonne Jacques **Bred** Natton House Thoroughbreds & Mark Woodall **Trained** Newmarket, Suffolk

**FOCUS**
Racing under the stands' rail, they appeared to go a reasonable gallop. The third has been rated as running a length pb.

## 6689 EBF STALLIONS KIER CONSTRUCTION AND FOUNDATION FILLIES' H'CAP — 6f
**5:55** (5:55) (Class 2) (0-100,98) 3-Y-O+

**£12,450** (£3,728; £1,864; £932; £466; £234) **Stalls** High

Form RPR

-104 **1** **Secret Hint**[23] 6006 3-8-5 84 oh4 DavidProbert 1 92
(Andrew Balding) *pressed ldrs: rdn and ev ch over 1f out: led wl ins fnl f: styd on wl* **9/2**[3]

2434 **2** *¾* **Remember**[21] 6068 3-9-2 95 RichardHughes 6 101
(Richard Hannon) *pressed ldr: rdn and ev ch over 1f out: drvn to ld 1f out: hdd and one pce wl ins fnl f* **3/1**[1]

-101 **3** *shd* **Aetna**[134] 2254 4-9-7 98 GrahamGibbons 5 104
(Michael Easterby) *in tch in midfield: effrt whn stmbld wl over 1f out: rallied ins fnl f: clsng whn forced to switch lft wl ins fnl f: styd on strly towards fin: nt rch ldrs* **7/2**[2]

3051 **4** *½* **Augusta Ada**[7] 6492 3-8-5 84 6ex PaulHanagan 4 88
(Ollie Pears) *stdd s: t.k.h: hld up in last pair: effrt over 1f out: styd on wl u.p ins fnl f: nt rch ldrs* **8/1**

6024 **5** *1* **Links Drive Lady**[30] 5784 6-8-11 88 WilliamBuick 2 89
(Dean Ivory) *hld up in tch: rdn and hdwy ent fnl f: no imp fnl 100yds* **16/1**

1061 **6** *½* **Athenian (IRE)**[25] 5965 5-9-6 97 (p) ChrisCatlin 7 96
(Sir Mark Prescott Bt) *lw: led: rdn 2f out: drvn and hdd 1f out: no ex: wknd towards fin* **17/2**

1431 **7** *3* **Refuse Colette (IRE)**[8] 6463 5-8-7 84 6ex PaoloSirigu 8 74
(Mick Quinn) *chsd ldrs: rdn ent fnl 2f: outpcd over 1f out: wknd 1f out* **20/1**

4221 **8** *6* **Cordial**[8] 6468 3-8-5 84 6ex AndreaAtzeni 3 54
(Stuart Williams) *rrd as stalls opened: hld up in rr: effrt 2f out: no hdwy and btn over 1f out: wknd fnl f* **6/1**

1m 11.45s (-0.75) **Going Correction** -0.025s/f (Good)
**WFA** 3 from 4yo+ 2lb **8** Ran SP% **112.0**
Speed ratings (Par 96): **104,103,102,102,100 100,96,88**
CSF £17.60 CT £51.35 TOTE £6.70: £1.80, £1.40, £1.30; EX 22.00 Trifecta £116.30.
**Owner** George Strawbridge **Bred** George Strawbridge **Trained** Kingsclere, Hants

**FOCUS**
This good-quality fillies' sprint handicap was run at an average pace and it saw something of a bunched finish, but those racing handily were at an advantage. The runner-up has been rated as running a small pb, with the third similar to her York win.
T/Plt: £400.90 to a £1 stake. Pool: £106,639.27 - 194.15 winning units T/Qpdt: £149.20 to a £1 stake. Pool: £6,312.02 - 31.30 winning units SP

# 6489 PONTEFRACT (L-H)
### Thursday, September 25

**OFFICIAL GOING: Good to firm (good in places; 7.9)**
Wind: Fresh; half behind Weather: Cloudy with sunny periods

## 6690 BRITISH STALLION STUDS EBF STRAWBERRY HILL MAIDEN STKS (BOBIS RACE) — 6f
**2:20** (2:22) (Class 4) 2-Y-O **£4,528** (£1,347; £673; £336) **Stalls** Low

Form RPR

022 **1** **Captain Revelation**[30] 5799 2-9-5 76 RichardKingscote 1 75
(Tom Dascombe) *led: hdd jst over 2f out: cl up on inner: rdn over 1f out: styd on to ld again last 100yds: hld on wl towards fin* **6/4**[1]

0230 **2** *hd* **Lackaday**[27] 5874 2-9-5 72 TomEaves 10 74
(Mick Channon) *prom: cl up 1/2-way: slt ld jst over 2f out: rdn over 1f out: hdd and drvn last 100yds: rallied wl towards fin* **11/1**

05 **3** *shd* **Its Gonna Be Me (IRE)**[22] 6039 2-9-5 0 JoeFanning 5 74+
(William Haggas) *in tch: pushed along wl over 2f out: rdn to chse ldrs whn edgd lft and green wl over 1f out: swtchd rt to outer ent fnl f: styd on strly towards fin* **13/2**[3]

5422 **4** *7* **Intruder**[15] 6222 2-9-5 73 TonyHamilton 6 53
(Richard Fahey) *cl up to 1/2-way: pushed along wl over 2f out: sn rdn and one pce fr wl over 1f out* **4/1**[2]

6 **5** *1½* **Normandy Barriere (IRE)**[21] 6058 2-9-5 0 JasonHart 8 49
(Nigel Tinkler) *in tch: pushed along 1/2-way: rdn over 2f out: sn no imp* **66/1**

**6** *8* **Humphry Repton** 2-9-5 0 JimmyQuinn 11 25+
(Mark H Tompkins) *s.i.s and bhd: green and pushed along 1/2-way: rdn and kpt on fnl 2f: nvr a factor* **80/1**

**7** *nk* **Regal Missile (IRE)** 2-9-5 0 GrahamLee 4 24
(William Haggas) *a towards rr: pushed along and green wl over 2f out: nvr a factor* **4/1**[2]

0 **8** *7* **Exact Science (IRE)**[8] 6462 2-9-5 0 RobertWinston 2 3
(David Brown) *chsd ldrs: rdn along wl over 2f out: sn wknd* **40/1**

05 **9** *10* **Rainbow Orse**[21] 6059 2-9-5 0 LiamJones 7
(Robert Cowell) *towards rr: pushed along 1/2-way: sn rdn: outpcd and bhd* **22/1**

1m 17.0s (0.10) **Going Correction** -0.125s/f (Firm) **9** Ran SP% **111.2**
Speed ratings (Par 97): **94,93,93,84,82 71,71,61,48**
CSF £18.56 TOTE £2.00: £1.10, £2.10, £2.40; EX 17.00 Trifecta £80.00.
**Owner** Cheshire Racing **Bred** Downfield Cottage Stud **Trained** Malpas, Cheshire

**FOCUS**
The opening contest was a fair juvenile maiden in which they went an even gallop on ground officially described as good to firm, good in places. Joe Fanning, rider of the third horse home, felt plain good would have been more accurate.

## 6691 BEST HORSE RACING - SKY CHANNEL 432 FILLIES' NURSERY H'CAP (BOBIS RACE) — 1m 4y
**2:55** (2:55) (Class 4) (0-85,84) 2-Y-O **£4,528** (£1,347; £673; £336) **Stalls** Low

Form RPR

4212 **1** **Abbey Angel (IRE)**[19] 6151 2-9-2 **84** JackGarritty(5) 6 89+
(Richard Fahey) *trckd ldrs: hdwy to ld jst over 2f out: rdn clr wl over 1f out: kpt on strly fnl f* **5/1**[3]

510 **2** *2¼* **Adelasia (IRE)**[40] 5436 2-9-5 **82** PaulMulrennan 5 82
(Charlie Appleby) *dwlt and in rr: hdwy 3f out: chsd wnr 2f out: sn rdn: kpt on fnl f: no imp towards fin* **7/1**

1522 **3** *1½* **Lady Moscou (IRE)**[9] 6436 2-9-5 **82** KierenFallon 3 78
(James Tate) *hld up: hdwy whn n.m.r 2f out: rdn to chse ldng pair over 1f out: sn drvn and kpt on same pce* **9/2**[2]

332 **4** *2¾* **Spring Dixie (IRE)**[12] 6317 2-8-4 **72** NoelGarbutt(5) 2 62
(Rae Guest) *trckd ldrs on inner: effrt and n.m.r over 2f out: sn rdn: swtchd rt wl over 1f out: sn one pce* **6/1**

4020 **5** *nse* **Our Kylie (IRE)**[67] 4467 2-8-0 **63** PatrickMathers 1 53
(Tony Coyle) *in rr: rdn along over 3f out: kpt on u.p fnl 2f: nrst fin* **50/1**

0123 **6** *6* **Binky Blue (IRE)**[18] 6165 2-8-0 **68** JoeDoyle(5) 4 43
(Brian Ellison) *led: rdn along and hdd 3f out: wknd over 2f out* **10/1**

32 **7** *7* **Tadpole**[19] 6148 2-8-11 **74** LiamJones 7 32
(William Haggas) *tardy s and sn rdn along to chse ldrs: hdwy and cl up after 1 1/2f: led 3f out: hdd and rdn along jst over 2f out: sn drvn and btn: eased fnl f* **7/4**[1]

1m 44.5s (-1.40) **Going Correction** -0.125s/f (Firm) **7** Ran SP% **109.0**
Speed ratings (Par 94): **102,99,98,95,95 89,82**
CSF £35.25 TOTE £5.40: £2.50, £3.90; EX 37.50 Trifecta £109.50.
**Owner** Mrs H Steel **Bred** Paul Hyland **Trained** Musley Bank, N Yorks

**FOCUS**
A fairly decent fillies' nursery in which they went a contested gallop.

## 6692 DOWNLOAD THE RACING UK IPAD APP H'CAP — 6f
**3:30** (3:30) (Class 4) (0-85,85) 3-Y-O+ **£6,469** (£1,925; £962; £481) **Stalls** Low

Form RPR

3040 **1** **Sunraider (IRE)**[11] 6369 7-9-0 78 GrahamLee 5 91
(Paul Midgley) *hld up in rr: hdwy on inner wl over 1f out: squeezed through to ld jst ins fnl f: sn rdn clr: readily* **25/1**

6001 **2** *5* **Evanescent (IRE)**[7] 6478 5-8-12 76 6ex IanBrennan 4 75
(John Quinn) *trckd ldrs on inner: hdwy whn nt clr run over 1f out: swtchd lft and sltly hmpd ent fnl f: sn rdn and kpt on: no ch w wnr* **2/1**[1]

3112 **3** *½* **Poyle Vinnie**[20] 6095 4-9-7 85 AndrewMullen 8 80
(Michael Appleby) *trckd ldrs: hdwy wl over 1f out: rdn ent fnl f: sn drvn and kpt on same pce* **3/1**[2]

3363 **4** *hd* **Available (IRE)**[24] 5986 5-8-13 77 (tp) FrannyNorton 2 72
(John Mackie) *slt ld: rdn along 2f out: drvn and edgd rt over 1f out: kpt on same pce fnl f* **9/1**[3]

0040 **5** *2½* **Tumblewind**[27] 5888 4-9-4 85 GeorgeChaloner(3) 3 72
(Richard Whitaker) *cl up: rdn along 2f out and ev ch tl drvn and wknd appr fnl f* **12/1**

0002 **6** *¾* **Teetotal (IRE)**[19] 6150 4-8-3 72 ShelleyBirkett(5) 6 56
(Nigel Tinkler) *chsd ldrs: rdn along wl over 1f out: grad wknd* **16/1**

3000 **7** *1¼* **Dark Castle**[14] 6260 5-9-0 78 KierenFallon 13 58
(Micky Hammond) *hmpd s and sn swtchd lft to inner: in rr: effrt and sme hdwy 2f out: sn rdn and n.d* **12/1**

3062 **8** *3* **Misplaced Fortune**[7] 6492 9-9-4 82 (v) JasonHart 10 53
(Nigel Tinkler) *hld up: effrt 2f out: sn rdn and n.d* **9/1**[3]

3421 **9** *hd* **Percy's Gal**[23] 5997 3-8-1 72 GemmaTutty(5) 9 42
(Karen Tutty) *cl up: rdn 2f out: sn wknd* **16/1**

0050 **10** *37* **Tasrih (USA)**[19] 6145 5-9-2 80................................(p) DanielTudhope 11
*(Alan McCabe) wnt rt s: prom on wd outside: rdn along over 2f out: sn wknd and bhd whn eased over 1f out* **40/1**

1m 15.03s (-1.87) **Going Correction** -0.125s/f (Firm)
**WFA** 3 from 4yo+ 2lb **10** Ran SP% **111.8**
Speed ratings (Par 105): **107,100,99,99,96 95,93,89,89,39**
CSF £72.12 CT £199.70 TOTE £22.20: £5.30, £1.10, £1.80; EX 87.60 Trifecta £769.80.
**Owner** David Mann **Bred** Lodge Park Stud **Trained** Westow, N Yorks

**FOCUS**
A decent sprint handicap won in a good time. The winner has run well here in the past and everything fell right for him this time.

## 6693 SIMON SCROPE DALBY SCREW-DRIVER H'CAP 1m 2f 6y
**4:05** (4:05) (Class 2) (0-105,99) 3-Y-O£12,450 (£3,728; £1,864; £932; £466) **Stalls** Low

Form RPR
0-40 **1** **Ennistown**[122] 2618 4-10-0 **99**................................ PhillipMakin 1 108
*(Charlie Appleby) t.k.h early: hld up in rr: hdwy wl over 2f out: effrt whn nt clr run ent fnl f: sn swtchd rt and rdn: styd on strly to ld nr line* **3/1**[2]

1122 **2** *hd* **Woodacre**[30] 5792 7-8-8 **82**................................ GeorgeChaloner(3) 3 90
*(Richard Whitaker) trckd ldng pair: hdwy and cl up over 2f out: chal over 1f out: sn rdn and edgd lft ent fnl f: sn led: drvn and edgd rt last 100yds: hdd and no ex nr fin* **11/4**[1]

5064 **3** *2 ¼* **Kelinni (IRE)**[14] 6257 6-9-10 **95**................................ GrahamLee 6 99
*(Marco Botti) led: jnd and pushed along 3f out: rdn 2f out: drvn and hdd ins fnl f: kpt on same pce* **11/4**[1]

5264 **4** *17* **Hit The Jackpot (IRE)**[33] 5695 5-9-11 **96**................................ DanielTudhope 7 80
*(David O'Meara) trckd ldr: cl up 1/2-way: rdn along jst over 2f out: sn wknd* **7/2**[3]

1030 **5** *82* **Epic Battle (IRE)**[19] 6156 4-8-12 **83**................................(v[1]) KierenFallon 4
*(George Margarson) trckd ldrs: pushed along 1/2-way: rdn 4f out: sn outpcd and bhd whn eased fnl 2f* **14/1**

2m 10.04s (-3.66) **Going Correction** -0.125s/f (Firm)
**WFA** 3 from 4yo+ 6lb **5** Ran SP% **107.2**
Speed ratings (Par 109): **109,108,107,93,27**
CSF £10.89 TOTE £4.60: £3.10, £1.70; EX 11.30 Trifecta £33.30.
**Owner** Godolphin **Bred** Darley **Trained** Newmarket, Suffolk

**FOCUS**
A good-class handicap in which they went a solid gallop. The winner has been rated as running a length pb.

## 6694 BRITISH STALLION STUDS EBF FRIER WOOD MAIDEN STKS (BOBIS RACE) 1m 4y
**4:40** (4:40) (Class 4) 2-Y-O £4,528 (£1,347; £673; £336) **Stalls** Low

Form RPR
43 **1** **Darrington**[21] 6056 2-9-5 0................................ TonyHamilton 6 74
*(Richard Fahey) trckd ldr: cl up 1/2-way: chal over 2f out: rdn wl over 1f out: drvn to ld ins fnl f: kpt on* **2/1**[1]

24 **2** *½* **Cymro (IRE)**[9] 6420 2-9-5 0................................ RichardKingscote 3 73
*(Tom Dascombe) led: jnd over 2f out: rdn over 1f out: drvn and hdd ins fnl f: kpt on wl u.p towards fin* **3/1**[2]

43 **3** *1* **Enville (IRE)**[20] 6108 2-9-5 0................................ GrahamLee 7 70
*(William Haggas) chsd ldrs on outer: rdn along 2f out: drvn over 1f out: kpt on u.p fnl f* **7/2**[3]

04 **4** *1 ¼* **Austin Friars**[58] 4750 2-9-5 0................................ PaulMulrennan 2 67
*(Charlie Appleby) trckd ldrs on inner: effrt over 2f out: rdn over 1f out: drvn and kpt on same pce ins fnl f* **8/1**

**5** *1 ¾* **Goneinaminute** 2-9-0 0................................ BarryMcHugh 8 58
*(Tony Coyle) in rr: pushed along 3f out: rdn over 2f out: styd on appr fnl f: nrst fin* **80/1**

00 **6** *2 ¼* **Snappy Guest**[8] 6462 2-9-5 0................................ KierenFallon 4 58
*(George Margarson) trckd ldrs: pushed along over 2f out: rdn wl over 1f out: sn wknd* **33/1**

6 **7** *nk* **Peeps**[47] 5187 2-9-0 0................................ JimmyQuinn 1 52
*(Mark H Tompkins) hld up in rr: pushed along and sme hdwy over 2f out: rdn along wl over 1f out and sn outpcd* **13/2**

0 **8** *7* **Almost Nowhere (IRE)**[8] 6448 2-9-0 0................................ AndrewMullen 5 35
*(Michael Appleby) in tch: rdn along 3f out: sn outpcd* **80/1**

1m 45.91s (0.01) **Going Correction** -0.125s/f (Firm) **8** Ran SP% **110.4**
Speed ratings (Par 97): **94,93,92,91,89 87,86,79**
CSF £7.50 TOTE £3.10: £1.40, £1.10, £1.40; EX 8.10 Trifecta £15.60.
**Owner** The G-Guck Group **Bred** Avenue Farm Stud **Trained** Musley Bank, N Yorks

**FOCUS**
An ordinary juvenile maiden in which they went an even gallop.

## 6695 100% RACING UK PROFITS RETURNED TO RACING H'CAP 5f
**5:15** (5:16) (Class 5) (0-75,78) 3-Y-O+ £3,234 (£962; £481; £240) **Stalls** Low

Form RPR
6001 **1** **Bondi Beach Boy**[8] 6451 5-9-7 78 6ex................................ GeorgeChaloner(3) 3 89
*(James Turner) mde most: rdn wl over 1f out: kpt on strly* **6/1**[3]

3302 **2** *1 ¾* **Boxing Shadows**[10] 6406 4-9-0 68................................ DavidAllan 1 73
*(Les Eyre) trckd ldrs on inner: swtchd rt and hdwy wl over 1f out: sn chsng wnr: drvn ins fnl f and no imp towards fin* **7/2**[1]

005 **3** *1 ½* **Thatcherite (IRE)**[8] 6452 6-9-4 72................................(t) BarryMcHugh 12 71+
*(Tony Coyle) hld up and bhd: hdwy wl over 1f out: rdn and styd on strly fnl f: nrst fin* **33/1**

2143 **4** *hd* **Flash City (ITY)**[8] 6451 6-9-4 72................................(p) JamesSullivan 4 71
*(Ruth Carr) towards rr: hdwy 2f out: rdn to chse ldrs over 1f out: kpt on same pce fnl f* **13/2**

0040 **5** *2 ¼* **Lastchancelucas**[15] 6235 4-9-3 74................................(b) NeilFarley(3) 6 64
*(Declan Carroll) chsd ldrs: n.m.r and hmpd after 1f: rdn along 2f out: drvn and kpt on same pce fr over 1f out* **12/1**

0221 **6** *¾* **It Must Be Faith**[7] 6495 4-9-1 69................................ AndrewMullen 11 57+
*(Michael Appleby) towards rr: rdn along 1/2-way: drvn and kpt on fr wl over 1f out: nvr nr ldrs* **9/2**[2]

4230 **7** *¾* **Whipphound**[12] 6346 6-9-1 69................................ GrahamLee 5 54
*(Mark Brisbourne) midfield: hdwy and in tch over 2f out: rdn wl over 1f out and sn no imp* **12/1**

0262 **8** *¾* **Captain Royale (IRE)**[26] 5913 9-9-4 75................................(p) JacobButterfield(3) 14 57
*(Tracy Waggott) qckly away and cl up: rdn along 2f out: grad wknd* **28/1**

0602 **9** *¾* **Sunny Side Up (IRE)**[8] 6451 5-8-3 62................................ GemmaTutty(5) 8 42
*(Karen Tutty) chsd ldrs whn n.m.r and hmpd after 1f: sn lost pl and in rr after* **12/1**

10-0 **10** *¾* **Omaha Gold (IRE)**[52] 4977 3-9-4 73................................ PaulMulrennan 2 50
*(Bryan Smart) chsd ldrs on inner: rdn along 2f out: wknd over 1f out* **17/2**

0300 **11** *1 ¼* **Jiroft (ITY)**[12] 6324 7-9-7 75................................ TonyHamilton 9 47
*(Ann Stokell) a towards rr* **40/1**

5465 **12** *3* **Ypres**[10] 6406 5-8-13 70................................(v) JoeyHaynes(3) 13 32
*(Jason Ward) a towards rr* **20/1**

055 **13** *7* **Three Pips**[24] 5987 3-8-10 65................................ DaleSwift 10
*(Ed McMahon) chsd ldrs: rdn along 1/2-way: sn lost pl and bhd* **50/1**

1m 2.14s (-1.16) **Going Correction** -0.125s/f (Firm)
**WFA** 3 from 4yo+ 1lb **13** Ran SP% **117.2**
Speed ratings (Par 103): **104,101,98,98,94 93,92,91,90,88 86,82,70**
CSF £25.18 CT £664.90 TOTE £7.60: £3.30, £2.10, £6.10; EX 25.20 Trifecta £888.90.
**Owner** G R Turner & H Turner **Bred** G R & H Turner **Trained** Norton-le-Clay, N Yorks

**FOCUS**
A fair sprint handicap in which they went a contested gallop. The runner-up has been rated to his C&D run in July.

## 6696 WATCH ON 3 DEVICES RACINGUK.COM/ANYWHERE APPRENTICE H'CAP 1m 4f 8y
**5:45** (5:46) (Class 5) (0-75,75) 3-Y-O+ £3,234 (£962; £481; £240) **Stalls** Low

Form RPR
056 **1** **Le Deluge (FR)**[25] 5950 4-9-1 64................................(t) GaryMahon(2) 5 73
*(Ann Stokell) mde all: clr after 2f: rdn along wl over 1f out: drvn and styd on strly fnl f* **10/1**

5221 **2** *2 ¼* **Saint Thomas (IRE)**[23] 6000 7-9-6 67................................ JennyPowell 1 72
*(John Mackie) trckd wnr: effrt over 2f out: rdn along to chse wnr over 1f out: drvn ins fnl f and kpt on same pce* **11/4**[1]

2042 **3** *shd* **Men Don't Cry (IRE)**[14] 6274 5-9-12 75................................(b) CharlieBennett(2) 2 80
*(Ed de Giles) trckd ldrs: hdwy 3f out: rdn to chse ldng pair 2f out: drvn ins fnl f and kpt on same pce* **9/2**[3]

0006 **4** *8* **Pertuis (IRE)**[21] 6062 8-8-12 63................................(p) RowanScott(4) 7 55
*(Micky Hammond) hld up towards rr: tk clsr order over 3f out: rdn along over 2f out: sn one pce* **12/1**

2200 **5** *3 ¼* **Mountain Kingdom (IRE)**[14] 6274 3-8-13 74................................ ManuelFernandes(6) 3 61
*(Sir Mark Prescott Bt) trckd ldng pair: effrt on outer 3f out: sn rdn along: wknd wl over 1f out* **7/2**[2]

4-U4 **6** *23* **Red Inca**[45] 5238 6-9-12 73................................ MeganCarberry 6 23
*(Brian Ellison) hld up in rr: hdwy 3f out: rdn along 2f out: sn btn* **11/4**[1]

2m 39.2s (-1.60) **Going Correction** -0.125s/f (Firm)
**WFA** 3 from 4yo+ 8lb **6** Ran SP% **110.5**
Speed ratings (Par 103): **100,98,98,93,90 75**
CSF £36.32 TOTE £8.40: £5.70, £1.90; EX 50.70 Trifecta £125.80.
**Owner** Stephen Arnold **Bred** J F Gribomont **Trained** Lincoln, Lincolnshire
■ Stewards' Enquiry : Charlie Bennett four-day ban; used whip above permitted level (9th-12th Oct)

**FOCUS**
An ordinary middle-distance handicap restricted to apprentice riders in which they went a respectable gallop. The winner has been rated back to his Redcar claimer win.
T/Jkpt: Not won. T/Plt: £41.90 to a £1 stake. Pool: £77,691.83 - 1,352.49 winning units T/Qpdt: £6.70 to a £1 stake. Pool: £6,355.12 - 699.32 winning units JR

# 6591 MAISONS-LAFFITTE (R-H)
### Thursday, September 25
**OFFICIAL GOING: Turf: good to soft**

## 6698a PRIX DE BURES SUR YVETTE (CLAIMER) (2YO FILLIES) (ROUND) (TURF) 1m (S)
**12:15** (12:15) 2-Y-O £9,583 (£3,833; £2,875; £1,916; £958)

RPR
**1** **Starsic (FR)**[61] 2-8-10 0................................ MllePaulineDominois(6) 9 80+
(Yves de Nicolay, France) **132/10**

**2** *4* **Gilded Lace**[10] 6400 2-8-9 0................................(p) MickaelBarzalona 4 64
*(J S Moore) led: hdd bef 1/2-way and pressed ldr on outer: regained ld passing 2 1/2f marker: kicked 2 l clr under 2f out: hdd appr fnl f: kpt on u.p but readily outpcd by wnr* **58/10**

**3** *½* **Kadla (FR)**[9] 2-8-9 0................................ GeraldMosse 5 63
(C Laffon-Parias, France) **57/10**[3]

**4** *snk* **Houteville**[48] 2-8-13 0................................ GregoryBenoist 2 67
(P Sogorb, France) **37/10**[2]

**5** *3* **Wild Wild West (FR)**[9] 2-8-9 0................................(b) StephanePasquier 6 56
(Yannick Fouin, France) **155/10**

**6** *¾* **Trust The Captain (FR)**[27] 5901 2-9-2 0................................ JimmyTastayre 10 62
(Robert Collet, France) **59/1**

**7** *½* **Why Whipping (FR)**[9] 2-8-13 0................................(b) ChristopheSoumillon 7 57
(Robert Collet, France) **92/10**

**8** *1 ½* **Fulki (FR)**[118] 2755 2-8-9 0................................ EddyHardouin 1 50
(J Heloury, France) **28/1**

**9** *5* **Turtle Beach (FR)** 2-8-9 0................................ GuillaumeMandel 11 39
(M Pimbonnet, France) **35/1**

**10** *20* **Belle Du Jour (FR)**[77] 2-9-4 0................................ CristianDemuro 8
(M Boutin, France) **99/10**

**11** *dist* **Balbec (FR)**[95] 2-9-2 0................................ AnthonyCrastus 3
(C Boutin, France) **5/2**[1]

1m 46.9s (4.60) **11** Ran SP% **119.5**
WIN (incl. 1 euro stake): 14.20. PLACES: 4.00, 3.00, 2.50. DF: 39.80. SF: 115.10.
**Owner** Mme Anita Louboutin **Bred** Mme A Louboutin **Trained** France

# 6131 HAYDOCK (L-H)
### Friday, September 26
**OFFICIAL GOING: Good (8.2) changing to good (good to soft in places) after race 1 (1.30)**
Wind: Moderate against Weather: Cloudy with sunny periods

## 6699 THREE SISTERS H'CAP 1m 3f 200y
**1:30** (1:31) (Class 5) (0-70,70) 3-Y-O+ £2,587 (£770; £384; £192) **Stalls** Centre

Form RPR
2236 **1** **Light Of Asia (IRE)**[25] 5975 3-9-4 70................................ PhillipMakin 3 79
*(Ed Dunlop) hld up towards rr: hdwy on inner 4f out: effrt to chse ldrs 2f out: swtchd rt and rdn jst ins fnl f: styd on to ld last 100yds* **12/1**

5254 **2** *nk* **Rex Whistler (IRE)**[33] 5716 4-9-10 68................................ PaulMulrennan 8 77
*(Julie Camacho) hld up in midfield: hdwy over 3f out: rdn to chse ldrs over 1f out: n.m.r on inner and swtchd rt ins fnl f: styd on strly towards fin* **7/1**[2]

0516 **3** *1* **Lochalsh (IRE)**[26] 5949 3-8-13 65........................................ ShaneKelly 9 72
(William Knight) *led: rdn over 2f out: drvn ent fnl f: hdd and no ex last 100yds* **14/1**

6552 **4** *3* **Red Dragon (IRE)**[24] 6007 4-9-7 65................................ DavidProbert 7 68
(Michael Blanshard) *hld up towards rr: hdwy over 4f out: rdn along to chse ldng pair wl over 1f out: drvn and one pce fnl f* **14/1**

6534 **5** *2 3/4* **Carraig Rock**[21] 6107 4-9-10 68........................................ RobertHavlin 4 66
(Hughie Morrison) *trckd ldrs on inner: hdwy to chse ldr 3f out: rdn along 2f out: sn drvn and kpt on same pce* **16/1**

60-4 **5** *dht* **Dancing Primo**[120] 2701 8-9-2 65........................................ EoinWalsh(5) 6 63
(Mark Brisbourne) *hld up in rr: hdwy 4f out: rdn along 2f out: styd on u.p appr fnl f: nrst fin* **20/1**

0266 **7** *3 3/4* **Grand Liaison**[3] 6651 5-9-3 61........................................ JamesSullivan 10 53
(James Given) *chsd ldrs: rdn along 3f out: drvn over 2f out and grad wknd* **25/1**

6-02 **8** *nk* **Ze King**[24] 6019 5-9-8 66........................................................ TedDurcan 5 60
(Chris Wall) *chsd ldrs: pushed along 4f out: rdn wl over 2f out: grad wknd* **7/1**[2]

0020 **9** *4 1/2* **Essanar**[20] 6157 3-8-4 56 oh4........................................ FrannyNorton 13 41
(Andrew Hollinshead) *prom on outer: rdn along over 3f out: wknd wl over 2f out* **40/1**

4516 **10** *nk* **Hallbeck**[15] 6252 3-9-4 70.................................................. DaneO'Neill 12 56
(Henry Candy) *nvr bttr than midfield* **6/1**[1]

6624 **11** *4* **Ferdy (IRE)**[16] 6223 5-8-12 56........................................ LukeMorris 1 34
(Paul Green) *towards rr: hdwy over 4f out: in tch 3f out: sn rdn along and wknd* **25/1**

**12** *2* **Silver Shuffle (IRE)**[16] 133 7-8-9 56 oh3.........(p) GeorgeChaloner(3) 17 30
(Malcolm Jefferson) *chsd ldrs on outer: rdn along wl over 3f out: sn drvn and wknd* **14/1**

6014 **13** *nse* **A Little Bit Dusty**[22] 6062 6-9-12 70..........................(p) HayleyTurner 14 44
(Conor Dore) *dwlt: a bhd* **12/1**

U021 **14** *2 1/2* **Slunovrat (FR)**[32] 5765 3-8-12 64........................................ RaulDaSilva 11 34
(David Menuisier) *chsd ldrs on outer: rdn along over 4f out: sn wknd* **15/2**[3]

4403 **15** *2 3/4* **Lyric Ballad**[41] 5414 4-9-12 70..........................................(b) JohnFahy 15 36
(Hughie Morrison) *dwlt and in rr: hdwy on outer to chse ldrs 7f out: rdn along over 4f out: sn wknd* **12/1**

5020 **16** *dist* **Cloud Monkey (IRE)**[16] 6223 4-9-11 69........................................ GrahamLee 16
(Martin Todhunter) *towards rr: lost pl and bhd 4f out: virtually p.u fr wl over 2f out* **10/1**

2m 34.33s (0.53) **Going Correction** +0.125s/f (Good)
**WFA** 3 from 4yo+ 8lb **16 Ran SP% 124.0**
Speed ratings (Par 103): **103,102,102,100,98 98,95,95,92,92 89,88,88,86,84**
CSF £91.00 CT £1217.69 TOTE £15.30: £3.10, £2.80, £4.00, £3.60; EX 126.80 Trifecta £961.40 Part won..

**Owner** The Hon R J Arculli & Robert Ng **Bred** Tullamaine Castle Stud And Partners **Trained** Newmarket, Suffolk

**FOCUS**
All races were run on the stands' side home straight, adding approximately 57 yards to the 1m-1m4f races and 107 yards to the 1m6f handicap. There had been no rain since Tuesday night but, given the winning time and the views of several riders, who stated the ground was on the easy side of good and softer in the back straight, the ground was eased to good, good to soft in places. Several exposed sorts in a modest handicap. An ordinary gallop increased passing the 3f marker. The winner was back to form.

## 6700 IRISH STALLION FARMS EBF VALE UK MAIDEN FILLIES' STKS (BOBIS RACE) (DIV I) 6f

**2:00** (2:01) (Class 5) 2-Y-O **£2,911** (£866; £432; £216) **Stalls** Centre

Form RPR

**1** **Lap Of Luxury (IRE)** 2-8-10 0........................................ RobertHavlin 6 80+
(John Gosden) *trckd ldrs: 2nd over 1f out: r.o to ld clsng stages* **10/1**

2 **2** *1/2* **Excilly**[70] 4389 2-9-0 0........................................ RichardKingscote 11 82+
(Tom Dascombe) *overall ldr stands' side: hdd and no ex clsng stages* **4/7**[1]

64 **3** *6* **Liberal Angel (FR)**[37] 5590 2-9-0 0........................................ MichaelStainton 5 64
(K R Burke) *chsd ldrs: effrt over 2f out: kpt on same pce appr fnl f* **25/1**

4 **4** *2* **Apache Storm**[9] 6453 2-9-0 0........................................ AndrewMullen 7 58
(Michael Appleby) *chsd ldrs: kpt on one pce over 1f out* **6/1**[2]

0 **5** *nk* **Rose Abella**[21] 6093 2-9-0 0........................................ GrahamLee 3 57
(Andrew Hollinshead) *chsd ldrs: outpcd over 2f out: kpt on fnl f* **20/1**

46 **6** *4* **Poyle Jessica**[23] 6032 2-9-0 0........................................ GrahamGibbons 9 45+
(Ralph Beckett) *s.i.s: sn chsng ldr stands' side: wknd over 1f out* **16/1**

**7** *1/2* **Ince Moss** 2-8-7 0........................................ GeorgeChaloner(3) 8 40
(Richard Fahey) *chsd ldrs: lost pl over 1f out* **28/1**

**8** *hd* **Spirit Of Sound (FR)** 2-8-10 0........................................ RobertWinston 2 39+
(Hugo Palmer) *dwlt: swtchd rt after s and racd stands' side: sn chsng ldrs: wknd over 1f out* **7/1**[3]

00 **9** *3/4* **La Favorita (IRE)**[34] 5667 2-8-9 0........................................ CamHardie(5) 10 41+
(Charles Hills) *chsd ldrs stands' side: lost pl over 1f out* **80/1**

00 **10** *3/4* **Anniversarie**[25] 5982 2-8-11 0........................................ JacobButterfield(3) 4 39
(John Norton) *sn outpcd and in rr: nvr on terms* **100/1**

1m 15.15s (1.35) **Going Correction** +0.125s/f (Good) **10 Ran SP% 119.7**
Speed ratings (Par 92): **96,95,87,84,84 78,78,78,77,76**
CSF £16.13 TOTE £12.00: £3.00, £1.10, £4.70; EX 19.60 Trifecta £323.00.

**Owner** M Tabor, D Smith & Mrs J Magnier **Bred** Smythson **Trained** Newmarket, Suffolk

**FOCUS**
Not a competitive event and one in which the first two pulled clear. The field split into two groups (stands' side and centre) but there seemed little advantage in track position. The gallop was reasonable. A nice start from the winner, the third helping with the level.

## 6701 IRISH STALLION FARMS EBF VALE UK MAIDEN FILLIES' STKS (BOBIS RACE) (DIV II) 6f

**2:30** (2:32) (Class 5) 2-Y-O **£2,911** (£866; £432; £216) **Stalls** Centre

Form RPR

4 **1** **Goodnightsuzy (IRE)**[21] 6093 2-9-0 0........................................ RichardKingscote 3 79+
(Ed Walker) *trckd ldng pair: hdwy to chse ldr over 2f out: rdn over 1f out: styd on wl fnl f to ld nr fin* **5/2**[1]

43 **2** *3/4* **Illogical**[10] 6435 2-9-0 0........................................ PaulMulrennan 10 77
(Ed Dunlop) *led: rdn clr wl over 1f out: drvn ins fnl f: hdd and no ex towards fin* **7/1**

**3** *2 3/4* **Lady Estella (IRE)** 2-8-10 0........................................ LukeMorris 4 65
(Marco Botti) *towards rr: pushed along 1/2-way: swtchd rt and hdwy over 2f out: rdn wl over 1f out: kpt on fnl f: nrst fin* **25/1**

4 **4** *1 1/2* **Emblaze**[49] 5128 2-9-0 0........................................ PhillipMakin 5 64
(Bryan Smart) *hld up: hdwy 2f out: sn rdn and kpt on fnl f: nrst fin* **10/1**

53 **5** *hd* **Mallymkun**[21] 6093 2-9-0 0........................................ PJMcDonald 9 63+
(K R Burke) *swtchd rt to r alone stands' rail: prom: rdn 2f out: kpt on same pce* **7/2**[3]

5 **6** *1 1/4* **The Fairy (IRE)**[21] 6093 2-9-0 0........................................ RobertHavlin 6 60
(John Gosden) *wnt rt s: in tch: hdwy 1/2-way: pushed along to chse ldrs over 2f out: sn rdn and one pce* **10/3**[2]

0 **7** *1 1/2* **Lucy The Painter (IRE)**[7] 6517 2-9-0 0........................................ SteveDrowne 1 55
(Peter Makin) *chsd ldrs: rdn along 2f out: grad wknd* **33/1**

0 **8** *6* **Camdora (IRE)**[79] 4075 2-9-0 0........................................ ShaneKelly 7 37
(Jamie Osborne) *dwlt: a towards rr* **66/1**

00 **9** *3 3/4* **Signorina Roseina**[11] 6408 2-8-11 0........................................ NeilFarley(3) 2 26
(Eric Alston) *chsd ldr: pushed along 1/2-way: rdn over 2f out: sn wknd* **100/1**

0 **10** *1 1/2* **Bipartisan (IRE)**[10] 6434 2-9-0 0........................................ WilliamTwiston-Davies 8 21
(Michael Bell) *chsd ldrs: rdn along 1/2-way: sn wknd* **11/1**

1m 15.34s (1.54) **Going Correction** +0.125s/f (Good) **10 Ran SP% 113.1**
Speed ratings (Par 92): **94,93,89,87,87 85,83,75,70,68**
CSF £19.49 TOTE £3.80: £1.20, £2.50, £5.20; EX 18.30 Trifecta £102.80.

**Owner** Chasemore Farm **Bred** Diomed Bloodstock Ltd **Trained** Newmarket, Suffolk

**FOCUS**
The second division of a fair maiden. The gallop was reasonable but, although only one elected to race near the stands' rail in the first half of the race, the field fanned across the track in the last quarter-mile. The form might be worth a bit more than rated.

## 6702 EBF VALE UK MAIDEN STKS (COLTS AND GELDINGS) 6f

**3:00** (3:02) (Class 5) 2-Y-O **£2,911** (£866; £432; £216) **Stalls** Centre

Form RPR

**1** **Fannaan (USA)** 2-9-0 0........................................ DaneO'Neill 3 85+
(John Gosden) *dwlt and wnt lft s: in rr: gd hdwy 1/2-way: chsd clr ldr wl over 1f out: rdn to ld jst ins fnl f: sn clr: readily* **5/2**[1]

0 **2** *3 1/2* **Stake Acclaim (IRE)**[35] 5646 2-9-0 0........................................ RobertWinston 1 74
(Dean Ivory) *racd towards far side: sn led and clr 1/2-way: rdn along over 1f out: hdd jst ins fnl f: kpt on: no ch w wnr* **10/1**

3 **3** *2 1/4* **Yazan (IRE)**[22] 6059 2-9-0 0........................................ RichardKingscote 8 67+
(Tom Dascombe) *trckd ldrs: pushed along and sltly outpcd over 2f out: rdn and hdwy over 1f out: hung lft ent fnl f: sn drvn and no imp* **5/2**[1]

53 **4** *1 3/4* **Manolito**[17] 6203 2-9-0 0........................................ JohnFahy 7 62
(Hughie Morrison) *prom: rdn along over 2f out: sn one pce* **8/1**[3]

**5** *nk* **Tunnel Creek** 2-9-0 0........................................ BenCurtis 12 61+
(Henry Candy) *towards rr: hdwy 2f out: styd on appr fnl f: nrst fin* **50/1**

**6** *hd* **Mujassam** 2-9-0 0........................................ JackMitchell 2 60+
(Roger Varian) *chsd ldrs: rdn 2f out: sn one pce* **12/1**

**7** *1 1/4* **Velociter (IRE)** 2-8-9 0........................................ CamHardie(5) 4 56
(Richard Hannon) *racd towards far side: prom: chsd ldr over 2f out: sn rdn and wknd appr fnl f* **20/1**

06 **8** *1* **Treaty Of York (IRE)**[23] 6038 2-9-0 0........................................ DavidProbert 9 53
(Henry Candy) *trckd ldrs: hdwy 1/2-way: rdn along over 2f out: sn drvn and one pce* **33/1**

**9** *1 1/2* **Major Pusey** 2-8-11 0........................................ JoeyHaynes(3) 5 49
(John Gallagher) *t.k.h early: a towards rr* **50/1**

**10** *7* **Good Judge (USA)** 2-9-0 0........................................ HarryBentley 11 28
(Saeed bin Suroor) *towards rr: hdwy and in tch 1/2-way: sn rdn along and wknd* **6/1**[2]

**11** *7* **Rockmount** 2-9-0 0........................................ GrahamGibbons 6
(Ed McMahon) *dwlt and wnt lft s: sn prom: rdn along wl over 2f out: sn wknd* **33/1**

**12** *15* **Broughtonian** 2-9-0 0........................................ LukeMorris 10
(Marco Botti) *chsd ldrs: rdn along 1/2-way: sn wknd* **16/1**

1m 14.61s (0.81) **Going Correction** +0.125s/f (Good) **12 Ran SP% 119.8**
Speed ratings (Par 95): **99,94,91,89,88 88,86,85,83,74 64,44**
CSF £29.28 TOTE £4.70: £1.70, £3.10, £1.10; EX 26.30 Trifecta £79.40.

**Owner** Hamdan Al Maktoum **Bred** Waterville Lake Stables Ltd Llc **Trained** Newmarket, Suffolk

**FOCUS**
An interesting maiden (that has thrown up several smart sorts in the past decade) featuring a couple of horses who had shown ability and several top stables were represented with newcomers. The gallop was reasonable and the action unfolded away from the main group towards the far side in the closing stages. This year's winner looks a decent prospect, capable of better still.

## 6703 BRYN NURSERY H'CAP (BOBIS RACE) 5f

**3:35** (3:35) (Class 2) 2-Y-O **£9,056** (£2,695; £1,346; £673) **Stalls** Centre

Form RPR

2556 **1** **Rosie's Premiere (IRE)**[34] 5694 2-8-11 89........................................ RobertWinston 6 94
(Dean Ivory) *hld up: hdwy wl over 1f out: rdn ent fnl f: styd on strly to ld nr line* **10/1**

3122 **2** *nk* **Profitable (IRE)**[20] 6128 2-8-9 90........................................ RyanTate(3) 7 94
(Clive Cox) *trckd ldrs: hdwy 2f out: led over 1f out: sn rdn and edgd lft: drvn and hung bdly lft ins fnl f: hdd nr line* **6/4**[1]

2041 **3** *1 3/4* **La Cuesta (IRE)**[11] 6408 2-8-4 87 6ex........................................ CamHardie(5) 5 85
(Jamie Osborne) *trckd ldrs: swtchd lft and hdwy wl over 1f out: rdn ent fnl f: kpt on same pce* **3/1**[2]

4013 **4** *1* **Clouds Rest**[24] 5998 2-8-5 88........................................ JackGarritty(5) 8 82
(Richard Fahey) *slt ld: pushed along and hdd over 2f out: rdn over 1f out: one pce fnl f* **16/1**

4503 **5** *nk* **Union Rose**[20] 6128 2-9-4 96..........................(p) WilliamTwiston-Davies 1 89
(Ronald Harris) *cl up: slt ld over 2f out: sn rdn and edgd lft: drvn and one pce fnl f* **16/1**

110 **6** *3/4* **Showing Character**[34] 5694 2-9-7 99........................................ RichardKingscote 2 89
(Tom Dascombe) *trckd ldrs: hdwy 2f out: rdn ent fnl f: sn wknd* **8/1**

1002 **7** *2 3/4* **Harry's Dancer (IRE)**[56] 4869 2-8-10 88........................................ IanBrennan 3 68
(John Quinn) *trckd ldrs: hdwy and swtchd lft over 1f out: sn rdn and btn* **13/2**[3]

1m 0.36s (-0.44) **Going Correction** +0.125s/f (Good) **7 Ran SP% 110.3**
Speed ratings (Par 101): **108,107,104,103,102 101,97**
CSF £23.75 CT £53.49 TOTE £13.30: £5.30, £1.10; EX 30.00 Trifecta £175.90.

**Owner** Mrs Heather Yarrow **Bred** Yeomanstown Stud **Trained** Radlett, Herts

**FOCUS**
A useful nursery in which the gallop was sound throughout and resulted in the best comparative time of the afternoon. The field raced in two small centre groups but the runner-up drifted to the far rail in the closing stages. Quite a taking effort from the winner.

## 6704 FRANK AND TOM FITZGERALD H'CAP 1m
**4:10** (4:10) (Class 3) (0-90,89) 3-Y-O+ **£8,086** (£2,406; £1,202; £601) **Stalls** Low

Form RPR

5132 **1** **No Poppy (IRE)**[22] 6057 6-9-0 79 DavidAllan 14 88
(Tim Easterby) *hld up towards rr: hdwy 3f out: pushed along over 2f out: rdn and styd on strly on outer ins fnl f to ld last 50yds* **12/1**

46 **2** *3/4* **Sweet Martoni**[29] 5849 4-8-10 75 TedDurcan 10 82
(William Knight) *trckd ldrs: hdwy over 2f out: rdn to chal ent fnl f: sn drvn and ev ch tl no ex last 50yds* **25/1**

4300 **3** *nk* **Showpiece**[48] 5177 3-8-4 78 (b) CamHardie(5) 1 85
(Richard Hannon) *in tch on inner: hdwy wl over 2f out: swtchd rt and rdn over 1f out: drvn and slt ld wl ins fnl f: hdd and no ex last 50yds* **16/1**

115 **4** *1/2* **Si Senor (IRE)**[20] 6140 3-9-5 88 GrahamLee 7 95+
(Ed Vaughan) *hld up in rr: swtchd lft to inner 2f out: n.m.r and swtchd rt jst over 1f out: effrt and nt clr run jst ins fnl f: rdn: squeezed through and kpt on towards fin* **9/2**[2]

2135 **5** *hd* **Wilde Inspiration (IRE)**[16] 6234 3-9-2 85 PaulMulrennan 6 90
(Julie Camacho) *trckd ldr: cl up over 3f out: led 2f out: sn rdn: drvn ent fnl f: hdd and no ex last 100yds* **5/1**[3]

1411 **6** *3/4* **Pearl Nation (USA)**[21] 6097 5-9-10 89 AndrewMullen 9 92
(Michael Appleby) *t.k.h: trckd ldrs: effrt 2f out: sn rdn: drvn ent fnl f: kpt on same pce* **11/2**

5300 **7** *1* **Dubai Hills**[48] 5178 8-9-7 86 TomEaves 13 87
(David O'Meara) *trckd ldrs: hdwy on outer over 3f out: effrt 2f out and sn chal: rdn over 1f out: kpt on same pce ins fnl f* **25/1**

3460 **8** *nse* **King Of Macedon (IRE)**[15] 6263 3-8-7 76 (b) FrannyNorton 3 77
(Mark Johnston) *trckd ldrs on inner: effrt 3f out: rdn along over 2f out: drvn appr fnl f: kpt on same pce* **16/1**

0000 **9** *3/4* **Chosen Character (IRE)**[14] 6281 6-9-5 89 (vt) JennyPowell(5) 15 88
(Tom Dascombe) *led: rdn along 3f out: narrowly hdd 2f out: sn drvn and grad wknd appr fnl f* **12/1**

-035 **10** *nk* **Nurpur (IRE)**[139] 2144 4-9-2 84 SamJames(3) 2 82
(David O'Meara) *hld up in rr: hdwy wl over 2f out: chsd ldrs wl over 1f out: keeping on whn nt clr run ins fnl f: no imp after* **14/1**

0200 **11** *5* **Victoire De Lyphar (IRE)**[17] 6207 7-9-9 88 (e) JamesSullivan 11 75
(Ruth Carr) *chsd ldng pair: rdn along wl over 2f out: sn wknd* **50/1**

3601 **12** *3/4* **Berlusca (IRE)**[22] 6057 5-9-6 85 DavidNolan 4 70
(David O'Meara) *hld up in rr: hdwy on outer 3f out: rdn along to chse ldrs over 2f out: sn drvn and wknd over 1f out* **14/1**

023 **13** *17* **Yourartisonfire**[21] 6097 4-9-5 87 (v) JoeyHaynes(3) 12 33
(K R Burke) *sn rdn along in rr: nvr striding out and a bhd* **4/1**[1]

1m 44.95s (1.25) **Going Correction** +0.125s/f (Good)
**WFA** 3 from 4yo+ 4lb **13** Ran SP% **120.4**
Speed ratings (Par 107): **98,97,96,96,96 95,94,94,93,93 88,87,70**
CSF £285.89 CT £4907.61 TOTE £11.70: £3.70, £9.20, £4.50; EX 328.10 Trifecta £1902.20 Part won..
**Owner** J Musgrave **Bred** Michael O'Mahony **Trained** Great Habton, N Yorks

**FOCUS**
A useful handicap in which the gallop was fair and the times again suggested the ground on the round course was slower than the sprint track. Ordinary but sound form.

## 6705 VALE UK H'CAP (BOBIS RACE) 1m 6f
**4:45** (4:45) (Class 3) (0-95,90) 3-Y-O **£8,086** (£2,406; £1,202; £601) **Stalls** Low

Form RPR

0021 **1** **William Of Orange**[21] 6099 3-8-13 82 LukeMorris 7 91+
(Sir Mark Prescott Bt) *hld up: hdwy to trck ldrs 7f out: led 2f out: drvn and wnt lft appr fnl f: styd on wl clsng stages* **13/8**[1]

3124 **2** *1* **Taws**[13] 6325 3-8-0 74 CamHardie(5) 1 81
(Rod Millman) *led 1f: chsd ldrs: pushed along 7f out: outpcd over 3f out: rallied over 1f out: hung lft and styd on same pce last 100yds* **12/1**

3153 **3** *nse* **Spectator**[20] 6137 3-8-8 77 (p) DavidProbert 2 84
(Andrew Balding) *hld up in rr: stdy hdwy over 3f out: sn trcking ldrs: styd on same pce last 100yds* **6/1**[3]

244 **4** *3/4* **Kashmiri Sunset**[20] 6137 3-8-11 80 PhillipMakin 4 85
(Ed de Giles) *mid-div: drvn over 6f out: chsng ldrs over 3f out: nt clr run fr over 2f out tl last 75yds: kpt on same pce* **7/2**[2]

0216 **5** *1 1/2* **Galizzi (USA)**[20] 6127 3-9-2 90 LouisSteward(5) 5 93
(Michael Bell) *trckd ldng pair: chsd ldr after 3f: carried lft appr fnl f: fdd last 75yds* **7/1**

1122 **6** *12* **Needless Shouting (IRE)**[13] 6325 3-8-8 77 SamHitchcott 6 64
(Mick Channon) *led after 1f: hdd 2f out: sn lost pl: bhd whn eased clsng stages* **20/1**

2242 **7** *3 1/2* **Cosette (IRE)**[21] 6099 3-8-10 79 DaneO'Neill 8 61
(Henry Candy) *hld up in rr: hdwy to chse ldrs over 3f out: wknd over 2f out: eased whn bhd* **8/1**

3m 3.24s (1.24) **Going Correction** +0.125s/f (Good) **7** Ran SP% **110.7**
Speed ratings (Par 105): **101,100,100,99,99 92,90**
CSF £21.04 CT £88.58 TOTE £2.30: £1.10, £5.20; EX 23.10 Trifecta £99.40.
**Owner** Nicholas Jones **Bred** Coln Valley Stud **Trained** Newmarket, Suffolk

**FOCUS**
A useful handicap in which a steady gallop only increased before the 2f pole and the first five finished in a bit of a heap. They are all possible improvers but the form has been rated at face value.

## 6706 BETDAQ HAYDOCK APPRENTICE TRAINING SERIES FINAL H'CAP (PART OF THE RACING EXCELLENCE INITIATIVE) 1m 2f 95y
**5:20** (5:20) (Class 5) (0-70,70) 3-Y-O+ **£3,234** (£962; £481; £240) **Stalls** Centre

Form RPR

1223 **1** **Dansili Dutch (IRE)**[16] 6232 5-9-7 69 JoshDoyle(5) 2 79
(David O'Meara) *hld up in midfield: hdwy 3f out: trckd ldrs 2f out: n.m.r and swtchd rt jst over 1f out: rdn and styd on strly to ld last 50yds* **6/1**[2]

0062 **2** *1 1/4* **King Of Paradise (IRE)**[4] 6597 5-9-0 60 RachelRichardson(3) 16 67
(Eric Alston) *led: pushed along wl over 2f out: rdn wl over 1f out: sn jnd: drvn ins fnl f: kpt on: hdd and no ex last 50yds* **9/2**[1]

4120 **3** *1/2* **Hallingham**[24] 6007 4-9-10 67 (b) CamHardie 5 73
(Jonathan Portman) *hld up towards rr: stdy hdwy 3f out: chsd ldr over 1f out: rdn to chal ent fnl f: ev ch tl drvn and no ex last 50yds* **22/1**

1501 **4** *1* **Pim Street (USA)**[15] 6267 4-9-5 62 JackGarritty 12 66
(David O'Meara) *hld up: hdwy 3f out: chsd ldrs over 1f out: rdn to chal ent fnl f: sn edgd lft and kpt on same pce* **8/1**

-610 **5** *3/4* **Marengo**[23] 6034 3-9-6 69 JacobButterfield 4 72
(Ed de Giles) *trckd ldrs: hdwy on inner wl over 2f out: rdn to chse ldrs over 1f out: drvn and no imp fnl f* **9/2**[1]

-640 **6** *1 3/4* **Gala Casino Star (IRE)**[68] 4470 9-9-5 65 (v) JennyPowell(3) 7 64
(Lawrence Mullaney) *chsd ldr: rdn along wl over 2f out: drvn wl over 1f out and grad wknd* **22/1**

4150 **7** *1 1/2* **Monopoli**[106] 3155 5-8-12 58 JordanNason(3) 10 55
(Shaun Harris) *chsd ldrs: rdn along wl over 2f out: drvn over 1f out and grad wknd* **20/1**

0205 **8** *4 1/2* **Market Puzzle (IRE)**[11] 6394 7-8-8 56 oh11 GaryMahon(5) 6 44
(Mark Brisbourne) *in rr: sme hdwy fr wl over 2f out: n.d* **66/1**

4113 **9** *3/4* **Frontline Phantom (IRE)**[16] 6223 7-9-8 70 PeterSword(5) 15 57
(K R Burke) *chsd ldrs: rdn along over 2f out: grad wknd* **7/1**[3]

3025 **10** *2 3/4* **Kudu Country (IRE)**[34] 5678 8-9-8 65 LouisSteward 9 46
(Tom Tate) *nvr bttr than midfield* **14/1**

4454 **11** *2 1/2* **Vicky Valentine**[11] 6403 4-9-6 63 (p) KevinStott 1 40
(Alistair Whillans) *trckd ldrs on inner: pushed along over 3f out: rdn wl over 2f out: sn wknd* **14/1**

4110 **12** *1 3/4* **Greyemkay**[21] 6086 6-9-3 60 DanielMuscutt 11 33
(Richard Price) *chsd ldrs: rdn along wl over 2f out: sn wknd* **20/1**

5501 **13** *1 1/4* **Thane Of Cawdor (IRE)**[23] 6031 5-9-2 62 MeganCarberry(3) 14 33
(Joseph Tuite) *a towards rr* **16/1**

5555 **14** *nk* **Bold Duke**[105] 3175 6-9-13 70 EoinWalsh 8 40
(Edward Bevan) *a in rr* **14/1**

2m 16.62s (1.12) **Going Correction** +0.125s/f (Good)
**WFA** 3 from 4yo+ 6lb **14** Ran SP% **119.9**
Speed ratings (Par 103): **100,99,98,97,97 95,94,91,90,88 86,84,83,83**
CSF £30.35 CT £567.33 TOTE £5.40: £1.80, £2.40, £6.10; EX 31.30 Trifecta £656.20.
**Owner** Direct Racing **Bred** Castlefarm Stud **Trained** Nawton, N Yorks

**FOCUS**
A modest handicap run at a reasonable gallop. Improvement from the winner.
T/Jkpt: Not won. T/Plt: £209.10 to a £1 stake. Pool: £71,823.05 - 250.69 winning units. T/Qpdt: £40.50 to a £1 stake. Pool: £4895.03 - 89.40 winning units. JR

# 6683 NEWMARKET (R-H)
Friday, September 26

**OFFICIAL GOING: Good (good to firm in places; 7.6; stands' side 7.4; centre 7.5; far side 7.8)**
Wind: fresh, behind Weather: dry, bright spells

## 6707 NAYEF ROSEMARY STKS (LISTED RACE) (F&M) 1m
**1:40** (1:42) (Class 1) 3-Y-O+
**£22,684** (£8,600; £4,304; £2,144; £1,076; £540) **Stalls** Low

Form RPR

114 **1** **Etaab (USA)**[49] 5151 3-8-12 89 PaulHanagan 3 107
(William Haggas) *hld up in tch in rr: pushed along 3f out: swtchd rt and hdwy 2f out: drvn and ev ch over 1f out: led ins fnl f: hung lft wl ins fnl f: hld on wl* **8/1**

-211 **2** *shd* **Belle D'Or (USA)**[83] 3983 3-8-12 104 WilliamBuick 6 106
(John Gosden) *lw: wl in tch in midfield: rdn and effrt 2f out: led over 1f out: hdd ins fnl f: battled on wl u.p: jst hld* **5/2**[2]

311 **3** *1 1/2* **Provenance**[48] 5177 3-8-12 98 RyanMoore 4 104+
(Sir Michael Stoute) *lw: chsd ldrs: rdn and effrt jst over 2f out: ev ch over 1f out tl ins fnl f: cl 3rd and keeping on same pce and hld whn pushed lft and hmpd towards fin* **9/4**[1]

6255 **4** *1 1/4* **Pelerin (IRE)**[44] 5312 3-8-12 96 (p) MartinHarley 5 100
(Marco Botti) *lw: hld up in tch in rr: hdwy to trck ldrs 2f out: effrt u.p to chal over 1f out tl no ex fnl 100yds: 4th and hld whn pushed lft and hmpd wl ins fnl f* **10/1**

4-30 **5** *2* **Zibelina (IRE)**[27] 5927 4-9-2 105 AdamKirby 8 95
(Charlie Appleby) *swtg: wl in tch in midfield: chsd ldr over 2f out: drvn and ev ch over 1f out tl 1f out: outpcd ins fnl f* **7/1**[3]

4200 **6** *2 1/2* **Gifted Girl (IRE)**[9] 6464 5-9-2 102 (b[1]) TomQueally 9 89
(Paul Cole) *racd keenly: chsd ldr tl led after 2f: rdn and hdd over 1f out: wknd fnl f* **10/1**

0464 **7** *4 1/2* **Amulet**[9] 6458 4-9-2 89 (b) JimmyFortune 1 79
(Eve Johnson Houghton) *led for 2f: chsd ldr tl struggling u.p over 2f out: wknd wl over 1f out* **25/1**

21 **8** *5* **Batrana**[35] 5648 3-8-12 84 PatCosgrave 7 67
(M F De Kock, South Africa) *hld up in tch in rr: rdn and effrt over 2f out: sn struggling and btn: bhd over 1f out* **14/1**

1m 35.52s (-3.08) **Going Correction** -0.05s/f (Good)
**WFA** 3 from 4yo+ 4lb **8** Ran SP% **111.6**
Speed ratings: **113,112,111,110,108 105,101,96**
CSF £27.00 TOTE £7.80: £2.50, £1.20, £1.40; EX 32.70 Trifecta £76.10.
**Owner** Hamdan Al Maktoum **Bred** Shadwell Farm LLC **Trained** Newmarket, Suffolk
■ Stewards' Enquiry : Paul Hanagan three-day ban: careless riding (Oct 10-12)

**FOCUS**
Far side track used. Stalls Far Side except 12f: Centre. It was dry overnight, there was no dew, and together with a strong cross wind the going had quickened up to good, good to firm in places (GoingStick 7.6). The result of this opening Listed contest confirmed the ground was riding on the fast side, as the time was just 0.42sec above standard. Ordinary Listed form, the winner an improver.

## 6708 PRINCESS ROYAL EBF SAKHEE STKS (FORMERLY THE HARVEST STAKES) (LISTED RACE) (F&M) 1m 4f
**2:10** (2:15) (Class 1) 3-Y-O+
**£22,684** (£8,600; £4,304; £2,144; £1,076; £540) **Stalls** Centre

Form RPR

5341 **1** **Queen Of Ice**[36] 5611 3-8-12 105 RichardHughes 12 108
(William Haggas) *lw: mde all: rdn and fnd ex 2f out: clr over 1f out: drvn and kpt on wl ins fnl f: all out* **7/1**

0051 **2** *3/4* **Jordan Princess**[33] 5723 3-8-9 93 AndreaAtzeni 6 104+
(Luca Cumani) *lw: hld up in midfield: swtchd rt and effrt 2f out: hdwy u.p to chse ldrs over 1f out: wnt 2nd ins fnl f: steadily clsd but nvr quite getting to wnr* **9/2**[2]

-536 **3** *1 1/2* **Vanity Rules**[44] 5312 4-9-3 96 FrederikTylicki 2 101
(Ed Vaughan) *travelled wl in midfield: effrt to chse clr wnr over 1f out: kpt on but no real imp: lost 2nd ins fnl f* **20/1**

3243 **4** *2 3/4* **Criteria (IRE)**[15] 6255 3-8-9 104 WilliamBuick 3 97
(John Gosden) *chsd ldrs: wnt 2nd 3f out tl over 1f out: kpt on same pce fnl f* **3/1**[1]

1132 **5** *1 ¼* **My Spirit (IRE)**[11] 6419 3-8-9 100 JoeFanning 8 95+
(William Haggas) *lw: taken down early: stdd s: t.k.h in midfield: rdn and outpcd over 2f out: rallied and styd on fnl f: no threat to ldrs* **5/1**[3]

-602 **6** *1 ¼* **Livia's Dream (IRE)**[13] 6321 5-9-3 95 GeorgeBaker 1 93
(Ed Walker) *hld up towards rr: racd alone against far rail in st: hdwy into midfield 1/2-way: rdn and wknd over 1f out* **16/1**

-504 **7** *1 ½* **Island Remede**[36] 5611 3-8-9 97 PaulHanagan 13 91
(Ed Dunlop) *hld up in tch in midfield: rdn and effrt over 2f out: sn outpcd: no imp but plugged on fr over 1f out* **20/1**

0-52 **8** *2 ½* **Zipp (IRE)**[45] 5288 4-9-3 85 JamesDoyle 4 87
(Ralph Beckett) *hld up towards rr: effrt u.p over 2f out: no imp* **20/1**

-210 **9** *1 ¼* **Miss Marjurie (IRE)**[34] 5668 4-9-3 93 OisinMurphy 11 85
(Denis Coakley) *lw: taken down early: chsd ldrs: rdn over 2f out: wknd u.p over 1f out* **10/1**

-335 **10** *7* **Familliarity**[77] 4160 4-9-3 79 MartinHarley 14 73
(Roger Varian) *chsd wnr tl 3f out: sn struggling: wknd 2f out* **66/1**

0006 **11** *3* **Agent Allison**[9] 6464 4-9-3 95 JimCrowley 7 69
(Peter Chapple-Hyam) *stdd s: hld up in rr: short-lived effrt over 2f out: sn btn and bhd over 1f out* **33/1**

-253 **12** *9* **Regal Hawk**[12] 6389 4-9-3 91 KierenFallon 9 54
(James Tate) *hld up towards rr: rdn over 2f out: sn btn and bhd fnl 2f: t.o* **25/1**

331 **13** *39* **Long View (IRE)**[25] 5976 3-8-9 88 RyanMoore 5
(Sir Michael Stoute) *in tch in midfield: rdn and lost pl over 4f out: lost tch and eased over 2f out: t.o* **11/1**

2m 27.55s (-4.45) **Going Correction** -0.05s/f (Good)
**WFA** 3 from 4yo+ 8lb **13** Ran SP% **118.2**
Speed ratings: **112,111,110,108,107 107,106,104,103,98 96,90,64**
CSF £34.37 TOTE £5.90: £2.10, £2.30, £7.10; EX 42.00 Trifecta £1696.80.
**Owner** Cheveley Park Stud **Bred** Cheveley Park Stud Ltd **Trained** Newmarket, Suffolk

**FOCUS**
This looked really competitive. The gallop was uneven, though, and Richard Hughes's injection of pace aboard the winner around 3f out caught the majority flat-footed. The form should be treated with a degree of caution, with the third the key. A good effort from the winner.

## 6709 SHADWELL ROCKFEL STKS (GROUP 2) (FILLIES) 7f
**2:40** (2:47) (Class 1) 2-Y-O

**£61,813** (£23,435; £11,728; £5,842; £2,932; £1,471) **Stalls** Low

Form RPR

22 **1** **Lucida (IRE)**[12] 6372 2-9-0 0 KevinManning 5 111+
(J S Bolger, Ire) *str: in tch: rdn and swtchd lft 2f out: drvn and gd hdwy over 1f out: led fnl 100yds: styd on strly: rdn out* **1/1**[1]

21 **2** *1* **Fadhayyil (IRE)**[22] 6066 2-9-0 0 PaulHanagan 2 108+
(B W Hills) *lw: in tch in midfield: effrt and hdwy to chal 2f out: led and rn green 1f out: hdd fnl 100yds: kpt on same pce after* **10/1**

1321 **3** *2* **New Providence**[22] 6067 2-9-0 102 JimCrowley 6 103
(Hugo Palmer) *lw: hld up towards rr: hdwy u.p over 1f out: wnt 3rd wl ins fnl f: no imp after* **5/1**[2]

1310 **4** *½* **Tigrilla (IRE)**[33] 5734 2-9-0 105 AndreaAtzeni 4 102
(Roger Varian) *swtg: chsd ldr: rdn and ev ch 2f out tl 1f out: one pce ins fnl f* **20/1**

3163 **5** *½* **Stroll Patrol**[22] 6067 2-9-0 98 OisinMurphy 1 100
(Philip McBride) *hld up in tch towards rr: rdn and effrt 2f out: swtchd lft and hdwy 1f out: styd on wl fnl 100yds: no threat to ldrs* **11/1**

41 **6** *3 ½* **What Say You (IRE)**[35] 5644 2-9-0 0 WilliamBuick 3 91
(K R Burke) *unf: scope: lengthy: led: rdn and pressed 2f out: hdd over 1f out: sn btn and wknd ins fnl f* **6/1**[3]

3102 **7** *2 ¾* **East Coast Lady (IRE)**[15] 6253 2-9-0 88 MartinHarley 9 83
(Robert Eddery) *stdd s: hld up in rr: shkn up and effrt over 1f out: sn outpcd and btn* **50/1**

2141 **8** *2 ¾* **Home Cummins (IRE)**[15] 6253 2-9-0 91 TonyHamilton 7 76
(Richard Fahey) *lengthy: chsd ldrs: rdn over 2f out: losing pl and towards rr whn sltly hmpd 2f out: no ch after* **33/1**

1122 **9** *4 ½* **Calypso Beat (USA)**[34] 5707 2-9-0 103 RyanMoore 8 65
(Kevin Ryan) *w'like: leggy: in tch in midfield: rdn: lost pl and bhd whn hmpd 2f out: no ch after* **14/1**

1m 22.82s (-2.58) **Going Correction** -0.05s/f (Good) **9** Ran SP% **114.7**
Speed ratings (Par 104): **112,110,108,108,107 103,100,97,92**
CSF £11.84 TOTE £1.90: £1.10, £2.50, £1.50; EX 14.00 Trifecta £69.80.
**Owner** Godolphin **Bred** Darley **Trained** Coolcullen, Co Carlow

**FOCUS**
A reliable Guineas trial over the past ten years, producing winners in Speciosa and Finsceal Beo and runners-up in Maids Causeway and Just The Judge, not to mention Lahaleeb and Music Show, who both placed in the Irish equivalent. Previously run in mid-October on Dewhurst day, this looks a better spot in the calendar for it as trainers can now use it as a stepping stone to the mile Group 1s in October. This is straightforward form, pretty much par for the race. The winner should have at least a little more to offer.

## 6710 SHADWELL JOEL STKS (BRITISH CHAMPIONS SERIES) (GROUP 2) 1m
**3:15** (3:18) (Class 1) 3-Y-O+

**£61,813** (£23,435; £11,728; £5,842; £2,932; £1,471) **Stalls** Low

Form RPR

1111 **1** **Custom Cut (IRE)**[34] 5690 5-9-4 114 DanielTudhope 11 120
(David O'Meara) *lw: mde all: rdn 2f out: kpt on finding for press: forged into ld and wnt clr ins fnl f: styd on strly* **15/2**

1131 **2** *2 ½* **Captain Cat (IRE)**[20] 6132 5-9-4 115 JamesDoyle 5 114
(Roger Charlton) *stdd s: hld up in tch in rr: rdn: edging rt and hdwy over 1f out: chsng ldrs and hung rt ins fnl f: sn chsng wnr: no imp* **3/1**[1]

1325 **3** *1 ¼* **Hors De Combat**[34] 5666 3-9-0 108 RyanMoore 3 111
(James Fanshawe) *lw: hld up in tch towards rr: hdwy 3f out: drvn to chse ldrs over 1f out: kpt on same pce ins fnl f: wnt 3rd cl home* **9/2**[3]

124 **4** *nk* **Tullius (IRE)**[101] 3317 6-9-4 117 JimmyFortune 10 111
(Andrew Balding) *lw: chsd ldrs: rdn and hung rt over 1f out: sn swtchd lft: styd on same pce u.p fnl f* **8/1**

2642 **5** *shd* **Producer**[9] 6458 5-9-4 110 RichardHughes 9 110
(Richard Hannon) *stdd s: hld up towards rr: hdwy into midfield 1/2-way: clsd to press ldrs and rdn 2f out: wnt 2nd 1f out: no ex and lost 3 pls fnl 100yds* **25/1**

2-06 **6** *1 ½* **Cable Bay (IRE)**[13] 6328 3-9-0 110 FrankieDettori 12 107
(Charles Hills) *chsd ldrs: rdn and hung lft over 1f out: outpcd 1f out: no imp after* **33/1**

5035 **7** *hd* **Anjaal**[43] 5354 3-9-0 111 PaulHanagan 4 107
(Richard Hannon) *stdd s: t.k.h early: hld up in tch towards rr: rdn 2f out: drvn 1f out: styd on ins fnl f: nvr threatened ldrs* **20/1**

-034 **8** *shd* **Outstrip**[58] 4779 3-9-0 118 AdamKirby 2 106
(Charlie Appleby) *in tch in midfield: effrt and n.m.r 2f out: a struggling for enough room after: styd on same pce ins fnl f* **10/1**

0013 **9** *1 ¼* **Ocean Tempest**[20] 6132 5-9-4 117 JoeDoyle 8 103
(John Ryan) *chsd ldr tl over 2f out: sn u.p and lost pl 2f out: kpt on but no threat to ldrs after* **25/1**

4305 **10** *1 ¼* **Professor**[13] 6328 4-9-4 108 KierenFallon 14 101
(Richard Hannon) *stdd s: hld up in tch in rr: pushed along 1/2-way: rdn and no hdwy 2f out* **33/1**

-111 **11** *1 ½* **Wannabe Yours (IRE)**[56] 4850 3-9-0 109 WilliamBuick 1 106
(John Gosden) *wl in tch in midfield: hdwy to chse ldrs 1/2-way: wnt 2nd and pressing wnr over 2f out: sn rdn: lost 2nd 1f out: btn whn squeezed for room and hmpd ins fnl f: eased after* **7/2**[2]

130 **12** *nk* **Master Carpenter (IRE)**[12] 6382 3-9-0 107 AndreaAtzeni 13 96
(Rod Millman) *in tch in midfield: rdn over 2f out: lost pl and bhd over 1f out* **50/1**

1m 35.66s (-2.94) **Going Correction** -0.05s/f (Good)
**WFA** 3 from 4yo+ 4lb **12** Ran SP% **117.7**
Speed ratings: **112,109,108,107,107 106,106,106,104,103 102,101**
CSF £27.64 TOTE £8.50: £2.80, £1.30, £2.40; EX 27.70 Trifecta £216.20.
**Owner** Gary Douglas & Pat Breslin **Bred** Moyglare Stud Farm Ltd **Trained** Nawton, N Yorks

**FOCUS**
An exciting edition of the Group 2 Joel Stakes and, while there was another winner on the day from the front, it provided one of the stories of the season as the hugely progressive Custom Cut landed a five-timer. The first two both confirmed their recent improved form.

## 6711 MAWATHEEQ GODOLPHIN STKS (LISTED RACE) 1m 4f
**3:45** (3:51) (Class 1) 3-Y-O+

**£22,684** (£8,600; £4,304; £2,144; £1,076; £540) **Stalls** Centre

Form RPR

3644 **1** **Nabucco**[16] 6233 5-9-5 103 WilliamBuick 5 111
(John Gosden) *chsd ldrs: c to r in centre 9f out: led 3f out: rdn over 1f out: sustained duel w rival after: edgd rt and bmpd rival wl ins fnl f: styd on: all out: jst prevailed* **9/2**[2]

5002 **2** *shd* **Red Galileo**[16] 6233 3-8-11 106 RyanMoore 8 110
(Ed Dunlop) *stdd and dropped in bhd after s: hld up in tch: rdn over 2f out: swtchd lft and hdwy 1f out: styd on strly u.p ins fnl f: wnt 2nd on post* **6/1**[3]

02 **3** *nse* **Ayrad (IRE)**[32] 5755 3-8-11 100 AndreaAtzeni 3 110
(Roger Varian) *lw: chsd ldrs: effrt over 2f out: rdn to chal over 1f out: sustained duel w wnr after: edgd lft and bmpd wnr wl ins fnl f: styd on: lost 2nd on post* **13/2**

2224 **4** *3 ¼* **Windshear**[13] 6329 3-8-11 112 RichardHughes 6 105
(Richard Hannon) *chsd ldr tl 3f out: sn drvn: 3rd and unable qck over 1f out: wknd ins fnl f* **5/4**[1]

01-5 **5** *2* **Flying The Flag (IRE)**[34] 5690 4-9-5 108 (t) PatCosgrave 7 101
(M F De Kock, South Africa) *hld up in last pair: rdn 3f out: outpcd and btn over 1f out* **8/1**

-000 **6** *nk* **Penglai Pavilion (USA)**[133] 2315 4-9-5 114 AdamKirby 4 101
(Charlie Appleby) *led: hdd 3f out: sn rdn: btn over 1f out: wknd ins fnl f* **12/1**

2m 28.97s (-3.03) **Going Correction** -0.05s/f (Good)
**WFA** 3 from 4yo+ 8lb **6** Ran SP% **109.0**
Speed ratings: **108,107,107,105,104 104**
CSF £28.63 TOTE £6.20: £2.40, £2.50; EX 29.10 Trifecta £154.60.
**Owner** HRH Princess Haya Of Jordan **Bred** Darley **Trained** Newmarket, Suffolk
■ Stewards' Enquiry : William Buick caution: careless riding.

**FOCUS**
There was a tight finish to this Listed race and a case could be made for any one of the first three being the best horse on the day. The form is rated around the winner.

## 6712 DERRINSTOWN EBF STALLIONS MAIDEN STKS (BOBIS RACE) (C&G) 7f
**4:25** (4:25) (Class 4) 2-Y-O **£5,175** (£1,540; £769; £384) **Stalls** Low

Form RPR

**1** **Consort (IRE)** 2-9-0 0 RyanMoore 1 86+
(Sir Michael Stoute) *leggy: athletic: mde all: rdn and qcknd clr over 1f out: in command and styd on wl fnl f* **13/2**

**2** *2 ¾* **Hathal (USA)** 2-9-0 0 FrankieDettori 13 79+
(William Haggas) *athletic: stdd s: hld up in tch in rr: rdn wl over 1f out: hdwy 1f out: str run to go 2nd wl ins fnl f: no threat to wnr* **5/1**[3]

**3** *½* **Spanish Squeeze (IRE)** 2-9-0 0 DanielTudhope 5 77+
(Hugo Palmer) *lengthy: tall: lw: chsd ldrs: chsd wnr 3f out: rdn and outpcd by wnr over 1f out: r.o same pce after: lost 2nd wl ins fnl f* **6/1**

**4** *1 ½* **Mutamakkin (USA)** 2-9-0 0 RichardHughes 2 73+
(Sir Michael Stoute) *scope: bit bkwd: hld up in tch: hdwy into midfield 1/2-way: rdn wl over 1f out: styd on same pce after* **20/1**

**5** *nk* **Mubtaahij (IRE)** 2-9-0 0 PatCosgrave 4 72+
(M F De Kock, South Africa) *tall: unf: stdd s: hld up in tch in rr: rdn and sme hdwy over 1f out: kpt on ins fnl f: nvr trbld ldrs* **20/1**

5 **6** *nk* **Navigate (IRE)**[28] 5881 2-9-0 0 FergusSweeney 12 72
(Martyn Meade) *str: awkward leaving stalls: in tch in midfield: hdwy to chse ldrs and rdn 2f out: outpcd over 1f out: kpt on same pce after* **12/1**

**7** *1 ¾* **Yamllik** 2-9-0 0 FrederikTylicki 9 67+
(Saeed bin Suroor) *lengthy: athletic: lw: dwlt and short of room sn after s: in tch towards rr: rdn and hdwy over 1f out: kpt on same pce ins fnl f* **9/2**[2]

**8** *1 ¾* **Algaith (USA)** 2-9-0 0 PaulHanagan 10 62+
(B W Hills) *str: scope: chsd ldrs: 3rd and rdn 2f out: outpcd over 1f out: wknd ins fnl f* **7/2**[1]

**9** *1 ¼* **Fibre Optic** 2-9-0 0 AdamKirby 8 59
(Luca Cumani) *str: scope: hld up in tch towards rr: outpcd and rdn 2f out: wl hld but plugged on ins fnl f* **25/1**

6 **10** *nk* **Nota Cambiata (USA)**[9] 6456 2-9-0 0 WilliamBuick 6 58
(John Gosden) *w'like: str: chsd ldr tl 3f out: no ex u.p and btn over 1f out: wknd ins fnl f* **20/1**

0 **11** *½* **Wisewit**[63] 4618 2-9-0 0 RobertTart 11 57
(James Toller) *leggy: in tch in midfield: rdn: rn green and lost pl over 1f out: bhd 1f out* **100/1**

**12** *3* **Zabeel Star (IRE)** 2-9-0 0 AndreaAtzeni 7 48
(Luca Cumani) *leggy: scope: in tch towards rr: rdn 1/2-way: sn struggling in last and wl btn fnl 2f* **20/1**

1m 26.5s (1.10) **Going Correction** -0.05s/f (Good) **12** Ran SP% **116.3**
Speed ratings (Par 97): **91,87,87,85,85 84,82,80,79,79 78,75**
CSF £33.97 TOTE £6.30: £1.80, £2.50, £3.30; EX 35.90 Trifecta £141.60.
**Owner** Highclere Thoroughbred Racing(Hardwicke) **Bred** Old Long Hill Ballinteskin Stud Ltd **Trained** Newmarket, Suffolk


The Form Book, Raceform Ltd, Newbury, RG14 5SJ

**FOCUS**
There was an ordinary early pace on in this interesting 2yo maiden, with the field splitting into two groups until merging 3f out. The winner is likely to rate a good bit higher, and there was prmise from plenty of others.

## 6713 SHADWELL FARM H'CAP (SILVER CAMBRIDGESHIRE) 1m 1f
5:00 (5:09) (Class 2) 3-Y-O+
£18,675 (£5,592; £2,796; £1,398; £699; £351) Stalls Low

Form RPR

0-11 **1** **Gm Hopkins**[14] 6301 3-9-6 91 4ex........ WilliamBuick 11 108+
(John Gosden) *lw: hld up in midfield: travelled strly: clsd to join ldrs on bit: racd towards stands' side 2f out: shkn up to ld over 1f out: rdn and r.o strly fnl f: readily* **7/1[2]**

3015 **2** *2 3/4* **Munaaser**[35] 5656 3-9-9 94........ PaulHanagan 2 105+
(Sir Michael Stoute) *hld up in midfield: effrt over 2f out: hdwy u.p over 1f out: chsd wnr ins fnl f: r.o but no threat to wnr* **15/2[3]**

1604 **3** *1/2* **Muharrer**[6] 6534 5-9-7 90........ ConnorBeasley(3) 8 99
(Michael Dods) *lw: hld up in midfield: hdwy over 2f out: rdn to chse ldrs over 1f out: chse wnr briefly ins fnl f: 3rd and one pce fnl 100yds* **16/1**

1512 **4** *1/2* **Mange All**[15] 6257 3-9-7 92........ LiamJones 24 101
(William Haggas) *lw: stdd s: t.k.h: hld up in rr: gd hdwy over 2f out: rdn and ev ch wl over 1f out: 2nd and outpcd by wnr 1f out: one pce and lost 2 pls ins fnl f* **5/2[1]**

00 **5** *1* **Ty Gwr**[7] 6523 5-8-10 83........ MikeyEnnis(7) 25 89
(Brian Ellison) *stdd and dropped in bhd after s: hld up in rr: swtchd lft and gd hdwy over 2f out: rdn and chal wl over 1f out: led over 1f out: sn hdd: wknd ins fnl f* **33/1**

4141 **6** *1 1/4* **Nanton (USA)**[34] 5678 12-9-2 82........ DanielTudhope 1 85
(Jim Goldie) *hld up in midfield: hdwy u.p 2f out: styd on same pce ins fnl f* **33/1**

4323 **7** *1* **Jodies Jem**[41] 5446 4-9-6 86........ JoeFanning 14 87
(William Jarvis) *hld up in midfield: hdwy over 2f out: drvn and unable qck wl over 1f out: styd on same pce after* **16/1**

4164 **8** *nk* **Eurystheus (IRE)**[14] 6292 5-8-9 80........(p) AlistairRawlinson(5) 23 80
(Michael Appleby) *hld up towards rr: hdwy and rdn over 3f out: no ex u.p 2f out: styd on same pce after* **14/1**

-412 **9** *3/4* **Ree's Rascal (IRE)**[47] 5213 6-9-10 90........ PatCosgrave 9 89
(Jim Boyle) *hld up in midfield: rdn and hdwy over 2f out: chsd ldrs and unable qck wl over 1f out: wknd ins fnl f* **25/1**

3120 **10** *1/2* **Angelic Upstart (IRE)**[15] 6257 6-9-6 86........ OisinMurphy 15 84
(Andrew Balding) *hld up towards rr: rdn and hdwy jst over 2f out: drvn and no hdwy over 1f out: plugged on same pce fnl f* **16/1**

1520 **11** *1 3/4* **Coincidently**[6] 6534 4-9-0 80........ SilvestreDeSousa 17 74
(Alan Bailey) *chsd ldrs: clsd on clr ldr over 2f out: ev ch but struggling to qckn whn short of room over 1f out: wknd 1f out* **20/1**

-221 **12** *nse* **Lacan (IRE)**[106] 3153 3-9-4 89........ AdamKirby 12 84
(Clive Cox) *hld up in midfield: rdn and hdwy to chse ldrs 2f out: no ex u.p over 1f out: wknd ins fnl f* **11/1**

2200 **13** *2 1/2* **Ansaab**[6] 6531 6-9-9 89........(t) TomQueally 18 78
(Alan McCabe) *hld up in midfield: rdn and effrt over 2f out: no prog and btn over 1f out: wknd fnl f* **28/1**

1115 **14** *nk* **Chain Of Events**[84] 3931 7-9-2 82........ RyanMoore 7 70
(Michael Wigham) *hld up in midfield: rdn and effrt over 2f out: outpcd 2f out: rallied u.p over 1f out: wknd ins fnl f* **16/1**

5040 **15** *nk* **Anton Chigurh**[23] 6035 5-8-6 75........ DannyBrock(3) 16 63
(Philip McBride) *chsd ldrs: rdn over 2f out: struggling and lost pl wl over 1f out: wknd ins fnl f* **14/1**

000 **16** *1 1/4* **Showboating (IRE)**[10] 6430 6-9-0 80........(tp) KierenFallon 5 65
(Alan McCabe) *taken down early: led and sn clr: rdn and c bk to field over 2f out: hdd wl over 1f out: sn wknd: eased wl ins fnl f* **33/1**

U626 **17** *2 1/2* **Border Bandit (USA)**[16] 6226 6-9-4 84........(p) JimmyQuinn 20 64
(Tracy Waggott) *racd in midfield: clsd over 2f out: sn rdn and outpcd 2f out: wknd over 1f out: eased wl ins fnl f* **66/1**

10 **18** *1* **Unison (IRE)**[29] 5849 4-8-11 77........ JamieSpencer 21 55
(Peter Makin) *chsd ldrs: lost pl and bhd 1/2-way: n.d after* **33/1**

2023 **19** *nk* **Miguel Grau (USA)**[33] 5730 4-8-13 79........(b) AndreaAtzeni 4 56
(Roger Varian) *lw: racd in midfield: rdn and struggling whn short of room over 2f: wknd wl over 1f out* **20/1**

1116 **20** *5* **Puzzle Time**[14] 6292 4-9-5 85........ WilliamCarson 22 51
(Giles Bravery) *hld up towards rr: hld up towards rr: rdn and lost tch over 2f out* **33/1**

1410 **21** *1* **Desert Ranger (IRE)**[9] 6466 3-8-7 78........ MartinLane 6 43
(James Tate) *taken down early: stdd s: t.k.h: hld up in rr: effrt u.p over 2f out: no prog over 1f out: wknd fnl f* **66/1**

1053 **22** *6* **Sheila's Buddy**[7] 6523 5-8-12 78........ RichardHughes 10 30
(J S Moore) *lw: chsd clr ldr tl over 2f out: sn dropped out: eased over 1f out* **20/1**

1m 49.57s (-2.13) **Going Correction** -0.05s/f (Good)
**WFA** 3 from 4yo+ 5lb **22 Ran SP% 137.3**
Speed ratings (Par 109): **107,104,104,103,102 101,100,100,99,99 97,97,95,95,95 93,91,90,90,86 85,79**
CSF £54.76 CT £869.87 TOTE £9.50: £3.10, £1.20, £4.20, £1.60; EX 56.70 Trifecta £1853.80 Part won..
**Owner** R J H Geffen **Bred** Cadran-Earl Blot-Scea Des Bissons **Trained** Newmarket, Suffolk
■ Stewards' Enquiry : Richard Hughes jockey said gelding lost its action

**FOCUS**
The consolation race to Saturday's feature handicap, but a good event in its own right and it produced a winner who will surely be going on to much better things. Three of the five 3yos in the race made the frame. They started off in two bunches but the centre group gradually eased across and joined the stands' side group. Strong form, rated a little positively.

## 6714 NEWMARKET CHALLENGE WHIP (H'CAP) 1m 2f
5:30 (5:40) (Class 6) (0-85,89) 3-Y-O+
£0Stalls Low

Form RPR

6622 **1** **Inspector Norse**[7] 6516 3-8-5 75........ SilvestreDeSousa 5 84
(Sylvester Kirk) *racd in far side gp: chsd ldrs tl led 3f out: mde rest: forged ahd u.p over 1f out: styd on wl* **13/2[3]**

3451 **2** *2* **Micras**[23] 6026 3-8-13 83........(v) RyanMoore 11 88
(Andrew Balding) *racd in centre trio: towards rr: rdn 3f out: hdwy u.p over 1f out: wnt 2nd fnl 75yds: styd on but no threat to wnr* **11/2[2]**

5/2- **3** *2 1/4* **Fremont (IRE)**[364] 6802 7-7-11 66........ NoelGarbutt(5) 3 67
(Hugo Palmer) *racd in far side gp: chsd ldr: ev ch and drvn over 2f out: 2nd and btn 1f out: one pce and lost 2nd fnl 75yds* **14/1**

4030 **4** *2 1/4* **Highland Castle**[13] 6330 6-9-11 89........ JamieSpencer 6 86
(David Elsworth) *racd in far side gp: hld up wl bhd: stl plenty to do whn hdwy u.p over 1f out: styd on to go 4th wl ins fnl f: nvr trbld ldrs* **10/1**

0621 **5** *1* **Moshe (IRE)**[4] 6611 3-8-9 79........ RichardHughes 2 74
(Hughie Morrison) *lw: racd in far side gp: chsd ldr: rdn and ev ch over 2f out: 3rd and btn over 1f out: wknd ins fnl f* **7/4[1]**

6340 **6** *hd* **Glasgow Central**[77] 4168 3-8-2 72........ JoeFanning 10 66
(Charles Hills) *racd in centre trio: in midfield overall: rdn and effrt to chse ldrs: no imp and btn over 1f out: plugged on* **16/1**

3622 **7** *7* **Swordbearer**[24] 6018 3-8-3 73........ MartinLane 4 54
(James Fanshawe) *lw: racd in far side gp: rdn and effrt 3f out: chsd ldrs and drvn 2f out: wknd over 1f out* **9/1**

0664 **8** *21* **Flemish School**[21] 6098 4-9-10 88........(p) WilliamBuick 7 63
(David Elsworth) *racd in far side gp: a towards rr: effrt 3f out: sme hdwy 2f out: wknd over 1f out: eased ins fnl f: t.o* **7/1**

3504 **9** *3 3/4* **Beauchamp Melba**[32] 5747 3-7-11 70 oh23........(b) DannyBrock(3) 1 4
(Paul Fitzsimons) *racd in far side gp: led tl 3f out: sn dropped out: t.o and eased ins fnl f* **100/1**

1000 **10** *4* **Compton Bird**[7] 6523 5-8-13 77........ FrankieDettori 9 4
(Paul Fitzsimons) *racd in far side gp: a wl off the pce in rr: lost tch 2f out: t.o and eased ins fnl f* **25/1**

1101 **11** *36* **Ancient Greece**[15] 6251 7-8-10 74........(t) PatCosgrave 8
(George Baker) *racd in centre trio: midfield: struggling and lost pl over 3f out: t.o and heavily eased ins fnl f* **25/1**

2m 3.37s (-2.43) **Going Correction** -0.05s/f (Good)
**WFA** 3 from 4yo+ 6lb **11 Ran SP% 117.9**
Speed ratings (Par 101): **107,105,103,101,101 100,95,78,75,72 43**
CSF £41.62 CT £489.60 TOTE £6.30: £1.80, £2.00, £3.90; EX 47.60 Trifecta £1002.40.
**Owner** J C Smith **Bred** Littleton Stud **Trained** Upper Lambourn, Berks

**FOCUS**
They split into two groups and the winner emerged from the far-side gathering. Fair form, with a 4lb best from the winner.
T/Plt: £74.40 to a £1 stake. Pool: £153,634.66 - 1507.11 winning units. T/Qpdt: £22.80 to a £1 stake. Pool: £9203.25 - 298.44 winning units. SP

# 6561 WOLVERHAMPTON (A.W) (L-H)
## Friday, September 26

**OFFICIAL GOING: Tapeta: standard**
Wind: Fresh across easing throughout the evening Weather: Cloudy with sunny spells

## 6715 BET TOTEPLACEPOT H'CAP (TAPETA) 1m 141y
5:45 (5:45) (Class 6) (0-60,60) 3-Y-O+ £2,264 (£673; £336; £168) Stalls Low

Form RPR

0344 **1** **Evacusafe Lady**[11] 6407 3-8-11 53........(t) RyanPowell(3) 9 63
(John Ryan) *chsd ldrs: rdn over 3f out: led ins fnl f: styd on u.p* **8/1**

6000 **2** *1* **Yawail**[58] 4472 3-8-8 54........(p) KevinLundie(7) 5 62
(Brian Rothwell) *chsd ldrs: rdn over 2f out: ev ch ins fnl f: kpt on* **40/1**

3424 **3** *1 1/4* **Abigails Angel**[11] 6396 7-9-4 52 ow2........ AmirQuinn 2 56
(Lee Carter) *s.i.s: sn rcvrd into mid-div: nt clr run over 2f out: hdwy over 1f out: rdn and ev ch ins fnl f: styd on same pce* **13/2**

6 **4** *1* **Bosstime (IRE)**[42] 5395 4-9-12 60........ RobertHavlin 12 62
(John Holt) *s.i.s: hdwy to chse ldr over 7f out: led 2f out: sn rdn: hdd and no ex ins fnl f* **10/1**

-001 **5** *1/2* **Thomas Blossom (IRE)**[18] 6195 4-8-7 48........(v) RobHornby(7) 4 49
(Patrick Chamings) *prom: rdn over 1f out: styd on same pce fnl f* **6/1[3]**

5144 **6** *1 1/4* **Appyjack**[27] 5908 6-9-8 56........ RaulDaSilva 10 54
(Tony Carroll) *hld up: hdwy over 2f out: sn rdn: styd on same pce fr over 1f out* **9/2[2]**

6000 **7** *2 1/4* **Pipers Piping (IRE)**[15] 6267 8-9-4 55........ RossAtkinson(3) 8 48
(Mandy Rowland) *hld up: rdn over 1f out: nvr trbld ldrs* **18/1**

0044 **8** *1/2* **Eastward Ho**[22] 6076 6-9-5 53........(p) DaleSwift 6 44
(Michael Herrington) *led: rdn 3f out: hdd 2f out: wknd ins fnl f* **7/2[1]**

1500 **9** *1/2* **Indus Valley (IRE)**[23] 6035 7-9-12 60........ AdamBeschizza 11 50
(Des Donovan) *s.i.s: hld up: rdn over 2f out: n.d* **16/1**

60-0 **10** *1 3/4* **Glasgon**[144] 2021 4-8-12 49........ NeilFarley(3) 13 35
(Declan Carroll) *prom: drvn along over 3f out: wknd over 2f out* **25/1**

3006 **11** *1/2* **Bajan Story**[32] 5751 5-9-1 49........ MartinHarley 7 34
(Michael Blanshard) *s.i.s: hld up: pushed along 4f out: a in rr* **12/1**

1m 50.51s (0.41) **Going Correction** +0.05s/f (Slow)
**WFA** 3 from 4yo+ 5lb **11 Ran SP% 113.3**
Speed ratings (Par 101): **100,99,98,97,96 95,93,93,92,91 90**
CSF £268.20 CT £2212.83 TOTE £8.90: £2.20, £11.00, £1.60; EX 237.80 Trifecta £646.40.
**Owner** J Ryan **Bred** Mrs Sarah Moorcroft **Trained** Newmarket, Suffolk

**FOCUS**
The favourite was disappointing in this minor handicap but the winner scored in decent style.

## 6716 TOTEPOOL BET ON ALL UK RACING FILLIES' H'CAP (TAPETA) 7f 32y
6:20 (6:22) (Class 5) (0-70,70) 3-Y-O+ £2,587 (£770; £384; £192) Stalls High

Form RPR

3600 **1** **Arabian Flight**[18] 6195 5-8-7 59........(p) RyanTate(3) 3 70
(Michael Appleby) *mde all: rdn over 1f out: styd on wl* **14/1**

3203 **2** *2* **See Clearly**[6] 6543 5-8-9 58........(p) DuranFentiman 5 64
(Tim Easterby) *chsd wnr: rdn over 1f out: styd on same pce ins fnl f* **8/1[3]**

0064 **3** *1/2* **Palace Princess (FR)**[92] 3627 3-8-7 59........ RobertHavlin 9 63
(Ed Dunlop) *s.i.s: hld up: hdwy over 1f out: r.o to go 3rd nr fin: nt rch ldrs* **14/1**

6300 **4** *nk* **Lilac Lace (IRE)**[28] 5887 4-9-7 70........ DavidAllan 8 74
(Tim Easterby) *a.p: rdn over 1f out: styd on* **6/4[1]**

6-50 **5** *hd* **Larghetto (USA)**[20] 6160 6-8-13 62........ StevieDonohoe 1 65
(Ian Williams) *chsd ldrs: rdn and nt clr run over 1f out: styd on same pce ins fnl f* **20/1**

-020 **6** *1 1/2* **Gracefilly**[16] 6243 3-8-8 60........ WilliamTwiston-Davies 4 59
(Ed Walker) *prom: rdn over 2f out: no ex fnl f* **20/1**

1250 **7** *2* **Grace Hull**[16] 6232 4-9-3 66........(p) JasonHart 6 60
(Garry Moss) *hld up: hdwy over 1f out: sn rdn: no ex ins fnl f* **8/1[3]**

2350 **8** *2 3/4* **Candy Kitten**[144] 2021 4-8-11 63........(t) AshleyMorgan(3) 7 50
(Paul Cole) *hld up: rdn over 2f out: hdwy over 1f out: wknd fnl f* **7/1[2]**

5040 **9** *1* **Romantic Bliss (IRE)**[21] 6121 3-8-1 56........(b) JoeyHaynes(3) 12 40
(K R Burke) *prom: rdn over 2f out: sn wknd* **20/1**

-360 **10** *1 3/4* **Dazza**[29] 5861 3-9-2 68........ MartinHarley 11 47
(Gary Moore) *s.i.s: hld up: plld hrd: rdn over 2f out: a in rr* **16/1**

000 **11** *17* **Greek Spirit (IRE)**[16] 6240 4-9-0 63........(p) ShaneKelly 10
(Alan McCabe) *s.i.s: hld up: rdn over 2f out: sn wknd* **28/1**

-060 12 11 **Bond's Gift**[58] 4791 4-8-13 62.......................................[1] BarryMcHugh 2
(Geoffrey Oldroyd) *sn pushed along in rr: rdn 4f out: wknd wl over 2f out* **25/1**

1m 28.67s (-0.13) **Going Correction** +0.05s/f (Slow)
**WFA** 3 from 4yo+ 3lb 12 Ran SP% **115.5**
Speed ratings (Par 100): **102,99,99,98,98 96,94,91,90,88 68,56**
CSF £107.95 CT £1634.77 TOTE £15.40: £4.40, £1.60, £3.90; EX 117.10 Trifecta £1184.80.

**Owner** Dallas Racing **Bred** Mr & Mrs A E Pakenham **Trained** Danethorpe, Notts

**FOCUS**
The pace was very not strong and the first two were always in first and second in this ordinary handicap.

## 6717 BET TOTEQUADPOT MEDIAN AUCTION MAIDEN STKS (TAPETA) 7f 32y
6:50 (6:51) (Class 6) 3-5-Y-O £2,264 (£673; £336; £168) Stalls High

Form RPR

04 1 **Resonated (USA)**[22] 6073 3-9-5 0.............................. DaleSwift 2 69
(Brian Ellison) *led 6f out: rdn over 2f out: styd on gamely u.p* **25/1**

3 2 ¾ **Mr Frankie**[22] 6073 3-9-2 0.............................. DeclanBates(3) 6 67
(Ed de Giles) *s.i.s: sn pushed along in rr: hdwy 5f out: chsd wnr 2f out: sn rdn and ev ch: kpt on* **13/8**[1]

0344 3 2 **Kubeba (IRE)**[8] 6484 3-9-5 70.............................. LukeMorris 8 62
(Paul Cole) *a.p: chsd wnr 5f out tl rdn 2f out: styd on same pce ins fnl f* **2/1**[2]

6055 4 ¾ **Borough Belle**[10] 6421 3-8-11 49.............................. AmyScott(3) 4 55
(Henry Candy) *mid-div: hdwy over 2f out: rdn over 1f out: styd on* **25/1**

3030 5 1¾ **Jessy Mae**[21] 6088 3-8-9 50.............................. TimClark(5) 1 50
(Derek Haydn Jones) *led 1f: chsd ldrs: rdn over 2f out: no ex fnl f* **25/1**

563 6 3¼ **Swilken**[10] 6437 3-9-5 67..............................(e) TedDurcan 7 47
(Mark H Tompkins) *hld up: effrt on outer and hung rt over 2f out: rdn and wknd over 1f out* **11/4**[3]

40F 7 3¼ **Dreaming Brave**[114] 2883 3-9-5 0.............................. RobertHavlin 3 38
(Amanda Perrett) *prom: rdn and hung rt over 2f out: sn wknd* **20/1**

-600 8 4 **My Stroppy Poppy**[10] 6421 5-9-3 45.............................. RaulDaSilva 5 24
(Alan Phillips) *hld up: rdn over 2f out: sn wknd* **66/1**

1m 29.78s (0.98) **Going Correction** +0.05s/f (Slow)
**WFA** 3 from 5yo 3lb 8 Ran SP% **115.9**
Speed ratings (Par 101): **96,95,92,92,90 86,82,78**
CSF £64.57 TOTE £32.40: £5.40, £1.20, £1.10; EX 73.60 Trifecta £327.00.

**Owner** The Acorn Partnership & Brian Ellison **Bred** Sienna Farms LLC **Trained** Norton, N Yorks

**FOCUS**
There was a surprise result in this maiden.

## 6718 BET TOTEEXACTA MAIDEN STKS (TAPETA) (DIV I) 7f 32y
7:20 (7:21) (Class 5) 2-Y-O £2,587 (£770; £384; £192) Stalls High

Form RPR

52 1 **Tadqeeq**[20] 6147 2-9-5 0.............................. DaneO'Neill 8 74
(William Haggas) *chsd ldr tl led over 1f out: sn rdn and hung lft: styd on* **9/4**[2]

2 ½ **Champagne Bob** 2-9-5 0.............................. RichardKingscote 4 73+
(Tom Dascombe) *trckd ldrs: shkn up over 2f out: chsd wnr fnl f: sn rdn and ev ch: unable qck nr fin* **14/1**

5233 3 2¼ **Ventriloquist**[21] 6101 2-9-5 85.............................. PaulMulrennan 5 67
(Charlie Appleby) *led: rdn and hdd over 1f out: no ex ins fnl f* **1/1**[1]

6 4 3 **Capsize**[21] 6103 2-9-5 0.............................. JamesDoyle 7 60
(Sir Michael Stoute) *sn pushed along and prom: rdn over 2f out: hung lft over 1f out: styd on same pce* **7/2**[3]

0 5 9 **Foxy Boris (FR)**[42] 5377 2-9-5 0..............................(t) JohnFahy 9 37
(Paul Cole) *prom: rdn over 2f out: wknd over 1f out* **40/1**

6 7 **Aruan** 2-9-0 0.............................. LiamKeniry 10 15
(Derek Haydn Jones) *s.i.s: sn pushed along in rr: bhd fr 1/2-way* **50/1**

7 6 **Naval Action** 2-9-5 0.............................. LukeMorris 2 5
(Sir Mark Prescott Bt) *sn pushed along in rr: bhd fnl 4f* **25/1**

8 ¾ **Princess P** 2-8-11 0.............................. BillyCray(3) 3
(Alan McCabe) *s.i.s: outpcd: bhd fnl 4f* **50/1**

1m 29.89s (1.09) **Going Correction** +0.05s/f (Slow) 8 Ran SP% **119.9**
Speed ratings (Par 95): **95,94,91,88,78 70,63,62**
CSF £31.66 TOTE £3.30: £1.10, £3.60, £1.10; EX 34.20 Trifecta £79.70.

**Owner** Hamdan Al Maktoum **Bred** Mildmay Bloodstock Ltd **Trained** Newmarket, Suffolk

**FOCUS**
There was a tight finish in this fair maiden but the rest of the runners finished strung out. Quite ordinary form.

## 6719 BET TOTEEXACTA MAIDEN STKS (TAPETA) (DIV II) 7f 32y
7:50 (7:50) (Class 5) 2-Y-O £2,587 (£770; £384; £192) Stalls High

Form RPR

56 1 **Hard To Handel**[15] 6271 2-9-5 0.............................. SebSanders 4 76
(Ralph Beckett) *hld up: hdwy over 2f out: rdn to ld ins fnl f: styd on* **6/1**

03 2 nk **Elis Eliz (IRE)**[15] 6271 2-9-0 0.............................. JamesDoyle 5 70
(Michael Wigham) *chsd ldrs: rdn to ld over 1f out: hdd ins fnl f: styd on* **8/1**

06 3 5 **Tamarin**[53] 4980 2-9-0 0.............................. ShaneKelly 2 58
(Sir Michael Stoute) *w ldr tl led 1/2-way: rdn and hdd over 1f out: no ex ins fnl f* **11/2**[3]

2 4 3 **Red Touch (USA)**[121] 2680 2-9-5 0.............................. MartinHarley 9 55
(Alan McCabe) *chsd ldrs: rdn over 1f out: wknd fnl f* **2/1**[2]

523 5 2½ **Cosmic Ray**[14] 6279 2-9-5 75.............................. DavidProbert 7 49
(Andrew Balding) *led: hung rt and hdd 1/2-way: wknd over 1f out* **6/4**[1]

0 6 nk **First Summer**[15] 6270 2-9-5 0.............................. PaulMulrennan 3 48
(Ed McMahon) *hld up: pushed along 1/2-way: n.d* **40/1**

7 nk **Rainbow Pride (IRE)** 2-9-5 0.............................. LukeMorris 1 48+
(Sir Mark Prescott Bt) *s.i.s: sn pushed along in rr: effrt on outer over 2f out: sn wknd* **40/1**

00 8 33 **Xander (IRE)**[24] 5995 2-9-5 0.............................. DavidAllan 6
(Tim Easterby) *prom: rdn 1/2-way: wknd over 2f out* **66/1**

1m 29.52s (0.72) **Going Correction** +0.05s/f (Slow) 8 Ran SP% **120.5**
Speed ratings (Par 95): **97,96,90,87,84 84,83,46**
CSF £54.12 TOTE £9.00: £4.10, £2.30, £2.10; EX 56.70 Trifecta £779.50.

**Owner** Melody Racing **Bred** Melody Bloodstock **Trained** Kimpton, Hants

**FOCUS**
The market leaders were disappointing but the first two pulled clear in this maiden. Improved form from the winner.

## 6720 BET TOTESWINGER H'CAP (TAPETA) 5f 216y
8:20 (8:21) (Class 6) (0-55,56) 3-Y-O+ £2,264 (£673; £336; £168) Stalls Low

Form RPR

0306 1 **Major Muscari (IRE)**[11] 6409 6-9-4 52..............................(p) MartinHarley 5 64
(Shaun Harris) *hld up in tch: shkn up to ld wl ins fnl f: hung lft: r.o* **15/2**[3]

6320 2 1¼ **Reginald Claude**[11] 6409 6-8-13 54.............................. CharlotteJenner(7) 9 62
(Mark Usher) *hld up: hdwy and swtchd lft over 1f out: styd on same pce wl ins fnl f* **16/1**

0545 3 1¾ **First Rebellion**[6] 6561 5-9-0 51..............................(b) JoeyHaynes(3) 8 53
(Tony Carroll) *led: rdn over 1f out: edgd rt and hdd wl ins fnl f: no ex* **12/1**

0000 4 hd **Queen Hermione (IRE)**[31] 5797 6-9-2 50..............................(vt) FrannyNorton 2 51
(Derek Shaw) *s.i.s: sn pushed along in rr: hdwy u.p over 1f out: r.o: nt rch ldrs* **33/1**

6500 5 ¾ **Prigsnov Dancer (IRE)**[15] 6272 9-9-0 55..............................(p) DavidParkes(7) 13 54
(Deborah Sanderson) *chsd ldrs: rdn over 1f out: styd on same pce fnl f* **25/1**

0-61 6 ½ **Indastar**[11] 6409 4-9-8 56 6ex.............................. DaleSwift 7 53
(Michael Herrington) *trckd racd keenly: wnt 2nd wl over 2f out: rdn and ev ch fr over 1f out tl bmpd and no ex wl ins fnl f* **1/1**[1]

6620 7 1 **Baltic Prince (IRE)**[16] 6227 4-9-5 53..............................(b[1]) RaulDaSilva 10 47
(Paul Green) *broke wl: sn lost pl: hdwy over 2f out: sn rdn: styd on same pce* **9/2**[2]

005- 8 4 **Kopenhagen (IRE)**[311] 7956 3-9-1 54..............................(p) DeclanBates(3) 3 35
(Ed de Giles) *mid-div: sn pushed along: nvr trbld ldrs* **18/1**

254 9 ¾ **Proper Charlie**[49] 5136 6-9-3 51..............................(b) StevieDonohoe 1 30
(Lee Carter) *mid-div: sn pushed along: hdwy 2f out: sn rdn: wknd fnl f* **16/1**

36-0 10 6 **Bountiful Forest**[15] 6272 3-9-2 55.............................. AshleyMorgan(3) 12 15
(Kevin Frost) *s.i.s: sn pushed along and a in rr* **50/1**

6- 11 2¾ **Slanderous**[377] 6383 3-9-3 53.............................. LukeMorris 4 4
(Scott Dixon) *chsd ldrs: rdn over 2f out: wknd and eased over 1f out* **20/1**

0000 P **Saga Lout**[6] 6561 4-9-4 52..............................(p) GrahamGibbons 6
(Andrew Hollinshead) *chsd ldr tl wl over 2f out: sn wknd: p.u and dismntd over 1f out* **66/1**

1m 14.63s (0.13) **Going Correction** +0.05s/f (Slow)
**WFA** 3 from 4yo+ 2lb 12 Ran SP% **119.7**
Speed ratings (Par 101): **101,99,97,96,95 95,93,88,87,79 75,**
CSF £113.50 CT £1434.28 TOTE £9.10: £4.20, £5.50, £3.10; EX 140.70 Trifecta £1194.50 Part won..

**Owner** J Morris **Bred** Simon Holt David Thorpe & R J Beggan **Trained** Carburton, Notts

**FOCUS**
The hot favourite was turned over and the first two came from some way back.

## 6721 BET TOTETRIFECTA H'CAP (TAPETA) 1m 5f 194y
8:50 (8:51) (Class 4) (0-80,79) 3-Y-O+ £4,690 (£1,395; £697; £348) Stalls Low

Form RPR

231- 1 **Sunblazer (IRE)**[17] 7510 4-9-12 78..............................(t) DougieCostello 7 86
(Kim Bailey) *hld up: hdwy over 2f out: sn chsng ldr: rdn over 1f out: styd on to ld post* **8/1**[3]

0-12 2 shd **Investissement**[79] 4080 8-9-11 77..............................(p) AmirQuinn 10 84
(Lee Carter) *hld up in tch: led over 2f out: rdn clr over 1f out: hdd post* **11/2**[2]

4343 3 2 **Wall Street Boss (USA)**[29] 5863 4-9-5 71.............................. DaneO'Neill 8 75
(James Fanshawe) *pushed along in rr early: hdwy over 2f out: rdn and hung lft over 1f out: nt run on* **2/1**[1]

2454 4 1¾ **Admirable Duque (IRE)**[15] 6252 8-9-2 68..............................(be) LiamKeniry 4 70
(Dominic Ffrench Davis) *hld up: hdwy over 2f out: rdn over 1f out: styd on* **14/1**

3020 5 6 **Lineman**[21] 6099 4-9-6 72..............................(p) ShaneKelly 9 65
(Andrew Hollinshead) *hld up: nt clr run over 2f out: nvr trbld ldrs* **11/2**[2]

4266 6 ¾ **Opera Buff**[30] 5825 5-9-10 76..............................(p) IrineuGoncalves 6 68
(Jose Santos) *chsd ldrs: rdn over 2f out: wknd over 1f out* **16/1**

0630 7 ¾ **Tappanappa (IRE)**[27] 5924 7-9-6 72.............................. AndrewMullen 3 63
(Michael Appleby) *s.i.s: sn drvn along in rr: hdwy over 8f out: rdn over 4f out: wknd wl over 1f out* **8/1**[3]

1105 8 ¾ **Kingscombe (USA)**[21] 6107 5-9-7 73.............................. RobertHavlin 2 63
(Linda Jewell) *sn led: rdn and hdd over 2f out: wknd over 1f out* **28/1**

30/5 9 14 **Regal Park (IRE)**[48] 5193 7-8-12 69.............................. GeorgeDowning(5) 5 39
(Miss Imogen Pickard) *chsd ldr tl drvn along 3f out: wknd 2f out* **66/1**

213- 10 ½ **Stentorian (IRE)**[535] 1454 6-9-13 79..............................(v) MartinHarley 1 49
(Gary Moore) *prom: nt clr run and lost pl 3f out: nt rcvr* **11/2**[2]

3m 2.7s (-2.10) **Going Correction** +0.05s/f (Slow) 10 Ran SP% **119.2**
Speed ratings (Par 105): **108,107,106,105,102 101,101,101,93,92**
CSF £52.81 CT £123.72 TOTE £11.00: £3.00, £2.50, £2.00; EX 79.40 Trifecta £292.20.

**Owner** Kim Bailey Racing Partnership X **Bred** Michael G Daly **Trained** Andoversford, Gloucs

**FOCUS**
There was an exciting finish in this staying handicap.

## 6722 RYDER CUP IN PLAY AT TOTESPORT.COM H'CAP (TAPETA) 1m 1f 103y
9:20 (9:20) (Class 5) (0-75,75) 3-Y-O £2,587 (£770; £384; £192) Stalls Low

Form RPR

5536 1 **Sbraase**[44] 5320 3-9-5 73.............................. MartinHarley 6 80
(James Tate) *prom: hmpd and lost pl after 1f: hdwy over 1f out: r.o to ld last strides* **6/1**[3]

3240 2 nk **Barye**[23] 6044 3-9-5 73.............................. MartinLane 9 79
(David Simcock) *trckd ldrs: wnt 2nd over 1f out: rdn over 1f out: styd on to ld wl ins fnl f: hdd last strides* **4/1**[2]

3652 3 ½ **Ghosting (IRE)**[8] 6484 3-9-3 71..............................(t) RichardKingscote 12 76+
(Tom Dascombe) *swtchd lft sn after s: hld up: rdn and r.o ins fnl f: nt rch ldrs* **3/1**[1]

3512 4 ½ **Bon Port**[45] 5280 3-8-4 65.............................. CharlieBennett(7) 4 69
(Hughie Morrison) *a.p: rdn over 2f out: edgd lft over 1f out: styd on* **9/1**

1405 5 nse **Rising Breeze (FR)**[30] 5818 3-9-4 75.............................. JoeyHaynes(3) 2 79
(K R Burke) *hld up: r.o ins fnl f: nt rch ldrs* **16/1**

6355 6 nk **Master Dancer**[23] 6044 3-9-1 69..............................(b[1]) TomEaves 7 73
(Philip Hide) *led: clr over 6f out tl rdn over 1f out: hdd and unable qck wl ins fnl f* **9/1**

6025 7 ¾ **Tullia (IRE)**[42] 5394 3-9-7 75..............................(v[1]) LukeMorris 10 77
(William Knight) *hld up: hdwy over 2f out: rdn over 1f out: styd on* **25/1**

8 1¼ **Jackie Ellis (IRE)**[31] 5805 3-8-9 63..............................[1] GrahamGibbons 1 62
(Paul W Flynn, Ire) *chsd ldrs: rdn over 3f out: outpcd over 2f out: styd on u.p fnl f* **14/1**

063 **9** *1 ¾* **Noble Descent**[23] 6033 3-9-1 69 ShaneKelly 11 65
(Sir Michael Stoute) *chsd ldrs: wnt 2nd over 3f out tl rdn over 2f out: wknd fnl f* **6/1**[3]

6034 **10** *3 ½* **Kantara Castle (IRE)**[41] 5420 3-9-0 68 (t) FrannyNorton 3 56
(John Mackie) *chsd ldr 6f: sn rdn: wknd over 1f out* **16/1**

2m 0.83s (0.03) **Going Correction** +0.05s/f (Slow) **10** Ran SP% **115.8**
Speed ratings (Par 101): **101,100,100,99,99 99,98,97,96,93**
CSF £30.03 CT £86.39 TOTE £6.10: £1.90, £1.90, £1.40; EX 30.70 Trifecta £159.00.
**Owner** Saeed Manana **Bred** Miss K Rausing **Trained** Newmarket, Suffolk

**FOCUS**
There was a bunch finish in this handicap, which was run at a good pace.
T/Plt: £191.90 to a £1 stake. Pool: £78,657.90 - 299.11 winning units. T/Qpdt: £26.10 to a £1 stake. Pool: £11,747.82 - 332.16 winning units. CR

6723 - 6734a (Foreign Racing) - See Raceform Interactive

6319
# CHESTER (L-H)
## Saturday, September 27

**OFFICIAL GOING: Good to soft (good in places; 6.8)**
Wind: light 1/2 against Weather: mainly fine

### 6735 GOLDEN SQUARE SHOPPING CENTRE MAIDEN FILLIES' STKS (BOBIS RACE) 7f 2y
**1:55** (1:56) (Class 4) 2-Y-O **£6,469** (£1,925; £962; £481) **Stalls** Low

Form RPR

5 **1** **Muffri'Ha (IRE)**[11] 6435 2-9-0 0 GrahamGibbons 1 84+
(William Haggas) *mde all: t.k.h: drvn clr over 1f out: eased towards fin* **4/1**[2]

**2** *5* **Fragile Earth (IRE)**[48] 5216 2-9-0 0 RonanWhelan 4 66
(John Patrick Shanahan, Ire) *w wnr: kpt on same pce over 1f out* **20/1**

42 **3** *3* **Tropicana Bay**[22] 6093 2-9-0 0 FrederikTylicki 5 58
(Roger Varian) *chsd ldng pair: upsides over 2f out: sn drvn: one pce over 1f out* **1/1**[1]

4600 **4** *½* **Alpha Spirit**[25] 6016 2-8-11 62 CharlesBishop(3) 6 57
(Mick Channon) *mid-div: t.k.h: kpt on over 1f out: nvr nrr* **25/1**

06 **5** *½* **Bling Ring (USA)**[36] 5643 2-9-0 0 SeanLevey 9 56
(Charles Hills) *dwlt: swtchd lft after s: hld up in rr: hdwy over 1f out: kpt on: nvr a factor* **20/1**

**6** *¾* **Cape Spirit (IRE)** 2-9-0 0 DavidProbert 8 54+
(Andrew Balding) *sn drvn along in rr: sme hdwy over 1f out: nvr a factor* **14/1**

4 **7** *hd* **Triple Dip (IRE)**[17] 6224 2-9-0 0 FrannyNorton 7 53
(Mark Johnston) *mid-div: drvn over 2f out: nvr a threat* **12/1**

42 **8** *nk* **Midnite Ride (IRE)**[17] 6224 2-9-0 0 DavidNolan 3 52
(Richard Fahey) *chsd ldrs: drvn over 2f out: fdd over 1f out* **11/2**[3]

**9** *3* **Minnie (IRE)** 2-9-0 0 StevieDonohoe 2 45
(Tim Pitt) *dwlt: sn chsng ldrs: wknd over 1f out* **33/1**

1m 26.28s (-0.22) **Going Correction** 0.0s/f (Good) **9** Ran SP% **116.1**
Speed ratings (Par 94): **101,95,91,91,90 89,89,89,85**
CSF £81.65 TOTE £5.10: £1.90, £6.90, £1.02; EX 116.50 Trifecta £407.90.
**Owner** Sheikh Juma Dalmook Al Maktoum **Bred** Lodge Park Stud **Trained** Newmarket, Suffolk

**FOCUS**
Track at innermost configuration and distances as advertised. There's a danger the winner could be flattered but he's in very good hands.

### 6736 ADVANCED INSULATION H'CAP 6f 18y
**2:30** (2:32) (Class 4) (0-80,80) 3-Y-O+ **£6,469** (£1,925; £962; £481) **Stalls** Low

Form RPR

400 **1** **Tagula Night (IRE)**[16] 6260 8-9-7 80 (vt) FrannyNorton 2 89
(Dean Ivory) *chsd ldrs: 2nd over 1f out: styd on to ld clsng stages* **8/1**[3]

406 **2** *½* **Pandar**[22] 6089 5-9-6 79 FrederikTylicki 10 86
(Milton Bradley) *led: hdd and no ex clsng stages* **25/1**

0341 **3** *2 ¼* **Al Manaal**[16] 6269 4-9-2 78 CharlesBishop(3) 9 78
(Mick Channon) *chsd ldrs: kpt on same pce to take 3rd 1f out* **16/1**

-043 **4** *2* **Ambitious Boy**[14] 6313 5-9-2 75 LiamJones 1 69+
(Andrew Hollinshead) *rr-div: hdwy on inner 2f out: nt clr run: kpt on fnl f: tk 4th nr fin* **5/1**[1]

010- **5** *hd* **Bethany Bay (IRE)**[48] 5220 4-9-4 77 RonanWhelan 3 70
(John Patrick Shanahan, Ire) *mid-div: hdwy over 2f out: one pce over 1f out* **6/1**[2]

3362 **6** *½* **Withernsea (IRE)**[43] 5381 3-9-0 80 JackGarritty(5) 5 72
(Richard Fahey) *in tch: effrt over 2f out: kpt on one pce over 1f out* **5/1**[1]

6130 **7** *2* **Meandmyshadow**[7] 6558 6-9-0 73 JamesSullivan 11 58
(Alan Brown) *chsd ldrs: one pce fnl 2f* **40/1**

1244 **8** *½* **Verus Delicia (IRE)**[27] 5958 5-8-11 75 EoinWalsh(5) 6 59
(Daniel Mark Loughnane) *mid-div: effrt and nt clr run over 1f out: hung lft and kpt on* **12/1**

26 **9** *hd* **Baby Strange**[22] 6094 10-9-6 79 TomEaves 15 62
(Derek Shaw) *s.s: in rr: sme hdwy over 1f out: nvr a factor* **25/1**

3253 **10** *½* **Surety (IRE)**[9] 6484 3-8-13 74 SeanLevey 4 55
(Clive Brittain) *chsd ldrs: wknd appr fnl f* **8/1**[3]

1654 **11** *2 ¼* **Gravitational (IRE)**[21] 6145 4-9-4 80 AshleyMorgan(3) 13 54
(Chris Wall) *dwlt: in rr: sme hdwy on outer over 1f out: nvr on terms* **10/1**

0030 **12** *shd* **Hadaj**[11] 6430 5-8-13 77 (b) KevinStott(5) 8 51
(Ruth Carr) *chsd ldrs: wknd fnl 2f* **16/1**

0-00 **13** *3 ½* **Chester Aristocrat**[8] 6511 5-9-4 77 JFEgan 14 40
(Eric Alston) *s.i.s: in rr: sme hdwy over 3f out: lost pl 2f out* **33/1**

3300 **14** *1* **Pushkin Museum (IRE)**[14] 6324 3-9-1 76 (v[1]) DavidNolan 7 35
(Richard Fahey) *chsd ldrs: lost pl wl over 1f out* **33/1**

3340 **15** *1 ½* **Dutch Breeze**[35] 5696 3-9-4 79 (p) GrahamGibbons 12 34
(Tim Easterby) *restless in stalls: s.v.s: a detached in last* **20/1**

1m 13.08s (-0.72) **Going Correction** 0.0s/f (Good)
**WFA** 3 from 4yo+ 2lb **15** Ran SP% **119.2**
Speed ratings (Par 105): **104,103,100,97,97 96,94,93,93,92 89,89,84,83,81**
CSF £203.30 CT £3164.01 TOTE £11.50: £4.70, £18.40, £6.90; EX 257.90 Trifecta £1963.30 Part won..
**Owner** Hufford & Papworth **Bred** Carpet Lady Partnership **Trained** Radlett, Herts

**FOCUS**
An inside draw is often key in sprint races around here and that proved the case again. The winner's best form since 2011.

### 6737 GOLDEN SQUARE SHOPPING CENTRE H'CAP (BOBIS RACE) 1m 2f 75y
**3:05** (3:06) (Class 2) (0-105,102) 3-Y-O **£31,125** (£9,320; £4,660; £2,330; £1,165; £585) **Stalls** High

Form RPR

0122 **1** **Empress Ali (IRE)**[55] 4941 3-8-1 82 JamesSullivan 5 91
(Tom Tate) *led 1f: chsd ldrs: styd on over 1f out: led clsng stages* **20/1**

3020 **2** *½* **Master Of Finance (IRE)**[32] 5792 3-8-5 86 JFEgan 6 94
(Mark Johnston) *led after 1f: drvn 3f out: hdd and no ex clsng stages* **12/1**

2053 **3** *½* **Ventura Quest (USA)**[7] 6548 3-8-1 82 PatrickMathers 1 89
(Richard Fahey) *mid-div: hdwy over 2f out: chsng ldrs over 1f out: styd on same pce last 50yds* **7/1**[3]

3211 **4** *½* **Potent Embrace (USA)**[9] 6490 3-8-3 84 FrannyNorton 2 90
(Mark Johnston) *trckd ldrs: t.k.h: effrt over 2f out: chsng ldrs over 1f out: styd on same pce last 75yds* **4/1**[2]

2024 **5** *hd* **Lesha (IRE)**[7] 6535 3-8-9 90 TomEaves 11 96
(Kevin Ryan) *hld up in rr: hdwy on ins over 2f out: styng on whn edgd lft and n.m.r last 50yds* **33/1**

3211 **6** *½* **Fire Fighting (IRE)**[9] 6479 3-9-7 102 (b) KierenFallon 14 107+
(Mark Johnston) *s.s: swtchd lft after s: in rr: hdwy on outside over 1f out: fin wl* **9/1**

122 **7** *1* **Potentate (IRE)**[15] 6284 3-8-1 82 KieranO'Neill 9 85
(Richard Hannon) *trckd ldr after 1f: t.k.h: wknd last 50yds* **16/1**

5402 **8** *nk* **Green Light**[29] 5884 3-8-0 81 oh1 HayleyTurner 15 87+
(Ralph Beckett) *s.s: hdwy on inner 3f out: keeping on whn nt clr run and snatched up clsng stages* **25/1**

1201 **9** *1 ¼* **Hostile Fire (IRE)**[11] 6431 3-7-9 81 oh2 (p) NoelGarbutt(5) 8 81
(Ed de Giles) *s.i.s: sn mid-div: t.k.h: chsng ldrs 5f out: wknd over 1f out* **28/1**

0165 **10** *¾* **Roskilly (IRE)**[15] 6284 3-8-0 81 (v[1]) DavidProbert 12 80
(Andrew Balding) *mid-div: hdwy over 3f out: one pce over 1f out* **25/1**

4303 **11** *¾* **Examiner (IRE)**[34] 5720 3-8-7 88 LiamJones 3 85
(William Haggas) *hld up in rr: hdwy on outer 3f out: drvn and no imp over 1f out* **11/4**[1]

1601 **12** *1 ¾* **Latenightrequest**[23] 6061 3-8-4 90 JackGarritty(5) 10 84
(Richard Fahey) *chsd ldrs: wknd over 1f out* **14/1**

1660 **13** *16* **Maid Of The Glens (IRE)**[14] 6350 3-9-2 97 RonanWhelan 4 60
(John Patrick Shanahan, Ire) *chsd ldrs: drvn over 4f out: lost pl over 2f out: sn bhd and eased* **20/1**

5122 **14** *2* **Zugzwang (IRE)**[14] 6323 3-8-3 87 ow2 DeclanBates(3) 7 47
(Ed de Giles) *chsd ldrs: lost pl over 2f out: bhd and eased over 1f out* **10/1**

2100 **15** *6* **Our Gabrial (IRE)**[21] 6127 3-8-10 91 SeanLevey 13 39
(Richard Fahey) *mid-div: drvn over 5f out: lost pl over 2f out: sn bhd and eased* **20/1**

2m 9.11s (-2.09) **Going Correction** 0.0s/f (Good) **15** Ran SP% **126.9**
Speed ratings (Par 107): **108,107,107,106,106 106,105,105,104,103 103,101,88,87,82**
CSF £234.18 CT £1877.54 TOTE £24.10: £5.60, £5.00, £2.30; EX 273.10 Trifecta £2005.50 Part won..
**Owner** T T Racing **Bred** Denis McDonnell **Trained** Tadcaster, N Yorks

**FOCUS**
Another strongly contested handicap and another close finish. Ordinary if sound form.

### 6738 SPORTINGBET MAIDEN STKS 1m 2f 75y
**3:40** (3:40) (Class 4) 3-Y-O+ **£6,469** (£1,925; £962; £481) **Stalls** High

Form RPR

3302 **1** **The Character (IRE)**[9] 6491 3-9-5 79 StephenCraine 5 84
(Tom Dascombe) *drvn early: sn chsng ldr: led 2f out: all out* **15/8**[1]

03 **2** *nse* **Bikini Island (USA)**[15] 6282 3-9-0 0 DavidProbert 1 79
(Andrew Balding) *trckd ldrs: cl 2nd over 1f out: upsides fnl 50yds: jst denied* **3/1**[2]

0332 **3** *¾* **Dolce N Karama (IRE)**[30] 5851 3-9-5 84 RonanWhelan 8 82
(John Patrick Shanahan, Ire) *rr-div: hdwy over 4f out: sn chsng ldrs: handy 3rd over 1f out: kpt on towards fin* **7/2**[3]

0504 **4** *10* **Miguela McGuire**[5] 6599 3-9-0 44 PatrickMathers 2 58?
(Eric Alston) *led: hdd 2f out: wknd fnl f* **50/1**

0 **5** *6* **Blue Valentino**[14] 6344 5-9-11 0 GrahamGibbons 7 52
(Andrew Hollinshead) *dwlt: in rr: drvn over 5f out: outpcd over 3f out: sn bhd* **50/1**

2 **6** *1* **Chauvelin**[145] 2031 3-9-5 0 SeanLevey 3 50
(Roger Charlton) *sn chsng ldrs: reminders over 5f out: lost pl over 2f out* **11/2**

4-0 **7** *2 ¼* **Trendsetter (IRE)**[22] 6092 3-9-5 0 FrannyNorton 9 46
(John Butler) *in rr: sme hdwy 4f out: nvr on terms: wknd over 1f out* **14/1**

05 **8** *14* **Gabrial's Lady (IRE)**[15] 6282 3-9-0 0 DavidNolan 6 14
(Richard Fahey) *rr-div: t.k.h: drvn over 4f out: lost pl 3f out: sn bhd* **25/1**

**9** *11* **I'Mwaitingforyou**[76] 5-9-1 0 DanielMuscutt(5) 4
(Peter Bowen) *dwlt: sn chsng ldrs: drvn 7f out: lost pl over 3f out: sn wl bhd* **33/1**

2m 10.45s (-0.75) **Going Correction** 0.0s/f (Good)
**WFA** 3 from 5yo 6lb **9** Ran SP% **114.8**
Speed ratings (Par 105): **103,102,102,94,89 88,86,75,66**
CSF £7.32 TOTE £3.50: £1.80, £1.20, £1.30; EX 10.60 Trifecta £30.50.
**Owner** Aykroyd And Sons Ltd **Bred** Tally-Ho Stud **Trained** Malpas, Cheshire
■ Stewards' Enquiry : Stephen Craine four-day ban: used whip above permitted level (Oct 11-14)

**FOCUS**
Sound form, the winner rated to his C&D run.

### 6739 CONTROLLED SOLUTIONS GROUP NURSERY H'CAP (BOBIS RACE) 5f 110y
**4:15** (4:17) (Class 2) 2-Y-O **£12,938** (£3,850; £1,924; £962) **Stalls** Low

Form RPR

232 **1** **Kinematic**[24] 6038 2-8-7 78 DavidProbert 2 83
(Andrew Balding) *mde all: clr over 1f out: pushed out* **9/4**[1]

414 **2** *1 ¼* **Hatchet Harry (IRE)**[50] 5134 2-8-5 76 JFEgan 4 77
(David Evans) *s.i.s: effrt over 2f out: styd on over 1f out: tk 2nd last 50yds* **15/2**

3104 **3** *hd* **Showstoppa**[14] 6322 2-8-4 75 FrannyNorton 10 77
(Mark Johnston) *mid-div: hdwy and nt clr run 2f out: styd on to take 3rd clsng stages* **16/1**

1300 **4** 1 1/4 **She's A Worldie (IRE)**[15] 6286 2-9-6 91 .......... DavidNolan 5 87
(Bryan Smart) *chsd ldrs: kpt on same pce fnl f* **5/1**[3]
3613 **5** 1 3/4 **Emef Rock (IRE)**[6] 6574 2-8-0 71 oh1 .......... PatrickMathers 7 61
(Mick Channon) *in rr: hdwy on outer over 2f out: one pce fnl f* **25/1**
210 **6** *nk* **Don Sigfredo (IRE)**[21] 6135 2-9-0 85 ..........(p) GrahamGibbons 3 74
(Tom Dascombe) *dwlt: in rr: hdwy and n.m.r over 1f out: styd on ins fnl f* **4/1**[2]
2145 **7** 2 1/2 **Paddy Again (IRE)**[131] 2403 2-8-3 79 .......... RyanWhile(5) 8 60
(Bill Turner) *chsd ldrs: wknd fnl 100yds* **25/1**
3552 **8** 3 3/4 **Steve Prescott**[14] 6322 2-8-10 86 ..........(b) JackGarritty(5) 6 54
(Richard Fahey) *dwlt: outpcd and a in rr* **6/1**
2133 **9** *11* **Fuwairt (IRE)**[17] 6230 2-9-7 92 .......... SeanLevey 9 84+
(Richard Hannon) *chsd ldrs: sddle slipped and rdr tk feet out of irons over 4f out: lost weight cloth over 2f out: heavily eased fnl f: virtually p.u* **11/1**

1m 6.39s (0.19) **Going Correction** 0.0s/f (Good) 2y crse rec **9** Ran SP% **115.4**
Speed ratings (Par 101): **98,96,96,94,92 91,88,83,**
CSF £19.88 CT £212.31 TOTE £3.00: £3.10, £2.20, £5.90; EX 15.90 Trifecta £88.60.
**Owner** The Queen **Bred** The Queen **Trained** Kingsclere, Hants

**FOCUS**
This was furiously run.

## 6740 LDF H'CAP 7f 2y
**4:50** (4:50) (Class 3) (0-95,95) 3-Y-O+ **£16,172** (£4,812; £2,405; £1,202) **Stalls** Low

Form RPR
2241 **1** **Lincoln (IRE)**[17] 6234 3-8-11 91 .......... CharlesBishop(3) 5 101
(Mick Channon) *mde all: clr over 2f out: drvn out* **6/1**[3]
6440 **2** 1 1/2 **Newstead Abbey**[7] 6531 4-9-4 92 .......... GrahamGibbons 2 99
(David Barron) *chsd ldrs: 2nd over 2f out: kpt on: no real imp* **11/2**[2]
3312 **3** *1* **Athletic**[7] 6535 5-8-8 87 ..........(v) JennyPowell(5) 12 91+
(Andrew Reid) *swtchd lft after s: hld up in rr: hdwy 2f out: styd on wl to take 3rd last 50yds* **7/1**
100 **4** 1 3/4 **Nakuti (IRE)**[17] 6234 3-8-5 87 .......... NoelGarbutt(5) 8 86
(Sylvester Kirk) *mid-div: effrt over 2f out: styd on fnl f: tk 4th post* **16/1**
4001 **5** *nk* **Marcret (ITY)**[14] 6320 7-9-4 92 .......... JamesSullivan 1 91
(Ruth Carr) *in tch: effrt over 2f out: styd on fnl f: tk 5th post* **9/2**[1]
4004 **6** *hd* **Dubai Dynamo**[2] 6688 9-8-12 86 .......... TomEaves 14 85
(Ruth Carr) *hld up in rr: hdwy on ins over 1f out: keeping on at fin* **25/1**
0301 **7** 2 1/4 **Regal Parade**[43] 5392 10-9-0 88 ..........(t) FrederikTylicki 4 81
(Milton Bradley) *chsd ldrs: wknd last 100yds* **20/1**
0220 **8** *2* **Gatepost (IRE)**[8] 6511 5-8-8 82 .......... FrannyNorton 11 70
(Richard Fahey) *in rr: sme hdwy over 1f out: nvr a factor* **16/1**
-502 **9** 3/4 **Mehdi (IRE)**[7] 6531 5-8-11 90 ..........(t) JackGarritty(5) 9 76
(Richard Fahey) *mid-div: effrt on outside over 1f out: nvr a factor* **8/1**
0265 **10** *4* **Secret Look**[22] 6097 4-9-0 88 .......... SeanLevey 3 63
(Ed McMahon) *chsd ldrs: wknd over 1f out* **10/1**
2000 **11** *1* **Royal Rascal**[37] 5612 4-9-3 91 ..........(tp) DavidNolan 13 64
(Tim Easterby) *swtchd lft after s: in rr and sn drvn along: nvr on terms* **33/1**
0142 **12** *6* **Maverik**[14] 6320 6-8-13 87 .......... DavidProbert 7 44
(William Knight) *mid-div: drvn 3f out: sn lost pl: bhd ewhn eased fnl f* **8/1**
4046 **13** *8* **Desert Law (IRE)**[21] 6159 6-9-7 95 .......... KierenFallon 6 31
(Saeed bin Suroor) *trckd wnr: t.k.h: wknd over 1f out: eased whn bhd clsng stages* **20/1**

1m 24.59s (-1.91) **Going Correction** 0.0s/f (Good)
**WFA** 3 from 4yo+ 3lb **13** Ran SP% **119.7**
Speed ratings (Par 107): **110,108,107,105,104 104,102,99,98,94 93,86,77**
CSF £36.96 CT £248.14 TOTE £6.30: £2.40, £3.20, £3.20; EX 47.80 Trifecta £404.40.
**Owner** Billy Parish **Bred** Tipper House Stud **Trained** West Ilsley, Berks

**FOCUS**
A decent handicap in which few were involved. Another personal best from the winner.

## 6741 INNOSPEC H'CAP (BOBIS RACE) 1m 5f 89y
**5:25** (5:26) (Class 4) (0-85,83) 3-Y-O **£6,469** (£1,925; £962; £481) **Stalls** Low

Form RPR
3211 **1** **Chesil Beach**[14] 6325 3-8-13 75 .......... DavidProbert 8 87
(Andrew Balding) *stdd s: hld up in rr: stdy hdwy over 3f out: nt clr run 2f out: led last 150yds: pushed out* **9/4**[2]
3424 **2** 2 3/4 **Rite To Reign**[92] 3673 3-9-1 77 .......... SeanLevey 3 84
(Philip McBride) *trckd ldng pair: chal 2f out: led briefly 1f out: kpt on same pce* **2/1**[1]
3140 **3** 1 3/4 **Classical Art (IRE)**[29] 5877 3-8-13 75 ..........(b[1]) FrederikTylicki 2 79
(Roger Varian) *led 3f: trckd ldr: led and edgd lft over 2f out: hdd 1f out: kpt on one pce* **8/1**
2130 **4** 3 1/4 **Artistic Muse (IRE)**[21] 6137 3-9-1 77 .......... KierenFallon 6 77
(Charles Hills) *hld up in rr: hdwy over 3f out: outpcd over 2f out* **10/1**
0 **5** 2 3/4 **Drummore Road (IRE)**[82] 4037 3-8-5 67 .......... FrannyNorton 5 62+
(John Patrick Shanahan, Ire) *chsd ldrs: drvn over 4f out: btn whn hmpd and hit rail 2f out* **11/2**[3]
2410 **6** 2 1/4 **Fiery Sunset**[35] 5691 3-9-2 83 .......... DanielMuscutt(5) 7 75
(Michael Bell) *trckd ldr: led after 3f: set stdy pce: increased gallop over 4f out: hdd over 2f out: hung rt and sn wknd* **8/1**

2m 53.08s (0.38) **Going Correction** 0.0s/f (Good) **6** Ran SP% **110.8**
Speed ratings (Par 103): **98,96,95,93,91 90**
CSF £6.96 CT £25.86 TOTE £2.80: £1.40, £1.10; EX 4.30 Trifecta £22.00.
**Owner** Kingsclere Racing Club **Bred** Kingsclere Stud **Trained** Kingsclere, Hants

**FOCUS**
The final race of Chester's season. The winner continued her progress in good style.
T/Plt: £171.60 to a £1 stake. Pool: £65,502.46 - 278.54 winning tickets T/Qpdt: £32.40 to £1 stake. Pool: £4,024.19 - 91.86 winning tickets WG

# 6699 HAYDOCK (L-H)
### Saturday, September 27

**OFFICIAL GOING: Good (good to soft in places; 8.4)**
Wind: Virtually nil Weather: Cloudy

## 6742 BRITISH STALLION STUDS EBF MAIDEN FILLIES' STKS (BOBIS RACE) 1m
**2:25** (2:25) (Class 5) 2-Y-O **£2,911** (£866; £432; £216) **Stalls** Low

Form RPR
**1** **Loaves And Fishes** 2-9-0 0 .......... AdamKirby 4 81+
(Clive Cox) *trckd ldrs: smooth hdwy 3f out: swtchd rt jst over 2f out: sn cl up on bit: led ins fnl f: sn pushed clr: readily* **9/4**[1]
0 **2** 2 3/4 **Sampera (IRE)**[23] 6066 2-9-0 0 .......... PaulMulrennan 2 71
(Michael Bell) *led: rdn 2f out: drvn and jnd over 1f out: hdd jst ins fnl f: kpt on: no ch w wnr* **10/1**
0 **3** 1 3/4 **Art Charter (FR)**[23] 6056 2-9-0 0 ..........(v[1]) DanielTudhope 5 67
(K R Burke) *prom: rdn along over 2f: kpt on same pce* **20/1**
4 **4** *4* **Galileano (IRE)**[31] 5827 2-9-0 0 .......... LukeMorris 6 58
(Marco Botti) *towards rr: pushed along wl over 2f out: rdn wl over 1f out: kpt on fnl f: nrst fin* **3/1**[2]
**5** 1/2 **Candella** 2-8-11 0 .......... RossAtkinson(3) 8 57+
(Roger Varian) *a towards rr* **7/1**
3 **6** *7* **Donna Graciosa (GER)**[9] 6497 2-9-0 0 .......... JoeFanning 9 41
(Mark Johnston) *trckd ldng pair: cl up 1/2-way: pushed along wl over 2f out: sn rdn and wknd wl over 1f out* **7/2**[3]
**7** 4 1/2 **Kallisima** 2-9-0 0 .......... DaleSwift 1 30
(Ed McMahon) *dwlt: green and a in rr* **14/1**
0405 **8** *nk* **Mistral**[34] 5712 2-9-0 55 .......... RussKennemore 7 29
(Steph Hollinshead) *in tch: rdn along on outer over 2f out: sn wknd* **25/1**

1m 45.18s (1.48) **Going Correction** +0.05s/f (Good) **8** Ran SP% **114.9**
Speed ratings (Par 92): **94,91,89,85,85 78,73,73**
CSF £26.11 TOTE £3.70: £1.60, £2.00, £4.00; EX 26.80 Trifecta £335.20.
**Owner** D J Burke **Bred** Whitley Stud **Trained** Lambourn, Berks

**FOCUS**
All races run on Stands side home straight. Races 1, 2 5 & 7 increased by 57yds and race 6 by 107yds. A modest maiden overall, but an impressive winner. The level is fluid.

## 6743 BRITISH STALLION STUDS EBF MAIDEN STKS (C&G) 1m
**3:00** (3:00) (Class 5) 2-Y-O **£2,911** (£866; £432; £216) **Stalls** Low

Form RPR
3 **1** **Mustard**[22] 6102 2-9-0 0 .......... ShaneKelly 6 82+
(Sir Michael Stoute) *cl up: effrt over 2f out: rdn to chse ldr wl over 1f out: swtchd rt jst ins fnl f: styd on wl u.p to ld last 20yds* **3/1**[2]
2 **2** 3/4 **Emirates Skywards (IRE)**[13] 6362 2-9-0 0 .......... AdamKirby 4 81+
(Charlie Appleby) *hld up in rr: gd hdwy 3f out: led 2f out: rdn clr over 1f out: edgd lft ent fnl f: sn shkn up: drvn wl ins fnl f: hdd and no ex last 20yds* **5/2**[1]
32 **3** *7* **The Lampo Genie**[34] 5718 2-9-0 0 .......... DanielTudhope 3 64
(K R Burke) *hld up in rr: hdwy 3f out: n.m.r and swtchd rt wl over 1f out: sn rdn and kpt on fnl f* **3/1**[2]
0 **4** *nk* **Town Council (IRE)**[29] 5881 2-9-0 0 .......... TonyHamilton 8 63+
(Richard Fahey) *in tch on outer: hdwy over 3f out: chsd ldrs over 2f out: sn rdn and kpt on same pce* **25/1**
6 **5** 1/2 **Convicted (FR)**[40] 5494 2-9-0 0 .......... RobertWinston 7 62
(Ian Williams) *dwlt and bhd: hdwy on outer 3f out: rdn to chse ldng pair wl over 1f out: sn edgd lft and one pce* **50/1**
40 **6** *nk* **Azzir (IRE)**[21] 6125 2-9-0 0 .......... BenCurtis 1 61
(Timothy Jarvis) *chsd ldrs on inner: rdn along 3f out: drvn 2f out: grad wknd* **66/1**
**7** *shd* **Deebaj (IRE)** 2-9-0 0 .......... DaneO'Neill 9 61
(Mark Johnston) *slt ld: pushed along 3f out: rdn and hdd 2f out: sn drvn and one pce* **16/1**
50 **8** 2 3/4 **Le Torrent**[36] 5625 2-9-0 0 .......... HarryBentley 10 55
(Henry Candy) *chsd ldng pair on outer: pushed along over 3f out: rdn over 2f out: grad wknd* **50/1**
42 **9** 2 1/2 **Marmalad (IRE)**[115] 2895 2-9-0 0 .......... RichardKingscote 2 49
(Tom Dascombe) *chsd ldrs: rdn along 3f out: wknd over 2f out* **6/1**[3]
**10** *8* **Newspeak (IRE)** 2-9-0 0 .......... PaulMulrennan 5 30
(Charlie Appleby) *chsd ldrs: rdn along 3f out: sn wknd* **12/1**

1m 44.68s (0.98) **Going Correction** +0.05s/f (Good) **10** Ran SP% **115.7**
Speed ratings (Par 95): **97,96,89,88,88 88,88,85,82,74**
CSF £10.60 TOTE £3.80: £2.20, £1.20, £1.60; EX 14.80 Trifecta £30.70.
**Owner** The Queen **Bred** The Queen **Trained** Newmarket, Suffolk

**FOCUS**
The time was 0.4sec quicker than the earlier fillies' maiden, and the first two finished clear.

## 6744 WATCH RACING UK ANYWHERE H'CAP 6f
**3:35** (3:36) (Class 3) (0-90,90) 3-Y-O+ **£8,086** (£2,406; £1,202; £601) **Stalls** Centre

Form RPR
0003 **1** **Barracuda Boy (IRE)**[10] 6467 4-9-6 89 .......... RichardKingscote 10 99
(Tom Dascombe) *cl up: led 1/2-way: rdn over 1f out: drvn and kpt on wl fnl f* **10/1**
1403 **2** 3/4 **My Name Is Rio (IRE)**[8] 6511 4-9-2 85 .......... PaulMulrennan 11 93
(Michael Dods) *trckd ldrs: hdwy 1/2-way: sn chsng wnr: chal over 1f out: rdn and ev ch ent fnl f tl drvn and no ex last 75yds* **5/1**[1]
5635 **3** 3/4 **Jamaican Bolt (IRE)**[28] 5925 6-9-5 88 .......... BarryMcHugh 6 93
(Geoffrey Oldroyd) *hld up in rr: hdwy over 2f out: rdn over 1f out: styd on fnl f: nrst fin* **12/1**
4005 **4** 3 1/4 **The Hooded Claw (IRE)**[20] 6170 3-8-13 84 .......... LukeMorris 5 79
(Tim Easterby) *towards rr: hdwy 1/2-way: rdn wl over 1f out: kpt on fnl f: nrst fin* **20/1**
4040 **5** 1 1/2 **Muir Lodge**[21] 6159 3-9-3 88 .......... PatCosgrave 2 78
(George Baker) *bmpd s and bhd: gd hdwy on wd outside 2f out: sn rdn and kpt on fnl f: nrst fin* **28/1**
203 **6** *nk* **Run With Pride (IRE)**[16] 6260 4-9-2 85 .......... DaleSwift 3 74
(Derek Shaw) *wnt lft s: sn trcking ldrs: hdwy over 2f out: rdn wl over 1f out: one pce appr fnl f* **10/1**
0511 **7** 1/2 **Expose**[8] 6511 6-8-13 87 .......... JordanNason(5) 12 74
(Shaun Harris) *dwlt: sn in tch: effrt 2f out: sn rdn and no imp appr fnl f* **7/1**[3]
3110 **8** 2 1/2 **Cruise Tothelimit (IRE)**[8] 6511 6-8-13 87 .......... GeorgeDowning(5) 1 66
(Ian Williams) *slt ld: hdd 1/2-way: cl up: rdn over 2f out: grad wknd* **18/1**
5415 **9** 1 1/4 **Bop It**[21] 6150 5-9-0 83 .......... DanielTudhope 15 58
(David O'Meara) *hld up in rr: sme hdwy over 2f out: sn rdn and n.d* **6/1**[2]
2143 **10** 3/4 **Captain Bob (IRE)**[44] 5348 3-9-4 89 .......... GeorgeBaker 4 62
(Charles Hills) *a towards rr* **8/1**
0031 **11** 1 3/4 **Apricot Sky**[22] 6096 4-9-4 87 .......... DaneO'Neill 9 54
(Henry Candy) *chsd ldrs: rdn along over 2f out: drvn wl over 1f out: sn wknd* **10/1**
0000 **12** 3/4 **Whozthecat (IRE)**[15] 6290 7-9-2 88 ..........(v) NeilFarley(3) 8 53
(Declan Carroll) *prom: rdn along 1/2-way: sn wknd* **33/1**
6500 **13** *5* **El Viento (FR)**[16] 6260 6-9-1 84 ..........(v) TonyHamilton 13 33
(Richard Fahey) *a towards rr* **8/1**
0000 **14** *2* **Secret Witness**[16] 6260 8-9-4 87 ..........(b) BenCurtis 16 30
(Ronald Harris) *a towards rr* **16/1**

-110 **15** *14* **New Bidder**[136] 2257 3-9-2 87 RussKennemore 7
(Jedd O'Keeffe) *chsd ldrs: rdn along 1/2-way: sn wknd* **20/1**
1m 12.37s (-1.43) **Going Correction** -0.075s/f (Good)
**WFA** 3 from 4yo+ 2lb **15** Ran SP% **127.7**
Speed ratings (Par 107): **106,105,104,99,97 97,96,93,91,90 88,87,80,77,59**
CSF £59.70 CT £634.27 TOTE £12.90: £3.40, £2.60, £5.30; EX 68.00 Trifecta £1396.10.
**Owner** Laurence A Bellman **Bred** Mount Coote Partnership **Trained** Malpas, Cheshire
**FOCUS**
A fair sprint handicap, in which the first three pulled away from the pack. The main action took place down the centre. The winner is rated to his old turf best.

## 6745 RACING UK ANYWHERE AVAILABLE NOW H'CAP 5f
**4:10** (4:12) (Class 2) (0-105,102) 3-Y-0+
**£28,012** (£8,388; £4,194; £2,097; £1,048; £526) **Stalls** Centre

Form RPR
030 **1** **High On Life**[14] 6327 3-9-3 96 AdamKirby 12 108
(Jamie Osborne) *racd towards stands' rail: prom: led 2f out: rdn and edgd lft ent fnl f: kpt on wl towards fin* **6/1**[2]
214 **2** *1 1/2* **Goldream**[14] 6327 5-9-10 102 (p) PatDobbs 8 109
(Robert Cowell) *a.p: effrt 2f out: sn rdn: drvn and kpt on ins fnl f: no imp towards fin* **11/2**[1]
6600 **3** *1 1/2* **See The Sun**[14] 6327 3-9-0 93 RobertWinston 9 95
(Tim Easterby) *prom: effrt 2f out and sn chsng wnr: rdn ent fnl f: kpt on same pce* **12/1**
2520 **4** *hd* **Long Awaited (IRE)**[10] 6467 6-8-11 89 (v[1]) DaneO'Neill 17 90
(David Barron) *stdd and swtchd lft s: hld up in rr: hdwy 2f out: sn rdn: styd on wl fnl f: nrst fin* **8/1**
1000 **5** *3/4* **Lexi's Hero (IRE)**[7] 6531 6-8-12 90 (v) BarryMcHugh 16 88
(Richard Fahey) *racd towards stands' rail: in tch: effrt wl over 1f out: sn rdn and styd on fnl f: nrst fin* **28/1**
0200 **6** *nk* **Elusivity (IRE)**[28] 5925 6-8-11 89 ShaneKelly 11 86
(Peter Crate) *hld up: hdwy wl over 1f out: sn rdn and kpt on fnl f: nrst fin* **20/1**
6515 **7** *hd* **Chilworth Icon**[14] 6327 4-9-2 94 SamHitchcott 4 90
(Mick Channon) *towards rr: pushed along over 2f out: switched rt 1f out: styd on: nvr nrr* **10/1**
0000 **8** *3/4* **Racy**[7] 6533 7-9-6 98 (p) HarryBentley 5 92
(Brian Ellison) *hld up: hdwy wl over 1f out: rdn and kpt on fnl f: n.d* **16/1**
0106 **9** *hd* **Judge 'n Jury**[28] 5925 10-8-13 91 (t) BenCurtis 10 84
(Ronald Harris) *led: rdn along and hdd 2f out: drvn and hld whn n.m.r jst ins fnl f: wknd after* **33/1**
330 **10** *nk* **Ballesteros**[7] 6533 5-9-3 95 TonyHamilton 1 87
(Richard Fahey) *hld up: hdwy 2f out: rdn and no imp fnl f* **7/1**[3]
1330 **11** *1/2* **Peterkin (IRE)**[38] 5575 3-8-13 92 JoeFanning 3 82
(Mark Johnston) *racd wd: prom: cl up 1/2-way: rdn 2f out: grad wknd* **16/1**
0000 **12** *1/2* **Smoothtalkinrascal (IRE)**[14] 6327 4-9-8 100 DanielTudhope 6 88
(David O'Meara) *hld up: a towards rr* **14/1**
3110 **13** *nk* **Algar Lad**[14] 6327 4-9-5 97 GeorgeBaker 2 84
(David O'Meara) *hld up: a towards rr* **10/1**
33 **14** *1 1/2* **Da'Quonde (IRE)**[119] 2766 6-8-12 90 PaulMulrennan 7 72
(Bryan Smart) *chsd ldrs: hdwy 2f out: sn rdn and wknd appr fnl f* **16/1**
0332 **15** *1/2* **Normal Equilibrium**[10] 6467 4-9-1 93 (p) RichardKingscote 13 73
(Robert Cowell) *chsd ldrs to 1/2-way: sn wknd* **9/1**
59.25s (-1.55) **Going Correction** -0.075s/f (Good)
**WFA** 3 from 4yo+ 1lb **15** Ran SP% **124.6**
Speed ratings (Par 109): **109,106,104,103,102 102,101,100,100,99 99,98,97,95,94**
CSF £39.18 CT £398.32 TOTE £6.50: £1.90, £2.70, £6.20; EX 38.60 Trifecta £939.40.
**Owner** Michael Buckley **Bred** Moyns Park Estate And Stud Ltd **Trained** Upper Lambourn, Berks
**FOCUS**
A valuable and competitive sprint handicap in which pace held up. A personal best from the winner.

## 6746 EBF "REPROCOLOR" FILLIES' H'CAP 1m 2f 95y
**4:45** (4:46) (Class 3) (0-90,88) 3-Y-0+ **£12,938** (£3,850; £1,924; £962) **Stalls** Centre

Form RPR
231 **1** **This Is The Day**[19] 6192 3-9-0 84 PaulMulrennan 5 96
(Charlie Fellowes) *trckd ldng pair on inner: hdwy 3f out: chal 2f out: rdn to ld appr fnl f: drvn out* **6/1**[2]
1240 **2** *3/4* **Lady Tiana**[59] 4782 3-8-11 81 LukeMorris 1 91
(Lucy Wadham) *in tch on inner: hdwy 3f out: swtchd rt and n.m.r over 2f out: sn led and rdn: hdd appr fnl f: sn drvn and kpt on* **10/1**
5221 **3** *3/4* **Bright Cecily (IRE)**[13] 6365 3-8-7 77 ow1 (p) SteveDrowne 6 86
(Clive Cox) *hld up: hdwy 4f out: effrt over 2f out: rdn to chse ldrs over 1f out: kpt on fnl f* **12/1**
3-10 **4** *2 1/2* **Shama (IRE)**[136] 2255 3-8-12 82 ShaneKelly 2 86
(Sir Michael Stoute) *trckd ldrs: pushed along and hdwy 2f out: n.m.r over 1f out: sn rdn and kpt on fnl f* **11/2**[1]
-565 **5** *3/4* **Lizzie Tudor**[15] 6292 4-9-0 81 ThomasBrown[(3)] 11 83
(Andrew Balding) *hld up and bhd: hdwy wl over 2f out: nt clr run and swtchd rt over 1f out: rdn and kpt on fnl f: nrst fin* **20/1**
0564 **6** *2 1/4* **Hot Coffee (IRE)**[16] 6258 3-9-2 86 RichardKingscote 3 84
(Tom Dascombe) *hld up towards rr: hdwy on inner 3f out: rdn along to chse ldrs 2f out: sn drvn and no imp appr fnl f* **8/1**
1433 **7** *nse* **Rosehill Artist (IRE)**[71] 4397 3-9-3 87 GeorgeBaker 10 85
(Charles Hills) *trckd ldrs: hdwy on outer 3f out: cl up and rdn 2f out: drvn and wknd over 1f out* **13/2**[3]
3211 **8** *2 1/4* **Gift Of Silence**[15] 6285 5-8-7 74 oh1 PhilipPrince[(3)] 8 68
(Bernard Llewellyn) *hld up: a towards rr* **12/1**
5135 **9** *nse* **Patterned**[42] 5448 3-8-10 80 DaneO'Neill 14 74
(Luca Cumani) *prom: effrt and cl up 3f out: rdn along over 2f out: drvn and wknd over 1f out* **8/1**
3032 **10** *shd* **Maven**[9] 6479 6-9-8 86 DanielTudhope 16 79
(Tim Easterby) *led: rdn along 3f out: hdd 2f out: grad wknd* **7/1**
3150 **11** *5* **Maracuja**[47] 5238 3-8-9 79 JoeFanning 12 63
(Mark Johnston) *cl up: rdn along 3f out: wknd over 2f out* **20/1**
-153 **12** *11* **Tears Of The Sun**[75] 4272 3-8-11 81 HarryBentley 15 44
(Roger Varian) *hld up: hdwy over 3f out: sn rdn along and wknd: bhd whn eased over 1f out* **10/1**
2m 14.02s (-1.48) **Going Correction** +0.05s/f (Good)
**WFA** 3 from 4yo+ 6lb **12** Ran SP% **120.8**
Speed ratings (Par 104): **107,106,105,103,103 101,101,99,99,99 95,86**
CSF £66.21 CT £698.89 TOTE £5.20: £2.20, £4.00, £5.00; EX 79.40 Trifecta £1367.00 Part won..
**Owner** A E Oppenheimer **Bred** Hascombe And Valiant Studs **Trained** Newmarket, Suffolk
■ Stewards' Enquiry : Shane Kelly one-day ban: careless riding (Oct 11)

**FOCUS**
An interesting fillies' handicap, and form to follow for the remainder of the turf season. The winner built again on her Brighton win.

## 6747 DOWNLOAD THE NEW RACINGUK IPAD APP H'CAP 1m 6f
**5:20** (5:20) (Class 2) (0-100,98) 3-Y-0+ **£17,789** (£5,293; £2,645; £1,322) **Stalls** Low

Form RPR
1004 **1** **Swivel**[9] 6501 3-8-12 92 JoeFanning 12 102
(Mark Johnston) *hld up in tch: hdwy 4f out: led 2f out: sn rdn: styd on wl u.p fnl f* **13/2**
5305 **2** *1* **Great Hall**[15] 6287 4-9-12 96 PhillipMakin 13 104
(John Quinn) *hld up towards rr: gd hdwy over 3f out: trckd ldrs 2f out: effrt to chse wnr ent fnl f: sn rdn and edgd lft: kpt on same pce after* **12/1**
5010 **3** *2 1/4* **Aramist (IRE)**[21] 6133 4-9-5 89 RobertWinston 3 94
(Alan Swinbank) *hld up in tch: hdwy 3f out: trckd ldrs whn n.m.r over 1f out: sn swtchd rt and rdn: no imp ins fnl f* **4/1**[1]
1004 **4** *nk* **Gabrial's Star**[15] 6283 5-9-0 84 (b) PatDobbs 11 88
(Richard Fahey) *midfield: hdwy 3f out: rdn along 2f out: kpt on fnl f: nrst fin* **16/1**
4544 **5** *2 1/4* **Dashing Star**[60] 4759 4-10-0 98 LiamKeniry 2 99
(David Elsworth) *trckd ldr: hdwy and cl up 3f out: rdn along 2f out: sltly outpcd and n.m.r over 1f out: kpt on fnl f* **4/1**[1]
600 **6** *1 1/4* **Sir Walter Scott (IRE)**[15] 6287 4-10-0 98 (b[1]) AdamKirby 10 98
(Luca Cumani) *hld up: hdwy to trck ldrs 6f out: cl up 3f out: chal over 2f out: sn rdn and wknd appr fnl f* **6/1**[3]
3315 **7** *1 1/2* **Glenard**[21] 6133 4-9-10 94 DanielTudhope 9 91
(Charles Hills) *trckd ldng pair: hdwy and cl up 3f out: disp ld 2f out: sn rdn and ev ch tl drvn and wknd appr fnl f* **5/1**[2]
2160 **8** *nk* **English Summer**[14] 6349 7-8-11 81 (t) TonyHamilton 6 78
(Richard Fahey) *chsd ldrs: rdn along over 3f out: wknd over 2f out* **20/1**
0402 **9** *1 3/4* **Number One London (IRE)**[17] 6228 4-8-11 81 (p) PaulMulrennan 5 76
(Brian Meehan) *led: rdn along 3f out: hdd 2f out and sn wknd* **12/1**
400- **10** *6* **Ile De Re (FR)**[378] 6385 8-9-13 97 StevieDonohoe 7 83
(Kevin Frost) *trckd ldrs: pushed along wl over 3f out: rdn wl over 2f out: sn wknd* **33/1**
5-20 **11** *26* **Sula Two**[111] 3034 7-8-12 85 PhilipPrince[(3)] 8 35
(Jo Hughes) *a towards rr: rn wd home bnd and bhd after* **33/1**
3000 **U** **Sirvino**[23] 6061 9-9-7 91 DaneO'Neill 1
(David Barron) *hld up: towards rr whn lost action and uns rdr 3f out: fatally injured* **28/1**
3m 2.65s (0.65) **Going Correction** +0.05s/f (Good)
**WFA** 3 from 4yo+ 10lb **12** Ran SP% **119.6**
Speed ratings (Par 109): **100,99,98,97,96 95,95,94,93,90 75,**
CSF £78.80 CT £353.54 TOTE £8.70: £2.50, £3.60, £1.50; EX 93.60 Trifecta £1311.90.
**Owner** Sheikh Hamdan bin Mohammed Al Maktoum **Bred** Stratford Place Stud And Watership Down **Trained** Middleham Moor, N Yorks
**FOCUS**
A good staying handicap, but not many arrived with a progressive profile. A clear personal best from the winner.

## 6748 BETDAQ £50 FREE BET H'CAP 1m
**5:50** (5:50) (Class 2) (0-105,99) 3-Y-0+ **£14,555** (£4,331; £2,164; £1,082) **Stalls** Low

Form RPR
5022 **1** **Big Baz (IRE)**[15] 6304 4-8-11 84 ow2 SteveDrowne 12 92
(William Muir) *hld up in rr: hdwy on outer 2f out: rdn over 1f out: styd on strly fnl f to ld nr fin* **11/4**[2]
0506 **2** *1/2* **Prince Of Johanne (IRE)**[14] 6332 8-9-9 96 (p) PhillipMakin 3 105
(Tom Tate) *hld up in rr: gd hdwy on outer 3f out: chal wl over 1f out: sn rdn and edgd lft: led ins fnl f: drvn: hdd and no ex nr fin* **8/1**
2522 **3** *2* **Bold Prediction (IRE)**[17] 6226 4-9-2 92 JoeyHaynes[(3)] 1 96+
(K R Burke) *wnt rt s: led: rdn along 2f out: drvn over 1f out: hdd ins fnl f: kpt on same pce* **5/1**[3]
0 **4** *6* **Energia Flavio (BRZ)**[49] 5163 4-9-5 97 MarcMonaghan[(5)] 4 88
(Marco Botti) *sltly hmpd s: trckd ldrs: hdwy 3f out: rdn along over 2f out: drvn wl over 1f out and one pce* **25/1**
0400 **5** *1 1/4* **Ifwecan**[33] 5771 3-9-2 93 JoeFanning 9 81
(Mark Johnston) *cl up: rdn along 3f out: drvn 2f out: sn one pce* **10/1**
1000 **6** *1* **Navajo Chief**[37] 5609 7-9-3 97 GaryMahon[(7)] 10 82
(Timothy Jarvis) *trckd ldrs: hdwy over 3f out: rdn to chse ldrs 2f out: sn drvn and one pce* **25/1**
-216 **7** *1/2* **Le Chat D'Or**[68] 4491 6-9-4 91 (bt) PaulMulrennan 5 75
(Michael Dods) *a towards rr* **7/1**
6006 **8** *11* **Global Thrill**[33] 5755 5-9-5 95 ThomasBrown[(3)] 6 54
(Bernard Llewellyn) *a towards rr* **50/1**
30-0 **9** *3/4* **Mister Music**[150] 1870 5-9-12 99 (b) DaneO'Neill 2 56
(Brian Meehan) *trckd ldrs: n.m.r and hmpd bnd after 2f: effrt on inner 3f out: rdn over 2f out: sn wknd* **25/1**
3103 **10** *10* **Balducci**[37] 5609 7-9-11 98 (v) DanielTudhope 11 32
(David O'Meara) *racd wd: cl up: swtchd rt to stands' rails over 4f out: rdn along 3f out: sn bhd* **5/2**[1]
1m 44.44s (0.74) **Going Correction** +0.05s/f (Good)
**WFA** 3 from 4yo+ 4lb **10** Ran SP% **118.1**
Speed ratings (Par 109): **98,97,95,89,88 87,86,75,75,65**
CSF £24.25 CT £108.67 TOTE £3.90: £1.80, £2.60, £1.70; EX 21.90 Trifecta £164.20.
**Owner** The Big Baz Partnership **Bred** Haras De La Perelle **Trained** Lambourn, Berks
■ Stewards' Enquiry : Steve Drowne three-day ban: weighed in 2lb heavy (Oct 11-13)
**FOCUS**
They went a strong gallop in this decent handicap and the first two came from a group of four which were detached from the others during the first part of the race. The winner rates back to his early form.
T/Jkpt: Not won. T/Plt: £300.70 to a £1 stake. Pool: £68,186.35 - 165.52 winning tickets T/Qpdt: £162.90 to a £1 stake. Pool: £5,549.23 - 25.20 winning tickets JR

# 6707 NEWMARKET (R-H)

Saturday, September 27

**OFFICIAL GOING: Good to firm (good in places; 7.8; stands' side 7.7; centre 7.5; far side 8.0)**

Wind: virtually nil Weather: dry, bright spells

## 6749 EBF STALLIONS BREEDING WINNERS "JERSEY LILY" FILLIES' NURSERY H'CAP (BOBIS RACE) 7f

**2:00** (2:02) (Class 2) 2-Y-O

**£18,675** (£5,592; £2,796; £1,398; £699) **Stalls** Low

Form RPR

11 **1** **Rosalie Bonheur**[23] 6064 2-8-8 73 ........ PaulHanagan 13 82+
(Clive Cox) *lw: mde virtually all: rdn over 1f out: jnd ins fnl f: fnd ex and styd on gamely fnl 75yds: rdn out* **4/1**[2]

044 **2** *nk* **Hawkin (IRE)**[23] 6065 2-8-7 72 ........ OisinMurphy 12 80
(Ralph Beckett) *chsd ldrs: effrt u.p over 1f out: hdwy and str chal ins fnl f: kpt on but jst outpcd fnl 75yds* **25/1**

031 **3** *4* **Conjuring (IRE)**[24] 6024 2-8-6 71 ........ RoystonFfrench 11 68
(Mike Murphy) *restless in stalls: in tch in midfield: hdwy and edgd rt u.p over 1f out: kpt on to snatch 3rd last strides: no threat to ldrs* **25/1**

3330 **4** *hd* **Assault On Rome (IRE)**[16] 6253 2-9-1 80 ........ SilvestreDeSousa 1 77
(Mark Johnston) *chsd ldrs: effrt u.p over 1f out: wnt 3rd 1f out: one pce and no imp: lost 3rd last strides* **16/1**

231 **5** *nse* **Runner Runner (IRE)**[37] 5604 2-9-0 79 ........ PatSmullen 6 76
(George Baker) *lw: chsd ldrs: rdn wl over 1f out: outpcd by wnr ent fnl f: battling for 3rd and one pce after* **16/1**

1014 **6** *1 ½* **Feeling Easy (IRE)**[16] 6253 2-9-7 86 ........ AndreaAtzeni 2 78
(Robert Eddery) *in tch in midfield: effrt wl over 1f out: no imp whn carried rt and hmpd over 1f out: hld and plugged on same pce after* **10/1**

0153 **7** *1 ¼* **Little Lady Katie (IRE)**[16] 6253 2-8-11 76 ........ JimCrowley 5 65
(K R Burke) *chsd wnr: rdn 2f out: no ex and btn ent fnl f: wknd fnl 150yds* **8/1**

603 **8** *½* **Maybe Now Baby (IRE)**[44] 5344 2-7-12 68 ........ JoeDoyle(5) 4 56
(David Simcock) *in tch towards rr: effrt 2f out: no imp over 1f out: nvr trbld ldrs* **12/1**

3135 **9** *3 ¾* **Gregoria (IRE)**[16] 6253 2-8-13 78 ........ (p) RyanMoore 8 56
(William Haggas) *hld up in last pair: rdn and sme hdwy 2f out: no imp and btn over 1f out: wknd fnl f* **15/2**[3]

3220 **10** *31* **Crystal Malt (IRE)**[64] 4604 2-8-10 75 ........ RichardHughes 3
(Richard Hannon) *hld up in tch towards rr: effrt 2f out: sn btn and eased: t.o* **14/1**

4461 **11** *2 ¼* **Tagtale (IRE)**[56] 4899 2-7-11 67 oh1 ow2 ........ CamHardie(5) 9
(Richard Fahey) *in tch in midfield: rdn 4f out: dropped to rr over 2f out: lost tch over 1f out: t.o and eased ins fnl f* **33/1**

61 **12** *hd* **Sandy Cay (USA)**[45] 5305 2-9-2 81 ........ JamesDoyle 10
(Sir Michael Stoute) *str: slowly into stride: hld up in rr: short-lived effrt 2f out: sn btn and eased: t.o* **9/4**[1]

1m 24.96s (-0.44) **Going Correction** +0.05s/f (Good) **12 Ran SP% 119.5**
Speed ratings (Par 98): **104,103,99,98,98 97,95,95,90,55 52,52**
CSF £105.08 CT £1552.49 TOTE £5.00: £1.90, £7.90, £9.50; EX 122.50 Trifecta £2229.20.
**Owner** Mrs Hugh Maitland-Jones **Bred** Mrs Hugh Maitland-Jones **Trained** Lambourn, Berks

**FOCUS**
Far side course used. Stalls: Far side except 12f: Centre. A decent enough fillies' nursery, but it paid to sit handy and the favourite bombed out. Solid form, though, with the first pair clear.

## 6750 JUDDMONTE ROYAL LODGE STKS (GROUP 2) (C&G) 1m

**2:35** (2:35) (Class 1) 2-Y-O

**£67,428** (£25,563; £12,793; £6,373; £3,198; £1,605) **Stalls** Low

Form RPR

311 **1** **Elm Park**[29] 5876 2-9-0 102 ........ AndreaAtzeni 4 111
(Andrew Balding) *lw: stmbld leaving stalls: in tch in midfield: rdn over 2f out: hdwy and tk false step over 1f out: hung lft but styd on to ld fnl 100yds: rdn out* **11/4**[2]

411 **2** *1* **Nafaqa (IRE)**[15] 6291 2-9-0 109 ........ PaulHanagan 3 109
(B W Hills) *chsd ldr: rdn over 2f out: drvn over 1f out and kpt on to chal 1f out: chsd wnr and styd on same pce fnl 100yds* **5/4**[1]

2151 **3** *4* **Salateen**[17] 6229 2-9-0 99 ........ JamieSpencer 1 99
(Kevin Ryan) *led: rdn over 2f out: wandered lft and hrd pressed 1f out: hdd fnl 100yds: sn wknd* **15/2**[3]

31 **4** *1 ½* **Misterioso (IRE)**[77] 4207 2-9-0 85 ........ RichardHughes 6 95
(Richard Hannon) *athletic: hld up in tch: hdwy and cl 4th 3f out: sn rdn: no ex u.p 1f out: wknd ins fnl f* **11/1**

41 **5** *1 ¾* **Lord Ben Stack (IRE)**[23] 6056 2-9-0 84 ........ JimCrowley 5 91
(K R Burke) *str: t.k.h: chsd ldrs: rdn over 2f out: unable qck and btn over 1f out: wknd fnl f* **8/1**

212 **6** *6* **Medrano**[21] 6136 2-9-0 97 ........ RyanMoore 2 77
(David Brown) *tall: str: a in rr: rdn jst over 2f out: no prog: wknd over 1f out* **14/1**

1m 37.1s (-1.50) **Going Correction** +0.05s/f (Good) **6 Ran SP% 109.0**
Speed ratings (Par 107): **109,108,104,102,100 94**
CSF £6.17 TOTE £3.30: £2.10, £1.30; EX 7.20 Trifecta £26.00.
**Owner** Qatar Racing & Kingsclere Racing **Bred** Kingsclere Stud **Trained** Kingsclere, Hants

**FOCUS**
Aidan O´Brien, who has won the Royal Lodge five times, didn't run any of his many entries, but even without Ballydoyle representation this was still an interesting race. Elm Park is progressive, and so is the runner-up.

## 6751 CONNOLLY'S RED MILLS CHEVELEY PARK STKS (GROUP 1) (FILLIES) 6f

**3:10** (3:12) (Class 1) 2-Y-O

**£117,673** (£44,612; £22,327; £11,122; £5,581; £2,801) **Stalls** Low

Form RPR

1211 **1** **Tiggy Wiggy (IRE)**[37] 5608 2-9-0 117 ........ RichardHughes 3 117
(Richard Hannon) *broke wl: mde all: qcknd up wl 2f out: in command after: pushed out: comf* **6/4**[1]

13 **2** *¾* **Anthem Alexander (IRE)**[37] 5608 2-9-0 0 ........ PatSmullen 1 115
(Edward Lynam, Ire) *lw: trckd wnr: rdn over 1f out: kpt on wl but nt pce to chal wnr* **5/1**[3]

21 **3** *1 ¼* **High Celebrity (FR)**[18] 6220 2-9-0 0 ........ MaximeGuyon 5 111
(A Fabre, France) *tall: str: lw: s.i.s: midfield early: stdd bk into last trio after 1f: pushed along and hdwy over 1f out: wnt 3rd ent fnl f: r.o but nvr threatening to get involved* **9/4**[2]

1 **4** *1 ½* **Terror (IRE)**[33] 5774 2-9-0 0 ........ AndreaAtzeni 4 107
(David Simcock) *settled bk into midfield after 1f: rdn 2f out: kpt on ins fnl f: wnt 4th nring fin but nt pce to get involved* **11/1**

01 **5** *shd* **Tendu**[24] 6032 2-9-0 0 ........ JamesDoyle 7 106
(John Gosden) *str: lengthy: lw: trckd wnr tl rdn 2f out: lost 3rd ent fnl f: kpt on same pce: lost 4th nring fin* **8/1**

1615 **6** *4 ½* **Arabian Queen (IRE)**[49] 5190 2-9-0 101 ........ SilvestreDeSousa 9 93
(David Elsworth) *trckd wnr tl rdn 2f out: sn hld: wknd ins fnl f* **25/1**

6210 **7** *4* **Tongue Twista**[15] 6286 2-9-0 85 ........ (b) JimCrowley 2 81
(Nick Littmoden) *mid-div: rdn 3f out: sn outpcd: wknd fnl f* **100/1**

40 **8** *hd* **Amaze Me**[23] 6067 2-9-0 0 ........ JackMitchell 10 80
(Nick Littmoden) *hld up: rdn 3f out: nvr any imp: wknd fnl f* **150/1**

13 **9** *1* **Zuhoor Baynoona (IRE)**[134] 2313 2-9-0 0 ........ RyanMoore 8 77
(Richard Fahey) *racd keenly: hld up: hdwy over 3f out: rdn 2f out: nvr threatened: wknd fnl f* **33/1**

1m 11.4s (-0.80) **Going Correction** +0.05s/f (Good) **9 Ran SP% 115.3**
Speed ratings (Par 106): **107,106,104,102,102 96,90,90,89**
CSF £9.40 TOTE £2.10: £1.10, £1.70, £1.20; EX 8.80 Trifecta £15.70.
**Owner** Potensis Ltd C Giles Merriebelle Stables **Bred** Cbs Bloodstock **Trained** East Everleigh, Wilts

**FOCUS**
This race has a mixed record for producing Guineas winners, not surprisingly given the distance, but two winners in the last ten years have done the double. This looked a strong renewal and the form is straightforward, Tiggy Wiggy posting the best figure in this race for 12 years.

## 6752 BETFRED CAMBRIDGESHIRE (HERITAGE H'CAP) 1m 1f

**3:50** (3:51) (Class 2) 3-Y-O+

**£99,600** (£22,368; £22,368; £7,456; £3,728; £1,872) **Stalls** Low

Form RPR

0042 **1** **Bronze Angel (IRE)**[14] 6332 5-8-8 99 ........ (b) LouisSteward(5) 11 111
(Marcus Tregoning) *far side gp: in tch in midfield: clsd to trck ldrs and travelling strly over 1f out: rdn to ld 1f out: wnt clr and r.o strly fnl 150yds: 1st of 16 in gp* **14/1**

0103 **2** *2 ¼* **Velox**[14] 6332 4-8-6 97 ........ CamHardie(5) 28 104
(Luca Cumani) *lw: nr side gp: hld up towards rr: pushed along and hdwy 3f out: swtchd rt over 1f out: led gp 1f out: styd on wl: no threat to wnr: 1st of 15 in gp* **8/1**[2]

-100 **2** *dht* **Niceofyoutotellme**[60] 4756 5-8-10 96 ........ JamesDoyle 14 103
(Ralph Beckett) *far side gp: hld up in rr: hdwy between rivals over 1f out: sltly hmpd ent fnl f: styd on wl ins fnl f: no threat to wnr: 2nd of 16 in gp* **10/1**

2123 **4** *¾* **Buckstay (IRE)**[21] 6140 4-8-6 92 ........ MaximeGuyon 10 97
(Peter Chapple-Hyam) *far side gp: in tch in midfield: effrt over 2f out: rdn to ld overall over 1f out: hdd 1f out: sn outpcd by wnr: one pce and lost 2 pls cl home: 3rd of 16 in gp* **25/1**

2011 **5** *nk* **Tenor (IRE)**[10] 6458 4-9-5 110 7ex ........ (t) JoeDoyle(5) 26 115
(John Ryan) *lw: nr side gp: chsd ldrs: rdn over 1f out: edgd rt and styd on same pce ins fnl f: 2nd of 15 in gp* **33/1**

0341 **6** *1* **Tigers Tale (IRE)**[21] 6140 5-8-2 91 4ex ........ (v) DannyBrock(3) 25 94
(Roger Teal) *nr side gp: gp ldr and prom: overall: led overall 3f out tl drvn and hdd over 1f out: hung rt 1f out: plugged on same pce ins fnl f: 3rd of 15 in gp* **25/1**

1301 **7** *nse* **Big Johnny D (IRE)**[17] 6226 5-8-5 96 4ex ........ ShaneGray(5) 5 99
(David Barron) *swtg: far side gp: in tch in midfield: effrt u.p over 1f out: kpt on but no threat to wnr ins fnl f: 4th of 16 in gp* **50/1**

-000 **8** *nk* **Quick Wit**[126] 2554 7-9-1 101 ........ (p) RichardHughes 1 103
(Saeed bin Suroor) *lw: far side gp: in tch in midfield: hdwy u.p over 1f out: kpt on but no imp ins fnl f: 5th of 16 in gp* **25/1**

0444 **9** *¾* **Educate**[49] 5175 5-9-10 110 ........ MickaelBarzalona 3 110
(Ismail Mohammed) *far side gp: hld up towards rr: hdwy u.p over 1f out: styd on same pce ins fnl f: 6th of 16 in gp* **20/1**

0-16 **10** *½* **Homage (IRE)**[31] 5824 4-8-8 94 ........ PaulHanagan 9 93
(William Haggas) *far side gp: in tch in midfield: n.m.r wl over 1f out: hdwy u.p ent fnl f: styd on same pce fnl 150yds: 7th of 16 in gp* **25/1**

0030 **11** *½* **Pacific Heights (IRE)**[21] 6124 5-8-13 99 ........ ChrisHayes 20 97
(Brian Ellison) *swtg: nr side gp: in tch: chsd ldrs 3f out: drvn and unable qck over 1f out: wknd ins fnl f: 4th of 15 in gp* **66/1**

2050 **12** *nk* **Ingleby Angel (IRE)**[14] 6332 5-8-10 96 ........ JimCrowley 24 94
(David O'Meara) *swtg: nr side gp: bhd: rdn 3f out: hdwy over 1f out: kpt on ins fnl f: nvr trbld ldrs: 5th of 15 in gp* **50/1**

1-13 **13** *nk* **Cornrow**[21] 6124 4-8-8 94 ........ WilliamBuick 30 91
(John Gosden) *lw: nr side gp: chsd ldrs: rdn and pressing overall ldrs over 1f out: no ex 1f out: wknd fnl 100yds: 6th of 15 in gp* **6/1**[1]

2620 **14** *½* **Dance And Dance (IRE)**[63] 4648 8-8-8 94 ........ SilvestreDeSousa 16 90
(Ed Vaughan) *far side gp: stdd s: hld up bhd: rdn wl over 2f out: hdwy over 1f out: kpt on: nvr trbld ldrs: 8th of 16 in gp* **33/1**

0604 **15** *½* **Fort Bastion (IRE)**[21] 6124 5-8-9 95 ........ (b) FrankieDettori 2 90
(Ruth Carr) *far side gp: hld up towards rr: rdn over 2f out: hdwy u.p over 1f out: no imp fnl f: 9th of 16 in gp* **25/1**

0162 **16** *½* **Forgotten Hero (IRE)**[14] 6330 5-8-7 93 ........ JamieSpencer 12 87
(Charles Hills) *far side gp: hld up towards rr: hdwy over 2f out: rdn over 1f out: sn btn: wknd ins fnl f: 10th of 16 in gp* **25/1**

1002 **17** *nk* **Balty Boys (IRE)**[21] 6132 5-9-0 100 ........ (b) PaulPickard 8 93
(Brian Ellison) *far side gp: chsd ldrs: led gp and chsd overall ldr 3f out: no ex u.p and wandered jst over 1f out: wknd ins fnl f: 11th of 16 in gp* **20/1**

0000 **18** *¾* **Chancery (USA)**[21] 6133 6-8-7 93 ........ SamJames 22 85
(David O'Meara) *nr side gp: hld up in midfield: effrt u.p over 2f out: no imp: plugged on fnl f: 7th of 15 in gp* **22/1**

4226 **19** *nk* **Spirit Of The Law (IRE)**[7] 6548 5-8-6 92 ........ JohnFahy 35 83
(Richard Fahey) *nr side gp: in tch in midfield: rdn and lost pl jst over 2f out: same pce and n.d fnl 2f: 8th of 15 in gp* **40/1**

5050 **20** *hd* **Bancnuanaheireann (IRE)**[35] 5695 7-8-9 95 ........ AndrewMullen 29 86
(Michael Appleby) *nr side gp: chsd ldrs: rdn 3f out: outpcd and wl btn over 1f out: 9th of 15 in gp* **20/1**

-200 **21** *1 ½* **Yeager (USA)**[63] 4648 4-8-7 93 ........ JimmyQuinn 13 80
(Jeremy Noseda) *far side gp: hld up towards rr: effrt u.p over 2f out: hrd drvn and no imp over 1f out: nvr trbld ldrs: 12th of 16 in gp* **33/1**

300- **22** *3 ¾* **Indian Chief (IRE)**[377] 6440 4-9-2 102 ........ MartinDwyer 17 83
(David Nicholls) *far side gp: midfield: struggling u.p and lost pl jst over 2f out: wl btn over 1f out: 13th of 16 in gp* **50/1**

124 **23** *1 ¼* **Maverick Wave (USA)**[14] 6332 3-8-7 **98**........................ RobertHavlin 31 77
(John Gosden) *nr side gp: hld up towards rr: effrt and swtchd rt jst over 2f out: sn btn: bhd over 1f out: 10th of 15 in gp* **16/1**

1033 **24** *1 ¼* **The Rectifier (USA)**[13] 6358 7-8-13 **106**....................(t) MikeyEnnis(7) 27 81
(Seamus Durack) *nr side gp: chsd ldrs: rdn and btn ent fnl 2f: wknd over 1f out: 11th of 15 in gp* **66/1**

4113 **25** *shd* **Bartack (IRE)**[17] 6226 4-8-9 **95**....................................(v) TomQueally 15 70
(David O'Meara) *lw: far side gp: chsd ldrs: lost pl u.p 2f out: wknd over 1f out: bhd fnl f: 14th of 16 in gp* **33/1**

3121 **26** *1 ½* **Extremity (IRE)**[21] 6149 3-8-7 **98** 4ex.........................(p) AndreaAtzeni 18 71
(Hugo Palmer) *lw: far side gp: in tch in midfield: rdn and little rspnse 2f out: btn over 1f out: wknd ent fnl f: 15th of 16 in gp* **9/1**[3]

4035 **27** *hd* **Gabrial's Kaka (IRE)**[37] 5609 4-9-3 **103**....................... PatSmullen 34 75
(Richard Fahey) *nr side gp: hld up in rr: effrt but stl plenty to do whn hmpd wl over 1f out: no ch after: 12th of 15 in gp* **20/1**

1100 **28** *3* **Genius Boy**[33] 5749 4-8-1 **94**................................ KieranShoemark(7) 21 59
(James Tate) *swtg: nr side gp: hld up towards rr: effrt and sme hdwy jst over 2f out: wknd over 1f out: bhd fnl f: 13th of 15 in gp* **50/1**

2150 **29** *1 ¼* **Sound Advice**[21] 6140 5-8-6 **92**........................................ IanBrennan 6 55
(Keith Dalgleish) *far side gp: overall ldr tl 3f out: sn struggling u.p: wknd 2f out: bhd 1f out: 16th of 16 in gp* **100/1**

0001 **30** *nk* **Queensberry Rules (IRE)**[35] 5695 4-9-2 **102**..............(p) RyanMoore 33 64
(William Haggas) *nr side gp: chsd ldrs: rdn ent fnl 2f: struggling whn unbalanced on downhill run wl over 1f out: sn dropped out and bhd: 14th of 15 in gp* **14/1**

4502 **31** *20* **God Willing**[8] 6519 3-8-6 **97**........................................... OisinMurphy 19 18
(Ed Dunlop) *nr side gp: hld up towards rr: last and struggling u.p 3f out: lost tch over 1f out: eased: t.o: 15th of 15 in gp* **33/1**

1m 48.68s (-3.02) **Going Correction** +0.05s/f (Good)
**WFA** 3 from 4yo+ 5lb **31** Ran SP% **139.1**
Speed ratings (Par 109): **115,113,113,112,112 111,111,110,110,109 109,109,108,108,107 107,107,106,106,106 104,101,100,99**
WIN: £15.30; PL: Bronze Angel £3.00, Niceofyoutotellme £3.00, Velox £3.80, Buckstay £5.90; EX: BA/V £38.30, BA/N £69.60; CSF: BA/V £46.17, BA/N £56.03; TC: BA/V/N £615.23, BA/N/V £625.40; TF: BA/V/N £332.00, BA/N/V £414.70.
**Owner** Lady Tennant **Bred** Rihana Partnership **Trained** Whitsbury, Hants

**FOCUS**
Ante-post favourite Air Pilot missed the cut by one, but there were four non-runners. They split into two groups, with the far-side coming out on top, but one from the stands' side dead-heated for second and there didn't look to be a bias. The form makes sense, with Bronze Angel better than ever.

## 6753 RACING UK MAIDEN FILLIES' STKS (BOBIS RACE) (DIV I) 7f
**4:25** (4:26) (Class 4) 2-Y-O **£5,175** (£1,540; £769; £384) **Stalls** Low

Form RPR

02 **1** **Taqneyya (IRE)**[16] 6246 2-9-0 0....................................... PaulHanagan 9 81
(Charles Hills) *led: 5 l clr 3f out: in command after: pushed out fnl f* **5/2**[1]

**2** *1* **Pamona (IRE)** 2-8-9 0...................................................... CamHardie(5) 4 78+
(Luca Cumani) *leggy: unf: trckd ldrs: rdn to chse wnr over 2f out: kpt on wl fnl 120yds but a being hld* **14/1**

**3** *3 ¼* **Jazzi Top** 2-9-0 0............................................................. WilliamBuick 8 70+
(John Gosden) *tall: unfL s.i.s: mid-div: pushed along and hdwy 2f out: wnt 3rd ent fnl f: kpt on same pce fnl 120yds* **5/2**[1]

23 **4** *1 ¼* **Quite Smart (IRE)**[33] 5774 2-9-0 0....................................... TedDurcan 3 66
(Robert Cowell) *w'like: str: trckd wnr tl rdn over 2f out: kpt on same pce fnl f* **14/1**

**5** *2* **Skip And Jump (USA)** 2-9-0 0......................................... JackMitchell 1 61
(Roger Varian) *tall: trckd ldrs: rdn over 2f out: kpt on same pce fnl f* **25/1**

**6** *nk* **Bella Lulu** 2-9-0 0............................................................ AndreaAtzeni 5 60
(Roger Varian) *lengthy: scope: bit bkwd: mid-div: rdn over 2f out: no imp tl kpt on ins fnl f* **6/1**[2]

**7** *2* **Entertainment** 2-9-0 0.................................................... RobertHavlin 10 55
(John Gosden) *lengthy: towards rr: sme late prog: nvr any threat* **14/1**

**8** *½* **Justice Belle (IRE)** 2-9-0 0............................................. AntonioFresu 2 53
(Ed Walker) *leggy: s.i.s: mid-div: rdn over 2f out: wknd fnl f* **40/1**

**9** *nse* **Light Glass (IRE)** 2-9-0 0................................................ OisinMurphy 7 53+
(Richard Hannon) *tall: mid-div: rdn over 2f out: wknd fnl f* **12/1**[3]

0 **10** *1 ¾* **Lipstickandpowder (IRE)**[36] 5643 2-9-0 0...................[1] JamesDoyle 6 48
(William Jarvis) *unf: towards rr of midfield: rdn over 2f out: nvr any imp* **33/1**

05 **11** *10* **Fridge Kid**[16] 6261 2-9-0 0............................................... RobertTart 11 21
(Dr Jon Scargill) *leggy: struggling 1/2-way: a bhd* **66/1**

**12** *16* **Kawaii** 2-9-0 0.................................................................. RichardHughes 12
(Philip McBride) *w'like: str: s.i.s: a towards rr: eased over 1f out* **12/1**[3]

1m 25.72s (0.32) **Going Correction** +0.05s/f (Good) **12** Ran SP% **117.5**
Speed ratings (Par 94): **100,98,95,93,91 91,88,88,88,86 74,56**
CSF £41.61 TOTE £3.30: £1.30, £4.80, £1.70; EX 39.50 Trifecta £243.60.
**Owner** Hamdan Al Maktoum **Bred** Shadwell Estate Company Limited **Trained** Lambourn, Berks

**FOCUS**
While this form is perhaps nothing special on the face of it, there were one or two noteworthy performances.

## 6754 RACING UK MAIDEN FILLIES' STKS (BOBIS RACE) (DIV II) 7f
**5:00** (5:02) (Class 4) 2-Y-O **£5,175** (£1,540; £769; £384) **Stalls** Low

Form RPR

**1** **Lady Correspondent (USA)** 2-9-0 0................................. JamesDoyle 5 78+
(John Gosden) *lengthy: scope: lw: mid-div: hdwy 2f out: str run ins fnl f to ld nring fin: readily* **7/4**[1]

**2** *½* **Alfajer** 2-9-0 0.................................................................. MartinHarley 8 74+
(Marco Botti) *str: trckd ldrs: shkn up to ld jst over 1f out: kpt on but nt pce of wnr whn hdd nring fin* **14/1**

**3** *1 ¼* **Colorada** 2-9-0 0............................................................... TomQueally 10 71+
(William Knight) *leggy: athletic: trckd ldr: rdn to ld briefly over 1f out: kpt on same pce ins fnl f* **25/1**

**4** *1 ¾* **Twitch (IRE)** 2-9-0 0......................................................... JimCrowley 4 66+
(Hugo Palmer) *leggy: unf: mid-div: pushed along 2f out: no imp tl styd on nicely fnl f: wnt 4th towards fin* **6/1**

0 **5** *nk* **Mrs Eve (IRE)**[22] 6093 2-9-0 0............................................ RobertTart 11 65
(Alan Bailey) *leggy: led: rdn and hdd over 1f out: kpt on same pce fnl f* **66/1**

**6** *1 ¾* **Hana Lina** 2-9-0 0............................................................ RichardHughes 6 60
(William Haggas) *str: unshipped jockey gng to s but sn ct: s.i.s: trckd ldrs after 1f: effrt 2f out: one pce fnl f* **4/1**[2]

**7** *nse* **Kip** 2-9-0 0........................................................................ RyanMoore 7 60
(Sir Michael Stoute) *tall: unf: in tch: hdwy over 2f out: sn rdn and outpcd: styd on ins fnl f but nt pce to threaten* **5/1**[3]

06 **8** *4 ½* **Luv U**[10] 6462 2-9-0 0........................................................ PaulHanagan 2 48
(Ed Dunlop) *towards rr: effrt into mid-div over 2f out: wknd over 1f out* **20/1**

**9** *6* **Bracken Brae** 2-9-0 0...................................................... JimmyQuinn 3 32+
(Mark H Tompkins) *lengthy: unf: s.i.s: a towards rr* **66/1**

0 **10** *6* **Resolve**[14] 6333 2-9-0 0...................................................... MartinLane 9 16
(David Simcock) *leggy: a towards rr* **20/1**

**11** *nk* **Shasag (IRE)** 2-9-0 0........................................................ AndreaAtzeni 1 15
(Roger Varian) *leggy: athletic: mid-div: rdn over 2f out: wknd over 1f out* **10/1**

1m 28.8s (3.40) **Going Correction** +0.05s/f (Good) **11** Ran SP% **119.4**
Speed ratings (Par 94): **82,81,80,78,77 75,75,70,63,56 56**
CSF £28.31 TOTE £2.80: £1.10, £4.60, £8.10; EX 34.30 Trifecta £447.80.
**Owner** K Abdullah **Bred** Juddmonte Farms Inc **Trained** Newmarket, Suffolk

**FOCUS**
Those with previous experience had shown little and unsurprisingly the finish was dominated by newcomers. The time was significantly slower than the other races at this trip, including 3.08secs off the first division.

## 6755 WANDERIN' JOHN H'CAP 7f
**5:35** (5:35) (Class 2) (0-100,97) 3-Y-O+
**£12,450** (£3,728; £1,864; £932; £466; £234) **Stalls** Low

Form RPR

1416 **1** **Accession (IRE)**[14] 6320 5-8-10 86...................................... MartinLane 9 95
(Charlie Fellowes) *chsd ldrs: wnt 2nd 2f out: rdn to ld over 1f out: hld on wl towards fin: all out* **16/1**

5524 **2** *nk* **Jack's Revenge (IRE)**[33] 5749 6-9-6 96.....................(bt) RyanMoore 10 104
(George Baker) *lw: in tch in midfield: effrt u.p to chse ldrs 1f out: chsd wnr fnl 100yds: kpt on wl u.p but a hld* **7/2**[1]

5350 **3** *¾* **Suzi's Connoisseur**[17] 6234 3-9-4 97..........................(b[1]) JamesDoyle 2 103
(Hugo Palmer) *lw: in tch in midfield: n.m.r over 1f out: swtchd lft and hdwy jst ins fnl f: wnt sharply lft u.p fnl 50yds: styd on to go 3rd nr fin* **13/2**

0253 **4** *¾* **Lady Frances**[5] 6598 3-8-11 90.................................... SilvestreDeSousa 7 93
(Mark Johnston) *led and set stdy gallop: rdn and qckna wl over 1f out: hdd over 1f out: styd on on same pce ins fnl f* **20/1**

0105 **5** *shd* **Joey's Destiny (IRE)**[36] 5623 4-9-5 95..........................(p) MartinDwyer 8 99
(George Baker) *in tch in midfield: nt room over 1f out: kpt on u.p ins fnl f: pushed lft and hmpd towards fin* **16/1**

-000 **6** *shd* **One Word More (IRE)**[18] 6207 4-9-2 92........................... WilliamBuick 5 95
(Charles Hills) *in tch towards rr: n.m.r wl over 1f out: drvn 1f out: styd on wl fnl 100yds: nt rch ldrs* **14/1**

0032 **7** *1 ¼* **Secretinthepark**[18] 6207 4-9-5 95.................................. RichardHughes 13 95
(Ed McMahon) *chsd ldr tl 2f out: clsd 3rd and rdn over 1f out: outpcd fnl 100yds* **5/1**[2]

0111 **8** *¾* **Take A Note**[18] 6207 5-9-1 91........................................(v) JimCrowley 1 89
(Patrick Chamings) *chsd ldrs: nt clr run on far rail over 1f out: nvr enough room and one pce ins fnl f* **6/1**[3]

0030 **9** *nse* **Pastoral Player**[18] 6207 7-9-2 92...................................... JohnFahy 15 90
(Hughie Morrison) *stdd and dropped in bhd after s: t.k.h: hld up in rr: swtchd rt and effrt 1f out: nt clr run and swtchd lft ins fnl f: kpt on: nvr trbld ldrs* **12/1**

0004 **10** *1* **Valbchek (IRE)**[11] 6440 5-9-3 93.................................(p) JamieSpencer 4 89
(Jane Chapple-Hyam) *s.i.s: hld up in rr: swtchd lft 2f out: sme hdwy u.p over 1f out: no prog fnl f* **25/1**

5405 **11** *3 ½* **King Torus (IRE)**[17] 6226 6-9-0 90................................. FrankieDettori 16 76
(Ruth Carr) *in tch in midfield: effrt and hung rt over 1f out: btn 1f out: eased fnl 100yds* **12/1**

6521 **12** *1 ¼* **Red Refraction (IRE)**[9] 6498 4-9-1 96............................ CamHardie(5) 14 79
(Richard Hannon) *in tch in midfield: effrt 2f out: sn drvn and outpcd: wknd fnl f* **15/2**

4300 **13** *20* **Steventon Star**[162] 1555 3-9-3 96................................... AndreaAtzeni 11 26
(Alan Bailey) *a towards rr: dropped to last and struggling 1/2-way: lost tch 2f out: t.o* **50/1**

1m 24.36s (-1.04) **Going Correction** +0.05s/f (Good)
**WFA** 3 from 4yo+ 3lb **13** Ran SP% **122.7**
Speed ratings (Par 109): **107,106,105,104,104 104,103,102,102,101 97,95,72**
CSF £71.89 CT £434.11 TOTE £21.20: £4.90, £1.60, £2.70; EX 113.10 Trifecta £1404.20.
**Owner** Lady De Ramsey **Bred** Corduff Stud Ltd **Trained** Newmarket, Suffolk

**FOCUS**
They raced towards the far-side fence and a few found trouble in a steadily run race. The winner was close to his old form.

## 6756 JUNCTION 17 PRESTIGE CARS H'CAP (BOBIS RACE) 1m 4f
**6:05** (6:09) (Class 2) (0-100,95) 3-Y-O **£12,938** (£3,850; £1,924; £962) **Stalls** Centre

Form RPR

4161 **1** **Famous Kid (USA)**[22] 6106 3-9-4 **92**............................... RichardHughes 3 104+
(Saeed bin Suroor) *lw: mde all: grad led field to stands' side in st: rdn over 2f out: forged clr 1f out: styd on wl* **11/4**[1]

3161 **2** *3* **High Church (IRE)**[18] 6206 3-9-2 **90**.............................. JamesDoyle 6 98+
(Roger Charlton) *hld up in tch: effrt against stands' rail to chse wnr over 2f out: no ex and btn ins fnl f* **11/4**[1]

2221 **3** *1* **Almashooqa (USA)**[15] 6282 3-8-13 **87**............................ AndreaAtzeni 1 93
(Roger Varian) *chsd ldrs: rdn over 2f out: 3rd and styd on same pce fnl f* **11/1**

2130 **4** *1 ½* **Captain Morley**[35] 5691 3-9-2 **90**.................................. JamieSpencer 7 94
(David Simcock) *in tch in midfield: effrt and chsd wnr briefly over 2f out: 4th and btn over 1f out: plugegd on* **4/1**[3]

0415 **5** *3* **Gothic**[21] 6127 3-9-3 **91**.................................................. RyanMoore 8 92
(Sir Michael Stoute) *stdd and dropped in bhd s: swtchd rt and effrt over 2f out: btn over 1f out: eased wl ins fnl f* **7/2**[2]

3321 **6** *46* **Saarrem (USA)**[22] 6092 3-8-13 **87**..............................(b) PaulHanagan 10 12
(John Gosden) *chsd wnr: upsides 5f out tl over 2f out: sn dropped out: t.o and eased fnl f* **12/1**

2m 32.93s (0.93) **Going Correction** +0.05s/f (Good) **6** Ran SP% **111.6**
Speed ratings (Par 107): **98,96,95,94,92 61**
CSF £10.38 CT £66.28 TOTE £3.70: £2.20, £1.40; EX 9.20 Trifecta £63.50.
**Owner** Godolphin **Bred** Darley **Trained** Newmarket, Suffolk

**FOCUS**
This race was decimated by non-runners but it was still not a bad little contest and it may have gone to a future Group horse. The runner-up is progressive too.

T/Plt: £42.70 to a £1 stake. Pool: £163,162.02 - 2788.51 winning tickets T/Qpdt: £8.80 to a £1 stake. Pool: £10,352.80 - 861.05 winning tickets SP

# [5788]RIPON (R-H)
## Saturday, September 27

**OFFICIAL GOING: Good (8.1)**
Wind: Breezy, half behind Weather: Overcast

## 6757 IRISH STALLION FARMS EBF MAIDEN STKS 6f
**2:10** (2:10) (Class 5) 2-Y-O **£4,528** (£1,347; £673; £336) **Stalls** High

Form RPR
1 **Them And Us (IRE)** 2-9-5 0 WilliamTwiston-Davies 13 76+
(Michael Bell) *midfield: rdn and swtchd rt over 2f out: hdwy to ld ins fnl f: rdn out* **16/1**
3 2 ½ **Especial**[23] 6058 2-9-5 0 PhillipMakin 4 74
(Bryan Smart) *in tch on outside: smooth hdwy to ld over 1f out: sn rdn: hdd ins fnl f: rallied: hld nr fin* **11/4**[2]
0 3 2½ **Etienne Gerard**[9] 6489 2-9-0 0 ShelleyBirkett(5) 8 67
(Nigel Tinkler) *in tch: hdwy and ev ch over 2f out to over 1f out: rdn and outpcd by first two ins fnl f* **100/1**
3 4 ¾ **Character Onesie (IRE)**[14] 6319 2-9-2 0 GeorgeChaloner(3) 11 64
(Richard Fahey) *prom: drvn and outpcd over 2f out: rallied fnl f: nvr able to chal* **9/4**[1]
5 ½ **Mustaqbal (IRE)** 2-9-5 0 AdrianNicholls 2 63
(Mark Johnston) *led and sn crossed over to stands' rail: hdd after 2f: rdn and led over 2f out to over 1f out: sn outpcd* **8/1**
6 2¾ **Father Bertie** 2-9-5 0 DavidAllan 5 55
(Tim Easterby) *midfield: drvn along over 3f out: rallied over 1f out: no imp fnl f* **25/1**
7 ½ **Big Red** 2-9-0 0 JasonHart 10 50+
(Robin Bastiman) *towards rr and sn pushed along: effrt 1/2-way: kpt on fnl f: nvr able to chal* **50/1**
8 ¾ **Mo Henry** 2-9-5 0 PaulQuinn 9 51
(Richard Whitaker) *hld up: drvn along 1/2-way: sme late hdwy: nvr rchd ldrs* **50/1**
5 9 3½ **Tortilla Jackson**[14] 6319 2-9-5 0 GrahamLee 6 40
(Tom Dascombe) *chsd ldrs: drvn and outpcd over 2f out: btn over 1f out* **5/1**[3]
3323 10 1½ **Doppler Effect**[7] 6537 2-9-5 74 (v[1]) PJMcDonald 1 36
(Ann Duffield) *t.k.h: cl up: led after 2f to over 2f out: wknd over 1f out* **15/2**
11 6 **Madam Mai Tai** 2-9-0 0 AdamBeschizza 14 13
(Robin Bastiman) *bhd and green: struggling 1/2-way: nvr on terms* **50/1**
12 15 **Agreeable Lady (IRE)** 2-9-0 0 DuranFentiman 3
(Tim Easterby) *dwlt: sn pushed along on outside in rr: struggling over 3f out: sn btn* **40/1**
0 13 10 **Chatty Man (IRE)**[16] 6259 2-9-5 0 FergalLynch 7
(David C Griffiths) *dwlt: bhd and outpcd: lost tch bef 1/2-way: eased* **50/1**

1m 13.06s (0.06) **Going Correction** -0.075s/f (Good) 13 Ran SP% **118.0**
Speed ratings (Par 95): **96,95,92,91,90 86,86,85,80,78 70,50,37**
CSF £57.50 TOTE £17.40: £2.70, £1.50, £19.40; EX 95.50 Trifecta £1217.70 Part won..
**Owner** W J & T C O Gredley **Bred** John Foley **Trained** Newmarket, Suffolk

**FOCUS**
Rail at innermost position and all distances as advertised. A fairly useful effort from the winner to bely market weakness. The pace was sound once the leaders had got across from their outside stalls. The fourth helps set the level.

## 6758 DAVID SONIA'S 40TH BIRTHDAY CELEBRATION APPRENTICE H'CAP 6f
**2:45** (2:45) (Class 5) (0-70,75) 3-Y-O+ **£3,234** (£962; £481; £240) **Stalls** High

Form RPR
2562 1 **Monarch Maid**[24] 6029 3-8-9 65 DavidParkes(5) 6 75
(Peter Hiatt) *mde all: rdn and clr over 1f out: edgd lft and kpt on wl fnl f: unchal* **13/2**[3]
04 2 2¼ **Election Night**[63] 4660 3-9-1 69 RachelRichardson(3) 5 72
(Tim Easterby) *prom: effrt and chsd wnr over 2f out: edgd lft and kpt on fnl f: nt pce to chal* **11/2**[1]
6000 3 1 **Mercers Row**[17] 6227 7-9-1 67 GemmaTutty(3) 2 67
(Karen Tutty) *in tch on outside: effrt and pushed along 2f out: kpt on same pce ins fnl f* **16/1**
5230 4 ½ **Diamond Blue**[9] 6475 6-9-2 65 (p) SammyJoBell 1 63
(Richard Fahey) *rrd and lost grnd s: hld up on outside: stdy hdwy 1/2-way: effrt over 1f out: kpt on same pce ins fnl f* **11/2**[1]
3006 5 1 **Amis Reunis**[5] 6595 5-8-7 56 oh4 (p) EmmaSayer 8 51
(Alan Berry) *hld up: rdn and hdwy wl over 1f out: edgd rt and no imp ent fnl f* **40/1**
1000 6 3¾ **Mandalay King (IRE)**[25] 6013 9-9-5 68 JacobButterfield 11 51
(Marjorie Fife) *chsd ldrs: effrt and edgd rt over 1f out: outpcd ins fnl f* **12/1**
0010 6 dht **Ambitious Icarus**[8] 6511 5-9-9 75 (e) AlistairRawlinson(3) 7 58
(Richard Guest) *awkward s: hld up: rdn over 2f out: no imp fr over 1f out* **6/1**[2]
0004 8 ½ **Toboggan Star**[30] 5853 3-8-4 60 RowanScott(5) 3 41
(Ann Duffield) *hld up: rdn over 3f out: outpcd fr 2f out* **10/1**
1 9 1 **Boy Wonder**[151] 1860 3-9-1 69 DanielCremin(3) 9 47
(Mick Channon) *chsd ldrs: drvn along 1/2-way: wknd wl over 1f out* **11/2**[1]
2404 10 2¾ **Ray Of Joy**[10] 6463 8-9-2 65 (v) ShelleyBirkett 4 34
(J R Jenkins) *t.k.h: hld up: struggling over 2f out: sn btn* **8/1**
1400 11 27 **Cadeaux Pearl**[45] 5298 6-8-13 62 MatthewHopkins 10
(Scott Dixon) *chsd wnr to over 2f out: sn outpcd: lost pl whn flyj. twice appr fnl f: sn lost tch* **14/1**

1m 12.1s (-0.90) **Going Correction** -0.075s/f (Good)
**WFA** 3 from 5yo+ 2lb 11 Ran SP% **116.7**
Speed ratings (Par 103): **103,100,98,98,96 91,91,91,89,86 50**
CSF £41.80 CT £552.07 TOTE £8.00: £2.90, £1.10, £12.60; EX 53.90 Trifecta £2163.50 Part won..
**Owner** Carl Demczak **Bred** Oakhill Stud **Trained** Hook Norton, Oxon

**FOCUS**
A modest apprentice event in few which ever threatened to land a serious blow. The winner was not an obvious improver but the time comes out well.

## 6759 RIPON LAND ROVER NURSERY H'CAP (BOBIS RACE) 1m
**3:20** (3:20) (Class 4) (0-85,80) 2-Y-O **£6,301** (£1,886; £943; £472; £235) **Stalls** Low

Form RPR
3052 1 **Laidback Romeo (IRE)**[28] 5929 2-8-12 74 RyanTate(3) 3 81
(Clive Cox) *prom: hdwy to chse clr ldr over 2f out: effrt and hung rt over 1f out: led ins fnl f: r.o wl* **15/8**[1]
4442 2 1 **Lear's Rock (IRE)**[23] 6064 2-8-9 71 GeorgeChaloner(3) 6 76
(Ralph Beckett) *t.k.h: led and crossed to ins rail after 1f: clr 1/2-way: rdn over 1f out: hdd ins fnl f: kpt on same pce* **3/1**[2]
3163 3 5 **Summer Stroll (IRE)**[18] 6211 2-8-9 68 GrahamLee 1 61
(David O'Meara) *hld up: stdy hdwy over 3f out: rdn and hung rt 2f out: kpt on: nt rch first two* **7/1**
0314 4 6 **Grey Sensation (IRE)**[17] 6229 2-9-0 76 JoeyHaynes(3) 4 55
(K R Burke) *chsd ldr tl rdn and lost 2nd over 2f out: sn btn* **7/2**[3]
3413 5 4½ **Bizzario**[15] 6280 2-9-7 80 AdrianNicholls 2 49
(Mark Johnston) *towards rr: rdn along 4f out: struggling over 2f out: sn btn* **9/1**
601 6 43 **Cape Hideaway**[21] 6147 2-9-2 75 JasonHart 5
(Mark Walford) *t.k.h: cl up: hung bdly lft bnd ent st: lost tch fr over 2f out: eased* **16/1**

1m 39.5s (-1.90) **Going Correction** -0.075s/f (Good) 6 Ran SP% **110.4**
Speed ratings (Par 97): **106,105,100,94,89 46**
CSF £7.41 TOTE £3.60: £1.80, £1.20; EX 8.90 Trifecta £30.60.
**Owner** Robin Craddock **Bred** Mrs B Gardiner **Trained** Lambourn, Berks

**FOCUS**
The leading pair came well clear in a race where most of the remainder ran well below form.

## 6760 RIPON CATHEDRAL CITY OF THE DALES H'CAP 6f
**3:55** (3:55) (Class 2) (0-105,103) 3-Y-O+
**£18,675** (£5,592; £2,796; £1,398; £699; £351) **Stalls** High

Form RPR
22 1 **Spinatrix**[41] 5467 6-9-7 103 (p) ConnorBeasley(3) 4 111
(Michael Dods) *dwlt: sn prom on outside: hdwy to ld over 1f out: hld on wl u.p towards fin* **7/2**[2]
0000 2 hd **Supplicant**[7] 6533 3-8-11 95 GeorgeChaloner(3) 5 102
(Richard Fahey) *towards rr: pushed along 1/2-way: hdwy u.p over 1f out: kpt on wl towards fin: jst hld* **4/1**[3]
0000 3 hd **Kimberella**[15] 6281 4-9-1 94 AdrianNicholls 9 101
(David Nicholls) *trckd ldrs: nt clr run over 2f out to over 1f out: kpt on wl fnl f: hld nr fin* **14/1**
2000 4 nse **Seeking Magic**[14] 6327 6-9-2 98 (t) RyanTate(3) 8 105
(Clive Cox) *hld up towards rr: rdn and hdwy 2f out: kpt on wl: hld towards fin* **10/3**[1]
0404 5 1¼ **Bondesire**[33] 5754 4-9-3 96 GrahamLee 2 99
(David O'Meara) *led and sn trckd over to stands' rail: rdn and hdd over 1f out: kpt on same pce ins fnl f* **14/1**
0202 6 ¾ **Clear Spring (IRE)**[11] 6440 6-9-2 95 FergalLynch 11 95
(John Spearing) *dwlt: bhd: swtchd rt over 2f out: effrt over 1f out: one pce ins fnl f* **17/2**
2030 7 nse **Confessional**[21] 6131 7-8-13 92 (e) DavidAllan 12 92
(Tim Easterby) *in tch: pushed along over 2f out: no imp tl styd on ins fnl f: n.d* **10/1**
0300 8 1¼ **Barkston Ash**[14] 6354 6-9-2 95 (p) JasonHart 6 91
(Eric Alston) *cl up: rdn 2f out: wknd ins fnl f* **16/1**
0154 9 1 **Avon Breeze**[35] 5677 5-8-6 85 (p) PJMcDonald 10 78
(Richard Whitaker) *towards rr: rdn along 1/2-way: no imp fr 2f out* **10/1**
0000 10 14 **Deeds Not Words (IRE)**[20] 6170 3-8-11 92 WilliamTwiston-Davies 1 40
(Mick Channon) *dwlt: hld up on outside: struggling over 2f out: sn btn* **20/1**

1m 10.94s (-2.06) **Going Correction** -0.075s/f (Good)
**WFA** 3 from 4yo+ 2lb 10 Ran SP% **118.0**
Speed ratings (Par 109): **110,109,109,109,107 106,106,105,103,85**
CSF £18.22 CT £175.80 TOTE £3.10: £1.10, £2.40, £2.10; EX 19.60 Trifecta £379.60.
**Owner** Mrs J W Hutchinson & Mrs P A Knox **Bred** T K & Mrs P A Knox **Trained** Denton, Co Durham

**FOCUS**
A decent sprint which was soundly run. The first four were all close to their best.

## 6761 CHS VEHICLES H'CAP 1m 4f 10y
**4:30** (4:30) (Class 4) (0-85,87) 3-Y-O+ **£6,301** (£1,886; £943; £472; £235) **Stalls** Low

Form RPR
4252 1 **Brigadoon**[11] 6433 7-9-9 82 JasonHart 9 90
(Michael Appleby) *led at ordinary gallop: pushed along over 2f out: kpt on wl fnl f* **8/1**[3]
-031 2 ½ **Saoi (USA)**[13] 6366 7-10-0 87 GrahamLee 4 94
(William Knight) *hld up: stdy hdwy over 3f out: plld out and chsd wnr appr fnl f: edgd rt: kpt on: hld towards fin* **11/4**[1]
2-50 3 2¼ **Ambleside**[20] 6171 4-9-5 78 FergalLynch 2 82
(Michael Easterby) *chsd wnr: rdn and outpcd over 3f out: rallied over 1f out: one pce ins fnl f* **11/1**
52 4 4 **Arizona John (IRE)**[6] 6579 9-9-2 78 ConnorBeasley(3) 7 75
(John Mackie) *prom: stdy hdwy over 3f out: sn rdn: wknd over 1f out* **10/1**
5100 5 nse **Itlaaq**[20] 6169 8-9-11 84 (t) DuranFentiman 8 81
(Michael Easterby) *chsd ldrs: rdn over 2f out: outpcd whn n.m.r briefly over 1f out: sn btn* **20/1**
6115 6 4 **Mambo Rhythm**[7] 6539 3-8-11 78 (v) AdrianNicholls 1 69
(Mark Johnston) *hld up in tch on ins: struggling over 4f out: n.d after* **8/1**[3]
043 7 2¼ **Rio's Rosanna (IRE)**[41] 5465 7-9-3 79 GeorgeChaloner(3) 6 66
(Richard Whitaker) *dwlt: t.k.h: hld up in tch on outside: outpcd over 3f out: btn fnl 2f* **7/2**[2]
0133 8 ¾ **Bayan Kasirga (IRE)**[9] 6480 4-8-7 71 oh1 SammyJoBell(5) 3 57
(Richard Fahey) *dwlt: hld up: pushed along over 4f out: edgd rt and btn fnl 2f* **7/2**[2]

2m 36.08s (-0.62) **Going Correction** -0.075s/f (Good)
**WFA** 3 from 4yo+ 8lb 8 Ran SP% **115.5**
Speed ratings (Par 105): **99,98,97,94,94 91,90,89**
CSF £30.67 CT £246.13 TOTE £8.10: £2.90, £1.70, £4.30; EX 22.90 Trifecta £301.90.
**Owner** Castle Racing **Bred** Biddestone Stud **Trained** Danethorpe, Notts

**FOCUS**
An above-average handicap. The winner dictated what looked no more than a fair pace for most of the way, and is rated to form.

## 6762 LISA MCLEAN'S 40TH BIRTHDAY PARAPHERNALIA MAIDEN STKS 1m 4f 10y
**5:05** (5:05) (Class 5) 3-Y-O+ **£4,528** (£1,347; £673; £336) **Stalls** Low

Form RPR
43 1 **Never Up (GER)**[11] 6432 3-9-3 75 GrahamLee 2 81+
(David O'Meara) *mde all: qcknd clr over 2f out: v easily* **8/11**[1]
2404 2 8 **Norse Light**[16] 6274 3-9-3 72 (b) SebSanders 3 69
(Ralph Beckett) *t.k.h: chsd wnr: drvn and outpcd over 3f out: hung rt and no imp fnl 2f* **2/1**[2]

0-04 **3** *6* **Sr Swing**[15] 6282 3-8-12 51 DuranFentiman 1 52
(Philip Kirby) *prom: drvn and outpcd over 3f out: n.d after* **25/1**
65 **4** *7* **Philosofy**[186] 1088 4-8-13 0 JoshDoyle(7) 5 41
(David O'Meara) *hld up in tch: rdn over 3f out: edgd rt and wknd over 2f out* **7/1**[3]
2m 38.25s (1.55) **Going Correction** -0.075s/f (Good)
**WFA** 3 from 4yo 8lb 4 Ran SP% **107.6**
Speed ratings (Par 103): **91,85,81,77**
CSF £2.40 TOTE £1.20; EX 1.50 Trifecta £5.00.
**Owner** Geoff & Sandra Turnbull & Partner **Bred** Wertheimer & Frere **Trained** Nawton, N Yorks
**FOCUS**
A very weak maiden, where the winner was always in control. There's better to come from the winner.

## 6763 SIS LIVE H'CAP 5f
5:40 (5:40) (Class 4) (0-85,85) 3-Y-O+ **£6,301** (£1,886; £943; £472; £235) **Stalls** High

Form RPR
3144 **1** **Meadway**[28] 5923 3-9-5 82 (p) GrahamLee 4 92
(Bryan Smart) *cl up far side: effrt and rdn over 1f out: led that gp ins fnl f: kpt on wl: 1st of 4 in gp* **16/1**
6204 **2** *nk* **Adam's Ale**[17] 6235 5-9-7 83 JasonHart 1 92
(Mark Walford) *trckd far side ldrs: effrt and rdn over 1f out: kpt on fnl f: hld towards fin: 2nd of 4 in gp* **9/2**[2]
0000 **3** *¾* **Captain Dunne (IRE)**[14] 6324 9-8-13 75 DavidAllan 2 81
(Tim Easterby) *led far side and overall ldr: rdn 2f out: hdd ins fnl f: kpt on same pce: 3rd of 4 in gp* **40/1**
5043 **4** *nk* **Singeur (IRE)**[17] 6235 7-9-7 83 AdamBeschizza 14 88
(Robin Bastiman) *hld up stands' side: rdn and swtchd rt over 1f out: led that gp ins fnl f: kpt on: nt rch far side ldrs: 1st of 12 in gp* **7/1**[3]
0011 **5** *¾* **Bondi Beach Boy**[2] 6695 5-9-6 85 6ex GeorgeChaloner(3) 13 88
(James Turner) *led stands' side: rdn over 1f out: hdd ins fnl f: kpt on same pce: 2nd of 12 in gp* **4/1**[1]
5264 **6** *hd* **Jofranka**[8] 6512 4-9-0 76 SebSanders 9 78
(David Barron) *cl up stands' side: rdn and ev ch over 1f out to ins fnl f: one pce: 3rd of 12 in gp* **12/1**
2160 **7** *¾* **Noodles Blue Boy**[17] 6235 8-9-0 76 (p) AndrewElliott 10 77
(Ollie Pears) *hld up on outside of stands' side gp: pushed along and edgd rt over 1f out: kpt on ins fnl f: nrst fin: 4th of 12 in gp* **25/1**
1124 **8** *nk* **Perfect Words (IRE)**[12] 6406 4-8-5 70 JacobButterfield(3) 16 68
(Marjorie Fife) *cl up stands' side: rdn and effrt over 1f out: kpt on same pce fnl f: 5th of 12 in gp* **9/1**
3060 **9** *nse* **Lexington Place**[8] 6512 4-9-4 80 PJMcDonald 7 78
(Ruth Carr) *hld up on outside of stands' side gp: rdn over 1f out: kpt on: n.d: 6th of 12 in gp* **20/1**
0300 **10** *¾* **Bispham Green**[57] 4859 4-9-7 83 (p) FergalLynch 8 78
(David O'Meara) *dwlt: bhd stands' side tl kpt on fnl f: nvr able to chal: 7th of 12 in gp* **22/1**
0213 **11** *nk* **Brother Tiger**[14] 6324 5-9-1 80 RyanTate(3) 15 74
(David C Griffiths) *hld up stands' side: rdn and effrt over 1f out: no imp fnl f: 8th of 12 in gp* **9/2**[2]
2320 **12** *1 ½* **Gowanharry (IRE)**[40] 5498 5-8-13 78 (tp) ConnorBeasley(3) 6 67
(Michael Dods) *prom stands' side tl rdn and wknd 1f out: 9th of 12 in gp* **16/1**
630 **13** *nse* **Perfect Blossom**[8] 6512 7-8-5 72 EmmaSayer(5) 12 60
(Alan Berry) *dwlt: hld up stands' side: rdn 2f out: nvr on terms: 10th of 12 in gp* **50/1**
-056 **14** *¾* **Kenny The Captain (IRE)**[91] 3704 3-9-4 81 DuranFentiman 5 67
(Tim Easterby) *bhd and outpcd far side: struggling 1/2-way: nvr on terms: last of 4 in gp* **25/1**
1500 **15** *2 ¼* **Mister Manannan (IRE)**[8] 6512 7-9-4 80 AdrianNicholls 3 58
(David Nicholls) *sn outpcd bhd far side ldrs: drifted to stands' side gp 2f out: sn wknd: 11th of 12 in gp* **25/1**
0116 **16** *1 ¼* **Pastureyes**[12] 6399 4-8-2 69 (p) MatthewHopkins(5) 11 42
(Scott Dixon) *chsd stands' side ldrs tl rdn and wknd wl over 1f out* **33/1**
58.6s (-1.40) **Going Correction** -0.075s/f (Good)
**WFA** 3 from 4yo+ 1lb 16 Ran SP% **126.3**
Speed ratings (Par 105): **108,107,106,105,104 104,103,102,102,101 100,98,98,97,93 91**
CSF £81.23 CT £1919.43 TOTE £20.50: £2.90, £1.60, £5.30, £1.90; EX 126.00 Trifecta £886.90 Part won..
**Owner** Michael Moses & Terry Moses **Bred** Bond Thoroughbred Corporation **Trained** Hambleton, N Yorks
**FOCUS**
A decent enough sprint. The field split from the stalls, with the first three home racing in the smaller far-side group. The winner rates a personal best.
T/Plt: £172.00 to a £1 stake. Pool: £52,374.00 - 222.19 winning tickets T/Qpdt: £11.70 to a £1 stake. Pool: £3,586.73 - 225.55 winning tickets RY

# 6715 WOLVERHAMPTON (A.W) (L-H)
Saturday, September 27

**OFFICIAL GOING: Tapeta: standard**
Wind: Almost nil Weather: Overcast

## 6764 TOTEPLACEPOT WIN WITHOUT BACKING A WINNER CLAIMING STKS 5f 20y
5:30 (5:30) (Class 6) 3-Y-O+ **£2,264** (£673; £336; £168) **Stalls** Low

Form RPR
1024 **1** **Desert Strike**[25] 6020 8-9-6 80 (p) HayleyTurner 2 86
(Conor Dore) *led: rdn and hdd ins fnl f: carried lft: rallied to ld nr fin* **15/2**
340 **2** *shd* **Peace Seeker**[10] 6467 6-9-6 88 (t) WilliamCarson 5 86
(Anthony Carson) *chsd wnr: edgd lft wl over 3f out: rdn to ld and hung lft ins fnl f: hdd nr fin* **5/4**[1]
0000 **3** *1 ½* **Fitz Flyer (IRE)**[8] 6511 8-8-12 75 (v) PaddyAspell 6 72
(David Nicholls) *pushed along in rr early: hdwy 1/2-way: rdn over 1f out: nt clr run wl ins fnl f: styd on* **9/2**[3]
350 **4** *3* **Dark Lane**[37] 5595 8-7-13 63 HollieDoyle(7) 7 55
(David Evans) *prom: pushed along 3f out: sn outpcd: styd on ins fnl f* **14/1**
60 **5** *2 ½* **Monty Fay (IRE)**[22] 6088 5-8-1 46 TimClark(5) 1 46
(Derek Haydn Jones) *sn prom: rdn over 1f out: wknd ins fnl f* **150/1**
640 **6** *2 ¼* **Profile Star (IRE)**[17] 6236 5-8-3 72 NoraLooby(7) 3 42
(Ann Stokell) *hood removed sltly late and s.i.s: outpcd* **33/1**

5000 **7** *2 ¼* **Ben Hall (IRE)**[20] 6170 3-9-7 95 (b) RoystonFfrench 4 46
(Mike Murphy) *sn pushed along to chse ldrs: hmpd wl over 3f out: rdn and wknd over 1f out* **3/1**[2]
1m 1.54s (-0.36) **Going Correction** 0.0s/f (Stan)
**WFA** 3 from 5yo+ 1lb 7 Ran SP% **109.7**
Speed ratings (Par 101): **102,101,99,94,90 87,83**
CSF £15.94 TOTE £5.90: £4.60, £1.10; EX 9.10 Trifecta £83.20.
**Owner** Andrew Page **Bred** Mrs Mary Rowlands **Trained** Hubbert's Bridge, Lincs
**FOCUS**
This was an above-average claimer, with the top three in the weights rated 80 and above.

## 6765 TOTEPOOL BET ON ALL UK RACING MEDIAN AUCTION MAIDEN STKS 5f 216y
6:00 (6:07) (Class 5) 3-Y-O **£2,911** (£866; £432; £216) **Stalls** Low

Form RPR
0552 **1** **La Napoule**[31] 5820 3-9-0 58 KieranO'Neill 7 68+
(Richard Hannon) *a.p: chsd ldr over 3f out: led 2f out: sn rdn clr: eased towards fin* **7/4**[1]
**2** *4* **Bailiwick** 3-9-5 0 RoystonFfrench 4 57
(Daniel Kubler) *s.s: hld up: r.o to go 2nd wl ins fnl f: no ch w wnr* **10/1**
06 **3** *3 ½* **Windy Miller**[38] 5570 3-9-5 0 WilliamCarson 1 46
(Robin Dickin) *hld up: hdwy over 2f out: sn rdn: wknd fnl f* **50/1**
02- **4** *shd* **Qatar Princess (IRE)**[360] 6947 3-9-0 0 LiamJones 3 41
(J R Jenkins) *plld hrd and prom: rdn over 1f out: wknd fnl f* **7/1**
3 **5** *1* **Satellite Express (IRE)**[66] 4539 3-9-0 0 ChrisCatlin 6 37
(David Evans) *sn led: hdd 5f out: pushed along over 3f out: sn lost pl: kpt on ins fnl f* **4/1**[2]
0524 **6** *hd* **Aphrilis (IRE)**[36] 5642 3-9-0 58 BenCurtis 8 37
(Brian Ellison) *sn pushed along in rr: rdn over 2f out: n.d* **9/2**[3]
-565 **7** *nk* **Tolly McGuiness**[54] 4972 3-9-0 47 ShelleyBirkett(5) 9 41
(Julia Feilden) *led 5f out: rdn and hdd 2f out: wknd fnl f* **8/1**
1m 14.61s (0.11) **Going Correction** 0.0s/f (Stan) 7 Ran SP% **109.2**
Speed ratings (Par 101): **99,93,89,88,87 87,86**
CSF £18.54 TOTE £2.30: £1.30, £3.90; EX 18.90 Trifecta £398.10.
**Owner** Guy Reed Racing **Bred** G Reed **Trained** East Everleigh, Wilts
**FOCUS**
The most experienced runner won this moderate maiden easily.

## 6766 TOTEQUADPOT FOUR PLACES IN FOUR RACES H'CAP (DIV I) 7f 32y
6:30 (6:30) (Class 5) (0-70,70) 3-Y-O+ **£2,911** (£866; £432; £216) **Stalls** High

Form RPR
5241 **1** **Lady Crossmar (IRE)**[5] 6617 3-9-4 70 KieranO'Neill 8 83
(Richard Hannon) *hld up: hdwy over 2f out: rdn over 1f out: r.o to ld nr fin* **7/4**[1]
0003 **2** *½* **Steelriver (IRE)**[86] 3880 4-9-6 69 DaleSwift 7 81
(Michael Herrington) *s.s: hld up: hdwy over 5f out: chsd ldr 1/2-way: led over 2f out: rdn clr over 1f out: hung lft wl ins fnl f: hdd nr fin* **2/1**[2]
2324 **3** *2 ¾* **Hipz (IRE)**[16] 6266 3-9-0 66 LiamJones 9 70
(Laura Mongan) *hld up: hdwy over 1f out: r.o to go 3rd nr fin: nt rch ldrs* **11/1**
1565 **4** *½* **Be Royale**[21] 6160 4-9-1 64 LukeMorris 2 68
(Michael Appleby) *chsd ldrs: wnt 2nd 2f out: sn rdn and hung lft: no ex ins fnl f* **11/2**[3]
0400 **5** *2 ½* **Sakhalin Star (IRE)**[17] 6232 3-9-2 68 ChrisCatlin 10 64
(Richard Guest) *plld hrd and prom: rdn over 1f out: wknd fnl f* **33/1**
6200 **6** *15* **Baltic Prince (IRE)**[1] 6720 4-8-7 56 oh3 RaulDaSilva 1 14
(Paul Green) *sn pushed along to ld: rdn and hdd over 2f out: wknd over 1f out* **20/1**
0/00 **7** *10* **Two Pancakes**[56] 4925 4-9-0 66 NeilFarley(3) 4
(Declan Carroll) *sn outpcd* **66/1**
2610 **8** *32* **Galatian**[17] 6240 7-9-7 70 HayleyTurner 3
(Rod Millman) *chsd ldr tl rdn 1/2-way: wknd over 2f out* **10/1**
1m 28.77s (-0.03) **Going Correction** 0.0s/f (Stan)
**WFA** 3 from 4yo+ 3lb 8 Ran SP% **111.7**
Speed ratings (Par 103): **100,99,96,95,92 75,64,27**
CSF £5.12 CT £24.91 TOTE £2.80: £1.10, £1.10, £3.20; EX 6.60 Trifecta £38.60.
**Owner** Middleham Park Racing Vi **Bred** Scuderia San Pancrazio **Trained** East Everleigh, Wilts
■ Stewards' Enquiry : Dale Swift two-day ban: used whip above permitted level (Oct 11-12)
**FOCUS**
A decent pace appeared to play a significant part, with the slow-starting runner-up paying the price for being over-keen and getting involved too early.

## 6767 TOTEQUADPOT FOUR PLACES IN FOUR RACES H'CAP (DIV II) 7f 32y
7:00 (7:01) (Class 5) (0-70,70) 3-Y-O+ **£2,911** (£866; £432; £216) **Stalls** High

Form RPR
0421 **1** **Plucky Dip**[7] 6568 3-9-1 67 AdamKirby 7 79
(John Ryan) *hld up: hdwy wl over 1f out: rdn to ld 1f out: sn hung lft: styd on u.p* **4/5**[1]
5644 **2** *1 ¼* **Footstepsintherain (IRE)**[19] 6191 4-9-0 70 (t) MikeyEnnis(7) 9 80
(David Dennis) *dwlt: hld up: hdwy wl over 1f out: ev ch whn hmpd 1f out: styd on same pce ins fnl f* **9/2**[2]
0003 **3** *3 ¼* **Bogsnog (IRE)**[7] 6544 4-9-2 65 RoystonFfrench 2 67
(Kristin Stubbs) *chsd ldrs: rdn to ld over 1f out: sn edgd lft and hdd: no ex ins fnl f* **10/1**[3]
6-06 **4** *½* **An Cat Dubh (IRE)**[14] 6346 5-9-7 70 (p) StevieDonohoe 4 70
(Tim Pitt) *mid-div: hdwy over 2f out: sn rdn: styd on u.p* **12/1**
0/5- **5** *2 ¾* **Sadiigah**[533] 1515 4-8-4 58 ShelleyBirkett(5) 3 51
(Julia Feilden) *prom: rdn over 1f out: wknd ins fnl f* **80/1**
1536 **6** *½* **Orpsie Boy (IRE)**[29] 5887 11-9-5 68 LukeMorris 5 60
(Ruth Carr) *hld up: styd on ins fnl f: nvr on terms* **12/1**
2100 **7** *2 ½* **Smalljohn**[74] 4291 8-8-13 67 (v) AdamCarter(5) 1 52
(Bryan Smart) *led 1f: chsd ldr: rdn over 2f out: wknd over 1f out* **20/1**
0400 **8** *½* **Llewellyn**[74] 4291 6-9-1 67 NeilFarley(3) 10 51
(Declan Carroll) *pushed along to ld 6f out: rdn clr over 2f out: edgd rt and hdd over 1f out: wknd ins fnl f* **33/1**
2450 **9** *4* **Ambella (IRE)**[151] 1846 4-9-1 64 HayleyTurner 6 38
(Ian Williams) *broke wl: sn lost pl: pushed along 1/2-way: wknd over 2f out* **20/1**
1m 28.26s (-0.54) **Going Correction** 0.0s/f (Stan)
**WFA** 3 from 4yo+ 3lb 9 Ran SP% **111.9**
Speed ratings (Par 103): **103,101,97,97,94 93,90,90,85**
CSF £3.92 CT £18.78 TOTE £2.00: £1.10, £1.30, £2.20; EX 5.10 Trifecta £30.00.
**Owner** Byron, Lavallin & Donnison **Bred** Cheveley Park Stud Ltd **Trained** Newmarket, Suffolk

**FOCUS**
A lively gallop set this up for a finisher, and the winner made no mistake.

## 6768 TRY A TOTETRIFECTA TODAY H'CAP — 2m 119y
**7:30** (7:30) (Class 6) (0-60,60) 3-Y-0+ **£2,264** (£673; £336; £168) **Stalls** Low

Form — RPR

3051 **1** **Alba Verde**[14] 6339 3-8-13 57 ... LukeMorris 2 — 71+
(Sir Mark Prescott Bt) *a.p: hmpd over 3f out: led over 2f out: rdn out* **1/1**[1]

3205 **2** 2 1/4 **Honest Strike (USA)**[152] 1806 7-9-9 60 ... EoinWalsh(5) 1 — 65
(Daniel Mark Loughnane) *hld up: nt clr run over 3f out: hdwy over 2f out: rdn to chse wnr and edgd rt over 1f out: styd on same pce ins fnl f* **28/1**

5306 **3** 3/4 **Lacey**[40] 5508 5-9-10 56 ... (p) AdamKirby 8 — 60
(Andrew Hollinshead) *mid-div: hdwy over 5f out: rdn over 3f out: chsd wnr over 2f out tl over 1f out: styd on same pce ins fnl f* **11/2**[2]

**4** 4 **Luso's Way (IRE)**[15] 6310 6-9-7 53 ... HayleyTurner 7 — 52
(John Joseph Hanlon, Ire) *hld up: hdwy u.p over 2f out: styd on same pce fr over 1f out* **12/1**

233 **5** 2 3/4 **William Hogarth**[22] 6117 9-9-0 46 oh1 ... BenCurtis 11 — 42
(Brian Ellison) *mid-div: hdwy over 5f out: hmpd over 3f out: sn rdn: styd on same pce fnl 2f* **6/1**[3]

5006 **6** 11 **Fire In Babylon (IRE)**[12] 6410 6-8-12 49 ... (b) TobyAtkinson(5) 4 — 32
(Noel Quinlan) *s.i.s: hld up: hdwy and edgd lft over 3f out: rdn and ev ch over 2f out: wknd over 1f out* **12/1**

3044 **7** 4 **Sawwala**[9] 6486 4-9-3 49 ... JoeFanning 6 — 27
(J R Jenkins) *prom: pushed along and hmpd over 3f out: wknd over 1f out* **11/1**

/003 **8** 5 **Osgood**[44] 3521 7-9-5 58 ... (v) JasonNuttall(7) 9 — 30
(Gary Moore) *s.i.s: hld up: a in rr: wknd over 2f out* **28/1**

0065 **9** 3 **Dubara Reef (IRE)**[32] 5794 7-9-0 46 oh1 ... (p) RaulDaSilva 12 — 14
(Paul Green) *sn pushed along to ld: clr after 3f tl over 6f out: rdn over 4f out: hdd over 2f out: wknd and eased wl over 1f out* **50/1**

1344 **10** 7 **Lady Percy (IRE)**[24] 6031 5-9-0 53 ... CharlotteJenner(7) 3 — 13
(Mark Usher) *chsd ldr over 5f: remained handy: wnt 2nd again over 6f out: rdn and ev ch wl over 2f out: sn wknd* **25/1**

0500 **11** 9 **Chief Executive (IRE)**[136] 2252 4-8-11 46 oh1 ... (t) RossAtkinson(3) 5
(Mandy Rowland) *hld up: wknd over 2f out* **50/1**

-430 **12** 19 **Vertueux (FR)**[28] 5904 9-9-7 53 ... (p) LiamKeniry 10
(Tony Carroll) *prom: chsd clr ldr 11f out tl over 6f out: rdn whn hmpd and wknd over 3f out* **33/1**

4000 **13** 27 **Petite Madame (IRE)**[35] 5682 3-8-1 50 ...[1] NoelGarbutt(5) 13
(David Thompson) *hld up: a in rr: bhd fnl 5f* **66/1**

3m 41.42s (-2.28) **Going Correction** 0.0s/f (Stan)
**WFA** 3 from 4yo+ 12lb — **13** Ran SP% **122.5**
Speed ratings (Par 101): **105,103,103,101,100 95,93,91,89,86 82,73,60**
CSF £44.78 CT £125.71 TOTE £1.90: £1.10, £6.40, £2.00; EX 33.40 Trifecta £172.20.
**Owner** Miss K Rausing **Bred** Miss K Rausing **Trained** Newmarket, Suffolk

**FOCUS**
In a low-grade event, the gallop was strong for 2m, and that brought out the best in the relatively unexposed winner.

## 6769 FOLLOW @TOTEPOOL ON TWITTER NURSERY H'CAP — 1m 141y
**8:00** (8:00) (Class 5) (0-75,75) 2-Y-0 **£2,911** (£866; £432; £216) **Stalls** Low

Form — RPR

5342 **1** **Water Thief (USA)**[13] 6364 2-9-7 75 ... JoeFanning 7 — 80+
(Mark Johnston) *led 1f: chsd ldr tl led again over 2f out: rdn out* **2/1**[1]

043 **2** 1 3/4 **Thanksgiving Day (IRE)**[16] 6268 2-9-3 71 ... ShaneKelly 8 — 71
(Jamie Osborne) *a.p: rdn to chse wnr 2f out: styd on same pce ins fnl f* **11/4**[2]

052 **3** 1 3/4 **Lexi's Red Devil (IRE)**[31] 5827 2-8-12 71 ... DanielMuscutt(5) 6 — 68
(Marco Botti) *chsd ldrs: rdn over 1f out: edgd lft: styd on same pce ins fnl f* **7/2**[3]

340 **4** 1 **Horsetracker**[4] 6648 2-8-11 65 ... (v[1]) StevieDonohoe 9 — 60
(Ian Williams) *hld up: styd on u.p fr over 1f out: nt trble ldrs* **28/1**

5316 **5** nk **Red Rebel**[45] 5310 2-9-7 75 ... AdamKirby 2 — 69
(Clive Cox) *trckd ldrs: rdn over 2f out: no ex ins fnl f* **8/1**

224 **6** 1/2 **Edge Of Heaven**[26] 5981 2-9-1 69 ... LukeMorris 1 — 62
(Jonathan Portman) *hld up: nt clr run over 2f out: hdwy over 1f out: sn rdn: no imp fnl f* **16/1**

1000 **7** 3 3/4 **Showcard**[36] 5626 2-8-9 70 ... HectorCrouch(7) 5 — 55
(Gary Moore) *s.i.s: hld up: rdn over 2f out: n.d* **12/1**

2523 **8** 10 **La Estatua**[13] 6364 2-9-0 68 ... KierenFallon 4 — 32
(James Tate) *w wnr tl led over 7f out: hung rt fr 1/2-way: hdd over 2f out: wknd over 1f out* **9/1**

1m 51.42s (1.32) **Going Correction** 0.0s/f (Stan) — **8** Ran SP% **120.4**
Speed ratings (Par 95): **94,92,90,90,89 89,85,77**
CSF £8.17 CT £18.36 TOTE £4.40: £1.70, £1.70, £1.30; EX 12.70 Trifecta £36.70.
**Owner** Sheikh Majid bin Mohammed Al Maktoum **Bred** B P Walden Jr, P W Madden Et Al **Trained** Middleham Moor, N Yorks

**FOCUS**
In a fair maiden, the gallop was medium at best.

## 6770 TOTEEXACTA PICK THE 1,2 H'CAP — 1m 141y
**8:30** (8:30) (Class 4) (0-85,85) 3-Y-0+ **£4,851** (£1,443; £721; £360) **Stalls** Low

Form — RPR

3411 **1** **Fiftyshadesfreed (IRE)**[21] 6160 3-9-5 85 ... (p) PatCosgrave 7 — 96
(George Baker) *hld up: hdwy 1/2-way: led over 1f out: edgd lft ins fnl f: r.o: comf* **11/4**[2]

4635 **2** 1 **Life And Times (USA)**[18] 6210 6-9-5 80 ... JoeFanning 3 — 88
(Mark Johnston) *dwlt: hld up: hdwy to chse wnr fnl f: sn rdn and hung lft: styd on same pce* **7/2**[3]

4023 **3** 5 **Party Royal**[9] 6490 4-9-3 78 ... JamesSullivan 5 — 75
(Ruth Carr) *chsd ldrs: rdn over 1f out: styd on same pce* **8/1**

4421 **4** shd **Postscript (IRE)**[29] 5895 6-9-10 85 ... DavidNolan 6 — 81
(David Simcock) *hld up: hdwy over 1f out: no ex ins fnl f* **5/2**[1]

34-0 **5** 1 **Gilmer (IRE)**[98] 3484 3-8-12 78 ... DougieCostello 4 — 73
(Laura Young) *racd keenly: w ldr: led over 6f out: rdn and hdd over 1f out: wknd ins fnl f* **66/1**

0331 **6** 1/2 **Instant Attraction (IRE)**[14] 6345 3-9-0 85 ... JackGarritty(5) 2 — 79
(Jedd O'Keeffe) *led: hdd over 6f out: chsd ldr tl over 3f out: wknd ins fnl f* **5/1**

56-3 **7** 2 **Mystery Bet (IRE)**[267] 32 4-9-0 75 ... TonyHamilton 8 — 63
(Richard Fahey) *trckd ldrs: wnt 2nd over 3f out: rdn and ev ch wl over 1f out: wknd fnl f* **20/1**

1m 48.74s (-1.36) **Going Correction** 0.0s/f (Stan)
**WFA** 3 from 4yo+ 5lb — **7** Ran SP% **111.5**
Speed ratings (Par 105): **106,105,100,100,99 99,97**
CSF £12.13 CT £63.99 TOTE £3.40: £1.70, £1.90; EX 12.10 Trifecta £76.20 Part won..
**Owner** Team Fifty **Bred** Bernard Cloney **Trained** Manton, Wilts

**FOCUS**
A solid gallop made this a good test, with the first two setting a decent standard.

## 6771 RYDER CUP IN PLAY AT TOTESPORT.COM H'CAP — 1m 1f 103y
**9:00** (9:00) (Class 6) (0-60,60) 3-Y-0+ **£2,264** (£673; £336; £168) **Stalls** Low

Form — RPR

6023 **1** **City Of Angkor Wat (IRE)**[29] 5893 4-9-3 53 ... (t) FrannyNorton 4 — 64
(Jo Hughes) *mid-div: hdwy over 3f out: rdn to ld over 1f out: edgd rt ins fnl f: styd on* **9/2**[3]

0006 **2** 1 1/4 **My Renaissance**[21] 6157 4-8-9 50 ... JackGarritty(5) 6 — 58
(Ben Case) *s.i.s: hld up: hdwy over 2f out: rdn to chse wnr fnl f: no ex towards fin* **50/1**

6060 **3** 1 3/4 **Divine Rule (IRE)**[9] 6481 6-8-11 52 ... (v) JennyPowell(5) 13 — 56
(Laura Mongan) *s.i.s: hld up: hdwy over 1f out: r.o: nt rch ldrs* **50/1**

0450 **4** 1 **Stanlow**[12] 6407 4-9-5 55 ... (p) ShaneKelly 9 — 57
(Daniel Mark Loughnane) *chsd ldr tl led 3f out: rdn and hdd over 1f out: no ex ins fnl f* **9/1**

-041 **5** 1 1/4 **Hidden Asset**[23] 6076 4-9-3 53 ... AndrewMullen 2 — 53
(Michael Appleby) *prom: rdn over 2f out: no ex fnl f* **7/4**[1]

0024 **6** 1 1/2 **Fiftyshadesdarker (IRE)**[7] 6567 3-9-3 58 ... PatCosgrave 10 — 55
(George Baker) *hld up: hdwy over 3f out: rdn over 1f out: wknd ins fnl f* **5/1**

006- **7** 2 3/4 **Ferngrove (USA)**[375] 6485 3-8-13 57 ... DannyBrock(3) 3 — 49
(Jonathan Portman) *led: racd keenly: rdn and hdd 3f out: wknd fnl f* **8/1**

0300 **8** 7 **Prostate Awareness (IRE)**[53] 4998 3-9-0 55 ... AndrewElliott 5 — 32
(Patrick Holmes) *chsd ldrs: pushed along and lost pl over 6f out: wknd over 3f out* **50/1**

5606 **9** 1 **Poor Duke (IRE)**[16] 6267 4-9-5 55 ... (be) JoeFanning 1 — 29
(Michael Mullineaux) *hld up: a in rr: eased ins fnl f* **20/1**

254 **10** 1/2 **Mr Lando**[40] 5502 5-9-10 60 ... LukeMorris 12 — 33
(Tony Carroll) *chsd ldrs: rdn over 3f out: sn wknd* **12/1**

5341 **11** 2 **Anginola (IRE)**[12] 6394 5-9-8 58 ... (b) KierenFallon 7 — 27
(David Dennis) *prom: rdn over 2f out: wknd over 1f out* **4/1**[2]

0030 **12** 10 **Delightful Sleep**[33] 5751 6-9-2 52 ... AdamKirby 8
(David Evans) *hld up: nt clr run over 3f out: hdwy u.p over 1f out: btn whn virtually p.u wl ins fnl f* **12/1**

2m 0.97s (0.17) **Going Correction** 0.0s/f (Stan)
**WFA** 3 from 4yo+ 5lb — **12** Ran SP% **138.4**
Speed ratings (Par 101): **99,97,96,95,94 93,90,84,83,83 81,72**
CSF £243.61 CT £9965.66 TOTE £4.10: £1.50, £15.40, £7.10; EX 292.60 Trifecta £2051.90.
**Owner** Mrs Joanna Hughes **Bred** T Jones **Trained** Lambourn, Berks

**FOCUS**
This moderate handicap was run at a decent gallop but there were plenty scrapping it out in the straight.
T/Plt: £4.30 to a £1 stake. Pool: £68,345.08 - 11,581.77 winning units. T/Qpdt: £1.70 to a £1 stake. Pool: £7997.30 - 3342.86 winning units. CR

6772 - 6777a (Foreign Racing) - See Raceform Interactive

# 4524 COLOGNE (R-H)
Saturday, September 27

**OFFICIAL GOING: Turf: soft**

## 6778a PREIS DES VERLAGES M. DUMONT SCHAUBERG - WINTERKONIGIN-TRIAL (LISTED RACE) (2YO FILLIES) (TURF) — 7f 110y
**3:30** (12:00) 2-Y-0 **£11,666** (£5,416; £2,500; £1,250)

RPR

**1** **Weichsel (GER)** 2-8-11 0 ... AHelfenbein 8 — 96
(Markus Klug, Germany) **13/10**[1]

**2** nse **Rose Rized (GER)** 2-8-11 0 ... DanielePorcu 3 — 96
(P Schiergen, Germany) **136/10**

**3** 1/2 **Amabelle (GER)** 2-8-11 0 ... APietsch 4 — 95
(Waldemar Hickst, Germany) **56/10**[3]

**4** 1 1/2 **Bailey (FR)** 2-8-11 0 ... EPedroza 7 — 91
(A Wohler, Germany) **44/5**

**5** 3 **Publilia**[35] 5664 2-9-2 0 ... IoritzMendizabal 6 — 89
(Mark Johnston) *led on rail: rdn 3f out: hdd ent fnl f: sn no ex and btn: fdd and dropped to 5th* **2/1**[2]

**6** 3/4 **Tuscany (GER)** 2-9-2 0 ... DennisSchiergen 1 — 87
(P Schiergen, Germany) **192/10**

**7** 3 **Sign Your Name (GER)**[67] 4524 2-9-0 0 ... StefanieHofer 2 — 78
(Mario Hofer, Germany) **116/10**

**8** 13 **Woomera** 2-9-2 0 ... WPanov 5 — 50
(H-J Groschel, Germany) **113/10**

1m 34.37s (94.37) — **8** Ran SP% **130.0**
WIN (incl. 10 euro stake): 23. PLACES: 14, 31, 18. SF: 165.
**Owner** Gestut Rottgen **Bred** Gestut Rottgen **Trained** Germany

6779 - 6782a (Foreign Racing) - See Raceform Interactive

# 6261 EPSOM (L-H)
Sunday, September 28

**OFFICIAL GOING: Good (good to firm in places in home straight; 8.0)**
Wind: Light; half behind Weather: Sunny and quite warm

## 6783 TOTEJACKPOT GO FOR THE BIG ONE NURSERY H'CAP (BOBIS RACE) — 7f
**2:10** (2:10) (Class 4) (0-85,85) 2-Y-0 **£7,115** (£2,117; £1,058; £529) **Stalls** Low

Form — RPR

6321 **1** **Fieldsman (USA)**[20] 6190 2-9-7 **85** ... GeorgeBaker 4 — 94+
(Ed Dunlop) *mde all: shkn up and readily asserted over 1f out: r.o wl: comf* **7/4**[1]

422 **2** 2 **Evening Rain (USA)**[29] 5921 2-9-2 **80** ... JamesDoyle 1 — 83
(Saeed bin Suroor) *chsd ldrs: rdn and effrt to chse wnr 2f out: drvn and styd on same pce fr over 1f out* **11/4**[2]

0105 **3** 1 1/4 **Guiding Light (IRE)**[33] 5782 2-8-10 **74** ... OisinMurphy 5 — 74
(Andrew Balding) *chsd ldr tl wl over 1f out: 3rd and kpt on same pce u.p after* **20/1**

2011 **4** 3/4 **Harlequin Striker (IRE)**[8] 6550 2-9-0 **81** ... CharlesBishop(3) 2 — 79
(Mick Channon) *hld up in midfield: swtchd rt and rdn over 3f out: 4th and styd on same pce fnl 2f* **5/1**[3]

1460 **5** *4 ½* **Ventura Shadow**[14] 6375 2-8-8 **72**.................................. PaulHanagan 8 57
(Richard Fahey) *stdd s: hld up in midfield: rdn outpcd 3f out: no ch fnl 2f* **16/1**

015 **6** *nk* **Pasticcio**[37] 5645 2-9-0 **78**.................................. WilliamBuick 7 63
(Charlie Appleby) *hld up in last pair: rdn 3f out: no hdwy: n.d* **6/1**

2252 **7** *2 ½* **Pivot Point (IRE)**[13] 6393 2-8-11 **75**..........................(b[1]) RichardHughes 6 53
(Brian Meehan) *hld up in last pair: pushed along and no hdwy over 2f out: n.d* **12/1**

1m 23.4s (0.10) **Going Correction** 0.0s/f (Good) **7** Ran SP% **112.3**
Speed ratings (Par 97): **99,96,95,94,89 88,86**
CSF £6.42 CT £64.26 TOTE £2.40: £1.10, £2.10; EX 5.80 Trifecta £84.20.
**Owner** Highclere Thoroughbred Racing- Hard Spun **Bred** H Sexton, S Sexton & Silver Fern Farm **Trained** Newmarket, Suffolk

**FOCUS**
Rail out up to 7yds from 1m to Winning Post and 7f races increased by 15yds and the rest by 20yds. In a decent nursery, the winner was allowed to bowl along in front doing his own thing and never looked like being overhauled. The runner-up helps set the opening level.

## 6784 TOTEPLACEPOT AVAILABLE ON ARC DAY CONDITIONS STKS (BOBIS RACE) 1m 114y

**2:45** (2:46) (Class 3) 2-Y-O **£8,715** (£2,609; £1,304; £652) **Stalls** Low

Form RPR

1 **1** **Christophermarlowe (USA)**[16] 6300 2-9-0 0.................. WilliamBuick 3 97+
(John Gosden) *hld up in 3rd: effrt over 2f out: rdn and hdwy over 1f out: led fnl 150yds: styd on wl and gng away towards fin: comf* **4/6**[1]

212 **2** *1* **Good Contact (USA)**[26] 6004 2-9-0 95.................. JamesDoyle 1 93
(Saeed bin Suroor) *led: rdn and hung rt 2f out: drvn and pressed over 1f out: hdd fnl 150yds: kpt on* **3/1**[2]

2312 **3** *5* **Marshall Jennings (IRE)**[15] 6331 2-8-11 88.............. RichardHughes 4 79
(Richard Hannon) *chsd ldrs: swtchd lft wl over 1f out: drvn and pressed wnr over 1f out tl ins fnl f: wknd* **7/2**[3]

**4** *8* **Henryhudsonbridge (USA)** 2-8-8 0.............................. MartinLane 2 58
(Brian Meehan) *in tch in rr: pushed along and no hdwy over 2f out: lost tch over 1f out* **50/1**

1m 44.52s (-1.58) **Going Correction** 0.0s/f (Good) **4** Ran SP% **109.2**
Speed ratings (Par 99): **107,106,101,94**
CSF £3.03 TOTE £1.50; EX 2.80 Trifecta £4.10.
**Owner** Michael Tabor **Bred** Dress Rehearsal Syndicate **Trained** Newmarket, Suffolk

**FOCUS**
The standard of this conditions event looks good and it was run at a solid pace. The runner-up has been rated to form.

## 6785 TOTEQUADPOT FOUR PLACES IN FOUR RACES H'CAP (BOBIS RACE) 1m 114y

**3:20** (3:21) (Class 3) (0-90,88) 3-Y-O
**£12,450** (£3,728; £1,864; £932; £466; £234) **Stalls** Low

Form RPR

1511 **1** **Gratzie**[17] 6262 3-8-9 79.................................. CharlesBishop(3) 3 88
(Mick Channon) *in tch in midfield: rdn and effrt 2f out: drvn and chsd ldr over 1f out: led ins fnl f: kpt on wl: rdn out* **13/2**[3]

0206 **2** *½* **Pupil (IRE)**[35] 5720 3-9-7 88.............................. RichardHughes 5 96
(Richard Hannon) *led: rdn and kicked clr ent fnl 2f: drvn and pressed 1f out: hdd and styd on same pce ins fnl f* **7/2**[1]

1014 **3** *1 ½* **Between Wickets**[16] 6301 3-9-5 86.............................. ShaneKelly 1 91
(Marcus Tregoning) *hld up in tch in last pair: swtchd lft and effrt 2f out: chsd ldng pair over 1f out: keeping on same pce whn swtchd rt wl ins fnl f* **4/1**[2]

4113 **4** *1 ¼* **Merry Me (IRE)**[16] 6301 3-9-4 85.............................. JimCrowley 7 87
(Andrew Balding) *hld up in tch in last pair: rdn and effrt 4f out: chsd ldng trio over 1f out: no imp fnl f* **7/2**[1]

0102 **5** *5* **Hiking (USA)**[37] 5627 3-9-5 86.............................. JamesDoyle 4 76
(Roger Charlton) *chsd ldr: rdn ent fnl 2f: lost pl over 1f out: wl btn and edgd lft ins fnl f: eased towards fin* **7/2**[1]

2051 **6** *2 ¼* **Lockhart (IRE)**[11] 6466 3-9-4 85..........................(b) FrannyNorton 2 70
(Mark Johnston) *chsd ldrs: effrt on inner 2f out: unable qck and btn over 1f out: bhd and eased wl ins fnl f* **8/1**

1m 44.39s (-1.71) **Going Correction** 0.0s/f (Good) **6** Ran SP% **111.1**
Speed ratings (Par 105): **107,106,105,104,99 97**
CSF £28.50 TOTE £6.60: £2.60, £2.20; EX 31.40 Trifecta £107.20.
**Owner** C Corbett, David Hudd, Chris Wright **Bred** John Troy & Robert Levitt **Trained** West Ilsley, Berks

**FOCUS**
Most of the field in this decent handicap were in good form beforehand. They went a medium pace until stepping it up in the straight.

## 6786 TOTEEXACTA PICK THE 1, 2 H'CAP 1m 2f 18y

**3:55** (3:56) (Class 3) (0-95,91) 3-Y-O+
**£15,562** (£4,660; £2,330; £1,165; £582; £292) **Stalls** Low

Form RPR

1153 **1** **Yaakooum (IRE)**[9] 6518 3-8-11 84.............................. RichardHughes 1 92
(Richard Hannon) *taken down early: chsd ldrs tl led over 8f out: mde rest: rdn 2f out: drvn ins fnl f: hld on gamely cl home* **10/3**[1]

0442 **2** *nk* **Pasaka Boy**[34] 5757 4-9-4 85.............................. RichardKingscote 9 92
(Jonathan Portman) *in tch in midfield: hdwy to chse wnr ent fnl 2f: drvn over 1f out: styd on u.p wl fnl 100yds: nt quite rch wnr* **5/1**

515 **3** *hd* **Lungarno Palace (USA)**[63] 4698 3-8-10 83.............................. MartinLane 4 89
(John Gallagher) *hld up in last pair: swtchd rt over 1f out: hdwy u.p 1f out: edging lft but str run ins fnl f: nt quite rch ldrs* **25/1**

6143 **4** *1* **Jalingo (IRE)**[14] 6357 3-8-10 83.............................. FrannyNorton 5 87
(Mark Johnston) *in tch in midfield: rdn and effrt to chse ldrs on inner 2f out: styd on same pce ins fnl f* **9/2**[3]

601 **5** *½* **Stormardal (IRE)**[33] 5792 3-9-4 91.............................. JimCrowley 3 94
(Ismail Mohammed) *wl in tch in midfield: rdn and clsd to chse ldrs over 1f out: nt clrest of runs and one pce fnl f* **8/1**

1541 **6** *hd* **Jakey (IRE)**[87] 3878 4-9-2 83.............................. TedDurcan 7 85
(Pat Phelan) *hld up in last pair: hdwy u.p 1f out: edging lft down camber ins fnl f: nt enough room and hld fnl 100yds* **4/1**[2]

4111 **7** *9* **Starwatch**[9] 6523 7-9-8 89..........................(v) WilliamCarson 6 74
(John Bridger) *t.k.h: led for over 1f: chsd wnr after tl lost pl u.p ent fnl 2f: wknd over 1f out* **12/1**

500 **8** *nk* **Weapon Of Choice (IRE)**[9] 6523 6-9-2 83..........................(t) TomQueally 2 68
(Stuart Kittow) *nt best away: sn rcvrd to chse ldrs: drvn and unable qck 2f out: wknd jst over 1f out* **20/1**

136 **9** *9* **Dolphin Village (IRE)**[26] 6005 4-9-6 87.............................. PaulHanagan 8 55
(Richard Fahey) *chsd ldrs: rdn and lost pl over 2f out: wl bhd fnl f* **10/1**

2m 7.78s (-1.92) **Going Correction** 0.0s/f (Good)
**WFA** 3 from 4yo+ 6lb **9** Ran SP% **114.4**
Speed ratings (Par 107): **107,106,106,105,105 105,98,97,90**
CSF £19.90 CT £351.79 TOTE £3.40: £1.30, £2.30, £6.70; EX 20.50 Trifecta £366.10.
**Owner** Saeed H Al Tayer **Bred** George Kent **Trained** East Everleigh, Wilts

**FOCUS**
In a competitive and above-average handicap, the pace was fair to all, with the front-running winner contesting the finish with two more patiently ridden rivals.

## 6787 TOTEPOOL IJF APPRENTICES' DERBY H'CAP 1m 4f 10y

**4:30** (4:31) (Class 4) (0-80,75) 3-Y-O+ **£7,762** (£2,310; £1,154; £577) **Stalls** Centre

Form RPR

4262 **1** **Majestic Sun (IRE)**[8] 6564 3-8-7 67.............................. JordanNason(5) 8 76
(Peter Chapple-Hyam) *taken down early: hld up in last pair: rdn and hdwy on outer over 1f out: chal ins fnl f: r.o wl to ld towards fin* **7/2**[2]

6612 **2** *½* **Whinging Willie (IRE)**[17] 6264 5-9-9 75.................... HectorCrouch(5) 3 83
(Gary Moore) *hld up in last pair: rdn and hdwy on outer over 1f out: led fnl 150yds: r.o u.p: hdd and no ex towards fin* **6/1**

0531 **3** *1 ½* **Right Of Appeal**[7] 6579 3-8-10 72 6ex................ AhmadAlSubousi(7) 10 77
(Mark Johnston) *hld up in midfield: rdn and hdwy to ld over 1f out: hdd fnl 150yds: no ex and outpcd fnl 100yds* **4/1**[3]

0405 **4** *nk* **Lady Of Yue**[34] 5756 4-9-5 66.............................. RobertTart 9 71
(Eugene Stanford) *hld up in last trio: rdn and effrt 2f out: no imp whn carried lft over 1f out: hdwy ins fnl f: styd on wl fnl 100yds: nt rch ldrs* **9/1**

1403 **5** *2 ¾* **Play Street**[14] 6365 5-9-5 71.............................. NedCurtis(5) 2 72
(Jonathan Portman) *in tch in midfield: swtchd rt and effrt over 2f out: chsd ldrs and drvn over 1f out: wknd ins fnl f* **20/1**

5105 **6** *1* **Highlife Dancer**[13] 6395 6-8-9 63..........................(v) PaddyPilley(7) 7 62
(Mick Channon) *led tl 9f out: rdn over 2f out: ev ch 2f out tl over 1f out: wknd ins fnl f* **25/1**

3325 **7** *nk* **Sandy Cove**[25] 6037 3-8-12 67.............................. RyanTate 4 66
(James Eustace) *chsd ldrs: rdn ent fnl 2f: outpcd and btn jst over 1f out: plugged on same pce* **10/1**

-140 **8** *½* **Panettone (IRE)**[65] 4617 5-9-3 67..........................(b) ShelleyBirkett(3) 1 65
(Roger Varian) *chsd ldr tl led 9f out: clr and rdn over 2f out: hdd and no ex over 1f out: wknd ins fnl f* **20/1**

2231 **9** *2 ½* **Eton Rambler (USA)**[17] 6264 4-9-13 74.............................. OisinMurphy 6 68
(George Baker) *hld up in midfield: effrt whn squeezed out and hmpd wl over 1f out: nvr able to rcvr: bhd and eased ins fnl f* **5/2**[1]

2m 40.08s (1.18) **Going Correction** 0.0s/f (Good)
**WFA** 3 from 4yo+ 8lb **9** Ran SP% **117.5**
Speed ratings (Par 105): **96,95,94,94,92 91,91,91,89**
CSF £24.46 CT £88.03 TOTE £6.00: £2.00, £1.70, £2.10; EX 33.00 Trifecta £123.00.
**Owner** The Horse Players Two **Bred** Jocelyn Targett **Trained** Newmarket, Suffolk

**FOCUS**
The early pace was stronger than ideal for this course and distance, and that had its effect at the finish, with the first two home in this middling handicap having occupied the last two places for much of the race.

## 6788 TOTETRIFECTA PICK THE 1, 2, 3 MAIDEN STKS 1m 2f 18y

**5:05** (5:05) (Class 5) 3-Y-O **£3,881** (£1,155; £577; £288) **Stalls** Low

Form RPR

032 **1** **Too The Stars (IRE)**[26] 6002 3-9-0 75.............................. WilliamBuick 4 75
(John Gosden) *chsd clr ldr: clsd and led gng wl ent fnl 2f: pushed along and readily asserted 1f out: in command and pushed along fnl 75yds: jst lasted* **11/4**[2]

3 **2** *nse* **Ghany (IRE)**[79] 4168 3-9-0 0.............................. PaulHanagan 3 75+
(William Haggas) *hld up in last pair: clsd whn short of room 2f out: swtchd rt and sn rdn: nt handling trck and looked wl hld in 3rd over 1f out: hdwy 1f out: wnt 2nd and r.o strly fnl 100yds: jst failed* **1/3**[1]

00 **3** *2 ¼* **Zynah (IRE)**[131] 2432 3-8-7 0.............................. AhmadAlSubousi(7) 5 71
(Saeed bin Suroor) *hld up in tch in last pair: clsd and rdn to chse wnr ent fnl 2f: btn 1f out: lost 2nd fnl 100yds* **20/1**[3]

00 **4** *20* **Satchville Flyer**[10] 6483 3-9-5 0.............................. WilliamTwiston-Davies 1 49
(Brett Johnson) *racd keenly: led and sn clr: rdn and hdd ent fnl 2f: sn btn: wl bhd fnl f* **66/1**

2m 10.01s (0.31) **Going Correction** 0.0s/f (Good) **4** Ran SP% **107.9**
Speed ratings (Par 101): **98,97,96,80**
CSF £4.12 TOTE £2.70; EX 4.10 Trifecta £4.40.
**Owner** George Strawbridge **Bred** Michael D Ryan **Trained** Newmarket, Suffolk

**FOCUS**
This was a muddle of a race, with the front-running outsider being ignored by the others and the odds-on favourite looking unlucky. The overall standard was nothing special but the runner-up can step up considerably.

## 6789 COLLECT TOTEPOOL WINNINGS AT BETFRED SHOPS H'CAP 7f

**5:40** (5:41) (Class 4) (0-85,85) 3-Y-O+ **£7,762** (£2,310; £1,154; £577) **Stalls** Low

Form RPR

111 **1** **Aqua Ardens (GER)**[17] 6263 6-9-6 84..........................(t) PatCosgrave 6 93
(George Baker) *off the pce and niggled along in midfield: clsd u.p over 1f out: drvn and styd on to ld fnl 50yds: jst prevailed* **5/1**[1]

4166 **2** *nse* **Mime Dance**[16] 6285 3-8-13 80..........................(p) OisinMurphy 10 88
(Andrew Balding) *hld up off the pce in midfield: clsd u.p over 1f out: str chal wl ins fnl f: jst hld* **6/1**[2]

22-4 **3** *1* **Ortac Rock (IRE)**[29] 5913 5-8-11 75..........................(t) PaulHanagan 4 81
(Richard Fahey) *off the pce in midfield: rdn over 2f out: clsd u.p and chsd ldr jst ins fnl f: led fnl 75yds: sn hdd and no ex* **5/1**[1]

0-02 **4** *hd* **Gigawatt**[13] 6414 4-8-10 74.............................. JimCrowley 9 79+
(Jim Boyle) *stdd s: hld up wl off the pce in rr: rdn and stl plenty to do 2f out: r.o strly ins fnl f: nt rch ldrs* **16/1**

5340 **5** *nk* **Eastern Dragon (IRE)**[17] 6249 4-8-4 73.............................. NoelGarbutt(5) 14 78
(Michael Scudamore) *hld up wl off the pce in rr: rdn 2f out: r.o strly ins fnl f: nt rch ldrs* **33/1**

4113 **6** *½* **Bayleyf (IRE)**[13] 6398 5-9-1 79..........................(p) StevieDonohoe 7 82+
(Lee Carter) *sn bustled along to chse ldr and clr of field: rdn to ld over 2f out: drvn over 1f out: hdd fnl 75yds: wknd cl home* **12/1**

1352 **7** *1* **Mister Musicmaster**[17] 6249 5-9-1 79.............................. FrannyNorton 1 80
(Ron Hodges) *chsd ldrs and clr of field: rdn over 2f out: styd on to go 2nd briefly 1f out: plugged on same pce fnl 150yds* **12/1**

6043 **8** *½* **Charles Molson**[12] 6424 3-9-1 85.............................. AmyScott(3) 13 86
(Henry Candy) *stdd s: hld up wl off the pce in last: pushed along on inner over 2f out: gd hdwy 1f out: clsng but nvr gng to rch ldrs whn cannoned into rival and hmpd towards fin* **12/1**

0000 **9** *nk* **Birdman (IRE)**[15] 6334 4-9-1 79....................................(be) MartinLane 3 78
(David Simcock) *taken down early: dwlt: sn in midfield but off the pce: rdn over 2f out: clsd over 1f out: keeping on same pce whn short of room ins fnl f* **25/1**

1604 **10** *1* **Dr Red Eye**[16] 6281 6-9-4 82....................................(p) TomQueally 2 78
(Scott Dixon) *led and sn clr w rival: hdd and rdn over 2f out: kpt on tl btn jst ins fnl f: wknd fnl 75yds* **6/1**[2]

0005 **11** *5* **Brocklebank (IRE)**[17] 6263 5-8-8 72............... WilliamTwiston-Davies 5 55
(Simon Dow) *stdd s: hld up wl off the pce in rr: effrt over 2f out: no real prog: n.d* **10/1**[3]

3315 **12** *6* **Ixelles Diamond (IRE)**[23] 6112 3-8-5 77................... SammyJoBell(5) 8 44
(Richard Fahey) *off the pce in midfield: rdn and no hdwy over 2f out: bhd over 1f out* **11/1**

3520 **P** **Intomist (IRE)**[17] 6263 5-8-7 71 oh1........................... WilliamCarson 11
(Jim Boyle) *chsd ldrs and clr in ldng quartet tl lost action and p.u 4f out: fatally injured* **20/1**

1m 23.04s (-0.26) **Going Correction** 0.0s/f (Good)
**WFA** 3 from 4yo+ 3lb **13** Ran SP% **119.8**
Speed ratings (Par 105): **101,100,99,99,99 98,97,96,96,95 89,82,**
CSF £33.20 CT £166.16 TOTE £5.00: £1.70, £2.20, £4.10; EX 33.70 Trifecta £137.50.
**Owner** C.E.S Baker **Bred** Gestut Karlshof **Trained** Manton, Wilts

**FOCUS**
The field in this competitive event was soon stretched out in the face of a furious gallop set by two confirmed front-runners. It took a long time for the complexion of the race to change, but a host of strong finishers from well off the pace made sure the race went the full distance.
T/Plt: £237.20 to a £1 stake. Pool: £79,656.88 - 245.05 winning units T/Qpdt: £59.50 to a £1 stake. Pool: £5,636.55 - 70.05 winning units SP

# 6400 MUSSELBURGH (R-H)

Sunday, September 28

**OFFICIAL GOING: Good to firm (good in places; 7.4)**
Wind: Fresh; across Weather: Cloudy; dry

## 6790 BRITISH STALLION STUDS EBF MAIDEN STKS (BOBIS RACE) 7f 30y
**2:00** (2:00) (Class 4) 2-Y-O **£4,204** (£1,251; £625; £312) **Stalls** Low

Form RPR

45 **1** **Best Example (USA)**[20] 6190 2-9-5 0........................... FrederikTylicki 2 74
(Saeed bin Suroor) *trckd ldr: rdn and led over 1f out: pushed along and edgd rt ins fnl f: kpt on strly* **3/1**[2]

242 **2** *2 3/4* **Manshaa (IRE)**[16] 6279 2-9-5 77.................................... JoeFanning 3 67
(Mark Johnston) *led at modest gallop: rdn and hdd over 1f out: kpt on same pce fnl f* **1/3**[1]

**3** *2* **Penelope Pitstop** 2-9-0 0.......................................... JasonHart 4 57
(Keith Dalgleish) *t.k.h: hld up in tch: pushed along over 2f out: rallied and wandered over 1f out: kpt on: nt rch ldrs* **20/1**[3]

0 **4** *3* **Frosty Flyer (FR)**[24] 6058 2-9-5 0............................... TonyHamilton 5 54
(Richard Fahey) *t.k.h: hld up in tch: pushed along and outpcd over 2f out: n.d after* **20/1**[3]

00 **5** *8* **Pafiya**[16] 6279 2-9-5 0.................................................. TomEaves 1 33
(Kristin Stubbs) *trckd ldrs: rdn over 2f out: wknd wl over 1f out* **50/1**

1m 30.74s (1.74) **Going Correction** -0.125s/f (Firm) **5** Ran SP% **111.5**
Speed ratings (Par 97): **85,81,79,76,67**
CSF £4.47 TOTE £4.20: £1.50, £1.02; EX 5.10 Trifecta £13.60.
**Owner** Godolphin **Bred** Darley **Trained** Newmarket, Suffolk

**FOCUS**
Stands bend moved out 4m, bottom bend moved in 3m. The runner-up has been rated a bit below form.

## 6791 ROYAL REGIMENT OF SCOTLAND NURSERY H'CAP 5f
**2:30** (2:30) (Class 6) (0-65,66) 2-Y-O **£3,234** (£962; £481; £240) **Stalls** High

Form RPR

5442 **1** **The Wispe**[31] 5845 2-9-7 64........................................ GrahamLee 8 70+
(Robert Cowell) *trckd ldrs: nt clr run wl over 1f out: led appr fnl f: rdn and r.o wl* **4/1**[3]

4440 **2** *1 1/4* **Surrey Pink (FR)**[25] 6040 2-7-13 47.......................(p) CamHardie(5) 3 48
(William Muir) *bhd: drvn after 2f: hdwy on outside over 1f out: chsd wnr ins fnl f: r.o* **14/1**

2651 **3** *1/2* **Classic Flyer**[5] 6643 2-9-9 66 6ex.......................... DanielTudhope 9 71+
(David O'Meara) *dwlt: hld up on ins: hdwy whn no room over 1f out to ins fnl f: kpt on wl: nt rch first two* **2/1**[1]

6500 **4** *2 1/2* **Shortmile Lady (IRE)**[37] 5637 2-8-11 57.................. ConnorBeasley(3) 6 47
(Michael Dods) *cl up: rdn and ev ch over 1f out: kpt on same pce fnl f* **20/1**

456 **5** *2 1/4* **Macarthurs Park (IRE)**[30] 5896 2-8-0 48........................ JoeDoyle(5) 7 30
(Alan Berry) *hld up in tch: effrt and rdn over 1f out: outpcd fnl f* **100/1**

4602 **6** *1 1/2* **Penalty Scorer**[5] 6645 2-8-2 48................................. NeilFarley(3) 5 25
(Richard Guest) *prom: drvn over 2f out: wknd fnl f* **12/1**

250 **7** *2 1/4* **Pickle Lilly Pearl**[27] 5985 2-9-0 57.......................... GrahamGibbons 4 26
(David C Griffiths) *led tl rdn and hdd appr fnl f: sn btn* **25/1**

0400 **8** *hd* **Little Sista**[13] 6401 2-8-12 55..................................... PaulMulrennan 1 23
(Bryan Smart) *disp ld tl rdn and wknd over 1f out* **14/1**

664 **9** *15* **Emirates Challenge (IRE)**[52] 5104 2-9-5 62...........(t[1]) FrederikTylicki 2
(Saeed bin Suroor) *dwlt: bhd on outside: rdn and hdwy after 2f: hung rt and wknd 2f out: eased whn no ch* **5/2**[2]

1m 1.31s (0.91) **Going Correction** +0.10s/f (Good) **9** Ran SP% **112.5**
Speed ratings (Par 93): **96,94,93,89,85 83,79,79,55**
CSF £54.19 CT £141.57 TOTE £5.00: £1.30, £3.50, £1.20; EX 60.50 Trifecta £197.10.
**Owner** Manor Farm Stud & Miss S Hoare **Bred** Manor Farm Stud (rutland) & Miss S Hoare **Trained** Six Mile Bottom, Cambs
■ Stewards' Enquiry : Daniel Tudhope one-day ban: careless riding (Oct 12)

**FOCUS**
A moderate nursery and a messy race.

## 6792 SAVE THE CHILDREN H'CAP (BOBIS RACE) 7f 30y
**3:05** (3:05) (Class 4) (0-85,85) 3-Y-O **£6,469** (£1,925; £962; £481) **Stalls** Low

Form RPR

41-2 **1** **Art Obsession (IRE)**[15] 6345 3-8-13 77..................... GrahamGibbons 2 88+
(David Barron) *t.k.h early: disp ld: rdn and led over 1f out: hung lft and hrd pressed ins fnl f: kpt on gamely* **7/2**[1]

5631 **2** *nk* **Beautiful Stranger (IRE)**[9] 6515 3-8-7 71.................(p) TomEaves 3 79
(Keith Dalgleish) *hld up: effrt on outside whn checked over 2f out: gd hdwy to dispute ld ins fnl f: kpt on: hld cl home* **12/1**

2203 **3** *2* **Crowdmania**[13] 6411 3-9-7 85.......................................... JoeFanning 4 88
(Mark Johnston) *trckd ldrs: effrt and rdn over 1f out: kpt on same pce ins fnl f* **9/2**[3]

1023 **4** *nse* **Mr McLaren**[12] 6431 3-9-4 82.................................(p) DanielTudhope 7 85
(David O'Meara) *prom: outpcd and edgd lft over 2f out: rallied ins fnl f: kpt on towards fin* **7/2**[1]

1614 **5** *1 1/4* **In Focus (IRE)**[15] 6345 3-8-11 75.................................... DavidAllan 8 74
(Alan Swinbank) *slt ld to over 1f out: drvn and kpt on same pce ins fnl f* **6/1**

3440 **6** *4 1/2* **Finn Class (IRE)**[99] 3480 3-9-2 80............................ PaulMulrennan 1 68
(Michael Dods) *hld up: outpcd 3f out: no imp fr 2f out* **4/1**[2]

0000 **7** *2* **Sandra's Diamond (IRE)**[9] 6512 3-8-9 76............(b) ConnorBeasley(3) 6 59
(Keith Dalgleish) *bmpd s: t.k.h: chsd ldrs: rdn over 3f out: outpcd and hung rt over 1f out: sn btn* **25/1**

1003 **8** *18* **Jacquotte Delahaye**[15] 6345 3-9-4 82............................ GrahamLee 5 18
(David Brown) *bmpd s: bhd: lost tch over 4f out: t.o* **16/1**

1m 28.24s (-0.76) **Going Correction** -0.125s/f (Firm) **8** Ran SP% **114.3**
Speed ratings (Par 103): **99,98,96,96,94 89,87,66**
CSF £45.59 CT £191.27 TOTE £4.10: £1.70, £2.80, £1.70; EX 45.30 Trifecta £122.00.
**Owner** D Pryde & J Cringan **Bred** Lynch Bages Ltd & Camas Park Stud **Trained** Maunby, N Yorks

## 6793 EBF STALLIONS BREEDING WINNERS FILLIES' H'CAP 1m
**3:40** (3:41) (Class 3) (0-90,90) 3-Y-O+
**£9,337** (£2,796; £1,398; £699; £349; £175) **Stalls** Low

Form RPR

14 **1** **Rekdhat (IRE)**[37] 5627 3-9-4 86.................................... GrahamLee 3 96
(Roger Varian) *prom: shkn up and hdwy to ld over 1f out: rdn and kpt on wl ins fnl f* **3/1**[1]

2113 **2** *1/2* **Who's That Chick (IRE)**[22] 6129 5-8-10 77.............. ConnorBeasley(3) 2 86
(Ralph J Smith) *t.k.h: hld up in tch: rdn over 2f out: hdwy to press wnr ins fnl f: kpt on: hld nr fin* **10/3**[2]

4600 **3** *3* **Shot In The Sun (IRE)**[10] 6476 3-8-8 81..................... JackGarritty(5) 6 83
(Richard Fahey) *prom on outside: rdn over 2f out: kpt on same pce appr fnl f* **9/2**[3]

4504 **4** *1/2* **Auction (IRE)**[22] 6129 4-9-7 90.................................. CamHardie(5) 5 91
(Ed Dunlop) *slowly away: hld: stdy hdwy after 3f: rdn and outpcd over 2f out: rallied and edgd rt over 1f out: kpt on towards fin: nvr able to chal* **3/1**[1]

5540 **5** *2 3/4* **Alpine Storm (IRE)**[6] 6616 3-8-4 72............................... JoeFanning 1 67
(Mark Johnston) *t.k.h: pressed ldr: ev ch over 2f out to over 1f out: wknd ins fnl f* **5/1**

U310 **6** *3 1/2* **Lilly Junior**[17] 6269 3-8-5 73......................................... BenCurtis 4 60
(Brian Ellison) *t.k.h: led: rdn and hdd over 1f out: sn wknd* **18/1**

1m 38.71s (-2.49) **Going Correction** -0.125s/f (Firm)
**WFA** 3 from 4yo+ 4lb **6** Ran SP% **113.2**
Speed ratings (Par 104): **107,106,103,103,100 96**
CSF £13.50 TOTE £3.10: £2.20, £1.90; EX 10.30 Trifecta £37.80.
**Owner** Sheikh Ahmed Al Maktoum **Bred** Darley **Trained** Newmarket, Suffolk

**FOCUS**
Just the top two in this 0-90 handicap boasted marks within 12lb of the ratings ceiling, but it still looked a decent contest and the pace was generous.

## 6794 ROYAL SCOTS H'CAP 1m 5f
**4:15** (4:15) (Class 3) (0-90,85) 3-Y-O+ **£10,997** (£3,272; £1,635; £817) **Stalls** Centre

Form RPR

0120 **1** **Hidden Gold (IRE)**[22] 6127 3-9-5 85............................ FrederikTylicki 8 95
(Saeed bin Suroor) *in tch on outside: hdwy and cl up after 4f: rdn to ld over 2f out: kpt on strly fnl f* **3/1**[2]

6021 **2** *1 3/4* **Buthelezi (USA)**[8] 6536 6-10-0 85.................................. BenCurtis 2 92
(Brian Ellison) *trckd ldrs: rdn and outpcd over 2f out: rallied to chse wnr ins fnl f: kpt on: no imp* **3/1**[2]

2053 **3** *2* **Dark Ruler (IRE)**[8] 6536 5-9-13 84................................ DavidAllan 5 88
(Alan Swinbank) *hld up: rdn and effrt over 2f out: kpt on ins fnl f: nvr able to chal* **4/1**[3]

1511 **4** *nk* **Leaderene**[11] 6450 3-8-12 78...................................... JoeFanning 4 82
(Mark Johnston) *t.k.h: chsd ldrs: n.m.r and lost pl bnd after 3f: effrt and ev ch over 2f out: lost 2nd and outpcd ins fnl f* **11/4**[1]

2306 **5** *3* **High Office**[73] 4361 8-9-2 78.................................. JackGarritty(5) 6 77
(Richard Fahey) *trckd ldrs: drvn and outpcd over 2f out: hung rt and no imp over 1f out* **25/1**

3015 **6** *nk* **Merchant Of Dubai**[8] 6536 9-8-12 72.......................... GaryBartley(3) 3 71
(Jim Goldie) *hld up in tch on ins: rdn over 2f out: sn no imp* **20/1**

4444 **7** *3 1/2* **Aleksandar**[7] 6579 5-8-13 70..............................(v[1]) GrahamLee 7 63
(Jim Goldie) *led at ordinary gallop: rdn and hdd over 2f out: hung rt and wknd over 1f out* **14/1**

2m 49.16s (-2.84) **Going Correction** -0.125s/f (Firm)
**WFA** 3 from 4yo+ 9lb **7** Ran SP% **111.9**
Speed ratings (Par 107): **103,101,100,100,98 98,96**
CSF £11.89 CT £34.32 TOTE £3.70: £2.20, £2.30; EX 13.40 Trifecta £52.10.
**Owner** Godolphin **Bred** Darley **Trained** Newmarket, Suffolk
■ Stewards' Enquiry : Ben Curtis two-day ban: used whip above permitted level (Oct 12-13)

**FOCUS**
Effectively a 0-85 class 3 event, and something of a rude awakening for Leaderene, who was deprived of the early lead of her recent victories by the first-time visored Aleksandar.

## 6795 PURVIS GROUP H'CAP 1m 1f
**4:50** (4:50) (Class 5) (0-70,68) 3-Y-O+ **£3,234** (£962; £481; £240) **Stalls** Low

Form RPR

3335 **1** **Pigeon Pie**[9] 6515 3-9-1 64.......................................(b[1]) JoeFanning 3 73
(Mark Johnston) *t.k.h: cl up: led over 2f out: clr whn edgd rt over 1f out: rdn out* **7/1**

6313 **2** *2 1/4* **Tectonic (IRE)**[7] 6578 5-9-10 68..............................(p) PhillipMakin 5 71
(Keith Dalgleish) *dwlt: hld up: stdy hdwy over 2f out: chsd wnr over 1f out: edgd rt and no imp ins fnl f* **11/4**[2]

4442 **3** *1 3/4* **Outlaw Torn (IRE)**[6] 6601 5-8-13 62..........................(e) CamHardie(5) 2 62
(Richard Guest) *t.k.h: led to over 2f out: rallied: kpt on same pce appr fnl f* **15/8**[1]

5304 **4** *1* **Edas**[5] 6628 12-8-10 54 oh6........................................... GrahamLee 6 52
(Thomas Cuthbert) *hld up: rdn over 2f out: rallied whn n.m.r briefly wl over 1f out: sn no imp* **28/1**

41-6 **5** *4 1/2* **Haymarket**[10] 6477 5-9-8 66...................................... DanielTudhope 7 54
(R Mike Smith) *prom: drvn over 2f out: wknd over 1f out* **5/1**[3]

4565 **6** *1 3/4* **Order Of Service**[10] 6478 4-9-6 67.............................. GaryBartley(3) 8 51
(Jim Goldie) *t.k.h: cl up: drvn and outpcd 1/2-way: rallied over 2f out: edgd rt and wknd over 1f out* **7/1**

4460 7 4 **Royal Straight**[6] 6597 9-9-1 62..............................(t) ConnorBeasley(3) 4 38
(Linda Perratt) *dwlt: sn in tch: drvn over 2f out: wknd wl over 1f out* **14/1**
1m 52.97s (-0.93) **Going Correction** -0.125s/f (Firm)
**WFA** 3 from 4yo+ 5lb 7 Ran SP% **113.2**
Speed ratings (Par 103): **99,97,95,94,90 89,85**
CSF £26.04 CT £50.18 TOTE £6.00: £2.90, £1.80; EX 24.10 Trifecta £71.00.
**Owner** Ready To Run Partnership **Bred** Coln Valley Stud **Trained** Middleham Moor, N Yorks
**FOCUS**
A reasonable contest for the grade.

## 6796 UNIBET MASTERS DARTS TICKETS AVAILABLE NOW APPRENTICE H'CAP 5f
**5:20** (5:20) (Class 6) (0-60,58) 3-Y-O+ **£3,234** (£962; £481; £240) **Stalls** High

Form RPR
422 1 **Irish Girls Spirit (IRE)**[32] 5819 5-9-5 58.................... JackGarritty(3) 7 67
(Paul Midgley) *mde all: qcknd over 1f out: kpt on wl fnl f* **1/1**[1]
1000 2 ¾ **Saxonette**[6] 6595 6-9-1 54.......................................... KevinStott(3) 9 60
(Linda Perratt) *in tch: rdn and chsd wnr over 1f out: kpt on fnl f: hld towards fin* **9/2**[2]
5350 3 1 **Findog**[48] 5236 4-9-0 55.......................................... MeganCarberry(5) 8 57
(Linda Perratt) *in tch: rdn over 2f out: hdwy and edgd rt over 1f out: kpt on* **5/1**[3]
4-00 4 3 **Myjestic Melody (IRE)**[82] 4042 6-8-2 45...................... AaronJones(7) 5 37
(Shaun Harris) *dwlt: bhd and sn pushed along: hdwy fnl f: nvr rchd ldrs* **33/1**
0/0- 5 1 **Henry Morgan**[326] 7772 7-8-9 52.................................. ClaireMurray(7) 2 40
(David Brown) *prom: rdn and outpcd over 1f out: sn no ex* **9/1**
00-0 6 1 **On The High Tops (IRE)**[23] 6120 6-8-8 47.................(t) JoeDoyle(3) 6 31
(Colin Teague) *cl up tl rdn and wknd over 1f out* **25/1**
0000 7 1¾ **Fife Jo**[39] 5565 4-8-6 45..........................................(b) CamHardie(3) 4 23
(Jim Goldie) *prom: rdn over 2f out: wknd over 1f out* **16/1**
0000 8 2½ **Classy Lassy (IRE)**[11] 6454 3-8-8 45......................(b) ConnorBeasley 1 14
(Brian Ellison) *bhd on outside: drvn along 1/2-way: wknd wl over 1f out* **20/1**
20 9 1 **Busy Bimbo (IRE)**[39] 5565 5-8-13 52.........................(b) EmmaSayer(3) 3 18
(Alan Berry) *bhd and outpcd: struggling 1/2-way: nvr on terms* **16/1**
1m 0.69s (0.29) **Going Correction** +0.10s/f (Good)
**WFA** 3 from 4yo+ 1lb 9 Ran SP% **118.2**
Speed ratings (Par 101): **101,99,98,93,91 90,87,83,81**
CSF £5.65 CT £16.10 TOTE £2.10: £1.10, £1.80, £1.50; EX 7.40 Trifecta £23.90.
**Owner** Sheard, Banks, Jackson & Johnson **Bred** Seamus McMullan **Trained** Westow, N Yorks
**FOCUS**
A weak event and a very straightforward repeat race win for the favourite.
T/Jkpt: £11,241.50 to a £1 stake. Pool: £102,915.85 - 6.50 winning units T/Plt: £20.00 to a £1 stake. Pool: £78,216.96 - 2,843.52 winning units T/Qpdt: £13.00 to a £1 stake. Pool: £4,973.01 - 281.95 winning units RY

6797 - (Foreign Racing) - See Raceform Interactive

# 6369 CURRAGH (R-H)
Sunday, September 28

**OFFICIAL GOING: Good to firm**

## 6798a C.L. & M.F. WELD PARK STKS (GROUP 3) (FILLIES) 7f
**2:25** (2:25) 2-Y-O **£36,562** (£10,687; £5,062; £1,687)

RPR
1 **Qualify (IRE)**[14] 6372 2-9-0 102.................................... JosephO'Brien 6 105
(A P O'Brien, Ire) *hld up in rr tl gd hdwy on outer over 1f out: led ins fnl f and pushed clr clsng stages* **9/4**[2]
2 3 **Lola Beaux**[21] 6175 2-9-0 ................................................. FMBerry 3 97
(Mrs John Harrington, Ire) *trckd ldrs in 3rd: rdn along 2f out: disp ld briefly appr fnl f but sn hdd: kpt on same pce: no imp on wnr clsng stages* **11/2**[3]
3 shd **Stellar Glow (IRE)**[15] 6347 2-9-0 .............................. KevinManning 7 97
(J S Bolger, Ire) *t.k.h in 4th tl tk clsr order in 2nd 2f out: disp ld briefly appr fnl f: sn rdn in 3rd: kpt on same pce* **10/11**[1]
4 5 **Stormfly (IRE)**[91] 3763 2-9-0 ........................................ PatSmullen 1 83
(D K Weld, Ire) *hld up in 5th: rdn along in rr under 2f out: kpt on one pce into 4th fnl 100yds: nvr on terms* **14/1**
5 ¾ **Ask Me Nicely (IRE)**[15] 6347 2-9-0 ....................(p) SeamieHeffernan 4 81
(A P O'Brien, Ire) *led narrowly tl hdd appr fnl f: sn no ex* **33/1**
6 1 **Queen Anne (IRE)**[13] 6415 2-9-0 87................................ WayneLordan 5 78
(W McCreery, Ire) *t.k.h and sn pressed ldr in 2nd: rdn along over 2f out and sn wknd* **20/1**
1m 22.65s (-8.15) **Going Correction** -0.85s/f (Hard) 6 Ran SP% **112.9**
Speed ratings: **112,108,108,102,101 100**
CSF £15.00 TOTE £2.70: £1.50, £2.10; DF 13.70 Trifecta £22.90.
**Owner** Louis Ronan & Mrs Kate Ronan **Bred** Whisperview Trading Ltd **Trained** Cashel, Co Tipperary
**FOCUS**
A smart Group 3 with a bizarre market, the third available at 7-2 on Friday and going off odds-on. The time was a good deal quicker than the opening maiden and the winner was not fully extended.

## 6800a JUDDMONTE BERESFORD STKS (GROUP 2) 1m
**3:30** (3:30) 2-Y-O **£54,166** (£15,833; £7,500; £2,500)

RPR
1 **Ol' Man River (IRE)**[28] 5952 2-9-3 ............................... JosephO'Brien 1 114+
(A P O'Brien, Ire) *chsd ldrs in 4th: tk clsr order over 2f out: qcknd wl to ld appr fnl f and sn clr: styd on wl* **1/2**[1]
2 2¾ **Clonard Street**[57] 4926 2-9-3 ............................................. FMBerry 2 105
(A J Martin, Ire) *hld up in 5th: rdn along under 2f out: prog into 4th 1f out: styd on wl into 2nd cl home: nt trble wnr* **20/1**
3 ¾ **Battle Of Marathon (USA)**[92] 3738 2-9-3 100....(b[1]) SeamieHeffernan 6 103
(A P O'Brien, Ire) *trckd ldrs in 3rd: sn pressed ldr in 2nd tl rdn and nt qckn in 3rd appr fnl f: kpt on same pce* **25/1**
4 hd **Convergence (IRE)**[35] 5735 2-9-3 105............................. GaryCarroll 4 103
(G M Lyons, Ire) *trckd ldr in 2nd: sn 3rd: rdn and nt qckn appr fnl f in 4th: kpt on same pce* **12/1**[3]
5 1 **Tombelaine (USA)**[15] 6348 2-9-3 105................................ PatSmullen 3 101
(D K Weld, Ire) *sn led narrowly: hdd appr fnl f and sn no match for wnr: no imp and dropped to 5th cl home where squeezed for room on inner* **5/2**[2]
6 2¾ **Solomon Northup (USA)**[66] 4596 2-9-3 ........................ WayneLordan 7 94
(Charles O'Brien, Ire) *slowaly away and in rr thrght: rdn and no imp appr fnl f: kpt on one pce* **100/1**
1m 39.38s (-6.62) **Going Correction** -0.85s/f (Hard) 6 Ran SP% **112.5**
Speed ratings: **99,96,95,95,94 91**
CSF £14.35 TOTE £1.30: £1.10, £3.70; DF 10.80 Trifecta £76.40.
**Owner** Mrs John Magnier & Michael Tabor & Derrick Smith **Bred** Michael D Ryan **Trained** Cashel, Co Tipperary
**FOCUS**
This looked a relatively winnable Beresford but, given the list of horses who have scored in this race, the winner always needs respecting.

6801 - 6805a (Foreign Racing) - See Raceform Interactive

# 6778 COLOGNE (R-H)
Sunday, September 28

**OFFICIAL GOING: Turf: good to soft**

## 6806a 52ND PREIS VON EUROPA (GROUP 1) (3YO+) (TURF) 1m 4f
**3:50** (12:00) 3-Y-0+ **£83,333** (£25,000; £12,500; £5,833; £2,500)

RPR
1 **Empoli (GER)**[28] 5962 4-9-6 0.......................................... AdriedeVries 1 112
(P Schiergen, Germany) *a.p on inner: rdn and running on whn nt clr run as ldr edgd rt 1 1/2f out: swtchd outside and rdn over 1f out: styd on gamely u.p to ld fnl 50yds* **103/10**
2 ½ **Earl Of Tinsdal (GER)**[49] 5231 6-9-6 0................................ EPedroza 5 111
(A Wohler, Germany) *led: set stdy gallop: kicked for home 2 1/2f out: edgd rt and blocked eventual wnr 1 1/2f out: hrd rdn but 2 l clr over 1f out: kpt on gamely u.p: hdd 50yds out: no ex* **63/10**
3 1½ **Night Wish (GER)**[21] 6180 4-9-6 0....................................... APietsch 9 109+
(W Figge, Germany) *w.w towards rr: hdwy 3f out: 6th and styng on 2f out: rdn 1 1/2f out: kpt on fnl f but nvr enough pce to trble first two* **69/10**
4 2½ **Girolamo (GER)**[43] 5432 5-9-6 0.................................... DanielePorcu 3 105
(P Schiergen, Germany) *midfield on inner: 5th and swtchd to outer 2 1/2f out: styd on u.p: run flattened out ins fnl f* **203/10**
5 2 **Wild Chief (GER)**[84] 4007 3-8-13 0.......................... IoritzMendizabal 12 102
(J Hirschberger, Germany) *tk v t.k.h: restrained bhd ldng pair on outer: sltly outpcd and rowed along over 3f out: sn rdn and effrt 2f out: run petered out appr fnl f: plugged on at one pce* **41/10**[2]
6 4 **Papagena Star (IRE)**[56] 4955 3-8-9 0.............................. AHelfenbein 7 92
(Markus Klug, Germany) *midfield between horses: lost pl 4f out: rallied u.p fr 1 1/2f out: nvr in contention* **149/10**
7 1¼ **Guardini (FR)**[14] 6379 3-8-13 0...................................... FilipMinarik 8 94
(Jean-Pierre Carvalho, Germany) *in fnl pair on outer: effrt over 3f out: drifted rt over 2f out and no further imp: nvr able to get into the r* **3/1**[1]
8 ½ **Vif Monsieur (GER)**[21] 6184 4-9-6 0................................. KClijmans 2 92
(S Smrczek, Germany) *trckd ldr: 2nd and scrubbed along 3f out: kpt on wout qckning tl wknd over 1f out* **145/10**
9 ½ **Sirius (GER)**[21] 6180 3-8-13 0.......................................(b) SHellyn 6 92
(Andreas Lowe, Germany) *in fnl pair on inner: hdwy into midfield over 4f out: rdn and plugged on fr 2 1/2f out tl run flattened out fnl f* **9/2**[3]
10 29 **Hey Little Gorl (GER)**[15] 4-9-3 0.................................. AnthonyCrastus 4 42
(Markus Klug, Germany) *towards rr: bhd fnl 3f* **117/10**
11 11 **Amazonit (GER)**[84] 4007 3-8-13 0.............................. AntoineHamelin 10 28
(J Hirschberger, Germany) *tk v t.k.h: hld up in midfield on outer: rdn and no hdwy fr 3f out: sn btn* **145/10**
2m 30.24s (-2.66)
**WFA** 3 from 4yo+ 8lb 11 Ran SP% **129.8**
WIN (incl. 10 euro stake): 113. PLACES: 32, 25, 27. SF: 574.
**Owner** Valentin Bukhtoyarov & Evgeny Kappushev **Bred** Gestut Ebbesloh **Trained** Germany

# 6590 SAN SIRO (R-H)
Sunday, September 28

**OFFICIAL GOING: Turf: good**

## 6807a PREMIO SERGIO CUMANI (GROUP 3) (3YO+ FILLIES & MARES) (TURF) 1m
**4:10** (12:00) 3-Y-0+ **£29,166** (£12,833; £7,000; £3,500)

RPR
1 **Ming Zhi Cosmos (FR)**[21] 3-8-9 0................................... ThierryThulliez 6 101
(N Clement, France) *t.k.h: hld up on ldr's quarters: shkn up to ld over 2f out: qcknd clr and edgd rt over 1f out: drvn out fnl f: readily* **20/21**[1]
2 ½ **Love Happens**[21] 5-9-0 0.............................................. RobertHavlin 7 101
(Ferdinand J Leve, Germany) *hld up towards rr: hdwy 2f out: sn rdn: r.o u.p fnl f: nvr quite on terms w wnr* **69/10**
3 ¾ **Lady Dutch**[21] 3-8-9 0.............................................. CristianDemuro 5 98
(B Grizzetti, Italy) *t.k.h: restrained in midfield: rdn to hold pl 2 1/2f out: no immediate imp: styd on u.p fnl f but nvr quite on terms w ldrs* **77/20**[3]
4 ½ **Vague Nouvelle (IRE)**[105] 3-8-11 0.................................. MircoDemuro 4 99
(R Biondi, Italy) *trckd ldng pair: cl 3rd and ev ch over 2f out: sn rdn and edgd lft over 1f out: kpt on at one pce fnl f* **31/10**[2]
5 2½ **Must Be Me**[21] 4-9-0 0............................................... LManiezzi 3 92
(Marco Gasparini, Italy) *settled in midfield on inner: rdn and edgd lft 1 1/2f out: kpt on fnl f: nvr in contention* **102/10**
6 nk **Summer Fall (USA)**[21] 5-9-0 0.................................... DarioVargiu 8 92
(B Grizzetti, Italy) *midfield on outer: rdn 2f out: kpt on at same pce fnl f: nt pce to get on terms w ldrs* **97/10**
7 2½ **Love's Secret**[21] 3-8-9 0................................................. FBossa 2 85
(Marco Gasparini, Italy) *towards rr: outpcd in last pl 2 1/2f out: sn hrd rdn: wknd fnl f* **44/1**
8 8 **Sweet Fede**[154] 1780 3-8-9 0...................................... FabioBranca 1 67
(Stefano Botti, Italy) *led: hdd over 2f out: sn wknd: eased fnl f* **216/10**
1m 40.5s (-1.60)
**WFA** 3 from 4yo+ 4lb 8 Ran SP% **133.8**
WIN (incl. 1 euro stake): 1.96. PLACES: 1.13, 1.86, 1.79. DF: 6.26.
**Owner** Teo Ah Khing **Bred** Suc. P Lepeudry **Trained** Chantilly, France

## 6808a PREMIO VITTORIO DI CAPUA (GROUP 1) (3YO+) (TURF) 1m

4:45 (12:00) 3-Y-O+ £79,166 (£34,833; £19,000; £9,500)

RPR

1 **Priore Philip (ITY)**[126] 2589 3-8-11 0 DarioVargiu 4 112+
(Stefano Botti, Italy) *trckd ldr on rail: c down centre of trck in st: rdn to chal over 1f out: r.o wl top ld 100yds out: won a shade cosily* **61/10**[3]

2 1 3/4 **Verdetto Finale**[91] 3776 4-9-2 0 MircoDemuro 2 109
(R Biondi, Italy) *led on rail: alone on ins fr 2 1/2f out: hrd pressed fr over 1f out: hdd fnl 100yds: no ex* **181/10**

3 2 **Calyxa**[35] 5742 4-8-13 0 RobertHavlin 3 101
(Ferdinand J Leve, Germany) *w.w in midfield: hrd rdn and styd on fr 2f out: kpt on wl fnl f: nvr on terms w front two* **97/10**

4 1/2 **Magic Artist (IRE)**[25] 6054 3-8-11 0 DavidProbert 11 102
(W Figge, Germany) *w.w towards rr: pushed along and hdwy 2 1/2f out: styd on u.p fr 1 1/2f out: nt rch ldrs* **41/5**

5 1 3/4 **Amaron**[25] 6054 5-9-2 0 CristianDemuro 10 99
(Andreas Lowe, Germany) *midfield on outer: sltly outpcd and lost pl 4f out: sn rdn: kpt on u.p fr over 1 1/2f out: nvr able to get into contention* **22/5**[2]

6 1 1/2 **Salford Secret (IRE)**[133] 2376 3-8-11 0 FabioBranca 1 95
(Riccardo Santini, Italy) *midfield on inner: rdn to chse ldrs over 2f out: 3rd and hrd rdn over 1f out: fdd ins fnl f* **107/10**

7 3/4 **Kaspersky (IRE)**[112] 3-8-11 0 UmbertoRispoli 9 93
(E Botti, Italy) *chsd ldrs: rdn and nt qckn over 2f out: one pce u.p tl eased whn hld wl ins fnl f* **133/10**

8 nse **Stellar Path (FR)**[22] 3-8-8 0 AlexisBadel 8 90
(X Thomas-Demeaulte, France) *chsd ldng gp: rdn and nt qckn 2f out: fdd fnl f* **7/1**

9 snk **L'Amour De Ma Vie (USA)**[56] 4954 5-8-13 0 MickaelBarzalona 7 91
(Mme Pia Brandt, France) *t.k.h: restrained in midfield: n.m.r fr 3f out: nt clr run over 1f out: no real imp whn in clr fnl f* **1/1**[1]

10 6 **Refuse To Bobbin (IRE)**[140] 2191 4-9-2 0 GArena 5 80
(A Giorgi, Italy) *a among bkmarkers: rdn and btn fr over 2f out* **38/1**

11 2 1/2 **Passaggio (ITY)**[126] 2589 6-9-2 0 PierantonioConvertino 12 74
(A Cascio, Italy) *towards rr on outer: rdn and no imp fr over 2f out: sn btn* **86/1**

12 1 3/4 **Mr Muzzare (USA)**[140] 5-9-2 0 LManiezzi 6 70
(M Massimi Jr, Italy) *chsd ldrs: rdn and lost pl 2 1/2f out: sn wknd: bhd whn eased fnl f* **68/1**

1m 36.5s (-5.60)
**WFA** 3 from 4yo+ 4lb 12 Ran SP% **141.3**
WIN (incl. 1 euro stake): 7.09. PLACES: 2.80, 4.92, 3.39. DF: 142.58.
**Owner** Scuderia Ste Ma **Bred** Azienda Agricola Luciani Loreto **Trained** Italy

6809 - 6810a (Foreign Racing) - See Raceform Interactive

# 6355 BATH (L-H)

## Monday, September 29

**OFFICIAL GOING: Firm (9.8)**
Wind: Light, half behind Weather: Sunny spells, mild

## 6811 ARC RACING SYNDICATES NURSERY H'CAP 1m 2f 46y

2:20 (2:20) (Class 5) (0-75,69) 2-Y-O £2,587 (£770; £384; £192) Stalls Low

Form RPR

0333 1 **Kifaaya**[19] 6225 2-9-7 69 DaneO'Neill 7 73
(Mark Johnston) *dwlt: sn prom: chsd ldr 3f out: drvn to ld over 1f out: styd on wl* **6/4**[1]

5455 2 1/2 **Offshore**[18] 6250 2-9-0 62 AdamKirby 2 65
(James Tate) *w ldr: led after 2f: rdn and qcknd 3f out: hdd over 1f out: styd on* **3/1**[2]

006 3 2 3/4 **Avenue Du Monde (FR)**[15] 6361 2-8-9 57 RichardHughes 5 55
(Richard Hannon) *stdd in rr s: eased outside and hdwy 2f out: wnt 3rd over 1f out: no imp* **6/1**

6044 4 1 1/4 **Mikandy (IRE)**[18] 6250 2-8-10 61 RyanTate(3) 4 56
(Clive Cox) *handy 4th tl rdn and btn 2f out: styd on same pce fnl f* **5/1**[3]

026 5 1 **Diamond Runner (IRE)**[41] 5519 2-8-9 62 (b[1]) NoelGarbutt(5) 1 56
(Hugo Palmer) *dwlt: wnt prom after 3f: wknd over 1f out* **14/1**

5004 6 3/4 **Activation**[20] 6205 2-8-9 57 SilvestreDeSousa 6 49
(Hughie Morrison) *hld up towards rr: sme hdwy in centre 2f out: wknd over 1f out* **20/1**

6660 7 2 1/4 **Smugglers Lane (IRE)**[18] 6250 2-8-2 50 FrannyNorton 3 38
(David Evans) *led for 2f: lost pl and rdn over 4f out: wknd 2f out* **33/1**

2m 9.93s (-1.07) **Going Correction** -0.275s/f (Firm) 7 Ran SP% **110.3**
Speed ratings (Par 95): **93,92,90,89,88 88,86**
CSF £5.60 TOTE £2.00: £1.10, £2.50; EX 6.80 Trifecta £23.10.
**Owner** Hamdan Al Maktoum **Bred** M B Hawtin **Trained** Middleham Moor, N Yorks

**FOCUS**
A warm day for the time of year and firm ground. This looked a moderate staying nursery and, with the first pair dominating the final furlong, the form looks straightforward enough.

## 6812 IRISH STALLION FARMS EBF MAIDEN STKS 1m 2f 46y

2:50 (2:50) (Class 5) 2-Y-O £2,911 (£866; £432) Stalls Low

Form RPR

1 **Phyllis Maud (IRE)** 2-9-0 0 FrannyNorton 5 65+
(Mark Johnston) *dwlt: sn trcking ldr: briefly pushed along over 4f out: led 2f out: drvn clr* **5/6**[1]

0 2 7 **Illya Kuryakin**[18] 6259 2-9-5 0 JimmyFortune 2 56
(Peter Chapple-Hyam) *hld up in 3rd: rdn 4f out: veered rt 2f out: kpt on to take modest 2nd ins fnl f* **5/1**[3]

6 3 2 1/4 **Imperial War (IRE)**[16] 6317 2-9-5 0 RichardHughes 1 52
(Richard Hannon) *led tl 2f out: hrd rdn and wknd over 1f out* **7/4**[2]

2m 10.48s (-0.52) **Going Correction** -0.275s/f (Firm) 3 Ran SP% **107.6**
Speed ratings (Par 95): **91,85,83**
CSF £4.67 TOTE £1.80; EX 4.40 Trifecta £4.40.
**Owner** Abdullah Saeed Belhab **Bred** Darley **Trained** Middleham Moor, N Yorks

**FOCUS**
A modest staying maiden.

## 6813 BATHWICK CAR AND VAN HIRE H'CAP 1m 2f 46y

3:20 (3:20) (Class 5) (0-75,73) 3-Y-O+ £2,911 (£866; £432; £216) Stalls Low

Form RPR

5340 1 **Avocadeau (IRE)**[24] 6110 3-8-10 65 (p) SamHitchcott 5 72
(William Muir) *chsd ldng pair: effrt over 2f out: led over 1f out: drvn clr* **7/1**

3501 2 2 1/4 **Ana Shababiya (IRE)**[28] 5975 4-9-7 70 RichardHughes 3 73
(Ismail Mohammed) *led for 1f: chsd ldr tl led again 2f out: hrd rdn and hdd over 1f out: kpt on* **9/2**[3]

-066 3 4 **Flashheart (IRE)**[70] 4501 4-9-10 73 (t[1]) GeorgeBaker 4 68
(Marcus Tregoning) *dwlt: hld up and bhd: laboured effrt 2f out: hanging and nt striding out: wnt modest 3rd fnl 50yds* **7/4**[1]

0601 4 nk **Zambeasy**[30] 5908 3-8-13 68 RichardKingscote 2 63
(Philip Hide) *dwlt: led after 1f and racd freely: hdd 2f out: sn wknd* **5/2**[2]

2051 5 28 **Medal Of Valour (JPN)**[26] 6028 6-9-1 67 (bt) DeclanBates(3) 6 8
(Mark Gillard) *hld up: disp 3rd 4f out: drvn along 3f out: sn wknd* **7/1**

2m 7.16s (-3.84) **Going Correction** -0.275s/f (Firm)
**WFA** 3 from 4yo+ 6lb 5 Ran SP% **108.1**
Speed ratings (Par 103): **104,102,99,98,76**
CSF £34.89 TOTE £5.50: £2.80, £2.40; EX 34.70 Trifecta £142.40.
**Owner** John O'Mulloy **Bred** Wiji Bloodstock & Ceka Ltd **Trained** Lambourn, Berks

**FOCUS**
This modest handicap began to take shape turning for home and the second sets the level.

## 6814 THORN BAKER CONSTRUCTION RECRUITMENT CUP H'CAP (BOBIS RACE) 5f 11y

3:50 (3:50) (Class 4) (0-80,80) 3-Y-O £4,690 (£1,395; £697; £348) Stalls Centre

Form RPR

1-50 1 **Royal Birth**[104] 3331 3-9-1 74 OisinMurphy 3 83
(Stuart Williams) *dwlt: in tch: smooth hdwy to press ldr over 1f out: drvn to ld fnl 100yds* **8/1**

1631 2 3/4 **Red Lady (IRE)**[15] 6355 3-9-7 80 JimmyFortune 6 86
(Brian Meehan) *sn led and travelled wl in front: hrd rdn and hdd fnl 100yds: kpt on* **2/1**[1]

6500 3 1 **Threetimesalady**[24] 6089 3-9-1 74 (p) LukeMorris 7 77
(Sir Mark Prescott Bt) *dwlt: towards rr: outpcd over 2f out: styd on u.p to take 3rd ins fnl f* **8/1**

2336 4 1 1/2 **Gulland Rock**[26] 6029 3-8-7 66 oh1 SamHitchcott 1 64
(William Muir) *prom: hrd rdn over 1f out: one pce* **8/1**

3210 5 3 3/4 **The Dandy Yank (IRE)**[9] 6562 3-9-3 76 (p) AdamKirby 5 61
(Jamie Osborne) *prom tl wknd over 1f out* **8/1**

3100 6 2 1/2 **Al Senad**[37] 5677 3-9-7 80 RichardHughes 4 56
(Peter Chapple-Hyam) *prom on outer tl wknd over 1f out* **5/1**[3]

0226 7 1 1/4 **Shilla (IRE)**[16] 6314 3-8-8 70 AmyScott(3) 2 41
(Henry Candy) *s.i.s: in rr: hrd rdn 2f out: sn wknd* **4/1**[2]

1m 0.94s (-1.56) **Going Correction** -0.175s/f (Firm) 7 Ran SP% **114.4**
Speed ratings (Par 103): **105,103,102,99,93 89,87**
CSF £24.51 TOTE £9.40: £4.90, £1.70; EX 25.80 Trifecta £212.70.
**Owner** Qatar Racing Limited **Bred** Old Mill Stud & S Williams & J Parry **Trained** Newmarket, Suffolk

**FOCUS**
Not a bad 3yo sprint handicap for the class and solid form.

## 6815 STONE KING H'CAP 5f 11y

4:20 (4:23) (Class 6) (0-65,65) 3-Y-O+ £2,264 (£673; £336; £168) Stalls Centre

Form RPR

02 1 **Haadeeth**[39] 5594 7-8-13 57 (bt) SilvestreDeSousa 11 68
(David Evans) *mde all at str pce: sn 4 l clr: hrd rdn 1f out: a holding on* **7/1**[3]

1003 2 1 1/4 **Mambo Spirit (IRE)**[9] 6562 10-9-6 64 OisinMurphy 2 71
(Tony Newcombe) *off the pce towards rr: hdwy in centre to chse wnr 1f out: clsng at fin: a wl hld* **7/1**[3]

2260 3 1 3/4 **Burnt Cream**[12] 6455 7-9-3 61 (t) RobertHavlin 9 62
(Martin Bosley) *wl off the pce in rr: r.o strly fnl f: nrest at fin* **10/1**

6026 4 3/4 **Lujeanie**[19] 6236 8-9-6 64 (p) ShaneKelly 4 62
(Peter Crate) *chsd ldrs: rdn over 1f out: one pce* **20/1**

0504 5 hd **Ecliptic Sunrise**[17] 6297 3-8-1 51 NoelGarbutt(5) 3 48
(Des Donovan) *wl bhd tl rdn and hdwy over 1f out: nt rch ldrs* **25/1**

30-0 6 1 3/4 **Best Be Careful (IRE)**[52] 5154 6-9-0 65 [1] GearoidBrouder(7) 7 56
(John James Feane, Ire) *chsd ldrs tl rdn and btn over 1f out* **6/1**[2]

203 7 shd **Our Grey Lady**[15] 6356 3-8-10 60 RyanWhile(5) 12 51
(Bill Turner) *chsd wnr tl wknd 1f out* **20/1**

510 8 1 **Spray Tan**[67] 4567 4-9-0 58 LukeMorris 6 45
(Tony Carroll) *off the pce in midfield: effrt 2f out: hrd rdn and btn over 1f out* **10/1**

4110 9 3 1/4 **My Meteor**[26] 6025 7-9-4 65 DeclanBates(3) 1 41
(Tony Newcombe) *off the pce in midfield: rdn and n.d fnl 2f* **14/1**

3501 10 5 **Bilash**[18] 6273 7-9-5 63 RichardHughes 10 21
(Andrew Hollinshead) *stdd s: outpcd: a wl bhd* **7/2**[1]

450 11 8 **Anytimeatall (IRE)**[32] 5860 3-8-4 54 NatashaEaton(5) 5
(Alan Bailey) *a towards rr: rdn and no ch fnl 2f* **50/1**

1m 1.29s (-1.21) **Going Correction** -0.175s/f (Firm)
**WFA** 3 from 4yo+ 1lb 11 Ran SP% **101.7**
Speed ratings (Par 101): **102,100,97,96,95 92,92,91,85,77 65**
CSF £38.42 CT £308.22 TOTE £4.60: £1.30, £2.60, £2.50; EX 41.80 Trifecta £281.50.
**Owner** Mrs I M Folkes **Bred** Bolton Grange **Trained** Pandy, Monmouths

■ Molly Jones was withdrawn. Price at time of withdrawal 6/1. Rule 4 applies to all bets - deduction 15p in the pound.
■ Stewards' Enquiry : Oisin Murphy two-day ban: careless riding (Oct 13-14)

**FOCUS**
A moderate sprint handicap and typically wide open for the class, but the winner dominated.

## 6816 MJ CHURCH "HANDS AND HEELS" APPRENTICE SERIES H'CAP (RACING EXCELLENCE INITIATIVE) 5f 161y

4:50 (4:50) (Class 6) (0-60,60) 3-Y-O £2,264 (£673; £336; £168) Stalls Centre

Form RPR

3214 1 **Captain Ryan**[14] 6399 3-9-7 60 ChrisMeehan 4 67
(Peter Makin) *stdd s: hld up in 4th: rdn and hdwy over 1f out: led fnl 100yds: pushed out* **6/4**[1]

0502 2 nk **Wedgewood Estates**[11] 6488 3-8-11 53 AhmadAlSubousi(3) 3 59
(Tony Carroll) *chsd ldng pair: rdn to ld 2f out: hdd fnl 100yds: kpt on: comf hld* **7/2**[3]

4303 **3** *7* **Lucky Clover**[24] 6090 3-8-7 46 (v[1]) JennyPowell 2 29
(Malcolm Saunders) *led at gd pce tl 2f out: wknd over 1f out* **9/2**

6020 **4** *1 1/2* **Dylan's Centenary**[11] 6488 3-8-12 56 SophieKilloran(5) 1 34
(Rod Millman) *s.s: last and outpcd: modest effrt over 1f out: nvr able to chal* **11/4**[2]

6506 **5** *17* **Countess Lupus (IRE)**[26] 6030 3-8-7 46 oh1 (v) RobHornby 5
(Lisa Williamson) *pressed ldr tl wknd and hung rt 2f out* **33/1**

1m 10.71s (-0.49) **Going Correction** -0.175s/f (Firm) 5 Ran SP% **110.0**
Speed ratings (Par 99): **96,95,86,84,61**
CSF £7.07 TOTE £2.00: £1.10, £1.70; EX 6.50 Trifecta £12.80.
**Owner** Og Partnership **Bred** Mrs C Lloyd **Trained** Ogbourne Maisey, Wilts

**FOCUS**
A typically ordinary handicap of its type, run at a solid pace.

## 6817 NEW ARC RACING SYNDICATES H'CAP (DIV I) 1m 5f 22y
**5:20** (5:20) (Class 6) (0-60,60) 3-Y-O+ **£2,264** (£673; £336; £168) **Stalls** High

Form RPR

00-1 **1** **High Secret (IRE)**[6] 6644 3-9-1 58 6ex LukeMorris 4 73+
(Sir Mark Prescott Bt) *t.k.h: trckd ldrs: wnt 2nd over 3f out: rdn to ld over 1f out: edgd lft: styd on* **1/2**[1]

3212 **2** *3 1/2* **Reach The Beach**[18] 6252 5-9-8 56 (t) AdamKirby 6 65
(Brendan Powell) *led: hrd rdn and hdd over 1f out: kpt on same pce* **8/1**[3]

3214 **3** *9* **Noor Al Haya (IRE)**[15] 6360 4-9-5 60 CharlotteJenner(7) 2 55
(Mark Usher) *hld up in rr: hrd rdn over 2f out: styd on to take modest 3rd over 1f out* **12/1**

5000 **4** *4 1/2* **Illegale (IRE)**[32] 5864 8-8-12 46 oh1 (bt) OisinMurphy 3 33
(Nikki Evans) *rdn s: hld up in 5th: rdn over 3f out: btn 2f out* **50/1**

5332 **5** *nk* **Tunnel Tiger (IRE)**[14] 6395 3-9-3 60 RichardHughes 5 47
(William Knight) *plld hrd in 4th: wnt 3rd 3f out: wknd wl over 1f out* **3/1**[2]

3631 **6** *15* **River Du Nord (FR)**[22] 6188 7-8-9 46 oh1 JemmaMarshall(3) 7 9
(Sue Gardner) *sn trcking ldr: rdn and wknd over 3f out* **33/1**

-000 **7** *1 1/2* **Vexillum (IRE)**[11] 6486 5-9-1 52 (t[1]) CharlesBishop(3) 1 13
(Simon Hodgson) *n.m.r after 1f: sn in rr: drvn along and lost tch over 3f out* **50/1**

2m 51.34s (-0.66) **Going Correction** -0.275s/f (Firm)
**WFA** 3 from 4yo+ 9lb 7 Ran SP% **117.3**
Speed ratings (Par 101): **91,88,83,80,80 71,70**
CSF £5.96 CT £24.14 TOTE £1.60: £1.10, £3.00; EX 6.60 Trifecta £24.20.
**Owner** Charles C Walker - Osborne House **Bred** Norelands, Marston & A V Nicoll **Trained** Newmarket, Suffolk

**FOCUS**
There was a sound early pace on in this moderate handicap, but it steadied down the back and the first pair were ideally placed at the top of the home straight.

## 6818 NEW ARC RACING SYNDICATES H'CAP (DIV II) 1m 5f 22y
**5:50** (5:51) (Class 6) (0-60,60) 3-Y-O+ **£2,264** (£673; £336; £168) **Stalls** High

Form RPR

000- **1** **Jolie Blonde**[320] 7853 3-8-10 53 LukeMorris 2 63+
(Sir Mark Prescott Bt) *prom: rdn 4f out: led over 1f out: drvn out* **5/2**[2]

5646 **2** *1 1/4* **Cabuchon (GER)**[20] 6210 7-9-7 55 (t) SilvestreDeSousa 1 61
(David Evans) *mid-div: drvn along and styng on whn edgd rt 1f out: chal ins fnl f: jst hld* **8/1**[3]

4052 **3** *2 1/4* **Just Duchess**[32] 5850 4-8-12 46 oh1 DavidProbert 3 49
(Michael Blanshard) *dwlt: towards rr: hdwy in centre and hrd rdn 2f out: one pce fnl f* **16/1**

3532 **4** *1* **Hallouella**[21] 6193 3-9-3 60 (p) RichardHughes 5 61
(David Elsworth) *dwlt: in tch on outer: pressed ldr 6f out tl hrd rdn and wknd 1f out* **7/4**[1]

0460 **5** *10* **Wild Desert (FR)**[105] 3309 9-9-9 57 AdamKirby 9 49
(Tony Carroll) *led: rdn over 3f out: hdd over 1f out: sn wknd and eased* **14/1**

506 **6** *1 1/4* **St Ignatius**[39] 5600 7-9-5 58 (v) NatashaEaton(5) 6 42
(Alan Bailey) *t.k.h in rr: sme hdwy 6f out: n.d fnl 3f* **20/1**

0004 **7** *3/4* **En Reve**[30] 5904 3-8-11 54 FergusSweeney 8 37
(Seamus Durack) *stdd s: hld up towards rr: outpcd and struggling 5f out* **12/1**

4244 **8** *3 1/4* **Evergreen Forest (IRE)**[19] 6027 6-9-5 53 (bt) GeorgeBaker 4 31
(Natalie Lloyd-Beavis) *in tch tl wknd 3f out* **12/1**

0066 **U** **Bowberry**[54] 5048 3-8-12 58 RyanTate(3) 7 57
(Clive Cox) *prom: outpcd over 3f out: 5th and trying to rally whn edgd lft: hmpd and stmbld jst ins fnl f: uns rdr* **10/1**

2m 50.64s (-1.36) **Going Correction** -0.275s/f (Firm)
**WFA** 3 from 4yo+ 9lb 9 Ran SP% **117.8**
Speed ratings (Par 101): **93,92,90,90,84 83,82,80,**
CSF £23.61 CT £268.78 TOTE £4.20: £3.60, £1.50, £3.10; EX 21.00 Trifecta £150.00.
**Owner** Miss K Rausing **Bred** Miss K Rausing **Trained** Newmarket, Suffolk

**FOCUS**
The second division of the staying handicap and a quick double for Sir Mark Prescott and Luke Morris with an unexposed filly.
T/Plt: £39.00 to a £1 stake. Pool: £48,195.18 - 900.33 winning tickets T/Qpdt: £15.50 to a £1 stake. Pool: £4,077.56 - 193.76 winning tickets LM

# 6594 HAMILTON (R-H)
### Monday, September 29

**OFFICIAL GOING: Good (7.0)**
Wind: Almost nil Weather: Overcast, mild

## 6819 MARIE CURIE CANCER CARE H'CAP 5f 4y
**2:10** (2:13) (Class 6) (0-65,63) 3-Y-O+ **£2,045** (£603; £302) **Stalls** Centre

Form RPR

221 **1** **Irish Girls Spirit (IRE)**[1] 6796 5-9-3 58 GrahamLee 10 75
(Paul Midgley) *mde all and overall ldr stands' side: shkn up and qcknd clr fnl f: eased nr fin: readily* **7/4**[1]

6000 **2** *5* **Bronze Beau**[14] 6406 7-9-8 63 (t) JamesSullivan 3 62
(Kristin Stubbs) *gd spd far side: rdn 2f out: hung lft and kpt on ins fnl f: nt rch eased-down stands' side wnr* **9/1**

0012 **3** *nk* **Simply Black (IRE)**[16] 6340 3-9-7 63 (p) SamJames 2 61
(David O'Meara) *cl up far side: rdn over 2f out: carried lft ins fnl f: kpt on towards fin* **12/1**

462 **4** *2 1/4* **Rylee Mooch**[8] 6580 6-9-8 63 (e) JasonHart 8 53
(Richard Guest) *chsd wnr stands' side: rdn over 2f out: outpcd appr fnl f* **3/1**[2]

4500 **5** *1 1/2* **Rock Canyon (IRE)**[7] 6595 5-8-8 49 (p) JoeFanning 9 33
(Linda Perratt) *dwlt: bhd stands' side: sme hdwy over 1f out: nvr able to chal* **9/1**

3002 **6** *shd* **Sewn Up**[11] 6475 4-9-0 58 (p) JoeyHaynes(3) 4 42
(Keith Dalgleish) *dwlt: bhd on outside of stands' side gp: hdwy over 2f out: no imp over 1f out* **6/1**[3]

0034 **7** *2 1/2* **Mossy Marie (IRE)**[79] 4193 3-8-3 48 NeilFarley(3) 5 23
(Eric Alston) *racd centre: prom: outpcd and drvn 2f out: wkng whn drifted to far side fnl f* **25/1**

1010 **8** *3/4* **Two Turtle Doves (IRE)**[12] 6455 8-9-0 62 LewisStones(7) 7 34
(Michael Mullineaux) *prom stands' side: drvn over 2f out: wknd wl over 1f out* **16/1**

0406 **9** *7* **Sherry For Nanny (IRE)**[32] 5858 3-7-13 46 oh1 (p) JoeDoyle(5) 6
(Marjorie Fife) *hmpd s: sn in tch on outside of stands' side gp: rdn and hung rt over 2f out: sn btn* **50/1**

59.28s (-0.72) **Going Correction** -0.05s/f (Good)
**WFA** 3 from 4yo+ 1lb 9 Ran SP% **115.0**
Speed ratings (Par 101): **103,95,94,90,88 88,84,83,71**
CSF £18.70 CT £146.43 TOTE £2.30: £1.10, £3.60, £2.20; EX 23.60 Trifecta £134.70.
**Owner** Sheard, Banks, Jackson & Johnson **Bred** Seamus McMullan **Trained** Westow, N Yorks

**FOCUS**
Races four, five and seven measured approximately 25yds less than the official distances due to fresh ground being provided on the loop. As advertised, the going was good. A modest sprint handicap won decisively by a progressive mare.

## 6820 MARIE CURIE GLASGOW HOSPICE AUCTION NURSERY H'CAP 6f 5y
**2:40** (2:40) (Class 5) 2-Y-O **£3,234** (£962; £481; £240) **Stalls** High

Form RPR

6452 **1** **Straightothepoint**[8] 6574 2-8-9 69 (v) PaulMulrennan 1 75
(Bryan Smart) *wnt rt s: mde all and sn tacked over to stands' rail: rdn and clr over 1f out: kpt on strly: unchal* **7/1**

1132 **2** *3 1/4* **White Vin Jan**[7] 6610 2-8-3 66 CamHardie(3) 5 62
(Michael Bell) *in tch: rdn over 2f out: hdwy and edgd lft appr fnl f: chsd wnr ins fnl f: no imp* **7/4**[1]

1 **3** *3/4* **Gabrial The Tiger (IRE)**[16] 6319 2-8-10 75 JackGarritty(5) 3 69
(Richard Fahey) *taken early to post: chsd wnr tl rdn and outpcd over 2f out: nt clr run appr fnl f: styd on strly towards fin* **4/1**[3]

2105 **4** *hd* **Doc Charm**[10] 6510 2-9-7 81 TomEaves 2 74
(Keith Dalgleish) *t.k.h: chsd ldrs: wnt 2nd and rdn over 2f out: kpt on same pce ins fnl f* **9/4**[2]

4352 **5** *1/2* **Poolstock**[14] 6401 2-8-4 67 ConnorBeasley(3) 4 59
(Les Eyre) *hld up in tch: effrt and plld out 2f out: sn rdn: outpcd fnl f* **12/1**

1m 12.59s (0.39) **Going Correction** -0.05s/f (Good) 5 Ran SP% **107.3**
Speed ratings (Par 95): **95,90,89,89,88**
CSF £18.74 TOTE £8.20: £3.20, £1.10; EX 24.30 Trifecta £46.10.
**Owner** Crossfields Racing **Bred** Crossfields Bloodstock Ltd **Trained** Hambleton, N Yorks

**FOCUS**
An interesting nursery in which the winner made all against the stands' rail.

## 6821 JACK WEBSTER CLASSIFIED CLAIMING STKS 6f 5y
**3:10** (3:11) (Class 6) 3-Y-O+ **£2,045** (£603; £302) **Stalls** High

Form RPR

-000 **1** **Feel The Heat**[79] 4194 7-9-3 67 (v) AdamCarter(5) 2 78
(Bryan Smart) *hld up in tch: hdwy on outside over 2f out: drvn to ld ins fnl f: kpt on strly* **50/1**

0000 **2** *1 1/4* **Tango Sky (IRE)**[10] 6512 5-8-3 68 JackGarritty(5) 5 60
(Richard Fahey) *t.k.h: cl up: rdn to ld over 1f out: hdd ins fnl f: kpt on same pce* **15/8**[1]

0360 **3** *4* **Emily Davison (IRE)**[5] 6671 3-8-3 61 (p) GemmaTutty(3) 3 49
(Karen Tutty) *taken early to post: hld up bhd ldng gp: rdn over 2f out: effrt and edgd lft over 1f out: kpt on fnl f: tk 3rd last stride* **12/1**

2200 **4** *nse* **Live Dangerously**[11] 6475 4-8-13 64 CamHardie(3) 6 55
(Keith Dalgleish) *cl up: rdn over 2f out: hung rt and outpcd over 1f out* **8/1**

0530 **5** *1 1/2* **Zaitsev (IRE)**[11] 6490 4-8-9 70 JacobButterfield(3) 1 46
(Ollie Pears) *led tl rdn and hdd over 1f out: sn outpcd* **7/2**[2]

0325 **6** *3* **Madagascar Moll (IRE)**[16] 6340 3-8-6 61 (p) SamJames 7 33
(David O'Meara) *s.s: bhd and pushed along: drvn over 2f out: sn no imp* **8/1**

0000 **7** *4 1/2* **Amenable (IRE)**[12] 6455 7-9-2 69 (p) HayleyTurner 4 26
(Conor Dore) *taken early to post: cl up: outpcd and hung rt over 2f out: sn btn* **10/1**

5044 **8** *1 1/4* **Here Now And Why (IRE)**[8] 6580 7-8-3 48 (p[1]) NeilFarley(3) 8 12
(Ian Semple) *sn pushed along in rr: drvn along 1/2-way: nvr on terms* **50/1**

0336 **9** *2 1/4* **Decent Fella (IRE)**[28] 5979 8-9-0 70 (t) JoeFanning 9 13
(Ann Stokell) *sn pushed along in rr: struggling 1/2-way: sn btn* **6/1**[3]

1m 11.1s (-1.10) **Going Correction** -0.05s/f (Good)
**WFA** 3 from 4yo+ 2lb 9 Ran SP% **114.2**
Speed ratings (Par 101): **105,103,98,97,95 91,85,84,81**
CSF £142.42 TOTE £73.20: £10.70, £1.10, £3.50; EX 219.70 Trifecta £1078.20.Tango Sky was claimed by Northern Line Racing Ltd for £5,000.
**Owner** B Smart **Bred** Bearstone Stud **Trained** Hambleton, N Yorks

**FOCUS**
A fair claimer though few ran close to their best.

## 6822 AVIA SIGNS H'CAP 1m 65y
**3:40** (3:41) (Class 5) (0-75,73) 3-Y-O+ **£4,090** (£1,207; £604) **Stalls** Low

Form RPR

612 **1** **Queens Park (FR)**[86] 3950 3-9-3 73 PJMcDonald 7 82
(John Davies) *midfield: hdwy over 2f out: drvn to ld ins fnl f: hld on wl cl home* **14/1**

4403 **2** *shd* **Ellaal**[6] 6626 5-9-5 71 PaulMulrennan 8 79
(Ruth Carr) *led after 1f: stdd pce after 2f: rdn over 2f out: hdd ins fnl f: rallied: jst hld* **7/2**[1]

3132 **3** *1* **Tectonic (IRE)**[1] 6795 5-9-2 68 (p) PhillipMakin 6 74
(Keith Dalgleish) *stdd s: hld up: stdy hdwy whn nt clr run over 1f out: kpt on fnl f: hld towards fin* **5/1**[2]

4300 **4** *1/2* **Al Muheer (IRE)**[16] 6341 9-9-2 68 (v) JamesSullivan 5 73
(Ruth Carr) *taken early to post: prom: drvn along over 2f out: kpt on same pce ins fnl f* **25/1**

6604 **5** *shd* **Mandy The Nag (USA)**[40] 5573 4-8-5 62 JackGarritty(5) 10 66
(Richard Fahey) *led at decent gallop 1f: pressed ldr: rdn over 3f out: kpt on same pce fnl f* **40/1**

6312 **6** *1 1/4* **Beautiful Stranger (IRE)**[1] 6792 3-9-1 71 (p) TomEaves 2 72
(Keith Dalgleish) *dwlt: hld up: swtchd lft over 1f out: hdwy over 1f out: no imp fnl f* **5/1**[2]

0450 **7** ½ **I'm Super Too (IRE)**[32] 5855 7-9-2 68 ............................ DavidAllan 9 68
(Alan Swinbank) *in tch: drvn along 3f out: outpcd over 1f out* **11/1**

3411 **8** 2¼ **Paddy's Rock (IRE)**[32] 5854 3-8-3 66 ........................(p) RowanScott(7) 1 61
(Ann Duffield) *dwlt: hld up: drvn along 3f out: no imp fr 2f out* **6/1**[3]

43 **9** 6 **Heavenly River (FR)**[49] 5246 3-8-2 61 .............................. JoeyHaynes(3) 4 42
(K R Burke) *t.k.h: hld up towards rr: rdn over 3f out: wknd 2f out* **7/1**

6010 **10** 2¾ **Disclosure**[13] 6431 3-9-3 73 ................................................ GrahamLee 3 48
(Les Eyre) *t.k.h: hld up: stdy hdwy 3f out: rdn and wknd 2f out* **13/2**

1m 46.3s (-2.10) **Going Correction** -0.225s/f (Firm)
**WFA** 3 from 4yo+ 4lb **10** Ran SP% **117.0**
Speed ratings (Par 103): **101,100,99,99,99 98,97,95,89,86**
CSF £62.87 CT £287.29 TOTE £13.00: £3.30, £1.90, £1.50; EX 50.80 Trifecta £208.70.
**Owner** Mr & Mrs R Scott **Bred** Ecurie Des Monceaux **Trained** Piercebridge, Durham

**FOCUS**
An open-looking handicap, albeit not the strongest for the grade.

## 6823 HAMILTON PARK APPRENTICE H'CAP (HAMILTON PARK APPRENTICE SERIES FINAL) 1m 1f 36y
**4:10** (4:10) (Class 6) (0-65,70) 3-Y-0+ **£1,940** (£577; £288; £144) **Stalls** Low

Form RPR

0050 **1** **Card High (IRE)**[24] 6122 4-8-12 50 oh5 .........................(t) EmmaSayer 5 56
(Wilf Storey) *hld up in tch: stdy hdwy over 3f out: rdn over 2f out: hung rt and chsd wnr over 1f out: styd on wl to ld nr fin* **25/1**

3000 **2** nk **Prostate Awareness (IRE)**[2] 6771 3-8-12 55 ...............(v[1]) JackGarritty 4 60
(Patrick Holmes) *led: rdn over 2f out: kpt on fnl f: hdd nr fin* **11/1**

3224 **3** 2¾ **Her Red Devil (IRE)**[18] 6267 3-9-3 60 ......................... GeorgeChaloner 3 59
(Richard Fahey) *trckd ldr: drvn and ev ch over 2f out: outpcd fnl f* **2/1**[1]

2600 **4** 4½ **Taxiformissbyron**[9] 6564 4-8-7 50 oh2 ........................ RowanScott(5) 8 39
(Iain Jardine) *prom: smooth hdwy over 3f out: rdn and ch over 2f out: wknd ins fnl f* **10/1**[3]

2653 **5** 2½ **Libra Romana (IRE)**[14] 6396 3-8-7 50 .........................(p) RosieJessop 7 35
(Sir Mark Prescott Bt) *t.k.h: hld up bhd ldng gp: rdn 3f out: wknd over 1f out* **2/1**[1]

0026 **6** 13 **Neuf Des Coeurs**[10] 6516 3-9-3 60 ...................................... JoeyHaynes 1 17
(Keith Dalgleish) *hld up: hdwy on outside 4f out: rdn and wknd qckly over 2f out: t.o* **7/2**[2]

1m 57.33s (-2.37) **Going Correction** -0.225s/f (Firm)
**WFA** 3 from 4yo+ 5lb **6** Ran SP% **110.2**
Speed ratings (Par 101): **101,100,98,94,92 80**
CSF £236.20 CT £762.56 TOTE £18.90: £7.80, £5.20; EX 243.00 Trifecta £877.50.
**Owner** Gremlin Racing **Bred** John Foley **Trained** Muggleswick, Co Durham

**FOCUS**
An uncompetitive handicap for apprentice riders.

## 6824 MCTEAR'S AUCTIONEERS H'CAP 6f 5y
**4:40** (4:44) (Class 4) (0-85,84) 3-Y-0+ **£6,469** (£1,925; £962; £481) **Stalls** High

Form RPR

1010 **1** **Baron Run**[10] 6511 4-8-12 75 ........................................ JoeyHaynes(3) 9 84
(K R Burke) *mde all in centre: rdn 1/2-way: jnd over 1f out: hld on gamely towards fin* **13/2**[3]

1645 **2** nk **Classy Anne**[10] 6512 4-8-13 73 ........................................ GrahamLee 3 81
(Jim Goldie) *prom centre: rdn over 2f out: hdwy to dispute ld over 1f out to wl ins fnl f: jst hld* **9/1**

2251 **3** nk **Alexandrakollontai (IRE)**[7] 6598 4-9-5 82 6ex....(b) ConnorBeasley(3) 7 89
(Alistair Whillans) *s.i.s: bhd centre: rdn and hdwy wl over 1f out: kpt on ins fnl f* **9/2**[1]

1200 **4** 2½ **Bajan Bear**[10] 6511 6-9-7 81 ........................................ AdrianNicholls 4 80
(David Nicholls) *dwlt: hdwy in centre 1/2-way: effrt and chsng ldrs over 1f out: rdn and hung rt ins fnl f: one pce* **11/2**[2]

-500 **5** 2 **Reposer (IRE)**[6] 6639 6-9-3 77 ........................................ TomEaves 11 70
(Keith Dalgleish) *bhd centre: rdn along over 2f out: kpt on fnl f: nvr able to chal* **33/1**

1000 **6** shd **Gold Beau (FR)**[10] 6511 4-9-4 78 .................................(p) AmyRyan 8 70
(Kristin Stubbs) *midfield centre: rdn and outpcd over 2f out: kpt on fnl f: no imp* **33/1**

002 **7** 1¼ **Tellovoi (IRE)**[9] 6558 6-9-10 84 ...............................(p) JoeFanning 1 72
(Ann Stokell) *racd alone far rail: rdn over 2f out: hung rt and outpcd over 1f out* **12/1**

5120 **8** ½ **Klynch**[27] 6013 8-9-5 79 ...............................(b) JamesSullivan 5 66
(Ruth Carr) *prom centre: drvn along over 2f out: wknd appr fnl f* **16/1**

350 **9** hd **King Of Eden (IRE)**[80] 4161 8-9-1 75 .............................. DavidAllan 13 61
(Eric Alston) *cl up stands' side: rdn and hung rt 2f out: sn outpcd* **14/1**

0350 **10** 1 **Rasaman (IRE)**[10] 6511 10-9-2 79 .............................. GaryBartley(3) 2 62
(Jim Goldie) *hld up centre: rdn over 2f out: nvr able to chal* **16/1**

6310 **11** 1 **Al Khan (IRE)**[17] 6285 5-9-6 83 ..........................(p) JacobButterfield(3) 15 63
(Ollie Pears) *dwlt: bhd stands' side: drvn along 1/2-way: nvr on terms* **9/1**

655- **12** hd **Indego Blues**[335] 7594 5-9-0 74 ........................................ PaulQuinn 12 53
(David Nicholls) *hld up towards centre: pushed along 2f out: sn btn* **33/1**

0022 **13** 1½ **Enderby Spirit (GR)**[20] 6213 8-8-9 69 .............................. PaulMulrennan 16 43
(Bryan Smart) *spd stands' side tl rdn and wknd over 1f out* **9/1**

0-00 **14** 2¼ **Rodrigo De Torres**[31] 5888 7-9-9 83 .............................. JasonHart 14 50
(John Murray) *spd stands' rail tl wknd fr over 2f out* **33/1**

1m 10.98s (-1.22) **Going Correction** -0.05s/f (Good) **14** Ran SP% **114.8**
Speed ratings (Par 105): **106,105,105,101,99 99,97,96,96,95 93,93,91,88**
CSF £56.02 CT £247.29 TOTE £9.10: £3.30, £2.60, £2.00; EX 58.90 Trifecta £328.90.
**Owner** Mrs Elaine M Burke **Bred** Mrs D Hughes **Trained** Middleham Moor, N Yorks
■ Rule 4 of 5p in the pound applies to all bets; Withdrawn: Chooseday

**FOCUS**
A competitive sprint handicap in which they were spread across the track and it paid to race prominently.

## 6825 JUSTGIVING.COM/HAMILTONPARKRACECOURSE H'CAP 1m 4f 17y
**5:10** (5:11) (Class 5) (0-70,76) 3-Y-0+ **£3,234** (£962; £481; £240) **Stalls** Low

Form RPR

2241 **1** **Stanarley Pic**[7] 6596 3-9-12 76 6ex ...................................... DavidAllan 8 85
(Alan Swinbank) *prom: smooth hdwy to ld over 2f out: rdn: edgd rt and hdd over 1f out: rallied to ld ins fnl f: hld on gamely* **5/4**[1]

023 **2** hd **Dhaular Dhar (IRE)**[7] 6597 12-9-0 59 .............................. GaryBartley(3) 3 67
(Jim Goldie) *hld up: hdwy over 2f out: led over 1f out: hdd ins fnl f: rallied: hld nr fin* **12/1**[3]

05 **3** 2½ **Schmooze (IRE)**[7] 6597 5-8-13 55 ...................................... PJMcDonald 4 59
(Linda Perratt) *hld up: drvn and outpcd 4f out: rallied 2f out: kpt on fnl f: nt rch first two* **12/1**[3]

3361 **4** 2¼ **Harrison's Cave**[11] 6480 6-9-4 60 ...................................... JoeFanning 5 60
(Keith Dalgleish) *t.k.h: hld up in tch: stdy hdwy to trck ldrs over 2f out: rdn over 1f out: outpcd ins fnl f* **5/1**[2]

5463 **5** 4 **Amazing Blue Sky**[6] 6627 8-8-9 51 oh1 .............................. JamesSullivan 1 45
(Ruth Carr) *chsd ldrs: drvn along over 3f out: outpcd fr 2f out* **22/1**

4441 **6** 1¼ **Eilean Mor**[7] 6597 6-8-11 56 6ex ...................................... ConnorBeasley(3) 9 48
(R Mike Smith) *led at stdy pce 2f: cl up: rdn over 3f out: rallied: wknd over 1f out* **5/1**[2]

606 **7** 3¼ **Vittachi**[69] 4520 7-8-11 53 ................................................(p) JasonHart 2 40
(Alistair Whillans) *hld up in tch: drvn and outpcd over 3f out: n.d after* **12/1**[3]

0005 **8** 3¼ **Hero's Story**[32] 5856 4-8-9 51 oh1 ..........................(v) GrahamLee 6 33
(Jim Goldie) *led after 2f and set stdy pce: qcknd over 4f out: rdn and hdd over 2f out: wknd wl over 1f out* **25/1**

500 **9** 71 **Legal Advisor**[64] 4713 3-7-12 51 oh1 .............................. JoeyHaynes(3) 7
(Philip Kirby) *s.i.s: hld up: struggling over 4f out: sn lost tch and eased* **22/1**

2m 34.43s (-4.17) **Going Correction** -0.225s/f (Firm)
**WFA** 3 from 4yo+ 8lb **9** Ran SP% **113.4**
Speed ratings (Par 103): **104,103,102,100,98 97,95,92,45**
CSF £16.98 CT £124.87 TOTE £2.80: £1.60, £2.50, £3.20; EX 16.90 Trifecta £118.60.
**Owner** The Twopin Partnership **Bred** J L Dunlop **Trained** Melsonby, N Yorks

**FOCUS**
A weak handicap for the grade, but it produced a thrilling finish. The winner was the one with potential.
T/Jkpt: Not won. T/Plt: £2,172.70 to a £1 stake. Pool: £70,390.14 - 23.65 winning tickets T/Qpdt: £1,475.50 to a £1 stake. Pool: £5,583.29 - 2.80 winning tickets R

6826 - 6829a (Foreign Racing) - See Raceform Interactive

6529

# AYR (L-H)
## Tuesday, September 30

**OFFICIAL GOING: Good to firm (8.7)**
Wind: Fresh, half against Weather: Cloudy, dry

## 6830 RACING UK NURSERY H'CAP 7f 50y
**2:10** (2:12) (Class 6) (0-65,64) 2-Y-0 **£1,940** (£577; £288; £144) **Stalls** High

Form RPR

0524 **1** **Dominic Cork**[9] 6574 2-9-7 64 ...............................(p) FergalLynch 1 69
(Kevin Ryan) *mde all: clr whn edgd rt over 1f out: rdn and r.o wl fnl f* **4/1**[2]

5246 **2** 1¼ **Dragline**[53] 5129 2-8-12 55 ...............................(e[1]) DavidAllan 5 57
(Tim Easterby) *dwlt and blkd s: hld up: hdwy to chse wnr over 1f out: sn rdn and hung lft: kpt on ins fnl f* **14/1**

5655 **3** 1½ **Miss Van Gogh**[53] 5141 2-8-13 56 ...................................... TonyHamilton 9 54
(Richard Fahey) *prom: effrt and chsd wnr over 2f out to over 1f out: rdn and one pce fnl f* **10/1**

004 **4** 6 **Auld Fyffee (IRE)**[12] 6473 2-9-1 61 .............................. RyanPowell(3) 7 44
(John Ryan) *hld up: rdn and hdwy on outside over 2f out: edgd lft over 1f out: sn outpcd* **4/1**[2]

0006 **5** 2 **Follow The Faith**[14] 6420 2-8-6 52 ow2 .............................. CharlesBishop(3) 3 30
(Mick Channon) *midfield: rdn over 2f out: no imp fr wl over 1f out* **5/1**[3]

006 **6** nk **Cassandane (IRE)**[29] 5981 2-8-12 55 ...................................... JoeFanning 8 33
(Mark Johnston) *midfield: drvn and outpcd over 2f out: n.d after* **7/1**

3506 **7** ½ **Call Me Crockett (IRE)**[6] 6669 2-9-3 60 .............................. DuranFentiman 4 36
(Richard Guest) *dwlt and wnt rt s: hld up: rdn over 2f out: btn over 1f out* **7/2**[1]

4664 **8** 5 **Little Houidini**[7] 6642 2-8-9 52 ...................................... TomEaves 2 16
(Keith Dalgleish) *cl up tl rdn and wknd fr 2f out* **33/1**

0553 **9** ¾ **Triggers Broom (IRE)**[59] 4899 2-7-11 45 .............................. JackGarritty(5) 6 7
(Richard Fahey) *chsd wnr to over 2f out: sn rdn and wknd* **25/1**

1m 31.04s (-2.36) **Going Correction** -0.40s/f (Firm) **9** Ran SP% **113.9**
Speed ratings (Par 93): **97,95,93,87,84 84,83,78,77**
CSF £57.04 CT £522.65 TOTE £4.30: £1.90, £2.80, £3.00; EX 27.70 Trifecta £142.90.
**Owner** Mrs Janis Macpherson **Bred** Dachel Stud **Trained** Hambleton, N Yorks

**FOCUS**
The ground had dried out a little and was now officially good to firm Rail movement meant that the race was run over 18yds further than advertised. All nine of these were maidens beforehand.

## 6831 RACINGUK.COM MAIDEN STKS 6f
**2:40** (2:42) (Class 5) 2-Y-0 **£2,911** (£866; £432; £216) **Stalls** Low

Form RPR

062 **1** **Juncart**[10] 6537 2-9-5 74 ................................................ PaulMulrennan 7 77
(Kevin Ryan) *mde all: pushed along and qcknd over 1f out: kpt on wl fnl f* **4/5**[1]

3243 **2** 1½ **Westhoughton**[13] 6453 2-9-5 75 ...................................... DanielTudhope 6 73
(David O'Meara) *chsd wnr: rdn over 2f out: kpt on ins fnl f* **9/4**[2]

**3** 13 **Competent** 2-9-5 0 ................................................ TomEaves 2 34
(Kristin Stubbs) *in tch: rdn and outpcd over 2f out: rallied to take modest 3rd ins fnl f: no ch w first two* **16/1**

5 **4** 1 **Missisipi Baileys (FR)**[8] 6594 2-9-0 0 .............................. JoeFanning 3 26
(Mark Johnston) *prom: drvn and outpcd over 2f out: no imp after* **12/1**

**5** ½ **Doctors Papers** 2-9-5 0 ................................................ GrahamLee 1 29
(David Brown) *s.i.s: outpcd and green in rr: hdwy 2f out: nvr rchd ldrs* **8/1**[3]

60 **6** nse **Don Ricardo (IRE)**[19] 6271 2-9-5 0 .............................. TonyHamilton 5 29
(Richard Fahey) *in tch: pushed along and outpcd over 2f out: btn over 1f out* **25/1**

**7** 5 **Royal Regent** 2-9-0 0 ................................................ MeganCarberry(5) 4 14
(Lucy Normile) *s.s: a outpcd and wl bhd* **50/1**

1m 10.84s (-1.56) **Going Correction** -0.40s/f (Firm) **7** Ran SP% **116.8**
Speed ratings (Par 95): **94,92,74,73,72 72,65**
CSF £2.91 TOTE £1.80: £1.10, £2.00; EX 2.50 Trifecta £24.60.
**Owner** Michael Beaumont **Bred** D R Tucker **Trained** Hambleton, N Yorks
■ It's Time For Bed was withdrawn. Price at time of withdrawal 66/1. Rule 4 does not apply.

**FOCUS**
This moderate maiden only ever concerned the two market leaders and they finished spread out all over Western Scotland.

## 6832 WEDDINGS AT WESTERN HOUSE HOTEL H'CAP 1m 7f
**3:15** (3:15) (Class 5) (0-75,71) 3-Y-0+ **£2,911** (£866; £432; £216) **Stalls** Low

Form RPR

5616 **1** **Miss Macnamara (IRE)**[20] 6228 5-9-9 71 ......................[1] KevinStott(5) 3 76
(Martin Todhunter) *hld up: rdn over 2f out: gd hdwy on outside over 1f out: styd on wl to ld last stride* **16/1**

-011 **2** shd **Scrafton**[10] 6539 3-8-9 66 ................................................ JoeyHaynes(3) 1 71+
(James Bethell) *t.k.h: in tch: stdy hdwy over 2f out: rdn to ld ins fnl f: idled: hdd last stride* **9/4**[1]

1634 **3** ¾ **La Bacouetteuse (FR)**[12] 6493 9-9-13 70 ...............(p) DanielTudhope 9 74
(Iain Jardine) *hld up: rdn and outpcd over 2f out: rallied on outside over 1f out: kpt on fnl f: nrst fin* **18/1**

342 **4** 3/4 **Jammy Moment**[7] 6622 3-8-13 67 JoeFanning 5 70
(Linda Perratt) *led at modest gallop: rdn along over 2f out: hdd ins fnl f: kpt on same pce towards fin* **12/1**

0213 **5** shd **Crakehall Lad (IRE)**[10] 6539 3-8-11 65 DavidAllan 6 68
(Alan Swinbank) *chsd ldr: rdn over 3f out: rallied: kpt on same pce fnl f* **4/1**[2]

3633 **6** 1/2 **Shadows Ofthenight (IRE)**[13] 6461 3-8-12 69 CharlesBishop(3) 7 71
(Mick Channon) *prom: effrt and pushed along over 2f out: one pce fr over 1f out* **4/1**[2]

6326 **7** 1 **In Vino Veritas (IRE)**[12] 6480 3-8-11 65 (v) PJMcDonald 4 66
(Ann Duffield) *trckd ldrs: drvn over 2f out: rallied: outpcd over 1f out* **14/1**

4454 **8** 1/2 **A Southside Boy (GER)**[12] 6480 6-9-3 60 GrahamLee 8 61
(Jim Goldie) *hld up in tch: pushed along over 2f out: no imp whn nt clr run ins fnl f* **11/2**[3]

2350 **9** nk **Grand Diamond (IRE)**[12] 6480 10-8-3 53 RachaelGrant(7) 2 53
(Jim Goldie) *hld up: rdn and effrt over 2f out: no imp whn nt clr run ins fnl f* **40/1**

3m 20.86s (0.46) **Going Correction** -0.40s/f (Firm)
**WFA** 3 from 5yo+ 11lb **9** Ran **SP% 114.1**
Speed ratings (Par 103): **82,81,81,81,81 80,80,80,79**
CSF £51.63 CT £674.16 TOTE £14.00: £4.10, £1.50, £4.40; EX 65.20 Trifecta £736.90.
**Owner** Javas Charvers **Bred** Airlie Stud **Trained** Orton, Cumbria

**FOCUS**
Despite what looked a decent-enough pace for this ordinary staying event, several had their chance and they finished in a bit of a heap.

## 6833 RACING UK ANYWHERE AVAILABLE NOW H'CAP (DIV I) 7f 50y
**3:50** (3:51) (Class 6) (0-60,60) 3-Y-O+ **£2,045** (£603; £302) **Stalls High**

Form RPR

-004 **1** **Pitt Rivers**[8] 6595 5-8-12 51 PaulMulrennan 10 58
(Linda Perratt) *hld up: effrt whn nt clr run and swtchd rt over 1f out: gd hdwy fnl f to ld towards fin* **20/1**

-043 **2** 1/2 **Llandanwg**[39] 5642 3-7-13 46 JoeDoyle(5) 8 51
(Bryan Smart) *dwlt: sn midfield on outside: drvn and outpcd over 3f out: rallied over 1f out: led ins fnl f: kpt on: hdd towards fin* **5/1**[3]

0004 **3** 1 1/2 **Rioja Day (IRE)**[8] 6601 4-9-4 57 (b) GrahamLee 2 59
(Jim Goldie) *in tch: rdn along over 2f out: effrt and ch ins fnl f: kpt on same pce last 75yds* **9/2**[2]

0002 **4** 1 1/4 **Berbice (IRE)**[8] 6595 9-8-4 48 SammyJoBell(5) 3 47
(Linda Perratt) *dwlt: hld up: smooth hdwy to chal over 2f out: led over 1f out to ins fnl f: sn no ex* **11/2**

1003 **5** 1/2 **Rust (IRE)**[8] 6600 4-9-7 60 (b) PJMcDonald 4 57
(Ann Duffield) *hld up: rdn and hdwy 2f out: edgd lft and no imp fnl f* **10/3**[1]

0360 **6** 3 1/4 **Torridon**[19] 6267 3-8-4 46 JoeFanning 7 34
(Mark Johnston) *cl up: led over 2f out to over 1f out: sn rdn and btn* **11/2**

6000 **7** 1 **Look On By**[10] 6543 4-8-13 52 (b) JamesSullivan 5 38
(Ruth Carr) *t.k.h: led tl rdn and hdd over 2f out: wknd appr fnl f* **16/1**

02U6 **8** shd **Copper To Gold**[50] 5233 5-8-4 46 oh1 NeilFarley(3) 1 32
(Robin Bastiman) *chsd ldrs: drvn and outpcd whn n.m.r wl over 1f out: sn n.d* **22/1**

4300 **9** 1 **Benidorm**[10] 6544 6-8-7 46 (e) JasonHart 6 29
(Richard Guest) *chsd ldr: drvn whn n.m.r briefly over 2f out: wknd over 1f out* **12/1**

5500 **10** 2 1/4 **Raise A Billion**[8] 6601 3-8-3 50 JackGarritty(5) 9 26
(Alan Berry) *hld up: struggling over 2f out: sn btn* **25/1**

1m 30.42s (-2.98) **Going Correction** -0.40s/f (Firm)
**WFA** 3 from 4yo+ 3lb **10** Ran **SP% 115.2**
Speed ratings (Par 101): **101,100,98,97,96 93,91,91,90,88**
CSF £113.21 CT £550.33 TOTE £21.80: £3.60, £1.60, £2.00; EX 75.30 Trifecta £601.90.
**Owner** Mrs Helen Perratt **Bred** Jnp Bloodstock Ltd **Trained** East Kilbride, S Lanarks
■ Stewards' Enquiry : Joe Doyle one-day ban: careless riding (Oct 14)

**FOCUS**
A moderate handicap full of horses that have proved hard to win with.

## 6834 RACING UK ANYWHERE AVAILABLE NOW H'CAP (DIV II) 7f 50y
**4:25** (4:26) (Class 6) (0-60,59) 3-Y-O+ **£2,045** (£603; £302) **Stalls High**

Form RPR

3104 **1** **Secret City (IRE)**[25] 6122 8-9-7 59 (b) DanielTudhope 2 68
(Robin Bastiman) *in tch: rdn over 2f out: hdwy over 1f out: led ins fnl f: styd on* **13/8**[1]

0025 **2** 1 1/4 **Clabare**[15] 6405 3-8-9 50 TomEaves 8 55
(Ian Semple) *in tch: gd hdwy to ld over 2f out: rdn: edgd rt and hdd ins fnl f: sn one pce* **6/1**[3]

5005 **3** 3 **Rock Canyon (IRE)**[1] 6819 5-8-11 49 JoeFanning 6 47
(Linda Perratt) *hld up: rdn and hdwy over 1f out: kpt on ins fnl f: nvr able to chal* **6/1**[3]

6064 **4** 2 1/2 **Princess Rose**[10] 6543 3-8-5 49 (v) JoeyHaynes(3) 5 39
(John Weymes) *chsd ldrs: rdn along and ev ch over 2f out: outpcd over 1f out* **9/1**

6000 **5** 1/2 **Echologic**[25] 6088 4-8-7 45 (p) DuranFentiman 7 35
(Brian Baugh) *led to over 2f out: rdn and wknd over 1f out* **66/1**

-400 **6** 1 1/2 **Stoneacre Oskar**[8] 6595 5-8-9 47 ow1 DavidAllan 9 33
(Peter Grayson) *bhd: rdn over 2f out: sme hdwy over 1f out: nvr able to chal* **16/1**

0065 **7** 1 1/2 **Amis Reunis**[3] 6758 5-8-9 52 (p) EmmaSayer(5) 1 34
(Alan Berry) *t.k.h: hld up in tch: struggling over 2f out: sn btn* **4/1**[2]

00 **8** 2 1/2 **Hazza The Jazza**[13] 6272 4-8-12 50 (v[1]) JasonHart 3 26
(Richard Guest) *dwlt: hld up: rdn over 2f out: sn btn* **8/1**

0630 **9** 30 **Bannock Town**[11] 6516 3-8-4 48 ow3 (p) ConnorBeasley(3) 4
(Linda Perratt) *cl up tl rdn and wknd fr 2f out: t.o* **66/1**

1m 30.36s (-3.04) **Going Correction** -0.40s/f (Firm)
**WFA** 3 from 4yo+ 3lb **9** Ran **SP% 116.6**
Speed ratings (Par 101): **101,99,96,93,92 91,89,86,52**
CSF £12.03 CT £47.16 TOTE £2.10: £1.50, £2.10, £1.50; EX 14.20 Trifecta £61.00.
**Owner** Ms M Austerfield **Bred** Miss Karen Theobald **Trained** Cowthorpe, N Yorks

**FOCUS**
More of the same. The time was fractionally quicker than the first division and this was another race in which the winner was delivered wide and late.

## 6835 RACING UK ANDROID APP RACINGUK.COM H'CAP 6f
**5:00** (5:01) (Class 5) (0-70,70) 3-Y-O+ **£2,911** (£866; £432; £216) **Stalls Low**

Form RPR

0144 **1** **Native Falls (IRE)**[17] 6346 3-9-4 69 DavidAllan 10 79
(Alan Swinbank) *mde all: clr over 2f out: sn pushed along: kpt on wl fnl f: unchal* **9/2**[2]

3514 **2** 1 1/4 **Manatee Bay**[13] 6451 4-9-4 67 (v) PaulMulrennan 2 73
(David Nicholls) *blkd s: hld up: hdwy over 1f out: chsd wnr wl ins fnl f: r.o* **7/1**

3666 **3** shd **Jinky**[12] 6475 6-9-5 68 JoeFanning 5 74
(Linda Perratt) *hld up: rdn and hdwy over 1f out: disp 2nd pl wl ins fnl f: hld towards fin* **6/1**[3]

3503 **4** 1/2 **Findog**[2] 6796 4-8-4 56 oh1 ConnorBeasley(3) 11 60
(Linda Perratt) *hld up in tch: effrt and chsd wnr over 1f out to wl ins fnl f: no ex* **11/1**

3332 **5** 1 1/2 **Exotic Guest**[6] 6674 4-9-2 65 (p) JamesSullivan 13 64
(Ruth Carr) *wnt rt s: hld up: rdn and hdwy over 1f out: kpt on ins fnl f* **4/1**[1]

0002 **6** 1/2 **Saxonette**[2] 6796 6-8-2 56 oh2 JoeDoyle(5) 9 54
(Linda Perratt) *prom: rdn over 2f out: wknd ins fnl f* **16/1**

3000 **7** 1 3/4 **The Nifty Fox**[6] 6674 10-8-7 56 oh3 (p) PJMcDonald 7 48
(Tim Easterby) *in tch: rdn and outpcd 2f out: n.d after* **14/1**

0026 **8** 3/4 **Sewn Up**[1] 6819 4-8-6 58 (p) JoeyHaynes(3) 3 48
(Keith Dalgleish) *t.k.h: hld up: rdn over 2f out: edgd lft and wknd over 1f out* **10/1**

1403 **9** 6 **Chookie's Lass**[9] 6575 3-9-3 68 TomEaves 4 38
(Keith Dalgleish) *prom tl rdn and wknd wl over 1f out* **33/1**

1134 **10** 2 1/4 **Rise To Glory (IRE)**[12] 6475 6-9-6 69 (tp) DuranFentiman 6 32
(Shaun Harris) *chsd ldrs: rdn over 2f out: wknd wl over 1f out* **14/1**

1550 **11** 1 **Goninodaethat**[12] 6477 6-9-1 64 GrahamLee 12 24
(Jim Goldie) *prom tl rdn and wknd fr 2f out* **8/1**

6400 **12** shd **Munjally**[14] 6431 3-9-5 70 DanielTudhope 1 30
(Patrick Holmes) *wnt rt s: chsd ldrs tl rdn and wknd over 2f out* **33/1**

1m 9.53s (-2.87) **Going Correction** -0.40s/f (Firm)
**WFA** 3 from 4yo+ 2lb **12** Ran **SP% 118.6**
Speed ratings (Par 103): **103,101,101,100,98 97,95,94,86,83 82,82**
CSF £36.18 CT £192.99 TOTE £8.10: £2.10, £2.50, £2.00; EX 34.30 Trifecta £181.50.
**Owner** Anthea Findlay & The Twopin Partnership **Bred** John Foley **Trained** Melsonby, N Yorks

**FOCUS**
An ordinary sprint handicap, but a powerful piece of front-running by the winner.

## 6836 BETFAIR SCOTTISH RACING MILE SERIES FINAL H'CAP 1m
**5:30** (5:30) (Class 3) 3-Y-O+ **£9,703** (£2,887; £1,443; £721) **Stalls Low**

Form RPR

3130 **1** **Camerooney**[21] 6214 11-8-12 72 (p) NathanAlison(5) 8 81
(Marjorie Fife) *mde all: jnd 1/2-way: rdn and styd on gamely fnl f* **16/1**

1610 **2** 1 1/4 **Hanalei Bay (IRE)**[12] 6476 4-9-10 79 PhillipMakin 5 85
(Keith Dalgleish) *cl up: smooth hdwy and ev ch over 1f out: sn rdn: kpt on same pce ins fnl f* **4/1**[1]

1244 **3** hd **Bahamian C**[7] 6649 3-9-1 77 (p) GeorgeChaloner(3) 12 83+
(Richard Fahey) *hld up on outside: rdn and hdwy over 2f out: edgd lft over 1f out: kpt on ins fnl f* **7/1**[3]

1600 **4** 1 1/4 **Porthos Du Vallon**[12] 6478 3-8-11 70 [1] TomEaves 4 73
(Keith Dalgleish) *plld hrd in midfield: effrt and hdwy over 1f out: kpt on fnl f: nrst fin* **16/1**

0260 **5** 1/2 **True Pleasure (IRE)**[32] 5887 7-9-9 78 PJMcDonald 6 80
(James Bethell) *prom: rdn over 2f out: kpt on same pce appr fnl f* **8/1**

3000 **6** hd **Opt Out**[12] 6478 4-8-5 63 ConnorBeasley(3) 2 64
(Alistair Whillans) *hld up: rdn and effrt 2f out: edgd lft: kpt on same pce fnl f* **22/1**

0565 **7** nk **Spavento (IRE)**[8] 6601 8-8-0 58 NeilFarley(3) 10 58
(Eric Alston) *t.k.h: in tch: rdn and outpcd over 2f out: rallied fnl f: nvr able to chal* **25/1**

0100 **8** nk **Ewell Place (IRE)**[26] 6074 5-8-8 68 (p) JackGarritty(5) 3 68
(Richard Fahey) *trckd ldrs: effrt and rdn wl over 1f out: outpcd fnl f* **12/1**

3601 **9** 1/2 **Lil Sophella (IRE)**[8] 6601 5-8-3 61 6ex JoeyHaynes(3) 1 60
(Patrick Holmes) *t.k.h: hld up on ins: rdn and hdwy over 1f out: nvr able to chal* **6/1**[2]

2210 **10** nk **Gambino (IRE)**[20] 6232 4-8-8 68 (p) JoeDoyle(5) 11 66
(John David Riches) *s.i.s: sn midfield: plld hrd and hdwy to dispute ld 1/2-way: rdn and outpcd fr over 1f out* **6/1**[2]

0041 **11** nk **Funding Deficit (IRE)**[8] 6600 4-8-10 65 6ex FergalLynch 14 62
(Jim Goldie) *s.i.s: hld up: rdn and outpcd over 2f out: n.d after* **16/1**

5026 **12** 3 1/2 **Ted's Brother (IRE)**[33] 5855 6-9-7 76 (e) JasonHart 13 65
(Richard Guest) *propped s: hld up: struggling over 2f out: sn btn* **20/1**

5060 **13** nse **Another For Joe**[12] 6476 6-9-8 77 GrahamLee 9 66
(Jim Goldie) *t.k.h: hld up: rdn over 2f out: sn wknd* **11/1**

1m 40.87s (-2.93) **Going Correction** -0.40s/f (Firm)
**WFA** 3 from 4yo+ 4lb **13** Ran **SP% 118.8**
Speed ratings (Par 107): **98,96,96,95,94 94,94,94,93,93 92,89,89**
CSF £76.47 CT £520.30 TOTE £26.20: £7.80, £4.20, £2.30; EX 131.90 Trifecta £2141.40.
**Owner** Mrs Jean Stapleton **Bred** Miss Dianne Hill **Trained** Stillington, N Yorks

**FOCUS**
A competitive final of this series on paper, but another all-the-way winner.

## 6837 WATCH ON 3 DEVICES RACINGUK.COM ANYWHERE APPRENTICE TRAINING SERIES H'CAP 1m
**6:00** (6:01) (Class 6) (0-65,65) 3-Y-O+ **£2,045** (£603; £302) **Stalls Low**

Form RPR

0232 **1** **Jersey Brown (IRE)**[7] 6647 3-9-5 64 DanielCremin 8 73
(Mick Channon) *hld up: hdwy 2f out: shkn up to ld ins fnl f: rdn out* **6/4**[1]

3330 **2** 3/4 **Indian Giver**[8] 6600 6-9-0 55 (p) JoeDoyle 4 62
(John David Riches) *led: jnd 1/2-way: rdn 2f out: hdd ins fnl f: kpt on* **11/1**

0342 **3** 3/4 **Staffhoss**[8] 6600 4-9-0 62 PaulaMuir(7) 2 67
(Mark Johnston) *in tch: effrt over 2f out: edgd lft over 1f out: styd on ins fnl f* **7/1**[3]

4460 **4** 2 1/4 **Tortoise**[15] 6407 3-8-6 51 oh1 (b) GemmaTutty 9 51
(Richard Guest) *t.k.h: prom: rdn over 2f out: one pce fnl f* **22/1**

4322 **5** hd **Kiss Of Spring (IRE)**[10] 6540 3-9-1 65 JoshDoyle(5) 3 65
(David O'Meara) *t.k.h: cl up: chal 1/2-way to over 2f out: one pce fnl f* **11/4**[2]

0524 **6** nk **Smile For Me (IRE)**[28] 6015 3-8-6 51 oh4 JackGarritty 1 50
(Alan Berry) *plld hrd: cl up: rdn over 2f out: one pce over 1f out* **17/2**

4000 **7** 2 3/4 **Maillot Jaune (IRE)**[13] 6454 4-8-5 51 oh6 RowanScott(5) 7 44
(Patrick Holmes) *hld up: rdn over 3f out: rallied over 1f out: no imp* **33/1**

056 **8** 3 **Exton**[14] 6429 5-8-10 51 oh6 RachelRichardson 5 37
(Shaun Harris) *hld up: rdn over 3f out: edgd rt wl over 1f out: nvr rchd ldrs* **25/1**

40 **9** 29 **Ebony Clarets**[86] 4000 5-8-10 51 oh6 (p) MeganCarberry 6
(Linda Perratt) *rrd s: hld up: struggling over 2f out: sn btn: t.o* **25/1**

1m 42.31s (-1.49) **Going Correction** -0.40s/f (Firm)
**WFA** 3 from 4yo+ 4lb **9** Ran **SP% 113.0**
Speed ratings (Par 101): **91,90,89,87,87 86,84,81,52**
CSF £17.75 CT £88.99 TOTE £2.40: £1.10, £2.70, £2.40; EX 18.10 Trifecta £87.60.

**Owner** Lakedale **Bred** Richard Frayne **Trained** West Ilsley, Berks
**FOCUS**
A moderate apprentice handicap.
T/Plt: £68.70 to a £1 stake. Pool of £49473.46 - 525.52 winning tickets. T/Qpdt: £14.00 to a £1 stake. Pool of £5229.10 - 274.60 winning tickets. RY

# 6764 WOLVERHAMPTON (A.W) (L-H)

Tuesday, September 30

**OFFICIAL GOING: Tapeta: standard**
Wind: Light behind Weather: Cloudy with sunny spells

## 6838 PRICE BOOSTS GALORE @ BOOKMAKERS.CO.UK MAIDEN AUCTION STKS (TAPETA) 7f 32y

**5:50** (5:52) (Class 5) 2-Y-O £2,911 (£866; £432; £216) Stalls High

Form RPR
5 **1** **Midtech Star (IRE)**[50] 5241 2-9-3 0 StevieDonohoe 8 78
(Ian Williams) *a.p: pushed along 1/2-way: r.o to ld wl ins fnl f* **10/3**[2]
002 **2** 1 ¾ **Simone On Time (IRE)**[7] 6646 2-8-8 0 RichardHughes 4 65
(Sylvester Kirk) *chsd ldrs: rdn to chse ldr over 1f out: led ins fnl f: sn hdd and unable qck* **2/1**[1]
5 **3** 1 ¾ **Eatsleepracerepeat**[46] 5391 2-9-1 0 [1] MartinHarley 2 68
(Lady Cecil) *led: rdn over 1f out: hdd and no ex ins fnl f* **2/1**[1]
**4** 2 **Sea Of Red** 2-8-11 0 LiamKeniry 6 59
(J S Moore) *s.i.s: sn pushed along in rr: r.o wl towards fin: nt rch ldrs* **33/1**
60 **5** nse **Onelastfling**[51] 5210 2-8-6 0 LukeMorris 3 54
(Sylvester Kirk) *hld up: rdn 1/2-way: r.o ins fnl f: nt trble ldrs* **40/1**
50 **6** hd **Cascading Stars (IRE)**[19] 6246 2-8-12 0 LiamJones 5 59
(J S Moore) *hld up: hdwy 2f out: sn rdn: styd on same pce fnl f* **25/1**
550 **7** 1 ½ **Shimmering Silver (IRE)**[19] 6270 2-8-8 60 FrankieMcDonald 7 52
(Daniel Mark Loughnane) *trckd ldr: racd keenly: rdn and ev ch over 2f out: hung lft fr over 1f out: wknd ins fnl f* **25/1**
**8** 3 ¼ **Oracolo (IRE)** 2-9-1 0 MartinLane 1 51
(David Simcock) *s.i.s: a in rr* **7/1**[3]
1m 29.76s (0.96) **Going Correction** +0.025s/f (Slow) 8 Ran SP% **115.3**
Speed ratings (Par 95): **95,93,91,88,88 88,86,83**
CSF £10.16 TOTE £4.30: £2.40, £1.10, £1.10; EX 11.90 Trifecta £24.50.
**Owner** Midtech **Bred** Denis McDonnell **Trained** Portway, Worcs
**FOCUS**
A modest maiden restricted to juveniles who cost no more than £21,000.

## 6839 EXCLUSIVE FREE BETS @ BOOKMAKERS.CO.UK H'CAP (TAPETA) 1m 1f 103y

**6:20** (6:21) (Class 4) (0-85,85) 3-Y-O+ **£5,670** (£1,697; £848; £424; £211) Stalls Low

Form RPR
333 **1** **Dream Child (IRE)**[84] 4052 3-8-9 **75** RichardHughes 2 86+
(Charlie Appleby) *led 1f: chsd ldrs: shkn up to ld ins fnl f: r.o: readily* **3/1**[3]
6053 **2** 1 ½ **Modernism**[6] 6664 5-9-4 **79** JamieSpencer 6 84
(David Simcock) *hld up: hdwy over 1f out: sn rdn: styd on to go 2nd nr fin* **5/2**[1]
3004 **3** ½ **God's Speed (IRE)**[10] 6566 3-9-5 **85** ChrisCatlin 4 90
(Rae Guest) *a.p: chsd ldr over 6f out: rdn to ld over 1f out: hdd and unable qck ins fnl f* **10/1**
4130 **4** 4 **Mazaaher**[11] 6523 4-9-0 **75** PaulHanagan 1 71
(B W Hills) *hld up in tch: rdn over 1f out: no ex ins fnl f* **11/4**[2]
4412 **5** 2 ¾ **Off The Pulse**[113] 3050 4-9-7 **82** GrahamGibbons 5 72
(John Mackie) *prom: rdn over 1f out: wknd fnl f* **10/1**
-200 **6** 3 **Mubtadi**[32] 5895 6-9-7 **82** AdamKirby 3 66
(Ismail Mohammed) *prom tl rdn and wknd over 1f out* **33/1**
4144 **7** 1 ¼ **Dutch Rifle**[12] 6500 3-8-13 **79** MartinHarley 7 61
(James Tate) *s.i.s: rcvrd to ld over 8f out: rdn and hdd over 1f out: wknd fnl f* **6/1**
1m 59.42s (-1.38) **Going Correction** +0.025s/f (Slow)
**WFA** 3 from 4yo+ 5lb 7 Ran SP% **115.6**
Speed ratings (Par 105): **107,105,105,101,99 96,95**
CSF £11.24 TOTE £3.80: £1.60, £2.20; EX 16.20 Trifecta £88.40.
**Owner** Godolphin **Bred** Darley **Trained** Newmarket, Suffolk
**FOCUS**
This looked to be run at a sound gallop thanks to Dutch Rifle and that set this up nicely for the closers. Three pulled clear in the final furlong and the form looks solid enough for the level.

## 6840 DOWNLOAD THE APP @ BOOKMAKERS.CO.UK MAIDEN FILLIES' STKS (BOBIS RACE) (TAPETA) 1m 141y

**6:50** (6:51) (Class 5) 2-Y-O £2,911 (£866; £432; £216) Stalls Low

Form RPR
0446 **1** **Heart Of Africa**[13] 6448 2-9-0 72 AdamKirby 5 75
(Charlie Appleby) *mde all: qckng over 2f out: sn rdn: edgd lft ins fnl f: styd on* **7/2**[2]
44 **2** ¾ **Shaw Ting**[21] 6208 2-9-0 0 RichardKingscote 3 73
(Tom Dascombe) *chsd wnr: rdn and edgd lft fr over 1f out: styd on* **1/1**[1]
3 **3** 2 ¾ **Madam Midnight**[34] 5827 2-9-0 0 FergusSweeney 2 68
(David Simcock) *trckd ldrs: racd keenly: rdn over 1f out: styd on same pce ins fnl f* **4/1**[3]
060 **4** 1 ¾ **Theydon Bois**[25] 6085 2-9-0 65 JimmyQuinn 4 64
(Peter Charalambous) *hld up: effrt over 2f out: styd on same pce fr over 1f out* **33/1**
**5** 1 ½ **Singoalla** 2-9-0 0 LukeMorris 1 61
(Sir Mark Prescott Bt) *dwlt: pushed along in rr early: rdn over 2f out: nt trble ldrs* **7/1**
1m 52.13s (2.03) **Going Correction** +0.025s/f (Slow) 5 Ran SP% **107.7**
Speed ratings (Par 92): **91,90,87,86,85**
CSF £7.13 TOTE £3.00: £1.10, £2.00; EX 6.80 Trifecta £14.90.
**Owner** Godolphin **Bred** Darley **Trained** Newmarket, Suffolk
**FOCUS**
Just ordinary maiden form by the looks of things.

## 6841 GET FREE BETTING TIPS @ BOOKIES.COM H'CAP (TAPETA) 1m 141y

**7:20** (7:20) (Class 5) (0-75,75) 3-Y-O+ £2,911 (£866; £432; £216) Stalls Low

Form RPR
3024 **1** **Al Mukhdam**[18] 6304 4-9-8 75 (p) JamieSpencer 4 83
(Ed de Giles) *mde all: rdn and drifted rt over 1f out: styd on u.p* **10/3**[2]
0240 **2** ½ **Dark Ocean (IRE)**[33] 5855 4-9-3 70 RussKennemore 7 77
(Jedd O'Keeffe) *hld up: hdwy over 2f out: rdn and hung lft fr over 1f out: r.o* **25/1**
511 **3** 2 ¼ **For Shia And Lula (IRE)**[15] 6414 5-9-3 75 EoinWalsh(5) 8 77
(Daniel Mark Loughnane) *a.p: rdn to chse wnr over 1f out: sn ev ch: no ex wl ins fnl f* **7/1**
0400 **4** 1 ¾ **Anton Chigurh**[4] 6713 5-9-4 74 DannyBrock(3) 6 72
(Philip McBride) *hld up: hdwy 5f out: chsd wnr over 3f out tl rdn over 1f out: no ex fnl f* **6/4**[1]
2134 **5** 2 **Law Keeper (IRE)**[22] 6192 3-9-2 74 MartinHarley 2 68
(James Tate) *chsd ldrs: rdn over 3f out: wknd ins fnl f* **4/1**[3]
3205 **6** 6 **Celtic Sixpence (IRE)**[18] 6285 6-9-2 69 MichaelStainton 5 48
(Nick Kent) *chsd wnr 5f: n.m.r over 2f out: wknd fnl f* **16/1**
0216 **7** 1 ½ **Blazeofenchantment (USA)**[27] 6035 4-9-3 73 JacobButterfield(3) 3 49
(John Wainwright) *dwlt: hld up: rdn and wknd over 2f out* **11/1**
1m 49.03s (-1.07) **Going Correction** +0.025s/f (Slow)
**WFA** 3 from 4yo+ 5lb 7 Ran SP% **113.6**
Speed ratings (Par 103): **105,104,102,101,99 93,92**
CSF £71.75 CT £547.01 TOTE £6.80: £3.10, £10.30; EX 66.50 Trifecta £261.20.
**Owner** T Gould **Bred** Galadari Sons Stud Company Limited **Trained** Ledbury, H'fords
**FOCUS**
Quite a competitive heat for the grade and the pace held up.

## 6842 SPORTING LISBON V CHELSEA PRICE BOOST @ BOOKIES.COM NURSERY H'CAP (TAPETA) 1m 141y

**7:50** (7:50) (Class 6) (0-60,60) 2-Y-O £1,940 (£577; £288; £144) Stalls Low

Form RPR
0660 **1** **New Abbey Dancer (IRE)**[7] 6646 2-8-6 45 (p) ChrisCatlin 11 50
(Gay Kelleway) *sn pushed along in rr: rdn over 2f out: hdwy over 1f out: r.o to ld nr fin* **18/1**
4650 **2** 1 **Goolagong Girl (IRE)**[34] 5823 2-8-13 52 LukeMorris 4 55
(Jane Chapple-Hyam) *a.p: rdn over 1f out: led and hung lft ins fnl f: hdd nr fin* **9/1**
3500 **3** ¾ **Stealing Thunder (IRE)**[6] 6662 2-9-3 56 (b) OisinMurphy 8 57
(Eve Johnson Houghton) *chsd ldr: rdn to ld over 2f out: hdd ins fnl f: styd on same pce* **5/1**[3]
500 **4** nk **Roman De Brut (IRE)**[62] 4787 2-9-0 53 StevieDonohoe 9 54
(Ian Williams) *hld up: hdwy over 1f out: sn rdn: styd on* **4/1**[2]
0550 **5** 3 **Blue Burmese (IRE)**[10] 6563 2-9-1 54 ow1 AdamKirby 10 48
(Mark Usher) *sn pushed along in rr: rdn over 2f out: edgd rt and styd on towards fin: nvr nrr* **28/1**
0055 **6** ½ **Dancing Moon (IRE)**[15] 6413 2-9-0 53 SamHitchcott 2 46
(Mick Channon) *prom: rdn over 1f out: no ex ins fnl f* **10/1**
0066 **7** hd **More Drama (IRE)**[20] 6237 2-8-10 49 LiamKeniry 7 42
(Sylvester Kirk) *led: rdn and hdd over 2f out: ev ch over 1f out: no ex ins fnl f* **10/1**
6045 **8** ½ **Diminutive (IRE)**[10] 6563 2-9-0 60 MikeyEnnis(7) 5 52
(Grace Harris) *prom: rdn over 2f out: no ex fnl f* **22/1**
3306 **9** 2 ½ **Kidmeforever**[32] 5885 2-8-9 55 JosephineGordon(7) 6 42
(J S Moore) *mid-div: rdn over 2f out: wknd fnl f* **28/1**
0065 **10** 1 **Noble Master**[15] 6412 2-8-13 52 RichardHughes 1 37
(Sylvester Kirk) *chsd ldrs: rdn over 1f out: wknd ins fnl f* **2/1**[1]
4000 **11** 3 **Tantric Lady**[6] 6669 2-8-11 53 (be[1]) BillyCray(3) 3 31
(Alan McCabe) *s.s: hld up: plld hrd: rdn over 2f out: nvr on terms* **50/1**
0040 **12** ½ **Saphira Silver (IRE)**[15] 6412 2-8-5 49 NoelGarbutt(5) 13 26
(James Evans) *a in rr* **100/1**
1m 52.11s (2.01) **Going Correction** +0.025s/f (Slow) 12 Ran SP% **117.6**
Speed ratings (Par 93): **92,91,90,90,87 87,86,86,84,83 80,80**
CSF £161.60 CT £955.90 TOTE £31.20: £8.90, £3.90, £1.40; EX 244.80 Trifecta £2054.30 Part won. Pool of £2739.15 - 0.77 winning units..
**Owner** A G MacLennan **Bred** Mrs Eleanor Commins **Trained** Exning, Suffolk
**FOCUS**
A wide open, low-grade handicap run at quite a strong pace and the winner burst onto the scene from off the pace close home.

## 6843 CHAMPIONS LEAGUE BETTING TIPS @ BOOKIES.COM H'CAP (TAPETA) 5f 216y

**8:20** (8:22) (Class 5) (0-70,70) 3-Y-O+ £2,911 (£866; £432; £216) Stalls Low

Form RPR
4560 **1** **Thataboy (IRE)**[17] 6346 3-9-5 70 RichardKingscote 5 81
(Tom Dascombe) *s.i.s: sn prom: shkn up to ld ins fnl f: r.o wl* **11/2**[3]
4300 **2** 2 ¼ **Red Cape (FR)**[6] 6674 11-9-2 65 (b) DaleSwift 8 69
(Ruth Carr) *a.p: rdn to ld over 1f out: hdd ins fnl f: styd on same pce* **25/1**
510 **3** ¾ **Logans Lad (IRE)**[6] 6674 4-9-2 65 (t) FrankieMcDonald 11 67+
(Daniel Mark Loughnane) *sn pushed along in rr: hdwy over 1f out: r.o: nt rch ldrs* **3/1**[1]
260 **4** 1 ½ **Scoreline**[13] 6452 3-9-5 70 SamJames 6 67
(David O'Meara) *a.p: rdn over 1f out: styd on same pce ins fnl f* **14/1**
3220 **5** ½ **Billy Red**[33] 5861 10-9-2 68 (bt) DannyBrock(3) 7 63
(J R Jenkins) *mid-div: rdn over 2f out: styd on ins fnl f: nt trble ldrs* **28/1**
4610 **6** 1 ½ **Dream Catcher (FR)**[19] 6266 6-9-0 66 AmyScott(3) 3 56
(Henry Candy) *chsd ldr tl led wl over 1f out: sn hdd: wknd ins fnl f* **4/1**[2]
4064 **7** nk **National Service (USA)**[13] 6455 3-9-4 69 (b[1]) OisinMurphy 13 58
(Stuart Williams) *s.s: hld up: hdwy over 1f out: nt clr run ins fnl f: styd on same pce* **3/1**[1]
4440 **8** 1 ¼ **Putin (IRE)**[20] 6240 6-9-2 65 (bt) AdamKirby 1 50
(Phil McEntee) *led: rdn and hdd wl over 1f out: wknd ins fnl f* **16/1**
1550 **9** ½ **Invigilator**[144] 2127 6-8-9 65 (t) AdamMcLean(7) 9 49
(Derek Shaw) *broke wl enough: sn lost pl: n.d after* **25/1**
6055 **10** 1 ¼ **Steel City Boy (IRE)**[159] 1679 11-8-5 48 ow3 AnnStokell(5) 2 39
(Ann Stokell) *chsd ldrs: rdn over 2f out: wknd fnl f* **100/1**
15 **11** 1 **Chellalla**[41] 5573 5-9-3 66 StevieDonohoe 10 43
(Ian Williams) *hld up: rdn over 2f out: a towards rr* **14/1**
3000 **12** 3 ½ **Black Caesar (IRE)**[113] 3067 3-9-5 70 LiamKeniry 12 35
(Philip Hide) *mid-div: rdn over 2f out: wknd over 1f out* **20/1**
4300 **13** 1 ½ **Prince Of Passion (CAN)**[153] 1892 6-8-6 58 JacobButterfield(3) 4 19
(Derek Shaw) *s.i.s: sn pushed along in rr: nvr on terms* **66/1**
1m 14.35s (-0.15) **Going Correction** +0.025s/f (Slow)
**WFA** 3 from 4yo+ 2lb 13 Ran SP% **123.0**
Speed ratings (Par 103): **102,99,98,96,95 93,92,91,90,88 87,82,80**
CSF £146.33 CT £511.29 TOTE £8.30: £2.90, £4.80, £2.30; EX 161.80 Trifecta £1275.80.
**Owner** David Lowe & Laurence Bellman **Bred** Mrs Brid Cosgrove **Trained** Malpas, Cheshire
**FOCUS**
Most of these came into this with questions to answer, but the winner was dropping in grade.
T/Plt: £103.60 to a £1 stake. Pool of £76211.84 - 536.53 winning units. T/Qpdt: £53.50 to a £1 stake. Pool of £7145.77 - 98.70 winning units. CR

6844 - 6850a (Foreign Racing) - See Raceform Interactive

[6675]
# KEMPTON (A.W) (R-H)
Wednesday, October 1

**OFFICIAL GOING: Polytrack: standard**
Wind: Moderate, across (away from stands), becoming almost nil Weather: Fine but cloudy, warm

## 6851 HAYMARKET SALES TEAM OF THE YEAR H'CAP 5f (P)
**5:45** (5:45) (Class 7) (0-50,50) 3-Y-0+ **£1,617** (£481; £240; £120) **Stalls** Low

Form RPR

5453 **1** **First Rebellion**[5] 6720 5-9-3 49.....................(b) RobertTart 3 58
(Tony Carroll) *mde all: rdn over 1f out: kpt on and a holding rival* **7/4[1]**

036- **2** *1 1/4* **Befortyfour**[43] 5540 9-9-4 50.....................(p) JFEgan 4 55
(Muredach Kelly, Ire) *pressed wnr: rdn over 1f out: nt qckn and a hld fnl f: kpt on* **5/2[2]**

4665 **3** *1 1/2* **Greek Islands (IRE)**[13] 6481 6-8-11 50..................... RobertPWalsh(7) 6 49
(Edward Creighton) *dwlt: wl off the pce: urged along 2f out: r.o fnl f to take 3rd last 75yds: nrst fin* **3/1[3]**

2060 **4** *1* **Volcanic Dust (IRE)**[11] 6561 6-9-4 50.....................(t) FrannyNorton 7 46
(Milton Bradley) *chsd ldng trio: carried wd bnd over 3f out: nt on terms w ldrs after: rdn over 1f out: disp 3rd at one pce ins fnl f* **14/1**

0002 **5** *nk* **Dont Tell Nan**[42] 5574 3-9-2 48..................... DaleSwift 5 43
(Derek Shaw) *t.k.h: trckd ldng pair: wd bnd over 3f out: no imp over 1f out: lost 3rd last 75yds* **6/1**

4665 **6** *nk* **Silken Poppy**[26] 6090 3-9-4 50..................... LiamJones 9 44+
(Patrick Chamings) *dropped in fr wd draw and towards rr: in tch 2f out: shkn up 1f out: kpt on one pce after* **25/1**

-000 **7** *5* **Mack's Sister**[35] 5833 7-9-2 48.....................(p) WilliamCarson 8 23+
(Michael Madgwick) *dwlt: sn rdn and struggling: no ch whn wd bnd 2f out* **33/1**

0/0- **8** *hd* **Ladydolly**[440] 4427 6-9-1 50.....................(p) DeclanBates(3) 1 25
(Roy Brotherton) *chsd ldrs to 1/2-way: sn wknd* **66/1**

4000 **9** *1* **Speedy Rio (IRE)**[21] 6243 3-9-2 48..................... SteveDrowne 2 20+
(Luke Dace) *dwlt: sn struggling in rr: nvr a factor* **50/1**

1m 0.33s (-0.17) **Going Correction** -0.025s/f (Stan) **9** Ran SP% **121.1**
Speed ratings (Par 97): **100,98,95,94,93 93,85,84,83**
CSF £6.58 CT £12.50 TOTE £3.60: £1.40, £1.50, £1.10; EX 7.60 Trifecta £24.40.
**Owner** Brian, Mark & Carolynn Day & Mayden Stud **Bred** Mayden Stud, J A And D S Dewhurst **Trained** Cropthorne, Worcs

**FOCUS**
A very ordinary race.

## 6852 BRITISH STALLION STUDS EBF MAIDEN STKS 6f (P)
**6:15** (6:16) (Class 5) 2-Y-0 **£2,911** (£866; £432; £216) **Stalls** Low

Form RPR

2433 **1** **Khawaater**[15] 6422 2-9-0 67.....................(t) DaneO'Neill 4 69
(Roger Varian) *hld up in tch: clsd on ldrs over 1f out: shkn up to ld ins fnl f: sn pressed: hld on wl* **5/2[1]**

0 **2** *hd* **Longside**[61] 4864 2-9-5 0..................... JamesDoyle 8 73
(Charles Hills) *dwlt: in tch in rr: prog wl over 2f out: clsd over 1f out: wnt 2nd and str chal last 100yds: a jst hld* **3/1[2]**

**3** *2 1/4* **Sharissima** 2-9-0 0..................... RobertHavlin 10 62+
(Lady Cecil) *pressed ldrs: shkn up to ld 2f out: hdd ins fnl f: fdd nr fin* **7/1**

**4** *3/4* **Francisco** 2-9-5 0..................... SeanLevey 7 64
(Richard Hannon) *t.k.h: trckd ldr 2f: styd cl up: shkn up briefly over 1f out: kpt on same pce* **7/2[3]**

60 **5** *1 1/4* **Londonia**[9] 6604 2-9-5 0..................... DavidProbert 3 61
(Paul Cole) *prom: led on inner wl over 2f out to 2f out: steadily outpcd after* **6/1**

**6** *shd* **Equleus** 2-9-5 0..................... SteveDrowne 11 60+
(Jeremy Gask) *s.s and swvd lft: t.k.h and rn green in last pair: shkn up over 2f out: kpt on quite wl fr over 1f out: nrst fin* **20/1**

0 **7** *3* **Epsom Poems**[102] 3467 2-9-5 0..................... JFEgan 6 51
(Pat Phelan) *in tch in midfield: pushed along over 2f out: no imp over 1f out: fdd fnl f* **20/1**

**8** *1 1/2* **Red House Rebel (IRE)** 2-9-5 0..................... HarryBentley 5 47
(Stuart Williams) *s.s: wl in rr: rdn and sme prog over 2f out: wknd jst over 1f out* **25/1**

06 **9** *1 3/4* **Courier**[16] 6408 2-9-0 0..................... MartinHarley 2 37
(Jeremy Noseda) *s.s: hld up in last: pushed along over 2f out: no significant prog* **12/1**

0 **10** *4* **Dotties Boy**[42] 5555 2-9-2 0..................... JemmaMarshall(3) 1 30
(Pat Phelan) *led to wl over 2f out: nudged along and steadily wknd* **50/1**

**11** *3* **Vejovis** 2-9-5 0..................... ChrisCatlin 9 21
(Sir Mark Prescott Bt) *dwlt: rn green and wd in rr: wknd over 2f out* **14/1**

1m 15.49s (2.39) **Going Correction** -0.025s/f (Stan) **11** Ran SP% **132.3**
Speed ratings (Par 95): **83,82,79,78,77 76,72,70,68,63 59**
CSF £11.12 TOTE £3.10: £1.10, £1.40, £3.70; EX 16.70 Trifecta £76.80.
**Owner** Hamdan Al Maktoum **Bred** Shadwell Estate Company Limited **Trained** Newmarket, Suffolk

**FOCUS**
A fair maiden run at a steady pace.

## 6853 BETDAQ 50% COMMISSION REFUND NOVICE STKS (BOBIS RACE) 1m (P)
**6:45** (6:46) (Class 3) 2-Y-0
**£6,225** (£1,864; £932; £466; £233; £117) **Stalls** Low

Form RPR

1 **1** **My Reward**[17] 6362 2-9-7 0..................... JamesDoyle 4 90
(Charles Hills) *trckd ldrs: shkn up to ld over 2f out: hrd pressed and drifted lft fnl f: jst hld on* **9/4[2]**

512 **2** *nse* **Sharp Sailor (USA)**[21] 6241 2-9-7 89..................... MartinHarley 2 90
(Marco Botti) *w.w in tch: rdn and prog 2f out: chal fnl f: carried lft but styd on: jst failed* **5/4[1]**

15 **3** *2* **Gibeon (IRE)**[12] 6520 2-9-7 0..................... RichardHughes 1 85
(Richard Hannon) *led 3f: chal and upsides wl over 2f out gng wl: rdn sn after: tried to press wnr over 1f out: nt qckn* **9/2[3]**

51 **4** *7* **Typhoon Season**[65] 4740 2-9-7 81..................... SeanLevey 6 68
(Richard Hannon) *stdd s: hld up in last and swtchd to inner: prog to chse ldrs 2f out: wknd over 1f out* **16/1**

41 **5** *3/4* **Nona Blu**[26] 6101 2-9-7 77..................... DaneO'Neill 3 66
(Harry Dunlop) *t.k.h early: hld up in tch: shkn up over 2f out: sn wknd* **10/1**

6040 **6** *2* **Chadic**[11] 6529 2-9-7 85..................... FrannyNorton 5 62
(Mark Johnston) *w ldr: led 5f out to over 2f out: sn wknd* **16/1**

1m 39.77s (-0.03) **Going Correction** -0.025s/f (Stan) **6** Ran SP% **114.3**
Speed ratings (Par 99): **99,98,96,89,89 87**
CSF £5.61 TOTE £3.00: £1.10, £2.80; EX 6.70 Trifecta £19.50.
**Owner** K Abdullah **Bred** Millsec Limited **Trained** Lambourn, Berks

■ Stewards' Enquiry : James Doyle caution: careless riding

**FOCUS**
An interesting little race and likeable efforts from the front pair.

## 6854 BETDAQ £200 GAMES BONUS NURSERY H'CAP (BOBIS RACE) 7f (P)
**7:15** (7:17) (Class 3) (0-95,86) 2-Y-0 **£6,225** (£1,864; £932; £466; £233) **Stalls** Low

Form RPR

41 **1** **Bravo Zolo (IRE)**[25] 6138 2-9-3 82..................... MartinHarley 1 87+
(Marco Botti) *reluctant to enter stalls: trckd ldrs: gng best over 2f out: sn rdn to cl: led over 1f out: fnd enough and in command fnl f* **4/6[1]**

1206 **2** *1* **Be Bold**[68] 4605 2-9-2 81..................... RichardHughes 4 83
(Richard Hannon) *t.k.h early: hld up in last: pushed along and prog over 2f out: rdn to press wnr fnl f: no imp last 100yds* **16/1**

5421 **3** *1 1/4* **Subversive (IRE)**[20] 6271 2-8-10 75.....................(b[1]) FrannyNorton 6 74
(Mark Johnston) *pressed ldr: rdn to ld over 2f out: hdd over 1f out: one pce ins fnl f* **8/1**

2512 **4** *1/2* **Flying Machine (IRE)**[39] 5672 2-9-7 86..................... DaneO'Neill 3 84
(Richard Fahey) *rousted along early: trckd ldrs: rdn over 2f out and sn in last: n.d after: kpt on fnl f* **4/1[2]**

3234 **5** *1/2* **Big Chill (IRE)**[49] 5310 2-8-13 78..................... JamesDoyle 2 74
(Charles Hills) *led: rdn and hdd over 2f out: sn btn but kpt on same pce fnl f* **6/1[3]**

1m 26.07s (0.07) **Going Correction** -0.025s/f (Stan) **5** Ran SP% **111.3**
Speed ratings (Par 99): **98,96,95,94,94**
CSF £12.66 TOTE £1.50: £1.10, £3.80; EX 12.90 Trifecta £38.10.
**Owner** Mohamed Albousi Alghufli **Bred** Tipper House Stud **Trained** Newmarket, Suffolk

**FOCUS**
With the topweight rated 9lb below the race ceiling, this wasn't the strongest race for the grade.

## 6855 BETDAQ 3% COMMISSION H'CAP (LONDON MIDDLE DISTANCE SERIES QUALIFIER) 1m 3f (P)
**7:45** (7:45) (Class 4) (0-85,85) 3-Y-0+ **£4,690** (£1,395; £697; £348) **Stalls** Low

Form RPR

/341 **1** **Daaree (IRE)**[20] 6274 4-8-13 **74**..................... DaneO'Neill 2 84+
(Saeed bin Suroor) *dwlt: sn in 6th: rdn and prog on wd outside 2f out: sustained effrt fnl f to ld last 75yds* **5/2[2]**

6142 **2** *3/4* **Masterpaver**[42] 5552 3-9-4 **85**..................... RichardHughes 4 94
(Alan Bailey) *trckd ldng trio: rdn over 2f out: clsd on outer to ld 1f out: styd on but hdd last 75yds* **5/1**

044 **3** *2 1/4* **Opera Box**[26] 6106 6-9-9 **84**..................... GeorgeBaker 8 89
(Marcus Tregoning) *trckd ldr: rdn to ld 2f out: hdd and one pce 1f out* **4/1[3]**

-005 **4** *1 3/4* **Topamichi**[32] 5931 4-8-11 **72**..................... HarryBentley 3 75
(Mark H Tompkins) *trckd ldng pair: rdn to chal and upsides 2f out to over 1f out: fdd fnl f* **33/1**

0055 **5** *1 1/2* **Kastini**[13] 6487 4-8-12 **73**.....................(v) MartinHarley 7 73
(Denis Coakley) *hld up in last pair: prog on inner to trck ldrs 2f out: rdn over 1f out: wknd fnl f* **20/1**

40/2 **6** *1* **Marzante (USA)**[62] 4808 6-8-12 **73**..................... JamesDoyle 5 72
(Roger Charlton) *led: rdn and hdd 2f out: steadily wknd* **12/1**

005 **7** *5* **Collaboration**[33] 5884 3-8-12 **79**.....................(t) OisinMurphy 6 70
(Andrew Balding) *hld up in last pair: rdn over 2f out: sn struggling and btn* **9/4[1]**

3/1- **8** *33* **Rosie Probert**[284] 3975 5-9-4 **79**..................... DavidProbert 1 17
(Tony Carroll) *s.i.s: pushed up into 5th: rdn 4f out: sn wknd: t.o and eased* **25/1**

2m 19.39s (-2.51) **Going Correction** -0.025s/f (Stan)
**WFA** 3 from 4yo+ 6lb **8** Ran SP% **115.2**
Speed ratings (Par 105): **108,107,105,104,103 102,99,75**
CSF £15.15 CT £47.97 TOTE £3.90: £1.70, £1.20, £2.90; EX 10.70 Trifecta £39.10.
**Owner** Godolphin **Bred** Shadwell Estate Company Limited **Trained** Newmarket, Suffolk

**FOCUS**
There were plenty in with a chance in the straight.

## 6856 BETDAQ £30 FREE BET H'CAP 1m 3f (P)
**8:15** (8:17) (Class 6) (0-60,60) 3-Y-0+ **£1,940** (£577; £288; £144) **Stalls** Low

Form RPR

4240 **1** **Celestial Bay**[9] 6617 5-9-8 58..................... RichardHughes 7 67
(Sylvester Kirk) *stdd s and hld up in last: prog on outer jst over 4f out: rdn over 2f out: clsd to ld jst over 1f out: drvn out* **8/1**

5602 **2** *1* **Dark Days**[31] 5949 3-8-11 53.....................(t) MartinLane 8 60+
(Paul Cole) *trckd ldr after 1f: rdn 3f out: hrd rdn to ld wl over 1f out: hdd jst over 1f out: styd on but wl hld by wnr* **3/1[1]**

3433 **3** *3* **Sweeping Rock (IRE)**[16] 6395 4-9-3 60..............(t) JordanVaughan(7) 12 63
(Marcus Tregoning) *in tch in midfield: rdn wl over 2f out: kpt on fr over 1f out to take 3rd ins fnl f* **6/1[3]**

6060 **4** *1/2* **Poor Duke (IRE)**[4] 6771 4-9-5 55..................... GeorgeBaker 6 57
(Michael Mullineaux) *led 1f: chsd ldng pair: rdn to chal 2f out: nt qckn over 1f out: fdd ins fnl f* **16/1**

1-20 **5** *1 1/4* **Brave Decision**[29] 6007 7-9-10 60..................... MartinHarley 9 60
(Suzy Smith) *short of room over 9f out and dropped to rr: prog on inner over 2f out: drvn over 1f out: one pce after* **4/1[2]**

0605 **6** *1 1/4* **Byronegetonefree**[29] 6015 3-8-12 54..................... OisinMurphy 14 52
(John E Long) *pushed up fr wdst draw to ld after 1f: drvn over 3f out: hdd over 1f out: wknd fnl f* **14/1**

6344 **7** *1 1/4* **Beep**[29] 6007 4-9-9 59..................... RobertHavlin 4 55
(Lydia Richards) *trckd ldrs: rdn and nt qckn over 2f out: steadily fdd* **14/1**

0-00 **8** *2 1/2* **Mad About Harry (IRE)**[13] 6485 4-9-10 60..................(v) SebSanders 1 52
(Linda Jewell) *hld up in last 4f out: rdn and no prog over 2f out: plugged on* **25/1**

2600 **9** *2 3/4* **Amourita (IRE)**[15] 6426 3-9-3 59..................... RichardKingscote 3 46
(Jonathan Portman) *a in rr: no prog u.p over 2f out: no ch after* **25/1**

52 **10** *2* **Ferryview Place**[28] 6031 5-9-1 51.....................(p) StevieDonohoe 10 35
(Ian Williams) *tk fierce hold: trckd ldrs: rdn wl over 2f out: wknd qckly over 1f out* **6/1[3]**

60-0 **11** *2 3/4* **Majnon Fajer (IRE)**[13] 6483 4-8-11 47..................... PatCosgrave 2 27
(Jane Chapple-Hyam) *trckd ldrs: rdn 4f out: lost pl over 2f out: wknd qckly over 1f out* **50/1**

-000 **12** *hd* **Cinnamon Spice**[49] 5313 3-9-4 60 DaneO'Neill 5 39
(Harry Dunlop) *hld up in rr: gng bttr than many 3f out: shkn up and fnd nil over 2f out: wknd* **20/1**

0526 **13** *nk* **Saturation Point**[18] 6338 3-9-3 59 ChrisCatlin 11 38
(James Toller) *hld up towards rr on outer: rdn and wknd over 2f out* **7/1**

2m 22.08s (0.18) **Going Correction** -0.025s/f (Stan)
**WFA** 3 from 4yo+ 6lb **13 Ran SP% 130.8**
Speed ratings (Par 101): **98,97,95,94,93 92,92,90,88,86 84,84,84**
CSF £34.07 CT £166.83 TOTE £7.90: £2.30, £2.70, £2.70; EX 51.40 Trifecta £559.90.

**Owner** Homebred Racing **Bred** Chris Wall **Trained** Upper Lambourn, Berks

**FOCUS**
They went fast early, slowed it down in the back straight, then quickened turning in. The form looks ordinary.

## 6857 BARN DANCE CHRISTMAS PARTIES ON 01932 753518 H'CAP (DIV I) 7f (P)

**8:45** (8:45) (Class 6) (0-65,65) 3-Y-O+ **£1,940** (£577; £288; £144) **Stalls** Low

Form RPR

5006 **1** **Diamonds A Dancing**[98] 3576 4-8-7 51 oh2 (be[1]) FrannyNorton 8 59
(Brian Gubby) *trckd ldr: clsd to ld over 1f out: sn hdd: rallied wl fnl f to ld last strides* **16/1**

0023 **2** *nse* **Princess Spirit**[21] 6242 5-9-0 58 (p) RichardHughes 7 66
(Edward Creighton) *chsd ldrs in 6th: pushed along 1/2-way: prog over 2f out: rdn to ld jst over 1f out: worn down last strides* **11/4**[1]

0000 **3** *3/4* **Settle For Red (IRE)**[21] 6243 4-8-11 55 (b[1]) SteveDrowne 3 61
(Jeremy Gask) *trckd ldrs: rdn over 2f out: kpt on to take 3rd ins fnl f: clsd at fin but nvr able to chal* **20/1**

0560 **4** *1 1/2* **Lord Of The Dance (IRE)**[16] 6414 8-9-6 64 GeorgeBaker 9 66
(Michael Mullineaux) *hld up in last pair: cajoled along and prog fr jst over 2f out: styd on to press for a pl ins fnl f: pushed along and effrt petered out nr fin* **9/2**[2]

0221 **5** *shd* **Celestial Knight**[21] 6243 3-9-3 63 (v) ShaneKelly 10 64
(James Fanshawe) *towards rr: hanging whn rdn over 2f out: kpt on fr over 1f out: nvr able to threaten* **11/4**[1]

4600 **6** *3 1/4* **Marweena (IRE)**[97] 3627 3-9-2 62 MartinLane 1 54
(Martin Smith) *trckd ldng pair: chal on ins 2f out: nt qckn over 1f out: wknd fnl f* **50/1**

6000 **7** *nk* **Officer In Command (USA)**[25] 6160 8-9-0 58 (p) LiamKeniry 4 50
(John Butler) *dwlt: wl in rr: shuffled along over 2f out: modest late prog: nvr involved* **33/1**

5536 **8** *1 1/4* **Lacock**[11] 6567 3-9-3 63 (b[1]) DaneO'Neill 5 51
(Henry Candy) *pushed up to ld and then set fast pce: rdn and hdd over 1f out: wknd and eased fnl f* **8/1**[3]

030 **9** *nk* **What A Dandy (IRE)**[19] 6297 3-9-4 64 (p[1]) PatCosgrave 12 51
(Jim Boyle) *chsd ldrs: hanging lft bnd 4f out: wknd over 2f out* **33/1**

6664 **10** *hd* **Queen Aggie (IRE)**[11] 6562 4-9-7 65 WilliamCarson 14 52
(Tony Carroll) *forced to r wd: towards rr: rdn and no prog over 2f out* **20/1**

555 **11** *1 1/2* **Mon Cigar (IRE)**[37] 5775 3-9-5 65 OisinMurphy 2 47
(Denis Coakley) *in tch: rdn on inner whn hmpd over 2f out: tried to rally over 1f out: sn wknd* **8/1**[3]

2050 **12** *14* **Russian Ice**[156] 1799 6-9-7 65 JimCrowley 11 10
(Dean Ivory) *a in last trio: rdn and wknd over 2f out: t.o* **10/1**

1m 26.07s (0.07) **Going Correction** -0.025s/f (Stan)
**WFA** 3 from 4yo+ 2lb **12 Ran SP% 126.1**
Speed ratings (Par 101): **98,97,97,95,95 91,91,89,89,89 87,71**
CSF £60.58 CT £942.83 TOTE £20.50: £6.00, £1.30, £6.10; EX 77.50 Trifecta £1567.20.

**Owner** Brian Gubby **Bred** Lady Caffyn-Parsons **Trained** Bagshot, Surrey

**FOCUS**
An ordinary handicap.

## 6858 BARN DANCE CHRISTMAS PARTIES ON 01932 753518 H'CAP (DIV II) 7f (P)

**9:15** (9:15) (Class 6) (0-65,65) 3-Y-O+ **£1,940** (£577; £288; £144) **Stalls** Low

Form RPR

0635 **1** **Buckland Beau**[49] 5304 3-9-3 63 FrederikTylicki 7 72
(Charlie Fellowes) *chsd ldr: rdn to ld jst over 2f out and sent for home: clr over 1f out: drvn and kpt on* **8/1**

0260 **2** *2* **Borough Boy (IRE)**[18] 6346 4-9-6 64 DaleSwift 10 68
(Derek Shaw) *dropped in fr wdst draw and hld up in last: t.k.h: prog 2f out: drvn and r.o to take 2nd last stride: too much to do* **25/1**

4561 **3** *shd* **Eager To Bow (IRE)**[46] 5423 8-9-4 62 (p) DavidProbert 6 66
(Patrick Chamings) *in tch in midfield: effrt but already outpcd 2f out: drvn and styd on to chse wnr nr fin: lost 2nd last stride* **8/1**

6001 **4** *nk* **Arabian Flight**[5] 6716 5-9-7 65 6ex (p) AndrewMullen 4 68
(Michael Appleby) *led at gd pce: rdn and hdd jst over 2f out: no ch w wnr 1f out: lost 2 pls nr fin* **3/1**[2]

6353 **5** *2* **George Baker (IRE)**[27] 6070 7-9-7 65 PatCosgrave 3 63
(George Baker) *chsd ldrs: outpcd fr over 2f out: tried to make prog over 1f out: one pce* **6/1**

3454 **6** *3 1/4* **Substantivo (IRE)**[49] 5303 4-9-1 59 JimCrowley 8 48
(Timothy Jarvis) *a in rr: rdn and no prog over 2f out* **9/4**[1]

0-00 **7** *1 1/2* **Henry Grace (IRE)**[224] 665 3-8-6 52 KieranO'Neill 9 36
(Jimmy Fox) *chsd ldng pair: rdn over 2f out: wknd over 1f out* **50/1**

0603 **8** *2 1/4* **Heinrich (USA)**[11] 6568 3-9-2 62 RichardHughes 1 40
(Sylvester Kirk) *chsd ldng pair: outpcd over 2f out: wknd over 1f out* **4/1**[3]

4430 **9** *3 1/2* **Connaught Water (IRE)**[19] 6297 3-8-11 57 RichardKingscote 2 25
(Jonathan Portman) *a in rr: struggling over 2f out: wknd* **33/1**

1m 25.77s (-0.23) **Going Correction** -0.025s/f (Stan)
**WFA** 3 from 4yo+ 2lb **9 Ran SP% 121.0**
Speed ratings (Par 101): **100,97,97,97,94 91,89,86,82**
CSF £184.29 CT £1673.44 TOTE £10.80: £2.20, £6.40, £3.40; EX 100.00 Trifecta £671.30.

**Owner** P S McNally **Bred** D G Hardisty Bloodstock **Trained** Newmarket, Suffolk

**FOCUS**
The faster of the two divisions by 0.3sec. The winner was well ridden.

T/Plt: £10.00 to a £1 stake. Pool: £62,537.52 - 4,545.04 winning tickets T/Qpdt: £6.40 to a £1 stake. Pool: £6,938.11 - 792.60 winning tickets JN

# 6637 NEWCASTLE (L-H)

Wednesday, October 1

**OFFICIAL GOING: Good to firm (good in places on round course; 7.7)**
Weather: Overcast

## 6859 PINPOINT RECRUITMENT/EBF MAIDEN STKS (BOBIS RACE) 1m 3y(S)

**2:00** (2:01) (Class 4) 2-Y-O **£4,075** (£1,212; £606; £303) **Stalls** Centre

Form RPR

0 **1** **Stravagante (IRE)**[33] 5881 2-9-5 0 GrahamGibbons 6 77+
(Sir Michael Stoute) *prom: smooth hdwy to ld over 2f out: pushed out ins fnl f* **9/1**

0 **2** *1 3/4* **Puissant (IRE)**[11] 6551 2-9-5 0 PhillipMakin 8 73
(Marco Botti) *t.k.h: in tch: hdwy to chse wnr 2f out: sn rdn along: kpt on ins fnl f* **11/4**[2]

**3** *shd* **Keble (IRE)** 2-9-5 0 WilliamBuick 5 73+
(John Gosden) *s.s: hld up: hdwy and prom 1/2-way: effrt and disp 2nd pl over 1f out: kpt on ins fnl f* **11/8**[1]

4 **4** *2 1/2* **Mezajy (IRE)**[22] 6204 2-9-5 0 GrahamLee 3 67
(Michael Bell) *trckd ldrs: effrt and pushed along over 1f out: outpcd ins fnl f* **11/2**[3]

**5** *3/4* **Murgan** 2-9-5 0 JamieSpencer 1 65+
(Peter Chapple-Hyam) *dwlt: hld up: pushed along over 2f out: hdwy over 1f out: kpt on fnl f: bttr for r* **8/1**

0 **6** *5* **Light Breaks (IRE)**[57] 5009 2-9-5 0 LukeMorris 7 57+
(Sir Mark Prescott Bt) *dwlt: t.k.h in rr: shkn up over 2f out: hdwy over 1f out: no imp fnl f: improve* **50/1**

55 **7** *2* **Ali Bin Nayef**[11] 6565 2-9-5 0 PaulHanagan 2 49
(Charles Hills) *cl up: effrt and ev ch over 2f out: wknd over 1f out* **14/1**

6 **8** *1* **Life Knowledge (IRE)**[10] 6577 2-9-0 0 JackGarritty[(5)] 4 47
(Patrick Holmes) *led to over 2f out: sn rdn and wknd* **100/1**

00 **F** **Parliament (IRE)**[14] 6449 2-9-5 0 PJMcDonald 9
(Ann Duffield) *bhd: outpcd whn fell over 2f out: fatally injured* **100/1**

1m 41.75s (-1.65) **Going Correction** -0.225s/f (Firm) **9 Ran SP% 115.9**
Speed ratings (Par 97): **99,97,97,94,93 88,86,85,**
CSF £34.22 TOTE £14.60: £3.10, £1.50, £1.10; EX 43.80 Trifecta £128.60.

**Owner** Michael Tabor **Bred** Chelston Ireland **Trained** Newmarket, Suffolk

**FOCUS**
Races on Round course increased by 10yds. An interesting maiden run at a fair pace. Several of these have the scope to do better.

## 6860 GOLDENSHEAF & DINAISH & CHIPS/EBF MAIDEN STKS (BOBIS RACE) (DIV I) 7f

**2:30** (2:30) (Class 4) 2-Y-O **£4,075** (£1,212; £606; £303) **Stalls** Centre

Form RPR

0 **1** **Dagher**[25] 6125 2-9-5 0 WilliamBuick 2 79+
(Peter Chapple-Hyam) *t.k.h: hld up in tch: pushed along over 2f out: hdwy over 1f out: led ins fnl f: hld on wl cl home* **5/2**[3]

5 **2** *hd* **Alnashama**[22] 6203 2-9-5 0 PaulHanagan 6 78+
(Charles Hills) *led: pushed along over 2f out: hdd over 1f out: rallied and disp ld ins fnl f: edgd lft: jst hld* **7/4**[1]

4 **3** *1 1/2* **Yorkindred Spirit**[14] 6448 2-9-0 0 JoeFanning 8 69
(Mark Johnston) *cl up: pushed along and led over 1f out: hdd ins fnl f: kpt on same pce* **15/8**[2]

0 **4** *7* **Arms Around Me (IRE)**[34] 5852 2-9-5 0 PhillipMakin 4 55
(Bryan Smart) *trckd ldrs: pushed along and outpcd over 2f out: n.d after* **25/1**

0 **5** *3/4* **Stoneboat Bill**[7] 6668 2-9-5 0 JasonHart 3 53
(Declan Carroll) *t.k.h: hld up bhd ldng gp: pushed along and outpcd 3f out: no imp fr 2f out* **25/1**

**6** *2* **Night Generation (GER)** 2-9-5 0 LukeMorris 1 48+
(Sir Mark Prescott Bt) *slowly away: rn green in rr: shkn up and stdy hdwy over 2f out: kpt on but no imp fnl f: bttr for r* **25/1**

0 **7** *2* **Tonto's Spirit**[37] 5760 2-9-5 0 PaulMulrennan 5 42
(Michael Dods) *plld hrd in tch: drvn and outpcd 3f out: sn btn* **33/1**

55 **8** *9* **Mister Archie**[10] 6577 2-9-0 0 GarryWhillans[(5)] 9 18
(Alistair Whillans) *hld up: pushed along 3f out: sn struggling* **50/1**

0 **9** *5* **Crown Green**[26] 6115 2-9-0 0 RussKennemore 7
(Karen Tutty) *dwlt: t.k.h and sn in tch: rdn over 3f out: wknd over 2f out* **66/1**

1m 28.37s (0.57) **Going Correction** -0.225s/f (Firm) **9 Ran SP% 117.7**
Speed ratings (Par 97): **87,86,85,77,76 73,71,61,55**
CSF £6.98 TOTE £3.30: £1.90, £1.10, £1.10; EX 8.30 Trifecta £15.30.

**Owner** Ziad A Galadari **Bred** Galadari Sons Stud Company Limited **Trained** Newmarket, Suffolk

**FOCUS**
The pace was honest for this fair maiden. The front three pulled clear.

## 6861 GOLDENSHEAF & DINAISH & CHIPS/EBF MAIDEN STKS (BOBIS RACE) (DIV II) 7f

**3:00** (3:05) (Class 4) 2-Y-O **£4,075** (£1,212; £606; £303) **Stalls** Centre

Form RPR

03 **1** **Capel Path (USA)**[19] 6300 2-9-5 0 GrahamLee 7 78+
(Sir Michael Stoute) *hld up in tch: smooth hdwy over 2f out: led over 1f out: pushed out fnl f: comf* **11/4**[2]

**2** *4* **Taysh (USA)** 2-9-5 0 (t) WilliamBuick 1 66+
(John Gosden) *t.k.h: in tch: hdwy and ev ch over 2f out to over 1f out: sn outpcd by wnr* **7/2**[3]

**3** *1/2* **Castle Talbot (IRE)** 2-9-5 0 JamieSpencer 5 65+
(Charles Hills) *s.v.s: hld up and wl bhd: stdy hdwy and shkn up over 1f out: kpt on wl fnl f: improve* **12/1**

2 **4** *3/4* **Bleu Astral (FR)**[25] 6146 2-9-5 0 TonyHamilton 9 63
(Richard Fahey) *t.k.h: prom: effrt and hung lft over 2f out: one pce whn hung both ways fr over 1f out* **11/10**[1]

4 **5** *1* **Hidden Rebel**[39] 5679 2-8-9 0 GarryWhillans[(5)] 4 55
(Alistair Whillans) *t.k.h: sn w ldr: led 1/2-way to over 1f out: sn outpcd* **40/1**

**6** *3 3/4* **Khafayya (IRE)** 2-9-5 0 PaulHanagan 3 50
(Mark Johnston) *chsd ldrs: outpcd and hung lft over 2f out: wknd over 1f out* **12/1**

**7** *10* **Bond Starprincess** 2-9-0 0 AndrewElliott 8 18
(George Moore) *s.i.s: bhd and outpcd: no ch fr 1/2-way* **100/1**

00 **8** *9* **Unforgettable You (IRE)**[14] 6453 2-9-0 0 JasonHart 2
(Declan Carroll) *t.k.h: led to 1/2-way: outpcd whn bmpd over 2f out: sn btn* **50/1**

1m 27.67s (-0.13) **Going Correction** -0.225s/f (Firm) **8** Ran SP% **117.3**
Speed ratings (Par 97): **91,86,85,85,83 79,68,57**
CSF £13.20 TOTE £2.90: £1.20, £1.30, £2.70; EX 11.50 Trifecta £76.90.
**Owner** The Queen **Bred** Darley **Trained** Newmarket, Suffolk

**FOCUS**
They went a fair pace for this interesting maiden. The winner was quite impressive.

## 6862 AAK FISH & CHIPS MAIDEN STKS 6f
**3:35** (3:40) (Class 5) 3-Y-0+ **£2,587** (£770; £384; £192) **Stalls** Centre

Form RPR

3- **1** **Direct Times (IRE)**[326] 7817 3-9-5 0 WilliamBuick 5 65+
(Peter Chapple-Hyam) *slowly away: t.k.h and sn prom: smooth hdwy to ld over 2f out: rdn and qcknd over 1f out: kpt on wl fnl f* **4/9**[1]

2 **2** *1 1/2* **Advance (FR)**[218] 739 3-9-5 0 JamesSullivan 9 60+
(Ruth Carr) *s.i.s: hld up: effrt and hdwy over 2f out: chsd wnr over 1f out: kpt on fnl f: no imp* **8/1**[3]

**3** *2 3/4* **Baileys Partytime** 3-9-0 0 JoeFanning 6 47+
(Mark Johnston) *w ldrs: ev ch over 2f out: sn rdn: kpt on same pce fr over 1f out* **7/1**[2]

3405 **4** *nk* **Vale Mentor (IRE)**[33] 5891 3-9-5 48 (p) DavidAllan 8 51
(Tim Easterby) *led to over 2f out: rdn and outpcd fr over 1f out* **25/1**

6052 **5** *6* **Stroll On (IRE)**[15] 6437 3-8-9 60 JackGarritty(5) 3 28
(Rae Guest) *hld up in tch: hung lft and outpcd over 3f out: n.d after* **8/1**[3]

0/00 **6** *3 3/4* **Morna's Glory**[106] 3334 5-9-1 45 PaulMulrennan 4 17
(Michael Herrington) *t.k.h: w ldrs tl hung lft and wknd 2f out* **50/1**

4-0 **7** *10* **Nonagon**[26] 6118 3-9-0 0 EmmaSayer(5) 7
(Wilf Storey) *s.i.s: outpcd in rr: no ch fr 1/2-way* **50/1**

3- **8** *1* **Livia Drusilla (IRE)**[540] 1449 3-8-9 0 MeganCarberry(5) 2
(Brian Ellison) *t.k.h: cl up tl hung lft and wknd 2f out* **33/1**

1m 14.29s (-0.31) **Going Correction** -0.225s/f (Firm)
**WFA** 3 from 4yo+ 1lb **8** Ran SP% **114.7**
Speed ratings (Par 103): **93,91,87,86,78 73,60,59**
CSF £4.46 TOTE £1.30: £1.02, £1.80, £2.00; EX 5.00 Trifecta £18.60.
**Owner** Allan Belshaw **Bred** Times Of Wigan Ltd **Trained** Newmarket, Suffolk
■ Thorntoun Lady was withdrawn. Price at time of withdrawal 10/1. Rule 4 applies to all bets deduction - 5p in the pound.

**FOCUS**
A fair pace for this uncompetitive maiden. Thorntoun Lady got very upset in the stalls and was withdrawn.

## 6863 COVERIS PACKAGING FISH & CHIPS FILLIES' H'CAP 7f
**4:10** (4:10) (Class 5) (0-70,71) 3-Y-0+ **£2,587** (£770; £384; £192) **Stalls** Centre

Form RPR

55-3 **1** **Breakable**[12] 6516 3-9-2 67 DavidAllan 3 77
(Tim Easterby) *cl up: led over 2f out: sn rdn: hrd pressed ins fnl f: drvn out towards fin* **4/1**[2]

3330 **2** *1/2* **Fleurtille**[109] 3237 5-9-7 70 RobertWinston 7 80
(Ray Craggs) *taken early to post: hld up: hdwy to chse wnr over 1f out: effrt and ev ch ins fnl f: hld towards fin* **20/1**

06 **3** *1 1/2* **Bint Dandy (IRE)**[8] 6633 3-9-1 69 ConnorBeasley(3) 2 74
(Chris Dwyer) *in tch: effrt and rdn 2f out: kpt on same pce fnl f* **16/1**

5550 **4** *1 3/4* **Spirit Of Alsace (IRE)**[12] 6515 3-8-10 61 GrahamLee 12 61
(Jim Goldie) *t.k.h: led to over 2f out: rdn and hung lft over 1f out: sn no ex* **12/1**

5260 **5** *2 1/2* **Sakhee's Rose**[7] 6674 4-8-13 62 (b) GrahamGibbons 8 56
(Ed McMahon) *dwlt: hld up: smooth hdwy and in tch over 2f out: rdn and one pce over 1f out* **12/1**

1-00 **6** *1 1/2* **Woodland Girl**[50] 5265 3-9-3 68 [1] TonyHamilton 10 57
(Richard Fahey) *hld up: pushed along and hung lft over 2f out: sn outpcd: no imp fr over 1f out* **8/1**

0016 **7** *3* **Graceful Act**[8] 6628 6-8-2 56 oh1 EmmaSayer(5) 6 38
(Ron Barr) *prom: rdn over 2f out: wknd over 1f out* **20/1**

1140 **8** *2 1/2* **Clumber Place**[21] 6232 8-9-4 67 JasonHart 4 42
(Shaun Harris) *w ldr: rdn over 2f out: wknd wl over 1f out* **17/2**

-031 **9** *1/2* **Abbotsfield (IRE)**[40] 5642 4-9-2 65 (p) AndrewElliott 13 39
(Ben Haslam) *in tch: rdn and hung lft over 2f out: sn outpcd: btn over 1f out* **5/2**[1]

0021 **10** *3/4* **Blue Maisey**[8] 6626 6-9-3 71 6ex JackGarritty(5) 1 43
(Edwin Tuer) *prom: rdn over 2f out: wknd over 1f out* **5/1**[3]

3400 **11** *1 1/2* **Gladsome**[42] 5573 6-8-7 56 oh5 (p) JoeFanning 5 24
(Michael Herrington) *t.k.h: hld up in tch: struggling and hung lft over 2f out: sn btn* **33/1**

1m 27.11s (-0.69) **Going Correction** -0.225s/f (Firm)
**WFA** 3 from 4yo+ 2lb **11** Ran SP% **120.6**
Speed ratings (Par 100): **94,93,91,89,86 85,81,78,78,77 75**
CSF £85.93 CT £1191.18 TOTE £4.30: £1.60, £6.30, £7.20; EX 100.90 Trifecta £1355.70.
**Owner** Ryedale Partners No 9 **Bred** Habton Farms **Trained** Great Habton, N Yorks

**FOCUS**
An open fillies' handicap, run at an honest pace.

## 6864 HENRY COLBECK FISH & CHIPS H'CAP 2m 19y
**4:40** (4:40) (Class 5) (0-75,78) 3-Y-0+ **£2,587** (£770; £384; £192) **Stalls** Low

Form RPR

1211 **1** **Moscato**[8] 6640 3-9-9 78 6ex (p) LukeMorris 8 91+
(Sir Mark Prescott Bt) *led after 2f and maintained stdy pce: shkn up and qcknd clr over 2f out: kpt on strly fnl f: easily* **4/6**[1]

4153 **2** *2 3/4* **Hurry Home Poppa (IRE)**[8] 6651 4-9-4 62 JoeFanning 11 68
(John Mackie) *hld up in tch: rdn and hdwy over 2f out: chsd (clr) wnr over 1f out: kpt on fnl f: no imp* **20/1**

6043 **3** *1* **Chevalgris**[13] 6493 4-9-12 70 DavidAllan 9 75
(Alan Swinbank) *cl up: wnt 2nd 1/2-way: effrt and rdn over 2f out: one pce whn lost 2nd over 1f out* **20/1**

4332 **4** *nk* **Arcamante (ITY)**[14] 6461 3-9-1 70 DanielTudhope 7 76+
(K R Burke) *hld up in midfield: pushed along over 3f out: hung lft and hdwy over 2f out: kpt on fnl f: no imp* **6/1**[2]

4423 **5** *3/4* **Wor Lass**[8] 6644 6-9-0 58 PaulMulrennan 14 62
(Iain Jardine) *hld up: hdwy whn nt clr run over 3f out to over 2f out: rdn and styd on fnl f: nvr able to chal* **20/1**

3406 **6** *3 1/2* **Bowdler's Magic**[13] 6493 7-9-8 66 (t) DavidNolan 15 65
(David Thompson) *hld up: rdn along 3f out: styd on fr 2f out: nvr able to chal* **40/1**

2355 **7** *1 1/4* **Jan Smuts (IRE)**[16] 6404 6-9-6 64 (tp) GrahamLee 12 62
(Wilf Storey) *t.k.h: hld up: pushed along 3f out: styd on fnl f: nrst fin* **25/1**

1126 **8** *1 1/2* **Precision Strike**[33] 5890 4-10-0 72 (v) JasonHart 3 68
(Richard Guest) *missed break: t.k.h in rr: rdn over 3f out: sme late hdwy: n.d* **25/1**

3163 **9** *hd* **Censorius**[29] 6019 3-8-13 68 (v) JamesSullivan 4 64
(Ed Walker) *midfield: rdn and outpcd whn nt clr run over 2f out: n.d after* **16/1**

4-26 **10** *shd* **Enchanted Garden**[48] 5334 6-9-9 67 PaulHanagan 13 63
(Malcolm Jefferson) *hld up: drvn and outpcd over 2f out: sn n.d* **15/2**[3]

/64- **11** *4 1/2* **Viva Colonia (IRE)**[173] 4343 9-8-11 60 MeganCarberry(5) 1 50
(Brian Ellison) *trckd ldrs: drvn over 2f out: wknd wl over 1f out* **33/1**

4331 **12** *1 1/2* **Beat The Shower**[45] 5466 8-9-1 59 RobertWinston 2 47
(Peter Niven) *t.k.h in midfield: hdwy and prom over 2f out: wknd wl over 1f out* **16/1**

6664 **13** *4 1/2* **My Escapade (IRE)**[26] 6117 3-8-1 56 oh5 ow1 RoystonFfrench 5 39
(Simon Waugh) *led at stdy pce 2f: cl up tl rdn and wknd over 2f out* **50/1**

/000 **14** *7* **Takaatuf (IRE)**[15] 6216 8-8-9 56 ConnorBeasley(3) 6 31
(Tina Jackson) *t.k.h: trckd ldrs tl wknd fr 3f out* **80/1**

3m 36.2s (-3.20) **Going Correction** -0.225s/f (Firm)
**WFA** 3 from 4yo+ 11lb **14** Ran SP% **128.4**
Speed ratings (Par 103): **99,97,97,96,96 94,94,93,93,93 91,90,88,84**
CSF £24.25 CT £193.86 TOTE £2.10: £1.50, £5.40, £3.00; EX 23.10 Trifecta £287.30.
**Owner** The Green Door Partnership **Bred** Miss K Rausing **Trained** Newmarket, Suffolk

**FOCUS**
A steady pace for this uncompetitive staying handicap. The winner was well ahead and enjoyed a big class edge.

## 6865 STP CONSTRUCTION H'CAP 1m 3y(S)
**5:10** (5:17) (Class 5) (0-70,70) 3-Y-0+ **£2,587** (£770; £384; £192) **Stalls** Centre

Form RPR

5363 **1** **Exclusive Waters (IRE)**[7] 6672 4-9-1 61 RobertWinston 9 69
(Tracy Waggott) *hld up: hdwy over 2f out: rdn to ld ins fnl f: styd on wl* **4/1**[1]

0003 **2** *1* **Woody Bay**[27] 6057 4-9-10 70 JasonHart 3 76
(Mark Walford) *t.k.h: prom: led over 2f out: rdn over 1f out: hdd ins fnl f: one pce* **6/1**[3]

4660 **3** *shd* **Patriotic (IRE)**[21] 6232 6-9-6 69 (p) ConnorBeasley(3) 5 74
(Chris Dwyer) *slowly away: hld up: hdwy gng wl over 2f out: effrt and ev ch ins fnl f: kpt on: hld nr fin* **16/1**

6430 **4** *nk* **Day Of The Eagle (IRE)**[11] 6543 8-9-2 62 PhillipMakin 15 67
(Michael Easterby) *hld up: stdy hdwy and in tch over 1f out: rdn ins fnl f: kpt on towards fin* **14/1**

1663 **5** *1/2* **Thankyou Very Much**[36] 5793 4-9-7 67 (b[1]) JoeFanning 8 71
(James Bethell) *dwlt: t.k.h in tch: effrt and pushed along over 1f out: kpt on ins fnl f* **8/1**

4423 **6** *2 1/4* **Outlaw Torn (IRE)**[3] 6795 5-9-2 62 (e) TonyHamilton 2 60
(Richard Guest) *t.k.h: led to over 2f out: rdn and one pce fr over 1f out* **5/1**[2]

3051 **7** *1 3/4* **Tanawar (IRE)**[11] 6544 4-9-3 63 (b) JamesSullivan 12 57
(Ruth Carr) *t.k.h: hld up: effrt over 2f out: edgd lft and no imp fr over 1f out* **12/1**

6600 **8** *4 1/2* **Presidente**[21] 6240 3-9-2 65 LukeMorris 13 49
(Ed Walker) *hld up in tch: stdy hdwy 3f out: rdn and wknd 2f out* **20/1**

1130 **9** *14* **Kuwait Star**[21] 6232 5-9-10 70 PaulMulrennan 7 22
(Michael Herrington) *t.k.h: cl up tl rdn and wknd 2f out* **13/2**

0114 **10** *3 1/4* **Broctune Papa Gio**[13] 6490 7-9-10 70 DavidNolan 14 14
(Keith Reveley) *prom: drvn along 3f out: wknd fr 2f out* **10/1**

50-2 **11** *51* **Venutius**[21] 6227 7-9-9 69 GrahamGibbons 1
(Ed McMahon) *cl up tl wknd over 2f out: virtually p.u fnl f* **7/1**

1m 40.91s (-2.49) **Going Correction** -0.225s/f (Firm)
**WFA** 3 from 4yo+ 3lb **11** Ran SP% **122.0**
Speed ratings (Par 103): **103,102,101,101,101 98,97,92,78,75 24**
CSF £28.87 CT £357.12 TOTE £5.60: £2.20, £3.00, £5.60; EX 33.10 Trifecta £537.50.
**Owner** Northumbria Leisure Ltd **Bred** M M Sammon **Trained** Spennymoor, Co Durham

**FOCUS**
They went a solid pace for this open handicap. The action unfolded towards the far side.

## 6866 NORTH SEA LOGISTICS H'CAP 5f
**5:40** (5:43) (Class 6) (0-60,60) 3-Y-0+ **£1,940** (£577; £288; £144) **Stalls** Centre

Form RPR

3313 **1** **Pavers Star**[16] 6406 5-9-1 54 (p) JoeFanning 10 64
(Noel Wilson) *mde all: rdn over 1f out: hrd pressed ins fnl f: hld on wl towards fin* **5/1**[2]

0-00 **2** *1/2* **Invincible Lad (IRE)**[119] 2890 10-9-7 60 (b) GrahamGibbons 12 68
(Ed McMahon) *dwlt: hld up in tch: smooth hdwy over 2f out: effrt and ev ch ins fnl f: kpt on: hld nr fin* **25/1**

0040 **3** *3* **Fujin**[38] 5715 3-9-3 56 (b[1]) PatrickMathers 7 54
(Shaun Harris) *prom: effrt and ev ch over 2f out to over 1f out: outpcd by first two fnl f* **12/1**

453 **4** *1/2* **Captain Scooby**[9] 6595 8-8-9 48 (v) TonyHamilton 2 44
(Richard Guest) *hld up: rdn and hdwy over 1f out: kpt on ins fnl f: nvr able to chal* **7/2**[1]

-005 **5** *1 1/4* **Lazy Sioux**[105] 3366 3-8-8 47 DuranFentiman 6 39
(Richard Guest) *hld up: pushed along over 2f out: hdwy over 1f out: nrst fin* **33/1**

6405 **6** *1* **Bondi Beach Babe**[16] 6409 4-8-9 53 JackGarritty(5) 11 41
(James Turner) *prom: rdn over 2f out: one pce over 1f out* **8/1**

0-06 **7** *nk* **On The High Tops (IRE)**[3] 6796 6-8-8 47 (p) RoystonFfrench 14 33
(Colin Teague) *hld up: rdn and hdwy over 1f out: kpt on: nvr rchd ldrs* **33/1**

0400 **8** *2 3/4* **Sunrise Dance**[40] 5636 5-8-10 52 ConnorBeasley(3) 3 29
(Robert Johnson) *prom far side: rdn over 2f out: outpcd fr over 1f out* **5/1**[2]

1000 **9** *shd* **Black Douglas**[7] 6674 5-8-12 58 (v[1]) RachaelGrant(7) 5 34
(Jim Goldie) *hld up: rdn and drifted lft to far side fr over 2f out: no imp over 1f out* **6/1**[3]

6235 **10** *3/4* **Arch Walker (IRE)**[28] 6023 7-8-9 48 (b) LukeMorris 13 21
(John Weymes) *prom: rdn over 2f out: wknd over 1f out* **25/1**

0300 **11** *3/4* **Foreign Rhythm (IRE)**[7] 6671 9-9-7 60 GrahamLee 16 31
(Ron Barr) *hld up: pushed along over 2f out: sn no imp* **12/1**

0000 **12** *2 3/4* **Chamberlain**[7] 6674 3-9-2 55 (b[1]) JasonHart 8 17
(John Murray) *chsd ldrs: drvn along and wknd fr 2f out* **25/1**

0060 **13** *shd* **Aspirant**[89] 3908 3-9-7 60 DanielTudhope 15 22
(Marjorie Fife) *bhd: outpcd over 2f out: sn btn* **11/1**

0606 **14** *3/4* **Chosen One (IRE)**[35] 5819 9-9-5 58 JamesSullivan 4 16
(Ruth Carr) *spd far side tl rdn and wknd wl over 1f out* **12/1**

1m 0.01s (-1.09) **Going Correction** -0.225s/f (Firm) **14** Ran SP% **129.8**
Speed ratings (Par 101): **99,98,93,92,90 89,88,84,83,82 81,77,77,75**
CSF £139.16 CT £1465.98 TOTE £5.20: £1.70, £9.40, £5.40; EX 213.70 Trifecta £1765.10.

**Owner** Mrs Michael John Paver **Bred** Mrs C K Paver **Trained** Middleham, N Yorks
**FOCUS**
A truly run sprint handicap. The winner was back to his best.
T/Plt: £14.50 to a £1 stake. Pool: £64,077.46 - 3,213.93 winning tickets T/Qpdt: £11.80 to a £1 stake. Pool: £5,291.30 - 330.10 winning tickets RY

## 6645 NOTTINGHAM (L-H)
Wednesday, October 1

**OFFICIAL GOING: Good to firm (8.1)**
Wind: Virtually nil Weather: Fine and dry

### 6867 EBF STALLIONS SLIP ANCHOR MAIDEN STKS — 5f 13y
**2:10** (2:10) (Class 5) 2-Y-O — **£3,234** (£962; £481; £240) **Stalls** Centre

Form / RPR
52 **1** **Just Us Two (IRE)**[19] 6299 2-9-5 0 FrederikTylicki 5 77
(Robert Cowell) *cl up: slt ld 2f out: rdn clr and edgd lft ent fnl f: kpt on* **1/1**[1]
0 **2** *2* **Krazy Paving**[12] 6517 2-9-5 0 WilliamTwiston-Davies 2 70+
(Mick Channon) *towards rr: hdwy 2f out: sn rdn: styd on to chse wnr ins fnl f: no imp towards fin* **5/1**[2]
05 **3** *1 3/4* **You're Cool**[7] 6659 2-9-5 0 TomEaves 7 64+
(James Given) *trckd ldrs: hdwy 1/2-way: rdn along wl over 1f out: kpt on same pce fnl f* **8/1**
00 **4** *1* **Kill Or Cure (IRE)**[12] 6517 2-9-2 0 CamHardie(3) 4 60+
(Charles Hills) *dwlt and in rr: pushed along 1/2-way: hdwy wl over 1f out: sn rdn and kpt on fnl f: nrst fin* **7/1**[3]
56 **5** *1 1/4* **Belle Nellie (IRE)**[14] 6453 2-8-9 0 ShelleyBirkett(5) 3 50
(Nigel Tinkler) *cl up: slt ld after 1 1/2f: hdd and rdn 2f out: grad wknd appr fnl f* **50/1**
4050 **6** *1/2* **Able Spirit**[8] 6629 2-9-5 71 MartinDwyer 6 54
(Brian Meehan) *t.k.h and carried hd high: led 1 1/2f: cl up: rdn along over 2f out: sn wknd* **8/1**
6260 **7** *nse* **Muhaarib Al Emarat (IRE)**[29] 6008 2-9-2 68 GeorgeChaloner(3) 9 53
(Richard Fahey) *chsd ldrs: rdn along over 2f out: sn no imp* **20/1**
6 **8** *1 3/4* **Taffetta**[48] 5332 2-9-0 0 BarryMcHugh 1 42
(Tony Coyle) *awkward and wnt lft s: a in rr* **25/1**
0 **9** *11* **Exceedwell**[15] 6434 2-8-9 0 JoeDoyle(5) 8 3
(John Ryan) *a towards rr* **100/1**
1m 0.66s (-0.84) **Going Correction** -0.175s/f (Firm) **9 Ran SP% 112.9**
Speed ratings (Par 95): **99,95,93,91,89 88,88,85,68**
CSF £5.68 TOTE £1.70: £1.10, £1.30, £2.70; EX 5.90 Trifecta £42.70.
**Owner** Abdulla Al Mansoori **Bred** Andy Macdonald & Sarah Wigley **Trained** Six Mile Bottom, Cambs
**FOCUS**
Outer track used. Rail stepped out 2m on home bend and races on Round course increased by 6yds. This was probably just an ordinary sprint maiden.

### 6868 EBF STALLIONS OH SO SHARP MAIDEN FILLIES' STKS (BOBIS RACE) — 1m 75y
**2:40** (2:40) (Class 5) 2-Y-O — **£3,234** (£962; £481; £240) **Stalls** Centre

Form / RPR
4 **1** **Elle Dorado**[96] 3642 2-9-0 0 RichardKingscote 4 70
(Tom Dascombe) *led: pushed along and hdd 3f out: cl up on inner: rdn to ld again ent fnl f: kpt on wl towards fin* **7/1**
**2** *1/2* **Waldnah** 2-9-0 0 RobertHavlin 8 69+
(John Gosden) *dwlt and bhd: gd hdwy over 2f out: chsd ldrs over 1f out: n.m.r and swtchd rt ent fnl f: sn rdn and styd on strly* **7/2**[1]
04 **3** *1 1/4* **Imperial Link**[15] 6434 2-9-0 0 JimCrowley 10 66
(Paul Cole) *cl up: slt ld 3f out: rdn wl over 1f out: hdd ent fnl f: sn drvn and kpt on same pce* **5/1**[3]
**4** *hd* **Chapel Choir** 2-9-0 0 TedDurcan 6 66+
(Sir Michael Stoute) *towards rr: hdwy on inner over 2f out: pushed along and green wl over 1f out: rdn and styd on ins fnl f: nrst fin* **9/1**
0 **5** *nse* **Amber Mile**[22] 6208 2-9-0 0 SilvestreDeSousa 5 66
(Ralph Beckett) *trckd ldrs: hdwy on outer 1/2-way: rdn to chse ldng trio wl over 1f out: drvn ent fnl f: kpt on same pce* **7/1**
0 **6** *1/2* **Asima (IRE)**[11] 6553 2-8-11 0 CamHardie(3) 2 65
(Charles Hills) *t.k.h: trckd ldrs on inner: hdwy over 2f out: rdn over 1f out: drvn and kpt on same pce fnl f* **10/1**
0 **7** *3 1/2* **Vivi's Charis (IRE)**[35] 5821 2-9-0 0 ShaneKelly 3 57
(Sir Michael Stoute) *trckd ldrs: hdwy to chse ldng pair over 3f out: rdn along 2f out: wknd appr fnl f* **50/1**
6 **8** *2* **Scots Fern**[11] 6554 2-9-0 0 FergusSweeney 1 52
(Andrew Balding) *dwlt: sn chsng ldrs: rdn along over 2f out: edgd lft and wknd over 1f out* **9/2**[2]
**9** *nk* **Honour Promise (IRE)** 2-9-0 0 MartinDwyer 11 52
(William Muir) *s.i.s: a in rr* **33/1**
**10** *1/2* **Hyphaema (IRE)** 2-9-0 0 SteveDrowne 7 51
(Clive Cox) *towards rr: effrt and sme hdwy 3f out: rdn along over 2f out: sn wknd* **14/1**
**11** *nk* **The Madding Crowd** 2-9-0 0[1] HayleyTurner 9 50
(Hughie Morrison) *t.k.h: hld up: a towards rr* **20/1**
1m 49.48s (0.48) **Going Correction** -0.175s/f (Firm) **11 Ran SP% 117.5**
Speed ratings (Par 92): **90,89,88,88,88 87,84,82,81,81 80**
CSF £31.10 TOTE £4.90: £1.50, £1.80, £1.30; EX 27.10 Trifecta £67.50.
**Owner** Manor House Racing Club **Bred** Newsells Park Stud **Trained** Malpas, Cheshire
**FOCUS**
The pace was steady. A couple of nice types have won this in recent years, so it's best to treat this form positively until proven otherwise.

### 6869 WATCH RACINGUK ON SKY CHANNEL 432 NURSERY H'CAP — 1m 2f 50y
**3:10** (3:10) (Class 5) (0-75,67) 2-Y-O — **£2,587** (£770; £384; £192) **Stalls** Low

Form / RPR
0205 **1** **Our Kylie (IRE)**[6] 6691 2-9-3 63 BarryMcHugh 6 68
(Tony Coyle) *led to 1/2-way: cl up on inner: led again 3f out: rdn along wl over 1f out: drvn ins fnl f: hld on gamely towards fin* **11/1**
6022 **2** *nk* **Hillgrove Angel (IRE)**[8] 6648 2-9-7 67 TomEaves 8 71
(David Evans) *hld up towards rr: stdy hdwy over 3f out: effrt wl over 1f out: rdn to chal and edgd lft ent fnl f: ev ch tl drvn and no ex towards fin* **5/1**[2]
044 **3** *3 3/4* **Philba**[14] 6456 2-9-6 66 AndrewMullen 2 63
(Michael Appleby) *trckd ldrs: effrt and n.m.r over 2f out: rdn to chse wnr wl over 1f out: drvn and one pce ent fnl f* **13/8**[1]
0603 **4** *nk* **North Bay Lady (IRE)**[7] 6669 2-8-3 49 RaulDaSilva 1 45
(John Wainwright) *in rr: hdwy on outer wl over 2f out: sn rdn: kpt on u.p fnl f: nrst fin* **14/1**
4456 **5** *1/2* **Diatomic (IRE)**[8] 6648 2-9-3 63 RichardKingscote 4 58
(Tom Dascombe) *hld up: hdwy 3f out: rdn along 2f out: swtchd rt and drvn appr fnl f: sn no imp* **6/1**[3]
300 **6** *4* **Bridgekeeper**[20] 6261 2-8-13 62 RyanTate(3) 7 50
(James Eustace) *trckd ldng pair: hdwy and cl up over 3f out: rdn along 2f out: sn drvn and wknd* **6/1**[3]
5400 **7** *7* **Starring Guest (IRE)**[7] 6663 2-8-13 59 SilvestreDeSousa 5 34
(Mick Channon) *cl up: led 1/2-way: pushed along and hdd 3f out: sn rdn and wknd 2f out* **7/1**
2m 15.08s (0.78) **Going Correction** -0.175s/f (Firm) 2y crse rec **7 Ran SP% 110.8**
Speed ratings (Par 95): **89,88,85,85,85 81,76**
CSF £60.24 CT £131.14 TOTE £14.60: £6.70, £1.70; EX 72.40 Trifecta £160.30.
**Owner** Morecool & Cool Racing **Bred** Lynn Lodge Stud **Trained** Norton, N Yorks
**FOCUS**
A modest handicap for staying types and another winner to make just about all on the round course.

### 6870 JOCKEY CLUB GRASSROOTS MIDDLE DISTANCE SERIES FINAL (A H'CAP) — 1m 2f 50y
**3:45** (3:46) (Class 3) 3-Y-O+
**£15,562** (£4,660; £2,330; £1,165; £582; £292) **Stalls** Low

Form / RPR
2401 **1** **Donny Rover (IRE)**[48] 5345 3-9-8 89 AndrewMullen 3 97
(Michael Appleby) *dwlt: sn trcking ldrs: effrt 2f out: rdn over 1f out: drvn to chal ent fnl f: led last 100yds: kpt on wl towards fin* **5/1**[3]
6040 **2** *1/2* **Ocean Applause**[20] 6264 4-8-9 76 (t) JoeDoyle(5) 8 83
(John Ryan) *trckd ldrs: hdwy 3f out: rdn wl over 1f out: drvn to chal ins fnl f: kpt on* **20/1**
614 **3** *1 1/4* **Cosmic Halo**[13] 6491 5-8-13 78 GeorgeChaloner(3) 13 83
(Richard Fahey) *hld up and bhd: hdwy wl over 2f out: rdn to chse ldrs over 1f out: kpt on u.p fnl f: nrst fin* **12/1**
6660 **4** *shd* **Artful Prince**[7] 6672 4-8-12 74 (b) TomEaves 2 78
(James Given) *sn slt ld: pushed along over 3f out: rdn wl over 1f out: drvn ent fnl f: hdd and no ex last 100yds* **25/1**
1314 **5** *1/2* **No Win No Fee**[39] 5676 4-9-0 76 FrederikTylicki 9 79
(Michael Appleby) *trckd ldng pair: hdwy 3f out: chal over 2f out: rdn over 1f out: drvn and kpt on same pce fnl f* **9/2**[2]
0320 **6** *1 1/4* **Maven**[4] 6746 6-9-3 86 RachelRichardson(7) 11 87+
(Tim Easterby) *hld up towards rr: hdwy on outer over 3f out: chsd ldrs over 2f out: sn rdn and no imp appr fnl f* **9/1**
3062 **7** *nse* **Beakers N Num Nums (IRE)**[14] 6460 3-8-6 73 MartinDwyer 5 74+
(William Jarvis) *hld up: effrt and hdwy wl over 2f out: rdn wl over 1f out: drvn and no imp fnl f* **8/1**
3133 **8** *4* **Excellent Puck (IRE)**[18] 6323 4-9-4 80 WilliamTwiston-Davies 7 73
(Shaun Lycett) *in tch: pushed along over 3f out: rdn wl over 2f out: sn drvn and btn* **8/1**
2234 **9** *1* **An Chulainn (IRE)**[17] 6365 3-8-2 69 (b) SilvestreDeSousa 4 61
(Mark Johnston) *in tch on inner: pushed along 3f out: rdn over 2f out: n.d* **16/1**
3501 **10** *hd* **Raise Your Gaze**[14] 6460 3-9-7 91 RyanTate(3) 12 82
(Clive Cox) *trckd ldrs: hdwy wl over 2f out: rdn wl over 1f out: drvn and wknd appr fnl f* **3/1**[1]
340 **11** *4* **Hydrant**[18] 6323 8-8-3 68 CamHardie(3) 10 52
(Richard Guest) *cl up: disp ld 1/2-way: rdn along wl over 2f out: drvn and wknd wl over 1f out* **25/1**
2m 10.83s (-3.47) **Going Correction** -0.175s/f (Firm)
**WFA** 3 from 4yo+ 5lb **11 Ran SP% 118.1**
Speed ratings (Par 107): **106,105,104,104,104 103,103,99,99,98 95**
CSF £103.29 CT £1131.19 TOTE £5.40: £2.30, £4.30, £3.40; EX 118.80 Trifecta £1378.70.
**Owner** C L Bacon **Bred** Lynn Lodge Stud **Trained** Danethorpe, Notts
**FOCUS**
A decent handicap, but the early pace looked only ordinary.

### 6871 SPONSOR A RACE AT NOTTINGHAM RACECOURSE H'CAP (BOBIS RACE) — 1m 75y
**4:20** (4:20) (Class 4) (0-85,83) 3-Y-O — **£5,498** (£1,636; £817; £408) **Stalls** Centre

Form / RPR
1240 **1** **Express Himself (IRE)**[22] 6214 3-9-4 80 JimCrowley 8 87
(Ed McMahon) *in tch and hld up in rr: stdy hdwy wl over 2f out: trckd ldrs wl over 1f out: rdn ent fnl f: led last 100yds* **6/1**
6235 **2** *3/4* **Weekendatbernies (IRE)**[11] 6552 3-9-6 82 FrederikTylicki 2 87
(Ed de Giles) *trckd ldng pair on inner: hdwy over 3f out: led over 2f out: rdn over 1f out: jnd and drvn ent fnl f: hdd and no ex last 100yds* **8/1**
4432 **3** *1/2* **Grevillea (IRE)**[33] 5882 3-9-4 80 WilliamTwiston-Davies 1 84
(Mick Channon) *in tch: hdwy over 2f out: rdn to chse ldr wl over 1f out: chal ent fnl f and ev ch: drvn and no ex last 100yds* **10/1**
5232 **4** *4 1/2* **Emef Diamond**[15] 6431 3-8-13 75 SilvestreDeSousa 5 69+
(Mick Channon) *led 1f: cl up: rdn along over 2f out: drvn wl over 1f out: sn one pce* **4/1**[3]
3066 **5** *4 1/2* **Know Your Name**[32] 5903 3-8-9 71 (v) TomEaves 3 55+
(David Evans) *hdwy to ld after 1f: pushed along over 3f out: hdd over 2f out and sn rdn: wknd over 1f out* **40/1**
3321 **6** *7* **Faure Island**[9] 6616 3-9-2 78 6ex FergusSweeney 7 47
(Henry Candy) *hld up in tch: hdwy over 3f out: pushed along to chse ldrs over 2f out: sn rdn: drvn wl over 1f out and sn wknd* **5/2**[1]
15 **7** *11* **Unforgiving Minute**[27] 6060 3-9-4 83 RyanTate(3) 6 28
(Clive Cox) *t.k.h: trckd ldrs: effrt 3f out: rdn along over 2f out: sn drvn and btn: eased over 1f out* **3/1**[2]
1010 **8** *2 1/4* **Green Zone (IRE)**[32] 5930 3-8-13 75 (p) HayleyTurner 4 15
(Nigel Tinkler) *in tch: effrt and sme hdwy on outer 4f out: rdn along 3f out: sn wknd* **20/1**
1m 45.89s (-3.11) **Going Correction** -0.175s/f (Firm) **8 Ran SP% 115.3**
Speed ratings (Par 103): **108,107,106,102,97 90,79,77**
CSF £52.96 CT £476.23 TOTE £8.50: £2.20, £3.60, £2.70; EX 49.10 Trifecta £308.00.
**Owner** Milton Express Limited **Bred** Barouche Stud Ireland Ltd **Trained** Lichfield, Staffs

**FOCUS**
A couple of the fancied runners ran poorly, but the first three came clear of the remainder.

## 6872 JOCKEY CLUB GRASSROOTS SPRINT SERIES FINAL (A H'CAP) 6f 15y
**4:50** (4:51) (Class 3) 3-Y-0+

**£15,562** (£4,660; £2,330; £1,165; £582; £292) **Stalls** Centre

Form RPR

4600 **1** **Mon Brav**[12] 6511 7-8-13 78........ SilvestreDeSousa 1 87
(Brian Ellison) *racd towards centre: hld up in rr: hdwy 2f out: swtchd lft to outer and rdn over 1f out: chal ins fnl f: drvn to ld last 75yds* **12/1**

1113 **2** *nk* **Guishan**[13] 6492 4-8-8 78........ AlistairRawlinson(5) 10 86
(Michael Appleby) *racd centre: slt ld: rdn wl over 1f out: drvn ent fnl f: hdd last 75yds: kpt on* **7/1**[3]

6403 **3** *nse* **Rocket Rob (IRE)**[14] 6455 8-8-4 69........ MartinDwyer 13 77+
(Willie Musson) *racd towards stands' rail: trckd ldrs: effrt and nt clr run over 1f out: sn swtchd lft and rdn: str run ins fnl f: ev ch whn hung bdly lft fnl 100yds: no ex* **10/1**

0111 **4** *3 1/2* **Triple Chocolate**[26] 6095 4-9-6 85........ JimmyQuinn 16 82
(Roger Ingram) *racd nr stands' rail: trckd ldrs: swtchd lft and hdwy wl over 1f out: sn rdn: edgd lft and kpt on same pce fnl f* **4/1**[1]

202 **5** *hd* **Diamond Lady**[18] 6336 3-9-0 80........ FrederikTylicki 2 77
(William Stone) *wnt rt s: cl up: rdn along wl over 1f out: grad wknd* **16/1**

0025 **6** *2 1/4* **Best Trip (IRE)**[25] 6155 7-9-6 85........ BarryMcHugh 17 75
(Brian Ellison) *cl up nr stands' rail: disp ld 1/2-way: rdn wl over 1f out: drvn appr fnl f and one pce* **12/1**

0011 **7** *3/4* **Amadeus Wolfe Tone (IRE)**[15] 6423 5-9-6 85.....(p) FergusSweeney 12 73
(Jamie Osborne) *racd towards stands' rail: hld up: hdwy 1/2-way: swtchd lft end effrt 2f out: rdn and edgd lft over 1f out: kpt on u.p fnl f: nvr nr ldrs* **14/1**

2201 **8** *1 1/2* **Shades Of Silk**[29] 5994 3-7-11 68........ JoeDoyle(5) 3 51
(James Given) *chsd ldrs: rdn along 2f out: drvn and wknd appr fnl f* **25/1**

410 **9** *hd* **Front Page News**[11] 6558 4-8-10 78........ GeorgeChaloner(3) 7 61
(Robert Eddery) *racd towards centre: chsd ldrs: rdn along over 2f out: grad wknd* **25/1**

0456 **10** *2* **Honey Meadow**[13] 6488 3-7-9 66 oh6........ NoelGarbutt(5) 8 43
(Robert Eddery) *awkward s: sn chsng ldrs: rdn along bef 1/2-way: wknd 2f out* **50/1**

0006 **11** *nse* **Lupo D'Oro (IRE)**[29] 6021 5-8-1 69........ CamHardie(3) 11 46
(John Best) *chsd ldrs: rdn along 2f out: wknd over 1f out* **25/1**

1362 **12** *1 1/4* **Dont Have It Then**[14] 6468 3-8-9 75........ JimCrowley 6 50
(Willie Musson) *in rr: pushed along and sme hdwy whn nt clr run 2f out: no prog after* **16/1**

3531 **13** *1 1/2* **Generalyse**[30] 5987 5-8-7 75........(b) RyanTate(3) 15 43
(Ben De Haan) *racd towards stands' rail: cl up: rdn along over 2f out: sn edgd lft and wknd over 1f out* **12/1**

2140 **14** *3/4* **Arctic Feeling (IRE)**[11] 6531 6-9-5 89........(v) SammyJoBell(5) 14 57
(Richard Fahey) *racd towards stands' rail: chsd ldrs: rkidden along and hld whn n.m.r and hmpd 2f out: bhd after* **9/2**[2]

3446 **15** *1 1/4* **Atlantis Crossing (IRE)**[40] 5650 5-8-4 69........ NickyMackay 9 31
(Jim Boyle) *in tch: hdwy to chse ldrs 1/2-way: rdn along over 2f out: sn wknd* **33/1**

2250 **16** *3 1/2* **Alpha Delta Whisky**[14] 6455 6-8-3 71........(v) JoeyHaynes(3) 4 23
(John Gallagher) *in tch on wd outside: rdn along over 2f out: sn wknd* **40/1**

2000 **17** *nk* **Shirley's Pride**[14] 6455 4-8-0 65........(t) AndrewMullen 5 16
(Michael Appleby) *midfield: rdn along and sme 1/2-way: drvn 2f out: sn wknd* **25/1**

1m 13.09s (-1.61) **Going Correction** -0.175s/f (Firm)
**WFA** 3 from 4yo+ 1lb **17 Ran SP% 124.0**
Speed ratings (Par 107): **103,102,102,97,97 94,93,91,91,88 88,86,84,83,82 77,77**
CSF £87.77 CT £921.02 TOTE £10.40: £3.40, £2.30, £3.40, £1.40; EX 98.10 Trifecta £2212.00.
**Owner** Koo's Racing Club **Bred** J D Graham **Trained** Norton, N Yorks

**FOCUS**
A competitive sprint handicap run at a sound gallop. The first two came down the middle of the track.

## 6873 JOIN US FOR CONSTRUCTION DAY 15TH OCTOBER H'CAP 5f 13y
**5:20** (5:22) (Class 5) (0-75,75) 3-Y-0+ **£2,587** (£770; £384; £192) **Stalls** Centre

Form RPR

0005 **1** **Royal Bajan (USA)**[7] 6671 6-8-11 65........(p) TomEaves 14 73
(James Given) *mde all on stands' rail: rdn over 1f out: drvn ins fnl f: jst hld on* **14/1**

4000 **2** *shd* **Eland Ally**[7] 6671 6-8-7 66........(p) JoeDoyle(5) 5 74
(Tom Tate) *racd towards centre: cl up: rdn over 1f out: ev ch ins fnl f: drvn and kpt on wl towards fin: jst hld* **11/2**[1]

0234 **3** *1* **Waseem Faris (IRE)**[7] 6658 5-9-4 72........ SilvestreDeSousa 6 76
(Mick Channon) *racd towards centre: towards rr: gd hdwy wl over 1f out: rdn to chal ins fnl f: drvn and no ex towards fin* **8/1**[3]

3331 **4** *1/2* **Eternitys Gate**[17] 6356 3-9-7 75........ JimCrowley 12 78
(Peter Chapple-Hyam) *racd towards stands' rail: hld up in rr: gd hdwy wl over 1f out: rdn and kpt on wl fnl f: nrst fin* **6/1**[2]

0256 **5** *1* **Touch The Clouds**[25] 6153 3-9-2 70........ FrederikTylicki 13 70
(William Stone) *racd towards stands' rail: trckd ldrs: hdwy 2f out: sn rdn and kpt on fnl f: nrst fin* **16/1**

0010 **6** *shd* **Oldjoesaid**[21] 6235 10-9-7 75........ BarryMcHugh 8 73
(Paul Midgley) *hld up in rr: swtchd rt to stands' rail 2f out: sn rdn and styd on fnl f: nrst fin* **16/1**

0360 **7** *3/4* **Whitecrest**[8] 6650 6-9-2 73........ CamHardie(3) 3 69
(John Spearing) *racd towards centre: chsd ldrs: rdn along 2f out: sn drvn and kpt on one pce* **33/1**

2405 **8** *nk* **Sleepy Blue Ocean**[21] 6235 8-9-0 73........(p) ShaneGray(5) 11 68
(John Balding) *racd towards stands' rail: chsd ldrs: rdn along 2f out: drvn over 1f out: sn one pce* **8/1**[3]

5501 **9** *nk* **Dusty Storm (IRE)**[16] 6399 4-9-3 74........ GeorgeChaloner(3) 10 67
(Ed McMahon) *in rr: hdwy wl over 1f out: sn rdn and kpt on fnl f: nrst fin* **10/1**

4202 **10** *3/4* **Tweety Pie (IRE)**[14] 6452 3-9-0 71........ NeilFarley(3) 9 63
(Declan Carroll) *prom towards stands' rail: rdn 2f out: sn drvn and grad wknd* **20/1**

3151 **11** *4* **Only Ten Per Cent (IRE)**[14] 6455 6-9-6 74........(v) FergalLynch 7 50
(J R Jenkins) *chsd ldrs: rdn along over 2f out: sn wknd* **10/1**

2450 **12** *3 1/2* **Vodka Time (IRE)**[7] 6674 3-8-8 62........ PaddyAspell 1 27
(Shaun Harris) *racd wd: in tch: rdn along over 2f out: sn wknd* **12/1**

1551 **13** *4* **Dishy Guru**[7] 6658 5-8-10 64........(b) FergusSweeney 2 13+
(Michael Blanshard) *rrd s and lost many l: a bhd* **6/1**[2]

1m 0.01s (-1.49) **Going Correction** -0.175s/f (Firm) **13 Ran SP% 118.2**
Speed ratings (Par 103): **104,103,102,101,99 99,98,98,97,96 89,84,77**
CSF £88.21 CT £691.63 TOTE £18.30: £5.20, £2.20, £2.70; EX 131.20 Trifecta £1009.30.
**Owner** The Cool Silk Partnership **Bred** West Wind Farm **Trained** Willoughton, Lincs

**FOCUS**
With four last-time-out winners taking their chance, this should be sound form for the level.
T/Jkpt: Not won. T/Plt: £320.00 to a £1 stake. Pool: £57,390.12 - 130.90 winning tickets T/Qpdt: £248.60 to a £1 stake. Pool: £3,864.80 - 11.50 winning tickets JR

# 6293 SALISBURY (R-H)
### Wednesday, October 1

**OFFICIAL GOING: Good (good to firm in places; 8.3)**
Wind: virtually nil Weather: overcast, warm

## 6874 FRANCIS CLARK BRITISH STALLION STUDS EBF MAIDEN STKS (BOBIS RACE) (DIV I) 1m
**1:45** (1:45) (Class 4) 2-Y-O **£4,204** (£1,251; £652; £312) **Stalls** Low

Form RPR

**1** **Moheet (IRE)** 2-9-5 0........ FrankieDettori 9 88+
(Richard Hannon) *s.i.s: impr to midfield 4f out: hdwy whn nt clr run 2f out: swtchd rt: led over 1f out: r.o strly to draw wl clr: easily* **8/1**[3]

3 **2** *7* **Gild Master**[65] 4731 2-9-5 0........ RichardHughes 4 71
(Alan King) *led: rdn 2f out: hdd over 1f out: sn outpcd by wnr: kpt on* **8/1**[3]

**3** *nk* **Open The Red** 2-9-5 0........ PatDobbs 11 70
(Amanda Perrett) *hld up towards rr fr poor draw: hdwy fr over 3f out: nt clr run over 2f out: r.o ins fnl f: chalng for 2nd nring fin* **33/1**

2 **4** *1 1/2* **Kisumu**[22] 6203 2-9-5 0........ JamesDoyle 5 67
(Sir Michael Stoute) *trckd ldrs: rdn whn swtchd lft 2f out: kpt on same pce fnl f* **4/5**[1]

**5** *hd* **Istinfaar (USA)** 2-9-5 0........ DaneO'Neill 7 66
(Roger Varian) *in tch: rdn over 2f out: styd on fnl f but nt gng pce to get involved* **12/1**

05 **6** *2 1/2* **The Twisler**[26] 6102 2-9-5 0........ GeorgeBaker 6 61
(Charles Hills) *prom: rdn and ev ch over 2f out tl over 1f out: fdd fnl f* **33/1**

3 **7** *3/4* **Brandon Castle**[18] 6317 2-9-5 0........ DavidProbert 8 59
(Andrew Balding) *trckd ldrs: rdn 2f out: wknd ent fnl f* **9/2**[2]

0 **8** *2* **Magic Circle (IRE)**[20] 6259 2-9-5 0........ OscarPereira 1 54
(Ralph Beckett) *a towards rr* **66/1**

**9** *3* **Brittleton** 2-9-5 0........ TomQueally 3 47
(Harry Dunlop) *s.i.s: a towards rr* **80/1**

**10** *11* **Farendole (USA)** 2-9-0 0........ RyanMoore 10 17
(Roger Charlton) *mid-div: effrt over 2f out: wknd over 1f out* **16/1**

0 **11** *44* **Lionel Joseph**[9] 6604 2-9-5 0........ PatCosgrave 2
(George Baker) *mid-div tl wknd 3f out* **150/1**

1m 42.85s (-0.65) **Going Correction** +0.025s/f (Good) **11 Ran SP% 118.8**
Speed ratings (Par 97): **104,97,96,95,95 92,91,89,86,75 31**
CSF £69.13 TOTE £12.80: £3.30, £2.60, £8.10; EX 58.30 Trifecta £2087.20 Part won..
**Owner** Al Shaqab Racing **Bred** Hascombe And Valiant Stud **Trained** East Everleigh, Wilts

**FOCUS**
This looked the stronger of the two divisions, run at a reasonable gallop, with the winner impressive and the time 0.55secs faster than the following race.

## 6875 FRANCIS CLARK BRITISH STALLION STUDS EBF MAIDEN STKS (BOBIS RACE) (DIV II) 1m
**2:20** (2:20) (Class 4) 2-Y-O **£4,204** (£1,251; £625; £312) **Stalls** Low

Form RPR

**1** **Chemical Charge (IRE)** 2-9-5 0........ OisinMurphy 1 80+
(Ralph Beckett) *trckd ldrs: pushed along to chal over 2f out: led wl over 1f out: kpt on strly fnl f: comf* **6/1**[2]

4 **2** *3* **Subcontinent (IRE)**[17] 6362 2-9-5 0........ MartinLane 4 73+
(Charlie Appleby) *trckd ldrs: rdn over 2f out: styd on nicely to go 2nd ins fnl f but no ch w wnr* **12/1**

6 **3** *1 3/4* **Chief Spirit**[13] 6497 2-9-5 0........ StevieDonohoe 5 69
(James Eustace) *in tch: rdn over 2f out: hdwy over 1f out: styd on to go 3rd ins fnl f* **66/1**

62 **4** *1* **Voice Control (IRE)**[26] 6101 2-9-5 0........ RyanMoore 3 67
(Sir Michael Stoute) *led for 1f: trckd ldr: rdn and ev ch 2f out: sn hld by wnr: no ex whn lost 2 pls ins fnl f* **5/4**[1]

**5** *3* **Rembrandt** 2-9-5 0........ RichardHughes 8 60+
(Richard Hannon) *s.i.s: towards rr: swtchd rt and hdwy over 1f out: styd on fnl f but nvr a threat* **8/1**[3]

**6** *nk* **Munstead Pride** 2-9-5 0........ DavidProbert 2 59+
(Andrew Balding) *s.i.s: sn mid-div: rdn over 2f out: little imp tl styd on fnl f* **20/1**

**7** *3 1/2* **Tatawu (IRE)** 2-9-5 0........ DaneO'Neill 9 51+
(Brian Meehan) *s.i.s: towards rr: sme minor late prog but nvr any danger* **50/1**

5 **8** *1 3/4* **Sleep Easy**[19] 6300 2-9-5 0........ JimmyFortune 7 47
(Hughie Morrison) *mid-div: rdn 3f out: nvr any imp: wknd ent fnl f* **6/1**[2]

**9** *3 1/4* **Parish (IRE)** 2-9-5 0........ AndreaAtzeni 6 40
(Roger Varian) *mid-div: mid-div: pushed along over 3f out: wknd ent fnl f* **14/1**

35 **10** *nk* **Dutch Robin (IRE)**[7] 6652 2-9-0 0........ SamHitchcott 10 34
(Mick Channon) *led after 1f: rdn and hdd wl over 1f out: sn wknd* **33/1**

**11** *nk* **Heart Locket** 2-9-0 0........ JamesDoyle 11 33
(Roger Charlton) *towards rr fr wd draw: rn green: pushed along wl over 3f out: wknd over 1f out* **12/1**

1m 43.4s (-0.10) **Going Correction** +0.025s/f (Good) **11 Ran SP% 117.3**
Speed ratings (Par 97): **101,98,96,95,92 91,88,86,83,83 82**
CSF £72.41 TOTE £9.00: £2.40, £3.10, £10.60; EX 75.90 Trifecta £2651.90 Part won..
**Owner** Qatar Racing Limited **Bred** Viktor Timoshenko **Trained** Kimpton, Hants

**FOCUS**
The lesser of the two divisions, but still a fair contest.

## 6876 BOOKER WHOLESALE BRITISH STALLION STUDS EBF NOVICE STKS (BOBIS RACE) 6f 212y
**2:50** (2:51) (Class 4) 2-Y-O **£6,792** (£2,021; £1,010) **Stalls** Centre

Form RPR

61 **1** **Best Of Times**[40] 5625 2-9-5 0........ JamesDoyle 3 95+
(Saeed bin Suroor) *trckd ldr: pushed along and edging rt wl over 1f out: rdn jst ins fnl f: r.o wl to ld nring fin* **4/9**[1]

15 **2** *nk* **Risen Sun**[19] 6291 2-9-0 0 ........ FrannyNorton 4 89
(Mark Johnston) *led: rdn ins fnl f: kpt on: hdd nring fin* **5/2**[2]

0 **3** *9* **Brutus (FR)**[20] 6259 2-8-12 0 ........ AndreaAtzeni 1 66+
(Richard Hannon) *little slowly away: trckd ldng pair: pushed along over 3f out: rdn 2f out: sn outpcd* **9/1**[3]

1m 29.81s (1.21) **Going Correction** +0.025s/f (Good) **3** Ran SP% **107.8**
Speed ratings (Par 97): **94,93,83**
CSF £1.86 TOTE £1.40; EX 1.70 Trifecta £2.10.
**Owner** Godolphin **Bred** Darley **Trained** Newmarket, Suffolk

**FOCUS**
The two who counted drew right away in this novice contest, with the picture changing late on.

## 6877 INSPIRE FOUNDATION CLAIMING STKS — 1m 1f 198y
**3:20** (3:20) (Class 5) 3-4-Y-O — **£2,749** (£818; £408; £204) **Stalls** Low

Form — RPR

1662 **1** **Penny's Boy**[9] 6615 3-8-9 72 ........ (t) LiamKeniry 6 76
(Sylvester Kirk) *trckd ldrs: squeezed through gap jst over 1f out: led jst ins fnl f: drvn and strly pressed thrght fnl f: hld on* **9/2**[3]

0400 **2** *shd* **Tobacco Road (IRE)**[64] 4756 4-9-10 86 ........ RichardHughes 4 86
(Richard Hannon) *trckd ldrs: chal 2f out: sn rdn: ev ch thrght fnl f: kpt on* **5/4**[1]

0603 **3** *3 ¼* **Elysian Prince**[8] 6633 3-9-0 70 ........ (t) MartinLane 7 75
(Paul Cole) *wnt lft s: trckd ldr: chal 2f out: rdn to ld over 1f out: hdd jst ins fnl f: no ex* **8/1**

3311 **4** *5* **Rough Courte (IRE)**[46] 5427 3-8-7 70 ........ SamHitchcott 2 58
(Mick Channon) *taken to s early: led: jinked lft jst over 4f out: rdn 2f out: hdd jst ins fnl f: no ex* **4/1**[2]

0333 **5** *14* **Rome**[28] 6042 4-9-5 77 ........ (b¹) RyanMoore 5 39
(Gary Moore) *hld up in last but in tch: rdn 3f out: nvr finding pce to get involved: wknd ent fnl f* **5/1**

**6** *2 ¼* **Lamubaaly (IRE)**[32] 3-8-7 0 ........ JohnFahy 8 27+
(Alexandra Dunn) *carried bdly lft s: rcvrd to chse ldrs after 2f: rdn over 3f out: sn lost pl and btn* **66/1**

2m 8.66s (-1.24) **Going Correction** +0.025s/f (Good)
**WFA** 3 from 4yo 5lb **6** Ran SP% **111.9**
Speed ratings (Par 103): **105,104,102,98,87 85**
CSF £10.54 TOTE £4.80: £2.60, £1.10; EX 11.60 Trifecta £59.90.Penny's Boy was claimed by Mr S. P. Hodgson for £10,000.
**Owner** Malcolm Brown & Mrs Penny Brown **Bred** Peter Webb **Trained** Upper Lambourn, Berks

**FOCUS**
Fair claiming form.

## 6878 WEATHERBYS HAMILTON INSURANCE H'CAP — 1m 1f 198y
**3:55** (3:55) (Class 2) (0-105,97) 3-Y-0+
**£12,450** (£3,728; £1,864; £932; £466; £234) **Stalls** Low

Form — RPR

020 **1** **Ajmany (IRE)**[32] 5928 4-9-12 **97** ........ (b) AndreaAtzeni 1 105
(Luca Cumani) *trckd ldrs: pushed along over 3f out: rdn and drifted lft fr over 1f out: led ins fnl f: fin on stands' side rails: styd on wl* **4/1**[2]

-310 **2** *1* **Soviet Rock (IRE)**[117] 2957 4-9-12 **97** ........ DavidProbert 4 103
(Andrew Balding) *trckd ldr: rdn 3f out: led narrowly jst ins fnl f: sn hdd: styd on* **5/1**[3]

3106 **3** *½* **Whispering Warrior (IRE)**[18] 6321 5-9-10 **95** ........ JamesDoyle 3 100
(David Simcock) *in tch: rdn over 2f out: hdwy ent fnl f: wnt 3rd towards fin: styd on* **11/1**

1413 **4** *½* **Alex Vino (IRE)**[15] 6438 3-9-0 **90** ........ (v) RyanMoore 5 94
(Sir Michael Stoute) *trckd ldrs: rdn wl over 2f out: wnt 3rd ins fnl f: no ex nring fin* **4/1**[2]

0015 **5** *1 ¼* **War Singer (USA)**[19] 6303 7-8-8 **79** ........ (bt) StevieDonohoe 2 81
(Johnny Farrelly) *led: 5 l clr 4f out: rdn 3f out: hdd jst ins fnl f: no ex fnl 120yds* **33/1**

121 **6** *nk* **Basem**[33] 5882 3-9-5 **95** ........ RichardHughes 6 96
(Saeed bin Suroor) *hld up in last pair: hdwy wl over 3f out: rdn to chse ldrs 2f out: sn drifted lft: fin on stands' side rails: fdd ins fnl f* **15/8**[1]

3546 **7** *15* **Presburg (IRE)**[13] 6479 5-9-3 **88** ........ OisinMurphy 7 61
(Joseph Tuite) *hld up in last: rdn 3f out: wknd over 1f out* **10/1**

2m 7.9s (-2.00) **Going Correction** +0.025s/f (Good)
**WFA** 3 from 4yo+ 5lb **7** Ran SP% **111.8**
Speed ratings (Par 109): **109,108,107,107,106 106,94**
CSF £22.96 TOTE £5.50: £3.30, £4.80; EX 26.20 Trifecta £181.80.
**Owner** Sheikh Mohammed Obaid Al Maktoum **Bred** Rockfield Farm **Trained** Newmarket, Suffolk

**FOCUS**
A good-quality handicap, in which they got racing a long way out, and despite drifting across to the stands' rail, along with the favourite, it was Ajmany who saw it out best.

## 6879 BATHWICK TYRES CONDITIONS STKS (BOBIS RACE) — 6f
**4:30** (4:33) (Class 2) 2-Y-O — **£9,703** (£2,887) **Stalls** Low

Form — RPR

11 **1** **Elysian Flyer (IRE)**[32] 5906 2-9-1 0 ........ RichardHughes 1 97
(Richard Hannon) *travelled wl trcking ldr: swtchd out for effrt ent fnl f: qcknd up wl: led fnl 75yds* **13/8**[2]

4212 **2** *¾* **Astrophysics**[19] 6286 2-9-1 105 ........ RyanMoore 3 95
(David Elsworth) *led: shkn up 2f out: rdn fnl f: no ex whn hdd fnl 75yds* **1/2**[1]

1m 16.25s (1.45) **Going Correction** +0.025s/f (Good) **2** Ran SP% **104.8**
Speed ratings (Par 101): **91,90**
TOTE £1.50.
**Owner** The Low Flyers **Bred** Tom Shirley **Trained** East Everleigh, Wilts

**FOCUS**
A minor upset in this two-runner race.

## 6880 VANARAMA CHALLENGE H'CAP — 6f
**5:00** (5:00) (Class 4) (0-85,85) 3-Y-0+ — **£4,851** (£1,443; £721; £360) **Stalls** Low

Form — RPR

5060 **1** **Musicora**[27] 6068 3-9-6 85 ........ (b¹) RichardHughes 11 94
(Richard Hannon) *prom: rdn to ld narrowly over 1f out: stands' side fnl f: drifted rt: kpt on: drvn rt out* **8/1**

0040 **2** *nk* **Slip Sliding Away (IRE)**[25] 6130 7-9-3 84 ........ ThomasBrown(3) 12 92
(Peter Hedger) *hld up: hdwy over 2f out: sn rdn: ev ch in centre thrght fnl f: jst hld* **9/2**[1]

1522 **3** *nk* **Royal Brave (IRE)**[17] 6355 3-8-13 78 ........ DougieCostello 2 85
(William Muir) *racd far side w one other: pressed ldr: rdn and edgd to stands' side w ev ch fr over 1f out: kpt on fnl f* **7/1**[2]

0614 **4** *1 ¼* **Red Aggressor (IRE)**[14] 6467 5-9-4 82 ........ (b) AndreaAtzeni 8 85
(Clive Brittain) *mid-div: hdwy 2f out: sn rdn: stands' side fnl f: kpt on* **9/1**

5205 **5** *hd* **Joe Packet**[11] 6558 7-8-12 79 ........ (p) DannyBrock(3) 9 82
(Jonathan Portman) *hld up: swtchd rt and hdwy 2f out: rdn and ev ch in centre fnl f: no ex nring fin* **8/1**

0000 **6** *½* **Daylight**[11] 6558 4-9-3 81 ........ (t) OisinMurphy 10 83
(Andrew Balding) *hld up: rdn 2f out: hdwy whn nt best of runs over 1f out: stands' side fnl f: kpt on* **14/1**

5155 **7** *1 ½* **My Inspiration (IRE)**[21] 6236 3-8-5 75 ........[1] DanielMuscutt(5) 3 72
(Amy Weaver) *mid-div: effrt 2f out: fdd in centre fnl 120yds* **25/1**

6034 **8** *hd* **Tamayuz Star (IRE)**[15] 6441 4-9-6 84 ........ TomQueally 13 80
(George Margarson) *mid-div: hdwy over 2f out: effrt wl over 1f out: stands' side fnl f: fdd fnl 120yds* **8/1**

0200 **9** *nk* **Vallarta (IRE)**[29] 6006 4-8-12 76 ........ LiamKeniry 5 71
(Mick Channon) *hld up: rdn over 2f out: kpt on in centre fnl f but nvr gng pce to get involved* **18/1**

1424 **10** *1 ¼* **Langley Vale**[16] 6398 5-9-0 78 ........ (p) SebSanders 6 70
(Roger Teal) *trckd ldrs: rdn and ev ch 2f out: wknd stands' side fnl f* **12/1**

112 **11** *¾* **Panther Patrol (IRE)**[16] 6398 4-9-2 80 ........ (v) JohnFahy 7 71
(Eve Johnson Houghton) *mid-div: rdn whn nt clr run and bmpd over 1f out: wknd on stands' side fnl f* **15/2**[3]

66 **12** *2 ½* **Tidentime (USA)**[18] 6313 5-9-2 80 ........ SamHitchcott 4 63
(Mick Channon) *chsd ldrs: rdn over 3f out: sn hld: wknd in centre fnl f* **20/1**

5004 **13** *2* **Harwoods Volante (IRE)**[9] 6607 3-8-12 77 ........ PatDobbs 1 53
(Amanda Perrett) *racd on far side: led: rdn and edgd lft over 2f out: hdd over 1f out: wknd in centre* **12/1**

1m 14.63s (-0.17) **Going Correction** +0.025s/f (Good)
**WFA** 3 from 4yo+ 1lb **13** Ran SP% **121.7**
Speed ratings (Par 105): **102,101,101,99,99 98,96,96,95,94 93,89,87**
CSF £44.66 CT £281.58 TOTE £9.00: £3.30, £2.10, £2.10; EX 56.00 Trifecta £438.20.
**Owner** The Three Points Partnership **Bred** Sir Eric Parker **Trained** East Everleigh, Wilts

**FOCUS**
Racing centre-field, this modest handicap had a competitive look to it.

## 6881 BATHWICK TYRES H'CAP — 1m 6f 21y
**5:30** (5:30) (Class 5) (0-75,75) 3-Y-0+ — **£2,911** (£866; £432; £216)

Form — RPR

3332 **1** **Russian Royale**[18] 6318 4-9-9 70 ........ (p) PatDobbs 3 76
(Stuart Kittow) *mid-div: hdwy over 2f out: led ins fnl f: edgd lft: styd on: rdn out* **4/1**[2]

4133 **2** *½* **Air Squadron**[26] 6107 4-9-5 66 ........ RichardHughes 9 71
(Ralph Beckett) *hld up: t.k.h: hdwy ent loop to ld over 7f out: hdd over 3f out: rdn to chse ldrs 2f out: styd on fnl f* **7/4**[1]

/660 **3** *2 ¼* **Musical Moon**[20] 6274 4-9-4 65 ........ JimmyFortune 6 67
(Lady Herries) *led tl over 7f out: trckd ldr tl rdn over 2f out: styd on to regain 3rd ins fnl f* **66/1**

3 **4** *½* **Earls Quarter (IRE)**[133] 1218 8-10-0 75 ........ StevieDonohoe 7 77
(Ian Williams) *hld up towards rr: struggling and detached 4f out: stl last w plenty to do 2f out: hdwy over 1f out: styd on wl fnl f: wnt 4th fnl strides* **20/1**

/14- **5** *½* **Street Entertainer (IRE)**[10] 3284 7-9-6 74 ........ (bt) MikeyEnnis(7) 2 75
(David Pipe) *trckd ldr: chal 3f out: led 2f out: sn rdn: hdd ins fnl f: no ex* **6/1**[3]

00-0 **6** *½* **Takeitfromalady (IRE)**[119] 2882 5-9-2 66 ........ ThomasBrown(3) 10 66+
(Lee Carter) *mid-div: rdn over 2f out: no imp tl styd on fnl f* **25/1**

3640 **7** *3 ¾* **Jezza**[18] 6343 8-9-2 63 ........ (bt) TomQueally 1 59
(Victor Dartnall) *mid-div: dropped to last trio 7f out: rdn 3f out: nvr any threat after* **16/1**

3554 **8** *8* **Dark Amber**[17] 6367 4-9-3 64 ........ SebSanders 4 49
(Brendan Powell) *sn trcking ldr: led over 3f out: rdn and hdd over 1f out: wknd fnl f* **10/1**

2023 **9** *3 ½* **Ultimate Act**[93] 3797 3-9-5 75 ........ DougieCostello 5 56
(Seamus Mullins) *hld up: hdwy 4f out: effrt 3f out: wknd over 1f out* **4/1**[2]

0526 **10** *7* **Juvenal (IRE)**[40] 5621 5-9-5 66 ........ (p) AdamBeschizza 8 38
(Paul Morgan) *trckd ldrs: rdn 3f out: wknd over 1f out* **50/1**

3m 10.82s (3.42) **Going Correction** +0.025s/f (Good)
**WFA** 3 from 4yo+ 9lb **10** Ran SP% **117.7**
Speed ratings (Par 103): **91,90,89,89,88 88,86,81,79,75**
CSF £11.14 CT £397.97 TOTE £3.60: £1.20, £1.10, £13.40; EX 12.40 Trifecta £309.30.
**Owner** P A & M J Reditt **Bred** Mrs P A & M J Reditt **Trained** Blackborough, Devon

**FOCUS**
A steady pace and modest staying form.
T/Plt: £2,701.70 to a £1 stake. Pool: £39,680.56 - 10.72 winning tickets T/Qpdt: £24.40 to a £1 stake. Pool: £3,272.17 - 99.01 winning tickets TM

# 6618 CHANTILLY (R-H)
## Wednesday, October 1
**OFFICIAL GOING: Turf: soft; polytrack: standard**

## 6882a PRIX CHARLES LAFFITTE (LISTED RACE) (3YO FILLIES) (TURF) — 1m 2f
**3:35** (3:35) 3-Y-O — **£22,916** (£9,166; £6,875; £4,583; £2,291)

RPR

**1** **Bocaiuva (IRE)**[62] 4840 3-8-13 0 ........ ChristopheSoumillon 10 104
(F Chappet, France) **114/10**

**2** *1* **Summer Surprice (FR)**[43] 5545 3-9-2 0 ........ TheoBachelot 3 105
(F-H Graffard, France) **228/10**

**3** *1 ½* **Jiayuguan (IRE)**[57] 3-8-13 0 ........ ThierryThulliez 2 99
(N Clement, France) **84/10**

**4** *snk* **Yonna (FR)**[30] 5992 3-8-13 0 ........ AnthonyCrastus 1 99
(E Lellouche, France) **188/10**

**5** *1 ½* **Felcine (IRE)**[93] 3808 3-8-13 0 ........ CristianDemuro 12 96
(G Botti, France) **74/10**[3]

**6** *nk* **Momo No Sekku (FR)**[39] 3-8-13 0 ........ NorihiroYokoyama 6 95
(S Kobayashi, France) **238/10**

**7** *1* **Game Zone (IRE)**[45] 5479 3-9-2 0 ........ Francois-XavierBertras 11 96
(F Rohaut, France) **19/10**[1]

**8** *½* **Anipa**[74] 4443 3-9-2 0 ........ GeraldMosse 5 95
(Roger Varian) *prom: chsd ldr bef 1/2-way: rdn to ld 1 1/2f out: hdd appr fnl f: sn wknd* **161/10**

**9** *snk* **Chocolatier (FR)**[30] 5992 3-8-13 0 ........ UmbertoRispoli 4 92
(M Delzangles, France) **202/10**

**10** *10* **Dancequest (IRE)**[30] 5992 3-8-13 0 ........ OlivierPeslier 7 72
(F Head, France) **123/10**

11 *13* **So In Love**[25] 3-8-13 0 ........ MaximeGuyon 8 46
(A Fabre, France) **18/5**[2]

12 *2 ½* **Saas Fee (FR)**[151] 3-8-13 0 ........ RemiCampos 9 41
(Mme Pia Brandt, France) **50/1**

2m 3.48s (-1.32) **12** Ran SP% **120.2**
WIN (incl. 1 euro stake): 9.90 (Bocaiuva coupled with Saas Fee). PLACES: 3.70, 6.10, 3.30. DF: 80.60. SF: 166.70.
**Owner** Meridian Racing & Haras d'Etreham **Bred** Janus Bloodstock **Trained** France

# 6851 KEMPTON (A.W) (R-H)

Thursday, October 2

**OFFICIAL GOING: Polytrack: standard**
Wind: Almost nil Weather: Fine

## 6883 DOWNLOAD THE BETVICTOR APP NOW H'CAP 1m (P)
**5:45** (5:47) (Class 6) (0-60,60) 3-Y-O+ **£1,940** (£577; £288; £144) **Stalls** Low

Form RPR

6064 **1** **Speedy Writer**[10] 6617 4-9-7 60 ........ DaneO'Neill 7 72
(Henry Candy) *sn in midfield: hdwy fr 2f out: led ins fnl f: rdn out: readily* **11/2**[2]

0320 **2** *2* **El Mirage (IRE)**[36] 5833 4-9-5 58 ........ JimCrowley 5 65
(Dean Ivory) *chsd ldrs: led 2f out tl ins fnl f: one pce* **10/1**

1446 **3** *shd* **Appyjack**[6] 6715 6-9-0 56 ........ CamHardie(3) 9 63+
(Tony Carroll) *hld up in rr: swtchd to outer over 2f out: gd late hdwy* **7/1**

6200 **4** *¾* **Eugenic**[28] 6070 3-9-1 57 ........ AndreaAtzeni 2 62
(Rod Millman) *cl up on rail: rdn to press ldrs 2f out: one pce fnl f* **12/1**

3436 **5** *2 ¼* **Polydamos**[17] 6407 5-8-12 51 ........(v) SilvestreDeSousa 4 51
(Tony Carroll) *mid-div on rail: hdwy to chse ldrs 2f out: no ex fnl f* **13/2**

0000 **6** *5* **Berrahri (IRE)**[19] 6342 3-9-1 57 ........(e[1]) RobertHavlin 8 45
(John Best) *towards rr: rdn and sme hdwy 2f out: nvr trbld ldrs* **12/1**

3060 **7** *1* **Rezwaan**[29] 6028 7-9-3 56 ........(be) ShaneKelly 6 42
(Murty McGrath) *s.i.s: towards rr: rdn over 2f out: nvr rchd ldrs* **4/1**[1]

5665 **8** *¾* **Baars Causeway (IRE)**[36] 5820 3-9-2 58 ........ KierenFallon 14 42
(Timothy Jarvis) *mid-div on outer: pushed along 4f out: no hdwy fnl 3f* **14/1**

46-0 **9** *nk* **Lexington Blue**[31] 5975 4-9-4 57 ........(p) JamieSpencer 1 41
(Seamus Mullins) *led after 1f: hrd rdn and hdd over 1f out: wknd* **20/1**

5066 **10** *nk* **Warbond**[14] 6481 6-8-12 51 ........(p) LukeMorris 12 34
(Michael Madgwick) *bhd: rdn over 2f out: nvr nr ldrs* **6/1**[3]

3500 **11** *1 ¾* **Southern Cross**[12] 6564 3-9-2 58 ........(p) JimmyFortune 3 37
(Hughie Morrison) *led for 1f: prom tl wknd wl over 1f out* **20/1**

000 **12** *5* **Severn Crossing**[58] 5006 3-9-4 60 ........ MartinDwyer 11 27
(William Muir) *prom: pushed along over 4f out: wknd over 3f out* **25/1**

006 **13** *1 ½* **Dream And Search (GER)**[18] 6367 3-9-3 59 ........(t) JoeFanning 13 23
(Anthony Honeyball) *a towards rr* **25/1**

1m 39.96s (0.16) **Going Correction** 0.0s/f (Stan)
**WFA** 3 from 4yo+ 3lb **13** Ran SP% **123.9**
Speed ratings (Par 101): **99,97,96,96,93 88,87,87,86,86 84,79,78**
CSF £58.44 CT £396.33 TOTE £6.70: £2.90, £2.50, £2.50; EX 49.60 Trifecta £195.10.
**Owner** Henry Candy **Bred** Northcombe Stud **Trained** Kingston Warren, Oxon

**FOCUS**
A modest handicap run at a fair pace. The winner built on his latest form.

## 6884 £25 FREE BET AT BETVICTOR.COM NURSERY H'CAP 1m (P)
**6:15** (6:15) (Class 5) (0-70,70) 2-Y-O **£2,587** (£770; £384; £192) **Stalls** Low

Form RPR

0301 **1** **Dark Wave**[8] 6669 2-9-3 66 6ex ........ GeorgeBaker 7 72
(Ed Walker) *mid-div: wd and plenty to do whn rdn 3f out: hdwy over 1f out: r.o to ld fnl stride* **4/1**[2]

0244 **2** *shd* **Dutch Portrait**[28] 6064 2-9-7 70 ........ JimCrowley 3 76
(Paul Cole) *dwlt: t.k.h: sn in tch: effrt 2f out: led ins fnl f: hrd rdn: hdd fnl stride* **3/1**[1]

5214 **3** *1* **Father Stone**[8] 6662 2-9-2 65 ........ LiamKeniry 11 69
(David Elsworth) *hld up towards rr: hdwy 2f out: chsd ldrs ins fnl f: kpt on* **10/1**

0034 **4** *2* **Ghalib (IRE)**[43] 5554 2-9-4 67 ........(t[1]) MartinHarley 6 66
(Marco Botti) *chsd ldrs: led 2f out tl ins fnl f: no ex fnl 75yds* **5/1**[3]

3403 **5** *2 ¾* **Grand Proposal**[15] 6449 2-9-5 68 ........(p) JamieSpencer 13 61
(Kevin Ryan) *in tch: rdn and lost pl over 2f out: styd on again fnl f* **10/1**

0600 **6** *¾* **Foylesideview (IRE)**[43] 5554 2-8-11 60 ........ TomQueally 10 51
(Luke Dace) *dwlt: hld up in rr: hdwy over 1f out: styd on same pce fnl f* **66/1**

550 **7** *shd* **New Brunswick (GER)**[58] 5009 2-9-4 67 ........ WilliamBuick 5 58
(John Gosden) *dwlt: t.k.h towards rr: pushed along and wd into st: effrt over 2f out: no imp* **7/1**

4524 **8** *1 ½* **Jet Mate (IRE)**[17] 6413 2-8-10 59 ........(p) MartinDwyer 4 46
(William Muir) *dwlt: sn pressing ldr: wknd 2f out* **25/1**

0315 **9** *½* **Seebeedee**[34] 5875 2-9-3 66 ........ LukeMorris 2 52
(Harry Dunlop) *led tl 2f out: sn wknd* **25/1**

231 **10** *6* **Little**[17] 6393 2-9-6 69 ........ JoeFanning 9 41
(Jamie Osborne) *s.i.s: t.k.h towards rr: hdwy 2f out: wknd qckly over 1f out: sddle slipped* **20/1**

0336 **11** *3 ½* **Euthenia**[18] 6359 2-9-2 65 ........ SamHitchcott 1 29
(Mick Channon) *chsd ldrs on rail tl wknd over 1f out: lost pl rapidly fnl f* **50/1**

6002 **12** *2* **Prince Of Paris**[8] 6663 2-9-2 65 ........ RobertHavlin 8 25
(Roger Ingram) *prom on outer tl wknd 3f out* **16/1**

0354 **13** *12* **Emperors Warrior (IRE)**[8] 6663 2-8-12 64 ........ CamHardie(3) 12
(Richard Hannon) *a bhd: no ch fnl 3f* **33/1**

1m 40.06s (0.26) **Going Correction** 0.0s/f (Stan) **13** Ran SP% **117.1**
Speed ratings (Par 95): **98,97,96,94,92 91,91,89,89,83 79,77,65**
CSF £14.70 CT £116.41 TOTE £6.60: £2.30, £1.70, £3.30; EX 21.70 Trifecta £165.80.
**Owner** F Ma **Bred** Lady Bland & Miss Anthea Gibson-Fleming **Trained** Newmarket, Suffolk

**FOCUS**
An open nursery run at a good pace and the from should work out.

## 6885 BETVICTOR.COM H'CAP (DIV I) 1m (P)
**6:45** (6:45) (Class 4) (0-85,85) 3-Y-O+ **£4,690** (£1,395; £697; £348) **Stalls** Low

Form RPR

0030 **1** **Lunar Deity**[20] 6285 5-8-9 73 ........ AndreaAtzeni 2 85
(Stuart Williams) *in tch on rail: effrt over 2f out: led over 1f out: rdn out* **12/1**

2450 **2** *2* **Silverheels (IRE)**[26] 6140 5-9-7 85 ........ LukeMorris 9 92
(Paul Cole) *chsd ldrs on outer: rdn over 2f out: kpt on to take 2nd ins fnl f* **9/2**[3]

1650 **3** *2 ¼* **Reedcutter**[70] 4580 3-9-0 81 ........ RobertTart 5 83
(James Toller) *prom: led after 2f tl over 1f out: one pce* **14/1**

420- **4** *1* **Faintly (USA)**[368] 6865 3-8-13 80 ........ JamesDoyle 6 80
(Amanda Perrett) *t.k.h in midfield: hdwy 2f out: styd on same pce fr over 1f out* **14/1**

324 **5** *hd* **Zain Empire**[33] 5930 3-8-12 79 ........ JamieSpencer 7 78
(Robert Cowell) *towards rr on outer: rdn and hanging over 2f out: c wd: nrest at fin* **7/2**[1]

0020 **6** *hd* **Obliteright (IRE)**[26] 6145 5-9-5 83 ........(p) GeorgeBaker 4 82
(William Knight) *bhd: rdn over 2f out: styd on fnl f* **25/1**

23-3 **7** *1* **Moonfaarid**[14] 6483 3-8-10 77 ........ PatCosgrave 3 73
(M F De Kock, South Africa) *led for 2f: stdd to dispute 2nd on rail and t.k.h: wknd jst over 1f out* **8/1**

6352 **8** *½* **Life And Times (USA)**[5] 6770 6-9-2 80 ........ JoeFanning 1 75
(Mark Johnston) *towards rr: effrt over 2f out: btn wl over 1f out* **7/2**[1]

3210 **9** *½* **Messila Star**[10] 6609 4-9-2 80 ........(v) WilliamBuick 8 74
(Jeremy Noseda) *sn disputing 2nd: wknd and hanging 2f out* **4/1**[2]

1m 39.21s (-0.59) **Going Correction** 0.0s/f (Stan)
**WFA** 3 from 4yo+ 3lb **9** Ran SP% **118.6**
Speed ratings (Par 105): **102,100,97,96,96 95,94,94**
CSF £67.04 CT £783.53 TOTE £16.20: £4.10, £2.00, £3.80; EX 84.90 Trifecta £657.40.
**Owner** The Morley Family **Bred** Hermes Services Ltd **Trained** Newmarket, Suffolk

**FOCUS**
An open handicap that turned into a sprint from 2f out. The form is taken at face value, through the runner-up.

## 6886 BETVICTOR.COM H'CAP (DIV II) 1m (P)
**7:15** (7:15) (Class 4) (0-85,84) 3-Y-O+ **£4,690** (£1,395; £697; £348) **Stalls** Low

Form RPR

1005 **1** **Ogbourne Downs**[10] 6609 4-9-4 84 ........ CamHardie(3) 2 93
(Charles Hills) *sltly outpcd towards rr: rdn and hdwy 2f out: led over 1f out: styd on* **16/1**

01 **2** *¾* **The Steward (USA)**[14] 6483 3-8-11 77 ........ LukeMorris 7 84+
(Sir Mark Prescott Bt) *mid-div: effrt over 2f out: drvn to chal over 1f out: r.o* **13/8**[1]

5451 **3** *1* **Barnmore**[29] 6035 6-8-11 77 ........ CharlesBishop(3) 8 82
(Peter Hedger) *dwlt: bhd: rdn 3f out: gd hdwy to press ldrs over 1f out: kpt on* **8/1**[3]

-144 **4** *shd* **Amood (IRE)**[41] 5649 3-8-13 79 ........ AndrewElliott 4 84
(Simon West) *led after 2f: hdd and hrd rdn over 1f out: kpt on same pce fnl f* **16/1**

2-25 **5** *hd* **Never To Be (USA)**[15] 6466 3-9-3 83 ........(t) WilliamBuick 5 87
(John Gosden) *towards rr: rdn and r.o fnl 2f: nrest at fin* **4/1**[2]

4340 **6** *1 ¼* **Nassau Storm**[19] 6334 5-9-6 83 ........(p) GeorgeBaker 1 84
(William Knight) *led for 2f: disp 2nd tl no ex ins fnl f* **20/1**

-200 **7** *2 ¼* **Secret Archive (USA)**[110] 3247 3-8-11 77 ........ JimCrowley 3 73
(Ralph Beckett) *in tch on rail: rdn 4f out: drvn and lost pl over 2f out: n.d after* **8/1**[3]

3004 **8** *¾* **Big Whiskey (IRE)**[10] 6609 4-9-3 80 ........(t) PatCosgrave 6 74
(Edward Creighton) *chsd ldrs tl wknd over 1f out* **10/1**

4416 **9** *7* **Tasmanian**[9] 6625 3-8-9 75 ........ JoeFanning 9 53
(Mark Johnston) *cl up: disp 2nd after 3f tl wknd 2f out* **14/1**

1m 38.44s (-1.36) **Going Correction** 0.0s/f (Stan)
**WFA** 3 from 4yo+ 3lb **9** Ran SP% **112.6**
Speed ratings (Par 105): **106,105,104,104,103 102,100,99,92**
CSF £41.25 CT £233.16 TOTE £18.40: £4.90, £3.20, £2.20; EX 51.90 Trifecta £1571.40.
**Owner** S W Group Logistics Limited **Bred** Bumble Bloodstock & Mrs S Nicholls **Trained** Lambourn, Berks

**FOCUS**
The winning time was marginally faster than the first division, but still ordinary form. A clear best from the winner.

## 6887 DOWNLOAD THE BETVICTOR INSTABET APP MAIDEN AUCTION STKS 6f (P)
**7:45** (7:46) (Class 5) 2-Y-O **£2,587** (£770; £384; £192) **Stalls** Low

Form RPR

2433 **1** **Little Palaver**[12] 6550 2-8-8 74 ........ RyanTate(3) 2 70
(Clive Cox) *mde all: hrd rdn and chal by two rivals 1f out: hld on wl* **11/8**[1]

4233 **2** *¾* **Clergyman**[9] 6623 2-9-0 78 ........ FergusSweeney 4 71
(Martyn Meade) *hld up towards rr: hdwy 2f out: drvn to chal 1f out: r.o* **11/4**[3]

3245 **3** *shd* **Framley Garth (IRE)**[8] 6663 2-8-13 62 ........ SilvestreDeSousa 5 69
(David Elsworth) *t.k.h towards rr: swtchd rt and hdwy to chal 1f out: r.o* **10/1**

3300 **4** *2 ¾* **Rockaroundtheclock (IRE)**[7] 6678 2-9-3 71 ........ LukeMorris 7 65
(Paul Cole) *chsd wnr tl over 1f out: one pce* **10/1**

00 **5** *1 ¼* **Cloak And Degas (IRE)**[27] 6115 2-9-0 0 ........ FrederikTylicki 8 58
(Scott Dixon) *in tch tl outpcd and btn 2f out* **25/1**

0234 **6** *1* **Grenade**[34] 5874 2-8-12 72 ........ CamHardie(3) 6 56
(Richard Hannon) *prom tl wknd over 1f out* **2/1**[2]

6 **7** *2 ¼* **Kodiac Krossing**[17] 6393 2-8-6 0 ........ JoeFanning 1 41
(Jamie Osborne) *dwlt: a bhd* **66/1**

1m 13.77s (0.67) **Going Correction** 0.0s/f (Stan) **7** Ran SP% **125.6**
Speed ratings (Par 95): **95,94,93,90,88 87,84**
CSF £6.45 TOTE £2.30: £1.10, £2.30; EX 5.30 Trifecta £16.30.
**Owner** Trevor Fox **Bred** Mrs Sandra Fox **Trained** Lambourn, Berks

**FOCUS**
An ordinary maiden.

## 6888 BARN DANCE CHRISTMAS PARTIES AT KEMPTON NURSERY H'CAP 6f (P)
**8:15** (8:16) (Class 6) (0-60,60) 2-Y-O **£1,940** (£577; £288; £144) **Stalls** Low

Form RPR

0002 **1** **Sparbrook (IRE)**[30] 6017 2-9-1 54 ........ HarryBentley 11 59
(Simon Dow) *led tl 2f out: pressed ldr after: rallied to get bk up fnl strides* **16/1**

0602 **2** *hd* **My Mo (FR)**[8] 6662 2-8-12 51 ........ MartinLane 4 55
(David Dennis) *trckd ldr: led 2f out: rdn along fnl f: hdd fnl strides* **10/3**[1]

0033 **3** *1* **Tommys Geal**[8] 6662 2-8-10 49 ........ WilliamCarson 1 50
(Michael Madgwick) *mid-div on rail: hdwy to chse ldrs over 1f out: kpt on fnl f* **8/1**

005 **4** *1* **Cherry Empress (IRE)**[18] 6361 2-9-5 58 ........ MartinDwyer 10 56
(Jo Hughes) *prom: rdn 2f out: one pce* **16/1**

2404 **5** *1 ½* **River Spirit**[15] 6447 2-9-7 60 ........ SamHitchcott 8 54
(Mick Channon) *mid-div on outer: drvn along over 2f out: styd on fnl f* **8/1**

5406 **6** *½* **Seamoor Secret**[71] 4529 2-9-3 56 ........ (t) OisinMurphy 3 48
(Alex Hales) *chsd ldrs tl hrd rdn and btn over 1f out* **20/1**

0642 **7** *2 ¼* **Go Gently (IRE)**[21] 6248 2-9-1 54 ........ (b) LiamKeniry 7 39
(George Baker) *s.i.s and rdn s: t.k.h towards rr: rdn and hdwy 2f out: no imp* **11/2**[3]

0000 **8** *1 ¾* **Senor Firecracker (IRE)**[22] 6237 2-8-9 48 ...... WilliamTwiston-Davies 2 28
(Brett Johnson) *dwlt: bhd: short-lived effrt 2f out: unable to chal* **16/1**

466 **9** *¾* **Icandi**[87] 4018 2-9-3 56 ........ RichardKingscote 6 34
(Tom Dascombe) *in tch tl outpcd over 2f out* **4/1**[2]

044 **10** *½* **Cape Point**[42] 5593 2-9-7 60 ........ DavidProbert 9 36
(Michael Blanshard) *dwlt: a bhd* **13/2**

000 **11** *1 ½* **Heavenlyfriendship**[92] 3858 2-8-12 56 ........ JennyPowell(5) 12 28
(Brendan Powell) *chsd ldrs tl wknd and eased over 2f out* **10/1**

1m 14.03s (0.93) **Going Correction** 0.0s/f (Stan) **11** Ran SP% **125.5**
Speed ratings (Par 93): **93,92,91,90,88 87,84,82,81,80 78**
CSF £73.54 CT £494.23 TOTE £16.10: £3.40, £2.50, £1.80; EX 70.60 Trifecta £530.80.
**Owner** Andrew Li **Bred** Henry O'Callaghan **Trained** Epsom, Surrey
■ Stewards' Enquiry : Harry Bentley two-day ban: used whip above permitted level (Oct 16,19)

**FOCUS**
A modest but competitive nursery in which it paid to race prominently.

## 6889 DOWNLOAD THE RACINGUK IPAD APP H'CAP 6f (P)
**8:45** (8:45) (Class 6) (0-65,65) 3-Y-O+ **£1,940** (£577; £288; £144) **Stalls** Low

Form RPR

4641 **1** **Reaffirmed (IRE)**[21] 6272 3-9-2 61 ........ LukeMorris 8 74+
(Ed Vaughan) *dwlt: hld up in rr: smooth hdwy over 1f out: disp ld ins fnl f: won on the nod* **5/1**[2]

0001 **2** *shd* **Varsovian**[8] 6666 4-9-3 61 6ex ........ SebSanders 3 73+
(Dean Ivory) *dwlt: t.k.h: sn chsng ldrs: drvn to ld ins fnl f: sn jnd by wnr: btn on the nod* **11/10**[1]

4340 **3** *1* **Coiste Bodhar (IRE)**[31] 5987 3-9-2 61 ........ (p) OisinMurphy 4 70
(Joseph Tuite) *led: hrd rdn and hdd ins fnl f: kpt on* **33/1**

2342 **4** *1 ¼* **Divine Call**[34] 5897 7-9-3 61 ........ (v) FrederikTylicki 7 66
(Milton Bradley) *dwlt: bhd: rapid hdwy over 1f out: nrest at fin* **7/1**[3]

2124 **5** *nk* **Ghost Train (IRE)**[105] 3393 5-9-7 65 ........ (p) HayleyTurner 6 69
(Tim McCarthy) *prom tl no ex over 1f out* **14/1**

1000 **6** *nk* **Meridius (IRE)**[32] 5951 4-9-6 64 ........ (p) JackMitchell 10 67
(Nick Littmoden) *in tch: rdn and outpcd over 2f out: styd on fnl f* **50/1**

1603 **7** *½* **Caminel (IRE)**[20] 6297 3-9-2 61 ........ (v) TomQueally 2 62
(Jeremy Gask) *mid-div: hdwy 2f out: no imp fnl f* **25/1**

0000 **8** *2* **Salvado (IRE)**[38] 5777 4-9-5 63 ........ (t[1]) DavidProbert 9 58
(Tony Carroll) *towards rr: effrt and nt clr run over 1f out: nvr rchd ldrs* **20/1**

05 **9** *2 ½* **Compton Prince**[105] 3393 5-9-3 61 ........ (b) BenCurtis 5 48
(Milton Bradley) *dwlt: sn chsng ldrs: wknd over 1f out* **50/1**

463 **10** *1 ½* **Four Cheers (IRE)**[57] 5044 3-9-3 62 ........ KierenFallon 11 44
(Clive Brittain) *chsd ldr tl wknd and n.m.r over 1f out* **7/1**[3]

400 **11** *4 ½* **Captain Kendall (IRE)**[22] 6240 5-9-1 64 ........[1] ShaneGray(5) 1 32
(Harry Chisman) *towards rr: modest effrt over 2f out: sn wknd* **33/1**

1m 12.6s (-0.50) **Going Correction** 0.0s/f (Stan)
**WFA** 3 from 4yo+ 1lb **11** Ran SP% **114.4**
Speed ratings (Par 101): **103,102,101,99,99 99,98,95,92,90 84**
CSF £9.81 CT £158.56 TOTE £5.50: £1.70, £1.10, £5.40; EX 13.50 Trifecta £289.20.
**Owner** Ballymore Downunder Syndicate **Bred** Floors Farming, S Roy & Admington Hall **Trained** Newmarket, Suffolk

**FOCUS**
A competitive handicap for the grade and the pace was solid throughout. The first two may prove better than the bare form.

## 6890 FOLLOW @BETVICTORRACING ON TWITTER H'CAP 7f (P)
**9:15** (9:15) (Class 5) (0-75,75) 3-Y-O+ **£2,587** (£770; £384; £192) **Stalls** Low

Form RPR

1112 **1** **Peace Accord**[14] 6495 4-9-6 75 ........ JimCrowley 3 85+
(Michael Wigham) *rrng s: sn in tch: effrt 2f out: led ins fnl f: drvn out* **2/1**[1]

-312 **2** *hd* **Aragosta**[21] 6269 4-9-6 75 ........ HayleyTurner 7 84+
(James Fanshawe) *in tch: rdn 2f out: r.o ins fnl f: clsng at fin* **11/4**[2]

3500 **3** *½* **Fantasy Gladiator**[29] 6035 8-9-2 71 ........ (p) ChrisCatlin 4 79
(John Quinn) *hld up towards rr: hdwy 2f out: kpt on fnl f* **25/1**

216 **4** *¾* **Enliven**[21] 6263 3-9-3 74 ........ OisinMurphy 5 79
(Andrew Balding) *cl up: rdn to press ldrs over 1f out: kpt on* **11/4**[2]

2116 **5** *1* **Darnathean**[39] 5729 5-9-2 71 ........ (p) LukeMorris 6 75
(Paul D'Arcy) *prom: rdn 2f out: kpt on same pce fnl f* **16/1**[3]

216- **6** *2 ½* **Archibald Thorburn (IRE)**[344] 7463 3-8-13 73 ...... CharlesBishop(3) 11 69
(Peter Hedger) *mid-div: hdwy to ld 2f out: hdd and no ex ins fnl f* **25/1**

250 **7** *2 ¼* **Polar Kite (IRE)**[61] 4907 6-9-5 74 ........ GeorgeBaker 1 65
(Roger Ingram) *dwlt: hld up in rr: sme hdwy 2f out: unable to chal* **20/1**

0305 **8** *nk* **Tidal's Baby**[31] 5986 5-9-6 75 ........ AndrewMullen 9 66
(Michael Appleby) *dwlt: nvr trbld ldrs* **16/1**[3]

0050 **9** *1* **Presumido (IRE)**[87] 4024 4-8-10 72 ........ TomasHarrigan(7) 10 60
(Simon Dow) *t.k.h: sn chsng ldr on outer: wknd 2f out* **50/1**

5100 **10** *2 ¼* **Shaunas Spirit (IRE)**[17] 6414 6-8-12 74 ........ PaulBooth(7) 14 56
(Dean Ivory) *a towards rr* **50/1**

-060 **11** *3 ½* **Plover**[86] 4053 4-9-6 75 ........ (p) RobertHavlin 2 48
(Michael Attwater) *led tl wknd 2f out* **33/1**

110- **12** *1* **Refreshestheparts (USA)**[444] 4348 5-9-4 73 ........ (t) PatCosgrave 13 43
(George Baker) *a towards rr* **33/1**

1m 25.95s (-0.05) **Going Correction** 0.0s/f (Stan)
**WFA** 3 from 4yo+ 2lb **12** Ran SP% **120.7**
Speed ratings (Par 103): **100,99,99,98,97 94,91,91,90,87 83,82**
CSF £7.03 CT £104.03 TOTE £3.00: £1.60, £1.20, £6.30; EX 8.50 Trifecta £179.00.
**Owner** D Hassan **Bred** Darley **Trained** Newmarket, Suffolk

**FOCUS**
A fair and competitive handicap that produced a thrilling finish. The winner rates better than the bare form.
T/Jkpt: Not won. T/Plt: £124.10 to a £1 stake. Pool: £96,003.39 - 564.69 winning units. T/Qpdt: £24.60 to a £1 stake. Pool: £8623.05 - 259.20 winning units. LM

# 6124 ASCOT (R-H)
### Friday, October 3

**OFFICIAL GOING: Straight course - good (good to firm in places); round course - good to firm (good in places) changing to good after race 2 (2.30)**
Wind: Almost nil Weather: Fine but cloudy, warm

## 6891 VEOLIA H'CAP 7f
**2:00** (2:00) (Class 4) (0-85,85) 3-Y-O+ **£6,469** (£1,925; £962; £481) **Stalls** High

Form RPR

431 **1** **Charter (IRE)**[13] 6558 4-9-1 79 ........ JimCrowley 16 92
(Michael Wigham) *stdd s: hld up in rr: prog on outer fr 3f out: rdn over 1f out: led ins fnl f: styd on wl* **9/2**[1]

1220 **2** *1 ½* **Lulu The Zulu (IRE)**[27] 6129 6-9-7 85 ........ AndrewMullen 8 93
(Michael Appleby) *trckd ldrs: chal 2f out: rdn to ld over 1f out: hdd ins fnl f: styd on but readily hld* **8/1**[2]

000 **3** *1 ¼* **Equity Risk (USA)**[48] 5446 4-9-0 78 ........ JamieSpencer 6 83
(Kevin Ryan) *hld up in rr: prog over 2f out and sn swtchd to outer: rdn and styd on fr over 1f out to take 3rd last strides: no ch to threaten* **14/1**

4132 **4** *hd* **Scottish Glen**[20] 6334 8-9-0 78 ........ DavidProbert 11 82
(Patrick Chamings) *rdn in 9th pl after 3f: responded to press to cl on ldrs 2f out: chal 1f out: one pce fnl f* **8/1**[2]

43P0 **5** *1 ¼* **Mujazif (IRE)**[15] 6476 4-9-5 83 ........ JoeFanning 17 84
(David Nicholls) *trckd ldrs gng wl: shkn up wl over 1f out: styd on same pce fnl f: nt gng pce to chal* **8/1**[2]

166 **6** *1 ¾* **Maraayill (IRE)**[43] 5603 3-8-12 78 ........ (tp) MartinHarley 5 73
(Marco Botti) *hld up in rr: prog over 2f out: tried to cl on ldrs 1f out: kpt on but nvr in chalng position* **16/1**

6213 **7** *nk* **Pretty Bubbles**[21] 6302 5-9-4 82 ........ PaddyAspell 15 77
(J R Jenkins) *trckd ldrs: clsd against rail fr 2f out: rdn and nt qckn over 1f out: one pce after* **25/1**

6232 **8** *3 ½* **Good Authority (IRE)**[17] 6424 7-9-6 84 ........ RichardHughes 1 70
(Victor Dartnall) *hld up and in last early: plenty to do whn prog wl over 2f out: trying to cl whn nowhere to go over 1f out: kpt on same pce after and no ch* **10/1**[3]

3010 **9** *3 ¼* **Kakatosi**[24] 6207 7-9-7 85 ........ PatDobbs 7 63
(Mike Murphy) *dwlt and stdd s: wl in rr: rdn and struggling bdly in last trio 3f out: kpt on past wkng rivals fnl 2f* **16/1**

0002 **10** *¾* **Nameitwhatyoulike**[17] 6430 5-9-4 82 ........ PaulMulrennan 2 58
(Bryan Smart) *led: crossed fr wd draw towards nr side rail after 1f: hdd & wknd over 1f out* **10/1**[3]

2500 **11** *2 ¾* **Constantine**[43] 5603 3-8-8 77 ........ CamHardie(3) 4 45
(Richard Hannon) *chsd ldrs but off the bridle bef 1/2-way: losing pl whn short of room 1f out* **50/1**

2002 **12** *3 ½* **Rogue Wave (IRE)**[27] 6144 3-9-1 81 ........ JamesDoyle 10 40
(Timothy Jarvis) *prom on outer: rt on terms w ldrs 2f out: wknd qckly jst over 1f out* **14/1**

6540 **13** *2* **Gravitational (IRE)**[6] 6736 4-8-13 80 ........ AshleyMorgan(3) 13 34
(Chris Wall) *pressed ldr: carried lft after 1f: lost pl and wknd qckly 2f out* **16/1**

0200 **14** *3 ¼* **Jammy Guest (IRE)**[28] 6097 4-9-7 85 ........ KierenFallon 14 31
(George Margarson) *pressed ldrs tl wknd qckly 2f out* **16/1**

6600 **15** *2 ¾* **Smarty Socks (IRE)**[17] 6430 10-9-4 82 ........ DanielTudhope 3 21
(David O'Meara) *dwlt: a in rr: struggling in last trio over 2f out: no prog* **12/1**

4310 **16** *4 ½* **Refuse Colette (IRE)**[8] 6689 5-9-3 81 ........ PaoloSirigu 18 8
(Mick Quinn) *cl up whn bdly hmpd against nr side rail after 1f: lost pl and nvr able to rcvr* **50/1**

3320 **17** *4 ½* **Palace Moon**[172] 1492 9-9-5 83 ........ (t) GeorgeBaker 9
(William Knight) *hld up in rr: prog on outer fr 3f out: cl enough 2f out: sn wknd qckly: heavily eased* **20/1**

1m 28.02s (0.42) **Going Correction** +0.075s/f (Good)
**WFA** 3 from 4yo+ 2lb **17** Ran SP% **126.8**
Speed ratings (Par 105): **100,98,96,96,95 93,92,88,85,84 81,77,74,71,68 62,57**
CSF £37.83 CT £499.98 TOTE £5.10: £1.70, £2.00, £4.10, £2.10; EX 44.70 Trifecta £1295.40.
**Owner** J Searchfield, D Hassan **Bred** Barouche Stud (IRE) Ltd **Trained** Newmarket, Suffolk
■ Stewards' Enquiry : Paul Mulrennan seven-day ban; careless riding (17th-23rd Oct)

**FOCUS**
Stands side rail on Straight course 7yds inside normal position. Rail on Round course was 4yds inside from 12f to start of home straight where it increased to 9yds until after the Winning Post. Races 4 &6 increased by 20yds. Stands' side rail on Straight course 7yds inside normal position. Rail on Round course was 4yds inside from 12f to start of home straight where it increased to 9yds until after the Winning Post. Races 4 &6 increased by 20yds. Riders in the first were of the opinion the ground was on the easy side, certainly softer than the official description, and the opening time would appear to back them up. A competitive handicap. The winner is progressive and the runner-up better than ever.

## 6892 REDCENTRIC EBF STALLIONS CLASSIFIED STKS 1m (S)
**2:30** (2:34) (Class 3) 3-Y-O+
**£9,337** (£2,796; £1,398; £699; £349; £175) **Stalls** High

Form RPR

0030 **1** **Excellent Guest**[55] 5189 7-9-2 87 ........ TomQueally 2 96
(George Margarson) *hld up in rr of centre gp: smooth prog to trck ldr over 2f out: drvn to ld narrowly 1f out: jst hld on* **33/1**

0001 **2** *hd* **Consign**[8] 6688 4-9-8 88 ........ (v) RyanMoore 9 101+
(Jeremy Noseda) *stdd s: hld up in last of nr side quartet: gng easily but stl same pl 2f out: shkn up wl over 1f out and sn led gp: drifted rt u.p but r.o wl fnl f: jst failed* **8/1**

2062 **3** *nse* **Pupil (IRE)**[5] 6785 3-8-13 88 ........ (p) RichardHughes 1 94
(Richard Hannon) *overall ldr in centre: taken to far rail and sent for home over 2f out: drvn and hdd 1f out: styd on wl and w wnr after: jst hld and lost 2nd last stride* **5/1**[2]

402 **4** *2* **Secret Art (IRE)**[27] 6140 4-9-2 89 ........ MartinHarley 6 90
(William Knight) *chsd overall ldr in centre to over 2f out: styd on same pce fr over 1f out* **6/1**[3]

-442 **5** *3* **Democretes**[15] 6498 5-8-9 90 ........ MikeyEnnis(7) 4 83
(Seamus Durack) *hld up in centre gp: gng wl enough over 2f out: urged along strly and kpt on at one pce fr over 1f out* **16/1**

2431 **6** *shd* **Compton**[27] 6144 5-9-2 88 ........ (t) GeorgeBaker 5 83
(Stuart Williams) *dwlt: hld up in last of centre gp: prog over 2f out: shkn up and no further hdwy over 1f out* **12/1**

3125 **7** ½ **You're Fired (IRE)**[69] 4647 3-8-13 89 .......... JimCrowley 10 82
(K R Burke) *trckd ldrs nr side: drvn to ld gp brefly wl over 1f out: drifted rt and fdd fnl f* **4/1**[1]

4212 **8** 5 **Chinese Jade**[28] 6111 3-8-13 86 .......... (p) LukeMorris 11 70
(Sir Mark Prescott Bt) *trckd nr side ldr: upsides and drvn 2f out: sn wknd* **10/1**

4120 **9** hd **Ree's Rascal (IRE)**[7] 6713 6-9-2 90 .......... PatCosgrave 3 70
(Jim Boyle) *prom in centre gp tl wknd over 2f out* **16/1**

6033 **10** 1½ **Oxsana**[47] 5468 3-8-10 90 .......... AndreaAtzeni 8 63
(William Haggas) *led nr side quartet: nt on terms w far side fr 3f out: lost ld and wknd wl over 1f out* **6/1**[3]

1101 **11** 14 **Meet Me Halfway**[63] 4866 4-8-13 87 .......... TedDurcan 7 31
(Chris Wall) *chsd ldrs in centre tl wknd qckly 2f out: t.o* **12/1**

1m 42.06s (1.26) **Going Correction** +0.075s/f (Good)
**WFA** 3 from 4yo+ 3lb 11 Ran SP% **115.5**
Speed ratings (Par 107): **96,95,95,93,90 90,90,85,84,83 69**
CSF £273.68 TOTE £32.10: £7.60, £3.10, £1.80; EX 380.20 Trifecta £2428.00.
**Owner** John Guest Racing **Bred** John Guest Racing Ltd **Trained** Newmarket, Suffolk

**FOCUS**
A typically open classified stakes. They divided into two groups and it was the larger bunch who emerged on top, the main action taking place near the far rail. The winner improved on this year's shaky form.

## 6893 FAITHDEAN H'CAP (BOBIS RACE) 6f
3:05 (3:06) (Class 2) (0-105,97) 3-Y-O
**£18,675** (£5,592; £2,796; £1,398; £699; £351) **Stalls** High

Form RPR

6114 **1** **Telmeyd**[55] 5165 3-9-7 97 .......... RyanMoore 7 109
(William Haggas) *dwlt: hld up in last trio: shkn up and prog on outer 2f out: drvn to ld ins fnl f: styd on strly* **13/8**[1]

351 **2** 1¼ **Red Pike (IRE)**[42] 5632 3-8-13 89 .......... PaulMulrennan 11 97
(Bryan Smart) *trckd ldng trio: produced between them to ld jst over 1f out: styd on but hdd and outpcd ins fnl f* **9/1**

6121 **3** 1½ **Mr Win (IRE)**[41] 5675 3-9-2 92 .......... TedDurcan 5 95
(Chris Wall) *hld up in rr: prog along w wnr 2f out: drvn to chal 1f out: nt qckn fnl f: jst hld on for 3rd* **13/2**[3]

1362 **4** hd **Golden Steps (FR)**[55] 5165 3-9-5 95 .......... MartinHarley 12 101
(Marco Botti) *dwlt: t.k.h: hld up in last pair: prog whn nt clr run over 1f out: rdn and styd on fnl f: unable to chal* **9/2**[2]

2225 **5** shd **Lexington Abbey**[13] 6531 3-8-13 89 .......... JamieSpencer 9 91
(Kevin Ryan) *hld up in last pair: stl there 2f out: prog over 1f out: hrd rdn and r.o fnl f: too much to do* **10/1**

1160 **6** 3 **Desert Ace (IRE)**[41] 5696 3-8-11 90 .......... (tp) RyanTate(3) 2 83
(Clive Cox) *trckd ldrs: clsd over 2f out: chal against far rail over 1f out: wknd fnl f* **33/1**

4131 **7** ½ **Munfallet (IRE)**[12] 6575 3-8-0 81 6ex .......... JoeDoyle(5) 10 72
(David Brown) *chsd ldng pair: shkn up and nt qckn 2f out: lost pl sn after: fdd fnl f* **20/1**

0000 **8** ¾ **Deeds Not Words (IRE)**[6] 6760 3-8-13 92 .......... CharlesBishop(3) 3 81
(Mick Channon) *trckd ldrs: clsd over 2f out: chal and upsides over 1f out: wknd fnl f* **33/1**

2105 **9** ½ **Little Shambles**[15] 6498 3-8-12 88 .......... JoeFanning 8 75
(Mark Johnston) *pressed ldr: led 2f out to jst over 1f out: wknd* **33/1**

0262 **10** 1¼ **Ventura Mist**[11] 6598 3-9-4 94 .......... (p) GrahamLee 6 77
(Tim Easterby) *settled in midfield: clsd on ldrs 2f out but nowhere to go bhd ldng line: lost pl fnl f* **20/1**

6044 **11** 2¾ **Expert (IRE)**[23] 6234 3-9-7 97 .......... RichardHughes 1 71
(Richard Hannon) *slowly away: hld up in rr: tried to make prog 2f out: sn shkn up and btn* **14/1**

34- **12** 3¾ **Boom The Groom (IRE)**[81] 3-9-5 95 .......... JamesDoyle 4 57
(Tony Carroll) *led to 2f out: wkng whn squeezed out over 1f out* **50/1**

1m 13.53s (-0.97) **Going Correction** +0.075s/f (Good) 12 Ran SP% **115.7**
Speed ratings (Par 107): **109,107,105,105,104 100,100,99,98,96 93,88**
CSF £14.75 CT £78.46 TOTE £2.50: £1.10, £2.70, £2.50; EX 19.20 Trifecta £58.00.
**Owner** Sheikh Ahmed Al Maktoum **Bred** Cheveley Park Stud Ltd **Trained** Newmarket, Suffolk

**FOCUS**
The official going became Good all round before this race, a warm sprint handicap. The field all raced centre-to-far side. The form is sound.

## 6894 LONDONMETRIC NOEL MURLESS STKS (LISTED RACE) 1m 6f
3:40 (3:41) (Class 1) 3-Y-O
**£20,982** (£7,955; £3,981; £1,983; £995; £499) **Stalls** Low

Form RPR

2141 **1** **Big Orange**[34] 5920 3-9-4 104 .......... TomQueally 5 112
(Michael Bell) *t.k.h: trckd ldrs: led over 2f out: jnd and drvn over 1f out: battled on wl: jst hld on* **10/3**[3]

3545 **2** shd **Marzocco (USA)**[20] 6329 3-9-1 110 .......... (b) WilliamBuick 4 109
(John Gosden) *trckd ldrs: shkn up over 2f out: prog to join wnr over 1f out: gd battle after and upsides: nt qckn last strides* **7/4**[1]

4111 **3** shd **Mizzou (IRE)**[27] 6137 3-9-1 98 .......... AndreaAtzeni 2 109
(Luca Cumani) *hld up in last pair: pushed along fr 4f out: rdn over 2f out: chsd ldng pair over 1f out: clsd fnl f: jst failed* **15/8**[2]

043 **4** 13 **Odeon**[44] 5577 3-9-1 103 .......... GrahamLee 7 91
(James Given) *sweating: trckd ldr: led 3f out to over 2f out: wknd qckly over 1f out* **7/1**

1124 **5** 9 **Statsminister**[20] 6318 3-8-10 77 .......... FergusSweeney 1 73
(Luke Dace) *hld up in last pair: rdn over 3f out: wknd over 2f out: sn bhd* **80/1**

0123 **6** 41 **Koliakhova (FR)**[35] 5877 3-8-10 78 .......... LiamKeniry 6 16
(John Flint) *sweating: led to 3f out: wknd rapidly: t.o* **100/1**

2m 59.36s (-1.64) **Going Correction** +0.175s/f (Good) 6 Ran SP% **108.9**
Speed ratings: **111,110,110,103,98 74**
CSF £9.00 TOTE £4.40: £2.10, £1.20; EX 9.70 Trifecta £14.90.
**Owner** W J & T C O Gredley **Bred** Stetchworth & Middle Park Studs **Trained** Newmarket, Suffolk
■ Stewards' Enquiry : Andrea Atzeni two-day ban; used whip above permitted level (19th-20th Oct)
William Buick two-day ban; used whip above permitted level (19th-20th Oct)

**FOCUS**
A fair Listed race, which was first run in 2011. The pace was reasonable and the time was quick, with the first three fighting out a close finish, well clear of the others. The winner reversed Royal Ascot form with the runner-up.

## 6895 TROY ASSET MANAGEMENT H'CAP (BOBIS RACE) 7f
4:15 (4:19) (Class 3) (0-95,94) 3-Y-O **£8,409** (£2,502; £1,250; £625) **Stalls** High

Form RPR

5135 **1** **Outback Traveller (IRE)**[24] 6207 3-9-6 93 .......... RyanMoore 2 110
(Jeremy Noseda) *cl up and a gng wl: led 2f out: sn rdn clr: r.o strly* **9/2**[1]

5052 **2** 7 **Sir Robert Cheval**[23] 6234 3-9-7 94 .......... MartinHarley 5 93
(Marco Botti) *hld up towards rr: prog over 2f out: rdn to take 2nd jst over 1f out: kpt on but no ch w wnr* **5/1**[2]

0405 **3** ½ **Muir Lodge**[6] 6744 3-9-1 88 .......... PatCosgrave 3 86
(George Baker) *awkward s: hld up in rr: prog whn n.m.r 3f out: hd at awkward angle fr 2f out: tk 3rd fnl f: one pce after* **16/1**

4011 **4** ½ **Comino (IRE)**[17] 6430 3-8-2 80 .......... ShaneGray(5) 1 76
(Kevin Ryan) *led to 2f out: sn outpcd by wnr: lost 2nd jst over 1f out and one pce after* **20/1**

5013 **5** hd **Outer Space**[11] 6607 3-9-0 87 .......... WilliamTwiston-Davies 14 83
(Jamie Osborne) *stdd s: hld up in last: prog over 2f out: rdn over 1f out: styd on but unable to rch plcd horses* **16/1**

3151 **6** ½ **Above The Rest (IRE)**[13] 6552 3-8-12 85 .......... JamesDoyle 6 79
(Timothy Jarvis) *trckd ldrs: rdn 2f out: kpt on to press for a pl tl no ex ins fnl f* **5/1**[2]

0053 **7** 1 **Nezar (IRE)**[23] 6234 3-8-12 85 .......... (v) WilliamBuick 11 77
(George Margarson) *hld up in rr: rdn over 2f out: kpt on fr over 1f out: nvr nrr but n.d* **12/1**

4066 **8** 3½ **Azagal (IRE)**[23] 6234 3-9-2 89 .......... GrahamLee 12 72
(Tim Easterby) *hld up wl in rr: shkn up over 2f out: no prog and wl btn over 1f out* **14/1**

3606 **9** shd **Cool Bahamian (IRE)**[58] 5031 3-8-4 80 oh3 .......... (b[1]) CamHardie(3) 7 62
(Eve Johnson Houghton) *awkward s: sn in midfield: trapped bhd wkng rivals fr jst over 2f out and dropped to last trio 1f out: rdn and kpt on fnl f but no ch* **16/1**

3621 **10** 1½ **Whaleweigh Station**[30] 6042 3-9-3 90 .......... JimCrowley 4 69
(J R Jenkins) *hld up towards rr: clsd fr 1/2-way: rdn to chal 2f out: sn no ch w wnr: wknd fnl f* **14/1**

55U3 **11** 4½ **Lawyer (IRE)**[8] 6688 3-8-10 83 .......... AndreaAtzeni 8 50
(Luca Cumani) *pressed ldr: wknd jst over 2f out* **6/1**[3]

00 **12** 2 **Sir Guy Porteous (IRE)**[42] 5656 3-9-4 91 .......... JoeFanning 9 53
(Mark Johnston) *trckd ldng pair: shkn up and wknd fr jst over 2f out* **25/1**

2103 **13** 2 **Baltic Brave (IRE)**[42] 5649 3-9-0 87 .......... (t) JimmyFortune 10 43
(Hughie Morrison) *trckd ldrs: rdn over 2f out: wknd wl over 1f out* **16/1**

1m 26.62s (-0.98) **Going Correction** +0.075s/f (Good) 13 Ran SP% **119.0**
Speed ratings (Par 105): **108,100,99,98,98 98,96,92,92,91 85,83,81**
CSF £26.07 CT £273.52 TOTE £3.70: £1.90, £2.00, £5.50; EX 16.30 Trifecta £348.30.
**Owner** Saeed Suhail **Bred** Tally-Ho Stud **Trained** Newmarket, Suffolk

**FOCUS**
They raced in one group in this decent handicap, ending up towards the far side. The winner impressed and the form is all about him.

## 6896 ASCOT CAMRA BEER FESTIVAL GORDON CARTER H'CAP 2m
4:50 (4:50) (Class 3) (0-95,87) 3-Y-O+ **£8,409** (£2,502; £1,250; £625) **Stalls** Low

Form RPR

1220 **1** **Quest For More (IRE)**[27] 6133 4-10-0 87 .......... (b) GeorgeBaker 1 95
(Roger Charlton) *trckd ldng pair: chal on inner 2f out: edgd lft over 1f out: led jst ins fnl f: sn hrd pressed: hld on wl* **7/2**[2]

12/3 **2** hd **Fire Fighter (IRE)**[67] 4746 6-9-5 78 .......... (t) RyanMoore 6 86
(Alan King) *hld up in 5th: rdn and looking for room jst over 2f out: prog to take 2nd ins fnl f: chal last 100yds: jst hld* **3/1**[1]

3512 **3** 3¼ **Le Maitre Chat (USA)**[19] 6366 3-9-1 85 .......... JimCrowley 2 93+
(Clive Cox) *slowly away: hld up in last: tried for run on inner over 2f out but nowhere to go: renewed effrt and tried to force wway through jst over 1f out and nowhere to go: styd on fnl f to take 3rd last strides* **4/1**[3]

3020 **4** nk **Buckland (IRE)**[21] 6287 6-9-11 84 .......... MartinLane 3 88
(Charlie Fellowes) *trckd ldr: chal over 2f out: drvn to ld over 1f out: edgd rt sn after: hdd and fdd jst ins fnl f* **6/1**

5235 **5** 2½ **Sir Frank Morgan (IRE)**[13] 6557 4-9-8 81 .......... JoeFanning 7 84
(Mark Johnston) *led and untrbld in front: rdn over 2f out: hdd over 1f out: cl up but hld whn bdly hmpd sn after: nt rcvr* **8/1**

4461 **6** ½ **Snowy Dawn**[21] 6283 4-9-3 76 .......... GrahamLee 8 76
(Ben Case) *trckd ldng trio: rdn over 2f out: nt qckn wl over 1f out* **6/1**[3]

2030 **7** ¾ **Ex Oriente (IRE)**[13] 6557 5-9-5 78 .......... AndreaAtzeni 4 77
(Stuart Williams) *hld up in 6th: shkn up over 2f out: no rspnse and sn btn* **14/1**

3m 33.34s (4.34) **Going Correction** +0.175s/f (Good)
**WFA** 3 from 4yo+ 11lb 7 Ran SP% **113.6**
Speed ratings (Par 107): **96,95,94,94,92 92,92**
CSF £14.23 CT £42.29 TOTE £5.10: £2.40, £1.90; EX 18.30 Trifecta £42.90.
**Owner** H R H Sultan Ahmad Shah **Bred** Epona Bloodstock Ltd **Trained** Beckhampton, Wilts
■ Stewards' Enquiry : Martin Lane two-day ban; careless riding (19th-20th Oct)

**FOCUS**
They went a fairly steady gallop in this staying handicap and it became a rough race in the home straight. The form is ordinary.
T/Jkpt: Not won. T/Plt: £30.60 to a £1 stake. Pool of £140372.28 - 3338.82 winning tickets.
T/Qpdt: £5.70 to a £1 stake. Pool of £9530.64 - 1233.61 winning tickets. JN

# 6838 WOLVERHAMPTON (A.W) (L-H)
Friday, October 3

**OFFICIAL GOING: Tapeta: standard**
Wind: Fresh behind Weather: Overcast

## 6897 ENJOY DAILY BETTING TIPS @ BOOKMAKERS.CO.UK H'CAP (TAPETA) 5f 20y
5:50 (5:50) (Class 6) (0-60,64) 3-Y-O+ **£2,264** (£673; £336; £168) **Stalls** Low

Form RPR

0105 **1** **Pearl Noir**[18] 6399 4-8-11 55 .......... (b) MatthewHopkins(5) 3 66
(Scott Dixon) *chsd ldrs: pushed along 1/2-way: rdn and swtchd rt over 1f out: r.o to ld wl ins fnl f* **11/1**

0562 **2** 1 **Give Us A Belle (IRE)**[22] 6273 5-9-5 58 .......... (vt) AdamBeschizza 12 65
(Christine Dunnett) *chsd ldr tl led wl over 1f out: sn rdn: hdd wl ins fnl f* **9/1**

5100 **3** ½ **Danzoe (IRE)**[13] 6561 7-8-8 52 (v) EoinWalsh(5) 2 58
(Christine Dunnett) *hld up: hdwy over 1f out: sn rdn: r.o* **16/1**

1040 **4** 2¼ **Douneedahand**[42] 5624 3-9-0 60 (p) GaryMahon(7) 6 59
(Seamus Mullins) *hld up: racd keenly: hdwy and nt clr run over 1f out: styd on: nt trble ldrs* **10/1**

4562 **5** *hd* **Spic 'n Span**[19] 6368 9-8-10 49 (p) LukeMorris 1 46
(Ronald Harris) *mid-div: pushed along 1/2-way: hdwy over 1f out: styd on* **12/1**

4525 **6** *nk* **College Doll**[10] 6631 5-5-5 58 (t) JimmyQuinn 5 54
(Christine Dunnett) *led early: trckd ldrs: plld hrd: rdn over 1f out: no ex ins fnl f* **20/1**

0300 **7** 1¼ **Interchoice Star**[35] 5897 9-9-5 58 (p) TonyHamilton 7 49
(Ray Peacock) *mid-div: rdn over 1f out: nt trble ldrs* **20/1**

3331 **8** ½ **Dream Sika (IRE)**[13] 6561 3-9-0 53 JamesSullivan 11 43
(Ruth Carr) *sn led: hdd wl over 1f out: wknd ins fnl f* **7/2**[2]

3304 **9** *hd* **Passionada**[22] 6273 5-9-6 59 (p) DaleSwift 10 48
(Ed McMahon) *sn pushed along to chse ldrs: rdn 1/2-way: wknd ins fnl f* **5/1**[3]

0060 **10** 2½ **My Time**[52] 5287 5-8-9 48 TomEaves 4 28
(Michael Mullineaux) *s.i.s: outpcd* **33/1**

4305 **11** *hd* **Insolenceofoffice (IRE)**[212] 841 6-8-13 59 (p) NicolaGrundy(7) 9 38
(Richard Ford) *sn pushed along and a in rr* **20/1**

36-2 **12** 1½ **Befortyfour**[2] 6851 9-8-11 50 (p) RobertWinston 8 24
(Muredach Kelly, Ire) *mid-div: effrt on outer 1/2-way: rdn and hung lft over 1f out: wknd fnl f* **10/3**[1]

1m 2.0s (0.10) **Going Correction** +0.025s/f (Slow) 12 Ran SP% **120.2**
Speed ratings (Par 101): **100,98,97,94,93 93,91,90,90,86 85,83**
CSF £101.68 CT £1618.48 TOTE £13.20: £4.60, £3.30, £7.20; EX 87.60 Trifecta £834.20 Part won. Pool of £1112.37 - 0.74 winning units..
**Owner** P J Dixon & Partners **Bred** Mrs Yvette Dixon **Trained** Babworth, Notts

**FOCUS**
Overcast and dry. A weak handicap with 16lb separating the peak from the foot of the weights. There was plenty of pace horses and it ultimately helped to be drawn low. The winner is rated to his 6f April run here.

## 6898 DOWNLOAD THE FREE APP @ BOOKMAKERS.CO.UK CLAIMING STKS (TAPETA) 5f 216y
**6:20** (6:23) (Class 6) 3-Y-O+ **£2,264** (£673; £336; £168) **Stalls** Low

Form RPR
0003 **1** **Fitz Flyer (IRE)**[6] 6764 8-8-9 75 (v) AnnaHesketh(7) 11 84
(David Nicholls) *mde virtually all: clr over 2f out: styd on wl* **12/1**

1310 **2** 3½ **Cape Of Hope (IRE)**[28] 6095 4-9-6 70 (v) RichardKingscote 1 77
(Tom Dascombe) *sn prom: chsd wnr 5f out: rdn over 1f out: styd on same pce fnl f* **12/1**

340 **3** *hd* **Hamoody (USA)**[20] 6313 10-9-2 75 OisinMurphy 5 72
(Joseph Tuite) *chsd wnr 1f: remained handy: rdn over 1f out: styd on same pce* **14/1**

3010 **4** *hd* **Regal Parade**[6] 6740 10-9-6 88 (t) FrederikTylicki 3 76
(Milton Bradley) *prom: lost pl over 4f out: shkn up over 1f out: hdwy: nt clr run and swtchd lft ins fnl f: nvr nr to chal* **5/2**[2]

3041 **5** ¾ **Sacha Park (IRE)**[13] 6562 3-9-9 80 PatDobbs 7 77
(Richard Hannon) *chsd ldrs: rdn over 1f out: no ex ins fnl f* **2/1**[1]

0330 **6** ½ **Arctic Lynx (IRE)**[17] 6441 7-8-12 73 (tp) AdamBeschizza 13 64
(Robert Cowell) *mid-div: rdn over 1f out: styd on ins fnl f: nvr trbld ldrs* **25/1**

3560 **7** ¾ **Head Space (IRE)**[27] 6150 6-9-4 77 (v) JamesSullivan 9 67
(Ruth Carr) *hld up: nt clr run over 1f out and ins fnl f: nvr nrr* **15/2**[3]

2652 **8** *shd* **Noverre To Go (IRE)**[23] 6236 8-9-4 73 (p) LukeMorris 6 67
(Ronald Harris) *mid-div: rdn over 1f out: n.d* **14/1**

1055 **9** 2 **Crisis Averted (IRE)**[69] 4660 3-9-9 77 (b[1]) TonyHamilton 8 66
(Richard Fahey) *hld up in tch: plld hrd: rdn over 1f out: wknd ins fnl f* **16/1**

60 **10** 1¾ **Point North (IRE)**[13] 6562 7-9-2 67 (bt) BenCurtis 10 53
(John Balding) *s.i.s: hld up: plld hrd: rdn over 1f out: nvr on terms* **66/1**

-200 **11** ½ **Speightowns Kid (USA)**[120] 2933 6-8-12 65 TomEaves 2 47
(Michael Herrington) *hld up: a in rr* **80/1**

1m 14.35s (-0.15) **Going Correction** +0.025s/f (Slow)
**WFA** 3 from 4yo+ 1lb 11 Ran SP% **114.8**
Speed ratings (Par 101): **102,97,97,96,95 95,94,94,91,89 88**
CSF £142.17 TOTE £22.90: £5.60, £4.40, £5.10; EX 194.60 Trifecta £1193.20.Head Space was claimed by M. J. Attwater for £9000.
**Owner** Mike Browne **Bred** Colin Kennedy **Trained** Sessay, N Yorks

**FOCUS**
The pace held up and the winner is rated back to his summer form.

## 6899 SUSAN BOX MEMORIAL H'CAP (TAPETA) (DIV I) 1m 5f 194y
**6:50** (6:50) (Class 6) (0-65,65) 3-Y-O+ **£2,264** (£673; £336; £168) **Stalls** Low

Form RPR
0164 **1** **Oracle Boy**[28] 6119 3-9-1 61 (p) MartinDwyer 2 72
(William Muir) *mde virtually all: pushed along 6f out: drvn along over 1f out: styd on* **5/1**[2]

3603 **2** 1½ **Lady Bingo (IRE)**[20] 6338 3-9-5 65 JamieSpencer 4 74
(Sir Mark Prescott Bt) *a.p: chsd wnr over 10f out: rdn over 3f out: styd on same pce fnl f* **1/1**[1]

6-23 **3** 3¼ **Sheila's Heart**[192] 1088 4-9-9 65 ShelleyBirkett(5) 9 69
(John E Long) *hld up: hdwy over 8f out: rdn over 2f out: styd on same pce fr over 1f out* **18/1**

00 **4** 12 **Sakhra**[20] 6343 3-9-0 60 GrahamGibbons 8 47
(Mark Brisbourne) *hld up: hdwy over 6f out: rdn over 3f out: wknd over 1f out* **80/1**

0254 **5** 6 **Nolecce**[20] 6343 7-9-1 59 AdamMcLean(7) 5 38
(Tony Forbes) *prom: lost pl over 6f out: hdwy over 3f out: rdn and wknd over 2f out* **14/1**

400 **6** 7 **Painted Tail (IRE)**[23] 6223 7-9-1 55 NeilFarley(3) 1 24
(Andrew Crook) *s.i.s: sn pushed along in rr: rdn over 7f out: lost tch fnl 5f* **40/1**

3505 **7** ½ **Uganda Glory (USA)**[80] 4296 4-9-4 62 (b[1]) ChrisMeehan(7) 7 30
(George Baker) *rn in snatches in rr and rdn at various stages: lost tch fnl 4f* **9/1**

0310 **8** 4½ **Ohio (IRE)**[25] 6193 3-8-10 56 LukeMorris 6 18
(Nick Littmoden) *s.i.s: sn pushed along and prom: rdn over 4f out: wknd over 3f out* **11/2**[3]

0630 **9** 31 **Rookery (IRE)**[42] 5628 3-9-3 63 FrederikTylicki 3
(Roger Ingram) *chsd wnr over 3f: remained handy: rdn over 4f out: wknd 3f out* **12/1**

3m 5.17s (0.37) **Going Correction** +0.025s/f (Slow)
**WFA** 3 from 4yo+ 9lb 9 Ran SP% **115.3**
Speed ratings (Par 101): **99,98,96,89,86 82,81,79,61**
CSF £10.31 CT £82.31 TOTE £6.30: £1.90, £1.02, £7.10; EX 14.70 Trifecta £157.50.
**Owner** The Epicureans **Bred** Newsells Park Stud **Trained** Lambourn, Berks

**FOCUS**
The two market leaders had this modest handicap to themselves for the last half mile. The slightly quicker division and the form is rated a little on the positive side.

## 6900 SUSAN BOX MEMORIAL H'CAP (TAPETA) (DIV II) 1m 5f 194y
**7:20** (7:23) (Class 6) (0-65,64) 3-Y-O+ **£2,264** (£673; £336; £168) **Stalls** Low

Form RPR
0-11 **1** **High Secret (IRE)**[4] 6817 3-9-7 64 12ex LukeMorris 5 85+
(Sir Mark Prescott Bt) *mde all: pushed clr over 2f out: eased thrght fnl f* **4/11**[1]

6021 **2** 6 **Kelamita (IRE)**[27] 6157 3-9-5 62 PatDobbs 7 70
(Hughie Morrison) *chsd wnr 8f: rdn to go 2nd again wl over 2f out: sn outpcd* **7/2**[2]

00/0 **3** 1¼ **Delagoa Bay (IRE)**[67] 4737 6-8-11 45 DaneO'Neill 3 51
(Sylvester Kirk) *mid-div: hdwy over 5f out: rdn over 2f out: sn outpcd* **50/1**

4525 **4** 10 **Well Owd Mon**[18] 6410 4-9-3 51 (p) GrahamGibbons 2 43
(Andrew Hollinshead) *s.i.s: sn mid-div: hdwy over 3f out: sn rdn: wknd over 2f out* **16/1**

3610 **5** 2 **Magicalmysterytour (IRE)**[20] 6339 11-9-7 55 RobertWinston 6 44
(Willie Musson) *hld up: rdn over 2f out: n.d* **20/1**

1402 **6** 2½ **Captain Oats (IRE)**[50] 5343 11-9-7 60 RachealKneller(5) 9 46
(Pam Ford) *hld up: bhd fnl 6f* **20/1**

4635 **7** 1¾ **Ice Apple**[44] 5547 6-8-12 46 (b) JimmyQuinn 4 30
(John E Long) *prom: racd keenly: chsd wnr 6f out tl rdn wl over 2f out: sn wknd* **28/1**

0430 **8** 12 **Keep Calm**[71] 4575 4-10-0 62 (b) FrannyNorton 1 29
(John Mackie) *prom: rdn over 4f out: wknd over 3f out* **12/1**[3]

304- **9** 86 **Tram Express (FR)**[455] 4036 10-9-8 56 (t) JamieSpencer 8
(Shaun Lycett) *hld up and bhd: lost tch fnl 7f* **25/1**

3m 6.75s (1.95) **Going Correction** +0.025s/f (Slow)
**WFA** 3 from 4yo+ 9lb 9 Ran SP% **127.9**
Speed ratings (Par 101): **95,91,90,85,84 82,81,74,25**
CSF £2.15 CT £33.77 TOTE £1.20: £1.02, £1.40, £19.00; EX 2.50 Trifecta £55.80.
**Owner** Charles C Walker - Osborne House **Bred** Norelands, Marston & A V Nicoll **Trained** Newmarket, Suffolk

**FOCUS**
The weaker of the two divisions of a modest staying handicap with two progressive 3yos taking on exposed elders and finishing as the market suggested it would. The second is rated in line with her 1m4f win here last time.

## 6901 STAY AT THE WOLVERHAMPTON HOLIDAY INN MAIDEN STKS (TAPETA) 1m 4f 50y
**7:50** (7:51) (Class 5) 3-Y-O+ **£2,911** (£866; £432; £216) **Stalls** Low

Form RPR
463 **1** **Two Jabs**[20] 6344 4-9-12 75 GrahamGibbons 1 81
(Mark Brisbourne) *chsd ldrs: rdn over 2f out: looked hld whn lft in ld over 1f out: drvn out* **6/1**[2]

3264 **2** 5 **Sealed (USA)**[41] 5705 3-9-5 82 (v[1]) LukeMorris 9 73
(Gay Kelleway) *a.p: rdn over 2f out: looked hld whn lft 3rd and hmpd over 1f out: styd on same pce* **6/1**[2]

60 **3** *hd* **Taweyla (IRE)**[28] 6092 3-9-0 0 JackMitchell 5 68
(Roger Varian) *led: rdn and hdd over 2f out: hmpd sn after: looked hld whn lft w ev ch over 1f out: no ex fnl f* **15/2**[3]

00 **4** 8 **Havana Girl (IRE)**[23] 6238 3-9-0 0 DaneO'Neill 8 55
(Harry Dunlop) *hld up: hdwy over 4f out: rdn and wknd over 2f out* **28/1**

0 **5** 13 **Mobhirr**[8] 6677 3-9-5 0 (p) PaoloSirigu 3 39
(Marco Botti) *hld up: rdn and wknd over 3f out* **14/1**

**6** 1¾ **Pretty Mobile (FR)** 3-9-0 0 MartinDwyer 12 32
(Paul Webber) *s.i.s: hld up: rdn and wknd over 3f out* **40/1**

**7** 3½ **Molko Jack (FR)**[143] 10-9-5 0 LewisStones(7) 4 31
(Michael Mullineaux) *s.s: a bhd* **66/1**

**8** 4 **Astrodiamond** 3-9-0 0 JimmyQuinn 6 20
(Mark H Tompkins) *prom tl rdn and wknd over 3f out* **66/1**

022 **U** **Rembrandt Van Rijn (IRE)**[15] 6485 3-9-5 84 ShaneKelly 7 87
(David Lanigan) *chsd ldr tl led and edgd lft over 2f out: sn pushed clr: reminder whn swvd rt and uns rdr over 1f out* **2/5**[1]

2m 40.76s (-0.04) **Going Correction** +0.025s/f (Slow)
**WFA** 3 from 4yo+ 7lb 9 Ran SP% **127.3**
Speed ratings (Par 103): **101,97,97,92,83 82,80,77,**
CSF £44.93 TOTE £11.10: £2.30, £2.30, £2.90; EX 39.80 Trifecta £319.20.
**Owner** Raymond Tooth **Bred** Paramount Bloodstock **Trained** Great Ness, Shropshire

**FOCUS**
An ordinary maiden and an extraordinary outcome. The lucky winner still rates a personal best.

## 6902 INJURED JOCKEYS FUND 50TH ANNIVERSARY H'CAP (TAPETA) 7f 32y
**8:20** (8:22) (Class 5) (0-75,77) 3-Y-O **£3,234** (£962; £481; £240) **Stalls** High

Form RPR
1251 **1** **Marmarus**[13] 6567 3-8-13 70 RyanTate(3) 5 81
(Clive Cox) *hld up in tch: racd keenly: shkn up to ld ins fnl f: sn rdn: r.o* **3/1**[1]

5514 **2** *hd* **Derbyshire (IRE)**[15] 6478 3-9-4 72 (v) JamieSpencer 11 82
(Kevin Ryan) *hld up: hdwy and hung lft fr over 1f out: rdn and ev ch ins fnl f: r.o* **6/1**[3]

4211 **3** 1½ **Plucky Dip**[6] 6767 3-9-0 73 6ex JoeDoyle(5) 10 83+
(John Ryan) *hld up: nt clr run over 2f out: hdwy and nt clr run over 1f out: hmpd thrght fnl f: nvr able to chal* **7/2**[2]

3451 **4** *nk* **Spreadable (IRE)**[10] 6633 3-9-9 77 6ex JackMitchell 12 82
(Nick Littmoden) *hld up: hdwy to ld over 1f out: rdn and hdd ins fnl f: edgd lft: styd on same pce* **8/1**

0160 **5** 1½ **Zman Awal (IRE)**[86] 4074 3-9-6 74 TomQueally 7 75
(James Fanshawe) *a.p: nt clr run over 1f out: styd on same pce ins fnl f* **8/1**

14 **6** 1½ **Artistic Queen**[40] 5726 3-9-6 74 MartinHarley 3 72
(James Tate) *s.i.s: hld up: hdwy and nt clr run over 2f out: nt clr run over 1f out: styd on same pce fnl f* **22/1**

0510 **7** 3 **Jolly Red Jeanz (IRE)**[34] 5923 3-8-12 66 RichardKingscote 4 56
(Tom Dascombe) *chsd ldr: rdn and ev ch over 1f out: wknd ins fnl f* **50/1**

4255 **8** *3* **Secret Suspect**[98] 3663 3-9-5 73 LukeMorris 9 55
(James Tate) *hld up: effrt over 2f out: hmpd over 1f out: wknd fnl f* **33/1**

1402 **9** *½* **Shingle**[8] 6680 3-9-4 75 DeclanBates(3) 2 56
(Ed de Giles) *led: rdn over 2f out: hdd over 1f out: wknd fnl f* **7/1**

6453 **10** *¾* **Valen (IRE)**[22] 6269 3-9-4 72 WilliamTwiston-Davies 1 51
(Michael Bell) *chsd ldrs: rdn over 2f out: wknd over 1f out* **14/1**

1640 **11** *7* **Seven Lucky Seven**[13] 6568 3-8-10 64 RobertWinston 8 24
(Michael Herrington) *chsd ldrs: rdn and ev ch over 2f out: wknd over 1f out* **28/1**

-320 **12** *1¼* **Notebook**[138] 2363 3-9-0 75 NatalieHambling-Yates(7) 6 32
(Martin Smith) *hld up: bhd fr 1/2-way* **80/1**

1m 28.37s (-0.43) **Going Correction** +0.025s/f (Slow) **12** Ran SP% **116.8**
Speed ratings (Par 101): **103,102,101,100,99 97,93,90,89,89 81,79**
CSF £19.79 CT £66.65 TOTE £3.90: £1.80, £1.90, £1.80; EX 16.10 Trifecta £89.60.
**Owner** Ms Gillian Khosla **Bred** Vimal And Gillian Khosla **Trained** Lambourn, Berks
■ Stewards' Enquiry : Jamie Spencer two-day ban; careless riding (19th-20th Oct)

**FOCUS**
A decent pace for this fair handicap and it suited the closers. The form looks solid.

## 6903 FREE BETS GALORE @ BOOKIES.COM MAIDEN AUCTION STKS (TAPETA) 1m 141y
**8:50** (8:52) (Class 5) 2-Y-O **£2,587** (£770; £384; £192) **Stalls** Low

Form RPR

4 **1** **Bold Appeal**[28] 6085 2-8-12 0 PatDobbs 3 71+
(Ralph Beckett) *sn prom: chsd ldr over 2f out: edgd lft over 1f out: rdn to ld ins fnl f: styd on* **9/4**[2]

6 **2** *1½* **Rock Lobster**[11] 6603 2-9-0 0 MartinHarley 8 69
(Ed Dunlop) *hld up in tch: rdn over 1f out: styd on* **7/2**[3]

65 **3** *2¼* **Three Gracez**[10] 6646 2-8-5 0 SamJames 5 56
(Noel Quinlan) *chsd ldr tl led over 3f out: rdn over 1f out: hdd and no ex ins fnl f* **5/1**

000 **4** *1¾* **Ocean Crystal**[18] 6412 2-7-13 50 JoeDoyle(5) 4 51
(John Ryan) *hld up: hdwy over 2f out: rdn over 1f out: styd on: nt rch ldrs* **25/1**

**5** *nk* **Life Less Ordinary (IRE)** 2-8-10 0 ow1 JamieSpencer 6 56+
(Jamie Osborne) *s.i.s and rn green in rr: hdwy over 2f out: sn rdn: styd on: nt trble ldrs* **15/8**[1]

600 **6** *19* **Red Stripes (USA)**[11] 6603 2-9-0 0 (b[1]) StevieDonohoe 7 20
(Brian Meehan) *hld up: rdn and wknd over 2f out* **33/1**

0 **7** *16* **Revision (FR)**[13] 6545 2-8-12 0 SteveDrowne 1
(John Best) *led: hdd over 3f out: rdn and wknd over 2f out* **20/1**

0 **8** *34* **Amadeus Dream (IRE)**[91] 3934 2-8-9 0 RichardKingscote 2
(Milton Bradley) *prom: pushed along over 5f out: wknd over 3f out* **66/1**

1m 51.2s (1.10) **Going Correction** +0.025s/f (Slow) **8** Ran SP% **117.5**
Speed ratings (Par 95): **96,94,92,91,90 73,59,29**
CSF £10.49 TOTE £2.70: £1.50, £1.10, £2.40; EX 13.70 Trifecta £45.90.
**Owner** Wood Street Syndicate II **Bred** J Repard & S Dibb **Trained** Kimpton, Hants

**FOCUS**
An uninspiring bunch of juveniles but the pace was genuine enough. The fourth helps with the level of the form.

## 6904 WEEKEND PRICE BOOSTS NOW LIVE @ BOOKMAKERS.CO.UK H'CAP (TAPETA) 1m 1f 103y
**9:20** (9:21) (Class 5) (0-75,75) 3-Y-0+ **£3,234** (£962; £481; £240) **Stalls** Low

Form RPR

2624 **1** **Dreaming Beauty**[22] 6265 3-9-1 **70** (p) PatDobbs 1 86
(Jeremy Noseda) *hld up in tch: nt clr run over 2f out: rdn to ld ins fnl f: r.o* **10/1**

51 **2** *3* **Santa Teresa (IRE)**[15] 6482 3-9-6 **75** MartinHarley 11 85
(William Haggas) *a.p: chsd ldr 7f out tl over 5f out: wnt 2nd again over 3f out: led wl over 2f out: rdn over 1f out: edgd lft: hdd and no ex ins fnl f* **10/11**[1]

00-6 **3** *1¾* **Starfield**[123] 2851 5-9-3 73 AlistairRawlinson(5) 3 78
(Michael Appleby) *chsd ldr over 2f: wnt 2nd again over 5f out tl over 3f out: rdn over 1f out: styd on same pce fnl f* **12/1**

5350 **4** *¾* **Super Moment (IRE)**[20] 6341 3-8-9 **67** MatthewLawson(3) 7 72
(Saeed bin Suroor) *mid-div: hdwy over 5f out: rdn over 2f out: edgd lft and no ex fnl f* **8/1**[2]

3200 **5** *¾* **Taro Tywod (IRE)**[20] 6323 5-9-4 **69** GrahamGibbons 9 71
(Mark Brisbourne) *chsd ldrs: rdn over 3f out: hung lft over 1f out: no ex fnl f* **33/1**

1062 **6** *nk* **Kindlelight Storm (USA)**[48] 5426 4-8-13 **71** (b) JordanVaughan(7) 4 73
(Nick Littmoden) *hld up: hdwy over 2f out: sn rdn: hung lft ins fnl f: nt trble ldrs* **9/1**[3]

2440 **7** *10* **Rocksee (IRE)**[44] 5573 3-8-10 **65** (p) RichardKingscote 10 47
(Tom Dascombe) *prom: rdn over 3f out: wknd over 2f out* **33/1**

0506 **8** *½* **Game Mascot**[22] 6251 4-9-2 **67** LukeMorris 6 46
(Peter Hiatt) *hld up: rdn over 3f out: wknd over 2f out* **100/1**

4104 **9** *½* **Aomen Rock**[30] 6035 4-9-8 **73** (v) DaneO'Neill 2 54
(James Fanshawe) *hld up: rdn over 2f out: hdwy over 1f out: wknd and eased fnl f* **8/1**[2]

-030 **10** *shd* **Mountain Range (IRE)**[20] 6341 6-8-12 **63** StevieDonohoe 13 41
(Willie Musson) *s.s: sn pushed along and a in rr* **66/1**

-605 **11** *14* **Falcon's Reign (FR)**[53] 5235 5-9-2 **67** AndrewMullen 5 16
(Michael Appleby) *led: rdn and hdd wl over 2f out: hmpd and wknd sn after* **25/1**

2m 0.36s (-0.44) **Going Correction** +0.025s/f (Slow)
**WFA** 3 from 4yo+ 4lb **11** Ran SP% **113.6**
Speed ratings (Par 103): **102,99,97,97,96 96,87,86,86,86 73**
CSF £18.28 CT £115.22 TOTE £6.10: £2.20, £1.10, £3.60; EX 18.40 Trifecta £245.80.
**Owner** Saeed Suhail **Bred** Cliveden Stud Ltd **Trained** Newmarket, Suffolk

**FOCUS**
The gallop was genuine for this fair handicap, which saw a couple of unexposed 3yos draw clear. A clear personal best from the winner.
T/Plt: £836.10 to a £1 stake. Pool of £89433.94 - 78.08 winning tickets. T/Qpdt: £9.00 to a £1 stake. Pool of £12091.58 - 989.20 winning tickets. CR

6905 - 6908a (Foreign Racing) - See Raceform Interactive

# 6723 DUNDALK (A.W) (L-H)
Friday, October 3

**OFFICIAL GOING: Polytrack: standard**

## 6909a DIAMOND STKS (GROUP 3) 1m 2f 150y(P)
**7:40** (7:41) 3-Y-0+ **£32,500** (£9,500; £4,500; £1,500)

RPR

**1** **Cat O'Mountain (USA)**[27] 6139 4-9-8 111 FMBerry 4 111+
(Charlie Appleby) *sn trckd ldrs in 3rd: prog to press ldr in 2nd 3f out: led appr fnl f: styd on wl* **2/1**[1]

**2** *½* **Prince Of All**[20] 6350 3-9-3 109 ChrisHayes 5 111
(P D Deegan, Ire) *trckd ldr in 2nd tl led over 3f out: strly pressed under 2f out and hdd appr fnl f: kpt on wl* **4/1**[3]

**3** *2¼* **Bayrir (FR)**[23] 6233 5-9-8 109 ColmO'Donoghue 3 106
(Marco Botti) *hld up: prog u.str.p in 5th over 1f out: styd on wl into 3rd ins fnl f: nt rch principals* **7/1**

**4** *½* **Magnolia Beach (IRE)**[40] 5733 3-9-3 100 ColinKeane 1 106
(G M Lyons, Ire) *bit slowly away and racd towards rr: prog towards inner fr 2f out: wnt 3rd appr fnl f: no imp and dropped to 4th ins fnl f: kpt on same pce* **9/1**

**5** *4¼* **Michaelmas (USA)**[20] 6352 3-9-3 104 MichaelHussey 2 97
(A P O'Brien, Ire) *racd in 5th tl prog into 3rd 3f out: rdn and nt qckn over 1f out: sn no ex* **33/1**

**6** *11* **Afonso De Sousa (USA)**[7] 6730 4-9-8 107 JosephO'Brien 7 75
(A P O'Brien, Ire) *hld up in rr: pushed along 3f out: c wd home turn and sn strly rdn in 7th: sn no imp* **11/4**[2]

**7** *2* **Paene Magnus (IRE)**[97] 3741 5-9-8 106 KevinManning 8 71
(J S Bolger, Ire) *chsd ldrs in 4th: rdn along 3f out: no imp 2f out and sn eased* **8/1**

**8** *28* **Indian Maharaja (IRE)**[7] 6730 3-9-3 90 EmmetMcNamara 6 17
(A P O'Brien, Ire) *led tl hdd over 3f out: dropped away qckly fr 2f out* **66/1**

2m 9.76s (129.76)
**WFA** 3 from 4yo+ 6lb **8** Ran SP% **118.0**
CSF £10.81 TOTE £3.00: £1.50, £1.20, £3.00; DF 12.30 Trifecta £75.10.
**Owner** Godolphin **Bred** Darley **Trained** Newmarket, Suffolk

**FOCUS**
This was run in a good time compared to the handicap over the same trip.

6910 - 6912a (Foreign Racing) - See Raceform Interactive

# ANGERS (R-H)
Friday, October 3

**OFFICIAL GOING: Turf: good to soft**

## 6913a PRIX CLAUDE ROUGET (CONDITIONS) (3YO) (TURF) 1m
**11:30** (11:30) 3-Y-O **£11,250** (£4,500; £3,375; £2,250; £1,125)

RPR

**1** **Pompilius (FR)**[13] 3-9-0 0 TonyPiccone 3 93
(C Lotoux, France) **15/2**[3]

**2** *¾* **Leisure Time Bowl**[158] 3-9-0 0 VincentVion 5 92
(Rod Collet, France) **17/2**

**3** *¾* **Silver Treasure (FR)**[82] 4252 3-9-0 0 RonanThomas 1 90
(Amy Weaver) *led: sn 3 l clr: rdn whn pressed over 1 1/2f out: rallied but hdd ins fnl f: kpt on u.p: lost 2nd cl home* **11/1**

**4** *1½* **Honeymoon Cocktail (FR)**[25] 3-8-13 0 ElliotCanal(5) 6 91
(J-C Rouget, France) **13/10**[1]

**5** *1* **Blue Bere (FR)**[25] 3-8-10 0 ChristopherGrosbois 9 80
(J Boisnard, France) **183/10**

**6** *2* **Vaudemont (IRE)**[23] 3-9-0 0 Pierre-CharlesBoudot 2 80
(A Fabre, France) **3/1**[2]

**7** *nk* **Mu Gamara** 3-8-6 0 RaphaelMarchelli 8 71
(Rod Collet, France) **214/10**

**8** *15* **Sainte Croix (FR)**[32] 3-8-10 0 AlexandreRoussel 4 40
(M Boutin, France) **117/10**

**9** *dist* **Prisenflag (FR)**[99] 3-8-10 0 FabriceVeron 7
(G Nicot, France) **36/1**

1m 40.23s (100.23) **9** Ran SP% **119.3**
WIN (incl. 1 euro stake): 8.50. PLACES: 2.30, 2.90, 3.30. DF: 26.50. SF: 59.50.
**Owner** Michel Delaunay **Bred** M Monfort **Trained** France

# 5231 HOPPEGARTEN (R-H)
Friday, October 3

**OFFICIAL GOING: Turf: good**

## 6914a PFERDEWETTEN.DE 24TH PREIS DER DEUTSCHEN EINHEIT (GROUP 3) 3YO+ (TURF) 1m 2f
**3:50** (3:49) 3-Y-0+

**£41,666** (£14,166; £6,250; £4,166; £2,916; £833)

RPR

**1** **Wake Forest (GER)**[23] 4-9-4 0 EPedroza 4 112
(A Wohler, Germany) *w.w in midfield: hdwy outside: horses to ld appr fnl f: drvn clr: readily* **9/5**[1]

**2** *1¾* **Daksha (FR)**[93] 3873 4-9-1 0 APietsch 6 105
(Waldemar Hickst, Germany) *towards rr on outer: rdn and prog over 1 1/2f out: styd on wl fnl f: nvr on terms w wnr* **115/10**

**3** *nse* **Bank Of Burden (USA)**[19] 6389 7-9-4 0 Per-AndersGraberg 2 108+
(Niels Petersen, Norway) *w.w towards rr: swtchd outside 2f out but nt clr run: stdd and swtchd wdr 1 1/2f out: hdwy appr 1f out: fin wl ins fnl f: jst missed 2nd* **36/5**

**4** *½* **Longina (GER)**[19] 6384 3-8-10 0 AdriedeVries 11 104
(P Schiergen, Germany) *sn cl up on outer: chsd ldr fr 3f out: kpt on at same pce fnl f* **14/5**[2]

**5** *1¼* **Without Fear (FR)**[19] 6389 6-9-4 0 RafaelSchistl 9 105
(Niels Petersen, Norway) *led: kicked 2 l clr 3 1/2f out: hdd ent fnl 2f: sn rdn and kpt on at same pce* **208/10**

6 ½ **Polish Vulcano (GER)**[34] 5938 6-9-4 0 ........ WPanov 7 104
(H-J Groschel, Germany) *racd in midfield: pushed along and effrt 2f out: sn rdn and outpcd: styd on again ins fnl f: nvr in contention* **155/10**
6 dht **Eric (GER)**[47] 5484 3-9-0 0 ........ SHellyn 12 105
(C Von Der Recke, Germany) *hld up in rr: rdn 2f out: styd on appr fnl f: nrest at fin* **5/1**[3]
8 hd **Gereon (GER)**[30] 6054 6-9-4 0 ........ DennisSchiergen 3 103
(C Zschache, Germany) *midfield on inner: hrd rdn and no imp over 1 1/2f out: kpt on at same pce fnl f* **22/1**
9 ½ **Szoff (GER)**[23] 4-9-4 0 ........ AHelfenbein 5 102
(A Kleinkorres, Germany) *t.k.h: restrained bhd ldng trio on inner: outpcd and lost pl 3f out: hrd rdn 1 1/2f out: kpt on again fnl f* **233/10**
10 nk **Si Luna (GER)**[12] 5-9-1 0 ........ FranciscoDaSilva 10 99
(Prof Dr G W Sybrecht, Germany) *chsd ldrs: gd prog on outer 2 1/2f out: led ent fnl 2f: sn rdn and hdd appr 1f out: wknd* **63/1**
11 1 ¼ **Belango (GER)**[40] 8-9-4 0 ........ RPiechulek 8 99
(R Dzubasz, Germany) *chsd ldr on inner: rdn and no imp 2f out: wknd fnl f* **32/1**
12 1 ¼ **Nicolosio (IRE)**[34] 5938 4-9-4 0 ........ FilipMinarik 1 97
(Waldemar Hickst, Germany) *welt: w.w towards rr: effrt on rail appr 1 1/2f out: sn hrd rdn: wknd fnl f* **169/10**

2m 2.4s (-4.30)
**WFA** 3 from 4yo+ 5lb **12 Ran SP% 128.2**
WIN (incl. 10 euro stake): 28. PLACES: 16, 35, 27. SF: 326.
**Owner** Klaus Allofs & Stiftung Gestut Fahrhof **Bred** Stiftung Gestut Fahrhof **Trained** Germany

## 1462 KEENELAND (L-H)
Friday, October 3

**OFFICIAL GOING: Dirt: fast**

### 6915a DARLEY ALCIBIADES STKS (GRADE 1) (2YO FILLIES) (DIRT) 1m 110y
10:13 (10:13) 2-Y-O
£144,578 (£48,192; £24,096; £12,048; £7,228; £688)

RPR
1 **Peace And War (USA)**[56] 5131 2-8-6 0 ........ JRLeparoux 10 102
(Olly Stevens) *dwlt: towards rr: 3rd last and hdwy 3f out: 7th and styng on 2f out: sltly hmpd and n.m.r 1f out: swtchd outside and r.o fnl f: led last 40yds: won gng away* **231/10**
2 ½ **Top Decile (USA)**[47] 2-8-6 0 ........ RosieNapravnik 8 101
(Albert M Stall Jr, U.S.A) *hld up towards rr: hdwy 3f out: 6th and styng on 2f out: rdn to chal 1 1/2f out: led ins fnl f: r.o u.p: hdd last 40yds: no ex* **5/1**[3]
3 1 ¾ **Paige (USA)**[19] 2-8-6 0 ........ CLanderos 9 97
(Donnie K Von Hemel, U.S.A) *in rr and detached: hdwy 3f out: 11th and styng on 2f out: c wd into st: kpt on wl fnl f to go 3rd 100yds out: run flattened out sn after* **65/1**
4 ¾ **Milehigh Butterfly (USA)**[27] 2-8-6 0 ........ BHernandezJr 2 95
(William R Connelly, U.S.A) *towards rr: 10th and scrubbed along 2f out: disputing 5th whn short of room and swtchd outside over 1f out: one pce u.p fnl f* **29/1**
5 1 **Naval Command (USA)**[27] 2-8-6 0 ........ JCLeyva 6 93+
(William Kaplan, U.S.A) *racd in 5th: cl 3rd 4f out: rdn and effrt 2 1/2f out: sn ev ch and led briefly ent fnl f: hdd sn after: no ex u.p* **129/10**
6 4 **Fashion Alert (USA)**[77] 2-8-6 0 ........ JRVelazquez 1 84+
(Todd Pletcher, U.S.A) *pressed ldr on inner: swtchd outside in bkstretch: shkn up to ld 2f out: hrd rdn over 1 1/2f out: hdd ent fnl f: no ex and fdd last 100yds* **3/1**[2]
7 nk **Gap Year (USA)**[42] 2-8-6 0 ........ JRosario 12 83
(Kiaran McLaughlin, U.S.A) *in midfield: tk clsr order 3f out: 5th and pushed along on outer 2f out: sn rdn and nt qckn 1 1/2f out: fdd ins fnl furlong* **23/10**[1]
8 3 ¼ **Take Charge Brandi (USA)**[27] 2-8-6 0 ........ LSaez 11 76+
(D Wayne Lukas, U.S.A) *led on outer: swtchd to rail in bkstretch: hdd 2f out: sn wknd* **34/1**
9 2 ¼ **Calamity Kate (USA)**[22] 2-8-6 0 ........ PLopez 4 71
(Kelly Breen, U.S.A) *midfield on outer: hdwy 4f out to press front three on outer: hrd rdn and nt qukcen 2f out: wkng whn short of room sn after: wl btn fnl f* **141/10**
10 4 ¼ **Taylor S (USA)**[19] 2-8-6 0 ........ CLanerie 5 62
(Dale Romans, U.S.A) *chsd ldng pair on inner: outpcd sn after 1/2-way: bhd fnl 1 1/2f* **61/10**
11 3 ¾ **Innovative Idea (USA)**[29] 2-8-6 0 ........ JamesGraham 7 54
(Eoin Harty, U.S.A) *midfield on inner: 8th 1/2-way: scrubbed along to hold pl 3f out: bhd fnl 2f* **121/10**
12 7 ½ **Slava (USA)**[19] 2-8-6 0 ........ JKCourt 3 37+
(Gennadi Dorochenko, U.S.A) *chsd ldng pair on outer: lost pl over 4f out: sn wl btn* **113/1**

1m 44.86s (104.86) **12 Ran SP% 120.2**
PARI-MUTUEL (all including 2 usd stake): WIN 48.20; PLACE (1-2) 13.20, 6.00; SHOW (1-2-3) 9.40, 4.80, 16.40; SF 364.00.
**Owner** Qatar Racing Limited **Bred** Sally J Anderson **Trained** Chiddingfold, Surrey

## 6734 SAINT-CLOUD (L-H)
Friday, October 3

**OFFICIAL GOING: Turf: good**

### 6916a PRIX DE LA LIGUE CONTRE LA CARDIOMYOPATHIE (PRIX NINO) (CONDITIONS) (2YO) (TURF) 1m
12:15 (12:15) 2-Y-O £14,166 (£5,666; £4,250; £2,833; £1,416)

RPR
1 **Kahouanne (FR)**[121] 2-9-0 0 ........ AntoineHamelin 3 95
(T Lemer, France) **22/5**[3]
2 2 ½ **Jargon (FR)**[20] 6331 2-9-0 0 ........ MaximeGuyon 2 89
(Michael Bell) *cl up in 3rd on inner: rowed along over 2f out: sn chsng ldr: kpt on wl fnl f but no imp on wnr* **69/10**
3 1 ¼ **Mister Dancer (IRE)**[32] 2-8-10 0 ........ ChristopheSoumillon 4 82
(C Lerner, France) **1/1**[1]
4 1 ½ **Enjeu (IRE)**[24] 2-8-10 0 ........ OlivierPeslier 5 79
(A Fabre, France) **23/10**[2]
5 1 ½ **La Mezcla (FR)**[37] 5844 2-8-10 0 ........ LouisBeuzelin 1 75
(Rod Collet, France) **126/10**
6 3 ½ **Le Bambou (FR)** 2-8-10 0 ........ (b[1]) CristianDemuro 6 67
(P Demercastel, France) **37/1**

1m 44.02s (-3.48) **6 Ran SP% 121.5**
WIN (incl. 1 euro stake): 5.40. PLACES: 2.80, 4.20. SF: 20.90.
**Owner** Louis Clair Crane **Bred** Mme Mette Campbell Andenaes **Trained** France

### 6917a PRIX SCARAMOUCHE (LISTED RACE) (3YO+) (TURF) 1m 6f
1:50 (1:50) 3-Y-O+ £21,666 (£8,666; £6,500; £4,333; £2,166)

RPR
1 **Andry Brusselles**[21] 6392 4-9-0 0 ........ StephanePasquier 8 96
(C Delcher-Sanchez, France) **194/10**
2 shd **Crystal Diamond**[68] 3-8-5 0 ........ AurelienLemaitre 6 96
(F Head, France) **58/10**[3]
3 ¾ **Hidden Cove (IRE)**[19] 6383 4-9-0 0 ........ GeraldMosse 3 95
(A De Royer-Dupre, France) **29/10**[2]
4 shd **Quiz Mistress**[24] 6218 6-9-2 0 ........ IoritzMendizabal 5 97
(Hughie Morrison) *t.k.h: hld up in midfield: tk clsr order 1/2-way: sltly impeded and swtchd outside 2 1/2f out: scrubbed along and r.o to ld over 1 1/2f out: sn rdn: hdd 130yds out and kpt on at same pce: dropped to 4th fnl strides* **5/2**[1]
5 2 **Swordshire (GER)** 3-8-8 0 ........ CristianDemuro 7 95
(Werner Glanz, Germany) **29/1**
6 1 ¼ **Tres Rock Danon (FR)**[27] 8-9-3 0 ........ (p) MickaelBarzalona 2 93
(Gerald Geisler, Germany) **118/10**
7 1 ¼ **Casar (IRE)**[37] 6-9-3 0 ........ AlexisBadel 10 92
(M Delcher Sanchez, France) **25/1**
8 3 ½ **Mitzi Blue (IRE)**[18] 5-9-0 0 ........ AntoineHamelin 1 84
(D Darlix, France) **49/1**
9 snk **Art Contemporain (USA)**[23] 4-9-3 0 ........ ChristopheSoumillon 9 86
(P Bary, France) **58/10**[3]
10 hd **Wevanella (FR)**[29] 6084 5-9-2 0 ........ AdrienFouassier 4 85
(Alain Couetil, France) **6/1**

3m 1.56s (-10.64)
**WFA** 3 from 4yo+ 9lb **10 Ran SP% 119.8**
WIN (incl. 1 euro stake): 20.40. PLACES: 4.30, 1.90, 1.60. DF: 58.00. SF: 123.70.
**Owner** M Garcia De La Calera **Bred** Peter Webb & Peter Lay **Trained** France

## 6891 ASCOT (R-H)
Saturday, October 4

**OFFICIAL GOING: Good to soft changing to soft after race 1 (2.05)**
Wind: Almost nil Weather: Raining until Race 2; becoming bright

### 6918 ALBERT BARTLETT STKS (REGISTERED AS THE ROUS STAKES) (LISTED RACE) 5f
2:05 (2:06) (Class 1) 3-Y-O+
£25,519 (£9,675; £4,842; £2,412; £1,210; £607) Stalls High

Form RPR
1052 1 **Justice Day (IRE)**[14] 6549 3-9-0 107 ........ JFEgan 2 110
(David Elsworth) *mde all: rdn over 1f out: kpt on stoutly fnl f* **9/2**[2]
4061 2 1 ¼ **Kickboxer (IRE)**[28] 6131 3-9-0 99 ........ SamHitchcott 9 106
(Mick Channon) *chsd ldrs: rdn 1/2-way: prog to take 2nd wl over 1f out: styd on but no imp on wnr fnl 100yds* **10/1**
1201 3 nk **Milly's Gift**[12] 6614 4-8-9 98 ........ RyanTate 6 98+
(Clive Cox) *taken down early: sltly awkward s: hld up in last pair: rdn and prog over 1f out: styd on to take 3rd ins fnl f: nrst fin* **10/1**
16 4 1 ¾ **Online Alexander (IRE)**[24] 6231 3-8-9 99 ........ FrannyNorton 10 93
(Kevin Ryan) *prom: rdn to dispute 2nd briefly wl over 1f out: fdd ins fnl f* **6/1**
610U 5 ¾ **Holley Shiftwell**[12] 6614 4-8-9 83 ........ MartinHarley 8 89
(Stuart Williams) *trckd ldrs: gng bttr than many whn disp 2nd wl over 1f out: sn rdn and nt qckn: fdd fnl f* **66/1**
1042 6 hd **Ladies Are Forever**[27] 6167 6-9-1 108 ........ (b) BarryMcHugh 3 95
(Geoffrey Oldroyd) *chsd ldrs: rdn over 2f out: no prog over 1f out: fdd* **8/1**
6503 7 ½ **Steps (IRE)**[24] 6231 6-9-3 110 ........ (b) AndreaAtzeni 11 95+
(Roger Varian) *hld up in last trio: rdn and trying to make prog whn nt clr run twice over 1f out: no ch after* **11/4**[1]
0013 8 1 ½ **Ajjaadd (USA)**[14] 6549 8-9-0 100 ........ WilliamTwiston-Davies 5 87
(Ted Powell) *reluctant to enter stalls: n.m.r s: hld up in last pair: effrt 2f out: no prog 1f out: wknd* **20/1**
3060 9 7 **Addictive Dream (IRE)**[21] 6327 7-9-0 100 ........ RobertWinston 7 61
(John Murray) *chsd wnr to wl over 1f out: wknd qckly: eased fnl f: t.o* **20/1**
1404 10 2 ¾ **Demora**[24] 6231 5-8-9 102 ........ AndrewMullen 13 46
(Michael Appleby) *v awkward s: racd alone against nr side rail: nvr on terms: t.o* **5/1**[3]

1m 2.11s (1.61) **Going Correction** +0.60s/f (Yiel) **10 Ran SP% 116.1**
Speed ratings: **111,109,108,105,104 104,103,101,89,85**
CSF £47.23 TOTE £6.10: £1.80, £3.00, £3.10; EX 50.50 Trifecta £517.60.
**Owner** Robert Ng **Bred** Gerry Kenny **Trained** Newmarket, Suffolk

**FOCUS**
Stands side rail on Straight course 7yds inside normal position. Rail on Round course was 4yds inside from 12f to start of home straight where it increased to 9yds until after the Winning Post. Second race increased by 16yds. This opening Listed event was weakened significantly by the absence of the impressive Portland winner Muthmir, who would have been sent off a very warm favourite had the ground not gone against him. The bulk of the field raced up the centre of the track, while one raced alone up the nearside rail. There are some doubts, but the winner is rated to form.

### 6919 BMW CUMBERLAND LODGE STKS (GROUP 3) 1m 4f
2:40 (2:40) (Class 1) 3-Y-O+ £34,026 (£12,900; £6,456; £3,216; £1,614) Stalls Low

Form RPR
3101 1 **Pether's Moon (IRE)**[27] 6184 4-9-6 112 ........ PatDobbs 4 117
(Richard Hannon) *trckd ldr: chal gng easily 2f out: pushed into ld jst over 1f out and sn a l in front: drvn and kpt on fnl f* **9/4**[2]
2136 2 nk **Parish Hall (IRE)**[21] 6352 5-9-4 112 ........ (t) KevinManning 5 113
(J S Bolger, Ire) *hld up in detached in last: rdn to cl fr 2f out: hanging rt but tk 2nd ins fnl f: clsd on wnr fin* **8/1**

1/23 **3** ¾ **Encke (USA)**[20] 6374 5-9-1 112 ........ PaulHanagan 2 108
(Charlie Appleby) *led at v stdy pce: tried to kick on 3f out: rdn 2f out: hdd jst over 1f out: styd on same pce* **6/5**[1]

3541 **4** 3¾ **Don't Stare**[22] 6292 4-9-1 93 ........ (t) AndreaAtzeni 3 102
(James Fanshawe) *trckd ldng trio: rdn to chal 2f out: nrly upsides over 1f out: wknd fnl f* **10/1**

1 **5** 6 **Energia Fribby (BRZ)**[21] 6321 4-8-11 108 ........ MartinHarley 1 89
(Marco Botti) *trckd ldng pair: rdn over 2f out: wknd qckly wl over 1f out* **7/1**[3]

2m 40.73s (8.23) **Going Correction** +0.60s/f (Yiel) **5** Ran SP% **108.9**
Speed ratings: **96,95,95,92,88**
CSF £18.28 TOTE £3.20: £1.50, £3.50; EX 19.70 Trifecta £22.80.
**Owner** John Manley **Bred** Michael G Daly **Trained** East Everleigh, Wilts

**FOCUS**
The going was changed to soft before this race. Rail movement meant that it was run over 16yds further than advertised. A fascinating Cumberland Lodge on paper, but they didn't go much of a pace and it developed into a sprint from the home bend. The winner rates a small personal best.

## 6920 JOHN GUEST BENGOUGH STKS (GROUP 3) 6f
**3:15** (3:17) (Class 1) 3-Y-0+

**£39,697** (£15,050; £7,532; £3,752; £1,883; £945) **Stalls** High

Form RPR

11 **1** **Lightning Moon (IRE)**[126] 2768 3-9-1 98 ........ GeorgeBaker 7 114
(Ed Walker) *t.k.h early: trckd ldrs: gng wl 2f out: rdn to chal jst over 1f out: carried lft fnl f but styd on to ld last strides* **13/2**[2]

1012 **2** hd **Danzeno**[22] 6290 3-9-5 109 ........ AndrewMullen 6 117
(Michael Appleby) *trckd ldrs: rdn and prog 2f out: led jst over 1f out: hung lft fnl f: hdd last strides* **8/1**

0001 **3** 2¼ **Louis The Pious**[14] 6533 6-9-2 112 ........ (v) DanielTudhope 3 106
(David O'Meara) *trckd ldrs: rdn 2f out: cl enough but nt qckn over 1f out: styd on to take 3rd nr fin* **7/1**[3]

0210 **4** hd **Tropics (USA)**[28] 6134 6-9-2 115 ........ RobertWinston 15 106
(Dean Ivory) *awkward s: hld up in rr: effrt whn checked 2f out: prog and swtchd sharply rt over 1f out: styd on to press for a pl fnl f* **5/1**[1]

-000 **5** ¾ **Caspar Netscher**[28] 6134 5-9-2 106 ........ MartinHarley 1 103
(David Simcock) *trckd ldr: led 2f out: drvn and hdd jst over 1f out: fdd fnl f* **20/1**

6104 **6** 3¾ **Aeolus**[34] 5963 3-9-1 107 ........ JimCrowley 16 91
(Ed McMahon) *nvr bttr than midfield: rdn 2f out: no prog and btn jst over 1f out* **25/1**

-063 **7** 3¼ **Brown Sugar (IRE)**[15] 6522 3-9-1 103 ........ KierenFallon 14 81
(Richard Hannon) *chsd ldrs: rdn 1/2-way: wknd over 1f out* **20/1**

1-1 **8** ½ **Intibaah**[147] 2149 4-9-2 108 ........ PaulHanagan 2 79
(Brian Meehan) *hld up in last pair: prog towards far rail 2f out: rdn and wknd over 1f out* **7/1**[3]

231 **9** 2 **Signs Of Blessing (IRE)**[34] 5966 3-9-5 113 ... Francois-XavierBertras 9 77
(F Rohaut, France) *led to 2f out: sn wknd* **14/1**

-421 **10** hd **Badr Al Badoor (IRE)**[22] 6290 4-8-13 96 ........ TomQueally 10 69
(James Fanshawe) *n.m.r s: a towards rr: rdn and no prog 2f out: wknd* **25/1**

3021 **11** 4 **Royal Rock**[18] 6440 10-9-2 104 ........ TedDurcan 17 59
(Chris Wall) *dwlt: hld up in last pair: rdn over 2f out: no prog and wl btn over 1f out* **40/1**

0222 **12** 3¼ **Green Door (IRE)**[11] 6624 3-9-1 102 ........ (p) OisinMurphy 11 49
(Olly Stevens) *hld up in rr: rdn and no prog over 2f out: wl btn after* **33/1**

5-32 **13** ½ **Reckless Abandon**[24] 6231 4-9-2 110 ........ KevinManning 12 47
(Charlie Appleby) *prom over 3f: wknd qckly* **5/1**[1]

530 **14** 1 **Boomerang Bob (IRE)**[62] 4937 5-9-2 97 ........ CamHardie 4 44
(Charles Hills) *hld up in rr: rdn over 2f out: no prog and wl btn over 1f out* **40/1**

-210 **15** 1¼ **Musical Comedy**[108] 3352 3-9-1 106 ........ PatDobbs 13 40
(Richard Hannon) *chsd ldrs: rdn and wknd over 2f out* **25/1**

1m 15.7s (1.20) **Going Correction** +0.60s/f (Yiel)
**WFA** 3 from 4yo+ 1lb **15** Ran SP% **118.3**
Speed ratings: **116,115,112,112,111 106,102,101,98,98 93,88,88,86,85**
CSF £49.41 TOTE £7.10: £2.70, £3.20, £2.80; EX 59.40 Trifecta £288.60.
**Owner** M Betamar **Bred** Michael Collins **Trained** Newmarket, Suffolk

**FOCUS**
An interesting Group 3 sprint in which there were two groups early, but they soon merged into one down the centre of the track. The first five home pulled clear of the rest. The winner took another big step up.

## 6921 TOTEPOOL CHALLENGE CUP (HERITAGE H'CAP) 7f
**3:50** (3:52) (Class 2) 3-Y-0+

**£93,375** (£27,960; £13,980; £6,990; £3,495; £1,755) **Stalls** High

Form RPR

0410 **1** **Intransigent**[42] 5665 5-9-4 **104** ........ OisinMurphy 10 115
(Andrew Balding) *stdd s: hld up in midfield: smooth prog over 2f out: led over 1f out and sn in command: rdn out: readily* **16/1**

3065 **2** 1½ **Empire Storm (GER)**[17] 6458 7-8-11 **104** ........ (t) MikeyEnnis(7) 9 111
(Michael Attwater) *pressed ldr: chal and upsides 2f out tl wnr swept by over 1f out: chsd after but no imp* **40/1**

4004 **3** ¾ **Heaven's Guest (IRE)**[14] 6533 4-9-2 **105** ........ GeorgeChaloner(3) 8 110
(Richard Fahey) *trckd ldrs: rdn over 2f out: cl up wl over 1f out: styd on same pce after* **7/1**[2]

6204 **4** ¾ **Sirius Prospect (USA)**[15] 6522 6-9-6 **106** ........ RobertWinston 13 109
(Dean Ivory) *trckd ldrs: pushed along 1/2-way: lost pl and urged along over 2f out: styd on again jst over 1f out* **10/1**

1013 **5** 2¾ **Blaine**[14] 6533 4-9-4 **104** ........ (b) AmyRyan 3 100
(Kevin Ryan) *racd freely: led: rdn and hdd over 1f out: wknd tamely* **12/1**

1150 **6** 1 **Highland Acclaim (IRE)**[14] 6533 3-8-12 **100** ........ DanielTudhope 7 92+
(David O'Meara) *hld up in rr: rdn over 2f out: nt clr run briefly wl over 1f out and swtchd: kpt on but nvr gng pce to threaten* **8/1**[3]

2000 **7** ¾ **Heavy Metal**[28] 6124 4-8-12 **98** ........ FrannyNorton 17 89
(Mark Johnston) *pressed ldrs: rdn 3f out: steadily fdd fnl 2f* **16/1**

6003 **8** ¾ **Brazos (IRE)**[49] 5434 3-9-7 **109** ........ AndreaAtzeni 18 97
(Clive Brittain) *pressed ldrs: rdn and nt qckn jst over 2f out: steadily wknd* **12/1**

5210 **9** hd **Eastern Impact (IRE)**[14] 6533 3-9-3 **105** ........ PaulHanagan 14 93
(Richard Fahey) *hld up towards rr: rdn and no prog over 2f out: n.d after* **20/1**

6040 **10** nk **Fort Bastion (IRE)**[7] 6752 5-8-12 **98** ........ (v[1]) TomQueally 2 86
(David O'Meara) *dwlt and swvd rt s: sn in tch in rr: pushed along over 2f out: reminders over 1f out: passed a few late on* **12/1**

620 **11** 2¾ **Redvers (IRE)**[14] 6531 6-8-12 **98** ........ (b) TedDurcan 4 79
(Ed Vaughan) *hld up in rr: rdn and no prog over 2f out: wl btn after* **10/1**

1256 **12** 2½ **Chil The Kite**[42] 5666 5-9-11 **111** ........ GeorgeBaker 1 86
(Hughie Morrison) *stdd s: hld up in last: rdn and no prog over 2f out: wl btn after* **8/1**[3]

10-1 **13** 2½ **Prince's Trust**[41] 5728 4-8-11 **100** ........ CamHardie(3) 11 68
(William Haggas) *chsd ldrs: rdn over 2f out: sn wknd qckly* **6/1**[1]

-114 **14** 4 **Grey Mirage**[169] 1558 5-9-3 **103** ........ (p) MartinHarley 16 61
(Marco Botti) *hld up towards rr: shkn up over 2f out: sn wknd* **16/1**

2413 **15** 10 **Morache Music**[30] 6060 6-9-6 **106** ........ SebSanders 12 38
(Peter Makin) *in tch: rdn 1/2-way: sn btn: t.o* **16/1**

1m 30.24s (2.64) **Going Correction** +0.60s/f (Yiel)
**WFA** 3 from 4yo+ 2lb **15** Ran SP% **121.0**
Speed ratings (Par 109): **108,106,105,104,101 100,99,98,98,98 94,92,89,84,73**
CSF £539.42 CT £4820.80 TOTE £22.50: £6.50, £15.30, £2.60; EX 1239.70 Trifecta £14552.40.
**Owner** Kingsclere Racing Club **Bred** Kingsclere Stud **Trained** Kingsclere, Hants

**FOCUS**
Considering this was an ultra-valuable and red-hot handicap, it was remarkable so few ever got into it and the conclusion must be that several talented performers failed to handle the conditions. The pace looked steady as well and although the field started off as one group up the centre, they tended to drift towards the far rail as the race progressed. The winner's penultimate form fits this level.

## 6922 TOTEPOOL EBF STALLIONS OCTOBER STKS (LISTED RACE) (F&M) 7f
**4:25** (4:27) (Class 1) 3-Y-0+

**£22,684** (£8,600; £4,304; £2,144; £1,076; £540) **Stalls** High

Form RPR

2003 **1** **Al Thakhira**[23] 6254 3-8-12 107 ........ MartinHarley 5 102+
(Marco Botti) *hld up in last: charmed run through rivals fr jst over 2f out: squeezed between ldng pair to ld ins fnl f: won decisively* **5/2**[1]

221 **2** ¾ **Meeting Waters**[29] 6112 3-8-12 91 ........ RobertWinston 9 99
(William Haggas) *t.k.h: disp ld: narrow advantage fr 2f out: hdd and outpcd ins fnl f* **14/1**

3241 **3** nk **Interception (IRE)**[21] 6336 4-9-0 88 ........ GeorgeBaker 2 99
(David Lanigan) *hld up in midfield: angled towards outer fr 2f out: rdn over 1f out: styd on to take 3rd nr fin* **10/1**

6520 **4** ½ **Dutch Rose (IRE)**[23] 6254 5-9-0 98 ........ DanielTudhope 8 100+
(David O'Meara) *prom: lost pl and hmpd after 2f and dropped to rr: nt clr run over 2f out: prog over 1f out: swtchd rt and styd on fnl f: nvr able to chal* **14/1**

1211 **5** nse **Felwah**[30] 6068 3-8-12 96 ........ PaulHanagan 3 97
(William Haggas) *disp ld to 2f out: pressed ldr after tl one pce last 150yds* **5/1**[3]

004 **6** ½ **Nakuti (IRE)**[7] 6740 3-8-12 87 ........ PatDobbs 14 95
(Sylvester Kirk) *pressed ldrs: rdn over 2f out: nt qckn over 1f out: kpt on same pce after* **16/1**

4231 **7** 4 **Moonvoy**[37] 5862 3-8-12 80 ........ KierenFallon 10 85
(Jeremy Noseda) *pressed ldrs: rdn over 2f out: stl cl up 1f out: hld whn short of room sn after: wknd and eased* **25/1**

3 **8** ¾ **Capelita**[72] 4590 3-8-12 0 ........ FrannyNorton 11 83
(Clive Brittain) *hld up in rr: rdn over 2f out: no prog and btn after: plugged on fnl f* **66/1**

0256 **9** 1½ **Queen Catrine (IRE)**[64] 4854 3-8-12 105 ........ OisinMurphy 12 79
(Charles Hills) *hld up in midfield: rdn over 2f out: nt qckn and no prog over 1f out: wknd* **4/1**[2]

1014 **10** 2 **Ishiamber**[16] 6492 4-9-0 87 ........ MartinDwyer 4 75
(George Baker) *trckd ldrs: rdn over 2f out: wknd qckly fnl f* **40/1**

1132 **11** 2½ **Who's That Chick (IRE)**[6] 6793 5-9-0 77 ........ RyanTate 1 69
(Ralph J Smith) *cl up bhd ldrs: rdn and stl cl up over 2f out: wknd qckly jst over 1f out* **25/1**

1350 **12** 6 **Perfect Blessings (IRE)**[85] 4171 3-8-12 92 ........ JimCrowley 7 52
(Clive Cox) *stdd s: hld up in rr: no prog over 2f out: wknd* **8/1**

60-6 **13** 13 **Tobougg Happy**[97] 3759 3-8-12 85 ........ DavidProbert 13 18
(Andrew Balding) *reluctant to go on to crse: prom to 1/2-way: sn wknd rapidly t.o* **66/1**

1m 30.41s (2.81) **Going Correction** +0.60s/f (Yiel)
**WFA** 3 from 4yo+ 2lb **13** Ran SP% **117.8**
Speed ratings: **107,106,105,105,105 104,100,99,97,95 92,85,70**
CSF £38.13 TOTE £3.80: £1.30, £4.30, £3.40; EX 40.60 Trifecta £382.20.
**Owner** Al Shaqab Racing **Bred** Qatar Bloodstock Ltd **Trained** Newmarket, Suffolk

**FOCUS**
A wide range of abilities in this fillies' and mares' Listed event which had been dominated by the 3yo generation in the past decade and that trend continued. The winner was the form pick and didn't need to match her best. The entire field made straight for the far rail this time.

## 6923 LES AMBASSADEURS CASINO H'CAP 5f
**5:00** (5:00) (Class 3) (0-95,93) 3-Y-0+

**£12,450** (£3,728; £1,864; £932; £466; £234) **Stalls** High

Form RPR

0042 **1** **Dungannon**[35] 5918 7-9-6 92 ........ (b) OisinMurphy 11 102
(Andrew Balding) *hld up in midfield: prog 2f out to chse ldr over 1f out: rdn to ld jst ins fnl f and sn a l clr: jst hld on* **7/2**[2]

0-06 **2** shd **Khubala (IRE)**[18] 6440 5-9-6 92 ........ (b) PaulHanagan 14 102
(Hugo Palmer) *hld up in last quartet: waiting for room over 1f out: gd prog fnl f: tk 2nd last 100yds: clsd on wnr qckly at fin* **16/1**

3256 **3** ¾ **Mission Approved**[14] 6531 4-9-3 89 ........ AndreaAtzeni 7 96
(Luca Cumani) *hld up in rr: waiting for room over 1f out: prog along w wnr fnl f: styd on to take 3rd nr fin but nvr quite pce to chal* **11/4**[1]

0332 **4** 1¼ **Taajub (IRE)**[12] 6614 7-9-2 88 ........ ShaneKelly 6 91
(Peter Crate) *chsd clr ldr to over 1f out: nt qckn and hld after: kpt on again nr fin* **12/1**

1000 **5** nk **Gladiatrix**[24] 6231 5-9-4 90 ........ RobertWinston 18 91
(Rod Millman) *chsd ldrs: rdn and nt qckn 2f out: kpt on again fnl f: n.d* **20/1**

-030 **6** nk **Duke Of Firenze**[14] 6533 5-9-7 93 ........ (p) TedDurcan 1 93
(Robert Cowell) *dwlt: hld up in last quartet: prog against far rail 2f out: tried to cl on ldrs 1f out: one pce after* **16/1**

2211 **7** nk **Secret Missile**[34] 5945 4-9-2 88 ........ (b) MartinDwyer 13 87
(William Muir) *led and at least 2 l clr: hdd & wknd jst ins fnl f* **8/1**[3]

1106 **8** nk **Iffranesia (FR)**[35] 5925 4-9-1 87 ........ TomQueally 15 85
(Robert Cowell) *prom: rdn 2f out: nt qckn wl over 1f out: one pce after* **10/1**

0004 **9** *1 3/4* **Major Crispies**[12] 6614 3-9-6 92 .......... StevieDonohoe 2 85
(James Eustace) *hld up in last quartet: urged along 2f out: nvr gng pce to threaten but plugged on fnl f* **33/1**

1060 **10** *hd* **Sandfrankskipsgo**[17] 6467 5-9-1 87 .......... JimCrowley 5 78
(Peter Crate) *prom: rdn wl over 1f out: wknd fnl f* **33/1**

-000 **11** *1 3/4* **Oeil De Tigre (FR)**[49] 5438 3-9-3 89 .......... DavidProbert 10 75
(Tony Carroll) *chsd ldrs: rdn 2f out: sn lost pl and wknd* **14/1**

1003 **12** *1/2* **Extrasolar**[12] 6614 4-9-2 88 .......... (t) PatDobbs 12 71
(Amanda Perrett) *chsd ldrs: rdn and wknd qckly wl over 1f out* **20/1**

-350 **13** *3 3/4* **Foxy Forever (IRE)**[28] 6130 4-9-0 86 .......... MartinHarley 17 56
(Michael Wigham) *stdd s: hld up in last quartet: shuffled along 2f out: no prog and nvr involved* **8/1**[3]

1m 2.91s (2.41) **Going Correction** +0.60s/f (Yiel) **13** Ran SP% **121.7**
Speed ratings (Par 107): **104,103,102,100,100 99,99,98,95,95 92,92,86**
CSF £56.69 CT £177.93 TOTE £4.00: £1.60, £5.30, £1.60; EX 68.50 Trifecta £332.00.
**Owner** Dr E Harris **Bred** J A E Hobby **Trained** Kingsclere, Hants

**FOCUS**
A race hit by five non-runners, but still a decent sprint handicap and there was no hanging about. Again the field started off racing up the centre, but gradually edged over to the far rail. The winner is rated in line with last year's form.
T/Jkpt: Not won. T/Plt: £351.30 to a £1 stake. Pool of £183845.27 - 381.94 winning tickets.
T/Qpdt: £27.60 to £1 stake. Pool of £13581.31- 363.78 winning tickets. JN

## 6749 NEWMARKET (R-H)

Saturday, October 4

**OFFICIAL GOING: Good to firm changing to good after race 2 (2.20)**
Wind: medium, behind Weather: rain early on

## 6924 £300,000 TATTERSALLS MILLIONS 2YO FILLIES' TROPHY (BOBIS RACE) 7f

**1:50** (1:51) (Class 2) 2-Y-O

**£168,198** (£68,821; £30,618; £15,262; £7,646; £3,046) **Stalls** Low

Form RPR

5115 **1** **Osaila (IRE)**[20] 6372 2-9-0 109 .......... FrankieDettori 6 95
(Richard Hannon) *hld up in midfield: rdn and hdwy to chse ldr over 2f out: chal and clr w rival over 1f out: led ins fnl f: styd on wl and forged ahd fnl 50yds* **4/5**[1]

3201 **2** *1 1/2* **Lacing**[14] 6555 2-9-0 84 .......... RyanMoore 7 91
(Richard Fahey) *led: clr w wnr and rdn over 1f out: hdd ins fnl f: no ex and wknd towards fin* **7/1**[3]

1 **3** *3/4* **Very Special (IRE)**[16] 6496 2-9-0 0 .......... JamesDoyle 3 89+
(Saeed bin Suroor) *hld up in midfield: clsd 1/2-way: wnt 3rd 2f out: no imp u.p tl swtchd lft and styd on wl fnl 100yds* **9/4**[2]

26 **4** *7* **Thunder In Myheart (IRE)**[65] 4825 2-9-0 0 .......... JamieSpencer 5 70
(Michael Bell) *hld up in last pair: rdn over 2f out: no ch w ldrs but plugged on to snatch 4th nr fin* **25/1**

5055 **5** *nk* **Star Of Spring (IRE)**[14] 6555 2-9-0 64 .......... RichardHughes 8 69
(Charles Hills) *chsd ldrs: rdn ent fnl 2f: outpcd and btn over 1f out: wknd and lost 4th nr fin* **50/1**

41 **6** *4 1/2* **Yorkidding**[13] 6577 2-9-0 76 .......... JoeFanning 4 57
(Mark Johnston) *chsd ldrs: lost pl and struggling over 2f out: no ch over 1f out* **14/1**

2040 **7** *3 1/2* **Anastazia**[14] 6555 2-9-0 70 .......... JimmyFortune 1 47
(Paul D'Arcy) *chsd ldr tl over 2f out: 4th and btn 2f out: wknd over 1f out* **66/1**

**8** *3/4* **Melodious** 2-9-0 0 .......... LiamKeniry 9 45+
(David Elsworth) *wnt lft s and s.i.s: a bhd: lost tch 2f out* **33/1**

313 **9** *11* **Light Fantastic**[29] 6105 2-9-0 80 .......... WilliamBuick 2 16
(Ed Dunlop) *hld up in midfield: rdn and btn over 2f out: wl bhd fnl f* **16/1**

1m 23.53s (-1.87) **Going Correction** -0.25s/f (Firm) **9** Ran SP% **121.6**
Speed ratings (Par 98): **100,98,97,89,89 83,79,76,66**
CSF £7.95 TOTE £1.50: £1.02, £1.60, £1.70; EX 7.40 Trifecta £17.10.
**Owner** Al Shaqab Racing **Bred** Mennetou Syndicate **Trained** East Everleigh, Wilts

**FOCUS**
Far side course used. Stalls: Far side except 12f: Centre.\n\x\x The going was officially good to firm but although it had been raining since around lunchtime, the winning time of this opener was only around a second slower than standard. The jockeys said afterwards that it felt a little bit loose on top but was still good to firm underneath.

## 6925 £500,000 TATTERSALLS MILLIONS 2YO TROPHY (BOBIS RACE) 7f

**2:20** (2:24) (Class 2) 2-Y-O

**£280,331** (£114,702; £51,030; £25,437; £12,744; £5,077) **Stalls** Low

Form RPR

6211 **1** **Secret Brief (IRE)**[14] 6556 2-9-3 99 .......... JoeFanning 14 95
(Mark Johnston) *in tch in midfield: hdwy to ld 2f out: shkn up and asserted ent fnl f: styd on: rdn out* **9/2**[1]

31 **2** *3/4* **Outlaw Country (IRE)**[25] 6203 2-9-3 0 .......... PatSmullen 9 93
(Charlie Appleby) *s.i.s: hld up in rr: hdwy over 2f out: rdn and chsng ldrs over 1f out: edgd rt ins fnl f: styd on to go 2nd towards fin* **8/1**

0122 **3** *nk* **Bossy Guest (IRE)**[14] 6556 2-9-3 101 .......... JamesDoyle 3 92+
(Mick Channon) *s.i.s: niggled along in rr: pushed and hdwy into midfield 1/2-way: chsd ldrs u.p over 1f out: wnt 2nd fnl 100yds: kpt on but lost 2nd towards fin* **7/1**

0216 **4** *hd* **Azmaam (IRE)**[9] 6684 2-9-3 81 .......... FrankieDettori 12 92
(Richard Hannon) *chsd ldrs: rdn and ev ch 2f out: unable qck ent fnl f: styd on same pce fnl 100yds* **33/1**

3123 **5** *1/2* **Ballymore Castle (IRE)**[14] 6556 2-9-3 90 .......... DavidNolan 4 90
(Richard Fahey) *in tch in midfield: hdwy u.p over 1f out: kpt on ins fnl f: nvr enough pce to rch ldrs* **12/1**

314 **6** *2 1/4* **Misterioso (IRE)**[7] 6750 2-9-3 95 .......... RichardHughes 15 84
(Richard Hannon) *led for 1f: chsd ldr tl led again over 2f out: rdn and hdd 2f out: stl ev ch tl unable qck 1f out: wknd fnl 100yds* **6/1**[3]

1 **7** *1 1/4* **Tannaaf (IRE)**[43] 5646 2-9-3 0 .......... PatCosgrave 2 81
(M F De Kock, South Africa) *in tch in midfield: effrt u.p over 2f out: no imp and edgd rt over 1f out: plugged on same pce after* **9/1**

6211 **8** *1 1/2* **Invincible Gold (IRE)**[27] 6165 2-9-3 89 .......... JimmyFortune 1 78
(Ed Walker) *chsd ldrs: rdn ent fnl 2f: outpcd over 1f out: wknd ins fnl f* **14/1**

**9** *3 1/2* **The Warrior (IRE)**[6] 6797 2-9-3 0 .......... JosephO'Brien 10 67
(A P O'Brien, Ire) *in tch towards rr: rdn and no hdwy jst over 2f out: wknd over 1f out* **10/1**

3032 **10** *hd* **Goring (GER)**[24] 6229 2-9-3 77 .......... MartinLane 11 67
(Eve Johnson Houghton) *hld up in tch in midfield: rdn and unable qck 2f out: sn btn and wknd over 1f out* **66/1**

1124 **11** *19* **Heartbreak Hero**[14] 6556 2-9-3 106 .......... RyanMoore 13 15
(William Haggas) *in tch in midfield: rdn and no hdwy 2f out: btn over 1f out: wl btn and eased ins fnl f* **5/1**[2]

20 **12** *1* **Swot**[43] 5655 2-9-3 0 .......... WilliamBuick 5 13
(John Gosden) *hld up in last trio: effrt u.p over 2f out: no hdwy and wl btn 2f out: bhd and eased ins fnl f: t.o* **25/1**

5002 **13** *2* **Pipe Bomb**[14] 6538 2-9-3 68 .......... (p) JamieSpencer 6 7
(Kevin Ryan) *hld up in rr: effrt and shifted lft over 2f out: sn btn: bhd and eased ins fnl f: t.o* **66/1**

030 **14** *13* **Yorkie Talkie (IRE)**[14] 6556 2-9-3 63 .......... FMBerry 7
(Mark Johnston) *in tch in midfield: rdn and lost pl over 2f out: t.o fnl f* **100/1**

55 **15** *6* **Greatest Journey**[12] 6603 2-9-3 0 .......... (v[1]) MickaelBarzalona 8
(Saeed bin Suroor) *wnt lft s and s.i.s: racd keenly and rcvrd to ld after 1f: hdd over 2f out: sn dropped out: t.o fnl f* **50/1**

1m 23.21s (-2.19) **Going Correction** -0.25s/f (Firm) **15** Ran SP% **118.9**
Speed ratings (Par 101): **102,101,100,100,100 97,96,94,90,90 68,67,64,50,43**
CSF £37.96 TOTE £4.80: £1.90, £3.30, £2.10; EX 48.50 Trifecta £422.90.
**Owner** Sheikh Hamdan bin Mohammed Al Maktoum **Bred** Airlie Stud **Trained** Middleham Moor, N Yorks

**FOCUS**
The rain began to fall more heavily ahead of Europe's richest two-year-old race. The bulk of the action took place middle to stands' side.

## 6926 TRICONNEX OH SO SHARP STKS (GROUP 3) (FILLIES) 7f

**2:55** (3:02) (Class 1) 2-Y-O

**£28,355** (£10,750; £5,380; £2,680; £1,345; £675) **Stalls** Low

Form RPR

411 **1** **Local Time**[24] 6241 2-9-0 89 .......... JamesDoyle 6 98
(Saeed bin Suroor) *stdd s: in tch in midfield: clsd to chse ldrs over 2f out: rdn to ld over 1f out: hld on wl fnl f: rdn out* **7/4**[1]

1140 **2** *nk* **Astrelle (IRE)**[22] 6289 2-9-0 88 .......... PaoloSirigu 7 98
(Marco Botti) *led: rdn ent fnl 2f: hdd over 1f out: battled on wl and ev ch after: unable qck and hld fnl 100yds* **14/1**

160 **3** *hd* **Prize Exhibit**[14] 6530 2-9-0 95 .......... JamieSpencer 11 97
(Jamie Osborne) *s.i.s: bhd and niggled along: rdn and effrt whn shifted rt 2f out: hdwy u.p over 1f out: chsd ldrs and swtchd lft ins fnl f: styd on strly towards fin* **5/1**[3]

2133 **4** *1 3/4* **Shagah (IRE)**[22] 6289 2-9-0 101 .......... FrankieDettori 4 92
(Richard Hannon) *stdd s: t.k.h: hld up in midfield: clsd to chse ldrs 1/2-way: rdn and ev ch over 1f out tl wknd fnl 100yds* **9/4**[2]

314 **5** *1/2* **Taaqah (USA)**[22] 6295 2-9-0 91 .......... RyanMoore 10 91
(James Tate) *t.k.h: in tch towards rr: rdn over 2f out: outpcd wl over 1f out: rallied and hdwy ins fnl f: styd on wl fnl 100yds: nt rch ldrs* **10/1**

2414 **6** *nk* **Russian Punch**[28] 6126 2-9-0 91 .......... JoeFanning 8 90
(James Given) *chsd ldrs: rdn over 2f out: stl pressing ldrs but unable qck over 1f out: wknd ins fnl f* **12/1**

1 **7** *1* **Jelly Monger (IRE)**[30] 6065 2-9-0 77 .......... FMBerry 9 87
(Dominic Ffrench Davis) *stdd s: hld up in last pair: rdn and effrt wl over 1f out: no imp: kpt on ins fnl f: nvr trbld ldrs* **10/1**

0146 **8** *5* **Feeling Easy (IRE)**[7] 6749 2-9-0 85 .......... JimmyQuinn 1 74
(Robert Eddery) *w ldr: rdn over 2f out: btn wl over 1f out: sn wknd* **25/1**

1m 25.26s (-0.14) **Going Correction** +0.075s/f (Good) **8** Ran SP% **120.2**
Speed ratings: **103,102,102,100,99 99,98,92**
CSF £29.85 TOTE £3.00: £1.30, £5.20, £1.80; EX 31.70 Trifecta £177.10.
**Owner** Godolphin **Bred** Darley **Trained** Newmarket, Suffolk

■ Yodelling (9-2) and Majestic Manner (6-1) were withdrawn. Rule 4 applies to bets struck prior to withdrawals. Deduction - 25p in the pound. New market formed.

**FOCUS**
A new slot for this Group 3 contest which used to be run on the Friday of the Cambridgeshire meeting and was won last year by subsequent 1,000 Guineas winner Miss France. It was an eventful build-up to this race with Yodelling being withdrawn at the start on account of the ground, which was officially changed to good ahead of this race. Then Majestic Manner broke through the stalls which meant the whole field had to be taken out of the gates. Unlikely we have seen another Miss France here with the first two home currently rated just 89 and 88 respectively.

## 6927 KINGDOM OF BAHRAIN SUN CHARIOT STKS (GROUP 1) (F&M) 1m

**3:30** (3:36) (Class 1) 3-Y-O+

**£113,420** (£43,000; £21,520; £10,720; £5,380; £2,700) **Stalls** Low

Form RPR

2113 **1** **Integral**[62] 4954 4-9-3 117 .......... RyanMoore 8 119
(Sir Michael Stoute) *sn led and dictated gallop: rdn and qcknd 2f out: edging rt but in command ins fnl f: r.o wl* **7/2**[1]

6152 **2** *1* **Miss France (IRE)**[62] 4954 3-9-0 115 .......... MaximeGuyon 6 117
(A Fabre, France) *racd keenly: chsd ldng pair: rdn 2f out: r.o to chse wnr fnl 100yds: kpt on but a hld* **7/2**[1]

11 **3** *nk* **Fintry (IRE)**[35] 5927 3-9-0 115 .......... MickaelBarzalona 3 116
(A Fabre, France) *chsd wnr: rdn 2f out: r.o but a hld by wnr: lost 2nd fnl 100yds* **7/2**[1]

1014 **4** *1 1/2* **Esoterique (IRE)**[20] 6382 4-9-3 117 .......... Pierre-CharlesBoudot 2 113
(A Fabre, France) *in tch in midfield: rdn and effrt in 4th over 1f out: r.o same pce fnl f* **7/2**[1]

6241 **5** *3 1/4* **Kiyoshi**[23] 6254 3-9-0 111 .......... (p) JamieSpencer 5 105
(Charles Hills) *hld up in tch in midfield: rdn over 2f out: no imp: outpcd ins fnl f* **10/1**[3]

0-55 **6** *1 3/4* **Sky Lantern (IRE)**[85] 4165 4-9-3 115 .......... RichardHughes 1 101
(Richard Hannon) *broke wl: sn stdd bk and hld up in last pair: rdn and hdwy over 2f out: btn over 1f out: wknd ins fnl f* **8/1**[2]

1141 **7** *2 3/4* **Etaab (USA)**[8] 6707 3-9-0 104 .......... WilliamBuick 7 95
(William Haggas) *s.i.s: hld up in tch in rr: rdn and effrt wl over 1f out: sn outpcd and btn* **25/1**

1m 37.52s (-1.08) **Going Correction** +0.075s/f (Good)
**WFA** 3 from 4yo 3lb **7** Ran SP% **112.9**
Speed ratings: **108,107,106,105,101 100,97**
CSF £15.19 TOTE £2.90: £1.20, £2.70; EX 15.40 Trifecta £47.30.
**Owner** Cheveley Park Stud **Bred** Cheveley Park Stud Ltd **Trained** Newmarket, Suffolk

**FOCUS**
A wide-open renewal of this Group 1 prize with Andree Fabre sending over three talented fillies to tackle Sky Lantern and Integral who finished first and second in this 12 months ago. Three-year-olds have dominated their older rivals in this race in the last four decades (won 32 of last 40 runnings) but Integral clawed one back for the older fillies.

## 6928 WILD DUCK NORFOLK WOODLAND RETREAT EBF STALLIONS MAIDEN STKS (BOBIS RACE) 1m
4:05 (4:08) (Class 4) 2-Y-O **£5,175** (£1,540; £769; £384) **Stalls** Low

Form RPR
1 **Aloft (IRE)**[13] 6582 2-9-5 0 JosephO'Brien 7 81+
(A P O'Brien, Ire) *chsd ldrs: rdn: rn green and wandering on downhill run wl over 1f out: drvn and rallied ins fnl f: r.o wl fnl 100yds to ld nr fin* **13/8**[1]
2 *nk* **Storm The Stars (USA)** 2-9-5 0 JoeFanning 4 80+
(William Haggas) *in tch: effrt on far rail to press ldrs over 1f out: ev ch ins fnl f: drvn to ld wl ins fnl f: hdd and no ex nr fin* **12/1**
3 *shd* **Legend's Gate (IRE)** 2-9-5 0 PatSmullen 2 80+
(Charlie Appleby) *w ldr tl led 1/2-way: hrd pressed and rdn wl over 1f out: battled on wl tl hdd and no ex wl ins fnl f* **20/1**
4 *shd* **Great Glen** 2-9-5 0 RichardHughes 9 80+
(Ralph Beckett) *t.k.h: led tl 1/2-way: styd upsides ldr: rdn wl over 1f out: ev ch after and r.o: no ex towards fin* **18/1**
5 *1/2* **Wardat Dubai** 2-9-0 0 LiamKeniry 5 74+
(B W Hills) *hld up in tch: clsd whn nt clr run and swtchd lft wl over 1f out: pushed along and pressed ldrs 1f out: kpt on same pce ins fnl f* **33/1**
3 6 *3 1/2* **Archery Peak**[23] 6259 2-9-5 0 RyanMoore 3 71
(Luca Cumani) *chsd ldrs: rdn 2f out: unable qck over 1f out: wknd ins fnl f* **7/4**[2]
5 7 *5* **Mubtaahij (IRE)**[8] 6712 2-9-5 0 PatCosgrave 8 61+
(M F De Kock, South Africa) *short of room and hmpd sn after s: t.k.h: rn green and hld up towards rr: rdn and wandered 2f out: sn wknd* **16/1**
8 *2 1/2* **Rare Rhythm** 2-9-5 0 WilliamBuick 10 53
(Charlie Appleby) *in tch in midfield: rdn and rn green ent fnl 2f: sn btn and bhd over 1f out* **11/1**[3]
9 *hd* **Sirheed (IRE)** 2-9-5 0 FrankieDettori 12 53
(Richard Hannon) *rn green: in tch on outer: rdn 2f out: rn green and btn on downhill run over 1f out: nt given a hrd time after* **20/1**
10 *15* **Save The Date** 2-9-5 0 JamesDoyle 11 18
(Charles Hills) *dwlt: sn in tch in midfield: lost pl wl over 2f out: lost tch 2f out* **33/1**
1m 39.83s (1.23) **Going Correction** +0.075s/f (Good) **10 Ran SP% 117.0**
Speed ratings (Par 97): **96,95,95,95,95 91,86,84,83,68**
CSF £21.01 TOTE £2.50: £1.10, £3.60, £5.10; EX 24.30 Trifecta £476.10.
**Owner** Derrick Smith & Mrs John Magnier & Michael Tabor **Bred** Southern Bloodstock **Trained** Cashel, Co Tipperary

**FOCUS**
A good-quality maiden and although they didn't appear to go very fast early on and only around a length separated the first five home, plenty of winners should emerge from this.

## 6929 EBF STALLIONS NATIONAL STUD BOADICEA FILLIES' STKS (LISTED RACE) 6f
4:40 (4:43) (Class 1) 3-Y-O+
**£22,684** (£8,600; £4,304; £2,144; £1,076; £540) **Stalls** Low

Form RPR
3200 1 **Inyordreams**[23] 6254 3-9-0 94 FrankieDettori 10 105
(James Given) *chsd ldr tl rdn to ld 2f out: styd on wl fnl f: rdn out* **20/1**
4342 2 *1* **Remember**[9] 6689 3-9-0 97 RichardHughes 5 102
(Richard Hannon) *hld up in last quartet: swtchd rt and hdwy over 1f out: chsd wnr 1f out: drvn and kpt on same pce ins fnl f* **4/1**[2]
2324 3 *1 1/2* **Penny Drops**[49] 5438 3-9-0 93 RyanMoore 11 97
(William Haggas) *t.k.h: hld up in tch in midfield: effrt wl over 1f out: styd on u.p 1f out: wnt 3rd wl ins fnl f: no threat to wnr* **11/4**[1]
3340 4 *1/2* **Indignant**[23] 6254 4-9-4 102 WilliamBuick 12 98
(Richard Hannon) *hld up in last quartet: effrt u.p wl over 1f out: no hdwy tl styd on wl ins fnl f: nvr trbld ldrs* **7/1**
1043 5 *1 1/2* **Mu'Ajiza**[48] 5467 4-9-1 100 PatSmullen 9 91
(Paul Midgley) *in tch in midfield: pushed along and hdwy to chse ldrs 1/2-way: drvn and chsd wnr over 1f out tl 1f out: wknd ins fnl f* **7/1**
0363 6 *2* **Hopes N Dreams (IRE)**[13] 6576 6-9-1 85 JamieSpencer 4 84
(Kevin Ryan) *broke fast: led: rdn and hdd 2f out: no ex over 1f out: wknd ins fnl f* **25/1**
6401 7 *shd* **Serenity Spa**[40] 5776 4-9-1 81 JoeyHaynes 2 84
(Tony Carroll) *travelled wl: wl in tch in midfield: rdn and no rspnse over 1f out: wknd ins fnl f* **40/1**
143 8 *1* **Danehill Revival**[124] 2840 3-9-0 94 JoeFanning 1 81
(William Haggas) *chsd ldrs tl 1/2-way: rdn and unable qck ent fnl 2f: wknd over 1f out* **9/1**
504 9 *17* **Artistic Jewel (IRE)**[27] 6167 5-9-1 100 JamesDoyle 8 26
(Ed McMahon) *t.k.h: hld up in tch in midfield: rdn over 2f out: sn struggling: wknd over 1f out* **9/2**[3]
45-5 10 *1/2* **Boston Rocker (IRE)**[25] 6209 4-9-1 97 (t) JimmyFortune 7 25
(Hughie Morrison) *wnt sharply lft leaving stalls and rdn along early a in rr: rdn over 2f out: sn btn and bhd* **28/1**
1m 10.52s (-1.68) **Going Correction** +0.075s/f (Good)
**WFA** 3 from 4yo+ 1lb **10 Ran SP% 114.3**
Speed ratings: **114,112,110,110,108 105,105,103,81,80**
CSF £93.45 TOTE £22.50: £4.70, £1.10, £1.50; EX 75.20 Trifecta £271.10.
**Owner** Bolton Grange **Bred** Exors Of The Late J Ellis **Trained** Willoughton, Lincs

**FOCUS**
An open fillies' Listed contest on paper but they went quite a good gallop here and most of these were under pressure by the two-pole.

## 6930 QIPCO FUTURE STARS APPRENTICE H'CAP 1m 4f
5:15 (5:15) (Class 2) (0-105,105) 3-Y-O+**£32,345** (£9,625; £4,810; £2,405) **Stalls** Centre

Form RPR
4115 1 **Winter Thunder**[49] 5440 3-9-7 **105** KevinStott[(3)] 5 114
(Saeed bin Suroor) *in tch in midfield: rdn and hdwy to ld wl over 1f out: hrd pressed wl ins fnl f: hld on wl u.p cl home* **4/1**[2]
2116 2 *nk* **Fire Fighting (IRE)**[7] 6737 3-9-7 **102** (b) JoeyHaynes 13 111
(Mark Johnston) *stdd and dropped in bhd after s: hld up in last pair: rdn: edgd rt and hdwy over 1f out: chsd wnr ins fnl f: str chal wl ins fnl f: hld cl home* **6/1**
2131 3 *2 3/4* **Ruwasi**[18] 6433 3-8-1 **87** KieranShoemark[(5)] 1 91
(James Tate) *chsd ldrs: effrt 2f out: drvn and chsd ldrs 1f out: styd on same pce ins fnl f* **7/1**
1116 4 *1/2* **Treasure The Ridge (IRE)**[14] 6532 5-9-0 **93** (b) JennyPowell[(5)] 10 96
(Andrew Reid) *in tch in midfield: clsd to chse ldrs over 2f out: rdn and sltly outpcd over 1f out: kpt on again ins fnl f* **18/1**
3004 5 *1* **Bureau (IRE)**[17] 6465 3-7-13 **83** JoeDoyle[(3)] 6 85
(Mark Johnston) *chsd ldr: led and stl travelling strly 2f out: led wl over 1f out: rdn and no rspnse over 1f out: lost 2nd and wknd ins fnl f* **16/1**
-122 6 *1/2* **Investissement**[8] 6721 8-8-5 **79** (p) ThomasBrown 3 80
(Lee Carter) *wl in tch in midfield: rdn and unable qck ent fnl 2f: kpt on but no threat to ldrs fnl f* **16/1**
0433 7 *1 1/4* **Manomine**[16] 6487 5-7-11 **74** oh3 NathanAlison[(3)] 11 73
(Clive Brittain) *chsd ldrs: outpcd wl over 1f out: no threat to ldrs and kpt on same pce after* **33/1**
1102 8 *5* **Kinshasa**[18] 6438 3-8-12 **93** CharlesBishop 7 84
(Luca Cumani) *in tch in midfield: clsd to trck ldrs 3f out: rdn and ev ch 2f out: no ex and btn whn pushed rt ent fnl f: fdd* **11/4**[1]
3334 9 *1* **Vainglory (USA)**[12] 6616 10-7-7 **74** SophieKilloran[(7)] 9 63
(David Simcock) *a towards rr: pushed along over 2f out: n.d fnl 2f* **33/1**
2133 10 *nk* **Yenhaab (IRE)**[35] 5914 3-8-9 **93** (p) JackGarritty[(3)] 4 82
(William Haggas) *led tl rdn and hdd ent fnl 2f: lost pl over 1f out: wknd fnl f* **11/2**[3]
2411 11 *1 1/4* **Soul Intent (IRE)**[10] 6664 4-8-3 **82** AdamMcLean[(5)] 12 69
(Charles Hills) *a towards rr: rdn and struggling 3f out: bhd fnl 2f* **20/1**
6060 12 *4 1/2* **Viewpoint (IRE)**[35] 5928 5-8-6 **87** JoshQuinn[(7)] 8 67
(Richard Hannon) *stdd s: hld up in rr: rdn 3f out: sn struggling: bhd 2f out* **25/1**
2m 29.83s (-2.17) **Going Correction** +0.075s/f (Good)
**WFA** 3 from 4yo+ 7lb **12 Ran SP% 120.4**
Speed ratings (Par 109): **110,109,107,107,106 106,105,102,101,101 100,97**
CSF £27.45 CT £164.38 TOTE £4.70: £1.90, £2.50, £2.70; EX 27.20 Trifecta £113.40.
**Owner** Godolphin **Bred** Darley **Trained** Newmarket, Suffolk

**FOCUS**
A competitive handicap run at what looked a steady enough gallop before the pace quickened around the two pole where a whole host of these appeared in with a chance. The two highest-rated runners in the race put daylight between themselves and their rivals up the hill so in that respect the form looks quite strong.
T/Plt: £13.90 to a £1 stake. Pool: £112,872.78 - 5,897.41 winning tickets. T/Qpdt: £6.70 to a £1 stake. Pool: £6,329.96 - 692.35 winning tickets. SP

# 6667 REDCAR (L-H)
Saturday, October 4

**OFFICIAL GOING: Good (good to firm in places; 9.0)**
Wind: Moderate across Weather: Overcast, light rain

## 6931 BRITISH STALLION STUDS SUPPORTING BRITISH RACING EBF MAIDEN STKS (DIV I) 7f
2:00 (2:03) (Class 5) 2-Y-O **£3,234** (£962; £481; £240) **Stalls** Centre

Form RPR
1 **Belle Travers** 2-9-0 0 TonyHamilton 14 73+
(Richard Fahey) *wnt rt s: sn trcking ldrs: styd on strly fnl 75yds: led last stride* **12/1**
064 2 *nse* **Awjab (IRE)**[15] 6517 2-9-5 79 DaneO'Neill 10 78
(Brian Meehan) *mde most: drvn over 1f out: hdd post* **5/2**[2]
4522 3 *1 1/4* **Shootingsta (IRE)**[12] 6594 2-9-5 77 PaulMulrennan 12 75
(Bryan Smart) *w ldr: upsides 3f out: hung lft and styd on same pce fnl f* **13/8**[1]
4 *3 1/2* **Mystic Miraaj** 2-9-5 0 DavidAllan 6 65+
(Tim Easterby) *chsd ldrs: kpt on same pce fnl 2f* **33/1**
34 5 *7* **Sekuras Girl (IRE)**[28] 6147 2-8-11 0 ConnorBeasley[(3)] 3 41
(Michael Dods) *swtchd rt after s: sn trcking ldrs: t.k.h: wknd fnl f* **11/1**
6 *2* **Layerthorpe (IRE)** 2-9-5 0 SeanLevey 13 41
(David Brown) *trckd ldrs: effrt over 2f out: wknd over 1f out* **16/1**
7 *1/2* **Ingleby Hollow** 2-9-5 0 SamJames 5 40
(David O'Meara) *wnt lft s: mid-div: hdwy 3f out: sn outpcd: wknd over 1f out* **10/1**[3]
8 *1 3/4* **Kaine Keira** 2-9-5 0 GrahamLee 9 35
(Paul Midgley) *s.i.s: in rr: sme hdwy over 2f out: nvr on terms* **25/1**
000 9 *1 3/4* **What Usain**[17] 6449 2-9-5 45 (p) PatrickMathers 7 30
(Geoffrey Oldroyd) *mid-div: drvn 4f out: lost pl 2f out* **100/1**
10 *28* **El Draque (USA)** 2-9-5 0 LukeMorris 4
(Sir Mark Prescott Bt) *swvd bdly lft s: a detached in last: t.o fnl 3f* **16/1**
0 P **Beatabout (IRE)**[30] 6058 2-9-5 0 RaulDaSilva 8
(Paul Green) *sn w ldrs: lost pl 3f out: sn heavily eased: p.u and dismntd ins fnl f: lame* **100/1**
1m 25.74s (1.24) **Going Correction** +0.075s/f (Good) **11 Ran SP% 112.3**
Speed ratings (Par 95): **95,94,93,89,81 79,78,76,74,42**
CSF £39.61 TOTE £13.00: £3.10, £1.10, £1.10; EX 5.30 Trifecta £118.80.
**Owner** H J P Farr **Bred** Worksop Manor Stud **Trained** Musley Bank, N Yorks
■ Don't Tell Bertie (25-1) was withdrawn. Rule 4 does not apply.

**FOCUS**
Fair form from the principals in a maiden which lacked depth.

## 6932 RACING UK ANYWHERE AVAILABLE NOW (S) STKS 1m 2f
2:30 (2:31) (Class 5) 3-5-Y-O **£3,234** (£962; £481; £240) **Stalls** Low

Form RPR
4420 1 **Innsbruck**[22] 6292 4-9-3 81 (b) PhillipMakin 1 73
(John Quinn) *trckd ldrs: chsd ldr 1/2-way: tk clsr order over 2f out: rdn over 1f out: drvn ins fnl f: kpt on to ld last 50yds* **1/2**[1]
1160 2 *3/4* **Mixed Message (IRE)**[10] 6672 4-9-4 65 (p) DaleSwift 5 72
(Brian Ellison) *set stdy pce: pushed clr 5f out: rdn 2f out: drvn ent fnl f: hdd and no ex last 50yds* **5/1**[2]
540 3 *11* **Scrutiny**[41] 5717 3-8-12 64 SamJames 3 50
(David O'Meara) *in tch: hdwy over 3f out: chsd ldng pair: rdn over 2f out: edgd lft wl over 1f out: sn drvn and no imp* **13/2**[3]
266 4 *3/4* **Exclusive Contract (IRE)**[14] 6539 3-8-10 61 JacobButterfield[(3)] 4 50
(Ollie Pears) *hld up in tch: hdwy on inner over 3f out: pushed along over 2f out: n.m.r and swtchd rt wl over 1f out: sn rdn and no imp* **14/1**
3-00 5 *1* **Miss Ella Jade**[30] 6076 5-8-9 45 ConnorBeasley[(3)] 2 42
(Richard Whitaker) *in tch: hdwy on outer 3f out: rdn along over 2f out: drvn wl over 1f out: sn one pce* **50/1**
0304 6 *28* **Flying By**[145] 2209 3-8-7 52 (b) ChrisCatlin 7
(Rae Guest) *cl up: rdn along 1/2-way: sn lost pl and bhd* **33/1**

0060 **7** *1 3/4* **Soviet Union (IRE)**[17] 6454 3-8-7 45.................................... JasonHart 6
(Mark Walford) *s.i.s: a bhd* **80/1**

2m 6.74s (-0.36) **Going Correction** +0.075s/f (Good)
**WFA** 3 from 4yo+ 5lb 7 Ran SP% **109.5**
Speed ratings (Par 103): **104,103,94,94,93 70,69**
CSF £2.94 TOTE £1.50: £1.10, £2.00; EX 3.30 Trifecta £8.50.No bid for the winner.
**Owner** Riverdee Stable,Acorn P'Ship,M Lindsay **Bred** New England, Stanley House & Mount Coote Studs **Trained** Settrington, N Yorks

**FOCUS**
The leading pair had this seller between them from a long way out.

## 6933 TOTEPOOL TWO-YEAR-OLD TROPHY (LISTED RACE) 6f
**3:05** (3:07) (Class 1) 2-Y-O

**£117,219** (£44,440; £22,240; £11,079; £5,560; £2,790) **Stalls** Centre

Form RPR
111 **1** **Limato (IRE)**[78] 4398 2-8-12 111.......................................... GrahamLee 3 116+
(Henry Candy) *w ldrs gng wl: led on bit over 1f out: smoothly* **6/5**[1]
113 **2** *1 1/2* **Mattmu**[23] 6256 2-8-3 95..............................................(p) DuranFentiman 15 95
(Tim Easterby) *chsd ldrs: 2nd over 1f out: kpt on wl: no ch w wnr* **7/1**[2]
031 **3** *1 1/4* **Wet Sail (USA)**[36] 5874 2-9-0 88.................................. FrederikTylicki 14 102
(Charlie Fellowes) *mid-div: hdwy over 2f out: chsng ldrs over 1f out: styd on to take 3rd last 100yds* **14/1**
2016 **4** *2 3/4* **Kasb (IRE)**[23] 6256 2-9-0 95.............................................. DaneO'Neill 21 94
(John Gosden) *s.s: hdwy over 2f out: hung lft and styd on fnl f: tk 4th clsng stages* **12/1**[3]
1404 **5** *1 1/4* **Fox Trotter (IRE)**[12] 6612 2-8-11 96 ow2.............................. RyanClark 9 87
(Brian Meehan) *chsd ldrs: kpt on same pce over 1f out* **33/1**
2110 **6** *nk* **Bronze Maquette (IRE)**[22] 6286 2-9-0 104............. GrahamGibbons 20 89
(Gary Moore) *in rr: hdwy over 2f out: styd on same pce* **14/1**
0040 **7** *1 1/2* **Roudee**[44] 5607 2-9-2 88............................................................ DavidAllan 4 87
(Tom Dascombe) *slipped s: mid-div: effrt over 2f out: kpt on same pce* **100/1**
0102 **8** *1/2* **Mind Of Madness (IRE)**[15] 6513 2-9-3 102..................... ColinKeane 12 86
(David Brown) *mid-div: effrt over 2f out: kpt on one pce* **14/1**
2543 **9** *nk* **Realtra (IRE)**[20] 6375 2-8-11 95.................................... TonyHamilton 2 79
(Richard Fahey) *slipped s: mid-div: effrt and swtchd lft over 1f out: kpt on same pce* **16/1**
3212 **10** *1 1/2* **Mythmaker**[22] 6280 2-8-6 79............................................... JamesSullivan 1 70
(Bryan Smart) *trckd ldrs far side: hung lft and one pce over 1f out* **100/1**
4312 **11** *hd* **Snap Shots (IRE)**[39] 5791 2-9-2 95......................... RichardKingscote 16 79
(Tom Dascombe) *mid-div: effrt over 2f out: one pce whn edgd rt over 1f out* **33/1**
1000 **12** *nk* **Vimy Ridge**[23] 6256 2-8-9 92........................................... PatrickMathers 6 71
(Richard Fahey) *chsd ldrs: drvn over 2f out: one pce* **40/1**
2013 **13** *1/2* **Grey Zeb (IRE)**[47] 5511 2-9-0 78........................................ JasonHart 22 75
(Keith Dalgleish) *in rr: sme hdwy over 2f out: nvr a factor* **100/1**
126 **14** *1 1/4* **George Dryden (IRE)**[22] 6286 2-9-0 98.......................... FergalLynch 8 71
(Ann Duffield) *hld up in mid-div: effrt over 2f out: wknd over 1f out* **20/1**
3410 **15** *nk* **Sea Wolf (IRE)**[22] 6291 2-8-6 94....................................... LukeMorris 17 62
(Michael Dods) *mid-div: drvn over 2f out: n.m.r over 1f out: nvr a factor* **33/1**
1100 **16** *3/4* **Primrose Valley**[15] 6513 2-8-4 87.....................................(p) ChrisCatlin 10 58
(Ed Vaughan) *s.i.s: effrt whn nt clr run over 1f out: nvr a threat* **33/1**
0540 **17** *1 1/4* **Diamond Creek (IRE)**[23] 6256 2-8-11 80.......................... DaleSwift 13 61
(Richard Fahey) *led: hdd & wknd over 1f out* **125/1**
2330 **18** *3/4* **Buccaneers Vault (IRE)**[20] 6375 2-8-12 83.............. PaulMulrennan 11 60
(Michael Dods) *mid-div: drvn and outpcd over 2f out* **125/1**
20 **19** *1/2* **Sors (IRE)**[8] 6723 2-9-2 0.......................................... DeclanMcDonogh 7 63
(Andrew Slattery, Ire) *chsd ldrs: drvn over 2f out: sn wknd* **33/1**
4110 **20** *2* **Lady Desire (IRE)**[14] 6530 2-8-11 85..............................(p) TomEaves 19 52
(Keith Dalgleish) *mid-div: drvn and outpcd over 2f out: sn lost pl* **100/1**
0244 **21** *2* **Prince Bonnaire**[24] 6230 2-8-12 92.................................... PhillipMakin 5 47
(David Brown) *chsd ldrs: wknd appr fnl f: bhd whn eased clsng stages* **80/1**
224 **22** *1 3/4* **Cockney Island**[23] 6256 2-8-1 88...................................(p) DannyBrock 18 30
(Philip McBride) *s.s: in rr: bhd whn hung bdly lft over 2f out* **20/1**
1330 **23** *6* **Fuwairt (IRE)**[7] 6739 2-9-0 92............................................ SeanLevey 23 25
(Richard Hannon) *mid-div: lost pl over 2f out: bhd whn eased clsng stages* **66/1**

1m 10.66s (-1.14) **Going Correction** +0.075s/f (Good) 23 Ran SP% **126.5**
Speed ratings (Par 103): **110,108,106,102,101 100,98,97,97,95 95,94,94,92,92 91,89,88,87,85 82,80,72**
CSF £7.40 TOTE £1.80: £1.10, £2.60, £3.80; EX 10.20 Trifecta £99.00.
**Owner** Paul G Jacobs **Bred** Seamus Phelan **Trained** Kingston Warren, Oxon

**FOCUS**
The 26th running of this valuable sales race and undoubtedly it's most impressive winner to date. Straightforward form.

## 6934 TOTESCOOP6 EBF GUISBOROUGH STKS (LISTED RACE) 7f
**3:45** (3:45) (Class 1) 3-Y-O+

**£22,684** (£8,600; £4,304; £2,144; £1,076; £540) **Stalls** Centre

Form RPR
1226 **1** **Muteela**[23] 6254 3-8-10 104............................................ DaneO'Neill 6 109
(Mark Johnston) *mde all: rdn clr over 1f out: styd on strly: readily* **9/4**[2]
05 **2** *3 1/2* **Tawhid**[98] 3723 4-9-0 110.............................................(p) GrahamLee 8 103
(Saeed bin Suroor) *hld up in tch: hdwy over 3f out: chsd wnr over 2f out: rdn and edgd lft over 1f out and again ins fnl f: no imp* **3/1**[3]
/0-0 **3** *1* **Linton (AUS)**[210] 902 8-9-0 110....................................(p) PaddyAspell 4 100
(Marco Botti) *awkward s and in rr: swtchd rt to outer and hdwy wl over 2f out: rdn to chse ldrs wl over 1f out: kpt on u.p fnl f: nrst fin* **14/1**
-451 **3** *nk* **Patentar (FR)**[21] 6335 3-8-12 108.................................... LukeMorris 1 99
(Marco Botti) *trckd ldrs: hdwy over 3f out: rdn along over 2f out: drvn wl over 1f out and sn one pce* **7/4**[1]
2020 **4** *4* **Dream Walker (FR)**[21] 6354 5-9-0 90................................ DaleSwift 2 89
(Brian Ellison) *chsd wnr: rdn along wl over 2f out: sn wknd* **20/1**
5050 **5** *shd* **Penitent**[21] 6328 8-9-5 106........................................... SamJames 5 94
(David O'Meara) *trckd ldng pair: pushed along over 3f out: rdn wl over 2f out: sn wknd* **16/1**

1m 23.41s (-1.09) **Going Correction** +0.075s/f (Good)
**WFA** 3 from 4yo+ 2lb 6 Ran SP% **109.4**
Speed ratings: **109,105,103,103,98 98**
CSF £8.90 TOTE £2.60: £1.20, £2.70; EX 12.20 Trifecta £73.20.
**Owner** Hamdan Al Maktoum **Bred** Shadwell Estate Company Limited **Trained** Middleham Moor, N Yorks

**FOCUS**
Not a particularly strong Listed event, but a taking performance from the winner. She posted a clear personal best at face value, but there are doubts over the form.

## 6935 BRITISH STALLION STUDS SUPPORTING BRITISH RACING EBF MAIDEN STKS (DIV II) 7f
**4:20** (4:21) (Class 5) 2-Y-O **£3,234** (£962; £481; £240) **Stalls** Centre

Form RPR
4 **1** **Purple Rock (IRE)**[14] 6551 2-9-5 0............................ GrahamGibbons 11 80
(Charles Hills) *trckd ldng pair: hdwy to ld 2f out: rdn and edgd rt ent fnl f: sn clr: kpt on strly* **11/8**[1]
**2** *5* **Structured Note (IRE)** 2-9-5 0............................. RussKennemore 6 67
(Jedd O'Keeffe) *in tch: hdwy 3f out: rdn to chse wnr whn n.m.r ent fnl f: sn rdn and kpt on same pce* **25/1**
**3** *1* **Whisky Marmalade (IRE)** 2-9-0 0.................................. GrahamLee 13 59+
(David O'Meara) *chsd ldrs: hdwy 2f out: rdn over 1f out: kpt on* **16/1**
**4** *nk* **Thankstomonty** 2-9-5 0................................................ SamJames 7 63
(David O'Meara) *chsd ldr: rdn along 2f out: ev ch tl drvn and one pce fnl f* **14/1**
**5** *2* **Polly Jackson** 2-8-9 0............................................... GemmaTutty[(5)] 12 53
(Karen Tutty) *dwlt: sn in midfield: hdwy over 2f out: sn rdn: kpt on fnl f: nrst fin* **66/1**
**6** *nk* **Lone Star Boy (IRE)** 2-9-5 0................................ RichardKingscote 4 57
(Tom Dascombe) *in rr and pushed along 1/2-way: hdwy over 2f out: styng on whn sltly hmpd over 1f out: kpt on: nrst fin* **5/1**[3]
**7** *5* **Muhtadim (IRE)** 2-9-5 0............................................... DaneO'Neill 3 47+
(William Haggas) *towards rr: sme hdwy wl over 2f out: n.d* **11/4**[2]
0 **8** *5* **The Name's Bond**[10] 6667 2-9-5 0.................................... TomEaves 10 30
(Keith Reveley) *wnt lft s: a towards rr* **66/1**
**9** *3/4* **Bond Mystery** 2-9-5 0..................................................... PaulQuinn 9 28+
(Richard Whitaker) *s.i.s: a in rr* **66/1**
0 **10** *nk* **Citisonsmith (IRE)**[30] 6059 2-9-5 0.................................(b[1]) RaulDaSilva 8 27
(Paul Green) *led: rdn alko9ng 3f out: hdd 2f out: sn hung lft and wknd* **100/1**
0 **11** *1* **Naval Action**[8] 6718 2-9-5 0............................................... LukeMorris 2 24+
(Sir Mark Prescott Bt) *midfield: rdn along 1/2-way: sn outpcd and bhd* **66/1**
**12** *nse* **Grand Depart** 2-9-0 0................................................ TonyHamilton 5 19
(James Bethell) *dwlt: a in rr* **33/1**
0 **13** *nk* **Mclovin Riverdance**[17] 6449 2-9-5 0................................. DaleSwift 1 23
(Ann Duffield) *chsd ldrs: rdn along bef 1/2-way: sn lost pl and bhd* **33/1**

1m 25.89s (1.39) **Going Correction** +0.075s/f (Good) 13 Ran SP% **114.7**
Speed ratings (Par 95): **95,89,88,87,85 79,73,72,72 71,71,71**
CSF £45.64 TOTE £1.70: £1.10, £10.60, £3.90; EX 43.40 Trifecta £508.40.
**Owner** Morecombe,Anderson,Sangster,Farquhar **Bred** Barronstown Stud **Trained** Lambourn, Berks

**FOCUS**
Doubtful there was much depth to this race, but the winner did it in good style, the rest well strung out in behind.

## 6936 WATCH RACING UK ON 3 DEVICES STRAIGHT-MILE CHAMPIONSHIP FINAL (H'CAP) 1m
**4:55** (4:55) (Class 2) 3-Y-O+

**£12,450** (£3,728; £1,864; £932; £466; £234) **Stalls** Centre

Form RPR
4431 **1** **Karaka Jack**[42] 5681 7-8-10 78............................................ GrahamLee 1 87
(Jim Goldie) *chsd ldrs on outer: drvn over 2f out: styd on to ld last 75yds: hld on nr fin* **11/1**
1453 **2** *hd* **Big Storm Coming**[11] 6639 4-8-6 77........................ JacobButterfield[(3)] 8 85
(Ruth Carr) *trckd ldrs: nt clr run and swtchd rt jst ins fnl f: kpt on wl towards fin* **12/1**
1500 **3** *1/2* **Sound Advice**[7] 6752 5-9-8 90.............................................. TomEaves 17 97
(Keith Dalgleish) *w ldr: led over 1f out: edgd lft: hdd and no ex last 75yds* **20/1**
3323 **4** *1/2* **Almuheet**[16] 6476 3-9-1 86................................................... DaleSwift 2 92
(Brian Ellison) *w ldrs: wandered 1f out: kpt on towards fin* **15/2**[2]
0312 **5** *nk* **Arrowzone**[41] 5713 3-8-13 84............................................ JasonHart 3 89
(Garry Moss) *led: hdd over 1f out: kpt on same pce* **14/1**
0460 **6** *shd* **Barren Brook**[16] 6476 7-8-10 78....................................... FergalLynch 4 83
(Michael Easterby) *in rr: hdwy over 2f out: chsng ldrs whn hung rt jst ins fnl f: kpt on towards fin* **10/1**
1525 **7** *1* **Kiwi Bay**[14] 6534 9-9-5 87.......................................... PaulMulrennan 15 90
(Michael Dods) *hld up towards rr: hdwy over 2f out: kpt on fnl f* **12/1**
0331 **8** *3/4* **Anderiego (IRE)**[16] 6476 6-9-8 90................................(v) SamJames 5 91
(David O'Meara) *mid-div: edgd rt over 1f out: kpt on ins fnl f* **9/1**[3]
1321 **9** *1 1/4* **No Poppy (IRE)**[8] 6704 6-9-0 82........................................ DavidAllan 7 80
(Tim Easterby) *chsd ldrs: one pce fnl 2f: n.m.r ins fnl f* **11/1**
4051 **10** *1/2* **Knight Owl**[25] 6214 4-9-4 86............................................. DaneO'Neill 13 83
(James Fanshawe) *hld up in rr: effrt and swtchd lft over 2f out: rdn to chse ldrs on outer 1f out: wknd fnl 75yds* **10/3**[1]
5110 **11** *2 3/4* **Green Howard**[14] 6531 6-9-10 92................................. AdamBeschizza 12 83
(Robin Bastiman) *s.i.s: hld up in rr: sme hdwy over 1f out: nvr a factor* **16/1**
4200 **12** *1* **Who's Shirl**[42] 5681 8-8-6 74.......................................... AndrewElliott 6 62
(Chris Fairhurst) *in rr: hmpd and lost pl over 3f out: sme hdwy 2f out: nvr a factor* **66/1**
061 **13** *1 1/2* **Dual Mac**[56] 5196 7-8-5 73................................................ LukeMorris 16 58
(Neville Bycroft) *dwlt: in rr: drvn over 3f out: nvr on terms* **12/1**
6260 **14** *1* **Border Bandit (USA)**[8] 6713 6-9-1 83...........................(p) IanBrennan 9 66
(Tracy Waggott) *trckd ldrs: effrt over 2f out: wknd over 1f out* **33/1**
3423 **15** *1* **Staffhoss**[4] 6837 4-8-0 68 oh6........................................ DuranFentiman 10 48
(Mark Johnston) *mid-div: lost pl over 2f out* **33/1**
0045 **16** *4* **Hakuna Matata**[16] 6490 7-8-5 76.........................(v) ConnorBeasley[(3)] 14 47
(Michael Dods) *a towards rr: sme hdwy over 2f out: wknd over 1f out: bhd whn eased clsng stages* **20/1**

1m 37.55s (0.95) **Going Correction** +0.075s/f (Good)
**WFA** 3 from 4yo+ 3lb 16 Ran SP% **123.1**
Speed ratings (Par 109): **98,97,97,96,96 96,95,94,93,92 90,89,87,86,85 81**
CSF £130.04 CT £2716.24 TOTE £12.10: £3.20, £4.50, £6.00, £1.60; EX 258.80 Trifecta £2064.20.
**Owner** M Mackay & J Fyffe **Bred** Tarworth Bloodstock Investments Ltd **Trained** Uplawmoor, E Renfrews



The Form Book, Raceform Ltd, Newbury, RG14 5SJ

**FOCUS**
A well-contested handicap. The gallop appeared sound enough but nothing was able to land a serious blow from off the pace.

## 6937 MARKET CROSS JEWELLERS H'CAP — 1m 2f
5:30 (5:31) (Class 4) (0-85,84) 3-Y-O+ £6,469 (£1,925; £962; £481) Stalls Low

Form RPR
33-1 **1** **Stetchworth (IRE)**[12] 6599 3-8-13 78.................. AdrianNicholls 7 87+
(Mark Johnston) *sn led: rdn clr over 1f out: drvn out* **9/4**[1]
-040 **2** 1 3/4 **Docs Legacy (IRE)**[14] 6566 5-9-6 80.................. TonyHamilton 10 86
(Richard Fahey) *trckd wnr: effrt 2f out and sn rdn: edgd lft ent fnl f: sn drvn and no imp* **6/1**[3]
1063 **3** 3/4 **Dance King**[16] 6479 4-9-8 82.................. DavidAllan 11 87
(Tim Easterby) *hld up towards rr: hdwy wl over 2f out: rdn to chse ldrs whn n.m.r and swtchd rt ent fnl f: sn drvn and kpt on* **6/1**[3]
205 **4** 1 1/2 **Rocket Ronnie (IRE)**[11] 6626 4-8-13 73.................. PaddyAspell 1 75
(David Nicholls) *t.k.h: trckd ldrs: hdwy over 2f out: rdn wl over 1f out: kpt on same pce fnl f* **16/1**
0226 **5** hd **Duke Of Yorkshire**[21] 6323 4-8-10 70.................. DuranFentiman 3 71
(Tim Easterby) *hld up in rr: hdwy on outer over 2f out: rdn wl over 1f out: styd on fnl f: nrst fin* **14/1**
U46 **6** 1 3/4 **Red Inca**[9] 6696 6-8-10 70.................. DaleSwift 9 68+
(Brian Ellison) *dwlt and bhd: rapid hdwy on outer 3f out: sn cl up: rdn 2f out: drvn over 1f out and wknd fnl f* **16/1**
5641 **7** nk **Ardmay (IRE)**[49] 5413 5-9-6 80.................. FergalLynch 6 77
(Kevin Ryan) *chsd ldrs: rdn along over 2f out: grad wknd* **5/1**[2]
1203 **8** 4 **Galactic Heroine**[28] 6152 3-9-0 79..................[1] GrahamLee 8 69
(James Given) *trckd ldrs: hdwy 4f out: rdn along over 2f out: wknd wl over 1f out* **6/1**[3]
020 **9** 1 3/4 **Argaki (IRE)**[16] 6476 4-9-2 76.................. TomEaves 5 63
(Keith Dalgleish) *prom: rdn along over 3f out: wknd jst over 2f out* **33/1**
6306 **10** 1 3/4 **Eeny Mac (IRE)**[11] 6626 7-8-10 70 oh1.................. AndrewElliott 4 53
(Neville Bycroft) *nvr bttr than midfield* **28/1**

2m 6.5s (-0.60) **Going Correction** +0.075s/f (Good)
**WFA** 3 from 4yo+ 5lb **10 Ran SP% 115.1**
Speed ratings (Par 105): **105,103,103,101,101 100,100,96,95,94**
CSF £15.45 CT £71.00 TOTE £3.20: £1.60, £2.70, £1.10; EX 18.40 Trifecta £103.80.
**Owner** Sheikh Hamdan bin Mohammed Al Maktoum **Bred** Lodge Park Stud **Trained** Middleham Moor, N Yorks

**FOCUS**
Not a particularly strong handicap but the winner is certainly going the right way and has more to offer. The pace steadied towards the end of the back straight before quickening again over 3f out. The runner-up sets the standard.

## 6938 BET WITH YOUR RACING UK APP H'CAP — 5f
6:05 (6:06) (Class 5) (0-70,71) 3-Y-O+ £3,234 (£962; £481; £240) Stalls Centre

Form RPR
6260 **1** **Haajes**[17] 6451 10-9-5 68..................(v) GrahamLee 6 77
(Paul Midgley) *in tch: hdwy 2f out: rdn ent fnl f: str run to ld nr line* **6/1**[2]
0002 **2** nk **Bronze Beau**[5] 6819 7-8-9 63..................(t) ShaneGray(5) 4 71
(Kristin Stubbs) *cl up: rdn to ld ent fnl f: sn edgd lft: drvn and hung rt last 75yds: hdd no line* **9/1**
0652 **3** 1 1/2 **Storyline (IRE)**[10] 6671 3-9-2 65.................. DuranFentiman 10 69
(Tim Easterby) *chsd ldrs: hdwy wl over 1f out: rdn ent fnl f: kpt on same pce towards fin* **9/1**
4201 **4** hd **Spring Bird**[19] 6406 5-9-2 65.................. PaulQuinn 9 67
(David Nicholls) *cl up: rdn and ev ch over 1f out: drvn and kpt on same pce ins fnl f* **14/1**
0-60 **5** 3/4 **Hello Beautiful (IRE)**[35] 5913 3-8-13 62.................. PaulMulrennan 2 62
(Brian Ellison) *chsd ldrs: rdn over 1f out: kpt on same pce* **16/1**
2540 **6** nk **Windforpower (IRE)**[19] 6406 4-8-11 63..................(p) ConnorBeasley(3) 14 61
(Tracy Waggott) *midfield: hdwy to chse ldrs wl over 1f out: sn rdn and one pce fnl f* **16/1**
0051 **7** shd **Royal Bajan (USA)**[3] 6873 6-9-8 71 6ex..................(p) TomEaves 5 69
(James Given) *led: rdn wl over 1f out: hdds ent fnl f: sn wknd* **7/1**[3]
4000 **8** 1 1/4 **Hazelrigg (IRE)**[16] 6475 9-9-4 67..................(e) DavidAllan 3 60
(Tim Easterby) *dwlt and in rr: rdn along over 2f out: sme late hdwy* **10/1**
0040 **9** nk **Blue Bullet (IRE)**[73] 4531 4-9-2 65.................. DaleSwift 8 57
(Brian Ellison) *towards rr: rdn along 2f out: n.d* **20/1**
1240 **10** 1 1/4 **Perfect Words (IRE)**[7] 6763 4-9-4 70..................(p) JacobButterfield(3) 12 58
(Marjorie Fife) *in tch on wd outside: effrt 2f out: sn rdn and no imp* **11/2**[1]
0041 **11** 2 1/2 **Little Eli**[10] 6671 4-9-0 66..................(p) NeilFarley(3) 13 45
(Eric Alston) *chsd ldrs: rdn wl over 1f out: wknd appr fnl f* **15/2**
5100 **12** 9 **Majestic Manannan (IRE)**[16] 6475 5-9-4 67.................. AdrianNicholls 1 13
(David Nicholls) *in tch on outer: rdn along 1/2-way: sn wknd* **12/1**

58.49s (-0.11) **Going Correction** +0.075s/f (Good) **12 Ran SP% 113.9**
Speed ratings (Par 103): **103,102,100,99,98 98,97,95,95,93 89,75**
CSF £56.69 CT £487.57 TOTE £5.70: £2.30, £3.90, £3.50; EX 67.30 Trifecta £549.20.
**Owner** Sandfield Racing **Bred** Irish National Stud **Trained** Westow, N Yorks

**FOCUS**
A run-of-the-mill sprint. The winner is rated to this year's form.
T/Plt: £23.10 to a £1 stake. Pool: £59,705.51 - 1,883.88 winning tickets. T/Qpdt: £16.70 to a £1 stake. Pool: £3,150.26 - 139.40 winning tickets. JR

# 6897 WOLVERHAMPTON (A.W) (L-H)
Saturday, October 4

**OFFICIAL GOING: Tapeta: standard**
Wind: Light half-behind Weather: Cloudy with sunny spells

## 6939 COLLECT TOTEPOOL WINNINGS AT BETFRED SHOPS H'CAP (TAPETA) (DIV I) — 1m 1f 103y
5:25 (5:25) (Class 6) (0-55,57) 3-Y-O £2,264 (£673; £336; £168) Stalls Low

Form RPR
3441 **1** **Evacusafe Lady**[8] 6715 3-9-6 57..................(t) RyanPowell(3) 10 73
(John Ryan) *chsd ldrs: led over 1f out: rdn clr fnl f* **7/2**[1]
4005 **2** 8 **Mercury Magic**[18] 6426 3-9-5 53.................. DavidNolan 12 52
(David Menuisier) *hld up: pushed along over 3f out: styd on to go 2nd wl ins fnl f: no ch w wnr* **12/1**
000 **3** 1 1/2 **Tsarglas**[37] 5862 3-8-12 46 oh1.................. SteveDrowne 1 42
(Stuart Williams) *prom: rdn over 2f out: outpcd fr over 1f out* **20/1**
0006 **4** 3/4 **Cascadia (IRE)**[52] 5321 3-9-4 52.................. RobertHavlin 11 46
(Alison Hutchinson) *chsd ldr 8f out: led over 2f out: rdn and hdd wl over 1f out: wknd ins fnl f* **33/1**
0-40 **5** 3 1/2 **Dream And Hope**[53] 5267 3-9-1 54.................. MarcMonaghan(5) 13 41
(Philip McBride) *s.i.s: hld up: effrt on outer 2f out: n.d* **8/1**
00 **6** 1 **L Ge R**[50] 5395 3-9-2 50.................. RobertTart 2 35
(Peter Charalambous) *hld up: sme hdwy u.p over 1f out: nvr on terms* **15/2**[3]
00-0 **7** 1/2 **Vaguely Spanish**[21] 6342 3-9-5 53.................. WilliamCarson 5 37
(Tony Carroll) *hld up: hdwy over 3f out: led wl over 1f out: sn rdn and hdd: wknd ins fnl f* **33/1**
6030 **8** 1 1/4 **Golly Miss Molly**[23] 6267 3-9-0 48..................(p) HayleyTurner 7 29
(Jeremy Gask) *led 1f: chsd ldrs: n.m.r over 2f out: wknd over 1f out* **9/1**
0424 **9** 4 1/2 **Patronella (IRE)**[38] 5833 3-9-7 55.................. MartinLane 6 27
(David Simcock) *hld up: effrt whn hmpd and lost pl over 2f out: n.d after* **15/2**[3]
3065 **10** 2 1/4 **Jayeff Herring (IRE)**[36] 5893 3-8-11 52.................. MichaelKenneally(7) 3 19
(Michael Bell) *hld up: hdwy u.p over 1f out: sn wknd* **8/1**
6535 **11** 9 **Libra Romana (IRE)**[5] 6823 3-9-2 50.................. LiamJones 8
(Sir Mark Prescott Bt) *led over 8f out: rdn and hdd over 2f out: wknd over 1f out* **5/1**[2]
0500 **12** 20 **Pepperello**[14] 6564 3-8-9 46.................. AmyScott(3) 4
(Tim Etherington) *mid-div: rdn 1/2-way: wknd over 3f out* **66/1**

2m 0.13s (-0.67) **Going Correction** 0.0s/f (Stan) **12 Ran SP% 114.5**
Speed ratings (Par 99): **102,94,93,92,89 88,88,87,83,81 73,55**
CSF £43.43 CT £729.16 TOTE £3.90: £1.50, £5.20, £6.40; EX 37.20 Trifecta £1123.80 Part won..
**Owner** J Ryan **Bred** Mrs Sarah Moorcroft **Trained** Newmarket, Suffolk

**FOCUS**
The first division of a moderate 3yo handicap in which they went a proper gallop on standard Tapeta.

## 6940 BET TOTEJACKPOT MAIDEN FILLIES' STKS (FILLIES AND MARES) (TAPETA) — 7f 32y
6:00 (6:00) (Class 5) 3-Y-O+ £2,264 (£673; £336; £168) Stalls High

Form RPR
**1** **Tawteen (USA)** 3-9-0 0.................. NickyMackay 1 67+
(John Gosden) *s.i.s: hld up: hdwy over 1f out: rdn to ld wl ins fnl f: r.o* **5/2**[2]
3 **2** 1 1/4 **Nightlight**[16] 6482 3-9-0 0.................. MartinLane 6 63
(Jeremy Noseda) *chsd ldr: rdn and hung rt over 2f out: led ins fnl f: sn hdd and unable qck* **5/2**[2]
32 **3** 1 1/2 **Emirates Joy (USA)**[31] 6033 3-9-0 0.................. RobertHavlin 5 60
(Charlie Appleby) *led: shkn up over 1f out: rdn and hdd ins fnl f: styd on same pce* **5/4**[1]
-606 **4** 2 1/2 **Natalia**[42] 5683 5-9-2 47.................. RobertTart 3 54?
(Andrew Hollinshead) *prom: rdn over 2f out: styd on same pce fr over 1f out* **40/1**[3]
60 **5** 4 **Barwah (USA)**[10] 6661 3-9-0 0..................(t) WilliamCarson 4 43
(Anthony Carson) *hld up: shkn up over 2f out: sn outpcd* **80/1**
4-50 **6** 1 **Zeteah**[31] 6028 4-9-2 45.................. GeorgeBaker 2 41
(David Lanigan) *chsd ldrs: rdn over 2f out: wknd over 1f out* **40/1**[3]

1m 30.28s (1.48) **Going Correction** 0.0s/f (Stan)
**WFA** 3 from 4yo+ 2lb **6 Ran SP% 107.7**
Speed ratings (Par 100): **91,89,87,85,80 79**
CSF £8.30 TOTE £3.00: £1.60, £1.70; EX 8.10 Trifecta £13.90.
**Owner** Hamdan Al Maktoum **Bred** Shadwell Farm LLC **Trained** Newmarket, Suffolk

**FOCUS**
An ordinary fillies' maiden, run at an even gallop.

## 6941 TOTEPOOL BET ON ALL UK RACING (S) STKS (TAPETA) — 5f 20y
6:30 (6:30) (Class 6) 2-Y-O £2,264 (£673; £336; £168) Stalls Low

Form RPR
3301 **1** **Ar Colleen Aine**[14] 6563 2-8-11 65.................. SamHitchcott 1 67
(Mick Channon) *led: hdd over 3f out: led again 1/2-way: rdn out* **5/2**[1]
510 **2** 1 **Rictrude (FR)**[9] 6679 2-8-11 70.................. WilliamCarson 2 63
(Tom Dascombe) *a.p: rdn to chse wnr and hung lft over 1f out: styd on* **5/2**[1]
6162 **3** 3/4 **Millar Rose (IRE)**[17] 6447 2-8-11 67.................. MichaelStainton 6 61
(K R Burke) *chsd ldrs: rdn over 1f out: no ex towards fin* **11/4**[2]
0464 **4** 1 1/4 **Foxtrot Knight**[80] 4313 2-8-11 62..................(b[1]) LiamJones 8 56
(Olly Stevens) *s.i.s: swtchd lft sn after s: hld up: hdwy 2f out: rdn and nt clr run over 1f out: styd on same pce ins fnl f* **13/2**[3]
4040 **5** 2 **Sunhill Lodge Lady**[17] 6447 2-7-13 45..................(b) RowanScott(7) 7 44
(Ann Duffield) *prom: rdn over 1f out: hung lft and no ex fnl f* **100/1**
2050 **6** 1 **Bannister Bell (IRE)**[11] 6642 2-8-11 63.................. JFEgan 9 45
(David Evans) *prom: lost pl over 3f out: wknd over 1f out* **10/1**
5360 **7** 3 **Decisive Rebel**[43] 5662 2-8-8 55..................(p) PhilipPrince(3) 4 35
(Jo Hughes) *bmpd jst after s: sn pushed along and lost pl: bhd fnl 3f* **50/1**
3000 **8** 2 1/2 **Johnny Sorrento**[9] 6676 2-8-11 53..................(tp) BenCurtis 3 26
(Tim Pitt) *bmpd jst after s: sn chsng ldr: led over 3f out tl 1/2-way: rdn and wknd over 1f out* **66/1**

1m 2.4s (0.50) **Going Correction** 0.0s/f (Stan) **8 Ran SP% 110.7**
Speed ratings (Par 93): **96,94,93,91,88 86,81,77**
.The winner was bought in for 4800gns. \n\x\x Foxtrot Knight bought by Mrs Ruth A. Carr for £6,000.\n\x\x Rictrude bought by Mr John P. Evitt for £6,000.
**Owner** Anne & Steve Fisher **Bred** Wansdyke Farms Ltd **Trained** West Ilsley, Berks

**FOCUS**
A modest juvenile seller.

## 6942 BET TOTEQUADPOT H'CAP (TAPETA) — 1m 4f 50y
7:00 (7:02) (Class 5) (0-70,70) 3-Y-O+ £3,234 (£962; £481; £240) Stalls Low

Form RPR
431- **1** **Dukes Delight (IRE)**[424] 5099 4-9-11 69.................. GeorgeBaker 10 79+
(David Lanigan) *trckd ldrs: racd keenly: wnt 2nd over 1f out: r.o u.p to ld nr fin* **2/1**[1]
3-43 **2** nk **Favorite Girl (GER)**[33] 5984 6-9-4 62.................. AndrewMullen 1 71
(Michael Appleby) *a.p: led over 2f out: rdn and edgd rt fnl f: hdd nr fin* **20/1**
0266 **3** 2 **All The Winds (GER)**[33] 5984 9-9-5 70..................(t) CiaranMckee(7) 2 76
(Shaun Lycett) *s.s: hld up and bhd: hdwy over 2f out: rdn over 1f out: styd on* **33/1**
2621 **4** 1 **Majestic Sun (IRE)**[6] 6787 3-8-11 67.................. JordanNason(5) 9 71
(Peter Chapple-Hyam) *hld up: hdwy and hung lft fr over 1f out: r.o* **5/2**[2]
0603 **5** 3 **Red Pilgrim (IRE)**[14] 6564 4-9-4 62.................. RobertTart 12 61
(James Toller) *dwlt: hld up: hdwy over 1f out: nt rch ldrs* **20/1**
3025 **6** 2 1/2 **Highway Code (USA)**[29] 6099 8-9-5 70..................(t) MikeyEnnis(7) 3 65
(Richard Lee) *mid-div: rdn over 2f out: no imp fr over 1f out* **12/1**

0060 **7** 1 1/2 **Guising**[16] 6487 5-9-12 70 ........ BenCurtis 11 63
(David Brown) *led: hdd over 7f out: chsd ldr tl led again wl over 2f out: sn rdn and hdd: wknd fnl f* **7/1**[3]

3503 **8** *shd* **Tingo In The Tale (IRE)**[39] 5786 5-9-0 61 ........ CamHardie(3) 6 54
(David Arbuthnot) *hld up in tch: rdn over 2f out: wknd over 1f out* **28/1**

034 **9** 1 1/4 **Henpecked**[12] 6597 4-9-1 59 ........ JamesSullivan 7 50
(Alistair Whillans) *chsd ldrs: rdn over 2f out: wknd over 1f out* **11/1**

540 **10** 6 **Mr Lando**[7] 6771 5-8-10 59 ........ GeorgeDowning(5) 4 40
(Tony Carroll) *plld hrd and prom: trckd ldr over 9f out tl led over 7f out: hdd wl over 2f out: wknd over 1f out* **66/1**

135- **11** 1 **Nine Iron (IRE)**[512] 2233 4-9-12 70 ........ DougieCostello 8 50
(Tim Vaughan) *mid-div: rdn over 2f out: wknd over 1f out* **16/1**

5130 **12** 9 **Incendo**[23] 6274 8-9-11 69 ........(v) HayleyTurner 5 34
(Conor Dore) *hld up: pushed along over 3f out: wknd over 2f out* **33/1**

2m 38.99s (-1.81) **Going Correction** 0.0s/f (Stan)
**WFA** 3 from 4yo+ 7lb **12** Ran SP% **116.7**
Speed ratings (Par 103): **106,105,104,103,101 100,99,99,98,94 93,87**
CSF £50.47 CT £1026.36 TOTE £4.00: £1.80, £4.50, £9.90; EX 42.60 Trifecta £1908.20 Part won..
**Owner** B E Nielsen **Bred** Bjorn Nielsen **Trained** Upper Lambourn, Berks
■ Stewards' Enquiry : James Sullivan one-day ban: careless riding (Oct 19)

**FOCUS**
A modest middle-distance handicap in which the sedate tempo picked up with a circuit remaining.

## 6943 BET TOTEEXACTA H'CAP (TAPETA) 1m 1f 103y
**7:30** (7:32) (Class 3) (0-95,95) 3-Y-O **£7,246** (£2,168; £1,084; £542; £270) **Stalls** Low

Form RPR

5301 **1** **Tinghir (IRE)**[14] 6566 4-9-10 95 ........(b) GeorgeBaker 4 106
(David Lanigan) *hld up: nt clr run and swtchd rt over 2f out: hdwy u.p and hung lft fr over 1f out: qcknd to ld nr fin* **13/8**[1]

4-00 **2** 1/2 **I'm Back (IRE)**[40] 5749 4-9-7 92 ........ FrederikTylicki 8 102
(Saeed bin Suroor) *a.p: rdn to ld ins fnl f: hdd nr fin* **13/2**

0123 **3** 1 1/4 **The Great Gabrial**[18] 6430 5-9-1 86 ........(p) AndrewMullen 9 93
(Michael Appleby) *hld up: racd keenly: hdwy over 3f out: chsd ldr over 2f out: sn rdn: styd on same pce ins fnl f* **16/1**

134 **4** 1/2 **Knavery (USA)**[80] 4323 3-8-13 88 ........ JoeFanning 5 95
(Roger Varian) *hld up: hdwy 3f out: rdn over 1f out: styd on* **5/1**[3]

6002 **5** 1 **Capo Rosso (IRE)**[19] 6411 4-9-10 95 ........ StephenCraine 10 99
(Tom Dascombe) *led at stdy pce tl qcknd over 2f out: rdn over 1f out: hdd and no ex ins fnl f* **14/1**

2523 **6** 1/2 **Devilment**[10] 6665 3-9-2 94 ........ CamHardie(3) 3 98
(Charlie Appleby) *dwlt: hld up: hdwy over 1f out: sn rdn: styd on same pce ins fnl f* **4/1**[2]

4013 **7** 1 1/4 **Spiritual Star (IRE)**[14] 6566 5-9-2 87 ........(t) RobertTart 12 87
(Anthony Carson) *s.i.s: hld up: rdn and r.o ins fnl f: nvr nrr* **12/1**

1220 **8** 4 **Zugzwang (IRE)**[7] 6737 3-8-10 85 ........ MartinLane 2 78
(Ed de Giles) *prom: nt clr run and lost pl over 2f out: n.d after* **28/1**

0 **9** 4 **Arc Lighter (USA)**[21] 6332 5-9-9 94 ........(t) FergusSweeney 11 77
(Seamus Durack) *hld up: hdwy over 2f out: wknd fnl f* **40/1**

6400 **10** 1 1/2 **Commissar**[56] 5196 5-8-10 81 oh1 ........ StevieDonohoe 7 61
(Ian Williams) *hld up: pushed along over 2f out: nvr on terms* **40/1**

6300 **11** 1/2 **San Cassiano (IRE)**[16] 6479 7-9-2 87 ........ JamesSullivan 1 66
(Ruth Carr) *chsd ldr tl n.m.r 4f out: sn pushed along: wkng whn hmpd 2f out* **50/1**

1104 **12** 12 **Uncle Dermot (IRE)**[97] 3759 6-8-10 81 oh5 ........ LiamJones 6 35
(Brendan Powell) *prom: racd keenly: chsd ldr and edgd lft 4f out: rdn and lost 2nd over 2f out: wknd wl over 1f out* **80/1**

1m 59.06s (-1.74) **Going Correction** 0.0s/f (Stan)
**WFA** 3 from 4yo+ 4lb **12** Ran SP% **119.9**
Speed ratings (Par 107): **107,106,105,105,104 103,102,99,95,94 93,83**
CSF £12.36 CT £130.30 TOTE £2.20: £1.10, £3.40, £5.30; EX 15.80 Trifecta £237.90.
**Owner** B E Nielsen **Bred** Bjorn Nielsen **Trained** Upper Lambourn, Berks
■ Stewards' Enquiry : Stephen Craine one-day ban: failed to ride to draw (Oct 19)

**FOCUS**
The feature contest was a good handicap in which the tempo increased leaving the back straight.

## 6944 BET TOTESWINGER NURSERY H'CAP (TAPETA) 1m 141y
**8:00** (8:00) (Class 5) (0-75,71) 2-Y-O **£2,587** (£770; £384; £192) **Stalls** Low

Form

0051 **1** **Andretti**[10] 6662 2-9-4 68 ........ FrederikTylicki 6 74+
(Roger Varian) *a.p: pushed along over 2f out: rdn to ld ins fnl f: r.o wl* **1/1**[1]

5051 **2** 2 1/2 **Invincible Wish (IRE)**[19] 6413 2-8-4 54 ........ JamesSullivan 7 54
(Brian Ellison) *hld up: hdwy over 1f out: nt clr run fr over 1f out tl swtchd rt ins fnl f: r.o to go 2nd nr fin: no ch w wnr* **7/2**[2]

001 **3** 1/2 **Thewaythewindblows (IRE)**[58] 5098 2-9-2 69 ....(t) ThomasBrown(3) 2 68
(Daniel Kubler) *trckd ldr 7f out: rdn to ld and hung lft over 1f out: hdd ins fnl f: styd on same pce* **9/1**[3]

333 **4** 1/2 **Siren's Cove**[33] 5973 2-8-10 67 ........ KieranShoemark(7) 8 65
(James Tate) *awkward leaving stalls: hld up: nt clr run over 1f out: swtchd rt and r.o ins fnl f: nt trble ldrs* **7/2**[2]

2316 **5** 1 3/4 **Spindle (IRE)**[52] 5306 2-9-7 71 ........ LiamKeniry 3 65
(Mark Usher) *led at stdy pce tl qcknd over 2f out: rdn and hdd over 1f out: no ex ins fnl f* **12/1**

404 **6** 2 1/4 **Horsetracker**[7] 6769 2-8-12 62 ........ StevieDonohoe 1 52
(Ian Williams) *trckd ldrs: racd keenly: cl up whn hmpd 1f out: nt rcvr* **16/1**

1m 52.24s (2.14) **Going Correction** 0.0s/f (Stan) **6** Ran SP% **118.0**
Speed ratings (Par 95): **90,87,87,86,85 83**
CSF £5.25 CT £20.13 TOTE £1.90: £1.50, £2.70; EX 6.20 Trifecta £27.60.
**Owner** Nurlan Bizakov **Bred** Hesmonds Stud Ltd **Trained** Newmarket, Suffolk
■ Stewards' Enquiry : Liam Keniry one-day ban: careless riding (Oct 19)

**FOCUS**
A modest nursery handicap, run at a muddling tempo.

## 6945 BET TOTETRIFECTA FILLIES' H'CAP (TAPETA) 1m 141y
**8:30** (8:31) (Class 4) (0-85,82) 3-Y-O+ **£5,175** (£1,540; £769; £384) **Stalls** Low

Form RPR

1401 **1** **Fruit Pastille**[21] 6337 3-8-5 74 ........(b) CharlieBennett(7) 4 85
(Hughie Morrison) *s.i.s: sn pushed along and prom: chsd ldr over 6f out: rdn to ld over 2f out: clr fr over 1f out* **7/2**[1]

5421 **2** 2 1/2 **Water Queen**[23] 6247 3-8-13 75 ........(p) LiamJones 7 80
(William Haggas) *prom: n.m.r and lost pl 7f out: rdn over 1f out: r.o ins fnl f: wnt 2nd nr fin: no ch w wnr* **5/1**[3]

4230 **3** *nk* **History Book (IRE)**[9] 6681 4-9-7 82 ........ CamHardie(3) 8 85
(Charlie Appleby) *hld up in tch: rdn to chse wnr over 1f out: styd on same pce ins fnl f* **5/1**[3]

5602 **4** 1/2 **Oddysey (IRE)**[16] 6490 5-9-10 82 ........ DavidNolan 5 84
(Michael Dods) *hld up: pushed along and nt clr run over 3f out: r.o ins fnl f: nvr nrr* **10/1**

3634 **5** 1 1/2 **Dalmarella Dancer (IRE)**[47] 5505 3-8-8 70 ........(p) BenCurtis 9 70
(K R Burke) *hld up: hdwy 6f out: rdn over 1f out: styd on same pce fnl f* **10/1**

1225 **6** 3 1/4 **Waveguide (IRE)**[84] 4182 5-8-11 76 ........ GeorgeBuckell(7) 1 67
(David Simcock) *led 6f: wknd ins fnl f* **9/1**

1043 **7** 3 **Polar Eyes**[49] 5448 3-9-3 79 ........ RichardKingscote 6 64
(Tom Dascombe) *s.i.s: hld up: rdn over 1f out: n.d* **4/1**[2]

431 **8** 2 **Brisk**[11] 6638 3-8-10 72 ........ JFEgan 2 53
(David Evans) *chsd ldrs: rdn over 3f out: n.m.r and wknd over 2f out* **22/1**

0525 **9** 1/2 **Outbacker (IRE)**[13] 6578 3-8-10 72 ........ JoeFanning 3 52
(Mark Johnston) *prom: n.m.r and lost pl 6f out: hdwy over 2f out: wknd over 1f out* **14/1**

1m 48.44s (-1.66) **Going Correction** 0.0s/f (Stan)
**WFA** 3 from 4yo+ 4lb **9** Ran SP% **114.8**
Speed ratings (Par 102): **107,104,104,104,102 99,97,95,94**
CSF £20.94 CT £87.00 TOTE £6.00: £2.00, £2.40, £2.40; EX 27.50 Trifecta £100.30.
**Owner** The Caledonian Racing Society **Bred** M E Broughton **Trained** East Ilsley, Berks

**FOCUS**
A fair fillies' handicap, run at an even tempo.

## 6946 COLLECT TOTEPOOL WINNINGS AT BETFRED SHOPS H'CAP (TAPETA) (DIV II) 1m 1f 103y
**9:00** (9:01) (Class 6) (0-55,55) 3-Y-O **£2,264** (£673; £336; £168) **Stalls** Low

Form RPR

6440 **1** **Stoneham**[60] 5005 3-8-13 50 ........ CharlesBishop(3) 6 55
(Mick Channon) *hld up: hdwy and nt clr run over 1f out: r.o u.p to ld nr fin* **20/1**

0020 **2** *nk* **Sarlat**[11] 6647 3-8-9 46 ........ AmyScott(3) 1 50
(Mark Brisbourne) *mid-div: hdwy over 2f out: rdn to ld ins fnl f: hdd nr fin* **33/1**

0445 **3** *hd* **Little Flo**[26] 6193 3-9-4 52 ........ LiamJones 2 56
(Brendan Powell) *hld up: hdwy over 1f out: rdn and n.m.r ins fnl f: r.o* **14/1**

0004 **4** *nk* **Noble Reach**[17] 6454 3-8-9 48 ........ JordanNason(5) 5 51
(Lawrence Mullaney) *a.p: rdn over 2f out: ev ch ins fnl f: styd on* **50/1**

0043 **5** 1/2 **Silken Waters**[37] 5865 3-9-5 53 ........ GeorgeBaker 12 55
(Eve Johnson Houghton) *chsd ldr tl led 2f out: rdn and hdd ins fnl f: no ex nr fin* **3/1**[1]

0000 **6** 1 1/2 **Scariff Hornet (IRE)**[107] 3389 3-9-1 54 ........ JoshBaudains(5) 9 53
(Sylvester Kirk) *hld up: hdwy over 2f out: rdn and hung lft ins fnl f: styd on* **100/1**

5505 **7** *nk* **Focail Mear**[17] 6454 3-8-10 47 ........ RyanPowell(3) 7 45
(John Ryan) *hld up: pushed along over 3f out: hdwy over 1f out: styd on* **16/1**

-500 **8** 1 1/4 **Percys Princess**[32] 6015 3-8-13 47 ........ SteveDrowne 4 42
(Pat Murphy) *s.i.s: hld up: rdn over 2f out: r.o ins fnl f: nvr nrr* **100/1**

0-60 **9** 1 1/2 **Wunderkind (USA)**[11] 6628 3-8-12 46 oh1 ........ LukeMorris 8 38
(Sir Mark Prescott Bt) *chsd ldrs: rdn over 2f out: no ex fnl f* **5/1**[2]

4050 **10** *nk* **Danglydontask**[26] 6193 3-9-4 52 ........(b) HayleyTurner 3 44
(David Arbuthnot) *hld up: rdn over 3f out: nt trble ldrs* **33/1**

5262 **11** 2 **Maid Of Tuscany (IRE)**[19] 6394 3-9-7 55 ........(p) LiamKeniry 11 43
(Neil Mulholland) *mid-div: hdwy on outer over 2f out: wknd over 1f out* **7/1**[3]

0525 **12** 6 **Key To Your Heart**[19] 6407 3-9-2 53 ........(p) CamHardie(3) 13 28
(Hughie Morrison) *chsd ldrs: rdn over 2f out: wknd over 1f out* **3/1**[1]

4660 **13** 7 **Spinning Cobblers**[52] 5321 3-9-5 53 ........(v[1]) RichardKingscote 10 13
(Stuart Williams) *led: rdn and hdd 2f out: hung lft and wknd over 1f out* **14/1**

2m 1.76s (0.96) **Going Correction** 0.0s/f (Stan) **13** Ran SP% **113.0**
Speed ratings (Par 99): **95,94,94,94,93 92,92,91,89,89 87,82,76**
CSF £507.94 CT £9124.03 TOTE £12.10: £3.60, £5.30, £3.90; EX 97.20 Trifecta £2305.20 Part won..
**Owner** Norman Court Stud **Bred** Norman Court Stud **Trained** West Ilsley, Berks

**FOCUS**
The concluding contest was the second division of a moderate 3yo handicap, and the comparative winning time was significantly slower.
T/Plt: £31.40 to a £1 stake. Pool of £68,489.89 - 1,590.27 winning tickets. T/Qpdt: £5.70 to a £1 stake. Pool of £11,372.70 - 1,471.94 winning tickets. CR

6947 - 6948a (Foreign Racing) - See Raceform Interactive

6772

# BELMONT PARK (L-H)
Saturday, October 4

**OFFICIAL GOING: Dirt: sloppy; turf: soft**

## 6949a HILL PRINCE STKS (GRADE 3) (TURF) 1m 1f (T)
**10:02** (10:02) 3-Y-O
**£180,722** (£60,240; £30,120; £15,060; £9,036; £1,506)

RPR

**1** **Ring Weekend (USA)**[33] 3-8-6 ........(b) IOrtizJr 1 107
(H Graham Motion, U.S.A) **37/20**[1]

**2** 1/2 **Daddy's Kid (USA)** 3-8-4 ........(b) TDunkelberger 9 104
(Reid Nagle, U.S.A) **40/1**

**3** 3/4 **Smooth Daddy (USA)**[33] 3-8-4 ........(b) JLOrtiz 4 102
(Thomas Albertrani, U.S.A) **132/10**

**4** 1 **Pumpkin Rumble (USA)**[21] 3-8-4 ........ RSantanaJr 6 100
(Danny Gargan, U.S.A) **45/1**

**5** *nk* **Blacktype (FR)**[123] 3-8-5 ow1 ........ CHVelasquez 3 101
(Christophe Clement, U.S.A) **26/5**[3]

**6** 4 1/4 **Mr Speaker (USA)**[42] 5710 3-8-11 ........ JLezcano 8 98
(Claude McGaughey III, U.S.A) **43/20**[2]

**7** *nse* **Sheldon (USA)**[49] 5458 3-8-4 ........(b) JJCastellano 5 91
(James J Toner, U.S.A) **43/5**

**8** 2 1/4 **Sloane Avenue (USA)**[38] 5824 3-8-4 ........ JAlvarado 2 86
(Jeremy Noseda) **143/10**

**9** 9 **Cabral (USA)**[38] 3-8-4 ........ JulienAuge 7 67
(C Ferland, France) **114/10**

1m 55.56s (115.56) **9** Ran SP% **119.6**

**Owner** St Elias Stable & West Point Thoroughbreds Inc **Bred** Gainesway Thoroughbreds Ltd **Trained** USA



The Form Book, Raceform Ltd, Newbury, RG14 5SJ

# FRANKFURT (L-H)

Saturday, October 4

**OFFICIAL GOING: Turf: good**

## 6950a QUOTENHAUS FRANKFURT - BBAG AUKTIONSRENNEN (CONDITIONS) (2YO FILLIES) (TURF) 1m

3:10 (3:10) 2-Y-O

£20,833 (£9,166; £5,000; £3,333; £1,666; £1,666)

RPR

1 **Attraction (GER)**[83] 2-9-2 0........................ SHellyn 4 81
(J D Hillis, Germany) **164/10**

2 3 **Night Melody (IRE)** 2-9-2 0........................ AStarke 6 74
(P Schiergen, Germany) **5/2**[1]

3 hd **Peri (GER)** 2-9-2 0........................ EPedroza 7 74
(A Wohler, Germany) **19/5**[3]

4 1 1/4 **Hot Shot (IRE)** 2-9-2 0........................(b) FranciscoDaSilva 9 71
(P Harley, Germany) **89/10**

5 4 **Aluette (FR)** 2-9-2 0........................ BGanbat 8 61
(S Smrczek, Germany) **172/10**

6 3 **Princess Alba (GER)** 2-9-2 0........................ StefanieHofer 3 55
(Mario Hofer, Germany) **17/2**

7 1 3/4 **Saving Grace (GER)** 2-9-2 0........................ FilipMinarik 10 51
(Waldemar Hickst, Germany) **159/10**

8 5 **Black Rose (GER)**[20] 6385 2-9-2 0........................ MartinSeidl 5 39
(Frau Marion Rotering, Germany) **175/10**

9 1 3/4 **Adele (GER)**[35] 5910 2-9-2 0........................ AHelfenbein 2 35+
(Mark Johnston) *sn prom on inner: rdn and lost pl bef st: sn btn: eased fnl f* **16/5**[2]

10 4 **Augusta (GER)** 2-9-2 0........................ APietsch 1 26
(Waldemar Hickst, Germany) **26/5**

1m 40.4s (100.40) 10 Ran SP% 132.5

WIN (incl. 10 euro stake): 174. PLACES: 33, 22, 16. SF: 571.

**Owner** Frau J Stadler **Bred** Frau Jeanette Stadler **Trained** Germany

6951 - 6953a (Foreign Racing) - See Raceform Interactive

6569

# LONGCHAMP (R-H)

Saturday, October 4

**OFFICIAL GOING: Turf: good**

## 6954a QATAR PRIX CHAUDENAY (GROUP 2) (3YO) (TURF) 1m 7f

1:30 (1:30) 3-Y-O £95,000 (£36,666; £17,500; £11,666; £5,833)

RPR

1 **Auvray (FR)**[27] 6183 3-9-2 0........................ GregoryBenoist 1 109
(E Lellouche, France) *w ldrs early: sn midfield: rdn 2f out: clsd and chal ent fnl f: styd on wl and led fnl 120yds: pushed out firmly and asserted* **11/2**[3]

2 1/2 **Vent De Force**[42] 5691 3-9-2 0........................ UmbertoRispoli 5 108
(Hughie Morrison) *a.p: rdn to chal and jnd ldr 2f out: led narrowly ent fnl f: styd on wl but hdd fnl 120yds and hld* **14/1**

3 shd **Baino Hope (FR)**[48] 5481 3-8-13 0........................ IoritzMendizabal 4 105
(J-C Rouget, France) *midfield: rdn 2f out: edgd rt u.p over 1f out: styd on wl fnl f and almost snatched 2nd post: nt quite pce of wnr* **7/2**[2]

4 1 3/4 **Rio Tigre (IRE)**[34] 5962 3-9-2 0........................ RaphaelMarchelli 3 106
(A Fabre, France) *w ldrs early: led briefly bef 1/2-way and remained prom once hdd: 3rd on rail 3f out: rdn 2f out: outpcd by ldrs fnl f: styd on but wl hld* **16/1**

5 hd **Doumaran (FR)**[27] 6183 3-9-2 0........................ GeraldMosse 2 106
(A De Royer-Dupre, France) *dwlt and pushed along in rr early: sn midfield: hdwy to ld bef 1/2-way: rdn and jnd 2f out: jst hdd but stl ev ch ent fnl f: kpt on tl no ex and fdd towards fin* **9/1**

6 1 1/4 **Glaring**[27] 6183 3-9-2 0........................ FlavienPrat 6 104
(A Fabre, France) *hld up: rdn 2f out: sn outpcd by ldrs: styd on fnl f but nvr threatened* **11/2**[3]

7 3/4 **Kaldera (GER)**[13] 6589 3-8-13 0........................ EddyHardouin 8 100+
(P Harley, Germany) *hld up in rr: rdn in last 2f out: sn outpcd by ldrs: styd on fnl f but nvr threatened* **8/1**

8 1 3/4 **Theme Astral (FR)**[27] 6183 3-9-2 0........................ ThierryJarnet 7 101+
(P Bary, France) *hld up in rr: rdn 2f out: outpcd and btn fnl f: nvr threatened* **20/1**

9 2 **Vazira (FR)**[46] 5545 3-8-13 0........................ ChristopheSoumillon 9 95
(A De Royer-Dupre, France) *difficult to load: t.k.h: sn tacked across fr wdst draw and w ldrs: midfield in tch fr bef 1/2-way: rdn and effrt over 2f out: no ex and btn over 1f out: wknd and dropped to last fnl f: eased* **3/1**[1]

3m 10.86s (-5.14) **Going Correction** +0.05s/f (Good) 9 Ran SP% 116.4

Speed ratings: **115,114,114,113,113 112,112,111,110**

WIN (incl. 1 euro stake): 6.60. PLACES: 2.00, 3.00, 1.50. DF: 39.90. SF: 81.00.

**Owner** G Augustin-Normand & Mme E Vidal **Bred** Franklin Finance S.A. & Mme E Vidal **Trained** Lamorlaye, France

**FOCUS**

Good ground was provided for the opening day of the Arc meeting. Several of them had a go at setting the pace in this 3yo staying event and a trio of the last-time-out winners dominated.

## 6955a QATAR PRIX DANIEL WILDENSTEIN (GROUP 2) (3YO+) (TURF) 1m

2:08 (2:08) 3-Y-O+ £95,000 (£36,666; £17,500; £11,666; £5,833)

RPR

1 **Solow**[34] 5960 4-9-1 0........................ OlivierPeslier 7 118+
(F Head, France) *hld up on outside: shkn up and hdwy over 1f out: qcknd to ld ins fnl f: pushed out: comf* **5/2**[1]

2 1/2 **Veda (FR)**[125] 2817 3-8-8 0........................ ChristopheSoumillon 3 113
(A De Royer-Dupre, France) *t.k.h early: prom: smooth hdwy 2f out: rdn to ld 1f out: hdd ins fnl f: kpt on: nt pce of wnr* **9/2**[2]

3 1 1/2 **Sommerabend**[20] 6382 7-9-3 0........................ TheoBachelot 12 116
(M Rulec, Germany) *t.k.h: pressed ldr: drvn to ld briefly over 1f out: kpt on same pce ins fnl f* **12/1**

4 shd **Kenhope (FR)**[21] 6351 4-8-11 0........................ Christophe-PatriceLemaire 2 109
(H-A Pantall, France) *hld up on ins: rdn: hdwy and swtchd lft over 1f out: kpt on ins fnl f: nvr able to chal* **17/2**

5 1 **Affaire Solitaire (IRE)**[46] 4-9-1 0........................ ThierryJarnet 1 111
(P Khozian, France) *trckd ldrs: effrt whn nt clr run briefly over 1f out: sn rdn: kpt on same pce ins fnl f* **50/1**

6 2 **High Spirit (IRE)**[30] 4-9-1 0........................(b) AntoineHamelin 10 106
(Mme Pia Brandt, France) *s.i.s: hld up: rdn and plenty to do 2f out: kpt on fnl f: nvr able to chal* **50/1**

7 nk **Matorio (FR)**[90] 4008 4-8-11 0........................ FabriceVeron 6 102
(H-A Pantall, France) *t.k.h: hld up towards rr: drvn over 2f out: styd on ins fnl f: no imp* **25/1**

8 shd **La Hoguette (FR)**[82] 4278 3-8-8 0........................ GregoryBenoist 14 102
(J-C Rouget, France) *t.k.h: hld up midfield on outside: effrt and hung rt over 1f out: outpcd fnl f* **5/1**[3]

9 nse **Decathlete (USA)**[20] 6382 3-8-11 0........................ FlavienPrat 4 104
(A Fabre, France) *t.k.h in midfield: drvn and hung rt over 1f out: btn fnl f* **20/1**

10 nk **Limario (GER)**[13] 4-9-1 0........................ AdriedeVries 8 105
(A Savujev, Czech Republic) *led tl drvn and hdd over 1f out: sn wknd* **33/1**

11 nk **Zhiyi (USA)**[30] 4-9-1 0........................ StephanePasquier 9 104
(P Bary, France) *hld up and bhd: drvn along on outside 2f out: nvr rchd ldrs* **8/1**

12 2 **Baltic Knight (IRE)**[30] 6060 4-9-1 0........................ GeraldMosse 5 99
(Richard Hannon) *hld up on ins: drvn along over 2f out: sn no imp: eased whn no ch fnl f* **20/1**

13 7 **Pinturicchio (IRE)**[55] 5223 6-9-1 0........................ AnthonyCrastus 11 83
(E Lellouche, France) *s.i.s: hld up: drvn along over 2f out: nvr on terms* **16/1**

14 6 **Emirate's Girl (ARG)**[223] 4-9-0 0........................ ThierryThulliez 13 69
(Takashi Kodama, Ire) *prom: drvn along over 2f out: wknd qckly wl over 1f out* **25/1**

1m 36.59s (-1.81) **Going Correction** +0.05s/f (Good)

**WFA** 3 from 4yo+ 3lb 14 Ran SP% 122.7

Speed ratings: **111,110,109,108,107 105,105,105,105,105 104,102,95,89**

WIN (incl. 1 euro stake): 2.80. PLACES: 1.60, 2.10, 3.20. DF: 8.50. SF: 11.90.

**Owner** Wertheimer & Frere **Bred** Wertheimer Et Frere **Trained** France

**FOCUS**

Run at a fair clip, this decent Group 2 was won in taking style by the highly progressive Solow.

## 6956a QATAR PRIX DE ROYALLIEU (GROUP 2) (3YO+ FILLIES & MARES) (TURF) 1m 4f 110y

2:40 (2:40) 3-Y-O+ £118,750 (£45,833; £21,875; £14,583; £7,291)

RPR

1 **Frine (IRE)**[49] 5462 4-9-1 0........................ GeraldMosse 11 110+
(C Laffon-Parias, France) *hld up in last pl: plld out over 2f out: drvn and hdwy over 1f out: kpt on wl fnl f to ld towards fin* **16/1**

2 snk **Mayhem (IRE)**[19] 6419 3-8-8 0 ow1........................ OlivierPeslier 12 111
(P Sogorb, France) *reluctant to enter stalls: t.k.h: cl up: led over 2f out: sn hrd pressed and rdn: kpt on fnl f: hdd towards fin* **4/1**[2]

3 hd **Zarshana (IRE)**[48] 5479 3-8-8 0 ow1........................(b) ChristopheSoumillon 8 111
(A De Royer-Dupre, France) *hld up: stdy hdwy to chse ldrs over 2f out: effrt and drvn over 1f out: ev ch wl ins fnl f: hld cl home* **9/4**[1]

4 2 1/2 **Shared Account**[25] 6218 4-9-1 0........................(b[1]) StephanePasquier 9 106
(P Bary, France) *s.i.s: hld up: hdwy to chse ldrs over 4f out: effrt and ev ch over 2f out: sn rdn: kpt on same pce fnl f* **10/1**

5 1 **All At Sea**[33] 5992 3-8-7 0........................ Jean-BernardEyquem 1 104
(A Fabre, France) *t.k.h: chsd ldrs on ins: nt clr run and lost pl 4f out: swtchd lft and rallied over 1f out: kpt on fnl f: nvr able to chal* **9/2**[3]

6 2 **Abys (FR)**[51] 5369 4-9-1 0........................ AntoineHamelin 6 101
(Mme Pia Brandt, France) *t.k.h: hld up: rdn along and hdwy over 2f out: no further imp fr over 1f out* **25/1**

7 3 **Euphrasia (IRE)**[41] 5742 5-9-1 0........................ GaryCarroll 10 96
(Joseph G Murphy, Ire) *in tch: drvn along and outpcd 2f out: sn n.d: btn fnl f* **16/1**

8 4 1/2 **Your Game (FR)**[32] 3-8-7 0........................ FlavienPrat 3 89
(A Fabre, France) *t.k.h: led at modest gallop 5f: cl up tl drvn and wknd fr 2f out* **20/1**

9 1 1/2 **Savanne (IRE)**[49] 5462 3-8-7 0........................ RaphaelMarchelli 7 86
(A Fabre, France) *racd keenly: cl up: led after 5f tl rdn and hdd over 2f out: sn wknd* **5/1**

10 3 **Berlin Berlin**[27] 6180 5-9-1 0........................ AdriedeVries 2 82
(Markus Klug, Germany) *hld up: drvn and struggling wl over 2f out: sn btn* **16/1**

2m 37.29s (-2.61) **Going Correction** +0.05s/f (Good)

**WFA** 3 from 4yo+ 7lb 10 Ran SP% 121.0

Speed ratings: **110,109,109,108,107 106,104,101,100,99**

WIN (incl. 1 euro stake): 13.00. PLACES: 2.60,1.60, 1.40. DF: 30.10. SF: 85.40.

**Owner** Duke Of Alburquerque **Bred** Duc D'Alburquerque **Trained** Chantilly, France

**FOCUS**

Although run at a steady gallop early, three of the first four home were held up in rear.

## 6957a QNB PRIX DOLLAR (GROUP 2) (3YO+) (TURF) 1m 1f 165y

3:15 (3:15) 3-Y-O+ £95,000 (£36,666; £17,500; £11,666; £5,833)

RPR

1 hd **Fractional (IRE)**[15] 6592 5-9-0 0........................ RaphaelMarchelli 4 110+
(A Fabre, France) *t.k.h: hld up in tch: effrt and hdwy over 1f out: disp ld ins fnl f: bmpd nr fin: jst hld: fin 2nd: awrdd r* **10/3**[2]

2 1 1/4 **Hippy (FR)**[41] 5742 6-8-10 0........................ ThierryJarnet 2 106
(E Libaud, France) *t.k.h: in tch: effrt and drvn over 1f out: kpt on ins fnl f: fin 3rd: plcd 2nd* **33/1**

3 hd **Calling Out (FR)**[14] 6571 3-8-9 0........................ GregoryBenoist 1 110
(J-P Gauvin, France) *t.k.h: trckd ldrs: effrt and rdn over 1f out: kpt on same pce ins fnl f: fin 4th: plcd 3rd* **16/1**

4 snk **Planetaire**[15] 6592 3-8-9 0........................ FlavienPrat 3 109
(C Laffon-Parias, France) *racd keenly: cl up: drvn over 1f out: one pce whn short of room wl ins fnl f: sn no ex: fin 5th: plcd 4th* **12/1**[3]

5 **Cirrus Des Aigles (FR)**[119] 2988 8-9-6 0........................ ChristopheSoumillon 6 115+
(Mme C Barande-Barbe, France) *led at stdy pce: rdn and qcknd over 1f out: hrd pressed whn hung lft and bmpd rival nr fin: all out: fin first: disqualified and plcd 5th* **1/2**[1]

6 1 1/2 **Pilote (IRE)**[49] 5461 4-9-0 0........................ OlivierPeslier 7 106
(A Fabre, France) *hld up in last pl in slowly run r: rdn and effrt over 1f out: no imp ins fnl f* **20/1**

2m 5.78s (2.88) **Going Correction** +0.05s/f (Good)

**WFA** 3 from 4yo+ 5lb 6 Ran SP% 111.0

Speed ratings: **89,88,88,88,90 87**

WIN (incl. 1 euro stake): 3.20. PLACES: 2.50, 6.80. SF: 52.10.

**Owner** Godolphin SNC **Bred** Darley Stud Management Co, Ltd **Trained** Chantilly, France

**FOCUS**
The result was changed around after original first past the post Cirrus Des Aigles gave Fractional, who was awarded the race, a bump nearing the line.

## 6958a PRIX HORSE RACING ABROAD (CLAIMER) (2YO) (TURF) 1m
**4:50** (4:50) 2-Y-O **£11,250** (£4,500; £3,375; £2,250; £1,125)

RPR
1 **Ideal Approach (IRE)**[79] 2-8-11 0 ........ CristianDemuro 7 76
(M Delcher Sanchez, France) **41/1**
2 *3/4* **Dulciadargent (FR)**[24] 6244 2-8-11 0 ........ ThierryThulliez 6 74
(N Clement, France) **5/1**[2]
3 *1 1/2* **Pink (FR)**[31] 2-8-8 0 ........ AurelienLemaitre 1 68
(S Kobayashi, France) **22/1**
4 *1 1/2* **Cheeky Lady (FR)**[52] 5329 2-8-9 0 ........ MllePaulineDominois(4) 15 69+
(F Rohaut, France) **9/1**
5 *1* **Portenio (FR)**[24] 6244 2-9-1 0 ........(p) MarcLerner 4 69
(C Lerner, France) **32/1**
6 *nk* **Kailong (FR)**[31] 2-8-13 0 ........ ThierryJarnet 2 66
(E Leenders, France) **11/1**
7 *hd* **Whole Lotta Love (FR)**[44] 5619 2-8-8 0 ........ FlavienPrat 3 61
(Y Barberot, France) **9/1**
8 *1 3/4* **Patong (FR)**[63] 4932 2-9-6 0 ........ UmbertoRispoli 16 69
(Y Gourraud, France) **17/1**
9 *hd* **Kunst Basel (FR)**[38] 5844 2-8-8 0 ........ FabriceVeron 10 56
(H-A Pantall, France) **22/1**
10 *3* **Oui Monsieur (FR)**[119] 3029 2-9-2 0 ........(p) EddyHardouin 12 58
(Robert Collet, France) **42/1**
11 *1 1/2* **Chester Deal**[24] 6245 2-9-2 0 ........ ThomasHenderson 14 54
(Jo Hughes) *w ldrs: led narrowly 3f out: rdn and hdd 2f out: sn no ex and btn: wknd: eased fnl 100yds* **10/1**
12 *1 1/2* **Jialing River (FR)**[45] 5590 2-8-8 0 ........ RonanThomas 8 43
(R Chotard, France) **66/1**
13 *nk* **Hey Joe (FR)**[42] 5706 2-9-6 0 ........(b[1]) AdriedeVries 9 54
(Mario Hofer, Germany) **34/1**
14 *snk* **Asantasana (FR)**[20] 2-8-8 0 ........ Jean-BernardEyquem 17 42
(C Ferland, France) **11/1**
15 *6* **Raiponce (FR)** 2-8-9 0 ow1 ........ ChristopheSoumillon 5 29
(C Lerner, France) **8/1**[3]
16 *dist* **Chicago Bere (FR)**[10] 6660 2-9-2 0 ........ OlivierPeslier 11
(Richard Hannon) *prom early: sn midfield: lost pl qckly and dropped to rr over 3f out: wknd and wl btn into st: eased and t.o* **19/5**[1]

1m 40.67s (2.27) **16 Ran SP% 120.7**
WIN (incl. 1 euro stake): 41.80. PLACES: 9.80, 2.40, 6.30. DF: 92.60. SF: 296.90.
**Owner** Maldon Racing SL **Bred** Wardstown Stud Ltd **Trained** France

6959 - 6962a (Foreign Racing) - See Raceform Interactive

# 5866 TIPPERARY (L-H)
Sunday, October 5

**OFFICIAL GOING: Flat course - good; jumps courses - good to yielding**

## 6963a COOLMORE STUD HOME OF CHAMPIONS CONCORDE STKS (GROUP 3) 7f 100y
**2:40** (2:41) 3-Y-O+ **£36,562** (£10,687; £5,062; £1,687)

RPR
1 **Big Break**[108] 3412 4-9-2 105 ........ LeighRoche 8 106
(D K Weld, Ire) *sn trckd ldrs in 3rd: clsd to press ldrs over 2f out: led over 1f out: strly pressed and kpt on wl* **3/1**[2]
2 *1/2* **Brendan Brackan (IRE)**[22] 6350 5-9-5 111 ........ GaryCarroll 1 108
(G M Lyons, Ire) *sn led: rdn fr 2f out: hdd over 1f out: rallied wl* **3/1**[2]
3 *1 1/4* **Sruthan (IRE)**[52] 5361 4-9-8 111 ........ ChrisHayes 10 108
(P D Deegan, Ire) *chsd ldrs in 5th: rdn along over 2f out: strly rdn into 3rd ins fnl 100yds: nt rch principals* **2/1**[1]
4 *nk* **Some Spirit (IRE)**[38] 5869 3-9-0 100 ........ ColinKeane 4 100
(G M Lyons, Ire) *bit slowly away and racd towards rr tl hdwy under 2f out: wnt 4th 1f out: kpt on same pce* **5/1**[3]
5 *4* **Dark Skies (IRE)**[46] 5584 3-9-0 88 ........(p) ConnorKing 5 90
(David Wachman, Ire) *sn trckd ldr in cl 2nd: rdn along in 3rd 1f out: wknd fnl 150yds* **66/1**
6 *3/4* **Booker**[147] 2186 3-9-0 98 ........(p) NGMcCullagh 7 88
(David Wachman, Ire) *sn chsd ldrs in 4th: nt qckn ent fnl f: kpt on one pce* **18/1**
7 *1 1/4* **Slipper Orchid (IRE)**[16] 6525 5-9-2 97 ........ ShaneFoley 3 86
(M Halford, Ire) *hld up: pushed along under 3f out: no imp appr fnl f* **20/1**
8 *2 1/2* **Leitir Mor (IRE)**[22] 6352 4-9-5 106 ........(tp) KevinManning 2 83
(J S Bolger, Ire) *sn in rr: rdn along 2f out: sn no imp* **14/1**

1m 36.82s (96.82)
**WFA** 3 from 4yo+ 2lb **8 Ran SP% 118.2**
CSF £12.99 TOTE £3.90: £1.20, £1.02, £1.40; DF 11.40 Trifecta £20.20.
**Owner** K Abdullah **Bred** Juddmonte Farms Ltd **Trained** Curragh, Co Kildare

**FOCUS**
A fairly compact field, but still a solid renewal of this Group 3, with last year's winner and beaten favourite in opposition.

6964 - (Foreign Racing) - See Raceform Interactive

# 6377 DUSSELDORF (R-H)
Sunday, October 5

**OFFICIAL GOING: Turf: good**

## 6965a GROSSER PREIS DER LANDESHAUPTSTADT DUSSELDORF (GROUP 3) (3YO+) (TURF) 1m 110y
**3:20** (3:20) 3-Y-O+
**£26,666** (£9,166; £4,583; £2,500; £1,666; £1,250)

RPR
1 **Flamingo Star (GER)**[34] 4-9-2 0 ........(b) SHellyn 3 115
(Waldemar Hickst, Germany) *mde all: rdn whn chal fr 1 1/2f out: drvn clr ins fnl f: won easing down* **7/2**
2 *3* **Boomshackerlacker (IRE)**[65] 4851 4-9-2 0 ........ FergusSweeney 1 108
(George Baker) *t.k.h: trckd ldng pair: rdn to chal eventual wnr 1 1/2f out: outpcd by wnr ins fnl f* **11/2**
3 *nk* **Peace At Last (IRE)**[32] 6054 4-9-2 0 ........ AurelienLemaitre 6 107
(H-A Pantall, France) *disp 4th on inner: rdn and styd on fr over 1f out: nvr plcd to chal* **29/10**[2]
4 *3* **Felician (GER)**[21] 6384 6-9-2 0 ........ RobertHavlin 7 101
(Ferdinand J Leve, Germany) *w.w in rr on outer: rdn and no imp fr 1 1/2f out: plugged on at one pce fnl f* **23/10**[1]
5 *nk* **Zazou (GER)**[36] 5938 7-9-2 0 ........ APietsch 5 100
(Waldemar Hickst, Germany) *disp 4th on outer: nt qckn whn asked fr 2f out: plugged on at one pce fnl f* **16/5**[3]
6 *6* **High Duty**[70] 3-8-13 0 ........ AStarke 4 89
(P Schiergen, Germany) *trckd ldr on outer: rdn and wknd over 1 1/2f out* **56/10**

1m 45.09s (-2.49)
**WFA** 3 from 4yo+ 3lb **6 Ran SP% 132.5**
WIN (incl. 10 euro stake): 45. PLACES: 25, 32. SF: 361.
**Owner** Frau Marlene Haller **Bred** Frau Marlene Haller **Trained** Germany

# 6954 LONGCHAMP (R-H)
Sunday, October 5

**OFFICIAL GOING: Turf: good**

## 6966a QNB PRIX DE L'ABBAYE DE LONGCHAMP (GROUP 1) (2YO+) (TURF) 5f (S)
**1:00** (1:00) 2-Y-O+ **£166,658** (£66,675; £33,337; £16,654; £8,341)

RPR
1 **Move In Time**[21] 6378 6-9-11 0 ........ DanielTudhope 12 115
(David O'Meara) *chsd ldng gp: nt clr run over 1f out: rdn and r.o wl fnl f: led fnl stride* **25/1**
2 *hd* **Rangali**[21] 6378 3-9-11 0 ........ MickaelBarzalona 5 115
(H-A Pantall, France) *hld up in midfield: pushed along and clsd 2f out: drvn to ld between horses 1f out: hrd rdn and 1 l clr 100yds out: hdd fnl stride* **16/1**
3 *hd* **Moviesta (USA)**[29] 6134 4-9-11 0 ........ PaulMulrennan 4 115+
(Bryan Smart) *towards rr: moved into midfield 1/2-way: pushed along and hdwy on rail whn nt clr run under 1 1/2f out: stdd and eased off rail ins fnl f: drvn and r.o wl* **12/1**[3]
4 *hd* **Spirit Quartz (IRE)**[18] 6-9-11 0 ........(p) GregoryBenoist 18 113
(X Nakkachdji, France) *sn dropped in fr wd draw: settled in midfield: pushed along and hdwy 1 1/2f out: rdn and r.o wl fnl f* **100/1**
5 *3/4* **Mirza**[21] 6378 7-9-11 0 ........(p) FrankieDettori 10 110
(Rae Guest) *w.w towards rr: prog over 2f out: nt clr run and stdd 1 1/2f out: styd on fnl f: nrest at fin* **18/1**
6 *hd* **Take Cover**[15] 6549 7-9-11 0 ........ AdamKirby 3 110
(David C Griffiths) *chsd ldrs on inner: rdn to chal 1 1/2f out: one pce u.p fnl f* **10/1**[2]
7 *nk* **Sir Maximilian (IRE)**[21] 6371 5-9-11 0 ........ StevieDonohoe 15 109
(Tim Pitt) *chsd ldng pair: sltly outpcd over 2f out: kpt on again u.p fnl f* **40/1**
8 *nse* **Sole Power**[29] 6134 7-9-11 0 ........ RichardHughes 11 112+
(Edward Lynam, Ire) *w.w in midfield: hdwy and short of room 1 1/2f out: nt clr run appr fnl f: r.o fnl 100yds* **13/8**[1]
9 *nk* **Stepper Point**[21] 6371 5-9-11 0 ........(p) MartinDwyer 14 107
(William Muir) *disp ld: led over 2f out: hdd 1 1/2f out and rallied u.p: wknd wl ins fnl f* **12/1**[3]
10 *shd* **Catcall (FR)**[21] 6378 5-9-11 0 ........ OlivierPeslier 19 107
(P Sogorb, France) *midfield on outer: outpcd 1/2-way: hrd rdn fr 1 1/2f out: kpt on fnl f: nvr able to chal* **16/1**
11 *nk* **Goken (FR)**[42] 5741 2-8-7 0 ........ FabriceVeron 17 101
(H-A Pantall, France) *chsd ldng pair on outer: rdn to hold pl over 1 1/2f out: fdd ins fnl f* **33/1**
11 *dht* **Maarek**[29] 6134 7-9-11 0 ........ WayneLordan 7 114+
(Miss Evanna McCutcheon, Ire) *upset in stalls: rrd and missed break: in rr: hdwy 2f out: r.o fnl f: nvr in contention* **25/1**
13 *nk* **Guerre (USA)**[21] 6371 3-9-11 0 ........ JosephO'Brien 1 106
(A P O'Brien, Ire) *outpcd on fr last: hdwy 2f out: nt clr run and stopped riding 1 1/2f out: swtchd ins and styng on wl ins fnl f: nvr nrr* **22/1**
14 *snk* **Pearl Secret**[29] 6134 5-9-11 0 ........ JamieSpencer 13 104
(David Barron) *hld up towards rr on outer: nowhere to go fr over 1 1/2f out: nvr got a run* **20/1**
15 *hd* **Hot Streak (IRE)**[29] 6134 3-9-11 0 ........ OisinMurphy 9 107+
(Kevin Ryan) *chsd ldng pair: scrubbed along to chal over 2f out: led 1 1/2f out tl hdd 1f out: wknd fnl f* **14/1**
16 *3/4* **Cotai Glory**[23] 6286 2-8-7 0 ........ RyanMoore 16 96
(Charles Hills) *disp ld on outer: hdd over 2f out: wknd fnl f* **10/1**[2]
17 *snk* **Justineo**[28] 6167 5-9-11 0 ........ AndreaAtzeni 6 100
(Roger Varian) *chsd ldrs: lost pl over 1 1/2f out: wknd fnl f* **40/1**
18 *2 1/2* **Hamza (IRE)**[15] 6533 5-9-11 0 ........(b) PatSmullen 2 91
(Kevin Ryan) *midfield on rail: lost pl 2f out: bhd fnl f* **25/1**

56.42s (0.12) **Going Correction** +0.35s/f (Good) **18 Ran SP% 124.8**
**Speed ratings: 113,112,112,112,110 110,110,109,109,109 108,108,108,108,107 106,106,102**
WIN (incl. 1 euro stake): 31.60. PLACES: 7.90, 6.40, 8.10. DF: 174.30. SF: 377.90.
**Owner** A Turton, J Blackburn & R Bond **Bred** Bond Thoroughbred Corporation **Trained** Nawton, N Yorks

**FOCUS**
Minimal rain overnight and genuine good ground was provided. A typical running of this prestigious sprint, run in a flash and any number holding their chance, with it being hard to tell who had won as they crossed the line. A bunch finish, and the third and fourth help with the standard.

## 6967a TOTAL PRIX MARCEL BOUSSAC - CRITERIUM DES POULICHES (GROUP 1) (2YO FILLIES) (TURF) 1m
**1:35** (1:35) 2-Y-O **£142,850** (£57,150; £28,575; £14,275; £7,150)

RPR
1 **Found (IRE)**[21] 6372 2-8-11 0 ........ RyanMoore 6 115+
(A P O'Brien, Ire) *t.k.h: sn midfield in tch: rdn and hdwy to chal ent fnl f: led fnl 120yds: qcknd clr: pushed out: readily* **9/4**[1]
2 *2 1/2* **Ervedya (FR)**[42] 5741 2-8-11 0 ........ ChristopheSoumillon 12 109
(J-C Rouget, France) *got across fr wdst draw and led: hdd 5f out and trckd ldr: chal gng wl 2f out and sn bk in front: rdn and strly pressed ent fnl f: hdd fnl 120yds: kpt on but nt pce of wnr and hld* **3/1**[2]

**3** 1½ **Jack Naylor**[35] 5953 2-8-11 0................................ FMBerry 8 106
(Mrs John Harrington, Ire) *midfield in tch: pushed along and effrt to chal on outer 2f out: edgd rt: 3rd ent fnl f: kpt on but nt pce of front pair* **6/1**[3]

**4** 1¼ **Malabar**[21] 6372 2-8-11 0................................ RichardHughes 3 106+
(Mick Channon) *hld up in last pair on inner: last 3f out: gng wl but stl in rr and looking for room over 1f out: rdn ent fnl f: r.o wl and wnt 4th cl home: nvr nrr* **13/2**

**5** snk **Queen Bee (FR)**[43] 5707 2-8-11 0................................ GregoryBenoist 11 103
(E Lellouche, France) *dwlt sltly and hld up in last pair: rdn and hdwy on outer over 1f out: r.o fnl f but nvr threatened: dropped to 5th cl home* **25/1**

**6** nk **Night Of Light (IRE)**[26] 6219 2-8-11 0................................ StephanePasquier 2 102
(P Bary, France) *plld hrd: broke wl and prom on inner early: sn midfield in tch: looking for room 2f out: rdn over 1f out: outpcd by ldrs fnl f and sn wl hld: kpt on but dropped to 6th cl home* **16/1**

**7** hd **Makweti**[32] 2-8-11 0................................ CristianDemuro 4 102
(F Doumen, France) *hld up in midfield: pushed along and looking for room over 2f out: rdn over 1f out: kpt on same pce fnl f and nvr threatened* **66/1**

**8** 1¾ **Light In Paris (IRE)**[42] 5740 2-8-11 0................................ Pierre-CharlesBoudot 1 97
(J-C Rouget, France) *midfield on inner: rdn and brief effrt on rail over 1f out: outpcd and btn fnl f: fdd* **25/1**

**9** ½ **Pink Rose**[28] 2-8-11 0................................ MickaelBarzalona 5 96
(A Fabre, France) *hld up towards rr: pushed along over 1f out: outpcd and btn fnl f* **16/1**

**10** 1¼ **Soft Drink (USA)**[28] 2-8-11 0................................ OlivierPeslier 9 93
(A Fabre, France) *t.k.h: hld up in midfield on outer: pushed along 2f out: outpcd over 1f out: sn btn* **33/1**

**11** ½ **Thank You Bye Bye (FR)**[26] 6219 2-8-11 0................................ AntoineHamelin 7 92
(J-P Gauvin, France) *t.k.h: midfield early: sn allowed to stride on and led 5f out: rdn and strly pressed 2f out: sn hdd: no ex and btn over 1f out: wknd* **50/1**

**12** 1½ **Shahah**[26] 6219 2-8-11 0................................ FrankieDettori 10 89
(A Fabre, France) *t.k.h: sn prom: cl 2nd 3f out: pushed along and effrt 2f out: no ex whn squeezed for room over 1f out: sn btn and wknd: eased fnl 120yds and dropped to last* **12/1**

1m 37.45s (-0.95) **Going Correction** +0.15s/f (Good) **12** Ran SP% **116.9**
Speed ratings: **110,107,106,104,104 104,104,102,101,100 100,98**
WIN (incl. 1 euro stake): 4.20. PLACES: 1.70, 1.50, 2.20. DF: 7.30. SF: 15.70.
**Owner** Michael Tabor & Derrick Smith & Mrs John Magnier **Bred** Roncon, Wynatt & Chelston **Trained** Cashel, Co Tipperary

**FOCUS**
A race that often produces a top filly and the right horses came to the fore, despite the steady early gallop. Found impressed and the runner-up is rated to her Morny form in this solid renewal.

## 6968a QATAR PRIX JEAN-LUC LAGARDERE (GRAND CRITERIUM) (GROUP 1) (2YO COLTS & FILLIES) (TURF) 7f

**2:10** (2:10) 2-Y-0 **£166,658** (£66,675; £33,337; £16,654; £8,341)

RPR

**1** ½ **Full Mast (USA)**[28] 6181 2-9-0 0................................ ThierryThulliez 6 112
(Mme C Head-Maarek, France) *t.k.h: trckd ldr: chal gng strly over 2f out and sn led: rdn and hdd ent fnl f: kpt on wl u.p but sltly hmpd towards fin and a jst hld: fin 2nd: awrdd the r* **11/2**[3]

**2** snk **Territories (IRE)**[28] 6181 2-9-0 0................................ MaximeGuyon 1 112
(A Fabre, France) *t.k.h: midfield in tch: pushed along and swtchd ins to rail over 1f out: rdn and kpt on wl for 3rd fnl f: bmpd towards fin and nt quite pce of front pair: fin 3rd plcd 2nd* **14/1**

**3** **Gleneagles (IRE)**[21] 6373 2-9-0 0................................ JosephO'Brien 9 114+
(A P O'Brien, Ire) *hld up towards rr: pushed along to cl 2f out: rdn to chal over 1f out and qcknd to ld ent fnl f: edgd rt but r.o wl and a doing enough: fin 1st: disqualified and plcd 3rd* **9/4**[2]

**4** nk **Burnt Sugar (IRE)**[29] 6142 2-9-0 0................................ GeraldMosse 4 111
(Richard Hannon) *hld up towards rr: rdn 2f out: r.o wl and wnt 4th fnl f: nt quite pce to chal* **20/1**

**5** snk **War Envoy (USA)**[22] 6326 2-9-0 0................................ RyanMoore 7 111
(A P O'Brien, Ire) *hld up in rr: pushed along and hdwy over 1f out: r.o wl fnl f but nt quite pce to chal* **25/1**

**6** 1¼ **Aktabantay**[36] 5926 2-9-0 0................................(b[1]) WilliamBuick 8 108
(Hugo Palmer) *midfield on inner: shuffled bk to rr 2f out: pushed along and swtchd lft to outer ent fnl f: rdn and kpt on but nvr able to chal* **20/1**

**7** ½ **Citron Spirit (IRE)**[30] 6123 2-9-0 0................................ AntoineHamelin 2 108
(Matthieu Palussiere, France) *t.k.h: trckd ldr on inner: shuffled bk and nt clr run 2f out: pushed along in rr ent fnl f: kpt on but wl hld* **14/1**

**8** 1¼ **Nucifera (USA)**[28] 6181 2-9-0 0................................ StephanePasquier 10 103
(J E Pease, France) *midfield in tch on outer: clsd 3f out: rdn to chal 2f out: no ex ent fnl f and sn btn: fdd* **16/1**

**9** 8 **The Wow Signal (IRE)**[42] 5741 2-9-0 0................................ FrankieDettori 3 81
(John Quinn) *led: pushed along and strly pressed over 2f out: sn hdd: qckly btn and wknd on rail: dropped to last ent fnl f: eased* **7/4**[1]

1m 20.11s (-0.59) **Going Correction** +0.025s/f (Good) **9** Ran SP% **116.0**
Speed ratings: **103,103,104,102,102 101,100,99,90**
WIN (incl. 1 euro stake): 4.90. PLACES: 1.90, 2.60, 1.60. DF: 20.50. SF: 44.90.
**Owner** K Abdullah **Bred** Juddmonte Farms Inc **Trained** Chantilly, France

**FOCUS**
This looked a good renewal of a race that contained the 2014 Poule d'Essai des Poulains winner last year, plus a dual Group 1 winner back in third. The pace appeared to be satisfactory even though a couple took a hold in behind but, even before the stewards intervened, the fact so many finished close up does cast a bit of doubt over the value of the form. Gleneagles did not need to improve on his best Irish efforts.

## 6969a PRIX DE L'OPERA LONGINES (GROUP 1) (3YO+ FILLIES & MARES) (TURF) 1m 2f

**2:45** (2:45) 3-Y-0+ **£190,466** (£76,200; £38,100; £19,033; £9,533)

RPR

**1** **We Are (IRE)**[15] 3-8-11 0................................ ThierryJarnet 7 114
(F Head, France) *trckd ldr: cl up in midfield 3f out: briefly short of room but wnt through gap 1 1/2f out: disputing 4th and styng on appr 1f out: sn rdn and r.o fnl f: led last 40yds: readily* **6/1**[2]

**2** nk **Ribbons**[42] 5742 4-9-2 0................................ FrankieDettori 5 113
(James Fanshawe) *w.w in 4th or 5th thrght: bhd front rnk and short of room 2f out: saw daylight and shkn up under 1 1/2f out: rdn and r.o to ld 100yds out: hdd last 40yds: no ex* **6/1**[2]

**3** nk **Hadaatha (IRE)**[18] 6464 3-8-11 0................................ PaulHanagan 9 113
(Roger Varian) *w.w towards rr: swtchd outside and shkn up 2f out: last and rdn 1 1/2f out: r.o and edgd rt fnl f: nvr quite on terms w front two* **9/1**

**4** nk **Tarfasha (IRE)**[21] 6370 3-8-11 0................................ PatSmullen 1 112
(D K Weld, Ire) *trckd ldr on inner: angled out and led 2f out: rdn and edgd lft appr last f: hdd 100yds out: no ex* **3/1**[1]

**5** ½ **Feodora (GER)**[63] 4955 3-8-11 0................................ EPedroza 2 111
(A Wohler, Germany) *towards rr: gd hdwy on rail 1 1/2f out: disputing 4th ins fnl f: run flattened out last 75yds* **16/1**

**6** hd **Lavender Lane (IRE)**[15] 3-8-11 0................................ GeraldMosse 11 111
(J E Hammond, France) *in rr: clsd under 2f out: bhd wall of horses and nowhere to go 1 1/2f out: styd on ins fnl f: nrest at fin* **14/1**

**7** snk **Shamkala (FR)**[50] 5462 3-8-11 0................................ MaximeGuyon 3 110
(A De Royer-Dupre, France) *midfield on inner: tk clsr order 2 1/2f out: chsd ldrs fr 2f out: kpt on at same pce fnl f* **10/1**

**8** 2½ **Narniyn (IRE)**[42] 5742 4-9-2 0................................ ChristopheSoumillon 8 105
(A De Royer-Dupre, France) *towards rr on outer: hdwy over 2 1/2f out: midfield and rdn 2f out: no immediate imp: eased whn hld wl ins fnl f* **8/1**[3]

**9** ½ **Nymphea (IRE)**[28] 6184 5-9-2 0................................ DennisSchiergen 4 104
(P Schiergen, Germany) *led: shkn up 2 1/2f out: hdd 2f out: rdn and wknd fr over 1f out* **50/1**

**10** nk **Sultanina**[21] 6380 4-9-2 0................................ WilliamBuick 10 104
(John Gosden) *w.w in 4th or 5th thrght: shkn up on outer 2f out and no immediate imp: fdd ins fnl f* **6/1**[2]

**11** 3 **Crisolles (FR)**[47] 5545 3-8-11 0................................ GregoryBenoist 6 98
(J-C Rouget, France) *trckd ldr on outer: pushed along over 2f out: rdn and nt qckn whn squeezed out between horses appr fnl f: sn btn and eased* **16/1**

2m 2.33s (-1.67) **Going Correction** +0.15s/f (Good)
**WFA** 3 from 4yo+ 5lb **11** Ran SP% **118.5**
Speed ratings: **112,111,111,111,110 110,110,108,108,107 105**
WIN (incl. 1 euro stake): 8.00. PLACES: 3.20, 2.20, 4.70. DF: 33.50. SF: 47.80.
**Owner** George Strawbridge **Bred** G Strawbridge **Trained** France

**FOCUS**
This didn't appear a really strong race for the level despite containing previous Group 1 winners. The early gallop set by Nymphea looked to be respectable (the winning time was faster than standard), and seemed to increase on entering the home straight.

## 6970a QATAR PRIX DE L'ARC DE TRIOMPHE (GROUP 1) (3YO+ NO GELDINGS) (TURF) 1m 4f

**3:30** (3:30) 3-Y-0 **£2,380,833** (£952,500; £476,250; £237,916; £119,166)

RPR

**1** **Treve (FR)**[21] 6380 4-9-2 0................................ ThierryJarnet 3 127
(Mme C Head-Maarek, France) *t.k.h: midfield in tch on inner: smooth hdwy to chal 2f out: sn shkn up and qcknd to ld: rdn and styd on strly fnl f: easily* **11/1**

**2** 2 **Flintshire**[21] 6381 4-9-5 0................................ MaximeGuyon 4 125
(A Fabre, France) *midfield in tch: rdn and swtchd ins for clr run 2f out: styd on and wnt 2nd ins fnl f: chsd wnr but no real imp and wl hld* **16/1**

**3** 1¼ **Taghrooda**[45] 5610 3-8-8 0................................ PaulHanagan 15 119
(John Gosden) *t.k.h: dwlt sltly but sn rcvrd: in tch on outer: rdn 2f out: styd on and wnt 3rd ins fnl f: no ch w wnr* **9/2**[1]

**4** ¾ **Kingston Hill**[22] 6329 3-8-11 0................................ AndreaAtzeni 20 121
(Roger Varian) *worked across fr wdst draw and trckd ldr: pushed along to chal into st: ev ch 2f out: rdn and outpcd by wnr over 1f out: styd on wl for 4th fnl f* **25/1**

**5** nk **Dolniya (FR)**[21] 6380 3-8-8 0................................ ChristopheSoumillon 5 117
(A De Royer-Dupre, France) *t.k.h: squeezed s but qckly rcvrd: midfield: rdn and hdwy over 1f out: styd on wl fnl f but nvr able to chal* **16/1**

**6** nk **Harp Star (JPN)**[42] 3-8-8 0................................ YugaKawada 12 119+
(Hiroyoshi Matsuda, Japan) *stdd and hld up in rr: last into st: fanned out and rdn 2f out: hung rt but styd on steadily and wnt 6th post: too much to do and nvr nrr* **8/1**

**7** hd **Prince Gibraltar (FR)**[51] 5406 3-8-11 0........(b[1]) Jean-BernardEyquem 9 119
(J-C Rouget, France) *dwlt sltly: hld up in midfield on inner: pushed along to cl into st: rdn and prom over 1f out: sn outpcd by wnr: styd on fnl f but dropped to 7th post* **28/1**

**8** shd **Just A Way (JPN)**[119] 5-9-5 0................................ YuichiFukunaga 14 120
(Naosuke Sugai, Japan) *hld up in midfield: rdn on rail 2f out: styd on: swtchd lft fnl f and fin quite wl but nvr able to chal* **7/1**[3]

**9** ¾ **Ruler Of The World (IRE)**[21] 6381 4-9-5 0................................(p) FrankieDettori 6 119
(A P O'Brien, Ire) *bmpd s: led early: sn hdd but remained prom: rdn and effrt over 2f out: styd on same pce after: wl hld fnl f* **12/1**

**10** nse **Al Kazeem**[22] 6353 6-9-5 0................................ JamesDoyle 7 119
(Roger Charlton) *wnt rt s: prom early: restrained and sn midfield: rdn 2f out: styd on same pce and n.d* **66/1**

**11** ¾ **Avenir Certain (FR)**[47] 5545 3-8-8 0........ Christophe-PatriceLemaire 1 114
(J-C Rouget, France) *prom on inner: 3rd 3f out: effrt to chal gng strly 2f out: rdn and outpcd by wnr over 1f out: stl jst 2nd ent fnl f: no ex and wknd fnl 150yds* **8/1**

**12** nse **Siljan's Saga (FR)**[21] 6380 4-9-2 0................................ Pierre-CharlesBoudot 16 115
(J-P Gauvin, France) *hld up towards rr: pushed along to cl 2f out: sn rdn and outpcd: styd on fnl f: nvr a factor* **100/1**

**13** 1 **Tapestry (IRE)**[22] 6351 3-8-8 0................................ RyanMoore 8 112
(A P O'Brien, Ire) *midfield: rdn over 2f out: outpcd and btn fnl f* **14/1**

**14** hd **Gold Ship (JPN)**[42] 5-9-5 0................................(b) NorihiroYokoyama 2 116
(Naosuke Sugai, Japan) *stdd and hld up in last: effrt to cl on outer into st: rdn and outpcd in rr again 2f out: plugged on and sme hdwy fnl f but nvr a factor* **12/1**

**15** 1½ **Chicquita (IRE)**[21] 6370 4-9-2 0................................ JosephO'Brien 18 110
(A P O'Brien, Ire) *hld up in midfield: fanned out and rdn into st: sn no imp and btn: nvr threatened* **40/1**

**16** nse **Spiritjim (FR)**[21] 6381 4-9-5 0................................ StephanePasquier 13 113
(P Bary, France) *midfield on outer: rdn into st: checked sltly 2f out: outpcd and btn fnl f* **66/1**

**17** ¾ **Ectot**[21] 6379 3-8-11 0................................ GregoryBenoist 10 111
(E Lellouche, France) *plld hrd: hld up towards rr: pushed along and effrt to cl 2f out: rdn and no imp over 1f out: wl btn fnl f* **6/1**[2]

**18** shd **Ivanhowe (GER)**[28] 6180 4-9-5 0................................ WilliamBuick 19 112
(Jean-Pierre Carvalho, Germany) *midfield in tch on outer: rdn into st: outpcd and lost pl over 1f out: sn btn* **25/1**

**19** 2 **Free Port Lux**[15] 6571 3-8-11 0................................ MickaelBarzalona 17 108
(F Head, France) *dwlt sltly: hld up and a towards rr: rdn and no imp in st: nvr a factor* **100/1**

20 *9* **Montviron (FR)**[102] 3597 3-8-11 0 CyrilleStefan 11 93
(E Lellouche, France) *sn led: rdn and strly pressed 2f out: sn hdd: no ex and immediately btn: wknd: dropped to last and eased fnl f* **200/1**

2m 26.05s (-4.35) **Going Correction** +0.15s/f (Good)
**WFA** 3 from 4yo+ 7lb **20** Ran SP% **128.4**
Speed ratings: **120,118,117,117,117 116,116,116,116,116 115,115,115,114,113 113,113,113,111,105**
WIN (incl. 1 euro stake): 4.00 (Treve coupled with Ectot & Ruler Of The World). PLACES: 3.80, 5.10, 3.20. DF: 114.30. SF: 219.20.
**Owner** Al Shaqab Racing **Bred** Haras Du Quesnay **Trained** Chantilly, France

**FOCUS**
Pacemaker Montviron ensured it wasn't a dawdle, although they hardly went a strong gallop and several took a keen grip. This year's edition of the autumn showpiece looked well up to scratch.

## 6971a QATAR PRIX DE LA FORET (GROUP 1) (3YO+) (TURF) 7f
**4:50** (4:50) 3-Y-O+ **£142,850** (£57,150; £28,575; £14,275; £7,150)

RPR

1 **Olympic Glory (IRE)**[49] 5480 4-9-2 0 (b) FrankieDettori 12 123+
(Richard Hannon) *outpcd in rr: last and pushed along 2f out: gd hdwy 1 1/2f out: r.o wl fnl f: led 75yds out: won gng away* **5/1**[2]

2 *2* **Gordon Lord Byron (IRE)**[22] 6352 6-9-2 0 WayneLordan 10 118
(T Hogan, Ire) *t.k.h: sn chsng ldng gp on outer: 4th and pushed along 2 1/2f out: rdn and hdwy 1 1/2f out: r.o to press ldr 100yds out: tk 2nd cl home but no ch w wnr* **11/2**[3]

3 *hd* **Noozhoh Canarias (SPA)**[28] 6182 3-9-0 0 ChristopheSoumillon 11 116
(C Laffon-Parias, France) *led: 2 l clr 2f out: sn rdn and kpt on: hdd 75yds out: no ex and lost 2nd cl home* **20/1**

4 *snk* **Vorda (FR)**[56] 5223 3-8-10 0 Christophe-PatriceLemaire 15 112
(P Sogorb, France) *hld up towards rr: gd hdwy on outer 1 1/2f out: styd on wl fnl f: nrest at fin* **16/1**

5 *2* **Anodin (IRE)**[49] 5480 4-9-2 0 OlivierPeslier 4 112
(F Head, France) *w.w bhd ldrs: 5th and pushed along 2f out: styng on whn nt clr run and snatched up ent fnl f and dropped bk to 9th: styd on again fnl 100yds* **3/1**[1]

6 *1/2* **Ansgar (IRE)**[22] 6328 6-9-2 0 JamesDoyle 8 110
(Sabrina J Harty, Ire) *trckd ldr on outer: rdn 1 1/2f out and nt qckn: kpt on at same pce u.p fnl f* **11/1**

7 *1 1/4* **Fiesolana (IRE)**[22] 6351 5-8-13 0 BillyLee 6 104
(W McCreery, Ire) *midfield: rowed along to hold pl 2f out: rdn and kpt on at same pce fnl f: nvr trbld ldrs* **7/1**

8 *snk* **Gammarth (FR)**[35] 5963 6-9-2 0 (b) MickaelBarzalona 1 107
(H-A Pantall, France) *t.k.h: trckd ldr on inner: pushed along and nt qckn fr 1 1/2f out: wknd ins fnl f* **66/1**

9 *shd* **Es Que Love (IRE)**[22] 6328 5-9-2 0 AdamKirby 13 106
(Clive Cox) *towards rr: hdwy between horses 1 1/2f out: sn rdn and no further imp ins fnl f* **20/1**

10 *shd* **That Is The Spirit**[44] 5653 3-9-0 0 DanielTudhope 2 105
(David O'Meara) *dwlt: towards rr on inner: hdwy on rail 2f out: hmpd and snatched up 1 1/2f out: no ch after but kpt on again ins fnl f tl nt clr run fnl 100yds* **33/1**

11 *1 1/4* **Karakontie (JPN)**[126] 2818 3-9-0 0 StephanePasquier 5 102
(J E Pease, France) *chsd ldrs: hmpd and squeezed out bef end of first f: towards rr: niggled along and nt clr run over 2f out: sltly impeded whn looking for gaps: swtchd outside and no imp fnl f* **5/1**[2]

12 *2* **Aljamaaheer (IRE)**[22] 6328 5-9-2 0 (p) PaulHanagan 14 97
(Roger Varian) *t.k.h: w.w towards rr on outer: midfield and shoved along 2 1/2f out: kpt on u.p but no real imp fr 1 1/2f out: btn ins fnl f* **12/1**

13 *shd* **Darwin (USA)**[22] 6352 4-9-2 0 JosephO'Brien 3 97
(A P O'Brien, Ire) *midfield on inner: 6th and pushed along over 2f out: no imp: grad dropped away ins fnl f* **20/1**

14 *10* **Speedrider (IRE)**[22] 4-9-2 0 AntoineHamelin 9 70
(Mme Pia Brandt, France) *midfield between horses: rdn and outpcd 2f out: sn wknd* **200/1**

1m 17.73s (-2.97) **Going Correction** +0.025s/f (Good)
**WFA** 3 from 4yo+ 2lb **14** Ran SP% **127.3**
Speed ratings: **117,114,114,114,112 111,110,109,109,109 108,105,105,94**
Win (incl. 1 euro stake): 5.50. PLACES: 2.00, 2.30, 4.40. DF: 15.80. SF: 27.00.
**Owner** Al Shaqab Racing **Bred** Denis McDonnell **Trained** East Everleigh, Wilts

**FOCUS**
A big field and open look to this quality contest. The early gallop appeared really quick (reportedly it was a course record), and it was no surprise to see something come off the pace to win.

## 6972a QATAR PRIX DU CADRAN (GROUP 1) (4YO+) (TURF) 2m 4f
**5:20** (5:20) 4-Y-O+ **£142,850** (£57,150; £28,575; £14,275; £7,150)

RPR

1 **High Jinx (IRE)**[21] 6383 6-9-2 0 RyanMoore 6 112
(James Fanshawe) *pushed along to go forwards and mde all: 4 l clr 5f out: rdn into st: reduced advantage 2f out: styd on wl and a doing enough fnl f despite being clsd down all the way to fin: gd ride* **5/1**[3]

2 *nk* **Bathyrhon (GER)**[21] 6383 4-9-2 0 ChristopheSoumillon 5 112
(Mme Pia Brandt, France) *stdd and hld up in rr: rdn and hdwy whn hung lft 2f out: styd on and wnt 2nd fnl f: clsd on wnr all the way to fin but nvr getting there* **5/1**[3]

3 *3/4* **Pale Mimosa (IRE)**[21] 6374 5-8-13 0 PatSmullen 10 108
(D K Weld, Ire) *midfield: clsd into st: pushed along and wnt 2nd 2f out: rdn to chse wnr over 1f out: styd on but a hld fnl f and dropped to 3rd* **7/4**[1]

4 *1 3/4* **Whiplash Willie**[23] 6288 6-9-2 0 (p) DavidProbert 7 109
(Andrew Balding) *midfield: pushed along whn nt clr run on rail 2f out: swtchd lft and squeezed through gap ent fnl f: rdn and styd on same pce for 4th: nvr able to chal* **4/1**[2]

5 *1/2* **Kicky Blue (GER)**[21] 6383 4-8-13 0 MickaelBarzalona 2 106
(T Clout, France) *midfield in tch: rdn into st: styd on same pce and nvr able to chal* **14/1**

6 *3/4* **Trip To Rhodos (FR)**[21] 6383 5-9-2 0 OlivierPeslier 8 108
(Pavel Tuma, Czech Republic) *trckd wnr: rdn and effrt into st: outpcd whn squeezed out over 1f out: plugged on fnl f but wl hld* **16/1**

7 *snk* **Going Somewhere (BRZ)**[21] 6383 5-9-2 0 GregoryBenoist 3 108
(D Smaga, France) *hld up in rr: rdn in last into st: sn outpcd and no imp: plugged on but nvr a factor* **20/1**

8 *2 1/2* **Fly With Me (FR)**[42] 5743 4-9-2 0 (b) MaximeGuyon 1 105
(E Libaud, France) *trckd wnr: rdn and effrt into st: kpt on same pce tl no ex and fdd fnl f: dropped to last towards fin* **8/1**

4m 12.22s (-5.78) **Going Correction** +0.15s/f (Good) **8** Ran SP% **118.1**
Speed ratings: **117,116,116,115,115 115,115,114**
WIN (incl. 1 euro stake): 5.00. PLACES: 1.70, 1.80, 1.80. DF: 11.90. SF: 20.90.
**Owner** Mr & Mrs W J Williams **Bred** Haras De La Perelle **Trained** Newmarket, Suffolk

**FOCUS**
This marathon trip saw another example of the tactical awareness Ryan Moore so often employs on his mounts.

# 6951 KEENELAND (L-H)
Sunday, October 5

**OFFICIAL GOING: Dirt: fast; turf: firm**

## 6973a JUDDMONTE SPINSTER STKS (GRADE 1) (3YO+ FILLIES & MARES) (DIRT) 1m 1f
**10:45** (10:45) 3-Y-O+
**£180,722** (£60,240; £30,120; £15,060; £9,036; £6,024)

RPR

1 **Don't Tell Sophia (USA)**[29] 6-8-12 0 JRoccoJr 5 112
(Philip A Sims, U.S.A) **57/10**[2]

2 *2 1/2* **Ria Antonia (USA)**[29] 3-8-9 0 (b) PLopez 1 109
(Thomas Amoss, U.S.A) **165/10**

3 *2 1/4* **Molly Morgan (USA)**[29] 5-8-12 0 CLanerie 6 102
(Dale Romans, U.S.A) **23/1**

4 *2 1/2* **Close Hatches (USA)**[44] 5663 4-8-12 0 JRosario 2 97
(William Mott, U.S.A) **1/5**[1]

5 *1/2* **Got Lucky (USA)**[50] 5463 3-8-9 0 (b) RosieNapravnik 3 98
(Todd Pletcher, U.S.A) **184/10**

6 *7 3/4* **Shuruq (USA)**[29] 6164 4-8-12 0 (p) JRLeparoux 4 79
(Saeed bin Suroor) **41/5**[3]

1m 49.8s (109.80)
**WFA** 3 from 4yo+ 4lb **6** Ran SP% **124.2**
PARI-MUTUEL (all including 2 usd stake): WIN 13.40; PLACE (1-2) 7.00, 20.00; SHOW (1-2-3) 14.60, 37.60, 30.20; SF 138.20.
**Owner** Philip A Sims & Jerry Namy **Bred** Stoneside Stable **Trained** USA

# 6690 PONTEFRACT (L-H)
Monday, October 6

**OFFICIAL GOING: Good to soft changing to soft after race 3 (3.10)**
Wind: Moderate across Weather: Heavy cloud and rain

## 6976 IRISH STALLION FARMS EBF MAIDEN STKS (BOBIS RACE) 1m 2f 6y
**2:10** (2:12) (Class 4) 2-Y-O **£5,175** (£1,540; £769; £384) Stalls Low

Form RPR

4 1 **Oceanographer**[24] 6300 2-9-5 0 MartinLane 10 76+
(Charlie Appleby) *trckd ldr: cl up 1/2-way: pushed along to ld 2f out: rdn over 1f out: clr ins fnl f: kpt on strly* **6/4**[1]

5 2 *2 1/2* **Mythical City (IRE)**[17] 6509 2-9-0 0 JoeFanning 6 66
(Mark Johnston) *trckd ldrs: hdwy 3f out: chsd ldng pair wl over 1f out: rdn to chse wnr ins fnl f: no imp towards fin* **5/1**[3]

4245 3 *2 1/4* **Oregon Gift**[65] 4885 2-9-5 72 FrannyNorton 9 67
(Mark Johnston) *led: jnd 1/2-way: rdn and hdd 2f out: drvn over 1f out: grad wknd fnl f* **14/1**

66 4 *7* **Passionate Appeal**[19] 6449 2-9-5 0 GrahamLee 3 54
(Ann Duffield) *t.k.h early: chsd ldrs: rdn along wl over 2f out: sn one pce* **12/1**

0 5 *hd* **Politico**[14] 6605 2-9-0 0 WilliamBuick 8 49
(John Gosden) *chsd ldng pair: rdn along 3f out: wknd fnl 2f* **28/1**

53 6 *shd* **Ventura Castle**[13] 6646 2-9-2 0 CamHardie(3) 11 54
(Richard Hannon) *hld up in rr: niggled along 1/2-way: rdn and sme hdwy 3f out: plugged on fnl 2f: n.d* **3/1**[2]

00 7 *2 3/4* **Almost Nowhere (IRE)**[11] 6694 2-9-0 0 AndrewMullen 4 44
(Michael Appleby) *a towards rr* **100/1**

00 8 *21* **Egmont**[38] 5886 2-9-5 0 DanielTudhope 1 11
(George Moore) *chsd ldrs on inner: pushed along 1/2-way: sn rdn along and lost pl over 3f out: bhd after* **100/1**

9 *23* **Dont Tell Chris (FR)** 2-9-5 0 PhillipMakin 7
(John Quinn) *a towards rr: rdn along over 3f out: sn outpcd and bhd* **16/1**

06 10 *8* **La Vien Zen (IRE)**[43] 5712 2-9-0 0 TomEaves 5
(Ann Duffield) *towards rr: racd wd fr 6f out: rdn along over 4f out: nvr a factor* **40/1**

11 *72* **Big Bad Jack** 2-9-5 0 PaulMulrennan 2
(David Brown) *slowly in to stride: a in rr: outpcd and wl bhd fnl 3f* **25/1**

2m 19.71s (6.01) **Going Correction** +0.425s/f (Yiel) **11** Ran SP% **113.6**
Speed ratings (Par 97): **92,90,88,82,82 82,80,63,44,38**
CSF £8.43 TOTE £2.50: £1.10, £2.00, £2.70; EX 9.00 Trifecta £83.70.
**Owner** Godolphin **Bred** Earle I Mack **Trained** Newmarket, Suffolk

**FOCUS**
A modest staying maiden.

## 6977 RACING UK CLUB DAY 20TH OCTOBER NURSERY H'CAP (BOBIS RACE) 6f
**2:40** (2:40) (Class 4) (0-85,80) 2-Y-O **£4,528** (£1,347; £673; £336) Stalls Low

Form RPR

4013 1 **Golden Spun (USA)**[20] 6427 2-9-2 75 PaulMulrennan 10 78
(Bryan Smart) *trckd ldng pair: hdwy 2f out: rdn to ld jst ins fnl f: sn drvn and jst hld on* **20/1**

224 2 *nse* **Russian Heroine**[43] 5725 2-8-12 71 GrahamGibbons 4 74
(Sir Michael Stoute) *in tch: hdwy on outer wl over 1f out: rdn and edgd lft ins fnl f: styd on strly towards fin: jst failed* **10/1**

2105 3 *1 1/2* **Arthur MartinLeake (IRE)**[23] 6322 2-9-4 77 DanielTudhope 1 76
(K R Burke) *trckd ldrs: hdwy 2f out: n.m.r and swiitched rt over 1f out: sn rdn: styng on whn edgd lft ins fnl f: kpt on* **7/4**[1]

51 4 *1/2* **Qatar Road (FR)**[33] 6039 2-9-2 75 MartinHarley 5 72
(Marco Botti) *hld up in tch: hdwy on outer over 2f out: rdn wl over 1f out: kpt on ins fnl f: nrst fin* **11/4**[2]

2221 5 *1 1/4* **Fingal's Cave (IRE)**[35] 5981 2-9-2 78 CharlesBishop(3) 7 71
(Mick Channon) *led: rdn along 2f out: drvn and hdd jst ins fnl f: grad wknd* **11/2**[3]

4331 6 *nse* **Scarlet Bounty (IRE)**[14] 6610 2-8-5 69 JackGarritty(5) 11 62
(Richard Fahey) *cl up: chal over 2f out: sn rdn: drvn and edgd lft jst over 1f out: sn drvn and wknd ins fnl f* **12/1**



The Form Book, Raceform Ltd, Newbury, RG14 5SJ

315 **7** *2* **Steal The Scene (IRE)**[11] 6678 2-8-13 75........................ CamHardie(3) 8 74
(Richard Hannon) *in rr: hdwy on inner 2f out: styng on to chse ldrs whn nt clr run and swtchd rt 1f out: sn rdn: hmpd and almost uns rdr ins fnl f: no ch after* **14/1**

6410 **8** *18* **Honeysuckle Lil (IRE)**[17] 6510 2-9-2 75........................ DavidAllan 6 8
(Tim Easterby) *hld up: hdwy on outer over 2f out: sn rdn and wknd wl over 1f out* **16/1**

1m 21.16s (4.26) **Going Correction** +0.425s/f (Yiel) **8** Ran SP% **112.5**
Speed ratings (Par 97): **88,87,85,85,83 83,80,56**
CSF £194.38 CT £537.25 TOTE £14.30: £4.90, £1.90, £1.10; EX 153.80 Trifecta £1501.00.
**Owner** Fiddes, Chappell & Unique Sports **Bred** Carl Schexnayder & Harold Babineaux **Trained** Hambleton, N Yorks
■ Stewards' Enquiry : Graham Gibbons two-day ban: used whip above permitted level (Oct 20-21)

**FOCUS**
A fair nursery but a messy finish clouds matters.

## 6978 £40 TOTEPOOL PACKAGE ON 20TH OCTOBER H'CAP (BOBIS RACE) 1m 4y
3:10 (3:11) (Class 3) (0-95,95) 3-Y-O
**£9,337** (£2,796; £1,398; £699; £349; £175) **Stalls** Low

Form RPR

1130 **1** **Moohaarib (IRE)**[45] 5656 3-9-5 **93**........................ MartinHarley 1 102
(Marco Botti) *trckd ldrs: hdwy over 2f out: effrt and n.m.r wl over 1f out: sn rdn and led ent fnl f: kpt on wl* **3/1**[2]

10 **2** *½* **Top Of The Glas (IRE)**[16] 6534 3-8-13 **87**........................ TomEaves 5 94
(Brian Ellison) *hld up in rr: gd hdwy on inner wl over 1f out: rdn ent fnl f: sn chsng wnr: kpt on* **10/1**

115 **3** *½* **Dream Spirit (IRE)**[16] 6560 3-9-7 **95**........................ GrahamLee 3 101
(William Haggas) *trckd ldr: cl up 1/2-way: rdn to ld wl over 1f out: hdd ent fnl f: sn drvn and kpt on* **2/1**[1]

2151 **4** *nk* **Momayyaz (IRE)**[21] 6411 3-8-11 **92**........................ AhmadAlSubousi(7) 7 97
(Saeed bin Suroor) *trckd ldrs: hdwy over 2f out: effrt and ev ch whn edgd lft over 1f out: swtchd rt ins fnl f: kpt on wl towards fin* **12/1**

1204 **5** *8* **Libran (IRE)**[93] 3965 3-8-8 **82**........................ KierenFallon 4 69
(Alan Swinbank) *trckd ldrs: swtchd rt to outer and hdwy to join ldrs over 5f out: cl up 1/2-way: rdn along wl over 2f out: wknd over 1f out* **9/2**[3]

2114 **6** *9* **Potent Embrace (USA)**[9] 6737 3-8-11 **85**........................ JoeFanning 2 51
(Mark Johnston) *led: jnd 1/2-way: rdn along over 2f out: hdd wl over 1f out: sn wknd* **9/2**[3]

1m 49.23s (3.33) **Going Correction** +0.425s/f (Yiel) **6** Ran SP% **111.5**
Speed ratings (Par 105): **100,99,99,98,90 81**
CSF £30.26 TOTE £5.30: £2.70, £4.20; EX 19.30 Trifecta £169.00.
**Owner** Sheikh Mohammed Bin Khalifa Al Maktoum **Bred** Watership Down Stud **Trained** Newmarket, Suffolk

**FOCUS**
An interesting 3yo handicap, containing a few progressive types. The second has been rated as matching his Chester form and the fourth as running close to her AW form.

## 6979 PHIL BULL TROPHY CONDITIONS STKS 2m 1f 216y
3:40 (3:40) (Class 3) 3-Y-O+
**£7,762** (£2,310; £1,154; £577) **Stalls** Low

Form RPR

0644 **1** **Statutory (IRE)**[34] 6005 4-9-3 96........................ FrederikTylicki 4 101
(Saeed bin Suroor) *set fair gallop: pushed clr 2f out: idled and shkn up ins fnl f: sn rdn and kpt on towards fin* **4/5**[1]

1600 **2** *nk* **Alwilda**[24] 6288 4-8-12 91........................ LukeMorris 5 95
(Sir Mark Prescott Bt) *a trcking wnr: pushed along over 2f out: rdn wl over 1f out: swtchd rt and drvn ins fnl f: kpt on wl towards fin* **7/2**[3]

0000 **3** *6* **Repeater**[16] 6557 5-9-3 96........................ DanielTudhope 3 93
(David O'Meara) *hld up in rr: tk clsr order over 4f out: rdn along to chse ldng pair over 2f out: drvn and one pce fr over 1f out* **11/4**[2]

6141 **4** *14* **Hell Hath No Fury**[18] 6493 5-8-12 59........................ AndrewMullen 2 73
(Michael Appleby) *trckd ldng pair: rdn along on outer 3f out: wknd 2f out: sn eased* **33/1**

4m 14.44s (18.24) **Going Correction** +0.425s/f (Yiel) **4** Ran SP% **107.4**
Speed ratings (Par 107): **76,75,73,66**
CSF £3.88 TOTE £1.60; EX 3.80 Trifecta £7.10.
**Owner** Godolphin **Bred** Darley **Trained** Newmarket, Suffolk

**FOCUS**
This was all about the winner. The runner-up has been rated to form.

## 6980 BOOK YOUR CHRISTMAS PARTY ON 0113 287 6387 CLAIMING STKS 1m 4y
4:10 (4:10) (Class 5) 3-Y-O
**£3,234** (£962; £481; £240) **Stalls** Low

Form RPR

3514 **1** **Rangi Chase (IRE)**[13] 6625 3-8-7 71........................ FrannyNorton 1 79
(Richard Fahey) *trckd ldng pair: hdwy 2f out: chal over 1f out: led ent fnl f: sn clr: styd on strly* **5/1**

204 **2** *3 ¼* **Solid Justice (IRE)**[17] 6516 3-8-2 64........................ JackGarritty(5) 4 72
(Jason Ward) *hld up in rr: hdwy over 2f out: rdn over 1f out: styd on to chse wnr ins fnl f: no imp* **14/1**

0234 **3** *2 ½* **Mr McLaren**[8] 6792 3-9-3 82........................ DanielTudhope 2 76
(David O'Meara) *trckd ldr: hdwy and cl up over 2f out: led wl over 1f out: sn rdn: hdd ent fnl f: sn drvn and one pce* **2/1**[1]

3114 **4** *¾* **Rough Courte (IRE)**[5] 6877 3-7-9 70........................ PaddyPilley(7) 6 60
(Mick Channon) *wnt rt s: sn led: rdn along over 2f out: hdd wl over 1f out: sn wknd* **4/1**[2]

2115 **5** *2 ¼* **Strictly Glitz (IRE)**[47] 5566 3-7-13 67........................ CamHardie(3) 3 54
(John Quinn) *trckd ldrs: pushed along wl over 2f out: rdn wl over 1f out: sn outpcd* **9/2**[3]

3351 **6** *25* **Pigeon Pie**[8] 6795 3-8-2 64........................(b) JoeFanning 5
(Mark Johnston) *hld up: hdwy on outer over 3f out: sn chsng ldrs: rdn along 2f out: sn wknd and eased over 1f out* **5/1**

1m 48.0s (2.10) **Going Correction** +0.425s/f (Yiel) **6** Ran SP% **111.5**
Speed ratings (Par 101): **106,102,100,99,97 72**
CSF £62.53 TOTE £7.60: £3.50, £6.50; EX 64.60 Trifecta £171.80.
**Owner** Dr Marwan Koukash **Bred** Tinnakill Bloodstock **Trained** Musley Bank, N Yorks

**FOCUS**
Not a bad claimer. The winner has been rated to form.

## 6981 RACING UK ANYWHERE H'CAP 1m 4f 8y
4:40 (4:40) (Class 5) (0-70,70) 3-Y-O
**£3,234** (£962; £481; £240) **Stalls** Low

Form RPR

06-2 **1** **Thunder Pass (IRE)**[11] 6682 3-9-1 64........................ WilliamBuick 3 76+
(Hughie Morrison) *mde all: rdn clr wl over 1f out: kpt on strly fnl f* **10/3**[1]

4-00 **2** *3* **Trendsetter (IRE)**[9] 6738 3-9-4 67........................ FrannyNorton 4 75
(John Butler) *hld up towards rr: stdy hdwy 3f out: rdn to chse wnr over 1f out: drvn and no imp fnl f* **25/1**

6406 **3** *1 ¾* **Cape Karli (IRE)**[19] 6461 3-8-13 62........................ PaulMulrennan 5 66
(Kevin Ryan) *a chsng wnr: rdn along 2f out: drvn wl over 1f out: kpt on same pce fnl f* **33/1**

3436 **4** *½* **Power Up**[16] 6564 3-8-8 57........................(v) JoeFanning 6 60
(Mark Johnston) *t.k.h early: bhd: stdy hdwy 3f out: rdn wl over 1f out: styd on: nrst fin* **14/1**

3103 **5** *¾* **Chivers (IRE)**[13] 6637 3-9-6 69........................(p) DavidAllan 9 71
(Tim Easterby) *in tch: hdwy over 2f out: rdn wl over 1f out: kpt on same pce fnl f* **4/1**[2]

0451 **6** *¾* **Lucky Jim**[16] 6564 3-9-4 70........................ AshleyMorgan(3) 2 71
(Chris Wall) *chsd ldrs: rdn along over 2f out: drvn wl over 1f out: one pce* **6/1**[3]

F634 **7** *3 ½* **Heska (IRE)**[14] 6608 3-9-5 68........................(tp) AndrewMullen 10 63
(Michael Appleby) *dwlt and bhd tl sme late hdwy* **10/1**

5312 **8** *4 ½* **Where's Tiger**[43] 5717 3-9-3 66........................ RussKennemore 12 54
(Jedd O'Keeffe) *t.k.h: hld up towards rr: hdwy wl over 1f out: sn rdn and one pce* **10/1**

0440 **9** *6* **Crystal Pearl**[26] 6239 3-9-6 69........................ PhillipMakin 11 47
(Mark H Tompkins) *nvr bttr than midfield* **16/1**

0400 **10** *9* **Gannicus**[24] 6303 3-9-6 69........................ KierenFallon 8 33
(Brendan Powell) *chsd ldrs: hdwy over 2f out: sn rdn and wknd over 1f out* **16/1**

2542 **11** *22* **Mister Uno (IRE)**[14] 6596 3-9-3 66........................(p) TomEaves 1
(Ann Duffield) *chsd ldng pair on inner: rdn along 3f out: sn wknd* **12/1**

3000 **12** *81* **Tiptree Lace**[23] 6337 3-8-13 62........................(v) FrederikTylicki 14
(William Knight) *chsd ldrs on outer: rdn along over 5f out: sn lost pl and bhd whn heavily eased fnl 2f* **14/1**

2m 44.94s (4.14) **Going Correction** +0.425s/f (Yiel) **12** Ran SP% **115.1**
Speed ratings (Par 101): **103,101,99,99,99 98,96,93,89,83 68,14**
CSF £87.68 CT £2323.27 TOTE £3.80: £1.60, £6.40, £9.40; EX 67.30 Trifecta £2013.70.
**Owner** Thurloe Thoroughbreds XXXIII **Bred** Lynch Bages Ltd **Trained** East Ilsley, Berks

**FOCUS**
A one-sided handicap, the progressive winner dominating throughout. The third has been rated as matching her maiden form, and the fourth in line with her recent AW best.

## 6982 BUY YOUR 2015 ANNUAL BADGE TODAY MAIDEN STKS 1m 4y
5:10 (5:12) (Class 5) 3-Y-O
**£3,234** (£962; £481; £240) **Stalls** Low

Form RPR

**1** **Dubai Star (IRE)** 3-9-5 0........................ RobertHavlin 10 88+
(John Gosden) *trckd ldrs: cl up on outer 3f out: chal 2f out: sn led: pushed clr over 1f out: readily* **11/2**[3]

40 **2** *6* **Tayma (IRE)**[34] 6018 3-9-0 0........................ AhmedAjtebi 5 66
(Saeed bin Suroor) *t.k.h early: led: pushed along and jnd over 2f out: hdd and rdn wl over 1f out: kpt on same pce* **9/1**

46 **3** *½* **Archipeligo**[14] 6599 3-9-5 0........................ DavidNolan 8 70
(Iain Jardine) *hld up in rr: stdy hdwy 3f out: rdn to chse ldng pair over 1f out: kpt on fnl f: nrst fin* **25/1**

2-4 **4** *5* **Tornesel**[77] 4500 3-9-5 0........................(t) JamesSullivan 6 59
(Brian Rothwell) *chsd ldrs: rdn along over 2f out: sn one pce* **9/1**

555 **5** *3 ½* **Guesshowmuchiloveu (IRE)**[34] 6018 3-9-5 75........................ FrederikTylicki 4 50
(Charlie Fellowes) *trckd ldng pair on inner: effrt 3f out: sn rdn along: wknd 2f out* **3/1**[2]

005 **6** *21* **Sea Whisper**[18] 6494 3-9-0 45........................ TonyHamilton 7
(Ann Stokell) *chsd ldr: rdn along 3f out: wknd over 2f out: sn bhd* **100/1**

**7** *3 ¼* **Wiskee Lil** 3-8-9 0........................ KevinStott(5) 1
(Edwin Tuer) *s.i.s: a bhd* **50/1**

020 **8** *9* **Fallen In Line (IRE)**[61] 5039 3-9-5 74........................(t) WilliamBuick 3
(John Gosden) *dwlt and sn pushed along: hdwy and in tch 6f out: rdn along 4f out: wknd 3f out: sn bhd* **5/4**[1]

**9** *17* **Astrocat** 3-9-0 0........................ JoeFanning 9
(Mark H Tompkins) *v s.i.s and bhd: sme hdwy and in tch over 4f out: rdn along over 3f out: sn lost pl and bhd* **40/1**

1m 49.59s (3.69) **Going Correction** +0.425s/f (Yiel) **9** Ran SP% **114.1**
Speed ratings (Par 101): **98,92,91,86,83 62,58,49,32**
CSF £50.61 TOTE £8.80: £2.00, £3.00, £3.70; EX 56.60 Trifecta £945.20.
**Owner** HRH Princess Haya Of Jordan **Bred** Blackwater Bloodstock Ltd & Corrin Stud **Trained** Newmarket, Suffolk

**FOCUS**
No depth to this 3yo maiden. The level is a bit fluid, but the runner-up has been rated in line with her debut AW run.
T/Plt: £277.50 to a £1 stake. Pool of £70177.09 - 184.56 winning tickets. T/Qpdt: £162.50 to a £1 stake. Pool of £4174.15 - 19.0 winning tickets. JR

# 5684 WINDSOR (R-H)
## Monday, October 6

**OFFICIAL GOING: Soft (6.8)**
Wind: Moderate, across Weather: rain/drizzle all afternoon

## 6983 THAMES MATERIALS FEGENTRI WORLD CUP OF NATIONS STKS (AN AMATEUR RIDERS' H'CAP) 5f 10y
1:50 (1:50) (Class 6) (0-65,63) 3-Y-O+
**£1,871** (£580; £290; £145) **Stalls** Low

Form RPR

5613 **1** **Pharoh Jake**[25] 6266 6-11-4 57........................ MissEilidhGrant 7 67
(John Bridger) *racd towards centre: led 2f: edgd lft fr 2f out: led again 1f out: urged along and hld on* **5/2**[1]

6653 **2** *shd* **Greek Islands (IRE)**[5] 6851 6-10-11 50........................ MrPhilipSonsteby 8 59
(Edward Creighton) *racd wdst of all: chsd ldrs: carried lft fr 2f out: chal fnl f: jst failed* **4/1**[3]

4531 **3** *1 ½* **First Rebellion**[5] 6851 5-11-3 56 7ex........................(b) MissMeganNicholls 1 59
(Tony Carroll) *racd against nr side rail: prom: led after 2f to 1f out: edgd lft and one pce* **7/2**[2]

5434 **4** *1 ¾* **Oscars Journey**[39] 5860 4-11-10 63........................(v[1]) MrQuentinFoulon 4 60
(J R Jenkins) *prom: on terms w ldr 1/2-way: urged along and nt qckn wl over 1f out: one pce after* **5/2**[1]

0000 **5** *2 ¼* **Quality Art (USA)**[13] 6631 6-11-4 57........................ MrDanieleZucca 2 46
(Simon Hodgson) *chsd ldrs: no imp u.str.p fr 2f out: fdd fnl f* **25/1**

3000 **6** *9* **Prince Of Passion (CAN)**[6] 6843 6-11-0 53......(v) MissMBlumenauer 3 9
(Derek Shaw) *slowly away: rdn to try to latch on to ldrs after 2f: wknd 2f out* **20/1**

0000 7 4 ½ **Speedy Rio (IRE)**[5] 6851 3-10-10 49 oh1.......(bt[1]) MrVinzenzSchiergen 6
(Luke Dace) *slowly away: a in rr: bhd fnl 2f* **33/1**

1m 3.34s (3.04) **Going Correction** +0.225s/f (Good) **7** Ran SP% **110.9**
Speed ratings (Par 101): **84,83,81,78,75 60,53**
CSF £11.92 CT £31.91 TOTE £3.90: £1.60, £1.80; EX 15.10 Trifecta £34.00.
**Owner** The Hair & Haberdasher Partnership **Bred** J J Bridger **Trained** Liphook, Hants
■ The first winner in Britain for American rider Eilidh Grant.

**FOCUS**
The inner of the straight was dolled out 2yds at the 6f and 2yds at the winning line. Top bend dolled out 3yds from normal inner configuration, adding 11yds to race distances of 1m and over. 7.5mm of rain in the day turned the ground soft and the main action unfolded centre-field in this low-grade amateur riders' handicap. The runner-up has been rated in line with his summer AW form.

## 6984 BRITISH STALLION STUDS EBF MAIDEN STKS (DIV I) 1m 67y
**2:20** (2:21) (Class 5) 2-Y-O **£2,911** (£866; £432; £216) **Stalls** Low

Form RPR

4 **1** **Rocky Rider**[32] 6056 2-9-5 0.......... AndreaAtzeni 4 79+
(Andrew Balding) *trckd ldng pair: wnt 2nd and chal over 2f out: rdn to take narrow ld fnl f: jst hld on* **4/6**[1]

**2** *nse* **Magic Dancer** 2-9-5 0.......... PatDobbs 3 79+
(Ralph Beckett) *mde most: hrd pressed fr over 2f out: narrowly hdd fnl f: kpt on wl: jst failed* **12/1**[3]

033 **3** *3* **Harbour Patrol (IRE)**[16] 6545 2-9-5 77.......... RichardHughes 9 72
(Richard Hannon) *trckd ldrs: cl enough and shkn up over 2f out: reminders over 1f out and nt qckn: pushed along and lost grnd fnl f* **3/1**[2]

0 **4** *3 ¼* **Step On It (IRE)**[24] 6293 2-9-5 0.......... JohnFahy 2 65
(Eve Johnson Houghton) *chsd ldrs: pushed along wl over 3f out: struggling and nvr on terms after: kpt on to take 4th nr fin* **12/1**[3]

60 **5** *½* **Saint Honore**[11] 6675 2-9-0 0.......... HarryBentley 11 59
(Pat Phelan) *chsd ldrs: shkn up over 2f out: tk 4th over 1f out but n.d: wknd fnl f* **100/1**

**6** *¾* **The Cashel Man (IRE)** 2-9-5 0.......... JimCrowley 7 62+
(David Simcock) *v.s.a: mostly in last trio: shkn up over 2f out: kpt on quite wl fr over 1f out: bttr for experience* **25/1**

0 **7** *nk* **Basoco**[27] 6203 2-9-5 0.......... DavidProbert 8 61
(Harry Dunlop) *s.i.s and pushed along in last pair early: rdn 1/2-way and looked like tailing off: plugged on fnl 2f* **66/1**

05 **8** *1 ¾* **Envisioning (IRE)**[23] 6317 2-9-5 0.......... RyanMoore 5 58
(Richard Hannon) *w ldr to wl over 2f out: wknd qckly over 1f out* **25/1**

**9** *21* **Topsy Turvy (IRE)** 2-9-5 0.......... GeorgeBaker 6 11
(Jeremy Noseda) *rn green early and pushed along in last trio: wknd over 3f out: t.o* **14/1**

1m 49.68s (4.98) **Going Correction** +0.225s/f (Good) **9** Ran SP% **117.2**
Speed ratings (Par 95): **84,83,80,77,77 76,76,74,53**
CSF £10.59 TOTE £1.80: £1.10, £3.40, £1.10; EX 12.80 Trifecta £33.10.
**Owner** Qatar Racing Limited **Bred** Fittocks Stud **Trained** Kingsclere, Hants

**FOCUS**
A fair maiden, with the front pair pulling clear late on, although the time was 1.32secs slower than the second division. The third has been rated just below his mark.

## 6985 BRITISH STALLION STUDS EBF MAIDEN STKS (DIV II) 1m 67y
**2:50** (2:50) (Class 5) 2-Y-O **£2,911** (£866; £432; £216) **Stalls** Low

Form RPR

32 **1** **Master Apprentice (IRE)**[24] 6300 2-9-5 0.......... DavidProbert 1 80+
(Andrew Balding) *mde all: pressed 3f out: rdn 2f out: drvn to assert over 1f out: styd on* **4/5**[1]

4 **2** *2* **Firmament**[19] 6462 2-9-5 0.......... JimmyFortune 2 76
(Jeremy Noseda) *chsd wnr: chal 3f out: rdn 2f out: nt qckn over 1f out: kpt on but wl hld after* **8/1**[3]

**3** *2 ¼* **Wonder Laish** 2-9-5 0.......... AndreaAtzeni 5 71+
(William Haggas) *s.i.s: racd in 7th early: pushed along over 3f out: prog to take 3rd over 1f out: styd on but no threat to ldng pair* **14/1**

0 **4** *1 ¾* **Dannyday**[25] 6259 2-9-5 0.......... RyanMoore 3 67
(Sir Michael Stoute) *chsd ldng pair: rdn 3f out: no imp after: wknd over 1f out* **9/4**[2]

0 **5** *½* **St Georges Rock (IRE)**[52] 5377 2-9-5 0.......... SteveDrowne 4 66
(Clive Cox) *trckd ldng trio: shkn up to dispute 3rd 2f out: fdd over 1f out* **20/1**

**6** *2 ¼* **Putting Green** 2-9-5 0.......... RichardHughes 11 61
(Richard Hannon) *towards rr: pushed along bef 1/2-way and struggling: nvr on terms after* **16/1**

**7** *3 ¼* **Intrude** 2-9-5 0.......... JimCrowley 6 54
(David Simcock) *chsd ldrs in 5th: shkn up and ch of a pl over 2f out: wknd wl over 1f out* **33/1**

**8** *2 ¾* **Amour De Nuit (IRE)** 2-9-5 0.......... ChrisCatlin 9 48
(Sir Mark Prescott Bt) *a in rr pushed along bef 1/2-way: bhd fnl 2f* **66/1**

**9** *20* **Muscadelle** 2-9-0 0.......... JohnFahy 8
(Eve Johnson Houghton) *in tch 3f: sn rdn and wknd: t.o* **100/1**

1m 48.36s (3.66) **Going Correction** +0.225s/f (Good) **9** Ran SP% **120.2**
Speed ratings (Par 95): **90,88,85,84,83 81,78,75,55**
CSF £8.85 TOTE £1.70: £1.10, £2.00, £3.00; EX 6.80 Trifecta £36.70.
**Owner** Jadara Stables Sl **Bred** Grangemore Stud **Trained** Kingsclere, Hants

**FOCUS**
Probably the stronger of the two divisions, with the time being 1.32secs faster than the first leg. The winner could rate 5lb higher, while the fourth has been rated as not improving on his debut effort on this different ground.

## 6986 JOE WARD HILL MEMORIAL CLAIMING STKS 1m 2f 7y
**3:20** (3:21) (Class 5) 3-4-Y-O **£2,587** (£770; £384; £192) **Stalls** Centre

Form RPR

2236 **1** **Dalgig**[38] 5898 4-9-4 77.......... AndreaAtzeni 9 81
(Jamie Osborne) *trckd ldr after 3f: led wl over 2f out and sent for home: drvn and styd on wl fr over 1f out* **2/1**[1]

3060 **2** *3* **Henry The Aviator (USA)**[16] 6566 4-9-2 78.......... RyanMoore 2 73
(Mark Johnston) *trckd ldrs: cl up 4f out: drvn to chse wnr 2f out: no imp over 1f out* **5/2**[2]

003 **3** *3 ½* **Desert Society (IRE)**[20] 6423 3-8-11 77..........(b) RichardHughes 6 67
(Richard Hannon) *reluctant to go to post: w.w in rr: rdn 4f out: kpt on fr 2f out to take 3rd ins fnl f: n.d* **9/2**

0-61 **4** *¾* **Rochelle (IRE)**[18] 6481 3-8-10 59.......... MartinDwyer 1 64
(William Muir) *trckd ldrs: rdn over 2f out: chsd ldng pair wl over 1f out to ins fnl f: one pce* **10/1**

5000 **5** *4* **Cabin Fever**[38] 5884 3-8-8 70..........(bt[1]) RichardKingscote 5 55
(Ralph Beckett) *t.k.h early: led after 2f to wl over 2f out: wknd wl over 1f out* **4/1**[3]

5000 **6** *10* **Movie Magic**[12] 6661 3-7-11 45.......... RyanPowell(3) 3 28
(John Bridger) *led 2f: wl in tch: rdn 3f out: wknd over 2f out* **100/1**

0536 **7** *5* **Dark Tsarina (IRE)**[49] 5491 3-7-11 50 ow1.......... HectorCrouch(7) 4 22
(Michael Madgwick) *a wl in rr: pushed along 3f out: no prog: eased ins fnl f* **50/1**

-000 **8** *16* **Desert Island Dusk**[28] 6194 3-8-5 45.......... WilliamCarson 10
(John Bridger) *nvr gng wl: a wl in rr: t.o* **100/1**

2m 9.99s (1.29) **Going Correction** +0.225s/f (Good)
**WFA** 3 from 4yo 5lb **8** Ran SP% **113.1**
Speed ratings (Par 103): **103,100,97,97,94 86,82,69**
CSF £7.06 TOTE £3.30: £1.10, £1.80, £2.00; EX 7.40 Trifecta £20.20.Dalgig was claimed by D Pipe for £12000.
**Owner** N A Jackson **Bred** Usk Valley Stud **Trained** Upper Lambourn, Berks

**FOCUS**
The right horses came to the fore in this fair claimer. The winner has been rated to form, and the fourth helps set the level as well.

## 6987 READING POST H'CAP 1m 3f 135y
**3:50** (3:50) (Class 3) (0-90,88) 3-Y-O+ **£7,439** (£2,213; £1,106; £553) **Stalls** Centre

Form RPR

-263 **1** **Norway Cross**[37] 5931 4-9-5 81.......... AndreaAtzeni 10 91+
(Luca Cumani) *hld up in rr: pushed along and prog to chse ldng pair 3f out: racd in centre in st: sustained effrt fr 2f out to ld ins fnl f* **2/1**[1]

4002 **2** *1* **Tobacco Road (IRE)**[5] 6877 4-9-10 86.......... RichardHughes 1 94
(Richard Hannon) *led: styd against nr side rail in st: hrd pressed fr 3f out: drvn 2f out: kpt on but hdd ins fnl f* **6/1**[3]

1160 **3** *nse* **Puzzle Time**[10] 6713 4-9-8 84.......... WilliamCarson 4 92
(Giles Bravery) *cl up: trckd ldr over 3f out: rdn to chal over 2f out: upsides over 1f out tl wnr wnt past ins fnl f* **25/1**

4005 **4** *18* **Festival Theatre (IRE)**[33] 6036 3-8-13 82..........(v[1]) RyanMoore 8 60
(Sir Michael Stoute) *trckd ldr to 5f out: rdn over 3f out: sn wknd: v modest 4th fr over 1f out* **7/2**[2]

12-4 **5** *4* **Stock Hill Fair**[17] 6518 6-9-7 83.......... PatDobbs 3 55
(Brendan Powell) *cl up: chsd ldr 5f out to over 3f out: sn wknd and bhd* **6/1**[3]

106- **6** *20* **Emerging**[373] 6841 4-9-9 85.......... LiamKeniry 6 24
(David Elsworth) *hld up in tch: rdn and wknd over 3f out: wl bhd whn lost action nr fin: dismntd after* **20/1**

0000 **7** *7* **Busatto (USA)**[16] 6548 4-9-8 84.......... DaneO'Neill 11 11
(Mark Johnston) *chsd ldrs: rdn 4f out: sn btn: t.o* **10/1**

-145 **8** *66* **Christopher Wren (USA)**[121] 2991 7-9-12 88.......... GeorgeBaker 7
(Nick Gifford) *hld up in last and sn detached: pushed along and no rspnse 5f out: wl t.o* **8/1**

2m 31.44s (1.94) **Going Correction** +0.225s/f (Good)
**WFA** 3 from 4yo+ 7lb **8** Ran SP% **112.9**
Speed ratings (Par 107): **102,101,101,89,86 73,68,24**
CSF £14.05 CT £222.43 TOTE £3.00: £1.30, £2.20, £5.40; EX 12.70 Trifecta £128.50.
**Owner** Bartisan Racing Ltd **Bred** Tsega Mares Sarl **Trained** Newmarket, Suffolk

**FOCUS**
They came home at long intervals behind the front three in what was a decent handicap run at a fair gallop. The runner-up has been rated back to the level of his reappearance win here over 1m.

## 6988 50 FREE SPINS AT UNIBET CASINO MAIDEN STKS 6f
**4:20** (4:20) (Class 5) 3-Y-O+ **£2,587** (£770; £384; £192) **Stalls** Low

Form RPR

025 **1** **Lady Brigid (IRE)**[122] 2967 3-9-0 75.......... PatDobbs 8 73
(Olly Stevens) *w ldrs: led 1/2-way: hung lft fr over 2f out and ended against far rail: drvn clr fr over 1f out* **5/2**[2]

0225 **2** *3* **Posh Bounty**[16] 6567 3-9-0 45.......... OisinMurphy 13 63
(Joseph Tuite) *taken down early: w ldrs: chal fr 1/2-way: carried lft over 2f out: one pce fnl f* **20/1**

2322 **3** *1 ¼* **Persian Bolt (USA)**[14] 6617 3-8-9 70..........(b) GeorgeDowning(5) 11 59
(Eve Johnson Houghton) *in tch: rdn 1/2-way: styd on u.p fr 2f out to take 3rd nr fin* **9/4**[1]

2224 **4** *¾* **Anna's Vision (IRE)**[51] 5417 3-9-0 73.......... RyanMoore 1 57
(Jeremy Noseda) *towards rr: rdn and prog over 2f out: no imp on ldrs but kpt on fr over 1f out* **5/2**[2]

0 **5** *hd* **Elhaam (IRE)**[47] 5548 3-9-0 0.......... TomQueally 15 56
(George Margarson) *dwlt: sn w ldrs: rdn to chal over 2f out: nt qckn over 1f out: fdd fnl f* **20/1**

**6** *¾* **Sir Billy Wright (IRE)** 3-9-5 0.......... GeorgeBaker 2 59+
(David Evans) *dwlt: rn green in last: pushed along 1/2-way: kpt on in encouraging manner fnl 2f: nrst fin* **16/1**[3]

35 **7** *2 ¼* **Satellite Express (IRE)**[9] 6765 3-9-0 0.......... ChrisCatlin 9 47
(David Evans) *prom: led after 2f to 1/2-way: short of room sn after: wknd wl over 1f out* **50/1**

**8** *3* **Great Storm** 3-9-0 0.......... FergusSweeney 3 37
(Gary Moore) *pushed along in rr after 2f: nvr really figured* **50/1**

64 **9** *3 ¼* **Kings Chapel (USA)**[22] 6356 3-9-5 0.......... SteveDrowne 14 32
(Jeremy Gask) *a towards rr: shkn up and off the pce over 2f out: steadily wknd* **25/1**

6 **10** *2* **Man Of Music**[20] 6421 3-9-5 0.......... LiamKeniry 4 25
(Tony Carroll) *s.i.s: a in rr: rdn and struggling fr 1/2-way* **20/1**

00 **11** *23* **Aduvee**[20] 6421 4-9-1 0.......... WilliamTwiston-Davies 6
(Ronald Harris) *led 2f: wknd 1/2-way: t.o* **100/1**

1m 14.1s (1.10) **Going Correction** +0.225s/f (Good)
**WFA** 3 from 4yo 1lb **11** Ran SP% **116.8**
Speed ratings (Par 103): **101,97,95,94,94 93,90,86,81,79 48**
CSF £54.38 TOTE £4.60: £2.00, £4.10, £1.10; EX 59.50 Trifecta £179.50.
**Owner** M H and Mrs G Tourle **Bred** Minch Bloodstock & Brittas Stud **Trained** Chiddingfold, Surrey
■ Stewards' Enquiry : Pat Dobbs two-day ban: careless riding (Oct 20-21)

**FOCUS**
Quite a modest maiden, with a 45-rated filly finishing second. The runner-up has been rated as running a clear pb, and the winner has been rated to form.

## 6989 IVOR LAWS MEMORIAL NURSERY H'CAP (BOBIS RACE) 5f 10y
**4:50** (4:50) (Class 4) (0-85,85) 2-Y-O **£3,752** (£1,116; £557; £278) **Stalls** Low

Form RPR

0104 **1** **Goldcrest**[38] 5879 2-8-13 77..........[1] DaneO'Neill 13 88
(Henry Candy) *mde all: drvn clr over 1f out: styd on wl* **8/1**

215 **2** *3* **Marigot Bay**[37] 5921 2-8-8 77.......... DanielMuscutt(5) 12 77
(Gay Kelleway) *t.k.h: hld up early but prog to chse wnr after 2f: rdn 2f out: outpcd fr over 1f out* **20/1**

0444 **3** *½* **Stinky Socks (IRE)**[13] 6629 2-8-0 64.......... JimmyQuinn 9 62
(Charles Hills) *taken steadily to post: plld hrd: hld up bhd ldrs: rdn 2f out: one pce after* **14/1**

0413 **4** *hd* **La Cuesta (IRE)**[10] 6703 2-9-7 85 ........ RichardHughes 11 82
(Jamie Osborne) *hld up in last trio: tried to cl on ldrs 2f out: rdn and one pce over 1f out* **2/1**[1]

0610 **5** *1 1/2* **Majestic Hero (IRE)**[30] 6128 2-9-5 83 ........ DavidProbert 5 75
(Ronald Harris) *chsd wnr 2f: sn rdn: fdd over 1f out* **3/1**[2]

0054 **6** *1* **Stone Roses (IRE)**[35] 5973 2-8-3 67 ........ AndreaAtzeni 3 55
(Michael Bell) *hld up in last trio: rdn and no prog 2f out* **8/1**

0031 **7** *2 1/4* **Tecumseh (IRE)**[21] 6401 2-8-9 73 ........ JimCrowley 4 53
(K R Burke) *hld up in last trio: rdn and struggling over 2f out: wknd over 1f out: eased last 75yds* **4/1**[3]

1m 1.88s (1.58) **Going Correction** +0.225s/f (Good) **7 Ran SP% 112.0**
Speed ratings (Par 97): **96,91,90,90,87 86,82**
CSF £132.41 CT £2169.55 TOTE £8.60: £3.80, £4.80; EX 65.60 Trifecta £719.40.
**Owner** Lady Whent **Bred** Lady Whent **Trained** Kingston Warren, Oxon

**FOCUS**
A fair nursery that produced a clear-cut winner. The form makes sense rated around the second and third.

## 6990 GET £10 FREE AT UNIBET POKER H'CAP 1m 67y

**5:20** (5:20) (Class 4) (0-80,80) 3-Y-O+ **£4,851** (£1,443; £721; £360) **Stalls Low**

Form RPR

31-2 **1** **Donncha (IRE)**[150] 2112 3-9-3 79 ........ AndreaAtzeni 12 93+
(Robert Eddery) *wl in tch: pushed along and prog 3f out: taken to far rail and clsd to chal over 1f out: drvn to ld ins fnl f: styd on* **7/2**[2]

233- **2** *3/4* **Melvin The Grate (IRE)**[127] 2810 4-9-5 78 ........ OisinMurphy 9 90
(Andrew Balding) *mde most: narrowly hdd over 3f out to over 2f out: clr w wnr over 1f out: hdd ins fnl f: styd on* **8/1**[3]

2010 **3** *4 1/2* **Hostile Fire (IRE)**[9] 6737 3-9-3 79 ........(p) DaneO'Neill 11 81
(Ed de Giles) *dwlt: hld up in last: shkn up and prog fr 3f out: styd on to take 3rd fnl f but ldng pair clr* **10/1**

4064 **4** *1 1/2* **Subtle Knife**[19] 6466 5-9-0 73 ........ WilliamCarson 10 71
(Giles Bravery) *in tch: rdn and struggling 3f out: sn dropped to rr: kpt on again and squeezed between rivals fnl f to take 4th nr fin* **10/1**

100 **5** *shd* **Unison (IRE)**[10] 6713 4-9-3 76 ........ SteveDrowne 2 74
(Peter Makin) *prom: rdn 3f out: nt qckn and outpcd fr 2f out: kpt on again fnl f* **20/1**

134 **6** *nse* **Craftsmanship (FR)**[63] 4982 3-9-0 76 ........ JimmyQuinn 6 74
(Robert Eddery) *hld up in midfield: gng bttr than sme 3f out: outpcd whn reminder and hung lft over 1f out: no ch after* **25/1**

0640 **7** *1 1/4* **Ice Slice (IRE)**[61] 5038 3-9-1 77 ........ StevieDonohoe 7 72
(James Eustace) *hld up in rr: shkn up wl over 2f out: limited prog and n.d* **33/1**

0000 **8** *1/2* **Set The Trend**[18] 6498 8-9-1 74 ........(p) FergusSweeney 13 68
(David Dennis) *dwlt: hld up in rr: shoved along 3f out: one pce after and no threat* **50/1**

0501 **9** *3/4* **Killing Time (IRE)**[14] 6609 3-9-3 79 ........(b) JimCrowley 8 71
(Ralph Beckett) *chsd ldr after 1f: narrow ld over 3f out to over 2f out: wknd over 1f out* **14/1**

2112 **10** *nse* **Wordismybond**[45] 5629 5-9-1 74 ........ RichardHughes 1 66
(Peter Makin) *trckd ldrs: cl enough and rdn over 2f out: wknd over 1f out* **8/1**[3]

213 **11** *1 1/4* **Shama's Crown (IRE)**[19] 6460 3-9-4 80 ........ RyanMoore 5 69
(Jeremy Noseda) *t.k.h: trckd ldrs: rdn 3f out: wknd 2f out* **9/4**[1]

006 **12** *14* **Malicho**[24] 6304 5-9-0 73 ........(e[1]) TomQueally 14 30
(Dean Ivory) *awkward s: a wl in rr: struggling 3f out: t.o* **50/1**

0306 **13** *3 1/4* **Soaring Spirits (IRE)**[91] 4028 4-9-4 77 ........(b) RobertWinston 3 26
(Dean Ivory) *t.k.h: prom: wkng whn hmpd wl over 1f out: eased and t.o* **16/1**

1m 45.41s (0.71) **Going Correction** +0.225s/f (Good)
**WFA** 3 from 4yo+ 3lb **13 Ran SP% 121.4**
Speed ratings (Par 105): **105,104,99,98,98 98,96,96,95,95 94,80,77**
CSF £30.52 CT £261.17 TOTE £5.40: £2.10, £3.20, £2.50; EX 40.10 Trifecta £194.10.
**Owner** David Bannon **Bred** Ballyhane Stud **Trained** Newmarket, Suffolk

**FOCUS**
The headed far side in the straight this time and the front pair pulled clear. The runner-up has been rated a length up from his 3yo form.
T/Jkpt: £285.70 to a £1 stake. Pool of £6767.16 - 24.85 winning tickets. T/Plt: £8.10 to a £1 stake. Pool of £84773.52 - 7578.89 winning tickets. T/Qpdt: £3.20 to a £1 stake. Pool of £6184.83 - 1427.46 winning tickets. JN

# 6882 CHANTILLY (R-H)

Monday, October 6

**OFFICIAL GOING: Turf: good to soft; polytrack: standard**

## 6991a PRIX DES USAGES (CONDITIONS) (2YO) (TURF) 5f 110y

**11:30** (11:30) 2-Y-O **£14,166** (£5,666; £4,250; £2,833; £1,416)

RPR

**1** **Something Lucky (IRE)**[5] 2-9-0 0 ........ AntoineHamelin 7 92
(Matthieu Palussiere, France) **118/10**

**2** *nk* **Lightscameraction (IRE)**[17] 6513 2-9-0 0 ........ Pierre-CharlesBoudot 3 91
(Gay Kelleway) *led: rdn whn chal 1 1/2f out: hdd ins fnl f and rallied: no ex cl home* **11/2**[3]

**3** *nk* **Connected (FR)**[33] 2-8-10 0 ........ GregoryBenoist 4 86
(E Lellouche, France) **9/1**

**4** *3 1/2* **Finsbury Square (IRE)**[27] 2-8-10 0 ........ CristianDemuro 6 74
(F Chappet, France) **7/5**[1]

**5** *snk* **Enough Paint (IRE)**[17] 2-8-10 0 ........ ThierryJarnet 2 74
(J Heloury, France) **10/1**

**6** *1/2* **Dr King (ITY)**[61] 2-9-0 0 ........ IoritzMendizabal 1 76
(J-C Rouget, France) **2/1**[2]

**7** *1 1/4* **Loose Cannon (FR)**[17] 2-8-10 0 ........(b) MickaelBarzalona 5 68
(D Windrif, France) **42/1**

1m 3.7s (-0.80) **7 Ran SP% 119.6**
WIN (incl. 1 euro stake): 12.80. PLACES: 3.70, 2.70, 3.30. DF: 34.40. SF: 68.80.
**Owner** Mrs Theresa Marnane **Bred** Rathasker Stud **Trained** France

## 6992a PRIX DU VERGALLY (CLAIMER) (4YO+) (POLYTRACK) 1m

**12:00** (12:00) 4-Y-O+ **£9,583** (£3,833; £2,875; £1,916; £958)

RPR

**1** **Silverheels (IRE)**[4] 6885 5-9-4 0 ........(b) IoritzMendizabal 13 91
(Paul Cole) *broke wl fr wd draw: sn trcking ldr on outer: eased into ld 1 1/2f out: drvn clr ins fnl f: in command fnl 100yds* **67/10**[3]

**2** *3/4* **Tostaky Blue (FR)**[67] 5-8-11 0 ........ EddyHardouin 10 82
(Y Gourraud, France) **29/1**

**3** *nk* **Lips Dancer (IRE)**[92] 5-9-6 0 ........ MaximeGuyon 9 90
(Andreas Lowe, Germany) **74/10**

**4** *1* **Tangatchek (IRE)**[29] 5-8-11 0 ........ FabriceVeron 5 79
(H-A Pantall, France) **188/10**

**5** *hd* **Sussudio (FR)**[20] 4-9-1 0 ........ FilipMinarik 7 83
(N Sauer, Germany) **103/10**

**6** *nk* **Courcy (FR)**[540] 1562 4-9-1 0 ........ CristianDemuro 8 82
(G Botti, France) **101/10**

**7** *hd* **Ship Rock (IRE)**[20] 4-9-1 0 ........ Pierre-CharlesBoudot 2 81
(Robert Collet, France) **128/10**

**8** *snk* **Louvain (FR)**[29] 5-9-4 0 ........(p) ChristopheSoumillon 11 84
(P Demercastel, France) **123/10**

**9** *3/4* **Liman (IRE)**[21] 4-8-11 0 ........ GregoryBenoist 6 75
(Mme Pia Brandt, France) **43/10**[2]

**10** *1/2* **New Outlook (USA)**[26] 6-9-1 0 ........ BenjaminPinard(7) 3 85
(F Chappet, France) **27/10**[1]

**11** *shd* **Dakar Style (FR)**[20] 4-8-9 0 ........ MllePaulineDominois(6) 4 78
(E Lellouche, France) **35/1**

**12** *1/2* **Chopsoave (FR)**[29] 6-8-9 0 ........(p) NicolasLarenaudie(6) 12 77
(N Caullery, France) **189/10**

1m 36.3s (96.30) **12 Ran SP% 119.6**
WIN (incl. 1 euro stake): 7.70. PLACES: 3.00, 8.40, 2.90. DF: 110.90. SF: 183.40.
**Owner** P F I Cole Ltd **Bred** Castlemartin Stud And Skymarc Farm **Trained** Whatcombe, Oxon

## 6994a PRIX DE BONNEVAL (LISTED RACE) (3YO+) (TURF) 5f 110y

**1:35** (1:35) 3-Y-O+ **£21,666** (£8,666; £6,500; £4,333; £2,166)

RPR

**1** **Farmah (USA)**[20] 6446 3-8-9 0 ........ Francois-XavierBertras 12 113
(F Rohaut, France) **57/10**[3]

**2** *3 1/2* **Robert Le Diable (FR)**[36] 5963 5-8-13 0 ........ FlavienPrat 8 104
(D Prod'Homme, France) **22/5**[2]

**3** *1/2* **Penmaen (IRE)**[22] 6378 4-8-9 0 ........ FabienLefebvre 1 98
(J E Hammond, France) **77/10**

**4** *hd* **B Fifty Two (IRE)**[26] 6231 5-8-13 0 ........(b) ChristopheSoumillon 9 102
(Charles Hills) *wnt sltly lft leaving stalls: sn led: rdn and hdd over 1f out: kpt on gamely u.p fnl f* **93/10**

**5** *nse* **Katawi**[52] 5381 3-8-9 0 ........ MaximeGuyon 4 99
(Chris Wall) *hld up in midfield: chsd ldng pair appr 1/2-way: rdn over 1f out: kpt on fnl f: no ex cl home* **209/10**

**6** *nk* **Caledonia Lady**[22] 6378 5-9-0 0 ........ AlexisBadel 6 102
(Mme M Bollack-Badel, France) **7/2**[1]

**7** *nk* **Frascata (FR)**[19] 5-8-13 0 ........ Pierre-CharlesBoudot 5 100
(Yves de Nicolay, France) **162/10**

**8** *1/2* **Inspiriter**[48] 3-8-9 0 ........ MickaelBarzalona 11 95
(H-A Pantall, France) *hld up towards rr: niggled along 1 1/2f out but no imp: kpt on ins fnl f: nvr in contention* **187/10**

**9** *nse* **Myasun (FR)**[36] 5963 7-8-13 0 ........ ThierryJarnet 3 98
(C Baillet, France) **135/10**

**10** *3/4* **Cambio De Planes**[22] 6378 5-8-13 0 ........(p) StephanePasquier 2 95
(C Delcher-Sanchez, France) **93/10**

**11** *nk* **Aksil (FR)**[19] 4-8-9 0 ........ Christophe-PatriceLemaire 10 90
(M Boutin, France) **156/10**

**12** *hd* **Fanoos**[19] 5-8-9 0 ........(b) MickaelForest 7 90
(Mme G Rarick, France) **61/1**

**13** *1 1/4* **Fresles (IRE)**[36] 5963 3-8-9 0 ........ GregoryBenoist 13 86
(Mme Pia Brandt, France) **41/1**

1m 2.66s (-1.84) **13 Ran SP% 118.9**
WIN (incl. 1 euro stake): 6.70. PLACES: 2.20, 2.00, 2.70. DF: 14.80. SF: 34.10.
**Owner** Hamdan Al Maktoum **Bred** Shadwell Farm LLC **Trained** Sauvagnon, France

6993 - 6994a (Foreign Racing) - See Raceform Interactive

# 6393 BRIGHTON (L-H)

Tuesday, October 7

**OFFICIAL GOING: Soft changing to heavy after race 4 (3.20)**
Wind: Strong, half against away from stand Weather: Blustery showers

## 6995 NEWLY REFURBISHED GENTING CASINO BRIGHTON H'CAP 5f 213y

**1:50** (1:51) (Class 6) (0-60,60) 3-Y-O+ **£1,940** (£577; £288; £144) **Stalls Low**

Form RPR

0006 **1** **Telegraph (IRE)**[68] 4820 3-9-3 57 ........ JFEgan 4 66
(David Evans) *sn led: c to stands' rail in st: hdd 2f out: rallied to ld again fnl 100yds: pushed out* **28/1**

5045 **2** *1/2* **Ecliptic Sunrise**[8] 6815 3-8-12 52 ow1 ........ PatCosgrave 3 59
(Des Donovan) *t.k.h: in tch: effrt over 2f out: led over 1f out: hdd and unable qck fnl 100yds: readily hld* **10/1**

5014 **3** *1 1/2* **Bookmaker**[13] 6666 4-9-6 59 ........(b) WilliamCarson 1 61
(John Bridger) *chsd ldr: slt ld 2f out tl over 1f out: one pce fnl f* **6/1**[3]

603 **4** *1* **Night Trade (IRE)**[34] 6030 7-8-8 50 ........(p) CamHardie(3) 2 49
(Ronald Harris) *prom: rdn over 2f out: n.m.r 1f out: swtchd lft: one pce* **6/1**[3]

4005 **5** *1 1/2* **Trigger Park (IRE)**[32] 6088 3-8-10 50 ........ PatDobbs 6 44
(Ronald Harris) *in tch: rdn and no hdwy fnl 2f* **20/1**

0040 **6** *2 1/4* **Port Lairge**[22] 6409 4-8-11 50 ........(b) ChrisCatlin 7 37
(John Gallagher) *s.i.s: outpcd and bhd: nvr rchd ldrs* **33/1**

5000 **7** *nk* **Lionheart**[22] 6397 4-8-13 59 ........ HectorCrouch(7) 11 45
(Peter Crate) *rrd s and missed break: towards rr: modest effrt and hung lft 2f out: n.d* **10/1**

0255 **8** *2 3/4* **Koharu**[26] 6266 4-9-4 60 ........(p) DeclanBates(3) 14 37
(Peter Makin) *hld up in rr: pushed along 3f out: nvr nr ldrs* **9/4**[1]

-023 **9** *3* **Saskia's Dream**[80] 4431 6-9-6 59 ........(v) RichardHughes 5 53
(Jane Chapple-Hyam) *hld up in midfield: swtchd lft and effrt towards centre over 1f out: hung lft and eased* **4/1**[2]

0005 **10** *1 3/4* **Crafty Business (IRE)**[35] 6022 3-9-2 59 ........(v) CharlesBishop(3) 12 21
(Gary Moore) *sn outpcd and bhd* **14/1**

1m 15.59s (5.39) **Going Correction** +0.85s/f (Soft)
**WFA** 3 from 4yo+ 1lb **10 Ran SP% 115.3**
Speed ratings (Par 101): **98,97,95,94,92 89,88,84,80,78**
CSF £275.60 CT £1342.79 TOTE £24.80: £4.30, £3.10, £2.30; EX 204.80 Trifecta £1237.50.
**Owner** The Drink Pink Partnership **Bred** Ronnie Boland **Trained** Pandy, Monmouths

**FOCUS**

Rail dolled out from 2.5f to Winning Post to provide fresh inner running line and distances increased by 5yds. 22mm of overnight rain saw the ground changed to soft, leading to a host of non-runners on the card. A low-grade sprint handicap to open proceedings and the field came stands' side in the straight, as is usually the case when the rain gets into the ground here. The winner has been rated close to his best and the runner-up to a length pb.

## 6996 GENTING CASINO BRIGHTON ROULETTE NURSERY H'CAP — 6f 209y

**2:20** (2:20) (Class 5) (0-75,75) 2-Y-O — £2,587 (£770; £384; £192) Stalls Low

Form — RPR

4030 **1** **Ciaras Cookie (IRE)**[15] 6610 2-8-8 62 ........ JFEgan 7 — 63
(David Evans) *mde most: jnd and strly chal on both sides ins fnl f: hld on gamely* — **16/1**

065 **2** *shd* **Bling Ring (USA)**[10] 6735 2-8-11 65 ........ [1] HarryBentley 6 — 66
(Charles Hills) *dwlt: hld up: hdwy and fnd gap over 1f out: str chal ins fnl f: r.o* — **13/2**[3]

545 **3** *nk* **Shipwright (IRE)**[19] 6496 2-9-7 75 ........ KierenFallon 8 — 75
(Mark Johnston) *prom: squeezed through on stands' rail and drvn level ins fnl f: unable qck fnl strides* — **7/2**[2]

5002 **4** *¾* **Tumut (IRE)**[12] 6676 2-8-8 65 ........ CharlesBishop(3) 12 — 63
(Mick Channon) *hld up in rr: rdn 3f out: hdwy in centre to press ldrs over 1f out: kpt on* — **14/1**

644 **5** *2½* **Haarib**[32] 6103 2-9-1 69 ........ PatCosgrave 5 — 61
(Ed Walker) *chsd ldrs: drvn to chal 2f out: one pce appr fnl f* — **13/2**[3]

043 **6** *6* **Bobbie's Girl (IRE)**[27] 6224 2-9-1 69 ........ [1] LiamJones 13 — 45
(William Haggas) *hld up towards rr: effrt and in tch 2f out: wknd over 1f out* — **9/1**

4042 **7** *½* **Beach Samba (IRE)**[13] 6668 2-9-5 73 ........ MartinHarley 2 — 48
(Ed Dunlop) *trckd ldrs: chal over 2f out: sn outpcd* — **13/8**[1]

3050 **8** *20* **Lunar Knot**[22] 6413 2-8-0 54 ........ KieranO'Neill 10
(Alan McCabe) *chsd ldrs for 2f: sn lost pl: struggling in rr fnl 3f* — **33/1**

1m 30.15s (7.05) **Going Correction** +0.85s/f (Soft) — **8** Ran SP% **112.5**
Speed ratings (Par 95): **93,92,92,91,88 81,81,58**
CSF £111.18 CT £450.13 TOTE £15.50: £2.70, £2.20, £1.60; EX 144.40 Trifecta £714.30.
**Owner** Mrs Emma Ambrose **Bred** River Downs Stud **Trained** Pandy, Monmouths
■ Stewards' Enquiry : Kieren Fallon four-day ban: used whip above permitted level (Oct 21-24)

**FOCUS**

A slow-motion finish to the nursery with the winner providing a quick double on the card for David Evans and John Egan.

## 6997 GENTING CASINO BRIGHTON BLACKJACK MAIDEN AUCTION STKS — 6f 209y

**2:50** (2:52) (Class 5) 2-Y-O — £2,587 (£770; £384; £192) Stalls Low

Form — RPR

2442 **1** **Vegas Rebel (IRE)**[13] 6667 2-9-0 77 ........ MartinHarley 6 — 77
(Peter Chapple-Hyam) *hld up in rr: hdwy 2f out: led 1f out: rdn out* — **5/4**[1]

0 **2** *3½* **Burma Bridge**[17] 6545 2-8-10 0 ........ RichardHughes 1 — 64
(Richard Hannon) *led: c to stands' rail in st: rdn and hdd 1f out: one pce* — **20/1**

3 **3** *13* **Delaire**[26] 6261 2-8-9 0 ........ JackMitchell 2 — 29
(Roger Varian) *s.i.s: sn in 4th: effrt in centre and hrd rdn 2f out: edgd rt: wknd over 1f out* — **5/4**[1]

44 **4** *½* **Inke (IRE)**[13] 6652 2-8-6 0 ........ WilliamCarson 4 — 25
(Jim Boyle) *prom tl wknd 2f out* — **14/1**[2]

0 **5** *1¾* **Rainbow Pride (IRE)**[11] 6719 2-9-1 0 ........ ChrisCatlin 7 — 29
(Sir Mark Prescott Bt) *hld up towards rr: n.d fnl 2f* — **40/1**

0550 **6** *hd* **Vinamar (IRE)**[13] 6662 2-8-7 57 ........ LiamJones 3 — 21
(Roger Teal) *t.k.h: prom tl wknd wl over 1f out* — **80/1**

4 **7** *6* **Fayreway (IRE)**[119] 3082 2-8-3 0 ........ [1] CamHardie(3) 5 — 4
(Martyn Meade) *reluctant to go to s: hld up in 6th: rdn and lost tch over 2f out* — **16/1**[3]

1m 27.44s (4.34) **Going Correction** +0.85s/f (Soft) — **7** Ran SP% **109.9**
Speed ratings (Par 95): **109,105,90,89,87 87,80**
CSF £27.40 TOTE £2.60: £1.30, £5.00; EX 16.40 Trifecta £40.80.
**Owner** Rebel Racing (2) **Bred** Cloughmealy Stud **Trained** Newmarket, Suffolk

**FOCUS**

An uncompetitive maiden.

## 6998 GENTING CASINO BRIGHTON THREE CARD POKER EBF MAIDEN STKS — 7f 214y

**3:20** (3:21) (Class 5) 2-Y-O — £2,911 (£866; £432; £216) Stalls Low

Form — RPR

**1** **Smile That Smile** 2-9-0 0 ........ JimmyQuinn 4 — 65
(Mark H Tompkins) *dwlt: bhd: rdn 3f out: rapid hdwy to ld ins fnl f: all out* — **66/1**

55 **2** *hd* **Toofeeg (IRE)**[14] 6621 2-9-5 0 ........ LiamJones 6 — 70
(William Haggas) *led after 1f and set gd pce: hdd 3f out: led again 1f out: sn hdd: rallied wl* — **12/1**

34 **3** *6* **Resonant (IRE)**[14] 6621 2-9-5 0 ........ KierenFallon 3 — 57
(Mark Johnston) *led for 1f: prom after: chal and hung lft 1f out: wknd ins fnl f* — **9/2**[3]

**4** *1¼* **Desert Encounter (IRE)** 2-9-5 0 ........ MartinHarley 1 — 54
(David Simcock) *dwlt: sn prom: wandered in centre over 1f out: sn wknd* — **9/4**[2]

533 **5** *7* **Aledaid (IRE)**[19] 6496 2-9-5 84 ........ FrankieDettori 5 — 39
(Richard Hannon) *hld up: rdn to ld 3f out: hdd & wknd qckly 1f out* — **1/1**[1]

1m 44.75s (8.75) **Going Correction** +0.85s/f (Soft) — **5** Ran SP% **108.1**
Speed ratings (Par 95): **90,89,83,82,75**
CSF £549.49 TOTE £16.60: £8.20, £4.00; EX 95.90 Trifecta £319.70.
**Owner** Dullingham Park **Bred** Dullingham Park **Trained** Newmarket, Suffolk

**FOCUS**

A big surprise in the maiden with the 66-1 outsider of five making a winning debut.

## 6999 GENTING CASINO BRIGHTON £10K JACKPOT SLOTS H'CAP (DIV I) — 7f 214y

**3:50** (3:51) (Class 6) (0-65,65) 3-Y-O+ — £1,940 (£577; £288; £144) Stalls Low

Form — RPR

5061 **1** **Improvized**[40] 5846 3-8-9 56 ........ (p) SteveDrowne 2 — 63
(William Muir) *sn rdn along and detached in last pl: drvn and hdwy over 1f out: styd on wl to ld fnl 75yds* — **15/8**[1]

0030 **2** *½* **Shifting Star (IRE)**[13] 6657 9-9-7 65 ........ (vt) WilliamCarson 8 — 71
(John Bridger) *led and set gd pce: c to stands' rail in st: hdd over 1f out: rallied gamely ins fnl f* — **7/1**

3645 **3** *nk* **Stybba**[27] 6242 3-8-13 60 ........ (v[1]) HarryBentley 7 — 65
(Andrew Balding) *hld up in 5th: hdwy in centre to ld over 1f out: hdd fnl 75yds: kpt on* — **9/2**[3]

0000 **4** *9* **Zaeem**[14] 6635 5-9-0 58 ........ (p) PatCosgrave 10 — 42
(Dean Ivory) *cl up: hmpd on stands' rail 3f out: rallied 2f out: wknd 1f out* — **20/1**

0200 **5** *11* **Bloodsweatandtears**[166] 1665 6-8-12 63 ........ CallumShepherd(7) 5 — 22
(William Knight) *dwlt: sn chsng ldr: rdn 3f out: wknd over 1f out* — **10/1**

5222 **6** *8* **Cape Summit**[19] 6483 3-9-4 65 ........ MartinHarley 9 — 6
(Ed Dunlop) *chsd ldrs tl wknd wl over 1f out* — **9/4**[2]

1m 42.28s (6.28) **Going Correction** +0.85s/f (Soft)
**WFA** 3 from 4yo+ 3lb — **6** Ran SP% **110.1**
Speed ratings (Par 101): **102,101,101,92,81 73**
CSF £14.69 CT £46.87 TOTE £3.10: £1.50, £3.40; EX 14.20 Trifecta £70.20.
**Owner** Foursome Thoroughbreds **Bred** Foursome Thoroughbreds **Trained** Lambourn, Berks
■ Stewards' Enquiry : William Carson two-day ban: careless riding (Oct 21-22)

**FOCUS**

Five non-runners here but the pace looked solid and the winner is an improving filly. The winner has been rated back to his debut win.

## 7000 GENTING CASINO BRIGHTON £10K JACKPOT SLOTS H'CAP (DIV II) — 7f 214y

**4:20** (4:20) (Class 6) (0-65,64) 3-Y-O+ — £1,940 (£577; £288; £144) Stalls Low

Form — RPR

6430 **1** **Byrd In Hand (IRE)**[37] 5950 7-9-0 57 ........ (v) WilliamCarson 4 — 67
(John Bridger) *chsd ldr: led 5f out: styd alone on far side in st and wnt 6 l clr: too far ahd to be ct: drvn out* — **7/1**[3]

0456 **2** *3* **Black Dave (IRE)**[15] 6616 4-9-5 62 ........ JFEgan 2 — 65+
(David Evans) *hld up towards rr: rdn and hdwy 2f out: styd on to take 2nd ins fnl f: unable to rch wnr* — **11/4**[1]

6000 **3** *3¼* **Dana's Present**[24] 6337 5-9-7 64 ........ PatCosgrave 1 — 60+
(George Baker) *t.k.h in rr: rdn 3f out: styd on wl fr over 1f out: wnt 3rd nr fin* — **7/1**[3]

6465 **4** *½* **Alphabetique**[36] 5975 3-8-13 64 ........ JordanNason(5) 8 — 58+
(Peter Chapple-Hyam) *towards rr: rdn 4f out: styd on u.p fnl 2f* — **14/1**

5636 **5** *6* **Swilken**[11] 6717 3-9-2 62 ........ JimmyQuinn 10 — 43+
(Mark H Tompkins) *prom in chsng gp tl wknd over 1f out* — **20/1**

5213 **6** *1½* **Plough Boy (IRE)**[24] 6337 3-8-11 57 ........ KierenFallon 9 — 34+
(Willie Musson) *led for 3f: 2nd whn led main gp to stands' side in st: a wl hld by wnr on far side: wknd over 1f out* — **9/2**[2]

520 **7** *13* **Aristocratic Duty**[17] 6567 3-9-1 61 ........ LiamKeniry 7 — +
(Sylvester Kirk) *chsd ldrs tl wknd and eased over 1f out* — **14/1**

6020 **8** *15* **Tax Reform (IRE)**[14] 6636 4-8-10 60 ........ (b) HectorCrouch(7) 6
(Gary Moore) *dwlt: in tch tl hrd rdn and wknd 3f out* — **12/1**

5512 **9** *2½* **Claude Greenwood**[22] 6396 4-8-6 52 oh1 ow2 ........ (b) CharlesBishop(3) 5
(Linda Jewell) *chsd ldrs: hrd rdn 3f out: wknd wl over 1f out: eased* — **9/2**[2]

1m 42.65s (6.65) **Going Correction** +0.85s/f (Soft)
**WFA** 3 from 4yo+ 3lb — **9** Ran SP% **113.8**
Speed ratings (Par 101): **100,97,93,93,87 85,72,57,55**
CSF £26.17 CT £129.79 TOTE £8.10: £2.70, £1.70, £1.90; EX 44.50 Trifecta £321.50.
**Owner** Marshall Bridger **Bred** Bricklow Ltd **Trained** Liphook, Hants

**FOCUS**

Another modest handicap. The well-backed winner has been rated close to his best.

## 7001 GENTING CASINO BRIGHTON LEARN TO PLAY H'CAP — 1m 1f 209y

**4:50** (4:52) (Class 6) (0-65,65) 3-Y-O+ — £1,940 (£577; £288; £144) Stalls High

Form — RPR

0136 **1** **Mister Mayday (IRE)**[15] 6617 3-9-5 65 ........ (b) PatCosgrave 5 — 74
(George Baker) *hld up in rr: c to stands' side in st: rdn and hdwy 2f out: led over 1f out: styd on wl* — **9/2**[3]

2365 **2** *1¾* **On Demand**[40] 5848 3-9-2 65 ........ (v[1]) ThomasBrown(3) 11 — 70
(Andrew Balding) *chsd ldr: led 6f out and wnt 5 l clr: c to stands' side in st: hdd 2f out: styd on fnl f* — **7/2**[1]

4615 **3** *nk* **Glennten**[24] 6341 5-9-4 59 ........ IrineuGoncalves 4 — 63
(Jose Santos) *prom: c to stands' side in st: led 2f out tl over 1f out: kpt on* — **12/1**

2013 **4** *9* **Sexy Secret**[14] 6635 3-9-2 65 ........ (v) SimonPearce(3) 6 — 52
(Lydia Pearce) *in tch: c to stands' side in st: outpcd fnl 3f* — **10/1**

1056 **5** *5* **Highlife Dancer**[9] 6787 6-9-1 63 ........ (v) DanielCremin(7) 12 — 41
(Mick Channon) *chsd ldrs: c to stands' side in st: wknd 3f out* — **12/1**

3516 **6** *5* **Fair Comment**[32] 6086 4-9-7 62 ........ MartinHarley 14 — 30
(Michael Blanshard) *in tch: c to stands' side in st: wknd 3f out* — **12/1**

0562 **7** *2½* **Hill Fort**[32] 6086 4-9-3 65 ........ (p) MikeyEnnis(7) 8 — 29
(Ronald Harris) *pushed along early: towards rr: hdwy 5f out: styd on far side in st: wknd and eased over 1f out* — **4/1**[2]

6000 **8** *4* **Top Set (IRE)**[15] 6616 4-9-5 60 ........ (b) HarryBentley 2 — 16
(Simon Dow) *towards rr: styd on far side in st: sme hdwy over 3f out: wknd and hung rt wl over 1f out* — **20/1**

0514 **9** *17* **Snow Conditions**[22] 6395 3-9-3 63 ........ JimmyQuinn 1
(Philip Hide) *towards rr: styd on far side in st: hrd rdn 3f out: bhd and eased fnl 2f* — **10/1**

3420 **10** *9* **Megalala (IRE)**[22] 6395 13-9-5 60 ........ WilliamCarson 10
(John Bridger) *led for 4f: lost pl and towards rr whn n.m.r 5f out: sn bhd* — **14/1**

2m 14.47s (10.87) **Going Correction** +0.85s/f (Soft)
**WFA** 3 from 4yo+ 5lb — **10** Ran SP% **113.1**
Speed ratings (Par 101): **90,88,88,81,77 73,71,67,54,47**
CSF £19.93 CT £173.45 TOTE £3.60: £1.10, £2.10, £5.00; EX 18.90 Trifecta £224.70.
**Owner** Asprey, Kane & Thomas **Bred** David Allan & Barnane Stud **Trained** Manton, Wilts

**FOCUS**

Another modest handicap and, although the gallop looked solid enough, the runner-up was never too far away. The runner-up has been rated to her maiden form.

## 7002 GENTING CASINO BRIGHTON LATE BAR "HANDS AND HEELS" APPRENTICE SERIES H'CAP — 1m 3f 196y

**5:20** (5:21) (Class 6) (0-55,55) 3-Y-O+ — £1,940 (£577; £288; £144) Stalls High

Form — RPR

000 **1** **Salient**[14] 6636 10-8-12 46 oh1 ........ KieranShoemark 6 — 64
(Michael Attwater) *prom: led 5f out: sn clr: in n.d fnl 3f* — **11/1**

5050 **2** *19* **Focail Mear**[3] 6946 3-8-6 47 ........ CamHardie 9 — 38
(John Ryan) *mid-div: wnt modest 3rd 2f out: kpt on same pce to take remote 2nd ins fnl f* — **5/4**[1]

0-00 **3** *nk* **King's Road**[79] 2614 9-9-0 48 ........ (t) CharlotteJenner 10 — 39
(Anabel K Murphy) *hld up towards rr: hdwy to chal for 2nd 3f out: wknd 2f out* — **10/1**

2346 **4** *6* **Indian Scout**[82] 4343 6-8-12 46 ........(b) GaryMahon 5 29
(Anabel K Murphy) *hld up towards rr: wnt 2nd 3f out: styd alone on far side in st: a wl hld by wnr on stands' side: wknd over 1f out* **7/1**[2]

4536 **5** *15* **Tamujin (IRE)**[39] 5873 6-8-12 46 ........ RobHornby 11 8
(Ken Cunningham-Brown) *hld up towards rr: n.d fnl 3f* **9/1**

060/ **6** *11* **Epsom Flyer**[663] 8093 4-8-10 47 oh1 ow1 ........ PaddyBradley(3) 13
(Pat Phelan) *s.i.s: a bhd: no ch fnl 3f* **16/1**

000- **7** *9* **Craftybird**[372] 6896 3-8-2 46 oh1 ........(b[1]) HectorCrouch(3) 2
(Gary Moore) *chsd ldrs tl wknd over 3f out* **8/1**[3]

2446 **8** *76* **Strategic Action (IRE)**[133] 1387 5-8-12 46 ........(t) AaronJones 1
(Linda Jewell) *prom tl wknd over 3f out: t.o fnl 2f* **20/1**

0340 **9** *5* **Soiree D'Ete**[45] 5682 3-7-11 46 ........(b[1]) ManuelFernandes(8) 3
(Sir Mark Prescott Bt) *led tl 5f out: wknd qckly 4f out: t.o fnl 2f* **8/1**[3]

2m 45.74s (13.04) **Going Correction** +0.85s/f (Soft)
**WFA** 3 from 4yo+ 7lb **9** Ran SP% **117.2**
Speed ratings (Par 101): **90,77,77,73,63 55,49, ,**
CSF £25.59 CT £151.62 TOTE £14.00: £3.10, £1.20, £2.00; EX 47.90 Trifecta £510.30.
**Owner** Canisbay Bloodstock **Bred** Hesmonds Stud Ltd **Trained** Epsom, Surrey

**FOCUS**
A 0-55 'hands and heels' event to round off the card but run at a strong pace and the field finished strung out across East Sussex. The winner has been rated to his best form from the past two years.
T/Plt: £4,086.10 to a £1 stake. Pool of £61291.96 - 10.95 winning tickets. T/Qpdt: £325.60 to a £1 stake. Pool of £5589.53 - 12.70 winning tickets. LM

# 6537 CATTERICK (L-H)
## Tuesday, October 7

**OFFICIAL GOING: Good to soft (good in places; 7.8)**
Wind: moderate 1/2 behind Weather: fine

## 7003 BHEST RACING TO SCHOOL NURSERY H'CAP 5f 212y
**2:00** (2:10) (Class 6) (0-65,65) 2-Y-O **£2,385** (£704; £352) **Stalls** Low

Form RPR

406 **1** **Alaskan Wing (IRE)**[31] 6158 2-8-13 57 ........ BarryMcHugh 9 63
(Tony Coyle) *swtchd lft after s: t.k.h: mde all: drvn over 1f out: jst lasted* **14/1**

505 **2** *nk* **Magh Meall**[14] 6643 2-8-8 52 ........ AdrianNicholls 10 57
(David Nicholls) *a chsng wnr: drvn over 2f out: styd on ins fnl f: jst hld* **11/2**[2]

003 **3** *hd* **Zaza Zest (IRE)**[28] 6212 2-9-2 65 ........ JackGarritty(5) 11 69
(Richard Fahey) *chsd ldrs: 3rd over 2f out: styd on ins fnl f: gng on at fin* **11/1**

0050 **4** *6* **Mullionheir**[35] 6016 2-9-1 59 ........ GrahamLee 7 45
(John Best) *mid-div: hdwy over 3f out: wknd over 1f out* **7/1**[3]

4403 **5** *3 ¼* **Poppy In The Wind**[14] 6643 2-8-11 55 ........ DaleSwift 4 31
(Alan Brown) *mid-div: hdwy over 2f out: wknd appr fnl f* **12/1**

000 **6** *1* **May Hill Rebel**[20] 6449 2-8-3 50 ........(t) NeilFarley(3) 3 23
(Richard Guest) *dwlt: in rr: sme hdwy 2f out: nvr a factor* **66/1**

5010 **7** *nk* **Secret Friend (IRE)**[26] 6253 2-9-1 59 ........(b) DuranFentiman 8 31
(Tim Easterby) *in rr: sme hdwy over 2f out: hung lft 1f out: nvr nr ldrs* **18/1**

6050 **8** *nse* **Perfect Girl (IRE)**[14] 6643 2-8-12 56 ........ JamesSullivan 5 28
(Tim Easterby) *mid-div: t.k.h: effrt over 2f out: nvr a factor* **22/1**

032 **9** *½* **Frozen Princess**[60] 5120 2-9-4 62 ........ DanielTudhope 1 33
(Jamie Osborne) *chsd ldrs: drvn over 2f out: wknd over 1f out* **11/8**[1]

4135 **10** *2 ¾* **Studio Star**[20] 6447 2-9-3 64 ........(p) JacobButterfield(3) 12 26
(Ollie Pears) *stmbld s: swtchd lft after s: in rr: sme hdwy on ins whn hmpd jst ins fnl f: sn eased* **7/1**[3]

1m 16.09s (2.49) **Going Correction** +0.35s/f (Good) **10** Ran SP% **116.3**
Speed ratings (Par 93): **97,96,96,88,84 82,82,82,81,77**
CSF £88.92 CT £653.04 TOTE £19.40: £3.40, £1.60, £2.40; EX 82.30 Trifecta £780.90.
**Owner** Michael Beaumont **Bred** Hyde Park Stud **Trained** Norton, N Yorks
■ Mr Specialbru was withdrawn. Price at time of withdrawal 25/1. Rule 4 does not apply.

**FOCUS**
Bend into home straight dolled out 3yds. Races between 6f and 14f increased by 7yds and 2m races increase by 14yds. This moderate nursery was run at a decent pace and the principals came clear in a tight three-way finish.

## 7004 IRISH STALLION FARMS EBF MAIDEN STKS 5f
**2:30** (2:34) (Class 5) 2-Y-O **£2,911** (£866; £432; £216) **Stalls** Low

Form RPR

22 **1** **Beau Eile (IRE)**[30] 6168 2-9-0 0 ........ GrahamGibbons 5 73
(David Barron) *chsd ldrs: drvn over 2f out: styd on to ld nr fin* **10/11**[1]

2620 **2** *½* **Zuzinia (IRE)**[15] 6610 2-9-0 66 ........ JoeFanning 10 71
(Mick Channon) *w ldr: led over 2f out: hdd and no ex in clsng stages* **14/1**

3022 **3** *6* **Compton River**[28] 6212 2-9-5 70 ........ PaulMulrennan 8 54
(Bryan Smart) *led tl over 2f out: wknd last 150yds* **15/2**[3]

42 **4** *1 ¾* **Gold Pursuit**[19] 6489 2-9-5 0 ........ RobertWinston 1 48
(Alan Swinbank) *chsd ldrs: drvn over 2f out: hung rt over 1f out: sn wknd* **9/4**[2]

0 **5** *2* **Deep Blue Diamond**[14] 6623 2-9-0 0 ........ IanBrennan 4 36
(Ollie Pears) *stmbld s: sn mid-div: wknd over 1f out* **100/1**

**6** *shd* **Desire** 2-9-0 0 ........ TonyHamilton 2 36
(Richard Fahey) *s.s: hdwy 3f out: wknd over 1f out* **18/1**

**7** *nk* **Yorkshire Nanny (IRE)** 2-9-0 0 ........ GrahamLee 3 34
(David Brown) *mid-div: n.m.r over 2f out: kpt on appr fnl f: nvr on terms* **25/1**

**8** *4* **Coursing** 2-9-0 0 ........ LukeMorris 7 20
(Sir Mark Prescott Bt) *dwlt and wnt bdly rt s: in rr: bhd fnl 2f* **25/1**

**9** *15* **Miss Ruby Royale** 2-9-0 0 ........ TomEaves 11
(Paul Midgley) *wnt rt s: in rr: bhd fnl 2f: eased clsng stages: t.o* **100/1**

00 **10** *2 ½* **Little Polyanna**[28] 6212 2-9-0 0 ........ PatrickMathers 6
(Alan Berry) *mid-div: hung lft over 2f out: sn lost pl: bhd whn eased clsng stages: t.o* **150/1**

1m 0.46s (0.66) **Going Correction** +0.10s/f (Good) **10** Ran SP% **117.2**
Speed ratings (Par 95): **98,97,87,84,81 81,80,74,50,46**
CSF £16.24 TOTE £1.90: £1.10, £3.90, £2.20; EX 13.90 Trifecta £51.70.
**Owner** S W D McIlveen & Miss Aisling Byrne **Bred** Dermot Cantillon & Forenaghts Stud **Trained** Maunby, N Yorks

**FOCUS**
Straightforward maiden form.

## 7005 WATCH ON 3 DEVICES RACINGUK.COM/ANYWHERE NURSERY H'CAP (BOBIS RACE) 7f
**3:00** (3:03) (Class 3) (0-95,77) 2-Y-O **£7,762** (£2,310; £1,154; £577) **Stalls** Low

Form RPR

1006 **1** **Tachophobia**[19] 6499 2-9-0 75 ........ JackGarritty(5) 2 77
(Richard Fahey) *chsd ldrs: drvn over 3f out: edgd rt and styd on fnl f: led post* **7/2**[1]

240 **2** *shd* **Special Venture (IRE)**[17] 6529 2-9-5 75 ........ GrahamLee 3 77
(Tim Easterby) *led: racd alone far side in home st: hdd last stride* **8/1**

635 **3** *shd* **Kelly's Finest (IRE)**[20] 6448 2-9-3 73 ........ DanielTudhope 5 74
(James Bethell) *chsd ldrs: outpcd and c wd over 2f out: hdwy over 1f out: fin wl* **4/1**[2]

5104 **4** *shd* **Pumaflor (IRE)**[14] 6643 2-8-9 65 ........ JasonHart 7 66
(Richard Guest) *swtchd lft after s: t.k.h in rr: lost pl over 3f out: hdwy and edgd rt 2f out: upsides fnl f: kpt on* **9/1**

3156 **5** *2* **Kylach Me If U Can**[30] 6165 2-9-3 73 ........ TomEaves 6 69
(Kevin Ryan) *sn chsng ldrs: drvn and c wd over 2f out: fdd fnl 150yds* **7/2**[1]

6156 **6** *½* **Stardrifter**[27] 6229 2-8-13 69 ........ TonyHamilton 1 63
(Richard Fahey) *dwlt: in rr: hdwy in centre over 2f out: chsng ldrs over 1f out: fdd fnl 150yds* **7/1**

1165 **7** *1 ¾* **Disavow**[60] 5147 2-9-7 77 ........ JoeFanning 4 67
(Mark Johnston) *chsd ldr: brought wd over 2f out: wknd fnl 150yds* **6/1**[3]

1m 29.32s (2.32) **Going Correction** +0.35s/f (Good) **7** Ran SP% **112.3**
Speed ratings (Par 99): **100,99,99,99,97 96,94**
CSF £30.18 CT £114.21 TOTE £5.00: £2.10, £3.80; EX 29.30 Trifecta £190.80.
**Owner** A Rhodes Haulage And P Timmins **Bred** Springcombe Park Stud **Trained** Musley Bank, N Yorks

**FOCUS**
This modest nursery, weakened by the non-runner, was run at a solid pace and there was a difference of opinion regards the going as the field spread across the track. Muddling form.

## 7006 SKYRAM H'CAP (DIV I) 1m 7f 177y
**3:30** (3:34) (Class 6) (0-60,59) 3-Y-O+ **£2,385** (£704; £352) **Stalls** Low

Form RPR

00-1 **1** **Jolie Blonde**[8] 6818 3-9-4 59 6ex ........ LukeMorris 12 73+
(Sir Mark Prescott Bt) *chsd ldrs: drvn over 5f out: styd on u.p to ld 2f out: edgd lft: forged clr fnl f: eased towards fin* **5/6**[1]

5004 **2** *1 ¾* **May Hay**[12] 6682 4-10-0 58 ........ GrahamLee 7 65
(Anthony Carson) *hld up in rr: racd wd: hdwy over 7f out: sn chsng ldrs: led briefly over 2f out: styd on same pce* **4/1**[2]

0060 **3** *1 ¼* **Yorkshireman (IRE)**[14] 6644 4-8-13 48 ........(b) JackGarritty(5) 10 53
(Lynn Siddall) *led: hdd over 2f out: kpt on wl fnl f* **66/1**

5502 **4** *3* **Mr Wickfield**[24] 6343 3-9-0 55 ........ DavidNolan 3 57
(John Best) *mid-div: hdwy over 3f out: kpt on same pce fnl 2f: tk 4th nr fin* **16/1**

3603 **5** *1* **Impeccability**[17] 6542 4-9-2 46 ........(p) PatrickMathers 2 47
(John Mackie) *chsd ldrs: effrt over 2f out: wknd in clsng stages* **16/1**

2205 **6** *2 ¾* **Cool Baranca (GER)**[17] 6542 8-9-0 49 ........ EmmaSayer(5) 8 46
(Dianne Sayer) *s.i.s: in rr: hdwy 3f out: kpt on one pce* **12/1**

0020 **7** *1* **Different Scenario**[50] 5495 3-8-5 46 ........ RoystonFfrench 9 42
(Mel Brittain) *chsd ldrs: drvn over 3f out: one pce* **25/1**

335 **8** *15* **William Hogarth**[10] 6768 9-9-1 45 ........(p) RobertWinston 6 23
(Brian Ellison) *mid-div: pushed along after 6f: outpcd over 3f out: sn lost pl: bhd whn eased in clsng stages* **6/1**[3]

0006 **9** *17* **Musikhani**[61] 5090 4-9-12 56 ........(tp) TonyHamilton 13 14
(Philip Kirby) *sn chsng ldrs: lost pl 8f out: bhd fnl 3f: t.o* **40/1**

5430 **10** *47* **Kastela Stari**[64] 4962 7-9-7 51 ........(t) TomEaves 5
(Tim Fitzgerald) *s.s: hdwy on wd outside after 4f: sn chsng ldrs: lost pl over 3f out: wl bhd whn eased over 1f out: virtually p.u: tailed rt off* **50/1**

3m 38.49s (6.49) **Going Correction** +0.35s/f (Good)
**WFA** 3 from 4yo+ 11lb **10** Ran SP% **118.0**
Speed ratings (Par 101): **97,96,95,94,93 92,91,84,75,52**
CSF £4.19 CT £121.66 TOTE £1.80: £1.02, £1.80, £7.40; EX 4.50 Trifecta £130.40.
**Owner** Miss K Rausing **Bred** Miss K Rausing **Trained** Newmarket, Suffolk

**FOCUS**
A weak staying handicap, rated around the fifth. The runner-up has been rated in line with her latest AW effort.

## 7007 SKYRAM H'CAP (DIV II) 1m 7f 177y
**4:00** (4:04) (Class 6) (0-60,57) 3-Y-O+ **£2,385** (£704; £352) **Stalls** Low

Form RPR

0200 **1** **Waltz Darling (IRE)**[17] 6542 6-9-9 57 ........ EmmaSayer(5) 8 69+
(Keith Reveley) *hld up in rr: hdwy over 5f out: 2nd over 2f out: rdn to ld over 1f out: styd on: eased in clsng stages* **12/1**

4152 **2** *2 ¾* **Eastern Magic**[38] 5909 7-9-7 55 ........ JackDuern(5) 5 62
(Andrew Hollinshead) *hld up in mid-div: hdwy 6f out: sn trcking ldrs: led 3f out: hdd over 1f out: kpt on same pce* **11/4**[1]

4265 **3** *18* **Stormy Morning**[14] 6644 8-9-8 51 ........(p) TonyHamilton 4 36
(Philip Kirby) *mid-div: reminders after 5f: drvn 6f out: outpcd over 3f out: kpt on fnl 2f: tk poor 3rd in clsng stages* **11/1**

3040 **4** *½* **Rocky Two (IRE)**[17] 6542 4-9-9 52 ........(p) JoeFanning 12 37
(Philip Kirby) *led tl over 8f out: led over 6f out: hdd 3f out: one pce* **15/2**

6000 **5** *½* **Spithead**[14] 6644 4-9-6 49 ........ JamesSullivan 6 33
(Mike Sowersby) *hld up in rr: hdwy over 5f out: chsng ldrs over 3f out: one pce* **28/1**

0304 **6** *39* **Cowslip**[42] 5794 5-9-5 48 ........ AndrewMullen 3
(George Moore) *chsd ldrs: pushed along after 4f: lost pl over 4f out: sn bhd: t.o whn eased ins fnl f* **13/2**

3345 **7** *2* **Nam Ma Prow**[38] 5917 3-8-11 51 ........(p) JasonHart 7
(Simon West) *chsd ldrs: drvn 4f out: lost pl over 2f out: bhd whn eased fnl f: t.o* **5/1**[3]

/0-4 **8** *½* **Jim Tango (FR)**[21] 4522 10-9-2 45 ........(b) GrahamLee 2
(Karen McLintock) *drvn to sn chse ldrs: led over 8f out: hdd over 6f out: lost pl over 4f out: bhd whn eased 2f out* **33/1**

654 **P** **Philosofy**[10] 6762 4-9-7 50 ........ DanielTudhope 10
(David O'Meara) *sn chsng ldrs: reminders after 8f out: lost pl over 5f out: sn bhd: t.o whn eased over 3f out: p.u over 2f out* **3/1**[2]

3m 39.98s (7.98) **Going Correction** +0.35s/f (Good)
**WFA** 3 from 4yo+ 11lb **9** Ran SP% **115.8**
Speed ratings (Par 101): **94,92,83,83,83 63,62,62,**
CSF £45.31 CT £383.63 TOTE £9.20: £2.80, £1.10, £3.90; EX 45.70 Trifecta £474.70.
**Owner** Mrs M B Thwaites & M E Foxton **Bred** Ms Natalie Cleary **Trained** Lingdale, Redcar & Cleveland

**FOCUS**
The second division of the weak staying handicap and there was a sound pace on. The winner has been rated in line with the better view of his early season form.

## 7008 VISIT CATTERICK SUNDAY MARKET EVERY WEEK H'CAP — 1m 3f 214y
**4:30** (4:33) (Class 5) (0-75,75) 3-Y-O+ — **£2,911** (£866; £432; £216) **Stalls** Centre

Form — RPR

0065 **1** — **Sioux Chieftain (IRE)**[48] 5572 4-9-7 70 ...................... AndrewMullen 14 — 82
(Michael Appleby) *hld up in mid-div: hdwy to trck ldrs after 3f: 3rd 3f out: led over 1f out: drvn out* **14/1**

5344 **2** *2¼* **Eltheeb**[62] 5052 7-9-12 75 ..................................(p) PaulMulrennan 9 — 83
(Michael Dods) *hld up in rr: hdwy 4f out: chsd wnr over 1f out: styd on same pce* **5/1**[2]

5364 **3** *2½* **Save The Bees**[13] 6672 6-9-12 75 .................................. JasonHart 1 — 79
(Declan Carroll) *led: hdd over 1f out: kpt on same pce* **12/1**

243 **4** *nk* **Chant (IRE)**[16] 6579 4-9-3 73 .................................. RowanScott(7) 7 — 77+
(Ann Duffield) *stmbld bdly s: in rr: effrt over 3f out: styd on fnl 2f: nt rch ldrs* **16/1**

5313 **5** *hd* **Right Of Appeal**[9] 6787 3-9-1 71 .................................. JoeFanning 12 — 75
(Mark Johnston) *hld up in mid-div: t.k.h: hmpd bnd after 3f: hdwy over 4f out: chsng ldrs over 2f out: kpt on same pce* **11/2**[3]

3256 **6** *3* **Royal Marskell**[26] 6264 5-9-3 71 .................................. JackDuern(5) 6 — 70
(Alison Hutchinson) *hld up in rr: hdwy on outer over 3f out: chsng ldrs over 2f out: wknd fnl f* **20/1**

-002 **7** *½* **Istimraar (IRE)**[17] 6539 3-9-5 75 ..............................(p) TonyHamilton 11 — 73
(Philip Kirby) *mid-div: hdwy over 5f out: chsng ldrs over 2f out: edgd lft and fdd over 1f out* **16/1**

325 **8** *1* **Molly Cat**[21] 6432 4-9-4 67 .................................. RobertWinston 10 — 63
(Alan Swinbank) *trckd ldrs: t.k.h: 2nd over 3f out: wknd appr fnl f* **3/1**[1]

2231 **9** *2* **Dansili Dutch (IRE)**[11] 6706 5-9-5 75 .................................. JoshDoyle(7) 3 — 68
(David O'Meara) *mid-div: drvn over 5f out: outpcd and lost pl over 4f out: no threat after* **10/1**

**10** *2* **Apollo Eleven (IRE)**[42] 5-9-5 68 .................................. GrahamLee 13 — 58
(Donald McCain) *hld up in rr: t.k.h: hdwy over 4f out: rdn over 3f out: wknd 2f out* **10/1**

1066 **11** *4½* **Tinseltown**[17] 6541 8-9-3 66 .................................. AmyRyan 4 — 49
(Brian Rothwell) *chsd ldrs: drvn 4f out: lost pl over 2f out: bhd whn eased clsng stages* **33/1**

3322 **12** *5* **Valantino Oyster (IRE)**[13] 6672 7-9-8 74 ............(p) ConnorBeasley(3) 5 — 49
(Tracy Waggott) *chsd ldr: reminders over 4f out: wknd 2f out: bhd whn eased clsng stages* **11/1**

2m 41.87s (2.97) **Going Correction** +0.35s/f (Good)
**WFA** 3 from 4yo+ 7lb — **12** Ran SP% **117.4**
Speed ratings (Par 103): **104,102,100,100,100 98,98,97,96,94 91,88**
CSF £81.79 CT £880.85 TOTE £16.80: £3.30, £2.80, £3.40; EX 108.20 Trifecta £1089.50.
**Owner** Ferrybank Properties Limited **Bred** Newsells Park Stud **Trained** Danethorpe, Notts

**FOCUS**
This modest handicap provided a decent test of the distance. The winner has been rated close to his best, while the runner-up has been rated to his Carlisle figure.

## 7009 RACING AGAIN SATURDAY 18TH OCTOBER AMATEUR RIDERS' H'CAP (DIV I) — 5f
**5:00** (5:03) (Class 6) (0-55,55) 3-Y-O+ — **£2,305** (£709; £354) **Stalls** Low

Form — RPR

200 **1** — **Busy Bimbo (IRE)**[9] 6796 5-10-4 52 ........................(b) MrLAMurtagh(7) 4 — 58
(Alan Berry) *chsd ldrs: edgd rt over 1f out: led last 150yds: drvn out* **33/1**

4534 **2** *½* **Captain Scooby**[6] 6866 8-10-7 48 ..................................(v) MrSWalker 3 — 52
(Richard Guest) *in rr-div: hdwy 2f out: styd on to take 2nd last 50yds* **7/4**[1]

0450 **3** *¾* **Tidal Beauty**[29] 6194 3-10-5 46 oh1 .............................. MissSBrotherton 5 — 49
(Michael Appleby) *dwlt: in rr-div: hdwy over 1f out: tk 3rd post* **11/1**

3222 **4** *nse* **Pull The Pin (IRE)**[38] 5907 5-11-0 55 ..........................(bt) MrsCBartley 10 — 56
(Ann Stokell) *led: edgd rt and racd towards stands' side over 2f out: hdd and no ex last 150yds* **5/2**[2]

3653 **5** *hd* **A J Cook (IRE)**[13] 6671 4-10-9 55 ..............................(v) MrsVDavies(5) 1 — 56
(Ron Barr) *half rrd s: sn prom: outpcd 3f out: hdwy over 1f out: kpt on ins fnl f* **7/2**[3]

-060 **6** *1¾* **On The High Tops (IRE)**[6] 6866 6-10-6 47 .................(p) MissCWalton 6 — 41
(Colin Teague) *towards rr: hdwy stands' side to join ldr over 3f out: one pce fnl f* **25/1**

0000 **7** *3* **Under Review (IRE)**[13] 6666 8-10-2 48 .......................... MissHHeal(5) 9 — 32
(Bernard Llewellyn) *chsd ldrs: wknd appr fnl f* **25/1**

0443 **8** *3½* **Skinny Latte**[40] 5853 3-10-5 46 ..........................................(p) MrWHogg 8 — 18
(Micky Hammond) *unruly in stalls: lost pl over 3f out: bhd fnl 2f* **20/1**

0650 **9** *2¾* **Rosie Hall (IRE)**[46] 5636 4-10-5 46 oh1 .......................... MissHBethell 2 — 7
(Les Eyre) *outpcd and lost pl over 3f out: bhd fnl 2f* **50/1**

1m 1.42s (1.62) **Going Correction** +0.10s/f (Good) — **9** Ran SP% **112.8**
Speed ratings (Par 101): **91,90,89,88,88 85,81,75,71**
CSF £85.82 CT £710.50 TOTE £16.80: £5.40, £1.10, £3.20; EX 73.40 Trifecta £1262.70.
**Owner** Alan Berry **Bred** Tally-Ho Stud **Trained** Cockerham, Lancs

**FOCUS**
A typically weak sprint handicap for amateur riders, run at a frantic pace and the main action developed down the centre late on. The runner-up has been rated to his recent form.

## 7010 RACING AGAIN SATURDAY 18TH OCTOBER AMATEUR RIDERS' H'CAP (DIV II) — 5f
**5:30** (5:33) (Class 6) (0-55,55) 3-Y-O+ — **£2,305** (£709; £354) **Stalls** Low

Form — RPR

6006 **1** — **Red Invader (IRE)**[35] 6014 4-10-7 53 .......................... MrsRWilson(5) 7 — 64
(Paul D'Arcy) *carried rt s: w ldrs: edgd rt and led appr fnl f: hld on wl* **7/1**[3]

0013 **2** *1¼* **Thewestwalian (USA)**[19] 6495 6-10-5 51 ................ MissMollyKing(5) 9 — 58
(Peter Hiatt) *wnt rt s: w ldrs: led over 2f out: hdd appr fnl f: kpt on same pce* **3/1**[2]

0055 **3** *1¼* **Lazy Sioux**[6] 6866 3-10-6 47 .................................................. MrSWalker 1 — 50
(Richard Guest) *in tch: effrt and handy 3rd over 1f out: kpt on same pce ins fnl f* **9/4**[1]

0660 **4** *4* **Kalani's Diamond**[32] 6114 4-10-0 48 .......................... MissJGillam(7) 5 — 36
(David O'Meara) *wnt rt s: led: hdd over 2f out: wknd fnl f* **18/1**

003 **5** *nk* **Rat Catcher (IRE)**[17] 6561 4-10-7 48 ....................(b) MissSBrotherton 3 — 35
(Lisa Williamson) *w ldrs: edgd lft and wknd fnl f* **3/1**[2]

064 **6** *4* **Byronaissance**[38] 5916 5-10-9 55 .................................. MrKWood(5) 4 — 27
(Neville Bycroft) *awkward s: sn trcking ldrs: outpcd and lost pl over 2f out* **14/1**

4000 **7** *12* **Lunesdale Buddy**[41] 5819 3-9-12 46 oh1 ..............(b[1]) MrLAMurtagh(7) 8
(Alan Berry) *carried rt sn after s: outpcd and lost pl over 3f out: edgd rt and bhd over 1f out* **22/1**

1m 1.28s (1.48) **Going Correction** +0.10s/f (Good) — **7** Ran SP% **109.5**
Speed ratings (Par 101): **92,90,88,81,81 74,55**
CSF £25.85 CT £56.69 TOTE £7.00: £4.50, £1.50; EX 27.80 Trifecta £105.90.
**Owner** C M Wilson **Bred** Tally-Ho Stud **Trained** Newmarket, Suffolk

**FOCUS**
This second division of the weak sprint handicap, confined to amateurs, again saw the main action develop centre of the home straight. It was just quicker than the preceding race. The runner-up has been rated close to his last effort.
T/Jkpt: Not won. T/Plt: £159.00 to a £1 stake. Pool of £58662.13 - 269.32 winning tickets.
T/Qpdt: £35.50 to a £1 stake. Pool of £4199.08 - 87.36 winning tickets. WG

# 6883 KEMPTON (A.W) (R-H)
Tuesday, October 7

**OFFICIAL GOING: Polytrack: standard**
Wind: light, half behind Weather: dry

## 7011 £25 FREE BET AT TITANBET.CO.UK MAIDEN FILLIES' STKS (BOBIS RACE) — 1m (P)
**5:35** (5:37) (Class 5) 2-Y-O — **£2,911** (£866; £432; £216) **Stalls** Low

Form — RPR

3 **1** — **Forte**[41] 5821 2-9-0 0 .................................................. RichardKingscote 9 — 77+
(Ralph Beckett) *racd keenly: mde all: gng best ent fnl 2f: rdn over 1f out: in command but racing lazily ins fnl f: kpt on* **6/4**[1]

**2** *1¼* **Yarrow (IRE)** 2-9-0 0 ........................................................ RyanMoore 5 — 74
(Sir Michael Stoute) *s.i.s: bustled along early: in rr: rdn over 3f out: gd hdwy to chse clr ldng pair over 1f out: r.o strly fnl 100yds to go 2nd nr fin: nvr quite getting to wnr* **5/1**

22 **3** *hd* **Jersey Jewel (FR)**[32] 6105 2-9-0 0 .............................. RichardHughes 1 — 74
(Richard Hannon) *chsd ldrs: effrt u.p to chse wnr 2f out: styd on same pce u.p fnl f: lost 2nd nr fin* **11/4**[2]

**4** *5* **Barqeyya (IRE)** 2-9-0 0 ........................................................ DaneO'Neill 7 — 62
(John Gosden) *s.i.s and pushed along early: hdwy into midfield after 3f: rdn and effrt over 2f out: wnt 4th over 1f out: no imp* **9/2**[3]

**5** *½* **Alla Breve** 2-9-0 0 .......................................................... PaddyAspell 3 — 61
(Sir Michael Stoute) *s.i.s: rn green and fashing tail on rr: stl last and u.p over 1f out: hdwy 1f out: styd on wl fnl f: nvr trbld ldrs* **33/1**

0 **6** *2¼* **Zebella**[17] 6551 2-9-0 0 .................................................. TedDurcan 4 — 56
(Rod Millman) *chsd ldng trio: rdn over 2f out: outpcd and btn 2f out: 6th and wl hld whn eased fnl 75yds* **66/1**

**7** *1½* **Sonic Rainbow (GR)** 2-9-0 0 .................................................. PatDobbs 8 — 52
(Amanda Perrett) *in tch in last quartet: rdn over 2f out: outpcd and btn 2f out: wknd 1f out* **33/1**

5 **8** *3* **Singoalla**[7] 6840 2-9-0 0 .................................................. ChrisCatlin 2 — 45
(Sir Mark Prescott Bt) *bustled along early: in tch in midfield: rdn 1/2-way: outpcd and btn 2f out: wknd 1f out* **33/1**

00 **9** *2* **Purple Surprise**[21] 6435 2-9-0 0 .............................. FergusSweeney 6 — 41
(Andrew Reid) *chsd wnr tl 2f out: sn outpcd u.p: lost pl and bhd 1f out: wknd fnl f* **66/1**

1m 39.57s (-0.23) **Going Correction** -0.025s/f (Stan) — **9** Ran SP% **113.3**
Speed ratings (Par 92): **100,98,98,93,93 90,89,86,84**
CSF £8.95 TOTE £2.40: £1.40, £1.80, £1.10; EX 8.80 Trifecta £28.30.
**Owner** J L Rowsell & M H Dixon **Bred** Ashbrittle Stud & M H Dixon **Trained** Kimpton, Hants

**FOCUS**
A potentially informative opener, though not many got into it.

## 7012 BET & WATCH AT TITANBET.CO.UK H'CAP (DIV I) — 1m (P)
**6:05** (6:05) (Class 5) (0-70,70) 3-Y-O+ — **£2,587** (£770; £384; £192) **Stalls** Low

Form — RPR

0334 **1** — **Semaral (IRE)**[84] 4303 3-9-3 **69** .............................................. TedDurcan 6 — 81+
(Chris Wall) *hld up in tch: effrt u.p on inner over 1f out: led ins fnl f: r.o wl: rdn out* **20/1**

666 **2** *1* **John Caesar (IRE)**[35] 6018 3-9-1 **67** ..............................(tp) RyanMoore 7 — 77+
(Jeremy Noseda) *sn chsng ldr: rdn to ld over 2f out: hdd and one pce ins fnl f* **13/8**[2]

050- **3** *1¾* **Embankment**[350] 7438 5-9-7 **70** .............................................. KierenFox 5 — 76
(Michael Attwater) *s.i.s: hld up in tch: hdwy on outer 1/2-way: rdn and ev ch 2f out tl ent fnl f: kpt on same pce after* **20/1**

055 **4** *3½* **Blue Army**[69] 4791 3-9-0 **66** .......................................... RichardHughes 8 — 64
(Saeed bin Suroor) *in tch in midfield: hdwy over 2f out: rdn and ev ch 2f out tl ent fnl f: wknd fnl 100yds* **6/4**[1]

2402 **5** *½* **Dark Ocean (IRE)**[7] 6841 4-9-7 **70** .............................. RussKennemore 2 — 67
(Jedd O'Keeffe) *t.k.h: hld up in tch towards rr: rdn and effrt over 2f out: edgd rt and one pce fr over 1f out* **10/1**[3]

5630 **6** *2* **Turnbury**[24] 6337 3-8-3 **62** ..................................(t) SophieRalston(7) 9 — 54
(Robert Mills) *stdd s: hld up in rr: snatched up over 1f out: pushed along 1f out: no threat to ldrs: eased fnl 100yds* **50/1**

4003 **7** *¾* **Captain Starlight (IRE)**[34] 6035 4-9-6 **69** .................. FergusSweeney 3 — 59
(Jo Crowley) *chsd ldrs: rdn and unable qck ent fnl 2f: wknd over 1f out* **14/1**

0540 **8** *1¾* **Toymaker**[27] 6240 7-9-3 **66** ..............................................[1] PaddyAspell 1 — 52
(Phil McEntee) *hld up in tch: effrt on inner over 2f out: no prog: wknd over 1f out* **14/1**

4553 **9** *17* **Blackthorn Stick (IRE)**[194] 1121 5-8-12 **61** ........................ ChrisCatlin 4 — 8
(John Butler) *led tl over 2f out: sn dropped out: t.o ins fnl f* **33/1**

1m 39.07s (-0.73) **Going Correction** -0.025s/f (Stan)
**WFA** 3 from 4yo+ 3lb — **9** Ran SP% **114.9**
Speed ratings (Par 103): **102,101,99,95,95 93,92,90,73**
CSF £51.19 CT £694.30 TOTE £17.30: £3.50, £1.10, £8.00; EX 68.50 Trifecta £2962.00 Part won..
**Owner** Moyns Park Stud **Bred** Moyns Park Estate And Stud Ltd **Trained** Newmarket, Suffolk
■ Stewards' Enquiry : Sophie Ralston 20-day ban: (2nd offence in 12mths) failed to take all reasonable and permissable measures to obtain best possible placing (Oct 21-25,27-Nov 1,3-8,10-13)



The Form Book, Raceform Ltd, Newbury, RG14 5SJ

**FOCUS**
Just a fair handicap. A clear pb from the winner but rather muddling form.

## 7013 BET & WATCH AT TITANBET.CO.UK H'CAP (DIV II) 1m (P)
**6:35** (6:36) (Class 5) (0-70,70) 3-Y-0+ **£2,587** (£770; £384; £192) **Stalls** Low

Form RPR

2330 **1** **Go For Broke**[33] 6070 3-9-3 69..........(b) RichardHughes 1 78
(Richard Hannon) *hld up in tch: hdwy over 2f out: drvn to chal over 1f out: led ins fnl f: styd on* **8/1**

2146 **2** *hd* **Biotic**[36] 5986 3-9-1 67.......... SteveDrowne 4 76
(Rod Millman) *chsd ldrs: wnt 2nd over 3f out: rdn and ev ch over 1f out: led 1f out: hdd ins fnl f: kpt on* **7/2**[3]

P054 **3** *3 1/4* **Rizal Park (IRE)**[26] 6262 3-9-3 69..........(t) OisinMurphy 6 71
(Andrew Balding) *hdwy to ld after 1f: rdn 2f out: hdd 1f out: wknd ins fnl f* **5/2**[2]

665 **4** *2 3/4* **Evident (IRE)**[41] 5834 4-9-7 70.......... RyanMoore 9 65
(Jeremy Noseda) *hld up in rr: effrt and hdwy into 4th over 2f out: no imp fr over 1f out* **9/4**[1]

5045 **5** *12* **Pashan Garh**[43] 5750 5-8-12 61.......... DaneO'Neill 5 29
(Pat Eddery) *hldn up tch: effrt 2f out: sn struggling: wknd over 1f out* **20/1**

1566 **6** *6* **Jonnie Skull (IRE)**[44] 5727 8-8-13 62..........(vt) PaddyAspell 3 16
(Phil McEntee) *led for 1f: chsd ldr tl 3f out: sn lost pl u.p: bhd 2f out* **25/1**

3150 **7** *3/4* **Hill Of Dreams (IRE)**[22] 6414 5-9-6 69.......... ChrisCatlin 7 21
(Dean Ivory) *chsd ldrs: rdn and lost pl 3f out: bhd 2f out* **12/1**

054R **R** **Scruffy Tramp (IRE)**[31] 6154 3-9-3 69.......... LiamKeniry 8
(John Butler) *ref to r* **16/1**

1m 38.26s (-1.54) **Going Correction** -0.025s/f (Stan)
**WFA** 3 from 4yo+ 3lb **8** Ran SP% **114.9**
Speed ratings (Par 103): **106,105,102,99,87 81,81,**
CSF £36.32 CT £91.61 TOTE £8.70: £2.30, £1.10, £1.70; EX 37.00 Trifecta £161.80.
**Owner** Lady Whent **Bred** Raffin Bloodstock **Trained** East Everleigh, Wilts

**FOCUS**
The quickest-run of the three 1m contests on the card, clocking in at over 1.3 seconds faster than the opening maiden. The winner ran a pb here last year and has posted another pb on this third AW start.

## 7014 DAY DELEGATE RATES FROM £39 NURSERY H'CAP 7f (P)
**7:05** (7:07) (Class 6) (0-60,60) 2-Y-O **£1,940** (£577; £288; £144) **Stalls** Low

Form RPR

050 **1** **Steevo (IRE)**[34] 6039 2-8-11 50..........(p) RyanMoore 1 53+
(Gary Moore) *wl in tch in midfield: rdn and effrt over 2f out: hrd drvn over 1f out: steadily clsd to ld fnl 75yds: drvn out* **5/4**[1]

5053 **2** *1/2* **Scent Of Power**[13] 6663 2-9-0 53.......... WilliamCarson 12 55
(Anthony Carson) *hld up in rr: hdwy ent fnl 2f: rdn to chal jst over 1f out: led fnl 100yds: sn hdd and one pce towards fin* **8/1**[3]

0055 **3** *nk* **Laura B**[13] 6662 2-9-2 55.......... TedDurcan 11 56
(Chris Wall) *hld up towards rr: hdwy u.p over 1f out: hanging rt but styd on u.p to snatch 3rd on post* **10/1**

4640 **4** *nse* **Piccadillo**[42] 5798 2-9-4 57..........(b[1]) RichardKingscote 14 58
(Daniel Kubler) *led: rdn and clr 2f out: hrd pressed jst over 1f out: hdd fnl 100yds: one pce after* **14/1**

0200 **5** *1* **Lady Charlie**[34] 6040 2-9-0 53.......... StevieDonohoe 4 51
(Jo Hughes) *hld up towards rr: hdwy u.p on inner 2f out: chsd ldrs 1f out: one pce* **33/1**

000 **6** *2* **Indomitable Spirit**[12] 6683 2-9-3 56.......... SteveDrowne 9 49
(Martin Smith) *chsd ldrs: wnt 2nd over 2f out tl over 1f out: wknd ins fnl f* **25/1**

0065 **7** *shd* **Decibelle**[27] 6237 2-8-13 52.......... PatDobbs 6 45
(Jane Chapple-Hyam) *chsd ldrs: effrt in 3rd over 2f out: wnt 2nd over 1f out tl 1f out: wknd ins fnl f* **20/1**

0500 **8** *2 1/4* **Arousal**[27] 6237 2-8-8 47 ow1..........(v[1]) LiamKeniry 3 34
(Michael Bell) *hld up in tch: effrt on inner 2f out: no prog over 1f out* **25/1**

600 **9** *3/4* **Excelling Oscar (IRE)**[17] 6563 2-8-11 50.......... HayleyTurner 8 35
(Conor Dore) *in tch in midfield: rdn and unable qck ent fnl 2f: wknd jst over 1f out* **50/1**

6006 **10** *3* **Foylesideview (IRE)**[5] 6884 2-9-7 60.......... FergusSweeney 10 36
(Luke Dace) *hld up in tch but stuck wd thrght: rdn over 2f out: no hdwy: wl hld over 1f out* **16/1**

000 **11** *4* **Quae Supra**[13] 6652 2-9-6 59.......... RichardHughes 2 25
(Richard Hannon) *s.i.s: nvr travelling and sn u.p in rr: n.d* **7/2**[2]

0000 **12** *2 1/2* **Birdie Must Fly**[25] 6294 2-8-7 46 oh1..........(b[1]) KieranO'Neill 5 5
(Jimmy Fox) *hld up towards rr: rdn and no hdwy over 2f out: bhd1f out* **50/1**

5206 **13** *8* **Cupulation**[17] 6563 2-9-4 57..........(b[1]) OisinMurphy 7
(Amy Weaver) *w ldr tl over 2f out: sn dropped out: bhd 1f out* **25/1**

1m 27.26s (1.26) **Going Correction** -0.025s/f (Stan) **13** Ran SP% **122.6**
Speed ratings (Par 93): **91,90,90,90,88 86,86,83,83,79 75,72,63**
CSF £11.17 CT £77.93 TOTE £1.90: £1.02, £3.10, £5.20; EX 13.50 Trifecta £92.20.
**Owner** S Curwen **Bred** P E Banahan **Trained** Lower Beeding, W Sussex

**FOCUS**
A big field and a generous-looking early pace, but a race that didn't concern too many.

## 7015 MOBILE LOYALTY BONUS AT TITANBET .CO.UK MAIDEN STKS 1m 4f (P)
**7:35** (7:35) (Class 5) 3-Y-O+ **£2,587** (£770; £384; £192) **Stalls** Centre

Form RPR

0422 **1** **Shining Glitter (IRE)**[27] 6238 3-8-11 75.......... CamHardie[(3)] 6 72
(James Fanshawe) *hld up in tch: hdwy on outer 3f out: rdn to chal 2f out: sn clr w ldr: led 1f out: kpt on and a jst holding rival after: rdn out* **2/1**[2]

04 **2** *nk* **Sea Vision (IRE)**[12] 6677 4-9-12 0.......... AdamBeschizza 1 77
(Jo Crowley) *led: rdn ent fnl 2f: clr w wnr over 1f out: hdd 1f out: battled on wl but a jst hld fnl f* **33/1**

6-22 **3** *3* **Galuppi**[164] 1720 3-9-5 80.......... RyanMoore 4 72
(Luca Cumani) *chsd ldr: 3rd and outpcd 2f out: styd on same pce u.p after* **4/5**[1]

05 **4** *3 1/4* **Mobhirr**[4] 6901 3-9-5 0..........(p) PaoloSirigu 2 67
(Marco Botti) *chsd ldrs: 4th and outpcd u.p 2f out: wl hld after* **33/1**

320 **5** *2 3/4* **Will**[32] 6092 3-9-5 70.......... JackMitchell 8 63
(Nick Littmoden) *stdd s: hld up in tch in rr: effrt on inner over 2f out: no hdwy: wknd over 1f out* **12/1**[3]

66 **6** *hd* **Hidden Power**[25] 6298 3-9-5 0.......... StevieDonohoe 5 62
(Jo Hughes) *t.k.h: hld up in tch in midfield: rdn and outpcd whn sltly hmpd 2f out: sn btn* **66/1**

6 **7** *2* **Arquimedes (IRE)**[75] 4587 3-9-5 0..........(t) RichardHughes 3 61
(Charles Hills) *in tch in last trio: rdn over 2f out: sn outpcd and struggling: wl btn over 1f out* **14/1**

2m 38.18s (3.68) **Going Correction** -0.025s/f (Stan)
**WFA** 3 from 4yo 7lb **7** Ran SP% **110.6**
Speed ratings (Par 103): **86,85,83,81,79 79,78**
CSF £54.85 TOTE £3.00: £1.40, £16.10; EX 64.90 Trifecta £133.00.
**Owner** Dragon Gate **Bred** Petra Bloodstock & Ecurie Des Monceaux **Trained** Newmarket, Suffolk

**FOCUS**
No sort of test at the trip, with the pace only lifting seriously in the final three furlongs. Muddling form, but the winner has been rated to his maiden latest.

## 7016 TITANBET.CO.UK H'CAP 1m 4f (P)
**8:05** (8:05) (Class 4) (0-80,78) 3-Y-O+ **£4,690** (£1,395; £697; £348) **Stalls** Centre

Form RPR

2113 **1** **King Calypso**[13] 6654 3-8-5 67.......... CamHardie[(3)] 3 78+
(Denis Coakley) *hld up in midfield: hdwy over 2f out: rdn to ld wl over 1f out: clr ins fnl f: r.o wl* **3/1**[2]

4602 **2** *3* **Castle Combe (IRE)**[19] 6487 3-9-0 73.......... PatDobbs 8 79
(Marcus Tregoning) *stdd s: hld up in rr: rdn and effrt 2f out: hdwy over 1f out: styd on to chse wnr ins fnl f: no imp* **7/1**

2150 **3** *1/2* **Bishop Of Ruscombe**[34] 6044 3-9-2 75..........[1] OisinMurphy 9 80
(Andrew Balding) *stdd s: hld up in last pair: c wd and hdwy over 1f out: kpt on u.p to go 3rd wl ins fnl f: no threat to wnr* **6/1**[3]

1053 **4** *1* **Morning Watch (IRE)**[31] 6141 3-9-5 78..........(p) RyanMoore 7 82
(Lady Cecil) *in tch in midfield: effrt u.p to chse ldr wl over 1f out: no imp 1f out: plugged on same pce and lost 2 pls ins fnl f* **6/4**[1]

3015 **5** *4 1/2* **Jarlath**[16] 5552 3-9-3 76..........(b) SteveDrowne 4 72
(Seamus Mullins) *led: rdn over 2f out: hdd over 1f out: no ex u.p and btn over 1f out: wknd 1f out* **16/1**

0413 **6** *1/2* **Karam Albaari (IRE)**[14] 6649 6-9-9 75..........(p) PaddyAspell 2 71
(J R Jenkins) *hld up in tch in midfield: switching lft and effrt ent fnl 2f: no imp over 1f out: wknd fnl f* **16/1**

0423 **7** *1* **Men Don't Cry (IRE)**[12] 6696 5-9-6 75..........(b) DeclanBates[(3)] 1 69
(Ed de Giles) *t.k.h: chsd ldrs: rdn and unable qck wl over 1f out: sn btn: wknd 1f out* **20/1**

53/3 **8** *9* **Castlemorris King**[16] 6367 6-9-0 66.......... WilliamTwiston-Davies 10 46
(Brian Barr) *chsd ldr: rdn over 2f out: lost 2nd and struggling ust over 2f out: wknd over 1f out* **20/1**

2m 33.33s (-1.17) **Going Correction** -0.025s/f (Stan)
**WFA** 3 from 5yo+ 7lb **8** Ran SP% **113.1**
Speed ratings (Par 105): **102,100,99,99,96 95,95,89**
CSF £23.65 CT £115.70 TOTE £4.30: £1.90, £2.30, £1.40; EX 22.20 Trifecta £124.20.
**Owner** Count Calypso Racing **Bred** Miss K Rausing **Trained** West Ilsley, Berks

**FOCUS**
A more satisfactory test at the 1m4f trip than the maiden which preceded it, and a winning time more than 4.8 seconds quicker. The winner continues to progress, while the second, third and fourth have been rated pretty much to form.

## 7017 £10 FREE MOBILE BET AT TITANBET.CO.UK H'CAP 6f (P)
**8:35** (8:35) (Class 4) (0-85,85) 3-Y-O+ **£4,690** (£1,395; £697; £348) **Stalls** Low

Form RPR

3402 **1** **Peace Seeker**[10] 6764 6-9-7 85..........(t) WilliamCarson 4 93
(Anthony Carson) *chsd ldrs: effrt u.p over 1f out: led 1f out: styd on wl: rdn out* **8/1**

0145 **2** *1/2* **Taquka (IRE)**[35] 6021 3-8-7 79.......... PatrickO'Donnell[(7)] 2 85
(Ralph Beckett) *hld up in midfield: rdn and gd hdwy on inner wl over 1f out: pressed ldrs 1f out: chsd wnr ins fnl f: r.o* **14/1**

340 **3** *nk* **Amygdala (USA)**[35] 6021 3-8-13 78.......... PatDobbs 9 83
(Stuart Williams) *in tch in midfield: effrt u.p over 1f out: kpt on wl fnl 100yds* **33/1**

5114 **4** *1/2* **Alnoomaas (IRE)**[12] 6680 5-8-13 77..........(v) FergusSweeney 3 81
(Luke Dace) *in tch in midfield: rdn and effrt over 1f out: chsd ldrs ins fnl f: kpt on* **10/1**

220 **5** *nk* **Dangerous Age**[27] 6235 4-9-3 81.......... SteveDrowne 8 84
(Charles Hills) *chsd ldrs: wnt 2nd over 3f out: ev ch u.p over 1f out tl no ex ins fnl f* **25/1**

3061 **6** *hd* **Dutch Interior**[12] 6680 3-9-1 80.......... RyanMoore 5 82
(Gary Moore) *stdd s: t.k.h: hld up in tch in last quartet: effrt but stl plenty to do 2f out: styd on u.p ins fnl f: nvr gng to rch ldrs* **6/4**[1]

650 **7** *1/2* **Noble Deed**[66] 4892 4-9-7 85.......... KierenFox 12 86
(Michael Attwater) *stdd s: t.k.h: hld up in tch in rr: effrt u.p wl over 1f out: styd on ins fnl f: nt rch ldrs* **25/1**

0006 **8** *1* **Daylight**[6] 6880 4-9-3 81..........(t) OisinMurphy 6 78
(Andrew Balding) *hld up in tch in last quartet: hdwy u.p over 1f out: kpt on: nvr trbld ldrs* **9/2**[2]

0241 **9** *1/2* **Desert Strike**[10] 6764 8-9-2 80..........(p) HayleyTurner 11 76
(Conor Dore) *led: rdn over 1f out: drvn and hdd 1f out: wknd ins fnl f* **16/1**

5400 **10** *2* **Gabbiano**[31] 6130 5-9-4 82.......... DaneO'Neill 7 71
(Jeremy Gask) *hld up in tch in last quartet: effrt but stl plenty to do 2f out: kpt on but no real imp* **6/1**[3]

2403 **11** *3 3/4* **La Tinta Bay**[17] 6552 3-8-10 75.......... RichardHughes 1 52
(Richard Hannon) *chsd ldr tl over 3f out: rdn and btn wl over 1f out: wknd fnl f* **20/1**

-060 **12** *1* **Storm Trooper (IRE)**[26] 6249 3-8-5 73.......... CamHardie[(3)] 10 47
(Richard Hannon) *in tch in midfield: rdn and no hdwy over 2f out: wknd over 1f out* **33/1**

1m 11.62s (-1.48) **Going Correction** -0.025s/f (Stan)
**WFA** 3 from 4yo+ 1lb **12** Ran SP% **123.6**
Speed ratings (Par 105): **108,107,106,106,105 105,104,103,102,100 95,93**
CSF £109.70 CT £3557.07 TOTE £8.70: £3.10, £3.90, £12.70; EX 157.60 Trifecta £2821.40 Part won..
**Owner** Hugh & Mindi Byrne **Bred** C J Mills **Trained** Newmarket, Suffolk

**FOCUS**
A competitive-looking finale on paper and in practice with under 2l separating the first six home. The runner-up, third and fourth have been rated pretty much to form.

T/Plt: £22.30 to a £1 stake. Pool of £74274.28 - 2422.05 winning tickets. T/Qpdt: £6.80 to a £1 stake. Pool of £8454.99 - 910.47 winning tickets. SP

# 6610 LEICESTER (R-H)

Tuesday, October 7

**OFFICIAL GOING: Good (good to firm in places) changing to good to soft (good in places) after race 1 (2.10)**

Wind: Light behind Weather: Showers clearing

## 7018 BRITISH STALLION STUDS EBF MAIDEN FILLIES' STKS (BOBIS RACE) (DIV I) 7f 9y

**2:10** (2:13) (Class 4) 2-Y-O **£5,175** (£1,540; £769; £384) **Stalls** High

Form RPR

1 **Goodyearforroses (IRE)** 2-9-0 0 PaulHanagan 8 79
(Rae Guest) *hld up: pushed along 1/2-way: hdwy over 1f out: str run to ld nr fin* **33/1**

2 *nk* **Redstart** 2-9-0 0 RichardKingscote 7 78
(Ralph Beckett) *chsd ldrs: shkn up over 1f out: led wl ins fnl f: hdd nr fin* **6/1**[3]

3 *1 3/4* **Star Of Seville** 2-9-0 0 WilliamBuick 1 73
(John Gosden) *chsd ldrs: shkn up to ld over 1f out: hdd and unable qck wl ins fnl f* **3/1**[2]

3442 4 *1 3/4* **Looking Good**[17] 6550 2-9-0 70 AndreaAtzeni 2 69
(David Brown) *led: rdn and hdd over 1f out: styd on same pce ins fnl f* **6/1**[3]

5 *1 3/4* **Forres (IRE)** 2-9-0 0 SeanLevey 10 64
(Richard Hannon) *s.i.s: hld up: rdn over 2f out: styd on fr over 1f out: nt trble ldrs* **25/1**

03 6 *2 1/4* **Chain Of Daisies**[21] 6420 2-9-0 0 DaneO'Neill 5 58
(Henry Candy) *s.i.s: sn trcking ldrs: rdn over 2f out: edgd rt over 1f out: no ex fnl f* **2/1**[1]

7 *1 3/4* **Percella** 2-9-0 0 JimmyFortune 6 53
(Hughie Morrison) *hld up: hdwy over 2f out: wknd fnl f* **50/1**

8 *1 1/4* **Merritt Island** 2-8-11 0 RosieJessop(3) 4 50
(Sir Mark Prescott Bt) *s.s: hdwy over 4f out: wknd fnl f* **100/1**

9 *shd* **Intimation** 2-9-0 0 RyanMoore 9 50
(Sir Michael Stoute) *mid-div: pushed along 1/2-way: wknd over 1f out* **8/1**

10 *11* **Don't Tell Louise** 2-9-0 0 MartinDwyer 11 20
(William Muir) *s.i.s: rn green and a in rr* **66/1**

6 11 *2 3/4* **Twice Certain (IRE)**[14] 6641 2-9-0 0 JamesDoyle 3 12
(Ed Walker) *w ldr to 1/2-way: wknd over 1f out* **10/1**

1m 25.54s (-0.66) **Going Correction** -0.075s/f (Good) **11 Ran SP% 118.3**
Speed ratings (Par 94): **100,99,97,95,93 91,89,87,87,74 71**
CSF £217.57 TOTE £18.40: £8.70, £1.60, £1.80; EX 360.70 Trifecta £1543.10.
**Owner** The Hornets **Bred** The Hornets **Trained** Newmarket, Suffolk

**FOCUS**
False rail from top of hill on back straight all the way to Winning Post and distances on Round course increased by 17yds. Despite the recent wet weather, the ground remained good, good to firm in places. The field raced up the centre in the first division of this fillies' maiden.

## 7019 BRITISH STALLION STUDS EBF MAIDEN FILLIES' STKS (BOBIS RACE) (DIV II) 7f 9y

**2:40** (2:43) (Class 4) 2-Y-O **£5,175** (£1,540; £769; £384) **Stalls** High

Form RPR

3 1 **Sympathy (USA)**[25] 6295 2-9-0 0 RyanMoore 3 87+
(Sir Michael Stoute) *w ldrs tl led 1/2-way: shkn up and c clr ins fnl f: comf* **4/9**[1]

2 *5* **Tutti Frutti** 2-9-0 0 WilliamBuick 10 70
(John Gosden) *s.i.s: hld up: hdwy over 2f out: rdn over 1f out: wnt 2nd ins fnl f: no ch w wnr* **6/1**[2]

5 3 *1/2* **Regal Ways (IRE)**[19] 6474 2-9-0 0 FrannyNorton 1 69
(Mark Johnston) *led to 1/2-way: rdn over 1f out: styd on same pce* **16/1**

4 *1 1/4* **Falconize (IRE)** 2-9-0 0 RichardKingscote 6 65
(Charles Hills) *s.i.s: hdwy over 5f out: rdn over 1f out: no ex ins fnl f* **25/1**

5 *1/2* **Mystery Code** 2-9-0 0 FergusSweeney 8 64
(Alan King) *hld up: plld hrd: hdwy over 1f out: nt rch ldrs* **50/1**

0 6 *1 1/4* **Beta Tauri (USA)**[14] 6641 2-9-0 0 MartinLane 7 61
(Charlie Appleby) *hld up in tch: racd keenly: rdn over 1f out: wknd ins fnl f* **20/1**

7 *1* **Moderah** 2-9-0 0 TomQueally 11 58
(James Fanshawe) *hld up: shkn up over 1f out: nvr on terms* **25/1**

00 8 *3/4* **Skylight (IRE)**[15] 6605 2-9-0 0 PaulHanagan 9 56
(William Haggas) *chsd ldrs: rdn over 2f out: wknd fnl f* **33/1**

9 *nk* **Hayba** 2-9-0 0 AndreaAtzeni 2 56
(Marco Botti) *prom: rdn over 2f out: wknd over 1f out* **12/1**[3]

10 *1 3/4* **Heavens Above (IRE)** 2-9-0 0 JimCrowley 4 51
(Ed Dunlop) *hld up: rdn over 2f out: nt clr run over 1f out: n.d* **33/1**

1m 26.35s (0.15) **Going Correction** -0.075s/f (Good) **10 Ran SP% 117.4**
Speed ratings (Par 94): **96,90,89,88,87 86,85,84,83,81**
CSF £2.81 TOTE £1.30: £1.02, £2.30, £4.30; EX 3.20 Trifecta £31.60.
**Owner** Highclere T'Bred Racing St James' Palace **Bred** Hargus & Sandra Sexton & Silver Fern Farm Llc **Trained** Newmarket, Suffolk

■ Sea Scent was withdrawn. Price at time of withdrawal 10/1. Rule 4 applies to all bets - deduct 5p in the pound.

**FOCUS**
The ground was changed to good to soft, good in places before this race and the winning time was 0.81sec slower than the first division. Unlike in the opener, the field came straight over to the nearside rail.

## 7020 JENNINGSBET.COM H'CAP (BOBIS RACE) 1m 3f 183y

**3:10** (3:11) (Class 4) (0-85,85) 3-Y-O **£4,690** (£1,395; £697; £348) **Stalls** Low

Form RPR

1521 1 **Serena Grae**[13] 6654 3-9-3 81 MartinDwyer 10 92
(Marcus Tregoning) *mde all: qcknd over 3f out: rdn over 1f out: styd on wl* **10/1**

0122 2 *2* **Knife Point (GER)**[12] 6685 3-9-6 84 (p) JamesDoyle 9 92
(Hugo Palmer) *a.p: chsd wnr over 8f out: rdn over 1f out: styd on same pce ins fnl f* **3/1**[2]

0604 3 *1 3/4* **From Frost**[13] 6656 3-9-3 81 (vt) DavidProbert 5 86
(Andrew Balding) *hld up in tch: rdn over 2f out: styd on same pce fnl f* **6/1**[3]

2142 4 *1 3/4* **Desert Snow**[17] 6559 3-9-7 85 FrederikTylicki 6 87
(Saeed bin Suroor) *prom: rdn over 2f out: no ex ins fnl f* **5/2**[1]

2361 5 *3/4* **Light Of Asia (IRE)**[11] 6699 3-8-9 73 JimCrowley 7 74
(Ed Dunlop) *hld up: hdwy u.p over 1f out: no ex ins fnl f* **10/1**

0104 6 *2 1/4* **Nam Hai (IRE)**[118] 3110 3-8-9 73 WilliamTwiston-Davies 4 71
(Michael Bell) *prom: rdn over 3f out: wknd fnl f* **9/1**

4134 7 *1 1/4* **Allegria (IRE)**[66] 4887 3-9-6 84 WilliamBuick 3 80
(John Gosden) *chsd wnr over 3f: remained handy: rdn over 3f out: wknd fnl f* **8/1**

6314 8 *3 1/4* **Hoist The Colours (IRE)**[19] 6502 3-9-4 82 (v[1]) GeorgeBaker 1 72
(David Lanigan) *s.i.s: hld up: rdn over 3f out: a in rr* **16/1**

2m 32.6s (-1.30) **Going Correction** +0.05s/f (Good) **8 Ran SP% 113.0**
Speed ratings (Par 103): **106,104,103,102,101 100,99,97**
CSF £39.24 CT £197.68 TOTE £10.20: £2.10, £1.10, £1.70; EX 56.20 Trifecta £315.00.
**Owner** Mrs Heather Raw **Bred** Heather Raw **Trained** Whitsbury, Hants

**FOCUS**
They didn't go much of a pace in this fair 3yo handicap and that very much played into the hands of the winner. The runner-up has been rated to his latest mark, and the third to his turf latest.

## 7021 STOAT (S) STKS 1m 1f 218y

**3:40** (3:41) (Class 6) 3-Y-O **£1,940** (£577; £288; £144) **Stalls** Low

Form RPR

0530 1 **Les Gar Gan (IRE)**[13] 6480 3-8-6 61 PaulHanagan 2 61
(Keith Dalgleish) *a.p: shkn up to ld 2f out: sn hdd: rallied to ld ins fnl f: styd on* **11/8**[1]

5000 2 *1/2* **Southern Cross**[5] 6883 3-8-6 58 HayleyTurner 3 60
(Hughie Morrison) *hld up: hdwy over 2f out: led over 1f out: sn rdn: hdd ins fnl f: kpt on* **6/1**[3]

0000 3 *7* **Hickster (IRE)**[81] 4411 3-8-6 54 AlistairRawlinson(5) 6 52
(Roy Bowring) *plld hrd: led 4f: chsd ldr tl led again over 2f out: sn rdn and hdd: wknd fnl f* **14/1**

0000 4 *6* **Exceed Policy**[29] 6193 3-8-11 45 (t) MartinLane 8 41
(David Dennis) *s.i.s: hld up: rdn over 3f out: hung rt over 1f out: n.d* **66/1**

664 5 *hd* **Exclusive Contract (IRE)**[3] 6932 3-8-11 61 (p) JimmyFortune 5 40
(Ollie Pears) *chsd ldrs: rdn over 2f out: wknd over 1f out* **11/4**[2]

0044 6 *shd* **Cueca (FR)**[15] 6613 3-8-3 48 (b) DannyBrock(3) 4 35
(Jonathan Portman) *plld hrd: w ldr tl led 6f out: hdd over 2f out: wknd over 1f out* **12/1**

5000 7 *4* **Mary's Prayer**[20] 6454 3-8-6 45 (b[1]) FrannyNorton 7 27
(John Holt) *s.s: sme hdwy 1/2-way: rdn and wknd over 2f out* **33/1**

0-56 8 *35* **Canary Lad (IRE)**[40] 5862 3-8-11 59 JimCrowley 1
(Timothy Jarvis) *chsd ldrs: rdn over 3f out: wknd over 2f out* **8/1**

2m 9.89s (1.99) **Going Correction** +0.05s/f (Good) **8 Ran SP% 113.0**
Speed ratings (Par 99): **94,93,88,83,83 82,79,51**
CSF £9.99 TOTE £2.60: £1.50, £2.00, £3.00; EX 9.60 Trifecta £105.30.There was no bid for the winner.
**Owner** Middleham Park Racing XLIII **Bred** Sean O'Sullivan **Trained** Carluke, S Lanarks

**FOCUS**
A poor seller and the front pair, who were the two most favoured on adjusted official ratings, pulled well clear. The runner-up has been rated to her earlier maiden form.

## 7022 SQUIRREL H'CAP 1m 60y

**4:10** (4:11) (Class 2) (0-112,104) 3-Y-O+ **£15,762** (£4,715; £2,357; £1,180; £587) **Stalls** Low

Form RPR

0005 1 **Loving Spirit**[18] 6522 6-9-2 98 RobertTart 6 103
(James Toller) *s.i.s: hld up: pushed along over 2f out: hdwy u.p and c centre to r alone over 1f out: r.o to ld nr fin* **7/1**

4021 2 *nk* **Dark Emerald (IRE)**[17] 6560 4-9-4 100 SebSanders 2 104
(Brendan Powell) *w ldr tl led over 3f out: rdn over 1f out: hdd nr fin* **9/2**[2]

550 3 *1/2* **Cordite (IRE)**[20] 6458 3-9-0 104 AlistairRawlinson(5) 9 107
(Michael Appleby) *s.i.s: hdwy over 6f out: rdn to chse ldr over 1f out: styd on* **8/1**

0430 4 *3/4* **Fire Ship**[15] 6620 5-9-8 104 AndreaAtzeni 4 105
(William Knight) *a.p: rdn over 3f out: styd on: nt clr run towards fin* **5/2**[1]

6004 5 *shd* **Boom And Bust (IRE)**[23] 6358 7-9-2 98 MartinDwyer 3 99
(Marcus Tregoning) *trckd ldrs: plld hrd: rdn over 2f out: styd on same pce ins fnl f* **10/1**

2040 6 *5* **Spa's Dancer (IRE)**[20] 6458 7-9-4 100 StevieDonohoe 1 90
(James Eustace) *s.i.s: sn pushed along in rr: rdn over 2f out: nt trble ldrs* **12/1**

5223 7 *5* **Bold Prediction (IRE)**[10] 6748 4-9-2 98 MichaelStainton 8 76
(K R Burke) *led over 4f: rdn and wknd over 1f out* **10/1**

-240 8 *2 3/4* **Day Of Conquest**[31] 6124 3-9-3 102 SeanLevey 5 74
(Richard Hannon) *hld up: plld hrd early: rdn over 2f out: wknd over 1f out* **11/2**[3]

1m 44.82s (-0.28) **Going Correction** +0.05s/f (Good)
**WFA** 3 from 4yo+ 3lb **8 Ran SP% 111.6**
Speed ratings (Par 109): **103,102,102,101,101 96,91,88**
CSF £36.54 CT £255.04 TOTE £7.90: £2.10, £1.40, £2.70; EX 21.00 Trifecta £470.90.
**Owner** Loving Spirit Partnership **Bred** Elsdon Farms **Trained** Newmarket, Suffolk

**FOCUS**
The feature handicap featuring a few who have been contesting Pattern races and, in a race run at a fair gallop, the winner managed to come from last. The winner has been rated in line with his best, minus his claim.

## 7023 RED DEER H'CAP 5f 218y

**4:40** (4:44) (Class 5) (0-70,75) 3-Y-O+ **£2,587** (£770; £384; £192) **Stalls** High

Form RPR

0222 1 **Smokethatthunders (IRE)**[24] 6346 4-9-2 70 DanielMuscutt(5) 13 80
(James Unett) *a.p: rdn to ld ins fnl f: edgd rt: r.o* **6/1**[2]

5142 2 *1* **Manatee Bay**[7] 6835 4-9-4 67 (v) FrannyNorton 14 74
(David Nicholls) *hld up: pushed along over 2f out: hdwy over 1f out: r.o* **13/2**[3]

6510 3 *nk* **Maymyo (IRE)**[19] 6488 3-8-13 63 JamesDoyle 10 69
(Sylvester Kirk) *w ldr: rdn over 1f out: led ins fnl f: sn hdd: styd on same pce* **25/1**

4511 4 *3/4* **Tahchee**[55] 5307 3-9-6 70 FrederikTylicki 11 73
(James Fanshawe) *a.p: rdn and ev ch over 1f out: styd on same pce ins fnl f* **11/2**[1]

432 5 *shd* **Lead A Merry Dance**[25] 6297 3-8-13 63 PaulHanagan 5 66
(Sylvester Kirk) *chsd ldrs: pushed along 1/2-way: rdn and ev ch over 1f out: styd on same pce ins fnl f* **16/1**

2021 6 *hd* **Birdie Queen**[29] 6189 4-9-7 70 GeorgeBaker 6 72
(Gary Moore) *led: rdn over 1f out: hdd and unable qck ins fnl f* **8/1**

42 7 *2* **Election Night**[10] 6758 3-9-5 69 PhillipMakin 1 65
(Tim Easterby) *hld up: hdwy over 2f out: rdn over 1f out: no ex ins fnl f* **10/1**

0000 8 *1* **Time Medicean**[34] 6025 8-9-1 64 SebSanders 7 57
(Tony Carroll) *hld up: pushed along over 2f out: styd on u.p ins fnl f: nvr nrr* **6/1**[2]

1001 **9** *1 ¼* **Half Way**[15] 6613 3-9-3 70 .......... AmyScott(3) 8 59
(Henry Candy) *mid-div: hdwy over 2f out: no ex ins fnl f* **10/1**
3544 **10** *1* **Italian Tom (IRE)**[43] 5777 7-9-4 67 .......... DavidProbert 18 53
(Ronald Harris) *w ldrs tl rdn over 2f out: wknd ins fnl f* **25/1**
052 **11** *1 ¼* **Roly Tricks**[90] 4086 3-9-6 70 .......... JimCrowley 4 52
(Olly Stevens) *prom: rdn over 2f out: wknd over 1f out* **20/1**
1204 **12** *½* **Climaxfortackle (IRE)**[43] 5776 6-9-2 65 .......... MartinLane 2 45
(Derek Shaw) *sn pushed along in rr: nvr on terms* **33/1**
10 **13** *4 ½* **Boy Wonder**[10] 6758 3-9-5 69 .......... WilliamTwiston-Davies 9 35
(Mick Channon) *sn pushed along and a in rr* **33/1**
4325 **14** *3* **Bint Malyana (IRE)**[31] 6154 3-9-5 69 .......... SeanLevey 17 25
(Paul D'Arcy) *hld up: rdn over 2f out: wknd over 1f out* **16/1**
2300 **15** *1 ½* **Whipphound**[12] 6695 6-9-4 67 .......... WilliamBuick 3 18
(Mark Brisbourne) *hld up: rdn over 2f out: wknd over 1f out: eased ins fnl f* **14/1**

1m 12.05s (-0.95) **Going Correction** -0.075s/f (Good)
**WFA** 3 from 4yo+ 1lb **15** Ran SP% **123.4**
Speed ratings (Par 103): **103,101,101,100,100 99,97,95,94,92 91,90,84,80,78**
CSF £42.50 CT £923.29 TOTE £7.60: £3.20, £2.20, £6.80; EX 54.20 Trifecta £1477.20.
**Owner** Northern Line Racing Ltd **Bred** P Doyle Bloodstock & J K Thoroughbred **Trained** Tedsmore Hall, Shropshire
■ Avonmore Star was withdrawn. Price at time of withdrawal 50/1. Rule 4 does not apply.

**FOCUS**
A modest sprint handicap. The field split into two groups with one racing up the centre and the other towards the nearside, but although there wasn't that much between the two groups at the line those that raced closer to the stands' rail appeared to have an advantage. The winner has been rated to his Wolverhampton latest, and the runner-up to form.

## 7024 BREEDERS BACKING RACING EBF DORMOUSE MAIDEN STKS 7f 9y
5:10 (5:14) (Class 5) 3-Y-0 £3,881 (£1,155; £577; £288) Stalls High

Form RPR
0432 **1** **Nathr (USA)**[33] 6073 3-9-5 74 .......... PaulHanagan 3 80
(Charles Hills) *mde all: rdn over 1f out: r.o* **3/1**[2]
042 **2** *1 ½* **Gharaaneej (IRE)**[14] 6638 3-9-0 68 .......... RobertHavlin 5 71
(John Gosden) *a.p: nt clr run ins fnl f tl hung rt and r.o towards fin* **10/1**
332 **3** *1* **New Identity (IRE)**[40] 5862 3-9-5 80 .......... JamesDoyle 2 73
(Denis Coakley) *w wnr tl rdn 2f out: styd on same pce ins fnl f* **2/1**[1]
2 **4** *4 ½* **Wu Zetian**[21] 6421 3-9-0 0 .......... DavidProbert 1 57
(Andrew Balding) *chsd ldrs: rdn over 1f out: wknd ins fnl f* **3/1**[2]
2 **5** *2 ½* **Semblance**[39] 5883 3-9-0 0 .......... WilliamBuick 9 50
(John Gosden) *hld up: hdwy over 4f out: rdn over 1f out: wknd fnl f* **7/1**[3]
6 **6** *1* **Otterbridge**[19] 6482 3-9-0 0 .......... DougieCostello 6 48
(Rod Millman) *prom: lost pl 4f out: n.d after* **100/1**
**7** *½* **Approaching (IRE)** 3-9-5 0 .......... (t) JimCrowley 11 51
(Amanda Perrett) *s.i.s: hdwy over 4f out: wknd over 1f out* **20/1**
0 **8** *1 ½* **Duke Of Dunton (IRE)**[19] 6482 3-9-5 0 .......... WilliamTwiston-Davies 10 47
(Tony Carroll) *hld up: rdn over 2f out: n.d* **100/1**

1m 25.96s (-0.24) **Going Correction** -0.075s/f (Good) **8** Ran SP% **111.7**
Speed ratings (Par 101): **98,96,95,90,87 86,85,83**
CSF £30.31 TOTE £4.00: £1.10, £2.00, £1.20; EX 33.30 Trifecta £108.90.
**Owner** Hamdan Al Maktoum **Bred** Courtlandt Farm **Trained** Lambourn, Berks
■ Stewards' Enquiry : Robert Havlin caution: careless riding

**FOCUS**
A modest 3yo maiden, though five of the seven to have raced before had finished runner-up in their most recent outings. The field raced nearside and again it was an advantage to have the rail. The winner has been rated as running a length pb, with the runner-up a big improver.

## 7025 LEVERET APPRENTICE H'CAP 7f 9y
5:40 (5:43) (Class 6) (0-60,60) 3-Y-0+ £1,940 (£577; £288; £144) Stalls High

Form RPR
0600 **1** **No Refund (IRE)**[50] 5510 3-8-11 53 .......... RyanWhile(3) 14 61
(Martin Smith) *hld up: swtchd rt and hdwy 2f out: shkn up to ld over 1f out: styd on* **33/1**
0033 **2** *½* **Keene's Pointe**[55] 5303 4-8-13 57 .......... (b) TylerSaunders(7) 16 64
(Charles Hills) *chsd ldrs: pushed along over 1f out: styd on* **10/1**
3033 **3** *2* **Burnhope**[22] 6397 5-9-1 52 .......... MatthewHopkins 2 54+
(Scott Dixon) *led 6f out: rdn: hung lft and hdd over 1f out: styd on same pce ins fnl f* **9/2**[1]
4632 **4** *½* **Swiss Lait**[15] 6613 3-9-4 57 .......... TimClark 10 57
(David Elsworth) *prom: pushed along 1/2-way: rdn and nt clr run over 1f out: styd on same pce ins fnl f* **7/1**[2]
4050 **5** *hd* **Distant High**[21] 6426 3-9-3 56 .......... [1] NathanAlison 12 55
(Richard Price) *hld up: r.o ins fnl f: nvr nrr* **12/1**
3205 **6** *1* **Very First Blade**[15] 6595 5-8-13 50 .......... (b) NoelGarbutt 9 47
(Michael Mullineaux) *got loose on the way to the s: hld up: pushed along 1/2-way: styd on fr over 1f out: nt trble ldrs* **16/1**
0004 **7** *½* **Iggy**[13] 6674 4-9-3 57 .......... (t) MeganCarberry(3) 1 53
(Michael Easterby) *chsd ldrs: rdn and hung lft over 1f out: no ex ins fnl f* **7/1**[2]
5300 **8** *1 ¼* **Slick Indian**[18] 6515 3-8-13 55 .......... (b) AnnaHesketh(3) 15 47
(Michael Easterby) *mid-div: rdn over 1f out: styd on same pce* **20/1**
3064 **9** *1 ¼* **Mad Endeavour**[21] 6421 3-9-7 60 .......... ShaneGray 5 49
(Stuart Kittow) *s.i.s: sn pushed along in rr: styd on ins fnl f: nvr nrr* **12/1**
5556 **10** *2* **It's A Yes From Me**[41] 5820 3-9-4 57 .......... DanielMuscutt 8 40
(James Fanshawe) *hld up: hdwy u.p over 1f out: wknd ins fnl f* **10/1**
5005 **11** *3 ½* **Prignsov Dancer (IRE)**[11] 6720 9-9-0 56 .......... (p) JackBudge(5) 3 31
(Deborah Sanderson) *led 1f: chsd ldrs: rdn over 2f out: wknd over 1f out* **16/1**
6520 **12** *½* **Tubeanie (IRE)**[22] 6397 3-9-5 58 .......... (p) MarcMonaghan 6 31
(Amy Weaver) *sn pushed along and a in rr* **20/1**
005- **13** *¾* **Sannibel**[518] 2130 6-8-13 53 .......... AlistairRawlinson(3) 4 25
(David Bridgwater) *chsd ldrs: rdn over 2f out: wknd over 1f out* **33/1**
5-04 **14** *3 ¾* **Opus Dei**[19] 6495 7-9-2 53 .......... (p) GeorgeDowning 18 15
(John Murray) *s.i.s: a in rr* **20/1**
/0-5 **15** *¾* **Henry Morgan**[9] 6796 7-8-10 52 .......... ClaireMurray(5) 13 12
(David Brown) *prom: rdn over 2f out: wknd over 1f out* **25/1**
4602 **16** *1* **Mysterious Wonder**[20] 6454 4-8-11 53 .......... PhillipDennis(5) 11 11
(Philip Kirby) *hld up: rdn and wknd over 2f out* **9/1**[3]

1m 26.35s (0.15) **Going Correction** -0.075s/f (Good)
**WFA** 3 from 4yo+ 2lb **16** Ran SP% **122.5**
Speed ratings (Par 101): **96,95,93,92,92 91,90,89,87,85 81,80,80,75,74 73**
CSF £313.15 CT £1862.64 TOTE £68.80: £10.50, £2.10, £1.30, £1.80; EX 469.20 Trifecta £1407.50.
**Owner** Macguire's Bloodstock Ltd **Bred** Bricklow Stud **Trained** Newmarket, Suffolk
■ Stewards' Enquiry : Nathan Alison two-day ban: failed to ride out for 4th (Oct 21-22)

**FOCUS**
A moderate apprentice handicap in which they again raced centre-to-nearside and those that raced closest to the rail were at an advantage. The well-placed runner-up has been rated in line with his recent form.
T/Plt: £70.10 to a £1 stake. Pool of £68155.89 - 709.74 winning tickets. T/Qpdt: £17.60 to a £1 stake. Pool of £6622.65 - 277.40 winning tickets. CR

# 6698 MAISONS-LAFFITTE (R-H)
Tuesday, October 7

**OFFICIAL GOING: Turf: soft**

## 7026a PRIX DES AUNETTES (H'CAP) (3YO+) (TURF) 6f (S)
12:50 (12:50) 3-Y-0+
£23,500 (£9,500; £7,000; £4,500; £2,750; £1,750)

RPR
**1** **Chief Hawkeye (IRE)**[21] 5-8-9 0 .......... AnthonyCrastus 8 89
(J-V Toux, France) **217/10**
**2** *¾* **Calrissian (GER)**[33] 10-8-9 0 .......... MlleSarahCallac 6 87
(F Foresi, France) **201/10**
**3** *nk* **Daring Storm (GER)**[33] 4-8-7 0 .......... (b) GregoryBenoist 5 84
(S Wattel, France) **51/10**[2]
**4** *2* **Ghor (FR)**[45] 6-8-13 0 .......... (b) StephanePasquier 13 83
(M Boutin, France) **94/10**
**5** *1 ½* **Pretty Panther (FR)**[45] 4-9-5 0 .......... Francois-XavierBertras 11 84
(F Rohaut, France) **9/1**[3]
**6** *½* **Belletriste (FR)**[21] 6446 3-8-10 0 .......... ThierryJarnet 4 75
(Sylvester Kirk) *a.p: rdn and nt qckn 1 1/2f out: kpt on at same pce fnl f* **176/10**
**7** *1 ¼* **Artplace (IRE)**[45] 4-9-4 0 .......... (b) DelphineSantiago 12 78
(S Smrczek, Germany) **137/10**
**8** *nk* **Elabela (IRE)**[45] 4-8-8 0 .......... FabienLefebvre 14 67
(J E Hammond, France) **4/1**[1]
**9** *nse* **Self Indulgence (FR)**[44] 3-8-9 0 .......... OlivierPeslier 2 69
(C Ferland, France) **51/10**[2]
**10** *4* **Jo De Vati (FR)**[30] 4-9-3 0 .......... TheoBachelot 9 63
(S Wattel, France) **42/1**
**11** *shd* **Wingate**[110] 4-9-1 0 .......... ThierryThulliez 10 61
(J-V Toux, France) **40/1**
**12** *1 ½* **Le Valentin (FR)**[45] 8-9-2 0 .......... EddyHardouin 7 57
(Mlle C Nicot, France) **235/10**
**13** *½* **Xotic (FR)**[30] 5-9-7 0 .......... Pierre-CharlesBoudot 16 60
(D Prod'Homme, France) **156/10**
**14** *¾* **Asulaman (GER)**[65] 7-9-4 0 .......... (b) AurelienLemaitre 1 55
(S Cerulis, France) **25/1**
**15** *7* **Moscow Eight (IRE)**[45] 8-8-9 0 .......... CristianDemuro 3 23
(E J O'Neill, France) **136/10**

1m 11.9s (-1.50)
**WFA** 3 from 4yo+ 1lb **15** Ran SP% **119.3**
WIN (incl. 1 euro stake): 22.70. PLACES: 6.30, 5.60, 2.90. DF: 182.30. SF: 411.30.
**Owner** John Arnou **Bred** Kenilworth House Stud **Trained** France

## 7027a PRIX D'ECQUEVILLY (CLAIMER) (2YO) (STRAIGHT) (TURF) 1m 1f
1:20 (1:20) 2-Y-0 £7,916 (£3,166; £2,375; £1,583; £791)

RPR
**1** **Wild Wild West (FR)**[12] 6698 2-9-2 0 .......... (b) StephanePasquier 4 75
(Yannick Fouin, France) **6/1**[2]
**2** *1 ¾* **Becquanaille (FR)** 2-9-1 0 .......... ThierryJarnet 5 71
(T Lemer, France) **9/1**[3]
**3** *8* **Against Rules (FR)**[21] 2-8-11 0 .......... JimmyTastayre 3 51
(Robert Collet, France) **52/1**
**4** *1 ¼* **Gilded Lace**[12] 6698 2-8-11 0 .......... (p) MickaelBarzalona 14 48
(J S Moore) *half-rrd and wnt rt leaving stalls: sn prom on outer: rdn to chse ldng pair under 2f out: kpt on appr 1f out: readily outpcd by ldrs ins fnl f and fdd last 100yds* **8/5**[1]
**5** *1 ½* **Snow Guest (FR)**[21] 2-8-8 0 .......... (b) FlavienPrat 16 42
(D Windrif, France) **92/10**
**6** *½* **Trust The Captain (FR)**[12] 6698 2-8-9 0 .......... NicolasLarenaudie(6) 15 48
(Robert Collet, France) **124/10**
**7** *4* **Dayaday (FR)**[27] 6244 2-9-5 0 .......... AnthonyCrastus 2 44
(C Boutin, France) **11/1**
**8** *½* **Ath Cliath (IRE)**[34] 2-8-8 0 .......... MllePaulineDominois(3) 10 35
(C Boutin, France) **196/10**
**9** *20* **Moncucay (FR)** 2-9-1 0 .......... (p) FranckForesi 11
(F Foresi, France) **58/1**
**10** *1 ½* **Cotil Red (FR)** 2-9-1 0 .......... AlexisBadel 1
(J-V Toux, France) **20/1**
**11** *2* **Reinor (FR)** 2-9-1 0 .......... ThomasMessina 6
(Mlle A Voraz, France) **74/1**
**12** *1* **Charly Chop (FR)**[12] 2-9-4 0 .......... (b[1]) EddyHardouin 13
(Matthieu Palussiere, France) **169/10**
**13** *1 ½* **Mylenachope (FR)**[21] 2-8-8 0 .......... AurelienLemaitre 8
(C Boutin, France) **28/1**
**14** *7* **Komtess Ka (FR)**[21] 2-8-8 0 .......... GregoryBenoist 7
(A Junk, France) **28/1**
**15** *4* **Kerlogot (FR)**[144] 2-8-11 0 .......... RaphaelMarchelli 12
(T Castanheira, France) **29/1**

1m 55.2s (0.50) **15** Ran SP% **118.7**
WIN (incl. 1 euro stake): 7.00. PLACES: 2.40, 3.20, 11.80. DF: 26.90. SF: 58.60.
**Owner** N Guarino & Y Fouin **Bred** Janus Bloodstock Inc. & G Lugon **Trained** France

# [7011]KEMPTON (A.W) (R-H)

Wednesday, October 8

**OFFICIAL GOING: Polytrack: standard**

Wind: fresh, half behind Weather: showers, breezy

## 7029 100% RACINGUK PROFITS RETURNED TO RACING CLAIMING STKS 6f (P)

5:55 (5:56) (Class 6) 2-Y-O **£1,940** (£577; £288; £144) Stalls Low

Form RPR

5340 **1** **Just The Tip (IRE)**[19] 6513 2-8-8 75.................................... TomEaves 9 73+
(Keith Dalgleish) *chsd ldr: upsides and gng best over 2f out: shkn up to ld over 1f out: r.o strly: readily* **9/2**[2]

0156 **2** *4 ½* **Classic Seniority**[37] 5974 2-9-5 70.................................... PatDobbs 7 70
(Richard Hannon) *chsd ldng trio: rdn over 1f out: styd on to go 2nd wl ins fnl f: no ch w wnr* **14/1**

0216 **3** *2 ½* **Designate (IRE)**[21] 6447 2-8-11 73......................(bt) RichardKingscote 1 55
(Ralph Beckett) *broke fast: led jnd and rdn over 2f out: hdd over 1f out: btn 1f out: hung rt and lost 2nd wl ins fnl f* **2/1**[1]

4556 **4** *nk* **Mylaporyours (IRE)**[47] 5620 2-8-7 66.......................... DavidProbert 4 50
(Rod Millman) *chsd ldng pair: rdn and effrt over 2f out: 3rd and btn over 1f out: plugged on* **16/1**

0310 **5** *¾* **Tinkers Kiss (IRE)**[14] 6662 2-8-1 62.......................... DannyBrock(3) 10 44
(Philip McBride) *racd off the pce in midfield: styd on same pce u.p fnl 2f* **6/1**

4540 **6** *3 ¼* **Come Uppence**[24] 6375 2-8-9 70.......................................... MartinLane 6 40
(David Evans) *t.k.h: hld up off the pce in midfield: no hdwy over 2f out: n.d* **5/1**[3]

5230 **7** *3 ¼* **Giannizzero (IRE)**[26] 6294 2-8-12 67.......................... DanielMuscutt(5) 3 38
(Marco Botti) *sn pushed along and wl off the pce in last trio: n.d* **8/1**

520 **8** *1 ¼* **Mister Arden (FR)**[16] 6619 2-8-13 67.......................... TomQueally 5 30
(Harry Dunlop) *stdd s: hld up wl off the pce in last pair: n.d* **33/1**

66 **9** *½* **Zebs Lad (IRE)**[44] 5779 2-8-11 72.......................................... ChrisCatlin 2 27
(Ronald Harris) *awkward leaving stalls: a wl off the pce in rr* **25/1**

1m 12.12s (-0.98) **Going Correction** -0.125s/f (Stan) **9 Ran SP% 112.9**
Speed ratings (Par 93): **101,95,91,91,90 85,81,79,79**
CSF £63.13 TOTE £4.40: £1.60, £2.60, £1.30; EX 44.30 Trifecta £147.40.
**Owner** Straightline Construction Ltd **Bred** Knocklong House Stud **Trained** Carluke, S Lanarks

**FOCUS**
A fair juvenile claimer in which they went a decent gallop on standard Polytrack.

## 7030 BRITISH STALLION STUDS EBF MAIDEN STKS (DIV I) 7f (P)

6:25 (6:26) (Class 5) 2-Y-O **£2,911** (£866; £432; £216) Stalls Low

Form RPR

0 **1** **Algaith (USA)**[12] 6712 2-9-5 0.......................................... PaulHanagan 11 78+
(B W Hills) *chsd ldr: rdn to chal 2f out: sn clr w wnr: led over 1f out: rn green and edgd rt 1f out: asserted u.p fnl 100yds: r.o wl* **9/4**[1]

2 **2** *1 ¾* **Gold Will (IRE)**[16] 6604 2-9-5 0.......................... RichardKingscote 12 73
(Ralph Beckett) *led: rdn and wnt clr w wnr wl over 1f out: hdd over 1f out: kpt on u.p and stl evu ch whn bmpd 1f out: no ex and btn fnl 100yds* **5/2**[2]

0 **3** *2* **Velociter (IRE)**[12] 6702 2-9-5 0.......................................... PatDobbs 4 68
(Richard Hannon) *chsd ldrs: rdn and outpcd 2f out: kpt on same pce fr over 1f out* **33/1**

3 **4** *nk* **Mister Brightside (IRE)**[21] 6457 2-9-5 0.......................... WilliamBuick 9 67
(Jeremy Noseda) *t.k.h: hld up towards rr on outer: rdn and effrt 2f out: styd on wl ins fnl f: no threat to ldrs* **7/2**[3]

0 **5** *1 ¾* **Boarding Party (USA)**[18] 6551 2-9-5 0.......................... MartinLane 5 62
(Charlie Fellowes) *wl in tch in midfield: rdn and unable qck ent fnl 2f: styd on same pce after* **16/1**

**6** *1* **Royal Albert Hall** 2-9-5 0.......................................... JimCrowley 2 59
(Olly Stevens) *s.i.s: towards rr: rdn and effrt on inner 2f out: kpt on wl ins fnl f: nvr trbld ldrs* **50/1**

4 **7** *hd* **Wind In My Sails**[16] 6604 2-9-5 0.......................... FrederikTylicki 13 59
(Ed de Giles) *t.k.h: sn chsng ldrs: rdn and outpcd ent fnl 2f: no threat to ldrs after: wknd ins fnl f* **20/1**

0 **8** *5* **Vejovis**[7] 6852 2-9-5 0.......................................... ChrisCatlin 1 45
(Sir Mark Prescott Bt) *in tch in midfield: rdn and unable qck over 2f out: wknd over 1f out* **100/1**

60 **9** *nse* **Kingston Sassafras**[27] 6261 2-9-5 0.......................... FergusSweeney 6 45
(Ed Walker) *hld up towards rr: hmpd after 1f: in last pair after and n.d* **66/1**

**10** *7* **Exit Europe** 2-9-0 0.......................................... JennyPowell(5) 10 26
(Andrew Reid) *stdd s: hld up towards rr: struggling u.p over 2f out: sn wknd* **100/1**

50 **11** *3 ½* **Red Unico (IRE)**[14] 6667 2-9-5 0.......................................... TomQueally 3 17
(Alan McCabe) *sn bhd: lost tch over 2f out* **100/1**

0 **U** **Sonnolento (IRE)**[18] 6551 2-9-5 0.......................................... DavidProbert 7
(Andrew Balding) *towards rr whn stmbld and uns rdr after 1f* **13/2**

1m 26.66s (0.66) **Going Correction** -0.125s/f (Stan) **12 Ran SP% 114.9**
Speed ratings (Par 95): **91,89,86,86,84 83,83,77,77,69 65,**
CSF £7.42 TOTE £3.30: £1.20, £2.10, £7.20; EX 9.90 Trifecta £136.70.
**Owner** Hamdan Al Maktoum **Bred** Shadwell Farm LLC **Trained** Upper Lambourn, Berks

**FOCUS**
The first division of a fair juvenile maiden in which they went an even gallop.

## 7031 BRITISH STALLION STUDS EBF MAIDEN STKS (DIV II) 7f (P)

6:55 (7:00) (Class 5) 2-Y-O **£2,911** (£866; £432; £216) Stalls Low

Form RPR

**1** **Convey** 2-9-5 0.......................................... JamesDoyle 1 90+
(Sir Michael Stoute) *trckd ldrs: clsd over 1f out: shkn up to ld 1f out: rn green and wnt rt but immediately qcknd clr: r.o strly: impressive* **4/6**[1]

**2** *5* **King To Be (IRE)** 2-9-5 0.......................................... JimCrowley 6 74
(Richard Hannon) *s.i.s: hld up towards rr: hdwy on inner over 2f out: ev ch briefly jst over 1f out: chsd clr wnr and one pce ins fnl f* **20/1**

40 **3** *1 ¾* **Lethal Legacy (IRE)**[67] 4896 2-9-5 0.......................................... PatDobbs 10 69
(Richard Hannon) *chsd ldr tl rdn to ld 2f out: hdd 1f out: sn outpcd: 3rd and plugged on same pce fnl f* **4/1**[2]

2 **4** *2* **Caught On The Bid (IRE)**[13] 6675 2-9-2 0.......................... DeclanBates(3) 2 64
(Ed de Giles) *hld up in tch in midfield: effrt ent fnl 2f: chsng ldrs whn nt clr run and swtchd rt over 1f out: 4th and wl hld ins fnl f* **16/1**

66 **5** *1* **Zamperini (IRE)**[46] 5671 2-9-5 0.......................................... FergusSweeney 5 61
(Mike Murphy) *led: hdd and rdn 2f out: outpcd over 1f out: 5th and wl hld ins fnl f* **33/1**

0 **6** *nse* **Full Of Speed (USA)**[76] 4570 2-9-5 0.......................... FrederikTylicki 12 61
(James Fanshawe) *in tch in midfield: rdn ent fnl 2f: outpcd and btn over 1f out: plugged on* **25/1**

**7** *1* **Rattling Jewel** 2-9-5 0.......................................... LiamKeniry 11 58
(Andrew Balding) *dwlt and short of room sn after s: hld up towards rr: effrt and hdwy on inner 2f out: kpt on but no ch w wnr* **25/1**

**8** *½* **Upstaging** 2-9-5 0.......................................... MartinLane 8 57
(Paul Cole) *hld up in midfield: rdn over 2f out: unable qck ent fnl 2f: wl hld over 1f out: plugged on* **12/1**[3]

00 **9** *4 ½* **Master Choice (IRE)**[16] 6604 2-9-5 0.......................................... LiamJones 13 45
(William Haggas) *dwlt: bustled along and sn rcvrd to chse ldrs: rdn over 2f out: wknd wl over 1f out* **100/1**

**10** *nk* **Muhaafiz (IRE)** 2-9-5 0.......................................... PaulHanagan 4 44
(Charles Hills) *s.i.s: detached last: clsd 4f out: rdn and btn over 2f out* **20/1**

24 **11** *nk* **Red Touch (USA)**[12] 6719 2-9-5 0.......................................... TomQueally 7 43
(Alan McCabe) *chsd ldrs: struggling over 2f out: wknd 2f out* **33/1**

0 **12** *3 ¼* **Marlot**[40] 5881 2-9-5 0.......................................... WilliamCarson 9 34
(Jim Boyle) *in tch in midfield on outer: rdn over 2f out: sn wknd* **100/1**

5 **13** *3 ¾* **Willow Jubilee**[60] 5184 2-9-0 0.......................................... OisinMurphy 3 19
(John E Long) *a towards rr: lost tch over 2f out* **100/1**

1m 25.72s (-0.28) **Going Correction** -0.125s/f (Stan) **13 Ran SP% 119.6**
Speed ratings (Par 95): **96,90,88,86,84 84,83,83,77,77 77,73,69**
CSF £22.69 TOTE £1.50: £1.10, £4.80, £1.60; EX 23.90 Trifecta £58.60.
**Owner** K Abdullah **Bred** Juddmonte Farms Ltd **Trained** Newmarket, Suffolk

**FOCUS**
The second division of a fair juvenile maiden in which they went a respectable gallop and the comparative winning time was significantly quicker.

## 7032 BETBRIGHT MONEYBACK OFFERS MEDIAN AUCTION MAIDEN STKS 1m 3f (P)

7:25 (7:27) (Class 5) 3-5-Y-O **£2,587** (£770; £384; £192) Stalls Low

Form RPR

2- **1** **Fair Share**[315] 8067 3-9-5 0.......................................... JamesDoyle 8 81+
(Lady Cecil) *racd in last pair and rn in snatches: rdn over 2f out: gd hdwy u.p over 1f out: wnt 2nd and swtchd lft ins fnl f: led wl ins fnl f: sn in command: pushed out* **9/4**[2]

043 **2** *¾* **Panatella**[13] 6677 3-9-0 71.......................................... AndreaAtzeni 1 74
(James Fanshawe) *chsd ldrs: rdn to ld over 1f out: drvn and wnt clr w wnr ins fnl f: hdd wl ins fnl f: kpt on* **11/4**[3]

3622 **3** *5* **Steppe Daughter (IRE)**[15] 6634 3-9-0 75.......................... MartinHarley 2 66
(Denis Coakley) *in tch in midfield: effrt on inner 2f out: chal over 1f out: 3rd and outpcd ins fnl f* **13/8**[1]

2633 **4** *½* **Black Label**[20] 6485 3-9-5 73.......................................... TomQueally 3 70
(Harry Dunlop) *mde most tl rdn and hdd ent fnl 2f: unable qck jst over 1f out: outpcd ins fnl f* **12/1**

00 **5** *shd* **Perfect Rhythm**[35] 6033 3-9-0 0.......................................... LiamKeniry 7 65
(Patrick Chamings) *chsd ldrs: effrt u.p 2f out: outpcd and btn 1f out: plugged on same pce after* **66/1**

4 **6** *1 ¼* **Jeremy's Jet (IRE)**[35] 6045 3-9-5 0.......................................... OisinMurphy 10 68
(Andrew Balding) *sn w ldr and t.k.h: rdn to ld ent fnl 2f: hdd over 1f out: wknd 1f out* **14/1**

46 **7** *13* **Emily Yeats**[82] 4413 3-9-0 0.......................................... MartinDwyer 9 42
(Paul Webber) *s.i.s: a in rr: rdn and lost tch over 2f out* **33/1**

040 **8** *11* **Field Force**[56] 3849 3-9-5 70.......................................... (t) SaleemGolam 4 30
(Sophie Leech) *in tch: rdn over 2f out: sn struggling and bhd* **33/1**

2m 20.46s (-1.44) **Going Correction** -0.125s/f (Stan) **8 Ran SP% 117.3**
Speed ratings (Par 103): **100,99,95,95,95 94,85,77**
CSF £9.10 TOTE £2.80: £1.70, £1.10, £1.10; EX 9.60 Trifecta £16.50.
**Owner** K Abdullah **Bred** Juddmonte Farms Ltd **Trained** Newmarket, Suffolk

**FOCUS**
An ordinary middle-distance maiden in which they went a muddling gallop. It's been rated around the runner-up and fifth and sixth.

## 7033 BETBRIGHT MOBILE APP H'CAP (LONDON MIDDLE DISTANCE SERIES QUALIFIER) 1m 3f (P)

7:55 (7:55) (Class 4) (0-85,85) 3-Y-O+ **£4,690** (£1,395; £697; £348) Stalls Low

Form RPR

032 **1** **Double Discount (IRE)**[14] 6664 4-9-10 **85**..........(p) RichardKingscote 3 97
(Tom Dascombe) *chsd ldr: effrt to chse ldr over 1f out: led 1f out: styd on wl and in command fnl 150yds* **7/1**

2230 **2** *2* **Jazz Master**[33] 6106 4-9-9 **84**..................................(b) AndreaAtzeni 4 93
(Luca Cumani) *in tch in midfield: swtchd lft and effrt 2f out: hdwy u.p jst over 1f out: chsd wnr ins fnl f: kpt on* **7/2**[2]

1422 **3** *2 ¼* **Masterpaver**[7] 6855 3-9-4 **85**.......................................... MartinHarley 8 90
(Alan Bailey) *hld up in tch: gd hdwy to ld 5f out: rdn ent fnl 2f: hdd 1f out: wknd ins fnl f* **11/2**[3]

2110 **4** *1 ¼* **Sweetheart Abbey**[25] 6325 3-9-1 **82**..........................(p) JamesDoyle 6 85+
(William Knight) *hld up in last trio: rdn over 2f out: styd on u.p ins fnl f: no threat to ldrs* **25/1**

5010 **5** *½* **Almerzem (USA)**[13] 6685 3-9-2 **83**.......................... PaulHanagan 10 85
(Saeed bin Suroor) *t.k.h: chsd ldrs: rdn and unable qck ent fnl 2f: wl hld and one pce fr over 1f out* **7/2**[2]

31 **6** *nk* **Clear Mind**[84] 4325 3-9-1 **82**.......................................... WilliamBuick 9 84
(John Gosden) *dwlt: steadily rcvrd and chsd ldr 8f out tl 5f out: wnt 2nd again over 2f out tl no ex u.p over 1f out: wl hld fnl f* **3/1**[1]

-241 **7** *2 ¼* **Sweeping Up**[28] 6238 3-9-0 **81**.......................................... (t) PatDobbs 5 79
(Hughie Morrison) *led tl 5f out: 3rd and unable qck u.p 2f out: wknd over 1f out* **8/1**

0/0- **8** *5* **Starluck (IRE)**[515] 585 9-9-8 **83**.......................................... LiamKeniry 2 73+
(David Arbuthnot) *stdd after s: hld up in rr: effrt over 2f out: sn btn* **66/1**

2140 **9** *10* **Choral Festival**[26] 6303 8-8-10 **71** oh2.......................... WilliamCarson 7 45+
(John Bridger) *hld up in last trio: struggling u.p over 2f out: sn btn and lost tch* **66/1**

2m 17.91s (-3.99) **Going Correction** -0.125s/f (Stan)
**WFA** 3 from 4yo+ 6lb **9 Ran SP% 115.3**
Speed ratings (Par 105): **109,107,105,105,104 104,102,99,91**
CSF £31.39 CT £144.66 TOTE £8.10: £3.00, £1.70, £2.70; EX 32.00 Trifecta £95.10.
**Owner** Laurence A Bellman **Bred** Bernard Cooke **Trained** Malpas, Cheshire

**FOCUS**
A fairly decent middle-distance handicap. The winner has been rated as running a small pb.

## 7034 BETBRIGHT.COM DOWNLOAD OUR APP/EBF CONDITIONS STKS 6f (P)
8:25 (8:27) (Class 3) 3-Y-0+ **£9,337** (£2,796; £1,398; £699; £349) **Stalls** Low

Form RPR
5006 **1** **Hallelujah**[31] 6167 6-8-11 98 HayleyTurner 1 105
(James Fanshawe) *chsd ldrs: effrt to chal 2f out: drvn to ld over 1f out: in command and styd on wl ins fnl f* **7/2**[2]

0431 **2** *2* **Krypton Factor**[17] 6576 6-9-7 100 (b) PaulMulrennan 3 109
(George Peckham) *led: rdn and pressed 2f out: hdd over 1f out: styd on same pce fnl f* **5/2**[1]

604P **3** *1 3/4* **Ballista (IRE)**[39] 5918 6-9-2 98 RichardKingscote 2 99
(Tom Dascombe) *t.k.h early: sn chsng ldr: rdn and ev ch 2f out: no ex 1f out* **9/2**[3]

0040 **4** *nk* **Valbchek (IRE)**[11] 6755 5-9-2 99 (p) PatCosgrave 4 98
(Jane Chapple-Hyam) *dwlt: in tch in rr: effrt u.p over 1f out: kpt on but no threat to ldrs* **9/1**

2200 **5** *1/2* **Hasopop (IRE)**[165] 1728 4-9-2 103 (p) MartinHarley 5 96
(Marco Botti) *t.k.h: hld up in tch: effrt over 1f out: fnd little for press and btn ins fnl f* **5/2**[1]

1m 11.06s (-2.04) **Going Correction** -0.125s/f (Stan)
**WFA** 3 from 4yo+ 1lb **5** Ran SP% **107.5**
Speed ratings (Par 107): **108,105,103,102,101**
CSF £11.94 TOTE £4.40: £2.40, £1.50; EX 14.50 Trifecta £62.30.
**Owner** CLS (Chippenham) Limited **Bred** Chippenham Lodge Stud Ltd **Trained** Newmarket, Suffolk

**FOCUS**
A good quality conditions sprint in which they went a decent clip. The winner has been rated pretty much to her best.

## 7035 BETBRIGHT - LIVE THE MOMENT H'CAP 7f (P)
8:55 (8:55) (Class 4) (0-80,80) 3-Y-0+ **£4,690** (£1,395; £697; £348) **Stalls** Low

Form RPR
2336 **1** **Brigliadoro (IRE)**[110] 3430 3-8-10 74 DannyBrock(3) 4 85+
(Philip McBride) *in tch: rdn and qcknd to ld over 1f out: drvn clr 1f out: r.o strly: readily* **7/1**[3]

2210 **2** *2* **Elizona**[37] 5986 3-9-5 80 FrederikTylicki 8 85
(James Fanshawe) *in tch in midfield: hdwy u.p over 1f out: chsd wnr ins fnl f: r.o* **10/1**

0564 **3** *3/4* **Dubawi Fun**[22] 6424 3-8-11 79 AhmadAlSubousi(7) 2 82
(Ismail Mohammed) *led: rdn and hdd 2f out: outpcd by wnr over 1f out: kpt on same pce and lost 2nd ins fnl f* **16/1**

2502 **4** *nk* **Champagne Sydney (IRE)**[18] 6552 3-9-4 79 SeanLevey 13 81
(Richard Hannon) *hld up in last trio: hdwy u.p over 1f out: styd on wl ins fnl f* **8/1**

1206 **5** *1 1/2* **Syrian Pearl**[21] 6468 3-8-11 79 SamuelClarke(7) 1 77
(Chris Wall) *hld up in rr: hdwy on inner 2f out: styd on same pce ins fnl f* **25/1**

0056 **6** *nk* **Twenty One Choice (IRE)**[32] 6144 5-9-3 79 DeclanBates(3) 6 77
(Ed de Giles) *in tch in midfield on outer: rdn 3f out: lost pl over 2f out: c wd and rallied u.p 1f out: styd on* **8/1**

6104 **7** *hd* **Baynunah (USA)**[46] 5685 3-8-13 74 TomQueally 3 71
(James Fanshawe) *hld up in tch in midfield: effrt u.p over 1f out: styd on same pce and no imp fnl f* **8/1**

1010 **8** *1/2* **Red Primo (IRE)**[48] 5603 3-9-3 78 PaulMulrennan 9 73
(Alan McCabe) *hld up in last trio: hdwy u.p 1f out: styd on: nvr trbld ldrs* **25/1**

1201 **9** *5* **Secret Success**[42] 5834 4-9-6 79 (t) LukeMorris 12 62
(Paul Cole) *chsd ldr tl 2f out: lost pl u.p over 1f out: wknd ins fnl f* **7/2**[1]

3-30 **10** *1 3/4* **Moonfaarid**[6] 6885 3-9-2 77 PatCosgrave 7 54
(M F De Kock, South Africa) *in tch in midfield: rdn and lost pl ent fnl 2f: wknd over 1f out* **9/1**

1030 **11** *40* **Battle Command (USA)**[82] 4404 3-9-4 79 MartinHarley 5
(Peter Chapple-Hyam) *t.k.h: in tch in midfield: rdn and unable qck jst over 2f out: wknd over 1f out: virtually p.u ins fnl f* **6/1**[2]

1m 24.79s (-1.21) **Going Correction** -0.125s/f (Stan)
**WFA** 3 from 4yo+ 2lb **11** Ran SP% **115.0**
Speed ratings (Par 105): **101,98,97,97,95 95,95,94,88,86 41**
CSF £73.35 CT £1087.90 TOTE £8.70: £1.80, £3.50, £3.30; EX 90.80 Trifecta £965.90 Part won..
**Owner** Serafino Agodino **Bred** D Naughton, Zubieta & Javier Salmean **Trained** Newmarket, Suffolk

**FOCUS**
A fair handicap in which they went an even gallop. The second has been rated as running a pb.

## 7036 BETBRIGHT.COM H'CAP 7f (P)
9:25 (9:26) (Class 6) (0-55,55) 3-Y-0+ **£1,940** (£577; £288; £144) **Stalls** Low

Form RPR
0061 **1** **Diamonds A Dancing**[7] 6857 4-9-7 55 6ex (be) FrannyNorton 6 69
(Brian Gubby) *w ldrs tl led 1/2-way: rdn and fnd ex over 1f out: styd on wl: rdn out* **7/2**[3]

4332 **2** *3 3/4* **Stapleford Lad**[14] 6666 3-9-3 53 (v) TomQueally 4 58
(Stuart Williams) *in tch in midfield: rdn to chse wnr wl over 1f out: styd on same pce fnl f: lost action cl home: fatally injured* **11/4**[1]

2263 **3** *hd* **Red Shadow**[23] 6409 5-9-3 51 (p) PaulPickard 8 54
(Alan Brown) *hld up in midfield on outer: effrt over 2f out: hdwy u.p over 1f out: styd on strly fnl f: nt rch ldrs* **25/1**

0603 **4** *hd* **Divine Rule (IRE)**[11] 6771 6-8-13 52 (v) JennyPowell(5) 11 55
(Laura Mongan) *stdd and collided w rival leaving stalls: hld up in rr: hdwy and n.m.r over 1f out: styd on strly ins fnl f: nt rch ldrs* **20/1**

1603 **5** *nk* **Rasselas (IRE)**[23] 6402 7-9-7 55 (b) AndrewMullen 5 57
(Michael Appleby) *sn drvn along and off the pce in last trio: hdwy u.p over 1f out: styd on: nt rch ldrs* **11/4**[1]

4631 **6** *1 1/4* **Pelagian (USA)**[30] 6194 3-9-4 54 SteveDrowne 1 52
(Michael Attwater) *in tch in midfield: effrt u.p to chse ldng pair over 1f out: no imp: lost 3 pls wl ins fnl f* **8/1**

603 **7** *1 3/4* **The Reel Way (GR)**[27] 6247 3-8-13 52 RyanTate(3) 13 45
(Patrick Chamings) *in tch in midfield: effrt u.p over 2f out: styd on same pce fr over 1f out* **25/1**

4250 **8** *5* **True Spirit**[45] 5729 4-9-7 55 SeanLevey 3 36
(Paul D'Arcy) *w ldrs tl no ex and btn over 1f out: wknd fnl f* **3/1**[2]

005 **9** *3/4* **Picnic In The Glen**[24] 6356 3-9-2 52 PatDobbs 14 29
(Sylvester Kirk) *hld up in rr: n.d* **66/1**

2020 **10** *3/4* **High Tone**[14] 6666 4-9-2 50 (p) HarryBentley 2 26
(Dean Ivory) *in tch in midfield: effrt u.p 2f out: sn struggling: wknd over 1f out* **25/1**

0006 **11** *3/4* **Nouvelle Ere**[14] 6661 3-9-3 53 SebSanders 7 26
(Tony Carroll) *led tl 1/2-way: w ldrs tl 2f out: sn wknd u.p* **25/1**

3500 **12** *10* **Forest Glen (IRE)**[14] 6666 3-9-3 53 LiamKeniry 12
(Sylvester Kirk) *in tch in midfield: rdn and no hdwy over 2f out: bhd over 1f out* **50/1**

-014 **13** *32* **Torres Del Paine**[203] 1009 7-8-13 54 RhiainIngram(7) 9
(Roger Ingram) *t.k.h: chsd ldrs tl over 2f out: t.o fnl f: b.b.v* **33/1**

1m 25.67s (-0.33) **Going Correction** -0.125s/f (Stan)
**WFA** 3 from 4yo+ 2lb **13** Ran SP% **138.2**
Speed ratings (Par 101): **96,91,91,91,90 89,87,81,80,80 79,67,31**
CSF £14.74 CT £237.72 TOTE £3.60: £1.20, £1.70, £6.80; EX 14.60 Trifecta £262.70.
**Owner** Brian Gubby **Bred** Lady Caffyn-Parsons **Trained** Bagshot, Surrey

**FOCUS**
The concluding contest was a moderate handicap in which they went an even gallop. The form is rated as ordinary behind the winner.
T/Plt: £9.70 to a £1 stake. Pool: £97,377.32 - 7,303.97 winning tickets T/Qpdt: £4.20 to a £1 stake. Pool: £8,739.70 - 1,519.85 winning tickets SP

# 6867 NOTTINGHAM (L-H)
Wednesday, October 8

**OFFICIAL GOING: Good changing to soft after race 1 (2:20)**

## 7037 32RED ON THE APP STORE EBF STALLIONS MAIDEN STKS 6f 15y
2:20 (2:23) (Class 5) 2-Y-0 **£3,234** (£962; £481; £240) **Stalls** Centre

Form RPR
65 **1** **Code Red**[24] 6363 2-9-5 0 MartinDwyer 7 89
(William Muir) *mde all: jnd and rdn over 1f out: drvn ins fnl f: styd on strly* **16/1**[3]

032 **2** *4 1/2* **Amazour (IRE)**[27] 6270 2-9-5 73 MartinHarley 6 76
(Ismail Mohammed) *a.p: cl up 1/2-way: chal over 1f out: rdn and ev ch ent fnl f: kpt on same pce* **10/1**[2]

6 **3** *6* **Mujassam**[12] 6702 2-9-5 0 DaneO'Neill 12 58
(Roger Varian) *trckd ldrs: pushed along 2f out: sn rdn and kpt on same pce fnl f* **10/1**[2]

**4** *1* **Mutarakez (IRE)** 2-9-5 0 PaulMulrennan 3 55+
(Brian Meehan) *dwlt and towards rr: hdwy over 2f out: rdn over 1f out: kpt on fnl f: nrst fin* **40/1**

0 **5** *1/2* **Dark War (IRE)**[33] 6115 2-9-5 0 GrahamLee 16 53
(James Given) *racd alone stands' rail: prom: rdn along 2f out: drvn and outpcd appr fnl f* **66/1**

02 **6** *1/2* **Spiriting (IRE)**[21] 6462 2-9-5 0 AndreaAtzeni 9 52
(Luca Cumani) *prom: pushed along over 2f out: rdn wl over 1f out: sn wknd* **4/9**[1]

**7** *4* **Nuno Tristan (USA)** 2-9-5 0 GrahamGibbons 2 40+
(William Jarvis) *chsd ldrs: rdn along 2f out: sn edgd lft and wknd* **20/1**

**8** *3/4* **Pat Mustard** 2-9-0 0 RachealKneller(5) 8 37
(Jamie Osborne) *in rr: sme hdwy wl over 1f out: kpt on fnl f: nvr a factor* **66/1**

**9** *1/2* **Vale Of Paris (IRE)** 2-9-0 0 ChrisCatlin 11 31
(Rae Guest) *in tch: rdn along wl over 2f out: no hdwy* **20/1**

B4 **10** *shd* **Star Fire**[14] 6659 2-9-0 0 JamesDoyle 1 30
(Roger Charlton) *in tch: hdwy to chse ldrs 1/2-way: rdn along 2f out: sn edgd lft and wknd* **22/1**

00 **11** *1/2* **Camdora (IRE)**[12] 6701 2-9-0 0 JoeFanning 5 29
(Jamie Osborne) *towards rr: hdwy and in tch 1/2-way: sn rdn along and n.d* **100/1**

0 **12** *8* **Come Up And See Me**[14] 6660 2-8-12 0 VictorSantos(7) 15 10
(J R Jenkins) *wnt lft s: a in rr* **150/1**

**13** *1/2* **Speedfit Rules (IRE)** 2-9-5 0 KierenFallon 13 8
(George Margarson) *dwlt: a in rr* **80/1**

**14** *1 1/2* **Qatar Success** 2-9-0 0 LiamJones 17
(Olly Stevens) *dwlt and swtchd lft s: a in rr* **33/1**

5 **15** *1 3/4* **Major Attitude**[39] 5906 2-9-5 0 SteveDrowne 14
(Clive Cox) *dwlt: a in rr* **16/1**[3]

1m 15.82s (1.12) **Going Correction** +0.15s/f (Good) **15** Ran SP% **124.3**
Speed ratings (Par 95): **98,92,84,82,82 81,76,75,74,74 73,62,62,60,57**
CSF £158.76 TOTE £18.30: £3.30, £1.70, £3.60; EX 96.70 Trifecta £525.60.
**Owner** Mrs Michelle Morgan **Bred** Carmel Stud **Trained** Lambourn, Berks

**FOCUS**
All races took place on the outer track and, with the home bend rail moved out 2m, races on the round course were 6yds further than advertised. Recent rain had softened the ground up, which was further exacerbated by heavy rain around 20 minutes prior to the opener. Martin Harley and Dane O'Neill both called it heavy after the first and the official description was changed to soft. Some interesting types in what looked like a fair maiden, but the market only wanted to know about one of these. However, the odds-on favourite was comprehensively turned over. The balance of the runner-up and third help set the level.

## 7038 32REDSPORT.COM NURSERY H'CAP 5f 13y
2:50 (2:51) (Class 4) (0-80,80) 2-Y-0 **£3,881** (£1,155; £577; £288) **Stalls** Centre

Form RPR
0432 **1** **Charlie Lad**[15] 6642 2-8-8 67 JoeFanning 4 72
(Ollie Pears) *trckd ldrs: cl up 1/2-way: led wl over 1f out: rdn ent fnl f: edgd rt and hld on wl towards fin* **15/2**[3]

41 **2** *1/2* **Snow Cloud (IRE)**[29] 6212 2-8-8 67 SamJames 7 70
(David O'Meara) *hld up towards rr: hdwy 1/2-way: swtchd rt and effrt to chse ldrs jst over 1f out: swtchd lft and rdn ins fnl f: kpt on wl towards fin* **8/1**

106 **3** *nk* **Youcouldntmakeitup (IRE)**[23] 6401 2-8-11 70 (b[1]) DavidAllan 9 72
(Tim Easterby) *a.p: effrt to chal jst over 1f out: sn rdn and ev ch: drvn wl ins fnl f: no ex towards fin* **12/1**

1032 **4** *3/4* **Polar Vortex (IRE)**[61] 5129 2-8-13 75 RyanTate(3) 8 74
(Clive Cox) *in tch whn stmbld sltly and lost pl after 1f: sn pushed along in rr: hdwy wl over 1f out: sn rdn: styd on fnl f: nrst fin* **6/1**[1]

2261 **5** *3/4* **Flicka's Boy**[15] 6623 2-9-0 73 BarryMcHugh 10 70
(Tony Coyle) *hld up towards rr: hdwy 2f out: rdn to chse ldng pair and ev ch ent fnl f: sn rdn and kpt on same pce* **15/2**[3]

3651 **6** *3/4* **Rita's Boy (IRE)**[49] 5569 2-8-12 71 MartinHarley 5 65
(K R Burke) *chsd ldrs: rdn along 2f out: drvn appr fnl f: sn one pce* **8/1**

1145 **7** *1/2* **Rise Up Lotus (IRE)**[43] 5790 2-9-2 75 DaneO'Neill 6 67
(Charles Hills) *dwlt and towards rr: pushed along and hdwy on outer 1/2-way: rdn to chse ldrs wl over 1f out: drvn and one pce appr fnl f* **12/1**

1450 **8** *1 ½* **Paddy Again (IRE)**[11] 6739 2-8-10 74........................ RyanWhile(5) 1 61
(Bill Turner) *led: rdn along over 2f out: hdd wl over 1f out and grad wknd* **20/1**

021 **9** *½* **Dad's Girl**[49] 5561 2-8-9 68........................ IanBrennan 16 53
(Ollie Pears) *racd cl to stands' rail: cl up: rdn along over 2f out: grad wknd* **12/1**

43 **10** *½* **Aussie Ruler (IRE)**[24] 6363 2-9-5 78........................ RobertWinston 11 61
(Ronald Harris) *chsd ldrs: rdn along jst over 2f out: sn wknd* **8/1**

15 **11** *nse* **Zebelini (IRE)**[23] 6401 2-8-11 70........................ LemosdeSouza 2 54
(Mrs Ilka Gansera-Leveque) *sn cl up: rdn along over 2f out: sn wknd* **25/1**

4100 **12** *½* **Honcho (IRE)**[32] 6135 2-9-3 76........................ GrahamLee 15 57
(David Elsworth) *racd nr stands' rail: a towards rr* **7/1**[2]

2305 **13** *¾* **Stanghow**[29] 6212 2-8-9 68........................ DuranFentiman 13 46
(Mel Brittain) *racd nr stands' rail: prom: rdn along over 2f out: grad wknd* **20/1**

1m 2.51s (1.01) **Going Correction** +0.15s/f (Good) **13** Ran SP% **120.1**
Speed ratings (Par 97): **97,96,95,94,93 92,91,88,88,87 87,86,85**
CSF £64.76 CT £723.85 TOTE £8.30: £4.10, £2.20, £5.50; EX 40.00 Trifecta £804.20.
**Owner** S & A Mares **Bred** Willie Musson Racing Ltd **Trained** Norton, N Yorks

**FOCUS**
Lots of these brought winning form to the table and it looked a competitive nursery for the grade. The runner-up is progressing well and the third has been rated back towards her debut effort.

## 7039 32RED CASINO EBF STALLIONS MAIDEN STKS (DIV I) 1m 75y
**3:20** (3:20) (Class 5) 2-Y-O **£3,234** (£962; £481; £240) **Stalls** Centre

Form RPR

42 **1** **Stoked (IRE)**[18] 6545 2-9-5 0........................ GeorgeBaker 10 81+
(Ed Walker) *mde all: styd on strly to forge clr over 1f out: readily* **5/2**[1]

6 **2** *4* **Winterval**[18] 6551 2-9-5 0........................ AndreaAtzeni 7 71
(Luca Cumani) *chsd ldrs: drvn 4f out: 2nd 1f out: no imp* **5/2**[1]

0 **3** *1 ½* **Chorus of Lies**[13] 6683 2-9-5 0........................ JamesDoyle 2 68
(Charlie Appleby) *mid-div: drvn and outpcd 4f out: swtchd rt over 2f out: styd on and tk 3rd nr line* **12/1**

**4** *1 ½* **Black Night (IRE)** 2-9-5 0........................ OisinMurphy 1 65+
(Stuart Williams) *chsd wnr: chal over 2f out: kpt on same pce fnl 2f* **14/1**

**5** *2 ¼* **Verismo** 2-9-5 0........................ PaulMulrennan 5 60+
(Ed Dunlop) *s.i.s: hdwy over 3f out: tk modest 5th 1f out* **25/1**

**6** *2 ½* **Hymn Of Hope (IRE)** 2-9-5 0........................ PatCosgrave 8 54+
(Noel Quinlan) *chsd ldrs: wknd over 1f out* **33/1**

**7** *3 ¾* **Dasaateer (IRE)** 2-9-5 0........................ DaneO'Neill 4 46+
(Roger Varian) *s.s: drvn 4f out: nvr on terms* **10/1**[3]

**8** *6* **Alhamareer (IRE)** 2-9-5 0........................ FrankieDettori 3 33+
(Richard Hannon) *mid-div: t.k.h: drvn over 3f out: sn wknd: eased fnl f* **7/2**[2]

**9** *20* **Poetic License (IRE)** 2-9-5 0........................ LukeMorris 6
(Sir Mark Prescott Bt) *in rr and sn pushed along: sme hdwy 6f out: lost pl over 4f out: sn bhd: tailed rt off 2f out* **50/1**

1m 52.15s (3.15) **Going Correction** +0.325s/f (Good) **9** Ran SP% **111.6**
Speed ratings (Par 95): **97,93,91,90,87 85,81,75,55**
CSF £8.14 TOTE £3.20: £1.20, £1.80, £3.50; EX 8.30 Trifecta £52.10.
**Owner** Marc Keller **Bred** Es Que Syndicate **Trained** Newmarket, Suffolk

**FOCUS**
This is normally a decent maiden and the first division played host to some well-bred, expensive newcomers. However, those with previous experience were the first three home. The winner could rate a lot higher, as could the race itself, but the suspicion is that this is a race horses will progress from, rather than the bare form being considerably better.

## 7040 32RED CASINO EBF STALLIONS MAIDEN STKS (DIV II) 1m 75y
**3:50** (3:50) (Class 5) 2-Y-O **£3,234** (£962; £481; £240) **Stalls** Centre

Form RPR

6 **1** **King Bolete (IRE)**[29] 6204 2-9-5 0........................ AndreaAtzeni 6 81
(Luca Cumani) *trckd ldrs: hdwy on outer 3f out: cl up over 1f out: rdn to chal ent fnl f: drvn to ld fnl 100yds: kpt on wl* **11/4**[2]

65 **2** *nk* **Felix De Vega (IRE)**[26] 6279 2-9-5 0........................ SeanLevey 4 80
(Richard Hannon) *trckd ldrs: pushed along and sltly outpcd 3f out: hdwy 2f out: rdn and slt ld ent fnl f: drvn and hdd last 100yds: no ex* **7/1**

2 **3** *5* **Bold**[41] 5847 2-9-5 0........................ JamesDoyle 7 69
(Roger Charlton) *dwlt: sn trcking ldrs: hdwy on outer and cl up 1/2-way: slt ld 3f out: hdd 2f out and sn rdn: kpt on same pce fnl f* **9/4**[1]

**4** *nk* **Borak (IRE)** 2-9-5 0........................ MartinHarley 3 69+
(Marco Botti) *s.i.s and in rr: gd hdwy on inner 1/2-way: sn trcking ldrs: led 2f out: rdn over 1f out: hdd ent fnl f: one pce* **14/1**

6 **5** *5* **Sea Of Heaven (IRE)**[18] 6565 2-9-5 0........................ LukeMorris 8 58
(Sir Mark Prescott Bt) *hld up in rr: hdwy over 2f out: pushed along wl over 1f out: n.d* **33/1**

4 **6** *1* **Rewritten**[20] 6497 2-9-5 0........................ RyanMoore 5 55+
(Charlie Appleby) *cl up: pushed along over 3f out: rdn wl over 2f out: grad wknd* **3/1**[3]

0 **7** *1 ¼* **Mr Morocco**[47] 5646 2-9-5 0........................ PatCosgrave 2 53
(Noel Quinlan) *trckd ldng pair on inner: rdn along wl over 3f out: sn wknd* **40/1**

02 **8** *2 ¾* **Illya Kuryakin**[9] 6812 2-9-5 0........................ RobertHavlin 9 47
(Peter Chapple-Hyam) *towards rr: effrt and sme hdwy over 3f out: sn rdn along and n.d* **40/1**

0 **9** *1* **Eagle Empire (IRE)**[22] 6420 2-9-2 0........................ CamHardie(3) 1 44
(Richard Hannon) *sn led: jnd and pushed along 1/2-way: hdd 3f out: sn rdn and wknd* **50/1**

1m 52.16s (3.16) **Going Correction** +0.325s/f (Good) **9** Ran SP% **111.4**
Speed ratings (Par 95): **97,96,91,91,86 85,84,81,80**
CSF £20.58 TOTE £4.50: £1.10, £3.80, £1.10; EX 19.70 Trifecta £89.20.
**Owner** Sheikh Mohammed Obaid Al Maktoum **Bred** Ship Commodities International **Trained** Newmarket, Suffolk

**FOCUS**
The second division of this maiden looked weaker than the first, for all that the time was comparable. It's doubtful the level will be too far out.

## 7041 EBF STALLIONS 32RED NURSERY H'CAP (BOBIS RACE) 1m 1f
**4:25** (4:25) (Class 3) (0-90,83) 2-Y-O **£9,703** (£2,887; £1,443; £721) **Stalls** Low

Form RPR

6411 **1** **Crafty Choice**[47] 5645 2-9-3 82........................ CamHardie(3) 5 87+
(Richard Hannon) *hld up: pushed along 4f out: hdwy wl over 2f out: sn chsng ldng pair: rdn over 1f out: styd on wl to ld last 120yds: sn clr* **11/2**[3]

4414 **2** *3* **Paddys Motorbike (IRE)**[19] 6520 2-9-3 79........................ JFEgan 1 78
(David Evans) *trckd ldr: hdwy and cl up over 2f out: rdn to ld over 1f out: drvn and hdd last 120yds: no ex* **13/2**

1133 **3** *2 ¼* **Alans Pride (IRE)**[18] 6529 2-9-2 81........................ ConnorBeasley(3) 6 76
(Michael Dods) *led: pushed along 3f out: rdn 2f out: hdd and drvn over 1f out: kpt on same pce* **15/2**

41 **4** *4 ½* **Shalimah (IRE)**[45] 5718 2-9-2 81........................ RyanTate(3) 3 67+
(Clive Cox) *in rr: niggled along after 2f: pushed along bef 1/2-way: rdn 4f out: plugged on u.p fnl 3f: n.d* **2/1**[1]

31 **5** *12* **Khusoosy (USA)**[25] 6317 2-9-6 82........................ DaneO'Neill 2 44+
(Saeed bin Suroor) *dwlt: hld up in tch: hdwy to chse ldrs 4f out: rdn along over 3f out: sn outpcd and bhd* **9/4**[2]

2345 **6** *5* **Big Chill (IRE)**[7] 6854 2-9-2 78........................(b[1]) SteveDrowne 7 30
(Charles Hills) *chsd ldng pair: rdn along wl over 3f out: sn wknd* **16/1**

1m 59.82s (2.22) **Going Correction** +0.325s/f (Good) **6** Ran SP% **110.5**
Speed ratings (Par 99): **103,100,98,94,83 79**
CSF £37.86 TOTE £5.00: £2.60, £2.90; EX 36.40 Trifecta £96.70.
**Owner** Middleham Park Racing CIII **Bred** Pevens Racing **Trained** East Everleigh, Wilts

**FOCUS**
Despite the late defection of Black Granite this still had the look of a decent nursery. They went a fair pace, but little got into it as they came up the centre of the track. The winner was well delivered from the back and the runner-up's performance helps set the level.

## 7042 £10 FREE BET AT 32RED SPORT H'CAP 1m 75y
**4:55** (4:57) (Class 5) (0-73,73) 3-Y-O+ **£2,726** (£805; £402) **Stalls** Low

Form RPR

S201 **1** **Lord Franklin**[17] 6578 5-9-6 72........................ JasonHart 14 82
(Eric Alston) *in tch: hdwy on wd outside over 3f out: chal over 2f out: rdn to ld over 1f out: drvn ins fnl f: kpt on wl towards fin* **8/1**[3]

2463 **2** *1 ¾* **Lady Guinevere**[41] 5848 4-9-1 67........................ SeanLevey 11 73
(Stuart Williams) *in tch: hdwy over 3f out: chsd ldng pair wl over 1f out: sn rdn: drvn and kpt on fnl f* **9/1**

6604 **3** *1 ¼* **Artful Prince**[7] 6870 4-9-6 72........................(b) GrahamLee 10 75
(James Given) *cl up: led over 4f out: jnd and rdn over 2f out: hdd narrowly and edgd lft over 1f out: drvn and kpt on same pce fnl f* **11/2**[1]

3100 **4** *5* **Unex Michelangelo (IRE)**[31] 6166 5-9-2 68........................ GrahamGibbons 3 60
(Michael Easterby) *in tch: hdwy 3f out: rdn to chse ldrs 2f out: drvn and no imp fr over 1f out* **10/1**

0460 **5** *8* **Sword Of The Lord**[63] 5031 4-9-5 71........................ KierenFallon 9 46
(George Margarson) *in rr and sn pushed along: rdn along 1/2-way: bhd on u.p fnl 2f: nvr nr ldrs* **14/1**

2100 **6** *2* **Gambino (IRE)**[8] 6836 4-9-2 68........................(p) DavidNolan 17 38
(John David Riches) *midfield: swtchd to outer and hdwy over 3f out: rdn along over 2f out: plugged on one pce* **18/1**

0365 **7** *¾* **Venus Grace**[105] 3586 3-9-4 73........................ HayleyTurner 4 42
(Ralph Beckett) *chsd ldrs: rdn along over 3f out: grad wknd fnl 2f* **16/1**

0112 **8** *1* **The Osteopath (IRE)**[14] 6670 11-9-6 72........................ PhillipMakin 5 41
(John Davies) *towards rr: pushed along bef 1/2-way rdn over 3f out: n.d* **10/1**

4032 **9** *¾* **Ellaal**[9] 6822 5-9-5 71........................ DaleSwift 15 36
(Ruth Carr) *trckd ldng pair: effrt over 3f out: rdn along wl over 2f out: drvn wl over 1f out and sn wknd* **13/2**[2]

00-3 **10** *½* **Watts Up Son**[44] 5750 6-8-8 67........................(t) KieranShoemark(7) 8 31
(Richard Price) *slt ld on inner: hdd over 4f out and sn rdn along: wknd wl over 2f out* **9/1**

2000 **11** *1 ½* **Naoise (IRE)**[15] 6625 6-8-13 68........................(t) JacobButterfield(3) 6 29
(Ollie Pears) *chsd ldrs: rdn along 3f out: sn wknd* **12/1**

0 **12** *12* **Rakaan (IRE)**[27] 6263 7-9-4 70........................ DougieCostello 16
(Brendan Powell) *a in rr: rdn along 1/2-way: bhd whn eased over 2f out: lame* **33/1**

50-2 **13** *3* **Tahaf (IRE)**[49] 5585 4-9-4 70........................(bt) LukeMorris 7
(Mark Brisbourne) *midfield: rdn along 1/2-way: sn outpcd and bhd whn eased fnl 2f* **16/1**

450 **14** *1 ¾* **Boboli Gardens**[42] 5834 4-8-10 67........................ TobyAtkinson(5) 2
(Noel Quinlan) *a in rr: bhd and eased over 2f out* **50/1**

0106 **15** *hd* **Imaginary World (IRE)**[27] 6269 6-9-2 73........................(e) ShaneGray(5) 13
(John Balding) *a towards rr: bhd and eased fr over 2f out* **33/1**

1m 51.35s (2.35) **Going Correction** +0.425s/f (Yiel)
**WFA** 3 from 4yo+ 3lb **15** Ran SP% **117.2**
Speed ratings (Par 103): **105,103,102,97,89 87,86,85,84,84 82,70,67,65,65**
CSF £74.50 CT £433.44 TOTE £12.50: £3.80, £3.50, £1.80; EX 109.30 Trifecta £333.30.
**Owner** Liam & Tony Ferguson **Bred** Tony Ferguson & Liam Ferguson **Trained** Longton, Lancs

**FOCUS**
A modest if competitive handicap, with 6lb covering the field. They finished well strung out with horses finding it hard to come from off the pace. The runner-up handles these conditions and, along with the third, helps set the level.

## 7043 32RED.COM H'CAP 1m 2f 50y
**5:25** (5:25) (Class 4) (0-85,82) 3-Y-O+ **£5,175** (£1,540; £769; £384) **Stalls** Low

Form RPR

00 **1** **Dame Lucy (IRE)**[56] 5319 4-9-3 75........................ AndrewMullen 8 86+
(Michael Appleby) *in tch: hdwy to trck ldrs over 3f out: pushed along 2f out: rdn jst over 1f out: chal ent fnl f: drvn to ld last 100yds: kpt on strly* **16/1**

1022 **2** *1 ¾* **Principle Equation (IRE)**[27] 6258 3-9-5 82........................ FrankieDettori 14 90
(Ralph Beckett) *hld up: hdwy to trck ldrs after 4f: cl up over 3f out: led over 2f out: rdn wl over 1f out: drvn ins fnl f: hdd and no ex last 100yds* **10/3**[2]

36-1 **3** *2 ½* **Beltor**[14] 6672 3-8-13 76........................ LukeMorris 7 80
(Sir Mark Prescott Bt) *led 1f: cl up: effrt 3f out: rdn to chal over 2f out: ev ch whn drvn and edgd lft jst over 1f out and again ins fnl f: kpt on one pce* **9/4**[1]

0143 **4** *shd* **Golden Spear**[41] 5849 3-9-1 78........................(p) PatCosgrave 9 81
(Noel Quinlan) *in rr: hdwy over 3f out: chsd ldrs 2f out: sn rdn and styng on whn sltly hmpd jst ins fnl f: sn swtchd rt and drvn: kpt on* **17/2**

4041 **5** *7* **Handheld**[63] 5058 7-9-0 77........................(p) ShelleyBirkett(5) 6 68
(Julia Feilden) *led after 1f: pushed along over 3f out: rdn and hdd over 2f out: grad wknd* **12/1**

3021 **6** *10* **The Character (IRE)**[11] 6738 3-9-3 80........................ StephenCraine 4 53
(Tom Dascombe) *dwlt and sn pushed along to chse ldrs after 1f: rdn along over 4f out: wknd over 3f out* **9/1**

3036 **7** *3 ¼* **Martinas Delight (USA)**[38] 5948 4-9-2 74........................ KierenFallon 13 41
(Timothy Jarvis) *chsd ldrs: effrt 3f out: rdn along over 2f out: drvn wl over 1f out and sn wknd* **25/1**

1032 **8** *5* **Tercel (IRE)**[19] 6523 3-9-1 78........................ RyanMoore 1 36
(Sir Michael Stoute) *in rr and detached after 3f: pushed along over 4f out: rdn over 3f out: nvr a factor* **7/2**[3]

12-0 **9** *12* **Bushel (USA)**[14] 6664 4-9-6 78........................................ GrahamLee 3 14
(James Given) *chsd ldrs on inner: styd alone on inner rail 4f out: rdn over 3f out: sn outpcd and bhd* **33/1**
2m 16.92s (2.62) **Going Correction** +0.425s/f (Yiel)
**WFA** 3 from 4yo+ 5lb **9** Ran SP% **117.0**
Speed ratings (Par 105): **106,104,102,102,96 88,86,82,72**
CSF £69.83 CT £170.99 TOTE £20.50: £4.40, £1.60, £1.10; EX 96.90 Trifecta £468.80.
**Owner** P A Cafferty **Bred** Tony Doyle **Trained** Danethorpe, Notts
**FOCUS**
This is usually a decent back-end handicap and, with a strong 3yo contingent this year, it looked up to scratch once more. Four came clear and the form looks solid through the likes of the third.

## 7044 RACING SPECIALS AT 32REDSPORT.COM APPRENTICE H'CAP 1m 2f 50y
**6:00** (6:01) (Class 5) (0-70,70) 3-Y-O+ **£2,587** (£770; £384; £192) **Stalls** Low

Form RPR
014 **1** **Polar Forest**[17] 6578 4-9-6 66.........................(e) JacobButterfield 12 75
(Richard Guest) *chsd ldrs: handy 3rd 3f out: led over 1f out: styd on towards fin* **16/1**
6406 **2** *nk* **Gala Casino Star (IRE)**[12] 6706 9-8-12 63..............(b) JordanNason(5) 2 71
(Lawrence Mullaney) *s.i.s: hdwy to chse ldrs 7f out: 2nd over 4f out: led over 2f out: hdd over 1f out: rallied ins fnl f: no ex clsng stages* **8/1**[3]
0622 **3** *6* **King Of Paradise (IRE)**[12] 6706 5-9-2 62........................... JasonHart 7 60
(Eric Alston) *led tl over 2f out: kpt on same pce: heavily eased whn wl hld clsng stages* **9/2**[1]
6456 **4** *6* **Prophesy (IRE)**[28] 6227 5-8-13 64..................(p) RachelRichardson(5) 11 51
(Tim Easterby) *in rr: sme hdwy over 2f out: modest 6th 1f out: tk 4th nr fin* **13/2**[2]
1203 **5** *1 1/4* **Hallingham**[12] 6706 4-9-8 68...........................................(b) CamHardie 10 53
(Jonathan Portman) *in rr: hdwy over 2f out: nvr nr ldrs* **12/1**
2300 **6** *hd* **Tight Lipped (IRE)**[26] 6303 5-9-9 69.......................... RosieJessop 6 53
(James Eustace) *chsd ldrs: wknd fnl 2f* **12/1**
2110 **7** *1* **City Ground (USA)**[15] 6626 7-9-7 70........................ JackGarritty(3) 8 52
(Michael Easterby) *chsd ldrs: wknd over 2f out* **25/1**
0400 **8** *15* **Boogangoo (IRE)**[15] 6633 3-8-11 67........................... RobHornby(5) 3 22
(Grace Harris) *prom: drvn over 3f out: wknd fnl 2f* **14/1**
5041 **9** *9* **Brockfield**[15] 6628 8-8-12 61...................................... KevinStott(3) 16
(Mel Brittain) *hld up in mid-div on outside: lost pl over 3f out* **8/1**[3]
056 **10** *2* **Curved**[28] 6238 3-9-2 67..............................(v[1]) WilliamTwiston-Davies 13 3
(Lady Cecil) *mid-div: reminders over 4f out: sn lost pl: bhd whn eased over 1f out* **11/1**
000 **11** *2* **Zarliman (IRE)**[42] 5831 4-9-7 67............................... AshleyMorgan 14
(Martyn Meade) *in rr: bhd whn eased over 1f out* **16/1**
3002 **12** *52* **Automotive**[45] 5721 6-8-13 62.................................... ShelleyBirkett(3) 5
(Julia Feilden) *mid-div: lost pl over 3f out: wl bhd whn heavily eased 2f out: tailed rt off* **11/1**
2m 21.9s (7.60) **Going Correction** +0.425s/f (Yiel)
**WFA** 3 from 4yo+ 5lb **12** Ran SP% **108.1**
Speed ratings (Par 103): **86,85,80,76,75 75,74,62,55,53 51,10**
CSF £114.65 CT £506.87 TOTE £15.30: £5.50, £2.60, £1.10; EX 180.60 Trifecta £625.50 Part won..
**Owner** Maze Rattan Limited **Bred** Worksop Manor Stud **Trained** Ingmanthorpe, W Yorks
■ Ana Shababiya was withdrawn. Price at time of withdrawal 8-1. Rule 4 applies to all bets - deduction 10p in the pound.
**FOCUS**
A wide open, modest apprentice handicap. Ran in driving rain, it turned into a war of attrition with the field well strung out. The runner-up helps set the level.
T/Jkpt: Not won. T/Plt: £916.70 to a £1 stake. Pool: £74,847.94 - 59.60 winning tickets T/Qpdt: £18.90 to a £1 stake. Pool: £7,688.43 - 300.31 winning tickets JR

7045 - 7053a (Foreign Racing) - See Raceform Interactive

# 6830 AYR (L-H)
Thursday, October 9

**OFFICIAL GOING: Soft (7.6)**
Wind: Almost nil Weather: Overcast

## 7054 SCOTTISH LEADER MAIDEN STKS (BOBIS RACE) 1m
**2:10** (2:13) (Class 4) 2-Y-O **£3,881** (£1,155; £577; £288) **Stalls** Low

Form RPR
0 **1** **Royal Regent**[9] 6831 2-9-0 0.................................. MeganCarberry(5) 3 75
(Lucy Normile) *dwlt: hld up in tch: hdwy against far rail to ld over 1f out: styd on strly to go clr fnl f* **80/1**
6422 **2** *3* **Sir Chauvelin**[19] 6529 2-9-5 71.......................................... GrahamLee 6 68
(Jim Goldie) *chsd ldrs: effrt and ev ch briefly over 1f out: sn chsng wnr: kpt on same pce ins fnl f* **1/1**[1]
30 **3** *2 3/4* **Go Dan Go (IRE)**[20] 6509 2-8-12 0........................... JamieGormley(7) 4 62
(Keith Dalgleish) *s.i.s: hld up: hdwy on outside over 2f out: rdn and no imp fr over 1f out* **22/1**
03 **4** *4* **Fortuna Glas (IRE)**[18] 6577 2-9-5 0................................ PJMcDonald 5 53
(Donald McCain) *chsd ldrs: drvn and edgd lft over 2f out: wknd over 1f out* **4/1**[2]
**5** *1 1/2* **Woofie (IRE)** 2-9-5 0........................................... TonyHamilton 7 50
(Richard Fahey) *t.k.h: hld up in tch: outpcd over 2f out: sn btn* **5/1**[3]
**6** *1 3/4* **Mon Gris (IRE)** 2-9-5 0.................................................. DanielTudhope 1 46
(Kristin Stubbs) *cl up tl rdn and wknd fr 2f out* **12/1**
5244 **7** *1 1/4* **Battleranger (IRE)**[73] 4723 2-9-5 72....................................... TomEaves 2 43
(Keith Dalgleish) *led: rdn over 2f out: hdd over 1f out: sn wknd* **9/1**
1m 47.9s (4.10) **Going Correction** +0.375s/f (Good) **7** Ran SP% **109.9**
Speed ratings (Par 97): **94,91,88,84,82 81,79**
CSF £150.50 TOTE £67.20: £27.40, £1.02; EX 238.20 Trifecta £1616.80.
**Owner** Steve Dick **Bred** Steve Dick **Trained** Duncrievie, Perth & Kinross
**FOCUS**
Stands side rail moved in 6metres. Back straight and bends moved in 6m, home straight in 5m and races of 7f and 1m increased by 18yds and 1m 7f race by 36yds. This is probably just modest form, if that.

## 7055 BRITVIC SOFT DRINKS NURSERY H'CAP 6f
**2:40** (2:42) (Class 5) (0-75,75) 2-Y-O **£2,911** (£866; £432; £216) **Stalls** Low

Form RPR
053 **1** **Explain**[22] 6462 2-9-0 68.................................................. FergusSweeney 7 77
(Martyn Meade) *mde all: rdn over 1f out: edgd lft ins fnl f: hld on wl* **11/4**[1]
660 **2** *hd* **Aprovado (IRE)**[45] 5759 2-8-1 55....................................... AndrewMullen 10 63
(Michael Dods) *in tch: hdwy and ev ch over 1f out: sn rdn and hung lft: kpt on ins fnl f: jst hld* **8/1**
535 **3** *5* **Named Asset**[22] 6453 2-9-0 68.................................. RussKennemore 4 61
(Jedd O'Keeffe) *taken early to post: wnt rt s: in tch: outpcd and edgd lft 2f out: kpt on fnl f: no ch w first two* **18/1**
6030 **4** *1* **Agadoo**[16] 6643 2-8-1 55............................................... PatrickMathers 6 45
(Shaun Harris) *chsd ldrs: drvn along 1/2-way: outpcd 2f out: kpt on same pce fnl f* **33/1**
2432 **5** *4* **Westhoughton**[9] 6831 2-9-7 75........................................ DanielTudhope 3 53
(David O'Meara) *cl up: drvn over 2f out: wknd fnl f* **10/1**
0221 **6** *1 1/4* **Captain Revelation**[14] 6690 2-9-7 75.................................. GrahamLee 8 50
(Tom Dascombe) *chsd ldrs: drvn along 1/2-way: wknd fr 2f out* **7/2**[2]
6513 **7** *1/2* **Classic Flyer**[11] 6791 2-8-10 64............................................. SamJames 9 37
(David O'Meara) *stmbld as stall opened: hld up in tch: effrt whn nt clr run briefly over 1f out: sn rdn and btn* **5/1**[3]
060 **8** *2 1/4* **Heading Home (FR)**[45] 5760 2-8-6 60.................................... IanBrennan 1 26
(John Quinn) *s.i.s: bhd and a drvn along: nvr on terms* **9/1**
5653 **9** *4 1/2* **Reassert**[29] 6222 2-8-0 54 oh2..............................(b[1]) DuranFentiman 5 7
(Tim Easterby) *cl up: rdn over 2f out: wknd over 1f out* **40/1**
2401 **10** *18* **Mighty Warrior**[16] 6642 2-9-7 75......................................(b) TonyHamilton 2
(Richard Fahey) *cl up: rdn along 1/2-way: wknd 2f out: eased whn no ch fnl f* **10/1**
1m 14.34s (1.94) **Going Correction** +0.375s/f (Good) **10** Ran SP% **115.5**
Speed ratings (Par 95): **102,101,95,93,88 86,86,83,77,53**
CSF £25.18 CT £337.25 TOTE £4.30: £2.00, £2.70, £6.00; EX 31.30 Trifecta £446.50.
**Owner** D Farrington **Bred** Tibthorpe Stud **Trained** Newmarket, Suffolk
**FOCUS**
An interesting nursery, but not many got into serious contention.

## 7056 COCA-COLA H'CAP (DIV I) 6f
**3:10** (3:13) (Class 6) (0-65,65) 3-Y-O+ **£1,940** (£577; £288; £144) **Stalls** Low

Form RPR
200 **1** **Lord Buffhead**[24] 6409 5-8-10 54.........................................(v) JasonHart 4 64
(Richard Guest) *taken early to post: cl up: led over 2f out: rdn and r.o strly fnl f* **14/1**
4360 **2** *1 1/2* **Monel**[21] 6478 6-9-6 64................................................. FergalLynch 1 69
(Jim Goldie) *s.i.s: hld up: rdn and hdwy over 1f out: chsd wnr ins fnl f: r.o* **17/2**[3]
0026 **3** *1/2* **Saxonette**[9] 6835 6-8-7 54.......................................... ConnorBeasley(3) 11 58
(Linda Perratt) *in tch: effrt and rdn over 1f out: kpt on same pce ins fnl f* **14/1**
3000 **4** *2 1/4* **Benidorm**[9] 6833 6-8-4 51 oh5......................................(v) NeilFarley(3) 12 47
(Richard Guest) *sn cl up: disp ld over 2f out to over 1f out: one pce fnl f* **40/1**
0260 **5** *hd* **Sewn Up**[9] 6835 4-9-0 58...................................................(p) JoeFanning 8 54
(Keith Dalgleish) *taken early to post: hld up bhd ldng gp: effrt and hung lft over 1f out: no imp fnl f* **8/1**[2]
6055 **6** *1/2* **Masked Dance (IRE)**[58] 5287 7-8-12 56..........................(p) PJMcDonald 10 50
(Scott Dixon) *in tch: drvn and outpcd 2f out: kpt on ins fnl f: no imp* **8/1**[2]
5442 **7** *3/4* **Jumbo Steps (IRE)**[24] 6405 7-9-6 64.................................. GrahamLee 15 56
(Jim Goldie) *prom: effrt and ch wl over 1f out: sn rdn and outpcd* **3/1**[1]
0630 **8** *3/4* **Abraham Monro**[34] 6120 4-8-7 51 oh5.................................. JamesSullivan 3 40
(Ruth Carr) *chsd ldrs: rdn over 2f out: wknd over 1f out* **20/1**
0210 **9** *3 1/4* **Methaaly (IRE)**[28] 6272 11-8-6 57.....................................(b) AnnaHesketh(7) 2 36
(Michael Mullineaux) *hld up in midfield: drvn 2f out: sn wknd* **28/1**
0024 **10** *1 1/4* **Berbice (IRE)**[9] 6833 9-8-2 51 oh3...................................... SammyJoBell(5) 14 26
(Linda Perratt) *fly-jmpd s: hld up: pushed along and shortlived effrt 2f out: sn btn* **16/1**
5504 **11** *nk* **Spirit Of Alsace (IRE)**[8] 6863 3-8-11 61.......................... JackGarritty(3) 13 35
(Jim Goldie) *t.k.h: hld up: rdn over 2f out: btn over 1f out* **8/1**[2]
504 **12** *3/4* **De Lesseps (USA)**[48] 5636 6-8-0 51 oh1............ RachelRichardson(7) 9 23
(James Moffatt) *midfield: struggling over 2f out: sn btn* **28/1**
055 **13** *8* **Dark Opal (IRE)**[56] 5333 4-9-2 65......................................(v[1]) JoeDoyle(5) 6 11
(John Weymes) *t.k.h: slt ld to over 2f out: wknd over 1f out* **9/1**
-406 **14** *7* **Bon Chance**[85] 4318 3-8-8 53...............................................(b[1]) TomEaves 5
(Michael Easterby) *s.i.s: bhd and outpcd: no ch fr 1/2-way* **33/1**
1m 14.32s (1.92) **Going Correction** +0.375s/f (Good)
**WFA** 3 from 4yo+ 1lb **14** Ran SP% **116.0**
Speed ratings (Par 101): **102,100,99,96,96 95,94,93,89,87 87,86,75,66**
CSF £115.42 CT £1748.35 TOTE £13.00: £3.60, £3.40, £4.20; EX 174.10 Trifecta £1630.70.
**Owner** Available For Sale Or Lease **Bred** T K & Mrs P A Knox **Trained** Ingmanthorpe, W Yorks
**FOCUS**
The first division of a mainly moderate sprint. The runner-up has been rated a shade off his best, with the third close to form.

## 7057 COCA-COLA H'CAP (DIV II) 6f
**3:40** (3:42) (Class 6) (0-65,64) 3-Y-O+ **£1,940** (£577; £288; £144) **Stalls** Low

Form RPR
3150 **1** **New Lease Of Life**[21] 6475 5-8-12 58.........................(p) GaryBartley(3) 12 68
(Jim Goldie) *hld up: stdy hdwy over 2f out: led appr fnl f: rdn out* **8/1**[2]
0053 **2** *1* **Rock Canyon (IRE)**[9] 6834 5-8-7 50 oh1............................ JoeFanning 7 56
(Linda Perratt) *hld up: rdn and hdwy over 1f out: chsd wnr ins fnl f: kpt on* **16/1**
2004 **3** *1 1/4* **Live Dangerously**[10] 6821 4-9-7 64....................................... TomEaves 5 66
(Keith Dalgleish) *t.k.h: cl up: ev ch and rdn over 1f out: kpt on same pce ins fnl f* **14/1**
3660 **4** *1/2* **Tadalavil**[21] 6475 9-8-4 52................................................ SammyJoBell(5) 9 52
(Linda Perratt) *chsd ldrs: effrt and pushed along whn nt clr run briefly over 1f out: sn rdn: one pce ins fnl f* **22/1**
5342 **5** *3 3/4* **Captain Scooby**[2] 7009 8-8-7 50 oh2.............................(p) TonyHamilton 11 38
(Richard Guest) *in tch: effrt and rdn wl over 1f out: outpcd fnl f* **9/2**[1]
0000 **6** *nk* **Black Douglas**[8] 6866 5-9-0 57............................................ FergalLynch 14 44
(Jim Goldie) *dwlt: bhd: hdwy and drifted lft over 1f out: no imp fnl f* **16/1**
0526 **7** *nk* **Cahal (IRE)**[42] 5853 3-9-0 58............................................... PaddyAspell 6 44
(David Nicholls) *prom: rdn and outpcd 2f out: n.d after* **12/1**
3403 **8** *1 1/4* **Coiste Bodhar (IRE)**[7] 6889 3-9-3 61.............................(p) DanielTudhope 10 43
(Joseph Tuite) *led tl rdn and hdd appr fnl f: sn btn* **9/2**[1]
1502 **9** *nk* **Incomparable**[60] 5207 9-8-5 53...............................(p) MatthewHopkins(5) 8 35
(Scott Dixon) *w ldr: rdn over 2f out: wknd fnl f* **14/1**
5006 **10** *3 1/2* **Celestial Dawn**[141] 2451 5-8-3 51 oh4 ow1..................... JordanNason(5) 3 21
(John Weymes) *missed break: bhd and outpcd: hdwy over 1f out: nvr rchd ldrs* **33/1**
0006 **11** *nk* **Spoken Words**[35] 6076 5-8-2 50 oh5..................................(p[1]) JoeDoyle(5) 13 19
(John David Riches) *in tch: rdn over 2f out: wknd over 1f out* **28/1**
5500 **12** *3/4* **Goninodaethat**[9] 6835 6-9-7 64.............................................. GrahamLee 4 31
(Jim Goldie) *prom tl rdn and wknd wl over 1f out* **10/1**[3]
6124 **13** *3/4* **Bearskin (IRE)**[18] 6575 3-9-6 64.........................................(b) PJMcDonald 1 29
(Ann Duffield) *s.i.s: bhd: struggling over 3f out: nvr on terms* **11/1**

634 **14** *nse* **Minty Jones**[60] 5207 5-8-2 52........(b) AnnaHesketh(7) 2 16
(Michael Mullineaux) *prom tl rdn and wknd 2f out* **25/1**

0000 **15** *2* **The Nifty Fox**[9] 6835 10-8-10 53........(p) JamesSullivan 15 11
(Tim Easterby) *hld up: rdn over 2f out: sn wknd* **12/1**

1m 14.93s (2.53) **Going Correction** +0.375s/f (Good)
**WFA** 3 from 4yo+ 1lb **15** Ran SP% **120.0**
Speed ratings (Par 101): **98,96,95,94,89 88,88,86,86,81 81,80,79,79,76**
CSF £122.42 CT £1810.05 TOTE £9.20: £3.30, £4.80, £5.80; EX 201.50 Trifecta £2723.30.
**Owner** David McKenzie **Bred** Jim Goldie **Trained** Uplawmoor, E Renfrews

**FOCUS**
The early leaders went off at a good gallop considering the conditions, so it wasn't surprising that the winner came from the off the gallop. The runner-up helps set the standard.

## 7058 GUINNESS DUBLIN PORTER H'CAP 5f
**4:10** (4:10) (Class 5) (0-70,70) 3-Y-O **£2,911** (£866; £432; £216) **Stalls** Low

Form RPR

6114 **1** **Fredricka**[15] 6671 3-9-4 67........ JasonHart 5 78
(Garry Moss) *prom: smooth hdwy to ld 1f out: rdn and r.o strly fnl f* **10/3**[2]

31 **2** *2* **Margrets Gift**[56] 5333 3-9-7 70........(p) DavidAllan 7 74
(Tim Easterby) *t.k.h: cl up: disp ld over 1f out to ins fnl f: rdn and kpt on same pce* **13/8**[1]

604 **3** *nk* **Scoreline**[9] 6843 3-9-7 70........(p) DanielTudhope 8 73
(David O'Meara) *led tl rdn and hdd 1f out: kpt on same pce ins fnl f* **6/1**[3]

263 **4** *2* **Red Forever**[40] 5923 3-9-0 63........ PatrickMathers 6 59
(Alan Berry) *plld hrd: cl up: rdn over 1f out: outpcd ins fnl f* **7/1**

2040 **5** *2* **Secret Applause**[34] 6122 3-8-4 56........[1] ConnorBeasley(3) 3 45
(Michael Dods) *missed break: bhd: struggling 1/2-way: sme late hdwy: nvr on terms* **15/2**

350 **6** *8* **Sleeper Class**[48] 5631 3-8-13 62........ GrahamLee 4 22
(Jim Goldie) *in tch: rdn and hung lft wl over 1f out: sn wknd* **11/1**

1m 0.93s (1.53) **Going Correction** +0.375s/f (Good) **6** Ran SP% **108.1**
Speed ratings (Par 101): **102,98,98,95,91 79**
CSF £8.45 CT £24.40 TOTE £3.50: £2.20, £1.20; EX 8.80 Trifecta £22.20.
**Owner** Ron Hull **Bred** J C Parsons & J J Gilmartin **Trained** Tickhill, S Yorks

**FOCUS**
A fair handicap run at a good pace. The third has been rated to form.

## 7059 GINGER GROUSE H'CAP 1m 5f 13y
**4:40** (4:40) (Class 6) (0-65,65) 3-Y-O+ **£1,940** (£577; £288; £144) **Stalls** Low

Form RPR

4350 **1** **Rockweiller**[103] 3699 7-9-4 57........ JasonHart 7 65
(Shaun Harris) *prom: hdwy on outside to ld over 2f out: rdn and edgd lft ins fnl f: r.o* **11/2**[3]

3614 **2** *1 1/4* **Harrison's Cave**[10] 6825 6-9-7 60........ JoeFanning 10 66
(Keith Dalgleish) *t.k.h: hld up in tch: stdy hdwy over 2f out: chsd wnr ins fnl f: kpt on: hld nr fin* **3/1**[1]

40/0 **3** *2 3/4* **Nay Secret**[21] 6480 6-8-12 51 oh2........ FergalLynch 8 53
(Jim Goldie) *hld up: outpcd and reminder 4f out: hdwy and reminders wl over 1f out: styd on strly under hands and heels fnl f: nt rch first two* **14/1**

2545 **4** *1* **Latin Rebel (IRE)**[21] 6480 7-8-13 55........(p) GaryBartley(3) 6 56
(Jim Goldie) *chsd ldr: ev ch briefly over 2f out: sn rdn: edgd lft and no ex ins fnl f* **7/2**[2]

6266 **5** *9* **Ronald Gee (IRE)**[17] 6597 7-9-9 62........ GrahamLee 3 50
(Jim Goldie) *led: rdn and hdd over 2f out: wknd over 1f out* **3/1**[1]

-650 **6** *2 1/4* **I Am Who I Am**[34] 6117 4-8-7 51 oh6........(t) JackGarritty(5) 4 36
(Iain Jardine) *in tch: drvn and outpcd over 3f out: btn fnl 2f* **33/1**

30-0 **7** *4 1/2* **Roc De Prince**[37] 6012 5-9-12 65........(t) PaulMulrennan 1 44
(James Ewart) *chsd ldrs tl rdn and wknd over 2f out* **12/1**

3500 **8** *1 1/2* **Grand Diamond (IRE)**[9] 6832 10-8-7 53........ RachaelGrant(7) 2 30
(Jim Goldie) *s.i.s: hld up: rdn over 4f out: sn n.d* **16/1**

3m 3.24s (9.24) **Going Correction** +0.375s/f (Good)
**WFA** 3 from 4yo+ 8lb **8** Ran SP% **110.8**
Speed ratings (Par 101): **86,85,83,82,77 76,73,72**
CSF £20.93 CT £206.44 TOTE £6.10: £1.70, £1.40, £4.70; EX 27.10 Trifecta £231.10.
**Owner** S A Harris **Bred** Exors Of The Late Mrs E A Hankinson **Trained** Carburton, Notts

**FOCUS**
The gallop was an even on for this staying handicap. The runner-up has been rated to his previous win here.

## 7060 TENNENT'S LAGER H'CAP 7f 50y
**5:10** (5:10) (Class 3) (0-95,92) 3-Y-O+ **£7,762** (£2,310; £1,154; £577) **Stalls** High

Form RPR

P026 **1** **Our Boy Jack (IRE)**[40] 5915 5-8-13 82........ GeorgeChaloner(3) 10 95
(Richard Fahey) *hld up in tch: effrt and hdwy 2f out: led 1f out: rdn clr fnl f* **8/1**[3]

0012 **2** *3* **Evanescent (IRE)**[14] 6692 5-8-9 80........ JoeDoyle(5) 8 85
(John Quinn) *t.k.h: w ldrs: stl gng wl over 1f out: sn rdn: kpt on ins fnl f: nt pce of wnr* **13/2**[2]

4040 **3** *nk* **Farlow (IRE)**[19] 6531 6-9-7 87........ DavidNolan 2 91
(Richard Fahey) *t.k.h: led: rdn 2f out: hdd 1f out: kpt on same pce* **8/1**[3]

1100 **4** *3/4* **Green Howard**[5] 6936 6-9-12 92........ GrahamLee 12 94
(Robin Bastiman) *hld up: hdwy and prom over 1f out: kpt on same pce ins fnl f* **12/1**

1112 **5** *1 1/4* **Trixie Malone**[136] 2608 4-8-11 77........ PJMcDonald 9 76
(K R Burke) *w ldrs: ev ch tl rdn and outpcd fnl f* **4/1**[1]

2000 **6** *hd* **Victoire De Lyphar (IRE)**[13] 6704 7-9-6 86........(e) JamesSullivan 4 85
(Ruth Carr) *midfield: rdn over 2f out: hdwy and edgd lft over 1f out: no imp fnl f* **25/1**

1006 **7** *3/4* **Silver Rime (FR)**[19] 6535 9-9-6 86........ JoeFanning 6 83
(Linda Perratt) *s.i.s: hld up: rdn and hdwy over 1f out: no imp fnl f* **33/1**

0501 **8** *1/2* **Bachotheque (IRE)**[21] 6477 4-8-10 76........ DavidAllan 7 71
(Tim Easterby) *hld up in tch: stdy hdwy over 2f out: rdn over 1f out: outpcd fnl f* **12/1**

0300 **9** *2 3/4* **Tiger Twenty Two**[48] 5656 3-8-6 79........ JackGarritty(5) 1 66
(Richard Fahey) *chsd ldrs: drvn and outpcd over 2f out: n.d after* **10/1**

0060 **10** *2 1/4* **Secret Recipe**[54] 5446 4-8-11 77........ PaddyAspell 14 59
(David Nicholls) *in tch tl pushed along and wknd over 1f out* **14/1**

0260 **11** *5* **Ted's Brother (IRE)**[9] 6836 6-8-10 76........(e) JasonHart 5 45
(Richard Guest) *hld up: rdn over 2f out: btn over 1f out* **28/1**

3065 **12** *7* **Escape To Glory (USA)**[21] 6476 6-9-2 82........ PaulMulrennan 13 33
(Michael Dods) *hld up: rdn along over 2f out: hung lft and sn btn* **14/1**

2513 **13** *nk* **Alexandrakollontai (IRE)**[10] 6824 4-8-13 82........(b) ConnorBeasley(3) 3 32
(Alistair Whillans) *hld up: struggling 3f out: nvr on terms* **8/1**[3]

5000 **P** **Regiment**[32] 6170 3-9-0 82........ TonyHamilton 11
(Richard Fahey) *prom on outside: lost action and p.u after 1f* **12/1**

1m 34.49s (1.09) **Going Correction** +0.375s/f (Good)
**WFA** 3 from 4yo+ 2lb **14** Ran SP% **122.4**
Speed ratings (Par 107): **108,104,104,103,101 101,100,100,97,94 88,80,80,**
CSF £59.12 CT £453.15 TOTE £8.10: £2.90, £2.70, £3.60; EX 68.50 Trifecta £427.60.
**Owner** Middleham Park Racing XXXVI **Bred** Mrs Ian Fox **Trained** Musley Bank, N Yorks

**FOCUS**
A good quality handicap, run at a respectable pace. The runner-up has been rated as matching his previous win here.

## 7061 CALEDONIA BEST H'CAP 7f 50y
**5:40** (5:42) (Class 6) (0-60,65) 3-Y-O+ **£1,940** (£577; £288; £144) **Stalls** High

Form RPR

-202 **1** **Royal Duchess**[59] 5233 4-8-11 54........ MeganCarberry(5) 11 64
(Lucy Normile) *hld up: hdwy to ld over 1f out: rdn and edgd lft ins fnl f: kpt on strly* **15/2**

660 **2** *3/4* **Uncle Brit**[59] 5244 8-9-1 53........(p) TomEaves 5 61
(Rebecca Menzies) *t.k.h: in tch: smooth hdwy and ev ch over 1f out: kpt on ins fnl f: hld nr fin* **25/1**

3665 **3** *1 1/4* **Pat's Legacy (USA)**[62] 5142 8-9-2 59........(p) JordanNason(5) 6 64
(Marjorie Fife) *dwlt: hld up in midfield: effrt over 2f out: edgd lft and kpt on ins fnl f* **4/1**[1]

0043 **4** *1 3/4* **Rioja Day (IRE)**[9] 6833 4-9-3 55........(b) GrahamLee 12 55
(Jim Goldie) *led: rdn and hdd over 1f out: outpcd ins fnl f* **13/2**

0041 **5** *hd* **Pitt Rivers**[9] 6833 5-9-5 57 6ex........ PaulMulrennan 13 57
(Linda Perratt) *s.i.s: hld up: stdy hdwy over 2f out: rdn over 1f out: outpcd ins fnl f* **5/1**[2]

3302 **6** *1 3/4* **Indian Giver**[9] 6837 6-8-11 54........(p) JoeDoyle(5) 8 49
(John David Riches) *w ldr: rdn over 2f out: wknd over 1f out* **8/1**

5620 **7** *3 3/4* **Blue Sonic**[17] 6601 4-9-5 57........ FergalLynch 7 42
(Jim Goldie) *hld up: rdn and outpcd over 2f out: n.d after* **18/1**

1041 **8** *1/2* **Secret City (IRE)**[9] 6834 8-9-13 65 6ex........(b) DanielTudhope 9 49
(Robin Bastiman) *chsd ldrs: rdn over 2f out: edgd lft and wknd over 1f out* **11/2**[3]

0040 **9** *1/2* **Toboggan Star**[12] 6758 3-9-5 59........(p) PJMcDonald 14 41
(Ann Duffield) *in tch: drvn and outpcd over 2f out: n.d after* **12/1**

6000 **10** *1* **Hab Reeh**[15] 6674 6-9-6 58........ JamesSullivan 10 38
(Ruth Carr) *dwlt: hld up on outside: rdn and hung lft over 2f out: sn btn* **18/1**

5034 **11** *nse* **Findog**[9] 6835 4-9-0 55........ ConnorBeasley(3) 4 35
(Linda Perratt) *prom: rdn over 2f out: wknd wl over 1f out* **12/1**

1m 37.47s (4.07) **Going Correction** +0.425s/f (Yiel)
**WFA** 3 from 4yo+ 2lb **11** Ran SP% **118.0**
Speed ratings (Par 101): **93,92,90,88,88 86,82,81,81,79 79**
CSF £177.57 CT £874.91 TOTE £8.40: £2.90, £7.00, £1.30; EX 222.20 Trifecta £1583.30.
**Owner** Steve Dick **Bred** Steve Dick **Trained** Duncrievie, Perth & Kinross

**FOCUS**
Just moderate form. The winner has been rated as running a pb.
T/Jkpt: Not won. T/Plt: £845.80 to a £1 stake. Pool: £79,595.13 - 68.69 winning units. T/Qpdt: £130.20 to a £1 stake. Pool: £6,967.35 - 39.58 winning units. RY

# 6939 WOLVERHAMPTON (A.W) (L-H)
### Thursday, October 9

**OFFICIAL GOING: Tapeta: standard**
Wind: Fresh behind Weather: Overcast

## 7062 EBF STALLIONS BETTING.CO.UK - TERRIFIC MAIDEN FILLIES' STKS (BOBIS RACE) (TAPETA) 5f 216y
**5:20** (5:23) (Class 5) 2-Y-O **£2,911** (£866; £432; £216) **Stalls** Low

Form RPR

33 **1** **Luna Mission (IRE)**[23] 6434 2-9-0 0........ MartinHarley 6 73
(Marco Botti) *a.p: rdn to ld over 1f out: r.o wl* **7/2**[2]

**2** *1 1/2* **Scent Of Summer (USA)** 2-9-0 0........ FrannyNorton 10 69
(William Haggas) *hld up: rdn and r.o wl ins fnl f: nt rch wnr* **7/2**[2]

04 **3** *1/2* **Mary's Secret**[24] 6408 2-9-0 0........ RichardKingscote 11 67
(Tom Dascombe) *hld up: hdwy over 1f out: r.o* **22/1**

5 **4** *nse* **Bonfire Heart**[28] 6271 2-9-0 0........ FrankieMcDonald 2 67
(Daniel Mark Loughnane) *a.p: rdn over 1f out: r.o* **22/1**

2 **5** *1/2* **Silvery Blue**[15] 6660 2-9-0 0........ JamesDoyle 9 65
(Hugo Palmer) *s.i.s: pushed along early in rr: hdwy over 1f out: r.o: nt rch ldrs* **9/4**[1]

56 **6** *nk* **The Fairy (IRE)**[13] 6701 2-9-0 0........ WilliamBuick 5 64
(John Gosden) *sn led: hdd 5f out: racd keenly: rdn and ev ch over 1f out: styd on same pce ins fnl f* **16/1**

0 **7** *1/2* **Exoplanet Blue**[54] 5429 2-9-0 0........ DaneO'Neill 7 63
(Henry Candy) *mid-div: rdn over 1f out: nt clr run ins fnl f: r.o* **10/1**

0 **8** *3/4* **Vixen Hill**[45] 5774 2-9-0 0........ GrahamGibbons 4 61
(Charles Hills) *chsd ldrs: cl up whn nt clr run fr over 1f out tl ins fnl f: styd on same pce* **50/1**

523 **9** *nk* **Simple Elegance (USA)**[17] 6606 2-8-11 76........ CamHardie(3) 8 60
(Charlie Appleby) *led 5f out: rdn and hdd over 1f out: wknd ins fnl f* **7/1**[3]

0 **10** *2 1/4* **Glenbuck Lass (IRE)**[33] 6158 2-9-0 0........ RobertTart 3 53
(Alan Bailey) *s.i.s: hld up: hdwy over 1f out: no ex fnl f* **33/1**

0 **11** *12* **Perfect Bounty**[36] 6032 2-8-11 0........ RyanTate(3) 12 17
(Clive Cox) *led early: remained handy: rdn over 2f out: sn hung rt and wknd* **100/1**

5 **12** *1 1/2* **Emma Bovary**[52] 5507 2-8-11 0........ JacobButterfield(3) 1 13
(John Norton) *sn pushed along and a in rr* **200/1**

1m 14.95s (0.45) **Going Correction** +0.05s/f (Slow) **12** Ran SP% **117.8**
Speed ratings (Par 92): **99,97,96,96,95 95,94,93,93,90 74,72**
CSF £15.20 TOTE £5.60: £2.90, £1.90, £4.60; EX 23.30 Trifecta £315.70.
**Owner** Jonny Allison **Bred** Yeomanstown Stud **Trained** Newmarket, Suffolk

**FOCUS**
A fairly modest maiden.

## 7063 A BET A, "THANKS-TO-ALL" OUR CUSTOMERS MAIDEN STKS (TAPETA) 7f 32y
**5:50** (5:50) (Class 5) 3-4-Y-O **£2,911** (£866; £432; £216) **Stalls** High

Form RPR

**1** **Pollination (IRE)** 3-9-5 0........ WilliamBuick 5 73+
(Charlie Appleby) *hld up: shkn up over 2f out: hdwy over 1f out: hung lft ins fnl f: r.o to ld towards fin* **5/6**[1]

05 **2** *1* **Yard Of Ale**[132] 2737 3-9-5 0........................................ GrahamGibbons 8 70
(Kristin Stubbs) *chsd ldr 6f out: rdn and ev ch ins fnl f: r.o* **40/1**

53 **3** *nk* **Copperbelt**[23] 6421 3-9-5 0........................................ FrannyNorton 6 69
(Mark Johnston) *led: qcknd 2f out: edgd rt over 1f out: sn rdn: hdd towards fin* **11/4[2]**

620 **4** *1* **Incredible Fresh (IRE)**[50] 5550 3-9-5 70..................... FrederikTylicki 2 67
(James Fanshawe) *chsd ldr 1f: remained handy: pushed along over 2f out: styd on same pce ins fnl f* **7/2[3]**

0 **5** *2 ¼* **Road Map (IRE)**[23] 6421 3-8-12 0.................................. LouiseDay(7) 1 61
(Daniel Mark Loughnane) *s.i.s: hld up: shkn up over 1f out: nt trble ldrs* **100/1**

1m 30.17s (1.37) **Going Correction** +0.05s/f (Slow) **5** Ran SP% **106.9**
Speed ratings (Par 103): **94,92,92,91,88**
CSF £27.99 TOTE £1.50: £1.10, £5.40; EX 11.50 Trifecta £31.90.
**Owner** Godolphin **Bred** Ringfort Stud & Tally Ho Stud **Trained** Newmarket, Suffolk

**FOCUS**
Those with previous experience didn't set a high standard. Muddling form, with the runner-up improving. The third and fourth have been rated close to form.

## 7064 2DB DISPLAY SYSTEMS CLAIMING STKS (TAPETA) 1m 141y
**6:20** (6:21) (Class 5) 2-Y-O **£2,911** (£866; £432; £216) **Stalls** Low

Form RPR

5240 **1** **Jet Mate (IRE)**[7] 6884 2-8-13 59..................................(p) MartinDwyer 9 59
(William Muir) *trckd ldr: rdn over 2f out: led over 1f out: styd on u.p* **13/2**

2453 **2** *½* **Framley Garth (IRE)**[7] 6887 2-8-13 65........................ JamesDoyle 7 58
(David Elsworth) *led: hung rt and hdd over 1f out: sn rdn and continued to hang rt: nt run on* **15/8[1]**

0046 **3** *shd* **Activation**[10] 6811 2-8-6 55............................................ JohnFahy 11 51
(Hughie Morrison) *chsd ldrs: rdn and edgd rt over 1f out: r.o* **16/1**

0660 **4** *nse* **More Drama (IRE)**[9] 6842 2-8-0 49.......................... DannyBrock(3) 6 48
(Sylvester Kirk) *hld up: hdwy over 1f out: r.o* **16/1**

3006 **5** *½* **Three Robins**[50] 5554 2-8-3 63...................................... CamHardie(3) 4 50
(Richard Hannon) *prom: rdn over 1f out: r.o* **4/1[2]**

0265 **6** *½* **Diamond Runner (IRE)**[10] 6811 2-8-1 62..............(b) NoelGarbutt(5) 1 49
(Hugo Palmer) *mid-div: rdn over 3f out: hdwy over 2f out: styd on* **13/2**

00 **7** *1 ¾* **Lexi Grady Alice**[30] 6205 2-8-5 0..................................... JimmyQuinn 2 44
(Mark H Tompkins) *s.i.s: hld up: styd on u.p ins fnl f: nt trble ldrs* **66/1**

530 **8** *¾* **Colours Of Glory (IRE)**[28] 6261 2-8-10 63................. WilliamBuick 8 47
(Charles Hills) *hld up: hdwy 2f out: no ex fnl f* **6/1[3]**

0500 **9** *1* **Verchild Lad (IRE)**[24] 6412 2-8-6 47.........................(v[1]) FrannyNorton 13 41
(David Evans) *s.s: swtchd lft sn after s: hdwy u.p over 1f out: no ex fnl f* **50/1**

0450 **10** *½* **Diminutive (IRE)**[9] 6842 2-8-4 60................................... DavidProbert 5 38
(Grace Harris) *hld up: hdwy over 1f out: no ex fnl f* **20/1**

000 **11** *3 ¾* **Deeper Magic (IRE)**[17] 6602 2-8-8 59......................(b[1]) StevieDonohoe 3 34
(J S Moore) *chsd ldrs: rdn over 2f out: wknd over 1f out* **28/1**

1m 51.68s (1.58) **Going Correction** +0.05s/f (Slow) **11** Ran SP% **119.2**
Speed ratings (Par 95): **94,93,93,93,92 92,90,90,89,88 85**
CSF £18.76 TOTE £9.80: £2.10, £1.40, £4.90; EX 19.80 Trifecta £295.50.
**Owner** Martin P Graham **Bred** Rathasker Stud **Trained** Lambourn, Berks

**FOCUS**
A fairly open claimer.

## 7065 BOS MAGAZINE H'CAP (TAPETA) 2m 119y
**6:50** (6:50) (Class 6) (0-65,65) 4-Y-O+ **£2,264** (£673; £336; £168) **Stalls** Low

Form RPR

2116 **1** **Mister Bob (GER)**[16] 6632 5-9-4 62................................(p) TedDurcan 8 71+
(James Bethell) *hld up: pushed along over 3f out: hdwy over 2f out: shkn up to ld ins fnl f: styd on wl* **9/4[1]**

2354 **2** *3* **Black Iceman**[16] 6632 6-8-6 50........................................ HarryBentley 7 55
(Lydia Pearce) *a.p: chsd ldr over 2f out: rdn to ld over 1f out: hdd and unable qck ins fnl f* **8/1**

3156 **3** *1 ½* **Annaluna (IRE)**[16] 6640 5-9-1 59................................(v) MartinHarley 6 62
(David Evans) *sn led: clr 12f out tl over 3f out: rdn and hdd over 1f out: styd on same pce ins fnl f* **6/1[3]**

0523 **4** *1 ½* **Just Duchess**[10] 6818 4-8-2 46 oh1.................................. DavidProbert 2 47
(Michael Blanshard) *prom: rdn over 2f out: styd on same pce fnl f* **12/1**

2052 **5** *½* **Honest Strike (USA)**[12] 6768 7-8-13 62.......................... EoinWalsh(5) 4 63
(Daniel Mark Loughnane) *hld up: hdwy u.p over 2f out: styd on same pce fr over 1f out* **13/2**

3063 **6** *1* **Lacey**[12] 6768 5-8-8 57................................................(p) JackDuern(5) 3 57
(Andrew Hollinshead) *chsd ldr over 8f: lft 2nd again over 6f out tl rdn over 2f out: wknd ins fnl f* **15/2**

-350 **7** *1* **Phoenix Flight (IRE)**[169] 818 9-9-7 65......................... StevieDonohoe 1 63
(James Evans) *hld up: rdn over 2f out: wknd fnl f* **28/1**

0505 **8** *50* **Azrag (USA)**[26] 6343 6-9-5 63................................(bt) FrederikTylicki 5
(Michael Attwater) *hld up: hdwy 11f out: chsd ldr 8f out tl drvn along: reluctant and lost pl over 6f out: sn wl bhd* **5/1[2]**

3m 43.66s (-0.04) **Going Correction** +0.05s/f (Slow) **8** Ran SP% **109.1**
Speed ratings (Par 101): **102,100,99,99,98 98,98,74**
CSF £18.81 CT £83.61 TOTE £3.30: £1.30, £3.90, £1.80; EX 20.70 Trifecta £76.50.
**Owner** Robert Gibbons **Bred** Newsells Park Stud Ltd **Trained** Middleham Moor, N Yorks

**FOCUS**
An ordinary staying handicap. The runner-up has been rated close to form.

## 7066 BIDS5 BOOKIES SCREEN SYSTEMS CONDITIONS STKS (TAPETA) 1m 141y
**7:20** (7:21) (Class 4) 3-Y-O+ **£4,725** (£1,414; £707; £354; £176) **Stalls** Low

Form RPR

5033 **1** **Complicit (IRE)**[47] 5687 3-8-13 97...................................... LukeMorris 6 101
(Paul Cole) *chsd ldr: rdn over 1f out: led and edgd lft ins fnl f: r.o* **7/2[2]**

1223 **2** *¾* **Emirates Flyer**[194] 1178 3-9-4 109.................................... JamesDoyle 2 104
(Saeed bin Suroor) *chsd ldrs: rdn and ev ch ins fnl f: styd on* **4/5[1]**

0-30 **3** *nk* **Premio Loco (USA)**[201] 1068 10-9-3 108......................... GeorgeBaker 7 98
(Chris Wall) *led: shkn up over 1f out: hdd and edgd lft ins fnl f: kpt on* **13/2[3]**

0144 **4** *½* **Mindurownbusiness (IRE)**[24] 6411 3-8-10 90............... CamHardie(3) 4 97
(David Simcock) *hld up: hdwy over 1f out: sn rdn: r.o* **22/1**

4111 **5** *nk* **Fiftyshadesfreed (IRE)**[12] 6770 3-8-13 91.....................(p) PatCosgrave 5 97
(George Baker) *hld up in tch: rdn over 1f out: styd on* **8/1**

-602 **6** *¾* **Dragon Falls (IRE)**[222] 808 5-9-3 0.................................. WilliamBuick 3 94
(Charlie Appleby) *hld up: hdwy and hung lft over 1f out: nt clr run ins fnl f: styd on same pce* **17/2**

000 **7** *12* **Energia Eros (BRZ)**[103] 3722 5-9-10 96..........................(b) TedDurcan 9 73
(John Berry) *hld up: rdn over 3f out: wknd over 1f out* **50/1**

1m 49.51s (-0.59) **Going Correction** +0.05s/f (Slow)
**WFA** 3 from 5yo+ 4lb **7** Ran SP% **119.1**
Speed ratings (Par 105): **104,103,103,102,102 101,91**
CSF £7.08 TOTE £7.00: £2.90, £1.50; EX 10.30 Trifecta £48.80.
**Owner** T A Rahman **Bred** Barouche Stud Ireland Ltd **Trained** Whatcombe, Oxon

**FOCUS**
A decent contest. The early pace wasn't strong, though, and it turned into a dash from the turn in. The fourth has been rated close to his latest handicap run.

## 7067 SIS LTD MEDIAN AUCTION MAIDEN STKS (TAPETA) 1m 4f 50y
**7:50** (7:50) (Class 5) 3-5-Y-O **£2,587** (£770; £384; £192) **Stalls** Low

Form RPR

4462 **1** **Strawberry Martini**[16] 6651 3-9-0 75................................ MartinDwyer 1 75
(William Muir) *mde all: rdn over 1f out: edgd lft ins fnl f: styd on* **2/1[2]**

2202 **2** *1* **Perspicace**[29] 6239 3-9-5 77............................................ JamesDoyle 2 78
(Roger Charlton) *chsd wnr: shkn up and hung lft fr over 2f out: rdn over 1f out: kpt on* **4/9[1]**

05 **3** *9* **Dukes Den**[14] 6677 3-9-5 0.............................................. LiamKeniry 5 64
(Sylvester Kirk) *prom: rdn over 3f out: outpcd fr over 2f out* **33/1[3]**

05 **4** *10* **Blue Valentino**[12] 6738 5-9-12 0................................... GrahamGibbons 3 48
(Andrew Hollinshead) *hld up: pushed along over 7f out: wknd 3f out* **33/1[3]**

0 **5** *58* **I'Mwaitingforyou**[12] 6738 5-9-2 0................................... DanielMuscutt(5) 4
(Peter Bowen) *chsd ldr: rdn over 5f out: wknd 3f out: eased* **66/1**

2m 40.59s (-0.21) **Going Correction** +0.05s/f (Slow)
**WFA** 3 from 5yo 7lb **5** Ran SP% **110.0**
Speed ratings (Par 103): **102,101,95,88,50**
CSF £3.25 TOTE £4.50: £1.20, £1.10; EX 3.30 Trifecta £9.20.
**Owner** Newsells Park Stud **Bred** Newsells Park Stud **Trained** Lambourn, Berks

**FOCUS**
As the betting had predicted, only two mattered here from some way out. The runner-up has been rated to his latest handicap form.

## 7068 BETTING SHOP SOLUTIONS POWERED BY BETCONSTRUCT H'CAP (TAPETA) 1m 1f 103y
**8:20** (8:21) (Class 6) (0-65,65) 3-Y-O+ **£2,264** (£673; £336; £168) **Stalls** Low

Form RPR

4411 **1** **Evacusafe Lady**[5] 6939 3-9-4 63 6ex.............................(t) MartinHarley 13 73
(John Ryan) *chsd ldrs: rdn to ld fnl f: r.o* **4/5[1]**

6422 **2** *½* **Classic Mission**[28] 6267 3-8-12 62.................................(b) NedCurtis(5) 7 71
(Jonathan Portman) *chsd ldr tl led wl over 1f out: rdn and hdd 1f out: r.o* **8/1[3]**

3055 **3** *nk* **Coillte Cailin (IRE)**[77] 4579 4-9-7 62........................... StevieDonohoe 12 69+
(Daniel Mark Loughnane) *hld up: hdwy over 2f out: rdn and edgd rt ins fnl f: r.o* **40/1**

3142 **4** *3 ¾* **Roger Thorpe**[127] 2894 5-9-4 64...................................... JackDuern(5) 6 63
(Deborah Sanderson) *a.p: rdn over 1f out: styd on same pce fnl f* **25/1**

0032 **5** *1 ¼* **Spirit Of Gondree (IRE)**[26] 6342 6-9-8 63...................(b) LukeMorris 8 60
(Milton Bradley) *a.p: rdn over 2f out: no ex ins fnl f* **25/1**

5124 **6** *¾* **Bon Port**[13] 6722 3-9-6 65.............................................. WilliamBuick 4 61
(Hughie Morrison) *led: rdn and hdd wl over 1f out: wknd ins fnl f* **11/2[2]**

2506 **7** *½* **Yourinthewill (USA)**[26] 6342 6-9-7 62....................... FrankieMcDonald 11 56
(Daniel Mark Loughnane) *s.i.s: hld up: r.o ins fnl f: nvr nrr* **12/1**

6000 **8** *2 ¾* **Teide Peak (IRE)**[51] 5529 5-9-3 58.................................. SeanLevey 10 46
(Paul D'Arcy) *hld up: hdwy over 2f out: rdn over 1f out: wknd ins fnl f* **25/1**

6060 **9** *hd* **Mcbirney (USA)**[55] 5395 7-9-8 63.............................. PatrickDonaghy 2 51
(Paul D'Arcy) *dwlt: hld up: rdn over 1f out: nt trble ldrs* **25/1**

5405 **10** *6* **Roxy Hart**[21] 6500 3-9-4 63........................................... GeorgeBaker 5 39
(Ed Vaughan) *hld up: wknd over 2f out* **12/1**

/60- **11** *6* **Exclusive Dancer**[327] 2280 5-8-11 52............................... LiamKeniry 3 15
(George Moore) *mid-div: rdn over 2f out: sn wknd* **100/1**

2m 0.69s (-0.11) **Going Correction** +0.05s/f (Slow)
**WFA** 3 from 4yo+ 4lb **11** Ran SP% **116.2**
Speed ratings (Par 101): **102,101,101,97,96 96,95,93,93,87 82**
CSF £6.65 CT £147.86 TOTE £2.00: £1.10, £2.80, £5.10; EX 8.90 Trifecta £154.20.
**Owner** J Ryan **Bred** Mrs Sarah Moorcroft **Trained** Newmarket, Suffolk

**FOCUS**
They didn't go that quick early, but three came clear and this is probably form to be positive about. The winner has been rated as matching her latest win, with the runner-up running a pb.
T/Plt: £13.80 to a £1 stake. Pool: £82,553.81 - 4361.86 winning units. T/Qpdt: £3.40 to a £1 stake. Pool: £9477.25 - 2010.30 winning units. CR

# 6916 SAINT-CLOUD (L-H)
Thursday, October 9

**OFFICIAL GOING: Turf: soft**

## 7069a PRIX THOMAS BRYON (GROUP 3) (2YO) (TURF) 1m
**12:15** (12:00) 2-Y-O **£33,333** (£13,333; £10,000; £6,666)

RPR

**1** **Alea Iacta**[38] 2-8-8 0.......................................................... MaximeGuyon 4 104+
(A Fabre, France) *hld up in tch: pushed along and crossed to r alone against nr side rail in st: rdn to ld fnl f: drew clr w jockey easing down: impressive* **5/2[3]**

**2** *6* **Alpha Bravo**[30] 2-8-11 0.................................................. ThierryThulliez 3 94
(Mme C Head-Maarek, France) *t.k.h: trckd ldr: chal into st and sn led: rdn 2f out: kpt on but hdd fnl f and no match for wnr: 1st of 3 in gp* **9/4[2]**

**3** *¾* **Karaktar (IRE)**[14] 2-8-11 0.......................................... ChristopheSoumillon 2 92
(A De Royer-Dupre, France) *dwlt sltly and hld up in last: rdn to chal into st: ev ch ent fnl f: kpt on but no match for wnr: 2nd of 3 in gp* **13/8[1]**

**4** *8* **Gomati**[14] 6697 2-8-11 0.................................................. AntoineHamelin 1 75
(Matthieu Palussiere, France) *led: rdn and strly pressed into st: sn hdd: squeezed for room and dropped to rr 2f out: eased whn btn fnl f: last of 3 in gp* **7/1**

1m 44.28s (-3.22) **4** Ran SP% **109.9**
WIN (incl. 1 euro stake): 2.50. PLACES: 1.60, 1.80. SF: 7.10.
**Owner** Miss K Rausing **Bred** Miss K Rausing **Trained** Chantilly, France

## 7070a PRIX DAHLIA - FONDS EUROPEEN DE L'ELEVAGE (LISTED RACE) (4YO+ FILLIES & MARES) (TURF) 1m 2f

1:20 (12:00) 4-Y-O+ **£20,000** (£8,000; £6,000; £4,000; £2,000)

RPR

1 **Sparkling Beam (IRE)**[54] 5459 4-8-10 0 ThierryJarnet 9 110
(J E Pease, France) **17/5**[2]

2 ½ **Dalayna (FR)**[19] 4-8-10 0 ChristopheSoumillon 6 109
(A De Royer-Dupre, France) **23/5**

3 ¾ **Fate (FR)**[139] 2631 5-8-10 0 StephanePasquier 8 108
(A De Royer-Dupre, France) **42/10**[3]

4 3 **Princess Loulou (IRE)**[46] 5742 4-9-3 0 AndreaAtzeni 2 109
(Roger Varian) *trckd ldr: pushed along to chal and led early in st: rdn and hdd over 1f out: no ex and fdd fnl f* **11/5**[1]

5 2 **Lady Liberty (IRE)**[33] 6162 4-8-10 0 IoritzMendizabal 3 98
(Andreas Lowe, Germany) **205/10**

6 1 ¾ **Alumna (USA)**[164] 1827 4-8-10 0 MaximeGuyon 5 94
(A Fabre, France) **105/10**

7 3 **Kyurem (IRE)**[30] 6218 4-8-10 0 FlavienPrat 1 88
(T Clout, France) **186/10**

8 3 **Holly Filly (IRE)**[36] 6055 4-8-10 0 CristianDemuro 4 82
(F Vermeulen, France) **165/10**

9 1 ¾ **Abilene**[33] 6162 4-8-10 0 OlivierPeslier 7 79
(F-H Graffard, France) **217/10**

2m 9.73s (-6.27) **9** Ran SP% **119.6**
WIN (incl. 1 euro stake): 4.40. PLACES: 1.70, 1.90, 1.90. DF: 13.50. SF: 29.10.
**Owner** George Strawbridge **Bred** George Strawbridge **Trained** Chantilly, France

# 7062 WOLVERHAMPTON (A.W) (L-H)

Friday, October 10

**OFFICIAL GOING: Tapeta: standard**
Wind: Light behind Weather: Fine

## 7071 LADBROKES H'CAP (TAPETA) 5f 216y

5:45 (5:51) (Class 5) (0-75,75) 3-Y-O+ **£2,911** (£866; £432; £216) **Stalls** Low

Form RPR

0034 1 **Realize**[27] 6334 4-9-7 75 (t) JamesDoyle 9 86+
(Hughie Morrison) *hld up: hdwy over 2f out: led over 1f out: rdn and hung lft ins fnl f: r.o* **2/1**[1]

2221 2 1 ¼ **Dominium (USA)**[27] 6346 7-8-13 74 (b) DavidParkes(7) 10 81
(Jeremy Gask) *hld up: hdwy over 1f out: sn rdn r.o* **13/2**

0434 3 hd **Ambitious Boy**[13] 6736 5-9-2 75 JackDuern(5) 12 81
(Andrew Hollinshead) *hld up: r.o ins fnl f: nt rch ldrs* **6/1**[3]

0300 4 2 ¾ **Hadaj**[13] 6736 5-9-2 75 KevinStott(5) 8 73
(Michael Herrington) *chsd ldrs: rdn and ev ch over 1f out: styd on same pce ins fnl f* **14/1**

6042 5 ¾ **Ashkari (IRE)**[20] 6562 3-9-6 75 (p) SteveDrowne 4 70
(Clive Cox) *sn pushed along to chse ldrs: nt clr run over 1f out: swtchd rt: styd on same pce ins fnl f* **5/1**[2]

3030 6 ½ **Punk**[15] 6680 3-9-4 73 (v[1]) LukeMorris 7 67
(George Peckham) *mid-div: hdwy and nt clr run over 1f out: rdn and hung lft ins fnl f: styd on same pce* **25/1**

326- 7 nse **Flicksta (USA)**[324] 7978 3-9-0 69 JackMitchell 1 62
(John Ryan) *s.i.s: hld up: hdwy over 1f out: nt clr run 1f out: swtchd rt ins fnl f: styd on same pce* **28/1**

3246 8 1 ¾ **Storm Lightning**[25] 6398 5-9-3 71 WilliamCarson 13 59
(Mark Brisbourne) *hld up: rdn over 2f out: nvr trbld ldrs* **16/1**

260 9 ½ **Baby Strange**[13] 6736 10-8-11 72 AdamMcLean(7) 2 58
(Derek Shaw) *hld up: rdn over 1f out: nvr on terms* **18/1**

0405 10 hd **Lastchancelucas**[15] 6695 4-9-4 72 (b) JasonHart 6 58
(Declan Carroll) *chsd ldr: rdn to ld over 1f out: sn hdd: wknd ins fnl f* **16/1**

3006 11 nk **Al's Memory (IRE)**[17] 6639 5-9-2 70 MartinLane 3 55
(David Evans) *sn pushed along to ld: rdr lost whip briefly over 2f out: rdn and hdd over 1f out: wknd ins fnl f* **10/1**

5 12 1 ¼ **Springlike (IRE)**[24] 6423 3-8-13 73 DanielMuscutt(5) 5 54
(Amy Weaver) *prom: rdn over 1f out: wknd ins fnl f* **100/1**

1m 13.23s (-1.27) **Going Correction** -0.10s/f (Stan)
**WFA** 3 from 4yo+ 1lb **12** Ran SP% **118.7**
Speed ratings (Par 103): **104,102,102,98,97 96,96,94,93,93 93,91**
CSF £14.53 CT £68.72 TOTE £2.80: £1.50, £1.90, £2.30; EX 18.70 Trifecta £85.50.
**Owner** Deborah Collett & M J Watson **Bred** M J Watson **Trained** East Ilsley, Berks

**FOCUS**
There was a fair pace on here. The winner was back to his Southwell reappearance form.

## 7072 DOWNLOAD THE NEW LADBROKES APP H'CAP (TAPETA) 1m 5f 194y

6:20 (6:20) (Class 5) (0-75,75) 3-Y-O+ **£2,911** (£866; £432; £216) **Stalls** Low

Form RPR

4431 1 **Atalanta Bay (IRE)**[27] 6338 4-9-5 67 RichardKingscote 7 77
(Marcus Tregoning) *chsd ldr: rdn over 3f out: styd on u.p to ld nr fin* **10/1**[3]

1133 2 ½ **Nyanza (GER)**[81] 4504 3-9-2 73 FergusSweeney 4 82
(Alan King) *chsd ldrs: rdn over 2f out: ev ch wl ins fnl f: styd on* **7/1**[2]

-111 3 nk **High Secret (IRE)**[7] 6900 3-9-2 73 12ex LukeMorris 5 82
(Sir Mark Prescott Bt) *led: rdn over 2f out: hdd nr fin* **4/11**[1]

4156 4 2 ¾ **Grayswood**[20] 6542 4-9-6 68 (p) MartinDwyer 6 73
(William Muir) *hld up: tk clsr order over 5f out: rdn over 2f out: sn outpcd: styd on ins fnl f* **20/1**

4544 5 5 **Admirable Duque (IRE)**[14] 6721 8-9-5 67 (be) MartinLane 2 65
(Dominic Ffrench Davis) *hld up: tk clsr order over 5f out: rdn over 4f out: outpcd fnl 3f* **20/1**

0205 6 nk **Lineman**[14] 6721 4-9-4 71 (p) JackDuern(5) 1 69
(Andrew Hollinshead) *hld up: rdn over 4f out: nvr on terms* **20/1**

5-0 7 14 **Paris Snow**[40] 5961 4-9-13 75 StevieDonohoe 3 53
(Ian Williams) *hld up: rdn over 3f out: sn wknd* **33/1**

3m 1.74s (-3.06) **Going Correction** -0.10s/f (Stan)
**WFA** 3 from 4yo+ 9lb **7** Ran SP% **112.1**
Speed ratings (Par 103): **104,103,103,101,99 98,90**
CSF £65.50 TOTE £7.40: £3.40, £3.50; EX 72.50 Trifecta £85.90.
**Owner** Miss S Sharp **Bred** Manister House Stud **Trained** Whitsbury, Hants

**FOCUS**
A fair handicap in which the favourite was a little disappointing.

## 7073 BET NOW WITH THE NEW LADBROKES APP H'CAP (TAPETA) 5f 20y

6:50 (6:51) (Class 4) (0-80,80) 3-Y-O+ **£5,175** (£1,540; £769; £384) **Stalls** Low

Form RPR

3314 1 **Eternitys Gate**[9] 6873 3-9-2 75 JimCrowley 7 87
(Peter Chapple-Hyam) *a.p: rdn over 1f out: r.o to ld nr fin* **9/2**[3]

1061 2 ½ **Clearing**[17] 4614 4-9-3 76 PatCosgrave 8 85
(Jim Boyle) *led: hdd over 3f out: chsd ldr: rdn to ld wl ins fnl f: hdd nr fin* **10/1**

1005 3 hd **Zac Brown (IRE)**[60] 5243 3-9-6 79 MartinDwyer 11 88+
(David Barron) *hld up: hdwy over 1f out: n.m.r ins fnl f: r.o* **10/1**

506 4 ¾ **Dreams Of Reality**[67] 4971 3-9-0 73 RichardKingscote 5 80
(Tom Dascombe) *mid-div: hdwy 1/2-way: rdn over 1f out: styd on* **10/1**

0050 5 ½ **Royal Acquisition**[44] 5830 4-8-13 72 (p) AdamBeschizza 10 76
(Robert Cowell) *sn pushed along to chse ldrs: led over 3f out: rdn: edgd lft and hdd wl ins fnl f: no ex* **40/1**

255 6 ½ **Angelito**[27] 6324 5-9-5 78 PaulMulrennan 2 80
(Ed McMahon) *hld up: rdn over 1f out: r.o ins fnl f: nt rch ldrs* **8/1**

3214 7 ½ **Newton's Law (IRE)**[35] 6096 3-9-5 78 (t) JamesDoyle 6 79
(Brian Meehan) *chsd ldrs: rdn over 1f out: styd on same pce ins fnl f* **5/2**[1]

4050 8 3 **Sleepy Blue Ocean**[9] 6873 8-9-7 80 (p) JasonHart 12 69
(John Balding) *hld up: rdn over 1f out: n.d* **25/1**

4040 9 1 ½ **Temple Road (IRE)**[143] 2414 6-9-0 73 LukeMorris 9 57
(Milton Bradley) *hld up: hdwy over 1f out: wknd ins fnl f* **25/1**

3010 10 1 ½ **Distant Past**[21] 6512 3-8-12 76 KevinStott(5) 3 56
(Kevin Ryan) *mid-div: pushed along over 3f out: sn lost pl: n.d after* **4/1**[2]

0450 11 6 **Clear Praise (USA)**[92] 4121 7-8-12 78 TomasHarrigan(7) 4 35
(Simon Dow) *s.s: a bhd* **40/1**

1m 0.91s (-0.99) **Going Correction** -0.10s/f (Stan) **11** Ran SP% **117.7**
Speed ratings (Par 105): **103,102,101,100,99 99,98,93,91,88 79**
CSF £46.85 CT £427.18 TOTE £5.10: £2.20, £2.90, £4.30; EX 44.30 Trifecta £591.30.
**Owner** Mrs Fitri Hay **Bred** Cheveley Park Stud Ltd **Trained** Newmarket, Suffolk

**FOCUS**
A fair sprint. The form makes sense among the first four.

## 7074 LADBROKES MEDIAN AUCTION MAIDEN STKS (TAPETA) 1m 141y

7:20 (7:23) (Class 5) 3-5-Y-O **£2,587** (£770; £384; £192) **Stalls** Low

Form RPR

1 **Persona Grata** 3-8-11 0 RichardKingscote 11 72+
(Ed Walker) *hld up: hdwy over 1f out: edgd lft and r.o to ld nr fin* **10/1**

3344 2 nk **Kicking The Can (IRE)**[39] 5976 3-9-2 80 RobertHavlin 10 76
(Peter Chapple-Hyam) *chsd ldr tl led over 3f out: rdn ins fnl f: hdd nr fin* **4/1**[2]

3443 3 1 ½ **Kubeba (IRE)**[14] 6717 3-9-2 69 LukeMorris 5 73
(Paul Cole) *a.p: rdn to chse ldr over 2f out: styd on* **9/2**[3]

4 1 ¾ **Galactic Halo** 3-8-11 0 JamesDoyle 8 64
(Lady Cecil) *a.p: rdn over 1f out: styd on same pce ins fnl f* **7/2**[1]

26 5 2 **Chauvelin**[13] 6738 3-9-2 0 GeorgeBaker 12 64
(Roger Charlton) *hld up: pushed along and hdwy over 2f out: no ex ins fnl f* **9/2**[3]

65 6 ¾ **So It's War (FR)**[18] 6599 3-9-2 0 TomEaves 9 62
(Keith Dalgleish) *hld up: hdwy 3f out: rdn over 1f out: no ex fnl f* **13/2**

00 7 ½ **Kirtling**[38] 6018 3-9-2 0 RobertTart 1 61
(Andi Brown) *hld up: rdn over 2f out: styd on fr over 1f out: nvr nrr* **40/1**

65 8 7 **Housewives Choice**[128] 2899 3-8-11 0 [1] TedDurcan 3 40
(James Bethell) *hld up: rdn over 2f out: sn wknd* **25/1**

9 2 **Honey Badger** 3-9-2 0 SteveDrowne 2 40
(Alison Hutchinson) *s.i.s: sn pushed along and a in rr* **14/1**

0040 10 2 ¼ **Seraphima**[35] 6121 4-9-1 45 (v) JasonHart 4 29
(Lisa Williamson) *plld hrd and prom: rdn and wknd over 2f out* **100/1**

-035 11 6 **Thrtypointstothree (IRE)**[43] 5862 3-8-13 55 PhilipPrince(3) 6 21
(Nikki Evans) *led: rdn and hdd over 3f out: wknd 2f out* **100/1**

12 1 **Hidden Ambition** 5-8-10 0 JackDuern(5) 7 13
(Steph Hollinshead) *s.s: a bhd* **100/1**

1m 50.08s (-0.02) **Going Correction** -0.10s/f (Stan)
**WFA** 3 from 4yo+ 4lb **12** Ran SP% **116.9**
Speed ratings (Par 103): **96,95,94,92,91 90,89,83,81,79 74,73**
CSF £48.37 TOTE £15.10: £3.60, £1.40, £1.40; EX 50.30 Trifecta £453.00.
**Owner** Miss K Rausing **Bred** Miss K Rausing **Trained** Newmarket, Suffolk

**FOCUS**
Those with previous form didn't set a great standard. The form is rated around the third and fourth.

## 7075 LADBROKES NURSERY H'CAP (TAPETA) 1m 141y

7:50 (7:51) (Class 6) (0-65,65) 2-Y-O **£2,264** (£673; £336; £168) **Stalls** Low

Form RPR

500 1 **Master Zephyr**[20] 6545 2-9-5 63 GeorgeBaker 9 69
(Roger Charlton) *s.i.s: hld up: hdwy over 1f out: r.o to ld nr fin* **7/2**[2]

5520 2 nk **Romance Story (IRE)**[17] 6648 2-9-2 65 (p) KevinStott(5) 8 70
(Saeed bin Suroor) *hld up: hdwy 2f out: rdn to ld wl ins fnl f: hdd nr fin* **10/3**[1]

063 3 2 **The Wee Barra (IRE)**[23] 6448 2-9-4 62 PaulMulrennan 12 63
(Kevin Ryan) *a.p: chsd ldr over 6f out: led over 1f out: rdn and hdd wl ins fnl f: styd on same pce* **8/1**

0444 4 ¾ **Mikandy (IRE)**[11] 6811 2-9-0 61 RyanTate(3) 11 60
(Clive Cox) *chsd ldrs: rdn over 1f out: styd on same pce ins fnl f* **25/1**

0512 5 ¾ **Invincible Wish (IRE)**[6] 6944 2-8-10 54 PaulPickard 2 52
(Brian Ellison) *plld hrd and prom: rdn over 1f out: ev ch ins fnl f: no ex towards fin* **4/1**[3]

6601 6 1 ¼ **Secret Lightning (FR)**[31] 6205 2-9-4 62 JamesDoyle 10 57
(Michael Appleby) *hld up: hdwy over 1f out: sn rdn: no ex ins fnl f* **6/1**

5004 7 nk **Roman De Brut (IRE)**[10] 6842 2-8-9 53 StevieDonohoe 1 47
(Ian Williams) *chsd ldrs: hmpd and lost pl 7f out: hdwy over 2f out: nt clr run fr over 1f out tl no ex ins fnl f* **14/1**

0600 8 7 **Avenue Des Champs**[17] 6646 2-8-12 56 (p) PatCosgrave 13 36
(Jane Chapple-Hyam) *hld up: hdwy on outer over 6f out: rdn over 3f out: wknd ins fnl f* **66/1**

0100 9 4 **Just Marion (IRE)**[16] 6662 2-9-4 62 MartinLane 6 33
(David Evans) *sn led: rdn and hdd over 1f out: wknd ins fnl f* **50/1**

4066 10 2 **Seamoor Secret**[8] 6888 2-8-9 56 (t) ConnorBeasley(3) 7 23
(Alex Hales) *prom: lost pl 6f out: pushed along and hdwy on outer over 2f out: rdn and wknd over 1f out* **50/1**

0065 11 3 ¼ **Kopassus (IRE)**[16] 6669 2-9-0 58 JimCrowley 3 18
(Peter Chapple-Hyam) *chsd ldrs: rdn over 3f out: wkng whn hmpd 2f out* **14/1**

044 **12** *6* **Auld Fyffee (IRE)**[10] 6830 2-9-3 **61** ............ KierenFallon 4 9
(John Ryan) *sn pushed along in rr: wknd over 3f out* **25/1**
1m 50.13s (0.03) **Going Correction** -0.10s/f (Stan) **12** Ran SP% **117.1**
Speed ratings (Par 93): **95,94,92,92,91 90,90,84,80,78 75,70**
CSF £14.70 CT £87.19 TOTE £4.20: £1.30, £1.10, £3.10; EX 18.00 Trifecta £94.90.
**Owner** Beckhampton 2 **Bred** Ashbrittle Stud **Trained** Beckhampton, Wilts

**FOCUS**
The gallop picked up heading to the turn out of the back straight and the first two came from off the pace.

## 7076 DOWNLOAD THE NEW LADBROKES APP MEDIAN AUCTION MAIDEN STKS (TAPETA) 7f 32y
**8:20** (8:20) (Class 6) 2-Y-O **£2,264** (£673; £336; £168) **Stalls** High

Form RPR
65 **1** **Gentlemusic (FR)**[17] 6641 2-8-9 0 ............ DanielMuscutt(5) 10 68
(Marco Botti) *a.p: rdn over 1f out: r.o to ld nr fin* **11/1**
5 **2** *nk* **Unnoticed**[16] 6668 2-9-5 0 ............ RobertWinston 11 72
(Ollie Pears) *plld hrd: trckd ldr 6f out: led over 1f out: rdn and hdd wl ins fnl f: r.o* **13/2**[2]
22 **3** *shd* **Excilly**[14] 6700 2-9-0 0 ............ RichardKingscote 1 67+
(Tom Dascombe) *led early: chsd ldrs: rdn to ld wl ins fnl f: hdd nr fin* **30/100**[1]
**4** *2 ¾* **Padlock (IRE)** 2-9-5 0 ............ JimCrowley 3 66+
(David Simcock) *prom: nt clr run ins fnl f: swtchd rt: styd on same pce* **8/1**[3]
00 **5** *2 ¼* **Mysterious Star (FR)**[17] 6646 2-9-5 0 ............ FergusSweeney 7 60
(Martyn Meade) *mid-div: hdwy over 2f out: rdn over 1f out: wknd ins fnl f* **50/1**
00 **6** *1* **Lonely Ranger (USA)**[29] 6270 2-9-5 0 ............ PatCosgrave 9 58
(Amy Weaver) *sn led: rdn over 2f out: hdd over 1f out: wknd ins fnl f* **66/1**
05 **7** *½* **Kerrymerry (IRE)**[23] 6462 2-8-12 0 ............ AhmadAlSubousi(7) 4 57
(Ismail Mohammed) *hld up: rdn over 1f out: nvr trbld ldrs* **33/1**
**8** *1 ¾* **Bangers (IRE)** 2-9-5 0 ............ StephenCraine 6 53
(Tom Dascombe) *s.s: rdn over 1f out: a in rr* **28/1**
06 **9** *½* **First Summer**[14] 6719 2-9-5 0 ............ PaulMulrennan 2 51
(Ed McMahon) *hld up: effrt over 1f out: n.d* **50/1**
6 **10** *¾* **Night Generation (GER)**[9] 6860 2-9-5 0 ............ LukeMorris 8 50
(Sir Mark Prescott Bt) *pushed along in rr early: shkn up over 2f out: nvr on terms* **28/1**
1m 30.69s (1.89) **Going Correction** -0.10s/f (Stan) **10** Ran SP% **125.0**
Speed ratings (Par 93): **85,84,84,81,78 77,77,75,74,73**
CSF £79.04 TOTE £12.40: £3.00, £2.40, £1.02; EX 108.90 Trifecta £130.30.
**Owner** Umberto Saini Fasanotti **Bred** Har De L'Hirondelle **Trained** Newmarket, Suffolk

## 7077 LADBROKES MOBILE APP H'CAP (TAPETA) (DIV I) 7f 32y
**8:50** (8:50) (Class 6) (0-65,65) 3-Y-O+ **£2,264** (£673; £336; £168) **Stalls** High

Form RPR
0505 **1** **Rich Again (IRE)**[16] 6674 5-9-6 64 ............(p) TedDurcan 9 74
(James Bethell) *hld up: hdwy over 1f out: edgd lft and r.o to ld nr fin* **8/1**
2222 **2** *½* **Slingsby**[20] 6567 3-8-11 57 ............(b) BarryMcHugh 11 65
(Michael Easterby) *sn chsng ldrs: led over 1f out: sn rdn: hdd nr fin* **7/2**[1]
-505 **3** *2 ¼* **Larghetto (USA)**[14] 6716 6-8-12 61 ............ GeorgeDowning(5) 5 64
(Ian Williams) *hld up: hdwy over 1f out: sn rdn: styd on same pce ins fnl f* **14/1**
0-00 **4** *1 ¾* **Nashmi**[112] 3430 3-9-2 62 ............(v[1]) LukeMorris 4 60
(George Peckham) *plld hrd and prom: rdn over 1f out: no ex ins fnl f* **25/1**
2432 **5** *½* **Orwellian**[20] 6543 5-8-12 56 ............ PaulMulrennan 1 53+
(Bryan Smart) *hld up: nt clr run fr over 2f out tl swtchd lft and r.o ins fnl f: nt trble ldrs* **7/1**
0003 **6** *nk* **Dimitar (USA)**[27] 6342 5-9-2 60 ............(p) StevieDonohoe 3 57
(Johnny Farrelly) *sn pushed along in rr: rdn and r.o ins fnl f: nrst fin* **9/2**[3]
5036 **7** *hd* **Unbridled Joy (IRE)**[38] 6022 3-8-11 60 ............ RyanTate(3) 8 55
(Clive Cox) *hld up: rdn over 2f out: styd on ins fnl f: nvr nrr* **10/1**
64 **8** *1 ¼* **Bosstime (IRE)**[14] 6715 4-9-2 60 ............(p) RobertHavlin 10 53
(John Holt) *hld up: hdwy 2f out: rdn over 1f out: no ex fnl f* **22/1**
4144 **9** *3* **Zed Candy Girl**[34] 6155 4-9-2 65 ............(p) EoinWalsh(5) 6 50
(John Stimpson) *sn chsng ldr: led 2f out: rdn and hdd over 1f out: wknd ins fnl f* **9/1**
0033 **10** *1 ¾* **Bogsnog (IRE)**[13] 6767 4-9-7 65 ............ TomEaves 2 45
(Kristin Stubbs) *racd keenly: trckd ldrs: rdn over 1f out: wknd fnl f* **4/1**[2]
4000 **11** *3 ¾* **Llewellyn**[13] 6767 6-9-4 65 ............ NeilFarley(3) 7 36
(Declan Carroll) *led: rdn and hdd 2f out: wknd over 1f out* **25/1**
1m 27.91s (-0.89) **Going Correction** -0.10s/f (Stan)
**WFA** 3 from 4yo+ 2lb **11** Ran SP% **121.8**
Speed ratings (Par 101): **101,100,97,95,95 94,94,93,89,87 83**
CSF £36.62 CT £399.55 TOTE £7.50: £3.80, £1.80, £3.80; EX 48.00 Trifecta £492.50.
**Owner** Clarendon Thoroughbred Racing **Bred** Mrs Sandra Maye **Trained** Middleham Moor, N Yorks

**FOCUS**
A moderate heat. The winner was back to his best, with the runner-up confirming his recent form.

## 7078 LADBROKES MOBILE APP H'CAP (TAPETA) (DIV II) 7f 32y
**9:20** (9:21) (Class 6) (0-65,65) 3-Y-O+ **£2,264** (£673; £336; £168) **Stalls** High

Form RPR
40-0 **1** **Dazeen**[168] 1689 7-9-1 59 ............ RobertWinston 4 72+
(Michael Herrington) *hld up: hdwy and nt clr run over 1f out: rdn to ld ins fnl f: edgd lft: r.o* **4/1**[2]
2310 **2** *2* **Pour La Victoire (IRE)**[16] 6657 4-9-7 65 ......(b) WilliamTwiston-Davies 9 73
(Tony Carroll) *s.i.s: hld up: hdwy over 1f out: rdn and ev ch ins fnl f: styd on same pce* **10/1**
4562 **3** *nk* **Black Dave (IRE)**[3] 7000 4-9-4 62 ............ MartinLane 6 69+
(David Evans) *chsd ldrs: rdn to ld 1f out: sn hdd: styd on same pce* **2/1**[1]
025 **4** *1* **Rememberance Day**[17] 6638 3-9-2 62 ............ DavidAllan 12 66
(Les Eyre) *hld up: pushed along and hdwy over 2f out: rdn over 1f out: styd on* **25/1**
1416 **5** *1 ½* **Clapperboard**[52] 5522 3-9-3 63 ............(b) WilliamCarson 7 63
(Paul Fitzsimons) *led: rdn: hung lft and hdd 1f out: no ex* **20/1**
5020 **6** *¾* **Malaysian Boleh**[18] 6617 4-9-7 65 ............ HarryBentley 10 64
(Simon Dow) *s.s: hld up: hdwy and edgd lft over 1f out: styd on: nt trble ldrs* **8/1**
0036 **7** *2 ¼* **Street Boss (IRE)**[22] 6495 3-8-12 58 ............(v) RussKennemore 11 50
(Jedd O'Keeffe) *sn pushed along to chse ldrs: rdn over 2f out: nt clr run 1f out: sn wknd* **20/1**
0643 **8** *2* **Palace Princess (FR)**[14] 6716 3-8-13 59 ............ PaulMulrennan 3 46
(Ed Dunlop) *mid-div: hdwy over 2f out: wknd fnl f* **11/2**[3]

2546 **9** *2 ¾* **Monsieur Royale**[25] 6405 4-9-6 64 ............(b) BarryMcHugh 1 45
(Geoffrey Oldroyd) *prom: rdn over 2f out: wknd fnl f* **16/1**
0014 **10** *shd* **Arabian Flight**[9] 6858 5-9-6 64 ............(p) AndrewMullen 8 44
(Michael Appleby) *chsd ldr: rdn over 2f out: wknd fnl f* **8/1**
3305 **11** *4 ½* **Eastlands Lad (IRE)**[79] 4534 5-8-9 53 oh3 ow2 ............ TomEaves 2 22
(Micky Hammond) *hld up: rdn over 2f out: wknd over 1f out* **40/1**
/000 **12** *15* **Two Pancakes**[13] 6766 4-8-13 60 ............ NeilFarley(3) 5
(Declan Carroll) *sn outpcd* **66/1**
1m 27.44s (-1.36) **Going Correction** -0.10s/f (Stan)
**WFA** 3 from 4yo+ 2lb **12** Ran SP% **123.2**
Speed ratings (Par 101): **103,100,100,99,97 96,94,91,88,88 83,66**
CSF £42.50 CT £107.10 TOTE £5.70: £2.60, £2.70, £1.60; EX 57.10 Trifecta £245.10.
**Owner** Darren & Annaley Yates **Bred** Bond Thoroughbred Corporation **Trained** Cold Kirby, N Yorks

**FOCUS**
The quicker of the two divisions by 0.47sec. The first two came from the rear and the form is rated through the second.
T/Plt: £81.60 to a £1 stake. Pool: £97,601.13 - 872.93 winning tickets T/Qpdt: £10.50 to a £1 stake. Pool: £11,626.26 - 814.38 winning tickets CR

# 6165 YORK (L-H)
### Friday, October 10

**OFFICIAL GOING: Soft (good to soft on both bends) changing to good to soft (soft in places) after race 3 (3:00)**
Wind: fresh 1/2 behind Weather: changeable, bright periods, occasional showers

## 7079 TSG STKS (NURSERY H'CAP) (BOBIS RACE) 6f
**2:00** (2:00) (Class 3) (0-95,92) 2-Y-O **£7,762** (£2,310; £1,154; £577) **Stalls** High

Form RPR
3136 **1** **Miami Carousel (IRE)**[77] 4625 2-8-5 **81** ............ JoeDoyle(5) 3 87
(John Quinn) *mde all: shkn up appr fnl f: rdn and hld on wl ins fnl f* **25/1**
0553 **2** *1 ¼* **George Bowen (IRE)**[21] 6510 2-8-11 **82** ............ RyanMoore 1 84
(Richard Fahey) *wnt lft s: hdwy to chse ldrs over 3f out: upsides and drvn over 1f out: no ex clsng stages* **4/1**[2]
010 **3** *2 ½* **Four Seasons (IRE)**[115] 3322 2-9-4 **89** ............ AdamKirby 8 84
(Charlie Appleby) *hld up towards rr: hdwy 2f out: kpt on same pce to take 3rd clsng stages* **7/1**[3]
1043 **4** *¾* **Showstoppa**[13] 6739 2-8-6 **77** ............ JoeFanning 6 70
(Mark Johnston) *chsd ldrs: kpt on one pce over 1f out* **10/1**
2334 **5** *1 ½* **Geordie George (IRE)**[21] 6510 2-9-7 **92** ............ PhillipMakin 10 80
(John Quinn) *hld up in rr: hdwy over 2f out: sn chsng ldrs: one pce appr fnl f* **15/2**
030 **6** *2* **Normandy Knight**[33] 6168 2-8-0 **71** ............ PatrickMathers 5 53
(Richard Fahey) *chsd ldrs: drvn over 2f out: wknd over 1f out* **22/1**
31 **7** *nk* **Acolyte (IRE)**[35] 6103 2-8-7 **78** ............ WilliamBuick 7 59
(Roger Charlton) *dwlt: in rr: hdwy over 2f out: drvn and hung lft over 1f out: sn fdd* **7/4**[1]
213 **8** *nk* **Charlie Croker (IRE)**[18] 6612 2-9-0 **90** ............ ShaneGray(5) 4 70
(Kevin Ryan) *mid-div: drvn and outpcd over 3f out: nvr a factor* **16/1**
0105 **9** *3 ¼* **Pillar Box (IRE)**[76] 4686 2-8-9 **87** ............ GeorgiaCox(7) 9 57
(William Haggas) *sn trcking ldrs: wknd over 1f out: eased whn bhd clsng stages* **20/1**
4421 **10** *2 ½* **The Wispe**[12] 6791 2-7-11 **71** 6ex ............ CamHardie(3) 2 34
(Robert Cowell) *sn chsng ldrs: lost pl over 1f out: bhd whn eased clsng stages* **20/1**
1m 13.34s (1.44) **Going Correction** +0.325s/f (Good) **10** Ran SP% **113.3**
Speed ratings (Par 99): **103,101,98,97,95 92,91,91,87,83**
CSF £114.00 CT £806.97 TOTE £33.40: £6.40, £1.60, £2.50; EX 195.00 Trifecta £900.60.
**Owner** Highfield Racing 5 **Bred** Lynn Lodge Stud **Trained** Settrington, N Yorks

**FOCUS**
Rail on innermost line and races of 1m and beyond decreased by 24yds. The going was described as soft, good to soft on the two bends and the winning time for the opener was 3.24sec outside standard. The jockeys variously described conditions as "soft", "very soft" and "slow - hard work." Despite the stalls being next to the stands' rail for this decent nursery, the runners came up the middle.

## 7080 BELL TRAILERS STKS (H'CAP) 5f
**2:30** (2:31) (Class 3) (0-95,95) 3-Y-O+ **£11,644** (£3,465; £1,731; £865) **Stalls** High

Form RPR
1400 **1** **Arctic Feeling (IRE)**[9] 6872 6-8-10 **89** ............ SammyJoBell(5) 4 99
(Richard Fahey) *towards rr: pushed along 2f out: rdn and hdwy over 1f out: styd on ins fnl f: led last 75yds: kpt on strly* **16/1**
030 **2** *1 ¼* **Free Zone**[41] 5925 5-9-0 **88** ............(p) FrederikTylicki 17 94
(Robert Cowell) *slt ld: hdd 2f out: cl up and sn rdn: drvn ent fnl f: kpt on wl u.p towards fin* **33/1**
6003 **3** *shd* **See The Sun**[13] 6745 3-9-5 **93** ............(p) DavidAllan 3 99
(Tim Easterby) *prom on outer: hdwy to ld wl over 1f out: rdn and edgd rt ins fnl f: hdd and no ex last 75yds* **20/1**
6353 **4** *hd* **Jamaican Bolt (IRE)**[13] 6744 6-9-1 **89** ............ BarryMcHugh 18 93
(Geoffrey Oldroyd) *towards rr: hdwy 2f out: sn rdn and kpt on ins fnl f: nrst fin* **8/1**[3]
6510 **5** *½* **Pearl Blue (IRE)**[41] 5925 6-9-6 **94** ............ GeorgeBaker 1 97
(Chris Wall) *towards rr: rdn along and hdwy on outer over 1f out: kpt on ins fnl f: nrst fin* **7/1**[2]
5204 **6** *½* **Long Awaited (IRE)**[13] 6745 6-9-1 **89** ............ GrahamGibbons 5 90
(David Barron) *chsd ldrs: rdn along wl over 1f out: drvn and wknd ins fnl f* **12/1**
0200 **7** *shd* **Pearl Acclaim (IRE)**[27] 6327 4-9-3 **91** ............ AdrianNicholls 7 91
(David Nicholls) *cl up: rdn to ld briefly 2f out: sn hdd & wknd ins fnl f* **40/1**
0000 **8** *nk* **Ancient Cross**[76] 4683 10-9-3 **91** ............(t) KierenFallon 15 90
(Michael Easterby) *dwlt and swtchd lft s: in rr: hdwy 2f out: rdn over 1f out: kpt on fnl f: nrst fin* **20/1**
3420 **9** *½* **Piazon**[55] 5438 3-9-1 **89** ............ WilliamBuick 11 88
(Michael Bell) *chsd ldrs: rdn along wl over 1f out: grad wknd ent fnl f* **14/1**
00 **10** *hd* **Magical Macey (USA)**[27] 6327 7-9-4 **92** ............(b) PhillipMakin 14 89
(David Barron) *cl up: rdn along over 2f out: drvn over 1f out: grad wknd ent fnl f* **25/1**
0065 **11** *nk* **Secret Asset (IRE)**[73] 4765 9-9-1 **89** ............ PatCosgrave 12 85
(Jane Chapple-Hyam) *towards rr: effrt 2f out: sn rdn and kpt on fnl f: n.d* **33/1**
304 **12** *hd* **Eccleston**[41] 5925 3-9-7 **95** ............ DanielTudhope 10 91
(David O'Meara) *towards rr: rdn along 2f out: sme late hdwy* **5/1**[1]
0005 **13** *½* **Gladiatrix**[6] 6923 5-9-2 **90** ............ RobertHavlin 6 83
(Rod Millman) *chsd ldrs: pushed along and sltly outpcd whn n.m.r over 1f out: rdn and n.m.r again ins fnl f: wknd after* **25/1**

1045 **14** *hd* **Silvanus (IRE)**[18] 6614 4-9-5 93........................ GrahamLee 13 86
(Paul Midgley) *chsd ldrs: rdn along 2f out: grad wknd* **40/1**

1000 **15** *½* **Top Boy**[18] 6614 4-9-0 88....................................(v) DaleSwift 16 79
(Derek Shaw) *a in rr* **20/1**

0100 **16** *2* **Asian Trader**[41] 5925 5-8-10 87........................ NathanAlison(3) 2 71
(William Haggas) *s.i.s and in rr whn swtchd markedly rt to stands' rail after 1f: a bhd* **16/1**

0 **17** *nk* **Graphic Guest**[20] 6549 4-9-4 92............................[1] AdamBeschizza 19 74
(Robert Cowell) *racd nr strnds' rail: in tch: rdn along over 2f out: sn outpcd* **25/1**

1060 **18** *7* **Judge 'n Jury**[13] 6745 10-9-1 89............................(t) AdamKirby 20 46
(Ronald Harris) *racd nr stands' rail: in tch: rdn along over 2f out: sn outpcd and bhd* **20/1**

0623 **U** **Bogart**[20] 6531 5-9-6 94............................................(p) AmyRyan 9
(Kevin Ryan) *got hd stuck in stalls and uns rdr s* **7/1**[2]

59.89s (0.59) **Going Correction** +0.325s/f (Good) **19** Ran SP% **125.5**
Speed ratings (Par 107): **108,106,105,105,104 103,103,103,102,102 101,101,100,100,99 96,95,84,**
CSF £473.42 CT £5089.87 TOTE £24.10: £4.10, £10.60, £2.70, £2.00; EX 764.30 Trifecta £2483.40 Part won..
**Owner** Percy / Green Racing 2 **Bred** John McEnery **Trained** Musley Bank, N Yorks

**FOCUS**
A decent sprint handicap and drama at the start when Bogart got his head over the next stall and was unable to exit the gates with the others as a result. When he did emerge, it was without Amy Ryan. The field raced centre-to-stands' side, but those that raced closest to the nearside rail were always up against it. The winner is rated back to his old best.

## 7081 THIS ISN'T THE "STAN JAMES CHAMPION HURDLE" STKS (H'CAP) 1m 110y
**3:00** (3:02) (Class 2) (0-100,100) 3-Y-O+**£16,172** (£4,812; £2,405; £1,202) **Stalls** Low

Form RPR

-160 **1** **Homage (IRE)**[13] 6752 4-9-0 93........................ RyanMoore 2 103
(William Haggas) *in rr: hdwy 3f out: 2nd over 1f out: edgd rt and styd on to ld last 75yds* **7/1**[2]

2260 **2** *1 ½* **Spirit Of The Law (IRE)**[13] 6752 5-8-6 90.............. JackGarritty(5) 9 97
(Richard Fahey) *trckd ldrs: led 3f out: hdd and no ex wl ins fnl f* **14/1**

3210 **3** *¾* **No Poppy (IRE)**[6] 6936 6-8-7 86 oh4........................ DavidAllan 8 91
(Tim Easterby) *in rr: hdwy on inner 3f out: chsng ldrs over 1f out: styd on same pce* **20/1**

-111 **4** *2* **Gm Hopkins**[14] 6713 3-9-3 100........................ WilliamBuick 4 102
(John Gosden) *mid-div: drvn and edgd rt 2f out: kpt on same pce* **6/4**[1]

0005 **5** *¾* **Levitate**[27] 6332 6-9-2 95....................................(v) PhillipMakin 13 95
(John Quinn) *s.i.s: hdwy into midfield 6f out: styd on wl fnl f* **12/1**

5102 **6** *½* **Don't Call Me (IRE)**[20] 6534 7-9-5 98........................(t) AdrianNicholls 7 96
(David Nicholls) *in rr: drvn and hdwy over 3f out: one pce over 1f out* **14/1**

2033 **7** *2 ¾* **Crowdmania**[12] 6792 3-8-3 86 oh1........................ JoeFanning 15 80
(Mark Johnston) *in rr-div: hdwy over 3f out: hung lft 2f out: one pce* **25/1**

0130 **8** *nse* **Osteopathic Remedy (IRE)**[20] 6534 10-8-8 90....(t) ConnorBeasley(3) 1 83
(Michael Dods) *sn chsng ldrs: drvn over 3f out: n.m.r 2f out: one pce* **33/1**

0614 **9** *½* **Storm King**[27] 6320 5-8-10 89....................................(p) OisinMurphy 14 81
(David C Griffiths) *chsd ldrs: hung rt and wknd over 1f out* **16/1**

4116 **10** *nse* **Pearl Nation (USA)**[14] 6704 5-8-10 89........................ AndrewMullen 11 80
(Michael Appleby) *chsd ldrs: drvn 3f out: fdd over 1f out* **20/1**

3310 **11** *2 ¼* **Anderiego (IRE)**[6] 6936 6-8-11 90............................(b) KierenFallon 18 77
(David O'Meara) *in rr: drvn over 4f out: sme hdwy on outside over 2f out: nvr a factor* **20/1**

0006 **12** *3 ¼* **Navajo Chief**[13] 6748 7-8-9 95........................ GaryMahon(7) 16 75
(Timothy Jarvis) *chsd ldrs: drvn over 3f out: lost pl over 1f out* **25/1**

6002 **13** *½* **Starboard**[46] 5749 5-9-0 93........................ JimCrowley 17 72
(David Simcock) *swtchd lft after s: hld up in rr: nvr on terms* **16/1**

3010 **14** *nk* **Big Johnny D (IRE)**[13] 6752 5-9-3 96........................ GrahamGibbons 6 74
(David Barron) *prom: drvn over 3f out: lost pl over 1f out* **11/1**[3]

1030 **15** *3 ½* **Balducci**[13] 6748 7-9-5 98....................................(v) DanielTudhope 5 69
(David O'Meara) *led: hdd 3f out: lost pl over 1f out: bhd whn eased clsng stages* **20/1**

1m 44.57s (-1.33) **Going Correction** +0.10s/f (Good)
**WFA** 3 from 4yo+ 3lb **15** Ran SP% **123.3**
Speed ratings (Par 109): **109,107,107,105,104 104,101,101,101,101 99,96,95,95,92**
CSF £91.17 CT £1929.91 TOTE £8.40: £2.70, £4.30, £4.40; EX 95.10 Trifecta £3201.70.
**Owner** Highclere Thoroughbred Racing - Dalmeny **Bred** J Hanly **Trained** Newmarket, Suffolk

**FOCUS**
A hot handicap run at a decent pace thanks to Balducci. The runners came away from the inside rail turning for home and came up the middle up the straight. The winner was back to his reappearance form.

## 7082 BRITTAINS VODKA EBF STALLIONS MAIDEN STKS (BOBIS RACE) 5f 89y
**3:30** (3:32) (Class 3) 2-Y-O **£6,792** (£2,021; £1,010; £505) **Stalls** High

Form RPR

5 **1** **Handsome Dude**[83] 4450 2-9-5 0........................ GrahamGibbons 4 85+
(David Barron) *wnt lft s: cl up: led over 1f out: sn rdn and edgd rt ins fnl f: drvn out* **8/1**

403 **2** *1 ¼* **Brando**[33] 6168 2-9-5 78........................ GrahamLee 1 81
(Kevin Ryan) *stmbld s: racd wd: prom: effrt 2f out: rdn to chse wnr ins fnl f: kpt on* **7/4**[1]

634 **3** *2 ¾* **Quintus Cerialis (IRE)**[26] 6363 2-9-5 79........................ AdamKirby 3 71
(Clive Cox) *hmpd s and bhd: hdwy 1/2-way: rdn to chse ldrs over 1f out: kpt on u.p fnl f* **5/1**[3]

35 **4** *3* **Wolfofwallstreet (IRE)**[122] 3082 2-9-5 0........................ GeorgeBaker 7 61
(Ed Walker) *led: rdn along 2f out: hdd over 1f out: drvn ent fnl f: wknd* **16/1**

50 **5** *1 ¾* **Granola**[29] 6271 2-9-0 0........................ OisinMurphy 2 50
(David Brown) *racd wd: towards rr: hdwy over 2f out: sn rdn and kpt on one pce* **33/1**

00 **6** *7* **Reflation**[28] 6293 2-9-5 0........................ PatDobbs 11 31
(Richard Hannon) *in tch: rdn along over 2f out: sn no imp* **33/1**

6202 **7** *½* **Zuzinia (IRE)**[3] 7004 2-9-0 66........................ JoeFanning 8 25
(Mick Channon) *chsd ldrs: rdn over 2f out: sn wknd* **8/1**

05 **8** *6* **Threatorapromise (IRE)**[58] 5297 2-9-0 0........................ BarryMcHugh 6 4
(Tony Coyle) *chsd ldrs: rdn along 1/2-way: sn wknd* **33/1**

**9** *shd* **Artist Cry** 2-9-5 0........................ RyanMoore 12 9
(Richard Fahey) *racd nr stands' rail: in tch: rdn along 1/2-way: sn wknd* **7/2**[2]

**10** *2 ¾* **Forest Missile (IRE)** 2-9-5 0........................ RaulDaSilva 9
(John Wainwright) *racd nr stands' rail: chsd ldrs: rdn along 1/2-way: sn wknd* **66/1**

03 **11** *hd* **Etienne Gerard**[13] 6757 2-9-0 0........................ ShelleyBirkett(5) 10
(Nigel Tinkler) *a in rr* **25/1**

0 **12** *5* **Kinloch Pride**[33] 6168 2-9-0 0........................ DuranFentiman 13
(Noel Wilson) *racd on stands' rail: in tch: rdn along 1/2-way: sn wknd* **66/1**

1m 5.88s (1.78) **Going Correction** +0.325s/f (Good) **12** Ran SP% **119.0**
Speed ratings (Par 99): **98,96,91,86,84 72,72,62,62,57 57,49**
CSF £21.45 TOTE £8.70: £2.80, £1.30, £1.80; EX 27.60 Trifecta £54.00.
**Owner** W D & Mrs D A Glover **Bred** Fifehead Farms M C Denning **Trained** Maunby, N Yorks

**FOCUS**
The ground was changed to good to soft, soft in places before this race. Probably not the strongest maiden for York and they finished well spread out.

## 7083 PARSONAGE HOTEL AND CLOISTERS SPA STKS (H'CAP) 1m 4f
**4:05** (4:05) (Class 2) (0-100,93) 3-Y-O+ **£12,938** (£3,850; £1,924; £962) **Stalls** Centre

Form RPR

0120 **1** **Old Town Boy**[15] 6685 3-9-1 89........................ RyanMoore 6 99
(Philip McBride) *led 1f: chsd ldrs: led 2f out: edgd rt ins fnl f: styd on towards fin* **11/2**[2]

2131 **2** *1* **Emerahldz (IRE)**[55] 5442 3-8-5 86........................ JackGarritty(5) 11 92
(Richard Fahey) *led after 1f: hdd 2f out: rallied and tk 2nd last 100yds* **6/1**[3]

0103 **3** *1 ¼* **Aramist (IRE)**[13] 6747 4-9-8 89........................ RobertWinston 12 95
(Alan Swinbank) *trckd ldrs: c stands' side over 3f out: styd on wl ins fnl f: tk 3rd nr fin* **5/1**[1]

25 **4** *nk* **Esteaming**[48] 5673 4-9-12 93........................ GrahamGibbons 13 99
(David Barron) *mid-div: effrt 4f out: chsng ldrs over 2f out: upsides over 1f out: wknd towards fin* **5/1**[1]

-005 **5** *¾* **Ardlui (IRE)**[104] 3717 6-9-10 91....................................(b) DavidAllan 1 95
(Tim Easterby) *mid-div: drvn to chse ldrs over 3f out: upsides 2f out: kpt on same pce* **16/1**

1105 **6** *¾* **Saved By The Bell (IRE)**[63] 5144 4-9-7 88........................ SamJames 5 91
(David O'Meara) *mid-div: rdn over 3f out: kpt on fnl f* **11/1**

2000 **7** *nse* **Kashmir Peak (IRE)**[70] 4349 5-9-2 83........................ PhillipMakin 7 86
(John Quinn) *trckd ldrs: c stands' side over 3f out and sn upsides: one pce appr fnl f* **25/1**

5104 **8** *2* **Kings Bayonet**[36] 6061 7-9-7 88........................ HayleyTurner 9 88
(Alan King) *dwlt: t.k.h in rr: stdy hdwy over 3f out: edgd rt and c stands' side 2f out: wknd last 150yds* **9/1**

0000 **9** *¾* **Chancery (USA)**[13] 6752 6-9-10 91........................(p) DanielTudhope 2 90
(David O'Meara) *mid-div: edgd rt and racd stands' side over 2f out: nvr a threat* **11/2**[2]

0600 **10** *1* **Hi There (IRE)**[22] 6479 5-9-10 91........................ BarryMcHugh 4 88
(Richard Fahey) *t.k.h in rr: hdwy 3f out: rdn 2f out: wknd fnl f* **18/1**

360 **11** *2* **Dolphin Village (IRE)**[12] 6786 4-9-3 87.............. GeorgeChaloner(3) 10 81
(Richard Fahey) *trckd ldrs: t.k.h: c stands' side over 3f out: wknd over 1f out* **25/1**

2m 39.23s (6.03) **Going Correction** +0.10s/f (Good)
**WFA** 3 from 4yo+ 7lb **11** Ran SP% **115.6**
Speed ratings (Par 109): **83,82,81,81,80 80,80,78,78,77 76**
CSF £37.79 CT £173.01 TOTE £6.50: £2.40, £2.00, £2.00; EX 36.10 Trifecta £217.50.
**Owner** Richard Wilson (Hertfordshire) **Bred** Wood Farm Stud (Waresley) **Trained** Newmarket, Suffolk

**FOCUS**
Not a strong handicap for the class with the top weight 7lb below the race ceiling, but the form is rated slightly positively. They only went a modest pace - a few were keen as a result - and it was crucial to be handy. The runners came centre-to-nearside up the straight.

## 7084 JIGSAW SPORTS BRANDING MAIDEN AUCTION STKS (BOBIS RACE) 1m
**4:40** (4:41) (Class 4) 2-Y-O **£6,469** (£1,925; £962; £481) **Stalls** Low

Form RPR

2 **1** **Storm Rock**[35] 6085 2-8-11 0........................ WilliamBuick 5 81+
(Harry Dunlop) *cl up: chal over 2f out: led wl over 1f out: rdn clr ent fnl f: readily* **11/4**[1]

334 **2** *3 ½* **Red Rubles (IRE)**[85] 4353 2-8-13 83............................[1] DavidProbert 9 75
(Andrew Balding) *led: rdn along over 2f out: hdd wl over 1f out: drvn and kpt on same pce fnl f* **6/1**

453 **3** *shd* **Cabelo (IRE)**[17] 6641 2-8-1 77........................ JoeDoyle(5) 4 68
(Brian Ellison) *trckd ldrs on inner: hdwy 3f out: rdn wl over 1f out: kpt on same pce fnl f* **7/2**[2]

0 **4** *3 ¼* **Who Dares Wins (IRE)**[20] 6551 2-9-3 0........................ PatDobbs 12 72
(Richard Hannon) *chsd ldrs: rdn along over 2f out: kpt on same pce* **16/1**

**5** *½* **Brosnan (IRE)** 2-8-6 0........................ SamJames 10 60
(Noel Quinlan) *towards rr: hdwy on outer 3f out: pushed along 2f out: kpt on fnl f: nrst fin* **33/1**

64 **6** *1 ¼* **Comanche Chieftain (CAN)**[39] 5982 2-9-1 0............ AndrewMullen 11 66
(Michael Appleby) *plld hrd: chsd ldng pair: rdn along wl over 2f out: grad wknd* **20/1**

**7** *1* **Sun Odyssey** 2-8-12 0........................ JoeFanning 1 61
(William Haggas) *in tch: rdn along 3f out: no imp* **14/1**

6 **8** *1* **Father Bertie**[13] 6757 2-8-11 0........................ DavidAllan 2 57
(Tim Easterby) *in tch: rdn along 3f out: sn no imp* **33/1**

**9** *¾* **Bletchley Park** 2-8-13 0........................ TonyHamilton 7 58
(Richard Fahey) *towards rr: rdn along and sme hdwy wl over 2f out: n.d* **14/1**

**10** *2 ¼* **Mythical Moment** 2-8-12 0........................ RyanMoore 13 52
(William Haggas) *dwlt: green and sn rdn along in rr: sme late hdwy* **4/1**[3]

00 **11** *3* **Mr Christopher (IRE)**[21] 6509 2-8-12 0........................ JoeyHaynes(3) 6 48
(Noel Wilson) *in tch: rdn along over 3f out: sn wknd* **66/1**

0 **12** *1 ¼* **Good Move (IRE)**[44] 5813 2-8-6 0........................ JamesSullivan 8 36
(Brian Rothwell) *a towards rr* **80/1**

**13** *nse* **Ghostly Arc (IRE)** 2-8-8 0........................ PeterSword(7) 15 45
(Noel Wilson) *s.i.s: a bhd* **66/1**

005 **14** *11* **Ponty Grigio (IRE)**[23] 6449 2-9-1 55........................ DuranFentiman 14 21
(Tim Easterby) *a towards rr* **50/1**

**15** *5* **Not Again** 2-8-13 0........................ GrahamLee 3 8
(Tim Easterby) *a in rr: bhd fnl 3f* **25/1**

1m 41.94s (2.94) **Going Correction** +0.10s/f (Good) **15** Ran SP% **123.1**
Speed ratings (Par 97): **89,85,85,82,81 80,79,78,77,75 72,71,71,60,55**
CSF £18.41 TOTE £3.20: £1.30, £2.30, £1.80; EX 25.10 Trifecta £46.50.
**Owner** Malcolm & Alicia Aldis **Bred** Kempsons Stud **Trained** Lambourn, Berks

**FOCUS**
Quite a test in the ground and they finished well spread out.

## 7085 FUTURE CLEANING SERVICES APPRENTICE STKS (H'CAP) 7f
5:10 (5:12) (Class 4) (0-85,85) 3-Y-O+ £6,469 (£1,925; £962; £481) Stalls Low

Form RPR
6435 1 **Zacynthus (IRE)**[17] 6639 6-8-13 78 JordanNason(3) 10 88
(Shaun Harris) *in rr: hdwy u.p over 2f out: styd on to ld towards fin* 25/1
0000 2 ½ **Whozthecat (IRE)**[13] 6744 7-9-3 84 LukeLeadbitter(5) 18 93
(Declan Carroll) *led: drvn over 3f out: hdd and no ex towards fin* 50/1
3316 3 ½ **Instant Attraction (IRE)**[13] 6770 3-9-1 82 MeganCarberry(3) 11 88
(Jedd O'Keeffe) *in rr-div: hdwy on outside over 2f out: styd on fnl f: tk 3rd nr fin* 14/1
5201 4 1¾ **Shouranour (IRE)**[53] 5496 4-9-4 85 (p) JoshDoyle(5) 8 88
(David O'Meara) *chsd ldrs: kpt on same pce fnl 100yds* 7/1[2]
2200 5 hd **Gatepost (IRE)**[13] 6740 5-9-5 81 JackGarritty 16 83
(Richard Fahey) *chsd ldrs: outpcd over 2f out: kpt on fnl f* 10/1
206 6 ½ **Personal Touch**[62] 5199 5-9-2 78 SammyJoBell 17 79
(Richard Fahey) *chsd ldrs: one pce over 1f out* 9/1[3]
1500 7 ¾ **Repetition**[20] 6531 4-9-8 84 ShaneGray 14 83
(Kristin Stubbs) *in rr: hdwy over 2f out: kpt on: nvr nr ldrs* 25/1
3030 8 ½ **Gran Canaria Queen**[21] 6511 5-9-0 79 RachelRichardson(5) 6 77
(Tim Easterby) *in rr: hdwy over 2f out: kpt on same pce fnl f* 20/1
4003 9 hd **Regal Dan (IRE)**[49] 5650 4-9-3 82 KieranShoemark(3) 15 79
(David O'Meara) *chsd ldrs: one pce fnl 2f* 11/1
000 10 ½ **Showboating (IRE)**[14] 6713 6-9-3 79 (tp) NoelGarbutt 13 75
(Alan McCabe) *s.i.s: in rr: hdwy on outer over 2f out: edgd lft: nvr a factor* 14/1
3P05 11 2¼ **Mujazif (IRE)**[7] 6891 4-9-4 83 AnnaHesketh(3) 9 73
(David Nicholls) *in rr: hdwy on ins 3f out: wknd over 1f out* 13/2[1]
1650 12 ¾ **Fieldgunner Kirkup (GER)**[20] 6535 6-9-3 82 GemmaTutty(3) 2 70
(David Barron) *chsd ldrs: wknd over 1f out* 22/1
2000 13 hd **Talent Scout (IRE)**[24] 6430 8-9-3 82 (p) PatMillman(3) 12 70
(Karen Tutty) *chsd ldr: wknd over 1f out* 50/1
0000 14 1¼ **Askaud (IRE)**[15] 6688 6-9-8 84 (p) MatthewHopkins 5 68
(Scott Dixon) *mid-div: effrt over 2f out: nvr a threat* 20/1
15 ¾ **Rousayan (IRE)**[123] 3069 3-9-1 79 MarcMonaghan 3 60
(David O'Meara) *in rr: sme hdwy 4f out: wknd over 1f out* 14/1
0132 16 1¾ **My Single Malt (IRE)**[28] 6285 6-9-4 80 (p) JoeDoyle 4 58
(Julie Camacho) *chsd ldrs: lost pl over 1f out* 10/1
6001 17 1 **Mon Brav**[9] 6872 7-9-5 84 6ex AlistairRawlinson(3) 1 59
(Brian Ellison) *s.i.s: drvn along and a in rr* 11/1
0540 18 1¼ **Norse Blues**[20] 6534 6-9-2 83 PaulMcGiff(5) 20 55
(David Barron) *a in rr* 16/1
3000 19 22 **Dubai Hills**[14] 6704 8-9-3 84 GaryMahon(5) 19
(David O'Meara) *mid-div on outer: lost pl over 2f out: heavily eased whn bhd: tailed rt off* 22/1

1m 27.76s (2.46) **Going Correction** +0.525s/f (Yiel)
**WFA** 3 from 4yo+ 2lb **19** Ran SP% **126.4**
Speed ratings (Par 105): **106,105,104,102,102 102,101,100,100,99 97,96,96,94,93 91,90,89,64**
CSF £920.50 CT £17042.19 TOTE £41.60: £8.90, £10.50, £3.90, £2.20; EX 2400.00 Trifecta £3727.70 Part won..
**Owner** Mrs June Bownes **Bred** Keatly Overseas Ltd **Trained** Carburton, Notts
■ Stewards' Enquiry : Jordan Nason four-day ban; used whip above permitted level (24th, 27th-29th Oct)

**FOCUS**
A competitive apprentice handicap and there was no hanging about. The winner is rated to his Newcastle May figure.
T/Jkpt: Not won. T/Plt: £268.30 to a £1 stake. Pool: £158,302.19 - 430.70 winning tickets T/Qpdt: £29.90 to a £1 stake. Pool: £11,480.63 - 283.95 winning tickets WG

7086 - 7093a (Foreign Racing) - See Raceform Interactive

# 6991 CHANTILLY (R-H)
Friday, October 10

**OFFICIAL GOING: Turf: soft; polytrack: standard**

## 7094a PRIX ECLIPSE (GROUP 3) (2YO) (TURF) 6f
1:50 (1:50) 2-Y-O £33,333 (£13,333; £10,000; £6,666; £3,333)

RPR
1 **Souvenir Delondres (FR)**[31] 6220 2-8-8 0 MaximeGuyon 1 105
(J E Pease, France) *hld up bhd ldrs: rdn 1 1/2f out: led appr fnl f: r.o u.p: asserted fnl 100yds* 3/1[2]
2 ½ **La Berma (IRE)**[21] 2-8-8 0 Christophe-PatriceLemaire 9 103
(F Chappet, France) *led: scrubbed along 1 1/2f out: hdd appr fnl f: flashed tail u.p: hld fnl 100yds* 5/1[3]
3 2½ **Royal Spring (FR)**[21] 2-8-11 0 (p) ThierryThulliez 7 99
(N Clement, France) *w.w towards rr on outer but wl in tch: shkn up and hdwy over 1f out: styd on u.p fnl f: nt pce to rch first two* 13/8[1]
4 1¼ **Malicieuse (IRE)**[47] 5741 2-8-8 0 StephanePasquier 2 92
(J E Pease, France) *t.k.h: hld up bhd front rnk: dropped towards rr bef 1/2-way: sn rdn and effrt to get on terms 1 1/2f out: kpt on at same pce u.p fnl f: nt trble ldrs* 7/1
5 shd **Kenouska (FR)**[31] 6220 2-8-8 0 FabriceVeron 3 91
(H-A Pantall, France) *trckd ldr: rdn and outpcd over 1 1/2f out: kpt on at same pce u.p fnl f* 12/1
6 ¾ **El Valle (FR)**[8] 2-8-11 0 MickaelBarzalona 8 92
(Mlle V Dissaux, France) *outpcd in rr: hdwy over 1 1/2f out: kpt on fnl f: nvr plcd to chal* 25/1
7 1¾ **Kindly Dismiss (FR)**[31] 6219 2-8-8 0 ThierryJarnet 5 84
(H-A Pantall, France) *w.w towards rr but in tch: rdn to chse ldrs over 2f out: sn no further imp: wknd ins fnl f* 20/1
8 1¼ **Immediate**[18] 6619 2-8-8 0 GregoryBenoist 4 80
(D Smaga, France) *w.w bhd front rnk: midfield and pushed along 1/2-way: dropped away fnl f* 8/1
9 20 **Mocklershill (FR)**[31] 6220 2-8-11 0 CristianDemuro 6 23
(F Chappet, France) *trckd ldng pair on outer: rdn and lost pl over 2f out: sn bhd: t.o fnl f* 33/1

1m 13.32s (1.92) **9** Ran SP% **122.6**
WIN (incl. 1 euro stake): 3.50. PLACES: 1.30, 1.50, 1.20. DF: 9.30. SF: 15.20.
**Owner** Christopher Wright **Bred** Stratford Place Stud **Trained** Chantilly, France

## 7095a PRIX DU RANELAGH (LISTED RACE) (3YO+) (TURF) 1m
2:55 (2:55) 3-Y-O+ £21,666 (£8,666; £6,500; £4,333; £2,166)

RPR
1 **Roero (FR)**[40] 5960 5-9-6 0 Francois-XavierBertras 5 111
(F Rohaut, France) 14/5[2]
2 2½ **Amulet**[14] 6707 4-9-0 0 (b) ThierryJarnet 3 99
(Eve Johnson Houghton) *broke wl: trckd ldr: pushed along 2f out and nt qckn: sn rdn and relegated to 3rd appr fnl f: rallied gamely u.p to regain 2nd cl home: no ch w wnr* 114/10
3 nk **Entree**[20] 4-9-3 0 StephanePasquier 6 101
(P Bary, France) 1/1[1]
4 3 **Alice's Dancer (IRE)**[18] 6620 5-9-0 0 Christophe-PatriceLemaire 4 91
(Mme G Rarick, France) 178/10
5 1½ **Silas Marner (FR)**[18] 6620 7-9-6 0 ChristopheSoumillon 2 94
(J-C Rouget, France) 37/10[3]
6 1 **Kenbella (FR)**[37] 6055 4-9-0 0 FabriceVeron 1 86
(H-A Pantall, France) 109/10

1m 44.48s (6.48) **6** Ran SP% **119.4**
WIN (incl. 1 euro stake): 3.80. PLACES: 2.70, 4.60. SF: 38.10.
**Owner** Scea Haras De Saint Pair & F Rohaut **Bred** 6 C Racing Ltd **Trained** Sauvagnon, France

7096 - (Foreign Racing) - See Raceform Interactive

# 6790 MUSSELBURGH (R-H)
Saturday, October 11

**OFFICIAL GOING: Good (good to soft in places on straight course; 7.0)**
Wind: Almost nil Weather: Cloudy

## 7097 IRISH STALLION FARMS EBF MAIDEN STKS (BOBIS RACE) 7f 30y
1:55 (1:56) (Class 4) 2-Y-O £4,204 (£1,251; £625; £312) Stalls Low

Form RPR
3242 1 **Henrytheaeroplane (USA)**[22] 6509 2-9-2 78 GeorgeChaloner(3) 7 82
(Richard Fahey) *chsd clr ldr: drvn to ld appr fnl f: kpt on strly to go clr ins fnl f* 11/8[1]
2226 2 4½ **Ythan Waters**[47] 5760 2-9-0 77 AdamCarter(5) 8 71
(Bryan Smart) *t.k.h: led and clr: rdn: hung lft and hdd appr fnl f: kpt on same pce* 6/1[3]
4 3 2 **Thankstomonty**[7] 6935 2-9-5 0 RonanWhelan 3 66
(David O'Meara) *in tch: effrt and drvn over 2f out: kpt on same pce fr over 1f out* 9/2[2]
3250 4 6 **Summer Times**[45] 5807 2-9-5 77 LiamJones 9 51
(Mark Johnston) *in tch: drvn and outpcd over 2f out: kpt on fnl f: nvr able to chal* 10/1
53 5 nse **Cyril**[17] 6668 2-9-5 0 BarryMcHugh 2 51+
(Kevin Ryan) *hld up: drvn whn hmpd over 3f out: no imp fr 2f out* 9/2[2]
5 6 1¾ **Mr Cool Cash**[44] 5852 2-9-5 0 PJMcDonald 4 47
(Ann Duffield) *prom: drvn along 3f out: wknd wl over 1f out* 33/1
3 7 5 **Penelope Pitstop**[13] 6790 2-9-0 0 TomEaves 6 30
(Keith Dalgleish) *hld up: rdn over 2f out: sn btn* 16/1
8 23 **Poniel** 2-9-5 0 DaleSwift 1
(Ian Semple) *s.i.s and sn wl bhd: t.o thrght* 66/1

1m 29.55s (0.55) **Going Correction** +0.225s/f (Good) **8** Ran SP% **112.2**
Speed ratings (Par 97): **105,99,97,90,90 88,82,56**
CSF £9.69 TOTE £1.90: £1.10, £1.70, £2.30; EX 11.90 Trifecta £46.70.
**Owner** Middleham Park Racing LXVI **Bred** Hinkle Farms **Trained** Musley Bank, N Yorks

**FOCUS**
All rails in normal position and distances as advertised. A bright dry day and just 1mm of overnight rain meant the ground remained good (going stick 7.0) with some slightly easier patches in the straight. Just ordinary maiden form in truth with the winner the pick of the weights and much the best.

## 7098 WILSONS RUBY WEDDING (S) H'CAP 1m 1f
2:30 (2:31) (Class 5) (0-70,70) 3-Y-O+ £3,234 (£962; £481; £240) Stalls Low

Form RPR
-064 1 **An Cat Dubh (IRE)**[14] 6767 5-9-3 68 (p) DanielMuscutt(5) 2 76
(Tim Pitt) *in tch: rdn to ld over 1f out: hld on wl fnl f* 9/1
0626 2 nk **Silver Duke (IRE)**[36] 6110 3-8-12 65 GaryBartley(3) 7 76+
(Jim Goldie) *dwlt: t.k.h in rr: effrt whn nt clr run fr over 2f out tl swtchd lft rnd whole field ins fnl f: str run last 100yds: kpt on: unlucky* 14/1
2425 3 1½ **Call Of Duty (IRE)**[24] 6223 9-8-7 58 EmmaSayer(5) 11 62
(Dianne Sayer) *s.i.s: bhd: rdn over 2f out: gd hdwy and cl up whn hung rt ins fnl f: one pce towards fin* 12/1
4230 4 ½ **Staffhoss**[7] 6936 4-9-2 62 RichardKingscote 9 65
(Mark Johnston) *midfield: effrt and pushed along over 2f out: kpt on same pce ins fnl f* 5/1[2]
3004 5 2¾ **Al Muheer (IRE)**[12] 6822 9-9-8 68 (v) JasonHart 12 65
(Michael Herrington) *in tch on outside: rdn over 2f out: outpcd appr fnl f* 9/1
1-00 6 2 **Megamunch (IRE)**[47] 5761 4-9-10 70 (p) TomEaves 13 63
(Kristin Stubbs) *sn pressing ldr: drvn and ev ch over 1f out: wknd ins fnl f* 40/1
-225 7 ½ **Brooke's Bounty**[23] 6477 4-9-3 66 GeorgeChaloner(3) 6 58
(Richard Fahey) *trckd ldrs: effrt whn n.m.r over 2f out: wknd fnl f* 4/1[1]
624 8 2¾ **Gabrial The Thug (FR)**[43] 5899 4-9-2 62 (t) BarryMcHugh 3 48
(Richard Fahey) *midfield on ins: pushed along after 2f: effrt over 2f out: wknd appr fnl f* 13/2[3]
3516 9 shd **Pigeon Pie**[5] 6980 3-9-6 70 (b) LiamJones 5 57
(Mark Johnston) *t.k.h: led to over 1f out: sn rdn and btn* 10/1
2035 10 2¼ **Mount Cheiron (USA)**[21] 6544 3-8-6 56 oh2 PJMcDonald 1 38
(Dianne Sayer) *bhd: drvn along over 3f out: nvr on terms* 14/1
600 11 1 **Royal Straight**[13] 6795 9-8-6 57 (t) SammyJoBell(5) 10 36
(Linda Perratt) *dwlt: bhd: rdn over 3f out: btn fnl 2f* 25/1
2460 12 16 **Iftikaar (IRE)**[26] 6405 4-9-2 62 DuranFentiman 8 8
(Philip Kirby) *prom tl rdn and wknd fr 2f out* 8/1

1m 54.8s (0.90) **Going Correction** +0.225s/f (Good)
**WFA** 3 from 4yo+ 4lb **12** Ran SP% **117.5**
Speed ratings (Par 103): **105,104,103,102,100 98,98,95,95,93 92,78**
CSF £127.31 CT £1544.92 TOTE £12.00: £2.90, £5.30, £3.40; EX 216.90 Trifecta £1594.90.The winner was bought in for £4,600.
**Owner** Paul Wildes **Bred** Kildare Racing Syndicate **Trained** Market Drayton, Shropshire
■ Stewards' Enquiry : Daniel Muscutt four-day ban: used whip above permitted level (Oct 27-30)
Gary Bartley jockey said gelding was denied a clear run

**FOCUS**
Quite a competitive event for the grade but, while the pace looked sound, the field grouped up towards the far rail in the straight and there were one or two hard-luck stories, most notably the runner-up. The winner's best form since last May.

## 7099 BRITISH STALLION STUDS EBF CONDITIONS STKS (BOBIS RACE) 5f
**3:00** (3:02) (Class 3) 2-Y-O £9,703 (£2,887; £1,443; £721) **Stalls** High

Form RPR
130 **1** **Zuhoor Baynoona (IRE)**[14] 6751 2-8-7 89 ow1..... GeorgeChaloner(3) 1 93+
(Richard Fahey) *cl up: carried rt for 1f: sn swtchd lft to r in stands' side gp: led 1/2-way: rdn clr fnl f* 11/2

4402 **2** 4 **Lightscameraction (IRE)**[5] 6991 2-8-9 95............... DanielMuscutt(5) 2 89+
(Gay Kelleway) *cl up: carried rt for nrly 2f: sn swtchd lft to r alone in centre: effrt and chsd wnr over 1f out: kpt on same pce fnl f* 11/4[1]

3004 **3** 1 1/2 **She's A Worldie (IRE)**[14] 6739 2-8-9 89....................... PJMcDonald 5 72
(Bryan Smart) *cl up stands' side: drvn and edgd rt 2f out: sn one pce* 11/4[1]

1106 **4** nk **Showing Character**[15] 6703 2-9-5 97....................... RichardKingscote 3 81
(Tom Dascombe) *hung bdly rt fr stalls and ended up on far rail after nrly 2f: overall ldr to 1/2-way: pushed along and wknd over 1f out* 9/2[3]

021 **5** 14 **Canny Kool**[24] 6453 2-9-0 84........................................ TomEaves 6 26
(Brian Ellison) *dwlt: prom stands' side tl rdn and wknd fr over 2f out* 7/2[2]

1m 0.4s **Going Correction** +0.225s/f (Good) **5 Ran SP% 109.1**
Speed ratings (Par 99): **109,102,100,99,77**
CSF £20.24 TOTE £5.70: £3.50, £1.10; EX 19.40 Trifecta £48.30.
**Owner** Jaber Abdullah **Bred** Rabbah Bloodstock Limited **Trained** Musley Bank, N Yorks

**FOCUS**
An open little conditions race but the start proved crucial. It's hard to pin the form down but it's very much in keeping with the winner's early profile.

## 7100 BETFAIR SCOTTISH STAYERS' SERIES FINAL (H'CAP) 1m 5f
**3:35** (3:35) (Class 3) 3-Y-O+ £9,703 (£2,887; £1,443; £721) **Stalls** Centre

Form RPR
0163 **1** **Titus Bolt (IRE)**[36] 6113 5-8-10 60............................... GaryBartley(3) 10 68
(Jim Goldie) *mde all: qcknd clr over 5f out: rdn over 2f out: edgd lft ins fnl f: hld on gamely* 9/1

1332 **2** nk **Clear Spell (IRE)**[18] 6637 3-9-4 73.............................. PJMcDonald 6 80
(Alistair Whillans) *hld up: rdn over 2f out: hdwy over 1f out: chsd wnr ins fnl f: kpt on: hld cl home* 6/1[2]

1650 **3** hd **Gold Chain (IRE)**[6] 6113 4-8-11 63............................. EmmaSayer(5) 7 70
(Dianne Sayer) *dwlt: hld up: rdn and hung rt over 3f out: hdwy on outside over 1f out: kpt on fnl f: hld towards fin* 16/1

4616 **4** 1 **Pressure Point**[21] 6536 4-9-10 71.................................. TomEaves 12 77
(Keith Dalgleish) *in tch on outside: hdwy to chse (clr) wnr 3f out: sn rdn and hung rt: lost 2nd over 1f out: kpt on same pce ins fnl f* 8/1

4146 **5** nk **Giovanni Jack**[36] 6113 4-9-7 68................................... DuranFentiman 9 73
(Alan Swinbank) *hld up: rdn 3f out: gd hdwy to chse wnr over 1f out to ins fnl f: sn outpcd* 16/1

5454 **6** hd **Latin Rebel (IRE)**[2] 7059 7-8-8 55.................................. JamesSullivan 2 60
(Jim Goldie) *midfield: rdn and outpcd 3f out: rallied over 1f out: no imp ins fnl f* 7/1[3]

060 **7** 2 **Vittachi**[12] 6825 7-7-11 51 ow1......................................(p) RowanScott(7) 5 53
(Alistair Whillans) *prom: hmpd bnd after 2f: rdn over 3f out: outpcd over 1f out* 22/1

4540 **8** 1 **A Southside Boy (GER)**[11] 6832 6-8-9 59............ GeorgeChaloner(3) 11 59
(Jim Goldie) *t.k.h: chsd wnr tl hmpd bnd after 2f: prom: rdn over 3f out: wknd appr fnl f* 8/1

232 **9** 1 1/4 **Dhaular Dhar (IRE)**[12] 6825 12-8-10 62.................... SammyJoBell(5) 3 60
(Jim Goldie) *dwlt: hld up: rdn and hung rt over 3f out: hdwy over 1f out: sn no imp* 12/1

1562 **10** 1/2 **Voice From Above (IRE)**[18] 6644 5-8-6 53...................... JasonHart 14 51
(Patrick Holmes) *prom: hmpd bnd after 2f: struggling wl over 2f out: sn btn* 20/1

2320 **11** 8 **Testa Rossa (IRE)**[23] 6480 4-8-13 60.............................. DaleSwift 13 46
(Jim Goldie) *hld up in midfield: drvn and outpcd 3f out: n.d after* 10/1

3135 **12** 2 1/4 **Right Of Appeal**[4] 7008 3-9-4 73.................................... LiamJones 1 55
(Mark Johnston) *t.k.h: cl up on ins: hmpd after 2f but sn chsng wnr: rdn 3f out: wknd 2f out* 4/1[1]

2m 53.93s (1.93) **Going Correction** +0.225s/f (Good)
**WFA** 3 from 4yo+ 8lb **12 Ran SP% 116.7**
Speed ratings (Par 107): **103,102,102,102,101 101,100,99,98 93,92**
CSF £61.15 CT £858.32 TOTE £10.60: £4.10, £1.20, £4.10; EX 69.80 Trifecta £833.10.
**Owner** Ian G M Dalgleish **Bred** Patrick Brady **Trained** Uplawmoor, E Renfrews

**FOCUS**
A wide-open stayers' series final which was run at a strong pace thanks to the winner. The compressed finish makes for an ordinary level of form.

## 7101 GRAPHIC IMPRESSIONS 21ST ANNIVERSARY CONDITIONS STKS 5f
**4:15** (4:15) (Class 2) 3-Y-O+ £12,938 (£3,850; £1,924; £962) **Stalls** High

Form RPR
506 **1** **One Chance (IRE)**[21] 6549 3-9-0 93........................(p) DanielMuscutt 6 87
(John Butler) *trckd ldrs: effrt and rdn over 1f out: edgd rt and led ins fnl f: drvn out* 6/1[2]

5045 **2** 1 1/2 **Borderlescott**[24] 6467 12-10-1 89................................ DaleSwift 2 95
(Robin Bastiman) *trckd ldrs: rdn over 2f out: hdwy and ev ch ins fnl f: kpt on same pce towards fin* 14/1

0612 **3** hd **Kickboxer (IRE)**[7] 6918 3-9-5 101................................ SamHitchcott 3 86
(Mick Channon) *dwlt: sn pushed along in tch: drvn 1/2-way: hdwy whn nt clr run and swtchd rt appr fnl f: kpt on u.p last 100yds* 4/5[1]

0010 **4** 3/4 **Doc Hay (USA)**[30] 6260 7-9-12 85................................ RonanWhelan 7 89
(David O'Meara) *s.i.s: bhd: hdwy on outside over 1f out: kpt on ins fnl f: nrst fin* 20/1

1100 **5** 1 3/4 **Searchlight**[22] 6511 3-9-5 85........................................ BarryMcHugh 5 77
(Kevin Ryan) *w ldr: rdn over 1f out: outpcd ins fnl f* 14/1

0024 **6** nse **Tangerine Trees**[18] 6624 9-10-1 95................................(v) TomEaves 4 86
(Bryan Smart) *led: rdn over 1f out: hdd ins fnl f: sn no ex* 8/1

5003 **7** 7 **Burning Thread (IRE)**[18] 6624 7-10-1 90.................(b) JamesSullivan 8 60
(Tim Etherington) *bhd: struggling 1/2-way: nvr on terms* 25/1

1-62 **8** 1/2 **Viva Verglas (IRE)**[155] 2116 3-9-8 96...........................(b) JasonHart 1 53
(David Barron) *in tch: drvn and outpcd 1/2-way: hung rt and wknd wl over 1f out* 7/1[3]

1m 0.97s (0.57) **Going Correction** +0.225s/f (Good) **8 Ran SP% 115.4**
Speed ratings (Par 109): **104,101,101,100,97 97,86,85**
CSF £84.05 TOTE £9.80: £2.20, £3.10, £1.10; EX 70.80 Trifecta £246.10.
**Owner** Recycled Products Limited **Bred** Mrs C Regalado-Gonzalez **Trained** Newmarket, Suffolk

**FOCUS**
This conditions event looked at the mercy of Kickboxer, but he disappointed. The winner did not need to be at her best.

## 7102 WILLIE PARK TROPHY (H'CAP) (BOBIS RACE) 1m 6f
**4:50** (4:53) (Class 2) (0-100,97) 3-Y-O £16,172 (£4,812; £2,405; £1,202) **Stalls** Centre

Form RPR
2111 **1** **Chesil Beach**[14] 6741 3-8-6 82...................................... SamHitchcott 5 92+
(Andrew Balding) *stdd in tch: effrt over 2f out: led appr fnl f: rdn and r.o wl fnl f* 7/2[2]

2222 **2** 1 **Altaayil (IRE)**[28] 6344 3-8-13 89..................................... TomEaves 1 97
(Sir Michael Stoute) *led at stdy pce: rdn and edgd lft over 2f out: hdd appr fnl f: kpt on: hld towards fin* 7/2[2]

2102 **3** 6 **Thorntoun Care**[21] 6536 3-8-2 78 oh2......................... JamesSullivan 6 78
(Jim Goldie) *hld up: drvn and outpcd over 3f out: rallied to chse clr ldng pair appr fnl f: no imp* 11/1

0041 **4** 3/4 **Swivel**[14] 6747 3-9-7 97................................................ LiamJones 7 96
(Mark Johnston) *t.k.h: chsd ldr: rdn and ev ch over 2f out: wknd over 1f out* 11/4[1]

2122 **5** 2 1/4 **Indira**[21] 6541 3-7-13 78................................................ RosieJessop(3) 3 73
(John Berry) *t.k.h: cl up: effrt and edgd lft over 2f out: wknd over 1f out* 5/1[3]

2411 **6** 2 1/2 **Stanarley Pic**[12] 6825 3-8-4 80...................................... DuranFentiman 4 72
(Alan Swinbank) *t.k.h: prom: drvn along over 2f out: wknd over 1f out* 8/1

424 **7** 3/4 **Jammy Moment**[11] 6832 3-7-11 78 oh12........................ SammyJoBell(5) 2 69
(Linda Perratt) *cl up tl rdn and wknd fr 2f out* 33/1

3m 6.46s (1.16) **Going Correction** +0.225s/f (Good) **7 Ran SP% 110.2**
Speed ratings (Par 107): **105,104,101,100,99 97,97**
CSF £14.89 TOTE £3.90: £2.80, £2.50; EX 11.90 Trifecta £101.60.
**Owner** Kingsclere Racing Club **Bred** Kingsclere Stud **Trained** Kingsclere, Hants

**FOCUS**
A competitive 3yo staying handicap for the track and, although the early gallop was only steady, the front two, led by the progressive winner, drew clear in the final two furlongs to prove well ahead of their rivals off their current marks.

## 7103 LUDDON-FRONT RUNNER IN CONSTRUCTION H'CAP 5f
**5:25** (5:27) (Class 5) (0-75,76) 3-Y-O+ £3,234 (£962; £481; £240) **Stalls** High

Form RPR
1434 **1** **Flash City (ITY)**[16] 6695 6-9-4 72........................(p) JamesSullivan 6 82
(Ruth Carr) *trckd ldrs: effrt and rdn over 1f out: led ins fnl f: rdn out* 13/2[3]

6452 **2** 1 **Classy Anne**[12] 6824 4-9-5 76........................................ GaryBartley(3) 2 82
(Jim Goldie) *cl up: rdn to ld over 1f out: hdd ins fnl f: kpt on same pce towards fin* 3/1[1]

6663 **3** 1 **Jinky**[11] 6835 6-9-0 68................................................ TomEaves 10 70
(Linda Perratt) *hld up in tch: rdn 1/2-way: hdwy and edgd rt over 1f out: kpt on ins fnl f* 6/1[2]

0022 **4** nk **Bronze Beau**[7] 6938 7-8-7 66.................................(t) ShaneGray(5) 5 67
(Kristin Stubbs) *led tl rdn and hdd over 1f out: kpt on same pce ins fnl f* 8/1

5600 **5** 1 **Bunce (IRE)**[22] 6512 6-9-5 73..................................... PJMcDonald 1 71
(Linda Perratt) *in tch on outside: rdn 2f out: kpt on same pce fnl f* 11/1

0106 **6** 3/4 **Ambitious Icarus**[14] 6758 5-9-6 74..............................(e) JasonHart 8 69
(Richard Guest) *hld up: hmpd after 2f: rdn and effrt over 1f out: kpt on: nvr rchd ldrs* 8/1

3100 **7** hd **Go Go Green (IRE)**[22] 6512 8-8-12 71........................ SammyJoBell(5) 4 65
(Jim Goldie) *blindfold slow to remove and missed break: bhd: hdwy on outside over 2f out: rdn and no imp fnl f* 9/1

1600 **8** 2 **Noodles Blue Boy**[14] 6763 8-9-7 75...........................(p) DaleSwift 11 62
(Ollie Pears) *cl up tl rdn and wknd over 1f out* 8/1

2133 **9** 2 3/4 **Eva Clare (IRE)**[173] 1615 3-8-7 68............................. PeterSword(7) 9 46
(K R Burke) *t.k.h: in tch: nt clr run and swtchd rt after 2f: n.m.r 2f out: sn rdn and btn* 20/1

6300 **10** 4 1/2 **Perfect Blossom**[14] 6763 7-8-13 70..................... GeorgeChaloner(3) 3 31
(Alan Berry) *dwlt: bhd and pushed along: struggling fr 2f out* 20/1

060- **11** 12 **Sandwith**[466] 3933 11-8-7 61........................................(p) BarryMcHugh 7
(Ian Semple) *t.k.h: cl up tl nt clr run and lost pl over 1f out: sn btn and eased* 50/1

1m 1.65s (1.25) **Going Correction** +0.225s/f (Good) **11 Ran SP% 115.8**
Speed ratings (Par 103): **99,97,95,95,93 92,92,89,84,77 58**
CSF £25.20 CT £126.27 TOTE £7.80: £3.40, £1.20, £2.30; EX 31.10 Trifecta £121.10.
**Owner** S R Jackson **Bred** G Riccioni Et Al **Trained** Huby, N Yorks

**FOCUS**
An open handicap full of exposed performers. The winner rates up a length on this year's form.
T/Plt: £71.00 to a £1 stake. Pool: £49,795.73 - 511.85 winning tickets T/Qpdt: £8.30 to a £1 stake. Pool: £3,341.95 - 297.42 winning tickets RY

# 6924 NEWMARKET (R-H)
Saturday, October 11

**OFFICIAL GOING: Good (7.5)**
Wind: light, behind Weather: overcast

## 7104 BETFRED GOALS GALORE AUTUMN STKS (GROUP 3) 1m
**2:05** (2:05) (Class 1) 2-Y-O
£28,355 (£10,750; £5,380; £2,680; £1,345; £675) **Stalls** Low

Form RPR
41 **1** **Commemorative**[30] 6259 2-9-1 0.................................... JamesDoyle 3 105
(Charles Hills) *mde virtually all: rdn and wnt clr wl over 1f out: drifing lft 1f out: drvn ins fnl f: styd on and in command fnl 75yds* 10/1

13 **2** 1 **Restorer**[31] 6241 2-9-1 84......................................... MartinDwyer 10 103
(William Muir) *dropped in bhd after s: hld up in rr: rdn and hdwy over 1f out: chsd wnr and hung rt 1f out: styd on but no imp towards fin* 33/1

12 **3** 1 1/2 **Future Empire**[42] 5926 2-9-1 0................................... RichardHughes 4 99
(Saeed bin Suroor) *chsd ldr tl over 6f out: chsd ldrs tl lost pl and rdn over 2f out: swtchd rt and rallied u.p over 1f out: styd on to go 3rd ins fnl f: no threat to wnr* 11/4[1]

21 **4** 3/4 **Strong Chemistry**[19] 6603 2-9-1 0................................ WilliamBuick 1 98
(Charlie Appleby) *t.k.h early: chsd ldrs: wnt 2nd and hung lft u.p 2f out: lost 2nd and no ex 1f out: wknd ins fnl f* 5/1[3]

**5** 1 3/4 **Order Of St George (IRE)**[58] 5360 2-9-1 0.............. JosephO'Brien 7 94+
(A P O'Brien, Ire) *in tch in midfield: bmpd and hmpd 2f out: effrt u.p over 1f out: styd on same pce fnl f* 3/1[2]

621 **6** *nk* **Jolievitesse (FR)**[31] 6225 2-9-1 87........................ JimCrowley 6 94
(K R Burke) *bmpd s: t.k.h: hld up in tch in last trio: effrt whn short of room and hmpd 2f out: pushed along and rallied 1f out: kpt on ins fnl f: nvr trbld ldrs* **14/1**

21 **7** *nk* **Bartholomew Fair**[23] 6497 2-9-1 0........................ AndreaAtzeni 9 92
(Luca Cumani) *in tch in midfield: effrt and hung rt 2f out: stl edging rt and no imp over 1f out: plugged on* **7/1**

611 **8** *nk* **Mukhayyam**[35] 6151 2-9-1 87........................ RyanMoore 2 91
(Sir Michael Stoute) *in tch towards rr: effrt 2f out: no imp fr over 1f out* **8/1**

5411 **9** *4* **Dance Of Fire**[28] 6331 2-9-1 81........................ OisinMurphy 5 82
(Andrew Balding) *wnt lft and bmpd rival s: rcvrd to chse wnr over 6f out tl 2f out: wknd over 1f out: bhd fnl f* **20/1**

1m 37.91s (-0.69) **Going Correction** +0.025s/f (Good) **9** Ran SP% **115.4**
Speed ratings: **104,103,101,100,99 98,98,98,94**
CSF £274.70 TOTE £11.40: £2.50, £7.00, £1.50; EX 709.40 Trifecta £779.40.
**Owner** K Abdullah **Bred** Juddmonte Farms Ltd **Trained** Lambourn, Berks
■ Stewards' Enquiry : Martin Dwyer two-day ban: used whip in incorrect place (Oct 27-28)

**FOCUS**
Stands' side course used. Stalls: All races Far side. Reposition of bend into home straight increased 12f and 18f races by 13m. Newmarket had avoided much of the rain in recent days and the ground was given as good. Last year's Autumn Stakes was won by subsequent Racing Post Trophy and St Leger hero Kingston Hill, while the 2012 running went to Trading Leather, who later landed the Irish Derby. This latest edition looked rank ordinary in comparison. The third is rated 5lb below his Solario form.

## 7105 BETFRED MOBILE PRIDE STKS (FORMERLY THE SEVERALS STAKES) (LISTED RACE) (F&M) 1m 2f

**2:40** (2:40) (Class 1) 3-Y-0+
**£22,684** (£8,600; £4,304; £2,144; £1,076; £540) **Stalls** Low

Form RPR

3U-2 **1** **Albasharah (USA)**[24] 6464 5-9-3 103........................ FrederikTylicki 5 113
(Saeed bin Suroor) *travelled wl thrght: in tch in midfield: hdwy to ld 4f out: rdn and readily asserted over 1f out: r.o strly: easily* **5/1**[1]

3130 **2** *3 1/2* **Talmada (USA)**[114] 3376 3-8-12 97........................ AndreaAtzeni 6 106
(Roger Varian) *in tch in midfield: hdwy to chse wnr over 2f out: drvn to press wnr wl over 1f out: brushed aside over 1f out: no ch w wnr but kpt on for clr 2nd fnl f* **8/1**[3]

3012 **3** *4 1/2* **Wahgah (USA)**[21] 6566 3-8-12 95........................ KierenFallon 4 98
(Saeed bin Suroor) *in tch in midfield: effrt u.p ent fnl 2f: 3rd but no threat to ldng pair over 1f out: battled on to hold 3rd fnl f* **20/1**

462- **4** *nse* **La Banderilla (FR)**[336] 7829 4-9-3 99........................ WilliamBuick 9 98
(John Gosden) *hld up in tch in midfield: hdwy over 3f out: drvn and chsd ldng pair 2f: no imp and battling for 3rd after: kpt on* **14/1**

113 **5** *shd* **Provenance**[15] 6707 3-8-12 102........................ RyanMoore 12 98
(Sir Michael Stoute) *in tch in midfield: rdn 3f out: swtchd rt and effrt u.p 2f out: no ch w ldrs but battling for 3rd 1f out: kpt on* **6/1**[2]

6403 **6** *2 1/2* **Mutatis Mutandis (IRE)**[21] 6532 3-8-12 94........................ LukeMorris 1 93
(Ed Walker) *wl in tch in midfield: rdn 3f out: unable qck u.p 2f out: wl hld and plugged on same pce after* **25/1**

2311 **7** *1/2* **This Is The Day**[14] 6746 3-8-12 92........................ MartinLane 18 92
(Charlie Fellowes) *wl in tch in midfield: u.p and unable qck over 2f out: wl hld and plugged on same pce fr over 1f out* **20/1**

1063 **8** *3/4* **Marsh Daisy**[17] 6655 3-9-1 102........................ JimmyFortune 19 93
(Hughie Morrison) *in tch in midfield: hdwy to chse ldrs and rdn over 2f out: btn and edgd rt over 1f out: sn wknd* **10/1**

0541 **9** *3 3/4* **Placidia (IRE)**[23] 6500 3-8-12 87........................ FrankieDettori 15 83
(David Lanigan) *hld up in tch in rr: effrt but stl plenty to do over 2f out: sme hdwy 2f out: no imp and wl hld whn hung rt over 1f out* **22/1**

5363 **10** *nk* **Vanity Rules**[15] 6708 4-9-3 98........................ JamesDoyle 8 83
(Ed Vaughan) *in tch in midfield: rdn and effrt over 2f out: sn btn: wknd over 1f out: eased ins fnl f* **9/1**

2211 **11** *3* **Blue Waltz**[30] 6258 3-8-12 94........................ RichardHughes 13 77
(Luca Cumani) *hld up in tch in midfield: effrt over 2f out: no prog and hung rt over 1f out: wknd: eased ins fnl f* **6/1**[2]

2421 **12** *1* **Toast Of The Town (IRE)**[51] 5606 4-9-3 94........................(p) RobertHavlin 3 75
(John Gosden) *in tch in midfield: hdwy to chse ldrs 3f out: rdn and unable qck 2f out: edgd lft and btn and over 1f out: wknd and eased ins fnl f* **25/1**

40 **13** *1 1/4* **Kallisha**[84] 4443 3-8-12 90........................ PatDobbs 17 73
(Ralph Beckett) *hld up in tch in rr: struggling u.p 4f out: bhd over 2f out* **33/1**

2100 **14** *3 1/4* **Cosseted**[30] 6257 4-9-3 91........................(v[1]) TomQueally 2 67
(James Fanshawe) *s.i.s: hld up towards rr: rdn and sme hdwy 4f out: lost pl over 2f out: sn wknd: bhd over 1f out* **25/1**

4624 **15** *1* **Magic Art (IRE)**[35] 6156 4-9-3 80........................ MartinHarley 16 65
(Marco Botti) *led tl 4f out: lost 2nd and struggling u.p over 2f out: wknd over 1f out: bhd and eased fnl f* **66/1**

5110 **16** *2 1/4* **Perfect Light (IRE)**[24] 6464 3-8-12 89........................ JoeFanning 10 60
(William Haggas) *chsd ldrs tl 3f out: sn lost pl u.p: bhd over 1f out: eased ins fnl f* **28/1**

302 **17** *3 1/4* **Nullarbor Sky (IRE)**[24] 6465 4-9-3 87........................(p) OisinMurphy 7 54
(Lucy Wadham) *chsd ldrs tl over 3f out: lost pl ent fnl 2f: wl btn and eased ins fnl f* **50/1**

2m 1.62s (-4.18) **Going Correction** +0.025s/f (Good)
**WFA** 3 from 4yo+ 5lb **17** Ran SP% **117.4**
Speed ratings: **117,114,110,110,110 108,108,107,104,104 101,101,100,97,96 94,92**
CSF £35.49 TOTE £6.10: £1.80, £2.70, £6.30; EX 39.40 Trifecta £1281.90.
**Owner** Godolphin **Bred** Darley **Trained** Newmarket, Suffolk

**FOCUS**
A high-quality Listed event. It will be interesting to see if the impressive winner can build on this.

## 7106 BETFRED TV STKS (HERITAGE H'CAP) (BOBIS RACE) 1m 4f

**3:10** (3:14) (Class 2) (0-105,106) 3-Y-0
**£62,250** (£18,640; £9,320; £4,660; £2,330; £1,170) **Stalls** Low

Form RPR

40 **1** **Farquhar (IRE)**[29] 6287 3-8-5 89........................ LukeMorris 10 100
(Peter Chapple-Hyam) *hld up towards rr: styd far side st: hdwy and nt clr run over 2f out: swtchd lft 2f out: drvn to ld over 1f out: battled on wl fnl f: all out* **40/1**

1626 **2** *hd* **Adventure Seeker (IRE)**[29] 6287 3-8-10 94........................ JimCrowley 5 105
(Ed Vaughan) *hld up towards rr: styd far side st: hdwy over 2f out: rdn to chal over 1f out: sustained duel w wnr fnl f: styd on wl: a jst hld* **22/1**

5311 **3** *1* **Cinnilla**[36] 6091 3-7-12 85........................ CamHardie(3) 16 94
(Ralph Beckett) *hld up in midfield: c centre st: effrt 3f out: drvn and chsd ldrs over 1f out: styd on ins fnl f* **25/1**

1222 **4** *1/2* **Knife Point (GER)**[4] 7020 3-8-1 85 ow1........................(p) MartinDwyer 21 93
(Hugo Palmer) *chsd ldrs: c centre st: effrt 3f out: pressing overall ldrs u.p 2f out: kpt on same pce fnl f* **25/1**

215 **5** *2* **Nabatean (IRE)**[91] 4183 3-8-1 85........................ HayleyTurner 13 90
(Andrew Balding) *chsd ldrs: c centre st: rdn and hdwy to chal 2f out: no ex over 1f out: wknd ins fnl f* **10/1**

5115 **6** *1 1/2* **Mistiroc**[23] 6479 3-8-6 90 ow1........................ FergalLynch 8 93
(Jim Goldie) *hld up in tch: styd far side st: rdn over 3f out: hdwy u.p over 1f out: styd on wl ins fnl f: nvr trbld ldrs* **33/1**

2-61 **7** *1/2* **Top Tug (IRE)**[134] 2748 3-8-10 94........................ RyanMoore 19 96+
(Sir Michael Stoute) *hld up in rr: c centre st: effrt and switching lft over 2f out: unbalanced and wnt sharply lft over 1f out: pushed along and styd on ins fnl f: nvr trbld ldrs* **10/1**

411 **8** *hd* **Rewaaya (IRE)**[21] 6559 3-8-11 95........................ FrankieDettori 4 97
(John Gosden) *dwlt and hmpd leaving stalls: in tch: styd far side st: effrt to press ldrs and flashed tail u.p 2f out: btn 1f out: wknd ins fnl f* **9/1**[3]

1113 **9** *1/2* **Connecticut**[49] 5691 3-9-6 104........................ AndreaAtzeni 2 105
(Luca Cumani) *in tch: styd far side st: rdn 3f out: drvn and unable qck over 1f out: wknd ins fnl f* **7/1**[1]

1162 **10** *shd* **Fire Fighting (IRE)**[7] 6930 3-9-8 106........................(b) JoeFanning 20 107
(Mark Johnston) *hld up in rr: c centre st: rdn and effrt 3f out: kpt on u.p fnl f: nvr trbld ldrs* **20/1**

1000 **11** *2 1/2* **Our Gabrial (IRE)**[14] 6737 3-8-7 91........................ JohnFahy 22 88
(Richard Fahey) *hld up towards rr: c centre st: effrt 3f out: sme hdwy over 1f out: kpt on: nvr trbld ldrs* **100/1**

2112 **12** *1* **Epsom Hill (SWE)**[35] 6133 3-9-0 98........................ JamesDoyle 6 93
(Charlie Fellowes) *chsd ldrs: styd far side st: rdn 3f out: struggling whn squeezed for room over 1f out: wknd fnl f* **14/1**

3-11 **13** *1* **Stetchworth (IRE)**[7] 6937 3-8-0 84........................ FrannyNorton 9 77
(Mark Johnston) *mde most: styd far side st: rdn 3f out: drvn and hdd over 1f out: wknd fnl f* **8/1**[2]

1160 **14** *1 3/4* **Penhill**[35] 6127 3-8-4 88........................ BenCurtis 18 79
(James Bethell) *hld up in midfield: c centre st: effrt u.p 3f out: wknd over 1f out* **33/1**

62-1 **15** *1 1/2* **Flag War (GER)**[28] 6344 3-8-8 92........................ FrederikTylicki 23 80
(Saeed bin Suroor) *hld up towards rr: c centre st: hdwy into midfield 4f out: drvn and btn 2f out: sn wknd* **25/1**

2165 **16** *1 1/2* **Galizzi (USA)**[15] 6705 3-8-0 89........................ JoeDoyle(5) 12 75
(Michael Bell) *chsd ldr tl 9f out: styd far side st and styd handy: no ex u.p 2f out: wknd over 1f out* **50/1**

1611 **17** *4* **Famous Kid (USA)**[14] 6756 3-9-2 100........................ RichardHughes 15 79
(Saeed bin Suroor) *restless in stalls: in tch in midfield: c centre st: rdn and no rspnse over 2f out: wknd and edgd rt over 1f* **12/1**

0533 **18** *3 1/2* **Ventura Quest (USA)**[14] 6737 3-8-0 84........................ FrankieMcDonald 11 58
(Richard Fahey) *in tch in midfield: c centre st: rdn and no rspnse over 2f out: btn whn hmpd over 1f out: wknd* **50/1**

5211 **19** *10* **Battersea**[35] 6127 3-9-2 100........................ GrahamLee 7 58
(Roger Varian) *in tch in midfield: c centre st: rdn 3f out: no hdwy and btn 2f out: sn wknd: eased ins fnl f: t.o* **8/1**[2]

3210 **20** *5* **Hesketh Bank**[91] 4183 3-8-0 84 oh1........................ JimmyQuinn 3 34
(Richard Fahey) *in tch in midfield: styd far side st: struggling u.p 3f out: wl bhd and eased over 1f out: t.o* **50/1**

5132 **21** *1 1/4* **Saab Almanal**[22] 6518 3-8-11 95........................ TomQueally 14 43
(James Fanshawe) *in tch toward rr: c centre sraight: rdn and hmpd over 2f out: sn btn: eased fnl f: t.o* **25/1**

2160 **22** *26* **Miner's Lamp (IRE)**[91] 4183 3-9-6 104........................ WilliamBuick 24 10
(Charlie Appleby) *midfield: hdwy to chse ldrs and racd centre: pressed overall ldr 9f out tl 3f out: sn dropped out: wl bhd and eased over 1f out: t.o* **25/1**

6010 **23** *1 1/4* **Latenightrequest**[14] 6737 3-8-5 89........................ ChrisCatlin 17
(Richard Fahey) *in tch: racd centre: rdn and lost pl 4f out: t.o and eased over 1f out* **66/1**

5 **24** *19* **Min Alemarat (IRE)**[55] 5481 3-8-11 95........................ MartinHarley 1
(Marco Botti) *chsd ldrs: styd far side st: lost pl qckly 4f out: bhd and eased 2f out: t.o* **16/1**

2m 30.42s (-1.58) **Going Correction** +0.025s/f (Good) **24** Ran SP% **128.2**
Speed ratings (Par 107): **106,105,105,104,103 102,102,102,101,101 100,99,98,97,96 95,92,90,83,80 79,62,61,48**
CSF £752.38 CT £20088.72 TOTE £51.30: £7.70, £5.40, £5.70, £6.00; EX 814.10 Trifecta £2991.80.
**Owner** T Elliott & P Cunningham **Bred** D G Iceton **Trained** Newmarket, Suffolk

**FOCUS**
A superb new £100,000 3yo handicap - really competitive - although several of the more interesting ones didn't fire and the finish was dominated by outsiders. They were spread all over the place in the closing stages, but with the winner and second far side, the third and fourth near side, and the fifth up the middle, there was no obvious bias. The first three had all raced over further and their stamina was a key asset.

## 7107 BETFRED CESAREWITCH (HERITAGE H'CAP) 2m 2f

**3:50** (3:57) (Class 2) 3-Y-0+
**£155,625** (£46,600; £23,300; £11,650; £5,825; £2,925) **Stalls** Low

Form RPR

00-2 **1** **Big Easy (GER)**[21] 6557 7-8-7 87........................(p) TomQueally 2 97
(Philip Hobbs) *trckd ldrs: rdn to hold pl over 3f out: styng on whn swtchd lft ent fnl f: str run to ld towards fin: drvn out* **10/1**[2]

1103 **2** *3/4* **De Rigueur**[42] 5920 6-9-7 101........................(tp) AndreaAtzeni 13 110
(Marco Botti) *hld up towards rr: stdy prog fr 4f out: rdn to chse ldrs 2f out: mounting chal whn squeezed up ent fnl f: styd on wl w wnr: wnt 2nd fnl strides* **25/1**

12-1 **3** *shd* **Quick Jack (IRE)**[75] 4746 5-9-0 94........................ RichardHughes 12 103
(A J Martin, Ire) *in tch: nudged along to take clsr order on far rails over 3f out: w.w upsides ldr: rdn to ld ent fnl f: no ex whn hdd towards fin* **5/1**[1]

5346 **4** *1* **Brass Ring**[29] 6288 4-9-9 103........................ JamesDoyle 22 111
(John Gosden) *mid-div: smooth hdwy fr 3f out: rdn and v ch over 1f out: styd on same pce fnl f* **16/1**

00 **5** *1/2* **Digeanta (IRE)**[28] 6349 7-8-7 87........................(t) WayneLordan 25 94
(W P Mullins, Ire) *s.i.s: towards rr: gd hdwy fr 5f out: rdn and ev ch 2f out: styd on but no ex fnl f* **25/1**

20 **6** *1/2* **Nearly Caught (IRE)**[49] 5693 4-9-5 99........................ RyanMoore 20 106
(Hughie Morrison) *trckd ldrs: led briefly over 3f out: led over 2f out: sn rdn: hdd ent fnl f: no ex fnl 120yds* **12/1**[3]

011 **7** *5* **Teak (IRE)**[20] 6360 7-8-4 84ex........................(p) ChrisHayes 27 85
(Ian Williams) *mid-div: gd hdwy 4f out: led 3f out tl rdn over 2f out: styng on at same pce in cl 6th whn hmpd ent fnl f* **16/1**

4510 **8** *1 ¾* **Villa Royale**[116] 3321 5-8-13 93 .......... AndrewMullen 11 92
(Michael Appleby) *in tch: pushed along over 5f out: rdn to chse ldrs 3f out: wknd ent fnl f* **33/1**

3303 **9** *nk* **Communicator**[35] 6133 6-8-13 93 .......... OisinMurphy 5 92
(Andrew Balding) *mid-div: rdn 3f out: styd on same pce* **16/1**

0002 **10** *nk* **Jonny Delta**[22] 6514 7-7-11 80 oh1 .......... JoeyHaynes(3) 16 79
(Jim Goldie) *mid-div: rdn 3f out: styd on fnl 2f but nvr gng pce to get on terms* **20/1**

3240 **11** *nk* **Sohar**[30] 6255 6-8-10 90 .......... WilliamBuick 36 88
(James Toller) *hld up bhd: midfield u.p 3f out: styd on same pce fnl 2f* **33/1**

0623 **12** *3* **Ray Ward (IRE)**[21] 6557 4-8-13 93 .......... JimCrowley 32 88
(David Simcock) *hld up towards rr: hdwy fr 4f out: rdn in midfield over 2f out: no further imp* **20/1**

/301 **13** *½* **Ted Spread**[140] 2558 7-8-11 91 .......... (t) LukeMorris 15 86
(Suzy Smith) *mid-div: hdwy 4f out: rdn and ev ch 3f out: wknd over 1f out* **33/1**

-200 **14** *½* **Sula Two**[14] 6747 7-8-2 85 .......... PhilipPrince(3) 9 79
(Jo Hughes) *nvr bttr than mid-div* **100/1**

5352 **15** *¾* **Groovejet**[30] 6255 3-8-4 96 .......... FrannyNorton 10 90
(Peter Chapple-Hyam) *hld up towards rr: rdn 3f out: midfield 2f out: no further imp fr over 1f out* **16/1**

4010 **16** *½* **Gabrial's King (IRE)**[21] 6557 5-8-12 92 .......... FrederikTylicki 18 85
(David Simcock) *hld up towards rr: midfield and rdn 3f out: no further imp fnl 2f* **50/1**

/0-0 **17** *shd* **Very Good Day (FR)**[29] 6288 7-8-10 90 .......... PatCosgrave 7 83
(Richard Fahey) *in tch: rdn 3f out: wknd 2f out* **66/1**

0153 **18** *2 ¼* **Moidore**[22] 6514 5-8-1 86 .......... JoeDoyle(5) 4 76
(John Quinn) *trckd ldrs: pushed along over 5f out: wknd over 2f out* **16/1**

3411 **19** *hd* **Rhombus (IRE)**[22] 6518 4-9-1 98 4ex .......... CamHardie(3) 35 88
(Ismail Mohammed) *hld up bhd: rdn and sme prog into midfield over 2f out: no further imp fr over 1f out* **25/1**

3002 **20** *1 ½* **Lady Kashaan (IRE)**[23] 6501 5-8-8 88 .......... BenCurtis 29 76
(Alan Swinbank) *mid-div: rdn 3f out: wknd wl over 1f out* **50/1**

0044 **21** *hd* **Gabrial's Star**[14] 6747 5-8-5 85 .......... (b) ChrisCatlin 21 73
(Richard Fahey) *a towards rr* **100/1**

5004 **22** *1 ¾* **Argent Knight**[21] 6557 4-7-10 81 .......... NoelGarbutt(5) 8 67
(William Jarvis) *a towards rr* **25/1**

6-15 **23** *4 ½* **Swnymor (IRE)**[75] 4746 5-9-1 95 .......... PhillipMakin 34 76
(John Quinn) *t.k.h: mid-div: effrt over 2f out: wknd over 1f out* **18/1**

-240 **24** *5* **Mubaraza (IRE)**[21] 6557 5-9-4 98 .......... GeorgeBaker 30 74
(Ed Dunlop) *a towards rr* **33/1**

0060 **25** *hd* **Saddler's Rock (IRE)**[114] 3377 6-9-10 104 .......... (t) GrahamLee 24 79
(Jonjo O'Neill) *a towards rr* **33/1**

2355 **26** *2* **Sir Frank Morgan (IRE)**[8] 6896 4-8-3 83 .......... JoeFanning 31 56
(Mark Johnston) *mid-div: hdwy over 4f out: rdn over 3f out: wknd over 2f out* **33/1**

004 **27** *3 ½* **Waterclock (IRE)**[18] 6640 5-8-2 82 .......... (b) JimmyQuinn 3 51
(Jedd O'Keeffe) *trckd ldrs: rdn to nrly chalover 4f out: squeezed up and lost pl 3f out: lost pl rapidly and sn eased* **33/1**

1435 **28** *7* **Noble Silk**[42] 5920 5-9-0 94 .......... (p) FrankieDettori 19 56
(Lucy Wadham) *mid-div: rdn 3f out: wknd over 1f out* **25/1**

-220 **29** *1 ¾* **Earth Amber**[63] 5161 5-9-4 98 .......... KierenFallon 33 58
(Nicky Henderson) *in tch: rdn to chse ldrs 3f out: wknd 2f out: eased* **33/1**

5440 **30** *13* **Debdebdeb**[30] 6255 4-8-10 90 ..........[1] HayleyTurner 26 35
(Andrew Balding) *a towards rr* **40/1**

0130 **31** *2* **Mr Burbidge**[176] 1556 6-8-4 84 .......... (b) WilliamCarson 17 27
(Neil Mulholland) *led tl over 3f out: sn wknd* **66/1**

1203 **32** *1* **Suegioo (FR)**[29] 6287 5-9-8 102 .......... (p) MartinHarley 23 44
(Marco Botti) *mid-div: rdn 4f out: sn wknd* **20/1**

5515 **33** *1 ¾* **Spice Fair**[39] 6005 7-8-8 88 .......... LiamKeniry 1 28
(Mark Usher) *s.i.s: hung bdly lft fr over 2f out: a towards rr* **66/1**

3m 49.1s (-2.90) **Going Correction** +0.025s/f (Good)
**WFA** 3 from 4yo+ 12lb **33** Ran SP% **138.0**
Speed ratings (Par 109): **107,106,106,106,105 105,103,102,102,102 102,101,100,100,100 100,99,98,98,98 98,97,95,93,93 92**
CSF £242.10 CT £1439.62 TOTE £9.90: £3.00, £5.90, £2.50, £4.30; EX 196.50 Trifecta £460.00.

**Owner** Terry Warner **Bred** Capricorn Stud **Trained** Withycombe, Somerset
■ Laughing Jack (66-1) was withdrawn. Rule 4 does not apply.
■ Stewards' Enquiry : Tom Queally two-day ban: careless riding (Oct 27-28)

**FOCUS**
A proper Cesarewitch. They went a solid pace from the start, with it beginning to wind up from 1m out and the form looks strong with the first sixth coming clear. The winner matched his trial figure. Once again a low draw counted for plenty.

## 7108 BETFRED SUPPORTS JACK BERRY HOUSE MAIDEN FILLIES' STKS (BOBIS RACE) 7f
**4:25** (4:32) (Class 4) 2-Y-O **£5,175** (£1,540; £769; £384) **Stalls** Low

Form RPR

**1** **Irish Rookie (IRE)** 2-9-0 0 .......... LiamKeniry 6 78+
(Martyn Meade) *dwlt: in tch: rdn and effrt to chal over 1f out: led ins fnl f: styd on wl: rdn out* **50/1**

**2** *nk* **Sharqeyih** 2-9-0 0 .......... JoeFanning 11 78+
(William Haggas) *in tch: effrt whn short of room and swtchd lft over 1f out: styd on u.p to chse wnr ins fnl f: steadily clsng but nvr quite getting to wnr* **10/1**

**3** *hd* **Tazffin (IRE)** 2-9-0 0 .......... AndreaAtzeni 16 77+
(Roger Varian) *in tch in midfield: hdwy over 1f out: chsd ldrs 1f out: kpt on wl to go 3rd wl ins fnl f: gng on fin but nvr quite getting to ldng pair* **20/1**

64 **4** *1* **Lashkaal**[86] 4346 2-9-0 0 .......... RobertHavlin 3 74
(John Gosden) *chsd ldr: ev ch and rdn 2f out: no ex and outpcd fnl 100yds* **6/1**[2]

3 **5** *1 ¼* **Colorada**[14] 6754 2-9-0 0 .......... TomQueally 1 71
(William Knight) *led: rdn and edgd lft wl over 1f out: hdd ins fnl f: no ex and wknd fnl 75yds* **7/1**[3]

**6** *shd* **Bella Nouf** 2-9-0 0 .......... RichardHughes 12 71+
(William Haggas) *chsd ldrs: rdn and effrt over 1f out: styd on same pce ins fnl f* **11/1**

**7** *1 ½* **Jasmine Blue (IRE)** 2-9-0 0 .......... JimCrowley 2 67
(Paul Cole) *in tch in midfield: rdn and rn green over 1f out: kpt on same pce ins fnl f* **16/1**

**8** *½* **Caelica (IRE)** 2-9-0 0 .......... JamesDoyle 9 65
(Charles Hills) *chsd ldrs: drvn and ev ch over 1f out tl jst ins fnl f: wknd fnl 100yds* **16/1**

4 **9** *1 ¾* **Twitch (IRE)**[14] 6754 2-9-0 0 .......... GrahamLee 10 61
(Hugo Palmer) *chsd ldrs: rdn and unable qck 2f out: edgd rt and btn over 1f out: wknd ins fnl f* **3/1**[1]

**10** *1 ¼* **Farletti** 2-9-0 0 .......... OisinMurphy 5 57
(Andrew Balding) *s.i.s: hld up in rr: rdn wl over 1f out: sme hdwy over 1f out: no imp ins fnl f* **33/1**

05 **11** *1* **Mrs Eve (IRE)**[14] 6754 2-9-0 0 .......... RobertTart 13 55
(Alan Bailey) *hld up in tch towards rr: rdn and unable qck ent fnl 2f: wknd over 1f out* **50/1**

**12** *nk* **Moruadh (IRE)** 2-9-0 0 .......... RyanMoore 7 54
(Sir Michael Stoute) *chsd ldrs: rdn wl over 2f out: unable qck and btn over 1f out: wknd fnl f* **8/1**

**13** *hd* **Colour Party (IRE)** 2-9-0 0 .......... WilliamBuick 14 53
(John Gosden) *hld up in tch in last quartet: effrt and no imp whn rn green and hung rt wl over 1f out: wl hld after* **9/1**

0 **14** *1 ¾* **Tocororo (IRE)**[21] 6553 2-9-0 0 .......... PhillipMakin 17 48
(Ed Dunlop) *hld up in rr: rdn and struggling over 2f out: wl btn over 1f out* **25/1**

**15** *2 ¾* **Frenzified** 2-9-0 0 .......... LemosdeSouza 8 41+
(Luca Cumani) *t.k.h: in tch in midfield: rdn and lost pl 3f out: bhd whn hmpd wl over 1f out* **40/1**

**16** *2* **Malice** 2-9-0 0 .......... PatDobbs 4 36
(Peter Chapple-Hyam) *in tch in midfield: rdn and struggling 3f out: bhd over 1f out* **28/1**

**17** *3 ¼* **Gilded Lili (IRE)** 2-8-11 0 .......... CamHardie(3) 15 27
(Charles Hills) *s.i.s: hld up in rr: rdn and no hdwy over 2f out: bhd and wnt rt over 1f out* **40/1**

1m 26.36s (0.96) **Going Correction** +0.025s/f (Good) **17** Ran SP% **125.9**
Speed ratings (Par 94): **95,94,94,93,91 91,90,89,87,86 84,84,84,82,79 76,73**
CSF £480.83 TOTE £57.30: £11.50, £2.80, £5.80; EX 1196.30 Trifecta £1653.20.
**Owner** Rick Barnes **Bred** Kevin & Meta Cullen **Trained** Newmarket, Suffolk

**FOCUS**
There was a bit of a bunched finish to this big-field fillies' maiden and it went to a 50-1 shot. The bare form is rated a bit below the race average.

## 7109 BETFRED "RACING'S BIGGEST SUPPORTER" EBF STALLIONS FILLIES' CONDITIONS STKS (BOBIS RACE) 6f
**5:05** (5:07) (Class 2) 2-Y-O **£12,938** (£3,850) **Stalls** Low

Form RPR

6132 **1** **Parsley (IRE)**[21] 6530 2-8-12 100 .......... RichardHughes 2 91+
(Richard Hannon) *mde all: sn clr: rdn 2f out: kpt on wl: eased cl home: unchal* **1/14**[1]

1322 **2** *8* **White Vin Jan**[12] 6820 2-8-12 69 .......... RyanMoore 3 68
(Michael Bell) *chsd wnr: nvr on terms: 4 l down and rdn 2f out: no imp: eased towards fin* **8/1**[2]

1m 12.76s (0.56) **Going Correction** +0.025s/f (Good) **2** Ran SP% **104.5**
Speed ratings (Par 98): **97,86**
TOTE £1.10.
**Owner** De La Warr Racing **Bred** Thomas Hassett **Trained** East Everleigh, Wilts

**FOCUS**
Just the two runners, after War Alert came out, and with 31lb separating them at the ratings it was no surprise 1-14 shot Parsley coasted home. She didn't need to be at her best.

## 7110 BETFRED RACING "FOLLOW US ON TWITTER" H'CAP 1m 2f
**5:40** (5:40) (Class 3) (0-95,92) 3-Y-O+ **£9,703** (£2,887; £1,443; £721) **Stalls** Low

Form RPR

4422 **1** **Pasaka Boy**[13] 6786 4-9-2 **87** .......... DannyBrock(3) 7 98
(Jonathan Portman) *in tch towards rr: rdn and effrt 3f out: hdwy u.p to chal 2f out: led over 1f out: styd on strly and drew clr fnl f: rdn out* **10/1**

50 **2** *4 ½* **Truth Or Dare**[30] 6257 3-9-5 **92** .......... MartinDwyer 13 94
(Richard Hannon) *s.i.s: sn in tch in midfield: effrt u.p to chse ldrs 2f out: no threat to wnr but styd on u.p fnl f: snatched 2nd on post* **14/1**

2231 **3** *nse* **Qanan**[24] 6465 5-9-5 **90** .......... AshleyMorgan(3) 12 92
(Chris Wall) *chsd ldr until led and rdn over 2f out: drvn and hdd over 1f out: no ex and btn ins fnl f: lost 2nd on post* **12/1**

5205 **4** *2 ¼* **Kikonga**[21] 6559 4-9-7 **89** .......... AndreaAtzeni 8 87
(Luca Cumani) *in tch towards rr: rdn and effrt to chse ldrs 2f out: drvn and unable qck over 1f out: 4th and outpcd fnl f* **5/1**[2]

151 **5** *hd* **Red Runaway**[35] 6141 4-8-12 80 .......... JimCrowley 11 78
(Ed Dunlop) *in tch in midfield: rdn 3f out: outpcd u.p 2f out: 5th and no imp over 1f out* **12/1**

0400 **6** *½* **Bantam (IRE)**[37] 6061 4-9-5 **87** .......... GrahamLee 5 84
(Ed Dunlop) *chsd ldrs: rdn and outpcd whn squeezed for room and hmpd 2f out: 6th and wl hld whn edgd rt 1f out* **25/1**

1416 **7** *2 ¾* **Nanton (USA)**[15] 6713 12-8-13 **81** .......... FergalLynch 1 73
(Jim Goldie) *hld up in rr: effrt over 2f out: nvr trbld ldrs* **20/1**

4-16 **8** *10* **Night Party (IRE)**[21] 6566 3-9-0 **87** .......... RichardHughes 3 60
(Saeed bin Suroor) *chsd ldrs: rdn 3f out: lost pl and btn 2f out: wknd over 1f out: no ch and eased ins fnl f* **13/2**

3522 **9** *6* **Enobled**[29] 6292 4-9-5 **87** .......... RyanMoore 6 48
(Sir Michael Stoute) *in tch in midfield: rdn and no hdwy over 2f out: sn btn: wl bhd and eased ins fnl f* **4/1**[1]

-104 **10** *1 ¾* **Shama (IRE)**[14] 6746 3-8-6 **82** .......... CamHardie(3) 4 40
(Sir Michael Stoute) *led tl rdn and hdd over 2f out: sn btn: bhd and eased ins fnl f* **11/2**[3]

-106 **11** *2 ¼* **Rock 'N' Roll Star**[147] 2347 3-8-5 **78** oh2 .......... JoeFanning 2 32
(Peter Chapple-Hyam) *v.s.a: hld up in rr: effrt over 3f out: sn btn: bhd and eased ins fnl f: t.o* **12/1**

5200 **12** *5* **Coincidently**[15] 6713 4-8-12 **80** .......... LiamKeniry 10 24
(Alan Bailey) *t.k.h: chsd ldrs tl 3f out: sn lost pl and bhd 2f out: eased ins fnl f: t.o* **20/1**

2m 3.76s (-2.04) **Going Correction** +0.025s/f (Good)
**WFA** 3 from 4yo+ 5lb **12** Ran SP% **117.6**
Speed ratings (Par 107): **109,105,105,103,103 103,100,92,88,86 84,80**
CSF £136.33 CT £1700.23 TOTE £14.80: £4.60, £4.10, £4.10; EX 225.10 Trifecta £948.80.
**Owner** RWH Partnership **Bred** G Wickens And J Homan **Trained** Upper Lambourn, Berks

**FOCUS**
A fair handicap, which was sound run and was won in dominant fashion. The form is not taken too literally.
T/Jkpt: Not won. T/Plt: £3,201.20 to a £1 stake. Pool: £177,000.85 - 40.36 winning tickets.
T/Qpdt: £586.20 to a £1 stake. Pool: £10,377.55 - 13.10 winning tickets. SP

# 7071 WOLVERHAMPTON (A.W) (L-H)

Saturday, October 11

**OFFICIAL GOING: Tapeta: standard**

Wind: Light behind, easing to almost nil Weather: Overcast, turning misty

## 7111 LADBROKES H'CAP (TAPETA) 5f 216y

**5:50** (5:51) (Class 6) (0-60,60) 3-Y-O+ **£2,264** (£673; £336; £168) **Stalls** Low

Form RPR

46-4 **1** **Random**[32] 6215 3-9-4 59........ StevieDonohoe 7 73
(Daniel Mark Loughnane) *sn pushed along in rr: rdn over 2f out: hung lft and r.o to ld wl ins fnl f* **16/1**

3061 **2** 1¾ **Major Muscari (IRE)**[15] 6720 6-9-3 57........(p) PaddyAspell 2 65
(Shaun Harris) *hld up in tch: led 1f out: sn rdn: hdd wl ins fnl f* **9/1**

0006 **3** 1 **Prince Of Passion (CAN)**[5] 6983 6-9-2 56........(v) RussKennemore 3 61
(Derek Shaw) *mid-div: hdwy over 1f out: sn rdn: r.o* **50/1**

0404 **4** ¾ **Douneedahand**[8] 6897 3-8-11 59........(p) GaryMahon(7) 5 61
(Seamus Mullins) *trckd ldrs: led wl over 1f out: hdd 1f out: styd on same pce* **14/1**

2100 **5** hd **Methaaly (IRE)**[2] 7056 11-9-3 57........(be) HarryBentley 11 59
(Michael Mullineaux) *awkward leaving stalls: sn bhd: hdwy over 1f out: r.o* **25/1**

1051 **6** 3¼ **Pearl Noir**[8] 6897 4-9-0 59........(b) MatthewHopkins(5) 4 50
(Scott Dixon) *led: rdn and hdd wl over 1f out: wknd ins fnl f* **8/1**

4560 **7** ½ **Honey Meadow**[10] 6872 3-9-5 60........ WilliamTwiston-Davies 9 50
(Robert Eddery) *sn pushed along in rr: hdwy u.p over 1f out: wknd ins fnl f* **11/2**[3]

3000 **8** 1½ **Interchoice Star**[8] 6897 9-8-13 56........(p) DeclanBates(3) 13 41
(Ray Peacock) *chsd ldrs: rdn over 2f out: wknd ins fnl f* **28/1**

3332 **9** ½ **Lucky Mark (IRE)**[21] 6561 5-9-3 57........(p) MartinLane 6 40
(John Balding) *chsd ldr: rdn and ev ch over 2f out: wknd ins fnl f* **7/2**[1]

3050 **10** 2 **Insolenceofoffice (IRE)**[8] 6897 6-8-11 58........(p) NicolaGrundy(7) 12 35
(Richard Ford) *s.i.s: sn pushed along in rr: n.d* **33/1**

550 **11** 2¼ **Three Pips**[16] 6695 3-9-5 60........ SebSanders 10 30
(Ed McMahon) *chsd ldrs: rdn over 2f out: hmpd over 1f out: sn wknd* **4/1**[2]

0046 **12** nk **Hit The Lights (IRE)**[37] 6077 4-9-0 57........(p) ThomasBrown(3) 8 26
(Patrick Chamings) *hld up: hdwy over 2f out: rdn and wknd over 1f out* **12/1**

0650 **13** 3½ **De Repente (IRE)**[67] 4994 3-8-10 58........ DanielCremin(7) 1 16
(Paul Green) *sn pushed along in rr: rdn and wknd over 2f out* **80/1**

1m 13.77s (-0.73) **Going Correction** -0.15s/f (Stan)
**WFA** 3 from 4yo+ 1lb **13** Ran SP% **112.4**
Speed ratings (Par 101): **98,95,94,93,93 88,88,86,85,82 79,79,74**
CSF £137.73 CT £6827.44 TOTE £16.60: £3.50, £3.30, £15.10; EX 182.40 Trifecta £1399.10.
**Owner** Ms A Quinn **Bred** Ed's Stud Ltd **Trained** Baldwin's Gate, Staffs

**FOCUS**
They went off very quickly. A clear personal best from the winner.

## 7112 LADBROKES NURSERY H'CAP (TAPETA) 5f 216y

**6:20** (6:20) (Class 6) (0-65,70) 2-Y-O **£2,264** (£673; £336; £168) **Stalls** Low

Form RPR

030 **1** **Cartmell Cleave**[43] 5874 2-9-3 61........ MartinLane 4 67
(Stuart Kittow) *a.p: rdn over 1f out: led ins fnl f: edgd lft: r.o* **12/1**

5252 **2** 2½ **Lyfka**[39] 6016 2-9-7 65........ LukeMorris 11 68
(Paul Cole) *hld up in tch: nt clr run fr over 1f out tl swtchd rt ins fnl f: r.o to go 2nd nr fin* **4/1**[3]

060 **3** nk **Treaty Of York (IRE)**[15] 6702 2-9-3 61........ HarryBentley 3 59
(Henry Candy) *trckd ldrs: wnt 2nd over 2f out: rdn to ld 1f out: sn hdd: styd on same pce* **7/2**[2]

3011 **4** 3 **Ar Colleen Aine**[7] 6941 2-9-5 70........ DanielCremin(7) 6 59
(Mick Channon) *led: rdn and hdd 1f out: no ex* **7/1**

444 **5** ½ **Buraug**[33] 6190 2-9-7 65........(p) StevieDonohoe 8 52
(William Muir) *chsd ldrs: rdn over 2f out: edgd lft and styd on same pce fr over 1f out* **3/1**[1]

353 **6** 3¾ **Tarando**[43] 5879 2-9-3 61........ MartinHarley 5 37
(Michael Bell) *prom: chsd ldr over 3f out tl over 2f out: sn rdn: wknd fnl f* **6/1**

5545 **7** 4 **Gamesters Lad**[96] 4012 2-8-13 57........ WilliamCarson 1 21+
(Tom Dascombe) *s.i.s: sn pushed along in rr: nvr on terms* **20/1**

043 **8** 2½ **Star Pursuits**[26] 6393 2-8-11 60........ TobyAtkinson(5) 10 16
(Noel Quinlan) *prom: lost pl over 3f out: wknd over 2f out* **40/1**

0506 **9** ½ **Bannister Bell (IRE)**[7] 6941 2-8-11 58........(b[1]) DeclanBates(3) 7 13
(David Evans) *chsd ldr tl rdn over 3f out: wknd over 1f out* **40/1**

0616 **10** 2½ **Ruby Rose (IRE)**[26] 6412 2-9-2 60........ FrannyNorton 2 7
(Kevin Ryan) *awkward leaving stalls and rdr lost iron briefly: a in rr: lost tch over 2f out* **16/1**

1m 14.08s (-0.42) **Going Correction** -0.15s/f (Stan) **10** Ran SP% **117.2**
Speed ratings (Par 93): **96,92,92,88,87 82,77,73,73,69**
CSF £58.95 CT £211.78 TOTE £18.80: £4.30, £1.40, £1.20; EX 119.60 Trifecta £328.80.
**Owner** G D C Jewell **Bred** D R Tucker **Trained** Blackborough, Devon

**FOCUS**
A lively betting heat, and straightforward, low-grade nursery form.

## 7113 LADBROKES EBF STALLIONS MAIDEN STKS (TAPETA) (DIV I) 5f 216y

**6:50** (6:52) (Class 5) 2-Y-O **£2,911** (£866; £432; £216) **Stalls** Low

Form RPR

20 **1** **Encore D'Or**[22] 6517 2-9-5 0........ SebSanders 1 88+
(Ralph Beckett) *led 5f out: pushed clr fr over 1f out: easily* **4/9**[1]

00 **2** 7 **Always Be Ready**[19] 6603 2-9-5 0........(t) MartinHarley 6 65
(Lady Cecil) *led 1f: chsd wnr: rdn and hung lft over 1f out: styd on same pce* **25/1**

562 **3** 3 **Medicean Bliss (IRE)**[26] 6408 2-9-0 68........ HarryBentley 7 51
(Jeremy Gask) *prom: sn pushed along: outpcd fnl 2f* **5/1**[2]

05 **4** 1½ **Bushtown Boy (IRE)**[107] 3626 2-9-5 0........ FrannyNorton 5 51
(Mark Johnston) *chsd ldrs: rdn over 2f out: wknd fnl f* **7/1**[3]

**5** 4 **Royal Blessing** 2-9-5 0........ LukeMorris 9 39
(George Peckham) *s.i.s: hld up: rdn over 2f out: nvr nrr* **10/1**

40 **6** ½ **Grumpy Angel**[35] 6158 2-9-0 0........ PaddyAspell 2 33
(Richard Fahey) *hld up: sme hdwy over 1f out: nvr on terms* **33/1**

00 **7** 2½ **On The Tiles**[100] 3881 2-9-5 0........ SeanLevey 3 30
(David Brown) *s.i.s: outpcd* **20/1**

05 **8** 1 **Kylies Wild Card**[44] 5859 2-9-0 0........ WilliamCarson 10 22
(Simon Hodgson) *prom: rdn 1/2-way: wknd over 2f out* **66/1**

0 **9** ½ **Viva Madiba (IRE)**[16] 6675 2-8-11 0........ ThomasBrown(3) 8 21
(Daniel Kubler) *prom: racd keenly: rdn and wknd over 2f out* **50/1**

**10** 14 **Beau Sparkle (IRE)** 2-8-9 0........ JackDuern(5) 4
(Steph Hollinshead) *s.i.s: outpcd* **50/1**

1m 13.24s (-1.26) **Going Correction** -0.15s/f (Stan) 2y crse rec **10** Ran SP% **124.5**
Speed ratings (Par 95): **102,92,88,86,81 80,77,76,75,56**
CSF £24.78 TOTE £1.40: £1.02, £4.00, £1.60; EX 17.40 Trifecta £52.00.
**Owner** Newsells Park Stud **Bred** Newsells Park Stud **Trained** Kimpton, Hants

**FOCUS**
An uncompetitive maiden in which the winner set a fair tempo and showed pretty useful form.

## 7114 LADBROKES EBF STALLIONS MAIDEN STKS (TAPETA) (DIV II) 5f 216y

**7:20** (7:20) (Class 5) 2-Y-O **£2,911** (£866; £432; £216) **Stalls** Low

Form RPR

432 **1** **Illogical**[15] 6701 2-9-0 75........ RobertHavlin 6 73
(Ed Dunlop) *mde virtually all: rdn over 1f out: styd on* **2/1**[2]

**2** ¾ **Magical Effect (IRE)** 2-9-5 0........ AdamKirby 8 76+
(Charlie Appleby) *s.i.s: hdwy over 3f out: rdn over 1f out: r.o* **15/8**[1]

0043 **3** ¾ **Winstanley (IRE)**[19] 6594 2-9-5 74........ TonyHamilton 2 74
(Richard Fahey) *a.p: chsd wnr over 3f out: rdn over 1f out: r.o: lost 2nd wl ins fnl f* **8/1**

**4** 2¾ **Tarragon** 2-9-5 0........ HarryBentley 7 65+
(Jeremy Gask) *s.i.s: sn pushed along in rr: hdwy over 1f out: hung lft ins fnl f: nt rch ldrs* **66/1**

**5** ½ **Seychelloise** 2-9-0 0........ LukeMorris 1 59+
(Sir Mark Prescott Bt) *s.i.s: sn pushed along in rr: rdn 1/2-way: r.o ins fnl f* **28/1**

**6** 1½ **Stamp Of Authority (IRE)** 2-9-5 0........ MartinHarley 5 59
(James Tate) *led early: sn lost pl: effrt over 1f out: edgd lft and no ex ins fnl f* **16/1**

5 **7** 6 **Mustaqbal (IRE)**[14] 6757 2-9-5 0........ FrannyNorton 3 41
(Mark Johnston) *chsd ldrs tl rdn and wknd over 1f out* **7/2**[3]

1m 14.39s (-0.11) **Going Correction** -0.15s/f (Stan) **7** Ran SP% **112.3**
Speed ratings (Par 95): **94,93,92,88,87 85,77**
CSF £5.91 TOTE £3.00: £1.60, £1.30; EX 7.50 Trifecta £20.50.
**Owner** R J & W J Gredley **Bred** Middle Park Stud Ltd **Trained** Newmarket, Suffolk

**FOCUS**
A fair Polytrack maiden. The third looks the best guide.

## 7115 DOWNLOAD THE NEW LADBROKES APP H'CAP (TAPETA) 1m 1f 103y

**7:50** (7:50) (Class 6) (0-55,55) 3-Y-O+ **£2,264** (£673; £336; £168) **Stalls** Low

Form RPR

4433 **1** **Lola Montez (IRE)**[18] 6636 3-9-3 55........(b) GeorgeBaker 9 65
(David Lanigan) *a.p: chsd ldr fnl f: r.o u.p to ld nr fin* **5/2**[1]

4504 **2** nk **Stanlow**[14] 6771 4-9-7 55........(p) MartinHarley 13 63
(Daniel Mark Loughnane) *a.p: chsd ldr over 2f out: led over 1f out: rdn ins fnl f: hdd nr fin* **5/1**[3]

5060 **3** 2¾ **Triple Star**[39] 6022 3-9-3 55........ JohnFahy 8 59
(Hughie Morrison) *hld up: hdwy over 1f out: r.o: nt rch ldrs* **50/1**

0604 **4** hd **Poor Duke (IRE)**[10] 6856 4-9-5 53........ HarryBentley 5 55
(Michael Mullineaux) *mid-div: hdwy 2f out: sn edgd lft: styd on* **25/1**

6004 **5** ½ **Taxiformissbyron**[12] 6823 4-8-9 50........(p) KieranShoemark(7) 4 51
(Iain Jardine) *hld up: hdwy over 1f out: r.o* **22/1**

6035 **6** ½ **Rasselas (IRE)**[3] 7036 7-9-7 55........[1] AndrewMullen 3 55
(Michael Appleby) *hld up: hdwy u.p over 1f out: no ex ins fnl f* **7/2**[2]

3-30 **7** 1½ **Cherry Tiger**[30] 6252 4-9-7 55........ AdamKirby 11 52
(Graeme McPherson) *hld up: rdn over 1f out: n.d* **11/2**

0300 **8** hd **Delightful Sleep**[14] 6771 6-9-1 52........ DeclanBates(3) 10 49
(David Evans) *hld up: hdwy and nt clr run over 1f out: nvr on terms* **25/1**

4050 **9** 1 **Super Duplex**[20] 5428 7-9-2 50........(t) StevieDonohoe 1 44
(Roger Teal) *chsd ldrs: rdn over 2f out: wknd fnl f* **40/1**

0000 **10** 1 **Strong Conviction**[18] 6636 4-9-4 55........(p) CharlesBishop(3) 12 47
(Simon Hodgson) *s.i.s: sn prom: chsd ldr 7f out: pushed along to ld over 3f out: rdn and hdd over 1f out: wknd fnl f* **40/1**

0-50 **11** ½ **Coastal Storm**[37] 2926 3-9-3 55........(t) OisinMurphy 7 47
(Jennie Candlish) *s.i.s: hld up: rdn over 3f out: a in rr* **50/1**

5650 **12** 2 **Spavento (IRE)**[11] 6836 8-9-4 55........ NeilFarley(3) 6 42
(Eric Alston) *led 6f: rdn and wknd over 1f out* **9/1**

4440 **13** 4 **Squirrel Wood (IRE)**[23] 6481 6-9-2 50........(b) WilliamTwiston-Davies 2 29
(Mary Hambro) *chsd ldrs: rdn over 2f out: hmpd and wknd over 1f out* **28/1**

2m 0.1s (-0.70) **Going Correction** -0.15s/f (Stan)
**WFA** 3 from 4yo+ 4lb **13** Ran SP% **117.1**
Speed ratings (Par 101): **97,96,94,94,93 93,91,91,90,89 89,87,84**
CSF £13.17 CT £488.18 TOTE £3.90: £1.90, £1.70, £8.30; EX 14.80 Trifecta £1177.60.
**Owner** Mrs David Lanigan & Partners **Bred** Tullamaine Castle Stud **Trained** Upper Lambourn, Berks

■ Stewards' Enquiry : Declan Bates two-day ban: careless riding (Oct 27-28)

**FOCUS**
The market proved the ideal guide to this weak handicap. It's rated around the runner-up.

## 7116 BET NOW WITH THE NEW LADBROKES APP NURSERY H'CAP (TAPETA) 7f 32y

**8:20** (8:21) (Class 5) (0-85,83) 2-Y-O **£4,725** (£1,414; £707; £354; £176) **Stalls** High

Form RPR

3310 **1** **Faraajh (IRE)**[37] 6064 2-9-1 77........ MartinHarley 9 84+
(James Tate) *hld up in tch: rdn to ld ins fnl f: r.o* **13/2**

1360 **2** 1¼ **Muqaawel (USA)**[34] 6165 2-9-2 78........ FrannyNorton 4 82
(Mark Johnston) *s.i.s: hld up: hdwy over 2f out: rdn over 1f out: r.o to go 2nd post* **28/1**

4612 **3** shd **Swift Approval (IRE)**[23] 6473 2-9-3 79........ OisinMurphy 8 83
(Kevin Ryan) *chsd ldrs: led over 2f out: rdn over 1f out: hdd and unable qck ins fnl f* **11/4**[1]

1330 **4** 1½ **Red Icon (IRE)**[71] 4853 2-9-7 83........ HayleyTurner 7 83
(Tom Dascombe) *hld up: plld hrd: hdwy over 1f out: sn rdn: styd on same pce ins fnl f* **15/2**

5220 **5** 1¼ **Saltarello (IRE)**[32] 6211 2-8-3 70........ JoeDoyle(5) 6 67
(John Quinn) *hld up: rdn over 1f out: r.o ins fnl f: nrst fin* **25/1**

032 **6** hd **Zigayani (IRE)**[47] 5752 2-9-1 77........ GrahamGibbons 10 73
(Sir Michael Stoute) *chsd ldr tl led 3f out: sn hdd: rdn over 1f out: no ex fnl f* **9/2**[2]

01 **7** ½ **Todegica**[30] 6268 2-8-11 73........ SeanLevey 2 68
(Ralph Beckett) *prom: pushed along 1/2-way: nt clr run and lost pl whn hmpd over 2f out: styd on ins fnl f* **5/1**[3]

4516 **8** *1 1/2* **Heaven's Secret (IRE)**[22] 6510 2-9-1 77........................ TonyHamilton 1 68
(Richard Fahey) *prom: lost pl 6f out: nt clr run over 2f out: nt trble ldrs* 12/1

2210 **9** *3/4* **Make On Madam (IRE)**[27] 6375 2-8-9 71........................ PaulPickard 11 61
(Brian Ellison) *chsd ldrs: rdn and lost pl 1/2-way: n.d after* 40/1

1354 **10** *1 3/4* **Alpine Affair**[35] 6135 2-8-13 75........................(b) MartinLane 5 60
(Brian Meehan) *s.i.s: hdwy over 4f out: rdn over 2f out: wknd over 1f out* 28/1

1032 **11** *3 1/2* **Jaganory (IRE)**[16] 6679 2-9-1 77........................[1] AdamKirby 3 53
(David Evans) *led 4f: sn rdn: wknd over 1f out* 11/1

1m 28.2s (-0.60) **Going Correction** -0.15s/f (Stan) **11 Ran SP% 115.8**
Speed ratings (Par 95): **97,95,95,93,92 92,91,89,88,86 82**
CSF £177.34 CT £624.81 TOTE £6.50: £1.60, £5.80, £6.80; EX 162.80 Trifecta £2198.70.
**Owner** Saeed Manana **Bred** Rabbah Bloodstock Limited **Trained** Newmarket, Suffolk

**FOCUS**
A competitive feature. The winner can do better again at this venue.

## 7117 DOWNLOAD THE NEW LADBROKES APP MAIDEN STKS (TAPETA) 5f 216y
8:50 (8:52) (Class 5) 3-Y-O+ £2,911 (£866; £432; £216) Stalls Low

Form RPR

2 **1** **Bailiwick**[14] 6765 3-9-4 0........................ RichardKingscote 2 67
(Daniel Kubler) *chsd ldrs: rdn over 1f out: r.o to ld nr fin* 7/1[3]

4300 **2** *hd* **Suitsus**[37] 6070 3-9-4 66........................(p) LukeMorris 5 66
(Peter Makin) *chsd ldrs: rdn to ld 1f out: hdd nr fin* 15/2

**3** *1 1/4* **Moiety** 3-8-13 0........................ MartinHarley 9 57
(Rae Guest) *prom: stdd and lost pl 4f out: hdwy over 1f out: no ex wl ins fnl f* 15/2

23 **4** *nse* **Foxcover (IRE)**[45] 5814 3-9-4 0........................ TonyHamilton 7 62
(Richard Fahey) *chsd ldrs: rdn over 2f out: styd on same pce ins fnl f* 7/4[1]

0046 **5** *1 1/4* **Aaranyow (IRE)**[21] 6561 6-9-5 46........................(t) RobertTart 8 58?
(Clifford Lines) *led: rdn and hdd 1f out: no ex ins fnl f* 40/1

305 **6** *shd* **Knockroon**[155] 2122 3-9-1 68........................ ThomasBrown(3) 3 58
(Andrew Balding) *hld up: hdwy over 1f out: sn rdn and swtchd lft: no imp ins fnl f* 2/1[2]

3/56 **7** *nse* **Pearl Bell (IRE)**[32] 6215 4-9-0 70........................ OisinMurphy 1 53
(Olly Stevens) *hld up: hdwy over 1f out: sn rdn: styd on* 18/1

0005 **8** *6* **Echologic**[11] 6834 4-9-5 45........................(e[1]) GrahamGibbons 4 38
(Brian Baugh) *w ldr tl pushed along over 1f out: wknd ins fnl f* 80/1

6 **9** *9* **Gifted Spirit**[105] 3695 4-8-11 0........................ DeclanBates(3) 6
(Mark Brisbourne) *dwlt: outpcd* 66/1

1m 14.11s (-0.39) **Going Correction** -0.15s/f (Stan)
**WFA** 3 from 4yo+ 1lb **9 Ran SP% 116.2**
Speed ratings (Par 103): **96,95,94,94,92 92,92,84,72**
CSF £57.97 TOTE £7.40: £1.70, £2.50, £2.10; EX 60.00 Trifecta £254.70.
**Owner** Mr & Mrs G Middlebrook **Bred** Mr & Mrs G Middlebrook **Trained** Whitsbury, Hants

**FOCUS**
This took little winning and with many of those towards the head of the market failing to run up to expectations, it's hard to get too excited. The fifth limits the form too.

## 7118 BET NOW WITH THE NEW LADBROKES APP H'CAP (TAPETA) 1m 4f 50y
9:20 (9:20) (Class 6) (0-60,75) 3-Y-O £2,264 (£673; £336; £168) Stalls Low

Form RPR

-040 **1** **Star Anise (FR)**[44] 5865 3-9-5 58........................ RichardKingscote 7 64
(Harry Dunlop) *hld up: hdwy over 4f out: led wl over 1f out: rdn and hung lft ins fnl f: styd on* 12/1

2234 **2** *2 3/4* **Rock Of Leon**[52] 5558 3-8-12 51........................(p) MartinHarley 1 53
(Michael Bell) *chsd ldrs: rdn over 3f out: nt clr run over 2f out: chsd wnr and hung lft fr over 1f out: styd on same pce ins fnl f* 11/4[2]

004 **3** *1/2* **Sakhra**[8] 6899 3-9-5 58........................ GeorgeBaker 5 59
(Mark Brisbourne) *chsd ldrs: lost pl 8f out: rdn over 3f out: hdwy u.p over 1f out: styd on same pce ins fnl f* 20/1

000 **4** *3/4* **Ballyfarsoon (IRE)**[121] 3153 3-8-8 47........................ StevieDonohoe 2 47
(Ian Williams) *dwlt: hld up: nt clr run over 1f out: styd on ins fnl f: nt rch ldrs* 8/1

-566 **5** *nse* **Stilla Afton**[33] 6194 3-8-7 53........................(p) CharlotteJenner(7) 8 53
(Marcus Tregoning) *hld up: rdn over 1f out: styd on ins fnl f: nt trble ldrs* 14/1

006 **6** *3 1/4* **Taanif**[165] 1847 3-9-1 54........................(p) GrahamGibbons 4 49
(Michael Easterby) *led 4f: chsd ldr: rdn over 1f out: no ex ins fnl f* 7/1[3]

3445 **7** *3 1/4* **Anjin (IRE)**[18] 6632 3-9-7 60........................(b[1]) LukeMorris 3 50
(Sir Mark Prescott Bt) *s.i.s: plld hrd and sn prom: swtchd rt 9f out: led 8f out: rdn and hdd wl over 1f out: wknd ins fnl f* 13/8[1]

0660 **8** *82* **Dover The Moon (IRE)**[37] 4042 3-8-5 47 oh1 ow1...... DeclanBates(3) 6
(Tom Gretton) *chsd ldr 4f: remained handy tl rdn and wknd over 4f out* 40/1

2m 39.3s (-1.50) **Going Correction** -0.15s/f (Stan) **8 Ran SP% 109.9**
Speed ratings (Par 99): **99,97,96,96,96 94,91,37**
CSF £41.72 CT £617.58 TOTE £10.90: £2.40, £1.20, £3.00; EX 54.20 Trifecta £186.30.
**Owner** The Astronomers 2 **Bred** S F Bloodstock LLC **Trained** Lambourn, Berks

**FOCUS**
A weak finale and something of a boil over. There are doubts over the form.
T/Plt: £107.40 to a £1 stake. Pool: £86,314.30 - 586.38 winning tickets. T/Qpdt: £4.80 to a £1 stake. Pool: £11,337.71 - 1,747.15 winning tickets. CR

# 7079 YORK (L-H)
Saturday, October 11

**OFFICIAL GOING: Good to soft (soft in places)**
Wind: Light half against Weather: Fine

## 7119 SPORTINGBET.COM STKS (H'CAP) (BOBIS RACE) 1m 208y
1:50 (1:50) (Class 2) (0-100,95) 3-Y-O £16,172 (£4,812; £2,405; £1,202) Stalls Low

Form RPR

1100 **1** **Imshivalla (IRE)**[23] 6476 3-8-2 81 oh1........................ JackGarritty(5) 2 91
(Richard Fahey) *slt ld: pushed clr wl over 1f out: jnd and rdn ins fnl f: kpt on gamely towards fin* 25/1

3030 **2** *1* **Examiner (IRE)**[14] 6737 3-8-13 87........................ RobertWinston 10 95
(William Haggas) *hld up in rr: hdwy on inner 3f out: chsd ldrs wl over 1f out: rdn to chal ent fnl f: sn disp ld and ev ch tl drvn and no ex last 75yds* 7/1[1]

6460 **3** *2* **Braidley (IRE)**[42] 5914 3-8-13 87........................ TedDurcan 4 91
(James Bethell) *hld up towards rr: hdwy 3f out: chsd ldrs wl over 1f out: sn rdn and kpt on fnl f* 8/1[3]

5020 **4** *nk* **God Willing**[14] 6752 3-9-6 94........................ PaulMulrennan 3 97
(Ed Dunlop) *trckd ldrs on inner: hdwy over 3f out: chsd wnr wl over 1f out: sn rdn: drvn appr fnl f and grad wknd* 16/1

1221 **5** *1/2* **Empress Ali (IRE)**[14] 6737 3-8-13 87........................ DeclanMcDonogh 5 89
(Tom Tate) *cl up: pushed along 3f out: rdn 2f out: edgd lft and grad wknd* 15/2[2]

0330 **6** *3/4* **End Of Line**[28] 6332 3-9-2 90........................(v[1]) DavidProbert 8 91
(Andrew Balding) *dwlt and in rr: hdwy over 3f out: rdn along over 2f out: chsd ldrs wl over 1f out: drvn and no imp appr fnl f* 17/2

2210 **7** *3* **Lacan (IRE)**[15] 6713 3-9-1 89........................ AdamKirby 6 83
(Clive Cox) *trckd ldrs: hdwy over 3f out: rdn wl over 2f out: drvn 2f and sn wknd* 15/2[2]

1-2 **8** *2 3/4* **Indy (IRE)**[135] 2706 3-9-7 95........................ GrahamGibbons 7 84
(David Barron) *trckd ldrs: pushed along 3f out: rdn over 2f out: grad wknd* 7/1[1]

6003 **9** *3* **Shot In The Sun (IRE)**[13] 6793 3-8-7 81 oh1........................ TonyHamilton 1 63
(Richard Fahey) *sn trcking ldng pair on inner: pushed along over 3f out: sn rdn and wknd 2f out* 9/1

0202 **10** *6* **Master Of Finance (IRE)**[14] 6737 3-9-1 89........................ JFEgan 9 59
(Mark Johnston) *in tch: pushed along 4f out: rdn 3f out: sn btn* 15/2[2]

2060 **11** *2* **Lily Rules (IRE)**[42] 5927 3-9-0 95........................ MikeyEnnis(7) 11 61
(Tony Coyle) *midfield: pushed along on outer 4f out: rdn over 3f out and sn wknd* 7/1[1]

1m 52.02s (0.02) **Going Correction** +0.225s/f (Good) **11 Ran SP% 114.2**
Speed ratings (Par 107): **108,107,105,105,104 103,101,98,96,90 89**
CSF £185.80 CT £1568.81 TOTE £27.10: £7.00, £2.50, £2.90; EX 267.10 Trifecta £1704.20.
**Owner** Pow Partnership **Bred** M Fahy & Rathbarry Stud **Trained** Musley Bank, N Yorks

**FOCUS**
The rail on the home bend had been moved 3 metres to provide fresh ground, so all races over 1m and further were run over 21 yards less than the official distance. After riding in the opener, Ted Durcan, David Probert and Robert Winston all described the ground as 'soft'. Eleven runners and they bet 7-1 the field in a wide-open handicap. A clear personal best from the winner.

## 7120 DOWNLOAD THE CORAL APP STKS (H'CAP) 1m 2f 88y
2:20 (2:22) (Class 2) (0-112,109) 3-Y-O+ £19,407 (£5,775; £2,886; £1,443) Stalls Low

Form RPR

1305 **1** **Sudden Wonder (IRE)**[85] 4385 3-9-1 103........................ AdamKirby 3 111
(Charlie Appleby) *prom: chsd ldr over 2f out: rdn wl over 1f out: drvn ins fnl f: styd on gamely to ld nr fin* 13/2[3]

413 **2** *hd* **Fattsota**[47] 5755 6-9-3 100........................ DanielTudhope 2 107
(David O'Meara) *led: pushed along over 2f out: rdn over 1f out: drvn and edgd lft ins fnl f: hdd and no ex nr fin* 5/1[2]

4440 **3** *1 1/2* **Educate**[14] 6752 5-9-5 109........................ AhmadAlSubousi(7) 9 113
(Ismail Mohammed) *hld up in tch: stdy hdwy wl over 2f out: chsd ldrs and edgd lft over 1f out: rdn and edgd lft again ins fnl f: kpt on: nrst fin* 8/1

0152 **4** *1/2* **First Flight (IRE)**[21] 6548 3-8-10 98........................ PaulMulrennan 7 101
(Saeed bin Suroor) *hld up: hdwy whn n.m.r over 3f out: sn swtchd lft: effrt over 2f out: rdn to chse ldr over 1f out: drvn ins fnl f: kpt on same pce towards fin* 10/3[1]

1305 **5** *6* **Magic Hurricane (IRE)**[31] 6233 4-9-1 98........................ GrahamGibbons 5 91
(James Fanshawe) *trckd ldrs: hdwy 4f out: edgd lft 3f out: effrt to chse ldng pair 2f out: sn rdn and wknd appr fnl f* 7/1

0644 **6** *6* **Gabrial (IRE)**[21] 6532 5-9-1 98........................ DavidNolan 10 80
(Richard Fahey) *in tch: hdwy on outer to chse ldrs 3f out: sn rdn: edgd lft and wknd 2f out* 14/1

3102 **7** *3/4* **Soviet Rock (IRE)**[10] 6878 4-9-1 98........................ DavidProbert 11 78
(Andrew Balding) *cl up: pushed along on outer over 3f out: rdn over 2f out: sn wknd* 5/1[2]

00-0 **8** *7* **Indian Chief (IRE)**[14] 6752 4-9-3 100........................ PaddyAspell 1 68
(David Nicholls) *hld up towards rr: hdwy on inner over 3f out: rdn along wl over 2f out: n.d* 25/1

1452 **9** *7* **Sennockian Star**[21] 6532 4-9-9 106........................(v) AdrianNicholls 8 61
(Mark Johnston) *prom: rdn along whn n.m.r wl over 3f out: sn wknd* 12/1

2m 11.88s (-0.62) **Going Correction** +0.225s/f (Good)
**WFA** 3 from 4yo+ 5lb **9 Ran SP% 111.6**
Speed ratings (Par 109): **111,110,109,109,104 99,99,93,87**
CSF £37.06 CT £257.41 TOTE £7.20: £2.20, £2.00, £2.20; EX 39.60 Trifecta £432.70.
**Owner** Godolphin **Bred** Rabbah Bloodstock Limited **Trained** Newmarket, Suffolk

■ Stewards' Enquiry : Daniel Tudhope two-day ban: used whip above permitted level (Oct 27-28)

**FOCUS**
There wasn't much pace on early and for much of the race it looked likely that another front-runner would make just about all. The runner-up is the key to the form.

## 7121 CORAL.CO.UK ROCKINGHAM STKS (LISTED RACE) 6f
2:55 (2:55) (Class 1) 2-Y-O
£25,519 (£9,675; £4,842; £2,412; £1,210; £607) Stalls High

Form RPR

1132 **1** **Mattmu**[7] 6933 2-9-1 93........................(p) DavidAllan 3 106
(Tim Easterby) *mde all: qcknd 2f out: rdn clr appr fnl f: kpt on strly* 2/1[1]

1041 **2** *2 1/4* **Bond's Girl**[30] 6256 2-8-10 94........................ PatrickMathers 10 94
(Richard Fahey) *chsd ldrs on outer: effrt 2f out: sn rdn: drvn to chse wnr and hung lft ent fnl f: sn no imp* 11/4[2]

3154 **3** *2* **Fanciful Angel (IRE)**[35] 6142 2-9-1 101........................ ColmO'Donoghue 6 93
(Marco Botti) *hmpd s: hdwy to trck ldrs after 2f: effrt 2f out: sn rdn: sltly hmpd ent fnl f: kpt on same pce* 5/1[3]

43 **4** *3/4* **Manofmanytalents**[29] 6299 2-9-1 0........................ AdamKirby 5 91
(Michael Squance) *hmpd s and towards rr: hdwy over 2f out: rdn to chse ldrs whn n.m.r and hmpd ent fnl f: sn drvn and one pce* 22/1

2150 **5** *3* **Cool Strutter (IRE)**[22] 6513 2-9-1 94........................ SeanLevey 8 82
(Richard Hannon) *chsd wnr: rdn along 2f out: hmpd ent fnl f: sn wknd* 12/1

611 **6** *2 1/4* **Park Glen (IRE)**[44] 5845 2-8-10 85........................ SamJames 4 70
(Noel Quinlan) *trckd ldrs: pushed along 2f out: rdn wl over 1f out: hld whn hmpd ent fnl f and wknd* 14/1

1201 **7** *5* **Teruntum Star (FR)**[35] 6135 2-9-1 95........................ DeclanMcDonogh 7 60
(Kevin Ryan) *wnt bdly lft s: chsd ldrs: rdn along over 2f out: wkng whn n.m.r ent fnl f* 5/1[3]

1m 14.43s (2.53) **Going Correction** +0.50s/f (Yiel) **7 Ran SP% 112.0**
Speed ratings: **103,100,97,96,92 89,82**
CSF £7.31 TOTE £2.50: £1.60, £1.70; EX 6.00 Trifecta £22.30.
**Owner** James Bowers **Bred** J Bowers **Trained** Great Habton, N Yorks


The Form Book, Raceform Ltd, Newbury, RG14 5SJ

**FOCUS**
A boost for the Redcar Two-Year-Old Trophy form here. Mattmu rfelished the conditions and is rated par for the level.

## 7122 CORAL SPRINT TROPHY (H'CAP) 6f
**3:30** (3:31) (Class 2) (0-105,105) 3-Y-O+

**£46,687** (£13,980; £6,990; £3,495; £1,747; £877) **Stalls** High

Form RPR
221 **1** **Spinatrix**[14] 6760 6-9-7 105............(p) ConnorBeasley(3) 9 114
(Michael Dods) *mde all: edgd rt fnl f: hld on wl* **12/1**
1506 **2** ¾ **Highland Acclaim (IRE)**[7] 6921 3-9-4 100............ SamJames 4 107
(David O'Meara) *mid-div: hdwy over 2f out: chsd wnr ins fnl f: no ex clsng stages* **14/1**
1262 **3** 2 ¼ **Another Wise Kid (IRE)**[20] 6576 6-9-4 99............ AdamKirby 16 98
(Paul Midgley) *chsd ldrs: styd on same pce last 150yds* **20/1**
1200 **4** ¾ **Rene Mathis (GER)**[21] 6533 4-9-5 100............ DavidNolan 6 97
(Richard Fahey) *chsd ldrs: styd on same pce last 150yds* **14/1**
4065 **5** *nse* **Highland Colori (IRE)**[50] 5653 6-9-8 103............ DavidProbert 13 100
(Andrew Balding) *w ldrs: edgd lft 2f out: styd on same pce last 150yds* **9/1**
0004 **6** *hd* **Seeking Magic**[14] 6760 6-9-0 98............(t) RyanTate(3) 19 94
(Clive Cox) *mid-div: effrt over 2f out: styd on fnl f* **16/1**
3504 **7** 1 ¼ **Arnold Lane (IRE)**[47] 5778 5-9-2 97............ TedDurcan 7 89
(Mick Channon) *mid-div: effrt over 2f out: kpt on fnl f* **33/1**
5310 **8** 1 **Out Do**[28] 6327 5-9-2 97............(v) SeanLevey 2 86
(David O'Meara) *chsd ldrs: one pce over 1f out* **25/1**
4005 **9** ½ **Fast Shot**[21] 6533 6-8-8 96............ RachelRichardson(7) 1 83
(Tim Easterby) *mid-div far side: hdwy over 2f out: edgd lft and one pce over 1f out* **16/1**
1013 **10** 1 ¼ **Aetna**[16] 6689 4-9-4 99............ GrahamGibbons 14 82
(Michael Easterby) *mid-div: hdwy over 2f out: sn chsng ldrs: outpcd over 1f out: kpt on clsng stages* **5/1**[1]
0100 **11** ½ **Compton Park**[21] 6531 7-9-0 95............(t) DavidAllan 8 77
(Les Eyre) *mid-div: effrt over 2f out: fdd fnl f* **33/1**
5150 **12** *nk* **Chilworth Icon**[14] 6745 4-8-10 94............ CharlesBishop(3) 18 75
(Mick Channon) *swtchd lft after s: in rr: sme hdwy 2f out: nvr a factor* **18/1**
3310 **13** 1 ½ **Watchable**[21] 6533 4-9-9 104............(p) DanielTudhope 10 80
(David O'Meara) *chsd ldrs: carried lft wl over 1f out: hung lft: wknd and eased last 100yds* **7/1**[2]
0002 **14** 1 ¼ **Supplicant**[14] 6760 3-8-9 96............ JackGarritty(5) 11 68
(Richard Fahey) *chsd ldrs: wkng whn n.m.r wl over 1f out* **9/1**
010 **15** ¾ **Fairway To Heaven (IRE)**[56] 5445 5-9-0 95............ JackMitchell 3 65
(Michael Wigham) *s.i.s: sme hdwy over 2f out: wknd over 1f out* **20/1**
000 **16** ½ **Mass Rally (IRE)**[21] 6533 7-9-7 102............(b) PaulMulrennan 5 70
(Michael Dods) *hld up in rr: nvr on terms* **8/1**[3]
0050 **17** ¾ **Ashpan Sam**[21] 6533 5-9-0 102............ KieranShoemark(7) 20 68
(John Spearing) *w ldrs stands' side: lost pl over 1f out* **25/1**
0035 **18** 3 ¾ **Rex Imperator**[25] 6440 5-9-0 95............ DeclanMcDonogh 12 49
(William Haggas) *mid-div: effrt over 2f out: lost pl over 1f out: bhd whn eased clsng stages* **25/1**
0000 **19** ½ **Racy**[14] 6745 7-9-2 97............(p) ColmO'Donoghue 17 49
(Brian Ellison) *in rr: eased whn bhd clsng stages* **50/1**

1m 13.26s (1.36) **Going Correction** +0.50s/f (Yiel)
**WFA** 3 from 4yo+ 1lb **19** Ran SP% **127.2**
Speed ratings (Par 109): **110,109,106,105,104 104,103,101,101,99 98,98,96,94,93 92,91,86,86**
CSF £156.10 CT £3428.05 TOTE £13.00: £2.60, £4.30, £3.10, £4.30; EX 260.20 Trifecta £9159.40.
**Owner** Mrs J W Hutchinson & Mrs P A Knox **Bred** T K & Mrs P A Knox **Trained** Denton, Co Durham
■ Stewards' Enquiry : Sam James nine-day ban: used whip above permitted level (Oct 25,27-31,Nov 1,3,4)

**FOCUS**
A typically competitive heat and, having originally split into two groups, the whole field merged within 2f of the start and came more or less centre to stands' side. A terrific effort under topweight from Spinatrix, with the pace holding up overall.

## 7123 CORAL.CO.UK EBF STALLIONS MAIDEN STKS (BOBIS RACE) 7f
**4:10** (4:11) (Class 3) 2-Y-O **£7,439** (£2,213; £1,106; £553) **Stalls** Low

Form RPR
4 **1** **Mutamakkin (USA)**[15] 6712 2-9-5 0............ GrahamGibbons 6 88+
(Sir Michael Stoute) *trckd ldrs: hdwy to ld 2f out: jnd and rdn over 1f out: clr ins fnl f: pushed out* **7/2**[2]
**2** 1 ¾ **Nebulla** 2-9-5 0............ SamJames 12 81+
(Noel Quinlan) *hld up towards rr: hdwy on wd outside 3f out: chsd ldrs wl over 1f out: sn rdn: swtchd lft ins fnl f and kpt on wl towards fin* **20/1**
56 **3** ½ **Navigate (IRE)**[15] 6712 2-9-5 0............ FergusSweeney 3 80
(Martyn Meade) *hld up in tch: hdwy on inner 3f out: chsd ldrs wl over 1f out: rdn to chse wnr ins fnl f: no imp* **17/2**
2 **4** 1 ¾ **Akeed Champion**[35] 6125 2-9-5 0............ TonyHamilton 11 76
(Richard Fahey) *trckd ldrs: hdwy on outer 1/2-way: cl up over 2f out: chal wl over 1f out and sn rdn: ev ch ent fnl f: sn wknd* **6/5**[1]
04 **5** 2 ½ **Cadeau Magnifique**[17] 6667 2-9-5 0............ DavidNolan 10 69
(Richard Fahey) *cl up: led 1/2-way: rdn along and hdd 2f out: grad wknd* **33/1**
**6** 1 ½ **Nortron (IRE)** 2-9-5 0............ DavidProbert 7 66
(Andrew Balding) *hld up towards rr: sme hdwy wl over 2f out: sn rdn and kpt on appr fnl f* **12/1**
66 **7** 1 **Montefalcon (IRE)**[17] 6668 2-9-0 0............ JackGarritty(5) 4 63
(Richard Fahey) *trckd ldrs: pushed along 1/2-way: rdn along wl over 2f out: grad wknd* **20/1**
6 **8** 1 ¼ **Count Montecristo (FR)**[22] 6509 2-9-5 0............ DeclanMcDonogh 1 60
(Kevin Ryan) *trckd ldrs: effrt and cl up over 2f out: rdn wl over 1f out: sn wknd* **7/1**[3]
65 **9** 4 **Normandy Barriere (IRE)**[16] 6690 2-9-5 0............ RobertWinston 8 50
(Nigel Tinkler) *slt ld: pushed along and hdd 1/2-way: rdn along wl over 2f out: sn wknd* **50/1**
0 **10** 12 **Kaine Keira**[7] 6931 2-9-5 0............ PaulMulrennan 13 20
(Paul Midgley) *a in rr: rdn over 3f out: sn outpcd and bhd* **40/1**
**11** 1 ½ **Satanic Mills (IRE)** 2-9-0 0............ ShelleyBirkett(5) 9 16
(Nigel Tinkler) *a in rr: rdn along 1/2-way: sn outpcd and bhd* **33/1**

1m 29.29s (3.99) **Going Correction** +0.50s/f (Yiel) **11** Ran SP% **118.2**
Speed ratings (Par 99): **97,95,94,92,89 87,86,85,80,67 65**
CSF £76.36 TOTE £4.10: £1.60, £6.10, £3.00; EX 106.40 Trifecta £333.10.
**Owner** Hamdan Al Maktoum **Bred** Helen K Groves Revocable Trust **Trained** Newmarket, Suffolk

**FOCUS**
A fair maiden, and the winner could improve again.

## 7124 EASYODDS "THE ODDS COMPARISON APP" STKS (H'CAP) 2m 2f
**4:45** (4:49) (Class 4) (0-85,84) 3-Y-O+ **£7,439** (£2,213; £1,106; £553) **Stalls** Low

Form RPR
2444 **1** **Kashmiri Sunset**[15] 6705 3-8-12 80............ DanielTudhope 2 93+
(Ed de Giles) *hld up in rr: hdwy 4f out: led over 2f out: edgd rt and drvn clr appr fnl f* **7/4**[1]
10-0 **2** 3 ¾ **Hidden Justice (IRE)**[149] 2289 5-9-9 79............ IanBrennan 13 85
(John Quinn) *mid-div: hdwy to r stands' side over 3f out: styd on to take 2nd post* **20/1**
021- **3** *shd* **Mister Pagan**[386] 6585 6-9-10 80............ PaulMulrennan 4 86
(Keith Dalgleish) *trckd ldrs: c wd to stands' side over 3f out: styd on to take 2nd last 50yds* **14/1**
05 **4** 1 ¼ **Caledonia**[18] 6640 7-8-10 71............ JordanNason(5) 11 76
(Jim Goldie) *hld up in rr: hdwy over 2f out: styd on wl fnl f* **10/1**[3]
3065 **5** *nk* **High Office**[13] 6794 8-9-0 75............ JackGarritty(5) 16 79
(Richard Fahey) *mid-div: c wd to r stands' side over 3f out: kpt on fnl f* **16/1**
2441 **6** *nk* **Deepsand (IRE)**[26] 6404 5-9-6 76............(p) DavidAllan 12 80
(Tim Easterby) *swtchd lft after s: hld up in rr: hdwy over 3f out: upsides over 2f out: one pce fnl f* **11/1**
5422 **7** 3 ¾ **Dr Irv**[18] 6640 5-9-1 76............(p) MeganCarberry(5) 3 76
(Philip Kirby) *dwlt: sn mid-div: effrt over 3f out: wnt rt and racd stands' side over 2f out: wknd fnl f* **14/1**
6161 **8** 6 **Miss Macnamara (IRE)**[11] 6832 5-8-12 73............ KevinStott(5) 6 68
(Martin Todhunter) *hld up in rr: swtchd wd to r towards stands' side over 3f out: sn chsng ldrs: wknd and eased last 150yds* **16/1**
6343 **9** 2 ¼ **La Bacouetteuse (FR)**[11] 6832 9-9-0 70............(p) ColmO'Donoghue 10 61
(Iain Jardine) *sn chsng ldrs: drvn 4f out: wknd over 1f out* **40/1**
46-0 **10** ½ **Montaff**[25] 6433 8-8-9 68............ JacobButterfield(3) 14 58
(Richard Guest) *swtchd lft after s: hld up in rr: sme hdwy over 2f out: nvr a factor* **40/1**
-004 **11** 1 ¼ **Rock On Bollinski**[25] 6432 4-8-13 72............ ConnorBeasley(3) 9 61
(Tim Fitzgerald) *mid-div: drvn 10f out: brought wd to r stands' side over 3f out: wknd 2f out* **33/1**
331 **12** ½ **Nashville (IRE)**[22] 6514 5-9-11 81............ DavidNolan 5 69
(Richard Fahey) *trckd ldrs: c wd and racd stands' side over 3f out: wknd 2f out* **8/1**[2]
/-05 **13** 7 **Cape Tribulation**[134] 2739 10-9-3 73............ DavidProbert 7 54
(Malcolm Jefferson) *sn prom: brought wd to r stands' side over 3f out: n.m.r over 2f out: sn wknd: eased whn bhd clsng stages* **12/1**
1012 **14** 2 **Hot Spice**[47] 5764 6-9-5 75............ GrahamGibbons 18 53
(Michael Easterby) *sn trcking ldrs: led after 5f: hdd over 2f out: sn wknd: eased whn bhd clsng stages* **14/1**
1306 **15** 15 **Albonny (IRE)**[22] 6514 5-9-0 70............ RobertWinston 8 32
(Timothy Jarvis) *mid-div: drvn to chse ldrs over 3f out: wknd 2f out: heavily eased fnl f: t.o* **33/1**
4200 **16** 9 **Be Perfect (USA)**[22] 6514 5-10-0 84............ AdrianNicholls 1 36
(David Nicholls) *led 5f: chsd ldrs: drvn 4f out: wknd wl over 1f out: sn heavily eased: t.o* **14/1**

4m 4.85s (9.45) **Going Correction** +0.225s/f (Good)
**WFA** 3 from 4yo+ 12lb **16** Ran SP% **126.5**
Speed ratings (Par 105): **88,86,86,85,85 85,83,81,80,79 79,79,76,75,68 64**
CSF £47.18 CT £408.85 TOTE £2.50: £1.50, £4.80, £3.20, £2.80; EX 57.80 Trifecta £600.40.
**Owner** Jennifer & Alex Viall **Bred** K F Fallon **Trained** Ledbury, H'fords
■ Longshadow was withdrawn. Price at time of withdrawal 25-1 - no Rule 4.

**FOCUS**
An extreme test. The winner improved and the second is rated back to last season's Pontefract win.

## 7125 COLDSTREAM GUARDS ASSOCIATION CUP (H'CAP) 1m 2f 88y
**5:20** (5:23) (Class 4) (0-85,85) 3-Y-O+ **£8,086** (£2,406; £1,202; £601) **Stalls** Low

Form RPR
0005 **1** **Open Eagle (IRE)**[55] 5465 5-9-7 82............ DanielTudhope 16 93
(David O'Meara) *trckd ldrs: hdwy and cl up over 3f out: led wl over 2f out: jnd and rdn over 1f out: hdd narrowly and drvn ent fnl f: regained ld last 100yds and kpt on gamely* **9/1**[2]
5660 **2** 1 ¼ **Ginger Jack**[84] 4453 7-9-6 81............ PaulMulrennan 3 90
(Keith Dalgleish) *in tch: smooth hdwy over 3f out: trckd ldrs over 2f out: sn cl up: led narrowly ent fnl f: sn drvn: hdd and one pce last 100yds* **12/1**
133 **3** *nk* **Ribblehead (USA)**[34] 6166 3-8-12 78............ DavidAllan 5 86
(Tim Easterby) *in rr: pushed along over 4f out: hdwy over 3f out: swtchd rt and rdn to chse ldrs over 1f out: drvn and kpt on same pce fnl f* **8/1**[1]
5153 **4** ½ **Lungarno Palace (USA)**[13] 6786 3-9-5 85............ FergusSweeney 18 92
(John Gallagher) *midfield: hdwy on wd outside 3f out: rdn along 2f out: styd on to chse ldng pair ins fnl f: kpt on* **20/1**
0-10 **5** ¾ **Pintrada**[25] 6433 6-9-5 80............ TedDurcan 20 86
(James Bethell) *stdd s and sn swtchd lft: hld up towards rr: gd hdwy over 3f out: chsd ldrs over 2f out: sn rdn and no imp fnl f* **25/1**
333 **6** 3 ½ **El Beau (IRE)**[29] 6284 3-8-10 76............ IanBrennan 13 75
(John Quinn) *midfield: hdwy over 3f out: chsd ldrs over 2f out: sn rdn and kpt on one pce* **12/1**
0230 **7** 2 ¼ **Ultimate Act**[10] 6881 3-8-7 73............ JFEgan 12 68
(Seamus Mullins) *prom on inner: rdn along over 3f out: drvn wl over 2f out and grad wknd* **10/1**[3]
6-30 **8** ½ **Mystery Bet (IRE)**[14] 6770 4-8-11 72............ PatrickMathers 4 66
(Richard Fahey) *trckd ldrs: hdwy over 4f out: sn cl up: disp ld and rdn along wl over 2f out: drvn over 1f out: wknd fnl f* **12/1**
4154 **9** 1 **Noble Alan (GER)**[25] 6433 11-9-2 82............ MeganCarberry(5) 8 74
(Nicky Richards) *hld up in rr: hdwy 3f out: rdn along over 2f out: plugged on: nvr nr ldrs* **14/1**
211 **10** *nse* **Giantstepsahead (IRE)**[64] 5150 5-9-5 80............ JackMitchell 14 72
(Denis Quinn) *led: pushed along over 3f out: rdn and hdd wl over 2f out: grad wknd* **8/1**[1]
6600 **11** 7 **Kalk Bay (IRE)**[49] 5681 7-9-5 80............ GrahamGibbons 7 59
(Michael Easterby) *hld up: a towards rr* **33/1**
6100 **12** ¾ **Aldborough (IRE)**[84] 4423 4-8-8 74............(p) JamesRogers(5) 9 51
(Ralph Beckett) *a midfield* **22/1**
215 **13** 2 ½ **Sophisticated Heir (IRE)**[23] 6491 4-9-7 82............ DavidNolan 17 55
(David O'Meara) *in tch: hdwy on outer over 3f out: rdn along wl over 2f out: sn wknd* **16/1**
1150 **14** *nk* **Chain Of Events**[15] 6713 7-9-4 82............ ConnorBeasley(3) 6 54
(Michael Wigham) *dwlt: a towards rr* **14/1**

2110 **15** *3* **Ingleby Symphony (IRE)**[23] 6479 4-9-4 84.............. JackGarritty(5) 10 50
(Richard Fahey) *a midfield* **14/1**

0540 **16** *6* **Fazza**[23] 6490 7-8-5 71.............................................. KevinStott(5) 15 26
(Edwin Tuer) *dwlt: a towards rr* **33/1**

110 **17** *1 1/4* **Only Orsenfoolsies**[55] 5465 5-9-1 83......................... MikeyEnnis(7) 1 36
(Micky Hammond) *a in rr* **20/1**

431 **18** *1 1/2* **Never Up (GER)**[14] 6762 3-9-0 80.................................. SamJames 19 30
(David O'Meara) *prom: rdn along 4f out: sn wknd* **14/1**

13 **19** *3/4* **War Poet**[133] 2790 7-9-5 80......................................... RobertWinston 11 28
(Brian Ellison) *hld up: a in rr* **11/1**

2m 13.66s (1.16) **Going Correction** +0.225s/f (Good)
**WFA** 3 from 4yo+ 5lb **19** Ran SP% **128.9**
Speed ratings (Par 105): **104,103,102,102,101 98,97,96,95,95 90,89,87,87,85 80,79,78,77**
CSF £105.82 CT £921.63 TOTE £10.60: £3.10, £3.00, £2.70, £6.20; EX 181.20 Trifecta £1638.90.
**Owner** Middleham Park Racing LXXIV & Partner **Bred** F Bayrou **Trained** Nawton, N Yorks

**FOCUS**
The betting suggested this was wide open, but the early pace wasn't strong, there was some bunching early on in midfield which hampered a few, and the upshot was that it paid to race prominently. The first two were both well in on their best form.
T/Plt: £1,104.50 to a £1 stake. Pool: £163,244.30 - 107.89 winning tickets. T/Qpdt: £66.20 to a £1 stake. Pool: £10,854.31 - 121.32 winning tickets. JR

## 6805 CAULFIELD (R-H)
### Saturday, October 11

**OFFICIAL GOING: Turf: good**

### 7126a SPORTINGBET HERBERT POWER STKS (GROUP 2 QUALITY H'CAP) (3YO+) (TURF) 1m 4f
5:20 (12:00) 3-Y-0+

**£65,053** (£19,354; £9,677; £4,838; £2,688; £2,150)

RPR

**1** **Big Memory (FR)**[15] 6733 4-8-5 0..............................(t) TommyBerry 1 105
(Tony McEvoy, Australia) **5/1**[2]

**2** *1/2* **Signoff (IRE)**[15] 6733 4-8-5 0........................................ GlenBoss 12 104
(Darren Weir, Australia) **16/5**[1]

**3** *hd* **Let's Make Adeal (AUS)**[7] 6975 5-8-5 0....................(b) DwayneDunn 5 104+
(Nigel Blackiston, Australia) **14/1**

**4** *nk* **Protectionist (GER)**[48] 5743 4-9-4 0.......................... CraigAWilliams 2 116+
(A Wohler, Germany) **5/1**[2]

**5** *1 1/4* **Lord Van Percy**[49] 5693 4-8-8 0................................. KerrinMcEvoy 3 104+
(Andrew Balding) *t.k.h: hld up towards rr on inner: pushed along and angled out 2f out: rdn into st: styd on wl fnl f and wnt 5th towards fin: nt pce to chal* **9/1**

**6** *3/4* **Albonetti (AUS)**[21] 5-8-5 0.......................................(t) DeanYendall 7 100+
(Sue Jaensch, Australia) **20/1**

**7** *1 1/4* **Bonfire**[21] 5-8-8 0................................................. JamesMcDonald 4 101
(Gai Waterhouse, Australia) **5/1**[2]

**8** *1 3/4* **Waltzing To Win (AUS)**[7] 5-8-5 0.................................. CoreyBrown 6 95
(David Huxtable, Australia) **100/1**

**9** *2 1/4* **Unchain My Heart (AUS)**[14] 8-8-5 0.......................(b) CraigNewitt 10 92
(David A Hayes & Tom Dabernig, Australia) **40/1**

**10** *1/2* **Ancient King (IRE)**[15] 6733 4-8-5 0................................. JimCassidy 8 91
(Peter G Moody, Australia) **30/1**

**11** *2 1/4* **Sangster (NZ)**[15] 6733 6-8-13 0...............................(t) HughBowman 9 95
(Trent Busuttin & Natalie Young, New Zealand) **7/1**[3]

**12** *3/4* **Renew (IRE)**[37] 6069 4-8-5 0...................................(p) ChrisSymons 13 86
(Marco Botti) *prom on outer early: wnt 2nd and trckd ldr bef 1/2-way: rdn and lost pl 3f out: no ex and btn in st: wknd* **30/1**

**13** *5 1/4* **Masked Marvel**[28] 6-8-5 0............................................. StevenKing 11 78
(Robert Hickmott, Australia) **30/1**

2m 26.68s (146.68) **13** Ran SP% **120.8**
PARI-MUTUEL (NSW TAB - all including 1 aud stake): WIN 6.60; PLACE 2.40, 2.00, 3.70; DF 11.20; SF 32.10.
**Owner** Pipeliner Bloodstock P/L, R & C Legh Racing P/L & **Bred** K Hoffman **Trained** Australia

### 7127a CATHAY PACIFIC CAULFIELD STKS (GROUP 1) (3YO+) (TURF) 1m 2f
5:55 (12:00) 3-Y-0+

**£130,107** (£38,709; £19,354; £9,677; £5,376; £4,301)

RPR

**1** **Fawkner (AUS)**[28] 7-9-4 0.................................(b) NicholasHall 4 118
(Robert Hickmott, Australia) **9/2**[2]

**2** *hd* **Criterion (NZ)**[21] 4-9-2 0....................................(b) HughBowman 3 116
(David Payne, Australia) **15/1**

**3** *1 3/4* **Side Glance**[56] 5460 7-9-4 0.......................................... JamieSpencer 5 115
(Andrew Balding) *led and allowed to dictate: rdn and strly pressed into st: kpt on but hdd fnl f and sn hld: dropped to 3rd towards fin* **25/1**

**4** *1/2* **Sacred Falls (NZ)**[21] 5-9-4 0..................................(b) ZacPurton 12 114+
(Chris Waller, Australia) **5/1**[3]

**5** *nk* **Happy Trails (AUS)**[7] 6975 7-9-4 0.................................. DamienOliver 6 113+
(Paul Beshara, Australia) **11/2**

**6** *hd* **Dissident (AUS)**[13] 6805 4-9-2 0............................(b) BenMelham 8 111+
(Peter G Moody, Australia) **3/1**[1]

**7** *1* **Dear Demi (AUS)**[15] 6731 5-9-0 0............................(b) JimCassidy 1 107
(Clarry Conners, Australia) **8/1**

**8** *1* **Foreteller**[21] 7-9-4 0.............................................(b) GlenBoss 10 109
(Chris Waller, Australia) **13/1**

**9** *3/4* **Sertorius (AUS)**[28] 7-9-4 0........................................ CraigAWilliams 7 107
(Jamie Edwards & Bruce Elkington, Australia) **40/1**

**10** *1 1/4* **Massiyn (IRE)**[364] 7212 5-9-4 0.......................................... StevenKing 2 105
(Robert Hickmott, Australia) **150/1**

**11** *1/2* **Kirramosa (NZ)**[14] 4-8-11 0....................................(b) TommyBerry 9 97
(John Sargent, Australia) **30/1**

**12** *7* **Crackerjack King (IRE)**[21] 6-9-4 0................................ MichaelWalker 11 90
(David A Hayes & Tom Dabernig, Australia) **18/1**

2m 1.68s (121.68) **12** Ran SP% **115.2**
PARI-MUTUEL (NSW TAB - all including 1 aud stake): WIN 5.20; PLACE 2.00, 4.20, 7.00; DF 39.20; SF 67.30.
**Owner** N C Williams & Mr & Mrs L J Williams **Bred** S Bennetts **Trained** Australia

### 7128a DAVID JONES NBCF TOORAK H'CAP (GROUP 1) (3YO+) (TURF) 1m
6:30 (12:00) 3-Y-0+

**£130,107** (£38,709; £19,354; £9,677; £5,376; £4,301)

RPR

**1** **Trust In A Gust (AUS)**[13] 6805 4-8-13 0.............................. BradRawiller 11 113
(Darren Weir, Australia) **18/5**[1]

**2** *3/4* **Speediness (AUS)**[13] 6805 7-9-1 0..........................(bt) HughBowman 3 113+
(Colin Scott, Australia) **18/1**

**3** *hd* **Desert Jeuney (AUS)**[175] 5-8-5 0.................................... JamesWinks 1 103+
(Nigel Blackiston, Australia) **60/1**

**4** *shd* **Akavoroun (AUS)**[13] 6805 5-8-5 0...........................(tp) MichellePayne 12 103+
(Ciaron Maher, Australia) **14/1**

**5** *hd* **Rhythm To Spare (NZ)**[13] 6805 5-8-5 0.....................(tp) DwayneDunn 9 102+
(Michael Moroney, Australia) **30/1**

**6** *nk* **Bull Point (AUS)**[13] 6805 4-8-8 0.......................................(b) JimCassidy 2 105
(Chris Waller, Australia) **6/1**[2]

**7** *hd* **Escado (AUS)**[175] 5-8-5 0.............................................(b) TommyBerry 4 101
(Matt Laurie, Australia) **30/1**

**8** *1* **Solicit (AUS)**[15] 6731 4-8-6 0............................................ CraigNewitt 14 100
(Mathew Ellerton & Simon Zahra, Australia) **6/1**[2]

**9** *1/2* **Guest Of Honour (IRE)**[91] 4180 5-9-2 0........................(p) DamienOliver 5 109
(Marco Botti) *hld up in rr: pushed along into st: rdn and kpt on fnl f but nvr threatened* **14/1**

**10** *3/4* **Commanding Jewel (AUS)**[15] 6731 5-8-13 0...............(t) CoreyBrown 10 104
(Leon & Troy Corstens, Australia) **12/1**

**11** *1* **Late Charge (AUS)**[13] 6805 4-8-5 0...........................(bt) GlenBoss 7 94
(Wendy Kelly, Australia) **14/1**

**12** *2 1/2* **Recite (NZ)**[42] 4-8-5 0..................................................... StephenBaster 15 88
(John Bary, New Zealand) **50/1**

**13** *1 1/4* **Tristram's Sun (NZ)** 6-8-5 0............................................. DarrenGauci 6 85
(Robbie Laing, Australia) **90/1**

**14** *3* **Arabian Gold (AUS)**[14] 4-8-7 0........................................ CraigAWilliams 13 80
(David Vandyke, Australia) **13/2**[3]

**15** *2* **Atlante (AUS)**[13] 6805 4-8-8 0.................................(bt) KerrinMcEvoy 8 77
(Michael, Wayne & John Hawkes, Australia) **9/1**

1m 35.2s (95.20) **15** Ran SP% **117.8**
PARI-MUTUEL (NSW TAB - all including 1 aud stake): WIN 4.30; PLACE 2.00, 5.30, 14.60; DF 55.40; SF 68.80.
**Owner** D G Speechley, W B Thomas Et Al **Bred** A Sangster **Trained** Australia

## 6652 GOODWOOD (R-H)
### Sunday, October 12

**OFFICIAL GOING: Soft (6.2)**
Wind: Moderate, across (towards stands) Weather: Cloudy, raining from Race 5 onwards, virtually dark final race

### 7129 ALDERBROOK STKS (H'CAP) (TO BE RIDDEN BY PROFESSIONAL NATIONAL HUNT JOCKEYS) 2m
2:00 (2:01) (Class 4) (0-80,80) 4-Y-0+ **£6,469** (£1,925; £962; £481) **Stalls** Low

Form RPR

6421 **1** **Aiyana**[19] 6632 4-11-2 70.............................................. RichardHughes 13 81
(Hughie Morrison) *trckd ldrs: rdn over 4f out: brought wd in st: chsd ldr over 1f out: clsd u.p fnl f: bmpd but led last strides* **9/2**[1]

**2** *nk* **Flying Light (IRE)**[363] 7259 8-10-11 65.................. WayneHutchinson 15 75
(Graeme McPherson) *s.s: mostly in last pair tl gd prog fr 4f out: led 2f out: drvn and hung lft fr over 1f out: bmpd wnr and hdd last strides* **13/2**[3]

03-0 **3** *4 1/2* **Valid Reason**[219] 292 7-10-12 66.................................... AlainCawley 1 71
(Dean Ivory) *hmpd after 2f and dropped to rr: rdn wl over 3f out: prog over 2f out: styd on to take 3rd last strides* **33/1**

2666 **4** *1/2* **Opera Buff**[16] 6721 5-11-6 74.....................................(p) JamesDavies 16 78
(Jose Santos) *trckd ldr: led after 7f: mde most after tl hdd u.p 2f out: steadily fdd* **9/1**

1352 **5** *3 1/4* **Underwritten**[27] 6404 5-11-1 69...................................... DaveCrosse 4 69
(Shaun Harris) *prom: rdn over 4f out: wnt 2nd u.p briefly over 3f out: fdd fnl 2f* **10/1**

0/50 **6** *8* **Regal Park (IRE)**[16] 6721 7-10-9 63................................ RobertDunne 8 54
(Miss Imogen Pickard) *wl in rr: rdn 4f out: prog fr 3f out: no imp on ldrs 2f out: wknd over 1f out* **50/1**

-154 **7** *1 1/4* **Coup De Grace (IRE)**[184] 1418 5-11-0 68.......................... ColinBolger 12 57
(Pat Phelan) *chsd ldrs: hrd rdn over 3f out: steadily wknd over 2f out* **16/1**

6/5- **8** *3/4* **Ya Hafed**[12] 119 6-10-13 67.........................................(t) MattieBatchelor 6 55
(Sheena West) *trckd ldrs: rdn over 3f out: wknd over 2f out* **50/1**

2343 **9** *shd* **Our Folly**[28] 6360 6-11-4 72...................................(b) DougieCostello 10 60
(Stuart Kittow) *dwlt: wl in rr: tried to make prog on outer over 3f out: wknd over 2f out* **8/1**

1223 **10** *3/4* **Wannabe Your Man**[26] 6439 4-11-8 76.....................(p) AndrewTinkler 11 63
(George Baker) *stdd s: hld up wl in rr: rdn 4f out: no prog and wl btn over 2f out* **5/1**[2]

2122 **11** *3* **Reach The Beach**[13] 6817 5-10-7 61 oh4.........................(t) RichieMcLernon 7 44
(Brendan Powell) *led 7f: w ldr: led briefly 5f out: wknd over 3f out* **14/1**

4020 **12** *6* **Number One London (IRE)**[15] 6747 4-11-12 80.....(p) GerardTumelty 9 56
(Brian Meehan) *hld up in rr: prog 6f out: rdn and no hdwy 4f out: sn wknd* **7/1**

2034 **13** *4 1/2* **Shalambar (IRE)**[40] 6019 8-10-10 64................................... LeeEdwards 5 35
(Tony Carroll) *in tch: rdn 6f out: wknd over 4f out: sn bhd* **25/1**

6-31 **14** *9* **Shalianzi (IRE)**[204] 581 4-11-3 71..........................(b) LeightonAspell 3 31
(Gary Moore) *hmpd after 2f and dropped to rr: rdn 4f out: wknd 3f out: t.o* **20/1**

3m 38.25s (9.25) **Going Correction** +0.70s/f (Yiel) **14** Ran SP% **118.9**
Speed ratings (Par 105): **104,103,101,101,99 95,95,94,94,94 92,89,87,83**
CSF £30.94 CT £862.17 TOTE £4.40: £1.60, £1.60, £13.10; EX 36.20 Trifecta £1219.20.
**Owner** The End-R-Ways Partnership & Partners **Bred** The Lavington Stud **Trained** East Ilsley, Berks

**FOCUS**
Outside running rail from 7f start to the top bend moved out 5yds to fresh ground, but no change to distances. Soft ground for the final meeting of Goodwood's season. This staying handicap was restricted to National Hunt jockeys but Richard Hughes holds a licence to ride over jumps and that enabled him to partner the winner.

## 7130 STEVE SMITH MEMORIAL MAIDEN AUCTION STKS 5f
**2:30** (2:30) (Class 5) 2-Y-O **£3,234** (£962; £481; £240) **Stalls** High

Form RPR

3 **1** **Fligaz (FR)**[18] 6659 2-8-5 0 ................................ LiamJones 3 83
(Martyn Meade) *in tch: pushed along over 2f out: fnd gap and rdn to cl over 1f out: led jst ins fnl f: drvn clr: decisively* **14/1**

3 **2** *2 ¼* **Lightning Charlie**[23] 6517 2-9-0 0 ................................ RichardHughes 1 84
(Amanda Perrett) *sltly awkard s: sn led: shkn up over 1f out: hdd and drvn jst ins fnl f: one pce* **8/11**[1]

**3** *1 ¼* **Magical Daze** 2-8-5 0 ................................ LukeMorris 4 70
(Sylvester Kirk) *w ldrs: stl upsides 1f out: rn green and no ex fnl f: decent debut* **14/1**

355 **4** *2 ½* **Signoret (IRE)**[24] 6489 2-8-6 70 ................................ JoeFanning 2 62
(Richard Fahey) *in tch: shkn up over 2f out: hanging and nt qckn wl over 1f out: fdd fnl f* **10/3**[2]

4224 **5** *hd* **Intruder**[17] 6690 2-8-9 71 ................................ RyanMoore 5 65
(Richard Fahey) *pressed ldr to 1/2-way: sn pushed along: fdd over 1f out* **11/2**[3]

59.21s (-0.99) **Going Correction** -0.20s/f (Firm) **5 Ran SP% 109.7**
Speed ratings (Par 95): **99,95,93,89,89**
CSF £25.24 TOTE £14.20: £5.70, £1.10; EX 24.70 Trifecta £69.20.
**Owner** Ladyswood Stud **Bred** Karine Belluteau **Trained** Newmarket, Suffolk

**FOCUS**
This might turn out to be a decent little maiden, because the first three pulled clear of the two more exposed runners and the time was quite a good one on this sort of ground. The beaten favourite is rated minor improvement.

## 7131 IRISH STALLION FARMS EBF NURSERY STKS (H'CAP) (BOBIS RACE) 7f
**3:05** (3:06) (Class 4) (0-85,85) 2-Y-O **£6,469** (£1,925; £962; £481) **Stalls** Low

Form RPR

4104 **1** **Popeswood (IRE)**[26] 6436 2-8-12 79 ................................ CharlesBishop(3) 2 83
(Mick Channon) *cl up: gng strly over 2f out: rdn to ld wl over 1f out: hrd pressed after: styd on wl and in command nr fin* **9/1**

3455 **2** *nk* **Percy Alleline**[17] 6684 2-9-6 84 ................................(v[1]) RichardKingscote 10 87
(Ralph Beckett) *w ldrs: rdn to chal 2f out: pressed wnr fr over 1f out: nt qckn last 100yds* **8/1**

053 **3** *1 ¼* **Its Gonna Be Me (IRE)**[17] 6690 2-8-10 74 ................................(p) RyanMoore 8 74
(William Haggas) *hld up in last: stl there 2f out: rdn and prog over 1f out: styd on to take 3rd nr fin: no ch to threaten* **7/2**[1]

2062 **4** *½* **Be Bold**[11] 6854 2-9-4 82 ................................ SeanLevey 4 81
(Richard Hannon) *trckd ldrs: drvn to chse ldng pair over 1f out: no imp: kpt on but lost 3rd nr fin* **16/1**

461 **5** *1 ½* **Finial**[31] 6246 2-9-0 78 ................................ AdamKirby 3 74
(Clive Cox) *wl in tch: rdn and nt clr run briefly wl over 1f out: one pce and no imp on ldrs after* **9/2**[3]

4415 **6** *2 ¾* **No One Knows**[79] 4619 2-8-12 76 ................................ WilliamBuick 6 64
(Charles Hills) *t.k.h: hld up: shkn up over 2f out: tried to make prog over 1f out: sn no hdwy* **16/1**

3304 **7** *1* **Assault On Rome (IRE)**[15] 6749 2-9-0 78 ................................ JoeFanning 9 64
(Mark Johnston) *led 2f: pressed ldr: upsides 2f out: wknd over 1f out* **10/1**

600 **8** *1 ¼* **Albecq**[23] 6517 2-7-10 65 ................................ NoelGarbutt(5) 5 47
(David Evans) *hld up towards rr: rdn over 2f out: no prog and btn over 1f out: fdd* **40/1**

5000 **9** *hd* **Burtonwood**[31] 6256 2-8-12 76 ................................ TonyHamilton 1 58
(Richard Fahey) *led after 2f to wl over 1f out: wknd qckly* **25/1**

421 **10** *4* **Desert Force**[23] 6517 2-9-7 85 ................................ RichardHughes 11 57
(Richard Hannon) *hld up fr wd draw: clsd and wl in tch bhd ldrs over 2f out: shkn up and no rspnse over 1f out: wknd and eased last 150yds* **4/1**[2]

1003 **11** *4 ½* **Kingsbridge**[38] 6064 2-8-11 78 ................................(b[1]) CamHardie(3) 7 39
(Rod Millman) *restless stalls: nvr really gng wl: in tch to 2f out: wknd qckly* **11/1**

1m 28.96s (1.96) **Going Correction** +0.70s/f (Yiel) **11 Ran SP% 117.0**
Speed ratings (Par 97): **116,115,114,113,111 108,107,106,106,101 96**
CSF £78.70 CT £307.40 TOTE £8.70: £2.80, £2.70, £1.50; EX 70.20 Trifecta £411.20.
**Owner** N J Hitchins **Bred** Mr & Mrs Nick Hitchins **Trained** West Ilsley, Berks

**FOCUS**
An open nursery in which the field came down the middle of the track in the straight. The pace held up quite well.

## 7132 SISTEMA STKS (H'CAP) 5f
**3:40** (3:42) (Class 3) (0-95,95) 3-Y-O+ **£9,703** (£2,887; £1,443; £721) **Stalls** High

Form RPR

1606 **1** **Desert Ace (IRE)**[9] 6893 3-9-1 89 ................................(tp) AdamKirby 3 99
(Clive Cox) *racd centre: mde all: rdn over 1f out: styd on wl fnl f* **16/1**

4022 **2** *1* **Ladweb**[23] 6512 4-8-8 85 ................................ JoeyHaynes(3) 4 90
(John Gallagher) *chsd wnr in centre: rdn 2f out: only threat over 1f out: kpt on but no imp last 100yds* **11/1**

2006 **3** *1 ¼* **Elusivity (IRE)**[15] 6745 6-9-0 88 ................................ RichardKingscote 1 89
(Peter Crate) *hld up in centre: prog 2f out: rdn to chse clr ldng pair jst over 1f out: kpt on but nvr able to chal* **8/1**[3]

5513 **4** *hd* **Humidor (IRE)**[29] 6327 7-9-6 94 ................................ JamesDoyle 8 94
(George Baker) *taken down early: hld up nr side: prog to ld gp over 1f out: kpt on fnl f and nrly snatched 3rd* **11/4**[1]

0306 **5** *1 ¼* **Duke Of Firenze**[8] 6923 5-9-4 92 ................................(p) TedDurcan 10 87
(Robert Cowell) *awkward s: hld up nr side: nt clr run briefly 2f out: nt racing in stforward fashion but kpt on fr over 1f out* **14/1**

-062 **6** *1* **Khubala (IRE)**[8] 6923 5-9-7 95 ................................(b) GeorgeBaker 5 87
(Hugo Palmer) *racd centre: nvr on terms w ldrs: rdn over 2f out: one pce and no imp over 1f out* **6/1**[2]

412 **7** *1 ¼* **Dominate**[37] 6089 4-8-9 83 ................................(b) RichardHughes 6 70
(Richard Hannon) *chsd ldng pair in centre: rdn 1/2-way: wknd jst over 1f out* **8/1**[3]

4062 **8** *½* **Pandar**[15] 6736 5-8-5 82 ................................ CamHardie(3) 7 67
(Milton Bradley) *racd alone between two gps: struggling fr 1/2-way: last over 1f out: kpt on again ins fnl f* **8/1**[3]

3320 **9** *1* **Normal Equilibrium**[15] 6745 4-9-5 93 ................................(p) OisinMurphy 2 75
(Robert Cowell) *chsd ldrs in centre: rdn over 2f out: wknd over 1f out* **10/1**

0005 **10** *1 ¾* **Lexi's Hero (IRE)**[15] 6745 6-9-1 89 ................................(v) RyanMoore 11 64
(Richard Fahey) *w ldr nr side to 2f out: sn btn: eased ins fnl f* **20/1**

0000 **11** *2 ¼* **Deeds Not Words (IRE)**[9] 6893 3-8-13 90 ................................ CharlesBishop(3) 9 58
(Mick Channon) *led nr side gp but nt on terms w those in centre: hdd & wknd over 1f out* **14/1**

58.87s (-1.33) **Going Correction** -0.20s/f (Firm) **11 Ran SP% 115.7**
Speed ratings (Par 107): **102,100,98,98,96 94,92,91,90,87 83**
CSF £177.84 CT £1033.79 TOTE £16.30: £4.80, £3.20, £2.40; EX 231.70 Trifecta £2010.60.
**Owner** Arabian Knights **Bred** Kildaragh Stud **Trained** Lambourn, Berks

**FOCUS**
A wide-open sprint handicap but nothing really got into it from off the pace and those who raced towards the stands' rail were clearly at a disadvantage and can be excused their runs.

## 7133 AMATEUR JOCKEYS' ASSOCIATION GENTLEMAN AMATEUR H'CAP (FOR GENTLEMAN AMATEUR RIDERS) 1m 4f
**4:15** (4:16) (Class 5) (0-75,75) 3-Y-O+ **£3,119** (£967; £483; £242) **Stalls** High

Form RPR

2630 **1** **My Lord**[69] 4985 6-10-13 67 ................................ MrJDoe(7) 3 76
(Luke Dace) *blindfold off sltly late and slowly away: racd in last to 1/2-way: trying to make prog whn hmpd 3f out: lot to do after: hdwy into 3rd over 1f out: styd on to ld last 75yds* **20/1**

4451 **2** *1 ½* **Yul Finegold (IRE)**[48] 5747 4-11-10 71 ................................ MrSWaley-Cohen 4 78
(George Baker) *s.s: in tch in rr: prog fr 5f out: rdn over 3f out: led in centre over 2f out: hung rt fr over 1f out: hdd and no ex last 75yds* **11/2**[3]

5524 **3** *½* **Red Dragon (IRE)**[16] 6699 4-10-11 65 ................................ MrHFNugent(7) 5 71
(Michael Blanshard) *t.k.h: trckd ldrs: styd in centre st and wnt 2nd jst over 2f out: chal and carried rt fr over 1f out: nt qckn and lost 2nd last 75yds* **12/1**

0411 **4** *7* **Last Echo (IRE)**[47] 5786 3-11-7 75 ................................ MrRBirkett 1 71
(Ralph Beckett) *prom: led over 4f out: steered towards nr side rail over 3f out: hdd & wknd over 2f out* **7/4**[1]

460 **5** *3 ¼* **Pandorica**[69] 4985 6-11-1 67 ................................(p) MrJPWilliams(5) 11 58
(Bernard Llewellyn) *t.k.h: hld up in tch: rdn 3f out: sn no imp: wknd wl over 1f out* **16/1**

002 **6** *½* **El Bravo**[27] 6403 8-11-4 70 ................................ MrAidenBlakemore(5) 9 60
(Shaun Harris) *disp ld over 5f: lost pl rapidly and last 5f out: no ch over 2f out: passed a few stragglers late on* **16/1**

2401 **7** *1 ¼* **Celestial Bay**[11] 6856 5-11-0 64 ................................ MrORJSangster(3) 7 52
(Sylvester Kirk) *hld up in rr: rdn and no prog over 3f out: wl btn fnl 2f* **10/1**

1355 **8** *½* **Gavlar**[20] 6608 3-11-4 72 ................................(b) MrSWalker 8 59
(William Knight) *hld up in tch: chsd ldrs 3f out: wknd 2f out* **4/1**[2]

4000 **9** *8* **Boston Blue**[24] 6486 7-10-11 63 ................................ MrCCarroll(5) 6 38
(Tony Carroll) *in tch: rdn to chse ldrs 3f out: wknd 2f out* **25/1**

5345 **10** *hd* **Carraig Rock**[16] 6699 4-11-1 67 ................................ MrRPooles(5) 2 42
(Hughie Morrison) *mde most to over 4f out: impeded by ldr towards nr side over 3f out: wknd qckly over 2f out* **12/1**

2m 48.86s (10.46) **Going Correction** +0.70s/f (Yiel) **10 Ran SP% 116.6**
**WFA** 3 from 4yo+ 7lb
Speed ratings (Par 103): **93,92,91,87,84 84,83,83,78,77**
CSF £126.39 CT £1399.19 TOTE £12.30: £3.80, £2.10, £2.60; EX 101.80 Trifecta £933.50.
**Owner** Robert E Lee Syndicate **Bred** Mrs Monica Teversham **Trained** Okehurst Lane, W Sussex
■ A first winner on his third ride for 43-year-old jockey Jason Doe.
■ Stewards' Enquiry : Mr S Waley-Cohen one-day ban: careless riding (Oct 27)

**FOCUS**
A steadily run amateur riders' handicap in which they spread all over the track in the straight and it is not hard to have reservations about this form.

## 7134 IRISH EBF MAIDEN STKS (BOBIS RACE) 1m 1f
**4:45** (4:46) (Class 4) 2-Y-O **£5,175** (£1,540; £769; £384) **Stalls** Low

Form RPR

0242 **1** **Shadow Rock (IRE)**[18] 6653 2-9-5 79 ................................ RichardHughes 6 80
(Richard Hannon) *trckd ldr: shkn up 3f out: led briefly wl over 1f out: pressed ldr after: rdn to ld ins fnl f: styd on wl* **5/1**[3]

04 **2** *nk* **Secateur**[17] 6683 2-9-5 0 ................................ WilliamBuick 11 79
(John Gosden) *sn trckd ldng pair: shkn up over 2f out: rdn to ld over 1f out: wandered in front: hdd and nt qckn ins fnl f* **2/1**[1]

0 **3** *3 ½* **Deebaj (IRE)**[15] 6743 2-9-5 0 ................................ JoeFanning 12 72+
(Mark Johnston) *hld up in midfield: prog to trck ldrs over 3f out: rdn and tried to chal over 1f out: styd on and drew clr of rest but lft bhd by ldng pair fnl f* **8/1**

0 **4** *5* **Prince Of Cardamom (IRE)**[22] 6545 2-9-5 0 ................................ OisinMurphy 2 62
(Andrew Balding) *chsd ldrs: shkn up 3f out: lft bhd over 2f out: no ch after: tk modest 4th nr fin* **16/1**

**5** *¾* **Not Never** 2-9-5 0 ................................ JamesDoyle 1 61+
(Hugo Palmer) *hld up in last: shkn up over 2f out: kpt on fr over 1f out: no ch but shaped w sme promise* **25/1**

55 **6** *hd* **Rosenbaum**[25] 6456 2-9-5 0 ................................ AdamKirby 9 61
(Charlie Appleby) *led: hdd and reminder wl over 1f out: steadily wknd and nt knocked abt: lost 2 pls nr fin* **20/1**

0 **7** *nk* **Hambletts (IRE)**[20] 6603 2-9-5 0 ................................ TedDurcan 10 60+
(Robert Mills) *hld up in last pair: pushed along and lft bhd by ldrs fr over 2f out: kpt on fr over 1f out: nt disgracd* **50/1**

06 **8** *1 ¾* **Kitten's Red (USA)**[17] 6683 2-9-5 0 ................................ JimCrowley 5 56+
(Ed Dunlop) *hld up towards rr: lft bhd fr over 2f out: pushed along and no real prog after: nvr involved* **20/1**

0 **9** *nse* **Major Mac**[30] 6293 2-9-5 0 ................................ RichardKingscote 3 56+
(Hughie Morrison) *hld up towards rr: pushed along and lft bhd fr over 2f out: no ch after* **50/1**

6 **10** *shd* **Atalan**[18] 6653 2-9-5 0 ................................ GeorgeBaker 8 56+
(Hughie Morrison) *hld up towards rr: shkn up 3f out: lost tch and wl btn 2f out* **40/1**

065 **11** *3 ½* **Jolie De Vivre (IRE)**[20] 6602 2-9-5 67 ................................(p) LukeMorris 7 49
(Sylvester Kirk) *chsd ldrs: pushed along 3f out: lost pl and wknd fr over 2f out* **40/1**

3 **12** *1* **Open The Red**[11] 6874 2-9-5 0 ................................ RyanMoore 13 47+
(Amanda Perrett) *hld up in last pair early and racd wd: prog 1/2-way to chse ldrs: wknd over 2f out: nt knocked abt* **9/4**[2]

2m 1.91s (5.61) **Going Correction** +0.70s/f (Yiel) **12 Ran SP% 119.9**
Speed ratings (Par 97): **103,102,99,95,94 94,94,92,92,92 89,88**
CSF £14.46 TOTE £4.80: £1.90, £1.60, £2.60; EX 16.00 Trifecta £116.50.
**Owner** Michael Daniels **Bred** Kilfrush Stud **Trained** East Everleigh, Wilts

**FOCUS**
Conditions were getting worse as the rain fell heavily and they finished well strung out in this maiden, with the front two drawing clear in the final furlong. Straightforward form.

## 7135 FURNITURE MAKERS STKS (H'CAP) (BOBIS RACE) 1m 4f
5:15 (5:20) (Class 3) (0-95,93) 3-Y-O £9,703 (£2,887; £1,443; £721) Stalls High

Form RPR

1531 **1** **Yaakooum (IRE)**[14] 6786 3-9-1 **87**........ RichardHughes 7 95
(Richard Hannon) *trckd ldr: rdn 3f out: chalng whn carried lft 2f out: brought to nr side and led jst over 1f out: drvn and jst hld on* **6/1**[2]

0502 **2** *nse* **Fun Mac (GER)**[20] 6608 3-8-9 **81**........(t) JimCrowley 6 89
(Hughie Morrison) *in tch: pushed along 4f out: clsd over 2f out: drvn to chal over 1f out: led in centre ins fnl f: jst pipped by nr side wnr* **8/1**[3]

421 **3** *½* **Soviet Courage (IRE)**[40] 6002 3-8-11 **83**........ RyanMoore 2 90
(William Haggas) *trckd ldrs: pushed along 4f out: rdn and looked to be struggling 3f out: rallied wl over 1f out: led in centre fnl f and w upsides wnr: hdd and nt qckn last 100yds* **11/8**[1]

0035 **4** *2¾* **Pack Leader (IRE)**[18] 6656 3-9-2 **88**........(b[1]) RichardKingscote 8 91
(Amanda Perrett) *restless stalls and slowly away: rapid prog to ld after 1f: rdn and hung lft 2f out: hung lft and hdd jst over 1f out: fdd* **16/1**

2040 **5** *6* **Black Shadow**[22] 6548 3-9-7 **93**........ TomQueally 5 87
(Amanda Perrett) *hld up in last pair: clsd on ldrs 3f out: rdn over 2f out: wknd over 1f out* **12/1**

1162 **6** *2½* **Tioga Pass**[49] 5723 3-9-6 **92**........(b) LukeMorris 3 82
(Paul Cole) *cl up: trckd ldng pair 5f out: brought to chal gng strly over 2f out: drvn and fnd nil wl over 1f out: hung rt and wknd fnl f* **10/1**

4020 **7** *½* **Cotton Club (IRE)**[20] 6608 3-8-4 **79** oh1........ CamHardie(3) 10 69
(Rod Millman) *nvr really gng wl: a in rr: struggling fr 3f out* **33/1**

125 **8** *17* **Arabian Revolution**[73] 4819 3-9-0 **86**........(p) KierenFallon 11 50
(Saeed bin Suroor) *in tch: pushed along 5f out: wknd over 3f out: t.o* **10/1**

2m 48.56s (10.16) **Going Correction** +0.70s/f (Yiel) **8** Ran SP% **102.2**
Speed ratings (Par 105): **94,93,93,91,87 86,85,74**
CSF £40.70 CT £72.98 TOTE £4.70: £1.80, £2.10, £1.40; EX 43.60 Trifecta £135.40.
**Owner** Saeed H Al Tayer **Bred** George Kent **Trained** East Everleigh, Wilts
■ Spectator (8-1) was withdrawn. Rule 4 applies to all bets. Deduction - 10p in the £.

**FOCUS**
A competitive 3yo handicap and it proved quite a test of stamina after Pack Leader set what looked a sound enough gallop in the conditions. The front two were wide apart as they hit the line.

## 7136 RIFLES CARE FOR CASUALTIES APPEAL STKS (H'CAP) 1m
5:45 (5:50) (Class 4) (0-85,88) 3-Y-O+ £6,469 (£1,925; £962; £481) Stalls Low

Form RPR

0155 **1** **War Singer (USA)**[11] 6878 7-9-0 78........(vt[1]) StevieDonohoe 15 89
(Johnny Farrelly) *wl away fr wd draw: mde all: styd centre st: rdn clr over 2f out: drvn out 1f out: styd on wl* **11/1**

1400 **2** *2¼* **Extraterrestrial**[24] 6476 10-9-0 78........ TonyHamilton 6 84
(Richard Fahey) *hld up towards rr: prog in centre over 2f out: drvn to chse clr wnr over 1f out: styd on but nvr able to chal* **16/1**

5404 **3** *6* **Moonday Sun (USA)**[22] 6560 5-9-0 85........ KieranShoemark(7) 3 77
(Amanda Perrett) *impeded s: chsd ldrs: rdn over 2f out: kpt on u.p in centre fnl f to take 3rd last strides* **9/2**[2]

361 **4** *nk* **First Post (IRE)**[30] 6304 7-8-11 75........ HayleyTurner 1 67
(Derek Haydn Jones) *t.k.h: trckd ldng pair: styd centre st: rdn over 2f out: nt qckn and no imp over 1f out: fdd and lost 3rd nr fin* **5/2**[1]

2352 **5** *1¾* **Weekendatbernies (IRE)**[11] 6871 3-9-2 83........ OisinMurphy 14 70
(Ed de Giles) *chsd ldrs: brought towards nr side 3f out: sn rdn: pressing for a pl over 1f out: no ex* **8/1**[3]

2000 **6** *½* **Monsieur Chevalier (IRE)**[22] 6548 7-9-6 84........(b) RobertTart 5 70
(P J O'Gorman) *towards rr: brought towards nr side 3f out: sn rdn: plugged on fnl 2f: n.d* **12/1**

3216 **7** *6* **Faure Island**[11] 6871 3-8-11 78........ FergusSweeney 8 51
(Henry Candy) *wnt lft s: chsd wnr: styd centre st: rdn over 2f out: lost 2nd and wknd over 1f out* **10/1**

5000 **8** *3* **Weapon Of Choice (IRE)**[14] 6786 6-9-2 80........(b[1]) TomQueally 10 46
(Stuart Kittow) *impeded s: wl in rr: prog on outer 1/2-way and hdd to nr side in st: sn struggling* **20/1**

414 **9** *2¾* **Seldom Seen**[17] 6681 3-9-1 82........ JamesDoyle 9 41
(Sir Michael Stoute) *impeded s: mostly in last pair: brought towards nr side in st: no prog and sn wl btn* **10/1**

0051 **10** *2½* **Ogbourne Downs**[10] 6886 4-9-7 88........ CamHardie(3) 12 42
(Charles Hills) *dwlt: hld up in last pair: brought towards nr side over 3f out: sn toiling and bhd* **20/1**

0333 **11** *1* **Whipper Snapper (IRE)**[20] 6609 4-9-2 80........ AdamKirby 7 31
(William Knight) *a in rr: brought towards nr side over 3f out: sn wl btn* **8/1**[3]

0000 **12** *2¾* **Birdman (IRE)**[14] 6789 4-9-1 79........(b) MartinLane 13 24
(David Simcock) *n.m.r s: chsd ldrs: wknd over 3f out: sn bhd* **20/1**

1m 44.06s (4.16) **Going Correction** +0.70s/f (Yiel)
**WFA** 3 from 4yo+ 3lb **12** Ran SP% **123.4**
Speed ratings (Par 105): **107,104,98,98,96 96,90,87,84,81 80,78**
CSF £175.29 CT £917.39 TOTE £15.30: £4.50, £4.70, £2.20; EX 292.90 Trifecta £3123.90 Part won. Pool: £4,165.33 - 0.81 winning tickets..
**Owner** The War Cabinet **Bred** Hertrich-McCarthy Livestock **Trained** Enmore, Somerset

**FOCUS**
A wide-open handicap to end Goodwood's season and the field came centre to stands' side in the straight, but those who raced closer to the stands' rail could make no sort of challenge and the first four home all stayed nearer the centre of the track.
T/Jkpt: Not won. T/Plt: £256.90 to a £1 stake. Pool: £128,759.75 - 365.87 winning tickets.
T/Qpdt: £83.80 to a £1 stake. Pool: £10,940.10 - 96.55 winning tickets. JN

# 6797 CURRAGH (R-H)
Sunday, October 12
**OFFICIAL GOING: Yielding (good to yielding in places)**

## 7140a GO RACING IN KILDARE WATERFORD TESTIMONIAL STKS (LISTED RACE) 6f
3:10 (3:10) 3-Y-O+ £21,666 (£6,333; £3,000; £1,000)

RPR

**1** **Viztoria (IRE)**[63] 5223 4-9-1 109........ PatSmullen 6 108+
(Edward Lynam, Ire) *chsd ldrs: 4th 1/2-way: impr to dispute travelling wl 2f out: sn led and rdn clr ins fnl f: easily* **15/8**[1]

**2** *3* **Gathering Power (IRE)**[50] 5699 4-9-1 99........ FergalLynch 10 98
(Edward Lynam, Ire) *w.w in rr: last 1/2-way: hdwy fr over 2f out into 2nd ent fnl f: no imp on easy wnr: kpt on same pce* **8/1**

**3** *3* **An Saighdiur (IRE)**[22] 6533 7-9-9 102........(p) BillyLee 7 96
(Andrew Slattery, Ire) *sn disp and gained narrow advantage bef 1/2-way: rdn and jnd 2f out: sn hdd and no ch w easy wnr: dropped to 3rd ent fnl f and kpt on one pce* **10/1**

**4** *¾* **Russian Soul (IRE)**[28] 6371 6-9-11 110........(p) ShaneFoley 9 96
(M Halford, Ire) *hld up: clsr in 5th 1/2-way: sn pushed along and n.m.r bhd horses over 1f out: rdn in 4th ins fnl f and kpt on one pce: nvr trbld ldrs* **4/1**[2]

**5** *hd* **Flight Risk (IRE)**[35] 6172 3-9-5 103........(t) KevinManning 11 90
(J S Bolger, Ire) *disp early: sn settled bhd ldrs in 3rd: rdn over 2f out and sn no imp on ldrs: kpt on one pce in 5th wl ins fnl f* **9/2**[3]

**6** *¾* **Ruwaiyan (USA)**[22] 6533 5-9-6 103........(p) MartinHarley 8 88
(James Tate) *chsd ldrs: 6th 1/2-way: sme hdwy bhd ldrs 1 1/2f out: nt clr run and swtchd rt ent fnl f: rdn and no ex ins fnl f: kpt on one pce in 6th towards fin* **11/2**

**7** *shd* **Texas Rock (IRE)**[59] 5358 3-9-5 79........ NGMcCullagh 2 88
(M C Grassick, Ire) *hld up: 8th 1/2-way: sn pushed along and no imp on ldrs u.p in rr 1f out: kpt on one pce towards fin* **66/1**

**8** *1½* **Lady Ultra (IRE)**[9] 6908 3-9-0 88........ RonanWhelan 5 78
(Ms Sheila Lavery, Ire) *chsd ldrs early: pushed along in 7th fr 1/2-way and sn no ex: one pce fnl f* **33/1**

**9** *¾* **Tylery Wonder (IRE)**[28] 6369 4-9-6 87........(be) JosephO'Brien 1 80
(W McCreery, Ire) *prom: cl 2nd bef 1/2-way: sn pushed along in 3rd and no ex 2f out: wknd and eased ins fnl f* **20/1**

1m 12.59s (-2.91) **Going Correction** +0.075s/f (Good)
**WFA** 3 from 4yo+ 1lb **9** Ran SP% **117.7**
Speed ratings: **111,107,103,102,101 100,100,98,97**
CSF £18.19 TOTE £2.40: £1.10, £2.50, £3.40; DF 17.10 Trifecta £127.30.
**Owner** Mrs K Lavery **Bred** Airlie Stud **Trained** Dunshaughlin, Co Meath

**FOCUS**
Ease in the ground was vital for Viztoria and she won easily. She probably did not need to be at her best, with the seventh a form doubt.

## 7142a IRISH CESAREWITCH (PREMIER H'CAP) 2m
4:20 (4:23) 3-Y-O+
£50,000 (£15,833; £7,500; £2,500; £1,666; £833) Stalls Far side

RPR

**1** **El Salvador (IRE)**[66] 5115 5-9-5 **102**........(p) DonnachaO'Brien(7) 108
(A P O'Brien, Ire) *hld up in mid-div: clsr in 7th 1/2-way: hdwy on outer 3f out to ld 2f out: rdn and strly pressed ent fnl f: kpt on wl to assert clsng stages* **25/1**

**2** *1* **Hidden Universe (IRE)**[75] 4772 8-8-8 **84**........ PatSmullen 89
(D K Weld, Ire) *hld up in mid-div: 10th 1/2-way: tk clsr order 5f out: pushed along in 5th over 3f out and sn clsd u.p: wnt cl 2nd over 1f out: kpt on wl towards fin wout matching wnr* **8/1**[2]

**3** *2¾* **Marchese Marconi (IRE)**[22] 6593 5-9-0 **90**........(b[1]) JosephO'Brien 92
(A P O'Brien, Ire) *hld up: 14th 1/2-way: tk clsr order in 9th 3f out and impr far side to chse ldrs in cl 3rd over 1f out: sn no ex u.p: kpt on same pce* **10/1**[3]

**4** *hd* **Asbury Boss (IRE)**[23] 6526 3-8-1 **91** oh6........ ConorHoban(3) 93
(M Halford, Ire) *trckd ldr: cl 2nd 1/2-way: sn niggled along in 3rd: rdn in 4th 3f out and no imp on ldrs over 1f out: kpt on same pce* **12/1**

**5** *hd* **Grecian Tiger (IRE)**[49] 5737 5-8-4 **80**........(b) LeighRoche 81
(D K Weld, Ire) *hld up: 11th 1/2-way: prog on outer fr 3f out to chse ldrs wl ins fnl f: kpt on towards fin: nvr a threat* **12/1**

**6** *nse* **He'llberemembered (IRE)**[25] 2183 11-7-11 **80** oh9........ TomMadden(7) 81+
(P G Fahey, Ire) *hld up: 12th 1/2-way: rdn towards rr over 3f out and sme late hdwy fnl 2f: nrst fin* **50/1**

**7** *½* **Cliff House (IRE)**[7] 6964 4-8-6 **82**........ RoryCleary 83
(John J Walsh, Ire) *chsd ldrs: 6th 1/2-way: rdn 2f out and sn no imp on ldrs: kpt on same pce ins fnl f* **25/1**

**8** *nk* **Blue Surf**[18] 6656 5-9-8 **98**........ PatDobbs 99
(Amanda Perrett) *hld up: 17th 1/2-way: rdn and sme late hdwy fr under 2f out: nvr nrr* **16/1**

**9** *1* **Massini's Trap (IRE)**[7] 6311 5-7-13 **80** oh6........ RobbieDowney(5) 79
(J A Nash, Ire) *hld up: 16th 1/2-way: rdn in rr 3f out and sme hdwy u.p fr 2f out: kpt on one pce in 9th wl ins fnl f* **25/1**

**10** *1½* **Saint Gervais (IRE)**[22] 6593 9-7-11 **80** oh1........ IanQueally(7) 78
(John E Kiely, Ire) *jinked and uns rdr on way to s and rn loose befhand: w.w in rr: last 1/2-way: sme hdwy far side fr under 3f out: kpt on one pce ins fnl f* **33/1**

**11** *1¼* **Winter Lion (IRE)**[29] 6349 4-8-5 **81**........(p) ChrisHayes 77
(Denis Gerard Hogan, Ire) *led: narrow advantage 1/2-way: rdn into st and hdd 2f out: no imp on ldrs on its ent fnl f: wknd* **14/1**

**12** *shd* **Ted Veale (IRE)**[13] 6593 7-9-2 **92**........ WayneLordan 88
(A J Martin, Ire) *hld up towards rr: 18th 1/2-way: tk clsr order in 13th 3f out: sn rdn and no ex u.p in 7th 1 1/2f out: wknd ins fnl f* **8/1**[2]

**13** *¾* **Eye Of The Tiger (GER)**[16] 6727 9-8-4 **80**........ NGMcCullagh 75
(J P Murtagh, Ire) *w.w towards rr: 20th 1/2-way: tk clsr order 3f out: rdn in mid-div 2f out and sn no ex u.p: wknd ins fnl f* **14/1**

**14** *shd* **Hassle (IRE)**[36] 6133 5-9-5 **95**........(p) BillyLee 90
(Clive Cox) *hld up: 15th 1/2-way: n.m.r over 2f out and swtchd lft: rdn and no imp over 1f out: kpt on one pce* **14/1**

**15** *2* **Zeus Magic**[22] 6541 4-8-8 **84**........ AndreaAtzeni 77
(Brian Ellison) *chsd ldrs: pushed along in 9th under 4f out and sn no imp on ldrs: wknd fnl f* **20/1**

**16** *1¼* **Rawnaq (IRE)**[15] 4223 7-8-10 **86**........ DeclanMcDonogh 78
(Matthew J Smith, Ire) *chsd ldrs: cl 3rd 1/2-way: rdn in 2nd over 3f out and sn wknd* **16/1**

**17** *1¾* **Morga (IRE)**[45] 4380 4-9-6 **96**........ KevinManning 86
(Desmond McDonogh, Ire) *chsd ldrs: 5th 1/2-way: tk clsr order and wnt 2nd appr st: rdn and wknd 2f out* **33/1**

**18** *6* **Clondaw Warrior (IRE)**[34] 6201 7-8-11 **87**........ ColinKeane 70
(W P Mullins, Ire) *hld up in mid-div: 13th 1/2-way: rdn and no ex over 2f out: sn wknd* **3/1**[1]

**19** *2½* **Majenta (IRE)**[9] 6910 4-8-13 **96**........ GaryHalpin(7) 76
(Kevin Prendergast, Ire) *a bhd: 19th 1/2-way: n.m.r bhd horses over 2f out and no imp* **14/1**

**20** *8* **Alhellal (IRE)**[76] 4746 8-7-13 **80** oh1........(t) SeanCorby(5) 52
(M Phelan, Ire) *chsd ldrs: 4th 1/2-way: rdn and no imp on ldrs in 8th 3f out: wknd* **50/1**



The Form Book, Raceform Ltd, Newbury, RG14 5SJ

21 *1* **Zaidiyn (FR)**[51] 5651 4-9-1 91 ColmO'Donoghue 62
(Brian Ellison) *in tch: racd keenly: 9th 1/2-way: rdn and no ex over 2f out: sn wknd and eased* **22/1**

3m 29.9s (-3.10) **Going Correction** +0.075s/f (Good)
**WFA** 3 from 4yo+ 11lb **21 Ran SP% 140.6**
Speed ratings: **110,109,108,108,107 107,107,107,107,106 105,105,105,105,104 103,102,99,98,94 93**
CSF £218.99 CT £2204.36 TOTE £46.70: £8.00, £2.40, £2.60, £3.80; DF 439.50 Trifecta £11495.30.
**Owner** Mrs A M O'Brien **Bred** Hascombe & Valiant Studs & Balmerino B/S **Trained** Cashel, Co Tipperary

**FOCUS**
A typically competitive renewal of this 170-year-old event. The form is rated around the third.

## 7144a FINALE STKS (LISTED RACE) 1m 4f
5:20 (5:23) 3-Y-O+ £21,666 (£6,333; £3,000; £1,000)

RPR

1 **Second Step (IRE)**[36] 6127 3-9-0 93 AndreaAtzeni 2 103
(Luca Cumani) *chsd ldrs: 4th 1/2-way: impr 2f out where n.m.r bhd horses and edgd lft: outpcd briefly and rdn: clsd u.p far side ins fnl f to ld cl home* **13/2**[3]

2 *½* **Chance To Dance (IRE)**[29] 6350 4-9-7 106 (t) KevinManning 13 102
(J S Bolger, Ire) *chsd ldrs: 8th 1/2-way: rdn 3f out and hdwy u.p on outer to dispute over 1f out: led narrowly ins fnl f tl hdd cl home* **15/2**

3 *½* **Altesse**[14] 6803 3-8-9 103 RoryCleary 12 96+
(J S Bolger, Ire) *in tch: 9th 1/2-way: pushed along in 11th into st and prog u.p to chse ldrs ent fnl f: kpt on wl to snatch 3rd fnl strides: nvr trbld ldrs* **13/2**[3]

4 *shd* **Blue Hussar (IRE)**[29] 6349 3-9-0 100 JosephO'Brien 14 101+
(A P O'Brien, Ire) *w.w in rr: last 1/2-way: brought wd into st and rdn 2f out: clsd u.p to chse ldrs ins fnl f: nvr trbld ldrs* **9/1**

5 *nk* **Emerita (IRE)**[91] 4236 3-8-9 102 PatSmullen 8 96
(D K Weld, Ire) *chsd ldrs: 5th 1/2-way: rdn to chal 2f out and sn disp tl hdd narrowly ins fnl f: no ex u.p in 3rd wl ins fnl f: dropped to 5th clsng stages* **5/1**[2]

6 *shd* **Tarana (IRE)**[25] 6471 4-9-5 108 DeclanMcDonogh 17 98
(John M Oxx, Ire) *hld up: 11th 1/2-way: rdn in 8th fr 3f out and impr on outer to chse ldrs over 1f out: no ex in 4th ins fnl f and one pce towards fin* **7/2**[1]

7 *nk* **Chapter Seven**[141] 2574 5-9-7 99 ColinKeane 10 100
(G M Lyons, Ire) *hld up: 10th 1/2-way: rdn and hdwy bhd horses 3f out: no ex u.p ins fnl f: kpt on one pce in 7th towards fin* **20/1**

8 *1* **Certerach (IRE)**[28] 6374 6-10-0 108 ShaneFoley 4 105
(M Halford, Ire) *dwlt: w.w in rr of mid-div: clsr in 9th after 1/2-way: rdn over 2f out and tk clsr order bhd horses over 1f out: kpt on one pce in 8th wl ins fnl f* **25/1**

9 *2¾* **Buonarroti (IRE)**[196] 1200 3-9-0 103 SeamieHeffernan 1 94
(A P O'Brien, Ire) *chsd ldrs: 6th 1/2-way: pushed along 3f out and no ex u.p 1 1/2f out: one pce fnl f* **14/1**

10 *2½* **Qewy (IRE)**[29] 6350 4-9-10 103 NGMcCullagh 6 93
(John M Oxx, Ire) *disp early tl sn settled bhd ldr: cl 2nd 1/2-way: disp 4f out and led narrowly into st: rdn and strly pressed: hdd 1f out and wknd* **33/1**

11 *nse* **Dragon Fei (IRE)**[52] 5615 4-9-2 77 ConnorKing 9 85?
(Dermot Anthony McLoughlin, Ire) *towards rr: 14th 1/2-way: pushed along in rr under 3f out and kpt on one pce u.p ins fnl f* **50/1**

12 *hd* **What Lies Ahead (IRE)**[44] 4951 4-9-2 75 WayneLordan 16 85?
(W McCreery, Ire) *hld up: 12th 1/2-way: rdn and no imp 2f out: kpt on one pce ins fnl f* **50/1**

13 *½* **Shell House (IRE)**[28] 6370 3-8-9 98 ColmO'Donoghue 11 84
(A P O'Brien, Ire) *in tch: 7th 1/2-way: clsr in 6th into st: rdn and n.m.r bhd horses 2f out: sn no imp and one pce* **16/1**

14 *4¾* **Inis Meain (USA)**[25] 6471 7-9-10 109 MartinHarley 7 84
(Denis Gerard Hogan, Ire) *sn led: narrow advantage 1/2-way: jnd 4f out and hdd into st: rdn and no ex over 2f out: wknd* **12/1**

15 *1¾* **Vivat Rex (IRE)**[34] 6202 3-9-0 (b) MichaelHussey 3 78
(A P O'Brien, Ire) *chsd ldrs: racd keenly: 3rd 1/2-way: rdn in 2nd over 2f out and sn no ex u.p: wknd over 1f out* **25/1**

2m 38.0s (-0.50) **Going Correction** +0.075s/f (Good)
**WFA** 3 from 4yo+ 7lb **15 Ran SP% 126.9**
Speed ratings: **104,103,103,103,103 103,102,102,100,98 98,98,98,94,93**
Pick Six: Not Won. Tote aggregate: 2014: 198,308.00 - 2013: 226,497.00 CSF £53.28 TOTE £7.00: £2.00, £3.20, £2.90; DF 53.90 Trifecta £289.00.
**Owner** Merry Fox Stud Limited **Bred** Merry Fox Stud Limited **Trained** Newmarket, Suffolk

**FOCUS**
A very tight finish for the trip. Second Step would have been a very unlucky loser and his superiority probably wasn't fully told by the half-length margin of success.
T/Jkpt: @588.50 Pool: @7,390.48 T/Plt: @85.90 Pool: @34,268.08 BF

7141 - 7144a (Foreign Racing) - See Raceform Interactive

# 6806 COLOGNE (R-H)
Sunday, October 12

**OFFICIAL GOING: Turf: soft**

## 7145a PREIS DES WINTERFAVORITEN (GROUP 3) (2YO) (TURF) 1m
3:35 (12:00) 2-Y-O
£70,833 (£25,833; £17,083; £8,583; £4,583; £2,250)

RPR

1 **Brisanto** 2-9-2 0 MartinSeidl 9 107
(M G Mintchev, Germany) *t.k.h: prom on outer: rdn to chal over 2f out: led over 1f out: edgd rt fnl f but kpt on wl and asserted* **173/10**

2 *2½* **Sherlock (GER)**[14] 2-9-2 0 AdriedeVries 8 102
(M Rulec, Germany) *disp ld on outer: rdn and hdd over 1f out: carried sltly rt fnl f: kpt on but nt pce of wnr* **31/10**[2]

3 *3* **Molly Le Clou (GER)**[28] 6377 2-9-2 0 FilipMinarik 5 95
(J Hirschberger, Germany) *midfield in tch on inner: rdn over 2f out: sn outpcd by ldrs: styd on for 3rd fnl f but nvr able to chal* **9/5**[1]

4 *¾* **Rock Academy (GER)** 2-9-2 0 APietsch 1 93
(Christian Sprengel, Germany) *disp ld on inner: rdn and hdd over 2f out: sn outpcd by front pair: plugged on but dropped to 4th fnl f and wl hld* **69/10**

5 *¾* **Ebeltoft (IRE)**[28] 6377 2-9-2 0 DennisSchiergen 3 92
(P Schiergen, Germany) *t.k.h: midfield: rdn over 2f out: kpt on same pce and nvr able to chal* **185/10**

6 *1* **Starwood (GER)**[37] 6123 2-9-2 0 AStarke 4 90
(P Schiergen, Germany) *midfield in tch: rdn into st: sn outpcd by ldrs: plugged on but wl btn* **16/5**[3]

7 *2* **Bleu Azur (FR)**[33] 2-9-2 0 FabriceVeron 2 85
(Mario Hofer, Germany) *midfield in tch: pushed along and lost pl 1/2-way: rdn into st: outpcd and sn no imp: plugged on but wl btn* **32/5**

8 *3* **Leonido**[14] 2-9-2 0 SHellyn 7 79
(M G Mintchev, Germany) *hld up in and a towards rr: rdn over 2f out: sn outpcd: eased whn btn fnl f* **241/10**

9 *7* **Sealord (GER)** 2-9-2 0 IoritzMendizabal 6 63
(Christian Sprengel, Germany) *sn pushed along in rr: rdn and no imp st: eased whn btn: nvr a factor* **171/10**

1m 42.87s (4.48) **9 Ran SP% 130.2**
WIN (incl. 10 euro stake): 183. PLACES: 31, 18, 15. SF: 1,504.
**Owner** Litex Commerce Ad **Bred** Litex Commerce **Trained** Germany

# 6807 SAN SIRO (R-H)
Sunday, October 12

**OFFICIAL GOING: Turf: soft**

## 7146a PREMIO VERZIERE-MEM. ALDO CIRLA (GROUP 3) (3YO+ FILLIES & MARES) (TURF) 1m 2f
3:30 (12:00) 3-Y-O+ £29,166 (£12,833; £7,000; £3,500)

RPR

1 **Quaduna**[35] 4-9-0 0 EPedroza 5 103
(A Wohler, Germany) *mde all: kicked 3 l clr over 2 1/2f out: drvn ent fnl f: unchal* **242/100**[2]

2 *2¼* **So Many Shots (IRE)**[112] 3513 3-8-11 0 DarioVargiu 3 100
(Stefano Botti, Italy) *w.w in tch: scrubbed along and hdwy over 2 1/2f out: chsd ldr over 1 1/2f out: kpt on fnl f: nvr on terms w wnr* **7/10**[1]

3 *6* **Lady Dutch**[14] 6807 3-8-9 0 MircoDemuro 4 86
(B Grizzetti, Italy) *trckd ldng pair on inner: rdn and no imp on ldr over 2f out: kpt on ins fnl f but readily outpcd by front two* **127/10**

4 *3* **Lili Moon (GER)**[58] 5-9-0 0 BClos 2 80
(Werner Glanz, Germany) *hld up next to last: hdwy to chse ldrs over 2f out: sn hrd rdn and no imp: plugged on at one pce fnl f* **7/2**[3]

5 *1¼* **Velum**[14] 4-9-0 0 LManiezzi 1 78
(Marco Gasparini, Italy) *chsd ldr: outpcd and rdn 2 1/2f out: lost tch w ldrs fr 1 1/2f out* **33/1**

6 *1* **Lady's Day (GER)**[14] 6810 5-9-0 0 CristianDemuro 7 76
(Werner Glanz, Germany) *t.k.h: trckd ldng pair on outer: pushed along to hold pl 3 1/2f out: wknd over 1 1/2f out* **154/10**

7 *10* **Summer Fall (USA)**[14] 6807 5-9-0 0 FabioBranca 6 56
(B Grizzetti, Italy) *w.w in rr: rdn and no imp over 2f out: sn wknd and eased ins fnl f* **225/10**

2m 10.5s (3.80)
**WFA** 3 from 4yo+ 5lb **7 Ran SP% 130.9**
WIN (incl. 1 euro stake): 3.42. PLACES: 1.45, 1.27. DF: 2.41.
**Owner** Stiftung Gestut Fahrhof **Bred** Stiftung Gestut Fahrhof **Trained** Germany

## 7147a GRAN CRITERIUM (GROUP 2) (2YO COLTS & FILLIES) (TURF) 7f 110y
4:50 (12:00) 2-Y-O £100,000 (£44,000; £24,000; £12,000)

RPR

1 **Hero Look (IRE)** 2-8-11 0 FabioBranca 2 108
(Stefano Botti, Italy) *trckd ldng pair on inner: smooth prog to press ldr 2f out: sn rdn and grad wore down runner-up to ld ent fnl f: drvn clr: in control fnl 75yds* **23/20**[1]

2 *1½* **Ginwar (ITY)**[21] 2-8-11 0 DarioVargiu 3 104
(Stefano Botti, Italy) *led: kicked 2 l clr 2 1/2f out: rallied u.p whn pressed 2f out: hdd ent fnl f: no ex fnl 75yds* **19/10**[2]

3 *3¾* **Azari**[21] 2-8-11 0 MircoDemuro 5 95
(B Grizzetti, Italy) *shared 4th on outer: 3rd and rdn 2f out: sn outpcd: rallied and kpt on u.p fnl f to regain 3rd cl home* **12/5**[3]

4 *snk* **Brex Drago (ITY)** 2-8-11 0 NicolaPinna 7 95
(Stefano Botti, Italy) *t.k.h: hld up next to last: hdwy on outer 2 1/2f out: 4th and styng on u.p over 1 1/2f out: sn hrd rdn and no further imp in 3rd appr 1f out: kpt on at same pce: lost 3rd cl home* **19/10**[2]

5 *14* **Farinacci** 2-8-11 0 UmbertoRispoli 6 62
(Stefano Botti, Italy) *hld up in rr: rdn and no imp fr 2 1/2f out: eased ins fnl f* **23/20**[1]

6 *1¼* **Paco Royale** 2-8-11 0 CristianDemuro 1 59
(Agostino Affe', Italy) *restrained in share of 4th on inner: rdn and nt qckn over 2f out: eased whn btn fnl f* **66/10**

7 *4½* **Kloud Gate (FR)**[17] 6697 2-8-11 0 (p) EPedroza 4 48
(J Heloury, France) *trckd ldr: rdn and lost pl 2 1/2f out: sn wknd: eased fnl f* **135/10**

1m 38.4s (2.90) **7 Ran SP% 211.5**
WIN (incl. 1 euro stake): 2.15 (Hero Look coupled with Farinacci) PLACES: 1.66, 1.89. DF: 4.34.
**Owner** Scuderia Effevi SRL **Bred** Kilfrush Stud **Trained** Italy

7148 - (Foreign Racing) - See Raceform Interactive

# 6874 SALISBURY (R-H)
Monday, October 13

**7149 Meeting Abandoned** - Waterlogged

# 6983 WINDSOR (R-H)
Monday, October 13

**OFFICIAL GOING: Heavy (5.1)**
Wind: Almost nil Weather: Overcast, drizzly, raining from Race 5 onwards

## 7155 LADBROKES BRITISH STALLION STUDS EBF MAIDEN STKS 6f
2:00 (2:02) (Class 5) 2-Y-O £3,557 (£1,058; £529; £264) Stalls Low

Form RPR

02 1 **Krazy Paving**[12] 6867 2-9-5 0 WilliamTwiston-Davies 4 73
(Mick Channon) *chsd ldrs: rdn over 2f out: prog to go 2nd over 1f out: drvn to ld ins fnl f: hld on* **11/4**[2]

44 **2** ½ **Winning Hunter**[21] 6603 2-9-5 0 ........................ GeorgeBaker 10 72
(Philip Hide) *led: racd alone in centre: tk field to far side fr 1/2-way: rdn 2f out: hdd ins fnl f: kpt on but a jst hld* **8/1**

5 **3** 2½ **Pressure**[78] 4695 2-9-5 0 ........................ AdamKirby 9 66
(Clive Cox) *chsd ldng pair: pushed along over 2f out: cl 3rd whn nt clr run 1f out: no ex* **4/1**[3]

444 **4** 4½ **Dear Bruin (IRE)**[29] 6361 2-9-0 65 ........................ LukeMorris 8 46
(John Spearing) *chsd ldrs: shkn up wl over 2f out: no imp wl over 1f out: kpt on to take 4th ins fnl f* **10/1**

00 **5** 2½ **The Olympus Man**[25] 6496 2-9-5 0 ........................ AndreaAtzeni 12 43
(Olly Stevens) *chsd ldrs in 6th: nt on terms fr 1/2-way: pushed along fr over 2f out: plugged on but nvr involved* **10/1**

4222 **6** ½ **Chevallier**[19] 6659 2-9-5 72 ........................ RichardHughes 2 42
(Richard Hannon) *t.k.h to post: racd against nr side rail to 1/2-way: pressed ldr: pushed along over 2f out: rdn and lost 2nd over 1f out: wknd* **5/2**[1]

0 **7** 1½ **Pat Mustard**[5] 7037 2-9-0 0 ........................ RachealKneller(5) 5 37
(Jamie Osborne) *pushed along and wl off the pce in last trio 1/2-way: modest effrt 2f out: sn no prog* **50/1**

06 **8** 2½ **Herecomestheband**[32] 6261 2-9-5 0 ........................ PatCosgrave 1 30
(George Baker) *a in last trio: struggling 1/2-way: no prog* **10/1**

0 **9** ½ **Catakanta**[18] 6675 2-9-2 0 ........................ CamHardie(3) 11 28
(Denis Coakley) *a in last trio: shkn up and struggling 1/2-way: no prog* **66/1**

1m 17.26s (4.26) **Going Correction** +0.60s/f (Yiel) **9** Ran SP% **117.1**
Speed ratings (Par 95): **95,94,91,85,81 81,79,75,75**
CSF £25.60 TOTE £4.60: £1.80, £2.00, £2.00; EX 27.60 Trifecta £123.20.
**Owner** Aiden Murphy & The Hon Mrs Foster **Bred** Trebles Holford Farm Thoroughbreds **Trained** West Ilsley, Berks

**FOCUS**
Inner of straight dolled out 2yds from 6f to Winning Post. Top bend out 6yds from normal inner configuration and races of 1m and beyond increased by 21yds. Testing ground and, as is normally the case when conditions are bad, they headed to the far side in the straight.

## 7156 LADBROKES NURSERY H'CAP 1m 67y
**2:30** (2:30) (Class 5) (0-75,75) 2-Y-O **£3,557** (£1,058; £529; £264) **Stalls** Low

Form RPR

5235 **1** **Cosmic Ray**[17] 6719 2-9-5 73 ........................ OisinMurphy 9 76+
(Andrew Balding) *t.k.h: led to 3f out: dropped to 4th over 2f out but stl cl up: rallied u.p over 1f out: drvn to ld last 75yds* **4/1**[1]

504 **2** ¾ **Little Riggs**[34] 6203 2-8-13 67 ........................ AntonioFresu 12 68
(Ed Walker) *trckd ldrs: chal 3f out: rdn to ld 2f out: kpt on but hdd last 75yds* **11/2**

3165 **3** ¾ **Spindle (IRE)**[9] 6944 2-9-1 69 ........................ LiamKeniry 6 69
(Mark Usher) *wl in tch: trckd ldrs 3f out and gng wl: cl 3rd and shkn up against far rail over 1f out: nt qckn* **8/1**

0044 **4** 1 **Pink Ribbon (IRE)**[31] 6294 2-8-2 56 ........................ LukeMorris 1 54
(Sylvester Kirk) *hld up in last pair: pushed along and prog 3f out: no imp on ldng quartet 2f out: drvn and stydd on fnl f* **8/1**

442 **5** 2½ **Shaw Ting**[13] 6840 2-9-4 72 ........................ RichardKingscote 10 64
(Tom Dascombe) *dwlt: rapid rcvry to chse ldr after 1f: narrow ldr 3f out to 2f out: wknd fnl f* **9/2**[2]

5146 **6** shd **Buckleberry**[39] 6064 2-8-13 70 ........................ DannyBrock(3) 7 62
(Jonathan Portman) *sn in rr: rdn 3f out: struggling after: stydd on fnl f: n.d* **5/1**[3]

5316 **7** 6 **Frosty Times (FR)**[39] 6072 2-8-1 55 ........................ JoeFanning 2 34
(Richard Fahey) *a in rr: shkn up in last 3f out: nvr a factor* **8/1**

3140 **8** 1¾ **Divine Law**[23] 6529 2-9-7 75 ........................ SeanLevey 8 50
(Richard Hannon) *chsd ldrs: rdn wl over 2f out: sn wknd* **10/1**

0510 **9** 2¼ **Vita Mina**[29] 6359 2-8-7 64 ........................(v) DeclanBates(3) 4 34
(David Evans) *chsd ldr 1f: wknd 3f out* **16/1**

1m 49.67s (4.97) **Going Correction** +0.60s/f (Yiel) **9** Ran SP% **118.5**
Speed ratings (Par 95): **99,98,97,96,94 93,87,86,83**
CSF £26.86 CT £171.35 TOTE £4.90: £1.30, £4.60, £3.40; EX 31.30 Trifecta £554.10.
**Owner** Winterbeck Manor Stud **Bred** Winterbeck Manor Stud **Trained** Kingsclere, Hants

**FOCUS**
This looked pretty open.

## 7157 LADBROKES MAIDEN STKS (DIV I) 1m 67y
**3:00** (3:01) (Class 5) 3-Y-O+ **£3,234** (£962; £481; £240) **Stalls** Low

Form RPR

5-02 **1** **Isabella Bird**[170] 1722 3-8-11 76 ........................ CharlesBishop(3) 5 84
(Mick Channon) *mde all: drew rt away fr over 2f out: rdn over 1f out: unchal* **7/1**

4642 **2** 8 **Heho**[54] 5570 3-9-0 70 ........................ TedDurcan 1 66
(Sir Michael Stoute) *chsd ldrs: rdn 3f out: wnt modest 2nd jst over 1f out: no imp on wnr* **7/1**

0455 **3** 2¾ **Pashan Garh**[6] 7013 5-9-8 66 ........................ JoeFanning 7 64
(Pat Eddery) *chsd ldrs: rdn 3f out: wnt 2nd 2f out to jst over 1f out: one pce* **20/1**

2- **4** 1½ **Miniskirt**[364] 7245 3-9-0 0 ........................ AdamKirby 2 56
(Rae Guest) *dwlt and pushed along to get in tch: rdn 3f out: ch of a pl over 1f out: no ex* **5/1**[3]

44 **5** 9 **Golden Emerald**[56] 5504 3-9-5 0 ........................[1] GeorgeBaker 6 40
(James Fanshawe) *trckd wnr: drvn over 2f out: sn lost 2nd and wknd* **9/2**[2]

4-5 **6** 99 **Nigel's Destiny (USA)**[168] 1795 3-9-5 0 ........................ MartinHarley 10
(Jeremy Noseda) *in tch in rr whn bdly hmpd after 2f: nt rcvr and allowed to coast home* **11/1**

4632 **B** **Lady Guinevere**[5] 7042 4-9-3 67 ........................ AndreaAtzeni 9
(Stuart Williams) *hld up in tch: b.d bnd after 2f* **7/4**[1]

0 **S** **Farmshop Boy**[27] 6421 3-8-12 0 ........................ CharlieBennett(7) 4
(Natalie Lloyd-Beavis) *disputing 3rd whn slipped up bnd after 2f* **100/1**

0 **B** **Great Storm**[7] 6988 3-8-7 0 ........................ JasonNuttall(7) 8
(Gary Moore) *trapped out wd: pushed along in rr whn b.d bnd after 2f* **66/1**

1m 49.63s (4.93) **Going Correction** +0.60s/f (Yiel)
**WFA** 3 from 4yo+ 3lb **9** Ran SP% **111.8**
Speed ratings (Par 103): **99,91,88,86,77 , , ,**
CSF £52.13 TOTE £7.50: £2.20, £2.20, £4.30; EX 43.20 Trifecta £293.70.
**Owner** Jon and Julia Aisbitt **Bred** Mr & Mrs J Davis & Cranford Stud **Trained** West Ilsley, Berks

**FOCUS**
This maiden was marred by a nasty incident on the bend, where Farmshop Boy fell, bringing down Lady Guinevere and Golden Emerald in the process, and badly hampering Nigel's Destiny. The quicker of the two divisions, but slow compared with the 2yo race. The winner could be worth more.

## 7158 LADBROKES MAIDEN STKS (DIV II) 1m 67y
**3:35** (3:43) (Class 5) 3-Y-O+ **£3,234** (£962; £481; £240) **Stalls** Low

Form RPR

02 **1** **Geordan Murphy**[19] 6661 3-9-5 0 ........................ OisinMurphy 9 81+
(Andrew Balding) *trckd ldng pair: wnt 2nd 3f out and led over 2f out: shkn up and drew clr over 1f out: comf* **9/4**[2]

2 **5** **Memoria** 3-9-0 0 ........................ ChrisCatlin 3 61
(Rae Guest) *in tch in rr: pushed along over 3f out: tried to mount an effrt over 2f out: no ch w wnr over 1f out but kpt on to take 2nd last strides* **8/1**

3335 **3** shd **Rome**[12] 6877 4-9-1 74 ........................ HectorCrouch(7) 8 66
(Gary Moore) *trckd ldr to 3f out: sn pushed along: wnt 2nd 2f out: sltly impeded over 1f out: fnd nil and btn after: lost 2nd last strides* **2/1**[1]

60 **4** 4 **Sea Tiger**[19] 6661 4-9-8 0 ........................ SamHitchcott 2 57
(Chris Gordon) *led: shkn up 3f out: hdd over 2f out: wknd over 1f out* **33/1**

0 **5** nk **Franco's Secret**[138] 2681 3-9-2 0 ........................ CharlesBishop(3) 1 56
(Peter Hedger) *trckd ldng trio: pushed along and lost tch wl over 2f out: no imp on ldrs after* **7/2**[3]

**6** 14 **Hope And Fortune (IRE)** 3-9-0 0 ........................ AdamKirby 4 19
(John Butler) *s.s: a in last pair: lost tch fr 3f out: t.o* **8/1**

1m 52.29s (7.59) **Going Correction** +0.60s/f (Yiel)
**WFA** 3 from 4yo 3lb **6** Ran SP% **111.5**
Speed ratings (Par 103): **86,81,80,76,76 62**
CSF £19.52 TOTE £2.20: £1.20, £3.90; EX 16.50 Trifecta £50.20.
**Owner** B P McGuire **Bred** M A L Evans **Trained** Kingsclere, Hants

**FOCUS**
This didn't look a particularly strong maiden, and the time on worsening ground was 2.66sec slower than the first division. A step up from the winner but the race rather fell apart.

## 7159 LADBROKES H'CAP 6f
**4:10** (4:12) (Class 4) (0-80,81) 3-Y-O+ **£5,822** (£1,732; £865; £432) **Stalls** Low

Form RPR

3000 **1** **Kinglami**[37] 6144 5-9-2 75 ........................(p) FrannyNorton 7 86
(Brian Gubby) *cl up: swvd over 4f out: rdn to ld wl over 1f out: in command fnl f: styd on* **8/1**[3]

3500 **2** ¾ **Midnight Rider (IRE)**[52] 5650 6-9-2 78 ........................ AshleyMorgan(3) 12 87
(Chris Wall) *hld up in rr: prog whn nt clr run 2f out: hdwy over 1f out: chsd wnr ins fnl f: styd on but nvr cl enough to chal* **14/1**

3626 **3** ¾ **Withernsea (IRE)**[16] 6736 3-9-6 80 ........................ PaulHanagan 4 86
(Richard Fahey) *towards rr: pushed along 1/2-way: prog on outer of gp 2f out: styd on to take 3rd ins fnl f: unable to chal* **7/1**[2]

2151 **4** 1½ **Abi Scarlet (IRE)**[105] 3793 5-9-4 77 ........................ LukeMorris 15 78
(Scott Dixon) *w ldrs: led over 2f out to wl over 1f out: fdd fnl f* **25/1**

1204 **5** nk **Ridge Ranger (IRE)**[21] 6598 3-9-3 77 ........................ JasonHart 14 77
(Eric Alston) *stdd s: hld up in rr: prog and pushed along 1/2-way: cl enough over 1f out: no ex fnl f* **20/1**

054 **6** 1 **Polski Max**[58] 5444 4-9-3 79 ........................ GeorgeChaloner(3) 11 76
(Richard Fahey) *chsd ldrs: rdn 1/2-way: kpt on u.p over 1f out but nvr gng pce to chal* **11/4**[1]

0251 **7** hd **Lady Brigid (IRE)**[7] 6988 3-9-7 81 6ex ........................ PatDobbs 5 78
(Olly Stevens) *pressed ldrs: rdn over 2f out: nt qckn over 1f out: steadily fdd* **12/1**

13 **8** ¾ **Crazy Chic (IRE)**[41] 6020 3-9-1 80 ........................ MarcMonaghan(5) 6 74
(Marco Botti) *chsd ldrs: rdn wl over 2f out: kpt on but nvr able to threaten* **12/1**

2452 **9** 2 **Pettochside**[47] 5817 5-9-2 75 ........................ KierenFallon 1 63
(Chris Gordon) *settled in rr: drvn and tried to cl on outer of gp 2f out: no hdwy fnl f* **10/1**

3520 **10** 5 **Mister Musicmaster**[15] 6789 5-9-6 79 ........................ AdamKirby 8 51
(Ron Hodges) *w ldr: led 1/2-way to over 2f out: wknd wl over 1f out* **25/1**

000 **11** ½ **Rocksilla**[23] 6558 4-9-4 77 ........................(b[1]) SebSanders 2 47
(Chris Wall) *racd alone against nr side rail: nt on terms w ldrs after 1/2-way: wl bhd fnl f* **16/1**

4-02 **12** 2½ **Half A Billion (IRE)**[72] 4925 5-9-4 80 ........................ ConnorBeasley(3) 10 42
(Michael Dods) *taken down early: mde most to 1/2-way: wknd 2f out* **10/1**

0310 **13** 1 **First In Command (IRE)**[38] 6096 9-9-3 76 ........................(t) FrankieMcDonald 13 35
(Daniel Mark Loughnane) *in tch: rdn 1/2-way: wknd wl over 1f out: eased ins fnl f* **50/1**

5226 **14** 4½ **Parisian Pyramid (IRE)**[19] 6657 8-9-2 75 ........................(p) AmirQuinn 3 20
(Lee Carter) *chsd ldrs: styd alone in centre fr 1/2-way: sn struggling* **16/1**

1550 **15** ½ **Baby Bush (IRE)**[78] 4697 3-9-5 79 ........................ RichardHughes 16 22
(Richard Hannon) *wl on terms w ldrs: racd against far rail over 2f out: wknd wl over 1f out: heavily eased* **10/1**

1m 15.81s (2.81) **Going Correction** +0.60s/f (Yiel)
**WFA** 3 from 4yo+ 1lb **15** Ran SP% **125.8**
Speed ratings (Par 105): **105,104,103,101,100 99,99,98,95,88 88,84,83,77,76**
CSF £114.66 CT £861.46 TOTE £9.30: £3.20, £6.30, £2.50; EX 112.70 Trifecta £2022.90.
**Owner** Brian Gubby **Bred** Cheveley Park Stud Ltd **Trained** Bagshot, Surrey

**FOCUS**
A competitive sprint. The first two have both run some of their best races here on soft ground.

## 7160 LADBROKES FILLIES H'CAP 1m 67y
**4:40** (4:42) (Class 4) (0-80,80) 3-Y-O+ **£5,822** (£1,732; £865; £432) **Stalls** Low

Form RPR

0250 **1** **Tullia (IRE)**[17] 6722 3-8-12 74 ........................(b[1]) LukeMorris 10 84
(William Knight) *trckd ldrs: drvn to ld 2f out: clr over 1f out: styd on u.p* **8/1**

462 **2** 3¼ **Sweet Martoni**[17] 6704 4-9-3 76 ........................ RichardHughes 8 79
(William Knight) *in tch: rdn and prog 3f out: chsd clr wnr over 1f out: styd on but no ch to threaten* **4/1**[1]

4323 **3** 4 **Grevillea (IRE)**[12] 6871 3-9-4 80 ........................ WilliamTwiston-Davies 2 73
(Mick Channon) *in tch: rdn to chse ldrs 3f out: no imp 2f out: kpt on to take 3rd fnl f* **9/2**[2]

5-10 **4** 3¾ **Lady Marl**[25] 6484 3-8-10 72 ........................ MartinHarley 1 57
(Gary Moore) *led at gd pce: rdn and racd awkwardly over 2f out: sn hdd: wknd over 1f out* **9/1**

1400 **5** ¾ **Choral Festival**[5] 7033 8-8-10 69 ........................ WilliamCarson 3 52
(John Bridger) *mostly in last pair: effrt and hmpd over 3f out: plugged on fnl 2f: no ch* **12/1**

2130 **6** *2* **Pretty Bubbles**[10] 6891 5-9-7 80 ........ PaddyAspell 9 58
(J R Jenkins) *trckd ldng trio: rdn 3f out: no imp 2f out: wknd over 1f out* **8/1**

2321 **7** *11* **Jersey Brown (IRE)**[13] 6837 3-8-5 67 ........ JoeFanning 6 20
(Mick Channon) *slowly away and awkward s: mostly in last trio: rdn and no prog 3f out: wknd 2f out* **11/2**[3]

0232 **8** *1 ½* **Cornish Path**[30] 6316 3-8-13 75 ........ FergusSweeney 7 25
(Henry Candy) *chsd ldng pair: rdn 3f out: wknd 2f out: eased fnl f* **4/1**[1]

035 **9** *24* **Lostintheclouds**[25] 6482 3-8-8 70 ow1 ........ OisinMurphy 5
(Mike Murphy) *chsd ldrs tl wknd sn after 1/2-way: t.o* **16/1**

1m 50.84s (6.14) **Going Correction** +0.90s/f (Soft)
**WFA** 3 from 4yo+ 3lb 9 Ran SP% **119.4**
Speed ratings (Par 105): **105,101,97,94,93 91,80,78,54**
CSF £41.46 CT £166.80 TOTE £9.60: £2.80, £1.70, £1.80; EX 36.70 Trifecta £151.00.

**Owner** Hot to Trot Racing Club & P Winkworth **Bred** Sc Archi Romani **Trained** Patching, W Sussex

**FOCUS**
The winner is rated back towards her early-season form.

## 7161 DOWNLOAD THE LADBROKES APP H'CAP — 1m 2f 7y
**5:10** (5:10) (Class 4) (0-85,85) 3-Y-O **£5,822** (£1,732; £865; £432) **Stalls** Centre

Form RPR

245 **1** **Latin Charm (IRE)**[27] 6438 3-8-11 **80** ow1 ........ (p) MarcMonaghan(5) 9 90
(Marco Botti) *dwlt: pushed along in last pair: rdn and prog fr 4f out to chse ldrs over 2f out: sustained effrt u.p to cl and ld ins fnl f: jst hld on* **7/2**[2]

1650 **2** *shd* **Roskilly (IRE)**[16] 6737 3-9-1 **79** ........ (vt) OisinMurphy 4 88
(Andrew Balding) *in tch: prog over 3f out: rdn to chal over 2f out against far rail: upsides whn wnr wnt past ins fnl f: kpt on wl nr fin: jst failed* **8/1**

3310 **3** *¾* **Loch Ma Naire (IRE)**[43] 5948 3-9-0 **78** ........ AdamKirby 8 86
(Ed Dunlop) *hld up in tch: prog 4f out: rdn to ld over 2f out: hrd pressed after: hdd ins fnl f: kpt on* **9/1**

2551 **4** *9* **Eddiemaurice (IRE)**[21] 6615 3-8-10 **74** ........ LukeMorris 12 65
(John Flint) *trckd ldng pair: led over 3f out to over 2f out: wknd over 1f out* **20/1**

-060 **5** *8* **Laugharne**[45] 5877 3-9-4 **82** ........ GeorgeBaker 5 59
(Roger Charlton) *hld up in last: shkn up 4f out: hanging and nt clr run 3f out: passed wkng rivals after but nvr a factor* **7/1**[3]

304 **6** *5* **Prairie Rose (GER)**[62] 5274 3-8-10 **74** ........ JoeFanning 10 42
(Olly Stevens) *led at gd pce: hdd over 3f out: wknd over 2f out* **25/1**

304 **7** *6* **All Talk N No Do (IRE)**[26] 6460 3-8-7 **76** ........ JoeDoyle(5) 1 33
(Seamus Durack) *chsd ldrs: rdn over 3f out: wknd over 2f out* **7/1**[3]

6221 **8** *30* **Inspector Norse**[17] 6714 3-9-3 **81** ........ LiamKeniry 11
(Sylvester Kirk) *chsd ldr: rdn 4f out: sn wknd: t.o* **8/1**

-304 **9** *3 ¼* **The Alamo (IRE)**[24] 6523 3-8-13 **77** ........ RichardHughes 6
(Richard Hannon) *trckd ldrs: shkn up 4f out: wknd 3f out: heavily eased fnl 2f: t.o* **3/1**[1]

0540 **10** *8* **Laurelita (IRE)**[45] 5884 3-8-12 **76** ........ PatCosgrave 2
(George Baker) *in tch: rdn and struggling bef 1/2-way: t.o over 2f out* **10/1**

2m 16.21s (7.51) **Going Correction** +0.90s/f (Soft) 10 Ran SP% **122.1**
Speed ratings (Par 103): **105,104,104,97,90 86,81,57,55,48**
CSF £33.57 CT £240.67 TOTE £4.70: £1.70, £2.90, £2.50; EX 34.10 Trifecta £229.40.

**Owner** Grundy Bloodstock Limited **Bred** Grundy Bloodstock Srl **Trained** Newmarket, Suffolk

■ Stewards' Enquiry : Marc Monaghan two-day ban: used whip above permitted level (Oct 27-28)

**FOCUS**
Bad ground. They went a decent pace here and finished well strung out behind the first three, the only ones to show their form.

## 7162 BET WITH THE NEW LADBROKES APP H'CAP — 1m 3f 135y
**5:40** (5:42) (Class 5) (0-70,70) 3-Y-O **£3,557** (£1,058; £529; £264) **Stalls** Centre

Form RPR

000 **1** **Rideonastar (IRE)**[89] 4325 3-9-4 67 ........ RichardKingscote 11 82+
(Ralph Beckett) *led 2f: styd prom: led again 4f out gng strly: hrd rdn 2f out against far rail: pressed over 1f out but kpt on wl* **6/1**[3]

023 **2** *1 ¼* **Gleese The Devil (IRE)**[38] 6118 3-9-7 70 ........ PaulHanagan 10 83+
(Richard Fahey) *hld up in tch: shkn up over 4f out: prog to chse wnr 3f out: drvn and tried to chal over 1f out: kpt on but nvr able to get there* **4/1**[2]

164 **3** *10* **Bella Varenna (IRE)**[30] 6338 3-9-5 68 ........ MartinHarley 6 65
(Marco Botti) *trckd ldrs: rdn to go 3rd 3f out: one pce and no imp on ldng pair fnl 2f* **7/1**

6105 **4** *nk* **Marengo**[17] 6706 3-9-6 69 ........ OisinMurphy 7 66
(Ed de Giles) *in tch: rdn over 3f out: no imp and btn 2f out: plugged on to press for 3rd nr fin* **3/1**[1]

1045 **5** *7* **Loving Your Work**[38] 6091 3-9-3 66 ........ PatCosgrave 4 51
(George Baker) *hld up: effrt and rdn over 3f out: no prog and wl btn 2f out* **6/1**[3]

2363 **6** *10* **Cincinnati Girl (IRE)**[30] 6341 3-9-0 66 ........ CamHardie(3) 1 35
(Denis Coakley) *t.k.h: led after 3f to 4f out: sn rdn: wknd wl over 2f out* **10/1**

0-54 **7** *15* **Heavens Eyes (IRE)**[33] 6238 3-9-6 69 ........ FrannyNorton 2 14
(Jo Hughes) *hld up in tch: rdn wl over 3f out: sn struggling: wl btn fnl 2f* **20/1**

6423 **8** *¾* **Travis Bickle (IRE)**[121] 3224 3-8-13 62 ........ LiamKeniry 3 6
(John Flint) *trckd ldrs: shkn up over 3f out: sn wknd: eased fnl 2f* **10/1**

5300 **9** *11* **Peacemaker (IRE)**[26] 6461 3-8-11 60 ........ (p) LukeMorris 8
(Eve Johnson Houghton) *led after 2f tl after 3f: rdn 1/2-way: sn struggling: bhd over 2f out* **10/1**

2m 44.05s (14.55) **Going Correction** +1.20s/f (Soft) 9 Ran SP% **118.1**
Speed ratings (Par 101): **99,98,91,91,86 79,69,69,62**
CSF £30.99 CT £174.57 TOTE £8.30: £2.70, £1.70, £2.10; EX 46.70 Trifecta £168.40.

**Owner** D & J Newell **Bred** Derek & Judith Newell **Trained** Kimpton, Hants

**FOCUS**
A one-two for the sire Manduro here, the first two clear. It's hard to know how literally to take the form.

T/Jkpt: £36,410.90 to a £1 stake. Pool: £102,566.13 - 2.00 winning tickets T/Plt: £220.50 to a £1 stake. Pool: £90,332.09 - 298.98 winning tickets T/Qpdt: £59.30 to a £1 stake. Pool: £9,205.48 - 114.76 winning tickets JN

# 4312 COMPIEGNE (L-H)
Monday, October 13

**OFFICIAL GOING: Turf: very heavy**

## 7163a PRIX DE PIERREFONDS (MAIDEN) (2YO FILLIES) (TURF) — 1m
**12:00** (12:00) 2-Y-O **£10,416** (£4,166; £3,125; £2,083; £1,041)

RPR

**1** **Passiflore (FR)**[27] 2-9-0 0 ........ MaximeGuyon 8 78
(Mme Pia Brandt, France) **12/5**[2]

**2** *nk* **Strelkita (FR)**[18] 2-9-0 0 ........ GregoryBenoist 2 77
(D Smaga, France) **6/4**[1]

**3** *6* **Sleekfonteine (FR)**[115] 2-9-0 0 ........ CristianDemuro 5 64
(F Doumen, France) **31/5**

**4** *4* **Graceland (FR)**[30] 6333 2-9-0 0 ........ ChristopheSoumillon 4 55
(Michael Bell) *broke wl: chsd ldng pair: shkn up to chal 1 1/2f out: sn rdn and nt qckn: wknd ins fnl f* **4/1**[3]

**5** *½* **Union Sacree (FR)** 2-8-10 0 ........ FabriceVeron 3 50
(H-A Pantall, France) **11/1**

**6** *7* **Dingari (FR)**[87] 2-9-0 0 ........ TheoBachelot 7 39
(Mario Hofer, Germany) **172/10**

**7** *2 ½* **Couleur Du Large (FR)** 2-8-3 0 ........ ClementLanfernini(7) 1 29
(C Lerner, France) **32/1**

1m 49.38s (109.38) 7 Ran SP% **120.2**
WIN (incl. 1 euro stake): 3.40. PLACES: 1.20, 1.10, 1.30. DF: 3.50. SF: 8.80.

**Owner** Ecurie Loick Fouchet **Bred** Ecurie Loick Fouchet **Trained** France

## 7164a PRIX DE CARLEPONT (MAIDEN) (3YO) (TURF) — 1m 6f
**2:05** (12:00) 3-Y-O **£8,333** (£3,333; £2,500; £1,666; £833)

RPR

**1** **Triptyka (IRE)** 3-8-13 0 ........ FlavienMasse 8 78
(J-M Beguigne, France) **49/10**[3]

**2** *5* **Agrapart (FR)**[162] 2003 3-9-2 0 ........ ValentinGambart 2 74
(Nick Williams) *dwlt: t.k.h and sn led: hdd after 2 1/2f and trckd new ldr: rdn to ld 2f out and edgd rt: hdd under 1 1/2f out: kpt on fnl f but no ch w wnr* **176/10**

**3** *6* **Koreen (IRE)**[165] 3-9-2 0 ........ MlleAmelieFoulon 4 66
(A Fabre, France) **2/1**[1]

**4** *nse* **Bodegas (FR)** 3-9-2 0 ........ RomainAuray 5 66
(M Figge, Germany) **133/10**

**5** *6* **Waldfest** 3-8-13 0 ........ AntoineCoutier 3 54
(A De Royer-Dupre, France) **31/10**[2]

**6** *5* **Affiche (USA)**[23] 3-8-13 0 ........ AnthonyCaramanolis 1 47
(N Clement, France) **67/10**

**7** *10* **Demoiselle (IRE)**[23] 3-8-13 0 ........ SoufyaneMoulin 6 33
(P Bary, France) **51/10**

**8** *dist* **Tonica (FR)**[172] 3-8-13 0 ........ JordanPlateaux 7
(J-J Chiozzi, France) **94/1**

**9** *¾* **Elassi (FR)** 3-8-13 0 ........ YohannBourgois 9
(Mme L Audon, France) **43/1**

3m 25.17s (205.17) 9 Ran SP% **119.7**
WIN (incl. 1 euro stake): 5.90. PLACES: 2.00, 3.20, 1.60. DF: 68.30. SF: 120.50.

**Owner** Patrick Fellous **Bred** Aleyrion Bloodstock Ltd **Trained** France

# 7018 LEICESTER (R-H)
Tuesday, October 14

**OFFICIAL GOING: Heavy (5.6)**
Wind: Light half-behind Weather: Overcast

## 7165 FOSSE WAY NURSERY H'CAP — 1m 60y
**2:10** (2:10) (Class 6) (0-60,60) 2-Y-O **£1,940** (£577; £288; £144) **Stalls** Low

Form RPR

0006 **1** **All My Love (IRE)**[46] 5875 2-9-4 58 ........ RichardHughes 1 68
(Richard Hannon) *sn w ldr: led over 3f out: rdn over 2f out: edgd lft fr over 1f out: styd on wl: eased nr fin* **7/1**

4454 **2** *3 ¾* **Star Ascending (IRE)**[27] 6449 2-9-4 58 ........ JamesDoyle 3 60
(Brian Ellison) *hld up: pushed along and hdwy over 2f out: rdn to chse wnr over 1f out: edgd lft ins fnl f: styd on same pce* **7/2**[2]

0000 **3** *2 ½* **Quae Supra**[7] 7014 2-9-5 59 ........ PatDobbs 7 55
(Richard Hannon) *led: hdd over 3f out: sn rdn: styd on same pce fr over 1f out* **25/1**

2051 **4** *1 ¼* **Chilworth Bells**[28] 6428 2-9-4 58 ........ GrahamGibbons 4 51
(David Barron) *chsd ldrs: rdn over 2f out: wknd wl ins fnl f* **3/1**[1]

060 **5** *1 ½* **Courier**[13] 6852 2-9-4 58 ........ RyanMoore 2 48
(Jeremy Noseda) *hld up: rdn over 3f out: hdwy over 2f out: wknd ins fnl f* **5/1**[3]

4046 **6** *¾* **Horsetracker**[10] 6944 2-9-1 60 ........ GeorgeDowning(5) 9 48
(Ian Williams) *chsd ldrs: rdn over 2f out: wknd over 1f out* **10/1**

000 **7** *1 ¾* **Sonar (IRE)**[43] 5981 2-9-4 58 ........ TomQueally 8 42
(Michael Bell) *hld up: rdn over 3f out: wknd over 1f out* **8/1**

3006 **8** *1 ½* **Bridgekeeper**[13] 6869 2-9-5 59 ........ StevieDonohoe 5 40
(James Eustace) *hld up in tch: rdn over 2f out: wknd over 1f out* **8/1**

1m 53.26s (8.16) **Going Correction** +0.725s/f (Yiel) 8 Ran SP% **111.5**
Speed ratings (Par 93): **88,84,81,80,79 78,76,75**
CSF £30.12 CT £569.75 TOTE £8.20: £2.00, £1.60, £4.40; EX 31.80 Trifecta £477.00.

**Owner** Mrs J Wood **Bred** Irish National Stud **Trained** East Everleigh, Wilts

**FOCUS**
False rail from the top of the hill on the back straight all the way to the winning post, this increased all the distances on the round course by 17 yards. After 15mm of overnight rain the going was eased to heavy (from soft, good to soft in places). A tight nursery with only 2lb covering the eight runners.

## 7166 EBFSTALLIONS.COM REFERENCE POINT MAIDEN STKS (BOBIS RACE) (C&G) — 7f 9y
**2:40** (2:40) (Class 4) 2-Y-O **£5,175** (£1,540; £769; £384) **Stalls** High

Form RPR

042 **1** **Maraakib (IRE)**[24] 6551 2-9-0 0 ........ PaulHanagan 2 83+
(Brian Meehan) *mde all: pushed clr fr over 1f out: eased nr fin* **10/11**[1]

2 2 ¾ **Conflicting Advice (USA)** 2-9-0 0 RyanMoore 8 72+
(Sir Michael Stoute) *hld up: pushed along over 2f out: hdwy to go 2nd over 1f out: styd on: no ch w wnr* **3/1**[2]

00 3 2 **Flying Fantasy**[22] 6603 2-9-0 0 GrahamGibbons 1 67+
(William Haggas) *hld up: hdwy: nt clr run and hit over hd by rivals whip over 1f out: styd on: nt trble ldrs* **12/1**

20 4 6 **Jewelled Prince**[25] 6509 2-9-0 0 PatrickMathers 9 52
(Richard Fahey) *chsd ldrs: nt clr run 4f out: rdn over 2f out: wknd ins fnl f* **16/1**

5 3 **Justice First** 2-9-0 0 JamesDoyle 5 45
(Ed Dunlop) *s.i.s: hld up: hdwy over 2f out: wknd fnl f* **20/1**

6 1 ¾ **Monna Valley** 2-9-0 0 HarryBentley 4 40
(Stuart Williams) *hld up: hdwy over 4f out: rdn over 2f out: wknd over 1f out* **40/1**

03 7 1 ¼ **Mutamid**[22] 6604 2-9-0 0 MartinHarley 7 37
(Ismail Mohammed) *chsd wnr: rdn over 2f out: wknd over 1f out* **7/1**[3]

1m 30.14s (3.94) **Going Correction** +0.675s/f (Yiel) 7 Ran SP% **110.7**
Speed ratings (Par 97): **104,100,98,91,88 86,84**
CSF £3.43 TOTE £1.70: £1.10, £3.00; EX 5.40 Trifecta £24.10.
**Owner** Hamdan Al Maktoum **Bred** Joe Fogarty **Trained** Manton, Wilts

**FOCUS**
An uncompetitive maiden run at a fair pace in the conditions.

## 7167 WHISSENDINE (S) STKS — 7f 9y
**3:10** (3:11) (Class 6) 3-4-Y-O **£1,940** (£577; £288; £144) **Stalls** High

Form RPR

5553 1 **Zain Zone (IRE)**[22] 6613 3-8-10 69 (p) JamesSullivan 7 76
(Ruth Carr) *mde all: rdn over 1f out: styd on* **9/2**[2]

6045 2 2 ¾ **Mandy The Nag (USA)**[15] 6822 4-8-7 62 PaulHanagan 5 65
(Richard Fahey) *chsd ldrs: pushed along and hung rt fr over 4f out: outpcd 1/2-way: rallied to chse wnr over 1f out: kpt on* **10/1**

51 3 8 **Admirable Art (IRE)**[39] 6087 4-8-12 60 (p) LiamKeniry 1 49
(Tony Carroll) *s.i.s: hdwy 3f out: rdn over 1f out: wknd fnl f* **5/1**[3]

00- 4 7 **Emperor Ferdinand (IRE)**[290] 8425 3-8-10 0 MartinDwyer 6 30
(Marcus Tregoning) *prom: lost pl 5f out: bhd fr 1/2-way* **16/1**

3102 5 shd **Cape Of Hope (IRE)**[11] 6898 4-9-3 69 (v) RichardKingscote 3 36
(Tom Dascombe) *chsd wnr: rdn over 2f out: wknd over 1f out* **5/2**[1]

042 6 11 **Emperor Julius (IRE)**[39] 6088 4-8-12 62 FergusSweeney 2
(Jo Crowley) *prom: rdn and hung rt over 2f out: wknd and eased fnl 2f* **9/2**[2]

4500 7 8 **Vodka Time (IRE)**[13] 6873 3-8-10 59 (be[1]) PaddyAspell 4
(Shaun Harris) *s.i.s: plld hrd and hdwy over 5f out: rdn and wknd over 2f out* **25/1**

0500 8 4 ½ **Robbian**[27] 6454 3-9-1 46 MartinLane 10
(Charles Smith) *sn pushed along in rr: bhd fnl 4f* **50/1**

0060 9 2 ¾ **Malachim Mist (IRE)**[11] 4501 3-8-11 72 ow1 (b) RichardHughes 9
(Oliver Sherwood) *sn bhd: eased fnl 2f* **8/1**

1m 29.64s (3.44) **Going Correction** +0.675s/f (Yiel)
**WFA** 3 from 4yo 2lb 9 Ran SP% **113.5**
Speed ratings (Par 101): **107,103,94,86,86 74,64,59,56**
CSF £47.64 TOTE £5.30: £1.20, £3.10, £2.50; EX 41.20 Trifecta £283.30.No bid for the winner. Mandy The Nag bought by Mrs Nikki Evans for £6,000.
**Owner** 21St Century Racing & Mrs R Carr **Bred** Tom Kelly **Trained** Huby, N Yorks

**FOCUS**
A weak seller run at a sound pace in the conditions. The winner is rated to the balance of his form.

## 7168 WREAKE H'CAP — 7f 9y
**3:40** (3:42) (Class 2) (0-110,104) 3-Y-O+ **£16,762** (£4,715; £2,357; £1,180; £587) **Stalls** High

Form RPR

3503 1 **Suzi's Connoisseur**[17] 6755 3-9-3 100 (b) JamesDoyle 2 107
(Hugo Palmer) *hld up: hdwy over 1f out: sn rdn: styd on u.p to ld nr fin* **5/1**[2]

3123 2 nk **Athletic**[17] 6740 5-8-10 96 (v) JennyPowell(5) 3 103
(Andrew Reid) *s.i.s: hld up: hdwy over 2f out: led over 1f out: rdn and hdd nr fin* **7/1**

0660 3 4 **Azagal (IRE)**[11] 6895 3-8-13 96 TedDurcan 10 92
(Tim Easterby) *sn pushed along in rr: styd on to go 2nd ins fnl f: nt trble ldrs* **20/1**

1055 4 2 ½ **Joey's Destiny (IRE)**[17] 6755 4-9-1 96 (p) MartinDwyer 4 87
(George Baker) *hld up in tch: racd keenly: rdn over 2f out: styd on same pce fr over 1f out* **8/1**

1005 5 nse **Kosika (USA)**[38] 6164 4-9-1 96 FrannyNorton 11 86
(Mark Johnston) *prom: rdn over 2f out: wknd ins fnl f* **8/1**

22-6 6 1 ½ **Modern Tutor**[129] 2984 5-9-1 96 DavidProbert 9 82
(Andrew Balding) *led: rdn: edgd rt and hdd over 1f out: wknd ins fnl f* **16/1**

0051 7 1 **Loving Spirit**[7] 7022 6-9-7 102 6ex RobertTart 5 86
(James Toller) *sn pushed along in rr: nvr on terms* **6/1**[3]

503 8 ½ **Cordite (IRE)**[7] 7022 3-9-2 104 AlistairRawlinson(5) 6 86
(Michael Appleby) *w ldr tl rdn over 2f out: wknd over 1f out* **3/1**[1]

3000 9 14 **Rufford (IRE)**[66] 5165 3-9-1 98 RyanMoore 8 43
(Richard Fahey) *w ldr 3f: rdn 1/2-way: wknd 2f out* **16/1**

0000 10 3 ¼ **Royal Rascal**[17] 6740 4-9-1 96 (bt) RobertWinston 1 34
(Tim Easterby) *s.i.s: hdwy over 5f out: rdn 1/2-way: wknd 2f out* **33/1**

1m 29.31s (3.11) **Going Correction** +0.675s/f (Yiel)
**WFA** 3 from 4yo+ 2lb 10 Ran SP% **110.1**
Speed ratings (Par 109): **109,108,104,101,101 99,98,97,81,78**
CSF £35.87 CT £563.72 TOTE £8.00: £1.80, £2.10, £6.90; EX 32.00 Trifecta £918.10.
**Owner** Greenstead Hall Racing Ltd **Bred** Greenstead Hall Racing Ltd **Trained** Newmarket, Suffolk
■ Seolan (14-1) was withdrawn. Rule 4 applies to all bets. Deduction - 5p in the £.

**FOCUS**
Not the most competitive contest for the grade with all but three racing off a higher mark than their official rating. It was run at a fair pace. The winner rates a length personal best.

## 7169 BRITISH STALLION STUDS EBF MAIDEN STKS (BOBIS RACE) (DIV I) — 1m 60y
**4:10** (4:10) (Class 4) 2-Y-O **£5,175** (£1,540; £769; £384) **Stalls** Low

Form RPR

5 1 **Atab (IRE)**[40] 6065 2-9-0 0 PaulHanagan 7 73+
(Charles Hills) *mde all: shkn up over 1f out: styd on wl: eased nr fin* **2/1**[1]

0 2 1 ½ **Fibre Optic**[18] 6712 2-9-5 0 TomQueally 9 72
(Luca Cumani) *hld up: hdwy over 2f out: chsd wnr over 1f out: styd on same pce ins fnl f* **8/1**

603 3 1 **Arcano Gold (IRE)**[60] 5386 2-9-5 76 PatrickMathers 4 70
(Richard Fahey) *chsd ldrs: rdn over 2f out: no ex ins fnl f* **11/4**[2]

4 ¾ **Scrutinise** 2-9-5 0 JamesDoyle 3 68+
(Ed Dunlop) *hld up: hdwy over 1f out: styd on same pce ins fnl f* **20/1**

6 5 ½ **Munstead Pride**[13] 6875 2-9-5 0 DavidProbert 6 67
(Andrew Balding) *prom: rdn over 2f out: no ex ins fnl f* **6/1**

6 6 ¾ **Doesyourdogbite (IRE)**[32] 6279 2-9-5 0 LiamKeniry 10 65
(Andrew Hollinshead) *w wnr tl rdn over 2f out: styd on same pce fr over 1f out* **33/1**

7 nse **I Zingari** 2-9-5 0 RyanMoore 5 65+
(Sir Michael Stoute) *s.i.s: hld up: pushed along over 1f out: nvr trbld ldrs* **9/2**[3]

1m 54.24s (9.14) **Going Correction** +0.725s/f (Yiel) 7 Ran SP% **111.3**
Speed ratings (Par 97): **83,81,80,79,79 78,78**
CSF £17.67 TOTE £2.90: £1.70, £3.40; EX 15.70 Trifecta £50.80.
**Owner** Hamdan Al Maktoum **Bred** Shadwell Estate Company Limited **Trained** Lambourn, Berks

**FOCUS**
Some nice types lined up for this maiden which was run at an honest pace.

## 7170 BRITISH STALLION STUDS EBF MAIDEN STKS (BOBIS RACE) (DIV II) — 1m 60y
**4:40** (4:40) (Class 4) 2-Y-O **£5,175** (£1,540; £769; £384) **Stalls** Low

Form RPR

2 1 **Shakopee**[36] 6190 2-9-5 0 TomQueally 3 78+
(Luca Cumani) *trckd ldrs: led 2f out: shkn up over 1f out: styd on* **8/13**[1]

0 2 ¾ **Searching (IRE)**[32] 6300 2-9-5 0 JackMitchell 2 74+
(Roger Varian) *chsd ldrs: rdn to chse wnr over 1f out: kpt on* **4/1**[2]

50 3 2 ¼ **Tortilla Jackson**[17] 6757 2-9-5 0 RichardKingscote 1 69
(Tom Dascombe) *w ldr tl led 5f out: rdn and hdd 2f out: styd on same pce fnl f* **14/1**

4 1 ¾ **Casila (IRE)** 2-9-0 0 FrannyNorton 6 61
(Mark Johnston) *led: hdd 5f out: hung rt 4f out: hmpd over 3f out: rdn over 1f out: styd on same pce* **7/1**[3]

5 5 **Duke Of Sonning** 2-9-5 0 JimmyFortune 8 61+
(Alan King) *hld up: hdwy whn hmpd over 3f out: sn lost pl: wknd ins fnl f* **12/1**

6 2 ½ **Spirit Rapping (IRE)** 2-9-5 0 LiamKeniry 7 49
(Andrew Hollinshead) *s.i.s: hld up: hdwy over 2f out: wknd fnl f* **50/1**

1m 57.27s (12.17) **Going Correction** +0.725s/f (Yiel) 6 Ran SP% **110.7**
Speed ratings (Par 97): **68,67,65,63,58 55**
CSF £3.25 TOTE £1.80: £1.10, £1.70; EX 3.70 Trifecta £18.00.
**Owner** Fittocks Stud **Bred** Fittocks Stud **Trained** Newmarket, Suffolk
■ Stewards' Enquiry : Franny Norton two-day ban: failed to ride to draw (Oct 28-29)

**FOCUS**
The pace was steady for this fair maiden.

## 7171 WYMESWOLD CONDITIONS STKS (BOBIS RACE) — 7f 9y
**5:10** (5:11) (Class 3) 2-Y-O **£6,469** (£1,925; £962; £481) **Stalls** High

Form RPR

13 1 **Johnny Barnes (IRE)**[42] 6004 2-9-2 0 WilliamBuick 1 99+
(John Gosden) *plld hrd and prom: led over 5f out: shkn up over 1f out: r.o wl* **10/11**[1]

1005 2 4 **Dougal (IRE)**[33] 6256 2-9-5 95 PatDobbs 2 92
(Richard Hannon) *prom: chsd wnr over 2f out: rdn over 1f out: sn outpcd* **7/4**[2]

4 3 10 **Henryhudsonbridge (USA)**[16] 6784 2-8-13 0 JimmyFortune 4 66
(Brian Meehan) *hld up in tch: pushed along 1/2-way: wknd over 1f out: eased ins fnl f* **12/1**[3]

51 4 15 **Midtech Star (IRE)**[14] 6838 2-8-13 79 StevieDonohoe 3 24
(Ian Williams) *led: hdd over 5f out: chsd wnr tl rdn over 2f out: sn wknd* **12/1**[3]

1m 30.84s (4.64) **Going Correction** +0.675s/f (Yiel) 4 Ran SP% **104.1**
Speed ratings (Par 99): **100,95,84,66**
CSF £2.49 TOTE £2.20; EX 2.50 Trifecta £6.20.
**Owner** Bermuda Thoroughbred Racing Limited **Bred** Citadel Stud **Trained** Newmarket, Suffolk

**FOCUS**
A disappointing turnout for this conditions event which was run at a steady pace.

## 7172 STEWARDS H'CAP — 1m 1f 218y
**5:40** (5:40) (Class 5) (0-75,75) 3-Y-O+ **£2,587** (£770; £384; £192) **Stalls** Low

Form RPR

3145 1 **No Win No Fee**[13] 6870 4-9-5 75 AlistairRawlinson(5) 13 86+
(Michael Appleby) *a.p: chsd ldr 6f out: led over 3f out: rdn and hdd over 1f out: rallied to ld nr fin* **6/1**[3]

6040 2 ¾ **Minstrel Lad**[43] 5975 6-8-10 64 SimonPearce(3) 15 73
(Lydia Pearce) *hld up: hdwy over 2f out: rdn to ld over 1f out: edgd lft: hdd nr fin* **16/1**

2414 3 2 ¼ **Scoppio Del Carro**[31] 6323 3-9-5 75 (t) DavidProbert 14 80
(Andrew Balding) *hld up: hdwy over 2f out: sn rdn: styd on: nt rch ldrs* **7/1**

6346 4 2 **Tucson Arizona**[22] 6608 3-9-4 74 (tp) WilliamCarson 7 75
(Anthony Carson) *s.i.s: hld up: swtchd rt and hdwy over 1f out: sn rdn: styd on same pce ins fnl f* **12/1**

0054 5 4 **Topamichi**[13] 6855 4-9-5 70 HarryBentley 1 63
(Mark H Tompkins) *chsd ldrs: rdn and ev ch 2f out: wknd ins fnl f* **5/1**[2]

6621 6 ¾ **Penny's Boy**[13] 6877 3-8-13 74 (t) TimClark(5) 4 66
(Simon Hodgson) *hld up: hdwy over 3f out: sn rdn: wknd ins fnl f* **25/1**

1361 7 5 **Mister Mayday (IRE)**[7] 7001 3-9-1 71 6ex (b) PatCosgrave 6 53
(George Baker) *hld up: hdwy over 2f out: sn rdn: wknd fnl f* **10/1**

5340 8 3 ¾ **Spiceupyourlife (IRE)**[21] 6626 3-9-2 72 PatrickMathers 8 47
(Richard Fahey) *chsd ldr 4f: remained handy tl rdn and wknd wl over 1f out* **25/1**

5-66 9 5 **Conflicting**[24] 6552 3-9-2 72 (t) JimmyFortune 11 38
(Charlie Fellowes) *s.s: bhd: nvr nrr* **50/1**

1260 10 6 **Sheriff Of Nawton (IRE)**[37] 6166 3-9-2 72 SamJames 2 26
(David O'Meara) *prom: rdn over 3f out: wknd over 2f out* **16/1**

4431 11 10 **Allergic Reaction (IRE)**[21] 6635 3-9-1 71 RichardKingscote 5 6
(William Knight) *led: rdn and hdd over 3f out: wknd over 2f out* **8/1**

3-1 12 17 **Lobster Pot**[60] 5388 3-9-1 71 JamesDoyle 16
(Hugo Palmer) *prom: rdn over 3f out: wknd over 2f out* **3/1**[1]

2m 13.93s (6.03) **Going Correction** +0.725s/f (Yiel)
**WFA** 3 from 4yo+ 5lb 12 Ran SP% **117.8**
Speed ratings (Par 103): **104,103,101,100,96 96,92,89,85,80 72,58**
CSF £95.04 CT £691.22 TOTE £4.60: £1.90, £8.40, £3.80; EX 136.50 Trifecta £1393.30.
**Owner** Stephen Almond **Bred** Bearstone Stud **Trained** Danethorpe, Notts
■ Stewards' Enquiry : Simon Pearce four-day ban: used whip above permitted level (Oct 28-31)

**FOCUS**
A competitive handicap run at a sound pace. The game winner could have been rated higher.
T/Plt: £53.60 to a £1 stake. Pool: £59,487.37 - 808.81 winning tickets. T/Qpdt: £16.20 to a £1 stake. Pool: £3,849.81 - 174.90 winning tickets. CR

# 6859 NEWCASTLE (L-H)

Tuesday, October 14

**OFFICIAL GOING: Good to soft (good in places; 6.9)**

Wind: Almost nil Weather: Overcast

## 7173 ROYAL MARINES 350TH ANNIVERSARY / EBF IRISH STALLION FARMS MAIDEN STKS (C&G) 1m 3y(S)

**2:00** (2:00) (Class 5) 2-Y-O **£2,911** (£866; £432; £216) **Stalls** Centre

Form RPR

4 **1** **Muqtaser (USA)**[38] 6125 2-9-0 0 ........ GrahamLee 3 86+
(Roger Varian) *in tch: stdy hdwy over 2f out: effrt and rdn over 1f out: led ins fnl f: qcknd clr: readily* **6/4**[2]

42 **2** *2 1/2* **Game Pie (IRE)**[19] 6683 2-9-0 0 ........ DanielTudhope 6 80
(Hugo Palmer) *trckd ldrs: hdwy to ld over 2f out: sn rdn: hdd ins fnl f: kpt on: nt pce of wnr* **8/13**[1]

0 **3** *12* **Ingleby Hollow**[10] 6931 2-9-0 0 ........ DavidNolan 2 52
(David O'Meara) *t.k.h: w ldr: rdn and outpcd over 3f out: rallied over 1f out: kpt on: no ch w first two* **22/1**[3]

60 **4** *2 1/4* **Life Knowledge (IRE)**[13] 6859 2-8-11 0 ........ JoeyHaynes(3) 7 47
(Patrick Holmes) *slt ld tl rdn and hdd over 2f out: wknd fnl f* **100/1**

5 **5** *1* **The Kurator (IRE)**[20] 6667 2-9-0 0 ........ PJMcDonald 5 45
(Ann Duffield) *dwlt: hld up: struggling wl over 2f out: sn btn* **33/1**

00 **6** *17* **Brightside**[60] 5386 2-8-11 0 ........ ConnorBeasley(3) 4 8
(Tracy Waggott) *in tch: struggling over 3f out: sn wknd* **100/1**

0 **7** *99* **Happy As Harry**[20] 6667 2-9-0 0 ........ PaulMulrennan 1
(Bryan Smart) *cl up: rdn and hung lft over 4f out: sn btn and eased: t.o* **33/1**

1m 41.2s (-2.20) **Going Correction** -0.075s/f (Good) 7 Ran SP% **114.1**
Speed ratings (Par 95): **108,105,93,91,90 73,**
CSF £2.72 TOTE £2.00: £1.40, £1.10; EX 3.00 Trifecta £10.10.
**Owner** Hamdan Al Maktoum **Bred** WinStar Farm LLC **Trained** Newmarket, Suffolk

**FOCUS**
Round course rail moved in 2yds and 12f races increased by 6yds and 2m race by 10yds. Ground on the slow side of good and this opener was run in a time around 3secs slower than standard, although they looked to go quite steady early on. No depth to this maiden and the front two, who dominated the market, proved different class to their rivals and drew a long way clear in the closing stages.

## 7174 PROTECTOR GROUP/EBF MAIDEN FILLIES' STKS (BOBIS RACE) 1m 3y(S)

**2:30** (2:32) (Class 5) 2-Y-O **£2,911** (£866; £432; £216) **Stalls** Centre

Form RPR

20 **1** **Sweet Dream**[24] 6553 2-9-0 0 ........ GrahamLee 4 75
(Ralph Beckett) *t.k.h: pressed ldr: led over 2f out: rdn and hrd pressed fr over 1f out: hld on wl fnl f* **7/4**[1]

**2** *nk* **Stella Etoile (IRE)** 2-9-0 0 ........ TonyHamilton 2 74+
(Richard Fahey) *t.k.h: hld up: hdwy over 2f out: shkn up to chse wnr ins fnl f: kpt on: hld nr fin* **20/1**

0 **3** *2* **Sperry (IRE)**[24] 6554 2-9-0 0 ........ RobertHavlin 1 70
(John Gosden) *t.k.h: trckd ldrs: smooth hdwy and ev ch over 1f out: sn rdn: one pce ins fnl f* **9/4**[2]

5 **4** *1 1/4* **Polly Jackson**[10] 6935 2-8-9 0 ........ GemmaTutty(5) 6 67
(Karen Tutty) *midfield on outside: effrt over 2f out: kpt on fnl f: nvr able to chal* **16/1**

02 **5** *6* **Sampera (IRE)**[17] 6742 2-9-0 0 ........ WilliamTwiston-Davies 13 54
(Michael Bell) *t.k.h: led to over 2f out: rallied: rdn and wknd over 1f out* **13/2**

**6** *shd* **Toboggan's Gift** 2-9-0 0 ........ PJMcDonald 9 54
(Ann Duffield) *bhd: rdn and outpcd over 3f out: sme hdwy over 1f out: kpt on: nrst fin* **50/1**

45 **7** *3 1/2* **Hidden Rebel**[13] 6861 2-8-9 0 ........ GarryWhillans(5) 10 46
(Alistair Whillans) *uns rdr on way to s: sn in tch: drvn along over 3f out: rallied: wknd over 1f out* **33/1**

0 **8** *5* **Bond Starprincess**[13] 6861 2-9-0 0 ........ AndrewElliott 3 35
(George Moore) *dwlt: bhd: drvn over 3f out: sn no imp* **66/1**

**9** *3 3/4* **Littlemissparton** 2-9-0 0 ........ IanBrennan 5 27
(Ollie Pears) *bhd: pushed along and green 1/2-way: nvr on terms* **33/1**

0 **10** *2 1/4* **La Hoofon**[21] 6641 2-9-0 0 ........ PaulMulrennan 11 22
(Michael Dods) *uns rdr bef s and unruly in stalls: midfield: struggling over 3f out: sn btn* **40/1**

3 **11** *3 1/4* **Whisky Marmalade (IRE)**[10] 6935 2-9-0 0 ........ DanielTudhope 7 15
(David O'Meara) *hld up: rdn over 3f out: sn wknd* **11/2**[3]

5 **12** *16* **Goneinaminute**[19] 6694 2-9-0 0 ........ BarryMcHugh 8
(Tony Coyle) *chsd ldrs tl rdn and wknd fr over 3f out: t.o* **33/1**

1m 43.41s (0.01) **Going Correction** -0.075s/f (Good) 12 Ran SP% **121.2**
Speed ratings (Par 92): **96,95,93,92,86 86,82,77,74,71 68,52**
CSF £44.42 TOTE £2.60: £1.40, £5.10, £1.40; EX 46.70 Trifecta £163.80.
**Owner** Britannia Thoroughbreds **Bred** Britannia Thoroughbreds **Trained** Kimpton, Hants

**FOCUS**
Not a bad fillies' maiden in which the pace looked sound from the outset.

## 7175 VICTORY SIGNS H'CAP 1m 4f 93y

**3:00** (3:00) (Class 6) (0-65,65) 3-Y-O+ **£2,264** (£673; £336; £168) **Stalls** Low

Form RPR

6-62 **1** **Rockawango (FR)**[42] 6012 8-9-8 62 ........(tp) PaulMulrennan 12 73+
(James Ewart) *hld up in tch: hdwy and swtchd ins over 2f out: plld out and led appr fnl f: sn rdn and edgd lft: hld on wl towards fin* **10/1**

3260 **2** *3/4* **In Vino Veritas (IRE)**[14] 6832 3-9-2 60 ........(v) PJMcDonald 1 71
(Ann Duffield) *hld up in tch: rdn over 2f out: hdwy to chse wnr ins fnl f: kpt on: hld towards fin* **7/1**[3]

500- **3** *3/4* **Lady Marmelo (IRE)**[526] 2094 4-9-6 60 ........ GrahamLee 11 67
(Philip Kirby) *hld up: rdn and edgd lft over 2f out: hdwy over 1f out: kpt on ins fnl f* **33/1**

6-46 **4** *2 1/4* **Mojolika**[50] 5764 6-9-10 64 ........ DanielTudhope 9 67
(Patrick Holmes) *pressed ldr: rdn and led over 2f out: hdd appr fnl f: outpcd last 100yds* **8/1**

6/30 **5** *shd* **Fisher**[150] 2327 5-9-6 60 ........(t) PhillipMakin 4 63
(John Quinn) *hld up towards rr: pushed along over 2f out: styd on fnl f: nvr able to chal* **13/2**[2]

340 **6** *nk* **Henpecked**[10] 6942 4-9-3 57 ........ TomEaves 6 60
(Alistair Whillans) *hld up: drvn over 3f out: rallied over 1f out: kpt on fnl f: no imp* **8/1**

4062 **7** *1 3/4* **Gala Casino Star (IRE)**[6] 7044 9-9-4 63 ........(b) JordanNason(5) 7 63
(Lawrence Mullaney) *in tch: effrt 2f out: rdn and wknd ins fnl f* **11/2**[1]

0-45 **8** *1* **Dancing Primo**[18] 6699 8-9-10 64 ........ LukeMorris 14 62
(Mark Brisbourne) *hld up: rdn over 2f out: sme late hdwy: nvr able to chal* **7/1**[3]

3310 **9** *2 1/2* **Gioia Di Vita**[24] 6542 4-9-10 64 ........ DavidNolan 3 58
(David Thompson) *t.k.h in midfield: rdn over 2f out: wknd over 1f out* **14/1**

4560 **10** *2 1/2* **Medieval Bishop (IRE)**[24] 6564 5-9-2 61 ........(p) JackGarritty(5) 10 51
(Mark Walford) *chsd ldrs: rdn 3f out: wknd over 1f out* **14/1**

6026 **11** *1* **Gabrial's Hope (FR)**[20] 6672 5-9-11 65 ........ TonyHamilton 2 54
(Tracy Waggott) *hld up on ins: drvn over 2f out: nvr on terms* **10/1**

2256 **12** *3/4* **Thackeray**[21] 6644 7-9-4 58 ........ MichaelStainton 13 45
(Chris Fairhurst) *missed break: bhd: rdn over 3f out: nvr on terms* **20/1**

5053 **13** *3/4* **Magnolia Ridge (IRE)**[35] 6210 4-9-7 61 ........(p) DougieCostello 5 47
(Kristin Stubbs) *prom: outpcd whn n.m.r over 2f out: wknd over 1f out* **20/1**

/60- **14** *3* **Mcvicar**[126] 7506 5-9-10 64 ........ SebSanders 8 45
(John Davies) *t.k.h: led to over 2f out: wknd over 1f out* **20/1**

2m 44.93s (-0.67) **Going Correction** 0.0s/f (Good)
**WFA** 3 from 4yo+ 7lb 14 Ran SP% **124.7**
Speed ratings (Par 101): **102,101,101,99,99 99,98,97,95,94 93,92,92,90**
CSF £77.00 CT £2267.46 TOTE £10.50: £4.10, £2.60, £8.30; EX 38.50 Trifecta £2471.70.
**Owner** Steve Murrills **Bred** E A R L Haras Du Camp Benard **Trained** Langholm, Dumfries & G'way

**FOCUS**
A wide-open handicap run at what looked an even enough gallop but quite a few of the lower drawn horses who had to drop in from their draws found it hard to get into it. The winner won more easily than the margin.

## 7176 GRASPAN FRANKTON MEDIAN AUCTION MAIDEN STKS 1m 4f 93y

**3:30** (3:30) (Class 6) 3-4-Y-O **£2,587** (£770; £384; £192) **Stalls** Low

Form RPR

3236 **1** **Interconnection**[39] 6091 3-9-5 65 ........(b) LukeMorris 11 77
(Ed Vaughan) *led at stdy pce 4f: chsd ldr: regained ld over 3f out: pushed clr fr 2f out* **11/2**

544 **2** *2 1/4* **Gale Force**[26] 6485 3-9-0 72 ........ HayleyTurner 1 68+
(James Fanshawe) *hld up in midfield on ins: pushed along over 4f out: hdwy and swtchd rt over 2f out: chsd (clr) wnr ins fnl f: r.o* **7/2**[2]

324 **3** *1 3/4* **Miss Tree**[99] 4020 3-9-0 71 ........ IanBrennan 7 66
(John Quinn) *prom: stdy hdwy to chse wnr 3f out: rdn 2f out: lost 2nd ins fnl f: one pce* **7/4**[1]

3250 **4** *1 1/2* **Molly Cat**[7] 7008 4-9-7 67 ........ DavidAllan 3 63
(Alan Swinbank) *plld hrd early: in tch: rdn and hdwy 3f out: rdn and one pce fr over 1f out* **4/1**[3]

**5** *1/2* **Lesson In Life** 3-9-0 0 ........ DanielTudhope 2 62+
(David O'Meara) *hld up: pushed along and hdwy over 2f out: edgd lft: kpt on sam pce fnl f* **8/1**

**6** *26* **Piper Bill** 3-9-5 0 ........ GrahamLee 4 26
(Jim Goldie) *dwlt: hld up: rdn and outpcd over 3f out: n.d after* **20/1**

000- **7** *hd* **Riponian**[11] 5139 4-9-12 45 ........ TonyHamilton 6 25
(Susan Corbett) *plld hrd: sn in tch on outside: rdn and wknd fr 3f out* **100/1**

0000 **8** *3/4* **Petite Madame (IRE)**[17] 6768 3-9-0 45 ........(b) DavidNolan 9 19
(David Thompson) *prom tl rdn and wknd over 3f out* **100/1**

0446 **9** *3/4* **Major Rowan**[52] 5682 3-9-0 46 ........(b) AdamCarter(5) 5 23
(Bryan Smart) *plld hrd: hld up: hdwy on outside to ld after 4f: hdd 3f out: sn rdn and wknd* **33/1**

05 **10** *43* **Pal Ella**[89] 4360 3-9-0 0 ........ TomEaves 8
(Keith Dalgleish) *chsd ldrs: struggling over 4f out: sn btn: t.o* **66/1**

6 **11** *3/4* **Magic Maisie**[32] 6282 3-8-9 0 ........ GarryWhillans(5) 10
(Alistair Whillans) *s.i.s: bhd: lost tch over 4f out: t.o* **50/1**

2m 45.92s (0.32) **Going Correction** 0.0s/f (Good)
**WFA** 3 from 4yo 7lb 11 Ran SP% **118.2**
Speed ratings (Par 101): **98,96,95,94,94 76,76,76,75,46 46**
CSF £24.34 TOTE £7.90: £1.60, £1.10, £1.10; EX 28.20 Trifecta £76.40.
**Owner** Salem Rashid **Bred** Newsells Park Stud **Trained** Newmarket, Suffolk

**FOCUS**
A modest fillies' maiden and not form to get too exited about. Several of these were keen in the early stages off what looked a very steady gallop until the free going Major Rowan took over and began to stretch on. The winner's effort is perhaps not as good as a literal reading of the form.

## 7177 M. R. STRATEGIC H'CAP 2m 19y

**4:00** (4:00) (Class 5) (0-75,75) 3-Y-O+ **£3,234** (£962; £481; £240) **Stalls** Low

Form RPR

1054 **1** **Lady Yeats**[59] 5449 3-8-12 70 ........ AndrewMullen 2 81
(George Moore) *in tch on inner: briefly n.m.r over 2f out: hdwy to chse ldr over 1f out: styd on: led towards fin* **11/2**[3]

3324 **2** *nk* **Arcamante (ITY)**[13] 6864 3-8-9 70 ........ JoeyHaynes(3) 15 80
(K R Burke) *trckd ldr: rdn over 4f out: led 2f out: kpt on: hdd towards fin* **5/1**[2]

0001 **3** *1/2* **Dan Emmett (USA)**[64] 5240 4-9-4 70 ........(p) JoeDoyle(5) 14 79
(John Wainwright) *hld up in midfield: rdn and hung lft over 2f out: hdwy over 1f out: chsd ldr jst ins fnl f: edgd lft: kpt on* **14/1**

4235 **4** *5* **Wor Lass**[13] 6864 6-8-10 57 ........ TomEaves 4 60
(Iain Jardine) *dwlt: hld up on inner: rdn over 3f out: styd on fr over 1f out: tk 4th nr fin: no threat to ldng trio* **9/1**

3550 **5** *hd* **Jan Smuts (IRE)**[13] 6864 6-8-11 63 ........(tp) EmmaSayer(5) 17 66
(Wilf Storey) *in tch on outer: rdn 3f out: chsd ldr 2f out: wknd ins fnl f: lost 4th nr fin* **20/1**

4066 **6** *1 1/2* **Bowdler's Magic**[13] 6864 7-9-3 64 ........(t) DavidNolan 13 65
(David Thompson) *chsd ldrs: rdn over 3f out: grad wknd over 1f out* **25/1**

6032 **7** *1* **Lady Bingo (IRE)**[11] 6899 3-8-9 67 ........ LukeMorris 12 67
(Sir Mark Prescott Bt) *dwlt: sn in tch: pushed along and lost pl over 5f out: rdn over 3f out: one pce* **4/1**[1]

355/ **8** *2 1/2* **Ryton Runner (IRE)**[20] 3337 6-9-7 68 ........(tp) GrahamLee 16 65
(Lucinda Russell) *led after 1f: rdn whn hdd over 2f out: grad wknd* **33/1**

1500 **9** *1* **Zamra (IRE)**[125] 3110 3-9-0 72 ........ DanielTudhope 5 68
(Brian Ellison) *in tch: rdn 3f out: briefly ev ch 2f out: wknd and eased fnl f* **25/1**

-605 **10** *hd* **Madam Lilibet (IRE)**[26] 6493 5-8-12 59 ........ PaulQuinn 9 54
(Sharon Watt) *hld up in rr: rdn over 3f out: minor late hdwy* **12/1**

10-4 **11** *1/2* **Rock Relief (IRE)**[141] 1485 8-9-6 67 ........ PaulMulrennan 1 62
(Chris Grant) *midfield on inner: rdn over 3f out: sn no imp* **12/1**

0433 **12** *shd* **Chevalgris**[13] 6864 4-9-9 70 ........ DavidAllan 10 65
(Alan Swinbank) *dwlt: hld up: hdwy on outer 12f out: sn prom: rdn over 3f out: led over 2f out: sn hdd: wknd over 1f out* **13/2**

-600 **13** *nk* **Georgian Firebird**[28] 6432 4-9-1 62 ........ BenCurtis 7 56
(Alan Swinbank) *hld up in midfield: rdn over 3f out: wknd 2f out* **40/1**

12-0 **14** ¾ **Attention Seaker**[21] 6640 4-9-9 70 ................................ DuranFentiman 3 63
(Tim Easterby) *hld up in rr: nvr threatened* **25/1**

22 **15** 1¾ **Zarosa (IRE)**[50] 5748 5-8-4 56 ................................ ShelleyBirkett(5) 11 47
(John Berry) *led for 1f: trckd ldr: rdn over 3f out: sn wknd* **16/1**

2425 **16** 8 **No Such Number**[27] 5863 6-9-3 64 ................................ DougieCostello 6 46
(Sandy Forster) *a in rr* **40/1**

3m 39.64s (0.24) **Going Correction** 0.0s/f (Good)
**WFA** 3 from 4yo+ 11lb **16** Ran SP% **127.4**
Speed ratings (Par 103): **99,98,98,96,96 95,94,93,93,92 92,92,92,92,91 87**
CSF £31.86 CT £380.83 TOTE £9.90: £1.40, £5.40, £2.60, £2.60; EX 44.70 Trifecta £1234.50.
**Owner** A Crute & Partners **Bred** Biddestone Stud **Trained** Middleham Moor, N Yorks

**FOCUS**
A competitive handicap featuring a few runners who aren't yet fully exposed. Another personal best from the winner.

## 7178 BOOTNECK 350 TARTAN H'CAP (DIV I) 6f
**4:30** (4:32) (Class 5) (0-75,74) 3-Y-O+ **£3,234** (£962; £481; £240) **Stalls** Centre

Form RPR

3122 **1** **Royal Connoisseur (IRE)**[23] 6575 3-9-3 74 ................ GeorgeChaloner(3) 16 83
(Richard Fahey) *taken early to post: prom: hdwy to ld over 1f out: drifted rt last 100yds: rdn out* **7/2**[1]

4210 **2** ½ **Percy's Gal**[19] 6692 3-8-13 72 ................................ GemmaTutty(5) 12 79
(Karen Tutty) *t.k.h: cl up: effrt and ev ch over 1f out: kpt on fnl f: hld towards fin* **8/1**[3]

5005 **3** nse **Reposer (IRE)**[15] 6824 6-9-7 74 ................................ TomEaves 11 81+
(Keith Dalgleish) *hld up: rdn and hdwy over 1f out: kpt on wl fnl f: nrst fin* **17/2**

0666 **4** 1 **Penny Garcia**[38] 6150 4-9-0 67 ................................ DavidAllan 13 71
(Tim Easterby) *hld up in tch: effrt and drvn over 1f out: kpt on same pce ins fnl f* **7/1**[2]

-060 **5** nk **Boris Grigoriev (IRE)**[25] 6512 5-9-1 68 ................(b) BarryMcHugh 2 71
(Michael Easterby) *hld up: stdy hdwy on far side of gp and ev ch over 1f out: sn rdn: one pce ins fnl f* **9/1**

3100 **6** ½ **Sleeping Apache (IRE)**[66] 5197 4-9-5 72 ................ PaulMulrennan 3 73
(Michael Dods) *prom: drvn and ev ch over 1f out: no ex ins fnl f* **25/1**

0350 **7** 3 **Penina (IRE)**[76] 4795 3-8-5 64 ................................ JoeDoyle(5) 8 55
(Brian Ellison) *wnt lft s: led tl rdn and hdd over 1f out: wknd ins fnl f* **16/1**

46-5 **8** ½ **Marciano (IRE)**[280] 75 4-9-5 72 ................................ DougieCostello 4 62
(Sue Smith) *cl up: drvn and ev ch over 2f out to over 1f out: wknd ins fnl f* **20/1**

106 **9** hd **Ella's Delight (IRE)**[53] 5641 4-9-5 72 ................................ GrahamLee 1 61
(Martin Todhunter) *hld up: rdn over 2f out: edgd lft and outpcd over 1f out* **16/1**

4500 **10** hd **Mowhoob**[26] 6477 4-9-2 69 ................................ FergalLynch 10 58
(Jim Goldie) *in tch: rdn over 2f out: wknd over 1f out* **20/1**

2440 **11** nk **Verus Delicia (IRE)**[17] 6736 5-9-7 74 ................................ DanielTudhope 15 62
(Daniel Mark Loughnane) *hld up: drvn along over 2f out: sn no imp* **7/1**[2]

0000 **12** ½ **Lewisham**[26] 6478 4-9-1 68 ................................ PaulQuinn 9 54
(David Nicholls) *dwlt: hld up: shkn up over 2f out: btn over 1f out* **12/1**

0 **13** 2½ **Walk Right Back (IRE)**[21] 6625 3-8-9 63 ................................ PJMcDonald 5 41
(Micky Hammond) *prom tl rdn and wknd fr 2f out* **50/1**

0006 **14** 3¾ **Mandalay King (IRE)**[17] 6758 9-8-9 67 ................................ JordanNason(5) 14 33
(Marjorie Fife) *hld up: drvn over 2f out: sn wknd* **14/1**

1013 **15** ¾ **Day Star Lad**[202] 1116 3-8-13 67 ................................(v) DaleSwift 7 31
(Derek Shaw) *hmpd s: bhd: rdn along over 2f out: sn btn* **33/1**

1m 13.51s (-1.09) **Going Correction** -0.075s/f (Good)
**WFA** 3 from 4yo+ 1lb **15** Ran SP% **123.3**
Speed ratings (Par 103): **104,103,103,101,101 100,96,96,95,95 95,94,91,86,85**
CSF £28.73 CT £229.88 TOTE £4.40: £2.10, £3.20, £3.10; EX 28.40 Trifecta £218.70.
**Owner** S & G Clayton, A Blower **Bred** Mrs Sheila Morrissey **Trained** Musley Bank, N Yorks
■ Alanos (25-1) was withdrawn. Rule 4 does not apply.

**FOCUS**
A wide-open sprint in which they raced down the middle of the track although the winner ended up drifting up across towards the stands side. The bare form can't be rated any higher than this.

## 7179 BOOTNECK 350 TARTAN H'CAP (DIV II) 6f
**5:00** (5:01) (Class 5) (0-75,75) 3-Y-O+ **£3,234** (£962; £481; £240) **Stalls** Centre

Form RPR

4030 **1** **Lucky Lodge**[35] 6213 4-8-7 61 ................................(b) DavidAllan 4 70
(Mel Brittain) *slowly away: hld up in rr: stl plenty to do whn briefly n.m.r wl over 1f out: pushed along and gd hdwy appr fnl f: rdn ins fnl f: kpt on to ld towards fin* **8/1**

3302 **2** ½ **Fleurtille**[13] 6863 5-9-5 73 ................................ PJMcDonald 11 80
(Ray Craggs) *midfield: rdn over 2f out: hdwy over 1f out: chal strly ins fnl f: kpt on* **11/2**[1]

210 **3** nse **Pennine Warrior**[33] 6260 3-9-6 75 ................................(p) LukeMorris 2 82
(Scott Dixon) *chsd ldrs towards outside: rdn 1/2-way: led 2f out: strly pressed ins fnl f: kpt on: hdd towards fin: lost 2nd post* **15/2**[3]

-001 **4** 1¾ **Chiswick Bey (IRE)**[20] 6674 6-8-10 69 ................................ SammyJoBell(5) 6 70
(Richard Fahey) *hld up: pushed along bef 1/2-way: hdwy over 1f out: kpt on* **8/1**

55-0 **5** 3½ **Indego Blues**[15] 6824 5-9-4 72 ................................ PaulQuinn 3 62
(David Nicholls) *hld up on outside: rdn 1/2-way: hdwy to chse ldrs 2f out: no ex ins fnl f* **16/1**

0000 **6** 2 **Sandra's Diamond (IRE)**[16] 6792 3-9-5 74 ................(v[1]) PhillipMakin 16 58
(Keith Dalgleish) *led against stands' rail: rdn whn hdd 2f out: grad wknd* **12/1**

0003 **7** ½ **Mercers Row**[17] 6758 7-8-8 67 ................................ GemmaTutty(5) 5 49
(Karen Tutty) *prom: rdn over 2f out: wknd appr fnl f* **16/1**

3044 **8** nk **Lothair (IRE)**[53] 5632 5-9-0 68 ................................ BenCurtis 10 49
(Alan Swinbank) *prom: rdn over 2f out: wknd fnl f* **7/1**[2]

4650 **9** 1¼ **Ypres**[19] 6695 5-8-10 67 ................................ JoeyHaynes(3) 8 44
(Jason Ward) *chsd ldrs: rdn and ev ch 2f out: wknd fnl f* **20/1**

1606 **10** ¾ **Banovallum**[27] 6451 4-9-3 71 ................................ BarryMcHugh 7 46
(Michael Easterby) *prom towards centre: rdn 1/2-way: wknd over 1f out* **20/1**

3314 **11** 1 **My Son Max**[40] 6082 6-9-3 71 ................................ GrahamLee 14 42
(Richard Ford) *midfield: rdn over 2f out: wknd over 1f out* **7/1**[2]

3644 **12** ½ **Heroique (IRE)**[50] 5769 3-9-1 70 ................................(e) DuranFentiman 12 40
(Tim Easterby) *prom towards stands' rail: rdn 1/2-way: wknd over 1f out* **16/1**

0026 **13** 1 **Teetotal (IRE)**[19] 6692 4-9-4 72 ................................ AndrewMullen 1 39
(Nigel Tinkler) *dwlt: hld up: nvr threatened* **9/1**

0000 **14** 5 **Lorimer's Lot (IRE)**[20] 6671 3-8-9 64 ................................(v[1]) TonyHamilton 13 15
(Mark Walford) *midfield: rdn 1/2-way: sn wknd* **33/1**

1m 14.11s (-0.49) **Going Correction** -0.075s/f (Good)
**WFA** 3 from 4yo+ 1lb **14** Ran SP% **122.2**
Speed ratings (Par 103): **100,99,99,96,92 89,88,88,86,85 84,83,82,75**
CSF £50.98 CT £362.21 TOTE £13.00: £2.90, £5.30, £2.30; EX 63.50 Trifecta £431.60.
**Owner** Mel Brittain **Bred** Mel Brittain **Trained** Warthill, N Yorks

**FOCUS**
Even more open the first division but the front three managed to put some daylight between themselves and the fourth, who was in turn well clear of the rest. The winner is rated to his best.

## 7180 ROYAL MARINES 350TH ANNIVERSARY H'CAP 7f
**5:35** (5:36) (Class 6) (0-65,65) 3-Y-O+ **£2,264** (£673; £336; £168) **Stalls** Centre

Form RPR

4325 **1** **Orwellian**[4] 7077 5-9-6 65 ................................ PaulMulrennan 10 75
(Bryan Smart) *dwlt: hld up centre: gd hdwy to ld 1f out: sn hrd pressed: hld on wl u.p cl home: 1st of 9 in gp* **15/2**[3]

0410 **2** hd **Funding Deficit (IRE)**[14] 6836 4-9-2 61 ................................ FergalLynch 4 70
(Jim Goldie) *prom: smooth hdwy and ev ch fr over 1f out: kpt on fnl f: hld cl home: 2nd of 9 in gp* **20/1**

2602 **3** 2½ **Borough Boy (IRE)**[13] 6858 4-9-5 64 ................................ DaleSwift 7 67
(Derek Shaw) *hld up bhd ldng gp centre: effrt and hdwy over 1f out: kpt on ins fnl f: nrst fin: 3rd of 9 in gp* **20/1**

134 **4** ¾ **Senor George (IRE)**[48] 5811 7-9-0 64 ................................(p) JoeDoyle(5) 13 65
(Brian Ellison) *hld up centre: rdn and hdwy over 2f out: kpt on ins fnl f: no imp: 4th of 9 in gp* **3/1**[1]

000 **5** 1½ **Steel Stockholder**[99] 4023 8-9-4 63 ................................ DavidAllan 8 60
(Mel Brittain) *cl up centre: effrt and led briefly appr fnl f: outpcd last 100yds: 5th of 9 in gp* **20/1**

3110 **6** 3½ **Jay Kay**[53] 5640 5-9-3 62 ................................ DanielTudhope 3 50
(K R Burke) *led centre and overall ldr after 2f: rdn and hdd appr fnl f: sn btn: 6th of 9 in gp* **11/2**[2]

-400 **7** 1½ **Destination Aim**[46] 5887 7-9-4 63 ................................ GrahamLee 16 47
(Frederick Watson) *prom stands' side: effrt over 2f out: led that gp ins fnl f: no ch w centre ldrs: 1st of 6 in gp* **33/1**

6404 **8** nse **Iceblast**[42] 6014 6-8-11 63 ................................ AnnaHesketh(7) 1 47
(Michael Easterby) *hld up in midfield centre: rdn over 2f out: wknd over 1f out: 7th of 9 in gp* **40/1**

0210 **9** nk **Gaelic Wizard (IRE)**[20] 6674 6-8-12 62 ................................ GemmaTutty(5) 2 45
(Karen Tutty) *t.k.h: cl up centre: rdn over 2f out: wknd over 1f out: 8th of 9 in gp* **25/1**

3106 **10** 1 **No Quarter (IRE)**[24] 6543 7-9-4 63 ................................ DougieCostello 9 44
(Tracy Waggott) *in tch centre: drvn over 2f out: sn wknd: last of 9 in gp* **25/1**

6412 **11** ½ **Old Man Clegg**[26] 6477 4-9-6 65 ................................(t) BarryMcHugh 5 44
(Michael Easterby) *overall ldr 2f: led stands' side gp: rdn over 2f out: no ch w centre ldrs whn hdd that gp ins fnl f: 2nd of 6 in gp* **8/1**

0623 **12** 7 **Royal Encounter**[21] 6647 3-9-2 63 ................................ LukeMorris 11 23
(Ed Vaughan) *chsd stands' side ldrs: drvn and outpcd over 2f out: sn btn: 3rd of 6 in gp* **8/1**

333 **13** nse **Dark Crystal**[22] 6601 3-8-11 63 ................................ MeganCarberry(5) 14 23
(Linda Perratt) *prom on outside of stands' side gp: drvn along 1/2-way: wknd over 2f out: 4th of 6 in gp* **16/1**

5164 **14** 5 **Bond Club**[63] 5265 4-9-6 65 ................................(b) TomEaves 15 13
(Geoffrey Oldroyd) *hld up stands' side: pushed along 3f out: sn struggling: 5th of 6 in gp* **14/1**

1400 **15** 14 **Clumber Place**[13] 6863 8-9-6 65 ................................ BenCurtis 6
(Shaun Harris) *in tch stands' side: struggling over 3f out: sn btn: last of 6 in gp* **14/1**

1m 27.44s (-0.36) **Going Correction** -0.075s/f (Good)
**WFA** 3 from 4yo+ 2lb **15** Ran SP% **120.9**
Speed ratings (Par 101): **99,98,95,95,93 89,87,87,87,86 85,77,77,71,55**
CSF £152.62 CT £2935.08 TOTE £6.70: £2.00, £8.50, £7.40; EX 242.80 Trifecta £1515.30.
**Owner** Rasio Cymru Racing 1 & B Smart **Bred** Mrs Fiona Denniff **Trained** Hambleton, N Yorks
■ Stewards' Enquiry : Barry McHugh two-day ban: careless riding (Oct 28-29)

**FOCUS**
The action unfolded down the middle of the track in this modest 7f handicap. A length best from the winner.
T/Jkpt: £7,100.00 to a £1 stake. Pool: £10,000.00 - 1.00 winning ticket. T/Plt: £30.40 to a £1 stake. Pool: £81,177.52 - 1,944.43 winning tickets. T/Qpdt: £17.70 to a £1 stake. Pool: £4,446.43 - 185.00 winning tickets. RY

# 7111 WOLVERHAMPTON (A.W) (L-H)
### Tuesday, October 14

**OFFICIAL GOING: Tapeta: standard**
Wind: light 1/2 against Weather: overcast

## 7181 ENJOY DAILY BETTING TIPS @ BOOKMAKERS.CO.UK MAIDEN AUCTION STKS (TAPETA) 5f 216y
**5:30** (5:33) (Class 5) 2-Y-O **£2,587** (£770; £384; £192) **Stalls** Low

Form RPR

032 **1** **Elis Eliz (IRE)**[18] 6719 2-8-12 73 ................................ RichardHughes 8 77
(Michael Wigham) *w ldrs on outer: led over 3f out: pushed out* **4/6**[1]

**2** 2¾ **Scalzo** 2-8-13 0 ................................ FergusSweeney 3 71+
(Martyn Meade) *hld up in mid-div: t.k.h: hdwy to trck ldrs over 2f out: styd on to take 2nd last 150yds* **7/1**[3]

550 **3** 4 **Entente**[46] 5874 2-9-3 72 ................................ SteveDrowne 7 62
(Peter Makin) *trckd ldrs: 2nd over 2f out: kpt on same pce* **10/1**

0 **4** nk **Vivre La Reve**[29] 6408 2-8-10 0 ................................ JasonHart 6 54
(Ed McMahon) *sn led: hdd over 3f out: one pce fnl 2f* **8/1**

05 **5** 2¾ **Ifittakesforever (IRE)**[102] 3934 2-8-10 0 ................ DanielMuscutt(5) 5 51
(Tim Pitt) *s.i.s: in rr: hdwy over 2f out: kpt on fnl f: nvr a factor* **22/1**

60 **6** 1¾ **Kodiac Krossing**[12] 6887 2-8-6 0 ................................ JoeFanning 4 36
(Jamie Osborne) *hld up in rr: bhd fnl 2f* **40/1**

05 **7** ¾ **Ventura Canyon (IRE)**[63] 5264 2-8-13 0 ................................ JamieSpencer 2 41
(Keith Dalgleish) *led early: chsd ldrs: lost pl over 2f out* **5/1**[2]

**8** 4½ **Military Music** 2-8-0 0 ow1 ................................ CharlotteJenner(7) 1 22
(Mark Usher) *dwlt: in rr: bhd whn hung rt 2f out* **50/1**

1m 15.14s (0.64) **Going Correction** -0.025s/f (Stan) **8** Ran SP% **118.1**
Speed ratings (Par 95): **94,90,85,84,80 78,77,71**
CSF £6.30 TOTE £1.50: £1.02, £2.20, £2.40; EX 5.20 Trifecta £40.10.
**Owner** T Akman & D Hassan **Bred** Irish National Stud **Trained** Newmarket, Suffolk



The Form Book, Raceform Ltd, Newbury, RG14 5SJ

**FOCUS**
A modest event.

## 7182 DOWNLOAD THE FREE APP @ BOOKMAKERS.CO.UK H'CAP (TAPETA) 1m 5f 194y
**6:00** (6:01) (Class 5) (0-70,70) 3-Y-0+ **£2,587** (£770; £384; £192) **Stalls** Low

| Form | | | | RPR |
|---|---|---|---|---|
| 0212 | 1 | | **Kelamita (IRE)**[11] 6900 3-8-12 65..........(b[1]) RichardHughes 11 (Hughie Morrison) *led after 2f: drvn 3f out: clr over 1f out: styd on wl* **4/1**[2] | 76 |
| 5230 | 2 | 2 ¼ | **By Jupiter**[34] 6239 3-9-3 70.......... JamieSpencer 2 (Michael Bell) *s.i.s: gd hdwy to chse wnr after 6f: drvn 3f out: styd on same pce over 1f out* **11/1** | 78 |
| 0534 | 3 | 3 ¼ | **Do Wah Diddy Diddy**[39] 6091 3-9-3 70.......... AdamKirby 10 (Clive Cox) *mid-div: hdwy to chse ldrs after 4f: drvn 3f out: kpt on same pce to take 3rd nr fin* **7/2**[1] | 73 |
| 424- | 4 | shd | **Handiwork**[194] 7278 4-9-0 65..........(p) MikeyEnnis(7) 1 (Steve Gollings) *trckd ldrs: kpt on same pce fnl 2f* **25/1** | 68 |
| 4054 | 5 | 1 ½ | **Lady Of Yue**[16] 6787 4-9-6 64.......... RobertTart 9 (Eugene Stanford) *hld up in rr: hdwy on outer over 5f out: one pce fnl 3f* **9/1** | 65 |
| 4333 | 6 | ½ | **Sweeping Rock (IRE)**[13] 6856 4-8-10 59..........(t) ShaneGray(5) 7 (Marcus Tregoning) *chsd ldrs: one pce fnl 3f* **14/1** | 60 |
| 2212 | 7 | 1 ½ | **Saint Thomas (IRE)**[19] 6696 7-9-9 67.......... JoeFanning 3 (John Mackie) *chsd ldrs: drvn 3f out: one pce* **11/1** | 65 |
| 4011 | 8 | 1 ½ | **Uncle Bernie (IRE)**[31] 6343 4-9-9 67..........(p) JamesSullivan 5 (Andrew Hollinshead) *s.s: hld up in rr: hdwy 5f out: one pce on outer over 2f out* **6/1** | 63 |
| 4354 | 9 | 1 | **Flying Cape (IRE)**[24] 6541 3-8-13 66..........(p) JasonHart 6 (Andrew Hollinshead) *hld up towards rr: t.k.h: sme hdwy over 2f out: kpt on fnl f* **9/2**[3] | 61 |
| | 10 | 10 | **Dusty Trail (IRE)**[58] 5365 10-9-1 64.......... DanielMuscutt(5) 8 (John Butler) *in rr: pushed along 4f out: sn bhd* **33/1** | 45 |
| 031/ | 11 | 9 | **Aldo**[949] 847 7-9-4 65..........(t) RossAtkinson(3) 4 (Sean Curran) *t.k.h: led 2f: trckd ldrs: lost pl over 3f out: wl bhd fnl 2f* **40/1** | 33 |

3m 4.8s **Going Correction** -0.025s/f (Stan)
**WFA** 3 from 4yo+ 9lb **11** Ran SP% **117.2**
Speed ratings (Par 103): **99,97,95,95,94 94,93,92,92,86 81**
CSF £46.46 CT £169.73 TOTE £3.60: £1.50, £3.80, £2.30; EX 46.10 Trifecta £318.80.
**Owner** M E Wates **Bred** M E Wates **Trained** East Ilsley, Berks

**FOCUS**
Nothing got into this modest staying handicap from the rear.

## 7183 FREE BETS GALORE @ BOOKIES.COM H'CAP (TAPETA) 7f 32y
**6:30** (6:32) (Class 4) (0-80,80) 3-Y-0+ **£4,725** (£1,414; £707; £354; £176) **Stalls** High

| Form | | | | RPR |
|---|---|---|---|---|
| 0032 | 1 | | **Steelriver (IRE)**[17] 6766 4-9-2 75.......... RobertWinston 9 (Michael Herrington) *mid-div: hdwy over 2f out: led over 1f out: styd on strly to go clr* **7/2**[2] | 94 |
| 2113 | 2 | 4 ½ | **Plucky Dip**[11] 6902 3-9-0 75.......... AdamKirby 4 (John Ryan) *trckd ldrs: nt clr run over 2f out: swtchd rt: styd on to take 2nd clsng stages* **11/4**[1] | 85 |
| 4343 | 3 | ¾ | **Ambitious Boy**[4] 7071 5-8-11 75.......... JackDuern(5) 8 (Andrew Hollinshead) *trckd ldrs: effrt over 2f out: kpt on to take 3rd post* **8/1** | 80 |
| 5113 | 4 | hd | **For Shia And Lula (IRE)**[14] 6841 5-8-11 75.......... EoinWalsh(5) 6 (Daniel Mark Loughnane) *chsd ldrs: drvn over 2f out: kpt on same pce over 1f out* **16/1** | 80 |
| 1435 | 5 | 2 | **Shamaheart (IRE)**[21] 6625 4-8-13 72..........(p) PaulHanagan 1 (Geoffrey Harker) *in rr: drvn 3f out: kpt on over 1f out: nvr nrr* **33/1** | 72 |
| 4100 | 6 | nse | **Desert Ranger (IRE)**[18] 6713 3-9-2 77.......... MartinHarley 3 (James Tate) *hld up in rr: drvn 3f out: styd on over 1f out: nvr nr to chal* **8/1** | 76 |
| 6442 | 7 | nk | **Footstepsintherain (IRE)**[17] 6767 4-8-13 72..........(t) RichardHughes 2 (David Dennis) *hld up in rr: drvn over 3f out: hdwy on wd outside wl over 1f out: nvr a threat* **7/1**[3] | 71 |
| 6044 | 8 | 1 ¾ | **Cara's Request (AUS)**[26] 6477 9-8-10 72.......... ConnorBeasley(3) 11 (Michael Dods) *w ldr: led over 3f out: hdd over 1f out: sn fdd* **16/1** | 66 |
| 5014 | 9 | ¾ | **Sakash**[29] 6414 4-9-1 74..........(p) FrederikTylicki 7 (J R Jenkins) *rr-div: hdwy on inner over 2f out: fdd fnl f* **9/1** | 66 |
| 000 | 10 | 1 ½ | **Skytrain**[28] 6424 4-9-7 80.......... JoeFanning 12 (Mark Johnston) *chsd ldrs: drvn over 2f out: wknd fnl f* **16/1** | 68 |
| -000 | 11 | 19 | **Chester Aristocrat**[17] 6736 5-9-2 75..........(b[1]) JasonHart 10 (Eric Alston) *led: hdd over 3f out: sn lost pl: bhd fnl 2f: eased: t.o* **50/1** | 14 |

1m 26.85s (-1.95) **Going Correction** -0.025s/f (Stan)
**WFA** 3 from 4yo+ 2lb **11** Ran SP% **116.2**
Speed ratings (Par 105): **110,104,104,103,101 101,101,99,98,96 74**
CSF £13.32 CT £71.11 TOTE £5.80: £1.80, £2.00, £2.10; EX 17.60 Trifecta £134.80.
**Owner** Darren & Annaley Yates **Bred** Kildaragh Stud **Trained** Cold Kirby, N Yorks

**FOCUS**
Ordinary handicap form, but the pace was solid.

## 7184 PRICE BOOSTS NOW AVAILABLE @ BOOKMAKERS.CO.UK MAIDEN FILLIES' STKS (BOBIS RACE) (TAPETA) 1m 141y
**7:00** (7:02) (Class 5) 2-Y-0 **£2,587** (£770; £384; £192) **Stalls** Low

| Form | | | | RPR |
|---|---|---|---|---|
| 43 | 1 | | **Stay Silent (IRE)**[53] 5643 2-9-0 0.......... RichardHughes 1 (Saeed bin Suroor) *mde all: drvn over 2f out: clr over 1f out: unchal* **3/1**[2] | 77+ |
| 2 | 2 | 2 ½ | **Waldnah**[13] 6868 2-9-0 0.......... RobertHavlin 4 (John Gosden) *chsd wnr: drvn over 2f out: edgd rt over 1f out: no imp* **11/8**[1] | 72 |
| | 3 | 1 ¾ | **Bittern (IRE)** 2-9-0 0..........[1] MartinLane 7 (Charlie Appleby) *hld up in mid-div: hdwy over 2f out: kpt on to take 3rd ins fnl f* **33/1** | 69+ |
| 5 | 4 | 1 ½ | **Tingleo**[35] 6208 2-9-0 0.......... TedDurcan 10 (Sir Michael Stoute) *chsd ldrs: drvn over 3f out: kpt on one pce fnl 2f* **20/1** | 65 |
| 3 | 5 | nk | **Light Of The World (IRE)**[22] 6605 2-9-0 0.......... JamieSpencer 5 (Jamie Osborne) *chsd ldrs: drvn over 3f out: one pce fnl 2f* **8/1** | 64 |
| 4 | 6 | nse | **Precast**[31] 6333 2-9-0 0.......... FergusSweeney 8 (David Simcock) *mid-div: drvn 3f out: kpt on over 1f out: nvr a factor* **66/1** | 64 |
| | 7 | 1 ¾ | **Radhaadh (IRE)** 2-9-0 0.......... PaulHanagan 12 (Sir Michael Stoute) *s.i.s: towards rr: sme hdwy over 2f out: kpt on over 1f out: nvr a factor* **14/1** | 61 |
| | 8 | ½ | **Callendula** 2-9-0 0.......... AdamKirby 11 (Clive Cox) *rr-div: sn drvn along: sme hdwy over 4f out: one pce fnl 2f* **66/1** | 59 |
| | 9 | 1 | **Melbourne Shuffle (USA)** 2-9-0 0.......... NickyMackay 9 (John Gosden) *s.i.s: in rr: sme hdwy over 1f out: edgd rt clsng stages: nvr a factor* **40/1** | 57 |
| 33 | 10 | 2 ½ | **Justify**[38] 6148 2-9-0 0.......... FrederikTylicki 13 (Roger Varian) *sn trcking ldrs: drvn over 2f out: wknd over 1f out* **15/2**[3] | 52 |
| 0 | 11 | 9 | **The Madding Crowd**[13] 6868 2-9-0 0.......... LiamKeniry 3 (Hughie Morrison) *in rr: bhd fnl 2f* **100/1** | 33 |
| | 12 | 2 | **Floweret (USA)** 2-8-11 0.......... CamHardie(3) 2 (Charlie Appleby) *mid-div: drvn over 5f out: lost pl over 3f out: sn bhd* **22/1** | 29 |

1m 49.98s (-0.12) **Going Correction** -0.025s/f (Stan) **12** Ran SP% **115.1**
Speed ratings (Par 92): **99,96,95,93,93 93,92,91,90,88 80,78**
CSF £6.74 TOTE £3.90: £2.10, £1.10, £5.10; EX 9.50 Trifecta £187.80.
**Owner** Godolphin **Bred** Darley **Trained** Newmarket, Suffolk

**FOCUS**
Some leading yards had representation in this fillies' maiden, which should supply winners.

## 7185 DOWNLOAD THE FREE APP @ BOOKIES.COM H'CAP (TAPETA) (DIV I) 1m 141y
**7:30** (7:30) (Class 4) (0-80,80) 3-Y-0+ **£4,725** (£1,414; £707; £354; £176) **Stalls** Low

| Form | | | | RPR |
|---|---|---|---|---|
| 2263 | 1 | | **Almanack**[26] 6478 4-8-12 72.......... NathanAlison(3) 7 (Ian Williams) *hld up in rr: gd hdwy on outside over 1f out: styd on to ld last 75yds* **20/1** | 79 |
| 3354 | 2 | ¾ | **Kingscroft (IRE)**[28] 6430 6-9-9 80..........(b) RobertWinston 4 (Michael Herrington) *mid-div: hdwy and nt clr run over 1f out tl ins fnl f: styd on to take 2nd nr fin* **4/1**[2] | 85 |
| 5405 | 3 | nk | **Alpine Storm (IRE)**[16] 6793 3-8-8 69.......... JoeFanning 9 (Mark Johnston) *sn trcking ldr: t.k.h: led over 1f out: hdd and no ex last 75yds* **16/1** | 74 |
| 2000 | 4 | hd | **Secret Archive (USA)**[12] 6886 3-9-0 75..........(p) RichardHughes 1 (Ralph Beckett) *trckd ldrs: drvn over 2f out: styd on same pce last 100yds* **12/1** | 80 |
| 1444 | 5 | ¾ | **Amood (IRE)**[12] 6886 3-9-4 79.......... AdamKirby 6 (Simon West) *t.k.h in rr: hdwy on outer over 3f out: kpt on ins fnl f* **15/2** | 82 |
| 200 | 6 | 1 ¼ | **Argaki (IRE)**[10] 6937 4-9-3 74..........[1] JimCrowley 8 (Keith Dalgleish) *mid-div: drvn over 3f out: outpcd over 2f out: kpt on outer fnl f* **12/1** | 73 |
| 6523 | 7 | hd | **Ghosting (IRE)**[18] 6722 3-8-11 72..........(t) RichardKingscote 3 (Tom Dascombe) *wnt lft s: sn trcking ldrs: t.k.h: kpt on same pce over 1f out* **7/1** | 72 |
| 2122 | 8 | shd | **Hesbaan (IRE)**[21] 6649 3-9-5 80..........(p) PaulHanagan 2 (Marcus Tregoning) *dwlt and hmpd s: in rr: hdwy on inner wl over 1f out: nvr nr ldrs* **7/2**[1] | 80 |
| 0241 | 9 | ½ | **Al Mukhdam**[14] 6841 4-9-8 79..........(p) JamieSpencer 5 (Ed de Giles) *led: reminders 3f out: hdd over 1f out: wknd and eased ins fnl f* **5/1**[3] | 76 |
| 003 | 10 | 2 ½ | **Zynah (IRE)**[16] 6788 3-8-10 71.......... FrederikTylicki 10 (Saeed bin Suroor) *trckd ldrs: wknd fnl f* **10/1** | 64 |

1m 48.75s (-1.35) **Going Correction** -0.025s/f (Stan)
**WFA** 3 from 4yo+ 4lb **10** Ran SP% **118.3**
Speed ratings (Par 105): **105,104,104,103,103 102,101,101,101,99**
CSF £99.96 CT £1378.36 TOTE £28.60: £6.60, £2.00, £6.40; EX 106.50 TRIFECTA Part won. Pool: £2,277.76 - 0.13 winning units..
**Owner** Phil Slater **Bred** Ed's Stud Ltd **Trained** Portway, Worcs

**FOCUS**
They went a decent pace in this modest handicap.

## 7186 DOWNLOAD THE FREE APP @ BOOKIES.COM H'CAP (TAPETA) (DIV II) 1m 141y
**8:00** (8:00) (Class 4) (0-80,80) 3-Y-0+ **£4,725** (£1,414; £707; £354; £176) **Stalls** Low

| Form | | | | RPR |
|---|---|---|---|---|
| 0530 | 1 | | **Toga Tiger (IRE)**[104] 3861 7-9-4 75.......... StevieDonohoe 9 (Kevin Frost) *dwlt: sn mid-div: hdwy on outer 2f out: rdr lost iron but styd on to ld last 100yds* **14/1** | 82 |
| 1050 | 2 | 1 | **Siouxperhero (IRE)**[22] 6616 5-9-1 72..........(b) MartinDwyer 10 (William Muir) *dwlt: sn chsng ldrs: 2nd 4f out: hung rt appr fnl f: sn led and wandered: hdd and no ex last 100yds* **33/1** | 77 |
| 5361 | 3 | nk | **Sbraase**[18] 6722 3-9-2 77.......... MartinHarley 4 (James Tate) *trckd ldrs: n.m.r 1f out: styd on same pce* **3/1**[2] | 82 |
| 0650 | 4 | ½ | **Mia's Boy**[168] 1834 10-9-9 80.......... LiamKeniry 3 (Chris Dwyer) *hld up in rr: effrt over 2f out: kpt on fnl f: gng on at fin* **18/1** | 83 |
| 6555 | 5 | ½ | **Like A Prayer**[26] 6484 3-8-3 67.......... CamHardie(3) 2 (Ralph Beckett) *in rr: hdwy over 2f out: kpt on same pce fnl f* **15/2** | 70 |
| 6123 | 6 | ½ | **Lean On Pete (IRE)**[182] 1495 5-9-2 76.......... JacobButterfield(3) 6 (Ollie Pears) *hld up in rr: hdwy on outer over 2f out: hmpd appr fnl f: kpt on* **10/1** | 77 |
| -533 | 7 | ½ | **Meteoroid (USA)**[117] 3383 3-9-1 76..........(p) RichardHughes 7 (Lady Cecil) *chsd ldrs: drvn 3f out: fdd last 150yds* **2/1**[1] | 76 |
| 0233 | 8 | 2 ¼ | **Party Royal**[17] 6770 4-9-6 77.......... JamesSullivan 8 (Ruth Carr) *led: clr over 3f out: hdd jst ins fnl f: hmpd and eased last 75yds* **12/1** | 71 |
| 5231 | 9 | 3 ¼ | **Ajig**[27] 6459 3-8-10 71..........(p) JohnFahy 5 (Eve Johnson Houghton) *chsd ldrs: outpcd over 2f out: wknd fnl f* **11/2**[3] | 59 |

1m 48.62s (-1.48) **Going Correction** -0.025s/f (Stan)
**WFA** 3 from 4yo+ 4lb **9** Ran SP% **117.1**
Speed ratings (Par 105): **105,104,103,103,102 102,102,100,97**
CSF £376.87 CT £1767.72 TOTE £24.40: £2.00, £5.30, £2.20; EX 468.20 Trifecta £1352.80 Part won. Pool: £1,803.78 - 0.18 winning units..
**Owner** Jan Mead Kelly Gould **Bred** Daniel Spaight **Trained** Red Hill, Warwickshire

**FOCUS**
This was run at a brisk pace, thanks to Party Royal, in a slightly quicker time than the first division. It was the fastest of the five C&D races.

## 7187 BETTING TIPS GALORE @ BOOKMAKERS.CO.UK H'CAP (TAPETA) (DIV I) 1m 141y
**8:30** (8:30) (Class 6) (0-58,58) 3-Y-0+ **£1,940** (£577; £288; £144) **Stalls** Low

| Form | | | | RPR |
|---|---|---|---|---|
| 0004 | 1 | | **Zaeem**[7] 6999 5-9-7 58..........(p) PatCosgrave 2 (Dean Ivory) *chsd ldrs: cl 2nd over 2f out: led wl over 1f out: styd on wl* **12/1** | 70 |
| 3000 | 2 | 1 ¾ | **Delightful Sleep**[3] 7115 6-8-12 52.......... DeclanBates(3) 1 (David Evans) *chsd ldrs: 2nd over 1f out: kpt on same pce* **16/1** | 60 |
| 0606 | 3 | 1 | **Crown Pleasure (IRE)**[22] 6613 3-8-13 57.......... DannyBrock(3) 11 (Willie Musson) *hld up in rr: hdwy on inner 2f out: kpt on same pce* **16/1** | 64 |

5212 **4** 3 1/4 **Flipping**38 6160 7-9-7 58 RichardHughes 9 56
(Stuart Kittow) *hld up in rr: hdwy on outer over 6f out: chsng ldrs over 2f out: one pce over 1f out* 5/4[1]
3526 **5** 1 1/2 **Dutch Lady**21 6647 3-9-3 58 FrannyNorton 6 54
(John Holt) *in rr: hdwy 3f out: one pce over 1f out* 8/1[3]
3421 **6** 2 1/4 **Elle Rebelle**29 6407 4-9-4 58 CamHardie(3) 13 48
(Mark Brisbourne) *hld up in mid-div: t.k.h: hdwy on outer over 1f out: nvr nr ldrs* 9/2[2]
4030 **7** 1 3/4 **Lady Bubbles**24 6564 3-8-7 48 JamesSullivan 5 35
(Michael Easterby) *chsd ldrs: effrt over 2f out: fdd over 1f out* 28/1
0000 **8** 1 1/4 **Pipers Piping (IRE)**18 6715 8-9-1 55 (t) RossAtkinson(3) 10 38
(Mandy Rowland) *chsd ldrs: drvn 3f out: wknd over 1f out* 20/1
0-06 **9** 3/4 **Savanna Spring (IRE)**46 5892 3-9-2 57 PaulHanagan 4 39
(Timothy Jarvis) *s.i.s: hdwy to chse ldrs 6f out: drvn over 3f out: lost pl over 1f out* 25/1
0-00 **10** nk **Smirfy's Silver**22 6601 10-8-9 46 oh1 HarryBentley 8 26
(Michael Mullineaux) *chsd ldr: led over 3f out: hdd wl over 1f out: sn wknd* 66/1
0643 **11** 2 **Zainda (IRE)**21 6628 4-8-10 47 JoeFanning 12 23
(Paul Midgley) *led: hdd over 3f out: wknd over 2f out* 10/1
0040 **12** 26 **Reflection**39 6088 3-8-5 46 JimmyQuinn 3
(Brian Baugh) *miud-div: lost pl over 3f out: bhd whn eased over 1f out: sn t.o* 66/1

1m 50.1s **Going Correction** -0.025s/f (Stan)
**WFA** 3 from 4yo+ 4lb 12 Ran SP% 117.3
Speed ratings (Par 101): **99,97,96,93,92 90,88,87,87,86 84,61**
CSF £174.33 CT £3103.77 TOTE £12.00: £3.00, £4.50, £5.70; EX 257.30 Trifecta £1570.70 Part won. Pool: £2,094.36 - 0.03 winning units..
**Owner** Richard Lewis & Steve Farmer **Bred** Umm Qarn Management Co Ltd **Trained** Radlett, Herts
**FOCUS**
A low-grade handicap.

## 7188 BETTING TIPS GALORE @ BOOKMAKERS.CO.UK H'CAP (TAPETA) (DIV II) 1m 141y
**9:00** (9:02) (Class 6) (0-58,58) 3-Y-0+ **£1,940** (£577; £288; £144) **Stalls** Low

Form RPR
6044 **1** **Poor Duke (IRE)**3 7115 4-9-2 53 HarryBentley 8 61
(Michael Mullineaux) *mid-div: drvn over 3f out: hdwy on ins over 2f out: styd on to ld last 100yds* 10/1
3202 **2** 1 1/4 **El Mirage (IRE)**12 6883 4-9-7 58 JimCrowley 3 63
(Dean Ivory) *chsd ldrs: led briefly jst ins fnl f: styd on same pce* 4/1[2]
0002 **3** hd **Yawail**18 6715 3-9-1 56 (p) JamesSullivan 4 62
(Brian Rothwell) *chsd ldrs: kpt on same pce fnl f* 12/1
0000 **4** 1/2 **Teide Peak (IRE)**5 7068 5-9-7 58 (p) AdamKirby 12 61
(Paul D'Arcy) *s.i.s: reminders after s: hdwy over 2f out: styd on ins fnl f* 11/4[1]
-406 **5** 3/4 **Crossley**27 6454 5-8-9 49 (p) CharlesBishop(3) 10 51
(Geoffrey Oldroyd) *w ldr: led over 3f out: hdd jst ins fnl f: one pce* 20/1
6650 **6** shd **Armourer (IRE)**36 6193 3-9-3 58 MartinDwyer 11 60
(William Muir) *chsd ldrs: kpt on one pce appr fnl f* 15/2
0202 **7** nse **Sarlat**10 6946 3-8-2 46 AmyScott(3) 6 48
(Mark Brisbourne) *hld up towards rr: hdwy on outer 2f out: kpt on: nt rch ldrs* 10/1
0000 **8** 1/2 **It's Taboo**29 6397 4-8-13 50 LiamKeniry 1 50
(Mark Usher) *chsd ldrs: nt clr run fr over 1f out: nt rcvr* 66/1
/3-6 **9** 1 1/4 **Flumps**36 6195 5-8-4 46 oh1 EoinWalsh(5) 7 43
(John Stimpson) *s.i.s: hdwy and nt clr run 2f out: n.m.r 1f out: nt rcvr* 16/1
424 **10** nse **Shiftin Bobbins**42 6010 3-8-6 50 (p) ConnorBeasley(3) 2 48
(Michael Dods) *led tl over 3f out: wknd jst ins fnl f* 20/1
0004 **11** 7 **Ballyfarsoon (IRE)**3 7118 3-8-7 48 ow1 StevieDonohoe 5 30
(Ian Williams) *s.i.s: bhd and drvn over 5f out* 8/1
6000 **12** 1 3/4 **Overrider**43 5977 4-9-2 53 (t) RichardHughes 9 30
(Shaun Lycett) *mid-div: drvn over 3f out: lost pl and eased 1f out* 6/1[3]

1m 50.34s (0.24) **Going Correction** -0.025s/f (Stan)
**WFA** 3 from 4yo+ 4lb 12 Ran SP% 126.6
Speed ratings (Par 101): **97,95,95,95,94 94,94,94,92,92 86,85**
CSF £52.26 CT £515.86 TOTE £10.80: £2.80, £2.80, £3.50; EX 102.30 Trifecta £417.20.
**Owner** Crewe And Nantwich Racing Club **Bred** Corrin Stud **Trained** Alpraham, Cheshire
**FOCUS**
This was the slightly slower division.
T/Plt: £55.20 to a £1 stake. Pool: £90,137.87 - 1,190.12 winning tickets T/Qpdt: £27.60 to a £1 stake. Pool: £10,164.21 - 272.00 winning tickets WG

# 3266 LYON PARILLY (R-H)
Tuesday, October 14
**OFFICIAL GOING: Turf: heavy**

## 7189a PRIX ANDRE BABOIN - MUSEE GALLO-ROMAIN DE SAINT-ROMAIN-EN-GAL (GROUP 3) (3YO+) (TURF) 1m 2f
**1:50** (1:50) 3-Y-0+ **£33,333** (£13,333; £10,000; £6,666; £3,333)

RPR
**1** **Dartagnan D'Azur (FR)**16 6810 5-8-13 0 MickaelBarzalona 1 110
(W Hefter, Germany) *w.w in rr on inner: hdwy 2f out: 3rd and styng on u.p 1 1/2f out: hrd rdn and edgd rt ent fnl f: r.o to ld 110yds out: sn clr* 8/1
**2** 4 **Le Ring (FR)**26 4-8-13 0 FranckBlondel 4 102
(F Rossi, France) *led: hdd after 2f: led single file trio on inner rail bk st: overall ldr whn gps merged over 3 1/2f out: kicked 2 1/2 l clr ins fnl 2f: sn rdn and kpt on: hdd 110yds out: readily outpcd by wnr* 5/4[1]
**3** 3/4 **Gaga A (URU)**25 6592 5-8-9 0 GregoryBenoist 2 97
(D Smaga, France) *trckd ldng pair on inner: 2nd of trio on inner rail bk st: chsd ldr whn gps merged over 3 1/2f out: 2nd and scrubbed along 2f out: hrd rdn over 1f out: one pce fnl f* 4/1[2]
**4** 12 **On Call Now**41 5-8-13 0 Christophe-PatriceLemaire 5 77
(X Thomas-Demeaulte, France) *hld up towards rr: wnt towards outer rail bk st: last whn gps merged over 3 1/2f out: pushed along and prog 1 1/2f out: kpt on at same pce fnl f: nvr in contention* 10/1
**5** 2 1/2 **Zand (IRE)**16 6810 4-8-13 0 MickaelForest 6 72
(Carmen Bocskai, Switzerland) *trckd ldr on outer: led after 2f: led single file trio towards outside rail bk st: chsd ldr on outer whn gps merged over 3 1/2f out: outpcd and sn btn* 5/1[3]
**6** 10 **Pachadargent (FR)**55 5591 3-8-8 0 ThierryThulliez 3 52
(F Rossi, France) *trckd ldng pair on outer: 2nd of trio towards outer rail bk st: chsd ldr between horses whn gps merged over 3 1/2f out: rdn and lost pl 2f out: wknd over 1f out* 14/1

2m 19.22s (139.22)
**WFA** 3 from 4yo+ 5lb 6 Ran SP% 108.0
WIN (incl. 1 euro stake): 5.80. PLACES: 2.30, 2.10. SF: 28.10.
**Owner** Stall Donna **Bred** Earl Haras Du Taillis **Trained** Germany
■ The first two are both sons of Slickly.

# 7029 KEMPTON (A.W) (R-H)
Wednesday, October 15
**OFFICIAL GOING: Polytrack: standard**
Wind: Light, across Weather: Raining

## 7190 RACINGUK.COM NURSERY H'CAP 5f (P)
**5:45** (5:46) (Class 6) (0-60,60) 2-Y-0 **£1,940** (£577; £288; £144) **Stalls** Low

Form RPR
0021 **1** **Sparbrook (IRE)**13 6888 2-9-6 59 HarryBentley 4 62
(Simon Dow) *trckd clr ldr: clsd to ld jst ins fnl f: drvn and hld on* 5/1[2]
0064 **2** hd **True Course**44 5985 2-9-7 60 WilliamBuick 5 62
(Charlie Appleby) *chsd ldng pair: pushed along 1/2-way: clsd over 1f out: wnt 2nd ins fnl f: grad clsd on wnr nr fin* 2/1[1]
650 **3** 3/4 **Most Tempting**29 6435 2-9-2 55 AdamBeschizza 2 56+
(Robert Cowell) *dwlt: stdy prog fr rr after 2f: clsng on ldrs whn nt clr run briefly 1f out and momentum checked: styd on last 100yds: nvr quite able to chal* 5/1[2]
1650 **4** 1 1/2 **Jimmy's Girl (IRE)**22 6645 2-9-4 57 (p) LiamKeniry 9 51
(Chris Dwyer) *taken down early: rousted to ld and crossed fr wd draw: sn 3 l clr: hdd and fdd jst ins fnl f* 25/1
060 **5** 1 **Auntie Dif**39 6158 2-7-13 45 AdamMcLean(7) 3 36
(Derek Shaw) *t.k.h: trckd ldng pair: shkn up on inner 1f out and fnd nil: fdd tamely* 50/1
540 **6** 1 **Ms Eboracum (IRE)**58 5509 2-8-6 48 CamHardie(3) 1 35+
(Edward Creighton) *nvr beyond midfield: rdn and outpcd fr 2f out: plugged on* 8/1
0030 **7** 1/2 **Air Of York (IRE)**29 6422 2-8-8 47 ow2 (b) WilliamTwiston-Davies 8 32+
(Ronald Harris) *wl in rr and racd wd: rdn bef 1/2-way: no ch 2f out: plugged on* 10/1
4045 **8** nk **River Spirit**13 6888 2-9-5 58 SamHitchcott 7 42+
(Mick Channon) *wl in rr: rdn 1/2-way: no ch fr 2f out: plugged on* 10/1
4402 **9** 3 3/4 **Surrey Pink (FR)**17 6791 2-8-9 48 (p) MartinDwyer 6 19+
(William Muir) *dwlt: a struggling in rr* 11/2[3]
0604 **10** 2 1/2 **Featsdontfailmenow**109 3692 2-8-6 45 JohnFahy 10 7
(Lisa Williamson) *chsd ldrs to 1/2-way: wknd wl over 1f out* 50/1

1m 0.73s (0.23) **Going Correction** -0.125s/f (Stan) 10 Ran SP% 119.1
Speed ratings (Par 93): **93,92,91,89,87 85,85,84,78,74**
CSF £15.58 CT £53.09 TOTE £5.80: £1.60, £1.10, £3.30; EX 17.60 Trifecta £91.80.
**Owner** Andrew Li **Bred** Henry O'Callaghan **Trained** Epsom, Surrey
**FOCUS**
They went a strong pace and there was a tight finish between the three market leaders in this nursery.

## 7191 COME JUMP RACING HERE ON SUNDAY H'CAP 5f (P)
**6:15** (6:15) (Class 6) (0-55,54) 3-Y-0+ **£1,940** (£577; £288; £144) **Stalls** Low

Form RPR
3440 **1** **Bubbly Bailey**50 5801 4-9-7 54 (v) RichardHughes 6 64
(J R Jenkins) *disp ld tl led on inner 2f out: in command 1f out: pushed out firmly* 11/4[1]
1003 **2** 1 1/2 **Danzoe (IRE)**12 6897 7-9-0 52 (v) EoinWalsh(5) 2 57
(Christine Dunnett) *chsd ldng quartet but nt on terms: rdn 2f out: r.o over 1f out to take 2nd last 100yds: no ch to threaten wnr* 9/2[3]
4000 **3** 1 1/2 **Mossgo (IRE)**22 6631 4-9-2 49 (t) MartinDwyer 8 48
(John Best) *disp ld to 2f out: nt qckn after: lost 2nd last 100yds* 10/1
300 **4** 1 3/4 **Imaginary Diva**30 6399 8-9-6 53 PaoloSirigu 3 46
(George Margarson) *sn wl in rr and off the pce: rdn over 2f out: nvr a factor but kpt on fnl f to take 4th last strides* 20/1
6532 **5** nk **Greek Islands (IRE)**9 6983 6-8-10 50 RobertPWalsh(7) 10 42
(Edward Creighton) *restless as stall opened: slowly away and impeded: tried to make up grnd fr 3f out but v wd bnd 2f out: styd on fnl f: nrly snatched 4th* 3/1[2]
5625 **6** hd **Spic 'n Span**12 6897 9-9-1 48 (p) WilliamTwiston-Davies 4 39
(Ronald Harris) *chsd ldng pair: urged along fr 2f out: fdd fnl f* 20/1
63/4 **7** 1/2 **Lucky Royale**22 6631 6-9-0 54 DavidParkes(7) 5 43
(Jeremy Gask) *sltly awkward s: hld up in last and wl off the pce: rdn over 1f out: kpt on fnl f: nvr a factor* 9/1
506 **8** nk **Nora Batty**79 4735 3-8-10 48 RyanWhile(5) 1 37
(Bill Turner) *sn off the pce towards rr: pushed along 2f out: one pce fr over 1f out: n.d* 50/1
4443 **9** 6 **Sylvan Spirit (IRE)**22 6631 3-9-3 50 LiamKeniry 9 18
(Roger Teal) *wnt lft s: chsd ldng trio: rdn 2f out: wknd over 1f out: eased ins fnl f* 16/1
422 **10** 2 1/2 **Lucky Surprise**22 6631 3-9-3 50 (b) SteveDrowne 7 9
(Jeremy Gask) *dwlt: a in rr: bhd over 1f out* 7/1

59.78s (-0.72) **Going Correction** -0.125s/f (Stan) 10 Ran SP% 118.8
Speed ratings (Par 101): **100,97,95,92,91 91,90,90,80,76**
CSF £15.36 CT £112.37 TOTE £3.40: £1.20, £2.00, £2.90; EX 19.00 Trifecta £202.90.
**Owner** Mrs S Bowmer **Bred** Bearstone Stud **Trained** Royston, Herts
**FOCUS**
The favourite scored in good style under a positive ride in this ordinary handicap and not many got involved. The runner-up helps with the level.

## 7192 BETDAQ £30 FREE BET MAIDEN FILLIES' STKS (BOBIS RACE) 6f (P)
**6:45** (6:46) (Class 5) 2-Y-0 **£2,587** (£770; £384; £192) **Stalls** Low

Form RPR
44 **1** **Apache Storm**19 6700 2-8-11 0 CamHardie(3) 11 78
(Michael Appleby) *wl away fr wd draw: mde all: hung bdly lft jst over 2f out and ended up against nr side rail: clr fnl f: rdn out* 16/1
0 **2** 3 1/2 **Dusty Blue**104 3888 2-9-0 0 (t) JohnFahy 6 67
(Paul Cole) *chsd wnr: rdn 2f out: one pce and no imp fnl f* 14/1
4 **3** shd **Slovak (IRE)**34 6270 2-9-0 0 MartinHarley 2 67
(James Tate) *chsd ldng trio: rdn 2f out: wnt 3rd over 1f out: drvn and styd on: nrly tk 2nd* 7/2[3]

4 nk **Engaging Smile** 2-9-0 0 PatDobbs 4 66+
(Ralph Beckett) *chsd ldrs in 5th: pushed along and styd on steadily fnl f: nrly tk 2nd* 3/1[2]

5 2 **Noblest** 2-9-0 0 RyanMoore 3 60+
(William Haggas) *slowly away: rn green and detached in last pair early: pushed along and kpt on fr over 2f out: nrst fin* 4/1

0 6 1 1/2 **Royal Silk**[26] 6517 2-9-0 0 JamesDoyle 10 56
(Roger Charlton) *in rr: pushed along and wd bnd 3f out: kpt on fnl 2f: nrst fin* 16/1

7 nk **Middle East Pearl** 2-9-0 0 JimCrowley 8 55
(James Tate) *chsd ldng pair: rdn 2f out: lost 3rd and steadily wknd over 1f out* 50/1

8 3/4 **Queen Zain (IRE)** 2-9-0 0 LiamJones 12 52+
(Robert Cowell) *slowly away: tried to rcvr over 4f out: nvr bttr than midfield: 7th over 1f out: no hdwy after* 66/1

9 nk **Darrell Rivers** 2-9-0 0 [1] HarryBentley 1 52
(Giles Bravery) *in tch in midfield: sme prog on inner 2f out: no hdwy over 1f out: fdd fnl f* 66/1

10 6 **Pacolita (IRE)** 2-9-0 0 LiamKeniry 9 34
(Sylvester Kirk) *t.k.h in midfield: no prog over 2f out: wknd qckly over 1f out* 33/1

0 11 12 **Coursing**[8] 7004 2-9-0 0 LukeMorris 7
(Sir Mark Prescott Bt) *blindfold off sltly late and slowly away: stl v green and pushed along in last pair: t.o* 66/1

053 12 19 **Raspberry Ripple**[41] 6066 2-9-0 82 RichardHughes 5
(Richard Hannon) *nt that wl away: a in rr: shkn up and no prog over 2f out: wknd and heavily eased: t.o* 5/2[1]

1m 12.17s (-0.93) **Going Correction** -0.125s/f (Stan) 12 Ran SP% 123.6
Speed ratings (Par 92): **101,96,96,95,93 91,90,89,89,81 65,40**
CSF £222.55 TOTE £17.30: £5.70, £3.70, £1.10; EX 166.00 Trifecta £1681.20.
**Owner** Ferrybank Properties Limited **Bred** Northmore Stud **Trained** Danethorpe, Notts

**FOCUS**
There was a surprise result in this maiden but the winner deserves extra credit for making all after setting a good pace from a wide draw.

## 7193 BETDAQ £200 GAMES BONUS MAIDEN FILLIES' STKS (BOBIS RACE) (DIV I) 7f (P)
7:15 (7:16) (Class 5) 2-Y-O £2,587 (£770; £384; £192) Stalls Low

Form RPR

66 1 **Music And Dance**[29] 6434 2-9-0 0 RyanMoore 14 76+
(Sir Michael Stoute) *w ldr: led over 2f out and kicked 2 l clr: hrd pressed ins fnl f: hld on wl* 8/1[3]

2 nk **Wild Storm** 2-9-0 0 JamesDoyle 6 75
(Saeed bin Suroor) *trckd ldrs: shkn up to chse wnr over 1f out: clsd to chal fnl f: styd on but a hld* 4/1[2]

3 3 1 1/2 **Jazzi Top**[18] 6753 2-9-0 0 WilliamBuick 4 73+
(John Gosden) *trckd ldrs: nt clr run jst over 2f out as wnr was sent for home: prog over 1f out: chsd ldng pair after: styd on same pce fnl f* 8/13[1]

4 3 3/4 **Faery Song (IRE)** 2-9-0 0 TedDurcan 8 61
(David Lanigan) *in tch in midfield: sme prog on inner over 2f out: reminder over 1f out: outpcd by ldng trio after* 33/1

4 5 3/4 **Lady Pinnacle**[23] 6605 2-9-0 0 DavidProbert 9 59
(Andrew Balding) *t.k.h: trckd ldrs: shkn up over 1f out: outpcd after* 10/1

6 1 **Lady Hare (IRE)** 2-9-0 0 JimCrowley 5 56
(David Simcock) *wl in rr: pushed along over 2f out: kpt on steadily fr over 1f out: nrst fin* 50/1

00 7 1 **Machiavelian Storm (IRE)**[20] 6675 2-9-0 0 PaulHanagan 1 53+
(Ed Dunlop) *hld up in last pair: nudged along and same pl over 2f out: pushed along and kpt on to sme effect fr over 1f out* 66/1

0 8 1 1/4 **Heavens Above (IRE)**[8] 7019 2-9-0 0 RobertHavlin 2 50+
(Ed Dunlop) *wl in rr: pushed along on inner over 2f out: one pce and no threat* 66/1

0 9 3/4 **Sonic Rainbow (GR)**[8] 7011 2-9-0 0 PatDobbs 10 48
(Amanda Perrett) *wl in tch in midfield: pushed along and no prog 2f out: n.d after* 66/1

10 shd **Fanny Again** 2-8-11 0 CamHardie(3) 7 48+
(Denis Coakley) *dwlt: wl in rr: pushed along over 2f out: no real prog but plugged on* 50/1

6 11 3/4 **Hana Lina**[18] 6754 2-9-0 0 JoeFanning 3 46
(William Haggas) *led to jst over 2f out: wknd rapidly over 1f out* 12/1

12 3 1/2 **Makramah (USA)** 2-9-0 0 RichardHughes 11 36
(Richard Hannon) *v.s.a: a in last pair* 20/1

13 4 **Bombalurina (IRE)** 2-9-0 0 KierenFallon 13 26
(George Peckham) *in tch in midfield on outer: pushed along 3f out: wknd over 2f out: eased* 66/1

1m 26.24s (0.24) **Going Correction** -0.125s/f (Stan) 13 Ran SP% 127.4
Speed ratings (Par 92): **93,92,90,86,85 84,83,82,81,81 80,76,71**
CSF £41.21 TOTE £11.40: £2.20, £2.10, £1.02; EX 52.00 Trifecta £111.80.
**Owner** Cheveley Park Stud **Bred** Cheveley Park Stud Ltd **Trained** Newmarket, Suffolk

**FOCUS**
The three market leaders pulled clear in this maiden. The winner had the run of the race and the hot favourite ran into some trouble at a crucial stage.

## 7194 BETDAQ £200 GAMES BONUS MAIDEN FILLIES' STKS (BOBIS RACE) (DIV II) 7f (P)
7:45 (7:49) (Class 5) 2-Y-O £2,587 (£770; £384; £192) Stalls Low

Form RPR

2 1 **Zari**[23] 6606 2-9-0 0 RyanMoore 10 78+
(Roger Varian) *mde all: kicked on over 2f out: pushed out firmly and wl in command fnl f* 9/4[1]

2 2 **Ershaadaat (IRE)** 2-9-0 0 JamesDoyle 2 73+
(Saeed bin Suroor) *trckd ldrs: prog over 2f out: rdn to chse wnr over 1f out: styd on but no imp* 5/1[2]

3 3 2 **Lady Estella (IRE)**[19] 6701 2-9-0 0 MartinHarley 11 67
(Marco Botti) *trckd wnr after 2f: rdn 2f out: lost 2nd and one pce over 1f out* 14/1[3]

5 4 1 1/4 **Eastern Romance**[25] 6553 2-9-0 0 JoeFanning 5 64+
(William Haggas) *hld up towards rr: pushed along and prog jst over 2f out: chsd ldrs over 1f out: kpt on same pce* 5/1[2]

0 5 1 **Nouveau Foret**[29] 6434 2-9-0 0 FergusSweeney 3 61+
(Ed Walker) *hld up towards rr: prog jst over 2f out to chse ldrs over 1f out: pushed along and one pce after* 66/1

6 1 **Naizah (IRE)** 2-9-0 0 PaulHanagan 9 58+
(Ed Dunlop) *in tch in midfield: no prog over 2f out: str reminder 1f out: kpt on fnl f* 33/1

06 7 nk **Asima (IRE)**[14] 6868 2-8-11 0 CamHardie(3) 4 58
(Charles Hills) *prom: pushed along over 2f out: steadily fdd fr over 1f out* 33/1

0 7 dht **Merritt Island**[8] 7018 2-9-0 0 LukeMorris 6 61+
(Sir Mark Prescott Bt) *awkward s: mostly in last pair: shkn up over 2f out: kpt on fr over 1f out: nrst fin* 100/1

32 9 1 3/4 **Rock Kristal (IRE)**[56] 5549 2-9-0 0 [1] WilliamBuick 13 53
(John Gosden) *dwlt: wl in rr: tried to make prog on wd outside 3f out but sn u.p: struggling after* 9/4[1]

10 1 1/2 **Flighty Filia (IRE)** 2-9-0 0 PatDobbs 8 51+
(Amanda Perrett) *hld up wl in rr: nt clr run over 2f out: modest prog 1f out: nvr a factor* 66/1

0 11 2 1/2 **Lady D's Rock (IRE)**[90] 4346 2-9-0 0 SteveDrowne 1 42
(Clive Cox) *wl in tch in midfield on inner: cl enough 2f out: wknd qckly over 1f out* 66/1

0 12 hd **Ninepins (IRE)**[41] 6065 2-9-0 0 RichardHughes 7 42
(Richard Hannon) *trckd wnr 2f: styd prom: shkn up over 2f out: wknd over 1f out: eased* 16/1

13 1 1/2 **Lilian Baylis (IRE)** 2-9-0 0 DavidProbert 14 38+
(Luca Cumani) *rn green in last pair: nudged along and no prog fnl 2f* 25/1

0 14 4 **Gentle Persuasion**[21] 6652 2-9-0 0 JimCrowley 12 27
(Amanda Perrett) *t.k.h: racd on outer: prom after 2f tl wknd over 2f out* 33/1

1m 26.01s (0.01) **Going Correction** -0.125s/f (Stan) 14 Ran SP% 125.6
Speed ratings (Par 92): **94,91,89,88,86 85,85,85,83,81 78,78,76,72**
CSF £13.90 TOTE £3.30: £1.10, £2.30, £5.10; EX 21.90 Trifecta £189.50.
**Owner** Saleh Al Homaizi & Imad Al Sagar **Bred** Saleh Al Homaizi & Imad Al Sagar **Trained** Newmarket, Suffolk

**FOCUS**
The winner was impressive in this maiden but there was also promise from a newcomer in second.

## 7195 DOWNLOAD THE BETDAQ+ APP MAIDEN STKS 1m 4f (P)
8:15 (8:17) (Class 5) 3-5-Y-O £2,587 (£770; £384; £192) Stalls Centre

Form RPR

1 **Kalaatah (USA)** 3-9-0 0 KierenFallon 2 77+
(Saeed bin Suroor) *slowly away: rcvrd and in tch: prog 3f out: led jst over 2f out: shkn up and hung lft fnl f: styd on* 9/1

022U 2 1 **Rembrandt Van Rijn (IRE)**[12] 6901 3-9-5 84 GeorgeBaker 6 80
(David Lanigan) *stdd s: hld up and sn in last: prog over 2f out: swtchd lft wl over 1f out and hd at awkward angle: sn in 3rd: cajoled along fnl f: styd on to take 2nd nr fin* 5/2[2]

653 3 1/2 **Cerutty (IRE)**[22] 6634 3-9-5 77 MartinHarley 1 79
(Marco Botti) *led to over 8f out: sn in 3rd: rdn to go 2nd again 2f out: drvn to chal over 1f out: carried lft and no ex ins fnl f* 7/1[3]

322 4 1 3/4 **Viceroyalty**[23] 6611 3-9-5 78 WilliamBuick 3 76
(Charlie Appleby) *hld up in rr: shkn up and outpcd over 2f out: pushed along and kpt on steadily fr over 1f out: n.d* 7/1[3]

32 5 1 1/2 **Ghany (IRE)**[17] 6788 3-9-0 0 PaulHanagan 7 69
(William Haggas) *trckd ldng pair tl quick move to ld over 8f out: rdn and hdd jst over 2f out: nt qckn: fdd fnl f* 5/4[1]

4263 6 1/2 **Dianora**[37] 6192 3-9-0 74 RyanMoore 4 68
(Sir Michael Stoute) *chsd ldrs: rdn 3f out: nt qckn over 2f out: wl hld after* 10/1

7 6 **Sea Rebelle** 5-9-7 0 AdamBeschizza 8 58
(Jo Crowley) *dwlt: in tch in rr: pushed along over 3f out: steadily wknd over 2f out* 100/1

5 8 11 **Tweedswood (IRE)**[23] 6611 3-9-5 0 JimCrowley 5 46
(Roger Varian) *mostly chsd ldr tl wknd qckly wl over 1f out* 50/1

2m 33.15s (-1.35) **Going Correction** -0.125s/f (Stan)
**WFA** 3 from 5yo 7lb 8 Ran SP% 120.1
Speed ratings (Par 103): **99,98,98,96,95 95,91,84**
CSF £33.54 TOTE £11.50: £2.80, £1.20, £3.80; EX 50.00 Trifecta £137.10.
**Owner** Godolphin **Bred** Shadwell Farm, Llc **Trained** Newmarket, Suffolk

**FOCUS**
The favourite was a bit disappointing but a Godolphin newcomer scored in decent style in this maiden. However it was falsely run and there are doubts over the bare form.

## 7196 BETDAQ 50% COMMISSION REFUND/CHOOSE EBF FILLIES' H'CAP 7f (P)
8:45 (8:47) (Class 4) (0-85,85) 3-Y-O+
£6,225 (£1,864; £932; £466; £233; £117) Stalls Low

Form RPR

2332 1 **Khatiba (IRE)**[33] 6302 3-8-13 79 JamesDoyle 6 93
(Roger Varian) *wl in tch: prog to trck ldrs 2f out: drvn to ld 1f out: styd on strly* 7/1[3]

2043 2 2 1/4 **Perfect Persuasion**[28] 6459 3-9-2 82 (p) RyanMoore 14 90
(William Haggas) *sn trckd ldr: rdn to ld 2f out: hdd 1f out: outpcd* 3/1[1]

1235 3 1 **Maggie Pink**[20] 6681 5-9-1 82 CamHardie(3) 9 88
(Michael Appleby) *taken down early: prom: rdn over 2f out: chsd ldng pair fnl f: kpt on same pce* 10/1

1224 4 1/2 **First Experience**[40] 6112 3-8-10 76 KierenFallon 8 80
(Rae Guest) *towards rr on outer: shkn up over 2f out: prog over 1f out: kpt on to take 4th fnl f: nt pce to threaten* 12/1

1 5 1/2 **Tawteen (USA)**[11] 6940 3-8-12 78 PaulHanagan 11 81+
(John Gosden) *dwlt: in last trio: shkn up on outer over 2f out: no prog tl styd on fr jst over 1f out: nrst fin* 9/2[2]

2U 6 3/4 **Artistic Charm**[55] 5612 3-9-4 84 JimCrowley 3 85
(David Simcock) *settled in midfield: rdn and sme prog to chse ldrs 2f out: no imp over 1f out: one pce after* 14/1

0635 7 2 1/2 **Welsh Sunrise**[21] 6657 4-8-10 74 HarryBentley 2 69
(Stuart Williams) *chsd ldrs: rdn over 2f out: no imp over 1f out: fdd* 25/1

2335 8 1/2 **Invoke (IRE)**[33] 6302 3-8-7 73 (p) LukeMorris 5 65
(Michael Bell) *t.k.h: chsd ldng pair: drvn 2f out: wknd jst over 1f out* 40/1

4500 9 3/4 **Our Queenie (IRE)**[23] 6607 3-9-4 84 RichardHughes 10 74
(Richard Hannon) *chsd ldrs on outer: rdn sn after 1/2-way: steadily wknd over 1f out* 25/1

0030 10 nk **Jacquotte Delahaye**[17] 6792 3-9-2 82 MartinHarley 1 72
(David Brown) *towards rr: tried to make prog fr 2f out: no hdwy jst over 1f out: wknd* 40/1

1432 11 hd **Rayoumti (IRE)**[53] 5685 3-8-11 77 TomQueally 7 66
(George Margarson) *rrd s: mostly in last trio: rdn 3f out: no great prog* 16/1

-400 12 3/4 **Mystical Sapphire**[36] 6207 4-9-7 85 FergusSweeney 13 74
(Jo Crowley) *dwlt: mostly in last trio: shkn up and nt clr run briefly over 2f out: no prog* 7/1[3]

323 **13** ½ **Emirates Joy (USA)**[11] 6940 3-8-11 **77**............................ MartinLane 4 63
(Charlie Appleby) *towards rr: rdn and no prog over 2f out: sn btn* **25/1**

-123 **14** 2 **Maria Bella (IRE)**[49] 5826 3-9-5 **85**............................ WilliamBuick 12 68
(Charlie Appleby) *sn led: hdd 2f out: wknd quicly jst over 1f out: eased* **10/1**

1m 23.91s (-2.09) **Going Correction** -0.125s/f (Stan)
**WFA** 3 from 4yo+ 2lb **14** Ran SP% **123.0**
Speed ratings (Par 102): **106,103,102,101,101 100,97,96,96,95 95,94,94,91**
CSF £27.24 CT £222.64 TOTE £5.70: £2.50, £2.20, £2.90; EX 33.90 Trifecta £228.90.
**Owner** Sheikh Ahmed Al Maktoum **Bred** Darley **Trained** Newmarket, Suffolk

**FOCUS**
The winner forged clear from the favourite in this interesting handicap. The winner may yet have more to offer.

## 7197 RACING UK ANYWHERE AVAILABLE NOW CLASSIFIED STKS 1m (P)
**9:15** (9:15) (Class 6) 3-Y-O+ **£1,940** (£577; £288; £144) **Stalls** Low

Form RPR

**1** **Succeed And Excel**[19] 6726 3-9-2 53............................ TomQueally 11 65+
(John Butler) *stdd s: hld up in last: stl there over 2f out: rapid prog after: led jst over 1f out: drvn clr* **5/1**[2]

5026 **2** 3¼ **Cadmium**[41] 6070 3-8-9 51............................ Leah-AnneAvery(7) 6 57
(Harry Dunlop) *hld up in last pair: stdy prog on inner over 2f out: trying to cl whn wnr shot by jst over 1f out: styd on but no ch* **20/1**

4634 **3** 2¾ **Nellies Quest**[197] 1228 5-9-5 46............................[1] AndrewMullen 9 51
(Michael Appleby) *racd wd in midfield: u.p fr 1/2-way: fnlly responded over 1f out: styd on to take 3rd nr fin* **16/1**

-405 **4** nk **Dream And Hope**[11] 6939 3-8-13 51............................ DannyBrock(3) 13 50+
(Philip McBride) *racd wd: chsd ldrs: prog arnd rivals to dispute ld 1/2-way to jst over 2f out: fdd jst over 1f out: did best of those racing promly* **9/1**

6316 **5** nk **Pelagian (USA)**[7] 7036 3-9-2 54............................ SteveDrowne 10 49
(Michael Attwater) *hld up in last trio: shkn up and prog 2f out: clsd to press for a pl ins fnl f: one pce nr fin* **9/2**[1]

3000 **6** 2 **Harwoods Star (IRE)**[29] 6426 4-9-5 54............................ PatDobbs 3 44+
(Amanda Perrett) *trckd ldr: mde most fr 1/2-way gng easily: def advantage 2f out: shkn up and hdd jst over 1f out: folded tamely* **5/1**[2]

5266 **7** 5 **Plauseabella**[31] 6356 3-9-2 51............................ MartinLane 2 32
(Stuart Kittow) *dwlt: pushed up to chse ldrs after 2f: struggling u.p over 2f out: btn over 1f out* **50/1**

0006 **8** 1¾ **Berrahri (IRE)**[13] 6883 3-9-2 54............................(e) RobertHavlin 7 28
(John Best) *chsd ldrs: drvn wl over 2f out: wknd over 1f out* **7/1**[3]

0046 **9** hd **Division Belle**[20] 6682 3-9-2 55............................ MartinDwyer 12 28+
(William Muir) *w ldrs: disp ld 1/2-way tl wknd u.p over 2f out* **9/2**[1]

-000 **10** ¾ **Wannabe Magic**[48] 5846 3-9-2 46............................ JohnFahy 5 26
(Geoffrey Deacon) *nvr beyond midfield: struggling over 2f out: sn btn* **50/1**

004 **11** 2 **Satchville Flyer**[17] 6788 3-9-2 53............................ RichardHughes 1 31+
(Brett Johnson) *led at str pce: hdd 1/2-way: wknd 2f out: heavily eased* **7/1**[3]

0000 **12** nk **Phantom Spirit**[33] 6297 3-9-2 45............................(p) PatCosgrave 8 20
(George Baker) *nvr on terms: rdn on outer over 3f out: sn btn* **66/1**

5030 **13** 2 **Heartstrings**[28] 6454 3-9-2 52............................(v) SamHitchcott 4 16
(Mick Channon) *nvr bttr than midfield: wknd over 2f out* **16/1**

1m 38.93s (-0.87) **Going Correction** -0.125s/f (Stan)
**WFA** 3 from 4yo+ 3lb **13** Ran SP% **126.6**
Speed ratings (Par 101): **99,95,93,92,92 90,85,83,83,82 80,80,78**
CSF £110.17 TOTE £5.90: £1.20, £7.80, £6.20; EX 143.90 Trifecta £1494.20.
**Owner** J Butler **Bred** Worksop Manor Stud **Trained** Newmarket, Suffolk

**FOCUS**
They went a fair pace in this modest classified and the first two came from a long way back. The winner improved a little on his Irish form.
T/Jkpt: Not won. T/Plt: £43.30 to a £1 stake. Pool: £92,255.51 - 1,554.38 winning tickets T/Qpdt: £16.00 to a £1 stake. Pool: £10,225.13 - 470.70 winning tickets JN

# 6629 LINGFIELD (L-H)
## Wednesday, October 15

**OFFICIAL GOING: Polytrack: standard**
Wind: virtually nil Weather: overcast, light rain from race 5

## 7198 £20 FREE BET AT WINNER.CO.UK MAIDEN AUCTION STKS 1m 1y(P)
**1:30** (1:31) (Class 6) 2-Y-O **£2,587** (£770; £384; £192) **Stalls** Low

Form RPR

3 **1** **Sarsted**[25] 6551 2-9-1 0............................ RichardHughes 6 74+
(Hughie Morrison) *str: lw: led after 1f: mde rest: rdn and qcknd 2f out: clr and in command fnl f: eased towards fin* **30/100**[1]

60 **2** ½ **Twice Certain (IRE)**[8] 7018 2-8-11 0............................ LukeMorris 8 67+
(Ed Walker) *leggy: in tch towards rr: hdwy u.p towards inner over 1f out: chsd clr wnr ins fnl f: kpt on u.p* **20/1**

4 **3** 2 **Sea Of Red**[15] 6838 2-8-11 0............................ LiamKeniry 7 62
(J S Moore) *w'like: chsd ldrs: rdn 2f out: sn chsng wnr: no imp: 3rd and one pce fnl 150yds* **10/1**

0 **4** 1½ **Jo Bibidia**[23] 6606 2-8-3 0............................ DannyBrock(3) 11 53
(Jonathan Portman) *w'like: s.i.s: sn rcvrd to chse ldrs: rdn and unable qck 2f out: styd on same pce fnl f* **16/1**

**5** ½ **Helmsman (IRE)** 2-9-0 0............................ LiamJones 2 60
(J S Moore) *w'like: str: wl in tch in midfield: rdn 2f out: no imp and one pce fr over 1f out* **66/1**

**6** hd **Littlemisspositive** 2-8-9 0 ow1............................ RobertTart 1 55
(Martin Smith) *leggy: in tch in midfield: rdn and outpcd wl over 1f out: styd on same pce after* **33/1**

03 **7** nk **Magical Thomas**[40] 6085 2-8-10 0............................ LouisSteward(3) 4 58
(Marcus Tregoning) *hld up in rr: pushed along and effrt 2f: nt clr run over 1f out: hmpd ins fnl f: kpt on but nvr a threat* **7/1**[2]

**8** nk **Dizzey Heights (IRE)** 2-8-3 0............................ ShelleyBirkett(5) 10 52+
(Stuart Kittow) *leggy: in tch in midfield: pushed along and outpcd 2f out: no imp and one pce fr over 1f out* **50/1**

00 **9** 2 **Epsom Poems**[14] 6852 2-8-9 0............................ JemmaMarshall(3) 3 51
(Pat Phelan) *w'like: led for 1f: chsd ldrs into lost pl and midfield 1/2-way: towards rr and rdn over 2f out: no hdwy* **66/1**

**10** nk **Rum Swizzle** 2-8-7 0............................ SamHitchcott 12 46
(Harry Dunlop) *leggy: unf: t.k.h: in tch but stuck wd: rdn and sme hdwy over 2f out: lost pl bnd 2f out: n.d after* **33/1**

0 **11** ½ **Honour Promise (IRE)**[14] 6868 2-8-7 0............................ MartinDwyer 9 45
(William Muir) *athletic: t.k.h: chsd wnr after 2f: rdn and edgd rt bnd 2f out: sn btn and wknd over 1f out* **8/1**[3]

1m 38.47s (0.27) **Going Correction** -0.15s/f (Stan) **11** Ran SP% **131.1**
Speed ratings (Par 93): **92,91,89,88,87 87,87,86,84,84 83**
CSF £17.24 TOTE £1.20: £1.02, £5.80, £2.20; EX 13.40 Trifecta £92.50.
**Owner** Annika Murjahn & Partners **Bred** Worksop Manor Stud **Trained** East Ilsley, Berks

**FOCUS**
An uncompetitive maiden auction to start. The winner had a soft lead and it's hard to rate the bare form any higher.

## 7199 DOWNLOAD THE WINNER.CO.UK APP NOW / IRISH EBF MAIDEN STKS (DIV I) 7f 1y(P)
**2:00** (2:01) (Class 5) 2-Y-O **£2,911** (£866; £432; £216) **Stalls** Low

Form RPR

**1** **Peterhof** 2-9-5 0............................ RyanMoore 4 80+
(Sir Michael Stoute) *str: scope: lw: in tch in midfield: effrt and swtchd out rt over 1f out: styd on wl to ld wl ins fnl f: gng away at fin* **6/1**[3]

03 **2** ½ **Brutus (FR)**[14] 6876 2-9-5 0............................ JimCrowley 5 79
(Richard Hannon) *w'like: tall: chsd ldrs: wnt 2nd after 2f: rdn and ev ch 2f out: sustained duel w ldr: kpt on same pce wl ins fnl f* **14/1**

32 **3** ¾ **Foreign Diplomat**[26] 6517 2-9-5 0............................ FrankieDettori 10 77
(William Haggas) *lw: led: rdn wl over 1f out: sustained duel w rival tl hdd wl ins fnl f: wknd cl home* **4/9**[1]

**4** hd **Tajathub** 2-9-5 0............................ PaulHanagan 3 77+
(Ed Dunlop) *leggy: athletic: t.k.h: chsd ldr for 2f: chsd ldrs after: effrt whn nt clr run on inner and hmpd ent fnl f: gap opened and rdn to press ldrs fnl 100yds: one pce* **14/1**

**5** 7 **Defence Event (USA)** 2-9-5 0............................ JamesDoyle 1 58
(John Gosden) *lengthy: s.i.s: in rr: rdn and outpcd ent fnl 2f: wl hld over 1f out* **4/1**[2]

05 **6** ½ **Rainbow Pride (IRE)**[8] 6997 2-9-5 0............................ LukeMorris 2 58+
(Sir Mark Prescott Bt) *w'like: t.k.h: hld up in tch in midfield: rdn 2f out: sn outpcd: wknd over 1f out* **50/1**

**7** 3¾ **Lahent** 2-9-5 0............................ TomQueally 9 46
(Charlie Fellowes) *w'like: v.s.a: in tch towards rr: rdn and outpcd ent fnl 2f: wknd wl over 1f out* **33/1**

00 **8** 11 **Now Say Boooom**[58] 5489 2-8-7 45............................ KieranShoemark(7) 8
(Luke Dace) *taken down early: chsd ldrs on outer: lost pl 1/2-way: bhd over 1f out* **100/1**

1m 24.44s (-0.36) **Going Correction** -0.15s/f (Stan) **8** Ran SP% **122.8**
Speed ratings (Par 95): **96,95,94,94,86 85,81,68**
CSF £85.64 TOTE £6.50: £1.80, £3.60, £1.02; EX 59.20 Trifecta £117.10.
**Owner** Lady Rothschild **Bred** Kincorth Investments Inc **Trained** Newmarket, Suffolk

**FOCUS**
This looked to be a decent maiden for the track, despite not much covering the front four at the line. Winners should emerge from it and Peterhof looks a potential big improver.

## 7200 DOWNLOAD THE WINNER.CO.UK APP NOW / IRISH EBF MAIDEN STKS (DIV II) 7f 1y(P)
**2:30** (2:32) (Class 5) 2-Y-O **£2,911** (£866; £432; £216) **Stalls** Low

Form RPR

2 **1** **Classic Collection**[141] 2642 2-9-5 0............................ RyanMoore 7 89+
(Saeed bin Suroor) *tall: athletic: chsd ldrs: effrt to press ldr 2f out: led over 1f out: sn clr: r.o strly: readily* **4/9**[1]

**2** 6 **Free One (IRE)** 2-9-5 0............................ FrankieDettori 3 72
(Jeremy Noseda) *leggy: chsd ldrs: rdn wl over 1f out: no ch w wnr but kpt on to go 2nd wl ins fnl f* **16/1**

330 **3** 2 **Chicago Bere (FR)**[11] 6958 2-9-5 0............................ RichardHughes 8 67
(Richard Hannon) *str: chsd ldr: rdn and ev ch wl over 1f out: 2nd and btn 1f out: wknd and lost 2nd wl ins fnl f* **7/1**[3]

60 **4** 2¼ **Nota Cambiata (USA)**[19] 6712 2-9-5 0............................ WilliamBuick 9 61+
(John Gosden) *in tch in midfield: rdn over 2f out: wl btn over 1f out: wnt modest 4th wl ins fnl f* **20/1**

3 **5** 1½ **Castle Talbot (IRE)**[14] 6861 2-9-5 0............................[1] JimCrowley 5 57
(Charles Hills) *w'like: lw: taken down early and led to post: hld up in rr: plenty to do and rdn ent fnl 2f: no real imp: n.d* **4/1**[2]

03 **6** shd **Toot Your Flute (IRE)**[22] 6630 2-9-5 0............................ JoeFanning 4 57
(William Haggas) *lw: broke fast: led: rdn and pressed 2f out: hdd over 1f out: sn btn: fdd ins fnl f* **8/1**

0 **7** 1 **Let Right Be Done**[21] 6668 2-9-5 0............................ PaulHanagan 2 54
(Ed McMahon) *leggy: t.k.h: hld up in tch in midfield: rdn and struggling over 2f out: sn wknd* **66/1**

00 **8** 13 **Naval Action**[11] 6935 2-9-5 0............................ LukeMorris 6 19
(Sir Mark Prescott Bt) *w'like: str: a in last pair and sn bustled: rdn and flashing tail 1/2-way: lost tch 2f out* **100/1**

1m 24.67s (-0.13) **Going Correction** -0.15s/f (Stan) **8** Ran SP% **126.0**
Speed ratings (Par 95): **94,87,84,82,80 80,79,64**
CSF £12.60 TOTE £1.60: £1.10, £4.50, £1.40; EX 11.20 Trifecta £55.60.
**Owner** Godolphin **Bred** Darley **Trained** Newmarket, Suffolk

**FOCUS**
The winning time was 0.23sec slower than the first division. The first two home were both non-runners at Leicester the previous day because of the ground and the Midlands track's loss was Lingfield's gain. The winner was very impressive.

## 7201 BET & WATCH AT WINNER.CO.UK NURSERY H'CAP (BOBIS RACE) 6f 1y(P)
**3:00** (3:00) (Class 4) (0-85,82) 2-Y-O **£4,269** (£1,270; £634; £317) **Stalls** Low

Form RPR

4222 **1** **Evening Rain (USA)**[17] 6783 2-9-2 **82**............................(p) KevinStott(5) 5 90+
(Saeed bin Suroor) *swtg: chsd ldr: rdn and sltly outpcd over 1f out: styd on u.p ins fnl f to ld fnl 50yds: rdn out* **3/1**[2]

431 **2** ¾ **Koptoon**[21] 6660 2-9-3 **78**............................(t) RichardKingscote 3 84
(Tom Dascombe) *lw: led: rdn over 1f out: sn hung lft but fnd ex: hdd fnl 50yds: sn btn* **9/4**[1]

2242 **3** 2¼ **Russian Heroine**[9] 6977 2-8-10 **71**............................ RyanMoore 4 70
(Sir Michael Stoute) *lw: in tch in midfield: clsd to chse ldrs 2f out: 3rd and no imp fnl f* **5/1**[3]

0612 **4** 2¼ **Gold Waltz**[40] 6104 2-8-9 **70**............................ PatDobbs 10 62
(Ralph Beckett) *hld up in tch in rr: hdwy over 2f out: drvn in 5th over 1f out: no imp: wnt modest 4th wl ins fnl f* **7/1**

6135 **5** 1 **Emef Rock (IRE)**[18] 6739 2-8-8 **69**............................ MartinDwyer 1 58
(Mick Channon) *chsd ldrs: cl 3rd and rdn 2f out: sn outpcd and btn: wknd 1f out* **33/1**

1304 **6** *1 ½* **L'Etacq**[25] 6550 2-8-13 **74**.............................. RichardHughes 6 59
(Richard Hannon) *hld up in tch in rr: rdn and sme hdwy over 1f out: sn no imp: n.d* **12/1**

1035 **7** *3 ¼* **Dittander**[47] 5879 2-9-1 **79**.............................. CamHardie(3) 9 54
(Richard Hannon) *v.s.a: detached in last and sn bustled along: n.d* **33/1**

165 **8** *1 ¾* **L'Addition**[44] 5974 2-8-9 **70**.............................. TedDurcan 7 40
(William Jarvis) *swtg: in tch in midfield but stuck wd: rdn and struggling over 2f out: wknd 2f out* **8/1**

5564 **9** *nk* **Mylaporyours (IRE)**[7] 7029 2-8-5 **66**..............................[1] DavidProbert 8 35
(Rod Millman) *chsd ldrs: rdn and struggling jst over 2f out: sn btn: wknd over 1f out* **66/1**

0300 **10** *5* **Yorkie Talkie (IRE)**[11] 6925 2-8-2 **63**.............................. JoeFanning 2 17
(Mark Johnston) *in tch in midfield: lost pl and in rr whn rdn 1/2-way: wknd 2f out* **16/1**

1m 10.93s (-0.97) **Going Correction** -0.15s/f (Stan) **10** Ran SP% **117.0**
Speed ratings (Par 97): **100,99,96,93,91 89,85,83,82,75**
CSF £10.08 CT £32.09 TOTE £5.20: £2.00, £1.10, £2.90; EX 10.90 Trifecta £48.30.
**Owner** Godolphin **Bred** Darley **Trained** Newmarket, Suffolk

**FOCUS**
A fair nursery though not many got into it. A step forward from the winner.

## 7202 HORSE RACING LOYALTY BONUS AT WINNER.CO.UK CLASSIFIED CLAIMING STKS 7f 1y(P)

**3:35** (3:36) (Class 6) 3-Y-O+ **£2,587** (£770; £384; £192) **Stalls** Low

Form RPR

3265 **1** **Lucky Di**[20] 6680 4-8-13 69.............................. CharlesBishop(3) 12 72
(Peter Hedger) *stdd and dropped in bhd after s: hld up in tch: hdwy towards inner over 1f out: r.o wl ins fnl f: led on post* **7/1**[3]

/335 **2** *nse* **Avertor**[51] 5751 8-8-6 62 ow1.............................. ThomasBrown(3) 2 65
(Robert Stephens) *mde most: edgd rt u.p over 1f out: kpt on gamely: hdd on post* **25/1**

0206 **3** *¾* **Malaysian Boleh**[5] 7078 4-9-6 65.............................. HarryBentley 4 74
(Simon Dow) *hld up in tch in rr: hdwy towards inner over 1f out: flashed tail u.p ins fnl f: styd on wl to go 3rd cl home: squeezed for room nr fin* **16/1**

5545 **4** *shd* **Fair Ranger**[54] 5624 3-8-10 68.............................. RichardHughes 3 65
(Richard Hannon) *lw: chsd ldrs: rdn and sltly outpcd 2f out: rallied u.p ins fnl f: kpt on: squeezed for room nr fin* **8/1**

0264 **5** *½* **Lujeanie**[16] 6815 8-8-2 70.............................. JoeFanning 8 54
(Peter Crate) *stdd s: hld up in tch in rr: effrt on outer wl over 1f out: kpt on u.p fnl f: nt rch ldrs* **8/1**

0415 **6** *½* **Concrete Mac**[34] 6251 3-8-10 64.............................. RichardKingscote 10 62
(Hughie Morrison) *in tch in midfield: hdwy on outer to chse ldrs 4f out: lost pl u.p bnd 2f out: rallied ins fnl f: kpt on* **7/1**[3]

2522 **7** *½* **Just Isla**[30] 6397 4-8-2 62 ow3..............................(p) SimonPearce(3) 7 55
(Peter Makin) *chsd ldrs: upsides ldr 3f out: rdn: and hung lft and sltly outpcd over 1f out: one pce fnl f* **12/1**

1165 **8** *1* **Darnathean**[13] 6890 5-8-8 70..............................(p) LukeMorris 5 55
(Paul D'Arcy) *in tch in midfield: rdn over 2f out: hrd drvn and sme hdwy over 1f out: no imp ins fnl f* **11/4**[1]

0336 **9** *1* **New Leyf (IRE)**[35] 6240 8-8-1 68..............................(b) CamHardie(3) 9 48
(Jeremy Gask) *taken down early: t.k.h: hld up towards rr: effrt u.p over 1f out: no imp fnl f* **6/1**[2]

1630 **10** *hd* **Double Czech (IRE)**[21] 6657 3-8-10 70..............................(v) DavidProbert 13 55
(Patrick Chamings) *in tch towards rr: rdn: hung lft and no hdwy over 1f out: kpt on fnl f: nvr trbld ldrs* **10/1**

2200 **11** *2 ½* **Paradise Spectre**[99] 4050 7-8-8 62..............................(p) JohnFahy 6 45
(Zoe Davison) *t.k.h: in tch in midfield: rdn and effrt 2f out: wknd ins fnl f* **66/1**

0400 **12** *30* **Field Force**[7] 7032 3-8-4 70..............................(p) LiamJones 1
(Sophie Leech) *t.k.h: w ldr tl 3f out: sn lost pl: wl bhd over 1f out: t.o* **33/1**

1m 23.93s (-0.87) **Going Correction** -0.15s/f (Stan)
**WFA** 3 from 4yo+ 2lb **12** Ran SP% **119.1**
Speed ratings (Par 101): **98,97,97,96,96 95,95,94,92,92 89,55**
CSF £171.92 TOTE £6.90: £2.70, £10.90, £3.60; EX 260.00 Trifecta £1980.20 Part won..Fair Ranger was claimed by Mrs Kate Digweed £10,000.
**Owner** P C F Racing Ltd **Bred** Cranford Stud **Trained** Eastergate, W Sussex

**FOCUS**
A modest classified claimer and a tight finish. The winner probably didn't need to quite match recent efforts.

## 7203 WINNER.CO.UK H'CAP (BOBIS RACE) 1m 4f (P)

**4:10** (4:10) (Class 2) (0-100,91) 3-Y-O **£12,938** (£3,850; £1,924; £962) **Stalls** Low

Form RPR

1201 **1** **Hidden Gold (IRE)**[17] 6794 3-9-2 **91**.............................. KevinStott(5) 5 101+
(Saeed bin Suroor) *detached in last: clsd onto bk of field 7f out: effrt but wdst on bnd 2f out: str run ent fnl f to ld fnl 75yds: sn in command: readily* **4/1**[2]

1534 **2** *1 ½* **Arab Dawn**[25] 6548 3-9-6 **90**.............................. RichardHughes 3 98
(Hughie Morrison) *lw: t.k.h: hld up in tch: hdwy to chse ldrs 7f out: rdn and ev ch 2f out: led ins fnl f: hdd fnl 75yds: no ex* **11/4**[1]

1434 **3** *1 ½* **Jalingo (IRE)**[17] 6786 3-8-13 **83**.............................. JoeFanning 7 88
(Mark Johnston) *t.k.h: in tch in midfield: hdwy to join ldr 8f out tl led 3f out: drvn over 1f out: hdd ins fnl f: sn outpcd: plugged on* **8/1**

2321 **4** *1* **Artful Rogue (IRE)**[27] 6485 3-9-1 **85**.............................. PatDobbs 4 89
(Amanda Perrett) *hld up in tch: nt clr run on inner 2f out: hdwy u.p on inner over 1f out: styd on same pce ins fnl f* **16/1**

2114 **5** *nk* **Scallop**[46] 5914 3-9-2 **86**.............................. JamesDoyle 6 89
(Sir Michael Stoute) *t.k.h: in tch in midfield: shuffled bk into last trio: hdwy u.p jst over 1f out: styd on ins fnl f: no threat ldrs* **7/1**[3]

0411 **6** *1 ¼* **Anglo Irish**[42] 6036 3-9-5 **89**.............................. WilliamBuick 9 90
(John Gosden) *lw: chsd ldrs: rdn ent fnl 2f: no ex 1f out: wknd ins fnl f* **4/1**[2]

2014 **7** *2 ½* **Erroneous (IRE)**[33] 6284 3-9-4 **88**.............................. JimCrowley 2 85
(David Simcock) *in tch in midfield: nt clr run jst over 2f out: sme hdwy u.p over 1f out: wknd ins fnl f* **25/1**

2013 **8** *1* **Invasor Luck (USA)**[23] 6608 3-8-11 **81**.............................. TomQueally 8 77
(James Fanshawe) *in tch towards rr: effrt towards outer bnd 2f out: no imp over 1f out: wknd ins fnl f* **10/1**

5211 **9** *1 ¾* **Serena Grae**[8] 7020 3-9-3 **87** 6ex.............................. MartinDwyer 1 80
(Marcus Tregoning) *led tl rdn and hdd over 2f out: sn struggling: wknd over 1f out* **20/1**

2m 28.43s (-4.57) **Going Correction** -0.15s/f (Stan) **9** Ran SP% **113.9**
Speed ratings (Par 107): **109,108,107,106,106 105,103,102,101**
CSF £15.17 CT £82.07 TOTE £4.50: £1.50, £1.30, £3.10; EX 13.50 Trifecta £117.30.
**Owner** Godolphin **Bred** Darley **Trained** Newmarket, Suffolk

**FOCUS**
A hot handicap with recent winning form in plentiful supply, but something of a stop-start gallop. The winner showed smart form and can do better still.

## 7204 RECOMMENDEDBOOKIES.CO.UK UK'S TOP BETTING SITE H'CAP 1m 7f 169y(P)

**4:45** (4:45) (Class 6) (0-65,65) 3-Y-O+ **£2,587** (£770; £384; £192) **Stalls** Low

Form RPR

0511 **1** **Alba Verde**[18] 6768 3-9-2 64.............................. LukeMorris 10 73+
(Sir Mark Prescott Bt) *mde all: rdn and kicked clr over 2f out: in command after: rdn out hands and heels fnl f* **8/11**[1]

2223 **2** *1 ¼* **Wintour Leap**[32] 6343 3-9-0 65.............................. ThomasBrown(3) 1 68
(Robert Stephens) *taken down early: in tch in midfield: rdn and effrt over 2f out: 3rd and no ch w wnr over 1f out: kpt on to go 2nd towards fin: no real threat to wnr* **20/1**

0135 **3** *½* **Mighty Mambo**[121] 992 7-9-9 60..............................(tp) RichardKingscote 4 62
(Lawney Hill) *chsd ldr for 4f: chsd ldrs after tl wnt 2nd again over 2f out: sn rdn and outpcd by wnr: kpt on fnl f: lost 2nd towards fin* **14/1**

5363 **4** *3 ¼* **Dr Finley (IRE)**[27] 6486 7-8-12 52..............................(v) SimonPearce(3) 6 51
(Lydia Pearce) *swtg: in tch in midfield: rdn over 2f out: modest 4th wl over 1f out: plugged on* **20/1**

431 **5** *2 ½* **Graylyn Ruby (FR)**[27] 6486 9-9-0 58.............................. KieranShoemark(7) 2 54
(Robert Eddery) *hld up in last pair: rdn and plenty to do over 2f out: hdwy into modest 5th over 1f out: n.d* **10/1**[3]

6644 **6** *2 ½* **Nelson Of The Nile**[54] 5628 3-8-10 61.............................. DannyBrock(3) 5 54
(Jonathan Portman) *chsd ldrs: lost pl 5f out: rdn and no hdwy over 2f out: 6th and wl btn over 1f out* **9/2**[2]

540/ **7** *½* **Ragdollianna**[1270] 7206 10-9-9 60.............................. SteveDrowne 3 52
(Mark Hoad) *hld up in rr: plenty to do and shkn up 2f out: no real imp: n.d* **50/1**

-233 **8** *1 ½* **Sheila's Heart**[12] 6899 4-9-9 65.............................. ShelleyBirkett(5) 9 55
(John E Long) *hld up towards rr: rdn and effrt over 2f out: sn struggling: wl btn fnl 2f* **16/1**

004 **9** *10* **Havana Girl (IRE)**[12] 6901 3-9-3 65.............................. TomQueally 8 43
(Harry Dunlop) *t.k.h: chsd ldrs: hdwy to go 2nd 12f out tl over 2f out: sn btn: fdd over 1f out* **20/1**

-000 **10** *5* **Mad About Harry (IRE)**[14] 6856 4-9-4 55..............................(v) SebSanders 7 27
(Linda Jewell) *swtg: hld up in last trio: rdn and struggling over 3f out: lost tch over 2f out: lame* **50/1**

3m 25.19s (-0.51) **Going Correction** -0.15s/f (Stan)
**WFA** 3 from 4yo+ 11lb **10** Ran SP% **115.9**
Speed ratings (Par 101): **95,94,94,92,91 90,89,89,84,81**
CSF £23.60 CT £120.48 TOTE £1.90: £1.10, £4.30, £2.80; EX 12.70 Trifecta £106.40.
**Owner** Miss K Rausing **Bred** Miss K Rausing **Trained** Newmarket, Suffolk

**FOCUS**
A weak and uncompetitive staying handicap which revolved around one horse. The winner was value for a greater margin.

## 7205 PLAY BLACKJACK AND ROULETTE AT WINNER.CO.UK H'CAP 1m 1y(P)

**5:15** (5:16) (Class 5) (0-75,75) 3-Y-O+ **£3,234** (£962; £481; £240) **Stalls** Low

Form RPR

3536 **1** **Fiftyshadesofgrey (IRE)**[37] 6191 3-9-2 73.............................. PatCosgrave 9 87+
(George Baker) *hld up in tch: hdwy to chse ldr and hung lft 2f: chal: hung lft and bmpd ldr over 1f out: sn led: clr fnl f: r.o* **6/1**

4246 **2** *2 ¼* **Royal Preserve**[23] 6609 3-9-3 74.............................. DavidProbert 3 83
(Andrew Balding) *in tch in midfield: nt clr run on inner 2f out: effrt over 1f out: styd on wl u.p to go 2nd wl ins fnl f: no threat to wnr* **7/2**[2]

-000 **3** *½* **Miss Buckshot (IRE)**[117] 3428 3-9-2 73.............................. TomQueally 4 81
(Rae Guest) *hld up in tch in last quartet: effrt jst over 2f out: styd on strly fnl f: no threat to wnr* **14/1**

212 **4** *1* **Stormbound (IRE)**[40] 6100 5-9-3 71.............................. LukeMorris 12 78
(Paul Cole) *in tch in midfield: hdwy to ld 2f out: sn rdn: jnd and bmpd over 1f out: sn hdd and outpcd: lost 2 pls wl ins fnl f* **11/4**[1]

264 **5** *1* **Gang Warfare**[86] 4501 3-9-2 73.............................. LiamJones 5 77
(Olly Stevens) *in tch in midfield: hdwy u.p over 1f out: hung lft 1f out: kpt on: nvr threatened ldrs* **16/1**

4240 **6** *1 ¼* **Silver Dixie (USA)**[39] 6141 4-9-2 73..............................(p) CharlesBishop(3) 10 74
(Peter Hedger) *swtg: w ldr tl squeezed for room 2f out: sn lost pl: wl hld and one pce after* **9/2**[3]

0000 **7** *¾* **Persepolis (IRE)**[42] 6035 4-9-5 73.............................. AmirQuinn 2 72+
(Lee Carter) *stdd s: t.k.h: hld up in rr: shkn up ent fnl f: styd on strly: nvr trbld ldrs* **16/1**

3050 **8** *¾* **Tidal's Baby**[13] 6890 5-9-3 74.............................. ThomasBrown(3) 1 72
(Lee Carter) *hld up in tch in last pair: effrt 2f out: sme hdwy over 1f out: kpt on same pce ins fnl f* **33/1**

1120 **9** *1* **Wordismybond**[9] 6990 5-8-13 74.............................. ChrisMeehan(7) 7 69
(Peter Makin) *led: hdd and rdn ent fnl 2f: 3rd and btn over 1f out: wknd fnl f* **12/1**

6330 **10** *5* **House Captain**[35] 6236 3-9-1 72.............................. PatDobbs 8 56
(Richard Hannon) *in tch in midfield: rdn and no rspnse over 2f out: wknd wl over 1f out* **25/1**

4460 **11** *½* **Club House (IRE)**[147] 2471 4-8-9 70.............................. SophieRalston(7) 6 53
(Robert Mills) *hld up in tch in last quartet: rdn wl over 1f out: no prog and wl btn after* **25/1**

0-50 **12** *3 ½* **Red Seventy**[13] 2991 5-9-0 75..............................(b) MikeyEnnis(7) 11 51
(Sarah Humphrey) *t.k.h: chsd ldrs: struggling whn squeezed for room: hmpd and lost pl 2f out: sn wknd* **66/1**

1m 36.2s (-2.00) **Going Correction** -0.15s/f (Stan)
**WFA** 3 from 4yo+ 3lb **12** Ran SP% **119.6**
Speed ratings (Par 103): **104,101,101,100,99 98,97,96,95,90 90,86**
CSF £26.61 CT £291.74 TOTE £7.70: £2.70, £1.30, £7.00; EX 31.30 Trifecta £198.30.
**Owner** Team Fifty **Bred** Doc Bloodstock **Trained** Manton, Wilts

**FOCUS**
An ordinary handicap. The winner is rated back to his best form.

T/Plt: £26.00 to a £1 stake. Pool: £68,654.26 - 1,925.53 winning tickets T/Qpdt: £28.10 to a £1 stake. Pool: £4,875.65 - 128.35 winning tickets SP

# 7037 NOTTINGHAM (L-H)

Wednesday, October 15

**OFFICIAL GOING: Soft (heavy in places)**

Wind: Light half behind Weather: Cloudy

## 7206 32RED ON THE APP STORE EBF STALLIONS MAIDEN STKS 1m 75y

1:40 (1:41) (Class 5) 2-Y-O £3,234 (£962; £481; £240) **Stalls** Centre

Form RPR

1 **Not So Sleepy** 2-9-5 0 ........ GeorgeBaker 5 81+
(Hughie Morrison) *dwlt: sn trcking ldrs on inner: hdwy over 2f out: chal over 1f out: rdn to ld ent fnl f: kpt on* **7/1**

2 1 3/4 **She Is No Lady** 2-9-0 0 ........ OisinMurphy 2 70+
(Ralph Beckett) *led: pushed along 3f out: jnd and rdn over 1f out: hdd ent fnl f: kpt on same pce* **11/4[1]**

3 8 **Laurence** 2-9-5 0 ........ AdamKirby 10 58
(Luca Cumani) *hld up in tch: hdwy on outer wl over 2f out: rdn to chse ldng pair over 1f out: sn one pce* **4/1[3]**

4 3/4 **Hope You Dance (FR)** 2-9-0 0 ........ MartinLane 6 51+
(David Simcock) *in tch: pushed along on inner 3f out: rdn over 2f out: kpt on fnl f: n.d* **10/1**

5 1 1/4 **Waaleef** 2-9-0 0 ........ DanielMuscutt(5) 9 53
(Marco Botti) *t.k.h early: sn cl up: pushed along 3f out: rdn over 2f out: wknd wl over 1f out* **7/1**

6 3 1/2 **Stars And Stripes** 2-9-5 0 ........ DanielTudhope 4 45
(Luca Cumani) *chsd ldrs: hdwy over 3f out: pushed along wl over 2f out: rdn wl over 1f out: sn wknd* **7/2[2]**

7 29 **Ashapurna (IRE)** 2-9-0 0 ........ GrahamLee 8
(William Knight) *s.i.s: green and sn rdn along in rr: detached and bhd fr 1/2-way* **10/1**

1m 55.43s (6.43) **Going Correction** +0.675s/f (Yiel) **7 Ran SP% 112.1**
Speed ratings (Par 95): **94,92,84,83,82 78,49**
CSF £25.49 TOTE £8.20: £4.20, £3.00; EX 31.40 Trifecta £113.30.
**Owner** Lady Blyth **Bred** Lord Blyth **Trained** East Ilsley, Berks
■ The 100th winner of the turf season for George Baker, his first century.

**FOCUS**
Outer track used. Rail stepped out 4m and races on Round course increased by 12yds. The ground may have been changed to soft, heavy in places following a dry night and a low water table, but conditions remained plenty testing enough and this was hard work for these previously unraced juveniles. The winner did it well.

## 7207 32REDSPORT.COM NURSERY H'CAP (DIV I) 1m 75y

2:10 (2:16) (Class 5) (0-70,70) 2-Y-O £2,587 (£770; £384; £192) **Stalls** Centre

Form RPR

0043 1 **Mywayalways (IRE)**[33] 6294 2-9-5 68 ........ AdamKirby 4 75
(David Evans) *led 2 1/2f: prom: effrt to chal over 2f out: rdn to ld wl over 1f out: clr ins fnl f* **7/2[2]**

000 2 2 **Youonlyliveonce (IRE)**[74] 4885 2-8-5 54 ........ IanBrennan 6 56
(John Quinn) *prom: pushed along and sltly outpcd over 2f out: sn rdn: styd on to chse wnr ins fnl f: nrst fin* **10/1**

0022 3 3 **Simone On Time (IRE)**[15] 6838 2-9-3 66 ........ RenatoSouza 8 61
(Sylvester Kirk) *prom: rdn along over 2f out: drvn over 1f out: kpt on same pce* **20/1**

660 4 1 1/2 **Duc De Seville (IRE)**[62] 5351 2-8-3 55 ........ RyanTate(3) 7 47
(Clive Cox) *dwlt: sn pushed along in rr: hdwy on outer over 2f out: sn rdn: styd on fnl f: nrst fin* **7/1**

0523 5 3/4 **Lexi's Red Devil (IRE)**[18] 6769 2-9-2 70 ........(p) DanielMuscutt(5) 11 60
(Marco Botti) *hld up towards rr: hdwy on outer 1/2-way: rdn to chse ldrs over 2f out: drvn wl over 1f out: no imp* **6/1[3]**

5500 6 5 **New Brunswick (GER)**[13] 6884 2-9-0 63 ........ RobertHavlin 9 42
(John Gosden) *chsd ldrs: led over 5f out: pushed along wl over 2f out: sn rdn and hdd wl over 1f out: wknd qckly fnl f* **3/1[1]**

0434 7 31 **Referendum (IRE)**[22] 6648 2-9-7 70 ........ GrahamGibbons 3
(Sir Michael Stoute) *trckd ldrs on inner: pushed along wl over 3f out: sn rdn and wknd: bhd and eased fnl 2f* **6/1[3]**

050 8 3 3/4 **Berkshire Beauty**[62] 5351 2-9-0 63 ........ OisinMurphy 1
(Andrew Balding) *a towards rr: rdn along over 3f out: sn outpcd and bhd whn eased fnl 2f* **8/1**

1m 55.29s (6.29) **Going Correction** +0.675s/f (Yiel) **8 Ran SP% 113.3**
Speed ratings (Par 95): **95,93,90,88,87 82,51,48**
CSF £37.00 CT £603.13 TOTE £4.50: £1.40, £4.30, £3.20; EX 49.90 Trifecta £327.70.
**Owner** E R Griffiths **Bred** Connal McGrath **Trained** Pandy, Monmouths

**FOCUS**
Conditions had been described as 'heavy' and as 'very testing' by Adam Kirby and George Baker respectively following the opener it's likely that the surface was again major factor in the outcome of this nursery. The winner was firmly on top.

## 7208 32REDSPORT.COM NURSERY H'CAP (DIV II) 1m 75y

2:40 (2:42) (Class 5) (0-70,70) 2-Y-O £2,587 (£770; £384; £192) **Stalls** Centre

Form RPR

054 1 **Perceived**[22] 6646 2-8-11 63 ........ AmyScott(3) 2 68
(Henry Candy) *hld up in tch: hdwy 3f out: rdn to chse ldng pair wl over 1f out: styd on ins fnl f to ld last 50yds* **3/1[1]**

4460 2 3/4 **Robben**[21] 6669 2-8-5 54 ........(p) JimmyQuinn 11 57
(Kevin Ryan) *dwlt and in rr: stdy hdwy over 4f out: cl up 3f out: led wl over 1f out: rdn ent fnl f: hdd and no ex last 50yds* **12/1**

105 3 1 1/4 **Honey Required**[27] 6499 2-8-12 61 ........ FrannyNorton 7 61
(Alan Bailey) *trckd ldrs: hdwy 1/2-way led wl over 2f out: jnd and rdn 2f out: sn hdd: drvn ent fnl f: kpt on towards fin* **7/2[2]**

550 4 10 **Mister Archie**[14] 6860 2-7-11 51 ow2 ........ JoeDoyle(5) 5 29
(Alistair Whillans) *in rr: pushed along 5f out: rdn over 2f out: kpt on u.p fnl 2f to take mod 4th nr fin* **20/1**

0013 5 1/2 **Thewaythewindblows (IRE)**[11] 6944 2-9-5 68 ........(t) RobertWinston 4 45
(Daniel Kubler) *t.k.h: trckd ldrs: effrt 3f out: rdn to chse ldrs 2f out: sn drvn and wknd appr fnl f* **4/1[3]**

5146 6 1/2 **Multiplier**[69] 5085 2-9-7 70 ........ JamesSullivan 6 46
(Kristin Stubbs) *hld up towards rr: sme hdwy 3f out: rdn along over 2f out: n.d* **14/1**

0500 7 1 **Phantasmo (IRE)**[21] 6669 2-8-2 51 ........ RaulDaSilva 1 25
(John Quinn) *chsd ldng pair: rdn along over 4f out: sn wknd* **5/1**

050 8 4 **Forcible**[109] 3701 2-9-7 70 ........ OisinMurphy 8 35
(David Brown) *led: rdn along over 3f out: hdd wl over 2f out and sn wknd* **16/1**

0060 9 8 **Bushranger Bay (IRE)**[30] 6412 2-8-6 55 ........ DuranFentiman 10 2
(Tim Easterby) *cl up: rdn along 4f out: sn wknd* **25/1**

1m 56.1s (7.10) **Going Correction** +0.675s/f (Yiel) **9 Ran SP% 112.7**
Speed ratings (Par 95): **91,90,89,79,78 78,77,73,65**
CSF £38.82 CT £130.00 TOTE £5.20: £2.10, £3.40, £1.10; EX 48.10 Trifecta £185.00.
**Owner** Candy, Pritchard & Thomas **Bred** J A E Hobby **Trained** Kingston Warren, Oxon

**FOCUS**
This was hard going in the conditions and three pulled well clear. Not form to get carried away with.

## 7209 32RED CASINO MEDIAN AUCTION MAIDEN FILLIES' STKS (BOBIS RACE) 1m 75y

3:10 (3:11) (Class 5) 2-Y-O £2,587 (£770; £384; £192) **Stalls** Centre

Form RPR

25 1 **Banzari**[33] 6289 2-9-0 0 ........ JamieSpencer 6 90+
(Michael Bell) *trckd ldrs: hdwy on wd outside 3f out: led over 2f out: rdn clr over 1f out: kpt on strly* **1/3[1]**

40 2 10 **Triple Dip (IRE)**[18] 6735 2-9-0 0 ........ FrannyNorton 4 67
(Mark Johnston) *led: rdn along and hdd over 2f out: drvn over 1f out: kpt on: no ch w wnr* **10/1[3]**

3 1 1/4 **Sky Rose** 2-9-0 0 ........ GrahamLee 1 64+
(William Knight) *chsd ldng pair: rdn along and outpcd over 2f out: plugged on u.p to take modest 3rd ins fnl f* **12/1**

4 5 **Miss Understood (IRE)** 2-9-0 0 ........ MartinLane 7 53
(David Simcock) *in tch: hdwy to chse ldrs 3f out: sn rdn: drvn over 1f out and sn wknd* **8/1[2]**

5 2 3/4 **Missandei** 2-8-9 0 ........ DanielMuscutt(5) 3 47
(Marco Botti) *in tch: sme hdwy 4f out: rdn along wl over 2f out: sn wknd* **20/1**

6034 6 5 **North Bay Lady (IRE)**[14] 6869 2-9-0 49 ........(p) RaulDaSilva 8 36
(John Wainwright) *chsd ldr: cl up 1/2-way: rdn along 3f out: drvn and wknd over 2f out* **33/1**

7 13 **Mercy Me** 2-8-9 0 ........ TobyAtkinson(5) 2 8
(Julia Feilden) *s.i.s: a bhd* **50/1**

1m 55.09s (6.09) **Going Correction** +0.675s/f (Yiel) **7 Ran SP% 112.6**
Speed ratings (Par 92): **96,86,84,79,77 72,59**
CSF £4.29 TOTE £1.30: £1.10, £2.80; EX 4.10 Trifecta £13.30.
**Owner** Bellbroughtondetterdingheadfortstafford **Bred** Barton Stud & New England Stud **Trained** Newmarket, Suffolk

**FOCUS**
This was painfully weak and proved a straightforward exercise for the long odds-on favourite. Not much to hang the form on.

## 7210 32RED MAIDEN STKS 1m 2f 50y

3:45 (3:47) (Class 5) 3-Y-O £4,851 (£1,443; £721; £360) **Stalls** Low

Form RPR

2- 1 **Flight Officer**[355] 7500 3-9-5 0 ........ FrederikTylicki 6 94+
(Saeed bin Suroor) *trckd ldrs: wd st: hdwy and cl up over 3f out: chal over 2f out: rdn to ld over 1f out: clr ins fnl f: kpt on strly* **5/6[1]**

2263 2 7 **Dalmatia (IRE)**[35] 6238 3-9-0 74 ........ GrahamGibbons 14 78
(Sir Michael Stoute) *racd wd: led: pushed along 3f out: rdn 2f out: hdd and drvn over 1f out: kpt on same pce* **7/1[3]**

46 3 3 1/4 **Peril**[22] 6634 3-9-5 0 ........ GeorgeBaker 11 76
(Lady Cecil) *hld up: hdwy over 4f out: jnd ldrs over 3f out: rdn 2f out: one pce appr fnl f* **8/1**

3 4 16 **Arsenale (GER)**[27] 6494 3-9-0 0 ........ AndrewMullen 12 42
(Michael Appleby) *stmbld in first f and lost pl: towards rr: gd hdwy 1/2-way: jnd ldrs on wd outside 4f out: rdn along wl over 2f out: sn outpcd* **25/1**

5 5 1 1/2 **Sail With Sultana**[34] 6247 3-9-0 0 ........ PaulMulrennan 16 39
(Mark Rimell) *chsd ldng pair: pushed along over 4f out: rdn 3f out: sn wknd* **100/1**

0-22 6 9 **Almuhalab**[33] 6298 3-9-5 81 ........ GrahamLee 9 28
(Charles Hills) *racd wd: chsd ldr: rdn along wl over 3f out: sn wknd* **5/1[2]**

7 1 1/2 **Burning Desire (IRE)** 3-9-5 0 ........ ChrisCatlin 1 25
(M F De Kock, South Africa) *s.i.s: a bhd* **14/1**

8 49 **Home Flyer (IRE)** 3-9-5 0 ........ JasonHart 2
(Mark Walford) *racd on inner: chsd ldrs: rdn along over 4f out: sn wknd and bhd* **66/1**

9 5 **Painted Black** 3-9-5 0 ........ WilliamCarson 3
(Jane Chapple-Hyam) *s.i.s: a bhd: t.o fnl 3f* **66/1**

00 10 1 3/4 **Bahama Dancer**[32] 6344 3-8-11 0 ........ JoeyHaynes(3) 10
(Jason Ward) *towards rr: rdn along and outpcd bef 1/2-way: t.o fnl 3f* **100/1**

2m 19.83s (5.53) **Going Correction** +0.675s/f (Yiel) **10 Ran SP% 110.3**
Speed ratings (Par 101): **104,98,95,83,81 74,73,34,30,28**
CSF £6.34 TOTE £2.50: £1.30, £1.70, £1.90; EX 7.50 Trifecta £29.30.
**Owner** Godolphin **Bred** Darley **Trained** Newmarket, Suffolk

**FOCUS**
Saeed Bin Suroor and Godolphin have targeted this maiden with tremendous success in past seasons and he made it six wins since 2007 as the strongly supported winner made light of lengthy absence. He recorded a fair time but the form has been rated with feet on the ground.

## 7211 £10 FREE BET AT 32RED SPORT H'CAP 1m 2f 50y

4:20 (4:21) (Class 3) (0-95,95) 3-Y-O+
£7,470 (£2,236; £1,118; £559; £279; £140) **Stalls** Low

Form RPR

2402 1 **Lady Tiana**[18] 6746 3-8-10 86 ........ GrahamLee 11 99+
(Lucy Wadham) *hld up in tch: smooth hdwy on outer 3f out: cl up 2f out: led on bit ent fnl f: sn shkn up and clr: readily* **4/1[2]**

005 2 3 **Ty Gwr**[19] 6713 5-8-11 82 ........ DaleSwift 1 88
(Brian Ellison) *hld up in rr: stdy hdwy over 3f out: chal wl over 1f out: sn rdn and ev ch tl drvn and kpt on same pce ins fnl f* **9/2[3]**

4020 3 nk **Green Light**[18] 6737 3-8-5 81 oh1 ........ HayleyTurner 5 86
(Ralph Beckett) *cl up: trckd ldrs: smooth hdwy 4f out: slt ld 3f out: rdn wl over 1f out: hdd ent fnl f: kpt on same pce* **7/2[1]**

6304 4 nse **Art Scholar (IRE)**[21] 6664 7-8-10 81 oh5 ........(p) OisinMurphy 2 86
(Michael Appleby) *hld up in rr: hdwy over 3f out: chsd ldrs wl over 1f out: sn rdn and kpt on fnl f: nrst fin* **10/1**

1130 5 4 **Bartack (IRE)**[18] 6752 4-9-9 94 ........(v) DanielTudhope 10 92
(David O'Meara) *trckd ldrs: hdwy on outer and cl up over 4f out: effrt to dispute ld 3f out: rdn 2f out: grad wknd* **8/1**

05/5 6 12 **Stand To Reason (IRE)**[26] 6518 6-9-4 89 ........ AdamKirby 9 65
(Tony Carroll) *trckd ldrs: effrt over 3f out: sn rdn and wknd wl over 2f out* **25/1**

44 **7** *5* **Missed Call (IRE)**[20] 6685 4-8-12 83 FrederikTylicki 7 50
(James Fanshawe) *hld up in rr: sme hdwy over 3f out: rdn along wl over 2f out: sn btn* **7/2**[1]

3000 **8** *½* **San Cassiano (IRE)**[11] 6943 7-9-0 85 JamesSullivan 3 51
(Ruth Carr) *cl up: led after 2f: rdn along and hdd 4f out: sn wknd* **33/1**

6- **9** *3* **Sublimation (IRE)**[480] 3563 4-8-11 82 RobertWinston 8 43
(Ian Williams) *led 2f: cl up tl led again 4f out: rdn and hdd 3f out: sn wknd* **20/1**

2m 19.03s (4.73) **Going Correction** +0.675s/f (Yiel)
**WFA** 3 from 4yo+ 5lb **9** Ran SP% **114.4**
Speed ratings (Par 107): **108,105,105,105,102 92,88,88,85**
CSF £21.52 CT £68.01 TOTE £4.80: £2.10, £2.00, £1.10; EX 22.80 Trifecta £96.50.
**Owner** The FOPS **Bred** Mr & Mrs A E Pakenham **Trained** Newmarket, Suffolk

**FOCUS**
A strongly run, competitive feature. The winner is rated better than ever.

## 7212 32RED.COM H'CAP 5f 13y
**4:55** (4:56) (Class 4) (0-85,85) 3-Y-0+ **£4,851** (£1,443; £721; £360) **Stalls** Centre

Form RPR

4400 **1** **Megaleka**[26] 6512 4-9-1 84 TimClark(5) 12 95
(Alan Bailey) *in tch: gd hdwy wl over 1f out: rdn to chal and hung lft ent fnl f: sn led and clr: kpt on* **16/1**

5001 **2** *2 ½* **Mutafaakir (IRE)**[22] 6650 5-9-7 85 (b) JamesSullivan 16 87
(Ruth Carr) *racd cl to stands' rail: prom: rdn and ev ch over 1f out: drvn and kpt on same pce fnl f* **10/1**[3]

5100 **3** *2* **Skye's The Limit**[26] 6512 3-9-0 78 TonyHamilton 13 74
(Richard Fahey) *swtchd rt to stands' rail after 1f: chsd ldrs: rdn wl over 1f out: kpt on fnl f* **8/1**[2]

000 **4** *1 ¼* **Even Stevens**[35] 6235 6-9-1 79 (v) TomEaves 9 69
(Scott Dixon) *racd towards centre: prom: rdn 2f out: drvn and kpt on same pce fnl f* **12/1**

1120 **5** *1 ¼* **Come On Dave (IRE)**[40] 6096 5-9-0 83 DanielMuscutt(5) 3 69
(John Butler) *racd towards centre: led: rdn over 1f out: hdd jst ins fnl f: wknd* **14/1**

4256 **6** *hd* **Scarborough (IRE)**[46] 5923 3-8-13 82 AlistairRawlinson(5) 8 68
(Michael Appleby) *racd towards centre: chsd ldrs: rdn wl over 1f out: kpt on same pce fnl f* **8/1**[2]

0560 **7** *shd* **Kenny The Captain (IRE)**[18] 6763 3-9-0 78 DuranFentiman 10 64
(Tim Easterby) *towards rr: hdwy 2f out: rdn and kpt on fnl f: nrst fin* **12/1**

0-50 **8** *2 ½* **Cheveton**[54] 5623 10-9-0 78 OisinMurphy 11 54
(Richard Price) *a towards rr* **8/1**[2]

0245 **9** *shd* **Signore Piccolo**[89] 4390 3-9-3 81 JasonHart 4 57
(Eric Alston) *racd towards centre: chsd ldrs: rdn along 2f out: sn wknd* **10/1**[3]

6100 **10** *4 ½* **Keep It Dark**[46] 5925 5-9-3 81 BarryMcHugh 17 40
(Tony Coyle) *a towards rr* **12/1**

20-0 **11** *½* **Shady McCoy (USA)**[164] 1967 4-9-2 80 RobertWinston 5 37
(Ian Williams) *racd towards centre: a towards rr* **16/1**

1110 **12** *½* **War Spirit**[74] 4898 3-9-5 83 SeanLevey 15 40
(Richard Hannon) *swtchd lft s: hld up: a in rr* **6/1**[1]

2133 **13** *½* **Clubland (IRE)**[32] 6346 5-9-0 78 JimmyQuinn 2 32
(Roy Bowring) *racd centre: chsd ldrs: rdn along over 2f out: sn wknd* **16/1**

5003 **14** *1 ¾* **Red Baron (IRE)**[26] 6512 5-9-3 84 (b) NeilFarley(3) 1 31
(Eric Alston) *racd wd: chsd ldrs: rdn 2f out: sn drvn and wknd over 1f out* **12/1**

1m 2.29s (0.79) **Going Correction** +0.325s/f (Good) **14** Ran SP% **120.9**
Speed ratings (Par 105): **106,102,98,96,94 94,94,90,90,82 82,81,80,77**
CSF £168.39 CT £930.35 TOTE £13.40: £4.50, £3.60, £2.70; EX 106.50 Trifecta £1787.60.
**Owner** North Cheshire Trading & Storage Ltd **Bred** North Cheshire Trading And Storage Ltd **Trained** Newmarket, Suffolk

**FOCUS**
A competitive sprint was turned into a procession as many appeared not to handle conditions. The winner is much improved this year.

## 7213 RACING SPECIALS AT 32REDSPORT.COM H'CAP 5f 13y
**5:25** (5:26) (Class 6) (0-65,65) 3-Y-0+ **£1,940** (£577; £288; £144) **Stalls** Centre

Form RPR

4344 **1** **Oscars Journey**[9] 6983 4-9-3 63 (v) AdamKirby 9 72
(J R Jenkins) *cl up centre: chal wl over 1f out: rdn to ld jst ins fnl f: edgd rt and drvn out* **6/1**[1]

624 **2** *¾* **Rylee Mooch**[16] 6819 6-9-3 63 (e) JasonHart 8 69
(Richard Guest) *racd centre: slt ld: rdn over 1f out: drvn and hdd ins fnl f: kpt on same pce towards fin* **8/1**[2]

0000 **3** *nk* **Hazelrigg (IRE)**[11] 6938 9-9-5 65 DavidAllan 5 70
(Tim Easterby) *racd centre: trckd ldrs: effrt wl over 1f out: sn rdn: kpt on fnl f* **8/1**[2]

0250 **4** *1 ½* **Picc Of Burgau**[48] 5860 4-9-2 62 StevieDonohoe 2 62+
(Geoffrey Deacon) *racd centre: chsd ldrs: rdn wl over 1f out: kpt on u.p fnl f: nrst fin* **25/1**

3046 **5** *½* **Dynamo Walt (IRE)**[25] 6562 3-9-5 65 (v) DaleSwift 13 64
(Derek Shaw) *chsd ldrs centre: rdn wl over 1f out: kpt on u.p fnl f: nrst fin* **16/1**

50 **6** *nk* **Sir Geoffrey (IRE)**[58] 5498 8-9-0 65 (p) MatthewHopkins(5) 3 62
(Scott Dixon) *racd wd: chsd ldrs: rdn along wl over 1f out: sn drvn and kpt on same pce* **25/1**

2040 **7** *hd* **Climaxfortackle (IRE)**[8] 7023 6-9-5 65 RussKennemore 10 61
(Derek Shaw) *in rr: hdwy wl over 1f out: sn rdn and kpt on fnl f: nrst fin* **25/1**

6640 **8** *nk* **Queen Aggie (IRE)**[14] 6857 4-8-12 63 GeorgeDowning(5) 11 58
(Tony Carroll) *in rr: hdwy wl over 1f out: sn rdn and kpt on fnl f: nrst fin* **33/1**

040- **9** *shd* **Mops Angel**[367] 7221 3-9-0 65 AlistairRawlinson(5) 6 61
(Michael Appleby) *dwlt and sn pushed along in rr: swtchd lft to outer and hdwy 1/2-way: rdn 2f out: drvn and kpt on fnl f: nrst fin* **20/1**

6106 **10** *1* **Dream Catcher (FR)**[15] 6843 6-9-2 65 AmyScott(3) 12 56
(Henry Candy) *racd towards centre: chsd ldrs: rdn along 2f out: grad wknd* **8/1**[2]

6150 **11** *1* **Pieman's Girl**[27] 6488 3-9-3 63 WilliamCarson 16 52
(Anthony Carson) *racd towards stands' rail: in rr: rdn and sme hdwy to chse ldrs over 1f out: no imp fnl f* **20/1**

50 **12** *1 ¼* **Cardinal**[48] 5861 9-9-4 64 HayleyTurner 15 47
(Robert Cowell) *a towards rr* **8/1**[2]

0400 **13** *2* **Finflash (IRE)**[33] 6297 3-9-2 62 GrahamLee 14 39
(Mick Channon) *racd towards stands' rail: in tch: rdn along 1/2-way: sn wknd* **10/1**[3]

-002 **14** *1 ¾* **Invincible Lad (IRE)**[14] 6866 10-9-3 63 GrahamGibbons 7 33
(Ed McMahon) *racd centre: chsd ldrs: rdn along 2f out: sn wknd* **16/1**

0000 **15** *nk* **Shirley's Pride**[14] 6872 4-9-2 62 (t) AndrewMullen 1 31
(Michael Appleby) *swtchd rt s to r centre: in tch: effrt and sme hdwy 2f out: sn rdn and wknd appr fnl f* **20/1**

2400 **16** *5* **New Decade**[103] 3935 5-9-3 63 (t) OisinMurphy 4 14
(Milton Bradley) *s.i.s: a bhd* **12/1**

3000 **17** *3* **Look Here's Al**[69] 5080 3-8-11 62 JackDuern(5) 17 3
(Andrew Hollinshead) *racd towards stands' rail: chsd ldrs: rdn over 2f out: sn wknd* **14/1**

1m 3.36s (1.86) **Going Correction** +0.325s/f (Good) **17** Ran SP% **122.7**
Speed ratings (Par 101): **98,96,96,93,93 92,92,91,91,90 88,86,83,80,80 72,67**
CSF £45.60 CT £396.62 TOTE £4.90: £1.10, £2.80, £2.20, £8.50; EX 52.90 Trifecta £325.00.
**Owner** Peter Watson **Bred** R B Hill **Trained** Royston, Herts

**FOCUS**
This may not have had the quality of the previous sprint handicap on the card but it was competitive and favoured those ridden up with the pace. The winner was close to his C&D nursery form in similar conditions.
T/Plt: £14.80 to a £1 stake. Pool: £48,203.36 - 2,372.20 winning tickets T/Qpdt: £2.80 to a £1 stake. Pool: £4,543.71 - 1,191.09 winning tickets JR

# 6995 BRIGHTON (L-H)
### Thursday, October 16

**OFFICIAL GOING: Heavy (soft in places; 5.2)**
Wind: light, across Weather: light cloud, brighter spells

## 7215 TM LEWIN SHIRTS, SUITS AND MORE H'CAP 5f 59y
**2:10** (2:10) (Class 5) (0-75,74) 3-Y-0+ **£3,234** (£962; £481; £240) **Stalls** Low

Form RPR

6131 **1** **Pharoh Jake**[10] 6983 6-8-10 63 6ex WilliamCarson 3 72
(John Bridger) *hld up in last pair: styd on far rail 1/2-way: hdwy and on terms w ldrs over 1f out: drvn to ld ins fnl f: kpt on wl* **10/1**

5130 **2** *nk* **Perfect Pastime**[35] 6266 6-8-9 62 (p) PatCosgrave 5 70
(Jim Boyle) *hld up in midfield: hdwy against stands' rail over 1f out: ev ch ins fnl f: kpt on wl but a jst hld* **12/1**

412 **3** *2 ¼* **Indian Tinker**[48] 5880 5-9-6 73 LiamJones 8 73
(Robert Cowell) *chsd ldr: c to stands' side 1/2-way: led over 1f out: sn hung lft: hdd ins fnl f: wknd towards fin* **9/2**[1]

1066 **4** *1* **Ambitious Icarus**[5] 7103 5-9-7 74 (e) JasonHart 6 71
(Richard Guest) *broke fast: sn stdd and hld up towards rr: c towards stands'side 1/2-way: hdwy u.p over 1f out: styd on ins fnl f: nvr threatened ldrs* **7/1**

0216 **5** *2 ¼* **Birdie Queen**[9] 7023 4-8-10 70 HectorCrouch(7) 11 59
(Gary Moore) *in tch in midfield: c to stands' side 1/2-way: sn lost pl: no ch but plugged on past btn horses ins fnl f* **5/1**[2]

06R6 **6** *1* **Steel Rain**[52] 5750 6-9-3 70 RobertWinston 1 55
(Nikki Evans) *in tch in midfield: c to stands' side 1/2-way: no imp in 4th over 1f out: wknd ins fnl f* **16/1**

2334 **7** *1 ¾* **Ginzan**[33] 6313 6-9-7 74 FergusSweeney 4 53
(Malcolm Saunders) *hld up in last trio: c to stands' side 1/2-way: effrt and nt clr run over 1f out: n.d* **8/1**

5412 **8** *½* **Lady Phill**[22] 6658 4-9-3 70 KierenFox 9 47
(Michael Attwater) *dropped to rr sn after s: c to stands' side 1/2-way: sme hdwy u.p 2f out: wknd over 1f out* **8/1**

3600 **9** *1 ¾* **Whitecrest**[15] 6873 6-9-4 71 WilliamTwiston-Davies 2 42
(John Spearing) *chsd ldrs: c to stands' side 1/2-way: struggling u.p 2f out: sn wknd* **11/1**

21 **10** *10* **By Rights**[47] 5923 3-9-5 72 RaulDaSilva 7 9
(Tony Carroll) *broke fast: led: c to stands' side 1/2-way: rdn and hdd over 1f out: sn dropped out: fdd fnl f* **11/2**[3]

1m 7.37s (5.07) **Going Correction** +1.10s/f (Soft) **10** Ran SP% **116.0**
Speed ratings (Par 103): **103,102,98,97,93 92,89,88,85,69**
CSF £122.40 CT £631.78 TOTE £10.10: £4.10, £5.00, £1.10; EX 172.60 Trifecta £1817.40 Part won. Pool of £2423.20 - 0.91 winning units..
**Owner** The Hair & Haberdasher Partnership **Bred** J J Bridger **Trained** Liphook, Hants

**FOCUS**
Rail moved out from 2.5f to the winning post, adding 5yds to race distances. The official going was heavy, soft in places (GoingStick 5.2) with the riders in the opener describing conditions as "heavy", "holding" and "sticky". The winning time was 6.97sec outside standard. As is traditional on testing ground here, the bulk of the field in this ordinary sprint handicap eventually came nearside, but the winner stayed on the inside. The winner rates better than ever at face value.

## 7216 WINNER RENTAL SERVICES EBF STALLIONS MAIDEN STKS 5f 213y
**2:40** (2:40) (Class 5) 2-Y-O **£3,557** (£1,058; £529) **Stalls** Low

Form RPR

2302 **1** **Lackaday**[21] 6690 2-9-5 74 CharlesBishop 1 74
(Mick Channon) *mde all: rdn ent fnl 2f: sn jnd: forged ahd ins fnl f: styd on* **6/5**[2]

5303 **2** *2 ½* **Burning The Clocks (IRE)**[40] 6158 2-9-5 76 GeorgeBaker 4 67
(Peter Chapple-Hyam) *chsd wnr: clsd over 2f out: upsides ldr and shkn up over 1f out: fnd little for press 1f out: wknd fnl 100yds* **10/11**[1]

**3** *23* **Monsieur Valentine** 2-9-5 0 WilliamCarson 2
(Tony Carroll) *a in last: lost tch 2f out: heavily eased wl ins fnl f* **14/1**[3]

1m 16.18s (5.98) **Going Correction** +1.10s/f (Soft) **3** Ran SP% **104.5**
Speed ratings (Par 95): **104,100,70**
CSF £2.57 TOTE £1.50; EX 1.90 Trifecta £3.30.
**Owner** A R Parrish **Bred** Andrew Parrish **Trained** West Ilsley, Berks

**FOCUS**
A weak maiden in which the trio stayed towards the inside. The two principals had similar profiles in that they had both been placed in three of their first five starts and just 2lb separated them. The form is given a token rating through the winner.

## 7217 IRISH STALLION FARMS EBF MEDIAN AUCTION MAIDEN STKS 7f 214y
**3:10** (3:10) (Class 5) 2-Y-O **£3,557** (£1,058; £529; £264) **Stalls** Low

Form RPR

0065 **1** **Follow The Faith**[16] 6830 2-9-0 47 CharlesBishop 2 59
(Mick Channon) *in tch in midfield: wnt 3rd 3f out: rdn to chal over 1f out: sustained duel w ldr fnl f: tired but led towards fin: all out* **16/1**

02 **2** *hd* **Burma Bridge**[9] 6997 2-9-5 0 SeanLevey 4 64
(Richard Hannon) *led: rdn and jnd over 2f out: battled on but tired ins fnl f: hdd and no ex towards fin* **2/1**[1]

30 **3** *1 ¼* **Brandon Castle**[15] 6874 2-9-5 0 DavidProbert 7 61
(Andrew Balding) *t.k.h: chsd ldr: rdn and ev ch over 2f out: no ex 1f out: 3rd and one pce ins fnl f* **2/1**[1]

0 **4** *3 3/4* **My Strategy (IRE)**[21] 6683 2-9-5 0.................................... TomQueally 3 53
(Michael Bell) *in tch in midfield: rdn 4f out: 4th and c towards centre over 2f out: drvn and btn over 1f out: wknd ins fnl f* **3/1**[2]

04 **5** *23* **Alexi (IRE)**[31] 6393 2-9-0 0.................................... OisinMurphy 5
(Harry Dunlop) *a in rr: lost tch 3f out* **33/1**

06 **6** *3/4* **Light Breaks (IRE)**[15] 6859 2-9-5 0.................................... ChrisCatlin 1
(Sir Mark Prescott Bt) *s.i.s: a in last pair: lost tch 3f out* **8/1**[3]

0 **7** *16* **Ocean Bentley (IRE)**[94] 4270 2-9-5 0.......................... WilliamCarson 6
(Tony Carroll) *t.k.h: hdwy to press ldrs over 6f out tl over 4f out: dropped out qckly 3f out: t.o fnl f* **66/1**

1m 44.88s (8.88) **Going Correction** +1.10s/f (Soft) **7** Ran SP% **113.1**
Speed ratings (Par 95): **99,98,97,93,70 70,54**
CSF £47.37 TOTE £12.80: £4.60, £1.80; EX 46.00 Trifecta £135.90.

**Owner** George Materna & Mark Barrett **Bred** M Barrett **Trained** West Ilsley, Berks

**FOCUS**
Another modest maiden and again the runners stayed towards the far side. The first four pulled miles clear of the other trio. The form is rated negatively.

## 7218 PLATINUM LACE H'CAP — 7f 214y
**3:40** (3:40) (Class 6) (0-60,62) 3-Y-O **£2,587** (£770; £384; £192) **Stalls** Low

Form RPR

3004 **1** **Rockie Road (IRE)**[23] 6647 3-8-11 50.................................... PaoloSirigu 7 57
(Mick Quinn) *in tch: hdwy against far rail over 2f out: drvn to chal 1f out: led fnl 75yds: styd on* **8/1**[3]

6306 **2** *3/4* **Turnbury**[9] 7012 3-8-12 58........................................(t) SophieRalston(7) 6 63
(Robert Mills) *taken down early: t.k.h: sn led: drifted rt off of rail over 2f out: rdn over 1f out: rdr dropped whip 1f out tl hdd and no ex fnl 75yds* **16/1**

6453 **3** *1* **Stybba**[9] 6999 3-9-7 60........................................(v) OisinMurphy 5 63
(Andrew Balding) *in tch in midfield: effrt u.p over 1f out: pressing ldrs but hung lft u.p 1f out: fnd little for press and one pce after* **2/1**[1]

0-00 **4** *2 1/2* **Vaguely Spanish**[12] 6939 3-8-10 49.................................... WilliamCarson 3 52
(Tony Carroll) *in tch in midfield: clsd to chse ldrs and stl gng okay whn swtchd lft and bdly hmpd 1f out: swtchd rt ins fnl f: nt rcvr and one pce after* **10/1**

0554 **5** *11* **Borough Belle**[20] 6717 3-8-8 50.................................... AmyScott(3) 1 22
(Henry Candy) *chsd ldrs: rdn over 1f out: jst beginning to struggle whn hmpd 1f out: sn wknd* **9/1**

6001 **6** *1/2* **No Refund (IRE)**[9] 7025 3-8-9 53.................................... RyanWhile(5) 4 24
(Martin Smith) *chsd ldr tl over 1f out: sn btn and wknd* **8/1**[3]

0611 **7** *4* **Improvized**[9] 6999 3-9-9 62 6ex........................................(p) SteveDrowne 9 24
(William Muir) *sn dropped to rr and nvr travelling in rr: wl bhd over 1f out* **3/1**[2]

4400 **8** *8* **Dancing Angel**[61] 5425 3-8-13 55.................................... RyanTate(3) 8
(James Eustace) *stdd s: hld up in rr: clsd 4f out: rdn wl over 1f out: sn wknd* **11/1**

1m 43.81s (7.81) **Going Correction** +1.10s/f (Soft) **8** Ran SP% **113.9**
Speed ratings (Par 99): **104,103,102,99,88 88,84,76**
CSF £120.89 CT £352.00 TOTE £9.10: £2.30, £5.90, £1.60; EX 180.00 Trifecta £1212.20.

**Owner** YNWA Partnership **Bred** Ms N O'Reilly **Trained** Newmarket, Suffolk

■ Stewards' Enquiry : Sophie Ralston two-day ban: careless riding (Nov 14-15)
William Carson three-day ban: careless riding (Oct 30-Nov 1)

**FOCUS**
A very moderate handicap and things got tight for a couple entering the last furlong. The winner is rated back to his best.

## 7219 CHOICEBET £500 PERMANENT MONEY BACKS H'CAP — 1m 1f 209y
**4:10** (4:13) (Class 6) (0-60,63) 3-Y-0+ **£2,587** (£770; £384; £192) **Stalls** High

Form RPR

6153 **1** **Glennten**[9] 7001 5-9-9 59.................................... IrineuGoncalves 8 68
(Jose Santos) *t.k.h: chsd ldrs: c towards stands' side 3f out: rdn to ld 2f out: kpt on wl: rdn out* **6/1**

0001 **2** *1 1/4* **Salient**[9] 7002 10-8-4 47 oh1 ow1.................................... KieranShoemark(7) 3 54
(Michael Attwater) *t.k.h: chsd ldr: c towards stands' side 3f out: rdn to ld over 2f out: sn hdd: sltly outpcd over 1f out: rallied and kpt on fnl 100yds: wnt 2nd towards fin* **11/4**[1]

1500 **3** *1/2* **Monopoli**[20] 6706 5-9-6 56........................................(p) RobertWinston 7 62
(Shaun Harris) *in tch in midfield: styd far side 3f out: chsd ldrs u.p over 1f out: wnt 2nd ins fnl f: one pce and lost 2nd towards fin* **4/1**[2]

00 **4** *3/4* **Lindsay's Dream**[122] 3308 8-8-10 46 oh1........................(p) LiamKeniry 6 51
(Zoe Davison) *t.k.h: in tch in midfield: styd far side 3f out: rdn to ld gp and chsd ldrs over 2f out: chsd wnr over 1f out: one pce and lost 2 pls ins fnl f* **40/1**

20 **5** *2* **With Hindsight (IRE)**[61] 5428 6-9-6 56.......................... SamHitchcott 4 57
(John Spearing) *hld up in rr: styd towards far side 3f out: swtchd rt and effrt 2f out: drifted towards stands' side and kpt on fnl f: nvr trbld ldrs* **16/1**

4301 **6** *6* **Byrd In Hand (IRE)**[9] 7000 7-9-13 63 6ex....................(v) WilliamCarson 9 53
(John Bridger) *t.k.h: hld up in tch towards rr: styd far side and effrt 3f out: no prog 2f out: sn wknd* **13/2**

0206 **7** *2 1/2* **Gracefilly**[20] 6716 3-9-3 58.......................... WilliamTwiston-Davies 5 44
(Ed Walker) *in tch in midfield: styd far side 3f out: effrt 2f out: no hdwy and sn wknd* **16/1**

3464 **8** *5* **Indian Scout**[9] 7002 6-8-10 46........................................(b) JohnFahy 1 23
(Anabel K Murphy) *dwlt: rcvrd to ld 9f out: styd far side 3f out: sn rdn and hdd: wknd and drifted rt over 1f out* **25/1**

462 **9** *6* **Numrood**[65] 5282 3-9-5 60........................................(v[1]) GeorgeBaker 11 26
(George Peckham) *in tch: c towards stands' side and effrt u.p 3f out: wknd 2f out* **16/1**

5050 **10** *13* **Uganda Glory (USA)**[13] 6899 4-9-9 59......................(v) PatCosgrave 10
(George Baker) *short of room and dropped to rr sn after s: a in rr: effrt and c towards stands' side 3f out: sn btn: t.o* **5/1**[3]

2m 14.31s (10.71) **Going Correction** +1.10s/f (Soft)
**WFA** 3 from 4yo+ 5lb **10** Ran SP% **114.9**
Speed ratings (Par 101): **101,100,99,99,97 92,90,86,81,71**
CSF £22.46 CT £73.95 TOTE £7.40: £2.50, £1.70, £1.60; EX 31.90 Trifecta £194.90.

**Owner** R Cooper Racing Ltd **Bred** The Hon Mrs R Pease **Trained** Upper Lambourn, Berks

**FOCUS**
A moderate and messy handicap with the field splitting into two groups of five coming to the last 3f. The front pair came nearside, but the third and fourth stayed far side and were not beaten far. Another turf best for the winner.

## 7220 NEW ACCOUNTS £300 FREE BETS CHOICEBET.NET H'CAP — 6f 209y
**4:40** (4:41) (Class 5) (0-75,74) 3-Y-0+ **£3,234** (£962; £481; £240) **Stalls** Low

Form RPR

3405 **1** **Eastern Dragon (IRE)**[18] 6789 4-9-1 73.......................... NoelGarbutt(5) 12 83
(Michael Scudamore) *hld up towards rr: rdn and hdwy against stands' rail 2f out: chsd ldrs and swtchd lft jst ins fnl f: led fnl 75yds: sn in command* **7/1**

0232 **2** *2* **Freddy With A Y (IRE)**[45] 5979 4-9-2 69.................(p) FergusSweeney 3 74
(Gary Moore) *chsd ldrs: effrt to chal over 2f out: ev ch and edgd rt over 1f out: sustained duel w rival tl one pce fnl 75yds* **10/1**

6100 **3** *1 3/4* **Comrade Bond**[64] 5320 6-9-4 71..............................(p) RobertWinston 11 71
(Mark H Tompkins) *chsd ldr: pushed along to ld 3f out: hrd pressed and drvn wl over 1f out: sustain duel w rival after tl no ex fnl 75yds: wknd towards fin* **22/1**

3223 **4** *7* **Persian Bolt (USA)**[10] 6988 3-9-1 70..............................(v) TomQueally 5 51
(Eve Johnson Houghton) *chsd ldrs: rdn over 2f out: sn struggling and lost pl 2f: rallied and kpt on ins fnl f: no threat to ldrs* **10/1**

2303 **5** *2 1/2* **Comanchero (IRE)**[24] 6616 3-9-0 69.................................... OisinMurphy 9 44
(Andrew Balding) *in tch: effrt to chse ldrs 2f out: 3rd and rdn over 1f out: btn ent fnl f: fdd ins fnl f* **4/1**[1]

6346 **6** *2 1/4* **Great Expectations**[30] 6424 6-8-13 73..........................(t) MikeyEnnis(7) 1 43
(J R Jenkins) *hld up in rr: effrt but stl plenty to do whn bmpd and pushed lft over 1f out: edgd rt and no prog sn after* **5/1**[3]

-024 **7** *1 1/2* **Gigawatt**[18] 6789 4-9-7 74.................................... GeorgeBaker 13 40
(Jim Boyle) *in tch in midfield: hdwy to join ldrs over 2f out: losing pl whn sltly short of room over 1f out: fdd and eased ins fnl f* **9/2**[2]

4536 **8** *1 1/4* **Olney Lass**[38] 6189 7-8-6 62.................................... SimonPearce(3) 2 25
(Lydia Pearce) *a towards rr: rdn and no prog over 2f out: wl hld but plugged on fnl f* **12/1**

**9** *3/4* **Bainne (IRE)**[140] 2691 4-9-6 73.................................... SteveDrowne 7 34
(Jeremy Gask) *hld up in rr: effrt but no hdwy over 2f out: wl bhd over 1f out* **25/1**

1510 **10** *15* **Mrs Warren**[33] 6346 4-9-6 73.................................... PatCosgrave 10
(George Baker) *in tch in midfield: rdn and no hdwy over 2f out: wknd over 1f out: wl btn and eased ins fnl f: t.o* **8/1**

0510 **11** *2 1/4* **Moonspring (IRE)**[21] 6680 3-9-2 71..............................(e) LiamJones 6
(Robert Cowell) *chsd ldrs: rdn and struggling over 2f out: sn btn: fading whn hung lft over 1f out: t.o* **20/1**

0000 **12** *2* **Black Caesar (IRE)**[16] 6843 3-8-13 68..........................(b[1]) LiamKeniry 8
(Philip Hide) *led tl 3f out: sn dropped out: wl bhd and eased fnl f: t.o: b.b.v* **40/1**

1m 29.97s (6.87) **Going Correction** +1.10s/f (Soft)
**WFA** 3 from 4yo+ 2lb **12** Ran SP% **119.7**
Speed ratings (Par 103): **104,101,99,91,88 86,84,83,82,65 62,60**
CSF £71.98 CT £1493.19 TOTE £8.50: £2.90, £3.30, £10.00; EX 121.20 Trifecta £2864.90 Part won. Pool of £3819.98 - 0.69 winning units..

**Owner** JCG Chua & CK Ong **Bred** James Mahon **Trained** Bromsash, H'fords

**FOCUS**
A modest handicap, but the pace was strong and this time the entire field came nearside inside the last half-mile. The front three pulled clear with few showing their form on the ground. A length best from the winner.

## 7221 CHOICEBET NUMBER ONE TELEPHONE BETTING 08000126499 H'CAP (DIV I) — 5f 213y
**5:10** (5:10) (Class 6) (0-55,60) 3-Y-0+ **£2,726** (£805; £402) **Stalls** Low

Form RPR

4503 **1** **Tidal Beauty**[9] 7009 3-8-8 45.................................... ThomasBrown(3) 5 59
(Lee Carter) *towards rr: hdwy over 2f out: chal over 1f out: clr w wnr 1f out: styd on and forged ahd cl home* **7/1**[3]

2252 **2** *nk* **Posh Bounty**[10] 6988 3-8-11 45.................................... OisinMurphy 8 58
(Joseph Tuite) *taken down early: in tch: hdwy to press ldrs 2f out: rdn to ld over 1f out: clr w wnr 1f out: hdd and no ex cl home* **7/4**[1]

4620 **3** *3 1/2* **Brean Splash Susie**[124] 3214 3-8-11 50.......................... RyanWhile(5) 7 52
(Bill Turner) *towards rr: styd far side 1/2-way: hdwy 2f out: chsd clr ldng pair over 1f out: no imp* **33/1**

0-50 **4** *5* **Trust Me Boy**[61] 5425 6-8-12 45.................................... FrankieMcDonald 2 31
(John E Long) *in tch in midfield: effrt u.p 2f out: plugged on to go modest 4th ins fnl f* **25/1**

-300 **5** *4 1/2* **Scommettitrice (IRE)**[267] 274 6-8-12 45...(t) WilliamTwiston-Davies 10 17
(Nigel Twiston-Davies) *in rr: hdwy and styd far side 1/2-way: hung rt u.p over 2f out: wknd over 1f out* **14/1**

300 **6** *1/2* **Senora Lobo (IRE)**[59] 5499 4-8-12 45..........................(p) PaddyAspell 11 15
(Lisa Williamson) *stdd after s: hld up in rr: effrt and hdwy ent fnl 2f: wknd over 1f out* **25/1**

034 **7** *3* **Night Trade (IRE)**[9] 6995 7-9-3 50..............................(p) RaulDaSilva 9 10
(Ronald Harris) *sn bustled along: in tch: hdwy u.pn over 2f out: no ex and btn over 1f out: fdd fnl f* **8/1**

440 **8** *1 1/2* **Frosted Off**[126] 3149 4-9-0 47.................................... SamHitchcott 3
(John Spearing) *led tl 3f out: lost pl 2f out: sn wknd: bhd fnl f* **25/1**

2001 **9** *1/2* **Lord Buffhead**[7] 7056 5-9-13 60 6ex..............................(v) JasonHart 6 14
(Richard Guest) *chsd ldr tl dropped to midfield 4f out: lost pl and bhd whn drvn 2f out: sn wknd* **11/4**[2]

556 **10** *24* **Prize**[97] 4155 3-9-5 53.................................... PatDobbs 4
(Sylvester Kirk) *chsd ldr tl led 3f out: rdn and hdd over 1f out: sn btn: fdd and eased ins fnl f: t.o* **12/1**

1m 16.85s (6.65) **Going Correction** +1.10s/f (Soft)
**WFA** 3 from 4yo+ 1lb **10** Ran SP% **115.5**
Speed ratings (Par 101): **99,98,93,87,81 80,76,74,73,41**
CSF £18.63 CT £384.32 TOTE £9.50: £2.70, £1.10, £7.40; EX 25.70 Trifecta £229.10.

**Owner** Mrs Bernadette Quinn **Bred** Mr & Mrs J Quinn **Trained** Epsom, Surrey



The Form Book, Raceform Ltd, Newbury, RG14 5SJ

**FOCUS**
A moderate handicap. The vast majority of the field came towards the nearside over 3f from home, but a couple stayed closer to the far side. It produced a thrilling finish between the front pair. A clear best from the winner.

## 7222 CHOICEBET NUMBER ONE TELEPHONE BETTING 08000126499 H'CAP (DIV II) 5f 213y
**5:40** (5:40) (Class 6) (0-55,55) 3-Y-O+ **£2,726** (£805; £402) **Stalls** Low

Form RPR
0406 **1** **Port Lairge**[9] 6995 4-9-2 50................................(b) ChrisCatlin 10 60
(John Gallagher) *reluctant early: sn detached in last and reminders: clsd and swtchd lft over 2f out: str run over 1f out: led ins fnl f: sn clr* **14/1**
0403 **2** 2 1/2 **Fujin**[15] 6866 3-9-6 55................................(b) RobertWinston 7 57
(Shaun Harris) *in tch in midfield: trcking ldrs and nt clr run over 1f out: squeezed through and rdn to ld ent fnl f: hdd and no ex ins fnl f* **11/4**[1]
1000 **3** 1 1/4 **Shaunas Spirit (IRE)**[14] 6890 6-9-4 52............................[1] PatCosgrave 6 50
(Dean Ivory) *pressed ldr: rdn to ld 2f out: hdd ent fnl f: kpt on same pce fnl 150yds* **13/2**[3]
2005 **4** 2 1/4 **Novalist**[55] 5636 6-8-12 46 oh1................................(b) AdamBeschizza 4 37
(Robin Bastiman) *in tch in midfield: lost pl and in rr 4f out: rdn 1/2-way: no threat to ldrs but styd on past btn horses fnl f* **9/1**
0004 **5** 1 1/2 **Benidorm**[7] 7056 6-8-9 46 oh1................................(v) NeilFarley(3) 3 32
(Richard Guest) *chsd ldrs: effrt and pressing ldrs u.p 2f out: wknd 1f out* **7/1**
0060 **6** 1 3/4 **Ficelle (IRE)**[52] 5751 5-8-12 46 oh1................................(b) OisinMurphy 8 26
(Nikki Evans) *in tch in midfield: effrt 2f out: no ex over 1f out: wknd fnl f* **10/1**
3425 **7** 2 3/4 **Captain Scooby**[7] 7057 8-8-13 47................................(b) JasonHart 9 19
(Richard Guest) **3/1**[2]
0000 **8** hd **Ishisoba**[70] 5075 4-8-12 46 oh1................................ SteveDrowne 1 17
(Mark Hoad) *led tl 2f out: no ex u.p over 1f out: wknd ins fnl f* **40/1**
3503 **9** 2 1/4 **Bold Max**[135] 2860 3-8-11 46 oh1................................(p) LiamJones 2 10
(Zoe Davison) *sn outpcd in last pair: rdn over 2f out: n.d* **25/1**
5240 **10** 2 1/4 **Diamond Vine (IRE)**[43] 6023 6-8-12 46........(p) WilliamTwiston-Davies 5 3
(Ronald Harris) *in rr of main gp and niggled along 4f out: no hdwy u.p 2f out: wknd over 1f out* **14/1**

1m 17.06s (6.86) **Going Correction** +1.10s/f (Soft)
**WFA** 3 from 4yo+ 1lb **10 Ran SP% 116.2**
Speed ratings (Par 101): **98,94,93,90,88 85,82,81,78,75**
CSF £52.36 CT £283.33 TOTE £22.00: £6.10, £1.10, £2.40; EX 83.50 Trifecta £829.50.
**Owner** Quench Racing Partnership **Bred** Theresa Fitsall **Trained** Chastleton, Oxon

**FOCUS**
This division looked even more dire than the first and the winning time was 0.21sec slower. Unconvincing form, but a dramatic race.
T/Plt: £259.80 to a £1 stake. Pool of £70639.18 - 198.46 winning tickets. T/Qpdt: £28.80 to a £1 stake. Pool of £4945.58 - 127.0 winning tickets. SP

# 7181 WOLVERHAMPTON (A.W) (L-H)
Thursday, October 16

**OFFICIAL GOING: Tapeta: standard**
Wind: Light behind Weather: Overcast

## 7223 EVENTMASTERS.CO.UK MAIDEN STKS (TAPETA) 5f 216y
**5:30** (5:30) (Class 5) 2-Y-O **£2,587** (£770; £384; £192) **Stalls** Low

Form RPR
253 **1** **Frognal Bear (IRE)**[22] 6652 2-9-5 74................................ RichardHughes 4 72
(Richard Hannon) *trckd ldrs: rdn to chse ldr over 1f out: styd on u.p to ld nr fin* **1/2**[1]
0 **2** hd **Dutch Law**[24] 6604 2-9-5 0................................ JimCrowley 2 71+
(Hughie Morrison) *s.i.s: hld up: hdwy over 1f out: sn rdn: r.o* **7/1**[3]
05 **3** nk **Dark War (IRE)**[8] 7037 2-9-5 0................................ GrahamLee 5 71
(James Given) *chsd ldr tl led over 1f out: rdn ins fnl f: hdd nr fin* **18/1**
**4** 1 3/4 **With Approval (IRE)** 2-8-12 0................................ TylerSaunders(7) 8 65+
(Charles Hills) *sn pushed along and prom: styd on: nt rch ldrs* **14/1**
**5** 3/4 **Danseur Noble** 2-9-5 0................................ MartinHarley 7 63+
(James Tate) *hld up: rdn over 2f out: styd on ins fnl f: nt trble ldrs* **13/2**[2]
00 **6** 5 **Vejovis**[8] 7030 2-9-5 0................................ LukeMorris 6 48
(Sir Mark Prescott Bt) *prom: sn pushed along: rdn over 1f out: wknd fnl f* **100/1**
0 **7** 1 **Rockmount**[20] 6702 2-9-5 0................................ GrahamGibbons 1 45
(Ed McMahon) *awkward leaving stalls: sn rcvrd to ld: rdn and hdd over 1f out: wknd ins fnl f* **50/1**

1m 15.22s (0.72) **Going Correction** -0.025s/f (Stan) **7 Ran SP% 107.4**
Speed ratings (Par 95): **94,93,93,91,90 83,82**
CSF £3.79 TOTE £1.30: £1.10, £2.70; EX 4.60 Trifecta £20.20.
**Owner** Martin Hughes **Bred** T Cahalan & D Cahalan **Trained** East Everleigh, Wilts

**FOCUS**
A fairly uncompetitive race in which the winner is rated to the balance of his form.

## 7224 MAXSTON NURSERY H'CAP (TAPETA) 5f 216y
**6:00** (6:00) (Class 3) (0-95,87) 2-Y-O **£6,225** (£1,864; £932; £466; £233; £117) **Stalls** Low

Form RPR
6263 **1** **Geological (IRE)**[33] 6312 2-9-2 82................................ RichardHughes 1 84
(Richard Hannon) *hld up: hdwy over 1f out: rdn to ld wl ins fnl f* **11/1**
3402 **2** nse **Billyoakes (IRE)**[21] 6678 2-8-5 71................................ LukeMorris 6 72
(Mick Channon) *hld up: hdwy over 1f out: rdn and hung lft ins fnl f: r.o: fin 3rd: plcd 2nd* **12/1**
034 **3** 1/2 **Dark Side Dream**[35] 6271 2-8-1 67................................ JimmyQuinn 2 69
(Chris Dwyer) *a.p: rdn to ld ins fnl f: sn edgd rt and hdd: r.o: fin 2nd: disqualified and plcd 3rd* **7/1**
6231 **4** 1 1/2 **Best Endeavour**[21] 6678 2-9-0 80................................ GrahamLee 8 76
(William Muir) *hld up: hdwy over 1f out: r.o: nt rch ldrs* **3/1**[1]
4213 **5** 1/2 **Subversive (IRE)**[15] 6854 2-8-7 73................................ JoeFanning 3 68
(Mark Johnston) *led: rdn over 1f out: hdd ins fnl f: styng on same pce whn hmpd sn after* **9/2**[2]
0130 **6** 1 **Grey Zeb (IRE)**[12] 6933 2-8-9 75................................ TomEaves 5 67
(Keith Dalgleish) *prom: rdn over 1f out: styd on same pce ins fnl f* **7/1**
1160 **7** 2 **Escalating**[40] 6142 2-9-7 87................................ JimCrowley 4 73
(Pat Eddery) *chsd ldr: rdn and ev ch wl over 1f out: wknd ins fnl f* **11/2**[3]
106 **8** 10 **Don Sigfredo (IRE)**[19] 6739 2-9-3 83................................(p) RichardKingscote 9 39
(Tom Dascombe) *sn pushed along in rr: hdwy over 4f out: rdn and edgd rt over 2f out: sn wknd* **10/1**
4521 **9** 4 1/2 **Straightothepoint**[17] 6820 2-8-9 75................................(v) PaulMulrennan 7 17
(Bryan Smart) *chsd ldrs: rdn over 2f out: wknd over 1f out* **25/1**

1m 14.08s (-0.42) **Going Correction** -0.025s/f (Stan) **9 Ran SP% 112.5**
Speed ratings (Par 99): **101,100,100,98,97 96,93,80,74**
CSF £129.56 CT £992.65 TOTE £7.00: £2.70, £3.50, £3.80; EX 57.00 Trifecta £458.20.
**Owner** The Royal Ascot Racing Club **Bred** Mrs Helen Keaveney **Trained** East Everleigh, Wilts

**FOCUS**
Quite a decent nursery with a few holding some sort of chance in the home straight. It was run at a strong pace.

## 7225 FACILITIES MANAGEMENT SERVICES LTD CLAIMING STKS (TAPETA) 1m 141y
**6:30** (6:30) (Class 6) 3-Y-O **£1,940** (£577; £288; £144) **Stalls** Low

Form RPR
6033 **1** **Elysian Prince**[15] 6877 3-9-7 73................................(t) LukeMorris 3 77
(Paul Cole) *hld up: rdn over 2f out: hdwy over 1f out: edgd lft ins fnl f: r.o to ld post* **6/4**[1]
2243 **2** shd **Her Red Devil (IRE)**[17] 6823 3-8-6 60................................ PatrickMathers 4 62
(Richard Fahey) *a.p: chsd ldr 2f out: rdn to ld wl ins fnl f: hdd post* **6/1**
-614 **3** 1/2 **Rochelle (IRE)**[10] 6986 3-8-12 59................................ GrahamLee 8 67
(William Muir) *jnd ldr after 1f: led over 5f out: rdn and hdd 1f out: rallied to ld ins fnl f: sn hdd: r.o* **5/1**[3]
2044 **4** 3/4 **Aran Sky (IRE)**[27] 6515 3-9-1 67................................ MartinHarley 2 68
(K R Burke) *chsd ldrs: rdn to ld 1f out: hdd and unable qck ins fnl f* **9/2**[2]
5160 **5** 1 3/4 **Pigeon Pie**[5] 7098 3-8-10 70................................(v[1]) JoeFanning 1 59
(Mark Johnston) *hld up: hdwy over 1f out: styd on same pce ins fnl f* **8/1**
4400 **6** 8 **Rocksee (IRE)**[13] 6904 3-8-8 62................................(p) RichardKingscote 7 38
(Tom Dascombe) *sn led: hdd over 5f out: chsd ldr tl rdn 2f out: wknd ins fnl f* **10/1**
0060 **7** 2 **Connexion Francais**[23] 6627 3-8-0 45................................(p) JoeyHaynes(3) 5 29
(Tim Etherington) *hld up: rdn over 3f out: wknd wl over 1f out* **200/1**

1m 51.03s (0.93) **Going Correction** -0.025s/f (Stan) **7 Ran SP% 109.8**
Speed ratings (Par 99): **94,93,93,92,91 84,82**
CSF £10.06 TOTE £2.30: £1.50, £2.50; EX 8.00 Trifecta £32.50.Her Red Devil was claimed by C. N. Kellett for £6000.
**Owner** D S Lee **Bred** D S Lee **Trained** Whatcombe, Oxon

**FOCUS**
The early gallop wasn't particularly quick for this modest event. The winner is rated to form.

## 7226 AUTOMATION EXPERTS LTD NURSERY H'CAP (BOBIS RACE) (TAPETA) 1m 141y
**7:00** (7:00) (Class 4) (0-85,84) 2-Y-O **£3,752** (£1,116; £557; £278) **Stalls** Low

Form RPR
6611 **1** **Black Granite (IRE)**[21] 6684 2-9-3 83................................(v) CamHardie(3) 7 91+
(Jeremy Noseda) *hld up: hdwy over 5f out: chsd ldr over 2f out: led over 1f out: sn rdn and hung lft: styd on wl* **5/1**[3]
552 **2** 2 **Giantouch (USA)**[24] 6603 2-8-12 75................................(t) MartinHarley 5 79+
(Marco Botti) *chsd ldrs: rdn over 2f out: styd on to go 2nd wl ins fnl f* **9/4**[1]
4412 **3** 1 1/4 **Muradif (IRE)**[64] 5306 2-9-2 79................................ SebSanders 1 80
(William Haggas) *chsd ldrs: nt clr run 2f out: rdn over 1f out: styd on same pce fnl f* **7/1**
4131 **4** 1 1/4 **Rotherwick (IRE)**[30] 6436 2-9-7 84................................ LukeMorris 6 83+
(Paul Cole) *hld up: hdwy over 1f out: sn rdn: r.o: nt rch ldrs* **6/1**
3521 **5** 2 1/4 **Here Now**[32] 6364 2-9-1 78................................ AdamKirby 2 72
(Charlie Appleby) *sn led: rdn and hdd over 1f out: no ex ins fnl f* **5/1**
41 **6** shd **Elle Dorado**[15] 6868 2-8-13 76................................ RichardKingscote 4 70
(Tom Dascombe) *chsd ldr tl rdn over 2f out: styd on same pce fr over 1f out* **66/1**
3421 **7** nk **Water Thief (USA)**[19] 6769 2-9-4 81................................ JoeFanning 10 74
(Mark Johnston) *hld up in tch: effrt on outer over 2f out: edgd lft and styd on same pce fr over 1f out* **20/1**
2223 **8** 8 **Silver Ranger**[55] 5625 2-9-3 80................................ RichardHughes 3 56
(Richard Hannon) *s.i.s: hld up: rdn over 2f out: wknd over 1f out* **7/2**[2]
0432 **9** 2 3/4 **Thanksgiving Day (IRE)**[19] 6769 2-8-10 73................................ JimCrowley 8 43
(Jamie Osborne) *hld up: rdn over 2f out: sn wknd* **25/1**
1054 **10** 1 1/2 **Doc Charm**[17] 6820 2-9-2 79................................ TomEaves 9 46
(Keith Dalgleish) *hld up: rdn and wknd over 2f out* **28/1**

1m 48.97s (-1.13) **Going Correction** -0.025s/f (Stan) **10 Ran SP% 124.3**
Speed ratings (Par 97): **104,102,101,100,98 97,97,90,88,86**
CSF £17.27 CT £85.77 TOTE £7.60: £2.50, £1.40, £2.00; EX 21.50 Trifecta £95.50.
**Owner** The ABC Partnership **Bred** Yeomanstown Stud **Trained** Newmarket, Suffolk

**FOCUS**
A fairly strong field for the class. The pace appeared respectable from the outset. The winner probably has more to offer.

## 7227 CHEMIQUE ADHESIVES H'CAP (BOBIS RACE) (TAPETA) 7f 32y
**7:30** (7:32) (Class 3) (0-95,95) 3-Y-O+ **£7,158** (£2,143; £1,071; £535; £267; £134) **Stalls** High

Form RPR
3221 **1** **Dutch Art Dealer**[40] 6145 3-8-11 87................................(p) LukeMorris 8 96+
(Paul Cole) *mid-div: pushed along over 2f out: hdwy over 1f out: rdn and edgd lft ins fnl f: r.o to ld nr fin* **11/8**[1]
3234 **2** hd **Almuheet**[12] 6936 3-8-10 86................................ TomEaves 1 94
(Brian Ellison) *chsd ldrs: rdn to ld wl ins fnl f: hdd nr fin* **14/1**
005 **3** 1 **Ifwecan**[19] 6748 3-9-1 91................................ JoeFanning 2 96
(Mark Johnston) *led: rdn over 1f out: hdd and unable qck wl ins fnl f* **10/1**
0025 **4** hd **Deauville Prince (FR)**[26] 6535 4-9-4 92................................ RichardKingscote 7 98
(Tom Dascombe) *a.p: rdn over 1f out: edgd lft ins fnl f: styd on: nt clr run towards fin* **12/1**
0040 **5** nk **Santefisio**[26] 6531 8-9-6 94................................(b) PhillipMakin 3 99+
(Keith Dalgleish) *s.i.s: hld up: hdwy and nt clr run over 1f out: styng on whn nt clr run wl ins fnl f* **9/1**[3]
531 **6** 2 **Verse Of Love**[30] 6424 5-8-12 86................................ JFEgan 6 86
(David Evans) *sn pushed along and prom: rdn over 2f out: styd on same pce fnl f* **20/1**
0046 **7** hd **Dubai Dynamo**[19] 6740 9-8-11 85................................ PJMcDonald 5 84
(Ruth Carr) *mid-div: hdwy over 1f out: sn rdn: no ex ins fnl f* **28/1**
1420 **8** 1 **Maverik**[19] 6740 6-8-13 87................................ MartinHarley 4 84
(William Knight) *chsd ldr: rdn and ev ch over 2f out: wknd fnl f* **28/1**
2363 **9** shd **George Cinq**[26] 6560 4-8-10 87................................ LouisSteward(3) 11 84
(Michael Bell) *hld up: nt clr run over 1f out: nt trble ldrs* **6/1**[2]
5210 **10** 3/4 **Red Refraction (IRE)**[19] 6755 4-9-7 95................................ RichardHughes 10 90
(Richard Hannon) *hld up: swtchd lft sn after s: rdn over 2f out: nvr on terms* **12/1**

200- **11** *1 1/4* **Secret Talent**[425] 5533 4-8-13 87......................(t) JimCrowley 9 78
(Hughie Morrison) *hld up: effrt on outer over 2f out: wknd over 1f out* **14/1**
3000 **12** *7* **Steventon Star**[19] 6755 3-9-4 94......................(v) AdamKirby 12 66
(Alan Bailey) *hld up: wknd over 2f out* **40/1**
1m 27.53s (-1.27) **Going Correction** -0.025s/f (Stan)
**WFA** 3 from 4yo+ 2lb **12** Ran SP% **118.3**
Speed ratings (Par 107): **106,105,104,104,104 101,101,100,100,99 98,90**
CSF £21.59 CT £150.75 TOTE £2.10: £1.20, £2.70, £5.60; EX 22.20 Trifecta £177.90.
**Owner** R A Green **Bred** Raymond Clive Tooth **Trained** Whatcombe, Oxon
**FOCUS**
There were plenty in with a chance heading into the home straight and it produced a tight finish. There's every chance the winner is better than the bare form.

## 7228 A-PLANT MAIDEN AUCTION STKS (TAPETA) 7f 32y
**8:00** (8:04) (Class 5) 2-Y-O **£2,587** (£770; £384; £192) **Stalls** High

Form RPR
5 **1** **Silver Rainbow (IRE)**[71] 5037 2-8-9 0...................... KierenFallon 5 74+
(Charles Hills) *trckd ldrs: racd keenly: shkn up to ld over 1f out: r.o wl* **5/4**[1]
0 **2** *6* **Poppet Rocket (IRE)**[27] 6517 2-8-10 0...................... PaulMulrennan 9 60
(Brian Meehan) *hld up: hdwy over 1f out: styd on to go 2nd nr fin: no ch w wnr* **6/1**
4422 **3** *nk* **Lear's Rock (IRE)**[19] 6759 2-9-1 74...................... RichardHughes 2 65
(Ralph Beckett) *led 3f: led again 2f out: sn rdn and hdd: no ex ins fnl f* **9/4**[2]
44 **4** *1 1/2* **Emblaze**[20] 6701 2-8-8 0...................... JoeFanning 8 54
(Bryan Smart) *prom: rdn and hung lft over 1f out: no ex* **11/2**[3]
0 **5** *1/2* **Amour De Nuit (IRE)**[10] 6985 2-9-2 0...................... LukeMorris 3 61
(Sir Mark Prescott Bt) *hld up: shkn up over 1f out: styd on ins fnl f: nvr nr to chal* **66/1**
00 **6** *1 1/4* **Play Nicely**[22] 6668 2-9-0 0...................... GrahamLee 4 56
(James Given) *w ldr: plld hrd: led 4f out: hdd 2f out: wknd ins fnl f* **80/1**
46 **7** *3/4* **Codger's Gift (IRE)**[50] 5807 2-8-11 0...................... TonyHamilton 1 51
(Richard Fahey) *wnt lft s: sn prom: rdn and wknd over 1f out* **25/1**
**8** *21* **Rialto Magic** 2-8-11 0...................... JimCrowley 6
(Jamie Osborne) *s.i.s: hld up: wknd over 2f out* **25/1**
**9** *25* **Titan Goddess** 2-8-11 0...................... MartinHarley 7
(Mike Murphy) *s.s: a in rr: wknd over 2f out: virtually p.u over 1f out* **16/1**
1m 29.72s (0.92) **Going Correction** -0.025s/f (Stan) **9** Ran SP% **121.2**
Speed ratings (Par 95): **93,86,85,84,83 82,81,57,28**
CSF £10.04 TOTE £2.00: £1.10, £2.50, £1.10; EX 12.80 Trifecta £55.70.
**Owner** R J Tufft **Bred** Austin Curran **Trained** Lambourn, Berks
**FOCUS**
The betting suggested only two of these would be involved in the final stages and the pair came away going to the furlong marker. The form is pretty ordinary.

## 7229 EVENTMASTERS H'CAP (TAPETA) 2m 119y
**8:30** (8:30) (Class 6) (0-60,65) 3-Y-O **£1,940** (£577; £288; £144) **Stalls** Low

Form RPR
-134 **1** **Gimme Five**[11] 2735 3-9-5 58......................(p) RichardHughes 4 67+
(Alan King) *a.p: rdn over 2f out: styd on to ld wl ins fnl f* **6/4**[1]
0040 **2** *1/2* **Deadline Day (IRE)**[21] 6682 3-9-2 55......................(p) JackMitchell 8 62
(Roger Varian) *in rr and rn in snatches: hdwy over 3f out: rdn to ld 1f out: hdd wl ins fnl f* **7/1**
6022 **3** *1/2* **Dark Days**[15] 6856 3-9-4 57......................(t) LukeMorris 2 64+
(Paul Cole) *hld up: rdn over 2f out: hdwy and hung lft over 1f out: r.o: nt rch ldrs* **9/4**[2]
6 **4** *1 1/4* **Lamubaaly (IRE)**[15] 6877 3-9-4 60...................... LouisSteward(3) 9 65
(Alexandra Dunn) *s.i.s: hld up: hdwy over 3f out: led over 2f out: hdd 1f out: styd on same pce* **66/1**
4352 **5** *2* **Oakbank (USA)**[28] 6486 3-8-11 50...................... KieranO'Neill 10 52
(Brett Johnson) *chsd ldr tl led over 4f out: rdn and hdd over 2f out: styd on same pce fnl f* **7/2**[3]
6000 **6** *3 3/4* **Amourita (IRE)**[15] 6856 3-8-12 54......................(b[1]) DannyBrock(3) 6 52
(Jonathan Portman) *trckd ldrs: racd keenly: chsd ldr over 3f out tl rdn over 2f out: edgd lft and no ex over 1f out* **20/1**
0600 **7** *1 3/4* **Born To Reign**[38] 6193 3-8-6 48...................... CamHardie(3) 1 44
(Michael Bell) *chsd ldrs: nt clr run and lost pl 4f out: nt rcvr* **14/1**
5060 **8** *8* **Archiebeau**[28] 6486 3-8-11 57...................... JackBudge(7) 3 43
(Jonathan Portman) *s.i.s: hld up: wknd over 3f out* **33/1**
-405 **9** *54* **L'Es Fremantle (FR)**[72] 4996 3-8-4 46 oh1...................... JoeyHaynes(3) 7
(Michael Chapman) *led: rdn and hdd over 4f out: wknd over 3f out* **100/1**
3m 44.41s (0.71) **Going Correction** -0.025s/f (Stan) **9** Ran SP% **122.3**
Speed ratings (Par 99): **97,96,96,95,95 93,92,88,63**
CSF £13.82 CT £24.97 TOTE £2.80: £1.20, £2.30, £1.30; EX 20.80 Trifecta £47.70.
**Owner** McNeill Family **Bred** Granham Farm Partnership **Trained** Barbury Castle, Wilts
**FOCUS**
The early pace was moderate and it developed into a dash for the line. The winner resumed his spring progress.
T/Plt: £12.00 to a £1 stake. Pool of £72602.91- 4386.89 winning tickets. T/Qpdt: £2.10 to a £1 stake. Pool of £11393.51 - 3925.03 winning tickets. CR

# 6742 HAYDOCK (L-H)
Friday, October 17
**OFFICIAL GOING: Soft (heavy in places back straight; 7.3)**
Wind: Light, across Weather: Mainly fine

## 7230 DAVID SMITH TRAVEL LTD MAIDEN STKS 1m 2f 95y
**2:00** (2:00) (Class 5) 2-Y-O **£2,587** (£770; £384; £192) **Stalls** Centre

Form RPR
4532 **1** **Framley Garth (IRE)**[8] 7064 2-9-5 72...................... SebSanders 2 73
(David Elsworth) *racd keenly: prom: rdn over 2f out: nt qckn: plld off rail over 1f out: styd on ins fnl f: led fnl 75yds: in command cl home* **16/1**
22 **2** *1 3/4* **Emirates Skywards (IRE)**[20] 6743 2-9-2 0...................... CamHardie(3) 4 69
(Charlie Appleby) *led: stl gng wl 2f out: rdn 1f out: hdd fnl 75yds: no ex cl home* **4/6**[1]
6020 **3** *hd* **Playboy Bay**[54] 5718 2-9-5 65...................... SamHitchcott 9 69
(Mick Channon) *hld up in rr: niggled along 5f out: rdn and hdwy 3f out: big effrt and hung lft over 1f out: ch ins fnl f: styd on cl home but nt pce of wnr* **33/1**
5 **4** *1 3/4* **Scarlet Minstrel**[23] 6653 2-9-5 0...................... DavidProbert 5 66
(Andrew Balding) *hld up: hdwy 3f out: rdn over 2f out: kpt on ins fnl f: nvr able to chal* **8/1**[3]
042 **5** *1/2* **Mister Rockandroll**[25] 6602 2-9-5 74...................... FrannyNorton 7 65
(Mark Johnston) *prom: chsd ldr after 2f tl rdn over 2f out: hung lft u.p over 1f out: styd on same pce ins fnl f* **5/1**[2]
6 **6** *5* **The Cashel Man (IRE)**[11] 6984 2-9-5 0...................... FergusSweeney 8 56
(David Simcock) *missed break: in rr: niggled along 5f out: u.p after: nvr a threat* **16/1**
03 **7** *1/2* **Art Charter (FR)**[20] 6742 2-9-0 0......................(v) DanielTudhope 3 50
(K R Burke) *midfield: hdwy 3f out: rdn and sn no imp: btn 2f out* **12/1**
0600 **8** *3 3/4* **Blythe Star (IRE)**[23] 6669 2-9-5 50......................(v[1]) GrahamLee 6 48
(Danielle McCormick) *trckd ldrs: rdn over 2f out: wknd over 1f out* **80/1**
44 **9** *6* **Galileano (IRE)**[20] 6742 2-9-0 0......................(p) PaoloSirigu 1 33
(Marco Botti) *midfield: rdn and wknd over 3f out: eased whn wl btn ins fnl f* **18/1**
2m 17.76s (2.26) **Going Correction** +0.35s/f (Good) **9** Ran SP% **116.7**
Speed ratings (Par 95): **104,102,102,101,100 96,96,93,88**
CSF £27.51 TOTE £13.20: £3.30, £1.02, £9.30; EX 43.20 Trifecta £373.20.
**Owner** D R C Elsworth **Bred** G Morrin **Trained** Newmarket, Suffolk
■ Stewards' Enquiry : Seb Sanders two-day ban; used whip above permitted level (31st Oct-1st Sep)
**FOCUS**
All races on Stands Side Home straight and 6yds added to 7, 8f and 10f races and 11yds to 2m race. In a routine maiden which was a severe test of stamina for these juveniles, the favourite was able to control things from the front but it didn't quite work out for him. The winner and third suggest this level of form is sensible.

## 7231 ST HELENS WINDOWS NURSERY H'CAP 5f
**2:35** (2:35) (Class 2) 2-Y-O **£9,056** (£2,695; £1,346; £673) **Stalls** Centre

Form RPR
0621 **1** **Juncart**[17] 6831 2-9-0 78...................... GrahamLee 3 88
(Kevin Ryan) *chsd ldr: led 2f out: rdn over 1f out: r.o ins fnl f: a in control* **3/1**[2]
412 **2** *1 1/2* **Snow Cloud (IRE)**[9] 7038 2-8-0 69 ow2...................... JackGarritty(5) 6 74
(David O'Meara) *chsd ldrs: wnt 2nd over 1f out: hung lft ins fnl f: kpt on but nt pce to chal wnr* **11/4**[1]
321 **3** *4 1/2* **Kinematic**[20] 6739 2-9-7 85...................... DavidProbert 7 73
(Andrew Balding) *led: hdd 2f out: rdn over 1f out: sn outpcd by front two: no ex fnl f: jst hld on for 3rd* **9/2**[3]
6516 **4** *hd* **Rita's Boy (IRE)**[9] 7038 2-8-4 71...................... CamHardie(3) 5 59
(K R Burke) *sn pushed along in rr: sme hdwy over 1f out: kpt on ins fnl f: chal for 3rd cl home: no ch w front two* **13/2**
3120 **5** *12* **Perardua**[34] 6322 2-8-12 79...................... GeorgeChaloner(3) 4 27
(Richard Fahey) *chsd ldrs: rdn over 2f out: wknd over 1f out: eased whn btn ins fnl f* **10/1**
5400 **6** *4 1/2* **Diamond Creek (IRE)**[13] 6933 2-9-2 80...................... DanielTudhope 1 12
(Richard Fahey) *hld up: rdn over 2f out: bhd over 1f out: eased whn wl btn ins fnl f* **9/1**
41 **7** *12* **Pearl's Azinger (IRE)**[133] 2949 2-9-5 83...................... GrahamGibbons 2
(David Barron) *in tch: lost pl 3f out: struggling over 2f out: wl bhd over 1f out: eased whn wl btn ins fnl f* **8/1**
1m 0.87s (0.07) **Going Correction** +0.25s/f (Good) **7** Ran SP% **113.4**
Speed ratings (Par 101): **109,106,99,99,79 72,53**
CSF £11.50 TOTE £4.90: £2.60, £1.70; EX 16.80 Trifecta £53.40.
**Owner** Michael Beaumont **Bred** D R Tucker **Trained** Hambleton, N Yorks
■ Stewards' Enquiry : Daniel Tudhope jockey said filly was never travelling.
**FOCUS**
Several of these, including the winner, had form at 6f, which in theory was useful considering the conditions. However, the pace was decent and in the end most of these speedy juveniles found it all too much. not form to take too literally.

## 7232 RACING UK TIPSTER PUNDIT COMPETITION EBF STALLIONS CONDITIONS STKS 6f
**3:10** (3:11) (Class 3) 2-Y-O **£9,703** (£2,887; £1,443; £721) **Stalls** Centre

Form RPR
1021 **1** **Portamento (IRE)**[70] 5134 2-8-11 96...................... CamHardie(3) 1 104
(Charlie Appleby) *mde all: rdn over 2f out: drew clr ins fnl f: pushed out whn wl in command* **2/7**[1]
2152 **2** *10* **Marigot Bay**[11] 6989 2-8-6 77...................... GeorgeChaloner(3) 2 69
(Gay Kelleway) *racd keenly: chsd wnr: rdn and nt qckn over 1f out: no ch w wnr fnl f* **20/1**[3]
1053 **3** *7* **Arthur MartinLeake (IRE)**[11] 6977 2-9-0 77......................(p) DanielTudhope 3 53
(K R Burke) *chsd ldrs: pushed along and outpcd 1/2-way: rdn and drifted rt over 2f out: no ch after and wknd* **10/3**[2]
4565 **4** *3 3/4* **Macarthurs Park (IRE)**[19] 6791 2-8-4 45...................... JackGarritty(5) 4 37
(Alan Berry) *rdn sn after s whn flashed tail and hung lft: wl bhd: nvr on terms w ldrs* **150/1**
1m 15.12s (1.32) **Going Correction** +0.25s/f (Good) **4** Ran SP% **106.3**
Speed ratings (Par 99): **101,87,78,73**
CSF £6.98 TOTE £1.30; EX 4.50 Trifecta £5.20.
**Owner** Godolphin **Bred** Darley **Trained** Newmarket, Suffolk
**FOCUS**
The winner had a 19lb advantage at the weights and he was always in charge at a solid pace. This is smart form.

## 7233 GRIFFITHS AND ARMOUR H'CAP 6f
**3:40** (3:40) (Class 3) (0-90,89) 3-Y-O+ **£8,086** (£2,406; £1,202; £601) **Stalls** Centre

Form RPR
30 **1** **Englishman**[62] 5444 4-9-3 88...................... CamHardie(3) 16 99
(Charles Hills) *hld up: hdwy 1/2-way: rdn and edgd lft fr 2f out: r.o to ld fnl 150yds: continued to go lft: kpt on wl* **10/1**
-111 **2** *1/2* **Shared Equity**[63] 5385 3-9-6 89...................... GrahamLee 10 98
(Jedd O'Keeffe) *trckd ldrs: rdn to ld over 1f out: edgd rt ins fnl f: hdd fnl 150yds: carried lft after whn stl ev ch: hld cl home* **3/1**[1]
3534 **3** *nk* **Jamaican Bolt (IRE)**[7] 7080 6-9-7 89...................... BarryMcHugh 14 97
(Geoffrey Oldroyd) *hld up: n.m.r briefly 2f out: rdn and hdwy over 1f out: r.o ins fnl f: gng on at fin* **11/2**[2]
0245 **4** *3/4* **Links Drive Lady**[22] 6689 6-9-5 87...................... KierenFallon 15 93
(Dean Ivory) *in rr: hdwy over 1f out: styd on to chse ldrs ins fnl f: n.m.r fnl strides* **18/1**
0402 **5** *1* **Slip Sliding Away (IRE)**[16] 6880 7-9-0 85...................... ThomasBrown(5) 5 88
(Peter Hedger) *hld up: hdwy 1/2-way: rdn 2f out: tried to chal over 1f out: no ex fnl 75yds* **10/1**
1452 **6** *2 1/2* **Iseemist (IRE)**[28] 6511 3-8-11 85...................... ShaneGray(5) 11 80
(John Gallagher) *led: rdn and hdd over 1f out: no ex ins fnl f* **8/1**[3]
001 **7** *3/4* **Tagula Night (IRE)**[20] 6736 8-9-3 85......................(vt) FrannyNorton 13 77
(Dean Ivory) *midfield: hdwy 2f out: chsd ldrs over 1f out: one pce fnl 100yds* **20/1**

0000 **8** 1 1/4 **Oeil De Tigre (FR)**[13] 6923 3-9-2 85 ........................ DavidProbert 8 73
(Tony Carroll) *chsd ldrs: rdn to chal 2f out: stl there over 1f out: wknd ins fnl f* **33/1**

0002 **9** 3/4 **Whozthecat (IRE)**[7] 7085 7-9-2 84 ........................ JasonHart 6 70
(Declan Carroll) *prom: rdn 1/2-way: wknd fnl f* **12/1**

1122 **10** 3 1/4 **Master Bond**[42] 6096 5-9-5 87 ........................ DanielTudhope 2 63
(David O'Meara) *in tch: rdn and lost pl over 2f out: eased whn btn ins fnl f* **12/1**

1100 **11** 7 **Cruise Tothelimit (IRE)**[20] 6744 6-8-13 86 ........ GeorgeDowning(5) 12 39
(Ian Williams) *prom: rdn 1/2-way: wknd over 1f out* **25/1**

1010 **12** 1/2 **Khelman (IRE)**[27] 6535 4-9-1 86 ........................ GeorgeChaloner(3) 4 38
(Richard Fahey) *sn pushed along towards rr: nvr on terms* **20/1**

2650 **13** 3 3/4 **Secret Look**[20] 6740 4-9-5 87 ........................ GrahamGibbons 3 27
(Ed McMahon) *midfield: rdn 2f out: sn wknd* **14/1**

4-00 **14** 1 1/4 **Poole Harbour (IRE)**[35] 6290 5-9-0 89 ........................ AnnaHesketh(7) 17 25
(David Nicholls) *hld up: struggling 2f out: nvr on terms* **50/1**

0050 **15** nk **Lexi's Hero (IRE)**[5] 7132 6-9-2 89 ........................(v) JackGarritty(5) 7 24
(Richard Fahey) *prom: lost pl and outpcd 1/2-way: wl btn* **25/1**

1100 **16** 8 **New Bidder**[20] 6744 3-9-2 85 ........................ RussKennemore 1
(Jedd O'Keeffe) *sn pushed along towards rr: outpcd 1/2-way* **25/1**

1m 14.19s (0.39) **Going Correction** +0.25s/f (Good)
**WFA** 3 from 4yo+ 1lb **16** Ran SP% **123.0**
Speed ratings (Par 107): **107,106,105,104,103 100,99,97,96,92 82,82,77,75,75 64**
CSF £36.60 CT £191.29 TOTE £13.70: £3.70, £1.40, £2.10, £4.00; EX 66.30 Trifecta £437.40.
**Owner** Qatar Racing Limited & P Winkworth **Bred** Peter Winkworth **Trained** Lambourn, Berks

**FOCUS**
This was a competitive sprint with an above-average field, many of whom had proved themselves in soft ground. The form looks sound.

## 7234 BRITISH STALLION STUDS EBF MAIDEN STKS 7f
**4:15** (4:15) (Class 5) 2-Y-O **£2,911** (£866; £432; £216) **Stalls** Low

Form RPR

**1** **Terhaal (IRE)** 2-9-5 0 ........................ GrahamGibbons 6 80+
(William Haggas) *chsd ldr tl over 2f out: rdn over 1f out: rallied ins fnl f: styd on to ld towards fin* **9/2**[2]

**2** 3/4 **Crown Command (IRE)** 2-9-5 0 ........................ MartinDwyer 5 78
(William Muir) *chsd ldrs: wnt 2nd over 2f out: sn chalng: led fnl 150yds: sn hdd: hld towards fin* **11/2**[3]

53 **3** 3/4 **Regal Ways (IRE)**[10] 7019 2-9-0 0 ........................ FrannyNorton 3 71
(Mark Johnston) *led: rdn 1f out: hdd fnl 150yds: styd on same pce after* **11/1**

22 **4** 3/4 **My Dream Boat (IRE)**[88] 4486 2-9-5 0 ........................ GrahamLee 2 75
(Donald McCain) *prom: effrt on inner over 1f out: styd on whn chsng ldrs clly ins fnl f: nt clr run and eased towards fin* **9/4**[1]

2 **5** 2 1/4 **Structured Note (IRE)**[13] 6935 2-9-5 0 ........................ RussKennemore 8 69
(Jedd O'Keeffe) *hld up: hdwy 3f out: rdn whn cl up chsng ldrs over 2f out: nt qckn over 1f out: one pce fnl 110yds* **9/2**[2]

**6** 3/4 **Tafahom (IRE)** 2-9-5 0 ........................ JimmyFortune 7 67+
(B W Hills) *rdn along early: in rr: rdn over 2f out: no imp whn hung lft over 1f out: one pce ins fnl f* **14/1**

6 **7** 1/2 **Lone Star Boy (IRE)**[13] 6935 2-9-5 0 ........................ HayleyTurner 4 65
(Tom Dascombe) *s.i.s and rdn along: sn in midfield: rdn 3f out: no imp on ldrs: one pce fnl f* **7/1**

0 **8** 19 **Doctor Watson**[151] 2386 2-9-5 0 ........................ JamesSullivan 1 18
(Tom Tate) *stdd s: hld up: pushed along 3f out: struggling fnl 2f: wl btn* **100/1**

1m 33.3s (2.60) **Going Correction** +0.35s/f (Good) **8** Ran SP% **111.0**
Speed ratings (Par 95): **99,98,97,96,93 93,92,70**
CSF £27.54 TOTE £5.90: £2.60, £1.10, £4.50; EX 31.20 Trifecta £493.90.
**Owner** Hamdan Al Maktoum **Bred** Norelands Bloodstock **Trained** Newmarket, Suffolk

**FOCUS**
It isn't easy to weigh up the standard of this late-developers' maiden, but the fourth is a decent yardstick so the form looks solid. The pace was ordinary on the testing ground.

## 7235 PAUL CROWLEY SOLICITORS H'CAP 2m 45y
**4:50** (4:51) (Class 4) (0-85,87) 3-Y-0+ **£5,175** (£1,540; £769; £384) **Stalls** Low

Form RPR

1260 **1** **Precision Strike**[16] 6864 4-9-0 71 ........................(v) RussKennemore 12 83
(Richard Guest) *hld up: hdwy over 4f out: led over 2f out: styd on: a doing enough towards fin* **20/1**

4242 **2** 1/2 **Rite To Reign**[20] 6741 3-8-10 77 ........................ KierenFallon 10 88
(Philip McBride) *midfield: rdn 1/2-way: hdwy on outer over 4f out: led 3f out: hdd over 2f out: continued to chal thrght fnl 2f: styd on: hld cl home* **15/8**[1]

416- **3** 7 **Spiritoftomintoul**[299] 8392 5-10-0 85 ........................(t) JimmyFortune 7 88
(Tony Carroll) *in rr: hdwy 3f out: chsd ldrs and hung lft fr 2f out: no imp on front pair over 1f out: kpt on* **33/1**

6224 **4** 5 **Mighty Missile (IRE)**[27] 6539 3-8-0 67 oh2 ........................ JamesSullivan 1 64
(Tom Tate) *chsd ldrs: rdn 5f out: one pce fnl 2f and no imp* **9/1**

1034 **5** 2 1/4 **Perfect Summer (IRE)**[51] 5825 4-9-6 80 ........................ CamHardie(3) 6 74
(Lady Cecil) *chsd ldrs: rdn over 3f out: one pce fnl 2f* **6/1**[2]

3310 **6** 1 3/4 **Nashville (IRE)**[6] 7124 5-9-7 81 ........................ GeorgeChaloner(3) 5 73
(Richard Fahey) *bustled along early: midfield: rdn 5f out: kpt on one pce fnl 2f: no imp* **10/1**

0105 **7** 4 **Stopped Out**[58] 5564 9-9-7 81 ........................(p) ConnorBeasley(3) 4 68
(Philip Kirby) *s.i.s: sn chsd ldrs: led after 3f: rdn and hdd 3f out: wknd wl over 1f out* **8/1**[3]

2-45 **8** 23 **Stock Hill Fair**[11] 6987 6-9-12 83 ........................ GrahamLee 2 42
(Brendan Powell) *led: hdd after 3f: remained prom: rdn and wknd 3f out: eased whn btn ins fnl f* **14/1**

060/ **9** 1 1/2 **Bothy**[20] 6642 8-8-13 70 ........................ PaulPickard 8 28
(Brian Ellison) *prom: pushed along over 5f out: rdn and wknd over 2f out: eased whn btn ins fnl f* **14/1**

-040 **10** 1/2 **Shrewd**[27] 6536 4-9-9 87 ........................(p) MikeyEnnis(7) 3 44
(Keith Dalgleish) *midfield: lost pl 6f out: bhd over 4f out: eased whn btn ins fnl f* **12/1**

440 **11** 8 **Mr Snoozy**[126] 3204 5-9-9 80 ........................(p) JasonHart 11 27
(Mark Walford) *midfield: rdn 5f out: sn wknd: eased whn wl btn over 1f out* **12/1**

1005 **12** 20 **Itlaaq**[20] 6761 8-9-12 83 ........................(t) GrahamGibbons 9 6
(Michael Easterby) *hld up: struggling 4f out: eased whn wl btn over 1f out* **25/1**

3m 39.2s (4.90) **Going Correction** +0.35s/f (Good)
**WFA** 3 from 4yo+ 10lb **12** Ran SP% **119.5**
Speed ratings (Par 105): **101,100,97,94,93 92,90,79,78,78 74,64**
CSF £56.93 CT £1312.28 TOTE £30.20: £6.90, £1.20, £8.50; EX 112.80 Trifecta £1873.20.
**Owner** Resdev **Bred** Mickley Stud **Trained** Ingmanthorpe, W Yorks

**FOCUS**
With the topweight rated 87, this was a decent stayers' race. The soft ground and solid pace made it an extreme test. Another personal best from the winner.

## 7236 ST HELENS COLLEGE SKILLS SHOW EXPERIENCE H'CAP 1m
**5:25** (5:27) (Class 3) (0-95,94) 3-Y-0+ **£8,086** (£2,406; £1,202; £601) **Stalls** Low

Form RPR

33-2 **1** **Melvin The Grate (IRE)**[11] 6990 4-8-7 80 oh2 ........................ DavidProbert 13 89+
(Andrew Balding) *midfield: hdwy over 2f out: rdn to ld over 1f out: jst hld on cl home* **7/2**[2]

0221 **2** nk **Big Baz (IRE)**[20] 6748 4-9-1 88 ........................ MartinDwyer 8 96+
(William Muir) *hld up: hdwy on outer over 2f out: sn rdn: r.o ins fnl f: fin wl* **11/4**[1]

0015 **3** 3/4 **Marcret (ITY)**[20] 6740 7-9-5 92 ........................ JamesSullivan 3 98
(Ruth Carr) *racd keenly: chsd ldrs: lost pl and sltly outpcd over 1f out: styd on ins fnl f: nt quite pce of front two* **16/1**

2005 **4** 1/2 **Gatepost (IRE)**[7] 7085 5-8-6 82 ow1 ........................ GeorgeChaloner(3) 12 87
(Richard Fahey) *racd keenly: chsd ldrs: rdn 2f out: chalng over 1f out: kpt on same pce fnl 75yds* **14/1**

0500 **5** 1 **Ingleby Angel (IRE)**[20] 6752 5-9-7 94 ........................ DanielTudhope 10 97
(David O'Meara) *racd keenly: hld up: hdwy 3f out: sn rdn: chsd ldrs 2f out: nt qckn over 1f out: kpt on same pce fnl 100yds* **11/1**

0630 **6** 1 1/4 **Silvery Moon (IRE)**[42] 6098 7-9-2 89 ........................ JasonHart 4 89
(Tim Easterby) *prom: rdn over 2f out: lost pl over 1f out: kpt on ins fnl f but nt get to ldrs* **22/1**

2160 **7** hd **Le Chat D'Or**[20] 6748 6-9-0 90 ........................(bt) ConnorBeasley(3) 9 89
(Michael Dods) *missed break: in rr: rdn over 2f out: swtchd rt over 1f out: kpt on ins fnl f: nt trble ldrs* **12/1**

4125 **8** 1 1/2 **Off The Pulse**[17] 6839 4-8-9 82 ........................ JimmyQuinn 14 78
(John Mackie) *prom: led wl over 1f out: rdn and sn hdd: fdd fnl 150yds* **20/1**

0-00 **9** 1/2 **Mister Music**[20] 6748 5-9-7 94 ........................(b) JimmyFortune 1 89
(Brian Meehan) *in rr: rdn bhd ldng bunch over 1f out: no imp* **66/1**

0261 **10** nse **Our Boy Jack (IRE)**[8] 7060 5-8-10 88 6ex ........................ JackGarritty(5) 2 83
(Richard Fahey) *midfield: effrt 2f out: nt clr run over 1f out: no imp* **10/1**[3]

0006 **11** 2 **Trail Blaze (IRE)**[29] 6476 5-8-5 83 ........................(p) ShaneGray(5) 15 73
(Kevin Ryan) *led: rdn over 2f out: hdd wl over 1f out: wknd fnl f* **16/1**

6-14 **12** 5 **Music In The Rain (IRE)**[167] 1957 6-9-4 91 ........................ KierenFallon 7 69
(David O'Meara) *towards rr: niggled along 5f out: hdwy over 3f out: rdn and wl there over 2f out: wknd over 1f out* **14/1**

5400 **13** 3 1/2 **Norse Blues**[7] 7085 6-8-10 83 ........................ GrahamGibbons 11 53
(David Barron) *racd keenly: chsd ldrs on outer: lost pl 3f out: bhd fnl 2f* **33/1**

1m 44.84s (1.14) **Going Correction** +0.35s/f (Good) **13** Ran SP% **112.6**
Speed ratings (Par 107): **108,107,106,106,105 104,104,102,102,101 99,94,91**
CSF £11.54 CT £119.85 TOTE £4.50: £1.70, £1.50, £5.10; EX 15.40 Trifecta £415.90.
**Owner** Fromthestables.Com & I A Balding **Bred** Barronstown Stud **Trained** Kingsclere, Hants
■ Uncle Dermot and Chosen Character were withdrawn. Prices at time of withdrawal 20/1 and 14/1 respectively. Rule 4 applies to all bets - deduction 5p in the pound.

**FOCUS**
There wasn't much between the first seven in this good-quality handicap, which is rated around the third and fourth.
T/Plt: £37.80 to a £1 stake. Pool: £54,836.43 - 1,056.92 winning tickets T/Qpdt: £11.40 to a £1 stake. Pool: £2,661.21 - 171.73 winning tickets DO

# 7104 NEWMARKET (R-H)
Friday, October 17

**OFFICIAL GOING: Soft (5.7)**
Wind: medium, across Weather: dry, mild

## 7237 DUBAI EUROPEAN BREEDERS' FUND FILLIES' NURSERY H'CAP (BOBIS RACE) 7f
**1:50** (1:53) (Class 2) 2-Y-O
**£37,350** (£11,184; £5,592; £2,796; £1,398; £702) **Stalls** High

Form RPR

1530 **1** **Little Lady Katie (IRE)**[20] 6749 2-8-2 75 ........ JordanVaughan(7) 16 86
(K R Burke) *hld up in midfield: rdn and hdwy to ld over 1f out: styd on wl and a holding rival fnl f: rdn out* **16/1**

51 **2** 1/2 **Pulcinella (IRE)**[34] 6333 2-9-1 81 ........................ WilliamBuick 10 91
(Charlie Appleby) *str: hld up in tch in midfield: swtchd rt and effrt over 1f out: chal wnr and clr ins fnl f: styd on but a hld* **7/1**[1]

2316 **3** 3 1/4 **Escrick (IRE)**[36] 6253 2-8-4 70 ........................ HarryBentley 14 72
(David Simcock) *in tch: clsd and travelling wl 3f out: rdn and ev ch over 1f out: no ex 1f out: outpcd but stl clr 3rd fnl f* **25/1**

0313 **4** 3 1/2 **Conjuring (IRE)**[20] 6749 2-8-3 69 ........................ RoystonFfrench 4 62
(Mike Murphy) *chsd ldr: wnt 2nd but racd awkwardly u.p 2f out: outpcd and btn over 1f out: plugged on* **14/1**

1020 **5** 3/4 **East Coast Lady (IRE)**[21] 6709 2-9-7 87 ........................ AndreaAtzeni 12 78
(Robert Eddery) *in tch in midfield: effrt and carried rt over 1f out: no threat to ldrs and kpt on same pce fnl f* **8/1**[2]

6030 **6** 3/4 **Maybe Now Baby (IRE)**[20] 6749 2-7-9 66 oh1 ........ NoelGarbutt(5) 6 56
(David Simcock) *in rr: rdn 1/2-way: hdwy u.p over 1f out: styd on past btn horses fnl f: nvr trbld ldrs* **20/1**

1300 **7** nse **Bimbo**[36] 6253 2-8-12 78 ........................ PaulHanagan 13 67
(Richard Fahey) *led: rdn and hung rt wl over 1f out: 4th and btn over 1f out: wknd ins fnl f* **16/1**

31 **8** shd **Majestic Manner**[44] 6041 2-9-2 82 ........................ RyanMoore 7 71
(William Haggas) *athletic: in tch in midfield: effrt 2f out: no imp u.p whn edgd rt over 1f out: wl hld and swtchd lft ins fnl f* **7/1**[1]

3510 **9** 1 1/2 **Only Joking**[37] 6229 2-8-10 76 ........................ JamesDoyle 9 61
(Hugo Palmer) *lw: in tch in midfield: effrt u.p over 2f out: no ex and btn over 1f out: wknd fnl f* **8/1**[2]

31 **10** 1/2 **Deep Blue Sea**[31] 6434 2-8-8 74 ........................ WilliamCarson 15 58
(Anthony Carson) *leggy: athletic: lw: wnt sharply lft s: hld up in rr: effrt but stl plenty to do whn hmpd wl over 1f out: no prog and wl hld whn eased ins fnl f* **7/1**[1]

21 **11** 2 1/4 **Fidelma Moon (IRE)**[43] 6071 2-8-10 79 ........................[1] JoeyHaynes(3) 11 58
(K R Burke) *leggy: chsd ldrs: rdn and unable qck 2f out: btn over 1f out: wknd fnl f* **33/1**

4053 **12** 3 3/4 **Hound Music**[25] 6610 2-8-0 69 ........................ DannyBrock(3) 8 38
(Jonathan Portman) *a towards rr: struggling u.p over 3f out: no ch fnl 2f* **11/1**[3]

322 **13** ¾ **Mystic Jade**[25] 6605 2-9-0 **80**............ RichardHughes 1 47
(Richard Hannon) *chsd ldr tl ent fnl 2f: sn btn: wknd over 1f out* **12/1**

2340 **14** 4 **Enlace**[28] 6510 2-9-5 **85**............ JoeFanning 3 42
(Mark Johnston) *wl in tch in midfield: rdn wl over 1f out: sn btn: fdd fnl f* **20/1**

264 **15** 7 **Thunder In Myheart (IRE)**[13] 6924 2-8-10 **76**............ JamieSpencer 5 16
(Michael Bell) *stdd s: t.k.h: hld up towards rr: pushed along jst over 2f out: sn btn and rdr looking down: eased* **11/1**[3]

1m 27.14s (1.74) **Going Correction** +0.475s/f (Yiel) **15** Ran SP% **118.8**
Speed ratings (Par 98): **109,108,104,100,99 99,98,98,97,96 93,89,88,84,76**
CSF £115.50 CT £2865.21 TOTE £28.00: £6.90, £3.00, £9.40; EX 311.20 Trifecta £2574.00 Part won..
**Owner** Ontoawinner 5, M Hulin & Mrs E Burke **Bred** Roger K Lee **Trained** Middleham Moor, N Yorks

**FOCUS**
Stands' side course used. Stalls: All races Stands' side. The fourth staging of Future Champions Day but despite further tweaking the programme remains unsatisfactory. It was already debatable whether the Middle Park and Dewhurst should be run on the same card (Diesis completed the double in 1982, and from 2000-2010 12 horses contested both races), and with the Cornwallis added to the mix there are now Group-race options at 5f, 6f and 7f for juvenile males. Only last season the Cornwallis winner Hot Streak ran second in the Middle Park seven days later. On a positive note, however, the Group 1 Fillies' Mile replacing the Group 2 Rockfel makes sense. Clerk of the Course Michael Prosser said: "We had 25mm of rain on Monday and 12mm of rain overnight on Wednesday, but have been dry since. The GoingStick reading was 6.0 at 10am this morning and it is proper soft ground. There is also a fresh strip of ground down the stands' side." This was a really competitive fillies' nursery, the most valuable of its type in Britain and the most valuable race supported by the EBF. The pace was strong and the first three raced nearest the stands' side. Pretty strong form.

## 7238 DUBAI CORNWALLIS STKS (GROUP 3) 5f
**2:25** (2:25) (Class 1) 2-Y-O

**£45,368** (£17,200; £8,608; £4,288; £2,152; £1,080) **Stalls** High

Form RPR

2154 **1** **Royal Razalma (IRE)**[27] 6530 2-8-12 **94**............ RichardKingscote 2 105
(Jonathan Portman) *swtg: racd towards centre: in tch: rdn and hdwy over 1f out: hung lft and led ins fnl f: r.o wl* **16/1**

124 **2** 1½ **Strath Burn**[27] 6547 2-9-1 0............ JamieSpencer 5 103
(Charles Hills) *racd in centre thrght: chsd ldrs: wnt 2nd 2f out: drvn over 1f out: ev ch ins fnl f: outpcd by wnr fnl 100yds: wnt 2nd last strides* **9/2**[1]

**3** nk **Volatile (SWE)**[30] 2-9-1 0............(b) AndreaAtzeni 12 102
(Jessica Long, Sweden) *tall: unf: racd against stands' rail: led: rdn jst over 1f out: hdd ins fnl f: kpt on same pce after: lost 2nd last strides* **15/2**[3]

3113 **4** nk **Squats (IRE)**[28] 6513 2-9-1 **97**............ RyanMoore 10 102
(William Haggas) *swtg: racd in stands' side: in tch in midfield: swtchd rt and effrt to chal over 1f out: keeping on same pce but ev ch of 2nd whn squeezed for room and hmpd wl ins fnl f* **9/2**[1]

1222 **5** ½ **Profitable (IRE)**[21] 6703 2-9-1 **93**............ AdamKirby 7 100
(Clive Cox) *lw: racd in stands' side gp: in tch in midfield: effrt over 1f out: hdwy and chsng ldrs whn hmpd and snatched up ins fnl f: nt rcvr and one pce after* **9/1**

5561 **6** ¾ **Rosie's Premiere (IRE)**[21] 6703 2-8-12 **93**............ RobertWinston 11 93
(Dean Ivory) *racd in stands' side gp: hld up in rr: swtchd rt and hdwy over 1f out: kpt on same pce ins fnl f* **11/1**

1230 **7** ½ **Al Fareej (IRE)**[28] 6513 2-8-12 **95**............ JimCrowley 1 92
(James Tate) *lw: racd towards centre: in tch in midfield: effrt over 1f out: styd on same pce u.p ins fnl f* **16/1**

1 **8** ¾ **Air Of Mystery**[33] 6361 2-8-12 0............ WilliamBuick 8 89
(Marcus Tregoning) *leggy: swtg: dwlt: swtchd to stands' side gp after 1f: in rr: rdn and effrt over 1f out: pushed along and styd on past btn horses ins fnl f: nvr trbld ldrs* **25/1**

0451 **9** hd **Accipiter**[28] 6513 2-8-12 **93**............ AshleyMorgan 6 88
(Chris Wall) *swtg: racd towards centre: chsd ldrs: rdn and unable qck over 1f out: wknd ins fnl f* **20/1**

1020 **10** 1 **Moonraker**[35] 6286 2-9-1 **101**............ RichardHughes 3 88
(Mick Channon) *lw: racd towards centre: bmpd and hmpd sn after s: rdn and hdwy over 1f out: no ex 1f out: wknd ins fnl f* **9/2**[1]

1105 **11** 1½ **Fendale**[28] 6513 2-9-1 **95**............ PaulHanagan 4 82
(Bryan Smart) *swtg: racd towards centre: bmpd sn after s: in tch in midfield: drifted towards stands' side gp and rdn 2f out: btn 1f out: wknd ins fnl f* **7/1**[2]

0204 **12** 12 **Secret Liaison (IRE)**[28] 6513 2-8-12 **91**............ JoeFanning 9 36
(James Tate) *racd in stands' side gp: chsd ldr tl 2f out: dropped out qckly over 1f out: bhd and eased ins fnl f* **40/1**

1m 0.55s (1.45) **Going Correction** +0.475s/f (Yiel) **12** Ran SP% **120.0**
Speed ratings: **107,104,104,103,102 101,100,99,99,97 95,76**
CSF £85.92 TOTE £22.20: £5.80, £1.60, £2.20; EX 166.90 Trifecta £718.20.
**Owner** David & Gwyn Joseph **Bred** Miss Eileen Farrelly **Trained** Upper Lambourn, Berks
■ Stewards' Enquiry : Richard Kingscote four-day ban; careless riding (31st Oct - 4th Nov)

**FOCUS**
Formerly run at Ascot, this year's Cornwallis Stakes looked wide open. There was a solid pace on and, after the field surprisingly neglected the fresh strip near the stands' rail in the opener, it was no big surprise to see the main action develop there late in the day. There was a compressed finish and it has been rated an ordinary renewal. The runner-up is a fair benchmark and the winning time suggested the surface was not too holding.

## 7239 VISION.AE MIDDLE PARK STKS (GROUP 1) (ENTIRE COLTS) 6f
**2:55** (2:55) (Class 1) 2-Y-O

**£123,344** (£46,762; £23,403; £11,658; £5,850; £2,936) **Stalls** High

Form RPR

211 **1** **Charming Thought**[25] 6612 2-9-0 **98**............ WilliamBuick 2 117
(Charlie Appleby) *w'like: stdd after s: wl in tch in midfield: swtchd out rt wl over 1f out: rdn ent fnl f: str chal ins fnl f: styd on wl u.p to ld wl ins fnl f: drvn out* **22/1**

111 **2** nse **Ivawood (IRE)**[78] 4822 2-9-0 **118**............ RichardHughes 1 117
(Richard Hannon) *lw: chsd ldrs: upsides ldr 2f out: led over 1f out: rdn ent fnl f: hrd pressed and drvn ins fnl f: kpt on: hdd wl ins fnl f: a jst hld after* **1/2**[1]

1331 **3** 1¼ **Muhaarar**[55] 5692 2-9-0 **111**............ PaulHanagan 5 113
(Charles Hills) *led: rdn over 2f out: hung rt over 1f out and no ex 1f out: styd on same pce ins fnl f* **8/1**[3]

2531 **4** ½ **Cappella Sansevero**[47] 5954 2-9-0 0............ AndreaAtzeni 4 112
(G M Lyons, Ire) *hld up in tch in rr: rdn and effrt over 1f out: wnt 4th ins fnl f: styd on but nvr gng pce to chal* **6/1**[2]

1126 **5** 1 **Kool Kompany (IRE)**[57] 5607 2-9-0 **111**............ RyanMoore 3 109
(Richard Hannon) *lw: sn pushed up to chse ldr: rdn 2f out: unable qck and lost pl over 1f out: hld and one pce fnl f* **9/1**

0 **6** ½ **The Warrior (IRE)**[13] 6925 2-9-0 0............(b[1]) JosephO'Brien 6 107
(A P O'Brien, Ire) *unf: shkn up leaving stalls: wl in tch in midfield: effrt 2f out: drvn and no ex over 1f out: one pce fnl f* **40/1**

1m 13.01s (0.81) **Going Correction** +0.475s/f (Yiel) **6** Ran SP% **108.9**
Speed ratings: **113,112,111,110,109 108**
CSF £32.36 TOTE £14.20: £4.20, £1.10; EX 40.40 Trifecta £140.20.
**Owner** Godolphin **Bred** Merry Fox Stud Limited **Trained** Newmarket, Suffolk
■ Charlie Appleby's first Group 1 winner in England.

**FOCUS**
A reasonable Middle Park, but we probably didn't quite see the best of Ivawood and this isn't form to get too excited about. The form has been rated at face value, with Charming Thought imptoving for his first run in a Group race but Ivawood unable to step up on his previous efforts. They raced stands' side, but the rail provided no obvious advantage.

## 7240 DUBAI FILLIES' MILE (GROUP 1) 1m
**3:25** (3:27) (Class 1) 2-Y-O

**£133,268** (£50,525; £25,286; £12,596; £6,321; £3,172) **Stalls** High

Form RPR

**1** **Together Forever (IRE)**[5] 7141 2-9-0 0............ JosephO'Brien 1 111
(A P O'Brien, Ire) *wl in tch in midfield: shkn up 2f out: rdn to ld over 1f out: edgd sltly ins fnl f: styd on wl: rdn out* **7/1**

21 **2** ½ **Agnes Stewart (IRE)**[35] 6289 2-9-0 0............ BillyLee 5 110
(Edward Lynam, Ire) *leggy: athletic: t.k.h: hld up in tch in last pair: swtchd rt wl over 1f out: hdwy u.p over 1f out: chsd wnr ins fnl f: kpt on wl but a hld* **5/1**[3]

134 **3** nse **Winters Moon (IRE)**[49] 5876 2-9-0 **98**............(p) JamesDoyle 7 110
(Saeed bin Suroor) *chsd ldr for 2f: chsd ldrs tl shuffled bk towards rr 2f out: swtchd rt and rallied 1f out: wnt 3rd wl ins fnl f: styd on wl towards fin* **20/1**

121 **4** 1¾ **Marsh Hawk**[28] 6521 2-9-0 **101**............ RichardHughes 4 106
(Richard Hannon) *lw: led: rdn and edgeing rt over 1f out: sn hdd: barging match w rival and no ex 1f out: wknd ins fnl f* **10/3**[2]

221 **5** shd **Lucida (IRE)**[21] 6709 2-9-0 0............ KevinManning 3 106
(J S Bolger, Ire) *wl in tch in midfield: clsd to join ldrs 2f out: rdn over 1f out: barging match w rival and finding little 1f out: wknd ins fnl f* **6/5**[1]

31 **6** 3 **Forte**[10] 7011 2-9-0 0............ RichardKingscote 2 99
(Ralph Beckett) *w'like: taken down early: t.k.h: hld up in tch in last pair: pushed rt and effrt wl over 1f out: no hdwy: wl hld fnl f* **25/1**

211 **7** 3 **Good Place (USA)**[41] 6126 2-9-0 **99**............ RyanMoore 6 93
(Saeed bin Suroor) *swtg: chsd ldr 6f out: rdn and ev ch 2f out: losing pl whn short of room over 1f out: sn wknd* **16/1**

1m 41.01s (2.41) **Going Correction** +0.475s/f (Yiel) **7** Ran SP% **112.2**
Speed ratings: **106,105,105,103,103 100,97**
CSF £39.73 TOTE £5.80: £2.90, £2.50; EX 35.90 Trifecta £470.60.
**Owner** Mrs John Magnier & Michael Tabor & Derrick Smith **Bred** Vimal And Gillian Khosla **Trained** Cashel, Co Tipperary

**FOCUS**
A falsely run Fillies' Mile, with Richard Hughes dictating up front, resulted in a muddling affair. The runner-up could be used as a positive guide for the form and Joseph O'Brien afterwards claimed it rode like a good race, but it should be treated with some caution and overall wasn't an overwhelming renewal. However the form is rated on the positive side with Together Forever making rapid strides.

## 7241 DUBAI DEWHURST STKS (GROUP 1) (ENTIRE COLTS & FILLIES) 7f
**4:00** (4:00) (Class 1) 2-Y-O

**£255,762** (£96,965; £48,527; £24,173; £12,131; £6,088) **Stalls** High

Form RPR

1414 **1** **Belardo (IRE)**[34] 6326 2-9-1 **107**............[1] AndreaAtzeni 6 119
(Roger Varian) *hld up in tch in last pair: rdn 2f out: nt clr run over 1f out: swtchd rt and forced way through 1f out: qcknd to ld ins fnl f: r.o strly: readily* **10/1**

251 **2** 2 **Kodi Bear (IRE)**[83] 4645 2-9-1 **109**............ AdamKirby 5 114
(Clive Cox) *lw: w ldr tl led after 1f: rdn 2f out: kpt on u.p tl hdd and outpcd by wnr ins fnl f: kpt on for clr 2nd* **7/1**

**3** 2½ **Smuggler's Cove (IRE)**[7] 7089 2-9-1 0............ JosephO'Brien 2 108
(A P O'Brien, Ire) *unf: scope: chsd ldrs: rdn and ev ch 2f out: drvn over 1f out: unable qck whn pushed rt 1f out: wknd ins fnl f* **7/2**[2]

2111 **4** ½ **Estidhkaar (IRE)**[34] 6326 2-9-1 **114**............ PaulHanagan 7 107
(Richard Hannon) *wnt sharply rt and nudged along leaving stalls: in tch in rr: hdwy over 2f out: pressing ldrs and rdn 2f out: unable qck and btn 1f out: wknd ins fnl f* **11/8**[1]

2121 **5** 1 **Maftool (USA)**[22] 6686 2-9-1 **112**............ RichardHughes 1 104
(Saeed bin Suroor) *wl in tch in midfield: rdn over 2f out: outpcd wl over 1f out: hld and plugged on same pce fnl f* **11/2**[3]

2111 **6** 1¼ **Secret Brief (IRE)**[13] 6925 2-9-1 **103**............ JoeFanning 4 101
(Mark Johnston) *swtg: led for 1f: pressed ldr after: rdn and ev ch 2f out tl outpcd hmpd 1f out: wknd* **9/1**

1m 27.31s (1.91) **Going Correction** +0.475s/f (Yiel) **6** Ran SP% **111.3**
Speed ratings: **108,105,102,102,101 99**
CSF £72.22 TOTE £13.40: £4.90, £2.90; EX 71.60 Trifecta £310.90.
**Owner** Prince A A Faisal **Bred** Ballylinch Stud **Trained** Newmarket, Suffolk

**FOCUS**
Jim Bolger had won five of the last eight Dewhursts but wasn't represented this time, while Aidan O'Brien (who has won this three times, including last season) relied solely on a dark horse who failed to make the step up, and the favourite disappointed. So too did Maftool, so it's fair to say this year's race wasn't a great one, but Belardo still showed himself a really smart sort under these conditions. His improved form puts him at the top of the 2yo colts rankings now. They raced stands' side.

## 7242 VISION.AE CHALLENGE STKS (GROUP 2) 7f
**4:35** (4:38) (Class 1) 3-Y-O+

**£56,710** (£21,500; £10,760; £5,360; £2,690; £1,350) **Stalls** High

Form RPR

501 **1** **Here Comes When (IRE)**[44] 6054 4-9-7 **113**............ JimCrowley 13 118
(Andrew Balding) *lw: hld up in rr: clsd and nt clr run over 1f out: swtchd rt and hdwy 1f out: str run to ld wl ins fnl f: gng away at fin* **8/1**[3]

-066 **2** 1 **Cable Bay (IRE)**[21] 6710 3-9-1 **105**............ WilliamBuick 12 110
(Charles Hills) *swtg: chsd ldrs: rdn to ld jst over 1f out: kpt on wl u.p tl hdd and no ex wl ins fnl f* **14/1**

3121 **3** hd **Breton Rock (IRE)**[62] 5434 4-9-7 **113**............ MartinLane 6 115
(David Simcock) *swtg: in tch in midfield: rdn and effrt 3f out: hdwy and ev ch over 1f out: no ex wl ins fnl f* **7/2**[1]



The Form Book, Raceform Ltd, Newbury, RG14 5SJ

52 **4** ½ **Tawhid**[13] 6934 4-9-3 109 ........ RichardHughes 8 110
(Saeed bin Suroor) *hld up in tch in last quartet: swtchd rt 2f out: hdwy u.p ent fnl f: pressed ldrs fnl 150yds: one pce towards fin* **8/1**[1]

0031 **5** 1 **Al Thakhira**[13] 6922 3-8-12 107 ........ FrankieDettori 11 103
(Marco Botti) *lw: stdd s: hld up in tch in last quartet: clsd and nt clr run 2f out: swtchd lft and hdwy over 1f out: drvn and chal 1f out: no ex ins fnl f: wknd fnl 75yds* **7/2**[1]

2200 **6** 1¼ **Joyeuse**[36] 6254 3-8-12 105 ........ JamesDoyle 10 100
(Lady Cecil) *stdd s: hld up in rr: clsd and nt clr run 2f out: swtchd rt over 1f out: kpt on u.p fnl f: no threat to ldrs* **12/1**

0655 **7** ½ **Highland Colori (IRE)**[6] 7122 6-9-3 103 ........ OisinMurphy 1 102
(Andrew Balding) *led: rdn 2f out: drvn and hdd jst over 1f out: no ex and wknd fnl 100yds* **14/1**

1050 **8** 2 **Amarillo (IRE)**[14] 5-9-3 110 ........ DennisSchiergen 4 97
(P Schiergen, Germany) *lw: t.k.h: hld up in tch in midfield: rdn and unable qck over 1f out: wknd ins fnl f* **16/1**

1-02 **9** 1¼ **Cape Factor (IRE)**[47] 5965 3-8-12 98 ........ ChrisCatlin 9 90
(Rae Guest) *racd keenly: chsd ldrs: lost pl and bhd 2f out: no ch w ldrs but styd on again past btn horses fnl f* **25/1**

0030 **10** 2¼ **Brazos (IRE)**[13] 6921 3-9-1 108 ........ HarryBentley 5 87
(Clive Brittain) *in tch in midfield: unable qck u.p over 1f out: wknd fnl f* **25/1**

2261 **11** 1¼ **Muteela**[13] 6934 3-8-12 111 ........ PaulHanagan 14 81
(Mark Johnston) *chsd ldrs: rdn and unable qck over 1f out: wknd fnl f* **13/2**[2]

0/40 **12** ¾ **Mogadishio (FR)**[33] 6382 7-9-3 96 ........ FrederikTylicki 2 83
(S Smrczek, Germany) *chsd ldr tl 2f out: losing pl whn sltly short of room over 1f out: wknd fnl f* **40/1**

3050 **13** ½ **Professor**[21] 6710 4-9-3 107 ........ SeanLevey 3 82
(Richard Hannon) *short of room leaving stalls: steadily rcvrd: in tch in midfield and rdn 1/2-way: lost pl 2f out: bhd fnl f* **28/1**

1m 26.53s (1.13) **Going Correction** +0.475s/f (Yiel)
**WFA** 3 from 4yo+ 2lb **13** Ran SP% **120.5**
Speed ratings: **112,110,110,110,108 107,106,104,103,100 99,98,97**
CSF £110.83 TOTE £10.10: £2.90, £4.90, £1.80; EX 133.50 Trifecta £713.40.
**Owner** Mrs Fitri Hay **Bred** Old Carhue & Graeng Bloodstock **Trained** Kingsclere, Hants

■ Stewards' Enquiry : Martin Lane four-day ban; used whip above permitted level (31st Oct - 4th Nov).

**FOCUS**
Although it's a shame Thawaany didn't turn up, this was still an extremely competitive contest. They went a fair enough pace, with those racing down the centre holding every chance, and threw up a tight finish. A smart effort from Here Comes When, with Cable Bay's best run since the Dewhurst.

## 7243 DARLEY STKS (GROUP 3) 1m 1f
**5:10** (5:13) (Class 1) 3-Y-O+
**£36,861** (£13,975; £6,994; £3,484; £1,748; £877) **Stalls** High

Form RPR

11-0 **1** **Berkshire (IRE)**[188] 1436 3-8-13 110 ........ JimCrowley 7 117+
(Paul Cole) *lw: stdd s: t.k.h: hld up in rr: swtchd rt and hdwy wl over 1f out: nt clr run over 1f out tl 1f out: str run ins fnl f to ld towards fin* **20/1**

2212 **2** ½ **Mutakayyef**[120] 3375 3-8-13 106 ........ PaulHanagan 12 116
(William Haggas) *travelled strly: chsd ldr tl led 3f out: rdn 2f out: sustained duel w rival after: kpt on wl tl hdd and no ex towards fin* **11/2**[2]

2121 **3** nk **Air Pilot**[27] 6548 5-9-3 105 ........ OisinMurphy 1 115
(Ralph Beckett) *in tch in midfield: rdn and hdwy 3f out: chal 2f out and sustained duel w rival after: clr w ldr 1f out: kpt on wl tl no ex towards fin* **11/4**[1]

3131 **4** 2¼ **Clon Brulee (IRE)**[37] 6233 5-9-3 107 ........ JamesDoyle 13 110
(Saeed bin Suroor) *lw: chsd ldrs: rdn over 2f out: 3rd and unable qck over 1f out: kpt on same pce fnl f* **15/2**

4403 **5** 1¼ **Educate**[6] 7120 5-9-3 109 ........ JoeFanning 6 110+
(Ismail Mohammed) *hld up in tch in last quartet: effrt over 2f out: hmpd wl over 1f out: rallied and styd on wl ins fnl f: no threat to ldrs* **6/1**[3]

0034 **6** nk **Zurigha (IRE)**[48] 5927 4-9-0 105 ........ RichardHughes 5 104
(Richard Hannon) *hld up in tch in last quartet: rdn 3f out: hdwy u.p wl over 1f out: no imp 1f out: wknd ins fnl f* **33/1**

3422 **7** 2¼ **Fencing (USA)**[125] 3252 5-9-3 110 ........ WilliamBuick 11 102
(John Gosden) *swtchd lft sn after s: in tch in midfield: rdn and effrt ent fnl 2f: no ex over 1f out: wknd ins fnl f* **12/1**

0130 **8** 2¾ **Ocean Tempest**[21] 6710 5-9-3 116 ........ AdamKirby 8 97
(John Ryan) *led: hdd and rdn 3f out: struggling u.p 2f out: wknd over 1f out* **10/1**

-021 **9** 2 **Code Of Honor**[28] 6519 4-9-3 108 ........ FrederikTylicki 4 92
(Saeed bin Suroor) *in tch in midfield: rdn and unable qck jst over 2f out: wknd over 1f out* **14/1**

6500 **10** 2 **Berling (IRE)**[18] 7-9-3 105 ........ AndreaAtzeni 10 88
(Jessica Long, Sweden) *chsd ldrs tl 4f out: rdn and lost pl over 3f out: bhd over 1f out* **50/1**

6015 **11** nse **Audacia (IRE)**[48] 5927 4-9-0 102 ........ FrankieDettori 2 85
(Hugo Palmer) *t.k.h: chsd ldrs: rdn and struggling over 3f out: lost pl and bhd wl over 1f out* **33/1**

421 **12** ½ **Grandeur (IRE)**[23] 6655 5-9-3 113 ........(p) RyanMoore 3 87
(Jeremy Noseda) *in tch in midfield: rdn over 2f out: swtchd rt wl over 1f out: no prog and sn btn: wknd 1f out* **17/2**

3011 **13** ½ **Tinghir (IRE)**[13] 6943 4-9-3 100 ........(b) GeorgeBaker 9 86
(David Lanigan) *stdd s: hld up in rr: short-lived effrt 2f out: sn btn* **20/1**

1m 53.4s (1.70) **Going Correction** +0.475s/f (Yiel)
**WFA** 3 from 4yo+ 4lb **13** Ran SP% **119.4**
Speed ratings: **111,110,110,108,107 106,104,102,100,98 98,98,97**
CSF £120.89 TOTE £22.40: £6.20, £2.00, £1.70; EX 148.60 Trifecta £653.10.
**Owner** H R H Sultan Ahmad Shah **Bred** Newsells Park Stud **Trained** Whatcombe, Oxon

**FOCUS**
A quality, competitive Group 3 and a good renewal, rated around the fourth.

T/Jkpt: Not won. T/Plt: £1,546.00 to a £1 stake. Pool: £160,828.94 - 75.94 winning tickets T/Qpdt: £89.50 to a £1 stake. Pool: £9,534.21 - 78.75 winning tickets SP

# 6931 REDCAR (L-H)
Friday, October 17

**OFFICIAL GOING: Good to soft changing to soft after race 1 (2:30)**
Wind: Breezy half behind Weather: Fine and sunny but breezy

## 7244 IJF 50TH ANNIVERSARY BRITISH STALLION STUDS EBF MAIDEN STKS 1m
**1:55** (1:56) (Class 5) 2-Y-O
**£3,408** (£1,006; £503) **Stalls** Centre

Form RPR

02 **1** **Puissant (IRE)**[16] 6859 2-9-5 0 ........ MartinHarley 13 90+
(Marco Botti) *led gng wl: shkn up appr fnl f: sn clr: eased clsng stages* **3/1**[2]

**2** 7 **New Strategy (IRE)** 2-9-2 0 ........ MatthewLawson(3) 12 75
(Saeed bin Suroor) *dwlt: hdwy 4f out: chsd wnr over 2f out: no imp* **16/1**

42 **3** 2¼ **Subcontinent (IRE)**[16] 6875 2-9-0 0 ........ KevinStott(5) 6 70
(Charlie Appleby) *chsd ldrs: 3rd over 1f out: kpt on one pce* **11/2**[3]

3 **4** 5 **Tawaasheeh (IRE)**[22] 6683 2-9-5 0 ........[1] TomEaves 2 59
(Roger Varian) *chsd ldrs: drvn 3f out: fdd appr fnl f* **4/5**[1]

4 **5** 2 **Mystic Miraaj**[13] 6931 2-9-5 0 ........ DavidAllan 4 54
(Tim Easterby) *s.i.s: in rr: sme hdwy over 1f out: nvr a factor* **20/1**

0 **6** 3¼ **Dont Tell Chris (FR)**[11] 6976 2-9-5 0 ........ PhillipMakin 7 47
(John Quinn) *chsd wnr: wknd over 1f out* **100/1**

**7** 1½ **Racing Spirit** 2-9-5 0 ........ IanBrennan 8 44+
(John Quinn) *dwlt: in rr: kpt on fnl 2f: nvr nr ldrs* **100/1**

5 **8** 1½ **Doctors Papers**[17] 6831 2-9-5 0 ........ PJMcDonald 1 41
(David Brown) *chsd ldrs on outer: drvn over 3f out: wknd over 1f out* **100/1**

433 **9** 2 **Drumkilbo**[81] 4740 2-9-5 76 ........(v[1]) RobertHavlin 3 36
(Lady Cecil) *chsd ldrs: lost pl over 1f out* **10/1**

05 **10** nk **Stoneboat Bill**[16] 6860 2-9-2 0 ........ NeilFarley(3) 10 35
(Declan Carroll) *dwlt: in rr: sme hdwy over 3f out: wknd 2f out* **66/1**

**11** 3½ **Hookergate Grammar** 2-9-5 0 ........ DavidNolan 5 28
(Keith Reveley) *s.i.s: sn bhd: sme hdwy over 2f out: nvr on terms* **100/1**

00 **12** hd **Mustique Dancer (IRE)**[41] 6148 2-9-0 0 ........ TonyHamilton 11 22
(Richard Fahey) *mid-div: drvn over 3f out: sn lost pl* **100/1**

00 **13** 39 **Chatty Man (IRE)**[20] 6757 2-9-5 0 ........(b[1]) AndrewMullen 9
(David C Griffiths) *in rr: lost pl over 4f out: sn wl bhd: tailed rt off* **100/1**

1m 40.09s (3.49) **Going Correction** +0.25s/f (Good) **13** Ran SP% **123.1**
Speed ratings (Par 95): **92,85,82,77,75 72,71,69,67,67 63,63,24**
CSF £49.59 TOTE £3.50: £1.50, £5.90, £1.60; EX 45.00 Trifecta £289.40.
**Owner** Puissant Stable **Bred** Elletelle Syndicate **Trained** Newmarket, Suffolk

**FOCUS**
Nearly an inch of rain fell on the track during the week and the ground was changed to soft after the opening maiden. Although the market leader disappointed, this was a reasonable maiden run at a fair gallop and the field finished well strung out. The winner is a very useful prospect and this was a big step forward.

## 7245 IJF JOHN OAKSEY MEMORIAL CLAIMING STKS 7f
**2:30** (2:31) (Class 6) 2-Y-O
**£2,045** (£603; £302) **Stalls** Centre

Form RPR

4605 **1** **Ventura Shadow**[19] 6783 2-9-0 70 ........ TonyHamilton 7 73
(Richard Fahey) *trckd ldrs: smooth hdwy and cl up 3f out: effrt to ld jst over 1f out: sn rdn and clr ins fnl f: kpt on wl* **7/2**[3]

1633 **2** 3¼ **Summer Stroll (IRE)**[20] 6759 2-9-0 66 ........(p) SamJames 12 65
(David O'Meara) *hld up: hdwy 3f out: chal 2f out: led briefly 1 1/2f out: sn rdn and hdd: drvn and one pce fnl f* **2/1**[1]

4430 **3** 3½ **Lord Of Words (IRE)**[56] 5645 2-8-11 55 ........ DaleSwift 6 53
(Brian Ellison) *in tch: pushed along 3f out: rdn over 1f out: styd on to chse ldng pair ins fnl f: no imp* **10/1**

0P0 **4** 1½ **Double K**[30] 6447 2-8-9 0 ........ PJMcDonald 8 47
(Paul Midgley) *towards rr: hdwy over 2f out: rdn wl over 1f out: kpt on fnl f: nrst fin* **50/1**

4300 **5** hd **Fazenda's Girl**[27] 6563 2-7-9 51 ........(b) JoeDoyle(5) 2 38
(Michael Easterby) *led: rdn 2f out: hung bdly lft and hdd 1 1/2f out: sn drvn and wknd* **16/1**

5520 **6** 1¾ **Snoway**[23] 6669 2-8-0 50 ........ PatrickMathers 3 34
(Tony Coyle) *racd wd: in tch: rdn along and sme hdwy over 2f out: drvn wl over 1f out: n.d* **14/1**

00 **7** 2¾ **Lilac Vale (IRE)**[24] 6623 2-9-0 0 ........(b[1]) DavidAllan 4 41
(Tim Easterby) *midfield: pushed along and hdwy 3f out: rdn to chse ldrs over 2f out: sn no imp* **40/1**

05 **8** 2 **Ty Ty**[60] 5493 2-8-7 0 ........(p) IanBrennan 9 29
(Michael Easterby) *towards rr: sme hdwy over 2f out: sn rdn and edgd lft wl over 1f out: n.d* **10/3**[2]

0 **9** 1 **Scottish Isles**[30] 6447 2-8-12 0 ........ DanielleMooney(7) 10 38
(Michael Easterby) *prom: rdn along 1/2-way: sn wknd* **10/1**

00 **10** 5 **Perfect Slipper**[31] 6435 2-8-6 0 ........ AdamBeschizza 11 13
(Noel Quinlan) *prom: rdn along 1/2-way: sn wknd* **20/1**

5043 **11** 1 **Tuebrook**[60] 5507 2-8-5 50 ........ DuranFentiman 1 9
(Michael Easterby) *chsd ldr: rdn along 3f out: sn wknd* **33/1**

00 **12** hd **Crown Green**[16] 6860 2-8-3 0 ........ NeilFarley(3) 5 10
(Karen Tutty) *a outpcd in rr* **100/1**

1m 27.3s (2.80) **Going Correction** +0.25s/f (Good) **12** Ran SP% **114.4**
Speed ratings (Par 93): **94,90,86,84,84 82,79,76,75,70 68,68**
CSF £9.92 TOTE £5.80: £1.70, £1.10, £3.30; EX 9.50 Trifecta £28.30.Ventura Shadow was subject to a friendly of £12,000.
**Owner** Middleham Park Racing LXXXVIII **Bred** Northmore Stud **Trained** Musley Bank, N Yorks

**FOCUS**
An ordinary claimer in which the gallop was sound and the two market leaders came to the fore in the last quarter mile. Straightforward form.

## 7246 MARKET CROSS JEWELLERS BRITISH STALLION STUDS EBF MAIDEN STKS 6f
**3:00** (3:00) (Class 5) 2-Y-O
**£3,234** (£962; £481; £240) **Stalls** Centre

Form RPR

44 **1** **Properus (IRE)**[28] 6509 2-9-5 0 ........ DavidNolan 5 79
(Kevin Ryan) *w ldr: led over 2f out: drvn out* **1/2**[1]

**2** 1¾ **Sir Domino (FR)** 2-9-5 0 ........ IanBrennan 4 74+
(Kevin Ryan) *chsd ldrs: cl 2nd over 1f out: styd on same pce* **10/1**

00 **3** 6 **Billy Bond**[24] 6623 2-9-5 0 ........ TonyHamilton 3 56
(Richard Fahey) *in rr: hdwy over 2f out: kpt on to take modest 3rd last 100yds* **33/1**

54 **4** 3 ½ **George Bailey (IRE)**[24] 6623 2-9-5 0 ........................ DuranFentiman 9 45
(Bryan Smart) *led: hdd over 2f out: wknd fnl 100yds* **9/1**[3]
5 **5** 1 **Spiritual Journey (IRE)**[24] 6623 2-9-0 0 ..................... PJMcDonald 7 37
(Ann Duffield) *mid-div: effrt over 2f out: fdd over 1f out* **12/1**
**6** nk **Makin Trouble (IRE)** 2-9-5 0 ............................... PhillipMakin 6 41
(John Quinn) *chsd ldrs: wknd over 1f out* **13/2**[2]
0 **7** ½ **Bracka Legend (IRE)**[30] 6453 2-9-5 0 ........................ AndrewMullen 8 40
(David Barron) *s.s: sn chsng ldrs: wknd over 1f out* **20/1**
0 **8** 1 ¾ **Agreeable Lady (IRE)**[20] 6757 2-9-0 0 ........................ DavidAllan 2 29
(Tim Easterby) *chsd ldrs on outside: lost pl over 1f out* **66/1**
0 **9** 2 **Lady Cordie**[60] 5493 2-8-11 0 .............................. GaryBartley(3) 11 23
(Jim Goldie) *in rr: hung lft over 1f out: nvr on terms* **66/1**
00 **10** 3 **The Name's Bond**[13] 6935 2-9-5 0 ............................ TomEaves 12 19
(Keith Reveley) *s.i.s: a in rr: hung lft thrght* **40/1**
**11** hd **Elmer J** 2-9-2 0 ......................................... NeilFarley(3) 10 19
(Declan Carroll) *s.i.s: in rr: reminders after 1f: sn bhd* **33/1**

1m 14.03s (2.23) **Going Correction** +0.25s/f (Good) **11** Ran SP% **122.9**
Speed ratings (Par 95): **95,92,84,80,78 78,77,75,72,68 68**
CSF £6.54 TOTE £1.80: £1.02, £4.90, £5.50; EX 9.10 Trifecta £229.10.
**Owner** Michael Beaumont **Bred** Marie & Mossy Fahy **Trained** Hambleton, N Yorks

**FOCUS**
An uncompetitive maiden run at a reasonable gallop and one in which the first two pulled clear in the closing stages. The winner is rated to a similar level as his previous run.

## 7247 SAM HALL MEMORIAL H'CAP — 1m 6f 19y
**3:30** (3:31) (Class 5) (0-75,74) 3-Y-O+ **£3,234** (£962; £481; £240) **Stalls** Low

Form RPR
2135 **1** **Crakehall Lad (IRE)**[17] 6832 3-8-10 65 .......................... BenCurtis 6 72
(Alan Swinbank) *sn trcking ldr: cl up 1/2-way: slt ld 3f out: rdn 2f out: drvn over 1f out: kpt on gamely u.p towards fin* **4/1**[2]
0112 **2** ¾ **Scrafton**[17] 6832 3-8-12 67 ................................. TonyHamilton 8 73
(James Bethell) *trckd ldrs: hdwy 4f out: effrt 3f out and sn cl up: rdn to chal over 1f out: ev ch tl drvn ins fnl f and no ex last 50yds* **5/2**[1]
5302 **3** ¾ **Choisan (IRE)**[29] 6480 5-9-11 71 ........................(tp) DavidAllan 2 76
(Tim Easterby) *trckd ldng pair: hdwy 3f out: rdn to chal 2f out: drvn and ev ch ent fnl f tl no ex last 50yds* **11/2**
01/3 **4** ½ **Fantasy King**[26] 732 8-9-9 74 ........................... MeganCarberry(5) 4 79
(James Moffatt) *trckd ldrs: hdwy on inner over 3f out: effrt and nt clr run 2f out and again over 1f out: rdn and n.m.r ins fnl f: nvr able to chal* **22/1**
2310 **5** nse **Eton Rambler (USA)**[19] 6787 4-10-0 74 ......................... TedDurcan 9 78
(George Baker) *stdd s and hld up in rr: hdwy 3f out: chsd ldrs whn n.m.r and swtchd rt to outer over 1f out: sn rdn and edgd lft: drvn and no imp fnl f* **5/1**[3]
2300 **6** 6 **Categorical**[126] 2739 11-9-10 70 .............................. DavidNolan 7 66
(Keith Reveley) *hld up: hdwy 3f out: rdn to chse ldrs wl over 1f out: wknd ent fnl f* **20/1**
0600 **7** nk **Jan De Heem**[24] 6628 4-8-12 58 ........................(p) PJMcDonald 1 53
(Tina Jackson) *set stdy pce: qcknd 6f out: rdn along and hdd 3f out: cl up tl drvn and wknd wl over 1f out* **28/1**
4402 **8** 10 **Madrasa (IRE)**[38] 6216 6-9-7 67 ........................(t[1]) TomEaves 3 48
(Keith Reveley) *hld up: a in rr* **10/1**

3m 10.19s (5.49) **Going Correction** +0.40s/f (Good)
**WFA** 3 from 4yo+ 9lb **8** Ran SP% **102.3**
Speed ratings (Par 103): **100,99,99,98,98 95,95,89**
CSF £11.35 CT £37.22 TOTE £5.00: £1.30, £1.10, £2.70; EX 10.00 Trifecta £64.50.
**Owner** G Brogan **Bred** Albert Conneally **Trained** Melsonby, N Yorks
■ The Ducking Stool was withdrawn. Price at time of withdrawal 9/1. Rule 4 applies to all bets - deduction 10p in the pound.

**FOCUS**
A couple of in-form types in a fair handicap but a steady gallop means this bare form isn't reliable. The first five, who finished in a heap, finished clear of the rest. The third helps with the standard.

## 7248 JOIN THE RACING UK CLUB H'CAP (DIV I) — 7f
**4:05** (4:07) (Class 5) (0-70,70) 3-Y-O+ **£3,234** (£962; £481; £240) **Stalls** Centre

Form RPR
5656 **1** **Order Of Service**[19] 6795 4-8-13 65 ......................(t) GaryBartley(3) 2 77
(Jim Goldie) *in rr: drvn and hdwy on wd outside over 2f out: upsides 1f out: kpt on to ld last 100yds* **10/1**
3004 **2** ½ **Lilac Lace (IRE)**[21] 6716 4-8-13 69 .................... RachelRichardson(7) 9 80
(Tim Easterby) *led: hdd last 100yds: edgd lft and no ex* **4/1**[2]
0115 **3** ½ **Strike A Light**[50] 5861 3-9-5 70 .............................. DavidAllan 6 79
(Rae Guest) *trckd ldrs: upsides over 1f out: styd on same pce last 50yds* **7/2**[1]
1422 **4** 5 **Manatee Bay**[10] 7023 4-9-4 67 ........................(v) AdrianNicholls 3 67
(David Nicholls) *fly-jmpd s: in rr: hdwy over 3f out: chsng ldrs over 2f out: eased whn wl hld clsng stages* **5/1**[3]
6063 **5** 3 **Magical Mischief**[24] 6638 4-8-7 56 oh1 ........................ DuranFentiman 1 45
(Chris Fairhurst) *chsd ldrs: one pce fnl 2f* **33/1**
560 **6** hd **Shushu Sugartown (IRE)**[30] 6463 3-8-12 63 .................... TonyHamilton 10 50
(Ian Williams) *chsd ldrs: wknd over 1f out* **25/1**
4005 **7** nk **Sakhalin Star (IRE)**[20] 6766 3-8-12 66 ...............(e[1]) JacobButterfield(3) 8 53
(Richard Guest) *wnt lft s: mid-div: drvn over 2f out: nvr a threat* **10/1**
0001 **8** 3 **The Blue Banana (IRE)**[27] 6543 5-8-6 60 ................(b) JoeDoyle(5) 16 40
(Edwin Tuer) *in rr: drvn and hung lft fnl 2f: nvr a factor* **11/1**
0-00 **9** 8 **Kerbaaj (USA)**[24] 6625 4-9-4 67 ................................ DaleSwift 15 26
(Ruth Carr) *mid-div: lost pl 2f out* **14/1**
06 **10** 3 **Opt Out**[17] 6836 4-8-13 62 ..............................(p) PJMcDonald 14 13
(Alistair Whillans) *s.i.s: r isolted towards stands' side: bhd fnl 2f* **14/1**
5340 **11** 1 **Niceonemyson**[23] 6674 5-8-10 59 ............................(b) TomEaves 7 8
(Christopher Wilson) *bmpd s: mid-div: effrt 3f out: wknd 2f out* **20/1**
0020 **12** 3 ¾ **Majestic Dream (IRE)**[46] 5987 6-9-5 68 ....................(v) IanBrennan 4 7
(Michael Easterby) *in rr: bhd fnl 2f* **33/1**
4065 **13** 5 **Crossley**[3] 7188 5-8-7 56 oh7 ........................(p) PatrickMathers 12
(Geoffrey Oldroyd) *chsd ldrs: sn drvn along: lost pl over 3f out* **25/1**
0/6- **14** 66 **Lord Avonbrook**[538] 1844 4-8-12 64 ........................ NeilFarley(3) 5
(Andrew Crook) *in rr: bhd and eased 2f out: sn tailed rt off: virtually p.u: lame* **100/1**

1m 25.69s (1.19) **Going Correction** +0.25s/f (Good)
**WFA** 3 from 4yo+ 2lb **14** Ran SP% **118.1**
Speed ratings (Par 103): **103,102,101,96,92 92,92,88,79,76 75,70,65,**
CSF £45.17 CT £177.34 TOTE £13.30: £3.40, £3.30, £1.10; EX 90.00 Trifecta £501.10.
**Owner** Whitestonecliffe Racing Partnership **Bred** Cheveley Park Stud Ltd **Trained** Uplawmoor, E Renfrews

**FOCUS**
A modest handicap in which the gallop was sound and the first three deserve credit for pulling clear. The time was quicker than division II.

## 7249 JOIN THE RACING UK CLUB H'CAP (DIV II) — 7f
**4:40** (4:41) (Class 5) (0-70,69) 3-Y-O+ **£3,234** (£962; £481; £240) **Stalls** Centre

Form RPR
141 **1** **Polar Forest**[9] 7044 4-9-1 66 .........................(e) JacobButterfield(3) 1 78
(Richard Guest) *cl up: led over 3f out: rdn over 1f out: jnd ent fnl f: sn drvn and kpt on gamely towards fin* **13/2**[3]
4102 **2** ½ **Funding Deficit (IRE)**[3] 7180 4-8-10 61 ...................... GaryBartley(3) 6 71
(Jim Goldie) *trckd ldrs on outer: hdwy 3f out: effrt over 1f out: rdn to chal ent fnl f: sn disputing ld and ev ch tl drvn edgd rt and no ex last 75yds* **7/2**[1]
0045 **3** 2 ½ **Al Muheer (IRE)**[6] 7098 9-9-6 68 ........................(v) PhillipMakin 3 71
(Michael Herrington) *hld up: hdwy 3f out: chsd ldrs 2f out: rdn to chse ldng pair appr fnl f: sn drvn: edgd rt and kpt on same pce* **8/1**
1140 **4** 3 ¾ **Broctune Papa Gio**[16] 6865 7-9-2 69 ............................ JoeDoyle(5) 14 62
(Keith Reveley) *in tch: hdwy on outer over 2f out: rdn to chse ldrs over 1f out: drvn and no imp ins fnl f* **6/1**[2]
213 **5** 1 ¼ **Smart Alec (IRE)**[51] 5816 3-9-0 64 .......................... DuranFentiman 12 53
(Alan Swinbank) *trckd ldrs: hdwy wl over 2f out: rdn wl over 1f out: sn drvn and one pce* **7/1**
4303 **6** 1 ¼ **King Pin**[53] 5761 9-8-12 60 ..............................(p) DavidAllan 9 47
(Tracy Waggott) *in rr: pushed along and hdwy on outer 2f out: sn rdn and kpt on fnl f: nvr nr ldrs* **8/1**
4410 **7** 1 **Munaawib**[242] 646 6-9-0 67 .......................(tp) AlistairRawlinson(5) 11 51
(Deborah Sanderson) *led: hdd over 3f out: cl up and sn pushed along: rdn 2f out and grad wknd* **40/1**
U466 **8** nk **Red Inca**[13] 6937 6-9-5 67 ..................................... TomEaves 8 51
(Brian Ellison) *in rr: sme hdwy wl over 2f out: sn rdn and n.d* **8/1**
0003 **9** 1 **Mitchum**[23] 6670 5-8-0 55 oh5 ......................(v) RachelRichardson(7) 13 36
(Ron Barr) *chsd ldrs: rdn along wl over 2f out: grad wknd* **25/1**
0410 **10** 3 ¼ **Secret City (IRE)**[8] 7061 8-9-2 64 ............................(b) DaleSwift 7 37
(Robin Bastiman) *chsd ldrs: rdn along wl over 2f out: sn wknd* **20/1**
150- **11** 3 ½ **Omanome (IRE)**[390] 6663 3-9-3 67 ............................... DavidNolan 10 29
(David O'Meara) *t.k.h early: chsd ldrs to 1/2-way: sn lost pl and bhd* **20/1**
-006 **12** hd **Woodland Girl**[16] 6863 3-9-1 65 ............................ TonyHamilton 15 27
(Richard Fahey) *towards rr: effrt and sme hdwy on wd outside 3f out: sn rdn and outpcd* **14/1**

1m 26.57s (2.07) **Going Correction** +0.25s/f (Good)
**WFA** 3 from 4yo+ 2lb **12** Ran SP% **118.2**
Speed ratings (Par 103): **98,97,94,90,88 87,86,85,84,81 77,76**
CSF £27.85 CT £164.66 TOTE £7.20: £2.50, £1.60, £3.20; EX 41.20 Trifecta £538.90.
**Owner** Maze Rattan Limited **Bred** Worksop Manor Stud **Trained** Ingmanthorpe, W Yorks

**FOCUS**
The second, and slower, division of an ordinary handicap. The gallop was reasonable and the first three pulled clear. The form makes sense.

## 7250 BET WITH YOUR RACING UK APP MAIDEN STKS — 6f
**5:15** (5:16) (Class 5) 3-Y-O+ **£3,234** (£962; £481; £240) **Stalls** Centre

Form RPR
2233 **1** **Another Royal**[23] 6674 3-9-0 60 ............................[1] PhillipMakin 3 55+
(Tim Easterby) *trckd ldrs: smooth hdwy to ld 1f out: drvn out: hld on towards fin* **5/2**[2]
22 **2** nk **Advance (FR)**[16] 6862 3-9-5 0 ............................... PJMcDonald 9 59
(Ruth Carr) *in rr: effrt over 2f out: hung lft: chsng ldrs over 1f out: 2nd last 100yds: no ex clsng stages* **4/1**[3]
4054 **3** ¾ **Vale Mentor (IRE)**[16] 6862 3-9-5 48 ............................. DavidAllan 5 57
(Tim Easterby) *led: hdd 2f out: styd on towards fin* **18/1**
0032 **4** 3 **Asha**[45] 5997 3-8-11 65 ................................ JacobButterfield(3) 4 42
(David C Griffiths) *chsd ldrs: sn drvn along: one pce fnl 2f* **7/1**
**5** 6 **Tijan (IRE)** 3-9-2 0 .................................. MatthewLawson(3) 1 28
(Saeed bin Suroor) *s.s: hdwy to trck ldrs over 3f out: led 2f out: hdd 1f out: wknd qckly* **9/4**[1]
0340 **6** 5 **Mossy Marie (IRE)**[18] 6819 3-8-11 46 ...................... NeilFarley(3) 8 7
(Eric Alston) *chsd ldrs: outpcd over 2f out: sn wknd* **50/1**
0252 **7** 9 **Clabare**[17] 6834 3-9-5 52 ......................................... TomEaves 6
(Ian Semple) *mid-div: t.k.h: lost pl over 2f out* **17/2**
-550 **8** 9 **Only For You**[42] 6120 4-9-1 45 ...........................(tp) DaleSwift 12
(Alan Brown) *chsd ldrs: lost pl 3f out: sn bhd* **25/1**
/00- **9** 15 **Misu Mac**[394] 6518 4-8-10 45 ......................... MeganCarberry(5) 11
(Neville Bycroft) *chsd ldrs: lost pl over 2f out: bhd whn eased fnl f: t.o* **66/1**
06-5 **10** 28 **Lady Calantha**[50] 5857 4-8-10 45 ............................ JoeDoyle(5) 2
(Alan Berry) *trckd ldrs: reminders over 3f out: lost pl over 3f out: sn bhd: eased: virtually p.u: tailed rt off* **100/1**

1m 14.35s (2.55) **Going Correction** +0.25s/f (Good)
**WFA** 3 from 4yo 1lb **10** Ran SP% **115.9**
Speed ratings (Par 103): **93,92,91,87,79 72,60,48,28,**
CSF £12.69 TOTE £3.20: £1.60, £1.70, £4.70; EX 12.70 Trifecta £249.10.
**Owner** C H Stevens **Bred** Habton Farms **Trained** Great Habton, N Yorks

**FOCUS**
A weak maiden run at a reasonable gallop but in a slow time. The winner was below his recent modest handicap form.

## 7251 RACING UK ANYWHERE AVAILABLE NOW LADIES' H'CAP (FOR LADY AMATEUR RIDERS) — 1m 2f
**5:45** (5:46) (Class 6) (0-65,65) 3-Y-O+ **£1,975** (£607; £303) **Stalls** Low

Form RPR
042 **1** **Solid Justice (IRE)**[11] 6980 3-10-1 64 .......................... MissCWalton 5 74
(Jason Ward) *hld up towards rr: stdy hdwy on inner 3f out: trckd ldrs 2f out: nt clr run and swtchd rt over 1f out: rdn to chal ent fnl f: drvn and edgd lft last 100yds: led nr line* **5/1**[2]
503 **2** shd **Tom Mann (IRE)**[31] 6429 3-9-13 62 ............................ MissADeniel 3 71
(David Barron) *in tch: hdwy on inner 3f out: led wl over 1f out: sn rdn: drvn ins fnl f: jnd last 100yds: sn hmpd and bmpd: hdd nr line* **8/1**
5056 **3** 1 ¾ **Angus Glens**[32] 6395 4-9-10 61 ........................(p) MissGFriswell(7) 7 67
(David Dennis) *prom: led after 2f: pushed clr 1/2-way: rdn along 3f out: hdd wl over 1f out: drvn and hld whn n.m.r and hmpd wl ins fnl f* **22/1**
0/2 **4** nse **Engai (GER)**[12] 6627 8-9-10 61 ........................ MissPBridgwater(7) 10 67
(David Bridgwater) *in tch: hdwy on wd outside 3f out: rdn over 2f out: kpt on u.p fnl f: nrst fin* **16/1**
3631 **5** 3 ½ **Exclusive Waters (IRE)**[16] 6865 4-10-6 64 ...................... MrsCBartley 1 63
(Tracy Waggott) *dwlt and in rr: swtchd rt and rdn 2f out: styd on wl fnl f: nrst fin* **7/2**[1]


The Form Book, Raceform Ltd, Newbury, RG14 5SJ

5404 6 *nk* **Dolphin Rock**[24] 6626 7-9-13 62..........................(p) MissLWilson(5) 15 61
(Brian Ellison) *led 2f: chsd l;eader: rdn along wl over 2f out: wknd over 1f out* 7/1
00 7 *3 1/2* **Hydrant**[16] 6870 8-10-7 65.......................... MissSBrotherton 14 57
(Richard Guest) *chsd ldng pair: rdn along 3f out: grad wknd fnl 2f* 13/2[3]
1/00 8 *3/4* **Artisan**[23] 6670 6-9-13 62.......................... MissJWalton(5) 11 53
(Brian Ellison) *nvr bttr than midfield* 33/1
1-65 9 *4 1/2* **Haymarket**[19] 6795 5-10-2 63.......................... MissJRRichards(3) 2 45
(R Mike Smith) *chsd ldrs: rdn along 3f out: wknd fnl 2f* 16/1
12 10 *3/4* **Barleycorn Lady (IRE)**[157] 2235 3-9-9 63.................. MissETodd(5) 13 44
(Mark Walford) *a towards rr* 10/1
4051 11 *4 1/2* **Tamayuz Magic (IRE)**[24] 6627 3-9-12 64.....(b) MissJoannaMason(3) 12 36
(Michael Easterby) *in tch: rdn along 3f out: sn wknd* 12/1
4310 12 *3* **Flag Of Glory**[24] 6636 7-10-0 63.......................... MissMEdden(5) 4 29
(Peter Hiatt) *midfield: sme hdwy on wd outside over 3f out: rdn along wl over 2f out: sn outpcd* 16/1
4 13 *7* **Jordaura**[134] 2913 8-9-7 58.......................... MissGCochrane(7) 9 11
(Alan Berry) *s.i.s: a bhd* 33/1

2m 10.58s (3.48) **Going Correction** +0.40s/f (Good)
**WFA** 3 from 4yo+ 5lb **13** Ran SP% **120.5**
Speed ratings (Par 101): **102,101,100,100,97 97,94,94,90,89 86,83,78**
CSF £44.33 CT £811.21 TOTE £7.30: £2.00, £4.40, £12.50; EX 73.30 Trifecta £759.50.
**Owner** Roger Naylor & Nicholas Carr **Bred** John O'Connor **Trained** Middleham, N Yorks
■ Stewards' Enquiry : Miss C Walton caution; careless riding

**FOCUS**
A couple of unexposed sorts finished 1-2 in an ordinary handicap . A modest gallop picked up turning for home.
T/Plt: £20.60 to a £1 stake. Pool: £51,003.02 - 1,806.29 winning tickets T/Qpdt: £4.40 to a £1 stake. Pool: £3,148.30 - 517.80 winning tickets WG

## 7223 WOLVERHAMPTON (A.W) (L-H)
### Friday, October 17

**OFFICIAL GOING: Tapeta: standard**
Wind: Light behind Weather: Overcast turning to rain after race 6

## 7252 HILLS EXPORT ALL AROUND THE WORLD APPRENTICE H'CAP (TAPETA) (DIV I) 5f 216y
**5:50** (5:51) (Class 6) (0-65,65) 3-Y-O+ **£2,264** (£673; £336; £168) **Stalls** Low

Form RPR
1054 1 **Backstage Gossip**[66] 5290 3-9-3 64.......................... KieranShoemark(3) 1 74
(Hughie Morrison) *chsd ldr tl led over 1f out: styd on wl* 6/1[2]
5103 2 *1 1/4* **Logans Lad (IRE)**[17] 6843 4-9-8 65..........................(vt) EoinWalsh 5 72
(Daniel Mark Loughnane) *hld up: hdwy over 1f out: nt clr run and swtchd rt ins fnl f: r.o to go 2nd towards fin: nt rch wnr* 85/40[1]
0003 3 *hd* **Settle For Red (IRE)**[16] 6857 4-8-11 57..........................(b) DavidParkes(3) 3 62
(Jeremy Gask) *hld up: hdwy over 1f out: r.o* 6/1[2]
3504 4 *1/2* **Dark Lane**[20] 6764 8-9-0 62.......................... HollieDoyle(5) 7 65
(David Evans) *a.p: rdn over 1f out: styd on* 8/1[3]
3424 5 *1 1/2* **Divine Call**[15] 6889 7-9-4 61..........................(v) NoelGarbutt 2 60
(Milton Bradley) *chsd ldrs: rdn over 1f out: no ex wl ins fnl f* 8/1[3]
3002 6 *1 1/2* **Red Cape (FR)**[17] 6843 11-9-5 65..........................(b) GemmaTutty(3) 6 59
(Ruth Carr) *sn prom: rdn over 1f out: edgd lft and no ex fnl f* 9/1
/5-5 7 *1 1/2* **Sadiigah**[20] 6767 4-8-11 54.......................... ShelleyBirkett 4 43
(Julia Feilden) *chsd ldrs: rdn over 1f out: wknd ins fnl f* 16/1
5500 8 *nk* **Invigilator**[17] 6843 6-9-4 64..........................(t) AdamMcLean(3) 12 52
(Derek Shaw) *broke wl: stdd and lost pl after 1f: n.d after* 18/1
-000 9 *shd* **Gauchita**[32] 6409 3-8-4 51 oh1.......................... JordanVaughan(3) 10 39
(K R Burke) *led: rdn: hung lft and hdd over 1f out: wknd ins fnl f* 33/1
1116 10 *shd* **Spider Lily**[24] 6631 3-8-11 60.......................... ChrisMeehan(5) 11 47
(Peter Makin) *s.s: rdn over 2f out: nvr on terms* 18/1
3040 11 *13* **Roomie**[88] 4495 3-8-2 53 oh4 ow2..........................[1] RyanHolmes(7) 9
(Barry Leavy) *mid-div: lost pl over 4f out: bhd fr 1/2-way* 50/1

1m 15.2s (0.70) **Going Correction** +0.025s/f (Slow)
**WFA** 3 from 4yo+ 1lb **11** Ran SP% **114.1**
Speed ratings (Par 101): **96,94,94,93,91 89,87,87,86,86 69**
CSF £18.41 CT £79.60 TOTE £10.60: £2.90, £1.30, £2.90; EX 26.20 Trifecta £126.50.
**Owner** Runs In The Family **Bred** Mrs A Plummer **Trained** East Ilsley, Berks

**FOCUS**
The going was standard. The first division of this apprentice handicap was run at a sound pace. The winner rates a personal best.

## 7253 HILLS EXPORT ALL AROUND THE WORLD APPRENTICE H'CAP (TAPETA) (DIV II) 5f 216y
**6:20** (6:21) (Class 6) (0-65,65) 3-Y-O+ **£2,264** (£673; £336; £168) **Stalls** Low

Form RPR
25-0 1 **Bush Beauty (IRE)**[62] 5427 3-9-7 65.......................... MarcMonaghan 3 73
(Philip McBride) *prom: n.m.r and lost pl wl over 3f out: hmpd over 2f out: hdwy over 1f out: rdn to ld wl ins fnl f: r.o* 10/1
4056 2 *1/2* **Bondi Beach Babe**[16] 6866 4-8-8 51.......................... JordanNason 8 57
(James Turner) *sn pushed along in rr: hdwy u.p over 1f out: r.o* 16/1
0005 3 *3/4* **Silver Mirage**[54] 5729 3-9-7 65.......................... LouisSteward 7 69
(Michael Bell) *chsd ldrs: rdn over 2f out: styd on* 7/2[2]
1005 4 *nk* **Methaaly (IRE)**[6] 7111 11-8-11 57..........................(b) AnnaHesketh(3) 12 60
(Michael Mullineaux) *a.p: led over 1f out: sn rdn and edgd lft: hdd and unable qck wl ins fnl f* 22/1
5054 5 *1 1/4* **Chester Deelyte (IRE)**[44] 6023 6-8-3 51 oh6............(v) RobHornby(5) 10 50
(Lisa Williamson) *prom: outpcd over 2f out: styd on ins fnl f* 50/1
0002 6 *hd* **Tango Sky (IRE)**[18] 6821 5-9-5 65.......................... DavidParkes(3) 4 63
(James Unett) *hld up: rdn over 2f out: styd on ins fnl f: nt rch ldrs* 9/2[3]
2141 7 *shd* **Captain Ryan**[18] 6816 3-9-0 63.......................... ChrisMeehan(5) 2 61
(Peter Makin) *plld hrd and prom: rdn over 1f out: styng on same pce whn n.m.r ins fnl f* 8/1
0004 8 *1 3/4* **Queen Hermione (IRE)**[21] 6720 6-8-5 51 oh3.......(vt) AdamMcLean(3) 9 43
(Derek Shaw) *dwlt: sn pushed along in rr: styd on ins fnl f: nvr nrr* 22/1
5020 9 *1 3/4* **Incomparable**[8] 7057 9-9-2 59..........................(p) MatthewHopkins 5 45
(Scott Dixon) *led: rdn and hdd over 1f out: wknd ins fnl f* 25/1
-616 10 *8* **Indastar**[21] 6720 4-9-2 59.......................... NathanAlison 1 20
(Michael Herrington) *plld hrd: w ldr: ev ch 2f out: sn rdn: wknd fnl f* 2/1[1]

1m 14.83s (0.33) **Going Correction** +0.025s/f (Slow)
**WFA** 3 from 4yo+ 1lb **10** Ran SP% **114.3**
Speed ratings (Par 101): **98,97,96,95,94 94,93,91,89,78**
CSF £142.41 CT £671.39 TOTE £13.30: £2.50, £6.30, £1.10; EX 145.60 Trifecta £1497.60 Part won..
**Owner** P J McBride **Bred** Lynn Lodge Stud **Trained** Newmarket, Suffolk

**FOCUS**
Plenty of pace for division two of this apprentice handicap, and the time was quicker than the first. The winner has the potential to do a bit better.

## 7254 EBF STALLIONS ULTRATEK - THE ULTIMATE NUMBER PLATE MEDIAN AUCTION MAIDEN STKS (TAPETA) 5f 216y
**6:50** (6:51) (Class 5) 2-Y-O **£2,911** (£866; £432; £216) **Stalls** Low

Form RPR
2332 1 **Clergyman**[15] 6887 2-9-5 73.......................... FergusSweeney 6 76
(Martyn Meade) *led 1f: chsd ldr tl led again 2f out: edgd rt ins fnl f: rdn out* 3/1[2]
433 2 *1 1/4* **Anonymous John (IRE)**[52] 5799 2-9-2 73.................. DeclanBates(3) 4 72
(David Evans) *plld hrd and prom: rdn over 1f out: chsd wnr ins fnl f.* 7/1[3]
3322 3 *4 1/2* **Red Perdita (IRE)**[33] 6361 2-9-0 75.......................... PatCosgrave 5 54
(George Baker) *chsd ldrs: rdn over 1f out: styd on same pce* 7/1[3]
2 4 *3/4* **Scent Of Summer (USA)**[8] 7062 2-9-0 0.......................... FrannyNorton 2 52
(William Haggas) *led 5f out: hdd 2f out: wknd ins fnl f* 8/11[1]
0 5 *3* **Miss Minuty**[46] 5973 2-9-0 0.......................... LukeMorris 1 43
(Sir Mark Prescott Bt) *chsd ldrs: shkn up over 1f out: wknd ins fnl f* 40/1
0 6 *2 1/4* **Mystify Me**[23] 6660 2-9-0 0.......................... MarcMonaghan(5) 9 41
(Ed McMahon) *sn pushed along in rr: nvr on terms* 12/1
00 7 *1* **Citisonsmith (IRE)**[13] 6935 2-9-5 0..........................(b) RaulDaSilva 10 38
(Paul Green) *prom: rdn 1/2-way: wknd over 2f out* 100/1
8 *9* **Jacksonfire** 2-9-5 0.......................... RobertHavlin 7 11
(Michael Mullineaux) *s.i.s: outpcd* 50/1
0P 9 *1/2* **Beatabout (IRE)**[13] 6931 2-9-2 0.......................... JoeyHaynes(3) 3 9
(Paul Green) *hld up: rdn 1/2-way: wknd over 2f out: hung lft over 1f out* 100/1

1m 14.71s (0.21) **Going Correction** +0.025s/f (Slow) **9** Ran SP% **122.0**
Speed ratings (Par 95): **99,97,91,90,86 83,82,70,69**
CSF £25.45 TOTE £3.90: £1.60, £2.50, £1.60; EX 32.50 Trifecta £70.50.
**Owner** Ladyswood Stud **Bred** Ladyswood Stud **Trained** Newmarket, Suffolk

**FOCUS**
The pace was fair for this uncompetitive maiden. The first pair were clear but the form is not rated positively.

## 7255 HILLS NUMBER PLATES GROUP NURSERY H'CAP (BOBIS RACE) (TAPETA) 5f 20y
**7:20** (7:21) (Class 4) (0-85,85) 2-Y-O **£5,175** (£1,540; £769; £384) **Stalls** Low

Form RPR
4443 1 **Stinky Socks (IRE)**[11] 6989 2-7-11 64.......................... CamHardie(3) 8 67
(Charles Hills) *chsd ldr tl led over 1f out: rdn out* 9/1
4221 2 *1 1/2* **Field Game**[23] 6659 2-9-7 85..........................(t) RobertHavlin 1 83
(Hughie Morrison) *a.p: rdn to chse wnr and hung lft fnl f: styd on* 3/1[1]
133 3 *hd* **Expensive Date**[48] 5906 2-9-7 85.......................... LukeMorris 6 82
(Paul Cole) *chsd ldrs: rdn 1/2-way: styd on u.p* 7/1[3]
0310 4 *1 1/2* **Flashy Diva**[34] 6312 2-9-0 78.......................... FergusSweeney 9 69
(Henry Candy) *hld up: pushed along over 3f out: r.o ins fnl f: nvr nrr* 14/1
1200 5 *nk* **Shamrock Sheila (IRE)**[28] 6513 2-8-2 73.......... JosephineGordon(7) 10 63
(J S Moore) *sn pushed along in rr: r.o ins fnl f: nrst fin* 33/1
100 6 *1/2* **Effusive**[27] 6530 2-9-7 85.......................... GrahamGibbons 2 74
(William Haggas) *bmpd s: sn pushed along in rr: hdwy over 1f out: styd on same pce ins fnl f* 4/1[2]
6623 7 *3/4* **Honest Bob'S**[30] 6447 2-9-2 83.......................... JoeyHaynes(3) 4 69
(Brian Ellison) *s.i.s: hdwy over 1f out: no ex fnl f* 11/1
521 8 *5* **Equally Fast**[41] 6158 2-9-3 81.......................... DougieCostello 5 49
(William Muir) *wnt lft and bmpd s: sn pushed along: hdwy over 3f out: rdn 1/2-way: wknd fnl f* 3/1[1]
4500 9 *nse* **Paddy Again (IRE)**[9] 7038 2-8-5 74..........................(p) RyanWhile(5) 7 42
(Bill Turner) *led: rdn and hdd over 1f out: wknd ins fnl f* 50/1

1m 2.03s (0.13) **Going Correction** +0.025s/f (Slow) **9** Ran SP% **112.4**
Speed ratings (Par 97): **99,96,96,93,93 92,91,83,83**
CSF £35.02 CT £201.90 TOTE £10.10: £4.30, £1.10, £2.70; EX 42.40 Trifecta £80.10 Part won..
**Owner** Plantation Stud **Bred** Highpark Bloodstock Ltd **Trained** Lambourn, Berks

**FOCUS**
A competitive sprint nursery run at a sound pace. Straightforward form.

## 7256 METATEK ALUMINIUM NUMBER PLATE SOLUTION CLASSIFIED STKS (TAPETA) 1m 1f 103y
**7:50** (7:53) (Class 6) 3-Y-O+ **£2,264** (£673; £336; £168) **Stalls** Low

Form RPR
0005 1 **I Am Not Here (IRE)**[47] 5949 3-8-5 55.......................... GaryMahon(7) 11 59
(Timothy Jarvis) *hld up: swtchd rt and hdwy over 1f out: r.o to ld post* 8/1
2000 2 *nk* **Innoko (FR)**[32] 6410 4-9-2 55..........................[1] WilliamTwiston-Davies 5 58
(Tony Carroll) *mid-div: hdwy over 1f out: rdn to ld ins fnl f: hdd post* 25/1
0415 3 *1/2* **Hidden Asset**[27] 6771 4-9-2 53.......................... AndrewMullen 10 57
(Michael Appleby) *hld up: hdwy over 2f out: led 1f out: sn rdn and hdd: r.o* 4/1[2]
6145 4 *3/4* **Why Not Now**[32] 6396 3-8-12 55.......................... DavidProbert 6 55
(Roger Charlton) *a.p: rdn over 1f out: edgd lft ins fnl f: r.o* 7/1[3]
4054 5 *2 1/4* **Dream And Hope**[2] 7197 3-8-9 51.......................... DannyBrock(3) 7 51
(Philip McBride) *mid-div: hdwy 6f out: rdn to ld over 1f out: sn edgd lft and hdd: styd on same pce* 10/3[1]
466 6 *1/2* **Rocky Hill Ridge**[96] 1452 3-8-9 45..........................(p) BillyCray(3) 9 50?
(Alan McCabe) *led: rdn over 2f out: hdd over 1f out: no ex ins fnl f* 100/1
400 7 *shd* **Dutch Lady Roseane**[52] 5796 3-8-12 45.......................... AdamBeschizza 8 49?
(James Unett) *chsd ldrs: rdn over 2f out: nt clr run over 1f out: hung lft and no ex ins fnl f* 50/1
0062 8 *1 3/4* **My Renaissance**[20] 6771 4-8-11 53.......................... JackDuern(5) 4 46
(Ben Case) *chsd ldrs: rdn over 1f out: wknd ins fnl f* 14/1
4401 9 *1 1/2* **Stoneham**[13] 6946 3-8-12 52.......................... CharlesBishop 3 43
(Mick Channon) *prom: nt clr run over 2f out: sn rdn: wknd ins fnl f* 11/1
003- 10 *3/4* **Namely (IRE)**[363] 7371 3-8-12 55.......................... LukeMorris 13 41
(Sir Mark Prescott Bt) *chsd ldr: rdn and ev ch over 1f out: wknd ins fnl f* 10/3[1]
0560 11 *6* **Exton**[17] 6837 5-9-2 45.......................... RobertWinston 1 28
(Shaun Harris) *s.s: hld up: rdn over 2f out: wknd over 1f out* 33/1
5000 12 *23* **Legal Advisor**[18] 6825 3-8-9 47..........................(v[1]) JoeyHaynes(3) 2
(Philip Kirby) *in rr: pushed along over 5f out: wknd over 2f out* 66/1
-060 13 *53* **Smirfys Blackcat (IRE)**[25] 6597 5-9-2 45.......................... HarryBentley 12
(Michael Mullineaux) *a in rr: bhd fnl 4f* 100/1

2m 1.79s (0.99) **Going Correction** +0.025s/f (Slow)
**WFA** 3 from 4yo+ 4lb **13** Ran SP% **117.0**
Speed ratings (Par 101): **96,95,95,94,92 92,92,90,89,88 83,62,15**
CSF £196.75 TOTE £7.70: £2.60, £6.40, £1.50; EX 219.80 Trifecta £1274.90 Part won..
**Owner** Jarvis Associates **Bred** John Reilly **Trained** Twyford, Bucks

**FOCUS**
A moderate classified stakes run at a steady pace, and low-grade, muddling form.

## 7257 HILLS NUMBERPLATES LTD UK INNOVATOR NURSERY H'CAP (TAPETA) (DIV I) 7f 32y

**8:20** (8:21) (Class 6) (0-65,65) 2-Y-O **£2,264** (£673; £336; £168) **Stalls** High

Form RPR
2330 1 **Wink Oliver**[23] 6663 2-9-1 59....(p) GrahamGibbons 4 62
(Kristin Stubbs) *a.p: rdn to ld over 1f out: edgd lft: styd on* **33/1**
0266 2 ½ **Ickymasho**[31] 6422 2-9-3 64.... DannyBrock(3) 10 66+
(Jonathan Portman) *sn outpcd: nt clr run over 2f out: hdwy over 1f out: rdn to chse wnr ins fnl f: r.o* **14/1**
5060 3 2 **Call Me Crockett (IRE)**[17] 6830 2-8-11 55....(e[1]) FrannyNorton 2 52
(Richard Guest) *racd keenly: trckd ldr 6f out tl over 3f out: remained handy: rdn over 1f out: styd on same pce ins fnl f* **14/1**
3334 4 ¾ **Siren's Cove**[13] 6944 2-9-0 65.... KieranShoemark(7) 1 61
(James Tate) *chsd ldrs: hmpd and lost pl over 2f out: rallied over 1f out: rdn and edgd rt ins fnl f: styd on same pce* **10/1**
0041 5 ½ **Gavarnie Encore**[23] 6663 2-9-0 58.... DavidProbert 12 52
(Michael Blanshard) *hld up: hdwy over 2f out: r.o: nt rch ldrs* **6/1[2]**
005 6 1¾ **Cloak And Degas (IRE)**[15] 6887 2-9-4 62.... LukeMorris 8 52
(Scott Dixon) *led: rdn and hdd over 1f out: no ex ins fnl f* **40/1**
4445 7 1¾ **Burauq**[6] 7112 2-9-7 65....(p) MartinDwyer 7 50
(William Muir) *hld up: hdwy over 1f out: sn rdn: hung lft and no ex fnl f* **15/2**
0500 8 3¼ **Splash Of Verve (IRE)**[24] 6642 2-9-2 60.... FrederikTylicki 5 37
(Philip Kirby) *chsd ldrs: rdn over 2f out: wknd ins fnl f* **20/1**
0024 9 nse **Tumut (IRE)**[10] 6996 2-9-7 65.... CharlesBishop 11 42
(Mick Channon) *hld up: rdn over 2f out: n.d* **12/1**
665 10 3½ **Finton Friend (IRE)**[44] 6038 2-9-4 65.... CamHardie(3) 6 34
(Charles Hills) *sn pushed along in rr: wknd over 2f out* **2/1[1]**
6404 11 1 **Piccadillo**[10] 7014 2-8-13 57....(b) RobertWinston 9 23
(Daniel Kubler) *prom: hung rt 6f out: rdn over 2f out: wknd wl over 1f out* **7/1[3]**

1m 29.52s (0.72) **Going Correction** +0.025s/f (Slow) 11 Ran SP% **112.1**
Speed ratings (Par 93): **96,95,93,92,91 89,87,84,83,79 78**
CSF £412.37 CT £6741.73 TOTE £15.50: £5.40, £3.20, £5.00; EX 201.30 Trifecta £874.10 Part won..
**Owner** P & L Partners **Bred** Norman Court Stud **Trained** Norton, N Yorks

**FOCUS**
Plenty of unexposed types in this nursery which was run at a fair pace.

## 7258 HILLS NUMBERPLATES LTD UK INNOVATOR NURSERY H'CAP (TAPETA) (DIV II) 7f 32y

**8:50** (8:51) (Class 6) (0-65,65) 2-Y-O **£2,264** (£673; £336; £168) **Stalls** High

Form RPR
653 1 **Three Gracez**[14] 6903 2-8-13 57.... SamJames 6 63
(Noel Quinlan) *a.p: r.o to ld wl ins fnl f: sn clr* **16/1**
5215 2 2¼ **Magic Mac**[25] 6610 2-9-0 58....(p) RobertHavlin 10 58
(Hughie Morrison) *chsd ldr 6f out: rdn to ld 1f out: hdd and unable qck wl ins fnl f* **16/1**
660 3 ½ **Zubaidah**[43] 6066 2-9-6 64.... PatCosgrave 1 63
(George Baker) *hld up: hdwy over 2f out: rdn over 1f out: styd on* **25/1**
6022 4 1½ **My Mo (FR)**[15] 6888 2-8-11 55.... KierenFallon 9 50
(David Dennis) *sn led: rdn and hdd 1f out: no ex* **9/2[1]**
1000 5 2 **Just Marion (IRE)**[7] 7075 2-9-1 62.... DeclanBates(3) 3 52
(David Evans) *mid-div: sn pushed along: hdwy over 1f out: nt trble ldrs* **33/1**
2310 6 3½ **Little**[15] 6884 2-9-4 65.... CamHardie(3) 12 47
(Jamie Osborne) *chsd ldrs: rdn over 2f out: hung lft over 1f out: wknd fnl f* **9/1**
040 7 nk **Overlord**[49] 5874 2-9-2 60....(b[1]) LukeMorris 7 41
(Sir Mark Prescott Bt) *hld up: rdn over 2f out: n.d* **15/2[3]**
5451 8 1½ **Mazoula (IRE)**[32] 6412 2-9-4 62.... RobertWinston 5 39
(Hugo Palmer) *hld up: rdn over 1f out: nvr on terms* **6/1[2]**
4322 9 ½ **Itsindebag**[27] 6563 2-8-5 56....(p) JosephineGordon(7) 11 32
(J S Moore) *s.i.s: rdn over 3f out: a in rr* **12/1**
5546 10 9 **Crikey (IRE)**[24] 6629 2-9-1 64.... KevinStott(5) 8 18
(Kevin Ryan) *mid-div: hdwy u.p over 2f out: wknd over 1f out* **17/2**
0652 11 6 **Bling Ring (USA)**[10] 6996 2-9-7 65.... HarryBentley 2 8
(Charles Hills) *sn pushed along in rr: rdn and wknd over 2f out: eased over 1f out* **8/1**
1044 12 ½ **Pumaflor (IRE)**[10] 7005 2-9-7 65.... JasonHart 4 3
(Richard Guest) *chsd ldrs: rdn over 2f out: wknd over 1f out* **9/2[1]**

1m 28.76s (-0.04) **Going Correction** +0.025s/f (Slow) 12 Ran SP% **120.3**
Speed ratings (Par 93): **101,98,97,96,93 89,89,87,87,76 70,69**
CSF £252.45 CT £6323.18 TOTE £23.10: £6.80, £4.80, £6.80; EX 262.90 Trifecta £796.90.
**Owner** Neil Hormann **Bred** Barton Stud **Trained** Newmarket, Suffolk

**FOCUS**
An open if modest nursery run at an honest pace. The runner-up fits in with the form.

## 7259 RAISE YOUR PROFILE WITH ULTRATEK H'CAP (TAPETA) 7f 32y

**9:20** (9:21) (Class 6) (0-60,65) 3-Y-O+ **£2,264** (£673; £336; £168) **Stalls** High

Form RPR
0611 1 **Diamonds A Dancing**[9] 7036 4-9-8 62 6ex....(be) FrannyNorton 10 74
(Brian Gubby) *a.p: chsd ldr wl over 2f out: rdn over 1f out: led wl ins fnl f: r.o* **5/2[2]**
0066 2 shd **On The Hoof**[23] 6670 5-9-4 58....(b) GrahamGibbons 5 69
(Michael Easterby) *chsd ldrs: rdn to ld over 1f out: hdd wl ins fnl f: r.o* **11/2**
0-66 3 1¼ **Humour (IRE)**[122] 3343 3-9-2 58.... FrederikTylicki 9 65+
(Roger Varian) *hld up: hung lft and r.o ins fnl f: wnt 3rd nr fin: nt rch ldrs* **3/1[3]**
0-01 4 2 **Dazeen**[7] 7078 7-9-11 65 6ex.... RobertWinston 2 68
(Michael Herrington) *hld up: hdwy over 2f out: rdn over 1f out: no ex ins fnl f* **2/1[1]**
0300 5 3 **Black Truffle (FR)**[23] 6666 4-8-9 56....(v) CharlotteJenner(7) 11 51
(Mark Usher) *hld up: hdwy over 2f out: no ex fnl f* **40/1**
5000 6 2¾ **Indus Valley (IRE)**[21] 6715 7-9-5 59....(p) DavidProbert 3 47
(Des Donovan) *hld up: hung lft fr over 1f out: n.d* **40/1**
6030 7 3 **Heinrich (USA)**[16] 6858 3-9-3 59....(t) LiamKeniry 1 38
(Sylvester Kirk) *hld up: rdn over 2f out: nvr on terms* **33/1**
-000 8 ½ **Tarquin (IRE)**[34] 6342 5-9-3 57.... DougieCostello 6 36
(Kristin Stubbs) *sn chsng ldr: led 4f out: rdn and hdd over 1f out: wknd ins fnl f* **25/1**
4063 9 6 **Applejack Lad**[27] 6567 3-9-0 59....(t) RyanPowell(3) 8 21
(John Ryan) *chsd ldrs: rdn 1/2-way: wknd over 2f out* **16/1**
5323 10 5 **Laughing Rock (IRE)**[207] 1080 4-9-2 56.... AndrewMullen 4 6
(Michael Appleby) *led: hdd 4f out: rdn whn hmpd and wknd 2f out* **10/1**

1m 29.42s (0.62) **Going Correction** +0.025s/f (Slow)
**WFA** 3 from 4yo+ 2lb 10 Ran SP% **128.9**
Speed ratings (Par 101): **97,96,95,93,89 86,83,82,75,70**
CSF £18.44 CT £45.96 TOTE £4.10: £1.70, £2.10, £1.70; EX 20.30 Trifecta £73.10.
**Owner** Brian Gubby **Bred** Lady Caffyn-Parsons **Trained** Bagshot, Surrey

**FOCUS**
A competitive handicap for the grade run at a sound pace. The fourth is rated slightly positively.
T/Plt: £3,703.10 to a £1 stake. Pool: £88,012.64 - 17.35 winning tickets T/Qpdt: £352.40 to a £1 stake. Pool: £10,716.90 - 22.50 winning tickets CR

# 7026 MAISONS-LAFFITTE (R-H)

Friday, October 17

**OFFICIAL GOING: Turf: heavy**

## 7268a PRIX DE SAINT-CYR (LISTED RACE) (3YO FILLIES) (STRAIGHT) (TURF) 7f (S)

**2:15** (12:00) 3-Y-0 **£22,916** (£9,166; £6,875; £4,583; £2,291)

RPR
1 **Mireille (IRE)**[42] 3-8-9 0....(b) AntoineHamelin 1 99
(Mme Pia Brandt, France) **16/1**
2 ¾ **Penny Drops**[13] 6929 3-8-10 0 ow1.... ChristopheSoumillon 8 98
(William Haggas) *trckd ldr: swtchd ins over 1 1/2f out: r.o u.p fnl f but a hld by wnr* **21/10[1]**
3 hd **Divina Comedia (FR)**[21] 6734 3-8-9 0.... ThierryThulliez 2 96
(N Clement, France) **26/5[3]**
4 shd **Raphinae**[14] 3-8-13 0.... MickaelBarzalona 3 100
(H-A Pantall, France) **98/10**
5 2 **This Time (FR)**[40] 6182 3-8-9 0.... FabriceVeron 6 91
(H-A Pantall, France) **17/5[2]**
6 hd **Sea Front (FR)**[41] 3-8-9 0.... MaximeGuyon 5 90
(E Libaud, France) **158/10**
7 nk **Kalsa (IRE)**[212] 3-8-9 0.... UmbertoRispoli 10 89
(Robert Collet, France) **56/1**
8 ½ **Caointiorn (FR)**[32] 3-8-9 0.... TheoBachelot 7 88
(S Wattel, France) **109/10**
9 1½ **Galaxe (FR)**[21] 6734 3-8-9 0.... StephanePasquier 9 84
(Rod Collet, France) **30/1**
10 8 **Celebre (FR)**[24] 3-8-9 0....(p) FranckBlondel 4 62
(F Rossi, France) **61/10**

1m 29.05s (1.05) 10 Ran SP% **119.7**
WIN (incl. 1 euro stake): 17.00. PLACES: 3.60, 1.70, 1.90. DF: 23.50. SF: 71.70.
**Owner** Ballygallon Stud Ltd **Bred** Ballygallon Stud Ltd **Trained** France

# 7069 SAINT-CLOUD (L-H)

Wednesday, October 15

**OFFICIAL GOING: Turf: soft**

## 7269a PRIX CARDMANIA (CLAIMER) (3YO COLTS & GELDINGS) (TURF) 1m

**12:30** (12:30) 3-Y-0 **£9,583** (£3,833; £2,875; £1,916; £958)

RPR
1 **Sahand (IRE)**[8] 3-9-0 0....(b) AntoineHamelin 12 91
(J Hirschberger, Germany) **4/1[2]**
2 2½ **Zamuja**[19] 3-9-0 0.... CristianDemuro 1 85
(G Botti, France) **19/5[1]**
3 3 **Cockney Bob**[20] 3-8-9 0.... FabriceVeron 9 73
(J Parize, France) **11/2**
4 1¼ **Mata Utu (IRE)** 3-8-9 0.... MaximeGuyon 11 70
(C Escuder, France) **10/1**
5 nse **Pissarro (GER)** 3-9-3 0.... FlavienPrat 6 78
(R Rohne, Germany) **67/10**
6 nk **Weeken (FR)**[19] 3-8-9 0.... ThierryThulliez 7 69
(Y Gourraud, France) **194/10**
7 1½ **Saon Risk (FR)**[27] 3-8-9 0....(b) RaphaelMarchelli 2 66
(T Castanheira, France) **188/10**
8 2½ **Race For Fame (IRE)**[25] 3-8-8 0.... NicolasLarenaudie(6) 3 65
(M Boutin, France) **30/1**
9 hd **The Artista (FR)**[4] 3-9-3 0.... RonanThomas 10 68
(J Phelippon, France) **5/1[3]**
10 2 **We'll Shake Hands (FR)**[41] 6057 3-9-3 0.... StephanePasquier 4 63
(K R Burke) *prom on inner: 4th and scrubbed along to hold pl 2 1/2f out: rdn and nt qckn over 1 1/2f out: eased whn btn fnl f* **134/10**
11 3 **Tocantins (IRE)**[8] 3-8-9 0.... Christophe-PatriceLemaire 5 48
(M Boutin, France) **39/1**
12 15 **Libido (FR)**[134] 3-8-2 0.... ValentinGambart(7) 8 14
(C Boutin, France) **57/1**

1m 43.31s (-4.19) 12 Ran SP% **119.3**
WIN (incl. 1 euro stake): 5.00. PLACES: 1.90, 1.50, 2.00. DF: 8.00. SF: 19.10.
**Owner** Darius Racing **Bred** Peter Henley **Trained** Germany

## 7270a PRIX MAJINSKAYA (CLAIMER) (3YO FILLIES) (TURF) 1m 2f 110y

**2:40** (2:40) 3-Y-0 **£9,583** (£3,833; £2,875; £1,916; £958)

RPR
1 **La Pyle (FR)**[80] 3-8-9 0....(b) GregoryBenoist 1 80
(Mme Pia Brandt, France) **13/5[1]**
2 2½ **Tout Va Bien (IRE)**[19] 3-8-6 0.... MllePaulineDominois(3) 8 75
(Yves de Nicolay, France) **6/1[3]**
3 1¼ **Stella D'Oroux (FR)**[11] 3-9-6 0.... EddyHardouin 6 84
(S Smrczek, Germany) **115/10**
4 2 **Baraka (GER)**[26] 3-9-0 0.... AStarke 13 74
(P Schiergen, Germany) **84/10**
5 ¾ **Solojorie (FR)**[26] 3-8-9 0....(b) FabriceVeron 7 67
(J Parize, France) **187/10**
6 ¾ **Dime Dancer (IRE)**[27] 3-9-4 0.... FrauTamaraHofer 12 75
(Werner Glanz, Germany) **83/10**


The Form Book, Raceform Ltd, Newbury, RG14 5SJ

7 1 1/4 **Like Me (IRE)**[19] 3-8-7 0.......................... Georges-AntoineAnselin(6) 11 67
(N Clement, France) **31/10**[2]

8 2 **Trigger Flash (FR)**[26] 3-8-4 0.......................................... LauraGrosso(5) 2 59
(N Caullery, France) **61/1**

9 2 **Selma Louise (FR)**[31] 3-8-9 0................................ MickaelBarzalona 14 56
(W Mongil, Germany) **159/10**

10 3 **Noctuelle (FR)**[103] 3-8-9 0.........................................(b) CesarPasserat 10 50
(N Caullery, France) **64/1**

11 3 1/2 **Zarnia (FR)**[46] 3-8-9 0.......................................... CristianDemuro 9 43
(Henk Grewe, Germany) **226/10**

12 1 1/4 **Zamarrila** 3-8-5 0........................................ JeremieCatineau(8) 5 44
(C Laffon-Parias, France) **60/1**

13 3 1/2 **Hortensia Diamond (FR)**[56] 5589 3-8-9 0..............(b[1]) AntoineHamelin 3 34
(K R Burke) *t.k.h: restrained bhd ldng gp: scrubbed along an no imp 2f out: sn lost pl: eased whn btn fnl f* **26/1**

2m 22.43s (2.83) **13** Ran SP% **119.6**
WIN (incl. 1 euro stake): 3.60. PLACES: 1.80, 2.00, 3.00. DF: 11.70. SF: 18.40.
**Owner** Gerard Augustin-Normand **Bred** Franklin Finance S A **Trained** France

# 6918 ASCOT (R-H)
## Saturday, October 18

**OFFICIAL GOING: Heavy (soft in places; stands' side 6.3, centre 6.3, far side 6.4; round course 5.0)**
Wind: Moderate, half against Weather: Overcast becoming bright

## 7271 QIPCO BRITISH CHAMPIONS LONG DISTANCE CUP (GROUP 2) 2m
**1:45** (1:46) (Class 1) 3-Y-O+

**£178,636** (£67,725; £33,894; £16,884; £8,473; £4,252) **Stalls** Low

Form RPR

1 **Forgotten Rules (IRE)**[78] 4880 4-9-7 0............................ PatSmullen 7 117+
(D K Weld, Ire) *hld up in last pair: prog on outer 3f out: hung rt 2f out causing carnage: drvn to ld 1f out: styd on wl* **3/1**[2]

055 2 1 3/4 **Biographer**[36] 6288 5-9-7 103..........................(b) GeorgeBaker 2 114
(David Lanigan) *hld up and sn in last: prog jst over 2f out: bmpd whn trying to cl over 1f out: styd on fnl f to take 2nd last strides* **25/1**

1401 3 nk **Pallasator**[23] 6687 5-9-7 110.................................. AndreaAtzeni 5 114
(Sir Mark Prescott Bt) *reluctant to go to s: last early: rapid prog to go 2nd after 3f: rdn to ld over 2f out: hdd and one pce 1f out: lost 2nd last strides* **8/1**[3]

224 4 2 **Whiplash Willie**[13] 6972 6-9-7 108..........................(p) DavidProbert 6 112
(Andrew Balding) *in tch: lost pl 4f: effrt whn nowhere to go over 2f out: swtchd to outer and styd on fr over 1f out: unable to threaten* **10/1**

1411 5 2 1/2 **Big Orange**[15] 6894 3-8-11 111................................ TomQueally 9 108
(Michael Bell) *led: urged along 4f out: hdd and steadily outpcd fr over 2f out* **14/1**

1-12 6 1/2 **Flying Officer (USA)**[23] 6687 4-9-7 109.......................... WilliamBuick 1 108
(John Gosden) *trckd ldrs: edgd lft wl over 2f out: rdn whn bmpd several times fr wl over 1f out: no ch after* **10/1**

1112 7 5 **Leading Light (IRE)**[34] 6374 4-9-7 118..................(p) JosephO'Brien 8 106
(A P O'Brien, Ire) *trckd ldrs but trapped out wd: rdn over 3f out: nudged by rival wl over 2f out: struggling whn bdly hmpd wl over 1f out: no ch after* **2/1**[1]

5452 8 3 3/4 **Marzocco (USA)**[15] 6894 3-8-11 110.......................(b) RobertHavlin 4 97
(John Gosden) *trckd ldr 3f: styd cl up: rdn 3f out: struggling whn bdly hmpd wl over 1f out: no ch after* **25/1**

2021 9 33 **Estimate (IRE)**[36] 6288 5-9-4 112................................ RyanMoore 3 55
(Sir Michael Stoute) *in tch: rdn and dropped to last pair over 4f out: sn btn: eased and t.o* **8/1**[3]

3m 36.77s (7.77) **Going Correction** +0.85s/f (Soft)
**WFA** 3 from 4yo+ 10lb **9** Ran SP% **113.1**
Speed ratings: **114,113,112,111,110 110,107,106,89**
CSF £70.99 CT £538.76 TOTE £4.30: £1.70, £6.20, £2.60; EX 73.40 Trifecta £539.50.
**Owner** Moyglare Stud Farm **Bred** Moyglare Stud Farm Ltd **Trained** Curragh, Co Kildare
■ Stewards' Enquiry : William Buick caution: careless riding
Pat Smullen three-day ban: careless riding (Nov 1,3,4)

**FOCUS**
Although the day was missing some notable stars of 2014, namely Kingman, Australia and The Grey Gatsby, every race for British Champions Day was full of quality. Seventeen Group 1 winners lined up during the afternoon. The leveller for everyone was the ground, as plenty of rain leading up to the weekend made for testing conditions. Pat Smullen said after the first: "It's heavy but consistent all the way round." George Baker's view: "It's bottomless. It's so loose out there and as bad as I've seen it." The opener was a prime example of the class on show, as it contained the last two winners of the Gold Cup staged at this course back in June, though neither was involved at the end. Forgotten Rules impressed, but the bare form is only rated to pre-race standard.

## 7272 QIPCO BRITISH CHAMPIONS SPRINT STKS (GROUP 2) 6f
**2:20** (2:23) (Class 1) 3-Y-O+

**£207,856** (£78,802; £39,438; £19,645; £9,859; £4,948) **Stalls** High

Form RPR

2232 1 **Gordon Lord Byron (IRE)**[13] 6971 6-9-2 118............ WayneLordan 14 121
(T Hogan, Ire) *chsd ldrs: rdn 2f out: looked hld tl drvn and squeezed between rivals to ld last 50yds: immediately clr* **5/1**[1]

2104 2 1 1/4 **Tropics (USA)**[14] 6920 6-9-2 115.......................... RobertWinston 16 117
(Dean Ivory) *t.k.h: hld up in midfield: prog towards nr side over 2f out: rdn to ld ins fnl f: hdd and outpcd last 50yds* **14/1**

0000 3 nk **Jack Dexter**[28] 6533 5-9-2 109.................................. GrahamLee 12 116
(Jim Goldie) *trckd ldr: led 2f out and sn grabbed nr side rail: hdd ins fnl f: outpcd last 50yds* **11/2**[2]

5000 4 1/2 **Maarek**[13] 6966 7-9-2 112........................................ JamieSpencer 13 114
(Miss Evanna McCutcheon, Ire) *in rr: rdn over 2f out: prog over 1f out: styd on but nvr pce to chal* **7/1**[3]

10 5 nse **Intibaah**[14] 6920 4-9-2 105........................................ PaulHanagan 11 114
(Brian Meehan) *pressed ldrs: rdn to chal 2f out: kpt on same pce fnl f* **20/1**

-133 6 1/2 **Eton Forever (IRE)**[112] 3723 7-9-2 108.......................... AndreaAtzeni 8 113
(Roger Varian) *in tch in midfield: rdn 1/2-way: prog towards outer 2f out: tried to cl over 1f out: one pce fnl f* **10/1**

6352 7 nk **Gathering Power (IRE)**[6] 7140 4-8-13 99....................... FergalLynch 2 109
(Edward Lynam, Ire) *t.k.h early: restrained bhd ldrs after 2f but on outer: rdn and prog 2f out: tried to cl on ldrs 1f out: one pce fnl f* **33/1**

0210 8 1 1/2 **Absolutely So (IRE)**[29] 6522 4-9-2 109.......................... OisinMurphy 9 107
(Andrew Balding) *dwlt and n.m.r s: wl in rr: rdn over 2f out: kpt on fr over 1f out: nt pce to threaten* **20/1**

-401 9 hd **Viztoria (IRE)**[6] 7140 4-8-13 109.................................. PatSmullen 7 103
(Edward Lynam, Ire) *wl in tch towards outer: rdn 2f out: nt qckn over 1f out: fdd fnl f* **5/1**[1]

5134 10 2 1/2 **Humidor (IRE)**[6] 7132 7-9-2 94.......................................... AdamKirby 4 98
(George Baker) *taken down early: racd towards outer in rr: brief effrt 2f out: sn no real prog* **66/1**

2104 11 1/2 **Baccarat (IRE)**[27] 6576 5-9-2 111................................ JamesDoyle 17 97
(Richard Fahey) *hld up in rr against nr side rail: sltly impeded over 1f out: no hdwy after* **14/1**

0554 12 1 1/4 **Joey's Destiny (IRE)**[4] 7168 4-9-2 95......................(p) MartinDwyer 10 93
(George Baker) *t.k.h: hld up in tch: wknd 2f out* **66/1**

4320 13 3 1/4 **Alben Star (IRE)**[28] 6533 6-9-2 109................................ RyanMoore 3 82
(Richard Fahey) *t.k.h early: racd wd and sn hld up: struggling 2f out: wl btn after* **33/1**

6003 14 1 1/2 **An Saighdiur (IRE)**[6] 7140 7-9-2 101........................(p) KierenFallon 6 77
(Andrew Slattery, Ire) *led and crossed to nr side rail: hdd & wknd 2f out: eased* **25/1**

2561 15 hd **G Force (IRE)**[42] 6134 3-9-1 118................................ DanielTudhope 1 77
(David O'Meara) *trapped out wdst of all: nvr on terms: wknd 2f out* **11/2**[2]

1m 17.3s (2.80) **Going Correction** +0.85s/f (Soft)
**WFA** 3 from 4yo+ 1lb **15** Ran SP% **121.3**
Speed ratings: **115,113,112,112,112 111,111,109,108,105 104,103,98,96,96**
CSF £69.69 CT £318.67 TOTE £5.70: £2.10, £5.10, £2.70; EX 83.70 Trifecta £714.70.
**Owner** Dr Cyrus Poonawalla & Morgan J Cahalan **Bred** Roland H Alder **Trained** Nenagh, Co Tipperary

**FOCUS**
The fourth running under its present guise of a race that will have Group 1 status next year. This edition contained three previous Group 1 winners but lacked the season's leading sprinter Slade Power (winner last year), while the unbeaten Lightning Moon was another notable absentee. A draw near the stands' rail proved beneficial, with the first five home coming from stalls 11 or higher, and the form is questionable given the testing conditions, but it still makes some sense. Gordon Lord Byron is rated to his best. The time was 4.9sec slower than standard.

## 7273 QIPCO BRITISH CHAMPIONS FILLIES & MARES STKS (GROUP 1) 1m 4f
**2:55** (2:57) (Class 1) 3-Y-O+

**£344,513** (£130,612; £65,367; £32,562; £16,341; £8,201) **Stalls** Low

Form RPR

-106 1 **Madame Chiang**[34] 6380 3-8-12 109.................................. JimCrowley 2 115
(David Simcock) *hld up in last pair: prog on inner wl over 2f out: drvn wl over 1f out: sustained effrt to ld last 100yds: styd on wl* **12/1**

3511 2 2 **Silk Sari**[37] 6255 4-9-5 108........................................ AndreaAtzeni 5 112
(Luca Cumani) *sn in rr and nt appearing to be gng wl: pushed along 1/2-way: last jst over 2f out: sme prog over 1f out: styd on wl fnl f to take 2nd nr fin* **9/2**[2]

1-20 3 3/4 **Chicquita (IRE)**[13] 6970 4-9-5 112........................ JosephO'Brien 8 113+
(A P O'Brien, Ire) *trckd ldrs: clsd 3f out: drvn to ld wl over 1f out: hanging bdly lft thrght fnl f: hdd last 100yds: lost 2nd nr fin: threw it away* **7/1**

1-30 4 nk **Pollyana (IRE)**[28] 5-9-5 110.................................. WilliamBuick 4 110
(J E Hammond, France) *hld up and sn in last: prog on outer over 3f out: drvn to chse ldrs 2f: disp 2nd briefly 1f out: one pce after* **16/1**

4034 5 3/4 **Seal Of Approval**[37] 6255 5-9-5 108.......................... GeorgeBaker 7 109
(James Fanshawe) *lost pl after 2f: in rr after: rdn over 3f out: struggling and no prog over 2f out: kpt on fnl f* **4/1**[1]

1003 6 1 **Cubanita**[28] 6546 5-9-5 109........................................ RyanMoore 6 108
(Ralph Beckett) *hld up in midfield: trckd ldrs 3f: rdn in cl 3rd 2f out: nt qckn over 1f out: fdd fnl f* **11/2**

U-21 7 1 1/2 **Albasharah (USA)**[7] 7105 5-9-5 108........................ FrederikTylicki 1 106
(Saeed bin Suroor) *trckd ldng pair: led over 3f out: drvn and hdd wl over 1f out: steadily wknd* **5/1**[3]

0234 8 1 **We'll Go Walking (IRE)**[40] 6200 4-9-5 99.......................... AdamKirby 9 105
(J P Murtagh, Ire) *led: clr 10f out to 7f out: hdd over 3f out: wl btn over 2f out* **40/1**

1313 9 47 **Hadaatha (IRE)**[13] 6969 3-8-12 114.......................... PaulHanagan 10 39
(Roger Varian) *t.k.h: trckd ldr: chal over 3f out: wknd qckly 2f out: eased fnl f: t.o* **7/1**

0132 10 14 **Tasaday (USA)**[28] 6546 4-9-5 109.......................... RichardHughes 3 19
(Saeed bin Suroor) *hld up towards rr: rdn over 3f out: wknd qckly over 2f out: sn heavily eased and t.o* **12/1**

2m 38.76s (6.26) **Going Correction** +0.85s/f (Soft)
**WFA** 3 from 4yo+ 7lb **10** Ran SP% **118.9**
Speed ratings: **113,111,111,110,110 109,108,108,76,67**
CSF £66.68 CT £417.92 TOTE £15.50: £3.30, £2.10, £2.80; EX 73.00 Trifecta £769.30.
**Owner** Miss K Rausing **Bred** Miss K Rausing **Trained** Newmarket, Suffolk
■ Stewards' Enquiry : Jim Crowley four-day ban: used whip above permitted level (Nov 1,3-5)

**FOCUS**
Even though most of the runners hadn't won a Group 1, as lots of these had run really well on their previous start. It still didn't look quite up to standard, and the form is rated a bit cautiously given the conditions. The pace set by We'll Go Walking seemed decent, which meant it was a proper test.

## 7274 QUEEN ELIZABETH II STKS SPONSORED BY QIPCO (BRITISH CHAMPIONS MILE) (GROUP 1) 1m (S)
**3:30** (3:33) (Class 1) 3-Y-O+

**£632,344** (£239,735; £119,979; £59,766; £29,994; £15,053) **Stalls** High

Form RPR

5111 1 **Charm Spirit (IRE)**[34] 6382 3-9-1 122.......................... OlivierPeslier 7 124
(F Head, France) *trckd ldrs: rdn and squeezed through to ld over 1f out: drvn fnl f: hld on* **5/1**[3]

1203 2 1/2 **Night Of Thunder (IRE)**[34] 6382 3-9-1 120.............. RichardHughes 10 123
(Richard Hannon) *hld up in rr against nr side rail: swtchd to outer over 3f out: prog over 1f out: nt clr run and swtchd bk ins fnl f: r.o to chse wnr last 100yds: nvr quite got there* **2/1**[1]

0623 3 1/2 **Toormore (IRE)**[41] 6185 3-9-1 113.......................... KierenFallon 11 122
(Richard Hannon) *tk fierce hold: hld up in midfield: stl keen but dropped to last 2f out: prog over 1f out: drvn and r.o to take 3rd nr fin: too much to do* **25/1**

244 4 1/2 **Tullius (IRE)**[22] 6710 6-9-4 117.............................. JimmyFortune 2 121
(Andrew Balding) *hld up in tch: prog over 2f out: led briefly wl over 1f out: chsd wnr to last 100yds: styd on same pce* **9/1**

1312 5 2 1/2 **Captain Cat (IRE)**[22] 6710 5-9-4 115.......................... JamesDoyle 6 115
(Roger Charlton) *dropped out in last: stdy prog on outer fr 3f out: clsd to chal jst over 1f out: effrt flattened out fnl f* **14/1**

-325 **6** *6* **Kingsbarns (IRE)**[34] 6381 4-9-4 113 JosephO'Brien 5 101
(A P O'Brien, Ire) *trckd ldrs: rdn to chal and upsides wl over 1f out: wknd qckly fnl f* **14/1**

1131 **7** *6* **Integral**[14] 6927 4-9-1 117 RyanMoore 9 85
(Sir Michael Stoute) *hld up towards rr: rdn and no prog whn nt clr run over 1f out: sn wknd* **9/2**[2]

1111 **8** *nk* **Custom Cut (IRE)**[22] 6710 5-9-4 117 DanielTudhope 1 87
(David O'Meara) *w ldr: led 3f out: drvn and hdd wl over 1f out: wknd qckly* **8/1**

3202 **9** *7* **Brendan Brackan (IRE)**[13] 6963 5-9-4 111 AndreaAtzeni 4 71
(G M Lyons, Ire) *pressed ldng pair: chal fr 3f out: upsides 2f out: wknd rapidly over 1f out* **66/1**

3624 **10** *shd* **Top Notch Tonto (IRE)**[35] 6352 4-9-4 111 DaleSwift 3 70
(Brian Ellison) *led and crossed to nr side rail: hdd 3f out: wknd over 2f out* **12/1**

2210 **11** *2* **Graphic (IRE)**[56] 5690 5-9-4 114 (p) FrankieDettori 8 66
(William Haggas) *t.k.h: hld up towards rr: cl enough whn n.m.r 2f out: sn wknd rapidly* **33/1**

1m 46.28s (5.48) **Going Correction** +0.85s/f (Soft)
**WFA** 3 from 4yo+ 3lb **11** Ran SP% **118.6**
Speed ratings: **106,105,105,104,102 96,90,89,82,82 80**
CSF £15.27 CT £232.48 TOTE £5.40: £1.80, £1.30, £6.40; EX 16.10 Trifecta £237.80.
**Owner** H H Sheikh Abdulla Bin Khalifa Al Thani **Bred** Ecurie Des Monceaux **Trained** France
■ Stewards' Enquiry : Richard Hughes four-day ban: used whip above permitted level (Nov 1,3-5)

**FOCUS**
A race lacking Kingman, the true star of the miling division this year, while the Al Shaqab/Richard Hannon pair Olympic Glory (successful last year) and Toronado were also missing. It was still a quality event, however, with five individual Group 1 winners on show, if slightly short of race standard. They went just a modest pace, and a couple met trouble. In the end the form makes plenty of sense, with the three 3yos in the line-up dominating the finish. Charm Spirit is perhaps the best of the rest behind Kingman, while Night Of Thunder is rated pretty much to his Guineas form.

## 7275 QIPCO CHAMPION STKS (BRITISH CHAMPIONS MIDDLE DISTANCE) (GROUP 1) 1m 2f
4:05 (4:08) (Class 1) 3-Y-O+
£770,547 (£292,131; £146,201; £72,829; £36,550; £18,343) Stalls Low

Form RPR

1122 **1** **Noble Mission**[83] 4720 5-9-5 117 JamesDoyle 5 123
(Lady Cecil) *mde all: rdn and jnd 2f out: battled on wl u.p: edgd sltly lft last 100yds: hld on most gamely* **7/1**

4150 **2** *nk* **Al Kazeem**[13] 6970 6-9-5 117 GeorgeBaker 8 122
(Roger Charlton) *trckd wnr: rdn to chal 2f out: upsides after and tremendous battle: sltly impeded and jst hld nr fin* **16/1**

2-1 **3** *1 ¼* **Free Eagle (IRE)**[35] 6350 3-9-0 120 PatSmullen 2 120
(D K Weld, Ire) *pushed along early to rch 6th: shkn up and prog to chse ldng pair 2f out: styd on but nvr able to bridge the gap* **5/2**[2]

1614 **4** *3 ½* **Western Hymn**[64] 5406 3-9-0 112 WilliamBuick 6 113
(John Gosden) *hld up in 7th: pushed along over 3f out: effrt on outer over 2f out: wandered u.p but kpt on to take 4th ins fnl f* **14/1**

1111 **5** *1* **Cirrus Des Aigles (FR)**[14] 6957 8-9-5 123 ChristopheSoumillon 9 112
(Mme C Barande-Barbe, France) *sn chsd ldng trio but trapped out wd thrght: rdn 3f out: no imp and btn 2f out: lost 4th ins fnl f* **7/4**[1]

2111 **6** *½* **Sheikhzayedroad**[34] 6390 5-9-5 113 MartinLane 3 111
(David Simcock) *hld up in last: detached and drvn 4f out: rdr persisted and styd on fr over 1f out to pass 3 rivals fnl f* **28/1**

1011 **7** *3 ½* **Pether's Moon (IRE)**[14] 6919 4-9-5 114 RichardHughes 7 104
(Richard Hannon) *hld up in midfield: pushed along 3f out: squeezed out over 2f out: no ch after* **25/1**

23 **8** *nk* **Ayrad (IRE)**[22] 6711 3-9-0 105 AndreaAtzeni 4 103
(Roger Varian) *hld up in 8th: rdn 3f out: no prog and wl btn 2f out: wknd* **50/1**

-010 **9** *2 ¼* **Ruler Of The World (IRE)**[13] 6970 4-9-5 122 (p) JosephO'Brien 1 99
(A P O'Brien, Ire) *trckd ldng pair: rdn 3f out: wknd 2f out* **6/1**[3]

2m 11.23s (3.83) **Going Correction** +0.85s/f (Soft)
**WFA** 3 from 4yo+ 5lb **9** Ran SP% **113.5**
Speed ratings: **118,117,116,113,113 112,109,109,107**
CSF £104.14 CT £354.58 TOTE £6.50: £2.00, £4.10, £1.30; EX 95.90 Trifecta £630.80.
**Owner** K Abdullah **Bred** Juddmonte Farms Ltd **Trained** Newmarket, Suffolk
■ Stewards' Enquiry : James Doyle caution: careless riding; seven-day ban, £10,000 fine: used whip above permitted level (Nov 1,3-8)
Joseph O'Brien two-day ban: careless riding (Nov 1,3)

**FOCUS**
A strong line-up was assembled for the showpiece race and it produced a wonderful and captivating duel down the home straight. While a couple of runners ran below expectations, this was a result to warm the heart, as it saw a fine training performance from Lady Cecil and a second win in the race for a colt out of the mare Kind who, famously, gave racing the brilliant Frankel. Noble Mission doesn't rate to the standard of the previous winners of the Champion Stakes at Ascot. Al Kazeem is still not quite at his 5yo level.

## 7276 BALMORAL H'CAP (SPONSORED BY QIPCO) 1m (S)
4:45 (4:48) (Class 2) 3-Y-O+
£155,625 (£46,600; £23,300; £11,650; £5,825; £2,925) Stalls High

Form RPR

0421 **1** **Bronze Angel (IRE)**[21] 6752 5-9-2 105 (b) LouisSteward(3) 10 116
(Marcus Tregoning) *hld up in midfield far side: smooth prog over 2f out: overall ldr jst over 1f out: rdn and styd on wl* **20/1**

1240 **2** *1 ¼* **Maverick Wave (USA)**[21] 6752 3-8-8 97 RobertHavlin 12 104
(John Gosden) *trckd far side ldrs: chsd ldr over 3f out to over 1f out: styd on to take 2nd again nr fin: 2nd of 13 in gp* **25/1**

0652 **3** *nk* **Empire Storm (GER)**[14] 6921 7-8-13 106 (t) MikeyEnnis(7) 13 113
(Michael Attwater) *prom far side: overall ldr 1/2-way: sent for home over 2f out: hdd jst over 1f out: kpt on but lost 2nd nr fin: 3rd of 13 in gp* **33/1**

0055 **4** *1 ¼* **Levitate**[8] 7081 6-8-4 95 (v) JoeDoyle(5) 6 100
(John Quinn) *cl up far side: rdn over 2f out: tried to mount a chal over 1f out: styd on same pce: 4th of 13 in gp* **10/1**[2]

0000 **5** *¾* **Heavy Metal**[14] 6921 4-8-11 97 KierenFallon 8 100
(Mark Johnston) *hld up in rr far side: taken to outer and gd prog over 2f out: tried to cl on ldrs 1f out: one pce after: 5th of 14 in gp* **28/1**

2560 **6** *3* **Chil The Kite**[14] 6921 5-9-10 110 OlivierPeslier 9 106
(Hughie Morrison) *hld up far side: gng bttr than many 3f out: nt qckn and lost ch over 2f out: hmpd over 1f out: kpt on fnl f: 6th of 13 in gp* **25/1**

0350 **7** *nk* **Gabrial's Kaka (IRE)**[21] 6752 4-9-2 102 JamieSpencer 22 97
(Richard Fahey) *hld up in rr nr side: prog 3f out: styd on to ld ins fnl f: no ch w far side: 1st of 14 in gp* **10/1**[2]

0406 **8** *1 ¼* **Russian Realm**[49] 5919 4-8-9 95 RyanMoore 25 87+
(Sir Michael Stoute) *hld up in rr nr side: prog against rail to ld gp 2f out: nvr on terms w far side: hdd ins fnl f: 2nd of 14 in gp* **10/1**[2]

1234 **9** *hd* **Buckstay (IRE)**[21] 6752 4-8-7 93 JimCrowley 20 85
(Peter Chapple-Hyam) *hld up in tch nr side: prog 3f out: chal for ld fr over 1f out: no ch w far side: 3rd of 14 in gp* **14/1**[3]

0603 **10** *nk* **Georgian Bay (IRE)**[35] 6335 4-8-2 95 (p) JordanVaughan(7) 3 86
(K R Burke) *prom far side: rdn over 2f out: wknd u.p jst over 1f out: 7th of 13 in gp* **33/1**

0036 **11** *¾* **Bold Thady Quill (IRE)**[31] 6458 7-9-1 101 (v) PatSmullen 5 90
(K J Condon, Ire) *hld up in rr far side: rdn and sme prog over 2f out: no hdwy wl over 1f out: 8th of 13 in gp* **20/1**

2103 **12** *8* **Chatez (IRE)**[91] 4448 3-8-8 97 FergusSweeney 4 67
(Alan King) *t.k.h: hld up in rr far side: rdn and no prog over 2f out: wl btn after: 9th of 13 in gp* **8/1**[1]

-130 **13** *½* **Cornrow**[21] 6752 4-8-11 97 WilliamBuick 16 67
(John Gosden) *hld up bhd ldrs nr side: cl up 3f out: outpcd by ldng trio fr 2f out: 4th of 14 in gp* **8/1**[1]

0506 **14** *2 ¾* **Belgian Bill**[41] 6185 6-9-2 102 (tp) FrankieDettori 1 66
(George Baker) *hld up in detached last far side: effrt over 2f out: no prog: 10th of 13 in gp* **25/1**

0403 **15** *½* **Farlow (IRE)**[9] 7060 6-8-1 87 PatrickMathers 27 49
(Richard Fahey) *prom nr side: led gp briefly over 3f out: wknd 2f out: 5th of 14 in gp* **25/1**

0400 **16** *2 ¼* **Fort Bastion (IRE)**[14] 6921 5-8-11 97 (p) DanielTudhope 2 54
(David O'Meara) *nvr beyond midfield far side: rdn and struggling in rr 3f out: 11th of 13 in gp* **25/1**

1311 **17** *5* **Baraweez (IRE)**[35] 6354 4-9-0 100 ColmO'Donoghue 15 46
(Brian Ellison) *prom nr side: rdn 3f out: wknd 2f out: 6th of 14 in gp* **14/1**[3]

0000 **18** *hd* **Askaud (IRE)**[8] 7085 6-8-0 86 oh2 (p) NickyMackay 24 31
(Scott Dixon) *pressed nr side ldrs to 3f out: sn btn: 7th of 14 in gp* **50/1**

3416 **19** *5* **Tigers Tale (IRE)**[21] 6752 5-8-5 94 (v) DannyBrock(3) 11 28
(Roger Teal) *prom far side: led gp after 2f to 1/2-way: wknd qckly 3f out: 12th of 13 in gp* **33/1**

0060 **20** *3 ½* **Hawkeyethenoo (IRE)**[28] 6533 8-8-13 99 GrahamLee 21 25
(Jim Goldie) *hld up wl in rr nr side: sme prog 3f out: wknd 2f out: 8th of 14 in gp* **20/1**

0205 **21** *1* **Dream Walker (FR)**[14] 6934 5-8-4 90 MartinLane 17 13
(Brian Ellison) *nvr beyond midfield nr side: wl btn over 2f out: 9th of 14 in gp* **25/1**

2044 **22** *3 ½* **Sirius Prospect (USA)**[14] 6921 6-9-4 104 RobertWinston 28 19
(Dean Ivory) *trckd nr side ldrs: led gp 3f out to 2f out: wknd rapidly and heavily eased: 10th of 14 in gp* **16/1**

0005 **23** *hd* **Abseil (USA)**[28] 6532 4-8-10 96 JamesDoyle 7 11
(Sir Michael Stoute) *t.k.h: led far side 2f: wknd rapidly 1/2-way: t.o and eased: last of 13 in gp* **25/1**

1032 **24** *7* **Velox**[21] 6752 4-8-10 99 CamHardie(3) 14
(Luca Cumani) *dwlt: chsd ldrs nr side tl wknd wl over 2f out: t.o: 11th of 14 in gp* **14/1**[3]

0/24 **25** *3 ¾* **Piri Wango (IRE)**[35] 6354 5-8-13 106 (p) TomMadden(7) 19
(G M Lyons, Ire) *led nr side to over 3f out: wknd qckly: t.o: 12th of 14 in gp* **25/1**

5242 **26** *4 ½* **Jack's Revenge (IRE)**[21] 6755 6-9-0 100 (bt) RichardHughes 23
(George Baker) *stdd s: hld up in detached last nr side: brief prog over 2f out: sn wknd and eased: t.o: 13th of 14 in gp* **16/1**

102 **27** *20* **Almargo (IRE)**[35] 6354 3-9-2 105 JoeFanning 26
(Mark Johnston) *prom nr side: disp ld briefly over 3f out: sn wknd rapidly: t.o: last of 14 in gp* **33/1**

1m 45.36s (4.56) **Going Correction** +0.85s/f (Soft)
**WFA** 3 from 4yo+ 3lb **27** Ran SP% **143.5**
Speed ratings (Par 109): **111,109,109,108,107 104,104,102,102,102 101,93,93,90,89 87,82,82,77,73 72,69,69,62,58 54,34**
CSF £451.92 CT £15181.52 TOTE £18.50: £4.10, £9.90, £12.80, £3.00; EX 1214.60 Trifecta £7638.70 Part won..
**Owner** Lady Tennant **Bred** Rihana Partnership **Trained** Whitsbury, Hants

**FOCUS**
This event, the richest mile handicap in Europe, replaces the 7f apprentice handicap run on the first three years of the fixture. The Balmoral handle was previously used for a 5f handicap at the Royal meeting which was discontinued in 2003. Runners had to qualify for this new race by finishing in the first six in any of 18 heritage handicaps during the season. The field split into two groups and the pace was on the far side, which provided the first six home. The next three finishers finished a long way clear of the remainder in the stands'-side group. Another personal best from Bronze Angel, with the runner-up nback to ealier form. The time comes out a stone quicker than the Queen Elizabeth Stakes, perhaps showing that the far side was quicker.
T/Jkpt: Not won. T/Plt: £435.80 to a £1 stake. Pool: £353,937.00 - 592.85 winning units. T/Qpdt: £50.10 to a £1 stake. Pool: £21,907.90 - 323.00 winning units. JN

# 7003 CATTERICK (L-H)
Saturday, October 18

**OFFICIAL GOING: Soft (6.9)**
Wind: Strong across Weather: Grey cloud and windy

## 7277 BET TOTEPLACEPOT MEDIAN AUCTION MAIDEN STKS 5f 212y
1:25 (1:26) (Class 6) 2-Y-O £2,726 (£805; £402) Stalls Low

Form RPR

5052 **1** **Magh Meall**[11] 7003 2-9-0 54 AdrianNicholls 2 67
(David Nicholls) *qckly away: mde all: rdn clr over 2f out: drvn ins fnl f: jst hld on* **8/1**

6203 **2** *nse* **Spirit Of Zeb (IRE)**[30] 6474 2-9-5 76 TonyHamilton 1 72
(Richard Fahey) *sn chsng wnr: effrt 2f out and sn rdn: drvn and styd on wl fnl f: jst failed* **11/8**[1]

334 **3** *2 ¾* **Rahmah (IRE)**[30] 6496 2-8-12 79 AhmadAlSubousi(7) 3 64
(Robert Cowell) *trckd ldng pair: pushed along wl over 2f out: rdn wl over 1f out: kpt on u.p fnl f* **11/4**[2]

63 **4** *9* **Makin A Statement (IRE)**[177] 1670 2-9-5 0 PhillipMakin 6 37
(John Quinn) *chsd ldrs: rdn over 2f out: sn drvn and btn* **6/1**[3]

**5** *3 ½* **Spinaminnie (IRE)** 2-9-0 0 FrannyNorton 4 21
(Mark Johnston) *towards rr: pushed along 3f out: rdn over 2f out: sn no hdwy* **17/2**

5 **6** *2 ½* **Captain Future**[52] 5813 2-9-5 0 DavidNolan 5 19
(Bryan Smart) *towards rr: rdn along wl over 2f out: sn outpcd* **25/1**

0655 **7** *8* **Oricano**[38] 6224 2-8-9 53........................ GemmaTutty(5) 7
(Karen Tutty) *dwlt: green and a in rr: outpcd and bhd fr over 2f out* **66/1**

1m 15.86s (2.26) **Going Correction** +0.325s/f (Good) **7** Ran SP% **110.0**
Speed ratings (Par 93): **97,96,93,81,76 73,62**
CSF £18.04 TOTE £6.10: £3.00, £1.50; EX 20.30 Trifecta £49.10.
**Owner** Dubelem (Racing) Limited **Bred** Bond Thoroughbred Corporation **Trained** Sessay, N Yorks

**FOCUS**
Rail on original line and all distances as advertised. An ordinary maiden, the winner dominating from the off under an aggressive ride. Jockeys described the ground as being "very soft". The form is rated a shade negatively.

## 7278 TOTESCOOP6 THE MILLIONAIRE MAKER MAIDEN FILLIES' STKS (BOBIS RACE) 7f
**1:55** (1:57) (Class 5) 2-Y-O £3,408 (£1,006; £503) **Stalls** Low

Form RPR

35 **1** **Caigemdar (IRE)**[93] 4357 2-9-0 0........................ GrahamGibbons 4 75
(David Barron) *mde all: rdn wl over 1f out: drvn ins fnl f: kpt on wl towards fin* **12/1**

6321 **2** *1 3/4* **Hollie Point**[25] 6641 2-9-0 76........................ PhillipMakin 6 71+
(Charlie Appleby) *dwlt: sn in tch: hdwy to trck ldrs on inner 1/2-way: chsd ldng pair and edgd lft continually: swtchd rt and drvn wl ins fnl f: no imp* **5/2**[1]

535 **3** *1 1/2* **Mallymkun**[22] 6701 2-9-0 71........................ MartinHarley 8 67
(K R Burke) *cl up: rdn along wl over 1f out: drvn ent fnl f: kpt on same pce* **8/1**[3]

2 **4** *7* **Opportuna**[71] 5128 2-9-0 0........................ WilliamCarson 3 50
(Tom Dascombe) *chsd ldrs: rdn along wl over 2f out: sn one pce* **5/2**[1]

43 **5** *1 3/4* **Yorkindred Spirit**[17] 6860 2-9-0 0........................ FrannyNorton 5 45
(Mark Johnston) *dwlt: a towards rr* **3/1**[2]

505 **6** *3 1/2* **Granola**[8] 7082 2-8-9 55........................ KevinStott(5) 1 36
(David Brown) *in tch: rdn along 3f out: sn outpcd* **20/1**

**7** *12* **Danzella** 2-9-0 0........................ MichaelStainton 2 6
(Chris Fairhurst) *dwlt: sn outpcd and bhd* **66/1**

**F** **Go Grazeon** 2-9-0 0........................ IanBrennan 9
(John Quinn) *in tch: pushed along whn slipped and fell bnd 2 1/2f out* **33/1**

1m 30.06s (3.06) **Going Correction** +0.325s/f (Good) **8** Ran SP% **110.1**
Speed ratings (Par 92): **95,93,91,83,81 77,63,**
CSF £39.13 TOTE £10.70: £3.40, £1.10, £2.50; EX 61.90 Trifecta £244.10.
**Owner** Home Farm Racing Limited **Bred** O & D Geraghty **Trained** Maunby, N Yorks

**FOCUS**
Fair form in this maiden, the winner the second 2yo to make all on the round course. She took a step forward.

## 7279 FOLLOW SCOOP6 AT TOTEPOOLLIVEINFO.COM CLAIMING STKS 1m 3f 214y
**2:30** (2:40) (Class 6) 3-Y-O+ £2,726 (£805; £402) **Stalls** Centre

Form RPR

1600 **1** **English Summer**[21] 6747 7-9-6 80........................(t) GeorgeChaloner 10 86
(Richard Fahey) *trckd ldrs: cl up 3f out: wd st to stands' rail and led 2f out: sn rdn: drvn ins fnl f: kpt on wl* **10/3**[2]

30 **2** *1* **War Poet**[7] 7125 7-8-10 79........................(p) MeganCarberry(5) 1 79
(Brian Ellison) *hld up: hdwy on inner over 3f out: rdn to chse wnr ent fnl f: ev ch tl drvn and no ex last 100yds* **9/2**

0655 **3** *2 1/2* **High Office**[7] 7124 8-9-4 74........................ TonyHamilton 7 78
(Richard Fahey) *trckd ldng pair: pushed along 3f out: wd st: sn outpcd and rdn: kpt on u.p fnl f* **7/2**[3]

3-11 **4** *4 1/2* **Reve De Nuit (USA)**[175] 1743 8-9-5 84........................ JoeyHaynes(3) 11 75
(K R Burke) *trckd ldr: cl up 1/2-way: led over 3f out: hdd 2f out and sn rdn: drvn and wknd ent fnl f* **9/4**[1]

6142 **5** *7* **Harrison's Cave**[9] 7059 6-9-1 60........................(p) TomEaves 9 57
(Keith Dalgleish) *hld up: sme hdwy 3f out: rdn over 2f out: n.d* **16/1**

3420 **6** *5* **Zafranagar (IRE)**[25] 6649 9-9-1 65........................(p) GeorgeDowning(5) 2 54
(Ian Williams) *a towards rr: rdn along 4f out: outpcd fnl 3f* **25/1**

0600 **7** *26* **Dabuki (FR)**[26] 6597 4-8-11 63........................(p) KevinStott(5) 4 8
(Geoffrey Harker) *led: pushed along over 4f out: rdn and hdd 3f out: sn wknd* **33/1**

56-0 **8** *22* **Street Artist (IRE)**[134] 2952 4-9-6 74........................ AdrianNicholls 5
(David Nicholls) *a in rr: bhd fnl 3f* **25/1**

2m 47.16s (8.26) **Going Correction** +0.425s/f (Yiel) **8** Ran SP% **110.8**
Speed ratings (Par 101): **89,88,86,83,79 75,58,43**
CSF £17.27 TOTE £4.60: £2.20, £2.10, £2.60; EX 19.40 Trifecta £71.70.High Office was claimed by C Dore for £8000. War Poet was claimed by C Chapman for £5000.
**Owner** Dr Marwan Koukash **Bred** Juddmonte Farms Ltd **Trained** Musley Bank, N Yorks

**FOCUS**
A fairly useful effort from the winner in this claimer. The winner is rated to the balance of this year's form.

## 7280 TOTEPOOL CATTERICK DASH (H'CAP) 5f
**3:05** (3:09) (Class 2) (0-100,98) 3-Y-O+ **£16,172** (£4,812; £2,405; £1,202) **Stalls** Low

Form RPR

3065 **1** **Duke Of Firenze**[6] 7132 5-9-1 92........................(p) MartinHarley 12 105
(Robert Cowell) *trckd ldrs: cl up 1/2-way: led 2f out: rdn clr over 1f out: readily* **9/1**[3]

0300 **2** *2 3/4* **Confessional**[21] 6760 7-8-13 90........................(e) DavidAllan 5 93
(Tim Easterby) *led: rdn and hdd 2f out: drvn and kpt on fnl f: no ch w wnr* **8/1**[2]

3300 **3** *3 3/4* **Ballesteros**[21] 6745 5-9-2 93........................ TonyHamilton 15 83
(Richard Fahey) *cl up on stands' rail: effrt 2f out: sn rdn and kpt on same pce appr fnl f* **6/1**[1]

4001 **4** *nk* **Arctic Feeling (IRE)**[8] 7080 6-8-12 94........................ SammyJoBell(5) 14 83
(Richard Fahey) *in rr: hdwy wl over 1f out: sn rdn and swtchd lft ent fnl f: nrst fin* **6/1**[1]

2046 **5** *1 3/4* **Long Awaited (IRE)**[8] 7080 6-8-11 88........................(b) PhillipMakin 6 70
(David Barron) *in tch: hdwy 2f out: rdn to chse ldrs over 1f out: no imp ins fnl f* **9/1**[3]

00 **6** *1 1/2* **Graphic Guest**[8] 7080 4-8-12 89........................ PJMcDonald 9 66
(Robert Cowell) *blind removed late: dwlt and in rr: hdwy on outer wl over 1f out: rdn and kpt on fnl f: n.d* **22/1**

000 **7** *nk* **Magical Macey (USA)**[8] 7080 7-8-8 90........................(b) ShaneGray(5) 2 66
(David Barron) *racd far side: prom: rdn along 2f out: sn one pce* **12/1**

-620 **8** *nk* **Viva Verglas (IRE)**[7] 7101 3-9-4 95........................(b) GrahamGibbons 7 71
(David Barron) *chsd ldrs: rdn along 1/2-way: hung rt 2f out: sn btn* **25/1**

0660 **9** *hd* **Inxile (IRE)**[28] 6531 9-8-12 89........................(p) FrannyNorton 4 63
(David Nicholls) *cl up: rdn along over 2f out: grad wknd* **20/1**

0010 **10** *1* **Colonel Mak**[63] 5445 7-9-3 94........................ JasonHart 8 64
(David Barron) *prom: rdn along whn hmpd 2f out: sn drvn and wknd* **20/1**

302 **11** *3/4* **Free Zone**[8] 7080 5-8-12 89........................(p) AdamBeschizza 1 57
(Robert Cowell) *racd far side: prom: rdn along 2f out: sn outpcd* **6/1**[1]

4045 **12** *1 1/4* **Bondesire**[21] 6760 4-9-4 95........................ SamJames 3 58
(David O'Meara) *in tch: rdn along 1/2-way: sn wknd* **6/1**[1]

2000 **13** *4* **Pearl Acclaim (IRE)**[8] 7080 4-8-13 90........................ AdrianNicholls 10 39
(David Nicholls) *chsd ldrs whn n.m.r and swtchd rt after 1f: effrt nr stands' rail: hanging rt whn nt clr run over 2f out: sn eased* **18/1**

59.76s (-0.04) **Going Correction** +0.20s/f (Good) **13** Ran SP% **118.9**
Speed ratings (Par 109): **108,103,97,97,94 91,91,90,90,89 87,85,79**
CSF £74.16 CT £487.53 TOTE £11.50: £4.40, £1.60, £3.00; EX 97.90 Trifecta £1137.00.
**Owner** Cheveley Park Stud **Bred** Cheveley Park Stud Ltd **Trained** Six Mile Bottom, Cambs
■ Addictive Dream was withdrawn. Price at time of withdrawal 40/1. Rule 4 does not apply.

**FOCUS**
What looked a competitive sprint ended up being anything but, the winner having the rest well strung out in behind. The main body of the field came stands' side, the pair who stayed far side ending up well beaten. The winner is rated back to his best.

## 7281 TOTEPOOL RACING'S BIGGEST SUPPORTER H'CAP 1m 3f 214y
**3:40** (3:40) (Class 4) (0-80,80) 3-Y-O+ £5,175 (£1,540; £769; £384) **Stalls** Centre

Form RPR

3351 **1** **Ebony Express**[38] 6228 5-9-10 78........................ BenCurtis 9 88+
(Alan Swinbank) *chsd ldrs: chal over 2f out: swtchd rt to stands' side rail over 1f out: led jst ins fnl f: hld on wl* **10/3**[2]

4564 **2** *3/4* **Prophesy (IRE)**[10] 7044 5-8-12 66 oh3........................(p) DavidAllan 4 75
(Tim Easterby) *led: hdd last 150yds: no ex* **22/1**

0651 **3** *1 1/2* **Sioux Chieftain (IRE)**[11] 7008 4-9-6 74........................ JasonHart 13 81+
(Michael Appleby) *in tch: chsng ldrs over 1f out: styd on same pce ins fnl f* **11/4**[1]

2265 **4** *3/4* **Duke Of Yorkshire**[14] 6937 4-9-0 68........................ DuranFentiman 6 73
(Tim Easterby) *chsd ldrs: kpt on same pce fnl f* **22/1**

3615 **5** *3 1/2* **Light Of Asia (IRE)**[11] 7020 3-8-12 73........................ PJMcDonald 12 73
(Ed Dunlop) *trckd ldrs: one pce fnl 2f* **7/1**[3]

4254 **6** *8* **Lexington Bay (IRE)**[28] 6536 6-9-6 74........................ GeorgeChaloner 11 61
(Richard Fahey) *hld up in rr: effrt over 4f out: one pce fnl 2f* **10/1**

3205 **7** *nk* **Engrossing**[91] 4427 5-9-2 70........................[1] BarryMcHugh 2 57
(Peter Niven) *dwlt: in rr: kpt on fnl 3f: nvr a factor* **33/1**

-320 **8** *1* **Magic Music Man**[43] 6092 3-9-0 75........................ MartinHarley 5 60
(K R Burke) *in tch: effrt over 3f out: wknd over 2f out* **12/1**

2434 **9** *hd* **Chant (IRE)**[11] 7008 4-8-11 72........................ RowanScott(7) 7 57
(Ann Duffield) *mid-div: lost pl over 3f out: no threat after* **14/1**

0525 **10** *1* **O Ma Lad (IRE)**[38] 6228 6-9-12 80........................ PhillipMakin 1 63
(John Quinn) *in rr: hdwy 6f out: chsng ldrs over 3f out: wknd over 2f out* **10/1**

-500 **11** *12* **Toptempo**[23] 6685 5-9-4 72........................ JimmyQuinn 8 36
(Mark H Tompkins) *in rr: bhd fnl 2f* **14/1**

-503 **12** *2 3/4* **Ambleside**[21] 6761 4-9-10 78........................ GrahamGibbons 3 37
(Michael Easterby) *in rr: hdwy 6f out: lost pl over 2f out* **25/1**

036/ **13** *22* **Dora's Gift**[770] 6037 5-8-7 66 oh1........................ KevinStott(5) 10
(Edwin Tuer) *in rr: bhd over 3f out: t.o* **50/1**

2m 45.64s (6.74) **Going Correction** +0.425s/f (Yiel)
**WFA** 3 from 4yo+ 7lb **13** Ran SP% **118.9**
Speed ratings (Par 105): **94,93,92,92,89 84,84,83,83,82 74,72,58**
CSF £82.87 CT £231.56 TOTE £3.30: £1.10, £9.70, £3.00; EX 119.00 Trifecta £579.40.
**Owner** Mrs T Blackett **Bred** Miss E J Wright **Trained** Melsonby, N Yorks

**FOCUS**
A fair handicap which the leading pair dominated throughout. The whole field came towards the stands' side in the straight. The runner-up is the key to the form.

## 7282 TOTEEXACTA AVAILABLE ON ALL RACES H'CAP 7f
**4:15** (4:19) (Class 4) (0-80,81) 3-Y-O+ £6,469 (£1,925; £962; £481) **Stalls** Low

Form RPR

0114 **1** **Comino (IRE)**[15] 6895 3-9-0 80........................ ShaneGray(5) 1 91
(Kevin Ryan) *trckd ldrs on inner: hdwy 2f out: rdn to chal ent fnl f: sn led: drvn and kpt on wl towards fin* **7/1**[2]

4200 **2** *nk* **Ready (IRE)**[39] 6214 4-9-7 80........................(p) DavidAllan 7 91
(Garry Moss) *prom: cl up over 2f out: rdn to chal over 1f out: drvn and ev ch ins fnl f: kpt on* **15/2**[3]

0122 **3** *1 1/2* **Evanescent (IRE)**[9] 7060 5-9-3 81........................ JackGarritty(5) 9 88
(John Quinn) *cl up: led over 2f out and c wd to stands' rail: rdn over 1f out: drvn and hdd ins fnl f: kpt on same pce* **8/1**

5516 **4** *2* **Conry (IRE)**[33] 6411 8-8-11 75........................ GeorgeDowning(5) 13 77
(Ian Williams) *in rr: wd st: hdwy 2f out: swtchd lft and rdn appr fnl f: kpt on: nrst fin* **8/1**

000 **5** *1 1/2* **Showboating (IRE)**[8] 7085 6-9-4 77........................(tp) PhillipMakin 3 75
(Alan McCabe) *in rr: hdwy 2f out: rdn over 1f out: kpt on fnl f: nrst fin* **11/2**[1]

6103 **6** *2* **Solar Spirit (IRE)**[42] 6150 9-9-3 76........................ JimmyQuinn 2 69
(Tracy Waggott) *chsd ldrs: rdn along over 2f out: grad wknd* **25/1**

1242 **7** *nk* **We'll Deal Again**[30] 6478 7-9-2 75........................ BarryMcHugh 8 67
(Michael Easterby) *chsd ldrs: hdwy over 2f out: swtchd rt to stands' rails wl over 1f out: sn rdn and no imp* **14/1**

6040 **8** *1* **Dr Red Eye**[20] 6789 6-9-7 80........................(p) AdamBeschizza 4 69
(Scott Dixon) *led: hdd and rdn along 2 1/2f out: drvn wl over 1f out: grad wknd* **12/1**

2600 **9** *1* **Ted's Brother (IRE)**[9] 7060 6-8-12 74........................(e) JacobButterfield(3) 6 61
(Richard Guest) *nvr bttr than midfield* **40/1**

2-43 **10** *1 1/4* **Ortac Rock (IRE)**[20] 6789 5-9-2 75........................(t) TonyHamilton 10 59
(Richard Fahey) *a towards rr* **11/1**

2605 **11** *3/4* **True Pleasure (IRE)**[18] 6836 7-9-4 77........................ PJMcDonald 11 59
(James Bethell) *in tch: rdn along over 2f out: sn drvn and wknd* **14/1**

1231 **12** *1 3/4* **Strong Man**[78] 4861 6-9-2 75........................ GrahamGibbons 14 52
(Michael Easterby) *a towards rr* **16/1**

2136 **13** *6* **Lord Of The Nile (IRE)**[133] 3002 3-9-2 77........................ SamJames 5 37
(David O'Meara) *chsd ldrs: rdn along bef 1/2-way: sn wknd* **16/1**

200- **14** *12* **Atlantic Affair (IRE)**[378] 7026 3-9-3 78........................ FrannyNorton 15 7
(Mark Johnston) *chsd ldrs: rdn along 1/2-way: sn wknd* **33/1**

3120 **15** *20* **Layla's Hero (IRE)**[29] 6511 7-9-5 78........................(v) AdrianNicholls 12
(David Nicholls) *dwlt and a bhd* **18/1**

1m 29.8s (2.80) **Going Correction** +0.525s/f (Yiel)
**WFA** 3 from 4yo+ 2lb **15** Ran SP% **117.5**
Speed ratings (Par 105): **105,104,102,100,98 96,96,95,94,92 91,89,82,69,46**
CSF £55.73 CT £442.42 TOTE £6.30: £2.10, £1.80, £3.00; EX 62.20 Trifecta £567.10.
**Owner** Exors of the late D W Barker **Bred** Tom Twomey **Trained** Hambleton, N Yorks

**FOCUS**
A pretty useful effort from the winner in another race which was dominated by those who raced prominently. The runner-up is the best guide.

## 7283 FOLLOW @TOTEPOOL ON TWITTER APPRENTICE H'CAP (DIV I) 1m 5f 175y
**4:50** (4:52) (Class 6) (0-60,60) 3-Y-0+ **£2,726** (£805; £402) **Stalls** Low

Form RPR
2056 **1** **Cool Baranca (GER)**[11] 7006 8-9-2 48 EmmaSayer 6 59+
(Dianne Sayer) *in rr: smooth hdwy to trck ldrs over 3f out: led centre over 1f out: v readily* **10/1**
3050 **2** *2* **Kashstaree**[124] 3303 3-8-6 47 ShaneGray 1 53
(David Barron) *in rr: hdwy over 4f out: styd on to take 2nd last 100yds* **4/1**[2]
6640 **3** *3 ¾* **My Escapade (IRE)**[17] 6864 3-8-9 50 JordanNason 4 51
(Simon Waugh) *chsd ldrs: drvn 4f out: one pce fnl f* **10/1**
05/0 **4** *1 ¾* **Salford Dream**[25] 6644 5-9-1 50 MeganCarberry(3) 2 49
(Pauline Robson) *dwlt: hld up in mid-div: hdwy 6f out: wnt 2nd over 3f out:sn wd on bnd: one pce fnl 2f* **12/1**
2630 **5** *1 ½* **Belle Peinture (FR)**[25] 6628 3-8-5 49 RachelRichardson(3) 8 45
(Alan Lockwood) *sn chsng ldrs: led over 8f out: hdd over 1f out: fdd ins fnl f* **12/1**
1231 **6** *8* **Midnight Warrior**[28] 6542 4-9-11 57 JackGarritty 7 42
(Ron Barr) *led: hdd over 8f out: outpcd over 3f out: wknd over 1f out* **5/2**[1]
0600 **7** *1 ¼* **Vittachi**[7] 7100 7-8-13 50 (p) RowanScott(5) 5 34
(Alistair Whillans) *chsd ldrs: drvn over 4f out: lost pl 3f out* **5/1**[3]
4400 **8** *¾* **Blue Top**[33] 6410 5-9-6 55 (p) NedCurtis(3) 10 37
(Mark Walford) *in rr: brief effrt over 4f out: sn btn* **14/1**
003 **9** *25* **Bold And Free**[24] 6673 4-9-0 51 JoshQuinn(5) 3
(David Thompson) *trckd ldrs t.k.h: lost pl over 3f out: sn bhd: tailed rt off* **20/1**
4300 **P** **Keep Calm**[15] 6900 4-10-0 60 (b) GeorgeDowning 9
(John Mackie) *drvn to sn chse ldrs: lost pl 4f out: t.o and eased over 2f out: sn p.u* **14/1**

3m 15.66s (12.06) **Going Correction** +0.525s/f (Yiel)
**WFA** 3 from 4yo+ 9lb **10** Ran **SP% 116.9**
Speed ratings (Par 101): **86,84,82,81,80 76,75,75,60,**
CSF £49.97 CT £418.41 TOTE £9.70: £3.40, £2.10, £3.70; EX 73.70 Trifecta £362.80.
**Owner** Dennis J Coppola **Bred** Stiftung Gestut Fahrhof **Trained** Hackthorpe, Cumbria

**FOCUS**
Front-runners had dominated most races on this card but the leaders seemed to overdo things here, the pace collapsing in the straight. The winner could still do a bit better yet given the right ground.

## 7284 FOLLOW @TOTEPOOL ON TWITTER APPRENTICE H'CAP (DIV II)1m 5f 175y
**5:20** (5:25) (Class 6) (0-60,59) 3-Y-0+ **£2,726** (£805; £402) **Stalls** Low

Form RPR
052 **1** **Bulas Belle**[30] 6494 4-9-11 56 KevinStott 7 65
(Edwin Tuer) *trckd ldrs: hdwy over 5f out: sn trcking ldr: effrt 2f out and sn cl up: rdn to ld jst ins fnl f: kpt on* **9/1**
4264 **2** *1* **Funky Munky**[8] 2455 9-9-2 50 (p) MeganCarberry(3) 1 57
(Alistair Whillans) *led: pushed along 3f out: wd st to stands' rail: rdn 2f out: drvn ent fnl f: sn hdd: kpt on* **11/2**[3]
0450 **3** *3 ½* **Fickle Feelings (IRE)**[95] 4304 3-8-10 50 ShaneGray 8 52
(David Barron) *hld up in rr: stdy hdwy 5f out: chsd ldng pair over 2f out: rdn wl over 1f out: kpt on same pce appr fnl f* **13/2**
360- **4** *3* **Omid**[168] 2991 6-9-5 50 (p) EmmaSayer 4 48
(Dianne Sayer) *trckd ldrs on inner: pushed along and lost pl 1/2-way: sn in rr: rdn along 3f out: styng on whn hung bdly rt over 1f out: nrst fin* **20/1**
043 **5** *nk* **Sound Of Life (IRE)**[94] 4321 3-8-8 48 (p) NoelGarbutt 6 45
(Rae Guest) *trckd ldrs: pushed along over 3f out: rdn over 2f out: sn one pce* **11/2**[3]
3501 **6** *6* **Rockweiller**[9] 7059 7-10-0 59 JordanNason 5 48
(Shaun Harris) *chsd ldrs: rdn along 4f out: drvn over 3f out and sn wknd* **3/1**[1]
0320 **7** *1 ¾* **First Sargeant**[46] 6015 4-9-6 54 AlistairRawlinson(3) 2 41
(Michael Appleby) *a towards rr* **9/2**[2]
5620 **8** *10* **Voice From Above (IRE)**[7] 7100 5-9-6 51 JackGarritty 9 24
(Patrick Holmes) *cl up on outer: pushed along 5f out: rdn 4f out: drvn 3f out and sn wknd* **14/1**
4010 **9** *6* **Think**[25] 6627 7-9-2 47 (p) SammyJoBell 3 11
(Clive Mulhall) *chsd ldrs: rdn along over 5f out: sn lost pl and bhd* **16/1**

3m 14.55s (10.95) **Going Correction** +0.625s/f (Yiel)
**WFA** 3 from 4yo+ 9lb **9** Ran **SP% 114.6**
Speed ratings (Par 101): **93,92,90,88,88 85,84,78,74**
CSF £57.28 CT £345.94 TOTE £7.50: £1.90, £2.20, £2.20; EX 43.00 Trifecta £320.80.
**Owner** E Tuer **Bred** E Tuer **Trained** Birkby, N Yorks

**FOCUS**
This was run at a more sedate pace than the first division. The winner had a bit in hand and this was an improved effort.
T/Plt: £89.80 to a £1 stake. Pool of £62804.78 - 510.16 winning tickets. T/Qpdt: £25.70 to a £1 stake. Pool of £4277.69 - 122.70 winning tickets. JR

# 7252 WOLVERHAMPTON (A.W) (L-H)
### Saturday, October 18

**OFFICIAL GOING: Tapeta: standard**
Wind: Light behind Weather: Cloudy

## 7285 BET365 MAIDEN STKS (TAPETA) 5f 20y
**5:45** (5:48) (Class 5) 3-Y-0+ **£2,911** (£866; £432; £216) **Stalls** Low

Form RPR
0465 **1** **Aaranyow (IRE)**[7] 7117 6-9-0 50 (t) TobyAtkinson(5) 5 63
(Clifford Lines) *chsd ldr: rdn to ld wl ins fnl f: edgd lft: jst hld on* **50/1**
30 **2** *nk* **Capelita**[14] 6922 3-9-0 0 HarryBentley 2 58+
(Clive Brittain) *hmpd s: sn pushed along towards rr: hdwy over 1f out: sn rdn: r.o wl* **11/8**[1]
03- **3** *1* **Extreme Supreme**[462] 4282 3-9-5 0 RussKennemore 4 60
(Derek Shaw) *chsd ldrs: rdn over 1f out: styd on* **13/2**[3]
0-40 **4** *¾* **Warm Order**[115] 3564 3-9-0 48 DavidProbert 3 52
(Tony Carroll) *led: rdn over 1f out: hdd and unable qck ins fnl f* **50/1**
6 **5** *½* **Sir Billy Wright (IRE)**[12] 6988 3-9-5 0 AdamKirby 6 55+
(David Evans) *s.i.s: sn pushed along in rr: rdn: edgd lft and r.o wl ins fnl f: nt rch ldrs* **15/2**
2-4 **6** *1 ½* **Qatar Princess (IRE)**[21] 6765 3-9-0 67 OisinMurphy 8 45
(J R Jenkins) *s.i.s: hld up: hdwy over 1f out: styd on same pce ins fnl f* **14/1**
3422 **7** *4* **Quick Touch**[34] 6356 3-9-5 65 SeanLevey 9 35
(Robert Cowell) *hld up: sme hdwy over 1f out: wknd fnl f* **7/2**[2]
2030 **8** *4* **Our Grey Lady**[19] 6815 3-8-9 58 RyanWhile(5) 10 16
(Bill Turner) *chsd ldrs: rdn over 1f out: wknd fnl f* **18/1**
60 **9** *1* **Gifted Spirit**[7] 7117 4-8-11 0 DeclanBates(3) 7 11
(Mark Brisbourne) *in tch: sn pushed along: lost pl over 3f out: wknd 1/2-way* **250/1**
-334 **10** *1 ½* **Resist**[43] 6116 3-8-11 57 ConnorBeasley(3) 1 7
(James Given) *chsd ldrs: rdn 1/2-way: wknd over 1f out* **22/1**

1m 1.81s (-0.09) **Going Correction** +0.05s/f (Slow) **10** Ran **SP% 110.0**
Speed ratings (Par 103): **102,101,99,98,97 95,89,82,81,78**
CSF £112.13 TOTE £31.70: £7.80, £1.10, £2.10; EX 138.50 Trifecta £2252.30.
**Owner** Prima Racing Partnership **Bred** Jeremy Gompertz **Trained** Exning, Suffolk

**FOCUS**
An ordinary sprint maiden in which they went an honest gallop on standard Tapeta. Weak form, rated around the winner and fourth.

## 7286 BET365 FILLIES' H'CAP (TAPETA) 5f 216y
**6:15** (6:16) (Class 5) (0-75,75) 3-Y-0+ **£3,234** (£962; £481; £240) **Stalls** Low

Form RPR
44 **1** **Autumns Blush (IRE)**[35] 6314 3-9-3 71 (v) AdamKirby 12 85
(Jeremy Noseda) *s.i.s: hld up: hdwy over 1f out: shkn up to ld wl ins fnl f: sn clr: comf* **5/1**[2]
1606 **2** *2 ¾* **Maria Montez**[23] 6680 5-9-3 70 SteveDrowne 8 75
(Charles Hills) *a.p: rdn to ld ins fnl f: sn hdd and unable qck* **22/1**
5100 **3** *1 ½* **Jolly Red Jeanz (IRE)**[15] 6902 3-8-11 65 (b) WilliamCarson 10 65
(Tom Dascombe) *chsd ldrs: rdn over 2f out: edgd lft and styd on same pce ins fnl f* **12/1**
6010 **4** *½* **Foxtrot Pearl (IRE)**[24] 6674 3-8-11 65 ChrisCatlin 3 63
(John Holt) *prom: rdn over 1f out: styd on same pce ins fnl f* **50/1**
2325 **5** *nse* **Poetic Choice**[31] 6468 3-9-7 75 LukeMorris 11 73
(Nick Littmoden) *mid-div: rdn on outer over 2f out: styd on u.p fnl f: nt trble ldrs* **7/2**[1]
5140 **6** *nk* **Majestic Song**[57] 5650 3-9-2 70 RobertTart 5 67
(James Toller) *s.i.s: hdwy over 1f out: styd on same pce fnl f* **7/1**[3]
6500 **7** *½* **Lexington Rose**[31] 6452 3-8-13 70 (v[1]) ConnorBeasley(3) 1 66
(Bryan Smart) *chsd ldr: led over 1f out: sn rdn: hdd and no ex ins fnl f* **25/1**
4550 **8** *1* **Milly's Secret (IRE)**[26] 6613 3-9-2 70 DavidNolan 6 62
(David O'Meara) *sn pushed along in rr: hdwy over 1f out: nt clr run and wknd ins fnl f* **7/1**[3]
0040 **9** *½* **Pull The Plug (IRE)**[38] 6235 3-8-13 74 LukeLeadbitter(7) 2 65
(Declan Carroll) *sn led: rdn and hdd 2f out: wknd fnl f* **11/1**
2040 **10** *1 ¼* **Medam**[44] 6074 5-8-11 67 NeilFarley(3) 9 54
(Shaun Harris) *prom: rdn 1/2-way: wknd fnl f* **18/1**
4165 **11** *1 ¾* **Joyous**[31] 6463 4-8-13 66 HarryBentley 4 47
(Dean Ivory) *chsd ldr tl led 2f out: rdn and hdd over 1f out: wknd ins fnl f* **7/1**[3]
4510 **12** *28* **Traditionelle**[24] 6671 3-9-1 69 AndrewElliott 7
(Tim Easterby) *bolted to post: hld up: racd keenly: wknd over 2f out* **9/1**

1m 14.39s (-0.11) **Going Correction** +0.05s/f (Slow)
**WFA** 3 from 4yo+ 1lb **12** Ran **SP% 117.8**
Speed ratings (Par 100): **102,98,96,95,95 95,94,93,92,90 88,51**
CSF £112.62 CT £1258.46 TOTE £5.20: £2.60, £7.20, £4.10; EX 94.20 Trifecta £2124.40.
**Owner** Fawzi Abdulla Nass **Bred** Lodge Park Stud **Trained** Newmarket, Suffolk

**FOCUS**
A fair fillies' handicap in which they went a strong, contested gallop. The winner posted the sort of figure that looked possible after her 2yo win.

## 7287 CASINO AT BET365 H'CAP (TAPETA) 2m 119y
**6:45** (6:46) (Class 6) (0-60,60) 3-Y-0+ **£2,264** (£673; £336; £168) **Stalls** Low

Form RPR
2342 **1** **Rock Of Leon**[7] 7118 3-8-10 52 (p) LukeMorris 5 59
(Michael Bell) *a.p: hung lft over 3f out: chsd ldr over 2f out: rdn to ld and hung lft fr over 1f out: all out* **5/2**[1]
0636 **2** *nk* **Lacey**[9] 7065 5-9-4 55 (p) JackDuern(5) 7 61
(Andrew Hollinshead) *hld up: hdwy over 2f out: rdn over 1f out: r.o* **6/1**[2]
0603 **3** *nk* **Yorkshireman (IRE)**[11] 7006 4-9-2 48 (b) PaddyAspell 8 53
(Lynn Siddall) *chsd ldr tl led over 3f out: rdn: whn hdd and hmpd over 1f out: hmpd again ins fnl f: swtchd rt: r.o* **16/1**
0042 **4** *2 ½* **May Hay**[11] 7006 4-10-0 60 WilliamCarson 3 62+
(Anthony Carson) *chsd ldrs: nt clr run fr over 3f out tl over 2f out: rdn over 1f out: styd on same pce fnl f* **5/2**[1]
3542 **5** *1* **Black Iceman**[9] 7065 6-9-2 51 SimonPearce(3) 4 52+
(Lydia Pearce) *hld up: nt clr run wl over 2f out: hdwy over 1f out: styd on: nt trble ldrs* **6/1**[2]
000/ **6** *½* **Peadar Miguel**[16] 6894 7-9-9 55 [1] HarryBentley 1 55
(Michael Mullineaux) *hld up: hdwy over 1f out: nt rch ldrs* **50/1**
/435 **7** *7* **Fade To Grey (IRE)**[13] 1485 10-8-12 51 (t) CiaranMckee(7) 6 43
(Shaun Lycett) *hld up: hdwy 6f out: rdn over 4f out: wknd over 2f out* **10/1**[3]
0000 **8** *25* **Uncle Muf (USA)**[25] 6632 4-9-13 59 (p) AdamKirby 2 21
(Ali Stronge) *led: rdn and hdd over 3f out: wknd over 2f out* **12/1**

3m 41.86s (-1.84) **Going Correction** +0.05s/f (Slow)
**WFA** 3 from 4yo+ 10lb **8** Ran **SP% 110.3**
Speed ratings (Par 101): **106,105,105,104,104 103,100,88**
CSF £16.72 CT £180.40 TOTE £2.40: £1.10, £2.30, £4.30; EX 15.30 Trifecta £143.00.
**Owner** Leon Caine & Mr & Mrs Ray Jenner **Bred** Worksop Manor Stud **Trained** Newmarket, Suffolk
■ Stewards' Enquiry : Jack Duern seven-day ban: used whip above permitted level (Nov 1,3-8)
Luke Morris two-day ban: careless riding (Nov 1,3)

**FOCUS**
A moderate staying handicap in which they went a muddling gallop. The form is rated around the second and third.

## 7288 POKER AT BET365 H'CAP (TAPETA) 1m 141y
**7:15** (7:15) (Class 6) (0-65,65) 3-Y-0+ **£2,264** (£673; £336; £168) **Stalls** Low

Form RPR
2136 **1** **Plough Boy (IRE)**[11] 7000 3-9-5 65 ChrisCatlin 10 73
(Willie Musson) *hld up: hdwy over 2f out: edgd lft an r.o u.p to ld nr fin* **7/2**[2]
5623 **2** *nk* **Black Dave (IRE)**[8] 7078 4-9-6 62 AdamKirby 9 69
(David Evans) *hld up: pushed along over 3f out: hdwy over 1f out: sn rdn: led briefly nr fin: r.o* **2/1**[1]

4236 3 shd **Outlaw Torn (IRE)**[17] 6865 5-9-6 62........................(e) RussKennemore 7 69
(Richard Guest) *chsd ldr: rdn over 2f out: r.o* **9/1**

1325 4 1/2 **Lynngale**[37] 6267 3-9-3 63.................................................. TomEaves 5 69
(Kristin Stubbs) *led: rdn over 1f out: hdd nr fin* **15/2**[3]

5014 5 nk **Pim Street (USA)**[22] 6706 4-8-13 62................................. JoshDoyle(7) 4 67
(David O'Meara) *a.p: rdn over 1f out: r.o* **10/1**

0020 6 3 3/4 **Born To Fly (IRE)**[46] 6022 3-9-2 62..............................(b) OisinMurphy 12 59
(Nick Littmoden) *hld up: rdn over 1f out: nt rch ldrs* **28/1**

5206 7 hd **Benandonner (USA)**[72] 5096 11-9-2 58................................ TedDurcan 3 54
(Mike Murphy) *chsd ldrs: rdn over 1f out: no ex ins fnl f: eased nr fin* **25/1**

3250 8 1 3/4 **Schottische**[35] 6342 4-9-3 59..............................................(v) LiamKeniry 2 51
(Derek Haydn Jones) *mid-div: rdn over 2f out: styd on same pce fr over 1f out* **28/1**

5604 9 2 3/4 **Lord Of The Dance (IRE)**[17] 6857 8-9-8 64.................(t) HarryBentley 6 50
(Michael Mullineaux) *hld up: rdn over 2f out: nvr on terms* **11/1**

4320 10 4 **Matraash (USA)**[60] 5521 8-9-9 65.............................(be) StephenCraine 8 42
(Daniel Mark Loughnane) *prom: rdn over 2f out: wknd over 1f out* **16/1**

0000 11 23 **Tevez**[73] 5041 9-9-7 63...................................................(p) TomQueally 1
(Des Donovan) *s.s: sn pushed along in rr: rdn and bhd fr 1/2-way* **40/1**

1m 49.66s (-0.44) **Going Correction** +0.05s/f (Slow)
**WFA** 3 from 4yo+ 4lb **11** Ran SP% **113.8**
Speed ratings (Par 101): **103,102,102,102,101 98,98,96,94,90 70**
CSF £9.99 CT £55.60 TOTE £3.70: £1.30, £2.80, £2.70; EX 13.40 Trifecta £52.80.
**Owner** K A Cosby & Partners **Bred** J P Keappock **Trained** Newmarket, Suffolk

**FOCUS**
A modest handicap in which they went an ordinary gallop. The form makes sense.

## 7289 BET365 H'CAP (TAPETA) 1m 4f 50y
7:45 (7:45) (Class 3) (0-95,94) 3-Y-O+ £7,246 (£2,168; £1,084; £542; £270) Stalls Low

Form RPR

1424 1 **Desert Snow**[11] 7020 3-8-10 **85**........................................ FrederikTylicki 6 94
(Saeed bin Suroor) *a.p: rdn to chse ldr over 1f out: edgd lft and r.o to ld wl ins fnl f* **4/1**[2]

0643 2 1 **Kelinni (IRE)**[23] 6693 6-9-11 **93**.......................................... MartinHarley 12 100
(Marco Botti) *hld up: hdwy over 3f out: led over 2f out: rdn and hdd wl ins fnl f* **9/1**

1114 3 1 3/4 **Ragged Robbin (FR)**[24] 6665 3-8-11 **86**...............................(t) TedDurcan 10 90
(David Lanigan) *prom: edgd lft after 1f: rdn over 1f out: styd on same pce ins fnl f* **8/1**[3]

515 4 nk **Red Runaway**[7] 7110 4-9-5 **87**........................................... RobertHavlin 5 91
(Ed Dunlop) *led 1f: chsd ldr tl led again 3f out: rdn and hdd over 2f out: no ex ins fnl f* **16/1**

2163 5 1/2 **Solidarity**[34] 6366 3-8-13 **88**................................................ TomEaves 11 91+
(Charlie Appleby) *hld up: nt clr run over 1f out: r.o ins fnl f: nt rch ldrs* **12/1**

2266 6 hd **Xinbama (IRE)**[44] 6061 5-9-1 **83**........................................... LukeMorris 7 86
(Charles Hills) *hld up: hmpd after 1f: rdn over 1f out: nt trble ldrs* **16/1**

2-6 7 nse **Plutocracy (IRE)**[140] 2779 4-9-10 **92**................................... GeorgeBaker 1 95+
(David Lanigan) *hld up: r.o ins fnl f: nt rch ldrs* **9/4**[1]

0162 8 1/2 **Gone Dutch**[43] 6106 4-9-7 **89**............................................... TomQueally 8 91
(James Fanshawe) *mid-div: hmpd after 1f: rdn over 2f out: styd on same pce fr over 1f out* **9/1**

0031 9 5 **Hunting Ground (USA)**[42] 6156 4-9-12 **94**........................... JoeFanning 3 88
(Mark Johnston) *chsd ldrs: hmpd after 1f: nt clr run over 2f out: rdn over 1f out: wknd ins fnl f: eased towards fin* **10/1**

3101 10 17 **Croquembouche (IRE)**[34] 6357 5-9-3 **85**.......................... OisinMurphy 4 52
(Ed de Giles) *led after 1f: rdn and hdd 3f out: wknd over 1f out* **33/1**

0313 11 3 3/4 **A Star In My Eye (IRE)**[39] 6206 4-8-6 **81**.................. AhmadAlSubousi(7) 9 42
(Kevin Ryan) *s.i.s: hld up: rdn and wknd over 2f out* **50/1**

2m 38.23s (-2.57) **Going Correction** +0.05s/f (Slow)
**WFA** 3 from 4yo+ 7lb **11** Ran SP% **115.3**
Speed ratings (Par 107): **110,109,108,107,107 107,107,107,103,92 89**
CSF £39.17 CT £274.93 TOTE £7.20: £2.90, £2.60, £2.10; EX 49.10 Trifecta £271.90.
**Owner** Godolphin **Bred** Darley **Trained** Newmarket, Suffolk
■ Stewards' Enquiry : Tom Queally two-day ban: careless riding (Nov 1,3)
Robert Havlin one-day ban: careless riding (Nov 1)

**FOCUS**
The feature contest was a good middle-distance handicap in which they went a muddling gallop, and it paid to be prominent. The winner resumed her progress.

## 7290 BET365.COM H'CAP (TAPETA) 1m 4f 50y
8:15 (8:15) (Class 6) (0-60,65) 3-Y-O+ £2,264 (£673; £336; £168) Stalls Low

Form RPR

0401 1 **Star Anise (FR)**[7] 7118 3-9-7 65........................................ GeorgeBaker 5 74+
(Harry Dunlop) *prom: lost pl over 3f out: hdwy over 2f out: nt clr run ins fnl f: shkn up to ld towards fin* **9/4**[1]

224 2 1/2 **Rowlestone Lass**[25] 6651 4-9-4 55...................................... MartinHarley 8 63
(Richard Price) *chsd ldrs: rdn and ev ch ins fnl f: styd on* **17/2**

3112 3 1/2 **Zinnobar**[35] 6339 4-9-6 60..............................................(p) DannyBrock(3) 1 67
(Jonathan Portman) *set stdy pce tl qcknd over 3f out: rdn over 1f out: hdd towards fin* **7/2**[2]

3233 4 1 1/2 **Give Us A Reason**[42] 6157 4-9-7 58....................................... LukeMorris 11 63
(James Toller) *prom: rdn over 2f out: styd on u.p* **11/2**[3]

0000 5 3/4 **Enzaal (USA)**[28] 6542 4-9-4 55.............................................. JoeFanning 2 59
(Philip Kirby) *hld up: hdwy over 1f out: r.o: nt rch ldrs* **11/1**

3004 6 1 1/4 **Candesta (USA)**[107] 3899 4-9-4 60..............................(p) ShelleyBirkett(5) 6 62
(Julia Feilden) *w ldr tl rdn over 2f out: no ex ins fnl f* **50/1**

3325 7 1/2 **Tunnel Tiger (IRE)**[19] 6817 3-9-2 60..................................... AdamKirby 3 61
(William Knight) *s.i.s: hld up: nt clr run over 2f out: rdn over 1f out: nt trble ldrs* **15/2**

0/ 8 4 **Osorios Trial**[42] 7-9-3 54..................................................(t) RussKennemore 9 49
(Kevin Frost) *hld up: hdwy over 3f out: sn rdn: wknd over 1f out* **20/1**

4123 9 nk **Giant Sequoia (USA)**[35] 6339 10-9-7 58.........................(t) DavidProbert 7 52
(Des Donovan) *hld up: hdwy over 3f out: rdn over 2f out: sn wknd* **17/2**

6305 10 1/2 **General Tufto**[25] 6627 9-9-2 53.......................................(b) TomQueally 4 46
(Charles Smith) *hld up: rdn over 2f out: a in rr* **28/1**

2m 46.73s (5.93) **Going Correction** +0.05s/f (Slow)
**WFA** 3 from 4yo+ 7lb **10** Ran SP% **119.7**
Speed ratings (Par 101): **82,81,81,80,79 79,78,76,75,75**
CSF £22.70 CT £67.60 TOTE £3.20: £1.40, £1.80, £2.80; EX 28.60 Trifecta £148.70.
**Owner** The Astronomers 2 **Bred** S F Bloodstock LLC **Trained** Lambourn, Berks

**FOCUS**
A moderate middle-distance handicap in which they went a steady gallop. The winner built on her modest latest win.

## 7291 BINGO AT BET365 H'CAP (TAPETA) (DIV I) 1m 1f 103y
8:45 (8:48) (Class 6) (0-60,59) 3-Y-O+ £2,264 (£673; £336; £168) Stalls Low

Form RPR

0033 1 **May Queen**[23] 6682 3-9-6 59................................................ TedDurcan 3 68
(Chris Wall) *a.p: chsd ldr 2f out: rdn to ld ins fnl f: r.o* **6/4**[1]

0/0P 2 nk **The Cash Generator (IRE)**[169] 1923 6-9-9 58............. OisinMurphy 10 66
(Ralph J Smith) *hld up: hdwy over 1f out: rdn and ev ch ins fnl f: r.o* **15/2**

0015 3 1 3/4 **Thomas Blossom (IRE)**[22] 6715 4-8-13 48..................(v) DavidProbert 8 53
(Patrick Chamings) *hld up: hdwy and nt clr run over 1f out: styd on* **5/1**[3]

620 4 3/4 **Perseverent Pete (USA)**[72] 5109 4-8-13 48........................... LukeMorris 1 51
(Christine Dunnett) *hld up in tch: rdn over 2f out: styd on same pce ins fnl f* **33/1**

0000 5 nk **Look On By**[18] 6833 4-9-1 50.......................................... JamesSullivan 5 52
(Ruth Carr) *led: hdd over 6f out: chsd ldr tl led again over 2f out: rdn over 1f out: hdd and no ex ins fnl f* **50/1**

0000 6 shd **Llyrical**[44] 6077 3-9-4 57...................................................... LiamKeniry 13 59
(Derek Haydn Jones) *hld up: rdn over 1f out: r.o ins fnl f: nt trble ldrs* **33/1**

/30- 7 1 1/4 **Fen Flyer**[310] 8258 5-8-12 47.............................................. PaddyAspell 11 47
(John Berry) *hld up: hdwy over 2f out: sn rdn: no ex ins fnl f* **66/1**

4000 8 5 **Hilali (IRE)**[117] 3526 5-9-10 59..........................................(t) GeorgeBaker 9 48
(Gary Brown) *mid-div: hdwy over 2f out: sn rdn: wknd fnl f* **9/2**[2]

3665 9 shd **Avidly**[25] 6636 4-9-2 56........................................... ShelleyBirkett(5) 7 45
(Julia Feilden) *hld up: nt clr run fr over 2f out tl 1f out: n.d* **10/1**

5565 10 hd **Saranta**[26] 6596 3-9-1 54...................................................... DavidNolan 2 42
(Richard Fahey) *hmpd s: hld up: rdn over 2f out: nvr on terms* **20/1**

464 11 2 **Hatton Springs (IRE)**[93] 4360 3-8-5 47.............................. NeilFarley(3) 12 31
(Stuart Coltherd) *prom: rdn over 3f out: wknd fnl f* **22/1**

6000 12 4 1/2 **Bajan Rebel**[57] 5640 3-9-3 56.............................................. TomEaves 6 31
(Michael Easterby) *chsd ldr tl led over 6f out: hdd over 2f out: wknd over 1f out* **28/1**

0044 13 3 1/4 **Noble Reach**[14] 6946 3-8-4 48........................................ JordanNason(5) 4 16
(Lawrence Mullaney) *trckd ldrs: plld hrd: sddle slipped over 6f out: hmpd over 2f out: sn wknd* **12/1**

2m 1.73s (0.93) **Going Correction** +0.05s/f (Slow)
**WFA** 3 from 4yo+ 4lb **13** Ran SP% **125.3**
Speed ratings (Par 101): **97,96,95,94,94 94,93,88,88,88 86,82,79**
CSF £13.16 CT £50.93 TOTE £3.80: £2.00, £3.40, £1.30; EX 17.30 Trifecta £124.20.
**Owner** Ms Aida Fustoq **Bred** Deerfield Farm **Trained** Newmarket, Suffolk

**FOCUS**
The first division of a moderate handicap in which they went an even gallop.

## 7292 BINGO AT BET365 H'CAP (TAPETA) (DIV II) 1m 1f 103y
9:15 (9:18) (Class 6) (0-60,60) 3-Y-O+ £2,264 (£673; £336; £168) Stalls Low

Form RPR

5260 1 **Saturation Point**[17] 6856 3-9-3 57....................................... JoeFanning 7 68
(James Toller) *hld up: nt clr run over 2f out: hdwy over 1f out: shkn up to ld ins fnl f: edgd lft: r.o wl* **14/1**

0340 2 2 1/2 **Norfolk Sound**[25] 6647 3-9-3 57............................................ TedDurcan 13 62
(Chris Wall) *hld up: hdwy over 2f out: rdn over 1f out: r.o* **2/1**[1]

0300 3 hd **Golly Miss Molly**[14] 6939 3-8-4 47.................................(b[1]) NeilFarley(3) 11 52
(Jeremy Gask) *hld up: hdwy on outer over 2f out: rdn over 1f out: r.o* **22/1**

5042 4 3/4 **Stanlow**[7] 7115 4-9-7 57...................................................(p) MartinHarley 8 60
(Daniel Mark Loughnane) *hld up: racd keenly: hdwy over 1f out: nt clr run ins fnl f: styd on* **5/2**[2]

520 5 nk **Ferryview Place**[17] 6856 5-9-0 50......................................(p) LukeMorris 2 53
(Ian Williams) *prom: rdn ovr 1f out: no ex ins fnl f* **11/1**

0006 6 1 1/4 **Scariff Hornet (IRE)**[14] 6946 3-8-12 52................................. LiamKeniry 10 52
(Sylvester Kirk) *chsd ldr tl led over 2f out: rdn and hdd ins fnl f: no ex* **40/1**

2020 7 3/4 **Sarlat**[4] 7188 3-8-3 46.......................................................... AmyScott(3) 4 45
(Mark Brisbourne) *prom: nt clr run 1f out: styd on same pce* **11/1**

0045 8 1 1/4 **Taxiformissbyron**[7] 7115 4-8-12 48...................................(p) TomEaves 6 44
(Iain Jardine) *chsd ldrs: nt clr run ovr 2f out: rdn and ev ch ovr 1f out: wknd ins fnl f* **20/1**

0441 9 12 **Poor Duke (IRE)**[4] 7188 4-9-8 58 6ex.............................. HarryBentley 3 29
(Michael Mullineaux) *hld up: rdn ovr 1f out: nvr dangerous* **9/1**[3]

000 10 5 **Severn Crossing**[16] 6883 3-9-1 55...............................(p) SteveDrowne 1 15
(William Muir) *led: rdn and hdd over 2f out: wknd over 1f out* **40/1**

2466 11 30 **Jazri**[54] 5747 3-9-6 60.......................................................... AdamKirby 9
(Milton Bradley) *hld up: rdn 1/2-way: wknd over 2f out* **16/1**

01-0 12 19 **Impertinent**[137] 2875 4-8-10 46........................................ WilliamCarson 12
(Anthony Carson) *prom: rdn over 3f out: wknd over 2f out* **25/1**

2m 1.46s (0.66) **Going Correction** +0.05s/f (Slow)
**WFA** 3 from 4yo+ 4lb **12** Ran SP% **119.0**
Speed ratings (Par 101): **99,96,96,95,95 94,93,92,82,77 51,34**
CSF £39.95 CT £639.31 TOTE £13.70: £2.10, £1.20, £6.40; EX 88.70 Trifecta £2089.60 Part won..
**Owner** Mr & Mrs P Pearce & S A Herbert **Bred** Burns Farm Stud **Trained** Newmarket, Suffolk

**FOCUS**
The concluding contest was the second division of a moderate handicap, and the winning time was marginally quicker off another even gallop.
T/Plt: £101.40 to a £1 stake. Pool of £91527.54 - 658.57 winning tickets. T/Qpdt: £12.60 to a £1 stake. Pool of £12307.43 - 717.70 winning tickets. CR

7293 - 7300a (Foreign Racing) - See Raceform Interactive

# 7126 CAULFIELD (R-H)
Saturday, October 18

**OFFICIAL GOING: Turf: good**

## 7301a CROWN GOLDEN ALE CAULFIELD CUP (GROUP 1 H'CAP) (3YO+) (TURF) 1m 4f
7:40 (12:00) 3-Y-O+
£1,021,505 (£228,494; £120,967; £67,204; £53,763; £40,322)

RPR

1 **Admire Rakti (JPN)**[167] 2002 6-9-2 0.................................... ZacPurton 7 119+
(Tomoyuki Umeda, Japan) *midfield: rdn 2f out: fanned wd into st: drifted lft but styd on strly fnl f: reeled in ldr fnl 100yds: led cl home* **10/1**

2 ½ **Rising Romance (NZ)**[14] 4-8-5 0........................ JamesMcDonald 14 109
(Donna Logan, New Zealand) *broke wl: led early and crossed to rail: sn hdd but remained prom: led again gng strly over 2f out: rdn and qcknd into st: 2 l clr ent fnl f: styd on but grad reeled in and hdd cl home* **11/1**

3 ½ **Lucia Valentina (NZ)**[14] [6975] 4-8-5 0........................ KerrinMcEvoy 10 108+
(Kris Lees, Australia) *hld up towards rr: rdn and fanned wdst of all into st: drifted lft but styd on wl fnl f: wnt 3rd fnl strides: nt pce of wnr* **3/1**[1]

4 hd **Brambles (NZ)**[14] [6975] 6-8-6 0........................(t) LukeNolen 9 107
(Peter G Moody, Australia) *sn led: hdd first turn and trckd ldr: pushed along to chal over 2f out: rdn in 2nd into st: outpcd by new ldr and 2 l down ent fnl f: styd on wl but dropped to 4th and hld* **9/1**

5 nk **Araldo**[14] [6961] 6-8-5 0........................ CraigAWilliams 15 105+
(Michael Moroney, Australia) *t.k.h: hld up in rr: pushed along and hdwy 2f out: swtchd rt and rdn over 1f out: styd on wl fnl f but nt quite pce to chal* **30/1**

6 ¾ **Lidari (FR)**[14] [6975] 5-8-6 0........................ BenMelham 3 105
(Peter G Moody, Australia) *midfield: rdn and clsd 2f out: styd on same pce in st and nvr able to chal* **15/2**[3]

7 shd **Junoob**[14] [6961] 6-8-10 0........................(b) DouglasWhyte 12 109
(Chris Waller, Australia) *sn prom: rdn and brief effrt over 2f out: sn outpcd and lost pl: rallied u.p and styd on again fnl f but wl hld* **7/1**[2]

8 nk **Hawkspur (AUS)**[14] [6975] 5-8-10 0........................(bt) DamienOliver 8 108
(Chris Waller, Australia) *midfield on outer: hdwy first turn and sn trcking ldr: pushed along to chal over 2f out: rdn in 3rd into st: outpcd by ldr over 1f out: styd on but hld whn sltly short of room and lost 2 pls towards fin* **18/1**

9 hd **Green Moon (IRE)**[14] [6975] 7-9-0 0........................(t) ChadSchofield 5 112
(Robert Hickmott, Australia) *hld up in midfield on inner: hdwy and prom over 2f out: rdn in 4th and ev ch into st: styd on same pce against rail fnl f and lost multiple pls* **40/1**

10 shd **Big Memory (FR)**[7] [7126] 4-8-3 0........................(t) CoreyBrown 17 101
(Tony McEvoy, Australia) *hld up in rr: rdn and fanned wd into st: styd on fnl f but nvr threatened* **25/1**

11 ¾ **The Offer (IRE)**[14] [6975] 5-8-13 0........................ TommyBerry 16 110+
(Gai Waterhouse, Australia) *stdd and hld up in rr: rdn in last and fanned wd into st: styd on fnl f but nvr threatened* **25/1**

12 ½ **Stipulate**[14] [6975] 5-8-7 0........................ DwayneDunn 4 103
(David A Hayes & Tom Dabernig, Australia) *t.k.h: hld up in midfield: rdn into st: styng on and stl ch whn squeezed out and lost momentum jst over 1f out: nt rcvr and fdd fnl f* **20/1**

13 shd **Who Shot Thebarman (NZ)**[14] 6-8-9 0........................ GlenBoss 13 105
(Chris Waller, Australia) *prom early: sn midfield in tch: swtchd out and pushed along to cl on outer over 2f out: rdn and outpcd into st: plugged on fnl f but wl hld* **10/1**

14 1 **Moriarty (IRE)**[14] 6-8-9 0........................(bt) MichaelRodd 6 103
(Chris Waller, Australia) *midfield: clsd 3f out: rdn and fanned wd into st: hung in and sn outpcd: allowed to coast home whn btn fnl f* **25/1**

15 shd **Seismos (IRE)**[63] [5432] 6-8-11 0........................(p) CraigNewitt 1 105
(Marco Botti) *pushed along to hold position early: midfield on inner: rdn 3f out: drvn and outpcd in st: eased whn btn nring fin* **25/1**

16 1 ¾ **Renew (IRE)**[7] [7126] 4-8-3 0........................(p) ReganBayliss 2 94
(Archie Alexander, Australia) *hmpd early: hld up in midfield: towards rr 1/2-way and sn last: rdn over 2f out: no imp and btn in st* **200/1**

17 2 **Unchain My Heart (AUS)**[7] [7126] 8-8-3 0........................(b) StephenBaster 11 91
(David A Hayes & Tom Dabernig, Australia) *hld up and a towards rr: rdn over 2f out: no imp and btn in st: nvr a factor* **150/1**

18 hd **Sea Moon**[14] 6-9-0 0........................ StevenArnold 18 102
(Robert Hickmott, Australia) *stdy hdwy fr wdst draw and led first turn: hdd over 2f out: sn rdn and btn: wknd: eased and dropped to last fnl f* **40/1**

2m 32.12s (152.12) **18 Ran SP% 120.5**
PARI-MUTUEL (NSW TAB - all including 1 aud stake): WIN 12.60; PLACE 4.40, 3.50, 2.10; DF 66.70; SF 133.70.
**Owner** Riichi Kondo **Bred** Northern Racing **Trained** Japan

# 6811 BATH (L-H)

## Sunday, October 19

**OFFICIAL GOING: Good to soft (soft in places; 6.9)**
Wind: strong against Weather: cloudy with sunny periods

## 7302 PROFAB WINDOWS FILLIES' H'CAP (DIV I) 1m 5y
**1:30** (1:30) (Class 5) (0-70,69) 3-Y-0+ **£3,234** (£962; £481; £240) **Stalls** Low

Form RPR

6430 1 **Palace Princess (FR)**[9] [7078] 3-8-7 55........................ JoeFanning 3 64
(Ed Dunlop) *in tch: nt clr run on heels of ldrs fr jst over 2f out tl swtchd lft ent fnl f: r.o wl to ld towards fin: pushed out* **10/1**

2241 2 ¾ **Mendacious Harpy (IRE)**[29] [6540] 3-9-4 66........................ PatCosgrave 6 73
(George Baker) *led: rdn ins fnl f: kpt on but no ex whn hdd towards fin* **4/1**[1]

3210 3 2 **Jersey Brown (IRE)**[6] [7160] 3-8-12 67........................ DanielCremin(7) 7 69
(Mick Channon) *s.i.s: towards rr: stdy prog fr over 2f out: wnt 3rd ent fnl f: styd on same pce* **5/1**[3]

5640 4 1 ½ **Tea In Transvaal (IRE)**[32] [6459] 3-9-4 66........................ LukeMorris 8 65
(John O'Shea) *prom: rdn over 2f out: kpt on same pce fnl f* **12/1**

102 5 ¾ **Raamz (IRE)**[28] [6578] 7-9-0 62........................(p) CamHardie(3) 9 60
(Kevin Morgan) *trckd ldrs: rdn over 2f out: kpt on same pce fr over 1f out* **9/2**[2]

4562 6 3 **Pink Lips**[56] [5731] 6-8-11 56........................(v) PaddyAspell 1 47
(J R Jenkins) *hld up: rdn 3f out: little imp: nvr a threat* **15/2**

5223 7 nk **Run Fat Lass Run**[27] [6615] 4-9-8 67........................(p) HayleyTurner 4 58
(Conor Dore) *in tch: effrt over 2f out: nt quite pce to get on chal: fdd ins fnl f* **6/1**

-202 8 18 **Princess Icicle**[52] [5848] 6-9-7 66........................ AdamKirby 5 15
(Jo Crowley) *trckd ldrs: rdn over 2f out: wkng whn hmpd jst over 1f out* **5/1**[3]

1m 44.26s (3.46) **Going Correction** +0.35s/f (Good)
**WFA** 3 from 4yo+ 3lb **8 Ran SP% 114.3**
Speed ratings (Par 100): **96,95,93,91,91 88,87,69**
CSF £49.71 CT £228.37 TOTE £10.10: £2.40, £1.80, £2.10; EX 103.80 Trifecta £646.70.
**Owner** Palace House Turf Club **Bred** Tsega Mares **Trained** Newmarket, Suffolk

**FOCUS**
This moderate fillies' handicap was run at a sound enough pace and the form ought to work out.

## 7303 PROFAB WINDOWS FILLIES' H'CAP (DIV II) 1m 5y
**2:00** (2:00) (Class 5) (0-70,68) 3-Y-0+ **£3,234** (£962; £481; £240) **Stalls** Low

Form RPR

4552 1 **Lady Bayside**[38] [6251] 6-9-10 68........................ SeanLevey 5 76
(Malcolm Saunders) *in tch: rdn and hdwy wl over 1f out: chalng whn hung lft ent fnl f: narrow advantage fnl 140yds: hld on* **6/1**[3]

4000 2 nk **Boogangoo (IRE)**[11] [7044] 3-9-4 65........................ DavidProbert 7 71
(Grace Harris) *led: rdn over 1f out: hdd fnl 140yds: kpt on* **7/1**

0422 3 1 ½ **Gharaaneej (IRE)**[12] [7024] 3-9-5 66........................ PaulHanagan 1 69
(John Gosden) *slowly away: sn trcking ldrs: rdn over 2f out: ch ent fnl f: kpt on same pce* **13/8**[1]

0505 4 hd **Distant High**[12] [7025] 3-8-6 56........................ JoeyHaynes(3) 2 58
(Richard Price) *trckd ldrs: rdn over 2f out: kpt on but nt pce to chal* **7/1**

4553 5 ½ **Sixties Love**[38] [6262] 3-9-6 67........................ SteveDrowne 9 68
(Simon Dow) *t.k.h: hld up: hdwy over 1f out: sn swtchd lft: kpt on same pce fnl f* **9/2**[2]

4500 6 1 ½ **Ambella (IRE)**[22] [6767] 4-9-2 60........................(v[1]) JimCrowley 6 59
(Ian Williams) *sn prom: rdn over 1f out: hld whn short of room ent fnl f: fdd fnl 120yds* **16/1**

0323 7 11 **Actonetaketwo**[34] [6407] 4-8-3 54 oh8........................ CallumShepherd(7) 8 28
(Ron Hodges) *s.i.s: sn in tch: effrt over 2f out: wknd over 1f out* **16/1**

064 8 ½ **Jethou Island**[25] [6661] 3-9-5 66........................ FergusSweeney 4 37
(Henry Candy) *in tch: effrt 2f out: sn wknd* **8/1**

1m 45.25s (4.45) **Going Correction** +0.35s/f (Good)
**WFA** 3 from 4yo+ 3lb **8 Ran SP% 118.4**
Speed ratings (Par 100): **91,90,89,89,88 87,76,75**
CSF £48.86 CT £100.51 TOTE £6.30: £2.00, £2.70, £1.10; EX 61.80 Trifecta £182.10.
**Owner** Biddestone Racing Partnership IV 1 **Bred** M Saunders & T Bostwick **Trained** Green Ore, Somerset

**FOCUS**
The second division of the fillies' handicap.

## 7304 WITHY KING SOLICITORS/EBF STALLIONS MAIDEN STKS 1m 3f 144y
**2:30** (2:31) (Class 5) 3-Y-O **£4,528** (£1,347; £673; £336) **Stalls** Low

Form RPR

4042 1 **Norse Light**[22] [6762] 3-9-5 69........................ SeanLevey 11 67
(Ralph Beckett) *mde virtually all: rdn along whn veered rt over 1f out: fnd more whn strly pressed insde fnl f: asserted towards fin* **8/1**

-360 2 ½ **What A Scorcher**[108] [3892] 3-9-0 73........................ AdamKirby 10 61
(Clive Cox) *trckd ldrs: wnt 2nd over 5f out: rdn over 2f out: hung lft over 1f out: str chal ins fnl f: no ex towards fin* **4/1**[2]

4240 3 1 **Past Forgetting (IRE)**[25] [6672] 3-8-11 72........................ CamHardie(3) 9 59
(Luca Cumani) *trckd ldrs: rdn over 2f out: drifted lft over 1f out: kpt on same pce fnl f* **5/1**[3]

4 4 3 **Western Bella**[37] [6298] 3-8-11 0........................ RyanTate(3) 5 54
(Clive Cox) *s.i.s: towards rr and pushed along early: rdn over 2f out: styd on fr over 1f out: wnt 4th towards fin* **10/1**

0200 5 hd **Essanar**[23] [6699] 3-9-0 52........................ JackDuern(5) 4 59
(Andrew Hollinshead) *mid-div: hdwy 3f out: rdn 2f out: styd on same pce* **50/1**

025 6 shd **Quenelle**[130] [3106] 3-9-0 72........................ PaulHanagan 8 54
(Ed Dunlop) *hld up: rdn over 2f out: hdwy over 1f out: styd on same pce fnl f* **10/1**

-320 7 8 **Freemason**[27] [6608] 3-9-5 75........................ JoeFanning 3 46
(Sir Michael Stoute) *trckd ldrs: rdn over 2f out: nt pce to get on terms: wknd fnl f* **7/2**[1]

03 8 3 ¼ **Gold Run**[27] [6611] 3-9-5 0........................ CharlesBishop 7 41
(Olly Stevens) *s.i.s: in tch after 2f: pushed along over 5f out: rdn to chse ldrs over 2f out: wknd fnl f* **16/1**

444 9 3 ½ **Obstinate (IRE)**[137] [2881] 3-9-5 77........................ JimCrowley 6 35
(Andrew Balding) *prom: rdn wl over 2f out: sn hld: wknd wl over 1f out* **4/1**[2]

10 12 **Renewing**[229] 3-9-5 0........................ LukeMorris 2 16
(Roy Brotherton) *mid-div tl dropped to rr u.p over 5f out: nt a threat after* **50/1**

0 11 2 ¾ **Dubai Skyline (USA)**[31] [6483] 3-9-0 0........................ FrannyNorton 1 7
(Clive Brittain) *mid-div tl struggling in last pair 4f out: no threat after* **33/1**

2m 33.67s (3.07) **Going Correction** +0.35s/f (Good) **11 Ran SP% 120.9**
Speed ratings (Par 101): **103,102,102,100,99 99,94,92,89,81 80**
CSF £40.89 TOTE £8.80: £3.50, £1.70, £1.80; EX 53.50 Trifecta £214.50.
**Owner** J C Smith **Bred** Littleton Stud **Trained** Kimpton, Hants

**FOCUS**
A typically ordinary maiden for the time of year in which the principals came clear.

## 7305 BATH ALES HARE FOUNDATION H'CAP 1m 3f 144y
**3:05** (3:05) (Class 4) (0-85,84) 3-Y-0+ **£4,690** (£1,395; £697; £348) **Stalls** Low

Form RPR

6004 1 **Full Moon Fever (IRE)**[77] [4947] 3-8-5 72........................ LukeMorris 6 83
(Ed Walker) *trckd ldrs: rdn over 2f out: led over 1f out: styd on wl* **6/1**[3]

3565 2 3 **Astra Hall**[75] [5003] 5-9-5 79........................ SeanLevey 5 85
(Ralph Beckett) *mid-div: hdwy over 2f out: sn rdn: styd on to chse wnr ent fnl f but a being hld* **12/1**

3040 3 1 ¼ **The Alamo (IRE)**[6] [7161] 3-8-7 77........................ CamHardie(3) 9 81
(Richard Hannon) *w ldr: led over 2f out: rdn and hdd over 1f out: no ex ins fnl f* **12/1**

0423 4 nk **Headline News (IRE)**[29] [6559] 5-9-10 84........................ ChrisCatlin 7 88
(Rae Guest) *s.i.s: in last pair: hdwy to chse ldrs over 2f out: sn rdn: styd on same pce fnl f* **7/2**[1]

2266 5 3 ½ **Samtu (IRE)**[51] [5878] 3-8-3 70........................ FrannyNorton 1 68
(Clive Brittain) *little slowly away: sn trcking ldrs: rdn over 2f out: sn one pce* **10/1**

032 6 3 ¼ **Bikini Island (USA)**[22] [6738] 3-8-8 75........................ DavidProbert 8 68
(Andrew Balding) *hld up in last pair: rdn over 2f out: little imp: wknd 1f out* **7/2**[1]

0-26 7 1 ½ **Rockfella**[100] [4144] 8-9-2 76........................ PatCosgrave 3 66
(Denis Coakley) *led: rdn and hdd over 2f out: wknd over 1f out* **10/1**

0206 8 1 **Bohemian Rhapsody (IRE)**[16] [4441] 5-9-10 84........................ AdamKirby 4 73
(Sean Curran) *trckd ldrs tl outpcd over 3f out: no threat after: wknd ent fnl f* **12/1**

314 **9** *6* **Authorized Too**[45] 6075 3-8-13 80.................................... JoeFanning 2 59
(William Haggas) *mid-div: rdn over 2f out: sn btn* **9/2**[2]

2m 32.86s (2.26) **Going Correction** +0.35s/f (Good)
**WFA** 3 from 5yo+ 7lb **9** Ran SP% **118.2**
Speed ratings (Par 105): **106,104,103,102,100 98,97,96,92**
CSF £76.43 CT £843.40 TOTE £8.00: £2.50, £4.20, £4.20; EX 105.60 Trifecta £1226.50.
**Owner** Bellman, Donald, Walker & Walker **Bred** T Boylan **Trained** Newmarket, Suffolk

**FOCUS**
A fair handicap, run at a sound enough pace.

## 7306 DRIBUILD.COM H'CAP — 2m 1f 34y
**3:35** (3:35) (Class 3) (0-95,87) 3-Y-0+ **£12,938** (£3,850; £1,924; £962) **Stalls** Centre

Form RPR

1242 **1** **Taws**[23] 6705 3-8-3 75.......................................... CamHardie(3) 8 86
(Rod Millman) *prom for 3f: trckd ldrs: rdn over 2f out: led over 1f out: styd on: rdn out* **7/2**[3]

5123 **2** *nk* **Le Maitre Chat (USA)**[16] 6896 3-9-3 86............................ AdamKirby 6 97
(Clive Cox) *nvr really travelling: in tch: pushed along over 4f out: hdwy 2f out: styd on to go 2nd ins fnl f: fin wl but a looking to be hld fnl 100yds* **2/1**[1]

2131 **3** *2 ¼* **Royal Warranty**[27] 6608 3-8-9 78.................................... DavidProbert 7 86
(Andrew Balding) *hld up: hdwy fr 3f out: rdn to chal 2f out: ev ch tl no ex fnl 120yds* **3/1**[2]

021 **4** *3 ½* **See And Be Seen**[29] 6557 4-9-1 79.......................... NoelGarbutt(5) 3 83
(Sylvester Kirk) *led tl over 6f out: chsd ldr: pushed along to ld over 2f out: hdd over 1f out: no ex ins fnl f* **7/1**

0505 **5** *hd* **Boite (IRE)**[37] 6283 4-10-0 87.......................................... LukeMorris 1 91
(Peter Chapple-Hyam) *trckd ldrs: rdn over 2f out: sn one pce* **15/2**

6163 **6** *½* **Mustamir (IRE)**[26] 6640 3-8-9 78.................................(b) JimCrowley 5 81
(James Tate) *trckd ldrs: jnd ldr after 2f: led over 6f out: rdn and hdd over 2f out: sn one pce* **12/1**

0211 **7** *28* **Saborido (USA)**[44] 6107 8-9-4 84...................(b) KieranShoemark(7) 2 53
(Amanda Perrett) *hld up: rdn over 3f out: sn btn* **16/1**

3m 57.62s (5.72) **Going Correction** +0.35s/f (Good)
**WFA** 3 from 4yo+ 10lb **7** Ran SP% **118.4**
Speed ratings (Par 107): **100,99,98,97,97 96,83**
CSF £11.57 CT £23.28 TOTE £4.40: £2.20, £2.10; EX 16.70 Trifecta £51.70.
**Owner** R K Arrowsmith **Bred** Harts Farm Stud **Trained** Kentisbeare, Devon

**FOCUS**
A modest staying handicap, run at an average pace.

## 7307 PREMIER ROMANS NETBALL TEAM H'CAP — 5f 161y
**4:10** (4:12) (Class 4) (0-80,79) 3-Y-0+ **£4,690** (£1,395; £697; £348) **Stalls** Centre

Form RPR

4245 **1** **Divine Call**[2] 7252 7-8-7 65 oh4.................................(v) ChrisCatlin 12 73
(Milton Bradley) *towards rr: hdwy fr 2f out: nt clr run and swtchd lft over 1f out: r.o wl to ld fnl 75yds: rdn out* **14/1**

1550 **2** *nk* **My Inspiration (IRE)**[18] 6880 3-9-1 74.............................. JoeFanning 6 81
(Amy Weaver) *trckd ldrs: rdn 2f out: led over 1f out: hdd fnl 75yds: kpt on* **12/1**

1600 **3** *shd* **Spellmaker**[38] 6263 5-8-11 69........................................ SteveDrowne 13 76
(Tony Newcombe) *hld up towards rr: hdwy fr 2f out: rdn for str chal ent fnl f: kpt on* **16/1**

5306 **4** *1 ¾* **Monsieur Jamie**[51] 5880 6-9-0 72.................................(v) PaddyAspell 10 73
(J R Jenkins) *trckd ldr: led after 2f: rdn and hdd over 1f out: ev ch ent fnl f: no ex fnl 120yds* **20/1**

0060 **5** *hd* **Daylight**[12] 7017 4-9-7 79.......................................(t) DavidProbert 16 79
(Andrew Balding) *mid-div: hdwy 2f out: sn rdn: chsd ldrs ent fnl f: no ex fnl 120yds* **11/2**[2]

1100 **6** *nk* **My Meteor**[20] 6815 7-8-4 65 oh1.................................. DeclanBates(3) 11 64
(Tony Newcombe) *in tch: rdn 2f out: ev ch ent fnl f: no ex fnl 120yds* **25/1**

16-0 **7** *1 ¼* **Clement (IRE)**[32] 6455 4-8-12 70.................................... FergusSweeney 2 65
(John O'Shea) *mid-div: styng on u.p whn squeezed up over 1f out: kpt on but no ch fnl f* **50/1**

2055 **8** *nk* **Joe Packet**[18] 6880 7-9-3 78.........................................(b[1]) DannyBrock(3) 1 72
(Jonathan Portman) *mid-div: hdwy 2f out: rdn and ev ch ent fnl f: fdd* **6/1**[3]

3000 **9** *¾* **Whipphound**[12] 7023 6-8-4 65........................................ CamHardie(3) 9 57
(Mark Brisbourne) *towards rr: hdwy over 2f out: swtchd lft over 1f out: no further imp* **10/1**

606- **10** *4* **Mount Hollow**[306] 8321 9-8-7 70.................................... JackDuern(5) 7 48
(Andrew Hollinshead) *mid-div: rdn over 2f out: wknd over 1f out* **33/1**

5121 **11** *nse* **Heartsong (IRE)**[137] 2890 5-8-10 71............................... JoeyHaynes(3) 4 49
(John Gallagher) *chsd ldrs rdn 2f out: wknd fnl f* **15/2**

4000 **12** *1 ½* **New Decade**[4] 7213 5-8-7 65 oh2...............................(t) FrannyNorton 14 38
(Milton Bradley) *stmbld v bdly leaving stalls: a towards rr* **25/1**

6350 **13** *5* **Sarangoo**[38] 6249 6-9-2 74............................................. SeanLevey 3 31
(Malcolm Saunders) *chsd ldrs tl wknd over 1f out* **10/1**

40-2 **14** *hd* **Threave**[68] 5275 6-9-4 76............................................... AdamKirby 17 32
(Jo Crowley) *mid-div: rdn wl over 2f out: sn wknd* **9/2**[1]

5320 **15** *1 ¼* **Dreams Of Glory**[25] 6658 6-8-13 71..............................(b) PatCosgrave 8 23
(Ron Hodges) *led for over 2f: edgd rt and wknd over 1f out* **14/1**

6R66 **16** *18* **Steel Rain**[3] 7215 6-8-7 70........................................... NoelGarbutt(5) 15
(Nikki Evans) *dwlt bdly: a wl bhd* **20/1**

1m 13.52s (2.32) **Going Correction** +0.35s/f (Good)
**WFA** 3 from 4yo+ 1lb **16** Ran SP% **126.8**
Speed ratings (Par 105): **98,97,97,95,94 94,92,92,91,86 86,84,77,77,75 51**
CSF £164.18 CT £2843.14 TOTE £13.10: £3.20, £3.30, £4.50, £4.80; EX 292.50 Trifecta £2499.70 Part won..
**Owner** E A Hayward **Bred** Cheveley Park Stud Ltd **Trained** Sedbury, Gloucs

**FOCUS**
A moderate sprint handicap in which the main action was towards the stands' side late in the day.

## 7308 SHAWBROOK BANK/IRISH EBF MAIDEN STKS (BOBIS RACE) — 5f 11y
**4:45** (4:46) (Class 4) 2-Y-0 **£4,528** (£1,347; £673; £336) **Stalls** Centre

Form RPR

06 **1** **Commodore (IRE)**[30] 6517 2-9-5 0.................................. PatCosgrave 1 74+
(George Baker) *wnt rt leaving stalls: mid-div: rdn over 2f out: hdwy over 1f out: kpt on wl to ld cl home* **7/1**[3]

3 **2** *hd* **Magical Daze**[7] 7130 2-9-0 0......................................... LiamKeniry 5 69
(Sylvester Kirk) *prom: led 2f out: sn rdn: kpt on: hdd cl home* **7/1**[3]

4042 **3** *hd* **Fujiano**[48] 5985 2-9-0 66................................................ DavidProbert 6 68
(Derek Haydn Jones) *trckd ldrs: rdn and ev ch ent fnl f: kpt on* **10/1**

0 **4** *2 ¾* **Takafol (IRE)**[30] 6517 2-9-5 0........................................ PaulHanagan 7 63
(Charles Hills) *outpcd towards rr: hdwy over 1f out: styd on to go 4th ins fnl f: nt pce to get on terms* **4/1**[2]

0 **5** *1 ½* **Yorkshire Nanny (IRE)**[12] 7004 2-9-0 0............................ FrannyNorton 4 53
(David Brown) *bmpd leaving stalls: mid-div: rdn to dispute 4th over 1f out: no ex fnl 120yds* **20/1**

5 **6** *2 ½* **Midnight Dance (IRE)**[25] 6660 2-9-0 0............................. SeanLevey 10 44
(Ralph Beckett) *trckd ldrs: rdn 2f out: wknd fnl f* **5/2**[1]

440 **7** *1 ¾* **John Joiner**[25] 6659 2-9-2 58...................................(b) DeclanBates(3) 2 42
(Peter Makin) *squeezed up leaving stalls: sn led: rdn and hdd 2f out: wknd fnl f* **25/1**

60 **8** *4* **Rubheira**[54] 5789 2-9-0 0............................................... SteveDrowne 9 23
(Hugo Froud) *outpcd towards rr: nvr on terms* **66/1**

2020 **9** *2* **Zuzinia (IRE)**[9] 7082 2-9-0 73....................................... JoeFanning 8 16
(Mick Channon) *trckd ldrs: rdn over 2f out: wknd over 1f out* **4/1**[2]

**10** *6* **Harley Rebel** 2-9-5 0.................................................... AdamKirby 3
(Neil Mulholland) *s.i.s: sn outpcd: a towards rr* **20/1**

**11** *35* **Liberty Rules (IRE)** 2-9-0 0.......................................... RyanWhile(5) 11
(Malcolm Saunders) *s.i.s: sn outpcd: eased whn no ch fnl 2f* **50/1**

1m 4.17s (1.67) **Going Correction** +0.35s/f (Good) **11** Ran SP% **119.5**
Speed ratings (Par 97): **100,99,99,94,92 88,85,79,76,66 10**
CSF £52.49 TOTE £10.30: £2.50, £2.30, £2.80; EX 51.80 Trifecta £363.90.
**Owner** Highclere Thoroughbred Racing - Trinity **Bred** Ringfort Stud **Trained** Manton, Wilts

**FOCUS**
A modest maiden in which the winner stepped up on his Newbury form.

## 7309 CLIP EXHIBITION AND DISPLAY H'CAP — 1m 2f 46y
**5:15** (5:16) (Class 5) (0-70,70) 3-Y-0+ **£2,587** (£770; £384; £192) **Stalls** Low

Form RPR

2251 **1** **Urban Space**[33] 6426 8-9-2 62.....................................(t) LiamKeniry 13 71
(John Flint) *in tch: rdn to chse ldrs over 2f out: chal 1f out: styd on wl to ld fnl 100yds* **10/1**

4005 **2** *½* **Strait Run (IRE)**[25] 6654 3-8-12 66................................ CamHardie(3) 7 74
(Richard Hannon) *mid-div: hdwy over 2f out: sn rdn and hung lft: led ent fnl f: hdd fnl 120yds: kpt on* **14/1**

6014 **3** *½* **Zambeasy**[20] 6813 3-9-2 67............................................ SteveDrowne 2 74
(Philip Hide) *led: rdn 2f out: hdd ent fnl f: kpt on but no ex* **8/1**

-404 **4** *2 ¼* **Be Seeing You**[50] 5903 3-9-3 68..............................(b[1]) GeorgeBaker 11 71
(Roger Charlton) *in tch: rdn to chse ldrs 2f out: ev ch ent fnl f: no ex fnl 120yds* **5/1**[1]

1054 **5** *1 ¼* **Marengo**[6] 7162 3-8-13 69.....................................(p) MeganCarberry(5) 5 69
(Ed de Giles) *trckd ldrs: rdn and hung lft fr 2f out: no ex fnl f* **7/1**[3]

000 **6** *1 ½* **Aurora Borealis (IRE)**[61] 5520 3-8-9 60........................... JimCrowley 12 58
(Ed Dunlop) *hld up towards rr: rdn over 2f out: hdwy over 1f out: styd on ins fnl f: nvr threatening to rch ldrs* **14/1**

2121 **7** *1 ½* **Daisy Boy (IRE)**[26] 6649 3-9-5 70.................................. SeanLevey 6 65
(Stuart Williams) *trckd ldr: rdn to chal over 2f out tl over 1f out: sn wknd* **6/1**[2]

3652 **8** *shd* **On Demand**[12] 7001 3-9-2 67.....................................(v) DavidProbert 14 62
(Andrew Balding) *rdn over 2f out: nvr bttr than mid-div* **7/1**[3]

0515 **9** *3* **Medal Of Valour (JPN)**[20] 6813 6-9-2 65.............(bt) DeclanBates(3) 15 54
(Mark Gillard) *mid-div: rdn over 2f out: nvr any imp: wknd fnl f* **33/1**

3434 **10** *3* **New Colours**[28] 4498 3-9-2 67...................................(b) MartinDwyer 8 50
(Marcus Tregoning) *a towards rr* **7/1**[3]

5550 **11** *1 ½* **Bold Duke**[23] 6706 6-9-1 68.......................................... DanielCremin(7) 9 48
(Edward Bevan) *mid-div: rdn over 3f out: sn btn* **25/1**

5560 **12** *4* **Dalasi (IRE)**[48] 5980 3-9-0 65...................................... FergusSweeney 3 38
(Henry Candy) *mid-div: struggling over 4f out: sn towards rr* **25/1**

3610 **13** *13* **Mister Mayday (IRE)**[5] 7172 3-9-5 70.........................(b) PatCosgrave 10 18
(George Baker) *towards rr of midfield: effrt over 2f out: wknd over 1f out* **10/1**

0630 **14** *2 ¾* **Template (IRE)**[58] 5621 3-8-7 65............................ KieranShoemark(7) 4 8
(Amanda Perrett) *mid-div: rdn over 2f out: sn wknd* **20/1**

5000 **15** *30* **Another Journey**[111] 3780 5-8-3 56 oh11.......................... RobHornby(7) 1
(Lisa Williamson) *a towards rr: virtually p.u fnl 2f* **66/1**

2m 13.33s (2.33) **Going Correction** +0.35s/f (Good)
**WFA** 3 from 5yo+ 5lb **15** Ran SP% **128.0**
Speed ratings (Par 103): **104,103,103,101,100 99,98,97,95,93 91,88,78,76,52**
CSF £142.17 CT £1202.28 TOTE £11.90: £4.80, £2.60, £3.60; EX 218.50 Trifecta £2466.50 Part won..
**Owner** Jason Tucker **Bred** Winterbeck Manor Stud **Trained** Kenfig Hill, Bridgend

**FOCUS**
A moderate handicap.
T/Jkpt: Not won. T/Plt: £5,358.00 to a £1 stake. Pool: £111,051.45 - 15.13 winning units. T/Qpdt: £415.90 to a £1 stake. Pool: £9,667.21 - 17.20 winning units. TM

7310 - 7314a (Foreign Racing) - See Raceform Interactive

6180
# BADEN-BADEN (L-H)
Sunday, October 19

**OFFICIAL GOING: Turf: soft**

## 7315a SOLDIER HOLLOW - PREIS DER WINTERKONIGIN (GROUP 3) (2YO FILLIES) (TURF) — 1m
**3:35** (12:00) 2-Y-0
**£50,000** (£19,166; £9,166; £5,000; £2,500; £1,666)

RPR

**1** **Bourree (GER)**[21] 2-9-2 0................................................ JBojko 2 100
(Andreas Lowe, Germany) *trckd ldr: rdn to chal into st and sn led: r.o: strly pressed and jnd towards fin: jst prevailed on hd bob post* **159/10**

**2** *shd* **Desiree Clary (GER)** 2-9-2 0........................................ EddyHardouin 13 100
(Waldemar Hickst, Germany) *hld up in rr: rdn and hdwy into st: wnt 2nd jst ins fnl f: r.o wl and jnd wnr towards fin: jst lost out on hd bob post* **113/10**

**3** *1 ¾* **Winnemark (GER)** 2-9-2 0............................................ DanielePorcu 1 96
(P Schiergen, Germany) *in tch: rdn to chal into st: kpt on wl but nt pce of front pair* **114/10**

**4** *¾* **Amabelle (GER)**[22] 6778 2-9-2 0...................................... SHellyn 7 94
(Waldemar Hickst, Germany) *led: rdn and strly pressed into st: sn hdd: kpt on same pce and dropped to 4th fnl f* **136/10**

**5** *1 ¼* **Pearl Diamond (GER)** 2-9-2 0....................................... JackMitchell 4 92
(Waldemar Hickst, Germany) *midfield in tch: pushed along over 3f out: rdn and effrt into st: kpt on same pce fr over 1f out and hld* **238/10**

**6** *hd* **Nymeria (GER)** 2-9-2 0................................................. APietsch 3 91
(Waldemar Hickst, Germany) *trckd ldr: rdn and effrt into st: kpt on same pce fr over 1f out and hld* **37/10**[1]

| | | | RPR |
|---|---|---|---|
| 7 | 3½ | **Ma Marie (FR)**[24] 2-9-2 0 ........ FrederikTylicki 12<br>(S Smrczek, Germany) *dwlt and in rr: rdn into st: plugged on but nvr a factor* **111/10** | 83 |
| 8 | 3 | **Peace Society (USA)**[46] [6053] 2-9-2 0 ........ EPedroza 5<br>(A Wohler, Germany) *t.k.h: midfield: rdn into st: outpcd and btn fnl f: wknd: eased nring fin* **69/10** | 77 |
| 9 | 1¼ | **Maha Kumari (GER)** 2-9-2 0 ........ MartinSeidl 10<br>(Markus Klug, Germany) *dwlt sltly and towards rr early: sn in tch on outer: rdn and brief effrt into st: outpcd and lost pl over 1f out: wknd and eased fnl f* **143/10** | 74 |
| 10 | 1¾ | **Rose Rized (GER)**[22] [6778] 2-9-2 0 ........ AStarke 9<br>(P Schiergen, Germany) *hld up: rdn into st: outpcd and no imp over 1f out: wknd fnl f* **48/10**[3] | 70 |
| 11 | 4 | **Weichsel (GER)**[22] [6778] 2-9-2 0 ........ AHelfenbein 11<br>(Markus Klug, Germany) *hld up: pushed along 1/2-way: rdn into st: no ex over 1f out: wknd and eased fnl f* **39/10**[2] | 61 |
| 12 | 8 | **Amona (IRE)** 2-9-2 0 ........ FilipMinarik 8<br>(Andreas Lowe, Germany) *midfield: rdn 1/2-way and sn dropped to rr: wl btn in st: eased fnl f* **92/10** | 44 |

1m 45.04s (5.93) — **12 Ran SP% 129.2**
WIN (incl. 10 euro stake): 169. PLACES: 38, 42, 35. SF: 3,053.
**Owner** Stall Lenau **Bred** Frau Claudia & Alexander Rom **Trained** Germany

## 7316a BADEN-WURTTEMBERG-TROPHY - DEFI DU GALOP (GROUP 3) (3YO+) (TURF) — 1m 2f

**4:45** (12:00) 3-Y-0+
**£26,666** (£9,166; £4,583; £2,500; £1,666; £1,250)

| | | | RPR |
|---|---|---|---|
| 1 | | **Ever Strong (GER)**[50] [5938] 6-9-0 0 ........ AdriedeVries 3<br>(Dr A Bolte, Germany) *trckd ldr: chal gng best into st: rdn to ld 2f out: styd on wl against rail and asserted: reduced advantage towards fin but a in control* **104/10** | 102 |
| 2 | nk | **Madurai (GER)**[105] [4007] 3-8-7 0 ........ EddyHardouin 2<br>(Waldemar Hickst, Germany) *w ldrs early: stdd and sn midfield in tch: rdn into st: wnt 2nd ent fnl f: styd on wl and clsd on wnr towards fin but a hld* **61/10**[3] | 99 |
| 3 | 1¼ | **Daytona Bay**[77] 4-8-8 0 ........ SHellyn 6<br>(Ferdinand J Leve, Germany) *hld up in last: rdn into st: styd on against rail fnl f and wnt 3rd cl home: nrst fin* **5/1**[2] | 93 |
| 4 | ½ | **Bermuda Reef (IRE)**[50] [5938] 4-9-2 0 ........ AStarke 5<br>(P Schiergen, Germany) *led: rdn and strly pressed into st: hdd 2f out: outpcd and dropped to 4th fnl f: styd on* **71/10** | 100 |
| 5 | nk | **Polish Vulcano (GER)**[16] [6914] 6-8-11 0 ........ JBojko 1<br>(H-J Groschel, Germany) *hld up in tch: rdn into st: brief effrt on outer over 1f out: kpt on same pce and hld fnl f* **67/10** | 94 |
| 6 | 1 | **Wake Forest (GER)**[16] [6914] 4-9-2 0 ........ EPedroza 4<br>(A Wohler, Germany) *t.k.h: midfield in tch: rdn into st: kpt on but nt pce to chal: lost 2 pls towards fin* **7/10**[1] | 97 |
| 7 | 12 | **Amazonit (GER)**[21] [6806] 3-8-9 0 ........ JackMitchell 7<br>(Waldemar Hickst, Germany) *hld up in tch: rdn and dropped to last into st: no ex and btn ent fnl f: wknd: eased* **147/10** | 71 |

2m 13.24s (8.25)
**WFA** 3 from 4yo+ 5lb — **7 Ran SP% 130.0**
WIN (incl. 10 euro stake): 114. PLACES: 55, 39. SF: 636.
**Owner** Frau Annette Christina Bolte **Bred** Danamore International Bloodstock Et Al **Trained** Germany

# [6966] LONGCHAMP (R-H)

Sunday, October 19

**OFFICIAL GOING: Turf: very soft**

## 7317a PRIX DE CONDE (GROUP 3) (2YO) (TURF) — 1m 1f

**1:30** (12:00) 2-Y-0 **£33,333** (£13,333; £10,000; £6,666; £3,333)

| | | | RPR |
|---|---|---|---|
| 1 | | **Epicuris**[48] 2-8-11 0 ........ ThierryThulliez 4<br>(Mme C Head-Maarek, France) *sn led and mde rest: rdn and qcknd over 1f out: 3 l advantage ent fnl f: styd on strly and in full control: pushed out: readily* **7/4**[1] | 106 |
| 2 | 2½ | **Big Blue**[17] 2-8-11 0 ........ MickaelBarzalona 7<br>(A Fabre, France) *hld up in midfield: rdn to try and cl 2f out: styd on and wnt 2nd ins fnl f: chsd wnr but no imp and wl hld* **15/8**[2] | 101 |
| 3 | 1¾ | **Capo Maximo**[34] 2-8-11 0 ........ Pierre-CharlesBoudot 5<br>(Yves de Nicolay, France) *t.k.h early: midfield in tch on outer: rdn over 2f out: outpcd in 5th ent fnl f: styd on and tk 3rd towards fin: nvr able to chal* **20/1** | 98 |
| 4 | nk | **Red Tornado (FR)**[27] [6618] 2-8-11 0 ........ MaximeGuyon 2<br>(Harry Dunlop) *hld up in last pair on inner: rdn over 2f out: styd on and wnt 4th cl home: nvr able to chal* **4/1**[3] | 97 |
| 5 | ¾ | **Winter Springs (FR)**[19] 2-8-11 0 ........ UmbertoRispoli 6<br>(J Reynier, France) *trckd wnr on outer: rdn to chal 2f out: outpcd in 2nd ent fnl f: sn no ex and fdd: dropped to 5th cl home* **14/1** | 95 |
| 6 | ½ | **Gentora (FR)**[26] 2-8-8 0 ........ StephanePasquier 8<br>(H-A Pantall, France) *hld up in last: rdn 2f out: sn outpcd and no imp: plugged on and wnt 6th post but nvr a factor* **22/1** | 91 |
| 7 | snk | **Cornwallville (IRE)**[13] [6993] 2-8-11 0 ........ GregoryBenoist 3<br>(F-H Graffard, France) *led early: trckd wnr on inner once hdd: rdn 2f out: outpcd in dispute of 3rd ent fnl f: no ex and btn sn after: fdd: dropped to 7th post* **16/1** | 94 |
| 8 | 8 | **Aldar (FR)**[21] 2-8-11 0 ........ ThierryJarnet 1<br>(A Savujev, Czech Republic) *midfield on inner: rdn 2f out: sn no ex and btn: dropped to last over 1f out: eased* **20/1** | 78 |

1m 56.89s (5.29) — **8 Ran SP% 117.6**
WIN (incl. 1 euro stake): 2.70. PLACES: 1.30, 1.50, 2.50. DF: 3.20. SF: 6.90.
**Owner** K Abdullah **Bred** Juddmonte Farms Ltd **Trained** Chantilly, France

## 7318a PRIX DU CONSEIL DE PARIS (GROUP 2) (3YO+) (TURF) — 1m 4f

**2:40** (12:00) 3-Y-0+ **£61,750** (£23,833; £11,375; £7,583)

| | | | RPR |
|---|---|---|---|
| 1 | | **Manatee**[20] 3-8-9 0 ........ MaximeGuyon 1<br>(A Fabre, France) *trckd ldr: rdn to chal over 1f out: jnd ldr ent fnl f: styd on wl and edgd ahd fnl 120yds: pushed out and in control at fin: shade cosily* **6/4**[1] | 115+ |
| 2 | ¾ | **Norse King (FR)**[140] [2819] 5-9-4 0 ........ AlexisBadel 4<br>(Mme M Bollack-Badel, France) *led: rdn and strly pressed over 1f out: jnd ent fnl f: styd on but hdd fnl 120yds and hld* **13/8**[2] | 116 |
| 3 | 1¼ | **Bodhi (FR)**[29] [6571] 3-8-11 0 ........ Jean-BernardEyquem 3<br>(J-F Bernard, France) *hld up in tch in last: pushed along 2f out: rdn and wnt 3rd fnl f: styd on but nvr able to chal* **3/1**[3] | 114+ |
| 4 | 2½ | **Garlingari (FR)**[12] [7028] 3-8-9 0 ........ (p) StephanePasquier 2<br>(Mme C Barande-Barbe, France) *midfield in tch in 3rd: rdn 2f out: outpcd and dropped to last fnl f: sn wl hld* **12/1** | 108 |

2m 40.96s (10.56)
**WFA** 3 from 5yo 7lb — **4 Ran SP% 110.8**
Win (incl. 1 euro stake): 2.50. PLACES: 1.20, 1.20. SF: 3.70.
**Owner** Godolphin SNC **Bred** Darley **Trained** Chantilly, France

## 7319a PRIX CASIMIR DELAMARRE (LISTED RACE) (3YO FILLIES) (TURF) — 1m 1f

**3:10** (12:00) 3-Y-0 **£22,916** (£9,166; £6,875; £4,583; £2,291)

| | | | RPR |
|---|---|---|---|
| 1 | | **Faufiler (IRE)**[34] 3-9-0 0 ........ StephanePasquier 9<br>(P Bary, France) **5/2**[1] | 111+ |
| 2 | 5 | **Brioniya** 3-9-0 0 ........ AntoineHamelin 4<br>(A De Royer-Dupre, France) **208/10** | 101 |
| 3 | 1 | **Graceful Grit (IRE)**[43] 3-9-0 0 ........ GregoryBenoist 12<br>(F-H Graffard, France) **42/1** | 98 |
| 4 | ½ | **Water Hole (IRE)**[32] [6464] 3-9-0 0 ........ OlivierPeslier 5<br>(John Gosden) *sn led: pushed along and strly pressed 2f out: rdn and hdd over 1f out: readily outpcd by wnr: styd on fnl f but dropped to 4th and wl hld* **63/10** | 97 |
| 5 | 1 | **No Wind No Rain**[80] [4840] 3-9-0 0 ........ Pierre-CharlesBoudot 1<br>(Yves de Nicolay, France) **67/10** | 95 |
| 6 | 1¼ | **Bereni Ka (FR)**[126] [3289] 3-9-0 0 ........ TonyPiccone 6<br>(L Tassart, France) **123/10** | 93 |
| 7 | ½ | **Petits Potins (IRE)**[43] 3-9-0 0 ........ VincentVion 8<br>(Rod Collet, France) **219/10** | 92 |
| 8 | 1¼ | **Straight Thinking (USA)**[23] [6734] 3-9-0 0 ........ (b[1]) MaximeGuyon 11<br>(A Fabre, France) **37/10**[2] | 89 |
| 9 | 1 | **Kozideh (FR)**[42] 3-9-0 0 ........ ThierryJarnet 3<br>(J-C Rouget, France) **57/10**[3] | 87 |
| 10 | ¾ | **Yonna (FR)**[18] [6882] 3-9-0 0 ........ AnthonyCrastus 2<br>(E Lellouche, France) **117/10** | 85 |
| 11 | 10 | **Local Hero (FR)**[84] [4721] 3-9-0 0 ........ JohanVictoire 7<br>(Y Durepaire, France) **46/1** | 64 |

1m 55.11s (3.51) — **11 Ran SP% 120.3**
WIN (incl. 1 euro stake): 3.50. PLACES: 1.80, 5.20, 6.90. DF: 41.60. SF: 53.10.
**Owner** Niarchos Family **Bred** Niarchos Family **Trained** Chantilly, France

# [7146] SAN SIRO (R-H)

Sunday, October 19

**OFFICIAL GOING: Turf: soft**

## 7320a PREMIO OMENONI (GROUP 3) (3YO+) (TURF) — 5f

**2:25** (12:00) 3-Y-0+ **£23,333** (£10,266; £5,600; £2,800)

| | | | RPR |
|---|---|---|---|
| 1 | | **Harlem Shake (IRE)**[14] 3-9-0 0 ........ FabioBranca 1<br>(Marco Gasparini, Italy) *chsd ldrs on stands' rail: shkn up to press ldr over 1f out: led ent fnl f: drvn out: readily* **13/5**[2] | 105 |
| 2 | 1½ | **Namera (GER)**[35] 5-8-10 0 ........ (b) CristianDemuro 3<br>(P Harley, Germany) *towards rr: hdwy 2f out: r.o u.str.p fnl f: tk 2nd fnl strides* **35/4** | 95 |
| 3 | hd | **Eldo River (IRE)**[14] 5-9-2 0 ........ (b) PBorrelli 2<br>(Luigi Biagetti, Italy) *pressed ldr: led 2f out: scrubbed along 1 1/2f out: hdd ent fnl f: kpt on at same pce: lost 2nd fnl strides* **15/2** | 100 |
| 4 | hd | **Universo Star (IRE)**[14] 4-8-10 0 ........ FBossa 5<br>(A Marcialis, Italy) *chsd ldrs towards centre: rdn and kpt on fnl f: nvr quite on terms* **103/20** | 93 |
| 5 | 1¼ | **Guinnevre (IRE)**[27] [6620] 4-8-10 0 ........ DarioVargiu 7<br>(A Wohler, Germany) *towards rr on outer: shkn up and sme prog 2f out: cl 5th and ev ch over 1f out: one pce fnl f* **97/10** | 89 |
| 6 | 5 | **Konkan (IRE)**[140] 3-8-10 0 ........ MircoDemuro 6<br>(L Riccardi, Italy) *midfield: rdn to chse ldrs 1/2-way: nt clrest of runs but qckly btn ent fnl f: sn eased* **69/20**[3] | 72 |
| 7 | nse | **Clorofilla (IRE)**[133] 4-9-1 0 ........ LManiezzi 9<br>(Marco Gasparini, Italy) *chsd ldrs on outer: rdn and nt qckn fr 2f out: eased whn btn fnl f* **13/5**[2] | 75 |
| 8 | 5 | **Omaticaya (IRE)**[92] 3-9-1 0 ........ GFois 4<br>(V Fazio, Italy) *chsd ldrs on outer: rdn and nt qckn fr 2f out: eased whn btn fnl f* **47/20**[1] | 58 |
| 9 | 2 | **Iftaar (IRE)**[114] [3672] 3-9-0 0 ........ SSulas 8<br>(D Grilli, Italy) *in rr: rdn and no imp 2f out: sn wknd* **165/10** | 50 |

1m 1.2s (2.00) — **9 Ran SP% 161.2**
WIN (incl. 1 euro stake): 3.58 (Harlem Shake coupled with Clorofilla). PLACES: 1.97, 3.11, 2.76. DF: 24.84.
**Owner** Vincenzo Caldarola **Bred** Ringfort Stud **Trained** Italy

## 7321a PREMIO DORMELLO (GROUP 3) (2YO FILLIES) (TURF) — 1m

**3:00** (12:00) 2-Y-0 **£37,500** (£16,500; £9,000; £4,500)

| | | | RPR |
|---|---|---|---|
| 1 | | **Fontanelice (IRE)**[112] [3775] 2-8-11 0 ........ CristianDemuro 5<br>(Stefano Botti, Italy) *mde all: hrd pressed fr 2f out: rdn and r.o fnl f: asserted last 100yds* **19/10**[2] | 102 |

2 1 ¼ **Marabea** 2-8-11 0 ......... FBossa 8 99
(R Rohne, Germany) *t.k.h: trckd ldr on outer: rdn to chal fr 2f out: kpt on under hrd driving fnl f: a hld last* **33/20**[1]

3 2 ¼ **Money Drop (ITY)**[21] 2-8-11 0 ......... CFiocchi 4 94
(Stefano Botti, Italy) *hld up towards rr: hdwy to chse ldng trio fr over 2f out: styd on to go 3rd 100yds out: nt rch front two* **61/20**[3]

4 hd **Aria Di Primavera** 2-8-11 0 ......... DarioVargiu 1 94
(Stefano Botti, Italy) *chsd ldrs on inner: rdn to chal between horses over 2f out: outpcd by front two over 1f out: one pce fnl f: lost 3rd 100yds out: no ex* **48/10**

5 3 **Evviva (ITY)** 2-8-11 0 ......... MEsposito 7 87
(Stefano Botti, Italy) *tk fierce hold: restrained in fnl pair: sme prog fr 1 1/2f out: nvr in contention* **106/10**

6 3 ½ **A Fari Spenti (IRE)** 2-8-11 0 ......... LManiezzi 2 80
(P L Giannotti, Italy) *w.w in fnl pair: hrd rdn and no imp fr 2f out: sn wl btn* **44/1**

7 11 **Torino (ITY)** 2-8-11 0 ......... FabioBranca 6 55
(L Riccardi, Italy) *chsd ldrs on outer: rdn and nt qckn fr 2f out: sn wknd and eased fnl f* **20/1**

1m 43.3s (1.20) **7 Ran SP% 129.8**
WIN (incl. 1 euro stake): 2.89. PLACES: 1.26, 1.20, 1.24. DF: 3.33.
**Owner** Stefano Botti **Bred** John Martin McLoughney **Trained** Italy

## 7322a PREMIO DEL PIAZZALE (GROUP 3) (3YO+) (TURF) 1m
4:10 (12:00) 3-Y-0+ **£23,333** (£10,266; £5,600; £2,800)

RPR

1 **Spoil The Fun (FR)**[49] 5960 5-8-11 0 ......... JulienAuge 4 112
(C Ferland, France) *settled in 5th on rail: gd hdwy on inner to chal 2f out: led 1 1/2f out: drvn clr appr fnl f: a in control* **11/5**[2]

2 3 **Felician (GER)**[14] 6965 6-8-11 0 ......... RobertHavlin 7 105
(Ferdinand J Leve, Germany) *towards rr on outer: rdn and hdwy over 1 1/2f out: kpt on ins fnl f: no ch w wnr* **81/10**[3]

3 ½ **Line Drummer (FR)**[30] 6592 4-8-11 0 ......... DarioVargiu 3 104
(J Reynier, France) *cl up bhd ldng pair on inner: rdn and outpcd 2 1/2f out: swtchd outside and hrd rdn over 1 1/2f out but no real imp: sn swtchd bk ins and styd on again fnl f* **89/10**

4 nk **Nordico (GER)**[35] 6384 3-8-11 0 ......... (p) CristianDemuro 2 105
(Mario Hofer, Germany) *trckd ldr: rdn to chal on outer 2f out: outpcd by wnr fr 1 1/2f out: kpt on at same pce fnl f* **11/5**[2]

5 5 **Musicante Di Breme (FR)** 4-8-11 0 ......... WGambarota 1 92
(M Amerio, Italy) *led: hrd pressed over 2f out: hdd 1 1/2f out: eased whn hld ins fnl f* **87/10**

6 1 ½ **Mujas**[21] 3-8-9 0 ......... CColombi 8 88
(F Turner, Italy) *hld up in rr: sme prog over 1 1/2f out: one pce fnl f: nvr in contention* **31/1**

7 7 **Salford Secret (IRE)**[21] 6808 3-8-11 0 ......... MircoDemuro 6 74
(Riccardo Santini, Italy) *cl up bhd ldng pair on outer: hrd rdn and wknd over 1 1/2f out* **39/20**[1]

8 ½ **Plusquemavie (IRE)** 3-8-9 0 ......... (b) GFois 5 71
(V Fazio, Italy) *towards rr on inner: rdn and no imp over 2f out: sn btn* **44/1**

1m 40.8s (-1.30)
**WFA** 3 from 4yo+ 3lb **8 Ran SP% 133.1**
WIN (incl. 1 euro stake): 3.20. PLACES: 1.61, 2.36, 2.34. DF: 15.53.
**Owner** Prime Equestrian S.A.R.L. **Bred** Snig Elevage **Trained** France

## 7323a GRAN PREMIO DEL JOCKEY CLUB (GROUP 1) (3YO+) (TURF) 1m 4f
4:50 (12:00) 3-Y-0+ **£79,166** (£34,833; £19,000; £9,500)

RPR

1 **Dylan Mouth (IRE)**[28] 6590 3-8-13 0 ......... FabioBranca 3 116
(Stefano Botti, Italy) *a cl up on inner: led 3 1/2f out: rdn and maintained gallop fr over 2f out: drvn out and wl in control fnl f* **30/100**[1]

2 4 **Duca Di Mantova**[182] 1603 5-9-4 0 ......... MircoDemuro 1 108
(R Biondi, Italy) *racd in fnl pair: hdwy to chse ldr over 2 1/2f out: kpt on fnl f but a wl hld by wnr: pair clr* **17/2**

3 14 **Biz The Nurse (IRE)**[28] 6590 4-9-4 0 ......... DarioVargiu 6 85
(Stefano Botti, Italy) *disp 4th on outer: rdn to chse ldrs over 3f out: sn no further imp and lost tch w front two fr 2f out: plugged on to go 3rd ins fnl f* **43/10**[2]

4 2 **Sopran Nicolo (IRE)**[154] 2376 3-8-13 0 ......... GArena 7 84
(B Grizzetti, Italy) *chsd ldr: pushed along to hold pl over 4f out: hrd rdn and no hdwy fr 2f out: plugged on fnl f* **27/1**

5 ½ **Refuse To Bobbin (IRE)**[21] 6808 4-9-4 0 ......... LManiezzi 4 81
(A Giorgi, Italy) *disp 4th on inner: rdn to chse eventual wnr over 3f out: 3rd and struggling u.p over 1f out: wknd ins fnl f* **29/1**

6 4 **Open Your Heart (GER)**[70] 5231 3-8-13 0 ......... CristianDemuro 2 77
(R Dzubasz, Germany) *w.w in fnl pair: rdn and brief effrt on outer 2 1/2f out: sn btn* **47/10**[3]

7 dist **Wild Wolf (IRE)**[133] 3047 5-9-4 0 ......... (b) CFiocchi 5
(Stefano Botti, Italy) *led: set str gallop: rdn over 4f out: hdd 3 1/2f out: sn wknd and heavily eased* **30/100**[1]

2m 34.5s (3.00)
**WFA** 3 from 4yo+ 7lb **7 Ran SP% 207.7**
WIN (incl. 1 euro stake): 1.31 (Dylan Mouth coupled with Wild Wolf). PLACES: 1.08, 1.59. DF: 4.64.
**Owner** Scuderia Effevi SRL **Bred** Azienda Agricola Mariano **Trained** Italy

# 6390 WOODBINE (R-H)
Sunday, October 19

**OFFICIAL GOING: Turf: good; polytrack: fast**

## 7324a PATTISON CANADIAN INTERNATIONAL STKS (GRADE 1) (3YO+) (TURF) 1m 4f (T)
8:32 (12:00) 3-Y-0+ **£340,909** (£113,636; £57,954; £28,409; £11,363; £5,681)

RPR

1 **Hillstar**[29] 6546 4-9-0 0 ......... RyanMoore 6 115
(Sir Michael Stoute) *settled in 5th: tk clsr order 3 1/2f out: drvn and hdwy on outer 2f out: led appr fnl f: punched clr and idled 120yds out: drvn and a holding runner-up* **5/4**[1]

2 ¾ **Big Blue Kitten (USA)**[22] 6776 6-9-0 0 ......... JRosario 8 114
(Chad C Brown, U.S.A) *hdd fnl quartet adrift of front five: pushed along and clsd 3 1/2f out: 5th and rdn over 2f out: swtchd outside 1 1/2f out and styd on u.p to go 2nd ins fnl f: kpt on but a hld by wnr* **11/4**[2]

3 2 **Dynamic Sky (CAN)**[35] 6390 4-9-0 0 ......... PHusbands 4 111
(Mark Casse, Canada) *in fnl quartet: hdwy on outer 3f out: 7th and styng on 1 1/2f out: swtchd outside and kpt on u.p fnl f: tk 3rd fnl strides* **138/10**

4 nse **The Pizza Man (USA)**[35] 6390 5-9-0 0 ......... FGeroux 2 111
(Roger Brueggemann, U.S.A) *led: hdd after 2f and trckd ldr: chal on outer over 2f out and regained ld sn after: rdn and hdd appr fnl f: no ex: lost 3rd fnl strides* **13/2**[3]

5 3 **Suntracer (USA)**[36] 6-9-0 0 ......... CHMarquezJr 3 106
(Chris Block, U.S.A) *in fnl quartet: hdwy 2 1/2f out: 8th and styaying on 1 1/2f out: kpt on u.p fnl f: nvr trbld ldrs* **35/1**

6 ½ **Reporting Star (USA)**[35] 6390 4-9-0 0 ......... JStein 9 105
(Pat Parente, Canada) *prom on outer: l;ed after 2f: rdn and hdd over 2f out: wekaned appr fnl f* **158/10**

7 ¾ **War Dancer (USA)**[36] 4-9-0 0 ......... LContreras 5 104
(Kenneth McPeek, U.S.A) *chsd ldng pair: hrd rdn and nt qckn 2f out: fdd fnl f* **126/10**

8 6 ¾ **Pyrite Mountain (CAN)**[36] 4-9-0 0 ......... JamieSpencer 7 93
(Todd Pletcher, U.S.A) *w.w in fnl quartet: hrd rdn and no real imprfession fr 2f out: wknd fnl f* **108/10**

9 17 ¼ **O'Prado Ole (USA)**[36] 4-9-0 0 ......... CHill 1 66
(Dale Romans, U.S.A) *settled in 4th: lost pl 3f out: sn bhd: t.o* **45/1**

2m 29.0s (-0.60) **9 Ran SP% 117.9**
PARI-MUTUEL (all including 2 cad stake): WIN 4.50; PLACE (1-2) 2.70, 2.80; SHOW (1-2-3) 2.50, 2.80, 4.50; SF 13.80.
**Owner** Sir Evelyn De Rothschild **Bred** Southcourt Stud **Trained** Newmarket, Suffolk

## 7325a NEARCTIC STKS (GRADE 2) (3YO+) (TURF) 6f
9:37 (12:00) 3-Y-0+
**£102,272** (£40,909; £17,045; £8,522; £4,772; £1,704)

RPR

1 **Caspar Netscher**[15] 6920 5-8-5 0 ......... AndrewMullen 7 109
(David Simcock) **48/10**[3]

2 ¾ **Black Hornet (CAN)**[36] 4-8-5 0 ......... JStein 8 107
(Pat Parente, Canada) **9/1**

3 nk **Calgary Cat (CAN)**[36] 4-8-7 0 ......... ERosaDaSilva 10 108
(Kevin Attard, Canada) **63/20**[1]

4 1 **Excaper (USA)**[70] 5-8-9 0 ......... (b) Emma-JayneWilson 5 107
(Ian Black, Canada) **16/5**[2]

5 4 ¼ **Paso Doble (USA)**[29] 8-8-5 0 ......... DJMoran 4 89
(Mark Fournier, Canada) **30/1**

6 ¾ **Lockout (USA)**[35] 6391 5-8-5 0 ......... GBoulanger 2 87
(Mark Casse, Canada) **705/100**

7 2 **Big Blue Spirit**[25] 5-8-6 0 ow1 ......... PHusbands 6 81
(Darrin Miller, U.S.A) **27/1**

8 1 **Dreamsgonewild (USA)**[22] 5-8-5 0 ......... (b) TrevorMcCarthy 9 77
(Bruce F Alexander, U.S.A) **705/100**

9 ½ **Langstaff (CAN)**[29] 4-8-5 0 ......... MRainford 3 76
(Scott H Fairlie, U.S.A) **67/1**

10 nse **Upgrade (USA)**[22] 7-8-5 0 ......... (b) JRosario 1 75
(Chad C Brown, U.S.A) **91/10**

1m 8.97s (68.97) **10 Ran SP% 118.2**
PARI-MUTUEL (all including 2 cad stake): WIN 11.60; PLACE (1-2) 7.70, 9.80; SHOW (1-2-3) 3.70, 6.30, 3.40; SF 141.50.
**Owner** Charles Wentworth **Bred** Meon Valley Stud **Trained** Newmarket, Suffolk

## 7326a E. P. TAYLOR STKS (GRADE 1) (3YO+ FILLIES & MARES) (TURF) 1m 2f (T)
10:41 (12:00) 3-Y-0+
**£170,454** (£56,818; £34,090; £14,204; £5,681; £2,840)

RPR

1 **Just The Judge (IRE)**[64] 5459 4-8-12 0 ......... JamieSpencer 3 109
(Charles Hills) **8/5**[1]

2 ½ **Odeliz (IRE)**[28] 6585 4-8-12 0 ......... RyanMoore 4 108
(K R Burke) **42/10**[3]

3 2 **Deceptive Vision (CAN)**[35] 4-8-12 0 ......... ERosaDaSilva 6 104
(Malcolm Pierce, Canada) **13/5**[2]

4 nk **Wall Of Sound**[32] 6464 4-8-12 0 ......... RichardKingscote 7 103
(Tom Dascombe) **43/5**

5 1 ½ **Eyeful**[23] 6734 3-8-7 0 ......... FlavienPrat 1 100
(A Fabre, France) **107/10**

6 1 ½ **Angel Terrace (USA)**[25] 5-8-12 0 ......... FGeroux 2 97
(Jonathan E Sheppard, U.S.A) **227/10**

7 1 ¼ **Royal Fury (USA)**[35] 5-8-12 0 ......... LContreras 5 95
(Brian A Lynch, Canada) **134/10**

8 3 **Meri Shika (FR)**[35] 4-8-12 0 ......... Emma-JayneWilson 8 89
(Roger L Attfield, Canada) **43/1**

2m 3.47s (-0.55)
**WFA** 3 from 4yo+ 5lb **8 Ran SP% 117.9**
PARI-MUTUEL (all including 2 cad stake): WIN 5.20; PLACE (1-2) 3.30, 4.20; SHOW (1-2-3) 2.30, 2.60, 2.40; SF 16.50.
**Owner** Qatar Racing Limited & Sangster Family **Bred** Mrs Joan Keaney Dempsey **Trained** Lambourn, Berks

# CHOLET (R-H)
Sunday, October 19

**OFFICIAL GOING: Turf: heavy**

## 7327a GRAND PRIX DE CHOLET (CONDITIONS) (3YO+) (TURF) 6f 165y
11:15 (12:00) 3-Y-0+ **£13,333** (£5,333; £4,000; £2,666; £1,333)

RPR

1 **Peace At Last (IRE)**[14] 6965 4-9-10 0 ......... FabriceVeron 6 107
(H-A Pantall, France) **1/1**[1]

2 2 **Dani Wallon (FR)**[33] 6446 3-9-6 0 ......... FabienLefebvre 4 98
(C Delcher-Sanchez, France) **43/10**[2]

**3** *1* **Aksil (FR)**[13] 6994 4-8-13 0 ValentinGambart(7) 2 94
(M Boutin, France) **61/10**
**4** *hd* **Silver Treasure (FR)**[16] 6913 3-9-0 0 JulienGuillochon 5 89
(Amy Weaver) *led: 2 l advantage into st: rdn over 1f out: strly pressed and hdd fnl f: no ex: dropped to 4th post* **11/1**
**5** *2* **Zayade (FR)**[27] 6620 5-8-9 0 (p) AlexandreRoussel 3 77
(J Boisnard, France) **73/10**
**6** *10* **Totxo (IRE)**[32] 6-9-5 0 (b) Roberto-CarlosMontenegro 1 58
(R Avial Lopez, Spain) **5/1**[3]
1m 28.72s (88.72)
**WFA** 3 from 4yo+ 2lb **6** Ran SP% **120.0**
WIN (incl. 1 euro stake): 2.00. PLACES: 1.50, 2.20. SF: 8.50.
**Owner** Guy Heald **Bred** G B Partnership **Trained** France

# 6976 PONTEFRACT (L-H)

Monday, October 20

**OFFICIAL GOING: Soft (good to soft in places; 7.0)**
Wind: moderate 1/2 behind Weather: changeable

## 7328 WIN BIG WITH THE TOTEJACKPOT NURSERY H'CAP — 1m 4y
**2:10** (2:10) (Class 5) (0-75,74) 2-Y-O **£3,234** (£962; £481; £240) **Stalls** Low

Form RPR
3011 **1** **Dark Wave**[18] 6884 2-9-3 70 GrahamLee 1 80+
(Ed Walker) *trckd ldrs: 2nd 2f out: led last 100yds: styd on wl* **4/1**[1]
242 **2** *6* **Cymro (IRE)**[25] 6694 2-9-7 74 GrahamGibbons 5 77
(Tom Dascombe) *led: hdd ins fnl f: heavily eased whn wl hld in clsng stages* **13/2**[3]
030 **3** *1* **Multellie**[26] 6667 2-8-9 62 DavidAllan 4 57+
(Tim Easterby) *in rr: hdwy 2f out: styd on wl to take 3rd last 50yds* **16/1**
0002 **4** *1½* **Youonlyliveonce (IRE)**[5] 7207 2-7-11 55 ow1 JoeDoyle(5) 8 47
(John Quinn) *trckd ldrs: kpt on same pce over 1f out* **9/2**[2]
0600 **5** *2½* **Seraffimo**[34] 6428 2-7-13 55 oh8 ow2 JoeyHaynes(3) 2 41
(Sharon Watt) *s.i.s: in rr: sme hdwy over 2f out: nvr nr ldrs* **100/1**
000 **6** *1½* **Master Choice (IRE)**[12] 7031 2-8-1 54 (p) JamesSullivan 6 37
(William Haggas) *in rr: kpt on appr fnl f: nvr nrr* **8/1**
6016 **7** *½* **Secret Lightning (FR)**[10] 7075 2-8-9 62 JasonHart 3 44
(Michael Appleby) *mid-div: effrt over 2f out: nvr a threat* **10/1**
000 **8** *¾* **Strong Flame**[27] 6641 2-8-4 57 FrannyNorton 7 37
(David Brown) *mid-div: effrt over 2f out: nvr a factor* **12/1**
4035 **9** *3¾* **Grand Proposal**[18] 6884 2-9-0 67 (p) TomEaves 11 39
(Kevin Ryan) *chsd ldrs: wknd fnl f* **14/1**
0346 **10** *5* **North Bay Lady (IRE)**[5] 7209 2-8-0 53 oh4 (p) RaulDaSilva 9 14
(John Wainwright) *in rr: drvn over 2f out: nvr a factor* **40/1**
3 **11** *½* **Percy Veer**[39] 6250 2-8-12 65 SeanLevey 10 25
(Sylvester Kirk) *in rr and sn drvn along: nvr on terms* **14/1**
1 **12** *15* **Phyllis Maud (IRE)**[21] 6812 2-9-0 67 JoeFanning 13
(Mark Johnston) *sn chsng ldrs on outer: lost pl 2f out: bhd whn eased ins fnl f* **8/1**
050 **13** *18* **Newgate Princess**[33] 6448 2-8-5 58 BarryMcHugh 12
(Tony Coyle) *s.i.s: sn drvn along: bhd whn eased over 1f out: t.o* **50/1**
1m 50.82s (4.92) **Going Correction** +0.675s/f (Yiel) **13** Ran SP% **115.1**
Speed ratings (Par 95): **102,96,95,93,91 89,89,88,84,79 79,64,46**
CSF £28.23 CT £299.14 TOTE £4.40: £2.00, £2.20, £6.50; EX 22.00 Trifecta £363.60.
**Owner** F Ma **Bred** Lady Bland & Miss Anthea Gibson-Fleming **Trained** Newmarket, Suffolk
**FOCUS**
Both Joe Fanning and Barry McHugh described the ground as "heavy" after the opener. What had looked quite a competitive nursery was won with ease by the favourite. They stuck to the inside rail in the straight.

## 7329 BET TOTEPLACEPOT ON ALL UK MEETINGS MAIDEN AUCTION STKS — 6f
**2:40** (2:40) (Class 5) 2-Y-O **£3,234** (£962; £481; £240) **Stalls** Low

Form RPR
342 **1** **Ocean Sheridan (IRE)**[27] 6623 2-9-0 68 AndrewMullen 4 70
(Michael Dods) *chsd ldrs: drvn over 2f out: styd on fnl f: led nr fin* **4/1**[2]
0 **2** *hd* **Regal Missile (IRE)**[25] 6690 2-9-2 0 JoeFanning 6 71
(William Haggas) *chsd ldrs: led 1f out: hdd and no ex towards fin* **12/1**
20 **3** *2¾* **Devious Spirit (IRE)**[36] 6375 2-8-13 0 TonyHamilton 11 60
(Richard Fahey) *w ldr: led 2f out: hdd 1f out: kpt on same pce* **15/8**[1]
0 **4** *1* **Mo Henry**[23] 6757 2-8-12 0 GeorgeChaloner 3 56
(Richard Whitaker) *chsd ldrs: effrt and nt clr run over 1f out: kpt on one pce* **11/2**[3]
4035 **5** *7* **Poppy In The Wind**[13] 7003 2-8-3 55 ConnorBeasley(3) 2 29
(Alan Brown) *s.i.s: in rr: sme hdwy over 2f out: nvr nr ldrs* **14/1**
56 **6** *1¼* **Mr Cool Cash**[9] 7097 2-8-13 0 PJMcDonald 8 32
(Ann Duffield) *s.i.s: in rr: kpt on fnl 2f: nvr a factor* **18/1**
00 **7** *1½* **Reckless Blue**[33] 6453 2-8-7 0 BarryMcHugh 7 22
(Michael Easterby) *led tl 2f out: wknd fnl f* **50/1**
00 **8** *6* **Out Of Aces**[32] 6474 2-8-8 0 KevinStott(5) 5 10
(Kevin Ryan) *in rr: drvn and sme hdwy over 2f out: wknd over 1f out* **50/1**
**9** *½* **Glorious Dancer** 2-8-9 0 CliffordLee(7) 12 11
(Ed Walker) *s.i.s: in rr: sme hdwy on wd outside over 1f out: nvr on terms* **20/1**
0 **10** *shd* **Big Red**[23] 6757 2-8-1 0 JoeDoyle(5) 9
(Robin Bastiman) *mid-div: lost pl over 2f out* **12/1**
00 **11** *1¼* **Illumination**[30] 6563 2-8-6 0 JamesSullivan 1
(Michael Easterby) *in rr: hdwy over 2f out: wknd over 1f out* **33/1**
0550 **12** *6* **Mister York**[86] 4684 2-8-11 62 TomEaves 10
(Mel Brittain) *chsd ldrs on outer: lost pl over 2f out* **20/1**
00 **13** *17* **Luvlylynnthomas**[143] 2725 2-8-11 0 GrahamLee 13
(Micky Hammond) *mid-div on outer: lost pl over 2f out: wl bhd whn eased: t.o* **66/1**
1m 21.79s (4.89) **Going Correction** +0.75s/f (Yiel) **13** Ran SP% **116.4**
Speed ratings (Par 95): **97,96,93,91,82 80,78,70,70,69 68,60,37**
CSF £45.64 TOTE £4.60: £1.90, £2.30, £1.40; EX 30.60 Trifecta £82.00.
**Owner** J Blackburn & A Turton **Bred** J Hernon **Trained** Denton, Co Durham
**FOCUS**
An ordinat maiden in which it paid to race handily, as was the case in the first race.

## 7330 TOTEQUADPOT FOUR PLACES IN FOUR RACES H'CAP — 5f
**3:10** (3:11) (Class 4) (0-85,85) 3-Y-O+ **£6,469** (£1,925; £962; £481) **Stalls** Low

Form RPR
0104 **1** **Doc Hay (USA)**[9] 7101 7-9-7 85 DavidNolan 10 97
(David O'Meara) *in rr: hdwy on ins over 2f out: hung rt over 1f out: styd on wl fnl f: led nr fin* **8/1**[3]
1101 **2** *½* **Perfect Muse**[38] 6296 4-9-7 85 AdamKirby 8 95+
(Clive Cox) *chsd ldrs: 2nd over 1f out: led last 150yds: hdd and no ex nr fin* **11/2**[1]
0434 **3** *2¾* **Singeur (IRE)**[23] 6763 7-9-5 83 DaleSwift 9 83
(Robin Bastiman) *in rr: hdwy over 1f out: carried rt: hmpd 1f out: edgd lft and styd on to take 3rd in clsng stages* **11/1**
1205 **4** *¾* **Come On Dave (IRE)**[5] 7212 5-9-5 83 LiamKeniry 1 80
(John Butler) *chsd ldrs: overall ldr on ins over 2f out: hdd jst ins fnl f: kpt on same pce* **11/1**
-000 **5** *½* **Hoofalong**[45] 6095 4-9-2 80 PhillipMakin 6 76
(Michael Easterby) *in rr: hdwy over 1f out: styng on at fin* **33/1**
1000 **6** *1½* **Keep It Dark**[5] 7212 5-9-3 81 BarryMcHugh 5 71
(Tony Coyle) *chsd ldrs: one pce fnl 2f* **20/1**
0012 **7** *¾* **Mutafaakir (IRE)**[5] 7212 5-9-7 85 (b) JamesSullivan 11 73
(Ruth Carr) *edgd rt s: overall ldr on outer: hdd over 2f out: one pce whn edgd lft and hmpd 1f out* **10/1**
4150 **8** *¾* **Bop It**[23] 6744 5-9-4 82 DanielTudhope 16 67
(David O'Meara) *in rr on outer: hdwy over 2f out: one pce over 1f out* **20/1**
2042 **9** *¾* **Adam's Ale**[23] 6763 5-9-7 85 JasonHart 12 67
(Mark Walford) *hmpd s: chsd ldrs on outer: fdd over 1f out* **12/1**
1441 **10** *2¼* **Meadway**[23] 6763 3-9-7 85 (p) GrahamLee 17 60
(Bryan Smart) *chsd ldrs on outer: wknd over 1f out* **20/1**
3660 **11** *2* **Jack Luey**[31] 6511 7-9-3 81 (v1) TomEaves 15 48
(Lawrence Mullaney) *in rr on outer: effrt over 2f out: lost pl over 1f out* **12/1**
0256 **12** *2½* **Best Trip (IRE)**[19] 6872 7-9-6 84 PaulPickard 14 42
(Brian Ellison) *chsd ldrs on outer: wknd over 1f out* **11/1**
0514 **13** *7* **Augusta Ada**[25] 6689 3-9-6 84 RobertWinston 13 18
(Ollie Pears) *mid-div: n.m.r over 2f out: wknd over 1f out: eased ins fnl f* **11/1**
0115 **14** *10* **Bondi Beach Boy**[23] 6763 5-9-2 85 JordanNason(5) 7
(James Turner) *dwlt: sn chsng ldrs: wknd over 2f out: bhd whn eased ins fnl f* **12/1**
1620 **15** *24* **Cheworee**[45] 6096 5-9-5 83 (tp) GrahamGibbons 2
(Tom Dascombe) *chsd ldr: wknd 2f out: bhd whn heavily eased fnl f: tailed rt off: b.b.v* **7/1**[2]
1m 6.57s (3.27) **Going Correction** +0.825s/f (Soft) **15** Ran SP% **121.7**
Speed ratings (Par 105): **106,105,100,99,98 96,95,94,92,89 86,82,70,54,16**
CSF £48.81 CT £497.98 TOTE £11.20: £3.70, £1.70, £4.40; EX 46.50 Trifecta £662.00.
**Owner** Baker, Hensby, Longden, Baker **Bred** Colts Neck Stables Llc **Trained** Nawton, N Yorks
**FOCUS**
They raced middle-to-far side in the straight, with Doc Hay finishing best down the centre.

## 7331 TOTEPOOL EBF STALLIONS SILVER TANKARD STKS (LISTED RACE) — 1m 4y
**3:40** (3:40) (Class 1) 2-Y-O
**£22,684** (£8,600; £4,304; £2,144; £1,076; £540) **Stalls** Low

Form RPR
3102 **1** **Prince Gagarin (IRE)**[25] 6684 2-9-3 92 AdamKirby 6 99
(Ed Dunlop) *hld up in mid-div: stdy hdwy over 2f out: led 1f out: styd on wl* **4/1**[1]
3 **2** *2¼* **Teofilo's Princess (IRE)**[30] 6554 2-8-12 0 FrannyNorton 2 89
(Clive Brittain) *dwlt: hdwy to trck ldrs over 6f out: nt clr run over 1f out: edgd rt and styd on fnl f: tk 2nd nr fin* **14/1**
11 **3** *½* **My Reward**[19] 6853 2-9-3 0 GeorgeBaker 4 93
(Charles Hills) *hld up in mid-div: hdwy over 2f out: styd on same pce ins fnl f* **4/1**[1]
146 **4** *1* **Carry On Deryck**[38] 6291 2-9-3 98 LiamKeniry 7 91
(Sylvester Kirk) *hld up in rr: effrt 2f out: sn rdn and outpcd: styd on wl last 100yds* **10/1**
5122 **5** *2½* **Sharp Sailor (USA)**[19] 6853 2-9-3 94 MartinHarley 8 85
(Marco Botti) *w ldr: effrt over 2f out: led briefly over 1f out: wknd fnl 150yds* **4/1**[1]
1311 **6** *3¼* **Power Play (IRE)**[30] 6529 2-9-3 93 SeanLevey 1 78
(Richard Hannon) *trckd ldrs: effrt over 2f out: wknd fnl f* **5/1**[2]
2406 **7** *nse* **Natural Order (USA)**[25] 6686 2-9-3 92 DanielTudhope 3 79
(K R Burke) *led: hdd over 1f out: edgd rt and wknd 1f out: eased and lost one pl nr line* **13/2**[3]
6311 **8** *3¼* **Natural Charm (IRE)**[36] 6359 2-8-12 82 GrahamLee 5 66
(Roger Varian) *in rr: drvn over 3f out: lost pl 2f out* **16/1**
1m 52.58s (6.68) **Going Correction** +0.825s/f (Soft) **8** Ran SP% **111.6**
Speed ratings: **99,96,96,95,92 89,89,86**
CSF £56.93 TOTE £4.40: £1.80, £3.90, £1.60; EX 63.10 Trifecta £424.60.
**Owner** Windflower Overseas & J L Dunlop OBE **Bred** Windflower Overseas **Trained** Newmarket, Suffolk
■ Stewards' Enquiry : Daniel Tudhope one-day ban: failed to take all reasonable and permissable measures to finish 6th (Nov 3)
**FOCUS**
Not a terribly strong Listed contest, but the winner did it well.

## 7332 TOTEEXACTA PICK THE 1,2 MAIDEN STKS — 1m 4f 8y
**4:10** (4:13) (Class 5) 3-Y-O+ **£3,234** (£962; £481; £240) **Stalls** Low

Form RPR
5 **1** **Instant Karma (IRE)**[32] 6485 3-9-5 0 WilliamTwiston-Davies 6 84
(Michael Bell) *trckd ldrs: 2nd over 2f out: led over 1f out: hung bdly lft: drvn out* **8/1**
-223 **2** *2¼* **Galuppi**[13] 7015 3-9-5 78 AdamKirby 1 80
(Luca Cumani) *trckd ldr: led over 2f out: hdd over 1f out: swtchd rt 100yds out: kpt on same pce* **10/11**[1]
22 **3** *15* **Shuriken (IRE)**[47] 6045 3-9-0 0 DanielTudhope 4 47
(Peter Chapple-Hyam) *led: hdd over 2f out: one pce* **11/4**[2]
**4** *3* **Harmonical** 3-9-0 0 TomEaves 3 41
(Mel Brittain) *s.i.s: hld up in rr: effrt over 2f out: hung rt and poor 4th over 1f out* **18/1**
0 **5** *2½* **The New Pharaoh (IRE)**[45] 6092 3-9-5 0 GeorgeBaker 5 41
(Chris Wall) *chsd ldrs: outpcd over 2f out: sn wknd* **9/2**[3]

0 **6** *8* **Moorsholm (IRE)**34 6429 3-9-5 0 BenCurtis 7 26
(Alan Swinbank) *t.k.h in rr: sme hdwy over 4f out: rdn and lost pl 3f out* **50/1**

**7** *13* **Dj Gerry** 3-9-5 0 MichaelStainton 9 1
(Nick Kent) *mid-div: drvn 6f out: chsng ldrs over 3f out: sn lost pl: eased ins fnl f* **66/1**

0 **8** *20* **Wiskee Lil**14 6982 3-8-9 0 KevinStott(5) 2
(Edwin Tuer) *s.i.s: in rr: lost pl 3f out: wl bhd whn eased over 1f out: t.o* **33/1**

00- **9** *1 3/4* **Rising Rainbow**421 5785 3-9-2 0 ConnorBeasley(3) 8
(Garry Woodward) *t.k.h in rr: hdwy over 3f out: lost pl over 2f out: bhd whn eased over 1f out: t.o* **100/1**

2m 49.29s (8.49) **Going Correction** +0.825s/f (Soft) **9** Ran SP% **121.0**
Speed ratings (Par 103): **104,102,92,90,88 83,74,61,60**
CSF £16.54 TOTE £8.90: £2.10, £1.10, £1.20; EX 24.40 Trifecta £85.90.
**Owner** L Caine & J Barnett **Bred** Glashare House Stud **Trained** Newmarket, Suffolk

**FOCUS**
The front two, who avoided the inside rail initially in the straight, pulled a long way clear in what was a fair maiden.

## 7333 TOTETRIFECTA BLUFF COVE H'CAP 2m 1f 216y
4:40 (4:41) (Class 5) (0-75,75) 3-Y-0+ £3,234 (£962; £481; £240) Stalls Low

Form RPR
6050 **1** **Madam Lilibet (IRE)**6 7177 5-8-9 59 JoeyHaynes(3) 1 74
(Sharon Watt) *dwlt: sn pushed along in rr: hdwy 4f out: led over 2f out: clr over 1f out: eased clsng stages* **7/1**3

0013 **2** *10* **Dan Emmett (USA)**6 7177 4-9-9 70 (p) DanielTudhope 9 74
(John Wainwright) *hld up in rr: hdwy over 5f out: chsng ldrs over 2f out: 3rd and hung lft over 1f: kpt on to take modest 2nd last 75yds* **9/2**2

1414 **3** *hd* **Hell Hath No Fury**14 6979 5-8-12 59 AndrewMullen 5 63
(Michael Appleby) *chsd ldr: led over 3f out: hdd over 2f out: kpt on same pce* **7/1**3

4-33 **4** *7* **Embsay Crag**93 3501 8-9-13 74 GrahamLee 11 71
(Philip Kirby) *trckd ldrs: t.k.h: effrt over 2f out: one pce and poor 4th ins fnl f* **8/1**

6-30 **5** *3 3/4* **Calculated Risk**158 2289 5-10-0 75 PhillipMakin 8 68
(John Quinn) *hld up in mid-div: effrt over 2f out: sn outpcd: wknd fnl f* **5/2**1

-330 **6** *3 1/4* **Big Time Billy (IRE)**43 6169 8-9-13 74 (v) JoeFanning 3 64
(Alan Phillips) *chsd ldrs: lost pl over 2f out* **10/1**

3310 **7** *7* **Beat The Shower**19 6864 8-8-11 58 RobertWinston 6 41
(Peter Niven) *hld up in rr: sme hdwy over 4f out: sn drvn: lost pl over 2f out* **12/1**

/506 **8** *6* **Regal Park (IRE)**8 7129 7-9-2 63 AdamKirby 10 40
(Miss Imogen Pickard) *mid-div: hdwy to chse ldrs 10f out: drvn over 7f out: lost pl 2f out* **33/1**

5024 **9** *15* **Mr Wickfield**13 7006 3-8-0 58 oh4 JimmyQuinn 7 21
(John Best) *led: hdd over 3f out: wknd over 2f out: eased over 1f out* **28/1**

0500 **P** **Arr' Kid (USA)**61 5564 4-9-9 70 TomEaves 4
(Keith Dalgleish) *hld up in mid-div: p.u over 3f out: fatally injured* **12/1**

4m 20.39s (24.19) **Going Correction** +0.825s/f (Soft)
**WFA** 3 from 4yo+ 11lb **10** Ran SP% **113.7**
Speed ratings (Par 103): **79,74,74,71,69 68,65,62,55,**
CSF £37.53 CT £228.60 TOTE £7.20: £2.30, £1.80, £2.10; EX 41.20 Trifecta £202.80.
**Owner** D H Montgomerie **Bred** Mrs Clodagh McStay **Trained** Brompton-on-Swale, N Yorks
■ Stewards' Enquiry : Joey Haynes two-day ban: used whip when clearly winning (Nov 3-4)

**FOCUS**
This was always likely to prove a thorough test and Madam Lilibet ran right away with it.

## 7334 TOTEPOOL RACING'S BIGGEST SUPPORTER H'CAP (DIV I) 1m 2f 6y
5:10 (5:11) (Class 4) (0-85,83) 3-Y-0+ £5,175 (£1,540; £769; £384) Stalls Low

Form RPR
0533 **1** **Dark Ruler (IRE)**22 6794 5-9-10 83 DavidAllan 4 94
(Alan Swinbank) *hld up in rr: hdwy over 2f out: swtchd lft wl over 1f out: led last 50yds: drvn out* **3/1**1

0402 **2** *1/2* **Docs Legacy (IRE)**16 6937 5-9-8 81 TonyHamilton 3 91
(Richard Fahey) *trckd ldrs: led and edgd lft jst ins fnl f: hdd last 50yds: no ex* **7/2**2

6410 **3** *3 1/2* **Ardmay (IRE)**16 6937 5-9-2 80 KevinStott(5) 2 83
(Kevin Ryan) *hld up in rr: hdwy on inner over 2f out: led and hung rt over 1f out: sn hdd: fdd last 100yds* **9/2**3

2011 **4** *9* **Lord Franklin**12 7042 5-9-5 78 JasonHart 6 64
(Eric Alston) *w ldr: led briefly wl over 2f out: wknd appr fnl f* **10/1**

0045 **5** *10* **Bureau (IRE)**16 6930 3-9-4 82 JoeFanning 1 49
(Mark Johnston) *trckd ldrs: led over 2f out: hdd and wkng whn n.m.r over 1f out* **7/2**2

6360 **6** *16* **Luv U Whatever**189 1493 4-8-10 69 oh1 AndrewMullen 9 6
(Michael Appleby) *chsd ldrs: lost pl 2f out: sn bhd* **11/1**

0610 **7** *6* **Dual Mac**16 6936 7-9-0 73 DaleSwift 8
(Neville Bycroft) *t.k.h in rr: hdwy over 5f out: lost pl over 2f out: sn bhd* **33/1**

5643 **8** *3 3/4* **Dubawi Fun**12 7035 3-9-1 79 MichaelStainton 10
(Ismail Mohammed) *racd wd: led: hdd wl over 2f out: sn lost pl and bhd* **25/1**

-P40 **9** *dist* **Pivotman**128 3254 6-8-10 69 GrahamGibbons 7
(Michael Easterby) *s.i.s: in rr: hdwy to chse ldrs 4f out: lost pl and heavily eased over 2f out: sn t.o: virtually p.u* **33/1**

2m 20.7s (7.00) **Going Correction** +0.825s/f (Soft)
**WFA** 3 from 4yo+ 5lb **9** Ran SP% **114.8**
Speed ratings (Par 105): **105,104,101,94,86 73,69,66,**
CSF £13.27 CT £44.47 TOTE £3.70: £1.50, £1.40, £2.20; EX 15.30 Trifecta £62.60.
**Owner** Kenneth Walters **Bred** John Thompson **Trained** Melsonby, N Yorks

**FOCUS**
The first division of a fair handicap.

## 7335 TOTEPOOL RACING'S BIGGEST SUPPORTER H'CAP (DIV II) 1m 2f 6y
5:40 (5:43) (Class 4) (0-85,82) 3-Y-0+ £5,175 (£1,540; £769; £384) Stalls Low

Form RPR
0052 **1** **Ty Gwr**5 7211 5-9-10 82 DaleSwift 6 92
(Brian Ellison) *s.i.s: hld up in rr: hdwy over 3f out: chal over 1f out: led ins fnl f: drvn rt out* **5/2**1

33 **2** *nk* **L'Inganno Felice (FR)**28 6599 4-8-11 69 GrahamLee 5 78
(Iain Jardine) *awkward to load: trckd ldrs: t.k.h: led appr 2f out: hdd ins fnl f: no ex* **14/1**

4606 **3** *7* **Barren Brook**16 6936 7-9-5 77 FergalLynch 2 73
(Michael Easterby) *s.i.s: hld up in rr: hdwy over 4f out: effrt over 2f out: kpt on same pce to take modest 3rd last 150yds* **4/1**2

0502 **4** *4 1/2* **Moccasin (FR)**69 5268 5-8-12 70 PJMcDonald 3 58
(Geoffrey Harker) *hld up in mid-div: chsng ldrs over 2f out: wknd fnl 100yds* **9/2**3

4263 **5** *2 3/4* **Endless Credit (IRE)**33 6465 4-9-7 79 AdamKirby 7 61
(Luca Cumani) *led 2f: trckd ldr: led briefly 3f out: wknd fnl f* **5/1**

0650 **6** *15* **Escape To Glory (USA)**11 7060 6-9-6 81 ConnorBeasley(3) 1 35
(Michael Dods) *unruly in stalls: hld up in rr: hdwy 4f out: wknd over 2f out: eased whn bhd clsng stages* **16/1**

1 **7** *2 1/4* **Harmonic Lady**146 2655 4-9-3 75 TomEaves 4 25
(Mel Brittain) *dwlt: hdwy to ld after 2f: hdd 3f out: sn wknd: eased whn bhd clsng stages* **16/1**

060- **8** *7* **Narcissist (IRE)**144 7498 5-8-11 69 GrahamGibbons 9 5
(Michael Easterby) *sn chsng ldrs: lost pl 3f out: eased whn bhd clsng stages* **40/1**

6620 **9** *13* **Sir Charlie Kunz**30 6541 3-9-2 79 JoeFanning 8
(Mark Johnston) *chsd ldrs: lost pl over 2f out: wl bhd whn heavily eased clsng stages* **12/1**

2m 21.85s (8.15) **Going Correction** +0.825s/f (Soft)
**WFA** 3 from 4yo+ 5lb **9** Ran SP% **112.0**
Speed ratings (Par 105): **100,99,94,90,88 76,74,68,58**
CSF £38.31 CT £133.89 TOTE £3.70: £1.50, £3.30, £1.50; EX 40.90 Trifecta £192.00.
**Owner** Kevin Corcoran Aaron Pierce Chris Weare **Bred** Mrs A E Simcock **Trained** Norton, N Yorks

**FOCUS**
The front pair dominated and the winner is rated back to his best.
T/Jkpt: Not won. T/Plt: £17.80 to a £1 stake. Pool of £91650.68- 3750.23 winning tickets. T/Qpdt: £9.10 to a £1 stake. Pool of £6667.30 - 539.73 winning tickets. WG

# 7155 WINDSOR (R-H)
Monday, October 20

**OFFICIAL GOING: Heavy (5.0)**
Wind: Moderate, behind Weather: Changeable - heavy shower during Race 6

## 7336 188BET MEDIAN AUCTION MAIDEN STKS 5f 10y
1:50 (1:50) (Class 5) 2-Y-O £3,039 (£904; £452; £226) Stalls Low

Form RPR
332 **1** **Anonymous John (IRE)**3 7254 2-9-5 73 DavidProbert 1 77
(David Evans) *pressed ldr led on inner 1/2-way: rdn and hung lft over 1f out: drvn and hld on wl fnl f* **7/4**1

354 **2** *1* **Wolfofwallstreet (IRE)**10 7082 2-9-5 65 LukeMorris 3 73
(Ed Walker) *trckd ldrs: rdn to go 2nd 2f out: tried to chal over 1f out: kpt on but a hld fnl f* **9/4**2

05P **3** *8* **Invisible Eye**56 5767 2-9-5 0 CharlesBishop 5 45
(Mick Channon) *bdly outpcd in last and pushed along: looked like fining t.o 1/2-way: shkn up and kpt on fr over 1f out to take 3rd last strides* **12/1**

0523 **4** *hd* **One Moment**35 6408 2-9-0 65 FrederikTylicki 2 39
(Robert Cowell) *led to 1/2-way: sltly impeded wl over 1f out: wknd qckly* **11/4**3

06 **5** *3 1/2* **Blackadder**25 6675 2-9-2 0 JemmaMarshall(3) 4 31
(Pat Phelan) *hld up and immediately wl outpcd in 5th: pushed along after 1f: nvr involved* **25/1**

200 **6** *2* **Mister Arden (FR)**12 7029 2-9-5 62 (b) JimCrowley 6 24
(Harry Dunlop) *pressed ldrs 2f out: wknd rapidly and eased* **20/1**

1m 2.78s (2.48) **Going Correction** +0.45s/f (Yiel) **6** Ran SP% **110.1**
Speed ratings (Par 95): **98,96,83,83,77 74**
CSF £5.70 TOTE £2.30: £1.10, £2.00; EX 4.90 Trifecta £23.40.
**Owner** Will Dawson **Bred** Tally-Ho Stud **Trained** Pandy, Monmouths

**FOCUS**
Inner of straight dolled out 9yds from 6f to intersection and 2yds to Winning Post. Top bend out 11yds from normal inner configuration and races of 1m and beyond increased by 42yds. The outer of the Home straight from the intersection moved in 6yds from line used a week ago. Testing conditions ahead of this weak opener, but it proved a profitable race for most punters.

## 7337 188BET CLASSIFIED CLAIMING STKS 6f
2:20 (2:22) (Class 5) 3-Y-O+ £2,911 (£866; £432; £216) Stalls Low

Form RPR
3600 **1** **Dazza**24 6716 3-8-10 65 FergusSweeney 10 72
(Gary Moore) *racd alone out wd and then against far rail: overall ldr after 2f: clr 2f out: drvn out* **14/1**

5000 **2** *1* **Constantine**17 6891 3-8-12 75 CamHardie(3) 8 74
(Richard Hannon) *in tch: prog to ld main gp wl over 1f out: drvn and kpt on but no imp on wnr last 100yds* **6/1**3

3125 **3** *3/4* **Spitfire**104 4050 9-8-4 70 (t) VictorSantos(7) 3 66
(J R Jenkins) *hld up and in last of main gp early: rdn and sme prog 2f out: styd on fnl f to take 3rd nr fin* **25/1**

010 **4** *nk* **Belle Bayardo (IRE)**26 6657 6-8-8 71 WilliamCarson 1 62
(Tony Carroll) *hld up in tch: prog to chal in main gp 2f out: hanging and nt qckn over 1f out: one pce fnl f* **8/1**

420 **5** *3/4* **Election Night**13 7023 3-8-12 69 OisinMurphy 7 65
(Tim Easterby) *hld up in main gp: rdn over 2f out: sme prog over 1f out: one pce fnl f* **5/1**2

6300 **6** *3 1/2* **Double Czech (IRE)**5 7202 3-8-10 70 (v) DavidProbert 4 52
(Patrick Chamings) *led 100yds: styd prom tl wknd over 1f out* **10/1**

4203 **7** *1* **Commanche**30 6558 5-8-10 74 ShaneGray(5) 9 53
(Chris Dwyer) *hld up in tch: pushed along over 2f out: no prog over 1f out: wknd fnl f* **11/4**1

-105 **8** *1 1/4* **Seal Rock**37 6346 6-8-9 71 (b) JimCrowley 2 43
(John Quinn) *prom: led main gp 1/2-way to wl over 1f out: wknd* **11/4**1

5630 **9** *35* **Loot**96 4324 3-8-5 52 RyanWhile(5) 6
(Bill Turner) *led main gp after 100yds tl 1/2-way: wknd rapidly over 2f out: t.o* **50/1**

1m 16.16s (3.16) **Going Correction** +0.45s/f (Yiel)
**WFA** 3 from 5yo+ 1lb **9** Ran SP% **117.0**
Speed ratings (Par 103): **96,94,93,93,92 87,86,84,37**
CSF £96.51 TOTE £16.70: £4.60, £2.50, £4.70; EX 149.40 Trifecta £2217.80 Part won..
**Owner** Galloping On The South Downs Partnership **Bred** Jeremy Hinds **Trained** Lower Beeding, W Sussex
■ Sister Guru was withdrawn. Price at time of withdrawal 25/1. Rule 4 does not apply.
■ Stewards' Enquiry : Jim Crowley one-day ban: careless riding (Nov 6)

**FOCUS**
David Probert had reported the ground to be riding slightly better down the centre of the track after partnering the winner of the opener and that seemed to play out again here as Fergus Sweeney excelled.

## 7338 R J CLYDE BUILDERS NURSERY H'CAP (BOBIS RACE) 1m 67y
**2:50** (2:50) (Class 4) (0-85,81) 2-Y-O **£4,690** (£1,395; £697; £348) **Stalls** Low

Form RPR

41 **1** **Yeenaan (FR)**[30] 6545 2-9-7 81 .......... LukeMorris 4 87+
(Marco Botti) *hld up in last: smooth prog to ld jst over 2f out: shkn up and drew clr fnl f* **2/5**[1]

1653 **2** *3* **Spindle (IRE)**[7] 7156 2-8-9 69 .......... OisinMurphy 3 65
(Mark Usher) *trckd ldr after 3f: rdn 3f out: n.m.r and loot footing briefly over 2f out and dropped to last: rallied to go 2nd 1f out: no ch w wnr* **5/1**[2]

0444 **3** *1* **Pink Ribbon (IRE)**[7] 7156 2-7-11 60 oh4 .......... CamHardie(3) 1 54
(Sylvester Kirk) *pressed ldr 3f: rdn to go 2nd again 2f out to 1f out: fdd fnl f* **8/1**[3]

0222 **4** *6* **Hillgrove Angel (IRE)**[19] 6869 2-8-9 69 .......... DavidProbert 2 50
(David Evans) *led: rdn over 2f out: sn hdd: wknd over 1f out* **8/1**[3]

1m 50.36s (5.66) **Going Correction** +0.80s/f (Soft) 4 Ran SP% **110.3**
Speed ratings (Par 97): **103,100,99,93**
CSF £2.93 TOTE £1.30; EX 3.30 Trifecta £5.40.
**Owner** Sheikh Mohammed Bin Khalifa Al Maktoum **Bred** Malcolm Parrish **Trained** Newmarket, Suffolk

**FOCUS**
Backing odds-on in bad ground does come with a health warning attached, but this proved relatively plain sailing for Marco Botti's colt, who made it 2-3 in his career.

## 7339 188BET CASINO H'CAP (DIV I) 1m 67y
**3:20** (3:20) (Class 5) (0-70,70) 3-Y-O+ **£3,234** (£962; £481; £240) **Stalls** Low

Form RPR

41 **1** **So Noble**[34] 6421 3-9-3 69 .......... MartinDwyer 9 80+
(William Muir) *trckd ldrs: pushed along 3f out: prog to go 2nd over 1f out: shkn up to ld ins fnl f: pushed out* **5/2**[1]

2060 **2** *½* **Chess Valley**[27] 6647 3-8-7 62 .......... CamHardie(3) 7 70
(Willie Musson) *hld up in last trio: stdy prog 3f out: rdn and eased to outer over 1f out: r.o fnl f: tk 2nd last 75yds and clsd on wnr fin* **16/1**

2412 **3** *1¼* **Mendacious Harpy (IRE)**[1] 7302 3-9-0 66 .......... PatCosgrave 10 71
(George Baker) *pressed ldr: led 3f out: rdn 2f out: hdd ins fnl f: one pce and lost 2nd last 75yds* **3/1**[2]

6603 **4** *1½* **Patriotic (IRE)**[19] 6865 6-9-2 70 .......... (p) ShaneGray(5) 4 73
(Chris Dwyer) *s.i.s: hld up in last: pushed along and stl last 3f out: prog and rdn over 1f out: styd on: nvr rchd ldrs* **9/2**[3]

2350 **5** *nse* **Bonjour Steve**[49] 5987 3-8-7 59 .......... (p) CharlesBishop 8 60
(Richard Price) *led to 3f out: styd wl there u.p tl steadily fdd over 1f out* **20/1**

6555 **6** *1* **Loud**[30] 6562 4-9-1 64 .......... (b) JimCrowley 1 64
(Amy Weaver) *hld up in last trio: shkn up and sme prog over 2f out: rdn and one pce fr over 1f out* **8/1**

4553 **7** *2* **Pashan Garh**[7] 7157 5-8-9 65 .......... (v[1]) KieranShoemark(7) 6 61
(Pat Eddery) *t.k.h: pressed ldrs: rdn 3f out: steadily fdd fnl 2f* **10/1**

0040 **8** *2½* **Silvee**[65] 5425 7-8-7 56 oh11 .......... WilliamCarson 3 46
(John Bridger) *prom: rdn over 3f out: lost pl and struggling in rr 2f out* **50/1**

5464 **9** *½* **Peak Storm**[20] 6423 5-8-13 62 .......... (p) LukeMorris 5 51
(John O'Shea) *t.k.h: in tch: rdn over 3f out: lost pl and struggling in rr 2f out* **8/1**

4500 **10** *½* **Chelwood Gate (IRE)**[26] 6658 4-9-4 67 .......... (v) DavidProbert 2 54
(Patrick Chamings) *in tch: shkn up 3f out: nt qckn and no prog 2f out: wknd over 1f out* **12/1**

1m 51.25s (6.55) **Going Correction** +0.80s/f (Soft)
**WFA** 3 from 4yo+ 3lb 10 Ran SP% **123.4**
Speed ratings (Par 103): **99,98,97,95,95 94,92,90,89,89**
CSF £48.08 CT £131.75 TOTE £3.10: £1.30, £5.40, £1.90; EX 64.50 Trifecta £315.30.
**Owner** Muir Racing Partnership - Windsor **Bred** Cheveley Park Stud Ltd **Trained** Lambourn, Berks

**FOCUS**
This was steadily run in the early stage as the jockeys attempted to conserve energy for the finish in these very testing conditions. The winner has the potential to rate higher.

## 7340 188BET CASINO H'CAP (DIV II) 1m 67y
**3:50** (3:50) (Class 5) (0-70,70) 3-Y-O+ **£3,234** (£962; £481; £240) **Stalls** Low

Form RPR

3531 **1** **Belle Park**[45] 6086 7-8-9 65 .......... KieranShoemark(7) 3 75
(Victor Dartnall) *dwlt: hld up in last pair: prog 3f out: squeezed out 2f out: rallied out wd over 1f out: rdn to ld last 150yds: styd on wl* **7/2**[2]

2124 **2** *1¼* **Flipping**[6] 7187 7-8-9 58 .......... FergusSweeney 2 65
(Stuart Kittow) *trckd ldrs: chal 3f out: rdn to take narrow ld 2f out: hdd and outpcd last 150yds* **9/4**[1]

0302 **3** *nk* **Shifting Star (IRE)**[13] 6999 9-9-3 66 .......... (vt) WilliamCarson 4 72
(John Bridger) *led at gd pce: rdn and narrowly hdd 2f out: pressed ldr after: edgd rt and nt qckn jst ins fnl f: outpcd last 100yds* **9/2**[3]

0-2 **4** *hd* **Ahoy There (IRE)**[70] 5245 3-8-13 65 .......... AndrewElliott 9 70
(Tom Tate) *trckd ldr: lost 2nd over 2f out: short of room twice sn after and dropped to 5th: rallied 1f out: one pce ins fnl f* **7/2**[2]

2404 **5** *4½* **Russian Remarque**[143] 2749 3-9-1 70 .......... DannyBrock(3) 6 65
(Jonathan Portman) *hld up in last pair: prog 3f out: tried to chal 2f out: wknd jst over 1f out* **6/1**

46-5 **6** *5* **Here For Good (IRE)**[275] 230 3-8-12 67 .......... CamHardie(3) 5 50
(Richard Hannon) *chsd ldrs: pushed along 1/2-way: dropped to last and struggling 3f out: sn btn* **12/1**

1m 50.41s (5.71) **Going Correction** +0.80s/f (Soft)
**WFA** 3 from 7yo+ 3lb 6 Ran SP% **115.4**
Speed ratings (Par 103): **103,101,101,101,96 91**
CSF £12.28 CT £35.11 TOTE £4.60: £2.50, £1.30; EX 13.10 Trifecta £73.90.
**Owner** V R A Dartnall **Bred** C A Green **Trained** Brayford, Devon

**FOCUS**
This second division of this handicap looked more competitive than the first and it served up a thrilling finish as the three older horses fought it out.

## 7341 188BET GREAT IN PLAY H'CAP 1m 2f 7y
**4:20** (4:20) (Class 4) (0-85,85) 3-Y-O+ **£5,983** (£1,780; £889; £444) **Stalls** Centre

Form RPR

0545 **1** **Topamichi**[6] 7172 4-8-10 71 oh1 .......... HarryBentley 2 80
(Mark H Tompkins) *prom: pressed ldr 3f out: rdn to ld over 1f out: drvn out* **7/1**

000 **2** *½* **Space Walker (IRE)**[27] 6633 3-8-8 74 .......... LukeMorris 7 82
(Harry Dunlop) *mde most: rdn 3f out: hdd over 1f out: kpt on wl u.p but a hld* **12/1**

-213 **3** *1* **Lunar Spirit**[56] 5768 3-8-3 72 .......... CamHardie(3) 3 78
(Ralph Beckett) *hld up in rr: prog 3f out: wnt 3rd 2f out but ldng pair clr: rdn and styd on but nvr quite able to chal* **11/4**[1]

2626 **4** *2½* **Little Buxted (USA)**[32] 6487 4-8-13 74 .......... DavidProbert 1 75
(Robert Mills) *hld up in rr: rdn 3f out: kpt on one pce fnl 2f: nvr able to threaten* **7/1**

1422 **5** *shd* **Calm Attitude (IRE)**[51] 5928 4-9-9 84 .......... ChrisCatlin 6 85
(Rae Guest) *hld up in last: rdn and prog 3f out: one pce and no imp on ldrs fnl 2f* **3/1**[2]

4512 **6** *2½* **Micras**[24] 6714 3-9-5 85 .......... (v) OisinMurphy 9 81
(Andrew Balding) *trckd ldrs: rdn 3f out: steadily wknd fr 2f out* **6/1**[3]

4043 **7** *6* **Moonday Sun (USA)**[8] 7136 5-9-3 85 .......... KieranShoemark(7) 4 70
(Amanda Perrett) *trckd ldrs: rdn and cl up 3f out: wknd jst over 2f out* **8/1**

610- **8** *24* **Take Two**[449] 4798 5-9-7 82 .......... HayleyTurner 8 21
(Alex Hales) *pressed ldr tl wknd qckly 3f out: t.o* **25/1**

040 **9** *3¾* **Exzachary**[101] 4156 4-8-7 71 .......... (t) PhilipPrince(3) 5 3
(Jo Hughes) *in tch in rr: rdn 3f out: wknd rapidly 2f out: eased and t.o fnl f* **25/1**

2m 15.18s (6.48) **Going Correction** +0.80s/f (Soft)
**WFA** 3 from 4yo+ 5lb 9 Ran SP% **117.4**
Speed ratings (Par 105): **106,105,104,102,102 100,95,76,73**
CSF £87.97 CT £285.12 TOTE £10.10: £3.30, £3.30, £1.50; EX 156.30 Trifecta £1761.70.
**Owner** Roalco Limited **Bred** Dullingham Park Stud & M P Bowring **Trained** Newmarket, Suffolk

**FOCUS**
They appeared to go plenty quick enough in the early stages of this feature and it required a dour, staying effort from Mark Tompkins' 4yo, who again proved his liking for extreme conditions.

## 7342 BEN WOOLLACOTT MEMORIAL H'CAP 5f 10y
**4:50** (4:50) (Class 5) (0-70,70) 3-Y-O+ **£3,234** (£962; £481; £240) **Stalls** Low

Form RPR

1302 **1** **Perfect Pastime**[4] 7215 6-8-13 62 .......... (p) PatCosgrave 4 75
(Jim Boyle) *sn settled towards rr: rdn and prog on outer 2f out: led 1f out: drvn clr* **5/2**[1]

500 **2** *2¼* **Cardinal**[5] 7213 9-9-1 64 .......... (p) HayleyTurner 6 69
(Robert Cowell) *s.i.s: sn pressed ldrs: pushed into ld against far rail 2f out: drvn and hdd 1f out: nt qckn* **8/1**

1311 **3** *¾* **Pharoh Jake**[4] 7215 6-9-5 68 6ex .......... WilliamCarson 5 70
(John Bridger) *prom: rdn to chal 2f out: nt qckn over 1f out: kpt on u.p* **7/2**[2]

1-44 **4** *nk* **Stellarta**[78] 4946 3-9-5 68 .......... DavidProbert 3 70
(Michael Blanshard) *hld up in last: sme prog on outer over 1f out: rdn and kpt on fnl f: nt gng pce to threaten* **8/1**

0224 **5** *1½* **Bronze Beau**[9] 7103 7-8-12 66 .......... (t) ShaneGray(5) 9 62
(Kristin Stubbs) *mde most to 2f out: steadily fdd jst over 1f out* **8/1**

0050 **6** *2½* **Rambo Will**[101] 4151 6-9-2 65 .......... OisinMurphy 1 52
(J R Jenkins) *towards rr: tried to make prog on outer 2f out: sn no hdwy and btn* **7/1**[3]

4120 **7** *hd* **Lady Phill**[4] 7215 4-9-7 70 .......... KierenFox 10 56
(Michael Attwater) *s.i.s: pressed ldrs after 2f but rdn: lost pl over 2f out: steadily wknd* **10/1**

4301 **8** *2¼* **West Coast Dream**[63] 5486 7-9-6 69 .......... LukeMorris 7 47
(Roy Brotherton) *pressed ldr to jst over 2f out: wknd jst over 1f out* **8/1**

1m 2.15s (1.85) **Going Correction** +0.45s/f (Yiel) 8 Ran SP% **116.8**
Speed ratings (Par 103): **103,99,98,97,95 91,91,87**
CSF £23.81 CT £70.70 TOTE £2.90: £1.20, £2.10, £1.70; EX 25.40 Trifecta £71.70.
**Owner** The Paddock Space Partnership 2 **Bred** R G & T E Levin **Trained** Epsom, Surrey

**FOCUS**
The market proved a good guide for this sprint handicap as Jim Boyle's bottom-weight turned the tables on his Brighton conqueror.

## 7343 JRL GROUP AMATEUR H'CAP (FOR GENTLEMAN AMATEUR RIDERS) 1m 3f 135y
**5:20** (5:20) (Class 5) (0-70,70) 3-Y-O+ **£3,119** (£967; £483; £242) **Stalls** Centre

Form RPR

51-4 **1** **Red Four**[171] 1915 4-11-1 61 .......... MrSWaley-Cohen 9 77
(George Baker) *hld up bhd ldrs: smooth prog to ld over 3f out: clr fnl 2f: comf* **7/1**

0250 **2** *9* **Kudu Country (IRE)**[24] 6706 8-11-3 63 .......... MrHAABannister 10 68
(Tom Tate) *hld up bhd ldrs: smooth prog to chal over 3f out: chsd wnr after: no ch fnl 2f but wl clr of rest* **10/1**

1046 **3** *8* **Nam Hai (IRE)**[13] 7020 3-10-12 70 .......... MrHStock(5) 1 60
(Michael Bell) *hld up towards rr: stdy prog over 4f out: styd against nr side rail in st: wl btn 3rd fnl 2f* **9/2**[2]

000 **4** *¾* **Eurato (FR)**[69] 5274 4-11-1 68 .......... (p) MrCHammond(7) 8 57
(John Spearing) *trckd ldrs: shoved along by 1/2-way: stl chsng 4f out: lft bhd fr 3f out: plugged on* **7/2**[1]

605 **5** *2* **Pandorica**[8] 7133 6-11-2 67 .......... (p) MrJPWilliams(5) 6 53
(Bernard Llewellyn) *w ldrs: urged along 5f out: lft bhd fr over 3f out: plugged on* **20/1**

5445 **6** *4* **Admirable Duque (IRE)**[10] 7072 8-10-9 58 .......... (b) MrChrisMartin(3) 11 38
(Dominic Ffrench Davis) *hld up in last trio: pushed along and passed struggling rivals fr 3f out: nvr a factor* **16/1**

050/ **7** *hd* **Malanos (IRE)**[661] 7018 6-10-5 56 oh2 .......... MrCCarroll(5) 2 36
(Tony Carroll) *sn in last: urged along 1/2-way: passed struggling rivals u.p fr 3f out* **66/1**

0565 **8** *9* **Highlife Dancer**[13] 7001 6-10-8 61 .......... (v) MrHJFCruickshank(7) 5 27
(Mick Channon) *mde most to over 3f out: wknd* **20/1**

5243 **9** *2¾* **Red Dragon (IRE)**[8] 7133 4-10-12 65 .......... MrHFNugent(7) 13 27
(Michael Blanshard) *w ldrs but racd v wd and lost pl bnd fr 6f out: styd nr side in st: sn btn* **6/1**[3]

3440 **10** *6* **Beep**[19] 6856 4-10-8 57 .......... MrMatthewBarber(3) 12 10
(Lydia Richards) *w ldrs tl rdn and wknd 4f out* **25/1**

4636 **11** *4½* **Palus San Marco (IRE)**[113] 3761 5-11-10 70 .......... MrSWalker 3 16
(Tony Carroll) *awkward s: wl in rr and sn nt gng wl: nvr a factor* **7/1**

-011 **12** *43* **Now What**[39] 6252 7-11-0 63 .......... MrJHarding(3) 7
(Jonathan Portman) *w ldrs: rdn 4f out: sn wknd rapidly: t.o* **8/1**

1034 **13** *1* **Roman Riches**[15] 5949 3-10-1 61 .......... (b) MrWRClarke(7) 4
(Gary Moore) *sn struggling in last trio: t.o* **20/1**

2m 41.09s (11.59) **Going Correction** +0.80s/f (Soft)
**WFA** 3 from 4yo+ 7lb 13 Ran SP% **125.4**
Speed ratings (Par 103): **93,87,81,81,79 77,77,71,69,65 62,33,32**
CSF £73.19 CT £360.17 TOTE £8.50: £3.60, £3.70, £2.30; EX 97.30 Trifecta £676.20.
**Owner** Lady Cobham **Bred** Lady Cobham **Trained** Manton, Wilts



The Form Book, Raceform Ltd, Newbury, RG14 5SJ

**FOCUS**
Not a race to dwell on with many of these failing to handle conditions.
T/Plt: £107.50 to a £1 stake. Pool of £63191.40 - 428.95 winning tickets. T/Qpdt: £6.60 to a £1 stake. Pool of £6034.78 - 675.45 winning tickets. JN

# 5661 CLAIREFONTAINE (R-H)
Monday, October 20

**OFFICIAL GOING: Turf: very soft**

## 7344a PRIX PARIS-TURF (PRIX FILIBERTO) (MAIDEN) (2YO COLTS & GELDINGS) (TURF) 1m
11:00 (12:00) 2-Y-O £10,416 (£4,166; £3,125; £2,083; £1,041)

RPR
1 **Plumetot (FR)** 2-9-2 0 ... GregoryBenoist 5 75
(J-C Rouget, France) 4/5[1]
2 ½ **What A Story (FR)**[10] 2-9-2 0 ... AlexisBadel 6 74
(C Boutin, France) 50/1
3 3 **Prince Du Goyen (FR)**[106] 2-9-2 0 ... RonanThomas 8 67
(A Bonin, France) 69/10
4 ½ **Catch Dream (FR)** 2-9-2 0 ... VincentVion 9 66
(L Baudron, France) 59/1
5 ¾ **Becquanaille (FR)**[13] 7027 2-9-2 0 ... Christophe-PatriceLemaire 1 64
(P Van De Poele, France) 57/10[2]
6 1 ¾ **Ruby's Teddy Bear (IRE)** 2-9-2 0 ... (b) TheoBachelot 4 60
(S Wattel, France) 214/10
7 ½ **Dawn Prayer**[156] 2-9-2 0 ... FabriceVeron 10 59
(H-A Pantall, France) 66/10[3]
8 7 **Mister Papy (FR)**[110] 3871 2-8-10 0 ... (b) SoufianeSaadi(6) 2 44
(C Plisson, France) 46/1
9 1 **Notre Archange (FR)** 2-9-2 0 ... StephanePasquier 7 42
(F Lemercier, France) 30/1
10 1 ¾ **Convicted (FR)**[23] 6743 2-9-2 0 ... MaximeGuyon 3 38
(Ian Williams) *t.k.h: led tl hld up bhd ldng pair after 2f: pushed along and n.m.r 2f out: hmpd and snatched up under 1 1/2f out and shuffled bk towards rr: heavily eased fnl 130yds* 77/10

1m 44.7s (104.70) 10 Ran SP% **121.2**
WIN (incl. 1 euro stake): 1.80. PLACES: 1.30, 6.70, 1.90. DF: 57.30. SF: 69.90.
**Owner** Gerard Augustin-Normand **Bred** Franklin Finance S.A. **Trained** Pau, France

# 7190 KEMPTON (A.W) (R-H)
Tuesday, October 21

**OFFICIAL GOING: Polytrack: standard**
Wind: Strong, against Weather: Cloudy

## 7345 £25 FREE BET AT TITANBET.CO.UK MAIDEN FILLIES' STKS (BOBIS RACE) 6f (P)
5:30 (5:32) (Class 5) 2-Y-O £2,587 (£770; £384; £192) Stalls Low

Form RPR
1 **Always Smile (IRE)** 2-9-0 0 ... FrederikTylicki 7 75+
(Saeed bin Suroor) *hld up in 6th: effrt 2f out: led over 1f out: rdn clr: comf* 7/4[1]
6 2 3 ½ **Marilyn Mon**[131] 3157 2-8-7 0 ... JoshuaBrowning(7) 5 65
(Jo Hughes) *hld up towards rr: nt clr run over 2f out: swtchd lft and gd hdwy to take 2nd jst ins fnl f: no ch w wnr* 66/1
0 3 1 ¼ **Hey You (IRE)**[92] 4499 2-9-0 0 ... SeanLevey 4 61
(Richard Hannon) *prom: rdn over 2f out: no ex fnl f* 10/1
06 4 shd **Beta Tauri (USA)**[14] 7019 2-8-11 0 ... CamHardie(3) 9 60
(Charlie Appleby) *hld up in 5th: effrt and hung rt over 2f out: styd on same pce* 7/1
00 5 1 ¾ **Lucy The Painter (IRE)**[25] 6701 2-9-0 0 ... SteveDrowne 3 55
(Peter Makin) *prom: n.m.r over 2f out: sn outpcd* 10/1
6 6 **Bahama Blue** 2-9-0 0 ... PaddyAspell 1 37
(James Eustace) *led tl over 2f out: wknd over 1f out* 20/1
3 7 6 **Sharissima**[20] 6852 2-9-0 0 ... MartinHarley 8 60+
(Lady Cecil) *plld hrd: sn chsng ldr: sddle slipped up horse's nk after 2f: led over 2f out tl over 1f out: jockey unable to ride fin and eased* 5/2[2]
8 ½ **Equilicious** 2-9-0 0 ... WilliamBuick 2 18
(Charles Hills) *a last: no ch fnl 3f* 5/1[3]

1m 14.61s (1.51) **Going Correction** +0.15s/f (Slow) 8 Ran SP% **118.5**
Speed ratings (Par 92): **95,90,88,88,86 78,70,69**
CSF £110.97 TOTE £2.30: £1.10, £5.90, £2.80; EX 59.70 Trifecta £509.70.
**Owner** Godolphin **Bred** Darley **Trained** Newmarket, Suffolk

**FOCUS**
An uncompetitive fillies' maiden that took less winning than seemed likely with the saddle slipping on the second favourite. The gallop was an ordinary one and the impressive winner raced in the centre in the straight.

## 7346 REWARDS4RACING.COM H'CAP (DIV I) 1m (P)
6:00 (6:00) (Class 6) (0-60,60) 3-Y-O+ £1,940 (£577; £288; £144) Stalls Low

Form RPR
2550 1 **Ostralegus**[29] 6617 4-9-7 60 ... BenCurtis 13 70
(John Gallagher) *hld up towards rr: hdwy over 2f out: led over 1f out: rdn out* 9/1
3330 2 1 **Baltic Fire (IRE)**[32] 6516 3-9-1 60 ... JoeyHaynes(3) 3 67
(K R Burke) *prom: rdn and chalng over 1f out: r.o* 11/4[1]
2004 3 1 ¼ **Eugenic**[19] 6883 3-9-1 57 ... RobertHavlin 12 61
(Rod Millman) *chsd ldr tl over 2f out: kpt on fnl f* 6/1[3]
-450 4 1 ½ **Robin Hood (IRE)**[67] 5395 6-9-7 60 ... JackMitchell 10 61
(Philip Mitchell) *led tl over 1f out: wknd fnl f* 5/1[2]
000 5 ½ **Haames (IRE)**[125] 3361 7-9-1 57 ... CamHardie(3) 7 57
(Kevin Morgan) *chsd ldrs: n.m.r and sltly lost pl over 2f out: no imp* 25/1
0444 6 ¾ **Bold Ring**[50] 5977 8-8-4 50 ... RobertPWalsh(7) 11 49
(Edward Creighton) *chsd ldrs on outer: outpcd 2f out: sn btn* 7/1
5600 7 ¾ **Honey Meadow**[10] 7111 3-9-2 58 ... MartinHarley 4 54
(Robert Eddery) *towards rr: drvn along fnl 2f: nvr rchd ldrs* 7/1
1006 8 1 ¼ **Little Indian**[70] 5280 4-9-7 60 ... FergusSweeney 5 54
(J R Jenkins) *hld up in rr: sme hdwy over 1f out: sn wknd* 9/1
5560 9 2 ½ **It's A Yes From Me**[14] 7025 3-8-13 55 ... FrederikTylicki 1 42
(James Fanshawe) *broke wl: stdd bk into midfield after 3f: effrt 2f out: wknd over 1f out* 5/1[2]
000 10 3 ½ **Frankie**[49] 6018 3-8-12 54 ... SteveDrowne 6 33
(Jimmy Fox) *s.i.s: a in rr: struggling over 2f out: fin lame* 16/1

1m 42.48s (2.68) **Going Correction** +0.15s/f (Slow)
**WFA** 3 from 4yo+ 3lb 10 Ran SP% **129.0**
Speed ratings (Par 101): **92,91,89,88,87 87,86,85,82,79**
CSF £37.80 CT £175.59 TOTE £10.50: £2.70, £1.80, £1.80; EX 45.40 Trifecta £268.60.
**Owner** The Oystercatcher Racing Syndicate **Bred** B Brookfield **Trained** Chastleton, Oxon

**FOCUS**
Division one of a very ordinary handicap. The gallop was an ordinary one and the winner came down the centre.

## 7347 REWARDS4RACING.COM H'CAP (DIV II) 1m (P)
6:30 (6:30) (Class 6) (0-60,60) 3-Y-O+ £1,940 (£577; £288; £144) Stalls Low

Form RPR
5366 1 **Dreaming Again**[62] 5560 4-8-7 46 oh1 ... KieranO'Neill 12 54
(Jimmy Fox) *rdn in rr s: pushed into midfield 4f out: styd on fnl 2f: led fnl strides* 25/1
4243 2 nk **Abigails Angel**[25] 6715 7-8-10 52 ... ThomasBrown(3) 8 59
(Lee Carter) *cl up: rdn to chse ldr over 2f out: led 50yds out: jst ct* 4/1[1]
205 3 1 ¾ **Ferryview Place**[3] 7292 5-8-11 50 ... (v) OisinMurphy 10 53
(Ian Williams) *w ldr: led after 2f: drvn along and hung rt fr 3f out: hdd and no ex fnl 50yds* 9/2[2]
0500 4 nk **Sebs Sensei (IRE)**[28] 6636 3-9-4 60 ... (b) RobertHavlin 7 62
(Mark Hoad) *mid-div: styd on u.p fnl 2f: nrest at fin* 25/1
0360 5 hd **Unbridled Joy (IRE)**[11] 7077 3-9-2 58 ... AdamKirby 3 59
(Clive Cox) *mid-div: rdn and hdwy fnl 2f: clsng at fin* 9/2[2]
0102 6 3 **Prim And Proper**[30] 5122 3-8-12 59 ... (p) JennyPowell(5) 13 53
(Brendan Powell) *s.i.s: outpcd and wl bhd: hdwy over 1f out: nvr nrr* 8/1
0000 7 1 ½ **Salvado (IRE)**[19] 6889 4-9-7 60 ... (t) LukeMorris 11 52
(Tony Carroll) *prom: chsd ldr after 2f tl over 2f out: wknd over 1f out* 7/1[3]
050- 8 3 **Crowning Star (IRE)**[596] 878 5-9-7 60 ... (t) JimCrowley 2 45
(Steve Woodman) *bhd: drvn along 3f out: n.d* 14/1
9 5 **Runaiocht (IRE)**[221] 969 4-9-0 53 ... LiamKeniry 9 26
(Paul Burgoyne) *led for 2f: prom tl wknd wl over 1f out* 8/1
0000 10 3 ¼ **Charlies Mate**[62] 5558 3-8-1 46 oh1 ... (v) CamHardie(3) 1 11
(John Best) *bhd: hrd rdn 3f out: no ch after* 66/1
0460 11 ½ **Hit The Lights (IRE)**[10] 7111 4-9-2 55 ... DavidProbert 5 20
(Patrick Chamings) *chsd ldrs tl hrd rdn and wknd over 2f out* 25/1
5530 12 2 **Blackthorn Stick (IRE)**[14] 7012 5-9-7 60 ... TomQueally 6 20
(John Butler) *towards rr: rdn 3f out: sn bhd* 10/1

1m 40.95s (1.15) **Going Correction** +0.15s/f (Slow)
**WFA** 3 from 4yo+ 3lb 12 Ran SP% **119.9**
Speed ratings (Par 101): **100,99,97,97,97 94,92,89,84,81 81,79**
CSF £120.76 CT £553.20 TOTE £40.70: £9.30, £1.10, £2.60; EX 225.30 Trifecta £1524.70.
**Owner** The Dancing Partners **Bred** The Dancing Partners **Trained** Collingbourne Ducis, Wilts
■ Stewards' Enquiry : Thomas Brown two-day ban: used whip above permitted level (Oct 4-5)

**FOCUS**
As with the first division, progressive performers were thin on the ground. The gallop was an ordinary one and the winner came down the centre in the straight.

## 7348 BET & WATCH AT TITANBET.CO.UK CONDITIONS STKS 1m (P)
7:00 (7:01) (Class 3) 2-Y-O £6,469 (£1,925; £962) Stalls Low

Form RPR
1 1 **Yodelling (USA)**[46] 6105 2-9-3 0 ... WilliamBuick 4 90+
(Charlie Appleby) *broke wl: stdd to trck ldr: led over 2f out: sn rdn: drew clr fnl f* 1/5[1]
652 2 3 ¼ **Felix De Vega (IRE)**[13] 7040 2-9-0 79 ... CamHardie(3) 1 79
(Richard Hannon) *sn led and set stdy pce: hdd over 2f out: rallied: outpcd by wnr 1f out* 4/1[2]
00 3 7 **Hambletts (IRE)**[9] 7134 2-9-3 0 ... TedDurcan 5 65
(Robert Mills) *dwlt: hld up in 3rd: brief effrt over 2f out: sn wknd* 25/1[3]

1m 47.15s (7.35) **Going Correction** +0.15s/f (Slow) 3 Ran SP% **107.2**
Speed ratings (Par 99): **69,65,58**
CSF £1.35 TOTE £1.10; EX 1.10 Trifecta £1.30.
**Owner** Godolphin **Bred** Darley **Trained** Newmarket, Suffolk

**FOCUS**
Two non-runners meant this was a very one-sided event and the slow pace to the intersection means the bare form isn't entirely reliable. The potentially smart winner came down the centre.

## 7349 MOBILE LOYALTY BONUS AT TITANBET.CO.UK MAIDEN STKS 1m 3f (P)
7:30 (7:30) (Class 5) 3-Y-O+ £2,587 (£770; £384; £192) Stalls Low

Form RPR
1 **Osaruveetil (IRE)** 3-9-5 0 ... JimCrowley 7 84+
(William Haggas) *dwlt: hld up off the pce towards rr: hdwy and in tch over 2f out: led 1f out: rdn out* 5/2[2]
0432 2 1 ¼ **Panatella**[13] 7032 3-9-0 71 ... FrederikTylicki 6 76
(James Fanshawe) *in tch: drvn to chal over 1f out: kpt on same pce fnl f* 13/8[1]
0330 3 ¾ **Frederic**[33] 6484 3-9-5 73 ... AdamKirby 9 80
(Luca Cumani) *led after 1f: hrd rdn and hdd 1f out: one pce* 7/2[3]
050 4 9 **Scillonian Sunset (IRE)**[127] 3315 3-9-0 60 ... WilliamBuick 10 58
(Charles Hills) *prom: chsd ldr 6f out tl over 2f out: sn wknd* 25/1
2642 5 13 **Sealed (USA)**[18] 6901 3-9-5 77 ... (b[1]) TomQueally 8 40
(Gay Kelleway) *prom: hrd rdn over 2f out: sn wknd* 10/1
3205 6 6 **Will**[14] 7015 3-9-5 69 ... GeorgeBaker 4 29
(Nick Littmoden) *led for 1f: chsd ldrs tl wknd 2f out* 12/1
0 7 2 ¼ **Sea Rebelle**[6] 7195 5-9-6 0 ... AdamBeschizza 2 20
(Jo Crowley) *mid-div: wknd and c wd on bnd into st: no ch after* 33/1
0 8 21 **Astrodiamond**[18] 6901 3-9-0 0 ... JimmyQuinn 1
(Mark H Tompkins) *sn wl bhd* 100/1
0 9 34 **Macs Scwar**[26] 6677 7-9-6 0 ... TimClark(5) 5
(Paul Morgan) *dwlt: sn wl bhd* 100/1
00 10 4 **Zand Man**[35] 6421 4-9-11 0 ... LukeMorris 3
(Milton Bradley) *towards rr: struggling 5f out: sn wl bhd* 100/1

2m 21.06s (-0.84) **Going Correction** +0.15s/f (Slow)
**WFA** 3 from 4yo+ 6lb 10 Ran SP% **115.4**
Speed ratings (Par 103): **109,108,107,101,91 87,85,70,45,42**
CSF £6.72 TOTE £5.20: £1.40, £1.10, £1.40; EX 7.00 Trifecta £21.10.
**Owner** Sheikh Mohammed Bin Khalifa Al Maktoum **Bred** George Grothier **Trained** Newmarket, Suffolk

**FOCUS**
Fair form from the first three, who pulled clear in the closing stages on the back of an ordinary gallop that picked up in the home straight. The winner came down the centre.

## 7350 TITANBET.CO.UK H'CAP 1m 3f (P)
**8:00** (8:00) (Class 4) (0-80,80) 3-Y-0+ **£4,690** (£1,395; £697; £348) **Stalls** Low

Form RPR
2450 **1** **Mymatechris (IRE)**[59] 5670 3-8-7 69 DavidProbert 4 83+
(Andrew Balding) *hld up in midfield: smooth hdwy 2f out: led over 1f out: rdn and styd on wl* **14/1**
2254 **2** *2 ¼* **Hedge End (IRE)**[38] 6315 3-8-13 78 CamHardie(3) 7 87
(Richard Hannon) *hld up in midfield: hdwy over 1f out: chsd wnr ins fnl f: one pce* **6/1**[3]
2006 **3** *3 ¼* **Mubtadi**[21] 6839 6-9-6 79 LouisSteward(3) 1 82+
(Ismail Mohammed) *hld up towards rr: weaved through and gd hdwy over 1f out: no ex fnl f* **14/1**
5330 **4** *1* **Meteoroid (USA)**[7] 7186 3-9-0 76 (p) MartinHarley 9 77
(Lady Cecil) *prom: drvn along 2f out: one pce* **8/1**
6143 **5** *1* **Cosmic Halo**[20] 6870 5-9-8 78 GeorgeChaloner 5 78
(Richard Fahey) *bhd: rdn over 2f out: styd on fnl f* **7/1**
4055 **6** *½* **Rising Breeze (FR)**[25] 6722 3-8-10 75 JoeyHaynes(3) 8 74
(K R Burke) *mid-div on outer: hdwy 4f out: hrd rdn 2f out: btn over 1f out* **8/1**
1110 **7** *nse* **Tizlove Regardless (USA)**[178] 1727 3-9-1 77 SilvestreDeSousa 6 76
(Mark Johnston) *chsd ldr: drew level over 2f out: sn hrd rdn and wknd* **7/2**[1]
2256 **8** *1* **Billy Blue (IRE)**[41] 6239 3-8-12 74 (b) WilliamBuick 10 71
(John Gosden) *sn led: hrd rdn 2f out: hdd & wknd over 1f out* **4/1**[2]
5000 **9** *1* **Royal Alcor (IRE)**[44] 6171 7-9-10 80 (t) TomQueally 2 75
(Gay Kelleway) *a bhd* **33/1**
006 **10** *7* **Argaki (IRE)**[7] 7185 4-9-4 74 JimCrowley 3 56
(Keith Dalgleish) *chsd ldrs tl hrd rdn and wknd 2f out* **10/1**

2m 21.69s (-0.21) **Going Correction** +0.15s/f (Slow)
**WFA** 3 from 4yo+ 6lb **10 Ran SP% 116.6**
Speed ratings (Par 105): **106,104,102,101,100 100,100,99,98,93**
CSF £95.65 CT £1211.53 TOTE £20.90: £4.80, £2.80, £3.90; EX 132.00 Trifecta £1514.00 Part won..
**Owner** David Brownlow **Bred** Derrick Fisher **Trained** Kingsclere, Hants
**FOCUS**
A fair handicap in which a couple of the market leaders disappointed. The gallop was an ordinary one to the home turn and the winner came down the centre.

## 7351 £10 FREE MOBILE BET AT TITANBET.CO.UK H'CAP (DIV I) 6f (P)
**8:30** (8:31) (Class 5) (0-75,75) 3-Y-0+ **£2,587** (£770; £384; £192) **Stalls** Low

Form RPR
3020 **1** **Salvatore Fury (IRE)**[32] 6512 4-9-4 72 (p) JimCrowley 7 83
(Keith Dalgleish) *patiently rdn towards rr: smooth hdwy over 1f out: shkn up and qcknd to ld fnl 50yds* **5/1**[3]
5114 **2** *½* **Tahchee**[14] 7023 3-9-1 70 FrederikTylicki 5 79
(James Fanshawe) *in tch: nt clr run and swtchd lft and rt over 1f out: qcknd to ld ins fnl f: kpt on: hdd fnl 50yds* **5/2**[1]
5310 **3** *1 ½* **Generalyse**[20] 6872 5-9-4 75 (b) RyanTate(3) 8 79
(Ben De Haan) *prom: hrd rdn 2f out: chal ent fnl f: one pce* **9/1**
0400 **4** *¾* **Temple Road (IRE)**[11] 7073 6-9-0 71 (t[1]) CamHardie(3) 9 73
(Milton Bradley) *stdd s: hld up in rr: rdn 2f out: styd on wl fnl f* **14/1**
0240 **5** *hd* **Gigawatt**[5] 7220 4-9-6 74 PatCosgrave 6 75
(Jim Boyle) *s.s: towards rr: sme hdwy over 1f out: kpt on fnl f* **4/1**[2]
5003 **6** *2 ½* **Threetimesalady**[22] 6814 3-9-5 74 LukeMorris 1 67+
(Sir Mark Prescott Bt) *chsd ldrs: slt ld 1f out tl wknd ins fnl f* **8/1**
4436 **7** *hd* **Exceeding Power**[101] 4206 3-9-3 72 RobertHavlin 2 65+
(Martin Bosley) *led tl hrd rdn and wknd 1f out* **10/1**
16-6 **8** *shd* **Archibald Thorburn (IRE)**[19] 6890 3-9-4 73 CharlesBishop 4 65+
(Peter Hedger) *mid-div: effrt on inner 2f out: no ex fnl f* **5/1**[3]
4000 **9** *hd* **Novellen Lad (IRE)**[26] 6680 9-9-5 73 TomQueally 3 65
(Willie Musson) *chsd ldr: drvn level 2f out: wknd 1f out* **16/1**

1m 13.57s (0.47) **Going Correction** +0.15s/f (Slow)
**WFA** 3 from 4yo+ 1lb **9 Ran SP% 124.7**
Speed ratings (Par 103): **102,101,99,98,98 94,94,94,94**
CSF £19.51 CT £115.86 TOTE £6.90: £2.10, £2.50, £2.60; EX 26.80 Trifecta £137.60.
**Owner** Prestige Thoroughbred Racing **Bred** Ken Harris & Dr Brid Corkery **Trained** Carluke, S Lanarks
■ Stewards' Enquiry : Jim Crowley caution: careless riding
**FOCUS**
Exposed performers in a fair handicap. The gallop was no more than fair and the winner was another to race down the centre in the straight.

## 7352 £10 FREE MOBILE BET AT TITANBET.CO.UK H'CAP (DIV II) 6f (P)
**9:00** (9:00) (Class 5) (0-75,75) 3-Y-0+ **£2,587** (£770; £384; £192) **Stalls** Low

Form RPR
5600 **1** **Head Space (IRE)**[18] 6898 6-9-7 75 (v) GeorgeBaker 2 85
(Michael Attwater) *towards rr: rdn and hdwy 2f out: styd on to ld ins fnl f* **6/1**[3]
0425 **2** *1 ½* **Ashkari (IRE)**[11] 7071 3-9-6 75 (p) AdamKirby 1 80
(Clive Cox) *chsd ldr: led over 1f out: hrd rdn and hdd ins fnl f: one pce* **7/2**[2]
1424 **3** *2 ¾* **Miss Brazil (IRE)**[43] 6189 3-9-2 74 CamHardie(3) 4 70
(Richard Hannon) *mid-div: rdn along fr 4f out: styd on wl fr over 1f out* **14/1**
2225 **4** *½* **Picks Pinta**[38] 6316 3-8-11 73 JoshuaBrowning(7) 9 68
(Jo Hughes) *in rr tl r.o steadily fnl 2f* **20/1**
0231 **5** *1 ¼* **Goodwood Storm**[35] 6437 3-9-3 72 LukeMorris 3 63
(William Knight) *in tch: wnt 3rd over 2f out: wknd fnl f* **3/1**[1]
0306 **6** *nse* **Punk**[11] 7071 3-9-2 71 (b[1]) JimCrowley 8 61
(George Peckham) *dwlt: bhd: swtchd lft 2f out: sme hdwy over 1f out: nt rch ldrs* **12/1**
5621 **7** *¾* **Monarch Maid**[24] 6758 3-8-10 72 DavidParkes(7) 10 60
(Peter Hiatt) *led tl hrd rdn and wknd over 1f out* **16/1**
62-0 **8** *1 ½* **Blue Jack**[49] 6020 9-9-7 75 LiamKeniry 6 58
(Zoe Davison) *towards rr: modest effrt 2f out: wknd over 1f out* **40/1**
6220 **9** *3 ½* **Sweet Talking Guy (IRE)**[26] 6680 4-9-1 72 (t) SimonPearce(3) 5 44
(Lydia Pearce) *prom tl wknd 2f out* **7/2**[2]
056 **10** *11* **Knockroon**[10] 7117 3-8-11 66 (v[1]) OisinMurphy 7 3
(Andrew Balding) *prom tl lost pl qckly 3f out* **10/1**

1m 12.47s (-0.63) **Going Correction** +0.15s/f (Slow)
**WFA** 3 from 4yo+ 1lb **10 Ran SP% 120.3**
Speed ratings (Par 103): **110,108,104,103,102 101,100,98,94,79**
CSF £28.24 CT £245.79 TOTE £8.50: £2.30, £3.80, £3.20; EX 36.50 Trifecta £384.70.
**Owner** J M Duggan & T P Duggan **Bred** Castlemartin Stud And Skymarc Farm **Trained** Epsom, Surrey
**FOCUS**
A couple of previous scorers in division two. The gallop was sound and the winner came down the centre in the straight.
T/Plt: £40.00 to a £1 stake. Pool: £65,941.44 - 1,203.43 winning tickets. T/Qpdt: £9.30 to a £1 stake. Pool: £7,742.63 - 611.66 winning tickets. LM

# 7198 LINGFIELD (L-H)
### Tuesday, October 21
**OFFICIAL GOING: Polytrack: standard**
Wind: strong across

## 7353 £20 FREE BET AT WINNER.CO.UK MAIDEN AUCTION STKS 7f 1y(P)
**2:00** (2:01) (Class 6) 2-Y-O **£2,037** (£606; £303; £151) **Stalls** Low

Form RPR
**1** **Easy Tiger** 2-8-9 0 SamHitchcott 5 72+
(William Muir) *in tch in midfield: effrt on inner to chse ldr wl over 1f out: led ins fnl f: r.o wl* **20/1**
53 **2** *1 ¼* **Eatsleepracerepeat**[21] 6838 2-8-11 0 MartinHarley 1 71
(Lady Cecil) *chsd ldrs tl led over 3f out: rdn wl over 1f out: hdd and one pce ins fnl f* **7/1**[2]
2246 **3** *hd* **Edge Of Heaven**[24] 6769 2-8-4 65 LukeMorris 8 63
(Jonathan Portman) *chsd ldng trio: rdn ent fnl 2f: wnt 3rd fnl 100yds: kpt on* **12/1**
46 **4** *1* **Mistamel (IRE)**[109] 3929 2-9-1 0 TomQueally 6 71
(Eve Johnson Houghton) *in tch in midfield: rdn and swtchd rt jst over 1f out: styd on wl ins fnl f: nvr trbld ldrs* **7/1**[2]
052 **5** *hd* **Dynamite Inventor (IRE)**[34] 6449 2-8-11 69 SilvestreDeSousa 7 67
(Kevin Ryan) *led tl 3f out: chsd ldr tl wl over 1f out: wknd ins fnl f* **8/1**[3]
4 **6** *¾* **Compton Mill**[31] 6545 2-8-13 0 WilliamBuick 4 67
(Hughie Morrison) *s.i.s: in tch towards rr: hdwy 4f out: styd on same pce fr over 1f out* **4/6**[1]
00 **7** *3 ½* **Artesana**[53] 5881 2-7-13 0 CallumShepherd(7) 2 50
(William Knight) *sn towards rr: rdn and struggling 3f out: no threat to ldrs but kpt on fnl f* **66/1**
0 **8** *nk* **Celtic Ava (IRE)**[26] 6675 2-8-3 0 JemmaMarshall(3) 9 49
(Pat Phelan) *t.k.h: hld up in tch in midfield: rdn jst over 2f out: wknd over 1f out* **100/1**
**9** *2 ¾* **Space Sheriff (IRE)** 2-8-11 0 JimCrowley 10 47
(Jamie Osborne) *s.i.s: hdwy to chse ldr 5f out tl over 3f out: lost pl bnd 2f out: sn wknd* **33/1**
**10** *20* **To The Victor (IRE)** 2-8-13 0 PatCosgrave 3
(Jim Boyle) *s.i.s: rn green in rr: struggling 3f out: lost tch 2f out* **66/1**

1m 26.09s (1.29) **Going Correction** 0.0s/f (Stan) **10 Ran SP% 115.5**
Speed ratings (Par 93): **92,90,90,89,88 88,84,83,80,57**
CSF £147.34 TOTE £31.30: £3.80, £2.10, £2.70; EX 173.50 Trifecta £1241.00.
**Owner** Miss E J Tanner **Bred** D J Weston **Trained** Lambourn, Berks
**FOCUS**
A modest maiden.

## 7354 DOWNLOAD THE WINNER.CO.UK APP NOW/BSS EBF MEDIAN AUCTION MAIDEN STKS 1m 1y(P)
**2:30** (2:33) (Class 5) 2-Y-O **£2,911** (£866; £432; £216) **Stalls** High

Form RPR
2 **1** **Taysh (USA)**[20] 6861 2-9-5 0 (t) FrankieDettori 3 79
(John Gosden) *t.k.h: chsd ldng pair: lft wl clr bnd 2f out: in n.d after: r.o: pushed out* **3/1**[2]
0 **2** *3 ½* **Tatawu (IRE)**[20] 6875 2-9-5 0 JimmyFortune 7 71
(Brian Meehan) *in tch in midfield: lft 4th bnd 2f out: chsd clr wnr jst over 1f out: kpt on but no threat to wnr* **16/1**
03 **3** *1 ¼* **Velociter (IRE)**[13] 7030 2-9-5 0 SeanLevey 5 68+
(Richard Hannon) *led: pressed whn cocked jaw: rn v wd and hdd bnd 2f out: lost all ch: racing against stands' rail and rallied ins fnl f to go 3rd fnl 75yds* **8/1**[3]
**4** *1 ¼* **Naady** 2-9-0 0 MartinHarley 10 60
(Ed Dunlop) *chsd ldng trio: lft 2nd and edgd rt bnd 2f out lost 2nd jst over 1f out: kpt on same pce after* **50/1**
**5** *hd* **Covert Love (IRE)** 2-8-9 0 NoelGarbutt(5) 12 60+
(Hugo Palmer) *s.i.s: in tch towards rr: rdn and hdwy over 1f out: styd on ins fnl f: nvr trbld ldrs* **33/1**
3 **6** *¾* **Perceus**[32] 6520 2-9-5 0 [1] WilliamBuick 8 68+
(Marcus Tregoning) *chsd ldr: rdn and pressed ldr over 2f out: carried v wd bnd 2f out: lost all ch but kpt on fnl f* **10/11**[1]
**7** *nk* **Whoopsy Daisy** 2-9-0 0 SilvestreDeSousa 11 57
(William Haggas) *hld up towards rr: sme hdwy over 1f out: kpt on ins fnl f: nvr trbld ldrs* **16/1**
04 **8** *½* **Step On It (IRE)**[15] 6984 2-9-5 0 GeorgeBaker 6 61
(Eve Johnson Houghton) *chsd ldrs: lft 3rd but struggling u.p bnd 2f out: wknd fnl f* **14/1**
0 **9** *2 ¼* **Brittleton**[20] 6874 2-9-5 0 TomQueally 4 56
(Harry Dunlop) *s.i.s: a towards rr: n.d* **100/1**
0 **10** *3 ½* **Beijing Star**[95] 4395 2-9-5 0 SteveDrowne 1 48
(Charles Hills) *s.i.s: t.k.h: hld up in tch in rr: struggling over 2f out: wknd over 1f out* **50/1**
5 **11** *¾* **Pyla (IRE)**[38] 6333 2-9-0 0 JimCrowley 9 41
(Ed Dunlop) *in tch in midfield: struggling 2f out: wknd over 1f out* **25/1**
0 **12** *19* **Funtime Barry (IRE)**[31] 6565 2-9-2 0 CamHardie(3) 2
(Richard Hannon) *in tch: lost pl and rdn over 3f out: bhd over 1f out: t.o* **66/1**

1m 39.51s (1.31) **Going Correction** 0.0s/f (Stan) **12 Ran SP% 120.1**
Speed ratings (Par 95): **93,89,88,87,86 86,85,85,83,79 78,59**
CSF £47.44 TOTE £3.70: £1.40, £5.90, £1.60; EX 61.20 Trifecta £291.50.
**Owner** Al Shaqab Racing **Bred** Normandy Farm Llc **Trained** Newmarket, Suffolk
**FOCUS**
No more than a fair maiden.

## 7355 BET AND WATCH AT WINNER.CO.UK (S) STKS 6f 1y(P)
**3:00** (3:00) (Class 6) 3-Y-O **£2,037** (£606; £303; £151) **Stalls** Low

Form RPR
4030 **1** **Coiste Bodhar (IRE)**[12] 7057 3-9-5 63 (p) OisinMurphy 8 71
(Joseph Tuite) *taken down early: mde all: rdn over 1f out: drvn ins fnl f: a jst holding on: all out* **14/1**

5004 **2** *hd* **Hagree (IRE)**[67] 5378 3-9-5 80 MartinHarley 5 70
(Marco Botti) *chsd ldrs: wnt 2nd over 4f out: rdn over 1f out: drvn ins fnl f: grad clsd but nvr doing enough to pass wnr* **4/7**[1]

2340 **3** *2* **Kodafine (IRE)**[39] 6297 3-9-0 64 SilvestreDeSousa 1 59
(David Evans) *in tch: effrt in 3rd 2f out: kpt on same pce u.p fnl f* **5/1**[2]

0 **4** *½* **Deftera Fantutte (IRE)**[99] 4265 3-8-6 0 PhilipPrince(3) 11 52
(Natalie Lloyd-Beavis) *hld up in midfield: rdn and hdwy towards inner over 1f out: styd on ins fnl f: nvr trbld ldrs* **100/1**

3256 **5** *½* **Madagascar Moll (IRE)**[22] 6821 3-8-9 60 (v) JimCrowley 4 55
(David O'Meara) *hld up towards rr: hdwy u.p over 1f out: kpt on ins fnl f: nvr trbld ldrs* **8/1**[3]

0520 **6** *½* **Roly Tricks**[14] 7023 3-8-6 68 (b[1]) CamHardie(3) 3 49
(Olly Stevens) *in tch in midfield: carried rt and lost pl bnd 2f out: rallied and kpt on u.p ins fnl f* **8/1**[3]

4044 **7** *shd* **El Duque**[96] 4365 3-9-0 60 (p) RyanWhile(5) 2 59
(Bill Turner) *in tch in midfield: 5th and effrt u.p over 1f out: kpt on ins fnl f: nvr trbld ldrs* **33/1**

0520 **8** *3¾* **Astral Rose**[29] 6613 3-8-6 48 (b) DannyBrock(3) 12 37
(Jonathan Portman) *v.s.a: a in rr: n.d* **33/1**

3500 **9** *1¾* **Orlando Star (CAN)**[73] 5183 3-8-7 53 (p) KieranShoemark(7) 6 36
(Roger Teal) *chsd wnr tl over 4f out: chsd ldrs tl hung rt and lost pl bnd 2f out: wknd over 1f out* **50/1**

0040 **10** *3* **Yankee Red**[31] 6561 3-9-0 47 (b) SteveDrowne 10 27
(John Best) *s.i.s: in rr: sme hdwy on outer over 2f out: wknd wl over 1f out* **66/1**

5065 **U** **Countess Lupus (IRE)**[22] 6816 3-8-2 45 (b) RobHornby(7) 7
(Lisa Williamson) *stmbld and uns rdr as stalls opened* **100/1**

1m 12.1s (0.20) **Going Correction** 0.0s/f (Stan) **11** Ran SP% **120.5**
Speed ratings (Par 99): **98,97,95,94,93 93,92,87,85,81**
.The winner was bought in 5,200gns. \n\x\x Hagree bought by Mr Declan Carroll for £6,000.
**Owner** Shefford Valley Racing **Bred** C Amerian **Trained** Great Shefford, Berks
■ Stewards' Enquiry : Oisin Murphy caution: careless riding

**FOCUS**
Few got into this modest seller.

## 7356 HORSE RACING LOYALTY BONUS AT WINNER.CO.UK H'CAP 6f 1y(P)
**3:30** (3:30) (Class 5) (0-70,70) 3-Y-0+ **£3,234** (£962; £481; £240) **Stalls** Low

Form RPR

5135 **1** **Top Offer**[36] 6398 5-9-3 66 GeorgeBaker 7 75
(Peter Crate) *chsd ldrs: lft clse 3rd bnd 2f out: led and edging rt 1f out: styd on: rdn out* **3/1**[2]

0055 **2** *1¼* **Prince Regal**[51] 5951 4-8-13 69 JordanVaughan(7) 3 74
(Timothy Jarvis) *chsd ldrs: rdn and effrt over 1f out: chsd wnr ins fnl f: kpt on but no imp* **14/1**

6411 **3** *1¾* **Reaffirmed (IRE)**[19] 6889 3-9-4 68 LukeMorris 2 67+
(Ed Vaughan) *in tch in midfield: hdwy u.p over 1f out: kpt on ins fnl f: nvr a threat to wnr* **11/4**[1]

-106 **4** *½* **For Ayman**[120] 3519 3-9-4 68 OisinMurphy 8 66
(Joseph Tuite) *racd in last quartet: rdn and hdwy over 1f out: kpt on ins fnl f: nt rch ldrs* **8/1**

0516 **5** *shd* **Pearl Noir**[10] 7111 4-8-5 59 (b) MatthewHopkins(5) 1 59+
(Scott Dixon) *led tl hung rt and v wd bnd 2f out: hdd 1f out: wknd ins fnl f* **20/1**

3243 **6** *2* **Hipz (IRE)**[24] 6766 3-8-11 66 JennyPowell(5) 6 57
(Laura Mongan) *racd off the pce in last quartet: hdwy u.p ent fnl f: kpt on: nvr trbld ldrs* **8/1**

0500 **7** *nse* **Presumido (IRE)**[19] 6890 4-9-0 70 TomasHarrigan(7) 9 61
(Simon Dow) *stdd and dropped in bhd s: wl off the pce in rr: hdwy on inner over 1f out: styd on: nvr trbld ldrs* **16/1**

0600 **8** *4* **Plover**[19] 6890 4-9-4 70 (p) LouisSteward(3) 10 48
(Michael Attwater) *in tch in midfield: struggling u.p over 2f out: wknd over 1f out* **20/1**

0160 **9** *3¼* **Le Laitier (FR)**[39] 6285 3-9-4 68 AdamBeschizza 5 36
(Scott Dixon) *racd in last pair: rdn over 3f out: wknd fnl f* **12/1**

-641 **10** *1½* **Findhorn Magic**[33] 6488 3-9-2 66 SteveDrowne 4 29
(Peter Makin) *chsd ldr: rdn over 2f out: lft w ev ch bnd 2f out: btn 1f out: fdd ins fnl f* **5/1**[3]

1m 11.26s (-0.64) **Going Correction** 0.0s/f (Stan)
**WFA** 3 from 4yo+ 1lb **10** Ran SP% **120.3**
Speed ratings (Par 103): **104,102,100,99,99 96,96,91,86,84**
CSF £46.40 CT £78.66 TOTE £6.60: £2.10, £4.10, £1.10; EX 70.70 Trifecta £249.60.
**Owner** Peter Crate **Bred** Juddmonte Farms Ltd **Trained** Newdigate, Surrey

**FOCUS**
A race run at a good pace and a gamble was landed.

## 7357 WINNER.CO.UK H'CAP 5f 6y(P)
**4:00** (4:03) (Class 5) (0-75,75) 3-Y-0+ **£3,234** (£962; £481; £240) **Stalls** High

Form RPR

0505 **1** **Royal Acquisition**[11] 7073 4-9-3 71 (p) AdamBeschizza 5 79
(Robert Cowell) *sn bustled along to chse ldr: rdn 2f out drvn and chal 1f out: led ins fnl f: styd on: drvn out* **20/1**

3403 **2** *1* **Hamoody (USA)**[18] 6898 10-9-6 74 OisinMurphy 9 78+
(Joseph Tuite) *in tch in midfield: lost pl and towards rr whn swtchd rt over 1f out: styd on wl u.p ins fnl f: wnt 2nd cl home* **12/1**

0523 **3** *nk* **Pucon**[27] 6658 5-9-5 73 GeorgeBaker 6 76
(Roger Teal) *led: rdn and hrd pressed 1f out: hdd ins fnl f: one pce after: lost 2nd cl home* **4/1**[2]

4350 **4** *nk* **Shamahan**[27] 6657 5-9-4 72 TomQueally 8 74
(Luke Dace) *in tch in midfield: effrt over 1f out: n.m.r briefly jst ins fnl f: kpt on wl u.p fnl 100yds* **7/1**[3]

6062 **5** *hd* **Maria Montez**[3] 7286 5-9-2 70 SteveDrowne 7 72
(Charles Hills) *broke wl: chsd ldrs: rdn and unable qck over 1f out: styd on same pce ins fnl f: burst blood vessel* **8/1**

1151 **6** *1* **Seamster**[47] 6078 7-9-4 75 (bt) CamHardie(3) 4 73+
(Richard Ford) *dwlt: in tch towards rr: effrt and c wd wl over 1f out: kpt on ins fnl f: nvr trbld ldrs* **7/2**[1]

415 **7** *shd* **Ask The Guru**[95] 4399 4-9-3 74 (v) LouisSteward(3) 2 72
(Michael Attwater) *in tch in midfield: unable qck u.p over 1f out: hld and one pce fnl f* **10/1**

0640 **8** *½* **National Service (USA)**[21] 6843 3-9-1 69 (b) MartinHarley 10 66+
(Stuart Williams) *slowly away: bhd: hdwy on outer into midfield 1/2-way: no prog u.p over 1f out* **7/1**[3]

2006 **9** *1* **Rebecca Romero**[55] 5830 7-9-6 74 LukeMorris 3 66
(Denis Coakley) *in tch towards rr: effrt towards inner over 1f out: no imp fnl f* **12/1**

5510 **10** *5* **Dishy Guru**[20] 6873 5-9-4 72 (b) LiamKeniry 1 46
(Michael Blanshard) *a towards rr: rdn and struggling 1/2-way: bhd and eased wl ins fnl f* **7/1**[3]

58.35s (-0.45) **Going Correction** 0.0s/f (Stan) **10** Ran SP% **120.1**
Speed ratings (Par 103): **103,101,100,100,100 98,98,97,95,87**
CSF £245.22 CT £1168.88 TOTE £22.00: £4.80, £4.00, £1.50; EX 432.70 Trifecta £1225.80.
**Owner** J Sargeant **Bred** Dunchurch Lodge Stud Co **Trained** Six Mile Bottom, Cambs

**FOCUS**
No hanging about here, but few got into it.

## 7358 RECOMMENDBOOKIES.CO.UK UK'S TOP BETTING SITE H'CAP (DIV I) 1m 2f (P)
**4:30** (4:31) (Class 5) (0-70,75) 3-Y-0+ **£3,234** (£962; £481; £240) **Stalls** Low

Form RPR

4600 **1** **Upper Street (IRE)**[48] 6026 3-8-11 62 DavidProbert 13 71
(Sir Michael Stoute) *in tch in midfield: rdn and effrt over 1f out: str run 1f out to ld wl ins fnl f: rdn out* **16/1**

-020 **2** *1* **Ze King**[25] 6699 5-9-5 65 TedDurcan 9 72+
(Chris Wall) *hld up in tch in midfield: stl travelling wl 2f out: nt clr run over 1f out: rdn and hdwy jst ins fnl f: str run to go 2nd wl ins fnl f: kpt on* **6/1**[2]

4044 **3** *1* **Darting**[50] 5975 3-9-1 66 OisinMurphy 2 71
(Andrew Balding) *led: rdn wl over 1f out: kpt on u.p tl hdd and no ex wl ins fnl f* **16/1**

3500 **4** *½* **Best Kept**[62] 5557 3-9-5 70 JimmyFortune 3 74
(Amanda Perrett) *chsd ldrs: wnt 2nd 5f out: drvn and ev ch over 1f out: no ex and outpcd fnl 50yds* **10/1**

1531 **5** *¾* **Glennten**[5] 7219 5-10-1 75 6ex SilvestreDeSousa 14 78
(Jose Santos) *hld up in tch in last quartet: hdwy over 1f out: kpt on ins fnl f: nvr gng to rch ldrs* **12/1**

1433 **6** *¾* **Cataria Girl (USA)**[35] 6426 5-8-11 64 (t) JordanVaughan(7) 10 65
(Marcus Tregoning) *hld up in last quartet: forced v wd and effrt bnd 2f out: kpt on u.p fnl f: nvr threatened ldrs* **16/1**

4122 **7** *½* **Pendo**[29] 6616 3-9-3 68 LukeMorris 1 68
(Paul Cole) *chsd ldr tl 5f out: styd chsng ldrs tl unable qck over 1f out: kpt on same pce and lost 4 pls fnl f* **7/2**[1]

200 **8** *nk* **Indian Trifone (IRE)**[45] 6141 4-9-9 69 (b[1]) GeorgeBaker 8 69
(Ed Walker) *hld up in tch in last quartet: effrt towards inner over 1f out: kpt on ins fnl f: nvr trbld ldrs* **7/2**[1]

555 **9** *1* **Guesshowmuchiloveu (IRE)**[15] 6982 3-9-5 70 PatCosgrave 11 68
(Charlie Fellowes) *wl in tch in midfield: rdn and effrt to chse ldrs 2f out: no ex 1f out: wknd ins fnl f* **8/1**[3]

140- **10** *1½* **Sail Home**[575] 1176 7-9-2 62 LiamKeniry 5 57
(John E Long) *in tch in midfield: rdn and effrt ent fnl 2f: no ex over 1f out: wknd ins fnl f* **66/1**

3344 **11** *hd* **Oyster (IRE)**[28] 6636 3-8-12 63 (b) JackMitchell 4 58
(Nick Littmoden) *in tch in midfield: effrt on inner wl over 1f out: no ex ent fnl f: wknd fnl 150yds* **10/1**

0300 **12** *5* **Mountain Range (IRE)**[18] 6904 6-9-1 61 TomQueally 6 46
(Willie Musson) *distracted by ernt neighbour in stalls and v.s.a: clsd on to bk of field after 2f: rdn and struggling 3f out: wknd 2f out* **25/1**

1166 **13** *2½* **Dozy Joe**[174] 1875 6-8-13 66 NoraLooby(7) 7 46
(Joseph Tuite) *plunged forward under stall jst bef stalls opened: sn in tch in midfield: lost pl ent fnl 2f: wknd over 1f out* **50/1**

44-0 **14** *3½* **Santadelacruze**[281] 154 5-9-3 63 RobertHavlin 12 37
(Mark Hoad) *in tch in midfield: rdn over 2f out: sn struggling: wknd qckly wl over 1f out* **50/1**

2m 6.69s (0.09) **Going Correction** 0.0s/f (Stan)
**WFA** 3 from 4yo+ 5lb **14** Ran SP% **122.6**
Speed ratings (Par 103): **99,98,97,97,96 95,95,95,94,93 93,89,87,84**
CSF £109.35 CT £1596.78 TOTE £14.50: £3.00, £2.50, £4.20; EX 106.30 Trifecta £2904.40 Part won..
**Owner** Ballymacoll Stud **Bred** Ballymacoll Stud Farm Ltd **Trained** Newmarket, Suffolk

**FOCUS**
A modest and muddling handicap, but the first two have the potential to do better.

## 7359 RECOMMENDBOOKIES.CO.UK UK'S TOP BETTING SITE H'CAP (DIV II) 1m 2f (P)
**5:00** (5:06) (Class 5) (0-70,70) 3-Y-0+ **£3,234** (£962; £481; £240) **Stalls** Low

Form RPR

2420 **1** **Kinema (IRE)**[41] 6239 3-9-2 70 (b[1]) AshleyMorgan(3) 2 79
(Ed Walker) *mde all: rdn and clr w rival 2f out: forged ahd and clr 1f out: hrd-pressed wl ins fnl f: jst hld on* **7/1**

4412 **2** *hd* **Sequester**[38] 6341 3-9-3 68 (p) GeorgeBaker 14 76
(David Lanigan) *hld up towards rr: hdwy on inner 2f out: wnt 3rd and swtchd rt jst over 1f out: wnt 2nd ins fnl f: styd on wl: nt quite rch wnr* **4/1**[2]

4400 **3** *2½* **Crystal Pearl**[15] 6981 3-9-2 67 JimmyQuinn 8 70
(Mark H Tompkins) *in tch in midfield: rdn and sltly outpcd over 2f out: rallied and styd on again ins fnl f: wnt 3rd towards fin* **16/1**

2212 **4** *nk* **Real Jazz (IRE)**[46] 6091 3-9-4 69 LukeMorris 6 72
(Sir Mark Prescott Bt) *in tch in midfield: outpcd over 2f out: drvn and edgd lft over 1f out: styd on ins fnl f: no threat to ldrs* **11/4**[1]

3636 **5** *hd* **Cincinnati Girl (IRE)**[8] 7162 3-9-1 66 PatCosgrave 3 68
(Denis Coakley) *chsd wnr: rdn to press wnr and clr of field 2f out: no ex and btn 1f out: wknd and lost 2 pls towards fin* **20/1**

00/0 **6** *1¼* **Cherry Street**[45] 6141 5-9-9 69 (p) AntonioFresu 1 69
(Denis Quinn) *chsd ldrs: 3rd and outpcd u.p over 1f out: hld and plugged on same pce after* **33/1**

0552 **7** *½* **Greeleys Love (USA)**[45] 6155 4-9-5 65 (t) JimmyFortune 13 64
(Luke Dace) *dwlt: hld up towards rr: hdwy u.p on inner over 1f out: kpt on same pce fnl f: nvr trbld ldrs* **20/1**

-041 **8** *½* **Sweet P**[28] 6636 3-8-12 70 JordanVaughan(7) 10 68
(Marcus Tregoning) *hld up in midfield: rdn 2f out: no imp and swtchd lft 1f out: kpt on but no threat to ldrs* **7/1**

620 **9** *hd* **Numrood**[5] 7219 3-8-9 66 (v) SilvestreDeSousa 12 58
(George Peckham) *chsd ldng trio: rdn and struggling over 2f out: wknd over 1f out* **33/1**

0046 **10** *½* **Bridge That Gap**[80] 4911 6-8-6 59 (p) RhiainIngram(7) 7 56
(Roger Ingram) *stdd s: hld up in rr: struggling in last 3f out: c wd bnd 2f out: styd on fnl f: nvr trbld ldrs* **50/1**

3556 **11** *½* **Master Dancer**[25] 6722 3-9-0 68 (b) LouisSteward(3) 5 64
(Philip Hide) *s.i.s: hld up in rr: rdn and effrt 2f out: kpt on fnl f: nvr trbld ldrs* **9/2**[3]

06 **12** *1½* **Planetoid (IRE)**[93] 990 6-9-8 68 (p) AmirQuinn 9 61
(Jim Best) *bustled along early: a towards rr: kpt on fr over 1f out but n.d* **10/1**

5030 **13** *14* **Tingo In The Tale (IRE)**17 6942 5-8-5 58.........(p) KieranShoemark(7) 4 24
(David Arbuthnot) *in tch in midfield: lost pl over 2f out: bhd fnl f* **20/1**

2m 3.85s (-2.75) **Going Correction** 0.0s/f (Stan)
**WFA** 3 from 4yo+ 5lb **13** Ran SP% **127.0**
Speed ratings (Par 103): **111,110,108,108,108 107,107,106,106,106 105,104,93**
CSF £34.33 CT £455.18 TOTE £7.90: £2.00, £1.90, £6.70; EX 60.20 Trifecta £1443.00.
**Owner** Marc Keller **Bred** Rockhart Trading Ltd **Trained** Newmarket, Suffolk
■ Fearless Lad (20-1) was withdrawn. Rule 4 does not apply.

**FOCUS**
A better pace and the faster of the two divisions by 2.84sec.

## 7360 PLAY BLACKJACK AND ROULETTE AT WINNER.CO.UK APPRENTICE H'CAP 1m 4f (P)
5:35 (5:36) (Class 6) (0-55,54) 3-Y-0+ **£2,587** (£770; £384; £192) **Stalls** Low

Form RPR
0013 **1** **Topaling**69 5318 3-9-0 52.......................... TimClark 8 63
(Mark H Tompkins) *in tch in midfield: rdn and effrt to chse ldrs 2f out: wnt 2nd and hrd drvn ins fnl f: styd on wl to ld last stride* **5/1**2

5140 **2** *shd* **Mazij**48 6028 6-9-0 45.......................... ShelleyBirkett 9 55
(Peter Hiatt) *led: rdn ent fnl 2f: looked to be holding rival ins fnl f: tired cl home and hdd last stride* **8/1**3

0-50 **3** *1 3/4* **Haines**138 2926 3-8-5 46.......................... KieranShoemark(3) 12 53
(Andrew Balding) *in tch: effrt 3f out: drvn and chsd ldr 2f out: kpt on same pce and lost 2nd ins fnl f* **4/1**1

06-0 **4** *4* **Rock Charm**78 4984 3-8-8 51.......................... AaronJones(5) 4 52+
(Stuart Williams) *chsd ldng trio: rdn over 2f out: plugged on same pce and no imp over 1f out* **12/1**

0004 **5** *1* **Illegale (IRE)**22 6817 8-9-0 45..........................(bt) PhilipPrince 5 44
(Nikki Evans) *dwlt: rdn along early: in rr: hdwy 1/2-way: 6th and stl plenty to do over 1f out: plugged on but nvr threatened ldrs* **33/1**

0502 **6** *6* **Focail Mear**14 7002 3-8-3 46.......................... JoshDoyle(5) 14 36
(John Ryan) *hld up towards rr: stl plenty to do and sme hdwy over 1f out: nvr trbld ldrs* **4/1**1

0006 **7** *2* **Movie Magic**15 6986 3-8-2 45.......................... HectorCrouch(5) 7 31
(John Bridger) *in tch in midfield: rdn and struggling over 3f out: wl hld fnl 2f* **50/1**

00-0 **8** *4* **Star Of Mayfair (USA)**67 5403 4-9-5 53.......................... JordanVaughan(3) 11 33
(Timothy Jarvis) *hld up towards rr: sme hdwy over 3f out: rdn and no prog over 2f out: no ch over 1f out* **25/1**

-600 **9** *1/2* **Wunderkind (USA)**17 6946 3-8-0 45..........................(p) ManuelFernandes(7) 3 24
(Sir Mark Prescott Bt) *chsd ldrs: wnt 2nd over 3f out tl over 2f out: wknd qckly over 1f out* **10/1**

0530 **10** *1 1/4* **Berwin (IRE)**33 6481 5-8-12 50..........................(p) JackDinsmore(7) 2 27
(Sylvester Kirk) *s.i.s: hld up in rr: hdwy but wd 8f out: rdn and btn over 2f out: wknd 2f out* **16/1**

00/0 **11** *19* **First Battalion (IRE)**28 6632 6-9-5 50.......................... GeorgeDowning 13
(Ian Williams) *chsd ldr tl over 3f out: sn lost pl: t.o over 1f out* **25/1**

5001 **12** *shd* **Edward Elgar**27 6673 3-8-11 54..........................(p) ChrisMeehan(5) 6
(Natalie Lloyd-Beavis) *nvr reallly travelling in rr: bhd and no rspnse whn rdn 4f out: t.o over 2f out* **25/1**

0-00 **13** *43* **Petale Noir**169 2028 3-8-7 45.......................... LouisSteward 10
(Jonathan Portman) *in tch in midfield: rdn and dropped away qckly 4f out: t.o over 2f out* **33/1**

00-0 **14** *2 3/4* **Gladstone (IRE)**26 6682 6-9-0 48.......................... DavidParkes(3) 1
(Jeremy Gask) *in tch in midfield: rdn and lost tch over 3f out: t.o over 2f out* **10/1**

2m 32.55s (-0.45) **Going Correction** 0.0s/f (Stan)
**WFA** 3 from 4yo+ 7lb **14** Ran SP% **118.9**
Speed ratings (Par 101): **101,100,99,97,96 92,91,88,88,87 74,74,45,44**
CSF £40.51 CT £177.82 TOTE £4.40: £2.20, £2.60, £2.40; EX 44.80 Trifecta £172.60.
**Owner** M P Bowring **Bred** Dullingham Park Stud & M P Bowring **Trained** Newmarket, Suffolk

**FOCUS**
Not a bad race of its type, with the first three finishing clear.
T/Plt: £498.70 to a £1 stake. Pool: £76,910.33 - 112.57 winning tickets. T/Qpdt: £18.50 to a £1 stake. Pool: £7,386.16 - 294.07 winning tickets. SP

# 7285 WOLVERHAMPTON (A.W) (L-H)
Tuesday, October 21

**OFFICIAL GOING: Tapeta: standard**
Wind: Strong behind Weather: Showers

## 7361 BRITISH STALLION STUDS EBF MAIDEN STKS (TAPETA) 5f 216y
2:20 (2:21) (Class 5) 2-Y-O **£2,911** (£866; £432; £216) **Stalls** Low

Form RPR
4 **1** **Darma (IRE)**27 6660 2-9-0 0.......................... FergusSweeney 6 71
(Martyn Meade) *mde all: rdn over 1f out: jst hld on* **4/1**3

4 **2** *hd* **Secret Glance**33 6489 2-9-5 0.......................... DaleSwift 1 75
(Ed McMahon) *chsd ldrs: rdn to chse wnr and edgd rt 1f out: styd on* **6/4**1

02 **3** *1 1/4* **Longside**20 6852 2-9-5 0.......................... PaulHanagan 2 71
(Charles Hills) *s.i.s: in rr: hdwy 2f out: rdn over 1f out: nt clr run and swtchd lft ins fnl f: styd on* **3/1**2

**4** *2 1/4* **Star Of The Stage** 2-9-5 0.......................... TonyHamilton 3 65
(Richard Fahey) *s.s: in rr: rdn over 1f out: styd on ins fnl f: nvr nrr* **16/1**

6 **5** *nk* **Bapak Asmara (IRE)**54 5852 2-9-5 0.......................... GrahamLee 5 64
(Kevin Ryan) *prom: rdn 1/2-way: lost pl over 2f out: styd on same pce fr over 1f out* **20/1**

54 **6** *nse* **Bonfire Heart**12 7062 2-9-0 0.......................... AndreaAtzeni 4 58
(Daniel Mark Loughnane) *chsd wnr: rdn over 2f out: lost 2nd and no ex 1f out* **15/2**

0 **7** *3 3/4* **Twinkle Twinkle**46 6115 2-8-11 0.......................... ConnorBeasley(3) 7 47
(Julie Camacho) *prom: rdn over 2f out: edgd lft over 1f out: wknd fnl f* **25/1**

1m 14.36s (-0.14) **Going Correction** -0.025s/f (Stan) **7** Ran SP% **111.3**
Speed ratings (Par 95): **99,98,97,94,93 93,88**
CSF £9.83 TOTE £6.00: £3.50, £1.10; EX 13.80 Trifecta £55.00.
**Owner** David Caddy **Bred** Di Lualdi Lucia & C **Trained** Newmarket, Suffolk

**FOCUS**
A fair maiden, albeit one lacking in depth.

## 7362 BOOK NOW FOR CHRISTMAS NURSERY H'CAP (TAPETA) (DIV I) 5f 216y
2:50 (2:51) (Class 5) (0-75,75) 2-Y-O **£2,587** (£770; £384; £192) **Stalls** Low

Form RPR
2522 **1** **Lyfka**10 7112 2-8-12 66.......................... MartinLane 1 86
(Paul Cole) *chsd ldrs: wnt 2nd over 2f out: led over 1f out: rdn clr fnl f* **5/2**1

0033 **2** *9* **Zaza Zest (IRE)**14 7003 2-8-13 67.......................... TonyHamilton 2 60
(Richard Fahey) *mid-div: hdwy over 2f out: rdn and swtchd rt ins fnl f: styd on: no ch w wnr* **8/1**

2440 **3** *nk* **Battleranger (IRE)**12 7054 2-9-1 69..........................(p) TomEaves 3 61
(Keith Dalgleish) *s.i.s: in rr and pushed along 1/2-way: styd on ins fnl f: nvr nrr* **20/1**

1433 **4** *nse* **Somedaysrdiamonds**36 6401 2-8-8 62..........................(p) LiamJones 10 54
(J S Moore) *broke wl: sn lost pl and swtchd lft: hdwy u.p over 1f out: nt rch ldrs* **14/1**

0114 **5** *3/4* **Ar Colleen Aine**10 7112 2-8-8 69.......................... DanielCremin(7) 4 59
(Mick Channon) *led: rdn and hdd over 1f out: wknd ins fnl f* **14/1**

601 **6** *3/4* **Savannah Beau**83 4790 2-8-12 66.......................... DanielTudhope 6 53
(Marjorie Fife) *plld hrd and prom: rdn over 2f out: wknd ins fnl f* **25/1**

6640 **7** *1* **Emirates Challenge (IRE)**23 6791 2-8-3 60.......... ConnorBeasley(3) 9 44
(Saeed bin Suroor) *hld up: hdwy and nt clr run over 1f out: n.d* **4/1**2

036 **8** *1 1/2* **Firgrove Bridge (IRE)**35 6427 2-9-7 75.......................... GrahamLee 8 55
(Kevin Ryan) *dwlt: outpcd* **11/1**

2152 **9** *3/4* **Zipedeedodah (IRE)**28 6629 2-9-4 72.......................... PaulHanagan 5 50
(Joseph Tuite) *chsd ldrs: pushed along 1/2-way: wkng whn nt clr run ins fnl f: eased* **11/2**3

054 **10** *2 1/4* **Bushtown Boy (IRE)**10 7113 2-8-9 63.......................... JoeFanning 7 34
(Mark Johnston) *chsd ldr tl rdn over 2f out: wknd fnl f* **9/1**

1m 13.5s (-1.00) **Going Correction** -0.025s/f (Stan) **10** Ran SP% **115.3**
Speed ratings (Par 95): **105,93,92,92,91 90,89,87,86,83**
CSF £22.81 CT £326.05 TOTE £3.90: £1.60, £2.60, £5.20; EX 22.90 Trifecta £334.10.
**Owner** A H Robinson **Bred** A H & C E Robinson **Trained** Whatcombe, Oxon

**FOCUS**
Only a modest nursery, but a good pace.

## 7363 BOOK NOW FOR CHRISTMAS NURSERY H'CAP (TAPETA) (DIV II) 5f 216y
3:20 (3:20) (Class 5) (0-75,73) 2-Y-O **£2,587** (£770; £384; £192) **Stalls** Low

Form RPR
040 **1** **British Embassy (IRE)**39 6294 2-9-0 66.......................... JohnFahy 5 70
(Eve Johnson Houghton) *hld up: hdwy over 1f out: r.o to ld wl ins fnl f* **7/1**

063 **2** *1 1/4* **Tamarin**25 6719 2-8-12 64.......................... ShaneKelly 2 64
(Sir Michael Stoute) *led 1f: chsd ldrs: rdn and ev ch ins fnl f: styd on* **11/4**1

1355 **3** *3/4* **Emef Rock (IRE)**6 7201 2-9-3 69.......................... MartinDwyer 10 67
(Mick Channon) *hld up: hdwy over 3f out: rdn over 1f out: led ins fnl f: sn hdd and unable qck* **6/1**

150 **4** *1 3/4* **Zebelini (IRE)**13 7038 2-9-1 67.......................... LemosdeSouza 7 60
(Mrs Ilka Gansera-Leveque) *w ldr tl led 5f out: rdn over 1f out: hdd and no ex ins fnl f* **12/1**

4443 **5** *2 1/2* **Charlie's Star**26 6676 2-8-11 63.......................... LiamJones 1 48
(Laura Mongan) *hld up: rdn over 2f out: nt trble ldrs* **10/1**

4044 **6** *hd* **Little Belter (IRE)**56 5790 2-9-3 69.......................... StephenCraine 8 54
(Tom Dascombe) *prom: rdn over 1f out: wknd ins fnl f* **4/1**2

5600 **7** *1* **Mutafarrej**42 6211 2-9-3 69.......................... PaulHanagan 9 51
(Mark Johnston) *prom: chsd ldr 4f out tl rdn over 1f out: wknd ins fnl f* **11/2**3

2005 **8** *1* **Shamrock Sheila (IRE)**4 7255 2-9-7 73.......................... JoeFanning 4 52
(J S Moore) *hld up in tch: plld hrd: rdn over 1f out: wknd ins fnl f* **8/1**

1m 15.19s (0.69) **Going Correction** -0.025s/f (Stan) **8** Ran SP% **116.7**
Speed ratings (Par 95): **94,92,91,89,85 85,84,82**
CSF £27.22 CT £104.79 TOTE £7.40: £4.30, £1.50, £1.40; EX 44.10 Trifecta £190.00.
**Owner** Eden Racing IV **Bred** Corduff Stud Ltd & T J Rooney **Trained** Blewbury, Oxon

**FOCUS**
The second division of this modest nursery was run 1.69sec slower than the first.

## 7364 FOLLOW US ON TWITTER @WOLVESRACES H'CAP (TAPETA) 5f 216y
3:50 (3:51) (Class 6) (0-60,60) 3-Y-O+ **£1,940** (£577; £288; £144) **Stalls** Low

Form RPR
0054 **1** **Methaaly (IRE)**4 7253 11-8-10 56..........................(b) AnnaHesketh(7) 13 64
(Michael Mullineaux) *a.p: chsd ldr 1/2-way: led over 1f out: pushed out* **22/1**

0032 **2** *hd* **Mambo Spirit (IRE)**22 6815 10-9-7 60.......................... MartinDwyer 6 67
(Tony Newcombe) *mid-div: hdwy over 1f out: rdn to chse wnr ins fnl f: r.o* **13/2**2

2605 **3** *1 1/4* **Sewn Up**12 7056 4-9-3 56..........................(p) JoeFanning 7 59
(Keith Dalgleish) *hld up: shkn up over 1f out: r.o ins fnl f: nt rch ldrs* **3/1**1

0165 **4** *3/4* **Catalinas Diamond (IRE)**27 6666 6-9-4 57..........................(t) SebSanders 12 58
(Pat Murphy) *mid-div: hdwy u.p over 1f out: r.o* **16/1**

5046 **5** *1/2* **Hamis Al Bin (IRE)**27 6666 5-9-2 55..........................(t) CharlesBishop 9 54
(Milton Bradley) *hld up: hdwy over 1f out: r.o: nt trble ldrs* **8/1**

3220 **6** *1/2* **Assertive Agent**27 6666 4-9-7 60.......................... PaulHanagan 10 58
(Tony Carroll) *hld up: pushed along 1/2-way: rdn and r.o ins fnl f: nt rch ldrs* **12/1**

0562 **7** *1 1/4* **Bondi Beach Babe**4 7253 4-8-7 51.......................... JordanNason(5) 1 45
(James Turner) *sn led: rdn and hdd over 1f out: no ex ins fnl f* **7/1**3

3202 **8** *hd* **Reginald Claude**25 6720 6-8-11 55.......................... RachealKneller(5) 11 48
(Mark Usher) *hld up: swtchd lft sn after s: r.o ins fnl f: nvr nrr* **10/1**

100 **9** *1* **Spray Tan**22 6815 4-9-4 57.......................... WilliamTwiston-Davies 8 47
(Tony Carroll) *prom: rdn over 1f out: no ex fnl f* **33/1**

050 **10** *nk* **Compton Prince**19 6889 5-9-7 60..........................(v1) FrannyNorton 4 49
(Milton Bradley) *prom: hmpd over 1f out: wknd ins fnl f* **16/1**

0230 **11** *3 1/4* **Saskia's Dream**14 6995 6-9-6 59..........................(v) GrahamLee 2 38
(Jane Chapple-Hyam) *chsd ldrs: rdn over 1f out: wknd ins fnl f* **16/1**

4044 **12** *1 1/4* **Douneedahand**10 7111 3-8-11 58..........................(p) GaryMahon(7) 5 33
(Seamus Mullins) *unruly to post: hld up in tch: rdn over 1f out: wknd ins fnl f* **8/1**

0500 **13** *1* **Insolenceofoffice (IRE)**10 7111 6-8-10 56..........................(p) NicolaGrundy(7) 3 27
(Richard Ford) *s.i.s: sn pushed along and prom: chsd ldr 5f out to 1/2-way: pushed along and edgd lft over 1f out: wknd ins fnl f* **66/1**

1m 14.87s (0.37) **Going Correction** -0.025s/f (Stan)
**WFA** 3 from 4yo+ 1lb **13** Ran SP% **116.3**
Speed ratings (Par 101): **96,95,94,93,92 91,90,89,88,88 83,82,80**
CSF £153.33 CT £562.03 TOTE £16.90: £6.20, £2.00, £1.50; EX 113.60 Trifecta £454.40.
**Owner** S A Pritchard **Bred** Scuderia Golden Horse S R L **Trained** Alpraham, Cheshire


The Form Book, Raceform Ltd, Newbury, RG14 5SJ

■ Stewards' Enquiry : Nicola Grundy caution: careless riding
**FOCUS**
A competitive sprint handicap for the grade, dominated by two old-timers.

## 7365 WOLVERHAMPTON-RACECOURSE.CO.UK H'CAP (TAPETA) 5f 216y
**4:20** (4:21) (Class 4) (0-85,85) 3-Y-O+ **£4,690** (£1,395; £697; £348) **Stalls Low**

Form RPR
0110 **1** **Amadeus Wolfe Tone (IRE)**[20] 6872 5-9-7 85......(p) DanielTudhope 10 95
(Jamie Osborne) *mid-div: hdwy over 3f out: led over 1f out: rdn out* **14/1**
1123 **2** *1 ¾* **Poyle Vinnie**[26] 6692 4-9-2 85.................... AlistairRawlinson(5) 6 89
(Michael Appleby) *a.p: rdn to chse wnr fnl f: styd on same pce ins fnl f* **9/2**[2]
3500 **3** *hd* **Foxy Forever (IRE)**[17] 6923 4-9-6 84...........................[1] AndreaAtzeni 7 88
(Michael Wigham) *hld up: hdwy over 1f out: r.o: nt rch ldrs* **10/1**
1452 **4** *hd* **Taquka (IRE)**[14] 7017 3-8-9 81........................ PatrickO'Donnell(7) 12 85+
(Ralph Beckett) *broke wl: sn stdd and lost pl: nt clr run over 1f out: r.o ins fnl f: nt rch ldrs* **10/1**
3535 **5** *½* **Lady Horatia**[38] 6336 3-9-4 83.............................. MartinDwyer 5 85
(William Muir) *mid-div: hdwy over 2f out: rdn over 1f out: styd on* **14/1**
3353 **6** *¾* **George Rooke (IRE)**[31] 6535 4-9-3 81.........................(p) JoeFanning 13 80
(Keith Dalgleish) *mid-div: hdwy over 3f out: rdn over 1f out: styd on same pce ins fnl f* **13/2**
0341 **7** *hd* **Realize**[11] 7071 4-9-2 80.........................................(t) GrahamLee 2 78
(Hughie Morrison) *prom: lost pl over 3f out: hdwy over 1f out: no ex ins fnl f* **3/1**[1]
3011 **8** *½* **Slim Chance (IRE)**[29] 6595 5-9-2 80.......................... AndrewElliott 8 77
(Simon West) *chsd ldr tl led 2f out: sn rdn and hdd: no ex ins fnl f* **28/1**
4500 **9** *1 ¼* **Clear Praise (USA)**[11] 7073 7-9-0 78.......................... SebSanders 1 71
(Simon Dow) *hld up: nt clr run over 1f out: nvr on terms* **100/1**
3403 **10** *2* **Amygdala (USA)**[14] 7017 3-9-0 79.................... WilliamTwiston-Davies 9 65
(Stuart Williams) *mid-div: rdn over 2f out: n.d* **20/1**
0100 **11** *5* **Dinneratmidnight**[60] 5650 3-9-5 84.......................... PaulHanagan 11 54
(Ralph Beckett) *sn pushed along in rr: n.d* **6/1**[3]
2410 **12** *2* **Desert Strike**[14] 7017 8-9-1 79.................................(p) HayleyTurner 4 43
(Conor Dore) *chsd ldr: ev ch 2f out: wknd fnl f* **25/1**
1005 **13** *11* **Baytown Kestrel**[98] 4282 3-9-5 84............................(p) RobertWinston 3 13
(Brian Ellison) *led 4f: wknd over 1f out* **33/1**

1m 13.13s (-1.37) **Going Correction** -0.025s/f (Stan)
**WFA** 3 from 4yo+ 1lb **13 Ran SP% 118.3**
Speed ratings (Par 105): **108,105,105,105,104 103,103,102,100,98 91,88,74**
CSF £71.39 CT £674.57 TOTE £10.20: £6.40, £1.90, £2.20; EX 105.50 Trifecta £1078.60.
**Owner** B T McDonald **Bred** Brian Williamson **Trained** Upper Lambourn, Berks
**FOCUS**
A competitive handicap for the grade in which the pace was solid throughout.

## 7366 WOLVERHAMPTON HOLIDAY INN H'CAP (TAPETA) 1m 4f 50y
**4:50** (4:50) (Class 5) (0-75,75) 3-Y-O+ **£2,587** (£770; £384; £192) **Stalls Low**

Form RPR
2542 **1** **Rex Whistler (IRE)**[25] 6699 4-9-4 70.................... ConnorBeasley(3) 10 81
(Julie Camacho) *hld up: hdwy over 3f out: led over 2f out: rdn clr over 1f out* **8/1**[3]
1350 **2** *2 ¼* **Right Of Appeal**[10] 7100 3-9-2 72.............................. JoeFanning 8 79
(Mark Johnston) *hld up: hdwy over 3f out: rdn to chse wnr fnl f: no imp* **9/1**
0300 **3** *1 ¾* **Ex Oriente (IRE)**[18] 6896 5-9-12 75.......................... GrahamLee 2 79
(Stuart Williams) *hld up: rdn over 1f out: r.o ins fnl f: nt rch ldrs* **15/2**[2]
6-21 **4** *1 ¾* **Thunder Pass (IRE)**[15] 6981 3-9-2 72.......................... AndreaAtzeni 11 73
(Hughie Morrison) *chsd ldrs: pushed along over 3f out: sn outpcd: styd on ins fnl f* **6/4**[1]
2663 **5** *½* **All The Winds (GER)**[17] 6942 9-9-0 70.....................(t) CiaranMckee(7) 9 71
(Shaun Lycett) *s.v.s: bhd: latched on to the bk of the field over 8f out: hdwy over 2f out: rdn over 1f out: wknd ins fnl f* **10/1**
1420 **6** *½* **Elegant Ophelia**[38] 6338 5-9-3 66...........................(t) RobertWinston 6 66
(Dean Ivory) *hld up: nt clr run over 2f out: hdwy and hmpd over 1f out: nvr trbld ldrs* **33/1**
0626 **7** *shd* **Kindlelight Storm (USA)**[18] 6904 4-9-7 70..(b) WilliamTwiston-Davies 7 70
(Nick Littmoden) *hld up: rdn over 3f out: styd on ins fnl f: nvr on terms* **16/1**
063 **8** *2* **Lady Lunchalot (USA)**[133] 3079 4-9-9 72...................... LiamJones 5 68
(Laura Mongan) *prom: chsd ldr 3f out: ev ch over 2f out: wknd fnl f* **25/1**
3643 **9** *½* **Save The Bees**[14] 7008 6-9-4 74.......................... LukeLeadbitter(7) 1 70
(Declan Carroll) *led: rdn and hdd over 2f out: wknd ins fnl f* **16/1**
2534 **10** *1 ¾* **Bold Runner**[34] 6461 3-9-5 75.............................. IrineuGoncalves 3 68
(Jose Santos) *prom: rdn over 3f out: wknd fnl f* **14/1**
3404 **11** *34* **Keep Kicking (IRE)**[129] 3234 7-9-4 67.......................... SebSanders 4 5
(Simon Dow) *hld up: rdn over 3f out: wknd over 2f out* **66/1**
6630 **12** *2* **Lovelocks (IRE)**[34] 6461 3-9-2 72.......................... PaulHanagan 12 7
(Charles Hills) *chsd ldr 9f: wknd over 2f out* **12/1**

2m 38.81s (-1.99) **Going Correction** -0.025s/f (Stan)
**WFA** 3 from 4yo+ 7lb **12 Ran SP% 116.4**
Speed ratings (Par 103): **105,103,102,101,100 100,100,99,98,97 74,73**
CSF £75.45 CT £565.09 TOTE £8.40: £3.20, £2.50, £2.30; EX 102.60 Trifecta £1346.60.
**Owner** Axom XXXVIII **Bred** Miss S Von Schilcher **Trained** Norton, N Yorks
**FOCUS**
A competitive handicap, but the pace was steady and it turned into a sprint up the straight.

## 7367 BREEDERS BACKING RACING EBF MAIDEN FILLIES' STKS (BOBIS RACE) (TAPETA) 1m 141y
**5:20** (5:24) (Class 5) 2-Y-O **£2,911** (£866; £432; £216) **Stalls Low**

Form RPR
5 **1** **Beautiful Ending**[32] 6517 2-9-0 0.............................. GrahamLee 7 73+
(Saeed bin Suroor) *hld up in tch: led over 1f out: sn hung rt: rdn out* **1/1**[1]
**2** *shd* **Pin Up (IRE)** 2-9-0 0.............................................. TonyHamilton 4 71+
(Richard Fahey) *a.p: rdn and ev ch fr over 1f out: r.o* **28/1**
**3** *1* **Nawaasy (USA)** 2-9-0 0.............................................. PaulHanagan 13 69+
(Charles Hills) *s.s: hld up: hdwy over 2f out: shkn up over 1f out: r.o* **15/2**
5 **4** *1 ¾* **Skip And Jump (USA)**[24] 6753 2-9-0 0.......................... AndreaAtzeni 11 65
(Roger Varian) *s.i.s: hld up: pushed along and hdwy over 2f out: styd on* **9/2**[3]
0 **5** *2 ¼* **Dominike (ITY)**[48] 6041 2-8-9 0.......................... MarcMonaghan(5) 1 60
(Marco Botti) *chsd ldr 6f: rdn over 1f out: styd on same pce ins fnl f* **25/1**
50 **6** *2 ¼* **Singoalla**[14] 7011 2-9-0 0.............................................. ChrisCatlin 10 56
(Sir Mark Prescott Bt) *chsd ldrs: wnt 2nd over 2f out: ev ch wl over 1f out: wknd ins fnl f* **100/1**
4 **7** *¾* **Chapel Choir**[20] 6868 2-9-0 0.............................................. ShaneKelly 9 54
(Sir Michael Stoute) *chsd ldrs: pushed along over 3f out: wknd fnl f* **4/1**[2]
0 **8** *nse* **Victorina**[110] 3888 2-9-0 0.............................................. MartinDwyer 5 54
(Stuart Kittow) *s.i.s: hld up: rdn over 2f out: wknd fnl f* **66/1**
00 **9** *nse* **Tocororo (IRE)**[10] 7108 2-9-0 0.............................................. PJMcDonald 6 54
(Ed Dunlop) *s.i.s: hld up: pushed along 3f out: wknd fnl f* **40/1**
6 **10** *1* **Aruan**[25] 6718 2-9-0 0.............................................. JoeFanning 2 52
(Derek Haydn Jones) *led: rdn and hdd over 1f out: wknd ins fnl f* **100/1**
**11** *1 ½* **Shifting Moon** 2-9-0 0.............................................. DanielTudhope 12 49
(Hughie Morrison) *s.s: a in rr* **33/1**
0 **12** *11* **Kallisima**[24] 6742 2-9-0 0.............................................. DaleSwift 3 25
(Ed McMahon) *mid-div: rdn over 3f out: wknd 2f out* **100/1**

1m 53.54s (3.44) **Going Correction** -0.025s/f (Stan) **12 Ran SP% 117.1**
Speed ratings (Par 92): **83,82,82,80,78 76,75,75,75,74 73,63**
CSF £41.81 TOTE £2.30: £1.10, £5.20, £2.60; EX 29.50 Trifecta £131.90.
**Owner** Godolphin **Bred** Darley **Trained** Newmarket, Suffolk
**FOCUS**
A steady pace, but still an interesting maiden that should produce winners.

## 7368 DOWNLOAD OUR IPHONE APP NOW H'CAP (TAPETA) 7f 32y
**5:50** (5:51) (Class 6) (0-65,65) 3-Y-O+ **£1,940** (£577; £288; £144) **Stalls High**

Form RPR
0332 **1** **Keene's Pointe**[14] 7025 4-9-2 60.................................(b) PaulHanagan 2 69
(Charles Hills) *a.p: rdn over 1f out: r.o to ld post* **13/2**[2]
3102 **2** *hd* **Pour La Victoire (IRE)**[11] 7078 4-9-7 65....(b) WilliamTwiston-Davies 11 73
(Tony Carroll) *chsd ldrs: led over 1f out: sn rdn: hdd post* **7/2**[1]
2120 **3** *hd* **Hawk Moth (IRE)**[36] 6397 6-9-3 61...........................(p) FrannyNorton 6 69
(John Spearing) *hld up: hdwy and nt clr run over 1f out: r.o* **12/1**
2063 **4** *hd* **Malaysian Boleh**[6] 7202 4-9-6 64.............................. GrahamLee 7 71
(Simon Dow) *hld up: rdn and r.o ins fnl f: nt quite rch ldrs* **7/2**[1]
1440 **5** *nk* **Zed Candy Girl**[11] 7077 4-9-1 64..............................(p) EoinWalsh(5) 5 70
(John Stimpson) *hld up: hdwy over 1f out: sn rdn: styd on* **16/1**
5053 **6** *1 ½* **Larghetto (USA)**[11] 7077 6-9-2 60...........................(t) DanielTudhope 3 62
(Ian Williams) *hld up: hdwy over 1f out: styd on same pce towards fin* **7/1**[3]
6000 **7** *1 ½* **Petergate**[57] 5761 3-8-3 54...........................(p) JackGarritty(5) 10 51
(Brian Rothwell) *hld up: hdwy over 2f out: rdn over 1f out: styd on same pce* **18/1**
0000 **8** *2 ¾* **Llewellyn**[11] 7077 6-8-12 63 ow1.......................... LukeLeadbitter(7) 8 54
(Declan Carroll) *chsd ldr: led over 2f out: rdn and hdd over 1f out: wknd ins fnl f* **20/1**
0500 **9** *2* **Russian Ice**[20] 6857 6-9-5 63.................................(p) RobertWinston 4 49
(Dean Ivory) *prom: rdn over 1f out: wknd fnl f* **16/1**
3454 **10** *1 ¼* **Skidby Mill (IRE)**[153] 2469 4-8-12 56.......................... LiamJones 9 39
(Laura Mongan) *s.i.s: hdwy over 2f out: wknd over 1f out* **16/1**
0043 **11** *17* **Live Dangerously**[12] 7057 4-9-6 64.......................... JoeFanning 1 3
(Keith Dalgleish) *led: racd keenly: sddle slipped sn after s: hung rt and rdr kicked feet out of irons over 4f out: swtchd rt and hdd over 2f out: eased* **15/2**

1m 29.09s (0.29) **Going Correction** -0.025s/f (Stan)
**WFA** 3 from 4yo+ 2lb **11 Ran SP% 117.4**
Speed ratings (Par 101): **97,96,96,96,95 94,92,89,87,85 66**
CSF £29.41 CT £275.79 TOTE £7.30: £2.40, £3.50, £2.90; EX 30.80 Trifecta £174.20.
**Owner** Mrs Paul Abberley **Bred** Christopher & Annabelle Mason **Trained** Lambourn, Berks
**FOCUS**
A thrilling finish to this competitive, albeit modest handicap.
T/Jkpt: Not won. T/Plt: £121.10 to a £1 stake. Pool: £87,267.34 - 525.72 winning tickets. T/Qpdt: £37.90 to a £1 stake. Pool: £5,933.96 - 115.75 winning tickets. CR

# 7345 KEMPTON (A.W) (R-H)
### Wednesday, October 22

**OFFICIAL GOING: Polytrack: standard**
Weather: dry

## 7369 ROCK AND GEM H'CAP 1m 2f (P)
**5:55** (5:55) (Class 6) (0-55,55) 3-Y-O+ **£1,940** (£577; £288; £144) **Stalls Low**

Form RPR
5400 **1** **Mr Lando**[18] 6942 5-9-4 55.............................................. RyanTate(3) 7 64
(Tony Carroll) *chsd ldrs: 3rd and swtchd lft and effrt over 1f out: r.o wl u.p to ld cl home* **7/1**
0055 **2** *nk* **Highly Likely (IRE)**[49] 6031 5-9-1 49.......................... SeanLevey 1 57
(Steve Woodman) *in tch in midfield: effrt wl over 1f out: gd hdwy on inner over 1f out: led ins fnl f: hdd and no ex cl home* **20/1**
5120 **3** *2 ¼* **Claude Greenwood**[15] 7000 4-9-1 49...........................(p) CharlesBishop 10 53
(Linda Jewell) *chsd ldrs: effrt u.p over 1f out: pressing ldrs 1f out: outpcd fnl 100yds* **20/1**
0052 **4** *1* **Mercury Magic**[18] 6939 3-8-13 52...........................(b) RaulDaSilva 14 54
(David Menuisier) *dwlt: pushed and rcvrd to r in midfield after 2f: pushed along and hdwy to chse ldrs 3f out: led over 1f out: hdd ins fnl f: wknd* **12/1**
3066 **5** *½* **Kingswinford (IRE)**[46] 6161 8-9-7 55...........................(p) PaddyAspell 4 56
(John Norton) *in tch in midfield: effrt 2f out: kpt on same pce ins fnl f* **20/1**
0435 **6** *hd* **Silken Waters**[18] 6946 3-8-13 52.............................. OisinMurphy 8 53
(Eve Johnson Houghton) *in tch in midfield: rdn over 2f out: styd on ins fnl f: nt rch ldrs* **6/1**[3]
4153 **7** *hd* **Hidden Asset**[5] 7256 4-9-2 53.............................. CamHardie(3) 2 54
(Michael Appleby) *stdd s: t.k.h: hld up in rr: hdwy but v wd 2f out: styd on ins fnl f: nt rch ldrs* **11/4**[1]
0060 **8** *2* **Berrahri (IRE)**[7] 7197 3-9-1 54...........................(v[1]) RobertHavlin 5 51
(John Best) *chsd ldr: led over 2f out: hdd over 1f out: wknd ins fnl f* **20/1**
0660 **9** *hd* **Warbond**[20] 6883 6-9-1 49...........................(v) LukeMorris 12 49
(Michael Madgwick) *hld up in tch towards rr: effrt whn bdly hmpd over 1f out: kpt on but nvr rcvrd* **16/1**
6-00 **10** *1 ¼* **Lexington Blue**[20] 6883 4-8-13 54...........................[1] GaryMahon(7) 9 52
(Seamus Mullins) *hld up in tch towards rr: effrt whn nt clr run and bdly hmpd over 1f out: nt rcvr* **33/1**
0/0 **11** *1 ¾* **Osorios Trial**[4] 7290 7-9-6 54...........................(t) DanielTudhope 6 45
(Kevin Frost) *in tch in midfield: effrt over 1f out: no hdwy' nvr trbld ldrs* **33/1**
0004 **12** *9* **Teide Peak (IRE)**[8] 7188 5-9-7 55...........................(p) AdamKirby 3 29
(Paul D'Arcy) *hld up towards rr: rdn 2f out: sn btn: wl bhd fnl f* **3/1**[2]
0060 **13** *10* **Nouvelle Ere**[14] 7036 3-8-11 50.............................. DavidProbert 11 5
(Tony Carroll) *hld up in last pair: lost tch 2f out* **40/1**

5560 **14** *2 ¾* **Purple Spot**27 6682 3-8-13 52....................(b1) SteveDrowne 13 3
(Rod Millman) *led tl over 2f out: losing pl qckly whn bdly hmpd over 1f out: wl bhd fnl f* **33/1**

2m 7.45s (-0.55) **Going Correction** 0.0s/f (Stan)
**WFA** 3 from 4yo+ 5lb **14** Ran SP% **122.3**
Speed ratings (Par 101): **102,101,99,99,98 98,98,96,96,95 94,87,79,76**
CSF £143.04 CT £2683.96 TOTE £6.50: £2.60, £5.90, £7.50; EX 145.30 Trifecta £1636.30 Part won. Pool of £2181.77 - 0.09 winning units..
**Owner** A W Carroll **Bred** Capitana Partnership **Trained** Cropthorne, Worcs

**FOCUS**
A desperately weak opener and not a race to over analyse.

## 7370 BETBRIGHT MONEYBACK OFFERS MEDIAN AUCTION MAIDEN STKS 6f (P)
**6:25** (6:25) (Class 5) 3-4-Y-O **£2,587** (£770; £384; £192) **Stalls** Low

Form RPR

3 **1** **Moiety**11 7117 3-9-0 0.................... MartinHarley 4 72+
(Rae Guest) *chsd ldr: clsd smoothly to ld over 1f out: shkn and sn wnt clr: v easily* **10/11**1

2365 **2** *4 ½* **Nelson's Pride**55 5853 3-8-7 56....................(b) RhiainIngram(7) 6 57
(Roger Ingram) *led: rdn and hdd over 1f out: sn btn: kpt on for clr 2nd* **8/1**

**3** *4 ½* **Kokovoko (IRE)** 3-9-2 0.................... ThomasBrown(3) 5 49+
(Andrew Balding) *v.s.a: rn green in detached last: sme hdwy over 1f out: wnt 3rd ins fnl f: nvr trbld ldrs* **7/2**2

00 **4** *1 ½* **Duke Of Dunton (IRE)**15 7024 3-9-2 0.................... JoeyHaynes(3) 1 44
(Tony Carroll) *racd in midfield: effrt over 2f out: no ch w ldrs but battling for 3rd over 1f out: no ex ins fnl f* **33/1**

**5** *½* **Prominna** 4-9-6 0.................... LukeMorris 8 43
(Tony Carroll) *wnt lft s and s.i.s: in rr: hdwy 3f out: no ch w ldrs but modest 3rd 2f out: no ex ins fnl f* **16/1**

60 **6** *1* **Man Of Music**16 6988 3-9-5 0.................... LiamKeniry 7 40
(Tony Carroll) *chsd ldrs: outpcd over 2f out: no ch w ldrs over 1f out: wknd ins fnl f* **16/1**

4636 **7** *2 ¾* **Templar Boy**48 6073 3-9-5 52.................... AdamKirby 2 31
(J R Jenkins) *chsd ldrs tl outpcd and lost 3rd 2f out: no ch after: wknd fnl f* **7/1**3

**8** *7* **Wattaboutsteve** 3-9-5 0.................... OisinMurphy 3 10
(Ralph J Smith) *midfield tl rdn and dropped to rr 4f out: lost tch over 2f out* **12/1**

1m 13.41s (0.31) **Going Correction** 0.0s/f (Stan)
**WFA** 3 from 4yo 1lb **8** Ran SP% **120.6**
Speed ratings (Par 103): **97,91,85,83,82 81,77,68**
CSF £10.13 TOTE £2.40: £1.10, £1.40, £2.20; EX 10.50 Trifecta £43.70.
**Owner** C J Mills **Bred** C J Mills **Trained** Newmarket, Suffolk
■ Stewards' Enquiry : Joey Haynes caution: careless riding.

**FOCUS**
A weak maiden. Favourites have an excellent record in this contest and that trend continued as Rae Guest's once-raced filly stretched clear for an authoritative success.

## 7371 BRITISH STALLION STUDS EBF MAIDEN STKS (BOBIS RACE) (DIV I) 1m (P)
**6:55** (6:57) (Class 4) 2-Y-O **£4,075** (£1,212; £606; £303) **Stalls** Low

Form RPR

0 **1** **Heatstroke (IRE)**81 4896 2-9-5 0.................... JimCrowley 4 84+
(Charles Hills) *hld up in midfield: effrt but stl plenty to do jst over 2f out: str run-in centre over 1f out: led ins fnl f: sn clr: readily* **16/1**

0 **2** *2 ¾* **Maxwell (IRE)**40 6293 2-9-5 0.................... OisinMurphy 10 77
(Ralph Beckett) *in tch in midfield: rdn and effrt jst over 2f out: chsd ldr jst over 1f out: 3rd ins fnl f: outpcd by wnr fnl 100yds: kpt on to go 2nd cl home* **7/1**

32 **3** *nk* **Natural Nine (IRE)**29 6621 2-9-5 0.................... FrederikTylicki 9 77
(Roger Varian) *chsd ldrs: rdn to ld wl over 1f out: drvn ent fnl f: hdd ins fnl f: sn outpcd and btn: lost 2nd cl home* **4/1**3

**4** *4 ½* **Assagher (USA)** 2-9-5 0.................... WilliamBuick 7 66
(John Gosden) *s.i.s: bhd: hdwy into midfield 1/2-way: switching rt and hdwy to chse ldrs over 1f out: outpcd fnl f* **5/1**

U32 **5** *5* **Wentworth Falls**41 6268 2-9-5 0.................... AdamKirby 11 54
(Charlie Appleby) *chsd ldr tl led 1/2-way: rdn and hdd wl over 1f out: sn btn: wknd 1f out* **7/2**2

0 **6** *1* **El Draque (USA)**18 6931 2-9-5 0....................(b1) LukeMorris 2 51
(Sir Mark Prescott Bt) *towards rr: u.p 1/2-way: sme hdwy past btn fnl f: n.d* **66/1**

**7** *2* **Global Force (IRE)** 2-9-5 0.................... PaulHanagan 1 47+
(Saeed bin Suroor) *hmpd and dropped to rr after 1f: hmpd again sn after and detached last after 2f: sme hdwy over 1f out: n.d* **5/2**1

6 **8** *hd* **Hymn Of Hope (IRE)**14 7039 2-9-5 0.................... PatCosgrave 5 46
(Noel Quinlan) *a towards rr: u.p over 2f out: no imp* **40/1**

0 **9** *½* **First Dream (IRE)**40 6300 2-9-5 0.................... SeanLevey 8 45
(Richard Hannon) *sn led: hdd 1/2-way: chsd ldrs tl struggling u.p jst over 2f out: wknd over 1f out* **50/1**

30 **10** *1* **Open The Red**10 7134 2-9-5 0.................... PatDobbs 12 43
(Amanda Perrett) *chsd ldrs: wnt 2nd over 3f out tl ent fnl 2f: wknd over 1f out* **16/1**

**11** *2 ¼* **Goodby Inheritence** 2-9-5 0.................... FergusSweeney 6 37
(Seamus Durack) *in tch in midfield: rdn over 2f out: sn struggling: wknd over 1f out* **66/1**

0 **12** *22* **Hayed**30 6606 2-8-7 0....................(b) RobertPWalsh(7) 3
(Edward Creighton) *s.i.s: sn rdn and nvr gng wl: lost tch over 2f out: t.o* **100/1**

1m 38.86s (-0.94) **Going Correction** 0.0s/f (Stan) **12** Ran SP% **120.1**
Speed ratings (Par 97): **104,101,100,96,91 90,88,88,87,86 84,62**
CSF £123.69 TOTE £13.10: £3.20, £3.10, £1.60; EX 150.90 Trifecta £1359.70.
**Owner** Mrs Fitri Hay **Bred** Mrs Fitriani Hay **Trained** Lambourn, Berks

**FOCUS**
The last three winners of this maiden have gone on to be rated in excess of 100 and, with some big yards represented yet again, it's likely this renewal took plenty of winning.

## 7372 BRITISH STALLION STUDS EBF MAIDEN STKS (BOBIS RACE) (DIV II) 1m (P)
**7:25** (7:27) (Class 4) 2-Y-O **£4,075** (£1,212; £606; £303) **Stalls** Low

Form RPR

3 **1** **Spanish Squeeze (IRE)**26 6712 2-9-5 0.................... DanielTudhope 10 83+
(Hugo Palmer) *hld up in tch in midfield: effrt and qcknd to ld 2f out: asserted ins fnl f: r.o wl* **3/1**3

3 **2** *1 ¾* **Legend's Gate (IRE)**18 6928 2-9-5 0.................... AdamKirby 8 79
(Charlie Appleby) *chsd ldrs: rdn to chal 2f out: sustained duel w wnr tl no ex fnl 100yds* **6/4**1

**3** *4* **China Club (IRE)** 2-9-5 0.................... WilliamBuick 2 69+
(John Gosden) *rn green early: in tch in midfield: effrt jst over 2f out: hdwy to chse clr ldng pair jst over 1f out: no threat but kpt on steadily fnl f* **5/2**2

05 **4** *3 ¾* **Foxy Boris (FR)**26 6718 2-9-5 0....................(t) LukeMorris 3 60
(Paul Cole) *in tch in midfield: rdn jst over 1f out: unable qck 2f out: 4th and wl hld over 1f out* **50/1**

00 **5** *2 ¼* **Vivi's Charis (IRE)**21 6868 2-9-0 0.................... PatDobbs 7 50
(Sir Michael Stoute) *stdd after s: hld up in last trio: swtchd lft and effrt over 2f out: no ch w ldrs and one pce fr over 1f out* **25/1**

46 **6** *hd* **Consortium (IRE)**28 6652 2-9-5 0.................... PatCosgrave 6 54
(David Simcock) *stdd s: hld up in rr: pushed along over 1f out: kpt on but nvr trbld ldrs* **14/1**

0 **7** *hd* **Giovanni Di Bicci**30 6604 2-9-5 0.................... MartinHarley 5 54
(Lady Cecil) *hld up in last trio: effrt u.p 2f out: no imp* **16/1**

0 **8** *2 ¾* **Top Pocket**40 6293 2-9-0 0.................... RyanWhile(5) 11 47
(Michael Madgwick) *led tl 2f out: sn drvn and outpcd by ldng pair: lost 3rd jst over 1f out: fdd fnl f* **100/1**

63 **9** *16* **Imperial War (IRE)**23 6812 2-9-2 0.................... CamHardie(3) 1 9
(Richard Hannon) *broke fast: chsd ldr tl jst over 2f out: lost pl qckly: wl bhd fnl f: t.o* **33/1**

1m 42.36s (2.56) **Going Correction** 0.0s/f (Stan) **9** Ran SP% **115.9**
Speed ratings (Par 97): **87,85,81,77,75 75,74,72,56**
CSF £7.75 TOTE £3.50: £1.10, £1.10, £2.00; EX 9.90 Trifecta £23.90.
**Owner** W Duff Gordon, J Bond, Rascals Racing **Bred** Camogue Stud Ltd **Trained** Newmarket, Suffolk

**FOCUS**
Things had failed to work out for the two Godolphin-owned runners in the first division of this maiden and it was a similar story here as their well supported favourite was readily gunned down.

## 7373 BETBRIGHT LIVE THE MOMENT H'CAP 1m (P)
**7:55** (7:55) (Class 5) (0-75,79) 3-Y-O+ **£2,587** (£770; £384; £192) **Stalls** Low

Form RPR

0000 **1** **Set The Trend**16 6990 8-9-2 70....................(p) FergusSweeney 7 85
(David Dennis) *dropped to rr after 1f: clsd 2f out: swtchd lft over 1f out: str run ins fnl f to ld cl home* **20/1**

5361 **2** *½* **Fiftyshadesofgrey (IRE)**7 7205 3-9-8 79 6ex.................... PatCosgrave 2 92+
(George Baker) *hld up in midfield: clsd and travelling wl 2f out: rdn to ld ent fnl f: clr and drvn ins fnl f: hdd and no ex cl home* **3/1**1

2226 **3** *4* **Cape Summit**15 6999 3-9-4 75.................... AdamKirby 8 79
(Ed Dunlop) *led for 1f: chsd ldrs: rdn to ld again wl over 1f out: hdd ent fnl f: outpcd fnl 150yds* **11/1**

4321 **4** *¾* **Nathr (USA)**15 7024 3-9-3 74.................... PaulHanagan 3 76
(Charles Hills) *chsd ldrs: rdn ent fnl 2f: drvn and unable qck over 1f out: outpcd fnl 150yds* **4/1**2

6220 **5** *nse* **Swordbearer**26 6714 3-9-2 73.................... FrederikTylicki 4 75
(James Fanshawe) *taken down early: in tch towards rr: effrt u.p 2f out: styd on ins fnl f: no threat to ldrs* **11/2**

0-63 **6** *1* **Starfield**19 6904 5-9-0 73.................... AlistairRawlinson(5) 1 74
(Michael Appleby) *chsd ldrs: rdn jst over 2f out: drvn and no ex over 1f out: outpcd ins fnl f* **7/1**

124 **7** *1* **Stormbound (IRE)**7 7205 5-9-3 71.................... LukeMorris 10 70
(Paul Cole) *towards rr: rdn and effrt on outer over 2f out: kpt on ins fnl f: nvr threatened ldrs* **9/2**3

0344 **8** *nk* **Living Leader**28 6657 5-9-0 68....................(tp) DavidProbert 13 66
(Grace Harris) *chsd ldrs: rdn ent fnl 2f: pressing ldrs but unable qck over 1f out: wknd ins fnl f* **20/1**

6040 **9** *nk* **Xanthos**76 5092 3-8-8 72.................... BradleyBosley(7) 14 68
(Ed Walker) *t.k.h: chsd ldrs: led over 3f out: rdn and hdd wl over 1f out: wknd fnl f* **25/1**

3126 **10** *¾* **Beautiful Stranger (IRE)**23 6822 3-9-4 75....................(p) TomEaves 12 69
(Keith Dalgleish) *stdd after s: hld up in rr: effrt 2f out: sme hdwy over 1f out: no imp fnl f* **14/1**

055 **11** *13* **Mr Matthews (IRE)**39 6334 3-9-1 72....................(v) DanielTudhope 6 37
(K R Burke) *t.k.h: hld up in tch: rdn over 2f out: sn btn: wknd over 1f out* **25/1**

4-05 **12** *7* **Gilmer (IRE)**25 6770 3-9-4 75.................... DougieCostello 5 23
(Laura Young) *in tch: struggling over 3f out: bhd fnl 2f* **50/1**

111- **13** *17* **It's Only Business**459 726 4-8-12 71.................... RyanWhile(5) 11
(Bill Turner) *led after 1f tl hdd over 3f out: sn dropped out: t.o fnl f* **33/1**

1m 38.22s (-1.58) **Going Correction** 0.0s/f (Stan)
**WFA** 3 from 4yo+ 3lb **13** Ran SP% **128.2**
Speed ratings (Par 103): **107,106,102,101,101 100,99,99,99,98 85,78,61**
CSF £79.77 CT £762.10 TOTE £27.70: £7.90, £2.20, £3.60; EX 228.70 Trifecta £760.70.
**Owner** Corbett Stud **Bred** Old Suffolk Stud **Trained** Hanley Swan, Worcestershire

**FOCUS**
This was competitive and it proved a difficult race to predict for most punters. The pace looked decent.

## 7374 BETBRIGHT MOBILE APP NURSERY H'CAP (BOBIS RACE) 7f (P)
**8:25** (8:25) (Class 4) (0-85,81) 2-Y-O **£3,752** (£1,116; £557; £278) **Stalls** Low

Form RPR

514 **1** **Qatar Road (FR)**16 6977 2-9-0 74.................... MartinHarley 2 87+
(Marco Botti) *t.k.h: chsd ldrs: rdn and qcknd to ld over 1f out: sn clr and r.o strly: readily* **9/2**3

1 **2** *2 ¾* **Mountain Rescue (IRE)**27 6675 2-9-3 77.................... OisinMurphy 3 82
(Roger Charlton) *hld up in midfield: effrt on outer 2f out: styd on to go 2nd fnl 75yds: no threat to wnr* **7/2**2

3304 **3** *1 ½* **Red Icon (IRE)**11 7116 2-9-7 81.................... HayleyTurner 7 82
(Tom Dascombe) *chsd ldr: rdn and ev ch 2f out: outpcd by wnr over 1f out: styd on same pce fnl f* **12/1**

0420 **4** *½* **Beach Samba (IRE)**15 6996 2-8-8 71.................... CamHardie(3) 8 71
(Ed Dunlop) *hld up in tch in rr: swtchd lft and hdwy jst over 2f out: no ch w wnr but kpt on fnl f* **20/1**

5241 **5** *1 ¾* **Dominic Cork**22 6830 2-8-9 69....................(p) FergalLynch 4 64
(Kevin Ryan) *led: rdn and jnd ent fnl 2f: hdd and outpcd by wnr over 1f out: wknd ins fnl f* **14/1**

3215 **6** *1 ½* **Dream Approval (IRE)**31 6574 2-8-13 73.................... LukeMorris 5 64
(Daniel Kubler) *stdd s: hld up towards rr: hdwy u.p on inner 2f out: no imp over 1f out* **33/1**

2442 **7** *4 ½* **Dutch Portrait**20 6884 2-8-13 73.................... JimCrowley 1 52
(Paul Cole) *pushed along early: in tch towards rr: hdwy u.p on inner 2f out: no imp over 1f out: wknd fnl f* **9/4**1

561 **8** *1¼* **Hard To Handel**[26] 6719 2-9-5 **79**................................ SebSanders 11 54
(Ralph Beckett) *taken down early: chsd ldrs: lost pl qckly u.p ent fnl 2f: wknd over 1f out* **7/1**

0642 **9** *3* **Awjab (IRE)**[18] 6931 2-9-5 **79**................................ PaulHanagan 10 46
(Brian Meehan) *midfield: dropped to rr 5f out: swtchd rt and drvn 2f out: no hdwy: bhd fnl f* **14/1**

0410 **10** *3¾* **Orlando Rogue (IRE)**[27] 6684 2-9-4 **78**.......................... PatCosgrave 9 35
(George Baker) *hld up towards rr: effrt on outer jst over 2f out: sn btn: bhd fnl f* **16/1**

1m 25.39s (-0.61) **Going Correction** 0.0s/f (Stan) **10** Ran SP% **118.3**
Speed ratings (Par 97): **103,99,98,97,95 93,88,87,83,79**
CSF £20.98 CT £179.17 TOTE £4.70: £1.60, £1.40, £3.70; EX 30.00 Trifecta £172.40.
**Owner** Mubarak Al Naemi **Bred** Scea De L'Aubay & Serge Bouvier **Trained** Newmarket, Suffolk

**FOCUS**
A fair race for the grade and hard not to be impressed as the winner breezed clear on his AW debut.

## 7375 BETBRIGHT.COM H'CAP 7f (P)
8:55 (8:55) (Class 4) (0-85,85) 3-Y-0+ **£4,690** (£1,395; £697; £348) **Stalls** Low

Form RPR

150 **1** **Unforgiving Minute**[21] 6871 3-9-3 83.............................. AdamKirby 9 96+
(Clive Cox) *hld up in midfield: hdwy 2f out: rdn and qcknd to ld over 1f out: clr fnl f: r.o wl: readily* **7/1**[3]

-255 **2** *3¼* **Never To Be (USA)**[20] 6886 3-9-3 83..........................(t) WilliamBuick 6 87
(John Gosden) *t.k.h: hld up in tch in midfield: rdn and hdwy over 1f out: chsd clr wnr ins fnl f: no imp* **6/1**[2]

3406 **3** *½* **Nassau Storm**[20] 6886 5-9-4 82................................ LukeMorris 12 86
(William Knight) *hld up in midfield: rdn and hdwy over 1f out: kpt on wl u.p fnl f: no threat to wnr* **14/1**

2000 **4** *1¼* **Jammy Guest (IRE)**[19] 6891 4-9-4 82.......................... MartinHarley 5 83
(George Margarson) *stdd s: hld up in rr: swtchd rt and gd hdwy on inner 2f out: chsd ldrs and drvn over 1f out: one pce fnl f* **10/1**

5401 **5** *½* **Good Luck Charm**[28] 6657 5-8-8 79......................(b) HectorCrouch(7) 14 78
(Gary Moore) *stdd and dropped in bhd after s: hld up in rr: hdwy on outer over 1f out: styd on: nvr threatened ldrs* **14/1**

-102 **6** *¾* **Exchequer (IRE)**[27] 6688 3-9-1 84.......................... CamHardie(3) 3 82
(Richard Hannon) *in tch in midfield: short of room and shuffled bk 2f out: kpt on again ins fnl f: no threat to wnr* **15/8**[1]

5003 **7** *½* **The Confessor**[34] 6498 7-9-3 81.............................. FergusSweeney 2 77
(Henry Candy) *chsd ldrs: rdn ent fnl 2f: chsd clr wnr over 1f out tl ins fnl f: wknd fnl 100yds* **10/1**

0415 **8** *½* **Sacha Park (IRE)**[19] 6898 3-9-0 80.............................. SeanLevey 13 74
(Richard Hannon) *hld up in rr: nt clr run 2f out: hdwy u.p 1f out: styd on: nvr trbld ldrs* **25/1**

3200 **9** *1¼* **Palace Moon**[19] 6891 9-9-4 82..................................(t) JimCrowley 1 73+
(William Knight) *chsd ldrs: hdwy u.p to chse ldrs 2f out: wknd fnl f* **20/1**

0050 **10** *1½* **Brocklebank (IRE)**[24] 6789 5-9-0 83.......................... JackDuern(5) 11 70
(Simon Dow) *stdd s: hld up in rr: effrt jst over 2f out: no imp over 1f out* **25/1**

0020 **11** *¾* **Rogue Wave (IRE)**[19] 6891 3-8-8 81.......................... GaryMahon(7) 7 65
(Timothy Jarvis) *hld up towards rr: c wd and effrt over 2f out: no prog* **16/1**

5000 **12** *½* **Repetition**[12] 7085 4-9-5 83.................................... TomEaves 10 67+
(Kristin Stubbs) *chsd ldrs: rdn to press ldr over 2f out: led 2f out: sn hdd & wknd* **25/1**

16-0 **13** *1¼* **Talksalot (IRE)**[56] 5824 3-9-5 85.............................. LiamJones 8 64+
(J S Moore) *chsd ldr tl over 2f out: losing pl whn hmpd 2f out: sn wknd* **66/1**

020 **14** *2½* **Tellovoi (IRE)**[23] 6824 6-9-6 84..............................(v) LiamKeniry 4 58+
(Ann Stokell) *led tl rdn and hdd 2f out: sn wknd* **16/1**

1m 24.64s (-1.36) **Going Correction** 0.0s/f (Stan)
**WFA** 3 from 4yo+ 2lb **14** Ran SP% **122.6**
Speed ratings (Par 105): **107,103,102,101,100 99,99,98,97,95 94,94,92,89**
CSF £46.46 CT £602.68 TOTE £9.20: £2.40, £2.20, £5.00; EX 52.70 Trifecta £601.50.
**Owner** P W Harris **Bred** Equine Breeding Ltd **Trained** Lambourn, Berks

**FOCUS**
They went quickly through the early stages and that set the race up for those with form over further.

## 7376 RAZOR RUDDOCK RACING CLUB CLASSIFIED STKS 7f (P)
9:25 (9:29) (Class 6) 3-Y-0+ **£1,940** (£577; £288; £144) **Stalls** Low

Form RPR

0262 **1** **Cadmium**[7] 7197 3-8-12 51.............................. Leah-AnneAvery(7) 1 56
(Harry Dunlop) *in tch in midfield: pushed along and effrt on inner 2f out: staedily clsd to ld wl ins fnl f: styd on* **15/8**[1]

0040 **2** *½* **Satchville Flyer**[7] 7197 3-9-2 53.............................. CamHardie(3) 8 55
(Brett Johnson) *chsd ldrs: rdn and effrt over 2f out: drvn and pressing ldr 1f out: kpt on: wnt 2nd last stride* **5/1**[3]

0300 **3** *hd* **Synonym (ITY)**[35] 6454 3-9-0 45.................. AlistairRawlinson(5) 12 54
(Michael Appleby) *led: rdn and clr 2f out: drvn over 1f out: hdd and no ex wl ins fnl f: lost 2nd last stride* **14/1**

641 **4** *1¼* **Copper Cavalier**[264] 411 3-9-5 49.......................(v) AdamBeschizza 14 51
(Robert Cowell) *in tch in midfield: effrt and rdn over 2f out: hrd drvn and styd on same pce fnl f* **8/1**

05-0 **5** *2½* **Sannibel**[15] 7025 6-9-7 50......................................(p) RobertTart 4 45
(David Bridgwater) *hld up in tch in midfield: effrt u.p over 2f out: sme hdwy over 1f out: no imp fnl f* **12/1**

655 **6** *4* **Forceful Beacon**[114] 3800 4-9-7 45.............................. LukeMorris 13 34
(Tony Carroll) *chsd ldrs: wnt 2nd wl over 2f out tl over 1f out: no ex u.p 1f out: wknd ins fnl f* **16/1**

3360 **7** *3* **Shamiana**[167] 2092 4-9-7 48..............................(b) SteveDrowne 9 26
(Daniel Kubler) *in tch in midfield: drvn and no hdwy over 2f out: wl hld fnl 2f* **16/1**

0204 **8** *2¼* **Dylan's Centenary**[23] 6816 3-8-12 55.................. SophieKilloran(7) 3 19+
(Rod Millman) *hld up wl off the pce in rr: pushed along and sme hdwy 2f out: n.d* **4/1**[2]

5050 **9** *5* **Ellingham (IRE)**[79] 4972 3-9-0 48.............................. EoinWalsh(5) 7 6
(Christine Dunnett) *t.k.h: chsd ldr tl wl over 2f out: lost pl 2f out: bhd fnl f* **50/1**

0/30 **10** *2¼* **Lady Cooper**[86] 4735 4-9-7 54.................................... ChrisCatlin 5
(Willie Musson) *hld up in last trio: rdn over 2f out: no hdwy: bhd fnl 2f* **16/1**

500/ **11** *45* **Welsh Dancer**[1007] 218 6-9-7 47.................................... AdamKirby 10
(John Butler) *restless in stalls: a towards rr: rdn and no rspnse over 2f out: t.o* **5/1**[3]

1m 26.98s (0.98) **Going Correction** 0.0s/f (Stan)
**WFA** 3 from 4yo+ 2lb **11** Ran SP% **133.2**
Speed ratings (Par 101): **94,93,93,91,88 84,80,78,72,70 18**
CSF £13.29 TOTE £3.60: £1.60, £1.90, £3.00; EX 17.00 Trifecta £209.30.
**Owner** Susan Abbott Racing **Bred** Bearstone Stud **Trained** Lambourn, Berks

**FOCUS**
This was as weak as you'll find and won't live long in the memory.
T/Plt: £154.00 to a £1 stake. Pool of £86351.15 - 409.25 winning tickets. T/Qpdt: £16.20 to a £1 stake. Pool of £12871.21 - 586.10 winning tickets. SP

# [7237] NEWMARKET (R-H)
Wednesday, October 22

**OFFICIAL GOING: Soft (6.6)**
Wind: Fresh behind Weather: Fine

## 7377 TURFTV MEDIAN AUCTION MAIDEN FILLIES' STKS (BOBIS RACE) 7f
1:30 (1:31) (Class 5) 2-Y-0 **£3,234** (£962; £481; £240) **Stalls** Low

Form RPR

2 **1** **Pamona (IRE)**[25] 6753 2-9-0 0.............................. AndreaAtzeni 13 90+
(Luca Cumani) *lw: chsd ldr tl led and edgd lft over 2f out: pushed out* **11/8**[1]

0 **2** *3¼* **Entertainment**[25] 6753 2-9-0 0.............................. WilliamBuick 15 82
(John Gosden) *lw: a.p: chsd wnr and hmpd over 2f out: rdn over 1f out: styd on same pce ins fnl f* **8/1**[3]

5 **3** *2½* **Wardat Dubai**[18] 6928 2-9-0 0.............................. PaulHanagan 10 76
(B W Hills) *leggy: unf: chsd ldrs: nt clr run over 2f out: rdn over 1f out: no ex ins fnl f* **5/2**[2]

0 **4** *2* **Run By Faith**[84] 4784 2-9-0 0.............................. TomQueally 14 71
(Roger Charlton) *unf: hld up: hdwy u.p over 1f out: nt trble ldrs* **25/1**

0 **5** *2* **Maybe Tomorrow**[32] 6553 2-9-0 0.............................. JoeFanning 5 66
(David Simcock) *leggy: scope: prom: hmpd over 2f out: sn rdn: no ex fnl f* **33/1**

**6** *hd* **Thanaaya (IRE)** 2-9-0 0.............................. GrahamLee 8 65+
(Ed Dunlop) *hld up: hdwy over 2f out: no ex fnl f* **20/1**

**7** *1¼* **Classical Rose** 2-9-0 0.............................. FrederikTylicki 1 62+
(Charlie Fellowes) *strong: bit bkwd: mid-div: hdwy over 1f out: nt trble ldrs* **33/1**

04 **8** *2* **Beach Walker**[32] 6554 2-9-0 0.............................. JimmyFortune 3 57
(Brian Meehan) *lw: chsd ldrs: rdn 1/2-way: wknd over 1f out* **16/1**

**9** *2* **J'Aspire** 2-9-0 0.............................. MartinHarley 9 52
(Stuart Williams) *unf: scope: on toes: s.i.s: sn pushed along in rr: hdwy whn stmbld over 1f out: nvr on terms* **66/1**

**10** *nk* **Perestroika** 2-9-0 0.............................. FergusSweeney 4 51
(Henry Candy) *sn pushed along in rr: styd on ins fnl f: nvr nrr* **16/1**

00 **11** *10* **This Is Too (IRE)**[149] 2615 2-8-9 0.............................. TimClark(5) 16 26
(Alan Bailey) *leggy: s.i.s: sn rcvrd into mid-div: rdn 1/2-way: wknd over 2f out* **100/1**

0 **12** *nk* **Newton Bomb (IRE)**[38] 6375 2-9-0 0.............................. LiamJones 11 26
(Conrad Allen) *led over 4f: wknd over 1f out* **40/1**

**13** *shd* **Authorized Spirit** 2-9-0 0.............................. ChrisCatlin 12 25
(Stuart Williams) *lengthy: scope: bit bkwd: s.i.s: sn outpcd* **66/1**

**14** *3¼* **Pandora's Pyx** 2-9-0 0.............................. TomEaves 7 17
(Philip Hide) *w'like: sn outpcd* **66/1**

**15** *shd* **Sweetly Does It** 2-9-0 0.............................. SteveDrowne 2 17
(Stuart Williams) *lengthy: bit bkwd: s.i.s: outpcd* **66/1**

1m 25.5s (0.10) **Going Correction** +0.175s/f (Good) **15** Ran SP% **117.4**
Speed ratings (Par 92): **106,102,99,97,94 94,93,90,88,88 76,76,76,72,72**
CSF £11.55 TOTE £1.90: £1.10, £1.50, £2.00; EX 14.20 Trifecta £38.80.
**Owner** Highclere Thoroughbred Racing (Albany) **Bred** Diomed Bloodstock Ltd **Trained** Newmarket, Suffolk

**FOCUS**
Stands side track used Stalls: Far side. Soft ground, but with a drying wind across the track it promised to become tacky. The winner was impressive.

## 7378 "GROUP 1 CREDIT MANAGEMENT" NURSERY H'CAP (DIV I) 7f
2:00 (2:00) (Class 5) (0-75,75) 2-Y-0 **£3,881** (£1,155; £577; £288) **Stalls** Low

Form RPR

1 **1** **Dark Kingdom (IRE)**[36] 6420 2-9-7 75.............................. GeorgeBaker 11 80+
(Ed Walker) *tall: athletic: hld up: racd towards stands' side tl swtchd to main gp wl over 2f out: hdwy: nt clr run and swtchd lft over 1f out: led ins fnl f: shkn up and r.o wl: readily* **15/8**[1]

644 **2** *1¼* **Lashkaal**[11] 7108 2-9-6 74.............................. PaulHanagan 5 76
(John Gosden) *lengthy: hld up: rdn over 2f out: hdwy over 1f out: r.o* **8/1**

355 **3** *1¼* **Jillanar (IRE)**[36] 6434 2-9-2 70.............................. WilliamBuick 6 69
(George Margarson) *hld up: plld hrd: hdwy u.p over 2f out: ev ch ins fnl f: styd on same pce towards fin* **7/1**[3]

1562 **4** *1¼* **Classic Seniority**[14] 7029 2-9-4 72.............................. RichardHughes 10 68
(Richard Hannon) *led duo towards stands' side: rdn to chse ldr and hung rt over 1f out: ev ch ins fnl f: styd on same pce* **20/1**

0020 **5** *½* **Pipe Bomb**[18] 6925 2-9-0 68..............................(p) OisinMurphy 9 62
(Kevin Ryan) *overall ldr: rdn over 1f out: hdd and no ex ins fnl f* **14/1**

030 **6** *1* **Yorkshire (IRE)**[66] 5464 2-8-9 63.............................. AndreaAtzeni 7 55
(Luca Cumani) *athletic: lw: prom: rdn over 1f out: ev ch ins fnl f: wknd towards fin* **5/1**[2]

2030 **7** *2¾* **Secret Spirit**[41] 6253 2-9-5 73.............................. AdamKirby 1 58
(Clive Cox) *chsd ldrs: rdn over 1f out: wknd ins fnl f* **11/1**

043 **8** *½* **Imperial Link**[21] 6868 2-8-12 71.............................. KevinStott(5) 3 55
(Paul Cole) *leggy: unf: chsd ldr: rdn over 2f out: wknd over 1f out* **14/1**

400 **9** *shd* **Never Easy (IRE)**[35] 6453 2-8-9 63.............................. TonyHamilton 2 47
(Richard Fahey) *tall: unf: prom: rdn over 2f out: wknd over 1f out* **25/1**

626 **10** *½* **Multistar**[29] 6646 2-8-12 66.............................. TedDurcan 8 48
(Chris Wall) *strong: s.i.s: a in rr* **12/1**

0001 **11** *¾* **Essaka (IRE)**[29] 6645 2-8-6 60.............................. CharlesBishop 4 40
(Mick Channon) *hld up: hdwy over 2f out: rdn and wknd over 1f out* **33/1**

1m 26.8s (1.40) **Going Correction** +0.175s/f (Good) **11** Ran SP% **116.0**
Speed ratings (Par 95): **99,97,96,94,94 93,89,89,89,88 87**
CSF £16.34 CT £89.26 TOTE £2.30: £1.60, £1.60, £3.40; EX 11.10 Trifecta £35.40.
**Owner** F Ma **Bred** David Harrison **Trained** Newmarket, Suffolk

**FOCUS**
The winner and fourth raced slightly apart from the main bunch, but whether they benefited from racing on better ground is open to question.

## 7379 "GROUP 1 CREDIT MANAGEMENT" NURSERY H'CAP (DIV II) 7f
**2:35** (2:35) (Class 5) (0-75,75) 2-Y-O **£3,881** (£1,155; £577; £288) **Stalls** Low

Form RPR

1053 **1** **Great Park (IRE)**[34] 6499 2-9-4 72 FergusSweeney 2 81+
(Martyn Meade) *chsd ldrs: led 5f out: rdn and edgd lft fr over 2f out: styd on wl* **8/1**

466 **2** *3 ¼* **Poyle Jessica**[26] 6700 2-8-10 64 OisinMurphy 3 65
(Ralph Beckett) *leggy: chsd ldrs: rdn over 1f out: styd on same pce ins fnl f* **14/1**

034 **3** *1 ½* **Captain Marmalade (IRE)**[27] 6675 2-9-4 72 GeorgeBaker 11 69
(Roger Charlton) *leggy: unf: lw: a.p: shkn up to chse ldr and nt clr run over 1f out: swtchd rt: no ex ins fnl f* **5/1**[3]

3150 **4** *1* **Steal The Scene (IRE)**[16] 6977 2-9-6 74 RichardHughes 10 69
(Richard Hannon) *leggy: scope: lw: w ldrs: rdn over 2f out: styd on same pce fr over 1f out* **9/2**[2]

5320 **5** *nse* **Outback Ruler (IRE)**[38] 6375 2-9-4 75 RyanTate(3) 5 70+
(Clive Cox) *hld up: rdn over 1f out: styd on ins fnl f: nt trble ldrs* **4/1**[1]

4602 **6** *1* **Robben**[7] 7208 2-8-0 54 (p) JimmyQuinn 4 46
(Kevin Ryan) *hld up: hdwy u.p 2f out: one pce fnl f* **7/1**

001 **7** *½* **Almoqatel (IRE)**[27] 6676 2-9-0 68 TomQueally 8 59
(James Fanshawe) *strong: prom: lost pl 4f out: hdwy over 1f out: no ex fnl f* **25/1**

643 **8** *1 ¼* **Dark Wonder (IRE)**[50] 5995 2-9-1 69 GrahamLee 1 57
(James Given) *w'like: lengthy: hld up: shkn up over 2f out: nvr trbld ldrs* **8/1**

5006 **9** *6* **New Brunswick (GER)**[7] 7207 2-8-9 63 RobertHavlin 6 36
(John Gosden) *prom: rdn over 2f out: wknd over 1f out* **11/1**

2520 **10** *½* **Pivot Point (IRE)**[24] 6783 2-9-3 71 JimmyFortune 9 42
(Brian Meehan) *chsd ldrs: hmpd wl over 1f out: wknd and eased fnl f* **14/1**

4610 **11** *16* **Tagtale (IRE)**[25] 6749 2-8-8 62 PaulHanagan 7
(Richard Fahey) *led 2f: remained handy tl wknd 2f out* **33/1**

1m 26.33s (0.93) **Going Correction** +0.175s/f (Good) **11** Ran SP% **118.0**
Speed ratings (Par 95): **101,97,95,94,94 93,92,91,84,83 65**
CSF £114.63 CT £632.16 TOTE £10.70: £2.90, £4.80, £1.30; EX 180.30 Trifecta £1128.70.
**Owner** David Caddy **Bred** Brinkley Stud, Ficomontanino, Bego Blu **Trained** Newmarket, Suffolk

**FOCUS**
The faster of the two divisions by 0.47sec. They gradually edged towards the stands' side, but the winner, who raced up the centre for much of the race, only reached the stands' rail through hanging.

## 7380 NEWMARKET EQUINE SECURITY MAIDEN STKS 7f
**3:10** (3:10) (Class 4) 2-Y-O **£4,528** (£1,347; £673; £336) **Stalls** Low

Form RPR

**1** **Ooty Hill** 2-9-0 0 AndreaAtzeni 7 84+
(Roger Charlton) *lengthy: tall: unf: lw: chsd ldr: carried lft and led over 1f out: shkn up and r.o wl* **7/2**[3]

52 **2** *2 ¼* **Alnashama**[21] 6860 2-9-0 0 PaulHanagan 3 78
(Charles Hills) *w'like: strong: led: shkn up and hung lft fr over 2f out tl hdd over 1f out: styd on same pce ins fnl f* **5/2**[1]

**3** *½* **Khalaas** 2-9-0 0 FrankieDettori 2 77+
(William Haggas) *leggy: athletic: a.p: rdn over 2f out: styd on same pce ins fnl f* **12/1**

**4** *¾* **Nayel (IRE)** 2-9-0 0 RichardHughes 6 75+
(Richard Hannon) *strong: bit bkwd: chsd ldrs: rdn over 2f out: styd on same pce ins fnl f* **10/1**

4 **5** *nk* **Bollihope**[91] 4550 2-9-0 0 WilliamBuick 10 74+
(John Gosden) *athletic: tall: hld up: hdwy over 2f out: rdn and edgd lft over 1f out: styd on wl towards fin* **10/3**[2]

**6** *1 ¾* **Pick Your Choice** 2-9-0 0 GrahamLee 4 70+
(William Haggas) *tall: lengthy: scope: prom: rdn over 2f out: no ex fnl f* **6/1**

**7** *4 ½* **Dutch Uncle** 2-9-0 0 JimmyFortune 1 59
(Ed Dunlop) *athletic: strong: bit bkwd: s.i.s: hld up: hdwy 3f out: wknd over 1f out* **33/1**

**8** *4 ½* **Captain Felix** 2-9-0 0 PatCosgrave 5 47
(Jane Chapple-Hyam) *strong: s.i.s: a towards rr: wknd over 2f out* **66/1**

0 **9** *4* **Red House Rebel (IRE)**[21] 6852 2-9-0 0 MartinHarley 8 37
(Stuart Williams) *s.i.s and wnt lft s: a in rr: wknd over 2f out* **66/1**

**10** *4 ½* **Ben Muir** 2-9-0 0 SteveDrowne 11 26
(Stuart Williams) *unf: scope: bit bkwd: s.s: in rr: wknd over 2f out* **80/1**

1m 27.41s (2.01) **Going Correction** +0.175s/f (Good) **10** Ran SP% **112.1**
Speed ratings (Par 97): **95,92,91,91,90 88,83,78,73,68**
CSF £11.97 TOTE £7.50: £1.50, £1.40, £3.10; EX 17.80 Trifecta £125.70.
**Owner** A E Oppenheimer **Bred** Hascombe Stud **Trained** Beckhampton, Wilts
■ Stewards' Enquiry : Paul Hanagan one-day ban: careless riding (Nov 5)

**FOCUS**
Those that had run set a fair standard so it was interesting that a couple of the newcomers were backed in opposition to them.

## 7381 AR LEGAL COLLECTIONS HOUGHTON CONDITIONS STKS (BOBIS RACE) 7f
**3:45** (3:47) (Class 2) 2-Y-O **£8,715** (£2,609; £1,304) **Stalls** Low

Form RPR

1 **1** **Fannaan (USA)**[26] 6702 2-9-3 0 PaulHanagan 2 100+
(John Gosden) *lw: athletic: mde all: shkn up and qcknd over 1f out: r.o wl: comf* **8/13**[1]

212 **2** *1 ½* **Hawkesbury**[67] 5431 2-9-3 104 WilliamBuick 3 92
(Charlie Appleby) *lengthy: trckd wnr: plld hrd: rdn over 1f out: styd on same pce fnl f* **11/8**[2]

43 **3** *6* **Henryhudsonbridge (USA)**[8] 7171 2-8-12 0 (b[1]) JimmyFortune 4 72
(Brian Meehan) *w'like: racd alone tl jnd rivals 5f out: w ldr tl shkn up over 2f out: wknd over 1f out* **40/1**[3]

1m 27.55s (2.15) **Going Correction** +0.175s/f (Good) **3** Ran SP% **106.5**
Speed ratings (Par 101): **94,92,85**
CSF £1.73 TOTE £1.40; EX 1.60 Trifecta £1.70.
**Owner** Hamdan Al Maktoum **Bred** Waterville Lake Stables Ltd Llc **Trained** Newmarket, Suffolk

**FOCUS**
For the first time since 2003 this race was run over 7f rather than a mile. The winner is very promising.

## 7382 BRITISH STALLION STUDS EBF MAIDEN STKS (BOBIS RACE) 1m
**4:20** (4:21) (Class 4) 2-Y-O **£4,528** (£1,347; £673; £336) **Stalls** Low

Form RPR

0 **1** **Rare Rhythm**[18] 6928 2-9-5 0 MartinLane 2 80+
(Charlie Appleby) *lengthy: tall: lw: a.p: chsd ldr over 5f: rdn over 1f out: edgd rt and styd on to ld nr fin* **14/1**

**2** *shd* **Wheat Sheaf** 2-9-5 0 GeorgeBaker 14 80+
(Roger Charlton) *athletic: lw: hld up in tch: led 2f out: shkn up and hung rt fr over 1f out: rdn ins fnl f: hdd nr fin* **8/1**

5 **3** *5* **Verismo**[14] 7039 2-9-5 0 GrahamLee 7 69
(Ed Dunlop) *strong: bit bkwd: a.p: rdn over 2f out: styd on same pce fnl f* **20/1**

**4** *1 ¼* **Afjaan (IRE)** 2-9-5 0 FrankieDettori 3 66+
(William Haggas) *lengthy: tall: lw: hld up: hdwy over 1f out: no ex ins fnl f* **9/1**

0 **5** *½* **Tempus Temporis (USA)**[27] 6683 2-9-5 0 WilliamBuick 12 65
(John Gosden) *lw: chsd ldrs: ev ch 2f out: sn rdn: no ex ins fnl f* **9/2**[2]

52 **6** *1 ½* **Mythical City (IRE)**[16] 6976 2-9-0 0 JoeFanning 9 57
(Mark Johnston) *leggy: athletic: chsd ldrs: rdn over 2f out: edgd lft and styd on same pce fr over 1f out* **15/2**[3]

**7** *4 ½* **Leoncavallo (IRE)** 2-9-5 0 SilvestreDeSousa 4 52
(Charlie Appleby) *strong: hld up: nt clr run over 4f out: nvr on terms* **11/1**

**8** *nk* **Etibaar (USA)** 2-9-5 0 PaulHanagan 15 51
(Brian Meehan) *lengthy: bit bkwd: s.i.s: sn pushed along in rr: styd on ins fnl f: nvr nrr* **16/1**

0 **9** *nk* **Topsy Turvy (IRE)**[16] 6984 2-9-5 0 JimmyFortune 13 50
(Jeremy Noseda) *prom: pushed along over 3f out: wknd over 1f out* **50/1**

6 **10** *nk* **Little Lord Nelson**[73] 5210 2-8-12 0 (t) AaronJones(7) 16 50
(Stuart Williams) *w'like: strong: s.i.s: hdwy over 5f out: wknd over 1f out* **66/1**

**11** *shd* **Racing History (IRE)** 2-9-5 0 FrederikTylicki 6 50
(Saeed bin Suroor) *athletic: s.i.s: sn pushed along in rr: n.m.r over 4f out: n.d* **7/2**[1]

0 **12** *½* **Sirheed (IRE)**[18] 6928 2-9-5 0 RichardHughes 8 48
(Richard Hannon) *tall: scope: led: rdn and hdd 2f out: wkng whn edgd rt fnl f* **16/1**

0 **13** *4* **London Mayor (IRE)**[47] 6102 2-9-5 0 AndreaAtzeni 10 46
(Roger Varian) *leggy: prom: rdn over 3f out: wknd wl over 1f out* **20/1**

**14** *3 ¾* **Rib Reserve (IRE)** 2-9-5 0 ShaneKelly 5 31
(Sir Michael Stoute) *lengthy: bit bkwd: hld up: pushed along over 2f out: sn wknd* **20/1**

00 **15** *4 ½* **Mr Morocco**[14] 7040 2-9-0 0 TobyAtkinson(5) 1 21
(Noel Quinlan) *strong: hld up: rdn over 3f out: wknd 2f out* **100/1**

**16** *7* **Cloud Seven** 2-9-5 0 TedDurcan 11
(Chris Wall) *lengthy: tall: bit bkwd: on toes: s.i.s: a in rr: wknd over 2f out* **33/1**

1m 40.18s (1.58) **Going Correction** +0.175s/f (Good) **16** Ran SP% **121.7**
Speed ratings (Par 97): **99,98,93,92,92 90,86,85,85,85 85,84,80,76,72 65**
CSF £113.49 TOTE £18.20: £3.90, £3.80, £6.60; EX 119.50 Trifecta £2902.20 Part won. Pool of £3869.62 - 0.51 winning units..
**Owner** Godolphin **Bred** Highclere Stud And Floors Farming **Trained** Newmarket, Suffolk

**FOCUS**
Two came clear in this maiden when once again they edged over to race stands' side.

## 7383 ZETLAND CONDITIONS STKS (BOBIS RACE) 1m 2f
**4:55** (4:56) (Class 3) 2-Y-O **£6,469** (£1,925; £962; £481) **Stalls** Low

Form RPR

4111 **1** **Crafty Choice**[14] 7041 2-9-0 88 RichardHughes 5 87+
(Richard Hannon) *lengthy: chsd ldr tl led over 1f out: shkn up and styd on wl* **1/1**[1]

5 **2** *1 ¼* **Captain Navarre**[27] 6683 2-8-11 0 SimonPearce(3) 6 83
(Lydia Pearce) *a.p: rdn and edgd lft over 1f out: chsd wnr ins fnl f: styd on* **12/1**

5 **3** *2 ½* **Murgan**[21] 6859 2-9-0 0 AndreaAtzeni 3 78
(Peter Chapple-Hyam) *strong: scope: lw: s.i.s: hld up: hdwy over 2f out: rdn to chse wnr over 1f out tl styd on same pce ins fnl f* **5/2**[2]

1155 **4** *3* **Pallister**[53] 5926 2-9-5 96 JoeFanning 2 78
(Mark Johnston) *led: rdn: edgd lft and hdd over 1f out: no ex ins fnl f* **10/3**[3]

0 **5** *9* **Speedfit Rules (IRE)**[14] 7037 2-9-0 0 PaoloSirigu 4 57
(George Margarson) *leggy: hld up: rdn over 3f out: wknd over 1f out* **100/1**

2m 10.61s (4.81) **Going Correction** +0.175s/f (Good) **5** Ran SP% **110.3**
Speed ratings (Par 99): **87,86,84,81,74**
CSF £13.79 TOTE £1.70: £1.20, £5.30; EX 15.20 Trifecta £32.00.
**Owner** Middleham Park Racing CIII **Bred** Pevens Racing **Trained** East Everleigh, Wilts

**FOCUS**
Quite a test in the ground for these 2yos.

## 7384 THOROUGHBRED BREEDERS' ASSOCIATION FILLIES' H'CAP 1m
**5:25** (5:28) (Class 2) (0-100,91) 3-Y-O+ **£12,938** (£3,850; £1,924; £962) **Stalls** Low

Form RPR

4011 **1** **Fruit Pastille**[18] 6945 3-8-11 81 (b) JimmyFortune 7 89+
(Hughie Morrison) *mde virtually all: rdn over 1f out: styd on wl* **15/2**[3]

1610 **2** *2* **Buredyma**[46] 6129 3-8-13 83 JoeFanning 8 87
(William Haggas) *lw: a.p: chsd wnr and edgd rt fr over 2f out: rdn over 1f out: styd on same pce fnl f* **9/2**[2]

5044 **3** *2 ¾* **Auction (IRE)**[24] 6793 4-9-8 89 RichardHughes 5 88+
(Ed Dunlop) *hld up: nt clr run over 2f out: hdwy over 1f out: nt trble ldrs* **9/2**[2]

2103 **4** *nk* **No Poppy (IRE)**[12] 7081 6-9-5 86 DavidAllan 1 84
(Tim Easterby) *hld up: rdn over 3f out: styd on fr over 1f out: nt trble ldrs* **3/1**[1]

5550 **5** *½* **Boonga Roogeta**[74] 5162 5-9-4 85 JimmyQuinn 4 82
(Peter Charalambous) *chsd wnr tl rdn over 2f out: styd on same pce fr over 1f out* **16/1**

0121 **6** *4* **Temptress (IRE)**[102] 4182 3-9-7 91 GeorgeBaker 6 78
(Roger Charlton) *prom: rdn over 1f out: wknd fnl f* **3/1**[1]

5130 **7** *1 ¼* **Alexandrakollontai (IRE)**[13] 7060 4-9-0 84 (b) ConnorBeasley(3) 3 69
(Alistair Whillans) *hld up: rdn over 2f out: wknd over 1f out* **16/1**

53-3 **8** *8* **Acclio (IRE)**[186] 1579 3-8-8 78 AndreaAtzeni 2 45
(Clive Brittain) *prom tl rdn and wknd over 1f out* **20/1**
1m 38.58s (-0.02) **Going Correction** +0.175s/f (Good)
**WFA** 3 from 4yo+ 3lb **8** Ran SP% **114.7**
Speed ratings (Par 96): **107,105,102,101,101 97,96,88**
CSF £41.21 CT £170.38 TOTE £8.30: £2.20, £2.10, £2.00; EX 35.00 Trifecta £269.60.
**Owner** The Caledonian Racing Society **Bred** M E Broughton **Trained** East Ilsley, Berks

**FOCUS**
Very few got into this, but the winner looks progressive.
T/Jkpt: £23,436.10 to a £1 stake. Pool of £412609.07 - 12.50 winning tickets. T/Plt: £211.50 to a £1 stake. Pool of £77593.83 - 267.78 winning tickets. T/Qpdt: £122.80 to a £1 stake. Pool of £5080.09 - 30.60 winning tickets. CR

7385 - 7392a (Foreign Racing) - See Raceform Interactive

## 5959 DEAUVILLE (R-H)
Wednesday, October 22

**OFFICIAL GOING: Turf: very soft: polytrack: standard**

### 7393a PRIX DES RESERVOIRS (GROUP 3) (2YO FILLIES) (ROUND) (TURF) 1m (R)
**1:20** (12:00) 2-Y-O **£33,333** (£13,333; £10,000; £6,666; £3,333)

RPR
**1** **Moonee Valley (FR)**[43] 6219 2-8-9 0 IoritzMendizabal 7 104
(Mario Hofer, Germany) *hld up in rr: hdwy on wd outside and prom 3f out: rdn to chal and edgd rt over 1f out: styd on wl and led towards fin* **168/10**
**2** *½* **Baltic Comtesse (FR)**[27] 2-8-9 0 MaximeGuyon 6 103
(A Fabre, France) *hld up in tch: rdn over 1f out and edgd rt: styd on and wnt 2nd cl home: nt quite pce of wnr* **17/10**[1]
**3** *½* **Tigrilla (IRE)**[26] 6709 2-8-10 0 ow1 ChristopheSoumillon 2 103
(Roger Varian) *sn led: rdn and strly pressed 2f out: styd on but worn down and hdd towards fin: dropped to 3rd and hld* **57/10**[3]
**4** *snk* **Lady Sybil (FR)**[33] 2-8-9 0 ThierryJarnet 4 102
(Y Barberot, France) *hld up on inner: in rr 2f out: gng wl but nt clr run fr over 1f out tl fnl 150yds: pushed along and r.o wl: short of room again cl home: unlucky* **30/1**
**5** *shd* **La Khaleesi (FR)**[60] 5707 2-8-9 0 StephanePasquier 9 101
(Y Gourraud, France) *hld up in rr: rdn 2f out: last ent fnl f: styd on down wd outside and wnt 5th cl home: fin strly but nvr able to chal* **37/1**
**6** *½* **Encore L'Amour**[58] 5746 2-8-9 0 ThierryThulliez 5 100
(David Simcock) *midfield in tch: rdn 2f out: outpcd whn hmpd ent fnl f and dropped to rr: rallied and kpt on wl u.p towards fin but nt rcvr* **78/10**
**7** *nk* **Makweti**[17] 6967 2-8-9 0 GregoryBenoist 8 100
(F Doumen, France) *in tch on outer: prom 3f out: rdn to chal 2f out: bmpd over 1f out: kpt on tl no ex and fdd fnl 150yds* **112/10**
**8** *snk* **Via Manzoni (IRE)**[49] 2-8-9 0 MickaelBarzalona 3 99
(A Fabre, France) *trckd ldr: rdn to chal 2f out: bmpd over 1f out: kpt on tl no ex and fdd fnl 100yds* **5/2**[2]
**9** *1* **Colonialiste (IRE)**[43] 6219 2-8-9 0 OlivierPeslier 1 97
(F Head, France) *t.k.h: in tch on inner: rdn and effrt 2f out: outpcd and lost pl over 1f out: dropped to last and hld fnl f* **109/10**
1m 46.76s (5.96) **9** Ran SP% **120.0**
WIN (incl. 1 euro stake): 17.80. PLACES: 3.50, 1.70, 2.00. DF: 27.60. SF: 97.30.
**Owner** Cocheese Bloodstock **Bred** Mme A Tamagni & Pat Chedeville **Trained** Germany

7394 - (Foreign Racing) - See Raceform Interactive

## GEELONG (L-H)
Wednesday, October 22

**OFFICIAL GOING: Turf: good**

### 7395a SPORTINGBET POWERED BY WILLIAM HILL GEELONG CUP (GROUP 3 H'CAP) (3YO+) (TURF) 1m 4f
**6:00** (12:00) 3-Y-O+
**£104,838** (£29,032; £14,516; £7,258; £4,032; £3,225)

RPR
**1** **Caravan Rolls On**[25] 6-8-7 0 (t) CraigAWilliams 2 105
(Danny O'Brien, Australia) **15/2**
**2** *¾* **Marksmanship (IRE)**[18] 6-8-7 0 (t) KerrinMcEvoy 1 104
(Ciaron Maher, Australia) **8/1**
**3** *½* **Like A Carousel (AUS)**[25] 5-8-7 0 (b) CraigNewitt 12 103
(Ken Keys, Australia) **17/2**
**4** *hd* **More Than Sacred (AUS)**[10] 5-8-7 0 GlenBoss 13 103
(Robert Smerdon, Australia) **5/1**[2]
**5** *3 ½* **Wish Come True (IRE)**[18] 6961 4-8-8 0 ChadSchofield 4 98
(Peter G Moody, Australia) **12/1**
**6** *shd* **Shoreham (AUS)**[18] 6975 5-8-9 0 ChrisSymons 10 99
(Saab Hasan, Australia) **5/1**[2]
**7** *2 ¼* **Pretty Blonde (AUS)** 6-8-7 0 DeanYendall 3 93
(Kym Healy, Australia) **70/1**
**8** *1 ¼* **Sertorius (AUS)**[11] 7127 7-9-2 0 RyanMaloney 11 100
(Jamie Edwards & Bruce Elkington, Australia) **19/5**[1]
**9** *hd* **Waltzing To Win (AUS)**[11] 7126 5-8-7 0 BenClaridge 8 91
(David Huxtable, Australia) **100/1**
**10** *2* **Ali Vital (NZ)**[10] 5-8-7 0 DarrenGauci 5 88
(Robbie Laing, Australia) **25/1**
**11** *6* **Zanbagh (AUS)**[17] 4-8-7 0 MichellePayne 6 80
(Patrick Payne, Australia) **6/1**[3]
**12** *15* **Correggio (NZ)**[17] 5-8-7 0 (bt) DeanHolland 7 54
(Murray Johnson, Australia) **50/1**
**P** **Ominous**[26] 6733 5-8-7 0 DwayneDunn 9
(Nigel Blackiston, Australia) **50/1**
2m 31.22s (151.22) **13** Ran SP% **119.7**
PARI-MUTUEL (NSW TAB - all including 1 aud stake): WIN 8.40; PLACE 2.90, 2.70, 3.50; DF 26.00; SF 87.50.
**Owner** Qatar Racing Limited **Bred** Miss K Rausing **Trained** Australia

## 7369 KEMPTON (A.W) (R-H)
Thursday, October 23

**OFFICIAL GOING: Polytrack: standard**
Wind: light to medium, half behind Weather: dry

### 7396 WATCH RACING UK ANYWHERE IPAD APP NURSERY H'CAP 1m (P)
**5:40** (5:40) (Class 6) (0-65,65) 2-Y-O **£1,940** (£577; £288; £144) **Stalls** Low

Form RPR
0020 **1** **Prince Of Paris**[21] 6884 2-9-7 65 MartinLane 14 70
(Roger Ingram) *s.i.s: bhd and pushed along: stl plenty to do and rdn over 2f out: str run fnl f to ld towards fin: won gng away* **14/1**
506 **2** *1* **Cascading Stars (IRE)**[23] 6838 2-9-4 62 SteveDrowne 1 65
(J S Moore) *chsd ldr for 2f: rdn to chse ldr again over 2f out: led over 1f out: clr ins fnl f: hdd and no ex cl home* **25/1**
444 **3** *½* **Inke (IRE)**[16] 6997 2-9-4 62 WilliamCarson 9 64
(Jim Boyle) *t.k.h: in tch in midfield: rdn over 2f out: no imp tl styd on wl ins fnl f: wnt 3rd wl ins fnl f* **10/1**
500 **4** *1 ¼* **Le Torrent**[26] 6743 2-9-2 60 FergusSweeney 12 59
(Henry Candy) *t.k.h: chsd ldrs: rdn over 2f out: kpt on ins fnl f: nvr enough pce to chal* **7/1**[3]
000 **5** *nse* **Skylight (IRE)**[16] 7019 2-9-2 60 (b[1]) AndreaAtzeni 3 59
(William Haggas) *in tch in midfield: flashed tail u.p and hdwy over 1f out: styd on same pce ins fnl f* **6/1**[2]
0005 **6** *¾* **Just Marion (IRE)**[6] 7258 2-9-4 62 GeorgeBaker 8 59
(David Evans) *led: clr and stl travelling wl 2f out: rdn and hdd over 1f out: wknd ins fnl f* **14/1**
2401 **7** *½* **Jet Mate (IRE)**[14] 7064 2-9-4 62 (p) MartinDwyer 13 58
(William Muir) *t.k.h: chsd ldrs: wnt 2nd 4f out tl over 2f out: no ex u.p: wknd ins fnl f* **7/1**[3]
605 **8** *1 ¼* **Saint Honore**[17] 6984 2-9-4 62 ShaneKelly 10 55
(Pat Phelan) *hld up in midfield: effrt u.p over 1f out: kpt on fnl f: nvr trbld ldrs* **25/1**
0630 **9** *1 ½* **Arthur's Way (IRE)**[55] 5875 2-9-7 65 LukeMorris 4 55
(Paul Cole) *sn dropped to rr and rdn along: sme hdwy u.p 2f out: no imp fnl f* **16/1**
0466 **10** *4 ½* **Horsetracker**[9] 7165 2-9-2 60 (b[1]) JimCrowley 7 39
(Ian Williams) *hld up in last trio: wd and effrt over 2f out: no imp* **16/1**
1053 **11** *1 ¼* **Honey Required**[8] 7208 2-9-3 61 [1] FrannyNorton 2 38
(Alan Bailey) *in tch in midfield: rdn and unable qck ent fnl 2f: wknd over 1f out* **9/2**[1]
006 **12** *½* **Lonely Ranger (USA)**[13] 7076 2-9-2 60 PatCosgrave 5 35
(Amy Weaver) *t.k.h: in tch in midfield: rdn and no hdwy over 2f out: wknd over 1f out* **50/1**
0420 **13** *12* **Keen Move**[37] 6420 2-9-6 64 MartinHarley 11 12
(Ismail Mohammed) *t.k.h: in tch in midfield: rdn and lost pl over 2f out: bhd fnl f* **7/1**[3]
3540 **14** *7* **Emperors Warrior (IRE)**[21] 6884 2-9-1 62 CamHardie[(3)] 6
(Richard Hannon) *a towards rr: last and lost tch 3f out: t.o* **14/1**
1m 40.6s (0.80) **Going Correction** 0.0s/f (Stan) **14** Ran SP% **120.5**
Speed ratings (Par 93): **96,95,94,93,93 92,91,90,89,84 83,82,70,63**
CSF £329.93 CT £3718.44 TOTE £13.60: £4.60, £7.90, £2.40; EX 687.90 Trifecta £1365.30 Part won..
**Owner** G E Ley **Bred** T G Roddick **Trained** Epsom, Surrey

**FOCUS**
An ordinary nursery, but the winner might be a bit better than this level.

### 7397 FOLLOW @BETVICTORRACING ON TWITTER FILLIES' H'CAP 1m (P)
**6:10** (6:10) (Class 5) (0-75,74) 3-Y-O+ **£2,587** (£770; £384; £192) **Stalls** Low

Form RPR
1500 **1** **Tides Reach (IRE)**[31] 6609 3-9-3 73 (p) GeorgeBaker 7 82
(Roger Charlton) *led for 3f: chsd ldr after: drvn and ev ch 1f out: led ins fnl f: hld on wl: all out* **6/1**[2]
2511 **2** *shd* **Lady Sylvia**[43] 6242 5-9-0 72 JennyPowell[(5)] 6 82
(Joseph Tuite) *in tch in midfield: rdn and hdwy over 1f out: ev ch fnl f: edgd lft ins fnl f: r.o: jst hld* **8/1**[3]
3341 **3** *hd* **Semaral (IRE)**[16] 7012 3-9-4 74 TedDurcan 9 83
(Chris Wall) *t.k.h: chsd ldrs: effrt 2f out: ev ch 1f out: r.o: no ex towards fin* **3/1**[1]
2136 **4** *2 ½* **White Russian**[41] 6302 3-8-12 71 AmyScott[(3)] 8 74
(Henry Candy) *pressed ldr for 3f: chsd ldrs: rdn to ld 2f out: hdd ins fnl f: stl ev ch but beginning to struggle whn squeezed for room and hmpd fnl 100yds: one pce after* **12/1**
3400 **5** *hd* **Real Tigress (IRE)**[30] 6626 5-9-2 69 (t[1]) DavidAllan 2 73
(Les Eyre) *t.k.h: hld up in tch in midfield: effrt u.p over 1f out: keeping on same pce whn sltly hmpd and swtchd rt wl ins fnl f* **10/1**
3310 **6** *1* **Lady Sparkler (IRE)**[42] 6262 3-9-4 74 AndreaAtzeni 3 74
(Roger Varian) *in tch in midfield: effrt u.p to chse ldrs over 1f out: styd on same pce fnl f* **8/1**[3]
2310 **7** *nk* **Ajig**[9] 7186 3-9-1 71 (p) JohnFahy 13 71
(Eve Johnson Houghton) *in tch in midfield: effrt 2f out: drvn and styd on same pce fr over 1f out* **12/1**
2260 **8** *nse* **Royal Connection**[45] 6191 3-9-1 71 PatDobbs 4 70
(Richard Hannon) *hld up in last quartet: hdwy u.p over 1f out: kpt on: nvr trbld ldrs* **25/1**
0644 **9** *½* **Miss Lillie**[30] 6633 3-8-12 71 DannyBrock[(3)] 12 69
(Roger Teal) *taken down early: towards rr: shkn up and hdwy on outer 1/2-way: kpt on but no imp fnl f* **14/1**
3226 **10** *nk* **Hala Hala (IRE)**[49] 6057 3-9-1 74 LouisSteward[(3)] 11 72
(Michael Bell) *t.k.h: chsd ldrs tl hdwy to ld 5f out: hdd and rdn 2f out: no ex and btn 1f out: wknd* **12/1**
10-0 **11** *hd* **Refreshestheparts (USA)**[21] 6890 5-9-5 72 PatCosgrave 14 70
(George Baker) *stdd bk after s: hld up in last quartet: effrt but stl plenty to do 2f out: kpt on fnl f: nvr trbld ldrs* **25/1**
060 **11** *dht* **High Drama (IRE)**[130] 3277 3-9-1 71 DavidProbert 1 68
(Andrew Balding) *in tch in midfield: effrt on inner 2f out: no prog u.p over 1f out: wknd ins fnl f* **10/1**
6 **13** *4 ½* **Elusive Ellen (IRE)**[116] 3755 4-9-0 67 FergusSweeney 10 55
(Brendan Powell) *hmpd and dropped to rr sn after s: rdn and no hdwy over 2f out: bhd over 1f out* **33/1**

-555 **14** *3 1/4* **Young Dottie**[84] 4808 8-8-12 68 ............................ JemmaMarshall(3) 5 48
(Pat Phelan) *hmpd and dropped to rr sn after s: hld up in rr: rdn over 2f out: sn btn* **40/1**

1m 39.32s (-0.48) **Going Correction** 0.0s/f (Stan)
**WFA** 3 from 4yo+ 3lb **14** Ran SP% **122.5**
Speed ratings (Par 100): **102,101,101,99,99 98,97,97,97,96 96,96,92,88**
CSF £52.43 CT £176.35 TOTE £6.90: £2.30, £2.30, £3.90; EX 51.20 Trifecta £196.30.
**Owner** D J Deer **Bred** D J And Mrs Deer **Trained** Beckhampton, Wilts
■ Stewards' Enquiry : Jenny Powell two-day ban: careless riding (Nov 6-7)

**FOCUS**
A competitive fillies' handicap and very little covered the first three home. It paid to race fairly handily.

## 7398 BETVICTOR.COM MAIDEN FILLIES' STKS (BOBIS RACE) (DIV I) 7f (P)
**6:40** (6:42) (Class 4) 2-Y-O **£3,752** (£1,116; £557; £278) **Stalls** Low

Form RPR
**1** **Roxy Star (IRE)** 2-9-0 0 ............................ AndreaAtzeni 5 75+
(William Haggas) *dwlt: hld up in rr: rdn and effrt on inner over 1f out: qcknd to ld ins fnl f: hld on cl home* **8/1**[2]
0 **2** *nk* **Melodious**[19] 6924 2-9-0 0 ............................ LiamKeniry 6 74
(David Elsworth) *t.k.h: hld up in midfield: hdwy u.p over 1f out: wnt 2nd wl ins fnl f: styd on wl* **8/1**[2]
0 **3** *3/4* **Perfect Orange**[84] 4825 2-9-0 0 ............................ MartinDwyer 2 72
(Marcus Tregoning) *wnt lft s: chsd ldr for 2f: rdn to press ldr 2f out: drvn to ld 1f out: sn hdd and styd on same pce after* **25/1**
0442 **4** *1 1/2* **Hawkin (IRE)**[26] 6749 2-9-0 79 ............................ OisinMurphy 3 68
(Ralph Beckett) *pushed lft s: hld up in last pair: rdn and effrt over 2f out: hdwy over 1f out: styd on same pce ins fnl f* **7/4**[1]
005 **5** *1 3/4* **Cascades (IRE)**[33] 6554 2-9-0 67 ............................ DavidProbert 1 63
(David Elsworth) *chsd ldrs: lost pl and pushed along 1/2-way: hdwy u.p over 1f out: r.o same pce fnl f* **12/1**[3]
032 **6** *1* **Its Lady Mary**[90] 4610 2-9-0 68 ............................ JimCrowley 9 60
(Paul Cole) *sn led: rdn over 1f out: drvn and hdd 1f out: wknd ins fnl f* **14/1**
0 **7** *2 1/4* **Farendole (USA)**[22] 6874 2-9-0 0 ............................ WilliamBuick 7 54
(Roger Charlton) *chsd ldrs: wnt 2nd after 2f tl 2f out: outpcd u.p over 1f out: wknd ins fnl f* **16/1**
66 **8** *nse* **Mandria (IRE)**[59] 5774 2-9-0 0 ............................ SteveDrowne 8 57+
(Daniel Kubler) *in tch in midfield: rdn and outpcd over 1f out: hld and one pce fnl f* **66/1**

1m 26.57s (0.57) **Going Correction** 0.0s/f (Stan) **8** Ran SP% **84.2**
Speed ratings (Par 94): **96,95,94,93,91 89,87,87**
CSF £33.13 TOTE £6.50: £1.90, £3.10, £6.50; EX 28.30 Trifecta £206.10.
**Owner** Mrs Deborah June James **Bred** Barronstown Stud **Trained** Newmarket, Suffolk
■ Wiener Valkyrie was withdrawn. Price at time of withdrawal 7-4. Rule 4 applies to all bets - deduction 35p in the pound.

**FOCUS**
A fair maiden and a nice start from the winner.

## 7399 BETVICTOR.COM MAIDEN FILLIES' STKS (BOBIS RACE) (DIV II) 7f (P)
**7:10** (7:11) (Class 4) 2-Y-O **£3,752** (£1,116; £557; £278) **Stalls** Low

Form RPR
**1** **Jellicle Ball (IRE)** 2-9-0 0 ............................ WilliamBuick 8 82+
(John Gosden) *dwlt: hld up in tch in last pair: clsd 2f out: swtchd lft and rdn over 1f out: str run to ld wl ins fnl f: pushed out towards fin* **7/2**[2]
0 **2** *1* **Lovely Memory (IRE)**[37] 6435 2-9-0 0 ............................ FrederikTylicki 1 78
(Saeed bin Suroor) *chsd ldr for 2f: rdn to chse ldr again over 2f out: drvn to chal 1f out: led fnl 150yds: hdd and no ex wl ins fnl f* **3/1**[1]
**3** *3/4* **Gold Sands (IRE)** 2-9-0 0 ............................ AndreaAtzeni 7 76+
(James Tate) *in tch in midfield: effrt 2f out: hdwy u.p to press ldrs 1f out: styd on same pce ins fnl f* **14/1**
03 **4** *3* **Spirited Acclaim (IRE)**[33] 6553 2-9-0 0 ............................ LiamKeniry 4 68
(David Elsworth) *led: drvn over 1f out: hdd fnl 150yds: sn btn: wknd fnl 100yds* **4/1**[3]
5 **5** *5* **Forres (IRE)**[16] 7018 2-9-0 0 ............................ PatDobbs 2 54
(Richard Hannon) *in tch in midfield: rdn and no hdwy ent fnl 2f: drvn and btn over 1f out: sn wknd* **9/2**
**6** *1/2* **Ashford (IRE)** 2-9-0 0 ............................ FergusSweeney 6 53
(Martyn Meade) *hld up in tch in last trio: effrt 2f out: sn struggling and outpcd: wknd fnl f* **16/1**
00 **7** *3 3/4* **Merritt Island**[8] 7194 2-9-0 0 ............................ LukeMorris 9 43
(Sir Mark Prescott Bt) *t.k.h: chsd ldrs: wnt 2nd 5f out tl over 2f out: wknd over 1f out* **40/1**
**8** *5* **Scimitarra** 2-9-0 0 ............................ JimCrowley 3 29
(Paul Cole) *hld up in tch: rdn and effrt on inner 2f out: sn btn: wknd over 1f out* **20/1**

1m 26.31s (0.31) **Going Correction** 0.0s/f (Stan) **8** Ran SP% **105.2**
Speed ratings (Par 94): **98,96,96,92,86 86,82,76**
CSF £12.13 TOTE £4.70: £1.70, £1.30, £3.70; EX 15.90 Trifecta £68.90.
**Owner** Lord Lloyd-Webber **Bred** Ennistown Stud **Trained** Newmarket, Suffolk
■ Misham was withdrawn. Price at time of withdrawal 8-1. Rule 4 applies to all bets - deduction 10p in the pound.

**FOCUS**
Marginally the quicker of the two divisions by 0.26sec and the winner made an impressive debut.

## 7400 £25 FREE BET AT BETVICTOR.COM MAIDEN STKS (BOBIS RACE) 6f (P)
**7:40** (7:42) (Class 4) 2-Y-O **£3,752** (£1,116; £557; £278) **Stalls** Low

Form RPR
32 **1** **Lightning Charlie**[11] 7130 2-9-5 0 ............................ WilliamBuick 6 81
(Amanda Perrett) *mde all: rdn wl over 1f out: in command and styd on wl fnl f: rdn out* **9/4**[1]
02 **2** *1 1/2* **British Art**[125] 3429 2-9-5 0 ............................ JimCrowley 9 77
(Paul Cole) *chsd ldrs: wnt 2nd after 2f: rdn wl over 1f out: styd on same pce ins fnl f* **9/2**[2]
0 **3** *shd* **Muqarred (USA)**[134] 3113 2-9-5 0 ............................ FrederikTylicki 1 76
(Saeed bin Suroor) *dwlt: sn pushed along and rcvrd to chse ldrs: rdn 2f out: battling for 2nd and kpt on same pce fnl f* **11/2**
03 **4** *1* **Sydney Ruffdiamond**[50] 6039 2-9-5 0 ............................ PatDobbs 12 73
(Richard Hannon) *stdd and dropped in bhd after s: hld up towards rr: rdn over 2f out: hdd over 1f out: kpt on same pce fnl f* **16/1**
**5** *2* **Wedlock** 2-9-0 0 ............................ LukeMorris 3 62+
(Sir Mark Prescott Bt) *in tch in midfield: rdn and effrt to chse ldrs over 1f out: no ex 1f out: outpcd fnl f* **33/1**
**6** *1 3/4* **Hurricane Alert** 2-9-5 0 ............................ OisinMurphy 10 62+
(Ralph Beckett) *t.k.h: hld up in tch in midfield: hdwy to chse ldrs over 3f out: rdn and racd awkwardly over 1f out: wknd fnl f* **13/2**

00 **7** *1/2* **Pat Mustard**[10] 7155 2-9-0 0 ............................ RachealKneller(5) 5 60
(Jamie Osborne) *hld up towards rr: swtchd rt and sme hdwy over 1f out: pushed along and styd on same pce fnl f* **66/1**
6 **8** *1 3/4* **Equleus**[22] 6852 2-9-5 0 ............................ SteveDrowne 4 55+
(Jeremy Gask) *v.s.a: t.k.h in rr: rdn ent fnl 2f: sn outpcd: wknd over 1f out* **12/1**
**9** *1 1/4* **Marasim** 2-9-5 0 ............................ AndreaAtzeni 7 51
(Roger Varian) *hld up in tch: rdn ent fnl 2f: sn outpcd: wknd over 1f out* **5/1**[3]
**10** *2 3/4* **Carron Valley** 2-9-5 0 ............................ TomEaves 8 43
(Keith Dalgleish) *sn dropped to rr: rdn and struggling over 3f out: n.d fnl 3f* **16/1**
**11** *4* **Aqdaar** 2-9-5 0 ............................ PaulHanagan 2 31
(Mark Johnston) *chsd ldr for 2f: hung rt bnd over 3f out: stl hanging and lost pl 2f out: bhd and eased ins fnl f* **16/1**

1m 13.52s (0.42) **Going Correction** 0.0s/f (Stan) **11** Ran SP% **124.1**
Speed ratings (Par 97): **97,95,94,93,90 88,87,85,83,80 74**
CSF £12.88 TOTE £3.60: £1.10, £1.30, £2.20; EX 13.60 Trifecta £73.50.
**Owner** Lightning Charlie Partnership **Bred** J A E Hobby **Trained** Pulborough, W Sussex

**FOCUS**
This was dominated by the uneasy (on the exchanges, at least) favourite and the pace held up well. The winner was very professional.

## 7401 DOWNLOAD THE BETVICTOR APP NOW MAIDEN STKS 1m 4f (P)
**8:10** (8:10) (Class 5) 3-Y-O+ **£2,587** (£770; £384; £192) **Stalls** Low

Form RPR
3020 **1** **Ridgeway Storm (IRE)**[54] 5924 4-9-12 77 ............................ TomQueally 7 85
(Alan King) *in tch in midfield: effrt over 2f out: rdn to ld over 1f out: sn clr and styd on wl: readily* **5/4**[1]
403 **2** *4* **Chatham House Rule**[126] 3385 3-9-5 75 ............................ GeorgeBaker 4 79
(Michael Bell) *led: rdn and pressed 2f out: sn hdd and outpcd: wl hld but clr 2nd after* **11/4**[2]
4 **3** *6* **Galactic Halo**[13] 7074 3-9-0 0 ............................ MartinHarley 2 64
(Lady Cecil) *chsd ldr tl 8f out: rdn over 2f out: sn outpcd and btn: 3rd and wl btn fnl 2f* **5/1**[3]
046 **4** *4 1/2* **Golden Bird (IRE)**[35] 6485 3-9-5 70 ............................ SteveDrowne 3 62
(Dean Ivory) *dwlt: rcvrd to chse ldrs after 2f: wnt 2nd 8f out tl over 2f out: sn btn* **14/1**
03-0 **5** *3 1/4* **Sharp Lookout**[114] 3814 3-9-5 73 ............................ WilliamTwiston-Davies 8 57
(Roger Charlton) *stdd and dropped in bhd after s: hld up in rr: effrt over 2f out: sn btn* **8/1**
425- **6** *16* **Al Guwair (IRE)**[414] 6116 4-9-12 65 ............................ RobertHavlin 1 31
(Mark Hoad) *in tch in last pair: rdn 3f out: sn lost tch: t.o* **33/1**

2m 34.27s (-0.23) **Going Correction** 0.0s/f (Stan)
**WFA** 3 from 4yo 7lb **6** Ran SP% **108.5**
Speed ratings (Par 103): **100,97,93,90,88 77**
CSF £4.45 TOTE £2.00: £1.60, £1.90; EX 4.50 Trifecta £9.10.
**Owner** W H Ponsonby **Bred** Mount Coote Stud **Trained** Barbury Castle, Wilts

**FOCUS**
This proved relatively straightforward for the winner.

## 7402 DOWNLOAD THE BETVICTOR INSTABET APP H'CAP 1m 4f (P)
**8:40** (8:40) (Class 4) (0-85,85) 3-Y-O+ **£4,690** (£1,395; £697; £348) **Stalls** Low

Form RPR
3411 **1** **Daaree (IRE)**[22] 6855 4-9-7 **80** ............................ PaulHanagan 8 89+
(Saeed bin Suroor) *chsd ldr over 10f out: rdn and fnd ex to ld 2f out: clr over 1f out: pressed ins fnl f: hld on wl: rdn out* **2/1**[1]
1131 **2** *1/2* **King Calypso**[16] 7016 3-8-4 **73** ............................ CamHardie(3) 7 81
(Denis Coakley) *t.k.h: hld up in tch in midfield: rdn and hdwy 2f out: chsd wnr 1f out: pressing wnr fnl 100yds: r.o but a hld* **9/2**[3]
1126 **3** *nk* **Sleeper**[33] 6559 3-9-1 **81** ............................ AndreaAtzeni 4 88
(Ralph Beckett) *led for 1f: chsd ldrs after: rdn ent fnl 2f: chsng ldrs and swtchd rt 1f out: r.o but nvr quite enough pce to rch wnr* **5/1**
2-1 **4** *1/2* **Fair Share**[15] 7032 3-9-5 **85** ............................ MartinHarley 3 91
(Lady Cecil) *stmbld leaving stalls: hld up in last pair: rdn hdwy on inner 2f out: chsd ldrs over 1f out: kpt on same pce fnl 100yds* **3/1**[2]
5522 **5** *3 1/4* **Jacob Cats**[29] 6656 5-9-9 **82** ............................(v) JimCrowley 5 83
(William Knight) *hld up in tch in last trio: rdn and effrt over 2f out: r.o but no imp fr over 1f out* **7/1**
1064 **6** *3* **Corton Lad**[35] 6479 4-9-10 **83** ............................(tp) TomEaves 6 79
(Keith Dalgleish) *dwlt: rcvrd to ld after 1f and set stdy gallop: rdn and hdd 2f out: outpcd over 1f out: wknd fnl f* **20/1**
3514 **7** *3* **Ssafa**[46] 6171 6-9-5 **78** ............................(p) LukeMorris 1 69
(Paul Cole) *in tch in midfield: rdn and outpcd jst over 2f out: wknd over 1f out* **25/1**
045 **8** *1/2* **The Gay Cavalier**[30] 6634 3-8-0 **71** oh1 ............................(t) JoeDoyle(5) 2 62
(John Ryan) *chsd ldrs: rdn jst over 2f out: outpcd and lost pl over 1f out: wknd 1f out* **25/1**
2230 **9** *1 3/4* **Wannabe Your Man**[11] 7129 4-9-3 **76** ............................(b[1]) PatCosgrave 9 64
(George Baker) *wnt lft s and slowly away: cajoled along early: in tch in rr: rdn over 2f out: sn btn* **33/1**

2m 32.73s (-1.77) **Going Correction** 0.0s/f (Stan)
**WFA** 3 from 4yo+ 7lb **9** Ran SP% **121.1**
Speed ratings (Par 105): **105,104,104,104,101 99,97,97,96**
CSF £11.46 CT £41.21 TOTE £4.00: £1.40, £1.80, £1.30; EX 10.00 Trifecta £43.50.
**Owner** Godolphin **Bred** Shadwell Estate Company Limited **Trained** Newmarket, Suffolk

**FOCUS**
Several in-form, progressive types lined up here and it's form to be positive about. They went quite steady though, and it was probably an advantage to be up there. The winner is continuing his progress.

## 7403 DOWNLOAD THE RACING UK IPAD APP H'CAP 7f (P)
**9:10** (9:10) (Class 5) (0-75,79) 3-Y-O+ **£2,587** (£770; £384; £192) **Stalls** Low

Form RPR
3612 **1** **Fiftyshadesofgrey (IRE)**[1] 7373 3-9-7 79 6ex ............................ PatCosgrave 13 90+
(George Baker) *hld up in tch: clsd smoothly over 1f out: led 1f out: sn rdn and qcknd: r.o wl: rdn out* **3/1**[1]
0053 **2** *3/4* **Reposer (IRE)**[9] 7178 6-9-4 74 ............................ TomEaves 8 83
(Keith Dalgleish) *hld up in tch in last trio: rdn and hdwy jst over 1f out: chsd wnr wl ins fnl f: r.o* **7/1**
2320 **3** *1 3/4* **Good Authority (IRE)**[20] 6891 7-8-11 74 ............................ KieranShoemark(7) 3 78
(Victor Dartnall) *hld up in tch: hdwy on inner 2f out: chsd ldrs and drvn 1f out: kpt on same pce ins fnl f* **9/2**[2]
500 **4** *shd* **King Of Eden (IRE)**[24] 6824 8-9-3 73 ............................ JasonHart 7 77
(Eric Alston) *chsd ldr: rdn to ld wl over 1f out: hdd 1f out: no ex and one pce fnl f* **33/1**


The Form Book, Raceform Ltd, Newbury, RG14 5SJ

3512 **5** *nk* **Bob**[30] 6639 4-9-3 73........................................ DavidAllan 14 76+
(Les Eyre) *hld up in tch in midfield: n.m.r and shuffled bk jst over 2f out: rallied and hdwy 1f out: styd on wl ins fnl f* **13/2**[3]

-001 **6** *½* **Hulcolt (IRE)**[30] 6625 3-8-13 74........................................ CamHardie(3) 12 75
(Garry Moss) *chsd ldrs: rdn and pressing ldrs 2f out: no ex and one pce ins fnl f* **25/1**

1003 **7** *¾* **Gone With The Wind (GER)**[28] 6680 3-9-3 75..........(p) MartinHarley 2 74
(Jeremy Noseda) *chsd ldrs: effrt u.p jst over 2f out: ev ch 1f out: wknd ins fnl f* **7/1**

2420 **8** *1* **Red Paladin (IRE)**[30] 6639 4-9-3 73........................................ TonyHamilton 10 71
(Kevin Ryan) *hld up in tch in rr: rdn and hdwy over 1f out: hung rt and nt clr run ins fnl f: swtchd lft and styd on fnl 100yds* **20/1**

3060 **9** *½* **Soaring Spirits (IRE)**[17] 6990 4-9-5 75..................(p) SteveDrowne 9 71
(Dean Ivory) *led: rdn over 1f out: stl ev ch 1f out: no ex and wknd ins fnl f* **33/1**

5100 **10** *2¾* **Mrs Warren**[7] 7220 4-8-10 73........................................ ChrisMeehan(7) 11 62
(George Baker) *s.i.s: hld up in rr: hdwy on outer into midfield 1/2-way: rdn and no hdwy over 2f out: wknd over 1f out* **66/1**

6112 **11** *shd* **Ganymede**[29] 6657 3-9-3 75........................................(p) JimCrowley 1 63
(Eve Johnson Houghton) *chsd ldrs: rdn ent fnl 2f: no ex and btn over 1f out: wknd ins fnl f* **9/2**[2]

4520 **12** *6* **Pettochside**[10] 7159 5-9-5 75........................................ PatDobbs 6 48
(Chris Gordon) *in tch in midfield: effrt on inner 2f out: no imp whn nt clr run and hmpd jst over 1f out: bhd and eased fnl f* **20/1**

1m 25.73s (-0.27) **Going Correction** 0.0s/f (Stan)
**WFA** 3 from 4yo+ 2lb 12 Ran SP% **120.4**
Speed ratings (Par 103): **101,100,98,98,97 97,96,95,94,91 91,84**
CSF £22.68 CT £97.02 TOTE £4.00: £1.80, £2.10, £4.00; EX 26.50 Trifecta £137.40.
**Owner** Team Fifty **Bred** Doc Bloodstock **Trained** Manton, Wilts

**FOCUS**
Things got a little tight in the closing stages and there were one or two hard-luck stories.
T/Jkpt: Not won. T/Plt: £2044.20 to a £1 stake. Pool: £79,889.44 - 28.52 winning units. T/Qpdt: £73.20 to a £1 stake. Pool: £12,022.38 - 121.45 winning units. SP

## 6326 DONCASTER (L-H)
### Friday, October 24

**OFFICIAL GOING: Good to soft (soft in places on round course) changing to soft after race 5 (4:05)**
Wind: Virtually nil Weather: Cloudy with sunny periods

## 7404 SOCIALITES ZERO STOPTOBER NURSERY H'CAP (BOBIS RACE) 1m (S)
**1:20** (1:22) (Class 3) (0-95,82) 2-Y-O **£7,762** (£2,310; £1,154; £577) **Stalls** High

Form RPR

0110 **1** **Stec (IRE)**[83] 4897 2-8-11 **77**........................................ JennyPowell(5) 2 87
(Tom Dascombe) *trckd ldr: led over 2f out: clr 1f out: swvd bdly rt 100yds out* **9/1**[3]

5321 **2** *6* **Framley Garth (IRE)**[7] 7230 2-9-1 **76** 6ex........................ GrahamLee 6 73
(David Elsworth) *led tl over 2f out: styd on same pce* **9/1**[3]

6353 **3** *2¼* **Kelly's Finest (IRE)**[17] 7005 2-8-12 **73**........................ PJMcDonald 3 65
(James Bethell) *hld up in mid-div: hdwy 3f out: sn swtchd rt: styd on fnl f: tk 3rd nr fin* **6/1**[2]

451 **4** *½* **Best Example (USA)**[26] 6790 2-9-1 **81**........................ KevinStott(5) 1 72
(Saeed bin Suroor) *trckd ldrs: effrt over 2f out: kpt on same pce* **6/1**[2]

41 **5** *2¾* **Bold Appeal**[21] 6903 2-8-8 **69**........................................ AndreaAtzeni 5 54
(Ralph Beckett) *trckd ldrs: effrt 3f out: wknd last 100yds* **11/4**[1]

0203 **6** *10* **Playboy Bay**[7] 7230 2-8-4 **65**........................................ JoeFanning 4 28
(Mick Channon) *dwlt: in rr: pushed along over 5f out: sme hdwy over 2f out: wknd fnl f: eased clsng stages* **9/1**[3]

631 **7** *5* **Lostock Hall (IRE)**[35] 6509 2-9-7 **82**........................ DanielTudhope 9 34
(K R Burke) *hld up towards rr: effrt over 3f out: wknd over 2f out: bhd whn eased* **11/4**[1]

1m 43.31s (4.01) **Going Correction** +0.45s/f (Yiel) 7 Ran SP% **111.9**
Speed ratings (Par 99): **97,91,88,88,85 75,70**
CSF £79.95 CT £521.13 TOTE £7.20: £3.30, £3.90; EX 42.20 Trifecta £243.60.
**Owner** D Ward **Bred** D G Iceton **Trained** Malpas, Cheshire

**FOCUS**
The ground seemed to be riding a bit slower than the official description, and the main action in this opening contest unfolded towards the stands' side.

## 7405 UNIVERSAL RECYCLING BRITISH STALLION STUDS EBF MAIDEN FILLIES' STKS (BOBIS RACE) (DIV I) 1m (S)
**1:50** (1:54) (Class 5) 2-Y-O **£3,881** (£1,155; £577; £288) **Stalls** High

Form RPR

3 **1** **Star Of Seville**[17] 7018 2-9-0 0........................................ WilliamBuick 9 81
(John Gosden) *mde all: pushed clr 2f out: rdn ins fnl f: kpt on strly: readily* **10/3**[2]

6 **2** *6* **Dreamlike**[34] 6553 2-9-0 0........................................ AndreaAtzeni 10 68
(Luca Cumani) *prom: hdwy to chse wnr 2f out: sn rdn and no imp appr fnl f* **11/2**

**3** *1½* **Speedy Boarding** 2-9-0 0........................................ FrederikTylicki 6 65
(James Fanshawe) *trckd ldrs: hdwy over 2f out: rdn along wl over 1f out: kpt on same pce fnl f* **20/1**

**4** *1½* **Libbard** 2-9-0 0........................................ MartinHarley 2 61
(Roger Charlton) *in rr: pushed along wl over 2f out: swtchd lft and rdn wl over 1f out: styd on strly fnl f: nrst fin* **25/1**

2 **5** *nk* **Yarrow (IRE)**[17] 7011 2-9-0 0........................................ ShaneKelly 1 61
(Sir Michael Stoute) *trckd ldrs: hdwy 3f out: rdn along 2f out: grad wknd* **2/1**[1]

**6** *1½* **Age Of Elegance (IRE)** 2-9-0 0........................................ JimCrowley 4 57
(Olly Stevens) *in tch on outer: green: pushed along and outpcd 1/2-way: hdwy wl over 2f out: rdn wl over 1f out: kpt on fnl f* **33/1**

05 **7** *½* **Amber Mile**[23] 6868 2-9-0 0........................................ SeanLevey 11 56
(Ralph Beckett) *prom: rdn along to chse wnr 3f out: wknd wl over 1f out* **20/1**

0 **8** *nk* **Mythical Moment**[14] 7084 2-9-0 0........................................ GrahamLee 12 56
(William Haggas) *racd nr stands' rail: prom: rdn along 3f out: sn outpcd* **9/2**[3]

0 **9** *½* **Hyphaema (IRE)**[23] 6868 2-9-0 0........................................ AdamKirby 5 55
(Clive Cox) *chsd ldrs: rdn and hung rt 3f out: sn wknd* **100/1**

**10** *1* **Bella Nostalgia (IRE)** 2-9-0 0........................................ DanielTudhope 8 52
(Hugo Palmer) *a towards rr* **12/1**

0 **11** *1* **Malice**[13] 7108 2-9-0 0........................................ PaulMulrennan 13 50
(Peter Chapple-Hyam) *racd nr stands' rail: pushed along over 3f out: swtchd lft: rdn and sme hdwy wl over 2f out: sn wknd* **66/1**

**12** *2½* **Desert Morning (IRE)** 2-9-0 0........................................ JoeFanning 3 45
(David Simcock) *dwlt and in rr: hdwy to chse ldrs 1/2-way: rdn along wl over 2f out: sn wknd* **33/1**

00 **13** *5* **Medicean Melody**[32] 6606 2-9-0 0........................................ MartinLane 7 34
(David Simcock) *dwlt: a in rr* **100/1**

1m 43.85s (4.55) **Going Correction** +0.525s/f (Yiel) 13 Ran SP% **120.4**
Speed ratings (Par 92): **98,92,90,89,88 87,86,86,85,84 83,81,76**
CSF £20.33 TOTE £4.00: £1.90, £2.20, £7.40; EX 20.10 Trifecta £221.50.
**Owner** Lady Bamford **Bred** Lady Bamford **Trained** Newmarket, Suffolk

**FOCUS**
This fillies' maiden has been contested by some decent sorts over the years, notably John Gosden's subsequent dual Group 1 winner Izzi Top, who ran second in the 2010 running. The same trainer sent out a winner wide-margin winner of division one this time around, although the time was slightly slower than the second leg, and also the opening nursery (action unfolded on different part of the track). The majority of these raced up the middle.

## 7406 UNIVERSAL RECYCLING BRITISH STALLION STUDS EBF MAIDEN FILLIES' STKS (BOBIS RACE) (DIV II) 1m (S)
**2:20** (2:23) (Class 5) 2-Y-O **£3,881** (£1,155; £577; £288) **Stalls** High

Form RPR

**1** **Beautiful Romance** 2-9-0 0........................................ FrederikTylicki 1 90+
(Saeed bin Suroor) *mid-div: hdwy over 3f out: upsides over 2f out: led over 1f out: drew wl clr last 150yds* **3/1**[2]

**2** *9* **Striding Out (IRE)** 2-9-0 0........................................ JimCrowley 7 70
(David Simcock) *s.i.s: in rr: hdwy 4f out: kpt on to take modest 2nd last 50yds* **12/1**

4 **3** *1* **Figment**[31] 6641 2-9-0 0........................................ WilliamBuick 4 68
(John Gosden) *trckd ldrs: led over 2f out: hdd over 1f out: fdd last 100yds* **7/4**[1]

0 **4** *4½* **Sylvette**[34] 6554 2-9-0 0........................................ AndreaAtzeni 9 58
(Roger Varian) *chsd ldrs: drvn over 2f out: edgd lft: one pce* **7/1**

**5** *2¼* **Sahara (IRE)** 2-9-0 0........................................ TedDurcan 12 53
(Chris Wall) *dwlt: in rr: drvn over 3f out: nvr a factor* **25/1**

2200 **6** *7* **Crystal Malt (IRE)**[27] 6749 2-8-11 0........................ CamHardie(3) 3 38
(Richard Hannon) *led: hdd over 2f out: wknd over 1f out* **12/1**

00 **7** *1¼* **Heavens Above (IRE)**[9] 7193 2-9-0 0........................ PaulMulrennan 8 35
(Ed Dunlop) *hld up towards rr: effrt over 3f out: wknd 2f out* **50/1**

**8** *17* **Armistice Day (IRE)** 2-9-0 0........................................ SeanLevey 10
(David Brown) *in rr: sn drvn along: bhd fnl 4f: t.o* **33/1**

0 **9** *4½* **Caelica (IRE)**[13] 7108 2-9-0 0........................................ RobertWinston 11
(Charles Hills) *chsd ldrs: lost pl over 1f out: sn heavily eased: t.o* **6/1**[3]

**10** *2* **Ambonnay Rouge (IRE)** 2-8-9 0........................ AlistairRawlinson(5) 2
(Michael Appleby) *sn chsng ldrs: lost pl over 2f out: sn bhd: t.o* **80/1**

1m 43.65s (4.35) **Going Correction** +0.525s/f (Yiel) 10 Ran SP% **113.5**
Speed ratings (Par 92): **99,90,89,84,82 75,74,57,52,50**
CSF £35.97 TOTE £4.10: £2.20, £3.10, £1.10; EX 35.80 Trifecta £201.30.
**Owner** Godolphin **Bred** Rabbah Bloodstock Limited **Trained** Newmarket, Suffolk

**FOCUS**
While it would be dangerous to get carried away by the winning margin on what was demanding ground (first two races on the card were both won by 6l), the time was only slightly slower than the opening nursery, and a bit quicker than the first division of this, and those winners had the benefit of experience. They raced up the middle.

## 7407 BETDAQ 3% COMMISSION IRISH STALLION FARMS EBF MAIDEN STKS 7f
**2:55** (2:58) (Class 5) 2-Y-O **£3,881** (£1,155; £577; £288) **Stalls** High

Form RPR

4 **1** **Mutarakez (IRE)**[16] 7037 2-9-5 0........................................ PaulHanagan 18 80
(Brian Meehan) *cl up: led 3f out: jnd and pushed along 2f out: rdn ent fnl f and sn edgd lft: wandered and hung rt last 75yds: kpt on* **6/1**[3]

**2** *hd* **Ice Lord (IRE)** 2-9-5 0........................................ AdamKirby 11 80
(Clive Cox) *trckd ldrs: hdwy and cl up 3f out: chal 2f out: rdn and ev ch ent fnl f: kpt on* **14/1**

**3** *2¾* **Thahab (IRE)** 2-9-5 0........................................ FrankieDettori 8 73
(Richard Hannon) *hld up in midfield: stdy hdwy 3f out: effrt 2f out: chal over 1f out: rdn and ev ch ent fnl f: kpt on same pce* **9/4**[1]

**4** *1½* **True Respect (IRE)** 2-9-5 0........................................ FrederikTylicki 16 69
(Saeed bin Suroor) *in tch: hdwy to trck ldrs 3f out: effrt over 2f out: rdn wl over 1f out: sn no imp* **4/1**[2]

0 **5** *1½* **Coolcalmcollected (IRE)**[119] 3671 2-9-0 0........................ TedDurcan 14 60
(Chris Wall) *hld up towards rr: stdy hdwy wl over 2f out: rdn over 1f out: kpt on fnl f: nrst fin* **16/1**

**6** *6* **Imperial March (IRE)** 2-9-5 0........................................ SteveDrowne 2 50
(Clive Cox) *dwlt and towards rr: hdwy 1/2-way: swtchd rt and styng on whn n.m.r and hmpd wl over 1f out: kpt on fnl f* **33/1**

**7** *½* **Penang Paparaja (IRE)** 2-9-5 0........................................ RobertWinston 17 49
(Michael Bell) *towards rr: hdwy over 2f out: sn rdn and kpt on fnl f* **16/1**

**8** *2¾* **Lightning Spree (IRE)** 2-9-0 0........................................ ShaneGray(5) 1 42
(Kevin Ryan) *chsd ldrs on outer: rdn along wl over 2f out: grad wknd* **25/1**

5 **9** *1¼* **Justice First**[10] 7166 2-9-5 0........................................ AndreaAtzeni 3 39
(Ed Dunlop) *in tch: hdwy to chse ldrs 3f out: rdn along over 2f out: sn wknd* **14/1**

**10** *¾* **Makzon (USA)** 2-9-5 0........................................ ShaneKelly 12 37
(Sir Michael Stoute) *v s.i.s: green and sn detached in rr: pushed along bef 1/2-way: sme late hdwy* **16/1**

06 **11** *1¼* **Rise To Power**[31] 6621 2-9-0 0........................(p[1]) KevinStott(5) 10 34
(Kevin Ryan) *slt ld: rdn along 1/2-way: sn hdd & wknd* **100/1**

**12** *hd* **Udododontu (IRE)** 2-9-2 0........................................ JacobButterfield(3) 5 33
(Richard Guest) *dwlt: a towards rr* **100/1**

**13** *1¼* **Isntshesomething** 2-9-0 0........................................ TomEaves 7 25
(Richard Guest) *dwlt: a towards rr* **66/1**

**14** *1* **Colourfilly** 2-9-0 0........................................ AntonioFresu 9 23
(Ed Walker) *prom: rdn along over 3f out: sn wknd* **33/1**

**15** *¾* **No Not Yet** 2-9-0 0........................................ PaulMulrennan 4 21
(Michael Dods) *chsd ldrs: rdn along over 3f out: sn wknd* **10/1**

6 **16** *½* **Layerthorpe (IRE)**[20] 6931 2-9-5 0........................................ SeanLevey 13 25
(David Brown) *a towards rr* **50/1**

**17** *½* **Show Me Baileys (FR)** 2-9-5 0........................................ GrahamLee 15 23
(James Given) *a towards rr* **50/1**

0 **18** *5* **Satanic Mills (IRE)**[13] 7123 2-9-0 0........................ ShelleyBirkett(5) 6
(Nigel Tinkler) *a towards rr* **100/1**

1m 30.64s (4.34) **Going Correction** +0.60s/f (Yiel) 18 Ran SP% **123.2**
Speed ratings (Par 95): **99,98,95,93,92 85,84,81,80,79 77,77,76,75,74 73,73,67**
CSF £82.61 TOTE £5.80: £2.00, £4.20, £1.60; EX 93.50 Trifecta £286.00.
**Owner** Hamdan Al Maktoum **Bred** John T Heffernan & Grainne Dooley **Trained** Manton, Wilts

**FOCUS**
A huge field of maidens and this ought to produce a few winners. They raced up the middle.

## 7408 RACING POST/SIS BETTING SHOP MANAGER H'CAP 6f
3:30 (3:34) (Class 2) (0-105,100) 3-Y-O+ **£12,938** (£3,850; £1,924; £962) **Stalls** High

Form RPR
5343 **1** **Jamaican Bolt (IRE)**[7] 7233 6-9-0 90 ........ WilliamBuick 10 100
(Geoffrey Oldroyd) *mid-div: hdwy 2f out: hmpd over 1f out: styd on wl: led towards fin* **11/2**[1]
512 **2** ¾ **Red Pike (IRE)**[21] 6893 3-9-1 92 ........ PaulMulrennan 9 100+
(Bryan Smart) *w ldrs: led over 1f out: hdd and no ex clsng stages* **7/1**[2]
0626 **3** *hd* **Khubala (IRE)**[12] 7132 5-9-5 95 ........(b) PaulHanagan 8 102
(Hugo Palmer) *hld up in mid-div: hdwy over 2f out: edgd rt over 1f out: cl 3rd wl ins fnl f: no ex* **10/1**[3]
623U **4** 2 **Bogart**[14] 7080 5-9-4 94 ........(p) AmyRyan 17 95
(Kevin Ryan) *trckd ldrs: led briefly 2f out: fdd clsng stages* **10/1**[3]
5040 **5** ½ **Arnold Lane (IRE)**[13] 7122 5-9-5 95 ........ SamHitchcott 5 94
(Mick Channon) *chsd ldrs: drvn over 2f out: kpt on same pce fnl f* **14/1**
0000 **6** *nse* **Mass Rally (IRE)**[13] 7122 7-9-10 100 ........(p) PJMcDonald 11 101
(Michael Dods) *in rr: hdwy whn nt clr run over 1f out: styd on fnl f* **14/1**
040 **7** ¾ **Eccleston**[14] 7080 3-9-3 94 ........(p) DanielTudhope 2 90
(David O'Meara) *in rr: kpt on over 1f out: nvr trbld ldrs* **14/1**
301 **8** *nk* **Englishman**[7] 7233 4-9-1 94 6ex ........ CamHardie[(3)] 4 89
(Charles Hills) *chsd ldrs: kpt on same pce appr fnl f* **11/1**
0050 **9** ¾ **Fast Shot**[13] 7122 6-8-12 95 ........(t) RachelRichardson[(7)] 22 88
(Tim Easterby) *hld up towards rr: hdwy over 1f out: nvr a factor* **12/1**
2623 **10** ½ **Another Wise Kid (IRE)**[13] 7122 6-9-9 99 ........ GrahamLee 20 90
(Paul Midgley) *hld up in mid-div: effrt over 2f out: kpt on fnl f* **11/1**
1000 **11** 1¾ **Compton Park**[13] 7122 7-9-4 94 ........(t) DavidAllan 13 80
(Les Eyre) *in rr: sme hdwy whn nt clr run over 1f out: nvr on terms* **20/1**
0500 **12** 1 **Ashpan Sam**[13] 7122 5-9-10 100 ........ AdamKirby 12 83
(John Spearing) *led: hdd 2f out: grad wknd* **25/1**
0100 **13** 2½ **Colonel Mak**[6] 7280 7-8-13 94 ........ ShaneGray[(5)] 16 69
(David Barron) *in rr: nvr on terms* **33/1**
0000 **14** 3¼ **Sleeper King (IRE)**[62] 5696 3-9-1 92 ........ AndreaAtzeni 1 56
(Luca Cumani) *chsd ldrs: drvn 3f out: lost pl 2f out* **12/1**
0515 **15** 2¼ **Pipers Note**[69] 5445 4-9-4 94 ........ GeorgeChaloner 18 51
(Richard Whitaker) *mid-div: effrt over 2f out: wknd over 1f out* **20/1**
0435 **16** 4½ **Mu'Ajiza**[20] 6929 4-9-10 100 ........ RobertWinston 3 43
(Paul Midgley) *chsd ldrs: wknd over 1f out: sn eased* **28/1**
0405 **17** *nse* **Love Island**[32] 6598 5-8-13 89 ........ PaulQuinn 14 32
(Richard Whitaker) *dwlt: a in rr: bhd whn eased clsng stages* **50/1**
0003 **18** 23 **Kimberella**[27] 6760 4-9-4 94 ........ AdrianNicholls 19
(David Nicholls) *in rr: bhd whn heavily eased fnl f: tailed rt off* **12/1**

1m 15.8s (2.20) **Going Correction** +0.60s/f (Yiel)
**WFA** 3 from 4yo+ 1lb **18 Ran SP% 127.5**
Speed ratings (Par 109): **109,108,107,105,104 104,103,102,101,101 98,97,94,89,86 80,80,50**
CSF £39.04 CT £392.32 TOTE £7.00: £2.10, £2.30, £3.10, £2.70; EX 37.50 Trifecta £213.40.
**Owner** R C Bond **Bred** Swordlestown Stud **Trained** Brawby, N Yorks

**FOCUS**
A typically competitive sprint handicap in which they raced up the middle. The winner has been rated as running his best race in two years, with the runner-up running another pb.

## 7409 BETDAQ BETTING EXCHANGE £30 FREE BET H'CAP 1m 6f 132y
4:05 (4:07) (Class 3) (0-95,95) 3-Y-O+ **£7,762** (£2,310; £1,154; £577) **Stalls** Low

Form RPR
533 **1** **Spectator**[28] 6705 3-8-2 78 ........(v[1]) DavidProbert 1 91+
(Andrew Balding) *trckd ldrs on inner: smooth hdwy 3f out: led wl over 1f out: sn pushed clr: eased towards fin: readily* **15/2**[3]
-343 **2** 3¾ **Novirak (IRE)**[29] 6687 6-9-8 89 ........ FrederikTylicki 5 96
(James Fanshawe) *hld up in midfield: hdwy over 3f out: rdn along 2f out: styd on u.p fnl f: no ch w wnr* **13/2**[2]
0055 **3** *nk* **Ardlui (IRE)**[14] 7083 6-9-10 91 ........(b) DavidAllan 19 98
(Tim Easterby) *cl up on outer: effrt 4f out: led 3f out: rdn and hdd wl over 1f out: drvn and kpt on same pce fnl f* **20/1**
2631 **4** 1 **Norway Cross**[18] 6987 4-9-5 86 ........ AndreaAtzeni 3 91
(Luca Cumani) *trckd ldrs: hdwy over 3f out: effrt 2f out: sn rdn and kpt on same pce* **10/3**[1]
1056 **5** 1½ **Saved By The Bell (IRE)**[14] 7083 4-9-6 87 ........ DanielTudhope 9 90
(David O'Meara) *chsd ldrs: hdwy over 3f out: rdn along over 2f out: drvn wl over 1f out and kpt on same pce* **14/1**
0330 **6** 2¼ **Linguine (FR)**[41] 6330 4-9-1 89 ........(t) MikeyEnnis[(7)] 4 89
(Seamus Durack) *led: jnd and pushed along 4f out: rdn and hdd 3f out: drvn over 2f out and grad wknd* **25/1**
0100 **7** *nse* **Gabrial's King (IRE)**[13] 7107 5-9-9 90 ........ AdamKirby 15 90
(David Simcock) *hld up in rr: hdwy over 3f out: swtchd rt to outer and rdn wl over 1f out: kpt on one pce* **25/1**
0020 **8** 3 **Lady Kashaan (IRE)**[13] 7107 5-9-4 85 ........ RobertWinston 14 81
(Alan Swinbank) *hld up in rr: swtchd rt to outer and hdwy 3f out: rdn 2f out: n.d* **9/1**
4114 **9** ¾ **Last Echo (IRE)**[12] 7133 3-7-11 76 oh1 ........ CamHardie[(3)] 7 71
(Ralph Beckett) *hld up towards rr: hdwy over 3f out: rdn along whn n.m.r 2f out: n.d* **14/1**
5030 **10** 2¼ **Ambleside**[6] 7281 4-8-11 78 ........ JamesSullivan 11 71
(Michael Easterby) *trckd ldrs: hdwy over 4f out: rdn along over 3f out: wkng whn hmpd wl over 1f out* **66/1**
00-0 **11** ½ **Ile De Re (FR)**[27] 6747 8-9-11 92 ........ JimCrowley 2 84
(Kevin Frost) *trckd ldng pair on inner: effrt over 3f out: rdn along wl over 2f out: sn drvn and wknd* **25/1**
-036 **12** 1 **Moontime**[153] 2566 3-8-11 87 ........ WilliamBuick 17 78
(Charlie Appleby) *a towards rr* **16/1**
0-00 **13** *nk* **Very Good Day (FR)**[13] 7107 7-9-6 87 ........ PaulHanagan 12 77
(Richard Fahey) *midfield: rdn along over 3f out: sn btn* **25/1**
-520 **14** ½ **Zipp (IRE)**[28] 6708 4-9-4 85 ........ SeanLevey 13 75
(Ralph Beckett) *hld up towards rr: effrt and sme hdwy on outer wl over 3f out: sn rdn and wknd wl over 2f out* **12/1**
4124 **15** 1¼ **Intense Tango**[31] 6637 3-8-0 79 ........ JoeyHaynes[(3)] 18 67
(K R Burke) *in tch on wd outside: hdwy 5f out: chsd ldrs 4f out: rdn along over 3f out: sn drvn and wknd* **15/2**[3]
-523 **16** 6 **Allnecessaryforce (FR)**[146] 2787 4-8-9 76 ........ JimmyQuinn 6 56
(Alex Hales) *midfield: hdwy 4f out: rdn along 3f out: sn wknd* **33/1**
5241 **17** *shd* **Almagest**[80] 5017 6-9-6 87 ........(p) SamJames 16 67
(David O'Meara) *a in rr* **28/1**

1150 **18** 4½ **Zeus Magic**[12] 7142 4-9-3 84 ........ TomEaves 10 58
(Brian Ellison) *dwlt and towards rr: hdwy on inner 5f out: in tch over 3f out: sn rdn along and wknd* **40/1**

3m 19.15s (11.75) **Going Correction** +0.975s/f (Soft)
**WFA** 3 from 4yo+ 9lb **18 Ran SP% 127.3**
Speed ratings (Par 107): **107,105,104,104,103 102,102,100,100,99 98,98,98,97,97 93,93,91**
CSF £50.50 CT £970.90 TOTE £9.40: £2.70, £2.10, £5.30, £1.20; EX 56.90 Trifecta £909.10.
**Owner** Kingsclere Racing Club **Bred** Kingsclere Stud **Trained** Kingsclere, Hants

**FOCUS**
This looked a wide-open handicap, but the winner bolted up. The third has been rated a bit closer to his old form.

## 7410 BETDAQ 50% COMMISSION FIRST 3 MONTHS H'CAP (BOBIS RACE) 1m 2f 60y
4:40 (4:42) (Class 3) (0-95,94) 3-Y-O **£7,762** (£2,310; £1,154; £577) **Stalls** Low

Form RPR
1104 **1** **Kleo (GR)**[37] 6464 3-9-5 92 ........ AndreaAtzeni 2 103
(Luca Cumani) *led early: trckd ldrs: led over 1f out: drvn out* **11/2**[3]
4513 **2** 2¾ **Cape Caster (IRE)**[29] 6685 3-9-0 87 ........ JimCrowley 10 93
(Ralph Beckett) *hld up in rr: hdwy 3f out: edgd lft and chsd wnr over 1f out: no imp* **9/2**[2]
1-20 **3** *nk* **Indy (IRE)**[13] 7119 3-9-6 93 ........ GrahamGibbons 6 98
(David Barron) *sn led: hdd after 2f: 3rd over 1f out: styd on same pce* **12/1**
02 **4** 1¾ **Top Of The Glas (IRE)**[18] 6978 3-9-1 88 ........ TomEaves 1 90
(Brian Ellison) *hld up towards rr: drvn over 3f out: edgd rt over 1f out: kpt on to take 4th nr fin* **12/1**
1320 **5** ½ **Master The World (IRE)**[29] 6688 3-9-7 94 ........(v) GrahamLee 3 95
(David Elsworth) *chsd ldrs: effrt over 2f out: one pce over 1f out* **15/2**
424 **6** 1 **Raven Ridge (IRE)**[60] 5757 3-8-12 85 ........ WilliamBuick 7 84
(Michael Bell) *chsd ldrs: one pce fnl 2f* **9/2**[2]
2020 **7** ½ **Master Of Finance (IRE)**[13] 7119 3-9-2 89 ........ JoeFanning 9 87
(Mark Johnston) *led after 2f: hdd over 1f out: fdd* **16/1**
1- **8** 9 **Ghazi (IRE)**[426] 5744 3-8-4 82 ........(p) KevinStott[(5)] 5 63
(Saeed bin Suroor) *dwlt: in rr: pushed along 7f out: drvn 4f out: nvr on terms: eased whn bhd clsng stages* **10/3**[1]
206 **9** 10 **Rainbow Rock (IRE)**[30] 6656 3-8-13 86 ........(v) DanielTudhope 4 48
(Mark Johnston) *hld up in rr: effrt 3f out: sn btn: eased whn bhd clsng stages* **12/1**

2m 16.66s (7.26) **Going Correction** +0.975s/f (Soft) **9 Ran SP% 115.6**
Speed ratings (Par 105): **109,106,106,105,104 103,103,96,88**
CSF £30.48 CT £285.54 TOTE £4.60: £1.90, £1.40, £5.30; EX 22.40 Trifecta £265.90.
**Owner** Mrs M Marinopoulos **Bred** Figaia Stud **Trained** Newmarket, Suffolk

**FOCUS**
A decent 3yo handicap. The third has been rated as running a pb off a stiff mark.

## 7411 BETDAQ NO PREMIUM CHARGE AMATEUR RIDERS' H'CAP 1m 2f 60y
5:10 (5:12) (Class 5) (0-75,75) 3-Y-O+ **£3,743** (£1,161; £580; £290) **Stalls** Low

Form RPR
2110 **1** **Gift Of Silence**[27] 6746 5-10-7 73 ........ MrJPWilliams[(5)] 13 86
(Bernard Llewellyn) *hld up in midfield: smooth hdwy over 3f out: chsd ldrs over 2f out: sn cl up: rdn to ld over 1f out: kpt on* **14/1**
3-56 **2** ½ **Mash Potato (IRE)**[151] 2607 4-10-2 68 ........(p) MrHStock[(5)] 12 80
(Michael Dods) *trckd ldrs: hdwy 4f out: cl up 3f out: led 2f out: sn rdn and hdd over 1f out: drvn and ev ch ins fnl f tl no ex last 75yds* **8/1**
4633 **3** 4½ **Aryizad (IRE)**[38] 6433 5-10-9 70 ........ MrSWalker 9 74
(Alan Swinbank) *hld up in rr: hdwy over 3f out: n.m.r and swtchd rt to outer over 2f out: rdn wl over 1f out: chsd ldng pair appr fnl f: sn no imp* **4/1**[1]
5000 **4** ¾ **Ruzeiz (USA)**[151] 2627 5-10-5 71 ........ MrJDoe[(5)] 16 73
(Peter Hedger) *hld up in rr: hdwy on outer 3f out: rdn 2f out: kpt on u.p fnl f: nrst fin* **33/1**
16-3 **5** 2¾ **Collodi (GER)**[27] 376 5-10-7 75 ........ MissPBridgwater[(7)] 10 72
(David Bridgwater) *v s.i.s and bhd: hdwy on outer wl over 2f out: sn rdn: styd on fnl f: nrst fin* **7/1**[3]
-120 **6** 1½ **Hussar Ballad (USA)**[150] 2654 5-10-3 64 ........ MissSBrotherton 5 58
(Mel Brittain) *towards rr: hdwy over 4f out: chsd ldrs 2f out: sn rdn and kpt on one pce* **14/1**
0026 **7** 1 **El Bravo**[12] 7133 8-10-4 70 ........(p) MrAidenBlakemore[(5)] 20 62
(Shaun Harris) *in tch: hdwy on outer 4f out: chsd ldrs 3f out: rdn over 2f out and sn one pce* **25/1**
6040 **8** 1½ **King Of The Celts (IRE)**[30] 6672 6-9-13 63 ........ MrWEasterby[(3)] 14 52
(Tim Easterby) *trckd ldr: hdwy 4f out: rdn to ld 3f out: hdd 2f out: sn drvn and wknd appr fnl f* **20/1**
1602 **9** *nk* **Mixed Message (IRE)**[20] 6932 4-10-1 67 ........(p) MrJohnWilley[(5)] 11 56
(Brian Ellison) *midfield: hdwy to chse ldrs over 6f out: rdn along over 3f out: grad wknd fnl 2f* **16/1**
433- **10** 1¼ **Scurr Mist (IRE)**[379] 7146 3-10-2 68 ........ MrWHogg 1 54
(Keith Dalgleish) *t.k.h: trckd ldng pair on inner: effrt 4f out: rdn along 3f out: wknd over 2f out* **14/1**
1004 **11** 3 **Unex Michelangelo (IRE)**[16] 7042 5-10-3 67(p) MissJoannaMason[(3)] 4 48
(Michael Easterby) *nvr bttr than midfield* **20/1**
550- **12** 2 **Raven's Tower (USA)**[181] 1614 4-10-2 63 ........ MrRBirkett 2 40
(Ben Pauling) *in tch on inner: hdwy over 4f out: chsd ldrs 3f out: rdn along over 2f out: sn wknd* **11/2**[2]
1324 **13** ¾ **Deep Resolve (IRE)**[141] 2934 3-9-10 69 ........ MrABartlett[(7)] 7 44
(Alan Swinbank) *led: rdn along 4f out: hdd 3f out and sn wknd* **16/1**
P400 **14** *nk* **Pivotman**[4] 7334 6-10-8 69 ........(t) MissHBethell 15 44
(Michael Easterby) *rrd and almost uns rdr s: a in rr* **33/1**
0340 **15** ¾ **Kantara Castle (IRE)**[28] 6722 3-10-1 67 ........(t) MrPCollington 3 40
(John Mackie) *chsd ldrs: rdn along over 4f out: wknd over 3f out* **33/1**
463 **16** *nse* **Archipeligo**[18] 6982 3-9-12 67 ........ MrTHamilton[(3)] 17 40
(Iain Jardine) *dwlt and towards rr: hdwy on inner and in tch over 4f out: rdn along 3f out: sn wknd* **9/1**
0210 **17** 2 **Blue Maisey**[23] 6863 6-10-2 70 ........ MissRMTaylor[(7)] 19 39
(Edwin Tuer) *towards rr: sme hdwy on outer 6f out: rdn along over 4f out: sn wknd* **33/1**

2m 19.76s (10.36) **Going Correction** +0.975s/f (Soft)
**WFA** 3 from 4yo+ 5lb **17 Ran SP% 125.9**
Speed ratings (Par 103): **97,96,93,92,90 89,88,87,86,85 83,81,81,80,80 80,78**
CSF £114.82 CT £538.74 TOTE £12.50: £2.50, £2.20, £1.60, £8.40; EX 126.80 Trifecta £758.60.
**Owner** Mrs E A Llewellyn **Bred** Henry And Mrs Rosemary Moszkowicz **Trained** Fochriw, Caerphilly

**FOCUS**
A massive field for this amateur riders' contest, and just modest form. The third has been rated close to form.

T/Jkpt: Not won. T/Plt: £92.10 to a £1 stake. Pool: £111,889.23 - 886.11 winning tickets T/Qpdt: £3.60 to a £1 stake. Pool: £14,080.96 - 2,835.32 winning tickets JR

# 6545 NEWBURY (L-H)

Friday, October 24

**OFFICIAL GOING: Soft (5.7)**

Wind: virtually nil Weather: overcast

## 7412 JOIN HOT TO TROT FOR 2015 EBF STALLIONS MAIDEN STKS (BOBIS RACE) 6f 110y

**1:35** (1:36) (Class 4) 2-Y-O **£4,075** (£1,212; £606; £303) **Stalls** Centre

Form RPR

63 **1** **Mujassam**[16] 7037 2-9-5 0 JackMitchell 2 79
(Roger Varian) *str: trckd ldrs: rdn to press ldr over 1f out: led fnl 120yds: styd on wl: pushed out* **8/1**[3]

**2** ½ **Mobsta (IRE)** 2-9-5 0 CharlesBishop 3 78
(Mick Channon) *w'like: lengthy: trckd ldr: led after 2f: rdn and strly pressed fr over 1f out: kpt on but no ex whn hdd fnl 120yds* **7/1**[2]

4 **3** 5 **With Approval (IRE)**[8] 7223 2-9-5 0 GeorgeBaker 10 64
(Charles Hills) *w'like: str: chsd ldrs: rdn over 2f out: sn hld by front pair: kpt on same pce fnl f* **7/1**[2]

**4** 5 **Green Tornado (IRE)** 2-9-5 0 RichardKingscote 6 50
(Ralph Beckett) *str: bit bkwd: hld up towards rr: stdy prog whn swtchd lft wl over 1f out: wnt 5th ent fnl f: styd on to take 4th towards fin: nvr trbld ldrs too* **12/1**

**5** *shd* **Calima Breeze** 2-9-0 0 WilliamCarson 7 45
(Charles Hills) *neat: hmpd s: in last pair: swtchd rt 2f out: hdwy sn after: styd on nicely fnl f but no ch w ldrs: nrly snatched 4th fnl stride* **25/1**

2 **6** ¾ **King To Be (IRE)**[16] 7031 2-9-5 0 RichardHughes 9 48
(Richard Hannon) *lengthy: mid-div: wnt 4th 2f out: sn rdn: fdd fnl 120yds: lame* **1/1**[1]

**7** 5 **Spanish Danser (IRE)** 2-9-0 0 FergusSweeney 8 29
(George Baker) *leggy: green: mid-div: rdn wl over 2f out: no imp: wknd fnl f* **33/1**

**8** 1¾ **Samsamsam** 2-9-5 0 PatDobbs 5 29
(Robert Cowell) *w'like: trckd ldrs: rdn over 2f out: nvr threatened: wknd ent fnl f* **20/1**

**9** 5 **Mugharred (USA)** 2-9-5 0 DaneO'Neill 13 15
(B W Hills) *w'like: bit bkwd: s.i.s: racd keenly towards rr: rdn over 2f out: nvr any imp* **16/1**

00 **10** 7 **Trixy**[112] 3933 2-8-11 0 PhilipPrince(3) 12
(Jo Hughes) *w'like: led for over 2f: sn rdn: wknd 2f out* **100/1**

**11** 1¾ **Lady Bee (IRE)** 2-9-0 0 PatCosgrave 4
(George Baker) *w'like: mid-div: rdn wl over 2f out: wknd wl over 1f out* **66/1**

0 **12** 6 **Silence In Court (IRE)**[34] 6556 2-9-5 0 JimmyFortune 1
(Eve Johnson Houghton) *lengthy: racd keenly trcking ldrs: rdn over 2f out: sn wknd* **33/1**

1m 23.34s (4.04) **Going Correction** +0.525s/f (Yiel) 12 Ran SP% **116.7**
Speed ratings (Par 97): **97,96,90,85,84 84,78,76,70,62 60,53**
CSF £57.68 TOTE £9.30: £1.90, £2.80, £2.20; EX 50.70 Trifecta £527.00.
**Owner** Hamdan Al Maktoum **Bred** Bumble Bs, D F Powell & S Nicholls **Trained** Newmarket, Suffolk

**FOCUS**

The ground was officially soft (GoingStick 5.7) and the jockeys in the opener concurred. The rail had been moved in so all races were over the measured distances. An interesting maiden to open with in which the field raced as a group up the centre, but this looked quite a test in the conditions and the front pair had it to themselves from some way out.

## 7413 AL BASTI EQUIWORLD MAIDEN STKS (BOBIS RACE) (DIV I) 1m (S)

**2:10** (2:12) (Class 4) 2-Y-O **£5,175** (£1,540; £769; £384) **Stalls** Centre

Form RPR

42 **1** **Firmament**[18] 6985 2-9-5 0 JimmyFortune 1 82
(Jeremy Noseda) *athletic: hld up in tch: hdwy 2f out: led ent fnl f: sn drifted rt and rdn: kpt on wl* **11/4**[1]

**2** ¾ **Duretto** 2-9-5 0 OisinMurphy 4 80
(Andrew Balding) *w'like: chunky: hld up in tch: hdwy over 2f out: rdn ins fnl f: chsd wnr fnl 120yds: kpt on but a being hld towards fin* **7/1**

6 **3** 1¼ **Scooner (USA)**[32] 6604 2-9-5 0 GeorgeBaker 3 78
(Roger Charlton) *leggy: athletic: travelled wl most of way: trckd ldr: led 2f out: rdn whn hdd ent fnl f: sn hmpd: kpt on same pce* **13/2**

5 **4** 6 **Miracle Ninetynine (IRE)**[34] 6551 2-9-5 0 RichardHughes 8 64
(Richard Hannon) *tall: hld up: hdwy over 2f out: rdn over 1f out: sn one pce* **3/1**[2]

**5** ¾ **Shell Bay (USA)** 2-9-5 0 PatDobbs 7 63
(Richard Hannon) *str: bit bkwd: trckd ldrs: rdn 2f out: sn one pce* **14/1**

00 **6** 6 **Magic Circle (IRE)**[23] 6874 2-9-5 0 RichardKingscote 10 50
(Ralph Beckett) *w'like: towards rr: struggling 3f out: sme late prog past btn horses: n.d* **20/1**

**7** ½ **Locommotion** 2-9-5 0 MartinDwyer 6 48
(Jo Hughes) *leggy: bit bkwd: plld hrd: trckd ldr after 2f tl rdn over 2f out: wknd ent fnl f* **50/1**

**8** 6 **Director (IRE)** 2-9-5 0 SilvestreDeSousa 5 35
(William Haggas) *str: lw: led tl rdn 2f out: sn wknd* **4/1**[3]

**9** 24 **Mr Bissto** 2-9-5 0 LukeMorris 9
(Ian Williams) *tall: bit bkwd: hld up: hdwy after 2f: rdn over 3f out: wknd over 2f out* **33/1**

1m 47.61s (7.91) **Going Correction** +0.875s/f (Soft) 9 Ran SP% **113.8**
Speed ratings (Par 97): **95,94,93,87,86 80,79,73,49**
CSF £21.66 TOTE £2.90: £1.20, £2.80, £2.00; EX 21.30 Trifecta £190.80.
**Owner** Cheveley Park Stud **Bred** Cheveley Park Stud Ltd **Trained** Newmarket, Suffolk

**FOCUS**

Quite a test for these youngsters in the conditions.

## 7414 AL BASTI EQUIWORLD MAIDEN STKS (BOBIS RACE) (DIV II) 1m (S)

**2:45** (2:46) (Class 4) 2-Y-O **£5,175** (£1,540; £769; £384) **Stalls** Centre

Form RPR

**1** **Milky Way (IRE)** 2-9-5 0 FergusSweeney 5 75
(Gary Moore) *unf: tall: mde all: shkn up and edgd sltly lft over 1f out: kpt on wl fnl f: pushed out* **4/1**[2]

**2** 1 **Perrault (IRE)** 2-9-5 0 OscarPereira 6 73
(Ralph Beckett) *leggy: scope: hld up in tch: rdn and hdwy wl over 1f out: edgd rt: styd on fnl f: wnt 2nd towards fin* **15/2**

00 **3** 1¼ **Major Mac**[12] 7134 2-9-5 0 JohnFahy 4 70
(Hughie Morrison) *trckd ldrs: rdn to chse wnr 2f out: kpt on tl no ex whn lost 2nd towards fin* **14/1**

0 **4** 2½ **Parish (IRE)**[23] 6875 2-9-5 0 DaneO'Neill 7 65
(Roger Varian) *str: lw: trckd ldrs: disp 2nd over 2f out: rdn over 1f out: edgd lft: no ex ins fnl f* **9/1**

**5** 11 **Knight Music** 2-9-5 0 KierenFox 9 40
(Michael Attwater) *w'like: bit bkwd: wnt rt s: trckd ldrs: rdn over 2f out: wknd ent fnl f* **33/1**

**6** 1½ **Idle Talker (IRE)**[71] 5360 2-9-5 0 IrineuGoncalves 2 37
(Jose Santos) *leggy: prom: rdn over 2f out: wknd over 1f out* **50/1**

**7** 1 **Fidelity** 2-8-12 0 ChrisMeehan(7) 1 35
(Jonathan Geake) *unf: swtg: dwlt: a towards rr* **33/1**

**8** 3½ **Smart (GER)** 2-9-5 0 RichardHughes 8 27
(Richard Hannon) *athletic: in tch: rdn 2f out: nvr threatened: wknd ent fnl f* **9/2**[3]

**9** 2 **Copperopolis** 2-9-5 0 GeorgeBaker 3 23
(Roger Charlton) *str: lengthy: hld up in last pair: rdn over 3f out: sn btn* **6/4**[1]

1m 47.59s (7.89) **Going Correction** +0.875s/f (Soft) 9 Ran SP% **114.5**
Speed ratings (Par 97): **95,94,92,90,79 77,76,73,71**
CSF £32.98 TOTE £4.50: £1.40, £3.10, £3.50; EX 41.90 Trifecta £302.30.
**Owner** Patterson Hinds & Curwen **Bred** Beauty Bright Syndicate **Trained** Lower Beeding, W Sussex

**FOCUS**

This looked the weaker division, even though the time was fractionally faster than the first, and the front four pulled miles clear.

## 7415 SIR GERALD WHENT MEMORIAL NURSERY H'CAP (BOBIS RACE) 6f 8y

**3:20** (3:20) (Class 3) (0-95,93) 2-Y-O **£6,469** (£1,925; £962; £481) **Stalls** Centre

Form RPR

4023 **1** **Billyoakes (IRE)**[8] 7224 2-8-0 72 oh1 SilvestreDeSousa 4 75
(Mick Channon) *trckd ldrs: led over 1f out: sn rdn: drifted rt fnl f: hld on wl* **10/1**

4421 **2** *nk* **Vegas Rebel (IRE)**[17] 6997 2-8-5 77 LukeMorris 1 79
(Peter Chapple-Hyam) *untidy leaving stalls: in last pair: swtchd rt and hdwy 2f out: rdn and ev ch ent fnl f: kpt on but no ex towards fin* **6/4**[1]

1064 **3** 1 **Showing Character**[13] 7099 2-9-7 93 (p) RichardKingscote 2 92
(Tom Dascombe) *in tch: hdwy 2f out: sn rdn: kpt on fnl f* **10/1**

1452 **4** 1¼ **Inniscastle Lad**[48] 6135 2-8-10 82 MartinDwyer 5 77
(William Muir) *lw: trckd ldr: rdn and ev ch over 1f out: kpt on same pce fnl f* **9/2**[2]

42 **5** 1 **Hatchet Harry (IRE)**[27] 6739 2-8-4 76 ChrisCatlin 6 68
(David Evans) *led: rdn and eged rt whn hdd over 1f out: no ex fnl f* **8/1**

1050 **6** 10 **Pillar Box (IRE)**[14] 7079 2-8-12 84 LiamJones 8 46
(William Haggas) *cl up: effrt 2f out: wknd over 1f out* **25/1**

2346 **7** 8 **Grenade**[22] 6887 2-8-0 72 oh4 KieranO'Neill 7 10
(Richard Hannon) *racd keenly: trckd ldr: rdn over 2f out: wknd over 1f out* **25/1**

4414 **8** 12 **St Brelades Bay (IRE)**[105] 4143 2-9-3 89 RichardHughes 3
(Richard Hannon) *squeezed up s: in last pair: effrt 2f out: wknd ent fnl f: eased* **5/1**[3]

1m 18.22s (5.22) **Going Correction** +0.875s/f (Soft) 8 Ran SP% **111.8**
Speed ratings (Par 99): **100,99,98,96,95 81,71,55**
CSF £24.36 CT £155.16 TOTE £7.50: £1.90, £1.90, £2.60; EX 25.70 Trifecta £281.40.
**Owner** Nick & Olga Dhandsa & John & Zoe Webster **Bred** Mrs M Cusack **Trained** West Ilsley, Berks

**FOCUS**

A decent nursery in which the runners gradually edged towards the nearside rail. The first five pulled well clear.

## 7416 SMITH & WILLIAMSON FILLIES' H'CAP 1m 2f 6y

**3:55** (3:55) (Class 4) (0-85,83) 3-Y-O+ **£4,851** (£1,443; £721; £360) **Stalls** Centre

Form RPR

0430 **1** **Polar Eyes**[20] 6945 3-8-13 **77** (p) RichardKingscote 1 87
(Tom Dascombe) *trckd ldrs: rdn to ld over 1f out: styd on wl fnl f: rdn out* **16/1**

001 **2** ¾ **Dame Lucy (IRE)**[16] 7043 4-9-7 **80** OisinMurphy 11 88
(Michael Appleby) *lw: w ldr: led over 2f out: sn rdn: hdd over 1f out: styd on gamely but hld fnl 100yds* **7/2**[1]

2145 **3** ¾ **Thatchereen (IRE)**[54] 5948 3-8-7 **74** LouisSteward(3) 5 81
(Michael Bell) *trckd ldrs: rdn over 2f out: styd on same pce fnl f* **14/1**

3331 **4** *nk* **Dream Child (IRE)**[24] 6839 3-9-2 **80** SilvestreDeSousa 8 86
(Charlie Appleby) *lw: in tch: tk clsr order 3f out: rdn 2f out: styd on same pce fnl f* **11/2**[2]

1052 **5** 1¾ **Palerma**[37] 6459 3-8-13 **77** CharlesBishop 7 80
(Mick Channon) *mid-div: rdn over 2f out: styd on ent fnl f: nvr threatened ldrs* **10/1**

3335 **6** *nk* **Miss Crystal (IRE)**[51] 6026 3-8-7 **71** MartinDwyer 2 74
(Charles Hills) *swtg: led: rdn and hdd over 2f out: kpt chsng ldrs tl no ex fnl 120yds* **25/1**

0644 **7** 2 **Subtle Knife**[18] 6990 5-8-13 **72** WilliamCarson 3 71
(Giles Bravery) *towards rr of midfield: rdn and stdy prog fr 2f out: styd on same pce fnl f* **12/1**

4315 **8** *hd* **Ligeia**[37] 6459 3-8-12 **76** PatDobbs 12 74
(Richard Hannon) *mid-div: rdn over 3f out: styd on fnl f: nvr trbld ldrs* **20/1**

0006 **9** 5 **Lady Tyne**[30] 6665 3-9-1 **79** LiamJones 14 68
(Roger Charlton) *mid-div: rdn 3f out: wknd over 1f out* **14/1**

0360 **10** ½ **Martinas Delight (USA)**[16] 7043 4-8-7 **73** GaryMahon(7) 4 61
(Timothy Jarvis) *hld up towards rr: hdwy in centre fr over 3f out: sn rdn: wknd over 1f out* **33/1**

5646 **11** 1 **Hot Coffee (IRE)**[27] 6746 3-9-5 **83** (p) GeorgeBaker 9 69
(Tom Dascombe) *a towards rr* **10/1**

3103 **12** ¾ **Loch Ma Naire (IRE)**[11] 7161 3-9-0 **78** JimmyFortune 6 63
(Ed Dunlop) *mid-div: effrt 3f out: nvr threatened: wknd ent fnl f* **7/1**[3]

6345 **13** 2¼ **Dalmarella Dancer (IRE)**[20] 6945 3-7-12 **69** (p) JordanVaughan(7) 15 49
(K R Burke) *swtg: trckd ldrs: rdn 3f out: wknd over 1f out* **25/1**

1- **14** 13 **Curious Mind**[309] 8348 4-8-13 **72** LukeMorris 10 28
(Sir Mark Prescott Bt) *s.i.s: sn mid-div: struggling to hold pl over 5f out: rdn over 3f out: sn btn* **7/1**[3]

2m 13.44s (4.64) **Going Correction** +0.625s/f (Yiel)
**WFA** 3 from 4yo+ 5lb 14 Ran SP% **123.1**
Speed ratings (Par 102): **106,105,104,104,103 102,101,101,97,96 95,95,93,83**
CSF £69.77 CT £840.06 TOTE £19.60: £4.80, £1.50, £4.70; EX 91.20 Trifecta £1989.50.
**Owner** The Illusionists **Bred** Societa Agricola Gem Srl **Trained** Malpas, Cheshire

**FOCUS**
A competitive fillies' handicap run at a fair pace. Those that raced handily were at an advantage. The fourth has been rated close to her AW win.

## 7417 TKP SURFACING H'CAP (BOBIS RACE) 1m 7y(R)
4:30 (4:31) (Class 4) (0-85,84) 3-Y-O £4,851 (£1,443; £721; £360) Stalls Centre

Form RPR
6400 1 **Ice Slice (IRE)**[18] 6990 3-8-9 75 RyanTate(3) 11 85
(James Eustace) *lw: hld up towards rr: c to centre ent st: gd hdwy over 2f out: led over 1f out: styd on strly: rdn out* 10/1
2501 2 3 **Tullia (IRE)**[11] 7160 3-9-3 80 6ex (b) LukeMorris 6 83
(William Knight) *led at decent pce: rdn and hdd over 1f out: kpt on but hld fnl f* 5/1[2]
512 3 3 3/4 **Santa Teresa (IRE)**[21] 6904 3-9-0 77 SilvestreDeSousa 7 71
(William Haggas) *lw: stdd s: c to centre ent st: hdwy over 3f out: rdn over 2f out: wnt 3rd ent fnl f: styd on same pce* 4/1[1]
3125 4 1/2 **Arrowzone**[20] 6936 3-9-7 84 JimmyFortune 10 77
(Garry Moss) *in tch: c to centre ent st: rdn and edgd lft 3f out: styd on to go 4th ins fnl f* 11/2[3]
1626 5 3/4 **Pageant Belle**[29] 6681 3-9-1 78 PatDobbs 3 70
(Roger Charlton) *lw: in tch: rdn to chse ldrs over 2f out: wnt 4th ent fnl f tl no ex towards fin* 12/1
0444 6 1 **Aran Sky (IRE)**[8] 7225 3-8-0 70 oh3 (v[1]) JordanVaughan(7) 4 59
(K R Burke) *trckd ldr: rdn 3f out: kpt chsng ldrs tl fdd ins fnl f* 22/1
0103 7 4 **Hostile Fire (IRE)**[18] 6990 3-9-2 79 (p) OisinMurphy 8 59
(Ed de Giles) *mid-div: hdwy over 2f out: sn rdn: wknd fnl f* 7/1
0410 8 2 3/4 **Brown Diamond (IRE)**[48] 6129 3-8-12 75 WilliamCarson 1 49
(Charles Hills) *swtg: hld up towards rr: hdwy on inner 3f out: sn rdn: wknd over 1f out* 12/1
3245 9 8 **Zain Empire**[22] 6885 3-9-2 79 (p) LiamJones 9 34
(Robert Cowell) *s.i.s: sn mid-div: rdn 3f out: sn btn* 8/1
3233 10 1 3/4 **Grevillea (IRE)**[11] 7160 3-9-3 80 WilliamTwiston-Davies 5 31
(Mick Channon) *swtg: chsd ldrs: rdn 3f out: wknd 2f out* 15/2
0460 11 10 **After The Goldrush**[63] 5629 3-8-10 73 (b) RichardHughes 2
(Richard Hannon) *rdn 3f out: a towards rr* 20/1

1m 42.49s (3.79) **Going Correction** +0.625s/f (Yiel) 11 Ran SP% 121.0
Speed ratings (Par 103): **106,103,99,98,98 97,93,90,82,80 70**
CSF £61.20 CT £244.89 TOTE £13.10: £2.40, £1.90, £2.00; EX 88.70 Trifecta £615.50.
**Owner** The MacDougall Two **Bred** Kilfrush Stud **Trained** Newmarket, Suffolk

**FOCUS**
A fair handicap in which those who made their challenges widest were at an advantage. The form has been rated cautiously, with the runner-up to her Windsor figure.

## 7418 INTERACTIVE MAIDEN STKS 1m 2f 6y
5:00 (5:01) (Class 4) 3-Y-O+ £4,690 (£1,395; £697; £348) Stalls Centre

Form RPR
42 1 **Court Room (IRE)**[204] 1258 3-9-5 0 RobertHavlin 7 79
(John Gosden) *leggy: unf: racd keenly: trckd ldr: rdn to chal over 1f out: led jst ins fnl f: styd on wl to assert fnl 100yds* 2/1[1]
46 2 1 1/4 **Jeremy's Jet (IRE)**[16] 7032 3-9-5 0 OisinMurphy 2 76
(Andrew Balding) *leggy: t.k.h early: in tch: hdwy 3f out: rdn to chal 2f out: led over 1f out: hdd jst ins fnl f: no ex fnl 100yds* 13/2
3 nk **Ocean Boulevard** 3-9-0 0 DaneO'Neill 3 70+
(Luca Cumani) *leggy: trckd ldrs: rdn 2f out: styd on wl ins fnl f: wnt 3rd towards fin* 6/1
4 1 1/4 **Lunasea (IRE)** 3-9-5 0 LemosdeSouza 6 73+
(Luca Cumani) *w'like: scope: str: lw: wnt lft s: in tch: pushed along and hdwy 3f out: led 2f out tl over 1f out: no ex fnl 120yds: lost 3rd towards fin* 7/2[2]
5 17 **Fawn** 3-9-0 0 LiamJones 4 35
(William Haggas) *cmpt: lw: led: rdn and hdd 2f out: sn wknd* 5/1[3]
6 1 **Hong Kong Joe** 4-9-10 0 CharlesBishop 5 38
(Lydia Richards) *w'like: bit bkwd: s.i.s: sn in tch: pushed along 4f out: btn 2f out* 33/1
4 7 4 **Wowee**[36] 6483 3-9-5 0 JimmyFortune 1 31
(Tony Carroll) *w'like: hld up: effrt 3f out: wknd over 1f out* 8/1

2m 18.46s (9.66) **Going Correction** +0.875s/f (Soft)
**WFA** 3 from 4yo 5lb 7 Ran SP% 113.9
Speed ratings (Par 105): **96,95,94,93,80 79,76**
CSF £15.52 TOTE £2.30: £1.30, £4.70; EX 17.30 Trifecta £66.60.
**Owner** HRH Princess Haya Of Jordan **Bred** Gerrardstown House Stud **Trained** Newmarket, Suffolk

**FOCUS**
Older-horse maidens at this time of year tend not to be strong affairs and this was no exception. The fact that the first three home managed to fill those positions despite all taking a strong hold at various stages suggests the form is modest. The front four pulled miles clear. The winner has been rated close to his spring AW form.

## 7419 RACINGUK.COM "HANDS AND HEELS" APPRENTICE SERIES FINAL H'CAP 2m
5:30 (5:30) (Class 5) (0-75,76) 4-Y-O+ £2,587 (£770; £384; £192) Stalls High

Form RPR
6400 1 **Jezza**[23] 6881 8-8-11 61 (bt) KieranShoemark 4 71+
(Victor Dartnall) *s.i.s: pushed along towards rr early: smooth hdwy fr 4f out: led over 2f out: sn in command: eased towards fin* 12/1
4211 2 3/4 **Aiyana**[12] 7129 4-9-12 76 6ex DavidParkes 5 82
(Hughie Morrison) *trckd ldrs: rdn and ev ch briefly over 2f out: sn no ch w wnr: styd on same pce* 5/2[1]
0410 3 1 1/4 **Medburn Cutler**[43] 6264 4-8-2 55 oh1 (p) AaronJones(3) 6 60
(Paul Henderson) *hld up towards rr: hdwy fr 4f out: rdn 3f out: styd on same pce fnl 2f: wnt 3rd fnl 100yds* 14/1
-45U 4 1/2 **Oetzi**[156] 2464 6-9-6 70 GaryMahon 8 74
(Timothy Jarvis) *trckd ldrs: led over 2f out tl rdn over 2f out: kpt chsng ldng pair tl no ex fnl 100yds* 20/1
220 5 8 **Zarosa (IRE)**[10] 7177 5-8-6 56 HectorCrouch 10 50
(John Berry) *mid-div: rdn 3f out: styd on same pce fnl 2f: nvr trbld ldrs* 8/1
003 6 3 3/4 **Bondi Mist (IRE)**[92] 4568 5-8-2 55 oh5 (v) PaddyPilley(3) 9 45
(Jonathan Geake) *hld up towards rr: midfield over 5f out: effrt 3f out: wknd over 1f out* 33/1
5161 7 2 3/4 **Glens Wobbly**[51] 6027 6-8-7 57 ChrisMeehan 2 44
(Jonathan Geake) *mid-div: hdwy 4f out: rdn 3f out: wknd over 1f out* 14/1
2143 8 nk **Noor Al Haya (IRE)**[25] 6817 4-8-10 60 AnnaHesketh 1 46
(Laura Mongan) *stdd s: last: sme hdwy 3f out: nvr threatened to get on terms: wknd over 1f out* 9/2[2]
6603 9 1/2 **Musical Moon**[23] 6881 4-8-11 64 JoshDoyle(3) 3 50
(Lady Herries) *trckd ldrs tl over 3f out: n.d in rr after* 9/1
000/ 10 1 1/2 **Promised Wings (GER)**[217] 521 7-8-6 56 (p) RobHornby 7 40
(Chris Gordon) *trckd ldr: jnd ldr over 5f out tl over 3f out: sn wknd* 12/1
6664 11 1 1/4 **Opera Buff**[12] 7129 5-9-7 74 (tp) PaddyBradley(3) 11 56
(Jose Santos) *led tl over 3f out: sn wknd* 5/1[3]

3m 48.71s (16.71) **Going Correction** +1.125s/f (Soft) 11 Ran SP% 121.0
Speed ratings (Par 103): **103,102,102,101,97 95,94,94,94,93 92**
CSF £43.33 CT £446.70 TOTE £11.40: £3.40, £1.70, £4.70; EX 41.10 Trifecta £1209.70.
**Owner** Mrs J Scrivens **Bred** C P Ranson **Trained** Brayford, Devon

**FOCUS**
A modest apprentice staying handicap run at something of a stop-start gallop. The first four came clear. The winner has been rated to his best form over the past wo years.
T/Plt: £256.30 to a £1 stake. Pool: £66,781.49 - 190.19 winning tickets T/Qpdt: £50.80 to a £1 stake. Pool: £6,804.57 - 99.00 winning tickets TM

# 7361 WOLVERHAMPTON (A.W) (L-H)
### Friday, October 24

**OFFICIAL GOING: Tapeta: standard**
Wind: Light across Weather: Overcast

## 7420 MONSTERBET CLASSIFIED STKS (TAPETA) 5f 216y
5:40 (5:41) (Class 6) 3-Y-O+ £2,264 (£673; £336; £168) Stalls Low

Form RPR
5022 1 **Wedgewood Estates**[25] 6816 3-9-0 55 LiamKeniry 11 62
(Tony Carroll) *hld up: hdwy over 1f out: rdn to ld wl ins fnl f: edgd rt: styd on* 9/2[2]
6306 2 1 1/2 **Redalani (IRE)**[31] 6638 4-9-1 49 (tp) ShaneKelly 1 57
(Alan Brown) *led: rdn over 1f out: hdd wl ins fnl f: sn hung rt: styd on same pce* 50/1
0540 3 1 1/4 **Encapsulated**[53] 5977 4-9-1 50 (p) MartinLane 5 53
(Roger Ingram) *prom: racd keenly: nt clr run over 3f out: rdn over 1f out: hung rt and styd on same pce wl ins fnl f: eased whn hld nr fin* 8/1[3]
0200 4 1 1/4 **High Tone**[16] 7036 4-9-1 49 (p) FrannyNorton 9 49
(Dean Ivory) *a.p: rdn to chse ldr over 2f out: no ex ins fnl f* 16/1
0405 5 3/4 **Secret Applause**[15] 7058 3-8-11 54 ConnorBeasley(3) 10 47
(Michael Dods) *hld up in tch: rdn over 1f out: styd on u.p* 11/1
4032 6 3/4 **Fujin**[8] 7222 3-9-0 55 (b) JasonHart 4 44
(Shaun Harris) *prom: hmpd 5f out: rdn over 1f out: styd on same pce* 3/1[1]
0644 7 1 3/4 **Princess Rose**[24] 6834 3-9-0 48 (v) BenCurtis 3 39
(John Weymes) *chsd ldr tl rdn over 2f out: wknd ins fnl f* 33/1
6203 8 1 **Brean Splash Susie**[8] 7221 3-8-9 50 RyanWhile(5) 13 35
(Bill Turner) *chsd ldrs: rdn over 2f out: wknd fnl f* 28/1
0132 9 nse **Thewestwalian (USA)**[17] 7010 6-8-10 52 ShelleyBirkett(5) 7 35
(Peter Hiatt) *hld up: rdn over 1f out: nvr on terms* 9/2[2]
00-3 10 nk **Kingsway Lad (IRE)**[232] 865 3-9-0 51 (t) DaleSwift 6 34
(Derek Shaw) *sn pushed along in rr: rdn over 1f out: n.d* 10/1
5246 11 1/2 **Aphrilis (IRE)**[27] 6765 3-8-9 55 (p) MeganCarberry(5) 12 33
(Brian Ellison) *hld up: rdn over 1f out: a in rr* 28/1
360 12 nse **Clear Focus (IRE)**[42] 6297 3-9-0 51 (v) DougieCostello 2 33
(Brendan Powell) *sn pushed along in mid-div: rdn and lost pl over 2f out* 25/1
2300 13 4 1/2 **Daneglow (IRE)**[203] 1282 4-8-12 47 DannyBrock(3) 8 18
(Mike Murphy) *hld up: rdn over 1f out: a in rr* 28/1

1m 14.45s (-0.05) **Going Correction** -0.025s/f (Stan)
**WFA** 3 from 4yo+ 1lb 13 Ran SP% 114.9
Speed ratings (Par 101): **99,97,95,93,92 91,89,88,87,87 86,86,80**
CSF £226.54 TOTE £5.40: £3.30, £19.50, £1.50; EX 290.20 Trifecta £1261.00.
**Owner** Wedgewood Estates **Bred** Wedgewood Estates **Trained** Cropthorne, Worcs

**FOCUS**
A modest contest run at a fair pace. The field headed stands' side. The winner has been rated as running a length pb.

## 7421 MONSTERBET (S) STKS (TAPETA) 5f 216y
6:15 (6:16) (Class 5) 2-Y-O £2,911 (£866; £432; £216) Stalls Low

Form RPR
3106 1 **Little**[7] 7258 2-8-11 65 TomQueally 4 65
(Jamie Osborne) *s.i.s: hld up: hdwy over 2f out: nt clr run over 1f out: rdn to ld ins fnl f: r.o* 5/1[3]
0240 2 1 1/4 **Tumut (IRE)**[7] 7257 2-8-11 65 LiamKeniry 3 61
(Mick Channon) *a.p: chsd ldr over 2f out: led over 1f out: rdn and hdd ins fnl f: styd on same pce* 8/1
30 3 1 3/4 **Penelope Pitstop**[13] 7097 2-8-6 0 JasonHart 12 51
(Keith Dalgleish) *hld up: swtchd lft and hdwy over 1f out: sn rdn: r.o: nt rch ldrs* 4/1[2]
0120 4 1 1/2 **Multi Quest**[78] 5119 2-8-11 62 FrannyNorton 6 52
(Jo Hughes) *a.p: rdn over 2f out: no ex fnl f* 10/1
0450 5 hd **River Spirit**[9] 7190 2-8-11 58 SamHitchcott 9 51
(Mick Channon) *mid-div: hdwy on outer over 2f out: sn rdn: styd on same pce fnl f* 22/1
1623 6 nk **Millar Rose (IRE)**[20] 6941 2-8-11 65 MichaelStainton 10 50
(K R Burke) *s.i.s: hld up: hdwy over 2f out: rdn over 1f out: styd on same pce fnl f* 15/2
0430 7 4 1/2 **Aqlette**[29] 6678 2-8-6 64 PaoloSirigu 13 32
(Marco Botti) *chsd ldrs: rdn and hung lft over 1f out: sn wknd* 3/1[1]
5103 8 hd **Smart Stepper (IRE)**[31] 6645 2-8-13 60 ConnorBeasley(3) 2 41
(Michael Dods) *chsd ldr tl led 1/2-way: rdn and hdd over 1f out: wknd ins fnl f* 14/1
0000 9 2 **Tantric Lady**[24] 6842 2-8-4 46 ow1 (be) BillyCray(3) 1 26
(Alan McCabe) *s.s: outpcd* 100/1
0000 10 1 1/2 **Soldier Sam (IRE)**[31] 6642 2-8-7 52 ow1 MeganCarberry(5) 5 26
(Brian Ellison) *hld up: rdn over 2f out: a in rr* 11/1
00 11 2 1/2 **Gleaming Princess**[40] 6363 2-8-6 0 BenCurtis 8 13
(Milton Bradley) *led to 1/2-way: wknd over 1f out* 100/1

1m 14.9s (0.40) **Going Correction** -0.025s/f (Stan) 11 Ran SP% 115.0
Speed ratings (Par 95): **96,94,92,90,89 89,83,83,80,78 75**
CSF £43.21 TOTE £5.20: £1.50, £3.30, £2.10; EX 44.50 Trifecta £293.60.There was no bid for the winner. Aqlette was claimed by David Evans for 7000gns.
**Owner** A F Tait **Bred** Highclere Stud Ltd **Trained** Upper Lambourn, Berks


The Form Book, Raceform Ltd, Newbury, RG14 5SJ

**FOCUS**
A fair pace for this open seller.

## 7422 MONSTERBET H'CAP (TAPETA) 1m 5f 194y
6:50 (6:50) (Class 4) (0-85,82) 3-Y-0+ £4,851 (£1,443; £721; £360) Stalls Low

Form RPR

3601 1 **Norab (GER)**[37] 6461 3-9-1 78 MartinLane 3 89+
(Marco Botti) *chsd ldr tl rdn to ld 1f out: edgd lft: styd on* 3/1[1]

0440 2 1 3/4 **Gabrial's Star**[13] 7107 5-10-0 82 (b) GeorgeChaloner 6 90+
(Richard Fahey) *hld up: hdwy over 2f out: rdn over 1f out: r.o to go 2nd post: nt rch wnr* 7/2[2]

2121 3 hd **Kelamita (IRE)**[10] 7182 3-8-8 71 6ex (b) RaulDaSilva 4 79
(Hughie Morrison) *led: rdn over 2f out: hdd 1f out: styd on same pce ins fnl f: lost 2nd post* 10/1

524 4 4 1/2 **Arizona John (IRE)**[27] 6761 9-9-9 77 FrannyNorton 8 79
(John Mackie) *chsd ldrs: rdn over 2f out: edgd lft and no ex ins fnl f* 15/2

4631 5 hd **Two Jabs**[21] 6901 4-9-10 78 PatCosgrave 5 79
(Mark Brisbourne) *plld hrd and prom: rdn over 2f out: styd on same pce fr over 1f out* 11/2[3]

31-1 6 1 1/4 **Sunblazer (IRE)**[8] 6721 4-9-13 81 (tp) DougieCostello 7 81
(Kim Bailey) *hld up in tch: rdn over 1f out: no ex fnl f* 8/1

3321 7 hd **Russian Royale**[23] 6881 4-9-6 74 (p) ShaneKelly 9 73
(Stuart Kittow) *hld up: sme hdwy over 1f out: sn rdn: no ex fnl f* 14/1

1104 8 3/4 **Sweetheart Abbey**[16] 7033 3-9-5 82 (p) TomQueally 2 80
(William Knight) *chsd ldrs: rdn over 3f out: wknd ins fnl f* 8/1

0400 9 3/4 **Back Burner (IRE)**[34] 6566 6-9-4 72 SamHitchcott 12 69
(Dai Burchell) *s.s: hld up: racd keenly: rdn over 2f out: hdwy and nt clr run over 1f out: wknd ins fnl f* 80/1

3142 10 11 **Last Minute Lisa (IRE)**[36] 6500 4-9-5 73 RobertWinston 1 55
(Sylvester Kirk) *s.i.s: hld up: rdn over 3f out: sn bhd* 14/1

6300 11 2 3/4 **Perennial**[24] 6099 5-9-9 77 (b) TonyHamilton 11 55
(Philip Kirby) *prom tl rdn and wknd over 2f out* 14/1

3m 5.16s (0.36) **Going Correction** -0.025s/f (Stan)
**WFA** 3 from 4yo+ 9lb 11 Ran SP% **118.1**
Speed ratings (Par 105): **97,96,95,93,93 92,92,91,91,85 83**
CSF £13.36 CT £93.65 TOTE £4.00: £1.80, £1.90, £2.30; EX 16.70.
**Owner** Marc Keller **Bred** Gestut Etzean **Trained** Newmarket, Suffolk

**FOCUS**
A competitive handicap run at a steady pace. It suited those prominent. The runner-up has been rated as matching his old Polytrack best.

## 7423 MONSTERBET.CO.UK H'CAP (TAPETA) (DIV I) 7f 32y
7:20 (7:21) (Class 6) (0-60,60) 3-Y-0+ £2,264 (£673; £336; £168) Stalls High

Form RPR

0002 1 **Kraka Gym (IRE)**[34] 6568 3-8-10 51 (b) GrahamGibbons 4 65
(Michael Easterby) *prom: hmpd and lost pl after 1f: nt clr run 1/2-way: hdwy and nt clr run over 1f out: shkn up to ld ins fnl f: rdn clr* 11/4[2]

-663 2 4 **Humour (IRE)**[7] 7259 3-9-3 58 FrederikTylicki 11 61
(Roger Varian) *hld up: hdwy 1/2-way: led over 1f out: rdn and hdd ins fnl f: styd on same pce* 11/8[1]

0536 3 1 1/4 **Larghetto (USA)**[3] 7368 6-9-7 60 LukeMorris 7 61
(Ian Williams) *hld up: hdwy over 2f out: rdn over 1f out: styd on same pce fnl f* 7/1[3]

0360 4 3/4 **Street Boss (IRE)**[14] 7078 3-9-0 55 (v) DougieCostello 3 53
(Jedd O'Keeffe) *hld up: rdn over 2f out: styd on u.p fr over 1f out: nvr nrr* 40/1

2014 5 1 **Rocky's Pride (IRE)**[32] 6600 8-9-2 55 GeorgeChaloner 6 51
(Richard Whitaker) *prom: rdn over 2f out: no ex fnl f* 22/1

3351 6 1/2 **Ice Mayden**[37] 6454 3-8-10 56 JoeDoyle(5) 8 50
(Bryan Smart) *hld up: rdn over 2f out: nvr on terms* 10/1

0640 7 3 **Mad Endeavour**[17] 7025 3-9-3 58 (b[1]) MartinLane 2 44
(Stuart Kittow) *sn led: hdd over 4f out: rdn over 2f out: wknd fnl f* 33/1

0305 8 1 **Jessy Mae**[28] 6717 3-8-4 50 (p) TimClark(5) 9 34
(Derek Haydn Jones) *chsd ldr tl led over 4f out: rdn and hdd over 1f out: wknd ins fnl f* 50/1

0050 9 4 1/2 **Prigsnov Dancer (IRE)**[17] 7025 9-8-8 52 TobyAtkinson(5) 12 25
(Deborah Sanderson) *prom: chsd ldr 1/2-way: rdn and ev ch over 2f out: wknd over 1f out* 40/1

0063 10 6 **Prince Of Passion (CAN)**[13] 7111 6-9-2 55 (v) RussKennemore 5 12
(Derek Shaw) *chsd ldrs: rdn over 2f out: sn wknd* 40/1

-004 11 4 **Nashmi**[14] 7077 3-9-5 60 (v) ShaneKelly 10 6
(George Peckham) *hld up: plld hrd: hdwy on outer over 2f out: sn rdn and wknd* 10/1

1m 28.31s (-0.49) **Going Correction** -0.025s/f (Stan)
**WFA** 3 from 6yo+ 2lb 11 Ran SP% **116.0**
Speed ratings (Par 101): **101,96,95,94,93 92,89,87,82,75 71**
CSF £6.33 CT £22.35 TOTE £3.60: £1.60, £1.02, £3.70; EX 9.70 Trifecta £43.60.
**Owner** S A Hollings **Bred** E Lonergan **Trained** Sheriff Hutton, N Yorks

**FOCUS**
A decent pace for division one of this modest handicap. The winner has been rated to the best view of her 3yo form.

## 7424 MONSTERBET.CO.UK H'CAP (TAPETA) (DIV II) 7f 32y
7:50 (7:51) (Class 6) (0-60,59) 3-Y-0+ £2,264 (£673; £336; £168) Stalls High

Form RPR

6053 1 **Sewn Up**[3] 7364 4-9-4 56 (p) PhillipMakin 12 64
(Keith Dalgleish) *sn prom: chsd ldr over 5f out: led over 1f out: sn rdn: jst hld on* 3/1[1]

2022 2 shd **El Mirage (IRE)**[10] 7188 4-9-6 58 (p) RobertWinston 1 65
(Dean Ivory) *chsd ldrs: rdn over 1f out: r.o* 4/1[2]

0630 3 1/2 **Applejack Lad**[7] 7259 3-9-5 59 (t) JackMitchell 8 63
(John Ryan) *hld up: hdwy u.p over 1f out: edgd lft: r.o* 10/1

132 4 nk **Wotalad**[36] 6481 4-9-6 58 (p) GeorgeChaloner 11 63
(Richard Whitaker) *led: rdn over 2f out: hdd over 1f out: styd on* 5/1[3]

2006 5 1/2 **Baltic Prince (IRE)**[27] 6766 4-9-0 52 RaulDaSilva 10 55
(Paul Green) *chsd ldrs: rdn over 2f out: styd on* 25/1

6324 6 1/2 **Swiss Lait**[17] 7025 3-8-13 56 CamHardie(3) 7 57
(David Elsworth) *hld up: rdn over 1f out: r.o ins fnl f: nt trble ldrs* 7/1

6064 7 3/4 **Natalia**[20] 6940 5-8-12 50 RobertTart 6 50
(Andrew Hollinshead) *hld up: rdn over 2f out: hdwy over 1f out: r.o* 14/1

6205 8 1/2 **Sweet Lily Pea (USA)**[31] 6647 3-8-6 51 (v[1]) TimClark(5) 4 49
(Mrs Ilka Gansera-Leveque) *hld up: hdwy over 2f out: rdn over 1f out: styd on* 14/1

6546 9 1/2 **Adimendis (IRE)**[56] 5893 3-8-12 55 ConnorBeasley(3) 2 52
(Michael Dods) *hld up: nt clr run and r.o ins fnl f: nvr trbld ldrs* 8/1

3000 10 5 **Monte Cassino (IRE)**[67] 5510 9-8-12 55 (e) AdamCarter(5) 5 40
(Bryan Smart) *hld up: rdn over 2f out: n.d* 22/1

0030 11 2 1/4 **La Danza**[34] 6543 4-8-10 48 (v) SamHitchcott 3 27
(Lisa Williamson) *mid-div: rdn over 2f out: wknd ins fnl f* 33/1

5000 12 5 **Bay Street Belle**[67] 5499 3-9-3 57 TomEaves 9 22
(Alison Hutchinson) *chsd ldrs: rdn over 2f out: wknd over 1f out* 80/1

1m 28.93s (0.13) **Going Correction** -0.025s/f (Stan)
**WFA** 3 from 4yo+ 2lb 12 Ran SP% **120.1**
Speed ratings (Par 101): **98,97,97,96,96 95,94,94,93,88 85,79**
CSF £14.24 CT £108.87 TOTE £4.60: £1.30, £1.70, £3.20; EX 19.90 Trifecta £234.10.
**Owner** John Kelly **Bred** M E Broughton **Trained** Carluke, S Lanarks

**FOCUS**
The second division of this modest handicap was run at a steady pace. The runner-up and fourth have been rated close to their recent marks.

## 7425 MONSTERBET BRITISH STALLION STUDS EBF MEDIAN AUCTION MAIDEN STKS (TAPETA) 1m 1f 103y
8:20 (8:22) (Class 5) 2-Y-O £2,911 (£866; £432; £216) Stalls Low

Form RPR

5 1 **Life Less Ordinary (IRE)**[21] 6903 2-9-5 0 TomQueally 1 72
(Jamie Osborne) *a.p: hmpd over 2f out: shkn up to ld over 1f out: rdn and edgd rt ins fnl f: r.o wl* 6/1[3]

5243 2 1 3/4 **Classic Villager**[32] 6602 2-9-5 72 RobertWinston 5 68
(Philip Hide) *chsd ldrs: rdn and ev ch over 1f out: hmpd ins fnl f: styd on same pce* 3/1[2]

3 5 **Moydin** 2-9-5 0 CharlesBishop 6 59
(Mick Channon) *hld up: hdwy over 1f out: styd on same pce fnl f* 15/2

6502 4 1 **Goolagong Girl (IRE)**[24] 6842 2-8-11 54 CamHardie(3) 3 52
(Jane Chapple-Hyam) *led 1f: led again 6f out: hdd over 4f out: led over 2f out: rdn and hdd over 1f out: wknd ins fnl f* 18/1

5 nk **Cocker** 2-9-5 0 RichardKingscote 8 56
(Tom Dascombe) *s.i.s: hld up: pushed along over 2f out: hung lft fr over 1f out: nvr on terms* 5/2[1]

6 3/4 **Inflexiball** 2-9-0 0 FrannyNorton 2 50
(John Mackie) *hld up: hdwy over 1f out: wknd ins fnl f* 66/1

5 7 1 3/4 **Brosnan (IRE)**[14] 7084 2-9-0 0 PatCosgrave 7 47
(Noel Quinlan) *prom: chsd ldr over 2f out: sn rdn and ev ch: wknd ins fnl f* 3/1[2]

0 8 5 **Poetic License (IRE)**[16] 7039 2-9-5 0 LukeMorris 4 42
(Sir Mark Prescott Bt) *racd keenly: led after 1f: hdd 6f out: led again over 4f out: hdd over 2f out: sn edgd lft: wknd over 1f out* 40/1

2m 1.59s (0.79) **Going Correction** -0.025s/f (Stan) 8 Ran SP% **113.8**
Speed ratings (Par 95): **95,93,89,88,87 87,85,81**
CSF £24.12 TOTE £5.10: £1.20, £1.10, £5.00; EX 24.70 Trifecta £136.90.
**Owner** Michael Buckley & Mrs Karima Burman **Bred** Aidan Sexton **Trained** Upper Lambourn, Berks

**FOCUS**
Not a strong maiden run at a steady pace.

## 7426 ENHANCED ODDS AT MONSTERBET H'CAP (TAPETA) 1m 1f 103y
8:50 (8:50) (Class 6) (0-60,60) 3-Y-0+ £2,264 (£673; £336; £168) Stalls Low

Form RPR

0002 1 **Innoko (FR)**[7] 7256 4-9-5 55 LukeMorris 1 64
(Tony Carroll) *hld up: nt clr run over 2f out: hdwy over 1f out: rdn to ld ins fnl f: jst hld on* 11/1

0460 2 hd **Bridge That Gap**[3] 7359 6-9-9 59 (p) JimmyQuinn 6 67
(Roger Ingram) *s.i.s: hld up: hdwy over 1f out: r.o* 8/1

54 3 2 3/4 **Assoluta (IRE)**[46] 6193 3-8-13 56 CamHardie(3) 9 58
(Sylvester Kirk) *chsd ldrs: rdn over 1f out: nt clr run ins fnl f: styd on* 22/1

0000 4 1/2 **Sabre Rock**[31] 6635 4-9-3 53 (t) SteveDrowne 12 54
(John Best) *chsd ldr: led over 7f out: hdd over 6f out: led again over 3f out: rdn and hdd over 1f out: styd on same pce* 50/1

0002 5 1/2 **Delightful Sleep**[10] 7187 6-8-11 50 DeclanBates(3) 2 50
(David Evans) *mid-div: hdwy over 2f out: rdn to ld over 1f out: hdd and no ex ins fnl f* 7/1[2]

240 6 1/2 **Gabrial The Thug (FR)**[13] 7098 4-9-10 60 (t) GeorgeChaloner 4 59
(Richard Fahey) *hld up: rdn over 1f out: hung lft and r.o ins fnl f: nt rch ldrs* 15/2[3]

5060 7 2 **Yourinthewill (USA)**[15] 7068 6-9-10 60 StephenCraine 5 55
(Daniel Mark Loughnane) *prom: hmpd wl over 1f out: edgd lft and no ex fnl f* 7/1[2]

0266 8 8 **Neuf Des Coeurs**[25] 6823 3-9-4 58 PhillipMakin 3 36
(Keith Dalgleish) *chsd ldrs: rdn over 3f out: wknd over 1f out* 12/1

4660 9 1 1/4 **Jazri**[6] 7292 3-9-6 60 BenCurtis 10 35
(Milton Bradley) *hld up: rdn over 2f out: a in rr* 80/1

0002 10 1/2 **Prostate Awareness (IRE)**[25] 6823 3-8-13 58 (v) JackGarritty(5) 8 32
(Patrick Holmes) *led: hdd over 7f out: led again over 6f out: rdn and hdd over 3f out: wknd over 1f out* 20/1

4331 11 6 **Lola Montez (IRE)**[13] 7115 3-9-4 58 (b) TedDurcan 11 20
(David Lanigan) *pushed along early in rr: hdwy to go prom over 7f out: rdn over 3f out: wknd over 1f out* 15/8[1]

-135 12 6 **Night's Watch**[263] 458 4-9-1 58 DavidPrichard(7) 7 7
(Dai Burchell) *hld up: rdn and wknd over 2f out* 28/1

1m 59.85s (-0.95) **Going Correction** -0.025s/f (Stan)
**WFA** 3 from 4yo+ 4lb 12 Ran SP% **114.4**
Speed ratings (Par 101): **103,102,100,99,99 99,97,90,89,88 83,77**
CSF £87.27 CT £1895.36 TOTE £13.40: £3.70, £2.50, £4.80; EX 96.60 Trifecta £753.00.
**Owner** Mill House Racing Syndicate **Bred** Marquise Soledad De Moratalla **Trained** Cropthorne, Worcs

**FOCUS**
They went a fair pace for this moderate handicap. The runner-up has been rated as running his best race since early 2013, while the third helps set the standard.

## 7427 EXCLUSIVE FREE BETS AT MONSTERBET H'CAP (TAPETA) 1m 141y
9:20 (9:21) (Class 6) (0-65,65) 3-Y-0+ £2,264 (£673; £366; £168) Stalls Low

Form RPR

0000 1 **Naoise (IRE)**[16] 7042 6-9-7 65 (t) JacobButterfield(3) 1 76+
(Ollie Pears) *hld up: hdwy over 1f out: rdn to ld towards fin* 8/1

6010 2 hd **Lil Sophella (IRE)**[24] 6836 5-9-0 60 JackGarritty(5) 2 70
(Patrick Holmes) *hld up in tch: rdn to ld ins fnl f: hdd towards fin* 25/1

004 3 3 **Welliesinthewater (IRE)**[64] 5605 4-9-5 60 (v) DaleSwift 11 63
(Derek Shaw) *hld up: hdwy over 1f out: r.o* 14/1

0325 4 1/2 **Spirit Of Gondree (IRE)**[15] 7068 6-9-7 62 (b) BenCurtis 4 64
(Milton Bradley) *chsd ldrs: rdn and ev ch fr over 1f out tl no ex ins fnl f* 12/1

4216 5 2 1/2 **Elle Rebelle**[10] 7187 4-9-0 58 CamHardie(3) 3 54
(Mark Brisbourne) *hld up: rdn over 1f out: styd on ins fnl f: nvr nrr* 16/1

1000 **6** *1* **Ewell Place (IRE)**[24] 6836 5-9-4 **59**.........................(p) GeorgeChaloner 5 53
(Richard Fahey) *led: rdn over 2f out: hdd & wknd ins fnl f* **12/1**

0000 **7** *hd* **Zarliman (IRE)**[16] 7044 4-9-8 **63**........................................ TedDurcan 6 56
(Martyn Meade) *chsd ldrs: rdn over 2f out: wknd ins fnl f* **4/1**[2]

2644 **8** *2* **The Firm (IRE)**[41] 6341 5-9-10 **65**............................ FrankieMcDonald 7 54
(Daniel Mark Loughnane) *prom: rdn over 2f out: wknd over 1f out* **9/2**[3]

0554 **9** *1 3/4* **Blue Army**[17] 7012 3-9-3 **65**...................................(p) MatthewLawson(3) 13 50
(Saeed bin Suroor) *mid-div: hdwy over 2f out: sn rdn: wknd fnl f* **11/4**[1]

6506 **10** *10* **Armourer (IRE)**[10] 7188 3-8-13 **58**................................ SteveDrowne 9 20
(William Muir) *hld up: rdn and wknd 3f out* **18/1**

430 **11** *1 1/2* **Heavenly River (FR)**[25] 6822 3-8-11 **59**......................(v[1]) JoeyHaynes(3) 12 17
(K R Burke) *chsd ldrs: rdn over 2f out: wknd over 1f out* **25/1**

00 **12** *18* **Boboli Gardens**[16] 7042 4-9-2 **62**............................ TobyAtkinson(5) 10
(Noel Quinlan) *s.s: a in rr: wknd over 3f out* **80/1**

1m 48.98s (-1.12) **Going Correction** -0.025s/f (Stan)
**WFA** 3 from 4yo+ 4lb **12** Ran SP% **118.1**
Speed ratings (Par 101): **103,102,100,99,97 96,96,94,93,84 82,66**
CSF £193.56 CT £2740.26 TOTE £9.80: £3.80, £8.10, £4.10; EX 257.00 Trifecta £1709.80.
**Owner** Terence Elsey **Bred** J S Bolger **Trained** Norton, N Yorks

**FOCUS**

An honest pace for this concluding handicap. The front two pulled clear. The third has been rated to his 7f latest here.

T/Plt: £61.00 to a £1 stake. Pool: £104,019.07 - 1,243.14 winning tickets T/Qpdt: £5.50 to a £1 stake. Pool: £13,194.36 - 1,766.75 winning tickets CR

## 7260 DUNDALK (A.W) (L-H)

Friday, October 24

**OFFICIAL GOING: Polytrack: standard**

### 7433a MERCURY STKS (LISTED RACE) 5f (P)

**8:10** (8:15) 2-Y-0+ **£21,666** (£6,333; £3,000; £1,000)

RPR

**1** **Sir Maximilian (IRE)**[19] 6966 5-10-2 108....................... StevieDonohoe 2 109+
(Ian Williams) *trckd ldrs: short of room between horses after 1f and pushed along in 5th briefly: hdwy on outer 2f out into 2nd ins fnl f: styd on wl to ld cl home* **7/4**[1]

**2** *hd* **Abstraction (IRE)**[77] 5154 4-9-13 106........................ SeamieHeffernan 3 105
(R K Watson, Ire) *wnt sltly rt s and led: over 1 l clr 1/2-way: rdn 1 1/2f out and stl clr ent fnl f: strly pressed u.p wl ins fnl f and hdd cl home: jst failed* **10/3**[3]

**3** *1 1/2* **Russian Soul (IRE)**[12] 7140 6-10-2 108...........................(p) ShaneFoley 4 103+
(M Halford, Ire) *led to post wout rdr: sltly impeded s and settled bhd ldrs: pushed along in 6th fr 1/2-way: hdwy u.p into 3rd ins fnl 150yds and kpt on wl towards fin wout ever troubling principals* **9/4**[2]

**4** *2 1/4* **Aerialist (IRE)**[16] 7045 3-9-13 ........................................ KevinManning 5 93
(J S Bolger, Ire) *trckd ldrs: 2nd 1/2-way: n.m.r and sltly hmpd into st: rdn and no imp on ldr in 3rd over 1f out: kpt on one pce in 4th ins fnl f* **25/1**

**5** *3/4* **My Good Brother (IRE)**[21] 6908 5-9-13 100...................(v) ColinKeane 1 89
(T G McCourt, Ire) *cl up early and dropped to 4th bef 1/2-way: swtchd to far side fr 1/2-way and sn rdn in 2nd: no imp on ldr in 3rd ins fnl f and wknd towards fin* **11/2**

**6** *nk* **Sylvan Mist (IRE)**[26] 6802 4-9-8 80..................................(tp) PatSmullen 7 83
(Edward Lynam, Ire) *w.w in rr: sme hdwy on outer fr 2f out: no imp on ldrs ent fnl f: kpt on one pce* **33/1**

**7** *1 1/4* **Master Speaker (IRE)**[2] 7386 4-9-13 91..........................(tp) SJHassett 6 84
(Martin Hassett, Ire) *chsd ldrs: clsr in 3rd bef 1/2-way: rdn 2f out and sn no ex u.p: wknd fnl f* **33/1**

58.2s (58.20) **7** Ran SP% **115.3**
CSF £8.03 TOTE £2.40: £1.02, £3.20; DF 7.60 Trifecta £15.10.
**Owner** Paul Wildes **Bred** Holborn Trust Co **Trained** Portway, Worcs

**FOCUS**

A decent contest.

### 7435a CHRISTMAS PARTY NIGHTS AT DUNDALK H'CAP 1m 2f 150y(P)

**9:10** (9:11) (50-75,75) 3-Y-0+ **£4,887** (£1,133; £495; £283)

RPR

**1** **Johann Bach (IRE)**[28] 6727 5-9-11 **72**............................ EmmetMcNamara 5 77
(Patrick G Harney, Ire) *in tch: clsr in 5th bef 1/2-way: hdwy over 2f out to chse ldrs in 4th: rdn over 1f out and clsd u.p to chal in 2nd ins fnl f: kpt on wl to ld fnl strides* **10/1**

**2** *nk* **Sharjah (IRE)**[25] 6829 4-9-6 **67**.................................... DeclanMcDonogh 6 71
(Andrew Slattery, Ire) *led tl hdd after 1f: remained prom tl rdn to ld narrowly under 2f out: strly pressed u.p wl ins fnl f and hdd fnl strides* **11/2**[2]

**3** *2* **Fanzine**[24] 6850 4-9-12 **73**.............................................. ColinKeane 2 73
(M D O'Callaghan, Ire) *chsd ldrs: 3rd 1/2-way: effrt in 2nd under 2f out: no ex u.p ins fnl f and dropped to 3rd: kpt on same pce* **7/1**[3]

**4** *1/2* **Pretty Angel (IRE)**[53] 5990 3-9-1 **72**............................. SeanCorby(5) 14 72
(M Halford, Ire) *dwlt and towards rr: last 1/2-way: rdn and brought wd into st: gd hdwy on outer into 7th ins fnl f and kpt on wl u.p into nvr threatening 4th fnl strides* **16/1**

**5** *hd* **An Cat Dubh (IRE)**[13] 7098 5-9-7 **75**........................(p) LukeDempsey(7) 9 74
(Ian Williams) *chsd ldrs: racd keenly: 6th 1/2-way: rdn 2f out and no imp on ldrs ent fnl f: kpt on one pce* **11/2**[2]

**6** *shd* **Elusive Laurence (IRE)**[14] 7087 3-8-9 **68**.................... TomMadden(7) 1 68
(Mrs John Harrington, Ire) *in tch: 9th 1/2-way: rdn and tk clsr order over 2f out: no imp on ldrs u.p ent fnl f: kpt on one pce* **12/1**

**7** *2 3/4* **You've Got It**[12] 7139 3-9-1 **67**...................................... ShaneFoley 13 61
(M Halford, Ire) *towards rr: 13th 1/2-way: sme hdwy over 1f out where n.m.r and checked: swtchd lft and kpt on towards fin* **12/1**

**8** *3/4* **Crown Of Aragon**[14] 7093 3-9-9 **75**...............................(v) ChrisHayes 3 68
(A Oliver, Ire) *pushed along to ld after 1f: racd keenly: 3 l clr 1/2-way: reduced advantage and pushed along bef st: hdd under 2f out and sn no ex: wknd ins fnl f* **33/1**

**9** *nk* **Grandma Dotty (IRE)**[8] 6179 5-9-7 **68**.............................. PatSmullen 12 59
(C F Swan, Ire) *w.w towards rr: clsr in 11th 1/2-way: rdn into st and sn no imp: kpt on one pce fnl 2f* **9/2**[1]

**10** *shd* **Waterloo Sunrise (IRE)**[14] 7091 9-9-5 **66**.................. ColmO'Donoghue 8 57
(S M Duffy, Ire) *hld up: 12th 1/2-way: rdn and no imp 2f out* **14/1**

**11** *1 1/4* **Regal Warrior (IRE)**[56] 4929 11-8-12 **69**..........(t) ChristinaSimpson(10) 4 57
(J J Lambe, Ire) *dwlt: hld up: 10th 1/2-way: rdn and no ex 2f out* **25/1**

**12** *nse* **Teochrios (IRE)**[28] 6727 4-9-4 **65**..................................(t) KevinManning 7 53
(J S Bolger, Ire) *chsd ldrs: 4th 1/2-way: rdn and no ex in 5th over 1f out: sn edgd rt u.p: wknd and eased* **14/1**

**13** *3 1/4* **Comedy Club (IRE)**[14] 7092 3-9-5 **71**............................ NGMcCullagh 10 54
(Charles O'Brien, Ire) *in tch: clsr in 7th bef 1/2-way: rdn under 3f out and no imp 2f out: wknd* **8/1**

**14** *1/2* **Little Arrows (IRE)**[113] 3903 8-9-7 **68**..................................(p) BillyLee 11 49
(K J Condon, Ire) *hld up: 12th 1/2-way: rdn and sme hdwy far side fr 2f out: no ex over 1f out: wknd and eased* **16/1**

2m 12.98s (132.98)
**WFA** 3 from 4yo+ 6lb **14** Ran SP% **128.9**
Pick Six. Not Won. Pool of 161.05 carried forward to Leopardstown on Saturday, 25th October.
Tote aggregate: 2014: 104,257.08 - 2013: 108,719.92. CSF £68.76 CT £429.88 TOTE £9.80: £2.60, £1.40, £1.70; DF 76.50 Trifecta £470.20.
**Owner** Mrs P Harney **Bred** T F Lacy **Trained** Rhode, Co. Offaly
■ Stewards' Enquiry : Declan McDonogh one-day ban: used whip without giving gelding time to respond (tbn)

**FOCUS**

The winner close to best back in trip.

T/Jkpt: Not Won. T/Plt: @34.10. Pool: @27,982.82. BF

7434 - 7436a (Foreign Racing) - See Raceform Interactive

## 7393 DEAUVILLE (R-H)

Thursday, October 23

**OFFICIAL GOING: Polytrack: standard, turf: soft**

### 7437a PRIX DE LA MOTTERAYE (CONDITIONS) (4YO+) (POLYTRACK) 6f 110y

**2:05** (12:00) 4-Y-0+ **£13,750** (£5,500; £4,125; £2,750; £1,375)

RPR

**1** **Majestic Mount**[22] 4-8-13 0.................................. MickaelBarzalona 11 102
(Rod Collet, France) **4/1**[2]

**2** *nk* **Grand Vintage (FR)**[18] 5-8-13 0.............................. StephanePasquier 12 101
(W Mongil, Germany) **181/10**

**3** *2* **Desert Blanc**[22] 6-8-13 0........................................... GregoryBenoist 1 95
(C Baillet, France) **17/5**[1]

**4** *shd* **Dastarhon (IRE)**[28] 4-8-13 0.......................................(p) MaximeGuyon 8 95
(Mme Pia Brandt, France) **58/10**[3]

**5** *shd* **Keravnos (FR)**[22] 4-8-13 0........................................ DavidMorrison 2 94
(C Gourdain, France) **121/10**

**6** *2 1/2* **Totxo (IRE)**[4] 7327 6-9-2 0.................................. ChristopheSoumillon 6 90
(R Avial Lopez, Spain) **96/10**

**7** *1/2* **Gengis (FR)**[46] 4-8-13 0............................................. ThierryThulliez 4 86
(G Doleuze, France) **10/1**

**8** *nk* **Bravo Echo**[29] 6657 8-8-13 0........................................ RobertHavlin 10 85
(Michael Attwater) **32/1**

**9** *snk* **Birthday Prince (GER)**[20] 6-9-5 0.........................................(p) APietsch 7 90
(Christian Sprengel, Germany) **206/10**

**10** *3/4* **Abu Sidra (FR)**[72] 5-8-13 0........................................... AlexisBadel 5 82
(G E Mikhalides, France) **179/10**

**11** *1* **Kool And The Gang (IRE)** 4-8-13 0............................ AnthonyCrastus 9 79
(J Albrecht, Czech Republic) **48/1**

**12** *1 3/4* **Valbchek (IRE)**[15] 7034 5-8-13 0.................................(p) OlivierPeslier 13 74
(Jane Chapple-Hyam) **215/10**

**13** *1 1/2* **Wahib (FR)**[18] 4-8-13 0.............................................(b) UmbertoRispoli 3 70
(M Delzangles, France) **41/5**

1m 15.72s (75.72) **13** Ran SP% **119.1**
WIN (incl. 1 euro stake): 5.00. Places: 1.60, 4.50, 1.80. DF: 45.40. SF: 84.90..
**Owner** Graham Robinson **Bred** G Robinson & Mme G Robinson **Trained** France

## 7404 DONCASTER (L-H)

Saturday, October 25

**OFFICIAL GOING: Soft (6.8)**

Wind: Moderate half against Weather: Cloudy with sunny periods

### 7438 SOCIALITES ZERO STOPTOBER APPRENTICE JOCKEYS' TRAINING SERIES FINAL H'CAP (BOBIS RACE) (DIV I) 7f

**1:40** (1:40) (Class 4) (0-85,85) 3-Y-0 **£5,175** (£1,540; £769; £384) **Stalls** High

Form RPR

6263 **1** **Withernsea (IRE)**[12] 7159 3-9-2 **80**................................ JackGarritty 7 93
(Richard Fahey) *hld up: smooth hdwy on outer 3f out: led 2f out: rdn clr over 1f out: kpt on* **7/2**[1]

5230 **2** *3 3/4* **Debit**[35] 6552 3-8-6 **73**..................................................(p) RobHornby(3) 5 76
(Clive Cox) *trckd ldrs: hdwy and cl up 3f out: chsd wnr 2f out: sn rdn and no imp fnl f* **8/1**

14 **3** *3/4* **Cornborough**[182] 1714 3-8-10 **74**..................................... AnnaHesketh 4 75
(Mark Walford) *hld up towards rr: hdwy over 2f out: sn rdn: styd on fnl f: nrst fin* **16/1**

3163 **4** *3/4* **Instant Attraction (IRE)**[15] 7085 3-9-7 **85**.................. MeganCarberry 6 84
(Jedd O'Keeffe) *trckd ldrs: hdwy and cl up 1/2-way: ev ch 2f out: sn rdn and grad wknd* **9/2**[2]

6503 **5** *6* **Reedcutter**[23] 6885 3-9-2 **80**.................................... KieranShoemark 3 64
(James Toller) *sn led: pushed along 1/2-way: rdn and hdd 2f out: sn wknd* **5/1**[3]

6410 **6** *1 1/2* **Syros (IRE)**[71] 5387 3-8-2 **71**................................ DanielleMooney(5) 10 51
(Michael Easterby) *a towards rr* **33/1**

3000 **7** *3* **Tiger Twenty Two**[16] 7060 3-8-13 **77**................................. JoeDoyle 8 49
(Richard Fahey) *cl up: pushed along over 3f out: rdn wl over 2f out: sn wknd* **8/1**

0330 **8** *5* **Crowdmania**[15] 7081 3-9-6 **84**.................................. AlistairRawlinson 1 43
(Mark Johnston) *towards rr: hdwy on outer to chse ldrs 1/2-way: rdn along over 2f out: sn wknd* **7/1**

4243 **9** *1 1/4* **Inflection (IRE)**[61] 5763 3-8-8 **72**..........................................(t) CamHardie 9 28
(Hugo Palmer) *t.k.h: cl up: rdn along 3f out: sn wknd* **8/1**

1m 30.8s (4.50) **Going Correction** +0.725s/f (Yiel) **9** Ran SP% **111.7**
Speed ratings (Par 103): **103,98,97,97,90 88,85,79,77**
CSF £30.37 CT £383.65 TOTE £3.30: £1.10, £2.00, £5.80; EX 41.50 Trifecta £588.70.
**Owner** City Vaults Racing 1 **Bred** Yeomanstown Stud **Trained** Musley Bank, N Yorks

**FOCUS**
The going was officially soft (GoingStick 6.8) and the winning rider in the opener agreed with that description. A fair first division of this apprentice handicap in which the runners raced centre-to-nearside. The pace looked ordinary. The winner has been rated as running a pb, with the second and third close to their marks.

## 7439 SCOTT DOBSON MEMORIAL DONCASTER STKS (LISTED RACE) 6f
**2:10** (2:10) (Class 1) 2-Y-O **£15,984** (£6,045; £3,021; £1,509) **Stalls** High

Form RPR
651 1 **Code Red**[17] 7037 2-9-1 85.................................................. MartinDwyer 5 100
(William Muir) *hld up in rr: swtchd rt towards stands' rail and gd hdwy 3f out: cl up 2f out: rdn to chal over 1f out: led last 150yds: styd on wl* **11/2**
0211 2 3/4 **Portamento (IRE)**[8] 7232 2-9-1 100.................................. WilliamBuick 1 98
(Charlie Appleby) *led: rdn along 2f out: drvn over 1f out: hdd and no ex last 150yds* **9/4**[1]
5616 3 1 1/2 **Rosie's Premiere (IRE)**[8] 7238 2-8-10 93................. RobertWinston 2 88
(Dean Ivory) *trckd ldrs: pushed along wl over 2f out: rdn wl over 1f out: kpt on u.p fnl f* **8/1**
34 4 1 1/4 **Manofmanytalents**[14] 7121 2-9-1 87................................... LukeMorris 8 89
(Michael Squance) *dwlt: hld up towards rr: hdwy 1/2-way: cl up and rdn 2f out: drvn and kpt on same pce ent fnl f* **16/1**
1 5 nk **Salt Island**[63] 5684 2-9-1 0................................................... SteveDrowne 4 88
(Charles Hills) *trckd ldr: hdwy and cl up over 2f out: rdn wl over 1f out: drvn appr fnl f and sn wknd* **4/1**[3]
3021 6 4 **Lackaday**[9] 7216 2-9-1 77........................................................ CharlesBishop 6 76
(Mick Channon) *chsd ldrs: rdn along over 2f out: sn one pce* **33/1**
3032 7 1 **Burning The Clocks (IRE)**[9] 7216 2-9-1 75...............[1] MartinHarley 3 73
(Peter Chapple-Hyam) *in tch: rdn along wl over 2f out: sn wknd* **50/1**
102 8 1/2 **Growl**[35] 6547 2-9-1 97.............................................(t) PaulMulrennan 7 72
(Brian Meehan) *cl up: rdn along 2f out: sn drvn and wknd over 1f out* **3/1**[2]
1m 17.17s (3.57) **Going Correction** +0.725s/f (Yiel) **8 Ran SP% 113.0**
Speed ratings: **105,104,102,100,99 94,93,92**
CSF £17.86 TOTE £6.00: £2.00, £1.10, £2.60; EX 15.50 Trifecta £112.50.
**Owner** Mrs Michelle Morgan **Bred** Carmel Stud **Trained** Lambourn, Berks

**FOCUS**
An interesting Listed event, taken by the 2,000 Guineas winner Night Of Thunder last season, and this year's winner looks a nice sort. Again they raced centre-to-nearside, although the winner came up the rail.

## 7440 BET THROUGH THE RACING POST APP H'CAP 1m 4f
**2:40** (2:40) (Class 2) (0-100,97) 3-Y-0+ **£12,938** (£3,850; £1,924; £962) **Stalls** Low

Form RPR
0100 1 **Latenightrequest**[14] 7106 3-8-10 88.............................. PaulHanagan 11 100
(Richard Fahey) *in tch: hdwy on outer over 3f out: cl up 2f out: sn led and rdn clr: hung bdly rt ins fnl f: kpt on wl* **14/1**
5445 2 4 1/2 **Dashing Star**[28] 6747 4-9-12 97.............................. AndreaAtzeni 4 102
(David Elsworth) *led: clr 1/2-way: rdn along 3f out: drvn and hdd wl over 1f out: rallied u.p fnl f: no ch w wnr* **6/1**[3]
1246 3 nk **Oasis Fantasy (IRE)**[30] 6685 3-8-8 86........................... OisinMurphy 1 90
(Ed Dunlop) *in tch: rdn along and outpcd 3f out: hdwy 2f out: styd on wl u.p fnl f: nrst fin* **6/1**[3]
0051 4 nse **Open Eagle (IRE)**[14] 7125 5-9-1 86.............................. DanielTudhope 9 90
(David O'Meara) *trckd ldrs: hdwy over 3f out: rdn to chse wnr over 1f out: drvn and kpt on same pce fnl f* **9/2**[1]
0000 5 1 1/4 **Kashmir Peak (IRE)**[15] 7083 5-8-12 83 oh1.................. PhillipMakin 7 85
(John Quinn) *hld up and bhd: hdwy on outer 3f out: rdn along to chse ldrs wl over 1f out: sn drvn and kpt on same pce* **14/1**
2000 6 hd **Proud Chieftain**[30] 6685 6-8-10 86.......................... TobyAtkinson(5) 8 88
(Clifford Lines) *in tch: hdwy to chse ldrs over 4f out: rdn along 3f out: drvn wl over 1f out and kpt on same pce* **20/1**
1312 7 1/2 **Emerahldz (IRE)**[15] 7083 3-8-4 87............................... JackGarritty(5) 2 88
(Richard Fahey) *chsd ldng pair: rdn along 3f out: drvn over 2f out and grad wknd* **6/1**[3]
2521 8 10 **Brigadoon**[28] 6761 7-9-2 87...................................................... JasonHart 10 72
(Michael Appleby) *hld up in rr: effrt 4f out: sn rdn along and nvr a factor* **16/1**
1620 9 12 **Forgotten Hero (IRE)**[28] 6752 5-9-10 95........................ WilliamBuick 5 61
(Charles Hills) *plld hrd: chsd ldr: rdn along wl over 3f out: wknd wl over 2f out* **8/1**
1313 P **Ruwasi**[21] 6930 3-8-9 87................................................................ DavidAllan 6
(James Tate) *a in rr: pushed along 4f out: rdn over 3f out: wknd qckly and wl bhd whn p.u over 2f out* **5/1**[2]
2m 38.69s (3.79) **Going Correction** +0.55s/f (Yiel)
**WFA** 3 from 4yo+ 7lb **10 Ran SP% 112.8**
Speed ratings (Par 109): **109,106,105,105,104 104,104,97,89,**
CSF £92.54 CT £561.87 TOTE £15.80: £3.20, £2.60, £2.50; EX 102.70 Trifecta £1323.40 Part won..
**Owner** Middleham Park Racing XVI & Partner **Bred** Mrs S J Walker **Trained** Musley Bank, N Yorks

**FOCUS**
A decent handicap and the runner-up made sure it was a proper test. The runners came out into the centre of the track on turning in. The third has been rated close to form.

## 7441 BETDAQ BETTING EXCHANGE £30 FREE BET H'CAP 5f
**3:15** (3:17) (Class 2) 3-Y-0+
**£31,125** (£9,320; £4,660; £2,330; £1,165; £585) **Stalls** High

Form RPR
0421 1 **Dungannon**[21] 6923 7-8-10 96........................................(b) OisinMurphy 4 106
(Andrew Balding) *racd towards far side: hld up towards rr: swtchd rt and hdwy in centre over 2f out: effrt over 1f out: rdn to chal ent fnl f: led last 100yds: kpt on wl* **13/2**[2]
0130 2 1 1/4 **Ajjaadd (USA)**[21] 6918 8-8-9 100.............................. KevinStott(5) 7 106
(Ted Powell) *racd towards far side: chsd ldrs: hdwy to ld 1 1/2f out: sn rdn: drvn ins fnl f: hdd and no ex last 100yds* **25/1**
4040 3 3/4 **Demora**[21] 6918 5-8-11 102...................................... AlistairRawlinson(5) 22 105+
(Michael Appleby) *racd towards stands' side: slt ld to 1/2-way: cl up and ev ch whn edgd lft jst over 1f out: drvn ins fnl f: kpt on same pce* **12/1**
3002 4 hd **Confessional**[7] 7280 7-8-6 92..............................................(e) DavidAllan 1 94
(Tim Easterby) *racd towards far side: cl up: slt ld 1/2-way: rdn and hdd 1 1/2f out: sn drvn and kpt on same pce ins fnl f* **16/1**
0000 5 shd **Lancelot Du Lac (ITY)**[105] 4179 4-8-13 99.................. RobertWinston 6 101
(Dean Ivory) *racd towards far side: chsd ldrs: hdwy 2f out: sn rdn: kpt on u.p fnl f* **16/1**
3624 6 1/2 **Golden Steps (FR)**[22] 6893 3-8-9 95.............................. MartinHarley 9 96+
(Marco Botti) *outpcd and in rr: rdn along and hdwy 2f out: styd on fnl f: nrst fin* **11/2**[1]
5030 7 1/2 **Steps (IRE)**[21] 6918 6-9-3 110..............................(b) KieranShoemark(7) 3 108
(Roger Varian) *awkward s anbd towards rr: rdn along 2f out: styd on wl u.p fnl f: nrst fin* **12/1**
0050 8 1 3/4 **Gladiatrix**[15] 7080 5-7-11 88 ow1........................................ JoeDoyle(5) 2 80
(Rod Millman) *racd towards far side: cl up: rdn along 2f out: drvn and wknd appr fnl f* **20/1**
6123 9 1/2 **Kickboxer (IRE)**[14] 7101 3-9-1 101................................... LukeMorris 17 92
(Mick Channon) *racd towards stands' side: towards rr: hdwy wl over 1f out: styd on fnl f: nt rch ldrs* **8/1**[3]
4001 10 1 **Megaleka**[10] 7212 4-7-13 90.................................................. TimClark(5) 5 76
(Alan Bailey) *racd towards far side: in tch: effrt 2f out: sn rdn and no imp* **20/1**
3300 11 hd **Peterkin (IRE)**[28] 6745 3-8-5 91........................................ JoeFanning 18 78
(Mark Johnston) *racd towards stands' side: chsd ldrs: rdn along 2f out: sn one pce* **33/1**
3003 12 hd **Ballesteros**[7] 7280 5-8-6 92............................................ PaulHanagan 12 77
(Richard Fahey) *prom in centre: rdn along 2f out: grad wknd* **10/1**
041 12 dht **Doc Hay (USA)**[5] 7330 7-8-5 91 6ex.................................... BenCurtis 20 76
(David O'Meara) *racd alone stands' rail: a towards rr* **11/1**
0000 14 3/4 **Magical Macey (USA)**[7] 7280 7-7-13 88..................(b) CamHardie(3) 16 70
(David Barron) *chsd ldrs: rdn along 2f out: sn wknd* **20/1**
0063 15 3/4 **Elusivity (IRE)**[13] 7132 6-8-2 88.................................... JimmyQuinn 21 68
(Peter Crate) *racd towards stands' side: in tch: hdwy to chse ldrs over 2f out: sn rdn and wknd wl over 1f out* **16/1**
0000 16 nk **Ancient Cross**[15] 7080 10-8-4 90...................................(t) JamesSullivan 19 69
(Michael Easterby) *racd towards stands' side: dwlt and a in rr* **20/1**
0001 17 6 **Sleepy Sioux**[39] 6441 3-8-5 91.......................................(p) DavidProbert 13 49
(David Elsworth) *sltly hmpd s: a towards rr* **20/1**
6200 18 1 **Viva Verglas (IRE)**[7] 7280 3-8-7 93......................(b) GrahamGibbons 15 47
(David Barron) *wnt lft s: a towards rr* **33/1**
3104 19 1 **B Fifty Two (IRE)**[19] 6994 5-9-3 103.............................(bt) FrannyNorton 14 53
(Charles Hills) *chsd ldrs: rdn along 1/2-way: sn wknd* **20/1**
1m 1.05s (0.55) **Going Correction** +0.40s/f (Good) **19 Ran SP% 128.6**
Speed ratings (Par 109): **111,109,107,107,107 106,105,102,102,100 100,99,99,98,97 97,87,85,84**
CSF £169.14 CT £1937.06 TOTE £6.80: £2.10, £5.40, £4.10, £4.30; EX 252.40 Trifecta £2538.90.
**Owner** Dr E Harris **Bred** J A E Hobby **Trained** Kingsclere, Hants

**FOCUS**
A red-hot sprint handicap, with the 2011 and 2013 winners back for another crack. The field were spread all over the track, but the main action unfolded up the centre. The winner has been rated to his best and the runner-up to a small pb.

## 7442 RACING POST TROPHY (GROUP 1) (ENTIRE COLTS & FILLIES) 1m (S)
**3:50** (3:50) (Class 1) 2-Y-O
**£122,493** (£46,440; £23,241; £11,577; £5,810; £2,916) **Stalls** High

Form RPR
3111 1 **Elm Park**[28] 6750 2-9-1 111.............................................. AndreaAtzeni 3 118
(Andrew Balding) *w ldr: led after 2f: drvn over 1f out: forged clr last 150yds: readily* **13/8**[1]
1 2 2 3/4 **Aloft (IRE)**[21] 6928 2-9-1 0.............................................. WilliamBuick 6 112
(A P O'Brien, Ire) *dwlt: hld up in rr: hdwy over 2f out: 3rd over 1f out: styd on to take 2nd last 50yds* **10/1**
11 3 1/2 **Celestial Path (IRE)**[49] 6136 2-9-1 0.................................. LukeMorris 7 111
(Sir Mark Prescott Bt) *trckd ldrs: drvn and 2nd over 2f out: kpt on same pce appr fnl f* **6/1**[3]
4 5 **Jacobean (IRE)**[13] 7138 2-9-1 0.................................. ColmO'Donoghue 1 100
(A P O'Brien, Ire) *hld up in mid-div: hdwy over 2f out: sn hung rt: swvd rt and wknd 150yds out* **3/1**[2]
011 5 6 **Snoano**[36] 6520 2-9-1 100................................................ PaulHanagan 5 87
(John Gosden) *led 2f: chsd ldrs: wknd over 1f out* **9/1**
132 6 3 1/2 **Restorer**[14] 7104 2-9-1 101............................................. MartinDwyer 2 79
(William Muir) *trckd ldrs: effrt 3f out: hmpd 2f out: sn lost pl* **11/1**
1235 7 1 1/4 **Tupi (IRE)**[57] 5876 2-9-1 102.............................................. SeanLevey 4 76
(Richard Hannon) *hld up in rr: effrt over 2f out: wknd wl over 1f out* **33/1**
2034 8 1 1/4 **Cock Of The North**[56] 5926 2-9-1 102................................ FrederikTylicki 8 74
(Scott Dixon) *chsd ldrs: drvn over 3f out: lost pl over 2f out* **20/1**
1m 43.82s (4.52) **Going Correction** +0.725s/f (Yiel) **8 Ran SP% 112.5**
Speed ratings: **106,103,102,97,91 88,87,85**
CSF £18.59 TOTE £2.20: £1.10, £3.10, £1.90; EX 16.80 Trifecta £76.90.
**Owner** Qatar Racing & Kingsclere Racing **Bred** Kingsclere Stud **Trained** Kingsclere, Hants

**FOCUS**
The Racing Post Trophy boasts an impressive roll of honour over the years, including three subsequent Derby winners in the previous ten runnings, namely Motivator (2004), Authorized (2006) and Camelot (2011), while St Nicholas Abbey (2009) went on eventually to prove top-class on an international stage and this season's St Leger winner and Derby runner-up Kingston Hill took it last year. In a race in which the eight runners stuck to the nearside throughout, the pace didn't look that strong and the winner had the run of things, but he could do no more than win like he did.

## 7443 CROWNHOTEL-BAWTRY.COM NURSERY H'CAP (BOBIS RACE) 7f
**4:25** (4:25) (Class 3) (0-95,89) 2-Y-O **£6,469** (£1,925; £962; £481) **Stalls** High

Form RPR
0061 1 **Tachophobia**[18] 7005 2-8-3 **76**........................................ JackGarritty(5) 1 80
(Richard Fahey) *mde all: rdn wl over 1f out: drvn ins fnl f: kpt on gamely* **8/1**
6033 2 nk **Arcano Gold (IRE)**[11] 7169 2-8-8 **76**.................................. PaulHanagan 6 79
(Richard Fahey) *towards rr: pushed along over 2f out: rdn wl over 1f out: styd on on strly fnl f: jst failed* **10/1**
1041 3 1/2 **Popeswood (IRE)**[13] 7131 2-9-2 **84**................................... CharlesBishop 4 86
(Mick Channon) *awkward s and towards rr: hdwy wl over 2f out: rdn to chse ldng pair over 1f out: drvn and kpt on fnl f* **5/1**[3]
0103 4 1 3/4 **Four Seasons (IRE)**[15] 7079 2-9-7 **89**............................... WilliamBuick 7 86
(Charlie Appleby) *trckd ldrs: hdwy 2f out: sn chsng wnr: rdn over 1f out: drvn and wknd ins fnl f* **7/2**[1]
3210 5 2 **Intiwin (IRE)**[44] 6256 2-9-3 **85**..................................... GeorgeChaloner 9 77
(Richard Fahey) *hld up in rr: hdwy wl over 2f out: rdn wl over 1f out: sn drvn and no imp* **8/1**
1 6 6 **Them And Us (IRE)**[28] 6757 2-8-9 **77**............... WilliamTwiston-Davies 2 54
(Michael Bell) *trckd ldng pair: pushed along over 2f out: rdn wl over 1f out: sn wknd* **4/1**[2]
1423 7 3/4 **When Will It End (IRE)**[45] 6229 2-9-2 **87**....................... CamHardie(3) 11 63
(Richard Hannon) *hld up: hdwy to chse ldrs 3f out: rdn over 2f out: sn wknd* **8/1**
204 8 11 **Jewelled Prince**[11] 7166 2-7-11 **70** oh2 ow2..................(p) JoeDoyle(5) 8 18
(Richard Fahey) *chsd wnr: rdn wl over 2f out: sn wknd* **20/1**

1100 9 4 **Lady Desire (IRE)**[21] 6933 2-9-1 **83**.................................. JimCrowley 5 21
(Keith Dalgleish) *in tch: rdn along 3f out: sn wknd* **12/1**

2402 10 3 ¼ **Special Venture (IRE)**[18] 7005 2-8-7 **75**.................................. DavidAllan 10 5
(Tim Easterby) *chsd ldrs: rdn along wl over 2f out: sn wknd* **16/1**

1m 30.99s (4.69) **Going Correction** +0.725s/f (Yiel) **10** Ran SP% **119.6**
Speed ratings (Par 99): **102,101,101,99,96 89,89,76,71,68**
CSF £87.32 CT £447.03 TOTE £9.40: £3.00, £2.80, £2.00; EX 89.80 Trifecta £1694.40.
**Owner** A Rhodes Haulage And P Timmins **Bred** Springcombe Park Stud **Trained** Musley Bank, N Yorks

**FOCUS**
A decent nursery, but the conditions seem to catch out a few and they finished very well spread out.

## 7444 RACING POST DAILY EDITION FOR IPAD CONDITIONS STKS 7f
**5:00** (5:00) (Class 3) 3-Y-O+

**£8,092** (£2,423; £1,211; £605; £302; £152) **Stalls** High

Form RPR

2202 1 **Lulu The Zulu (IRE)**[22] 6891 6-8-3 88.................................. RyanTate(3) 4 103
(Michael Appleby) *hld up in rr: hdwy over 2f out: nt clr run appr fnl f: styd on wl to ld fnl 75yds* **14/1**

6240 2 1 **Top Notch Tonto (IRE)**[7] 7274 4-8-11 111.................................. DaleSwift 3 105
(Brian Ellison) *rr-div: drvn over 2f out: styd on and upsides 75yds out: no ex* **7/2**[2]

4220 3 ½ **Fencing (USA)**[8] 7243 5-8-11 110.................................. WilliamBuick 6 104
(John Gosden) *dwlt: t.k.h: sn trcking ldrs: led appr fnl f: hdd and no ex fnl 75yds* **7/2**[2]

2004 4 nse **Rene Mathis (GER)**[14] 7122 4-8-11 100.................................. PaulHanagan 7 104
(Richard Fahey) *w ldr: t.k.h: led over 5f out: edgd rt and hdd appr fnl f: upsides 75yds out: kpt on same pce* **8/1**

0013 5 3 **Louis The Pious**[21] 6920 6-8-11 111..........................(v) DanielTudhope 8 96
(David O'Meara) *hld up towards rr: hdwy 3f out: n.m.r 2f out: sltly hmpd over 1f out: wknd fnl 150yds* **10/3**[1]

2002 6 ½ **Jallota**[36] 6522 3-8-9 103.................................. JimCrowley 1 94
(Charles Hills) *trckd ldrs: wknd over 1f out* **9/1**

6550 7 7 **Highland Colori (IRE)**[8] 7242 6-9-0 102.................................. DavidProbert 9 80
(Andrew Balding) *led tl over 5f out: drvn over 2f out: lost pl over 1f out: bhd whn eased clsng stages* **5/1**[3]

1m 29.28s (2.98) **Going Correction** +0.725s/f (Yiel)
**WFA** 3 from 4yo+ 2lb **7** Ran SP% **112.0**
Speed ratings (Par 107): **111,109,109,109,105 105,97**
CSF £59.66 TOTE £10.90: £3.00, £2.70; EX 53.00 Trifecta £239.40.
**Owner** The Ab Kettlebys **Bred** Hong Kong Breeders Club **Trained** Danethorpe, Notts

**FOCUS**
An interesting conditions event and something of a surprise result. Another pb from the winner, while the fourth has been rated to form.

## 7445 SOCIALITES ZERO STOPTOBER APPRENTICE JOCKEYS' TRAINING SERIES FINAL H'CAP (BOBIS RACE) (DIV II) 7f
**5:30** (5:31) (Class 4) (0-85,85) 3-Y-O **£5,175** (£1,540; £769; £384) **Stalls** High

Form RPR

2004 1 **Alquimia (IRE)**[53] 5999 3-8-9 73.................................. JackGarritty 5 82
(Richard Fahey) *n.m.r after s: in rr: hdwy 2f out: effrt over 1f out: rdn to chal ent fnl f: styd on to ld last 75yds* **9/1**

5-31 2 ½ **Breakable**[24] 6863 3-8-8 72.................................. RachelRichardson 2 79
(Tim Easterby) *cl up: rdn to ld over 1f out: drvn ent fnl f: hdd and no ex last 75yds* **5/1**[3]

0430 3 ¾ **Charles Molson**[27] 6789 3-9-7 85.................................. CamHardie 1 90
(Henry Candy) *cl up on outer: rdn along wl over 1f out: drvn and ev ch ins fnl f tl no ex last 75yds* **7/2**[1]

-145 4 1 ¼ **Bold Captain (IRE)**[62] 5713 3-8-11 75.................................. JoeDoyle 9 77
(John Quinn) *led: rdn along and hdd 3f out: sn sltly outpcd: swtchd lft over 1f out: kpt on u.p ins fnl f* **7/1**

2324 5 ½ **Emef Diamond**[24] 6871 3-8-10 74.................................. DanielCremin 7 74
(Mick Channon) *trckd ldrs: effrt over 2f out: sn rdn and kpt on same pce fnl f* **9/2**[2]

3012 6 shd **Can't Change It (IRE)**[65] 5603 3-8-9 80.................................. SophieKilloran(7) 3 80
(David Simcock) *trckd ldrs: hdwy to ld 3f out: rdn 2f out: hdd over 1f out: wknd ins fnl f* **9/2**[2]

0030 7 12 **Shot In The Sun (IRE)**[14] 7119 3-9-1 79.................................. MeganCarberry 4 48
(Richard Fahey) *towards rr: rdn along bef 1/2-way: sn outpcd and bhd* **11/2**

1m 30.88s (4.58) **Going Correction** +0.725s/f (Yiel) **7** Ran SP% **113.1**
Speed ratings (Par 103): **102,101,100,99,98 98,84**
CSF £51.60 CT £188.01 TOTE £9.20: £3.90, £2.40; EX 65.00 Trifecta £280.70.
**Owner** Sir Robert Ogden **Bred** Sir Robert Ogden **Trained** Musley Bank, N Yorks
■ Stewards' Enquiry : Sophie Killoran caution: failed to take all reasonable and permissable measures to obtain the best possible placing

**FOCUS**
A rather messy affair and the winning time was slightly slower than the first division at the start of the card, though the ground was a bit more chewed up by now. The winner has been rated as running a small pb.
T/Jkpt: Not won. T/Plt: £178.50 to a £1 stake. Pool: £164,542.79 - 672.63 winning units. T/Qpdt: £45.50 to a 31 stake. Pool: £7834.28 - 127.25 winning units. JR

# 7412 NEWBURY (L-H)
Saturday, October 25

**OFFICIAL GOING: Soft (5.4)**
Wind: Fresh, half against Weather: Sunny intervals

## 7446 WORTHINGTON'S WHIZZ KIDZ STKS (REGISTERED AS THE HORRIS HILL STAKES) (GROUP 3) (C&G) 7f (S)
**1:50** (1:50) (Class 1) 2-Y-O

**£22,684** (£8,600; £4,304; £2,144; £1,076; £540) **Stalls** Centre

Form RPR

0313 1 **Smaih (GER)**[49] 6136 2-9-0 90.................................. FrankieDettori 4 102
(Richard Hannon) *w ldr: led over 1f out: rdn out: readily* **7/1**

4045 2 1 **Fox Trotter (IRE)**[21] 6933 2-9-0 94.................................. JimmyFortune 2 100
(Brian Meehan) *t.k.h and covered up in tch: nt clr run 2f out: swtchd rt and hdwy over 1f out: clsd on wnr but a hld* **11/2**[3]

40 3 1 ¼ **King Of Normandy (FR)**[44] 6259 2-9-0 0.................................. PatDobbs 1 96
(Richard Hannon) *led: rdn and hdd over 1f out: one pce* **12/1**

3330 4 1 ¼ **Lexington Times (IRE)**[44] 6256 2-9-0 102.................................. RichardHughes 5 93
(Richard Hannon) *hdwy to press ldrs after 3f: no ex ins fnl f* **2/1**[1]

6110 5 nk **Mukhayyam**[14] 7104 2-9-0 92.................................. DaneO'Neill 6 93
(Sir Michael Stoute) *prom tl hrd rdn and btn over 1f out* **4/1**[2]

1 6 1 **Not So Sleepy**[10] 7206 2-9-0 0.................................. GeorgeBaker 3 90
(Hughie Morrison) *restrained and rrd s: t.k.h in rr: hdwy 3f out: wknd over 1f out* **4/1**[2]

1m 32.45s (6.75) **Going Correction** +0.925s/f (Soft) **6** Ran SP% **108.9**
Speed ratings: **98,96,95,94,93 92**
CSF £40.95 TOTE £5.90: £2.70, £3.50; EX 43.40 Trifecta £69.10.
**Owner** Al Shaqab Racing **Bred** Stiftung Gestut Fahrhof **Trained** East Everleigh, Wilts

**FOCUS**
Rail moved from Friday between 8f and 5f and distances on Round course increased by 24yds. Just 0.5mm of rain overnight and the ground was soft. This looked a weak Group 3, highlighted by the performance of the maiden in third.

## 7447 WORTHINGTON'S BURLISON INNS STKS (REGISTERED AS THE ST SIMON STAKES) (GROUP 3) 1m 4f 5y
**2:20** (2:20) (Class 1) 3-Y-O+

**£34,026** (£12,900; £6,456; £3,216; £1,614; £810) **Stalls** Centre

Form RPR

-461 1 **Sky Hunter**[35] 6532 4-9-4 109.................................. JamesDoyle 6 117
(Saeed bin Suroor) *hld up in 4th: rdn to chse ldr 3f out: led over 1f out: sn clr* **7/2**[1]

040 2 9 **Island Remede**[29] 6708 3-8-8 97.................................. RichardKingscote 5 100
(Ed Dunlop) *hld up in 5th: effrt 3f out: styd on to take 2nd fnl strides: nvr trbld wnr* **25/1**

1053 3 ½ **Battalion (IRE)**[49] 6139 4-9-4 108..........................(p) SilvestreDeSousa 4 102
(William Haggas) *led and sn setting decent pce: 3 l clr 3f out: hdd & wknd over 1f out: lost 2nd fnl strides* **11/2**

5014 4 2 ½ **Quiz Mistress**[22] 6917 6-9-1 103.................................. RichardHughes 2 95
(Hughie Morrison) *dwlt: hld up in rr: hdwy into modest 3rd 2f out: no imp* **8/1**

0114 5 2 ¾ **Glorious Protector (IRE)**[35] 6546 4-9-4 105.................................. GeorgeBaker 3 93
(Ed Walker) *s.s: hld up in rr: rdn and sme hdwy over 2f out: wknd over 1f out* **4/1**[2]

0022 6 ½ **Red Galileo**[29] 6711 3-8-11 105.................................. GrahamLee 7 93
(Ed Dunlop) *hld up in 6th: rdn 3f out: wknd 2f out* **9/2**[3]

0006 7 20 **Penglai Pavilion (USA)**[29] 6711 4-9-4 103.................................. AdamKirby 1 61
(Charlie Appleby) *chsd ldrs: disp 2nd 7f out tl 5f out: wknd wl over 2f out* **14/1**

4461 8 7 **Rawaki (IRE)**[51] 6069 6-9-4 107.................................. LiamKeniry 8 49
(Andrew Balding) *chsd ldr tl 3f out: sn wknd* **6/1**

2m 44.52s (9.02) **Going Correction** +1.10s/f (Soft)
**WFA** 3 from 4yo+ 7lb **8** Ran SP% **111.7**
Speed ratings: **113,107,106,105,103 102,89,84**
CSF £81.87 TOTE £3.60: £1.60, £4.90, £1.90; EX 90.60 Trifecta £920.40.
**Owner** Godolphin **Bred** Darley **Trained** Newmarket, Suffolk

**FOCUS**
Just 6lb covered seven of the the eight runners on adjusted official ratings and this looked quite competitive on paper, but it was turned into a procession by the winner. The winner has been rated back to his best, and a small pb from the runner-up.

## 7448 AL BASTI EQUIWORLD CELEBRATION STKS (REGISTERED AS THE RADLEY STAKES) (LISTED RACE) (FILLIES) 7f (S)
**2:50** (2:50) (Class 1) 2-Y-O

**£17,013** (£6,450; £3,228; £1,608; £807; £405) **Stalls** Centre

Form RPR

4146 1 **Russian Punch**[21] 6926 2-9-0 92.................................. GrahamLee 2 98
(James Given) *hld up in rr: rdn 3f out: styd on to ld 1f out: slt advantage fnl f: hld on wl* **9/1**

1334 2 nk **Shagah (IRE)**[21] 6926 2-9-0 101.................................. FrankieDettori 1 97
(Richard Hannon) *dwlt: t.k.h towards rr: smooth hdwy over 2f out: c to stands' rail and rdn to join wnr 1f out: r.o* **7/2**[1]

201 3 3 ¼ **Sweet Dream**[11] 7174 2-9-0 77.................................. RichardKingscote 4 89
(Ralph Beckett) *led for over 2f: remained prom: one pce fnl f* **11/1**

1402 4 ½ **Astrelle (IRE)**[21] 6926 2-9-0 98.................................. PaoloSirigu 3 88
(Marco Botti) *prom: rdr lost iron and led over 4f out: hrd rdn and hdd 1f out: no ex* **5/1**[2]

51 5 4 **Muffri'Ha (IRE)**[28] 6735 2-9-0 85.................................. JamesDoyle 5 78
(William Haggas) *chsd ldrs tl outpcd and btn over 2f out* **7/2**[1]

2012 6 11 **Lacing**[21] 6924 2-9-0 98.................................. TonyHamilton 8 50
(Richard Fahey) *prom tl hrd rdn and wknd qckly over 1f out* **5/1**[2]

51 7 15 **Silver Rainbow (IRE)**[9] 7228 2-9-0 82.................................. RichardHughes 6 13
(Charles Hills) *racd alone on stands' rail: chsd ldrs tl wknd over 2f out* **8/1**[3]

2130 8 2 ¾ **Disprove (IRE)**[35] 6530 2-9-0 83.................................. DaneO'Neill 7 6
(Hugo Palmer) *dwlt: t.k.h in rr: rdn 3f out: sn wknd* **20/1**

1m 31.81s (6.11) **Going Correction** +0.925s/f (Soft) **8** Ran SP% **112.0**
Speed ratings: **102,101,97,97,92 80,63,59**
CSF £38.85 TOTE £9.20: £3.10, £1.50, £3.30; EX 59.50 Trifecta £477.10.
**Owner** Lovely Bubbly Racing **Bred** Mrs Deborah O'Brien **Trained** Willoughton, Lincs

**FOCUS**
Just one of these came into the race rated in three figures and this doesn't look strong form. The pace was pretty good and the first two came from the back of the field.

## 7449 BATHWICK TYRES H'CAP 1m 2f 6y
**3:30** (3:30) (Class 2) (0-105,104) 3-Y-O+

**£12,450** (£3,728; £1,864; £932; £466; £234) **Stalls** Centre

Form RPR

0546 1 **Burano (IRE)**[30] 6688 5-8-9 **87**.................................. HayleyTurner 2 96
(Brian Meehan) *prom: wnt 2nd after 3f and tk ldr on at gd pce: led 4f out: drvn and hld on gamely fnl 2f* **7/1**[3]

6306 2 1 ¼ **Silvery Moon (IRE)**[8] 7236 7-8-9 **87**.................................. TedDurcan 6 94
(Tim Easterby) *in tch: drvn to chse wnr 1f out: styd on: a hld* **8/1**

6000 3 ¾ **Hi There (IRE)**[15] 7083 5-8-5 **88**.................................. SammyJoBell(5) 9 94
(Richard Fahey) *s.s: towards rr: effrt in centre 3f out: styd on fnl f* **15/2**

0331 4 3 ¼ **Complicit (IRE)**[16] 7066 3-9-4 **101**.................................. GeorgeBaker 3 100
(Paul Cole) *prom: gng wl and wnt 2nd over 2f out: hrd rdn and wandered over 1f out: wknd fnl f* **5/1**[2]

1110 5 ½ **Starwatch**[27] 6786 7-8-10 **88**..........................(v) WilliamCarson 1 86
(John Bridger) *sluggish s: sn rushed up to ld and set gd pce: jnd after 3f: hdd 4f out: wknd over 1f out* **8/1**

-401 6 hd **Ennistown**[30] 6693 4-9-10 **102**.................................. AdamKirby 8 100
(Charlie Appleby) *in tch tl hrd rdn and btn over 2f out* **5/2**[1]

1600 **7** *12* **Miner's Lamp (IRE)**[14] 7106 3-9-7 **104**.................. MartinLane 5 79
(Charlie Appleby) *sn towards rr: drvn along and struggling fnl 3f* **9/1**

0406 **8** *3* **Spa's Dancer (IRE)**[18] 7022 7-9-6 **98**.................. GrahamLee 4 68
(James Eustace) *s.s: a bhd: no ch fnl 3f* **8/1**

2m 17.13s (8.33) **Going Correction** +1.10s/f (Soft)
**WFA** 3 from 4yo+ 5lb **8** Ran SP% **112.8**
Speed ratings (Par 109): **110,109,108,105,105 105,95,93**
CSF £59.28 CT £429.61 TOTE £7.60: £2.50, £2.70, £2.00; EX 65.60 Trifecta £436.60.
**Owner** Jonathan Harvey **Bred** Sir E J Loder **Trained** Manton, Wilts

**FOCUS**
There was a steady early pace and that played against those held up. The runner-up has been rated to his best.

## 7450 AL BASTI EQUIWORLD EBF STALLIONS MAIDEN FILLIES' STKS (BOBIS RACE) 1m (S)

**4:05** (4:07) (Class 4) 2-Y-O **£5,175** (£1,540; £769; £384) **Stalls** Centre

Form RPR

5 **1** **Lulani (IRE)**[51] 6066 2-9-0 0.................. TomQueally 6 79+
(Harry Dunlop) *trckd ldrs: effrt on bit and led over 1f out: shkn up and hung lft: cajoled home: all out* **8/1**

04 **2** *nse* **Bellajeu**[79] 5078 2-9-0 0..................[1] PatDobbs 8 79
(Ralph Beckett) *led tl over 1f out: rallied and level w wnr ins fnl f: r.o: jst denied* **6/1**[3]

0 **3** *3 1/4* **Gilded Lili (IRE)**[14] 7108 2-9-0 0.................. DaneO'Neill 1 72
(Charles Hills) *mid-div: effrt and swtchd lft 2f out: styd on to take 3rd ins fnl f* **33/1**

**4** *1* **L'Ingenue** 2-9-0 0.................. RichardHughes 11 70+
(Ralph Beckett) *hld up in midfield: rdn and styd on fnl 2f: nvr rchd ldrs* **4/1**[1]

**5** *4 1/2* **Merry Dancer (IRE)** 2-9-0 0.................. PatCosgrave 3 60
(Paul Webber) *towards rr: rdn and sme hdwy over 2f out: in tch over 1f out: no ex* **22/1**

**6** *1/2* **Sweet Selection** 2-9-0 0.................. SilvestreDeSousa 7 59
(Hughie Morrison) *dwlt: towards rr: rdn over 3f out: hdwy and c to stands' rail 2f out: no imp fnl f* **10/1**

0 **7** *1 1/2* **Sun Odyssey**[15] 7084 2-9-0 0.................. GrahamLee 9 55
(William Haggas) *wnt rt and bmpd s: chsd ldrs: rdn over 3f out: wknd over 1f out* **11/2**[2]

**8** *1* **Melodica** 2-9-0 0.................. JamesDoyle 4 53
(Roger Charlton) *mid-div: rdn and sltly hmpd 2f out: no hdwy after* **7/1**

**9** *4* **Fieldmouse** 2-9-0 0.................. JimmyFortune 15 44
(Eve Johnson Houghton) *bhd tl shkn up and kpt on past btn rivals fnl 2f* **14/1**

00 **10** *1 1/2* **The Madding Crowd**[11] 7184 2-9-0 0.................. JohnFahy 2 41
(Hughie Morrison) *w ldrs tl wknd 2f out* **66/1**

0005 **11** *shd* **Eileen Gray (IRE)**[41] 6359 2-9-0 47..................(p) WilliamCarson 13 41
(Charles Hills) *w ldrs tl wknd over 2f out* **50/1**

**12** *1 1/4* **Estournel** 2-9-0 0.................. HayleyTurner 12 38
(Harry Dunlop) *mid-div: rdn 3f out: sn wknd* **25/1**

**13** *1* **Alert** 2-8-9 0.................. NedCurtis(5) 14 36
(Jonathan Portman) *dwlt: a bhd* **25/1**

0 **14** *4 1/2* **Shifting Moon**[4] 7367 2-9-0 0.................. FergusSweeney 5 26
(Hughie Morrison) *mid-div: rdn 3f out: wknd over 1f out* **50/1**

06 **15** *1/2* **Almaardiyah (IRE)**[70] 5416 2-9-0 0.................. FrankieDettori 10 25
(Richard Hannon) *bmpd s: a bhd: eased whn no ch over 1f out* **7/1**

1m 47.16s (7.46) **Going Correction** +0.925s/f (Soft) **15** Ran SP% **121.9**
Speed ratings (Par 94): **99,98,95,94,90 89,88,87,83,81 81,80,79,74,74**
CSF £52.28 TOTE £9.10: £2.80, £2.20, £10.30; EX 83.30 Trifecta £2379.90 Part won..
**Owner** Mr & Mrs James Blyth Currie **Bred** Oak Lodge Bloodstock **Trained** Lambourn, Berks

**FOCUS**
There were one or two noteworthy performances in this fillies' maiden.

## 7451 WORTHINGTON'S HIGHFIELD SOCIAL CLUB EBF STALLIONS H'CAP (F&M) 7f (S)

**4:40** (4:42) (Class 3) (0-95,94) 3-Y-O+ **£8,733** (£2,598; £1,298; £649) **Stalls** Centre

Form RPR

0042 **1** **Lilac Lace (IRE)**[8] 7248 4-8-7 80 oh7.................. DuranFentiman 8 87
(Tim Easterby) *mde all: hrd rdn fnl f: jst hld on by diminishing margin* **5/1**[3]

3430 **2** *shd* **Dusky Queen (IRE)**[35] 6534 4-8-11 89.................. SammyJoBell(5) 3 96
(Richard Fahey) *chsd ldrs: wnt 2nd 2f out: clsd steadily on wnr fnl f: jst failed* **9/2**[2]

5000 **3** *3* **Our Queenie (IRE)**[10] 7196 3-8-7 82.................. HarryBentley 1 80
(Richard Hannon) *in tch: rdn 3f out: styd on fr over 1f out* **10/1**

1430 **4** *2 1/2* **Danehill Revival**[21] 6929 3-9-3 92..................(p) GrahamLee 5 84
(William Haggas) *chsd wnr tl 2f out: sn outpcd* **9/2**[2]

0605 **5** *4 1/2* **Dutch Courage**[51] 6068 3-9-0 89.................. TonyHamilton 4 69
(Richard Fahey) *chsd ldrs tl wknd 2f out* **13/2**

5500 **6** *3/4* **Baby Bush (IRE)**[12] 7159 3-8-5 80 oh2.................. KieranO'Neill 2 58
(Richard Hannon) *bhd: modest effrt 2f out: no imp* **25/1**

6603 **7** *1 1/4* **Azagal (IRE)**[11] 7168 3-8-12 87.................. TedDurcan 9 62
(Tim Easterby) *a bhd* **7/2**[1]

6134 **8** *6* **Stosur (IRE)**[41] 6388 3-9-5 94..................(b) TomQueally 6 53
(Gay Kelleway) *chsd ldrs: brought wd towards stands' rail 4f out: hrd rdn and hung lft 2f out: sn wknd* **16/1**

2534 **9** *14* **Lady Frances**[28] 6755 3-9-1 90.................. SilvestreDeSousa 7 13
(Mark Johnston) *racd mainly alone on stands' rail: bhd fnl 3f* **10/1**

1m 30.74s (5.04) **Going Correction** +0.925s/f (Soft)
**WFA** 3 from 4yo 2lb **9** Ran SP% **116.5**
Speed ratings (Par 107): **108,107,104,101,96 95,94,87,71**
CSF £28.05 CT £219.05 TOTE £6.60: £2.40, £1.80, £4.00; EX 34.20 Trifecta £427.10.
**Owner** S A Heley **Bred** Robert Ryan, Brendan Quinn & Joan Quinn **Trained** Great Habton, N Yorks
■ Stewards' Enquiry : Sammy Jo Bell four-day ban: used whip above permitted level (Nov 8,10,12,13)

**FOCUS**
Not many took to this test in the ground. The winner has been rated not far off her best, while the runner-up is solid and helps set the standard.

## 7452 RAYNER BOSCH CAR SERVICE H'CAP (FOR LADY AMATEUR RIDERS) 1m 4f 5y

**5:10** (5:10) (Class 5) (0-75,74) 4-Y-O+ **£2,495** (£774; £386; £193) **Stalls** Centre

Form RPR

00-1 **1** **Low Key (IRE)**[276] 278 7-9-12 65.................. MissAliceMills 2 89+
(David Pipe) *hld up towards rr: hdwy on bit to ld over 3f out: easily drew clr: rdr motionless thrght: canter* **3/1**[1]

2050 **2** *8* **Shades Of Grey**[57] 5878 7-9-11 64.................. MissADeniel 9 67
(Clive Cox) *hld up in midfield: hdwy 3f out: wnt 2nd over 2f out: nvr nr easy wnr* **11/2**[3]

50-5 **3** *7* **Our Phylli Vera (IRE)**[176] 1910 5-10-4 74.......... MissMeganNicholls(3) 6 67
(Alan King) *bhd: hdwy in centre and rdn 4f out: modest 3rd fnl 2f* **9/1**

/0-5 **4** *1 1/2* **Asker (IRE)**[141] 2966 6-9-10 68..................(p) MissAWallace(5) 7 58
(Zoe Davison) *dwlt: outpcd and wl bhd tl styd on to take modest 4th over 1f out* **25/1**

-450 **5** *1 3/4* **Dancing Primo**[11] 7175 8-9-4 62.................. MissPFuller(5) 8 50
(Mark Brisbourne) *chsd clr ldrs: effrt 3f out: wknd 2f out* **15/2**

0563 **6** *1 1/2* **Angus Glens**[8] 7251 4-9-1 61..................(p) MissGFriswell(7) 1 46
(David Dennis) *led at gd pce tl 6f out: rdn and btn over 3f out* **8/1**

3506 **7** *7* **Hi Note**[3] 6360 6-9-10 70.................. MissFHickman(7) 4 45
(Sheena West) *sn taking on ldr at gd pce: led 6f out tl over 3f out: hrd rdn and wknd over 2f out* **7/1**

2110 **8** *1/2* **The Quarterjack**[139] 3034 5-10-5 72.................. MissSBrotherton 5 46
(Ron Hodges) *mid-div: lost pl 5f out: sn struggling* **4/1**[2]

6553 **9** *1 1/4* **High Office**[7] 7279 8-10-7 74.................. MissEJJones 3 46
(Conor Dore) *chsd clr ldrs tl hrd rdn and wknd 3f out* **10/1**

0/ **10** *21* **Golan Guy (IRE)**[17] 5872 9-9-0 60 oh6..................(bt) MissLLJenkins(7) 10
(Sean Curran) *towards rr on outer: rdn and no ch fnl 4f* **40/1**

2m 50.62s (15.12) **Going Correction** +1.10s/f (Soft) **10** Ran SP% **121.1**
Speed ratings (Par 103): **93,87,83,82,80 79,75,74,74,60**
CSF £20.53 CT £137.48 TOTE £4.90: £2.00, £1.80, £2.70; EX 27.10 Trifecta £321.70.
**Owner** M C Pipe **Bred** Christoph Berglar **Trained** Nicholashayne, Devon

**FOCUS**
This was run at a decent gallop given the conditions. The runner-up has been rated close to form.
T/Plt: £799.30 to a £1 stake. Pool: £93,129.32 - 85.05 winning units. T/Qpdt: £103.70 to a 31 stake. Pool: £4933.26 - 35.18 winning units. LM

# 7420 WOLVERHAMPTON (A.W) (L-H)

Saturday, October 25

**OFFICIAL GOING: Tapeta: standard**
Wind: Fresh behind Weather: Overcast

## 7453 GET LIVE SCORE UPDATES @ FOOTBALLSCORES.COM NURSERY H'CAP (TAPETA) 5f 20y

**5:45** (5:47) (Class 6) (0-60,63) 2-Y-O **£2,264** (£673; £336; £168) **Stalls** Low

Form RPR

00 **1** **Toni's A Star**[133] 3215 2-8-6 45..................(b[1]) RaulDaSilva 8 50
(Paul Green) *mde all: pushed clr 2f out: rdn over 1f out: all out* **33/1**

6503 **2** *hd* **Most Tempting**[10] 7190 2-9-3 56.................. AdamBeschizza 7 60
(Robert Cowell) *mid-div: hdwy 1/2-way: rdn over 1f out: r.o wl ins fnl f: nt quite get up* **11/4**[1]

0326 **3** *1* **Sky Steps (IRE)**[31] 6663 2-8-7 49..................(v) DannyBrock(3) 12 49
(Philip McBride) *s.i.s: hld up: r.o ins fnl f: wnt 3rd nr fin: nt rch ldrs* **11/4**[1]

6026 **4** *1/2* **Penalty Scorer**[27] 6791 2-8-8 50.................. NeilFarley(3) 6 49
(Richard Guest) *chsd ldrs: rdn to go 2nd over 1f out tl wl ins fnl f: styd on* **16/1**

600 **5** *3/4* **Junior Ben**[31] 6659 2-8-11 50.................. TomEaves 3 46
(Derek Shaw) *chsd ldrs: rdn over 1f out: styd on same pce wl ins fnl f* **25/1**

050 **6** *3/4* **Kylies Wild Card**[14] 7113 2-8-6 45.................. LiamJones 11 38
(Simon Hodgson) *sn pushed along in mid-div: hdwy u.p over 1f out: nt trble ldrs* **80/1**

606 **7** *nk* **Don Ricardo (IRE)**[25] 6831 2-9-1 54.................. DavidNolan 2 46
(Richard Fahey) *s.i.s: outpcd: r.o wl ins fnl f: nvr nrr* **7/1**[3]

0211 **8** *1* **Sparbrook (IRE)**[10] 7190 2-9-3 63.................. TomasHarrigan(7) 5 52
(Simon Dow) *prom: pushed along 1/2-way: rdn over 1f out: styd on same pce* **13/2**[2]

0300 **9** *1 1/4* **Air Of York (IRE)**[10] 7190 2-8-6 45..................(b) ChrisCatlin 13 29
(Ronald Harris) *mid-div: sn pushed along: nvr on terms* **28/1**

5654 **10** *nk* **Macarthurs Park (IRE)**[8] 7232 2-8-6 45..................(b) PatrickMathers 10 28
(Alan Berry) *sn pushed along in rr: hdwy and nt clr run over 1f out: sn rdn and flashed tail: n.d* **50/1**

6040 **11** *8* **Featsdontfailmenow**[10] 7190 2-8-6 45..................(t) PJMcDonald 1
(Lisa Williamson) *a in rr* **125/1**

6504 **12** *1 1/4* **Jimmy's Girl (IRE)**[10] 7190 2-9-0 56..................(p) ConnorBeasley(3) 4 6
(Chris Dwyer) *w wnr 2f: sn rdn: wknd over 1f out* **15/2**

000 **13** *1 1/4* **Lydiate Lady**[50] 6093 2-8-9 48.................. JasonHart 9
(Paul Green) *prom tl hung rt and lost pl over 3f out* **16/1**

1m 2.42s (0.52) **Going Correction** -0.10s/f (Stan) **13** Ran SP% **116.9**
Speed ratings (Par 93): **91,90,89,88,87 85,85,83,81,81 68,66,64**
CSF £117.33 CT £347.70 TOTE £36.60: £13.60, £1.20, £1.60; EX 301.80 Trifecta £1620.00.
**Owner** A Star Recruitment Ltd **Bred** Paul Green **Trained** Lydiate, Merseyside

**FOCUS**
A modest nursery in which not many arrived in good form. The gallop was sound throughout and the winner raced towards the far rail in the straight.

## 7454 EBF STALLIONS ENJOY DAILY BETTING TIPS @ BOOKMAKERS.CO.UK MAIDEN STKS (TAPETA) 5f 20y

**6:15** (6:16) (Class 5) 2-Y-O **£2,911** (£866; £432; £216) **Stalls** Low

Form RPR

2642 **1** **Exceedingly**[39] 6435 2-9-0 76.................. RobertHavlin 2 68
(John Gosden) *led 1f: chsd ldr tl rdn to ld 1f out: edgd lft: r.o* **5/4**[1]

55 **2** *1 1/2* **Shackled N Drawn (USA)**[114] 3889 2-9-5 0..................(t) LiamJones 6 68
(Olly Stevens) *trckd ldrs: hmpd over 3f out: rdn and ev ch 1f out: styd on same pce ins fnl f* **3/1**[2]

B40 **3** *1/2* **Star Fire**[17] 7037 2-9-0 0.................. RichardKingscote 3 61
(Roger Charlton) *s.i.s: plld hrd and sn prom: hmpd and lost pl over 3f out: hdwy over 1f out: n.m.r ins fnl f: r.o* **8/1**

0506 **4** *hd* **Able Spirit**[24] 6867 2-9-5 66.................. JoeFanning 1 65
(Brian Meehan) *plld hrd: led after 1f: rdn and hdd 1f out: styd on same pce* **16/1**

**5** *1* **Kodiac Lady (IRE)** 2-9-0 0.................. PaulMulrennan 5 56
(James Tate) *prom: swtchd lft over 3f out: rdn over 1f out: styd on* **6/1**[3]

00 **6** *hd* **Coursing**[10] 7192 2-8-11 0.................. RosieJessop(3) 7 56
(Sir Mark Prescott Bt) *chsd ldrs: pushed along 1/2-way: styd on same pce wl ins fnl f* **50/1**

**7** *1 1/4* **Mon Petit Fleur** 2-8-7 0.................. ThomasHemsley(7) 8 51
(Chris Dwyer) *s.i.s: hld up: r.o towards fin: nvr nrr* **66/1**

0 **8** *nse* **Show Boat**[63] 5679 2-9-5 0.................. PJMcDonald 4 56
(Ann Duffield) *s.i.s: sn pushed along in rr: r.o ins fnl f: nt trble ldrs* **18/1**

9 *1* **More Spice (IRE)** 2-9-5 0........................ AdamBeschizza 9 52
(Robert Cowell) *s.i.s: hld up: rdn 1/2-way: nt trble ldrs* **9/1**

1m 2.23s (0.33) **Going Correction** -0.10s/f (Stan) **9** Ran SP% **119.4**
Speed ratings (Par 95): **93,90,89,89,87 87,85,85,83**
CSF £5.23 TOTE £2.10: £1.10, £1.40, £2.20; EX 5.90 Trifecta £28.50.
**Owner** Cheveley Park Stud **Bred** Cheveley Park Stud Ltd **Trained** Newmarket, Suffolk
**FOCUS**
An uncompetitive maiden run at a reasonable gallop. The winner raced centre-to-far side in the in the straight.

## 7455 DOWNLOAD THE FREE APP @ BOOKMAKERS.CO.UK H'CAP (TAPETA) 7f 32y

**6:45** (6:46) (Class 3) (0-95,95) 3-Y-0+ **£7,439** (£2,213; £1,106; £553) **Stalls** High

Form RPR
0025 **1** **Capo Rosso (IRE)**[21] 6943 4-9-6 **94**........................ RichardKingscote 3 105
(Tom Dascombe) *a.p: chsd ldr over 1f out: sn rdn: led ins fnl f: styd on wl* **9/2**[2]
3630 **2** *2 1/4* **George Cinq**[9] 7227 4-8-10 **87**........................ LouisSteward(3) 1 92
(Michael Bell) *mid-div: hdwy 2f out: rdn over 1f out: styd on same pce ins fnl f* **11/1**
0031 **3** *1/2* **Earth Drummer (IRE)**[35] 6535 4-9-7 **95**........................ DavidNolan 9 99
(David O'Meara) *mid-div: hdwy and nt clr run over 1f out: sn rdn: styd on: nt rch ldrs* **9/2**[2]
31-0 **4** *shd* **Pretend (IRE)**[261] 505 3-9-5 **95**........................[1] AdamKirby 2 98
(Charlie Appleby) *chsd ldrs: led over 2f out: sn pushd along: rdn: hdd and no ex ins fnl f* **4/1**[1]
1233 **5** *3/4* **The Great Gabrial**[21] 6943 5-8-12 **86**........................(p) JasonHart 4 88
(Michael Appleby) *hld up: hdwy over 1f out: r.o: nt rch ldrs* **9/2**[2]
1004 **6** *2 1/4* **Green Howard**[16] 7060 6-9-3 **91**........................ PaulMulrennan 7 87
(Robin Bastiman) *hld up: hdwy and n.m.r over 1f out: sn rdn: no ex ins fnl f* **18/1**
4041 **7** *3/4* **Bluegrass Blues (IRE)**[42] 6334 4-9-0 **88**........................ LukeMorris 8 82
(Paul Cole) *hld up: rdn over 2f out: styd on: nt trble ldrs* **11/2**[3]
00 **8** *2 1/4* **Sir Guy Porteous (IRE)**[22] 6895 3-8-13 **89**........................ JoeFanning 10 76
(Mark Johnston) *chsd ldrs: rdn over 2f out: no ex fnl f* **22/1**
5110 **9** *1 1/4* **Expose**[28] 6744 6-8-13 **87**........................ RobertWinston 11 72
(Shaun Harris) *s.i.s: hld up: nvr on terms* **14/1**
0020 **10** *1 3/4* **Whozthecat (IRE)**[8] 7233 7-8-10 **91** ow3........................ LukeLeadbitter(7) 5 71
(Declan Carroll) *led: rdn and hdd over 2f out: wkng whn n.m.r ent fnl f* **33/1**
1400 **11** *11* **Silverware (USA)**[132] 3272 6-8-13 **87**........................ TomEaves 6 39
(Kristin Stubbs) *chsd ldr tl rdn over 2f out: wknd over 1f out* **66/1**

1m 26.44s (-2.36) **Going Correction** -0.10s/f (Stan) course record
**WFA** 3 from 4yo+ 2lb **11** Ran SP% **119.0**
Speed ratings (Par 107): **109,106,105,105,104 102,101,98,97,95 82**
CSF £52.96 CT £238.78 TOTE £6.90: £2.00, £3.30, £1.80; EX 49.10 Trifecta £377.90.
**Owner** Deva Racing Red Clubs Partnership **Bred** Michael Wiley **Trained** Malpas, Cheshire
**FOCUS**
A good-quality handicap but one in which progressive sorts were in a minority. The gallop was reasonable and the winner came down the centre in the straight.

## 7456 FREE BETS GALORE @ BOOKIES.COM CLAIMING STKS (TAPETA) 1m 141y

**7:15** (7:16) (Class 6) 3-Y-0+ **£2,264** (£673; £336; £168) **Stalls** Low

Form RPR
2446 **1** **Dialogue**[40] 6402 8-8-11 77........................ SilvestreDeSousa 1 65
(Geoffrey Harker) *a.p: rdn to chse ldr over 1f out: styd on to ld nr fin* **11/1**
000 **2** *nk* **Skytrain**[11] 7183 4-9-9 78........................ JoeFanning 8 76
(Mark Johnston) *led: rdn and edgd rt over 1f out: hdd nr fin* **6/1**[3]
644 **3** *1 1/2* **Choice Of Destiny**[42] 6342 3-8-5 63........................ DannyBrock(3) 6 62
(Philip McBride) *s.i.s: hld up: r.o u.p ins fnl f: nt rch ldrs* **11/1**
0453 **4** *1/2* **Al Muheer (IRE)**[8] 7249 9-8-6 68........................(v) ConnorBeasley(5) 10 57
(Michael Herrington) *hld up: hdwy over 1f out: r.o: nt rch ldrs* **15/2**
1101 **5** *1* **Tee It Up Tommo (IRE)**[98] 4432 5-9-13 82........................ RobertWinston 4 73
(Michael Wigham) *hld up in tch: rdn over 1f out: styd on same pce ins fnl f* **2/1**[1]
0062 **6** *hd* **Kimbali (IRE)**[32] 6626 5-8-10 74........................ LukeLeadbitter(7) 5 63
(Declan Carroll) *mid-div: hdwy over 1f out: nt clr run 1f out: kpt on* **8/1**
0000 **7** *1 3/4* **Calrissian (IRE)**[53] 6019 3-9-5 60........................ BenCurtis 3 65
(Timothy Jarvis) *prom: chsd ldr over 6f out tl rdn over 1f out: no ex ins fnl f* **100/1**
6233 **8** *shd* **Jackpot**[48] 6188 4-8-1 45........................ JemmaMarshall(3) 7 45
(Brendan Powell) *w ldr 2f: remained handy: rdn over 1f out: no ex ins fnl f* **100/1**
5200 **9** *1 3/4* **Mister Musicmaster**[12] 7159 5-9-1 78........................ AdamKirby 9 52
(Ron Hodges) *hld up: rdn 3f out: n.d* **5/2**[2]

1m 49.09s (-1.01) **Going Correction** -0.10s/f (Stan)
**WFA** 3 from 4yo+ 4lb **9** Ran SP% **117.7**
Speed ratings (Par 101): **100,99,98,97,97 96,95,95,93**
CSF £76.79 TOTE £10.00: £3.40, £2.30, £2.00; EX 62.60 Trifecta £399.70.Dialogue was claimed by Andrew Reid for £4,000. Mister Musicmaster was subject to a friendly claim of £6,000
**Owner** P I Harker **Bred** Darley **Trained** Thirkleby, N Yorks
**FOCUS**
A reasonable event of its type. The gallop soon steadied and it proved difficult to make up ground from off the pace.

## 7457 EVERY GOAL SCORER @ FOOTBALLSCORES.COM H'CAP (TAPETA) 5f 20y

**7:45** (7:45) (Class 6) (0-65,68) 3-Y-0 **£2,264** (£673; £336; £168) **Stalls** Low

Form RPR
0123 **1** **Simply Black (IRE)**[26] 6819 3-9-5 63........................(p) DavidNolan 4 72
(David O'Meara) *chsd ldr tl led 2f out: rdn and edgd rt over 1f out: all out* **8/1**
0465 **2** *shd* **Dynamo Walt (IRE)**[10] 7213 3-9-6 64........................(v) DaleSwift 5 73
(Derek Shaw) *trckd ldrs: plld hrd: rdn to chse wnr over 1f out: r.o* **11/8**[1]
0553 **3** *2* **Lazy Sioux**[18] 7010 3-8-4 46........................ NeilFarley(3) 6 53
(Richard Guest) *hld up: rdn over 1f out: styd on u.p ins fnl f* **14/1**
5-01 **4** *1* **Bush Beauty (IRE)**[8] 7253 3-9-7 68........................ DannyBrock(3) 7 66
(Philip McBride) *hld up: rdn over 1f out: nt trble ldrs* **9/4**[2]
634 **5** *1 1/2* **Red Forever**[16] 7058 3-9-3 61........................ PatrickMathers 3 54
(Alan Berry) *s.i.s: plld hrd and sn prom: rdn over 1f out: no ex fnl f* **12/1**
2014 **6** *hd* **Meebo (IRE)**[42] 6340 3-9-7 65........................(vt) JoeFanning 1 57
(J R Jenkins) *led 3f: sn rdn: wknd ins fnl f* **15/2**[3]

1m 2.07s (0.17) **Going Correction** -0.10s/f (Stan) **6** Ran SP% **110.1**
Speed ratings (Par 99): **94,93,90,89,86 86**
CSF £18.85 TOTE £5.20: £3.00, £1.10; EX 24.40 Trifecta £148.00.
**Owner** Sterling Racing **Bred** Liam Ormsby **Trained** Nawton, N Yorks
**FOCUS**
A modest handicap run at a fair gallop. The winner came down the centre in the straight.

## 7458 PRICE BOOSTS NOW AVAILABLE @ BOOKMAKERS.CO.UK H'CAP (TAPETA) 1m 4f 50y

**8:15** (8:15) (Class 6) (0-65,70) 3-Y-O **£2,264** (£673; £336; £168) **Stalls** Low

Form RPR
0064 **1** **Cascadia (IRE)**[21] 6939 3-8-8 52 oh1 ow1........................ TomEaves 7 61
(Alison Hutchinson) *mde all: rdn over 1f out: all out* **33/1**
066U **2** *nk* **Bowberry**[26] 6818 3-8-11 58........................ RyanTate(3) 9 66
(Clive Cox) *hld up: hdwy u.p over 1f out: r.o wl towards fin: jst failed* **16/1**
3421 **3** *1/2* **Rock Of Leon**[7] 7287 3-8-12 56........................(p) LukeMorris 1 63
(Michael Bell) *chsd wnr over 3f: remained handy: rdn to chse wnr again 2f out: ev ch fr over 1f out: unable qck nr fin* **5/2**[1]
0043 **4** *2 1/4* **Sakhra**[14] 7118 3-9-0 58........................ GrahamGibbons 3 61
(Mark Brisbourne) *a.p: chsd wnr over 8f out tl rdn 2f out: styd on same pce ins fnl f* **14/1**
000 **5** *2* **Kirtling**[15] 7074 3-9-4 62........................ AdamKirby 10 62
(Andi Brown) *s.s: hld up: plld hrd: hdwy over 5f out: rdn over 2f out: styd on same pce fnl f* **5/1**[3]
4364 **6** *7* **Power Up**[19] 6981 3-8-13 57........................(v) JoeFanning 4 46
(Mark Johnston) *prom: rdn over 2f out: wknd over 1f out* **5/1**[3]
006 **7** *nk* **Aurora Borealis (IRE)**[6] 7309 3-9-2 60........................(b[1]) PaulMulrennan 6 48
(Ed Dunlop) *prom: rdn over 3f out: wknd over 1f out* **3/1**[2]
0-06 **8** *13* **Sweet Charlie**[37] 6483 3-8-7 51 oh1........................ SilvestreDeSousa 5 18
(Mike Murphy) *s.i.s: hld up: plld hrd: rdn and wknd over 2f out* **8/1**

2m 39.72s (-1.08) **Going Correction** -0.10s/f (Stan) **8** Ran SP% **113.5**
Speed ratings (Par 99): **99,98,98,96,95 90,90,82**
CSF £452.34 CT £1804.91 TOTE £18.10: £2.90, £7.20, £1.10; EX 212.80 Trifecta £1972.30.
**Owner** Miss A L Hutchinson **Bred** John Wholey **Trained** Exning, Suffolk
**FOCUS**
A couple of previous winners in a modest handicap. An ordinary gallop only lifted on the approach to the home turn and the winner came down the centre.

## 7459 DOWNLOAD THE FREE APP @ BOOKIES.COM FILLIES' H'CAP (TAPETA) 1m 1f 103y

**8:45** (8:45) (Class 5) (0-75,74) 3-Y-0+ **£2,911** (£866; £432; £216) **Stalls** Low

Form RPR
2124 **1** **Real Jazz (IRE)**[4] 7359 3-9-1 **69**........................ LukeMorris 7 84+
(Sir Mark Prescott Bt) *led: hdd 8f out: chsd ldr tl led again over 2f out: rdn out* **10/3**[1]
402 **2** *2 1/4* **Tayma (IRE)**[19] 6982 3-8-9 **63**........................ SilvestreDeSousa 8 73
(Saeed bin Suroor) *a.p: chsd wnr 2f out: rdn and hung lft over 1f out: styd on same pce fnl f* **7/2**[2]
5250 **3** *2 1/2* **Outbacker (IRE)**[21] 6945 3-9-2 **70**........................ JoeFanning 6 75
(Mark Johnston) *hld up in tch: rdn over 1f out: styd on same pce* **20/1**
4111 **4** *1 3/4* **Evacusafe Lady**[16] 7068 3-9-1 **69**........................(t) AdamKirby 1 70
(John Ryan) *mid-div: hdwy u.p over 1f out: nt trble ldrs* **7/2**[2]
3060 **5** *2 1/4* **Saltwater Creek (IRE)**[32] 6633 3-9-3 **74**........................ LouisSteward(3) 9 70
(Michael Bell) *hld up: rdn over 2f out: nt trble ldrs* **11/2**
2310 **6** *1* **Dansili Dutch (IRE)**[18] 7008 5-9-3 **74**........................ JoshDoyle(7) 2 68
(David O'Meara) *hld up: rdn over 1f out: nvr nrr* **22/1**
-300 **7** *1/2* **Mystery Bet (IRE)**[14] 7125 4-9-6 **70**........................ DavidNolan 3 63
(Richard Fahey) *chsd ldrs: rdn over 2f out: wknd over 1f out* **14/1**
1605 **8** *6* **Pigeon Pie**[9] 7225 3-8-13 **67**........................(b) FrannyNorton 4 48
(Mark Johnston) *plld hrd and prom: rdn over 2f out: wknd over 1f out* **33/1**
3105 **9** *2* **Diletta Tommasa (IRE)**[31] 6672 4-9-2 **71**........................(p) EoinWalsh(5) 10 47
(John Stimpson) *s.i.s: outpcd: rdn over 2f out: n.d* **16/1**
1345 **10** *13* **Law Keeper (IRE)**[25] 6841 3-9-4 **72**........................(b[1]) RichardKingscote 11 21
(James Tate) *led 8f out: rdn and hdd over 2f out: wknd over 1f out* **12/1**
4650 **11** *37* **French Flirt**[36] 6515 3-8-11 **65**........................ BenCurtis 5
(Timothy Jarvis) *s.i.s: outpcd* **66/1**

1m 58.37s (-2.43) **Going Correction** -0.10s/f (Stan)
**WFA** 3 from 4yo+ 4lb **11** Ran SP% **125.7**
Speed ratings (Par 100): **106,104,101,100,98 97,96,91,89,78 45**
CSF £15.82 CT £213.62 TOTE £4.20: £1.40, £2.10, £5.50; EX 18.70 Trifecta £367.20.
**Owner** Timothy J Rooney **Bred** Alan Dargan **Trained** Newmarket, Suffolk
**FOCUS**
A reasonable handicap run at an ordinary gallop. The winner raced just off the far rail throughout.
T/Plt: £116.10 to a £1 stake. Pool: £85,801.19 - 539.48 winning tickets T/Qpdt: £94.70 to a £1 stake. Pool: £9,043.44 - 70.60 winning tickets CR

7460 - 7461a (Foreign Racing) - See Raceform Interactive

# 6347 LEOPARDSTOWN (L-H)

Saturday, October 25

**OFFICIAL GOING: Yielding to soft**

## 7462a KILLAVULLAN STKS (GROUP 3) 7f

**3:10** (3:10) 2-Y-O **£32,500** (£9,500; £4,500; £1,500)

RPR
**1** **Steip Amach (IRE)**[3] 7388 2-9-0 89........................ KevinManning 2 100
(J S Bolger, Ire) *w.w in rr of quartet: hdwy on outer into 3rd fr 2f out: effrt in 2nd ins fnl f and r.o wl u.p to ld ins fnl 100yds* **12/1**[3]
**2** *3/4* **Royal Navy Ship (USA)**[13] 7138 2-9-3........................ SeamieHeffernan 3 101
(A P O'Brien, Ire) *sn led: narrow advantage 1/2-way: hdd briefly into st: sn rdn w narrow advantage: strly pressed u.p wl ins fnl f and hdd ins fnl 100yds: no ex* **1/6**[1]
**3** *2 1/2* **Cocoon (IRE)**[13] 7141 2-9-0 94........................ AnaO'Brien 1 92
(A P O'Brien, Ire) *settled bhd ldrs in 3rd: dropped to rr fr 2f out: rdn into 3rd jst ins fnl f and swtchd rt: no imp on ldrs towards fin: kpt on same pce* **10/1**[2]
**4** *2 1/2* **Mandamus (IRE)**[7] 7296 2-9-3 88........................ PatSmullen 4 89
(Ms Sheila Lavery, Ire) *wnt sltly rt s: settled bhd ldr in cl 2nd: led briefly into st: sn rdn in 2nd and no imp on ldr u.p ent fnl f: no ex and dropped to rr ins fnl f* **10/1**[2]

1m 32.96s (4.26) **Going Correction** +0.425s/f (Yiel) **4** Ran SP% **111.6**
Speed ratings: **92,91,88,85**
CSF £15.93 TOTE £10.10; DF 33.60 Trifecta £51.80.
**Owner** Mrs J S Bolger **Bred** J S Bolger **Trained** Coolcullen, Co Carlow
**FOCUS**
A somewhat disappointing turnout and a 1-6 favourite beaten.


The Form Book, Raceform Ltd, Newbury, RG14 5SJ

7463 - 7466a (Foreign Racing) - See Raceform Interactive

## 7436 MOONEE VALLEY (L-H)

Saturday, October 25

**OFFICIAL GOING: Turf: good**

### 7467a SPORTINGBET COX PLATE (GROUP 1) (3YO+) (TURF) 1m 2f 44y

7:40 (12:00) 3-Y-O+

**£992,043** (£236,559; £118,279; £69,892; £59,139; £53,763)

RPR

1 **Adelaide (IRE)**[41] 6379 3-8-11 0 RyanMoore 13 114
(A P O'Brien, Ire) *hld up in last: clsd steadily on wd outside fr 5f out: rdn 2f out and chal into st: led ins fnl f: styd on wl and a doing enough* **7/1**[3]

2 *snk* **Fawkner (AUS)**[14] 7127 7-9-4 0 (b) NicholasHall 4 116
(Robert Hickmott, Australia) *stmbld s: sn midfield in tch: clsd and rdn to chal 2f out: led into st: styd on wl but hdd fnl f and jst hld: almost lost 2nd post* **17/5**[1]

3 *shd* **Silent Achiever (NZ)**[21] 6975 6-9-0 0 (b) NashRawiller 11 111
(Roger James, New Zealand) *midfield: rdn and clsd 2f out: effrt into st: styd on wl and wnt 3rd fnl f: almost snatched 2nd post: nt quite pce of wnr* **25/1**

4 *nk* **Side Glance**[14] 7127 7-9-4 0 JamieSpencer 7 115
(Andrew Balding) *pushed along to go forward and sn w ldrs: hdd after first turn but remained prom: rdn 2f out: styd on wl fnl f but nt quite pce of ldng trio* **20/1**

5 *shd* **Foreteller**[14] 7127 7-9-4 0 (b) TommyBerry 1 115
(Chris Waller, Australia) *midfield in tch on inner: had to wait for run and shuffled bk 2f out: rdn into st: nt clr run again jst ins fnl f: styd on strly once clr: unlucky* **30/1**

6 *shd* **Happy Trails (AUS)**[14] 7127 7-9-4 0 DamienOliver 2 115
(Paul Beshara, Australia) *dwlt but qckly rcvrd: hld up towards rr on inner: angled out and rdn over 2f out: styd on wl fnl f but nt quite pce to chal* **11/1**

7 *3/4* **Criterion (NZ)**[14] 7127 4-9-1 0 (b) JamesMcDonald 6 110+
(David Payne, Australia) *dwlt sltly and hld up towards rr: rdn 3f out: effrt to cl on wd outside into st: styd on wl towards fin but nvr able to chal* **5/1**[2]

8 *1/2* **Sweynesse (AUS)**[14] 3-7-11 0 (p) ChadSchofield 12 107
(J O'Shea, Australia) *hld up in rr: last 3f out: rdn into st: styd on wl fnl f but hld whn short of room toward fin* **16/1**

9 *1 1/2* **The Cleaner (AUS)**[29] 6733 7-9-4 0 (bt) StevenArnold 14 109
(Mick Burles, Australia) *sent forward fr wdst draw and sn w ldrs on outer: led after first turn: rdn and kicked on 3f out: strly pressed fr 2f out: hdd into st: no ex and fdd fnl 120yds* **14/1**

10 *hd* **Wandjina (AUS)**[14] 3-7-11 0 (b) DeanYendall 5 104
(Gai Waterhouse, Australia) *led early: sn jnd and hdd after first turn: in tch after: clsd again and rdn to chal over 1f out: ev ch into st: no ex fnl f: fdd* **30/1**

11 *3* **Sacred Falls (NZ)**[14] 7127 5-9-4 0 (b) ZacPurton 9 103
(Chris Waller, Australia) *hld up towards rr on inner: rdn 2f out: kpt on same pce and no imp in st: eased whn btn towards fin* **15/2**

12 *2* **Royal Descent (AUS)**[21] 6959 5-9-0 0 (t) GlenBoss 3 95
(Chris Waller, Australia) *midfield: rdn and effrt to improve on outer over 2f out: no ex and lost pl into st: eased whn btn fnl f* **10/1**

13 *20* **Almalad (AUS)**[14] 3-7-11 0 (b) CraigNewitt 8 54
(Gai Waterhouse, Australia) *sn w ldrs: hdd after first turn and trckd ldr: rdn and lost pl over 2f out: dropped to rr and btn into st: eased: t.o* **10/1**

P **Guest Of Honour (IRE)**[14] 7128 5-9-4 0 (p) CraigAWilliams 10
(Marco Botti) *t.k.h: sn midfield: lost pl and dropped to last over 2f out: t.o and p.u* **80/1**

2m 3.76s (123.76)
**WFA** 3 from 4yo+ 5lb **14** Ran SP% **113.2**
PARI-MUTUEL (NSW TAB - all including 1 aud stake): WIN 8.30; PLACE 3.00, 2.10, 5.30; DF 19.50; SF 39.90.
**Owner** Mrs J Magnier, W H Webb Et Al **Bred** Elletelle Syndicate **Trained** Cashel, Co Tipperary

**FOCUS**
A good field competed for Australasia's weight-for-age championship but, as is often the case in races in that part of the world, plenty of runners finished close up on passing the post - Damien Oliver said afterwards that it was 'probably the most exciting finish I've ridden in a Cox Plate'. The race proved to be another triumph in the saddle for Ryan Moore who, from a difficult draw, made all the right moves at the right time. It was also a second win for an International runner in the space of a week, after Admire Rakti's win in the Caulfield Cup.

## 3810 NANTES (R-H)

Saturday, October 25

**OFFICIAL GOING: Turf: heavy**

### 7468a PRIX DES SABLONNETS (LISTED RACE) (2YO) (TURF) 1m

12:15 (12:00) 2-Y-O **£22,916** (£9,166; £6,875; £4,583; £2,291)

RPR

1 **Jolly Good Kitten (USA)** 2-9-2 0 CristianDemuro 8 100+
(Gianluca Bietolini, Italy) **54/10**[3]

2 *hd* **Leader Writer (FR)**[33] 6618 2-9-2 0 AntoineWerle 1 99
(H-A Pantall, France) **17/2**

3 *4* **Biraaj (IRE)** 2-9-2 0 AntoineHamelin 9 90
(Matthieu Palussiere, France) **33/10**[2]

4 *2 1/2* **Stand Up In Paris (FR)**[39] 2-8-13 0 RaphaelMarchelli 4 81
(H Fortineau, France) **20/1**

5 *5* **Texalila (FR)**[81] 2-8-13 0 MathieuAndrouin 2 70
(Mme A-M Poirier, France) **40/1**

6 *10* **Groor**[41] 6377 2-9-2 0 IoritzMendizabal 5 51
(James Tate) *chsd ldrs on outer: rdn 2f out and no imp: wknd over 1f out: eased ins fnl f* **5/2**[1]

7 *8* **Synthese (IRE)**[32] 2-8-13 0 AlexandreRoussel 3 31
(J Boisnard, France) **7/1**

8 *dist* **Carry Out (FR)** 2-9-2 0 FabriceVeron 7
(H-A Pantall, France) **63/10**

9 *dist* **Arystyn Gouli (FR)**[23] 2-8-13 0 MaximeGuyon 6
(X Thomas-Demeaulte, France) **10/1**

1m 45.37s (105.37) **9** Ran SP% **120.5**
PARI-MUTUEL (all including 1 euro stake): WIN 6.40; PLACE 2.30, 2.40, 1.70; DF 21.70; SF 45.20.
**Owner** Kenneth L & Sarah K Ramsey **Bred** Kenneth L Ramsey & Sarah K Ramsey **Trained** Italy

## 7320 SAN SIRO (R-H)

Saturday, October 25

**OFFICIAL GOING: Turf: good**

### 7469a ST LEGER ITALIANO (GROUP 3) (3YO+) (TURF) 1m 6f

3:25 (12:00) 3-Y-O+ **£23,333** (£10,266; £5,600; £2,800)

RPR

1 **Rock Of Romance (IRE)**[34] 6589 4-8-13 0 EPedroza 2 100+
(A Wohler, Germany) *trckd ldr: rdn to ld 2f out: drvn appr fnl f and forged clr: readily* **13/20**[1]

2 *2 1/2* **Salut (GER)**[370] 7407 6-8-13 0 AStarke 3 97
(P Schiergen, Germany) *t.k.h: hld up in midfield: rdn to chse ldr over 1 1/2f out: kpt on u.p fnl f: nt pce to go w wnr* **16/5**[2]

3 *2* **Vado Di Siella (ITY)** 3-8-5 0 DarioVargiu 5 95
(Stefano Botti, Italy) *w.w towards rr: clsd on inner 3 1/2f out: rdn to chse ldng trio 2f out: sltly outpcd by front two over 1f out: kpt on at same pce fnl f* **36/5**

4 *1/2* **Victory Song (IRE)**[367] 7479 4-8-13 0 LManiezzi 6 93
(W Figge, Germany) *hld up in last: rdn and outpcd 2 1/2f out: kpt on ins fnl f: nt pce to get involved* **61/10**[3]

5 *nse* **Targaryen (IRE)**[188] 1603 4-8-13 0 (p) FBossa 4 93
(G Marras, Italy) *t.k.h early: sn settled bhd ldng pair: rdn and nt qckn 2 1/2f out: fdd ins fnl f* **219/10**

6 *nse* **Donn Halling (IRE)**[87] 6-8-13 0 VJanacek 7 93
(V Luka Jr, Czech Republic) *w.w towards rr on outer: pushed along and sltly outpcd 3f out: plugged on at one pce u.p fnl f: nvr in contention* **68/10**

7 *1/2* **Roncalli (IRE)**[405] 5-8-13 0 AntonioFresu 1 92
(Klaudia Freitag, Italy) *t.k.h: led: hdd 2f out: wknd fnl f* **46/1**

3m 6.9s (186.90)
**WFA** 3 from 4yo+ 9lb **7** Ran SP% **130.0**
WIN (incl. 1 euro stake): 1.64. PLACES: 1.10, 1.52. DF: 2.65.
**Owner** Hans-Georg Stihl **Bred** Brendan Corbett **Trained** Germany

7470 - 7475a (Foreign Racing) - See Raceform Interactive

## 7460 LEOPARDSTOWN (L-H)

Sunday, October 26

**OFFICIAL GOING: Yielding (soft in places)**

### 7476a TOTE NOVEMBER H'CAP (PREMIER HANDICAP) 1m 7f

3:25 (3:27) 3-Y-O+

**£50,000** (£15,833; £7,500; £2,500; £1,666; £833)

RPR

1 **Clondaw Warrior (IRE)**[14] 7142 7-8-8 **86** JFEgan 8 90
(W P Mullins, Ire) *in tch: 7th 4f out: tk clsr order into st and rdn in 3rd 1 1/2f out: clsd u.p on outer to ld ins fnl 150yds: all out towards fin to hold on* **16/1**

2 *nk* **Spacious Sky (USA)**[43] 6349 5-8-2 **85** (t) SeanCorby(5) 20 88+
(A J Martin, Ire) *dwlt and settled towards rr: plenty to do into st: gd hdwy far side fr 2f out to chse ldrs in 4th ins fnl f: swtchd rt and r.o wl into 2nd clsng stages: jst hld* **16/1**

3 *1/2* **Albert Bridge**[57] 5924 6-8-4 **82** SilvestreDeSousa 22 85
(Ralph Beckett) *sn chsd ldrs tl tk clsr order in 2nd after 2f: 3rd 1/2-way: rdn to chal under 2f out and sn led narrowly: hdd u.p ins fnl 150yds and no ex in 3rd clsng stages* **14/1**

4 *3/4* **Hisaabaat (IRE)**[87] 4139 6-8-8 **86** LeighRoche 2 88
(D K Weld, Ire) *led tl hdd after 6f: rdn in 2nd into st and sn led: hdd u.p 1 1/2f out and no ex in 4th wl ins fnl f* **20/1**

5 *1/2* **Hidden Universe (IRE)**[14] 7142 8-8-8 **86** PatSmullen 7 87
(D K Weld, Ire) *chsd ldrs: 5th 1/2-way: rdn in 4th 1 1/2f out and sn no imp on ldrs: kpt on same pce* **9/2**[2]

6 *1/2* **Waydownsouth (IRE)**[21] 6588 7-7-11 **82** IanQueally(7) 1 82
(Patrick J Flynn, Ire) *in rr of mid-div: 16th 3f out: hdwy far side into st to chse ldrs in 6th 1f out: no ex and one pce towards fin* **33/1**

7 *1/2* **Cliff House (IRE)**[14] 7142 4-7-11 **82** TomMadden(7) 4 82
(John J Walsh, Ire) *chsd ldrs: rdn in 6th under 2f out and no imp on ldrs ent fnl f: kpt on same pce* **16/1**

8 *3/4* **Coolfighter (GER)**[26] 6849 6-8-1 **84** (p) GaryPhillips(5) 6 83
(N Dooly, Ire) *in tch: 10th over 3f out: rdn into 7th 1 1/2f out and no imp on ldrs ins fnl f: kpt on one pce* **20/1**

9 *1 1/4* **Artful Artist (IRE)**[42] 6376 5-8-12 **90** RichardHughes 16 87
(A J Martin, Ire) *hld up: last 4f out: hdwy fr 2f out where short of room and swtchd rt: kpt on wl ins fnl f: nvr a threat* **9/1**[3]

10 *3/4* **Sailors Warn (IRE)**[106] 3768 7-8-3 **84** ConorHoban(3) 11 80
(E J O'Grady, Ire) *racd in mid-div: rdn in 12th under 2f out and no imp ent fnl f: kpt on one pce* **40/1**

11 *1 1/4* **Stomachion (IRE)**[44] 6287 4-9-7 **99** BillyLee 21 94
(Sir Michael Stoute) *in tch: pushed along in 9th 3f out and no ex u.p 1 1/2f out: one pce fnl f* **7/2**[1]

12 *1 3/4* **Digeanta (IRE)**[15] 7107 7-8-10 **88** (tp) ShaneFoley 19 80
(W P Mullins, Ire) *w.w towards rr: pushed along in 17th over 3f out and sme late hdwy fnl 2f* **12/1**

13 *hd* **Ballyadam Brook (IRE)**[120] 3740 10-8-5 **83** RoryCleary 5 75
(Terence O'Brien, Ire) *in tch tl tk clsr order after 5f: sn led and extended advantage: reduced advantage and pushed along fr 4f out: hdd 2f out and sn wknd* **50/1**

14 *1 1/4* **Massini's Trap (IRE)**[14] 7142 5-8-0 **83** oh5 ow1 RobbieDowney(5) 13 73
(J A Nash, Ire) *in rr of mid-div: pushed along in 14th 3f out and no imp under 2f out: kpt on one pce* **28/1**

15 *hd* **Gentleman Duke (IRE)**[7] 6141 6-8-6 **84** (e[1]) NGMcCullagh 15 74
(A L T Moore, Ire) *reluctant to load: settled in mid-div: pushed along over 4f out and tk clsr order on outer 3f out: no ex u.p into st: wknd fnl 2f* **25/1**

16 *1 3/4* **Blue Hussar (IRE)**[7] 7314 3-8-11 **105** DonnachaO'Brien(7) 17 93
(A P O'Brien, Ire) *dwlt and settled in rr: tk clsr order on outer towards rr 3f out and brought wd into st: kpt on one pce fnl 2f* **16/1**

17 *shd* **Sir Ector (USA)**[22] 4880 7-9-9 **101** (b) RonanWhelan 23 89
(J J Lambe, Ire) *nvr bttr than mid-div: rdn and no imp 3f out* **16/1**

18 *shd* **Street Party (IRE)**[189] 8255 4-8-6 **84** oh12 ow2.........(t) MichaelHussey 3 72
(Mrs Julie Cashin, Ire) *chsd ldrs: 4th 1/2-way: rdn and no ex over 2f out: wknd* **50/1**

19 *3/4* **Eye Of The Tiger (GER)**[14] 7142 9-8-4 **82** oh2.................... BenCurtis 9 69
(J P Murtagh, Ire) *chsd ldrs: 6th 1/2-way: rdn and wknd fr 3f out* **20/1**

20 *2* **Orgilgo Bay (IRE)**[11] 5842 4-8-12 **90**........................ GaryCarroll 10 74
(John C McConnell, Ire) *racd in mid-div: rdn over 4f out and no imp bef st: wknd* **14/1**

21 *15* **Majenta (IRE)**[14] 7142 4-9-0 **92**........................... ChrisHayes 18 56
(Kevin Prendergast, Ire) *in rr of mid-div: rdn and wknd fr under 4f out* **25/1**

22 *24* **Cosmic Cannonball (IRE)**[42] 6370 4-9-12 **104**......... KevinManning 14 37
(J S Bolger, Ire) *ponied to s: in tch: 9th 4f out: sn rdn and wknd bef st: eased* **20/1**

3m 14.06s (-1.94) **Going Correction** +0.125s/f (Good)
**WFA** 3 from 4yo+ 9lb **22** Ran SP% **140.3**
Speed ratings: **110,109,109,109,108 108,108,107,107,106 106,105,105,104,104 103,103,103,102,101 93,81**
CSF £243.32 CT £3713.24 TOTE £22.80: £4.30, £4.10, £3.20, £5.70; DF 378.70 Trifecta £7296.80.
**Owner** Act D Wagg Syndicate **Bred** John & Miriam Murphy **Trained** Muine Beag, Co Carlow

**FOCUS**
A big disappointment when favourite for the Irish Cesarewitch in which he raced far too freely.

7477 - 7478a (Foreign Racing) - See Raceform Interactive

## 2374 CAPANNELLE (R-H)
Sunday, October 26

**OFFICIAL GOING: Turf: good**

### 7479a PREMIO GUIDO BERARDELLI (GROUP 3) (2YO) (TURF) 1m 1f
**1:25** (12:00) 2-Y-O **£29,166** (£12,833; £7,000; £3,500)

RPR

1 **Misterious Boy (IRE)**[119] 2-8-11 0.............................. DarioVargiu 3 100
(Stefano Botti, Italy) *cl up in 3rd on outer: shkn up 2 1/2f out: hrd rdn and chal on outer 2f out: led ins fnl f: drvn out and asserted last 100yds* **4/9**[1]

2 *1* **Panther Cat (ITY)** 2-8-11 0.............................. GBietolini 2 98
(Gianluca Bietolini, Italy) *trckd ldr: rdn and r.o fnl f: pressed wnr but no match fnl 100yds* **166/10**

3 *snk* **Yucatan (ITY)** 2-8-11 0.............................. MircoDemuro 4 98
(Stefano Botti, Italy) *settled in rr: outpcd and niggled along over 3f out: hdwy on inner 2f out: kpt on u.p fnl f: nvr quite on terms* **41/10**[3]

4 *2* **Altroquando (IRE)** 2-8-11 0.............................. CFiocchi 1 94
(Stefano Botti, Italy) *led: rdn and rallied whn chal 2f out: hdd ins fnl f: no ex* **9/5**[2]

1m 50.1s (-4.60) **4** Ran SP% **130.3**
WIN (incl. 1 euro stake): 1.44. PLACES: 1.18, 2.52. DF: 9.20.
**Owner** Scuderia Aleali Srl **Bred** Massimo Parri **Trained** Italy

### 7480a PREMIO LONGINES LYDIA TESIO (GROUP 1) (3YO+ FILLIES & MARES) (TURF) 1m 2f
**3:35** (12:00) 3-Y-O+ **£91,666** (£40,333; £22,000; £11,000)

RPR

1 **Final Score (IRE)**[129] 3376 3-8-10 0.............................. FabioBranca 11 107
(Stefano Botti, Italy) *mde all: jnd 2 1/2f out and hdd briefly 2f out: sn regained ld: hrd rdn and r.o fnl f: gamely responded whn chal on either side ins fnl f: jst hld on* **25/12**[2]

2 *nse* **Lacy (GER)**[50] 6162 3-8-10 0.............................. AndreaAtzeni 2 107
(Waldemar Hickst, Germany) *racd in 4th: rdn and chsd wnr on rail fr 2f out: hrd rdn and chal thrght fnl f: jst failed* **4/1**[3]

3 *3/4* **Calyxa**[28] 6808 4-9-0 0.............................. RobertHavlin 1 104
(Ferdinand J Leve, Germany) *trckd wnr: rdn and chal on outer fr 1 1/2f out: kpt on u.p ins fnl f: no ex fnl 75yds* **41/10**

4 *1 1/4* **Mayhem (IRE)**[22] 6956 3-8-10 0.............................. OlivierPeslier 10 103+
(P Sogorb, France) *racd in midfield: 6th and sltly outpcd 3f out: rdn and no immediate imp over 2f out: 5th and styng on fr over 1f out: kpt on fnl f: nt rch ldrs* **17/10**[1]

5 *1 3/4* **So Many Shots (IRE)**[14] 7146 3-8-10 0.............................. DarioVargiu 6 99+
(Stefano Botti, Italy) *racd in midfield: cl 5th and sltly outpcd fr 3f out: hrd rdn and no immediate imp fr 2f out: kpt on again fnl f: nvr in contention* **10/1**

6 *nk* **Vague Nouvelle (IRE)**[28] 6807 3-8-10 0.............................. MircoDemuro 8 99
(R Biondi, Italy) *a cl up: hdwy on outer to join wnr 2 1/2f out: led narrowly and briefly over 2f out: sn hdd: cl 4th and fading whn squeezed out and snatched up 100yds out: nt persevered w* **143/10**

7 *nse* **Summer Surprice (FR)**[25] 6882 3-8-10 0.............................. NicolaPinna 7 99
(F-H Graffard, France) *towards rr: pushed along and no real imp 2 1/2f out: sn rdn: styd on fr 1 1/2f out: kpt on wl ins fnl f: nrest at fin* **13/1**

8 *shd* **Lady Dutch**[14] 7146 3-8-10 0.............................. MEsposito 4 99
(B Grizzetti, Italy) *towards rr on inner: rdn and btn fr over 2f out* **51/1**

9 *1 3/4* **Lucky Serena (IRE)**[28] 4-9-0 0.............................. CFiocchi 5 94
(Agostino Affe', Italy) *in rr: rdn and no imp fnl 3f* **179/10**

10 *6* **Bridge Arabrab (IRE)**[28] 3-8-10 0.............................. CDiStasio 3 83
(Pierpaolo Sbariggia, Italy) *tk a t.k.h: restrained in rr: rdn and btn fr 2 1/2f out* **173/1**

11 *1 3/4* **Dark Ray (IRE)**[28] 5-9-0 0..............................(b) FrancescoDettori 9 79
(L Riccardi, Italy) *restrained in midfield on outer: rdn and btn fr 2f out* **61/1**

2m 2.0s (-1.30)
**WFA** 3 from 4yo+ 5lb **11** Ran SP% **141.3**
WIN (incl. 1 euro stake): 3.09. PLACES: 1.47, 1.60, 1.66. DF: 18.93.
**Owner** Scuderia Effevi SRL **Bred** Razza Del Velino Srl **Trained** Italy

## 4247 HANOVER (L-H)
Sunday, October 26

**OFFICIAL GOING: Turf: soft**

### 7481a GROSSER PREIS DES GESTUT ETZEAN (LISTED RACE) (2YO FILLIES) (TURF) 7f
**12:00** (12:00) 2-Y-O **£11,666** (£5,416; £2,500; £1,250)

RPR

1 **Fuscetta (GER)** 2-8-11 0.............................. APietsch 8 92
(Waldemar Hickst, Germany) **122/10**

2 *1 1/4* **Runner Runner (IRE)**[29] 6749 2-8-11 0.............................. LukeMorris 3 89
(George Baker) *wnt rt s: midfield in tch: rdn to chal into st: w ldrs and ev ch ent fnl f: r.o wl but nt pce of wnr towards fin and hld* **3/1**[2]

3 *3* **Damour (GER)** 2-9-0 0.............................. AHelfenbein 10 84
(Markus Klug, Germany) **21/10**[1]

4 *hd* **Rosy Blush** 2-8-11 0.............................. FabriceVeron 2 81
(A Wohler, Germany) **53/10**

5 *1/2* **Majestic Hope (GER)**[51] 6123 2-8-11 0.............................. JBojko 5 80
(A Wohler, Germany) **47/10**[3]

6 *nk* **Tuscany (GER)**[29] 6778 2-8-11 0.............................. AStarke 4 79
(P Schiergen, Germany) **99/10**

7 *5* **Universal Star (GER)** 2-8-11 0.............................. JackMitchell 1 66
(R Dzubasz, Germany) **108/10**

8 *2 1/2* **Hot Chilli Kiss (FR)**[31] 2-8-11 0.............................. AdriedeVries 9 60
(K Demme, Germany) **119/10**

9 *1* **Guavia (GER)** 2-8-11 0.............................. DanielePorcu 7 58
(P Schiergen, Germany) **96/10**

1m 31.93s (91.93) **9** Ran SP% **133.1**
WIN (incl. 10 euro stake): 132. PLACES: 29, 18, 13. SF: 1,008.
**Owner** Gestut Ittlingen **Bred** Gestut Hof Ittlingen **Trained** Germany

### 7482a GROSSER PREIS DER MEHL-MULHENS-STIFTUNG GESTUT ROTTGEN (GROUP 3) (3YO+ FILLIES & MARES) (TURF) 1m 3f
**1:05** (12:00) 3-Y-O+ **£26,666** (£9,166; £4,583; £2,500; £1,666; £1,250)

RPR

1 **Good Donna (GER)**[21] 3-8-13 0.............................. JackMitchell 6 104
(J Hirschberger, Germany) *t.k.h: hld up towards rr: hdwy into midfield 5f out: rdn into st: chal 2f out: led over 1f out: styd on wl fnl f and grad asserted* **11/2**[3]

2 *1 1/2* **Special Meaning**[35] 6589 4-9-4 0.............................. FrannyNorton 5 100
(Mark Johnston) *sn led: rdn into st: strly pressed 2f out: hdd over 1f out: styd on wl against rail fnl f but nt pce of wnr and hld towards fin* **117/10**

3 *3 1/2* **Abraxa (IRE)**[35] 3-8-13 0.............................. JulienAuge 3 95
(C Ferland, France) *prom: rdn and effrt into st: styd on for 3rd: nt pce of front pair* **9/1**

4 *3/4* **Heartily (IRE)**[21] 3-8-13 0.............................. FabriceVeron 7 93
(H-A Pantall, France) *midfield: rdn into st: short of room whn attempting to chal on rail over 1f out: swtchd lft and effrt sn after: styd on but readily outpcd by front pair fnl f* **13/5**[1]

5 *1/2* **Daksha (FR)**[23] 6914 4-9-4 0.............................. APietsch 10 91
(Waldemar Hickst, Germany) *midfield on outer: rdn 3f out: sn outpcd and dropped to rr: rallied u.p and styd on to go 5th cl home: nvr able to chal* **41/10**[2]

6 *1/2* **Emily Of Tinsdal (GER)**[35] 5-9-4 0.............................. AdriedeVries 8 91
(P Harley, Germany) *hld up in rr: rdn and hdwy 2f out: effrt over 1f out: outpcd by ldrs fnl f: no ex and dropped to 6th cl home* **6/1**

7 *1 1/2* **Seperate Opinion**[14] 5-9-4 0.............................. KKerekes 9 88
(C Zala, Hungary) *hld up in midfield: rdn into st: outpcd in rr over 1f out: plugged on but wl btn* **114/10**

8 *3* **Lutindi (GER)**[21] 3-8-13 0.............................. AStarke 4 83
(P Schiergen, Germany) *midfield on inner: rdn 3f out: outpcd over 1f out: eased whn btn fnl f* **201/10**

9 *1/2* **Alaskakonigin (GER)**[21] 3-8-13 0.............................. AHelfenbein 2 83
(Markus Klug, Germany) *led early: restrained and sn hdd: trckd ldr: rdn and brief effrt into st: outpcd and lost pl 2f out: eased whn btn fnl f* **7/1**

10 *4* **Lady Liberty (IRE)**[17] 7070 4-9-4 0.............................. SHellyn 11 74
(Andreas Lowe, Germany) *hld up and a in rr: rdn into st: no imp fnl 2f: eased whn btn fnl f* **135/10**

11 *4 1/2* **Early Morning (GER)**[21] 5-9-4 0.............................. FilipMinarik 1 66
(Dr A Bolte, Germany) *prom on inner: rdn 3f out: no ex and lost pl qckly over 1f out: last and wl btn fnl f: eased* **168/10**

2m 27.14s (147.14)
**WFA** 3 from 4yo+ 6lb **11** Ran SP% **132.7**
WIN (incl. 10 euro stake): 65. PLACES: 27, 27, 27. SF: 1,173.
**Owner** Gestut Auenquelle **Bred** Gestut Auenquelle **Trained** Germany

### 7483a GROSSER PREIS DER DEUTSCHEN BANK (LISTED RACE) (3YO+ FILLIES & MARES) (TURF) 7f
**2:10** (12:00) 3-Y-O+ **£11,666** (£5,416; £2,500; £1,250)

RPR

1 **Goiania**[28] 3-8-11 0..............................(p) AStarke 12 98
(P Schiergen, Germany) **12/1**

2 *nk* **Iveagh Gardens (IRE)**[217] 1074 3-8-11 0.............................. AdriedeVries 13 97+
(Charles O'Brien, Ire) *dwlt sltly and racd in rr: rdn 3f out: swtchd rt then lft for run 2f out: styd on wl and wnt 2nd towards fin: nt quite rch wnr* **26/5**[3]

3 *1 1/2* **Malka (FR)**[28] 3-8-11 0..............................(p) JackMitchell 6 93
(Frau Erika Mader, Germany) **18/1**

4 *3/4* **Al Queena (GER)** 3-8-11 0.............................. MichaelCadeddu 8 91
(Frau C Barsig, Germany) **128/10**

5 *3* **Alpha (GER)**[56] 5966 5-9-0 0..............................(b) PJWerning 15 85
(R Werning, Germany) **30/1**

6 *1* **Si Luna (GER)**[23] 6914 5-9-0 0.............................. FranciscoDaSilva 2 82
(Prof Dr G W Sybrecht, Germany) **176/10**

7 *1 1/2* **Chesturo (IRE)**[63] 3-8-11 0.............................. JBojko 14 76
(A Wohler, Germany) **15/2**

8 *6* **Athenian (IRE)**[31] 6689 5-9-3 0..............................(p) LukeMorris 3 65
(Sir Mark Prescott Bt) *chsd ldr on inner: rdn 3f out: outpcd and btn over 1f out: wknd and eased fnl f* **4/1**[1]

9 *hd* **Sugar Love (GER)**[56] 5965 3-8-11 0.............................. FilipMinarik 7 60
(P Schiergen, Germany) **38/1**
10 *1* **Agama (GER)**[126] 4-9-0 0.............................. EFrank 1 59
(F Kurz, Germany) **57/1**
11 *2* **Rosa Rot (GER)**[179] 3-8-11 0.............................. WPanov 16 51
(Mario Hofer, Germany) **49/1**
12 *6* **Librettista (FR)**[49] 4-9-0 0.............................. MartinSeidl 4 37
(Frau S Weis, Germany) **30/1**
13 *1* **Sovalla**[42] 3-8-11 0.............................. DanielePorcu 5 33
(P Schiergen, Germany) **156/10**
14 *1* **Al Quintana (GER)**[56] 5965 5-9-3 0.............................. SHellyn 11 35
(S Richter, Germany) **87/10**
15 *2 ½* **Antalya (GER)** 3-8-11 0.............................. AHelfenbein 10 23
(Markus Klug, Germany) **77/10**
16 *15* **Tender Emotion**[33] 3-8-11 0.............................. FabriceVeron 9
(H-A Pantall, France) *dwlt sltly and a towards rr: rdn over 3f out: eased qckly as if smething amiss 2f out: dropped to last and t.o* **43/10**[2]

1m 30.65s (90.65)
**WFA** 3 from 4yo+ 2lb **16** Ran SP% **132.9**
WIN (incl. 10 euro stake): 130. PLACES: 61, 26, 55. SF: 802.
**Owner** Stiftung Gestut Fahrhof **Bred** Gestut Faehrhof **Trained** Germany

7484 - (Foreign Racing) - See Raceform Interactive

# 7317 LONGCHAMP (R-H)

Sunday, October 26

**OFFICIAL GOING: Turf: very soft**

## 7485a CRITERIUM DE VITESSE (LISTED RACE) (2YO) (TURF) 5f (S)

1:30 (12:00) 2-Y-O £22,916 (£9,166; £6,875; £4,583; £2,291)

RPR
1 **Dikta Del Mar (SPA)**[47] 6220 2-8-13 0.............................. ChristopheSoumillon 6 98+
(T Martins, Spain) **29/10**[2]
2 *2 ½* **Something Lucky (IRE)**[20] 6991 2-9-2 0.............................. AntoineHamelin 3 92
(Matthieu Palussiere, France) **16/5**[3]
3 *¾* **Malicieuse (IRE)**[16] 7094 2-8-13 0.............................. MaximeGuyon 1 86
(J E Pease, France) **8/5**[1]
4 *snk* **Cool Strutter (IRE)**[15] 7121 2-9-2 0.............................. OisinMurphy 5 89
(David O'Meara) **13/2**
5 *nk* **Banana Split**[53] 6053 2-8-13 0.............................. MartinHarley 2 85
(P Harley, Germany) **61/10**
6 *5* **Cheik Bere (FR)**[37] 2-9-2 0.............................. AlexisBadel 4 70
(M Figge, Germany) **186/10**

58.66s (2.36) **6** Ran SP% **120.4**
WIN (incl. 1 euro stake): 3.90. PLACES: 1.80, 2.00. SF: 12.20.
**Owner** Cuadra Nortenha **Bred** Jose Simo **Trained** Spain

## 7486a PRIX ROYAL-OAK (GROUP 1) (3YO+) (TURF) 1m 7f 110y

2:40 (12:00) 3-Y-O+ £166,658 (£66,675; £33,337; £16,654; £8,341)

RPR
1 **Tac De Boistron (FR)**[163] 2315 7-9-4 0.............................. MartinHarley 3 114+
(Marco Botti) *travelled strly in midfield: angled out into st: rdn and hdwy 2f out: chal over 1f out and sn led: edgd rt u.p but styd on strly and asserted fnl f: pushed out towards fin: readily* **7/4**[1]
2 *1* **High Jinx (IRE)**[21] 6972 6-9-4 0.............................. JamesDoyle 11 113
(James Fanshawe) *led: rdn over 2f out: hdd over 1f out and sn dropped to 3rd: nt pce of wnr fnl f but styd on gamely u.p and got bk up for 2nd post* **8/1**[3]
3 *nse* **Narrow Hill (GER)**[48] 6-9-4 0.............................. ChristopheSoumillon 6 113
(P Sogorb, France) *a.p: pushed along 2f out: rdn to chal and ev ch over 1f out: cl 2nd ent fnl f: styd on wl but nt pce of wnr: dropped to 3rd post* **10/1**
4 *½* **Pale Mimosa (IRE)**[21] 6972 5-9-1 0.............................. WilliamBuick 9 109
(D K Weld, Ire) *a.p: rdn and effrt over 2f out: styd on wl for 4th but nt quite pce to chal and hld* **6/1**[2]
5 *1* **Siljan's Saga (FR)**[21] 6970 4-9-1 0.............................. GregoryBenoist 4 108
(J-P Gauvin, France) *travelled strly in midfield: pushed along and clsd 2f out: rdn and ev ch whn short of room and lost sme momentum as wnr edgd rt over 1f out: styd on same pce after and hld* **16/1**
6 *2 ½* **Frine (IRE)**[22] 6956 4-9-1 0.............................. FrankieDettori 2 105
(C Laffon-Parias, France) *hld up in midfield: rdn over 2f out: outpcd by ldrs over 1f out: plugged on for wl hld 6th fnl f* **12/1**
7 *1* **Zarshana (IRE)**[22] 6956 3-8-6 0..............................(b) ThierryJarnet 8 105
(A De Royer-Dupre, France) *dwlt and hld up towards rr: fanned wd into st: rdn 2f out: plugged on u.p and tk n.d 7th fnl f* **10/1**
8 *2* **Altano (GER)**[63] 5743 8-9-4 0.............................. EPedroza 1 104
(A Wohler, Germany) *in tch: 5th 5f out: rdn into st: outpcd and lost pl 2f out: no ex and btn fnl f: eased nring fin* **14/1**
9 *5* **Fly With Me (FR)**[21] 6972 4-9-4 0..............................(p) MaximeGuyon 5 97
(E Libaud, France) *midfield: pushed along and reminders bef st: rdn over 2f out: outpcd over 1f out: no imp and btn fnl f: eased* **14/1**
10 *1 ¼* **Domeside**[42] 6383 8-9-4 0.............................. CristianDemuro 10 96
(M Delcher Sanchez, France) *hld up: rdn 3f out: no imp and btn fnl 2f: nvr a factor* **20/1**
11 *½* **Vent De Force**[22] 6954 3-8-9 0.............................. UmbertoRispoli 12 96
(Hughie Morrison) *trckd ldr: rdn and brief effrt to chal over 2f out: no ex and btn over 1f out: wknd: eased fnl f* **14/1**
12 *nk* **Satanicjim (IRE)**[36] 5-9-4 0.............................. AdrienFouassier 7 95
(Alain Couetil, France) *dwlt and hld up in last: rdn 3f out: edgd lft and no imp in st: eased whn btn: nvr a factor* **50/1**
13 *5* **Andry Brusselles**[23] 6917 4-9-1 0.............................. Francois-XavierBertras 13 85
(C Delcher-Sanchez, France) *hld up and a towards rr: rdn and no imp in st: last and wl btn whn eased fnl f: nvr a factor* **40/1**

3m 32.73s (11.23) **Going Correction** +1.15s/f (Soft)
**WFA** 3 from 4yo+ 9lb **13** Ran SP% **122.7**
Speed ratings: **117,116,116,116,115 114,113,112,110,109 109,109,106**
WIN (incl. 1 euro stake): 3.40. PLACES: 1.50, 2.40, 2.00. DF: 15.50. SF: 21.50.
**Owner** Australian Thoroughbred Bloodstock **Bred** Mme Isabelle Reverseau **Trained** Newmarket, Suffolk

**FOCUS**
There was strength in depth to this Group 1 and it looks solid 2m form. The front-running second helps set the standard.

# 7165 LEICESTER (R-H)

Monday, October 27

**OFFICIAL GOING: Soft (good to soft in places; 6.0)**
Wind: Fresh half-behind Weather: Overcast

## 7487 HAYMARKET NURSERY H'CAP (DIV I) 7f 9y

1:00 (1:00) (Class 6) (0-65,65) 2-Y-O £1,940 (£577; £288; £144) Stalls High

Form RPR
0304 1 **Agadoo**[18] 7055 2-8-7 51.............................. DavidProbert 5 61
(Shaun Harris) *a.p: chsd ldr 1/2-way: rdn to ld over 1f out: styd on* **6/1**
6006 2 *2 ¼* **Red Stripes (USA)**[24] 6903 2-8-1 45..............................(b) HayleyTurner 6 49
(Brian Meehan) *s.i.s: sn prom: rdn to chse wnr over 1f out: hung rt and styd on same pce ins fnl f* **25/1**
000 3 *7* **Machiavelian Storm (IRE)**[12] 7193 2-9-2 60.............................. PaulHanagan 1 47
(Ed Dunlop) *s.i.s: hld up: pushed along over 2f out: hdwy u.p over 1f out: styd on to go 3rd ins fnl f: nt trble ldrs* **5/1**[2]
005 4 *2 ¼* **The Olympus Man**[14] 7155 2-9-7 65.............................. AndreaAtzeni 4 46
(Olly Stevens) *trckd ldrs: rdn over 1f out: wknd fnl f* **11/2**[3]
0540 5 *1 ½* **Bushtown Boy (IRE)**[6] 7362 2-9-5 63.............................. SilvestreDeSousa 8 41
(Mark Johnston) *led: rdn over 2f out: hdd over 1f out: wknd ins fnl f* **6/1**
000 6 *¾* **Overstone Lass (IRE)**[128] 3467 2-7-12 45.............................. JoeyHaynes(3) 2 21
(John Spearing) *prom: rdn over 2f out: wknd over 1f out* **66/1**
0003 7 *nse* **Quae Supra**[13] 7165 2-8-9 56.............................. CamHardie(3) 7 32
(Richard Hannon) *chsd ldr to 1/2-way: sn rdn: wknd 2f out* **8/1**
0306 8 *1 ½* **Maybe Now Baby (IRE)**[10] 7237 2-9-6 64.............................. LukeMorris 3 36
(David Simcock) *sn pushed along and a in rr: wknd 2f out* **7/2**[1]
5206 9 *1* **Snoway**[10] 7245 2-8-5 49.............................. JamesSullivan 10 18
(Tony Coyle) *hld up: a in rr: rdn over 2f out: sn wknd* **10/1**
0355 10 *11* **Poppy In The Wind**[7] 7329 2-8-11 55..............................(p) GrahamLee 9
(Alan Brown) *prom: rdn over 2f out: sn wknd* **16/1**

1m 28.11s (1.91) **Going Correction** +0.20s/f (Good) **10** Ran SP% **114.3**
Speed ratings (Par 93): **97,94,86,83,82 81,81,79,78,65**
CSF £138.57 CT £801.31 TOTE £6.50: £2.00, £5.30, £1.30; EX 155.10 Trifecta £678.10.
**Owner** John E Rose **Bred** J E Rose **Trained** Carburton, Notts

**FOCUS**
False rail from top of hill in back straight to the Winning Post and distances on Round course increased by about 17yds. This looked a weak race on paper, so although the front two pulled well clear, this probably isn't great form. The winner has been rated back to form, with a small step forward from the runner-up.

## 7488 HAYMARKET NURSERY H'CAP (DIV II) 7f 9y

1:30 (1:30) (Class 6) (0-65,64) 2-Y-O £1,940 (£577; £288; £144) Stalls High

Form RPR
6553 1 **Miss Van Gogh**[27] 6830 2-8-11 54.............................. PaulHanagan 7 58
(Richard Fahey) *a.p: rdn over 1f out: led ins fnl f: styd on wl* **3/1**[1]
404 2 *1 ¾* **Picture Postcard**[37] 6563 2-8-9 55..............................(p) NathanAlison(3) 4 55
(William Haggas) *a.p: chsd ldr over 5f out: led 1/2-way: rdn and hung lft over 1f out: hdd and unable qck ins fnl f* **14/1**
6005 3 *4* **Seraffimo**[7] 7328 2-7-13 45.............................. JoeyHaynes(3) 5 35
(Sharon Watt) *plld hrd: trckd ldr tl over 5f out: remained handy: drvn along 1/2-way: styd on same pce fr over 1f out* **14/1**
5003 4 *1 ½* **Stealing Thunder (IRE)**[27] 6842 2-8-13 56..............................(b) AndreaAtzeni 2 42
(Eve Johnson Houghton) *mid-div: pushed along and lost pl 5f out: hdwy u.p over 1f out: nt trble ldrs* **4/1**[3]
01 5 *2 ½* **Ragtime Dancer**[96] 4541 2-9-3 63.............................. DannyBrock(3) 9 43
(Jonathan Portman) *prom: chsd ldr over 2f out: rdn and edgd rt over 1f out: wknd fnl f* **7/2**[2]
0650 6 *4* **Cerise Firth**[67] 5593 2-8-7 50..............................[1] HayleyTurner 8 20
(Steph Hollinshead) *s.i.s: sn pushed along in rr: nvr on terms* **25/1**
0301 7 *3* **Ciaras Cookie (IRE)**[20] 6996 2-9-7 64.............................. AdamKirby 6 26
(David Evans) *led to 1/2-way: sn rdn: wknd over 2f out* **5/1**
050 8 *hd* **Envisioning (IRE)**[21] 6984 2-9-2 62.............................. CamHardie(3) 1 24
(Richard Hannon) *s.i.s: sn prom: rdn and wknd over 2f out* **8/1**
0000 9 *7* **Just No Rules**[33] 6669 2-8-2 45.............................. JamesSullivan 3
(Tony Coyle) *a in rr: drvn along 1/2-way: wknd over 2f out* **50/1**

1m 27.9s (1.70) **Going Correction** +0.20s/f (Good) **9** Ran SP% **114.1**
Speed ratings (Par 93): **98,96,91,89,86 82,78,78,70**
CSF £45.59 CT £506.90 TOTE £3.50: £1.90, £3.60, £4.90; EX 48.50 Trifecta £707.60.
**Owner** Dyson Racing & D Powell **Bred** Mrs D O Joly **Trained** Musley Bank, N Yorks

**FOCUS**
The combination of modest horses going a solid pace on tiring ground meant most of these were off the bridle by halfway and they finished strung out like 3m chasers. Not form to pay much attention to. A minor pb from the winner.

## 7489 GUMLEY CLAIMING STKS 7f 9y

2:00 (2:00) (Class 6) 3-4-Y-O £1,940 (£577; £288; £144) Stalls High

Form RPR
0554 1 **Swift Cedar (IRE)**[46] 6251 4-8-11 72..............................(v[1]) SilvestreDeSousa 3 71
(David Evans) *hld up: hdwy over 2f out: rdn to ld 1f out: r.o* **5/2**[2]
3246 2 *2* **Swiss Lait**[3] 7424 3-8-8 56..............................(p) DavidProbert 2 64
(David Elsworth) *a.p: chsd ldr over 2f out: sn edgd rt: rdn and ev ch fr over 1f out tl styd on same pce ins fnl f* **14/1**
5531 3 *1* **Zain Zone (IRE)**[13] 7167 3-8-13 72..............................(p) JamesSullivan 5 66
(Ruth Carr) *led: rdn and hdd 1f out: styd on same pce ins fnl f* **7/2**[3]
6004 4 *3* **Porthos Du Vallon**[14] 6836 3-8-9 69.............................. PaulHanagan 4 55
(Keith Dalgleish) *hld up: hdwy 1/2-way: rdn over 2f out: styd on same pce fnl f* **12/1**
1125 5 *3 ½* **Trixie Malone**[18] 7060 4-9-1 77.............................. JoeyHaynes(3) 7 54
(K R Burke) *chsd ldrs: lost pl over 4f out: hdwy over 1f out: wknd fnl f* **9/4**[1]
4030 6 *nse* **La Tinta Bay**[20] 7017 3-7-11 72.............................. CamHardie(3) 6 36
(Richard Hannon) *chsd ldr over 4f: sn rdn: wknd fnl f* **15/2**
0000 7 *16* **Hidden Talent**[76] 5273 4-8-7 45..............................(p) HayleyTurner 1
(Steph Hollinshead) *prom: rdn over 2f out: sn wknd* **100/1**

1m 26.71s (0.51) **Going Correction** +0.20s/f (Good)
**WFA** 3 from 4yo 2lb **7** Ran SP% **108.7**
Speed ratings (Par 101): **105,102,101,98,94 94,75**
CSF £31.85 TOTE £3.00: £2.00, £3.20; EX 35.00 Trifecta £107.70.
**Owner** J E Abbey **Bred** Carlingford Breeding Syndicate **Trained** Pandy, Monmouths

**FOCUS**
A reasonably competitive claimer in which the pace was strong thanks to Zain Zone. That set things up nicely for a couple of the hold-up horses. A clear pb from the runner-up on face value, but not obvious on profile and the race has been rated cautiously.

## 7490 SIS H'CAP 1m 60y
**2:30** (2:30) (Class 2) (0-100,99) 3-Y-O+ **£12,938** (£3,850; £1,924; £962) **Stalls** Low

Form RPR

6446 **1** **Gabrial (IRE)**[16] 7120 5-9-2 94 PaulHanagan 10 105
(Richard Fahey) *trckd ldrs: racd keenly: shkn up to join ldr over 1f out: rdn to ld and edgd rt ins fnl f: styd on* **6/1**[3]

0204 **2** 1 ½ **God Willing**[16] 7119 3-8-13 94 AndreaAtzeni 4 101
(Ed Dunlop) *chsd ldr: rdn to ld wl over 1f out: sn edgd lft: hdd and unable qck ins fnl f* **4/1**[1]

1300 **3** 2 ½ **Osteopathic Remedy (IRE)**[17] 7081 10-8-8 89....(t) ConnorBeasley(3) 9 91
(Michael Dods) *plld hrd: a.p: rdn over 2f out: styd on* **16/1**

1600 **4** nk **Le Chat D'Or**[10] 7236 6-8-11 89 (bt) GrahamLee 5 91
(Michael Dods) *hld up in tch: racd keenly: rdn over 2f out: styd on* **6/1**[3]

5005 **5** ¾ **Ingleby Angel (IRE)**[10] 7236 5-9-1 93 DanielTudhope 3 93
(David O'Meara) *hld up: rdn over 1f out: styd on fnl f: nt trble ldrs* **5/1**[2]

0510 **6** 1 ¼ **Loving Spirit**[13] 7168 6-9-7 99 RobertTart 8 96
(James Toller) *hld up: hdwy in centre 2f out: sn rdn: edgd lft and no ex ins fnl f* **10/1**

2610 **7** hd **Our Boy Jack (IRE)**[10] 7236 5-8-11 89 GeorgeChaloner 2 86
(Richard Fahey) *hld up: rdn over 2f out: nvr nrr* **10/1**

-140 **8** 1 ½ **Music In The Rain (IRE)**[10] 7236 6-8-12 90 WilliamBuick 1 83
(David O'Meara) *prom: racd keenly: rdn over 3f out: wknd fnl f* **16/1**

2051 **9** 3 ½ **Stand My Ground (IRE)**[42] 6402 7-8-13 91 DavidNolan 7 76
(David O'Meara) *hld up: rdn over 2f out: nvr on terms* **11/1**

0055 **10** 1 ¼ **Kosika (USA)**[13] 7168 4-9-2 94 SilvestreDeSousa 6 76
(Mark Johnston) *led: rdn and hdd wl over 1f out: wknd fnl f* **10/1**

1m 48.86s (3.76) **Going Correction** +0.60s/f (Yiel)
**WFA** 3 from 4yo+ 3lb **10** Ran SP% **112.6**
Speed ratings (Par 109): **105,103,101,100,99 98,98,97,93,92**
CSF £29.10 CT £360.87 TOTE £7.00: £1.80, £1.50, £3.50; EX 17.30 Trifecta £300.40.
**Owner** Dr Marwan Koukash **Bred** B Kennedy **Trained** Musley Bank, N Yorks

**FOCUS**
A competitive-enough handicap, but they got quite well strung out early and several were quite keen. Two drew clear in the closing stages. The runner-up has been rated pretty much to his best.

## 7491 BRITISH STALLION STUDS EBF MAIDEN STKS (BOBIS RACE) 5f 218y
**3:00** (3:00) (Class 4) 2-Y-O **£4,851** (£1,443; £721; £360) **Stalls** High

Form RPR

2 **1** **Sir Domino (FR)**[10] 7246 2-9-5 0 GrahamLee 1 79+
(Kevin Ryan) *mde all: shkn up over 1f out: pushed out* **1/1**[1]

6343 **2** 2 **Quintus Cerialis (IRE)**[17] 7082 2-9-5 77 AdamKirby 2 70
(Clive Cox) *chsd wnr: rdn over 1f out: styd on same pce ins fnl f* **7/4**[2]

5 **3** 2 ¾ **Seychelloise**[12] 7114 2-9-0 0 LukeMorris 6 57
(Sir Mark Prescott Bt) *chsd ldrs: pushed along whn stmbld wl over 2f out: edgd rt over 1f out: styd on same pce fnl f* **14/1**

00 **4** 1 **Picket Line**[91] 4740 2-9-5 0 JohnFahy 4 59
(Geoffrey Deacon) *trckd ldrs: racd keenly: pushed along 1/2-way: styd on same pce fnl f* **100/1**

**5** 4 ½ **Ertidaad (IRE)** 2-9-5 0 JamesSullivan 5 46
(Pat Eddery) *s.i.s: outpcd* **7/1**[3]

**6** 11 **Irish Belle (IRE)** 2-8-11 0 JoeyHaynes(3) 3 8
(Tony Carroll) *pushed along in rr: wnt rt over 4f out: hdwy over 3f out: rdn and wknd over 1f out* **33/1**

1m 15.49s (2.49) **Going Correction** +0.20s/f (Good) **6** Ran SP% **109.5**
Speed ratings (Par 97): **91,88,84,83,77 62**
CSF £2.76 TOTE £1.70: £1.10, £1.70; EX 3.80 Trifecta £9.80.
**Owner** Hambleton Racing Ltd XXXV **Bred** Jean-Yves Payet Descombes & Jocelyne Payet Descomb **Trained** Hambleton, N Yorks

**FOCUS**
No depth to this maiden. A small step forward from the winner, with the third close to her debut form.

## 7492 SIR GORDON RICHARDS H'CAP 1m 3f 183y
**3:30** (3:30) (Class 2) (0-112,105) 3-Y-O+ **£18,903** (£5,658; £2,829; £1,416; £705) **Stalls** Low

Form RPR

4110 **1** **Rewaaya (IRE)**[16] 7106 3-9-0 100 PaulHanagan 4 107+
(John Gosden) *hld up: hdwy and hung rt fr over 3f out: rdn to ld over 1f out: styd on* **7/4**[1]

-005 **2** 1 ¼ **Harris Tweed**[127] 3500 7-9-12 105 (p) GeorgeBaker 5 109
(William Haggas) *sn w ldr: led 7f out: hdd over 2f out: sn rdn: n.m.r over 1f out: hung rt and styd on same pce ins fnl f* **6/1**

**3** 6 **Blue Rambler**[483] 3912 4-9-10 103 WilliamBuick 6 99
(Charlie Appleby) *prom: chsd ldr 5f out: led over 2f out: rdn and hdd over 1f out: nt clr run sn after: wknd and eased ins fnl f* **11/4**[2]

0004 **4** nk **Shwaiman (IRE)**[32] 6687 4-9-7 100 AndreaAtzeni 1 94
(James Fanshawe) *prom: rdn over 2f out: wknd over 1f out* **12/1**

4132 **5** 6 **Fattsota**[16] 7120 6-9-9 102 DanielTudhope 3 86
(David O'Meara) *led 5f: rdn over 3f out: wknd wl over 1f out* **7/2**[3]

06- **6** 15 **Cardinal Palace (IRE)**[71] 5477 4-9-7 100 AdamKirby 2 60
(John Joseph Murphy, Ire) *hld up: rdn over 3f out: wknd over 2f out* **50/1**

2m 37.85s (3.95) **Going Correction** +0.60s/f (Yiel)
**WFA** 3 from 4yo+ 7lb **6** Ran SP% **109.2**
Speed ratings (Par 109): **110,109,105,104,100 90**
CSF £12.01 TOTE £2.80: £1.10, £2.80; EX 11.30 Trifecta £39.30.
**Owner** Hamdan Al Maktoum **Bred** Shadwell Estate Company Limited **Trained** Newmarket, Suffolk

**FOCUS**
A good-quality handicap, but the pace didn't look overly strong despite the presence of two confirmed front-runners. The runner-up posted his first real form of the year.

## 7493 COSSINGTON MEDIAN AUCTION MAIDEN FILLIES' STKS (BOBIS RACE) 5f 218y
**4:00** (4:01) (Class 5) 2-Y-O **£2,587** (£770; £384; £192) **Stalls** High

Form RPR

2200 **1** **Pastoral Girl**[37] 6530 2-9-0 99 GrahamLee 2 70+
(James Given) *led 1f: chsd ldr tl over 3f out: shkn up to ld over 1f out: idled and drifted rt ins fnl f: comf* **1/4**[1]

60 **2** 1 **Paloma Dancer**[32] 6675 2-9-0 0 LukeMorris 1 67
(Harry Dunlop) *w ldr tl led 5f out: rdn: edgd rt and hdd over 1f out: styd on same pce ins fnl f* **12/1**[3]

5 **3** 1 ¾ **Spinaminnie (IRE)**[9] 7277 2-9-0 0 SilvestreDeSousa 3 62
(Mark Johnston) *prom: chsd ldr over 3f out: rdn and ev ch over 1f out: styng on same pce whn hmpd wl ins fnl f* **5/1**[2]

0 **4** 8 **Beau Sparkle (IRE)**[16] 7113 2-9-0 0 HayleyTurner 5 38
(Steph Hollinshead) *prom: rdn 1/2-way: wknd over 1f out* **50/1**

**5** 2 ¼ **Outlaw Kate (IRE)** 2-9-0 0 RobertTart 4 31
(Michael Mullineaux) *dwlt: sn pushed along in rr: wknd over 2f out* **16/1**

1m 16.24s (3.24) **Going Correction** +0.20s/f (Good) **5** Ran SP% **112.2**
Speed ratings (Par 92): **86,84,82,71,68**
CSF £4.76 TOTE £1.20: £1.02, £5.00; EX 4.30 Trifecta £8.40.
**Owner** The Cool Silk Partnership **Bred** Alvediston Stud **Trained** Willoughton, Lincs

**FOCUS**
A desperately weak maiden. The level is very fluid.

## 7494 FOSSE WAY AMATEUR RIDERS' H'CAP (FOR GENTLEMAN AMATEUR RIDERS) 7f 9y
**4:30** (4:30) (Class 5) (0-70,70) 3-Y-O+ **£2,634** (£810; £405) **Stalls** High

Form RPR

6435 **1** **Echo Of Lightning**[77] 5233 4-10-8 57 (p[1]) MrDannyBurton 2 67+
(Brian Ellison) *racd far side: led that trio tl overall ldr over 4f out: rdn over 1f out: styd on wl: 1st of 3 that side* **12/1**

2322 **2** ¾ **Freddy With A Y (IRE)**[11] 7220 4-10-13 69 (p) MrWRClarke(7) 10 77
(Gary Moore) *racd centre: sn pushed along in rr: hdwy and edgd rt over 1f out: chsd wnr ins fnl f: styd on: 1st of 14 in gp* **8/1**[3]

0565 **3** 1 ¾ **Edge (IRE)**[25] 6615 3-10-1 57 (b) MrJPWilliams(5) 7 59
(Bernard Llewellyn) *dwlt: racd centre: bhd: r.o ins fnl f: wnt 3rd post: nt rch ldrs: 2nd of 14 in gp* **40/1**

4123 **4** ½ **Mendacious Harpy (IRE)**[7] 7339 3-11-1 66 MrSWalker 14 67
(George Baker) *racd centre: a.p: rdn to ld centre gp ins fnl f: styd on: 3rd of 14 in gp* **5/1**[1]

5530 **5** ¾ **Pashan Garh**[7] 7339 5-10-13 65 MrDavidTurner(3) 9 65
(Pat Eddery) *racd centre: prom: rdn 1/2-way: styd on u.p: 4th of 14 in gp* **25/1**

2106 **6** shd **The Dukkerer (IRE)**[48] 6217 3-11-3 68 MrWHogg 13 67
(Garry Moss) *racd centre: chsd ldrs: led that gp over 2f out tl ins fnl f: styd on same pce: 5th of 14 in gp* **20/1**

4504 **7** ½ **Robin Hood (IRE)**[6] 7346 6-10-4 60 MrCharlieMarshall(7) 12 59
(Philip Mitchell) *racd centre: outpcd: styd on fr over 1f out: nt rch ldrs: 6th of 14 in gp* **16/1**

0055 **8** ¾ **Powerful Pierre**[63] 5777 7-11-2 65 (b) MrPCollington 16 62
(Noel Quinlan) *s.i.s: racd centre: in rr: rdn over 2f out: styd on fr over 1f out: nt trble ldrs: 7th of 14 in gp* **40/1**

4120 **9** ¾ **Old Man Clegg**[13] 7180 4-10-11 65 (t) MrZBaker(5) 6 60
(Michael Easterby) *racd centre: prom: rdn over 2f out: wknd ins fnl f: 8th of 14 in gp* **12/1**

5654 **10** 1 **Be Royale**[30] 6766 4-10-11 63 MrWEasterby(3) 11 55
(Michael Appleby) *hld up: hdwy 4f out: rdn over 1f out: wknd ins fnl f: 9th of 14 in gp* **12/1**

4000 **11** 5 **Clumber Place**[13] 7180 8-10-11 65 MrAidenBlakemore(5) 15 44
(Shaun Harris) *overall ldr in centre tl over 4f out: hdd that gp over 2f out: wknd over 1f out: 10th of 14 in gp* **25/1**

5020 **12** shd **Alanos (IRE)**[133] 3299 5-11-2 70 MrLAMurtagh(5) 5 49
(James Ewart) *racd centre: prom: rdn over 2f out: wknd over 1f out: 11th of 14 in gp* **33/1**

2522 **13** ¾ **Mfiftythreedotcom (IRE)**[38] 6515 3-11-1 69 (p) MrTHamilton(3) 4 45
(Richard Fahey) *racd centre: chsd ldrs: rdn over 2f out: wknd over 1f out: 12th of 14 in gp* **7/1**[2]

**14** ¾ **St James Gate (IRE)**[9] 7293 3-10-11 62 MrMichaelJMurphy 18 36
(John Joseph Murphy, Ire) *racd centre: a in rr: 13th of 14 in gp* **12/1**

3335 **15** ¾ **Irondale Express**[37] 6540 3-10-10 66 (v[1]) MrKWood(5) 17 38
(Tony Coyle) *racd centre: s.i.s: a in rr: last of 14 in gp* **10/1**

5650 **16** 6 **Kung Hei Fat Choy (USA)**[39] 6477 5-11-4 67 (b) MrHAABannister 1 24
(James Given) *racd far side: chsd ldrs: rdn over 4f out: sn wknd: 2nd of 3 that side* **14/1**

4530 **17** shd **Valen (IRE)**[24] 6902 3-11-0 70 MrHStock(5) 3 26
(Michael Bell) *racd far side: chsd ldrs: rdn over 4f out: wknd 1/2-way: last of 3 that side* **9/1**

1m 28.74s (2.54) **Going Correction** +0.20s/f (Good)
**WFA** 3 from 4yo+ 2lb **17** Ran SP% **123.0**
Speed ratings (Par 103): **93,92,90,89,88 88,88,87,86,85 79,79,78,77,76 69,69**
CSF £96.85 CT £3720.19 TOTE £25.20: £4.60, £1.90, £9.70, £1.60; EX 169.70 Trifecta £2078.70.
**Owner** Victoria Greetham & Emily Beasley **Bred** Gracelands Stud **Trained** Norton, N Yorks

**FOCUS**
They were spread right across the track in this wide-open handicap. There's a good chance the winner is a bit better than the bare form.
T/Plt: £127.00 to a £1 stake. Pool: £63,503.52 - 364.87 winning tickets T/Qpdt: £11.00 to a £1 stake. Pool: £6,136.86 - 409.22 winning tickets CR

# 7244 REDCAR (L-H)
Monday, October 27

**OFFICIAL GOING: Good to soft changing to good to soft (good in places) after race 1 (12:40) changing to good after race 4 (2:10)**
Wind: blustery, half behind Weather: dry

## 7495 BRITISH STALLION STUDS SUPPORTING BRITISH RACING EBF MAIDEN STKS (DIV I) 6f
**12:40** (12:42) (Class 5) 2-Y-O **£3,234** (£962; £481; £240) **Stalls** Centre

Form RPR

2262 **1** **Ythan Waters**[16] 7097 2-9-5 75 PaulMulrennan 9 75
(Bryan Smart) *mde all: clr w 2 rivals 1/2-way: forged ahd u.p 1f out: clr ins fnl f: drvn out* **6/4**[1]

**2** 1 ½ **Highest Level (IRE)** 2-9-5 0 FrederikTylicki 4 71
(Saeed bin Suroor) *in tch in midfield: rdn and outpcd by ldng trio 1/2-way: rallied and hdwy over 1f out: styd on wl to go 2nd fnl 50yds: no threat to wnr* **2/1**[2]

**3** 1 ½ **Free Radical** 2-9-5 0 (b[1]) PatCosgrave 5 66
(Noel Quinlan) *chsd ldng pair: kicked clr w 2 rivals 1/2-way: drvn over 1f out: styd on same pce fnl f* **20/1**

00 **4** 1 **Bracka Legend (IRE)**[10] 7246 2-9-5 0 GrahamGibbons 1 63
(David Barron) *pressed wnr: kicked clr w 2 rivals 1/2-way: no ex u.p 1f out: wknd and lost 2 pls wl ins fnl f* **16/1**

45 **5** *3* **Mystic Miraaj**[10] 7244 2-9-5 0............................................ DavidAllan 12 54+
(Tim Easterby) *s.i.s: in rr: pushed along and outpcd 1/2-way: hdwy over 1f out: styd on steadily ins fnl f: no threat to ldrs* **13/2**[3]

0 **6** *1* **Bond Mystery**[23] 6935 2-9-5 0............................................ PaulQuinn 8 51
(Richard Whitaker) *towards rr: struggling and outpcd 1/2-way: sme prog over 1f out: kpt on: nvr trbld ldrs* **80/1**

0 **7** *3* **Marsoomah**[34] 6641 2-9-0 0............................................ TonyHamilton 10 37
(Richard Fahey) *s.i.s: sn pushed along in rr: modest last hdwy: n.d* **50/1**

0 **8** *shd* **Riverlynx (IRE)**[112] 4018 2-9-0 0............................................ AndrewElliott 2 37
(Ben Haslam) *chsd ldng trio: rdn and outpcd 1/2-way: hung lft and wknd 2f out* **66/1**

00 **9** *3/4* **Tonto's Spirit**[26] 6860 2-9-5 0............................................ TomEaves 11 39
(Michael Dods) *s.i.s: a bhd* **50/1**

00 **10** *nk* **Doctor Watson**[10] 7234 2-9-5 0............................................ FrannyNorton 7 39
(Tom Tate) *in tch in midfield: outpcd 1/2-way and no threat to ldrs after: wknd ins fnl f* **100/1**

**11** *1* **Rennie Mackintosh (IRE)** 2-9-5 0............................................ JoeFanning 6 36
(Mark Johnston) *s.i.s: sn pushed along and rn green in rr: bhd fnl 2f* **12/1**

00 **12** *1 1/2* **Good Move (IRE)**[17] 7084 2-9-0 0............................................ PatrickMathers 3 26
(Brian Rothwell) *in tch in midfield: struggling u.p at 1/2-way: hung lft and wknd 2f out* **100/1**

1m 9.82s (-1.98) **Going Correction** -0.45s/f (Firm) **12** Ran SP% **113.6**
Speed ratings (Par 95): **95,93,91,89,85 84,80,80,79,78 77,75**
CSF £4.09 TOTE £2.30: £1.10, £1.10, £7.90; EX 5.90 Trifecta £47.50.
**Owner** BEFG Partnership **Bred** Southill Stud **Trained** Hambleton, N Yorks

**FOCUS**
The going was good to soft after a dry night, and there was a strong tailwind in the straight. There was little strength in depth in this maiden and not many got involved but the favourite delivered and his main market rival stayed on for second. The time was only 0.32 seconds slower than standard. The winner has been rated close to form.

## 7496 BRITISH STALLION STUDS SUPPORTING BRITISH RACING EBF MAIDEN STKS (DIV II) 6f
**1:10** (1:14) (Class 5) 2-Y-O **£3,234** (£962; £481; £240) **Stalls** Centre

Form RPR

25 **1** **Silvery Blue**[18] 7062 2-9-0 0............................................ GrahamGibbons 11 70
(Hugo Palmer) *chsd ldrs: rdn and ev ch 1/2-way: led over 1f out: sustained duel w runner-up after: battled on wl: drvn out* **7/2**[2]

60 **2** *nk* **Father Bertie**[17] 7084 2-9-5 0............................................ DavidAllan 7 74
(Tim Easterby) *led: rdn and hrd pressed 1/2-way: hdd over 1f out: ev ch and sustained duel wnr after: battled on wl tl no ex cl home* **14/1**

32 **3** *1 1/2* **Especial**[30] 6757 2-9-5 0............................................ PhillipMakin 6 70
(Bryan Smart) *nt best away: sn in tch in midfield: effrt to chse ldng trio 1/2-way: 3rd and drvn over 1f out: kpt on same pce* **5/4**[1]

43 **4** *6* **Thankstomonty**[16] 7097 2-9-5 0............................................ PaulMulrennan 8 52
(David O'Meara) *pressed ldr: rdn and ev ch 1/2-way tl no ex wl over 1f out: 4th and wknd 1f out* **4/1**[3]

0 **5** *3 3/4* **Charlie's Approval (IRE)**[39] 6489 2-9-0 0............................................ AndrewElliott 5 35
(Ben Haslam) *chsd ldrs tl outpcd u.p 1/2-way: 5th and wknd over 1f out* **100/1**

6 **6** *5* **Desire**[20] 7004 2-9-0 0............................................ TonyHamilton 1 20
(Richard Fahey) *s.i.s: hld up in rr of main gp: struggling u.p 1/2-way: sn wknd* **14/1**

**7** *1* **Desert Chief** 2-9-5 0............................................ PaulQuinn 9 22+
(Richard Whitaker) *v.s.a: rn green and sn pushed along in detached last: n.d* **50/1**

030 **8** *1/2* **Etienne Gerard**[17] 7082 2-9-0 69............................................ ShelleyBirkett(5) 3 21
(Nigel Tinkler) *in tch in midfield: struggling u.p 1/2-way: lost tch 2f out* **25/1**

**9** *1 1/2* **Joey Black** 2-9-5 0............................................ PaddyAspell 10 16
(Susan Corbett) *s.i.s: rn green and a towards rr: wandered u.p and wknd 2f out* **100/1**

6 **10** *nk* **Makin Trouble (IRE)**[10] 7246 2-9-5 0............................................ TomEaves 2 15
(John Quinn) *in tch in midfield: rdn and struggling 1/2-way: sn wknd* **16/1**

1m 9.87s (-1.93) **Going Correction** -0.45s/f (Firm) **10** Ran SP% **113.7**
Speed ratings (Par 95): **94,93,91,83,78 71,70,69,67,67**
CSF £48.07 TOTE £4.80: £1.40, £4.60, £1.10; EX 48.20 Trifecta £119.20.
**Owner** Mrs Mary Taylor & James Taylor **Bred** Mrs M F Taylor & James F Taylor **Trained** Newmarket, Suffolk

**FOCUS**
The going was changed to good to soft, good in places. The first two were always prominent in this ordinary maiden and the first three pulled clear. Ordinary form, with the winner being rated a tad higher than her Polytrack form.

## 7497 DOWNLOAD YOUR RACING UK APP NURSERY H'CAP 5f
**1:40** (1:42) (Class 6) (0-65,65) 2-Y-O **£2,264** (£673; £336; £168) **Stalls** Centre

Form RPR

3542 **1** **Wolfofwallstreet (IRE)**[7] 7336 2-9-7 65............................................(t) PatCosgrave 11 77+
(Ed Walker) *in tch in midfield: hdwy 1/2-way: rdn to ld over 1f out: styd on strly and drew clr ins fnl f: readily* **7/4**[1]

4061 **2** *3* **Alaskan Wing (IRE)**[20] 7003 2-9-3 61............................................ BarryMcHugh 10 62
(Tony Coyle) *chsd ldrs: effrt u.p 2f out: chsd wnr 1f out: outpcd by wnr fnl 150yds: kpt on and hld on for 2nd* **6/1**[2]

565 **3** *1/2* **Belle Nellie (IRE)**[26] 6867 2-8-12 56............................................ JasonHart 13 55
(Nigel Tinkler) *pushed rt s and slowly away: sn swtchd lft: hdwy into midfield 1/2-way: styd on strly u.p fnl f: wnt 3rd cl home: no threat to wnr* **14/1**

0004 **4** *1/2* **Pancake Day**[34] 6645 2-8-8 52............................................ AndrewElliott 4 50
(Jason Ward) *led: wnt sharply rt sn after s: rdn 1/2-way: hdd over 1f out: styd on same pce ins fnl f* **66/1**

0466 **5** *3/4* **Maid In Rome (IRE)**[34] 6623 2-8-12 56............................................ DavidAllan 9 51
(Tim Easterby) *chsd ldrs: rdn 2f out: drvn and no ex over 1f out: kpt on same pce fnl f* **28/1**

440 **6** *1/2* **Brindle**[52] 6093 2-9-0 63............................................ JackGarritty(5) 3 56
(Richard Fahey) *wnt rt s: racd keenly and sn rcvrd to press ldr: no ex u.p over 1f out: one pce ins fnl f* **6/1**[2]

0264 **7** *1 3/4* **Penalty Scorer**[2] 7453 2-8-6 50............................................ DuranFentiman 6 37
(Richard Guest) *short of room sn after s: hld up in tch in midfield: effrt and no imp over 1f out: wknd ins fnl f* **18/1**

3525 **8** *shd* **Poolstock**[28] 6820 2-9-1 64............................................ KevinStott(5) 8 50
(Les Eyre) *bmpd sn after s: in tch in midfield: rdn and unable qck over 1f out: wknd ins fnl f* **16/1**

050 **9** *1* **Ventura Canyon (IRE)**[13] 7181 2-9-3 61............................................ TomEaves 12 44
(Keith Dalgleish) *wnt rt and bmpd rival s: towards rr: u.p 1/2-way: nvr trbld ldrs* **33/1**

0344 **10** *1 1/4* **Lady Marita (IRE)**[41] 6422 2-9-5 63............................................ GrahamGibbons 2 41
(David Evans) *in tch in midfield: u.p at 1/2-way: wknd ent fnl f* **11/1**

050 **11** *2* **Threatorapromise (IRE)**[17] 7082 2-9-0 58............................................ PJMcDonald 14 29
(Tony Coyle) *a outpcd towards rr: u.p 1/2-way: nvr trbld ldrs* **66/1**

0430 **12** *nse* **Star Pursuits**[16] 7112 2-8-12 56............................................ PhillipMakin 15 27
(Noel Quinlan) *a outpcd towards rr: no hdwy u.p 1/2-way: nvr trbld ldrs* **20/1**

406 **13** *2* **Charles Messier**[71] 5464 2-9-3 61............................................ PaulMulrennan 1 25
(Bryan Smart) *press ldrs tl no ex u.p over 1f out: sn wknd: eased ins fnl f* **10/1**[3]

0000 **14** *1 1/2* **Shamkhani**[48] 6211 2-8-3 47 ow2............................................ PatrickMathers 7
(Alan Berry) *short of room sn after s: a in rr* **125/1**

56.88s (-1.72) **Going Correction** -0.45s/f (Firm) 2y crse rec **14** Ran SP% **115.1**
Speed ratings (Par 93): **95,90,89,88,87 86,83,83,82,80 76,76,73,71**
CSF £10.13 CT £110.57 TOTE £2.50: £1.10, £2.70, £7.30; EX 10.20 Trifecta £66.20.
**Owner** Alpine Racing **Bred** Hyde Park Stud **Trained** Newmarket, Suffolk

**FOCUS**
The well-backed favourite powered clear in this nursery. Ordinary form behind the winner.

## 7498 EUROPEAN BREEDERS' FUND - DOUBLE TRIGGER MAIDEN STKS (FOR THE DOUBLE TRIGGER TROPHY) 1m 1f
**2:10** (2:13) (Class 5) 2-Y-O **£3,234** (£962; £481; £240) **Stalls** Low

Form RPR

5 **1** **Not Never**[15] 7134 2-9-5 0............................................ GrahamGibbons 4 76
(Hugo Palmer) *mde all: rdn and clr w 2 rivals over 2f out: drvn and hld on wl u.p fnl f: all out* **13/2**[3]

0 **2** *hd* **Yamllik**[31] 6712 2-9-5 0............................................ FrederikTylicki 7 76
(Saeed bin Suroor) *chsd ldrs: wnt 3rd 3f out and sn clr w 2 rivals: str chal u.p over 1f out: kpt on wl but a jst hld* **11/8**[1]

03 **3** *3 1/2* **Chorus of Lies**[19] 7039 2-9-5 0............................................ MartinLane 6 70
(Charlie Appleby) *chsd ldrs: wnt 2nd 3f out and sn clr w 2 rivals: 3rd and no ex over 1f out: one pce fnl f* **9/2**[2]

**4** *1 3/4* **Perche** 2-9-5 0............................................ PaulMulrennan 9 66+
(Charlie Appleby) *in tch in midfield: effrt to go 4th 2f out: kpt on steadily: nvr threatened ldrs* **7/1**

54 **5** *4* **Polly Jackson**[13] 7174 2-8-9 0............................................ GemmaTutty(5) 12 53+
(Karen Tutty) *hld up towards rr: effrt into modest 7th 3f out: kpt on but no imp after* **10/1**

6 **6** *4 1/2* **Toboggan's Gift**[13] 7174 2-9-0 0............................................ PJMcDonald 14 44
(Ann Duffield) *in tch in midfield: rdn and outpcd 3f out: 5th and wl btn over 1f out: wknd fnl f* **25/1**

0 **7** *3* **Artistic Flare**[34] 6641 2-9-0 0............................................ PhillipMakin 11 38
(John Quinn) *in tch in midfield: drvn and outpcd 3f out: wl btn fnl 2f* **50/1**

6 **8** *nk* **Mon Gris (IRE)**[18] 7054 2-9-5 0............................................ TomEaves 5 42
(Kristin Stubbs) *chsd wnr tl 3f out: sn struggling: 5th and wkng 2f out* **50/1**

0 **9** *2* **Hookergate Grammar**[10] 7244 2-9-5 0............................................ DaleSwift 13 38
(Keith Reveley) *hld up in last trio: plugged on past btn horses fnl 2f: n.d* **100/1**

0 **10** *1* **Ghostly Arc (IRE)**[17] 7084 2-9-5 0............................................ DuranFentiman 15 36
(Noel Wilson) *a towards rr: drvn and no hdwy 5f out: wl btn fnl 3f* **100/1**

0 **11** *3/4* **Not Again**[17] 7084 2-9-5 0............................................ DavidAllan 2 34
(Tim Easterby) *in tch in midfgield: rdn and outpcd over 3f out: sn wknd* **100/1**

0 **12** *nk* **Poniel**[16] 7097 2-9-5 0............................................ JasonHart 1 34
(Ian Semple) *stdd s: t.k.h: hld up in last quartet: lost tch 4f out* **150/1**

0 **13** *1 1/2* **Racing Spirit**[10] 7244 2-9-5 0............................................ BarryMcHugh 3 31
(John Quinn) *hld up in midfield: rdn and btn over 3f out: sn wknd* **40/1**

**14** *16* **Wolf Albarari** 2-9-5 0............................................ PaoloSirigu 10
(Marco Botti) *rn green: sn struggling in rr: t.o fnl 4f* **14/1**

**15** *10* **Mighty Bond** 2-9-2 0............................................ JacobButterfield(3) 8
(Tracy Waggott) *v.s.a: a bhd: t.o fnl 4f* **66/1**

1m 52.82s (-0.18) **Going Correction** -0.10s/f (Good) **15** Ran SP% **117.2**
Speed ratings (Par 95): **96,95,92,91,87 83,80,80,78,78 77,77,75,61,52**
CSF £14.75 TOTE £8.80: £2.10, £1.10, £2.60; EX 17.70 Trifecta £29.60.
**Owner** Mrs Denis Haynes **Bred** Wretham Stud **Trained** Newmarket, Suffolk

**FOCUS**
The first two had a good battle and pulled clear in this fair maiden. The level is fluid.

## 7499 RACING UK ANYWHERE AVAILABLE NOW (S) STKS 1m 2f
**2:40** (2:42) (Class 6) 3-5-Y-O **£2,385** (£704; £352) **Stalls** Low

Form RPR

6020 **1** **Mixed Message (IRE)**[3] 7411 4-8-12 67............................................(p) DaleSwift 4 63+
(Brian Ellison) *drvn along early: hdwy to press ldr over 8f out: led 1/2-way: rdn over 2f out: qcknd and in command 1f out: kpt up to work fnl f* **5/6**[1]

5301 **2** *1 1/2* **Les Gar Gan (IRE)**[20] 7021 3-8-7 61............................................ JoeFanning 5 60+
(Keith Dalgleish) *t.k.h: chsd ldrs: wnt 2nd 4f out: sn clr w wnr: rdn and pressing wnr 3f out: no ex and btn 1f out: kpt on* **15/8**[2]

1040 **3** *3* **Aseela (IRE)**[52] 6119 4-8-12 55............................................ AndrewElliott 7 55
(George Moore) *s.i.s and pushed along early: bhd: hdwy to press for modest 3rd 3f out: wnt 3rd over 1f out: kpt on and clsng fnl f: nvr trbld ldrs* **8/1**[3]

030 **4** *3* **Bold And Free**[9] 7283 4-9-3 48............................................ JimmyQuinn 1 54
(David Thompson) *in tch in midfield: rdn and swtchd rt 4f out: battling for modest 3rd 3f out: 4th plugged on same pce fr over 1f out* **28/1**

0000 **5** *4* **Maillot Jaune (IRE)**[27] 6837 4-8-7 45............................................ JackGarritty(5) 6 41
(Patrick Holmes) *stdd s: hld up in last pair: swtchd rt and effrt 4f out: modest 3rd 3f out: no imp: wknd over 1f out* **28/1**

00-0 **6** *20* **Riponian**[13] 7176 4-9-3 45............................................ TonyHamilton 3 8
(Susan Corbett) *t.k.h: chsd ldrs tl lost pl u.p 4f out: bhd fnl 2f: t.o* **100/1**

4050 **7** *5* **L'Es Fremantle (FR)**[11] 7229 3-8-5 45............................................ BradleyBosley(7) 2
(Michael Chapman) *led tl 1/2-way: hung lft and struggling u.p 4f out: wknd 3f out: t.o* **200/1**

2m 5.21s (-1.89) **Going Correction** -0.10s/f (Good)
**WFA** 3 from 4yo 5lb **7** Ran SP% **108.8**
Speed ratings (Par 101): **103,101,99,97,93 77,73**
CSF £2.25 TOTE £1.50: £1.10, £2.40; EX 2.50 Trifecta £5.60.
**Owner** W I Bloomfield **Bred** J Costello **Trained** Norton, N Yorks

**FOCUS**
The two clear market leaders dominated in this weak seller and the going was changed to good. Neither the first two were at their best and the fourth and fifth are better guides to the level.

## 7500 MARKET CROSS JEWELLERS H'CAP 1m 6f 19y
**3:10** (3:12) (Class 5) (0-70,70) 3-Y-O **£3,234** (£962; £481; £240) **Stalls** Low

Form RPR
-002 1 **Trendsetter (IRE)**[21] 6981 3-9-7 70.................... FrannyNorton 10 80+
(John Butler) *stdd and dropped in bhd after s: hld up in last trio: hdwy to chse ldrs but nt clr run 3f out: forced way through wl over 1f out: sn drvn to chal: led ins fnl f: hld on u.p towards fin* **13/2**[3]
243 2 *hd* **Miss Tree**[13] 7176 3-9-1 69.................... JoeDoyle(5) 6 78
(John Quinn) *wl in tch in midfield: effrt and rdn to chal 3f out: led 2f out: hrd pressed over 1f out: hdd ins fnl f: rallied wl cl home: jst hld* **9/2**[2]
240 3 2 ½ **Jammy Moment**[16] 7102 3-9-3 66.................... JoeFanning 12 71
(Linda Perratt) *wl in tch in midfield: clsd to chse ldrs 3f out: n.m.r 2f out: sn swtchd rt: kpt on u.p fnl f: wnt 3rd towards fin* **12/1**
1630 4 ½ **Censorius**[26] 6864 3-9-4 67....................(v) PatCosgrave 7 71
(Ed Walker) *rousted along leaving stalls: chsd ldrs: wnt wd bnd after 2f: rdn and pressing ldrs 3f out: no ex 1f out: kpt on same pce after* **15/2**
0210 5 ¾ **Slunovrat (FR)**[31] 6699 3-8-12 61.................... RaulDaSilva 8 64
(David Menuisier) *t.k.h: chsd ldr: rdn and ev ch 3f tl wl over 1f out: styd on same pce after* **14/1**
5000 6 3 **Zamra (IRE)**[13] 7177 3-9-7 70.................... DaleSwift 3 69
(Brian Ellison) *in tch in midfield: effrt on inner 4f out: chsng ldrs and keeping on whn bdly hmpd wl over 1f out: nt rcvr: hld and eased wl ins fnl f* **20/1**
0353 7 *hd* **Rokeby**[62] 5794 3-8-2 51 oh2.................... DuranFentiman 5 50
(George Moore) *hld up in last trio: effrt u.p 3f out: styd on same pce fr over 1f out* **50/1**
4023 8 1 ½ **Bentons Lad**[65] 5682 3-8-2 51.................... PatrickMathers 11 48
(George Moore) *in tch in midfield: unable qck u.p over 3f out: wknd wl over 1f out* **12/1**
054 9 2 ¼ **Mobhirr**[20] 7015 3-9-3 66....................(p) PaoloSirigu 4 60
(Marco Botti) *s.i.s: a towards rr: effrt and racing wd of rivals 4f out: nvr a threat to ldrs* **10/1**
4063 10 ½ **Cape Karli (IRE)**[21] 6981 3-9-0 63....................(p) TomEaves 2 56
(Kevin Ryan) *led: hrd pressed and rdn 3f out: hdd 2f out: bdly hmpd and snatched up wl over 1f out: nt rcvr and wl btn after* **14/1**
0502 11 3 ½ **Kashstaree**[9] 7283 3-8-2 51 oh3.................... JimmyQuinn 1 39
(David Barron) *hld up in rr: n.d* **14/1**
1351 12 9 **Crakehall Lad (IRE)**[10] 7247 3-9-4 67.................... BenCurtis 9 42
(Alan Swinbank) *chsd ldrs tl 4f out: sn struggling: bhd fnl 2f* **4/1**[1]
3m 1.92s (-2.78) **Going Correction** -0.10s/f (Good) **12 Ran SP% 114.5**
Speed ratings (Par 101): **103,102,101,101,100 99,98,98,96,96 94,89**
CSF £34.46 CT £342.92 TOTE £6.90: £2.50, £3.60, £3.20; EX 34.20 Trifecta £174.30.
**Owner** Maxilead Limited **Bred** Denis McDonnell **Trained** Newmarket, Suffolk
■ Stewards' Enquiry : Joe Doyle two-day ban: used whip above permitted level (Nov 10,12)

**FOCUS**
The went a steady pace and the favourite was very disappointing, but the unexposed winner scored with a bit in hand and the form could work out. A small pb from the runner-up, with the third close to her Ayr form.

## 7501 RACING UK SUBSCRIBER CLUB DAYS MAIDEN STKS 7f
**3:40** (3:45) (Class 5) 3-Y-O+ **£3,234** (£962; £481; £240) **Stalls** Centre

Form RPR
2502 1 **Millkwood**[41] 6429 4-9-7 73....................(b) PhillipMakin 8 65
(John Davies) *chsd ldr tl led 1/2-way: mde rest: wnt clr u.p over 1f out: styd on: rdn out* **11/8**[1]
05 2 2 **Elhaam (IRE)**[21] 6988 3-9-0 0.................... MartinLane 9 52
(George Margarson) *chsd ldrs: chsd wnr and rdn 1/2-way: no ex over 1f out: edgd rt but hld on to 2nd ins fnl f* **8/1**[3]
0635 3 ¾ **Magical Mischief**[10] 7248 4-9-2 53.................... MichaelStainton 11 52
(Chris Fairhurst) *led tl 1/2-way: 3rd and outpcd 2f out: no threat to wnr but kpt on again ins fnl f* **9/1**
3060 4 *hd* **Lady Liz**[62] 5793 3-9-0 46....................(b) TomEaves 6 50
(George Moore) *in tch in midfield: modest 5th and wnt lft u.p wl over 1f out: no threat to wnr and edgd lft ins fnl f: kpt on* **50/1**
5 2 ¼ **Polly's Rose**[40] 5-9-2 0.................... JasonHart 7 45
(Ian Semple) *chsd ldrs: struggling u.p 3f out: kpt on same pce u.p fr over 1f out* **66/1**
6 *shd* **Mambo Fever** 3-9-0 0.................... AndrewElliott 12 44
(David C Griffiths) *s.i.s: rn green and wl off the pce in rr: sme hdwy and hung lft 1/2-way: wnt 6th over 1f out: got the hang of things and gng on wl ins fnl f: nvr trbld ldrs* **25/1**
4-00 7 7 **Nonagon**[26] 6862 3-9-0 46.................... EmmaSayer(5) 10 31
(Wilf Storey) *midfield: struggling u.p 1/2-way: n.d fnl 2f* **150/1**
6 8 1 ½ **Hope And Fortune (IRE)**[14] 7158 3-9-0 0.................... PatCosgrave 1 22
(John Butler) *pushed lft s: in tch in midfield but sn bustled along: struggling 1/2-way: n.d after* **40/1**
-350 9 *nk* **Master Clockmaker (IRE)**[119] 3789 3-9-5 67...........(v[1]) PJMcDonald 5 26
(Ann Duffield) *chsd ldrs tl 1/2-way: sn dropped out u.p: no ch over 1f out* **5/1**[2]
00-0 10 2 ¾ **Misu Mac**[10] 7250 4-9-2 45.................... RaulDaSilva 14 15
(Neville Bycroft) *hld up off the pce in last quartet: n.d* **150/1**
0-25 11 ¾ **Danzki (IRE)**[157] 2516 3-9-5 62.................... ChrisCatlin 13 17
(Gay Kelleway) *off the pce in midfield: struggling and btn 1/2-way* **10/1**
46 12 1 ¼ **Byronaissance**[20] 7010 5-9-7 52.................... DavidAllan 2 15
(Neville Bycroft) *wnt lft s: chsd ldrs: losing pl u.p 1/2-way: bhd over 1f out* **40/1**
3-30 13 11 **Penny Pursuits**[140] 3054 3-9-0 50.................... PatrickMathers 15
(Alan Berry) *a wl off pce in rr: t.o* **125/1**
14 1 ½ **Alpha Delphini** 3-9-5 0.................... PaulMulrennan 4
(Bryan Smart) *s.i.s: a wl off pce in rr: t.o* **9/1**
4640 15 1 **Hatton Springs (IRE)**[9] 7291 3-9-0 46.................... TonyHamilton 3
(Stuart Coltherd) *chsd ldrs for 2f: sn struggling u.p: wl bhd over 1f out: t.o* **50/1**
1m 22.79s (-1.71) **Going Correction** -0.45s/f (Firm)
**WFA** 3 from 4yo+ 2lb **15 Ran SP% 115.2**
Speed ratings (Par 103): **91,88,87,87,85 84,76,75,74,71 70,69,56,55,54**
CSF £11.29 TOTE £2.50: £1.10, £2.40, £3.20; EX 12.80 Trifecta £78.60.
**Owner** Pipeline Precision Engineering Limited **Bred** G Lambert **Trained** Piercebridge, Durham

**FOCUS**
The well-backed winner finally got off the mark in this modest maiden. A poor maiden, the winner being rated a stone off his best.

## 7502 100% RACINGUK PROFITS RETURNED TO RACING APPRENTICE H'CAP 6f
**4:10** (4:14) (Class 6) (0-65,65) 3-Y-O+ **£1,940** (£577; £288; £144) **Stalls** Centre

Form RPR
2331 1 **Another Royal**[10] 7250 3-8-13 60.................... MeganCarberry(3) 13 71
(Tim Easterby) *a gng wl: hld up in tch: wnt 2nd and carried rt wl over 1f out: pushed along and qcknd to ld ins fnl f: r.o: comf* **5/1**[1]
0311 2 1 ¼ **Armelle (FR)**[65] 5683 3-8-13 60....................(p) DavidParkes(3) 19 67
(Scott Dixon) *racd towards stands' rail: chsd ldrs: effrt u.p over 1f out: styd on to snatch 2nd on post: no threat to wnr* **7/1**[2]
0041 3 *nse* **Red Tide (IRE)**[60] 5853 3-9-3 61.................... JackDuern 3 68
(Marjorie Fife) *led: rdn and edgd rt wl over 1f out: hdd and one pce ins fnl f: lost 2nd on post* **16/1**
0061 4 ¾ **Telegraph (IRE)**[20] 6995 3-9-4 62.................... JoeDoyle 2 67
(David Evans) *dwlt: hld up towards rr: hdwy in to midfield at 1/2-way: styd on wl u.p ins fnl f: no threat to wnr* **16/1**
5120 5 1 ½ **White Flag**[42] 6409 3-8-12 59.................... RachelRichardson(3) 11 59
(Tim Easterby) *chsd ldng pair: rdn wl over 1f out: no ex and one pce ins fnl f* **20/1**
0430 6 *nk* **Live Dangerously**[6] 7368 4-9-4 64.................... KieranShoemark(3) 12 63
(Keith Dalgleish) *in tch in midfield: drvn 1f out: kpt on ins fnl f: nvr gng pce to chal* **8/1**
1640 7 ½ **Bond Club**[13] 7180 4-9-4 64....................(b) AdamMcLean(3) 7 61
(Geoffrey Oldroyd) *sn outpcd in rr: hdwy towards far rail over 1f out: kpt on wl u.p ins fnl f: nvr trbld ldrs* **20/1**
3030 8 ¾ **Two Shades Of Grey (IRE)**[72] 5437 3-9-5 63.........(p) SammyJoBell 16 58
(Richard Fahey) *midfield: effrt 1/2-way: hdwy ent fnl f: kpt on ins fnl f: nvr trbld ldrs* **12/1**
0643 9 *shd* **Space War**[34] 6625 7-9-2 62.................... AnnaHesketh(3) 17 57
(Michael Easterby) *towards rr: rdn 2f out: hdwy 1f out: styd on wl ins fnl f: nvr threatened ldrs* **11/1**
0030 10 1 **Mercers Row**[13] 7179 7-9-5 65.................... GemmaTutty(3) 18 56
(Karen Tutty) *in tch midfield: rdn and no hdwy over 1f out: hld and one pce fnl f* **12/1**
2104 11 1 ¼ **Mission Impossible**[55] 5996 9-9-8 65....................(p) KevinStott 14 52
(Tracy Waggott) *in tch in midfield: rdn and no hdwy 2f out: wknd fnl f* **25/1**
0010 12 *nse* **Lord Buffhead**[11] 7221 5-8-9 59....................(v) MelissaThompson(7) 8 46
(Richard Guest) *in tch in midfield: pushed along and no hdwy over 1f out: wknd ins fnl f* **20/1**
3620 13 1 ¾ **Cash Is King**[33] 6674 4-9-5 62.................... GeorgeDowning 5 44
(Robert Johnson) *chsd ldr tl wl over 1f out: sn struggling u.p: wknd fnl f* **33/1**
3000 14 ¾ **Foreign Rhythm (IRE)**[26] 6866 9-8-9 57.................... PhillipDennis(5) 20 36
(Ron Barr) *midfield: rdn and no hdwy 2f out: wknd ent fnl f* **33/1**
3400 15 ½ **Niceonemyson**[10] 7248 5-8-9 57.................... RowanScott(5) 9 35
(Christopher Wilson) *a off the pce towards rr: n.d* **25/1**
1501 16 *nk* **New Lease Of Life**[18] 7057 5-9-7 64....................(p) JackGarritty 4 41
(Jim Goldie) *in tch in midfield: struggling u.p wl over 1f out: sn wknd* **15/2**[3]
4040 17 5 **Iceblast**[13] 7180 6-9-0 62....................(v) DanielleMooney(5) 15 23
(Michael Easterby) *s.i.s: a bhd: n.d* **25/1**
1300 18 ½ **Betty Boo (IRE)**[86] 4891 4-9-1 58.................... ShelleyBirkett 6 17
(Shaun Harris) *a towards rr: bhd fr 1/2-way* **20/1**
1m 9.72s (-2.08) **Going Correction** -0.45s/f (Firm)
**WFA** 3 from 4yo+ 1lb **18 Ran SP% 124.0**
Speed ratings (Par 101): **95,93,93,92,90 89,89,88,88,86 85,85,82,81,81 80,73,73**
CSF £31.30 CT £547.65 TOTE £5.60: £1.80, £1.60, £4.40, £3.70; EX 27.90 Trifecta £396.90.
**Owner** C H Stevens **Bred** Habton Farms **Trained** Great Habton, N Yorks

**FOCUS**
Most of the runners raced centre to stands' side in this handicap and the favourite delivered in good style. A pb from the winner, while the runner-up has been rated to her C&D win in August.
T/Jkpt: £3,785.90 to a £1 stake. Pool: £1,33308.27 - 25.00 winning tickets T/Plt: £3.80 to a £1 stake. Pool: £52,249.91 - 9,797.32 winning tickets T/Qpdt: £3.80 to a £1 stake. Pool: £3,656.18 - 709.90 winning tickets SP

# 7277 CATTERICK (L-H)
### Tuesday, October 28

**OFFICIAL GOING: Good to soft (7.3) changing to good to soft (soft in places) after race 5 (2.50)**
Wind: Breezy half behind Weather: Overcast and showers

## 7503 CATTERICKBRIDGE.CO.UK NOVICE STKS 5f
**12:50** (12:51) (Class 5) 2-Y-O **£6,469** (£1,925; £962; £481) **Stalls** Low

Form RPR
2212 1 **Field Game**[11] 7255 2-9-7 86....................(t) GrahamLee 5 90
(Hughie Morrison) *chsd ldrs: pushed along and sltly outpcd 1/2-way: sn swtchd lft to inner rail and hdwy over 1f out: rdn to ld ent fnl f: kpt on* **4/1**[2]
4032 2 ½ **Brando**[18] 7082 2-8-9 82.................... ShaneGray(5) 4 81
(Kevin Ryan) *cl up: rdn to take slt ld wl over 1f out: hdd ent fnl f: sn drvn and edgd lft: no ex towards fin* **1/1**[1]
116 3 3 ¾ **Park Glen (IRE)**[17] 7121 2-9-3 85.................... PJMcDonald 7 71
(Noel Quinlan) *prom on outer: rdn along 2f out: kpt on u.p fnl f* **7/1**[3]
6230 4 *nk* **Honest Bob'S**[11] 7255 2-8-9 79.................... JackGarritty(5) 1 67
(Brian Ellison) *slt ld: rdn along 1/2-way: hdd wl over 1f out: grad wknd* **7/1**[3]
1522 5 2 ¾ **Marigot Bay**[11] 7232 2-8-8 77.................... JoeDoyle(5) 3 56
(Gay Kelleway) *cl up: rdn along 2f out: sn wknd* **9/1**
6 23 **Good Boy Alex** 2-9-0 0.................... PatrickMathers 6
(Alan Berry) *dwlt: green and sn rdn along in rr: a outpcd and bhd* **250/1**
0 P **Ince Moss**[32] 6700 2-8-9 0.................... TonyHamilton 2
(Richard Fahey) *chsd ldrs: lost action and p.u qckly after 1f* **33/1**
1m 0.4s (0.60) **Going Correction** 0.0s/f (Good) **7 Ran SP% 108.3**
Speed ratings (Par 95): **95,94,88,87,83 46,**
CSF £7.46 TOTE £4.40: £2.40, £1.10; EX 8.70 Trifecta £21.40.
**Owner** Lord Carnarvon **Bred** Earl Of Carnarvon **Trained** East Ilsley, Berks

**FOCUS**
A useful effort from the winner to concede upwards of 4lb all round. It was run at a good pace. The runner-up has been rated to his mark in defeat. Rail on far bend moved out 4yds and races between 6f and 14f increased by 12yds and 2m race by 24yds

## 7504 RACING UK ON SKY 432 H'CAP — 1m 3f 214y
1:20 (1:20) (Class 4) (0-85,81) 3-Y-O+ — £5,453 (£1,610; £805) Stalls Centre

Form — RPR

6001 **1** **English Summer**[10] 7279 7-9-11 80 (t) GeorgeChaloner 5 — 89
(Richard Fahey) *hld up towards rr: rapid hdwy on wd outside home turn and sn cl up: rdn to dispute ld wl over 1f out: drvn and edgd lft ins fnl f: kpt on wl to ld nr fin* **6/1**

6513 **2** *shd* **Sioux Chieftain (IRE)**[10] 7281 4-9-5 74 BenCurtis 2 — 83
(Michael Appleby) *trckd ldrs: hdwy 3f out: sn rdn and hung rt over 1f out: drvn ins fnl f: hdd and no ex nr fin* **3/1**[2]

16-1 **3** *¾* **Forced Family Fun**[206] 1307 4-9-10 79 PhillipMakin 6 — 87
(John Quinn) *trckd ldrs: hdwy whn n.m.r over 2f out: effrt whn nt clr run and swtchd lft over 1f out: rdn to chal ins fnl f: ev ch tl no ex nr fin* **5/1**[3]

2050 **4** *3* **Engrossing**[10] 7281 5-8-13 68 BarryMcHugh 7 — 71
(Peter Niven) *hld up towards rr: hdwy over 4f out: wd st and jnd ldrs over 2f out: rdn whn n.m.r over 1f out: sn drvn and kpt on same pce* **22/1**

0-06 **5** *nk* **Freewheel (IRE)**[199] 1444 4-9-12 81 GrahamLee 8 — 84
(Frederick Watson) *trckd ldr: cl up 1/2-way: led 3f out: sn rdn hdd 2f out: drvn and edgd lft wl over 1f out: grad wknd* **25/1**

0041 **6** *1¾* **Full Moon Fever (IRE)**[9] 7305 3-9-2 78 6ex LukeMorris 9 — 78
(Ed Walker) *trckd ldng pair: pushed along over 4f out: rdn 3f out: wkng whn n.m.r and sltly hmpd over 1f out* **2/1**[1]

02 **7** *5* **War Poet**[10] 7279 7-9-4 78 (p) KevinStott[(5)] 3 — 70
(Clive Mulhall) *hld up: a towards rr* **18/1**

4310 **8** *nk* **Never Up (GER)**[17] 7125 3-9-2 78 DavidNolan 4 — 69
(David O'Meara) *led: jnd 1/2-way: rdn along and hdd 3f out: sn wknd* **20/1**

4340 **9** *2¾* **Chant (IRE)**[10] 7281 4-8-8 70 RowanScott[(7)] 1 — 57
(Ann Duffield) *a towards rr: pushed along 4f out: rdn 3f out: sn outpcd* **25/1**

2m 42.39s (3.49) **Going Correction** +0.425s/f (Yiel)
**WFA** 3 from 4yo+ 7lb — 9 Ran SP% **111.4**
Speed ratings (Par 105): **105,104,104,102,102 101,97,97,95**
CSF £22.04 CT £93.12 TOTE £4.70: £2.00, £1.40, £1.80; EX 23.10 Trifecta £89.60.
**Owner** Dr Marwan Koukash **Bred** Juddmonte Farms Ltd **Trained** Musley Bank, N Yorks
■ Stewards' Enquiry : Ben Curtis one-day ban; careless riding (12th Nov)

**FOCUS**
A fair handicap which was soundly run. A small pb from the third off a tough mark.

## 7505 DAVID BARKER MEMORIAL H'CAP (DIV I) — 5f 212y
1:50 (1:50) (Class 4) (0-80,79) 3-Y-O+ — £5,175 (£1,540; £769; £384) Stalls Low

Form — RPR

546 **1** **Polski Max**[15] 7159 4-9-7 79 (p) DaleSwift 4 — 89
(Brian Ellison) *chsd ldrs: carried rt over 1f out: led jst ins fnl f: edgd lft: drvn out* **5/1**[2]

0664 **2** *½* **Ambitious Icarus**[12] 7215 5-8-12 73 (e) JacobButterfield[(3)] 2 — 81
(Richard Guest) *mid-div: hdwy on inner over 2f out: chsng ldrs over 1f out: edgd rt and tk 2nd last 50yds: no ex* **16/1**

2102 **3** *1* **Percy's Gal**[14] 7178 3-8-9 73 GemmaTutty[(5)] 7 — 78
(Karen Tutty) *in rr: effrt over 2f out: styd on wl fnl f: tk 3rd cl home* **9/1**

0300 **4** *nk* **Gran Canaria Queen**[18] 7085 5-9-6 78 DavidAllan 12 — 82
(Tim Easterby) *mid-div: hdwy on outer over 2f out: kpt on fnl f* **9/1**

0220 **5** *shd* **Pea Shooter**[39] 6512 5-9-7 79 PaddyAspell 8 — 83
(David Nicholls) *t.k.h: trckd ldrs: led over 2f out: edgd rt over 1f out: hdd jst ins fnl f: fdd last 50yds* **12/1**

1221 **6** *shd* **Royal Connoisseur (IRE)**[14] 7178 3-9-4 77 GeorgeChaloner 3 — 81
(Richard Fahey) *trckd ldrs: effrt over 2f out: kpt on same pce fnl f* **4/1**[1]

5600 **7** *1* **Kenny The Captain (IRE)**[13] 7212 3-9-2 75 DuranFentiman 10 — 75
(Tim Easterby) *dwlt: in rr: hdwy on outer over 2f out: kpt on one pce fnl f* **7/1**[3]

103 **8** *1¼* **Pennine Warrior**[14] 7179 3-9-2 75 (p) LukeMorris 11 — 71
(Scott Dixon) *chsd ldrs: effrt outer over 2f out: one pce* **7/1**[3]

6060 **9** *1¼* **Banovallum**[14] 7179 4-8-11 69 (b[1]) GrahamGibbons 5 — 61
(Michael Easterby) *mid-div: effrt over 2f out: nvr a threat* **33/1**

5-05 **10** *1¼* **Indego Blues**[14] 7179 5-8-12 70 PaulQuinn 1 — 58
(David Nicholls) *dwlt: hmpd on inner and lost pl after 2f: nvr a factor after* **8/1**

0-00 **11** *2* **Shady McCoy (USA)**[13] 7212 4-9-5 77 RobertWinston 9 — 59
(Ian Williams) *w ldr: hung rt and lost pl over 2f out: wknd fnl f* **25/1**

6012 **12** *3* **Camanche Grey (IRE)**[85] 4974 3-8-9 68 AndrewElliott 6 — 40
(Ben Haslam) *led: hdd over 2f out: sn wknd* **33/1**

1m 16.17s (2.57) **Going Correction** +0.425s/f (Yiel)
**WFA** 3 from 4yo+ 1lb — 12 Ran SP% **116.1**
Speed ratings (Par 105): **99,98,97,96,96 96,95,93,91,90 87,83**
CSF £78.57 CT £702.32 TOTE £7.90: £2.20, £5.30, £4.10; EX 104.20 Trifecta £1068.70.
**Owner** Market Avenue Racing & Tremousser **Bred** Mike J Beadle **Trained** Norton, N Yorks
■ Stewards' Enquiry : Paddy Aspell one-day ban; careless riding.

**FOCUS**
A modest sprint handicap. The leaders looked to go pretty hard. The winner has been rated as running his best race since his 2yo/early 3yo days, and the third has been rated close to form.

## 7506 DAVID BARKER MEMORIAL H'CAP (DIV II) — 5f 212y
2:20 (2:20) (Class 4) (0-80,79) 3-Y-O+ — £5,175 (£1,540; £769; £384) Stalls Low

Form — RPR

6664 **1** **Penny Garcia**[14] 7178 4-8-8 66 (p) DavidAllan 8 — 75
(Tim Easterby) *midfield: rdn along wl over 2f out: hdwy to chse ldrs over 1f out: drvn to chal ins fnl f: kpt on wl to ld nr fin* **11/2**[2]

2620 **2** *shd* **Captain Royale (IRE)**[33] 6695 9-9-0 75 (p) JacobButterfield[(3)] 9 — 83
(Tracy Waggott) *trckd ldrs: hdwy 1/2-way: wd st: cl up on outer 2f out: rdn and slt ld appr fnl f: sn drvn: hdd and no ex nr fin* **28/1**

1210 **3** *½* **Heartsong (IRE)**[9] 7307 5-8-10 71 JoeyHaynes[(3)] 10 — 77
(John Gallagher) *hld up in rr: wd st: gd hdwy over 2f out: rdn to chal over 1f out: drvn ins fnl f and ev ch tl no ex last 50yds* **18/1**

3022 **4** *3* **Fleurtille**[14] 7179 5-8-10 73 GemmaTutty[(5)] 11 — 70
(Ray Craggs) *towards rr: hdwy over 2f out: and sn rdn: styd on fnl f: nrst fin* **7/1**

1200 **5** *1* **Layla's Hero (IRE)**[10] 7282 7-9-5 77 (v) PaulMulrennan 12 — 71
(David Nicholls) *chsd ldrs: led 1/2-way: rdn wl over 1f out: hdd appr fnl f: grad wknd* **11/1**

0605 **6** *2¼* **Boris Grigoriev (IRE)**[14] 7178 5-8-9 67 (b) GrahamLee 2 — 53
(Michael Easterby) *towards rr: hdwy on inner 2f out: sn rdn and kpt on fnl f* **13/2**[3]

1514 **7** *2¼* **Abi Scarlet (IRE)**[15] 7159 5-9-5 77 LukeMorris 7 — 56
(Scott Dixon) *slt ld 2f: cl up: rdn along wl over 2f out: grad wknd* **17/2**

-020 **8** *1* **Half A Billion (IRE)**[15] 7159 5-9-4 79 ConnorBeasley[(3)] 6 — 55
(Michael Dods) *chsd ldrs: rdn along wl over 2f out: sn wknd* **11/1**

1166 **9** *hd* **Jamesbo's Girl**[40] 6492 4-9-7 79 GrahamGibbons 1 — 54
(David Barron) *cl up on inner: led 4f out: hdd 1/2-way: rdn along over 2f out: sn wknd* **9/2**[1]

6-50 **10** *3* **Marciano (IRE)**[14] 7178 4-8-12 70 RussKennemore 5 — 36
(Sue Smith) *a towards rr* **12/1**

3004 **11** *3¼* **Hadaj**[18] 7071 5-9-2 74 TomEaves 4 — 29
(Michael Herrington) *chsd ldrs on inner: rdn along 1/2-way: sn wknd* **12/1**

1300 **12** *5* **Meandmyshadow**[31] 6736 6-9-0 72 DaleSwift 3 — 11
(Alan Brown) *sn rdn along: a in rr: bhd fr 1/2-way* **20/1**

1m 15.86s (2.26) **Going Correction** +0.425s/f (Yiel) — 12 Ran SP% **115.5**
Speed ratings (Par 105): **101,100,100,96,94 91,88,87,87,83 78,72**
CSF £143.77 CT £2567.40 TOTE £7.20: £1.80, £5.00, £4.30; EX 167.90 Trifecta £1651.70.
**Owner** James Bowers **Bred** J Bowers **Trained** Great Habton, N Yorks

**FOCUS**
The second division of the modest sprint handicap. The third has been rated to her best since last summer.

## 7507 DAVID T BROWN "LORD HOVIS" H'CAP — 7f
2:50 (2:52) (Class 4) (0-85,85) 3-Y-O+ — £6,469 (£1,925; £962; £481) Stalls Low

Form — RPR

1223 **1** **Evanescent (IRE)**[10] 7282 5-8-12 81 JoeDoyle[(5)] 8 — 90
(John Quinn) *hld up in mid-div: hdwy over 2f out: chsng ldrs over 1f out: styd on to ld nr fin* **7/1**[2]

1141 **2** *¾* **Comino (IRE)**[10] 7282 3-8-13 84 ShaneGray[(5)] 7 — 90+
(Kevin Ryan) *chsd ldrs: 2nd over 2f out: led over 1f out: hdd and no ex clsng stages* **4/1**[1]

P050 **3** *nse* **Mujazif (IRE)**[18] 7085 4-9-4 82 PaddyAspell 12 — 89
(David Nicholls) *in rr: hdwy over 2f out: swtchd rt appr fnl f: styng on at fin* **16/1**

6500 **4** *¾* **Fieldgunner Kirkup (GER)**[18] 7085 6-9-2 80 GrahamGibbons 10 — 85
(David Barron) *hld up in rr: hdwy and c stands' side rail over 2f out: styd on fnl f* **18/1**

0U40 **5** *½* **Johnny Cavagin**[47] 6260 5-9-4 82 (t) TomEaves 9 — 86
(Richard Guest) *hld up in mid-div: hdwy over 2f out: chsng ldrs 1f out: kpt on same pce* **15/2**[3]

0006 **6** *nk* **Victoire De Lyphar (IRE)**[19] 7060 7-9-7 85 (e) PJMcDonald 13 — 88
(Ruth Carr) *chsd ldrs: kpt on same pce appr fnl f* **20/1**

0400 **7** *½* **Dr Red Eye**[10] 7282 6-9-1 79 (p) DaleSwift 15 — 81
(Scott Dixon) *led: swtchd lft sn after s: hdd over 1f out: fdd and eased nr fin* **18/1**

6000 **8** *4* **Kalk Bay (IRE)**[17] 7125 7-9-0 78 (t) PaulMulrennan 14 — 69
(Michael Easterby) *s.i.s: in rr: hdwy over 2f out: wknd appr fnl f* **25/1**

025 **9** *shd* **Piceno (IRE)**[75] 5346 6-9-4 82 (p) LukeMorris 1 — 73
(Scott Dixon) *chsd ldr: wknd over 1f out* **8/1**

-000 **10** *6* **Rodrigo De Torres**[29] 6824 7-9-0 78 GrahamLee 6 — 53
(Frederick Watson) *chsd ldrs: hmpd sn after s: lost pl over 1f out* **80/1**

2002 **11** *1* **Ready (IRE)**[10] 7282 4-9-5 83 (p) DavidAllan 11 — 56
(Garry Moss) *rr-div: drvn 3f out: chsng ldrs over 1f out: wknd and eased last 75yds* **4/1**[1]

1500 **12** *7* **Bop It**[8] 7330 5-9-4 82 (p) DavidNolan 2 — 37
(David O'Meara) *chsd ldrs: drvn over 3f out: lost pl wl over 1f out* **25/1**

0620 **13** *6* **Pandar**[16] 7132 5-9-1 82 JoeyHaynes[(3)] 3 — 21
(Milton Bradley) *in rr: lost pl over 2f out: sn bhd* **14/1**

-000 **14** *nk* **Poole Harbour (IRE)**[11] 7233 5-9-6 84 PaulQuinn 5 — 22
(David Nicholls) *hmpd sn after s: chsd ldrs: lost pl over 3f out: sn bhd: eased over 1f out* **50/1**

1m 29.93s (2.93) **Going Correction** +0.425s/f (Yiel)
**WFA** 3 from 4yo+ 2lb — 14 Ran SP% **114.1**
Speed ratings (Par 105): **100,99,99,98,97 97,96,92,92,85 84,76,69,68**
CSF £31.14 CT £432.33 TOTE £7.70: £2.80, £1.40, £5.70; EX 26.90 Trifecta £466.00.
**Owner** Mrs S Quinn **Bred** Oliver Donlon **Trained** Settrington, N Yorks
■ Stewards' Enquiry : Dale Swift three-day ban; careless riding (12th-14th Nov)

**FOCUS**
A fairly useful handicap. Not for the first time during the afternoon, the leaders seemed to go hard enough, setting it up for those coming from off the pace, the performance of the second probably worth marking up slightly. A small pb from the winner.

## 7508 BOOK NOW FOR NEW YEAR'S DAY H'CAP (DIV I) — 1m 7f 177y
3:20 (3:20) (Class 5) (0-70,70) 3-Y-O+ — £2,911 (£866; £432; £216) Stalls Low

Form — RPR

24-4 **1** **Handiwork**[14] 7182 4-9-8 64 (p) JoeFanning 6 — 78+
(Steve Gollings) *trckd ldrs: hdwy 4f out: led 3f out: wd st to stands' rail and sn clr: kpt on strly: unchal* **9/2**[1]

5060 **2** *8* **Regal Park (IRE)**[8] 7333 7-8-13 60 TimClark[(5)] 13 — 61
(Miss Imogen Pickard) *hld up towards rr: hdwy 5f out: chsd ldrs 3f out: wd st and rdn 2f out: sn drvn and kpt on: no ch w wnr* **25/1**

-621 **3** *nk* **Rockawango (FR)**[14] 7175 8-9-10 66 (tp) PaulMulrennan 2 — 67
(James Ewart) *trckd ldrs: hdwy to chse wnr 3f out: rdn over 2f out: sn one pce* **10/1**

0521 **4** *2¾* **Bulas Belle**[10] 7284 4-9-3 64 KevinStott[(5)] 10 — 62
(Edwin Tuer) *hld up towards rr: hdwy over 3f out: rdn to chse ldrs 2f out: sn drvn and no imp* **6/1**[2]

14-4 **5** *2¾* **Iron Butterfly**[165] 1359 5-9-2 58 LukeMorris 3 — 52
(James Eustace) *chsd ldrs: rdn along over 3f out: outpcd over 2f out: plugged on u.p fnl f* **13/2**[3]

2354 **6** *1½* **Wor Lass**[14] 7177 6-9-1 57 DavidNolan 8 — 50
(Iain Jardine) *hld up: effrt and sme hdwy over 3f out: rdn wl over 2f out: n.d* **9/1**

3046 **7** *2½* **Cowslip**[21] 7007 5-8-10 52 oh5 (b[1]) AndrewElliott 4 — 42
(George Moore) *trckd ldrs: pushed along over 4f out: rdn 3f out: sn drvn and wknd over 2f out* **50/1**

300- **8** *¾* **Generous Dream**[319] 8268 6-8-12 54 TomEaves 9 — 43
(Mel Brittain) *trckd ldr: cl up 1/2-way: led 5f out: rdn along and hdd 3f out: sn wknd* **66/1**

5-00 **9** *5* **Paris Snow**[18] 7072 4-10-0 70 RobertWinston 12 — 53
(Ian Williams) *a bhd* **18/1**

325- **10** *2½* **Beyeh (IRE)**[194] 2545 6-9-1 62 AlistairRawlinson[(5)] 7 — 42
(Michael Appleby) *a towards rr* **9/1**

0561 **11** *3¼* **Cool Baranca (GER)**[10] 7283 8-8-9 56 EmmaSayer[(5)] 11 — 32
(Dianne Sayer) *hld up: a in rr: bhd fnl 3f* **14/1**

4440 **12** *6* **Aleksandar**[30] 6794 5-9-12 68 .......... GrahamLee 5 37
(Jim Goldie) *midfield: pushed along on inner over 4f out: rdn over 3f out and sn wknd* **9/1**

2642 **13** *7* **Funky Munky**[10] 7284 9-8-10 52 .......... (p) PJMcDonald 1 12
(Alistair Whillans) *led: pushed along 7f out: rdn 6f out: sn hdd & wknd* **8/1**

3m 41.39s (9.39) **Going Correction** +0.425s/f (Yiel) **13** Ran SP% **115.2**
Speed ratings (Par 103): **93,89,88,87,86 85,84,83,81,79 78,75,71**
CSF £119.77 CT £1066.75 TOTE £5.30: £1.60, £7.60, £3.30; EX 121.80 Trifecta £1151.60 Part won..
**Owner** C Johnstone **Bred** The Queen **Trained** Scamblesby, Lincs

**FOCUS**
A moderate and one-sided handicap. The third and fourth have been rated a little off their latest wins.

## 7509 BOOK NOW FOR NEW YEAR'S DAY H'CAP (DIV II) 1m 7f 177y
**3:50** (3:51) (Class 5) (0-70,69) 3-Y-0+ **£2,911** (£866; £432; £216) **Stalls** Low

Form RPR

40/ **1** *nse* **Dara Tango (FR)**[723] 5864 7-9-3 58 .......... GrahamLee 7 68
(A J Martin, Ire) *hld up in mid-div: t.k.h: trckd ldrs 6f out: swtchd lft over 1f out: upsides whn carried bdly lft fnl 75yds: jst failed: fin 2nd, nse: awrdd r* **2/1**[1]

0-11 **2** **Jolie Blonde**[21] 7006 3-9-4 69 .......... LukeMorris 9 79
(Sir Mark Prescott Bt) *sn chsng ldrs: drvn over 4f out: led over 2f out: edgd rt over 1f out: edgd lft last 100yds: all out: disqualified and pl 2nd* **2/1**[1]

5505 **3** *2 ¼* **Jan Smuts (IRE)**[14] 7177 6-9-2 62 .......... (tp) ShaneGray(5) 13 69
(Wilf Storey) *hld up in mid-div: hdwy over 4f out: chsng ldrs 3f out: kpt on same pce to take 3rd clsng stages* **20/1**

4-04 **4** *2 ¼* **Come On Sunshine**[101] 2198 3-8-13 64 .......... DaleSwift 6 68
(Brian Ellison) *chsd ldrs: drvn over 5f out: one pce over 1f out: eased nr fin* **8/1**[2]

5025 **5** *2 ¼* **Authentication**[80] 5200 5-8-11 52 .......... PJMcDonald 4 54
(Mel Brittain) *led: hdd over 2f out: fdd fnl 150yds* **25/1**

6-00 **6** *1* **Montaff**[17] 7124 8-9-8 66 .......... JacobButterfield(3) 1 66
(Richard Guest) *dwlt: in rr: hdwy 5f out: chsng ldrs 3f out: one pce over 1f out* **20/1**

2001 **7** *7* **Waltz Darling (IRE)**[21] 7007 6-9-2 62 .......... EmmaSayer(5) 10 54
(Keith Reveley) *hld up in rr: hdwy to trck ldrs after 6f: lost pl over 3f out: kpt on fnl 2f* **12/1**[3]

205 **8** *nk* **Zarosa (IRE)**[4] 7419 5-9-0 55 .......... RobertWinston 8 47
(John Berry) *t.k.h in mid-div: hdwy 4f out: sn chsng ldrs: wknd fnl f* **16/1**

3430 **9** *21* **La Bacouetteuse (FR)**[17] 7124 9-10-0 69 .......... (p) DavidAllan 2 35
(Iain Jardine) *s.i.s: hld up towards rr: reminders after 3f: drvn 6f out: lost pl over 4f out: bhd whn eased over 1f out: t.o* **25/1**

**10** *27* **Balboni (IRE)**[70] 5541 6-8-10 51 oh6 .......... TonyHamilton 11
(Mark Michael McNiff, Ire) *s.i.s: t.k.h: sn mid-div: hdwy to chse ldrs 6f out: lost pl over 3f out: bhd whn eased over 1f out: t.o* **28/1**

3454 **11** *4 ½* **Pixie Cut (IRE)**[153] 2678 4-9-10 68 .......... ConnorBeasley(3) 3
(Alistair Whillans) *hld up in mid-div: lost pl over 5f out: bhd whn eased over 1f out: t.o* **16/1**

624- **12** *31* **Brasingaman Eric**[448] 5109 7-9-10 65 .......... AndrewElliott 5
(George Moore) *trckd ldrs: lost pl over 5f out: bhd whn eased 2f out: virtually p.u: tailed rt off* **50/1**

3m 47.52s (15.52) **Going Correction** +0.425s/f (Yiel)
**WFA** 3 from 4yo+ 10lb **12** Ran SP% **119.9**
Speed ratings (Par 103): **77,78,76,75,74 74,70,70,59,46 44,28**
CSF £4.80 CT £60.54 TOTE £3.80: £3.30, £5.60; EX 7.70 Trifecta £146.20.
**Owner** A Shiels & Niall Reilly **Bred** Sarl Ecurie Haras De Quetieville **Trained** Summerhill, Co. Meath
■ Stewards' Enquiry : Luke Morris two-day ban; careless riding (12th-13th Nov)

**FOCUS**
A moderate staying handicap with a dramatic finish. Muddling form rated around the third.

## 7510 JUMP SEASON NEXT ON DECEMBER 3RD H'CAP 5f
**4:20** (4:21) (Class 6) (0-65,64) 3-Y-0+ **£2,385** (£704; £352) **Stalls** Low

Form RPR

0030 **1** **Ingenti**[34] 6671 6-8-10 58 .......... KevinStott(5) 14 67
(Christopher Wilson) *in tch: hdwy wl over 1f out: rdn to chal ent fnl f: drvn to ld and edgd lft last 100yds: kpt on* **8/1**[3]

3131 **2** *½* **Pavers Star**[27] 6866 5-9-2 59 .......... (p) JoeFanning 13 66
(Noel Wilson) *cl up: led 1/2-way: rdn over 1f out: drvn ins fnl f: hdd and carried sltly lft last 100yds: no ex towards fin* **11/2**[2]

242 **3** *½* **Rylee Mooch**[13] 7213 6-9-7 64 .......... (e) AndrewElliott 8 69
(Richard Guest) *led to 1/2-way: cl up: rdn wl over 1f out: drvn and ev ch ent fnl f: no ex last 75yds* **5/1**[1]

40 **4** *¾* **Minty Jones**[19] 7057 5-8-2 50 .......... (v) TimClark(5) 12 53
(Michael Mullineaux) *towards rr: rdn along 2f out: swtchd rt over 1f out: styd on strly fnl f: nrst fin* **11/1**

4000 **5** *hd* **Sunrise Dance**[27] 6866 5-8-4 50 .......... (p) ConnorBeasley(3) 5 52
(Robert Johnson) *dwlt and in rr: hdwy wl over 1f out: sn swtchd rt to stands' rail and rdn: styd on strly fnl f: nrst fin* **10/1**

5406 **6** *½* **Windforpower (IRE)**[24] 6938 4-9-5 62 .......... (v) TonyHamilton 11 62
(Tracy Waggott) *prom: hdwy and cl up 2f out: rdn over 1f out: wkng whn n.m.r wl ins fnl f* **10/1**

5436 **7** *1 ¼* **Straight Gin**[108] 4193 3-8-2 50 oh2 .......... JoeDoyle(5) 15 46
(Alan Berry) *racd towards stands' rail: chsd ldrs: cl up over 2f out: rdn wl over 1f out: wknd ins fnl f* **28/1**

0000 **8** *2 ½* **Shirley's Pride**[13] 7213 4-8-11 59 .......... (vt[1]) AlistairRawlinson(5) 7 45
(Michael Appleby) *chsd ldrs: rdn along wl over 1f out: wknd appr fnl f* **8/1**[3]

3016 **9** *2 ¾* **Lucky Times**[65] 5715 3-9-7 64 .......... PJMcDonald 2 42
(Mel Brittain) *racd towards far side: prom: rdn along jst over 2f out: wknd over 1f out* **10/1**

506 **10** *1 ½* **Sir Geoffrey (IRE)**[13] 7213 8-9-7 64 .......... (p) LukeMorris 4 35
(Scott Dixon) *racd towards far side: prom: rdn along 2f out: sn wknd* **8/1**[3]

006 **11** *2* **Senora Lobo (IRE)**[12] 7221 4-8-7 50 oh5 .......... (p) GeorgeChaloner 9 14
(Lisa Williamson) *chsd ldrs: rdn along over 2f out: sn wknd* **100/1**

0-00 **12** *2 ¾* **Fama Mac**[35] 6627 7-8-12 55 .......... DaleSwift 3 9
(Neville Bycroft) *racd towards far side: a bhd* **22/1**

550 **13** *nk* **Dark Opal (IRE)**[19] 7056 4-9-6 63 .......... (v) BenCurtis 6 16
(John Weymes) *a towards rr* **16/1**

60-0 **14** *1 ½* **Sandwith**[17] 7103 11-9-3 60 .......... (p) DuranFentiman 1 8
(Ian Semple) *racd towards far side: a in rr* **100/1**

1m 0.84s (1.04) **Going Correction** 0.0s/f (Good) **14** Ran SP% **116.6**
Speed ratings (Par 101): **91,90,89,88,87 87,85,81,76,74 71,66,66,63**
CSF £48.70 CT £244.38 TOTE £11.30: £2.90, £4.10, £2.00; EX 70.30 Trifecta £307.10.
**Owner** David Bartlett **Bred** Mrs Andrea Bartlett **Trained** Manfield, N Yorks

**FOCUS**
A run-of-the-mill sprint to conclude proceedings. Straightforward form rated around the first three.
T/Jkpt: Not won. T/Plt: £309.50 to a £1 stake. Pool: £57,992.22 - 136.77 winning tickets. T/Qpdt: £115.20 to a £1 stake. Pool: £4,164.79 - 26.75 winning tickets. JR

# 7336 WINDSOR (R-H)
## Tuesday, October 28

**OFFICIAL GOING: Soft (good to soft in places; 6.3)**
Wind: Almost nil Weather: Sunny, warm!

## 7511 BRITISH STALLION STUDS EBF MAIDEN STKS 6f
**1:00** (1:03) (Class 5) 2-Y-O **£2,911** (£866; £432; £216) **Stalls** Low

Form RPR

563 **1** **Navigate (IRE)**[17] 7123 2-9-5 84 .......... FergusSweeney 4 79
(Martyn Meade) *trckd ldng pair: pushed along to cl 2f out: led over 1f out: shkn up fnl f: styd on* **4/7**[1]

6 **2** *1 ½* **Nortron (IRE)**[17] 7123 2-9-5 0 .......... DavidProbert 2 75
(Andrew Balding) *pressed ldr: led 2f out to over 1f out: kpt on same pce* **5/2**[2]

0 **3** *¾* **Pacolita (IRE)**[13] 7192 2-8-11 0 .......... CamHardie(3) 6 67
(Sylvester Kirk) *chsd ldrs in 5th but nt on terms: pushed along 1/2-way: styd on to take 3rd over 1f out: clsd on ldng pair fnl f: nrst fin* **33/1**

05P3 **4** *7* **Invisible Eye**[8] 7336 2-9-5 0 .......... CharlesBishop 3 51
(Mick Channon) *led to 2f out: wknd qckly* **10/1**

0 **5** *1 ½* **Harley Rebel**[9] 7308 2-9-5 0 .......... LiamKeniry 7 47
(Neil Mulholland) *s.i.s: hld up in last trio: nvr a factor: tk modest 5th over 1f out: nt disgracd* **50/1**

00 **6** *11* **Catakanta**[15] 7155 2-9-5 0 .......... PatCosgrave 5 14
(Denis Coakley) *nvr on terms w ldrs: pushed along and no ch over 2f out: t.o* **100/1**

**7** *5* **Avail (IRE)** 2-9-0 0 .......... NedCurtis(5) 9
(Jonathan Portman) *s.i.s: rn green and a bhd: t.o* **33/1**

**8** *34* **Beauchamp Diamond** 2-9-0 0 .......... WilliamCarson 8
(Paul Fitzsimons) *s.s: rn green and a bhd: wl t.o* **66/1**

**P** **Harmony Bowl (IRE)** 2-9-0 0 .......... JimmyFortune 1
(Gary Moore) *spd over 2f: wknd qckly: wl bhd whn p.u ins fnl f* **7/1**[3]

1m 13.82s (0.82) **Going Correction** +0.05s/f (Good) **9** Ran SP% **124.1**
Speed ratings (Par 95): **96,94,93,83,81 67,60,15,**
CSF £2.47 TOTE £1.50: £1.10, £1.30, £7.30; EX 2.90 Trifecta £30.20.
**Owner** Richard Morecombe **Bred** Tom McDonald **Trained** Newmarket, Suffolk

**FOCUS**
Meeting transferred from Yarmouth. All rails had been moved. The inner of straight was dolled out 14yds at 6f and 2yds at the winning line. The top bend was dolled out 2yds from normal inner configuration, adding 14yds to race distances of 1m and over. As is often the case here on soft ground, the runners headed far side in this opening contest, which was an ordinary maiden. The winner has been rated to his latest York form.

## 7512 EBFSTALLIONS.COM MAIDEN STKS 1m 67y
**1:30** (1:33) (Class 5) 2-Y-O **£2,911** (£866; £432; £216) **Stalls** Low

Form RPR

2 **1** **Magic Dancer**[22] 6984 2-9-5 0 .......... PatDobbs 6 79+
(Ralph Beckett) *mde virtually all: sltly green bnd over 5f out: shkn up and drew clr over 1f out: comf* **10/11**[1]

0 **2** *2 ½* **Justice Belle (IRE)**[31] 6753 2-9-0 0 .......... AntonioFresu 11 66
(Ed Walker) *wl in tch in midfield: pushed along over 3f out: nt qckn over 2f out: hrd rdn and styd on fnl 2f to take 2nd nr fin* **12/1**

05 **3** *½* **St Georges Rock (IRE)**[22] 6985 2-9-5 0 .......... SteveDrowne 2 69
(Clive Cox) *trckd ldrs gng wl: shkn up to chse wnr over 2f out: hanging and nt qckn over 1f out: kpt on but lost 2nd nr fin* **14/1**

02 **4** *1* **Searching (IRE)**[14] 7170 2-9-5 0 .......... JackMitchell 12 67
(Roger Varian) *fractious bef ent stalls: wl plcd bhd ldrs: pushed along 3f out: disp 3rd over 1f out: one pce after* **7/2**[2]

4 **5** *½* **Scrutinise**[14] 7169 2-9-5 0 .......... JimmyFortune 14 68
(Ed Dunlop) *wl in rr early: prog on outer 1/2-way: pushed along to chse ldrs 3f out: disputing 3rd whn short of room briefly ins fnl f: one pce after* **10/1**[3]

5 **6** *½* **Duke Of Sonning**[14] 7170 2-9-5 0 .......... FergusSweeney 9 65
(Alan King) *trckd ldrs: pushed along 3f out: ev ch of a pl fr 2f out: pushed along and one pce after* **20/1**

4 **7** *1 ¼* **Miss Understood (IRE)**[13] 7209 2-9-0 0 .......... MartinLane 3 57
(David Simcock) *s.i.s: wl in rr: pushed along and kpt on steadily fr over 2f out: nrst fin* **16/1**

0 **8** *½* **Jakodima (IRE)**[40] 6497 2-9-2 0 .......... CamHardie(3) 8 61
(Richard Hannon) *pressed wnr: hung lft bnd over 5f out and urged along: lost 2nd over 2f out and then lost pl qckly: one pce over 1f out* **33/1**

6 **9** *8* **Littlemisspositive**[13] 7198 2-9-0 0 .......... RobertTart 5 39
(Martin Smith) *a in rr: wd bnd over 5f out: no ch w ldrs fnl 2f* **33/1**

**10** *6* **Beausant** 2-9-5 0 .......... PatCosgrave 7 30
(George Baker) *slowly away: wl in rr: sme prog on outer 1/2-way: wknd 3f out* **50/1**

50 **11** *3* **Willow Jubilee**[20] 7031 2-9-0 0 .......... JimmyQuinn 4 19
(John E Long) *wl in rr: pushed along and rn green 3f out: sn bhd* **100/1**

**12** *9* **Artistic Flight (IRE)** 2-9-5 0 .......... WilliamCarson 10 4
(Jim Boyle) *wl in rr: brief effrt on wd outside 1/2-way: sn wknd: t.o* **66/1**

00 **13** *15* **Basoco**[22] 6984 2-9-5 0 .......... DavidProbert 13
(Harry Dunlop) *prom: wd bnd over 5f out and sn lost pl: wknd 3f out: wl t.o* **66/1**

1m 46.26s (1.56) **Going Correction** +0.05s/f (Good) **13** Ran SP% **120.5**
Speed ratings (Par 95): **94,91,91,90,89 89,87,87,79,73 70,61,46**
CSF £13.33 TOTE £1.80: £1.10, £3.80, £3.60; EX 17.80 Trifecta £110.90.
**Owner** J C Smith **Bred** Littleton Stud **Trained** Kimpton, Hants

**FOCUS**
The favourite set a leisurely gallop and won well. The winner didn't need to improve and the form looks sensible.

## 7513 HAPPY 75TH BIRTHDAY DAVID NICHOLSON H'CAP (DIV I) 1m 67y
**2:00** (2:06) (Class 5) (0-75,75) 3-Y-0+ **£2,652** (£789; £394; £197) **Stalls** Low

Form RPR

021 **1** **Geordan Murphy**[15] 7158 3-9-4 75 .......... DavidProbert 5 82
(Andrew Balding) *hld up in midfield: prog to chse ldr 3f out and styd in centre: rdn to cl over 1f out: led ins fnl f: hld on wl* **10/3**[1]

0602 **2** *nk* **Chess Valley**[8] 7339 3-8-2 62 .......... CamHardie(3) 8 68
(Willie Musson) *hld up and sn in last: prog in centre 2f out: rdn to chal fnl f: nt qckn last 100yds* **7/2**[2]



The Form Book, Raceform Ltd, Newbury, RG14 5SJ

3016 **3** 1/2 **Byrd In Hand (IRE)**[12] 7219 7-8-8 62........................(v) WilliamCarson 2 68
(John Bridger) *led: clr over 3f out: styd against nr side rail in st: hdd ins fnl f: kpt on* **12/1**

4323 **4** 1 1/4 **Piccadilly Jim (IRE)**[71] 5497 3-8-11 68................................ PatDobbs 6 70+
(Richard Fahey) *hld up in last trio: taken to r alone on far side fr 3f out: nt far bhd ldrs fr 2f out but nvr quite on terms* **5/1**[3]

3466 **5** 3/4 **Great Expectations**[12] 7220 6-9-4 72........................(t) JimmyFortune 7 73
(J R Jenkins) *slowly away: t.k.h and hld up in last trio: rdn to chse ldrs in centre over 1f out: no imp fnl f* **10/1**

0622 **6** 3 3/4 **Solo Hunter**[42] 6423 3-9-2 73........................................ FergusSweeney 3 65
(Martyn Meade) *chsd ldrs: styd against nr side rail and rdn 3f out: fdd fnl 2f* **7/2**[2]

6216 **7** hd **Penny's Boy**[14] 7172 3-9-3 74........................................(t) HayleyTurner 4 65
(Simon Hodgson) *trckd ldng pair: rdn 3f out: lost pl and fdd fr 2f out* **8/1**

3200 **8** 3 1/2 **Notebook**[25] 6902 3-9-1 72................................................ SteveDrowne 9 55
(Martyn Smith) *chsd ldr: rdn 3f out and styd against nr side rail in st: wknd 2f out* **50/1**

1m 44.35s (-0.35) **Going Correction** +0.05s/f (Good)
**WFA** 3 from 5yo+ 3lb **8** Ran **SP% 114.0**
Speed ratings (Par 103): **103,102,102,100,100 96,96,92**
CSF £15.19 CT £121.84 TOTE £2.90: £1.60, £1.40, £3.10; EX 14.80 Trifecta £112.20.
**Owner** B P McGuire **Bred** M A L Evans **Trained** Kingsclere, Hants

**FOCUS**
In contrast to the first two races, the runners, with the exception of Picadilly Jim, headed centre-to-stands' side. They got racing a fair way out. The winner has been rated to his maiden win, and the runner-up to her C&D latest.

## 7514 HAPPY 75TH BIRTHDAY DAVID NICHOLSON H'CAP (DIV II) 1m 67y
**2:30** (2:34) (Class 5) (0-75,75) 3-Y-O+ **£2,652** (£789; £394; £197) **Stalls** Low

Form RPR

346 **1** **Craftsmanship (FR)**[22] 6990 3-9-4 75........................(p) JimmyQuinn 3 82
(Robert Eddery) *hld up in 5th: shkn up wl over 2f out: clsd on ldrs over 1f out: drvn to ld last 100yds: hld on* **5/1**[3]

0545 **2** 1/2 **Marengo**[9] 7309 3-8-8 68....................................(p) RyanTate(3) 6 74
(Ed de Giles) *hld up in 4th: shkn up 3f out: clsd on ldrs u.p jst over 1f out: kpt on to take 2nd nr fin: jst hld* **5/1**[3]

-301 **3** shd **Rolling Dice**[59] 5903 3-9-1 72........................................ LiamKeniry 7 78
(Dominic Ffrench Davis) *reluctant to enter stalls: led: rdn over 2f out: kpt on but hdd and one pce last 100yds* **12/1**

5141 **4** hd **Rangi Chase (IRE)**[22] 6980 3-9-3 74........................ JimmyFortune 2 79
(Richard Fahey) *trckd ldng pair: rdn to go 2nd over 1f out and sn chalng: upsides jst ins fnl f: nt qckn last 100yds* **3/1**[2]

411 **5** 2 **So Noble**[8] 7339 3-9-4 75 6ex........................................ SteveDrowne 8 76
(William Muir) *hld up in 6th: rdn and no prog 3f out: plugged on fr over 1f out: nvr rchd ldrs* **7/4**[1]

0005 **6** 3/4 **Multitask**[52] 6145 4-8-7 61 oh1.................................. WilliamCarson 1 61
(Michael Madgwick) *t.k.h: hld up in 7th: impeded after 100yds: shkn up 3f out: nvr on terms but plugged on fnl f* **25/1**

5626 **7** 1 3/4 **Pink Lips**[9] 7302 6-8-7 61 oh5........................................(v) DavidProbert 9 57
(J R Jenkins) *awkward s: mostly in last: rdn 1/2-way: detached over 2f out: hrd drvn and plugged on fnl f* **16/1**

-104 **8** 1 **Lady Marl**[15] 7160 3-8-13 70........................................ ShaneKelly 4 63
(Gary Moore) *trckd ldr to over 1f out: wknd qckly fnl f* **10/1**

1m 44.67s (-0.03) **Going Correction** +0.05s/f (Good)
**WFA** 3 from 4yo+ 3lb **8** Ran **SP% 121.2**
Speed ratings (Par 103): **102,101,101,101,99 98,96,95**
CSF £32.10 CT £292.30 TOTE £7.80: £2.00, £1.60, £3.80; EX 29.70 Trifecta £395.30.
**Owner** Trisha Keane & Julia Rayment **Bred** Haras Du Logis Saint Germain **Trained** Newmarket, Suffolk

**FOCUS**
They raced centre-field in a race run at a steady gallop. The first four have all been rated within a length of their pre-race ratings.

## 7515 188BET NURSERY H'CAP 6f
**3:00** (3:11) (Class 5) (0-75,73) 2-Y-O **£2,652** (£789; £394; £197) **Stalls** Low

Form RPR

2600 **1** **Muhaarib Al Emarat (IRE)**[27] 6867 2-8-12 64............. JimmyFortune 9 70
(Richard Fahey) *dwlt: racd wdst of all: prog fr rr 1/2-way: rdn to ld over 1f out: in command fnl f: styd on wl* **16/1**

5056 **2** 2 **Granola**[10] 7278 2-8-3 55............................................... DavidProbert 5 55
(David Brown) *chsd ldrs: shkn up over 2f out: tried to cl over 1f out: kpt on to take 2nd ins fnl f: no threat to wnr* **10/1**[3]

3553 **3** 1/2 **Emef Rock (IRE)**[7] 7363 2-8-9 68........................... DanielCremin(7) 2 67
(Mick Channon) *cl up: chsd ldr over 2f out and rdn to ld v briefly over 1f out: nt qckn after: lost 2nd ins fnl f* **8/1**[2]

5140 **4** hd **Sallabeh**[54] 6064 2-9-4 70............................................... MartinLane 6 68
(George Margarson) *dwlt: immediately rdn and struggling in rr: prog u.p on outer 1/2-way: chsd ldrs over 1f out: one pce after* **12/1**

40 **5** 2 **As A Dream (IRE)**[36] 6610 2-9-1 67........................... SilvestreDeSousa 10 59
(David Evans) *pressed ldrs on outer: rdn 1/2-way: lost pl over 2f out: no hdwy after* **20/1**

4331 **6** 3/4 **Little Palaver**[26] 6887 2-9-4 73........................................ RyanTate(3) 1 63
(Clive Cox) *led: styd against nr side rail 1/2-way: hung lft and hdd over 1f out: wknd* **5/2**[1]

6004 **7** 3 **Q Twenty Girl (IRE)**[55] 6040 2-8-0 55 ow2................... PhilipPrince(3) 3 38
(Mark Usher) *s.i.s: wl in rr: rdn over 2f out: hanging and no prog over 1f out* **20/1**

1040 **8** 10 **Jersey Bull (IRE)**[33] 6679 2-9-0 66................................ LiamKeniry 4 17
(Michael Madgwick) *chsd ldr to over 2f out: wknd qckly: t.o* **33/1**

1m 14.88s (1.88) **Going Correction** +0.05s/f (Good) **8** Ran **SP% 74.8**
Speed ratings (Par 95): **89,86,85,85,82 81,77,64**
CSF £68.42 CT £369.17 TOTE £11.50: £2.60, £1.90, £2.00; EX 64.10 Trifecta £751.00.
**Owner** Al Shira'aa Stable **Bred** Miss Annmarie Burke **Trained** Musley Bank, N Yorks
■ Winning Hunter (7-4f) and Crosse Fire (12-1) were withdrawn. Rule 4 applies to all bets. Deduction - 40p in the pound.

**FOCUS**
They headed stands' side in what was a competitive nursery. The winner has been rated back to form. The runner-up is limited and thie third consistent but exposed.

## 7516 188BET GREAT IN PLAY H'CAP 1m 2f 7y
**3:30** (3:34) (Class 4) (0-80,80) 3-Y-O+ **£4,690** (£1,395; £697; £348) **Stalls** Centre

Form RPR

1204 **1** **Gaelic Silver (FR)**[147] 2862 8-8-8 71........................ HectorCrouch(7) 12 80
(Gary Moore) *hld up in rr: stdy prog on wd outside over 3f out: clsd on ldrs 2f out: led jst ins fnl f: pushed along and hung rt 50yds out: hld on* **25/1**

4512 **2** nk **Yul Finegold (IRE)**[16] 7133 4-9-2 72................................ PatCosgrave 7 80
(George Baker) *towards rr: prog 3f out: rdn to go 3rd 1f out: sltly impeded 50yds out: sn chsd wnr and clsd last strides* **5/1**[3]

2164 **3** 1 **Bertie Moon**[75] 5345 4-9-7 77........................................ SteveDrowne 8 83
(Geoffrey Deacon) *fast away: led: shkn up and hdd over 2f out: led again over 1f out: hdd jst ins fnl f: hld whn impeded last 50yds and lost 2nd* **16/1**

0002 **4** 2 1/4 **Space Walker (IRE)**[8] 7341 3-8-13 74............................ JimmyFortune 6 76
(Harry Dunlop) *trckd ldr: led over 2f out: hdd and nt qckn over 1f out: fdd fnl f* **4/1**[2]

3044 **5** 2 1/4 **Art Scholar (IRE)**[13] 7211 7-9-10 80....................(p) SilvestreDeSousa 3 77
(Michael Appleby) *dwlt: wl in rr: shkn up and sme prog 3f out: rdn and no imp on ldrs over 1f out* **3/1**[1]

2361 **6** 3/4 **Dalgig**[22] 6986 4-9-1 78........................................[1] MikeyEnnis(7) 2 74
(David Pipe) *wl in tch: rdn to go 3rd 3f out: nt qckn over 2f out: hung lft and fdd jst over 1f out* **4/1**[2]

2511 **7** 2 1/2 **Urban Space**[9] 7309 8-8-12 68 6ex........................(t) LiamKeniry 10 59
(John Flint) *trckd ldrs: rdn 3f out: wknd fr 2f out* **8/1**

0326 **8** nk **Bikini Island (USA)**[9] 7305 3-9-0 75............................ DavidProbert 1 66
(Andrew Balding) *wl in tch: rdn 3f out: no prog over 2f out: wknd wl over 1f out* **6/1**

0-30 **9** 4 **Watts Up Son**[20] 7042 6-8-10 66................................(bt) JimmyQuinn 5 49
(Richard Price) *chsd ldng pair to 3f out: sn lost pl u.p: wknd* **50/1**

4005 **10** 1 3/4 **Choral Festival**[15] 7160 8-8-12 68........................ WilliamCarson 11 48
(John Bridger) *a towards rr: rdn on outer 3f out: no prog over 2f out: wknd* **25/1**

2-44 **11** 1/2 **Song And Dance Man**[239] 827 4-9-2 72........................ ShaneKelly 13 51
(Gary Moore) *slowly away: a in last: detached 3f out: no prog* **33/1**

2m 7.87s (-0.83) **Going Correction** +0.05s/f (Good)
**WFA** 3 from 4yo+ 5lb **11** Ran **SP% 125.5**
Speed ratings (Par 105): **105,104,103,102,100 99,97,97,94,92 92**
CSF £151.34 CT £2128.01 TOTE £30.10: £7.30, £1.10, £4.50; EX 187.40 Trifecta £3058.90.
**Owner** The Winning Hand **Bred** Earl Haras Du Camp Bernard Et Al **Trained** Lower Beeding, W Sussex

**FOCUS**
The pace soon steadied in this fair handicap, the runners heading centre-field in the straight. The winner has been rated as running his best race in Britain on his return from a break.

## 7517 188BET CASINO H'CAP 1m 2f 7y
**4:00** (4:01) (Class 6) (0-60,60) 3-Y-O **£2,005** (£596; £298; £149) **Stalls** Centre

Form RPR

-004 **1** **Vaguely Spanish**[12] 7218 3-8-10 49................................ WilliamCarson 4 57
(Tony Carroll) *hld up towards rr: prog 2f out: nt clr run briefly over 1f out: squeezed through sn after: drvn and r.o to ld last 75yds* **7/1**[3]

3062 **2** 3/4 **Turnbury**[12] 7218 3-9-7 60........................................(t) JackMitchell 12 66
(Robert Mills) *trckd ldrs: gd prog on outer to ld wl over 1f out: edgd rt after: hdd and nt qckn last 75yds* **9/2**[1]

0300 **3** 1/2 **Heartstrings**[13] 7197 3-8-10 49................................ CharlesBishop 14 54
(Mick Channon) *w.w in midfield: prog over 2f out: rdn to chal fnl f: upsides 100yds out: nt qckn* **10/1**

0310 **4** 1/2 **Benoordenhout (IRE)**[35] 6636 3-9-1 59....................(p) NedCurtis(5) 11 59
(Jonathan Portman) *led after 2f: racd awkwardly and hdd over 3f out: styd w ldrs tl fdd jst over 1f out: fin 5th: plcd 4th* **10/1**

5055 **5** shd **Softly She Treads (IRE)**[9] 4812 3-9-2 55.............(b[1]) FergusSweeney 3 55
(Pat Phelan) *led 2f: pressed ldr: led over 3f out to wl over 1f out: fdd fnl f: fin 6th: plcd 5th* **33/1**

0400 **6** 3/4 **Lingfield Lupus (IRE)**[45] 6339 3-8-7 46 oh1.............(v) JimmyQuinn 13 44
(John Best) *trckd ldng pair: pushed along and lost pl 2f out: bdly hmpd over 1f out: no ch after: kpt on: fin 7th: plcd 6th* **50/1**

0500 **7** nk **Danglydontask**[24] 6946 3-8-5 49.................................[1] JennyPowell(5) 9 47
(David Arbuthnot) *hld up in rr: pushed along over 2f out: last whn swtchd lft jst over 1f out: passed a few late on: nvr involved: fin 8th: plcd 7th* **16/1**

0300 **8** 1/2 **Heinrich (USA)**[11] 7259 3-8-13 55........................(t) CamHardie(3) 6 52
(Sylvester Kirk) *wl in tch in midfield: rdn over 2f out: edgd rt and fdd over 1f out: fin 9th: plcd 8th* **25/1**

0603 **9** nk **Triple Star**[17] 7115 3-9-1 56........................................ JimmyFortune 5 50
(Hughie Morrison) *stdd s: hld up in rr: pushed along over 2f out: no imp on ldrs over 1f out: nvr a threat: fin 10th: plcd 9th* **10/1**

1400 **10** 1 1/4 **Lucky Dottie**[161] 2416 3-8-7 46 oh1........................ FrankieMcDonald 1 40
(Pat Phelan) *a in rr: rdn and no prog over 3f out: one pce after: fin 11th: plcd 10th* **66/1**

2005 **11** nk **Essanar**[9] 7304 3-8-13 52........................................ RobertHavlin 10 45
(Andrew Hollinshead) *prom: rdn 3f out: sn lost pl and btn: fin 12th: plcd 11th* **5/1**[2]

0066 **12** 3/4 **Scariff Hornet (IRE)**[10] 7292 3-8-11 50........................ PatDobbs 2 42
(Sylvester Kirk) *chsd ldrs: rdn over 2f out: hmpd 1f out and no ch: fin 13th: plcd 12th* **33/1**

0041 **13** 3/4 **Rockie Road (IRE)**[12] 7218 3-9-1 54............................ PaoloSirigu 7 45
(Mick Quinn) *dwlt: hld up in last: pushed along over 2f out: reminder over 1f out and hmpd on inner sn after: allowed to come home in own time after: fin 14th: plcd 13th* **5/1**[2]

0002 **D** 2 **Southern Cross**[21] 7021 3-9-5 58................................ HayleyTurner 8 59
(Hughie Morrison) *hld up in last trio: shkn up 3f out: sme prog on outer over 2f out: styd on to take 4th nr fin: nvr really involved* **10/1**

2m 11.9s (3.20) **Going Correction** +0.05s/f (Good) **14** Ran **SP% 119.4**
Speed ratings (Par 99): **89,88,88,86,85 85,85,84,84,83 83,82,82,86**
CSF £36.64 CT £321.62 TOTE £9.30: £2.90, £1.90, £3.60; EX 49.30 Trifecta £485.60.
**Owner** D Boocock **Bred** D Boocock **Trained** Cropthorne, Worcs
■ Stewards' Enquiry : Hayley Turner three-day ban; jockey failed to weigh-in (12th-14th Nov)

**FOCUS**
Plenty had their chance in what was a moderate handicap. The winner is perhaps a bit better than the bare form after not getting a clear run through.

## 7518 188BET H'CAP 1m 3f 135y
**4:30** (4:30) (Class 6) (0-55,55) 3-Y-O+ **£1,940** (£577; £288; £144) **Stalls** Centre

Form RPR

3200 **1** **First Sargeant**[10] 7284 4-9-5 53........................(p) SilvestreDeSousa 2 62
(Michael Appleby) *s.v.s: sn in tch in last trio: rdn and prog fr 3f out: racd awkwardly but clsd on ldrs over 1f out: drvn ahd ins fnl f* **9/2**[2]

0012 **2** 1 **Salient**[12] 7219 10-9-7 55........................................ KierenFox 1 62
(Michael Attwater) *trckd ldng pair: led 3f out and sent for home: hdd and nt qckn ins fnl f* **10/1**

-503 **3** 1 1/4 **Haines**[7] 7360 3-8-5 46........................................ HayleyTurner 6 51
(Andrew Balding) *t.k.h: trckd ldr to 4f out: sn shkn up: outpcd fr 3f out: tried to rally u.p 2f out: one pce fnl f* **7/4**[1]

5234 **4** *nk* **Just Duchess**[19] 7065 4-8-12 45 DavidProbert 7 50
(Michael Blanshard) *chsd ldrs: rdn 3f out: outpcd 2f out: kpt on again fnl f: nrly snatched 3rd* **10/1**
162 **5** *3* **Crouching Harry (IRE)**[81] 5121 5-9-4 52 (p) JohnFahy 11 51
(Anabel K Murphy) *hld up wl in rr: rdn and outpcd over 3f out: kpt on fr over 1f out: n.d* **12/1**
6105 **6** *1/2* **Magicalmysterytour (IRE)**[25] 6900 11-9-5 53 ChrisCatlin 10 52
(Willie Musson) *hld up in rr: outpcd and pushed along 3f out: kpt on fr over 1f out: n.d* **8/1**[3]
60/6 **7** *3* **Epsom Flyer**[21] 7002 4-8-12 45 (v[1]) FergusSweeney 9 40
(Pat Phelan) *t.k.h in midfield: rdn 3f out: sn outpcd and btn* **33/1**
-300 **8** *nk* **Cherry Tiger**[17] 7115 4-9-5 53 CharlesBishop 13 46
(Graeme McPherson) *t.k.h: hld up and sn in last: urged along and no rspnse 4f out: no prog after tl consented to keep on fr over 1f out* **12/1**
-600 **9** *1/2* **Vera Lou (IRE)**[133] 3333 3-8-2 45 (b) CamHardie(3) 3 38
(Pat Eddery) *t.k.h: hld up in midfield: outpcd and rdn 3f out: no ch after* **33/1**
3440 **10** *nse* **Lady Percy (IRE)**[31] 6768 5-8-10 51 CharlotteJenner(7) 15 43
(Mark Usher) *towards rr: rdn 3f out: trying to make prog but no ch whn hmpd over 1f out* **10/1**
0060 **11** *3/4* **Movie Magic**[7] 7360 3-8-5 45 WilliamCarson 12 37
(John Bridger) *racd freely: led to 3f out: wknd qckly 2f out* **40/1**
-003 **12** *1 1/2* **King's Road**[21] 7002 9-8-13 47 (t) JimmyFortune 5 36
(Anabel K Murphy) *rrd s: sn in midfield: rdn 3f out: wknd 2f out* **25/1**
5000 **R** **In Seine**[33] 6682 3-8-9 50 ow1 SteveDrowne 4
(John Best) *c out of the stalls but ref to r* **66/1**

2m 33.26s (3.76) **Going Correction** +0.05s/f (Good)
**WFA** 3 from 4yo+ 7lb **13** Ran SP% **122.0**
Speed ratings (Par 101): **89,88,87,87,85 84,82,82,82,82 81,80,**
CSF £47.90 CT £109.88 TOTE £7.10: £2.10, £2.60, £2.80; EX 54.30 Trifecta £171.90.
**Owner** Rothmere Racing Limited **Bred** Rothmere Racing Ltd **Trained** Danethorpe, Notts

**FOCUS**
The front four pulled a little way clear in what was a low-grade handicap. The pace was a steady one. Muddling form.
T/Plt: £667.10 to a £1 stake. Pool: £67,478.06 - 73.83 winning tickets. T/Qpdt: £326.60 to a £1 stake. Pool: £5,429.59 - 12.30 winning tickets. JN

# 7453 WOLVERHAMPTON (A.W) (L-H)
## Tuesday, October 28

**OFFICIAL GOING: Tapeta: standard**
Wind: Fresh half-behind Weather: Overcast

## 7519 DOWNLOAD THE FREE APP @ BOOKIES.COM H'CAP (TAPETA) (DIV I) 5f 20y
**4:40** (4:41) (Class 6) (0-55,54) 3-Y-O+ **£2,264** (£673; £336; £168) **Stalls** Low

Form RPR
0032 **1** **Danzoe (IRE)**[13] 7191 7-9-0 52 (v) EoinWalsh(5) 5 62
(Christine Dunnett) *sn pushed along in rr: hdwy 1/2-way: rdn to ld 1f out: styd on* **7/2**[1]
0000 **2** *1 1/2* **Interchoice Star**[17] 7111 9-9-7 54 (v[1]) GeorgeBaker 2 59
(Ray Peacock) *prom: rdn over 1f out: styd on* **9/2**[2]
6354 **3** *1/2* **Your Gifted (IRE)**[38] 6561 7-9-0 52 (v) JackGarritty(5) 9 55
(Lisa Williamson) *hld up: r.o ins fnl f: wnt 3rd post: nt rch ldrs* **10/1**
5533 **4** *nk* **Lazy Sioux**[3] 7457 3-8-10 46 NeilFarley(3) 4 49
(Richard Guest) *chsd ldrs: rdn over 1f out: styd on* **6/1**
4540 **5** *1 1/2* **Play The Blues (IRE)**[57] 5972 7-8-9 45 (t) DannyBrock(3) 3 42
(Dominic Ffrench Davis) *sn prom: chsd ldr over 3f out: led wl over 1f out: sn rdn: hdd 1f out: no ex ins fnl f* **25/1**
3310 **6** *1 3/4* **Dream Sika (IRE)**[25] 6897 3-9-6 53 JamesSullivan 7 44
(Ruth Carr) *led: rdn and hdd wl over 1f out: wknd ins fnl f* **11/2**[3]
1030 **7** *1 1/2* **Ichimoku**[74] 5390 4-8-11 49 AdamCarter(5) 8 34
(Bryan Smart) *chsd ldr tl pushed along over 3f out: wknd over 1f out* **12/1**
000 **8** *1* **Lizzy's Dream**[37] 6580 6-9-3 50 (b[1]) AdamBeschizza 1 31
(Robin Bastiman) *s.i.s: sn pushed along in rr: nvr on terms* **6/1**
540 **9** *3/4* **Little Briar Rose**[38] 6561 3-8-13 46 LiamJones 6 26
(John Spearing) *hld up: rdn over 1f out: nvr on terms* **50/1**
0606 **10** *4 1/2* **On The High Tops (IRE)**[21] 7009 6-8-12 45 (p) FrederikTylicki 11 7
(Colin Teague) *prom: rdn 1/2-way: wknd over 1f out* **25/1**

1m 1.71s (-0.19) **Going Correction** -0.025s/f (Stan) **10** Ran SP% **110.8**
Speed ratings (Par 101): **100,97,96,96,93 91,88,87,85,78**
CSF £17.50 CT £133.81 TOTE £3.50: £3.30, £1.60, £2.60; EX 17.20 Trifecta £56.20.
**Owner** One For All **Bred** Miss Anne Ormsby **Trained** Hingham, Norfolk
■ Stewards' Enquiry : Eoin Walsh two-day ban; used whip above permitted level (12th-13th Nov)

**FOCUS**
They went a strong pace with Dream Sika and Play The Blues duelling for the lead but they only served to set it up for the closers. The winner has been rated as running his best race since his C&D Polytrack win last November, while the third helps set the level.

## 7520 DOWNLOAD THE FREE APP @ BOOKIES.COM H'CAP (TAPETA) (DIV II) 5f 20y
**5:10** (5:10) (Class 6) (0-55,54) 3-Y-O+ **£2,264** (£673; £336; £168) **Stalls** Low

Form RPR
500 **1** **Gypsy Rider**[34] 6666 5-8-8 46 EoinWalsh(5) 2 54
(Henry Tett) *a.p: rdn over 1f out: r.o to ld wl ins fnl f* **4/1**[1]
4250 **2** *3/4* **Captain Scooby**[12] 7222 8-9-2 49 (b) JasonHart 1 54
(Richard Guest) *prom: n.m.r and lost pl 3f out: nt clr run 2f out: hdwy over 1f out: r.o* **9/2**[2]
0005 **3** *1 1/4* **Quality Art (USA)**[22] 6983 6-9-7 54 LiamJones 5 55
(Simon Hodgson) *hld up: hdwy over 1f out: r.o* **8/1**
0600 **4** *hd* **Diamond Solitaire (IRE)**[82] 5080 3-8-12 52 GaryMahon(7) 4 53
(Timothy Jarvis) *led: rdn over 1f out: hdd wl ins fnl f: styd on same pce* **25/1**
0035 **5** *1 1/4* **Rat Catcher (IRE)**[21] 7010 4-8-7 47 (b) RobHornby(7) 3 42
(Lisa Williamson) *s.i.s: hld up: r.o ins fnl f: nt rch ldrs* **4/1**[1]
0300 **6** *3/4* **Hellolini**[78] 5237 4-8-12 45 (p) AdamBeschizza 6 38
(Robin Bastiman) *prom: rdn over 1f out: no ex ins fnl f* **66/1**
0000 **7** *1/2* **Under Review (IRE)**[21] 7009 8-9-1 53 (tp) JackGarritty(5) 7 44
(Bernard Llewellyn) *s.i.s: hld up: rdn over 1f out: nvr trbld ldrs* **15/2**[3]
0440 **8** *hd* **Here Now And Why (IRE)**[29] 6821 7-8-13 46 (p) DougieCostello 10 36
(Ian Semple) *hld up: rdn over 1f out: n.d* **8/1**
3004 **9** *2 3/4* **Imaginary Diva**[13] 7191 8-9-5 52 MartinHarley 9 32
(George Margarson) *prom: chsd ldr over 3f out tl rdn over 1f out: wknd ins fnl f* **9/2**[2]
/0-0 **10** *1* **Ladydolly**[27] 6851 6-8-13 49 (p) DeclanBates(3) 8 26
(Roy Brotherton) *chsd ldrs: rdn over 1f out: wknd ins fnl f* **66/1**

1m 2.55s (0.65) **Going Correction** -0.025s/f (Stan) **10** Ran SP% **117.2**
Speed ratings (Par 101): **93,91,89,89,87 86,85,85,80,79**
CSF £21.99 CT £137.09 TOTE £5.40: £1.40, £1.20, £2.80; EX 24.00 Trifecta £176.90.
**Owner** The Racing 4 Fun Partnership **Bred** Mr And Mrs L Baker **Trained** Lambourn, Berks
■ Henry Tett's first training success.

**FOCUS**
None of these had been showing much in recent starts and they didn't look to go as hard as in the first division (winning time was nearly a second slower than previous race), so this doesn't have the feel of form that will hold up. The runner-up helps set the standard.

## 7521 FREE BETS GALORE @ BOOKIES.COM H'CAP (TAPETA) 5f 216y
**5:40** (5:41) (Class 4) (0-78,81) 3-Y-O+ **£5,040** (£1,508; £754; £377; £188) **Stalls** Low

Form RPR
3433 **1** **Ambitious Boy**[14] 7183 5-9-1 77 JackDuern(5) 5 87
(Andrew Hollinshead) *s.i.s: hld up: hdwy on outer over 1f out: edgd lft and r.o to ld wl ins fnl f* **17/2**
0612 **2** *1 1/2* **Clearing**[18] 7073 4-9-7 78 DaneO'Neill 4 84
(Jim Boyle) *led: rdn over 1f out: hdd and unable qck ins fnl f* **18/1**
5601 **3** *1/2* **Thataboy (IRE)**[28] 6843 3-9-3 75 RichardKingscote 6 79
(Tom Dascombe) *chsd ldrs: rdn over 1f out: styd on* **5/1**[2]
0000 **4** *nk* **Stonefield Flyer**[38] 6535 5-9-6 77 PhillipMakin 10 80
(Keith Dalgleish) *a.p: rdn over 2f out: styd on* **8/1**[3]
2221 **5** *3/4* **Smokethatthunders (IRE)**[21] 7023 4-9-4 75 StevieDonohoe 13 76
(James Unett) *mid-div: hdwy over 2f out: rdn and nt mcuh room over 1f out: styd on towards fin* **11/1**
4032 **6** *1* **Hamoody (USA)**[7] 7357 10-9-3 74 MartinHarley 7 71
(Joseph Tuite) *prom: pushed along over 2f out: styd on same pce fnl f* **16/1**
640 **7** *nse* **Breccbennach**[66] 5677 4-9-6 77 (tp) GeorgeBaker 1 74
(Seamus Durack) *chsd ldr tl rdn over 1f out: no ex ins fnl f* **9/2**[1]
2212 **8** *nk* **Dominium (USA)**[18] 7071 7-8-12 76 (b) DavidParkes(7) 2 72
(Jeremy Gask) *mid-div: effrt over 1f out: styd on same pce fnl f* **12/1**
2506 **9** *nse* **Khajaaly (IRE)**[102] 4415 7-8-8 72 (tp) GaryMahon(7) 3 68
(Michael Appleby) *hld up: rdn over 1f out: nvr on terms* **33/1**
5223 **10** *nse* **Royal Brave (IRE)**[27] 6880 3-9-6 78 DougieCostello 9 74
(William Muir) *s.i.s: hld up: rdn over 2f out: n.d* **8/1**[3]
6001 **11** *1 3/4* **Head Space (IRE)**[7] 7352 6-9-10 81 6ex (v) FrederikTylicki 8 78
(Michael Attwater) *s.i.s: hld up: effrt over 1f out: no ch whn nt clr run ins fnl f* **9/2**[1]

1m 13.62s (-0.88) **Going Correction** -0.025s/f (Stan)
**WFA** 3 from 4yo+ 1lb **11** Ran SP% **115.9**
Speed ratings (Par 105): **104,102,101,100,99 98,98,98,98,98 95**
CSF £148.15 CT £847.47 TOTE £13.20: £3.30, £3.60, £2.50; EX 169.30 Trifecta £2066.50 Part won..
**Owner** C W Wardle & Mrs J E Wardle **Bred** Cecil W Wardle & Mrs Janet E Wardle **Trained** Upper Longdon, Staffs
■ Stewards' Enquiry : Phillip Makin one-day ban; careless riding (12th Nov)

**FOCUS**
A wide open handicap run at a strong pace thanks to Clearing, who went off fast and tried to kick again off the home turn. A pb from the winner.

## 7522 DOWNLOAD THE FREE APP @ BOOKMAKERS.CO.UK H'CAP (TAPETA) 1m 1f 103y
**6:10** (6:10) (Class 5) (0-70,70) 3-Y-O+ **£3,150** (£943; £471; £236; £117) **Stalls** Low

Form RPR
0553 **1** **Coillte Cailin (IRE)**[19] 7068 4-9-3 63 StevieDonohoe 5 72+
(Daniel Mark Loughnane) *a.p: shkn up to ld 1f out: sn rdn: all out* **9/2**[2]
0145 **2** *shd* **Pim Street (USA)**[10] 7288 4-8-9 62 JoshDoyle(7) 9 71
(David O'Meara) *hld up: hdwy over 1f out: edgd lft ins fnl f: r.o: jst failed* **8/1**
-303 **3** *1 1/4* **Hernando Torres**[120] 3785 6-9-0 60 (t) JamesSullivan 2 66
(Michael Easterby) *prom: lost pl 7f out: nt clr run 3f out: hdwy 2f out: sn rdn: r.o* **20/1**
4020 **4** *3/4* **St Paul De Vence (IRE)**[39] 6523 4-9-8 68 MartinLane 7 73
(Paul Cole) *prom: rdn over 2f out: styd on* **7/2**[1]
2363 **5** *3/4* **Outlaw Torn (IRE)**[10] 7288 5-9-3 63 (e) RussKennemore 4 66
(Richard Guest) *plld hrd and prom: led over 2f out: rdn and hdd 1f out: styd on same pce* **8/1**
0060 **6** *1* **Apache Glory (USA)**[45] 6341 6-9-1 66 (p) EoinWalsh(5) 8 67
(John Stimpson) *s.i.s: hld up: hdwy over 1f out: styd on same pce ins fnl f* **20/1**
0561 **7** *7* **Le Deluge (FR)**[33] 6696 4-9-0 67 (t) DavidParkes(7) 11 53
(Ann Stokell) *prom: jnd ldr over 6f out: led over 3f out: rdn and hdd over 2f out: wknd over 1f out* **11/1**
0036 **8** *2 1/4* **Idol Deputy (FR)**[129] 3472 8-9-3 68 (p) RachealKneller(5) 6 49
(James Bennett) *hld up: hdwy 2f out: rdn over 1f out: sn edgd lft and wknd* **25/1**
6223 **9** *7* **King Of Paradise (IRE)**[20] 7044 5-9-2 62 JasonHart 10 29
(Eric Alston) *led: hdd over 3f out: sn rdn: wknd over 1f out* **6/1**
5012 **10** *2 1/4* **Ana Shababiya (IRE)**[29] 6813 4-9-3 70 KieranShoemark(7) 3 32
(Ismail Mohammed) *awkward leaving stalls: sn chsng ldrs: rdn and wknd over 2f out* **11/2**[3]

1m 59.0s (-1.80) **Going Correction** -0.025s/f (Stan)
**WFA** 3 from 4yo+ 4lb **10** Ran SP% **114.0**
Speed ratings (Par 103): **107,106,105,105,104 103,97,95,89,87**
CSF £37.95 CT £647.53 TOTE £6.50: £2.00, £2.60, £6.50; EX 56.50 Trifecta £789.70.
**Owner** Peter J Moran **Bred** Whisperview Trading Ltd **Trained** Baldwin's Gate, Staffs

**FOCUS**
Another strongly run handicap and this looks reasonable form for the grade. The winner has been rated to form.

## 7523 ENJOY DAILY BETTING TIPS @ BOOKMAKERS.CO.UK MEDIAN AUCTION MAIDEN STKS (TAPETA) 1m 141y
**6:40** (6:42) (Class 5) 2-Y-O **£3,150** (£943; £471; £236; £117) **Stalls** Low

Form RPR
02 **1** **Royal Altitude**[40] 6497 2-9-5 0 TedDurcan 2 81+
(Chris Wall) *mde all: set stdy pce tl qcknd 2f out: clr fnl f: easily* **8/13**[1]
532 **2** *5* **Eatsleepracerepeat**[7] 7353 2-9-5 0 MartinHarley 4 70
(Lady Cecil) *plld hrd: w wnr tl over 6f out: lost 2nd over 5f out: chsd wnr again over 1f out: sn outpcd* **7/4**[2]
04 **3** *2 3/4* **Jo Bibidia**[13] 7198 2-8-11 0 DannyBrock(3) 5 59
(Jonathan Portman) *prom: chsd wnr over 5f out: rdn over 2f out: lost 2nd over 1f out: no ex* **16/1**[3]

55 **4** *10* **The Kurator (IRE)**[14] 7173 2-9-5 0 .......................... TomEaves 3 43
(Ann Duffield) *s.i.s: hld up: wknd over 2f out* **28/1**

00 **5** *2 1/4* **Mullion Cove**[42] 6434 2-9-0 0 .......................... FrederikTylicki 7 33
(John Best) *s.i.s: hld up: wknd over 2f out* **100/1**

000 **6** *1/2* **Illumination**[8] 7329 2-8-7 0 .......................... DanielleMooney(7) 6 32
(Michael Easterby) *prom tl wknd over 2f out* **100/1**

1m 50.29s (0.19) **Going Correction** -0.025s/f (Stan) **6** Ran SP% **109.6**
Speed ratings (Par 95): **98,93,91,82,80 79**
CSF £1.78 TOTE £1.60: £1.10, £1.10; EX 2.20 Trifecta £4.60.
**Owner** Follow The Flag Partnership **Bred** Miss J Chaplin **Trained** Newmarket, Suffolk

**FOCUS**
A modest maiden. The winner enjoyed the run of the race but suspect there's more to come from him. The runner-up and those in behind set the level.

## 7524 BETTING TIPS GALORE @ BOOKMAKERS.CO.UK H'CAP (TAPETA) 2m 119y
**7:10** (7:10) (Class 6) (0-60,60) 3-Y-0+ **£2,264** (£673; £336; £168) **Stalls** Low

Form RPR

2242 **1** **Rowlestone Lass**[10] 7290 4-9-11 57 .......................... MartinHarley 9 70
(Richard Price) *set stdy pce tl hdd 13f out: chsd ldr tl led again over 2f out: rdn clr over 1f out: eased towards fin* **4/1**[1]

0/03 **2** *6* **Delagoa Bay (IRE)**[25] 6900 6-9-0 46 .......................... DaneO'Neill 1 51
(Sylvester Kirk) *chsd ldrs: rdn over 2f out: styd on same pce: wnt 2nd wl ins fnl f* **28/1**

6035 **3** *1 1/4* **Impeccability**[21] 7006 4-8-11 46 oh1 .......................... (p) JoeyHaynes(3) 3 49
(John Mackie) *chsd wnr 3f: remained handy: rdn over 2f out: no ex fnl f* **18/1**

0525 **4** *3/4* **Honest Strike (USA)**[19] 7065 7-9-9 60 .......................... (t) EoinWalsh(5) 8 62
(Daniel Mark Loughnane) *hld up in tch: lost pl over 4f out: rdn and nt clr run over 2f out: styd on same pce fr over 1f out* **4/1**[1]

**5** *1 3/4* **Ring Of Fire (GER)**[135] 5-9-6 52 .......................... TomEaves 10 52
(Brian Ellison) *hld up: hdwy over 4f out: rdn over 1f out: wknd ins fnl f* **4/1**[1]

6362 **6** *hd* **Lacey**[10] 7287 5-9-5 56 .......................... (p) JackDuern(5) 7 56
(Andrew Hollinshead) *hld up: rdn over 2f out: nvr trbld ldrs* **6/1**[2]

6035 **7** *1 1/4* **Red Pilgrim (IRE)**[24] 6942 4-10-0 60 .......................... RobertTart 5 58
(James Toller) *s.i.s: hld up: rdn over 2f out: n.d* **4/1**[1]

0-00 **8** *2 1/4* **Star Of Mayfair (USA)**[7] 7360 4-9-0 53 .......................... GaryMahon(7) 6 49
(Timothy Jarvis) *hld up: rdn over 3f out: nvr on terms* **66/1**

64 **9** *19* **Lamubaaly (IRE)**[12] 7229 3-9-0 59 .......................... LouisSteward(3) 2 32
(Alexandra Dunn) *chsd ldrs: led 13f out: rdn and hdd over 2f out: wknd over 1f out* **7/1**[3]

3m 44.76s (1.06) **Going Correction** -0.025s/f (Stan)
**WFA** 3 from 4yo+ 10lb **9** Ran SP% **117.0**
Speed ratings (Par 101): **96,93,92,92,91 91,90,89,80**
CSF £121.91 CT £1811.63 TOTE £6.20: £1.90, £3.80, £4.60; EX 69.50 Trifecta £823.80.
**Owner** Ocean's Five **Bred** G E Amey **Trained** Ullingswick, H'fords

**FOCUS**
They didn't go that hard. A clear pb from the winner, the runner-up has been rated to her latest, and the third close to form.

## 7525 PRICE BOOSTS NOW AVAILABLE @ BOOKMAKERS.CO.UK NURSERY H'CAP (TAPETA) 7f 32y
**7:40** (7:41) (Class 5) (0-70,73) 2-Y-0 **£3,150** (£943; £471; £236; £117) **Stalls** High

Form RPR

5202 **1** **Romance Story (IRE)**[18] 7075 2-8-13 **69** .......... (p) KieranShoemark(7) 10 74
(Saeed bin Suroor) *s.i.s: hld up: hdwy over 1f out: rdn to ld 1f out: r.o* **11/2**[3]

420 **2** *1 3/4* **Marmalad (IRE)**[31] 6743 2-9-7 **70** .......................... RichardKingscote 1 71
(Tom Dascombe) *led 1f: chsd ldrs: rdn and ev ch 1f out: styd on same pce* **14/1**

534 **3** *1/2* **Manolito**[32] 6702 2-9-6 **69** .......................... (t) GeorgeBaker 7 68
(Hughie Morrison) *s.i.s: hld up: hmpd wl over 1f out: hdwy and nt clr run ins fnl f: r.o: nt rch ldrs* **15/8**[2]

604 **4** *nk* **Nota Cambiata (USA)**[13] 7200 2-9-4 **67** .......................... (b[1]) RobertHavlin 8 66
(John Gosden) *prom: lost pl over 2f out: rallied and edgd lft fnl f: r.o* **10/1**

046 **5** *nk* **Forza Blacky**[36] 6602 2-9-4 **70** .......................... DannyBrock(3) 5 68
(Philip McBride) *hld up: hdwy and forced to r wd 1/2-way: rdn over 1f out: styd on* **9/1**

5221 **6** *hd* **Lyfka**[7] 7362 2-9-10 **73** 7ex .......................... MartinLane 3 77
(Paul Cole) *hld up: nt clr run over 2f out: hdwy: hmpd and stmbld over 1f out: nt rcvr* **7/4**[1]

4403 **7** *4* **Battleranger (IRE)**[7] 7362 2-9-6 **69** .......................... (p) TomEaves 9 56+
(Keith Dalgleish) *led 6f out: rdn and hdd 1f out: edgd rt and no ex ins fnl f* **28/1**

665 **8** *4* **Zamperini (IRE)**[20] 7031 2-9-5 **68** .......................... ShaneKelly 6 45+
(Mike Murphy) *prom: chsd ldr 5f out: rdn over 2f out: looked btn whn hmpd and eased ins fnl f* **20/1**

0010 **9** *1 1/4* **Almoqatel (IRE)**[6] 7379 2-9-5 **68** .......................... FrederikTylicki 2 42
(James Fanshawe) *prom: rdn over 2f out: nt clr run over 1f out: wkng whn hmpd ins fnl f* **20/1**

1m 29.39s (0.59) **Going Correction** -0.025s/f (Stan) **9** Ran SP% **125.3**
Speed ratings (Par 95): **95,93,92,92,91 91,86,82,80**
CSF £81.27 CT £202.46 TOTE £6.20: £1.70, £3.30, £1.60; EX 66.00 Trifecta £326.50.
**Owner** Godolphin **Bred** Darley **Trained** Newmarket, Suffolk
■ Stewards' Enquiry : Martin Lane three-day ban; careless riding (12th-14th Nov)

**FOCUS**
A rough race with the favourite enjoying no luck at all. There was a strong pace and the winner and third came from the rear.
T/Plt: £117.50 to £1 stake. Pool: £92,252.63 - 572.89 winning tickets. T/Qpdt: £23.20 to £1 stake. Pool: £10,981.58 - 350.00 winning tickets. CR

# 7396 KEMPTON (A.W) (R-H)
Wednesday, October 29

**OFFICIAL GOING: Polytrack: standard**
Wind: Light, across Weather: rain/drizzle

## 7526 BOOK CHRISTMAS FESTIVAL TICKETS NOW H'CAP (DIV I) 1m 2f (P)
**4:55** (4:55) (Class 6) (0-65,69) 3-Y-0+ **£1,940** (£577; £288; £144) **Stalls** Low

Form RPR

0004 **1** **Gentlemax (FR)**[39] 6564 4-9-7 62 .......................... (b) PatCosgrave 10 69
(Jim Boyle) *trckd ldr: rdn over 2f out: led wl over 1f out: hrd pressed nr fin: jst hld on* **8/1**

-205 **2** *nse* **Brave Decision**[28] 6856 7-9-4 59 .......................... MartinHarley 1 66
(Suzy Smith) *trckd ldng pair: rdn over 2f out: wnt 2nd jst over 1f out: clsd on wnr fnl f: jst failed* **2/1**[1]

0004 **3** *1 1/4* **Sabre Rock**[5] 7426 4-8-9 53 .......................... (t) LouisSteward(3) 7 58
(John Best) *taken down early: trckd ldng pair: rdn over 2f out: tried to cl over 1f out: nt qckn* **8/1**

5140 **4** *1 1/2* **Snow Conditions**[22] 7001 3-9-1 61 .......................... TomEaves 2 63
(Philip Hide) *dwlt: chsd ldrs disputing 5th: rdn over 2f out: hung lft over 1f out: kpt on to take 4th ins fnl f* **16/1**

0510 **5** *1 1/4* **Always Resolute**[41] 6480 3-8-12 65 .......................... GaryMahon(7) 5 64
(Timothy Jarvis) *sn in 7th: rdn and outpcd 3f out: wd bnd 2f out: no ch but kpt on fnl f* **6/1**[3]

126- **6** *shd* **Mr Fickle (IRE)**[141] 7091 5-8-13 61 .......................... JasonNuttall(7) 9 60
(Gary Moore) *dwlt: rn in snatches in last: outpcd 3f out: prog on inner over 1f out but no ch: plugged on* **25/1**

43 **7** *3 1/4* **Assoluta (IRE)**[5] 7426 3-8-10 56 .......................... LiamKeniry 8 49
(Sylvester Kirk) *pushed up to ld: rdn and hdd wl over 1f out: wknd qckly fnl f* **11/2**[2]

004- **8** *1 1/4* **Warden Bond**[331] 8121 6-9-4 59 .......................... (p) FrederikTylicki 6 50
(William Stone) *chsd ldrs disputing 5th: rdn 3f out: wknd wl over 1f out* **14/1**

**9** *11* **Highsalvia Cosmos**[122] 3-9-3 63 .......................... FrannyNorton 4 33
(Mark Hoad) *a in last trio: wknd over 2f out: t.o* **9/1**

2m 6.62s (-1.38) **Going Correction** -0.05s/f (Stan)
**WFA** 3 from 4yo+ 5lb **9** Ran SP% **111.6**
Speed ratings (Par 101): **103,102,101,100,99 99,97,96,87**
CSF £23.22 CT £130.31 TOTE £10.40: £2.30, £1.60, £2.50; EX 31.90 Trifecta £218.20.
**Owner** Allen B Pope **Bred** Bernard Leclere & Mme Raymonde Leclere **Trained** Epsom, Surrey
■ Stewards' Enquiry : Pat Cosgrave two-day ban: used whip above permitted level (Nov 12-13)

**FOCUS**
An ordinary handicap. It was run at an uneven pace as it steadied on the far side and those racing handy were at an advantage.

## 7527 BOOK CHRISTMAS FESTIVAL TICKETS NOW H'CAP (DIV II) 1m 2f (P)
**5:25** (5:25) (Class 6) (0-65,65) 3-Y-0+ **£1,940** (£577; £288; £144) **Stalls** Low

Form RPR

0313 **1** **Archie's Advice**[78] 5269 3-9-3 63 .......................... FrederikTylicki 6 74
(Keith Dalgleish) *in tch: rdn and prog into 4th over 2f out: hanging and racd awkwardly over 1f out: drvn and clsd to ld last 150yds: sn clr* **3/1**[1]

4222 **2** *2 1/4* **Classic Mission**[20] 7068 3-8-13 64 .......................... (b) NedCurtis(5) 4 71
(Jonathan Portman) *trckd ldr: styd cl up whn pce lifted 3f out: rdn to ld over 1f out: idled bdly and hdd 150yds out: one pce* **7/2**[2]

0134 **3** *1 1/4* **Sexy Secret**[22] 7001 3-9-5 65 .......................... (v) MartinHarley 10 70
(Lydia Pearce) *hld up in last pair: gd prog fr 3f out but plenty to do: rdn to go 3rd jst ins fnl f: effrt flattened out after* **13/2**

1400 **4** *2 1/2* **Panettone (IRE)**[31] 6787 5-9-1 63 .......................... KieranShoemark(7) 2 63
(Roger Varian) *sn towards rr: rdn and prog fr 3f out: tried to cl on ldrs over 1f out: one pce after* **14/1**

-000 **5** *3* **Henry Grace (IRE)**[28] 6858 3-8-5 51 oh2 .......................... KieranO'Neill 9 45
(Jimmy Fox) *hld up in last pair: outpcd 3f out: tried to make prog 2f out: plugged on same pce* **50/1**

6504 **6** *1/2* **Understory (USA)**[36] 6635 7-9-3 58 .......................... LiamKeniry 3 51
(Tim McCarthy) *led: kicked on 3f out: hdd & wknd over 1f out* **8/1**

-500 **7** *5* **Bowsers Bold**[139] 3144 3-8-8 57 .......................... LouisSteward(3) 1 41
(Marcus Tregoning) *trckd ldrs: rdn whn pce lifted 3f out: wknd over 1f out* **20/1**

4001 **8** *8* **Mr Lando**[7] 7369 5-9-3 61 6ex .......................... RyanTate(3) 8 30
(Tony Carroll) *trckd ldrs but trapped out wd: rdn and wknd qckly wl over 2f out: eased* **4/1**[3]

0000 **9** *5* **Top Set (IRE)**[22] 7001 4-9-0 55 .......................... (b) TomEaves 7 14
(Simon Dow) *prom: rdn and wknd rapidly jst over 3f out* **33/1**

2m 6.13s (-1.87) **Going Correction** -0.05s/f (Stan)
**WFA** 3 from 4yo+ 5lb **9** Ran SP% **108.0**
Speed ratings (Par 101): **105,103,102,100,97 97,93,87,83**
CSF £11.83 CT £52.34 TOTE £4.20: £1.60, £2.00, £2.20; EX 12.70 Trifecta £55.10.
**Owner** G L S Partnership **Bred** G L S Partnership **Trained** Carluke, S Lanarks
■ Aldo was withdrawn. Price at time of withdrawal 50/1. Rule 4 does not apply.

**FOCUS**
The second division of the ordinary 1m2f handicap and it was run at a fairer pace. The runner-up sets the level

## 7528 BETBRIGHT MOBILE MAIDEN STKS 7f (P)
**5:55** (5:55) (Class 5) 3-Y-0+ **£2,587** (£770; £384; £192) **Stalls** Low

Form RPR

4-56 **1** **Nigel's Destiny (USA)**[16] 7157 3-9-5 0 .......................... MartinHarley 2 82+
(Jeremy Noseda) *mde all: rdn 2f out: jnd over 1f out: fnd enough and asserted ins fnl f* **2/1**[1]

5 **2** *1* **Tijan (IRE)**[12] 7250 3-9-5 0 .......................... [1] FrederikTylicki 1 79
(Saeed bin Suroor) *t.k.h: trckd wnr 2f and again over 2f out: rdn to chal and upsides over 1f out: nt qckn ins fnl f* **7/2**[2]

24 **3** *1 1/4* **Wu Zetian**[22] 7024 3-9-0 0 .......................... HayleyTurner 8 71
(Andrew Balding) *trckd ldrs: prog to go 3rd 2f out: rdn and nt qckn over 1f out: styd on but unable to chal* **7/1**[3]

6 **4** *2 1/4* **Elysian Fields (GR)**[145] 2967 3-8-7 0 .......................... KieranShoemark(7) 11 65
(Amanda Perrett) *mostly in 7th: shkn up over 2f out and no prog: styd on fnl f to take 4th last stride* **7/1**[3]

32 **5** *nse* **Mr Frankie**[33] 6717 3-9-2 0 .......................... DeclanBates(3) 7 70
(Ed de Giles) *t.k.h: trckd wnr after 2f to over 2f out: nt qckn after: one pce fr over 1f out* **7/1**[3]

25 **6** *shd* **Semblance**[22] 7024 3-9-0 0 .......................... SteveDrowne 4 65
(John Gosden) *trckd ldrs: shkn up over 2f out: sn outpcd: one pce fr over 1f out* **20/1**

3 **7** *nse* **Scarlet Sash**[114] 4029 3-8-11 0 .......................... AmyScott(3) 3 65+
(Henry Candy) *dwlt: settled in last quartet: pushed along over 2f out: styd on encouragingly after: nrst fin* **14/1**

05 **8** *1 1/2* **Franco's Secret**[16] 7158 3-9-5 0 .......................... CharlesBishop 10 66
(Peter Hedger) *awkward s: a in midfield: looking for room over 2f out: swtchd rt and urged along sn after: reminder over 1f out: kpt on: possible improver* **25/1**

0 **9** *1* **Divine Warrior (IRE)**[117] 3925 3-8-12 0 .......................... GaryMahon(7) 6 63
(Timothy Jarvis) *trckd ldrs: drvn over 2f out: wknd over 1f out* **66/1**

0 **10** *2* **Approaching (IRE)**[22] 7024 3-9-5 0 .......................... (t[1]) PatCosgrave 5 58
(Amanda Perrett) *dwlt: settled in 10th: pushed along on outer over 2f out: reminders and kpt on one pce over 1f out: rdr dropped whip ins fnl f* **25/1**

05 **11** *1* **Road Map (IRE)**[20] 7063 3-8-12 0 LouiseDay(7) 14 55
(Daniel Mark Loughnane) *a in last quartet: rdn over 2f out: one pce and no prog* **100/1**

0B **12** *4 ½* **Great Storm**[16] 7157 3-9-0 0 FergusSweeney 9 39
(Gary Moore) *nvr bttr than midfield: rdn and wknd over 1f out* **100/1**

00 **13** *5* **Macs Scwar**[8] 7349 7-9-4 0 RyanTate(3) 12 32
(Paul Morgan) *a in last quartet: wknd 2f out* **100/1**

**14** *17* **Irish Sweetheart (IRE)** 3-9-0 0 KierenFox 13
(Christine Dunnett) *slowly away: a in last: t.o* **100/1**

1m 26.96s (0.96) **Going Correction** -0.05s/f (Stan)
**WFA** 3 from 7yo 2lb **14** Ran SP% **117.6**
Speed ratings (Par 103): **92,90,89,86,86 86,86,84,83,81 80,75,69,50**
CSF £7.79 TOTE £3.20: £1.10, £3.80, £2.40; EX 10.70 Trifecta £74.60.
**Owner** Nigel O'Sullivan **Bred** DATTT Farm LLC **Trained** Newmarket, Suffolk

**FOCUS**
Not a bad maiden, rated around the third.

## 7529 BETBRIGHT - LIVE THE MOMENT NURSERY H'CAP 6f (P)
**6:25** (6:26) (Class 6) (0-60,60) 2-Y-O **£1,940** (£577; £288; £144) **Stalls** Low

Form RPR

0502 **1** **Chetan**[43] 6422 2-9-3 56 FrannyNorton 5 59
(Milton Bradley) *chsd ldng pair: shkn up to go 2nd over 2f out: led over 1f out: hrd pressed after: drvn and kpt on wl* **6/1**[3]

006 **2** *nk* **Reflation**[19] 7082 2-9-3 59 CamHardie(3) 3 61
(Richard Hannon) *chsd ldrs: rdn and prog 2f out: wnt 2nd ins fnl f and racd on inner: chal last 100yds: jst hld* **9/2**[1]

4505 **3** *¾* **River Spirit**[5] 7421 2-9-3 56 ChrisCatlin 7 56
(Mick Channon) *chsd ldrs: rdn over 2f out: cl enough over 1f out: one pce fnl f* **12/1**

3105 **4** *1* **Tinkers Kiss (IRE)**[21] 7029 2-9-4 60 DannyBrock(3) 6 57
(Philip McBride) *prog on outer fr midfield over 3f out: clsd to chal over 1f out: nt qckn and lost pl ins fnl f* **6/1**[3]

4040 **5** *nse* **Piccadillo**[12] 7257 2-9-5 58 (b) MartinHarley 10 55
(Daniel Kubler) *gd spd to ld fr wd draw: 2 l up and gng strly over 2f out: rdn and hdd over 1f out: steadily lost pl* **6/1**[3]

5042 **6** *nse* **Lady Atlas**[36] 6643 2-9-5 58 MichaelStainton 9 55+
(David Brown) *dwlt: mostly in last trio: rdn and no prog over 2f out: hanging bdly over 1f out: fnlly styd on ins fnl f* **5/1**[2]

0010 **7** *¾* **Essaka (IRE)**[7] 7378 2-9-7 60 CharlesBishop 4 54
(Mick Channon) *hld up towards rr: gng wl enough whn nt clr run over 2f out: shkn up and one pce over 1f out: nvr involved* **10/1**

0240 **8** *1 ¾* **Margot Rose**[48] 6248 2-8-13 59 Leah-AnneAvery(7) 1 48
(Harry Dunlop) *a abt same pl: nudged along on inner fnl 2f and no imp on ldrs* **25/1**

0055 **9** *1 ¾* **Recover (USA)**[89] 4857 2-9-4 57 HayleyTurner 2 41
(Brian Meehan) *chsd ldrs but pushed along after 2f: rdn and no prog over 2f out: wl btn over 1f out* **12/1**

0000 **10** *nse* **Heavenlyfriendship**[27] 6888 2-9-3 56 FergusSweeney 12 40
(Brendan Powell) *gd spd fr wdst draw to chse ldr: lost 2nd over 2f out: sn btn* **40/1**

5500 **11** *¾* **Shimmering Silver (IRE)**[29] 6838 2-9-4 57 SteveDrowne 8 39
(Daniel Mark Loughnane) *a in last trio: rdn and no prog over 2f out* **25/1**

600 **12** *nk* **Indian Joe**[64] 5799 2-8-13 55 (b[1]) LouisSteward(3) 11 36
(J S Moore) *a in last trio: struggling over 2f out* **33/1**

1m 13.24s (0.14) **Going Correction** -0.05s/f (Stan) **12** Ran SP% **115.3**
Speed ratings (Par 93): **97,96,95,94,94 94,93,90,88,88 87,87**
CSF £30.84 CT £314.57 TOTE £7.40: £2.80, £2.10, £3.70; EX 28.60 Trifecta £231.30.
**Owner** Roger & Val Miles,Colin Miles,Tony Stamp **Bred** Andrew W Robson **Trained** Sedbury, Gloucs

**FOCUS**
A weak nursery, run at a sound pace. Ordinary form, with the winner rated to his mark.

## 7530 BETBRIGHT.COM H'CAP 7f (P)
**6:55** (6:55) (Class 4) (0-80,80) 3-Y-O+ **£4,690** (£1,395; £697; £348) **Stalls** Low

Form RPR

6060 **1** **Cool Bahamian (IRE)**[26] 6895 3-9-2 77 (b) JohnFahy 1 85
(Eve Johnson Houghton) *trckd ldng pair: rdn to ld over 1f out and sn a l in front: drvn and hld on fnl f* **8/1**[3]

4445 **2** *¾* **Amood (IRE)**[15] 7185 3-9-4 79 LiamKeniry 7 85
(Simon West) *trckd ldr: rdn to chal 2f out: upsides as wnr wnt past over 1f out: chsd after: kpt on but a hld* **5/1**[2]

4420 **3** *nk* **Footstepsintherain (IRE)**[15] 7183 4-8-13 72 FergusSweeney 4 78+
(David Dennis) *in tch in mdfield: rdn 2f out: prog over 1f out: kpt on fnl f but nvr quite able to chal* **10/1**

2145 **4** *½* **Doctor Sardonicus**[46] 6345 3-9-5 80 FrederikTylicki 6 84
(David Simcock) *led: rdn 2f out: hdd and nt qckn over 1f out: one pce after* **10/1**

0532 **5** *hd* **Reposer (IRE)**[6] 7403 6-9-2 75 JoeFanning 5 79
(Keith Dalgleish) *trckd ldng trio: rdn and nt qckn 2f out: kpt on fnl f: nvr able to chal* **6/4**[1]

5003 **6** *shd* **Fantasy Gladiator**[27] 6890 8-9-0 73 (p) ChrisCatlin 3 77
(John Quinn) *settled in rr: urged along and nt clr run over 2f out: prog over 1f out: styd on but nvr quite able to chal* **12/1**

0050 **7** *2 ½* **Lord Ofthe Shadows (IRE)**[47] 6304 5-9-1 77 CamHardie(3) 8 75
(Richard Hannon) *towards rr: rdn and struggling 3f out: nvr on terms after: plugged on* **16/1**

4100 **8** *2* **Front Page News**[28] 6872 4-9-4 77 MartinHarley 10 69
(Robert Eddery) *hld up in last trio: stl there though gng wl enough 2f out: no ch whn rdn fnl f: nvr involved* **16/1**

0003 **9** *½* **Shaunas Spirit (IRE)**[13] 7222 6-8-6 72 PaulBooth(7) 11 63
(Dean Ivory) *in tch in midfield: rdn and no prog over 2f out: sn btn* **33/1**

3000 **10** *1 ¾* **Sheikh The Reins (IRE)**[49] 6240 5-8-8 70 (v) LouisSteward(3) 2 57
(John Best) *a in rr: rdn and no prog over 2f out* **50/1**

0000 **11** *1 ¼* **Birdman (IRE)**[17] 7136 4-9-2 75 (be) MartinLane 9 58
(David Simcock) *awkward s: a last: rdn and struggling 3f out* **14/1**

1m 24.59s (-1.41) **Going Correction** -0.05s/f (Stan)
**WFA** 3 from 4yo+ 2lb **11** Ran SP% **117.0**
Speed ratings (Par 105): **106,105,104,104,104 103,101,98,98,96 94**
CSF £47.50 CT £419.59 TOTE £12.50: £3.00, £1.70, £3.00; EX 69.60 Trifecta £569.70.
**Owner** L R Godfrey & R F Johnson Houghton **Bred** Kildaragh Stud **Trained** Blewbury, Oxon

**FOCUS**
A competitive handicap for the class and another race where it paid to be prominent.

## 7531 BETBRIGHT MONEYBACK OFFERS H'CAP (LONDON MIDDLE DISTANCE SERIES QUALIFIER) 1m 3f (P)
**7:25** (7:26) (Class 4) (0-85,84) 3-Y-O+ **£4,690** (£1,395; £697; £348) **Stalls** Low

Form RPR

440 **1** **Missed Call (IRE)**[14] 7211 4-9-7 81 FrederikTylicki 9 90
(James Fanshawe) *trckd ldng trio: rdn over 2f out: tk 2nd 1f out: styd on wl after to ld last strides* **8/1**[3]

2321 **2** *nk* **Tabjeel**[36] 6634 3-9-0 80 (p) PaulHanagan 1 88
(Saeed bin Suroor) *led at mod pce: wound it up fr 3f out: lugged lft fr 2f out: 2 l up and looked in command fnl f: collared last strides* **85/40**[1]

134 **3** *1* **Charlie Wells (IRE)**[47] 6303 3-8-6 72 (b) JohnFahy 6 79+
(Eve Johnson Houghton) *hld up in last trio: rdn over 2f out: prog over 1f out: styd on to take 3rd nr fin: did best of those to come fr off the pce* **11/1**

443 **4** *¾* **Opera Box**[28] 6855 6-9-7 84 LouisSteward(3) 4 89
(Marcus Tregoning) *chsd ldr: rdn over 2f out: no imp over 1f out: lost 2nd and one pce fnl f* **9/2**[2]

3464 **5** *½* **Tucson Arizona**[15] 7172 3-8-4 73 (tp) CamHardie(3) 3 77
(Anthony Carson) *a abt same pl: rdn over 2f out: styd on fnl f: nvr able to chal* **9/2**[2]

264 **6** *2 ¼* **Yojojo (IRE)**[39] 6559 5-9-6 80 MartinHarley 8 80
(Gay Kelleway) *hld up in 6th: shuffled along over 2f out: no imp on ldrs: nvr involved* **14/1**

5655 **7** *1 ½* **Lizzie Tudor**[32] 6746 4-9-7 81 JimCrowley 2 79
(Andrew Balding) *trckd ldng pair: rdn over 2f out: disp 2nd pl to 1f out: wknd* **8/1**[3]

6010 **8** *shd* **Chapter And Verse (IRE)**[52] 6166 8-9-9 83 ShaneKelly 5 80
(Mike Murphy) *stdd s: hld up in last trio: pushed along and sme prog on inner 2f out: shkn up over 1f out: wknd fnl f* **25/1**

2-13 **9** *1 ½* **Devon Drum**[27] 1219 6-9-2 76 WilliamTwiston-Davies 7 71
(Paul Webber) *dwlt: hld up and sn in last: rdn and no rspnse over 2f out: wl btn after* **20/1**

2m 21.08s (-0.82) **Going Correction** -0.05s/f (Stan)
**WFA** 3 from 4yo+ 6lb **9** Ran SP% **114.2**
Speed ratings (Par 105): **100,99,99,98,98 96,95,95,94**
CSF £25.07 CT £189.53 TOTE £8.80: £2.50, £1.30, £3.40; EX 30.90 Trifecta £416.60.
**Owner** Malcolm C Denmark **Bred** Francois Drion & Ptns **Trained** Newmarket, Suffolk

**FOCUS**
A fair handicap, rated around the fourth.

## 7532 BOOK THE RESTAURANT FOR BOXING DAY H'CAP 1m 4f (P)
**7:55** (7:57) (Class 6) (0-60,60) 3-Y-O+ **£1,940** (£577; £288; £144) **Stalls** Centre

Form RPR

0340 **1** **Shalambar (IRE)**[17] 7129 8-9-10 60 (v) JimCrowley 5 69
(Tony Carroll) *trckd ldr to over 5f out: wnt 2nd again over 4f out: rdn to ld wl over 2f out: drvn clr over 1f out: styd on wl* **13/8**[1]

0500 **2** *3 ½* **Uganda Glory (USA)**[13] 7219 4-9-6 56 PatCosgrave 7 60
(George Baker) *trckd ldrs: rdn to go 2nd jst over 2f out: no imp on wnr over 1f out: one pce* **14/1**

5324 **3** *½* **Hallouella**[30] 6818 3-9-3 60 (p) LiamKeniry 2 63
(David Elsworth) *hld up: t.k.h 1/2-way: rdn over 2f out: wnt 3rd wl over 1f out: kpt on same pce after* **7/2**[2]

1666 **4** *4* **Novel Dancer**[27] 5558 6-9-3 53 RobertHavlin 1 50
(Lydia Richards) *urged along early: in tch: rdn and outpcd over 2f out: tk modest 4th over 1f out: n.d* **10/1**

1220 **5** *¾* **Reach The Beach**[17] 7129 5-9-7 57 (t) AdamKirby 3 52
(Brendan Powell) *chsd ldng pair: lost pl 5f out and sn pushed along: detached in last over 2f out: plugged on* **6/1**

00-4 **6** *8* **Awesome Rock (IRE)**[62] 5864 5-8-7 46 CamHardie(3) 6 29
(Roger Ingram) *led: stdd pce 1/2-way: hdd over 5f out: wknd qckly over 2f out* **5/1**[3]

0045 **7** *¾* **Illegale (IRE)**[8] 7360 8-8-10 46 oh1 (bt) JohnFahy 4 27
(Nikki Evans) *stdd s: hld up in last: t.k.h after 5f and rushed up to ld over 5f out: hdd & wknd qckly wl over 2f out* **25/1**

2m 34.34s (-0.16) **Going Correction** -0.05s/f (Stan)
**WFA** 3 from 4yo+ 7lb **7** Ran SP% **110.9**
Speed ratings (Par 101): **98,95,95,92,92 86,86**
CSF £24.54 CT £67.27 TOTE £2.90: £3.50, £6.00; EX 29.90 Trifecta £78.80.
**Owner** B J Millen **Bred** His Highness The Aga Khan's Studs S C **Trained** Cropthorne, Worcs

**FOCUS**
There was an uneven gallop on in this moderate staying handicap.

## 7533 BETBRIGHT - LIVE THE MOMENT H'CAP 1m (P)
**8:25** (8:27) (Class 5) (0-70,76) 3-Y-O+ **£2,587** (£770; £384; £192) **Stalls** Low

Form RPR

2215 **1** **Celestial Knight**[28] 6857 3-8-13 65 (v) ShaneKelly 9 74
(James Fanshawe) *trckd ldrs: wnt 2nd over 2f out: drvn to ld jst over 1f out: jst hld on* **7/1**[3]

0001 **2** *shd* **Set The Trend**[7] 7373 8-9-13 76 6ex (p) FergusSweeney 7 85
(David Dennis) *hld up in midfield: prog fr 2f out: drvn on inner to take 2nd fnl f: clsd on wnr fin: jst failed* **3/1**[1]

0500 **3** *1 ¼* **Flamborough Breeze**[36] 6635 5-8-13 62 (bt) LiamKeniry 5 68
(Ed Vaughan) *hld up in tch: prog gng strly over 2f out: rdn and nt qckn over 1f out: styd on to take 3rd nr fin* **25/1**

3105 **4** *hd* **Hardy Black (IRE)**[36] 6633 3-9-1 67 AdamKirby 2 72
(Jamie Osborne) *led: edgd lft fr 2f out: hdd and nt qckn jst over 1f out: one pce* **5/1**[2]

6023 **5** *3* **Borough Boy (IRE)**[15] 7180 4-9-1 64 DaleSwift 13 63
(Derek Shaw) *stdd s: plld hrd in rr: rdn and prog fr 2f out: styd on to take 5th ins fnl f: nvr on terms* **16/1**

1323 **6** *½* **Tectonic (IRE)**[30] 6822 5-9-6 69 (p) PhillipMakin 6 67
(Keith Dalgleish) *t.k.h: hld up bhd ldrs: rdn 2f out: nt qckn over 1f out: no prog after* **8/1**

4402 **7** *1 ¼* **Foxford**[119] 3849 3-9-1 67 DavidProbert 4 61
(Patrick Chamings) *pressed ldrs: wnt 2nd 3f out to over 2f out: wknd over 1f out* **20/1**

0003 **8** *1 ¾* **Dana's Present**[22] 7000 5-8-13 62 PatCosgrave 11 53
(George Baker) *mounted on crse: stdd s: t.k.h and hld up in rr: prog out wd 4f out: hanging and no hdwy 2f out* **8/1**

4600 **9** *hd* **Club House (IRE)**[14] 7205 4-9-5 68 RobertTart 1 59
(Robert Mills) *s.v.s: wl off the pce in last trio: pushed along over 2f out: passed a few rivals after: nvr involved* **33/1**


The Form Book, Raceform Ltd, Newbury, RG14 5SJ

5454 **10** 1 1/4 **Fair Ranger**[14] 7202 3-8-11 66 CamHardie(3) 14 53
(Chris Gordon) *nvr beyond midfield: rdn over 3f out: no prog and btn 2f out* **50/1**

00 **11** 1/2 **Rakaan (IRE)**[21] 7042 7-9-2 70 JennyPowell(5) 10 57
(Brendan Powell) *s.v.s: wl off the pce in last: shkn up over 2f out: no great prog* **10/1**

0060 **12** 1 1/4 **Malicho**[23] 6990 5-9-4 67 (e) SebSanders 8 51
(Dean Ivory) *chsd ldr to 3f out: sn wknd u.p* **33/1**

4131 **13** 1 1/2 **Jumbo Prado (USA)**[46] 6342 5-8-9 63 (p) EoinWalsh(5) 3 43
(John Stimpson) *trckd ldrs to over 2f out: sn rdn and wknd* **20/1**

6454 **14** 1 1/2 **Kagami**[56] 6043 3-9-2 68 [1] JimCrowley 12 44
(Simon Dow) *stdd s: a in last trio: rdn and btn wl over 2f out* **16/1**

1m 39.33s (-0.47) **Going Correction** -0.05s/f (Stan)
**WFA** 3 from 4yo+ 3lb **14** Ran SP% **118.5**
Speed ratings (Par 103): **100,99,98,98,95 94,93,91,91,90 90,88,87,85**
CSF £25.24 CT £507.62 TOTE £7.20: £1.90, £3.70, £6.70; EX 24.00 Trifecta £201.70.
**Owner** Carivalis, Eady, Papworth & Swinburn **Bred** G B Balding & Whitsbury Manor Stud **Trained** Newmarket, Suffolk

**FOCUS**
The field were strung out early in this competitive handicap yet they didn't go tearing off by any means.
T/Plt: £53.00 to a £1 stake. Pool of £75960.57 - 1044.71 winning tickets. T/Qpdt: £26.70 to a £1 stake. Pool of £9109.41 - 251.70 winning tickets. JN

## 7206 NOTTINGHAM (L-H)
Wednesday, October 29

**OFFICIAL GOING: Good to soft (soft in places; 6.9)**

## 7534 32RED ON THE APP STORE H'CAP (DIV I) 5f 13y
1:30 (1:34) (Class 5) (0-75,75) 3-Y-O+ £2,587 (£770; £384; £192) **Stalls** Centre

Form RPR

1105 **1** **Dawn Catcher**[36] 6650 4-9-7 75 GeorgeBaker 6 84
(Geoffrey Deacon) *racd towards far side: trckd ldr: effrt to chal over 1f out: rdn to ld ent fnl f: kpt on wl towards fin* **8/1**[3]

3022 **2** 1/2 **Boxing Shadows**[34] 6695 4-9-2 70 DavidAllan 7 77
(Les Eyre) *racd towards far side: trckd ldng pair: swtchd rt and hdwy 2f out: rdn to chal over 1f out: sn ev ch: drvn ins fnl f: no ex last 50yds* **7/1**[2]

0410 **3** nk **Little Eli**[25] 6938 4-8-12 66 (v[1]) JasonHart 3 72
(Eric Alston) *sn led nr far rail: rdn along and jnd over 1f out: hdd ent fnl f: kpt on wl u.p towards fin* **20/1**

1006 **4** 1/2 **Sleeping Apache (IRE)**[15] 7178 4-9-2 70 PaulMulrennan 1 74
(Michael Dods) *racd towards far side: in tch: hdwy 2f out: rdn over 1f out: styd on wl fnl f: nrst fin* **10/1**

0003 **5** nk **Hazelrigg (IRE)**[14] 7213 9-8-11 65 GrahamGibbons 12 68
(Tim Easterby) *racd towards centre: chsd ldrs: rdn along wl over 1f out: kpt on same pce fnl f* **8/1**[3]

510 **6** 3/4 **Only Ten Per Cent (IRE)**[28] 6873 6-9-6 74 (v) AdamKirby 2 75
(J R Jenkins) *racd towards far side: chsd ldrs: rdn over 1f out: kpt on same pce fnl f* **20/1**

6043 **7** nk **Scoreline**[20] 7058 3-9-1 69 (p) DanielTudhope 17 69
(David O'Meara) *racd towards centre: towards rr: hdwy 2f out: sn rdn along: kpt on fnl f: nrst fin* **12/1**

6642 **8** nk **Ambitious Icarus**[1] 7505 5-9-2 73 (e) JacobButterfield(3) 9 71
(Richard Guest) *dwlt and towards rr centre: sn pushed along: hdwy 2f out: sn rdn: styd on fnl f: nrst fin* **11/2**[1]

4-10 **9** shd **Macdillon**[42] 6455 8-9-0 75 MikeyEnnis(7) 4 73
(Stuart Kittow) *racd towards far side chsd ldrs: rdn along 2f out: no imp fnl f* **14/1**

R660 **10** 1/2 **Steel Rain**[10] 7307 6-8-11 68 MatthewCosham(3) 11 64
(Nikki Evans) *racd centre: in midfield: pushed along 2f out: sn rdn and kpt on fnl f* **25/1**

002 **11** 3/4 **Cardinal**[9] 7342 9-8-8 62 (p) HayleyTurner 10 56
(Robert Cowell) *in tch towards centre: rdn along 2f out: sn no imp* **10/1**

5256 **12** 2 1/2 **College Doll**[26] 6897 5-8-7 61 oh9 (t) JimmyQuinn 13 46
(Christine Dunnett) *racd towards centre: in tch: rdn along 1/2-way: sn outpcd* **66/1**

2601 **13** 1 **Haajes**[25] 6938 10-9-4 72 (v) GrahamLee 8 53
(Paul Midgley) *racd towards far side: in tch: rdn along over 2f out: sn wknd* **10/1**

0-55 **14** 1/2 **Rock On Candy**[152] 2727 5-9-0 71 CamHardie(3) 14 50
(John Spearing) *racd towards centre: a towards rr* **8/1**[3]

3240 **15** 1 1/2 **Shawkantango**[216] 1127 7-9-0 68 (v) DaleSwift 15 42
(Derek Shaw) *racd towards centre: dwlt: a towards rr* **33/1**

040 **16** 3/4 **Bay Knight (IRE)**[243] 777 8-9-7 75 (p) TonyHamilton 16 46
(Ann Stokell) *a in rr: bhd fr 1/2-way* **40/1**

59.47s (-2.03) **Going Correction** -0.50s/f (Hard) **16** Ran SP% **123.1**
Speed ratings (Par 103): **96,95,94,93,93 92,91,91,91,90 89,85,83,82,80 79**
CSF £58.55 CT £749.11 TOTE £9.90: £2.20, £1.70, £5.60, £3.70; EX 66.70 Trifecta £1321.10.
**Owner** Mayden Stud & Associates **Bred** Mayden Stud, J A And D S Dewhurst **Trained** Compton, Berks

**FOCUS**
With no measurable rain overnight, the going remained good to soft, soft in places. The inner track was in use for the first time since April and race distances were as advertised. The field split into two early in the first division of this ordinary sprint handicap, but eventually those drawn high edged towards the far side to join the others. Few got into it and those that raced up the far rail dominated. The runner-up and third have been rated close to their marks.

## 7535 32RED ON THE APP STORE H'CAP (DIV II) 5f 13y
2:00 (2:01) (Class 5) (0-75,75) 3-Y-O+ £2,587 (£770; £384; £192) **Stalls** Centre

Form RPR

2216 **1** **It Must Be Faith**[34] 6695 4-9-2 70 HayleyTurner 15 88
(Michael Appleby) *racd cl to stands' rail: cl up: led 1/2-way: rdn and qcknd clr wl over 1f out: readily* **9/2**[1]

423 **2** 3 1/2 **Rylee Mooch**[1] 7510 6-8-10 64 (e) AndrewElliott 12 69
(Richard Guest) *racd towards stands' rail: led 2f: cl up: rdn along wl over 1f out: kpt on fnl f: no ch w wnr* **7/1**[2]

123 **3** 1 1/4 **Indian Tinker**[13] 7215 5-9-5 73 (v[1]) LiamJones 1 74
(Robert Cowell) *racd towards far side: a.p: rdn along wl over 1f out: kpt on* **7/1**[2]

-444 **4** 3/4 **Stellarta**[9] 7342 3-9-0 68 DavidProbert 7 67
(Michael Blanshard) *racd towards far side: chsd ldrs: hdwy 2f out: sn rdn and kpt on same pce fnl f* **11/1**

2600 **5** nk **Baby Strange**[19] 7071 10-9-0 75 AdamMcLean(7) 8 72
(Derek Shaw) *dwlt and rr towards far side: hdwy wl over 1f out: sn rdn and styd on fnl f: nrst fin* **14/1**

3064 **6** 1 **Monsieur Jamie**[10] 7307 6-9-4 72 (v) AdamKirby 14 65
(J R Jenkins) *dwlt: sn chsng ldng pair on stands' rail: rdn along 2f out: sn one pce* **7/1**[2]

1141 **7** 3/4 **Fredricka**[20] 7058 3-9-6 74 JasonHart 16 65
(Garry Moss) *towards rr stands' rail: rdn along 2f out: kpt on fnl f: n.d* **15/2**[3]

0060 **8** nse **Lupo D'Oro (IRE)**[28] 6872 5-8-12 66 (v) SteveDrowne 6 56
(John Best) *racd towards far side: in tch: rdn along 2f out: sn no imp* **20/1**

6000 **9** hd **Whitecrest**[13] 7215 6-8-12 69 CamHardie(3) 11 59
(John Spearing) *chsd ldng pair towards stands' rail: rdn along 1/2-way: sn wknd* **16/1**

0106 **10** 3/4 **Oldjoesaid**[28] 6873 10-9-7 75 GrahamLee 5 62
(Paul Midgley) *racd towards far rail: a towards rr* **12/1**

1000 **11** 1/2 **Go Go Green (IRE)**[18] 7103 8-8-13 70 GaryBartley(3) 4 55
(Jim Goldie) *racd towards far side: dwlt: a towards rr* **12/1**

6001 **12** shd **Dazza**[9] 7337 3-9-3 71 6ex FergusSweeney 10 57
(Gary Moore) *racd towards far side: prom: rdn along 2f out: sn wknd* **12/1**

1340 **13** nse **Rise To Glory (IRE)**[29] 6835 6-9-0 68 (tp) DuranFentiman 2 52
(Shaun Harris) *racd nr far rail: chsd ldrs: rdn along over 2f out: sn wknd* **25/1**

58.49s (-3.01) **Going Correction** -0.50s/f (Hard) course record **13** Ran SP% **118.2**
Speed ratings (Par 103): **104,98,96,95,94 93,91,91,91,90 89,89,89**
CSF £33.88 CT £227.01 TOTE £5.80: £2.90, £2.40, £2.30; EX 57.50 Trifecta £242.30.
**Owner** Michael Appleby **Bred** Matthew Sharkey & Newsells Park Stud Ltd **Trained** Danethorpe, Notts

**FOCUS**
The winning time was almost a second quicker than the first division. A complete turnaround in terms of which side was favoured from the first leg with the first two home sticking to the stands' rail from their high draws. Another clear pb from the winner, with the runner-up rated close to his penultimate C&D run.

## 7536 32REDSPORT.COM (S) STKS 1m 75y
2:30 (2:31) (Class 6) 2-Y-O £1,940 (£577; £288; £144) **Stalls** Centre

Form RPR

6006 **1** **Weardiditallgorong**[46] 6333 2-8-6 48 (b[1]) DavidProbert 8 50
(Des Donovan) *towards rr: hdwy on outer 4f out: effrt over 2f out: rdn to chse ldr over 1f out: styd on wl u.p ins fnl f to ld nr line* **16/1**

0514 **2** hd **Chilworth Bells**[15] 7165 2-9-2 58 GrahamGibbons 12 60
(David Barron) *trckd ldrs: hdwy over 3f out: led jst over 2f out: rdn clr over 1f out: drvn ins fnl f: edgd rt last 50yds: hdd and no ex nr line* **10/3**[2]

060 **3** 3/4 **First Summer**[19] 7076 2-8-11 55 PaulMulrennan 9 55
(Ed McMahon) *hld up in rr: hdwy over 2f out: rdn wl over 1f out: styd on wl fnl f: nrst fin* **8/1**

0000 **4** 6 **Soldier Sam (IRE)**[5] 7421 2-8-11 52 BenCurtis 6 40
(Brian Ellison) *trckd ldr: hdwy and cl up over 4f out: rdn along over 2f out: drvn wl over 1f out: sn one pce* **16/1**

05 **5** hd **Speedfit Rules (IRE)**[7] 7383 2-8-11 0 PaoloSirigu 10 39
(George Margarson) *in tch: hdwy on outer 4f out: rdn and cl up over 2f out: drvn wl over 1f out and sn one pce* **11/2**[3]

6300 **6** 8 **Arthur's Way (IRE)**[6] 7396 2-8-11 65 (p) MartinLane 1 22
(Paul Cole) *trckd ldrs on inner: pushed along over 3f out: rdn wl over 2f out: sn wknd* **3/1**[1]

2006 **7** 1/2 **Mister Arden (FR)**[9] 7336 2-8-11 62 TomQueally 5 21
(Harry Dunlop) *led: rdn along over 3f out: hdd jst over 2f out: sn drvn and wknd* **10/1**

045 **8** 1/2 **Alexi (IRE)**[13] 7217 2-8-6 46 (b[1]) JoeFanning 2 14
(Harry Dunlop) *dwlt: a in rr* **25/1**

05 **9** 1 3/4 **Kicking Leaves (IRE)**[34] 6676 2-8-11 0 (b) LiamJones 4 16
(J S Moore) *trckd ldrs: hdwy 4f out: cl up 3f out: sn rdn and wknd fnl 2f* **33/1**

1m 48.24s (-0.76) **Going Correction** -0.225s/f (Firm) **9** Ran SP% **102.2**
Speed ratings (Par 93): **94,93,93,87,86 78,78,77,76**
CSF £54.83 TOTE £19.10: £4.20, £1.10, £2.90; EX 96.50 Trifecta £505.70.There was no bid for winner. First Summer was claimed by S A Harris for £6500.
**Owner** The Wednesday Club **Bred** Mr & Mrs J Davis & P Mitchell B'Stock **Trained** Newmarket, Suffolk

■ Double K was withdrawn. Price at time of withdrawal 8/1. Rule 4 applies to all bets - deduct 10p in the pound. This Is Too was withdrawn. Price at time of withdrawal 33/1. Rule 4 does not apply.

**FOCUS**
A modest seller weakened further when Double K was withdrawn after getting upset in the stalls and This Is Too was also withdrawn after bursting out of her gate. The first three pulled well clear and the winning time suggested that the ground was riding much slower on the round course. A typical seller, with the penalised runner-up helping to set the level.

## 7537 32RED EBF STALLIONS OATH MAIDEN STKS (BOBIS RACE) (C&G) 1m 75y
3:00 (3:01) (Class 4) 2-Y-O £6,469 (£1,925; £962; £481) **Stalls** Centre

Form RPR

**1** **Golden Horn** 2-9-0 0 WilliamBuick 5 83+
(John Gosden) *s.i.s and bhd: tk clsr order 4f out: swtchd rt to wd outside 3f out: str run fr wl over 1f out: to ld ins fnl f: sn edgd lft and green: rdn last 50yds and kpt on* **15/8**[2]

2 **2** hd **Storm The Stars (USA)**[25] 6928 2-9-0 0 JoeFanning 4 83+
(William Haggas) *trckd ldng pair: hdwy over 3f out: sn cl up: led 2f out: rdn and hdd ins fnl f: rallied wl u.p and ev ch tl no ex nr fin* **1/1**[1]

2 **3** 7 **Champagne Bob**[33] 6718 2-9-0 0 RichardKingscote 7 67
(Tom Dascombe) *led: pushed along 4f out: jnd and rdn over 2f out: sn hdd: drvn appr fnl f: kpt on same pce* **8/1**

3 **4** 3 1/2 **Al**[54] 6103 2-9-0 0 AdamKirby 3 59
(Luca Cumani) *trckd ldrs: hdwy 4f out: rdn along over 2f out: sn one pce* **7/1**[3]

**5** 1 **Master Of Speed (IRE)** 2-9-0 0 JackMitchell 8 57
(Roger Varian) *trckd ldrs: pushed along over 4f out: hdwy to chse ldrs 3f out: rdn over 2f out: sn one pce* **25/1**

**6** shd **Leonardo (GER)** 2-9-0 0 TomQueally 2 57
(James Fanshawe) *in tch: hdwy on inner over 3f out: chsd ldrs over 2f out: sn rdn and one pce* **40/1**

**7** 1/2 **Countermand** 2-9-0 0 DavidProbert 6 56
(Andrew Balding) *in rr: hdwy on outer 3f out: rdn along over 2f out: sn wknd* **50/1**

6 **8** *12* **Spirit Rapping (IRE)**[15] 7170 2-9-0 0 GrahamLee 1 30
(Andrew Hollinshead) *chsd ldr: hdwy and cl up over 3f out: sn rdn along and wknd over 2f out* **66/1**

1m 46.69s (-2.31) **Going Correction** -0.225s/f (Firm) 2y crse rec 8 Ran SP% **118.1**
Speed ratings (Par 97): **102,101,94,91,90 90,89,77**
CSF £4.18 TOTE £2.70: £1.10, £1.10, £2.80; EX 4.50 Trifecta £14.70.
**Owner** A E Oppenheimer **Bred** Hascombe & Valiant Studs **Trained** Newmarket, Suffolk

**FOCUS**
An informative 2yo maiden run at a decent pace resulting in a 2yo course record. The first two, both of whom we will be hearing a lot more of, pulled clear. The runner-up helps set the level.

## 7538 32RED CASINO H'CAP — 1m 75y
**3:30** (3:33) (Class 4) (0-85,85) 3-Y-0+ **£5,433** (£1,617; £808; £404) **Stalls** Centre

Form RPR
1- **1** **Lightning Spear**[426] 5924 3-9-4 85 JimCrowley 11 94+
(Olly Stevens) *trckd ldrs: drvn over 2f out: led over 1f out: styd on wl* **5/1**[2]

6043 **2** *1 ¼* **Artful Prince**[21] 7042 4-8-9 73 (b) GrahamLee 2 80
(James Given) *led over 1f: chsd ldrs: led briefly on inner 2f out: styd on same pce last 100yds* **8/1**[3]

032 **3** *hd* **Woody Bay**[28] 6865 4-8-7 71 (t) JasonHart 8 78
(Mark Walford) *s.s: in rr: gd hdwy on outside wl over 1f out: fin wl* **10/1**

2443 **4** *¾* **Bahamian C**[29] 6836 3-8-11 78 (p) GeorgeChaloner 14 82
(Richard Fahey) *mid-div: hdwy on outer 3f out: sn chsng ldrs: kpt on same pce fnl f* **12/1**

3614 **5** *½* **First Post (IRE)**[17] 7136 7-8-11 75 DavidProbert 13 79
(Derek Haydn Jones) *in tch: chsng ldrs 2f out: kpt on one pce* **12/1**

4002 **6** *¾* **Extraterrestrial**[17] 7136 10-9-1 79 TonyHamilton 5 81
(Richard Fahey) *mid-div: hdwy 3f out: chsng ldrs over 1f out: one pce* **12/1**

054 **7** *hd* **Rocket Ronnie (IRE)**[25] 6937 4-8-7 71 PaulQuinn 9 72
(David Nicholls) *in rr: hdwy over 2f out: styd on ins fnl f* **25/1**

4000 **8** *½* **Norse Blues**[12] 7236 6-9-2 80 GrahamGibbons 16 80
(David Barron) *in rr: hdwy over 2f out: nt clr run over 1f out: styd on ins fnl f* **25/1**

1250 **9** *nk* **Off The Pulse**[12] 7236 4-9-2 80 BenCurtis 1 80
(John Mackie) *chsd ldrs: wknd over 1f out* **16/1**

0350 **10** *1 ¾* **Nurpur (IRE)**[33] 6704 4-9-4 82 (p) DanielTudhope 12 78
(David O'Meara) *mid-div: effrt on outer over 3f out: nvr a factor* **20/1**

6024 **11** *¾* **Oddysey (IRE)**[25] 6945 5-9-3 81 DavidNolan 6 75
(Michael Dods) *mid-div: effrt 3f out: fdd over 1f out* **20/1**

0626 **12** *¾* **Kimbali (IRE)**[4] 7456 5-8-10 74 DavidAllan 3 66
(Declan Carroll) *s.v.s: in rr: sme hdwy on inner over 2f out: wknd over 1f out* **25/1**

6000 **13** *hd* **Ted's Brother (IRE)**[11] 7282 6-8-5 72 (e) JacobButterfield(3) 15 64
(Richard Guest) *s.i.s: nvr on terms* **33/1**

6050 **14** *¾* **Falcon's Reign (FR)**[26] 6904 5-8-7 71 oh8 (p) AndrewElliott 4 61
(Michael Appleby) *in tch: effrt 3f out: wknd over 1f out* **25/1**

6-0 **15** *2 ¼* **Sublimation (IRE)**[14] 7211 4-9-1 79 RobertWinston 17 64
(Ian Williams) *chsd ldrs: wknd wl over 1f out* **33/1**

1 **16** *11* **Dubai Star (IRE)**[23] 6982 3-9-3 84 RobertHavlin 7 43
(John Gosden) *lost hind shoe on way to s: w ldr: led 7f out: hdd 2f out: sn wknd: bhd whn eased in clsng stages: b.b.v* **5/2**[1]

1m 45.84s (-3.16) **Going Correction** -0.225s/f (Firm)
**WFA** 3 from 4yo+ 3lb 16 Ran SP% **125.2**
Speed ratings (Par 105): **106,104,104,103,103 102,102,101,101,99 99,98,98,97,95 84**
CSF £40.21 CT £413.68 TOTE £5.30: £1.50, £2.80, £2.70, £2.00; EX 57.00 Trifecta £595.00.
**Owner** Qatar Racing Limited **Bred** Newsells Park Stud **Trained** Chiddingfold, Surrey

**FOCUS**
A decent handicap run at a good pace and the betting was dominated by two horses that had won their only previous starts. It's been rated around the placed horses.

## 7539 £10 FREE BET AT 32REDSPORT H'CAP — 1m 6f 15y
**4:00** (4:01) (Class 4) (0-85,85) 3-Y-0+ **£5,175** (£1,540; £769; £384) **Stalls** Low

Form RPR
155 **1** **Nabatean (IRE)**[18] 7106 3-9-5 85 DavidProbert 6 97+
(Andrew Balding) *hld up: stdy hdwy over 3f out: trckd ldrs 2f out: sn cl up: led appr fnl f: rdn towards fin: readily* **5/4**[1]

6215 **2** *1 ¼* **Moshe (IRE)**[33] 6714 3-8-13 79 WilliamBuick 11 85
(Hughie Morrison) *trckd ldrs: hdwy on outer over 3f out: led 2f out: jnd and rdn over 1f out: sn hdd: kpt on wl u.p fnl f* **7/1**[3]

0-02 **3** *½* **Hidden Justice (IRE)**[18] 7124 5-9-9 80 PhillipMakin 14 85
(John Quinn) *dwlt and reminders s: in rr: hdwy on outer 3f out: rdn along over 2f out: kpt on u.p fr over 1f out: nrst fin* **16/1**

2300 **4** *nse* **Ultimate Act**[18] 7125 3-8-3 72 [1] JoeyHaynes(3) 4 77
(Seamus Mullins) *trckd ldrs: hdwy over 3f out: cl up 2f out: sn rdn: kpt on same pce fnl f* **10/1**

2400 **5** *1 ¼* **Mister Fizz**[39] 6536 6-9-8 84 EoinWalsh(5) 7 87
(Miss Imogen Pickard) *in tch: hdwy over 3f out: pushed along 2f out: sn rdn: kpt on u.p fnl f* **16/1**

5340 **6** *½* **Bold Runner**[8] 7366 3-8-6 72 (p) IrineuGoncalves 3 75
(Jose Santos) *led: pushed along over 3f out: rdn and hdd 2f out: cl up tl drvn and grad wknd fnl f* **33/1**

4416 **7** *hd* **Deepsand (IRE)**[18] 7124 5-9-5 76 (p) DavidAllan 8 79
(Tim Easterby) *hld up: hdwy over 3f out: rdn to chse ldrs 2f out: drvn appr fnl and sn no imp* **8/1**

0120 **8** *12* **Hot Spice**[18] 7124 6-9-3 74 JamesSullivan 12 60
(Michael Easterby) *chsd ldr: effrt and cl up over 3f out: rdn along wl over 2f out: sn wknd* **50/1**

11 **9** *1 ¾* **Civil War (IRE)**[171] 1941 5-9-9 80 GeorgeBaker 13 63
(Gary Moore) *a in rr* **13/2**[2]

6301 **10** *¾* **My Lord**[17] 7133 6-8-13 70 TomQueally 10 52
(Luke Dace) *a in rr* **33/1**

1131 **11** *5* **Meetings Man (IRE)**[13] 6439 7-9-11 82 (p) AdamKirby 1 57
(Ali Stronge) *chsd ldng pair: rdn along over 3f out: sn wknd* **20/1**

1165 **12** *14* **Arashi**[112] 4076 8-8-5 69 (p) GeorginaBaxter(7) 2 25
(Derek Shaw) *t.k.h: trckd ldrs on inner: hdwy to chse ldng pair 1/2-way: rdn along wl over 3f out: sn wknd* **100/1**

3m 7.26s (0.26) **Going Correction** -0.225s/f (Firm)
**WFA** 3 from 5yo+ 9lb 12 Ran SP% **115.8**
Speed ratings (Par 105): **90,89,89,88,88 87,87,81,80,79 76,68**
CSF £9.14 CT £95.86 TOTE £2.30: £1.70, £1.70, £3.30; EX 11.10 Trifecta £91.80.
**Owner** Lord Blyth **Bred** Lord Blyth **Trained** Kingsclere, Hants

**FOCUS**
A fair staying handicap, run at a good pace, in which the 3yos came to to fore. The winner has been rated as running a pb.

## 7540 32RED.COM LONGINES WORLD FEGENTRI CHAMPIONSHIP GENTLEMEN AMATEUR RIDERS' H'CAP — 1m 2f 50y
**4:30** (4:30) (Class 6) (0-60,59) 3-Y-0+ **£1,871** (£580; £290; £145) **Stalls** Low

Form RPR
0501 **1** **Card High (IRE)**[30] 6823 4-11-2 54 (t) MrFTett 7 62
(Wilf Storey) *mid-div: effrt on outer over 3f out: sn drvn: styd on to ld appr fnl f: kpt on* **9/1**

6343 **2** *1* **Nellies Quest**[14] 7197 5-10-8 46 MrNicolasDeJulian 9 52
(Michael Appleby) *trckd ldrs: drvn 4f out: kpt on same pce fnl f* **4/1**[2]

5003 **3** *hd* **Monopoli**[13] 7219 5-11-5 57 (p) MrJindrichFabris 4 63
(Shaun Harris) *trckd ldrs: effrt on ins over 2f out: led briefly over 1f out: kpt on same pce* **10/3**[1]

1060 **4** *3* **Time Square (FR)**[161] 2464 7-11-7 59 MrSWalker 1 59
(Tony Carroll) *w ldrs: t.k.h: led after 2f: hdd over 1f out: sn wknd* **5/1**[3]

4006 **5** *3* **Cabal**[103] 4381 7-10-7 45 (b) MrVinzenzSchiergen 2 39
(Andrew Crook) *s.i.s: hld up in rr: drvn and sme hdwy 4f out: modest 5th over 2f out: one pce* **33/1**

-220 **6** *shd* **Ptolomeos**[36] 6644 11-10-7 45 MrAntonioFerramosca 5 39
(Sean Regan) *hld up in rr: effrt over 3f out: sn outpcd: kpt on fnl f* **6/1**

0000 **7** *8* **Valentine's Gift**[36] 6628 6-10-12 50 MrKevinTobin 6 29
(Neville Bycroft) *hld up in rr: effrt over 3f out: nvr on terms* **6/1**

6464 **8** *5* **Monzino (USA)**[85] 4996 6-10-9 47 MrMaxDenuault 3 16
(Michael Chapman) *mid-div: drvn 7f out: reminders and lost pl over 4f out: bhd whn eased ins fnl f* **16/1**

6645 **9** *28* **Kyllachykov (IRE)**[182] 1891 6-11-0 52 MrHAABannister 8
(Robin Bastiman) *led 2f: drvn over 5f out: lost pl 4f out: sn bhd: t.o whn virtually p.u over 1f out* **12/1**

2m 17.14s (2.84) **Going Correction** -0.225s/f (Firm) 9 Ran SP% **114.8**
Speed ratings (Par 101): **79,78,78,75,73 73,66,62,40**
CSF £44.66 CT £146.06 TOTE £7.70: £1.80, £2.10, £1.20; EX 45.30 Trifecta £160.50.
**Owner** Gremlin Racing **Bred** John Foley **Trained** Muggleswick, Co Durham
■ Stewards' Enquiry : Mr F Tett two-day ban: used whip above permitted level (Nov 19,25)
Mr Max Denuault two-day ban: used whip above shoulder height (Nov 19,25)

**FOCUS**
A moderate amateur riders' handicap in which the front four had it to themselves from some way out. The runner-up and third have been rated to form.
T/Jkpt: Not won. T/Plt: £58.00 to a £1 stake. Pool of £66687.93 - 839.21 winning tickets. T/Qpdt: £11.60 to a £1 stake. Pool of £5526.08 - 350.90 winning tickets. JR

# 7526 KEMPTON (A.W) (R-H)
Thursday, October 30

**OFFICIAL GOING: Polytrack: standard**
Wind: Light, across Weather: Fine, very mild

## 7541 COME JUMP RACING AT KEMPTON 03.11.14 (S) STKS — 1m 3f (P)
**4:30** (4:33) (Class 6) 3-Y-0 **£1,940** (£577; £288; £144) **Stalls** Low

Form RPR
4340 **1** **New Colours**[11] 7309 3-9-5 67 MartinDwyer 4 67
(Marcus Tregoning) *trckd ldr: led wl over 2f out and encouraged along: rdn and styd on fnl f* **4/5**[1]

3012 **2** *1 ¾* **Les Gar Gan (IRE)**[3] 7499 3-9-0 61 PhillipMakin 2 59
(Keith Dalgleish) *hld up in last: effrt over 2f out: rdn to chse wnr over 1f out: styd on but nvr able to chal* **6/4**[2]

00-4 **3** *5* **Emperor Ferdinand (IRE)**[16] 7167 3-9-0 55 HayleyTurner 1 50
(Marcus Tregoning) *hld up in 3rd: shkn up wl over 2f out: sn lft bhd: tk modest 3rd fnl f* **12/1**[3]

030- **4** *2 ¾* **Worcharlie'slass**[305] 8434 3-8-9 45 TonyHamilton 3 40
(Michael Herrington) *led at modest pce: rdn and hdd wl over 2f out: wknd over 1f out* **50/1**

2m 27.3s (5.40) **Going Correction** -0.10s/f (Stan) 4 Ran SP% **105.2**
Speed ratings (Par 99): **76,74,71,69**
CSF £2.10 TOTE £1.70; EX 2.30 Trifecta £2.50.New Colours was bought by Linda Perratt for £9,600
**Owner** J A Tabet **Bred** Mr & Mrs G Middlebrook **Trained** Whitsbury, Hants

**FOCUS**
Moderate stuff. It's been rated negatively.

## 7542 BETVICTOR.COM MAIDEN STKS — 6f (P)
**5:00** (5:01) (Class 5) 2-Y-0 **£2,587** (£770; £384; £192) **Stalls** Low

Form RPR
0 **1** **Upstaging**[22] 7031 2-9-5 0 JimCrowley 4 78
(Paul Cole) *chsd ldr: shkn up over 2f out: clsd and rdn to ld 1f out: styd on wl* **5/1**[2]

6 **2** *1 ½* **Absolute Champion (USA)**[36] 6660 2-9-5 0 GeorgeBaker 1 74
(Jamie Osborne) *led: hld together 2f out: hdd and shkn up 1f out: nt qckn* **5/1**[2]

022 **3** *1 ¼* **British Art**[7] 7400 2-9-5 0 LukeMorris 7 70
(Paul Cole) *chsd ldng trio: shkn up over 2f out: drvn to take 3rd over 1f out: styd on but unable to threaten* **4/6**[1]

03 **4** *5* **Hey You (IRE)**[9] 7345 2-9-0 0 KieranO'Neill 11 50
(Richard Hannon) *in tch: outpcd and shkn up over 2f out: kpt on fr over 1f out to take 4th last strides* **10/1**[3]

06 **5** *½* **Blackasyourhat (IRE)**[99] 4542 2-9-5 0 (t) KierenFox 3 53
(Roger Ingram) *wnt rt s: chsd ldng pair: drvn and cl up 2f out: lost 3rd over 1f out: wknd qckly* **50/1**

0 **6** *1 ¾* **Speculator**[115] 4025 2-9-5 0 GrahamLee 6 48
(David Menuisier) *nvr bttr than midfield: outpcd and shkn up over 2f out: nvr on terms after* **66/1**

0 **7** *½* **Captain Felix**[8] 7380 2-9-5 0 FrederikTylicki 9 47
(Jane Chapple-Hyam) *mostly in last pair: shkn up and struggling over 2f out: kpt on fnl f* **20/1**

**8** *2* **Ripinto (IRE)** 2-9-5 0 PatCosgrave 2 41
(Jim Boyle) *s.s: mostly wl in rr: brief effrt on inner 2f out: sn no prog* **12/1**

50 **9** *1* **Major Attitude**[22] 7037 2-9-5 0 AdamKirby 10 38
(Clive Cox) *a towards rr and racd wd: hanging whn rdn over 2f out: no prog* **25/1**

3 **10** *1 ¼* **Monsieur Valentine**[14] 7216 2-9-2 0 JoeyHaynes(3) 5 34
(Tony Carroll) *chsd ldrs in 5th: shkn up 3f out: wknd wl over 1f out* **33/1**


The Form Book, Raceform Ltd, Newbury, RG14 5SJ

00 **11** 2 1/2 **Ocean Bentley (IRE)**[14] 7217 2-9-5 0 ........ LiamKeniry 8 26
(Tony Carroll) *tk fierce hold: hld up in rr: wknd 2f out* **100/1**

1m 12.51s (-0.59) **Going Correction** -0.10s/f (Stan) **11 Ran SP% 126.1**
Speed ratings (Par 95): **99,97,95,88,88 85,85,82,81,79 76**
CSF £30.78 TOTE £6.00: £1.80, £2.00, £1.10; EX 29.60 Trifecta £58.80.
**Owner** H R H Sultan Ahmad Shah **Bred** Glebe Stud **Trained** Whatcombe, Oxon
**FOCUS**
The main players were to the fore throughout. The level is fluid, but the first two are improvers.

## 7543 £25 FREE BET AT BETVICTOR.COM H'CAP 6f (P)
**5:30** (5:32) (Class 3) (0-95,94) 3-Y-O+
**£7,158** (£2,143; £1,071; £535; £267; £134) **Stalls** Low

Form RPR
0321 **1** **Steelriver (IRE)**[16] 7183 4-9-0 87 ........ ShaneKelly 6 100+
(Michael Herrington) *stdd s: hld up in last trio: smooth prog fr 2f out: nudged along and clsd to ld 120yds out: comf* **7/1[3]**
5150 **2** 3/4 **Pipers Note**[6] 7408 4-9-7 94 ........ GeorgeChaloner 1 103
(Richard Whitaker) *trckd ldrs: pushed along and prog to ld jst over 2f out: drvn and hdd last 120yds: styd on but readily hld* **14/1**
0003 **3** 2 1/4 **Secondo (FR)**[69] 5623 4-9-2 89 ........ (v[1]) PaulHanagan 9 91
(Robert Stephens) *hld up in last pair: rdn and no reponse over 2f out: prog over 1f out: styd on fnl f to take 3rd last stride* **12/1**
02 **4** shd **Counter Ridge (SAF)**[49] 6260 5-9-2 89 ........ MartinHarley 8 90
(Marco Botti) *chsd ldng trio: rdn over 2f out: cl enough after: disp 2nd briefly 1f out: one pce* **10/1**
2563 **5** 1 1/2 **Mission Approved**[26] 6923 4-9-3 90 ........ AdamKirby 3 87
(Luca Cumani) *in tch in midfield shkn up jst over 2f out: nt qckn over 1f out: one pce and no imp after* **7/4[1]**
321 **6** nk **Marmalady (IRE)**[47] 6313 4-9-3 90 ........ GeorgeBaker 12 86
(Gary Moore) *gd spd to ld fr wdst draw: hdd jst over 2f out: chsd ldr to 1f out: wl hld whn squeezed for room sn after* **10/1**
2454 **7** 1 1/2 **Links Drive Lady**[13] 7233 6-9-0 87 ........ GrahamLee 7 78
(Dean Ivory) *patiently rdn on outer: shkn up over 2f out: sme prog over 1f out: one pce fnl f* **25/1**
1043 **8** 1 **Money Team (IRE)**[53] 6170 3-9-0 88 ........ GrahamGibbons 2 76
(David Barron) *stmbld s: nvr bttr than midfield: struggling u.p over 2f out* **11/2[2]**
100 **9** nk **Fairway To Heaven (IRE)**[19] 7122 5-9-6 93 ........ JimCrowley 4 80
(Michael Wigham) *hld up in last pair: shkn up over 2f out: modest prog on inner over 1f out: sn btn* **12/1**
006 **10** 2 3/4 **Zero Money (IRE)**[54] 6130 8-9-2 89 ........ (b) MartinDwyer 5 67
(Hugo Palmer) *chsd ldng pair: u.p over 2f out: wknd qckly over 1f out* **16/1**
121- **11** nk **Zhiggy's Stardust**[407] 6526 5-8-11 87 ........ AmyScott(3) 11 64
(Henry Candy) *chsd ldr to over 2f out: sn wknd* **20/1**
0000 **12** 7 **Steventon Star**[14] 7227 3-9-4 92 ........ (b) LukeMorris 10 47
(Alan Bailey) *a towards rr on outer: struggling over 2f out: wknd qckly over 1f out* **66/1**

1m 10.94s (-2.16) **Going Correction** -0.10s/f (Stan)
**WFA** 3 from 4yo+ 1lb **12 Ran SP% 120.5**
Speed ratings (Par 107): **110,109,106,105,103 103,101,100,99,96 95,86**
CSF £100.29 CT £1183.15 TOTE £9.90: £2.60, £5.80, £4.10; EX 121.10 Trifecta £1853.80.
**Owner** Darren & Annaley Yates **Bred** Kildaragh Stud **Trained** Cold Kirby, N Yorks
■ Stewards' Enquiry : Shane Kelly caution: careless riding
**FOCUS**
This was more open than the betting suggested. The runner-up has been rated as running a pb and the third as close to this year's form.

## 7544 DOWNLOAD THE BETVICTOR INSTABET APP NURSERY H'CAP (BOBIS RACE) 1m (P)
**6:00** (6:03) (Class 4) (0-85,79) 2-Y-O **£4,528** (£1,347; £673; £336) **Stalls** Low

Form RPR
315 **1** **Khusoosy (USA)**[22] 7041 2-9-7 79 ........ (v[1]) PaulHanagan 5 85
(Saeed bin Suroor) *trckd ldr: led 2f out and veered sharply rt: drvn and styd on stoutly fr over 1f out* **7/2[2]**
4623 **2** 1 1/2 **Landwade Lad**[35] 6684 2-9-3 75 ........ ShaneKelly 2 78
(James Fanshawe) *hld up in 6th: prog on outer 2f out: drvn and styd on to take 2nd ins fnl f: no real imp on wnr* **9/4[1]**
010 **3** 1 **Todegica**[19] 7116 2-8-13 71 ........ SilvestreDeSousa 3 71
(Ralph Beckett) *chsd ldrs in 4th: pushed along wl over 2f out and sn struggling: rallied u.p over 1f out w tail swishing: kpt on same pce fnl f* **8/1**
4123 **4** 2 1/4 **Muradif (IRE)**[14] 7226 2-9-7 79 ........ JoeFanning 1 74
(William Haggas) *hld up in 5th: prog 2f out: pressed wnr over 1f out: sn nt qckn and hld: wknd ins fnl f* **7/2[2]**
5042 **5** 1 1/4 **Little Riggs**[17] 7156 2-8-11 69 ........ GrahamLee 4 63
(Ed Walker) *chsd ldng pair: cl up whn impeded on inner 2f out: outpcd over 1f out* **4/1[3]**
0223 **6** 2 3/4 **Simone On Time (IRE)**[15] 7207 2-8-7 65 ........ LukeMorris 7 51
(Sylvester Kirk) *mostly in last and nvr gng that wl: drvn and no prog over 2f out* **33/1**
3324 **7** 2 **Spring Dixie (IRE)**[35] 6691 2-8-4 67 ........ JackGarritty(5) 6 48+
(Rae Guest) *led: hdd and bmpd 2f out: wknd over 1f out* **20/1**

1m 38.57s (-1.23) **Going Correction** -0.10s/f (Stan) **7 Ran SP% 114.0**
Speed ratings (Par 97): **102,100,99,97,96 93,91**
CSF £11.76 TOTE £4.20: £2.20, £1.20; EX 12.50 Trifecta £62.80.
**Owner** Godolphin **Bred** Shadwell Farm LLC **Trained** Newmarket, Suffolk
**FOCUS**
The top-weight came in 6lb below the ceiling for the race. A messy race, with the winner rated back to his debut level in the first-time visor.

## 7545 DOWNLOAD THE BETVICTOR APP NOW H'CAP 1m (P)
**6:30** (6:33) (Class 3) (0-95,95) 3-Y-O+
**£7,158** (£2,143; £1,071; £535; £201; £201) **Stalls** Low

Form RPR
1625 **1** **Billingsgate (IRE)**[35] 6688 3-9-4 95 ........ AdamKirby 11 104
(Charlie Appleby) *trckd ldng trio: rdn 2f out: chal 1f out: drvn ahd on outer ins fnl f: styd on* **11/2[3]**
4160 **2** 3/4 **Tigers Tale (IRE)**[12] 7276 5-9-3 94 ........ (v) DannyBrock(3) 7 102
(Roger Teal) *t.k.h: trckd ldrs in 5th: clsd on inner 2f out: drvn and styd alone against far rail and chal jst over 1f out: styd on but a jst hld* **13/2**
21 **3** hd **Heisman (IRE)**[185] 1795 3-8-7 84 ........ (t) LiamJones 2 91
(Olly Stevens) *led after 1f: drvn 2f out: kpt on but hdd and no ex ins fnl f* **5/1[2]**
0510 **4** 3/4 **Knight Owl**[26] 6936 4-8-12 86 ........ ShaneKelly 6 92+
(James Fanshawe) *hld up in rr: pushed along over 2f out: stl wl in rr over 1f out: rdn and styd on wl fnl f: tk 4th nr fin and clsd on ldrs: too much to do* **14/1**
3230 **5** 1/2 **Jodies Jem**[34] 6713 4-8-11 85 ........ GrahamLee 14 90
(William Jarvis) *trckd ldrs: rdn over 2f out: kpt on fr over 1f out: nvr quite pce to chal* **16/1**
1514 **5** dht **Momayyaz (IRE)**[24] 6978 3-8-10 92 ........ KevinStott(5) 10 96+
(Saeed bin Suroor) *racd wd in midfield: wdst of all bnd 3f out: lost pl and in rr 2f out: styd on again fnl f* **3/1[1]**
5021 **7** 1 1/4 **Silverheels (IRE)**[24] 6992 5-8-11 85 ........ LukeMorris 3 87
(Paul Cole) *chsd ldng pair: drvn 2f out: upsides u.p over 1f out: nt qckn and fdd ins fnl f* **12/1**
0130 **8** nk **Spiritual Star (IRE)**[26] 6943 5-8-13 87 ........ PatCosgrave 5 88
(Anthony Carson) *t.k.h: hld up in tch in midfield: shkn up 2f out: nt pce to cl on ldrs after but kpt on* **33/1**
4-00 **9** shd **Frog Hollow**[40] 6535 5-8-13 87 ........ DanielTudhope 13 88
(David O'Meara) *t.k.h: hld up in last trio: prog on inner fr 2f out: one pce fnl f: n.d* **33/1**
0510 **10** 1/2 **Ogbourne Downs**[18] 7136 4-8-11 88 ........ CamHardie(3) 8 88
(Charles Hills) *s.i.s: hld up in last pair: pushed along and prog into midfield over 1f out: rdn and no hdwy fnl f* **25/1**
0405 **11** 1/2 **Santefisio**[14] 7227 8-9-6 94 ........ (p) PhillipMakin 1 93
(Keith Dalgleish) *t.k.h: hld up bhd ldrs: drvn 2f out: no imp 1f out: wknd* **10/1**
4223 **12** 1 **Masterpaver**[22] 7033 3-8-11 88 ........ MartinHarley 4 83
(Alan Bailey) *a towards rr: rdn and no prog over 2f out* **20/1**
5003 **13** 4 **Sound Advice**[26] 6936 5-9-3 91 ........ JoeFanning 9 78
(Keith Dalgleish) *led 1f: chsd ldr to over 2f out: nt qckn but stl cl up over 1f out: wknd rapidly fnl f* **16/1**
1115 **14** 1 1/2 **Top Diktat**[152] 2783 6-9-1 89 ........ FergusSweeney 12 73
(Gary Moore) *a in last pair: shkn up and no prog over 2f out* **33/1**

1m 37.38s (-2.42) **Going Correction** -0.10s/f (Stan)
**WFA** 3 from 4yo+ 3lb **14 Ran SP% 123.0**
Speed ratings (Par 107): **108,107,107,106,105 105,104,104,104,103 103,102,98,96**
CSF £39.48 CT £196.22 TOTE £6.30: £2.10, £2.50, £5.50; EX 46.60 Trifecta £292.60.
**Owner** Godolphin **Bred** Darley **Trained** Newmarket, Suffolk
**FOCUS**
A good, competitive handicap. A small pb from the winner, with the runner-up running better than ever and the third also improving on his maiden form.

## 7546 FOLLOW @BETVICTORRACING ON TWITTER H'CAP 1m (P)
**7:00** (7:02) (Class 6) (0-55,57) 3-Y-O+ **£1,940** (£577; £288; £144) **Stalls** Low

Form RPR
2621 **1** **Cadmium**[8] 7376 3-8-13 57 6ex ........ Leah-AnneAvery(7) 1 64+
(Harry Dunlop) *prog into midfield after 3f: stdy hdwy on inner over 2f out: led wl over 1f out: pushed along and styd on wl* **4/1[3]**
0400 **2** 1 3/4 **Silvee**[10] 7339 7-8-12 46 oh1 ........ (b[1]) LukeMorris 10 50
(John Bridger) *prom thrght: rdn over 2f out: kpt on fr over 1f out to take 2nd ins fnl f: no real threat to wnr* **20/1**
3-60 **3** 1 1/4 **Flumps**[16] 7188 5-8-7 46 oh1 ........ (b) EoinWalsh(5) 2 47
(John Stimpson) *dwlt: wl in rr: rdn wl over 2f out: prog u.p over 1f out: styd on to take 3rd nr fin* **20/1**
2355 **4** 3/4 **Brown Pete (IRE)**[149] 2874 6-8-12 46 ........ (p) TonyHamilton 5 45
(Ann Stokell) *urged along early: wl in rr: drvn 3f out: styd on u.p fr 2f out: nrst fin* **8/1**
0000 **5** 1 1/4 **It's Taboo**[16] 7188 4-9-2 50 ........ LiamKeniry 3 47
(Mark Usher) *led 1f: styd prom: drvn to chal wl over 1f out: chsd wnr after tl wknd ins fnl f* **8/1**
6034 **6** 2 1/2 **Divine Rule (IRE)**[22] 7036 6-8-13 52 ........ (b) JennyPowell(5) 9 43
(Laura Mongan) *s.s: t.k.h and hld up in last pair: shkn up and kpt on fnl 2f: nvr involved* **3/1[2]**
3005 **7** 1 3/4 **Scommettitrice (IRE)**[14] 7221 6-8-12 46 oh1(t) WilliamTwiston-Davies 4 33
(Nigel Twiston-Davies) *chsd ldrs: drvn over 2f out: nt qckn over 1f out: fdd* **20/1**
0003 **8** 3 **Tsarglas**[26] 6939 3-8-9 46 oh1 ........ SteveDrowne 7 25
(Stuart Williams) *nvr beyond midfield: rdn and no prog over 2f out: wl btn after* **2/1[1]**
0000 **9** 4 **Cuthbert (IRE)**[83] 5138 7-8-12 46 oh1 ........ (b) KierenFox 6 17
(Michael Attwater) *reluctant to enter stalls: prog to ld after 1f and sn 3 l clr: hdd & wknd wl over 1f out* **50/1**
0340 **10** 1 1/4 **Jenny Sparks**[78] 5321 3-8-9 46 oh1 ........ JoeFanning 8 13
(Mick Channon) *hld up in rr: nt clr run over 2f out: no ch after* **20/1**
000U **11** 4 **Water For Life**[52] 6194 3-8-4 46 oh1 ........ JackGarritty(5) 13 4
(Dave Morris) *chsd ldr over 6f out to 2f out: wknd rapidly* **33/1**
/00- **12** 5 **Superior Duchess**[360] 7728 9-8-5 46 oh1 ........ KieranShoemark(7) 12
(Michael Blanshard) *a in rr on outer: struggling fr 3f out* **100/1**

1m 39.63s (-0.17) **Going Correction** -0.10s/f (Stan)
**WFA** 3 from 4yo+ 3lb **12 Ran SP% 125.5**
Speed ratings (Par 101): **96,94,93,92,91 88,86,83,79,78 74,69**
CSF £87.01 CT £1498.55 TOTE £5.50: £3.40, £4.60, £5.10; EX 56.00 Trifecta £711.90.
**Owner** Susan Abbott Racing **Bred** Bearstone Stud **Trained** Lambourn, Berks
**FOCUS**
An ordinary race in which eight of the 12 runners were out of the handicap. They went a good pace. The winner is in career-best form but the race has been rated cautiously.

## 7547 BOOK CHRISTMAS FESTIVAL TICKETS NOW H'CAP (DIV I) 7f (P)
**7:30** (7:30) (Class 6) (0-55,61) 3-Y-O+ **£1,940** (£577; £288; £144) **Stalls** Low

Form RPR
6600 **1** **Spinning Cobblers**[26] 6946 3-9-0 50 ........ (v) GrahamGibbons 4 67
(Stuart Williams) *mde all shifted lft fr 2f out but sn clr: styd on wl: unchal* **12/1**
0145 **2** 6 **Rocky's Pride (IRE)**[6] 7423 8-9-7 55 ........ GeorgeChaloner 10 57
(Richard Whitaker) *chsd wnr: rdn over 2f out: sn lft bhd: kpt on* **11/4[2]**
0300 **3** 1 1/4 **Genax (IRE)**[55] 6121 3-8-13 49 ........ StevieDonohoe 11 47
(Ian Williams) *trckd ldng trio: rdn over 2f out and racd awkwardly: no imp tl styd on u.p to take 3rd ins fnl f* **2/1[1]**
-004 **4** 3/4 **Myjestic Melody (IRE)**[32] 6796 6-8-12 46 oh1 ........ BenCurtis 5 43
(Shaun Harris) *settled in midfield: rdn over 2f out: hanging rt and no prog over 1f out: styd on ins fnl f* **25/1**
0100 **5** nse **Wimboldsley**[48] 6297 3-9-2 52 ........ AdamKirby 7 48
(Scott Dixon) *slowly away: wl in rr: prog 2f out: kpt on same pce fnl f* **8/1**
0040 **6** 1/2 **Queen Hermione (IRE)**[13] 7253 6-9-0 48 ........ (vt) DaleSwift 6 43
(Derek Shaw) *towards rr: rdn over 2f out: sn struggling: plugged on fr over 1f out* **14/1**

0221 **7** *1¼* **Wedgewood Estates**[6] 7420 3-9-11 61 6ex...................... LiamKeniry 3 52
(Tony Carroll) *trckd ldrs: shkn up to chse ldng pair 2f out: no imp after: wknd fnl f* **3/1**[3]

350 **8** *hd* **Compton Silver**[225] 1015 4-9-0 48..............................(b) PaddyAspell 2 40
(Miss Joey Ellis) *chsd ldng pair to 2f out: wknd* **16/1**

0060 **9** *11* **Bajan Story**[34] 6715 5-8-7 48................................. KieranShoemark(7) 1 11
(Michael Blanshard) *sn urged along and dropped to last: wknd 2f out: t.o* **20/1**

-050 **10** *13* **Sakuramachi**[55] 6087 3-8-10 46 oh1.................................. LukeMorris 8
(Nikki Evans) *in tch 5f: wknd rapidly and eased: wl t.o* **66/1**

1m 25.16s (-0.84) **Going Correction** -0.10s/f (Stan)
**WFA** 3 from 4yo+ 2lb **10** Ran SP% **126.5**
Speed ratings (Par 101): **100,93,91,90,90 90,88,88,76,61**
CSF £48.34 CT £101.63 TOTE £14.00: £3.40, £1.20, £1.70; EX 64.50 Trifecta £331.30.
**Owner** Brian Piper & David Cobill **Bred** L Ellinas & Old Mill Stud **Trained** Newmarket, Suffolk

**FOCUS**

The early pace wasn't strong and the winner made every yard. The form is all about the winner and whether he can repeat this.

## 7548 BOOK CHRISTMAS FESTIVAL TICKETS NOW H'CAP (DIV II) 7f (P)

**8:00** (8:00) (Class 6) (0-55,55) 3-Y-O+ **£1,940** (£577; £288; £144) **Stalls** Low

Form RPR

0545 **1** **Dream And Hope**[13] 7256 3-8-11 50............................ DannyBrock(3) 9 60
(Philip McBride) *patiently rdn off the pce in 7th: rdn and prog 2f out: led jst ins fnl f: styd on wl* **2/1**[1]

414 **2** *1* **Copper Cavalier**[8] 7376 3-8-13 49..........................(v) AdamBeschizza 6 56
(Robert Cowell) *t.k.h early: led 1f: settled bhd rivals: rdn and renewed effrt 2f out: led briefly 1f out: kpt on but nt pce of wnr last 100yds* **5/1**

400 **3** *2* **Clary (IRE)**[111] 4156 4-9-0 48........................................(t) PatCosgrave 10 51
(James Unett) *prom: trckd ldr over 4f out: led over 2f out: drvn and hdd 1f out: no ex* **8/1**

0402 **4** *2½* **Satchville Flyer**[8] 7376 3-8-11 50.............................. CamHardie(3) 4 45
(Brett Johnson) *trckd ldrs: wnt 2nd jst over 2f out and looked a threat: rdn and nt qckn wl over 1f out: fdd fnl f* **3/1**[2]

2500 **5** *6* **True Spirit**[22] 7036 4-9-5 53..........................................(p) LukeMorris 11 34
(Paul D'Arcy) *chsd ldrs in 5th: rdn 1/2-way: wknd 2f out* **9/2**[3]

3005 **6** *1* **Black Truffle (FR)**[13] 7259 4-9-0 55....................(v) CharlotteJenner(7) 8 33
(Mark Usher) *racd freely: led after 1f to over 2f out: wknd over 1f out* **10/1**

0050 **7** *6* **Picnic In The Glen**[22] 7036 3-8-13 49.......................... RenatoSouza 2 11
(Sylvester Kirk) *in tch tl wknd over 2f out* **50/1**

5030 **8** *6* **Bold Max**[14] 7222 3-8-10 46 oh1..................................(b) LiamJones 5
(Zoe Davison) *plld hrd: hld up: n.m.r after 1f: n.m.r again after 2f and stmbld: bhd fnl 3f: t.o* **33/1**

506- **9** *2¼* **Kaahen (USA)**[348] 7929 4-8-9 46 oh1............................(v) JoeyHaynes(3) 1
(Pat Eddery) *dwlt: a in last trio: bhd fr over 2f out: t.o* **33/1**

0-30 **10** *1½* **Kingsway Lad (IRE)**[6] 7420 3-9-1 51.............................(t) DaleSwift 7
(Derek Shaw) *a in last trio: wknd u.p wl over 2f out: t.o* **20/1**

1m 25.81s (-0.19) **Going Correction** -0.10s/f (Stan)
**WFA** 3 from 4yo 2lb **10** Ran SP% **126.0**
Speed ratings (Par 101): **97,95,93,90,83 82,75,69,66,64**
CSF £13.31 CT £71.84 TOTE £3.60: £4.80, £1.90, £2.30; EX 17.30 Trifecta £142.00.
**Owner** P J McBride **Bred** Newsells Park Stud **Trained** Newmarket, Suffolk

**FOCUS**

The early pace was stronger here but the final time was the slower of the two divisions by 0.65sec. The winner has the potential to rate higher for this yard.

T/Plt: £112.50 to a £1 stake. Pool: £65,761.80 - 426.51 winning units. T/Qpdt: £115.40 to a £1 stake. Pool: £10,376.76 - 66.52 winning units. JN

# 7353 LINGFIELD (L-H)

### Thursday, October 30

**OFFICIAL GOING: Polytrack: standard**

Wind: light, half behind Weather: dry, mild

## 7549 32RED CASINO/BRITISH STALLION STUDS EBF MAIDEN FILLIES' STKS (BOBIS RACE) (DIV I) 7f 1y(P)

**12:50** (12:51) (Class 5) 2-Y-O **£2,911** (£866; £432; £216) **Stalls** Low

Form RPR

3 **1** **Crystal Zvezda**[41] 6521 2-9-0 0.................................... ShaneKelly 1 77+
(Sir Michael Stoute) *chsd ldrs: carried rt bnd 2f out: pushed along and qcknd to ld 1f out: in command and pushed out fnl f: comf* **4/7**[1]

0 **2** *1½* **Nancy Astor**[153] 2744 2-9-0 0......................................... RobertHavlin 8 70
(John Gosden) *t.k.h: hld up in midfield: rdn and effrt over 1f out: hdwy to chse ldr fnl 100yds: r.o but no imp* **12/1**

**3** *½* **Fine View (USA)** 2-8-11 0................................... MatthewLawson(3) 10 69+
(Saeed bin Suroor) *s.i.s: in rr: rdn 2f out: hdwy on inner over 1f out: styd on wl ins fnl f: no threat to wnr* **5/1**[2]

35 **4** *¾* **Colorada**[19] 7108 2-9-0 0................................................ TomQueally 4 67
(William Knight) *s.i.s: hld up in last trio: rdn and hdwy ent fnl f: nt clr run fnl 150yds: swtchd rt and styd on strly fnl 100yds: no threat to ldrs* **7/1**[3]

0 **5** *shd* **Farletti**[19] 7108 2-9-0 0................................................... LiamKeniry 5 67
(Andrew Balding) *in tch in last quartet: hdwy towards inner and pressing ldrs over 1f out: no ex and outpcd fnl 150yds* **50/1**

00 **6** *1¼* **Vixen Hill**[21] 7062 2-9-0 0............................................ RobertWinston 3 63
(Charles Hills) *led: hung rt fr 3f out: rdn and hrd pressed wl over 1f out: hdd 1f out: wknd ins fnl f* **33/1**

533 **7** *nse* **Regal Ways (IRE)**[13] 7234 2-9-0 72..................................... JoeFanning 2 63
(Mark Johnston) *chsd ldrs: rdn to press ldrs 2f out: ev ch over 1f out tl jst ins fnl f: btn and n.m.r fnl 100yds: wknd* **8/1**

0 **8** *¾* **Makramah (USA)**[15] 7193 2-8-11 0............................... CamHardie(3) 7 61
(Richard Hannon) *in tch in midfield on outer: rdn over 2f out: outpcd and btn over 1f out: styd on same pce fnl f* **66/1**

6 **9** *½* **Lady Hare (IRE)**[15] 7193 2-9-0 0..................................... JimCrowley 9 60
(David Simcock) *chsd ldr tl widish and lost pl bnd 2f out: n.d and one pce fr over 1f out* **25/1**

**10** *3* **Rock Heroine** 2-9-0 0................................................... JimmyFortune 11 52
(Hughie Morrison) *dwlt: a in last pair: rdn and wd bnd 2f out: n.d* **100/1**

1m 24.96s (0.16) **Going Correction** -0.15s/f (Stan) **10** Ran SP% **122.9**
Speed ratings (Par 92): **93,91,90,89,89 88,88,87,86,83**
CSF £9.87 TOTE £1.60: £1.02, £3.80, £2.00; EX 12.90 Trifecta £56.10.
**Owner** Sir Evelyn De Rothschild **Bred** Southcourt Stud **Trained** Newmarket, Suffolk

**FOCUS**

The meeting marked the 25th anniversary of the first AW fixture to be run in this country (on Equitrack) at Lingfield on October 30th 1989. The first division of this fillies' maiden was a one-horse affair according to the market and so it proved. Ordinary form, but a step forward from the runner-up and the fourth helps set the level.

## 7550 32RED CASINO/BRITISH STALLION STUDS EBF MAIDEN FILLIES' STKS (BOBIS RACE) (DIV II) 7f 1y(P)

**1:20** (1:22) (Class 5) 2-Y-O **£2,911** (£866; £432; £216) **Stalls** Low

Form RPR

2 **1** **Alfajer**[33] 6754 2-9-0 0.................................................... MartinHarley 6 75+
(Marco Botti) *mde all: rdn and asserted jst over 1f out: in command and pushed out ins fnl f: readily* **7/4**[2]

2 **2** *2¼* **Sharqeyih**[19] 7108 2-9-0 0......................................... PaulHanagan 10 68+
(William Haggas) *in tch in midfield: effrt 2f out: no prog tl styd on fnl 100yds to snatch 2nd last strides: no threat to wnr* **11/10**[1]

**3** *nk* **Sur Empire** 2-9-0 0.............................................................. JoeFanning 9 67
(Mark Johnston) *sn in tch and t.k.h: effrt in 3rd 2f out: hung lft jst ins fnl f: outpcd by wnr but wnt 2nd towards fin: lost 2nd last strides* **20/1**

4 **4** *nk* **Faery Song (IRE)**[15] 7193 2-9-0 0.................................... TedDurcan 7 66
(David Lanigan) *chsd wnr: rdn 2f out: outpcd jst over 1f out: one pce fnl f: lost 2 pls towards fin* **7/1**[3]

**5** *4* **Vanishing** 2-9-0 0................................................................. GrahamLee 8 56+
(Ed Walker) *in tch in midfield: 6th and outpcd over 2f out: no threat to ldrs but kpt on ins fnl f* **25/1**

**6** *½* **Krafty One** 2-9-0 0............................................................. RobertHavlin 2 54
(John Gosden) *s.i.s: sme hdwy but no threat to ldrs 2f out: kpt on: nvr trbld ldrs* **10/1**

60 **7** *nk* **Gumhrear (IRE)**[106] 4320 2-8-11 0 ow2.................[1] HarryPoulton(5) 11 55
(James Tate) *taken down early: swtchd lft after s: hld up towards rr: outpcd over 2f out: n.d after but plugged on ins fnl f* **66/1**

05 **8** *2* **Miss Minuty**[13] 7254 2-9-0 0............................................ LukeMorris 3 48
(Sir Mark Prescott Bt) *chsd ldrs: clr in ldng quintet 2f out: shkn up and outpcd over 1f out: btn 1f out: pushed along and wknd fnl f* **66/1**

06 **9** *2¼* **Zebella**[23] 7011 2-9-0 0..................................................... SteveDrowne 1 42
(Rod Millman) *in tch in midfield: outpcd over 2f out: n.d after* **50/1**

**10** *1¾* **Solveig's Song** 2-9-0 0.................................................. JackMitchell 5 37
(Steve Woodman) *s.i.s: rn green in rr: n.d* **100/1**

0 **11** *¾* **Equilicious**[9] 7345 2-9-0 0............................................ RobertWinston 4 35
(Charles Hills) *t.k.h: hld up in last trio: outpcd over 2f out: n.d after* **66/1**

1m 26.77s (1.97) **Going Correction** -0.15s/f (Stan) **11** Ran SP% **121.1**
Speed ratings (Par 92): **82,79,79,78,74 73,73,70,68,66 65**
CSF £3.98 TOTE £3.20: £1.10, £1.10, £3.50; EX 4.80 Trifecta £34.80.
**Owner** Saleh Al Homaizi & Imad Al Sagar **Bred** Newsells Park Stud **Trained** Newmarket, Suffolk

**FOCUS**

The betting for the second division of this maiden was dominated by two fillies that had finished runner-up on their debuts. They finished 1-2, but only one of the pair was ever going to win. The time was a whopping 1.81sec slower than the first leg. The level is fluid, but the runner-up shaped quite well despite being rated below her debut effort.

## 7551 32RED ON THE APP STORE/IRISH EBF MAIDEN STKS 7f 1y(P)

**1:50** (1:56) (Class 5) 2-Y-O **£2,911** (£866; £432; £216) **Stalls** Low

Form RPR

0 **1** **Rattling Jewel**[22] 7031 2-9-5 0...................................... LiamKeniry 11 75
(Andrew Balding) *mde all: rdn and fnd ex over 1f out: hrd pressed ins fnl f: hld on wl: rdn out* **25/1**

020 **2** *nk* **Hills And Dales (IRE)**[36] 6667 2-9-5 79............................ AdamKirby 3 74
(Charlie Appleby) *t.k.h: chsd wnr for 1f: chsd ldrs after tl rdn to chse wnr again over 1f out: str chal 1f out: kpt on but hld towards fin* **5/2**[1]

40 **3** *1¾* **Wind In My Sails**[22] 7030 2-9-5 0.............................. FrederikTylicki 5 69+
(Ed de Giles) *t.k.h: in tch in midfield: effrt over 1f out: kpt on u.p to go 3rd wl ins fnl f: no imp on ldrs* **5/1**[3]

**4** *nse* **Horseshoe Bay (IRE)** 2-9-5 0........................................ ShaneKelly 10 69+
(Sir Michael Stoute) *hld up in tch in last quartet: pushed along 2f out: swtchd rt over 1f out: styd on wl under hands and heels riding ins fnl f: no threat to ldrs* **5/1**[3]

023 **5** *nk* **Longside**[9] 7361 2-9-5 0................................................ GeorgeBaker 12 68
(Charles Hills) *dwlt: sn rcvrd and chsd wnr after 1f tl unable qck over 1f out: one pce fnl f and lost 2 pls wl ins fnl f* **9/2**[2]

200 **6** *1¼* **Swot**[26] 6925 2-9-5 77..................................................... RobertHavlin 9 65
(John Gosden) *chsd ldrs but stuck wd: rdn and unable qck bnd 2f out: outpcd and btn 1f out: one pce after* **9/2**[2]

54 **7** *1½* **Dubawi Diamond**[66] 5745 2-9-5 0............................... MartinHarley 1 61
(James Tate) *in tch in midfield: rdn and no rspnse over 1f out: wknd ins fnl f* **16/1**

06 **8** *3* **Full Of Speed (USA)**[22] 7031 2-9-5 0............................. TomQueally 2 53
(James Fanshawe) *in tch in last trio: rdn over 1f out: sn btn* **14/1**

00 **9** *1½* **Wisewit**[34] 6712 2-9-5 0.................................................. RobertTart 7 49
(James Toller) *in tch in midfield: rdn and lost pl ent fnl 2f: wknd over 1f out* **66/1**

**10** *¾* **Skimp** 2-9-5 0.................................................................. SteveDrowne 6 47
(John Gosden) *stdd s: a in rr: rdn and no rspnse over 1f out* **20/1**

1m 24.67s (-0.13) **Going Correction** -0.15s/f (Stan) **10** Ran SP% **120.9**
Speed ratings (Par 95): **94,93,91,91,91 89,88,84,82,82**
CSF £89.10 TOTE £31.50: £7.20, £1.30, £2.50; EX 115.20 Trifecta £1883.90.
**Owner** Mick and Janice Mariscotti **Bred** Robert Pocock **Trained** Kingsclere, Hants

■ Stewards' Enquiry : Liam Keniry one-day ban: failed to ride to draw (Nov 13)

**FOCUS**

This looked an ordinary event, though the winning time was faster than both divisions of the fillies' maiden. The field was reduced by one when Alfie The Pug was withdrawn after getting out underneath his stall. The runner-up has been rated near his pre-race form.

## 7552 CORAL APP DOWNLOAD FROM THE APP STORE H'CAP 1m 2f (P)

**2:20** (2:20) (Class 5) (0-75,74) 3-Y-O+ **£3,654** (£1,087; £543; £271) **Stalls** Low

Form RPR

3040 **1** **All Talk N No Do (IRE)**[17] 7161 3-9-5 74...........................(tp) AdamKirby 1 83
(Seamus Durack) *chsd ldr: rdn and wnt clr w wnr 2f out: drvn to ld jst ins fnl f: styd on: in command whn drifted rt cl home* **8/1**

6264 **2** *1* **Little Buxted (USA)**[10] 7341 4-9-10 74...........................(p) GrahamLee 6 81
(Robert Mills) *hld up in tch in midfield: effrt in 5th 2f out: clsng and swtchd rt 1f out: chsd wnr wl ins fnl f: kpt on* **3/1**[1]

12- **3** *¾* **Leonard Thomas**[349] 7898 4-9-10 74.............................. GeorgeBaker 4 80+
(David Lanigan) *hld up in last trio: effrt but stl plenty to do 2f out: c to centre and hdwy over 1f out: styd on ins fnl f to go 3rd wl ins fnl f: nvr threatened wnr* **3/1**[1]

2406 **4** 1 ¼ **Silver Dixie (USA)**[15] 7205 4-9-7 71............................(v[1]) CharlesBishop 2 74
(Peter Hedger) *wnt rt s: led: rdn and kicked clr w wnr 2f out: drvn and hdd ins fnl f: no ex and lost 2 pls ins fnl f* **6/1**[3]

6440 **5** hd **Miss Lillie**[7] 7397 3-8-13 71.......................................... DannyBrock(3) 3 74
(Roger Teal) *taken down early: in tch in midfield: effrt to chse ldng pair 2f out: pressing ldrs 1f out: outpcd ins fnl f* **25/1**

-636 **6** 1 ¼ **Starfield**[8] 7373 5-9-9 73................................................. PaulHanagan 5 74
(Michael Appleby) *squeezed for room sn after s: t.k.h: hld up in tch in midfield: effrt over 1f out: r.o same pce: hld whn nt clr run wl ins fnl f* **5/1**[2]

0324 **7** 2 ½ **Starlit Cantata**[36] 6654 3-9-3 72....................................(p) JohnFahy 10 68
(Eve Johnson Houghton) *hld up in tch in last trio: forced to go v wd and effrt 2f out: kpt on fnl f: nvr a threat* **10/1**

3336 **8** 2 ¼ **Gracious George (IRE)**[41] 6523 4-9-7 71....................(p) KieranO'Neill 9 63
(Jimmy Fox) *chsd ldrs: rdn 3f out: struggling 2f out: wknd over 1f out* **14/1**

3353 **9** 2 ½ **Rome**[17] 7158 4-9-10 74............................................ JimmyFortune 8 61
(Gary Moore) *chsd ldrs: rdn over 2f out: lost pl and btn over 1f out: wknd fnl f* **20/1**

4030 **10** 3 ¾ **Moontown**[88] 4948 3-9-4 73.......................................... RobertWinston 7 53
(Charles Hills) *s.i.s: nvr travelling wl and a last: lost tch 2f out* **20/1**

2m 4.01s (-2.59) **Going Correction** -0.15s/f (Stan)
**WFA** 3 from 4yo+ 5lb **10** Ran SP% **121.2**
Speed ratings (Par 103): **104,103,102,101,101 100,98,96,94,91**
CSF £32.70 CT £91.80 TOTE £13.30: £2.90, £1.90, £1.60; EX 46.70.
**Owner** Mrs Anne Cowley **Bred** John Kirby **Trained** Upper Lambourn, Berkshire

**FOCUS**
An ordinary handicap run at a fair pace. The winner has been rated to form, with the runner-up a length off.

## 7553 32RED/EBFSTALLIONS.COM FLEUR DE LYS FILLIES' STKS (LISTED RACE) (FAST TRACK QUALIFIER) 1m 1y(P)
**2:50** (2:54) (Class 1) 3-Y-O+
**£22,684** (£8,600; £4,304; £2,144; £1,076; £540) **Stalls** High

Form RPR

110 **1** **Tearless**[78] 5312 4-9-1 97.............................................. AdamKirby 5 102+
(Charlie Appleby) *chsd ldrs: rdn to chse ldr over 1f out: clr w ldr and ev ch 1f out: led and wnt rt fnl 100yds: asserting whn wnt bk lft towards fin: r.o* **4/1**[2]

4050 **2** 1 ¼ **Lamar (IRE)**[134] 3357 3-8-12 92........................................ LukeMorris 7 98
(James Tate) *chsd ldrs: wnt 2nd over 2f out: rdn to ld wl over 1f out: hrd drvn and clr w wnr 1f out: hdd and no ex fnl 100yds* **20/1**

0123 **3** ½ **Wahgah (USA)**[19] 7105 3-8-12 95...............................(p) PaulHanagan 11 97
(Saeed bin Suroor) *hld up in tch in rr: effrt but stl plenty to do wl over 1f out: hdwy 1f out: r.o strly ins fnl f: wnt 3rd last strides: nvr gng to rch wnr* **9/4**[1]

046 **4** hd **Nakuti (IRE)**[26] 6922 3-8-12 90........................................ MartinHarley 8 97
(Sylvester Kirk) *in tch in midfield: effrt u.p over 1f out: chsd clr ldng pair 1f out: kpt on u.p: lost 3rd last strides* **50/1**

0443 **5** ¾ **Auction (IRE)**[8] 7384 4-9-1 89........................................ CamHardie 6 96
(Ed Dunlop) *hld up in tch in last trio: stl plenty to do and effrt over 1f out: hdwy 1f out: styd on wl: nt rch ldrs* **33/1**

5204 **6** 2 **Dutch Rose (IRE)**[26] 6922 5-9-1 98.................................. DanielTudhope 2 91
(David O'Meara) *led for 2f: settled bk and wl in tch in midfield: effrt over 1f out: no imp: wknd ins fnl f* **12/1**

2006 **7** ½ **Gifted Girl (IRE)**[34] 6707 5-9-1 98............................(tp) TomQueally 1 90
(Paul Cole) *hld up in tch in last trio: effrt wl over 1f out: clsng but stl plenty to do whn nt clr run and hmpd 1f out: swtchd rt and styd on ins fnl f: nvr trbld ldrs* **8/1**

0121 **8** 1 ½ **Saucy Minx (IRE)**[48] 6302 4-9-1 91..............................(b) JimCrowley 4 87
(Amanda Perrett) *hld up in tch in midfield: effrt over 1f out: no imp 1f out: wknd ins fnl f* **20/1**

0302 **9** 3 **Crowley's Law**[54] 6164 3-8-12 99.................................... MartinDwyer 3 79
(Tom Dascombe) *chsd ldr tl led 6f out: rdn ent fnl 2f: hdd wl over 1f out: no ex and btn 1f out: wknd* **7/1**

0111 **10** 1 **Fruit Pastille**[8] 7384 3-8-12 81.................................(b) JimmyFortune 10 76
(Hughie Morrison) *dwlt: steadily rcvrd to chse ldrs 5f out: wd and lost pl u.p 2f out: wknd over 1f out* **12/1**

1304 **11** 1 ¼ **Water Hole (IRE)**[11] 7319 3-8-12 103................................ RobertHavlin 9 74
(John Gosden) *in tch in midfield on outer: lost pl whn wd bnd 2f out: sn rdn: edgd lft and hmpd: bhd and no ch after* **9/2**[3]

1m 35.03s (-3.17) **Going Correction** -0.15s/f (Stan)
**WFA** 3 from 4yo+ 3lb **11** Ran SP% **122.4**
Speed ratings: **109,107,107,107,106 104,103,102,99,98 97**
CSF £87.86 TOTE £5.00: £1.80, £5.00, £1.40; EX 107.20 Trifecta £917.80.
**Owner** Godolphin **Bred** Darley **Trained** Newmarket, Suffolk

**FOCUS**
An interesting fillies' Listed event and the first fast-track qualifier for the Fillies and Mares AW Championship next Easter. There was no hanging about with a three-horse battle for the early lead. Ordinary form rated around the fourth and fifth.

## 7554 32RED.COM/CHOOSE EBF NOMINATED RIVER EDEN FILLIES' STKS (LISTED RACE) 1m 5f (P)
**3:20** (3:22) (Class 1) 3-Y-O+
**£22,684** (£8,600; £4,304; £2,144; £1,076; £540) **Stalls** Low

Form RPR

2011 **1** **Hidden Gold (IRE)**[15] 7203 3-8-10 98.............................. FrederikTylicki 9 101+
(Saeed bin Suroor) *hld up in tch in last quartet: hdwy on outer 4f out: rdn to chse ldr over 2f out: led over 1f out: sn clr: styd on wl: rdn out* **5/4**[1]

2100 **2** 1 ¾ **Miss Marjurie (IRE)**[34] 6708 4-9-4 93.............................. PatCosgrave 4 98+
(Denis Coakley) *taken down early: hld up in tch in midfield: nt clr run and shuffled bk over 2f out: swtchd rt and hdwy over 1f out: styd on wl to go 2nd last strides: no threat to wnr* **25/1**

6002 **3** nk **Alwilda**[24] 6979 4-9-4 91................................................... LukeMorris 6 98
(Sir Mark Prescott Bt) *in tch in midfield: hdwy u.p to chse ldrs 2f out: wnt 2nd fnl 100yds: kpt on same pce: lost 2nd last strides* **33/1**

6026 **4** ½ **Livia's Dream (IRE)**[34] 6708 5-9-4 95.............................. GeorgeBaker 3 97
(Ed Walker) *in tch in midfield: hdwy on inner to chse ldrs over 1f out: battling for placings and kpt on u.p fnl f* **14/1**

11-0 **5** 2 ½ **Speckled (USA)**[103] 4443 4-9-4 95.................................. AdamKirby 14 93
(Charlie Appleby) *hld up in tch in last quartet: gd hdwy on outer to chse ldrs 4f out: rdn to ld over 2f out: hdd and no ex over 1f out: lost 2nd and wknd fnl 100yds* **8/1**[3]

1 **6** ½ **Tamasha**[48] 6298 3-8-10 87...................................... SilvestreDeSousa 11 92
(Ralph Beckett) *hld up in tch in last pair: rdn over 4f out: hdwy over 1f out: styd on ins fnl f: nvr trbld ldrs* **9/4**[2]

1420 **7** 2 **Last Minute Lisa (IRE)**[6] 7422 4-9-4 73.......................... JimmyFortune 12 89?
(Sylvester Kirk) *stdd s: hld up in rr: hdwy and swtchd lft over 1f out: styd on: nvr trbld ldrs* **100/1**

12 **8** ½ **Spacelab**[36] 6654 3-8-10 85............................................ RobertHavlin 1 89+
(Amanda Perrett) *chsd ldrs: rdn and unable qck wl over 1f out: wknd ins fnl f* **20/1**

5130 **9** 3 ¼ **Cascading**[49] 6255 3-8-10 97........................................... JimCrowley 7 84
(Hughie Morrison) *in tch in midfield: rdn and unable qck ent fnl 2f: wknd over 1f out* **12/1**

2530 **10** 3 **Regal Hawk**[34] 6708 4-9-4 100........................................ MartinHarley 5 83
(James Tate) *wl in tch in midfield: shuffled bk and nt clr run over 2f out: n.d after: wl hld and eased ins fnl f* **33/1**

2054 **11** 1 ¼ **Kikonga**[19] 7110 4-9-4 87............................................. DanielTudhope 13 77
(Luca Cumani) *stuck wd early: hdwy to chse ldr 10f out tl led over 2f out: sn hdd and rdn: wknd over 1f out* **25/1**

1603 **12** 5 **Puzzle Time**[24] 6987 4-9-4 85........................................ GrahamLee 10 70
(Giles Bravery) *wl in tch in midfield: lost pl an dsltly hmpd over 2f out: sn btn: bhd fnl f* **66/1**

-016 **13** 3 **Rawoof (IRE)**[51] 6218 3-8-10 85..................................... ChrisCatlin 2 65
(Rae Guest) *sn led: rdn and hdd over 2f out: wknd over 1f out: fdd fnl f* **66/1**

1626 **14** ½ **Tioga Pass**[18] 7135 3-8-10 90...................................(p) MartinLane 8 65
(Paul Cole) *chsd ldr tl 10f out: rdn and lost pl over 2f out: bhd fnl f* **66/1**

2m 39.7s (-6.30) **Going Correction** -0.15s/f (Stan) course record
**WFA** 3 from 4yo+ 8lb **14** Ran SP% **124.5**
Speed ratings: **113,111,111,111,109 109,108,108,106,104 103,100,98,98**
CSF £46.76 TOTE £2.40: £1.10, £6.00, £6.20; EX 55.50 Trifecta £1433.20.
**Owner** Godolphin **Bred** Darley **Trained** Newmarket, Suffolk

**FOCUS**
Another interesting Listed fillies' event, this time for stayers, including last year's first and second. Six of the eight previous winners of this race had been 3yos, the exception being dual-winner Baila Me in 2009 and 2010. This wasn't as competitive as the numbers would suggest as a few of these had plenty to find on official ratings. The winning time was a new course record, though this distance isn't used that often and this would be the classiest race run over it. The proximity of the seventh takes some believing but the time backs it up to a fair degree, and the fourth helps set the standard.

## 7555 LADBROKES H'CAP 7f 1y(P)
**3:50** (3:54) (Class 2) (0-105,105) 3-Y-O+ **£12,291** (£3,657; £1,827; £913) **Stalls** Low

Form RPR

0-10 **1** **Prince's Trust**[26] 6921 4-9-5 **100**.................................... ShaneKelly 12 112+
(William Haggas) *hld up in midfield: nt clr run wl over 1f out: clsd and nt clr run 1f out: gap opened ins fnl f: pushed along and qcknd readily to ld towards fin: cleverly* **5/1**[2]

13-0 **2** ½ **Music Theory (IRE)**[103] 4442 3-9-6 **103**.......................... MartinLane 5 111
(Charlie Appleby) *wl in tch in midfield: squeezed for room and hmpd wl over 1f out: hdwy u.p over 1f out: r.o to ld wl ins fnl f: hdd and no ex towards fin* **14/1**

4101 **3** ½ **Intransigent**[26] 6921 5-9-7 **105**.............................. ThomasBrown(3) 10 113
(Andrew Balding) *hld up off the pce towards rr: hdwy on outer jst over 1f out: r.o wl ins fnl f: wnt 3rd towards fin* **9/4**[1]

3155 **4** ¾ **Alejandro (IRE)**[48] 6290 5-9-2 **97**................................ DanielTudhope 4 103
(David O'Meara) *led: rdn jst over 2f out: battled on wl u.p tl hdd wl ins fnl f: lost 2 pls towards fin* **14/1**

2005 **5** nse **Hasopop (IRE)**[22] 7034 4-9-6 **101**................................. MartinHarley 1 107
(Marco Botti) *wl in tch in midfield: clsd to chse ldrs over 1f out: rdn and effrt ins fnl f: styd on same pce* **12/1**

1232 **6** 1 ¼ **Athletic**[16] 7168 5-8-9 **95**......................................(v) JennyPowell(5) 3 101+
(Andrew Reid) *hld up off the pce in last pair: swtchd lft and gd hdwy jst over 1f out: nvr enough room and one pce ins fnl f* **7/1**[3]

053 **7** 1 ¾ **Ifwecan**[14] 7227 3-8-8 **91**............................................... JoeFanning 7 88
(Mark Johnston) *pressed ldr: rdn and ev ch ent 2f out tl ins fnl f: wknd fnl 100yds* **8/1**

0300 **8** ¾ **Brazos (IRE)**[13] 7242 3-9-8 **105**.................................. JimmyFortune 2 100
(Clive Brittain) *chsd ldrs: effrt and unable to quicken over 1f out: hld and one pce fnl f* **20/1**

2600 **9** 1 ½ **George Guru**[35] 6688 7-9-3 **98**.................................... RobertHavlin 6 90
(John Bridger) *chsd ldrs: unable qck u.p over 1f out: wknd fnl f* **25/1**

05 **10** ¾ **Swiss Cross**[54] 6159 7-9-0 **95**.................................(t) StevieDonohoe 8 85
(Phil McEntee) *chsd ldrs on outer: rdn and unable qck 2f out: btn over 1f out: wknd fnl f* **50/1**

2100 **11** ½ **Red Refraction (IRE)**[14] 7227 4-8-10 **94**........................ CamHardie(3) 9 83
(Richard Hannon) *in tch in midfield: drvn and no hdwy 2f out: no threat to ldrs and one pce after* **25/1**

316 **12** 9 **Verse Of Love**[14] 7227 5-8-5 **86**.............................. SilvestreDeSousa 11 52
(David Evans) *dropped in bhd after: a bhd: eased ins fnl f* **25/1**

2050 **13** 6 **Passing Star**[70] 5609 3-9-5 **102**................................... RobertWinston 14 51
(Charles Hills) *hld up off the pce towards rr: sme hdwy 3f out: v wd and lost pl bnd 2f out: bhd and eased 1f out* **10/1**

1m 22.17s (-2.63) **Going Correction** -0.15s/f (Stan)
**WFA** 3 from 4yo+ 2lb **13** Ran SP% **119.4**
Speed ratings (Par 109): **109,108,107,107,106 105,103,102,100,100 99,89,82**
CSF £67.31 CT £202.37 TOTE £5.90: £2.40, £5.20, £1.80; EX 108.00 Trifecta £461.80.
**Owner** The Queen **Bred** The Queen **Trained** Newmarket, Suffolk
■ Stewards' Enquiry : Silvestre De Sousa five-day ban: improper riding (Nov 13-15,17-18)

**FOCUS**
A hot handicap and a typically dramatic Lingfield finish. The third has been rated close to his turf form, and the fourth close to form as well.

## 7556 DOWNLOAD THE LADBROKES APP APPRENTICE H'CAP 7f 1y(P)
**4:20** (4:21) (Class 6) (0-65,65) 3-Y-O+ **£3,008** (£895; £447; £223) **Stalls** Low

Form RPR

1022 **1** **Pour La Victoire (IRE)**[9] 7368 4-9-7 65..................(b) GeorgeDowning 2 74+
(Tony Carroll) *chsd ldng trio and in tch: effrt to chse ldr over 1f out: drvn to ld ins fnl f: jst lasted home* **5/2**[1]

5550 **2** hd **Mon Cigar (IRE)**[29] 6857 3-9-2 62........................................ JoeDoyle 8 68
(Denis Coakley) *off the pce in 5th: clsd 2f out: racd awkwardly u.p but wnt 3rd over 1f out: no imp tl str burst fnl 100yds: wnt 2nd and clsng rapidly on ldr towards fin: nt quite get up* **20/1**

6310 **3** 1 ½ **Meddling**[133] 3390 4-9-2 60......................................... ShelleyBirkett 14 63
(Julia Feilden) *chsd ldng pair and in tch: wnt 2nd and clsd to join ldr 2f out: sn led and rdn: drvn and hdd ins fnl f: one pce fnl 75yds* **25/1**

0143 **4** 2 ¼ **Bookmaker**[23] 6995 4-8-12 59..........................(b) CharlotteJenner(3) 5 56
(John Bridger) *racd off the pce in midfield: edgd rt on bnd 2f out: battling for modest 4th jst ins fnl f: kpt on: no threat to ldrs* **7/1**

0126 **5** *hd* **Chevise (IRE)**[69] 5624 6-8-12 61...........................(b) HectorCrouch(5) 11 58
(Steve Woodman) *hld up off the pce in rr: hdwy into midfield over 2f out: battling for modest 4th jst ins fnl f: kpt on: nvr trbld ldrs* **14/1**

1026 **6** *1 ¾* **Prim And Proper**[9] 7347 3-8-10 59...........................(p) JennyPowell(3) 9 50
(Brendan Powell) *s.i.s: wl off the pce in rr and bustled along: hdwy over 1f out: styd on wl fnl f: nvr trbld ldrs* **25/1**

6443 **7** *½* **Choice Of Destiny**[5] 7456 3-8-12 63........................... GaryMahon(5) 12 53
(Philip McBride) *off the pce in midfield: effrt whn nt clr run and bdly hmpd over 1f out: nt rcvr and no hdwy after* **6/1**[3]

-440 **8** *¾* **Berkeley Vale**[45] 6397 3-8-12 63..................................... RobHornby(5) 7 51
(Roger Teal) *dwlt: wl off the pce towards rr: rdn over 2f out: styd on ins fnl f: nvr trbld ldrs* **25/1**

0050 **9** *¾* **Afkar (IRE)**[43] 6466 6-9-4 65.................................. KieranShoemark(3) 10 52
(Clive Brittain) *racd off the pce in midfield: trying to cl whn hmpd jst over 2f out: no threat after* **5/1**[2]

2550 **10** *hd* **Koharu**[23] 6995 4-8-10 59............................................(p) ChrisMeehan(5) 1 45
(Peter Makin) *racd off the pce in midfield: lost pl and bhd over 2f out: no ch after but kpt on fnl f* **33/1**

0150 **11** *1* **Bertie Blu Boy**[55] 6122 6-9-4 62.......................................(b) EoinWalsh 6 46
(Lisa Williamson) *led: jnd and rdn 2f out: 4th and btn 1f out: fdd ins fnl f* **8/1**

4165 **12** *1 ½* **Clapperboard**[20] 7078 3-9-2 62...................................(b) JordanNason 3 41
(Paul Fitzsimons) *chsd ldr tl over 2f out: wkng whn edgd lft over 1f out: fdd fnl f* **8/1**

1m 23.31s (-1.49) **Going Correction** -0.15s/f (Stan)
**WFA** 3 from 4yo+ 2lb **12 Ran SP% 120.2**
Speed ratings (Par 101): **102,101,100,97,97 95,94,93,92,92 91,89**
CSF £62.70 CT £1047.92 TOTE £2.60: £2.00, £6.00, £7.70; EX 62.50 Trifecta £2751.70 Part won..
**Owner** Curry House Corner **Bred** L Fox **Trained** Cropthorne, Worcs

**FOCUS**
Despite what looked a breakneck pace, those that raced handily were at an advantage in this moderate apprentice handicap. The third has been rated close to her win over 1m here in May.
T/Jkpt: Not won. T/Plt: £12.30 to a £1 stake. Pool: £68,372.34 - 4038.90 winning units. T/Qpdt: £10.70 to a £1 stake. Pool: £5475.50 - 377.70 winning units. SP

# 7269 SAINT-CLOUD (L-H)
## Thursday, October 30

**OFFICIAL GOING: Turf: soft**

## 7557a CRITERIUM INTERNATIONAL (GROUP 1) (2YO COLTS & FILLIES) (TURF) 1m
**1:20** (12:00) 2-Y-O **£119,041** (£47,625; £23,812; £11,895; £5,958)

RPR

**1** **Vert De Grece (IRE)**[67] 5735 2-9-0 0.................... UmbertoRispoli 3 116+
(Roger Varian) *midfield in tch on inner: pushed along to chal 2f out: rdn to ld ent fnl f: qcknd clr smartly and sn in command: impressive* **7/2**[2]

**2** *4* **Johnny Barnes (IRE)**[16] 7171 2-9-0 0......................... WilliamBuick 2 106
(John Gosden) *dwlt and in rr early: hdwy to trck ldr on inner after 2f: t.k.h: shkn up to chal 2f out: led narrowly over 1f out: rdn and hdd ent fnl f: readily outpcd by wnr but kpt on for distant 2nd* **10/1**

**3** *¾* **Sherlock (GER)**[18] 7145 2-9-0 0..................................... AStarke 5 104
(M Rulec, Germany) *hld up in last pair: rdn over 1f out: kpt on fnl f and tk nvr nrr 3rd cl home: no ch w wnr* **25/1**

**4** *nk* **Cherek (FR)**[40] 6570 2-9-0 0...........................(p) ChristopheSoumillon 4 104
(J-C Rouget, France) *midfield in tch on outer: shkn up 2f out and nt qckn: towards rr whn rdn ent fnl f: rallied and kpt on u.p towards fin: tk wl hld 4th post* **9/1**

**5** *shd* **Alea Iacta**[21] 7069 2-8-10 0........................................... MaximeGuyon 8 99
(A Fabre, France) *trckd ldr on outer: chal gng strly and ev ch early in st: rdn and nt qckn over 1f out: kpt on same pce fnl f and wl hld* **5/4**[1]

**6** *shd* **Wag'n Tail (SPA)**[24] 6993 2-9-0 0........................ StephanePasquier 1 103
(C Delcher-Sanchez, France) *hld up towards rr on inner: rdn 2f out: effrt over 1f out: readily outpcd by wnr fnl f: kpt on but lost 2 pls cl home* **16/1**

**7** *nk* **Kenfreeze (FR)**[40] 6570 2-9-0 0..............................(p) ThierryJarnet 6 103
(H-A Pantall, France) *hld up towards rr on outer: clsd gng wl into st: rdn and nt qckn over 1f out: kpt on same pce fnl f and wl hld* **25/1**

**8** *nk* **Burnt Sugar (IRE)**[25] 6968 2-9-0 0........................ MickaelBarzalona 9 102
(Richard Hannon) *stdd and hld up in last: pushed along into st: rdn and effrt on outer over 1f out: ev ch ent fnl f: sn outpcd by wnr: no ex and fdd* **5/1**[3]

**9** *1 ¾* **Master Apprentice (IRE)**[24] 6985 2-9-0 0.................... DavidProbert 7 98
(Andrew Balding) *led: rdn and strly pressed 2f out: hdd over 1f out: sn no ex and btn: wknd and dropped to last fnl f* **16/1**

1m 43.16s (-4.34) **9 Ran SP% 121.9**
WIN (incl. 1 meuro stake): 4.80. PLACES: 2.10, 3.50, 5.00. DF: 19.30. SF: 42.70.
**Owner** Britannia Thoroughbreds 1 **Bred** Katy Murphy **Trained** Newmarket, Suffolk

**FOCUS**
Some classy horses have won this race in the past, most notably subsequent Prix de l'Arc de Triomphe winners Dalakhani and Bago. Last year it went to Ectot. Vert De Grece rates one of the stronger winners.

## 7558a PRIX DE FLORE (GROUP 3) (3YO+ FILLIES & MARES) (TURF) 1m 2f 110y
**1:50** (12:00) 3-Y-O+ **£33,333** (£13,333; £10,000; £6,666; £3,333)

RPR

**1** **Fate (FR)**[21] 7070 5-8-11 0.......................... StephanePasquier 1 105
(A De Royer-Dupre, France) *hld up in rr: pushed along and hdwy to chal 2f out: led narrowly jst ins fnl f: strly pressed all the way to fin: styd on and jst prevailed on hd bob post* **5/2**[1]

**2** *nse* **Bocaiuva (IRE)**[29] 6882 3-8-9 0 ow2................ ChristopheSoumillon 11 109
(F Chappet, France) *hld up towards rr: rdn and hdwy over 2f out: swtchd out and styd on strly fnl f: wnt 2nd and chal towards fin: jst denied on hd bob post* **7/1**

**3** *hd* **Sparkling Beam (IRE)**[21] 7070 4-8-11 0.......................... ThierryJarnet 9 105
(J E Pease, France) *hld up in midfield: smooth hdwy early in st: rdn to chal and ev ch fnl f: styd on wl: jst failed* **7/2**[2]

**4** *1 ¼* **Regardez**[39] 6585 3-8-7 0............................ MickaelBarzalona 2 104
(Ralph Beckett) *prom on inner: rdn to chal 2f out: led over 1f out: hdd jst ins fnl f: styd on but nt pce of ldng trio towards fin and hld* **11/2**

**5** *snk* **Gaga A (URU)**[16] 7189 5-8-11 0........................... GregoryBenoist 3 102
(D Smaga, France) *midfield on inner: rdn 2f out: styd on wl but nt quite pce to chal and hld* **20/1**

**6** *hd* **Vally Jem (FR)**[41] 6592 5-8-11 0...........................(b) IoritzMendizabal 6 101
(D Sepulchre, France) *hld up in midfield on inner: rdn early in st: effrt over 1f out: styd on same pce fnl f and hld* **20/1**

**7** *snk* **All At Sea**[26] 6956 3-8-7 0.......................... MaximeGuyon 4 103
(A Fabre, France) *midfield in tch: rdn and effrt over 1f out: keeping on same pce whn squeezed for room fnl f: hld after* **5/1**[3]

**8** *nk* **No News (FR)**[160] 2631 4-8-11 0.......................... ThomasMessina 10 101
(X Nakkachdji, France) *hld up in last: rdn over 1f out: styd on fnl f but nvr threatened* **25/1**

**9** *4 ½* **Abys (FR)**[26] 6956 4-8-11 0.............................. AntoineHamelin 7 92
(Mme Pia Brandt, France) *wnt rt s: midfield: rdn 2f out: outpcd and lost pl over 1f out: no ex and btn fnl f* **12/1**

**10** *3* **Lili Moon (GER)**[18] 7146 5-8-11 0......................... CristianDemuro 12 86
(Werner Glanz, Germany) *midfield on outer: rdn into st: outpcd and lost pl over 1f out: no ex and btn fnl f: eased towards fin* **25/1**

**11** *hd* **Honeysuckle Rose (FR)**[20] 3-8-9 0 ow2...................... FreddyDiFede 8 90
(F Chappet, France) *bmpd s: sn led: 5 l clr into st: rdn and reduced advantage 2f out: hdd over 1f out: no ex and btn: wknd and eased fnl f* **50/1**

**12** *10* **Adriana (GER)**[117] 6-8-11 0........................................ AStarke 5 66
(M Rulec, Germany) *trckd ldr: rdn and lost pl 2f out: sn no ex and btn: wknd and dropped to last ent fnl f: eased* **25/1**

2m 15.37s (-4.23)
**WFA** 3 from 4yo+ 5lb **12 Ran SP% 126.1**
WIN (incl. 1 euro stake): 3.90. PLACES: 1.50, 2.10, 1.70. DF: 16.10. SF: 29.90.
**Owner** Fair Salinia Ltd **Bred** Fair Salinia Ltd **Trained** Chantilly, France

## 7559a PRIX PERTH (GROUP 3) (3YO+) (TURF) 1m
**2:20** (12:00) 3-Y-O+ **£33,333** (£13,333; £10,000; £6,666; £3,333)

RPR

**1** **Flamingo Star (GER)**[25] 6965 4-9-4 0..............................(b) APietsch 2 117
(Waldemar Hickst, Germany) *pushed along to go forward and sn led: mde rest: rdn 2f out: strly pressed ent fnl f: r.o wl and asserted towards fin* **20/1**

**2** *1 ¼* **Pinturicchio (IRE)**[26] 6955 6-9-4 0.......................... AnthonyCrastus 3 114
(E Lellouche, France) *hld up towards rr: rdn 2f out: kpt on wl fr over 1f out: swtchd rt fnl 120yds and wnt 2nd fnl strides: nrst fin* **16/1**

**3** *hd* **Visoriyna (FR)**[40] 3-8-8 0.............................. ThierryJarnet 11 106
(J-C Rouget, France) *sn trcking wnr: gng best 2f out: rdn to chal over 1f out: kpt on same pce fnl f and sn hld: dropped to 3rd fnl strides* **8/1**[3]

**4** *nk* **Graphic (IRE)**[12] 7274 5-9-4 0..............................(p) IoritzMendizabal 10 113
(William Haggas) *prom on inner: rdn into st: kpt on same pce and nvr able to chal* **6/1**[2]

**5** *½* **Red Dubawi (IRE)**[57] 6054 6-9-6 0.......................... EddyHardouin 6 114
(Frau Erika Mader, Germany) *dwlt and hld up in rr: hdwy 2f out: rdn over 1f out: kpt on same pce fnl f and nvr able to chal* **20/1**

**6** *½* **Matorio (FR)**[26] 6955 4-8-11 0.............................. FabriceVeron 1 104
(H-A Pantall, France) *dwlt and pushed along to rcvr: hld up in midfield on inner: rdn into st: kpt on same pce and nvr able to chal* **16/1**

**7** *hd* **Hippy (FR)**[26] 6957 6-9-1 0.................................. MickaelBarzalona 9 107
(E Libaud, France) *stdd and hld up in rr: rdn over 2f out: kpt on against rail fnl f and sme late hdwy: wnt 7th post but nvr a factor* **8/1**[3]

**8** *hd* **Dalayna (FR)**[21] 7070 4-8-11 0.......................... ChristopheSoumillon 7 103
(A De Royer-Dupre, France) *midfield in tch: rdn 2f out: rn arnd u.p and sn outpcd: kpt on wout threatening fnl f: dropped to 8th post* **5/1**[1]

**9** *1* **Affaire Solitaire (IRE)**[26] 6955 4-9-1 0.......................... GregoryBenoist 4 104
(P Khozian, France) *midfield on inner: rdn 2f out: carried lft over 1f out: kpt on same pce and wl hld whn sltly hmpd fnl 120yds* **12/1**

**10** *½* **Zhiyi (USA)**[26] 6955 4-9-1 0.............................. StephanePasquier 5 103
(P Bary, France) *dwlt sltly: sn midfield: rdn 2f out: hmpd over 1f out and nt clr run again fnl f: nt rcvr and nvr able to chal* **14/1**

**11** *snk* **Lord Of The Land (IRE)**[19] 3-8-11 0.......................... MaximeGuyon 13 101
(A Fabre, France) *midfield on outer: rdn 2f out: outpcd and wl hld whn sltly short of room towards fin: nvr able to chal* **5/1**[1]

**12** *2* **Kenhope (FR)**[26] 6955 4-8-11 0.............................. AurelienLemaitre 12 94
(H-A Pantall, France) *prom on outer: rdn and effrt 2f out: outpcd and btn over 1f out: fdd fnl f: eased* **5/1**[1]

**13** *1 ¼* **Dylar (FR)**[25] 7-9-1 0........................................ VincentVion 8 95
(L Nyffels, France) *hld up towards rr: rdn 2f out: no imp and dropped to last ent fnl f: sn btn and eased* **14/1**

1m 41.72s (-5.78)
**WFA** 3 from 4yo+ 3lb **13 Ran SP% 128.8**
WIN (incl. 1 euro stake): 22.70. PLACES: 7.40, 6.40, 3.60. DF: 200.10. SF: 387.70.
**Owner** Frau Marlene Haller **Bred** Frau Marlene Haller **Trained** Germany

# 7377 NEWMARKET (R-H)
## Friday, October 31

**OFFICIAL GOING: Good to soft (6.9)**
Wind: medium, half-against Weather: sunny, dry and mild

## 7560 IN LOVING MEMORY OF VAL CHANDLER EBF STALLIONS MAIDEN STKS (BOBIS RACE) (COLTS/GELDINGS) (DIV I) 7f
**12:30** (12:30) (Class 4) 2-Y-O **£4,528** (£1,347; £673; £336) **Stalls** Low

Form RPR

2 **1** **New Strategy (IRE)**[14] 7244 2-9-0 0.......................... FrederikTylicki 7 77+
(Saeed bin Suroor) *mde all: rdn and fnd ex over 1f out: clr: rn green and wandered ins fnl f: styd on* **7/4**[1]

**2** *1* **Greatest Hits (USA)** 2-9-0 0.......................... RobertHavlin 5 74+
(John Gosden) *dwlt: rn green but sn rcvrd and in tch in midfield: effrt to chse clr wnr and drifted rt 1f out: kpt on* **8/1**

0 **3** *1 ¾* **Sir Henry Raeburn (IRE)**[109] 4270 2-9-0 0.......................(t) LukeMorris 3 70
(Paul Cole) *t.k.h: hld up wl in tch in midfield: rdn 2f hdwy to chse ldng pair 1f out: one pce fnl f* **33/1**

**4** *1* **Druot** 2-9-0 0.................................................. SteveDrowne 9 67+
(Peter Makin) *dwlt: hld up in tch: rdn: drifted rt and outpcd wl over 1f out: rallied and styd on wl fnl 100yds: no threat to wnr* **100/1**

6 **5** *shd* **Tafahom (IRE)**[14] 7234 2-9-0 0.......................... PaulHanagan 6 67
(B W Hills) *chsd ldr tl rdn and unable qck wl over 1f out: kpt on same pce fnl f* **7/1**[3]

**6** *½* **Goathland (IRE)** 2-9-0 0.......................................... ShaneKelly 8 66
(Peter Chapple-Hyam) *hld up in tch in last pair: pushed along and outpcd wl over 1f out: rallied and styd on again fnl 100yds: no threat to wnr* **33/1**

7 *nk* **Awesome Power** 2-9-0 0 JoeFanning 4 65
(William Haggas) *t.k.h: chsd ldng pair: rdn 2f out: outpcd over 1f out: hld and one pce fnl f* **7/1**3

4 **8** *hd* **Borak (IRE)**23 7040 2-9-0 0 AdamKirby 10 64
(Marco Botti) *chsd ldrs: rdn to go 2nd briefly but struggling to qckn wl over 1f out: lost pl 1f out: one pce after* **9/4**2

**9** *50* **Sporting Bob** 2-9-0 0 JimmyQuinn 2
(Robert Eddery) *a in rr: rdn and struggling 1/2-way: lost tch over 2f out: t.o* **25/1**

1m 28.97s (3.57) **Going Correction** +0.375s/f (Good) **9** Ran SP% **114.0**
Speed ratings (Par 97): **94,92,90,89,89 89,88,88,31**
CSF £15.81 TOTE £2.30: £1.10, £2.90, £5.50; EX 19.80 Trifecta £236.70.
**Owner** Godolphin **Bred** Airlie Stud **Trained** Newmarket, Suffolk

**FOCUS**
The ground had dried up a touch and the going was given as good to soft all round. The early pace was sedate in this maiden.Stands Side course and Stalls: Far Side. Repositioning of bend into home straight increased distances of 12f & 16f races by 15yds. The level is very fluid and the form isn't to be taken too literally.

## 7561 IN LOVING MEMORY OF VAL CHANDLER EBF STALLIONS MAIDEN STKS (BOBIS RACE) (COLTS/GELDINGS) (DIV II) 7f
**1:00** (1:02) (Class 4) 2-Y-O **£4,528** (£1,347; £673; £336) **Stalls** Low

Form RPR
**1** **Suddyan (IRE)** 2-9-0 0 ShaneKelly 9 84+
(Sir Michael Stoute) *stdd s: in tch in midfield: rdn over 2f out: styd on to cl on ldrs ent fnl f: swtchd lft ins fnl f: led fnl 75yds: pushed out* **10/1**

6 **2** *1/2* **Stars And Stripes**16 7206 2-8-11 0 CamHardie(3) 6 83
(Luca Cumani) *chsd ldrs: rdn over 2f out: styd on u.p ent fnl f: led ins fnl f: sn hdd and kpt on same pce* **7/1**

**3** *3 1/2* **Flying Hammer** 2-9-0 0 JoeFanning 5 74
(William Haggas) *chsd ldrs: rdn 2f out: drvn and pressing ldrs over 1f out tl no ex ins fnl f: wknd fnl 100yds* **7/2**2

2 **4** *nk* **Crown Command (IRE)**14 7234 2-9-0 0 MartinDwyer 2 73
(William Muir) *w ldr: rdn and ev ch wl over 1f out tl no ex ins fnl f: wknd fnl 100yds* **2/1**1

02 **5** *1 3/4* **Crack Shot (IRE)**90 4885 2-9-0 0 SilvestreDeSousa 4 68
(Clive Brittain) *mde most: rdn 2f out: battled on wl u.p tl hdd ins fnl f: wknd fnl 100yds* **6/1**3

**6** *2 1/2* **Tawdeea** 2-9-0 0 PaulHanagan 7 62+
(Richard Hannon) *s.i.s: rn green and sn rdn along in rr: 7th and wl hld over 1f out: plugged on* **6/1**3

00 **7** *7* **Giovanni Di Bicci**9 7372 2-8-11 0 AshleyMorgan(3) 8 44
(Lady Cecil) *hld up in rr: effrt into 6th but nt on terms 2f out: no hdwy over 1f out: wknd fnl f* **40/1**

**8** *13* **Zingiber** 2-9-0 0 PatCosgrave 1 10
(Noel Quinlan) *s.i.s: a in rr: rdn and lost tch over 2f out* **66/1**

**9** *6* **Royal Normandy** 2-9-0 0 DavidProbert 3
(Andrew Balding) *sn dropped to rr and nvr striding out: t.o fnl 3f* **16/1**

1m 28.27s (2.87) **Going Correction** +0.375s/f (Good) **9** Ran SP% **115.5**
Speed ratings (Par 97): **98,97,93,93,91 88,80,65,58**
CSF £77.86 TOTE £13.10: £3.30, £2.80, £1.10; EX 103.30 Trifecta £702.30.
**Owner** Prince A A Faisal **Bred** Mrs Brid Cosgrove **Trained** Newmarket, Suffolk

**FOCUS**
There was a better pace on here and it was the faster of the two divisions by 0.7sec. It's been rated to the race average.

## 7562 GEORGE ROGERS MOBILE CATERING H'CAP 1m 2f
**1:30** (1:30) (Class 4) (0-85,85) 3-Y-O+ **£5,175** (£1,540; £769; £384) **Stalls** Low

Form RPR
1005 **1** **Unison (IRE)**25 6990 4-9-0 75 SteveDrowne 7 82
(Peter Makin) *mde all: rdn 2f out: hrd pressed but hld on wl u.p fnl f: all out* **20/1**

0415 **2** *hd* **Handheld**23 7043 7-8-11 77 (p) ShelleyBirkett(5) 9 83
(Julia Feilden) *hld up in tch in last pair: rdn and hdwy over 2f out: ev ch fnl f: r.o but a jst hld* **10/1**

1534 **3** *shd* **Lungarno Palace (USA)**20 7125 3-9-5 85 BenCurtis 5 90
(John Gallagher) *s.i.s: hld up in tch in last pair: rdn and hdwy over 1f out: nvr enough room ins fnl f tl swtchd rt and styd on wl towards fin* **10/3**2

5330 **4** *3/4* **Ventura Quest (USA)**20 7106 3-9-4 84 PaulHanagan 4 88
(Richard Fahey) *in tch in midfield: rdn over 2f out: pressing ldrs over 1f out: styd on same pce ins fnl f* **5/2**1

500 **5** *3/4* **Thecornishcowboy**58 6036 5-9-0 80 (t) JoeDoyle(5) 8 83
(John Ryan) *hld up wl in tch in midfield: rdn over 2f out: chsng ldrs and n.m.r ins fnl f: styd on same pce fnl 100yds* **25/1**

1451 **6** *1 3/4* **No Win No Fee**17 7172 4-9-1 81 AlistairRawlinson(5) 1 80
(Michael Appleby) *w ldr: rdn over 2f out: no ex jst ins fnl f: wknd fnl 100yds* **7/2**3

1330 **7** *4 1/2* **Excellent Puck (IRE)**30 6870 4-9-3 78 (b1) LukeMorris 10 69
(Shaun Lycett) *racd along on stands' rail: chsd ldrs: rdn over 2f out: drvn and btn over 1f out: wl hld and eased wl ins fnl f* **8/1**

1500 **8** *9* **Chain Of Events**20 7125 7-9-6 81 JimCrowley 3 55
(Michael Wigham) *hld up in tch in midfield: rdn 3f out: sn struggling u.p: wl bhd 1f out* **10/1**

2m 7.82s (2.02) **Going Correction** +0.375s/f (Good)
**WFA** 3 from 4yo+ 5lb **8** Ran SP% **111.8**
Speed ratings (Par 105): **106,105,105,105,104 103,99,92**
CSF £191.99 CT £831.85 TOTE £21.60: £3.70, £3.00, £1.40; EX 173.20 Trifecta £1219.70 Part won..
**Owner** J P Carrington **Bred** Alan Dargan **Trained** Ogbourne Maisey, Wilts

**FOCUS**
They finished in a bit of a heap. Ordinary form at best, with the first three rated to their best.

## 7563 IRISH STALLION FARMS "BOSRA SHAM" EBF FILLIES' STKS (LISTED RACE) 6f
**2:00** (2:02) (Class 1) 2-Y-O
**£17,013** (£6,450; £3,228; £1,608; £807; £405) **Stalls** Low

Form RPR
14 **1** **Terror (IRE)**34 6751 2-9-0 0 JimCrowley 1 98+
(David Simcock) *led for 1f: trckd ldr after: upsides and gng best 2f out: shkn up to ld ins fnl f: easily* **1/5**1

31 **2** *1 1/2* **Fligaz (FR)**19 7130 2-9-0 75 FergusSweeney 5 87
(Martyn Meade) *dwlt: t.k.h and hdwy to ld after 1f: rdn wl over 1f out: drvn 1f out: hdd ins fnl f: sn btn and one pce* **7/1**2

333 **3** *3/4* **Expensive Date**14 7255 2-9-0 85 LukeMorris 4 85
(Paul Cole) *broke wl: sn restrained and std ldng pair: rdn 2f out: drvn and outpcd ent fnl f: no ch w wnr but kpt on again towards fin* **25/1**

0 **4** *3 3/4* **Haalan**70 5644 2-9-0 0 SilvestreDeSousa 2 74
(Clive Brittain) *s.i.s: bhd: rdn over 3f out: struggling u.p over 2f out: no ch w wnr but styd on past btn horses ins fnl f* **50/1**

6 **5** *1 1/4* **Avenue Montaigne (IRE)**69 5701 2-9-0 0 AdamKirby 3 70
(John Joseph Murphy, Ire) *in tch: rdn 2f out: drvn and outpcd over 1f out: wknd fnl f* **8/1**3

2100 **6** *2 3/4* **Tongue Twista**34 6751 2-9-0 85 JFEgan 6 62
(Nick Littmoden) *in tch: rdn over 2f out: struggling u.p wl over 1f out: wknd fnl f* **33/1**

1m 14.08s (1.88) **Going Correction** +0.375s/f (Good) **6** Ran SP% **115.7**
Speed ratings: **102,100,99,94,92 88**
CSF £2.45 TOTE £1.20: £1.10, £1.90; EX 2.10 Trifecta £18.00.
**Owner** Qatar Racing Limited **Bred** Tally-Ho Stud **Trained** Newmarket, Suffolk

**FOCUS**
This proved straightforward for the odds-on favourite. The winner was in a different league and won with lots in hand. It's been rated around the third.

## 7564 THAI STREET CAFE & CROWN ROOMS NEWMARKET CONDITIONS STKS (BOBIS RACE) 6f
**2:35** (2:35) (Class 3) 2-3-Y-O
**£7,470** (£2,236; £1,118; £559; £279; £140) **Stalls** Low

Form RPR
5122 **1** **Red Pike (IRE)**7 7408 3-9-13 92 PaulMulrennan 6 96
(Bryan Smart) *chsd ldrs: pushed along 1/2-way: hdwy u.p to ld ent fnl f: styd on: rdn out* **5/6**1

025 **2** *1 1/4* **Diamond Lady**30 6872 3-9-5 79 RobertTart 5 84
(William Stone) *in tch: effrt over 2f out: hdwy u.p to chse wnr 1f out: styd on same pce fnl 100yds* **12/1**

441 **3** *2* **Apache Storm**16 7192 2-8-0 79 CamHardie(3) 4 76
(Michael Appleby) *sn led: rdn 2f out: hdd ent fnl f: wknd fnl 100yds* **3/1**2

11-0 **4** *1 1/2* **Evening Attire**51 6234 3-9-13 90 JoeFanning 2 81
(William Stone) *in tch: lost pl and pushed along 2f out: no ch w ldrs but styd on past btn horses ins fnl f* **33/1**

34-0 **5** *1/2* **Boom The Groom (IRE)**28 6893 3-9-13 88 AdamKirby 3 79
(Tony Carroll) *w ldr: rdn and ev ch 2f out tl ent fnl f: wknd ins fnl f* **33/1**

6121 **6** *2 1/4* **Fiftyshadesofgrey (IRE)**8 7403 3-9-13 79 PatCosgrave 1 72
(George Baker) *s.i.s: bhd: effrt 2f out: drvn and no hdwy over 1f out: wknd ins fnl f* **5/1**3

1m 13.64s (1.44) **Going Correction** +0.375s/f (Good) **6** Ran SP% **109.8**
Speed ratings: **105,103,100,98,98 95**
CSF £11.82 TOTE £1.60: £1.10, £4.60; EX 9.00 Trifecta £27.50.
**Owner** Sir A Ferguson, P Deal & G Lowe **Bred** Mrs M Marnane **Trained** Hambleton, N Yorks

**FOCUS**
Nine of the previous ten winners, including the last eight, had been 2yos, but Apache Storm couldn't take advantage of the weight concession this time and the streak was broken. The winner was the form pick and didn't need to quite match his best to score. The third has been rated close to her AW win.

## 7565 EBF STALLIONS MOBILE PIMM'S BARS FILLIES' H'CAP 1m 4f
**3:10** (3:11) (Class 3) (0-90,86) 3-Y-O+
**£8,092** (£2,423; £1,211; £605; £302; £152) **Stalls** Low

Form RPR
4234 **1** **Headline News (IRE)**12 7305 5-9-5 84 JackGarritty(5) 13 94
(Rae Guest) *dropped in bhd after s: hld up in rr: smooth hdwy 3f out: led 2f out: rdn and kicked clr over 1f out: kpt up to work and a doing enough fnl f* **4/1**2

4006 **2** *1/2* **Bantam (IRE)**20 7110 4-9-10 84 GrahamLee 5 93
(Ed Dunlop) *wl in tch in midfield: effrt to chse wnr wl over 1f out: kpt on u.p ins fnl f* **10/1**

0345 **3** *2* **Perfect Summer (IRE)**14 7235 4-9-2 79 CamHardie(3) 8 85
(Lady Cecil) *t.k.h: hld up in last quartet: rdn and hdwy 3f out: 4th and drvn over 1f out: kpt on to go 3rd cl home* **20/1**

4330 **4** *1/2* **Rosehill Artist (IRE)**34 6746 3-9-5 86 SilvestreDeSousa 11 91
(Charles Hills) *t.k.h: hld up in tch in midfield: rdn 3f out: hdwy to join ldrs 2f out: 3rd and outpcd over 1f out: kpt on same pce after: lost 3rd cl home* **12/1**

5000 **5** *7* **Toptempo**13 7281 5-8-12 72 oh3 TedDurcan 4 66
(Mark H Tompkins) *hld up in last quartet: rdn over 3f out: hdwy into modest 6th over 1f out: plugged but no ch w ldrs* **33/1**

-166 **6** *3 3/4* **Asia Minor (IRE)**37 6664 5-9-0 74 (t) RobertTart 2 62
(Dr Jon Scargill) *stdd s: hld up in rr: rdn and hdwy 3f out: 5th and no imp over 1f out: wknd fnl f* **33/1**

316 **7** *10* **Clear Mind**23 7033 3-9-0 81 RobertHavlin 12 53
(John Gosden) *in tch in midfield: rdn and struggling over 2f out: wknd wl over 1f out* **15/2**3

3005 **8** *1/2* **Duchess Of Gazeley (IRE)**180 1981 4-9-9 83 SebSanders 6 54
(Dean Ivory) *chsd ldrs: wnt 2nd 3f out tl over 2f out: sn lost pl u.p: wknd over 1f out* **12/1**

5505 **9** *4 1/2* **Boonga Roogeta**9 7384 5-9-8 85 RosieJessop(3) 1 49
(Peter Charalambous) *led tl hdd and rdn 3f out: lost pl over 2f out: wknd wl over 1f out* **33/1**

0012 **10** *nk* **Dame Lucy (IRE)**7 7416 4-9-3 80 RyanTate(3) 10 44
(Michael Appleby) *chsd ldr: led 3f out tl rdn and hdd jst over 2f out: sn btn and wknd* **9/4**1

0006 **11** *3 1/4* **Zamra (IRE)**4 7500 3-8-0 72 oh2 JoeDoyle(5) 7 30
(Brian Ellison) *in tch in midfield: rdn over 3f out: sn struggling: wknd 2f out: t.o* **33/1**

5114 **12** *2* **Leaderene**33 6794 3-8-11 78 JoeFanning 9 33
(Mark Johnston) *chsd ldrs: rdn and no rspnse over 3f out: lost pl and bhd 2f out: t.o* **17/2**

2160 **13** *18* **Spiritoftheunion**41 6559 3-8-7 77 LouisSteward(3) 3 3
(Michael Bell) *wl in tch in midfield: losing pl and rdn over 4f out: bhd and lost tch over 2f out: t.o* **22/1**

2m 35.6s (3.60) **Going Correction** +0.375s/f (Good)
**WFA** 3 from 4yo+ 7lb **13** Ran SP% **118.4**
Speed ratings (Par 104): **103,102,101,101,96 93,87,86,83,83 81,80,68**
CSF £39.00 CT £700.40 TOTE £5.20: £1.80, £3.70, £3.90; EX 54.90 Trifecta £814.70.
**Owner** Chestnuts **Bred** Airlie Stud **Trained** Newmarket, Suffolk

**FOCUS**
A fairly open fillies' handicap. The winner's penultimate C&D run had been franked by the winner and second since and she's been rated to a similar level to that effort. The third and fourth have been rated close to their marks.

## 7566 ROUTEMASTER BUS BAR AND SHARDLOW BREWING H'CAP — 2m
**3:45** (3:47) (Class 3) (0-90,88) 3-Y-0+ **£7,762** (£2,310; £1,154; £577) **Stalls** Low

Form — RPR

2422 **1** **Rite To Reign**[14] 7235 3-8-12 82 ............ SilvestreDeSousa 2 91
(Philip McBride) *in tch in midfield: hdwy 4f out: rdn to chse ldr over 1f out: led ins fnl f: styd on: rdn out* **11/4**[1]

2400 **2** *3/4* **Sohar**[20] 7107 6-10-0 88 ............ JoeFanning 4 97
(James Toller) *stdd s: hld up in rr: hdwy 5f out: rdn to chse ldrs over 1f out: swtchd lft 1f out: chsd wnr wl ins fnl f: kpt on* **11/2**[2]

4616 **3** *1 1/4* **Snowy Dawn**[28] 6896 4-9-1 75 ............ GrahamLee 12 82
(Ben Case) *led: rdn over 2f out: drvn over 1f out: hdd and one pce ins fnl f* **16/1**

3430 **4** *2 1/4* **Our Folly**[19] 7129 6-8-11 71 ............(b) PatCosgrave 13 75
(Stuart Kittow) *hld up towards rr: hdwy 5f out: chsd ldrs and rdn 2f out: no ex 1f out: wknd ins fnl f* **33/1**

364 **5** *6* **Kleitomachos (IRE)**[20] 5924 6-9-1 75 ............ JimCrowley 8 72
(Stuart Kittow) *hld up in midfield: effrt 3f out: 6th and no imp u.p over 1f out* **12/1**

51-5 **6** *nk* **Cool Sky**[34] 4940 5-9-7 81 ............ StevieDonohoe 1 78
(Ian Williams) *chsd ldrs: wnt 2nd over 2f out tl over 1f out: wknd ins fnl f* **16/1**

2601 **7** *5* **Precision Strike**[14] 7235 4-9-3 77 ............(v) RobertHavlin 10 68
(Richard Guest) *stdd s: hld up in rr: hdwy over 3f out: rdn and no hdwy 2f out: wknd over 1f out* **20/1**

6216 **8** *5* **Entihaa**[41] 6557 6-9-8 82 ............ BenCurtis 3 67
(Alan Swinbank) *chsd ldrs: rdn 3f out: no ex and btn 2f out: wknd over 1f out* **14/1**

2-01 **9** *7* **Deficit (IRE)**[65] 5825 4-8-13 80 ............ MikeyEnnis(7) 6 56
(Steve Gollings) *chsd ldrs: wnt 2nd 1/2-way tl over 2f out: sn btn: wknd over 1f out* **14/1**

054 **10** *2* **Caledonia**[20] 7124 7-8-6 71 ............ JordanNason(5) 7 45
(Jim Goldie) *stdd s: hld up in rr: rdn 4f out: sn struggling: bhd fnl 2f* **8/1**

3242 **11** *hd* **Arcamante (ITY)**[17] 7177 3-8-0 73 ............ JoeyHaynes(3) 5 47
(K R Burke) *chsd ldrs tl lost pl u.p 3f out: sn wl btn: wknd wl over 1f out* **10/1**

21-3 **12** *18* **Mister Pagan**[20] 7124 6-9-7 81 ............ PaulMulrennan 9 33
(Keith Dalgleish) *chsd ldrs: rdn and lost pl 5f out: bhd and lost tch 2f out: t.o: lame* **7/1**[3]

/31- **13** *46* **Harry Hunt**[199] 7217 7-9-11 85 ............ AdamKirby 11
(Graeme McPherson) *chsd ldr tl 1/2-way: steadily lost pl: bhd and eased 2f out: t.o* **25/1**

3m 31.46s (0.96) **Going Correction** +0.375s/f (Good)
**WFA** 3 from 4yo+ 10lb — **13 Ran SP% 119.1**
Speed ratings (Par 107): **112,111,111,109,106 106,104,101,98,97 97,88,65**
CSF £15.96 CT £207.88 TOTE £3.50: £1.30, £2.30, £3.20; EX 17.20 Trifecta £306.20.
**Owner** Maelor Racing **Bred** Oscar Stud **Trained** Newmarket, Suffolk

**FOCUS**
A fair test at the trip. The winner continues to progress, while the runner-up is on a fair mark and has been rated to form.

## 7567 EXPRESS COFFEE CARS & WARRENS OF WARWICK H'CAP — 1m
**4:15** (4:18) (Class 4) (0-85,85) 3-Y-0+ **£5,175** (£1,540; £769; £384) **Stalls** Low

Form — RPR

1640 **1** **Eurystheus (IRE)**[35] 6713 5-8-10 79 ............(p) AlistairRawlinson(5) 12 93
(Michael Appleby) *dwlt: sn rcvrd to chse ldrs: wnt 2nd after 2f: led over 2f out: rdn and kicked clr wl over 1f out: in n.d after: rdn out* **9/4**[1]

5521 **2** *5* **Duelling Dragon (USA)**[83] 5195 3-8-8 75 ............ PatCosgrave 3 77
(Stuart Kittow) *in tch in midfield: effrt over 2f out: drvn and chsd clr wnr over 1f out: kpt on but no imp* **12/1**

4051 **3** *1/2* **Eastern Dragon (IRE)**[15] 7220 4-8-13 77 ........ WilliamTwiston-Davies 1 78
(Michael Scudamore) *swtchd lft and dropped in bhd after s: hdwy 3f out: drvn and battling for placings over 1f out: no imp on wnr: wnt 3rd ins fnl f* **7/1**[2]

524 **4** *3/4* **World Record (IRE)**[39] 6615 4-8-4 71 oh1 ............ CamHardie(3) 10 71
(Mick Quinn) *racd keenly: led tl over 2f out: rdn and outpcd by wnr wl over 1f out: kpt on same pce after* **20/1**

4025 **5** *1 1/4* **Dark Ocean (IRE)**[24] 7012 4-8-8 72 ............ PJMcDonald 4 69
(Jedd O'Keeffe) *t.k.h: hld up in tch: effrt u.p and swtchd lft wl over 1f out: no ch w wnr but kpt on ins fnl f* **14/1**

2/30 **6** *2* **Jamhoori**[65] 5824 6-9-7 85 ............(p) AdamKirby 7 77
(Jeremy Gask) *s.i.s: in rr: rdn 3f out: hdwy u.p past btn horses over 1f out: nvr trbld ldrs* **50/1**

1416 **7** *2 1/4* **Special Miss**[44] 6459 3-8-6 73 ............ JoeFanning 8 59
(Ali Stronge) *in tch in midfield: rdn and lost pl over 2f out: no ch but kpt on past btn horses ins fnl f* **10/1**

0402 **8** *2* **Ocean Applause**[30] 6870 4-8-9 78 ............(t) JoeDoyle(5) 2 60
(John Ryan) *t.k.h early: hld up in tch in midfield: effrt u.p over 2f out: no real hdwy: wknd over 1f out* **8/1**[3]

6034 **9** *2 3/4* **Patriotic (IRE)**[11] 7339 6-8-7 71 oh1 ............(p) SilvestreDeSousa 11 47
(Chris Dwyer) *in tch: rdn 3f out: drvn and no hdwy 2f out: wknd over 1f out* **8/1**[3]

0600 **10** *3/4* **Another For Joe**[31] 6836 6-8-6 75 ............ JordanNason(5) 5 49
(Jim Goldie) *stdd after s: hld up in tch towards rr: rdn and no hdwy whn sltly hmpd wl over 1f out: n.d after* **16/1**

1200 **11** *1/2* **Wordismybond**[16] 7205 5-8-9 73 ............ SteveDrowne 9 46
(Peter Makin) *chsd ldr for 2f: chsd ldrs tl lost pl 2f out: no ex and sn btn: wknd fnl f* **20/1**

4622 **12** *nk* **Sweet Martoni**[18] 7160 4-8-12 76 ............ JimCrowley 6 48
(William Knight) *in tch in midfield: chsd ldrs and rdn over 2f out: lost pl and squeezed for room over 1f out: wknd fnl f* **7/1**[2]

1m 41.18s (2.58) **Going Correction** +0.375s/f (Good)
**WFA** 3 from 4yo+ 3lb — **12 Ran SP% 118.8**
Speed ratings (Par 105): **102,97,96,95,94 92,90,88,85,84 84,83**
CSF £30.43 CT £171.29 TOTE £3.20: £1.20, £3.00, £2.60; EX 30.60 Trifecta £151.20.
**Owner** Midest Partnership **Bred** Calley House Uk **Trained** Danethorpe, Notts

**FOCUS**
There was a gamble landed here. The winner, who was well backed, has been rated as running a career-best.
T/Plt: £193.30 to a £1 stake. Pool: £60,181.45 - 227.18 winning tickets T/Qpdt: £18.40 to a £1 stake. Pool: £5,137.78 - 206.07 winning tickets SP

# 7519 WOLVERHAMPTON (A.W) (L-H)
Friday, October 31

**OFFICIAL GOING: Tapeta: standard**
Wind: Fresh behind Weather: Overcast

## 7568 LADBROKES H'CAP (TAPETA) (DIV I) — 1m 141y
**4:25** (4:27) (Class 5) (0-70,76) 3-Y-0+ **£2,911** (£866; £432; £216) **Stalls** Low

Form — RPR

4022 **1** **Tayma (IRE)**[6] 7459 3-8-8 **63** ............ KevinStott(5) 3 75
(Saeed bin Suroor) *a.p: chsd ldr over 6f out: led over 2f out: rdn and flashed tail over 1f out: styd on wl* **2/1**[1]

1006 **2** *2* **Gambino (IRE)**[23] 7042 4-9-2 **65** ............ ConnorBeasley(3) 6 72
(John David Riches) *s.s: hld up: hdwy over 1f out: r.o to go 2nd post: nt rch wnr* **12/1**

5315 **3** *hd* **Glennten**[10] 7358 5-9-2 **69** ............ KieranShoemark(7) 7 76
(Jose Santos) *a.p: rdn to chse wnr over 1f out: styd on* **11/2**[2]

0041 **4** *1* **Zaeem**[17] 7187 5-9-4 **64** ............(p) RobertWinston 10 68
(Dean Ivory) *hld up: hdwy over 1f out: nt trble ldrs* **9/1**[3]

0012 **5** *hd* **Set The Trend**[2] 7533 8-9-11 **76** 6ex ............(p) GeorgeDowning(5) 9 80
(David Dennis) *hld up: swtchd rt over 3f out: hdwy on outer 2f out: sn rdn: r.o: nt rch ldrs* **2/1**[1]

4501 **6** *3* **Toto Skyllachy**[37] 6670 9-9-5 **68** ............ JacobButterfield(3) 4 65
(Marjorie Fife) *prom: rdn over 2f out: wknd ins fnl f* **20/1**

0045 **7** *1* **Mysterial**[81] 5244 4-8-13 **62** ............ NeilFarley(3) 8 57
(Declan Carroll) *led: racd keenly: rdn and hdd over 2f out: wknd ins fnl f* **50/1**

0-20 **8** *1/2* **Tahaf (IRE)**[23] 7042 4-9-8 **68** ............(tp) GeorgeBaker 2 61
(Mark Brisbourne) *chsd ldr tl over 6f out: remained handy: rdn over 1f out: wknd ins fnl f* **20/1**

005 **9** *shd* **Steel Stockholder**[17] 7180 8-9-2 **62** ............ DavidAllan 1 55
(Mel Brittain) *prom: racd keenly: rdn over 2f out: wknd over 1f out* **33/1**

1m 49.72s (-0.38) **Going Correction** +0.025s/f (Slow)
**WFA** 3 from 4yo+ 4lb — **9 Ran SP% 114.2**
Speed ratings (Par 103): **102,100,100,99,98 96,95,94,94**
CSF £27.38 CT £114.95 TOTE £1.60: £1.02, £4.80, £2.60; EX 34.40 Trifecta £217.50.
**Owner** Godolphin **Bred** Darley **Trained** Newmarket, Suffolk

**FOCUS**
They went a steady pace and the hold-up performers were never dangerous but the winner powered clear. The runner-up has been rated close to his best.

## 7569 LADBROKES H'CAP (TAPETA) (DIV II) — 1m 141y
**4:55** (4:57) (Class 5) (0-70,71) 3-Y-0+ **£2,911** (£866; £432; £216) **Stalls** Low

Form — RPR

0001 **1** **Naoise (IRE)**[7] 7427 6-9-9 71 6ex ............(t) JacobButterfield(3) 4 83+
(Ollie Pears) *hld up in tch: a gng wl: led on bit 1f out: r.o: readily* **11/4**[2]

0/06 **2** *1 1/4* **Cherry Street**[10] 7359 5-9-10 69 ............(p) LiamKeniry 3 73
(Denis Quinn) *chsd ldr tl led over 2f out: rdn and hdd 1f out: styd on same pce* **33/1**

26-0 **3** *1/2* **Flicksta (USA)**[21] 7071 3-9-4 67 ............ JackMitchell 5 70
(John Ryan) *awkward leaving stalls: hld up: hdwy and nt clr run 2f out: rdn ins fnl f: styd on same pce* **12/1**

1452 **4** *3/4* **Pim Street (USA)**[3] 7522 4-8-10 62 ............ JoshDoyle(7) 7 63
(David O'Meara) *hld up: hdwy over 1f out: rdn and swtchd lft ins fnl f: nt rch ldrs* **7/2**[3]

2103 **5** *nk* **Reggie Bond**[76] 5415 4-9-9 68 ............(b) CharlesBishop 9 69
(Geoffrey Oldroyd) *s.i.s: hld up: nt clr run 2f out: hdwy sn after: rdn and no ex ins fnl f* **9/4**[1]

260 **6** *10* **Mister Marcasite**[76] 5415 4-9-5 64 ............ DavidAllan 1 42
(Mel Brittain) *prom: rdn over 2f out: wknd over 1f out* **40/1**

0-20 **7** *1/2* **Venutius**[30] 6865 7-9-10 69 ............ GrahamGibbons 2 45
(Ed McMahon) *led: rdn and hdd over 2f out: wknd over 1f out* **25/1**

6603 **8** *9* **Harry Bosch**[39] 6617 4-9-1 67 ............(b) Keely-JoPhillips(7) 8 23
(Gay Kelleway) *chsd ldrs: racd on outer: pushed along over 2f out: wknd over 1f out* **14/1**

1m 50.42s (0.32) **Going Correction** +0.025s/f (Slow)
**WFA** 3 from 4yo+ 4lb — **8 Ran SP% 103.2**
Speed ratings (Par 103): **99,97,97,96,96 87,87,79**
CSF £72.82 CT £685.14 TOTE £3.60: £1.70, £5.80, £3.10; EX 59.20 Trifecta £424.50.
**Owner** Terence Elsey **Bred** J S Bolger **Trained** Norton, N Yorks
■ Boogangoo was withdrawn. Price at time of withdrawal 8/1. Rule 4 applies to all bets - deduction 10p in the pound.

**FOCUS**
They went a stop-start gallop but one before the market leaders scored with plenty in hand. Muddling form, with the runner-up rated as running his best race since his return.

## 7570 CORAL H'CAP (TAPETA) — 1m 1f 103y
**5:25** (5:25) (Class 6) (0-60,60) 3-Y-0 **£2,264** (£673; £336; £168) **Stalls** Low

Form — RPR

2442 **1** **Mary Le Bow**[45] 6426 3-8-13 59 ............(p) KieranShoemark(7) 11 71+
(Victor Dartnall) *hld up: hdwy over 3f out: led over 1f out: sn clr: idled ins fnl f: jst hld on* **3/1**[1]

6063 **2** *nse* **Crown Pleasure (IRE)**[17] 7187 3-9-1 57 ............ DannyBrock(3) 8 66
(Willie Musson) *hld up: hdwy over 1f out: sn rdn: edgd rt ins fnl f: r.o* **9/2**[2]

1300 **3** *1/2* **Sooqaan**[63] 5891 3-9-6 59 ............ DavidAllan 9 67
(Mel Brittain) *chsd ldrs: rdn over 1f out: r.o* **25/1**

0436 **4** *6* **Vied (USA)**[55] 6160 3-8-13 52 ............(v[1]) GrahamGibbons 13 47
(David O'Meara) *chsd ldrs: rn wd 7f out: shkn up to ld over 2f out: rdn and hdd over 1f out: wknd ins fnl f* **16/1**

6000 **5** *1 3/4* **Tohaveandtohold**[138] 3281 3-9-0 53 ............(p) PaulHanagan 10 45
(William Haggas) *hld up: hdwy u.p over 1f out: edgd lft and no ex fnl f* **8/1**

5044 **6** *2 3/4* **Miguela McGuire**[34] 6738 3-9-0 53 ............ PatrickMathers 3 39
(Eric Alston) *s.i.s: plld hrd and sn trcking ldrs: rdn and edgd lft over 2f out: wknd fnl f* **33/1**

4356 **7** *3* **Silken Waters**[9] 7369 3-8-13 52 ............(p) RobertWinston 5 32
(Eve Johnson Houghton) *w ldr tl led 3f out: sn rdn and hdd: wknd fnl f* **15/2**[3]

005 **8** *3/4* **Keeper's Ring (USA)**[43] 6483 3-9-7 60 ............ FrederikTylicki 4 38
(Roger Varian) *prom: rdn over 3f out: wknd over 2f out* **9/2**[2]

0004 **9** *3/4* **Tableforten**[41] 6568 3-9-6 59 ............(p) LiamJones 12 35
(J S Moore) *s.i.s: hld up: nvr on terms* **33/1**

2015 **10** *hd* **Suni Dancer**[51] 6227 3-9-0 53 ............ RaulDaSilva 7 29
(Paul Green) *hld up: hdwy on outer 3f out: sn rdn: wknd 2f out* **22/1**


The Form Book, Raceform Ltd, Newbury, RG14 5SJ

0006 **11** *2* **Llyrical**[13] 7291 3-9-3 56........................................[1] LiamKeniry 1 28
(Derek Haydn Jones) *mid-div: plld hrd: hmpd 7f out: rdn and wknd wl over 1f out* **28/1**

2432 **12** *8* **Her Red Devil (IRE)**[15] 7225 3-9-1 59........................ JackDuern(5) 2 14
(Christopher Kellett) *led: rdn and hdd 3f out: hmpd over 2f out: sn wknd* **16/1**

2m 1.67s (0.87) **Going Correction** +0.025s/f (Slow) **12** Ran SP% **113.5**
Speed ratings (Par 99): **97,96,96,91,89 87,84,83,83,83 81,74**
CSF £13.95 CT £272.77 TOTE £4.00: £1.60, £2.40, £7.60; EX 20.40 Trifecta £456.30.
**Owner** Mrs J Scrivens **Bred** Mr & Mrs A E Pakenham **Trained** Brayford, Devon

**FOCUS**
There was an exciting finish in this low-grade handicap. The winner got off the mark on her 15th attempt and the first three pulled a long way clear. The runner-up has been rated as building slightly on her latest effort.

## 7571 £20 RISK-FREE BET AT UNIBET NURSERY H'CAP (BOBIS RACE) (TAPETA) 5f 20y
**5:55** (5:55) (Class 2) 2-Y-O **£9,056** (£2,695; £1,346; £673) **Stalls** Low

Form RPR

0231 **1** **Billyoakes (IRE)**[7] 7415 2-8-10 79 6ex........................ CharlesBishop 1 84
(Mick Channon) *hld up: shkn up and nt clr run over 1f out: sn rdn: qcknd to ld wl ins fnl f: sn clr* **7/1**

4022 **2** *1 3/4* **Lightscameraction (IRE)**[20] 7099 2-9-2 90.................. JackDuern(5) 5 89
(Gay Kelleway) *hld up: plld hrd: hung rt 1/2-way: hdwy over 1f out: rdn to ld wl ins fnl f: sn edgd lft and hdd: styd on same pce* **11/4**[2]

2110 **3** *1 3/4* **Johnny B Goode (IRE)**[42] 6510 2-8-9 78.................... PaulHanagan 3 70
(Richard Fahey) *led: rdn over 1f out: hdd and unable qck wl ins fnl f* **4/1**[3]

4334 **4** *1* **Somedaysrdiamonds**[10] 7362 2-8-0 69 oh7................(p) JimmyQuinn 6 58
(J S Moore) *swtchd lft sn after s: plld hrd and sn w ldr: rdn and ev ch ins fnl f: no ex* **50/1**

1145 **5** *1 3/4* **Ar Colleen Aine**[10] 7362 2-8-0 69........................................ LukeMorris 4 52
(Mick Channon) *trckd ldrs: hmpd sn after s: rdn over 1f out: wknd ins fnl f* **16/1**

4312 **6** *1* **Koptoon**[16] 7201 2-9-0 83..........................................(tp) StephenCraine 2 62
(Tom Dascombe) *prom: hmpd sn after s: rdn over 1f out: wknd fnl f* **11/8**[1]

1m 2.08s (0.18) **Going Correction** +0.025s/f (Slow) **6** Ran SP% **109.1**
Speed ratings (Par 101): **99,96,93,91,89 87**
CSF £24.95 TOTE £5.70: £3.80, £1.50; EX 21.80 Trifecta £54.50.
**Owner** Nick & Olga Dhandsa & John & Zoe Webster **Bred** Mrs M Cusack **Trained** West Ilsley, Berks

■ Stewards' Enquiry : Paul Hanagan two-day ban: careless riding (14-15 Nov)
Jack Duern five-month ban (of which seven weeks will be deferred for three months): had committed four whip breaches warranting a suspension of seven days of more since 15 June 2014

**FOCUS**
They went a steady pace but the winner forged clear under a hold-up ride. The winner has been rated better than ever.

## 7572 32RED ON THE APP STORE H'CAP (TAPETA) 2m 119y
**6:25** (6:25) (Class 6) (0-60,59) 3-Y-O+ **£2,264** (£673; £336; £168) **Stalls** Low

Form RPR

0223 **1** **Dark Days**[15] 7229 3-9-2 57..........................................(t) LukeMorris 6 72+
(Paul Cole) *chsd ldrs: wnt 2nd over 3f out: led over 2f out: drvn clr and edgd lft fr over 1f out: eased wl ins fnl f* **11/10**[1]

6033 **2** *7* **Yorkshireman (IRE)**[13] 7287 4-9-4 49........................(b) PaddyAspell 3 54
(Lynn Siddall) *chsd ldr tl led 5f out: rdn and hdd over 2f out: sn outpcd* **8/1**[3]

-605 **3** *nse* **Weybridge Light**[31] 6117 9-9-1 46..............................(b) JimmyQuinn 8 51
(David Thompson) *hld up: hdwy 3f out: hmpd 2f out: styd on same pce* **20/1**

1563 **4** *6* **Annaluna (IRE)**[22] 7065 5-10-0 59.................................(v) JFEgan 5 57
(David Evans) *prom: rdn over 2f out: wknd over 1f out* **9/2**[2]

40-3 **5** *4 1/2* **Iguacu**[8] 5748 10-9-0 45........................................ CharlesBishop 2 37
(Richard Price) *hld up: rdn and wknd over 2f out* **22/1**

0064 **6** *13* **Volcanic Jack (IRE)**[34] 5403 6-8-12 50.................... CiaranMckee(7) 4 27
(Michael Chapman) *hld up: rdn and wknd 3f out* **40/1**

5425 **7** *3/4* **Black Iceman**[13] 7287 6-9-6 51........................................ JackMitchell 1 27
(Lydia Pearce) *chsd ldrs: rdn over 3f out: wknd over 2f out* **8/1**[3]

300 **8** *33* **Vertueux (FR)**[23] 6768 9-9-3 48....................................(p) LiamKeniry 7
(Tony Carroll) *led: hdd 5f out: rdn and wknd over 3f out* **8/1**[3]

3m 40.82s (-2.88) **Going Correction** +0.025s/f (Slow)
**WFA** 3 from 4yo+ 10lb **8** Ran SP% **110.7**
Speed ratings (Par 101): **107,103,103,100,98 92,92,76**
CSF £9.64 CT £102.42 TOTE £1.60: £1.10, £2.00, £4.30; EX 9.10 Trifecta £166.40.
**Owner** Mrs E A Bass **Bred** Mrs E A Bass **Trained** Whatcombe, Oxon

**FOCUS**
The favourite hammered his rivals in this staying handicap. The runner-up has been rated to his C&D latest.

## 7573 32RED CASINO MEDIAN AUCTION MAIDEN STKS (TAPETA) 7f 32y
**6:55** (6:56) (Class 6) 2-Y-O **£2,264** (£673; £336; £168) **Stalls** High

Form RPR

0320 **1** **Goring (GER)**[27] 6925 2-9-5 77........................................ JohnFahy 10 75
(Eve Johnson Houghton) *chsd ldrs: shkn up over 1f out: rdn: edgd lft and r.o to ld wl ins fnl f: comf* **3/1**[3]

52 **2** *1 1/4* **Unnoticed**[21] 7076 2-9-5 0........................................ RobertWinston 11 72
(Ollie Pears) *hld up: hdwy over 2f out: rdn and ev ch ins fnl f: styd on same pce* **6/1**

04 **3** *hd* **Vivre La Reve**[17] 7181 2-9-0 0........................................ AdamBeschizza 9 66
(James Unett) *led: rdn over 1f out: hdd and unable qck wl ins fnl f* **50/1**

5 **4** *2* **Marmot**[49] 6293 2-9-5 0........................................ GeorgeBaker 3 67
(Roger Charlton) *hld up: hdwy 2f out: rdn over 1f out: styd on same pce ins fnl f* **5/2**[2]

0 **5** *1 1/4* **Rialto Magic**[15] 7228 2-8-9 0........................................ RachealKneller(5) 5 58
(Jamie Osborne) *hld up: nt clr run over 2f out: r.o ins fnl f: nvr nrr* **100/1**

24 **6** *nk* **Bleu Astral (FR)**[30] 6861 2-9-5 0........................................ PaulHanagan 4 63
(Richard Fahey) *hung lft sn after s: chsd ldr: rdn over 1f out: hung lft and no ex ins fnl f* **7/4**[1]

0 **7** *4 1/2* **Minnie (IRE)**[34] 6735 2-9-0 0........................................ StevieDonohoe 7 47
(Johnny Farrelly) *plld hrd and prom: rdn over 1f out: wknd fnl f* **33/1**

60 **8** *1 3/4* **Night Generation (GER)**[21] 7076 2-9-5 0........................................ LukeMorris 6 47
(Sir Mark Prescott Bt) *hld up: shkn up over 2f out: nvr nr to chal* **100/1**

**9** *5* **Dippinganddiving (IRE)**[100] 4554 2-9-0 0........................................ IrineuGoncalves 2 30
(Jose Santos) *hmpd sn after s: prom: rdn over 2f out: wknd over 1f out* **100/1**

0 **10** *6* **Bangers (IRE)**[21] 7076 2-9-5 0........................................ StephenCraine 1 20
(Tom Dascombe) *s.i.s: sn pushed along in rr: rdn and wknd over 2f out* **50/1**

1m 30.33s (1.53) **Going Correction** +0.025s/f (Slow) **10** Ran SP% **114.1**
Speed ratings (Par 93): **92,90,90,88,86 86,81,79,73,66**
CSF £19.98 TOTE £3.60: £1.40, £2.10, £4.90; EX 21.70 Trifecta £398.10.
**Owner** G C Stevens **Bred** Westminster Race Horses Gmbh **Trained** Blewbury, Oxon

**FOCUS**
The winner scored with some authority in this fair maiden. Straightforward form rated around the front pair.

## 7574 32RED NOVICE STKS (TAPETA) 7f 32y
**7:25** (7:26) (Class 5) 2-Y-O **£6,469** (£1,925; £962; £481) **Stalls** High

Form RPR

01 **1** **Algaith (USA)**[23] 7030 2-9-7 0........................................ PaulHanagan 4 85+
(B W Hills) *mde all: racd keenly: shkn up over 1f out: rdn and edgd lft ins fnl f: r.o wl* **9/4**[2]

**2** *5* **Merhoob (IRE)** 2-9-0 0........................................ LukeMorris 1 68+
(Marco Botti) *s.i.s: hdwy and in tch over 5f out: chsd wnr over 1f out: sn rdn: no ex ins fnl f* **16/1**[3]

643 **3** *5* **Liberal Angel (FR)**[35] 6700 2-8-6 0........................................ JoeyHaynes(3) 3 49
(K R Burke) *chsd ldrs: wnt 2nd over 2f out tl rdn wl over 1f out: wknd fnl f* **50/1**

21 **4** *41* **Classic Collection**[16] 7200 2-9-7 0........................................ FrederikTylicki 2
(Saeed bin Suroor) *plld hrd: trckd wnr tl rdn 3f out: wknd 2f out: eased* **1/2**[1]

1m 29.08s (0.28) **Going Correction** +0.025s/f (Slow) **4** Ran SP% **105.3**
Speed ratings (Par 95): **99,93,87,40**
CSF £22.77 TOTE £2.90; EX 23.40 Trifecta £44.20.
**Owner** Hamdan Al Maktoum **Bred** Shadwell Farm LLC **Trained** Upper Lambourn, Berks

**FOCUS**
The hot favourite was very disappointing in this novice but the winner scored in good style and looks useful. The winner had a soft lead, while the favourite failed to run his race so the form is hard to quantify.

## 7575 32RED.COM FILLIES H'CAP (TAPETA) 7f 32y
**7:55** (7:55) (Class 5) (0-75,75) 3-Y-O+ **£3,234** (£962; £481; £240) **Stalls** High

Form RPR

063 **1** **Bint Dandy (IRE)**[30] 6863 3-8-10 **69**........................ ConnorBeasley(3) 5 81
(Chris Dwyer) *hld up in tch: rdn to chse ldr over 1f out: r.o to ld nr fin* **16/1**

1605 **2** *nk* **Zman Awal (IRE)**[28] 6902 3-9-3 **73**........................ FrederikTylicki 4 84
(James Fanshawe) *chsd ldrs: led 2f out: rdn and hdd nr fin* **7/4**[1]

3/30 **3** *2 3/4* **Don't Be**[99] 4593 4-8-12 **66**........................................ LukeMorris 12 71
(Sir Mark Prescott Bt) *s.i.s: hld up: hdwy 2f out: sn rdn: styd on: nt rch ldrs* **8/1**

1066 **4** *2* **The Dukkerer (IRE)**[4] 7494 3-8-12 **68**........................ JasonHart 7 67
(Garry Moss) *s.i.s: hld up: hdwy u.p over 1f out: nt rch ldrs* **7/1**[3]

3250 **5** *1 1/2* **Bint Malyana (IRE)**[24] 7023 3-8-11 **67**........................ JFEgan 8 62
(Paul D'Arcy) *heold up: hdwy 2f out: rdn over 1f out: no ex ins fnl f* **16/1**

0102 **6** *1* **Lil Sophella (IRE)**[7] 7427 5-8-2 **61** oh1........................ JackGarritty(5) 1 54
(Patrick Holmes) *hld up: hdwy over 1f out: wknd ins fnl f* **5/1**[2]

0030 **7** *1 1/4* **Zynah (IRE)**[17] 7185 3-8-9 **70**........................(p) KevinStott(5) 2 59
(Saeed bin Suroor) *hld up: rdn over 2f out: nvr on terms* **10/1**

2010 **8** *3/4* **Simply Shining (IRE)**[55] 6129 4-9-2 **75**........................ SammyJoBell(5) 9 63
(Richard Fahey) *chsd ldrs: hmpd over 2f out: wknd over 1f out* **16/1**

5500 **9** *1 3/4* **Milly's Secret (IRE)**[13] 7286 3-8-11 **67**........................ GrahamGibbons 3 50
(David O'Meara) *led: rdn and hdd 2f out: wknd fnl f* **22/1**

100 **10** *1 1/4* **Cool Music (IRE)**[74] 5496 4-9-4 **72**........................ DavidAllan 10 52
(Mel Brittain) *chsd ldr 6f out tl rdn and hung rt over 2f out: wknd over 1f out* **40/1**

165 **11** *1 1/2* **Byron's Gold**[53] 6189 3-8-13 **72**........................ RyanTate(3) 11 47
(Ben De Haan) *hld up: rdn and wknd over 1f out* **33/1**

2020 **12** *1 3/4* **Tweety Pie (IRE)**[30] 6873 3-8-10 **69**........................ NeilFarley(3) 6 40
(Declan Carroll) *plld hrd and prom: rdn and wknd over 1f out* **50/1**

1m 28.14s (-0.66) **Going Correction** +0.025s/f (Slow)
**WFA** 3 from 4yo+ 2lb **12** Ran SP% **115.1**
Speed ratings (Par 103): **104,103,100,98,96 95,93,93,91,89 87,85**
CSF £41.71 CT £252.47 TOTE £16.70: £4.00, £1.10, £2.70; EX 55.60 Trifecta £443.40.
**Owner** M M Foulger **Bred** Ballyhane Stud **Trained** Newmarket, Suffolk

**FOCUS**
The went a fair pace and first two pulled clear in this handicap. There are doubts over most of these but the form looks sound enough among the principals.
T/Jkpt: £7,958.40 to a £1 stake. Pool: £28,022.68 - 2.50 winning tickets T/Plt: £93.20 to a £1 stake. Pool: £96,397.03 - 754.44 winning tickets T/Qpdt: £13.00 to a £1 stake. Pool: £11,910.49 - 677.10 winning tickets CR

# 7428 DUNDALK (A.W) (L-H)
Friday, October 31

**OFFICIAL GOING: Polytrack: standard**

## 7579a IRISH STALLION FARMS EUROPEAN BREEDERS FUND COOLEY FILLIES STKS (LISTED RACE) 1m (P)
**7:10** (7:11) 3-Y-O+ **£27,083** (£7,916; £3,750; £1,250)

RPR

**1** **Pelerin (IRE)**[35] 6707 3-9-0 98........................(p) MartinHarley 6 107+
(Marco Botti) *racd in mid-div tl tk clsr order under 2f out: rdn to ld 1f out and sn pushed clr: styd on wl* **10/3**[1]

**2** *2 1/4* **Sea Coast (IRE)**[12] 7313 3-9-0 94........................[1] ShaneFoley 9 101
(M Halford, Ire) *hld up tl prog over 1f out to chse ldrs: styd on wl into 2nd clsng strides: nt trble wnr* **8/1**

**3** *hd* **Slipper Orchid (IRE)**[14] 7263 5-9-3 100........................(p) ConorHoban 7 102
(M Halford, Ire) *racd in mid-div tl prog to chse ldrs appr fnl f: kpt on wl into 2nd fnl 100yds: dropped to 3rd clsng strides* **11/2**[3]

**4** *1* **Some Spirit (IRE)**[26] 6963 3-9-0 104........................ ColinKeane 11 99
(G M Lyons, Ire) *hld up in rr tl prog appr fnl f: styd on wl into 4th clsng stages: nvr nrr* **5/1**[2]

**5** *1* **Fastnet Mist (IRE)**[12] 7313 3-9-0 96........................ ColmO'Donoghue 13 96
(David Wachman, Ire) *chsd ldrs in 3rd: rdn along in 2nd under 2f out: no imp ins fnl f and wknd fnl 100yds* **8/1**

**6** *2 1/2* **Stereo Love (FR)**[36] 6681 3-9-0 88........................ KevinManning 2 91
(Clive Cox) *racd in mid-div towards inner: prog over 1f out: sn no imp: kpt on one pce* **12/1**

7 *nk* **Beyond Brilliance (IRE)**[6] 7463 3-9-0 98 ................... MichaelHussey 4 90
(A P O'Brien, Ire) *hld up towards rr: rdn over 2f out: kpt on wl ins fnl f: nvr nrr* **16/1**

8 *1 1/4* **Shanooan (USA)**[14] 7265 3-9-0 93 ................................ RonanWhelan 14 87
(George Kent, Ire) *chsd ldrs: rdn along in 4th 2f out: sn no ex: wknd fnl f* **66/1**

9 *1 1/4* **Harpist (IRE)**[12] 7313 4-9-3 91 ..........................................(p) ConnorKing 3 85
(David Wachman, Ire) *racd in mid-div: pushed along 3f out: no imp under 2f out* **40/1**

10 *shd* **Adeste Fideles (USA)**[7] 7428 3-9-0 83 .................... SeamieHeffernan 1 84
(A P O'Brien, Ire) *trckd ldr in 2nd tl led 2f out: hdd 1f out and wknd qckly* **16/1**

11 *3/4* **Harry's Princess (IRE)**[12] 7313 3-9-0 97 ....................... NGMcCullagh 5 82
(John M Oxx, Ire) *chsd ldrs in 4th: rdn along 2f out: wknd appr fnl f* **16/1**

12 *3* **Elegant Peace (IRE)**[5] 7474 3-9-0 92 ...........................(b) ChrisHayes 12 75
(D K Weld, Ire) *a towards rr: no threat under 2f out* **33/1**

13 *2 1/2* **Maontri (IRE)**[14] 7263 7-9-3 94 ..........................................(p) RoryCleary 10 71
(M J Tynan, Ire) *led to 2f out: sn wknd* **25/1**

14 *2 3/4* **Stars So Bright (IRE)**[173] 2186 3-9-0 .................(t) DeclanMcDonogh 8 63
(John M Oxx, Ire) *a towards rr: no imp and dropped to rr under 2f out: eased* **10/1**

1m 35.13s (95.13)
**WFA** 3 from 4yo+ 3lb **14** Ran SP% **122.5**
CSF £29.67 TOTE £3.50: £1.10, £3.50, £1.80; DF 38.10 Trifecta £133.40.
**Owner** Newsells Park Stud **Bred** Rabbah Bloodstock Limited **Trained** Newmarket, Suffolk

**FOCUS**
A well spotted opportunity in the calendar for a winner coming back to her best and the way she won over this trip should open up more opportunities for her. The third to fifth set the standard.

7580 - 7589a (Foreign Racing) - See Raceform Interactive

# 6974 SANTA ANITA (L-H)

Friday, October 31

**OFFICIAL GOING: Dirt: fast; turf: firm**

## 7590a BREEDERS' CUP JUVENILE TURF (GRADE 1) (2YO COLTS & GELDINGS) (TURF) 1m (T)

**9:25** (12:00) 2-Y-O **£331,325** (£108,433; £60,240; £36,144; £18,072)

RPR

1 **Hootenanny (USA)**[68] 5741 2-8-10 0 ..........................(b) FrankieDettori 5 110+
(Wesley A Ward, U.S.A) *t.k.h early: chsd ldrs: effrt and drvn 2f out: edgd lft and led last 110yds: kpt on strly* **4/1**[2]

2 *3/4* **Luck Of The Kitten (USA)**[26] 2-8-10 0 ...............................(b) MESmith 3 108
(Wesley A Ward, U.S.A) *led: 3 l clr after 2f: rdn along 2f out: hdd last 110yds: kpt on same pce* **11/1**

3 *1 1/2* **Daddy D T (USA)**[34] 6780 2-8-10 0 ...................................... CNakatani 2 105
(John W Sadler, U.S.A) *prom: drvn along 2f out: kpt on u.p ins fnl f* **20/1**

4 *hd* **Conquest Typhoon (CAN)**[26] 2-8-10 0 .......................... PHusbands 6 104
(Mark Casse, Canada) *midfield on outside: rdn and sltly outpcd 2f out: kpt on ins fnl f* **14/1**

5 *nse* **Faithful Creek (IRE)**[48] 6348 2-8-10 0 ........................(b[1]) KierenFallon 15 104+
(Brian Meehan) *hld up on ins: rdn over 2f out: hdwy over 1f out: kpt on ins fnl f: nt pce to rch ldrs* **33/1**

6 *nse* **Lawn Ranger (USA)**[26] 2-8-10 0 ..................................... CLanderos 13 104
(Kenneth McPeek, U.S.A) *chsd ldr: effrt and drvn 2f out: blkd ins fnl f: outpcd last 100yds* **33/1**

7 *hd* **Commemorative**[20] 7104 2-8-10 0 ...................................... JamesDoyle 4 103
(Charles Hills) *hld up in tch: rdn over 2f out: effrt and angled rt over 1f out: kpt on same pce ins fnl f* **8/1**

8 *1/2* **Danny Boy (USA)**[26] 2-8-10 0 ........................................ JRLeparoux 14 102
(Dale Romans, U.S.A) *hld up in rr: effrt whn n.m.r over 1f out and ent fnl f: kpt on last 100yds: nrst fin* **25/1**

9 *nk* **International Star (USA)**[26] 2-8-10 0 ........................(b) JRVelazquez 12 102
(Michael J Maker, U.S.A) *hld up on outside: pushed along over 3f out: effrt on outside whn hung lft and bmpd over 1f out and ins fnl f: kpt on fin* **33/1**

10 *1/2* **Imperia (USA)**[33] 2-8-10 0 ............................................... JJCastellano 11 100
(Kiaran McLaughlin, U.S.A) *blkd sn after s: hld up towards rr: stdy hdwy on ins 3f out: effrt and rdn whn no room and hmpd over 1f out: repeatedly denied room ins fnl f: nt rcvr* **6/1**[3]

11 *nse* **Startup Nation (USA)**[33] 2-8-10 0 ..................................... JRosario 10 100
(Chad C Brown, U.S.A) *s.i.s: bhd: rdn and c wdst into home st: sme late hdwy: nvr on terms* **10/1**

12 *hd* **War Envoy (USA)**[26] 6968 2-8-10 0 ................................. RyanMoore 7 100
(A P O'Brien, Ire) *midfield: drvn and outpcd over 2f out: no imp whn nt clr run ins fnl f: eased whn hld last 100yds* **7/2**[1]

13 *3/4* **Offering Plan (USA)**[33] 2-8-10 0 ......................................... IOrtizJr 8 98
(Chad C Brown, U.S.A) *hld up towards rr: rdn and plenty to do whn bmpd appr fnl f: nvr able to chal* **33/1**

14 *1 1/4* **Wet Sail (USA)**[27] 6933 2-8-10 0 ................................... JamieSpencer 1 95
(Charlie Fellowes) *in tch on ins: effrt and drvn 2f out: wknd ins fnl f* **16/1**

1m 34.79s (0.92) **14** Ran SP% **118.0**
PARI-MUTUEL (all including 2 usd stake): WIN 14.00; PLACE (1-2) 7.80, 9.20; SHOW (1-2-3) 5.60, 7.00, 11.00; SF 100.00.
**Owner** Derrick Smith & Mrs John Magnier & Michael Tabor **Bred** Barronstown **Trained** North America

**FOCUS**
The field were soon strung out behind the front-running Luck Of The Kitten, but the pace turned out to be slower than the later Juvenile Fillies Turf and few got involved behind the Wesley Ward-trained one-two. Here are the splits with the fillies' event in brackets: 22.71 (22.66), 46.91 (46.46), 1:11.36 (1:10.48), 1:23.14 (1:21.98). The final time was 1.38secs slower. The winner was the pick on the figures.

## 7591a BREEDERS' CUP DIRT MILE (GRADE 1) (3YO+) (DIRT) 1m

**10:05** (12:00) 3-Y-O+ **£331,325** (£108,433; £60,240; £36,144; £18,072)

RPR

1 **Goldencents (USA)**[26] 6974 4-9-0 0 ................................. RBejarano 1 123
(Leandro Mora, U.S.A) *pushed along to go forward and sn led: mde rest: set v fast pce: saw off rival sn after 1/2-way and 3 l clr over 2f out: rdn and reduced advantage in st: kpt on wl u.p fnl f and a doing enough* **8/13**[1]

2 *1 1/4* **Tapiture (USA)**[41] 6573 3-8-11 0 ........................... RosieNapravnik 8 119
(Steven Asmussen, U.S.A) *midfield: clsd and wnt 2nd over 2f out: rdn and effrt in st: kpt on wl wout matching wnr fnl f* **6/1**[2]

3 *5* **Pants On Fire (USA)**[40] 6-9-0 0 ............................................ PLopez 4 109
(Kelly Breen, U.S.A) *chsd clr ldrs: rdn and clsd over 2f out: kpt on for wl hld 3rd in st* **12/1**

4 *3/4* **Bronzo (CHI)**[126] 5-9-0 0 .................................................. LuisTorres 6 107
(Jorge Andres Inda, Chile) *hld up: rdn in rr 2f out: plugged on against rail in st and tk n.d 4th ins fnl f: edgd rt towards fin* **25/1**

5 *2 3/4* **Big Bane Theory (USA)**[26] 5-9-0 0 ...................................... JTalamo 9 101
(Carla Gaines, U.S.A) *midfield: rdn 3f out: plugged on same pce in st and nvr threatened* **33/1**

6 *1* **Carve (USA)**[34] 4-9-0 0 ..................................................(b) MESmith 2 98
(Brad H Cox, U.S.A) *midfield: effrt to cl over 2f out: rdn and outpcd in st: sn btn: lost two pls fnl f* **25/1**

7 *3 1/2* **Fed Biz (USA)**[34] 6782 5-9-0 0 ..................................... MartinAGarcia 7 90
(Bob Baffert, U.S.A) *midfield: lost pl over 3f out: rdn in rr into st and sn btn: n.d* **7/1**[3]

8 *2 1/2* **Golden Ticket (USA)**[34] 6772 5-9-0 0 ................................ JRosario 5 85
(Kenneth McPeek, U.S.A) *hld up in last: rdn over 2f out: no imp and wl btn in st: nvr a factor* **20/1**

9 *19* **Vicar's In Trouble (USA)**[26] 3-8-11 0 .........................(b) JRVelazquez 3 40
(Michael J Maker, U.S.A) *broke wl and led early: sn hdd and pressed ldr on outer: no ex sn after 1/2-way: wknd bk through field and dropped to last into st: eased and t.o* **20/1**

1m 35.16s (95.16)
**WFA** 3 from 4yo+ 3lb **9** Ran SP% **116.6**
PARI-MUTUEL (all including 2 usd stake): WIN 3.40; PLACE (1-2) 2.60, 3.80; SHOW (1-2-3) 2.10, 3.00, 4.00; SF 14.20.
**Owner** W C Racing **Bred** Rosecrest Farm & Karyn Pirrello **Trained** North America

**FOCUS**
Another stunning performance from the winner, who is rated to last year's mark.

## 7592a BREEDERS' CUP JUVENILE FILLIES TURF (GRADE 1) (2YO FILLIES) (TURF) 1m (T)

**10:50** (12:00) 2-Y-O **£331,325** (£108,433; £60,240; £36,144; £18,072)

RPR

1 **Lady Eli (USA)**[33] 2-8-10 0 ............................................... IOrtizJr 4 113+
(Chad C Brown, U.S.A) *prom on ins: shkn up and qcknd to ld over 1f out: rdn and drifted rt ins fnl f: edgd lft and kpt on strly towards fin: readily* **5/2**[1]

2 *2 3/4* **Sunset Glow (USA)**[61] 5967 2-8-10 0 .......................(b) VictorEspinoza 3 107
(Wesley A Ward, U.S.A) *led: rdn and hdd over 1f out: kpt on and clr of rest ins fnl f: nt pce of ready wnr* **5/1**[2]

3 *2 1/4* **Osaila (IRE)**[27] 6924 2-8-10 0 ......................................... FrankieDettori 2 102
(Richard Hannon) *hld up in midfield: pushed along briefly over 4f out: drvn whn n.m.r briefly over 2f out: rallied over 1f out: kpt on fnl f: nt rch first two* **6/1**[3]

4 *1/2* **Prize Exhibit**[27] 6926 2-8-10 0 ...................................... JamieSpencer 12 100
(Jamie Osborne) *t.k.h: stdd in last pl: rdn whn plenty to do ent st: hrd rdn and styd on strly fnl f: nvr able to chal* **33/1**

5 *1/2* **Sivoliere (IRE)**[69] 5707 2-8-10 0 ...................................... GaryStevens 6 99
(Chad C Brown, U.S.A) *t.k.h: hld up in midfield: stdy hdwy over 2f out: sn rdn: one pce fr over 1f out* **12/1**

6 *3/4* **Partisan Politics (USA)**[33] 2-8-10 0 ................................ JJCastellano 1 97
(Chad C Brown, U.S.A) *t.k.h in midfield: effrt and drvn over 2f out: edgd rt ent fnl f: sn outpcd* **14/1**

7 *nk* **Tammy The Torpedo (USA)**[33] 2-8-10 0 .......................... RBejarano 11 97
(Chad C Brown, U.S.A) *hld up towards rr: drvn along and outpcd over 2f out: kpt on fnl f: nvr able to chal* **33/1**

8 *1/2* **Qualify (IRE)**[33] 6798 2-8-10 0 ........................................ RyanMoore 13 96
(A P O'Brien, Ire) *hld up: rdn along and plenty to do whn hmpd bnd ent st: sn swtchd lft and no imp: allowed to coast home fnl f* **6/1**[3]

9 *nse* **Rainha Da Bateria (USA)**[23] 2-8-10 0 ................................ JRosario 7 96
(H Graham Motion, U.S.A) *hld up: rdn along on wd outside over 2f out: sme late hdwy: nvr rchd chalng position* **12/1**

10 *nse* **Quality Rocks (USA)**[23] 2-8-10 0 ....................................... JLezcano 9 95
(William Mott, U.S.A) *in tch: effrt whn hung lft over 1f out: wknd ins fnl f* **33/1**

11 *1/2* **Conquest Harlanate (CAN)**[26] 2-8-10 0 .......................... PHusbands 10 94
(Mark Casse, Canada) *t.k.h: in tch on outside: drvn along and outpcd 2f out: sn btn* **20/1**

12 *1 1/4* **Isabella Sings (USA)**[48] 2-8-10 0 ................................. JRVelazquez 5 91
(Todd Pletcher, U.S.A) *t.k.h: chsd ldr tl lost pl over 2f out: wknd over 1f out* **16/1**

13 *8 1/4* **Nicky's Brown Miss (USA)**[33] 2-8-10 0 .................................. FTorres 8 72
(Savino A Capilupi, U.S.A) *prom: drvn along and lost pl 2f out: sn struggling* **100/1**

1m 33.41s (-0.46) **13** Ran SP% **116.3**
PARI-MUTUEL (all including 2 usd stake): WIN 6.80; PLACE (1-2) 4.20, 5.20; SHOW (1-2-3) 3.00, 3.40, 3.60; SF 35.00.
**Owner** Sheep Pond Partners **Bred** Runnymede Farm Inc & Catesby W Clay **Trained** USA

**FOCUS**
A stronger pace than in the earlier Juvenile Turf and the time was 1.38secs quicker, but the winner was never far away and the pacesetter finished clear of the others in second. The form is rated around the fourth to seventh.

## 7593a LONGINES BREEDERS' CUP DISTAFF (GRADE 1) (3YO+ FILLIES & MARES) (DIRT) 1m 1f (D)

**11:35** (12:00) 3-Y-O+ **£662,650** (£216,867; £120,481; £72,289; £36,144)

RPR

1 **Untapable (USA)**[41] 6572 3-8-9 0 ........................... RosieNapravnik 10 119
(Steven Asmussen, U.S.A) *midfield in tch: hdwy on outer and rdn to chal into st: lugged lft and bmpd rival whn taking ld over 1f out: kpt on wl u.p and asserted towards fin* **2/1**[1]

2 *1 1/4* **Don't Tell Sophia (USA)**[26] 6973 6-8-12 0 .......................... JRoccoJr 7 115
(Philip A Sims, U.S.A) *hld up in last: rdn and hdwy on outer 2f out: kpt on wl u.p in st and wnt 2nd post: nvr nrr* **6/1**[3]

3 *nse* **Iotapa (USA)**[34] 6779 4-8-12 0 .............................................. JTalamo 3 115
(John W Sadler, U.S.A) *pressed ldr on outer: led narrowly 3f out: rdn ent st: bmpd and hdd over 1f out: kpt on wl but hld by wnr towards fin and dropped to 3rd post* **8/1**

4 *4 1/2* **Ria Antonia (USA)**[26] 6973 3-8-9 0 ..........................................(b) PLopez 9 106
(Thomas Amoss, U.S.A) *midfield early: clsd and prom on rail 1/2-way: rdn and effrt 2f out: angled out into st: outpcd by ldng trio fnl f: kpt on and jst hld on for 4th* **14/1**

5 hd **Unbridled Forever (USA)**[26] 3-8-9 0 ........ JRVelazquez 5 106
(Dallas Stewart, U.S.A) *hld up in last trio: rdn and clsd on rail over 2f out: outpcd by ldrs in st: swtchd rt ent fnl f: kpt on and almost snatched 4th but nvr able to chal* **50/1**

6 3 1/2 **Tiz Midnight (USA)**[34] 6779 4-8-12 0 ........ VictorEspinoza 2 98
(Bob Baffert, U.S.A) *led: pushed along and jst hdd 3f out: rdn and outpcd by ldrs into st: no ex and fdd fnl f* **9/1**

7 1 1/4 **Stanwyck (USA)**[34] 6773 5-8-12 0 ........ CNakatani 6 95
(John Shirreffs, U.S.A) *hld up in last trio: rdn and effrt to cl over 2f out: no imp and wl btn in st: nvr threatened* **33/1**

8 1 3/4 **Valiant Emilia (PER)**[131] 5-8-12 0 ........ RBejarano 8 91
(Gary Mandella, U.S.A) *prom: lost pl 1/2-way: rdn and towards rr 3f out: outpcd and wl btn in st* **40/1**

9 1 **Belle Gallantey (USA)**[34] 6773 5-8-12 0 ........ (b) JLOrtiz 4 89
(Rudy Rodriguez, U.S.A) *midfield: dropped to rr and last 2f out: sme hdwy under v tender handling in st but nvr plcd to chal: strnge ride* **14/1**

10 4 1/4 **L'Amour De Ma Vie (USA)**[33] 6808 5-8-12 0 ........ MaximeGuyon 1 80
(Mme Pia Brandt, France) *t.k.h: trckd ldrs on inner: moved off rail 1/2-way: rdn and brief effrt over 2f out: lost pl into st and sn btn: wknd* **16/1**

11 3/4 **Close Hatches (USA)**[26] 6973 4-8-12 0 ........ JRosario 11 79
(William Mott, U.S.A) *trapped wd first turn: sn prom: brief effrt 3f out: rdn and lost pl over 2f out: sn btn and wknd: dropped to last ent fnl f* **3/1[2]**

1m 48.68s (-0.22)
**WFA** 3 from 4yo+ 4lb **11** Ran SP% **120.3**
PARI-MUTUEL (all including 2 usd stake): WIN 5.20; PLACE (1-2) 3.40, 4.60; SHOW (1-2-3) 2.60, 3.40, 4.00; SF 27.00.
**Owner** Winchell Thoroughbreds LLC **Bred** Winchell Thoroughbreds, Llc **Trained** USA
■ Jockey Rosie Napravnik announced after this win that she's about to retire.

**FOCUS**
Last year's winner Beholder was missing, but the race still went to a genuinely high-class filly. The splits were 22.93, 46.73, 1:10.95 and 1:35.77.

7560 **NEWMARKET** (R-H)
## Saturday, November 1
**OFFICIAL GOING: Good to soft changing to good after race 4 (2:00)**
Wind: Light across Weather: Fine

## 7594 EBF STALLIONS PRESTIGE VEHICLES MAIDEN FILLIES' STKS (BOBIS RACE) 7f
**12:20** (12:21) (Class 4) 2-Y-O **£4,528** (£1,347; £673; £336) **Stalls** High

Form RPR

1 **Suffused** 2-9-0 0 ........ WilliamTwiston-Davies 11 75+
(Roger Charlton) *hld up in tch: shkn up over 1f out: edgd rt and r.o to ld nr fin* **8/1**

0 2 1/2 **Colour Party (IRE)**[21] 7108 2-9-0 0 ........ JimmyFortune 12 74
(John Gosden) *chsd ldrs: led over 1f out: rdn and hdd nr fin* **10/1**

0 3 1 1/4 **Frenzified**[21] 7108 2-9-0 0 ........ AdamKirby 5 71
(Luca Cumani) *chsd ldrs: rdn and ev ch over 1f out: edgd lft and styd on same pce ins fnl f* **25/1**

4 2 1/4 **Rive Gauche** 2-9-0 0 ........ GrahamLee 14 65+
(William Haggas) *hld up: hdwy 1/2-way: rdn over 1f out: r.o* **7/1[3]**

5 nk **Saraha** 2-9-0 0 ........ PaulHanagan 6 64+
(William Haggas) *rn green towards rr: hdwy over 1f out: r.o* **13/2[2]**

06 6 3/4 **Red Words (IRE)**[46] 6435 2-9-0 0 ........ TomQueally 4 62
(George Margarson) *chsd ldr tl led over 2f out: rdn and hdd over 1f out: no ex ins fnl f* **40/1**

7 3/4 **Bishara (USA)** 2-9-0 0 ........ ShaneKelly 13 61+
(Sir Michael Stoute) *prom: shkn up and hung lft over 1f out: styd on same pce* **8/1**

00 8 1 3/4 **Exceedwell**[31] 6867 2-8-9 0 ........ JoeDoyle(5) 10 56
(John Ryan) *led over 4f: rdn over 1f out: wknd ins fnl f* **100/1**

9 1/2 **Raddeh** 2-9-0 0 ........ JoeFanning 1 55+
(Sir Michael Stoute) *s.i.s: hdwy over 2f out: styd on same pce fr over 1f out* **9/1**

10 nk **Devonshire Place (IRE)** 2-8-11 0 ........ CamHardie(3) 15 54+
(Roger Charlton) *dwlt: hld up: nvr on fnl f: nvr nrr* **16/1**

11 1/2 **Dream Job** 2-9-0 0 ........ FrederikTylicki 8 53+
(Saeed bin Suroor) *s.i.s: pushed along over 2f out: n.d* **7/2[1]**

12 1/2 **Stubbins** 2-9-0 0 ........ RobertHavlin 3 52+
(John Gosden) *hld up: shkn up over 1f out: nvr on terms* **17/2**

13 3/4 **Take Note (IRE)** 2-9-0 0 ........ HayleyTurner 7 50
(James Toller) *s.i.s: pushed along 1/2-way: wknd over 1f out* **33/1**

14 1 3/4 **Oakley Star** 2-9-0 0 ........ ChrisCatlin 9 45
(Gay Kelleway) *mid-div: rdn 1/2-way: wknd 2f out* **66/1**

15 1 1/2 **Raseel** 2-9-0 0 ........ MartinHarley 2 42
(Peter Chapple-Hyam) *prom: rdn over 2f out: wknd over 1f out* **20/1**

1m 29.18s (3.78) **Going Correction** +0.15s/f (Good) **15** Ran SP% **122.2**
Speed ratings (Par 95): **84,83,82,79,79 78,77,75,74,74 73,73,72,70,68**
CSF £81.40 TOTE £11.50: £3.90, £2.80, £9.70; EX 99.80 Trifecta £1355.40.
**Owner** K Abdullah **Bred** Juddmonte Farms Ltd **Trained** Beckhampton, Wilts

**FOCUS**
Stands side course and Stalls: Stands side. It was dry overnight and the going remained good to soft. Those that had already run hadn't shown a great deal and it was no surprise to see this maiden won by a newcomer. It's been rated cautiously.

## 7595 NOBLE HOUSE SERVICES NURSERY H'CAP (BOBIS RACE) 1m 1f
**12:50** (12:50) (Class 4) (0-85,83) 2-Y-O **£5,175** (£1,540; £769; £384) **Stalls** High

Form RPR

1314 1 **Rotherwick (IRE)**[16] 7226 2-9-7 83 ........ AdamKirby 1 88
(Paul Cole) *w ldr tl led over 2f out: rdn and hung lft over 1f out: hung rt and lft u.p ins fnl f: styd on* **5/2[1]**

402 2 1 3/4 **Triple Dip (IRE)**[17] 7209 2-8-6 68 ........ FrannyNorton 7 70
(Mark Johnston) *led: hdd over 2f: rdn over 1f out: styd on* **25/1**

0431 3 1 1/4 **Mywayalways (IRE)**[17] 7207 2-9-0 76 ........ JFEgan 6 75
(David Evans) *chsd ldrs: rdn over 2f out: styd on same pce ins fnl f* **10/1**

0111 4 1 **Dark Wave**[12] 7328 2-9-4 80 ........ GeorgeBaker 5 77
(Ed Walker) *hld up in tch: rdn and hung lft over 1f out: swtchd lft ins fnl f: styd on* **11/4[2]**

416 5 1 1/2 **Yorkidding**[28] 6924 2-8-9 71 ........ JoeFanning 3 65
(Mark Johnston) *chsd ldrs: ev ch over 2f out: shkn up over 1f out* **5/1[3]**

2421 6 13 **Shadow Rock (IRE)**[20] 7134 2-9-2 78 ........ JimmyFortune 2 46
(Richard Hannon) *in rr: pushed along 5f out: sme hdwy over 3f out: wknd over 1f out* **11/2**

0443 7 1 **Philba**[31] 6869 2-8-3 65 ........ (p) SilvestreDeSousa 4 31
(Michael Appleby) *s.i.s: hld up: rdn over 3f out: wknd 2f out* **9/1**

1m 53.04s (1.34) **Going Correction** +0.15s/f (Good) **7** Ran SP% **110.2**
Speed ratings (Par 98): **100,98,97,96,95 83,82**
CSF £54.67 CT £498.11 TOTE £3.50: £1.60, £6.60; EX 91.60 Trifecta £609.70.
**Owner** H R H Sultan Ahmad Shah **Bred** Brian O'Neill **Trained** Whatcombe, Oxon

**FOCUS**
An open nursery. The runner-up has been rated as improving a little on her nursery debut.

## 7596 EBF STALLIONS MONTROSE FILLIES' STKS (LISTED RACE) 1m
**1:25** (1:25) (Class 1) 2-Y-O
**£17,013** (£6,450; £3,228; £1,608; £807; £405) **Stalls** High

Form RPR

1 1 **Irish Rookie (IRE)**[21] 7108 2-9-0 77 ........ FergusSweeney 6 95+
(Martyn Meade) *a.p: shkn up to ld over 1f out: edgd rt towards fin: rdn out* **10/1**

031 2 1/2 **Lady Of Dubai**[42] 6554 2-9-0 87 ........ TomQueally 2 94
(Luca Cumani) *chsd ldrs: wnt 2nd over 2f out: led wl over 1f out: sn rdn and hdd: styd on* **15/8[1]**

22 3 1 **Kodiva (IRE)**[82] 5232 2-9-0 0 ........ MartinHarley 1 92
(Charles Hills) *led: hdd wl over 1f out: sn rdn and hung lft: no ex towards fin* **25/1**

1 4 1 **Sagaciously (IRE)**[53] 6208 2-9-0 0 ........ PaulHanagan 7 89
(Ed Dunlop) *hld up: hdwy 1/2-way: rdn and ev ch over 1f out: styd on same pce fnl f* **11/1**

1 5 3/4 **Toujours L'Amour**[42] 6553 2-9-0 0 ........ JoeFanning 4 88
(William Haggas) *hld up: shkn up over 1f out: r.o towards fin: nvr nrr* **5/1[2]**

10 6 1 **Bitter Lake (USA)**[134] 3415 2-9-0 0 ........ AdamKirby 5 85
(Charlie Appleby) *hld up: hdwy over 2f out: rdn and hung lft over 1f out: no ex ins fnl f* **5/1[2]**

2 7 1 3/4 **She Is No Lady**[17] 7206 2-9-0 0 ........ SilvestreDeSousa 8 81
(Ralph Beckett) *chsd ldr tl rdn over 2f out: styd on same pce fr over 1f out* **12/1**

3416 8 1 3/4 **Encore L'Amour**[10] 7393 2-9-0 81 ........ FrederikTylicki 3 77
(David Simcock) *chsd ldrs: rdn over 2f out: styd on same pce appr fnl f* **11/2[3]**

1m 39.69s (1.09) **Going Correction** +0.15s/f (Good) **8** Ran SP% **112.5**
Speed ratings: **100,99,98,97,96 95,94,92**
CSF £28.23 TOTE £10.80: £2.70, £1.10, £5.10; EX 29.80 Trifecta £215.20.
**Owner** Rick Barnes **Bred** Kevin & Meta Cullen **Trained** Newmarket, Suffolk

**FOCUS**
Not a strong Listed race on the face of it, but there were three in the line-up who came here on the back of debut maiden wins, and it was one of their number that came out on top. The early pace didn't look that hot and the filly with the best turn of foot won it. It's been rated as an ordinary renewal.

## 7597 WOODHURST CONSTRUCTION H'CAP 1m
**2:00** (2:01) (Class 3) (0-95,93) 3-Y-O+
**£7,470** (£2,236; £1,118; £559; £279; £140) **Stalls** High

Form RPR

2050 1 **Dream Walker (FR)**[14] 7276 5-9-2 88 ........ (t) DaleSwift 10 96
(Brian Ellison) *hld up in tch: rdn over 1f out: styd on to ld post* **14/1**

0500 2 hd **Bancnuanaheireann (IRE)**[35] 6752 7-9-4 93 ........ RyanTate(3) 4 101
(Michael Appleby) *hld up: hdwy 1/2-way: rdn to ld over 1f out: edgd lft: hdd post* **11/2[3]**

6602 3 shd **Ginger Jack**[21] 7125 7-8-10 82 ........ PaulMulrennan 9 89
(Keith Dalgleish) *chsd ldrs: led over 2f out: rdn and hdd over 1f out: ev ch whn hmpd ins fnl f: styd on* **4/1[2]**

0300 4 3 1/4 **Pastoral Player**[35] 6755 7-9-4 90 ........ JohnFahy 5 90
(Hughie Morrison) *s.i.s: hld up: hdwy over 1f out: styd on same pce ins fnl f* **14/1**

1026 5 3 1/2 **Exchequer (IRE)**[10] 7375 3-8-10 84 ........ JoeFanning 6 76
(Richard Hannon) *prom: rdn over 2f out: edgd lft over 1f out: no ex* **9/1**

1-21 6 3 3/4 **Donncha (IRE)**[26] 6990 3-8-12 86 ........ MartinHarley 8 69
(Robert Eddery) *prom: rdn over 2f out: wknd fnl f* **7/4[1]**

1551 7 1 **War Singer (USA)**[20] 7136 7-8-12 84 ........ (vt) StevieDonohoe 7 65
(Johnny Farrelly) *chsd ldr tl led over 5f out: rdn and hdd over 2f out: wknd over 1f out* **9/1**

0301 8 nk **Excellent Guest**[29] 6892 7-9-5 91 ........ TomQueally 2 71
(George Margarson) *hld up: rdn over 2f out: wknd over 1f out* **16/1**

1040 9 9 **Uncle Dermot (IRE)**[28] 6943 6-9-1 87 ........[1] AdamKirby 1 46
(Brendan Powell) *led: hdd over 5f out: rdn and wknd 3f out* **25/1**

1m 37.86s (-0.74) **Going Correction** +0.15s/f (Good)
**WFA** 3 from 5yo+ 2lb **9** Ran SP% **114.8**
Speed ratings (Par 107): **109,108,108,105,101 98,97,96,87**
CSF £88.38 CT £372.25 TOTE £16.40: £3.80, £2.50, £2.00; EX 94.70 Trifecta £797.40.
**Owner** Keith Brown **Bred** John Berry **Trained** Norton, N Yorks
■ Stewards' Enquiry : Dale Swift four-day ban: used whip above permitted level (Nov 15,17-19)

**FOCUS**
A tight three-way finish to this handicap.

## 7598 AGMA HOLDINGS JAMES SEYMOUR STKS (LISTED RACE) 1m 2f
**2:35** (2:37) (Class 1) 3-Y-O+
**£20,982** (£7,955; £3,981; £1,983; £995; £499) **Stalls** High

Form RPR

1213 1 **Air Pilot**[15] 7243 5-9-3 110 ........ GrahamLee 6 115
(Ralph Beckett) *prom: nt clr run and lost pl over 3f out: swtchd rt and hdwy 2f out: shkn up to ld ins fnl f: r.o wl* **15/8[2]**

3051 2 2 **Sudden Wonder (IRE)**[21] 7120 3-8-13 106 ........ AdamKirby 3 111
(Charlie Appleby) *chsd ldrs: wnt 2nd over 2f out: led wl over 1f out tl hdd ins fnl f: styd on same pce* **11/2[3]**

2122 3 nk **Mutakayyef**[15] 7243 3-8-13 111 ........ PaulHanagan 4 111
(William Haggas) *hld up: plld hrd: hdwy over 2f out: rdn and ev ch fr over 1f out tl no ex ins fnl f* **5/4[1]**

4035 4 7 **Educate**[15] 7243 5-9-3 109 ........ DanielTudhope 2 97
(Ismail Mohammed) *chsd ldr tl led 4f out: rdn and hdd wl over 1f out: wknd ins fnl f* **8/1**

0006 5 11 **Proud Chieftain**[7] 7440 6-9-3 84 ........ JimmyQuinn 5 76
(Clifford Lines) *led: rdn and hdd 4f out: wknd over 2f out: lame* **66/1**

5450 6 1 3/4 **Running Deer (IRE)**[42] 6548 5-8-12 89 ........ LouisSteward 1 68
(Eve Johnson Houghton) *hld up in tch: shkn up and wknd 2f out* **33/1**

2m 4.34s (-1.46) **Going Correction** +0.15s/f (Good)
**WFA** 3 from 5yo+ 4lb **6** Ran SP% **110.2**
Speed ratings: **111,109,109,103,94 93**
CSF £11.97 TOTE £2.50: £1.20, £2.70; EX 10.00 Trifecta £24.60.
**Owner** Lady Cobham **Bred** Lady Cobham **Trained** Kimpton, Hants

**FOCUS**
The going was changed to good before this race. The early pace wasn't strong and the race developed into a bit of a dash to the line.

## 7599 BEN MARSHALL STKS (LISTED RACE) 1m
3:10 (3:12) (Class 1) 3-Y-O+

£20,982 (£7,955; £3,981; £1,983; £995; £499) Stalls High

Form RPR
2311 1 **French Navy**148 2958 6-9-7 115 AdamKirby 6 118
(Charlie Appleby) *hld up: hdwy over 1f out: rdn: hung lft and r.o to ld wl ins fnl f* **2/1**2
4304 2 *nk* **Fire Ship**25 7022 5-9-1 103 GrahamLee 7 111
(William Knight) *led: rdn over 1f out: hdd wl ins fnl f* **16/1**
4211 3 *2 3/4* **Bronze Angel (IRE)**14 7276 5-9-1 111 (b) LouisSteward 2 105
(Marcus Tregoning) *hld up in tch: chsd ldr over 2f out: rdn over 1f out: edgd lft and no ex ins fnl f* **13/8**1
0-00 4 *4* **Linton (AUS)**28 6934 8-9-1 108 (p) MartinHarley 5 96
(Marco Botti) *hld up: hdwy u.p over 1f out: no ex ins fnl f* **10/1**
010 5 *1/2* **Baltic Knight (IRE)**28 6955 4-9-1 107 JimmyFortune 3 95
(Richard Hannon) *prom: rdn over 2f out: no ex fnl f* **14/1**
1300 6 *1 1/2* **Ocean Tempest**15 7243 5-9-4 115 JoeDoyle 8 94
(John Ryan) *chsd ldrs: rdn over 2f out: wknd over 1f out* **8/1**3
0243 7 *2 1/4* **Emell**45 6458 4-9-1 105 JoeFanning 1 86
(Richard Hannon) *prom tl rdn and wknd over 1f out* **14/1**
0045 8 *2 1/2* **Boom And Bust (IRE)**25 7022 7-9-1 96 ShaneKelly 4 80
(Marcus Tregoning) *chsd ldr tl rdn over 2f out: wknd over 1f out* **33/1**
1m 37.44s (-1.16) **Going Correction** +0.15s/f (Good) **8** Ran SP% **113.8**
Speed ratings: **111,110,107,103,103 101,99,97**
CSF £33.11 TOTE £2.80: £1.20, £3.50, £1.10; EX 32.40 Trifecta £123.10.
**Owner** Godolphin **Bred** Darley **Trained** Newmarket, Suffolk
**FOCUS**
For the fifth time in the last nine years Godolphin captured this Listed event.

## 7600 TURFTV H'CAP (DIV I) 7f
3:45 (3:49) (Class 4) (0-85,85) 3-Y-O+ £5,175 (£1,540; £769; £384) Stalls High

Form RPR
2353 1 **Maggie Pink**17 7196 5-8-13 82 AlistairRawlinson(5) 5 96+
(Michael Appleby) *mde all: qcknd clr over 2f out: rdn over 1f out: eased nr fin* **6/1**2
0005 2 *2* **Showboating (IRE)**14 7282 6-8-13 77 (tp1) TomQueally 7 84
(Alan McCabe) *s.i.s: hld up: hdwy u.p over 1f out: wnt 2nd ins fnl f: r.o: no ch w wnr* **5/1**1
0014 3 *3* **Chiswick Bey (IRE)**18 7179 6-8-2 71 oh2 SammyJoBell(5) 10 70
(Richard Fahey) *a.p: rdn over 1f out: styd on same pce fnl f* **8/1**
6064 4 *nse* **Crew Cut (IRE)**77 5437 6-8-6 77 AaronJones(7) 11 76
(Stuart Williams) *chsd ldrs: rdn over 2f out: styd on same pce fnl f* **10/1**
2034 5 *2 3/4* **Silver Treasure (FR)**13 7327 3-9-6 85 RobertHavlin 4 76
(Amy Weaver) *s.i.s: sn prom: rdn over 2f out: wknd ins fnl f* **20/1**
2400 6 *1/2* **Trojan Rocket (IRE)**42 6531 6-9-7 85 (p) GeorgeBaker 8 76
(Michael Wigham) *prom: chsd wnr over 2f out: rdn and edgd lft over 1f out: wknd ins fnl f* **10/1**
3150 7 *5* **Ixelles Diamond (IRE)**34 6789 3-8-10 75 PaulHanagan 1 52
(Richard Fahey) *hld up: pushed along 1/2-way: nvr on terms* **8/1**
2530 8 *3* **Surety (IRE)**35 6736 3-8-5 73 CamHardie(3) 3 42
(Clive Brittain) *chsd wnr over 4f: rdn and wknd over 1f out* **12/1**
0004 9 *1 1/2* **Jammy Guest (IRE)**10 7375 4-9-4 82 MartinHarley 6 48
(George Margarson) *hld up: rdn over 2f out: wknd over 1f out* **8/1**
5305 10 *3 1/2* **Pashan Garh**5 7494 5-8-7 71 oh8 (v) JoeFanning 9 28
(Pat Eddery) *chsd ldrs tl rdn and wknd over 2f out* **12/1**
1132 11 *21* **Plucky Dip**18 7183 3-9-0 79 AdamKirby 2
(John Ryan) *mid-div: rdn over 3f out: wknd over 2f out* **7/1**3
1m 25.43s (0.03) **Going Correction** +0.15s/f (Good)
**WFA** 3 from 4yo+ 1lb **11** Ran SP% **115.1**
Speed ratings (Par 105): **105,102,99,99,96 95,89,86,84,80 56**
CSF £35.25 CT £246.73 TOTE £5.60: £2.30, £2.10, £2.90; EX 36.60 Trifecta £332.00.
**Owner** A W Bult **Bred** Harcourt Stud **Trained** Danethorpe, Notts
**FOCUS**
This was dominated from the start by the winner, who set a good gallop out in front. It was the faster of the two divisions by 0.62sec.

## 7601 TURFTV H'CAP (DIV II) 7f
4:15 (4:18) (Class 4) (0-85,84) 3-Y-O+ £5,175 (£1,540; £769; £384) Stalls High

Form RPR
066 1 **Personal Touch**22 7085 5-9-0 77 PaulHanagan 5 87
(Richard Fahey) *led to 1/2-way: led again over 2f out: rdn over 1f out: styd on gamely* **7/2**2
4534 2 *nk* **Al Muheer (IRE)**7 7456 9-8-4 70 oh2 (v) ConnorBeasley(3) 2 79
(Michael Herrington) *hld up: hdwy over 2f out: rdn and ev ch ins fnl f: styd on* **20/1**
3203 3 *1 3/4* **Good Authority (IRE)**9 7403 7-9-0 84 KieranShoemark(7) 7 89
(Victor Dartnall) *hld up: hdwy over 1f out: sn rdn and edgd rt: styd on same pce ins fnl f* **10/1**
1441 4 *3/4* **Tiger Jim**39 6639 4-8-12 75 FergalLynch 9 78
(Jim Goldie) *hld up: hdwy 2f out: no ex wl ins fnl f* **2/1**1
0000 5 *1 3/4* **Ted's Brother (IRE)**3 7538 6-8-6 72 (e) JacobButterfield(3) 8 70
(Richard Guest) *s.i.s: hld up: hdwy u.p over 1f out: nt rch ldrs* **25/1**
1324 6 *nse* **Scottish Glen**29 6891 8-9-1 78 DavidProbert 10 76
(Patrick Chamings) *hld up: rdn over 1f out: r.o ins fnl f: nt rch ldrs* **5/1**3
1003 7 *1 3/4* **Comrade Bond**16 7220 6-8-2 70 (p) TimClark(5) 6 63
(Mark H Tompkins) *w wnr tl led 1/2-way: hdd over 2f out: sn rdn: no ex ins fnl f* **16/1**
0100 8 *2 1/4* **Kakatosi**29 6891 7-9-7 84 ShaneKelly 3 72
(Mike Murphy) *chsd ldrs: rdn over 2f out: wknd fnl f* **20/1**
0020 9 *shd* **Nameitwhatyoulike**29 6891 5-9-5 82 PaulMulrennan 4 69
(Bryan Smart) *prom: racd keenly: rdn over 1f out: wknd fnl f* **8/1**
3361 10 *1 1/2* **Brigliadoro (IRE)**24 7035 3-9-0 81 DannyBrock(3) 1 63
(Philip McBride) *chsd ldrs: rdn over 1f out: eased whn btn ins fnl f* **12/1**
1m 26.05s (0.65) **Going Correction** +0.15s/f (Good)
**WFA** 3 from 4yo+ 1lb **10** Ran SP% **119.4**
Speed ratings (Par 105): **102,101,99,98,96 96,94,92,92,90**
CSF £75.23 CT £668.11 TOTE £4.20: £1.40, £4.70, £2.40; EX 100.30 Trifecta £926.80.
**Owner** Nicholas Wrigley & Kevin Hart **Bred** Cheveley Park Stud Ltd **Trained** Musley Bank, N Yorks
**FOCUS**
The early pace was steadier in this division, and the final time slower, but once again the leader didn't come back.

T/Jkpt: Not won. T/Plt: £493.70 to a £1 stake. Pool: £73,775.00 - 109.07 winning tickets T/Qpdt: £18.10 to a £1 stake. Pool: £8,700.00 - 354.80 winning tickets CR

# 6975 FLEMINGTON (L-H)
Saturday, November 1

**OFFICIAL GOING: Turf: good**

## 7602a LONGINES MACKINNON STKS (GROUP 1) (3YO+) (TURF) 1m 2f
4:00 (12:00) 3-Y-O+

£323,924 (£96,774; £48,387; £24,193; £13,440; £10,752)

RPR
1 **Happy Trails (AUS)**7 7467 7-9-4 0 DamienOliver 12 116
(Paul Beshara, Australia) *hld up towards rr: rdn 2f out: styd on and chal ent fnl f: drvn to ld post: jst prevailed* **6/1**3
2 *shd* **He's Your Man (FR)**28 6959 5-9-4 0 (t) JoaoMoreira 5 116
(Chris Waller, Australia) *midfield on outer: rdn 2f out: chal ent fnl f: led narrowly fnl 100yds: styd on but hdd post: jst denied* **5/1**2
3 *3/4* **Farraaj (IRE)**70 5690 5-9-4 0 AndreaAtzeni 14 114+
(Roger Varian) *sn prom on outer: chal into st: rdn to ld 2f out: strly pressed ent fnl f: styd on but hdd fnl 100yds: dropped to 3rd and hld* **11/1**
4 *1 1/2* **Spillway**28 6961 4-9-4 0 (b1) KerrinMcEvoy 13 111
(David A Hayes & Tom Dabernig, Australia) *stdd and hld up in rr: rdn over 2f out: styd on down wd outside and wnt 4th towards fin: nt pce to chal* **20/1**
5 *1 1/4* **Criterion (NZ)**7 7467 4-9-3 0 (b) CoreyBrown 1 108
(David Payne, Australia) *midfield: clsd into st: rdn and effrt 2f out: kpt on same pce fr over 1f out: hld fnl f but got up to snatch 5th post* **9/2**1
6 *shd* **Rising Romance (NZ)**14 7301 4-8-13 0 JamesMcDonald 11 104
(Donna Logan, New Zealand) *hld up in midfield: rdn 2f out: hdwy and effrt over 1f out: nt pce of ldng trio fnl f: no ex and fdd towards fin: dropped to 6th post* **7/1**
7 *1 1/4* **Mourinho (AUS)**20 7-9-4 0 (bt) CraigNewitt 10 106
(Peter Gelagotis, Australia) *sn trcking ldr on outer: chal and led narrowly into st: hdd 2f out and immediately rdn: no ex and lost pl jst over 1f out: fdd fnl f* **50/1**
8 *1 1/2* **Moriarty (IRE)**14 7301 6-9-4 0 (bt) JimCassidy 3 103
(Chris Waller, Australia) *hld up towards rr: clsd and swtchd to rail 2f out: rdn and effrt over 1f out: outpcd fnl f: fdd* **25/1**
9 *nk* **Brambles (NZ)**14 7301 6-9-4 0 (t) LukeNolen 8 103
(Peter G Moody, Australia) *sn led: hdd into st: sn rdn: no ex ent fnl f: fdd* **14/1**
10 *2* **Star Rolling (AUS)**28 6959 5-9-4 0 (b) StephenBaster 6 99
(Peter Morgan & Craig Widdison, Australia) *in tch: rdn over 2f out: no ex and btn over 1f out: wknd* **50/1**
11 *hd* **Hawkspur (AUS)**14 7301 5-9-4 0 (bt) TyeAngland 7 98
(Chris Waller, Australia) *led early: sn hdd and dropped to midfield on inner: angled out and rdn into st: outpcd ent fnl f: sn btn* **20/1**
12 *4* **Costume (NZ)**28 5-9-0 0 (b) BlakeShinn 2 86
(Graeme & Debbie Rogerson, New Zealand) *hld up in midfield: rdn over 2f out: no imp and btn over 1f out: n.d* **40/1**
13 *3/4* **Foreteller**7 7467 7-9-4 0 (b) GlenBoss 9 89
(Chris Waller, Australia) *hld up and a in rr: rdn 3f out: no imp and wl btn in st: nvr a factor* **9/1**
14 *2* **Amralah (IRE)**84 5175 4-9-4 0 ChadSchofield 4 85
(Robert Hickmott, Australia) *in tch: rdn over 2f out: lost pl and btn over 1f out: wknd and eased: dropped to last ins fnl f* **10/1**
2m 2.28s (122.28) **14** Ran SP% **115.5**
PARI-MUTUEL (NSW TAB - all including 1 aud stake): WIN 5.90; PLACE 2.30, 2.30, 4.30; DF 23.20; SF 43.50.
**Owner** P & Mrs E Dickmann Et Al **Bred** B K Parker **Trained** Australia

# 6384 MUNICH (L-H)
Saturday, November 1

**OFFICIAL GOING: Turf: soft**

## 7603a PASTORIUS - GROSSER PREIS VON BAYERN (GROUP 1) (3YO+) (TURF) 1m 4f
2:35 (12:00) 3-Y-O+ £83,333 (£25,000; £12,500; £5,833; £2,500)

RPR
1 **Ivanhowe (GER)**27 6970 4-9-6 0 FilipMinarik 8 118+
(Jean-Pierre Carvalho, Germany) *midfield: rdn and hdwy 2f out: styd on and chal ins fnl f: led fnl 150yds and qcknd clr: readily* **17/10**1
2 *2 1/2* **Cubanita**14 7273 5-9-3 0 MartinLane 11 111
(Ralph Beckett) *hld up in midfield: rdn and hdwy 2f out: styd on and chal ins fnl f: wnt 2nd fnl 150yds: readily outpcd by wnr towards fin* **77/10**
3 *3* **Earl Of Tinsdal (GER)**34 6806 6-9-6 0 EPedroza 4 109
(A Wohler, Germany) *led: rdn and effrt to kick on into st: strly pressed ins fnl f: hdd fnl 150yds: no ex after and jst hld on for 3rd* **56/10**2
4 *shd* **Feodora (GER)**27 6969 3-8-11 0 CristianDemuro 10 106
(A Wohler, Germany) *hld up: rdn 3f out: styd on steadily in st and wnt 4th ins fnl f: almost snatched 3rd post but nvr able to chal* **67/10**3
5 *2* **Wild Chief (GER)**34 6806 3-9-1 0 AdriedeVries 13 107
(J Hirschberger, Germany) *hld up in rr: rdn 2f out: plugged on and tk n.d 5th post* **171/10**
6 *shd* **Eric (GER)**29 6914 3-9-1 0 SHellyn 12 107
(C Von Der Recke, Germany) *t.k.h: sn prom: rdn into st: outpcd by ldrs fnl f: plugged on but dropped to 6th post* **34/1**
7 *7* **Feuerblitz (GER)**43 6592 5-9-6 0 ThierryThulliez 6 94
(M Figge, Germany) *prom: rdn to chal 2f out: no ex ent fnl f: wknd and eased* **198/10**
8 *1 1/4* **Night Wish (GER)**34 6806 4-9-6 0 APietsch 9 92
(W Figge, Germany) *sn midfield: rdn over 2f out: outpcd and btn fnl f: eased towards fin* **116/10**
9 *6* **Virginia Sun (GER)**41 6589 3-8-11 0 AnthonyCrastus 7 80
(J Hirschberger, Germany) *hld up towards rr: rdn over 2f out: outpcd and btn fnl f: eased: n.d* **131/10**

10 *10* **Daytona Bay**[13] 7316 4-9-3 0........................ FrederikTylicki 14 64
(Ferdinand J Leve, Germany) *t.k.h: sn trcking ldr: rdn over 2f out: lost pl and qckly btn: wknd: eased fnl f* **26/1**

11 *3* **Quinzieme Monarque (USA)**[63] 5938 4-9-6 0... MrVinzenzSchiergen 5 62
(P Schiergen, Germany) *dwlt sltly and hld up in last: rdn 3f out: no imp and wl btn in st: nvr a factor* **173/10**

12 *4* **Papagena Star (IRE)**[34] 6806 3-8-11 0........................ AHelfenbein 3 53
(Markus Klug, Germany) *hld up in midfield: rdn and outpcd over 2f out: sn btn: eased over 1f out* **49/1**

13 *2* **Girolamo (GER)**[34] 6806 5-9-6 0........................ AStarke 2 52
(P Schiergen, Germany) *in tch: rdn into st: no ex and btn fnl 2f: wknd and eased* **151/10**

14 *3/4* **Born To Run (GER)**[145] 3073 3-9-1 0........................(b) JackMitchell 1 52
(R Dzubasz, Germany) *in tch: rdn 3f out: lost pl early in st: sn btn and wknd: eased and dropped to last fnl f* **31/1**

2m 38.33s (158.33)
**WFA** 3 from 4yo+ 6lb **14** Ran SP% **125.4**
win (incl. 10 euro stake): 27. PLACES: 13, 20, 15, 17. SF: 209.
**Owner** Gestut Schlenderhan **Bred** Gestut Schlenderhan **Trained** Germany

## 7469 SAN SIRO (R-H)
### Saturday, November 1

**OFFICIAL GOING: Turf: good**

### 7604a PREMIO CHIUSURA (GROUP 3) (2YO+) (TURF) 7f
**2:50** (12:00) 2-Y-O+ **£23,333** (£10,266; £5,600; £2,800)

RPR

1 **Gothic Dance (IRE)**[139] 5-9-1 0........................ IRossi 10 99
(B Grizzetti, Italy) *hld up in tch: rdn to cl 2f out: r.o and chal wl ins fnl f: drvn to ld cl home* **73/10**

2 *snk* **Falest (IRE)**[146] 5-9-4 0........................ SMulas 6 102
(D Crisanti, Italy) *led: rdn clr over 1f out: kpt on but steadily reeled in fnl f and strly pressed towards fin: hdd cl home* **68/10**

3 *nk* **Regarde Moi**[181] 6-9-4 0........................ DarioVargiu 9 101
(Stefano Botti, Italy) *midfield in tch: rdn 2f out: r.o wl for 3rd fnl f but nt quite pce to chal* **13/10**[1]

4 *hd* **Birthday Prince (GER)**[9] 7437 6-9-4 0........................ DanielePorcu 2 100
(Christian Sprengel, Germany) *hld up in last: pushed along 1/2-way: rdn and hdwy over 1f out: kpt on wl fnl f but nt quite pce to chal* **363/100**[2]

5 *2 1/2* **Universo Star (IRE)**[13] 7320 4-9-1 0........................ UmbertoRispoli 1 90
(A Marcialis, Italy) *midfield in tch: rdn 2f out: kpt on same pce fnl f and hld* **26/5**[3]

6 *hd* **Psichedelic (IRE)** 4-9-4 0........................ SUrru 8 93
(M Manili, Italy) *hld up in tch: rdn 2f out: kpt on same pce fnl f and nvr able to chal* **26/1**

7 *2 1/2* **Grand Oriente (ITY)**[521] 3-9-4 0........................ GArena 5 86
(Luciano Vitabile, Italy) *trckd ldr: rdn 2f out: sn outpcd: no ex and wknd fnl f* **132/10**

8 *nk* **Kitten's Lady (USA)**[188] 1780 3-9-1 0........................ GBietolini 7 82
(Gianluca Bietolini, Italy) *trckd ldr: rdn 2f out: lost pl over 1f out: no ex and btn fnl f* **124/10**

9 *4* **Mr Muzzare (USA)**[34] 6808 5-9-4 0........................ FrancescoDettori 4 75
(M Massimi Jr, Italy) *in tch: rdn and lost pl ins fnl 2f: sn btn: eased towards fin* **159/10**

10 *2 1/2* **Meaning Of Life (IRE)**[238] 892 3-9-4 0........................ FabioBranca 3 68
(Stefano Botti, Italy) *hld up in tch: rdn over 1f out: in rr whn nt clr run on rail fnl f: eased and btn after* **81/10**

1m 23.8s (-4.40)
**WFA** 3 from 4yo+ 1lb **10** Ran SP% **141.2**
WIN (incl. 1 euro stake): 8.29. PLACES: 2.53, 1.93, 1.26. DF: 108.72.
**Owner** Allevamento La Nuova Sbarra **Bred** Ennistown Stud **Trained** Italy

## 7590 SANTA ANITA (L-H)
### Saturday, November 1

**OFFICIAL GOING: Dirt: fast; turf: good changing to firm before race 11 (23:40)**

### 7605a JUVENILE TURF SPRINT STKS (LISTED RACE) (2YO) (DIRT) 6f 110y
**5:15** (12:00) 2-Y-O
**£36,144** (£12,048; £7,228; £3,614; £1,204; £150)

RPR

1 **Ocho Ocho Ocho (USA)** 2-8-6 0........................ JTalamo 2 104
(James Cassidy, U.S.A) **4/5**[1]

2 *5 3/4* **Peacenluvpeacenluv (USA)**[27] 2-8-6 0........................(b) ASolis 7 87
(George Papaprodromou, U.S.A) **114/10**

3 *2 1/4* **Tizcano (USA)**[18] 2-8-6 0........................(b[1]) TBaze 6 80
(Peter Miller, U.S.A) **37/10**[2]

4 *3/4* **Metaboss (USA)** 2-8-6 0........................ AQuinonez 1 78
(Jeff Bonde, U.S.A) **118/10**

5 *9 1/2* **Gambler's Roll (USA)** 2-8-6 0........................(b) FHPerez 4 51
(Philip D'Amato, U.S.A) **15/1**

6 *1 1/2* **War Alert (USA)**[42] 6530 2-8-8 0........................ JamieSpencer 5 48
(David Brown) *dwlt and scrubbed along in rr: pushed along and effrt 3f out: sn rdn and no further imp: sn wknd* **22/5**[3]

7 *9 1/4* **Not Enough Eddie (USA)** 2-8-6 0........................(b) MGutierrez 3 20
(Leandro Mora, U.S.A) **27/1**

1m 14.57s (74.57) **7** Ran SP% **121.0**
PARI-MUTUEL (all including 2 usd stake): WIN 3.60; PLACE (1-2) 2.80, 6.80; SHOW (1-2-3) 2.10, 3.60, 2.80; SF 31.00.
**Owner** DP Racing LLC **Bred** Siena Farms LLC **Trained** USA

### 7606a 14 HANDS WINERY BREEDERS' CUP JUVENILE FILLIES (GRADE 1) (2YO FILLIES) (DIRT) 1m 110y(D)
**7:05** (12:00) 2-Y-O **£662,650** (£216,867; £120,481; £72,289; £36,144)

RPR

1 **Take Charge Brandi (USA)**[29] 6915 2-8-10 0........................ VictorEspinoza 6 108
(D Wayne Lukas, U.S.A) *mde all: rdn along over 2f out: hld on gamely fnl f* **66/1**

2 *1/2* **Top Decile (USA)**[29] 6915 2-8-10 0........................ RosieNapravnik 11 107+
(Albert M Stall Jr, U.S.A) *hld up in midfield: stdy hdwy over 3f out: effrt and drvn along 2f out: edgd lft over 1f out: styd on wl fnl f to take 2nd cl home* **8/1**

3 *1/2* **Wonder Gal (USA)**[28] 6947 2-8-10 0........................ MESmith 10 106
(Leah Gyarmati, U.S.A) *hld up in tch: stdy hdwy over 4f out: rdn along over 2f out: kpt on u.p and disp 2nd wl ins fnl f: hld cl home* **14/1**

4 *nse* **Feathered (USA)**[28] 6947 2-8-10 0........................ JJCastellano 1 106
(Todd Pletcher, U.S.A) *t.k.h early: trckd ldrs: rdn to go 2nd over 2f out: kpt on fnl f: no ex and lost two pls towards fin* **12/1**

5 *1/2* **Danette (USA)**[34] 6809 2-8-10 0........................ KDesormeaux 3 105
(J Keith Desormeaux, U.S.A) *broke wl but sn hmpd and dropped to last pl: stdy hdwy on ins and in tch over 2f out: hrd rdn wl over 1f out: one pce ins fnl f* **25/1**

6 *1 1/2* **Puca (USA)**[31] 2-8-10 0........................ JRosario 8 101+
(William Mott, U.S.A) *s.i.s: hld up in rr: hdwy and plenty to do over 2f out: styng on whn nt clr run last 100yds: no imp and eased towards fin* **6/1**[3]

7 *4 1/2* **Conquest Eclipse (USA)**[34] 6809 2-8-10 0........................ CNakatani 4 98+
(Mark Casse, Canada) *hld up towards rr: pushed along over 3f out: drvn and no imp fr 2f out* **9/2**[2]

8 *1 1/2* **By The Moon (USA)**[28] 6947 2-8-10 0........................ JLOrtiz 12 95
(Michelle Nevin, U.S.A) *cl up on outside: effrt and chsd wnr over 3f out to over 2f out: hung lft and wknd over 1f out* **10/1**

9 *4 1/4* **Majestic Presence (USA)**[34] 6809 2-8-10 0........................ ElvisTrujillo 7 86
(Jerry Hollendorfer, U.S.A) *hld up: drvn along over 2f out: hung lft over 1f out: nvr on terms* **20/1**

10 *nk* **Angela Renee (USA)**[34] 6809 2-8-10 0........................(b) JRVelazquez 2 85
(Todd Pletcher, U.S.A) *midfield on ins: struggling over 3f out: btn fr 2f out* **3/1**[1]

11 *4 1/4* **Cristina's Journey (USA)**[56] 2-8-10 0........................ MMena 5 76
(Dale Romans, U.S.A) *prom: pushed along over 4f out: wknd over 3f out* **8/1**

12 *4 1/4* **Hennythelovepenny (USA)**[19] 2-8-10 0........................(b) FHPerez 9 66
(Peter Miller, U.S.A) *chsd wnr to over 3f out: sn lost pl: btn ent st* **40/1**

1m 41.95s (-0.47) **12** Ran SP% **115.7**
PARI-MUTUEL (all including 2 usd stake): WIN 125.40; PLACE (1-2) 51.40, 7.20; SHOW (1-2-3) 24.80, 5.40, 9.40; SF 1557.20.
**Owner** Willis D Horton **Bred** Charming Syndicate **Trained** USA

**FOCUS**
On the clock this unfolded in much the same way as the later Juvenile, but that set up for the closers whereas Take Charge Brandi made all. Not a strong renewal.

### 7607a BREEDERS' CUP FILLY & MARE TURF (GRADE 1) (3YO+ FILLIES & MARES) (TURF) 1m 2f (T)
**7:43** (12:00) 3-Y-O+ **£662,650** (£216,867; £120,481; £72,289; £36,144)

RPR

1 **Dayatthespa (USA)**[28] 6951 5-8-12 0........................ JJCastellano 4 114
(Chad C Brown, U.S.A) *broke wl and mde all: shkn up and qcknd over 1f out: 2 l advantage ent fnl f: rdn and styd on strly: readily* **7/1**[3]

2 *1 1/4* **Stephanie's Kitten (USA)**[35] 6774 5-8-12 0........................ JRVelazquez 10 112+
(Chad C Brown, U.S.A) *hld up in midfield: rdn and effrt to improve on outer into st: styd on steadily and wnt 2nd towards fin: no ch w wnr* **4/1**[2]

3 *1/2* **Just The Judge (IRE)**[13] 7326 4-8-12 0........................ JamieSpencer 2 111
(Charles Hills) *prom on inner: rdn 2f out: styd on against rail in st but nt pce of wnr and dropped to 3rd towards fin* **9/1**

4 *hd* **Dank**[136] 3354 5-8-12 0........................ RyanMoore 3 110
(Sir Michael Stoute) *t.k.h: midfield in tch: rdn into st: styd on steadily but nvr able to chal* **7/4**[1]

5 *nk* **Secret Gesture**[69] 5742 4-8-12 0........................ PatSmullen 5 110
(Ralph Beckett) *prom: rdn and effrt over 2f out: outpcd by wnr in st: styd on but wl hld* **8/1**

6 *2 1/4* **Parranda (USA)**[35] 6781 5-8-12 0........................(b) ElvisTrujillo 9 105
(Jerry Hollendorfer, U.S.A) *trckd wnr on outer: rdn and effrt to chal 2f out: outpcd by wnr in st: no ex and fdd fnl f* **33/1**

7 *nk* **Abaco (USA)**[35] 6774 6-8-12 0........................(b) JLOrtiz 1 104
(Claude McGaughey III, U.S.A) *stdd and hld up in last: rdn 2f out: stl in rr ent fnl f: styd on and tk nvr nrr 7th post* **22/1**

8 *hd* **Fiesolana (IRE)**[27] 6971 5-8-12 0........................ BillyLee 6 104
(W McCreery, Ire) *midfield on inner: angled out and rdn into st: nt qckn: no imp and wl hld fnl f: dropped to 8th post* **12/1**

9 *1/2* **Emollient (USA)**[35] 6781 4-8-12 0........................(b) RosieNapravnik 7 103
(William Mott, U.S.A) *hld up towards rr: clsd on rail 3f out: ct on heels early in st: rdn and swtchd rt over 1f out: outpcd and btn fnl f: fdd* **14/1**

10 *1/2* **Rusty Slipper (USA)**[35] 6781 4-8-12 0........................ AGryder 11 102
(H Graham Motion, U.S.A) *midfield: lost pl after 1/2-way: towards rr whn rdn 2f out: outpcd and no imp in st* **40/1**

11 *1/2* **Irish Mission (CAN)**[35] 6781 5-8-12 0........................ JRosario 8 101
(Christophe Clement, U.S.A) *hld up and sn towards rr: effrt to improve on wd outside 3f out: rdn into st: sn no imp: dropped to last fnl f* **33/1**

2m 0.12s (0.84) **11** Ran SP% **117.0**
PARI-MUTUEL (all including 2 usd stake): WIN 13.00; PLACE (1-2) 6.60, 5.20; SHOW (1-2-3) 4.60, 3.80, 4.60; SF 54.20.
**Owner** Jerry Frankel, Ronald Frankel et al **Bred** Castellare Di Cracchiolo Stable, Cracchiolo & Gold **Trained** USA

**FOCUS**
Chad Brown, who trained the first two home, had this race covered from a pace angle, with front-runner Dayatthespa holding off the best closer in Stephanie's Kitten. The gallop was steady, the leader setting splits of 23.89 and 48.37 before finishing in 1:13.12. A small pb from the winner.

### 7608a DRAFTKINGS BREEDERS' CUP FILLY & MARE SPRINT (GRADE 1) (3YO+ FILLIES & MARES) (DIRT) 7f
**8:21** (12:00) 3-Y-O+ **£331,325** (£108,433; £60,240; £36,144; £18,072)

RPR

1 **Judy The Beauty (CAN)**[76] 5-8-12 0........................ MESmith 7 116
(Wesley A Ward, U.S.A) *midfield in tch: rdn and hdwy on wd outside into st: chal over 1f out and led ent fnl f: r.o wl: strly pressed towards fin but a jst doing enough* **7/2**[1]

2 *hd* **Better Lucky (USA)**[28] 6951 5-8-12 0........................ JJCastellano 8 115+
(Thomas Albertrani, U.S.A) *in rr: clsd steadily fr 1/2-way: rdn on rail over 2f out: swtchd rt to wd outside into st: r.o wl and wnt 2nd ins fnl f: clsd on wnr and chal towards fin: jst hld* **25/1**

3 *3 1/2* **Thank You Marylou (USA)**[14] 3-8-10 0........................(b) JRVelazquez 4 104
(Michael J Maker, U.S.A) *midfield in tch: rdn over 2f out: kpt on in st: swtchd lft to rail fnl f and wnt 3rd towards fin: nt pce of front pair* **33/1**

4 1 **Stonetastic (USA)**[28] 3-8-10 0................................................ PLopez 3 101
(Kelly Breen, U.S.A) *led: set solid pce: rdn and tried to kick on into st: strly pressed over 1f out: hdd ent fnl f: no ex and fdd: dropped to 4th towards fin* **4/1**[2]

5 3/4 **Leigh Court (USA)**[28] 4-8-12 0........................................ GBoulanger 6 101
(Josie Carroll, Canada) *prom on outer: rdn and effrt into st: outpcd by ldrs ent fnl f: fdd* **11/2**

6 3/4 **Southern Honey (USA)**[28] 3-8-10 0.......................................... JRLeparoux 10 97
(George R Arnold II, U.S.A) *chsd ldr: rdn and effrt into st: no ex ent fnl f: fdd* **33/1**

7 1/2 **Artemis Agrotera (USA)**[42] 3-8-10 0........................................ JLOrtiz 5 96
(Michael Hushion, U.S.A) *sn outpcd towards rr: rdn 3f out: plugged on in st: swtchd rt fnl f and tk n.d 7th towards fin* **4/1**[2]

8 2 1/4 **Sweet Reason (USA)**[42] 6572 3-8-10 0...................................... IOrtizJr 1 90
(Leah Gyarmati, U.S.A) *midfield on inner: rdn and brief effrt into st: no ex ent fnl f: wknd and eased* **5/1**[3]

9 1/2 **Little Alexis (USA)**[42] 6572 3-8-10 0....................................... JRosario 2 88
(Carlo Vaccarezza, U.S.A) *a in rr: rdn in last 2f out: no imp and btn in st: nvr a factor* **20/1**

10 1/2 **Living The Life (IRE)**[53] 4-8-12 0.....................................(b) RBejarano 9 89
(Gary Mandella, U.S.A) *a towards rr: rdn and effrt to improve 3f out: no further imp in st: dropped to last nring fin* **16/1**

1m 21.92s (81.92)
**WFA** 3 from 4yo+ 1lb **10** Ran SP% **114.6**
PARI-MUTUEL (all including 2 usd stake): WIN 8.20; PLACE (1-2) 4.60, 16.40; SHOW (1-2-3) 3.60, 10.00, 13.80; SF 136.00.
**Owner** Wesley A Ward **Bred** Adena Springs **Trained** North America

**FOCUS**
The principals closed off fractions of 22.51, 44.97 and 1:09.35. The winner is rated similarly to her second in this a year ago.

## 7609a BREEDERS' CUP TURF SPRINT (GRADE 1) (3YO+) (TURF) 6f 110y
**9:05** (12:00) 3-Y-0+ **£331,325** (£108,433; £60,240; £36,144; £18,072)

RPR

1 **Bobby's Kitten (USA)**[48] 6391 3-8-12 0.................................... JRosario 6 112
(Chad C Brown, U.S.A) *sn bhd: last and plenty to do ent st: str run on wd outside fnl f: led cl home* **7/1**[3]

2 1/2 **No Nay Never (USA)**[28] 3-8-12 0.................................... FrankieDettori 13 111
(Wesley A Ward, U.S.A) *sn chsng ldr: effrt and rdn over 1f out: led ins fnl f: edgd lft and hdd cl home* **7/2**[1]

3 nse **Undrafted (USA)**[38] 4-9-0 0............................................. JRVelazquez 10 112
(Wesley A Ward, U.S.A) *towards rr: rdn and plenty to do ent st: kpt on strly fnl f: tk 3rd cl home* **9/1**

4 nk **Ageless (USA)**[22] 5-8-11 0............................................... JRLeparoux 14 109
(Arnaud Delacour, U.S.A) *prom: effrt and rdn 2f out: chsd ldr ins fnl f: no ex and lost two pls towards fin* **66/1**

5 hd **Sweet Swap (USA)**[201] 5-9-0 0............................................. CNakatani 3 111
(John W Sadler, U.S.A) *midfield: rdn over 2f out: edgd lft and rallied towards far side over 1f out: kpt on u.p ins fnl f: nrst fin* **16/1**

6 1/2 **Tightend Touchdown (USA)**[61] 5-9-0 0.........................(b) JJCastellano 4 110
(Jason Servis, U.S.A) *in tch: effrt towards far side 2f out: kpt on same pce ins fnl f* **14/1**

7 1 1/2 **Ambitious Brew (USA)**[35] 4-9-0 0...................................... MESmith 5 105
(Martin F Jones, U.S.A) *towards rr: drvn along 3f out: hdwy over 1f out: kpt on: nvr able to chal* **8/1**

8 nse **Caspar Netscher**[13] 7325 5-9-0 0...................................... PatSmullen 12 105
(David Simcock) *midfield: hdwy on outside and in tch over 1f out: sn drvn: no ex ins fnl f* **16/1**

9 1/2 **Reneesgotzip (USA)**[59] 5-8-11 0.................................(b) EMaldonado 1 101
(Peter Miller, U.S.A) *led at str gallop: rdn over 2f out: edgd rt and hdd ins fnl f: sn btn* **13/2**[2]

10 nse **Something Extra (USA)**[38] 6-9-0 0.............................(b) ERosaDaSilva 8 103
(Gail Cox, Canada) *disp 2nd pl: rdn and edgd rt over 2f out: wknd ins fnl f* **33/1**

11 1/2 **Home Run Kitten (USA)**[35] 3-8-12 0........................................ JTalamo 9 100
(David Hofmans, U.S.A) *hld up towards rr: rdn and outpcd wl over 2f out: sme hdwy towards far rail over 1f out: sn no imp* **10/1**

12 3/4 **Dimension**[38] 6-9-0 0........................................................ RyanMoore 11 100
(Conor Murphy, U.S.A) *s.i.s and n.m.r sn after s: bhd: struggling over 2f out: nvr on terms* **25/1**

13 1/2 **Marchman (USA)**[28] 4-9-0 0............................................... KDesormeaux 7 98
(J Keith Desormeaux, U.S.A) *midfield: drvn over 2f out: outpcd whn blkd over 1f out: btn and eased last 150yds* **33/1**

14 3 1/4 **Silentio (USA)**[68] 5-9-0 0............................................... VictorEspinoza 2 89
(Gary Mandella, U.S.A) *midfield: drvn and struggling 3f out: btn fnl 2f* **11/1**

1m 12.73s (72.73) **14** Ran SP% **116.2**
PARI-MUTUEL (all including 2 usd stake): WIN 16.40; PLACE (1-2) 8.00, 6.60; SHOW (1-2-3) 6.20, 4.80, 7.60; SF 108.20.
**Owner** Kenneth L & Sarah K Ramsey **Bred** Kenneth L & Sarah K Ramsey **Trained** USA

**FOCUS**
Unsurprisingly they went fast up front here, recording splits of 21.69 and 43.67, before the winner, who had been dropped out last, came home in 1:12.73. The form is rated around the winner and seventh.

## 7610a SENTIENT JET BREEDERS' CUP JUVENILE (GRADE 1) (2YO COLTS & GELDINGS) (DIRT) 1m 110y(D)
**9:43** (12:00) 2-Y-0 **£662,650** (£216,867; £120,481; £72,289; £36,144)

RPR

1 **Texas Red (USA)**[35] 6780 2-8-10 0.................................... KDesormeaux 5 120
(J Keith Desormeaux, U.S.A) *dwlt sltly: hld up and sn detached in last: hdwy 3f out: rdn and fanned out to chal into st: edgd lft and led over 1f out: continued to drift lft but r.o strly and forged clr fnl f: v easily* **14/1**

2 6 1/2 **Carpe Diem (USA)**[28] 6952 2-8-10 0.................................. JRVelazquez 7 106
(Todd Pletcher, U.S.A) *hld up in rr in main body of field: rdn over 2f out: outpcd in st: plugged on and tk distant 2nd post: no ch w wnr* **5/2**[1]

3 nse **Upstart (USA)**[28] 6948 2-8-10 0.............................................. JLOrtiz 11 106
(Richard Violette Jr, U.S.A) *dwlt sltly: sn in midfield: rdn over 2f out: effrt to chal ent st: squeezed for room and bmpd over 1f out: wnt 2nd but readily outpcd by wnr fnl f: plugged on but dropped to 3rd post* **9/1**[2]

4 1 3/4 **The Great War (USA)**[34] 6799 2-8-10 0............................ RyanMoore 3 102
(A P O'Brien, Ire) *t.k.h: chsd ldrs: rdn and effrt on inner whn bmpd 2f out: ev ch over 1f out: readily outpcd by wnr fnl f: plugged on* **11/1**[3]

5 nse **Mr. Z (USA)**[28] 6952 2-8-10 0...........................................(b[1]) MESmith 8 102
(D Wayne Lukas, U.S.A) *sn prom: rdn and effrt 2f out: w ldrs and ev ch into st: bmpd over 1f out: readily outpcd by wnr fnl f: plugged on* **20/1**

6 1 1/4 **One Lucky Dane (USA)**[28] 2-8-10 0...................................(b) RBejarano 9 99
(Bob Baffert, U.S.A) *sn prom: ct on heels and dropped to midfield after 3f: rdn over 2f out: outpcd in st: plugged on but wl btn* **9/1**[2]

7 3 1/4 **Souper Colossal (USA)**[62] 2-8-10 0....................................... PLopez 6 92
(Edward Plesa Jr, U.S.A) *pressed ldr: rdn to chal over 2f out and sn led: strly pressed into st: bmpd and hdd over 1f out: no ex and btn: wknd fnl f* **11/1**[3]

8 3 1/2 **Lucky Player (USA)**[56] 2-8-10 0....................................... RSantanaJr 4 84
(Steven Asmussen, U.S.A) *hld up in rr in main body of field: rdn and dropped to last over 2f out: no imp and wl btn in st* **25/1**

9 1 1/4 **Private Prospect (USA)**[56] 2-8-10 0......................(b) JesseMCampbell 1 81
(Michael B Campbell, U.S.A) *chsd ldrs on inner: rdn and lost pl over 2f out: no ex and btn over 1f out: wknd* **33/1**

10 4 1/4 **Blue Dancer (USA)**[19] 2-8-10 0...................................(b) RicoWWalcott 2 72
(Greg Tracy, Canada) *led: set str pce: rdn and hdd over 2f out: bmpd sn after: no ex and btn 1f out: wknd* **40/1**

11 4 1/2 **Daredevil (USA)**[28] 6948 2-8-10 0...................................... JJCastellano 10 62
(Todd Pletcher, U.S.A) *sn prom on outer: rdn and lost pl over 2f out: last into st: bhd and wl btn fnl f* **5/2**[1]

1m 41.91s (-0.51) **11** Ran SP% **114.5**
PARI-MUTUEL (all including 2 usd stake): WIN 29.80; PLACE (1-2) 9.80, 3.80; SHOW (1-2-3) 5.60, 2.80, 3.60; SF 100.60.
**Owner** Erich Brehm, Wayne Detmar Et Al **Bred** Stonestreet Throughbred Holdings Llc **Trained** USA

**FOCUS**
The winner had previously finished third to the now sidelined pair American Pharoah (favourite until withdrawn) and Calculator. The fractions (22.37, 45.66, 1:10.17 and 1:35.69) were much the same as the earlier Juvenile Fillies, but this time the principals came from well behind. The form is rated around the fourth, fifth and sixth.

## 7611a LONGINES BREEDERS' CUP TURF (GRADE 1) (3YO+) (TURF) 1m 4f (T)
**10:22** (12:00) 3-Y-0+ **£993,975** (£325,301; £180,722; £108,433; £54,216)

RPR

1 **Main Sequence (USA)**[35] 6776 5-9-0 0................................ JRVelazquez 12 118
(H Graham Motion, U.S.A) *hld up: effrt and hdwy on outside 2f out: qcknd to ld last 150yds: pushed out: comf* **7/1**[3]

2 1/2 **Flintshire**[27] 6970 4-9-0 0............................................... MaximeGuyon 7 117
(A Fabre, France) *s.i.s: sn in tch: effrt and hdwy to ld appr fnl f: sn rdn and edgd lft: hdd last 150yds: rallied: hld towards fin* **11/4**[2]

3 1 1/4 **Twilight Eclipse (USA)**[35] 6776 5-9-0 0.............................. JJCastellano 2 115
(Thomas Albertrani, U.S.A) *hld up towards rr: pushed along and hdwy over 1f out: kpt on ins fnl f: nt rch first two* **25/1**

4 1/2 **Telescope (IRE)**[73] 5578 4-9-0 0......................................... RyanMoore 1 114
(Sir Michael Stoute) *trckd ldrs on ins: squeezed through and ev ch 1f out: kpt on same pce u.p last 150yds* **7/4**[1]

5 nk **Chicquita (IRE)**[14] 7273 4-8-11 0................................... FrankieDettori 11 111
(A P O'Brien, Ire) *t.k.h in midfield: effrt and rdn over 2f out: hdwy over 1f out: kpt on ins fnl f* **10/1**

6 1 1/4 **Hangover Kid (USA)**[35] 6776 6-9-0 0...................................(b) JLezcano 5 112
(Jason Servis, U.S.A) *s.i.s: hld up: rdn and hdwy over 1f out: kpt on fnl f: nt pce to chal* **65/1**

7 1/2 **Imagining (USA)**[35] 6776 6-9-0 0....................................(b) JRosario 3 111
(Claude McGaughey III, U.S.A) *led at ordinary gallop 4f: cl up: effrt and ev ch over 1f out: no ex last 150yds* **25/1**

8 1/2 **Hardest Core (USA)**[77] 5460 4-9-0 0........................................ EVaz 9 110
(Edward Graham, U.S.A) *t.k.h: cl up on outside: led and maintained ordinary gallop after 4f: rdn and hdd appr fnl f: wknd last 100yds* **9/1**

9 1/2 **Big John B (USA)**[34] 5-9-0 0............................................. MESmith 13 110
(Philip D'Amato, U.S.A) *hld up: rdn along over 2f out: no imp fr over 1f out* **33/1**

10 hd **Finnegans Wake (USA)**[34] 5-9-0 0.......................................... JTalamo 6 109
(Peter Miller, U.S.A) *hld up: pushed along over 2f out: nvr able to chal* **66/1**

11 nk **Brown Panther**[48] 6374 6-9-0 0................................ RichardKingscote 4 109
(Tom Dascombe) *prom: drvn and outpcd over 1f out: btn fnl f* **14/1**

12 14 1/2 **Starspangled Heat (USA)**[34] 6-9-0 0..................................... CNakatani 10 86
(Barry Abrams, U.S.A) *cl up tl rdn and wknd over 2f out: eased whn no ch over 1f out* **66/1**

2m 24.91s (-1.74) **12** Ran SP% **116.4**
PARI-MUTUEL (all including 2 usd stake): WIN 14.40; PLACE (1-2) 5.80, 4.80; SHOW (1-2-3) 4.20, 3.60, 6.40; SF 64.80.
**Owner** Flaxman Holdings Ltd **Bred** Flaxman Holdings Ltd **Trained** USA

## 7612a XPRESSBET BREEDERS' CUP SPRINT (GRADE 1) (3YO+) (DIRT) 6f (D)
**11:01** (12:00) 3-Y-0+ **£496,987** (£162,650; £90,361; £54,216; £27,108)

RPR

1 **Work All Week (USA)**[29] 5-9-0 0........................................... FGeroux 13 121
(Roger Brueggemann, U.S.A) *trckd ldr on outer: rdn to ld into st: r.o wl: reduced advantage towards fin but a doing enough* **20/1**

2 1/2 **Secret Circle (USA)**[27] 6974 5-9-0 0................................ MartinAGarcia 4 119
(Bob Baffert, U.S.A) *a.p: rdn 2f out: r.o and wnt 2nd ins fnl 120yds: chsd wnr and clsd towards fin but nvr getting there* **5/1**[2]

3 1 1/4 **Private Zone (CAN)**[35] 6775 5-9-0 0........................(b) MartinAPedroza 5 115
(Alfredo Velazquez, U.S.A) *a.p: rdn 2f out: r.o and wnt 3rd cl home: nt quite pce of front pair* **8/1**

4 nk **Bourbon Courage (USA)**[29] 5-9-0 0...................................... RSantanaJr 14 114+
(Kellyn Gorder, U.S.A) *dwlt and racd in rr: rdn over 2f out: last and toiling over 1f out: responded to press and str run down wd outside fnl f: wnt 4th fnl strides: nrst fin* **33/1**

5 1/2 **Fast Anna (USA)**[42] 3-8-12 0.....................................(b) JRVelazquez 12 111
(Kathy Ritvo, U.S.A) *sn led and crossed to rail: set searing pce: rdn and hdd into st: kpt on tl no ex fnl f: fdd and lost 3 pls fnl 120yds* **16/1**

6 1/2 **Palace (USA)**[35] 6775 5-9-0 0.......................................... CHVelasquez 8 111
(Linda Rice, U.S.A) *midfield: rdn 3f out: kpt on same pce in st and nvr able to chal* **7/1**[3]

7 nse **Salutos Amigos (USA)**[7] 4-9-0 0................................(b) JJCastellano 9 111
(David Jacobson, U.S.A) *hld up: rdn 3f out: kpt on u.p in st but nvr able to chal* **16/1**

8 1/2 **Bakken (USA)**[30] 4-9-0 0.................................................... GaryStevens 11 109
(Chad C Brown, U.S.A) *midfield: rdn over 2f out: kpt on same pce in st and nvr able to chal* **16/1**

9 3/4 **Big Macher (USA)**[68] 4-9-0 0...........................................(b) TBaze 10 107
(Richard Baltas, U.S.A) *dwlt and racd in rr: last 2f out: kpt on and sme hdwy in st but nvr threatened* **16/1**

10 1 1/4 **Indianapolis (USA)**[35] 3-8-12 0........................................(b) MESmith 2 101
(Bob Baffert, U.S.A) *sn towards rr: rdn over 2f out: kpt on steadily under tender handling fnl f but nvr threatened* **12/1**

11 2 1/2 **Seeking The Sherif (USA)**[41] 5-9-0 0................................ EMaldonado 1 95
(Ronald W Ellis, U.S.A) *broke wl and led early: sn hdd and chsd ldr on inner: rdn 3f out: outpcd and lost pl into st: no ex and btn fnl f: wknd: eased* **25/1**

12 1/2 **Mico Margarita (USA)**[34] 4-9-0 0............................(b) RosieNapravnik 7 93
(Steven Asmussen, U.S.A) *sn towards rr: rdn 3f out: outpcd and no imp in st: n.d* **20/1**

13 3 3/4 **Wind Fire (USA)**[48] 6378 3-8-9 0.................................. JamieSpencer 3 76
(David Brown) *midfield on inner: rdn over 2f out: angled out into st: no ex and btn fnl f: wknd and eased* **25/1**

14 7 1/4 **Rich Tapestry (IRE)**[27] 6974 6-9-0 0...............................(b) ODoleuze 6 58
(C W Chang, Hong Kong) *dwlt sltly: sn in midfield: rdn 3f out: outpcd and lost pl into st: btn and dropped to last ent fnl f: eased* **7/2**[1]

1m 8.28s (0.02) **14** Ran SP% **113.9**
PARI-MUTUEL (all including 2 usd stake): WIN 40.20; PLACE (1-2) 18.40, 6.40; SHOW (1-2-3) 11.00, 4.60, 5.80; SF 245.40.
**Owner** Midwest Thoroughbreds Inc **Bred** Midwest Thoroughbreds **Trained** North America

**FOCUS**
There was no big pace battle this time and the winner sat second through splits of 21.19, 43.34 and 55.38.

## 7613a BREEDERS' CUP MILE (GRADE 1) (3YO+) (TURF) 1m (T)
**11:40** (12:00) 3-Y-O+ **£662,650** (£216,867; £120,481; £72,289; £36,144)

RPR

1 **Karakontie (JPN)**[27] 6971 3-8-11 0........................ StephanePasquier 14 120
(J E Pease, France) *hld up towards rr: stdy hdwy 3f out: effrt and rdn over 1f out: qckned to ld fnl 100yds: keeping on strly whn edgd rt towards fin* **16/1**

2 1 **Anodin (IRE)**[27] 6971 4-9-0 0........................................ OlivierPeslier 9 119+
(F Head, France) *hld up: rdn along 2f out: plld out fnl f and kpt on strly to take 2nd pl last 50yds: hld whn crossed by wnr towards fin* **7/1**[3]

3 1 **Trade Storm**[48] 6391 6-9-0 0........................................ JamieSpencer 8 116
(David Simcock) *s.i.s: hld up: hdwy whn nt clr run briefly 2f out: gd hdwy over 1f out: kpt on strly fnl f: nrst fin* **16/1**

4 hd **Summer Front (USA)**[103] 5-9-0 0.................................. JJCastellano 10 116
(Christophe Clement, U.S.A) *hld up: stdy hdwy over 2f out: rdn and kpt on ins fnl f: nt pce to chal* **66/1**

5 3/4 **Obviously (IRE)**[69] 6-9-0 0............................................... JTalamo 2 114
(Philip D'Amato, U.S.A) *led after 1f and set str gallop: hrd rdn fr 2f out: hdd fnl 100yds: sn btn* **10/1**

6 1 3/4 **Mustajeeb**[49] 6352 3-8-11 0.............................................. PatSmullen 4 109
(D K Weld, Ire) *t.k.h early: in tch: effrt and drvn along over 2f out: no ex ins fnl f* **5/1**[2]

7 1/2 **Tom's Tribute (USA)**[69] 4-9-0 0.......................................... MESmith 6 109
(James Cassidy, U.S.A) *hld up in midfield: effrt and pushed along over 2f out: no imp fr over 1f out* **18/1**

8 nk **Toronado (IRE)**[48] 6382 4-9-0 0................................. RichardHughes 5 108
(Richard Hannon) *led 1f: chsd ldr: hrd rdn and hung rt fr 2f out: lost 2nd and wknd ins fnl f* **2/1**[1]

9 3/4 **Seek Again (USA)**[28] 6953 4-9-0 0........................................ JRosario 12 107
(William Mott, U.S.A) *bhd and nvr gng wl: swtchd to outside and hdwy over 1f out: kpt on fnl f: nvr able to chal* **12/1**

10 1 **Kaigun (CAN)**[28] 6953 4-9-0 0........................................ PHusbands 7 104
(Mark Casse, Canada) *hld up: drvn along appr st: nvr rchd chalng position* **40/1**

11 1 **Grand Arch (USA)**[28] 6953 5-9-0 0................................ JRVelazquez 1 102
(Brian A Lynch, Canada) *midfield on ins: struggling 3f out: btn fnl 2f* **40/1**

12 nk **Veda (FR)**[28] 6955 3-8-8 0.................................. ChristopheSoumillon 3 97
(A De Royer-Dupre, France) *chsd ldrs: effrt and drvn over 2f out: wknd over 1f out: eased last 150yds* **10/1**

13 3/4 **Tourist (USA)**[77] 5458 3-8-11 0............................(b) RosieNapravnik 13 99
(William Mott, U.S.A) *in tch on outside: drvn over 2f out: wknd wl over 1f out* **25/1**

14 3 3/4 **Sayaad (USA)**[28] 6953 4-9-0 0........................................ JRLeparoux 11 91
(Kiaran McLaughlin, U.S.A) *t.k.h early: in tch tl rdn and wknd over 2f out* **40/1**

1m 32.88s (-0.99)
**WFA** 3 from 4yo+ 2lb **14** Ran SP% **118.1**
PARI-MUTUEL (all including 2 usd stake): WIN 62.00; PLACE (1-2) 33.00, 12.60; SHOW (1-2-3) 19.40, 7.20, 12.80; SF 663.40.
**Owner** Niarchos Family **Bred** Flaxman Holdings Limited **Trained** Chantilly, France

**FOCUS**
It paid to be held up here, as the early pace was frantic, the first quarter being run in 21.95. The following splits were 45.16 and 1:08.82, while the winner crossed the line in 1:32.88. The winner is rated to a best view of his form.

# 7605 SANTA ANITA (L-H)
Sunday, November 2

**OFFICIAL GOING: Dirt: fast; turf: firm**

## 7614a BREEDERS' CUP CLASSIC (GRADE 1) (3YO+) (DIRT) 1m 2f (D)
**12:35** (12:00) 3-Y-O£**1,656,626** (£542,168; £301,204; £180,722; £90,361)

RPR

1 **Bayern (USA)**[43] 6573 3-8-10 0...............................(b) MartinAGarcia 7 123
(Bob Baffert, U.S.A) *mde all: broke wl and wnt sharply lft across shared belief first stride leaving stalls: rallied whn pressed fr over 1 1/2f out: r.o u.p fnl f: hld on gamely* **7/1**

2 nse **Toast Of New York (USA)**[69] 5781 3-8-10 0............... JamieSpencer 9 123
(Jamie Osborne) *trckd ldr on outer: rdn to cl fr 2f out: r.o u.p fnl f: clsd all way to line: jst missed out* **12/1**

3 nk **California Chrome (USA)**[43] 6573 3-8-10 0..........(b) VictorEspinoza 13 122+
(Art Sherman, U.S.A) *chsd ldrs on outer: 3rd and rdn on outer over 1 1/2f out: styd on u.p fnl f: no ex fnl 50yds* **5/1**[3]

4 3 1/2 **Shared Belief (USA)**[36] 6782 3-8-10 0.................................. MESmith 6 115+
(Jerry Hollendorfer, U.S.A) *hmpd s: disp 5th on outer: scrubbed along 2 1/2f out: abt 6l 5th 1 1/2f out: sn rdn and kpt on fnl f but nt pce to bridge gap to front three* **5/2**[1]

5 1 1/4 **Tonalist (USA)**[36] 6777 3-8-10 0........................................ JRosario 11 113+
(Christophe Clement, U.S.A) *w.w in rr: pushed along and sme hdwy 3 1/2f out: 10th and hrd rdn over 1 1/2f out: swtchd outside sn after: styd on wl fnl f: nvr on terms w ldrs* **9/2**[2]

6 1/2 **Candy Boy (USA)**[43] 6573 3-8-10 0................................ CNakatani 12 112+
(John W Sadler, U.S.A) *settled towards fnl 3rd: pushed along and prog 3f out: styd on u.p to go 5th ins fnl f: run flattened out and dropped a pl cl home* **25/1**

7 3 1/2 **Cigar Street (USA)**[36] 5-9-0 0.................................... JRVelazquez 2 105+
(William Mott, U.S.A) *chsd ldrs on inner: outpcd and pushed along 3f out: grad lft bhd by ldrs fr 2f out: wknd fnl f* **12/1**

8 1 1/2 **Zivo (USA)**[36] 6777 5-9-0 0............................................ JLezcano 8 102+
(Chad C Brown, U.S.A) *outpcd in rr: last and detached 4f out: rowed along fr sme way out: last and styng on turning for home over 1 1/2f out: kpt on fnl f: nvr plcd to chal* **14/1**

9 nk **Imperative (USA)**[36] 6782 4-9-0 0..............................(b) FrankieDettori 3 101+
(George Papaprodromou, U.S.A) *towards rr: rdn and sme prog over 3f out: hrd rdn and no further imp fr 1 1/2f out: fdd u.p fnl f* **50/1**

10 hd **Footbridge (USA)**[36] 6782 4-9-0 0.................................. RBejarano 10 101+
(Eoin Harty, U.S.A) *racd in midfield: clsng in 6th and niggled along 3f out: rdn and no imp fr 1 1/2f out: one pce fnl f* **50/1**

11 hd **V. E. Day (USA)**[36] 6777 3-8-10 0........................................ JTalamo 5 100+
(James Jerkens, U.S.A) *racd in fnl trio: scrubbed along and no imp 3f out: plugged on u.p fr over 1 1/2f out: nvr in contention* **25/1**

12 nse **Prayer For Relief (USA)**[64] 5944 6-9-0 0...................(b) IOrtizJr 1 100+
(Dale Romans, U.S.A) *midfield: outpcd towards rr 1/2-way: sme prog under hrd riding over 1 1/2f out: nvr a factor* **50/1**

13 3 1/2 **Majestic Harbor (USA)**[36] 6782 6-9-0 0................................ TBaze 14 93+
(Sean McCarthy, U.S.A) *midfield on outer: rdn and lost pl over 2 1/2f out: bhd fnl 1 1/2f* **25/1**

14 22 **Moreno (USA)**[36] 6777 4-9-0 0..............................(b) JJCastellano 4 49+
(Eric J Guillot, U.S.A) *hmpd s: disp 5th on outer: rdn and outpcd 3f out: sn wknd and eased fnl f* **25/1**

1m 59.88s
**WFA** 3 from 4yo+ 4lb **14** Ran SP% **119.2**
PARI-MUTUEL (all including 2 usd stake): WIN 14.20; PLACE (1-2) 8.00, 18.00; SHOW (1-2-3) 5.20, 10.80, 5.40; SF 249.80.
**Owner** Kaleem Shah Inc **Bred** Helen Alexander **Trained** USA

**FOCUS**
A controversial running of the Breeders' Cup Classic as many felt Bayern should have been disqualified for causing interference when swerving violently left on leaving the stalls. While he didn't bother the second or third, he did badly hamper the favourite who in turn bumped Moreno, a potential pace rival for the need-to-lead Bayern, and that completely changed the complexion of the race. It's not difficult to argue the stewards, who apparently voted unanimously for the winner to keep the race, got it wrong. With the Baffert horse left to control a pace to suit (23.12, 46.44, 1:10.22, 1:34.16), the first three raced one-two-three more or less throughout. Bayern is rated to his mark.

## 7615a GOLDIKOVA STKS (GRADE 2) (3YO+ FILLIES & MARES) (TURF) 1m (T)
**11:59** (12:19) 3-Y-O+
**£72,289** (£24,096; £14,457; £7,228; £2,409; £150)

RPR

1 **Filimbi (USA)**[29] 6951 4-8-7 0........................................ JRosario 1 106
(William Mott, U.S.A) **8/5**[1]

2 1/2 **Strathnaver**[36] 6774 5-8-7 0........................................ RBejarano 4 105
(H Graham Motion, U.S.A) *fin 3rd: plcd 2nd* **48/10**

3 3/4 **Wall Of Sound**[14] 7326 4-8-7 0.............................. RichardKingscote 2 103
(Tom Dascombe) *broke wl: chsd ldrs: scrubbed along and effrt over 2f out: c wd into st: styd on wl fnl f: chalng for 3rd whn squeezed out and snatched up 100yds out: fin 5th: plcd 3rd* **136/10**

4 1 1/4 **Emotional Kitten (USA)**[63] 4-8-9 0................................ FrankieDettori 5 102
(Wesley A Ward, U.S.A) *fin 2nd: disqualified and plcd 4th* **119/10**

5 hd **I'm Already Sexy (USA)**[50] 4-8-7 0................................(b) FGeroux 6 100
(Wayne Catalano, U.S.A) *fin 4th: disqualified and plcd 5th* **42/10**[3]

6 2 3/4 **Rhagori**[159] 2659 5-8-7 0............................................... JTalamo 3 93
(Simon Callaghan, U.S.A) **217/10**

7 3 1/4 **Pontchatrain (USA)**[258] 4-8-9 0............................................. MESmith 8 88
(Thomas F Proctor, U.S.A) **33/10**[2]

8 6 1/4 **Legacy (USA)**[167] 4-8-7 0........................................ VictorEspinoza 7 72
(John W Sadler, U.S.A) **50/1**

1m 34.13s (0.26) **8** Ran SP% **119.2**
PARI-MUTUEL (all including 2 usd stake): WIN 5.20; PLACE (1-2) 3.20, 4.20; SHOW (1-2-3) 2.60, 3.00, 4.80; SF 19.60.
**Owner** Juddmonte Farms Inc **Bred** Juddmonte Farms Inc **Trained** USA

# 7479 CAPANNELLE (R-H)
Sunday, November 2

**OFFICIAL GOING: Turf: good**

## 7616a PREMIO RIBOT (GROUP 2) (3YO+) (TURF) 1m
**2:40** (12:00) 3-Y-O+ **£39,583** (£17,416; £9,500; £4,333)

RPR

1 **Porsenna (IRE)**[126] 3776 4-9-2 0...............................(b) DarioVargiu 11 105
(Stefano Botti, Italy) *w.w in rr: tk clsr order after 1/2-way: gd hdwy on outer over 2f out: r.o to ld ins fnl f: drvn out* **122/10**

2 1/2 **Kramulkie (IRE)**[126] 3776 4-9-2 0..........................(p) UmbertoRispoli 6 104
(A Marcialis, Italy) *t.k.h: hld up towards rr: effrt and n.m.r 2 1/2f out: in clr and rdn under 2f out: qckned to chal ldr ins fnl f: run flattened out fnl 75yds* **59/10**

3 1 1/2 **Dancing Sands (IRE)**[35] 3-8-11 0................................ MickaelBarzalona 4 98
(H-A Pantall, France) *w.w in midfield: chsd ldng pair fr 3f out: sn rdn and n.m.r fr 2 1/2f out: angled out appr fnl f: styd on u.p: nt pce to rch front two* **152/100**[1]

4 snk **Kaspersky (IRE)**[35] 6808 3-9-1 0........................................ FabioBranca 5 101
(E Botti, Italy) *racd in midfield: hdwy on outer 3f out: led over 2f out: sn rdn: hdd ins fnl f: wknd last 100yds* **152/10**

5 1 1/4 **Lucky Serena (IRE)**[7] 7480 4-8-13 0.................................... CFiocchi 10 94
(Agostino Affe', Italy) *hld up towards rr: rdn and styd on fr 2f out: kpt on wl fnl f: nrest at fin* **232/10**

6 3/4 **Verdetto Finale**[35] 6808 4-9-2 0..................................(p) FBossa 3 96
(R Biondi, Italy) *trckd ldr: rdn and rallied u.p fr 2f out: wknd ins fnl f* **21/10**[2]

7 4 **Rimbaud (GER)**[203] 6-9-2 0 SDiana 1 86
(Alfredino Sauli, Italy) *chsd ldrs: rdn and nt qckn 2 1/2f out: wknd over 1f out* **59/1**

8 2 **Love Happens**[35] 6807 5-8-13 0 RobertHavlin 7 79
(Ferdinand J Leve, Germany) *towards rr: outpcd and rdn in last fr 3f out: sme prog passed btn horses fnl f: nvr in contention* **81/10**

9 1 1/2 **Musicante Di Breme (FR)**[14] 7322 4-9-2 0 WGambarota 9 78
(M Amerio, Italy) *cl up in 3rd: rdn and sltly outpcd 2 1/2f out: wknd fnl f* **235/10**

10 3/4 **Monte Fanum (ITY)** 4-9-2 0 APolli 8 77
(C Felaco, Italy) *led: hdd over 2f out: tightened up on rail sn after and squeezed out: sn wknd: eased fnl f* **26/1**

11 1/2 **Salford Secret (IRE)**[14] 7322 3-9-1 0 CColombi 2 76
(Riccardo Santini, Italy) *hld up in fnl 3rd: gd hdwy on rail 3f out: chsd ldrs fr 2f out: n.m.r and shuffled bk sn after: eased ins fnl f* **26/5**[3]

1m 36.0s (-3.80)
**WFA** 3 from 4yo+ 2lb **11** Ran SP% **140.9**
WIN (incl. 1 euro stake): 13.16. PLACES: 2.91, 2.19, 1.62. DF: 138.20.
**Owner** Scuderia Aleali Srl **Bred** Gennaro Stimola & Vito Colonna **Trained** Italy

## 7617a PREMIO ROMA GBI RACING (GROUP 1) (3YO+) (TURF) 1m 2f
**3:15** (12:00) 3-Y-O+ **£79,166** (£34,833; £19,000; £9,500)

RPR

1 **Priore Philip (ITY)**[35] 6808 3-9-0 0 DarioVargiu 7 118+
(Stefano Botti, Italy) *midfield: smooth hdwy 3f out: chal gng strly 2f out: shkn up and qcknd to ld over 1f out: rdn and styd on strly fnl f: v easily* **31/20**[1]

2 6 **Cleo Fan (ITY)**[35] 3-9-0 0 UmbertoRispoli 8 106
(Stefano Botti, Italy) *led: rdn over 2f out: hdd over 1f out and lft bhd by wnr: kpt on for wl btn 2nd* **41/10**[3]

3 1 3/4 **Dartagnan D'Azur (FR)**[19] 7189 5-9-2 0 MickaelBarzalona 2 101
(W Hefter, Germany) *stdd and hld up in last: fanned out and rdn in st: plugged on down wd outside and wnt 3rd ins fnl f: no ch w wnr* **19/10**[2]

4 2 **Refuse To Bobbin (IRE)**[14] 7323 4-9-2 0 LManiezzi 3 97
(A Giorgi, Italy) *hld up: rdn 4f out: plugged on for n.d 4th* **26/1**

5 1 **Oil Of England (GER)**[42] 6590 3-9-0 0 MEsposito 6 97
(Werner Glanz, Germany) *prom: rdn over 3f out: outpcd and btn fnl 2f: fdd* **183/20**

6 snk **Slowpoke (IRE)**[35] 3-9-0 0 PAragoni 4 96
(L Riccardi, Italy) *hld up and sn towards rr: rdn and hdwy 2f out: edgd rt u.p: no further imp and btn fnl f* **35/1**

7 2 **Lodovico Il Moro (IRE)**[147] 3047 4-9-2 0 CristianDemuro 10 90
(L Riccardi, Italy) *midfield in tch: clsd gng wl 3f out: rdn and brief effrt over 2f out: sn outpcd: no ex and fdd fnl f* **57/10**

8 5 **Duca Di Mantova**[14] 7323 5-9-2 0 FBossa 11 80
(R Biondi, Italy) *dwlt: pushed along to rcvr and sn midfield: rdn 4f out: keeping on but no imp and wl hld whn eased over 1f out* **66/10**

9 1 1/2 **Occhio Della Mente (IRE)**[147] 3047 7-9-2 0 (b) CFiocchi 1 77
(E Botti, Italy) *hld up towards rr: rdn 4f out: sn outpcd and no imp: eased whn btn fnl f* **57/10**

10 15 **Awake My Soul (IRE)**[42] 6590 5-9-2 0 GBietolini 9 47
(Gianluca Bietolini, Italy) *trckd ldr: rdn into st: lost pl over 3f out: sn no ex: eased whn btn over 2f out: t.o* **28/1**

11 1/2 **Dark Sea (IRE)**[35] 3-9-0 0 (b) FabioBranca 5 48
(E Botti, Italy) *hld up towards rr: rdn 3f out: outpcd and no imp whn eased over 2f out: t.o and dropped to last* **57/10**

1m 58.4s (-4.90)
**WFA** 3 from 4yo+ 4lb **11** Ran SP% **171.0**
WIN (incl. 1 euro stake): 2.55. PLACES: 1.27, 1.44, 1.37. DF: 10.72.
**Owner** Scuderia Ste Ma **Bred** Azienda Agricola Luciani Loreto **Trained** Italy

# 6950 FRANKFURT (L-H)
### Sunday, November 2
**OFFICIAL GOING: Turf: good to soft**

## 7618a HESSEN-POKAL (LISTED RACE) (3YO+) (TURF) 1m
**2:30** (12:00) 3-Y-O+ **£11,666** (£5,416; £2,500; £1,250)

RPR

1 **Boomshackerlacker (IRE)**[28] 6965 4-9-3 0 FergusSweeney 1 108
(George Baker) *midfield: clsd 1/2-way: 3rd into st: swtchd rt and rdn 2f out: r.o wl and chal ins fnl f: led nr fin: pushed out firmly* **17/10**[1]

2 3/4 **Gereon (GER)**[30] 6914 6-9-3 0 DennisSchiergen 9 106
(C Zschache, Germany) **77/10**

3 7 **Laeyos (GER)**[173] 5-9-0 0 AnthonyCrastus 6 87
(P Harley, Germany) **63/10**[3]

4 3/4 **Royal Fox**[140] 4-9-0 0 (b) AStarke 5 85
(P Schiergen, Germany) **106/10**

5 3/4 **Maningrey (GER)**[41] 6620 5-9-3 0 APietsch 7 87
(Waldemar Hickst, Germany) **27/10**[2]

6 1 3/4 **Sanjii Danon (GER)**[130] 8-9-0 0 FilipMinarik 11 80
(Gerald Geisler, Germany) **146/10**

7 1 **All In (GER)**[102] 6-9-0 0 MiguelLopez 8 77
(Claudia Erni, Switzerland) **129/10**

8 1 3/4 **Swingdream (GER)**[21] 3-8-8 0 DanielePorcu 4 69
(M Figge, Germany) **132/10**

9 2 **Leonard (GER)** 5-9-0 0 (b) AlexanderWeis 10 69
(Frau S Weis, Germany) **18/1**

10 2 **Commander Kirk (IRE)**[542] 4-9-0 0 MartinSeidl 3 64
(Markus Klug, Germany) **156/10**

11 2 1/2 **Librettista (FR)**[7] 7483 4-8-10 0 BGanbat 2 54
(Frau S Weis, Germany) **42/1**

1m 42.4s (102.40)
**WFA** 3 from 4yo+ 2lb **11** Ran SP% **132.1**
WIN (incl. 10 euro stake): 27. PLACES: 15, 24, 22. SF: 117.
**Owner** PJL Racing **Bred** Miss Elaine Marie Smith **Trained** Manton, Wilts

# 7094 CHANTILLY (R-H)
### Friday, October 31
**OFFICIAL GOING: Turf: soft; polytrack: standard**

## 7619a PRIX DE MONTLEVEQUE (CONDITIONS) (3YO) (POLYTRACK) 1m
**1:50** (12:00) 3-Y-O **£14,166** (£5,666; £4,250; £2,833; £1,416)

RPR

1 **Complicit (IRE)**[6] 7449 3-9-0 0 IoritzMendizabal 5 101
(Paul Cole) *sn trcking ldr on outer: shkn up to chal over 1 1/2f out: led appr fnl f: drvn out* **3/1**[1]

2 snk **Plaisanciere (FR)**[61] 3-8-10 0 Francois-XavierBertras 9 97
(F Rohaut, France) **3/1**[1]

3 2 **Bernay (IRE)**[140] 3-9-0 0 GregoryBenoist 8 96
(C Ferland, France) **26/5**[3]

4 2 **Pompilius (FR)**[28] 6913 3-9-0 0 TonyPiccone 4 91
(C Lotoux, France) **129/10**

5 nse **Dominandros (FR)**[72] 5591 3-9-4 0 UmbertoRispoli 2 95
(Gay Kelleway) *w.w towards rr: n.m.r fr over 2f out: in clr and effrt appr 1f out: sn rdn and one pce fnl f* **239/10**

6 3/4 **Muharaaj (IRE)**[10] 3-9-0 0 (b) AntoineHamelin 7 90
(Matthieu Palussiere, France) **11/2**

7 shd **Rosebay (GER)**[54] 3-8-10 0 TheoBachelot 3 85
(Markus Klug, Germany) **30/1**

8 1 **Zenobios (USA)**[24] 7028 3-9-0 0 MickaelBarzalona 1 87
(A Fabre, France) **39/10**[2]

9 1 1/2 **Vedeux (IRE)**[20] 3-9-0 0 ThierryThulliez 6 84
(C Lerner, France) **45/1**

1m 37.96s (97.96) **9** Ran SP% **118.5**
WIN (incl. 1 euro stake): 3.90. PLACES: 1.40, 1.40, 1.70. DF: 5.50. SF: 11.80.
**Owner** T A Rahman **Bred** Barouche Stud Ireland Ltd **Trained** Whatcombe, Oxon

## 7620a PRIX DU BOIS TURQUET (CLAIMER) (4YO+) (POLYTRACK) 1m 5f 110y
**2:20** (12:00) 4-Y-O+ **£7,916** (£3,166; £2,375; £1,583; £791)

RPR

1 **Varadero (IRE)**[9] 6-9-0 0 NicolasBarzalona(5) 6 82
(L Baudron, France) **11/5**[2]

2 5 **Jason Bournes (FR)**[69] 7-8-9 0 MllePaulineDominois(6) 3 70
(E Lellouche, France) **37/10**[3]

3 4 **Vardaris (IRE)**[9] 4-9-0 0 (p) NicolasLarenaudie(5) 2 68
(P Adda, France) **9/1**

4 2 1/2 **Ssafa**[8] 7402 6-9-5 0 IoritzMendizabal 7 64
(Paul Cole) *trckd ldr on outer: led over 4f out: rdn and hdd 2f out: grad lft bhd fnl 1 1/2f* **21/10**[1]

5 5 **Vasias (FR)**[20] 6-9-1 0 TonyPiccone 5 53
(C Lotoux, France) **13/2**

6 dist **Plaine Monceau (FR)**[18] 4-8-8 0 CristianDemuro 4
(Braem Horse Racing Sprl, Belgium) **15/2**

2m 56.73s (176.73) **6** Ran SP% **119.9**
WIN (incl. 1 euro stake): 3.20. PLACES: 1.70, 2.20. SF: 9.90.
**Owner** Louis Baudron **Bred** Aleyrion Bloodstock Ltd **Trained** France

# 7568 WOLVERHAMPTON (A.W) (L-H)
### Monday, November 3
**OFFICIAL GOING: Tapeta: standard**
Wind: Fresh half-behind Weather: Fine

## 7621 £20 RISK-FREE BET AT UNIBET H'CAP (TAPETA) (DIV I) 5f 216y
**1:45** (1:47) (Class 6) (0-65,65) 3-Y-O+ **£2,264** (£673; £336; £168) **Stalls** Low

Form RPR

0531 1 **Sewn Up**[10] 7424 4-9-1 59 (p) PhillipMakin 3 67
(Keith Dalgleish) *sn pushed along and prom: shkn up over 1f out: r.o to ld nr fin* **4/1**[2]

1003 2 hd **Jolly Red Jeanz (IRE)**[16] 7286 3-9-6 64 (b) WilliamCarson 9 71
(Tom Dascombe) *chsd ldrs: rdn over 1f out: edgd rt and led ins fnl f: hdd nr fin* **11/1**

6400 3 hd **Seven Lucky Seven**[31] 6902 3-9-4 62 TomEaves 5 68
(Michael Herrington) *s.i.s: hld up: hdwy over 2f out: rdn to ld 1f out: sn hdd: r.o* **9/1**

1032 4 1 **Logans Lad (IRE)**[17] 7252 4-9-2 65 (vt) EoinWalsh(5) 7 68
(Daniel Mark Loughnane) *sn pushed along to chse ldrs: rdn over 1f out: bmpd ins fnl f: styd on* **9/4**[1]

6030 5 3/4 **Caminel (IRE)**[32] 6889 3-9-1 59 (b[1]) SteveDrowne 6 59
(Jeremy Gask) *hld up: rdn over 1f out: r.o wl ins fnl f: nt rch ldrs* **25/1**

0026 6 3/4 **Tango Sky (IRE)**[17] 7253 5-9-5 63 LukeMorris 4 61
(James Unett) *mid-div: hdwy over 2f out: rdn over 1f out: styd on* **8/1**[3]

6500 7 nse **Ypres**[20] 7179 5-9-7 65 PaulMulrennan 10 63
(Jason Ward) *mid-div: hdwy over 2f out: sn rdn: styd on* **14/1**

0000 8 1/2 **Whipphound**[15] 7307 6-9-5 63 GeorgeBaker 2 61
(Mark Brisbourne) *s.i.s: hld up: effrt and nt clr run over 1f out: nt trble ldrs* **11/1**

2160 9 1 3/4 **Goadby**[70] 5777 3-9-3 61 RobertHavlin 13 52
(John Holt) *led: hdd over 3f out: led again over 2f out: rdn and hdd 1f out: wknd ins fnl f* **66/1**

0000 10 nk **Look Here's Al**[19] 7213 3-9-5 63 GrahamGibbons 11 53
(Andrew Hollinshead) *hld up: rdn over 1f out: n.d* **10/1**

5000 11 8 **Invigilator**[17] 7252 6-9-4 62 (t) DaleSwift 8 26
(Derek Shaw) *mid-div: rdn and lost pl over 2f out: sn wknd* **20/1**

0000 12 10 **New Decade**[15] 7307 5-9-2 60 (t) RobertWinston 1
(Milton Bradley) *sn pushed along to join ldr: led over 3f out tl rdn and hdd over 2f out: wknd and eased over 1f out* **40/1**

1m 14.5s **Going Correction** -0.075s/f (Stan) **12** Ran SP% **116.8**
Speed ratings (Par 101): **97,96,96,95,94 93,93,92,90,89 79,65**
CSF £44.87 CT £376.15 TOTE £4.30: £1.70, £3.10, £2.40; EX 37.60 Trifecta £268.40.
**Owner** John Kelly **Bred** M E Broughton **Trained** Carluke, S Lanarks
■ Stewards' Enquiry : Dale Swift two-day ban: careless riding (Nov 20-21)


The Form Book, Raceform Ltd, Newbury, RG14 5SJ

**FOCUS**
Mainly exposed sorts in a modest handicap. The gallop was reasonable and the winner raced towards the far rail in the straight. The winner got closer to his old form.

## 7622 £20 RISK-FREE BET AT UNIBET H'CAP (TAPETA) (DIV II) 5f 216y
**2:15** (2:18) (Class 6) (0-65,65) 3-Y-O+ **£2,264** (£673; £336; £168) **Stalls** Low

Form RPR
000 **1** **Avonmore Star**[46] 6495 6-9-4 62........................(p) BenCurtis 3 70
(Alan McCabe) *a.p: chsd ldr over 2f out: rdn over 1f out: styd on u.p to ld wl ins fnl f* **50/1**
0400 **2** ½ **Medam**[16] 7286 5-9-7 65........................ RobertWinston 13 71+
(Shaun Harris) *mid-div: hdwy over 2f out: rdn over 1f out: r.o to go 2nd towards fin: nt rch wnr* **11/1**
5165 **3** ¾ **Pearl Noir**[13] 7356 4-9-0 58........................(b) LukeMorris 6 62
(Scott Dixon) *led: rdn over 1f out: hdd and unable qck wl ins fnl f* **10/3**[1]
3403 **4** 1¼ **Kodafine (IRE)**[13] 7355 3-9-4 62........................ AdamKirby 9 62
(David Evans) *a.p: rdn over 2f out: styd on same pce ins fnl f* **6/1**[2]
0026 **5** ½ **Red Cape (FR)**[17] 7252 11-9-7 65........................(b) JamesSullivan 12 63
(Ruth Carr) *chsd ldrs: rdn over 1f out: no ex ins fnl f* **16/1**
0541 **6** 1 **Methaaly (IRE)**[13] 7364 11-8-9 60........................(b) AnnaHesketh(7) 8 55+
(Michael Mullineaux) *hld up: nt clr run wl over 1f out: r.o ins fnl f: nrst fin* **8/1**
00-0 **7** ¾ **Scatty Cat (IRE)**[60] 6078 4-9-5 63........................(t) ShaneKelly 10 55
(Daniel Mark Loughnane) *sn pushed along towards rr: rdn over 1f out: r.o ins fnl f: nvr nrr* **20/1**
0400 **8** ¾ **Climaxfortackle (IRE)**[19] 7213 6-9-5 63........................ JoeFanning 5 53
(Derek Shaw) *pushed along in rr early: hdwy over 1f out: styd on same pce fnl f* **7/1**
640 **9** 1¼ **Kings Chapel (USA)**[28] 6988 3-9-3 61........................ SteveDrowne 7 47
(Jeremy Gask) *s.i.s: sn mid-div: rdn 1/2-way: n.d* **18/1**
0432 **10** 1½ **Dancing Maite**[109] 4344 9-8-10 59........................(b) EoinWalsh(5) 11 40
(Roy Bowring) *s.i.s: hld up: nvr on terms* **13/2**[3]
50-0 **11** 1¼ **Omanome (IRE)**[17] 7249 3-9-7 65........................ DanielTudhope 2 42
(David O'Meara) *mid-div: rdn 1/2-way: n.d* **12/1**
0104 **12** 2½ **Foxtrot Pearl (IRE)**[16] 7286 3-9-6 64........................ RobertHavlin 4 33
(John Holt) *chsd ldr over 3f: wknd over 1f out* **14/1**
550 **13** 1¾ **Volito**[114] 4206 8-9-5 63........................ GeorgeBaker 1 27
(Anabel K Murphy) *s.i.s: hld up: a in rr* **16/1**

1m 14.69s (0.19) **Going Correction** -0.075s/f (Stan) **13** Ran SP% **120.8**
Speed ratings (Par 101): **95,94,93,91,91 89,88,87,86,84 82,79,76**
CSF £538.59 CT £2361.89 TOTE £40.70: £9.70, £4.30, £1.30; EX 2367.00 Trifecta £3460.10 Part won. Pool of £4613.46 - 0.29 winning units..
**Owner** McCabe, Timms & Timms **Bred** Miss J R Tooth **Trained** Averham Park, Notts

**FOCUS**
Division two of an ordinary event, and slightly slower than the first The gallop was reasonable but, as is often the case in sprints on Tapeta, not many figured and those held up were again at a disadvantage. The winner raced centre-to-far side in the straight and got back to his early-season form.

## 7623 UNIBET OFFER DAILY JOCKEY/TRAINER SPECIALS CLASSIFIED (S) STKS (TAPETA) 5f 20y
**2:50** (2:50) (Class 6) 3-Y-O+ **£2,264** (£673; £336; £168) **Stalls** Low

Form RPR
/4-6 **1** **Invincible Ridge (IRE)**[64] 5958 6-9-0 75........................(t) LukeMorris 2 76
(Eric Alston) *chsd ldrs: shkn up to ld 1f out: r.o* **11/8**[1]
3000 **2** 1¼ **Thorpe Bay**[163] 2552 5-8-11 70........................ RyanTate(3) 5 72
(Michael Appleby) *a.p: chsd ldr 1/2-way: rdn over 1f out: styd on same pce ins fnl f* **16/1**
0031 **3** hd **Fitz Flyer (IRE)**[31] 6898 8-8-13 74........................(v) AnnaHesketh(7) 1 77
(David Nicholls) *led 4f out: rdn and hdd 1f out: styd on same pce* **9/4**[2]
0326 **4** 1¼ **Hamoody (USA)**[6] 7521 10-9-3 75........................ ThomasBrown(3) 7 72
(Joseph Tuite) *hld up: hdwy over 1f out: styd on same pce ins fnl f* **9/2**[3]
1650 **5** 1 **Joyous**[16] 7286 4-9-6 64........................ RobertWinston 3 69
(Dean Ivory) *hld up: swtchd rt and hdwy over 1f out: no ex ins fnl f* **22/1**
3000 **6** 8 **Jiroft (ITY)**[39] 6695 7-9-0 72........................(t) JoeFanning 6 34
(Ann Stokell) *s.i.s: a in rr: wknd 2f out* **12/1**
406 **7** 2¼ **Profile Star (IRE)**[37] 6764 5-9-6 69........................ TonyHamilton 4 32
(Ann Stokell) *led 1f: chsd ldr tl pushed along 1/2-way: wknd over 1f out* **50/1**

1m 1.11s (-0.79) **Going Correction** -0.075s/f (Stan) **7** Ran SP% **110.9**
Speed ratings (Par 101): **103,101,100,98,97 84,80**
CSF £23.67 TOTE £2.70: £1.60, £6.30; EX 21.30 Trifecta £71.70.There was no bid for the winner. Profile Star was claimed by V M. Jordan for £6000.
**Owner** Edges Farm Racing Stables Ltd **Bred** Con Harrington **Trained** Longton, Lancs

**FOCUS**
A fair race of its type, but the usual doubts over the form. The gallop was fair and the winner raced just off the far rail in the straight.

## 7624 DAILY PRICE BOOSTS AT UNIBET H'CAP (TAPETA) 5f 216y
**3:20** (3:22) (Class 4) (0-85,85) 3-Y-O+ **£4,851** (£1,443; £721; £360) **Stalls** Low

Form RPR
0053 **1** **Zac Brown (IRE)**[24] 7073 3-9-3 81........................ GrahamGibbons 9 98
(David Barron) *hld up in tch: shkn up to chse ldr over 1f out: rdn to ld ins fnl f: r.o wl* **7/2**[2]
6144 **2** 3 **Dissent (IRE)**[45] 6511 5-8-11 78........................(b) ConnorBeasley(3) 11 85
(James Given) *led: rdn over 1f out: hdd and unable qck ins fnl f* **4/1**[3]
1036 **3** ½ **Solar Spirit (IRE)**[16] 7282 9-8-11 75........................ JoeFanning 5 80
(Tracy Waggott) *hld up: hdwy over 1f out: styd on* **20/1**
1100 **4** nk **Expose**[9] 7455 6-9-7 85........................ DavidNolan 6 89
(Shaun Harris) *mid-div: hdwy over 1f out: styd on* **11/1**
0010 **5** 1 **Tagula Night (IRE)**[17] 7233 8-9-7 85........................(tp) FrannyNorton 4 86
(Dean Ivory) *prom: chsd ldr 1/2-way tl rdn over 1f out: no ex ins fnl f* **33/1**
4355 **6** 1¼ **Shamaheart (IRE)**[20] 7183 4-8-7 71........................(v) SilvestreDeSousa 10 68
(Geoffrey Harker) *s.i.s: sn pushed along in rr: edgd lft and hmpd over 2f out: styd on ins fnl f: nvr nrr* **6/1**
141 **7** 1 **Sleep Walk**[61] 6025 3-9-6 84........................ GeorgeBaker 8 78
(Roger Charlton) *chsd ldrs: rdn over 1f out: wknd ins fnl f* **2/1**[1]
0000 **8** 5 **Secret Witness**[37] 6744 8-9-7 85........................(p) LukeMorris 7 63
(Ronald Harris) *hld up: rdn whn hmpd over 2f out: n.d* **25/1**
6204 **9** 4 **Drive On (IRE)**[50] 6355 3-9-1 79........................(v[1]) JohnFahy 1 44
(Eve Johnson Houghton) *mid-div: lost pl over 2f out: sn wknd* **14/1**
032 **10** 11 **Diamond Charlie (IRE)**[75] 5559 6-9-5 83........................ SebSanders 3 13
(Simon Dow) *chsd ldr to 1/2-way: rdn and hung rt over 2f out: sn wknd* **20/1**

1m 13.24s (-1.26) **Going Correction** -0.075s/f (Stan) **10** Ran SP% **121.2**
Speed ratings (Par 105): **105,101,100,99,98 96,95,88,83,68**
CSF £17.74 CT £251.13 TOTE £4.70: £1.60, £1.70, £7.20; EX 20.00 Trifecta £430.00.
**Owner** R G Toes **Bred** Tally-Ho Stud **Trained** Maunby, N Yorks

**FOCUS**
A useful handicap in which the pace was sound. The winner came down the centre in the straight and the form is rated around the second and third.

## 7625 32RED MAIDEN AUCTION STKS (TAPETA) 1m 141y
**3:50** (3:51) (Class 6) 2-Y-O **£2,264** (£673; £336; £168) **Stalls** Low

Form RPR
602 **1** **Twice Certain (IRE)**[19] 7198 2-8-12 72........................ LukeMorris 9 71
(Ed Walker) *a.p: rdn over 2f out: led ins fnl f: styd on wl* **2/1**[1]
**2** 1½ **Quest For Wonder** 2-8-13 0........................ MartinHarley 4 69
(James Tate) *hld up: pushed along and hdwy over 2f out: ev ch ins fnl f: styd on same pce* **16/1**
2463 **3** hd **Edge Of Heaven**[13] 7353 2-8-4 63........................ DannyBrock(3) 5 62
(Jonathan Portman) *chsd ldrs: wnt 2nd over 2f out: rdn to ld over 1f out: hdd ins fnl f: styd on same pce* **7/2**[3]
5 **4** 1½ **Missandei**[19] 7209 2-8-9 0........................ PaoloSirigu 6 61+
(Marco Botti) *s.i.s: hdwy over 6f out: outpcd over 2f out: edgd lft and styd on ins fnl f* **25/1**
0 **5** 1¾ **Rum Swizzle**[19] 7198 2-8-7 0 ow2........................ ThomasBrown(3) 1 59
(Harry Dunlop) *hld up: hdwy over 1f out: no ex ins fnl f* **33/1**
0 **6** ½ **Callendula**[20] 7184 2-8-5 0........................ RyanTate(3) 7 56
(Clive Cox) *hld up: rdn over 1f out: no ex ins fnl f* **5/1**
0 **7** 3½ **Space Sheriff (IRE)**[13] 7353 2-9-1 0........................(b[1]) AdamKirby 3 55
(Jamie Osborne) *led over 7f out: rdn 2f out: hdd over 1f out: wknd ins fnl f* **16/1**
022 **8** 3¼ **Burma Bridge**[18] 7217 2-8-10 69........................ CamHardie(3) 8 46
(Richard Hannon) *led: hung rt and hdd over 7f out: remained w ldr tl rdn over 3f out: wknd fnl f* **11/4**[2]
00 **9** 4½ **Resolve**[37] 6754 2-8-13 0........................ FergusSweeney 2 37
(David Simcock) *s.i.s: a in rr: rdn and wknd over 2f out* **66/1**

1m 50.36s (0.26) **Going Correction** -0.075s/f (Stan) **9** Ran SP% **118.9**
Speed ratings (Par 94): **95,93,93,92,90 90,87,84,80**
CSF £37.28 TOTE £3.70: £1.10, £3.20, £3.10; EX 43.00 Trifecta £252.30.
**Owner** Bobby Donworth **Bred** Round Hill Stud **Trained** Newmarket, Suffolk

**FOCUS**
A modest and uncompetitive maiden and one run at a modest gallop to the home turn. The winner raced centre-to-far side in the straigh and built on his latest promise.

## 7626 DOWNLOAD THE CORAL APP H'CAP (TAPETA) 1m 1f 103y
**4:25** (4:26) (Class 5) (0-70,70) 3-Y-O+ **£2,911** (£866; £432; £216) **Stalls** Low

Form RPR
4000 **1** **Pivotman**[10] 7411 6-9-2 **65**........................(bt) GrahamGibbons 6 76
(Michael Easterby) *mde all: clr 6f out tl over 3f out: shkn up and qcknd clr again over 2f out: styd on u.p* **28/1**
0202 **2** 1¾ **Ze King**[13] 7358 5-9-4 **67**........................ TedDurcan 3 74
(Chris Wall) *chsd wnr: rdn over 2f out: no imp ins fnl f* **9/4**[2]
5531 **3** 2¼ **Coillte Cailin (IRE)**[6] 7522 4-9-6 **69** 6ex........................ StevieDonohoe 10 71
(Daniel Mark Loughnane) *hld up in tch: rdn over 1f out: styd on same pce fnl f* **8/1**
5024 **4** hd **Moccasin (FR)**[14] 7335 5-9-6 **69**........................ SilvestreDeSousa 9 71
(Geoffrey Harker) *chsd ldrs: rdn over 1f out: styd on same pce fnl f* **5/1**[3]
6-56 **5** 3½ **Here For Good (IRE)**[14] 7340 3-8-10 **65**........................ CamHardie(3) 11 61
(Richard Hannon) *mid-div: rdn 1/2-way: styd on fr over 1f out: nt trble ldrs* **66/1**
0221 **6** 4½ **Tayma (IRE)**[3] 7568 3-8-13 **70** 6ex........................ KevinStott(5) 2 56
(Saeed bin Suroor) *s.i.s: sn rcvrd into mid-div: hdwy 2f out: wknd fnl f* **7/4**[1]
0421 **7** nse **Solid Justice (IRE)**[17] 7251 3-9-2 **68**........................ TomEaves 7 54
(Jason Ward) *hld up: rdn over 2f out: n.d* **16/1**
3236 **8** 4½ **Tectonic (IRE)**[5] 7533 5-9-6 **69**........................(p) PhillipMakin 13 45
(Keith Dalgleish) *hld up: plld hrd: a in rr: eased over 1f out* **9/1**
0360 **9** nk **Idol Deputy (FR)**[6] 7522 8-9-0 **68**........................(p) RachealKneller(5) 1 43
(James Bennett) *chsd ldrs tl wknd wl over 1f out* **40/1**
3200 **10** 4 **Matraash (USA)**[16] 7288 8-8-13 **62**........................(be) ShaneKelly 12 28
(Daniel Mark Loughnane) *prom tl wknd over 2f out* **40/1**
00 **11** 4 **Boboli Gardens**[10] 7427 4-8-8 **62**........................ TobyAtkinson(5) 5 20
(Noel Quinlan) *s.i.s: hld up: rdn and wknd 3f out* **100/1**
2354 **12** 14 **Aldeburgh**[186] 1899 5-9-3 **66**........................ GeorgeBaker 4
(Claire Dyson) *hld up: wknd wl over 2f out* **28/1**

1m 59.0s (-1.80) **Going Correction** -0.075s/f (Stan)
**WFA** 3 from 4yo+ 3lb **12** Ran SP% **125.1**
Speed ratings (Par 103): **105,103,101,101,98 94,94,90,89,86 82,70**
CSF £93.54 CT £597.73 TOTE £30.10: £7.30, £1.50, £2.80; EX 120.20 Trifecta £1617.80.
**Owner** K Wreglesworth **Bred** Cheveley Park Stud Ltd **Trained** Sheriff Hutton, N Yorks

**FOCUS**
Mainly exposed sorts in a modest handicap. A reasonable gallop steadied around halfway and those held up were at a disadvantage. The winner raced close to the inside rail throughout. The winner is rated to his form of the past year or so.

## 7627 BET IN PLAY AT CORAL MAIDEN STKS (TAPETA) 1m 4f 50y
**4:55** (4:55) (Class 5) 3-Y-O+ **£2,587** (£770; £384; £192) **Stalls** Low

Form RPR
6533 **1** **Cerutty (IRE)**[19] 7195 3-9-4 80........................ MartinHarley 4 78+
(Marco Botti) *chsd ldr tl led 2f out: easily* **2/7**[1]
5262 **2** 2¼ **Master Dan**[60] 6075 3-9-4 73........................ GrahamLee 2 71
(James Given) *sn led: hung rt and given reminders over 7f out: rdn and hdd 2f out: styd on same pce* **5/2**[2]
55 **3** 8 **Sail With Sultana**[19] 7210 3-8-13 0........................ PaulMulrennan 7 53?
(Mark Rimell) *hld up: hdwy u.p over 3f out: outpcd fr over 2f out* **25/1**[3]
0 **4** nk **Renewing**[15] 7304 3-9-4 0........................ TomEaves 6 58?
(Roy Brotherton) *hld up: rdn over 3f out: sn outpcd* **50/1**
**5** 26 **Direct Approach (IRE)**[250] 10-9-10 0........................ PaddyAspell 3 16
(Lynn Siddall) *s.i.s: sn prom: rdn and wknd 3f out* **28/1**

2m 42.43s (1.63) **Going Correction** -0.075s/f (Stan)
**WFA** 3 from 10yo 6lb **5** Ran SP% **115.6**
Speed ratings (Par 103): **91,89,84,83,66**
CSF £1.43 TOTE £1.20: £1.10, £1.10; EX 1.50 Trifecta £3.40.
**Owner** Mrs Clodagh McStay **Bred** Tinnakill Bloodstock & E Cantillon **Trained** Newmarket, Suffolk

**FOCUS**
Effectively a match between the two market leaders, who pulled clear in the last quarter mile. The gallop was on the steady side and the winner came down the centre. He didn't need to improve.

## 7628 CORAL.CO.UK H'CAP (TAPETA) 1m 4f 50y
5:25 (5:25) (Class 6) (0-65,65) 3-Y-O+ £2,264 (£673; £336; £168) Stalls Low

Form RPR

5232 1 **Royal Trooper (IRE)**[49] 6410 8-8-13 61 BeckyBrisbourne(7) 9 69
(Mark Brisbourne) *s.i.s: hld up and bhd: hdwy on outer over 2f out: led over 1f out: rdn and edgd lft ins fnl f: styd on* 7/1

0625 2 1 3/4 **Dire Straits (IRE)**[47] 6461 3-9-4 65 (p) TedDurcan 3 70
(Chris Wall) *chsd ldrs: rdn over 1f out: styd on* 5/2[1]

3540 3 1/2 **Flying Cape (IRE)**[20] 7182 3-9-3 64 (p) GrahamLee 8 68
(Andrew Hollinshead) *hld up: hdwy over 3f out: rdn over 1f out: styd on same pce ins fnl f* 5/1[2]

0434 4 hd **Sakhra**[9] 7458 3-8-11 58 GrahamGibbons 2 62
(Mark Brisbourne) *hld up: nt clr run over 2f out: hdwy and nt clr run over 1f out: rdn and r.o ins fnl f: nt rch ldrs* 25/1

5636 5 1/2 **Angus Glens**[9] 7452 4-9-5 60 (p) FergusSweeney 7 63
(David Dennis) *mid-div: hdwy over 3f out: rdn over 1f out: styd on* 28/1

6000 6 hd **Dabuki (FR)**[16] 7279 4-9-6 61 (p) SilvestreDeSousa 10 64
(Geoffrey Harker) *chsd ldr 10f out: led over 2f out: rdn and hdd over 1f out: no ex wl ins fnl f* 50/1

1425 7 1 1/4 **Harrison's Cave**[16] 7279 6-9-2 60 JoeyHaynes(3) 5 61
(Sharon Watt) *hld up: rdn over 1f out: r.o ins fnl f: nvr nrr* 20/1

0005 8 1 1/2 **Enzaal (USA)**[16] 7290 4-8-13 54 JoeFanning 12 52
(Philip Kirby) *hld up: hdwy over 2f out: rdn over 1f out: no ex fnl f* 5/1[2]

4505 9 1 1/2 **Dancing Primo**[9] 7452 8-9-5 60 GeorgeBaker 4 56
(Mark Brisbourne) *prom: pushed along whn hmpd 2f out: no ch after* 14/1

2230 10 6 **King Of Paradise (IRE)**[6] 7522 5-9-2 62 KevinStott(5) 6 48
(Eric Alston) *led: rdn and hdd over 2f out: wknd fnl f* 11/1

5540 11 3 1/2 **Dark Amber**[33] 6881 4-9-7 62 (t) SebSanders 11 43
(Brendan Powell) *chsd ldrs: rdn and ev ch over 2f out: wknd and eased fnl f* 16/1

4206 12 31 **Elegant Ophelia**[13] 7366 5-9-10 65 (t) AdamKirby 1
(Dean Ivory) *prom: pushed along 3f out: wknd over 2f out* 6/1[3]

2m 38.76s (-2.04) **Going Correction** -0.075s/f (Stan)
**WFA** 3 from 4yo+ 6lb 12 Ran SP% **123.6**
Speed ratings (Par 101): **103,101,101,101,101 100,100,99,98,94 91,71**
CSF £24.91 CT £100.79 TOTE £9.20: £2.50, £2.30, £1.50; EX 41.10 Trifecta £156.70.
**Owner** Mark Brisbourne **Bred** Western Bloodstock **Trained** Great Ness, Shropshire

**FOCUS**
Exposed sorts in a modest handicap. The gallop was fair and the winner came down the centre before edging towards the far side late on. There are one or two doubts over the form.
T/Jkpt: Not won. T/Plt: £236.40 to a £1 stake. Pool of £87483.49 - 270.04 winning tickets.
T/Qpdt: £19.80 to a £1 stake. Pool of £9018.60 - 337.0 winning tickets. CR

# 7619 CHANTILLY (R-H)
Monday, November 3
**OFFICIAL GOING: Turf: very soft; polytrack: standard**

## 7629a PRIX ISOLA BELLA (LISTED RACE) (3YO+ FILLIES & MARES) (TURF) 1m
1:05 (12:00) 3-Y-O+ £21,666 (£8,666; £6,500; £4,333; £2,166)

RPR

1 **Coco Sun (FR)**[36] 4-9-0 0 TheoBachelot 2 107
(W Mongil, Germany) 14/1

2 2 **Amulet**[24] 7095 4-9-0 0 (b) ThierryJarnet 4 102
(Eve Johnson Houghton) *chsd ldrs: stuck bhd wall of horses fr 3f out: swtchd outside and shkn up 2f out: nt clr run appr 1 1/2f out: styd on wl fnl f to take 2nd cl home: no ch w wnr* 58/10[2]

3 nk **Raphinae**[17] 7268 3-8-11 0 MickaelBarzalona 8 100
(H-A Pantall, France) *dwlt: t.k.h and restrained in midfield on outer: hdwy over 2f out: rdn to chse ldr 1 1/2f out: kpt on ins fnl f: lost 2nd cl home* 114/10

4 nk **Hestia (FR)**[49] 3-8-11 0 MaximeGuyon 7 100
(A Fabre, France) 43/5

5 2 **Brioniya**[15] 7319 3-8-11 0 AntoineHamelin 13 95
(A De Royer-Dupre, France) 23/5[1]

6 1/2 **So In Love**[33] 6882 3-8-11 0 FlavienPrat 3 94
(A Fabre, France) 135/10

7 2 **More Than Sotka (FR)**[42] 6620 4-9-0 0 EddyHardouin 1 90
(Matthieu Palussiere, France) 104/10

8 snk **Having A Blast (USA)**[61] 6055 3-8-11 0 UmbertoRispoli 14 89
(M Delzangles, France) 205/10

9 3/4 **Artwork Genie (IRE)**[50] 6384 3-8-11 0 GeraldPardon 10 87
(Jean-Pierre Carvalho, Germany) 132/10

10 hd **Sosia (GER)**[38] 6734 3-8-11 0 OlivierPeslier 6 87
(C Laffon-Parias, France) 13/2[3]

11 6 **Ice Love (FR)**[38] 6734 3-8-11 0 RaphaelMarchelli 5 73
(T Castanheira, France) 218/10

12 1/2 **Holly Filly (IRE)**[25] 7070 4-9-0 0 CristianDemuro 15 73
(F Vermeulen, France) 239/10

13 1 3/4 **Si Luna (GER)**[8] 7483 5-9-0 0 AnthonyCrastus 11 69
(Prof Dr G W Sybrecht, Germany) 29/1

14 2 **Alice's Dancer (IRE)**[24] 7095 5-9-0 0 MickaelForest 12 64
(Mme G Rarick, France) 25/1

15 nse **Cape Factor (IRE)**[17] 7242 3-8-11 0 ChrisCatlin 9 63
(Rae Guest) *broke wl: w ldrs early: sn racing in midfield: outpcd and scrubbed along 2 1/2f out: wknd appr fnl f* 189/10

1m 42.67s (4.67)
**WFA** 3 from 4yo+ 2lb 15 Ran SP% **119.0**
WIN (incl. 1 euro stake): 15.00. PLACES: 4.40, 2.70, 4.00. DF: 51.00. SF: 110.40.
**Owner** German Racing Club **Bred** Haras De Bernesq **Trained** Germany

## 7630a PRIX DE LA FORET DE CARNELLE (CLAIMER) (3YO) (POLYTRACK) 1m 1f
1:35 (12:00) 3-Y-O £9,583 (£3,833; £2,875; £1,916; £958)

RPR

1 **Elysian Prince**[18] 7225 3-9-8 0 ChristopheSoumillon 6 84
(Paul Cole) *led after 1f: mde rest: c stands' side st (followed by jst one other): rdn and qckned 1 1/2f out: drvn out fnl f: readily* 19/10[1]

2 1 1/4 **Like Me (IRE)**[19] 7270 3-8-7 0 (p) Georges-AntoineAnselin(4) 10 70
(N Clement, France) 66/10[2]

3 nse **Dark Dream (FR)**[38] 3-8-11 0 CesarPasserat 13 70
(N Caullery, France) 30/1

4 1 3/4 **Dime Dancer (IRE)**[19] 7270 3-9-3 0 CristianDemuro 3 72
(Werner Glanz, Germany) 107/10

5 2 1/2 **Surspenders (FR)**[13] 3-9-1 0 (p) OlivierPeslier 1 65
(S Wattel, France) 41/5

6 3 1/2 **Finglass (IRE)**[6] 3-8-13 0 ThierryThulliez 12 56
(Y Gourraud, France) 238/10

7 3 **Erkis De La Vis (FR)**[124] 3-8-4 0 JulienMagniez(7) 11 47
(Mme C Barande-Barbe, France) 41/1

8 nse **Pissarro (GER)**[19] 7269 3-9-5 0 UmbertoRispoli 4 55
(R Rohne, Germany) 8/1

9 10 **Baojun (FR)**[19] 3-8-11 0 MickaelBarzalona 5 26
(R Rohne, Germany) 11/1

10 3 1/2 **German Rules**[137] 3-8-11 0 EddyHardouin 7 19
(Yasmin Almenrader, Germany) 98/10

11 dist **Southampton (GER)** 3-8-11 0 MaximeGuyon 9
(S Smrczek, Germany) 71/10[3]

12 2 **Vite Princesse (FR)** 3-8-9 0 ow1 ThomasMessina 8
(Frau M Weber, Germany) 72/1

1m 50.24s (110.24) 12 Ran SP% **119.1**
WIN (incl. 1 euro stake): 2.90. PLACES: 1.80, 2.40, 5.70. DF: 13.10. SF: 21.10.
**Owner** D S Lee **Bred** D S Lee **Trained** Whatcombe, Oxon

# 7541 KEMPTON (A.W) (R-H)
Tuesday, November 4
**OFFICIAL GOING: Polytrack: standard**
Wind: Light, half against Weather: Rain

## 7631 £25 FREE BET AT TITANBET.CO.UK MAIDEN AUCTION STKS 7f (P)
4:35 (4:37) (Class 5) 2-Y-O £2,911 (£866; £432; £216) Stalls Low

Form RPR

3004 1 **Rockaroundtheclock (IRE)**[33] 6887 2-9-3 68 GeorgeBaker 9 71
(Paul Cole) *chsd ldr: led over 2f out: hld on wl fnl f: rdn out* 3/1[1]

3223 2 1/2 **Red Perdita (IRE)**[18] 7254 2-8-13 69 PatCosgrave 5 66
(George Baker) *chsd ldrs: drvn to chal ins fnl f: r.o* 7/2[2]

05 3 1 1/4 **Rialto Magic**[4] 7573 2-8-6 0 RachealKneller(5) 1 60
(Jamie Osborne) *prom: rdn to chal over 1f out: one pce ins fnl f* 8/1

0200 4 3/4 **Chefchaouen (IRE)**[67] 5901 2-8-4 0 CamHardie(3) 12 54
(J S Moore) *led: rdn and hdd over 2f out: kpt on same pce* 12/1

5 1/2 **Robins Pearl (FR)** 2-8-12 0 LiamJones 6 58+
(Olly Stevens) *mid-div: effrt over 2f out: styd on* 8/1

00 6 1/2 **Italian Beauty (IRE)**[60] 6093 2-8-2 0 JordanVaughan(7) 4 54
(Timothy Jarvis) *chsd ldrs: shkn up over 2f out: one pce* 50/1

7 2 1/4 **Whitchurch** 2-9-0 0 DavidProbert 10 52
(Andrew Balding) *mid-div: rdn 1/2-way: nvr able to chal* 5/1[3]

00 8 hd **Brittleton**[14] 7354 2-9-3 0 TomQueally 3 55
(Harry Dunlop) *dwlt: towards rr: rdn 1/2-way: n.d* 33/1

0 9 nk **Titan Goddess**[19] 7228 2-8-11 0 ShaneKelly 8 48
(Mike Murphy) *dwlt: outpcd and bhd: modest hdwy over 1f out: nt rch ldrs* 25/1

00 10 3 **Revision (FR)**[32] 6903 2-9-3 0 MartinDwyer 2 46
(John Best) *in tch: rdn 3f out: wknd wl over 1f out* 33/1

5406 11 3 1/4 **Ms Eboracum (IRE)**[20] 7190 2-7-13 45 RobertPWalsh(7) 13 26
(Edward Creighton) *plld hrd towards rr: rdn and n.d fnl 3f* 33/1

05 12 1 **Amour De Nuit (IRE)**[19] 7228 2-9-2 0 [1] ChrisCatlin 7 34
(Sir Mark Prescott Bt) *s.s: outpcd: a bhd* 16/1

13 3/4 **Casius** 2-9-2 0 SteveDrowne 11 32+
(Harry Dunlop) *s.s: outpcd and rn green: sn wl bhd* 12/1

1m 27.21s (1.21) **Going Correction** -0.025s/f (Stan) 13 Ran SP% **122.0**
Speed ratings (Par 96): **92,91,90,89,88 88,85,85,84,81 77,76,75**
CSF £12.86 TOTE £3.60: £1.50, £1.40, £2.90; EX 11.80 Trifecta £78.40.
**Owner** Chris Wright & PFI Cole Ltd **Bred** Lisieux Stud **Trained** Whatcombe, Oxon

**FOCUS**
A very modest maiden for this track with the main form contenders only rated in the high 60s, and this isn't form to get carried away with. It says plenty about the others that the two most exposed runners dominated the finish. The winner is rated to his pre-race level.

## 7632 REWARDS4RACING.COM CLASSIFIED STKS 1m (P)
5:10 (5:11) (Class 6) 3-Y-O+ £1,940 (£577; £288; £144) Stalls Low

Form RPR

2060 1 **Gracefilly**[19] 7219 3-9-0 55 AntonioFresu 5 64
(Ed Walker) *chsd ldrs: led over 2f out: rdn clr over 1f out: comf* 7/1

3632 2 3 3/4 **Carrera**[50] 6407 4-8-9 55 ChrisMeehan(7) 3 55
(Michael Blanshard) *towards rr: rdn over 2f out: gd hdwy to chse wnr over 1f out: no imp* 7/2[1]

0446 3 1/2 **Cueca (FR)**[28] 7021 3-8-9 48 (b) NedCurtis(5) 8 54
(Jonathan Portman) *sn chsng ldr: chal 2f out: kpt on same pce* 33/1

0 4 1 1/4 **Runaiocht (IRE)**[14] 7347 4-9-2 51 JimmyQuinn 11 51
(Paul Burgoyne) *prom on outer: outpcd and hrd rdn 2f out: kpt on again fnl f* 20/1

0552 5 hd **Highly Likely (IRE)**[13] 7369 5-8-13 53 CamHardie(3) 4 51
(Steve Woodman) *mid-div: rdn to chse ldrs over 1f out: one pce* 4/1[2]

6650 6 nse **Avidly**[17] 7291 4-9-2 54 GeorgeBaker 9 50
(Julia Feilden) *stdd s: t.k.h in rr: brought wd home turn: cajoled along and hung rt fnl 3f: styd on* 5/1[3]

3600 7 1 3/4 **Stun Gun**[56] 6210 4-9-2 55 (v[1]) TomQueally 10 46
(Derek Shaw) *outpcd and bhd: effrt and nt clr run 2f out: sme hdwy and hrd rdn over 1f out: no further prog* 11/2

005 8 1 **Haames (IRE)**[14] 7346 7-9-2 55 ShaneKelly 12 47
(Kevin Morgan) *hld up in midfield: promising hdwy whn nt clr run over 1f out: pushed along and unable to chal* 14/1

054- 9 3 **Hija**[351] 7945 3-9-0 48 SteveDrowne 6 37
(Rod Millman) *towards rr: rdn over 3f out: n.d* 50/1

6650 10 12 **Baars Causeway (IRE)**[33] 6883 3-8-7 55 JordanVaughan(7) 1 10
(Timothy Jarvis) *prom tl wknd 2f out* 16/1

03-0 11 2 3/4 **Namely (IRE)**[18] 7256 3-9-0 53 ChrisCatlin 7 3
(Sir Mark Prescott Bt) *in tch: rdn 4f out: struggling towards rr fnl 3f* 12/1

2660 **12** 3/4 **Plauseabella**[20] 7197 3-9-0 49 (b[1]) PatCosgrave 2 2
(Stuart Kittow) *sn led: hdd over 2f out: sn wknd* **50/1**

1m 39.48s (-0.32) **Going Correction** -0.025s/f (Stan)
**WFA** 3 from 4yo+ 2lb **12** Ran SP% **118.6**
Speed ratings (Par 101): **100,96,95,94,94 94,92,91,88,76 73,73**
CSF £30.74 TOTE £11.10: £3.80, £1.10, £15.20; EX 36.80 Trifecta £1645.50.
**Owner** Laurence A Bellman **Bred** Vimal And Gillian Khosla **Trained** Newmarket, Suffolk

**FOCUS**
A weak 0-55 classified event on paper but the pace looked even enough and the winner was quite impressive so this might not be bad form for the grade.

## 7633 TITANBET.CO.UK H'CAP 1m (P)
**5:40** (5:42) (Class 5) (0-70,70) 3-Y-0+ **£2,911** (£866; £432; £216) **Stalls** Low

Form RPR
0-03 **1** **Ertikaan**[55] 6240 7-9-7 70 GeorgeBaker 5 81+
(Miss Joey Ellis) *hld up towards rr: rapid hdwy on bit 2f out: led over 1f out: pushed out* **11/4**[2]

4000 **2** 3/4 **Gannicus**[29] 6981 3-9-2 67 (p) MartinDwyer 4 75
(Brendan Powell) *chsd ldrs: wnt 2nd jst over 1f out: pressed wnr fnl f: a hld* **20/1**

1240 **3** 1 3/4 **Stormbound (IRE)**[13] 7373 5-9-7 70 DavidProbert 7 76+
(Paul Cole) *hld up in midfield: squeezed for room over 2f out: rdn and r.o wl fr over 1f out* **9/4**[1]

1220 **4** 2 1/4 **Pendo**[14] 7358 3-9-3 68 ShaneKelly 10 67
(Paul Cole) *led after 1f: 2 l in front but rdn 2f out: hdd over 1f out: wknd fnl f* **6/1**[3]

0030 **5** 4 **Captain Starlight (IRE)**[28] 7012 4-9-5 68 FergusSweeney 2 58
(Jo Crowley) *chsd ldrs: rdn and carried hd high 2f out: wknd over 1f out* **20/1**

3023 **6** 1 3/4 **Shifting Star (IRE)**[15] 7340 9-9-3 66 (vt) WilliamCarson 8 52
(John Bridger) *led for 1f: prom tl hrd rdn and wknd over 1f out* **12/1**

6404 **7** 3/4 **Tea In Transvaal (IRE)**[16] 7302 3-8-10 64 CamHardie(3) 3 48
(John O'Shea) *mid-div on rail: rdn and sme hdwy over 2f out: no further prog* **16/1**

0040 **8** 2 1/4 **Don't**[78] 5492 3-8-9 65 ShelleyBirkett(5) 9 44
(Julia Feilden) *mid-div: struggling to hold pl and drvn along 3f out: n.d after* **33/1**

-445 **9** hd **Joyful Risk (IRE)**[229] 1024 4-9-0 63 SteveDrowne 6 41
(Martin Bosley) *bhd: rdn 3f out: nvr trbld ldrs* **66/1**

0000 **10** nk **Snow King (USA)**[92] 4968 4-9-4 67 WilliamTwiston-Davies 13 45
(Ted Powell) *towards rr: drvn along 3f out: nvr nr ldrs* **25/1**

2005 **11** 1 **Bloodsweatandtears**[28] 6999 6-8-13 62 JimmyQuinn 11 37
(William Knight) *t.k.h: w ldrs on outer: hung rt and wknd qckly 2f out* **20/1**

5501 **12** 6 **Ostralegus**[14] 7346 4-9-2 65 TomQueally 14 26
(John Gallagher) *mid-div on outer: wknd over 2f out* **6/1**[3]

1660 **13** 1 3/4 **Dozy Joe**[14] 7358 6-8-9 65 (b) NoraLooby(7) 12 22
(Joseph Tuite) *s.i.s: drvn along 3f out: a bhd* **33/1**

1m 38.32s (-1.48) **Going Correction** -0.025s/f (Stan)
**WFA** 3 from 4yo+ 2lb **13** Ran SP% **125.1**
Speed ratings (Par 103): **106,105,103,101,97 95,94,92,92,92 91,85,83**
CSF £64.21 CT £150.71 TOTE £4.10: £1.30, £5.60, £2.10; EX 93.00 Trifecta £288.20.
**Owner** Mrs Angela Ellis **Bred** Floors Farming And Dominic Burke **Trained** Newmarket, Suffolk

**FOCUS**
A soundly run handicap.

## 7634 MOBILE LOYALTY BONUS AT TITANBET.CO.UK H'CAP 1m (P)
**6:10** (6:10) (Class 4) (0-85,85) 3-Y-0+ **£4,851** (£1,443; £721; £360) **Stalls** Low

Form RPR
0003 **1** **Miss Buckshot (IRE)**[20] 7205 3-8-7 **73** DavidProbert 7 82
(Rae Guest) *hld up disputing 5th: rdn and hdwy over 1f out: r.o to ld ins fnl f* **6/1**

3251 **2** 1 1/2 **Glorious Sun**[41] 6661 3-9-2 **82** GeorgeBaker 3 87
(Ed Walker) *led for 3f: led again 2f out: hdd and outpcd ins fnl f* **9/4**[1]

630 **3** 1 **Cricklewood Green (USA)**[53] 6301 3-9-0 **80** TomQueally 8 83
(Richard Hannon) *t.k.h towards rr: dropped to last and struggling 3f out: styd on wl fr over 1f out* **16/1**

3003 **4** hd **Showpiece**[39] 6704 3-8-9 **78** (b) CamHardie(3) 1 80
(Richard Hannon) *hld up disputing 5th: rdn to press ldrs over 1f out: kpt on* **10/1**

1-0 **5** 1 3/4 **Ghazi (IRE)**[11] 7410 3-8-11 **82** (v[1]) KevinStott(5) 6 80
(Saeed bin Suroor) *dwlt and rdn s: bhd: sme hdwy and drvn over 1f out: no imp* **3/1**[2]

6102 **6** 1 1/4 **Hanalei Bay (IRE)**[35] 6836 4-9-2 **80** ShaneKelly 5 75
(Keith Dalgleish) *chsd ldr: led 5f out tl 2f out: wknd 1f out* **4/1**[3]

6050 **7** hd **True Pleasure (IRE)**[17] 7282 7-8-11 **75** TedDurcan 2 70
(James Bethell) *prom: chal 2f out: wknd fnl f* **33/1**

/306 **8** hd **Jamhoori**[4] 7567 6-9-7 **85** (p) LukeMorris 4 79
(Jeremy Gask) *chsd ldrs tl outpcd and btn 2f out* **25/1**

1m 39.11s (-0.69) **Going Correction** -0.025s/f (Stan)
**WFA** 3 from 4yo+ 2lb **8** Ran SP% **111.8**
Speed ratings (Par 105): **102,100,99,99,97 96,96,95**
CSF £19.00 CT £201.67 TOTE £10.70: £2.00, £1.10, £4.90; EX 22.50 Trifecta £158.60.
**Owner** Buckhurst Chevaliers **Bred** Mrs S M Rogers & Sir Thomas Pilkington **Trained** Newmarket, Suffolk

**FOCUS**
This 0-85 was run in a slightly slower time than the previous 0-70 mile contest, but that is because this was run at a stop-start gallop.

## 7635 BET & WATCH AT TITANBET.CO.UK H'CAP 1m 3f (P)
**6:40** (6:40) (Class 6) (0-60,60) 3-Y-0+ **£1,940** (£577; £288; £144) **Stalls** Low

Form RPR
0021 **1** **Innoko (FR)**[11] 7426 4-9-10 60 LukeMorris 1 69
(Tony Carroll) *hld up in 6th: hdwy over 2f out: drvn to chse clr ldr 1f out: styd on to ld nr fin* **9/2**[3]

0600 **2** nk **Mcbirney (USA)**[26] 7068 7-9-10 60 GeorgeBaker 3 68
(Paul D'Arcy) *confidently rdn in rr: smooth hdwy to ld 2f out: sn rdn 3 l clr: drvn and fnd little fnl f: ct nr fin* **9/4**[1]

3554 **3** 3 1/2 **Brown Pete (IRE)**[5] 7546 6-8-7 46 (p) CamHardie(3) 8 48
(Ann Stokell) *sn w ldr: led over 3f out tl 2f out: sn outpcd* **8/1**

0600 **4** 11 **Rezwaan**[33] 6883 7-9-6 56 (be) ShaneKelly 5 38
(Murty McGrath) *in tch: wnt 3rd 4f out: wknd 2f out* **14/1**

4000 **5** 2 **Lingfield Lupus (IRE)**[7] 7517 3-8-5 46 oh1 (v) MartinDwyer 6 25
(John Best) *dwlt: towards rr: rdn and n.d fnl 3f* **11/1**

3402 **6** 1 1/2 **Norfolk Sound**[17] 7292 3-9-3 58 TedDurcan 2 34
(Chris Wall) *prom: hrd rdn over 2f out: sn wknd* **5/2**[2]

4000 **7** 18 **Dutch Lady Roseane**[18] 7256 3-8-7 48 AdamBeschizza 4
(James Unett) *led tl over 3f out: wknd qckly over 2f out* **16/1**

000 **8** 27 **Officer In Command (USA)**[34] 6857 8-9-6 56 (p) LiamKeniry 7
(John Butler) *s.s: sn chsng ldrs: rdn 5f out: wknd over 3f out: sn bhd* **25/1**

2m 20.85s (-1.05) **Going Correction** -0.025s/f (Stan)
**WFA** 3 from 4yo+ 5lb **8** Ran SP% **113.4**
Speed ratings (Par 101): **102,101,99,91,89 88,75,55**
CSF £14.78 CT £76.73 TOTE £6.00: £1.70, £1.10, £1.80; EX 12.20 Trifecta £81.90.
**Owner** Mill House Racing Syndicate **Bred** Marquise Soledad De Moratalla **Trained** Cropthorne, Worcs

**FOCUS**
The front three pulled clear in what was a modest contest.

## 7636 £10 FREE MOBILE BET AT TITAN.CO.UK H'CAP 7f (P)
**7:10** (7:11) (Class 4) (0-80,80) 3-Y-0+ **£4,851** (£1,443; £721; £360) **Stalls** Low

Form RPR
0004 **1** **Stonefield Flyer**[7] 7521 5-9-4 77 (p) GeorgeBaker 8 86
(Keith Dalgleish) *chsd ldr: rdn over 2f out: kpt on to ld fnl 100yds* **15/8**[1]

0040 **2** 3/4 **Another Try (IRE)**[47] 6477 9-8-3 69 JordanVaughan(7) 1 76
(Timothy Jarvis) *led: hrd rdn over 1f out: hdd fnl 100yds: kpt on* **33/1**

5051 **3** nk **Rich Again (IRE)**[25] 7077 5-8-9 68 (p) TedDurcan 9 74+
(James Bethell) *towards rr: rdn over 2f out: gd late hdwy* **5/1**[3]

3542 **4** 1 3/4 **Kingscroft (IRE)**[21] 7185 6-9-7 80 (b) ShaneKelly 11 82
(Michael Herrington) *chsd ldrs: rdn over 2f out: styd on fnl f* **3/1**[2]

6500 **5** shd **Kung Hei Fat Choy (USA)**[8] 7494 5-9-6 79 (b) TomQueally 7 80
(James Given) *bhd: hrd rdn over 2f out: hdwy over 1f out: nt rch ldrs* **10/1**

1200 **6** 2 1/4 **Exceedexpectations (IRE)**[54] 6263 5-9-4 77 (v) AmirQuinn 2 73
(Lee Carter) *prom tl wknd jst over 1f out* **16/1**

500 **7** 1/2 **Polar Kite (IRE)**[33] 6890 6-9-0 73 AdamBeschizza 5 67
(Roger Ingram) *s.s: towards rr: gd hdwy 2f out: wknd over 1f out* **25/1**

0040 **8** 1 **Big Whiskey (IRE)**[33] 6886 4-9-5 78 PatCosgrave 10 70
(Edward Creighton) *in tch on outer tl outpcd and btn 2f out* **7/1**

6-00 **9** 2 1/4 **Clement (IRE)**[16] 7307 4-8-9 68 FergusSweeney 6 54
(John O'Shea) *a bhd* **25/1**

6-00 **10** 1 3/4 **Talksalot (IRE)**[13] 7375 3-8-13 80 (p) JosephineGordon(7) 4 60
(J S Moore) *dwlt: sn in 5th: hrd rdn over 2f out: sn wknd* **66/1**

0301 **11** nk **Frankthetank (IRE)**[153] 2906 3-8-13 73 (p) JimmyQuinn 3 53
(Keith Dalgleish) *mid-div tl wknd 2f out* **20/1**

1m 24.81s (-1.19) **Going Correction** -0.025s/f (Stan)
**WFA** 3 from 4yo+ 1lb **11** Ran SP% **120.8**
Speed ratings (Par 105): **105,104,103,101,101 99,98,97,94,92 92**
CSF £83.79 CT £291.41 TOTE £2.50: £1.10, £14.20, £2.20; EX 103.80 Trifecta £694.80.
**Owner** G R Leckie **Bred** Ian Crawford And Gordon Leckie **Trained** Carluke, S Lanarks

**FOCUS**
An open handicap run at what looked an even gallop.
T/Jkpt: £14,378.90 to a £1 stake. Pool: £50,630.15 - 2.50 winning units. T/Plt: £21.80 to a £1 stake. Pool: £85,302.79 - 2850.16 winning units. T/Qpdt: £6.40 to a £1 stake. Pool: £10,629.98 - 1218.90 winning units. LM

# 7495 REDCAR (L-H)
Tuesday, November 4

**OFFICIAL GOING: Soft (7.4)**

## 7637 IRISH STALLION FARMS EBF MAIDEN STKS (DIV I) 7f
**12:30** (12:30) (Class 5) 2-Y-O **£3,234** (£962; £481; £240) **Stalls** Centre

Form RPR
32 **1** **Wiener Valkyrie**[45] 6554 2-9-0 0 GrahamLee 7 73+
(Ed Walker) *trckd ldrs: hdwy over 2f out: cl up over 1f out: rdn to ld ins fnl f: styd on* **4/5**[1]

**2** 1 3/4 **Brotherly Company (IRE)** 2-9-5 0 PaulHanagan 9 72+
(Richard Fahey) *in tch: green and pushed along 3f out: rdn wl over 1f out: styd on wl fnl f: nrst fin* **13/2**[3]

4 **3** hd **Lewis Valentine (IRE)**[41] 6668 2-9-5 0 PhillipMakin 11 71
(Bryan Smart) *prom: cl up 1/2-way: chal over 2f out: rdn to ld briefly jst over 1f out: hdd and edgd lft ins fnl f: kpt on same pce* **9/2**[2]

53 **4** 2 1/2 **Spinaminnie (IRE)**[8] 7493 2-9-0 0 JoeFanning 4 60
(Mark Johnston) *slt ld: rdn along 2f out: edgd lft and hdd jst over 1f out: wknd fnl f* **16/1**

0 **5** 3 1/2 **Intrude**[29] 6985 2-9-5 0 TomEaves 5 56
(David Simcock) *towards rr: hdwy 2f out: rdn and kpt on fnl f: nrst fin* **16/1**

03 **6** 1 1/2 **Ingleby Hollow**[21] 7173 2-9-5 0 DanielTudhope 6 52
(David O'Meara) *chsd ldrs: rdn along 2f out: drvn and no imp fr over 1f out* **8/1**

00 **7** 3 1/4 **Racing Spirit**[8] 7498 2-9-0 0 JoeDoyle(5) 2 44
(John Quinn) *in tch: rdn along wl over 2f out: grad wknd* **66/1**

66 **8** 2 3/4 **Toboggan's Gift**[8] 7498 2-9-0 0 PJMcDonald 3 32
(Ann Duffield) *cl up: rdn along wl over 2f out: sn wknd* **33/1**

**9** 1/2 **Bridget Gem** 2-9-0 0 JasonHart 10 31
(Nigel Tinkler) *a toward rr* **66/1**

**10** 11 **Dazzling Display** 2-9-0 0 AndrewElliott 8 4
(Richard Guest) *s.i.s: a bhd* **100/1**

0P0 **11** 13 **Beatabout (IRE)**[18] 7254 2-9-5 0 RaulDaSilva 1
(Paul Green) *in tch: pushed along bef 1/2-way: sn rdn and outpcd: bhd fnl 3f* **250/1**

1m 26.27s (1.77) **Going Correction** +0.225s/f (Good) **11** Ran SP% **117.3**
Speed ratings (Par 96): **98,96,95,92,88 87,83,80,79,67 52**
CSF £6.48 TOTE £1.40: £1.02, £1.90, £1.60; EX 7.20 Trifecta £23.20.
**Owner** Car Colston Hall Stud Syndicate **Bred** Car Colston Hall Stud **Trained** Newmarket, Suffolk

**FOCUS**
The official going remained soft. Only a fair maiden and it was dominated by the market leaders. The winner's previous form is working out well and she may have more to offer.

## 7638 IRISH STALLION FARMS EBF MAIDEN STKS (DIV II) 7f
**1:00** (1:05) (Class 5) 2-Y-O **£3,234** (£962; £481; £240) **Stalls** Centre

Form RPR
**1** **Flashy Memories** 2-9-5 0 TonyHamilton 8 75+
(Richard Fahey) *prom gng wl: plld out and shkn up to ld appr fnl f: edgd lft and kpt on strly last 100yds: readily* **5/1**[3]

0 **2** 3 **Udodontu (IRE)**[11] 7407 2-9-5 0 AndrewElliott 9 64
(Richard Guest) *dwlt: cl up: led wl over 2f out: rdn: hung lft and hdd appr fnl f: kpt on: nt pce of wnr* **50/1**

0 **3** *shd* **Oracolo (IRE)**[35] 6838 2-9-5 0 .......... TomEaves 4 63
(David Simcock) *cl up: chal wl over 2f out to appr fnl f: kpt on u.p last 100yds* **20/1**

2 **4** *5* **Ershaadaat (IRE)**[20] 7194 2-9-0 0 .......... PaulHanagan 5 46
(Saeed bin Suroor) *dwlt: t.k.h and sn cl up: disp ld over 2f out to over 1f out: wknd ins fnl f* **1/1**[1]

602 **5** *4½* **Father Bertie**[8] 7496 2-9-5 0 .......... DuranFentiman 7 40
(Tim Easterby) *in tch: drvn along 3f out: wknd over 1f out* **11/4**[2]

00 **6** *3* **Anneani (IRE)**[69] 5807 2-9-0 0 .......... PJMcDonald 6 27
(Paul Green) *hld up: drvn and outpcd over 2f out: n.d after* **100/1**

6 **7** *1¼* **Kyllach Me (IRE)**[45] 6537 2-9-0 0 .......... AdamCarter(5) 10 29
(Bryan Smart) *slt ld to over 2f out: sn rdn: wknd over 1f out* **25/1**

**8** *½* **Ultima Ora (IRE)** 2-9-0 0 .......... JoeFanning 11 23
(Mark Johnston) *dwlt: hld up: pushed along and hung lft over 3f out: sn struggling* **11/1**

0 **9** *5* **Joey Black**[8] 7496 2-8-12 0 .......... MikeyEnnis(7) 3 15
(Susan Corbett) *s.i.s: hld up: struggling 1/2-way: sn btn* **100/1**

**10** *12* **Eric The Viking** 2-9-5 0 .......... JasonHart 2
(Richard Guest) *slowly away and sn wl bhd: nvr on terms* **40/1**

1m 26.65s (2.15) **Going Correction** +0.225s/f (Good) **10** Ran SP% **116.7**
Speed ratings (Par 96): **96,92,92,86,81 78,76,76,70,56**
CSF £220.53 TOTE £8.10: £2.10, £12.70, £6.00; EX 594.70 Trifecta £1638.60 Part won..
**Owner** Jaber Abdullah **Bred** Rabbah Bloodstock Limited **Trained** Musley Bank, N Yorks

**FOCUS**
The second division of this maiden was run 0.38secs slower than the first leg. Ordinary form. The winner was value for extra.

## 7639 HOLD YOUR CHRISTMAS PARTY HERE (S) STKS 1m
1:30 (1:34) (Class 6) 3-5-Y-O £2,385 (£704; £352) Stalls Centre

Form RPR

2250 **1** **Brooke's Bounty**[24] 7098 4-9-0 65 .......... PaulHanagan 1 59
(Richard Fahey) *trckd ldrs: pushed along 3f out: hdwy and cl up 2f out: rdn to ld jst over 1f out: kpt on* **7/4**[1]

0030 **2** *1* **Mitchum**[18] 7249 5-9-0 50 .......... (v) GrahamLee 9 57
(Ron Barr) *chsd clr ldr: hdwy and cl up 3f out: rdn 2f out and sn slt ld: hdd jst over 1f out: sn drvn and kpt on* **16/1**

0500 **3** *3* **Eium Mac**[107] 4468 5-8-9 45 .......... (b1) JoeDoyle(5) 12 50
(Neville Bycroft) *led and sn clr: jnd and pushed along 3f out: rdn 2f out: sn hdd and kpt on same pce* **33/1**

-006 **4** *2¾* **Megamunch (IRE)**[24] 7098 4-9-0 68 .......... (p) TomEaves 11 44
(Kristin Stubbs) *chsd ldrs: rdn over 2f out: drvn over 1f out: kpt on one pce* **8/1**[3]

211- **5** *nk* **Idyllic Star (IRE)**[469] 4615 5-8-9 67 .......... (p) FergalLynch 2 38
(Jim Goldie) *slipped s and s.i.s: hdwy 1/2-way: rdn to chse ldrs swl over 1f out: no imp fnl f* **11/4**[2]

0010 **6** *½* **The Blue Banana (IRE)**[18] 7248 5-9-6 60 .......... (p) PJMcDonald 8 48
(Edwin Tuer) *in tch: effrt over 2f out: sn rdn and no imp* **12/1**

11-0 **7** *hd* **It's Only Business**[13] 7373 4-9-0 69 .......... (p) JoeFanning 5 41
(Bill Turner) *chsd ldrs: rdn along over 2f out: sn no imp* **8/1**[3]

0604 **8** *nk* **Lady Liz**[8] 7501 3-8-7 46 .......... (b) DuranFentiman 3 36
(George Moore) *hld up and bhd: sme hdwy wl over 2f out: rdn along wl over 1f out: n.d* **25/1**

026 **9** *1½* **Nelson's Bay**[43] 6600 5-8-9 57 .......... ShaneGray(5) 7 37
(Wilf Storey) *a towards rr* **10/1**

000 **10** *1¾* **Nonagon**[8] 7501 3-8-7 46 .......... EmmaSayer(5) 4 33
(Wilf Storey) *dwlt: a in rr* **100/1**

0000 **P** **Kaytom**[102] 4627 3-8-7 50 .......... (b1) RaulDaSilva 6
(John Wainwright) *chsd ldng pair: pushed along bef 1/2-way: sn lost pl and bhd: t.o whn p.u and dismntd ins fnl f* **25/1**

1m 39.9s (3.30) **Going Correction** +0.225s/f (Good)
**WFA** 3 from 4yo+ 2lb **11** Ran SP% **119.5**
Speed ratings (Par 101): **92,91,88,85,84 84,84,83,82,80**
CSF £32.60 TOTE £3.30: £1.50, £1.80, £12.60; EX 31.40 Trifecta £623.90.
**Owner** James Gaffney **Bred** East Layton Stud Ltd **Trained** Musley Bank, N Yorks

**FOCUS**
A modest seller.

## 7640 DOWNLOAD YOUR RACING UK APP H'CAP 7f
2:00 (2:05) (Class 5) (0-75,75) 3-Y-O £2,587 (£770; £384; £192) Stalls Centre

Form RPR

3-30 **1** **Acclio (IRE)**[13] 7384 3-9-4 75 .......... LouisSteward(3) 1 87
(Clive Brittain) *in tch: smooth hdwy to ld over 1f out: pushed along and edgd rt ins fnl f: sn clr: comf* **20/1**

-312 **2** *2½* **Breakable**[10] 7445 3-9-6 74 .......... (p) DuranFentiman 9 79
(Tim Easterby) *hld up in tch: hdwy 1/2-way: effrt and chsd wnr ins fnl f: kpt on: no imp* **7/1**[3]

222 **3** *¾* **Advance (FR)**[18] 7250 3-8-8 62 .......... JamesSullivan 6 65
(Ruth Carr) *t.k.h: hld up: rdn and hdwy over 1f out: edgd lft and kpt on fnl f: tk 3rd cl home* **9/2**[2]

1153 **4** *nk* **Strike A Light**[18] 7248 3-9-0 73 .......... JackGarritty(5) 8 75
(Rae Guest) *t.k.h: hld up: stdy hdwy over 3f out: shkn up: edgd lft and chsd wnr over 1f out to ins fnl f: one pce* **5/2**[1]

1260 **5** *shd* **Beautiful Stranger (IRE)**[13] 7373 3-9-6 74 .......... (p) JoeFanning 7 76
(Keith Dalgleish) *stdd s: t.k.h: hld up: nt clr run briefly over 2f out: effrt over 1f out: edgd lft and no imp ins fnl f* **8/1**

143 **6** *1* **Cornborough**[10] 7438 3-9-6 74 .......... JasonHart 2 73
(Mark Walford) *led: rdn over 2f out: hdd over 1f out: sn outpcd* **9/2**[2]

5030 **7** *2½* **White Rose Runner**[72] 5717 3-8-7 61 oh4 .......... PJMcDonald 3 54
(Mel Brittain) *chsd ldrs: outpcd and lost pl over 2f out: n.d after* **33/1**

1454 **8** *¾* **Bold Captain (IRE)**[10] 7445 3-9-6 74 .......... PhillipMakin 4 65
(John Quinn) *sn w ldr: drvn over 2f out: hung lft and wknd wl over 1f out* **15/2**

0610 **9** *hd* **Sartori**[90] 5055 3-8-8 67 .......... JordanNason(5) 5 57
(Marjorie Fife) *t.k.h early: cl up: disp ld 1/2-way out to over 1f out: sn wknd* **33/1**

1m 25.8s (1.30) **Going Correction** +0.225s/f (Good) **9** Ran SP% **111.0**
Speed ratings (Par 102): **101,98,97,96,96 95,92,91,91**
CSF £144.34 CT £728.16 TOTE £16.40: £4.00, £2.50, £1.90; EX 116.90 Trifecta £227.90.
**Owner** Saeed Manana **Bred** E Mulryan **Trained** Newmarket, Suffolk

**FOCUS**
A fair and competitive 3yo handicap.

## 7641 RACING UK TIPSTER PUNDIT COMPETITION H'CAP 1m 2f
2:30 (2:34) (Class 3) (0-95,91) 3-Y-O+ £7,439 (£2,213; £1,106; £553) Stalls Low

Form RPR

0514 **1** **Open Eagle (IRE)**[10] 7440 5-9-5 86 .......... DanielTudhope 2 97
(David O'Meara) *trckd ldrs: hdwy over 3f out: cl up over 2f out: rdn to ld jst over 1f out: kpt on* **7/2**[1]

3206 **2** *2* **Maven**[34] 6870 6-8-12 84 .......... JackGarritty(5) 11 91
(Tim Easterby) *led: pushed clr over 4f out: rdn along over 2f out: hdd and drvn jst over 1f out: kpt on* **25/1**

0521 **3** *½* **Ty Gwr**[15] 7335 5-9-0 88 .......... MikeyEnnis(7) 4 94
(Brian Ellison) *hld up towards rr: smooth hdwy over 3f out: trckd ldrs on bit over 2f out: effrt over 1f out: sn rdn and kpt on same pce* **6/1**[3]

0203 **4** *1¼* **Green Light**[20] 7211 3-8-9 80 .......... GrahamGibbons 12 84
(Ralph Beckett) *hld up in rr: hdwy 3f out: chsd ldrs whn n.m.r wl over 1f out: rdn and edgd lft ent fnl f: no imp* **9/2**[2]

1146 **5** *2* **Potent Embrace (USA)**[29] 6978 3-9-0 85 .......... JoeFanning 8 85
(Mark Johnston) *chsd ldr: hdwy and cl up 3f out: rdn along and ev ch 2f out: drvn and wknd appr fnl f* **33/1**

6-60 **6** *2½* **King's Warrior (FR)**[174] 2253 7-9-5 91 .......... JordanNason(5) 7 86
(Peter Chapple-Hyam) *dwlt and in rr: hdwy on inner 1/2-way: chsd ldrs 3f out: rdn along over 2f out: sn no imp* **28/1**

4022 **7** *1½* **Docs Legacy (IRE)**[15] 7334 5-9-4 85 .......... PaulHanagan 3 77
(Richard Fahey) *midfield: effrt and hdwy 4f out: rdn along 3f out: n.d* **7/2**[1]

1540 **8** *hd* **Noble Alan (GER)**[24] 7125 11-8-13 80 .......... TomEaves 6 72
(Nicky Richards) *in tch: hdwy on inner 4f out: chsd ldrs 3f out: sn rdn and one pce fnl 2f* **25/1**

4301 **9** *1¼* **Polar Eyes**[11] 7416 3-8-5 81 .......... (p) JennyPowell(5) 9 71
(Tom Dascombe) *awkward s: a in rr* **12/1**

0003 **10** *hd* **Hi There (IRE)**[10] 7449 5-9-7 88 .......... BarryMcHugh 13 77
(Richard Fahey) *a towards rr* **14/1**

5-00 **11** *3* **Quixote**[227] 1071 5-8-10 80 .......... (b) LouisSteward(3) 5 64
(Clive Brittain) *trckd ldrs: pushed along 4f out: rdn over 3f out: sn wknd* **100/1**

1034 **12** *4* **No Poppy (IRE)**[13] 7384 6-9-5 86 .......... RobertWinston 1 62
(Tim Easterby) *a in rr* **20/1**

4311 **13** *1¾* **Karaka Jack**[31] 6936 7-9-0 81 .......... GrahamLee 10 54
(Jim Goldie) *chsd ldrs on outer: pushed along 4f out: rdn 3f out and sn wknd* **20/1**

2m 6.08s (-1.02) **Going Correction** +0.175s/f (Good)
**WFA** 3 from 5yo+ 4lb **13** Ran SP% **115.9**
Speed ratings (Par 107): **111,109,109,108,106 104,103,103,102,101 99,96,94**
CSF £98.29 CT £512.01 TOTE £4.40: £1.40, £7.30, £2.30; EX 98.90 Trifecta £648.10.
**Owner** Middleham Park Racing LXXIV & Partner **Bred** F Bayrou **Trained** Nawton, N Yorks

**FOCUS**
A competitive handicap, albeit not the strongest for the grade.

## 7642 RACING UK ANYWHERE AVAILABLE NOW CLAIMING STKS 1m 2f
3:00 (3:03) (Class 6) 3-4-Y-O £2,385 (£704; £352) Stalls Low

Form RPR

4600 **1** **Iftikaar (IRE)**[24] 7098 4-9-2 59 .......... JoeFanning 2 62
(Philip Kirby) *chsd clr ldrs: smooth hdwy to ld 2f out: shkn up: edgd lft and sn clr* **11/2**

0440 **2** *3¾* **Noble Reach**[17] 7291 3-8-5 48 .......... JordanNason(5) 6 53
(Lawrence Mullaney) *chsd ldr and sn clr of rest: led briefly over 2f out: kpt on same pce fnl f* **25/1**

0-06 **3** *2¾* **Riponian**[8] 7499 4-8-12 45 .......... TonyHamilton 5 46
(Susan Corbett) *led: qcknd 1/2-way: rdn and hdd over 2f out: sn outpcd* **100/1**

2406 **4** *2¾* **Gabrial The Thug (FR)**[11] 7426 4-9-1 59 .......... (t) PaulHanagan 7 44
(Richard Fahey) *hld up: rdn and outpcd over 4f out: rallied and hung lft over 2f out: sn no imp* **11/4**[3]

3003 **5** *nk* **Heartstrings**[7] 7517 3-8-8 49 .......... CharlesBishop 1 40
(Mick Channon) *dwlt: t.k.h: hld up: effrt 3f out: sn rdn along: wknd over 1f out* **9/4**[1]

3350 **6** *2¾* **Irondale Express**[8] 7494 3-8-9 66 .......... BarryMcHugh 3 36
(Tony Coyle) *hld up: pushed along 1/2-way: hdwy over 3f out: hung lft and wknd 2f out* **5/2**[2]

0-6 **7** *3¾* **Lucky North**[47] 6494 4-9-0 0 .......... PJMcDonald 4 30
(Mel Brittain) *prom: drvn and struggling over 3f out: btn fnl 2f* **66/1**

2m 8.51s (1.41) **Going Correction** +0.175s/f (Good)
**WFA** 3 from 4yo 4lb **7** Ran SP% **107.7**
Speed ratings (Par 101): **101,98,95,93,93 91,88**
CSF £89.51 TOTE £8.70: £3.20, £5.20; EX 103.00 Trifecta £683.70.Heartstrings was claimed by Michael Wigham for £8000
**Owner** C B Construction (Cleveland) Limited **Bred** S P Tindall **Trained** Middleham, N Yorks

**FOCUS**
A moderate claimer and the form is questionable.

## 7643 100% RACING UK PROFITS RETURNED TO RACING H'CAP 1m 6f 19y
3:30 (3:33) (Class 6) (0-65,63) 3-Y-O+ £2,358 (£704; £176; £176) Stalls Low

Form RPR

1532 **1** **Hurry Home Poppa (IRE)**[34] 6864 4-10-0 63 .......... JoeFanning 10 69+
(John Mackie) *in tch: hdwy to trck ldrs 3f out: chal wl over 1f out: rdn to take slt ld ins fnl f: edgd lft and kpt on wl towards fin* **6/1**[1]

0666 **2** *nk* **Bowdler's Magic**[21] 7177 7-9-13 62 .......... (bt1) GrahamLee 3 67
(David Thompson) *hld up in midfield: hdwy on inner 3f out: rdn to chse ldrs 2f out: squeezed through to chal ent fnl f: sn drvn and ev ch tl no ex nr fin* **12/1**

5053 **3** *hd* **Jan Smuts (IRE)**[7] 7509 6-9-8 62 .......... (tp) EmmaSayer(5) 16 68
(Wilf Storey) *hld up towards rr: hdwy on inner 3f out: n.m.r and swtchd rt wl over 1f out: rdn but ev ch whn nt clr run and swtchd rt wl ins fnl f: styd on wl towards fin* **10/1**

0054 **3** *dht* **Time Of My Life (IRE)**[17] 6644 5-8-10 50 .......... (t) JackGarritty(5) 1 55+
(Patrick Holmes) *led: rdn along and jnd over 2f out: hdd jst over 1f out: rallied u.p and ev ch ins fnl f tl no ex towards fin* **20/1**

2000 **5** *½* **Sirpertan**[20] 6644 3-8-6 54 .......... JordanNason(5) 15 58
(Marjorie Fife) *chsd ldr: hdwy 3f out: chal 2f out: sn rdn and slt ld jst over 1f out: sn drvn and hdd ins fnl f: hld whn nt much towards fin* **8/1**[2]

0/03 **6** *hd* **Nay Secret**[26] 7059 6-9-0 49 .......... FergalLynch 5 53
(Jim Goldie) *hld up: hdwy 3f out: rdn wl over 1f out: drvn and kpt on fnl f: nrst fin* **10/1**

0602 **7** *shd* **Regal Park (IRE)**[7] 7508 7-9-1 55 ........................ TimClark(5) 14 59
(Miss Imogen Pickard) *hld up: hdwy on outer over 4f out: chsd ldrs wl over 2f out: rdn to chal over 1f out and ev ch tl drvn and no ex wl ins fnl f* **9/1**[3]

00-3 **8** *2 1/2* **Lady Marmelo (IRE)**[21] 7175 4-9-12 61 ........................ PaulHanagan 12 61
(Philip Kirby) *towards rr: hdwy 3f out: rdn to chse ldrs over 1f out: drvn and one pce fnl f* **8/1**[2]

0255 **9** *1 1/2* **Authentication**[7] 7509 5-9-3 52 ........................ TomEaves 4 50
(Mel Brittain) *chsd ldrs: rdn along 3f out: drvn over 2f out and grad wknd* **20/1**

6403 **10** *3/4* **My Escapade (IRE)**[17] 7283 3-8-1 49 ........................ JoeDoyle(5) 8 46
(Simon Waugh) *chsd ldrs: rdn along 3f out: drvn wl over 1f out and grad wknd* **14/1**

3406 **11** *4 1/2* **Henpecked**[21] 7175 4-9-7 56 ........................ PJMcDonald 13 47
(Alistair Whillans) *a towards rr* **11/1**

2560 **12** *nse* **Thackeray**[21] 7175 7-9-7 56 ........................ MichaelStainton 11 47
(Chris Fairhurst) *a in rr* **25/1**

0050 **13** *3/4* **That Be Grand**[47] 6480 3-9-0 57 ........................ JasonHart 9 47
(Shaun Harris) *a towards rr* **10/1**

**14** *1* **Birthday Guest (GER)**[11] 5-8-11 46 ........................ TonyHamilton 7 34
(Philip Kirby) *chsd ldrs: rdn along wl over 2f out: sn drvn and wknd* **14/1**

5460 **15** *22* **Destiny Blue (IRE)**[47] 6490 7-9-10 59 ........................ (t) RaulDaSilva 6 17
(Suzzanne France) *dwlt: a in rr: bhd fnl 3f* **40/1**

6200 **16** *30* **Voice From Above (IRE)**[17] 7284 5-9-0 49 ........................ (v) DuranFentiman 2
(Patrick Holmes) *chsd ldng pair: rdn along 4f out: sn wknd and bhd fnl 2f* **33/1**

3m 7.9s (3.20) **Going Correction** +0.175s/f (Good)
**WFA** 3 from 4yo+ 8lb **16** Ran SP% **121.9**
Speed ratings (Par 101): **97,96,96,96,96 96,96,94,93,93 90,90,90,89,77 60**
WIN: £5.10; PL: £1.60 Hurry Home Poppa, £4.20 Bowdler's Magic, £6.50 Time Of My Life, £1.70 Jan Smuts; EX: £70.30; CSF: £71.46; TC: HHP/BM/JS £360.98, HHP/BM/T £686.90; TF: HHP/BM/JS £224.40, HHP/BM/T £910.60;.

**Owner** D Ward **Bred** Kilcarn Stud **Trained** Church Broughton , Derbys

■ Stewards' Enquiry : Tim Clark four-day ban: use of whip (18 - 21 Oct)

**FOCUS**
A modest but wide open staying handicap, which produced a bunched finish.

## 7644 THANKS & SEE YOU NEXT SEASON H'CAP 6f
**4:00** (4:05) (Class 6) (0-60,60) 3-Y-0+ **£2,385** (£704; £352) **Stalls** Centre

Form RPR

0226 **1** **Ad Vitam (IRE)**[41] 6674 6-9-3 56 ........................ (bt) RaulDaSilva 2 65
(Suzzanne France) *sn rdn along towards rr: hdwy fr 1/2-way: led ins fnl f: kpt on* **14/1**

0100 **2** *1 1/2* **Lord Buffhead**[8] 7502 5-9-3 59 ........................ (v) NeilFarley(3) 5 63
(Richard Guest) *led: hdd over 3f out: rdn to ld again over 1f out: hdd ins fnl f: one pce* **20/1**

3440 **3** *1 1/2* **McCarthy Mor (IRE)**[46] 6516 3-9-2 55 ........................ (v) PaulHanagan 3 54
(Richard Fahey) *in tch: rdn over 2f out: kpt on* **11/1**[3]

3112 **4** *hd* **Armelle (FR)**[8] 7502 3-9-4 60 ........................ (p) LouisSteward(3) 20 59+
(Scott Dixon) *chsd ldrs: rdn 1/2-way: kpt on* **3/1**[1]

0601 **5** *3/4* **Liliargh (IRE)**[78] 5499 5-8-10 49 ........................ (v) AndrewElliott 12 45
(Ben Haslam) *hld up: rdn over 3f out: bhd tl r.o fnl f* **20/1**

2056 **6** *nk* **Very First Blade**[28] 7025 5-8-5 49 ........................ (b) TimClark(5) 17 44
(Michael Mullineaux) *midfield: rdn 1/2-way: kpt on fnl f* **12/1**

0452 **7** *hd* **Ecliptic Sunrise**[28] 6995 3-9-2 55 ........................ JoeFanning 6 50
(Des Donovan) *dwlt: hld up: rdn and hdwy 2f out: one pce fnl f* **16/1**

0033 **8** *hd* **Settle For Red (IRE)**[18] 7252 4-9-4 57 ........................ (b) DanielTudhope 1 51
(Jeremy Gask) *hld up in rr: rdn over 3f out: kpt on fnl f: nvr threatened* **12/1**

2224 **9** *nse* **Pull The Pin (IRE)**[28] 7009 5-9-2 55 ........................ (bt) CharlesBishop 15 49
(Ann Stokell) *w ldr: led over 3f out: hdd over 1f out: wknd ins fnl f* **14/1**

4220 **10** *3/4* **Lucky Surprise**[20] 7191 3-9-2 55 ........................ (b) RobertWinston 4 46
(Jeremy Gask) *chsd ldrs: rdn over 2f out: wknd ins fnl f* **40/1**

5620 **11** *nk* **Bondi Beach Babe**[14] 7364 4-8-8 52 ........................ JordanNason(5) 16 42
(James Turner) *midfield: rdn 1/2-way: no imp* **25/1**

2502 **12** *1/2* **Captain Scooby**[7] 7520 8-8-10 49 ........................ (v) JasonHart 10 38
(Richard Guest) *hld up: rdn 1/2-way: nvr threatened* **9/1**[2]

0650 **13** *nse* **Amis Reunis**[35] 6834 5-8-5 49 ........................ (p) JoeDoyle(5) 11 38
(Alan Berry) *prom: rdn 1/2-way: wknd fnl f* **20/1**

1205 **14** *shd* **White Flag**[8] 7502 3-9-6 59 ........................ DuranFentiman 18 47
(Tim Easterby) *midfield: rdn 1/2-way: nvr threatened* **20/1**

3603 **15** *hd* **Emily Davison (IRE)**[36] 6821 3-9-4 57 ........................ (p) TonyHamilton 7 45
(Ann Stokell) *midfield: rdn 1/2-way: nvr threatened* **28/1**

0556 **16** *1/2* **Masked Dance (IRE)**[26] 7056 7-9-2 55 ........................ (p) TomEaves 13 41
(Scott Dixon) *chsd ldrs: sn pushed along: lost pl 1/2-way: no threat after* **16/1**

4330 **17** *nk* **Lendal Bridge**[89] 5089 3-9-1 54 ........................ (b[1]) BarryMcHugh 14 39
(Tony Coyle) *dwlt: hld up: rdn 1/2-way: sn struggling* **20/1**

0060 **18** *1* **Sleeping Star**[78] 5497 3-9-0 53 ........................ PJMcDonald 19 35
(Mel Brittain) *midfield: rdn 1/2-way: wknd fnl f* **33/1**

0600 **19** *6* **Aspirant**[34] 6866 3-9-2 55 ........................ MichaelStainton 8 18
(Marjorie Fife) *chsd ldrs: wknd 2f out* **50/1**

0434 **20** *8* **Rioja Day (IRE)**[26] 7061 4-9-3 56 ........................ (b) FergalLynch 9
(Jim Goldie) *hld up: bhd fr 1/2-way: eased* **14/1**

1m 13.17s (1.37) **Going Correction** +0.225s/f (Good) **20** Ran SP% **128.9**
Speed ratings (Par 101): **99,97,95,94,93 93,93,92,92,91 91,90,90,90,90 89,89,87,79,69**
CSF £274.63 CT £1840.61 TOTE £19.50: £3.90, £5.70, £2.60, £1.70; EX 460.00 Trifecta £2922.30 Part won..

**Owner** Arc Racing Yorkshire I **Bred** Michelle Morgan **Trained** Norton, N Yorks

■ Stewards' Enquiry : Raul Da Silva four-day ban: use of whip (18-21 Nov)

**FOCUS**
A modest but competitive sprint handicap.

T/Plt: £4,473.30 to a £1 stake. Pool: £47,490.94 - 7.75 winning units. T/Qpdt: £146.70 to a £1 stake. Pool: £5413.79 - 27.30 winning units. JR

# 5568 SOUTHWELL (L-H)
Tuesday, November 4

**OFFICIAL GOING: Standard**
Wind: almost nil Weather: fine and sunny

## 7645 LADBROKES H'CAP (DIV I) 1m (F)
**12:40** (12:41) (Class 6) (0-55,55) 3-Y-0+ **£1,940** (£577; £288; £144) **Stalls** Low

Form RPR

0034 **1** **Master Of Song**[77] 5530 7-8-9 48 ........................ (p) EoinWalsh(5) 4 60
(Roy Bowring) *trckd ldrs: led last 150yds: drvn out* **4/1**[2]

13 **2** *1 3/4* **Admirable Art (IRE)**[21] 7167 4-9-7 55 ........................ (p) AdamKirby 10 63
(Tony Carroll) *sn trcking ldrs: led over 1f out: hdd jst ins fnl f: styd on same pce* **7/2**[1]

-504 **3** *nse* **Trust Me Boy**[19] 7221 6-8-5 46 oh1 ........................ VictorSantos(7) 13 54
(John E Long) *w ldrs: led over 3f out: hdd over 1f out: styd on same pce: eased nr fin and lost 2nd line* **40/1**

0410 **4** *4 1/2* **Rockie Road (IRE)**[7] 7517 3-9-1 51 ........................ LukeMorris 7 49
(Mick Quinn) *dwlt: hdwy to chse ldrs over 3f out: one pce fnl 2f* **7/2**[1]

0432 **5** *3* **Llandanwg**[35] 6833 3-8-12 48 ........................ PaulMulrennan 9 39
(Bryan Smart) *mid-div: hdwy on outside to chse ldrs over 2f out: one pce* **7/1**

0155 **6** *10* **Nifty Kier**[72] 5731 5-9-2 53 ........................ DannyBrock(3) 6 21
(Phil McEntee) *trckd ldrs: wknd over 1f out: sn heavily eased* **11/1**

0000 **7** *1 1/4* **Bajan Rebel**[17] 7291 3-9-4 54 ........................ DavidNolan 2 19
(Michael Easterby) *in rr: hdwy on ins over 2f out: wknd over 1f out* **20/1**

00U0 **8** *1* **Water For Life**[5] 7546 3-8-10 46 oh1 ........................ (b) StevieDonohoe 3 8
(Dave Morris) *led 2f: chsd ldrs: lost pl over 2f out* **40/1**

3300 **9** *3* **Bitaphon (IRE)**[190] 1800 5-9-2 55 ........................ (t) AlistairRawlinson(5) 1 11
(Michael Appleby) *in rr: sme hdwy on inner over 2f out: sn wknd* **11/2**[3]

06-0 **10** *2* **The Bunny Catcher**[63] 6010 3-8-10 46 oh1 ........................ PaddyAspell 5
(Sharon Watt) *s.i.s: a in rr* **50/1**

-006 **11** *11* **Fair Bunny**[83] 5300 7-8-12 46 oh1 ........................ (b) SilvestreDeSousa 11
(Alan Brown) *swtchd lft after s: led after 2f: hdd over 3f out: sn lost pl and bhd* **50/1**

4500 **P** **Kneesy Earsy Nosey**[273] 474 8-8-7 46 oh1 ........................ (be[1]) AnnStokell(5) 8
(Ann Stokell) *in rr whn p.u 5f out; fatally injured* **100/1**

1m 44.68s (0.98) **Going Correction** +0.025s/f (Slow)
**WFA** 3 from 4yo+ 2lb **12** Ran SP% **115.2**
Speed ratings (Par 101): **96,94,94,89,86 76,75,74,71,69 58,**
CSF £16.90 CT £482.16 TOTE £3.90: £1.50, £1.50, £11.30; EX 18.20 Trifecta £632.00.

**Owner** S R Bowring **Bred** S R Bowring **Trained** Edwinstowe, Notts

■ Stewards' Enquiry : Victor Santos seven-day ban: failed to ride out for second place (18-25 Nov)
Danny Brock trainer said the gelding was unsuited by the fibresand surface on this occasion

**FOCUS**
The opening contest was the first division of a moderate handicap in which they went a respectable gallop on standard Fibresand. The first two were both on good marks.

## 7646 LADBROKES H'CAP (DIV II) 1m (F)
**1:10** (1:11) (Class 6) (0-55,55) 3-Y-0+ **£1,940** (£577; £288; £144) **Stalls** Low

Form RPR

0025 **1** **Delightful Sleep**[11] 7426 6-9-6 54 ........................ AdamKirby 7 64
(David Evans) *hld up in mid-div: hdwy to trck ldrs over 3f out: nt clr run tl swtchd rt over 1f out: led last 100yds: all out* **9/2**[2]

0566 **2** *hd* **Im Dapper Too**[45] 6544 3-8-8 49 ........................ KevinStott(5) 9 58
(John Davies) *trckd ldrs: dropped bk after 3f: hdwy on outer to chse ldrs 3f out: led over 1f out: hdd ins fnl f: kpt on wl: no ex nr fin* **6/1**

305 **3** *6* **Chez Vrony**[180] 2092 8-8-12 46 oh1 ........................ StevieDonohoe 2 41
(Dave Morris) *sn detached in rr and drvn along: hdwy on wd outside over 2f out: kpt on to take modest 3rd last 50yds* **16/1**

0000 **4** *1 3/4* **Flying Applause**[71] 5761 9-8-7 46 oh1 ........................ (bt) EoinWalsh(5) 1 37
(Roy Bowring) *in rr: drvn 4f out: hdwy over 1f out: kpt on* **25/1**

3516 **5** *shd* **Ice Mayden**[11] 7423 3-9-5 55 ........................ PaulMulrennan 10 46
(Bryan Smart) *chsd ldrs on outer: one pce fnl 2f* **11/2**[3]

4364 **6** *nk* **Vied (USA)**[4] 7570 3-9-2 52 ........................ (v) SilvestreDeSousa 11 42
(David O'Meara) *chsd ldrs: led over 2f out: hdd over 1f out: one pce* **2/1**[1]

0005 **7** *3 1/4* **Look On By**[17] 7291 4-9-1 49 ........................ LukeMorris 4 32
(Ruth Carr) *led 1f: led again over 3f out: hdd over 2f out: wknd over 1f out* **10/1**

0045 **8** *2 1/4* **Benidorm**[3] 7222 6-8-9 46 ........................ (e) JacobButterfield(3) 3 24
(Richard Guest) *chsd ldrs: wknd fnl 150yds* **12/1**

0500 **9** *nk* **L'Es Fremantle (FR)**[8] 7499 3-8-3 46 oh1 ........................ (p) BradleyBosley(7) 12 23
(Michael Chapman) *s.i.s: hdwy to ld after 1f: hdd and reminders over 3f out: wknd over 2f out* **100/1**

0005 **10** *3 1/4* **Maillot Jaune (IRE)**[8] 7499 4-8-9 46 oh1 ........................ (v[1]) DeclanBates(3) 6 15
(Patrick Holmes) *s.i.s: in rr: sme hdwy over 2f out: sn wknd* **22/1**

050 **11** *7* **Pal Ella**[21] 7176 3-8-3 46 oh1 ........................ JamieGormley(7) 5
(Keith Dalgleish) *prom: lost pl after 3f: sn bhd* **20/1**

1m 45.56s (1.86) **Going Correction** +0.025s/f (Slow)
**WFA** 3 from 4yo+ 2lb **11** Ran SP% **117.8**
Speed ratings (Par 101): **91,90,84,83,82 82,79,77,76,73 66**
CSF £30.30 CT £400.29 TOTE £5.30: £1.90, £3.50, £4.90; EX 38.10 Trifecta £545.70.

**Owner** Mrs E Evans **Bred** Theresa Fitsall **Trained** Pandy, Monmouths

**FOCUS**
The second division of a moderate handicap, and the winning time was nearly a second slower off a respectable gallop. The winner is rated to his summer turf form.

## 7647 DOWNLOAD THE LADBROKES APP H'CAP 7f (F)
**1:40** (1:40) (Class 5) (0-70,70) 3-Y-0+ **£2,587** (£770; £384; £192) **Stalls** Low

Form RPR

5016 **1** **Toto Skyllachy**[4] 7568 9-9-2 68 ........................ JacobButterfield(3) 7 85
(Marjorie Fife) *reluctant to go to post: chsd ldrs: sn drvn along: hung lft and led over 1f out: forged clr last* **9/1**

5556 **2** *6* **Loud**[15] 7339 4-8-10 62 ........................ (b) ConnorBeasley(3) 12 63
(Amy Weaver) *s.i.s: in rr on outer: hdwy on outside over 1f out: kpt on to take 2nd nr fin* **11/4**[1]

5060 **3** *nk* **Game Mascot**[32] 6904 4-8-13 62 ........................ (bt) LukeMorris 8 63
(Peter Hiatt) *s.i.s: hdwy to chse ldrs over 3f out: kpt on one pce over 1f out* **14/1**

0140 **4** *4* **Arabian Flight**[25] 7078 5-9-1 64 ........................ (p) SilvestreDeSousa 6 54
(Michael Appleby) *led: hdd over 2f out: wknd fnl 150yds* **13/2**[3]

3251 **5** *5* **Orwellian**[21] 7180 5-8-11 60 ........................ PaulMulrennan 9 37
(Bryan Smart) *t.k.h in mid-div: hdwy over 2f out: hung lft and wknd appr fnl f* **9/2**[2]

4100 **6** *2* **Munaawib**[18] 7249 6-9-4 67....................(tp) AdamKirby 11 39
(Deborah Sanderson) *chsd ldrs on outer tl over 3f out: hung lft and wknd over 1f out* **10/1**

2120 **7** *1 ¼* **Black Vale (IRE)**[42] 6633 3-9-6 70.................... FrederikTylicki 5 38
(Ralph J Smith) *w ldrs: led over 2f out: hdd over 1f out: sn wknd* **16/1**

4400 **8** *½* **Putin (IRE)**[35] 6843 6-8-11 63....................(bt) DannyBrock(3) 2 30
(Phil McEntee) *chsd ldrs: wknd over 1f out* **33/1**

3255 **9** *hd* **It's All A Game**[20] 6543 3-7-13 56..........(e) MelissaThompson(7) 10 22
(Richard Guest) *chsd ldrs on outer tl over 3f out: lost pl 2f out* **25/1**

6232 **10** *nk* **Black Dave (IRE)**[17] 7288 4-8-11 63.................... DeclanBates(3) 1 29
(David Evans) *in rr: nvr on terms* **8/1**

0130 **11** *2 ¼* **Day Star Lad**[21] 7178 3-9-1 65....................(v) DaleSwift 3 24
(Derek Shaw) *chsd ldrs: hung rt and wknd over 2f out* **25/1**

1253 **12** *7* **Spitfire**[15] 7337 9-9-0 70....................(t) VictorSantos(7) 4 12
(J R Jenkins) *dwlt: in rr: bhd fnl 2f* **22/1**

1m 29.15s (-1.15) **Going Correction** +0.025s/f (Slow)
**WFA** 3 from 4yo+ 1lb **12** Ran SP% **115.9**
Speed ratings (Par 103): **107,100,99,95,89 87,85,85,85,84 82,74**
CSF £31.58 CT £350.94 TOTE £9.90: £2.90, £2.40, £7.60; EX 42.60 Trifecta £1322.00 Part won..
**Owner** Richard Walker **Bred** Mrs G Slater **Trained** Stillington, N Yorks

**FOCUS**
A modest handicap in which they went a proper gallop, and it was the standout time on the round course. The winner was back to something like this year's turf form.

## 7648 32RED CASINO NURSERY H'CAP — 7f (F)
**2:10** (2:10) (Class 6) (0-60,58) 2-Y-O **£1,940** (£577; £288; £144) **Stalls** Low

Form RPR

0063 **1** **Pyrocumulus (IRE)**[49] 6428 2-9-0 **51**....................(p[1]) BenCurtis 4 61
(Alan McCabe) *s.i.s: in rr: hdwy on outside over 2f out: styd on to ld jst ins fnl f: forged clr* **8/1**[3]

6000 **2** *3* **Excelling Oscar (IRE)**[28] 7014 2-8-10 **47**....................(p) HayleyTurner 1 49
(Conor Dore) *chsd ldrs: sn drvn along: kpt on to take 2nd last 150yds* **50/1**

0603 **3** *3 ½* **Sparkling Sapphire**[42] 6642 2-8-8 **45**....................(p) PaulQuinn 6 38
(Richard Whitaker) *chsd ldr: led 2f out: hdd jst ins fnl f: fdd* **33/1**

050 **4** *½* **Kerrymerry (IRE)**[25] 7076 2-9-4 **55**.................... AdamKirby 7 46
(Ismail Mohammed) *chsd ldrs: wknd appr fnl f* **4/1**[1]

303 **5** *¾* **Penelope Pitstop**[11] 7421 2-9-6 **57**.................... DavidNolan 14 46
(Keith Dalgleish) *chsd ldrs on outer: one pce over 1f out* **4/1**[1]

5125 **6** *¾* **Invincible Wish (IRE)**[25] 7075 2-9-2 **53**.................... PaulPickard 5 40
(Brian Ellison) *in rr: hdwy over 1f out: nrst fin* **4/1**[1]

6400 **7** *½* **Emirates Challenge (IRE)**[14] 7362 2-9-5 **56**.................... FrederikTylicki 8 42
(Saeed bin Suroor) *led: hdd 2f out: wknd fnl f* **5/1**[2]

0560 **8** *nse* **Madame Ascension**[78] 5489 2-8-6 **46** ow1..........(v[1]) DeclanBates(3) 3 32
(David Evans) *mid-div: sme hdwy over 1f out: nvr a factor* **40/1**

460 **9** *1 ¼* **Sweet Talker**[67] 5886 2-9-1 **52**.................... PaulMulrennan 10 34
(Tim Easterby) *trckd ldrs: lost pl over 4f out: no threat after* **14/1**

6640 **10** *3 ¼* **Little Houidini**[35] 6830 2-8-3 **47**.................... JamieGormley(7) 12 21
(Keith Dalgleish) *chsd ldrs on outside: lost pl over 4f out* **20/1**

000 **11** *nse* **Almost Nowhere (IRE)**[29] 6976 2-9-2 **53**.................... SilvestreDeSousa 2 29
(Michael Appleby) *chsd ldrs: sn drvn along: wknd and eased over 1f out* **14/1**

600 **12** *3* **Rubheira**[16] 7308 2-8-9 **46** ow1.................... StevieDonohoe 9 16
(Hugo Froud) *rr-div: effrt over 2f out: lost pl over 1f out* **50/1**

1m 31.8s (1.50) **Going Correction** +0.025s/f (Slow) **12** Ran SP% **115.2**
Speed ratings (Par 94): **92,88,84,84,83 82,81,81,80,76 76,73**
CSF £362.74 CT £11739.07 TOTE £10.40: £2.40, £7.30, £8.10; EX 364.40 Trifecta £1976.60 Part won..
**Owner** Shropshire Wolves **Bred** R P Ryan **Trained** Averham Park, Notts

**FOCUS**
A moderate nursery handicap in which they went a perfectly respectable gallop. Another step forward from the winner.

## 7649 DAILY PRICE BOOSTS AT UNIBET EBF MAIDEN STKS — 5f (F)
**2:40** (2:41) (Class 5) 2-Y-O **£2,911** (£866; £432; £216) **Stalls** High

Form RPR

2032 **1** **Spirit Of Zeb (IRE)**[17] 7277 2-9-5 74.................... DavidNolan 5 74
(Richard Fahey) *chsd ldrs: 2nd over 1f out: styd on to ld last 75yds: drvn rt out* **11/10**[1]

4026 **2** *1* **Crosse Fire**[72] 5714 2-9-5 70....................(p) DaleSwift 8 70
(Scott Dixon) *led to post: chsd ldrs: led over 3f out: hung lft: hdd and no ex last 75yds* **15/2**

53 **3** *2* **Seychelloise**[8] 7491 2-9-0 0.................... LukeMorris 1 58
(Sir Mark Prescott Bt) *s.i.s: outpcd over 2f out: hung rt and kpt on to take 3rd over 1f out* **8/1**

5234 **4** *5* **One Moment**[15] 7336 2-9-0 63....................(p) FrederikTylicki 2 40
(Robert Cowell) *led over 1f: chsd ldrs: wknd over 1f out* **7/1**[3]

500 **5** *½* **Pickle Lilly Pearl**[37] 6791 2-9-0 54.................... StevieDonohoe 7 38
(David C Griffiths) *mid-div: outpcd over 2f out: wknd over 1f out* **33/1**

0223 **6** *5* **Compton River**[28] 7004 2-9-5 70.................... PaulMulrennan 6 25
(Bryan Smart) *chsd ldrs: wknd over 1f out* **5/1**[2]

0 **7** *shd* **Ambonnay Rouge (IRE)**[11] 7406 2-8-9 0.................... AlistairRawlinson(5) 3 20
(Michael Appleby) *chsd ldrs: lost pl over 2f out* **14/1**

0 **8** *nse* **Mon Petit Fleur**[10] 7454 2-8-7 0.................... ThomasHemsley(7) 9 19
(Chris Dwyer) *mid-div: outpcd over 2f out: wknd over 1f out* **50/1**

0030 **9** *5* **Rocco's Delight**[42] 6623 2-9-5 62....................(p) PaddyAspell 4 6
(John Wainwright) *in rr: outpcd and bhd over 3f out* **33/1**

1m 0.62s (0.92) **Going Correction** +0.025s/f (Slow) **9** Ran SP% **114.2**
Speed ratings (Par 96): **95,93,90,82,81 73,73,73,65**
CSF £9.71 TOTE £1.90: £1.10, £3.30, £2.10; EX 10.30 Trifecta £45.70.
**Owner** IMEJ Racing **Bred** Tally-Ho Stud **Trained** Musley Bank, N Yorks

**FOCUS**
A fair juvenile sprint maiden in which they went a proper gallop. Straightforward form.

## 7650 32RED H'CAP — 2m (F)
**3:10** (3:12) (Class 4) (0-85,84) 3-Y-O+ **£4,690** (£1,395; £697; £348) **Stalls** Low

Form RPR

1050 **1** **Kingscombe (USA)**[15] 6721 5-9-0 **70**.................... RobertHavlin 6 83
(Linda Jewell) *awkward to load: trckd ldrs: upsides over 3f out: led narrowly appr fnl f: fnd ex nr fin* **7/1**

2135 **2** *nk* **Cousin Khee**[41] 6664 7-9-13 **83**.................... SilvestreDeSousa 1 95
(Hughie Morrison) *w ldr: led after 5f: drvn 3f out: hdd appr fnl f: upsides last 100yds: jst hld* **13/8**[1]

1530 **3** *14* **Moidore**[24] 7107 5-10-0 **84**.................... PaulMulrennan 2 79
(John Quinn) *trckd ldrs: drvn over 4f out: wknd over 1f out* **7/2**[3]

1250 **4** *7* **Arabian Revolution**[23] 7135 3-9-5 **84**....................(v[1]) FrederikTylicki 3 71
(Saeed bin Suroor) *dwlt: hld up: hdwy 7f out: sn trcking ldrs: drvn over 3f out: wknd over 2f out* **5/2**[2]

11-0 **5** *26* **Bathwick Street**[44] 5276 5-9-6 **76**.................... AdamKirby 5 32
(David Evans) *led 5f: w ldrs: drvn 5f out: lost pl 3f out: eased whn bhd: t.o* **20/1**

-022 **6** *nk* **Cropley (IRE)**[182] 2055 5-8-6 **67**....................(p) AnnStokell(5) 4 22
(Ann Stokell) *in rr: pushed along after 4f: reminders 6f out: lost pl over 4f out: sn wl bhd: t.o* **33/1**

3m 43.57s (-1.93) **Going Correction** +0.025s/f (Slow)
**WFA** 3 from 5yo+ 9lb **6** Ran SP% **109.1**
Speed ratings (Par 105): **105,104,97,94,81 81**
CSF £17.84 TOTE £8.20: £3.70, £1.10; EX 15.00 Trifecta £38.30.
**Owner** Peter Oppenheimer **Bred** Juddmonte Farms Inc **Trained** Sutton Valence, Kent

**FOCUS**
The feature contest was a decent staying handicap in which they went an, at best, even gallop. Similar form from the winner to his last start here.

## 7651 CORAL.CO.UK CLAIMING STKS — 1m 3f (F)
**3:40** (3:40) (Class 6) 3-Y-O+ **£2,045** (£603; £302) **Stalls** Low

Form RPR

-114 **1** **Reve De Nuit (USA)**[17] 7279 8-9-7 92.................... SilvestreDeSousa 2 99
(K R Burke) *led tl over 4f out: led over 3f out: drvn wl clr over 2f out: eased last 50yds* **8/15**[1]

155 **2** *15* **Layline (IRE)**[99] 4744 7-9-5 73.................... AdamKirby 3 72
(Gay Kelleway) *hld up in mid-div: hdwy to trck ldrs over 5f out: drvn to chse wnr over 2f out: kpt on same pce* **14/1**

1236 **3** *1* **Lean On Pete (IRE)**[21] 7186 5-9-3 75.................... JacobButterfield(3) 5 71
(Ollie Pears) *in rr: drvn over 4f out: chsng ldrs over 2f out: 3rd and one pce over 1f out* **10/3**[2]

0306 **4** *4 ½* **Sofias Number One (USA)**[52] 6341 6-8-13 68..........(b) EoinWalsh(5) 7 62
(Roy Bowring) *hld up in rr: drvn and lost pl over 4f out: one pce fnl 3f* **9/1**[3]

1056 **5** *4* **Anjuna Beach (USA)**[108] 4433 4-9-7 62.................... AnnStokell(5) 1 64
(Ann Stokell) *trckd ldrs: t.k.h: led over 4f out: hdd over 3f out: wknd over 1f out* **50/1**

2230 **6** *4* **Run Fat Lass Run**[16] 7302 4-9-0 66....................(p) HayleyTurner 4 45
(Conor Dore) *chsd ldrs: drvn over 4f out: wknd over 1f out* **33/1**

006/ **7** *63* **Simplified**[11] 129 11-7-13 45....................(tp) BradleyBosley(7) 6
(Michael Chapman) *half-rrd s: sn chsng ldrs: drvn 7f out: lost pl 5f out: t.o and eased 3f out: eventually completed* **150/1**

2m 26.48s (-1.52) **Going Correction** +0.025s/f (Slow) **7** Ran SP% **110.5**
Speed ratings (Par 101): **106,95,94,91,88 85,39**
CSF £9.06 TOTE £1.50: £1.10, £2.50; EX 6.40 Trifecta £11.00.
**Owner** Mrs Z Wentworth **Bred** Ecurie Du Haras De Meautry **Trained** Middleham Moor, N Yorks

**FOCUS**
A fair middle-distance claimer in which they went a proper gallop. The wasy winner is rated to his January reappearance figure.

## 7652 £20 RISK-FREE BET AT UNIBET MAIDEN STKS — 5f (F)
**4:10** (4:10) (Class 5) 3-Y-O+ **£2,587** (£770; £384; £192) **Stalls** High

Form RPR

03-3 **1** **Extreme Supreme**[17] 7285 3-9-5 65.................... DaleSwift 1 60+
(Derek Shaw) *chsd ldrs: drvn and outpcd over 3f out: hdwy over 2f out: led wl over 1f out: styd on* **4/5**[1]

330 **2** *1 ¼* **Big City Boy (IRE)**[57] 6195 6-9-2 45.................... DannyBrock(3) 7 55
(Phil McEntee) *chsd ldrs: 2nd over 1f out: kpt on same pce* **8/1**[3]

4 **3** *3 ½* **Saved My Bacon (IRE)**[77] 5531 3-9-0 0.................... SilvestreDeSousa 4 37
(Chris Dwyer) *led: hdd wl over 1f out: one pce* **12/1**

-43 **4** *3 ½* **Black Widow**[76] 5568 3-9-0 0.................... StevieDonohoe 2 25
(Pat Eddery) *chsd ldrs: lost pl over 3f out: kpt on fnl f* **12/1**

6360 **5** *1* **Templar Boy**[13] 7370 3-9-5 49....................(v[1]) PaddyAspell 5 26
(J R Jenkins) *in rr: kpt on fnl f: nvr a factor* **16/1**

0560 **6** *shd* **Tinchy Ryder**[58] 5853 3-9-5 45....................(p) PaulMulrennan 3 26
(Bryan Smart) *chsd ldrs: drvn over 2f out: edgd rt and wknd over 1f out* **10/1**

5300 **7** *¾* **Island Express (IRE)**[42] 6631 7-9-0 48....................(bt) AnnStokell(5) 6 23
(Ann Stokell) *hmpd s: outpcd in rr: kpt on fnl 150yds* **50/1**

-46 **8** *1 ½* **Qatar Princess (IRE)**[17] 7285 3-9-0 62.................... FrederikTylicki 9 13
(J R Jenkins) *chsd ldrs: wknd appr fnl f* **15/2**[2]

3-0 **9** *4* **Livia Drusilla (IRE)**[34] 6862 3-9-0 0.................... PaulPickard 8
(Brian Ellison) *chsd ldrs: lost pl over 1f out* **16/1**

1m 1.1s (1.40) **Going Correction** +0.025s/f (Slow) **9** Ran SP% **116.6**
Speed ratings (Par 103): **91,89,83,77,76 76,74,72,66**
CSF £8.00 TOTE £1.80: £1.50, £3.10, £3.40; EX 9.40 Trifecta £97.90.
**Owner** Mrs Lyndsey Shaw **Bred** Derek Shaw **Trained** Sproxton, Leics

**FOCUS**
A modest sprint maiden run in a relatively slow time. The winner is rated in line with his reappearance effort.
T/Plt: £664.60 to a £1 stake. Pool: £52,095.76 - 57.22 winning units. T/Qpdt: £74.10 to a £1 stake. Pool: £4842.19 - 48.35 winning units. WG

# 7602 FLEMINGTON (L-H)
Tuesday, November 4

**OFFICIAL GOING: Turf: good**

## 7653a EMIRATES MELBOURNE CUP (GROUP 1 H'CAP) (3YO+) (TURF) — 2m
**4:00** (12:00) 3-Y-O+
**£2,043,010** (£483,870; £241,935; £134,408; £94,086; £67,204)

RPR

**1** **Protectionist (GER)**[24] 7126 4-8-13 **0**.................... RyanMoore 10 122+
(A Wohler, Germany) *hld up and sn towards rr: pushed along and clsd 3f out: rdn and fnd gap between horses 2f out: chal over 1f out and led ent fnl f: qckd clr: styd on strly: v readily* **7/1**[3]

**2** *4* **Red Cadeaux**[59] 6139 8-9-0 **0**.................... GeraldMosse 14 119
(Ed Dunlop) *midfield: clsd steadily and prom 3f out: rdn to chal and disputing ld jst over 2f out: hdd ent fnl f: styd on wl for 2nd but readily outpcd by wnr* **20/1**

**3** *½* **Who Shot Thebarman (NZ)**[17] 7301 6-8-9 **0**.................... GlenBoss 12 113
(Chris Waller, Australia) *w ldrs early: sn stdd and settled in midfield: rdn and clsd into st: swtchd lft to rail and ev ch over 1f out: readily outpcd by wnr fnl f but styd on wl for 3rd* **20/1**



The Form Book, Raceform Ltd, Newbury, RG14 5SJ

4 1 1/2 **Signoff (IRE)**[3] 4-8-2 0 ow2 ........................(b) JoaoMoreira 15 104
(Darren Weir, Australia) *sn dropped in and hld up in midfield: clsd steadily and wl in tch 4f out: prom into st: rdn to chal and disputing ld jst over 2f out: hdd ent fnl f: dropped to 4th and hld: styd on* **7/1**[3]

5 1 **Willing Foe (USA)**[51] 6374 7-8-9 0 ........................ JamesMcDonald 16 110
(Saeed bin Suroor) *midfield: rdn into st: effrt over 1f out: styd on same pce and wl hld fnl f* **30/1**

6 1 **Precedence (NZ)**[10] 9-8-8 0 ........................(t) MichaelRodd 18 108
(Bart & James Cummings, Australia) *hld up in rr: fanned out and rdn to cl into st: styd on down wd outside and tk n.d 6th towards fin* **80/1**

7 1 1/4 **Araldo**[17] 7301 6-8-5 0 ........................ DwayneDunn 22 104
(Michael Moroney, Australia) *t.k.h: sn dropped in fr wdst draw and hld up towards rr: fanned out and clsd gng wl into st: rdn 2f out: nt qckn and hung lft: styd on wout threatening after* **20/1**

8 1 1/2 **Au Revoir (IRE)**[10] 4-8-6 0 ........................ GlynSchofield 21 103
(A Fabre, France) *midfield on outer: smooth hdwy and prom into st: rdn to chal and ev ch 2f out: outpcd by ldrs over 1f out: no ex and fdd fnl f* **70/1**

9 1 3/4 **Seismos (IRE)**[17] 7301 6-8-11 0 ........................ CraigNewitt 1 106
(Marco Botti) *pushed along but unable to go forward early and sn hld up in rr: last over 3f out: rdn into st: kpt on wout ever threatening fnl 2f* **90/1**

10 1/2 **Fawkner (AUS)**[10] 7467 7-9-0 0 ........................(b) NicholasHall 8 109
(Robert Hickmott, Australia) *wnt rt s: led early: dropped bk once hdd and sn prom in midfield: rdn and brief effrt over 2f out: outpcd by ldrs over 1f out: no ex and fdd fnl f* **15/2**

11 2 1/4 **Opinion (IRE)**[10] 5-8-6 0 ........................(t) TyeAngland 13 98
(Chris Waller, Australia) *hld up in midfield: rdn and effrt to cl on outer into st: outpcd fnl 2f: fdd* **70/1**

12 hd **Gatewood**[65] 5962 6-8-9 0 ........................ WilliamBuick 20 101
(John Gosden) *hld up towards rr: clsd into midfield 1/2-way: rdn into st: outpcd over 1f out: sn btn: fdd* **60/1**

13 nk **Lucia Valentina (NZ)**[17] 7301 4-8-5 0 ........................ KerrinMcEvoy 2 101
(Kris Lees, Australia) *sn midfield on inner: rdn and angled out into st: outpcd and btn fnl 2f: nvr able to chal* **6/1**[2]

14 1 3/4 **Mutual Regard (IRE)**[73] 5693 5-8-9 0 ........................(p) DamienOliver 11 99
(J P Murtagh, Ire) *t.k.h: midfield: rdn and effrt to improve 2f out: no ex and btn ent fnl f: wknd: eased* **8/1**

15 3 1/4 **Brambles (NZ)**[3] 7602 6-8-7 0 ........................(t) LukeNolen 19 93
(Peter G Moody, Australia) *t.k.h: midfield: clsd and prom sn after 1/2-way: chal gng strly 3f out: w ldr into st: hdd jst over 2f out: no ex and btn: wknd* **80/1**

16 2 3/4 **Unchain My Heart (AUS)**[17] 7301 8-8-2 0 ........................(v[1]) DeanYendall 4 85
(David A Hayes & Tom Dabernig, Australia) *midfield on inner: shuffled bk and towards rr 1/2-way: rdn and angled out 3f out: outpcd and btn in st: wknd and eased* **100/1**

17 1 1/4 **My Ambivalent (IRE)**[128] 3766 5-8-8 0 ........................ AndreaAtzeni 3 90
(Roger Varian) *t.k.h: sn led: rdn and strly pressed 3f out: hdd jst over 2f out: no ex and btn: wknd on rail: eased fnl f* **30/1**

18 4 **Junoob**[17] 7301 6-8-10 0 ........................(b) HughBowman 6 87
(Chris Waller, Australia) *prom in midfield on inner: rdn and effrt 3f out: no ex and qckly btn 2f out: wknd: eased* **20/1**

19 3 **Lidari (FR)**[17] 7301 5-8-6 0 ........................ BenMelham 9 80
(Peter G Moody, Australia) *bmpd s: t.k.h: sn restrained in midfield on inner: rdn into st: no ex and btn 2f out: wknd: eased* **70/1**

20 16 **Royal Diamond (IRE)**[51] 6374 8-8-10 0 ........................ StevenArnold 5 67
(J P Murtagh, Ire) *t.k.h: prom: lost pl bef st: rdn over 2f out: qckly btn: wknd and eased: t.o* **100/1**

21 1/2 **Mr O'Ceirin (NZ)**[23] 7-8-7 0 ........................(vt) ChadSchofield 17 63
(Ciaron Maher, Australia) *hld up towards rr: rdn and dropped to last bef st: lost tch and btn 2f out: eased: t.o* **200/1**

22 25 **Admire Rakti (JPN)**[17] 7301 6-9-3 0 ........................ ZacPurton 7 45
(Tomoyuki Umeda, Japan) *restrained early and trckd ldr: rdn and effrt to chal over 3f out: fnd little and btn bef st: wknd: eased and dropped to last: tailed rt off: collapsed and fatally injured after r* **9/2**[1]

3m 17.71s (-1.93) **22 Ran SP% 117.8**
PARI-MUTUEL (NSW TAB - all including 1 aud stake): WIN 8.20; PLACE 3.00, 5.60, 3.30; DF 92.70; SF (Exacta) 154.30; TRIFECTA 2202.40.
**Owner** Narola Stables, Australian Bloodstock Et Al **Bred** Dr Christoph Berglar **Trained** Germany

**FOCUS**
This didn't look to be one of the strongest renewals in recent years, but what it did have was a strong pace throughout, which is often missing. My Ambivalent was quickly into stride and got on with things in front. She set good fractions but was done with heading into the final half a mile. This ensured the race didn't have any unlucky in-running stories, and should produce form that is reliable.

## 7268 MAISONS-LAFFITTE (R-H)
Tuesday, November 4
**OFFICIAL GOING: Turf: very soft**

### 7654a PRIX MIESQUE (GROUP 3) (2YO FILLIES) (STRAIGHT) (TURF) 7f (S)
**12:15** (12:00) 2-Y-O **£33,333** (£13,333; £10,000; £6,666; £3,333)

RPR

1 **Ameenah (FR)**[40] 6697 2-8-11 0 ........................ FranckBlondel 6 105
(F Rossi, France) *w.w in 4th of single file field: rdn and hdwy to join ldrs ent fnl f: r.o u.p to ld 100yds out: sn clr* **4/1**[3]

2 2 **Night Of Light (IRE)**[30] 6967 2-8-11 0 ........................ StephanePasquier 5 100
(P Bary, France) *led: rdn 1 1/2f out: chal on either side appr fnl f: rallied u.p: hdd 100yds out: no ex* **11/8**[1]

3 1 1/4 **Kenouska (FR)**[25] 7094 2-8-11 0 ........................(p) FabriceVeron 2 97
(H-A Pantall, France) *trckd ldr: rdn to chal over 1f out: one pce u.p fnl f* **12/1**

4 2 1/2 **Niyama (GER)**[60] 6123 2-8-11 0 ........................ ChristopheSoumillon 3 91
(Mario Hofer, Germany) *trckd front two: reminder over 2f out: effrt to try and chal appr 1f out: wknd ins fnl f* **11/4**[2]

5 shd **Tres Forte (FR)**[27] 7053 2-8-11 0 ........................ AdrienFouassier 1 90
(M Delzangles, France) *dwlt: towards rr: rdn 1 1/2f out: plugged on u.p ins fnl f: nvr on terms* **10/1**

6 9 **Connected (FR)**[29] 6991 2-8-11 0 ........................ GregoryBenoist 4 68
(E Lellouche, France) *in rr: rdn over 1 1/2f out: no imp: bhd whn eased ins fnl f* **9/1**

1m 30.49s (2.49) **6 Ran SP% 115.6**
WIN (incl. 1 euro stake): 3.70. PLACES: 1.50, 1.50. SF: 10.40.
**Owner** Jean-Claude Seroul **Bred** Sheikh Abdulla Bin Khalifa Al Thani **Trained** France

### 7655a CRITERIUM DE MAISONS-LAFFITTE (GROUP 2) (2YO) (TURF) 6f (S)
**1:20** (12:00) 2-Y-O **£90,250** (£34,833; £16,625; £11,083; £5,541)

RPR

1 **Mattmu**[24] 7121 2-9-0 0 ........................(p) DavidAllan 5 112
(Tim Easterby) *broke wl: mde all: 1 l clr and rdn over 1 1/2f out: edgd lft ins fnl f: drvn out: readily* **6/1**[3]

2 1 **Queen Bee (FR)**[30] 6967 2-8-10 0 ........................ GregoryBenoist 10 105
(E Lellouche, France) *w.w in rr: hdwy on outer 2f out: rdn to chse ldr ins fnl f: r.o u.p: nvr quite on terms w wnr* **9/1**

3 1 3/4 **Goken (FR)**[30] 6966 2-9-0 0 ........................ FabriceVeron 8 104
(H-A Pantall, France) *chsd ldrs: pushed along and pressed ldr 2f out: sn rdn and nt qckn: kpt on at same pce fnl f* **10/1**

4 5 **Pivotal Rio (IRE)**[25] 2-9-0 0 ........................ CristianDemuro 6 89
(Manila Illuminati, Italy) *towards rr: rdn and hdwy between horses 2 1/2f out: n.m.r over 2f out: styd on u.p fr over 1f out: nvr plcd to chal* **33/1**

5 3/4 **Souvenir Delondres (FR)**[25] 7094 2-8-10 0 ........................ MaximeGuyon 11 83
(J E Pease, France) *t.k.h: hld up towards rr: rdn and effrt to chse ldrs 2f out: outpcd by ldrs fr over 1f out: plugged on at one pce* **5/1**[2]

6 2 1/2 **Avabin (IRE)**[37] 2-9-0 0 ........................ WGambarota 4 79
(M Gonnelli, Italy) *chsd ldr between horses: rdn and nt qckn w ldrs over 1 1/2f out: wandered and wknd u.p fnl f* **33/1**

7 1 1/4 **Shepherd's Purse**[65] 5954 2-9-0 0 ........................ GaryCarroll 3 75
(Joseph G Murphy, Ire) *racd in fnl trio: prog into midfield 1/2-way: hemmed in 2f out: rdn and effrt over 1f out: swtchd ins and bmpd rival 1f out: no imp fnl f* **8/1**

8 20 **City Money (IRE)**[56] 6220 2-9-0 0 ........................ StephanePasquier 7 15
(M Delcher Sanchez, France) *towards rr on inner: rdn and outpcd in last over 2f out: eased whn btn ins fnl f* **8/1**

9 3 1/2 **Shamal (FR)**[14] 2-9-0 0 ........................ OlivierPeslier 1 5
(Y-M Porzier, France) *showed gd spd and prom on inner: lost pl and rdn along 2f out: wkng whn bmpd and knocked into anther rival 1f out: eased ins fnl f* **7/4**[1]

10 snk **Parsley (IRE)**[24] 7109 2-8-10 0 ........................ FrankieDettori 2
(Richard Hannon) *w.w in midfield: rdn 1/2-way and no imp: next to last and btn whn bmpd 1f out: eased ins fnl f* **7/1**

1m 13.35s (-0.05) **10 Ran SP% 127.0**
WIN (incl. 1 euro stake): 8.70. PLACES: 2.90, 3.10, 3.40. DF: 44.60. SF: 75.20.
**Owner** James Bowers **Bred** J Bowers **Trained** Great Habton, N Yorks

**FOCUS**
Some didn't give their running but the form fits the race average.

### 7656a PRIX DE SEINE-ET-OISE (GROUP 3) (3YO+) (TURF) 6f (S)
**1:50** (12:00) 3-Y-O+ **£33,333** (£13,333; £10,000; £6,666; £3,333)

RPR

1 **Gammarth (FR)**[30] 6971 6-8-11 0 ........................(b) MickaelBarzalona 12 110
(H-A Pantall, France) *chsd ldng pair on outer: rowed along to chse ldr under 2f out: sn chal and led ent fnl f: drvn out* **11/1**

2 3/4 **Caledonia Lady**[29] 6994 5-8-8 0 ........................ AlexisBadel 3 105
(Mme M Bollack-Badel, France) *chsd ldng pair between horses: cl 4th and hrd rdn 1 1/2f out: r.o u.p fnl f: nvr quite on terms w wnr* **16/1**

3 shd **Catcall (FR)**[30] 6966 5-9-0 0 ........................ OlivierPeslier 10 111
(P Sogorb, France) *hld up in midfield: n.m.r over 2f out: niggled along and swtchd rnd horses over 1 1/2f out: r.o u.p fnl f: nt pce to chal wnr* **9/2**[2]

4 1 **Robert Le Diable (FR)**[29] 6994 5-8-11 0 ........................ FlavienPrat 1 104
(D Prod'Homme, France) *trckd ldng pair on stands' side: scrubbed along and sltly outpcd 1 1/2f out: kpt on u.p fnl f: nvr able to chal* **7/1**

5 3/4 **Kolonel (GER)**[22] 5-8-11 0 ........................ ChristopheSoumillon 4 102
(Mario Hofer, Germany) *led or disp ld: rdn and hdd under 2f out: kpt on gamely fnl f* **11/1**

6 1 1/4 **Bamiyan (FR)**[58] 6182 4-9-0 0 ........................ ThierryJarnet 8 101
(T Lemer, France) *hld up in fnl quartet: hdwy 2f out: sltly impeded bef switching outside appr 1f out: kpt on u.p fnl f: nvr plcd to chal* **10/1**

7 3/4 **Justice Day (IRE)**[31] 6918 3-8-11 0 ........................ JFEgan 9 96
(David Elsworth) *led or disp ld: led under 2f out: hdd ent fnl f: sn wknd* **6/1**[3]

8 3/4 **Aksil (FR)**[16] 7327 4-8-8 0 ........................ GregoryBenoist 7 90
(M Boutin, France) *w.w in fnl quartet: kpt on u.p fnl 1 1/2f: nvr in contention* **25/1**

9 2 **Ming Zhi Cosmos (FR)**[37] 6807 3-8-10 0 ........................(p) ThierryThulliez 2 86
(N Clement, France) *settled in midfield: rdn and hung rt 1 1/2f out: sn btn and eased ins fnl f* **14/1**

10 1 1/2 **Penmaen (IRE)**[29] 6994 4-8-8 0 ........................ FabienLefebvre 11 79
(J E Hammond, France) *racd in midfield: rowed along and brief effrt 1 1/2f out: sn btn* **9/1**

11 1 3/4 **Maarek**[17] 7272 7-9-2 0 ........................ BillyLee 5 81
(Miss Evanna McCutcheon, Ire) *got away on terms: in rr: scrubbed along in last pl 2f out: sn rdn and no imp: nt persevered w whn hld ins fnl f* **3/1**[1]

12 1 1/2 **Fanoos**[29] 6994 5-8-8 0 ........................(p) MickaelForest 13 69
(Mme G Rarick, France) *midfield: rdn and no imp 2f out: wknd fr 1 1/2f out: eased ins fnl f* **50/1**

13 hd **Frascata (FR)**[29] 6994 5-8-11 0 ........................ StephanePasquier 6 71
(Yves de Nicolay, France) *outpcd in fnl quartet: rdn and no imp fr 2f out: eased ins fnl f* **25/1**

1m 13.38s (-0.02) **13 Ran SP% 127.9**
WIN (incl. 1 euro stake): 14.70. PLACES: 4.30, 3.90, 3.00. DF: 95.50. SF: 277.90.
**Owner** Gerard Mimouni **Bred** Madame Marie-Therese Mimouni **Trained** France

## 7631 KEMPTON (A.W) (R-H)
Wednesday, November 5
**OFFICIAL GOING: Polytrack: standard**
Wind: fresh, half against Weather: Fine but cloudy

### 7657 BOOK CHRISTMAS FESTIVAL TICKETS NOW H'CAP 2m (P)
**4:35** (4:38) (Class 6) (0-60,60) 3-Y-O+ **£1,940** (£577; £288; £144) **Stalls Low**

Form RPR

/032 1 **Delagoa Bay (IRE)**[8] 7524 6-8-12 46 ........................ MartinDwyer 10 53
(Sylvester Kirk) *mde all: set mod pce tl 6f out: drvn over 2f out: kpt finding and hld on wl* **33/1**

4103 **2** ½ **Medburn Cutler**[12] 7419 4-9-7 55................................(p) PaulHanagan 11 61
(Paul Henderson) *slowly away: hld up in last pair: shoved along 4f out: gng nowhere in 10th 3f out: styd on fr wl over 1f out: fin wl to take 2nd last strides and cl on wnr* **7/1**

1353 **3** ¾ **Mighty Mambo**[21] 7204 7-9-12 60................................(tp) GeorgeBaker 3 66
(Lawney Hill) *restless in stalls: t.k.h: hld up in 9th: gng bttr than most 3f out: rdn and rather laboured prog fr jst over 2f out: chsd wnr ins fnl f: kpt on but lost 2nd last strides* **4/1**[2]

0424 **4** 1½ **May Hay**[18] 7287 4-9-12 60.................................................. LukeMorris 5 64
(Anthony Carson) *trckd ldr after 6f: rdn to chal over 2f out: nt qckn wl over 1f out: one pce and lost 2 pls ins fnl f* **6/1**[3]

2344 **5** 2½ **Just Duchess**[8] 7518 4-8-12 46 oh1.................................. GrahamLee 7 47
(Michael Blanshard) *trckd ldr 6f: styd prom: pushed along over 4f out: one pce u.p over 2f out: fdd fnl f* **20/1**

/000 **6** ½ **Artisan**[19] 7251 6-9-6 59...................................................... KevinStott(5) 1 59
(Brian Ellison) *slowly away: hld up in last pair: rdn and tried to make prog on inner over 2f out: no hdwy jst over 1f out* **7/2**[1]

5002 **7** 1¾ **Uganda Glory (USA)**[7] 7532 4-9-8 56.............................. PatCosgrave 4 54
(George Baker) *trckd ldrs: rdn over 3f out: nt qckn over 2f out: wknd over 1f out* **14/1**

3634 **8** 3¾ **Dr Finley (IRE)**[21] 7204 7-9-0 51................................(v) SimonPearce(3) 9 45
(Lydia Pearce) *chsd ldrs: rdn over 3f out: wknd over 2f out* **14/1**

5-R0 **9** 1¾ **Red Current**[53] 6343 10-8-12 46 oh1................. WilliamTwiston-Davies 2 37
(Michael Scudamore) *hld up in midfield: rdn and rchd 4th over 2f out: wknd qckly wl over 1f out* **66/1**

5254 **10** 13 **Honest Strike (USA)**[8] 7524 7-9-12 60..........................(bt) AdamKirby 8 36
(Daniel Mark Loughnane) *t.k.h: hld up in midfield: shkn up over 3f out: hanging v bdly and wknd 2f out: virtually p.u* **8/1**

4315 **P** **Graylyn Ruby (FR)**[21] 7204 9-9-2 57........................... ChrisMeehan(7) 6 +
(Robert Eddery) *in tch: sddle slipped bdly 1/2-way: last and tailing off over 4f out: p.u ins fnl f* **7/1**

3m 36.03s (5.93) **Going Correction** +0.025s/f (Slow) 11 Ran SP% **115.1**
Speed ratings (Par 101): **86,85,85,84,83 83,82,80,79,73**
CSF £242.05 CT £1142.32 TOTE £27.80: £5.60, £3.60, £1.80; EX 223.90 Trifecta £1008.20.
**Owner** Homebred Racing **Bred** J Ryan **Trained** Upper Lambourn, Berks

**FOCUS**
A weak staying handicap, run at an ordinary pace. The winner only had to step up slightly on her latest form.

## 7658 BETDAQ £30 FREE BET 3% COMMISSION MAIDEN FILLIES' STKS (BOBIS RACE) (DIV I) 1m (P)
**5:10** (5:13) (Class 5) 2-Y-O **£2,587** (£770; £384; £192) **Stalls** Low

Form RPR

**1** **Fey** 2-9-0 0............................................................ AdamKirby 6 75+
(Charlie Appleby) *trckd ldrs: wnt 2nd over 2f out: no imp tl rdn and clsd the gap fnl f: led last strides* **11/1**

22 **2** nk **Waldnah**[22] 7184 2-9-0 0............................................. RobertHavlin 4 74
(John Gosden) *led: gng strly and 2 l clr 2f out: shkn up over 1f out: kpt on fnl f but hdd last strides* **4/1**[1]

**3** 3¼ **Alhania (USA)** 2-9-0 0.............................................. PaulHanagan 10 67+
(Saeed bin Suroor) *t.k.h: hld up in midfield: pushed along and rn green over 2f out: prog to take 3rd over 1f out: styd on but no imp on ldng pair* **5/1**[2]

**4** 3¼ **Michaela** 2-9-0 0.............................................................. MartinDwyer 2 59
(Paul Webber) *hld up in midfield: pushed along and outpcd over 2f out: kpt on fr over 1f out to take 4th ins fnl f: nt disgracd* **66/1**

**5** 2 **Pensionnat (IRE)** 2-9-0 0........................................ OscarPereira 1 54+
(Ralph Beckett) *dwlt: sn in last: rn green and pushed along fr 1/2-way: kpt on fr over 1f out to take 5th ins fnl f* **10/1**

00 **6** 2¾ **Lady D's Rock (IRE)**[21] 7194 2-9-0 0........................ SteveDrowne 5 48
(Clive Cox) *chsd ldr to over 2f out: wknd qckly over 1f out* **66/1**

24 **7** ½ **Opportuna**[18] 7278 2-9-0 0........................................ WilliamCarson 8 47
(Tom Dascombe) *dwlt: a in rr: rdn and no prog wl over 2f out* **7/1**[3]

0 **8** shd **Scimitarra**[13] 7399 2-9-0 0........................................ LukeMorris 3 47
(Paul Cole) *chsd ldng pair to over 2f out: wknd qckly over 1f out* **66/1**

**9** 4 **Beccabuddyblues (GR)** 2-9-0 0.................................. PatCosgrave 9 38
(Amanda Perrett) *t.k.h: hld up in rr: pushed along over 2f out: wknd qckly* **66/1**

1m 39.92s (0.12) **Going Correction** +0.025s/f (Slow) 9 Ran SP% **72.6**
Speed ratings (Par 93): **100,99,96,93,91 88,87,87,83**
CSF £19.98 TOTE £6.80: £2.70, £1.40, £1.40; EX 20.90 Trifecta £48.80.
**Owner** Godolphin **Bred** Darley **Trained** Newmarket, Suffolk

■ Tazffin was withdrawn. Price at time of withdrawal 11-10. Rule 4 applies to all bets - deduction 45p in the pound.

**FOCUS**
This interesting if ordinary 2yo fillies' maiden was markedly weakened when Tazffin refused to load up. There was something of an uneven pace on and the form is rated around the second.

## 7659 BETDAQ £30 FREE BET 3% COMMISSION MAIDEN FILLIES' STKS (BOBIS RACE) (DIV II) 1m (P)
**5:40** (5:43) (Class 5) 2-Y-O **£2,587** (£770; £384; £192) **Stalls** Low

Form RPR

**1** **Namhroodah (IRE)** 2-9-0 0...................................... LukeMorris 10 72+
(James Tate) *pressed ldng pair but trapped out wd: led over 2f out but lugged rt and rn green: hdd over 1f out: rallied to ld ins fnl f: styd on wl and a holding on* **11/4**[1]

0 **2** hd **Melbourne Shuffle (USA)**[22] 7184 2-9-0 0................. RobertHavlin 8 71
(John Gosden) *hld up in midfield: prog over 2f out: shkn up to ld over 1f out: hdd ins fnl f: styd on wl but a jst hld* **10/1**

00 **3** 3¼ **Ninepins (IRE)**[21] 7194 2-9-0 0.................................... SeanLevey 7 63+
(Richard Hannon) *hld up in 8th: pushed along over 2f out: stdy prog to take 3rd 1f out: no ch w ldng pair but styd on* **33/1**

**4** 4½ **Cracker** 2-9-0 0............................................................ SebSanders 5 54+
(Ralph Beckett) *trckd ldrs: cl up 2f out: shkn up and outpcd after: lost 3rd 1f out: wknd* **7/2**[2]

**5** 1 **Sabha (IRE)** 2-9-0 0...................................................... GrahamLee 9 50+
(Timothy Jarvis) *towards rr: pushed along over 2f out: sn outpcd: kpt on same pce fr over 1f out* **50/1**

**6** ¾ **Included** 2-9-0 0.......................................................... PatCosgrave 1 49
(Amanda Perrett) *trckd ldrs: outpcd fr 2f out: shkn up over 1f out: wknd fnl f* **12/1**

**7** 1¾ **Prying** 2-9-0 0............................................................ AdamKirby 3 45
(Charlie Appleby) *sn pushed along in last pair and rn green: nvr a factor* **4/1**[3]

526 **8** ½ **Mythical City (IRE)**[14] 7382 2-9-0 0............................ JoeFanning 4 44
(Mark Johnston) *pressed ldr: upsides over 2f out: sn rdn and nt qckn: wknd over 1f out* **9/2**

**9** 1½ **Caroline Norton (USA)** 2-9-0 0................................ SteveDrowne 6 40
(John Gosden) *rn green in last pair and sn pushed along: nvr any prog* **10/1**

00 **10** nk **Victorina**[15] 7367 2-9-0 0........................................... MartinDwyer 2 39
(Stuart Kittow) *mde most to over 2f out: wknd qckly over 1f out* **66/1**

1m 41.05s (1.25) **Going Correction** +0.025s/f (Slow) 10 Ran SP% **119.3**
Speed ratings (Par 93): **94,93,90,86,85 84,82,82,80,80**
CSF £32.33 TOTE £3.30: £1.20, £3.20, £10.10; EX 35.10 Trifecta £1954.30.
**Owner** Saeed Manana **Bred** Gevi International Bv **Trained** Newmarket, Suffolk

**FOCUS**
The second division of the fillies' maiden. It was run at an average pace, resulting in a notably slower time than the preceding contest, and fell apart in the home straight as two pulled clear. It's hard to enthuse over the bare form.

## 7660 IRISH STALLION FARMS EBF MAIDEN STKS 7f (P)
**6:10** (6:12) (Class 5) 2-Y-O **£2,911** (£866; £432; £216) **Stalls** Low

Form RPR

0 **1** **Victory Megastar**[46] 6545 2-9-5 0.............................. AdamKirby 9 79
(Clive Cox) *chsd ldng trio: shkn up to chal over 2f out: led over 1f out whn veered rt and bmpd runner-up: hrd pressed after: hld on wl* **5/2**[1]

**2** ½ **Feng Shui** 2-9-5 0.................................................... GeorgeBaker 1 78+
(Jamie Osborne) *trckd ldng pair: led gng easily over 2f out: hdd and bmpd over 1f out: pressed wnr after: jst hld nr fin* **8/1**

03 **3** 1½ **Muqarred (USA)**[13] 7400 2-9-5 0............................. PaulHanagan 14 74
(Saeed bin Suroor) *t.k.h: trckd ldr: pushed along and dropped to 4th 2f out: shkn up over 1f out: kpt on to take 3rd ins fnl f* **4/1**[3]

0 **4** ½ **Wally's Wisdom**[60] 6125 2-9-2 0.............................. CamHardie(3) 5 73
(William Haggas) *led to over 2f out: shkn up and nt qckn but kpt on fr over 1f out* **5/1**

**5** 2¾ **Estikhraaj** 2-9-5 0......................................................... GrahamLee 4 65
(Roger Varian) *in tch in 7th: shkn up over 2f out: nvr on terms w ldrs but kpt on* **14/1**

04 **6** 1¼ **My Strategy (IRE)**[20] 7217 2-9-5 0........................... TomQueally 12 62+
(Michael Bell) *restrained after s and sn in last pair: pushed along over 2f out: reminders and prog over 1f out: kpt on and nvr nrr: possible improver* **33/1**

0 **7** 1 **Penang Paparaja (IRE)**[12] 7407 2-9-5 0.................. RobertWinston 2 59
(Michael Bell) *trckd ldrs in 5th: cl up and shuffled along 2f out: steadily wknd over 1f out* **33/1**

**8** nk **Parole (IRE)** 2-9-5 0............................................... JimmyFortune 11 58+
(Hughie Morrison) *dwlt: settled in last quartet: pushed along and prog on inner over 2f out: no hdwy over 1f out: fdd* **33/1**

**9** 1¼ **Keep In Line (GER)** 2-9-0 0.................................... KevinStott(5) 8 55+
(Saeed bin Suroor) *dwlt: towards rr and trapped out wd: pushed along over 2f out and no great prog* **3/1**[2]

0 **10** 1 **Carron Valley**[13] 7400 2-9-5 0.................................. SeanLevey 6 52
(Keith Dalgleish) *t.k.h early: chsd ldrs in 6th: shkn up and no imp over 2f out: wknd jst over 1f out* **25/1**

**11** hd **Thames Knight** 2-9-2 0........................................ LouisSteward(3) 10 52
(Marcus Tregoning) *sn in last trio: pushed along and no real prog on outer fnl 2f* **40/1**

P **12** ¾ **Lady Spangles (IRE)**[61] 6105 2-9-0 0..................... StevieDonohoe 7 45
(J S Moore) *dwlt: nvr beyond midfield: wknd over 2f out* **66/1**

0 **13** 10 **Georgia's Gamble (IRE)**[46] 6551 2-9-5 0..................... AmirQuinn 13 23
(Lee Carter) *sn in last pair: shoved along bef 1/2-way: t.o* **66/1**

**14** 3 **Boston Two Step** 2-9-5 0.......................................... JoeFanning 3 15
(Mark Johnston) *nvr beyond midfield: wknd over 2f out: t.o* **25/1**

1m 27.04s (1.04) **Going Correction** +0.025s/f (Slow) 14 Ran SP% **130.0**
Speed ratings (Par 96): **95,94,92,92,89 87,86,86,84,83 83,82,71,67**
CSF £24.05 TOTE £3.50: £2.80, £1.70, £2.20; EX 17.90 Trifecta £140.70.
**Owner** One Carat Partnership **Bred** Highbank Stud **Trained** Lambourn, Berks

**FOCUS**
They didn't go too hard up front in this 2yo maiden yet were still fairly strung out early and it paid to be handy. Improvement from the winner.

## 7661 DOWNLOAD THE BETDAQ+ APP NURSERY H'CAP (BOBIS RACE) 7f (P)
**6:40** (6:40) (Class 3) (0-95,89) 2-Y-O **£6,469** (£1,925; £962; £481) **Stalls** Low

Form RPR

1034 **1** **Four Seasons (IRE)**[11] 7443 2-9-5 **87**.......................... AdamKirby 4 99+
(Charlie Appleby) *hld up in 4th: clsd qckly fr 2f out to ld over 1f out: shkn up and readily drew clr* **13/8**[1]

0624 **2** 3½ **Be Bold**[24] 7131 2-8-11 **82**........................................ CamHardie(3) 1 83
(Richard Hannon) *t.k.h: hld up in 5th: last 2f out: pushed along and prog over 1f out: reminder and tk 2nd jst ins fnl f: kpt on but no ch w wnr* **8/1**[3]

0320 **3** 1½ **Jaganory (IRE)**[25] 7116 2-8-9 **77**.......................... GrahamGibbons 5 74
(David Evans) *led: rdn and hdd 2f out: outpcd fr over 1f out* **25/1**

2221 **4** ¾ **Evening Rain (USA)**[21] 7201 2-9-2 **89**...................(p) KevinStott(5) 3 84
(Saeed bin Suroor) *pressed ldr: led 2f out but nt racing stforwardly: hdd over 1f out: fdd* **13/8**[1]

0000 **5** 1¼ **Vimy Ridge**[32] 6933 2-9-2 **89**...................................... TimClark(5) 6 81
(Alan Bailey) *hld up in last: effrt on outer jst over 2f out: shkn up and no prog over 1f out* **14/1**

2422 **6** 10 **Manshaa (IRE)**[38] 6790 2-8-7 **75**............................... PaulHanagan 2 40
(Mark Johnston) *mostly chsd ldng pair to over 2f out: wknd rapidly wl over 1f out: t.o* **6/1**[2]

1m 25.25s (-0.75) **Going Correction** +0.025s/f (Slow) 6 Ran SP% **112.1**
Speed ratings (Par 100): **105,101,99,98,97 85**
CSF £15.89 TOTE £3.30: £2.20, £3.00; EX 15.90 Trifecta £97.70.
**Owner** Godolphin **Bred** Michael E Wates **Trained** Newmarket, Suffolk

**FOCUS**
They went a sound pace in this fair nursery and the winning time was below the standard, so it's strong form. The runner-up and third set the level.

## 7662 BETDAQ 50% COMMISSION REFUND FLOODLIT STKS (LISTED RACE) 1m 4f (P)
**7:10** (7:10) (Class 1) 3-Y-O+

**£20,982** (£7,995; £3,981; £1,983; £995; £499) **Stalls** Centre

Form RPR

1222 **1** **Grendisar (IRE)**[201] 1553 4-9-4 102..............................(p) MartinHarley 8 105+
(Marco Botti) *hld up in last pair: waiting for room jst over 2f out: smooth prog over 1f out: pushed into narrow ld ins fnl f: hrd pressed after: urged along and edgd rt nr fin: hld on* **10/3**[3]

1620 **2** *nk* **Fire Fighting (IRE)**[25] 7106 3-8-12 106 (b) JoeFanning 7 105
(Mark Johnston) *dwlt: t.k.h: hld up in last pair: gd prog to chal wl over 1f out: rdn: nt pick up jst over 1f out: rallied to press wnr last 100yds: edgd lft and jst hld* **2/1**[2]

3401 **3** *1* **Rydan (IRE)**[42] 6665 3-8-12 97 TomQueally 3 104
(Robert Mills) *trckd ldrs: lost pl sltly 4f out: eased out and smooth prog 2f out to ld over 1f out: immediately pressed: hdd ins fnl f: cl up but hld whn bdly squeezed out last strides* **15/8**[1]

3012 **4** *4½* **Carnevale**[42] 6665 3-8-7 86 PaulHanagan 4 91
(Ralph Beckett) *t.k.h: prom: trckd ldr 1/2-way to 2f out: hld whn short of room over 1f out: outpcd after* **10/1**

6640 **5** *nse* **Flemish School**[40] 6714 4-8-13 87 (v[1]) GrahamLee 1 91
(David Elsworth) *racd freely: led: hdd over 1f out: sn wl btn in 4th: wknd ins fnl f* **25/1**

1241 **6** *4½* **Real Jazz (IRE)**[11] 7459 3-8-7 75 LukeMorris 2 83
(Sir Mark Prescott Bt) *trckd ldr to over 5f out: styd cl up: drvn 2f out: wknd over 1f out* **25/1**

0 **7** *2½* **Vivat Rex (IRE)**[24] 7144 3-8-12 0 (b) LiamKeniry 6 84
(Alan Bailey) *in tch: rdn to chse ldng trio 3f out: wknd over 2f out* **50/1**

364- **8** *2¾* **Chiberta King**[341] 7193 8-9-4 0 (p) JimmyFortune 5 80
(Andrew Balding) *in tch: pushed along on outer over 3f out: wknd over 2f out* **25/1**

2m 32.78s (-1.72) **Going Correction** +0.025s/f (Slow)
**WFA** 3 from 4yo+ 6lb **8 Ran SP% 113.8**
Speed ratings: **106,105,105,102,102 99,97,95**
CSF £9.97 TOTE £4.30: £1.70, £1.10, £1.30; EX 11.70 Trifecta £22.30.
**Owner** Mohamed Albousi Alghufli **Bred** Old Carhue & Graeng Bloodstock **Trained** Newmarket, Suffolk

**FOCUS**
This Listed contest provided a fair test and threw up a tight three-way finish as the principals forged clear of the rest. The winner picked up the thread after a break.

## 7663 BETDAQ COMMISSION FREE FOOTBALL ON SATURDAY H'CAP 7f (P)
**7:40** (7:42) (Class 3) (0-95,95) 3-Y-O+
**£7,158** (£2,143; £1,071; £535; £267; £134) **Stalls** Low

Form RPR

1230 **1** **Musaddas**[60] 6140 4-8-7 **86** (p) KevinStott(5) 6 94
(Saeed bin Suroor) *urged along early and racd w hd high: trckd ldr to 3f out: styd cl up: drvn to chal over 1f out: led last 100yds: jst hld on* **9/2**[3]

3321 **2** *hd* **Khatiba (IRE)**[21] 7196 3-8-10 **85** GrahamLee 5 91
(Roger Varian) *hld up in tch: pushed along in 7th wl over 1f out: rdn and r.o fnl f: clsd on wnr and tk 2nd nr fin: line c too sn* **3/1**[2]

1000 **3** *nk* **Lawmans Thunder**[41] 6688 4-9-2 **95** TimClark(5) 11 102
(Ismail Mohammed) *prom: trckd ldr 3f out: rdn to ld 2f out but hrd pressed all sides after: hdd last 100yds: kpt on* **20/1**

0135 **4** *nk* **Outer Space**[33] 6895 3-8-12 **87** WilliamTwiston-Davies 1 92
(Jamie Osborne) *stdd s: hld up in rr: prog on inner over 2f out: drvn to chal over 1f out: nt qckn ins fnl f* **14/1**

0410 **5** *¾* **Bluegrass Blues (IRE)**[11] 7455 4-9-0 **88** (b) LukeMorris 7 92
(Paul Cole) *trckd ldrs: rdn 2f out: cl up u.p 1f out: one pce after* **14/1**

522 **6** *¾* **Sir Robert Cheval**[33] 6895 3-9-5 **94** MartinHarley 3 95
(Marco Botti) *trckd ldrs: cl up but nt clr run fr 2f out to 1f out: one pce and no imp after* **11/4**[1]

4050 **7** *¾* **Santefisio**[6] 7545 8-9-6 **94** (b) JimmyFortune 2 95
(Keith Dalgleish) *awkward s: hld up in last pair: shkn up 2f out: kpt on same pce fr over 1f out: n.d* **5/1**

302 **8** *2¼* **Capelita**[18] 7285 3-8-5 **83** CamHardie(3) 4 76
(Clive Brittain) *t.k.h: hld up in rr and racd on outer: shkn up over 2f out: wknd over 1f out* **25/1**

0254 **9** *½* **Deauville Prince (FR)**[20] 7227 4-9-4 **92** GeorgeBaker 10 84
(Tom Dascombe) *won battle for ld: hdd 2f out: wknd qckly jst over 1f out* **8/1**

0040 **10** *½* **Forceful Appeal (USA)**[109] 4447 6-8-12 **86** HayleyTurner 8 77
(Simon Dow) *stdd s: t.k.h in last pair: urged along wl over 2f out: no prog* **50/1**

1m 24.43s (-1.57) **Going Correction** +0.025s/f (Slow)
**WFA** 3 from 4yo+ 1lb **10 Ran SP% 121.5**
Speed ratings (Par 107): **109,108,108,108,107 106,105,102,102,101**
CSF £18.91 CT £260.02 TOTE £5.10: £1.50, £3.10, £4.90; EX 25.50 Trifecta £367.30.
**Owner** Godolphin **Bred** Highbury Stud Ltd **Trained** Newmarket, Suffolk

**FOCUS**
Competitive stuff and there was a very tight finish off an ordinary pace. The winner was well treated on his 1m form.

## 7664 BOOK THE RESTAURANT FOR CHRISTMAS FESTIVAL H'CAP 1m 4f (P)
**8:10** (8:11) (Class 6) (0-55,55) 3-Y-O **£1,940** (£577; £288; £144) **Stalls** Centre

Form RPR

340 **1** **San Quentin (IRE)**[151] 2694 3-9-0 48 (p) LukeMorris 7 57
(Tony Carroll) *awkward s: hld up in last pair: rdn and prog over 2f out: tk 2nd 1f out: styd on u.p to ld narrowly last 75yds* **4/1**[3]

-060 **2** *hd* **Reimpose (USA)**[102] 4658 3-9-7 55 StevieDonohoe 4 63
(Pat Eddery) *trckd clr ldng trio: clsd fr 4f out: led over 2f out and drvn for home: kpt on but hdd and jst hld last 75yds* **14/1**

6000 **3** *1½* **Born To Reign**[20] 7229 3-8-12 46 (v[1]) TomQueally 10 52
(Michael Bell) *towards rr: u.p 4f out: responded and prog fr 3f out: kpt on for driving to take 3rd ins fnl f: nvr quite able to chal* **10/1**

4503 **4** *2* **Fickle Feelings (IRE)**[18] 7284 3-9-2 50 GrahamGibbons 1 53
(David Barron) *awkward st s: hld up in last pair: rdn on outer over 2f out: plugged on fr over 1f out: nt pce to threaten* **7/4**[1]

5026 **5** *3½* **Focail Mear**[15] 7360 3-8-12 46 oh1 JackMitchell 6 43
(John Ryan) *w.w in midfield: prog over 3f out: wnt 2nd and tried to chal over 2f out: wknd fnl f* **7/2**[2]

0600 **6** *11* **Movie Magic**[8] 7518 3-8-12 46 oh1 WilliamCarson 5 25
(John Bridger) *led at decent pce: hdd & wknd over 2f out* **66/1**

000 **7** *1½* **Flying Author (IRE)**[31] 4261 3-8-9 46 oh1 (tp) DannyBrock(3) 2 26
(Phil McEntee) *nvr bttr than midfield: rdn 4f out: struggling whn stmbld jst over 3f out: no ch after* **33/1**

5040 **8** *3½* **Beauchamp Melba**[40] 6714 3-8-13 47 GrahamLee 8 18
(Paul Fitzsimons) *chsd clr ldng pair: rdn 4f out: wknd 3f out* **20/1**

06 **9** *11* **L Ge R**[12] 6939 3-8-10 47 RosieJessop(3) 9
(Peter Charalambous) *chsd ldr and clr of rest: lost 2nd and wknd rapidly 3f out: t.o* **20/1**

5360 **S** **Dark Tsarina (IRE)**[30] 6986 3-8-13 50 CamHardie(3) 3
(Michael Madgwick) *hld up in rr: 8th whn hmpd and fell jst over 2f out* **14/1**

2m 34.69s (0.19) **Going Correction** +0.025s/f (Slow) **10 Ran SP% 115.0**
Speed ratings (Par 98): **100,99,98,97,95 87,86,84,77,**
CSF £53.55 CT £522.33 TOTE £6.40: £1.50, £2.00, £2.80; EX 62.30 Trifecta £427.00.
**Owner** Stephen Louch **Bred** London Thoroughbred Services Ltd **Trained** Cropthorne, Worcs

**FOCUS**
A weak 3yo handicap, run at a brisk early pace, which suited the closers.
T/Plt: £38.20 to a £1 stake. Pool: £85,906.08 - 1638.04 winning units. T/Qpdt: £15.00 to a £1 stake. Pool: £7995.22 - 393.90 winning units. JN

# [7534] NOTTINGHAM (L-H)
Wednesday, November 5

**OFFICIAL GOING: Good (good to soft in places) changing to good to soft (soft in places) after race 2 (12.50).**

## 7665 BOOK 2015 HOSPITALITY NOW AT NOTTINGHAM NURSERY H'CAP (BOBIS RACE) 5f 13y
**12:20** (12:21) (Class 4) (0-85,77) 2-Y-O **£3,881** (£1,155; £577; £288) **Stalls** High

Form RPR

10 **1** **Uptight (FR)**[77] 5580 2-9-1 76 KevinStott(5) 5 79
(Kevin Ryan) *mde all: jnd over 2f out: shkn up wl over 1f out: rdn ent fnl f: kpt on wl towards fin* **13/8**[1]

4122 **2** *hd* **Snow Cloud (IRE)**[19] 7231 2-9-2 72 DanielTudhope 3 74
(David O'Meara) *t.k.h early: trckd wnr: pushed along 1/2-way and sn outpcd: rdn over 1f out: swtchd lft ent fnl f: styd on strly: jst failed* **7/4**[2]

31 **3** *shd* **Rio Ronaldo (IRE)**[55] 6270 2-9-7 77 ShaneKelly 2 79
(Mike Murphy) *prom: hdwy and cl up 1/2-way: chal 2f out: rdn ent fnl f: ev ch tl drvn and no ex towards fin* **9/4**[3]

6005 **4** *10* **Junior Ben**[11] 7453 2-8-0 56 oh9 RaulDaSilva 4 22
(Derek Shaw) *t.k.h early: hld up: pushed along in rr 1/2-way: sn rdn along and outpcd fr wl over 1f out* **50/1**

1m 0.77s (-0.73) **Going Correction** -0.025s/f (Good) **4 Ran SP% 107.2**
Speed ratings (Par 98): **104,103,103,87**
CSF £4.74 TOTE £3.60; EX 5.10 Trifecta £7.10.
**Owner** Matt & Lauren Morgan **Bred** Madame Antonia Devin **Trained** Hambleton, N Yorks

**FOCUS**
Inner track used and all distances as advertised. The opening contest was a fair little nursery despite the lack of numbers, in which they went a proper gallop on ground officially described as good, good to soft in places.

## 7666 B&M INSTALLATIONS MAIDEN STKS (DIV I) 1m 75y
**12:50** (12:51) (Class 5) 2-Y-O **£2,587** (£770; £384; £192) **Stalls** Centre

Form RPR

0332 **1** **Arcano Gold (IRE)**[11] 7443 2-9-5 79 DanielTudhope 9 80
(Richard Fahey) *trckd ldr: led 3f out: rdn wl over 1f out: kpt on strly fnl f* **7/2**[1]

4 **2** *1¾* **Desert Encounter (IRE)**[29] 6998 2-9-5 0 MartinHarley 3 76
(David Simcock) *trckd ldrs on inner: effrt 2f out and sn n.m.r: rdn over 1f out: kpt on wl u.p towards fin* **20/1**

36 **3** *hd* **Perceus**[15] 7354 2-9-5 0 MartinDwyer 15 76
(Marcus Tregoning) *trckd ldng pair: hdwy wl over 2f out: rdn to chse wnr over 1f out: drvn and kpt on fnl f* **9/2**[2]

**4** *½* **Making Shapes** 2-9-5 0 JimmyFortune 7 74+
(Peter Chapple-Hyam) *in tch: hdwy to trck ldrs over 3f out: effrt 2f out: rdn to chse wnr jst over 1f out: drvn and kpt on same pce fnl f* **25/1**

**5** *1¾* **Entitling (IRE)** 2-9-5 0 ShaneKelly 2 70+
(James Fanshawe) *hld up in midfield: stdy hdwy on inner 3f out: nt clr run and swtchd rt wl over 1f out: rdn and kpt on fnl f: nrst fin* **15/2**

**6** *1¼* **Mojawiz** 2-9-2 0 CamHardie(3) 10 67+
(Charlie Appleby) *in rr: hdwy 3f out: chsd ldrs 2f: sn rdn and kpt on same pce fnl f* **12/1**

02 **7** *2¼* **Fibre Optic**[22] 7169 2-9-5 0 TomQueally 1 62
(Luca Cumani) *in tch: hdwy wl over 2f out: rdn along wl over 1f out: kpt on same pce appr fnl f* **5/1**[3]

**8** *4* **Excellent Team** 2-9-5 0 FrederikTylicki 6 53+
(Saeed bin Suroor) *towards rr: hdwy 3f out: rdn along over 2f out: sn one pce* **6/1**

**9** *1½* **Diamond Joel** 2-9-5 0 CharlesBishop 5 50
(Mick Channon) *hld up: hdwy on inner: 3f out: rdn along 2f out: sn no imp* **66/1**

60 **10** *nk* **Atalan**[24] 7134 2-9-5 0 HayleyTurner 4 49
(Hughie Morrison) *chsd ldrs: rdn along over 3f out: sn wknd* **100/1**

40 **11** *¾* **Le Rouquin (FR)**[67] 5922 2-9-5 0 WilliamTwiston-Davies 11 47
(Michael Bell) *a towards rr* **50/1**

**12** *shd* **Counterproof (IRE)** 2-9-5 0 RobertHavlin 14 47
(John Gosden) *a towards rr* **16/1**

**13** *¾* **Scottish (IRE)** 2-9-5 0 DavidProbert 12 45+
(Andrew Balding) *dwlt: a towards rr* **12/1**

00 **14** *2¼* **Lipstickandpowder (IRE)**[39] 6753 2-9-0 0 JoeFanning 16 35
(William Jarvis) *towards rr: hdwy on outer over 3f out: sn in tch: rdn over 2f out and sn wknd* **100/1**

0 **15** *9* **Lady Vellyn**[102] 4676 2-9-0 0 LiamKeniry 8 14
(Derek Haydn Jones) *t.k.h: led: rdn along and hdd 3f out: sn wknd* **100/1**

66 **16** *1¼* **Doesyourdogbite (IRE)**[22] 7169 2-9-5 0 BarryMcHugh 17 17
(Andrew Hollinshead) *a in rr: bhd fnl 3f* **100/1**

**17** *16* **Konnos Bay** 2-9-5 0 BenCurtis 13
(Shaun Harris) *a in rr: rdn along 1/2-way: bhd fnl 3f* **100/1**

1m 50.27s (1.27) **Going Correction** -0.025s/f (Good) **17 Ran SP% 121.4**
Speed ratings (Par 96): **92,90,90,89,87 86,84,80,78,78 77,77,76,74,65 64,48**
CSF £79.95 TOTE £4.40: £1.50, £7.40, £2.30; EX 85.20 Trifecta £588.10.
**Owner** Middleham Park Racing XL & Partner **Bred** Trevor Reilly **Trained** Musley Bank, N Yorks

**FOCUS**
The first division of a fair juvenile maiden in which they went a sensible gallop on ground officially changed to good to soft, soft in places after this contest. Pace held up well.

## 7667 B&M INSTALLATIONS MAIDEN STKS (DIV II) 1m 75y
**1:20** (1:24) (Class 5) 2-Y-O **£2,587** (£770; £384; £192) **Stalls** Centre

Form RPR
2 **1** **Nebulla**[25] 7123 2-9-5 0 PatCosgrave 9 83
(Noel Quinlan) *trckd ldrs: smooth hdwy to join ldr wl over 2f out: led wl over 1f out: rdn ent fnl f: kpt on* **9/4**[1]
0 **2** ½ **Global Force (IRE)**[14] 7371 2-9-5 0 FrederikTylicki 10 82
(Saeed bin Suroor) *trckd ldr: led 3f out: sn jnd and rdn: hdd wl over 1f out: drvn and rallied ins fnl f: no ex towards fin* **5/2**[2]
3 **3** 8 **Laurence**[21] 7206 2-9-5 0 TomQueally 15 63
(Luca Cumani) *hld up: hdwy over 3f out: rdn along to chse ldrs 2f out: kpt on same pce u.p fnl f* **8/1**[3]
**4** nk **Higher Power** 2-9-5 0 ShaneKelly 14 63+
(James Fanshawe) *hld up in rr: stdy hdwy on outer 3f out: rdn over 1f out: kpt on wl fnl f: nrst fin* **20/1**
4 **5** 1½ **Casila (IRE)**[22] 7170 2-9-0 0 JoeFanning 2 54
(Mark Johnston) *led: rdn along and hdd 3f out: drvn and grad wknd fnl 2f* **20/1**
**6** 3¾ **Bank Of Gibraltar** 2-9-5 0 JimmyFortune 5 51+
(Peter Chapple-Hyam) *chsd ldrs: rdn along over 2f out: sn one pce* **40/1**
0 **7** ½ **Leoncavallo (IRE)**[14] 7382 2-9-2 0 CamHardie(3) 7 50
(Charlie Appleby) *t.k.h early: prom: rdn along 3f out: drvn over 2f out: grad wknd* **11/1**
05 **8** 1 **Politico**[30] 6976 2-9-0 0 RobertHavlin 13 42
(John Gosden) *midfield on inner: rdn along over 3f out: no hdwy* **66/1**
**9** hd **Welsh Rebel** 2-9-2 0 MatthewCosham(3) 11 47
(Nikki Evans) *in tch: hdwy to chse ldrs on outer over 3f out: rdn along wl over 2f out: sn wknd* **100/1**
**10** ½ **Darkening Night** 2-9-5 0 DavidAllan 16 46
(James Tate) *towards rr: sme hdwy on inner over 3f out: sn rdn along and n.d* **66/1**
66 **11** nk **The Cashel Man (IRE)**[19] 7230 2-9-5 0 MartinHarley 12 45
(David Simcock) *a towards rr* **33/1**
56 **12** ½ **Duke Of Sonning**[8] 7512 2-9-5 0 FergusSweeney 6 44
(Alan King) *a towards rr* **20/1**
5 **13** 9 **Cocker**[12] 7425 2-9-5 0 StephenCraine 8 23
(Tom Dascombe) *a towards rr* **33/1**
**14** nk **St Saviour** 2-9-5 0 DavidProbert 3 22
(Andrew Balding) *trckd ldrs: pushed along over 3f out: rdn wl over 2f out and sn wknd* **16/1**
**15** ¾ **Down To Earth** 2-9-5 0 WilliamTwiston-Davies 4 21
(Michael Bell) *s.i.s: a bhd* **100/1**
0 **16** hd **Copperopolis**[12] 7414 2-9-5 0 TedDurcan 17 20
(Roger Charlton) *dwlt: a in rr* **12/1**
**17** 21 **Marymalade** 2-9-0 0 LiamKeniry 1
(Harry Dunlop) *s.i.s and in rr: hdwy on inner to chse ldrs after 2f: rdn along over 3f out: sn wknd and bhd* **100/1**

1m 49.4s (0.40) **Going Correction** -0.025s/f (Good) **17** Ran SP% **120.9**
Speed ratings (Par 96): **97,96,88,88,86 82,82,81,81,80 80,79,70,70,69 69,48**
CSF £6.69 TOTE £3.20: £1.50, £1.60, £2.80; EX 9.40 Trifecta £41.50.
**Owner** Newtown Anner Stud Farm **Bred** The Lavington Stud **Trained** Newmarket, Suffolk

**FOCUS**
The second division of a fair juvenile maiden in which they went a sensible gallop on ground changed to good to soft, soft in places before this race, and the winning time was nearly a second quicker. It was all about the front pair and the winner is the type to rate higher again.

## 7668 THANKS FOR EVERYTHING PIP KIRKBY H'CAP 1m 75y
**1:50** (1:51) (Class 2) (0-112,107) 3-Y-O+**£16,172** (£4,812; £2,405; £1,202) **Stalls** Centre

Form RPR
0105 **1** **Baltic Knight (IRE)**[4] 7599 4-9-11 107 JimmyFortune 2 114
(Richard Hannon) *trckd ldng pair: effrt over 2f out and sn pushed along: rdn to chse ldr jst over 1f out: drvn to ld ins fnl f: kpt on strly* **9/2**[3]
1301 **2** 1¾ **Moohaarib (IRE)**[30] 6978 3-9-2 97 MartinHarley 1 103
(Marco Botti) *chsd ldr: led over 4f out: pushed along 2f out: jnd and rdn jst over 1f out: hdd and drvn ins fnl f: kpt on same pce* **5/2**[2]
1114 **3** 1¼ **Gm Hopkins**[26] 7081 3-9-2 100 RobertHavlin 3 100
(John Gosden) *trckd ldrs: hdwy on outer 3f out: cl up 2f out: rdn to chal over 1f out: drvn and kpt on same pce ins fnl f* **13/8**[1]
030 **4** 1¼ **Cordite (IRE)**[22] 7168 3-9-5 103 FrederikTylicki 5 102
(Michael Appleby) *led early gng freely and clr whn rn wd home turn: sn hdd: cl up: rdn over 2f out: drvn and one pce appr fnl f* **13/2**
4130 **5** 21 **Morache Music**[32] 6921 6-9-9 105 TedDurcan 4 56
(Peter Makin) *hld up in rr: pushed along over 3f out: rdn wl over 2f out: sn outpcd* **10/1**

1m 48.23s (-0.77) **Going Correction** -0.025s/f (Good)
**WFA** 3 from 4yo+ 2lb **5** Ran SP% **107.3**
Speed ratings (Par 109): **102,100,99,97,76**
CSF £15.14 TOTE £5.20: £2.40, £6.00; EX 15.30 Trifecta £50.90.
**Owner** Thurloe Thoroughbreds XXX **Bred** Henry O'Callaghan **Trained** East Everleigh, Wilts

**FOCUS**
The feature contest was a good class small-field handicap in which they went a proper gallop. A slight improvement on the winner's previous best.

## 7669 B&M INSTALLATIONS H'CAP 5f 13y
**2:20** (2:21) (Class 4) (0-85,85) 3-Y-O+ **£5,175** (£1,540; £769; £384) **Stalls** High

Form RPR
2161 **1** **It Must Be Faith**[7] 7535 4-8-12 76 6ex HayleyTurner 10 89
(Michael Appleby) *racd towards stands' rail: prom: led 2f out: rdn clr appr fnl f: edgd lft and kpt on strly* **13/8**[1]
4522 **2** 1¾ **Classy Anne**[25] 7103 4-8-10 79 JackGarritty(5) 4 86
(Jim Goldie) *racd towards centre: in tch: hdwy wl over 1f out: swtchd lft and rdn ent fnl f: sn chsng wnr: kpt on* **10/1**
4343 **3** 2 **Singeur (IRE)**[16] 7330 7-9-5 83 DanielTudhope 5 83
(Robin Bastiman) *towards rr: rdn along 1/2-way: gd hdwy towards centre over 1f out: styd on wl fnl f: nrst fin* **13/2**
0006 **4** nk **Keep It Dark**[16] 7330 5-9-1 79 BarryMcHugh 7 77
(Tony Coyle) *racd towards centre: chsd ldrs: rdn wl over 1f out: kpt on same pce fnl f* **20/1**
000 **5** shd **Rothesay Chancer**[47] 6511 6-8-13 77 FergalLynch 2 75
(Jim Goldie) *racd centre: in tch: hdwy on outer wl over 1f out: sn rdn and kpt on fnl f: nrst fin* **18/1**
1000 **6** ¾ **Cruise Tothelimit (IRE)**[19] 7233 6-9-2 85 GeorgeDowning(5) 13 80
(Ian Williams) *racd towards stands' rail: prom: rdn along over 2f out: grad wknd* **25/1**
1330 **7** 1 **Clubland (IRE)**[21] 7212 5-8-11 75 JimmyQuinn 8 67
(Mandy Rowland) *racd towards stands' rail: in tch: hdwy over 2f out: rdn along over 1f out: sn no imp* **33/1**
302 **8** nk **Angel Way (IRE)**[70] 5830 5-8-11 75 ShaneKelly 1 66
(Mike Murphy) *racd centre: cl up on wd outside: rdn along 2f out: sn wknd* **25/1**
4120 **9** nk **Dominate**[24] 7132 4-8-12 83 (b) JoshQuinn(7) 6 73
(Richard Hannon) *s.i.s: a towards rr* **16/1**
2054 **10** 1¾ **Come On Dave (IRE)**[16] 7330 5-9-4 82 LiamKeniry 14 65
(John Butler) *racd cl to stands' rail: led: rdn along 1/2-way: hdd 2f out and sn wknd* **8/1**[3]
6600 **11** nk **Steel Rain**[7] 7534 6-8-2 71 oh3 JoeDoyle(5) 11 53
(Nikki Evans) *racdd towards stands' rail: chsd ldrs: rdn along over 2f out: sn wknd* **66/1**
5502 **12** 1½ **My Inspiration (IRE)**[17] 7307 3-8-11 75 MartinHarley 15 52
(Amy Weaver) *racd towards stands' rail: a towards rr* **10/1**
0001 **13** 3 **Feel The Heat**[37] 6821 7-8-4 73 ow1 (v) AdamCarter(5) 3 39
(Bryan Smart) *wnt rt s: a in rr* **25/1**
3116 **14** 21 **Gregori (IRE)**[187] 1922 4-9-5 83 (tp) JimmyFortune 9
(Brian Meehan) *towards rr: pushed along whn stmbld and lost action wl over 1f out: sn eased and bhd* **50/1**

59.95s (-1.55) **Going Correction** -0.025s/f (Good) **14** Ran SP% **114.6**
Speed ratings (Par 105): **111,108,105,104,104 103,101,101,100,97 97,94,90,56**
CSF £15.14 CT £86.90 TOTE £2.60: £2.20, £2.30, £2.30; EX 13.60 Trifecta £49.50.
**Owner** Michael Appleby **Bred** Matthew Sharkey & Newsells Park Stud Ltd **Trained** Danethorpe, Notts

**FOCUS**
A decent sprint handicap in which they went a contested gallop with the main action unfolding up the favoured nearside rail. The winner could rate a bit higher still.

## 7670 ROA GOLD NOTTINGHAM RACECOURSE AWARD WINNERS H'CAP (DIV I) 5f 13y
**2:50** (2:51) (Class 6) (0-65,65) 3-Y-O+ **£1,940** (£577; £288; £144) **Stalls** High

Form RPR
0506 **1** **Rambo Will**[16] 7342 6-9-5 63 FergalLynch 13 71
(J R Jenkins) *mde virtually all stands' side: hld on towards fin* **16/1**
5334 **2** hd **Lazy Sioux**[8] 7519 3-8-4 51 oh3 NeilFarley(3) 4 58
(Richard Guest) *w wnr: no ex nr fin* **20/1**
40-0 **3** nk **Mops Angel**[21] 7213 3-9-1 64 AlistairRawlinson(5) 5 70
(Michael Appleby) *s.i.s: hdwy and swtchd towards stands' side over 2f out: styd on fnl f* **8/1**
0321 **4** ¾ **Danzoe (IRE)**[8] 7519 7-8-9 58 6ex (v) JoeDoyle(5) 11 62
(Christine Dunnett) *hld up in mid-div: hdwy to chse ldrs over 1f out: kpt on same pce last 100yds* **10/1**
04 **5** ½ **Minty Jones**[8] 7510 5-8-2 51 oh1 (v) TimClark(5) 8 53
(Michael Mullineaux) *chsd ldrs: hung rt appr fnl f: kpt on same pce last 150yds* **10/1**
4651 **6** hd **Aaranyow (IRE)**[18] 7285 6-8-4 53 (t) TobyAtkinson(5) 9 54
(Clifford Lines) *w ldrs: upsides over 2f out: edgd lft appr fnl f: kpt on same pce last 150yds* **25/1**
03 **7** 1 **Maymyo (IRE)**[29] 7023 3-9-7 65 ShaneKelly 3 65
(Sylvester Kirk) *s.i.s: hdwy in centre of over 2f out: nt clr run over 1f out: styd on ins fnl f* **8/1**
2504 **8** nse **Picc Of Burgau**[21] 7213 4-9-3 61 StevieDonohoe 15 58
(Geoffrey Deacon) *in rr: hdwy stands' side over 1f out: nt rch ldrs* **5/1**[1]
0000 **9** hd **Time Medicean**[29] 7023 8-9-5 63 DavidProbert 10 60
(Tony Carroll) *chsd ldrs: keeping on same pce whn nt clr run 1f out* **7/1**[3]
4652 **10** ¾ **Dynamo Walt (IRE)**[11] 7457 3-9-6 64 (v) DaleSwift 2 58
(Derek Shaw) *chsd ldrs centre: wknd fnl f* **15/2**
5-50 **11** 6 **Sadiigah**[19] 7252 4-8-3 52 ShelleyBirkett(5) 6 24
(Julia Feilden) *in tch: lost pl over 1f out* **50/1**
0326 **12** ¾ **Fujin**[12] 7420 3-8-11 55 DuranFentiman 1 24
(Shaun Harris) *chsd ldrs centre: wknd fnl f* **16/1**
1065 **13** ¾ **Fathom Five (IRE)**[111] 4344 10-9-1 59 PaddyAspell 12 26
(Shaun Harris) *chsd ldrs: wknd 2f out* **25/1**
1002 **14** 5 **Lord Buffhead**[1] 7644 5-9-1 59 (v) JasonHart 16 8
(Richard Guest) *s.i.s: in rr: bhd whn eased clsng stages* **11/2**[2]

1m 1.21s (-0.29) **Going Correction** -0.025s/f (Good) **14** Ran SP% **122.9**
Speed ratings (Par 101): **101,100,100,99,98 97,96,96,95,94 85,83,82,74**
CSF £312.65 CT £2819.45 TOTE £24.80: £8.90, £5.90, £3.10; EX 465.30 Trifecta £2309.00 Part won..
**Owner** Mrs S Bambridge **Bred** T H Bambridge **Trained** Royston, Herts

**FOCUS**
The first division of a modest sprint handicap in which they went a contested gallop. Solid enough form.

## 7671 ROA GOLD NOTTINGHAM RACECOURSE AWARD WINNERS H'CAP (DIV II) 5f 13y
**3:25** (3:25) (Class 6) (0-65,65) 3-Y-O+ **£1,940** (£577; £288; £144) **Stalls** High

Form RPR
5020 **1** **Captain Scooby**[1] 7644 8-8-7 51 oh2 (b) JasonHart 3 62+
(Richard Guest) *swtchd rt towards stands' side s and hld up: hdwy over 2f out: rdn over 1f out: led ins fnl f: kpt on strly* **8/1**[3]
4232 **2** 2½ **Rylee Mooch**[7] 7535 6-9-6 64 (e) AndrewElliott 2 66
(Richard Guest) *racd centre: dwlt: sn chsng ldrs: hdwy on outer 2f out: rdn to ld over 1f out: hdd and drvn ins fnl f kpt on* **5/1**[2]
5313 **3** 1¼ **First Rebellion**[30] 6983 5-8-9 56 (b) JoeyHaynes(3) 16 54
(Tony Carroll) *racd cl to stands' rail: slt ld: rdn along 2f out: hdd and drvn over 1f out: kpt on same pce* **8/1**[3]
0146 **4** ¾ **Meebo (IRE)**[11] 7457 3-9-5 63 (vt) FergalLynch 14 58
(J R Jenkins) *racd towards stands' rail: hld up: hdwy whn nt clr run and swtchd rt wl over 1f out: sn rdn: styd on fnl f: nrst fin* **20/1**
3230 **5** 1 **Laughing Rock (IRE)**[19] 7259 4-8-10 59 AlistairRawlinson(5) 9 50
(Michael Appleby) *racd towards stands' rail: dwlt and hmpd s: in rr: hdwy whn n.m.r wl over 1f out: swtchd rt and sn rdn: styd on fnl f* **5/1**[2]
0000 **6** hd **Invigilator**[2] 7621 6-8-11 55 (t) DaleSwift 12 45
(Derek Shaw) *trckd ldrs nr stands' rail: hdwy and cl up 1/2-way: rdn and ev ch wl over 1f out: drvn and wknd appr fnl f* **10/1**
3000 **7** nk **Betty Boo (IRE)**[9] 7502 4-9-0 58 BenCurtis 1 47
(Shaun Harris) *dwlt: racd wd in centre: a towards rr* **33/1**
0035 **8** ½ **Hazelrigg (IRE)**[7] 7534 9-9-7 65 DavidAllan 8 53
(Tim Easterby) *racd towards stands' rail: prom: rdn along over 2f out: sn wknd* **9/2**[1]

0100 **9** *hd* **Two Turtle Doves (IRE)**[37] 6819 8-9-0 61 DannyBrock(3) 6 48
(Michael Mullineaux) *racd towards centre: trckd ldrs: hdwy and cl up 1/2-way: rdn 2f out and grad wknd* **20/1**

0301 **10** *3/4* **Ingenti**[8] 7510 6-9-1 64 6ex MeganCarberry(5) 7 48
(Christopher Wilson) *cl up towards centre: rdn along over 2f out: grad wknd* **8/1**[3]

2560 **11** *nk* **College Doll**[7] 7534 5-8-3 52 (t) JoeDoyle(5) 5 35
(Christine Dunnett) *cl up centre: rdn along 2f out: sn wknd* **14/1**

2030 **12** *1 1/4* **Brean Splash Susie**[12] 7420 3-8-5 54 oh4 ow3 RyanWhile(5) 4 33
(Bill Turner) *racd centre: chsd ldrs: rdn along over 2f out: sn edgd rt and wkng whn n.m.r wl over 1f out* **50/1**

1m 1.05s (-0.45) **Going Correction** -0.025s/f (Good) **12** Ran SP% **115.0**
Speed ratings (Par 101): **102,98,96,94,93 92,92,91,91,90 89,87**
CSF £44.14 CT £337.40 TOTE £7.50: £2.50, £2.80, £1.70; EX 38.00 Trifecta £231.70.
**Owner** Available For Sale Or Lease **Bred** Hellwood Stud Farm & Paul Davies (h'Gate) **Trained** Ingmanthorpe, W Yorks

**FOCUS**
The second division of a modest sprint handicap in which they went another contested gallop, and the winning time was a shade quicker. The winner was in total command and the form makes sense.

## 7672 AJA GENTLEMEN AMATEUR RIDERS' H'CAP 1m 2f 50y
4:00 (4:01) (Class 5) (0-75,75) 3-Y-O+ **£2,495** (£774; £386; £193) **Stalls** Low

Form RPR

4533 **1** **Stybba**[20] 7218 3-9-13 60 MrHHunt(5) 12 68+
(Andrew Balding) *stdd s: hld up in rr: hdwy over 4f out: swtchd wd 3f out: styd on to ld last 75yds* **5/1**[2]

3223 **2** *1* **The Ducking Stool**[48] 6500 7-11-4 70 MrRBirkett 6 76
(Julia Feilden) *hld up in mid-div: hdwy 4f out: styd on to ld over 1f out: hdd and no ex last 75yds* **9/1**

411 **3** *2 1/4* **Polar Forest**[19] 7249 4-11-7 73 (e) MrSWalker 7 75
(Richard Guest) *hld up in rr: hdwy over 2f out: kpt on fnl f* **5/1**[2]

0-01 **4** *shd* **Carragold**[147] 3095 8-10-12 69 MrLAMurtagh(5) 9 71
(Mel Brittain) *mid-div: hdwy over 3f out: upsides 1f out: kpt on one pce* **18/1**

-562 **5** *2* **Mash Potato (IRE)**[12] 7411 4-11-2 73 (p) MrHStock(5) 8 71
(Michael Dods) *hld up in mid-div: hdwy 4f out: led over 2f out: hdd over 1f out: sn fdd* **5/2**[1]

6430 **6** *2 3/4* **Zainda (IRE)**[22] 7187 4-10-0 59 oh13 [1] MrAFrench(7) 1 52
(Paul Midgley) *t.k.h in rr: hdwy to trck ldrs after 2f: led 6f out: hdd 4f out: one pce fnl 2f* **100/1**

0004 **7** *3* **Ruzeiz (USA)**[12] 7411 5-11-1 70 MrFTett(3) 2 58
(Peter Hedger) *dwlt: hld up in rr: hdwy over 3f out: nt clr run and swtchd ins over 2f out: wknd over 1f out* **9/1**

06 **8** *8* **Shirocco Passion**[82] 5387 3-10-1 62 MrKWood(5) 4 36
(Tony Coyle) *led tl 6f out: lost pl over 1f out* **14/1**

2150 **9** *2 1/2* **Daydreamer**[44] 6608 3-11-5 75 MrMichaelJMurphy 11 44
(William Haggas) *trckd ldrs: t.k.h: led 4f out: hdd over 2f out: wknd over 1f out* **8/1**[3]

2105 **10** *1/2* **Bobby Benton (IRE)**[119] 4077 3-10-10 71 MrJDoe(5) 3 39
(Luke Dace) *trckd ldrs: effrt outside 3f out: lost pl over 1f out* **12/1**

2m 19.93s (5.63) **Going Correction** -0.025s/f (Good)
**WFA** 3 from 4yo+ 4lb **10** Ran SP% **113.6**
Speed ratings (Par 103): **76,75,73,73,71 69,67,60,58,58**
CSF £48.05 CT £234.91 TOTE £5.00: £1.70, £2.00, £1.60; EX 36.40 Trifecta £251.50.
**Owner** Qatar Racing Limited **Bred** W And R Barnett Ltd **Trained** Kingsclere, Hants

**FOCUS**
The concluding contest was an ordinary handicap, restricted to gentleman amateur riders, in which they went a steady gallop. Straightforward form.
T/Jkpt: £7,100.00 to a £1 stake. Pool: £10,000.00 - 0.5 winning units. T/Plt: £102.60 to a £1 stake. Pool: £47,917.45 - 340.83 winning units. T/Qpdt: £22.30 to a £1 stake. Pool: £4956.04 - 164.00 winning units. JR

# 3089 LE CROISE-LAROCHE
Wednesday, November 5
**OFFICIAL GOING: Turf: very soft**

## 7681a PRIX DE LA MARQUE (CONDITIONS) (3YO) (TURF) 1m 4f 110y
7:05 (12:00) 3-Y-O **£7,500** (£3,000; £2,250; £1,500; £750)

RPR

**1** **Agrapart (FR)**[23] 7164 3-8-11 0 FlavienMasse 4 83
(Nick Williams) *chsd clr ldr: steadily clsd on rail to ld over 2 1/2f out: hrd rdn 1 1/2f out: sed to draw clr appr fnl f: comf* **36/5**

**2** *6* **Bryce Canyon (IRE)** 3-8-8 0 CesarPasserat 5 71
(F-H Graffard, France) **31/5**[3]

**3** *nk* **It's Not It (IRE)**[25] 3-9-2 0 (p) AntoineCoutier 6 79
(S Wattel, France) **19/10**[1]

**4** *2 1/2* **Duncan (GER)**[25] 3-9-2 0 (p) JimmyTastayre 11 75
(F Chappet, France) **114/10**

**5** *1/2* **Camondo (IRE)**[155] 3-8-11 0 YohannBourgois 1 70
(Y-M Porzier, France) **145/10**

**6** *9* **Grazie Mille (FR)** 3-8-11 0 MlleLauraPoggionovo 3 56
(Yannick Fouin, France) **70/1**

**7** *3/4* **Laura (GER)**[26] 3-8-13 0 WilliamsSaraiva 2 57
(Waldemar Hickst, Germany) **18/5**[2]

**8** *5 1/2* **Nerfair Premier (FR)**[19] 3-8-11 0 MlleRoxanneDessaint 7 47
(T Castanheira, France) **113/10**

**9** *dist* **Black Tie Dancer (IRE)**[23] 3-8-11 0 (b) MatthieuAutier 12
(B Duchemin, France) **62/1**

**10** *dist* **Tanguero (FR)** 3-8-11 0 FlorentMalbran 9
(Mlle A Bretel, France) **76/1**

**11** *1* **Quelamour (FR)** 3-8-8 0 AurelienMalenfant 8
(Robert Collet, France) **40/1**

**12** *1* **Born To Be Alive (FR)**[26] 3-9-2 0 LouisBeuzelin 10
(Robert Collet, France) **118/10**

2m 51.8s (171.80) **12** Ran SP% **119.5**
PARI-MUTUEL (all including 1 euro stake): WIN 8.20PLACE 2.10, 1.90, 1.40 DF 20.10 SF 45.90..
**Owner** The Gascoigne Brookes Partnership Iii **Bred** J-M Lucas **Trained** George Nympton, Devon

# 7621 WOLVERHAMPTON (A.W) (L-H)
Thursday, November 6
**OFFICIAL GOING: Tapeta: standard**

## 7682 LADBROKES MAIDEN STKS (TAPETA) 7f 32y
4:35 (4:36) (Class 5) 3-Y-O+ **£2,587** (£770; £384; £192) **Stalls** High

Form RPR

4223 **1** **Gharaaneej (IRE)**[18] 7303 3-9-0 66 (b1) PaulHanagan 8 65
(John Gosden) *midfield: pushed along over 2f out: rdn to chse ldrs over 1f out: r.o fnl 75yds: led post* **15/8**[1]

32 **2** *hd* **Nightlight**[33] 6940 3-9-0 0 GrahamLee 6 64
(Jeremy Noseda) *in tch: rdn 2f out: led 110yds out: kpt on: hdd post* **3/1**[3]

**3** *3/4* **Memorial Day (IRE)** 3-9-5 0 FrederikTylicki 1 67+
(Saeed bin Suroor) *dwlt: sn in midfield: pushed along 2f out: angled to outer appr fnl f: kpt on wl fnl 110yds* **5/2**[2]

6544 **4** *3/4* **Song Of Norway**[64] 6042 3-9-0 68 (p) SteveDrowne 11 60
(Peter Makin) *in tch: rdn to chse ldr over 1f out: wandered u.p ins fnl f: one pce* **14/1**

04 **5** *shd* **Deftera Fantutte (IRE)**[16] 7355 3-8-11 0 PhilipPrince(3) 7 60
(Natalie Lloyd-Beavis) *trckd ldr: rdn to ld over 2f out: hdd 110yds out: no ex* **80/1**

-500 **6** *1/2* **Mississippi Queen (USA)**[49] 6483 3-9-0 0 WilliamTwiston-Davies 4 59
(Michael Bell) *hld up: rdn 2f out: kpt on fnl f* **40/1**

**7** *1/2* **Intimidator (IRE)** 3-9-5 0 TomQueally 5 62+
(Clive Brittain) *s.i.s: rn green in rr: stl in last appr fnl f: kpt on ins fnl f: nrst fin* **28/1**

052 **8** *1/2* **Yard Of Ale**[28] 7063 3-9-5 68 GrahamGibbons 2 65+
(Kristin Stubbs) *trckd ldr: rdn and effrt whn n.m.r ins fnl f: eased* **10/1**

54 **9** *2* **Katie Taylor (IRE)**[87] 5246 4-9-1 0 ChrisCatlin 10 52
(Rae Guest) *stdd s: hld up: rdn 2f out: nvr threatened* **20/1**

5 **10** *2 1/4* **Prominna**[15] 7370 4-9-6 0 LiamKeniry 9 51
(Tony Carroll) *racd keenly: in midfield on outer: rdn over 2f out: wknd over 1f out* **100/1**

6- **11** *6* **Zaria**[395] 7078 3-9-0 0 JoeFanning 3 29
(Richard Price) *led: rdn whn hdd over 2f out: wknd* **100/1**

1m 29.7s (0.90) **Going Correction** -0.025s/f (Stan)
**WFA** 3 from 4yo 1lb **11** Ran SP% **118.0**
Speed ratings (Par 103): **93,92,91,91,90 90,89,89,86,84 77**
CSF £7.39 TOTE £3.10: £2.40, £1.30, £1.20; EX 9.80 Trifecta £22.30.
**Owner** Hamdan Al Maktoum **Bred** T Stewart **Trained** Newmarket, Suffolk
■ Stewards' Enquiry : Frederik Tylicki one-day ban: careless riding (Nov 20)

**FOCUS**
A modest maiden, and unconvincing form with the fifth beaten in a seller latest.

## 7683 32RED CASINO NURSERY H'CAP (TAPETA) (DIV I) 5f 216y
5:10 (5:11) (Class 6) (0-65,65) 2-Y-O **£2,264** (£673; £336; £168) **Stalls** Low

Form RPR

005 **1** **Lucy The Painter (IRE)**[16] 7345 2-9-2 60 SteveDrowne 5 64
(Peter Makin) *hld up: kpt to ins rail in st: rdn over 1f out: r.o: led 75yds out* **28/1**

3263 **2** *1/2* **Sky Steps (IRE)**[12] 7453 2-8-2 49 (v) DannyBrock(3) 6 51
(Philip McBride) *hld up: rdn and hdwy on wd outside fr over 2f out: pressed ldr over 1f out: led 110yds out: sn hdd: kpt on* **5/2**[2]

0603 **3** *1/2* **Treaty Of York (IRE)**[26] 7112 2-9-5 63 FergusSweeney 4 64
(Henry Candy) *trckd ldng pair: rdn to take narrow ld over 1f out: hdd 110yds out: one pce* **3/1**[3]

005 **4** *1 1/4* **Pafiya**[39] 6790 2-8-10 54 GrahamGibbons 7 51
(Kristin Stubbs) *midfield: rdn and outpcd over 1f out: kpt on ins fnl f* **33/1**

053 **5** *1/2* **You're Cool**[36] 6867 2-9-7 65 GrahamLee 3 60
(James Given) *midfield: hdwy and in tch 2f out: rdn over 1f out: one pce* **13/8**[1]

660 **6** *3/4* **Mandria (IRE)**[14] 7398 2-9-0 58 RichardKingscote 1 51
(Daniel Kubler) *led narrowly: rdn whn hdd over 1f out: wknd ins fnl f* **25/1**

2110 **7** *2* **Sparbrook (IRE)**[12] 7453 2-9-5 63 SebSanders 8 50
(Simon Dow) *pressed ldr: rdn over 2f out: wknd over 1f out* **25/1**

6060 **8** *hd* **Don Ricardo (IRE)**[12] 7453 2-8-9 53 PaulHanagan 9 39
(Richard Fahey) *midfield: rdn 1/2-way: wknd fnl f* **12/1**

500 **9** *1/2* **Lunar Knot**[30] 6996 2-8-7 51 BenCurtis 2 36
(Alan McCabe) *dwlt: hld up in rr: rdn 1/2-way: nvr threatened* **50/1**

1m 15.27s (0.77) **Going Correction** -0.025s/f (Stan) **9** Ran SP% **115.4**
Speed ratings (Par 94): **93,92,91,90,89 88,85,85,84**
CSF £94.05 CT £284.35 TOTE £31.80: £5.40, £1.10, £2.60; EX 159.70 Trifecta £724.80.
**Owner** J P Carrington **Bred** Bakewell Bloodstock **Trained** Ogbourne Maisey, Wilts

**FOCUS**
This nursery was run at a good gallop and the first two were in the last three turning into the straight.

## 7684 32RED CASINO NURSERY H'CAP (TAPETA) (DIV II) 5f 216y
5:40 (5:40) (Class 6) (0-65,63) 2-Y-O **£2,264** (£673; £336; £168) **Stalls** Low

Form RPR

566 **1** **The Fairy (IRE)**[28] 7062 2-9-6 62 RobertHavlin 9 69+
(John Gosden) *stdd s: hld up in tch: stl on bit over 1f out: pushed along and hdwy whn hmpd appr fnl f: swtchd rt: r.o wl to ld nr fin* **7/4**[1]

546 **2** *hd* **Bonfire Heart**[16] 7361 2-9-7 63 StevieDonohoe 2 67
(Daniel Mark Loughnane) *chsd ldr: rdn to ld over 1f out: kpt on: hdd nr fin* **5/1**[3]

000 **3** *2 3/4* **Purple Surprise**[30] 7011 2-8-7 52 DannyBrock(3) 4 48
(Andrew Reid) *hld up: rdn and hdwy over 1f out: kpt on* **40/1**

3301 **4** *1 1/2* **Wink Oliver**[20] 7257 2-9-7 63 (p) GrahamGibbons 6 55
(Kristin Stubbs) *chsd ldr: rdn 2f out: one pce in 4th ins fnl f* **2/1**[2]

4500 **5** *3 1/2* **Diminutive (IRE)**[28] 7064 2-9-1 57 (b1) DavidProbert 1 38
(Grace Harris) *led: rdn whn hdd over 1f out: wknd* **40/1**

5450 **6** *2 1/4* **Gamesters Lad**[26] 7112 2-8-11 53 (v1) RichardKingscote 3 27
(Tom Dascombe) *slowly away: sn pushed in rr: a bhd* **5/1**[3]

0506 **7** *1/2* **Kylies Wild Card**[12] 7453 2-8-4 46 ow1 WilliamCarson 7 19
(Simon Hodgson) *in tch: rdn over 2f out: wknd over 1f out* **33/1**

1m 15.15s (0.65) **Going Correction** -0.025s/f (Stan) **7** Ran SP% **110.8**
Speed ratings (Par 94): **94,93,90,88,83 80,79**
CSF £10.19 CT £229.73 TOTE £3.20: £1.10, £3.20; EX 11.60 Trifecta £183.80.
**Owner** Anthony Rogers **Bred** Airlie Stud **Trained** Newmarket, Suffolk

**FOCUS**
Marginally the quicker of the two divisions by 0.12sec.

## 7685 32RED.COM MAIDEN AUCTION STKS (TAPETA) 5f 216y
6:10 (6:11) (Class 6) 2-Y-O £2,264 (£673; £336; £168) Stalls Low

Form RPR
236 1 **Cumbrianna**[49] 6489 2-8-8 64 PaulHanagan 8 64
(Bryan Smart) *mde all: rdn 2f out: kpt on* **5/2**[2]
0 2 1 ½ **Rennie Mackintosh (IRE)**[10] 7495 2-8-13 0 JoeFanning 6 65
(Mark Johnston) *sn in tch on outer: rdn to chse ldr over 1f out: edgd lft ent fnl f: kpt on* **5/1**[3]
0 3 2 **Percella**[30] 7018 2-9-0 0 DanielTudhope 7 60
(Hughie Morrison) *sn prom: rdn 2f out: one pce in 3rd fnl f* **4/5**[1]
0 4 1 ½ **Military Music**[23] 7181 2-8-0 0 CharlotteJenner(7) 2 48
(Mark Usher) *in tch: rdn 2f out: no ex ins fnl f* **25/1**
4600 5 ½ **Invincible Zeb (IRE)**[63] 6064 2-9-3 62 WilliamTwiston-Davies 3 57
(Ronald Harris) *s.i.s: hld up in rr: rdn 2f out: sme late hdwy: nvr threatened* **20/1**
00 6 4 **Magic Round (IRE)**[145] 3210 2-8-11 0 RyanWhile(5) 4 44
(Bill Turner) *in tch: rdn over 2f out: wknd over 1f out* **28/1**
0 7 ¾ **Misu Pete**[120] 4079 2-8-12 0 LiamKeniry 1 37
(Mark Usher) *hld up: rdn over 2f out: sn btn* **50/1**
8 3 **Spirit Of Rosanna** 2-8-10 0 HayleyTurner 5 26
(Steph Hollinshead) *midfield: rdn and outpcd 1/2-way: bhd fnl 2f* **16/1**
1m 15.41s (0.91) **Going Correction** -0.025s/f (Stan) 8 Ran SP% 120.7
Speed ratings (Par 94): **92,90,87,85,84 79,78,74**
CSF £15.57 TOTE £2.50: £1.10, £2.70, £1.02; EX 14.80 Trifecta £22.80.
**Owner** The Smart Positivity Partnership **Bred** Mrs Fiona Denniff **Trained** Hambleton, N Yorks
■ Stewards' Enquiry : Paul Hanagan one-day ban: failed to ride to draw (Nov 20)
**FOCUS**
An ordinary contest.

## 7686 32RED MAIDEN FILLIES' STKS (TAPETA) 1m 141y
6:40 (6:41) (Class 5) 3-Y-O+ £2,587 (£770; £384; £192) Stalls Low

Form RPR
2 1 **Memoria**[24] 7158 3-8-12 0 ChrisCatlin 9 78
(Rae Guest) *prom: rdn to take slt ld over 1f out: kpt on* **9/1**
325 2 1 **Ghany (IRE)**[22] 7195 3-8-12 74 PaulHanagan 6 76
(William Haggas) *led: rdn whn hdd over 1f out: kpt on but a jst hld* **10/11**[1]
4-4 3 nk **Jacqueline Jouliac**[64] 6033 3-8-12 0 (t[1]) RobertHavlin 5 75
(John Gosden) *trckd ldng pair: rdn 2f out: sn edgd rt: kpt on fnl f* **9/2**[3]
30 4 2 **Scarlet Sash**[8] 7528 3-8-12 0 FergusSweeney 3 71
(Henry Candy) *trckd ldng pair: rdn 2f out: sn one pce* **10/3**[2]
0- 5 4 ½ **Synaesthesia (FR)**[380] 7435 3-8-12 0 MartinHarley 11 60+
(Lady Cecil) *hld up in rr: rdn over 1f out: kpt on fnl f* **16/1**
6 1 **Undulate** 3-8-12 0 TomEaves 1 58
(Peter Niven) *s.i.s: hld up: rdn 2f out: kpt on fnl f* **66/1**
34 7 ½ **Arsenale (GER)**[22] 7210 3-8-7 0 AlistairRawlinson(5) 4 57
(Michael Appleby) *dwlt: hld up: rdn over 2f out: one pce and nvr threatened* **16/1**
0 8 ½ **The French Grey (FR)**[168] 2489 3-8-5 0 CallumShepherd(7) 8 56
(Ron Hodges) *racd keenly in midfield: rdn over 2f out: nvr threatened* **100/1**
0 9 9 **Shanghai Sunrise**[144] 3276 3-8-5 0 DavidParkes(7) 10 35
(Keiran Burke) *in tch: rdn over 2f out: sn wknd* **100/1**
000 10 11 **Bahama Dancer**[22] 7210 3-8-9 45 JoeyHaynes(3) 2 10
(Jason Ward) *in tch: rdn 3f out: wknd* **150/1**
0 11 99 **Hidden Ambition**[27] 7074 5-9-1 0 [1] HayleyTurner 7
(Steph Hollinshead) *midfield: pushed along and dropped to rr 4f out: sn t.o and eased* **100/1**
1m 50.69s (0.59) **Going Correction** -0.025s/f (Stan)
**WFA** 3 from 5yo 3lb 11 Ran SP% 120.5
Speed ratings (Par 100): **96,95,94,93,89 88,87,87,79,69**
CSF £18.33 TOTE £12.30: £2.40, £1.02, £2.80; EX 22.00 Trifecta £51.40.
**Owner** C J Mills **Bred** C J Mills **Trained** Newmarket, Suffolk
**FOCUS**
They didn't go much of a gallop here, but the first four were clear and the form has been given a chance.

## 7687 £20 RISK-FREE BET AT UNIBET CLAIMING STKS (TAPETA) 5f 216y
7:10 (7:11) (Class 6) 3-Y-O+ £2,264 (£673; £336; £168) Stalls Low

Form RPR
3410 1 **Realize**[16] 7365 4-9-7 80 (t) DanielTudhope 7 88
(Hughie Morrison) *midfield: rdn and hdwy 2f out: sn chsd ldr: kpt on: led ins fnl f* **9/4**[1]
1005 2 2 **Searchlight**[26] 7101 3-9-2 84 ShaneGray(5) 10 82
(Kevin Ryan) *trckd ldr: led 2f out: sn rdn: hdd ins fnl f: no ex* **7/2**[2]
0000 3 5 **Lewisham**[23] 7178 4-9-0 65 (v[1]) PaddyAspell 8 59
(David Nicholls) *chsd ldr on outer: rdn over 2f out: sltly hmpd by faller wl over 1f out: sn one pce and hld in 3rd* **25/1**
2030 4 1 ¾ **Commanche**[17] 7337 5-9-2 73 ConnorBeasley(3) 12 58
(Chris Dwyer) *dwlt: hld up in rr: rdn over 2f out: wnt 4th ins fnl f: nvr threatened* **25/1**
2560 5 10 **Best Trip (IRE)**[17] 7330 7-9-5 77 PaulPickard 9 26
(Brian Ellison) *led: rdn whn hdd 2f out: wknd* **25/1**
4100 6 4 ½ **Desert Strike**[16] 7365 8-9-7 77 (p) HayleyTurner 6 14
(Conor Dore) *prom: rdn over 2f out: already lost pl btn whn hmpd wl over 1f out: eased* **33/1**
2000 7 24 **Appease**[132] 3670 5-8-13 72 TomQueally 1
(John Butler) *hld up: bdly hmpd wl over 1f out: no ch after and eased* **50/1**
0313 F **Fitz Flyer (IRE)**[3] 7623 8-8-10 74 (v) JordanNason(5) 3
(David Nicholls) *racd keenly in tch: smooth hdwy whn clipped heels and fell wl over 1f out: fatally injured* **11/1**
0550 U **Powerful Pierre**[10] 7494 7-8-10 77 (b) TobyAtkinson(5) 13
(Noel Quinlan) *slowly away: hld up in rr: rdn over 3f out: wl btn whn uns wl over 1f out* **33/1**
-430 B **Ortac Rock (IRE)**[19] 7282 5-9-2 75 (t) PaulHanagan 11
(Richard Fahey) *hld up: jst pushed along whn b.d wl over 1f out* **11/2**[3]
6200 B **Pandar**[9] 7507 5-8-13 82 FrederikTylicki 4
(Milton Bradley) *chsd ldrs: pushed along and jst lost pl whn b.d wl over 1f out* **10/1**
1025 B **Cape Of Hope (IRE)**[23] 7167 4-9-2 69 (v) RichardKingscote 2
(Tom Dascombe) *midfield: pushed along whn b.d wl over 1f out* **14/1**
1m 12.78s (-1.72) **Going Correction** -0.025s/f (Stan) 12 Ran SP% 111.8
Speed ratings (Par 101): **110,107,100,98,85 79,47,,,**
CSF £8.09 TOTE £2.50: £1.10, £2.00, £8.20; EX 10.30 Trifecta £212.60.Realize was claimed by K. A. Ryan for £15000. Searchlight was subject to a friendly claim.
**Owner** Deborah Collett & M J Watson **Bred** M J Watson **Trained** East Ilsley, Berks
**FOCUS**
There was a pile-up on the turn in as the keen-going Fitz Flyer clipped heels with the weakening Best Trip, fell heavily and brought down Cape Of Hope and Pandar, who in turn brought down Ortac Rock and badly hampered Appease. Powerful Pierre also jinked and unseated his rider. The winner is rated as improving from his penultimate C&D win.

## 7688 DOWNLOAD THE CORAL APP H'CAP (TAPETA) 1m 1f 103y
7:40 (8:04) (Class 2) (0-105,104) 3-Y-£01,971 (£3,583; £1,791; £896; £446) Stalls Low

Form RPR
0220 1 **Docs Legacy (IRE)**[2] 7641 5-8-5 85 DavidProbert 8 94
(Richard Fahey) *midfield: rdn and hdwy 2f out: led ins fnl f: kpt on* **16/1**
0313 2 1 ¾ **Earth Drummer (IRE)**[12] 7455 4-9-1 95 DanielTudhope 7 100
(David O'Meara) *hld up: pushed along and hdwy over 2f out: rdn over 1f out: kpt on: wnt 2nd nr fin* **4/1**[3]
2402 3 nk **Maverick Wave (USA)**[19] 7276 3-9-3 100 RobertHavlin 10 106
(John Gosden) *prom: led over 2f out: sn rdn: hdd ins fnl f: no ex: lost 2nd nr fin* **7/4**[1]
04 4 1 ¼ **Energia Flavio (BRZ)**[40] 6748 4-8-12 95 RyanTate(3) 4 97
(Marco Botti) *trckd ldng pair: rdn over 2f out: one pce in 4th ins fnl f* **16/1**
5644 5 ¾ **Solar Deity (IRE)**[202] 1559 5-9-10 104 MartinHarley 5 104+
(Marco Botti) *midfield: pushed along whn briefly n.m.r 2f out: kpt on for hand riding fnl f* **5/2**[2]
6023 6 4 ½ **Ginger Jack**[5] 7597 7-8-5 85 oh3 JimmyQuinn 1 76
(Keith Dalgleish) *trckd ldng pair: rdn over 2f out: wknd over 1f out* **10/1**
0200 7 1 ¾ **Master Of Finance (IRE)**[13] 7410 3-8-4 87 JoeFanning 2 75
(Mark Johnston) *hld up: rdn over 2f out: nvr threatened* **28/1**
0030 8 2 **Sound Advice**[7] 7545 5-8-12 92 ow1 PhillipMakin 9 75
(Keith Dalgleish) *led: rdn whn hdd over 2f out: wknd over 1f out* **25/1**
0000 9 4 ½ **Uramazin (IRE)**[171] 2405 8-9-1 95 LiamKeniry 6 69
(Philip Hide) *s.i.s: hld up in rr: a bhd* **50/1**
1000 10 3 ¾ **The Lock Master (IRE)**[161] 2700 7-8-7 92 AlistairRawlinson(5) 3 58
(Michael Appleby) *sn pushed along in rr: a bhd* **40/1**
1m 57.15s (-3.65) **Going Correction** -0.025s/f (Stan) course record
**WFA** 3 from 4yo+ 3lb 10 Ran SP% 117.5
Speed ratings (Par 109): **115,113,113,112,111 107,105,104,100,96**
CSF £77.46 CT £173.05 TOTE £15.50: £3.50, £1.50, £1.10; EX 104.40 Trifecta £349.80.
**Owner** D Bardsley **Bred** Miss Mary Davison **Trained** Musley Bank, N Yorks
**FOCUS**
A really good handicap. The winner rates better than ever.

## 7689 BET IN PLAY AT CORAL H'CAP (BOBIS RACE) (TAPETA) 1m 4f 50y
8:10 (8:32) (Class 4) (0-85,81) 3-Y-O £4,851 (£1,443; £721; £360) Stalls Low

Form RPR
1 1 **Kalaatah (USA)**[22] 7195 3-9-7 81 MartinHarley 5 97+
(Saeed bin Suroor) *hld up: gng wl whn briefly n.m.r 2f out: swtchd to outer over 1f out: qcknd up wl to ld ins fnl f: pushed out: comf* **13/8**[1]
1530 2 2 **Tears Of The Sun**[40] 6746 3-9-5 79 GrahamLee 1 87
(Roger Varian) **11/1**
6340 3 ¾ **Heska (IRE)**[31] 6981 3-8-4 67 (tp) RyanTate(3) 6 74
(Michael Appleby) *pressed ldr: rdn to ld 2f out: hdd ins fnl f: no ex* **6/1**[3]
1100 4 ¾ **Tizlove Regardless (USA)**[16] 7350 3-9-2 76 JoeFanning 2 82
(Mark Johnston) *in tch: rdn over 2f out: one pce* **15/2**
232 5 1 **Gleese The Devil (IRE)**[24] 7162 3-9-1 75 GeorgeChaloner 3 79
(Richard Fahey) *hld up: rdn over 2f out: one pce and nvr threatened* **2/1**[2]
042 6 4 ½ **Westerly**[62] 6110 3-8-8 68 DavidProbert 4 65
(Luke Dace) **20/1**
2m 39.11s (-1.69) **Going Correction** -0.025s/f (Stan) 6 Ran SP% 110.6
Speed ratings (Par 104): **104,102,102,101,101 98**
CSF £19.03 TOTE £2.90: £1.70, £4.20; EX 13.00 Trifecta £85.20.
**Owner** Godolphin **Bred** Shadwell Farm, Llc **Trained** Newmarket, Suffolk
**FOCUS**
A fair handicap won in good style. A big step up from the winner, who looked better than the bare form.
T/Plt: £5.70 to a £1 stake. Pool of £99207.69 - 12599.41 winning tickets. T/Qpdt: £2.70 to a £1 stake. Pool of £9566.34 - 2557.60 winning tickets. AS

7690 - 7696a (Foreign Racing) - See Raceform Interactive

7682
# WOLVERHAMPTON (A.W) (L-H)
Friday, November 7

**OFFICIAL GOING: Tapeta: standard**
Wind: Fresh behind Weather: Overcast

## 7697 £20 RISK-FREE BET AT UNIBET APPRENTICE H'CAP (TAPETA) (DIV I) 5f 216y
4:35 (4:38) (Class 5) (0-70,70) 3-Y-O+ £2,911 (£866; £432; £216) Stalls Low

Form RPR
6001 1 **Spinning Cobblers**[8] 7547 3-8-0 56 6ex (v) AaronJones(7) 6 66
(Stuart Williams) *a.p: edgd lft over 1f out: r.o to ld wl ins fnl f* **3/1**[2]
1406 2 nk **Majestic Song**[20] 7286 3-9-5 68 WilliamTwiston-Davies 7 77
(James Toller) *hld up: hdwy over 1f out: nt clr run and swtchd rt ins fnl f: r.o wl* **16/1**
2010 3 1 ¼ **Shades Of Silk**[37] 6872 3-9-0 68 MeganCarberry(5) 8 73
(James Given) *led: rdn over 1f out: hdd and unable qck wl ins fnl f* **12/1**
1210 4 ¾ **Chapellerie (IRE)**[48] 6562 5-9-1 69 (b) JennyPowell(5) 3 72
(Brendan Powell) *s.i.s: hld up: r.o ins fnl f: nt rch ldrs* **6/1**[3]
4030 5 ½ **Chookie's Lass**[38] 6835 3-9-3 66 JoeyHaynes 9 67
(Keith Dalgleish) *chsd ldr: rdn and ev ch fr over 2f out tl hung rt and no ex ins fnl f* **12/1**
0222 6 1 ¾ **Boxing Shadows**[9] 7534 4-9-2 70 KieranShoemark(5) 2 65
(Les Eyre) *chsd ldrs: rdn over 1f out: no ex fnl f* **9/1**
-014 7 ½ **Dazeen**[21] 7259 7-8-12 64 KevinStott(3) 10 58
(Michael Herrington) *hld up: pushed along and hdwy 2f out: no ex fnl f* **6/4**[1]
452 8 2 ¼ **Mey Blossom**[64] 6077 9-8-10 59 (p) GeorgeChaloner 5 46
(Richard Whitaker) *prom: drvn along 1/2-way: wknd over 1f out* **33/1**
0000 9 ½ **Look Here's Al**[4] 7621 3-8-9 63 RobHornby(5) 1 48
(Andrew Hollinshead) *sn pushed along and prom: rdn over 2f out: wknd over 1f out* **22/1**

1006 **10** *4* **My Meteor**[19] 7307 7-9-0 63 DannyBrock 4 35
(Tony Newcombe) *s.i.s: hld up: plld hrd: wknd over 2f out* **40/1**
1m 13.52s (-0.98) **Going Correction** -0.10s/f (Stan) 10 Ran SP% **120.3**
Speed ratings (Par 103): **102,101,99,98,98 95,95,92,91,86**
CSF £50.46 CT £519.36 TOTE £4.50: £1.70, £4.50, £3.70; EX 69.30 Trifecta £581.10.
**Owner** Brian Piper & David Cobill **Bred** L Ellinas & Old Mill Stud **Trained** Newmarket, Suffolk

**FOCUS**
A fair but competitive sprint for apprentice riders, which was run at a sound pace. The winner backed up his Kempton win.

## 7698 £20 RISK-FREE BET AT UNIBET APPRENTICE H'CAP (TAPETA) (DIV II) 5f 216y

**5:10** (5:11) (Class 5) (0-70,69) 3-Y-0+ **£2,911** (£866; £432; £216) **Stalls** Low

Form RPR
06-0 **1** **Mount Hollow**[19] 7307 9-9-1 68 (p) RobHornby(5) 9 78
(Andrew Hollinshead) *hld up: hdwy over 1f out: rdn and r.o to ld nr fin* **14/1**
5363 **2** *nk* **Larghetto (USA)**[14] 7423 6-8-7 59 (b[1]) GeorgeDowning(3) 6 68
(Ian Williams) *hld up: hdwy over 2f out: rdn over 1f out: led ins fnl f: edgd lft: hdd nr fin* **13/2**[3]
2304 **3** *1 ½* **Diamond Blue**[41] 6758 6-8-13 64 (p) SammyJoBell(3) 4 68
(Richard Fahey) *hld up: hdwy over 1f out: r.o* **16/1**
1350 **4** *hd* **Classic Pursuit**[48] 6552 3-9-7 69 (p) WilliamTwiston-Davies 1 72
(Ronald Harris) *a.p: rdn to chse ldr 2f out: styd on same pce ins fnl f* **13/2**[3]
4103 **5** *nk* **Little Eli**[9] 7534 4-9-4 66 (v) JasonHart 10 69
(Eric Alston) *led 5f out: rdn over 1f out: hdd and no ex ins fnl f* **3/1**[1]
-014 **6** *½* **Bush Beauty (IRE)**[13] 7457 3-9-1 68 GaryMahon(5) 5 69
(Philip McBride) *mid-div: hdwy over 2f out: rdn over 1f out: styd on same pce fnl f* **3/1**[1]
1160 **7** *5* **Pastureyes**[41] 6763 4-9-3 68 (p) TimClark(3) 3 54
(Scott Dixon) *led 1f: chsd ldr tl rdn over 2f out: wknd fnl f* **50/1**
2000 **8** *1* **Speightowns Kid (USA)**[35] 6898 6-8-12 63 KevinStott(3) 2 46
(Michael Herrington) *hld up: pushed along over 2f out: nvr nrr* **8/1**
0400 **9** *6* **Roomie**[21] 7252 3-8-0 55 oh8 RyanHolmes(7) 7 20
(Barry Leavy) *prom: lost pl 4f out: sn rdn: wknd over 2f out* **150/1**
0322 **10** *4 ½* **Mambo Spirit (IRE)**[17] 7364 10-9-1 63 LouisSteward 8 15
(Tony Newcombe) *chsd ldrs: rdn over 2f out: wknd over 1f out* **6/1**[2]
1m 14.14s (-0.36) **Going Correction** -0.10s/f (Stan) 10 Ran SP% **117.2**
Speed ratings (Par 103): **98,97,95,95,94 94,87,86,78,72**
CSF £102.65 CT £1485.88 TOTE £18.30: £4.80, £2.40, £1.90; EX 145.90 Trifecta £2943.40 Part won..
**Owner** A N Hollinshead **Bred** G Robinson **Trained** Upper Longdon, Staffs

**FOCUS**
The second division of this apprentice handicap was run 0.62 secs slower than the first leg. The winner was still 8lb off his best.

## 7699 UNIBET OFFER DAILY JOCKEY/TRAINER SPECIALS MAIDEN STKS (TAPETA) 5f 216y

**5:40** (5:41) (Class 5) 3-Y-0 **£2,911** (£866; £432; £216) **Stalls** Low

Form RPR
22 **1** **Jan Van Hoof (IRE)**[63] 6116 3-9-5 0 TonyHamilton 6 74+
(Richard Fahey) *a.p: led on bit over 1f out: drvn out* **5/2**[2]
65 **2** *1 ¼* **Sir Billy Wright (IRE)**[20] 7285 3-9-2 0 DeclanBates(3) 3 67+
(David Evans) *chsd ldrs: rdn over 1f out: edgd lft and chsd wnr ins fnl f: r.o* **9/4**[1]
0053 **3** *1 ¼* **Silver Mirage**[21] 7253 3-9-0 64 AdamKirby 1 58
(Michael Bell) *led 1f: chsd ldrs: rdn and ev ch over 1f out: edgd lft and no ex ins fnl f* **9/4**[1]
2520 **4** *1 ¼* **Clabare**[21] 7250 3-9-5 52 TomEaves 7 59
(Ian Semple) *s.i.s: hld up: hdwy over 1f out: sn rdn: styd on same pce ins fnl f* **14/1**
**5** *4* **Two Turns** 3-8-11 0 SimonPearce(3) 4 41
(Lydia Pearce) *sn outpcd: styd on fr over 1f out: nvr on terms* **8/1**[3]
3652 **6** *hd* **Nelson's Pride**[16] 7370 3-8-7 56 (b) RhiainIngram(7) 5 41
(Roger Ingram) *led 5f out: hdd over 1f out: wknd fnl f* **10/1**
0 **7** *2 ½* **Wattaboutsteve**[16] 7370 3-9-5 0 JoeFanning 2 38
(Ralph J Smith) *hld up: rdn over 1f out: wknd fnl f* **50/1**
246 **8** *13* **Smile For Me (IRE)**[38] 6837 3-9-0 47 PaulMulrennan 8
(Alan Berry) *w ldr tl rdn wl over 2f out: sn hung rt: wknd over 1f out* **50/1**
1m 13.74s (-0.76) **Going Correction** -0.10s/f (Stan) 8 Ran SP% **120.9**
Speed ratings (Par 102): **101,99,97,96,90 90,87,69**
CSF £9.20 TOTE £2.20: £1.10, £1.10, £1.30; EX 8.60 Trifecta £20.60.
**Owner** Mark A Leatham **Bred** Old Carhue Stud **Trained** Musley Bank, N Yorks

**FOCUS**
An ordinary maiden, but the winner has plenty of scope. The time was relatively quick, but the form is rated a bit cautiously.

## 7700 DAILY PRICE BOOSTS AT UNIBET H'CAP (TAPETA) 5f 216y

**6:10** (6:13) (Class 2) (0-105,100) 3-Y-£11,971 (£3,583; £1,791; £896; £446) **Stalls** Low

Form RPR
2024 **1** **Foxtrot Romeo (IRE)**[48] 6531 5-9-4 97 (b) MartinHarley 10 109
(Marco Botti) *hld up: hdwy over 1f out: led wl ins fnl f: r.o: comf* **7/2**[1]
1502 **2** *1 ½* **Pipers Note**[8] 7543 4-9-0 93 GeorgeChaloner 1 100
(Richard Whitaker) *a.p: chsd ldr over 2f out: rdn to ld and hung rt 1f out: hdd and unable qck wl ins fnl f* **6/1**[3]
0024 **3** *shd* **Confessional**[13] 7441 7-8-13 92 (e) DavidAllan 11 99
(Tim Easterby) *hld up: rdn over 1f out: r.o ins fnl f: nt rch ldrs* **9/1**
1101 **4** *hd* **Amadeus Wolfe Tone (IRE)**[17] 7365 5-8-11 90 (p) TomQueally 2 96
(Jamie Osborne) *hld up in tch: rdn over 1f out: styd on same pce wl ins fnl f* **10/1**
1160 **5** *1 ¼* **Go Far**[48] 6533 4-9-7 100 (v) AdamKirby 8 102
(Alan Bailey) *prom: sn lost pl: bhd and rdn 1/2-way: r.o ins fnl f* **6/1**[3]
0000 **6** *shd* **Compton Park**[14] 7408 7-8-6 92 (t) KieranShoemark(7) 4 94
(Les Eyre) *s.i.s: hld up: hdwy over 1f out: styd on* **25/1**
04P3 **7** *nse* **Ballista (IRE)**[30] 7034 6-9-4 97 GrahamGibbons 7 99
(Tom Dascombe) *led: rdn and edgd rt over 1f out: hdd 1f out: no ex ins fnl f* **12/1**
0061 **8** *½* **Hallelujah**[30] 7034 6-9-5 98 HayleyTurner 9 98
(James Fanshawe) *chsd ldrs: rdn over 2f out: styd on same pce fnl f* **11/2**[2]
0650 **9** *½* **Secret Asset (IRE)**[28] 7080 9-8-8 87 (p) LukeMorris 6 85
(Jane Chapple-Hyam) *stmbld sn after s: sn pushed along into mid-div: rdn over 1f out: no ex ins fnl f* **28/1**
1050 **10** *2* **Little Shambles**[35] 6893 3-8-8 87 JoeFanning 13 79
(Mark Johnston) *prom: rdn over 2f out: no ex fnl f* **50/1**
3100 **11** *½* **Out Do**[27] 7122 5-9-3 96 (v) DanielTudhope 5 86
(David O'Meara) *chsd ldrs: rdn over 2f out: hung lft over 1f out: no ex fnl f* **15/2**
0030 **12** *¾* **Ballesteros**[13] 7441 5-8-11 90 TonyHamilton 3 78
(Richard Fahey) *chsd ldr: rdn over 2f out: wknd ins fnl f* **20/1**
1m 12.5s (-2.00) **Going Correction** -0.10s/f (Stan) course record 12 Ran SP% **118.7**
Speed ratings (Par 109): **109,107,106,106,104 104,104,104,103,100 100,99**
CSF £22.92 CT £177.21 TOTE £5.30: £1.90, £1.80, £4.20; EX 27.30 Trifecta £183.30.
**Owner** Andrew Tinkler **Bred** Barronstown Stud **Trained** Newmarket, Suffolk

**FOCUS**
A good-quality sprint handicap run at a good pace. The winner built on a good effort here in September.

## 7701 £20 RISK-FREE BET AT UNIBET MAIDEN AUCTION STKS (TAPETA) 5f 20y

**6:40** (6:41) (Class 6) 2-Y-0 **£2,264** (£673; £336; £168) **Stalls** Low

Form RPR
0320 **1** **Frozen Princess**[31] 7003 2-8-10 62 TomQueally 3 64+
(Jamie Osborne) *chsd ldrs: nt clr run and swtchd lft over 1f out: rdn to ld wl ins fnl f: r.o* **7/2**
3000 **2** *1 ¾* **Air Of York (IRE)**[13] 7453 2-8-12 45 (b) WilliamTwiston-Davies 1 60
(Ronald Harris) *chsd ldr: led over 1f out: sn rdn: hdd and unable qck wl ins fnl f* **66/1**
4 **3** *¾* **Miss Jonh (FR)**[179] 2206 2-8-9 0 FergusSweeney 4 54
(Martyn Meade) *mid-div: hdwy over 1f out: rdn ins fnl f: styd on same pce* **9/4**[1]
024 **4** *3 ½* **Wiseton (IRE)**[72] 5813 2-9-0 62 GrahamGibbons 2 46
(David Barron) *led: hung rt thrght: rdn and hdd over 1f out: wknd ins fnl f* **11/4**[3]
544 **5** *1 ¼* **George Bailey (IRE)**[21] 7246 2-9-1 64 PaulMulrennan 5 43
(Bryan Smart) *chsd ldrs: rdn over 1f out: wknd fnl f* **5/2**[2]
**6** *nk* **Desert Apostle (IRE)** 2-8-11 0 DaleSwift 7 38
(Derek Shaw) *s.s: styd on fr over 1f out: nt trble ldrs* **20/1**
4660 **7** *3* **Icandi**[36] 6888 2-8-3 54 ow1 KieranShoemark(7) 8 26
(Alan Berry) *sn pushed along in rr: nvr on terms* **50/1**
**8** *¾* **Magical Peak** 2-8-8 0 JasonHart 6 21
(Eric Alston) *sn outpcd* **50/1**
1m 2.2s (0.30) **Going Correction** -0.10s/f (Stan) 8 Ran SP% **118.4**
Speed ratings (Par 94): **93,90,89,83,81 80,76,74**
CSF £196.66 TOTE £3.50: £1.10, £8.00, £1.30; EX 67.70 Trifecta £311.30.
**Owner** Barratt & Johnsons **Bred** Mrs Mary Taylor & Kirtlington Stud **Trained** Upper Lambourn, Berks

**FOCUS**
No more than a fair maiden.

## 7702 CORAL CASINO H'CAP (TAPETA) 1m 4f 50y

**7:10** (7:10) (Class 4) (0-85,85) 3-Y-0+ **£4,851** (£1,443; £721; £360) **Stalls** Low

Form RPR
4402 **1** **Gabrial's Star**[14] 7422 5-9-10 85 (b) GeorgeChaloner 1 94
(Richard Fahey) *hld up in tch: shkn up over 2f out: swtchd lft over 1f out: rdn to ld ins fnl f: jst hld on* **9/2**[2]
-105 **2** *shd* **Pintrada**[27] 7125 6-9-5 80 TedDurcan 2 88
(James Bethell) *hld up: hdwy over 1f out: rdn and nt clr run ins fnl f: r.o wl* **6/1**[3]
0201 **3** *1* **Ridgeway Storm (IRE)**[15] 7401 4-9-4 79 TomQueally 9 85
(Alan King) *hld up: hdwy on outer over 2f out: rdn over 1f out: r.o* **13/8**[1]
0646 **4** *nk* **Corton Lad**[15] 7402 4-9-6 81 (tp) PhillipMakin 5 87
(Keith Dalgleish) *a.p: rdn and ev ch 1f out: styd on* **14/1**
0455 **5** *½* **Bureau (IRE)**[18] 7334 3-8-13 80 JoeFanning 8 85
(Mark Johnston) *chsd ldrs: shkn up to ld over 1f out: rdn and hdd ins fnl f: styd on same pce* **20/1**
4200 **6** *1 ¼* **Last Minute Lisa (IRE)**[8] 7554 4-8-12 73 LukeMorris 11 76
(Sylvester Kirk) *hld up: rdn over 1f out: r.o ins fnl f: nt trble ldrs* **10/1**
3606 **7** *nk* **Luv U Whatever**[18] 7334 4-8-11 77 AlistairRawlinson(5) 6 79
(Michael Appleby) *led: rdn and hdd over 1f out: no ex ins fnl f* **10/1**
-000 **8** *¾* **Very Good Day (FR)**[14] 7409 7-9-7 82 DavidNolan 3 83
(Richard Fahey) *prom: chsd ldr over 8f out: rdn and ev ch 2f out: nt clr run 1f out: no ex ins fnl f* **14/1**
-000 **9** *1 ½* **Quixote**[3] 7641 5-9-2 80 LouisSteward(3) 7 79
(Clive Brittain) *chsd ldr over 3f: remained handy: rdn and ev ch 1f out: wknd ins fnl f* **25/1**
10-0 **10** *4* **Take Two**[18] 7341 5-9-5 80 HayleyTurner 4 72
(Alex Hales) *s.s: hld up: rdn over 3f out: nvr on terms* **66/1**
2660 **11** *3 ¼* **Cathedral**[135] 3582 5-8-8 72 JoeyHaynes(3) 10 59
(Philip Kirby) *hld up: hdwy over 6f out: rdn over 2f out: wknd over 1f out* **50/1**
3000 **12** *2 ½* **Perennial**[14] 7422 5-8-11 72 TonyHamilton 12 55
(Philip Kirby) *hld up: rdn over 3f out: sn wknd* **33/1**
2m 37.01s (-3.79) **Going Correction** -0.10s/f (Stan) course record
**WFA** 3 from 4yo+ 6lb 12 Ran SP% **117.1**
Speed ratings (Par 105): **108,107,107,107,106 105,105,105,104,101 99,97**
CSF £29.51 CT £61.69 TOTE £5.10: £1.80, £2.40, £1.50; EX 38.10 Trifecta £55.70.
**Owner** Dr Marwan Koukash **Bred** Miss K Rausing **Trained** Musley Bank, N Yorks

**FOCUS**
A useful middle distance handicap and again the pace was strong. The bare form is only ordinary.

## 7703 32RED H'CAP (TAPETA) 1m 5f 194y

**7:40** (7:40) (Class 2) (0-105,97) 3-Y-£11,971 (£3,583; £1,791; £896; £446) **Stalls** Low

Form RPR
2230 **1** **Masterpaver**[8] 7545 3-8-11 **88** MartinHarley 4 97
(Alan Bailey) *a.p: rdn to ld jst over 1f out: sn hung lft: styd on u.p* **20/1**
1000 **2** *1 ¾* **Gabrial's King (IRE)**[14] 7409 5-9-6 **89** AdamKirby 5 96
(David Simcock) *hld up: hmpd over 3f out: hdwy over 2f out: styd on u.p to go 2nd towards fin: nt rch wnr* **25/1**
6011 **3** *¾* **Norab (GER)**[14] 7422 3-8-7 **84** LukeMorris 3 90
(Marco Botti) *a.p: chsd ldr over 8f out tl over 3f out: wnt 2nd again over 2f out: led wl over 1f out: sn rdn and hung lft: hdd ent fnl f: styd on same pce* **7/2**[2]
4350 **4** *hd* **Noble Silk**[27] 7107 5-9-3 **93** (p) KieranShoemark(7) 6 99
(Lucy Wadham) *hld up: hmpd over 3f out: hdwy over 1f out: r.o: nt rch ldrs* **11/2**[3]
0000 **5** *6* **Our Gabrial (IRE)**[27] 7106 3-8-12 **89** GeorgeChaloner 10 86
(Richard Fahey) *s.i.s: hld up: rdn over 2f out: n.d* **10/1**
-034 **6** *nk* **I'm Fraam Govan**[55] 6330 6-9-11 **94** PatCosgrave 8 91
(George Baker) *hld up: hdwy 2f out: sn rdn: wknd fnl f* **6/1**

0565 **7** *1* **Saved By The Bell (IRE)**[14] 7409 4-9-3 86................. DanielTudhope 1 81
(David O'Meara) *led after 1f: rdn and hdd wl over 1f out: wknd fnl f* **16/1**

1400 **8** *7* **Masterful Act (USA)**[61] 6169 7-10-0 97.................. TomQueally 9 83
(Alan McCabe) *led 1f: chsd ldr tl over 8f out: wnt 2nd again over 3f out tl rdn over 2f out: wknd over 1f out* **40/1**

4111 **P** **Daaree (IRE)**[15] 7402 4-9-3 86.................................. GrahamLee 2
(Saeed bin Suroor) *s.i.s: sn prom: disputing cl 4th whn broke down and p.u over 3f out: fatally injured* **2/1**[1]

2m 58.4s (-6.40) **Going Correction** -0.10s/f (Stan) course record
**WFA** 3 from 4yo+ 8lb **9** Ran SP% **111.2**
Speed ratings (Par 109): **114,113,112,112,109 108,108,104,**
CSF £389.59 CT £2108.19 TOTE £18.10: £3.10, £4.70, £1.40; EX 203.90 Trifecta £992.40.
**Owner** Mrs A M Riney **Bred** Mrs A M Riney **Trained** Newmarket, Suffolk

**FOCUS**
A competitive staying handicap, albeit not the strongest for the grade, but the favourite broke down fatally and the first pair were not obvious.

## 7704 LADBROKES H'CAP (TAPETA) 7f 32y
**8:10** (8:11) (Class 6) (0-62,62) 3-Y-0+ **£2,264** (£673; £336; £168) **Stalls** High

Form RPR

6400 **1** **Queen Aggie (IRE)**[23] 7213 4-9-0 62........................ GeorgeDowning(5) 5 74
(Tony Carroll) *hld up in tch: rdn to ld ins fnl f: r.o wl* **9/4**[1]

0222 **2** *3 ¼* **El Mirage (IRE)**[14] 7424 4-9-3 60.............................(p) RobertWinston 6 64
(Dean Ivory) *a.p: rdn over 2f out: styd on* **9/2**[2]

1203 **3** *1 ½* **Hawk Moth (IRE)**[17] 7368 6-9-5 62..............................(p) LukeMorris 10 62
(John Spearing) *hld up: hdwy over 1f out: styd on u.p to go 3rd nr fin: nt trble ldrs* **9/2**[2]

4630 **4** *nk* **Four Cheers (IRE)**[36] 6889 3-9-1 62.................... LouisSteward(3) 2 60
(Clive Brittain) *chsd ldr: led over 2f out: rdn over 1f out: hdd ins fnl f: wknd towards fin* **8/1**

5606 **5** *shd* **Shushu Sugartown (IRE)**[21] 7248 3-9-2 60................ StevieDonohoe 8 58
(Ian Williams) *mid-div: rdn over 2f out: r.o ins fnl f: nvr nrr* **22/1**

5000 **6** *shd* **Russian Ice**[17] 7368 6-9-4 61.......................................(b) SebSanders 7 60
(Dean Ivory) *sn pushed along in rr: rdn over 2f out: styd on ins fnl f: nrst fin* **33/1**

3321 **7** *½* **Keene's Pointe**[17] 7368 4-9-5 62..................................(b) TomEaves 3 60
(Kristin Stubbs) *chsd ldrs: rdn over 1f out: wknd ins fnl f* **9/1**

0003 **8** *½* **Hickster (IRE)**[31] 7021 3-9-1 62................................... RossAtkinson(3) 1 57
(Mandy Rowland) *sn led: hdd over 2f out: rdn and ev ch over 1f out: wknd ins fnl f* **33/1**

350 **9** *1 ½* **Satellite Express (IRE)**[32] 6988 3-9-4 62...................... AdamKirby 11 53
(David Evans) *hld up: shkn up over 1f out: nvr on terms* **25/1**

0324 **10** *1 ¼* **Asha**[21] 7250 3-9-2 60................................................ AndrewElliott 4 48
(David C Griffiths) *mid-div: rdn 1/2-way: wknd over 1f out* **12/1**

4654 **11** *9* **Alphabetique**[31] 7000 3-9-4 62...................................... MartinHarley 12 27
(Peter Chapple-Hyam) *hdwy over 5f out: rdn and wknd over 2f out* **15/2**[3]

1m 27.93s (-0.87) **Going Correction** -0.10s/f (Stan)
**WFA** 3 from 4yo+ 1lb **11** Ran SP% **121.8**
Speed ratings (Par 101): **100,96,94,94,94 94,93,92,91,89 79**
CSF £12.03 CT £42.84 TOTE £4.60: £2.00, £1.70, £3.30; EX 20.20 Trifecta £89.00.
**Owner** Shropshire Wolves 4 **Bred** Mrs Marion Daly **Trained** Cropthorne, Worcs

**FOCUS**
A modest handicap but it was wide open, with only 2lb separating the field on official ratings. The winner is rated close to last winter's form.
T/Jkpt: Not won. T/Plt: £102.40 to a £1 stake. Pool: £122,785.20 - 874.80 winning tickets T/Qpdt: £3.40 to a £1 stake. Pool: £14,826.87 - 3159.20 winning tickets CR

7705 - 7711a (Foreign Racing) - See Raceform Interactive

# 7438 DONCASTER (L-H)
Saturday, November 8

**OFFICIAL GOING: Soft (heavy in places) changing to heavy after race 2 (12:40)**
Wind: Moderate half against Weather: Heavy cloud and rain

## 7712 BETFRED MOBILE COCK O'THE NORTH EBF MAIDEN STKS (DIV I) 6f
**12:10** (12:13) (Class 5) 2-Y-0 **£5,175** (£1,540; £769; £384) **Stalls** High

Form RPR

02 **1** **Stake Acclaim (IRE)**[43] 6702 2-9-5 0.......................... RobertWinston 9 80
(Dean Ivory) *trckd ldr: led over 1f out: drvn clr* **6/4**[1]

65 **2** *3 ¼* **Bapak Asmara (IRE)**[18] 7361 2-9-5 0........................ JamieSpencer 8 72
(Kevin Ryan) *led: hdd over 1f out: kpt on same pce* **14/1**

**3** *1 ¾* **What Could She Be (IRE)** 2-9-0 0.............................. PaulMulrennan 1 60+
(Bryan Smart) *chsd ldrs: kpt on same pce over 1f out* **10/1**

**4** *nk* **Sacred Bond** 2-9-0 0...................................................... TonyHamilton 2 59+
(Richard Fahey) *chsd ldrs: kpt on same pce over 1f out* **6/1**[3]

**5** *6* **Wisteria** 2-9-0 0............................................................. LiamJones 10 41
(David C Griffiths) *dwlt: read-div: hdwy over 2f out: fdd fnl f* **100/1**

**6** *1* **Racing Angel (IRE)** 2-9-0 0.......................................... PhillipMakin 5 38
(John Quinn) *trckd ldrs: t.k.h: wknd appr fnl f* **14/1**

02 **7** *4 ½* **Regal Missile (IRE)**[19] 7329 2-9-5 0.............................. JasonHart 14 30
(Mark Walford) *chsd ldrs: drvn over 2f out: sn wknd* **7/2**[2]

**8** *4* **Invectus Hero** 2-9-5 0..................................................... DaleSwift 6 18
(Derek Shaw) *solwy into stride: hld up in rr: hdwy 3f out: hung rt and wknd over 1f out* **33/1**

0 **9** *¾* **Dazzling Display**[4] 7637 2-8-11 0........................ JacobButterfield(3) 7 10
(Richard Guest) *dwlt: in rr: sme hdwy 3f out: sn wknd* **100/1**

60 **10** *nk* **Kyllach Me (IRE)**[4] 7638 2-9-5 0.................................. JoeFanning 3 14
(Bryan Smart) *prom: drvn over 2f out: sn wknd* **40/1**

5 **11** *nse* **Outlaw Kate (IRE)**[12] 7493 2-9-0 0.............................. RobertTart 4 9
(Michael Mullineaux) *chsd ldrs: wknd 2f out* **66/1**

0 **12** *hd* **Glorious Dancer**[19] 7329 2-9-5 0.............................. AntonioFresu 11 14
(Ed Walker) *dwlt: in rr: drvn 3f out: sn bhd* **20/1**

1m 19.35s (5.75) **Going Correction** +0.875s/f (Soft) **12** Ran SP% **112.5**
Speed ratings (Par 96): **96,91,89,88,80 79,73,68,67,66 66,66**
CSF £22.56 TOTE £2.10: £1.10, £3.70, £3.40; EX 21.80 Trifecta £180.50.
**Owner** M J Yarrow **Bred** G Devlin **Trained** Radlett, Herts

**FOCUS**
After riding in the opener, jockeys all agreed the ground was heavy. The opening time was 8.85sec slower than standard, and 0.59sec slower than the second division. A modest maiden in which the first two had drawn clear before the furlong pole.

## 7713 BETFRED MOBILE COCK O'THE NORTH EBF MAIDEN STKS (DIV II) 6f
**12:40** (12:42) (Class 5) 2-Y-0 **£5,175** (£1,540; £769; £384) **Stalls** High

Form RPR

2 **1** **Mobsta (IRE)**[15] 7412 2-9-5 0........................................ CharlesBishop 9 86+
(Mick Channon) *cl up: led wl over 1f out: rdn clr jst over 1f out: edgd rt fnl f: styd on* **6/4**[1]

**2** *3 ¼* **Beardwood** 2-9-5 0......................................................... TonyHamilton 6 75+
(Richard Fahey) *wnt lft s: green and hld up in rr: hdwy 3f out: chsd ldrs 2f out: rdn and kpt on wl fnl f* **14/1**

3 **3** *4 ½* **Thahab (IRE)**[15] 7407 2-9-5 0....................................... FrankieDettori 12 62
(Richard Hannon) *racd nr stands' rail: sn led: jnd over 2f out and sn pushed along: hdd and rdn wl over 1f out: kpt on same pce* **13/8**[2]

F **4** *2 ¾* **Go Grazeon**[21] 7278 2-9-0 0....................................... PhillipMakin 10 49
(John Quinn) *chsd ldng pair: rdn along over 2f out: sn one pce* **66/1**

30 **5** *5* **Monsieur Valentine**[9] 7542 2-9-5 0............................... LukeMorris 7 39
(Tony Carroll) *towards rr: rdn along bef 1/2-way: kpt on u.p fr over 2f out: nvr nr ldrs* **66/1**

4 **6** *1* **Green Tornado (IRE)**[15] 7412 2-9-5 0............................. PatSmullen 11 36
(Ralph Beckett) *chsd ldrs: rdn along over 2f out: sn wknd* **7/1**[3]

**7** *1 ½* **Cooper** 2-9-5 0................................................................ TomEaves 1 31
(Kevin Ryan) *dwlt: sn in tch on outer: rdn along 1/2-way and sn btn* **20/1**

56 **8** *hd* **Captain Future**[21] 7277 2-9-5 0.................................. PaulMulrennan 4 30
(Bryan Smart) *chsd ldrs: rdn along 3f out: sn btn* **66/1**

**9** *2* **Best Boy** 2-9-5 0........................................................... AndrewElliott 2 24
(David C Griffiths) *dwlt: towards rr and a edging lft: bhd fr 1/2-way* **50/1**

0 **10** *4 ½* **Ben Muir**[17] 7380 2-9-5 0............................................... SteveDrowne 3 11
(Stuart Williams) *in tch towards outer: rdn along 1/2-way: sn wknd* **66/1**

**11** *5* **Gerrard's Slip** 2-9-0 0............................................ AdamCarter(5) 13
(Bryan Smart) *dwlt: a towards rr* **20/1**

0 **12** *4 ½* **Isntshesomething**[15] 7407 2-8-11 0....................... JacobButterfield(3) 8
(Richard Guest) *midfield: rdn along 1/2-way: sn outpcd and bhd* **100/1**

0 **13** *4 ½* **Forest Missile (IRE)**[29] 7082 2-9-5 0............................. RaulDaSilva 5
(John Wainwright) *in tch: rdn along and lost pl bef 1/2-way: bhd whn swtchd lft to outer and rdn 3f out: nvr a factor* **66/1**

1m 18.73s (5.13) **Going Correction** +0.875s/f (Soft) **13** Ran SP% **117.2**
Speed ratings (Par 96): **100,95,89,86,79 78,76,75,73,67 60,54,48**
CSF £21.25 TOTE £2.40: £1.10, £3.10, £1.10; EX 22.90 Trifecta £47.80.
**Owner** Billy Parish **Bred** P J Gleeson **Trained** West Ilsley, Berks

**FOCUS**
This looked the stronger of the two divisions on paper and that impression was backed up by the time, which was 0.62secs faster than the first race. The ground was officially changed to heavy following this race.

## 7714 BETFRED "RACING'S BIGGEST SUPPORTER" NURSERY H'CAP (BOBIS RACE) 6f
**1:15** (1:15) (Class 4) (0-85,78) 2-Y-0 **£5,175** (£1,540; £769; £384) **Stalls** High

Form RPR

321 **1** **Anonymous John (IRE)**[19] 7336 2-9-3 74.................... DavidProbert 3 89+
(David Evans) *trckd ldrs: smooth hdwy over 2f out: sn led: shkn up and wnt wl clr appr fnl f* **13/8**[1]

1103 **2** *10* **Johnny B Goode (IRE)**[8] 7571 2-9-2 78................... JackGarritty(5) 4 63
(Richard Fahey) *led 1f: w ldr: led briefly over 2f out: kpt on same pce* **5/2**[2]

0562 **3** *8* **Granola**[11] 7515 2-8-0 57 oh1........................................ JamesSullivan 6 18
(David Brown) *sn outpcd in last: kpt on to take poor 3rd last 100yds: nvr on terms* **9/1**

262 **4** *3* **Crosse Fire**[4] 7649 2-8-13 70..........................................(p) LukeMorris 1 22
(Scott Dixon) *chsd ldrs: wknd fnl f* **4/1**[3]

5210 **5** *9* **Straightothepoint**[23] 7224 2-9-2 73..........................(v) PaulMulrennan 2
(Bryan Smart) *led after 1f: hdd over 2f out: wknd over 1f out* **7/1**

1m 19.02s (5.42) **Going Correction** +0.875s/f (Soft) **5** Ran SP% **109.2**
Speed ratings (Par 98): **98,84,74,70,58**
CSF £5.81 TOTE £2.40: £1.40, £1.40; EX 5.60 Trifecta £21.60.
**Owner** Will Dawson **Bred** Tally-Ho Stud **Trained** Pandy, Monmouths

**FOCUS**
The ground description was changed to heavy before this race. They came home at wide margins in this uncompetitive nursery, and it may pay not to take the form too literally for all that the winner impressed.

## 7715 BETFRED SUPPORTING JACK BERRY HOUSE H'CAP 7f
**1:50** (1:51) (Class 2) (0-105,104) 3-Y-0+ **£12,938** (£3,850; £1,924; £962) **Stalls** High

Form RPR

0554 **1** **Levitate**[21] 7276 6-9-1 95..........................................(v) MartinHarley 3 106
(John Quinn) *prom: hdwy wl over 2f out: chal wl over 1f out: led appr fnl f: sn rdn clr and styd on strly* **4/1**[1]

2021 **2** *3* **Lulu The Zulu (IRE)**[14] 7444 6-9-1 98........................ RyanTate(3) 7 101+
(Michael Appleby) *wnt lft s: prom: led over 3f out: rdn wl over 1f out: hdd appr fnl f: sn drvn and kpt on same pce* **7/1**[3]

4050 **3** *1* **King Torus (IRE)**[42] 6755 6-8-8 88............................... SamJames 1 89
(David O'Meara) *towards rr: pushed along over 3f out: sn swtchd lft to outer: rdn to chse ldrs wl over 1f out: drvn and edgd rt ent fnl f: kpt on* **33/1**

2326 **4** *2 ¼* **Athletic**[9] 7555 5-8-10 95......................................(v) JennyPowell(5) 13 90+
(Andrew Reid) *trckd ldrs: smooth hdwy over 2f out: rdn wl over 1f out and ev ch: sn drvn and one pce appr fnl f* **12/1**

5100 **5** *nse* **Roachdale House (IRE)**[84] 5410 3-8-8 89.................. TonyHamilton 4 83
(Richard Fahey) *in tch: hdwy wl over 2f out: sn chsng ldrs: rdn wl over 1f out: sn no imp* **16/1**

4030 **6** *1 ¾* **Farlow (IRE)**[21] 7276 6-8-2 87...........................(b[1]) JackGarritty(5) 11 77
(Richard Fahey) *slt ld: pushed along 1/2-way: sn hdd and rdn: drvn and edgd lft 2f out: sn wknd* **12/1**

410 **7** *4 ½* **Doc Hay (USA)**[14] 7441 7-8-11 91............................... DanielTudhope 15 69
(David O'Meara) *racd towards stands' rail: hld up in rr: hdwy over 2f out: rdn to chse ldrs over 1f out: sn drvn and n.d* **25/1**

2631 **8** *¾* **Withernsea (IRE)**[14] 7438 3-8-6 87............................. AndreaAtzeni 6 62
(Richard Fahey) *hmpd s: a towards rr* **11/2**[2]

0501 **9** *hd* **Dream Walker (FR)**[7] 7597 5-8-11 91..........................(t) DaleSwift 2 67
(Brian Ellison) *chsd ldrs: rdn along wl over 2f out: sn wknd* **12/1**

0440 **10** *1 ¼* **Sirius Prospect (USA)**[21] 7276 6-9-10 104............... RobertWinston 14 77
(Dean Ivory) *hld up towards rr: sme hdwy over 2f out: swtchd lft and rdn wl over 1f out: n.d* **10/1**

3431 **11** *4 1/2* **Jamaican Bolt (IRE)**[15] 7408 6-9-1 95 ........ WilliamBuick 8 56
(Geoffrey Oldroyd) *hmpd s: in tch: pushed along and sme hdwy wl over 2f out: rdn wl over 1f out: sn btn* **8/1**

2-66 **12** *12* **Modern Tutor**[25] 7168 5-8-12 92 ........ DavidProbert 16 22
(Andrew Balding) *racd towards stands' rail: prom: pushed along 1/2-way: sn rdn and wknd* **16/1**

313- **13** *2 3/4* **Voice Of A Leader (IRE)**[421] 6351 3-9-2 97 ........ JimCrowley 5 19
(Peter Chapple-Hyam) *wnt rt s: hld up in rr: rdn along over 2f out: sn bhd* **25/1**

4161 **14** *16* **Accession (IRE)**[42] 6755 5-8-11 91 ........ MartinLane 9
(Charlie Fellowes) *trckd ldrs: pushed along over 3f out: rdn wl over 2f out: sn wknd* **14/1**

1m 33.42s (7.12) **Going Correction** +1.275s/f (Soft)
**WFA** 3 from 5yo+ 1lb **14** Ran SP% **120.2**
Speed ratings (Par 109): **110,106,105,102,102 100,95,94,94,93 88,74,71,52**
CSF £30.06 CT £824.39 TOTE £4.70: £1.90, £2.60, £8.90; EX 31.40 Trifecta £1070.70.
**Owner** Charles Wentworth **Bred** Cheveley Park Stud Ltd **Trained** Settrington, N Yorks

**FOCUS**
Two proven soft-ground performers came to the fore in what was a useful handicap. A similar effort from Levitate as when winning this last year.

## 7716 BETFRED "GOALS GALORE" WENTWORTH STKS (LISTED RACE) 6f
**2:25** (2:27) (Class 1) 3-Y-O+ **£26,116** (£9,896; £4,945; £2,470) **Stalls** High

Form RPR
0130 **1** **Aetna**[28] 7122 4-8-12 99 ........ GrahamGibbons 9 111
(Michael Easterby) *trckd ldrs centre: led 1f out: styd on wl* **8/1**

0005 **2** *2 3/4* **Lancelot Du Lac (ITY)**[14] 7441 4-9-3 99 ........ JimCrowley 2 108
(Dean Ivory) *edgd lft after 1f: led 2 on far side: led overall over 3f out: hdd 1f out: styd on same pce* **14/1**

2211 **3** *1 1/2* **Spinatrix**[28] 7122 6-8-12 110 ........(p) ConnorBeasley 3 98
(Michael Dods) *racd centre: w ldrs: kpt on same pce fnl f* **4/1**[2]

0003 **4** *nk* **Jack Dexter**[21] 7272 5-9-3 110 ........ GrahamLee 10 102+
(Jim Goldie) *swtchd rt after s: chsd ldrs stands' side: edgd lft and kpt on same pce fnl f* **15/8**[1]

1042 **5** *6* **Tropics (USA)**[21] 7272 6-9-6 115 ........ RobertWinston 7 87
(Dean Ivory) *edgd lft after 1f: trckd ldrs far side: wknd fnl f* **9/2**[3]

2001 **6** *8* **Inyordreams**[35] 6929 3-9-1 100 ........ FrankieDettori 12 58+
(James Given) *overall ldr stands' side: hdd over 3f out: wknd over 1f out* **20/1**

4211 **7** *4 1/2* **Dungannon**[14] 7441 7-9-3 102 ........(b) JimmyFortune 8 47
(Andrew Balding) *chsd ldrs centre: wknd and eased appr fnl f* **8/1**

1015 **8** *16* **Katawi**[33] 6994 3-8-12 97 ........ TedDurcan 11
(Chris Wall) *hld up in rr stands' side: drvn over 2f out: sn wl bhd: eased: t.o* **20/1**

5105 **9** *29* **Pearl Blue (IRE)**[29] 7080 6-8-12 94 ........ AshleyMorgan 13
(Chris Wall) *chsd ldrs stands' side: wknd 2f out: sn wl bhd and eased: tailed rt off* **33/1**

2210 **10** *7* **Cordial**[44] 6689 3-8-12 83 ........ AndreaAtzeni 1
(Stuart Williams) *edgd rt after s: trckd ldrs centre: lost pl 2f out: eased whn wl bhd: tailed rt off* **66/1**

4540 **P** **Links Drive Lady**[9] 7543 6-8-12 87 ........ WilliamBuick 5
(Dean Ivory) *edgd lft after 1f: chsd ldr frar side: wknd rapidly appr fnl f: heavily eased: t.o whn p.u last 50yds* **50/1**

1m 19.12s (5.52) **Going Correction** +1.275s/f (Soft) **11** Ran SP% **117.8**
Speed ratings: **114,110,108,107,99 89,83,61,23,13**
CSF £104.48 TOTE £11.80: £2.40, £4.30, £1.80; EX 119.00 Trifecta £910.30.
**Owner** B Padgett **Bred** Bearstone Stud **Trained** Sheriff Hutton, N Yorks

**FOCUS**
A decent Listed event, but with the ground continuing to deteriorate, conditions clearly paid a major part. The field soon split into three distinct groups, with the winner coming down the middle. Only the first two showed their form.

## 7717 BETFRED TV EBF STALLIONS BREEDING WINNERS GILLIES FILLIES' STKS (LISTED RACE) 1m 2f 60y
**3:00** (3:00) (Class 1) 3-Y-O+ **£26,048** (£9,851; £4,923; £2,459) **Stalls** Low

Form RPR
4021 **1** **Lady Tiana**[24] 7211 3-8-12 94 ........ GrahamLee 5 107
(Lucy Wadham) *trckd ldrs: smooth hdwy 2f out: chal on bit over 1f out: led ent fnl f: pushed out* **4/1**[2]

3024 **2** *1* **Princess Loulou (IRE)**[30] 7070 4-9-2 110 ........ AndreaAtzeni 3 104
(Roger Varian) *trckd ldrs on inner: effrt over 2f out: sn pushed along effrt and n.m.r over 1f out: sn swtchd rt and rdn: styd on to chse wnr ins fnl f: no imp towards fin* **9/4**[1]

1134 **3** *1 1/2* **Merry Me (IRE)**[41] 6785 3-8-12 85 ........ JimCrowley 8 101
(Andrew Balding) *sn trcking ldr: hdwy and cl up 3f out: led on bit wl over 1f out: sn jnd and shkn up: rdn and hdd ent fnl f: kpt on same pce* **16/1**

1220 **4** *3 1/4* **Raskova (USA)**[52] 6464 4-9-2 95 ........ JoeFanning 11 95
(William Jarvis) *hld up: hdwy 4f out: rdn over 2f out: sn chsng ldrs: drvn and kpt on same pce fnl f* **25/1**

1210 **5** *5* **Melrose Abbey (IRE)**[58] 6255 3-8-12 89 ........ RichardHughes 10 86
(Ralph Beckett) *hld up in rr: hdwy on wd outside 3f out: rdn along 2f out: sn drvn and no imp* **7/1**[3]

62-4 **6** *4 1/2* **La Banderilla (FR)**[28] 7105 4-9-2 95 ........ WilliamBuick 1 78
(John Gosden) *midfield: hdwy on inner 4f out: rdn along over 2f out: sn drvn and n.d* **4/1**[2]

0150 **7** *nk* **Audacia (IRE)**[22] 7243 4-9-5 100 ........ DanielTudhope 6 80
(Hugo Palmer) *led: rdn along and jnd wl over 2f out: drvn 2f out: sn hdd & wknd* **14/1**

00 **8** *14* **Kallisha**[28] 7105 3-8-12 90 ........(p) GrahamGibbons 2 52
(Ralph Beckett) *reminders s: a towards rr* **16/1**

4210 **9** *1 3/4* **Toast Of The Town (IRE)**[28] 7105 4-9-2 93 ........(p) RobertHavlin 9 49
(John Gosden) *a towards rr* **25/1**

5410 **10** *8* **Placidia (IRE)**[28] 7105 3-8-12 87 ........ PatSmullen 4 35
(David Lanigan) *hld up towards rr: hdwy 4f out: rdn along wl over 2f out: sn btn* **20/1**

-301 **11** *38* **Acclio (IRE)**[4] 7640 3-8-12 75 ........ RobertWinston 7
(Clive Brittain) *trckd ldrs: hdwy on outer 5f out: rdn along over 3f out: sn wknd* **33/1**

2m 26.46s (17.06) **Going Correction** +1.375s/f (Soft)
**WFA** 3 from 4yo 4lb **11** Ran SP% **117.1**
Speed ratings: **86,85,84,81,77 73,73,62,60,54 24**
CSF £12.62 TOTE £4.20: £1.80, £1.60, £3.50; EX 14.50 Trifecta £176.50.
**Owner** The FOPS **Bred** Mr & Mrs A E Pakenham **Trained** Newmarket, Suffolk

**FOCUS**
Not a terribly strong Listed event, but it was won by a thoroughly progressive filly. The form is not entirely convincing.

## 7718 BETFRED NOVEMBER H'CAP 1m 4f
**3:35** (3:37) (Class 2) 3-Y-O+
**£43,575** (£13,048; £6,524; £3,262; £1,631; £819) **Stalls** Low

Form RPR
5141 **1** **Open Eagle (IRE)**[4] 7641 5-8-12 90 4ex ........ DanielTudhope 18 106
(David O'Meara) *sn taken v wd and racd lone: trckd ldrs: led on bit over 2f out: sn clr: easily* **15/2**[1]

1033 **2** *12* **Aramist (IRE)**[29] 7083 4-8-12 90 ........ RobertWinston 21 89
(Alan Swinbank) *chsd ldrs: styd on to take modest 2nd last 150yds* **20/1**

4452 **3** *1* **Dashing Star**[14] 7440 4-9-6 98 ........ JamieSpencer 11 96
(David Elsworth) *led: hdd over 2f out: kpt on same pce* **14/1**

3030 **4** *1 1/4* **Communicator**[28] 7107 6-9-0 92 ........ DavidProbert 22 88
(Andrew Balding) *in rr: hdwy over 3f out: kpt on same pce fnl 2f* **25/1**

5331 **5** *7* **Dark Ruler (IRE)**[19] 7334 5-8-10 88 ........ JoeFanning 3 74
(Alan Swinbank) *chsd ldrs: drvn over 3f out: one pce* **20/1**

0553 **6** *1 1/4* **Ardlui (IRE)**[15] 7409 6-8-13 91 ........(b) DavidAllan 23 76
(Tim Easterby) *chsd ldrs on outer: hdwy over 3f out: one pce* **20/1**

0300 **7** *7* **First Mohican**[141] 3416 6-9-7 102 ........(p) LouisSteward(3) 16 77
(Alan King) *chsd ldrs: effrt 3f out: fdd over 1f out* **16/1**

4110 **8** *1* **Rhombus (IRE)**[28] 7107 4-9-6 98 ........ MartinHarley 14 71
(Ismail Mohammed) *in rr: hdwy 3f out: nvr nr ldrs* **25/1**

1201 **9** *9* **Old Town Boy**[29] 7083 3-8-11 95 ........ JimCrowley 1 56
(Philip McBride) *chsd ldrs: drvn over 3f out: lost pl over 2f out: eased over 1f out* **11/1**[3]

2341 **10** *1 3/4* **Headline News (IRE)**[8] 7565 5-8-6 89 ........ JackGarritty(5) 15 47
(Rae Guest) *in rr: swtchd rt after 1f: sme hdwy 4f out: wknd over 2f out* **11/1**[3]

1001 **11** *26* **Latenightrequest**[14] 7440 3-8-12 96 ........ TonyHamilton 9 18
(Richard Fahey) *in rr: hdwy 4f out: in tch over 2f out: wknd over 1f out* **12/1**

6401 **12** *7* **Eurystheus (IRE)**[8] 7567 5-8-5 88 ........(p) AlistairRawlinson(5) 2
(Michael Appleby) *mid-div: effrt over 4f out: wknd 3f out* **33/1**

1331 **13** *2 3/4* **Mount Logan (IRE)**[56] 6330 3-9-5 103 ........ AndreaAtzeni 13 11
(Luca Cumani) *in rr: sme hdwy over 2f out: nvr a factor* **10/1**[2]

54 **14** *13* **Esteaming**[29] 7083 4-9-1 93 ........ GrahamGibbons 20
(David Barron) *mid-div: drvn 4f out: sn btn* **16/1**

**15** *1 1/4* **Manhattan Swing (IRE)**[28] 2189 4-9-1 93 ........ DaleSwift 19
(Brian Ellison) *mid-div: sn drvn along: nvr a factor* **14/1**

01 **16** *1 3/4* **Farquhar (IRE)**[28] 7106 3-8-13 97 ........ LukeMorris 5
(Peter Chapple-Hyam) *dwlt: hld up in mid-div: lost pl over 3f out* **12/1**

434 **17** *15* **Odeon**[36] 6894 3-9-3 101 ........ GrahamLee 7
(James Given) *trckd ldrs: t.k.h: drvn 4f out: sn lost pl: t.o* **20/1**

1164 **18** *4 1/2* **Treasure The Ridge (IRE)**[35] 6930 5-8-11 92 ........(b) DannyBrock(3) 4
(Andrew Reid) *chsd ldrs: lost pl over 3f out: t.o* **33/1**

-60 **19** *9* **Plutocracy (IRE)**[21] 7289 4-9-0 92 ........(p) PatSmullen 12
(David Lanigan) *chsd ldrs: lost pl over 4f out: sn bhd: t.o* **12/1**

2221 **20** *8* **One Pekan (IRE)**[75] 5757 4-8-10 88 ........ JackMitchell 17
(Roger Varian) *in rr: bhd and reminders 5f out: t.o* **20/1**

4016 **21** *13* **Ennistown**[14] 7449 4-9-10 102 ........ WilliamBuick 6
(Charlie Appleby) *hld up in rr: bhd whn eased over 3f out: t.o* **33/1**

1040 **22** *68* **Kings Bayonet**[29] 7083 7-8-9 87 ........ HayleyTurner 8
(Alan King) *hld up in rr: bhd 4f out: sn t.o and virtually p.u: tailed rt off* **33/1**

6006 **P** **Sir Walter Scott (IRE)**[42] 6747 4-9-5 97 ........(b) RichardHughes 10
(Luca Cumani) *in tch: lost pl over 6f out: bhd and heavily eased over 5f out: tailed rt off and p.u over 2f out* **25/1**

2m 48.22s (13.32) **Going Correction** +1.375s/f (Soft)
**WFA** 3 from 4yo+ 6lb **23** Ran SP% **132.8**
Speed ratings (Par 109): **110,102,101,100,95 95,90,89,83,82 65,60,58,50,49 48,38,35,29,23 15,,**
CSF £156.91 CT £2078.41 TOTE £7.40: £2.50, £6.40, £3.90, £5.80; EX 236.00 Trifecta £5503.20.
**Owner** Middleham Park Racing LXXIV & Partner **Bred** F Bayrou **Trained** Nawton, N Yorks

**FOCUS**
The 50th running of the race since it was switched from Manchester, although that total includes one edition apiece at Thirsk and Windsor. It looked typically open, but few got into it in the desperate ground. The majority of the field came down the middle in the home straight. The level of the form is pitched around the easy winner.

## 7719 BETFRED BINGO APPRENTICE H'CAP 7f
**4:05** (4:09) (Class 3) (0-90,92) 3-Y-O+ **£16,172** (£4,812; £2,405; £1,202) **Stalls** High

Form RPR
0503 **1** **Mujazif (IRE)**[11] 7507 4-9-2 84 ........ JacobButterfield 1 95
(David Nicholls) *racd wd on far side: chsd ldrs: hdwy to ld 3f out: rdn clr wl over 1f out: rdr dropped whip last 100yds: styd on strly* **10/1**[3]

2014 **2** *2 3/4* **Shouranour (IRE)**[29] 7085 4-8-10 85 ........(p) JoshDoyle(7) 17 89+
(David O'Meara) *in tch towards stands' rail: hdwy wl over 2f out: rdn wl over 1f out: styd on to chse wnr ent fnl f: sn drvn: edgd lft and no imp* **10/1**[3]

4351 **3** *2 1/2* **Zacynthus (IRE)**[29] 7085 6-9-1 83 ........ WilliamTwiston-Davies 5 80
(Shaun Harris) *racd towards far side: in tch: hdwy over 2f out: sn rdn and styd on fnl f* **20/1**

5250 **4** *shd* **Kiwi Bay**[35] 6936 9-9-4 86 ........ ConnorBeasley 2 83
(Michael Dods) *racd towards far side: chsd ldrs: hdwy 3f out: rdn wl over 1f out: drvn and kpt on same pce fnl f* **33/1**

2231 **5** *1/2* **Evanescent (IRE)**[11] 7507 5-9-0 85 ........ JoeDoyle(3) 21 81
(John Quinn) *trckd ldrs towards stands' side: pushed along over 2f out: rdn wl over 1f out: kpt on same pce appr fnl f* **14/1**

0066 **6** *3/4* **Victoire De Lyphar (IRE)**[11] 7507 7-8-13 84 ........(e) KevinStott(3) 10 78
(Ruth Carr) *rrd s and s.i.s: bhd and rdn along towards far side 3f out: hdwy on wd outside wl over 1f out: kpt on fnl f: nrst fin* **20/1**

1634 **7** *1/2* **Instant Attraction (IRE)**[14] 7438 3-8-10 84 ........ MeganCarberry(5) 7 76
(Jedd O'Keeffe) *in tch centre: rdn along and hdwy 2f out: sn drvn and no imp fnl f* **25/1**

3531 **8** *3/4* **Maggie Pink**[7] 7600 5-9-5 92 ........ AlistairRawlinson(5) 13 83
(Michael Appleby) *racd centre: led: hdd 3f out and sn pushed along: rdn 2f out and grad wknd* **10/1**[3]

661 **9** *3/4* **Personal Touch**[7] 7601 5-8-11 82 ........ JackGarritty(3) 4 71
(Richard Fahey) *chsd ldrs centre: rdn along over 2f out: grad wknd* **9/1**[2]

2150 **10** *1 1/2* **Sophisticated Heir (IRE)**[26] 7125 4-8-13 81 ........(p) LouisSteward 8 66
(David O'Meara) *towards rr: sme hdwy wl over 2f out: sn rdn and n.d* **20/1**

0046 **11** *1 ½* **Green Howard**[14] 7455 6-9-8 90............................................ NeilFarley 6 71
(Robin Bastiman) *in tch: rdn along wl over 2f out: sn no hdwy* **50/1**

3-21 **12** *3 ¼* **Melvin The Grate (IRE)**[22] 7236 4-8-10 83.......... KieranShoemark(5) 15 55
(Andrew Balding) *towards rr centre tl rdn and plugged on fnl 2f: nvr a factor* **4/1**[1]

0400 **13** *4* **Uncle Dermot (IRE)**[7] 7597 6-8-12 85...................... JennyPowell(5) 14 47
(Brendan Powell) *chsd ldrs centre: rdn along 3f out: sn wknd* **33/1**

2235 **14** *1 ¼* **Mishaal (IRE)**[50] 6511 4-8-13 81...................................... JoeyHaynes 3 40
(Michael Herrington) *racd towards far side: prom: rdn along wl over 2f out: sn wknd* **20/1**

3004 **15** *nk* **Pastoral Player**[7] 7597 7-9-1 88................................ DavidParkes(5) 12 46
(Hughie Morrison) *rrd s and s.i.s: a bhd* **12/1**

1400 **16** *12* **Music In The Rain (IRE)**[12] 7490 6-9-6 88.................... SamJames 18 15
(David O'Meara) *a towards rr* **25/1**

0020 **17** *3 ½* **Ready (IRE)**[11] 7507 4-9-1 83.......................................(p) JasonHart 19 1
(Garry Moss) *racd nr stands' rail: chsd ldrs to 1/2-way: sn wknd* **33/1**

6100 **18** *shd* **Our Boy Jack (IRE)**[12] 7490 5-9-6 88............... GeorgeChaloner 11 5
(Richard Fahey) *a towards rr* **12/1**

0000 **19** *1* **Norse Blues**[10] 7538 6-8-3 78................................... PaulMcGiff(7) 16
(David Barron) *racd towards centre: a in rr* **25/1**

1412 **20** *14* **Comino (IRE)**[11] 7507 3-9-0 86...................................... ShaneGray(3) 20
(Kevin Ryan) *chsd ldrs towards stands' rail: rdn along 1/2-way: sn wknd and eased fr wl over 1f out* **12/1**

5004 **21** *31* **Fieldgunner Kirkup (GER)**[11] 7507 6-8-12 80.......... CharlesBishop 22
(David Barron) *racd nr stands' rail: chsd ldrs: rdn along 3f out: sn wknd: bhd and eased wl over 1f out* **25/1**

1m 34.56s (8.26) **Going Correction** +1.375s/f (Soft)
**WFA** 3 from 4yo+ 1lb **21** Ran SP% **132.2**
Speed ratings (Par 107): **107,103,101,100,100 99,98,98,97,95 93,90,85,84,83 69,65,65,64,48 13**
CSF £91.96 CT £2018.43 TOTE £13.40: £3.60, £3.60, £4.80, £7.40; EX 217.20 Trifecta £1102.30.
**Owner** George D Taylor **Bred** Wardstown Stud Ltd **Trained** Sessay, N Yorks

**FOCUS**
What had looked a competitive handicap was won in commanding style. The winner was close to his old best.
T/Jkpt: £8,718.90 to a £1 stake. Pool: £30,700.44 - 2.50 winning tickets T/Plt: £29.00 to a £1 stake. Pool: £156,447.12 - 3,932.69 winning tickets T/Qpdt: £17.50 to a £1 stake. Pool: £12,649.67 - 531.97 winning tickets JR

# 7557 SAINT-CLOUD (L-H)
## Saturday, November 8

**OFFICIAL GOING: Turf: heavy**

## 7720a PRIX SOLITUDE (LISTED RACE) (3YO FILLIES) (TURF) 1m 2f
**1:00** (12:00) 3-Y-O **£22,916** (£9,166; £6,875; £4,583; £2,291)

RPR

**1** **Secret Pursuit (IRE)**[143] 3357 3-8-11 0............................. ThierryJarnet 10 106
(Marcus Tregoning) *pressed ldr on outer: c stands' side st: shkn up to ld under 2f out: drvn clr fnl f: comf* **241/10**

**2** *2 ½* **Sahrawi (GER)**[54] 6419 3-8-13 0 ow2.............................. OlivierPeslier 9 103
(M Delzangles, France) **7/2**[1]

**3** *½* **Great Virtues (IRE)**[160] 2816 3-8-11 0........................ MaximeGuyon 6 100
(A Fabre, France) **123/10**

**4** *2 ½* **Graceful Grit (IRE)**[20] 7319 3-8-11 0........................ AntoineHamelin 1 95
(F-H Graffard, France) **57/10**

**5** *snk* **La Gohanniere (FR)**[32] 3-8-11 0................................ GregoryBenoist 4 95
(F Rohaut, France) **126/10**

**6** *nk* **Petits Potins (IRE)**[20] 7319 3-8-11 0....................... MickaelBarzalona 7 94
(Rod Collet, France) **164/10**

**7** *2* **Mandalaya (USA)**[26] 3-8-13 0 ow2.......................... ChristopheSoumillon 8 92
(A De Royer-Dupre, France) **49/10**[2]

**8** *4 ½* **Laseen (IRE)**[11] 3-8-11 0.............................................(p) ThierryThulliez 3 81
(N Clement, France) **51/10**[3]

**9** *½* **Green Speed (FR)**[10] 3-8-11 0.......................................(p) AlexisBadel 11 80
(Mme M Bollack-Badel, France) **147/10**

**10** *2 ½* **No Wind No Rain**[20] 7319 3-8-11 0......................... StephanePasquier 5 75
(Yves de Nicolay, France) **97/10**

**11** *6* **Bereni Ka (FR)**[20] 7319 3-9-2 0................................ IoritzMendizabal 2 68
(L Tassart, France) **111/10**

2m 16.16s (0.16) **11** Ran SP% **119.1**
WIN (incl. 1 euro stake): 25.10. PLACES: 5.90, 1.80, 4.30. DF: 42.30. SF: 166.70.
**Owner** Guy Brook **Bred** Petra Bloodstock Agency Ltd **Trained** Whitsbury, Hants

## 7721a CRITERIUM DE SAINT-CLOUD (GROUP 1) (2YO COLTS & FILLIES) (TURF) 1m 2f
**1:30** (12:00) 2-Y-O **£119,041** (£47,625; £23,812; £11,895; £5,958)

RPR

**1** **Epicuris**[20] 7317 2-9-0 0........................................... ThierryThulliez 3 112
(Mme C Head-Maarek, France) *mde all: led field over to stands' side in st: shkn up and responded 2f out: reminder over 1f out: drvn clr fnl f: comf* **10/11**[1]

**2** *2 ½* **Palang (USA)**[27] 2-9-0 0........................................... CristianDemuro 2 107
(Andreas Lowe, Germany) *hld up towards rr: shkn up and prog under 2 1/2f out: rdn to chse ldr fr 1 1/2f out: kpt on u.p fnl f: no match for wnr* **14/1**

**3** *hd* **Big Blue**[20] 7317 2-9-0 0........................................ MickaelBarzalona 4 107
(A Fabre, France) *trckd ldr: 3rd and shkn up 2 1/2f out: rdn and nt qckn 1 1/2f out: kpt on at same pce fnl f* **11/2**

**4** *2* **Crafty Choice**[17] 7383 2-9-0 0............................. ChristopheSoumillon 6 103
(Richard Hannon) *cl up on outer: 2nd and rdn on stands' rail over 2f out: grad lft bhd by ldrs fr over 1f out* **5/1**[3]

**5** *3* **Capo Maximo**[20] 7317 2-9-0 0................................ StephanePasquier 5 98
(Yves de Nicolay, France) *in rr: clsd up fr 1/2-way: rdn to chse ldrs 3f out: sn outpcd and dropped to rr: plugged on fnl f* **33/1**

**6** *3* **Clonard Street**[41] 6800 2-9-0 0...................................... FMBerry 1 93
(A J Martin, Ire) *hld up towards rr but in tch: cl 4th and pushed along 2f out: rdn and no imp over 1 1/2f out: wknd fnl f* **9/2**[2]

2m 17.41s (1.41) **6** Ran SP% **112.2**
Win (incl. 1 euro stake): 1.90. PLACES: 1.40, 3.40. SF: 15.00.
**Owner** K Abdullah **Bred** Juddmonte Farms Ltd **Trained** Chantilly, France

**FOCUS**
Not a strong race for the level, but a classy winner. The form is rated in line with the ten-year average.

## 7722a PRIX DE GRISY (H'CAP) (3YO FILLIES) (TURF) 7f
**3:10** (12:00) 3-Y-O **£12,500** (£5,000; £3,750; £2,500; £1,250)

RPR

**1** **Graciously**[54] 3-9-2 0.......................................... VincentCheminaud(3) 11 90
(A De Royer-Dupre, France) **15/2**

**2** *1 ¼* **Irradiance (IRE)**[55] 3-8-13 0................................ MickaelBarzalona 2 81
(H-A Pantall, France) **45/1**

**3** *1 ¾* **Cosima (FR)**[33] 3-9-6 0........................................ ThierryThulliez 16 83
(G Doleuze, France) **158/10**

**4** *¾* **Sea Flower (FR)**[32] 3-8-0 0...................................... EddyHardouin 14 61
(J-M Beguigne, France) **31/1**

**5** *nk* **Diana D'Aumont (FR)**[76] 3-8-9 0............................. AntoineHamelin 8 69
(Mme C Rondele, France) **106/10**

**6** *shd* **Excellent View**[62] 3-9-3 0......................................... FabriceVeron 10 77
(H-A Pantall, France) **31/1**

**7** *¾* **Hasturianita (IRE)**[33] 3-9-2 0..............................(b[1]) UmbertoRispoli 3 74
(Mme Pia Brandt, France) **29/1**

**8** *1* **Belletriste (FR)**[32] 7026 3-9-5 0.................................... ThierryJarnet 1 74
(Sylvester Kirk) *chsd ldrs on inner. 4th and rdn 2f out: kpt on at same pce press: fdd ins fnl 100yds* **74/10**[3]

**9** *snk* **Lys Des Aigles (FR)**[65] 3-9-2 0................................. FredericSpanu 6 71
(Mme C Barande-Barbe, France) **41/10**[1]

**10** *¾* **Palabre (USA)**[16] 3-9-3 0............................................ FlavienPrat 7 70
(F Head, France) **116/10**

**11** *¾* **Pise (IRE)**[24] 3-7-11 0...........................................(p) PierreBazire(3) 13 51
(J-P Gallorini, France) **195/10**

**12** *1 ½* **Tea Gown (IRE)**[47] 3-9-7 0.........................................(b[1]) MaximeGuyon 4 68
(A Fabre, France) **48/10**[2]

**13** *nk* **Raffinee (FR)**[18] 3-8-6 0........................................ GregoryBenoist 5 52
(D Smaga, France) **231/10**

**14** *nk* **Princess Kiara (FR)**[24] 3-8-4 0..................................... AlexisBadel 15 49
(N Caullery, France) **166/10**

**15** *2 ½* **Pink Chalice**[24] 3-8-2 0 ow2...................................(b) CristianDemuro 12 41
(F Doumen, France) **15/1**

**16** *4* **Haswell (SPA)**[111] 3-8-2 0......................................... JeromeClaudic 9 30
(M Delcher Sanchez, France) **26/1**

1m 32.25s (0.05) **16** Ran SP% **119.4**
WIN (incl. 1 euro stake): 8.50. PLACES: 3.20, 8.70, 5.30. DF: 159.40. SF: 179.20.
**Owner** Marquesa De Moratalla **Bred** Haras De La Perelle **Trained** Chantilly, France

# 7629 CHANTILLY (R-H)
## Friday, November 7

**OFFICIAL GOING: Polytrack: standard**

## 7723a PRIX DU ROND DU CHENE (CONDITIONS) (2YO COLTS & GELDINGS) (POLYTRACK) 1m 1f
**12:20** (12:20) 2-Y-O **£14,166** (£5,666; £4,250; £2,833; £1,416)

RPR

**1** **War Dispatch (USA)**[64] 2-9-0 0.......................... ChristopheSoumillon 2 88
(J-C Rouget, France) **9/10**[1]

**2** *2* **Beyond Henry (USA)**[27] 2-9-0 0.................................... ThierryJarnet 4 84
(J E Pease, France) **17/10**[2]

**3** *3* **Mount Isa (IRE)**[65] 2-9-0 0......................................(p) MaximeGuyon 3 78
(Mme Pia Brandt, France) **49/10**[3]

**4** *¾* **Helmsman (IRE)**[23] 7198 2-8-10 0............................ MickaelBarzalona 1 72
(J S Moore) *pushed along to ld: hdd after 2f and chsd ldr: 3 l 2nd and scrubbed along 3f out: brief effrt 2f out: outpcd by ldrs appr fnl f: kpt on at same pce last 150yds* **218/10**

**5** *¾* **Swingking (FR)**[17] 2-8-13 0 ow3................................... OlivierPeslier 5 73
(M Figge, Germany) **102/10**

1m 51.7s (111.70) **5** Ran SP% **119.9**
WIN (incl. 1 euro stake): 1.90. PLACES: 1.10, 1.30. SF: 3.80.
**Owner** Joseph Allen **Bred** Joseph Allen **Trained** Pau, France

# 7690 FLEMINGTON (L-H)
## Saturday, November 8

**OFFICIAL GOING: Turf: good changing to good to firm after darley classic**

## 7724a DARLEY CLASSIC (GROUP 1) (3YO+) (TURF) 6f
**4:40** (12:00) 3-Y-O+
**£323,924** (£96,774; £48,387; £24,193; £13,440; £10,752)

RPR

**1** **Terravista (AUS)**[15] 7436 5-9-3 0.................................. HughBowman 6 126
(Joseph Pride, Australia) *hld up in rr: clsd and rdn over 1f out: r.o and chal fnl 100yds: led towards fin and a doing enough* **9/1**[3]

**2** *nk* **Chautauqua (AUS)**[35] 4-9-3 0........................................ DwayneDunn 3 125
(Michael, Wayne & John Hawkes, Australia) *t.k.h: hld up: clsd over 1f out: rdn ent fnl f: r.o and wnt 2nd cl home: nt quite pce of wnr* **29/20**[1]

**3** *¾* **Lankan Rupee (AUS)**[15] 7436 5-9-3 0........................ ChadSchofield 11 123
(Mick Price, Australia) *sn disputing ld: rdn 2f out: led jst ins fnl f: r.o but hdd towards fin: dropped to 3rd and hld* **4/1**[2]

**4** *1 ¾* **Buffering (AUS)**[15] 7436 7-9-3 0...........................(b) DamianBrowne 1 117
(Robert Heathcote, Australia) *led: sn jnd: rdn 2f out: hdd jst ins fnl f: no ex and fdd fnl 100yds* **14/1**

**5** *nk* **Moment Of Change (AUS)**[15] 7436 6-9-3 0........................ LukeNolen 2 116
(Peter G Moody, Australia) *t.k.h: prom: rdn and effrt 2f out: kpt on same pce fr over 1f out and nvr able to chal* **40/1**

**6** *½* **Famous Seamus (NZ)**[15] 7436 6-9-3 0........................ TimothyClark 7 114
(Noel Mayfield-Smith, Australia) *midfield: dropped to rr and rdn over 2f out: kpt on fnl f but nvr able to chal* **20/1**

**7** *hd* **Rebel Dane (AUS)**[15] 7436 5-9-3 0.......................... CraigAWilliams 8 114
(Gary Portelli, Australia) *hld up in rr: rdn over 1f out: kpt on fnl f but nvr threatened* **18/1**

8 ½ **Sidestep (AUS)**[203] 4-9-3 0........................................ JamesMcDonald 5 112
(J O'Shea, Australia) *midfield: dropped to rr and rdn 2f out: outpcd and btn fnl f* **30/1**

9 ¾ **Platelet (AUS)**[15] 7436 6-8-13 0........................................ BenMelham 13 106
(Darren Weir, Australia) *trckd ldrs: rdn and effrt 2f out: no ex and btn ent fnl f: wknd* **40/1**

10 nk **Driefontein (AUS)**[7] 5-8-13 0........................................(bt) VladDuric 10 105
(Gai Waterhouse, Australia) *pushed along early and sn prom: rdn and lost pl 2f out: sn btn* **40/1**

11 nk **Slade Power (IRE)**[119] 4201 5-9-3 0........................................ WayneLordan 4 108
(Edward Lynam, Ire) *dwlt: sn rcvrd and travelled strly on rail: rdn 2f out: fnd little and btn ent fnl f: wknd: eased fnl 50yds: lame after r* **9/1**[3]

12 3¼ **Temple Of Boom (AUS)**[15] 7436 8-9-3 0..................(b) TeganHarrison 9 98
(Tony Gollan, Australia) *midfield: rdn over 2f out: no ex and btn over 1f out: wknd: eased towards fin* **60/1**

13 nk **Cluster (AUS)**[41] 6805 4-9-3 0..................(bt[1]) DamienOliver 12 97
(Peter & Paul Snowden, Australia) *midfield: rdn 2f out: no ex and btn over 1f out: wknd and dropped to last: eased fnl f* **25/1**

1m 8.79s (68.79) **13** Ran SP% **113.5**
PARI-MUTUEL (NSW TAB - all including 1 aud stake): WIN 8.70; PLACE 2.40, 1.40, 1.90; DF 10.80; SF 27.10.
**Owner** N B Couper, A J Rix Et Al **Bred** M Ryan **Trained** Australia

## 7616 CAPANNELLE (R-H)
Sunday, November 9

**OFFICIAL GOING: Turf: heavy**

### 7725a PREMIO CARLO E FRANCESCO ALOISI (GROUP 3) (2YO+) (TURF) 6f
**3:10** (12:00) 2-Y-O+ **£23,333** (£10,266; £5,600; £2,800)

RPR

1 **Farmah (USA)**[34] 6994 3-9-1 0........................ Francois-XavierBertras 2 115
(F Rohaut, France) *mde all against stands' rail: shkn up: edgd lft and qckncd clr over 1f out: readily* **13/8**[1]

2 6 **Guinnevre (IRE)**[21] 7320 4-9-1 0........................ MichaelCadeddu 6 96
(A Wohler, Germany) *in tch: effrt and pushed along over 2f out: chsd (clr) wnr ins fnl f: kpt on: no imp* **219/10**

3 1½ **Rosendhal (IRE)**[60] 7-9-4 0........................ CristianDemuro 9 94
(G Botti, France) *prom on outside: hdwy to chse wnr over 2f out: sn rdn: one pce and lost 2nd ins fnl f* **11/5**[2]

4 1 **Harlem Shake (IRE)**[21] 7320 3-9-8 0........................ LManiezzi 5 95
(Marco Gasparini, Italy) *cl up: wnt 2nd briefly 1/2-way: rdn and no ex fr over 1f out* **13/4**[3]

5 2 **Traditional Chic (IRE)**[364] 7830 6-9-4 0........................ PAragoni 3 84
(L Riccardi, Italy) *bhd and sn outpcd: hdwy and edgd rt over 1f out: kpt on fnl f: nvr able to chal* **13/1**

6 hd **Namera (GER)**[21] 7320 5-9-1 0........................ AnthonyCrastus 8 81
(P Harley, Germany) *chsd ldng gp: drvn and outpcd over 2f out: n.d after* **49/10**

7 2 **Pride And Joy (IRE)**[154] 5-9-4 0........................ CColombi 1 77
(Riccardo Santini, Italy) *s.i.s: bhd and sn pushed along: nvr on terms* **93/10**

8 4 **Heige (ITY)**[56] 2-8-0 0........................ ManuelPorcu 4 61
(Pietro Sbariggia, Italy) *t.k.h: chsd wnr to 1/2-way: rdn and wknd over 1f out* **39/1**

9 1½ **Konkan (IRE)**[21] 7320 3-9-1 0........................ FrancescoDettori 7 57
(L Riccardi, Italy) *awkward s: hld up: shortlived effrt over 2f out: btn over 1f out* **123/10**

10 2 **Clorofilla (IRE)**[21] 7320 4-9-5 0........................ FabioBranca 10 54
(Marco Gasparini, Italy) *chsd ldrs on outside: struggling over 2f out: sn btn* **13/4**[3]

1m 8.2s (-2.10) **10** Ran SP% **164.6**
WIN (incl. 1 euro stake): 2.63. PLACES: 1.42, 3.83, 1.52. DF: 71.79.
**Owner** Hamdan Al Maktoum **Bred** Shadwell Farm LLC **Trained** Sauvagnon, France

## 5484 KREFELD (R-H)
Sunday, November 9

**OFFICIAL GOING: Turf: soft**

### 7726a HERZOG VON RATIBOR-RENNEN KREFELD (GROUP 3) (2YO) (TURF) 1m 110y
**12:30** (12:00) 2-Y-O

**£26,666** (£9,166; £4,583; £2,500; £1,666; £1,250)

RPR

1 **Los Cerritos (SWI)**[28] 2-8-13 0........................ MartinSeidl 7 104
(K Demme, Germany) *sn led: rdn and jnd into st: hdd narrowly over 1f out: kpt on gamely and battled bk to ld again ins fnl f: asserted towards fin* **26/1**

2 1¾ **Liberry Gold (GER)** 2-8-13 0........................ MartinHarley 5 100
(P Harley, Germany) *dwlt sltly: sn rcvrd and trckd wnr on outer: rdn 3f out: chal and led narrowly over 1f out: hdd ins fnl f: kpt on but hld towards fin* **6/5**[1]

3 2 **Ebeltoft (IRE)**[28] 7145 2-9-2 0........................ DanielePorcu 9 99
(P Schiergen, Germany) *plld hrd: hld up in tch: rdn over 2f out: kpt on and wnt 3rd wl ins fnl f: nt pce of front pair* **27/1**

4 2 **Molly Le Clou (GER)**[28] 7145 2-9-2 0........................ JackMitchell 8 95
(J Hirschberger, Germany) *hld up in rr: rdn and hdwy on outer into st: kpt on same pce fnl 2f and nvr able to chal* **9/2**

5 ¾ **Nabhan**[56] 6377 2-8-13 0........................ JBojko 6 90
(A Wohler, Germany) *restrained and trckd wnr on inner: rdn and disputing ld into st: hdd over 1f out: no ex and fdd fnl f* **123/10**

6 2 **Lovato (GER)**[38] 2-8-13 0........................ AStarke 2 86
(P Schiergen, Germany) *restrained early: sn midfield in tch: rdn 3f out: outpcd fnl 2f: eased whn btn nring fin* **18/5**[2]

7 3½ **Ajalo (FR)** 2-9-2 0........................ SHellyn 3 82
(Waldemar Hickst, Germany) *dwlt sltly: hld up in rr: rdn 3f out: outpcd and btn fnl 2f: eased towards fin: nvr a factor* **4/1**[3]

8 10 **Rock Academy (GER)**[28] 7145 2-9-2 0........................ APietsch 1 61
(Christian Sprengel, Germany) *awkward s and dwlt sltly: qckly rcvrd and prom on inner early: sn midfield: rdn 3f out: no ex and btn over 1f out: wknd: eased fnl f* **11/1**

9 31 **Le Tiger Still (GER)**[65] 6123 2-9-2 0........................ FilipMinarik 4
(P Vovcenko, Germany) *stdd early and sn midfield: rdn and dropped to rr 3f out: btn early in st: wknd: eased and t.o* **29/1**

1m 55.08s (8.48) **9** Ran SP% **131.8**
WIN (incl. 10 euro stake): 273. PLACES: 41, 18, 55. SF: 1,231.
**Owner** Stall Leon **Bred** Gestut Sohrenhof **Trained** Germany

### 7727a PREIS DER DEUTSCHEN BESITZER - NIEDERRHEIN-POKAL (GROUP 3) (3YO+) (TURF) 1m 2f 55y
**2:10** (12:00) 3-Y-O+

**£26,666** (£9,166; £4,583; £2,500; £1,666; £1,250)

RPR

1 **Vif Monsieur (GER)**[42] 6806 4-9-1 0........................ KClijmans 3 110
(S Smrczek, Germany) *mde virtually all: rdn along 2f out: styd on strly fnl f: unchal* **18/5**[2]

2 2½ **Kerosin (GER)**[14] 3-8-8 0........................ FilipMinarik 7 102+
(Jean-Pierre Carvalho, Germany) *hld up: rdn and hdwy over 2f out: edgd rt and kpt on fnl f: wnt 2nd last stride* **124/10**

3 nk **Vanishing Cupid (SWI)**[52] 4-8-13 0..................(b) FabriceVeron 2 102
(H-A Pantall, France) *t.k.h: cl up: chsd wnr over 3f out: effrt and rdn over 2f out: kpt on same pce ins fnl f: lost 2nd last stride* **123/10**

4 9 **Diamond Dove (GER)**[71] 5927 3-8-7 0........................ EPedroza 5 82
(Andreas Lowe, Germany) *t.k.h: prom: rdn over 2f out: edgd rt and no ex over 1f out: eased whn hld ins fnl f* **12/5**[1]

5 3 **Nicolosio (IRE)**[37] 6914 4-9-1 0........................ SHellyn 11 80
(Waldemar Hickst, Germany) *hld up: rdn and hdwy over 2f out: edgd rt and no imp over 1f out* **125/10**

6 2 **Szoff (GER)**[37] 6914 4-8-13 0........................ IFerguson 9 74
(A Kleinkorres, Germany) *t.k.h: hld up: rdn along over 3f out: no imp fnl 2f* **30/1**

7 hd **Polish Vulcano (GER)**[21] 7316 6-8-13 0........................ JBojko 6 74
(H-J Groschel, Germany) *hld up in midfield on outside: outpcd over 4f out: no imp fr over 2f out* **135/10**

8 8 **Abendwind (GER)**[119] 4247 3-8-9 0 ow1........................ APietsch 4 58
(Waldemar Hickst, Germany) *hld up in midfield: rdn and outpcd over 2f out: sn btn* **87/10**

9 6 **Bermuda Reef (IRE)**[21] 7316 4-9-3 0........................ AStarke 13 50
(P Schiergen, Germany) *t.k.h early: in tch on outside: drvn along over 3f out: wknd over 2f out* **119/10**

10 25 **Pas De Deux (GER)**[42] 4-9-1 0........................ MartinSeidl 12
(Yasmin Almenrader, Germany) *chsd wnr to over 3f out: rdn and wknd wl over 2f out* **7/1**[3]

11 6 **Emily Of Tinsdal (GER)**[14] 7482 5-8-11 0........................ MartinHarley 8
(P Harley, Germany) *hld up towards rr: rdn along 4f out: wknd over 2f out* **25/1**

12 1¼ **Dorado (GER)**[49] 4-9-1 0........................ AHelfenbein 10
(Markus Klug, Germany) *dwlt: hld up: drvn along over 3f out: nvr on terms: eased whn no ch over 1f out* **136/10**

13 2 **Ever Strong (GER)**[21] 7316 6-9-3 0........................ DanielePorcu 1
(Dr A Bolte, Germany) *t.k.h early: cl up: struggling 4f out: btn and eased fr 2f out* **149/10**

2m 13.14s (133.14)
**WFA** 3 from 4yo+ 4lb **13** Ran SP% **131.2**
WIN (incl. 10 euro stake): 46. PLACES: 20, 56, 37. SF: 1,403.
**Owner** Frank Maria Van Gorp **Bred** Frau Ursula Herberts **Trained** Germany

## 7657 KEMPTON (A.W) (R-H)
Monday, November 10

**OFFICIAL GOING: Polytrack: standard**
Wind: Moderate, across (away from stands) Weather: Overcast becoming fine

### 7728 DOWNLOAD THE BETVICTOR APP NOW NURSERY H'CAP 6f (P)
**2:15** (2:16) (Class 5) (0-70,69) 2-Y-O **£3,234** (£721; £721; £240) **Stalls** Low

Form RPR

0400 1 **Anastazia**[37] 6924 2-9-5 **67**........................ LukeMorris 4 74
(Paul D'Arcy) *hld up towards rr: prog and squeezed between rivals fr 2f out: drvn to ld jst ins fnl f: styd on wl* **10/1**

2606 2 1½ **Stocking**[51] 6555 2-9-7 **69**........................ WilliamBuick 1 71
(Roger Varian) *trckd ldrs: prog on inner 2f out: drvn to chal 1f out: one pce last 100yds* **4/1**[2]

0453 2 dht **Oriental Splendour (IRE)**[48] 6629 2-9-6 **68**........................ JimCrowley 9 70
(Roger Charlton) *hld up in last pair: shkn up over 2f out: prog over `1f out: styd on wl fnl f: nrst fin* **11/4**[1]

2226 4 1¾ **Chevallier**[28] 7155 2-9-7 **69**........................ SeanLevey 2 66
(Richard Hannon) *prom: chsd ldr over 2f out to over 1f out: one pce fnl f* **13/2**[3]

0642 5 ½ **True Course**[26] 7190 2-8-8 **63**........................ KieranShoemark[(7)] 10 58
(Charlie Appleby) *trckd ldrs: rdn and nt qckn jst over 2f out: kpt on same pce fnl f* **8/1**

0535 6 ½ **You're Cool**[4] 7683 2-9-3 **65**........................(b[1]) TomQueally 8 59
(James Given) *hld up towards rr: pushed along 1/2-way: racd awkwardly and no prog 2f out: styd on ins fnl f* **15/2**

1554 7 1 **The Dapper Tapper (IRE)**[70] 5974 2-9-4 **66**..................(v) JohnFahy 3 57
(Eve Johnson Houghton) *drvn to ld: kicked 2 l clr over 2f out: hdd & wknd jst ins fnl f* **13/2**[3]

5503 8 shd **Entente**[27] 7181 2-9-7 **69**........................ SteveDrowne 6 59
(Peter Makin) *t.k.h: trckd ldrs: rdn over 2f out: disp 2nd briefly wl over 1f out: wknd* **25/1**

0655 9 3 **Just Because**[48] 6629 2-8-10 **65**........................ RobertWalsh[(7)] 5 46
(Edward Creighton) *plld hrd: hld up in last pair: shkn up and no prog over 2f out* **66/1**

050 10 ½ **Mrs Eve (IRE)**[30] 7108 2-9-5 **67**........................ CharlesBishop 7 47
(Alan Bailey) *chsd ldr to over 2f out: sn btn* **25/1**

1m 12.88s (-0.22) **Going Correction** +0.05s/f (Slow) **10** Ran SP% **114.5**
Speed ratings (Par 96): **103,101,101,98,98 97,96,95,91,91**
WIN: £14.00 Anastazia; PL £2.00; Stocking, £4.10 Anastazia; Oriental Splendour£1.10 ; EX: A/S £31.30, A/OS £25.60; CSF: A/S £24.06, A/OS £18.22; TC: A/S/OS £72.00, A/OS/S £66.38; TRIFECTA: A/S/OS £205.40, A/OS/S £204.50.
**Owner** K Snell **Bred** K Snell **Trained** Newmarket, Suffolk

**FOCUS**
A modest nursery in which they avoided the far rail in the straight.

## 7729 BETVICTOR.COM H'CAP 7f (P)
2:50 (2:50) (Class 4) (0-78,78) 3-Y-0+ £4,690 (£1,395; £697; £348) Stalls Low

Form RPR
0311 1 **Holiday Magic (IRE)**[53] 6484 3-9-6 78 ................ WilliamBuick 11 88
(Charlie Appleby) *pressed ldr: led wl over 2f out: pushed 2 l clr sn after: rdn out fnl f* **6/4**[1]

0225 2 1 ¼ **Smart Salute**[93] 5197 3-9-2 74 ................(b) LukeMorris 3 81
(Ed Walker) *hld up in 6th: rdn and prog fr 2f out: chsd wnr fnl f: styd on but nvr able to chal* **8/1**[2]

5004 3 1 **King Of Eden (IRE)**[18] 7403 8-9-1 72 ................ JasonHart 7 77
(Eric Alston) *prom: rdn to chse wnr over 2f out to 1f out: one pce* **20/1**

4015 4 ½ **Good Luck Charm**[19] 7375 5-9-7 78 ................(b) FergusSweeney 2 82
(Gary Moore) *hld up towards rr: rdn and prog fr 2f out: kpt on same pce fnl f* **8/1**[2]

2254 5 hd **Picks Pinta**[20] 7352 3-9-1 73 ................ MartinDwyer 5 76
(Jo Hughes) *bmpd s: in tch in midfield but pushed along bef 1/2-way: prog 2f out: kpt on same pce fnl f* **8/1**[2]

1504 6 1 ¾ **A Legacy Of Love (IRE)**[118] 4282 3-9-3 75 ................ TedDurcan 4 73
(Amanda Perrett) *hld up towards rr: nt clr run v briefly 2f out: pushed along and reminder over 1f out: kpt on but nvr involved* **25/1**

2405 7 nk **Gigawatt**[20] 7351 4-9-2 73 ................ PatCosgrave 12 71
(Jim Boyle) *s.v.s: sn in tch in last pair: rdn on outer over 2f out: sme prog after but nvr able to threaten* **10/1**[3]

000 8 1 ¾ **Rocksilla**[28] 7159 4-9-3 74 ................(b) SebSanders 1 68
(Chris Wall) *dwlt: mostly in last pair: tried to make prog on inner over 2f out: no hdwy over 1f out* **25/1**

5005 9 13 **Kung Hei Fat Choy (USA)**[6] 7636 5-9-7 78 ................(p) JimCrowley 6 38
(James Given) *wnt rt s: in tch: rdn and no prog over 2f out: sn wknd: t.o* **8/1**[2]

-000 10 shd **Shady McCoy (USA)**[13] 7505 4-9-2 73 ................ RobertWinston 13 33
(Ian Williams) *chsd ldng pair but racd wd and hanging: lost grnd bnd 4f out to 3f out: wknd 2f out: t.o* **20/1**

6102 11 1 ¾ **Angel Flores (IRE)**[79] 5675 3-9-3 75 ................ AmirQuinn 8 29
(Lee Carter) *chsd ldrs: rdn over 2f out: wknd qckly wl over 1f out: t.o* **14/1**

044- 12 21 **Mahlah (IRE)**[437] 5955 3-9-5 77 ................ TomQueally 9
(John Butler) *led to wl over 2f out: hanging bdly and wknd qckly: t.o and eased* **33/1**

RR0R R **Caramack**[56] 6414 4-8-13 73 ................ DeclanBates(3) 10
(David Evans) *ref to leave the stalls: tk no part* **33/1**

1m 26.05s (0.05) **Going Correction** +0.05s/f (Slow)
**WFA** 3 from 4yo+ 1lb 13 Ran SP% **123.3**
Speed ratings (Par 105): **101,99,98,97,97 95,95,93,78,78 76,52,**
CSF £12.50 CT £186.69 TOTE £2.50: £1.90, £2.20, £4.00; EX 15.60 Trifecta £231.80.
**Owner** Godolphin **Bred** Mrs Ann Fortune **Trained** Newmarket, Suffolk

**FOCUS**
Two of the 3yos came to the fore in what was an average handicap, but the winner continues to improve.

## 7730 IRISH STALLION FARMS EBF MAIDEN STKS (BOBIS RACE) (DIV I) 1m (P)
3:20 (3:21) (Class 4) 2-Y-0 £4,075 (£1,212; £606; £303) Stalls Low

Form RPR
1 **Balios (IRE)** 2-9-5 0 ................ PatCosgrave 11 83+
(David Simcock) *hld up in midfield: pushed along and prog on outer over 2f out: led over 1f out: shkn up and r.o wl* **9/1**

2 1 ¼ **Pathway To Honour** 2-9-5 0 ................ MartinLane 6 80
(Charlie Appleby) *hld up towards rr: gd prog fr 2f out: chsd wnr 1f out: r.o and drew clr of rest but unable to chal* **11/2**[3]

3 4 **Arabian Illusion (FR)** 2-9-5 0 ................ JimCrowley 9 71
(Andrew Balding) *prom: shkn up to ld narrowly over 2f out: hdd and easily outpcd fr over 1f out* **7/1**

6 4 1 ¼ **Azilian**[51] 6545 2-9-5 0 ................(t) LukeMorris 7 68
(Paul Cole) *prom: shkn up and cl up 2f out: easily outpcd fr over 1f out* **7/2**[1]

50 5 hd **Justice First**[17] 7407 2-9-5 0 ................ PaulMulrennan 3 68
(Ed Dunlop) *hld up in midfield: pushed along over 2f out: outpcd over 1f out: styd on quite wl fnl f* **33/1**

0 6 ½ **I Zingari**[27] 7169 2-9-5 0 ................ TedDurcan 12 66+
(Sir Michael Stoute) *hld up in last quartet: shoved along over 2f out: sn outpcd: styd on again ins fnl f* **10/1**

32 7 2 ½ **Gild Master**[40] 6874 2-9-5 0 ................ FergusSweeney 4 61
(Alan King) *led: narrowly hdd over 2f out: pressed ldr to over 1f out: wknd* **5/1**[2]

8 1 ½ **Peterhouse (USA)** 2-9-5 0 ................ WilliamBuick 5 57
(John Gosden) *dwlt: rn green in last pair: pushed along over 2f out: no great prog* **11/2**[3]

00 9 ½ **Celtic Ava (IRE)**[20] 7353 2-9-0 0 ................ ShaneKelly 8 51
(Pat Phelan) *broke w ldrs but sn restrained into last quartet: pushed along and no prog fr over 2f out: nvr involved* **66/1**

10 ¾ **Goodwood Moonlight** 2-9-5 0 ................ TomQueally 2 54
(William Knight) *v s.i.s: rn green in last pair: nvr a factor* **33/1**

003 11 ½ **Major Mac**[17] 7414 2-9-5 0 ................ RobertHavlin 1 53
(Hughie Morrison) *trckd ldrs: cl up on inner over 2f out: wknd over 1f out* **20/1**

0 12 nk **Alhamareer (IRE)**[33] 7039 2-9-5 0 ................ FrankieDettori 10 52
(Richard Hannon) *trckd ldr: chal over 2f out tl wknd rapidly over 1f out* **12/1**

1m 41.37s (1.57) **Going Correction** +0.05s/f (Slow) 12 Ran SP% **121.1**
Speed ratings (Par 98): **94,92,88,87,87 86,84,82,82,81 81,80**
CSF £57.32 TOTE £13.20: £3.50, £2.20, £3.20; EX 66.90 Trifecta £958.30.
**Owner** Al Asayl Bloodstock Ltd **Bred** Sheikh Sultan Bin Khalifa Al Nahyan **Trained** Newmarket, Suffolk

**FOCUS**
The front pair pulled clear in what was a fair maiden that should produce winners.

## 7731 IRISH STALLION FARMS EBF MAIDEN STKS (BOBIS RACE) (DIV II) 1m (P)
3:50 (3:51) (Class 4) 2-Y-0 £4,075 (£1,212; £606; £303) Stalls Low

Form RPR
1 **Pacify** 2-9-5 0 ................ SebSanders 11 71
(Ralph Beckett) *racd on outer: in tch: prog over 2f out: rdn and r.o fr over 1f out to ld last strides* **16/1**

6 2 nk **Royal Albert Hall**[33] 7030 2-9-5 0 ................ JimCrowley 7 70
(Olly Stevens) *trckd ldrs: pushed along 2f out: prog jst over 1f out: r.o to take 2nd last stride* **7/1**[2]

3 hd **Dark Deed** 2-9-5 0 ................ ShaneKelly 6 70+
(Sir Michael Stoute) *hld up in last pair: pushed along 2f out: gd prog jst over 1f out: styd on to take promising 3rd last strides* **8/1**[3]

00 4 nse **Sirheed (IRE)**[19] 7382 2-9-5 0 ................ FrankieDettori 4 70
(Richard Hannon) *led at mod pce: jnd 2f out: drvn over 1f out: styd on but hdd and lost pls nr fin* **20/1**

3 5 nk **China Club (IRE)**[19] 7372 2-9-5 0 ................ WilliamBuick 1 69
(John Gosden) *t.k.h: trckd ldng pair: chal over 2f out and sn upsides: drvn over 1f out: stl upsides 100yds out: nt qckn and lost pls nr fin* **4/11**[1]

0 6 ¾ **Dutch Uncle**[19] 7380 2-9-5 0 ................ PaulMulrennan 3 70+
(Ed Dunlop) *hld up towards rr: gng strly whn appeared nt to have clr run 2f out: swtchd rt over 1f out: pushed along and kpt on encouragingly: nvr cl enough to chal* **25/1**

7 ½ **Molten Lava (IRE)** 2-9-5 0 ................ LukeMorris 9 66
(Paul Cole) *t.k.h: trckd ldrs: tried to cl 2f out: nt qckn 1f out: one pce after* **50/1**

8 2 ¾ **Arthenus** 2-9-5 0 ................ TomQueally 2 60
(James Fanshawe) *in tch in midfield: pushed along towards inner 2f out: no prog over 1f out: wl hld after* **12/1**

50 9 2 **Sleep Easy**[40] 6875 2-9-5 0 ................ RobertHavlin 10 55
(Hughie Morrison) *sn hld up in last pair: effrt on inner 2f out: no prog over 1f out: wknd* **33/1**

0 10 2 ¾ **Admiral's Gold (IRE)**[49] 6604 2-9-5 0 ................ PatCosgrave 8 49
(Edward Creighton) *trckd ldr: shkn up over 2f out: sn wknd and eased* **66/1**

11 2 ½ **Harold Lloyd** 2-9-5 0 ................ FergusSweeney 5 43
(Henry Candy) *rn green and sn in last: detached over 2f out: no prog after* **25/1**

1m 43.23s (3.43) **Going Correction** +0.05s/f (Slow) 11 Ran SP% **129.3**
Speed ratings (Par 98): **84,83,83,83,83 82,81,79,77,74 71**
CSF £124.72 TOTE £28.40: £7.40, £2.20, £2.40; EX 266.30 Trifecta £3379.00.
**Owner** Prince Of Wales And Duchess Of Cornwall **Bred** The Prince Of Wales & The Duchess Of Cornwall **Trained** Kimpton, Hants

**FOCUS**
Probably the lesser of the two divisions and the pace was a steady one. They finished in a heap.

## 7732 DOWNLOAD THE BETVICTOR INSTABET APP H'CAP 1m (P)
4:20 (4:20) (Class 4) (0-80,80) 3-Y-0+ £4,690 (£1,395; £697; £348) Stalls Low

Form RPR
-561 1 **Nigel's Destiny (USA)**[12] 7528 3-9-2 77 ................ FrankieDettori 8 87+
(Jeremy Noseda) *trckd ldng pair: clsd on outer 2f out: drvn to ld 1f out: kpt on and a holding on* **7/4**[1]

3413 2 nk **Semaral (IRE)**[18] 7397 3-9-2 77 ................(p) TedDurcan 9 86+
(Chris Wall) *hld up in last trio: prog jst over 2f out: hd at awkward angle but sustained effrt to go 2nd last 75yds: clsng on wnr fin* **7/1**[3]

4200 3 ¾ **Jack Of Diamonds (IRE)**[72] 5931 5-9-7 80 ................ RobertWinston 1 87
(Roger Teal) *sn w ldr: led 2f out: drvn and hdd 1f out: one pce and lost 2nd last 75yds* **16/1**

5301 4 1 ¾ **Toga Tiger (IRE)**[27] 7186 7-9-4 77 ................ JimCrowley 2 80
(Kevin Frost) *in tch in midfield: rdn and nt qckn over 2f out: kpt on to take 4th ins fnl f: n.d* **8/1**

0000 5 ½ **Birdman (IRE)**[12] 7530 4-8-13 72 ................(b) MartinLane 3 74
(David Simcock) *slowly away: t.k.h: hld up in last: prog on inner 2f out: drvn and kpt on: nt pce to threaten* **25/1**

5164 6 ½ **Conry (IRE)**[23] 7282 8-8-13 72 ................ StevieDonohoe 11 73
(Ian Williams) *hld up in last trio: urged along over 2f out: no prog tl kpt on fnl f: nrst fin* **25/1**

0 7 1 ¼ **Dynamite Dixie (IRE)**[17] 7431 5-9-0 76 ................(p) DannyBrock(3) 7 74
(Phil McEntee) *mde most in narrow ld to 2f out: sn wknd* **33/1**

5405 8 nse **Westminster (IRE)**[81] 5603 3-8-12 78 ................ AlistairRawlinson(5) 5 76
(Michael Appleby) *trckd ldng pair: shkn up and cl enough 2f out: wknd over 1f out* **8/1**

461 9 3 ¼ **Craftsmanship (FR)**[13] 7514 3-9-2 77 ................(p) JimmyQuinn 4 67
(Robert Eddery) *wl in tch: rdn on inner over 2f out: no prog over 1f out: wknd* **20/1**

0125 10 ½ **Set The Trend**[10] 7568 8-9-6 79 ................(p) FergusSweeney 6 68
(David Dennis) *in tch in midfield: shkn up and no prog over 2f out: wknd over 1f out* **13/2**[2]

4406 11 6 **Finn Class (IRE)**[43] 6792 3-9-3 78 ................ PaulMulrennan 12 53
(Michael Dods) *racd on outer in midfield: shkn up over 2f out: sn wknd* **8/1**

1m 38.53s (-1.27) **Going Correction** +0.05s/f (Slow)
**WFA** 3 from 4yo+ 2lb 11 Ran SP% **116.8**
Speed ratings (Par 105): **108,107,106,105,104 104,102,102,99,99 93**
CSF £13.06 CT £152.20 TOTE £2.80: £2.40, £2.00, £3.10; EX 13.30 Trifecta £158.80.
**Owner** Nigel O'Sullivan **Bred** DATTT Farm LLC **Trained** Newmarket, Suffolk

**FOCUS**
A race in which it paid to sit handily.

## 7733 FOLLOW @BETVICTORRACING ON TWITTER MAIDEN STKS 1m (P)
4:50 (4:54) (Class 4) 3-Y-0+ £4,690 (£1,395; £697; £348) Stalls Low

Form RPR
- 1 **Mahsoob** 3-9-5 0 ................ WilliamBuick 2 91+
(John Gosden) *trckd ldng quartet: clsd 2f out: led over 1f out on outer: shkn up and styd on wl* **11/8**[2]

32 2 1 **Razor Wind (IRE)**[122] 4168 3-9-5 0 ................ MartinLane 4 85+
(Charlie Appleby) *trckd ldng pair: clsd to chal on inner 2f out: chsd wnr over 1f out: styd on but readily hld ins fnl f* **1/1**[1]

445 3 3 ¼ **Golden Emerald**[28] 7157 3-9-5 77 ................ ShaneKelly 10 78
(Mike Murphy) *v awkward to load into stalls: trckd ldr: led over 2f out w hd at awkward angle: hdd over 1f out: readily outpcd* **12/1**

4 2 ½ **John Reel (FR)**[340] 5-9-4 0 ................ DeclanBates(3) 12 72+
(David Evans) *hld up in 10th and wl off the pce: pushed along over 2f out: prog wl over 1f out: styd on wl to take 4th last strides* **50/1**

5 ½ **Poyle Toby (IRE)** 4-9-7 ................ OscarPereira 7 71
(Ralph Beckett) *trckd ldrs in 6th: nudged along over 2f out: tk 4th and reminder over 1f out: outpcd and no hdwy after* **16/1**

00 6 1 **Approaching (IRE)**[12] 7528 3-9-5 0 ................(t) JimCrowley 1 69
(Amanda Perrett) *in tch in 7th: pushed along over 2f out: tk 5th over 1f out but outpcd: one pce after* **33/1**

7 1 ¾ **Greenside** 3-9-5 0 ................ FergusSweeney 11 65
(Henry Candy) *dwlt: wl off the pce in last trio: pushed along over 2f out: passed a few fr over 1f out* **33/1**

3323 **8** *1 1/4* **New Identity (IRE)**[34] 7024 3-9-5 80........................ PatCosgrave 9 62
(Denis Coakley) *t.k.h: hld up in 8th pushed along on outer over 2f out: no prog after* **8/1**[3]

00 **9** *hd* **Divine Warrior (IRE)**[12] 7528 3-9-5 0........................ LukeMorris 8 61
(Timothy Jarvis) *chsd ldng trio to 2f out: sn wknd* **50/1**

**10** *2 1/4* **Arrayan**[8] 9-9-7 0........................ JohnFahy 3 56
(Alexandra Dunn) *a wl in rr and off the pce: no prog fnl 2f* **66/1**

6 **11** *1* **Hong Kong Joe**[17] 7418 4-9-7 0........................(e[1]) CharlesBishop 13 54
(Lydia Richards) *racd in 9th but off the pce: effrt over 2f out: sn no prog and btn* **66/1**

00 **12** *10* **Famous Tales**[53] 6482 4-9-2 0........................ ChrisCatlin 6 26
(Edward Creighton) *led to over 2f out: sn wknd rapidly* **66/1**

**13** *78* **Copper Ern** 5-9-7 0........................ KieranO'Neill 5
(Jimmy Fox) *slowly away: t.o after 2f* **66/1**

1m 39.52s (-0.28) **Going Correction** +0.05s/f (Slow)
**WFA** 3 from 4yo+ 2lb **13** Ran SP% **132.6**
Speed ratings (Par 105): **103,102,98,96,95 94,93,91,91,89 88,78,**
CSF £3.41 TOTE £3.40: £1.80, £1.02, £3.50; EX 4.40 Trifecta £32.20.
**Owner** Hamdan Al Maktoum **Bred** Shadwell Estate Company Limited **Trained** Newmarket, Suffolk

**FOCUS**
The big two in the market dominated what was probably a decent little maiden.

## 7734 £25 FREE BET AT BETVICTOR.COM H'CAP 1m 4f (P)
**5:20** (5:22) (Class 5) (0-75,75) 3-Y-O+ **£2,587** (£770; £384; £192) **Stalls** Centre

Form RPR

6304 **1** **Censorius**[14] 7500 3-8-7 67........................ ThomasBrown(3) 10 76+
(Lee Carter) *hld up and in last early: stl wl in rr and pushed along 2f out: rapid prog on outer over 1f out and reminder: fin strly to ld post* **15/2**

0256 **2** *shd* **Quenelle**[22] 7304 3-8-12 69........................ PaulMulrennan 5 77
(Ed Dunlop) *trckd ldrs: shkn up over 2f out: wnt 3rd over 1f out: clsd on ldng pair fnl f: led last strides: hdd post* **20/1**

2632 **3** *1/2* **Dalmatia (IRE)**[26] 7210 3-9-3 74........................ ShaneKelly 8 81
(Sir Michael Stoute) *led 1f: trckd ldng pair after: led and sent for home over 2f out: hdd over 1f out: kpt on and upsides 50yds out: nt qckn* **3/1**[2]

4322 **4** *3/4* **Panatella**[20] 7349 3-9-0 71........................ TomQueally 1 77
(James Fanshawe) *trckd ldng pair after 1f: nt clr run over 2f out and had to barge way through: drvn to ld over 1f out: hdd and wilted last strides* **9/4**[1]

042 **5** *4 1/2* **Sea Vision (IRE)**[34] 7015 4-9-10 75........................ AdamBeschizza 7 74
(Jo Crowley) *in tch in midfield: pushed along briefly after 3f: shkn up over 3f out: no prog tl kpt on one pce fr over 1f out* **10/1**

4136 **6** *3/4* **Karam Albaari (IRE)**[34] 7016 6-9-9 74........................(p) FergalLynch 2 71
(J R Jenkins) *in tch in midfield: shkn up 4f out: tried to make prog 2f out: effrt flattened out fnl f* **7/1**[3]

004 **7** *1/2* **Eurato (FR)**[21] 7343 4-9-2 67........................ LiamJones 6 64
(John Spearing) *nvr bttr than midfield: rdn over 2f out: plugged on fr over 1f out* **33/1**

5230 **8** *nk* **Allnecessaryforce (FR)**[17] 7409 4-9-10 75........................ JimmyQuinn 4 71
(Alex Hales) *dwlt: sn wl in tch: cl up on inner over 2f out: nt qckn and outpcd wl over 1f out: no hdwy after* **12/1**

425 **9** *1 3/4* **Haydn's Lass**[70] 5976 3-8-9 66........................ MartinDwyer 3 59
(Marcus Tregoning) *led after 1f to over 2f out: lost 3rd and wknd over 1f out* **14/1**

5550 **10** *nk* **Young Dottie**[18] 7397 8-9-2 67........................ FergusSweeney 9 60
(Pat Phelan) *t.k.h: hld up in last trio: sme prog over 2f out: no hdwy and pushed along over 1f out* **66/1**

1350 **11** *3/4* **Night's Watch**[17] 7426 4-8-10 61 oh6........................ JohnFahy 11 53
(Dai Burchell) *dwlt: a wl in rr: struggling 4f out* **66/1**

4000 **12** *8* **Back Burner (IRE)**[17] 7422 6-9-2 67........................ ChrisCatlin 13 46
(Dai Burchell) *racd on outer towards rr: wknd over 2f out* **25/1**

-225 **13** *1 1/2* **Silk Train**[136] 3681 4-9-5 70........................ LukeMorris 12 46
(Alexandra Dunn) *trckd ldr after 1f to wl over 2f out: losing pl whn hmpd sn after: wknd qckly* **20/1**

2m 35.02s (0.52) **Going Correction** +0.05s/f (Slow)
**WFA** 3 from 4yo+ 6lb **13** Ran SP% **122.8**
Speed ratings (Par 103): **100,99,99,99,96 95,95,95,93,93 93,87,86**
CSF £156.51 CT £555.66 TOTE £12.00: £2.90, £5.70, £1.50; EX 195.20 Trifecta £1967.30.
**Owner** Clear Racing **Bred** Langham Hall Stud **Trained** Epsom, Surrey

**FOCUS**
A modest handicap in which the front four, all 3yos, came clear. The winner looks capable of better on the AW.

## 7735 BOOK CHRISTMAS FESTIVAL TICKETS NOW H'CAP 6f (P)
**5:50** (5:50) (Class 6) (0-60,60) 3-Y-O+ **£1,940** (£577; £288; £144) **Stalls** Low

Form RPR

3632 **1** **Larghetto (USA)**[3] 7698 6-9-4 59........................(b) StevieDonohoe 4 69
(Ian Williams) *trckd ldrs: gng strly whn clsd fr 2f out: led jst over 1f out: drvn clr* **15/8**[1]

0000 **2** *3* **Time Medicean**[5] 7670 8-9-3 58........................ RobertWinston 9 58
(Tony Carroll) *settled off the pce towards rr: taken to outer and prog 2f out: rdn and styd on to take 2nd last strides: nvr really a threat* **15/8**[1]

6030 **3** *nk* **Emily Davison (IRE)**[6] 7644 3-9-2 57........................(p) CharlesBishop 1 56
(Ann Stokell) *t.k.h: trckd ldng pair: rdn to ld over 1f out to jst over 1f out: one pce* **33/1**

000- **4** *1/2* **Hatta Stream (IRE)**[474] 4636 8-9-0 58........................ SimonPearce(3) 11 56
(Lydia Pearce) *trckd ldrs: rdn 2f out: tried to chal over 1f out: one pce fnl f* **33/1**

5300 **5** *nk* **Blackthorn Stick (IRE)**[20] 7347 5-9-4 59........................ TomQueally 7 56
(John Butler) *hld up in last and off the pce: prog 2f out: drvn over 1f out: kpt on but nvr able to threaten* **33/1**

4401 **6** *2 1/2* **Bubbly Bailey**[26] 7191 4-9-4 59........................(v) FergalLynch 2 48
(J R Jenkins) *led at gd pce to over 1f out: wknd fnl f* **6/1**[3]

1434 **7** *3* **Bookmaker**[11] 7556 4-9-4 59........................(b) WilliamCarson 3 38
(John Bridger) *mostly chsd ldr: chal and upsides over 1f out: wknd qckly fnl f* **4/1**[2]

506 **8** *1/2* **Swendab (IRE)**[48] 6650 6-8-12 60........................(p) CiaranMckee(7) 5 38
(John O'Shea) *dwlt: wl in rr and off the pce: urged along and no prog over 2f out: sn no ch* **16/1**

2000 **9** *3/4* **Paradise Spectre**[26] 7202 7-9-5 60........................(p) LiamKeniry 12 35
(Zoe Davison) *a in rr and off the pce: struggling over 2f out* **50/1**

0440 **10** *3 1/4* **El Duque**[20] 7355 3-8-12 58........................(p) RyanWhile(5) 8 23
(Bill Turner) *pressed ldrs but racd wd: lost pl over 2f out: sn btn* **33/1**

1m 12.28s (-0.82) **Going Correction** +0.05s/f (Slow) **10** Ran SP% **123.5**
Speed ratings (Par 101): **107,103,102,101,101 98,94,93,92,88**
CSF £5.44 CT £89.53 TOTE £2.80: £1.90, £1.20, £4.50; EX 9.50 Trifecta £304.40.
**Owner** Ian Williams Racing Club **Bred** Barr Inman & Giant's Causeway Syndicate **Trained** Portway, Worcs

**FOCUS**
They went a decent gallop and the race set up for the closers. The form looks weak.
T/Jkpt: Not won. T/Plt: £205.70 to a £1 stake. Pool of £61695.64 - 218.94 winning tickets.
T/Qpdt: £44.70 to a £1 stake. Pool of £5197.83 - 85.90 winning tickets. JN

# TOULOUSE
## Tuesday, November 11
**OFFICIAL GOING: Turf: good to soft**

## 7736a PRIX FILLE DE L'AIR (GROUP 3) (3YO+ FILLIES & MARES) (TURF) 1m 2f 110y
**1:20** (12:00) 3-Y-O+ **£33,333** (£13,333; £10,000; £6,666; £3,333)

RPR

**1** **Gaga A (URU)**[12] 7558 5-8-11 0........................ AlexisBadel 1 104
(D Smaga, France) *cl up on inner: rdn to chse ldr 1 1/2f out: r.o u.p fnl f: led 50yds out: readily* **4/1**[3]

**2** *1/2* **Peut Etre (IRE)**[21] 3-8-8 0........................ StephanePasquier 4 105
(P Sogorb, France) *led: kicked 2 l clr over 1 1/2f out: sn rdn: r.o fnl f: hdd 50yds out: no ex* **43/5**

**3** *2* **Heartily (IRE)**[16] 7482 3-8-8 0........................ FabriceVeron 2 101
(H-A Pantall, France) *w.w in midfield: cl 5th and n.m.r 1 1/2f out: drvn through emerging gap appr 1f out: kpt on fnl f: nvr on terms w front two* **39/10**[2]

**4** *2 1/2* **Beautiful Heroine (IRE)**[32] 7096 3-8-8 0........................ MaximeGuyon 6 96
(F-H Graffard, France) *hld up towards rr: outpcd and scrubbed along fr 2f out: no imp tl styd on fnl f: nrest at fin* **21/10**[1]

**5** *3/4* **No News (FR)**[12] 7558 4-8-11 0........................ ThomasMessina 7 93
(X Nakkachdji, France) *w.w towards rr: effrt 1 1/2f out: run petered out ent fnl f: kpt on at same pce* **112/10**

**6** *hd* **Navarra (SPA)**[16] 4-8-11 0........................ VJanacek 3 92
(G Arizkorreta Elosegui, Spain) *w.w in midfield: tk clsr order on outer 1/2-way: rdn and nt qckn 2f out: bmpd 1 1/2f out and sn lost pl: rallied u.p fnl f: nvr really in contention* **226/10**

**7** *nse* **Daksha (FR)**[16] 7482 4-9-4 0........................ ThierryThulliez 5 99
(Waldemar Hickst, Germany) *trckd ldr on outer: rowed along to hold pl over 2f out: wknd fnl f* **58/10**

**8** *1/4* **Oriental Magic (GER)**[32] 7096 3-8-8 0........................ JulienAuge 8 94
(C Ferland, France) *dwlt: t.k.h in rr: rdn and effrt on outer over 1 1/2f out: sn no further imp: one pce fnl f* **19/2**

2m 13.7s (133.70)
**WFA** 3 from 4yo+ 4lb **8** Ran SP% **119.7**
WIN (incl. 1 euro stake): 5.00. PLACES: 1.90, 2.40, 1.70. DF: 18.10. SF: 36.90.
**Owner** Benjamin Steinbruch **Bred** Haras Phillipson **Trained** Lamorlaye, France

7728

# KEMPTON (A.W) (R-H)
## Wednesday, November 12
**OFFICIAL GOING: Polytrack: standard**
Wind: light to medium, half behind Weather: dry

## 7737 BIRKY'S BARBADOS BASH H'CAP 5f (P)
**4:20** (4:20) (Class 7) (0-50,56) 3-Y-O+ **£1,617** (£481; £240; £120) **Stalls** Low

Form RPR

3003 **1** **Synonym (ITY)**[21] 7376 3-8-13 50........................ AlistairRawlinson(5) 2 56
(Michael Appleby) *chsd ldrs: rdn over 1f out: styd on wl ins fnl f to ld cl home* **10/3**[1]

2004 **2** *nk* **High Tone**[19] 7420 4-9-3 49........................(p) RobertWinston 5 54
(Dean Ivory) *led: rdn over 1f out: kpt on wl tl hdd and no ex cl home* **11/2**[3]

0201 **3** *nk* **Captain Scooby**[7] 7671 8-9-3 56 6ex........................(b) KieranShoemark(7) 1 60
(Richard Guest) *hld up in midfield: hdwy over 1f out: styd on wl ins fnl f: nt quite rch ldrs* **7/2**[2]

0003 **4** *nk* **Mossgo (IRE)**[28] 7191 4-9-2 48........................(t) MartinDwyer 10 51
(John Best) *w ldr: rdn over 1f out: kpt on u.p: no ex and losty 2 pls towards fin* **15/2**

5-05 **5** *3/4* **Sannibel**[21] 7376 6-9-2 48........................(p) RobertTart 3 48
(David Bridgwater) *v.s.a: bhd: stl 9th and plenty to do over 1f out: styd on strly ins fnl f: nt rch ldrs* **14/1**

3000 **6** *1* **Island Express (IRE)**[8] 7652 7-8-11 48........................(bt) AnnStokell(5) 9 44
(Ann Stokell) *s.i.s: bhd: pushed along and hdwy into midfield 1/2-way: kpt on fnl f: nvr enough pce to chal* **50/1**

404 **7** *3 1/4* **Warm Order**[25] 7285 3-9-2 48........................(t) WilliamCarson 8 33
(Tony Carroll) *chsd ldrs: rdn and unable qck over 1f out: wknd fnl f* **13/2**

5001 **8** *nk* **Gypsy Rider**[15] 7520 5-8-13 50........................ NedCurtis(5) 7 34
(Henry Tett) *midfield: rdn and unable qck over 1f out: wknd fnl f* **6/1**

0604 **9** *1 1/4* **Volcanic Dust (IRE)**[42] 6851 6-9-3 49........................(t) ChrisCatlin 4 28
(Milton Bradley) *awkward as stalls opened and slowly away: a bhd* **16/1**

1m 0.24s (-0.26) **Going Correction** -0.10s/f (Stan) **9** Ran SP% **114.6**
Speed ratings (Par 97): **98,97,97,96,95 93,88,88,86**
CSF £21.79 CT £67.60 TOTE £3.20: £1.30, £2.10, £1.50; EX 22.20 Trifecta £102.20.
**Owner** Almond Appleby Harris Woodward **Bred** Rz Pian Del Lago Di Fattoria Marcianella Srl **Trained** Danethorpe, Notts

**FOCUS**
The opening contest was a moderate sprint handicap in which they went a strong gallop.

## 7738 BETBRIGHT - LIVE THE MOMENT H'CAP 5f (P)
**4:50** (4:52) (Class 3) (0-95,95) 3-Y-O+
**£7,158** (£2,143; £1,071; £535; £267; £134) **Stalls** Low

Form RPR

0010 **1** **Sleepy Sioux**[18] 7441 3-9-3 91........................(p) SilvestreDeSousa 2 100
(David Elsworth) *hld up in midfield: swtchd lft and effrt over 1f out: str run ins fnl f to ld last strides* **5/1**[3]

4-05 **2** *hd* **Boom The Groom (IRE)**[12] 7564 3-8-9 83........................ WilliamCarson 5 91
(Tony Carroll) *pushed rt leaving stalls: sn rcvrd and chsd ldrs: styd on u.p fnl f: led fnl 50yds: hdd last strides* **11/1**

0004 **3** *1* **Even Stevens**[28] 7212 6-9-7 95........................(v) TomEaves 8 99
(Scott Dixon) *led: clr after 2f: rdn over 1f out: hdd fnl 50yds: wknd towards fin* **11/1**

10U5 **4** *nse* **Holley Shiftwell**[39] 6918 4-8-9 83 WilliamTwiston-Davies 3 87
(Stuart Williams) *in tch in midfield: swtchd lft and effrt over 1f out: styd on u.p ins fnl f: nt rch ldrs* **3/1**[1]

0630 **5** *hd* **Elusivity (IRE)**[18] 7441 6-8-13 87 ShaneKelly 4 91
(Peter Crate) *squeezed and bdly hmpd sn after s: dropped to rr: clsd 1/2-way: rdn and effrt 1f out: styd on: nt rch ldrs* **7/2**[2]

0010 **6** *1* **Megaleka**[18] 7441 4-8-11 90 TimClark(5) 1 90
(Alan Bailey) *chsd ldrs: rdn to chse clr ldr over 1f out tl ins fnl f: wknd fnl 50yds* **8/1**

2000 **7** *1 ½* **Viva Verglas (IRE)**[18] 7441 3-9-3 91 GrahamGibbons 6 85
(David Barron) *wnt sharply rt leaving stalls: chsd ldr tl over 1f out: wknd ins fnl f* **6/1**

1000 **8** *8* **Captain Secret**[51] 6607 3-9-4 92 (p) PaddyAspell 7 57
(Marco Botti) *a towards rr: rdn over 1f out: sn wknd* **12/1**

59.19s (-1.31) **Going Correction** -0.10s/f (Stan) **8 Ran SP% 113.6**
Speed ratings (Par 107): **106,105,104,104,103 102,99,86**
CSF £56.64 CT £578.33 TOTE £6.20: £2.00, £3.10, £3.10; EX 77.50 Trifecta £791.10.
**Owner** Ten Green Bottles I **Bred** New Hall Stud **Trained** Newmarket, Suffolk

**FOCUS**
A decent sprint handicap in which they went a proper gallop, and those played centrally in the straight did best again.

## 7739 BETBRIGHT.COM DOWNLOAD OUR APP MEDIAN AUCTION MAIDEN STKS 1m (P)

**5:20** (5:21) (Class 6) 2-Y-O **£1,940** (£577; £288; £144) **Stalls** Low

Form RPR

64 **1** **Camagueyana**[82] 5644 2-9-0 0 SilvestreDeSousa 1 75+
(Ralph Beckett) *led for 1f: chsd ldr after tl rdn to ld 2f out: clr 1f out: r.o wl: readily* **11/4**[2]

2453 **2** *4 ½* **Oregon Gift**[37] 6976 2-9-5 70 JoeFanning 10 68
(Mark Johnston) *chsd wnr tl led after 1f: hdd and wandered 2f out: sn outpcd: kpt on to hold 2nd fnl f* **5/1**

**3** *1 ½* **Postbag** 2-9-0 0 FergusSweeney 7 60
(Henry Candy) *racd in midfield: rdn over 3f out: hdwy into modest 5th over 1f out: styd on steadily to go 3rd wl ins fnl f: no ch w wnr* **50/1**

5 **4** *1 ¼* **Waaleef**[28] 7206 2-9-5 0 PaddyAspell 4 62
(Marco Botti) *chsd ldrs: effrt 2f out: drvn and outpcd over 1f out: wl hld and one pce fnl f* **9/2**[3]

2 **5** *shd* **Free One (IRE)**[28] 7200 2-9-5 0 TomQueally 2 61
(Jeremy Noseda) *wl in tch in midfield: swtchd lft and effrt jst over 2f out: no prog over 1f out: wl hld and one pce fnl f* **9/4**[1]

64 **6** *2 ½* **Capsize**[47] 6718 2-9-5 0 ShaneKelly 12 56
(Sir Michael Stoute) *in tch in midfield: rdn and no rspnse over 2f out: 6th and wl hld fr over 1f out* **8/1**

00 **7** *¾* **Eagle Empire (IRE)**[35] 7040 2-9-5 0 SeanLevey 14 54+
(Richard Hannon) *stdd bk to rr sn after s: hld up wl in rr: rdn and sme hdwy over 1f out: styd on ins fnl f: nvr trbld ldrs* **100/1**

60 **8** *hd* **Layerthorpe (IRE)**[19] 7407 2-9-5 0 KieranO'Neill 5 54
(David Brown) *in tch in midfield: pushed along 4f out: rdn and struggling over 2f out: sn wknd* **100/1**

**9** *nk* **Light Of Love** 2-9-0 0 BenCurtis 11 48+
(Henry Candy) *s.i.s: rn green and rdn along in last trio: hdwy past btn horses ins fnl f: hmpd and wnt lft nr fin: nvr trbld ldrs* **33/1**

0 **10** *½* **Artistic Flight (IRE)**[15] 7512 2-9-5 0 WilliamCarson 8 52
(Jim Boyle) *off the pce in midfield: rdn and struggling 1/2-way: n.d fnl 2f* **100/1**

**11** *2 ½* **Man Look** 2-9-5 0 LiamKeniry 6 46
(Andrew Balding) *pushed along leaving stalls: in tch in midfield: rdn and no hdwy over 2f out: wknd 2f out* **25/1**

0 **12** *3 ¼* **Oakley Star**[11] 7594 2-9-0 0 ChrisCatlin 9 33
(Gay Kelleway) *a off the pce towards rr: rdn and struggling over 3f out: bhd 2f out* **100/1**

0 **13** *2* **Any Given Time (IRE)**[49] 6660 2-9-5 0 LiamJones 13 34
(David Simcock) *s.i.s: rn green and a rdn along in rr: n.d* **100/1**

6 **14** *¾* **Leonardo (GER)**[14] 7537 2-9-5 0 TonyHamilton 3 32
(James Fanshawe) *wl in tch in midfield: rdn jst over 2f out: sn btn: wknd over 1f out* **16/1**

1m 39.28s (-0.52) **Going Correction** -0.10s/f (Stan) **14 Ran SP% 123.0**
Speed ratings (Par 94): **98,93,92,90,90 88,87,87,86,86 83,80,78,77**
CSF £17.01 TOTE £3.80: £2.30, £1.70, £7.90; EX 23.70 Trifecta £665.60.
**Owner** Miss K Rausing **Bred** Miss K Rausing **Trained** Kimpton, Hants

**FOCUS**
An ordinary juvenile maiden in which they went a solid gallop and the pace held up

## 7740 BETBRIGHT MOBILE APP NURSERY H'CAP 1m (P)

**5:50** (5:51) (Class 6) (0-60,60) 2-Y-O **£1,940** (£577; £288; £144) **Stalls** Low

Form RPR

4444 **1** **Mikandy (IRE)**[33] 7075 2-9-3 59 RyanTate(3) 14 66
(Clive Cox) *in tch in midfield: clsd to chse ldrs over 2f out: rdn to chal over 1f out: led 1f out: r.o wl* **8/1**[3]

0605 **2** *1 ½* **Courier**[29] 7165 2-8-10 52 ThomasBrown(3) 6 56
(Lee Carter) *in tch in midfield: effrt towards inner over 1f out: chsd wnr fnl 150yds: kpt on but no imp: eased last strides* **10/1**

0603 **3** *hd* **First Summer**[14] 7536 2-9-2 55 RobertWinston 12 59+
(Shaun Harris) *hld up in last trio: hdwy on outer over 1f out: styd on wl ins fnl f: wnt 3rd towards fin: no threat to wnr* **10/1**

4443 **4** *¾* **Pink Ribbon (IRE)**[23] 7338 2-9-5 58 LiamKeniry 11 60
(Sylvester Kirk) *led: rdn jst over 2f out: hdd 1f out: no ex and lost 2 pls fnl 150yds* **6/1**[2]

000 **5** *¾* **La Favorita (IRE)**[47] 6700 2-8-8 50 DannyBrock(3) 2 50
(Phil McEntee) *in tch in midfield: rdn and effrt over 1f out: n.m.r 1f out: kpt on same pce* **33/1**

060 **6** *shd* **Luv U**[46] 6754 2-8-13 52 JimmyQuinn 5 52+
(Ed Dunlop) *dwlt: hld up in last trio: rdn and effrt over 1f out: styd on strly fnl 100yds: nt rch ldrs* **16/1**

0005 **7** *½* **Skylight (IRE)**[20] 7396 2-9-6 59 (v[1]) CharlesBishop 9 58
(Mick Channon) *in tch in midfield: effrt u.p over 1f out: drvn and styd on same pce fnl f* **8/1**[3]

0030 **8** *1 ¼* **Wolf Of Windlesham (IRE)**[75] 5875 2-9-7 60 SteveDrowne 1 56
(Charles Hills) *in tch in midfield: effrt u.p to chse ldrs 2f out: no ex 1f out: wknd ins fnl f* **10/1**

0463 **9** *nk* **Activation**[34] 7064 2-9-1 54 JohnFahy 3 49
(Hughie Morrison) *wl in tch in midfield: effrt and rdn to chse ldrs 2f out: no ex 1f out: wknd ins fnl f* **16/1**

0532 **10** *hd* **Scent Of Power**[36] 7014 2-8-9 55 KieranShoemark(7) 10 50
(Anthony Carson) *in tch in midfield: rdn to chse ldrs 2f out: no hdwy and n.m.r 1f out: one pce after* **7/2**[1]

605 **11** *3 ¾* **Cahar Fad (IRE)**[98] 5056 2-8-12 56 (p) JackDuern(5) 7 42
(Steph Hollinshead) *chsd ldrs: rdn wl over 2f out: struggling to qckn whn short of room and shuffled bk jst over 1f out: no rcvr and bhd fnl f* **66/1**

0030 **12** *3* **Quae Supra**[16] 7487 2-9-3 56 SeanLevey 4 35
(Richard Hannon) *w ldr: rdn and ev ch 2f out tl jst over 1f out: fdd ins fnl f* **33/1**

0606 **13** *1* **El Campeon**[77] 5823 2-8-11 50 SilvestreDeSousa 13 27
(Simon Dow) *s.i.s: a in rr: swtchd lft and tried to cl 2f out: no real hdwy: eased wl ins fnl f* **12/1**

065 **14** *4* **Blackadder**[23] 7336 2-9-1 54 FergusSweeney 8 22
(Pat Phelan) *t.k.h: in tch in midfield on outer: rdn and lost pl 3f out: bhd over 1f out* **8/1**[3]

1m 40.31s (0.51) **Going Correction** -0.10s/f (Stan) **14 Ran SP% 123.9**
Speed ratings (Par 94): **93,91,91,90,89 89,89,87,87,87 83,80,79,75**
CSF £87.43 CT £846.59 TOTE £11.50: £3.30, £4.00, £3.10; EX 183.80 Trifecta £2157.70 Part won..
**Owner** The Mikandy Partnership **Bred** A Thompson & M O'Brien **Trained** Lambourn, Berks

**FOCUS**
A moderate nursery handicap in which they went a respectable gallop.

## 7741 IRISH STALLION FARMS EBF MAIDEN STKS (BOBIS RACE) (DIV I) 6f (P)

**6:20** (6:21) (Class 4) 2-Y-O **£4,075** (£1,212; £606; £303) **Stalls** Low

Form RPR

06 **1** **Royal Silk**[28] 7192 2-9-0 0 WilliamTwiston-Davies 3 76+
(Roger Charlton) *stdd s: hld up in last pair: rdn and swtchd lft wl over 1f out: hdwy to chse clr ldr jst ins fnl f: str run to ld fnl 50yds: sn clr* **33/1**

42 **2** *2* **Secret Glance**[22] 7361 2-9-5 0 GrahamGibbons 10 75
(Ed McMahon) *led: rdn and kick clr over 1f out: drvn and hdd fnl 50yds: sn btn but stl clr 2nd* **2/1**[1]

0202 **3** *2 ¼* **Hills And Dales (IRE)**[13] 7551 2-8-12 79 KieranShoemark(7) 11 68
(Charlie Appleby) *t.k.h: dropped in bhd after s: clsd over 1f out: rdn and effrt in 3rd jst over 1f out: no imp* **5/2**[2]

0333 **4** *2 ¾* **Harbour Patrol (IRE)**[37] 6984 2-9-5 77 SeanLevey 6 60
(Richard Hannon) *in tch in midfield: swtchd lft and effrt 2f out: outpcd over 1f out: 4th and no imp fnl f* **4/1**[3]

60 **5** *2* **Hana Lina**[28] 7193 2-9-0 0 (b[1]) SilvestreDeSousa 2 49+
(William Haggas) *s.i.s: towards rr: swtchd ins and effrt u.p 2f out: n.d but kpt on fnl f* **20/1**

03 **6** *1* **Sir Henry Raeburn (IRE)**[12] 7560 2-9-5 0 (t) FergusSweeney 7 51
(Paul Cole) *chsd ldr: rdn and outpcd over 1f out: wknd fnl f* **8/1**

0 **7** *½* **Artist Cry**[33] 7082 2-9-5 0 TonyHamilton 4 50
(Richard Fahey) *in tch in midfield: rdn and no rspnse wl over 1f out: wknd fnl f* **12/1**

00 **8** *¾* **Perfect Bounty**[34] 7062 2-8-11 0 RyanTate(3) 5 42
(Clive Cox) *hld up in last trio: effrt 2f out: drvn and no hdwy over 1f out: wknd ins fnl f* **66/1**

02 **9** *5* **Rennie Mackintosh (IRE)**[6] 7685 2-9-5 0 JoeFanning 1 32
(Mark Johnston) *chsd ldng trio: outpcd u.p wl over 1f out: wknd jst over 1f out* **20/1**

**10** *1 ¼* **Tranquil Glen** 2-8-9 0 AlistairRawlinson(5) 8 24
(Michael Appleby) *chsd ldrs tl jst over 2f out: sn lost pl: bhd fnl f* **66/1**

**11** *3 ¼* **Arkansas Slim (IRE)** 2-9-5 0 RobertWinston 9 19
(Charles Hills) *s.i.s: rn green and a in rr* **50/1**

1m 12.13s (-0.97) **Going Correction** -0.10s/f (Stan) **11 Ran SP% 118.1**
Speed ratings (Par 98): **102,99,96,92,90 88,87,86,80,78 74**
CSF £95.94 TOTE £26.40: £6.00, £2.50, £1.70; EX 150.20 Trifecta £1030.20.
**Owner** D J Deer **Bred** D J And Mrs Deer **Trained** Beckhampton, Wilts

**FOCUS**
The first division of a fair juvenile maiden, in which they went a proper gallop, and the winning time was quicker than the second.

## 7742 IRISH STALLION FARMS EBF MAIDEN STKS (BOBIS RACE) (DIV II) 6f (P)

**6:50** (6:52) (Class 4) 2-Y-O **£4,075** (£1,212; £606; £303) **Stalls** Low

Form RPR

62 **1** **Absolute Champion (USA)**[13] 7542 2-9-5 0 TomQueally 7 71+
(Jamie Osborne) *mde all: pressed and rdn jst over 1f out: styd on wl and asserted ins fnl f: rdn out* **7/4**[1]

534 **2** *1 ¼* **Spinaminnie (IRE)**[8] 7637 2-9-0 0 JoeFanning 9 62
(Mark Johnston) *sn chsng wnr: rdn and pressing wnr over 1f out: no ex and outpcd fnl 100yds* **14/1**

4 **3** *1 ¼* **Star Of The Stage**[22] 7361 2-9-5 0 TonyHamilton 2 64+
(Richard Fahey) *t.k.h: hld up in tch in midfield: effrt to chse ldng pair over 1f out: drvn and styd on same pce fnl f* **8/1**

53 **4** *2 ½* **Pressure**[30] 7155 2-9-5 0 SteveDrowne 1 59+
(Clive Cox) *chsd ldrs: rdn and outpcd over 1f out: 4th and one pce fnl f* **10/3**[2]

43 **5** *1 ¼* **With Approval (IRE)**[19] 7412 2-9-5 0 RobertWinston 5 52
(Charles Hills) *t.k.h: rdn and lost pl jst over 2f out: wknd over 1f out* **6/1**[3]

505 **6** *hd* **Moon River (IRE)**[105] 4781 2-9-0 58 SeanLevey 8 47+
(Brian Meehan) *hld up in last trio: effrt 2f out: drvn and no hdwy over 1f out: kpt on same pce fnl f* **8/1**

**7** *nse* **Glorious Asset** 2-9-5 0 AntonioFresu 6 52+
(Ed Walker) *in tch in last trio: rdn and outpcd jst over 2f out: rallied and kpt on same pce ins fnl f: no threat to ldrs* **7/1**

5 **8** *nk* **Ertidaad (IRE)**[16] 7491 2-9-2 0 JoeyHaynes(3) 10 51+
(Pat Eddery) *wnt lft s: hld up in tch in midfield on outer: rdn and lost pl 2f out: bhd but kpt on fnl f* **66/1**

**9** *nse* **Mildmay Arms** 2-9-5 0 LiamJones 3 50+
(Simon Hodgson) *dwlt: pushed along in last pair: sme hdwy 2f out: no imp fnl f: eased cl home* **66/1**

1m 12.87s (-0.23) **Going Correction** -0.10s/f (Stan) **9 Ran SP% 118.1**
Speed ratings (Par 98): **97,95,93,90,88 88,88,87,87**
CSF £30.35 TOTE £2.40: £1.10, £2.60, £2.20; EX 25.20 Trifecta £182.90.
**Owner** Eddie M C Wong **Bred** Tada Nobutaka **Trained** Upper Lambourn, Berks


The Form Book, Raceform Ltd, Newbury, RG14 5SJ

**FOCUS**
The weaker division of a fair juvenile maiden, in which the winner made all at a respectable tempo, and the time was slower than the first.

## 7743 BETBRIGHT.COM CONDITIONS STKS 7f (P)
**7:20** (7:20) (Class 2) 3-Y-O+ **£11,827** (£3,541; £1,770; £885; £442) **Stalls** Low

Form RPR
2333 **1** **Magic City (IRE)**[81] 5665 5-8-11 100 SeanLevey 2 107
(Richard Hannon) *in tch: clsd to join ldrs over 1f out: rdn and qcknd to ld 1f out: r.o wl* **7/1**
4210 **2** 1 1/2 **Badr Al Badoor (IRE)**[39] 6920 4-8-6 96 JoeFanning 5 98
(James Fanshawe) *stdd s: hld up in tch in rr: effrt between horses to press wnr 1f out: one pce fnl 100yds* **7/2**[3]
4514 **3** 1 **Patentar (FR)**[39] 6934 3-9-4 108 (t) ShaneKelly 3 107
(Marco Botti) *chsd ldr: rdn 2f out: drvn and stl pressing ldrs but unable qck 1f out: one pce fnl f* **9/4**[2]
2100 **4** 1 1/2 **Frontier Fighter**[187] 2113 6-8-11 103 SamJames 6 96
(David O'Meara) *led: rdn 2f out: hdd and no ex 1f out: outpcd ins fnl f* **10/1**
6030 **5** 1/2 **Georgian Bay (IRE)**[25] 7276 4-8-11 99 (p) SilvestreDeSousa 4 95
(K R Burke) *chsd ldrs: nudged along and dropped to 4th 3f out: rdn over 2f out: last and no prog fnl f* **7/4**[1]
1m 24.04s (-1.96) **Going Correction** -0.10s/f (Stan)
**WFA** 3 from 4yo+ 1lb 5 Ran SP% **110.9**
Speed ratings (Par 109): **107,105,104,102,101**
CSF £30.74 TOTE £4.90: £3.30, £2.50; EX 25.30 Trifecta £57.80.
**Owner** Barker, Ferguson, Mason, Hassiakos, Done **Bred** Miss Annmarie Burke **Trained** East Everleigh, Wilts
**FOCUS**
A good-quality conditions contest in which they went an even gallop.

## 7744 BETBRIGHT MONEYBACK OFFERS H'CAP 1m 3f (P)
**7:50** (7:51) (Class 6) (0-65,65) 3-Y-O+ **£1,940** (£577; £288; £144) **Stalls** Low

Form RPR
4336 **1** **Cataria Girl (USA)**[22] 7358 5-9-8 64 (t) MartinDwyer 6 72
(Marcus Tregoning) *led for 1f: chsd ldrs tl effrt to ld again 2f out: drvn 1f out: kpt on and a holding rival: drvn out* **16/1**
2222 **2** nk **Classic Mission**[14] 7527 3-8-13 65 (b) NedCurtis(5) 8 73
(Jonathan Portman) *chsd ldrs: wnt 2nd 9f out: upsides wnr and stl on bit over 1f out: rdn 1f out: kpt on but a hld* **13/2**[2]
005 **3** 3 1/2 **Perfect Rhythm**[35] 7032 3-9-2 63 LiamKeniry 3 65
(Patrick Chamings) *chsd ldrs: effrt 2f out: 3rd and outpcd jst ins fnl f: kpt on* **25/1**
6002 **4** nse **Mcbirney (USA)**[8] 7635 7-9-4 60 JimCrowley 4 62+
(Paul D'Arcy) *hld up in tch towards rr: hdwy 2f out: nt clr run over 1f out: hdwy 1f out: battling for 3rd towards fin: kpt on: no threat to ldrs* **6/4**[1]
4010 **5** 1 1/2 **Celestial Bay**[31] 7133 5-9-7 63 ShaneKelly 1 62+
(Sylvester Kirk) *hld up in tch: effrt 2f out: drvn and chsd ldrs over 1f out: outpcd fnl f* **16/1**
2430 **6** shd **Red Dragon (IRE)**[23] 7343 4-9-1 64 ChrisMeehan(7) 7 63
(Michael Blanshard) *trckd ldrs: rdn and outpcd over 2f out: rallied 1f out: kpt on but nvr enough pce to chal* **13/2**[2]
4602 **7** nse **Bridge That Gap**[19] 7426 6-9-7 63 (p) JimmyQuinn 10 62
(Roger Ingram) *t.k.h: chsd ldrs 8f out: rdn 2f out: unable qck jst over 1f out: outpcd ins fnl f* **10/1**
4421 **8** 3/4 **Mary Le Bow**[12] 7570 3-8-10 64 (p) KieranShoemark(7) 11 62
(Victor Dartnall) *in tch in midfield: rdn and effrt jst over 2f out: no prog and one pce fr over 1f out* **7/1**[3]
5010 **9** nk **Thane Of Cawdor (IRE)**[47] 6706 5-9-2 63 JennyPowell(5) 2 61+
(Joseph Tuite) *hld up in rr: sme hdwy on inner over 1f out: nvr trbld ldrs* **14/1**
-200 **10** 1/2 **Laura Secord (CAN)**[68] 6091 4-9-9 65 SeanLevey 13 62
(Heather Main) *s.i.s: hdwy to ld and slowed pce after 2f: rdn and hdd 2f out: outpcd jst over 1f out: wknd ins fnl f* **50/1**
0233 **11** 1 1/4 **Maison Brillet (IRE)**[151] 3234 7-9-5 61 (p) RobertHavlin 5 60
(Clive Drew) *in tch in midfield: effrt and nt clr run over 1f out tl ins fnl f: lost all ch and eased wl ins fnl f* **33/1**
-110 **12** 3 **Reality Show (IRE)**[286] 382 7-9-6 62 RobertWinston 9 52+
(Shaun Harris) *stdd s: hld up in tch in rr: effrt 2f out: no hdwy* **14/1**
06-5 **13** 9 **Guards Chapel**[161] 818 6-9-9 65 FergusSweeney 14 41+
(Gary Moore) *hld up in tch towards rr: hdwy into midfield 7f out: rdn and lost pl over 2f out: bhd fnl f* **25/1**
2m 27.18s (5.28) **Going Correction** -0.10s/f (Stan)
**WFA** 3 from 4yo+ 5lb 13 Ran SP% **125.9**
Speed ratings (Par 101): **76,75,73,73,72 72,72,71,71,70 69,67,61**
CSF £119.17 CT £2641.65 TOTE £20.70: £4.70, £4.50, £6.60; EX 143.40 Trifecta £1604.40.
**Owner** Mr And Mrs A E Pakenham **Bred** Shadwell Farm LLC **Trained** Whitsbury, Hants
**FOCUS**
A modest middle-distance handicap in which they went a particularly steady gallop, with the contest effectively turning into a 3f sprint and the prominent runners being massively favoured.
T/Jkpt: Not won. T/Plt: £266.10 to a £1 stake. Pool: £85,524.74 - 234.60 winning tickets. T/Qpdt: £30.00 to a £1 stake. Pool: £10,932.70 - 269.32 winning tickets. SP

# 7737 KEMPTON (A.W) (R-H)
Thursday, November 13

**OFFICIAL GOING: Polytrack: standard**
Wind: medium, half behind Weather: dry

## 7752 DOWNLOAD THE BETVICTOR APP MEDIAN AUCTION MAIDEN STKS 7f (P)
**4:20** (4:20) (Class 5) 2-Y-O **£2,587** (£770; £384; £192) **Stalls** Low

Form RPR
05 **1** **Nouveau Foret**[29] 7194 2-9-0 0 LukeMorris 8 72
(Ed Walker) *in tch in midfield: effrt on inner to chse ldrs 2f out: led ins fnl f: r.o wl: rdn out* **12/1**
45 **2** 1 1/2 **Lady Pinnacle**[29] 7193 2-9-0 0 LiamKeniry 14 68
(Andrew Balding) *chsd ldr: rdn to chal over 1f out: led 1f out: sn hdd and r.o same pce* **6/1**[3]
03 **3** 1 **Pacolita (IRE)**[16] 7511 2-9-0 0 MartinDwyer 4 65
(Sylvester Kirk) *chsd ldng pair: rdn 2f out: short of room and hmpd jst over 1f out: rallied ins fnl f: wnt 3rd fnl 100yds: kpt on* **8/1**
5 **4** hd **Shell Bay (USA)**[20] 7413 2-9-5 0 SeanLevey 2 70
(Richard Hannon) *in tch on midfield: rdn 2f out: no imp tl styd on ins fnl f: nvr enough pce to chal* **3/1**[1]
00 **5** 1 3/4 **You Be Lucky (IRE)**[52] 6605 2-9-0 0 JimCrowley 13 60
(Jo Crowley) *led: rdn 2f out: hdd 1f out: no ex: wknd fnl 100yds* **20/1**
**6** 1 3/4 **Kaufmann** 2-9-5 0 WilliamBuick 1 60+
(John Gosden) *in tch in midfield: rdn and effrt jst over 2f out: 6th and plenty to do over 1f out: kpt on but nvr threatened ldrs* **3/1**[1]
**7** 2 1/4 **Logorrheic** 2-9-5 0 SebSanders 11 54
(Ralph Beckett) *in tch in midfield: rdn and effrt jst over 2f out: 7th and plenty to do over 1f out: kpt on but no imp* **5/1**[2]
4 **8** 3 3/4 **Tarragon**[33] 7114 2-9-5 0 SteveDrowne 5 44
(Jeremy Gask) *chsd ldrs: struggling u.p over 2f out: sn btn: wknd over 1f out* **20/1**
0 **9** 5 **Fanny Again**[29] 7193 2-9-0 0 ShaneKelly 7 26
(Denis Coakley) *hld up off the pce in last pair: n.d* **25/1**
50 **10** 2 1/2 **Doctors Papers**[27] 7244 2-9-5 0 TomQueally 10 24
(David Brown) *chsd ldrs tl 1/2-way: sn lost pl: wknd 2f out: bhd fnl f* **50/1**
**11** 2 **Onorina (IRE)** 2-9-0 0 PatCosgrave 9 13
(Jim Boyle) *a towards rr: n.d* **25/1**
**12** 6 **Selfrespect** 2-9-0 0 FergusSweeney 3
(Henry Candy) *s.i.s: rn green and a bhd* **16/1**
6 **13** 4 1/2 **Irish Belle (IRE)**[17] 7491 2-9-0 0 WilliamCarson 6
(Tony Carroll) *a towards rr: rdn 1/2-way: bhd fnl 2f* **50/1**
1m 26.73s (0.73) **Going Correction** -0.025s/f (Stan) 13 Ran SP% **126.8**
Speed ratings (Par 96): **94,92,91,90,88 86,84,80,74,71 69,62,57**
CSF £80.76 TOTE £10.80: £3.50, £1.90, £2.70; EX 70.60 Trifecta £1134.90.
**Owner** N M Bowden **Bred** Cap Jaluca Pty Ltd **Trained** Newmarket, Suffolk
**FOCUS**
Just a modest maiden.

## 7753 DOWNLOAD THE RACINGUK IPAD APP NURSERY H'CAP 7f (P)
**4:50** (4:50) (Class 6) (0-65,65) 2-Y-O **£1,940** (£577; £288; £144) **Stalls** Low

Form RPR
000 **1** **Pat Mustard**[21] 7400 2-9-1 59 TomQueally 5 63
(Jamie Osborne) *in tch in midfield: effrt u.p 2f out: str chal ins fnl f: r.o wl u.p to ld on post* **8/1**
5021 **2** nse **Chetan**[15] 7529 2-9-2 60 WilliamTwiston-Davies 2 64
(Milton Bradley) *led: rdn 2f out: battled on gamely u.p: hdd on post* **14/1**
0062 **3** 1 1/4 **Reflation**[15] 7529 2-9-4 62 SeanLevey 4 63
(Richard Hannon) *wl in tch in midfield: hdwy to chse ldrs and effrt u.p over 1f out: no ex and one pce fnl 100yds* **7/1**[3]
6650 **4** 1/2 **Finton Friend (IRE)**[27] 7257 2-9-7 65 (b[1]) JimCrowley 9 64
(Charles Hills) *chsd ldrs: rdn over 2f out: unable qck and outpcd over 1f out: rallied and styd on again ins fnl f* **16/1**
1054 **5** nk **Tinkers Kiss (IRE)**[15] 7529 2-8-7 58 KieranShoemark(7) 6 56
(Philip McBride) *hld up in tch in last quartet: hdwy on inner 2f out: drvn to chse ldrs 1f out: styd on same pce ins fnl f* **16/1**
4435 **6** 1/2 **Charlie's Star**[23] 7363 2-9-2 60 LiamJones 10 57
(Laura Mongan) *in tch in midfield: rdn 2f out: hdwy 1f out: styd on wl fnl 100yds: nt rch ldrs* **33/1**
055 **7** 1/2 **Beauty Of The Sea**[58] 6420 2-9-6 64 WilliamBuick 8 60
(Roger Varian) *chsd ldrs: c towards centre and rdn jst over 2f out: styd on same pce and no imp after* **11/4**[1]
050 **8** hd **Miss Minuty**[14] 7550 2-9-2 60 LukeMorris 7 58
(Sir Mark Prescott Bt) *hld up in last pair: rdn over 2f out: hdwy 1f out: running on wl whn nt clr run fnl 75yds: nowhere to go and eased after* **25/1**
015 **9** 1 1/2 **Ragtime Dancer**[17] 7488 2-9-0 63 NedCurtis(5) 1 54
(Jonathan Portman) *chsd ldr: rdn and ev ch 2f out: no ex jst ins fnl f: sn wknd* **9/2**[2]
000 **10** 3 1/2 **On The Tiles**[33] 7113 2-9-5 63 KieranO'Neill 12 45
(David Brown) *hld up in tch in last quartet: effrt jst over 2f out: no prog: n.d* **66/1**
0054 **11** shd **The Olympus Man**[17] 7487 2-9-4 62 JamieSpencer 3 43
(Olly Stevens) *stdd s: hld up in tch in last quartet: effrt 2f out: no prog: n.d* **20/1**
6603 **12** 1 1/2 **Zubaidah**[27] 7258 2-9-7 65 PatCosgrave 13 42
(George Baker) *in tch in midfield on outer: rdn wl over 2f out: sn lost pl: bhd 1f out* **9/2**[2]
1m 26.84s (0.84) **Going Correction** -0.025s/f (Stan) 12 Ran SP% **118.1**
Speed ratings (Par 94): **94,93,92,91,91 91,90,90,88,84 84,82**
CSF £108.90 CT £828.12 TOTE £12.30: £3.10, £2.30, £2.00; EX 107.40 Trifecta £1734.60.
**Owner** B T McDonald **Bred** Triple H Stud Ltd **Trained** Upper Lambourn, Berks
**FOCUS**
A competitive nursery.

## 7754 DOWNLOAD THE BETVICTOR APP CLAIMING STKS 1m 4f (P)
**5:20** (5:20) (Class 6) 3-4-Y-O **£1,940** (£577; £288; £144) **Stalls** Centre

Form RPR
3616 **1** **Dalgig**[16] 7516 4-9-3 70 MikeyEnnis(7) 1 70
(David Pipe) *chsd ldr: rdn 2f out: led over 1f out: in command but kpt up to work fnl f* **4/9**[1]
5610 **2** 2 **Le Deluge (FR)**[16] 7522 4-9-5 66 (t) DavidParkes(7) 2 69
(Ann Stokell) *led: rdn jst over 2f out: hdd over 1f out: kpt on same pce fnl f* **7/2**[2]
4230 **3** 2 3/4 **Travis Bickle (IRE)**[31] 7162 3-8-10 57 (b) LiamKeniry 3 54
(John Flint) *a in 3rd: effrt jst over 2f out: no ex 1f out: one pce fnl f* **8/1**[3]
6056 **4** 7 **Roy Rocket (FR)**[107] 4769 4-9-0 45 JimCrowley 4 41
(John Berry) *hld up in last: rdn 3f out: sme hdwy u.p 2f out: wknd 1f out* **25/1**
2m 36.55s (2.05) **Going Correction** -0.025s/f (Stan)
**WFA** 3 from 4yo 6lb 4 Ran SP% **106.4**
Speed ratings (Par 101): **92,90,88,84**
CSF £2.18 TOTE £1.30; EX 2.00 Trifecta £3.00.
**Owner** Mrs Donna Hopkins **Bred** Usk Valley Stud **Trained** Nicholashayne, Devon
**FOCUS**
This proved straightforward enough for the favourite in this muddling claimer. The winner was the clear form pick but the third wasn't beaten far.

## 7755 £25 FREE BET AT BETVICTOR.COM NURSERY H'CAP 6f (P)
**5:50** (5:51) (Class 4) (0-85,82) 2-Y-O **£4,528** (£1,347; £673; £336) **Stalls** Low

Form RPR
2216 **1** **Lyfka**[16] 7525 2-9-5 80 LukeMorris 3 90+
(Paul Cole) *stdd s: hld up in rr: rdn and effrt over 1f out: led 1f out: r.o strly and drew clr: readily* **9/4**[1]
1031 **2** 4 **Spring Loaded (IRE)**[49] 6679 2-9-7 82 SeanLevey 2 80
(Paul D'Arcy) *chsd ldrs: effrt 2f out: press ldrs over 1f out: outpcd by wnr 1f out: kpt on same pce after: wnt 2nd fnl 100yds* **5/2**[2]

442 **3** *hd* **Winning Hunter**[31] 7155 2-8-12 73 ....(p) LiamKeniry 4 70
(Philip Hide) *w ldr: rdn to ld 2f out: hdd 1f out: sn outpcd by wnr: kpt on same pce and lost 2nd fnl 100yds* **10/1**

6242 **4** *3 ¼* **Be Bold**[8] 7661 2-9-7 82 .... WilliamBuick 5 70
(Richard Hannon) *chsd ldrs: rdn 2f out: outpcd and dropped to rr over 1f out: wl hld fnl f* **3/1**[3]

0343 **5** *nk* **Captain Marmalade (IRE)**[22] 7379 2-8-10 71 .... JimCrowley 1 58
(Roger Charlton) *led tl rdn and hdd 2f out: styd pressing ldrs tl btn 1f out: sn wknd* **4/1**

1m 12.41s (-0.69) **Going Correction** -0.025s/f (Stan) **5** Ran SP% **113.4**
Speed ratings (Par 98): **103,97,97,93,92**
CSF £8.50 TOTE £2.90: £1.40, £1.40; EX 9.30 Trifecta £25.00.
**Owner** A H Robinson **Bred** A H & C E Robinson **Trained** Whatcombe, Oxon

**FOCUS**
Despite the small field this looked a fair nursery, the gallop was solid and the form looks reliable.

## 7756 IRISH STALLION FARMS EBF MAIDEN FILLIES' STKS (BOBIS RACE) 1m (P)
**6:20** (6:25) (Class 4) 2-Y-O **£4,075** (£1,212; £606; £303) **Stalls** Low

Form RPR

**1** **Light And Shade** 2-9-0 0 .... LukeMorris 11 76
(James Tate) *chsd ldr: rdn and ev ch over 1f out: led 1f out: styd on wl: rdn out* **20/1**

03 **2** *1 ¾* **Perfect Orange**[21] 7398 2-9-0 0 .... MartinDwyer 5 72
(Marcus Tregoning) *led: rdn and hung lft over 1f out: hdd 1f out: styd on same pce fnl f* **3/1**[1]

**3** *nk* **Perfect Glance (USA)** 2-9-0 0 .... ShaneKelly 6 71+
(Sir Michael Stoute) *racd in midfield: clr in ldng sextet and pushed along 2f out: styd on steadily ins fnl f: pressing for 2nd cl home* **7/1**[2]

**4** *2* **Lovely Surprise (IRE)** 2-9-0 0 .... JimCrowley 3 67
(Ismail Mohammed) *chsd ldrs: rdn and effrt in 3rd over 1f out: styd on same pce after: lost 3rd ins fnl f* **20/1**

0 **5** *5* **Fieldmouse**[19] 7450 2-9-0 0 .... TomQueally 1 55
(Eve Johnson Houghton) *in tch in midfield: clr in ldng sextet and rdn 2f out: btn jst over 1f out: wknd ins fnl f* **33/1**

**6** *2 ¼* **Miss Giler** 2-9-0 0 ....(t) NickyMackay 7 50+
(John Gosden) *sn off the pce in rr: sme hdwy into modest 7th 2f out: no imp: n.d* **33/1**

**7** *¾* **Noble Vision (IRE)** 2-8-7 0 .... KieranShoemark(7) 13 48+
(John Gosden) *s.i.s: wl off the pce in rr: styd on past btn horses over 1f out: n.d* **25/1**

0 **8** *8* **Prying**[8] 7659 2-9-0 0 .... JamieSpencer 2 30
(Charlie Appleby) *chsd ldng pair: rdn 2f out: btn over 1f out: sn eased* **8/1**[3]

0 **9** *¾* **Beccabuddyblues (GR)**[8] 7658 2-9-0 0 ....[1] PatCosgrave 9 28
(Amanda Perrett) *t.k.h: hld up off the pce in midfield: modest 7th and struggling over 2f out: wknd 2f out* **100/1**

0 **10** *2 ¾* **Solveig's Song**[14] 7550 2-9-0 0 .... JackMitchell 10 22
(Steve Woodman) *a off the pce towards rr: rdn over 3f out: struggling over 2f out: no ch after* **100/1**

**11** *2 ½* **Oakling** 2-9-0 0 .... LiamKeniry 12 16
(Sylvester Kirk) *sn rdn along and outpcd in last pair: n.d* **100/1**

**12** *10* **Neath Abbey** 2-9-0 0 .... SteveDrowne 4
(William Muir) *in tch in midfield on outer: rdn 1/2-way: lost pl 3f out: t.o fnl f* **50/1**

1m 40.35s (0.55) **Going Correction** -0.025s/f (Stan) **12** Ran SP% **72.8**
Speed ratings (Par 95): **96,94,93,91,86 84,83,75,75,72 69,59**
CSF £27.84 TOTE £10.50: £2.80, £1.30, £1.70; EX 46.20 Trifecta £138.00.
**Owner** Saeed Manana **Bred** M H And Mrs G Tourle **Trained** Newmarket, Suffolk
■ Journey was withdrawn. Price at time of withdrawal 5/4F. Rule 4 applies to all bets - deduct 40p in the pound.

**FOCUS**
The first two dominated throughout.

## 7757 DOWNLOAD THE BETVICTOR.COM INSTABET APP H'CAP 1m (P)
**6:50** (6:52) (Class 5) (0-75,75) 3-Y-O+ **£2,587** (£770; £384; £192) **Stalls** Low

Form RPR

0000 **1** **Persepolis (IRE)**[29] 7205 4-9-5 73 .... AmirQuinn 7 85
(Lee Carter) *hld up in tch in midfield: hdwy to chse ldrs 2f out: led over 1f out: sn hrd pressed and rdn: fnd enough u.p and asserted fnl 75yds: r.o* **7/4**[1]

4203 **2** *½* **Footstepsintherain (IRE)**[15] 7530 4-9-4 72 .... FergusSweeney 1 83
(David Dennis) *hld up in tch towards rr: hdwy to chse ldrs 2f out: drvn and str chal 1f out: r.o but a jst hld fnl 75yds* **4/1**[2]

0665 **3** *7* **Know Your Name**[43] 6871 3-8-8 67 ....(v) DeclanBates(3) 3 62
(David Evans) *led for 2f: chsd ldr after tl rdn to ld again 2f out: sn hdd: outpcd fnl f* **33/1**

5230 **4** *1 ¾* **Ghosting (IRE)**[30] 7185 3-9-1 71 ....(t) JimCrowley 9 62
(Tom Dascombe) *s.i.s: hld up in rr: hdwy jst over 2f out: kpt on to go 4th ins fnl f: no threat to ldrs* **6/1**[3]

0600 **5** *2 ¼* **High Drama (IRE)**[21] 7397 3-8-12 68 .... LiamKeniry 10 54
(Andrew Balding) *in tch in midfield: rdn and effrt over 2f out: sn outpcd: wl hld over 1f out* **16/1**

5112 **6** *1* **Lady Sylvia**[21] 7397 5-9-2 75 .... JennyPowell(5) 11 58
(Joseph Tuite) *dwlt: towards rr: hdwy into midfield but stuck v wd bnd over 3f out: rdn and outpcd 2f out: wl hld after* **8/1**

2310 **7** *1* **Lindart (ITY)**[64] 6236 3-8-9 72 ....(b) GaryMahon(7) 2 53
(Richard Hannon) *sn rdn along in midfield: outpcd over 2f out: no threat to ldrs fnl 2f* **50/1**

6000 **8** *nse* **Club House (IRE)**[15] 7533 4-8-13 67 .... RobertTart 6 48
(Robert Mills) *hld up in last quartet: rdn and sme hdwy 2f out: nvr trbld ldrs* **25/1**

0502 **9** *1 ¾* **Siouxperhero (IRE)**[30] 7186 5-9-4 72 ....(b) MartinDwyer 4 49
(William Muir) *nvr travelling wl and sn pushed along towards rr: bhd fnl 2f* **10/1**

0500 **10** *hd* **Tidal's Baby**[29] 7205 5-9-1 72 .... ThomasBrown(3) 8 49
(Lee Carter) *nt best away: dashed up to ld after 2f: rdn and hdd 2f out: sn btn: fdd fnl f* **25/1**

2000 **11** *23* **Notebook**[16] 7513 3-8-12 68 ....[1] SteveDrowne 13
(Martin Smith) *chsd ldrs tl lost pl u.p over 2f out: sn bhd: t.o fnl f* **66/1**

0140 **12** *14* **Well Painted (IRE)**[87] 5487 5-9-2 73 ....(tp) RossAtkinson(3) 14
(Andy Turnell) *a in rr: rdn 1/2-way: lost tch over 2f out: t.o fnl f* **33/1**

0016 **13** *14* **Hulcolt (IRE)**[21] 7403 3-9-4 74 .... LukeMorris 5
(Garry Moss) *chsd ldrs tl lost pl and rdr looking down over 2f out: eased after and t.o over 1f out: fin lame* **12/1**

1m 37.92s (-1.88) **Going Correction** -0.025s/f (Stan)
**WFA** 3 from 4yo+ 2lb **13** Ran SP% **121.5**
Speed ratings (Par 103): **108,107,100,98,96 95,94,94,92,92 69,55,41**
CSF £7.76 CT £181.76 TOTE £3.20: £1.70, £1.40, £10.00; EX 14.60 Trifecta £548.90.
**Owner** John Joseph Smith **Bred** Avington Manor Stud **Trained** Epsom, Surrey
■ Stewards' Enquiry : Amir Quinn four-day ban: used whip above permitted level (Nov 27-29,Dec 1)

**FOCUS**
This was a strongly run handicap, two came clear and a gamble was landed. The winner was well treated on his 3yo form.

## 7758 BETVICTOR.COM H'CAP (DIV I) 7f (P)
**7:20** (7:20) (Class 5) (0-70,70) 3-Y-O+ **£2,587** (£770; £288; £288) **Stalls** Low

Form RPR

0056 **1** **Multitask**[16] 7514 4-9-6 69 .... LiamKeniry 5 77
(Michael Madgwick) *bmpd s: stdd and hld up in rr: swtchd ins and gd hdwy 2f out: str run to ld ins fnl f: in command and shifting lft towards fin* **8/1**[3]

3222 **2** *¾* **Freddy With A Y (IRE)**[17] 7494 4-9-7 70 ....(p) FergusSweeney 9 76
(Gary Moore) *chsd ldrs: rdn over 2f out: clsd on ldr 1f out: chsd wnr fnl 100yds: kpt on* **13/2**[2]

4 **3** *nk* **Until Midnight (IRE)**[180] 2341 4-9-4 67 .... RobertTart 13 72
(Eugene Stanford) *hld up towards rr: hdwy u.p over 1f out: styd on wl ins fnl f: nt rch ldrs* **13/2**[2]

4231 **3** *dht* **Tychaios**[63] 6266 4-9-3 66 .... SeanLevey 12 71
(Stuart Williams) *hld up in midfield: hdwy u.p over 1f out: styd on wl ins fnl f: nt rch ldrs* **10/1**

3440 **5** *½* **Living Leader**[22] 7373 5-9-4 67 ....(tp) PatCosgrave 11 71
(Grace Harris) *hld up in last trio: hdwy u.p 1f out: styd on wl ins fnl f: nt rch ldrs* **16/1**

0-20 **6** *1* **Oasis Spirit**[209] 1554 4-9-0 70 .... RobHornby(7) 3 71+
(Andrew Balding) *chsd ldrs: wnt 2nd and clsd on ldr over 1f out: pressed ldrs briefly ins fnl f: no ex fnl 100yds: b.b.v* **14/1**

0221 **7** *½* **Pour La Victoire (IRE)**[14] 7556 4-9-1 69 ....(b) GeorgeDowning(5) 8 69+
(Tony Carroll) *t.k.h: chsd ldrs: wnt 2nd 5f out: led 1/2-way and sn clr: stl clr but tiring u.p 1f out: hdd ins fnl f: sn wknd* **5/1**[1]

2436 **8** *1 ½* **Hipz (IRE)**[23] 7356 3-9-2 66 .... LiamJones 4 61
(Laura Mongan) *in tch in midfield: hmpd and hit rail 5f out: effrt and sme hdwy over 1f out: no imp ins fnl f* **28/1**

1054 **9** *¾* **Hardy Black (IRE)**[15] 7533 3-9-4 68 .... TomQueally 10 61
(Jamie Osborne) *s.i.s: hld up in rr: effrt u.p over 1f out: kpt on: nvr trbld ldrs* **5/1**[1]

2651 **10** *1 ¼* **Lucky Di**[29] 7202 4-9-6 69 .... CharlesBishop 1 60
(Peter Hedger) *hld up towards rr: hdwy u.p 2f out: no prog ins fnl f* **10/1**

5044 **11** *¾* **Dark Lane**[27] 7252 8-8-10 62 .... DeclanBates(3) 6 51
(David Evans) *hld up towards rr: rdn and effrt 2f out: no real imp: nvr trbld ldrs* **33/1**

2436 **12** *4 ½* **Kakapuka**[97] 5125 7-9-3 66 .... LukeMorris 2 43
(Anabel K Murphy) *led early: sn stdd bk to chse ldrs: hmpd 5f out: rdn 2f out: wknd over 1f out* **14/1**

0600 **13** *½* **Lupo D'Oro (IRE)**[15] 7535 5-9-1 64 .... SteveDrowne 7 40
(John Best) *in tch in midfield: hmpd 5f out: rdn and wknd 2f out* **25/1**

4306 **14** *1 ¾* **Live Dangerously**[17] 7502 4-9-0 63 .... WilliamCarson 14 34
(John Bridger) *sn led: hdd 1/2-way: chsd ldr tl over 1f out: sn btn: wknd fnl f* **66/1**

1m 25.42s (-0.58) **Going Correction** -0.025s/f (Stan)
**WFA** 3 from 4yo+ 1lb **14** Ran SP% **120.2**
Speed ratings (Par 103): **102,101,100,100,100 99,98,96,95,94 93,88,87,85**
WIN: Multitask £14.40 ; PL: Tychaios £2.00, Freddy With A Y £2.20, Until Midnight £1.30, Multitask £3.00; EX: £65.20; CSF: £57.32; TC: M/F/U : £187.50, M/F/T £274.77, TF: M/F/U £277.30, M/F/U £40160.00.
**Owner** Mrs L N Harmes **Bred** Mrs L N Harmes **Trained** Denmead, Hants

**FOCUS**
A bit of a messy race, but ultimately it paid to be ridden with some patience off a strong pace. The winner was on a good mark on last winter's form.

## 7759 BETVICTOR.COM H'CAP (DIV II) 7f (P)
**7:50** (7:50) (Class 5) (0-70,70) 3-Y-O+ **£2,587** (£770; £384; £192) **Stalls** Low

Form RPR

60 **1** **Elusive Ellen (IRE)**[21] 7397 4-9-2 65 .... FergusSweeney 2 72
(Brendan Powell) *hld up in rr: swtchd ins 2f out: gd hdwy over 1f out: led ins fnl f: hld on wl* **25/1**

6-03 **2** *shd* **Flicksta (USA)**[13] 7569 3-9-2 66 .... JackMitchell 4 72
(John Ryan) *in tch in midfield: effrt u.p over 1f out: drvn and led ins fnl f: sn hdd: ev ch after: jst hld* **7/1**[3]

4360 **3** *nse* **Exceeding Power**[23] 7351 3-8-13 70 .... MikeyEnnis(7) 9 76
(Martin Bosley) *in tch in midfield: effrt u.p over 1f out: hdwy ins fnl f: str chal cl home: jst hld* **25/1**

1064 **4** *nse* **For Ayman**[23] 7356 3-9-3 67 .... SteveDrowne 13 73
(Joseph Tuite) *hld up in tch: effrt on outer over 1f out: str run ins fnl f: nt quite rch ldrs* **16/1**

5050 **5** *½* **The Happy Hammer (IRE)**[61] 6337 8-8-13 62 .... RobertTart 5 68
(Eugene Stanford) *hld up towards rr: hdwy on inner over 1f out: ev ch ins fnl f: no ex cl home* **14/1**

0060 **6** *nk* **Al's Memory (IRE)**[34] 7071 5-9-1 67 .... DeclanBates(3) 11 72
(David Evans) *chsd ldrs: drvn to ld 2f out: hdd ins fnl f: no ex towards fin* **14/1**

0146 **7** *nse* **Bush Beauty (IRE)**[6] 7698 3-8-11 68 .... GaryMahon(7) 3 72
(Philip McBride) *in tch in midfield: short of room and shuffled bk 2f out: rallied u.p ins fnl f: styd on* **8/1**

300 **8** *nk* **What A Dandy (IRE)**[43] 6857 3-8-12 62 ....(p) PatCosgrave 1 67+
(Jim Boyle) *hld up in tch: hmpd and swtchd rt over 1f out: hdwy ins fnl f: styd on wl towards fin: nt rch ldrs* **25/1**

0163 **9** *2* **Byrd In Hand (IRE)**[16] 7513 7-9-1 64 ....(b) WilliamCarson 6 63
(John Bridger) *chsd ldrs: rdn and pressing ldrs 2f out: no ex 1f out: wknd ins fnl f* **20/1**

6-60 **10** *¾* **Archibald Thorburn (IRE)**[23] 7351 3-9-6 70 ....(p) CharlesBishop 12 66
(Peter Hedger) *s.i.s: t.k.h: hld up in rr: hdwy u.p over 1f out: no ex ins fnl f: wknd fnl 100yds* **16/1**

104 **11** *shd* **Belle Bayardo (IRE)**[24] 7337 6-9-7 70 .... TomQueally 8 66
(Tony Carroll) *t.k.h: chsd ldrs: rdn and struggling to qckn whn hmpd wl over 1f out: styd on same pce after* **20/1**

0552 **12** ½ **Prince Regal**[23] [7356] 4-9-6 69 ............ LukeMorris 7 64
(Timothy Jarvis) *t.k.h: led tl rdn and hdd 2f out: wknd ins fnl f* **3/1**[2]

6111 **13** 2 **Diamonds A Dancing**[27] [7259] 4-9-3 66....(be) WilliamTwiston-Davies 10 56
(Brian Gubby) *in tch in midfield: rdn 2f out: struggling to qckn whn short of room and shuffled bk over 1f out: n.d fnl f* **9/4**[1]

0000 **14** 9 **Sheikh The Reins (IRE)**[15] [7530] 5-9-5 68................(v) MartinDwyer 14 35
(John Best) *s.i.s: hdwy into midfield: rdn and lost pl over 2f out: bhd 1f out* **25/1**

1m 26.0s **Going Correction** -0.025s/f (Stan)
**WFA** 3 from 4yo+ 1lb **14** Ran SP% **129.4**
Speed ratings (Par 103): **99,98,98,98,98 97,97,97,95,94 94,93,91,81**
CSF £189.39 CT £4539.23 TOTE £35.40: £10.40, £2.20, £4.70; EX 389.70 Trifecta £1995.60 Part won..
**Owner** Con Harrington **Bred** Mrs Chris Harrington **Trained** Upper Lambourn, Berks
**FOCUS**
They finished in a heap here and it was the slower of the two divisions by 0.58sec. The second to fifth were close to their marks.
T/Jkpt: Not won. T/Plt: £42.80 to a £1 stake. Pool of £69329.39 - 1179.97 winning tickets.
T/Qpdt: £3.50 to a £1 stake. Pool of £9060.87 - 1868.14 winning tickets. SP

## 7645 SOUTHWELL (L-H)
Thursday, November 13

**OFFICIAL GOING: Fibresand: standard**
Wind: Moderate against Weather: Heavy cloud

### 7760 CORAL MOBILE JUST THREE CLICKS TO BET H'CAP 1m 4f (F)
12:20 (12:20) (Class 5) (0-70,70) 3-Y-O+ £2,587 (£770; £384; £192) Stalls Low

Form RPR
2205 **1** **Reach The Beach**[15] [7532] 5-8-10 56..........................(tp) BenCurtis 7 67
(Brendan Powell) *slt ld: pushed clr 3f out: jnd and rdn 2f out: drvn appr fnl f and kpt on strly* **25/1**

2566 **2** 4 **Royal Marskell**[37] [7008] 5-9-7 70........................ ConnorBeasley(3) 11 75
(Alison Hutchinson) *trckd ldrs: hdwy 4f out: effrt to chse wnr 2f out: swtchd rt and chal wl over 1f out: sn rdn and ev ch tl drvn and one pce ent fnl f* **9/4**[1]

2330 **3** 2 ¼ **Sheila's Heart**[29] [7204] 4-9-4 64........................................ PaddyAspell 13 65
(John E Long) *midfield: hdwy 5f out: chsd ldrs over 3f out: rdn 2f out: swtchd lft wl over 1f out: sn drvn and kpt on fnl f* **10/1**

45U4 **4** 1 **Oetzi**[20] [7419] 6-8-10 63................................................ GaryMahon(7) 5 63
(Timothy Jarvis) *dwlt and sn pushed along to chse ldrs: rdn 4f out: drvn 3f out: swtchd rt wl over 1f out: kpt on one pce* **9/1**

6520 **5** nk **On Demand**[25] [7309] 3-8-10 65......................(v) ThomasBrown(3) 2 64
(Andrew Balding) *t.k.h early: disp ld on inner: pushed along over 4f out: rdn 3f out: sn drvn and edgd rt wl over 1f out: one pce* **11/4**[2]

3563 **6** 10 **Yasir (USA)**[89] [5101] 6-9-1 61..................................(b) PaulMulrennan 3 44
(Conor Dore) *hld up in rr: swtchd rt to outer and sme hdwy 5f out: rdn along wl over 3f out: wd st and sn outpcd* **9/1**

0630 **7** ¾ **Cape Karli (IRE)**[17] [7500] 3-8-10 62.........................(p) TomEaves 8 44
(Kevin Ryan) *chsd ldng pair: cl up after 4f: rdn along over 4f out: wknd over 3f out* **12/1**

-006 **8** 2 ½ **Montaff**[16] [7509] 8-9-1 64..............................(e[1]) JacobButterfield(3) 9 42
(Richard Guest) *in rr: effrt on outer and sme hdwy 5f out: rdn along wl over 3f out: sn outpcd* **8/1**[3]

4210 **9** 16 **Solid Justice (IRE)**[10] [7626] 3-9-2 68..................... AndrewElliott 1 21
(Jason Ward) *hld up on inner: pushed along 1/2-way: rdn along 5f out: sn outpcd and bhd* **10/1**

2m 40.02s (-0.98) **Going Correction** +0.10s/f (Slow)
**WFA** 3 from 4yo+ 6lb **9** Ran SP% **118.3**
Speed ratings (Par 103): **107,104,102,102,101 95,94,93,82**
CSF £83.29 CT £634.56 TOTE £31.00: £4.40, £2.10, £3.80; EX 69.30 Trifecta £406.70.
**Owner** Winterbeck Manor Stud **Bred** Winterbeck Manor Stud **Trained** Upper Lambourn, Berks
■ Stewards' Enquiry : Thomas Brown one-day ban: careless riding (Nov 27)
**FOCUS**
An ordinary middle-distance handicap. The form is rated around the second.

### 7761 UNIBET OFFER DAILY JOCKEY TRAINER SPECIALS H'CAP (DIV I) 5f (F)
12:50 (12:51) (Class 4) (0-85,85) 3-Y-O+ £4,690 (£1,395; £697; £348) Stalls High

Form RPR
4410 **1** **Meadway**[24] [7330] 3-9-7 85...........................................(p) PaulMulrennan 2 94
(Bryan Smart) *slt ld: pushed along 2f out: rdn over 1f out: kpt on wl towards fin* **5/4**[1]

233 **2** ½ **Indian Tinker**[15] [7535] 5-8-8 72..................................(v) AdamBeschizza 1 79
(Robert Cowell) *prom: effrt 2f out: sn chal: rdn ent fnl f: ev ch tl drvn and no ex last 50yds* **5/1**[2]

106 **3** shd **Only Ten Per Cent (IRE)**[15] [7534] 6-8-11 75..................(v) FergalLynch 9 82
(J R Jenkins) *trckd ldrs: hdwy 2f out: rdn to chal jst over 1f out: ev ch tl drvn ins fnl f and no ex last 50yds* **8/1**

0050 **4** 3 ¼ **Baytown Kestrel**[23] [7365] 3-8-13 82.........................(p) RachealKneller(5) 4 77
(Jamie Osborne) *towards rr: hdwy over 2f out: rdn wl over 1f out: edgd lft and kpt on fnl f: nrst fin* **16/1**

3110 **5** ½ **Harrogate Fair**[126] [4128] 4-8-4 71 oh1.........................(p) DannyBrock(3) 7 65
(Michael Squance) *sn outpcd and bhd: hdwy 1/2-way: rdn and edgd lft towards far rail wl over 1f out: kpt on: nrst fin* **33/1**

5060 **6** nse **Sir Geoffrey (IRE)**[16] [7510] 8-8-4 71 oh2............(p) ConnorBeasley(3) 10 64
(Scott Dixon) *chsd ldrs: rdn along 2f out: sn one pce* **16/1**

2506 **7** 1 **Naabegha**[128] [4061] 7-8-13 77.................................................. JasonHart 3 67
(John Balding) *a towards rr* **14/1**

0510 **8** 2 **Royal Bajan (USA)**[40] [6938] 6-9-7 85..........................(p) TomEaves 5 68
(James Given) *cl up: rdn along over 2f out: drvn and wknd over 1f out* **15/2**[3]

0064 **9** 1 ¾ **Keep It Dark**[8] [7669] 5-9-1 79.............................................. BarryMcHugh 8 55
(Tony Coyle) *dwlt and swtchd rt s: a in rr* **12/1**

2032 **10** 5 **Bapak Bangsawan**[154] [3138] 4-8-5 74............................(bt) AnnStokell(5) 6 32
(Ann Stokell) *chsd ldrs: rdn along 1/2-way: sn wknd* **25/1**

1m 1.71s (2.01) **Going Correction** +0.475s/f (Slow) **10** Ran SP% **116.9**
Speed ratings (Par 105): **102,101,101,95,95 94,93,90,87,79**
CSF £7.38 CT £35.94 TOTE £2.50: £1.10, £1.90, £2.80; EX 9.00 Trifecta £55.10.
**Owner** Michael Moses & Terry Moses **Bred** Bond Thoroughbred Corporation **Trained** Hambleton, N Yorks

**FOCUS**
A decent sprint handicap, featuring several CD winners, and the main action unfolded up the middle. It was the slower division by 0.71sec. The winner rates a small personal best.

### 7762 £20 RISK-FREE BET AT UNIBET CLAIMING STKS 6f (F)
1:20 (1:21) (Class 6) 2-Y-O £1,940 (£577; £288; £144) Stalls Low

Form RPR
1061 **1** **Little**[20] [7421] 2-8-3 67 ow1................................................ JennyPowell(5) 2 65
(Jamie Osborne) *dwlt: hld up in rr: hdwy on outer wl over 2f out: led 1 1/2f out: rdn clr and edgd lft jst ins fnl f: kpt on* **11/8**[1]

0044 **2** 2 ¼ **Pancake Day**[17] [7497] 2-8-8 50........................................ AndrewElliott 3 55
(Jason Ward) *trckd ldng pair: hdwy on inner 3f out: cl up 2f out: sn ev ch: rdn over 1f out: swtchd rt ins fnl f: kpt on same pce* **6/1**

660 **3** 1 ½ **Zebs Lad (IRE)**[36] [7029] 2-8-9 69.................... WilliamTwiston-Davies 6 52
(Ronald Harris) *chsd ldrs: rdn along over 2f out: kpt on fnl f* **5/1**[3]

05 **4** 1 ¾ **As A Dream (IRE)**[16] [7515] 2-8-3 64 ow1.............................. BenCurtis 5 41
(David Evans) *cl up: rdn along over 2f out: drvn wl over 1f out and sn one pce* **9/4**[2]

000 **5** 2 **Striking Stone**[117] [4429] 2-8-4 0..................................(b[1]) PhilipPrince(3) 4 39
(Jo Hughes) *led: rdn along 2f out: hdd 1 1/2f out and grad wknd* **20/1**

1m 18.51s (2.01) **Going Correction** +0.10s/f (Slow) **5** Ran SP% **108.6**
Speed ratings (Par 94): **90,87,85,82,80**
CSF £9.65 TOTE £1.40: £1.10, £5.40; EX 7.30 Trifecta £24.30.As A Dream was claimed by N Evans for £4000.
**Owner** A F Tait **Bred** Highclere Stud Ltd **Trained** Upper Lambourn, Berks
**FOCUS**
A modest juvenile claimer which became a one-horse race.

### 7763 32RED MAIDEN AUCTION STKS 7f (F)
1:50 (1:51) (Class 5) 2-Y-O £2,587 (£770; £384; £192) Stalls Low

Form RPR
0332 **1** **Zaza Zest (IRE)**[23] [7362] 2-8-10 67.................................... TonyHamilton 7 71
(Richard Fahey) *trckd ldng pair: hdwy and cl up 3f out: led 2f out: sn rdn clr: readily* **1/1**[1]

00 **2** 8 **Space Sheriff (IRE)**[10] [7625] 2-8-10 0........................ RachealKneller(5) 2 54
(Jamie Osborne) *cl up: rdn to ld wl over 2f out: hdd and drvn 2f out: sn one pce* **4/1**[2]

043 **3** 4 ½ **Vivre La Reve**[13] [7573] 2-8-12 68.......................................... AdamBeschizza 1 39
(James Unett) *slt ld on inner: rdn along 3f out: sn hdd & wknd fnl 2f* **6/1**[3]

0333 **4** 3 **Fast Scat (USA)**[104] [4846] 2-8-12 57........................................ BenCurtis 3 31
(David Evans) *in tch: rdn along bef 1/2-way: sn outpcd* **6/1**[3]

0 **5** 21 **Eric The Viking**[9] [7638] 2-8-11 0.............................................. JasonHart 5
(Richard Guest) *in tch: rdn along wl over 3f out: sn outpcd and bhd* **66/1**

**6** 10 **Ace Of Marmalade (IRE)** 2-9-5 0........................................ TomEaves 4
(Brian Ellison) *sn rdn along and a outpcd in rr: bhd fr 1/2-way* **10/1**

1m 30.74s (0.44) **Going Correction** +0.10s/f (Slow) **6** Ran SP% **109.2**
Speed ratings (Par 96): **101,91,86,83,59 47**
CSF £4.90 TOTE £1.20: £1.10, £3.30; EX 6.30 Trifecta £47.20.
**Owner** Andrea & Graham Wylie **Bred** Yeomanstown Stud **Trained** Musley Bank, N Yorks
**FOCUS**
A weak and uncompetitive maiden.

### 7764 LADBROKES MAIDEN STKS 7f (F)
2:20 (2:21) (Class 5) 3-Y-O £2,587 (£770; £348; £192) Stalls Low

Form RPR
6 **1** **Mambo Fever**[17] [7501] 3-9-0 0........................................... AndrewElliott 4 61
(David C Griffiths) *trckd ldrs: hdwy 3f out: chsd ldr over 2f out: chal wl over 1f out: sn rdn: drvn ent fnl f: led last 120yds: styd on* **6/1**

0520 **2** 2 ¼ **Yard Of Ale**[7] [7682] 3-9-5 68.............................................. GrahamGibbons 2 59
(Kristin Stubbs) *slt ld: hdd narrowly 4f out: led again 3f out: rdn and wandered over 1f out: drvn and hung rt ent fnl f: hdd and one pce last 120yds* **2/1**[1]

3300 **3** ½ **Lendal Bridge**[9] [7644] 3-9-5 54.......................................... BarryMcHugh 9 58
(Tony Coyle) *midfield: hdwy 3f out: chsd ldrs 2f out: rdn whn carried lft towards far rail ent fnl f: n.m.r wl ins fnl f: styd on towards fin* **11/1**

5662 **4** ¾ **Im Dapper Too**[9] [7646] 3-9-5 49......................................... PhillipMakin 10 56
(John Davies) *chsd ldrs: hdwy on wd outside wl over 2f out: rdn wl over 1f out: swtchd lft and drvn ent fnl fuyrlong: sn edgd lft and one pce* **9/4**[2]

250 **5** 10 **Danzki (IRE)**[17] [7501] 3-9-5 57..................................(b[1]) ChrisCatlin 7 30
(Gay Kelleway) *towards rr: rdn along 1/2-way: plugged on fnl 2f: n.d* **20/1**

0000 **6** 7 **Bay Street Belle**[20] [7424] 3-9-0 52........................................ TomEaves 5 7
(Alison Hutchinson) *prom: rdn along over 3f out: sn wknd* **66/1**

003 **7** ½ **Tasaaboq**[106] [4785] 3-9-2 60...................................(vt[1]) DannyBrock(3) 6 11
(Phil McEntee) *cl up: slt ld 4f out: hdd 3f out: sn rdn and wknd* **5/1**[3]

0-0 **8** 10 **Perspicacity**[163] [2877] 3-9-0 0............................................... FergalLynch 1
(J R Jenkins) *outpcd and bhd fr 1/2-way* **33/1**

**9** 2 ½ **Minister Of Fun** 3-9-5 0.................................................. PaulMulrennan 3 23
(Scott Dixon) *unruly bef s: dwlt and in rr: gd hdwy on outer to chse ldrs 1/2-way: wd st: sn rdn and wknd* **40/1**

1m 31.19s (0.89) **Going Correction** +0.10s/f (Slow) **9** Ran SP% **115.0**
Speed ratings (Par 102): **98,95,94,94,82 74,74,62,59**
CSF £17.86 TOTE £10.20: £2.20, £2.00, £2.00; EX 24.80 Trifecta £126.10.
**Owner** Norcroft Park Stud **Bred** Norcroft Park Stud **Trained** Bawtry, S Yorks
**FOCUS**
A modest 3yo maiden and the front four pulled well clear, but there is probably more to come from the winner. The form is rated around the second and third.

### 7765 LADBROKES H'CAP 1m (F)
2:50 (2:50) (Class 6) (0-65,71) 3-Y-O+ £1,940 (£577; £288; £144) Stalls Low

Form RPR
0422 **1** **Royal Holiday (IRE)**[72] [6009] 7-9-6 65..........................(b) RobertWinston 8 80
(Marjorie Fife) *cl up: led over 3f out: rdn wl over 1f out: drvn ent fnl f: kpt on wl towards fin* **7/2**[2]

0161 **2** 2 ¾ **Toto Skyllachy**[9] [7647] 9-9-9 71 6ex..................... JacobButterfield(3) 1 80
(Marjorie Fife) *trckd ldrs on inner: hdwy over 3f out: sn chsng wnr: rdn over 1f out: drvn ins fnl f: no imp* **5/2**[1]

1344 **3** 1 ¼ **Senor George (IRE)**[30] [7180] 7-9-5 64.........................(p) StephenCraine 9 70
(Brian Ellison) *towards rr: hdwy 3f out: rdn wl over 1f out: styd on fnl f: nrst fin* **5/1**[3]

4000 **4** ¾ **Putin (IRE)**[9] [7647] 6-8-13 63.................................(tp) RachealKneller(5) 13 67
(Phil McEntee) *slt ld: pushed along and hdd over 3f out: cl up tl rdn wl over 1f out and grad wknd* **50/1**

0500 **5** ¾ **Falcon's Reign (FR)**[15] [7538] 5-8-13 63...........(p) AlistairRawlinson(5) 14 65
(Michael Appleby) *cl up on outer: hdwy to chal over 3f out: rdn along over 2f out: drvn wl over 1f out: kpt on same pce* **7/1**

5400 **6** 3 1/4 **Toymaker**[37] 7012 7-9-4 63....(t) PaddyAspell 10 58
(Phil McEntee) *dwlt: hdwy on wd outside over 3f out: wd st: rdn over 2f out and sn no imp* **16/1**

0452 **7** shd **Mandy The Nag (USA)**[30] 7167 4-9-0 62.... MatthewCosham(3) 2 57
(Nikki Evans) *chsd ldrs: rdn along 3f out: drvn over 2f out and sn outpcd* **33/1**

1106 **8** 2 1/4 **Jay Kay**[30] 7180 5-8-12 60.... JoeyHaynes(3) 6 49
(K R Burke) *chsd ldrs: rdn along 3f out: wknd over 2f out* **20/1**

0614 **9** 5 **Telegraph (IRE)**[17] 7502 3-9-1 62.... BenCurtis 4 40
(David Evans) *in tch: hdwy to chse ldrs over 3f out: rdn along wl over 2f out: sn wknd* **25/1**

0565 **10** 1 **Anjuna Beach (USA)**[9] 7651 4-8-12 62.... AnnStokell(5) 5 38
(Ann Stokell) *dwlt: a in rr* **25/1**

0060 **11** 2 3/4 **Little Indian**[23] 7346 4-8-13 58.... FergalLynch 7 27
(J R Jenkins) *a towards rr* **16/1**

640 **12** 1 **Bosstime (IRE)**[34] 7077 4-8-13 58....(p) PhillipMakin 3 25
(John Holt) *a towards rr* **20/1**

3254 **13** 1 1/2 **Lynngale**[26] 7288 3-9-2 63.... TomEaves 12 27
(Kristin Stubbs) *in tch: rdn along over 3f out: sn wknd* **8/1**

1m 44.46s (0.76) **Going Correction** +0.10s/f (Slow)
**WFA** 3 from 4yo+ 2lb **13** Ran SP% **125.0**
Speed ratings (Par 101): **100,97,96,95,94 91,91,88,83,82 80,79,77**
CSF £12.06 CT £46.11 TOTE £4.10: £2.10, £1.40, £2.40; EX 14.00 Trifecta £56.40.
**Owner** Mrs Marion Turner **Bred** E Tynan **Trained** Stillington, N Yorks

**FOCUS**
A moderate handicap dominated by the top weights. It paid to be handy and it resulted in a 1-2 for trainer Marjorie Fife. The winner rates a small pb.

## 7766 LADBROKES ALL-WEATHER "HANDS AND HEELS" APPRENTICE SERIES H'CAP (RACING EXCELLENCE INITIATIVE) 7f (F)
**3:20** (3:21) (Class 6) (0-60,60) 3-Y-0+ **£2,045** (£603; £302) **Stalls** Low

Form RPR

4060 **1** **Best Tamayuz**[81] 5715 3-8-4 49....[1] RussellHarris(7) 8 65
(Scott Dixon) *prom: led 1/2-way: pushed clr wl over 2f out: rdn and kpt on fnl f* **25/1**

0566 **2** 5 **Very First Blade**[9] 7644 5-8-5 49....(be) AlfieDavies(7) 10 53
(Michael Mullineaux) *in tch: hdwy 1/2-way: chsd ldrs wl over 2f out: rdn to chse wnr over 1f out: kpt on same pce* **7/1**[3]

132 **3** nk **Admirable Art (IRE)**[9] 7645 4-9-4 55....(p) ChrisMeehan 3 58+
(Tony Carroll) *dwlt and bhd: hdwy over 2f out: rdn and styd on fr over 1f out: nrst fin* **7/4**[1]

5560 **4** 2 **Masked Dance (IRE)**[9] 7644 7-8-5 49....(p) SophieKilloran(7) 1 47
(Scott Dixon) *led: hdd 1/2-way and sn pushed along: rdn over 2f out: plugged on same pce* **16/1**

4320 **5** 1 1/2 **Dancing Maite**[10] 7622 9-9-5 59....(b) PaulBooth(3) 11 53
(Roy Bowring) *prom: chsd wnr wl over 2f out: sn rdn along: wknd over 1f out* **14/1**

2550 **6** nse **It's All A Game**[9] 7647 3-8-11 56....(b) MelissaThompson(7) 12 49
(Richard Guest) *dwlt sltly and pushed along towards rr: hdwy 1/2-way: wd st: rdn and hung lft wl over 1f out: sn one pce* **12/1**

6000 **7** 6 **Stun Gun**[9] 7632 4-8-11 55....(v) GeorginaBaxter(7) 9 33
(Derek Shaw) *dwlt: a towards rr* **15/2**

00 **8** 1 **La Paiva (FR)**[178] 2387 3-8-2 45.... CallumShepherd(5) 13 20
(Scott Dixon) *midfield: effrt 3f out: sn rdn along and no hdwy* **33/1**

010 **9** 2 1/2 **Honiton Lace**[77] 5846 3-9-4 56....(tp) RobHornby 6 24
(Phil McEntee) *in tch: rdn along 3f out: sn wknd* **25/1**

3124 **10** 1 1/2 **Miami Gator (IRE)**[259] 755 7-8-12 54....(v) PeterSword(5) 5 19
(K R Burke) *chsd ldrs to 1/2-way: sn wknd* **6/1**[2]

0-06 **11** 12 **Moissanite**[234] 1086 5-8-5 45....(t) DanielleMooney(3) 4
(Sean Regan) *a towards rr: bhd fnl 3f* **100/1**

0251 **12** 59 **Delightful Sleep**[9] 7646 6-9-4 60 6ex.... HarryBurns(5) 2
(David Evans) *a towards rr: wknd qckly wl over 1f out: bled fr nose* **8/1**

1m 30.69s (0.39) **Going Correction** +0.10s/f (Slow)
**WFA** 3 from 4yo+ 1lb **12** Ran SP% **117.9**
Speed ratings (Par 101): **101,95,94,92,90 90,84,82,80,78 64,**
CSF £186.06 CT £475.88 TOTE £49.40: £9.80, £2.10, £1.20; EX 428.40 Trifecta £3216.30 Part won..
**Owner** Paul J Dixon **Bred** Rabbah Bloodstock Limited **Trained** Babworth, Notts
■ Russell Harris's first winner.
■ Stewards' Enquiry : Chris Meehan seven-day ban: used whip down shoulder in the backhand (Nov 27,Dec 2,4,5,10,16,17)

**FOCUS**
A very strange contest in which three appeared to have gone off much too fast, but they included the easy winner. The form looks suspect, with the winner posting a clear best.

## 7767 UNIBET OFFER DAILY JOCKEY TRAINER SPECIALS H'CAP (DIV II) 5f (F)
**3:50** (3:51) (Class 4) (0-85,85) 3-Y-0+ **£4,690** (£1,395; £697; £348) **Stalls** High

Form RPR

1232 **1** **Poyle Vinnie**[23] 7365 4-9-2 85.... AlistairRawlinson(5) 1 98
(Michael Appleby) *dwlt: sn trcking ldrs: hdwy on outer and cl up 1/2-way: led 1 1/2f out: rdn and clr whn hung bdly rt ins fnl f: kpt on* **11/10**[1]

0 **2** 2 3/4 **Bainne (IRE)**[28] 7220 4-8-4 71 oh1....[1] RyanTate(3) 2 74
(James Eustace) *dwlt and in rr: hdwy on wd outside 2f out: sn rdn and styd on fnl f: nrst fin* **20/1**

030 **3** 1 1/4 **Bedloe's Island (IRE)**[211] 1506 9-9-6 84.... BenCurtis 3 83
(Alan McCabe) *chsd ldrs: hdwy 2f out: sn rdn and kpt on fnl f* **10/1**

1410 **4** 2 1/2 **Fredricka**[15] 7535 3-8-10 74.... JasonHart 9 64
(Garry Moss) *in tch: hdwy 1/2-way: rdn wl over 1f out: kpt on same pce appr fnl f* **33/1**

0500 **5** 1/2 **Sleepy Blue Ocean**[34] 7073 8-9-0 78....(p) RobertWinston 6 66
(John Balding) *chsd ldrs: rdn along over 2f out: sn one pce* **16/1**

5140 **6** nk **Abi Scarlet (IRE)**[16] 7506 5-9-2 80.... PJMcDonald 7 67
(Scott Dixon) *chsd ldrs: rdn along over 2f out: wknd over 1f out* **10/1**

0003 **7** 1 1/2 **Captain Dunne (IRE)**[47] 6763 9-8-4 75.... RachelRichardson(7) 5 56
(Tim Easterby) *cl up: led after 2f: rdn along and hdd 1 1/2f out: sn wknd* **7/2**[2]

0646 **8** 1 3/4 **Monsieur Jamie**[15] 7535 6-8-7 71 oh1....(v) FergalLynch 10 46
(J R Jenkins) *a towards rr* **9/1**[3]

00 **9** 7 **Six Wives**[91] 5333 7-8-12 76....(p) GrahamGibbons 8 26
(Scott Dixon) *led 2f: rdn along 1/2-way: sn wknd* **25/1**

1m 1.0s (1.30) **Going Correction** +0.475s/f (Slow) **9** Ran SP% **115.5**
Speed ratings (Par 105): **108,103,101,97,96 96,93,91,79**
CSF £29.94 CT £155.64 TOTE £2.00: £1.30, £4.50, £2.80; EX 32.20 Trifecta £203.90.
**Owner** Dallas Racing & C L Bacon **Bred** Cecil And Miss Alison Wiggins **Trained** Danethorpe, Notts

**FOCUS**
The winning time was 0.71sec quicker than the first division. Once again the centre of the track was the place to be. There's a good chance the winner can rate higher still.
T/Plt: £6.20 to a £1 stake. Pool of £54594.45 - 6359.91 winning tickets. T/Qpdt: £4.20 to a £1 stake. Pool of £4404.21 - 761.63 winning tickets. JR

# 7720 SAINT-CLOUD (L-H)
### Thursday, November 13

**OFFICIAL GOING: Turf: heavy**

## 7768a PRIX BELLE DE NUIT (LISTED RACE) (3YO+ FILLIES & MARES) (TURF) 1m 4f 110y
**1:05** (12:00) 3-Y-0+ **£21,666** (£8,666; £6,500; £4,333; £2,166)

RPR

**1** **Crystal Diamond**[22] 7394 3-8-9 0.... AurelienLemaitre 7 105
(F Head, France) **47/10**[2]

**2** 1/2 **Hidden Cove (IRE)**[41] 6917 4-9-2 0.... ChristopheSoumillon 5 104
(A De Royer-Dupre, France) **49/10**[3]

**3** 2 **Chasse Maree (FR)**[33] 3-8-9 0.... AdrienFouassier 1 101
(Alain Couetil, France) **71/10**

**4** 1 **Island Remede**[19] 7447 3-8-10 0 ow1.... OlivierPeslier 9 100
(Ed Dunlop) *trckd ldrs: rdn to chal into st: ev ch 2f out: outpcd by ldrs over 1f out: styd on for 4th* **66/10**

**5** 3/4 **Sanaija**[22] 7394 3-8-9 0.... AntoineHamelin 3 98
(A De Royer-Dupre, France) **193/10**

**6** 3/4 **Game Zone (IRE)**[43] 6882 3-8-9 0.... Francois-XavierBertras 8 97
(F Rohaut, France) **43/10**[1]

**7** 1/2 **Rewaaya (IRE)**[17] 7492 3-8-9 0.... RobertHavlin 4 96
(John Gosden) *dwlt sltly and wnt rt s but qckly rcvrd: sn w ldr on inner: led over 4f out: rdn and strly pressed into st: hdd 2f out: outpcd and fdd* **11/2**

**8** 15 **Cinnilla**[33] 7106 3-8-9 0.... IoritzMendizabal 10 72
(Ralph Beckett) *hld up: pushed along bef 1/2-way: rdn and clsd on outer bef st: outpcd and no further imp fr over 2f out: eased whn btn fnl f* **127/10**

**9** 4 **Kyurem (IRE)**[35] 7070 4-9-2 0.... FlavienPrat 2 66
(T Clout, France) **28/1**

**10** 1 1/2 **Bella Duchessa (GER)**[32] 4-9-2 0.... AStarke 11 63
(P Schiergen, Germany) **215/10**

**11** 3 **Norway Cross**[20] 7409 4-9-2 0.... MaximeGuyon 6 58
(Luca Cumani) *led: hdd over 4f out: rdn and lost pl into st: qckly btn: eased and dropped to last: t.o* **187/10**

2m 49.15s (169.15)
**WFA** 3 from 4yo 6lb **11** Ran SP% **119.4**
WIN (incl. 1 euro stake): 5.70. PLACES: 1.90, 2.00, 2.20. DF: 7.90. SF: 23.90.
**Owner** Jaber Abdullah **Bred** E Puerari, Oceanic Bloodstock Inc & Haras D'Etreha **Trained** France

## 7769a PRIX DENISY (LISTED RACE) (3YO+) (TURF) 1m 7f 110y
**2:05** (12:00) 3-Y-0+ **£21,666** (£8,666; £6,500; £4,333; £2,166)

RPR

**1** **Windy King**[16] 5-9-1 0.... StephanePasquier 4 99
(J Bertran De Balanda, France) **23/1**

**2** 2 1/2 **Salut (GER)**[19] 7469 6-9-1 0.... AStarke 7 96
(P Schiergen, Germany) **17/2**

**3** 1 1/4 **Swordshire (GER)**[41] 6917 3-8-7 0.... AntoineHamelin 3 95
(Werner Glanz, Germany) **192/10**

**4** 1/2 **Storm (GER)** 3-8-7 0.... CristianDemuro 9 94
(Frau C Barsig, Germany) **165/10**

**5** 1/2 **Alwilda**[14] 7554 4-8-11 0.... Jean-BernardEyquem 10 89
(Sir Mark Prescott Bt) *midfield: clsd and prom bef st: rdn and effrt 3f out: outpcd fnl 2f: styd on but hld: lost 2 pls towards fin* **8/1**[3]

**6** nk **A Soldier's Life (IRE)**[22] 7394 3-8-10 0.... MaximeGuyon 2 96
(A Fabre, France) *t.k.h: sn midfield on inner: rdn and effrt into st: styd on same pce fnl 2f and hld* **13/10**[1]

**7** 20 **Green Byron (FR)**[45] 4-9-1 0.... IoritzMendizabal 12 68
(Mme Pia Brandt, France) **151/10**

**8** 2 1/2 **Balu**[45] 4-9-1 0.... FabienLefebvre 5 65
(Mme J Romich, France) **58/1**

**9** 1 1/4 **La Femme Fatale (GER)**[22] 7394 3-8-4 0.... FlavienPrat 8 62
(M Munch, Germany) **242/10**

**10** 7 **Baroness Daniela**[32] 4-9-1 0.... FabriceVeron 1 56
(H-A Pantall, France) **83/10**

**11** 3 1/2 **Mombasa (GER)**[32] 7-8-11 0.... DanielePorcu 11 47
(P Schiergen, Germany) **86/1**

**12** 1 1/4 **Quidamo**[19] 7-9-1 0.... ChristopheSoumillon 6 50
(Frau J Mayer, Germany) **26/5**[2]

3m 34.78s (-3.92)
**WFA** 3 from 4yo+ 8lb **12** Ran SP% **119.9**
WIN (incl. 1 euro stake): 24.00. Places: 6.80, 3.40, 5.60. DF: 114.30. SF: 319.80..
**Owner** Jean Boniche **Bred** Stall Sohrenhof **Trained** France

# 7549 LINGFIELD (L-H)
### Friday, November 14

**OFFICIAL GOING: Polytrack: standard**
Wind: light, half behind Weather: dry after morning rain

## 7770 32RED CASINO NURSERY H'CAP 7f 1y(P)
**11:55** (11:57) (Class 5) (0-75,75) 2-Y-0 **£2,587** (£770; £384; £192)

Form RPR

1 **1** **Easy Tiger**[24] 7353 2-9-1 69.... MartinDwyer 8 73
(William Muir) *pressed ldr: rdn over 1f out: styd on wl ins fnl f to ld cl home: rdn out* **7/4**[1]

5062 **2** nk **Cascading Stars (IRE)**[22] 7396 2-8-11 65.... SteveDrowne 7 68
(J S Moore) *led: rdn over 1f out: drvn ins fnl f: kpt on but hdd and no ex cl home* **8/1**

4060 **3** 1 1/4 **Ms Eboracum (IRE)**[10] 7631 2-8-0 54 oh9.... JimmyQuinn 1 54
(Edward Creighton) *t.k.h: chsd ldrs: effrt on inner over 1f out: styd on same pce ins fnl f* **100/1**

0223 **4** 1/2 **British Art**[15] 7542 2-9-7 75 LukeMorris 4 73
(Paul Cole) *chsd ldrs: rdn and effrt over 1f out: kpt on same pce ins fnl f* **2/1**[2]

053 **5** *shd* **Dark War (IRE)**[29] 7223 2-9-1 69 JimCrowley 2 67
(James Given) *hld up in rr: effrt over 1f out: kpt on fnl f: nvr gng pce to chal* **5/1**[3]

6001 **6** *19* **Muhaarib Al Emarat (IRE)**[17] 7515 2-9-3 71 GeorgeChaloner 3 18
(Richard Fahey) *chsd ldrs on outer: rdn and hung rt bnd 2f out: sn wl btn: eased ins fnl f* **7/1**

1m 25.51s (0.71) **Going Correction** -0.025s/f (Stan) **6** Ran SP% **111.0**
Speed ratings (Par 96): **94,93,92,91,91 69**
CSF £15.69 CT £932.40 TOTE £2.10: £1.10, £3.60; EX 20.60 Trifecta £131.90.
**Owner** Miss E J Tanner **Bred** D J Weston **Trained** Lambourn, Berks

**FOCUS**
Due to a collapse of a section of the M25 in Surrey, the stalls handlers weren't able to make it in time for this opening contest, so it was started by flag instead. The form may not be rock-solid as a result, but the front two dominated throughout and the best horse won.

## 7771 UNIBET/BRITISH STALLION STUDS EBF MAIDEN STKS 5f 6y(P)
**12:25** (12:26) (Class 5) 2-Y-O **£2,911** (£866; £432; £216) **Stalls** High

Form RPR
5 **1** **Wedlock**[22] 7400 2-9-0 0 LukeMorris 5 69
(Sir Mark Prescott Bt) *chsd ldrs: effrt jst over 1f out: drvn 1f out: styd on wl to ld fnl 50yds* **12/1**

6 **2** 3/4 **Hurricane Alert**[22] 7400 2-9-5 0 JamieSpencer 3 71
(Ralph Beckett) *chsd ldrs: awkward bnd 2f out: rdn over 1f out: hdwy ins fnl f: wnt 2nd towards fin: no imp* **2/1**[1]

552 **3** 1/2 **Shackled N Drawn (USA)**[20] 7454 2-9-5 69 (t) JimCrowley 7 70
(Olly Stevens) *racd keenly: pressed ldr: rdn to ld 1f out: drvn ins fnl f: hdd and lost 2 pls fnl 50yds* **9/4**[2]

2006 **4** *hd* **Brazen Spirit**[62] 6312 2-9-5 74 SteveDrowne 9 69
(Clive Cox) *in tch in 5th: rdn 2f out: no imp tl str run ins fnl f: nt rch ldrs* **5/2**[3]

5 **5** 1 1/4 **Kodiac Lady (IRE)**[20] 7454 2-9-0 0 JoeFanning 2 59
(James Tate) *led: hdd 1f out: sn rdn and unable qck: wknd fnl 100yds* **12/1**

4400 **6** 4 1/2 **John Joiner**[26] 7308 2-9-2 56 (b) DeclanBates(3) 6 48
(Peter Makin) *dwlt: a struggling in last pair: wknd over 1f out* **33/1**

065 **7** 2 1/4 **Blackasyourhat (IRE)**[15] 7542 2-8-12 60 (t) MikeyEnnis(7) 8 40
(Roger Ingram) *awkward leaving stalls: a outpcd in last pair: wknd over 1f out* **33/1**

58.91s (0.11) **Going Correction** -0.025s/f (Stan) **7** Ran SP% **113.9**
Speed ratings (Par 96): **98,96,96,95,93 86,82**
CSF £36.19 TOTE £10.90: £4.80, £3.40; EX 40.80 Trifecta £93.60.
**Owner** Cheveley Park Stud **Bred** Cheveley Park Stud Ltd **Trained** Newmarket, Suffolk

**FOCUS**
Thankfully the stalls had arrived in time for this contest, an ordinary sprint maiden.

## 7772 DOWNLOAD THE CORAL APP MAIDEN STKS 1m 4f (P)
**12:55** (12:56) (Class 5) 3-Y-O+ **£2,587** (£770; £384; £192) **Stalls** Low

Form RPR
5533 **1** **Elpida (USA)**[77] 5898 3-9-0 69 [1] JimCrowley 6 75
(David Simcock) *in tch in midfield: rdn over 4f out: 3rd and no imp over 1f out: swtchd lft 1f out: led ins fnl f: idling in front but a jst doing enough: rdn out* **4/1**[3]

**2** 1 1/4 **Al Destoor**[482] 4552 4-9-11 80 (t) SteveDrowne 2 78
(Anthony Middleton) *stdd s: hld up in tch: pushed along and outpcd 3f out: wnt 4th 2f out: clsd over 1f out: styd on under mainly hands and heels riding ins fnl f: wnt 2nd last strides* **16/1**

3 **3** *nk* **Ocean Boulevard**[21] 7418 3-9-0 0 TomQueally 1 73
(Luca Cumani) *chsd ldrs: wnt 2nd over 2f out: rdn and fnd little over 1f out: plugged on same pce ins fnl f: lost 2nd last strides* **5/4**[1]

2302 **4** *nk* **By Jupiter**[31] 7182 3-9-0 72 WilliamTwiston-Davies 4 72
(Michael Bell) *led: rdn wl over 1f out: hdd ins fnl f: no ex and lost pls after* **3/1**[2]

044/ **5** *27* **Let's Confer**[684] 8297 5-9-6 60 JimmyQuinn 3 29
(Michael Attwater) *stdd s: hld up in tch: rdn and struggling 4f out: lost tch 3f out: t.o over 1f out* **66/1**

32 **6** *12* **Rohesia**[286] 434 3-9-0 0 JamieSpencer 5 10
(Sir Mark Prescott Bt) *chsd ldr: reminder over 4f out: drvn and dropped out rapidly over 2f out: t.o fnl f* **6/1**

0- **7** *35* **Loafer**[503] 3821 4-9-11 0 (p) LiamKeniry 7
(Zoe Davison) *a in rr: rdn 8f out: sn lost tch: t.o 4f out* **100/1**

2m 30.51s (-2.49) **Going Correction** -0.025s/f (Stan)
**WFA** 3 from 4yo+ 6lb **7** Ran SP% **112.1**
Speed ratings (Par 103): **107,106,105,105,87 79,56**
CSF £58.52 TOTE £6.20: £4.00, £4.80; EX 49.20 Trifecta £189.70.
**Owner** St Albans Bloodstock LLP **Bred** Capital Bloodstock **Trained** Newmarket, Suffolk

**FOCUS**
A slow-motion finish to this middle-distance maiden and the form looks ordinary. It has been rated a bit cautiously.

## 7773 32RED/BRITISH STALLION STUDS EBF FILLIES' H'CAP (BOBIS RACE) 1m 2f (P)
**1:30** (1:30) (Class 3) (0-90,85) 3-Y-O **£6,085** (£6,085; £1,394; £697) **Stalls** Low

Form RPR
2213 **1** **Wrood (USA)**[72] 6044 3-9-5 **83** TomQueally 6 93+
(James Fanshawe) *hld up in tch in rr: nt clr run and swtchd lft over 1f out: r.o wl u.p fnl f: jnd ldr on line* **5/4**[1]

6422 **1** *dht* **Heho**[32] 7157 3-8-7 **71** oh3 JoeFanning 2 79
(Sir Michael Stoute) *chsd ldrs: effrt on inner over 1f out: drvn to ld ins fnl f: jnd on line* **8/1**

3304 **3** *1* **Rosehill Artist (IRE)**[14] 7565 3-9-7 **85** WilliamCarson 5 91
(Charles Hills) *led: rdn and qcknd 2f out: hdd ins fnl f: no ex and btn whn short of room nr fin* **6/1**[3]

0222 **4** *2* **Principle Equation (IRE)**[37] 7043 3-9-6 **84** JimCrowley 7 86
(Ralph Beckett) *sn pressing ldr: rdn wl over 1f out: drvn and no ex 1f out: one pce fnl f* **7/4**[2]

1114 **5** 2 3/4 **Evacusafe Lady**[20] 7459 3-8-4 **71** oh2 (t) DannyBrock(3) 4 68
(John Ryan) *t.k.h: in tch: effrt to press ldrs over 2f out: outpcd over 1f out: styd on same pce fnl f* **16/1**

2m 8.5s (1.90) **Going Correction** -0.025s/f (Stan) **5** Ran SP% **112.1**
Speed ratings (Par 103): **91,91,90,88,86**
WIN: 3.00 Heho, 1.20 Wrood; PL: 2.50 Heho, 1.50 Wrood; EX: 5.80 Heho & Wrood, 8.30 Heho & Wrood; CSF: 5.91 Heho & Wrood, 9.53 Wrood & Heho. TF: 24.10 Wrood & Heho & Rosehill Artist, 34.80 Heho & Wrood & Rosehill Artist.
**Owner** Lady Rothschild **Bred** Whitley Stud **Trained** Newmarket, Suffolk

**Owner** Mohamed Obaida **Bred** Rabbah Bloodstock Llc **Trained** Newmarket, Suffolk
■ Stewards' Enquiry : Joe Fanning one-day ban: careless riding (Nov 28)

**FOCUS**
A valuable fillies' handicap, but a small field due to the non-runners and the pace was modest until picking up racing towards the home bend. Not surprisingly it resulted in a tight finish and the first two could not be split by the judge. The third is the best guide.

## 7774 LADBROKES H'CAP 1m 1y(P)
**2:05** (2:05) (Class 4) (0-85,85) 3-Y-O+ **£4,690** (£1,395; £697; £348) **Stalls** High

Form RPR
213 **1** **Heisman (IRE)**[15] 7545 3-9-5 85 (t) JamieSpencer 3 95+
(Olly Stevens) *sn led and mde rest: rdn and asserted over 1f out: kpt on u.p fnl f: rdn out* **4/5**[1]

1300 **2** 3/4 **Spiritual Star (IRE)**[15] 7545 5-9-7 85 (t) WilliamCarson 4 93
(Anthony Carson) *hld up in tch in midfield: effrt on inner to chse ldrs over 1f out: drvn to go 2nd jst ins fnl f: r.o but a hld* **5/1**[2]

2631 **3** 2 3/4 **Almanack**[31] 7185 4-8-5 74 ShaneGray(5) 2 76
(Ian Williams) *stdd s: hld up in rr: rdn and hdwy towards inner over 1f out: styd on wl ins fnl f: snatched 3rd last stride* **8/1**

0400 **4** *shd* **Big Whiskey (IRE)**[10] 7636 4-9-0 78 (t) PatCosgrave 7 79
(Edward Creighton) *chsd ldr: ev ch 2f out: rdn and unable qck over 1f out: 3rd and outpcd fnl 150yds: lost 3rd last stride* **20/1**

0500 **5** 1/2 **Brocklebank (IRE)**[23] 7375 5-9-2 80 TomQueally 8 80
(Simon Dow) *stdd after s: hld up in tch in last pair: nt clr run over 1f out: swtchd lft jst ins fnl f: styd on: no threat to wnr* **16/1**

4461 **6** 1 1/2 **Dialogue**[20] 7456 8-8-10 74 (t) JimCrowley 5 71
(Andrew Reid) *in tch in midfield: rdn and outpcd wl over 1f out: one pce and hld fnl f* **16/1**

2000 **7** *shd* **Red Warrior (IRE)**[88] 5487 4-9-4 82 WilliamTwiston-Davies 9 79
(Ismail Mohammed) *in tch in midfield on outer: rdn over 3f out: lost pl u.p wl over 1f out: one pce and wl hld after* **25/1**

-400 **8** 4 1/2 **Quickaswecan**[190] 2090 3-9-1 81 JoeFanning 1 67
(Mark Johnston) *t.k.h: chsd ldrs: unable qck u.p and struggling over 1f out: hld and one pce fnl f* **7/1**[3]

1m 36.79s (-1.41) **Going Correction** -0.025s/f (Stan)
**WFA** 3 from 4yo+ 2lb **8** Ran SP% **116.2**
Speed ratings (Par 105): **106,105,102,102,101 100,100,95**
CSF £5.22 CT £19.20 TOTE £1.50: £1.10, £1.70, £2.00; EX 5.10 Trifecta £29.00.
**Owner** Qatar Racing Limited **Bred** Keatly Overseas Ltd **Trained** Chiddingfold, Surrey

**FOCUS**
A decent handicap, but not that competitive with a short-priced favourite. The gallop looked sound and the winner built on his latest run.

## 7775 UNIBET H'CAP (DIV I) 6f 1y(P)
**2:40** (2:42) (Class 5) (0-75,75) 3-Y-O+ **£2,587** (£770; £384; £192) **Stalls** Low

Form RPR
0012 **1** **Varsovian**[43] 6889 4-8-13 67 JimmyQuinn 1 75
(Dean Ivory) *chsd ldr: rdn to ld over 1f out: hld on gamely fnl f: drvn out* **5/1**

1351 **2** *nk* **Top Offer**[24] 7356 5-9-2 70 JamieSpencer 11 77
(Peter Crate) *chsd ldrs: rdn to chal and edgd rt 1f out: ev ch fnl f: a jst hld* **3/1**[2]

3620 **3** *hd* **Dont Have It Then**[44] 6872 3-9-7 75 TomQueally 9 81+
(Willie Musson) *hld up in last trio: effrt on outer over 1f out: styd on strly ins fnl f: snatched 3rd last stride: nt quite rch ldrs* **7/1**

0561 **4** *shd* **Multitask**[1] 7758 4-9-7 75 6ex LiamKeniry 5 81
(Michael Madgwick) *t.k.h: hld up in tch: clsd on ldrs over 1f out: swtchd lft 1f out: rdn to chal ins fnl f: no imp fnl 50yds: lost 3rd last stride* **9/4**[1]

0460 **5** 2 1/4 **Welease Bwian (IRE)**[64] 6266 5-8-5 66 AaronJones(7) 3 65
(Stuart Williams) *dwlt: hld up in tch in last trio: effrt over 1f out: kpt on same pce ins fnl f* **25/1**

31 **6** 1/2 **Moiety**[23] 7370 3-9-2 70 JimCrowley 8 69
(Rae Guest) *chsd ldrs: effrt on inner over 1f out: keeping on same pce whn hmpd 1f out: unable to rcvr and no imp after* **7/2**[3]

3306 **7** *hd* **Arctic Lynx (IRE)**[42] 6898 7-9-4 72 (p) PatCosgrave 10 69
(Robert Cowell) *in tch in midfield: effrt u.p over 1f out: no imp fnl f* **25/1**

05-0 **8** 1/2 **Summerinthecity (IRE)**[184] 2254 7-9-5 73 GeorgeChaloner 6 68
(Richard Fahey) *hld up in rr: rdn and sme hdwy over 1f out: no imp 1f out: wknd ins fnl f* **10/1**

6136 **9** *6* **Amosite**[87] 5535 8-9-4 72 (v) NickyMackay 2 48
(J R Jenkins) *led: rdn and hdd over 1f out: no ex 1f out: sn wknd* **33/1**

6000 **10** 2 1/2 **Plover**[24] 7356 4-8-11 65 (p) JoeFanning 12 33
(Michael Attwater) *stdd s: hld up in tch: pushed along and lost pl 2f out: hung lft and wknd over 1f out* **66/1**

1m 11.04s (-0.86) **Going Correction** -0.025s/f (Stan) **10** Ran SP% **128.4**
Speed ratings (Par 103): **104,103,103,103,100 99,99,98,90,87**
CSF £22.09 CT £112.80 TOTE £6.30: £2.30, £1.10, £2.00; EX 23.10 Trifecta £179.20.
**Owner** Geoff Copp & Radlett Racing **Bred** Darley **Trained** Radlett, Herts

**FOCUS**
An ordinary sprint handicap, but a competitive race annd the form may turn out to be a bit better than it looks.

## 7776 UNIBET H'CAP (DIV II) 6f 1y(P)
**3:15** (3:16) (Class 5) (0-75,74) 3-Y-O+ **£2,587** (£770; £384; £192) **Stalls** Low

Form RPR
0600 **1** **Soaring Spirits (IRE)**[22] 7403 4-9-5 72 (p) PatCosgrave 5 80
(Dean Ivory) *mde all: rdn over 1f out: r.o wl u.p fnl f: rdn out* **10/1**

0000 **2** 1/2 **Novellen Lad (IRE)**[24] 7351 9-9-2 69 JimCrowley 7 76
(Willie Musson) *hld up in last pair: c wdst over 1f out: str run ins fnl f: wnt 2nd last strides: nvr quite getting to wnr* **7/1**[3]

524 **3** 1/2 **Blue Bounty**[57] 6488 3-8-12 65 (b[1]) JimmyQuinn 6 70
(Mark H Tompkins) *hld up wl in tch in midfield: swtchd rt but wating to hang lft over 1f out: drvn and pressing ldrs 1f out: one pce u.p ins fnl f* **2/1**[1]

5000 **4** *shd* **Presumido (IRE)**[24] 7356 4-9-3 70 SebSanders 1 75
(Simon Dow) *hld up in tch: rdn and hdwy on inner over 1f out: wnt 2nd fnl 75yds: kpt on same pce after: lost 2 pls nr fin* **12/1**

3504 **5** *nse* **Shamahan**[24] 7357 5-9-5 72 TomQueally 12 77
(Luke Dace) *chsd ldr: rdn over 1f out: stl pressing wnr 1f out: no ex and jst outpcd fnl 100yds* **6/1**[2]

6210 **6** *shd* **Monarch Maid**[24] 7352 3-9-3 70 WilliamCarson 4 74
(Peter Hiatt) *chsd ldrs: rdn and pressing ldrs and drvn 1f out: wnt 2nd fnl 100yds: no ex and lost 4 pls towards fin* **8/1**

0020 **7** 1 1/2 **Cardinal**[16] 7534 9-8-11 64 (p) LiamKeniry 2 63
(Robert Cowell) *hld up in tch in last trio: rdn and hdwy over 1f out: styd on same pce ins fnl f* **33/1**

2645 **8** ½ **Lujeanie**[30] 7202 8-9-1 68 JamieSpencer 3 66
(Peter Crate) *stdd s: hld up in rr: pushed along and hdwy towards inner 1f out: n.m.r and no imp ins fnl f* **10/1**

1200 **9** *hd* **Lady Phill**[25] 7342 4-9-2 69 JoeFanning 9 66
(Michael Attwater) *chsd ldrs: rdn and no ex over 1f out: wknd ins fnl f* **25/1**

1516 **10** 3 ¼ **Seamster**[24] 7357 7-9-2 74 (bt) JackDuern(5) 8 61
(Richard Ford) *fly-jmpd as stalls opened and bmpd sn after s: bhd: t.k.h: hdwy into midfield but stuck wd: rdn and btn over 1f out: wknd* **7/1**[3]

1m 11.55s (-0.35) **Going Correction** -0.025s/f (Stan) **10** Ran SP% **116.4**
Speed ratings (Par 103): **101,100,99,99,99 99,97,96,96,92**
CSF £78.05 CT £198.11 TOTE £14.90: £3.50, £2.30, £1.70; EX 106.70 Trifecta £480.20.
**Owner** Mrs Doreen Carter **Bred** Kevin & Meta Cullen **Trained** Radlett, Herts

**FOCUS**
The winning time was around half a second slower than the first division. The winner was back to his ealy summer level.

## 7777 32RED.COM APPRENTICE H'CAP — 1m 5f (P)
**3:50** (3:50) (Class 6) (0-65,67) 3-Y-0+ **£2,587** (£577; £577; £192) **Stalls** Low

Form RPR

2250 **1** **Comedy House**[25] 6635 6-9-10 63 (v) HectorCrouch 13 70
(Michael Madgwick) *hld up towards rr: hdwy 5f out: chsd ldng pair and rdn over 1f out: styd on wl ins fnl f to ld cl home* **5/1**[3]

1123 **2** ½ **Zinnobar**[27] 7290 4-9-3 61 (p) JackBudge(5) 8 67
(Jonathan Portman) *wirh ldr: rdn to ld 2f out: sustained duel w rival after: hdd and no ex cl home* **7/2**[1]

6365 **2** *dht* **Angus Glens**[11] 7628 4-9-2 60 (p) JosephineGordon(5) 7 66
(David Dennis) *led: rdn and hdd 2f out: sustained duel w rival after: no ex cl home* **5/1**[3]

0464 **4** 2 **Golden Bird (IRE)**[22] 7401 3-9-2 65 PaulBooth(3) 12 68
(Dean Ivory) *awkward leaving stalls: hld up in tch: hdwy over 2f out: chsd clr ldng trio1f out: styd on but nvr enough pce to chal* **8/1**

5665 **5** 1 ½ **Stilla Afton**[34] 7118 3-8-6 52 (p) ChrisMeehan 11 53
(Marcus Tregoning) *chsd ldr: rdn and racd awkwardly bnd 2f out: one pce and no imp fr over 1f out* **9/2**[2]

-565 **6** 2 **Here For Good (IRE)**[11] 7626 3-8-12 65 TomMarquand(7) 6 63
(Richard Hannon) *hld up in tch in last trio: hdwy on outer over 4f out: rdn and struggling 2f out: one pce and no threat to ldrs after* **8/1**

0000 **7** 1 **Flying Author (IRE)**[9] 7664 3-8-0 51 oh6 (tp) PatrickO'Donnell(5) 9 47
(Phil McEntee) *hld up in midfield: hdwy to chse ldrs 9f out: rdn and no ex 2f out: 4th and btn over 1f out: wknd ins fnl f* **50/1**

4040 **8** *shd* **Keep Kicking (IRE)**[24] 7366 7-9-6 64 TomasHarrigan(5) 4 60
(Simon Dow) *stdd s: hld up in midfield: shuffled bk to rr 4f out: stl bhd and hmpd 2f out: swtchd rt and rdn over 1f out: kpt on: nvr trbld ldrs* **14/1**

053 **9** *nse* **Dukes Den**[36] 7067 3-8-11 64 JackDinsmore(7) 2 60
(Sylvester Kirk) *in tch in midfield: lost pl and rdn over 2f out: kpt on but no threat to ldrs after* **10/1**

600- **10** 13 **Astrowolf**[389] 7418 3-8-10 59 JoshQuinn(3) 5 36
(Mark H Tompkins) *t.k.h: hld up in tch in midfield: rdn and struggling over 2f out: wknd wl over 1f out* **16/1**

-050 **11** 1 ½ **Summerling (IRE)**[85] 5600 3-9-5 65 AaronJones 1 39
(Phil McEntee) *chsd ldrs tl 8f out: in tch in midfield after tl lost pl over 2f out: bhd fnl f* **33/1**

2m 45.78s (-0.22) **Going Correction** -0.025s/f (Stan)
**WFA** 3 from 4yo+ 7lb **11** Ran SP% **122.5**
Speed ratings (Par 101): **99,98,98,97,96 95,94,94,94,86 85**
WIN: 4.40 Comedy House; PL: 1.90 Comedy House, 2.70 Angus Glens, 1.50 Zinnobar; EX: 10.60 Comedy House & Zinnobar, 18.20 Comedy House & Angus Glens; CSF: 15.83 CH & AG, 11.95 CH & Z; TC: 47.75, 50.92; TF: 60.40 CH&Z&AG, 69.00 CH&AG&Z.
**Owner** Los Leader **Bred** Giles W Pritchard-Gordon (farming) Ltd **Trained** Denmead, Hants
■ Stewards' Enquiry : Josephine Gordon two-day ban: careless riding (Nov 28-29)

**FOCUS**
They didn't go much of a pace in this moderate apprentice handicap. A small pb from the winner.
T/Plt: £116.30 to a £1 stake. Pool: £45,305.48 - 284.19 winning tickets T/Qpdt: £28.00 to a £1 stake. Pool: £4,719.11 - 124.70 winning tickets SP

# 7697 WOLVERHAMPTON (A.W) (L-H)
Friday, November 14

**OFFICIAL GOING: Tapeta: standard**
Wind: Light behind easing to almost nil Weather: Cloudy

## 7778 32RED.COM MAIDEN STKS (TAPETA) — 1m 141y
**4:00** (4:01) (Class 5) 2-Y-O **£2,911** (£866; £432; £216) **Stalls** Low

Form RPR

**1** **Yeats Magic (IRE)** 2-9-5 0 RobertHavlin 9 82+
(John Gosden) *s.i.s: hld up: hdwy over 1f out: rdn and edgd rt ins fnl f: r.o to ld nr fin* **12/1**

2 **2** ½ **Pin Up (IRE)**[24] 7367 2-9-0 0 TonyHamilton 7 75+
(Richard Fahey) *mid-div: pushed along and hdwy over 2f out: rdn to ld and edgd rt ins fnl f: hdd nr fin* **3/1**[2]

6 **3** 3 ¼ **Mojawiz**[9] 7666 2-9-5 0 PhillipMakin 1 73
(Charlie Appleby) *a.p: chsd ldr over 3f out: rdn over 1f out: ev ch whn hung rt ins fnl f: sn hung lft and no ex* **9/2**

**4** 1 ½ **Fiesole** 2-9-5 0 ShaneKelly 11 70
(Luca Cumani) *s.i.s: hld up: hdwy over 1f out: r.o: nt trble ldrs* **12/1**

23 **5** ½ **Champagne Bob**[16] 7537 2-9-5 0 GrahamGibbons 12 69
(Tom Dascombe) *led: rdn: edgd rt and hdd ins fnl f: wknd towards fin* **7/2**[3]

4 **6** ½ **Amadeity (IRE)**[118] 4429 2-9-5 0 MartinDwyer 6 68
(Jo Hughes) *chsd ldrs: rdn over 2f out: no ex fnl f* **50/1**

0 **7** ½ **Cloud Seven**[23] 7382 2-9-2 0 AshleyMorgan(3) 2 67
(Chris Wall) *s.s: hld up: hdwy over 1f out: nt rch ldrs* **66/1**

00 **8** 4 ½ **London Mayor (IRE)**[23] 7382 2-9-5 0 JackMitchell 13 57
(Roger Varian) *hld up: pushed along over 2f out: n.d* **18/1**

**9** 12 **Sneaking Budge** 2-9-5 0 TedDurcan 5 32
(David Lanigan) *rn green in rr: drvn along 1/2-way: wkng whn nt clr run over 2f out* **11/4**[1]

0 **10** 14 **Beauchamp Diamond**[17] 7511 2-9-0 0 LiamJones 8
(Paul Fitzsimons) *chsd ldr tl rdn over 3f out: wknd over 2f out* **100/1**

**11** 15 **Merton Place (USA)** 2-9-5 0 TomEaves 4
(Charlie Appleby) *prom tl rdn and wknd over 2f out* **20/1**

1m 48.79s (-1.31) **Going Correction** -0.05s/f (Stan) 2y crse rec **11** Ran SP% **121.9**
Speed ratings (Par 96): **103,102,99,98,97 97,97,93,82,69 56**
CSF £49.12 TOTE £12.80: £3.70, £1.10, £2.70; EX 42.60 Trifecta £259.10.
**Owner** Lady Bamford **Bred** Lady Bamford **Trained** Newmarket, Suffolk

**FOCUS**
An interesting juvenile maiden featuring several well-bred runners from good yards

## 7779 32RED MAIDEN STKS (TAPETA) — 7f 32y
**4:30** (4:32) (Class 5) 2-Y-O **£2,911** (£866; £432; £216) **Stalls** High

Form RPR

203 **1** **Biting Bullets (USA)**[64] 6270 2-9-5 74 MartinDwyer 3 70+
(Jo Hughes) *hld up: hdwy over 2f out: rdn to ld wl ins fnl f: r.o* **7/2**[2]

0 **2** 1 ¼ **Beauty Prince**[56] 6517 2-9-5 0 SteveDrowne 7 67
(Clive Cox) *a.p: chsd ldr 2f out: rdn to ld ins fnl f: sn hdd and unable qck* **16/1**

**3** 1 ½ **Time Flies** 2-9-5 0 RobertHavlin 5 63+
(John Gosden) *s.i.s: hld up: hdwy over 1f out: r.o* **9/2**[3]

2 **4** 1 **Conflicting Advice (USA)**[31] 7166 2-9-5 0 ShaneKelly 2 61+
(Sir Michael Stoute) *hld up: shkn up over 1f out: r.o ins fnl f: nt rch ldrs* **1/2**[1]

00 **5** *hd* **Let Right Be Done**[30] 7200 2-9-5 0 GrahamGibbons 8 60
(Ed McMahon) *led: qcknd over 2f out: sn rdn: hdd and no ex ins fnl f* **50/1**

5 **6** 1 **Woofie (IRE)**[36] 7054 2-9-5 0 TonyHamilton 6 58
(Richard Fahey) *chsd ldr tl rdn 2f out: no ex fnl f* **20/1**

05 **7** 1 **Fit The Bill (IRE)**[69] 6147 2-9-5 0 LukeMorris 4 55
(James Tate) *chsd ldrs: rdn over 2f out: no ex fr over 1f out* **20/1**

**8** 6 **Show Me The Bar** 2-9-2 0 PhilipPrince(3) 1 41
(Jo Hughes) *s.i.s: a in rr: wknd over 2f out* **50/1**

1m 29.46s (0.66) **Going Correction** -0.05s/f (Stan) **8** Ran SP% **126.4**
Speed ratings (Par 96): **94,92,90,89,89 88,87,80**
CSF £53.86 TOTE £5.00: £1.10, £3.70, £1.70; EX 87.00 Trifecta £370.00.
**Owner** Merriebelle Irish Farm Limited **Bred** Daniel J Burke **Trained** Lambourn, Berks

**FOCUS**
Just an ordinary gallop to this maiden which was won by the most exposed member of the field.

## 7780 £20 RISK-FREE BET AT UNIBET NURSERY H'CAP (TAPETA) — 5f 20y
**5:00** (5:01) (Class 5) (0-75,74) 2-Y-O **£2,911** (£866; £432; £216) **Stalls** Low

Form RPR

3344 **1** **Somedaysrdiamonds**[14] 7571 2-8-9 62 (p) LiamJones 1 65
(J S Moore) *led: rdn and hdd ins fnl f: rallied to ld sn after: r.o* **15/2**[3]

5032 **2** ½ **Most Tempting**[20] 7453 2-8-6 59 AdamBeschizza 5 60
(Robert Cowell) *s.i.s: hld up: hdwy over 1f out: rdn to ld ins fnl f: sn hdd: styd on* **5/2**[2]

3151 **3** ¾ **Low Cut Affair (IRE)**[88] 5507 2-9-7 74 ChrisCatlin 3 72
(Gay Kelleway) *chsd ldrs: rdn over 1f out: styd on u.p* **12/1**

B403 **4** *shd* **Star Fire**[20] 7454 2-8-8 61 ShaneKelly 8 59
(Roger Charlton) *hld up: plld hrd: racd on outer: hdwy over 1f out: rdn ins fnl f: styd on* **5/4**[1]

1204 **5** 3 **Multi Quest**[21] 7421 2-8-7 60 MartinDwyer 6 47
(Jo Hughes) *prom: rdn over 1f out: no ex fnl f* **16/1**

006 **6** 3 ¾ **Coursing**[20] 7454 2-8-5 58 LukeMorris 2 32+
(Sir Mark Prescott Bt) *s.i.s: sn pushed along in rr: nvr on terms* **9/1**

4440 **7** 1 ½ **Celestial Vision (USA)**[119] 4410 2-9-3 70 StephenCraine 4 38
(Tom Dascombe) *chsd ldr tl rdn over 1f out: wknd fnl f* **25/1**

1m 2.24s (0.34) **Going Correction** -0.05s/f (Stan) **7** Ran SP% **112.2**
Speed ratings (Par 96): **95,94,93,92,88 82,79**
CSF £25.59 CT £221.58 TOTE £8.50: £3.80, £2.00; EX 27.20 Trifecta £110.40.
**Owner** G V March & J S Moore **Bred** Manor Farm Stud (rutland) **Trained** Upper Lambourn, Berks

**FOCUS**
An ordinary nursery in which the well-supported favourite raced too keenly and just over a length covered the first four home.

## 7781 UNIBET OFFER DAILY JOCKEY/TRAINER SPECIALS H'CAP (TAPETA) — 5f 20y
**5:30** (5:30) (Class 6) (0-55,55) 3-Y-O+ **£2,264** (£673; £336; £168) **Stalls** Low

Form RPR

3543 **1** **Your Gifted (IRE)**[17] 7519 7-8-13 52 (v) AlistairRawlinson(5) 6 62
(Lisa Williamson) *hmpd s: hld up: hdwy over 1f out: rdn to ld ins fnl f: r.o* **9/2**[2]

0355 **2** 1 ¾ **Rat Catcher (IRE)**[17] 7520 4-8-5 46 (b) RobHornby(7) 2 50
(Lisa Williamson) *a.p: rdn to ld 1f out: sn hdd: styd on same pce* **8/1**

0053 **3** 1 ¼ **Quality Art (USA)**[17] 7520 6-9-5 53 LiamJones 12 52
(Simon Hodgson) *hld up: hdwy over 1f out: r.o* **13/2**[3]

00 **4** ½ **Spray Tan**[24] 7364 4-9-7 55 LukeMorris 7 52
(Tony Carroll) *mid-div: hmpd wl over 1f out: hdwy sn after: styd on u.p: nt rch ldrs* **17/2**

045 **5** 1 ½ **Minty Jones**[9] 7670 5-8-9 48 (v) TimClark(5) 8 40
(Michael Mullineaux) *mid-div: hdwy u.p over 1f out: nt trbld ldrs* **8/1**

0010 **6** 2 **Gypsy Rider**[2] 7737 5-8-11 50 NedCurtis(5) 3 35+
(Henry Tett) *sn pushed along in mid-div: lost pl after 1f: nt clr run 1/2-way: hdwy whn nt clr run and swtchd rt over 1f out: r.o: nvr trbld ldrs* **10/3**[1]

4360 **7** 1 **Straight Gin**[17] 7510 3-9-0 48 BarryMcHugh 1 29
(Alan Berry) *chsd ldrs: rdn and edgd lft over 1f out: wknd fnl f* **22/1**

0-40 **8** *hd* **Nine Before Ten (IRE)**[161] 2955 6-8-9 46 (t) ConnorBeasley(3) 4 26
(Deborah Sanderson) *led: hdd over 3f out: rdn and ev ch 1f out: sn wknd* **33/1**

/50- **9** 1 **Wreningham**[668] 213 9-9-4 55 JoeyHaynes(3) 10 32
(Pat Eddery) *chsd ldr tl led over 3f out: rdn and hdd 1f out: sn wknd* **40/1**

6256 **10** *nk* **Spic 'n Span**[30] 7191 9-8-13 47 (p) ChrisCatlin 5 23
(Ronald Harris) *edgd rt s: a in rr* **14/1**

5-00 **11** 8 **Maltease Ah**[193] 2008 5-9-0 55 AlfieWarwick(7) 11
(Andrew Reid) *mid-div: wknd 1/2-way* **33/1**

6004 **12** 4 **Diamond Solitaire (IRE)**[17] 7520 3-9-3 51 BenCurtis 13
(Timothy Jarvis) *chsd ldrs: rdn 1/2-way: wknd over 1f out* **11/1**

1m 1.63s (-0.27) **Going Correction** -0.05s/f (Stan) **12** Ran SP% **115.0**
Speed ratings (Par 101): **100,97,95,94,92 88,87,86,85,84 72,65**
CSF £37.45 CT £232.75 TOTE £5.60: £1.80, £2.40, £2.80; EX 34.50 Trifecta £136.60.
**Owner** Anthony Thomas Sykes **Bred** Rathasker Stud **Trained** Saighton, Cheshire

**FOCUS**
A low-grade sprint featuring mainly exposed performers, but it was run at a fair gallop. The winner was close to his best post-2011 form.

## 7782 DAILY PRICE BOOSTS AT UNIBET H'CAP (TAPETA) (DIV I) — 5f 216y
**6:00** (6:03) (Class 6) (0-55,56) 3-Y-O+ **£2,264** (£673; £336; £168) **Stalls** Low

Form RPR

5000 **1** **Insolenceofoffice (IRE)**[24] 7364 6-9-3 54 (p) ConnorBeasley(3) 5 68
(Richard Ford) *chsd ldrs: led over 1f out: rdn clr fnl f* **11/2**

0465 **2** 5 **Hamis Al Bin (IRE)**[24] 7364 5-9-6 54 (t) LukeMorris 11 52
(Milton Bradley) *broke wl: sn std and lost pl: hdwy over 1f out: rdn and nt clr run ins fnl f: styd on to go 2nd towards fin: no ch w wnr* **9/2**[3]


The Form Book, Raceform Ltd, Newbury, RG14 5SJ

0200 3 nk **Knockamany Bends (IRE)**[70] 6120 4-9-4 52 PaddyAspell 4 49
(John Wainwright) *s.i.s: plld hrd and sn prom: rdn over 1f out: styd on same pce fnl f* 11/1
0042 4 ½ **High Tone**[2] 7737 4-9-1 49 (p) ChrisCatlin 2 44
(Dean Ivory) *sn pushed along to ld: rdn and hdd over 1f out: no ex ins fnl f* 5/2[1]
340 5 1 **Night Trade (IRE)**[29] 7221 7-8-8 49 (p) DavidParkes(7) 9 41
(Ronald Harris) *broke wl: sn lost pl: r.o ins fnl f: nt trble ldrs* 33/1
0600 6 ½ **Sleeping Star**[10] 7644 3-9-5 53 PJMcDonald 1 44
(Mel Brittain) *s.i.s: hld up: hdwy over 1f out: wknd ins fnl f* 33/1
3450 7 1 ¾ **Divertimenti (IRE)**[57] 6495 10-8-12 51 (b) EoinWalsh(5) 13 36
(Roy Bowring) *chsd ldrs: rdn 1/2-way: wknd over 1f out* 12/1
0000 8 ½ **Under Review (IRE)**[17] 7520 8-8-13 50 (tp) JoeyHaynes(3) 8 33
(Bernard Llewellyn) *mid-div: sn drvn along: wknd over 1f out* 16/1
5403 9 3 ½ **Encapsulated**[21] 7420 4-9-2 50 (p) RobertHavlin 7 22
(Roger Ingram) *prom: chsd ldr over 4f out: rdn and ev ch 2f out: wknd over 1f out* 7/2[2]
0630 10 1 ¾ **Prince Of Passion (CAN)**[21] 7423 6-9-7 55 (v) TonyHamilton 10 22
(Derek Shaw) *prom tl rdn and wknd over 2f out* 16/1
1m 13.79s (-0.71) **Going Correction** -0.05s/f (Stan) 10 Ran SP% 118.0
Speed ratings (Par 101): **102,95,94,94,92 92,89,89,84,82**
CSF £30.91 CT £263.01 TOTE £13.50: £3.80, £1.80, £3.90; EX 53.90.
**Owner** CCCNLP **Bred** Gerard Kennedy **Trained** Garstang, Lancs

**FOCUS**
A low-grade sprint handicap run at a decent pace and a convincing winner. The winner was back to his best form for the past year or so.

## 7783 DAILY PRICE BOOSTS AT UNIBET H'CAP (TAPETA) (DIV II) 5f 216y
6:30 (6:32) (Class 6) (0-55,55) 3-Y-O+ £2,264 (£673; £336; £168) Stalls Low

Form RPR
0500 1 **Prigsnov Dancer (IRE)**[21] 7423 9-8-9 50 (p) DavidParkes(7) 1 59
(Deborah Sanderson) *wnt rt s: led: hdd over 4f out: led again 1/2-way: shkn up over 1f out: jst hld on* 25/1
2020 2 shd **Reginald Claude**[24] 7364 6-9-2 55 RachealKneller(5) 13 63
(Mark Usher) *hld up: n.m.r and r.o wl ins fnl f: nt quite get there* 14/1
550- 3 1 **Done Dreaming (IRE)**[400] 7149 4-9-4 52 TonyHamilton 2 57
(Richard Fahey) *chsd ldrs: rdn over 2f out: edgd lft over 1f out: styd on* 20/1
0002 4 1 ½ **Interchoice Star**[17] 7519 9-9-6 54 (p) ChrisCatlin 11 54
(Ray Peacock) *a.p: rdn over 1f out: styd on same pce ins fnl f* 8/1
202 5 nk **Littlecote Lady**[240] 1009 5-8-12 53 (v) CharlotteJenner(7) 3 52
(Mark Usher) *s.i.s and hmpd s: hld up: rdn over 1f out: n.m.r and styd on ins fnl f: nt trble ldrs* 25/1
0000 6 ¾ **Quantum Dot (IRE)**[80] 5795 3-8-13 50 (p) DeclanBates(3) 5 47
(Ed de Giles) *s.i.s: hld up: swtchd rt and hdwy over 1f out: styd on: nt rch ldrs* 15/8[1]
0640 7 hd **Natalia**[21] 7424 5-9-0 48 GrahamGibbons 4 44
(Andrew Hollinshead) *hmpd s: sn mid-div: hdwy over 1f out: no ex ins fnl f* 4/1[3]
6500 8 shd **Amis Reunis**[10] 7644 5-9-1 49 (p) PatrickMathers 6 45
(Alan Berry) *chsd ldrs: rdn over 1f out: styd on same pce fnl f* 33/1
3062 9 nse **Redalani (IRE)**[21] 7420 4-9-5 53 (tp) ShaneKelly 8 49
(Alan Brown) *prom: racd keenly: rdn over 1f out: no ex ins fnl f* 8/1
5662 10 1 **Very First Blade**[1] 7766 5-9-1 49 (be) RobertHavlin 12 41
(Michael Mullineaux) *hld up: pushed along over 2f out: nvr on terms* 7/2[2]
4400 11 1 ¼ **Balinka**[91] 5390 4-9-2 50 PJMcDonald 7 38
(Mel Brittain) *chsd wnr tl led over 4f out: hdd 1/2-way: rdn over 1f out: wknd ins fnl f* 50/1
000P 12 7 **Kaytom**[10] 7639 3-9-2 50 (b) PaddyAspell 10 16
(John Wainwright) *hld up: rdn over 2f out: wknd over 1f out* 66/1
1m 14.37s (-0.13) **Going Correction** -0.05s/f (Stan) 12 Ran SP% 124.7
Speed ratings (Par 101): **98,97,96,94,94 93,92,92,92,91 89,80**
CSF £329.25 CT £6990.43 TOTE £34.90: £9.50, £3.70, £4.50; EX 321.00 Trifecta £1733.70 Part won..
**Owner** J M Lacey **Bred** Tom Radley **Trained** Tickhill, S Yorks

**FOCUS**
Just an ordinary sprint, and 0.56sec slower than the first division. The winner was on a good mark on his early-summer form.

## 7784 CORAL.CO.UK H'CAP (TAPETA) 1m 1f 103y
7:00 (7:00) (Class 3) (0-90,90) 3-Y-O- £7,246 (£2,168; £1,084; £542; £270) Stalls Low

Form RPR
1635 1 **Solidarity**[27] 7289 3-9-2 88 PhillipMakin 7 101
(Charlie Appleby) *hld up: hdwy 2f out: led 1f out: shkn up and r.o wl: comf* 7/4[1]
3613 2 3 ½ **Sbraase**[31] 7186 3-8-5 77 LukeMorris 3 83
(James Tate) *a.p: chsd ldr over 3f out: led over 1f out: sn rdn and hdd: styd on same pce* 9/2[2]
0445 3 ½ **Art Scholar (IRE)**[17] 7516 7-8-7 79 RyanTate(3) 9 83
(Michael Appleby) *bhd and pushed along over 7f out: hdwy over 1f out: rdn and hmpd ins fnl f: styd on: nt rch ldrs* 17/2
6010 4 ½ **Berlusca (IRE)**[49] 6704 5-9-2 85 GrahamGibbons 8 88
(David O'Meara) *hld up: nt clr run over 2f out: hdwy over 1f out: rdn: edgd rt and styd on same pce ins fnl f* 14/1
332 5 6 **L'Inganno Felice (FR)**[25] 7335 4-8-4 76 oh2 ConnorBeasley(3) 2 66
(Iain Jardine) *w ldr tl led 7f out: rdn and hdd over 1f out: wknd fnl f* 5/1[3]
6060 6 1 ½ **Luv U Whatever**[7] 7702 4-8-8 77 LiamJones 6 64
(Michael Appleby) *chsd ldrs: rdn over 2f out: wknd over 1f out* 6/1
6504 7 3 **Mia's Boy**[31] 7186 10-8-11 80 LiamKeniry 4 61
(Chris Dwyer) *mid-div: hdwy over 6f out: rdn over 1f out: wknd fnl f* 16/1
0000 8 7 **Energia Eros (BRZ)**[36] 7066 5-9-7 90 (b) TedDurcan 11 56
(John Berry) *in rr and pushed along 7f out: effrt over 2f out: wknd wl over 1f out* 50/1
0000 9 8 **Shahdaroba (IRE)**[52] 6639 4-9-0 83 (p) PJMcDonald 5 32
(Micky Hammond) *led: hdd 7f out: chsd ldr tl rdn over 3f out: wknd over 2f out* 66/1
3500 10 6 **Nurpur (IRE)**[16] 7538 4-8-11 80 SamJames 10 17
(David O'Meara) *prom: rdn 1/2-way: wknd over 2f out* 22/1
1m 57.43s (-3.37) **Going Correction** -0.05s/f (Stan)
**WFA** 3 from 4yo+ 3lb 10 Ran SP% 116.4
Speed ratings (Par 107): **112,108,108,108,102 101,98,92,85,80**
CSF £9.28 CT £52.48 TOTE £2.70: £1.10, £1.50, £2.40; EX 9.60 Trifecta £56.50.
**Owner** Godolphin **Bred** Darley **Trained** Newmarket, Suffolk

**FOCUS**
A competitive handicap run at a decent gallop and a decisive winner in a race in which the first four finished clear. The race lacked depth for the grade.

## 7785 CORAL MOBILE "JUST THREE CLICKS TO BET" CLASSIFIED STKS (TAPETA) 1m 1f 103y
7:30 (7:31) (Class 6) 3-Y-O+ £2,264 (£673; £336; £168) Stalls Low

Form RPR
0041 1 **Vaguely Spanish**[17] 7517 3-8-12 52 LukeMorris 11 63
(Tony Carroll) *hld up: hdwy over 1f out: rdn: edgd lft and r.o to ld wl ins fnl f* 11/4[2]
0601 2 ½ **Gracefilly**[10] 7632 3-9-4 55 AntonioFresu 4 68
(Ed Walker) *chsd ldr: rdn over 1f out: ev ch ins fnl f: r.o* 9/2[3]
1530 3 ¾ **Hidden Asset**[23] 7369 4-8-10 54 AlistairRawlinson(5) 2 59
(Michael Appleby) *hld up in tch: racd keenly: led wl over 1f out: rdn and hdd wl ins fnl f: styd on same pce* 15/8[1]
3500 4 2 ¼ **Caledonia Laird**[55] 6568 3-8-12 55 ShaneKelly 13 55
(Jo Hughes) *hld up: rdn over 1f out: r.o ins fnl f: nt rch ldrs* 16/1
3600 5 hd **Shamiana**[23] 7376 4-9-1 47 (b) SteveDrowne 9 54
(Daniel Kubler) *hld up in tch: rdn over 1f out: styd on same pce fnl f* 50/1
6506 6 hd **Avidly**[10] 7632 4-8-10 54 ShelleyBirkett(5) 12 53
(Julia Feilden) *hld up: rdn over 1f out: edgd lft and r.o ins fnl f: nt rch ldrs* 20/1
0524 7 1 **Mercury Magic**[23] 7369 3-8-12 52 (b) RaulDaSilva 6 52
(David Menuisier) *hld up: hdwy u.p over 1f out: no ex ins fnl f* 8/1
604 8 ½ **Sea Tiger**[32] 7158 4-9-1 55 LiamKeniry 8 50
(Chris Gordon) *chsd ldr tl led over 2f out: hdd wl over 1f out: no ex fnl f* 33/1
500 9 2 ¾ **Tight Knit (USA)**[141] 3623 4-8-8 55 PhillipDennis(7) 5 45
(John Weymes) *prom: rdn over 1f out: wknd fnl f* 33/1
0000 10 1 ¼ **Dutch Lady Roseane**[10] 7635 3-8-12 48 LiamJones 10 43
(James Unett) *hld up: rdn over 2f out: nvr on terms* 50/1
204 11 nk **Perseverent Pete (USA)**[27] 7291 4-8-10 47 EoinWalsh(5) 7 41
(Christine Dunnett) *led: rdn and hdd over 2f out: wknd fnl f* 33/1
000 12 22 **Macs Scwar**[16] 7528 7-8-12 45 RyanTate(3) 3
(Paul Morgan) *s.i.s: hld up: rdn and wknd over 2f out* 80/1
2m 1.59s (0.79) **Going Correction** -0.05s/f (Stan)
**WFA** 3 from 4yo+ 3lb 12 Ran SP% 115.4
Speed ratings (Par 101): **94,93,92,90,90 90,89,89,86,85 85,65**
CSF £14.06 TOTE £4.70: £1.50, £1.70, £1.50; EX 16.90 Trifecta £39.20.
**Owner** D Boocock **Bred** D Boocock **Trained** Cropthorne, Worcs

**FOCUS**
A slow gallop to this 0-55 classified event, but the right trio came clear.
T/Plt: £1,592.70 to a £1 stake. Pool: £80,185.36 - 36.75 winning tickets T/Qpdt: £94.70 to a £1 stake. Pool: £11,663.24 - 91.10 winning tickets CR

7786 - 7797a (Foreign Racing) - See Raceform Interactive

# 7770 LINGFIELD (L-H)
Saturday, November 15

**OFFICIAL GOING: Polytrack: standard**
Wind: virtually nil Weather: dry, overcast

## 7798 32RED/BRITISH STALLION STUDS EBF NOVICE STKS 1m 1y(P)
11:50 (11:51) (Class 5) 2-Y-O £3,234 (£962; £481; £240) Stalls High

Form RPR
1 1 **Chemical Charge (IRE)**[45] 6875 2-9-7 0 JamieSpencer 4 93+
(Ralph Beckett) *sn led: rdn and readily asserted over 1f out: r.o: comf* 2/7[1]
323 2 3 ¾ **Natural Nine (IRE)**[24] 7371 2-9-0 79 WilliamBuick 2 73
(Roger Varian) *t.k.h: chsd ldr: rdn wl over 1f out: unable qck and btn 1f out: one pce* 11/4[2]
0 3 ¾ **Take Note (IRE)**[14] 7594 2-8-9 0 HayleyTurner 1 66
(James Toller) *awkward leaving stalls: t.k.h: hld up in tch: rdn and outpcd over 1f out: kpt on same pce after* 66/1
0201 4 ½ **Prince Of Paris**[23] 7396 2-9-4 71 MartinLane 3 74
(Roger Ingram) *broke wl: sn stdd and hld up in tch: rdn and effrt over 1f out: r.o same pce* 33/1[3]
1m 38.18s (-0.02) **Going Correction** -0.025s/f (Stan) 4 Ran SP% 108.9
Speed ratings (Par 96): **99,95,94,94**
CSF £1.38 TOTE £1.30; EX 1.30 Trifecta £12.10.
**Owner** Qatar Racing Limited **Bred** Viktor Timoshenko **Trained** Kimpton, Hants

**FOCUS**
An uncompetitive novice event to start with and all very straightforward for the long odds-on favourite.

## 7799 BET NOW WITH LADBROKES APP CLAIMING STKS 1m 1y(P)
12:20 (12:20) (Class 6) 3-Y-O £1,940 (£577; £288; £144) Stalls High

Form RPR
0000 1 **Steventon Star**[16] 7543 3-9-2 87 (b) LukeMorris 3 72
(Alan Bailey) *in tch in midfield: wnt 3rd 3f out: rdn and effrt over 1f out: drvn to ld fnl 100yds: r.o: drvn out* 11/4[2]
1343 2 1 ¼ **Sexy Secret**[17] 7527 3-9-0 64 (v) RobertHavlin 2 67
(Lydia Pearce) *chsd ldrs: wnt 2nd 4f out: rdn over 1f out: drvn to ld 1f out: hdd and one pce fnl 100yds* 2/1[1]
030 3 nk **Tasaaboq**[2] 7764 3-8-6 60 (vt) DannyBrock(3) 7 61
(Phil McEntee) *stdd s: hld up in last pair: effrt on outer jst over 1f out: styd on wl u.p ins fnl f* 12/1
6006 4 1 ¾ **Movie Magic**[10] 7664 3-8-3 45 (v[1]) WilliamCarson 1 51
(John Bridger) *racd keenly: led: drvn jst over 2f out: hdd 1f out: no ex: wknd fnl 100yds* 66/1
5206 5 ¾ **Roly Tricks**[25] 7355 3-8-3 62 ow1 LiamJones 6 50
(Olly Stevens) *stdd s: t.k.h: hld up in last pair: effrt on inner over 1f out: no imp fnl f* 6/1
4540 6 2 ¾ **Kagami**[17] 7533 3-9-0 65 HayleyTurner 4 54
(Simon Dow) *chsd ldr tl 4f out: rdn and lost pl 3f out: bhd whn jostled wl over 1f out: wknd 1f out* 14/1
33 7 ½ **Muzaahim (IRE)**[56] 6540 3-8-8 0 KieranShoemark(7) 5 54
(Kevin Morgan) *in tch in midfield: rdn and lost pl jst over 1f out: bhd over 1f out* 7/2[3]
1m 37.39s (-0.81) **Going Correction** -0.025s/f (Stan) 7 Ran SP% 112.4
Speed ratings (Par 98): **103,101,101,99,98 96,95**
CSF £8.35 TOTE £4.00: £1.30, £2.00; EX 8.70 Trifecta £63.90.
**Owner** John Stocker **Bred** The National Stud **Trained** Newmarket, Suffolk

**FOCUS**
A moderate claimer.

## 7800 UNIBET MEDIAN AUCTION MAIDEN STKS — 6f 1y(P)
12:50 (12:52) (Class 6) 3-5-Y-O £1,940 (£577; £288; £144) Stalls Low

Form RPR
3002 1 **Suitsus**[35] [7117] 3-9-5 66..........(p) LukeMorris 3 73+
(Peter Makin) *chsd ldrs: clsd and gng best 2f out: rdn to ld 1f out: sn in command: eased cl home: easily* 4/9[1]
045 2 2 ½ **Deftera Fantutte (IRE)**[9] [7682] 3-8-11 64.......... PhilipPrince(3) 2 57
(Natalie Lloyd-Beavis) *stdd s: hld up in midfield: clsd and lft 4th whn rdr dropped rein and rn wd bnd 2f out: rallied 1f out: styd on to go 2nd ins fnl f: no ch w wnr* 9/2[2]
6526 3 2 ½ **Nelson's Pride**[8] [7699] 3-8-7 55..........(b) RhiainIngram(7) 7 49
(Roger Ingram) *t.k.h: chsd ldrs: jnd ldr over 4f out: rdn to ld over 1f out: sn hdd and outpcd* 12/1
5650 4 3 ¾ **Tolly McGuiness**[49] [6765] 3-9-0 45.......... ShelleyBirkett(5) 6 42
(Julia Feilden) *t.k.h: chsd ldr tl led over 4f out: rdn 2f out: hdd over 1f out: sn wknd* 20/1
-434 5 nk **Black Widow**[11] [7652] 3-9-0 46.......... TomQueally 4 36
(Pat Eddery) *a last trio: rdn and outpcd 3f out: n.d after* 20/1
0S 6 7 **Farmshop Boy**[33] [7157] 3-8-12 0.......... CharlieBennett(7) 9 19
(Natalie Lloyd-Beavis) *wnt rt s and s.i.s: a bhd* 33/1
505 7 ¾ **Tilsworth Annalisa**[60] [6437] 3-8-7 45.......... VictorSantos(7) 5 11
(J R Jenkins) *a last trio: rdn over 2f out: sn btn: lost tch over 1f out* 25/1
5 P **Two Turns**[8] [7699] 3-8-11 0.......... SimonPearce(3) 1
(Lydia Pearce) *led tl over 4f out: chsd ldrs: 4th and struggling whn lost action and p.u 2f out: fatally injured* 6/1[3]

1m 12.01s (0.11) **Going Correction** -0.025s/f (Stan) 8 Ran SP% 125.7
Speed ratings (Par 101): **98,94,91,86,85 76,75,**
CSF £3.21 TOTE £1.50: £1.10, £1.50, £1.60; EX 3.70 Trifecta £18.40.
**Owner** Suitsus Partnership **Bred** Mrs Susan Cole & Miss Lesley McGrath **Trained** Ogbourne Maisey, Wilts

**FOCUS**
An uncompetitive sprint maiden.

## 7801 LADBROKES H'CAP — 1m 1y(P)
1:25 (1:26) (Class 2) (0-105,100) 3-Y-O+ £12,291 (£3,657; £1,827; £913) Stalls High

Form RPR
2212 1 **Big Baz (IRE)**[29] [7236] 4-9-0 90.......... MartinDwyer 3 101+
(William Muir) *dwlt: sn rcvrd and chsd ldrs after 2f: wnt 2nd wl over 1f out: pushed into ld 1f out: rdn clr: and r.o wl: comf* 5/2[1]
0055 2 1 ½ **Ingleby Angel (IRE)**[19] [7490] 5-9-1 91.......... JimCrowley 4 97
(David O'Meara) *hld up in tch in last pair: effrt u.p on inner over 1f out: styd on on fnl f: wnt 2nd towards fin: no threat to wnr* 8/1
2042 3 ½ **God Willing**[19] [7490] 3-9-5 97.......... JamieSpencer 8 102
(Ed Dunlop) *in tch in midfield: hdwy to go 2nd over 2f out: drvn and unable qck over 1f out: kpt on ins fnl f* 7/2[3]
0000 4 ½ **Rebellious Guest**[113] [4608] 5-9-6 96.......... TomQueally 1 100
(George Margarson) *hld up in tch in last trio: effrt over 1f out: kpt on u.p ins fnl f: no threat to wnr* 16/1
530 5 shd **Ifwecan**[16] [7555] 3-8-13 91.......... JoeFanning 2 94
(Mark Johnston) *sn led: rdn and hrd pressed over 1f out: hdd 1f out: sn outpcd by wnr: wknd and lost 3 pls towards fin* 12/1
4200 6 ½ **Alfred Hutchinson**[70] [6124] 6-9-10 100.......... WilliamBuick 5 102
(Geoffrey Oldroyd) *hld up wl in tch in midfield: rdn over 2f out: no hdwy and widish bnd 2f out: kpt on same pce fr over 1f out* 3/1[2]
0251 7 2 ½ **Capo Rosso (IRE)**[21] [7455] 4-9-10 100.......... StephenCraine 7 97
(Tom Dascombe) *broke fast: sn hdd: chsd ldr: rdn over 3f out: lost pl over 2f out: wknd ins fnl f* 8/1
6000 8 3 ¾ **George Guru**[16] [7555] 7-9-6 96.......... RobertHavlin 6 84
(John Bridger) *hld up in tch in rr: effrt u.p over 1f out: no prog: wknd ins fnl f* 33/1

1m 35.4s (-2.80) **Going Correction** -0.025s/f (Stan)
**WFA** 3 from 4yo+ 2lb 8 Ran SP% 114.5
Speed ratings (Par 109): **113,111,111,110,110 109,107,103**
CSF £23.31 CT £69.51 TOTE £3.20: £1.70, £2.80, £1.90; EX 25.90 Trifecta £132.70.
**Owner** The Big Baz Partnership **Bred** Haras De La Perelle **Trained** Lambourn, Berks

**FOCUS**
A decent handicap and a good pace always looked likely. The form looks solid.

## 7802 UNIBET GOLDEN ROSE STKS (FAST TRACK QUALIFIER) (LISTED RACE) — 6f 1y(P)
2:00 (2:01) (Class 1) 3-Y-O+
£22,684 (£8,600; £4,304; £2,144; £1,076; £540) Stalls Low

Form RPR
1013 1 **Intransigent**[16] [7555] 5-9-5 107.......... JamieSpencer 8 105
(Andrew Balding) *in tch in midfield: rdn and hdwy jst over 1f out: styd on wl to ld towards fin: rdn out* 9/4[1]
0300 2 nk **Fresles (IRE)**[40] [6994] 3-8-12 0.......... WilliamBuick 3 97
(Mme Pia Brandt, France) *led: rdn over 1f out: kpt on wl tl hdd and no ex towards fin* 20/1
5151 3 1 **Polybius**[54] [6607] 3-9-3 102.......... TedDurcan 11 98
(David Lanigan) *hld up in midfield: rdn and effrt over 1f out: styd on wl fnl 100yds: wnt 3rd last strides* 7/2[2]
6246 4 shd **Golden Steps (FR)**[21] [7441] 3-9-3 95.......... JimCrowley 9 98
(Marco Botti) *taken down early: dwlt and niggled along early: hld up in tch in last pair: hdwy between horses 1f out: styd on wl fnl 100yds* 5/1
1440 5 nse **Medicean Man**[147] [3451] 8-9-3 107..........(tp) MartinLane 10 98
(Jeremy Gask) *in tch in midfield: hdwy to chse ldrs 1f out: r.o same pce u.p fnl 100yds: lost 2 pls last strides* 6/1
4010 6 1 ¼ **Serenity Spa**[42] [6929] 4-8-12 81.......... WilliamTwiston-Davies 6 89
(Tony Carroll) *stdd s: hld up in last pair: rdn and hdwy jst over 1f out: nt clr run and swtchd rt wl ins fnl f: nvr trbld ldrs* 66/1
1100 7 ½ **Aertex (IRE)**[119] [4436] 3-8-12 87.......... SeanLevey 1 87
(Richard Hannon) *in tch in midfield: lft 3rd wl over 1f out: sn chsng ldr: no imp and lost 2nd 1f out: wknd ins fnl f* 25/1
046 8 nse **Seeking Magic**[35] [7122] 6-9-3 97..........(t) RyanTate 2 92
(Clive Cox) *taken down early: t.k.h: chsd ldrs: lft 2nd briefly wl over 1f out: lost pl u.p 1f out: wknd ins fnl f* 9/2[3]
024 9 1 **Counter Ridge (SAF)**[16] [7543] 5-8-12 89.......... LukeMorris 4 84
(Marco Botti) *chsd ldr tl rn v wd bnd 2f out and lost pl: bhd and no prog over 1f out* 25/1

1m 9.98s (-1.92) **Going Correction** -0.025s/f (Stan) 9 Ran SP% 116.1
Speed ratings: **111,110,109,109,109 107,106,106,105**
CSF £52.48 TOTE £3.20: £1.10, £4.40, £1.90; EX 32.90 Trifecta £181.40.
**Owner** Kingsclere Racing Club **Bred** Kingsclere Stud **Trained** Kingsclere, Hants

**FOCUS**
A decent Listed sprint and a fast-track qualifier for the All-Weather Championships Sprint Final next Easter. As might have been expected, they went a serious pace.

## 7803 CORAL CHURCHILL STKS (FAST TRACK QUALIFIER) (LISTED RACE) — 1m 2f (P)
2:35 (2:41) (Class 1) 3-Y-O+
£25,519 (£9,675; £4,842; £2,412; £1,210; £607) Stalls Low

Form RPR
0533 1 **Battalion (IRE)**[21] [7447] 4-9-2 106.......... TomQueally 1 108+
(William Haggas) *hld up in tch in midfield: rdn and gd hdwy on inner over 1f out: qcknd to ld ins fnl f: sn in command and r.o strly* 4/1[2]
0354 2 1 ½ **Educate**[14] [7598] 5-9-2 108.......... WilliamBuick 4 104
(Ismail Mohammed) *chsd ldrs: rdn and effrt over 1f out: ev ch 1f out: carried rt ins fnl f: outpcd by wnr but kpt on to go 2nd cl home* 3/1[1]
30 3 nk **Energia Fox (BRZ)**[65] [6255] 4-8-11 96.......... TedDurcan 9 98
(Marco Botti) *chsd ldr: rdn to ld wl over 1f out: hdd and outpcd by wnr ins fnl f: lost 2nd cl home* 25/1
410 4 ¾ **Energia Davos (BRZ)**[56] [6548] 6-9-2 105.......... LukeMorris 5 101+
(Marco Botti) *hld up in tch in last trio: hdwy on inner jst over 1f out: styd on wl fnl 100yds: no threat to wnr* 5/1[3]
5002 5 ½ **Bancnuanaheireann (IRE)**[14] [7597] 7-9-2 95.......... HayleyTurner 6 100
(Michael Appleby) *t.k.h: hld up in tch in midfield: rdn 2f out: carried rt ins fnl f: r.o same pce fnl 100yds* 16/1
6202 6 shd **Fire Fighting (IRE)**[10] [7662] 3-8-12 106..........(b) JoeFanning 7 100
(Mark Johnston) *s.i.s: hdwy on outer to chse ldrs 8f out: rdn wl over 1f out: keeping on same pce whn carried rt ins fnl f* 5/1[3]
2301 7 shd **Masterpaver**[8] [7703] 3-8-12 94.......... ShaneKelly 2 100
(Alan Bailey) *hld up wl in tch in midfield: effrt over 1f out: kpt on ins fnl f: nvr enough pce to chal* 33/1
1063 8 hd **Whispering Warrior (IRE)**[45] [6878] 5-9-2 95.......... JimCrowley 8 100
(David Simcock) *stdd and dropped in after s: hld up in tch in last trio: effrt but wd bnd 2f out: styd on same pce fnl f* 16/1
9 1 **Snowmane (IRE)**[43] [6910] 3-8-12 98..........(p) JamieSpencer 10 98
(James Given) *led: rdn 2f out: hdd ins fnl f: no ex: btn and eased wl ins fnl f* 10/1
1002 10 nk **Niceofyoutotellme**[49] [6752] 5-9-2 98.......... SeanLevey 11 97
(Ralph Beckett) *taken down early: stdd s: hld up in tch in rr: effrt over 1f out: sme hdwy fnl 100yds: nvr threatened ldrs* 7/1
3026 11 2 ½ **Tinshu (IRE)**[64] [6303] 8-8-11 87..........(p) LiamKeniry 3 87
(Derek Haydn Jones) *hld up in tch towards rr: rdn wl over 1f out: bhd whn nt clr run 1f out: no hdwy: eased towards fin* 66/1

2m 5.21s (-1.39) **Going Correction** -0.025s/f (Stan)
**WFA** 3 from 4yo+ 4lb 11 Ran SP% 120.0
Speed ratings: **104,102,102,101,101 101,101,101,100,100 98**
CSF £16.55 TOTE £4.60: £2.30, £1.50, £7.10; EX 18.70 Trifecta £465.50.
**Owner** Sheikh Juma Dalmook Al Maktoum **Bred** Kildaragh Stud **Trained** Newmarket, Suffolk

**FOCUS**
A fast-track qualifier for the All-Weather Championships Middle Distance Final back here next April, but an interesting Listed event in its own right. The early pace didn't look that strong, but the winner was very impressive.

## 7804 CORAL CONNECT H'CAP (DIV I) — 1m 2f (P)
3:10 (3:11) (Class 6) (0-65,76) 3-Y-O+ £1,940 (£577; £288; £144) Stalls Low

Form RPR
0020 1 **Automotive**[38] [7044] 6-9-2 62.......... ShelleyBirkett(5) 5 72
(Julia Feilden) *hld up in last trio: hdwy 3f out: chsd clr ldr 2f out: rdn and steadily clsd to ld ins fnl f: kpt on* 20/1
3105 2 ½ **Benoordenhout (IRE)**[18] [7517] 3-8-11 59..........(p) DannyBrock(3) 3 68
(Jonathan Portman) *led: clr 7f out: drvn over 1f out: hdd ins fnl f: battled on u.p but a hld* 7/1[3]
2601 3 ¾ **Saturation Point**[28] [7292] 3-9-4 63.......... JoeFanning 9 71
(James Toller) *hld up in midfield: nt clr run and swtchd rt jst over 2f out: chsd clr ldng pair 1f out: styd on: nvr quite getting to ldrs* 3/1[1]
2052 4 ¾ **Brave Decision**[17] [7526] 7-9-5 60.......... LukeMorris 10 66
(Suzy Smith) *racd in midfield: effrt u.p over 2f out: 4th and kpt on u.p fnl f: nvr enough pce to rch ldrs* 7/2[2]
0640 5 4 ½ **Jethou Island**[27] [7303] 3-9-5 64.......... WilliamBuick 4 61
(Henry Candy) *hld up in rr: pushed along over 2f out: rdn and plugged on past btn horses 1f out: nvr trbld ldrs* 8/1
0041 6 3 ¾ **Gentlemax (FR)**[17] [7526] 4-9-9 64..........(b) PatCosgrave 8 54
(Jim Boyle) *t.k.h: chsd ldrs: wnt 2nd 8f out tl 2f out: wknd over 1f out* 7/2[2]
043- 7 nk **Percybelle**[352] [8085] 3-9-4 63.......... ShaneKelly 2 52
(William Knight) *racd in midfield: effrt over 2f out: btn 2f out: wknd over 1f out* 8/1
4002 8 6 **Silvee**[16] [7546] 7-8-10 51 oh5..........(b) WilliamCarson 7 28
(John Bridger) *chsd ldr for 2f: styd chsng ldrs tl lost pl over 2f out: bhd fnl f* 33/1
3000 9 5 **Mountain Range (IRE)**[25] [7358] 6-9-5 60.......... ChrisCatlin 11 27
(Willie Musson) *s.i.s: hld up in last trio: rdn and struggling in last 3f out: wl bhd fnl 2f* 12/1

2m 4.68s (-1.92) **Going Correction** -0.025s/f (Stan)
**WFA** 3 from 4yo+ 4lb 9 Ran SP% 119.6
Speed ratings (Par 101): **106,105,105,104,100 97,97,92,88**
CSF £157.73 CT £550.90 TOTE £27.80: £6.20, £2.60, £1.60; EX 204.50 Trifecta £1379.60 Part won..
**Owner** Stowstowquickquickstow Partnership **Bred** Juddmonte Farms Ltd **Trained** Exning, Suffolk

**FOCUS**
A moderate handicap which threatened to be slowly run until the second horse soon quickened things up. The winning time was faster than the Churchill Stakes.

## 7805 CORAL CONNECT H'CAP (DIV II) — 1m 2f (P)
3:45 (3:49) (Class 6) (0-65,64) 3-Y-O+ £1,940 (£577; £288; £144) Stalls Low

Form RPR
0043 1 **Sabre Rock**[17] [7526] 4-8-7 52..........(t) ShelleyBirkett(5) 8 58
(Julia Feilden) *taken down early: in tch: stdy hdwy on outer 1/2-way: rdn to chal 1f out: drvn to ld towards fin* 9/2[2]
0622 2 ½ **Turnbury**[18] [7517] 3-9-5 63..........(t) JackMitchell 1 68
(Robert Mills) *chsd ldrs: rdn and effrt over 1f out: ev ch fnl f: led towards fin: sn hdd and no ex* 5/1[3]
400 3 nse **Seaside Rock (IRE)**[187] [2219] 4-9-3 57..........(p) SeanLevey 11 62
(Keith Dalgleish) *chsd ldr: rdn and ev ch 2f out: led over 1f out: kpt on wl tl hdd and no ex towards fin* 8/1


The Form Book, Raceform Ltd, Newbury, RG14 5SJ

000 **4** *nse* **What A Dandy (IRE)**2 7759 3-9-4 62 ............ PatCosgrave 2 67
(Jim Boyle) *stdd s: hld up in rr: hdwy 3f out: hrd drvn 1f out: styd on wl u.p ins fnl f* **6/1**

0211 **5** *1* **Innoko (FR)**11 7635 4-9-10 64 ............ LukeMorris 4 69+
(Tony Carroll) *hld up in tch: effrt over 1f out: clsd to chse ldrs but nt clr run thrght fnl f: eased towards fin* **3/1**1

4540 **6** *nk* **Fair Ranger**17 7533 3-9-6 64 ............ JimCrowley 6 66
(Chris Gordon) *wl in tch in midfield: effrt 2f out: chsd ldrs 1f out: nt clr run ins fnl f: kpt on same pce towards fin* **25/1**

6450 **7** *nk* **Dark Phantom (IRE)**53 6647 3-8-6 50 oh5 ............(b1) LiamJones 3 52
(Peter Makin) *in tch in midfield: effrt u.p over 1f out: kpt on same pce ins fnl f* **33/1**

0005 **8** *hd* **Kirtling**21 7458 3-9-3 61 ............ MartinLane 5 62
(Andi Brown) *s.i.s: pushed along at times: effrt u.p on outer bnd 2f out: kpt on ins fnl f: nvr trbld ldrs* **14/1**

-056 **9** *½* **Storm Runner (IRE)**260 780 6-9-8 62 ............ TomQueally 7 62
(George Margarson) *hld up in tch in midfield: drvn over 1f out: kpt on same pce ins fnl f* **16/1**

0600 **10** *¾* **Malicho**17 7533 5-9-8 62 ............(t1) SebSanders 10 61
(Dean Ivory) *led: rdn jst over 2f out: hdd over 1f out: no ex ins fnl f: wknd towards fin* **16/1**

40-0 **11** *1* **Sail Home**25 7358 7-9-6 60 ............ LiamKeniry 9 57
(John E Long) *dropped in towards rr after s: hld up in tch in last trio: rdn and effrt over 1f out: kpt on: nvr trbld ldrs* **16/1**

2m 7.67s (1.07) **Going Correction** -0.025s/f (Stan)
**WFA** 3 from 4yo+ 4lb **11** Ran SP% **116.3**
Speed ratings (Par 101): **94,93,93,93,92 92,92,92,91,91 90**
CSF £26.99 CT £175.42 TOTE £6.80: £2.30, £2.30, £2.30; EX 32.40 Trifecta £185.20.
**Owner** Miss J Feilden **Bred** J H Mayne **Trained** Exning, Suffolk

**FOCUS**
They didn't go anything like as quick in this division (the winning time was around 3sec slower) resulting in a bunch finish. It provided a double for the winning trainer and rider having won the first leg with Automotive.
T/Plt: £8.80 to a £1 stake. Pool: £49,144.85 - 4,052.85 winning tickets T/Qpdt: £3.80 to a £1 stake. Pool: £5290.89 - 1021.10 winning tickets SP

# 7778 WOLVERHAMPTON (A.W) (L-H)
Saturday, November 15

**OFFICIAL GOING: Tapeta: standard**
Wind: Light against Weather: Overcast

## 7806 £20 RISK-FREE AT UNIBET H'CAP (TAPETA) 5f 20y
**5:45** (5:45) (Class 5) (0-70,69) 3-Y-O+ **£2,911** (£866; £432; £216) **Stalls** Low

Form RPR
6520 **1** **Dynamo Walt (IRE)**10 7670 3-9-5 67 ............(v) TonyHamilton 6 79
(Derek Shaw) *a.p: rdn to ld ins fnl f: edgd lft: r.o* **7/2**1

5010 **2** *1 ¼* **Bilash**47 6815 7-8-10 63 ............ JackDuern(5) 8 70
(Andrew Hollinshead) *hld up: hdwy over 1f out: rdn to chse wnr ins fnl f: styd on* **18/1**

2500 **3** *½* **Alpha Delta Whisky**45 6872 6-9-3 68 ............(v) JoeyHaynes(3) 7 73
(John Gallagher) *hld up: hdwy and nt clr run over 1f out: rdn and edgd lft ins fnl f: r.o* **25/1**

1231 **4** *½* **Simply Black (IRE)**21 7457 3-9-5 67 ............(p) SamJames 1 70
(David O'Meara) *sn pushed along and prom: n.m.r and lost pl after 1f: hdwy over 1f out: r.o* **7/1**

2565 **5** *1 ¼* **Touch The Clouds**45 6873 3-9-0 69 ............ KieranShoemark(7) 11 70
(William Stone) *sn pushed along towards rr: nt clr run 1f out: running on whn hmpd ins fnl f: nt trble ldrs* **9/2**2

0636 **6** *nk* **Howyadoingnotsobad (IRE)**52 6658 6-8-11 64 ............ RyanWhile(5) 3 62
(Bill Turner) *chsd ldrs: led over 2f out: rdn over 1f out: hdd and no ex ins fnl f* **18/1**

3010 **7** *½* **West Coast Dream**26 7342 7-9-7 69 ............ TomEaves 5 65
(Roy Brotherton) *w ldrs: rdn and ev ch over 1f out: no ex ins fnl f* **16/1**

60-0 **8** *½* **Oil Strike**317 8 7-9-4 66 ............ GrahamGibbons 12 60
(Michael Easterby) *hld up: effrt over 1f out: nt trble ldrs* **9/1**

4034 **9** *1 ¼* **Kodafine (IRE)**12 7622 3-8-13 61 ............ JFEgan 2 51
(David Evans) *sn drvn along and prom: hmpd wl over 3f out: no ex fnl f* **12/1**

0000 **10** *2 ¾* **Electric Qatar**151 3338 5-9-3 65 ............(p) BenCurtis 4 45
(Alan McCabe) *led: hdd over 2f out: wknd fnl f* **14/1**

5000 **11** *nk* **Lexington Rose**28 7286 3-9-6 68 ............(v) PaulMulrennan 13 47
(Bryan Smart) *chsd ldrs: rdn 1/2-way: wknd over 1f out* **14/1**

6505 **12** *11* **Joyous**12 7623 4-9-2 64 ............(p) RobertWinston 9 3
(Dean Ivory) *sn pushed along and prom: rdn over 1f out: sn wknd and eased* **5/1**3

1m 0.83s (-1.07) **Going Correction** -0.10s/f (Stan) **12** Ran SP% **120.9**
Speed ratings (Par 103): **104,102,101,100,98 97,97,96,94,89 89,71**
CSF £71.60 CT £1392.88 TOTE £5.00: £1.70, £5.10, £8.40; EX 63.00 Trifecta £2122.50 Part won..
**Owner** Brian Johnson (Northamptonshire) **Bred** Dan Major **Trained** Sproxton, Leics

**FOCUS**
Only a Class 5, but interesting and competitive enough.

## 7807 UNIBET OFFER DAILY JOCKEY/TRAINER SPECIALS NURSERY H'CAP (BOBIS RACE) (TAPETA) 5f 216y
**6:15** (6:15) (Class 2) 2-Y-O **£8,821** (£2,640; £1,320; £660; £329) **Stalls** Low

Form RPR
4130 **1** **Ticks The Boxes (IRE)**86 5607 2-9-1 86 ............ RyanTate(3) 5 90
(Clive Cox) *chsd ldrs: sn lost pl: hdwy to chse ldr over 1f out: rdn and swtchd rt ins fnl f: edgd rt and r.o to ld whn rdr dropped whip towards fin* **11/4**2

1222 **2** *nk* **Snow Cloud (IRE)**10 7665 2-8-4 72 ............ SamJames 7 75+
(David O'Meara) *sn pushed along in rr: hdwy over 1f out: rdn and ev ch ins fnl f: r.o* **6/1**

0342 **3** *1* **Dark Side Dream**30 7224 2-7-12 69 ............ JoeyHaynes(3) 1 69
(Chris Dwyer) *sn led: rdn over 1f out: hdd towards fin* **8/1**

51 **4** *6* **Bamboccianti**69 6168 2-9-0 82 ............ TonyHamilton 3 64
(Richard Fahey) *s.i.s: hdwy 1/2-way: rdn to chse ldr 2f out: edgd rt: wknd fnl f* **9/4**1

3203 **5** *4* **Jaganory (IRE)**10 7661 2-8-7 75 ............ JFEgan 4 45
(David Evans) *chsd ldr: rdn over 2f out: wknd over 1f out* **10/1**

1610 **6** *3* **Son Of Africa**57 6510 2-9-7 89 ............ FergusSweeney 2 50
(Henry Candy) *chsd ldrs: rdn over 2f out: wknd wl over 1f out* **9/2**3

1m 13.5s (-1.00) **Going Correction** -0.10s/f (Stan) **6** Ran SP% **110.1**
Speed ratings (Par 102): **102,101,100,92,86 82**
CSF £18.30 TOTE £4.00: £2.90, £2.40; EX 29.60 Trifecta £159.70.
**Owner** Miss J Deadman & S Barrow **Bred** John B Hughes **Trained** Lambourn, Berks

**FOCUS**
A strongly run nursery in which the first two came from the last two positions.

## 7808 32RED EBF STALLIONS MAIDEN FILLIES' STKS (BOBIS RACE) (TAPETA) (DIV I) 7f 32y
**6:45** (6:47) (Class 5) 2-Y-O **£2,911** (£866; £432; £216) **Stalls** High

Form RPR
02 **1** **Colour Party (IRE)**14 7594 2-9-0 0 ............ RobertHavlin 7 73+
(John Gosden) *mde all: qcknd over 1f out: r.o: comf* **5/6**1

**2** *2* **Pure Line** 2-9-0 0 ............ GrahamGibbons 4 67+
(Ralph Beckett) *s.i.s: hld up: hdwy over 1f out: r.o to go 2nd wl ins fnl f: no ch w wnr* **6/1**3

62 **3** *1 ¼* **Marilyn Mon**25 7345 2-9-0 0 ............ MartinDwyer 3 64
(Jo Hughes) *trckd ldrs: racd keenly: rdn over 1f out: styd on same pce ins fnl f* **20/1**

435 **4** *nk* **Yorkindred Spirit**28 7278 2-9-0 64 ............ JoeFanning 5 63
(Mark Johnston) *chsd ldrs: rdn over 1f out: edgd lft and styd on same pce ins fnl f* **10/1**

05 **5** *1* **Coolcalmcollected (IRE)**22 7407 2-9-0 0 ............ TedDurcan 1 61
(Chris Wall) *s.i.s: sn mid-div: swtchd rt and hdwy over 1f out: styd on same pce ins fnl f* **13/2**

**6** *1 ½* **Kinnara** 2-9-0 0 ............ ShaneKelly 2 57+
(Sylvester Kirk) *s.i.s: hld up: styd on fr over 1f out: nt trble ldrs* **33/1**

**7** *¾* **Misham** 2-9-0 0 ............ LukeMorris 9 55
(Marco Botti) *chsd wnr: rdn and ev ch over 2f out: wknd fnl f* **11/2**2

**8** *11* **Lady Antonios (IRE)** 2-8-7 0 ............ ThomasHemsley(7) 6 28
(Chris Dwyer) *hld up: rdn over 2f out: wknd over 1f out* **80/1**

00 **9** *2* **Stellar Jet (IRE)**54 6605 2-8-11 0 ............ RossAtkinson(3) 8 23
(Roger Varian) *hld up: rdn and wknd 2f out* **33/1**

1m 29.72s (0.92) **Going Correction** -0.10s/f (Stan) **9** Ran SP% **118.5**
Speed ratings (Par 93): **90,87,86,85,84 83,82,69,67**
CSF £6.31 TOTE £1.70: £1.10, £4.30, £2.00; EX 8.70 Trifecta £67.50.
**Owner** Mount Brilliant Farm & Ranch, LLC **Bred** Mount Brilliant Farm & Ranch Llc **Trained** Newmarket, Suffolk

**FOCUS**
The pace was slow and the 1st, 2nd, 3rd and 4th-placed finishers were positioned 1st, 8th, 3rd and 4th at halfway.

## 7809 32RED EBF STALLIONS MAIDEN FILLIES' STKS (BOBIS RACE) (TAPETA) (DIV II) 7f 32y
**7:15** (7:16) (Class 5) 2-Y-O **£2,911** (£866; £432; £216) **Stalls** High

Form RPR
03 **1** **Sperry (IRE)**32 7174 2-9-0 0 ............ RobertHavlin 5 82+
(John Gosden) *mde virtually all: racd keenly: qcknd clr fr over 1f out: comf* **1/2**1

04 **2** *7* **Sylvette**22 7406 2-9-0 0 ............ JackMitchell 7 65
(Roger Varian) *hld up: hdwy over 1f out: styd on to go 2nd wl ins fnl f: no ch w wnr* **5/1**2

**3** *½* **Salma Gondis (IRE)** 2-9-0 0 ............1 SamJames 9 64
(David O'Meara) *prom: rdn over 2f out: styd on same pce fr over 1f out: wnt 3rd nr fin* **16/1**

5330 **4** *½* **Regal Ways (IRE)**16 7549 2-9-0 71 ............ JoeFanning 4 62
(Mark Johnston) *prom: chsd wnr 1/2-way: rdn over 1f out: no ex fnl f* **9/1**3

**5** *nk* **Crystalin (IRE)** 2-9-0 0 ............ LukeMorris 1 62
(Marco Botti) *mid-div: outpcd 4f out: hdwy u.p over 1f out: no ex ins fnl f* **12/1**

50 **6** *2 ½* **Brosnan (IRE)**22 7425 2-9-0 0 ............(b1) PatCosgrave 2 56+
(Noel Quinlan) *hld up: nt clr run over 2f out: rdn over 1f out: wknd fnl f* **14/1**

**7** *24* **Lamyaa** 2-9-0 0 ............ PaulMulrennan 3
(Charles Hills) *s.s: a in rr: lost tch over 2f out* **12/1**

0630 **8** *2 ½* **Keep 'r Lit**163 2928 2-8-9 45 ............ TimClark(5) 6
(Miss Imogen Pickard) *chsd wnr tl rdn 1/2-way: wknd 2f out* **80/1**

1m 27.79s (-1.01) **Going Correction** -0.10s/f (Stan) 2y crse rec **8** Ran SP% **122.5**
Speed ratings (Par 93): **101,93,92,91,91 88,61,58**
CSF £3.96 TOTE £1.50: £1.02, £2.00, £4.10; EX 5.90 Trifecta £56.40.
**Owner** HRH Princess Haya Of Jordan **Bred** Corduff Bloodstock Ltd & David Egan **Trained** Newmarket, Suffolk

**FOCUS**
A stronger pace than in the slowly run first division, but still sensible and the time was almost 2sec faster. The result was much the same, though, with the winner making all for John Gosden and Robert Havlin.

## 7810 32RED.COM NURSERY H'CAP (TAPETA) 1m 141y
**7:45** (7:48) (Class 5) (0-70,69) 2-Y-O **£2,911** (£866; £432; £216) **Stalls** Low

Form RPR
0021 **1** **Winter Queen**80 5823 2-8-11 **66** ............ KieranShoemark(7) 6 71
(Charlie Appleby) *hld up: nt clr run over 2f out: hdwy over 1f out: rdn to ld ins fnl f: edgd lft: r.o* **6/4**1

4320 **2** *½* **Thanksgiving Day (IRE)**30 7226 2-9-7 **69** ............ ShaneKelly 7 73
(Jamie Osborne) *a.p: rdn over 2f out: styd on u.p to ld 1f out: hdd ins fnl f: kpt on* **11/4**2

5000 **3** *¾* **Splash Of Verve (IRE)**29 7257 2-8-6 **57** ............ JoeyHaynes(3) 3 60
(Philip Kirby) *hld up: nt clr run over 2f out: hdwy over 1f out: r.o u.p: nt rch ldrs* **28/1**

540 **4** *1* **Dubawi Diamond**16 7551 2-9-7 **69** ............ LukeMorris 1 69
(James Tate) *s.i.s: sn prom: rdn and ev ch 1f out: styd on same pce ins fnl f* **7/2**3

330 **5** *2 ¼* **Sands Chorus**52 6667 2-9-4 **69** ............ ConnorBeasley(3) 8 64
(James Given) *w ldr tl led 7f out: rdn and hdd 1f out: no ex ins fnl f* **9/2**

0000 **6** *1* **Strong Flame**26 7328 2-8-5 **53** ............ JoeFanning 5 46
(David Brown) *trckd ldrs: racd keenly: rdn over 2f out: hmpd wl over 1f out: no ex fnl f* **20/1**

5100 **7** *4* **Vita Mina**33 7156 2-9-2 **64** ............(v) JFEgan 2 48
(David Evans) *led: hdd 7f out: chsd ldr tl over 3f out: sn rdn: wknd fnl f* **25/1**

1m 49.53s (-0.57) **Going Correction** -0.10s/f (Stan) **7** Ran SP% **119.1**
Speed ratings (Par 96): **98,97,96,96,94 93,89**
CSF £6.14 CT £79.51 TOTE £3.00: £1.80, £2.20; EX 7.80 Trifecta £70.30.
**Owner** Godolphin **Bred** S Boucheron **Trained** Newmarket, Suffolk

**FOCUS**
A modest nursery.

## 7811 32RED CASINO EBF STALLIONS MAIDEN STKS (TAPETA) 1m 1f 103y
8:15 (8:17) (Class 5) 2-Y-O £2,911 (£866; £432; £216) Stalls Low

Form RPR
0 **1** **Wolf Albarari**[19] 7498 2-9-5 0 (b[1]) LukeMorris 10 73
(Marco Botti) *mid-div: hdwy over 2f out: rdn and nt clr run 1f out: r.o to ld nr fin* 14/1

**2** *3/4* **Inexes** 2-9-5 0 RobertHavlin 11 72
(John Gosden) *trckd ldrs: racd keenly and hung rt almost thrght: rdn to ld over 1f out: hdd nr fin* 8/1

0 **3** *1* **Counterproof (IRE)**[10] 7666 2-9-5 0 NickyMackay 1 70
(John Gosden) *chsd ldrs: rdn over 2f out: unable qck wl ins fnl f* 12/1

4 **4** *2 1/4* **Perche**[19] 7498 2-9-5 0 MartinLane 5 66
(Charlie Appleby) *led after 1f: hdd 4f out: led again over 2f out: rdn and hdd over 1f out: wknd towards fin* 7/4[1]

54 **5** *1 1/2* **Skip And Jump (USA)**[25] 7367 2-9-0 0 JackMitchell 3 58
(Roger Varian) *mid-div: hdwy and nt clr run over 1f out: no ex ins fnl f* 5/1[3]

**6** *3/4* **Zac Truth (USA)** 2-9-5 0 ChrisCatlin 4 62
(Gay Kelleway) *prom: rdn over 3f out: sn outpcd: styd on ins fnl f* 33/1

46 **7** *5* **Rewritten**[38] 7040 2-8-12 0 (t) KieranShoemark(7) 2 52
(Charlie Appleby) *s.i.s: hld up: rdn over 2f out: sn hung rt and wknd* 12/1

**8** *hd* **Monsart (IRE)** 2-9-5 0 MartinDwyer 9 52
(Jo Hughes) *hld up: rdn and wknd over 2f out* 80/1

**9** *2 1/4* **Mr Sundowner (USA)** 2-9-5 0 PatCosgrave 6 47
(Noel Quinlan) *led 1f: chsd ldr tl led 4f out: rdn and hdd over 2f out: wknd over 1f out* 50/1

**10** *54* **Christmas Hamper (IRE)** 2-9-5 0 ShaneKelly 8
(Sir Michael Stoute) *s.s: rn green and a in rr: lost tch 1/2-way* 7/2[2]

2m 1.51s (0.71) **Going Correction** -0.10s/f (Stan) 10 Ran SP% **114.6**
Speed ratings (Par 96): **92,91,90,88,87 86,82,81,79,31**
CSF £117.71 TOTE £11.80: £3.90, £1.70, £3.70; EX 98.20 Trifecta £1132.50.
**Owner** Mrs A Dasmal-Fox **Bred** W And R Barnett Ltd **Trained** Newmarket, Suffolk

**FOCUS**
A relatively interesting maiden, with some decent connections represented. John Gosden had won the two earlier juvenile maidens on this card, but had to settle for second and third this time behind an improving half-brother to one of his stable stars.

## 7812 LADBROKES MAIDEN STKS (TAPETA) 1m 141y
8:45 (8:45) (Class 5) 3-Y-O+ £2,911 (£866; £432; £216) Stalls Low

Form RPR
3432 **1** **Park Place**[54] 6599 4-9-8 74 PhillipMakin 1 76
(John Quinn) *a.p: swtchd rt over 1f out: rdn to ld wl ins fnl f: jst hld on* 6/4[1]

4 **2** *shd* **John Reel (FR)**[5] 7733 5-9-8 0 JFEgan 2 75
(David Evans) *s.i.s: rcvrd to chse ldr over 7f out: rdn over 3f out: ev ch wl ins fnl f: r.o* 9/2

2636 **3** *1* **Dianora**[31] 7195 3-9-0 73 (v[1]) ShaneKelly 5 69
(Sir Michael Stoute) *sn led: rdn clr 2f out: hdd and unable qck wl ins fnl f* 11/4[2]

0 **4** *2* **Home Flyer (IRE)**[31] 7210 3-9-5 0 (t) DuranFentiman 3 69
(Mark Walford) *hld up: rdn over 3f out: hdwy over 1f out: nt rch ldrs* 40/1

3234 **5** *6* **Piccadilly Jim (IRE)**[18] 7513 3-9-5 67 TonyHamilton 4 55
(Richard Fahey) *chsd ldrs: rdn over 2f out: wknd fnl f* 4/1[3]

1m 48.16s (-1.94) **Going Correction** -0.10s/f (Stan)
**WFA** 3 from 4yo+ 3lb 5 Ran SP% **107.3**
Speed ratings (Par 103): **104,103,103,101,95**
CSF £8.09 TOTE £2.70: £1.80, £1.20; EX 8.90 Trifecta £22.30.
**Owner** Crowe Partnership **Bred** Juddmonte Farms Ltd **Trained** Settrington, N Yorks

**FOCUS**
An ordinary maiden.

## 7813 DOWNLOAD THE LADBROKES APP H'CAP (TAPETA) 1m 141y
9:15 (9:17) (Class 6) (0-60,60) 3-Y-O+ £2,264 (£673; £336; £168) Stalls Low

Form RPR
000 **1** **Oak Bluffs (IRE)**[128] 4108 3-8-12 54 TonyHamilton 3 65
(Richard Fahey) *a.p: rdn to ld ins fnl f: jst hld on* 12/1

2255 **2** *hd* **Company Secretary (USA)**[102] 5027 3-9-1 57 (p) MartinDwyer 8 67
(Jo Hughes) *bmpd s: mid-div: hdwy over 1f out: sn rdn: r.o* 5/1[1]

0600 **3** *3/4* **Act Your Shoe Size**[99] 5142 5-9-5 58 JoeFanning 6 65
(Keith Dalgleish) *chsd ldrs: rdn and ev ch ins fnl f: unable qck nr fin* 5/1[1]

4410 **4** *3/4* **Poor Duke (IRE)**[28] 7292 4-9-4 57 RobertHavlin 11 62
(Michael Mullineaux) *hld up: rdn over 1f out: hung lft and r.o ins fnl f: nt rch ldrs* 14/1

6534 **5** *1 1/4* **Yorksters Prince (IRE)**[53] 6627 7-9-2 55 (p) RobertWinston 4 57
(Marjorie Fife) *led: rdn over 1f out: hdd and no ex ins fnl f* 14/1

04-0 **6** *nk* **Warden Bond**[17] 7526 6-9-4 57 (p) RobertTart 2 59
(William Stone) *chsd ldrs: rdn and ev ch ins fnl f: no ex towards fin* 20/1

3026 **7** *3/4* **Indian Giver**[37] 7061 6-8-13 55 (v[1]) ConnorBeasley(3) 10 55
(John David Riches) *bmpd s: hld up: hdwy over 3f out: rdn over 1f out: no ex ins fnl f* 16/1

3505 **8** *hd* **Bonjour Steve**[26] 7339 3-9-2 58 (p) LukeMorris 5 59
(Richard Price) *trckd ldr: plld hrd: rdn over 1f out: no ex fnl f* 9/1[3]

5040 **9** *hd* **Robin Hood (IRE)**[19] 7494 6-9-5 58 JackMitchell 7 57
(Philip Mitchell) *hld up: hdwy over 1f out: styd on same pce fnl f* 9/1[3]

2261 **10** *nk* **Ad Vitam (IRE)**[11] 7644 6-9-7 60 (bt) RaulDaSilva 13 58
(Suzzanne France) *hld up: effrt on outer over 2f out: n.d* 13/2[2]

2165 **11** *1 1/4* **Elle Rebelle**[22] 7427 4-8-11 57 KieranShoemark(7) 9 55
(Mark Brisbourne) *s.i.s and hmpd s: hld up: running on whn nt clr run ins fnl f: nvr able to chal* 13/2[2]

4061 **12** *1 1/4* **Port Lairge**[30] 7222 4-9-3 56 (b) ChrisCatlin 1 49
(John Gallagher) *hld up: rdn over 2f out: nvr on terms* 33/1

2060 **13** *3 3/4* **Benandonner (USA)**[28] 7288 11-9-3 56 ShaneKelly 12 40
(Mike Murphy) *prom: rdn over 2f out: wknd fnl f* 20/1

1m 49.46s (-0.64) **Going Correction** -0.10s/f (Stan)
**WFA** 3 from 4yo+ 3lb 13 Ran SP% **119.4**
Speed ratings (Par 101): **98,97,97,96,95 95,94,94,94,93 92,91,88**
CSF £69.11 CT £348.02 TOTE £16.70: £4.20, £2.80, £2.10; EX 125.10 Trifecta £1001.00.
**Owner** Mrs Una Towell **Bred** C Mac Hale And J Hyland **Trained** Musley Bank, N Yorks

**FOCUS**
A moderate handicap, but some horses of interest.
T/Plt: £457.90 to a £1 stake. Pool: £103,215.16 - 164.54 winning units. T/Qpdt: £24.30 to a £1 stake. Pool: £8504.83 - 258.02 winning units. CR

7814 - (Foreign Racing) - See Raceform Interactive

# [7806] WOLVERHAMPTON (A.W) (L-H)
Monday, November 17

**OFFICIAL GOING: Tapeta: standard**
Wind: Light across Weather: overcast

## 7815 32RED ON THE APP STORE NURSERY H'CAP (TAPETA) 1m 1f 103y
2:10 (2:10) (Class 6) (0-65,65) 2-Y-O £2,102 (£625; £312; £156) Stalls Low

Form RPR
4441 **1** **Mikandy (IRE)**[5] 7740 2-9-5 65 6ex RyanTate(3) 6 73
(Clive Cox) *mde all: rdn clr 2f out: kpt on* 7/2[1]

4552 **2** *2* **Offshore**[49] 6811 2-9-6 63 (p) GrahamGibbons 2 67+
(James Tate) *trckd ldng pair: rdn over 2f out: briefly n.m.r 2f out: wnt 2nd 1f out: kpt on but nvr rching wnr* 4/1[2]

000 **3** *3* **Naval Action**[33] 7200 2-8-2 45 (p) LukeMorris 7 44
(Sir Mark Prescott Bt) *prom: rdn 3f out: sn outpcd by wnr: lost 2nd 1f out: one pce* 16/1

6600 **4** *3* **Smugglers Lane (IRE)**[49] 6811 2-8-0 46 DannyBrock(3) 1 39
(David Evans) *dwlt: sn in tch on inner: rdn over 2f out: one pce and nvr threatened ldrs* 33/1

4200 **5** *hd* **Keen Move**[25] 7396 2-9-4 61 (b[1]) GrahamLee 12 53
(Ismail Mohammed) *trckd ldng pair: rdn over 2f out: wknd ins fnl f* 22/1

0650 **6** *3/4* **Jolie De Vivre (IRE)**[36] 7134 2-9-7 64 LiamKeniry 10 55
(Sylvester Kirk) *hld up: rdn over 2f out: kpt on ins fnl f: nrst fin* 16/1

6000 **7** *nk* **Avenue Des Champs**[38] 7075 2-8-7 50 (p) WilliamCarson 9 40
(Jane Chapple-Hyam) *hld up: rdn over 2f out: one pce and nvr threatened* 25/1

0024 **8** *nse* **Youonlyliveonce (IRE)**[28] 7328 2-8-12 55 TomEaves 4 45
(John Quinn) *midfield: rdn over 2f out: sn no imp* 16/1

5004 **9** *1* **Le Torrent**[25] 7396 2-9-2 59 BenCurtis 8 47
(Henry Candy) *racd keenly in midfield: rdn over 2f out: sn no imp* 9/2[3]

601 **10** *hd* **New Abbey Dancer (IRE)**[48] 6842 2-8-7 50 (p) ChrisCatlin 11 38
(Gay Kelleway) *hld up: pushed along 4f out: rdn over 2f out: nvr threatened* 14/1

600 **11** *1 3/4* **Kingston Sassafras**[40] 7030 2-9-5 62 AntonioFresu 3 47
(Ed Walker) *midfield: rdn over 2f out: wknd over 1f out* 6/1

000 **12** *2 1/4* **Heavens Above (IRE)**[24] 7406 2-9-0 57 PaulMulrennan 13 37
(Ed Dunlop) *hld up in rr: a bhd* 12/1

0000 **13** *1 3/4* **Almost Nowhere (IRE)**[13] 7648 2-8-2 50 TimClark(5) 5 27
(Michael Appleby) *hld up in midfield on outer: sme hdwy 3f out: wknd over 1f out* 100/1

2m 0.64s (-0.16) **Going Correction** -0.10s/f (Stan) 2y crse rec 13 Ran SP% **118.8**
Speed ratings (Par 94): **96,94,91,88,88 88,87,87,86,86 85,83,81**
CSF £16.35 CT £200.32 TOTE £4.10: £1.50, £2.60, £2.60; EX 12.30 Trifecta £102.70.
**Owner** The Mikandy Partnership **Bred** A Thompson & M O'Brien **Trained** Lambourn, Berks

**FOCUS**
A moderate nursery.

## 7816 32RED CASINO CLAIMING STKS (TAPETA) 1m 141y
2:40 (2:40) (Class 6) 2-Y-O £2,102 (£625; £312; £156) Stalls Low

Form RPR
6604 **1** **More Drama (IRE)**[39] 7064 2-8-6 51 LukeMorris 4 50
(Sylvester Kirk) *chsd ldr: rdn over 2f out: led jst ins fnl f: kpt on* 11/2[3]

0062 **2** *1 3/4* **Red Stripes (USA)**[21] 7487 2-9-5 49 (b) SeanLevey 2 59
(Brian Meehan) *led: hdd over 6f out: remained prom: rdn to ld again 2f out: hdd jst ins fnl f: one pce* 33/1

050 **3** *hd* **Politico**[12] 7667 2-8-9 56 RobertHavlin 1 49
(John Gosden) *trckd ldr: led over 6f out: rdn whn hdd 2f out: kpt on same pce* 13/2

0005 **4** *2* **La Favorita (IRE)**[5] 7740 2-8-1 50 DannyBrock(3) 5 39
(Phil McEntee) *hld up: pushed along over 2f out: kpt on fr over 1f out* 5/1[2]

5142 **5** *3 1/4* **Chilworth Bells**[19] 7536 2-8-12 62 GrahamGibbons 7 41+
(David Barron) *hld up: bmpd on bnd after 1f: sme hdwy on outer 4f out: hrd rdn over 2f out: sn no imp: btn over 1f out* 11/8[1]

6506 **6** *1/2* **Cerise Firth**[21] 7488 2-8-2 45 HayleyTurner 3 30
(Steph Hollinshead) *midfield: rdn over 2f out: no imp* 80/1

40 **7** *2 1/2* **Sheila Belle (IRE)**[56] 6602 2-8-9 0 (p) LiamKeniry 9 31
(J S Moore) *hld up in rr: rdn over 2f out: nvr threatened* 66/1

30 **8** *3 3/4* **Whisky Marmalade (IRE)**[34] 7174 2-9-0 0 SamJames 8 28+
(David O'Meara) *hld up: rdn 3f out: sn btn* 11/2[3]

060 **9** *1* **Lady Ballantrae (IRE)**[115] 4610 2-8-11 45 GrahamLee 6 23
(Simon Dow) *in tch: rdn over 3f out: wknd over 1f out* 100/1

1m 51.13s (1.03) **Going Correction** -0.10s/f (Stan) 9 Ran SP% **109.5**
Speed ratings (Par 94): **91,89,89,87,84 84,81,78,77**
CSF £142.08 TOTE £6.00: £1.90, £3.80, £2.30; EX 58.10 Trifecta £643.90.
**Owner** Ms Carol Cleary **Bred** Miss Carol Cleary **Trained** Upper Lambourn, Berks

**FOCUS**
A typically weak affair of its type.

## 7817 32RED.COM H'CAP (TAPETA) 2m 119y
3:10 (3:11) (Class 5) (0-75,75) 3-Y-O+ £2,911 (£866; £432; £216) Stalls Low

Form RPR
4143 **1** **Hell Hath No Fury**[28] 7333 5-8-12 59 HayleyTurner 4 70
(Michael Appleby) *in tch: rdn to chse ldr over 2f out: led jst ins fnl f: kpt on* 15/2

1161 **2** *nk* **Mister Bob (GER)**[39] 7065 5-9-8 69 (p) GrahamLee 8 79
(James Bethell) *midfield: smooth hdwy 4f out: pushed along to chse ldr over 2f out: rdn and ev ch ins fnl f: kpt on* 5/2[1]

2421 **3** *2* **Rowlestone Lass**[20] 7524 4-9-3 64 JoeFanning 2 72
(Richard Price) *trckd ldng pair: led wl over 2f out: sn rdn: hdd jst ins fnl f: no ex* 8/1

2232 **4** *5* **Wintour Leap**[33] 7204 3-8-7 66 ThomasBrown(3) 12 68
(Robert Stephens) *in tch: led 3f out: sn hdd: grad wknd* 12/1

1100 **5** *hd* **The Quarterjack**[23] 7452 5-9-3 71 (p) CallumShepherd(7) 11 73
(Ron Hodges) *midfield: rdn 3f out: one pce and nvr threatened ldrs* 33/1

1552 **6** *1 1/4* **Layline (IRE)**[13] 7651 7-9-11 72 RobertWinston 3 72
(Gay Kelleway) *slowly away: hld up in rr: rdn over 2f out: kpt on: nvr threatened* 20/1

0005 **7** *1 3/4* **Toptempo**[17] 7565 5-9-8 69 JimmyQuinn 10 67
(Mark H Tompkins) *hld up: twice short of room over 2f out: stl plenty to do over 1f out: kpt on fnl f* 14/1

0533 **8** *2 1/4* **Jan Smuts (IRE)**[13] 7643 6-8-12 64 (tp) EmmaSayer(5) 7 59
(Wilf Storey) *hld up: pushed along in rr 1/2-way: plugged on fr over 1f out* 16/1



The Form Book, Raceform Ltd, Newbury, RG14 5SJ

1650 **9** *1 ½* **Arashi**[19] 7539 8-9-6 67....................(v) TonyHamilton 9 61
(Derek Shaw) *hld up: nvr threatened* **66/1**
1213 **10** *22* **Kelamita (IRE)**[24] 7422 3-8-12 75....................(b) CharlieBennett(7) 6 42
(Hughie Morrison) *w ldr: rdn over 3f out: sn wknd* **9/2[2]**
0320 **11** *2* **Lady Bingo (IRE)**[34] 7177 3-8-10 66....................(p) LukeMorris 13 31
(Sir Mark Prescott Bt) *trckd ldng pair: rdn to ld over 4f out: hdd 3f out: sn wknd* **5/1[3]**
4400 **12** *29* **Aleksandar**[20] 7508 5-9-1 65.................... GaryBartley(3) 5
(Jim Goldie) *led narrowly: rdn whn hdd over 4f out: wknd and eased* **28/1**
3m 36.62s (-7.08) **Going Correction** -0.10s/f (Stan)
**WFA** 3 from 4yo+ 9lb **12** Ran SP% **119.2**
Speed ratings (Par 103): **112,111,110,108,108 107,107,106,105,94 94,80**
CSF £25.74 CT £159.56 TOTE £11.00: £2.70, £1.30, £2.40; EX 34.70 Trifecta £187.70.
**Owner** C L Bacon **Bred** K F Fallon **Trained** Danethorpe, Notts
**FOCUS**
Not a bad staying handicap for the class with the first three all having positives. The winner is progressing.

## 7818 32RED MAIDEN FILLIES' STKS (TAPETA) 7f 32y
**3:40** (3:43) (Class 5) 3-Y-O+ **£2,911** (£866; £432; £216) **Stalls** High

Form RPR
5 **1** **Polly's Rose**[21] 7501 5-9-0 0.................... JasonHart 6 75
(Ian Semple) *mde all: rdn 2f out: kpt on* **17/2**
243 **2** *1 ¼* **Wu Zetian**[19] 7528 3-8-13 67.................... HayleyTurner 2 71
(Andrew Balding) *trckd ldr: stl on bit 2f out: rdn over 1f out: drvn ins fnl f: one pce* **9/4[2]**
354 **3** *1* **Two Smart (IRE)**[55] 6638 3-8-13 70.................... LukeMorris 11 68
(Daniel Kubler) *trckd ldr: rdn 2f out: hung lft ins fnl f: one pce* **4/1[3]**
322 **4** *¾* **Nightlight**[11] 7682 3-8-13 69.................... GrahamLee 4 66
(Jeremy Noseda) *chsd ldrs: rdn over 2f out: one pce* **2/1[1]**
5444 **5** *5* **Song Of Norway**[11] 7682 3-8-13 66....................(p) SteveDrowne 3 53
(Peter Makin) *in tch: rdn 3f out: wknd ins fnl f* **15/2**
6-0 **6** *3 ½* **Zaria**[11] 7682 3-8-13 0.................... JoeFanning 1 44
(Richard Price) *midfield: rdn over 2f out: sn outpcd by ldrs* **100/1**
6 **7** *hd* **Undulate**[11] 7686 3-8-13 0.................... TomEaves 7 44
(Peter Niven) *dwlt: hld up: sme hdwy over 2f out: pushed along over 1f out: nvr threatened ldrs* **20/1**
66 **8** *2 ¼* **Otterbridge**[41] 7024 3-8-13 0....................(t) RobertHavlin 10 38
(Rod Millman) *hld up: pushed along over 2f out: nvr threatened* **50/1**
00 **9** *7* **The French Grey (FR)**[11] 7686 3-8-6 0.................... CallumShepherd(7) 5 20
(Ron Hodges) *hld up: a bhd* **80/1**
0- **10** *7* **Courtezan**[518] 3414 3-8-8 0.................... RachealKneller(5) 8 2
(Jamie Osborne) *slowly away: hld up in rr: a bhd* **100/1**
**11** *7* **Double First** 3-8-13 0.................... StevieDonohoe 9
(Kevin Frost) *slowly away: hld up in rr: a bhd* **80/1**
0 **12** *3 ½* **Irish Sweetheart (IRE)**[19] 7528 3-8-13 0.................... ChrisCatlin 12
(Christine Dunnett) *midfield: wknd over 3f out* **100/1**
1m 29.81s (1.01) **Going Correction** -0.10s/f (Stan)
**WFA** 3 from 5yo 1lb **12** Ran SP% **118.6**
Speed ratings (Par 100): **90,88,87,86,80 76,76,74,66,58 50,46**
CSF £27.62 TOTE £10.00: £2.00, £1.70, £3.30; EX 33.50 Trifecta £141.70.
**Owner** Keith Pollock **Bred** Wickham Stud **Trained** Haddington, East Lothian
**FOCUS**
Straightforward maiden form, with the winner a big improver.

## 7819 DOWNLOAD THE LADBROKES APP CLASSIFIED (S) STKS (TAPETA) 7f 32y
**4:10** (4:10) (Class 6) 3-Y-O+ **£2,102** (£625; £312; £156) **Stalls** High

Form RPR
3140 **1** **My Son Max**[34] 7179 6-9-7 75....................(v) GrahamLee 3 83
(Richard Ford) *hld up in tch: pushed along and hdwy over 1f out: rdn to ld 110yds out: kpt on* **9/2[3]**
5342 **2** *½* **Al Muheer (IRE)**[16] 7601 9-8-12 74....................(v) ConnorBeasley(3) 1 76
(Michael Herrington) *trckd ldr: rdn over 1f out: drvn and ev ch ins fnl f: edgd lft and one pce fnl 75yds* **5/4[1]**
0000 **3** *nse* **Appease**[11] 7687 5-9-1 72.................... LiamKeniry 5 76
(John Butler) *in tch: rdn over 1f out: kpt on* **9/1**
5605 **4** *2* **Best Trip (IRE)**[11] 7687 7-9-1 73.................... GrahamGibbons 7 70
(Brian Ellison) *led: rdn over 1f out: hdd 110yds out: wknd* **7/4[2]**
0440 **5** *12* **Buxton**[90] 5523 10-9-1 45....................(t) MartinLane 2 39
(Roger Ingram) *hld up in rr: rdn over 2f out: sn btn* **66/1**
6-00 **6** *13* **Misty Eyes**[277] 592 5-9-1 45....................(v) TomEaves 6 5
(Geoffrey Harker) *trckd ldr: rdn over 2f out: sn wknd* **100/1**
1m 27.39s (-1.41) **Going Correction** -0.10s/f (Stan) **6** Ran SP% **111.5**
Speed ratings (Par 101): **104,103,103,101,87 72**
CSF £10.45 TOTE £5.50: £3.20, £1.20; EX 9.30 Trifecta £24.20.Al Muheer was claimed by T Dascombe for £6000.
**Owner** The Four Aces **Bred** Mrs Fiona Denniff **Trained** Garstang, Lancs
**FOCUS**
A fair seller, run at a sound pace in a reasonable time.

## 7820 LADBROKES H'CAP (TAPETA) (DIV I) 7f 32y
**4:40** (4:40) (Class 4) (0-85,84) 3-Y-O+ **£4,851** (£1,443; £721; £360) **Stalls** High

Form RPR
4-16 **1** **Shyron**[202] 1861 3-9-2 80.................... MartinLane 4 91
(George Margarson) *midfield: rdn and hdwy over 1f out: led jst ins fnl f: kpt on* **13/2[3]**
244 **2** *1 ½* **First Experience**[33] 7196 3-8-12 76.................... GrahamLee 6 83
(Rae Guest) *trckd ldr: pushed along over 1f out: rdn jst ins fnl f: one pce and sn hld in 2nd* **15/8[1]**
3500 **3** *1* **Rasaman (IRE)**[49] 6824 10-8-11 77.................... GaryBartley(3) 1 82
(Jim Goldie) *trckd ldr: rdn over 1f out: one pce* **33/1**
5060 **4** *¾* **Khajaaly (IRE)**[20] 7521 7-8-9 72.................... HayleyTurner 2 75
(Michael Appleby) *midfield: rdn 2f out: kpt on same pce* **7/1**
0000 **5** *¾* **Repetition**[26] 7375 4-9-5 82.................... TomEaves 9 84
(Kristin Stubbs) *led: rdn 2f out: hdd jst ins fnl f: wknd* **7/1**
0040 **6** *1 ¾* **Fieldgunner Kirkup (GER)**[9] 7719 6-9-3 80.................... GrahamGibbons 5 77
(David Barron) *hld up in tch: pushed along over 1f out: nvr threatened* **9/1**
0520 **7** *nk* **Loyalty**[165] 2922 7-9-7 84....................(v) JoeFanning 3 80
(Derek Shaw) *dwlt: hld up: rdn over 1f out: nvr threatened* **16/1**
-110 **8** *½* **Dreese (IRE)**[159] 3122 3-9-5 83.................... LukeMorris 7 77
(James Tate) *slowly away: hld up: rdn over 2f out: sn btn* **7/2[2]**
1m 27.75s (-1.05) **Going Correction** -0.10s/f (Stan)
**WFA** 3 from 4yo+ 1lb **8** Ran SP% **114.2**
Speed ratings (Par 105): **102,100,99,98,97 95,95,94**
CSF £19.06 CT £374.16 TOTE £5.90: £1.50, £1.10, £5.50; EX 20.40 Trifecta £457.90.
**Owner** F Butler **Bred** F Butler **Trained** Newmarket, Suffolk
**FOCUS**
A modest but competitive handicap and the form looks sound enough. It was the slower division.

## 7821 LADBROKES H'CAP (TAPETA) (DIV II) 7f 32y
**5:10** (5:10) (Class 4) (0-85,83) 3-Y-O+ **£4,851** (£1,443; £721; £360) **Stalls** High

Form RPR
6561 **1** **Order Of Service**[31] 7248 4-8-10 75....................(t) GaryBartley(3) 1 85
(Jim Goldie) *dwlt: hld up: rdn 3f out: hdwy 2f out: led ins fnl f: kpt on* **25/1**
0601 **2** *½* **Cool Bahamian (IRE)**[19] 7530 3-9-3 80....................(b) JohnFahy 7 88
(Eve Johnson Houghton) *midfield: hdwy over 2f out: rdn to ld over 1f out: hdd ins fnl f: kpt on but a jst hld* **10/3[2]**
2350 **3** *2* **Mishaal (IRE)**[9] 7719 4-9-5 81.................... PaulMulrennan 8 85
(Michael Herrington) *led: pushed along over 2f out: rdn whn hdd over 1f out: one pce* **11/4[1]**
0036 **4** *2* **Fantasy Gladiator**[19] 7530 8-8-10 72....................(p) ChrisCatlin 9 70
(John Quinn) *midfield: rdn and outpcd 1/2-way: plugged on fr over 1f out* **7/1**
0030 **5** *1 ¼* **The Confessor**[26] 7375 7-9-3 79.................... BenCurtis 3 74
(Henry Candy) *trckd ldr: rdn 2f out: wknd ins fnl f* **7/1**
1015 **6** *¾* **Two Moons**[151] 3402 4-9-2 78.................... PaulPickard 2 71
(Brian Ellison) *hld up: rdn over 2f out: nvr threatened* **12/1**
4331 **7** *1 ¾* **Ambitious Boy**[20] 7521 5-9-2 83.................... JackDuern(5) 6 72
(Andrew Hollinshead) *dwlt: hld up: rdn over 2f out: nvr threatened* **9/2[3]**
0200 **8** *9* **Ready (IRE)**[9] 7719 4-9-6 82....................(p) RobertWinston 5 60
(Garry Moss) *trckd ldr: rdn over 2f out: wknd over 1f out: eased* **9/1**
1m 26.6s (-2.20) **Going Correction** -0.10s/f (Stan)
**WFA** 3 from 4yo+ 1lb **8** Ran SP% **114.5**
Speed ratings (Par 105): **108,107,105,102,101 100,98,88**
CSF £107.01 CT £311.97 TOTE £14.90: £3.60, £1.10, £1.80; EX 152.40 Trifecta £967.30.
**Owner** Whitestonecliffe Racing Partnership **Bred** Cheveley Park Stud Ltd **Trained** Uplawmoor, E Renfrews
**FOCUS**
The second division of the modest 7f handicap and the pick of the four 7f times. A length best from the winner.

## 7822 CORAL H'CAP (TAPETA) 1m 4f 50y
**5:40** (5:40) (Class 5) (0-75,75) 3-Y-O+ **£2,911** (£866; £432; £216) **Stalls** Low

Form RPR
6-00 **1** **Street Artist (IRE)**[30] 7279 4-9-6 71.................... JoeFanning 12 85
(David Nicholls) *mde all: qcknd pce 2f out: kpt on and wl in command ins fnl f* **16/1**
5132 **2** *3* **Sioux Chieftain (IRE)**[20] 7504 4-9-10 75.................... BenCurtis 11 84
(Michael Appleby) *trckd ldr: rdn to chse wnr over 1f out: edgd lft and hld in 2nd ins fnl f* **11/8[1]**
0000 **3** *4 ½* **Royal Alcor (IRE)**[27] 7350 7-9-5 75.................... ShelleyBirkett(5) 4 77
(Gay Kelleway) *midfield: rdn and hdwy 2f out: wnt 3rd appr fnl f: kpt on but no threat to ldng pair* **11/1**
0244 **4** *shd* **Moccasin (FR)**[14] 7626 5-9-2 67.................... TomEaves 1 69
(Geoffrey Harker) *midfield: stl gng wl whn n.m.r 2f out tl over 1f out: rdn and kpt on fr appr fnl f* **10/1**
6635 **5** *1 ¾* **All The Winds (GER)**[27] 7366 9-9-4 69.................... LukeMorris 7 70
(Shaun Lycett) *v.s.a: hld up in rr: stl plenty to do over 1f out: kpt on ins fnl f* **5/1[2]**
66U2 **6** *½* **Bowberry**[23] 7458 3-8-2 62.................... RyanTate(3) 2 60
(Clive Cox) *in tch: rdn over 2f out: wknd appr fnl f* **8/1[3]**
4U20 **7** *nk* **Triple Eight (IRE)**[17] 6597 6-8-9 67....................(p) PhillipDennis(7) 5 65
(Philip Kirby) *midfield: rdn 2f out: one pce and no imp* **40/1**
0402 **8** *½* **Minstrel Lad**[34] 7172 6-9-0 68.................... SimonPearce(3) 6 65
(Lydia Pearce) *hld up: pushed along and sme hdwy on wd outside over 2f out: rdn over 1f out: no further imp* **12/1**
0000 **9** *3 ¼* **Perennial**[10] 7702 5-9-2 67.................... TonyHamilton 8 59
(Philip Kirby) *midfield: rdn over 2f out: wknd over 1f out* **40/1**
0140 **10** *hd* **A Little Bit Dusty**[52] 6699 6-9-10 75....................(p) HayleyTurner 9 66
(Conor Dore) *chsd ldng pair: rdn 3f out: wknd over 1f out* **10/1**
**11** *1 ¾* **Wyoyo (IRE)**[25] 6913 4-9-10 75....................(t) GrahamLee 10 63
(Tim Vaughan) *chsd ldng pair: rdn over 2f out: wknd wl over 1f out* **25/1**
-000 **12** *1 ¼* **Paris Snow**[20] 7508 4-9-0 65.................... StevieDonohoe 3 51
(Ian Williams) *hld up: a towards rr* **33/1**
2m 39.3s (-1.50) **Going Correction** -0.10s/f (Stan)
**WFA** 3 from 4yo+ 6lb **12** Ran SP% **121.6**
Speed ratings (Par 103): **101,99,96,95,94 94,94,93,91,91 90,89**
CSF £38.36 CT £274.93 TOTE £18.80: £4.70, £1.40, £3.50; EX 64.90 Trifecta £475.50.
**Owner** J A Rattigan **Bred** Darley **Trained** Sessay, N Yorks
**FOCUS**
An ordinary handicap where it paid to be handy due to a moderate pace. There was no depth to it and the winner was hard to find.
T/Jkpt: Not won. T/Plt: £57.60 to a £1 stake. Pool of £85269.48 - 1079.41 winning tickets.
T/Qpdt: £7.10 to a £1 stake. Pool of £9185.14 - 952.97 winning tickets. AS

# 7760 SOUTHWELL (L-H)
Tuesday, November 18
**OFFICIAL GOING: Fibresand: standard**
Wind: Virtually nil Weather: Cloudy with sunny periods

## 7823 CORAL.CO.UK BEST ODDS GUARANTEED ON RACING H'CAP 1m 4f (F)
**12:10** (12:10) (Class 6) (0-55,55) 3-Y-O+ **£1,940** (£577; £288; £144) **Stalls** Low

Form RPR
0341 **1** **Master Of Song**[14] 7645 7-8-13 52....................(p) EoinWalsh(5) 6 62
(Roy Bowring) *hld up in rr: stdy hdwy over 3f out: chsd ldrs over 2f out: rdn to chse wnr over 1f out: chal ent fnl f: led last 100yds: styd on* **7/2[2]**
0066 **2** *nk* **Fire In Babylon (IRE)**[52] 6768 6-8-8 47....................(b) TobyAtkinson(5) 11 56+
(Noel Quinlan) *hld up in midfield: smooth hdwy on outer 1/2-way: trckd ldrs 4f out: led over 2f out: rdn and wandered jst over 1f out: jnd and drvn ent fnl f: sn edgd rt and hdd last 100yds: rallied towards fin* **3/1[1]**
0440 **3** *2* **Sawwala**[52] 6768 4-8-13 47.................... TonyHamilton 9 53
(J R Jenkins) *cl up: led over 3f out: rdn along over 2f out: sn hdd: drvn and kpt on same pce fr over 1f out* **16/1**
0050 **4** *1 ¼* **Enzaal (USA)**[15] 7628 4-9-5 53.................... JoeFanning 14 57
(Philip Kirby) *cl up: effrt over 3f out: sn rdn: drvn 2f out and kpt on same pce* **9/2**
04-6 **5** *1 ¾* **Shirls Son Sam**[286] 73 6-8-13 47.................... MichaelStainton 8 48
(Chris Fairhurst) *trckd ldrs: pushed along 3f out: rdn 2f out: drvn over 1f out and kpt on one pce* **80/1**

3000 **6** *6* **Cherry Tiger**[21] 7518 4-9-3 51 RobertTart 1 43
(Graeme McPherson) *in rr: pushed along and hdwy over 3f out: rdn wl over 2f out: plugged on: n.d* **25/1**
3432 **7** *shd* **Nellies Quest**[20] 7540 5-8-13 47 HayleyTurner 12 38
(Michael Appleby) *chsd ldrs: pushed along and lost pl 1/2-way: sn rdn along and n.d after* **4/1**[3]
30-0 **8** *6* **Fen Flyer**[31] 7291 5-8-12 46 PaddyAspell 3 28
(John Berry) *in tch: pushed along in midfield 1/2-way: rdn over 4f out and sn outpcd* **16/1**
3330 **9** *shd* **Goldmadchen (GER)**[190] 2199 6-9-3 54 ConnorBeasley(3) 4 36
(James Given) *slt ld: rdn along 4f out: hdd over 3f out and sn wknd* **9/1**
1056 **10** *nse* **Magicalmysterytour (IRE)**[21] 7518 11-9-4 52 ChrisCatlin 2 34
(Willie Musson) *chsd ldrs: rdn along over 5f out: wknd 4f out* **25/1**
6450 **11** *5* **Kyllachykov (IRE)**[20] 7540 6-9-4 52 PaulMulrennan 13 26
(Robin Bastiman) *trckd ldrs on outer: reminders 1/2-way: rdn along 4f out: sn wknd* **25/1**
3125 **12** *2* **Aureate**[217] 1501 10-8-8 49 (p) CharlotteJenner(7) 5 19
(Brian Forsey) *in rr: pushed along bef 1/2-way: sn outpcd and bhd* **22/1**

2m 38.78s (-2.22) **Going Correction** -0.175s/f (Stan) **12** Ran SP% **124.3**
Speed ratings (Par 101): **100,99,98,97,96 92,92,88,88,88 84,83**
CSF £14.30 CT £155.73 TOTE £5.00: £1.30, £2.10, £6.70; EX 21.20 Trifecta £274.30.
**Owner** S R Bowring **Bred** S R Bowring **Trained** Edwinstowe, Notts

**FOCUS**
There was a decent enough pace on. The first two were both on good marks based on their old form round here.

## 7824 £20 RISK-FREE BET AT UNIBET NURSERY H'CAP 6f (F)
**12:40** (12:40) (Class 6) (0-60,58) 2-Y-O **£1,940** (£577; £288; £144) **Stalls** Low

Form RPR
0600 **1** **Milady Eileen (IRE)**[56] 6643 2-8-10 47 TonyHamilton 9 50
(Richard Fahey) *cl up: chal wl over 2f out: rdn to ld 1 1/2f out: drvn ent fnl f: kpt on* **3/1**[2]
0003 **2** *3/4* **Purple Surprise**[12] 7684 2-8-9 49 DannyBrock(3) 5 50
(Andrew Reid) *a.p: cl up 1/2-way: chal over 2f out: rdn and ev ch over 1f out: drvn ins fnl f: no ex last 75yds* **5/1**
6033 **3** *4* **Sparkling Sapphire**[14] 7648 2-8-8 45 (p) PaulQuinn 7 34
(Richard Whitaker) *trckd ldrs: hdwy on outer 3f out: chal over 2f out: rdn wl over 1f out and ev ch tl drvn and oven pce ent fnl f* **11/4**[1]
0002 **4** *1/2* **Air Of York (IRE)**[11] 7701 2-9-7 58 (b) WilliamTwiston-Davies 3 45
(Ronald Harris) *led: rdn over 2f out: hdd 1 1/2f out: sn drvn and wknd* **9/1**
5060 **5** *nk* **Bannister Bell (IRE)**[38] 7112 2-9-0 54 DeclanBates(3) 6 40
(David Evans) *towards rr: rdn along 1/2-way: kpt on fnl 2f: nrst fin* **16/1**
6540 **6** *6* **Macarthurs Park (IRE)**[24] 7453 2-8-8 45 PatrickMathers 4 13
(Alan Berry) *chsd ldrs: rdn along wl over 2f out: grad wknd* **66/1**
0400 **7** *9* **Saphira Silver (IRE)**[49] 6842 2-8-9 46 ow1 StevieDonohoe 8
(James Evans) *sn rdn along and a in rr: bhd fr 1/2-way* **66/1**
0054 **8** *nk* **Cherry Empress (IRE)**[47] 6888 2-9-6 57 MartinDwyer 2
(Jo Hughes) *chsd ldrs on inner: rdn along 1/2-way: sn wknd* **9/2**[3]
006 **9** *1/2* **Magic Round (IRE)**[12] 7685 2-8-11 48 JoeFanning 1
(Bill Turner) *sn outpcd in rr: bhd fr 1/2-way* **20/1**

1m 16.46s (-0.04) **Going Correction** -0.175s/f (Stan) **9** Ran SP% **110.1**
Speed ratings (Par 94): **93,92,86,86,85 77,65,65,64**
CSF £16.86 CT £41.14 TOTE £4.30: £1.40, £1.70, £1.40; EX 17.70 Trifecta £43.30.
**Owner** Mrs H Steel **Bred** Herbertstown House Stud **Trained** Musley Bank, N Yorks

**FOCUS**
Two came clear in this moderate nursery.

## 7825 UNIBET OFFER DAILY JOCKEY/TRAINER SPECIALS H'CAP (DIV I) 6f (F)
**1:10** (1:11) (Class 6) (0-65,66) 3-Y-0+ **£1,940** (£577; £288; £144) **Stalls** Low

Form RPR
0413 **1** **Red Tide (IRE)**[22] 7502 3-9-5 63 (p) RobertWinston 11 74
(Marjorie Fife) *cl up: led 1/2-way: rdn wl over 1f out: drvn and hdd wl ins fnl f: rallied gamely to ld nr fin* **4/1**[3]
0225 **2** *hd* **Musical Molly (IRE)**[60] 6516 3-9-7 65 (p) GrahamGibbons 3 75
(Brian Ellison) *trckd ldrs on inner: hdwy and cl up over 2f out: sn chal and rdn over 1f out: drvn to take slt ld wl ins fnl f: hdd and no ex towards fin* **11/4**[1]
0006 **3** *2 3/4* **Invigilator**[13] 7671 6-9-2 60 (t) TomEaves 1 61
(Derek Shaw) *in tch on inner: hdwy over 2f out: rdn wl over 1f out: swtchd rt ent fnl f: sn drvn and kpt on: nrst fin* **50/1**
6321 **4** *1 3/4* **Larghetto (USA)**[8] 7735 6-9-8 66 6ex (b) StevieDonohoe 10 62
(Ian Williams) *dwlt and in rr: hdwy over 2f out: sn rdn: swtchd rt jst over 1f out: sn drvn and kpt on same pce* **7/2**[2]
5000 **5** *3/4* **Milly's Secret (IRE)**[18] 7575 3-9-7 65 SamJames 9 58
(David O'Meara) *chsd ldrs: rdn along over 2f out: swtchd lft and drvn over 1f out: no imp* **20/1**
1124 **6** *1 1/2* **Armelle (FR)**[14] 7644 3-9-4 62 (p) LukeMorris 8 50
(Scott Dixon) *slt ld: hdd 1/2-way and sn pushed along: rdn over 2f out: grad wknd* **8/1**
0303 **7** *1* **Emily Davison (IRE)**[8] 7735 3-8-11 55 (p) TonyHamilton 12 40
(Ann Stokell) *prom on outer: rdn along wl over 2f out: sn wknd* **20/1**
0600 **8** *1/2* **Walta (IRE)**[123] 4411 3-8-11 60 (bt) EoinWalsh(5) 6 44
(Roy Bowring) *s.i.s and in rr: gd hdwy over 3f out: chsd ldrs whn swtchd lft over 2f out: sn rdn and wknd wl over 1f out* **12/1**
-500 **9** *7* **Sadiigah**[13] 7670 4-8-7 51 oh2 (p) MartinLane 2 12
(Julia Feilden) *nvr bttr than midfield* **40/1**
3540 **10** *1 3/4* **Greenhead High**[106] 4960 6-9-5 63 (v) JoeFanning 7 19
(David Nicholls) *chsd ldrs on outer: rdn along wl over 2f out: sn wknd* **9/1**
302 **11** *2* **Big City Boy (IRE)**[14] 7652 6-8-4 51 DannyBrock(3) 5
(Phil McEntee) *towards rr: sme hdwy and wd st: rdn over 2f out and n.d* **16/1**
6-50 **12** *32* **Lady Calantha**[32] 7250 4-8-7 51 oh6 PatrickMathers 4
(Alan Berry) *a towards rr: bhd fr 1/2-way* **100/1**

1m 16.12s (-0.38) **Going Correction** -0.175s/f (Stan) **12** Ran SP% **118.5**
Speed ratings (Par 101): **95,94,91,88,87 85,84,83,74,72 69,26**
CSF £14.57 CT £480.98 TOTE £5.40: £2.20, £1.70, £9.10; EX 15.80 Trifecta £919.60.
**Owner** Mrs Jo McHugh **Bred** Rathasker Stud **Trained** Stillington, N Yorks

**FOCUS**
Ordinary form, and 0.87sec slower than the first division.

## 7826 UNIBET OFFER DAILY JOCKEY/TRAINER SPECIALS H'CAP (DIV II) 6f (F)
**1:40** (1:40) (Class 6) (0-65,65) 3-Y-0+ **£1,940** (£577; £288; £144) **Stalls** Low

Form RPR
0601 **1** **Best Tamayuz**[5] 7766 3-8-7 51 oh2 LukeMorris 1 71
(Scott Dixon) *cl up on inner: led wl over 1f out: sn rdn clr: readily* **9/4**[1]
3320 **2** *4* **Lucky Mark (IRE)**[38] 7111 5-8-8 57 (p) ShaneGray(5) 10 64
(John Balding) *dwlt: sn chsng ldrs: hdwy wl over 2f out: rdn wl over 1f out: kpt on fnl f: no ch w wnr* **16/1**
2100 **3** *3/4* **Gaelic Wizard (IRE)**[35] 7180 6-8-11 60 GemmaTutty(5) 4 65
(Karen Tutty) *midfield: hdwy wl over 2f out: rdn to chse ldrs over 1f out: kpt on same pce* **12/1**
2240 **4** *1 3/4* **Pull The Pin (IRE)**[14] 7644 5-9-5 63 (bt) TonyHamilton 2 62
(Ann Stokell) *slt ld: rdn over 2f out: hdd wl over 1f out: sn drvn and one pce* **14/1**
0-03 **5** *1 1/4* **Mops Angel**[13] 7670 3-9-2 65 AlistairRawlinson(5) 8 60
(Michael Appleby) *chsd ldrs on outer: wd st: rdn over 2f out: drvn wl over 1f out and sn one pce* **3/1**[2]
1464 **6** *nse* **Meebo (IRE)**[13] 7671 3-9-4 62 (vt) JoeFanning 11 57
(J R Jenkins) *chsd ldrs: wd st: swtchd lft and rdn 2f out: sn drvn and wknd* **9/1**
405 **7** *1 1/2* **Night Trade (IRE)**[4] 7782 7-8-7 51 oh2 (p) ChrisCatlin 5 41
(Ronald Harris) *in rr: rdn along 1/2-way: n.d* **66/1**
0003 **8** *3/4* **Lewisham**[12] 7687 4-9-7 65 (v) PaulMulrennan 3 53
(David Nicholls) *dwlt: a in rr* **7/2**[3]
0-00 **9** *2 1/4* **Scatty Cat (IRE)**[15] 7622 4-9-4 62 (t) ShaneKelly 9 42
(Daniel Mark Loughnane) *prom: rdn along wl over 2f out: sn wknd* **33/1**
05-0 **10** *3* **Kopenhagen (IRE)**[53] 6720 3-8-8 52 (p) MartinLane 7 23
(Ed de Giles) *dwlt: a in rr* **50/1**

1m 15.25s (-1.25) **Going Correction** -0.175s/f (Stan) **10** Ran SP% **114.6**
Speed ratings (Par 101): **101,95,94,92,90 90,88,87,84,80**
CSF £39.84 CT £362.90 TOTE £2.70: £1.40, £2.00, £3.40; EX 31.90 Trifecta £291.80.
**Owner** Paul J Dixon **Bred** Rabbah Bloodstock Limited **Trained** Babworth, Notts

**FOCUS**
The quicker of the two divisions by 0.87sec. The winner more than confirmed last week's surprise win.

## 7827 32RED IRISH STALLION FARMS EBF MAIDEN STKS 1m (F)
**2:10** (2:11) (Class 5) 2-Y-O **£2,911** (£866; £432; £216) **Stalls** Low

Form RPR
65 **1** **Munstead Pride**[35] 7169 2-9-5 0 LiamKeniry 4 76+
(Andrew Balding) *trckd ldr whn bmpd and lft in ld after 3f: jnd and rdn over 2f out: drvn and edgd lft ent fnl f: kpt on u.p towards fin* **5/2**[2]
**2** *1* **Reetaj** 2-9-5 0 PaulMulrennan 1 74
(Peter Chapple-Hyam) *dwlt: sn trcking ldrs on inner: hdwy and cl up over 3f out: chal over 2f out: rdn wl over 1f out and ev ch tl drvn ins fnl f and no ex last 100yds* **7/1**
552 **3** *11* **Toofeeg (IRE)**[42] 6998 2-9-5 76 (p) LiamJones 3 48+
(William Haggas) *led tl jinked bdly rt: rdr lost iron and hdd after 3f: sn lost pl: rcvrd to chse ldrs over 3f out: rdn over 2f out: kpt on to take modest 3rd appr fnl f* **2/1**[1]
**4** *1/2* **Crusading (USA)** 2-9-5 0 JoeFanning 8 47+
(Mark Johnston) *prom whn sltly hmpd after 3f: chsd ldng pair: rdn over 2f out and sn one pce* **3/1**[3]
00 **5** *1 3/4* **Carron Valley**[13] 7660 2-9-5 0 PhillipMakin 5 43
(Keith Dalgleish) *chsd ldrs: rdn along 3f out: sn rdn and outpcd fnl 2f* **9/1**
05 **6** *27* **Eric The Viking**[5] 7763 2-9-5 0 JasonHart 2
(Richard Guest) *sn outpcd in rr: bhd fr 1/2-way* **80/1**
**7** *1/2* **Sunfyre (IRE)** 2-9-5 0 StevieDonohoe 6
(James Evans) *dwlt: sn outpcd and a bhd* **50/1**
0 **8** *4 1/2* **Arcanman (IRE)**[55] 6652 2-9-5 0 LukeMorris 7
(Ronald Harris) *chsd ldrs on outer whn sltly hmpd and lost pl after 3f: sn bhd* **50/1**

1m 43.32s (-0.38) **Going Correction** -0.175s/f (Stan) **8** Ran SP% **114.6**
Speed ratings (Par 96): **94,93,82,81,79 52,52,47**
CSF £20.16 TOTE £5.80: £2.30, £1.30, £1.10; EX 19.40 Trifecta £55.50.
**Owner** Sir Gordon Brunton **Bred** Sir Gordon Brunton **Trained** Kingsclere, Hants

**FOCUS**
A modest maiden.

## 7828 32RED CASINO (S) STKS 7f (F)
**2:40** (2:41) (Class 6) 2-Y-O **£2,045** (£603; £302) **Stalls** Low

Form RPR
0002 **1** **Excelling Oscar (IRE)**[14] 7648 2-8-12 50 (b[1]) HayleyTurner 3 54
(Conor Dore) *mde all: pushed clr jst over 2f out: rdn wl over 1f out: kpt on wl u.p fnl f* **7/1**
1256 **2** *1 1/2* **Invincible Wish (IRE)**[14] 7648 2-9-3 53 GrahamGibbons 7 55
(Brian Ellison) *trckd ldrs on outer: hdwy to chse wnr over 2f out: rdn and edgd lft over 1f out: drvn ins fnl f: no imp towards fin* **9/4**[2]
4630 **3** *1* **Activation**[6] 7740 2-8-5 54 CharlieBennett(7) 6 47
(Hughie Morrison) *prom: chsd ldng pair 3f out: rdn over 2f out: kpt on fnl f* **7/2**[3]
**4** *8* **Sweet Midnight** 2-8-8 0 ow1 StevieDonohoe 8 22
(John Holt) *s.i.s and bhd: hdwy wl over 2f out: sn rdn and kpt on fnl f: nrst fin* **16/1**
0530 **5** *2 3/4* **Honey Required**[26] 7396 2-8-12 61 JoeFanning 4 18
(Alan Bailey) *cl up: rdn along 3f out: sn drvn and wknd over 2f out* **13/8**[1]
00 **6** *15* **Dazzling Display**[10] 7712 2-8-5 0 ow1 JacobButterfield(3) 2
(Richard Guest) *sn rdn along and a outpcd in rr* **66/1**
6600 **7** *nse* **Icandi**[11] 7701 2-8-7 49 PatrickMathers 5
(Alan Berry) *chsd ldrs: rdn along 3f out: sn drvn and wknd* **66/1**
**8** *nk* **Edw Gold (IRE)** 2-8-9 0 DeclanBates(3) 1
(David Evans) *s.i.s: sn rdn along and a in rr* **25/1**

1m 29.97s (-0.33) **Going Correction** -0.175s/f (Stan) **8** Ran SP% **116.3**
Speed ratings (Par 94): **94,92,91,82,78 61,61,61**
CSF £23.47 TOTE £7.50: £1.90, £1.40, £1.60; EX 23.20 Trifecta £73.50.Winner bought in 6,000gns.
**Owner** Mrs Jennifer Marsh **Bred** Miss Hilary McLoughlin **Trained** Hubbert's Bridge, Lincs

**FOCUS**
This didn't take much winning.

## 7829 DOWNLOAD THE LADBROKES APP H'CAP 1m (F)
**3:10** (3:11) (Class 5) (0-70,71) 3-Y-0+ **£2,911** (£866; £432; £216) **Stalls** Low

Form RPR
6366 **1** **Starfield**[19] 7552 5-9-2 70 (v[1]) AlistairRawlinson(5) 14 80+
(Michael Appleby) *prom on outer: cl up 1/2-way: led 3f out: sn rdn clr: hung lft wl over 1f out: drvn fnl f and kpt on* **7/2**[2]
0004 **2** *1* **Putin (IRE)**[5] 7765 6-8-7 61 (tp) RachealKneller(5) 1 69
(Phil McEntee) *in tch on inner: swtchd rt after 3f: hdwy 3f out: rdn 2f out: styd on to chse wnr over 1f out: kpt on wl towards fin* **25/1**

4500 **3** 2 1/4 **I'm Super Too (IRE)**[50] 6822 7-9-3 66 MartinDwyer 5 69
(Alan Swinbank) *hld up: hdwy on inner 3f out: rdn along 2f out: chsd ldrs over 1f out: kpt on fnl f: nrst fin* **14/1**

4524 **4** 1 **Pim Street (USA)**[18] 7569 4-9-1 64 SamJames 6 65
(David O'Meara) *chsd ldrs: rdn along wl over 2f out: drvn over 1f out: kpt on same pce* **20/1**

140 **5** hd **Dandarrell**[81] 5899 7-8-13 62 (p) PaulMulrennan 4 62
(Julie Camacho) *towards rr: hdwy towards outer st: rdn 2f out: kpt on fnl f: nrst fin* **33/1**

5313 **6** 1 **Coillte Cailin (IRE)**[15] 7626 4-9-4 67 StevieDonohoe 8 65
(Daniel Mark Loughnane) *towards rr: hdwy over 2f out: styd on appr fnl f: nrst fin* **16/1**

4221 **7** nk **Royal Holiday (IRE)**[5] 7765 7-9-5 71 6ex (b) JacobButterfield(3) 12 68
(Marjorie Fife) *sn prom: chsd ldng pair fr 1/2-way: rdn wl over 2f out: drvn wl over 1f out: grad wknd* **3/1**[1]

4053 **8** shd **Alpine Storm (IRE)**[35] 7185 3-9-4 69 JoeFanning 9 65
(Mark Johnston) *led: jnd 1/2-way: rdn along and hdd 3f out: drvn 2f out: grad wknd* **8/1**

315 **9** 1/2 **Exclusive Waters (IRE)**[32] 7251 4-9-7 70 RobertWinston 7 66
(Tracy Waggott) *dwlt and towards rr: wd st: sn rdn and kpt on: n.d* **4/1**[3]

244 **10** 3 **World Record (IRE)**[18] 7567 4-9-7 70 PatCosgrave 3 59
(Mick Quinn) *chsd ldrs on inner: rdn along 3f out: drvn 2f out: sn wknd* **20/1**

0060 **11** 5 **Argaki (IRE)**[28] 7350 4-9-5 68 (b1) PhillipMakin 10 45
(Keith Dalgleish) *nvr bttr than midfield* **16/1**

2204 **12** 1/2 **Pendo**[14] 7633 3-9-2 67 LukeMorris 11 42
(Paul Cole) *chsd ldrs: rdn along over 3f out: sn wknd* **10/1**

1m 41.85s (-1.85) **Going Correction** -0.175s/f (Stan)
**WFA** 3 from 4yo+ 2lb **12 Ran SP% 122.2**
Speed ratings (Par 103): **102,101,98,97,97 96,96,96,95,92 87,87**
CSF £97.23 CT £1123.72 TOTE £6.90: £1.70, £5.00, £5.80; EX 137.50 Trifecta £2367.80 Part won. Pool: £3,157.07 - 0.13 winning units..
**Owner** Dallas Racing **Bred** Dunchurch Lodge Stud Co **Trained** Danethorpe, Notts

**FOCUS**
The winner scored despite setting a strong pace and there's every chance he's still capable of better.

## 7830 LADBROKES H'CAP 7f (F)
**3:40** (3:42) (Class 5) (0-70,70) 3-Y-O+ **£2,587** (£770; £384; £192) **Stalls Low**

Form RPR

6540 **1** **Be Royale**[22] 7494 4-8-8 62 AlistairRawlinson(5) 9 74+
(Michael Appleby) *in tch: hdwy 3f out: chsd ldng pair wl over 1f out and sn rdn: swtchd lft and drvn appr fnl f: hung lft to far rail u.p ins fnl f: styd on wl to ld nr fin* **4/1**[1]

0333 **2** nk **Burnhope**[42] 7025 5-8-11 60 PaulMulrennan 11 71
(Scott Dixon) *chsd ldr and sn cl up: led 3f out: rdn 2f out: drvn ent fnl f: hdd and no ex towards fin* **10/1**

1404 **3** 1 1/4 **Arabian Flight**[14] 7647 5-8-11 63 (p) RyanTate(3) 12 71
(Michael Appleby) *sn led: jnd after 3f: rdn along 1/2-way and sn hdd: drvn wl over 1f out: ev ch tl no ex last 150yds* **8/1**[3]

0440 **4** 4 **Cara's Request (AUS)**[35] 7183 9-9-4 70 ConnorBeasley(3) 7 68
(Michael Dods) *chsd ldng pair: rdn along wl over 2f out: drvn and kpt on same pce fr over 1f out* **9/1**

5230 **5** 3/4 **Tin Pan Alley**[106] 4964 6-9-2 65 AndrewElliott 5 61
(David C Griffiths) *chsd ldng pair: rdn along 3f out: drvn 2f out and sn one pce* **10/1**

0235 **6** 2 1/4 **Borough Boy (IRE)**[20] 7533 4-9-1 64 TomEaves 14 54
(Derek Shaw) *in tch: hdwy on outer wl over 2f out: rdn to chse ldrs wl over 1f out: sn no imp* **10/1**

2250 **7** 1 3/4 **Hellbender (IRE)**[132] 4072 8-9-2 65 RobertWinston 2 50
(Shaun Harris) *chsd ldrs: rdn along wl over 2f out: sn no imp* **16/1**

0000 **8** hd **Amenable (IRE)**[50] 6821 7-8-13 62 (p) HayleyTurner 10 47
(Conor Dore) *chsd ldrs: rdn along wl over 2f out: sn one pce* **20/1**

0143 **9** nse **Chiswick Bey (IRE)**[17] 7600 6-9-3 66 TonyHamilton 3 51
(Richard Fahey) *a towards rr* **8/1**[3]

0603 **10** hd **Game Mascot**[14] 7647 4-8-12 61 (bt) LukeMorris 6 45
(Peter Hiatt) *reminders s and a towards rr* **9/2**[2]

4100 **11** 5 **Fantasy Justifier (IRE)**[55] 6657 3-9-6 70 ChrisCatlin 4 40
(Ronald Harris) *a in rr* **33/1**

1016 **12** 10 **Sam Spade (IRE)**[169] 2841 4-9-4 67 (v) JoeFanning 1 12
(Derek Shaw) *a towards rr* **12/1**

050 **13** 5 **Road Map (IRE)**[20] 7528 3-8-12 62 ShaneKelly 13
(Daniel Mark Loughnane) *s.i.s: in rr and swtchd rt after s: wd st: a bhd* **50/1**

1m 28.29s (-2.01) **Going Correction** -0.175s/f (Stan)
**WFA** 3 from 4yo+ 1lb **13 Ran SP% 120.9**
Speed ratings (Par 103): **104,103,102,97,96 94,92,92,91,91 86,74,68**
CSF £44.00 CT £313.33 TOTE £7.60: £2.20, £3.10, £2.20; EX 46.20 Trifecta £394.60.
**Owner** Wayne Brackstone, Steve Whitear **Bred** W Brackstone & S J Whitear **Trained** Danethorpe, Notts

**FOCUS**
The pace held up pretty well and only the winner was able to get to the leading duo. She's getting back towards her best.
T/Jkpt: Not won. T/Plt: £41.70 to a £1 stake. Pool: £72,010.63 - 1,259.31 winning tickets. T/Qpdt: £9.30 to a £1 stake. Pool: £5,506.01 - 437.44 winning tickets. JR

# 7752 KEMPTON (A.W) (R-H)
## Wednesday, November 19

**OFFICIAL GOING: Polytrack: standard**
Wind: Almost nil Weather: Fine

## 7831 BETDAQ £30 FREE BET AND 3% COMM H'CAP 1m 2f (P)
**3:50** (3:51) (Class 5) (0-75,75) 3-Y-O+ **£2,587** (£770; £384; £192) **Stalls Low**

Form RPR

2041 **1** **Gaelic Silver (FR)**[22] 7516 8-9-1 75 HectorCrouch(7) 9 84+
(Gary Moore) *w.w in rr: clsr order over 2f out: shkn up and gd prog on outer to ld 1f out: surged clr* **12/1**

2642 **2** 1 3/4 **Little Buxted (USA)**[20] 7552 4-9-8 75 (p) GrahamLee 6 81
(Robert Mills) *in tch in midfield: pushed along 4f out: prog over 2f out: clsd over 1f out but wnr sn swept past: styd on to take 2nd last 150yds: no ch* **5/1**[2]

030 **3** 1 1/2 **Lu's Buddy (GR)**[93] 5504 3-9-4 75 RobertHavlin 13 78
(Amanda Perrett) *chsd ldrs in 5th: clsd over 2f out: rdn to ld over 1f out: hdd and outpcd 1f out* **8/1**

3360 **4** 3 1/2 **Gracious George (IRE)**[20] 7552 4-9-2 69 (p) KieranO'Neill 7 66
(Jimmy Fox) *rdn to go prom and sn chsd ldng pair: wnt 2nd 3f out: led over 2f out to over 1f out: outpcd* **20/1**

1450 **5** nk **Thanks Harry**[128] 4263 3-9-2 73 JimmyFortune 2 69
(Andrew Balding) *chsd ldng pair: rdn over 2f out: outpcd fr over 1f out* **6/1**[3]

1366 **6** 3/4 **Karam Albaari (IRE)**[9] 7734 6-9-7 74 (p) FrankieDettori 14 69
(J R Jenkins) *stdd s: hld up and last for 4f: rdn in 11th 3f out: kpt on fr over 1f out: n.d* **14/1**

12-3 **7** nk **Leonard Thomas**[20] 7552 4-9-7 74 GeorgeBaker 11 68
(David Lanigan) *chsd ldrs in 6th: drvn 3f out: nvr gng pce to threaten: plugged on* **7/4**[1]

1366 **8** 1 1/4 **Stockhill Diva**[93] 5503 4-9-2 69 LiamKeniry 10 61
(Brendan Powell) *t.k.h: hld up in midfield: tried to make prog on outer bnd 2f out: no hdwy over 1f out: fdd* **20/1**

**9** 3 1/4 **Leyland (IRE)**[434] 6112 5-8-10 70 CharlieBennett(7) 4 55
(Natalie Lloyd-Beavis) *nvr gng wl: last and rdn 1/2-way: modest late prog* **100/1**

/062 **10** nk **Cherry Street**[19] 7569 5-9-2 69 (p) JackMitchell 8 54+
(Denis Quinn) *pressed ldr at str pce: led over 3f out to over 2f out: sn wknd* **16/1**

5620 **11** 3 3/4 **Hill Fort**[43] 7001 4-9-4 71 WilliamTwiston-Davies 3 49
(Ronald Harris) *restless stalls: wl in rr: rdn over 4f out: nvr a factor* **50/1**

0-00 **12** 3 **Refreshestheparts (USA)**[27] 7397 5-9-5 72 PatCosgrave 5 50+
(George Baker) *hld up in midfield: pushed along 3f out: nt clr run twice sn after: wknd* **33/1**

0540 **13** 10 **Syncopate**[62] 6487 5-9-4 71 AdamKirby 12 24
(Pam Sly) *racd wd towards rr: wknd over 2f out: t.o* **16/1**

00 **14** 6 **Sublimation (IRE)**[21] 7538 4-9-8 75 RobertWinston 1 17+
(Ian Williams) *led at gd pce: hdd over 3f out: wknd rapidly: t.o* **20/1**

2m 4.89s (-3.11) **Going Correction** -0.125s/f (Stan)
**WFA** 3 from 4yo+ 4lb **14 Ran SP% 124.7**
Speed ratings (Par 103): **107,105,104,101,101 100,100,99,96,96 93,91,83,78**
CSF £68.38 CT £528.81 TOTE £14.20: £4.80, £2.90, £4.50; EX 54.90 Trifecta £1262.20.
**Owner** The Winning Hand **Bred** Earl Haras Du Camp Bernard Et Al **Trained** Lower Beeding, W Sussex

**FOCUS**
This was run at a strong pace and played into the hands of those ridden with a bit of patience. The second helps set a straightforward level.

## 7832 GILLIAN NOBLE MEMORIAL NURSERY H'CAP 7f (P)
**4:25** (4:25) (Class 6) (0-65,65) 2-Y-O **£1,940** (£557; £288; £144) **Stalls Low**

Form RPR

0056 **1** **Just Marion (IRE)**[27] 7396 2-9-1 59 SilvestreDeSousa 6 64
(David Evans) *trckd ldrs: rdn over 2f out: clsd to ld over 1f out: drvn out* **5/1**[3]

0540 **2** 3/4 **The Olympus Man**[6] 7753 2-9-4 62 JimCrowley 12 65
(Olly Stevens) *nt that wl away but rcvrd to press ldr after 2f: led over 2f out: drvn and hdd over 1f out: one pce* **25/1**

0415 **3** 1 **Gavarnie Encore**[33] 7257 2-8-13 57 SteveDrowne 7 57
(Michael Blanshard) *chsd ldrs: rdn over 2f out: swtchd lft over 1f out: tk 3rd sn after: kpt on but nvr able to chal* **6/1**

0001 **4** 1/2 **Pat Mustard**[6] 7753 2-9-7 65 6ex (p) AdamKirby 11 64
(Jamie Osborne) *in tch in midfield but racd on outer: rdn over 2f out: prog over 1f out: kpt on but nvr able to challenghe* **9/4**[1]

034 **5** 1/2 **Hey You (IRE)**[20] 7542 2-9-7 65 SeanLevey 9 63
(Richard Hannon) *hld up in last trio: rdn over 2f out: prog over 1f out: kpt on same pce fnl f: n.d* **7/1**

4356 **6** nk **Charlie's Star**[6] 7753 2-9-2 60 LiamJones 5 57
(Laura Mongan) *towards rr: pushed along 1/2-way: struggling over 2f out: styd on fr jst over 1f out* **10/1**

006 **7** 1/2 **Italian Beauty (IRE)**[15] 7631 2-9-1 59 BenCurtis 2 54
(Timothy Jarvis) *chsd ldr 2f: styd cl up: rdn over 2f out: lost pl over 1f out: steadily fdd* **33/1**

060 **8** 1 3/4 **Almaardiyah (IRE)**[25] 7450 2-9-7 65 FrankieDettori 3 60
(Richard Hannon) *in tch in midfield but racd on outer: rdn over 2f out: edgd rt wl over 1f out: no hdwy after: fdd fnl f* **9/2**[2]

0400 **9** nk **Jersey Bull (IRE)**[22] 7515 2-9-4 62 LiamKeniry 8 52
(Michael Madgwick) *stdd s: hld up in last trio: trying to make prog whn hmpd over 1f out: no ch after: kpt on* **66/1**

000 **10** 2 **Exceedwell**[18] 7594 2-9-1 59 JackMitchell 1 43
(John Ryan) *trckd ldrs on inner: rdn over 2f out: no hdwy over 1f out: wknd fnl f* **25/1**

000 **11** 3 **Pisces**[95] 5416 2-8-6 57 RyanHolley(7) 13 33
(David Elsworth) *slowly away: detached in last: latched on to rr 1/2-way: wd bnd sn after and wl detached again: fnlly r.o last 150yds* **25/1**

654 **12** shd **Powerfulstorm**[69] 6246 2-9-0 58 LukeMorris 10 34
(Ronald Harris) *led to over 2f out: wknd rapidly over 1f out* **33/1**

1m 27.13s (1.13) **Going Correction** -0.125s/f (Stan) **12 Ran SP% 120.4**
Speed ratings (Par 94): **88,87,86,85,84 84,83,81,81,79 75,75**
CSF £131.45 CT £789.00 TOTE £8.20: £2.50, £8.30, £1.70; EX 205.50 Trifecta £1433.90.
**Owner** D E Edwards **Bred** M A Doyle **Trained** Pandy, Monmouths
■ Stewards' Enquiry : Frankie Dettori two-day ban: careless riding (Dec 3-4)

**FOCUS**
Ordinary nursery form. The early gallop wasn't strong and it suited those ridden close to the pace.

## 7833 IRISH STALLION FARMS EBF MAIDEN STKS (BOBIS RACE) 7f (P)
**4:55** (4:57) (Class 4) 2-Y-O **£4,075** (£1,212; £606; £303) **Stalls Low**

Form RPR

0 **1** **Ripinto (IRE)**[20] 7542 2-9-5 0 PatCosgrave 8 74
(Jim Boyle) *t.k.h: trckd ldr: rdn to chal wl over 1f out: led last 150yds: jst hld on* **20/1**

0U **2** nse **Sonnolento (IRE)**[42] 7030 2-9-5 0 LiamKeniry 4 74+
(Andrew Balding) *sn trckd ldrs: rdn over 2f out: wnt 3rd u.p 1f out: r.o to take 2nd last 75yds: clsd on wnr fin: jst failed* **4/1**[2]

**3** nk **Cilento (IRE)** 2-9-5 0 RobertHavlin 3 73+
(John Gosden) *s.s: in last trio to 1/2-way: stl only 6th 1f out and wl off the pce: tk off ins fnl f: flashed home and needed two more strides* **13/8**[1]

**4** 1 1/2 **White Dog (IRE)** 2-9-5 0 RobertTart 2 69+
(Eugene Stanford) *chsd ldng pair: rdn and nt qckn over 2f out: lost 3rd 1f out: kpt on* **25/1**

6 **5** shd **Stamp Of Authority (IRE)**[39] 7114 2-9-5 0 LukeMorris 10 69
(James Tate) *t.k.h: led: kicked for home over 2f out: drvn over 1f out: hdd last 150yds: lost pls nr fin* **8/1**

| | 6 | nk | **Special Code (IRE)** 2-9-5 0 ... NickyMackay 5 | 68+ |
|---|---|---|---|---|
| | | | (John Gosden) *dwlt: wl in rr: pushed along on inner over 2f out: kpt on steadily fr over 1f out: nrst fin* **10/1** | |
| 0 | 7 | 5 | **Rock Heroine**[20] 7549 2-9-0 0 ... JoeFanning 9 | 49 |
| | | | (Hughie Morrison) *nvr bttr than midfield: outpcd over 2f out: no ch after* **33/1** | |
| | 8 | ½ | **Packed House** 2-9-0 0 ... SebSanders 11 | 48 |
| | | | (Ralph Beckett) *s.s: a in rr: no prog 2f out* **5/1**[3] | |
| 00 | 9 | 13 | **Shifting Moon**[25] 7450 2-9-0 0 ... HayleyTurner 7 | 13 |
| | | | (Hughie Morrison) *chsd ldrs: urged along 3f out: wknd over 2f out: t.o* **66/1** | |

1m 27.95s (1.95) **Going Correction** -0.125s/f (Stan) **9** Ran SP% **108.0**
Speed ratings (Par 98): **83,82,82,80,80 80,74,74,59**
CSF £84.92 TOTE £17.00: £4.20, £1.30, £1.10; EX 119.50 Trifecta £334.40.
**Owner** The 'In Recovery' Partnership **Bred** Redpender Stud Ltd **Trained** Epsom, Surrey

■ Donetsk was withdrawn. Price at time of withdrawal 10-1. Rule 4 applies to all bets - deduction 5p in the pound.

**FOCUS**
A few were keen early off a steady gallop, and the winner benefited from being towards the fore, in contrast with the placed horses. Rip Van Winkle sired the first two home. Due to the slow pace it's doubtful this will prove a good literal guide.

## 7834 RACING UK ANYWHERE MEDIAN AUCTION MAIDEN STKS (DIV I) 1m (P)
**5:25** (5:29) (Class 6) 2-Y-O **£1,940** (£577; £288; £144) **Stalls** Low

| Form | | | | RPR |
|---|---|---|---|---|
| 2 | 1 | | **Duretto**[26] 7413 2-9-5 0 ... JimmyFortune 8 | 80+ |
| | | | (Andrew Balding) *trckd ldng pair: wnt 2nd over 2f out and clsd on ldr: shkn up to ld over 1f out: drvn and steadily asserted fnl f* **8/13**[1] | |
| 4532 | 2 | 1½ | **Oregon Gift**[7] 7739 2-9-5 70 ... JoeFanning 1 | 77 |
| | | | (Mark Johnston) *led at decent pce: 4 l clr over 3f out: pressed and edgd lft 2f out: hdd over 1f out: styd on but hld fnl f* **4/1**[2] | |
| 0 | 3 | 7 | **Diamond Joel**[14] 7666 2-9-5 0 ... CharlesBishop 4 | 60 |
| | | | (Mick Channon) *chsd ldr to over 2f out: rdn and nt qckn after: lft bhd by ldng pair over 1f out* **25/1** | |
| 54 | 4 | 2½ | **Missandei**[16] 7625 2-9-0 0 ... MartinHarley 6 | 50 |
| | | | (Marco Botti) *chsd ldrs: no imp on ldng trio fr over 2f out: kpt on* **8/1** | |
| | 5 | 2¼ | **Noro Lim (IRE)** 2-9-5 0 ... AdamKirby 5 | 50+ |
| | | | (Luca Cumani) *dwlt: in rr: outpcd over 3f out: pushed along over 2f out: kpt on* **14/1** | |
| 4 | 6 | ½ | **Naady**[29] 7354 2-9-0 0 ... FrankieDettori 7 | 43 |
| | | | (Ed Dunlop) *in tch towards rr: rdn over 3f out: one pce and no real prog fnl 2f* **7/1**[3] | |
| | 7 | 6 | **Kissy Suzuki** 2-9-0 0 ... JimCrowley 11 | 30+ |
| | | | (Hughie Morrison) *s.s: rn green and wl off the pce in last: sme prog 3f out: wknd over 1f out* **33/1** | |
| | 8 | nk | **Strait Of Magellan (IRE)** 2-9-5 0 ... HayleyTurner 9 | 34 |
| | | | (Michael Bell) *awkward s: mostly in last pair and pushed along: nvr on terms* **33/1** | |
| 500 | 9 | 11 | **Willow Jubilee**[22] 7512 2-9-0 45 ... PaddyAspell 2 | |
| | | | (John E Long) *chsd ldrs: wknd qckly over 3f out: t.o* **66/1** | |
| 00 | 10 | 12 | **Georgia's Gamble (IRE)**[14] 7660 2-9-5 0 ... AmirQuinn 10 | |
| | | | (Lee Carter) *chsd ldrs: wknd rapidly over 3f out: wl t.o* **66/1** | |

1m 38.64s (-1.16) **Going Correction** -0.125s/f (Stan) **10** Ran SP% **124.9**
Speed ratings (Par 94): **100,98,91,89,86 86,80,79,68,56**
CSF £3.59 TOTE £1.60: £1.10, £1.20, £6.40; EX 4.60 Trifecta £64.70.
**Owner** Lord Blyth **Bred** Lord Blyth **Trained** Kingsclere, Hants

**FOCUS**
This was much the quicker of the two divisions, being 2.19sec faster, and the first two finished well clear. The winner stood out on debut form and the second took a step forward.

## 7835 RACING UK ANYWHERE MEDIAN AUCTION MAIDEN STKS (DIV II) 1m (P)
**5:55** (5:57) (Class 6) 2-Y-O **£1,940** (£577; £288; £144) **Stalls** Low

| Form | | | | RPR |
|---|---|---|---|---|
| 40 | 1 | | **Miss Understood (IRE)**[22] 7512 2-9-0 0 ... MartinLane 8 | 72+ |
| | | | (David Simcock) *cl up whn n.m.r and snatched up over 6f out: towards rr tl rdn and prog wl over 1f out: sustained effrt to ld last 75yds: styd on wl* **4/1**[2] | |
| | 2 | ½ | **Niblawi (IRE)** 2-9-5 0 ... GeorgeBaker 3 | 74+ |
| | | | (Michael Bell) *hld up towards rr: stdy prog on outer to ld narrowly 2f out: hrd pressed after: hdd last 75yds: kpt on* **12/1** | |
| 6 | 3 | hd | **Sweet Selection**[25] 7450 2-9-0 0 ... SilvestreDeSousa 10 | 68+ |
| | | | (Hughie Morrison) *s.i.s: pushed along to rcvr and be prom: drvn to chal 2f out: pressed ldr after: upsides ins fnl f: outpcd last 75yds* **2/1**[1] | |
| 05 | 4 | 4 | **Rum Swizzle**[16] 7625 2-9-0 0 ... MartinHarley 4 | 59 |
| | | | (Harry Dunlop) *towards rr: nudged along on inner fr 2f out: n.d but kpt on in encouraging style to take 4th fnl f* **14/1** | |
| 5 | 5 | ½ | **Robins Pearl (FR)**[15] 7631 2-9-0 0 ... JimCrowley 6 | 58 |
| | | | (Olly Stevens) *trckd ldrs: cl up whn nt clr run 2f out: outpcd over 1f out: no ch after: plugged on* **4/1**[2] | |
| 406 | 6 | 1¾ | **Azzir (IRE)**[53] 6743 2-9-5 66 ... BenCurtis 2 | 59 |
| | | | (Timothy Jarvis) *led 2f: chsd ldrs after: cl up 2f out: sn shkn up and fdd* **12/1** | |
| | 7 | 7 | **Tokomaro (IRE)** 2-9-5 0 ... SeanLevey 5 | 43 |
| | | | (Richard Hannon) *led after 2f to 2f out: sn wknd qckly* **10/1**[3] | |
| 00 | 8 | 2 | **Honour Promise (IRE)**[35] 7198 2-9-0 0 ... MartinDwyer 11 | 33 |
| | | | (William Muir) *pressed ldr after 2f to over 2f out: sn wknd qckly* **33/1** | |
| 0 | 9 | 2¼ | **Ultima Ora (IRE)**[15] 7638 2-9-0 0 ... JoeFanning 1 | 28 |
| | | | (Mark Johnston) *dropped to rr after 2f: struggling over 2f out* **12/1** | |
| 0 | 10 | 6 | **Sporting Bob**[19] 7560 2-9-5 0 ... (v[1]) JimmyQuinn 9 | 19 |
| | | | (Robert Eddery) *chsd ldrs on outer: rdn over 2f out: sn wknd* **50/1** | |
| | 11 | 14 | **Falmouth Harbour** 2-9-5 0 ... LukeMorris 7 | |
| | | | (Paul Cole) *slowly away: bdly outpcd and detached in last: t.o: lame* **10/1**[3] | |

1m 40.83s (1.03) **Going Correction** -0.125s/f (Stan) **11** Ran SP% **126.2**
Speed ratings (Par 94): **89,88,88,84,83 82,75,73,70,64 50**
CSF £55.76 TOTE £5.60: £2.00, £3.40, £1.50; EX 46.30 Trifecta £313.70.
**Owner** Mrs Julia Annable **Bred** Swersky & Associates **Trained** Newmarket, Suffolk

**FOCUS**
This looked the weaker of the two divisions on paper, and was run in a time 2.19sec slower. The winner looks a bit better than the bare facts.

## 7836 CASH OUT ON THE BETDAQ+ APP/EBF STALLIONS HYDE STKS (FAST TRACK QUALIFIER) (LISTED RACE) 1m (P)
**6:25** (6:27) (Class 1) 3-Y-O+
**£22,684** (£8,600; £4,304; £2,144; £1,076; £540) **Stalls** Low

| Form | | | | RPR |
|---|---|---|---|---|
| 510 | 1 | | **Sloane Avenue (USA)**[46] 6949 3-9-0 98 ... FrankieDettori 9 | 109+ |
| | | | (Jeremy Noseda) *s.i.s: t.k.h: hld up in rr: prog on outer jst over 2f out: clsd to ld last 150yds: pushed out firmly and hld on* **8/1**[3] | |
| 00 | 2 | nk | **Cladocera (GER)**[96] 5407 3-8-11 102 ... AntoineHamelin 8 | 105+ |
| | | | (A De Royer-Dupre, France) *t.k.h: hld up in midfield: prog to go 3rd jst over 1f out: drvn fnl f: tk 2nd nr fin and clsd on wnr last strides* **20/1** | |
| 1004 | 3 | ½ | **Graphic (IRE)**[20] 7559 5-9-6 114 ... (p) SebSanders 10 | 112 |
| | | | (William Haggas) *mde most: rdn 2f out: hdd last 150yds: lost 2nd and short of room nr fin* **20/1** | |
| 3125 | 4 | 1 | **Captain Cat (IRE)**[32] 7274 5-9-6 115 ... JamesDoyle 4 | 110 |
| | | | (Roger Charlton) *sn restrained into last: stl there whn asked to make prog over 2f out: hd high but hdwy over 1f out: rchd 4th ins fnl f: no imp after: too much to do* **6/5**[1] | |
| 1051 | 5 | hd | **Baltic Knight (IRE)**[14] 7668 4-9-2 110 ... JimmyFortune 5 | 105 |
| | | | (Richard Hannon) *s.i.s: mostly in last pair: rdn over 2f out: prog over 1f out: styd on fnl f: nvr able to chal* **20/1** | |
| 1336 | 6 | 1½ | **Eton Forever (IRE)**[32] 7272 7-9-4 108 ... GrahamLee 6 | 104 |
| | | | (Roger Varian) *short of room after 2f: rdn 2f out: sme prog over 1f out: one pce fnl f* **10/1** | |
| -101 | 7 | ½ | **Prince's Trust**[20] 7555 4-9-2 107 ... ShaneKelly 12 | 100 |
| | | | (William Haggas) *trckd ldrs: rdn over 2f out: nt qckn and lost pl wl over 1f out: one pce after* **7/2**[2] | |
| 3116 | 8 | ½ | **Stereo Love (FR)**[19] 7579 3-8-9 91 ... LukeMorris 11 | 93 |
| | | | (Clive Cox) *prom: rdn to chse ldr jst over 2f out to wl over 1f out: wknd fnl f* **50/1** | |
| 3006 | 9 | ½ | **Ocean Tempest**[18] 7599 5-9-4 112 ... JackMitchell 3 | 100 |
| | | | (John Ryan) *prom: rdn over 2f out: wknd jst over 1f out* **33/1** | |
| -303 | 10 | 29 | **Premio Loco (USA)**[41] 7066 10-9-2 105 ... GeorgeBaker 2 | 31 |
| | | | (Chris Wall) *chsd ldrs: wknd rapidly 2f out: eased and t.o* **33/1** | |
| 0115 | 11 | nk | **Tenor (IRE)**[53] 6752 4-9-4 110 ... (t) AdamKirby 1 | 33 |
| | | | (John Ryan) *chsd ldr to jst over 2f out: wknd rapidly and eased: t.o* **10/1** | |
| 2430 | 12 | ½ | **Emell**[18] 7599 4-9-2 105 ... SeanLevey 7 | 30 |
| | | | (Richard Hannon) *t.k.h: racd wd: prom: wknd rapidly over 2f out: eased and t.o* **66/1** | |

1m 36.34s (-3.46) **Going Correction** -0.125s/f (Stan)
**WFA** 3 from 4yo+ 2lb **12** Ran SP% **120.6**
Speed ratings: **112,111,111,110,110 108,108,107,107,78 77,77**
CSF £156.85 TOTE £9.60: £2.90, £6.50, £4.20; EX 166.70 Trifecta £4092.10.
**Owner** Mrs Susan Roy **Bred** Claiborne Farm & Adele B Dilschneider **Trained** Newmarket, Suffolk

**FOCUS**
A strong Listed contest and a qualifier for the Mile Final on Good Friday. There was a good pace and it paid to be held up. Sloane Avenue can rate higher again.

## 7837 BETDAQ 50% COMMISSION REFUND H'CAP 2m (P)
**6:55** (6:57) (Class 2) (0-105,97) 3-Y-O+
**£11,827** (£3,541; £1,770; £885; £442; £222) **Stalls** Low

| Form | | | | RPR |
|---|---|---|---|---|
| 4241 | 1 | | **Desert Snow**[32] 7289 3-8-12 **90** ... JamesDoyle 6 | 99+ |
| | | | (Saeed bin Suroor) *hld up in 5th: prog over 2f out: pushed into ld 1f out: easily drew clr* **1/1**[1] | |
| 0204 | 2 | 3¾ | **Buckland (IRE)**[47] 6896 6-9-3 **86** ... (t) MartinLane 4 | 91 |
| | | | (Charlie Fellowes) *pushed up to chse ldr: led 3f out: drvn 2f out: hdd 1f out: easily outpcd* **7/1** | |
| 3010 | 3 | 2½ | **Masterpaver**[4] 7803 3-9-2 **94** ... MartinHarley 1 | 96 |
| | | | (Alan Bailey) *hld up in 4th: prog to trck ldr over 2f out: drvn and lost 2nd over 1f out: outpcd after* **11/4**[2] | |
| 0-05 | 4 | 17 | **Flashman**[16] 1581 5-8-12 **78** oh1 ... HectorCrouch(7) 3 | 59 |
| | | | (Gary Moore) *chsd ldng pair: rdn over 3f out: wknd over 2f out* **25/1** | |
| 64-0 | 5 | 4½ | **Chiberta King**[14] 7662 8-10-0 **97** ... (p) JimmyFortune 2 | 73 |
| | | | (Andrew Balding) *led: urged along 4f out: hdd 3f out: sn wl btn* **16/1** | |
| 5231 | 6 | dist | **Noble Gift**[56] 6656 4-9-8 **91** ... AdamKirby 5 | |
| | | | (William Knight) *t.k.h: hld up in last: lost action and eased 5f out: allowed to trot home after* **13/2**[3] | |

3m 25.07s (-5.03) **Going Correction** -0.125s/f (Stan)
**WFA** 3 from 4yo+ 9lb **6** Ran SP% **112.2**
Speed ratings (Par 109): **107,105,103,95,93**
CSF £8.84 TOTE £1.70: £1.20, £3.20; EX 8.40 Trifecta £19.70.
**Owner** Godolphin **Bred** Darley **Trained** Newmarket, Suffolk

**FOCUS**
A straightforward enough win for the favourite in a handicap in which the top-weight weighed in 8lb below the ceiling. The winner is progressive and the second is a solid guide.

## 7838 BETDAQ COMMISSION FREE FOOTBALL ON SATURDAYS H'CAP 1m 4f (P)
**7:25** (7:28) (Class 4) (0-85,85) 3-Y-O+ **£4,690** (£1,395; £697; £348) **Stalls** Centre

| Form | | | | RPR |
|---|---|---|---|---|
| 2451 | 1 | | **Latin Charm (IRE)**[37] 7161 3-9-3 84 ... (p) AdamKirby 1 | 93 |
| | | | (Marco Botti) *trckd ldrs: drvn to chal towards inner 2f out: w ldr after: gd battle and gained narrow ld nr fin* **10/3**[1] | |
| 2666 | 2 | hd | **Xinbama (IRE)**[32] 7289 5-9-7 82 ... FrankieDettori 7 | 91 |
| | | | (Charles Hills) *hld up in rr: prog on inner fr 4f out: drvn to ld 2f out: sn jnd: gd battle after: hdd and jst hld last strides* **10/1** | |
| 1-16 | 3 | 2 | **Sunblazer (IRE)**[26] 7422 4-9-5 80 ... (tp) WilliamTwiston-Davies 2 | 86 |
| | | | (Kim Bailey) *hld up towards rr: sme prog over 3f out: drvn over 2f out: hdwy wl over 1f out: tk 3rd ins fnl f: unable to chal* **20/1** | |
| 1052 | 4 | ½ | **Pintrada**[12] 7702 6-9-7 82 ... TedDurcan 8 | 87 |
| | | | (James Bethell) *hld up in midfield: prog over 3f out: rdn and tried to cl on ldrs fr 2f out: kpt on same pce* **5/1**[3] | |
| -450 | 5 | 1½ | **Stock Hill Fair**[33] 7235 6-9-4 79 ... (t) LiamKeniry 6 | 82 |
| | | | (Brendan Powell) *prom: prog to go 2nd jst over 3f out: led briefly jst over 2f out: chsd ldng pair after tl ins fnl f: one pce* **33/1** | |
| 5200 | 6 | 1¼ | **Zipp (IRE)**[26] 7409 4-9-6 81 ... (p) JamesDoyle 4 | 82 |
| | | | (Ralph Beckett) *wl in tch in midfield: rdn over 3f out: lost pl and struggling wl over 2f out: kpt on again fr over 1f out: nrst fin* **6/1** | |
| 2646 | 7 | 6 | **Yojojo (IRE)**[21] 7531 5-9-4 79 ... RobertWinston 5 | 70 |
| | | | (Gay Kelleway) *hld up in last pair: shuffled along over 2f out then couple of reminders: kpt on fr over 1f out: nvr involved* **25/1** | |

2000 **8** ¾ **Coincidently**[39] 7110 4-9-3 78 MartinHarley 13 68
(Alan Bailey) *dwlt: wl in rr: sme prog 3f out but nt on terms: no hdwy fr 2f out* **25/1**

640- **9** *nk* **Willie Wag Tail (USA)**[455] 5655 5-9-7 82 JimCrowley 10 71
(Ed Walker) *dwlt: hld up in last pair: limited prog 3f out: no hdwy fr 2f out* **7/2**[2]

1310 **10** *11* **Meetings Man (IRE)**[21] 7539 7-9-6 81 (p) JoeFanning 3 53
(Ali Stronge) *prom: chsd ldr 4f out to jst over 3f out: sn wknd: bhd fnl f* **40/1**

6120 **11** ½ **Purple Spectrum**[74] 6137 3-9-4 85 StevieDonohoe 12 56
(J R Jenkins) *led: clr 5f out: hdd & wknd qckly jst over 2f out* **25/1**

1226 **12** *4* **Investissement**[46] 6930 8-9-3 78 (p) AmirQuinn 9 43
(Lee Carter) *in tch in midfield on outer: pushed along 5f out: wknd 3f out: sn bhd* **10/1**

0416 **13** *28* **Full Moon Fever (IRE)**[22] 7504 3-8-12 79 LukeMorris 11
(Ed Walker) *chsd ldrs on outer tl wknd over 3f out: t.o* **14/1**

102 **14** *15* **Jupiter Storm**[16] 6425 5-9-9 84 (p) GeorgeBaker 14
(Gary Moore) *chsd ldr to 4f out: wknd rapidly: t.o* **20/1**

2m 30.12s (-4.38) **Going Correction** -0.125s/f (Stan)
**WFA** 3 from 4yo+ 6lb **14 Ran SP% 127.5**
Speed ratings (Par 105): **109,108,107,107,106 105,101,100,100,93 93,90,71,61**
CSF £35.94 CT £611.40 TOTE £4.50: £1.40, £3.40, £7.30; EX 38.20 Trifecta £447.00.
**Owner** Grundy Bloodstock Limited **Bred** Grundy Bloodstock Srl **Trained** Newmarket, Suffolk

**FOCUS**
A solid handicap for the grade and the form looks pretty reliable. Improvement from the runner-up.
T/Jkpt: Not won. T/Plt: £297.50 to a £1 stake. Pool: £86,631.68 - 212.57 winning tickets T/Qpdt: £42.20 to a £1 stake. Pool: £1,1650.60 - 204.15 winning tickets JN

# 7798 LINGFIELD (L-H)

## Wednesday, November 19

**OFFICIAL GOING: Polytrack: standard**
Wind: Light, across away from stand Weather: Hazy sun

## 7839 32RED.COM NURSERY H'CAP 1m 1y(P)
**12:00** (12:00) (Class 5) (0-75,71) 2-Y-O **£2,587** (£770; £384; £192) **Stalls High**

Form RPR

4202 **1** **Marmalad (IRE)**[22] 7525 2-9-7 71 GeorgeBaker 8 77
(Tom Dascombe) *cl up: pressed ldrs 3f out: led over 1f out: pushed out* **11/4**[1]

0622 **2** 1¾ **Cascading Stars (IRE)**[5] 7770 2-9-1 65 SteveDrowne 6 67
(J S Moore) *hld up towards rr: wnt 4th 3f out: chsd wnr ins fnl f: a hld* **5/1**

2236 **3** 1½ **Simone On Time (IRE)**[20] 7544 2-8-12 62 RenatoSouza 5 61
(Sylvester Kirk) *led for 2f: prom tl lost pl 3f out: r.o again fnl f* **14/1**

2224 **4** *1* **Hillgrove Angel (IRE)**[30] 7338 2-9-4 68 AdamKirby 9 64
(David Evans) *slt ld after 2f tl over 1f out: sn wknd* **4/1**[3]

5322 **5** 2¼ **Eatsleepracerepeat**[22] 7523 2-9-4 68 MartinHarley 7 59
(Lady Cecil) *dwlt: hdwy to join ldr after 2f: wknd over 1f out* **3/1**[2]

5506 **6** 1¼ **Vinamar (IRE)**[43] 6997 2-8-1 54 DannyBrock(3) 1 42
(Roger Teal) *restless in stalls and missed break: bhd: rdn 3f out: n.d* **50/1**

054 **7** *2* **Foxy Boris (FR)**[28] 7372 2-9-5 69 (t) LukeMorris 2 53
(Paul Cole) *bhd: rdn 3f out: nvr trbld ldrs* **6/1**

3060 **8** 1¾ **Kidmeforever**[50] 6842 2-7-10 53 ow1 JosephineGordon(7) 4 33
(J S Moore) *hld up on inner: lost tch 3f out* **66/1**

1m 38.08s (-0.12) **Going Correction** -0.05s/f (Stan) **8 Ran SP% 112.7**
Speed ratings (Par 96): **98,96,94,93,91 90,88,86**
CSF £16.43 CT £158.55 TOTE £3.90: £1.60, £1.40, £3.70; EX 18.50 Trifecta £123.30.
**Owner** Caroline, Dave, Lol, Lyn & Nick **Bred** Manister House Stud **Trained** Malpas, Cheshire

**FOCUS**
An ordinary nursery, and pretty straightforward form.

## 7840 32RED/BRITISH STALLION STUDS EBF MAIDEN STKS 6f 1y(P)
**12:30** (12:30) (Class 5) 2-Y-O **£2,911** (£866; £432; £216) **Stalls Low**

Form RPR

5462 **1** **Bonfire Heart**[13] 7684 2-9-0 67 StevieDonohoe 7 64
(Daniel Mark Loughnane) *prom: drvn to ld ins fnl f: all out* **3/1**[2]

533 **2** *hd* **Seychelloise**[15] 7649 2-9-0 63 LukeMorris 5 63
(Sir Mark Prescott Bt) *led: hrd rdn over 1f out: hdd ins fnl f: rallied wl* **7/2**[3]

0 **3** 1½ **Thames Knight**[14] 7660 2-9-5 0 MartinDwyer 6 64
(Marcus Tregoning) *hld up in 6th: shkn up over 1f out: r.o to take 3rd ins fnl f* **8/1**

0 **4** ½ **Azamaara (IRE)**[157] 3267 2-9-0 0 MartinHarley 2 57
(James Tate) *hld up in 5th: effrt over 1f out: kpt on fnl f* **33/1**

00 **5** ½ **Glorious Dancer**[11] 7712 2-9-5 0 AntonioFresu 1 61+
(Ed Walker) *hld up in rr: rdn over 2f out: styd on wl fnl f* **20/1**

**6** 1¼ **Souk Al Tahab (IRE)** 2-9-5 0 AdamKirby 8 57
(Ed Dunlop) *s.i.s: plld hrd: sn prom on outer: wnt cl 2nd 3f out tl wknd 1f out* **6/1**

0 **7** 3½ **Samsamsam**[26] 7412 2-9-5 0 JimCrowley 3 47
(Robert Cowell) *t.k.h: trckd ldr tl 3f out: hrd rdn and wknd over 1f out* **2/1**[1]

**8** ½ **Pyroclastic (IRE)** 2-9-5 0 PatCosgrave 4 45
(Jim Boyle) *hld up in rr: rdn and n.d fnl 2f* **50/1**

1m 13.48s (1.58) **Going Correction** -0.05s/f (Stan) **8 Ran SP% 115.6**
Speed ratings (Par 96): **87,86,84,84,83 81,77,76**
CSF £13.87 TOTE £3.10: £1.30, £1.40, £2.20; EX 8.30 Trifecta £51.40.
**Owner** Ms A Quinn **Bred** Bostwick Bloodstock **Trained** Baldwin's Gate, Staffs

**FOCUS**
A modest maiden which resulted in a tight finish between the two most experienced juveniles. The time was slow and the form is rated around the front pair.

## 7841 CORAL APP DOWNLOAD FROM THE APP STORE MAIDEN STKS 1m 2f (P)
**1:00** (1:01) (Class 5) 3-Y-O+ **£2,587** (£770; £384; £192) **Stalls Low**

Form RPR

4 **1** **Lunasea (IRE)**[26] 7418 3-9-5 0 AdamKirby 3 85+
(Luca Cumani) *led for 1f: prom: rdn over 4f out: led on inner ent st: styd on wl: pushed out* **6/4**[1]

6223 **2** *1* **Steppe Daughter (IRE)**[42] 7032 3-9-0 75 LukeMorris 1 76
(Denis Coakley) *in tch: drvn to chse wnr over 1f out: r.o* **7/1**[3]

3252 **3** 2¾ **Ghany (IRE)**[13] 7686 3-9-0 73 (p) SilvestreDeSousa 2 74
(William Haggas) *chsd ldrs: squeezed for room and lost pl over 2f out: rallied into 3rd 1f out: kpt on* **9/2**[2]

05- **4** ¾ **Salmon Sushi**[378] 7766 3-9-5 0 [1] GeorgeBaker 10 74
(David Lanigan) *stdd s: hld up wl in rr tl shkn up and r.o fr over 1f out* **12/1**

4 **5** ½ **Priors Brook**[62] 6482 3-9-5 0 LiamKeniry 12 73
(Andrew Balding) *chsd ldr after 1f tl 2f out: sn outpcd* **16/1**

0- **6** 1¾ **Squire**[508] 3833 3-9-5 0 JimCrowley 9 70+
(Michael Attwater) *hld up off the pce towards rr: shkn up and styd on steadily fr over 1f out* **66/1**

64 **7** *nse* **Elysian Fields (GR)**[21] 7528 3-9-0 0 PaulMulrennan 5 65
(Amanda Perrett) *in tch: effrt over 2f out: btn over 1f out* **20/1**

4-43 **8** *nse* **Jacqueline Jouliac**[13] 7686 3-9-0 73 (t) RobertHavlin 7 65
(John Gosden) *led after 1f tl wl over 1f out: sn btn* **14/1**

4 **9** 1¼ **Stonecutter (IRE)**[183] 2422 3-9-5 0 MartinHarley 6 68
(Marco Botti) *mid-div most of way: towards rr and n.d fnl 3f* **9/2**[2]

00 **10** *23* **Sea Rebelle**[29] 7349 5-9-4 0 PatCosgrave 8 19
(Jo Crowley) *chsd ldrs tl wknd 2f out* **100/1**

**11** *38* **Centralized** 3-9-2 0 JoeyHaynes(3) 11
(Eric Wheeler) *outpcd: sn rdn along and wl bhd* **200/1**

0 **P** **Painted Black**[35] 7210 3-9-5 0 WilliamCarson 4
(Jane Chapple-Hyam) *dwlt: towards rr tl broke down and p.u over 3f out* **150/1**

2m 3.39s (-3.21) **Going Correction** -0.05s/f (Stan)
**WFA** 3 from 5yo 4lb **12 Ran SP% 117.5**
Speed ratings (Par 103): **110,109,107,106,106 104,104,104,103,85 54,**
CSF £12.33 TOTE £3.50: £1.60, £2.30, £1.40; EX 12.80 Trifecta £40.80.
**Owner** Jon S Kelly **Bred** Rathbarry Stud **Trained** Newmarket, Suffolk

**FOCUS**
A modest older-horse maiden.

## 7842 LADBROKES H'CAP 7f 1y(P)
**1:30** (1:30) (Class 6) (0-65,65) 3-Y-O+ **£1,940** (£577; £288; £144) **Stalls Low**

Form RPR

0634 **1** **Malaysian Boleh**[29] 7368 4-9-7 65 PaulMulrennan 10 74
(Simon Dow) *dwlt: mid-div on outer: hdwy 4f out: led 1f out: drvn along fnl f: jst hld on* **6/1**[3]

5502 **2** *hd* **Mon Cigar (IRE)**[20] 7556 3-9-6 65 PatCosgrave 6 72
(Denis Coakley) *swvd lft s: mid-div: hrd rdn and hdwy over 1f out: edgd lft and str run fnl f: jst failed* **5/2**[1]

325 **3** 1½ **Lead A Merry Dance**[43] 7023 3-9-4 63 MartinDwyer 5 67
(Sylvester Kirk) *bmpd s: cl up: pressed ldrs on inner over 1f out: one pce* **7/1**

1245 **4** ½ **Ghost Train (IRE)**[48] 6889 5-9-6 64 (p) LukeMorris 4 69
(Tim McCarthy) *dwlt and hmpd s: towards rr: rdn and hdwy over 1f out: disputing 4th and styng on whn hmpd ins fnl f* **9/2**[2]

0236 **5** *nse* **Shifting Star (IRE)**[15] 7633 9-9-7 65 (vt) WilliamCarson 11 68
(John Bridger) *sn led and c across fr wd stall after 1f: hrd rdn and hdd 1f out: no ex* **12/1**

0000 **6** 1¾ **Plover**[5] 7775 4-9-7 65 RobertHavlin 7 64
(Michael Attwater) *bhd: rdn and r.o fr over 1f out: nvr nrr* **50/1**

5010 **7** ¾ **Ostralegus**[15] 7633 4-9-6 64 (v[1]) BenCurtis 2 61
(John Gallagher) *chsd ldr: drew level 2f out: 6th and btn whn squeezed ins fnl f* **8/1**

0400 **8** *1* **Don't**[15] 7633 3-8-10 60 ShelleyBirkett(5) 3 53
(Julia Feilden) *bdly bmpd s: in tch: effrt on inner over 1f out: sn wknd* **25/1**

4020 **9** *6* **Foxford**[21] 7533 3-9-5 64 LiamKeniry 9 41
(Patrick Chamings) *prom tl wknd 2f out* **12/1**

2306 **10** 3½ **Run Fat Lass Run**[15] 7651 4-9-4 62 (p) HayleyTurner 1 31
(Conor Dore) *dwlt: a bhd* **20/1**

0000 **11** *11* **Black Caesar (IRE)**[34] 7220 3-9-6 65 GeorgeBaker 8 5+
(Philip Hide) *chsd ldrs tl wknd 2f out* **16/1**

1m 24.64s (-0.16) **Going Correction** -0.05s/f (Stan)
**WFA** 3 from 4yo+ 1lb **11 Ran SP% 116.5**
Speed ratings (Par 101): **98,97,96,95,95 93,92,91,84,80 68**
CSF £20.64 CT £108.66 TOTE £6.90: £2.30, £1.60, £3.00; EX 27.10 Trifecta £100.60.
**Owner** JCG Chua & CK Ong **Bred** John & Sue Davis **Trained** Epsom, Surrey
■ Stewards' Enquiry : Pat Cosgrave three-day ban: careless riding (Dec 3-5)

**FOCUS**
A moderate handicap. The winner had a very solid chance at these weights on recent form.

## 7843 UNIBET H'CAP 6f 1y(P)
**2:00** (2:02) (Class 3) (0-95,95) 3-Y-O+ **£7,439** (£2,213; £1,106; £553) **Stalls Low**

Form RPR

0031 **1** **Barracuda Boy (IRE)**[53] 6744 4-9-7 95 GeorgeBaker 1 104
(Tom Dascombe) *mde all: kicked 3 l clr 2f out: hrd rdn fnl f: jst hld on* **3/1**[1]

1531 **2** *nk* **Major Jack**[78] 6020 3-8-12 86 JamesDoyle 11 94+
(Roger Charlton) *hld up and bhd: gd hdwy on inner over 1f out: wnt 2nd and clsd on wnr fnl 100yds: jst failed* **5/1**[3]

1200 **3** 1¾ **Baddilini**[199] 1975 4-9-0 88 (p) MartinHarley 3 91
(Alan Bailey) *chsd ldrs: hrd rdn over 1f out: kpt on same pce* **25/1**

000 **4** *nk* **Fairway To Heaven (IRE)**[20] 7543 5-9-4 92 JimCrowley 10 94
(Michael Wigham) *dwlt and dropped in to rail: in midfield after 2f: drvn to chse wnr over 1f out: lost 2nd and one pce fnl 100yds* **12/1**

0252 **5** ¾ **Diamond Lady**[19] 7564 3-8-9 81 oh1 ow2 RobertTart 5 86
(William Stone) *hld up towards rr: shkn up over 1f out: styd on wl fnl f* **14/1**

6305 **6** *1* **Elusivity (IRE)**[7] 7738 6-8-13 87 ShaneKelly 4 84
(Peter Crate) *in tch: lost pl over 2f out: no imp after* **8/1**

205 **7** *shd* **Dangerous Age**[43] 7017 4-8-7 81 JoeFanning 12 77
(Charles Hills) *mid-div on outer: effrt and wd into st: nvr able to chal* **25/1**

1004 **8** ½ **Expose**[16] 7624 6-8-10 84 BenCurtis 9 81
(Shaun Harris) *towards rr: hrd rdn and unable to rch ldrs fnl 2f* **10/1**

0006 **9** ½ **Compton Park**[12] 7700 7-8-10 91 (t) KieranShoemark(7) 7 84
(Les Eyre) *towards rr: sme hdwy 2f out: wknd fnl f* **8/1**

1014 **10** ½ **Amadeus Wolfe Tone (IRE)**[12] 7700 5-9-2 90 (p) AdamKirby 6 82
(Jamie Osborne) *a bhd* **7/2**[2]

5025 **11** ¾ **Golden Amber (IRE)**[193] 2161 3-9-2 90 SebSanders 8 80
(Dean Ivory) *prom tl wknd 2f out* **33/1**

060 **12** *11* **Zero Money (IRE)**[20] 7543 8-8-13 87 LiamKeniry 2 44
(Hugo Palmer) *chsd wnr tl wknd over 2f out* **50/1**

1m 10.63s (-1.27) **Going Correction** -0.05s/f (Stan) **12 Ran SP% 122.2**
Speed ratings (Par 107): **106,105,103,102,101 100,100,99,99,98 97,82**
CSF £17.98 CT £326.60 TOTE £5.50: £2.20, £1.90, £5.00; EX 15.10 Trifecta £162.80.
**Owner** Laurence A Bellman **Bred** Mount Coote Partnership **Trained** Malpas, Cheshire

**FOCUS**
A hot sprint handicap and contrasting fortunes for the first two home. The form has a pretty straightforward feel.

## 7844 DOWNLOAD THE LADBROKES APP H'CAP (DIV I) 1m 1y(P)
2:30 (2:31) (Class 6) (0-55,55) 3-Y-O+ £1,940 (£577; £288; £144) Stalls High

Form RPR

-000 1 **Lexington Blue**[28] 7369 4-9-4 52 SteveDrowne 6 58
(Seamus Mullins) *bhd: cajoled along and hdwy 1f out: str run u.p to ld on line* **14/1**

0064 2 *shd* **Movie Magic**[4] 7799 3-8-10 46 oh1 (v) WilliamCarson 7 51
(John Bridger) *led: 3 l clr and rdn 2f out: tired fnl f: jst ct* **16/1**

0000 3 *nk* **Top Set (IRE)**[21] 7527 4-9-2 50 SebSanders 11 55
(Simon Dow) *bhd: styd on strly u.p fr over 1f out: clsng fast at fin* **14/1**

2432 4 *nse* **Abigails Angel**[29] 7347 7-9-7 55 AmirQuinn 10 60
(Lee Carter) *s.i.s: towards rr: hdwy on inner over 1f out: pressed ldr ins fnl f: no ex nr fin* **7/2**[2]

2546 5 *1 3/4* **Lewamy (IRE)**[75] 6122 4-8-13 47 (p) LukeMorris 2 48
(Michael Bell) *chsd ldrs: hrd rdn over 1f out: one pce* **2/1**[1]

0346 6 *3/4* **Divine Rule (IRE)**[20] 7546 6-9-4 52 (p) LiamJones 1 51
(Laura Mongan) *bhd: rdn over 2f out: styd on fnl f* **10/1**

1556 7 *2 1/2* **Nifty Kier**[15] 7645 5-9-0 51 DannyBrock(3) 5 45
(Phil McEntee) *chsd ldr tl wknd jst over 1f out* **20/1**

0660 8 *2 1/2* **Scariff Hornet (IRE)**[22] 7517 3-8-12 48 MartinHarley 8 35
(Sylvester Kirk) *mid-div: effrt on outer over 2f out: wknd over 1f out* **10/1**

0000 9 *nse* **Charlies Mate**[29] 7347 3-8-10 46 oh1 (v) MartinDwyer 3 33
(John Best) *a towards rr* **100/1**

0600 10 *1/2* **Bajan Story**[20] 7547 5-8-12 46 oh1 HayleyTurner 4 33
(Michael Blanshard) *chsd ldrs: outpcd 3f out: sn btn* **50/1**

5525 11 *4* **Highly Likely (IRE)**[15] 7632 5-9-5 53 (b) JamesDoyle 12 30
(Steve Woodman) *sn c across fr wd stall and chal for 2nd: wknd 2f out* **6/1**[3]

4460 12 *13* **Strategic Action (IRE)**[30] 7002 5-8-12 46 oh1 (p) RobertHavlin 9
(Linda Jewell) *plld hrd in rr: hung rt and rn wd on bnd 4f out: eased* **33/1**

1m 37.55s (-0.65) **Going Correction** -0.05s/f (Stan)
**WFA** 3 from 4yo+ 2lb 12 Ran SP% **117.9**
Speed ratings (Par 101): **101,100,100,100,98 98,95,93,93,92 88,75**
CSF £210.16 CT £3174.08 TOTE £19.10: £6.70, £5.30, £7.20; EX 285.70 Trifecta £2687.70 Part won..
**Owner** Church Racing Partnership **Bred** The National Stud Blakeney Club **Trained** Wilsford-Cum-Lake, Wilts

**FOCUS**
A dramatic finish to this poor handicap. The runer-up confirmed her latest run didn't flatter her.

## 7845 DOWNLOAD THE LADBROKES APP H'CAP (DIV II) 1m 1y(P)
3:00 (3:00) (Class 6) (0-55,55) 3-Y-O+ £1,940 (£577; £288; £144) Stalls High

Form RPR

600 1 **Habeshia**[75] 6121 4-8-12 46 oh1 LukeMorris 9 55+
(Michael Bell) *chsd ldrs: led over 2f out tl wl over 1f out: drvn to regain ld 1f out: styd on* **7/4**[1]

0600 2 *1 3/4* **Nouvelle Ere**[28] 7369 3-8-7 46 [1] JoeyHaynes(3) 6 50
(Tony Carroll) *led for 3f: led again on inner ent st: hrd rdn and hdd 1f out: one pce* **25/1**

0265 3 *1* **Focail Mear**[14] 7664 3-8-7 46 oh1 DannyBrock(3) 1 48
(John Ryan) *prom: lost pl over 4f out: rallied 2f out: r.o fnl f* **6/1**[3]

4540 4 *1/2* **Skidby Mill (IRE)**[29] 7368 4-9-7 55 LiamJones 2 57
(Laura Mongan) *mid-div on rail: hdwy on inner to press ldrs over 1f out: one pce* **12/1**

1203 5 *1 3/4* **Claude Greenwood**[28] 7369 4-9-1 49 (b) CharlesBishop 4 47
(Linda Jewell) *in tch: effrt on outer and hrd rdn over 2f out: wd and btn ent st* **5/1**[2]

3003 6 *3/4* **Golly Miss Molly**[32] 7292 3-8-12 48 (b) MartinLane 5 43
(Jeremy Gask) *bhd: rdn over 2f out: styd on fnl f* **10/1**

000 7 *1 1/2* **Heinrich (USA)**[22] 7517 3-9-2 52 (t) MartinDwyer 7 43
(Sylvester Kirk) *towards rr: rdn over 1f out: n.d* **7/1**

0460 8 *3 3/4* **Rosie Prospects**[77] 6030 3-8-10 46 oh1 (p) JimmyQuinn 3 29
(Roger Ingram) *mid-div: hrd rdn 3f out: nvr able to chal* **100/1**

0543 9 *1* **Vale Mentor (IRE)**[33] 7250 3-8-12 55 (v[1]) MichaelKenneally(7) 8 35
(Denis Quinn) *dwlt: sn prom: led 5f out tl over 2f out: sn wknd* **16/1**

0000 10 *3* **Overrider**[36] 7188 4-9-4 52 (t) SteveDrowne 12 27
(Shaun Lycett) *s.s: a bhd: no ch fnl 3f* **25/1**

0020 11 *nk* **Silvee**[4] 7804 7-8-12 46 (v) MartinHarley 11 20
(John Bridger) *chsd ldr on outer tl wknd over 2f out* **16/1**

054- 12 *1 3/4* **Just Rubie**[336] 8325 3-8-11 54 ChrisMeehan(7) 10 23
(Michael Blanshard) *dwlt: mid-div on outer: outpcd over 2f out: sn bhd* **50/1**

1m 37.14s (-1.06) **Going Correction** -0.05s/f (Stan)
**WFA** 3 from 4yo+ 2lb 12 Ran SP% **119.0**
Speed ratings (Par 101): **103,101,100,99,98 97,95,92,91,88 87,85**
CSF £59.06 CT £229.96 TOTE £2.90: £1.10, £13.90, £2.00; EX 74.70 Trifecta £564.70.
**Owner** Brian Goodyear **Bred** Haras Du Mezeray **Trained** Newmarket, Suffolk

**FOCUS**
The winning time was 0.41sec quicker than the first division. Very rordinary for, the winner improving for the change of yard.

## 7846 CORAL MOBILE "JUST THREE CLICKS TO BET" AMATEUR RIDERS' H'CAP 1m 4f (P)
3:30 (3:31) (Class 6) (0-65,65) 3-Y-O+ £1,871 (£580; £290; £145) Stalls Low

Form RPR

0122 1 **Salient**[22] 7518 10-10-0 58 MrEdwardSibbick(7) 8 64
(Michael Attwater) *chsd ldrs: led 3f out: hld on gamely fnl f* **10/1**

0224 2 *3/4* **Qibtee (FR)**[47] 5301 4-10-7 58 (b[1]) MissHBethell 13 62
(Les Eyre) *dwlt: plld hrd towards rr: smooth hdwy over 2f out: hrd rdn over 1f out: r.o wl to snatch 2nd nr fin* **8/1**

5520 3 *hd* **Greeleys Love (USA)**[29] 7359 4-10-7 63 MrJDoe(5) 11 67
(Luke Dace) *dwlt: hld up and bhd: rdn and hdwy over 1f out: r.o* **8/1**

6462 4 *nk* **Cabuchon (GER)**[51] 6818 7-10-6 57 (vt) MrHAABannister 7 61
(David Evans) *mid-div: hdwy 5f out: drvn to chal 1f out: unable qck nr fin* **7/2**[1]

0604 5 *nk* **Time Square (FR)**[21] 7540 7-10-7 58 MrSWalker 6 61
(Tony Carroll) *plld hrd: cl up: chsd wnr 3f out tl 1f out: kpt on same pce* **4/1**[2]

2232 6 *2 1/4* **The Ducking Stool**[14] 7672 7-11-0 65 MrRBirkett 16 64
(Julia Feilden) *chsd ldrs: rdn and wd on bnd into st: one pce* **7/1**[3]

6600 7 *1 1/2* **Dozy Joe**[15] 7633 6-10-9 63 (bt) MrChrisMartin(3) 5 60
(Joseph Tuite) *dwlt: bhd tl rdn and styd on fnl 2f* **33/1**

3646 8 *1* **Power Up**[25] 7458 3-9-6 56 MissGFriswell(7) 9 51
(Jane Chapple-Hyam) *towards rr: rdn over 2f out: nvr rchd ldrs* **16/1**

5150 9 *hd* **Medal Of Valour (JPN)**[16] 7309 6-10-6 64 (bt) MrTGillard(7) 3 59
(Mark Gillard) *led after 1f tl 3f out: wknd over 1f out* **50/1**

10 *hd* **Green Du Ciel (FR)**[554] 9-10-9 65 (t) MissHHeal(5) 10 60
(Brian Barr) *mid-div: hrd rdn on rail over 2f out: nvr able to chal* **33/1**

5016 11 *1/2* **Rockweiller**[18] 7284 7-10-3 59 MrAidenBlakemore(5) 2 53
(Shaun Harris) *led for 1f: chsd ldrs: rdn and btn 3f out* **16/1**

4306 12 *1 1/2* **Zainda (IRE)**[14] 7672 4-9-7 51 oh2 MrAFrench(7) 1 43
(Paul Midgley) *mid-div on rail: rdn 4f out: sn outpcd* **33/1**

0/24 13 *2 1/2* **Engai (GER)**[33] 7251 8-10-3 61 MissPBridgwater(7) 14 49
(David Bridgwater) *sn chsng ldr: wnt level 5f out tl 3f out: sn wknd* **10/1**

4435 14 *2* **Sutton Sid**[101] 5208 4-10-2 58 (p) MissMBryant(5) 4 42
(Paddy Butler) *dwlt: a wl bhd* **25/1**

15 *2* **Daidaidai (FR)**[178] 4-10-8 64 MrWRussell(5) 12 45
(Gary Moore) *mid-div on outer: lost pl 1/2-way: sn bhd* **25/1**

1404 16 *nk* **Snow Conditions**[21] 7526 3-9-10 60 MrJamieCoates(7) 15 41
(Philip Hide) *dwlt: sn in tch on outer: wknd over 4f out: sn bhd* **14/1**

2m 32.43s (-0.57) **Going Correction** -0.05s/f (Stan)
**WFA** 3 from 4yo+ 6lb 16 Ran SP% **131.1**
Speed ratings (Par 101): **99,98,98,98,97 96,95,94,94,94 94,93,91,90,88 88**
CSF £89.23 CT £696.26 TOTE £11.50: £2.90, £4.20, £2.70, £1.60; EX 171.50 Trifecta £2154.10 Part won..
**Owner** Canisbay Bloodstock **Bred** Hesmonds Stud Ltd **Trained** Epsom, Surrey
■ Edward Sibbick's first winner.

**FOCUS**
A big field for this moderate amateurs' handicap, but despite a fair pace it resulted in a tight finish. Straightforward form.
T/Plt: £264.30 to a £1 stake. Pool: £62,563.93 - 172.78 winning tickets T/Qpdt: £85.70 to a £1 stake. Pool: £5,925.51 - 51.16 winning tickets LM

# 7831 KEMPTON (A.W) (R-H)
### Thursday, November 20

**OFFICIAL GOING: Polytrack: standard**
Wind: virtually nil Weather: dry

## 7847 RACINGUK.COM/FREETRIAL START YOURS TODAY CLAIMING STKS 6f (P)
4:10 (4:10) (Class 6) 3-Y-O+ £1,940 (£577; £288; £144) Stalls Low

Form RPR

4006 1 **Trojan Rocket (IRE)**[19] 7600 6-9-11 87 (p) GeorgeBaker 11 92
(Michael Wigham) *chsd ldrs: upsides ldr and travelling best over 2f out: pushed into ld over 1f out: kpt on: rdn out* **13/8**[1]

4100 2 *1* **Doc Hay (USA)**[12] 7715 7-9-11 90 DavidNolan 5 89
(David O'Meara) *taken down early: hld up in rr of main gp: hdwy u.p on inner 2f out: chsd clr wnr fnl 150yds: styd on* **5/2**[2]

5002 3 *1* **Midnight Rider (IRE)**[38] 7159 6-9-4 80 PatMillman(7) 6 86
(Rod Millman) *hld up in rr of main gp: swtchd lft 2f out: stl plenty to do whn hdwy over 1f out: wnt 3rd ins fnl and styd on strly: nt rch ldrs* **10/1**

3352 4 *5* **Avertor**[36] 7202 8-9-3 60 (v[1]) LiamJones 9 62
(Robert Stephens) *in tch in midfield: hdwy to chse ldrs and drvn 2f out: outpcd and btn over 1f out: plugged on to snatch 4th last strides* **33/1**

0340 5 *nk* **Kodafine (IRE)**[5] 7806 3-8-1 61 DannyBrock(3) 4 48
(David Evans) *sn led: rdn over 2f out: hdd and outpcd over 1f out: lost 2nd fnl 150yds: wknd* **20/1**

3060 6 *nk* **Arctic Lynx (IRE)**[6] 7775 7-8-13 72 (p) MartinHarley 7 56
(Robert Cowell) *hld up towards rr of main gp: effrt and sme hdwy over 2f out: styd on same pce fr over 1f out* **13/2**[3]

0440 7 *1 1/2* **Dark Lane**[7] 7758 8-8-5 62 JFEgan 8 43
(David Evans) *chsd ldrs: rdn 1/2-way: outpcd and btn over 1f out: wl hld fnl f* **20/1**

0304 8 *3 1/2* **Commanche**[14] 7687 5-9-11 70 AdamKirby 1 52
(Chris Dwyer) *chsd ldrs tl unable qck u.p jst over 2f out: wknd over 1f out* **16/1**

3100 9 *1 1/4* **Lindart (ITY)**[7] 7757 3-8-4 72 (b) GaryMahon(7) 10 34
(Richard Hannon) *sn outpcd and rdn in detached last: n.d* **25/1**

0010 10 *1/2* **Dazza**[22] 7535 3-7-13 70 HectorCrouch(7) 12 27
(Gary Moore) *towards rr of main gp and stuck wd: lost pl u.p over 2f out: no ch fnl 2f* **16/1**

0306 11 *6* **La Tinta Bay**[24] 7489 3-7-13 69 TomMarquand(7) 3 8
(Richard Hannon) *in tch in midfield: rdn and struggling 1/2-way: wl bhd fnl f* **33/1**

1m 11.22s (-1.88) **Going Correction** -0.10s/f (Stan) 11 Ran SP% **120.1**
Speed ratings (Par 101): **108,106,105,98,98 97,95,91,89,88 80**
CSF £5.22 TOTE £2.70: £1.30, £1.10, £3.90; EX 6.70 Trifecta £20.10.Doc Hay was claimed by L. A. Carter for £12000.
**Owner** G Linder, D Hassan, R Warner **Bred** J G F Fox **Trained** Newmarket, Suffolk

**FOCUS**
Straightforward claiming form, with the first three coming home in market order. The winner was close to his AW best.

## 7848 DOWNLOAD YOUR RACING UK APP NURSERY H'CAP 6f (P)
4:40 (4:40) (Class 6) (0-65,64) 2-Y-O £1,940 (£577; £288; £144) Stalls Low

Form RPR

0212 1 **Chetan**[7] 7753 2-9-3 60 LukeMorris 4 63
(Milton Bradley) *in tch in midfield: n.m.r jst over 2f out: drvn and hdwy to chal over 1f out: led ins fnl f: drvn out* **6/5**[1]

0056 2 *1/2* **Cloak And Degas (IRE)**[34] 7257 2-9-3 60 PaulMulrennan 3 62
(Scott Dixon) *sn led: rdn wl over 1f out: sn hrd pressed: hdd ins fnl f: kpt on wl but a hld* **8/1**

053 3 *2* **Rialto Magic**[16] 7631 2-9-7 64 AdamKirby 1 60
(Jamie Osborne) *hld up in tch: swtchd lft and effrt wl over 1f out: chsd ldrs and one pce fnl f* **3/1**[2]

5060 4 *1/2* **Kylies Wild Card**[14] 7684 2-8-0 46 ow1 JoeyHaynes(3) 7 40
(Simon Hodgson) *hld up in tch in rr: hdwy u.p jst over 1f out: kpt on same pce ins fnl f* **66/1**

0333 5 *7* **Tommys Geal**[49] 6888 2-8-0 50 HectorCrouch(7) 5 29
(Michael Madgwick) *in tch in midfield: rdn over 3f out: no ex u.p and btn 1f out: wknd fnl f* **15/2**[3]

3440 6 *1 1/2* **Lady Marita (IRE)**[24] 7497 2-9-6 63 JFEgan 6 32
(David Evans) *chsd ldrs: wnt 2nd 4f out tl over 1f out: wknd fnl f* **8/1**

0550 7 *2 1/4* **Recover (USA)**[22] 7529 2-9-0 57 SeanLevey 2 19
(Brian Meehan) *t.k.h: chsd ldr for 2f: shuffled bk on inner wl over 2f out: wknd over 1f out* **25/1**


The Form Book, Raceform Ltd, Newbury, RG14 5SJ

1100 **8** *2* **Sparbrook (IRE)**[14] 7683 2-8-12 62 TomasHarrigan(7) 8 18
(Simon Dow) *chsd ldrs tl lost pl 2f out: wknd over 1f out* **16/1**

1m 12.64s (-0.46) **Going Correction** -0.10s/f (Stan) **8** Ran SP% **115.7**
Speed ratings (Par 94): **99,98,95,95,85 83,80,78**
CSF £12.18 CT £24.56 TOTE £2.00: £1.10, £2.00, £1.50; EX 11.60 Trifecta £41.90.
**Owner** Roger & Val Miles,Colin Miles,Tony Stamp **Bred** Andrew W Robson **Trained** Sedbury, Gloucs

**FOCUS**
A weak nursery, run at a sound pace.

## 7849 TITANBET.CO.UK NURSERY H'CAP (BOBIS RACE) 7f (P)
**5:10** (5:10) (Class 4) (0-85,86) 2-Y-O **£4,528** (£1,347; £673; £336) **Stalls** Low

Form RPR
055 **1** **Gleaming Girl**[59] 6605 2-8-1 67 SophieKilloran(7) 1 71
(David Simcock) *in tch in 3rd: effrt over 1f out: ev ch ins fnl f: styd on wl to ld towards fin* **16/1**

4212 **2** *nk* **Vegas Rebel (IRE)**[27] 7415 2-9-3 76 MartinHarley 2 79
(Peter Chapple-Hyam) *chsd ldrs: chal 2f out: rdn to ld over 1f: kpt on wl tl hdd and no ex towards fin* **11/8**[2]

2161 **3** *shd* **Lyfka**[7] 7755 2-9-13 86 6ex LukeMorris 4 89
(Paul Cole) *wnt lft s: hld up in tch in rr: effrt 2f out: drvn and ev ch fnl f: kpt on* **11/10**[1]

5624 **4** *1 ¾* **Classic Seniority**[29] 7378 2-8-12 71 SeanLevey 3 69
(Richard Hannon) *t.k.h: led: rdn 2f out: hdd over 1f out: no ex and btn ins fnl f: wknd fnl 75yds* **8/1**[3]

1m 27.09s (1.09) **Going Correction** -0.10s/f (Stan) **4** Ran SP% **106.7**
Speed ratings (Par 98): **89,88,88,86**
CSF £37.58 TOTE £10.30; EX 35.00 Trifecta £70.80.
**Owner** Tick Tock Partnership **Bred** Rabbah Bloodstock Limited **Trained** Newmarket, Suffolk

**FOCUS**
Not a bad little nursery. It was run at an uneven pace, though, and produced a blanket three-way finish.

## 7850 TITANBET.CO.UK H'CAP (LONDON MIDDLE DISTANCE SERIES QUALIFIER) 1m 3f (P)
**5:40** (5:40) (Class 3) (0-95,94) 3-Y-O+ **£7,158** (£2,143; £1,071; £535; £267; £134) **Stalls** Low

Form RPR
6351 **1** **Solidarity**[6] 7784 3-9-7 **94** 6ex AdamKirby 8 103+
(Charlie Appleby) *hld up in tch in last trio: rdn and gd hdwy wl over 1f out: led fnl 100yds: r.o wl and gng away at fin* **7/4**[1]

0321 **2** *1* **Double Discount (IRE)**[43] 7033 4-9-10 **92** (p) GeorgeBaker 1 99
(Tom Dascombe) *led: rdn wl over 1f out: kpt on wl tl hdd and no ex fnl 100yds* **7/2**[2]

310 **3** *1 ¼* **Elbereth**[63] 6487 3-8-5 **78** oh1 DavidProbert 4 83
(Andrew Balding) *chsd ldr: rdn and ev ch 2f out tl ins fnl f: no ex and outpcd fnl 100yds* **12/1**[3]

542 **4** *3 ½* **Hedge End (IRE)**[30] 7350 3-8-7 **80** KieranO'Neill 2 79
(Richard Hannon) *chsd ldrs: effrt u.p over 2f out: 4th and outpcd jst over 1f out: one pce and wl hld fnl f* **20/1**

0346 **5** *1* **I'm Fraam Govan**[13] 7703 6-9-10 **92** (t) PatCosgrave 3 89
(George Baker) *hld up in tch in midfield: effrt over 2f out: no imp and n.m.r 2f out: wl hld and one pce fr over 1f out* **7/2**[2]

6405 **6** *½* **Flemish School**[15] 7662 4-9-5 **87** (v) JimCrowley 7 83
(David Elsworth) *hld up in tch in midfield: rdn and no rspnse over 2f out: no ch but plugged on past btn horses fnl f* **16/1**

6030 **7** *1 ¾* **Puzzle Time**[21] 7554 4-9-2 **84** WilliamCarson 6 77
(Giles Bravery) *in tch in midfield: unable qck u.p jst over 2f out: wknd over 1f out* **33/1**

-606 **8** *2 ¾* **King's Warrior (FR)**[16] 7641 7-9-6 **88** MartinHarley 5 77
(Peter Chapple-Hyam) *in tch in midfield: rdn and no hdwy jst over 2f out: wknd over 1f out* **14/1**

5/56 **9** *2 ½* **Stand To Reason (IRE)**[36] 7211 6-9-4 **86** (p) WilliamTwiston-Davies 9 70
(Tony Carroll) *hld up in rr: rdn and no hdwy over 2f out: n.d* **40/1**

1150 **10** *21* **Top Diktat**[21] 7545 6-8-12 **87** HectorCrouch(7) 10 36
(Gary Moore) *in tch in midfield: wd and lost pl bnd 3f out: lost tch 2f out: t.o* **33/1**

2m 17.73s (-4.17) **Going Correction** -0.10s/f (Stan)
**WFA** 3 from 4yo+ 5lb **10** Ran SP% **114.1**
Speed ratings (Par 107): **111,110,109,106,106 105,104,102,100,85**
CSF £7.18 CT £53.34 TOTE £2.80: £1.30, £1.30, £3.30; EX 8.50 Trifecta £54.60.
**Owner** Godolphin **Bred** Darley **Trained** Newmarket, Suffolk

**FOCUS**
A good-quality and competitive handicap. The pace suited those racing handily and the winner confirmed his Wolverhampton form.

## 7851 £25 FREE BET AT TITANBET.CO.UK H'CAP 7f (P)
**6:10** (6:10) (Class 2) (0-105,104) 3-Y-O+ **£11,827** (£3,541; £1,770; £664; £664; £222) **Stalls** Low

Form RPR
4400 **1** **Sirius Prospect (USA)**[12] 7715 6-9-9 103 JimCrowley 3 113
(Dean Ivory) *hld up in midfield: rdn and gd hdwy over 1f out: led ins fnl f: r.o strly* **11/4**[1]

1320 **2** *1 ½* **Plucky Dip**[19] 7600 3-8-1 85 oh6 DannyBrock(3) 4 90
(John Ryan) *chsd ldng trio: rdn to ld over 1f out: hdd ins fnl f: outpcd by wnr but kpt on for clr 2nd* **20/1**

1554 **3** *3 ¼* **Alejandro (IRE)**[21] 7555 5-9-3 97 DavidNolan 10 95
(David O'Meara) *chsd ldr after 2f: rdn and ev ch jst over 2f out: led over 1f out: sn hdd and no ex: outpcd but hld on for 3rd fnl f* **8/1**

1305 **4** *1* **Morache Music**[15] 7668 6-9-10 104 LukeMorris 6 99
(Peter Makin) *dwlt: hld up in tch in last trio: hdwy u.p on inner 2f out: r.o same pce and wl hld fnl f* **20/1**

-660 **4** *dht* **Modern Tutor**[12] 7715 5-8-9 89 DavidProbert 5 84
(Andrew Balding) *wnt lft s: stdd and hld up in rr: hdwy and nt clr run over 1f out: swtchd lft 1f out: styd on but no ch w wnr* **9/1**

0550 **6** *1 ½* **Kosika (USA)**[24] 7490 4-8-12 92 JoeFanning 2 85
(Mark Johnston) *led for 1f: chsd ldrs: nt clr run and bdly hmpd over 1f out: rdn 1f out: r.o same pce fnl f* **16/1**

1005 **7** *nk* **Roachdale House (IRE)**[12] 7715 3-8-7 88 GeorgeChaloner 1 77
(Richard Fahey) *in tch in midfield: rdn 2f out: drvn and no hdwy over 1f out: one pce and wl hld fnl f* **8/1**

140 **8** *5* **Grey Mirage**[47] 6921 5-9-2 103 KieranShoemark(7) 7 80
(Marco Botti) *in tch in midfield: lost pl u.p over 2f out: bhd over 1f out* **3/1**[2]

0055 **9** *1 ½* **Hasopop (IRE)**[21] 7555 4-9-7 101 MartinHarley 9 74
(Marco Botti) *hld up in last trio: rdn over 2f out: sn struggling: bhd over 1f out* **6/1**[3]

50 **10** *nk* **Swiss Cross**[21] 7555 7-8-13 93 (bt) StevieDonohoe 8 66
(Phil McEntee) *dwlt: rdn to rcvr and ld after 1f: drvn and hdd over 1f out: fdd fnl f* **33/1**

1m 23.1s (-2.90) **Going Correction** -0.10s/f (Stan) course record
**WFA** 3 from 4yo+ 1lb **10** Ran SP% **116.5**
Speed ratings (Par 109): **112,110,106,105,105 103,103,97,95,95**
CSF £61.40 CT £406.38 TOTE £3.50: £1.50, £2.20, £3.20; EX 78.50 Trifecta £527.40.
**Owner** Miss N Yarrow **Bred** Brookdale And Dr Ted Folkerth **Trained** Radlett, Herts

**FOCUS**
A strongly run handicap that produced a new course record time. The third rates a solid benchmark and the winner was close to his old best.

## 7852 BET AND WATCH AT TITANBET.CO.UK H'CAP 1m (P)
**6:40** (6:40) (Class 3) (0-90,90) 3-Y-O+ **£7,158** (£2,143; £1,071; £535; £267; £134) **Stalls** Low

Form RPR
1501 **1** **Unforgiving Minute**[29] 7375 3-9-5 90 AdamKirby 6 99+
(Clive Cox) *t.k.h: hld up in tch in midfield: rdn and hdwy to ld jst over 1f out: r.o wl: hld on cl home* **5/4**[1]

1111 **2** *nk* **Aqua Ardens (GER)**[53] 6789 6-9-4 87 (t) PatCosgrave 3 95
(George Baker) *hld up in midfield: clsd to chse ldrs whn nt clr run and swtchd lft 1f out: chsd wnr ins fnl f: r.o wl nt quite rch wnr* **20/1**

1354 **3** *1* **Outer Space**[15] 7663 3-9-2 87 WilliamTwiston-Davies 4 92
(Jamie Osborne) *stdd s: hld up in tch in rr: hdwy wdst over 1f out: str run ins fnl f: nt rch ldrs* **16/1**

0211 **4** *¾* **Geordan Murphy**[23] 7513 3-8-8 79 DavidProbert 11 82
(Andrew Balding) *in tch in last quartet: rdn 2f out: clsng whn sltly hmpd and swtchd lft 1f out: kpt on ins fnl f* **7/1**[3]

2512 **5** *1 ½* **Glorious Sun**[16] 7634 3-8-13 84 LukeMorris 5 84
(Ed Walker) *chsd ldrs: drvn to press ldr over 1f out tl unable qck jst over 1f out: wknd fnl 100yds* **15/2**

2305 **6** *nk* **Jodies Jem**[21] 7545 4-9-1 84 JoeFanning 7 84
(William Jarvis) *chsd ldng pair: effrt to chal 2f out: rdn to ld over 1f out: sn hdd: wknd fnl 100yds* **15/2**

6465 **7** *2* **Directorship**[102] 5213 8-9-3 86 LiamKeniry 10 82
(Patrick Chamings) *stdd s: hld up in tch in rr: rdn and hdwy jst over 1f out: no imp fnl 100yds* **20/1**

5104 **8** *nk* **Knight Owl**[21] 7545 4-9-3 86 GeorgeBaker 12 81
(James Fanshawe) *hld up in tch in midfield: swtchd lft and effrt over 2f out: no imp: kpt on same pce fnl f* **7/2**[2]

6210 **9** *2 ¼* **Whaleweigh Station**[48] 6895 3-9-3 88 PaulMulrennan 8 77
(J R Jenkins) *led: rdn 2f out: hdd over 1f out: wknd ins fnl f* **33/1**

2003 **10** *1 ¼* **Jack Of Diamonds (IRE)**[10] 7732 5-8-11 80 StevieDonohoe 9 67
(Roger Teal) *in tch in midfield: rdn over 2f out: sn outpcd: bhd over 1f out* **20/1**

4340 **11** *¾* **Nonno Giulio (IRE)**[124] 4447 3-9-0 85 HayleyTurner 2 69
(Simon Dow) *hld up in tch in midfield: rdn and no hdwy 2f out: bhd 1f out* **66/1**

410 **12** *1* **Ishikawa (IRE)**[159] 3244 6-8-13 85 JoeyHaynes(3) 1 68
(K R Burke) *chsd ldr tl 2f out: wknd u.p over 1f out* **20/1**

1m 37.66s (-2.14) **Going Correction** -0.10s/f (Stan)
**WFA** 3 from 4yo+ 2lb **12** Ran SP% **132.1**
Speed ratings (Par 107): **106,105,104,103,102 102,100,99,97,96 95,94**
CSF £40.52 CT £333.92 TOTE £2.60: £1.50, £3.60, £3.70; EX 43.60 Trifecta £377.40.
**Owner** P W Harris **Bred** Equine Breeding Ltd **Trained** Lambourn, Berks

**FOCUS**
Competitive stuff. There was a fair pace on and the form should work out. The unexposed winner progressed again.

## 7853 TITANBET H'CAP (DIV I) 1m (P)
**7:10** (7:11) (Class 6) (0-60,60) 3-Y-O+ **£1,940** (£577; £288; £144) **Stalls** Low

Form RPR
1262 **1** **Olivers Mount**[127] 4327 4-9-6 59 (t) LukeMorris 3 65
(Ed Vaughan) *hld up in tch: smooth hdwy to join ldr 2f out: rdn over 1f out: drvn to ld fnl 100yds: a doing enough: drvn out* **11/4**[1]

3661 **2** *nk* **Dreaming Again**[30] 7347 4-8-11 50 KieranO'Neill 1 55
(Jimmy Fox) *hld up in tch in midfield: effrt and carried rt over 1f out: str run ins fnl f: wnt 2nd cl home: nvr quite getting to wnr* **7/1**

1452 **3** *½* **Rocky's Pride (IRE)**[21] 7547 8-9-0 53 GeorgeChaloner 8 57
(Richard Whitaker) *led: jnd and rdn 2f out: battled on wl tl hdd fnl 100yds: styd on same pce towards fin* **7/2**[2]

1240 **4** *shd* **Cherry Princess**[66] 6396 4-9-3 56 MartinHarley 7 60
(Stuart Williams) *t.k.h: chsd ldrs: rdn 2f out: unable qck u.p over 1f out: kpt on u.p fnl 100yds* **6/1**[3]

0000 **5** *½* **Paradise Spectre**[10] 7735 7-9-7 60 (p) LiamKeniry 10 63
(Zoe Davison) *stdd s: hld up in tch in rr: clsd 2f out: drvn and effrt over 1f out: kpt on same pce ins fnl f* **33/1**

-603 **6** *¾* **Flumps**[21] 7546 5-8-2 46 oh1 (b) EoinWalsh(5) 2 47
(John Stimpson) *hld up in tch: hdwy on inner 2f out: styd on same pce u.p ins fnl f* **16/1**

0006 **7** *2* **Russian Ice**[13] 7704 6-9-5 58 (b) AdamKirby 9 54
(Dean Ivory) *in tch in midfield: rdn over 2f out: edging rt and no imp over 1f out: r.o same pce fnl f* **7/2**[2]

0-00 **8** *1* **Luna Sunrise**[127] 4329 3-9-2 57 BenCurtis 5 50
(Timothy Jarvis) *in tch towards rr: rdn and no imp over 2f out: no threat to ldrs but kpt on steadily ins fnl f* **33/1**

306- **9** *1* **Malih**[337] 8329 5-9-1 57 JoeyHaynes(3) 11 49
(Eric Wheeler) *chsd ldrs: rdn and effrt over 2f out: no ex over 1f out: wknd ins fnl f* **20/1**

000 **10** *1 ¾* **Boboli Gardens**[17] 7626 4-8-13 57 TobyAtkinson(5) 4 45
(Noel Quinlan) *stdd s: hld up in last trio: effrt wl over 1f out: no prog: n.d* **33/1**

000 **11** *26* **Zand Man**[30] 7349 4-8-7 46 oh1 (b[1]) JimmyQuinn 12
(Milton Bradley) *t.k.h: styd wd early: chsd ldr tl lost pl qckly over 1f out: t.o fnl f* **66/1**

1m 40.3s (0.50) **Going Correction** -0.10s/f (Stan)
**WFA** 3 from 4yo+ 2lb **11** Ran SP% **118.9**
Speed ratings (Par 101): **93,92,92,92,91 90,88,87,86,85 59**
CSF £21.74 CT £71.50 TOTE £3.00: £1.40, £2.20, £1.30; EX 21.20 Trifecta £59.10.
**Owner** A M Pickering **Bred** Mrs A D Bourne **Trained** Newmarket, Suffolk

■ Stewards' Enquiry : Kieran O'Neill four-day ban: used whip above permitted level (Dec 4-6,8)

**FOCUS**
An ordinary handicap. There was a bunch finish but the form looks solid for the class.

## 7854 TITANBET H'CAP (DIV II) 1m (P)
7:40 (7:40) (Class 6) (0-60,60) 3-Y-0+ £1,940 (£577; £288; £144) Stalls Low

Form RPR

005 **1** **Barbary (IRE)**[71] 6243 3-9-2 57 MartinLane 1 63
(Charlie Fellowes) *hld up in tch: effrt u.p over 1f out: led 1f out: styd on wl: drvn out* 9/4[1]

6322 **2** *nk* **Carrera**[16] 7632 4-8-8 54 ChrisMeehan(7) 9 60
(Michael Blanshard) *stdd s: hld up in tch in last pair: rdn and hdwy over 1f out: styd on wl to chse wnr wl ins fnl f: hld cl home* 5/1[3]

5000 **3** *nk* **Bowsers Bold**[22] 7527 3-8-13 54 ShaneKelly 12 58
(Marcus Tregoning) *stdd s: t.k.h: hld up in tch in last pair: clsd on outer 2f out: rdn jst over 1f out: kpt on to go 3rd wl ins fnl f* 20/1

0600 **4** *3/4* **Little Indian**[7] 7765 4-9-5 58 JoeFanning 11 62
(J R Jenkins) *in tch in midfield: hdwy u.p over 1f out: pressing ldrs ins fnl f: one pce fnl 100yds* 16/1

5004 **5** *nk* **Sebs Sensei (IRE)**[30] 7347 3-9-4 59 (b) RobertHavlin 3 61
(Mark Hoad) *hld up in tch towards rr: hdwy u.p over 1f out: kpt on same pce fnl 100yds* 8/1

2330 **6** *1* **Jackpot**[26] 7456 4-8-7 46 oh1 HayleyTurner 2 47
(Brendan Powell) *in tch in midfield: effrt on inner 2f out: drvn and pressing ldrs over 1f out: no ex and outpcd fnl 100yds* 20/1

5006 **7** *1* **Ambella (IRE)**[32] 7303 4-9-4 57 (v) StevieDonohoe 10 55
(Ian Williams) *chsd ldrs: rdn to chse ldr 2f out tl jst over 1f out: wknd fnl 100yds* 5/1[3]

50-0 **8** *3/4* **Crowning Star (IRE)**[30] 7347 5-9-5 58 (t) SeanLevey 7 55
(Steve Woodman) *sn led: set stdy gallop: rdn and qcknd jst over 2f out: hdd 1f out: wknd ins fnl f* 33/1

060 **9** *1/2* **L Ge R**[15] 7664 3-8-5 46 oh1 JimmyQuinn 8 40
(Peter Charalambous) *hld up in tch in last trio: effrt over 2f out: r.o same pce and no imp fr over 1f out* 33/1

2222 **10** *2* **El Mirage (IRE)**[13] 7704 4-9-7 60 (p) JimCrowley 4 51
(Dean Ivory) *t.k.h: chsd ldr tl 1/2-way: rdn 2f out: wknd fnl f* 3/1[2]

54-0 **11** *hd* **Hija**[16] 7632 3-8-7 48 LukeMorris 5 37
(Rod Millman) *chsd ldrs: wnt 2nd 1/2-way tl 2f out: lost pl over 1f out: wknd fnl f* 20/1

0000 **12** *1 1/2* **Mack's Sister**[50] 6851 7-8-7 46 oh1 WilliamCarson 6 33
(Michael Madgwick) *in tch in midfield: rdn over 2f out: no ex 2f out: lost pl and bhd 1f out* 50/1

1m 40.19s (0.39) **Going Correction** -0.10s/f (Stan)
**WFA** 3 from 4yo+ 2lb 12 Ran SP% 128.2
Speed ratings (Par 101): **94,93,93,92,92 91,90,89,89,87 86,85**
CSF £13.83 CT £197.49 TOTE £3.70: £1.60, £1.60, £5.60; EX 19.20 Trifecta £224.20.
**Owner** Graham Mills **Bred** Brinkley Stud, Ficomontanino, Bego Blu **Trained** Newmarket, Suffolk
■ Stewards' Enquiry : Chris Meehan four-day ban: used whip in incorrect place (Dec 6,8,9,11)
Martin Lane two-day ban: used whip above permitted level (Dec 4-5)

**FOCUS**
This second and slightly quicker division of the moderate 1m handicap saw a muddling finish with plenty involved. A minor best from the winner.
T/Jkpt: £4,342.90 to a £1 stake. Pool: £33642.42 - 5.50 winning tickets. T/Plt: £172.20 to a £1 stake. Pool of £89566.42 - 379.48 winning tickets. T/Qpdt: £147.00 to a £1 stake. Pool of £9738.78 - 49.0 winning tickets. SP

# 1207 FONTAINEBLEAU
Thursday, November 20
**OFFICIAL GOING: Turf: very soft**

## 7855a PRIX ZEDDAAN (LISTED RACE) (2YO) (TURF) 6f
1:20 (12:00) 2-Y-0 £22,916 (£9,166; £6,875; £4,583; £2,291)

RPR

**1** **Biraaj (IRE)**[26] 7468 2-8-11 0 AntoineHamelin 7 98
(Matthieu Palussiere, France) 68/10

**2** *1* **El Valle (FR)**[41] 7094 2-8-13 0 ow2 ChristopheSoumillon 2 97
(Mlle V Dissaux, France) 9/1

**3** *1 1/4* **Finsbury Square (IRE)**[20] 2-8-11 0 CristianDemuro 6 91
(F Chappet, France) 9/2[3]

**4** *3/4* **Kindly Dismiss (FR)**[41] 7094 2-8-8 0 FabriceVeron 4 86
(H-A Pantall, France) 105/10

**5** *1* **Svoul (FR)**[95] 5478 2-8-11 0 OlivierPeslier 1 86
(F-H Graffard, France) 68/10

**6** *3/4* **Something Lucky (IRE)**[25] 7485 2-8-11 0 TomEaves 5 84
(Kristin Stubbs) *t.k.h: trckd ldrs: rdn and nt qckn 1 1/2f out: edgd lft over 1f out: wknd ins fnl f* 42/10[2]

**7** *1 3/4* **Fligaz (FR)**[20] 7563 2-8-8 0 MaximeGuyon 3 76
(Martyn Meade) *w.w in fnl trio: rdn and effrt on outer over 1 1/2f out: wknd ins fnl f* 8/5[1]

1m 12.0s (72.00) 7 Ran SP% 120.2
PARI-MUTUEL (all including 1 euro stake): WIN 7.80 PLACE 4.10, 4.60 SF 57.90.
**Owner** Zalim Bifov **Bred** Mrs E Bifova **Trained** France

## 7856a PRIX CONTESSINA (LISTED RACE) (3YO+) (TURF) 6f
1:50 (12:00) 3-Y-0+ £21,666 (£8,666; £5,416; £5,416; £2,166)

RPR

**1** **Inspiriter**[45] 6994 3-8-8 0 AntoineWerle 2 100
(H-A Pantall, France) *w.w in tch: rdn to chse ldrs over 1f out: r.o to ld last 80yds: drvn out* 36/1

**2** *1 1/2* **Guinnevre (IRE)**[11] 7725 4-8-13 0 CristianDemuro 7 100
(G Botti, France) 194/10

**3** *shd* **Revedargent (FR)**[22] 3-8-8 0 FabriceVeron 11 95
(H-A Pantall, France) 172/10

**3** *dht* **Dani Wallon (FR)**[32] 7327 3-8-11 0 StephanePasquier 14 98
(C Delcher-Sanchez, France) 127/10

**5** *3/4* **Fanny (FR)**[30] 4-8-8 0 FranckBlondel 12 92
(F Rossi, France) 36/5

**6** *3/4* **Spinatrix**[12] 7716 6-8-8 0 (p) ConnorBeasley 4 90
(Michael Dods) *chsd ldrs: n.m.r between horses 1 1/2f out and snatched up and lost pl: styd on u.p fnl f* 48/10[2]

**7** *hd* **Kolonel (GER)**[16] 7656 5-8-13 0 ow2 ChristopheSoumillon 9 94
(Mario Hofer, Germany) 89/10

**8** *hd* **Robert Le Diable (FR)**[16] 7656 5-8-11 0 MaximeGuyon 5 92
(D Prod'Homme, France) 7/2[1]

**9** *hd* **Catcall (FR)**[16] 7656 5-9-6 0 OlivierPeslier 16 100
(P Sogorb, France) 5/1[3]

**10** *1/2* **Quirinus**[17] 7-8-11 0 (p) DelphineSantiago 6 90
(S Smrczek, Germany) 26/1

**11** *3/4* **Aksil (FR)**[16] 7656 4-8-8 0 GregoryBenoist 13 84
(M Boutin, France) 247/10

**12** *3/4* **Kilava (FR)**[17] 3-8-8 0 NicolasLarenaudie 3 82
(T Clout, France) 269/10

**13** *1/2* **Murcielago (GER)**[17] 7-8-11 0 EddyHardouin 15 83
(M Keller, Germany) 62/1

**14** *hd* **Silver Treasure (FR)**[19] 7600 3-8-11 0 AlexandreRoussel 10 83
(Amy Weaver) *racd in fnl trio: last and outpcd 2f out: kpt on u.p fnl f: nvr in contention* 32/1

**15** *1 1/2* **Fanoos**[16] 7656 5-8-8 0 (p) MickaelForest 8 75
(Mme G Rarick, France) 108/1

**16** *20* **Chief Hawkeye (IRE)**[16] 5-8-11 0 AnthonyCrastus 1 14
(J-V Toux, France) 29/1

1m 11.8s (71.80) 16 Ran SP% 118.9
PARI-MUTUEL (all including 1 euro stake): WIN 36.50 PLACE 10.40, 6.60, 2.90 (Dani Wallon), 3.40 (Revedargent) DF 248.90 SF 500.00.
**Owner** Godolphin SNC **Bred** Darley **Trained** France

## 7857a PRIX CERES (LISTED RACE) (3YO FILLIES) (TURF) 7f
2:20 (12:00) 3-Y-0 £22,916 (£9,166; £6,875; £4,583; £2,291)

RPR

**1** **Kalsa (IRE)**[34] 7268 3-9-0 0 RonanThomas 8 102
(Robert Collet, France) 36/1

**2** *3/4* **Paola Lisa (FR)**[22] 3-9-0 0 ThierryThulliez 11 100
(N Clement, France) 79/10[3]

**3** *3/4* **Winshine (FR)**[22] 3-9-0 0 DelphineSantiago 3 98
(S Smrczek, Germany) 142/10

**4** *1 3/4* **Nakuti (IRE)**[21] 7553 3-9-0 0 MaximeGuyon 13 93
(Sylvester Kirk) *w.w in midfield on outer: hdwy 2f out: styd on fnl f: nt pce to rch ldrs* 27/1

**5** *1 1/2* **Divina Comedia (FR)**[34] 7268 3-9-0 0 StephanePasquier 9 89
(N Clement, France) 6/1[1]

**6** *3/4* **Source D'Honneur (FR)**[152] 3-9-0 0 ThomasHenderson 2 87
(D De Watrigant, France) 145/10

**7** *hd* **Witches Brew (IRE)**[25] 7474 3-9-0 0 GregoryBenoist 5 87
(Edward Lynam, Ire) *trckd ldrs: 4th and ev ch 2 1/2f out: scrubbed along and nt qckn 1 1/2f out: one pce u.p fnl f* 7/1[2]

**8** *snk* **Graceful Grit (IRE)**[12] 7720 3-9-0 0 AntoineHamelin 6 86
(F-H Graffard, France) 167/10

**9** *3* **Jusquiame Noire (IRE)**[67] 3-9-0 0 ChristopheSoumillon 16 78
(Y Gourraud, France) 83/10

**10** *3/4* **Onirique (IRE)**[404] 3-9-0 0 ThierryJarnet 12 76
(X Nakkachdji, France) 211/10

**11** *hd* **Iveagh Gardens (IRE)**[25] 7483 3-9-0 0 FMBerry 15 76
(Charles O'Brien, Ire) *towards rr: rdn and effrt over 1 1/2f out: no further imp sn after: one pce fnl f* 87/10

**12** *shd* **Tender Emotion**[25] 7483 3-9-0 0 AntoineWerle 4 75
(H-A Pantall, France) *cl up on inner: 3rd and rdn 2 1/2f out: sn no imp: wknd fr over 1f out* 46/1

**13** *1 3/4* **La Petite Maison (FR)**[40] 3-9-0 0 PaulineProd'homme 1 71
(D Prod'Homme, France) 195/10

**14** *nk* **Zylpha (IRE)**[17] 3-9-0 0 (b) FabriceVeron 17 70
(H-A Pantall, France) 243/10

**15** *shd* **Raceness (FR)**[16] 3-9-0 0 TheoBachelot 14 70
(S Wattel, France) 28/1

**16** *snk* **Zakiyyah (FR)**[74] 3-9-0 0 OlivierPeslier 18 69
(N Clement, France) 103/10

**17** *nk* **Graciously**[12] 7722 3-9-0 0 EddyHardouin 10 68
(A De Royer-Dupre, France) 179/10

**18** *1 3/4* **Moonvoy**[47] 6922 3-9-0 0 IoritzMendizabal 7 64
(Jeremy Noseda) *midfield: rdn over 2f out but no imp: wknd over 1f out: eased whn btn fnl f* 46/1

1m 32.7s (92.70) 18 Ran SP% 119.2
PARI-MUTUEL (all including 1 euro stake): WIN 36.70 PLACE 11.80, 3.10, 4.80 DF 209.10 SF 455.80.
**Owner** James Anthony Oldham **Bred** Citadel Stud **Trained** Chantilly, France

# 7815 WOLVERHAMPTON (A.W) (L-H)
Friday, November 21
**OFFICIAL GOING: Tapeta: standard**
Wind: Light across Weather: Raining

## 7864 £20 RISK-FREE BET AT UNIBET APPRENTICE H'CAP (TAPETA) 5f 216y
4:10 (4:10) (Class 6) (0-60,60) 3-Y-0+ £2,102 (£625; £312; £156) Stalls Low

Form RPR

0655 **1** **Spowarticus**[95] 5499 5-8-2 46 (v) RussellHarris(5) 8 64
(Scott Dixon) *mde all: clr 1/2-way: rdn over 1f out: styd on* 6/1

6430 **2** *4 1/2* **Little Choosey**[106] 5071 4-8-7 46 oh1 (bt[1]) AaronJones 9 50
(Roy Bowring) *a.p: chsd wnr 2f out: rdn over 1f out: edgd lft and styd on same pce fnl f* 12/1

0001 **3** *nk* **Insolenceofoffice (IRE)**[7] 7782 6-9-0 60 6ex (p) NicolaGrundy(7) 4 63
(Richard Ford) *hld up: hdwy over 1f out: nt rch ldrs* 3/1[1]

0404 **4** *1/2* **Foie Gras**[136] 4050 4-9-1 59 ThomasHemsley(5) 6 60
(Chris Dwyer) *s.i.s: hld up: hdwy over 1f out: nrst fin* 20/1

0031 **5** *2* **Synonym (ITY)**[9] 7737 3-9-3 56 6ex GaryMahon 7 51+
(Michael Appleby) *s.s: hld up: hdwy over 1f out: sn rdn: nt rch ldrs* 11/2[3]

056 **6** *1/2* **Studfarmer**[83] 5907 4-8-3 47 oh1 ow1 (p) Leah-AnneAvery(5) 5 40
(Polly Gundry) *prom: nt clr run and lost pl over 2f out: n.d after* 50/1

-000 **7** *1 1/2* **Forzarzi (IRE)**[78] 6077 10-8-3 47 HarryBurns(5) 13 35
(John David Riches) *hld up: rdn over 1f out: nvr nrr* 66/1

-055 **8** *3/4* **Sannibel**[9] 7737 6-8-9 48 (p) ChrisMeehan 10 34
(David Bridgwater) *prom: rdn over 1f out: wknd fnl f* 7/1

3/40 **9** *1 3/4* **Lucky Royale**[37] 7191 6-8-6 52 AlfieDavies(7) 3 32
(Jeremy Gask) *mid-div: wknd over 1f out* 22/1



The Form Book, Raceform Ltd, Newbury, RG14 5SJ

0500 **10** *2* **Picnic In The Glen**[22] 7548 3-8-3 49 oh1 ow3......... JackDinsmore(7) 12 23
(Sylvester Kirk) *chsd wnr tl over 4f out: wnt 2nd again briefly over 2f out: wknd over 1f out* **66/1**

5416 **11** *hd* **Methaaly (IRE)**[18] 7622 11-9-0 60..............................(b) LewisStones(7) 2 33
(Michael Mullineaux) *mid-div: wknd 2f out* **11/1**

0000 **12** *3* **Salvado (IRE)**[31] 7347 4-9-5 58...............................(t) RobHornby 1 22
(Tony Carroll) *s.i.s: hdwy to chse wnr over 4f out tl over 2f out: sn wknd* **4/1**[2]

1m 14.1s (-0.40) **Going Correction** -0.10s/f (Stan) **12 Ran SP% 117.3**
Speed ratings (Par 101): **98,92,91,90,88 87,85,84,82,79 79,75**
CSF £70.57 CT £258.27 TOTE £7.50: £2.10, £4.00, £1.30; EX 90.80 Trifecta £867.20.
**Owner** Paul J Dixon **Bred** Mrs Yvette Dixon **Trained** Babworth, Notts

**FOCUS**
An ordinary apprentice handicap in which very few featured and it paid to race handy. The winner scored in a fast time and showed much improved form.

## 7865 UNIBET OFFER DAILY JOCKEY/TRAINER SPECIALS MAIDEN STKS (TAPETA) 5f 216y
**4:40** (4:40) (Class 5) 3-4-Y-0 **£2,587** (£770; £384; £192) **Stalls** Low

Form RPR

32-6 **1** **Mukaynis (IRE)**[56] 3-9-0 63.............................. ShaneGray(5) 4 75
(Kevin Ryan) *hld up in tch: rdn over 2f out: chsd ldr over 1f out: styd on to ld and edgd lft wl ins fnl f* **5/6**[1]

0533 **2** *½* **Silver Mirage**[14] 7699 3-9-1 63 ow1............................ AdamKirby 5 69
(Michael Bell) *sn led: rdn: hung lft and hdd wl ins fnl f* **3/1**[3]

5243 **3** *2* **Blue Bounty**[7] 7776 3-9-5 65..............................(b) JimmyQuinn 8 67
(Mark H Tompkins) *hld up: hdwy over 2f out: rdn over 1f out: styd on same pce ins fnl f* **5/2**[2]

43 **4** *5* **Saved My Bacon (IRE)**[17] 7652 3-8-11 0............... ConnorBeasley(3) 3 46
(Chris Dwyer) *chsd ldrs: wnt 2nd over 2f out tl rdn over 1f out: wknd ins fnl f* **20/1**

0666 **5** *½* **Aussie Sky (IRE)**[69] 6340 3-9-0 46........................ StevieDonohoe 9 44
(Daniel Mark Loughnane) *plld hrd: trckd ldr tl over 2f out: rdn and wknd over 1f out* **33/1**

50 **6** *5* **Prominna**[15] 7682 4-9-5 0.......................................... LukeMorris 7 33
(Tony Carroll) *hld up: pushed along over 2f out: nvr on terms* **20/1**

0500 **7** *1* **Ellingham (IRE)**[30] 7376 3-9-0 46..............................(v[1]) ChrisCatlin 2 25
(Christine Dunnett) *sn pushed along in rr: bhd fr 1/2-way* **50/1**

00 **8** *8* **Wattaboutsteve**[14] 7699 3-9-5 0............................... JoeFanning 6 4
(Ralph J Smith) *prom tl wknd 2f out* **40/1**

1m 14.01s (-0.49) **Going Correction** -0.10s/f (Stan) **8 Ran SP% 125.0**
Speed ratings (Par 103): **99,98,95,89,88 81,80,69**
CSF £4.00 TOTE £1.90: £1.10, £1.40, £1.10; EX 4.80 Trifecta £7.70.
**Owner** Mubarak Al Naemi **Bred** Peter & Ann Gibbons & Derek Gibbons **Trained** Hambleton, N Yorks
■ Stewards' Enquiry : Jimmy Quinn trainers representative said gelding was struck into
Stevie Donohoe one-day ban; did not keep mount straight leaving stalls (5th Dec)

**FOCUS**
Probably no more than an ordinary maiden in which the first three home who are all rated in the sixties and are exposed sorts, dominated the market as well as the race. The winner was back to something like his best.

## 7866 32RED H'CAP (TAPETA) 1m 5f 194y
**5:15** (5:16) (Class 5) (0-75,73) 3-Y-O+ **£2,749** (£818; £408; £204) **Stalls** Low

Form RPR

0131 **1** **Topaling**[31] 7360 3-8-4 57.......................................... JimmyQuinn 10 66
(Mark H Tompkins) *hld up: nt clr run over 2f out: rdn: hdwy and hung lft fr over 1f out: styd on to ld wl ins fnl f* **8/1**[3]

0-15 **2** *¾* **Watt Broderick (IRE)**[29] 848 5-9-12 71................ StevieDonohoe 9 79
(Ian Williams) *hld up: hdwy over 1f out: sn rdn: styd on* **9/2**[2]

2056 **3** *1¾* **Lineman**[42] 7072 4-9-10 69..............................(p) ShaneKelly 5 75
(Andrew Hollinshead) *hld up: hdwy on outer over 2f out: rdn and ev ch ins fnl f: styd on same pce* **12/1**

2562 **4** *hd* **Quenelle**[11] 7734 3-9-2 69.................................. PaulMulrennan 3 74
(Ed Dunlop) *hld up: hdwy on outer over 3f out: chsd ldr over 2f out: led over 1f out: rdn and hdd wl ins fnl f* **9/4**[1]

0545 **5** *¾* **Lady Of Yue**[38] 7182 4-9-3 62.................................. RobertTart 8 66
(Eugene Stanford) *chsd ldrs: rdn and ev ch over 1f out: no ex ins fnl f* **8/1**[3]

3652 **6** *3¼* **Angus Glens**[7] 7777 4-9-0 59..............................(p) FergusSweeney 2 59
(David Dennis) *led: rdn and hdd over 1f out: wknd ins fnl f* **10/1**

021 **7** *2¾* **Aneedh**[59] 6622 4-9-11 70..............................(b) PJMcDonald 7 66
(Clive Mulhall) *hld up: rdn over 1f out: nt trble ldrs* **33/1**

-130 **8** *4½* **Devon Drum**[23] 7531 6-10-0 73...................... WilliamTwiston-Davies 11 63
(Paul Webber) *hld up in tch: rdn and nt clr run over 2f out: wknd over 1f out* **11/1**

2120 **9** *1¾* **Saint Thomas (IRE)**[38] 7182 7-9-7 66.................. GrahamGibbons 1 53
(John Mackie) *chsd ldr tl rdn over 2f out: wknd over 1f out* **22/1**

0606 **10** *3¼* **Ascendant**[43] 5137 8-9-8 70..............................(v) DannyBrock(3) 4 53
(Andrew Reid) *prom: rdn over 3f out: wknd over 1f out* **20/1**

5403 **11** *2½* **Flying Cape (IRE)**[18] 7628 3-8-11 64...................(tp) TomEaves 12 43
(Andrew Hollinshead) *sn chsng ldrs: rdn over 2f out: wknd over 1f out* **10/1**

3m 1.44s (-3.36) **Going Correction** -0.10s/f (Stan)
**WFA** 3 from 4yo+ 8lb **11 Ran SP% 117.4**
Speed ratings (Par 103): **105,104,103,103,103 101,99,97,96,94 92**
CSF £42.73 CT £436.51 TOTE £8.10: £2.10, £2.00, £3.00; EX 58.70 Trifecta £295.50.
**Owner** M P Bowring **Bred** Dullingham Park Stud & M P Bowring **Trained** Newmarket, Suffolk
■ Stewards' Enquiry : Jimmy Quinn two-day ban; used whip above permitted level (5th-6th Dec)

**FOCUS**
No more than a fair gallop to this ordinary staying handicap but the main protagonists came from off the pace. The winner progressed again.

## 7867 32RED.COM MAIDEN AUCTION STKS (TAPETA) 7f 32y
**5:50** (5:52) (Class 6) 2-Y-O **£2,264** (£673; £336; £168) **Stalls** High

Form RPR

03 **1** **Oracolo (IRE)**[17] 7638 2-8-13 0................................ TomEaves 12 75+
(David Simcock) *pushed along in rr early: hdwy on outer over 2f out: jnd ldr 1f out: edgd lft and styd on u.p to ld post* **9/2**[2]

53 **2** *shd* **Cape Cay**[164] 3082 2-8-8 0.................................. GrahamGibbons 5 70+
(Ralph Beckett) *a.p: rdn to ld and edgd lft ins fnl f: n.m.r after: hdd post* **5/2**[1]

3303 **3** *2½* **Chicago Bere (FR)**[37] 7200 2-8-13 69...................... KieranO'Neill 6 69
(Richard Hannon) *chsd ldrs: rdn to ld over 1f out: hdd ins fnl f: styd on same pce* **6/1**[3]

0 **4** *1* **Colourfilly**[28] 7407 2-8-8 0.......................................... LukeMorris 11 62
(Ed Walker) *mid-div: pushed along and hdwy over 2f out: rdn over 1f out: styd on same pce ins fnl f* **13/2**

2004 **5** *2¾* **Chefchaouen (IRE)**[17] 7631 2-7-13 0................. JosephineGordon(7) 4 53
(J S Moore) *w ldr tl led over 2f out: rdn and hdd over 1f out: wknd ins fnl f* **33/1**

**6** *hd* **Charlton Heights (IRE)** 2-8-11 0............................... LiamJones 10 57+
(J S Moore) *sn pushed along in rr: hdwy over 1f out: nt trble ldrs* **66/1**

**7** *2¾* **Thermal Column (IRE)** 2-8-13 0.............................. TonyHamilton 9 53
(Richard Fahey) *s.s: nvr nrr* **25/1**

020 **8** *2¼* **Rennie Mackintosh (IRE)**[9] 7741 2-8-11 0................. JoeFanning 1 45
(Mark Johnston) *chsd ldrs: nt clr run over 2f out: wknd over 1f out* **16/1**

00 **9** *5* **Misu Pete**[15] 7685 2-8-11 0.................................... RobertHavlin 8 33
(Mark Usher) *mid-div: pushed along 1/2-way: wknd over 2f out* **100/1**

6 **10** *6* **Kinnara**[6] 7808 2-8-8 0.......................................... LiamKeniry 7 15
(Sylvester Kirk) *prom tl rdn and wknd 2f out* **10/1**

0 **11** *4½* **Signs And Signals (IRE)**[104] 5187 2-8-10 0............ FergusSweeney 3 6
(Ed Vaughan) *s.s: a in rr: bhd fr 1/2-way* **20/1**

**12** *4* **Kyrenia Castle (GER)** 2-9-1 0.................................. SeanLevey 2
(Richard Hannon) *led over 4f: wknd wl over 1f out* **7/1**

1m 28.09s (-0.71) **Going Correction** -0.10s/f (Stan) **12 Ran SP% 115.9**
Speed ratings (Par 94): **100,99,97,95,92 92,89,86,81,74 69,64**
CSF £14.95 TOTE £5.20: £2.00, £1.60, £2.70; EX 17.70 Trifecta £84.40.
**Owner** Ali Saeed **Bred** Jeddah Bloodstock **Trained** Newmarket, Suffolk
■ Stewards' Enquiry : Tom Eaves three-day ban; used whip above permitted level (6th-8th Dec)

**FOCUS**
A race lacking in strength but a decent gallop and fair form from the first two.

## 7868 CORAL.CO.UK H'CAP (TAPETA) (DIV I) 1m 1f 103y
**6:20** (6:21) (Class 6) (0-60,59) 3-Y-O+ **£2,102** (£625; £312; £156) **Stalls** Low

Form RPR

0200 **1** **Sarlat**[34] 7292 3-8-2 46.......................................... AmyScott(3) 11 54
(Mark Brisbourne) *hld up: hdwy on outer over 2f out: led ins fnl f: r.o* **16/1**

0231 **2** *nk* **City Of Angkor Wat (IRE)**[55] 6771 4-9-0 59.......(t) JoshuaBrowning(7) 6 66+
(Jo Hughes) *a.p: rdn to ld over 1f out: shkn up ins fnl f: r.o* **15/8**[1]

4440 **3** *nk* **Snow Dancer (IRE)**[60] 6597 10-8-8 49................. ConnorBeasley(3) 5 55
(John David Riches) *hld up: hdwy and nt clr run over 1f out: r.o* **15/2**

0424 **4** *2* **Stanlow**[34] 7292 4-9-5 57..............................(p) ShaneKelly 10 59
(Daniel Mark Loughnane) *hld up: hdwy on outer over 2f out: led over 1f out: rdn and hdd ins fnl f: styd on same pce* **7/2**[2]

4104 **5** *1¾* **Poor Duke (IRE)**[6] 7813 4-9-5 57............................. RobertHavlin 4 55
(Michael Mullineaux) *chsd ldrs: rdn over 3f out: ev ch over 1f out: no ex ins fnl f* **9/2**[3]

0004 **6** *2* **Flying Applause**[17] 7646 9-8-2 45..............................(bt) EoinWalsh(5) 2 39
(Roy Bowring) *s.s: hld up: rdn over 1f out: nvr on terms* **50/1**

5116 **7** *hd* **Catching Zeds**[156] 1428 7-9-1 53..............................(b) StevieDonohoe 3 47
(Kevin Frost) *s.i.s: sn pushed along into mid-div: rdn over 3f out: nvr trbld ldrs* **25/1**

0030 **8** *1¼* **Hickster (IRE)**[14] 7704 3-9-3 58.............................. JimmyQuinn 8 49
(Mandy Rowland) *chsd ldrs: rdn over 3f out: wknd fnl f* **28/1**

2205 **9** *7* **Tukitinyasok (IRE)**[100] 5300 7-9-3 55...................... GeorgeChaloner 1 31
(Clive Mulhall) *led: rdn and hdd over 2f out: wknd fnl f* **22/1**

2040 **10** *5* **Perseverent Pete (USA)**[7] 7785 4-8-9 47................ LukeMorris 7 13
(Christine Dunnett) *chsd ldr tl rdn to ld over 2f out: hdd over 1f out: sn wknd* **28/1**

205 **11** *½* **With Hindsight (IRE)**[36] 7219 6-9-4 56.................... ChrisCatlin 9 21
(John Spearing) *hld up: rdn over 3f out: sn wknd* **16/1**

2m 0.18s (-0.62) **Going Correction** -0.10s/f (Stan)
**WFA** 3 from 4yo+ 3lb **11 Ran SP% 115.8**
Speed ratings (Par 101): **98,97,97,95,94 92,92,91,84,80 79**
CSF £43.24 CT £261.19 TOTE £17.00: £4.70, £1.10, £2.30; EX 71.20 Trifecta £544.00.
**Owner** The Bourne Connection **Bred** Mr & Mrs J Laws **Trained** Great Ness, Shropshire

**FOCUS**
A medium gallop to a low-grade handicap which didn't take a great deal of winning as few came into it in much form. A 4lb best from the winner.

## 7869 CORAL.CO.UK H'CAP (TAPETA) (DIV II) 1m 1f 103y
**6:50** (6:50) (Class 6) (0-60,59) 3-Y-O+ **£2,102** (£625; £312; £156) **Stalls** Low

Form RPR

6030 **1** **Triple Star**[24] 7517 3-8-12 53.................................. HayleyTurner 2 63
(Hughie Morrison) *hld up and bhd: hdwy over 1f out: shkn up and edgd lft ins fnl f: styd on to ld post* **14/1**

0620 **2** *hd* **My Renaissance**[35] 7256 4-8-10 53......................... JackDuern(5) 9 62
(Ben Case) *hld up: hdwy on outer over 3f out: led over 2f out: rdn ins fnl f: hdd post* **25/1**

5543 **3** *2* **Brown Pete (IRE)**[17] 7635 6-8-7 45..............................(p) CharlesBishop 4 49
(Ann Stokell) *chsd ldr tl over 6f out: remained handy: rdn over 1f out: styd on same pce ins fnl f* **11/2**[3]

4224 **4** *nk* **Royal Mizar (SPA)**[67] 6394 4-8-8 49..................... ConnorBeasley(3) 10 53
(Ralph J Smith) *a.p: rdn and ev ch 2f out: no ex ins fnl f* **10/1**

0000 **5** *1¾* **Dutch Lady Roseane**[7] 7785 3-8-5 46......................... LiamJones 3 46
(James Unett) *s.i.s: sn pushed along into mid-div: n.m.r and lost pl over 3f out: rallied and edgd lft ins fnl f: styd on* **100/1**

0600 **6** *1* **Yourinthewill (USA)**[28] 7426 6-9-5 57........................ ShaneKelly 6 55
(Daniel Mark Loughnane) *prom: rdn over 1f out: hung lft and no ex ins fnl f* **2/1**[1]

3310 **7** *1½* **Lola Montez (IRE)**[28] 7426 3-9-3 58..............................(b) GeorgeBaker 11 53
(David Lanigan) *hld up: hdwy on outer over 2f out: rdn and hung lft fr over 1f out: nt run on* **5/1**[2]

1650 **8** *2¼* **Elle Rebelle**[6] 7813 4-9-5 57...................................... LukeMorris 1 47
(Mark Brisbourne) *s.i.s: hld up: shkn up over 1f out: nvr on terms* **14/1**

2400 **9** *½* **Merchant Of Medici**[60] 6597 7-9-7 59........................ PJMcDonald 5 48
(Micky Hammond) *chsd ldrs: rdn over 3f out: wknd over 1f out* **16/1**

0122 **10** *6* **Les Gar Gan (IRE)**[22] 7541 3-9-4 59.......................... JoeFanning 7 35
(Keith Dalgleish) *led: rdn and hdd over 2f out: wknd fnl f* **11/2**[3]

5003 **11** *2* **Eium Mac**[17] 7639 5-8-5 46..............................(b) JacobButterfield(3) 8 18
(Neville Bycroft) *trckd ldrs: plld hrd: wnt 2nd over 6f out tl rdn wl over 2f out: wknd over 1f out* **18/1**

2m 0.04s (-0.76) **Going Correction** -0.10s/f (Stan)
**WFA** 3 from 4yo+ 3lb **11 Ran SP% 119.2**
Speed ratings (Par 101): **99,98,97,96,95 94,93,91,90,85 83**
CSF £319.62 CT £2207.91 TOTE £13.60: £2.50, £6.90, £3.00; EX 276.80 Trifecta £1523.80 Part won..
**Owner** Lady Hardy **Bred** Lady Hardy **Trained** East Ilsley, Berks

**FOCUS**
Mainly exposed sorts in a moderate handicap. The gallop was sound and the first two finished a few lengths clear. the winner ties in with division I form.

## 7870 CORAL H'CAP (TAPETA) 1m 1f 103y
**7:20** (7:20) (Class 4) (0-85,85) 3-Y-0+ **£4,851** (£1,443; £721; £360) **Stalls** Low

Form RPR
3314 1 **Dream Child (IRE)**[28] 7416 3-8-13 **80** PhillipMakin 8 91
(Charlie Appleby) *led 1f: chsd ldrs: led again over 1f out: hdd ins fnl f: rallied to ld towards fin* **11/10**[1]
1-05 2 *shd* **Ghazi (IRE)**[17] 7634 3-8-5 **79** (p) KieranShoemark(7) 7 89
(Saeed bin Suroor) *hld up: hdwy on outer over 2f out: jnd wnr over 1f out: rdn to ld ins fnl f: hdd towards fin* **7/2**[2]
0340 3 *1 1/2* **Patriotic (IRE)**[21] 7567 6-8-12 **79** (p) ConnorBeasley(3) 6 86
(Chris Dwyer) *hld up: hdwy over 1f out: r.o: nt rch ldrs* **25/1**
0100 4 *3/4* **Chapter And Verse (IRE)**[23] 7531 8-9-2 **80** ShaneKelly 1 85
(Mike Murphy) *hld up in tch: rdn over 1f out: styd on same pce ins fnl f* **33/1**
0104 5 *1 3/4* **Berlusca (IRE)**[7] 7784 5-9-7 **85** SamJames 13 86
(David O'Meara) *hld up: r.o ins fnl f: nvr nrr* **18/1**
0026 6 *hd* **Extraterrestrial**[23] 7538 10-9-0 **78** TonyHamilton 10 79
(Richard Fahey) *hld up: nt clr run over 2f out: hdwy over 1f out: styd on same pce ins fnl f* **22/1**
4152 7 *6* **Handheld**[21] 7562 7-8-7 **77** (p) ShelleyBirkett(5) 4 65
(Julia Feilden) *prom: rdn over 2f out: wknd fnl f* **22/1**
3014 8 *1 1/4* **Toga Tiger (IRE)**[11] 7732 7-8-13 **77** PJMcDonald 5 63
(Kevin Frost) *hld up in tch: rdn whn hmpd over 2f out: wknd over 1f out* **12/1**
303 9 *1/2* **Cricklewood Green (USA)**[17] 7634 3-8-13 **80** SeanLevey 12 65
(Richard Hannon) *led after 1f: hdd over 6f out: chsd ldr tl led again over 2f out: rdn and hdd over 1f out: wknd ins fnl f* **10/1**[3]
0000 10 *1 1/2* **Very Good Day (FR)**[14] 7702 7-9-1 **79** GeorgeChaloner 2 60
(Richard Fahey) *s.s: outpcd* **12/1**
0050 11 *1* **Kung Hei Fat Choy (USA)**[11] 7729 5-8-13 **77** (b) TomEaves 9 56
(James Given) *chsd ldrs: led over 6f out: rdn and hdd over 2f out: wknd over 1f out* **50/1**
2160 P **Like A Diamond (IRE)**[27] 5487 4-9-2 **80** JoeFanning 3
(Ann Stokell) *prom: lost pl 1/2-way: sn bhd: p.u 2f out* **25/1**

1m 58.15s (-2.65) **Going Correction** -0.10s/f (Stan)
**WFA** 3 from 4yo+ 3lb 12 Ran SP% **120.9**
Speed ratings (Par 105): **107,106,105,104,103 103,97,96,96,94 94,**
CSF £4.18 CT £62.85 TOTE £1.60: £1.10, £1.60, £7.30; EX 6.50 Trifecta £115.70.
**Owner** Godolphin **Bred** Darley **Trained** Newmarket, Suffolk

**FOCUS**
Just an ordinary gallop to this competitive handicap which was dominated by the two Godolphin horses and the first six were clear. The form looks strong for the grade, rated around the third.

## 7871 LADBROKES H'CAP (TAPETA) 1m 141y
**7:50** (7:51) (Class 5) (0-75,75) 3-Y-0+ **£2,749** (£818; £408; £204) **Stalls** Low

Form RPR
0062 1 **Gambino (IRE)**[21] 7568 4-8-10 67 ConnorBeasley(3) 12 76
(John David Riches) *hld up: plld hrd: hdwy over 3f out: rdn to ld ins fnl f: styd on* **9/1**
0001 2 *nk* **Pivotman**[18] 7626 6-9-2 70 (bt) GrahamGibbons 1 78
(Michael Easterby) *led: rdn and hung lft over 1f out: hdd ins fnl f: styd on* **7/2**[2]
2032 3 *hd* **Footstepsintherain (IRE)**[8] 7757 4-9-4 72 FergusSweeney 2 80
(David Dennis) *chsd ldrs: rdn and ev ch whn hmpd over 1f out: styd on* **7/4**[1]
21 4 *1* **Memoria**[15] 7686 3-9-4 75 ChrisCatlin 5 80
(Rae Guest) *chsd ldrs: rdn over 2f out: r.o* **9/2**[3]
2363 5 *4* **Lean On Pete (IRE)**[17] 7651 5-9-1 72 (p) JacobButterfield(3) 7 68
(Ollie Pears) *hld up: hdwy over 2f out: rdn over 1f out: wknd wl ins fnl f* **9/1**
4006 6 *1 1/4* **Wannabe King**[64] 6490 8-9-6 74 (v) DavidAllan 11 67
(Geoffrey Harker) *prom: chsd ldr over 2f out: sn rdn: wknd ins fnl f* **20/1**
3106 7 *shd* **Dansili Dutch (IRE)**[27] 7459 5-8-10 71 JoshDoyle(7) 10 64
(David O'Meara) *sn pushed along in rr: styd on fr over 1f out: nvr on terms* **25/1**
3200 8 *1 3/4* **Prime Exhibit**[70] 6285 9-8-13 72 (t) EoinWalsh(5) 13 61
(Daniel Mark Loughnane) *s.i.s: hld up: hdwy on outer over 2f out: wknd over 1f out* **50/1**
2-00 9 *9* **Bushel (USA)**[44] 7043 4-9-7 75 TomEaves 4 43
(James Given) *sn pushed along in rr: rdn 1/2-way: n.d* **50/1**
00 10 *4 1/2* **Rakaan (IRE)**[23] 7533 7-9-0 68 StevieDonohoe 9 26
(Brendan Powell) *s.s: outpcd* **22/1**
1256 11 *3/4* **Madame Mirasol (IRE)**[64] 6484 3-9-0 71 (p) TonyHamilton 8 27
(Kevin Ryan) *hld up: wknd 2f out* **33/1**
3010 12 *3/4* **Frankthetank (IRE)**[17] 7636 3-9-0 71 (p) JoeFanning 3 25
(Keith Dalgleish) *chsd ldr tl rdn over 2f out: wknd wl over 1f out* **25/1**

1m 48.12s (-1.98) **Going Correction** -0.10s/f (Stan)
**WFA** 3 from 4yo+ 3lb 12 Ran SP% **120.4**
Speed ratings (Par 103): **104,103,103,102,99 98,97,96,88,84 83,83**
CSF £38.15 CT £82.47 TOTE £9.00: £2.10, £2.20, £1.10; EX 42.50 Trifecta £120.60.
**Owner** J D Riches **Bred** Messrs M Quinn & P Slattery **Trained** Pilling, Lancashire

**FOCUS**
A fair handicap in which the gallop was reasonable and a race in which the first four finished clear. The winner continues to progress.
T/Jkpt: Not won. T/Plt: £217.70 to a £1 stake. Pool: £135,560.06 - 454.53 winning tickets T/Qpdt: £56.80 to a £1 stake. Pool: £12,543.96 - 163.40 winning tickets CR

7872 - (Foreign Racing) - See Raceform Interactive

# 7786 DUNDALK (A.W) (L-H)
Friday, November 21
**OFFICIAL GOING: Polytrack: standard**

## 7873a DUNDALK STADIUM - LIGHT UP YOUR NIGHT H'CAP 6f (P)
**6:10** (6:13) 3-Y-0+ **£5,750** (£1,333; £583; £333)

RPR
1 **Serenity Spa**[6] 7802 4-9-6 **81** PatSmullen 11 89
(Tony Carroll) *hld up in tch: hdwy in 7th appr st to chse ldrs: rdn into 2nd ins fnl f and kpt on wl u.p to ld cl home: all out* **5/1**[2]
2 *hd* **Kimbay (IRE)**[14] 7705 4-8-8 **69** RoryCleary 13 76
(Noel Lawlor, Ire) *chsd ldrs: 4th 1/2-way: rdn in 3rd ins fnl f and kpt on wl clsng stages into 2nd on line: jst hld* **9/1**
3 *shd* **Chillie Billie**[9] 7749 5-7-12 **69** (p) KeithMoriarty(10) 5 76
(J Larkin, Ire) *attempted to make all: over 2 l clr 1/2-way: reduced advantage fr under 2f out: strly pressed u.p ins fnl f and hdd cl home: dropped to 3rd on line* **25/1**
4 *1/2* **Strategic Heights (IRE)**[69] 6324 5-9-0 **75** FMBerry 10 80+
(John James Feane, Ire) *hld up: 10th 1/2-way: rdn 2f out and kpt on wl nr side ins fnl f: nrst fin* **10/1**
5 *3/4* **Antiquus (IRE)**[7] 7790 5-9-4 **79** (p) BillyLee 4 82
(Ms Joanna Morgan, Ire) *hld up: rdn in rr 2f out and kpt on wl ins fnl f: nvr nrr* **7/1**
6 *1* **Maontri (IRE)**[21] 7579 7-9-6 **88** DonnachaO'Brien(7) 1 88
(M J Tynan, Ire) *trckd ldr in 2nd: rdn over 2f out and sn no ex u.p: one pce fnl f* **12/1**
7 *1* **Grey Danube (IRE)**[132] 4219 5-9-4 **79** (t) DeclanMcDonogh 2 76
(D J Bunyan, Ire) *towards rr: sme hdwy far side fr under 2f out: no imp in 9th ins fnl f: kpt on towards fin* **22/1**
8 *nk* **Whaileyy (IRE)**[9] 7749 6-10-1 **90** ShaneFoley 6 86
(M Halford, Ire) *chsd ldrs: rdn 2f out and no imp on ldrs u.p in 4th ins fnl f: wknd towards fin* **7/4**[1]
9 *1/2* **Tennessee Wildcat (IRE)**[21] 7577 4-9-9 **84** ColinKeane 7 78
(G M Lyons, Ire) *hld up: 11th 1/2-way: rdn and no imp 2f out: kpt on one pce* **6/1**[3]
10 *nse* **Ask Dad**[9] 7749 4-8-5 **66** (tp) ChrisHayes 9 60
(Damian Joseph English, Ire) *upset in stalls: chsd ldrs: rdn in 3rd appr st and no ex over 1f out: wknd* **16/1**
11 *1* **Harry Trotter (IRE)**[21] 7577 5-9-4 **82** ConnorKing(3) 12 73
(David Marnane, Ire) *hooded to load: towards rr: rdn in 10th 2f out and sn no imp: one pce fnl f* **16/1**
12 *1 1/4* **Burren View Lady (IRE)**[21] 7578 4-8-12 **73** LeighRoche 3 60
(Denis Gerard Hogan, Ire) *towards rr: 12th 1/2-way: rdn and no imp 2f out: one pce fnl f* **33/1**
13 *2 3/4* **Catwilldo (IRE)**[132] 4219 4-8-4 **65** (b) NGMcCullagh 8 43
(Garvan Donnelly, Ire) *hld up in tch: pushed along in 6th fr 1/2-way: no ex u.p 1 1/2f out: wknd* **20/1**

1m 11.48s (71.48) 13 Ran SP% **134.3**
CSF £53.83 CT £1127.55 TOTE £5.30: £2.30, £2.50, £6.30; DF 26.40 Trifecta £1459.90.
**Owner** Seasons Holidays **Bred** Barry Hurley **Trained** Cropthorne, Worcs

**FOCUS**
A competitive contest run at a strong enough gallop.

## 7877a CROWNE PLAZA LEADING JOCKEY & TRAINER CHAMPIONSHIP H'CAP (DIV I) 1m 4f (P)
**8:10** (8:13) (47-65,68) 3-Y-0+ **£4,312** (£1,000; £437; £250)

RPR
1 **Innoko (FR)**[6] 7805 4-10-0 **65** JosephO'Brien 2 71
(Tony Carroll) *hld up in rr of mid-div: pushed along in 10th over 3f out: n.m.r briefly into st: hdwy u.p far side to chal 1 1/2f out: kpt on wl in 2nd ins fnl f to ld cl home: all out* **5/2**[1]
2 *shd* **House Limit (IRE)**[17] 6311 5-8-7 **49** (t) RobbieDowney(5) 8 55
(J Larkin, Ire) *chsd ldrs: 5th 1/2-way: effrt in 2nd 2f out and led narrowly u.p ins fnl f: hdd cl home* **20/1**
3 *2* **Doux Douce (IRE)**[16] 7679 7-9-0 **51** (b) GaryCarroll 14 54
(S M Duffy, Ire) *chsd ldrs: racd keenly: clsr in 2nd 1/2-way and led over 3f out: rdn 2f out and sn strly pressed: hdd u.p ins fnl f and sn no ex in 3rd: kpt on same pce* **6/1**[3]
4 *2* **Minot Street (CAN)**[9] 7750 4-9-10 **68** (bt) TomMadden(7) 12 68
(John C McConnell, Ire) *sn trckd ldr: 3rd 1/2-way: rdn 2f out and no ex u.p in 4th ent fnl f: kpt on one pce* **5/1**[2]
5 *3 1/4* **Tight Times (IRE)**[16] 7679 5-9-6 **57** (p) PatSmullen 11 51
(B R Hamilton, Ire) *in tch: rdn 2f out and no imp on ldrs in 6th ent fnl f: kpt on one pce* **7/1**
6 *3/4* **Diamond Dame (IRE)**[6] 5453 5-9-8 **59** DannyMullins 4 52
(John Joseph Hanlon, Ire) *in tch: rdn 2f out and no imp on ldrs in 5th ent fnl f: kpt on one pce* **5/1**[2]
7 *1 3/4* **Noble Call (IRE)**[17] 330 6-9-1 **52** (tp) ColinKeane 9 42
(P J Rothwell, Ire) *in rr of mid-div: rdn into 8th over 1f out and no imp on ldrs: kpt on one pce* **22/1**
8 *1* **Balofilo**[26] 5261 4-8-10 **47** NGMcCullagh 1 36
(P A Fahy, Ire) *chsd ldrs: 4th 1/2-way: rdn and wknd fr 2f out* **33/1**
9 *3 3/4* **Kilruane Shea (IRE)**[28] 7429 3-8-8 **51** MichaelHussey 5 34
(S Curling, Ire) *towards rr: rdn in 10th 3f out and tk clsr order far side 2f out: sn no imp on ldrs disputing 6th: one pce fnl f* **20/1**
10 *5 1/2* **General Bunching (USA)**[35] 7267 6-9-3 **54** (t) RoryCleary 7 28
(Thomas Cleary, Ire) *in rr of mid-div: rdn and no imp fr 2f out: kpt on one pce* **20/1**
11 *7* **Halarath (IRE)**[35] 7267 5-9-0 **58** DonnachaO'Brien(7) 6 21
(C Moore, Ire) *rrd sltly s: nvr bttr than mid-div: rdn towards rr over 2f out and no ex* **14/1**
12 *5* **Buccaneer Bob (IRE)**[16] 7679 6-9-1 **51** ow1 BillyLee 13 7
(Miss Susan A Finn, Ire) *towards rr early tl impr into 5th over 5f out: racd keenly: rdn and wknd 3f out* **14/1**
13 *12* **Bogha Baisti (IRE)**[56] 6728 4-8-10 **47** LeighRoche 3
(Mrs Y Dunleavy, Ire) *led: t.k.h: rdn and hdd over 3f out: sn wknd* **33/1**
14 *2* **The Drunken Dr (IRE)**[16] 7679 6-8-3 **47** (b) IanQueally(7) 10
(Niall Moran, Ire) *a bhd: rdn detached in rr 4f out and no imp* **40/1**

2m 33.91s (153.91)
**WFA** 3 from 4yo+ 6lb 14 Ran SP% **129.0**
CSF £64.95 CT £296.66 TOTE £4.10: £1.90, £7.00, £2.30; DF 148.50 Trifecta £1304.20.
**Owner** Mill House Racing Syndicate **Bred** Marquise Soledad De Moratalla **Trained** Cropthorne, Worcs

**FOCUS**
This looked much the stronger of the two divisions. Several had a chance hitting the straight.

7878 - 7879a (Foreign Racing) - See Raceform Interactive

## 7839 LINGFIELD (L-H)

Saturday, November 22

**OFFICIAL GOING: Polytrack: standard**

Wind: virtually nil Weather: overcast, showers

### 7880 32RED CASINO (S) STKS — 1m 1y(P)
11:50 (11:50) (Class 6) 2-Y-O — £1,940 (£577; £288; £144) Stalls High

| Form | | | | RPR |
|---|---|---|---|---|
| 0050 | 1 | | **Skylight (IRE)**[10] 7740 2-8-6 58 (v) CharlesBishop 6<br>(Mick Channon) *sn led and mde virtually all: wnt clr w runner-up 3f out: asserted over 1f out: styd on: rdn out* **6/4**[1] | 58 |
| 0054 | 2 | 1½ | **La Favorita (IRE)**[5] 7816 2-8-3 50 DannyBrock(3) 5<br>(Phil McEntee) *sn w wnr: wnt clr w wnr 3f out: rdn 2f out: no ex and one pce fnl f* **5/1** | 55 |
| 0440 | 3 | 2¾ | **Auld Fyffee (IRE)**[43] 7075 2-8-6 57 ChrisCatlin 4<br>(John Ryan) *in tch in midfield: rdn and outpcd over 3f out: wnt modest 3rd u.p over 1f out: plugged on but no threat to ldrs* **8/1** | 48 |
| 0 | 4 | 2 | **Tokomaro (IRE)**[3] 7835 2-8-11 0 SeanLevey 1<br>(Richard Hannon) *hld up in tch in rr: rdn over 3f out: outpcd by ldrs 3f out: no threat to ldrs after: plugged on fnl f* **9/2**[3] | 49 |
| 4400 | 5 | 5 | **Celestial Vision (USA)**[8] 7780 2-8-11 67 (t) JimCrowley 3<br>(Tom Dascombe) *broke wl: sn restrained to chse ldrs: 3rd and outpcd 3f out: wl hld after: lost 3rd and wknd over 1f out* **7/2**[2] | 37 |
| 00 | 6 | 40 | **Funtime Barry (IRE)**[32] 7354 2-8-11 0 MartinDwyer 2<br>(Richard Hannon) *in tch in midfield: rdn and reminder over 4f out: dropped to rr over 3f out: sn lost tch: t.o* **33/1** | |

1m 40.73s (2.53) **Going Correction** 0.0s/f (Stan) — **6** Ran SP% **111.1**

Speed ratings (Par 94): **87,85,82,80,75 35**

CSF £9.23 TOTE £2.50: £1.80, £2.90; EX 8.30 Trifecta £25.60.The winner was bought in for 3,600gns.

**Owner** Mrs T Burns **Bred** Paul, Ben & Charlie Cartan **Trained** West Ilsley, Berks

■ Stewards' Enquiry : Chris Catlin two-day ban; used whip above permitted level (6th,8th Dec)

**FOCUS**

A typically modest event for the grade, in which all the runners were dropping into a seller for the first time.

### 7881 UNIBET/EBF STALLIONS MAIDEN STKS — 5f 6y(P)
12:20 (12:21) (Class 5) 2-Y-O — £2,911 (£866; £432; £216) Stalls High

| Form | | | | RPR |
|---|---|---|---|---|
| 5523 | 1 | | **Shackled N Drawn (USA)**[8] 7771 2-9-5 69 (t) JimCrowley 5<br>(Olly Stevens) *t.k.h early: hld up in tch in midfield: rdn and qcknd to ld 1f out: styd on wl u.p fnl 100yds* **5/2**[2] | 72 |
| 40 | 2 | ½ | **Lady Kyllar**[131] 4269 2-9-0 0 PaoloSirigu 2<br>(George Margarson) *in tch: rdn and gd hdwy on inner over 1f out: chsd wnr fnl 150yds: kpt on and pressing wnr fnl 100yds: r.o but a hld* **14/1** | 65 |
| | 3 | 1¼ | **Lamps Of Heaven (IRE)** 2-9-0 0 LiamJones 9<br>(Olly Stevens) *stdd after s: hld up in last pair: pushed along and hdwy whn swtchd rt 1f out: chsd ldng pair fnl 100yds: kpt on and gng on fin* **8/1**[3] | 61 |
| 00 | 4 | 2½ | **Mon Petit Fleur**[18] 7649 2-8-7 0 ThomasHemsley(7) 4<br>(Chris Dwyer) *dwlt: sn rcvrd and chsd ldng trio: rdn and unable qck over 1f out: 4th and one pce fnl f* **50/1** | 52 |
| 00 | 5 | 1 | **Glenbuck Lass (IRE)**[44] 7062 2-8-9 0 (e[1]) TimClark(5) 8<br>(Alan Bailey) *taken down early: stdd s: hld up in tch in rr: wdst and effrt bnd 2f out: styd on ins fnl f: nvr trbld ldrs* **25/1** | 48+ |
| 0 | 6 | ½ | **Dippinganddiving (IRE)**[22] 7573 2-8-7 0 CharlotteJenner(7) 3<br>(Jose Santos) *chsd ldr: rdn 2f out: unable qck and lost pl over 1f out: wknd ins fnl f* **50/1** | 46 |
| 0 | 7 | ½ | **Equita**[59] 6659 2-9-0 0 DavidProbert 1<br>(Robert Stephens) *sn led: rdn 2f out: drvn and hdd 1f out: wknd and hung rt ins fnl f* **40/1** | 45 |
| 06 | 8 | ½ | **Mary Ann Bugg (IRE)**[130] 4302 2-8-11 45 DannyBrock(3) 7<br>(Phil McEntee) *in tch in midfield: effrt wl over 1f out: no prog: wl hld whn short of room and hmpd towards fin* **66/1** | 43 |
| 62 | 9 | ½ | **Hurricane Alert**[8] 7771 2-9-5 0 JamesDoyle 6<br>(Ralph Beckett) *chsd ldrs: rdn and finding little whn edgd rt and lost pl on bnd 2f out: drvn and no rspnse over 1f out: bhd ins fnl f* **1/2**[1] | 46 |

59.58s (0.78) **Going Correction** 0.0s/f (Stan) — **9** Ran SP% **124.7**

Speed ratings (Par 96): **93,92,90,86,84 83,83,82,81**

CSF £35.74 TOTE £3.20: £1.10, £4.00, £2.90; EX 51.20 Trifecta £160.10.

**Owner** Clipper Logistics **Bred** Pam & Martin Wygod **Trained** Chiddingfold, Surrey

■ Stewards' Enquiry : David Probert two-day ban; careless riding (6th,8th Dec)

**FOCUS**

Only a modest maiden, but the pace seemed sound throughout.

### 7882 32RED CONDITIONS STKS (BOBIS RACE) (FAST TRACK QUALIFIER) — 7f 1y(P)
12:55 (12:56) (Class 2) 2-Y-O — £9,056 (£2,695; £1,346; £673) Stalls Low

| Form | | | | RPR |
|---|---|---|---|---|
| 0341 | 1 | | **Four Seasons (IRE)**[17] 7661 2-9-3 96 AdamKirby 5<br>(Charlie Appleby) *stdd s: hld up in tch in last pair: clsd 2f out: rdn and str run over 1f out: led fnl 50yds: r.o wl* **1/1**[1] | 93 |
| 31 | 2 | 1 | **Super Kid**[135] 4117 2-9-3 0 JamesDoyle 3<br>(Saeed bin Suroor) *in tch in midfield: pushed along and clsd to join ldrs over 2f out: rdn to ld over 1f out: hdd and no ex fnl 50yds* **11/4**[2] | 90 |
| 5141 | 3 | nk | **Qatar Road (FR)**[31] 7374 2-9-3 84 MartinHarley 6<br>(Marco Botti) *stdd s: hld up in tch in rr: hdwy on outer over 1f out: edging lft and hdwy to go 3rd fnl 75yds: kpt on* **8/1** | 89 |
| 3211 | 4 | 2¼ | **Fieldsman (USA)**[55] 6783 2-9-3 92 GeorgeBaker 7<br>(Ed Dunlop) *chsd ldrs: led 2f out: hdd and shkn up over 1f out: no ex 1f out: wknd ins fnl f* **6/1**[3] | 83 |
| 0005 | 5 | shd | **Vimy Ridge**[17] 7661 2-9-0 86 JimCrowley 2<br>(Alan Bailey) *chsd ldrs: nt clr run 2f out: swtchd lft and hdwy over 1f out: drvn to chse ldrs 1f out: no ex and wknd fnl 100yds* **66/1** | 80 |
| 01 | 6 | ¾ | **Rattling Jewel**[23] 7551 2-9-3 80 LiamKeniry 4<br>(Andrew Balding) *led tl hdd and rdn 2f out: no ex over 1f out: wknd ins fnl f* **33/1** | 81 |
| 3101 | 7 | 2 | **Faraajh (IRE)**[42] 7116 2-8-9 81 LukeMorris 1<br>(James Tate) *in tch in midfield: rdn jst over 2f out: lost pl over 1f out: wknd fnl f* **20/1** | 67 |

1m 23.15s (-1.65) **Going Correction** 0.0s/f (Stan) — **7** Ran SP% **111.3**

Speed ratings (Par 102): **109,107,107,104,104 103,101**

CSF £3.59 TOTE £2.00: £1.20, £1.50; EX 4.30 Trifecta £15.20.

**Owner** Godolphin **Bred** Michael E Wates **Trained** Newmarket, Suffolk

**FOCUS**

An interesting conditions event and a 1-2 for Godolphin, with the winner qualifying for the 3-y-o final which will again be held on Good Friday in 2015.

### 7883 DOWNLOAD THE LADBROKES APP H'CAP (DIV I) — 7f 1y(P)
1:25 (1:26) (Class 6) (0-60,60) 3-Y-O+ — £2,587 (£770; £384; £192) Stalls Low

| Form | | | | RPR |
|---|---|---|---|---|
| 3466 | 1 | | **Divine Rule (IRE)**[3] 7844 6-8-13 52 (p) LiamJones 4<br>(Laura Mongan) *hld up in tch in midfield: rdn and effrt over 1f out: str run to ld wl ins fnl f: sn in command* **8/1** | 61 |
| 324 | 2 | 1½ | **Wotalad**[29] 7424 4-9-5 58 (p) GeorgeChaloner 7<br>(Richard Whitaker) *led: rdn 2f out: drvn and hrd pressed over 1f out: kpt on wl tl hdd and no ex wl ins fnl f* **5/1**[3] | 63 |
| 142 | 3 | nk | **Copper Cavalier**[23] 7548 3-8-11 51 (v) JimCrowley 6<br>(Robert Cowell) *chsd ldr: rdn and ev ch over 1f out tl no ex and one pce fnl 75yds* **5/1**[3] | 54 |
| 6632 | 4 | nk | **Humour (IRE)**[29] 7423 3-9-4 58 AdamKirby 2<br>(Christine Dunnett) *chsd ldrs: drvn and ev ch 1f out: styd on same pce fnl 100yds* **11/4**[1] | 60 |
| 6303 | 5 | hd | **Applejack Lad**[29] 7424 3-9-6 60 (t) JackMitchell 1<br>(John Ryan) *chsd ldrs: effrt on inner over 1f out: kpt on same pce u.p ins fnl f* **3/1**[2] | 62 |
| 0006 | 6 | 2 | **Indus Valley (IRE)**[36] 7259 7-9-4 57 (b) DavidProbert 10<br>(Des Donovan) *t.k.h: hld up in tch towards rr: effrt on outer over 1f out: kpt on but no real imp fnl f* **12/1** | 55 |
| 666 | 7 | ½ | **Jonnie Skull (IRE)**[46] 7013 8-8-13 59 (vt) PatrickO'Donnell(7) 3<br>(Phil McEntee) *broke wl: sn restrained and hld up in midfield: effrt over 1f out: r.o same pce and no imp fnl f* **33/1** | 55 |
| 100 | 8 | 1 | **Honiton Lace**[9] 7766 3-9-1 55 (tp) LukeMorris 8<br>(Phil McEntee) *s.i.s: hld up in last pair: niggled along 5f out: r.o same pce u.p fr over 1f out* **50/1** | 48 |
| 3003 | 9 | ¾ | **Genax (IRE)**[23] 7547 3-8-7 47 (v[1]) StevieDonohoe 9<br>(Ian Williams) *s.i.s: in tch in rr: effrt on inner over 1f out: no imp fnl f* **8/1** | 38 |
| 5405 | 10 | 4½ | **Play The Blues (IRE)**[25] 7519 7-8-4 46 oh1 (t) DannyBrock(3) 5<br>(Dominic Ffrench Davis) *plld hrd: hld up in tch in midfield: lost pl over 1f out: wknd fnl f* **33/1** | 26 |

1m 24.22s (-0.58) **Going Correction** 0.0s/f (Stan)

**WFA** 3 from 4yo+ 1lb — **10** Ran SP% **122.8**

Speed ratings (Par 101): **103,101,100,100,100 98,97,96,95,90**

CSF £49.82 CT £227.79 TOTE £10.10: £3.80, £1.50, £2.10; EX 67.90 Trifecta £445.00.

**Owner** Mrs L J Mongan **Bred** Car Colston Hall Stud **Trained** Epsom, Surrey

**FOCUS**

A modest but competitive sprint handicap. Straightforward form to rate, with the second and third pretty much to their marks.

### 7884 DOWNLOAD THE LADBROKES APP H'CAP (DIV II) — 7f 1y(P)
2:00 (2:00) (Class 6) (0-60,60) 3-Y-O+ — £2,587 (£770; £384; £192) Stalls Low

| Form | | | | RPR |
|---|---|---|---|---|
| 0011 | 1 | | **Spinning Cobblers**[15] 7697 3-9-6 60 (v) GeorgeBaker 2<br>(Stuart Williams) *mde all: rdn over 1f out: asserted 1f out: kpt on: rdn out* **11/10**[1] | 67 |
| 0612 | 2 | ½ | **Major Muscari (IRE)**[42] 7111 6-9-5 58 (p) MartinHarley 3<br>(Shaun Harris) *rrd as stalls opened: hld up in tch in rr: hdwy on outer over 1f out: hanging lft but r.o wl to go 2nd wl ins fnl f: nvr quite getting to wnr* **6/1**[3] | 65+ |
| 4523 | 3 | ¾ | **Rocky's Pride (IRE)**[2] 7853 8-9-0 53 GeorgeChaloner 9<br>(Richard Whitaker) *w wnr: rdn and ev ch 2f out: no ex 1f out: r.o same pce and lost 2nd wl ins fnl f* **4/1**[2] | 58 |
| 5360 | 4 | ¾ | **Olney Lass**[37] 7220 7-8-4 46 SimonPearce(3) 4<br>(Lydia Pearce) *chsd ldrs: effrt u.p on inner over 1f out: r.o same pce ins fnl f* **25/1** | 49 |
| 5404 | 5 | ¾ | **Skidby Mill (IRE)**[3] 7845 4-9-2 55 (v[1]) LiamJones 7<br>(Laura Mongan) *t.k.h: hld up in tch in midfield: rdn and effrt over 1f out: drvn 1f out: r.o same pce* **6/1**[3] | 56 |
| 0056 | 6 | 2¼ | **Black Truffle (FR)**[23] 7548 4-8-13 52 (v) LiamKeniry 8<br>(Mark Usher) *stdd and dropped in bhd after s: hld up in rr: shkn up over 1f out: kpt on past btn horses: nvr trbld ldrs* **20/1** | 47 |
| 3000 | 7 | nk | **Daneglow (IRE)**[29] 7420 4-8-8 47 (e) LukeMorris 6<br>(Mike Murphy) *t.k.h: hld up in tch in midfield: rdn and unable qck 2f out: wknd ins fnl f* **50/1** | 41 |
| 4405 | 8 | hd | **Buxton**[5] 7819 10-8-7 46 oh1 (t) MartinLane 1<br>(Roger Ingram) *hld up in tch in last trio: effrt u.p on inner over 1f out: no hdwy: wknd ins fnl f* **33/1** | 40 |
| 540 | 9 | ¾ | **Katie Taylor (IRE)**[16] 7682 4-9-5 58 ChrisCatlin 10<br>(Rae Guest) *chsd ldrs: drvn 2f out: sn struggling and lost pl: wknd fnl f* **16/1** | 50 |

1m 25.79s (0.99) **Going Correction** 0.0s/f (Stan)

**WFA** 3 from 4yo+ 1lb — **9** Ran SP% **115.6**

Speed ratings (Par 101): **94,93,92,91,90 88,87,87,86**

CSF £7.75 CT £20.15 TOTE £1.80: £1.10, £1.90, £2.20; EX 8.20 Trifecta £25.00.

**Owner** Brian Piper & David Cobill **Bred** L Ellinas & Old Mill Stud **Trained** Newmarket, Suffolk

**FOCUS**

The second division of this modest sprint handicap was run 1.57 seconds slower than the first leg, and if paid to race prominently. Muddling form.

### 7885 32RED.COM/BRITISH STALLION STUDS EBF FILLIES' H'CAP — 1m 1y(P)
2:35 (2:35) (Class 4) (0-85,82) 3-Y-O+ — £6,630 (£1,973; £986; £493) Stalls High

| Form | | | | RPR |
|---|---|---|---|---|
| 4132 | 1 | | **Semaral (IRE)**[12] 7732 3-9-3 **80** (p) GeorgeBaker 2<br>(Chris Wall) *in tch in midfield: rdn and effrt over 1f out: clsd u.p and swtchd lft ins fnl f: sn chalng: r.o to ld towards fin* **3/1**[2] | 88 |
| 2303 | 2 | ½ | **History Book (IRE)**[49] 6945 4-9-7 **82** AdamKirby 6<br>(Charlie Appleby) *sn led: rdn and qcknd jst over 2f out: drvn ins fnl f: hdd and no ex towards fin* **5/1** | 89 |
| 0031 | 3 | nk | **Miss Buckshot (IRE)**[18] 7634 3-9-1 **78** DavidProbert 3<br>(Rae Guest) *hld up in last pair: clsd whn nt clr run and swtchd rt jst ins fnl f: r.o strly fnl 100yds: nt quite rch ldrs* **7/2**[3] | 83 |
| -352 | 4 | nk | **Starlight Symphony (IRE)**[186] 2415 4-8-13 **74** (p) JimCrowley 1<br>(Eve Johnson Houghton) *bhd: clsd over 3f out: effrt u.p over 1f out: clsng and pushed lft ins fnl f: r.o: nt rch ldrs* **20/1** | 80 |
| 5001 | 5 | ¾ | **Tides Reach (IRE)**[30] 7397 3-9-0 **77** (b[1]) JamesDoyle 4<br>(Roger Charlton) *chsd ldrs: rdn over 2f out: drvn and chsd wnr 1f out: no imp: lost 3 pls fnl 100yds* **10/1** | 80 |
| 1145 | 6 | 1½ | **Evacusafe Lady**[8] 7773 3-8-2 **68** (t) DannyBrock(3) 7<br>(John Ryan) *chsd wnr: rdn over 2f out: unable qck and lost 2nd 1f out: outpcd ins fnl f* **33/1** | 67 |

5123 7 2 1/4 **Santa Teresa (IRE)**29 7417 3-9-0 77 MartinHarley 5 71
(William Haggas) *in tch in midfield: unable qck and lost pl over 1f out: wknd 1f out* 2/1[1]
1306 8 2 1/4 **Pretty Bubbles**40 7160 5-9-5 80 PaddyAspell 8 70
(J R Jenkins) *in tch in midfield: rdn: lost pl and hmpd over 1f out: wknd 1f out* 25/1

1m 36.45s (-1.75) **Going Correction** 0.0s/f (Stan)
**WFA** 3 from 4yo+ 2lb 8 Ran SP% 117.9
Speed ratings (Par 102): **108,107,107,106,106 104,102,100**
CSF £18.53 CT £55.00 TOTE £5.00: £1.30, £1.70, £2.20; EX 18.40 Trifecta £117.80.
**Owner** Moyns Park Stud **Bred** Moyns Park Estate And Stud Ltd **Trained** Newmarket, Suffolk
■ Stewards' Enquiry : George Baker two-day ban; careless riding (6th,8th Dec)

**FOCUS**
A reasonably competitive fillies' handicap. The fourth has been rated to her C&D form off another break.

## 7886 UNIBET H'CAP 5f 6y(P)
**3:10** (3:11) (Class 4) (0-80,80) 3-Y-0+ **£5,175** (£1,540; £769; £384) **Stalls** High

Form RPR
0052 1 **Searchlight**16 7687 3-9-0 78 ShaneGray(5) 7 90
(Kevin Ryan) *chsd ldrs: clsd u.p over 1f out: chal ins fnl f: led fnl 75yds: r.o wl: rdn out* 9/4[1]
6122 2 1 1/2 **Clearing**25 7521 4-9-6 79 PatCosgrave 2 86
(Jim Boyle) *chsd ldr: swtchd lft and clsd u.p over 1f out: drvn to ld ins fnl f: sn hdd and one pce* 9/2[2]
5000 3 2 **Clear Praise (USA)**32 7365 7-8-11 77 TomasHarrigan(7) 1 77
(Simon Dow) *stdd s: wl off the pce in rr: rdn and hdwy 1f out: r.o strly fnl f to go 3rd fnl 50yds: nvr trbld ldrs* 33/1
5051 4 3/4 **Royal Acquisition**32 7357 4-9-2 75 (p) JimCrowley 4 72
(Robert Cowell) *chsd ldrs: rdn 2f out: styd on same pce and no imp ins fnl f* 8/1
0540 5 1/2 **Come On Dave (IRE)**17 7669 5-9-7 80 (v1) LiamKeniry 6 75
(John Butler) *led and set fast gallop: clr over 3f out: rdn over 1f out: hdd ins fnl f: sn btn: wknd and lost 2 pls towards fin* 6/1[3]
00 6 1/2 **Triple Dream**131 4267 9-9-7 80 (tp) JimmyQuinn 10 74
(Milton Bradley) *off the pce in midfield: rdn over 2f out: kpt on same pce fnl f: nvr threatened ldrs* 50/1
3046 7 hd **Fair Value (IRE)**151 3551 6-9-7 80 GeorgeBaker 3 73
(Simon Dow) *stdd s: wl off the pce in last quartet: sme hdwy anjd rdn over 1f out: kpt on: nvr trbld ldrs* 7/1
5233 8 3/4 **Pucon**32 7357 5-9-0 73 JamesDoyle 5 63
(Roger Teal) *off the pce in midfield: rdn wl over 1f out: kpt on same pce fr over 1f out: nvr threatened ldrs* 10/1
4033 9 4 **Rocket Rob (IRE)**52 6872 8-8-13 72 ChrisCatlin 9 48
(Willie Musson) *dwlt: sn pushed along and outpcd in last quartet: n.d* 7/1
020 10 3 1/4 **Roy's Legacy**135 4114 5-9-0 73 MartinHarley 8 37
(Shaun Harris) *off the pce in last quartet: bhd 3f out: n.d* 25/1

57.79s (-1.01) **Going Correction** 0.0s/f (Stan) 10 Ran SP% 117.2
Speed ratings (Par 105): **108,105,102,101,100 99,99,98,91,86**
CSF £11.98 CT £260.74 TOTE £4.20: £1.20, £1.70, £6.70; EX 14.90 Trifecta £534.00.
**Owner** Elite Racing Club **Bred** Elite Racing Club **Trained** Hambleton, N Yorks

**FOCUS**
A useful and competitive sprint handicap and, despite the strong pace, those ridden prominently had the advantage. The winner has been rated to his turf mark.

## 7887 UNIBET £20 RISK FREE BET H'CAP 6f 1y(P)
**3:45** (3:48) (Class 6) (0-60,60) 3-Y-0+ **£2,587** (£770; £384; £192) **Stalls** Low

Form RPR
1265 1 **Chevise (IRE)**23 7556 6-9-7 60 (b) JamesDoyle 4 68
(Steve Woodman) *chsd ldrs: rdn 2f out: styd on u.p to ld fnl 75yds: drvn out* 9/2[3]
0003 2 1/2 **New Rich**59 6666 4-9-3 56 (b) JohnFahy 6 62+
(Eve Johnson Houghton) *hld up in tch in last trio: hdwy towards inner over 1f out: styd on wl u.p to go 2nd towards fin* 7/2[2]
4016 3 nk **Bubbly Bailey**12 7735 4-9-6 59 (v) GeorgeBaker 5 64
(J R Jenkins) *led: rdn over 1f out: drvn and hdd ins fnl f: no ex and lost 2nd towards fin* 5/2[1]
2300 4 1/2 **Saskia's Dream**32 7364 6-9-4 57 (v) PatCosgrave 9 61
(Jane Chapple-Hyam) *hld up wl in tch in midfield: shkn up jst over 1f out: swtchd lft and drvn ins fnl f: r.o same pce fnl 100yds* 25/1
1654 5 nk **Catalinas Diamond (IRE)**32 7364 6-9-3 56 (t) JimCrowley 2 59
(Pat Murphy) *hld up in tch in midfield: hdwy and swtchd lft 1f out: styd on same pce ins fnl f* 6/1
0500 6 3/4 **Compton Prince**32 7364 5-9-5 58 (v) LiamKeniry 10 58+
(Milton Bradley) *hld up in last trio: clsd and nt clr run over 1f out: gap opened briefly and hdwy ins fnl f: nt clr run again and no imp wl ins fnl f* 20/1
4520 7 shd **Ecliptic Sunrise**18 7644 3-9-1 54 (p) DavidProbert 12 54
(Des Donovan) *chsd ldrs: rdn and chsd ldr briefly over 1f out: no ex and lost 3 pls wl ins fnl f* 20/1
000 8 hd **Captain Kendall (IRE)**51 6889 5-9-2 60 ShaneGray(5) 3 60
(Harry Chisman) *t.k.h: hld up in tch in midfield: effrt over 1f out: kpt on ins fnl f: nvr enough pce to rch ldrs* 20/1
0202 9 3/4 **Reginald Claude**8 7783 6-8-12 58 CharlotteJenner(7) 8 55
(Mark Usher) *hld up in tlouch: widish and lost pl bnd wl over 1f out: r.o same pce ins fnl f* 8/1
4046 10 3 1/4 **Purford Green**234 1238 5-8-8 47 (v) JimmyQuinn 7 34
(Michael Attwater) *chsd ldr tl no ex u.p and lost 2nd over 1f out: wkng whn n.m.r ins fnl f* 33/1
2200 11 1 **Lucky Surprise**18 7644 3-8-10 49 (b) MartinLane 1 33
(Jeremy Gask) *in tch in last trio: sme hdwy u.p on inner over 1f out: wknd ins fnl f* 20/1
0060 12 6 **Pastoral Dancer**155 3422 5-8-7 46 oh1 (t) ChrisCatlin 11 10
(Richard Rowe) *in tch in midfield on outer: lost pl bnd 2f out: bhd and no hdwy over 1f out: wknd fnl f* 50/1

1m 12.16s (0.26) **Going Correction** 0.0s/f (Stan) 12 Ran SP% 122.2
Speed ratings (Par 101): **98,97,96,96,95 94,94,94,93,89 87,79**
CSF £19.11 CT £49.34 TOTE £6.50: £2.30, £1.70, £1.80; EX 19.90 Trifecta £80.70.
**Owner** The Chevise Partnership **Bred** Paul And Mrs Jenny Green **Trained** East Lavant, W Sussex

**FOCUS**
A weak handicap. The winner has been rated to her best form over the past year.
T/Plt: £49.30 to a £1 stake. Pool: £54,626.85 - 808.21 winning tickets T/Qpdt: £6.10 to a £1 stake. Pool: £5,787.83 - 694.34 winning tickets SP

# 7864 WOLVERHAMPTON (A.W) (L-H)
### Saturday, November 22

**OFFICIAL GOING: Tapeta: standard**
Wind: Light, half behind Weather: Overcast

## 7888 £20 RISK-FREE BET AT UNIBET H'CAP (TAPETA) 5f 216y
**5:45** (5:47) (Class 5) (0-75,75) 3-Y-0+ **£2,749** (£818; £408; £204) **Stalls** Low

Form RPR
2033 1 **Good Authority (IRE)**21 7601 7-8-12 73 KieranShoemark(7) 6 86
(Victor Dartnall) *chsd clr ldng pair: clsd over 1f out: led jst ins fnl f: rdn out* 9/4[1]
4-61 2 1 1/4 **Invincible Ridge (IRE)**19 7623 6-9-7 75 (t) LukeMorris 3 84
(Eric Alston) *chsd clr ldng pair: clsd w wnr and chal 1f out: kpt on same pce* 5/2[2]
2215 3 1 3/4 **Smokethatthunders (IRE)**25 7521 4-9-7 75 PaulMulrennan 13 78
(James Unett) *in tch on outer: effrt and wd st: styd on fnl f* 17/2
0002 4 shd **Thorpe Bay**19 7623 5-8-13 70 RyanTate(3) 12 73
(Michael Appleby) *chsd ldr: led over 2f out tl wknd jst ins fnl f* 14/1
0000 5 3/4 **Rodrigo De Torres**25 7507 7-9-7 75 GrahamLee 11 76
(Frederick Watson) *led at str pce tl over 2f out: wknd 1f out* 33/1
-100 6 hd **Macdillon**24 7534 8-9-6 74 MartinDwyer 9 74
(Stuart Kittow) *mid-div: rdn over 2f out: styd on fnl f* 25/1
6013 7 3/4 **Thataboy (IRE)**25 7521 3-9-2 75 EoinWalsh(5) 4 73
(Tom Dascombe) *s.s: towards rr: rdn 3f out: sme hdwy on inner over 1f out: no further prog* 5/1[3]
6520 8 1/2 **Noverre To Go (IRE)**50 6898 8-9-4 72 (p) WilliamTwiston-Davies 5 68
(Ronald Harris) *s.s: towards rr: hrd rdn over 1f out: nvr able to chal* 28/1
2451 9 hd **Divine Call**34 7307 7-9-0 68 (v) BenCurtis 8 63
(Milton Bradley) *outpcd towards rr: n.d* 25/1
6-01 10 nk **Mount Hollow**15 7698 9-8-12 71 (p) JackDuern(5) 1 65
(Andrew Hollinshead) *a towards rr* 16/1
5366 11 2 1/4 **Honeymoon Express (IRE)**66 6463 4-8-13 72 (p) ShelleyBirkett(5) 10 59
(Julia Feilden) *chsd clr ldng pair tl wknd over 2f out* 50/1
01 12 1/2 **Pensax Lad (IRE)**95 5526 3-9-4 72 SteveDrowne 7 58
(Ronald Harris) *outpcd: a bhd* 25/1
3100 13 3 1/4 **First In Command (IRE)**40 7159 9-9-0 75 (t) LouiseDay(7) 2 50
(Daniel Mark Loughnane) *mid-div tl wknd 2f out* 80/1

1m 13.48s (-1.02) **Going Correction** -0.15s/f (Stan) 13 Ran SP% 120.2
Speed ratings (Par 103): **100,98,96,95,94 94,93,92,92,92 89,88,84**
CSF £7.30 CT £40.71 TOTE £3.70: £1.90, £1.30, £3.00; EX 11.10 Trifecta £57.70.
**Owner** Mrs J Scrivens **Bred** Mountarmstrong Stud **Trained** Brayford, Devon

**FOCUS**
A fair handicap run at a sound gallop and this form should prove reliable. The winner came down the centre in the straight.

## 7889 UNIBET OFFER DAILY JOCKEY/TRAINER SPECIALS H'CAP (TAPETA) 5f 20y
**6:15** (6:17) (Class 3) (0-95,95) 3-Y-0 **£7,246** (£2,168; £1,084; £542; £270) **Stalls** Low

Form RPR
-052 1 **Boom The Groom (IRE)**10 7738 3-8-12 86 WilliamCarson 2 99
(Tony Carroll) *cl up: chsd ldr 3f out: drvn to ld 1f out: sn clr* 15/2
0316 2 2 **Smart Daisy K**61 6614 4-9-2 90 ShaneKelly 5 96
(Andrew Hollinshead) *dwlt: patiently rdn in rr: hdwy over 1f out: r.o wl to snatch 2nd nr fin* 22/1
0043 3 nk **Even Stevens**10 7738 6-9-7 95 (v) TomEaves 1 100
(Scott Dixon) *led at gd pce tl 1f out: sn btn: lost 2nd nr fin* 5/1[2]
1220 4 1 1/2 **Master Bond**36 7233 5-8-13 87 SamJames 11 86
(David O'Meara) *rdn along towards rr: styd on fnl f: nrest at fin* 33/1
0303 5 hd **Bedloe's Island (IRE)**9 7767 9-8-9 83 BenCurtis 3 82
(Alan McCabe) *sn pushed along: chsd ldrs: hrd rdn over 1f out: one pce* 50/1
1611 6 nk **It Must Be Faith**17 7669 4-8-9 83 HayleyTurner 10 81
(Michael Appleby) *bmpd s: in tch on outer: effrt 2f out: no imp* 15/8[1]
0101 7 1/2 **Sleepy Sioux**10 7738 3-9-7 95 (p) GrahamLee 9 91
(David Elsworth) *dwlt and hmpd s: rdn along towards rr: sme late hdwy* 10/1
6500 8 3/4 **Secret Asset (IRE)**15 7700 9-8-11 85 (p) LukeMorris 13 78
(Jane Chapple-Hyam) *rdn along and bhd: hung lft over 1f out: n.d* 25/1
0000 9 3/4 **Viva Verglas (IRE)**10 7738 3-8-13 87 (b) GrahamGibbons 7 77
(David Barron) *prom tl wknd over 1f out* 15/2
0106 10 nk **Megaleka**10 7738 4-8-10 89 TimClark(5) 4 78
(Alan Bailey) *mid-div: effrt on inner 2f out: wknd 1f out* 40/1
6061 11 2 3/4 **Desert Ace (IRE)**41 7132 3-9-6 94 (tp) PaulMulrennan 8 73
(Michael Dods) *in tch on outer: pushed wd on bnd 3f out: wknd 2f out* 6/1[3]
1160 12 20 **Gregori (IRE)**17 7669 4-8-9 83 (tp) SeanLevey 6
(Brian Meehan) *chsd ldr for 2f: wknd over 2f out: bhd whn eased over 1f out* 40/1

1m 0.25s (-1.65) **Going Correction** -0.15s/f (Stan) course record 12 Ran SP% 116.3
Speed ratings (Par 107): **107,103,103,100,100 100,99,98,96,96 92,60**
CSF £163.99 CT £904.90 TOTE £6.10: £2.40, £6.10, £2.80; EX 192.40 Trifecta £1520.10.
**Owner** Gary Attwood **Bred** John Foley **Trained** Cropthorne, Worcs

**FOCUS**
A very useful and valuable handicap and a decent gallop but, as is usually the case in sprints on the new Tapeta surface, not many figured. The winner came down the centre in the straight.

## 7890 32RED.COM NURSERY H'CAP (TAPETA) 5f 216y
**6:45** (6:47) (Class 5) (0-75,74) 2-Y-O **£2,749** (£818; £408; £204) **Stalls** Low

Form RPR
4001 1 **Anastazia**12 7728 2-9-5 72 LukeMorris 3 75
(Paul D'Arcy) *in tch: effrt over 1f out: drvn to ld ins fnl f* 7/2[3]
5016 2 3/4 **Barchan (USA)**58 6679 2-9-4 71 (t) AdamKirby 4 72
(Charlie Appleby) *in tch: effrt in centre over 1f out: drvn to press ldrs ins fnl f: r.o* 5/2[2]
6244 3 3/4 **Classic Seniority**2 7849 2-8-11 71 JoshQuinn(7) 5 70
(Richard Hannon) *chsd ldr: rdn to ld 2f out: hdd ins fnl f: kpt on* 18/1
5661 4 shd **The Fairy (IRE)**16 7684 2-9-2 69 RobertHavlin 2 67
(John Gosden) *cl up in 3rd: chal 2f out: hung lft over 1f out: kpt on* 11/8[1]
0611 5 1/2 **Little**9 7762 2-8-9 67 RachealKneller(5) 6 64
(Jamie Osborne) *bhd: rdn and sme hdwy on inner over 1f out: nvr quite able to chal* 6/1


The Form Book, Raceform Ltd, Newbury, RG14 5SJ

1513 **6** *8* **Low Cut Affair (IRE)**[8] 7780 2-9-2 **74**.............................. JackDuern(5) 1 47
(Gay Kelleway) *led: rdn and hdd 2f out: sn wknd* **28/1**

1m 13.91s (-0.59) **Going Correction** -0.15s/f (Stan) **6** Ran SP% **115.9**
Speed ratings (Par 96): **97,96,95,94,94 83**
CSF £13.24 TOTE £4.10: £2.20, £2.00; EX 11.40 Trifecta £97.50.
**Owner** K Snell **Bred** K Snell **Trained** Newmarket, Suffolk

**FOCUS**
A fair nursery in which the gallop was an ordinary one. The winner raced against the inside rail in the straight.

## 7891 32RED IRISH STALLION FARMS EBF MAIDEN STKS (TAPETA) (DIV I) 1m 141y

**7:15** (7:17) (Class 5) 2-Y-O **£2,911** (£866; £432; £216) **Stalls** Low

Form RPR

**1** **Aabir (IRE)** 2-9-5 0.............................. MartinHarley 10 75+
(Marco Botti) *hld up towards rr: gd hdwy and fnd gap 1f out: r.o to ld ins fnl f* **33/1**

53 **2** *½* **Mountainside**[130] 4301 2-9-5 0.............................. AdamKirby 6 74
(Charlie Appleby) *in tch: effrt on outer 2f out: hung lft and drvn to join ldrs ins fnl f: kpt on* **9/2[3]**

5 **3** *hd* **Vanishing**[23] 7550 2-9-0 0.............................. LukeMorris 7 69
(Ed Walker) *mid-div: effrt 2f out: styd on u.p fnl f* **20/1**

363 **4** *1 ¼* **Perceus**[17] 7666 2-9-5 78.............................. MartinDwyer 4 71
(Marcus Tregoning) *in tch: pressed ldr 5f out: slt ld over 1f out tl bmpd ins fnl f: one pce* **7/2[2]**

5 **5** *hd* **Estikhraaj**[17] 7660 2-9-5 0.............................. GrahamLee 9 71
(Roger Varian) *mid-div on outer: struggling to hold pl 6f out: hdwy in centre and hrd rdn over 1f out: unable to rch ldrs* **11/2**

4 **6** *½* **Assagher (USA)**[31] 7371 2-9-5 0.............................. RobertHavlin 3 72
(John Gosden) *prom: chal and leant on by rival fr over 1f out: 5th and hld whn squeezed ins fnl f* **11/8[1]**

0 **7** *2 ½* **Devonshire Place (IRE)**[21] 7594 2-9-0 0........ WilliamTwiston-Davies 5 60
(Roger Charlton) *mid-div: rdn over 3f out: btn 2f out* **25/1**

3304 **8** *5* **Regal Ways (IRE)**[7] 7809 2-9-0 68.............................. JoeFanning 1 49
(Mark Johnston) *led tl wknd over 1f out* **50/1**

**9** *4* **Takahiro** 2-9-5 0.............................. SeanLevey 2 46
(Richard Hannon) *prom tl wknd wl over 1f out* **66/1**

**10** *17* **Become Aware** 2-9-5 0.............................. TomEaves 8
(Tim Etherington) *stdd s: outpcd and bhd: no ch fnl 3f* **100/1**

1m 49.04s (-1.06) **Going Correction** -0.15s/f (Stan) **10** Ran SP% **113.9**
Speed ratings (Par 96): **98,97,97,96,96 95,93,88,85,70**
CSF £164.98 TOTE £27.20: £4.90, £1.60, £4.00; EX 153.90 Trifecta £844.90.
**Owner** Sheikh Mohammed Bin Khalifa Al Maktoum **Bred** Patrick Byrnes **Trained** Newmarket, Suffolk

**FOCUS**
A fair maiden but one in which the gallop was on the steady side to the home turn.

## 7892 32RED IRISH STALLION FARMS EBF MAIDEN STKS (TAPETA) (DIV II) 1m 141y

**7:45** (7:46) (Class 5) 2-Y-O **£2,911** (£866; £432; £216) **Stalls** Low

Form RPR

**1** **Malaf (USA)** 2-9-5 0.............................. RobertHavlin 5 76+
(John Gosden) *dwlt: trckd ldrs in 4th: effrt and wd st: hung lft and led 1f out: rdn out* **8/11[1]**

6 **2** *1 ½* **Putting Green**[47] 6985 2-9-5 0.............................. SeanLevey 6 73
(Richard Hannon) *led: rdn over 2f out: edgd rt and hdd 1f out: kpt on same pce* **22/1**

40 **3** *2 ¼* **Borak (IRE)**[22] 7560 2-9-5 0.............................. MartinHarley 7 69
(Marco Botti) *wnt rt s: chsd ldr: drvn and trying to chal whn squeezed out jst over 1f out: nt rcvr* **10/1**

**4** *nk* **Stay Strong (GER)** 2-9-5 0.............................. GrahamLee 1 67
(Saeed bin Suroor) *in tch: rdn over 2f out: styd on same pce* **9/2[3]**

**5** *shd* **Sparring (IRE)** 2-9-5 0.............................. AdamKirby 4 67
(Charlie Appleby) *stdd s: hld up in 6th: rdn over 2f out: no prog tl styng on at fin* **4/1[2]**

**6** *2* **Dexterous** 2-9-0 0.............................. WilliamTwiston-Davies 2 58
(Roger Charlton) *dwlt: hld up in rr: rdn and n.d fnl 2f* **25/1**

0 **7** *shd* **Parole (IRE)**[17] 7660 2-9-5 0.............................. JoeFanning 3 65
(Hughie Morrison) *cl 3rd tl hung lft and wknd wl over 1f out* **33/1**

1m 50.74s (0.64) **Going Correction** -0.15s/f (Stan) **7** Ran SP% **116.3**
Speed ratings (Par 96): **91,89,87,87,87 85,85**
CSF £23.24 TOTE £1.50: £1.10, £6.50; EX 22.00 Trifecta £175.70.
**Owner** Hamdan Al Maktoum **Bred** Anthony Grey **Trained** Newmarket, Suffolk
■ Stewards' Enquiry : Martin Harley two-day ban: careless riding (6, 8 Dec)

**FOCUS**
Division two and a ready winner, who overcame inexperience to win with something in hand. The gallop was just an ordinary one and the winner edged towards the far side late on.

## 7893 32RED CASINO H'CAP (TAPETA) 2m 119y

**8:15** (8:17) (Class 6) (0-60,60) 3-Y-O+ **£2,264** (£673; £336; £168) **Stalls** Low

Form RPR

0332 **1** **Yorkshireman (IRE)**[22] 7572 4-9-1 49.............................. (b) PaddyAspell 10 58
(Lynn Siddall) *prom: led 4f out: rdn clr wl over 1f out: comf* **12/1**

3626 **2** *3* **Lacey**[25] 7524 5-9-7 55.............................. (p) AdamKirby 13 60
(Andrew Hollinshead) *mid-div: hdwy 5f out: styd on same pce fnl 2f: tk 2nd fnl strides* **10/1**

0321 **3** *nk* **Delagoa Bay (IRE)**[17] 7657 6-9-0 48.............................. MartinDwyer 9 53
(Sylvester Kirk) *hld up disputing 4th: jnd ldr 5f out: one pce fnl 2f: lost 2nd fnl strides* **9/1**

2540 **4** *nk* **Honest Strike (USA)**[17] 7657 7-9-10 58.............................. (bt) ShaneKelly 12 62
(Daniel Mark Loughnane) *stdd s: hld up in rr: rdn and hdwy 2f out: styd on same pce fnl f* **14/1**

/036 **5** *1 ¾* **Nay Secret**[18] 7643 6-9-1 49.............................. GaryBartley 1 51
(Jim Goldie) *mid-div: rdn 5f out: hdwy on inner over 2f out: hrd rdn over 1f out: one pce* **7/1[3]**

1522 **6** *1 ½* **Eastern Magic**[46] 7007 7-9-3 56.............................. JackDuern(5) 5 56
(Andrew Hollinshead) *s.s: bhd: rdn and styd on fnl 2f: nvr nrr* **15/2**

3243 **7** *nk* **Hallouella**[24] 7532 3-9-2 59.............................. (p) GrahamLee 7 59
(David Elsworth) *dwlt: towards rr: rdn and sme hdwy over 1f out: nvr rchd ldrs* **3/1[1]**

6053 **8** *nk* **Weybridge Light**[16] 7572 9-8-12 46.............................. (b) JimmyQuinn 11 46
(David Thompson) *hld up towards rr: rdn and unable to trble ldrs fnl 3f* **33/1**

0006 **9** *3* **Artisan**[17] 7657 6-9-9 57.............................. (t) PaulPickard 6 53
(Brian Ellison) *towards rr: effrt out wd 5f out: hung to stands' rail in st: n.d* **9/2[2]**

0543 **10** *6* **Time Of My Life (IRE)**[18] 7643 5-9-0 51.............................. (t) DeclanBates(3) 2 40
(Patrick Holmes) *broke wl: stdd bk to dispute 4th: rdn 5f out: wknd over 2f out* **25/1**

054 **11** *3* **Blue Valentino**[44] 7067 5-9-7 55.............................. GrahamGibbons 4 40
(Andrew Hollinshead) *sn chsng ldr: jnd ldr after 5f: lost pl over 5f out: n.d after* **33/1**

4605 **12** *32* **Wild Desert (FR)**[54] 6818 9-9-5 53.............................. (p) LukeMorris 3
(Tony Carroll) *led tl 4f out: wknd 3f out: bhd and eased fnl 2f* **14/1**

3m 38.83s (-4.87) **Going Correction** -0.15s/f (Stan)
**WFA** 3 from 4yo+ 9lb **12** Ran SP% **117.3**
Speed ratings (Par 101): **105,103,103,103,102 101,101,101,100,97 95,80**
CSF £122.87 CT £1132.40 TOTE £15.20: £3.10, £3.30, £3.40; EX 106.60 Trifecta £1207.90.
**Owner** Miss J M Slater **Bred** Ossiana Partnership **Trained** Colton, N Yorks
■ Stewards' Enquiry : Jack Duern jockey said that the blindfold had become stuck on the bridle and he had to have two attempts at removing it=
Paul Pickard jockey said the gelding hung badly right throughout

**FOCUS**
A moderate handicap run at a stop-start gallop. The winner raced centre-to-far side in the straight.

## 7894 LADBROKES CLAIMING STKS (TAPETA) 1m 141y

**8:45** (8:46) (Class 6) 3-Y-O+ **£2,264** (£673; £336; £168) **Stalls** Low

Form RPR

0006 **1** **Monsieur Chevalier (IRE)**[41] 7136 7-9-8 82.............................. AdamKirby 8 87
(Jamie Osborne) *s.s: bhd: rdn and hdwy over 1f out: styd on to ld ins fnl f* **7/4[1]**

0002 **2** *1 ¼* **Boogangoo (IRE)**[34] 7303 3-8-12 68.............................. StevieDonohoe 6 77
(Grace Harris) *led after 1f: kicked clr ent st: hrd rdn and hdd ins fnl f: kpt on* **28/1**

0011 **3** *1* **Naoise (IRE)**[22] 7569 6-9-2 76.............................. (t) JacobButterfield(3) 5 79
(Ollie Pears) *stdd s: hld up in tch: effrt and hung lft wl over 1f out: styd on same pce* **5/2[2]**

1015 **4** *hd* **Tee It Up Tommo (IRE)**[28] 7456 5-9-2 82.............................. LukeMorris 3 75
(Michael Wigham) *in tch: rdn over 2f out: styd on fnl f* **4/1**

1612 **5** *3 ¼* **Toto Skyllachy**[9] 7765 9-8-13 75.............................. (p) SamJames 1 65
(David O'Meara) *led for 1f: styd cl up: hrd rdn 3f out: wknd 2f out* **7/2[3]**

11-5 **6** *1 ¼* **Idyllic Star (IRE)**[18] 7639 5-8-8 65.............................. JoeFanning 4 57
(Jim Goldie) *dwlt: sn prom: chsd ldr after 2f tl wl over 1f out: sn wknd* **20/1**

**7** *33* **Newforge House (IRE)**[20] 6-8-9 0.............................. EoinWalsh(5) 2
(Dai Burchell) *missed break and lost 12 l: a detached in last pl: drvn along 5f out: sn t.o* **100/1**

1m 48.04s (-2.06) **Going Correction** -0.15s/f (Stan)
**WFA** 3 from 4yo+ 3lb **7** Ran SP% **116.4**
Speed ratings (Par 101): **103,101,101,100,97 96,67**
CSF £52.08 TOTE £3.30: £1.70, £5.30; EX 39.20 Trifecta £204.30.
**Owner** J A Osborne **Bred** Tally-Ho Stud **Trained** Upper Lambourn, Berks
■ Stewards' Enquiry : Eoin Walsh jockey said that the gelding was slowly away

**FOCUS**
A useful claimer but one run at an ordinary gallop. The winner came down the centre in the straight.

## 7895 DOWNLOAD THE CORAL APP H'CAP (TAPETA) 1m 4f 50y

**9:15** (9:16) (Class 6) (0-60,60) 3-Y-O+ **£2,264** (£673; £336; £168) **Stalls** Low

Form RPR

5254 **1** **Well Owd Mon**[50] 6900 4-8-9 50.............................. (p) JackDuern(5) 1 57
(Andrew Hollinshead) *s.s: hld up in rr: hrd rdn over 1f out: rapid hdwy to ld fnl 30yds* **11/2[3]**

5650 **2** *½* **Anjuna Beach (USA)**[9] 7765 4-9-4 59.............................. AnnStokell(5) 3 65
(Ann Stokell) *dwlt: hld up in midfield: smooth hdwy 3f out: kpt on u.p fnl f to take 2nd nr fin* **50/1**

4344 **3** *nk* **Sakhra**[19] 7628 3-9-2 58.............................. GrahamGibbons 9 64
(Mark Brisbourne) *towards rr: rdn and hdwy 2f out: drvn to chal ins fnl f: unable qck nr fin* **5/2[1]**

31/0 **4** *1* **Aldo**[39] 7182 7-9-10 60.............................. (t) AdamKirby 8 64
(Sean Curran) *chsd ldrs: wnt cl 2nd 5f out: drvn to ld over 1f out tl no ex fnl 30yds* **4/1[2]**

0641 **5** *¾* **Cascadia (IRE)**[28] 7458 3-9-1 57.............................. TomEaves 5 60
(Alison Hutchinson) *led tl over 1f out: no ex ins fnl f* **9/1**

5050 **6** *1* **Dancing Primo**[19] 7628 8-9-1 58.............................. BeckyBrisbourne(7) 7 59
(Mark Brisbourne) *dwlt: bhd tl c wd and hdwy u.p over 1f out: unable to rch ldrs* **18/1**

320 **7** *¾* **Dhaular Dhar (IRE)**[16] 7100 12-9-10 60.............................. GaryBartley 11 60
(Jim Goldie) *hld up in rr: hld up in midfield on outer: hdwy 6f out: one pce fnl 2f* **16/1**

4250 **8** *1 ½* **Harrison's Cave**[19] 7628 6-9-9 59.............................. JoeFanning 2 57
(Sharon Watt) *in tch tl outpcd 2f out* **8/1**

0304 **9** *1 ¼* **Bold And Free**[26] 7499 4-9-0 50.............................. JimmyQuinn 4 46
(David Thompson) *prom tl wknd over 2f out* **33/1**

4520 **10** *4 ½* **Dark And Dangerous (IRE)**[118] 2770 6-9-7 57.............................. (t) LiamKeniry 10 45
(Brendan Powell) *a bhd* **33/1**

000 **11** *9* **Pahente**[85] 5898 6-9-0 50.............................. (p) WilliamCarson 12 24
(Tony Carroll) *mid-div: struggling 3f out: sn bhd* **20/1**

0006 **12** *99* **Dabuki (FR)**[19] 7628 4-9-10 60.............................. (p) PJMcDonald 6
(Geoffrey Harker) *chsd ldr tl 6f out: qckly lost pl: sn bhd* **8/1**

2m 39.38s (-1.42) **Going Correction** -0.15s/f (Stan)
**WFA** 3 from 4yo+ 6lb **12** Ran SP% **119.9**
Speed ratings (Par 101): **98,97,97,96,96 95,95,94,93,90 84,18**
CSF £268.40 CT £862.37 TOTE £7.50: £3.00, £8.20, £1.60; EX 485.10 Trifecta £1924.10.
**Owner** The Giddy Gang **Bred** Mr & Mrs W Hodge **Trained** Upper Longdon, Staffs
■ Stewards' Enquiry : Graham Gibbons two-day ban: use of whip (6, 8 Dec)
Jack Duern used whip above the permitted level (TBA)

**FOCUS**
A moderate handicap in which an ordinary gallop picked up on the approach to the straight.
T/Plt: £967.90 to a £1 stake. Pool of £135963.34 - 102.54 winning tickets. T/Qpdt: £136.30 to a £1 stake. Pool of £8696.85 - 47.20 winning tickets. LM

## [2004]SHA TIN (R-H)

Sunday, November 23

**OFFICIAL GOING: Turf: good to firm**

### 7897a BOCHK WEALTH MANAGEMENT JOCKEY CLUB SPRINT (GROUP 2) (3YO+) (TURF) 6f

**7:30** (12:00) 3-Y-0+ **£172,021** (£66,394; £34,706; £18,107; £10,562)

RPR

1 **Peniaphobia (IRE)**[35] 3-8-11 0 ....(tp) DouglasWhyte 14 118+
(A S Cruz, Hong Kong) **13/2**

2 ½ **Smart Volatility (AUS)**[28] 6-8-11 0 .... GeraldMosse 4 116
(K W Lui, Hong Kong) **33/10**[2]

3 1 **Flagship Shine (AUS)**[28] 5-8-11 0 ....(p) NashRawiller 6 113+
(J Moore, Hong Kong) **29/1**

4 nk **Golden Harvest (AUS)**[28] 6-8-11 0 ....(t) UmbertoRispoli 10 112
(A T Millard, Hong Kong) **28/1**

5 ¾ **Lucky Nine (IRE)**[189] 2378 7-9-2 0 ....(b) BrettPrebble 2 115
(C Fownes, Hong Kong) **31/5**

6 ½ **Super Jockey (NZ)**[28] 6-8-11 0 .... AndreaAtzeni 3 108
(A T Millard, Hong Kong) **26/1**

7 shd **Exciting Dream** 4-8-11 0 ....(p) ChristianReith 12 108
(J Moore, Hong Kong) **130/1**

8 shd **Amber Sky (AUS)**[53] 5-9-2 0 ....(t) MircoDemuro 9 112
(P F Yiu, Hong Kong) **47/1**

9 shd **Charles The Great (IRE)**[28] 5-8-11 0 ....(t) NeilCallan 11 107
(J Moore, Hong Kong) **47/1**

10 ½ **Bundle Of Joy (AUS)**[28] 5-8-11 0 .... KTeetan 8 105
(D J Hall, Hong Kong) **61/1**

10 dht **Frederick Engels**[28] 5-8-11 0 ....(t) MatthewChadwick 5 105+
(J Moore, Hong Kong) **105/1**

12 1¼ **Sterling City (AUS)**[28] 6-9-2 0 ....(t) JoaoMoreira 7 113+
(J Moore, Hong Kong) **18/1**

13 shd **Spalato (NZ)**[28] 5-9-2 0 .... JamesMcDonald 13 106
(John F O'Hara, Singapore) **59/10**[3]

14 1 **Aerovelocity (NZ)**[28] 6-8-11 0 ....(bt) ZacPurton 1 119+
(P O'Sullivan, Hong Kong) **19/10**[1]

1m 8.08s (68.08) **14** Ran SP% **122.7**
PARI-MUTUEL (all including 10 hkd stake): WIN 75.00; PLACE 27.00, 17.00, 69.50; DF 197.00.
**Owner** Huang Kai Wen **Bred** Aidan Fogarty **Trained** Hong Kong

### 7898a BOCHK WEALTH MANAGEMENT JOCKEY CLUB MILE (GROUP 2) (3YO+) (TURF) 1m

**8:05** (12:00) 3-Y-0+ **£172,021** (£66,394; £34,706; £18,107; £10,562)

RPR

1 **Able Friend (AUS)**[28] 5-8-11 0 ....(p) JoaoMoreira 8 120+
(J Moore, Hong Kong) **19/20**[1]

2 2¼ **Gold-Fun (IRE)**[28] 5-9-2 0 ....(b) DouglasWhyte 4 120
(R Gibson, Hong Kong) **13/5**[2]

3 ½ **Ambitious Dragon (NZ)**[28] 8-8-11 0 ....(b) GeraldMosse 3 114
(A T Millard, Hong Kong) **33/10**[3]

4 1 **Secret Sham (AUS)**[8] 5-8-11 0 .... NeilCallan 7 111
(J Moore, Hong Kong) **44/1**

5 1 **Rainbow Chic (IRE)**[14] 5-8-11 0 ....(bt[1]) JamesMcDonald 5 109+
(C Fownes, Hong Kong) **153/1**

6 ½ **Rewarding Hero**[28] 5-8-11 0 .... AndreaAtzeni 6 108
(J Moore, Hong Kong) **15/1**

7 2½ **Lord Sinclair (USA)**[962] 1208 5-8-11 0 ....(b) BrettPrebble 10 102+
(S Woods, Hong Kong) **104/1**

8 nk **Same World**[14] 6-8-11 0 .... ChristianReith 9 101
(J Moore, Hong Kong) **166/1**

9 7½ **Hana's Goal (JPN)**[49] 5-8-12 0 .... NashRawiller 2 85
(Kazuhiro Kato, Japan) **34/1**

10 6 **Packing Whiz (IRE)**[28] 6-8-11 0 ....(b[1]) ZacPurton 1 70
(C Fownes, Hong Kong) **14/1**

1m 33.46s (-1.24) **10** Ran SP% **122.5**
PARI-MUTUEL (all including 10 hkd stake): WIN 19.50; PLACE 12.00, 13.00, 13.50; DF 38.50.
**Owner** Dr & Mrs Cornel Li Fook Kwan **Bred** Ramsey Pastoral Co Pty Ltd **Trained** Hong Kong

### 7899a LONGINES JOCKEY CLUB CUP (GROUP 2) (3YO+) (TURF) 1m 2f

**8:40** (12:00) 3-Y-0+ **£172,021** (£66,394; £34,706; £18,107; £10,562)

RPR

1 **Blazing Speed**[28] 5-9-2 0 ....(t) NeilCallan 6 121
(A S Cruz, Hong Kong) **74/10**

2 hd **Military Attack (IRE)**[28] 6-9-2 0 .... ZacPurton 4 120
(C Fownes, Hong Kong) **11/5**[2]

3 hd **Endowing (IRE)**[28] 5-8-11 0 ....(e) BrettPrebble 7 115
(J Size, Hong Kong) **9/1**

4 ½ **California Memory (USA)**[28] 8-8-11 0 .... MatthewChadwick 2 114
(A S Cruz, Hong Kong) **14/1**

5 shd **Designs On Rome (IRE)**[28] 4-9-2 0 ....(t) JoaoMoreira 10 119+
(J Moore, Hong Kong) **8/5**[1]

6 1 **Bubble Chic (FR)**[14] 6-8-11 0 .... KTeetan 1 112
(D J Hall, Hong Kong) **110/1**

7 ½ **Willie Cazals (IRE)**[14] 6-8-11 0 ....(p) DouglasWhyte 9 111
(A S Cruz, Hong Kong) **31/5**[3]

8 ½ **Mr Gnocchi (AUS)**[14] 5-8-11 0 ....(bt) UmbertoRispoli 5 110
(C S Shum, Hong Kong) **51/1**

9 shd **Helene Super Star (USA)**[14] 4-8-11 0 ....(t) MircoDemuro 8 110
(A S Cruz, Hong Kong) **26/1**

10 1¾ **Sunny Ying**[14] 5-8-11 0 .... NashRawiller 3 106
(J Moore, Hong Kong) **179/1**

11 4¼ **Dominant (IRE)**[28] 6-9-2 0 .... GeraldMosse 12 103
(J Moore, Hong Kong) **40/1**

12 10 **Travel Brand**[14] 6-8-11 0 ....(bt) AndreaAtzeni 11 78
(C H Yip, Hong Kong) **350/1**

2m 1.71s (0.31) **12** Ran SP% **122.0**
PARI-MUTUEL (all including 10 hkd stake): WIN 84.00; PLACE 25.00, 12.00, 29.00; DF 89.50.
**Owner** Fentons Racing Syndicate **Bred** J Sankey **Trained** Hong Kong

## [7888]WOLVERHAMPTON (A.W) (L-H)

Monday, November 24

**OFFICIAL GOING: Tapeta: standard**

Wind: Light behind Weather: Fine

### 7900 £20 RISK-FREE BET AT UNIBET H'CAP (TAPETA) 5f 20y

**2:00** (2:01) (Class 6) (0-60,60) 3-Y-0+ **£2,264** (£673; £336; £168) **Stalls** Low

Form RPR

5622 1 **Give Us A Belle (IRE)**[52] 6897 5-9-5 59 ....(vt) AdamKirby 4 67
(Christine Dunnett) *mde all: pushed along 1/2-way: rdn and edgd rt fr over 1f out: all out* **9/2**[2]

3214 2 ½ **Danzoe (IRE)**[19] 7670 7-8-12 57 ....(v) EoinWalsh[(5)] 2 63
(Christine Dunnett) *hld up: hdwy over 1f out: rdn and ev ch ins fnl f: r.o* **10/1**

0060 3 shd **My Meteor**[17] 7697 7-9-1 58 .... DannyBrock[(3)] 9 64
(Tony Newcombe) *s.i.s: hdwy and nt clr run over 1f out: r.o* **50/1**

5431 4 nse **Your Gifted (IRE)**[10] 7781 7-8-11 58 ....(v) RobHornby[(7)] 3 63
(Lisa Williamson) *a.p: rdn over 1f out: r.o* **7/1**

0000 5 nk **Shirley's Pride**[27] 7510 4-8-12 57 ....(tp) AlistairRawlinson[(5)] 11 61
(Michael Appleby) *s.i.s: hdwy and nt clr run over 1f out: r.o* **6/1**[3]

6516 6 ½ **Aaranyow (IRE)**[19] 7670 6-9-0 59 ....(t) TobyAtkinson[(5)] 7 62
(Clifford Lines) *chsd wnr: rdn and ev ch fr over 1f out: hmpd ins fnl f: no ex towards fin* **14/1**

2040 7 1 **Master Of Disguise**[245] 1082 8-9-4 58 .... PhillipMakin 10 57
(Brian Baugh) *mid-div: lost pl 1/2-way: rdn over 1f out: r.o ins fnl f: nt rch ldrs* **12/1**

3133 8 ¾ **First Rebellion**[19] 7671 5-9-2 56 ....(b) DavidProbert 5 52
(Tony Carroll) *hld up in tch: rdn over 1f out: styd on same pce ins fnl f* **14/1**

0616 9 1¾ **Louis Vee (IRE)**[74] 6273 6-9-6 60 ....(t) TomEaves 6 50
(Roy Brotherton) *hld up: rdn over 1f out: nt trble ldrs* **40/1**

1653 10 nse **Pearl Noir**[21] 7622 4-9-4 58 ....(b) LukeMorris 8 48
(Scott Dixon) *chsd ldrs: rdn over 1f out: wknd ins fnl f* **3/1**[1]

6-40 11 3½ **Pavers Bounty**[157] 3440 3-9-5 59 .... JoeFanning 1 36
(Noel Wilson) *chsd ldrs: rdn 2f out: wknd fnl f* **11/1**

5600 12 nk **College Doll**[19] 7671 5-9-3 57 ....(t) JimmyQuinn 13 33
(Christine Dunnett) *hld up: rdn over 1f out: n.d* **125/1**

532 13 11 **Dancing Juice**[110] 5061 3-9-3 57 ....(v) GrahamGibbons 12
(Brian Ellison) *chsd ldrs tl rdn and wknd 1/2-way* **16/1**

1m 1.24s (-0.66) **Going Correction** -0.15s/f (Stan) **13** Ran SP% **119.5**
Speed ratings (Par 101): **99,98,98,97,97 96,95,93,91,91 85,84,67**
CSF £48.98 CT £2000.72 TOTE £5.40: £2.10, £3.40, £9.30; EX 32.60 Trifecta £1322.80.
**Owner** F Butler & Mrs C Dunnett **Bred** Audrey Frances Stynes **Trained** Hingham, Norfolk
■ Stewards' Enquiry : Adam Kirby two-day ban: careless riding (8-9 Dec)

**FOCUS**
Last year Christine Dunnett won both divisions of this race with Give US A Belle and Danzoe, and remarkably the same pair came back to finish one-two this time. Sound, straightforward form.

### 7901 DOWNLOAD THE CORAL APP MAIDEN STKS (TAPETA) 1m 1f 103y

**2:35** (2:36) (Class 5) 3-Y-0+ **£2,911** (£866; £432; £216) **Stalls** Low

Form RPR

322 1 **Razor Wind (IRE)**[14] 7733 3-9-5 84 .... AdamKirby 10 89
(Charlie Appleby) *trckd ldrs: shkn up to ld over 2f out: rdn clr fr over 1f out* **1/3**[1]

2 3¾ **Westwood Hoe** 3-9-5 0 .... RobertHavlin 7 81
(John Gosden) *a.p: rdn to chse wnr over 1f out: styd on same pce* **5/1**[3]

3224 3 hd **Panatella**[14] 7734 3-9-0 72 .... ShaneKelly 1 76
(James Fanshawe) *mid-div: hdwy over 2f out: rdn over 1f out: no imp fnl f* **7/2**[2]

4 1¼ **Urban Castle (USA)** 3-9-0 0 .... LukeMorris 8 73
(James Tate) *hld up: rdn over 1f out: styd on ins fnl f: nt trble ldrs* **16/1**

450 5 4½ **The Gay Cavalier**[32] 7402 3-9-5 68 ....(t) JackMitchell 11 69
(John Ryan) *mid-div: hdwy 3f out: rdn over 1f out: wknd ins fnl f* **28/1**

6 3½ **Mustafiz (USA)** 3-9-5 0 .... SamJames 9 62
(Noel Quinlan) *chsd ldr tl led 3f out: rdn and hdd over 2f out: wknd over 1f out* **33/1**

7 5 **Baileys En Premier (FR)**[158] 3-9-5 60 .... BenCurtis 5 51
(Chris Dwyer) *hld up: wknd over 2f out* **100/1**

8 2¼ **Roxy Madam**[134] 5-9-0 0 .... RossAtkinson[(3)] 4 41
(Mandy Rowland) *s.s: hld up: rdn and wknd 2f out* **100/1**

0 9 nk **Vilaz**[179] 2690 3-9-5 0 .... HayleyTurner 3 46
(Brian Meehan) *chsd ldrs tl rdn and wknd over 2f out* **40/1**

00 10 ½ **Norman's Star**[279] 649 3-9-2 0 .... ConnorBeasley[(3)] 6 45
(Chris Dwyer) *sn led: hdd 3f out: rdn and wknd 2f out* **100/1**

11 38 **Kaaber (USA)** 3-9-5 0 .... TomEaves 2
(Roy Brotherton) *s.s: outpcd* **100/1**

1m 59.4s (-1.40) **Going Correction** -0.15s/f (Stan)
**WFA** 3 from 5yo 3lb **11** Ran SP% **132.6**
Speed ratings (Par 103): **100,96,96,95,91 88,83,81,81,81 47**
CSF £3.43 TOTE £1.30: £1.10, £1.50, £1.30; EX 4.00 Trifecta £9.00.
**Owner** Godolphin **Bred** Stone Ridge Farm **Trained** Newmarket, Suffolk

**FOCUS**
The winner had already shown himself to be useful and this was uncompetitive. He only needed to run to form.

### 7902 32RED.COM NURSERY H'CAP (TAPETA) 1m 141y

**3:05** (3:05) (Class 5) (0-75,74) 2-Y-O **£2,911** (£866; £432; £216) **Stalls** Low

Form RPR

550 1 **Greatest Journey**[51] 6925 2-8-3 **63** .... KieranShoemark[(7)] 6 75+
(Saeed bin Suroor) *s.i.s: hld up: hdwy to ld over 1f out: r.o* **5/2**[2]

5522 2 1¾ **Offshore**[7] 7815 2-8-10 **63** ....(p) LukeMorris 7 71+
(James Tate) *chsd ldr: rdn to ld 2f out: hdd wl over 1f out: styd on same pce ins fnl f* **7/4**[1]

0622 3 2½ **Red Stripes (USA)**[7] 7816 2-8-0 **53** oh4 ....(b) HayleyTurner 5 56
(Brian Meehan) *trckd ldrs: led wl over 1f out: sn rdn and hdd: edgd lft and no ex ins fnl f* **10/1**

0041 4 2¾ **Rockaroundtheclock (IRE)**[20] 7631 2-9-2 **74** .... JackDuern[(5)] 4 71
(Paul Cole) *led: rdn and hdd 2f out: wknd fnl f* **12/1**

6036 5 2¼ **Digital Rebellion (IRE)**[90] 5782 2-9-6 **73** .... AdamKirby 3 66+
(Charlie Appleby) *dwlt: hld up: rdn and wknd over 1f out* **4/1**[3]

0550 6 1 1/4 **Beauty Of The Sea**[11] 7753 2-8-9 62 MartinDwyer 1 52
(Roger Varian) *prom: rdn over 2f out: wknd fnl f* 17/2

1m 49.97s (-0.13) **Going Correction** -0.15s/f (Stan) 6 Ran SP% 112.2
Speed ratings (Par 96): **94,92,90,87,85 84**
CSF £7.30 TOTE £3.10: £1.50, £1.40; EX 6.80 Trifecta £38.90.
**Owner** Godolphin **Bred** Meon Valley Stud **Trained** Newmarket, Suffolk

**FOCUS**
There were some good yards represented, but this was easy for the improved winner, who didn't require the whip.

## 7903 32RED H'CAP (TAPETA) 2m 119y
3:35 (3:35) (Class 4) (0-85,78) 3-Y-0+ £5,175 (£1,540; £769; £384) Stalls Low

Form RPR
0110 1 **Uncle Bernie (IRE)**[41] 7182 4-9-2 66 RobertTart 6 79
(Andrew Hollinshead) *hld up: hdwy over 2f out: led over 1f out: r.o wl: comf* 9/1

43-1 2 3 3/4 **Rutherglen**[255] 591 4-10-0 78 PhillipMakin 5 86
(John Quinn) *a.p: nt clr run and swtchd rt 2f out: sn rdn: styd on* 11/8[1]

3 4 1/2 **Call Me Pj (IRE)**[12] 7750 7-9-6 70 SamJames 3 73
(Oliver McKiernan, Ire) *prom: chsd ldr over 12f out: led 7f out: rdn: hung lft and hdd over 1f out: wknd ins fnl f* 8/1[3]

0050 4 3 1/2 **Toptempo**[7] 7817 5-9-5 69 (b[1]) JimmyQuinn 2 67
(Mark H Tompkins) *prom: chsd ldr over 2f out tl rdn over 1f out: wknd fnl f* 14/1

1-05 5 1 1/4 **Bathwick Street**[20] 7650 5-9-9 73 AdamKirby 8 70
(David Evans) *hld up: rdn over 2f out: wknd over 1f out* 50/1

3525 6 10 **Underwritten**[15] 7129 5-9-4 68 WilliamCarson 4 53
(Shaun Harris) *led over 9f: rdn whn n.m.r over 4f out: wknd 3f out* 14/1

6416 7 shd **Jacobs Son**[151] 3624 6-9-9 78 AlistairRawlinson[(5)] 7 63
(Michael Appleby) *prom: rdn over 3f out: wknd over 2f out* 16/1

5111 8 4 1/2 **Alba Verde**[40] 7204 3-8-12 71 LukeMorris 1 50
(Sir Mark Prescott Bt) *chsd ldr 4f: remained handy: wnt 2nd again 1/2-way tl rdn over 2f out: hung lft and wknd over 1f out* 9/4[2]

3m 37.02s (-6.68) **Going Correction** -0.15s/f (Stan)
**WFA** 3 from 4yo+ 9lb 8 Ran SP% 115.2
Speed ratings (Par 105): **109,107,105,103,102 98,98,96**
CSF £22.04 CT £106.85 TOTE £7.70: £2.60, £1.20, £2.30; EX 25.30 Trifecta £128.20.
**Owner** Graham Brothers Racing Partnership **Bred** Roundhill Stud & Gleadhill House Stud Ltd **Trained** Upper Longdon, Staffs

**FOCUS**
A fair staying handicap even with Alba Verde bombing out, and they went a sound pace. The winner took his form to a new high.

## 7904 32RED CASINO NURSERY H'CAP (TAPETA) 7f 32y
4:05 (4:07) (Class 6) (0-60,58) 2-Y-0 £2,264 (£673; £336; £168) Stalls High

Form RPR
0060 1 **Celestine Abbey**[98] 5489 2-8-13 50 JackMitchell 1 54
(John Ryan) *mid-div: hdwy over 1f out: rdn to ld wl ins fnl f: r.o* 50/1

0553 2 nk **Laura B**[48] 7014 2-9-5 56 GeorgeBaker 2 59
(Chris Wall) *led 1f: chsd ldrs tl led again over 1f out: rdn and hdd wl ins fnl f: r.o* 5/2[1]

3334 3 1 1/4 **Fast Scat (USA)**[11] 7763 2-9-4 55 (v[1]) AdamKirby 4 56
(David Evans) *s.i.s: hld up: hdwy and nt clr run fr over 1f out: swtchd lft wl ins fnl f: r.o* 16/1

3035 4 nk **Penelope Pitstop**[20] 7648 2-9-3 54 JoeFanning 11 53
(Keith Dalgleish) *a.p: chsd ldr 2f out: sn rdn: styd on same pce ins fnl f* 4/1[3]

0021 5 1 **Excelling Oscar (IRE)**[6] 7828 2-9-5 56 6ex (b) HayleyTurner 9 53
(Conor Dore) *led 6f out: rdn and hdd over 1f out: styd on same pce ins fnl f* 7/1

2632 6 nk **Sky Steps (IRE)**[18] 7683 2-8-7 51 (v) GaryMahon[(7)] 8 47
(Philip McBride) *hld up: hdwy 1/2-way: rdn over 1f out: styd on same pce ins fnl f* 11/4[2]

6050 7 3 1/4 **Cahar Fad (IRE)**[12] 7740 2-8-12 54 JackDuern[(5)] 5 42
(Steph Hollinshead) *mid-div: rdn over 2f out: nt trble ldrs* 40/1

0600 8 3 1/2 **Orobas (IRE)**[70] 6413 2-8-8 48 AmyScott[(3)] 7 28
(Harry Whittington) *hld up: rdn 1/2-way: nvr on terms* 12/1

3006 9 4 1/2 **Arthur's Way (IRE)**[26] 7536 2-9-2 58 (p) EoinWalsh[(5)] 10 27
(Lisa Williamson) *s.i.s: sn pushed along and a in rr* 50/1

002 10 4 1/2 **Space Sheriff (IRE)**[11] 7763 2-9-2 58 (b) RachealKneller[(5)] 3 16
(Jamie Osborne) *s.i.s: hdwy to join ldr over 5f out tl rdn over 2f out: wknd over 1f out* 13/2

1m 29.11s (0.31) **Going Correction** -0.15s/f (Stan) 10 Ran SP% 121.0
Speed ratings (Par 94): **92,91,90,89,88 88,84,80,75,70**
CSF £178.80 CT £2198.91 TOTE £33.50: £5.80, £2.00, £2.80; EX 323.90 Trifecta £3452.30.
**Owner** A Dee **Bred** P M Cunningham **Trained** Newmarket, Suffolk

**FOCUS**
They went a strong enough pace in this moderate nursery.

## 7905 LADBROKES H'CAP (TAPETA) (DIV I) 7f 32y
4:35 (4:36) (Class 5) (0-70,73) 3-Y-0+ £2,911 (£866; £432; £216) Stalls High

Form RPR
/303 1 **Don't Be**[24] 7575 4-9-3 66 LukeMorris 2 79
(Sir Mark Prescott Bt) *hld up in tch: led over 1f out: rdn and edgd rt ins fnl f: r.o* 9/2[2]

5311 2 1 1/4 **Sewn Up**[21] 7621 4-8-12 61 (p) PhillipMakin 4 71
(Keith Dalgleish) *a.p: rdn to chse wnr and edgd lft ins fnl f: styd on* 6/1

0513 3 2 3/4 **Rich Again (IRE)**[20] 7636 5-9-6 69 (p) JoeFanning 9 72
(James Bethell) *hld up: hdwy over 1f out: r.o to go 3rd towards fin: nt rch ldrs* 10/3[1]

0606 4 3/4 **Al's Memory (IRE)**[11] 7759 5-9-3 66 AdamKirby 10 67
(David Evans) *led to 1/2-way: rdn to ld again 2f out: hdd over 1f out: no ex ins fnl f* 10/3[1]

3210 5 1 1/2 **Keene's Pointe**[17] 7704 4-8-8 62 (p) ShaneGray[(5)] 6 59
(Kristin Stubbs) *hld up: nt clr run over 2f out: hdwy over 1f out: no ex ins fnl f* 33/1

0535 6 3/4 **Piddie's Power**[109] 5079 7-9-7 70 (t) StevieDonohoe 3 65
(Kevin Frost) *mid-div: rdn over 2f out: nt trble ldrs* 16/1

0030 7 2 1/4 **Comrade Bond**[23] 7601 6-9-0 68 TimClark[(5)] 7 57
(Mark H Tompkins) *plld hrd and prom: wnt 2nd over 5f out tl led 1/2-way: hdd 2f out: wknd fnl f* 18/1

3504 8 1/2 **Classic Pursuit**[17] 7698 3-9-4 68 (p) GeorgeBaker 11 55
(Ronald Harris) *s.i.s: nvr on terms* 11/2[3]

4360 9 5 **Kakapuka**[11] 7758 7-8-9 65 KieranShoemark[(7)] 5 40
(Anabel K Murphy) *chsd ldr tl over 5f out: remained handy tl rdn over 2f out: wknd over 1f out* 33/1

-500 10 1 3/4 **Marciano (IRE)**[27] 7506 4-9-4 67 TonyHamilton 12 37
(Sue Smith) *sn pushed along and prom: rdn over 2f out: sn wknd* 14/1

1m 26.86s (-1.94) **Going Correction** -0.15s/f (Stan)
**WFA** 3 from 4yo+ 1lb 10 Ran SP% 117.7
Speed ratings (Par 103): **105,103,100,99,97 97,94,93,88,86**
CSF £32.07 CT £100.65 TOTE £5.20: £2.00, £1.70, £1.70; EX 29.30 Trifecta £61.60.
**Owner** Mrs Olivia Hoare **Bred** P E Barrett **Trained** Newmarket, Suffolk

**FOCUS**
A reasonable race for the grade run at a fair pace. The time was marginally faster than the second division, and for what it's worth it was the fourth quickest of 63 races to be run over this trip on the new Tapeta, with the surface evidently riding fast. Sound form, rated slightly positively.

## 7906 LADBROKES H'CAP (TAPETA) (DIV II) 7f 32y
5:05 (5:05) (Class 5) (0-70,71) 3-Y-0+ £2,911 (£866; £432; £216) Stalls High

Form RPR
6341 1 **Malaysian Boleh**[5] 7842 4-9-3 71 6ex JackDuern[(5)] 1 80
(Simon Dow) *s.i.s: hld up: hdwy 1/2-way: led over 1f out: rdn out* 11/1

5401 2 1/2 **Be Royale**[6] 7830 4-9-0 68 6ex AlistairRawlinson[(5)] 11 76
(Michael Appleby) *s.i.s: hld up: hdwy on outer over 2f out: rdn and ev ch over 1f out: edgd lft ins fnl f: styd on* 11/4[1]

4001 3 hd **Queen Aggie (IRE)**[17] 7704 4-9-1 69 GeorgeDowning[(5)] 12 76
(Tony Carroll) *hld up: hdwy over 1f out: r.o* 8/1

3556 4 1 **Shamaheart (IRE)**[21] 7624 4-9-7 70 (p) JoeFanning 5 74
(Geoffrey Harker) *s.i.s: hld up: hdwy over 2f out: ev ch over 1f out: styd on same pce ins fnl f* 3/1[2]

0664 5 1 **The Dukkerer (IRE)**[24] 7575 3-9-3 67 AdamKirby 8 68
(Garry Moss) *hld up: hdwy and nt clr run over 1f out: r.o: nt trble ldrs* 10/1

0300 6 nk **Two Shades Of Grey (IRE)**[28] 7502 3-8-11 61 (p) TonyHamilton 9 61
(Richard Fahey) *mid-div: rdn 1/2-way: r.o ins fnl f: nt trble ldrs* 20/1

6-41 7 1/2 **Random**[44] 7111 3-9-2 66 StevieDonohoe 10 65
(Daniel Mark Loughnane) *hld up: pushed along 1/2-way: r.o ins fnl f: nvr nrr* 11/2[3]

1500 8 1 3/4 **Hill Of Dreams (IRE)**[48] 7013 5-9-4 67 (b) PatCosgrave 3 62
(Dean Ivory) *chsd ldrs: wnt 2nd 1/2-way: rdn to ld wl over 1f out: sn hdd: no ex ins fnl f* 50/1

0103 9 2 **Shades Of Silk**[17] 7697 3-9-1 68 ConnorBeasley[(3)] 7 57
(James Given) *chsd ldrs: rdn and ev ch over 1f out: wknd ins fnl f* 16/1

2103 10 nk **Heartsong (IRE)**[27] 7506 5-9-0 66 JoeyHaynes[(3)] 6 55
(John Gallagher) *mid-div: rdn over 2f out: wknd fnl f* 25/1

1500 11 nk **Bertie Blu Boy**[25] 7556 6-8-13 62 (b) MartinDwyer 4 50
(Lisa Williamson) *led: clr over 5f out tl over 2f out: hdd wl over 1f out: wknd fnl f* 33/1

0330 12 5 **Bogsnog (IRE)**[45] 7077 4-9-0 63 TomEaves 2 38
(Kristin Stubbs) *chsd ldr to 1/2-way: rdn over 2f out: wknd wl over 1f out* 18/1

1m 26.97s (-1.83) **Going Correction** -0.15s/f (Stan)
**WFA** 3 from 4yo+ 1lb 12 Ran SP% 120.2
Speed ratings (Par 103): **104,103,103,102,100 100,100,98,95,95 95,89**
CSF £40.44 CT £266.95 TOTE £13.90: £3.70, £1.30, £3.20; EX 49.60 Trifecta £204.80.
**Owner** JCG Chua & CK Ong **Bred** John & Sue Davis **Trained** Epsom, Surrey

**FOCUS**
A similar time to the first division, but they went off faster and came home slower in this one. It paid to be held up, and the form seems sound.

## 7907 DOWNLOAD THE LADBROKES APP H'CAP (TAPETA) 1m 141y
5:35 (5:35) (Class 6) (0-65,64) 3-Y-0+ £2,264 (£673; £336; £168) Stalls Low

Form RPR
4042 1 **Loraine**[62] 6635 4-9-6 63 GeorgeBaker 12 75
(Jamie Osborne) *hld up: hdwy over 1f out: led ins fnl f: r.o wl* 13/8[1]

1310 2 3 1/4 **Jumbo Prado (USA)**[26] 7533 5-9-1 63 (p) EoinWalsh[(5)] 2 67
(John Stimpson) *chsd ldrs: rdn and ev ch ins fnl f: styd on same pce* 14/1

6003 3 hd **Act Your Shoe Size**[9] 7813 5-9-2 59 JoeFanning 9 63
(Keith Dalgleish) *led: rdn over 1f out: hdd and unable qck ins fnl f* 8/1[3]

4430 4 shd **Choice Of Destiny**[25] 7556 3-8-10 63 GaryMahon[(7)] 4 66
(Philip McBride) *chsd ldrs: rdn over 1f out: styd on* 14/1

4520 5 shd **Mandy The Nag (USA)**[11] 7765 4-9-1 61 MatthewCosham[(3)] 7 64
(Nikki Evans) *mid-div: pushed along over 3f out: rdn over 1f out: r.o* 50/1

0414 6 shd **Zaeem**[24] 7568 5-9-7 64 (p) PatCosgrave 6 67
(Dean Ivory) *prom: nt clr run fr over 2f out tl swtchd lft over 1f out: sn rdn: styd on same pce ins fnl f* 9/2[2]

6222 7 2 1/4 **Turnbury**[9] 7805 3-9-3 63 (t) JackMitchell 8 61
(Robert Mills) *hld up: hdwy 1/2-way: rdn and hung lft over 1f out: no ex ins fnl f* 9/2[2]

0000 8 nse **Look Here's Al**[17] 7697 3-8-7 58 JackDuern[(5)] 5 56
(Andrew Hollinshead) *hld up: rdn over 1f out: nvr on terms* 20/1

3060 9 2 1/4 **Run Fat Lass Run**[5] 7842 4-9-5 62 (p) HayleyTurner 3 54
(Conor Dore) *hld up: n.d* 40/1

5006 10 2 1/4 **Mississippi Queen (USA)**[18] 7682 3-9-3 63 WilliamTwiston-Davies 1 50
(Michael Bell) *hood removed sltly late and s.i.s: hld up: nt clr run over 2f out: wknd over 1f out* 20/1

060- 11 2 **Ri Na Si**[389] 7643 4-8-4 50 oh1 RyanTate[(3)] 11 33
(Michael Appleby) *chsd ldr: rdn over 2f out: wknd fnl f* 33/1

5060 12 1 **Tijuca (IRE)**[138] 4073 5-9-5 62 LukeMorris 10 42
(Ed de Giles) *hld up: hdwy over 2f out: wknd over 1f out* 28/1

1m 48.65s (-1.45) **Going Correction** -0.15s/f (Stan)
**WFA** 3 from 4yo+ 3lb 12 Ran SP% 119.2
Speed ratings (Par 101): **100,97,96,96,96 96,94,94,92,90 88,87**
CSF £25.32 CT £150.53 TOTE £3.40: £1.60, £2.50, £2.20; EX 25.40 Trifecta £131.60.
**Owner** Mrs F Walwyn, Lady Aitken, A Taylor **Bred** Mr & Mrs A E Pakenham **Trained** Upper Lambourn, Berks

**FOCUS**
A modest handicap all about the gambled-on winner, who showed improved form.

T/Jkpt: Not won. T/Plt: £28.40 to a £1 stake. Pool: £103,408.37 - 2653.90 winning units. T/Qpdt: £6.20 to a £1 stake. Pool: £8444.69 - 996.45 winning units. CR

# [7823]SOUTHWELL (L-H)

Tuesday, November 25

**OFFICIAL GOING: Fibresand: standard**

Wind: Virtually nil Weather: Cloudy and dry

## 7908 LADBROKES AMATEUR RIDERS' H'CAP (DIV I) 1m (F)

**12:10** (12:10) (Class 6) (0-60,59) 3-Y-0+ **£1,871** (£580; £290; £145) **Stalls** Low

Form RPR

5506 **1** **It's All A Game**[12] 7766 3-10-8 55........................(b) MrSWalker 3 63
(Richard Guest) *trckd ldrs: hdwy 3f out: swtchd rt to outer and rdn wl over 1f out: drvn ent fnl f: styd on to ld nr line* **7/4**[1]

2552 **2** *nse* **Company Secretary (USA)**[10] 7813 3-10-7 59(p) MrJamesHughes(5) 7 67
(Jo Hughes) *trckd ldrs: hdwy on inner 1/2-way: cl up over 3f out: led over 2f out: rdn over 1f out: edgd rt and hdd nr fin* **9/4**[2]

0000 **3** *1 3/4* **Moxey**[93] 5717 3-9-5 45........................ MissAMcCormick(7) 6 49
(Danielle McCormick) *slt ld on outer: rdn along 3f out: hdd over 2f out: cl up and ev ch tl no ex ins fnl f* **50/1**

660 **4** *1* **Jonnie Skull (IRE)**[3] 7883 8-11-0 59........................(vt) MissSBrotherton 1 62
(Phil McEntee) *trckd ldrs: effrt wl over 2f out: sn rdn along and kpt on same pce appr fnl f* **7/1**[3]

0300 **5** *8* **La Danza**[32] 7424 4-9-11 47........................ MrAidenBlakemore(5) 2 31
(Shaun Harris) *cl up: rdn along 3f out: wknd over 2f out* **16/1**

6030 **6** *nk* **Supa Seeker (USA)**[71] 6407 8-9-12 50........................ MissSAColl(7) 5 33
(Tony Carroll) *dwlt and in rr: sme hdwy 3f out: plugged on fnl 2f: n.d* **12/1**

00- **7** *8* **Mazovian (USA)**[376] 7886 6-10-7 52........................ MrMichaelJMurphy 8 17
(Michael Chapman) *a towards rr: bhd fnl 3f* **16/1**

622- **8** *3* **Angelena Ballerina (IRE)**[571] 1987 7-10-5 55....(v) MissBHampson(5) 9 13
(Andy Turnell) *dwlt: a in rr: bhd fnl 3f* **10/1**

1m 43.5s (-0.20) **Going Correction** -0.175s/f (Stan)
**WFA** 3 from 4yo+ 2lb **8** Ran **SP% 110.1**
Speed ratings (Par 101): **94,93,92,91,83 82,74,71**
CSF £5.28 CT £113.36 TOTE £3.10: £1.10, £1.10, £15.00; EX 6.10 Trifecta £185.80.
**Owner** Viscount Environmental Ltd **Bred** Mrs G Sainty **Trained** Ingmanthorpe, W Yorks

**FOCUS**
Very weak form and leading amateur Simon Walker just managed to get the market leader up in the final strides. The winner returned to form.

## 7909 LADBROKES AMATEUR RIDERS' H'CAP (DIV II) 1m (F)

**12:40** (12:41) (Class 6) (0-60,59) 3-Y-0+ **£1,871** (£580; £290; £145) **Stalls** Low

Form RPR

602 **1** **Uncle Brit**[47] 7061 8-10-10 55........................(p) MissCWalton 9 67
(Rebecca Menzies) *trckd ldrs: pushed along and hdwy on outer over 2f out: rdn over 1f out: led ent fnl f: drvn and kpt on wl towards fin* **7/2**[2]

2312 **2** *nk* **City Of Angkor Wat (IRE)**[4] 7868 4-10-9 59......(t) MrJamesHughes(5) 7 70+
(Jo Hughes) *s.i.s and bhd: hdwy over 3f out: clsd on ldrs over 1f out: chal ins fnl f: sn rdn and ev ch tl no ex towards fin* **11/8**[1]

6620 **3** *7* **Very First Blade**[11] 7783 5-10-0 48........................(be) MissMMullineaux(3) 5 43
(Michael Mullineaux) *prom: cl up over 3f out: rdn along wl over 2f out: ev ch wl over 1f out: wknd ent fnl f* **12/1**

1240 **4** *1/2* **Miami Gator (IRE)**[12] 7766 7-10-8 53........................(v) MrsCBartley 1 47
(K R Burke) *set sound pce: pushed clr wl over 2f out: rdn along wl over 1f out: hdd & wknd ent fnl f* **10/1**

0061 **5** *3* **Red Invader (IRE)**[49] 7010 4-10-8 58........................ MrsRWilson(5) 2 45
(Paul D'Arcy) *t.k.h: chsd ldrs on inner: cl up 1/2-way: rdn over 2f out: grad wknd* **13/2**[3]

100- **6** *2* **Young Jackie**[479] 5002 6-10-5 55........................(b) MissKMargarson(5) 4 38
(George Margarson) *v.s.a and sn wl bhd: rdn and wd st: styd on fnl 2f: n.d* **20/1**

5560 **7** *14* **Nifty Kier**[6] 7844 5-9-13 51........................ MissEmmaJack(7) 8
(Phil McEntee) *dwlt: sn chsng ldrs: hdwy to chse ldng pair 1/2-way: rdn along 3f out: sn wknd* **33/1**

0-40 **8** *2* **Pink Cadillac (IRE)**[118] 4796 4-9-7 45........................ MissLSanders(7) 3
(Ben Haslam) *t.k.h: in tch: rdn along 1/2-way: sn outpcd and bhd* **25/1**

006- **9** *1* **Paint It Red (IRE)**[417] 6999 3-9-12 45........................ MrSWalker 6
(Richard Guest) *sn outpcd and a bhd* **12/1**

1m 43.25s (-0.45) **Going Correction** -0.175s/f (Stan)
**WFA** 3 from 4yo+ 2lb **9** Ran **SP% 113.7**
Speed ratings (Par 101): **95,94,87,87,84 82,68,66,65**
CSF £8.29 CT £48.53 TOTE £4.40: £1.40, £1.30, £2.80; EX 10.50 Trifecta £68.90.
**Owner** Panther Racing Ltd **Bred** Heather Raw **Trained** Stearsby, N Yorks

**FOCUS**
No depth to this handicap and the top two in the market drew clear in the closing stages. Slightly the quicker division. The winner is rated close to CD form this year.

## 7910 DOWNLOAD THE LADBROKES APP MAIDEN STKS 1m (F)

**1:10** (1:10) (Class 5) 3-Y-0+ **£3,234** (£962; £481; £240) **Stalls** Low

Form RPR

2432 **1** **Wu Zetian**[8] 7818 3-9-0 67........................ HayleyTurner 8 72
(Andrew Balding) *trckd ldr: cl up 1/2-way: led wl over 2f out: jnd and rdn wl over 1f out: drvn ins fnl f: kpt on gamely towards fin* **10/11**[1]

2222 **2** *hd* **Whispering Star (USA)**[132] 4321 3-9-0 65........................ JimCrowley 3 71
(David Simcock) *trckd ldrs: smooth hdwy over 2f out: chal on bit wl over 1f out: shkn up wl ins fnl f: sn rdn and nt qckn* **9/4**[2]

0/ **3** *10* **Dark Diamond (IRE)**[722] 7963 4-9-7 0........................ GrahamLee 5 54
(Robert Cowell) *in tch: outpcd and wd st: rdn along over 2f out: styd on appr fnl f* **25/1**

4460 **4** *nk* **Major Rowan**[42] 7176 3-9-0 46........................ AdamCarter(5) 1 52?
(Bryan Smart) *in rr: pushed along 1/2-way: hdwy wl over 2f out: sn rdn and kpt on same pce* **20/1**

3003 **5** *shd* **Lendal Bridge**[12] 7764 3-9-5 54........................ BarryMcHugh 2 52
(Tony Coyle) *chsd ldrs: rdn along over 2f out: sn drvn and plugged on one pce* **5/1**[3]

0056 **6** *2 3/4* **Sea Whisper**[50] 6982 3-9-0 45........................ TonyHamilton 4 40?
(Ann Stokell) *led: rdn along 3f out: hdd wl over 2f out: sn wknd* **66/1**

0- **7** *5* **Disco Dale (IRE)**[341] 8346 3-9-0 0........................ SammyJoBell(5) 6 34
(Richard Fahey) *a in rr* **20/1**

2505 **8** *8* **Danzki (IRE)**[12] 7764 3-9-5 54........................(b) AdamKirby 7 15
(Gay Kelleway) *sn rdn along and prom on outer: lost pl over 3f out and sn bhd* **16/1**

1m 41.22s (-2.48) **Going Correction** -0.175s/f (Stan)
**WFA** 3 from 4yo 2lb **8** Ran **SP% 120.6**
Speed ratings (Par 103): **105,104,94,94,94 91,86,78**
CSF £3.19 TOTE £1.50: £1.10, £1.02, £7.10; EX 3.20 Trifecta £35.80.
**Owner** Mrs Johnny McKeever **Bred** Aston House Stud **Trained** Kingsclere, Hants

**FOCUS**
No depth to this maiden and the front two drew right away from the rest. The winner is rated to form.

## 7911 32RED NOVICE STKS 7f (F)

**1:40** (1:40) (Class 5) 2-Y-0 **£2,587** (£770; £384; £192) **Stalls** Low

Form RPR

4 **1** **Padlock (IRE)**[46] 7076 2-9-0 0........................ JimCrowley 1 78+
(David Simcock) *trckd ldrs: hdwy over 2f out: led ent fnl f: sn rdn clr: readily* **6/4**[1]

**2** *4* **High Intensity** 2-9-0 0........................ LukeMorris 5 63
(Scott Dixon) *trckd ldrs: hdwy on outer 3f out: rdn to chal and ev ch over 1f out: edgd lft and kpt on same pce fnl f* **6/1**

6532 **3** *nk* **Spindle (IRE)**[36] 7338 2-9-2 69........................ LiamKeniry 3 64
(Mark Usher) *slt ld 3f: cl up: led again 3f out: rdn and hdd 1 1/2f out: drvn and one pce ent fnl f* **9/4**[2]

6430 **4** *2 3/4* **Dark Wonder (IRE)**[34] 7379 2-9-0 67........................ GrahamLee 2 55
(James Given) *cl up on inner: slt ld after 3f: hdd and rdn 3f out: drvn 2f out and grad wknd* **4/1**[3]

F4 **5** *hd* **Go Grazeon**[17] 7713 2-8-9 0........................ TomEaves 4 49
(John Quinn) *cl up: rdn along wl over 2f out: wknd over 1f out* **16/1**

1m 29.46s (-0.84) **Going Correction** -0.175s/f (Stan) **5** Ran **SP% 110.9**
Speed ratings (Par 96): **97,92,92,88,88**
CSF £10.89 TOTE £2.00: £1.10, £3.30; EX 9.90 Trifecta £32.00.
**Owner** Malih Lahej Al Basti **Bred** Limestone And Tara Studs **Trained** Newmarket, Suffolk

**FOCUS**
Modest form in all likelihood.

## 7912 32RED CASINO CLAIMING STKS 7f (F)

**2:10** (2:10) (Class 6) 2-Y-0 **£2,045** (£603; £302) **Stalls** Low

Form RPR

2562 **1** **Invincible Wish (IRE)**[7] 7828 2-8-13 53........................(p) PaulMulrennan 3 65
(Brian Ellison) *cl up: slt ld 1/2-way: rdn clr wl over 1f out: readily* **8/15**[1]

1425 **2** *7* **Chilworth Bells**[8] 7816 2-9-1 62........................ GrahamGibbons 5 48
(David Barron) *chsd ldrs: pushed along over 3f out: rdn wl over 2f out: kpt on u.p to take 2nd towards fin* **9/4**[2]

0005 **3** *1 1/4* **Striking Stone**[12] 7762 2-8-9 45........................(b) JoeFanning 1 39
(Jo Hughes) *slt ld: hdd 1/2-way: rdn wl over 2f out: drvn and one pce appr fnl f: lost 2nd towards fin* **25/1**

0540 **4** *1/2* **Reet Petite (IRE)**[62] 6663 2-8-2 45........................ LukeMorris 4 31
(James Evans) *chsd ldrs: rdn along wl over 2f out: sn one pce* **14/1**[3]

5066 **5** *10* **Cerise Firth**[8] 7816 2-8-6 45........................ HayleyTurner 2 8
(Steph Hollinshead) *in tch: rdn along and outpcd fr 1/2-way* **40/1**

1m 29.46s (-0.84) **Going Correction** -0.175s/f (Stan) **5** Ran **SP% 109.0**
Speed ratings (Par 94): **97,89,87,87,75**
CSF £1.89 TOTE £1.60: £1.10, £1.30; EX 2.30 Trifecta £8.80.
**Owner** Brian Ellison **Bred** Cyril Ryan **Trained** Norton, N Yorks

**FOCUS**
A weak claimer.

## 7913 CORAL APP DOWNLOAD FROM THE APP STORE MAIDEN STKS 1m 4f (F)

**2:40** (2:40) (Class 5) 3-Y-0+ **£2,587** (£770; £384; £192) **Stalls** Low

Form RPR

2622 **1** **Master Dan**[22] 7627 3-9-5 73........................ GrahamLee 3 81
(James Given) *trckd ldng pair: hdwy on inner to trck ldr after 4f: cl up over 4f out: led 2f out: rdn over 1f out: wandered ins fnl f: rdn out* **5/4**[1]

0443 **2** *4 1/2* **Darting**[35] 7358 3-9-0 66........................ DavidProbert 2 69
(Andrew Balding) *led: jnd over 4f out: rdn along and hdd 2f out: sn drvn and kpt on same pce* **11/4**[3]

2232 **3** *8* **Galuppi**[36] 7332 3-9-5 79........................ AdamKirby 1 61
(J R Jenkins) *t.k.h: hld up: hdwy to chse ldng pair 1/2-way: rdn along 3f out: sn one pce* **7/4**[2]

0226 **4** *6* **Cropley (IRE)**[21] 7650 5-9-6 64........................(b) AnnStokell(5) 4 52
(Ann Stokell) *hld up: hdwy 1/2-way: rdn along 4f out: sn outpcd* **33/1**

0000 **5** *26* **Sweet Summer**[93] 5717 3-9-0 45........................ StevieDonohoe 5 5
(John Holt) *chsd ldng pair: pushed along and lost pl 1/2-way: sn outpcd and bhd* **100/1**

2m 38.61s (-2.39) **Going Correction** -0.175s/f (Stan)
**WFA** 3 from 5yo 6lb **5** Ran **SP% 111.4**
Speed ratings (Par 103): **100,97,91,87,70**
CSF £5.20 TOTE £2.10: £1.10, £2.00; EX 5.80 Trifecta £12.00.
**Owner** The Cool Silk Partnership **Bred** Ed's Stud Ltd **Trained** Willoughton, Lincs

**FOCUS**
With Galuppi not running to anything like his mark, the way was clear for the winner to finally get off the mark. The form is rated around the runner-up.

## 7914 CORAL MOBILE "JUST THREE CLICKS TO BET" H'CAP 1m 4f (F)

**3:10** (3:10) (Class 5) (0-75,77) 3-Y-0+ **£2,587** (£770; £384; £192) **Stalls** Low

Form RPR

-001 **1** **Street Artist (IRE)**[8] 7822 4-9-12 77 6ex........................ JoeFanning 3 93+
(David Nicholls) *led 1f: trckd ldng pair: hdwy to ld over 4f out: rdn clr over 1f out: styd on strly* **7/2**[2]

0606 **2** *3 1/4* **Luv U Whatever**[11] 7784 4-9-4 74........................ AlistairRawlinson(5) 1 83
(Michael Appleby) *t.k.h early: trckd ldrs: hdwy over 3f out: chsd wnr 2f out: sn rdn: drvn and no imp whn hung rt ins fnl f* **7/4**[1]

5526 **3** *3 3/4* **Layline (IRE)**[8] 7817 7-9-7 72........................ AdamKirby 6 75
(Gay Kelleway) *hld up towards rr: hdwy 3f out: rdn along 2f out: kpt on u.p fnl f: nrst fin* **16/1**

2051 **4** *2* **Reach The Beach**[12] 7760 5-8-11 62........................(tp) BenCurtis 2 62
(Brendan Powell) *prom: rdn along and outpcd on inner over 4f out: swtchd rt and drvn 3f out: plugged on u.p fnl 2f* **8/1**

5662 **5** *1 1/4* **Royal Marskell**[12] 7760 5-9-5 70........................ TomEaves 8 68
(Alison Hutchinson) *trckd ldrs: hdwy over 7f out and sn cl up: rdn along over 3f out: drvn and wknd over 2f out* **9/2**[3]

5122 **6** *2 1/2* **Yul Finegold (IRE)**[28] 7516 4-9-2 74........................ ChrisMeehan(7) 5 68
(George Baker) *hld up towards rr: effrt over 4f out: sn rdn along and n.d* **5/1**

0-10 **7** *19* **Classic Colori (IRE)**[23] 5258 7-9-10 75........................ WilliamTwiston-Davies 7 38
(Martin Keighley) *a in rr: bhd fnl 4f* **40/1**

0201 **8** *1 1/2* **Mixed Message (IRE)**[29] 7499 4-9-0 65........................(p) GrahamGibbons 4 26
(Brian Ellison) *pushed along sn after s and led after 1f: rdn along over 5f out: hdd over 4f out: wknd over 3f out* **14/1**

2m 36.17s (-4.83) **Going Correction** -0.175s/f (Stan) **8** Ran **SP% 119.5**
Speed ratings (Par 103): **109,106,104,103,102 100,87,86**
CSF £10.58 CT £87.30 TOTE £4.70: £1.60, £1.10, £2.90; EX 13.10 Trifecta £132.00.
**Owner** J A Rattigan **Bred** Darley **Trained** Sessay, N Yorks



The Form Book, Raceform Ltd, Newbury, RG14 5SJ

**FOCUS**
Quite a competitive handicap, with several of these coming here in good order, and the form looks fairly strong for the grade. The winner was value for a bit extra than the bare form.

## 7915 £20 RISK-FREE BET AT UNIBET H'CAP — 6f (F)
**3:40** (3:41) (Class 6) (0-65,65) 3-Y-0+ **£1,940** (£577; £288; £144) **Stalls** Low

Form RPR

3202 **1** **Lucky Mark (IRE)**[7] 7826 5-8-8 57 ........(p) ShaneGray(5) 7 66
(John Balding) *slt ld: rdn wl over 1f out: hdd ent fnl f: sn drvn: rallied wl to ld again nr line* **8/1**[3]

0000 **2** *shd* **Speightowns Kid (USA)**[18] 7698 6-9-2 60 ........(b) GrahamLee 12 68
(Michael Herrington) *cl up on outer: chal 2f out: rdn to take slt ld ent fnl f: sn drvn: hdd and no ex nr line* **14/1**

6011 **3** *hd* **Best Tamayuz**[7] 7826 3-9-6 64 6ex ........ LukeMorris 1 71
(Scott Dixon) *cl up on inner: rdn along 2f out: drvn ent fnl f: ev ch tl no ex towards fin* **2/1**[1]

2356 **4** *4 1/2* **Borough Boy (IRE)**[7] 7830 4-9-6 64 ........ TonyHamilton 10 57
(Derek Shaw) *towards rr: hdwy and wd st: rdn to chse ldrs whn edgd lft over 1f out: kpt on same pce fnl f* **11/1**

2305 **5** *2 3/4* **Laughing Rock (IRE)**[20] 7671 4-8-6 55 ........(p) AlistairRawlinson(5) 6 39
(Michael Appleby) *chsd ldrs: rdn along over 2f out: drvn and wknd over 1f out* **8/1**[3]

0063 **6** *3 1/4* **Invigilator**[7] 7825 6-9-2 60 ........(t) TomEaves 2 33
(Derek Shaw) *in rr: hdwy on inner over 2f out: sn rdn and no imp* **20/1**

2252 **7** *1 1/2* **Musical Molly (IRE)**[7] 7825 3-9-7 65 ........(p) GrahamGibbons 5 34
(Brian Ellison) *towards rr: pushed along 1/2-way: rdn along over 2f out: n.d* **9/4**[2]

650 **8** *5* **Fathom Five (IRE)**[20] 7670 10-8-7 58 ........ KevinLundie(7) 4 11
(Shaun Harris) *cl up: rdn along 1/2-way: drvn over 2f out: sn wknd* **50/1**

030 **9** *12* **Art Dzeko**[220] 1573 5-8-12 56 ........ PaulMulrennan 9
(Brian Baugh) *s.i.s and in rr: hdwy and wd st: rdn wl over 2f out and sn wknd* **20/1**

1m 14.83s (-1.67) **Going Correction** -0.175s/f (Stan) **9** Ran SP% **112.8**
Speed ratings (Par 101): **104,103,103,97,93 89,87,80,64**
CSF £104.73 CT £307.28 TOTE £7.00: £1.90, £3.10, £1.30; EX 95.40 Trifecta £427.90.
**Owner** Chris Priestley **Bred** Mrs Lisa Kelly **Trained** Scrooby, S Yorks

**FOCUS**
Not much got into this. The winner and third were closely matched on CD form last week.
T/Jkpt: £457.30 to a £1 stake. Pool: £60,978.37 - 94.67 winning units. T/Plt: £5.50 to a £1 stake. Pool: £68,020.84 - 8900.34 winning units. T/Qpdt: £3.90 to a £1 stake. Pool: £4361.21 - 815.80 winning units. JR

# 7723 CHANTILLY (R-H)
Tuesday, November 25

**OFFICIAL GOING: Turf: heavy; polytrack: standard**

## 7916a PRIX TANTIEME (LISTED RACE) (3YO+) (TURF) — 1m
**3:25** (12:00) 3-Y-0+ **£21,666** (£8,666; £6,500; £4,333; £2,166)

RPR

**1** **Menardais (FR)**[39] 5-9-0 0 ........ StephanePasquier 8 111
(P Bary, France) **74/10**

**2** *2* **Dalayna (FR)**[26] 7559 4-8-10 0 ........ MaximeGuyon 4 102
(A De Royer-Dupre, France) **51/10**[3]

**3** *2 1/2* **Debutante (FR)**[181] 3-8-8 0 ........ CristianDemuro 2 96
(A De Royer-Dupre, France) **139/10**

**4** *shd* **Boomshackerlacker (IRE)**[23] 7618 4-9-4 0 ........ FergusSweeney 11 104
(George Baker) *t.k.h: restrained cl up on outer: 4th and shkn up 1 1/2f out: kpt on at same pce u.p fnl f* **37/10**[2]

**5** *1* **Amulet**[22] 7629 4-8-10 0 ........(b) ThierryJarnet 6 94
(Eve Johnson Houghton) *trckd ldrs: sltly outpcd over 1 1/2f out: rdn and kpt on ins fnl f* **17/5**[1]

**6** *3/4* **Raphinae**[22] 7629 3-8-13 0 ........ IoritzMendizabal 1 96
(H-A Pantall, France) *prom on inner: n.m.r over 1 1/2f out: rdn and nt qckn fr over 1f out: grad dropped away ins fnl f* **171/10**

**7** *snk* **Madame Defarge (IRE)**[39] 4-8-10 0 ........ AntoineHamelin 5 92
(J E Hammond, France) **197/10**

**8** *nse* **Baba O'Riley (IRE)**[31] 4-9-0 0 ........ FabienLefebvre 7 96
(R Le Dren Doleuze, France) **201/10**

**9** *3/4* **Pearlside (FR)**[94] 4-8-11 0 ow1 ........ OlivierPeslier 9 91
(M Delcher Sanchez, France) **26/1**

**10** *3/4* **Pont Neuilly (FR)**[61] 4-9-0 0 ........ JeromeCabre 3 92
(Yves de Nicolay, France) **28/1**

**11** *1* **Dancing Sands (IRE)**[23] 7616 3-9-1 0 ........ AnthonyCrastus 10 92
(H-A Pantall, France) *hld up towards rr: pushed along and no imp over 1 1/2f out: nvr in contention* **91/10**

**12** *1/2* **Matorio (FR)**[26] 7559 4-9-3 0 ........ AntoineWerle 12 92
(H-A Pantall, France) **11/1**

1m 45.53s (7.53)
**WFA** 3 from 4yo+ 2lb **12** Ran SP% **119.5**
WIN (incl. 1 euro stake): 8.40. PLACES: 2.80, 2.30, 4.30. DF: 23.20. SF: 54.60..
**Owner** Mme Georges Sandor **Bred** Georges Sandor **Trained** Chantilly, France

# 7847 KEMPTON (A.W) (R-H)
Wednesday, November 26

**OFFICIAL GOING: Polytrack: standard**
Wind: Almost nil Weather: Overcast, misty

## 7917 BETBRIGHT MOBILE APP MAIDEN AUCTION STKS — 5f (P)
**4:15** (4:17) (Class 5) 2-Y-0 **£2,587** (£770; £384; £192) **Stalls** Low

Form RPR

562 **1** **Jebediah Shine**[105] 5297 2-8-8 64 ........ SamJames 2 64
(David O'Meara) *mde all: rdn and fended off rivals fr over 1f out: kpt on* **7/2**[2]

0 **2** *3/4* **Kyrenia Castle (GER)**[5] 7867 2-9-3 0 ........ JimCrowley 5 70
(Richard Hannon) *chsd ldrs but sn pushed along: outpcd 1/2-way: clsd on inner fr jst over 1f out: tk 2nd last strides: nt rch wnr* **15/2**

6440 **3** *nk* **Jimmy's Hall**[68] 6591 2-8-13 0 ........(p) LiamJones 6 65
(J S Moore) *cl up in 3rd: pushed along and clr of rest 1/2-way: chsd wnr over 1f out and sn chalng: hld last 100yds: lost 2nd nr fin* **12/1**

624 **4** *2 3/4* **Crosse Fire**[18] 7714 2-9-2 70 ........(p) LukeMorris 4 58
(Scott Dixon) *pressed wnr: rdn and nt qckn over 1f out: sn lost 2nd and fdd* **11/10**[1]

6 **5** *2 3/4* **Desert Apostle (IRE)**[19] 7701 2-8-9 0 ........ JoeFanning 3 41
(Derek Shaw) *stdd s: t.k.h and hld up in rr: wd bnd over 3f out: nvr on terms but plugged on: possible improver* **25/1**

0 **6** *3 1/2* **Spirit Of Rosanna**[20] 7685 2-8-9 0 ........ GrahamGibbons 1 29
(Steph Hollinshead) *a struggling in rr: wl bhd over 1f out* **50/1**

43 **7** *1/2* **Miss Jonh (FR)**[19] 7701 2-8-8 0 ........ FergusSweeney 7 26
(Martyn Meade) *slowly away: racd on outer: nvr on terms w ldrs: wknd over 1f out* **11/2**[3]

1m 0.14s (-0.36) **Going Correction** -0.10s/f (Stan) **7** Ran SP% **110.5**
Speed ratings (Par 96): **98,96,96,91,87 81,81**
CSF £27.20 TOTE £5.50: £1.80, £3.40; EX 25.30 Trifecta £144.70.
**Owner** Sterling Racing **Bred** Whatton Manor Stud **Trained** Nawton, N Yorks

**FOCUS**
As is often the case over this CD, early speed from a low draw proved a winning combination. Straightforward, low-grade form.

## 7918 BETBRIGHT MONEYBACK OFFERS H'CAP — 1m 2f (P)
**4:45** (4:45) (Class 5) (0-70,70) 3-Y-0+ **£2,587** (£770; £384; £192) **Stalls** Low

Form RPR

3131 **1** **Archie's Advice**[28] 7527 3-9-2 69 ........ JoeFanning 5 76+
(Keith Dalgleish) *settled in midfield: forced to check lft wl over 1f out: gd prog sn after: r.o to ld last 120yds: rdn out* **5/2**[1]

2403 **2** *1/2* **Past Forgetting (IRE)**[38] 7304 3-9-3 70 ........ AdamKirby 11 76
(Luca Cumani) *hld up in last trio: stl there 2f out: gd prog jst over 1f out: r.o to take 2nd last 50yds: unable to threaten wnr* **7/1**[3]

0040 **3** *3/4* **Ruzeiz (USA)**[21] 7672 5-9-5 68 ........ CharlesBishop 1 73+
(Peter Hedger) *trckd ldng pair: gap appeared on inner and led over 1f out: hdd last 120yds: styd on* **8/1**

1456 **4** *3/4* **Evacusafe Lady**[4] 7885 3-9-1 68 ........(t) JackMitchell 7 71
(John Ryan) *settled towards rr: prog wl over 1f out: nt clrest of runs but kpt on to take 4th nr fin* **25/1**

1246 **5** *1 1/4* **Next Stop**[81] 6152 3-9-3 70 ........ PaulMulrennan 10 71
(David Nicholls) *mde most to over 1f out: steadily outpcd* **25/1**

0002 **6** *1/2* **Gannicus**[22] 7633 3-9-2 69 ........(p) MartinDwyer 6 69
(Brendan Powell) *trckd ldng trio: rdn over 1f out: nt qckn and one pce after: kpt on* **6/1**[2]

2304 **7** *shd* **Ghosting (IRE)**[13] 7757 3-9-3 70 ........(t) MartinHarley 4 73
(Tom Dascombe) *t.k.h: hld up in last trio: gng wl whn nt clr run over 1f out to ins fnl f: kpt on but no ch to be involved* **12/1**

4433 **8** *nk* **Kubeba (IRE)**[47] 7074 3-9-2 69 ........ LukeMorris 3 68
(Paul Cole) *trckd ldrs in 5th: rdn over 1f out: one pce and no imp after* **33/1**

2022 **9** *nk* **Ze King**[23] 7626 5-9-3 69 ........ AshleyMorgan(3) 13 68
(Chris Wall) *hld up in last: stl there and hanging over 1f out: pushed along and styd on fnl f: no ch of being involved* **14/1**

4064 **10** *2 1/2* **Silver Dixie (USA)**[27] 7552 4-9-6 69 ........[1] ShaneKelly 8 63
(Peter Hedger) *racd wd 1st 3f and sn in rr: prog 1/2-way to dispute 3rd 3f out: wknd over 1f out* **20/1**

3-10 **11** *7* **Lobster Pot**[43] 7172 3-9-3 70 ........(t) JimCrowley 14 52
(Hugo Palmer) *sn chsd ldr: rdn and lost 2nd 2f out: wkng whn hmpd 1f out* **9/1**

6440 **12** *nk* **Subtle Knife**[33] 7416 5-9-7 70 ........ WilliamCarson 2 50
(Giles Bravery) *towards rr on inner: drvn 3f out: prog over 1f out: keeping on one pce whn hmpd jst ins fnl f: nt rcvr and heavily eased* **16/1**

6161 **P** **Dalgig**[13] 7754 4-9-7 70 ........ GrahamLee 12
(David Pipe) *ref to leave the stalls tl rest had covered 1f: ambled 2f and then p.u* **16/1**

2m 6.16s (-1.84) **Going Correction** -0.10s/f (Stan)
**WFA** 3 from 4yo+ 4lb **13** Ran SP% **118.0**
Speed ratings (Par 103): **103,102,102,101,100 100,99,99,99,97 91,91,**
CSF £17.70 CT £124.45 TOTE £2.80: £1.60, £2.20, £3.50; EX 16.60 Trifecta £117.20.
**Owner** G L S Partnership **Bred** G L S Partnership **Trained** Carluke, S Lanarks

**FOCUS**
A modest handicap. The pace did not hold up. The winner continues to progress.

## 7919 IRISH STALLION FARMS EBF MAIDEN STKS (BOBIS RACE) (DIV I) — 6f (P)
**5:15** (5:15) (Class 4) 2-Y-0 **£4,075** (£1,212; £606; £303) **Stalls** Low

Form RPR

0064 **1** **Brazen Spirit**[12] 7771 2-9-5 72 ........ AdamKirby 6 75
(Clive Cox) *trckd ldng pair and clr of the rest: hrd rdn to go 2nd over 1f out: led jst ins fnl f: hanging lft and drvn out* **15/8**[1]

**2** *1 1/4* **Ershaad (IRE)** 2-9-5 0 ........ JackMitchell 2 71+
(Roger Varian) *hld up off the pce: chsd clr ldng trio 1/2-way: clsd fr 2f out: tk 3rd jst over 1f out: rdn and styd on into 2nd last stride* **3/1**[2]

5342 **3** *nse* **Spinaminnie (IRE)**[14] 7742 2-9-0 65 ........ JoeFanning 8 66
(Mark Johnston) *led at decent pce: rdn 2f out: hdd jst ins fnl f: edgd lft and one pce: lost 2nd last stride* **9/2**[3]

40 **4** *5* **Tarragon**[13] 7752 2-9-5 0 ........ SteveDrowne 9 56
(Jeremy Gask) *chsd clr ldng trio to 1/2-way: sn wl off the pce: pushed along and kpt on again fr over 1f out* **40/1**

**5** *nse* **Optimystic (IRE)** 2-9-0 0 ........ DavidProbert 7 51+
(Andrew Balding) *plld hrd: pressed ldr: rdn and lost 2nd over 1f out: wknd fnl f* **16/1**

**6** *1/2* **Sammy's Choice** 2-8-12 0 ........ DavidParkes(7) 3 54
(Paul Burgoyne) *sn off the pce in midfield: pushed along 2f out: kpt on but nvr a threat* **100/1**

**7** *1/2* **Sample (FR)** 2-9-0 0 ........ JamesDoyle 1 48
(Roger Charlton) *wl off the pce in rr: pushed along fr 2f out: kpt on steadily: bttr for experience* **11/1**

**8** *1 3/4* **Step Into The Tide (IRE)** 2-9-5 0 ........ LukeMorris 5 48
(Joseph Tuite) *v.s.a: wl bhd in last pair: urged along over 2f out: no great prog* **11/2**

05 **9** *7* **Harley Rebel**[29] 7511 2-9-5 0 ........ LiamKeniry 4 27
(Neil Mulholland) *s.s: a bhd in last pair: wknd over 1f out* **66/1**

1m 12.33s (-0.77) **Going Correction** -0.10s/f (Stan) **9** Ran SP% **112.5**
Speed ratings (Par 98): **101,99,99,92,92 91,91,88,79**
CSF £7.22 TOTE £3.90: £1.60, £1.40, £1.40; EX 10.10 Trifecta £28.20.
**Owner** Trevor Fox **Bred** Mr & Mrs C A H Villiers **Trained** Lambourn, Berks

**FOCUS**
Not a strong maiden. The winner is rated back to early-season form.

## 7920 IRISH STALLION FARMS EBF MAIDEN STKS (BOBIS RACE) (DIV II) 6f (P)
5:45 (5:45) (Class 4) 2-Y-O £4,075 (£1,212; £606; £303) Stalls Low

Form RPR
U325 1 **Wentworth Falls**[35] 7371 2-9-5 74..............................(b[1]) AdamKirby 4 83+
(Charlie Appleby) *trckd ldng pair: cruised up to ld jst over 1f out: easily drew clr* **7/2**[2]
422 2 3 ½ **Secret Glance**[14] 7741 2-9-5 78.............................. GrahamGibbons 3 73
(Ed McMahon) *led: shkn up 2f out: hdd jst over 1f out: kpt on but no ch w wnr* **5/6**[1]
50 3 1 **Ertidaad (IRE)**[14] 7742 2-9-5 0.............................. GrahamLee 5 69
(Pat Eddery) *chsd ldrs in 5th: wnt 4th over 2f out: rdn over 1f out: kpt on to take 3rd ins fnl f: n.d* **66/1**
02 4 ¾ **Dusty Blue**[42] 7192 2-9-0 0..............................(t) LukeMorris 9 61
(Paul Cole) *chsd ldr: rdn over 2f out: lost 2nd over 1f out: one pce* **9/2**[3]
5 2 **Showtime Blues** 2-9-5 0.............................. PaulMulrennan 7 60+
(Amanda Perrett) *chsd ldng trio tl over 2f out: nt on terms after but pushed along and kpt on: nt disgracd* **25/1**
0 6 6 **Qatar Success**[49] 7037 2-9-0 0..............................(bt[1]) LiamJones 6 37
(Olly Stevens) *s.s: sn in 6th: no imp on ldrs 2f out: fdd* **50/1**
0350 7 1 **Grand Proposal**[37] 7328 2-9-5 66.............................. PatCosgrave 2 39
(Jim Boyle) *dwlt: mostly in 8th and nvr on terms: bhd fnl 2f* **16/1**
0 8 ½ **Boston Two Step**[21] 7660 2-9-5 0.............................. JoeFanning 1 38
(Mark Johnston) *mostly in 7th pushed along and no prog over 2f out: bhd after* **25/1**
9 1 ½ **Lucky Leyf** 2-9-0 0.............................. JimCrowley 8 28
(Gary Moore) *s.s: a in last: bhd fnl 2f* **25/1**

1m 12.45s (-0.65) **Going Correction** -0.10s/f (Stan) **9** Ran SP% **115.8**
Speed ratings (Par 98): **100,95,94,93,90 82,81,80,78**
CSF £6.50 TOTE £3.20: £1.20, £1.10, £7.40; EX 8.30 Trifecta £130.30.
**Owner** Godolphin **Bred** Newsells Park Stud **Trained** Newmarket, Suffolk
**FOCUS**
Very marginally the slower of the two divisions. The winner built on previous promise, with the second a bit below form.

## 7921 BETBRIGHT.COM DOWNLOAD OUR APP MEDIAN AUCTION MAIDEN STKS 7f (P)
6:15 (6:16) (Class 6) 3-5-Y-O £1,940 (£577; £288; £144) Stalls Low

Form RPR
050 1 **Franco's Secret**[28] 7528 3-9-5 67..............................(p) CharlesBishop 1 74
(Peter Hedger) *broke wl but restrained bhd ldng pair: shkn up to chse ldr over 1f out but 2 l down: little imp tl surged last 50yds: led post* **3/1**[2]
2 nk **Rightway (IRE)**[45] 7143 3-9-5 76.............................. JimCrowley 5 73
(Tony Carroll) *disp ld tl led jst over 2f out: sn kicked for home and 2 l up over 1f out: looked like holding on tl collared last stride* **8/11**[1]
3 3 3 **Kokovoko (IRE)**[35] 7370 3-9-5 0.............................. DavidProbert 3 65
(Andrew Balding) *dwlt and awkward s: t.k.h in 6th: pushed along and prog 2f out: styd on one pce to take 3rd 1f out* **9/2**[3]
4 3 ¼ **Summersault (IRE)** 3-9-5 0.............................. FergusSweeney 4 56
(Jamie Osborne) *disp ld to jst over 2f out: lost 2nd over 1f out: and steadily wknd* **6/1**
0 5 10 **Beggers Luck**[305] 341 4-8-12 0.............................. JoeyHaynes(3) 7 25
(Eric Wheeler) *chsd ldrs: drvn over 2f out: sn wknd* **100/1**
50 6 ¾ **Scafell Pike**[169] 3074 3-9-5 0.............................. RobertTart 6 27
(Dr Jon Scargill) *dwlt: mostly in last: rdn and no prog over 2f out: bhd after* **100/1**
0-0 7 1 ¾ **Courtezan**[9] 7818 3-8-9 0.............................. RachealKneller(5) 2 18
(Jamie Osborne) *t.k.h: prom 4f: sn lost pl and struggling* **100/1**
8 2 ¼ **Devils In My Head** 4-8-8 0.............................. DavidParkes(7) 8 12
(Keiran Burke) *dwlt: a in rr: rdn and no prog over 2f out: sn bhd* **25/1**

1m 25.92s (-0.08) **Going Correction** -0.10s/f (Stan)
**WFA** 3 from 4yo 1lb **8** Ran SP% **122.2**
Speed ratings (Par 101): **96,95,92,88,77 76,74,71**
CSF £6.01 TOTE £5.30: £1.50, £1.10, £1.50; EX 7.80 Trifecta £18.30.
**Owner** P C F Racing Ltd **Bred** J J Whelan **Trained** Eastergate, W Sussex
**FOCUS**
This didn't take much winning. The early pace was sedate and the winner produced a marginal pb.

## 7922 BETBRIGHT.COM WILD FLOWER STKS (LISTED RACE) 1m 4f (P)
6:45 (6:46) (Class 1) 3-Y-O+
£22,684 (£8,600; £4,304; £2,144; £1,076; £540) Stalls Centre

Form RPR
0264 1 **Livia's Dream (IRE)**[27] 7554 5-9-1 92.............................. LukeMorris 1 99
(Ed Walker) *trckd ldr: led 2f out: drvn and hrd pressed over 1f out: forged ahd ins fnl f* **14/1**
2221 2 1 ¼ **Grendisar (IRE)**[21] 7662 4-9-8 104..............................(p) MartinHarley 4 104
(Marco Botti) *stdd s but sn wl in tch disputing 5th: cruised through fr 2f out to chal over 1f out: drvn and nt qckn fnl f* **10/3**[3]
3 nk **Billabong (MOR)**[26] 5-9-6 93.............................. CristianDemuro 6 102
(P Bary, France) *s.i.s: hld up towards rr: rdn and nt qckn over 2f out and outpcd: styd on fr over 1f out to take 3rd last strides* **14/1**
11 4 hd **Kalaatah (USA)**[20] 7689 3-8-9 89.............................. JamesDoyle 2 96
(Saeed bin Suroor) *dwlt but sn trckd ldng pair: rdn and tried to chal 2f out: kpt on one pce fr over 1f out* **9/4**[1]
4610 5 ¾ **Rawaki (IRE)**[32] 7447 6-9-6 103..............................(p) ThomasBrown 8 100
(Andrew Balding) *hld up disputing 5th: rdn 2f out: hanging and nt qckn over 1f out: kpt on fnl f* **3/1**[2]
2026 6 nk **Fire Fighting (IRE)**[11] 7803 3-9-0 103..............................(b) JoeFanning 10 100+
(Mark Johnston) *hld up in last pair: prog jst over 2f out: to cl on ldrs over 1f out: effrt flattened out fnl f* **11/2**
0052 7 1 ¾ **Harris Tweed**[30] 7492 7-9-6 105..............................(p) GeorgeBaker 5 97
(William Haggas) *led but nt at str pce: tried to kick on over 2f out: sn hdd: fdd over 1f out* **6/1**
0 8 1 **Snowmane (IRE)**[11] 7803 3-9-0 98..............................(p) GrahamLee 3 95
(James Given) *chsd ldng pair: rdn over 2f out: lost pl and fdd over 1f out* **33/1**
0-42 9 shd **Pernica**[184] 2628 4-9-1 72..............................(p) DavidProbert 9 90?
(Lucy Wadham) *hld up towards rr: clsd on ldrs 2f out: wknd fnl f* **100/1**
1666 10 nk **Asia Minor (IRE)**[26] 7565 5-9-1 74.............................. RobertTart 7 89?
(Dr Jon Scargill) *s.i.s: hld up in last pair: wd bnd 3f out: no prog and btn 2f out: kpt on* **66/1**

2m 34.43s (-0.07) **Going Correction** -0.10s/f (Stan)
**WFA** 3 from 4yo+ 6lb **10** Ran SP% **127.3**
Speed ratings: **96,95,94,94,94 94,92,92,92,92**
CSF £65.90 TOTE £15.60: £4.40, £1.10, £4.20; EX 69.70 Trifecta £707.30.
**Owner** Mrs Olivia Hoare **Bred** Mount Coote Stud And M H Dixon **Trained** Newmarket, Suffolk
**FOCUS**
A decent race, but there was a muddling gallop and it developed into a sprint up the straight. A literal interpretation of the form is obviously dangerous.

## 7923 BETBRIGHT CASINO H'CAP 6f (P)
7:15 (7:15) (Class 2) (0-100,103) 3-Y-O+
£11,827 (£3,541; £1,770; £885; £442; £222) Stalls Low

Form RPR
1000 1 **Out Do**[19] 7700 5-9-1 94..............................(v) SamJames 3 103
(David O'Meara) *trckd ldrs: clsd over 1f out: prog to ld last 150yds: sn jnd: styd on wl* **25/1**
0610 2 shd **Hallelujah**[19] 7700 6-9-4 97.............................. HayleyTurner 8 106
(James Fanshawe) *racd wd in midfield: wound up wl over 2f out: rdn and prog over 1f out: r.o to join wnr ins fnl f: jst pipped* **12/1**
0052 3 1 **Lancelot Du Lac (ITY)**[18] 7716 4-9-10 103.............................. JimCrowley 7 109
(Dean Ivory) *hld up in last trio shkn up and no real prog over 1f out: rdn and r.o fnl f to take 3rd nr fin: unable to chal* **5/2**[2]
5312 4 shd **Major Jack**[7] 7843 3-8-7 86.............................. DavidProbert 9 91
(Roger Charlton) *hld up in rr: rdn over 1f out: r.o fnl f to press for 3rd nr fin: nvr able to chal* **2/1**[1]
3211 5 hd **Steelriver (IRE)**[27] 7543 4-9-1 94.............................. ShaneKelly 12 99
(Michael Herrington) *slowly away: hld up in last: stl there jst over 2f out: hanging rt whn asked for effrt over 1f out: r.o wl fnl f: gaining at fin* **5/1**[3]
1040 6 nk **Upavon**[186] 2562 4-8-10 89.............................. LiamKeniry 5 93
(David Elsworth) *towards rr: shkn up 2f out: no real prog ovger 1f out: styd on fnl f: nt pce to chal* **33/1**
3300 7 nk **Hoof It**[123] 4683 7-9-9 102.............................. GrahamGibbons 11 105
(Michael Easterby) *rousted fr wd draw and led over 4f out: drvn over 1f out: hdd & wknd last 150yds* **9/1**
5022 8 ½ **Pipers Note**[19] 7700 4-9-2 95.............................. GeorgeChaloner 10 97
(Richard Whitaker) *t.k.h: trckd ldng pair: rdn to chal 2f out: nt qckn over 1f out: wknd ins fnl f* **8/1**
3056 9 ½ **Elusivity (IRE)**[7] 7843 6-8-1 87.............................. HectorCrouch(7) 4 87
(Peter Crate) *in tch in midfield: effrt against ins rail over 1f out: one pce after* **25/1**
2110 10 1 **Dungannon**[18] 7716 7-9-4 102..............................(b) KieranShoemark(5) 1 99
(Andrew Balding) *settled in midfield: effrt on inner and cl up over 1f out: fdd fnl f* **16/1**
240 11 1 **Counter Ridge (SAF)**[11] 7802 5-8-10 89..............................(p) MartinHarley 6 83
(Marco Botti) *led to over 4f out: chsd ldr: tried to chal 2f out: wknd fnl f* **33/1**
5340 12 8 **Lady Frances**[32] 7451 3-8-11 90.............................. JoeFanning 2 60
(Mark Johnston) *t.k.h: prom tl wknd qckly jst over 2f out* **20/1**

1m 10.85s (-2.25) **Going Correction** -0.10s/f (Stan) **12** Ran SP% **131.6**
Speed ratings (Par 109): **111,110,109,109,109 108,108,107,107,105 104,93**
CSF £309.02 CT £1052.28 TOTE £42.00: £12.50, £3.40, £1.30; EX 451.70 Trifecta £1997.40 Part won..
**Owner** Evan M Sutherland **Bred** Equibreed S R L **Trained** Nawton, N Yorks
**FOCUS**
A good, competitive sprint handicap, and straightforward form.

## 7924 BETHANY AND JACK GILBERT ALL WEATHER "HANDS AND HEELS" APPRENTICE SERIES H'CAP 1m (P)
7:45 (7:45) (Class 7) (0-50,51) 3-Y-O+ £1,617 (£481; £240; £120) Stalls Low

Form RPR
6001 1 **Habeshia**[7] 7845 4-9-5 51 6ex.............................. MichaelKenneally(3) 11 58+
(Michael Bell) *prog out wd to ld after 3f: mde rest: jnd over 2f out: battled on wl and fnly gained upper hand ins fnl f* **5/2**[1]
5433 2 ½ **Brown Pete (IRE)**[5] 7869 6-8-13 45..............................(p) CallumShepherd(3) 9 51
(Ann Stokell) *dwlt: quick prog to trck ldrs after 2f: wnt 2nd and urged along to chal over 2f out: w wnr after: nt qckn ins fnl f* **6/1**
5300 3 hd **Berwin (IRE)**[36] 7360 5-8-11 45.............................. JackDinsmore(5) 4 50
(Sylvester Kirk) *dwlt: hld up in rr: prog towards inner over 2f out: clsd on ldrs over 1f out: chal fnl f: nt qckn last 75yds* **25/1**
6400 4 shd **Navajo Dream**[162] 3333 3-8-9 45.............................. TomMarquand(5) 1 49
(Michael Appleby) *trckd ldrs: clsd fr 2f out: chal jst over 1f out: nt qckn last 75yds* **20/1**
0564 5 1 **Roy Rocket (FR)**[13] 7754 4-9-2 45.............................. HectorCrouch 14 48
(John Berry) *broke wl but sn restrained into last trio: tried to make prog on wd outside over 2f out: no hdwy tl kpt on fnl f* **33/1**
6002 6 shd **Nouvelle Ere**[7] 7845 3-8-12 46.............................. PaddyBradley(3) 2 48
(Tony Carroll) *led 3f: chsd wnr to over 2f out: styd cl up: one pce fnl f* **9/2**[2]
0003 7 1 ½ **Top Set (IRE)**[7] 7844 4-9-4 50.............................. TomasHarrigan(3) 7 49
(Simon Dow) *in tch in midfield: pushed along and cl up bhd ldrs fr 2f out tl fdd fnl f* **11/2**[3]
0005 8 4 **Henry Grace (IRE)**[28] 7527 3-9-2 47.............................. GaryMahon 3 36
(Jimmy Fox) *prom: lost pl 2f out: steadily fdd* **6/1**
000 9 hd **La Paiva (FR)**[13] 7766 3-8-11 45..............................[1] RussellHarris(3) 12 34
(Scott Dixon) *t.k.h in midfield: no prog 2f out: wknd over 1f out* **25/1**
00-5 10 1 ¾ **Magic Ice**[134] 4306 4-9-1 47.............................. PaddyPilley(3) 6 32
(John Berry) *dwlt: towards rr: prog on inner over 2f out: wknd over 1f out* **33/1**
5550 11 nk **Buzz Law (IRE)**[32] 6481 6-9-3 49..............................(t) JoshDoyle(3) 10 34
(John Weymes) *racd wd in midfield: no prog 2f out: sn wknd* **33/1**
5365 12 1 **Tamujin (IRE)**[50] 7002 6-9-2 45.............................. RobHornby 5 28
(Ken Cunningham-Brown) *dwlt: a in rr: nvr a factor* **25/1**
4100 13 5 **Fire King**[239] 1215 8-9-4 50..............................(p) JoshQuinn(3) 8 21
(Paul Burgoyne) *slowly away and then rel to r: a detached in last* **20/1**

1m 40.51s (0.71) **Going Correction** -0.10s/f (Stan)
**WFA** 3 from 4yo+ 2lb **13** Ran SP% **120.6**
Speed ratings (Par 97): **92,91,91,91,90 90,88,84,84,82 82,81,76**
CSF £15.34 CT £308.34 TOTE £4.60: £1.60, £2.50, £8.10; EX 20.40 Trifecta £541.20.
**Owner** Brian Goodyear **Bred** Haras Du Mezeray **Trained** Newmarket, Suffolk
**FOCUS**
A weak race and a bunched finish off a steady pace. Straightforward, very limited form.
T/Jkpt: Not won. T/Plt: £13.90 to a £1 stake. Pool: £88,757.98 - 4,631.98 winning tickets T/Qpdt: £2.30 to a £1 stake. Pool: £10,068.14 - 3,141.74 winning tickets JN

7880 **LINGFIELD** (L-H)
Wednesday, November 26

**OFFICIAL GOING: Polytrack: standard**
Wind: virtually nil Weather: drizzly, gloomy

## 7925 CORAL MOBILE "JUST THREE CLICKS TO BET" H'CAP 1m 2f (P)
**12:00** (12:00) (Class 6) (0-65,65) 3-Y-O+ **£1,940** (£577; £288; £144) **Stalls** Low

Form RPR
500- **1** **Young Dottie**16 7734 8-9-10 65 FergusSweeney 1 72
(Pat Phelan) *hld up in tch in midfield: gd hdwy towards inner over 1f out: ev ch and sustained duel w wnr fnl f: r.o wl to ld towards fin* **25/1**
/00- **2** *hd* **Santadelacruze**36 7358 5-9-5 60 RobertHavlin 4 67
(Mark Hoad) *hld up in tch in midfield: effrt and lft chsng ldrs wl over 1f out: drvn to ld 1f out: sustained duel w wnr fnl f: hdd nr fin* **50/1**
166- **3** *1 1/2* **Fair Comment**50 7001 4-9-5 60 DavidProbert 12 64
(Michael Blanshard) *chsd ldr tl 1/2-way: rdn to chse ldr again and clsng whn carried rt on bnd 2f out: rallied over 1f out: kpt on same pce ins fnl f* **20/1**
000- **4** *nk* **Matraash (USA)**23 7626 8-9-5 60 (p) ShaneKelly 11 66+
(Daniel Mark Loughnane) *stdd s: hld up in tch in rr: clsd on bit over 1f out: nt clr run 1f out tl ins fnl f: pushed along and styd on fnl 100yds: nvr trbld ldrs* **20/1**
6/0- **5** *3/4* **Buster Brown (IRE)**235 1302 5-9-10 65 GeorgeBaker 9 67
(Gary Moore) *chsd ldrs: effrt in 4th bnd 2f out: pressing ldrs 1f out: no ex ins fnl f* **5/1**2
024- **6** *hd* **Mcbirney (USA)**14 7744 7-9-8 63 LukeMorris 13 65
(Paul D'Arcy) *stdd s: hld up in tch towards rr: hdwy and wl in tch whn carried lft jst over 1f out: kpt on ins fnl f: nvr able to chal* **5/1**2
006- **7** *nk* **Toymaker**13 7765 7-8-12 60 (t) DonnaAspell(7) 6 61
(Phil McEntee) *in tch in midfield: rdn and sme hdwy over 1f out: kpt on but no real imp ins fnl f* **20/1**
201- **8** *3* **Automotive**11 7804 6-9-4 64 ShelleyBirkett(5) 10 59
(Julia Feilden) *t.k.h: hld up in tch in midfield: shuffled bk towards rr and rdn wl over 1f out: plugged on fnl f: no threat to ldrs* **5/1**2
656- **9** *nk* **Here For Good (IRE)**12 7777 3-9-1 60 RichardHughes 14 55
(Richard Hannon) *chsd ldrs tl rdn and lost pl over 1f out: wknd fnl f* **10/1**
000- **10** *1* **Snow King (USA)**22 7633 4-9-5 60 WilliamTwiston-Davies 7 53
(Ted Powell) *led tl over 5f out: chsd ldr tl jst over 2f out: lft in ld wl over 1f out: drvn and hdd 1f out: wknd ins fnl f* **20/1**
050- **11** *shd* **Munsarim (IRE)**85 6019 7-9-5 60 (b) AmirQuinn 5 52
(Lee Carter) *v.s.a and bustled along early: grad rcvrd and hdwy on outer to ld over 5f out: sn clr: coming bk to field and hung rt bnd 2f out: sn hdd: hung lft u.p over 1f out: wknd fnl f* **9/2**1
020- **12** *nk* **Bridge That Gap**14 7744 6-9-0 62 (p) RhiainIngram(7) 8 54
(Roger Ingram) *stdd s: hld up in last pair: pushed along wl over 1f out: nvr trbld ldrs* **14/1**
000- **13** *13* **Divine Warrior (IRE)**16 7733 3-9-4 63 JimCrowley 2 30
(Timothy Jarvis) *chsd ldrs: rdn and btn 2f out: fdd over 1f out* **8/1**3

2m 6.06s (-0.54) **Going Correction** -0.05s/f (Stan)
**WFA** 3 from 4yo+ 4lb **13 Ran SP% 119.9**
Speed ratings (Par 101): **100,99,98,98,97 97,97,95,94,93 93,93,83**
CSF £889.10 CT £22493.65 TOTE £25.70: £6.00, £7.50, £8.20; EX 662.50 Trifecta £1751.80 Part won..
**Owner** Tony Smith **Bred** Tony J Smith **Trained** Epsom, Surrey
■ Stewards' Enquiry : Amir Quinn two-day ban: careless riding (Dec 10-11)

**FOCUS**
A modest handicap and very straightforward form.

## 7926 UNIBET/IRISH STALLION FARMS EBF MAIDEN STKS (DIV I) 1m 1y(P)
**12:30** (12:31) (Class 5) 2-Y-O **£2,911** (£866; £432; £216) **Stalls** High

Form RPR
0- **1** **Awesome Power**26 7560 2-9-5 0 RichardHughes 7 73+
(William Haggas) *chsd ldr tl led and travelling strly jst over 2f out: rdn over 1f out: r.o wl and in command fnl f* **6/4**1
62- **2** *1 1/2* **Royal Albert Hall**16 7731 2-9-5 0 JimCrowley 8 70
(Olly Stevens) *t.k.h: chsd ldng trio: rdn and effrt to chse wnr 2f out: kpt on wl for clr 2nd: a hld by wnr* **3/1**2
**3** *4 1/2* **Crisscrossed** 2-9-5 0 PaulMulrennan 1 61+
(Amanda Perrett) *s.i.s: hld up in rr: hdwy into midfield and shkn up 2f out: no ch w ldng pair but styd on wl ins fnl f to go 3rd towards fin* **10/1**
0- **4** *3/4* **Goodwood Moonlight**16 7730 2-9-5 0 GeorgeBaker 6 59
(William Knight) *t.k.h: in tch in midfield: effrt and outpcd 2f out: wnt 3rd but no threat to ldng pair 1f out: kpt on same pce: lost 3rd wl ins fnl f* **25/1**
**5** *hd* **Singular Quest** 2-9-5 0 JamesDoyle 5 59+
(Ralph Beckett) *in tch towards rr: hdwy over 2f out: modest 7th and rn green over 1f out: no ch w ldrs but kpt on ins fnl f* **7/2**3
00- **6** *1 1/4* **Artistic Flight (IRE)**14 7739 2-9-5 0 PatCosgrave 10 56
(Jim Boyle) *dwlt: in tch in midfield on outer: pushed along and outpcd wl over 1f out: no threat to ldrs and keeping on same pce whn n.m.r and eased towards fin* **100/1**
0- **7** *2 3/4* **Peterhouse (USA)**16 7730 2-9-5 0 RobertHavlin 11 50
(John Gosden) *s.i.s: in tch but a towards rr: shkn up and outpcd wl over 1f out: plugged on but no threat to ldrs fnl f* **20/1**
00- **8** *3/4* **Top Pocket**35 7372 2-9-0 0 KieranShoemark(5) 2 49
(Michael Madgwick) *led: rdn and hdd over 2f out: 3rd and struggling u.p 2f out: lost 3rd 1f out: fdd fnl f* **100/1**
**9** *4 1/2* **No Backchat (IRE)** 2-9-5 0 GrahamLee 4 39
(Kevin Ryan) *in tch in midfield: lost pl and bhd wl over 1f out: sn wknd: fin lame* **16/1**
**10** *1* **Obsidian Rock (USA)** 2-9-5 0 LiamJones 9 37
(J S Moore) *s.i.s: rn green: in tch in rr: wknd wl over 1f out* **33/1**
00- **11** *4* **Ultima Ora (IRE)**7 7835 2-9-0 0 JoeFanning 3 24
(Mark Johnston) *chsd ldrs: losing pl whn bdly hmpd bnd jst over 1f out: bhd and no ch after* **66/1**

1m 39.57s (1.37) **Going Correction** -0.05s/f (Stan) **11 Ran SP% 117.2**
Speed ratings (Par 96): **91,89,85,84,84 82,80,79,74,73 69**
CSF £5.62 TOTE £2.40: £1.30, £1.10, £2.10; EX 6.20 Trifecta £36.60.
**Owner** The Queen **Bred** The Queen **Trained** Newmarket, Suffolk

**FOCUS**
The visibility wasn't great for the first division of this maiden. The front pair pulled clear and there's every chance the winner has better to come. It was much the slower of the two divisions.

## 7927 UNIBET/IRISH STALLION FARMS EBF MAIDEN STKS (DIV II) 1m 1y(P)
**1:00** (1:02) (Class 5) 2-Y-O **£2,911** (£866; £432; £216) **Stalls** High

Form RPR
322- **1** **Oregon Gift**7 7834 2-9-5 70 JoeFanning 3 78
(Mark Johnston) *mde all: rdn clr 2f out: in command over 1f out: styd on wl: rdn out* **5/1**2
02- **2** *3* **Justice Belle (IRE)**29 7512 2-9-0 0 AntonioFresu 6 66
(Ed Walker) *in tch in midfield: effrt and wdst bnd 2f out: no threat to wnr but kpt on wl u.p ins fnl f: wnt 2nd towards fin* **25/1**
64- **3** *1/2* **Azilian**16 7730 2-9-5 0 (t) LukeMorris 9 70
(Paul Cole) *chsd wnr: rdn over 3f out: drvn and outpcd by wnr 2f out: hld but battled on wl u.p after: lost 2nd towards fin* **25/1**
0- **4** *hd* **Melodica**32 7450 2-9-0 0 JamesDoyle 7 64
(Roger Charlton) *chsd ldng trio: outpcd and rdn wl over 1f out: no threat to wnr but battling for placings fnl f: kpt on* **7/1**3
63- **5** *hd* **Mojawiz**12 7778 2-9-5 0 (p) AdamKirby 2 69
(Charlie Appleby) *broke wl: stdd bk to chse ldrs: 3rd and outpcd by wnr 2f out: hld and battling for placings after: one pce* **9/4**1
05- **6** *1/2* **Tempus Temporis (USA)**35 7382 2-9-5 0 RobertHavlin 10 68+
(John Gosden) *hld up in last trio: shkn up jst over 1f out: no threat to wnr but hdwy under hands and heels ins fnl f: kpt on: n.m.r towards fin* **8/1**
04- **7** *1 1/4* **Wally's Wisdom**21 7660 2-9-5 0 RichardHughes 5 65+
(William Haggas) *in tch in midfield: pushed along and unable qck over 1f out: one pce and wl hld fnl f* **5/1**2
5- **8** *7* **Knight Music**33 7414 2-9-5 0 JimCrowley 1 49
(Michael Attwater) *in tch in midfield: rdn and struggling 2f out: sn lost pl and btn: wknd fnl f* **100/1**
**9** *nk* **Silken Ocean** 2-9-0 0 OscarPereira 8 43
(Ralph Beckett) *s.i.s: sn niggled along and rn green: a in rr* **10/1**
**10** *1 1/2* **Bernhard (IRE)** 2-9-5 0 ShaneKelly 4 45
(Sir Michael Stoute) *s.i.s: rn green and sn pushed along in rr: n.d* **5/1**2

1m 36.57s (-1.63) **Going Correction** -0.05s/f (Stan) **10 Ran SP% 122.2**
Speed ratings (Par 96): **106,103,102,102,102 101,100,93,93,91**
CSF £125.81 TOTE £6.70: £2.00, £4.40, £5.20; EX 117.00 Trifecta £950.70.
**Owner** N Browne,M Bradford,R Frosell,S Richards **Bred** Bearstone Stud **Trained** Middleham Moor, N Yorks

**FOCUS**
The winning time was exactly 3sec quicker than the first division. The winner matched his Kempton form.

## 7928 LADBROKES CLAIMING STKS 7f 1y(P)
**1:30** (1:30) (Class 6) 3-Y-O+ **£1,940** (£577; £288; £144) **Stalls** Low

Form RPR
405- **1** **Living Leader**13 7758 5-9-1 67 (tp) PatCosgrave 3 75
(Grace Harris) *chsd ldng pair: rdn and effrt 2f out: chsd clr wnr ins fnl f: styd on u.p to ld on post* **6/1**3
006- **2** *nse* **Exceedexpectations (IRE)**22 7636 5-8-8 75 (v) ThomasBrown(3) 6 71
(Lee Carter) *chsd ldr and clr of field: clsd and upsides over 2f out: led 2f out: rdn clr and pricking ears 1f out: drvn ins fnl f: kpt on: hdd on post* **6/4**1
005- **3** *1 1/4* **Birdman (IRE)**16 7732 4-9-1 71 (b) MartinLane 1 71
(David Simcock) *racd off the pce in midfield: effrt on inner 2f out: wnt 3rd 1f out: kpt on but no imp wl ins fnl f* **4/1**2
401- **4** *3/4* **My Son Max**9 7819 6-8-13 75 (v) GrahamLee 4 67
(Richard Ford) *racd off the pce in 4th: rdn over 2f out: no real imp tl styd on fnl 100yds: nvr enough pce to chal* **4/1**2
524- **5** *1 3/4* **Avertor**6 7847 8-8-13 60 (v) LiamJones 10 63
(Robert Stephens) *racd keenly: led: sn clr: hdd and rdn 2f out: lost 2nd ins fnl f: wknd fnl 100yds* **20/1**
0- **6** *1 3/4* **Expensive Taste (IRE)**57 6846 3-8-7 76 (t) DannyBrock(3) 8 55
(Phil McEntee) *s.i.s: hld up off the pce in last trio: pushed along and hdwy jst over 1f out: kpt on fnl f: nvr trbld ldrs* **10/1**
100- **7** *2* **Dazza**6 7847 3-7-12 70 ow1 HectorCrouch(7) 7 45
(Gary Moore) *racd off the pce in midfield: pushed along and no hdwy over 2f out: plugged on same pce after: nvr trbld ldrs* **16/1**
50U- **8** *3/4* **Powerful Pierre**20 7687 7-9-0 75 (b) MartinHarley 2 52
(Noel Quinlan) *s.i.s: hld up off the pce in last trio: sme hdwy over 1f out: nvr trbld ldrs* **33/1**
005- **9** *1* **Soul Instinct**85 5994 3-8-10 52 TomasHarrigan(7) 9 52
(Simon Dow) *wd and a off the pce in last trio: last and moved to inner jst over 2f out: n.d* **50/1**

1m 23.08s (-1.72) **Going Correction** -0.05s/f (Stan)
**WFA** 3 from 4yo+ 1lb **9 Ran SP% 118.9**
Speed ratings (Par 101): **107,106,105,104,102 100,98,97,96**
CSF £15.67 TOTE £8.50: £2.00, £1.10, £2.20; EX 37.30 Trifecta £144.20.Birdman was claimed by Mr D. O'Meara £10,000. Exceedexpectations was claimed by Gay Kelleway £6,000. My Son Max was claimed by Nikki Evans for £8,000.
**Owner** Mrs Michelle Harris **Bred** D J And Mrs Deer **Trained** Shirenewton, Monmouthshire

**FOCUS**
They went a decent pace here and few ever got into this claimer. The winner is rated around his better efforts of recent years.

## 7929 UNIBET OFFER DAILY JOCKEY/TRAINER SPECIALS MAIDEN STKS 6f 1y(P)
**2:00** (2:00) (Class 5) 3-Y-O **£2,587** (£770; £384; £192) **Stalls** Low

Form RPR
052- **1** **Elhaam (IRE)**30 7501 3-9-0 64 MartinLane 3 67+
(George Margarson) *led tl 1/2-way: rdn to ld again on inner jst over 1f out: in command fnl f: r.o* **5/4**2
543- **2** *1 3/4* **Two Smart (IRE)**9 7818 3-9-0 70 LukeMorris 2 62
(Daniel Kubler) *hld up in tch: cl 4th and effrt 2f out: chsd wnr jst ins fnl f: sn drvn: r.o same pce fnl 100yds* **4/5**1
263- **3** *5* **Nelson's Pride**11 7800 3-8-7 54 (b) RhiainIngram(7) 5 47
(Roger Ingram) *stdd s: keen and dashed up to press ldrs after 2f: led over 2f out tl rdn and hdd jst over 1f out: wknd ins fnl f* **20/1**
460- **4** *1/2* **Qatar Princess (IRE)**22 7652 3-9-0 55 JoeFanning 4 45
(J R Jenkins) *chsd ldr for 2f: cl 3rd and rdn 2f out: unable qck and btn 1f out: wknd ins fnl f* **16/1**3

600- **5** 3 ¾ **Kitty Bequick**[73] 6356 3-9-0 45 CharlesBishop 1 34
(Peter Hedger) *in tch in rr: rdn and struggling 2f out: wknd over 1f out* **66/1**

1m 12.04s (0.14) **Going Correction** -0.05s/f (Stan) 5 Ran SP% **112.1**
Speed ratings (Par 102): **97,94,88,87,82**
CSF £2.61 TOTE £3.50: £1.10, £1.10; EX 2.80 Trifecta £11.40.
**Owner** Saleh Al Homaizi & Imad Al Sagar **Bred** Saleh Al Homaizi & Imad Al Sagar **Trained** Newmarket, Suffolk

**FOCUS**
Five fillies went to post for this modest maiden even though the race was open to colts and geldings, but it was only a two-horse race according to the market. The time was slow and it's a race to be negative about.

## 7930 CORAL APP DOWNLOAD FROM THE APP STORE H'CAP 1m 2f (P)
**2:35** (2:35) (Class 2) (0-100,100) 3-Y-O+ **£12,291** (£3,657; £1,827; £913) **Stalls** Low

Form RPR
023- **1** **Maverick Wave (USA)**[20] 7688 3-9-6 100 RobertHavlin 2 106
(John Gosden) *mde all: set stdy gallop: rdn and qcknd over 1f out: kpt on wl u.p ins fnl f: rdn out* **4/5**[1]
100- **2** ¾ **Lyn Valley**[76] 6257 3-9-2 96 JoeFanning 1 101
(Mark Johnston) *chsd ldrs: effrt 2f out: wnt 2nd and pressing wnr ins fnl f: r.o but hld towards fin* **7/1**[3]
105- **3** 1 **Dominandros (FR)**[26] 7619 3-8-13 93 DavidProbert 5 96
(Gay Kelleway) *hld up wl in tch in midfield: rdn and effrt 2f out: 3rd and styd on same pce ins fnl f* **16/1**
514- **4** ½ **Castilo Del Diablo (IRE)**[222] 1556 5-8-13 96 SophieKilloran(7) 6 98
(David Simcock) *stdd s: hld up in tch in last pair: effrt over 1f out: sltly hmpd and swtchd lft ins fnl f: kpt on* **12/1**
600- **5** nk **Viewpoint (IRE)**[53] 6930 5-9-7 97 RichardHughes 3 98
(Richard Hannon) *stdd: short of room and hmpd s: hld up in tch in last pair: clsd and rdn 2f out: kpt on same pce ins fnl f* **12/1**
303- **6** 1 **Energia Fox (BRZ)**[11] 7803 4-9-6 96 MartinHarley 4 95
(Marco Botti) *chsd wnr: rdn wl over 1f out: lost 2nd ins fnl f: outpcd fnl 100yds* **7/2**[2]

2m 3.6s (-3.00) **Going Correction** -0.05s/f (Stan)
**WFA** 3 from 4yo+ 4lb 6 Ran SP% **111.5**
Speed ratings (Par 109): **110,109,108,108,107 107**
CSF £7.01 TOTE £1.70: £1.10, £2.30; EX 7.60 Trifecta £83.30.
**Owner** HRH Princess Haya Of Jordan **Bred** Jim Plemmons & Darley **Trained** Newmarket, Suffolk

**FOCUS**
The fog continued to thicken. They only went a modest pace in this decent handicap and not much covered the six runners at the line, with the 3yos dominating. There could be more to come from the first two.

## 7931 £20 RISK-FREE BET AT UNIBET H'CAP 6f 1y(P)
**3:10** (3:11) (Class 5) (0-75,75) 3-Y-O+ **£2,587** (£770; £384; £192) **Stalls** Low

Form RPR
121- **1** **Varsovian**[12] 7775 4-9-1 69 JimmyQuinn 11 77+
(Dean Ivory) *in tch in midfield: drvn and shifting lft 1f out: r.o wl ins fnl f to ld on post* **3/1**[1]
105- **2** nse **Harrogate Fair**[13] 7761 4-9-2 70 (p) AdamKirby 3 78
(Michael Squance) *chsd ldr: rdn to ld 1f out: kpt on u.p: hdd on post* **14/1**
006- **3** ½ **Desert Strike**[20] 7687 8-9-7 75 (p) HayleyTurner 10 81
(Conor Dore) *led: rdn over 1f out: hdd 1f out: kpt on wl u.p ins fnl f* **16/1**
004- **4** ¾ **Temple Road (IRE)**[36] 7351 6-9-2 70 (t) GrahamLee 6 74+
(Milton Bradley) *hld up in tch in midfield: shkn up and hdwy jst over 1f out: chsd ldrs ins fnl f: kpt on* **7/1**[3]
062- **5** 2 ¼ **Majestic Song**[19] 7697 3-9-2 70 WilliamTwiston-Davies 12 67
(James Toller) *dwlt: in tch towards rr: effrt and swtchd rt over 1f out: kpt on ins fnl f: nvr trbld ldrs* **10/1**
000- **6** ½ **Tidal's Baby**[13] 7757 5-9-4 72 AmirQuinn 8 68
(Lee Carter) *s.i.s: in tch in last pair: effrt on outer bnd 2f out: kpt on ins fnl f: nvr trbld ldrs* **5/1**[2]
200- **7** nk **Sweet Talking Guy (IRE)**[36] 7352 4-8-13 70 (t) SimonPearce(3) 1 65
(Lydia Pearce) *in tch in midfield: effrt in 4th over 1f out: no hdwy 1f out: wknd ins fnl f* **8/1**
402- **8** 2 ¼ **Another Try (IRE)**[22] 7636 9-8-9 70 JordanVaughan(7) 9 58
(Timothy Jarvis) *chsd ldrs tl lost pl u.p over 1f out: wknd ins fnl f* **10/1**
363- **9** 1 ¾ **Costa Filey**[117] 4862 3-9-3 71 GeorgeBaker 7 54
(Ed Vaughan) *t.k.h: hld up in tch in rr: effrt on inner and hung lft over 1f out: wknd fnl f* **3/1**[1]

1m 10.85s (-1.05) **Going Correction** -0.05s/f (Stan) 9 Ran SP% **121.0**
Speed ratings (Par 103): **105,104,104,103,100 99,99,96,93**
CSF £50.82 CT £596.01 TOTE £3.30: £1.40, £3.40, £6.80; EX 34.90 Trifecta £159.40.
**Owner** Geoff Copp & Radlett Racing **Bred** Darley **Trained** Radlett, Herts

**FOCUS**
An ordinary if competitive sprint handicap. There's every chance the winner can do better again.

## 7932 CORAL.CO.UK BEST ODDS GUARANTEED ON RACING APPRENTICE H'CAP 1m 4f (P)
**3:40** (3:40) (Class 6) (0-65,65) 3-Y-O+ **£1,940** (£577; £288; £144) **Stalls** Low

Form RPR
60- **1** **Planetoid (IRE)**[21] 7359 6-9-10 65 (b¹) WilliamTwiston-Davies 2 71
(Jim Best) *dwlt: in tch in rr: hdwy 2f out: swtchd lft ins fnl f and qcknd to ld wl ins fnl f: r.o* **7/1**
105- **2** hd **Celestial Bay**[14] 7744 5-9-5 63 TimClark(3) 13 69
(Sylvester Kirk) *in tch in midfield: hdwy u.p over 1f out: ev ch u.p ins fnl f: r.o* **20/1**
153- **3** ½ **Thomas Blossom (IRE)**[39] 7291 4-8-5 51 oh3 (v) RobHornby(5) 7 56
(Patrick Chamings) *in tch in midfield: hdwy u.pr over 1f out: styd on wl ins fnl f to go 3rd nr fin: nt rch ldrs* **5/1**[2]
402- **4** ½ **Mazij**[36] 7360 6-8-7 51 oh2 ShelleyBirkett(3) 11 55
(Peter Hiatt) *chsd ldr tl rdn to ld 2f out: kpt on u.p tl hdd and one pce wl ins fnl f* **10/1**
400- **5** ½ **Keep Kicking (IRE)**[12] 7777 7-9-2 64 TomasHarrigan(7) 5 67+
(Simon Dow) *stdd and dropped in bhd s: hld up in rr: clsd and nt clr run 1f out: swtchd rt ins fnl f: r.o wl fnl 100yds: nt reaxch ldrs* **16/1**
624- **6** hd **Cabuchon (GER)**[7] 7846 7-8-9 57 (t) HarryBurns(7) 8 60+
(David Evans) *hld up in tch in rr: effrt on outer over 1f out: styd on wl u.p ins fnl f: nt rch ldrs* **5/1**[2]
/30- **7** ½ **Josie's Dream (IRE)**[282] 640 6-8-10 51 oh1 ConnorBeasley 12 53
(Jo Hughes) *in tch in midfield: rdn over 1f out: kpt on same pce u.p ins fnl f* **33/1**
004- **8** shd **Panettone (IRE)**[28] 7527 5-9-6 61 (b) RossAtkinson 4 63
(Roger Varian) *t.k.h: chsd ldrs: rdn 2f out: keeping on same pce whn nt clr run and hmpd 1f out: r.o same pce fnl 100yds* **12/1**
100- **9** 1 ¼ **Reality Show (IRE)**[14] 7744 7-8-13 61 KevinLundie(7) 1 61
(Shaun Harris) *in tch in midfield: hdwy on inner whn nt clr run jst over 1f out: swtchd rt ins fnl f: kpt on: nvr trbld ldrs* **16/1**
040- **10** ½ **Eurato (FR)**[16] 7734 4-9-7 65 EoinWalsh(3) 10 64
(John Spearing) *hld up in tch in rr: effrt on outer 1f out: kpt on ins fnl f: nvr trbld ldrs* **6/1**[3]
000- **11** ½ **Flying Author (IRE)**[12] 7777 3-8-4 51 oh6 (tp) DannyBrock 6 49
(Phil McEntee) *led: hdd 2f out: kpt on and ev ch tl ins fnl f: wknd wl ins fnl f* **50/1**
040- **12** ¾ **Teide Peak (IRE)**[35] 7369 5-9-3 58 (p) RobertTart 9 55
(Grace Harris) *in tch: hdwy on outer to chse ldrs 7f out: unable qck u.p over 1f out: wknd ins fnl f* **20/1**
306- **13** ½ **Red Dragon (IRE)**[14] 7744 4-9-3 63 ChrisMeehan(5) 3 59+
(Michael Blanshard) *chsd ldrs: rdn and effrt on inner 2f out: styng on same pce and hld whn nt clr run and shuffled bk ins fnl f* **4/1**[1]

2m 33.7s (0.70) **Going Correction** -0.05s/f (Stan)
**WFA** 3 from 4yo+ 6lb 13 Ran SP% **123.1**
Speed ratings (Par 101): **95,94,94,94,93 93,93,93,92,92 91,91,91**
CSF £147.07 CT £775.94 TOTE £7.10: £2.30, £4.80, £2.30; EX 201.90 Trifecta £2413.40.
**Owner** Planetoid Partnership **Bred** Bjorn Nielsen **Trained** Lewes, E Sussex

**FOCUS**
The visibility was particularly poor for this moderate apprentice handicap. From what could be seen they only went a modest pace and they finished in a heap. The winner can rate a bit higher in the short term.
T/Plt: £820.70 to a £1 stake. Pool: £65,208.72 - 58.00 winning tickets T/Qpdt: £12.90 to a £1 stake. Pool: £9,585.65 - 548.63 winning tickets SP

7933 - 7939a (Foreign Racing) - See Raceform Interactive

# 7917 KEMPTON (A.W) (R-H)
Thursday, November 27

**OFFICIAL GOING: Polytrack: standard**
Wind: Almost nil Weather: Cloudy

## 7940 MIX BUSINESS AND PLEASURE AT KEMPTON APPRENTICE H'CAP 6f (P)
**3:55** (3:55) (Class 7) (0-50,50) 3-Y-O+ **£1,617** (£360; £360; £120) **Stalls** Low

Form RPR
405- **1** **Waabel**[99] 5574 7-9-7 50 (t) JordanVaughan 7 58
(Ann Stokell) *hld up in midfield: prog wl over 1f out: rdn to ld last 100yds: styd on* **6/4**[1]
540- **2** 1 **Fairy Wing (IRE)**[181] 2723 7-9-0 50 (b) TomMarquand(7) 11 55
(Ann Stokell) *w ldr at str pce: led 1/2-way: 2 l clr 2f out: rdn over 1f out: hdd and no ex last 100yds* **25/1**
030- **2** dht **Encapsulated**[13] 7782 4-8-13 49 (p) RhiainIngram(7) 10 54
(Roger Ingram) *wl in rr: shkn up over 2f out: prog wl over 1f out: kpt on fnl f: nrst fin* **8/1**
500- **4** 1 ¼ **Compton Silver**[28] 7547 4-9-3 46 DanielCremin 1 47
(Miss Joey Ellis) *rousted fr s: chsd ldng pair: wnt 2nd wl over 1f out tl fnl f: one pce* **5/1**[3]
000- **5** 2 **Mack's Sister**[7] 7854 7-8-13 45 HectorCrouch(3) 4 40
(Michael Madgwick) *towards rr: rdn over 2f out: tried to make prog over 1f out: kpt on but n.d* **20/1**
440- **6** shd **Princess Rose**[34] 7420 3-9-4 47 (v) KieranShoemark 6 41
(John Weymes) *chsd ldrs: rdn over 2f out: tried to cl over 1f out: fdd ins fnl f* **9/1**
006- **7** nk **Quantum Dot (IRE)**[13] 7783 3-9-7 50 (p) DavidParkes 12 43
(Ed de Giles) *s.s: off the pce in last trio: rdn over 2f out: plugged on fr over 1f out: no ch* **5/2**[2]
665- **8** ½ **Aussie Sky (IRE)**[6] 7865 3-9-3 46 PatMillman 2 38
(Daniel Mark Loughnane) *in tch: rdn on inner 2f out: no prog over 1f out: fdd* **11/1**
000- **9** 10 **Under Review (IRE)**[13] 7782 8-9-0 48 (bt) CallumShepherd(5) 9 8
(Bernard Llewellyn) *s.s: a bhd and wd bnds: t.o* **16/1**
040- **10** 14 **Diamond Solitaire (IRE)**[13] 7781 3-9-3 49 GaryMahon(3) 5
(Timothy Jarvis) *led at str pce to 1/2-way: wknd rapidly 2f out: wl t.o* **33/1**

1m 13.22s (0.12) **Going Correction** +0.025s/f (Slow) 10 Ran SP% **132.1**
Speed ratings (Par 97): **100,98,98,97,94 94,93,93,79,61**
WIN: 3.10 Waabel; PL: 1.10 Waabel, 7.70 Fairy Wing, 2.30 Encapsulated; EX: 38.90 W&FW, 14.70 W&E; CSF: 27.80 W&FW, 8.60 W&E; TC: 124.92 W&FW&E, 136.11 W&E&FW; TF: 379.60 W&FW&E, 221.20 W&E&FW.
**Owner** Stephen Arnold **Bred** Shadwell Estate Company Limited **Trained** Lincoln, Lincolnshire

**FOCUS**
A low-grade handicap run at a good pace.

## 7941 DOWNLOAD THE BETVICTOR APP MAIDEN AUCTION STKS 1m (P)
**4:25** (4:27) (Class 5) 2-Y-O **£2,587** (£770; £384; £192) **Stalls** Low

Form RPR
0- **1** **Logorrheic**[14] 7752 2-9-3 0 SeanLevey 11 78
(Ralph Beckett) *t.k.h: pressed ldr: led wl over 2f out: rdn over 1f out: pressed last 100yds: pushed out firmly* **7/1**[3]
2- **2** ½ **Quest For Wonder**[24] 7625 2-8-12 0 LukeMorris 10 72
(James Tate) *trckd ldng pair: drvn to go 2nd over 1f out: clsd on wnr 100yds out: no imp nr fin* **5/1**[2]
0- **3** 2 ½ **Whitchurch**[23] 7631 2-8-9 0 (t) KieranShoemark(5) 14 68
(Andrew Balding) *sn in midfield: 7th over 3f out: stdy prog on outer fr 2f out: rdn to go 3rd ins fnl f: no imp on ldng pair* **12/1**
2- **4** ¾ **Niblawi (IRE)**[8] 7835 2-9-0 0 AdamKirby 7 67+
(Michael Bell) *dwlt: wl in rr: stl only disputing 9th over 3f out: tried to make prog on outer over 2f out: rdn over 1f out: kpt on: n.d* **10/11**[1]
06- **5** nk **Callendula**[24] 7625 2-8-4 0 RyanTate(3) 1 59
(Clive Cox) *chsd ldrs in 6th: rdn 2f out: kpt on same pce: nvr able to threaten* **20/1**
045- **6** nk **Chefchaouen (IRE)**[6] 7867 2-8-0 0 (p) JosephineGordon(7) 3 58
(J S Moore) *chsd ldng trio: rdn over 2f out: no imp over 1f out: one pce after* **25/1**
0- **7** 1 ½ **Alfie The Pug**[83] 6101 2-8-11 0 ShaneKelly 13 59
(Pat Phelan) *chsd ldng quartet: rdn and tried to cl 2f out: no hdwy 1f out: wknd* **100/1**
5- **8** 2 ¼ **Candella**[61] 6742 2-8-6 0 RossAtkinson(3) 9 52
(Roger Varian) *led to over 2f out: chsd wnr to over 1f out: wknd qckly* **33/1**
**9** nse **Faith Matters (IRE)** 2-8-11 0 MartinHarley 5 53+
(Marco Botti) *dwlt: wl in rr: rdn and detached in last quartet over 3f out: kpt on fnl 2f: n.d* **16/1**


The Form Book, Raceform Ltd, Newbury, RG14 5SJ

6- **10** *1* **Ashford (IRE)**[35] 7399 2-8-7 0 FergusSweeney 2 47
(Martyn Meade) *nvr bttr than midfield: pushed along firmly and no hdwy over 2f out: wl btn after* **12/1**

0- **11** *2 1/4* **Casius**[23] 7631 2-9-2 0 SteveDrowne 12 51
(Harry Dunlop) *s.i.s: a wl in rr: detached in last quartet sn after 1/2-way: no prog* **50/1**

**12** *1/2* **Albert Herring** 2-8-9 0 DannyBrock(3) 8 46
(Jonathan Portman) *sn in midfield: drvn over 2f out: wknd* **66/1**

0- **13** *4 1/2* **Oakling**[14] 7756 2-8-7 0 MartinDwyer 4 30
(Sylvester Kirk) *s.i.s: a wl in rr: struggling and detached in last quartet over 3f out* **66/1**

0- **14** *18* **Falmouth Harbour**[8] 7835 2-8-12 0 MartinLane 6
(Paul Cole) *s.s: rn green and sn last: t.o* **66/1**

1m 39.92s (0.12) **Going Correction** +0.025s/f (Slow) **14** Ran SP% **121.8**
Speed ratings (Par 96): **100,99,97,96,95 95,94,91,91,90 88,88,83,65**
CSF £40.18 TOTE £7.20: £2.50, £1.60, £4.40; EX 52.90 Trifecta £463.20.
**Owner** Frewen & Ahkong **Bred** Mrs D. Camacho **Trained** Kimpton, Hants
■ Stewards' Enquiry : Sean Levey one-day ban: failed to ride to draw (Dec 11)

**FOCUS**
A fairly ordinary maiden.

## 7942 DOWNLOAD THE BETVICTOR APP H'CAP 1m (P)
4:55 (4:55) (Class 6) (0-65,64) 3-Y-0+ **£1,940** (£577; £288; £144) **Stalls** Low

Form RPR

004- **1** **What A Dandy (IRE)**[12] 7805 3-9-3 62 (p) PatCosgrave 9 70
(Jim Boyle) *t.k.h early: chsd ldng trio after 3f: shkn up over 2f out whn others gng much bttr: prog to ld over 1f out but sn jnd: styd on wl: jst hld on* **13/2**

000- **2** *hd* **Tevez**[40] 7288 9-9-4 61 (p) DavidProbert 6 69
(Des Donovan) *w.w in rr: prog over 2f out: chal and w wnr fr over 1f out: gd battle after: jst hld* **25/1**

000- **3** *3/4* **Chelwood Gate (IRE)**[38] 7339 4-9-7 64 (v) JimCrowley 4 71+
(Patrick Chamings) *hld up in midfield: dropped to rr 1/2-way: gng easily wl over 1f out and nt clr run briefly: prog jst over 1f out but ldng pair had flown: wnt 3rd ins fnl f and clsd at fin: too much to do* **6/1**

003- **4** *3/4* **Flamborough Breeze**[29] 7533 5-9-5 62 (t) LukeMorris 7 66
(Ed Vaughan) *slowly away: in last pair: pushed along over 3f out: asked to make prog but hung in bhd rival over 1f out: drvn and r.o to take 4th ins fnl f: no ch* **2/1**[1]

630- **5** *2* **Byrd In Hand (IRE)**[14] 7759 7-9-7 64 (v) WilliamCarson 3 64
(John Bridger) *led at decent pce: hdd over 1f out: sn btn* **25/1**

254- **6** *nk* **Spirit Of Gondree (IRE)**[34] 7427 6-9-4 61 (b) AdamKirby 5 60
(Milton Bradley) *trckd ldr 3f: styd prom: poised to chal gng easily 2f out: shkn up and no rspnse over 1f out: immediately btn* **3/1**[2]

211- **7** *nk* **Cadmium**[28] 7546 3-8-9 61 Leah-AnneAvery(7) 2 58
(Harry Dunlop) *trckd ldrs: pushed along and cl enough 2f out: fdd* **4/1**[3]

065- **8** *2 1/2* **Roly Tricks**[12] 7799 3-8-13 58 CharlesBishop 1 50
(Natalie Lloyd-Beavis) *s.s: a in last trio: nvr a factor* **33/1**

405- **9** *nk* **Zed Candy Girl**[37] 7368 4-9-2 64 (p) EoinWalsh(5) 10 56
(John Stimpson) *trckd ldr after 3f to 2f out: sn wknd* **11/1**

1m 39.95s (0.15) **Going Correction** +0.025s/f (Slow)
**WFA** 3 from 4yo+ 2lb **9** Ran SP% **124.9**
Speed ratings (Par 101): **100,99,99,98,96 96,95,93,92**
CSF £159.73 CT £1051.89 TOTE £7.90: £2.40, £4.70, £2.30; EX 133.90 Trifecta £1341.30.
**Owner** Inside Track Racing Club **Bred** Pat Beirne **Trained** Epsom, Surrey

**FOCUS**
A modest but competitive handicap and a thrilling finish.

## 7943 £25 FREE BET AT BETVICTOR.COM MAIDEN FILLIES' STKS (BOBIS RACE) (DIV I) 7f (P)
5:25 (5:26) (Class 4) 2-Y-0 **£3,881** (£1,155; £577; £288) **Stalls** Low

Form RPR

4- **1** **Engaging Smile**[43] 7192 2-9-0 0 JimCrowley 4 77+
(Ralph Beckett) *trckd ldrs: led 2f out: clr 1f out: pushed out firmly: comf* **1/1**[1]

405- **2** *1 3/4* **Rastanora (USA)**[66] 6606 2-9-0 72 RobertHavlin 3 70
(John Gosden) *chsd ldrs: shkn up 2f out: prog after: styd on to take 2nd ins fnl f* **9/2**[2]

00- **3** *1/2* **Hyphaema (IRE)**[34] 7405 2-9-0 0 (t) AdamKirby 9 69
(Clive Cox) *led after 1f: tried to kick on over 2f out: sn hdd: one pce and lost 2nd ins fnl f* **20/1**

**4** *2 1/4* **Lahayeb** 2-9-0 0 SeanLevey 7 64+
(Richard Hannon) *hld up in rr: shkn up 2f out: prog to take 4th fnl f: sltly green but kpt on* **16/1**

35- **5** *3/4* **Light Of The World (IRE)**[44] 7184 2-8-9 0 RachealKneller(5) 8 61
(Jamie Osborne) *prom: pushed along 2f out: sn outpcd: no hdwy after* **11/2**

00- **6** *1* **Fanny Again**[14] 7752 2-9-0 0 PatCosgrave 6 58+
(Denis Coakley) *hld up in last pair: outpcd over 2f out: no ch after: kpt on ins fnl f* **33/1**

00- **7** *nk* **Titan Goddess**[23] 7631 2-9-0 0 ShaneKelly 1 57
(Mike Murphy) *t.k.h: hld up in 6th: nudged along 2f out: losing grnd whn light reminder 1f out* **66/1**

430- **8** *shd* **Imperial Link**[36] 7378 2-9-0 67 LukeMorris 2 57
(Paul Cole) *led 1f: trckd ldrs after: shkn up 2f out: wknd over 1f out* **5/1**[3]

**9** *3 1/4* **Brean Golf Birdie** 2-8-9 0 KieranShoemark(5) 5 48
(Bill Turner) *t.k.h: hld up in last pair: outpcd over 2f out: no ch after* **66/1**

1m 28.17s (2.17) **Going Correction** +0.025s/f (Slow) **9** Ran SP% **116.8**
Speed ratings (Par 95): **88,86,85,82,82 80,80,80,76**
CSF £5.66 TOTE £2.00: £1.10, £1.80, £4.00; EX 7.00 Trifecta £66.80.
**Owner** Qatar Racing Ltd & N H Wrigley **Bred** Carmel Stud **Trained** Kimpton, Hants

**FOCUS**
Little depth to this fillies' maiden.

## 7944 £25 FREE BET AT BETVICTOR.COM MAIDEN FILLIES' STKS (BOBIS RACE) (DIV II) 7f (P)
5:55 (5:56) (Class 4) 2-Y-0 **£3,881** (£1,155; £577; £288) **Stalls** Low

Form RPR

2- **1** **Redstart**[51] 7018 2-9-0 0 AdamKirby 6 79+
(Ralph Beckett) *trckd ldr: shkn up briefly to ld over 2f out: pushed along and wl in command fnl f* **5/6**[1]

3- **2** *2 1/4* **Althania (USA)**[106] 5305 2-9-0 0 RobertHavlin 8 73
(John Gosden) *led and dictated ordinary pce: tried to step it up over 2f out: sn hdd: readily outpcd by wnr* **2/1**[2]

**3** *1 1/2* **Plaisir (IRE)** 2-9-0 0 MartinHarley 3 69+
(Marco Botti) *trckd ldrs in 5th: prog to take 3rd wl over 1f out: sn outpcd by ldng pair: kpt on steadily after* **9/1**[3]

**4** *5* **Omotenashi (USA)** 2-9-0 0 JackMitchell 9 55+
(Roger Varian) *dwlt: mostly in last: pushed along over 2f out: sn outpcd: kpt on to take modest 4th fnl f* **16/1**

**5** *1 1/4* **Rustique** 2-9-0 0 AntonioFresu 7 52
(Ed Walker) *mostly in last trio: rdn over 2f out: sn outpcd: nvr on terms after* **33/1**

**6** *shd* **Jaiyana** 2-9-0 0 LukeMorris 1 52
(James Tate) *chsd ldng pair to wl over 1f out: wknd* **12/1**

P0- **7** *1* **Lady Spangles (IRE)**[22] 7660 2-9-0 0 StevieDonohoe 4 49
(J S Moore) *dwlt: a in rr: rdn over 2f out: sn lft bhd* **66/1**

0- **8** *2 3/4* **Shamazing**[126] 4570 2-9-0 0 TonyHamilton 5 42
(Kevin Ryan) *chsd ldng trio: rdn wl over 2f out: sn wknd* **33/1**

1m 27.03s (1.03) **Going Correction** +0.025s/f (Slow) **8** Ran SP% **118.8**
Speed ratings (Par 95): **95,92,90,85,83 83,82,79**
CSF £2.77 TOTE £2.10: £1.10, £1.10, £2.40; EX 2.90 Trifecta £12.00.
**Owner** A D G Oldrey **Bred** A D G Oldrey **Trained** Kimpton, Hants

**FOCUS**
This looked the stronger of the two divisions and the time was 1.14secs quicker than the first leg.

## 7945 BETVICTOR.COM NURSERY H'CAP (BOBIS RACE) 7f (P)
6:25 (6:26) (Class 2) 2-Y-O
**£8,715** (£2,609; £1,304; £652; £326; £163) **Stalls** Low

Form RPR

222- **1** **Cascading Stars (IRE)**[8] 7839 2-8-7 65 LukeMorris 2 69
(J S Moore) *trckd ldng pair: drvn to chal over 1f out: led last 120yds: kpt on wl and a jst holding on* **12/1**

16- **2** *1/2* **Them And Us (IRE)**[33] 7443 2-9-3 75 GeorgeBaker 5 78
(Michael Bell) *hld up in 5th: prog 2f out: rdn to chal jst over 1f out: pressed wnr last 100yds: nt qckn* **4/1**

021- **3** *1/2* **Colour Party (IRE)**[12] 7808 2-9-4 76 RobertHavlin 3 77
(John Gosden) *trckd ldr: led 2f out: drvn and hrd pressed fr over 1f out: hdd and one pce last 120yds* **11/4**[2]

122- **4** *1* **Vegas Rebel (IRE)**[7] 7849 2-9-4 76 MartinHarley 4 75
(Peter Chapple-Hyam) *hld up in last: prog 2f out: rchd 4th and cl enough over 1f out: styd on but nvr quite pce to chal* **7/2**[3]

321- **5** *4* **Zaza Zest (IRE)**[14] 7763 2-8-10 68 TonyHamilton 1 56
(Richard Fahey) *led: rdn and hdd 2f out: wknd jst over 1f out* **10/1**

234- **6** *3/4* **Muradif (IRE)**[28] 7544 2-9-7 79 (p) AdamKirby 6 65
(William Haggas) *trckd ldng trio: rdn over 2f out: wknd over 1f out* **9/4**[1]

100- **7** *9* **Almoqatel (IRE)**[30] 7525 2-8-7 65 ChrisCatlin 7 26
(Tony Newcombe) *a in last pair: wknd over 2f out: t.o* **50/1**

1m 25.77s (-0.23) **Going Correction** +0.025s/f (Slow) **7** Ran SP% **118.4**
Speed ratings (Par 102): **102,101,100,99,95 94,84**
CSF £61.86 TOTE £9.70: £4.90, £2.70; EX 42.20 Trifecta £463.10.
**Owner** S & A Mares **Bred** M Fahy & Rathbarry Stud **Trained** Upper Lambourn, Berks

**FOCUS**
A fair nursery.

## 7946 DOWNLOAD THE BETVICTOR.COM INSTABET APP H'CAP 2m (P)
6:55 (6:57) (Class 5) (0-75,75) 3-Y-0+ **£2,587** (£770; £384; £192) **Stalls** Low

Form RPR

621- **1** **Strawberry Martini**[49] 7067 3-9-5 75 MartinDwyer 1 84
(William Muir) *trckd ldrs: pushed along and prog on inner 3f out: led 2f out: drvn over 1f out: jnd ins fnl f: won on the nod* **7/1**

343- **2** *nse* **Charlie Wells (IRE)**[29] 7531 3-9-3 73 (b) JohnFahy 8 82
(Eve Johnson Houghton) *hld up in last: stl only 9th 3f out and pce had lifted: prog over 2f out: tk 2nd 1f out and sn chalng: w wnr 100yds out and hung fire sltly: jst pipped* **7/2**[1]

0/2- **3** *1 1/4* **Shadarpour (IRE)**[26] 214 5-9-1 62 (b) FergusSweeney 3 70
(Alan King) *trckd ldrs: wl pl whn pce lifted 4f out: rdn and nt qckn over 2f out: styd on to take 3rd ins fnl f* **5/1**[3]

002- **4** *3 1/4* **Java Rose**[35] 6107 5-9-12 73 (p) AdamKirby 4 77
(Charlie Longsdon) *led: kicked on strly 4f out: hdd 2f out: grad outpcd* **4/1**[2]

001- **5** *1* **Jezza**[34] 7419 8-9-1 67 (bt) KieranShoemark(5) 7 69
(Victor Dartnall) *hld up towards rr: rdn and nt qckn 3f out: kpt on one pce u.p after: nvr able to rch ldrs* **14/1**

060- **6** *4 1/2* **Albonny (IRE)**[47] 7124 5-9-7 68 LukeMorris 2 65
(Timothy Jarvis) *trckd ldr 4f and again 3f out to over 2f out: wknd over 1f out* **5/1**[3]

530- **7** *hd* **Dukes Den**[13] 7777 3-8-2 61 CamHardie(3) 5 58
(Sylvester Kirk) *moslty in last pair and nt gng wl: struggling once pce lifted 4f out: no ch over 2f out* **25/1**

406- **8** *2* **Bold Runner**[29] 7539 3-9-0 70 (p) PatCosgrave 10 64
(Jose Santos) *wl in tch on outer: rdn over 3f out: no prog over 2f out: sn wknd* **7/1**

062- **9** *3 1/2* **Ermyn Lodge**[65] 6632 8-9-3 64 (bt[1]) JackMitchell 9 54
(Pat Phelan) *in tch: rdn over 3f out: struggling and btn over 2f out* **8/1**

100- **10** *3/4* **King's Request (IRE)**[33] 6264 4-10-0 75 LiamJones 6 64
(Laura Mongan) *chsd ldr after 4f to 3f out: wknd qckly* **16/1**

3m 30.48s (0.38) **Going Correction** +0.025s/f (Slow)
**WFA** 3 from 4yo+ 9lb **10** Ran SP% **128.1**
Speed ratings (Par 103): **100,99,99,97,97 94,94,93,92,91**
CSF £35.09 CT £141.99 TOTE £9.80: £3.60, £1.80, £2.30; EX 34.60 Trifecta £263.10.
**Owner** Newsells Park Stud **Bred** Newsells Park Stud **Trained** Lambourn, Berks
■ Stewards' Enquiry : Martin Dwyer four-day ban: used whip above permitted level (Dec 11-13,15)

**FOCUS**
A fair staying handicap, dominated by a couple of 3yos.

## 7947 FOLLOW @BETVICTORRACING ON TWITTER H'CAP 6f (P)
7:25 (7:27) (Class 4) (0-85,85) 3-Y-0+ **£4,690** (£1,395; £697; £348) **Stalls** Low

Form RPR

503- **1** **Mishaal (IRE)**[10] 7821 4-9-3 81 PaulMulrennan 9 94
(Michael Herrington) *mde virtually all: at least 2 l clr fr over 2f out: urged along over 1f out: kpt on wl: unchal* **11/2**[2]

021- **2** *2 1/4* **Spring Fling**[171] 3067 3-9-2 80 FergusSweeney 10 86
(Henry Candy) *t.k.h: prom: chsd wnr wl over 1f out: hung lft and nt qckn sn after: kpt on but nvr able to bridge the gap* **8/1**[3]

202- **3** *3/4* **Plucky Dip**[7] 7851 3-9-1 79 AdamKirby 3 83+
(John Ryan) *hld up in midfield: nt clr run over 2f out to over 1f out: drvn and prog to take 3rd ins fnl f: nvr able to threaten* **1/1**[1]

050- **4** *1* **Dangerous Age**[8] 7843 4-9-3 81 GeorgeBaker 8 81
(Charles Hills) *stdd s: hld up in last pair: stl there over 2f out: prog over 1f out: rdn and styd on fnl f: too much to do* **16/1**

430- **5** *1* **Corporal Maddox**[68] 6558 7-9-5 83 (p) LukeMorris 5 80
(Ronald Harris) *dwlt: in last pair tl rdn and prog on inner over 2f out: chsd ldrs 1f out: effrt flattened out after* **20/1**

120- **6** *½* **Panther Patrol (IRE)**[57] 6880 4-9-2 80 (b[1]) JohnFahy 6 76
(Eve Johnson Houghton) *in tch in midfield: gng wl enough 2f out: shuffled along over 1f out: nvr really involved* **14/1**

200- **7** *1¾* **Dominate**[22] 7669 4-9-2 83 CamHardie[(3)] 2 73
(Richard Hannon) *hld up in last quartet: prog on inner 2f out: no hdwy jst over 1f out: fdd* **20/1**

000- **8** *1¼* **Secret Witness**[24] 7624 8-9-4 82 (b) WilliamTwiston-Davies 1 68
(Ronald Harris) *prom tl wknd over 1f out* **25/1**

350- **9** *2½* **Oriental Relation (IRE)**[66] 6607 3-9-2 83 (v) ConnorBeasley[(3)] 7 61
(James Given) *chsd ldrs: rdn and no prog 2f out: wknd over 1f out* **20/1**

000- **10** *¾* **Clockmaker (IRE)**[75] 6320 8-9-2 80 HayleyTurner 12 56
(Conor Dore) *racd wdst of all fr outer draw: rchd midfield over 3f out: pushed along and dropped to last 2f out: running on nr fin* **33/1**

/40- **11** *1¾* **Foxtrot Jubilee (IRE)**[217] 1678 4-8-13 82 JamesRogers[(5)] 4 52
(Ralph Beckett) *nvr beyond midfield: rdn over 2f out: wknd over 1f out* **16/1**

123- **12** *5* **Mia San Triple**[71] 6468 3-9-7 85 MartinHarley 11 39
(Jeremy Noseda) *chsd wnr to wl over 1f out: wknd rapidly and eased* **8/1**[3]

1m 10.95s (-2.15) **Going Correction** +0.025s/f (Slow) 12 Ran SP% **127.1**
Speed ratings (Par 105): **115,112,111,109,108 107,105,103,100,99 97,90**
CSF £48.53 CT £82.14 TOTE £5.00: £2.00, £3.50, £1.30; EX 61.50 Trifecta £203.70.
**Owner** Kelvyn Gracie & Lawrence McCaughey **Bred** Darley **Trained** Cold Kirby, N Yorks

**FOCUS**
A useful sprint handicap that proved more competitive than the betting suggested.
T/Jkpt: £4,542.70 to a £1 stake. Pool: £15,995.54 - 2.50 winning tickets T/Plt: £259.00 to a £1 stake. Pool: £89,385.48 - 251.90 winning tickets T/Qpdt: £32.00 to a £1 stake. Pool: £1,2632.76 - 291.80 winning tickets JN

# 7900 WOLVERHAMPTON (A.W) (L-H)
## Friday, November 28

**OFFICIAL GOING: Tapeta: standard**
Wind: Light against Weather: Overcast

## 7948 DAILY PRICE BOOSTS AT UNIBET NURSERY H'CAP (TAPETA) 5f 20y
**3:55** (3:55) (Class 6) (0-65,65) 2-Y-0 **£2,102** (£625; £312; £156) **Stalls** Low

Form RPR

425- **1** **True Course**[18] 7728 2-9-4 **62** AdamKirby 2 66+
(Charlie Appleby) *hld up: hdwy over 1f out: rdn to ld ins fnl f: edgd rt: r.o* **9/4**[2]

540- **2** *nk* **The Dapper Tapper (IRE)**[18] 7728 2-9-2 **65** (v) GeorgeDowning[(5)] 9 68
(Eve Johnson Houghton) *hld up: hdwy over 1f out: r.o* **13/2**

442- **3** *¾* **Pancake Day**[15] 7762 2-8-6 **50** AndrewElliott 13 50
(Jason Ward) *w ldr tl led over 3f out: rdn and hdd ins fnl f: styd on* **16/1**

000- **4** *nse* **Lydiate Lady**[34] 7453 2-8-5 **49** ow1 (p) JFEgan 4 49
(Paul Green) *chsd ldrs: rdn over 1f out: styd on* **50/1**

201- **5** *1½* **Frozen Princess**[21] 7701 2-9-4 **62** GeorgeBaker 5 57
(Jamie Osborne) *chsd ldrs: rdn over 1f out: styd on same pce ins fnl f* **2/1**[1]

005- **6** *hd* **Diminutive (IRE)**[22] 7684 2-8-10 **54** (b) StevieDonohoe 6 48
(Grace Harris) *in rr: rdn over 1f out: r.o ins fnl f: nvr nrr* **80/1**

066- **7** *1* **Coursing**[14] 7780 2-8-13 **57** LukeMorris 1 47+
(Sir Mark Prescott Bt) *s.i.s: sn pushed along in rr: rdn and r.o ins fnl f: nt trble ldrs* **25/1**

033- **8** *1* **Robin Hill**[92] 5859 2-9-6 **64** MartinDwyer 3 51
(William Muir) *prom: rdn over 1f out: wknd ins fnl f* **11/2**[3]

024- **9** *½* **Air Of York (IRE)**[10] 7824 2-9-0 **58** (b) WilliamTwiston-Davies 8 43
(Ronald Harris) *led: hdd over 3f out: rdn and ev ch over 1f out: wknd ins fnl f* **28/1**

01- **10** *68* **Toni's A Star**[34] 7453 2-8-7 **51** (b) RaulDaSilva 10
(Paul Green) *reluctant to s: a bhd* **16/1**

1m 1.86s (-0.04) **Going Correction** -0.10s/f (Stan) 10 Ran SP% **115.1**
Speed ratings (Par 94): **96,95,94,94,91 91,89,88,87,**
CSF £16.57 CT £187.12 TOTE £3.30: £1.60, £2.30, £4.60; EX 19.70 Trifecta £208.20.
**Owner** Godolphin **Bred** W A Tinkler **Trained** Newmarket, Suffolk
■ Stewards' Enquiry : George Baker caution; careless riding.

**FOCUS**
They went a good gallop here and the first two came from off the pace.

## 7949 £20 RISK-FREE BET WITH UNIBET H'CAP (TAPETA) 5f 20y
**4:25** (4:26) (Class 5) (0-75,75) 3-Y-0+ **£2,749** (£818; £408; £204) **Stalls** Low

Form RPR

612- **1** **Invincible Ridge (IRE)**[6] 7888 6-9-7 75 (t) LukeMorris 6 85
(Eric Alston) *mid-div: hdwy over 1f out: shkn up to ld wl ins fnl f: r.o* **6/4**[1]

024- **2** *nk* **Thorpe Bay**[6] 7888 5-8-11 70 AlistairRawlinson[(5)] 9 79
(Michael Appleby) *chsd ldrs: rdn and ev ch ins fnl f: r.o* **11/2**[2]

201- **3** *1½* **Dynamo Walt (IRE)**[13] 7806 3-9-4 72 (v) TonyHamilton 4 76
(Derek Shaw) *trckd ldr: rdn to ld 1f out: hdd wl ins fnl f: sn hung lft and no ex* **6/1**[3]

000- **4** *hd* **Mayfield Girl (IRE)**[102] 5498 4-8-13 67 PJMcDonald 7 70
(Mel Brittain) *s.i.s: hdwy over 1f out: r.o* **40/1**

314- **5** *1¼* **Simply Black (IRE)**[13] 7806 3-8-6 67 (p) JoshDoyle[(7)] 5 65
(David O'Meara) *prom: rdn over 1f out: styng on same pce whn hmpd nr fin* **10/1**

205- **6** *nse* **Flighty Clarets (IRE)**[160] 3462 4-8-12 66 GrahamLee 11 64
(Richard Fahey) *hld up: hdwy over 1f out: styd on same pce ins fnl f* **40/1**

100- **7** *1¼* **West Coast Dream**[13] 7806 7-9-0 68 TomEaves 1 62
(Roy Brotherton) *led: rdn and hdd 1f out: no ex whn hmpd wl ins fnl f* **28/1**

400- **8** *nk* **Shawkantango**[30] 7534 7-8-7 68 (v) GeorginaBaxter[(7)] 10 61
(Derek Shaw) *s.s: hung lft and styd on ins fnl f: nvr nrr* **80/1**

040- **9** *1* **Hadaj**[31] 7506 5-9-4 72 PaulMulrennan 12 61
(Michael Herrington) *prom: lost pl after 1f: n.d after* **11/2**[2]

02- **10** *½* **Bainne (IRE)**[15] 7767 4-8-13 70 RyanTate[(3)] 2 57
(James Eustace) *s.i.s: rdn over 1f out: nvr on terms* **9/1**

625- **11** *¾* **Maria Montez**[38] 7357 5-9-3 71 SteveDrowne 3 56
(Charles Hills) *prom: rdn over 1f out: wknd and eased ins fnl f* **33/1**

320- **12** *6* **Bapak Bangsawan**[15] 7761 4-9-0 73 (bt) AnnStokell[(5)] 8 36
(Ann Stokell) *t.k.h: sn w ldrs: pushed along 1/2-way: wknd over 1f out* **50/1**

1m 0.94s (-0.96) **Going Correction** -0.10s/f (Stan) 12 Ran SP% **118.6**
Speed ratings (Par 103): **103,102,100,99,97 97,95,95,93,92 91,82**
CSF £9.24 CT £40.18 TOTE £2.10: £1.10, £2.10, £2.90; EX 11.00 Trifecta £50.30.
**Owner** Paul Buist & John Thompson **Bred** Con Harrington **Trained** Longton, Lancs

**FOCUS**
A modest handicap.

## 7950 UNIBET OFFER DAILY JOCKEY/TRAINER SPECIALS H'CAP (TAPETA) 5f 216y
**4:55** (4:56) (Class 6) (0-65,65) 3-Y-0+ **£2,102** (£625; £312; £156) **Stalls** Low

Form RPR

536/ **1** **Shotgun Start**[437] 6502 4-9-5 65 GeorgeBaker 10 77+
(Michael Wigham) *chsd ldr tl led 2f out: rdn and hung lft over 1f out: styd on* **2/1**[1]

003- **2** *2* **Seven Lucky Seven**[25] 7621 3-9-3 63 TomEaves 3 69+
(Michael Herrington) *hld up: nt clr run and swtchd rt over 1f out: rdn and r.o wl ins fnl f: nt rch wnr* **14/1**

032- **3** *hd* **Jolly Red Jeanz (IRE)**[25] 7621 3-9-5 65 (b) WilliamCarson 5 70
(Tom Dascombe) *trckd ldrs: nt clr run and swtchd rt 1f out: r.o* **10/1**

150- **4** *hd* **Imperator Augustus (IRE)**[104] 5415 6-9-1 64 DeclanBates[(3)] 11 69
(Patrick Holmes) *chsd ldrs: rdn and ev ch over 1f out: styd on same pce ins fnl f* **50/1**

305- **5** *shd* **Chookie's Lass**[21] 7697 3-9-2 65 JoeyHaynes[(3)] 6 69
(Keith Dalgleish) *prom: n.m.r 1/2-way: nt clr run and lost pl over 2f out: r.o ins fnl f* **15/2**[3]

040- **6** *1* **Foxtrot Pearl (IRE)**[25] 7622 3-9-2 62 RobertHavlin 9 63
(John Holt) *led: rdn and hdd 2f out: styd on same pce fnl f* **66/1**

324- **7** *shd* **Logans Lad (IRE)**[25] 7621 4-9-0 65 (bt) EoinWalsh[(5)] 1 66
(Daniel Mark Loughnane) *hld up in tch: rdn over 1f out: styd on same pce ins fnl f* **13/2**[2]

320- **8** *1* **Black Dave (IRE)**[24] 7647 4-9-3 63 JFEgan 12 61
(David Evans) *hld up: styd on ins fnl f: nvr nrr* **15/2**[3]

620/ **9** *nk* **John Coffey (IRE)**[409] 7283 5-8-11 62 AlistairRawlinson[(5)] 8 59
(Michael Appleby) *mid-div: rdn over 2f out: hdwy over 1f out: sn hung lft: no ex ins fnl f* **11/1**

505- **10** *1¼* **Bint Malyana (IRE)**[28] 7575 3-9-5 65 AdamKirby 2 58
(Paul D'Arcy) *hld up: rdn over 1f out: nt trble ldrs* **10/1**

440- **11** *1* **Italian Tom (IRE)**[52] 7023 7-9-5 65 LukeMorris 7 55
(Ronald Harris) *chsd ldrs: rdn over 1f out: wknd ins fnl f* **25/1**

000- **12** *nse* **Whipphound**[25] 7621 6-9-2 62 PaulMulrennan 4 51
(Mark Brisbourne) *s.i.s: hld up: hdwy over 2f out: wknd ins fnl f* **22/1**

500- **13** *5* **Volito**[25] 7622 8-9-2 62 MartinHarley 13 35
(Anabel K Murphy) *s.i.s: hld up: a in rr* **100/1**

1m 14.31s (-0.19) **Going Correction** -0.10s/f (Stan) 13 Ran SP% **116.0**
Speed ratings (Par 101): **97,94,94,93,93 92,92,90,90,88 87,87,80**
CSF £30.49 CT £230.97 TOTE £3.20: £2.00, £4.30, £2.20; EX 39.60 Trifecta £233.90.
**Owner** Palatinate Thoroughbred Racing Limited **Bred** Clive Dennett **Trained** Newmarket, Suffolk

**FOCUS**
They didn't go that quick early, the winner came clear and the rest finished in a bunch in behind.

## 7951 32RED.COM MAIDEN STKS (TAPETA) 1m 5f 194y
**5:25** (5:25) (Class 5) 3-Y-0+ **£2,587** (£770; £384; £192) **Stalls** Low

Form RPR

42- **1** **John Reel (FR)**[13] 7812 5-9-13 0 JFEgan 6 82
(David Evans) *hld up: hdwy over 4f out: led over 3f out: c clr fnl f* **1/1**[1]

0- **2** *11* **Royal Battalion**[133] 4407 3-9-5 0 GeorgeBaker 4 72
(Stuart Williams) *led: hdd over 11f out: chsd ldrs: wnt 2nd 2f out: eased whn btn fnl f* **11/10**[2]

4- **3** *5* **Harmonical**[39] 7332 3-9-0 0 PJMcDonald 5 55
(Mel Brittain) *prom: led 4f out: hdd over 3f out: wknd over 1f out* **33/1**

264- **4** *7* **Cropley (IRE)**[3] 7913 5-9-8 64 (b) AnnStokell[(5)] 1 50
(Ann Stokell) *prom tl wknd 3f out* **25/1**[3]

5- **5** *43* **Direct Approach (IRE)**[25] 7627 10-9-13 0 PaddyAspell 7
(Lynn Siddall) *trckd ldrs: plld hrd: led over 11f out: rdn and hdd 4f out: wknd wl over 2f out* **100/1**

**6** *99* **Silver Songstress**[17] 4-9-8 0 LukeMorris 2
(John Weymes) *prom: chsd ldr 10f out tl rdn over 5f out: wknd over 3f out* **33/1**

3m 1.23s (-3.57) **Going Correction** -0.10s/f (Stan)
**WFA** 3 from 4yo+ 8lb 6 Ran SP% **108.3**
Speed ratings (Par 103): **106,99,96,92,68 11**
CSF £2.15 TOTE £1.40: £1.02, £1.40; EX 3.00 Trifecta £13.90.
**Owner** Walters Plant Hire Ltd **Bred** Ecurie Biraben **Trained** Pandy, Monmouths

**FOCUS**
An uncompetitive maiden.

## 7952 32RED FILLIES' CONDITIONS STKS (FAST TRACK QUALIFIER) (TAPETA) 7f 32y
**5:55** (5:55) (Class 2) 3-Y-0+
**£11,827** (£3,541; £1,770; £885; £442; £222) **Stalls** High

Form RPR

212- **1** **Khatiba (IRE)**[23] 7663 3-9-0 86 GrahamLee 3 97
(Roger Varian) *a.p: rdn to ld ins fnl f: r.o* **15/2**

360- **2** *hd* **Majeyda (USA)**[163] 3357 3-9-0 103 AdamKirby 2 97
(Charlie Appleby) *hld up: hdwy over 1f out: rdn and ev ch ins fnl f: styd on* **8/11**[1]

102- **3** *½* **Badr Al Badoor (IRE)**[16] 7743 4-9-1 96 JoeFanning 6 96
(James Fanshawe) *hld up: hdwy over 1f out: rdn and ev ch ins fnl f: styd on* **11/4**[2]

340- **4** *½* **Stosur (IRE)**[34] 7451 3-9-0 90 (b) LukeMorris 5 94
(Gay Kelleway) *chsd ldr 2f: remained handy: rdn over 2f out: ev ch ins fnl f: kpt on* **66/1**

432- **5** *3½* **Penny Drops**[42] 7268 3-9-0 96 (b[1]) GrahamGibbons 4 85
(William Haggas) *led: rdn over 1f out: hdd, edgd rt and no ex ins fnl f* **6/1**[3]

310- **6** *4½* **Maggie Pink**[20] 7719 5-9-1 90 AlistairRawlinson 1 74
(Michael Appleby) *prom: chsd ldr 5f out: rdn over 2f out: lost 2nd over 1f out: wknd fnl f* **12/1**

1m 26.62s (-2.18) **Going Correction** -0.10s/f (Stan)
**WFA** 3 from 4yo+ 1lb 6 Ran SP% **119.8**
Speed ratings (Par 96): **108,107,107,106,102 97**
CSF £14.65 TOTE £6.40: £2.60, £1.30; EX 18.50 Trifecta £70.80.
**Owner** Sheikh Ahmed Al Maktoum **Bred** Darley **Trained** Newmarket, Suffolk

**FOCUS**
The winner was the lowest rated filly in the race but she's an improving type.

## 7953 DOWNLOAD THE LADBROKES APP H'CAP (TAPETA) (DIV I) 7f 32y
**6:25** (6:26) (Class 5) (0-75,75) 3-Y-O+ **£2,749** (£818; £408; £204) **Stalls** High

Form RPR

653- **1** **Know Your Name**[15] 7757 3-8-10 65....................(v) JFEgan 3 74
(David Evans) *chsd ldrs: led over 2f out: rdn over 1f out: jst hld on* **9/2**[3]

153- **2** *nk* **Smokethatthunders (IRE)**[6] 7888 4-9-7 75.............. PaulMulrennan 7 83
(James Unett) *a.p: nt clr run over 2f out: rdn over 1f out: r.o* **7/2**[2]

050- **3** *nk* **Dream Scenario**[126] 4629 4-9-4 72..............................(v) PJMcDonald 6 79
(Mel Brittain) *hld up: hdwy over 2f out: rdn over 1f out: r.o* **66/1**

000- **4** *1 ½* **Smalljohn**[62] 6767 8-8-7 66...............................(v) AdamCarter(5) 1 69
(Bryan Smart) *led: hdd over 6f out: chsd clr ldr: rdn over 2f out: styd on same pce ins fnl f* **33/1**

240- **5** *2 ¼* **Hierarch (IRE)**[89] 5950 7-8-7 68............................ MillyNaseb(7) 9 65
(David Simcock) *hld up: swtchd rt over 2f out: styd on ins fnl f: nt trble ldrs* **28/1**

052- **6** *¾* **Showboating (IRE)**[27] 7600 6-9-4 72....................(tp) MartinHarley 8 68
(Alan McCabe) *dwlt: hld up: pushed along 3f out: styd on ins fnl f: nvr nrr* **11/8**[1]

/00- **7** *¾* **Summerinthecity (IRE)**[14] 7775 7-9-2 70...................... TonyHamilton 2 64
(Richard Fahey) *hld up: hdwy over 1f out: no ex ins fnl f* **20/1**

422- **8** *nk* **Al Muheer (IRE)**[11] 7819 9-8-13 74......................[1] PatrickVaughan(7) 4 67
(Tom Dascombe) *hld up: nvr on terms* **12/1**

100- **9** *5* **Disclosure**[60] 6822 3-9-0 72..........................(b[1]) ConnorBeasley(3) 10 51
(Les Eyre) *plld hrd: led over 6f out: sn clr: hdd over 2f out: wknd over 1f out* **16/1**

00- **10** *8* **Dynamite Dixie (IRE)**[18] 7732 5-9-5 73......................(tp) PaddyAspell 5 32
(Phil McEntee) *prom: rdn over 2f out: wknd over 1f out* **25/1**

1m 27.91s (-0.89) **Going Correction** -0.10s/f (Stan)
**WFA** 3 from 4yo+ 1lb **10 Ran SP% 112.6**
Speed ratings (Par 103): **101,100,100,98,96 95,94,93,88,79**
CSF £18.55 CT £888.59 TOTE £4.10: £1.10, £1.20, £12.90; EX 22.80 Trifecta £889.40.
**Owner** Livvys Racing Group **Bred** Mill Farm Stud **Trained** Pandy, Monmouths

**FOCUS**
This was run at a fair gallop and it suited those ridden just off the pace.

## 7954 DOWNLOAD THE LADBROKES APP H'CAP (TAPETA) (DIV II) 7f 32y
**6:55** (6:58) (Class 5) (0-75,75) 3-Y-O+ **£2,749** (£818; £408; £204) **Stalls** High

Form RPR

301- **1** **Lucky Lodge**[45] 7179 4-8-9 63.............................(b) PJMcDonald 10 71
(Mel Brittain) *hld up: shkn up over 1f out: str run ins fnl f: led post* **28/1**

510- **2** *nse* **Woodbridge**[157] 3559 3-8-12 67.................................. TonyHamilton 2 74
(Richard Fahey) *led: rdn over 1f out: edgd lft ins fnl f: hdd post* **7/2**[1]

605- **3** *hd* **Beautiful Stranger (IRE)**[24] 7640 3-9-3 72..................(p) JoeFanning 3 78
(Keith Dalgleish) *hld up in tch: rdn over 1f out: r.o* **7/1**

146- **4** *1* **Artistic Queen**[56] 6902 3-9-5 74.......................................... LukeMorris 8 78
(James Tate) *chsd ldr to 1/2-way: rdn over 1f out: styd on* **7/1**

032- **5** *2 ¾* **Flicksta (USA)**[15] 7759 3-8-12 67.................................. JackMitchell 5 64
(John Ryan) *prom: chsd ldr 1/2-way: rdn and ev ch over 1f out: no ex ins fnl f* **5/1**[3]

604- **6** *hd* **Khajaaly (IRE)**[11] 7820 7-8-13 72......................(tp) AlistairRawlinson(5) 1 69
(Michael Appleby) *hld up: rdn over 2f out: hdwy over 1f out: styd on same pce ins fnl f* **9/2**[2]

042- **7** *3* **Hagree (IRE)**[38] 7355 3-9-6 75..........................................(t) GrahamLee 9 63
(Declan Carroll) *s.i.s: hld up: shkn up over 1f out: nvr nr to chal* **9/1**

560- **8** *hd* **Madame Mirasol (IRE)**[7] 7871 3-9-2 71............................(p) TomEaves 4 59
(Kevin Ryan) *mid-div: hdwy u.p over 2f out: wknd fnl f* **40/1**

043- **9** *½* **King Of Eden (IRE)**[18] 7729 8-9-4 72..............................(t) JFEgan 2 59
(Eric Alston) *prom: rdn over 2f out: wknd fnl f* **7/1**

000- **10** *nse* **Prime Exhibit**[7] 7871 9-8-13 72..........................(t) EoinWalsh(5) 7 59
(Daniel Mark Loughnane) *hld up: rdn 1/2-way: n.d* **28/1**

1m 27.6s (-1.20) **Going Correction** -0.10s/f (Stan)
**WFA** 3 from 4yo+ 1lb **10 Ran SP% 113.9**
Speed ratings (Par 103): **102,101,101,100,97 97,93,93,92,92**
CSF £119.82 CT £781.91 TOTE £27.80: £6.30, £2.40, £1.60; EX 164.40 Trifecta £1248.00.
**Owner** Mel Brittain **Bred** Mel Brittain **Trained** Warthill, N Yorks

**FOCUS**
The quicker of the two divisions by 0.31sec and a good performance from the winner, who came from well back in a race where otherwise the pace held up.

## 7955 LADBROKES H'CAP (TAPETA) 1m 141y
**7:25** (7:26) (Class 3) (0-90,90) 3-Y-O **£7,246** (£2,168; £1,084; £542; £270) **Stalls** Low

Form RPR

005- **1** **Brocklebank (IRE)**[14] 7774 5-8-6 78........................... JackDuern(3) 11 90
(Simon Dow) *hld up: hdwy over 1f out: r.o to ld nr fin* **16/1**

100- **2** *½* **Lacan (IRE)**[48] 7119 3-9-1 87.................................... MartinHarley 5 98+
(Marco Botti) *chsd ldrs: led over 1f out: sn rdn: hdd nr fin* **9/4**[1]

313- **3** *2 ¾* **Almanack**[14] 7774 4-8-7 76 oh2.......................................... LukeMorris 9 81
(Ian Williams) *hld up: hdwy u.p over 1f out: r.o: nt rch ldrs* **12/1**

045- **4** *nk* **Berlusca (IRE)**[7] 7870 5-9-1 84........................................ SamJames 6 88
(David O'Meara) *hld up: hdwy over 1f out: styd on same pce ins fnl f* **10/1**

050- **5** *nk* **Westminster (IRE)**[18] 7732 3-8-4 76........................... HayleyTurner 3 79
(Michael Appleby) *chsd ldr: pushed along over 3f out: led wl over 1f out: sn rdn and hdd: edgd lft 1f out: no ex ins fnl f* **16/1**

040- **6** *hd* **Mia's Boy**[14] 7784 10-8-6 78..................................... ConnorBeasley(3) 10 81
(Chris Dwyer) *hld up: r.o ins fnl f: nt rch ldrs* **25/1**

110- **7** *½* **Spes Nostra**[204] 2091 6-9-7 90.................................... GrahamGibbons 2 92
(David Barron) *chsd ldrs: rdn over 1f out: no ex ins fnl f* **9/1**

026- **8** *1 ¼* **Hanalei Bay (IRE)**[24] 7634 4-8-12 81 ow1......................... PhillipMakin 4 80
(Keith Dalgleish) *mid-div: hdwy u.p over 1f out: wknd ins fnl f* **20/1**

424- **9** *nk* **Kingscroft (IRE)**[24] 7636 6-8-11 80..............................(b) GrahamLee 7 78
(Michael Herrington) *hld up in tch: nt clr run over 1f out: wknd ins fnl f* **11/2**[3]

000- **10** *2 ½* **Silverware (USA)**[34] 7455 6-9-2 85........................... TomEaves 1 77
(Kristin Stubbs) *led: rdn and hdd wl over 1f out: wknd ins fnl f* **66/1**

200- **11** *1 ¾* **Loyalty**[11] 7820 7-9-1 84..........................................(v) TonyHamilton 12 72
(Derek Shaw) *hld up: rdn over 2f out: nvr on terms* **40/1**

430- **12** *9* **Moonday Sun (USA)**[39] 7341 5-9-6 89............................ AdamKirby 8 57
(Andy Turnell) *hld up: effrt on outer over 2f out: sn wknd* **9/2**[2]

000- **13** *1* **Quickaswecan**[14] 7774 3-8-6 78.................................. JoeFanning 13 43
(Mark Johnston) *mid-div: hdwy over 2f out: rdn and wknd over 1f out* **33/1**

1m 47.37s (-2.73) **Going Correction** -0.10s/f (Stan) course record
**WFA** 3 from 4yo+ 3lb **13 Ran SP% 118.4**
Speed ratings (Par 107): **108,107,105,104,104 104,103,102,102,100 98,90,89**
CSF £49.17 CT £470.38 TOTE £20.50: £4.80, £1.10, £2.40; EX 77.00 Trifecta £2120.50 Part won..
**Owner** J C G Chua **Bred** Vincent Reen **Trained** Epsom, Surrey

**FOCUS**
This was run at a good gallop and it suited those held up.
T/Plt: £24.60 to a £1 stake. Pool: £124,961.07 - 3696.30 winning units. T/Qpdt: £7.10 to a £1 stake. Pool: £12,260.12 - 1261.74 winning units. CR

7956 - 7958a (Foreign Racing) - See Raceform Interactive

# 7933 DUNDALK (A.W) (L-H)
Friday, November 28

**OFFICIAL GOING: Polytrack: standard**

## 7959a FLOODLIT FRIDAY NIGHTS AT DUNDALK APPRENTICE H'CAP 7f (P)
**7:40** (7:41) 3-Y-O+ **£4,887** (£1,133; £495; £283)

RPR

**1** **Marble Statuette (USA)**[21] 7707 4-9-13 69.................. ColinKeane 6 76+
(A J Martin, Ire) *dwlt and settled in rr: last into st: swtchd to outer and hdwy travelling wl fr 2f out: rdn ent fnl f and clsd u.p and hung lft ins fnl f to ld clsng stages* **2/1**[1]

**2** *½* **Your Pal Tal**[7] 7874 4-9-6 66.......................... DonaghO'Connor(4) 2 72
(J F Levins, Ire) *led: over 1 l clr 1/2-way: rdn 2f out and stl in front wl ins fnl f: hdd clsng stages: no ex* **8/1**

**3** *1 ¾* **Erelight (IRE)**[21] 7707 6-8-1 47..............................(p) TomMadden(7) 11 48
(S Donohoe, Ire) *dwlt sltly: sn chsd ldrs on outer and wnt 2nd after 2f: rdn 2f out and no imp on ldr u.p in 3rd wl ins fnl f: kpt on same pce* **33/1**

**4** *hd* **Queen Aggie (IRE)**[4] 7906 4-10-0 70............................ ConorHoban 10 71
(Tony Carroll) *restrained s and settled towards rr: 7th 1/2-way: hdwy 2f out to chse ldrs in 5th ins fnl f where hmpd between horses: no imp after: kpt on* **3/1**[2]

**5** *½* **Belle Bayardo (IRE)**[15] 7759 6-9-12 70................. RobbieDowney(2) 3 69
(Tony Carroll) *chsd ldrs: 3rd 1/2-way: rdn 2f out and sn no imp on ldr: kpt on one pce ins fnl f* **10/1**

**6** *hd* **Sandy Smile (IRE)**[139] 4227 3-8-10 55........................ SeanCorby(2) 5 53
(M Halford, Ire) *dwlt sltly and racd towards rr: 9th 1/2-way: swtchd over 2f out and tk clsr order bhd ldrs in 5th over 1f out: no ex ins fnl f: kpt on one pce* **14/1**

**7** *1 ¼* **Norville (IRE)**[23] 7677 7-9-6 62...................................(b) ConnorKing 1 57
(Lee Smyth, Ire) *chsd ldrs: pushed along early: 4th 1/2-way: rdn far side fr 2f out and no imp on ldrs ins fnl f: wknd and eased towards fin* **10/1**

**8** *1 ¼* **Affectionate Lady (IRE)**[23] 7678 3-8-11 54...............(b[1]) LeighRoche 8 45
(W McCreery, Ire) *hld up in tch: 6th 1/2-way: rdn on outer 2f out and no imp on ldrs ins fnl f: one pce* **20/1**

**9** *1* **Burren View Lady (IRE)**[7] 7873 4-10-0 70...................... RonanWhelan 9 59
(Denis Gerard Hogan, Ire) *hld up: 8th 1/2-way: rdn and no imp fr 2f out: kpt on one pce* **25/1**

**10** *¾* **Art Scene (IRE)**[35] 7430 4-8-1 47...........................(v) IanQueally(4) 4 34
(Patrick J Flynn, Ire) *chsd ldrs: 5th 1/2-way: rdn and wknd 2f out* **5/1**[3]

1m 24.7s (84.70)
**WFA** 3 from 4yo+ 1lb **10 Ran SP% 122.5**
CSF £19.76 CT £436.24 TOTE £2.90: £1.30, £2.30, £6.30; DF 20.80 Trifecta £431.60.
**Owner** Glen Devlin **Bred** Moyglare Stud **Trained** Summerhill, Co. Meath

**FOCUS**
Apparently the plan wasn't to come from last to first on the winner, but it couldn't have been more executed to perfection if it was.

## 7961a DUNDALK STADIUM ON FACEBOOK H'CAP 1m 2f 150y(P)
**8:40** (8:41) (47-65,65) 4-Y-O+ **£4,312** (£1,000; £437; £250)

RPR

**1** **Alvar (USA)**[14] 7789 6-9-11 65........................... ShaneBKelly(3) 7 75
(M Halford, Ire) *chsd ldrs: 4th 4f out: rdn into 2nd 1 1/2f out and clsd u.p wl ins fnl f to ld cl home: all out: jst* **4/1**[2]

**2** *shd* **Manorov**[7] 7878 4-8-7 47.................................. ConorHoban(3) 2 57
(T G McCourt, Ire) *in rr of mid-div: tk clsr order bhd ldrs gng wl 2f out: sn nt clr run between horses and swtchd rt: rdn into 4th ins fnl f and r.o wl towards fin: jst hld* **3/1**[1]

**3** *½* **Muck 'N' Brass (IRE)**[103] 5476 5-8-3 50..............(t) KeithMoriarty(10) 6 59+
(J Larkin, Ire) *hld up in mid-div: 7th 4f out: hdwy into st and clsd u.p on outer to ld under 2f out: strly pressed wl ins fnl f and hdd cl home* **8/1**

**4** *2 ½* **General Bunching (USA)**[7] 7877 6-8-13 50...............(t) RoryCleary 12 54
(Thomas Cleary, Ire) *hld up in mid-div: hdwy bhd horses 2f out: rdn in 3rd over 1f out and sn no imp on ldr: kpt on one pce in 4th wl ins fnl f* **14/1**

**5** *½* **Elusive Award (USA)**[28] 7580 7-8-3 47...............(tp) TomMadden(7) 10 50
(T J O'Mara, Ire) *s.i.s and pushed along towards rr early: rdn appr st and sme late hdwy u.p on outer fr under 2f out: nvr nrr* **25/1**

**6** *1 ¾* **Stynes (IRE)**[14] 7792 4-9-6 57....................(t) EmmetMcNamara 11 57
(John C McConnell, Ire) *chsd ldrs: 6th 4f out: rdn 2f out and sn no imp on ldrs disputing 3rd: one pce fnl f* **5/1**

**7** *hd* **The Nutcracker (IRE)**[7] 7878 4-8-10 47......................... LeighRoche 4 46
(Thomas Gibney, Ire) *upset in stalls: in rr of mid-div: rdn and no imp fr 2f out: kpt on one pce ins fnl f* **25/1**

**8** *nk* **Cristy's Call (IRE)**[14] 7792 5-9-6 57..................(p) DeclanMcDonogh 9 56
(Gavin Cromwell, Ire) *chsd ldrs: 3rd 1/2-way: clsr in 2nd 4f out: impr to dispute over 2f out: sn rdn and no ex u.p: wknd over 1f out* **9/2**[3]

**9** *4 ¾* **Horsewithnoname (IRE)**[14] 7792 7-8-10 50...........(p) ConnorKing(3) 8 39
(T G McCourt, Ire) *in rr of mid-div: rdn and no imp 2f out* **16/1**

**10** *4 ¾* **Chinanigans (IRE)**[114] 5067 4-8-3 47.............. GearoidBrouder(7) 5 27
(D T Kelly, Ire) *sn led tl hdd after 3f: regained advantage 1/2-way: rdn into st and jnd: hdd 2f out and wknd* **66/1**

**11** *2* **Sterling Cooper (IRE)**[7] 7876 6-8-9 53.......................... IanQueally(7) 3 29
(P J Rothwell, Ire) *s.i.s and racd in rr: rdn under 4f out and no imp into st: kpt on one pce fnl 2f* **33/1**

**12** *2 ¾* **Halarath (IRE)**[7] 7877 5-9-6 57..................................(p) GaryCarroll 1 28
(C Moore, Ire) *chsd ldrs: 5th 4f out: rdn 2f out and n.m.r on inner briefly: sn wknd and eased* **12/1**

**13** *22* **Mr Lando**[11] 7527 5-9-9 60....................................... JosephO'Brien 13
(Tony Carroll) *chsd ldrs on outer tl led after 3f: hdd narrowly 1/2-way: pushed along in 3rd 4f out and wknd into st: eased* **8/1**

2m 13.24s (133.24) **13 Ran SP% 134.4**
CSF £18.21 CT £101.89 TOTE £6.80: £1.70, £1.60, £3.10; DF 39.80 Trifecta £337.90.

**Owner** Paul Rooney **Bred** Dreamfields Inc, Tuition Stable & Kerry Cauthen **Trained** Doneany, Co Kildare

**FOCUS**
A race that changed complexion completely in the last furlong as an old servant delivered once more.

## 7962a FUND RAISING MADE EASY AT DUNDALK H'CAP 1m 4f (P)
9:10 (9:14) (47-70,70) 3-Y-O+ £4,887 (£1,133; £495; £283)

RPR

1 **Minot Street (CAN)**[7] 7877 4-9-5 68........................(bt) TomMadden(7) 4 78+
(John C McConnell, Ire) *chsd ldrs: 4th 1/2-way: rdn 2f out and clsd u.p to ld over 1f out: styd on wl* 7/1

2 2 ¾ **Sharjah (IRE)**[21] 7711 4-10-0 70........................ DeclanMcDonogh 6 74
(Andrew Slattery, Ire) *attempted to make all: gng wl over 1 l clr into st where edgd rt: rdn and hdd over 1f out and sn no ch w wnr in 2nd: kpt on same pce* 5/1[3]

3 hd **Timjoe (IRE)**[7] 7878 7-8-6 48........................ RoryCleary 3 52
(Thomas Cleary, Ire) *chsd ldrs: 3rd 1/2-way: rdn 2f out and no imp on wnr u.p in 3rd wl ins fnl f: kpt on same pce* 20/1

4 1 ½ **Shalambar (IRE)**[30] 7532 8-9-10 66........................(v) JosephO'Brien 5 68
(Tony Carroll) *chsd ldrs: 6th 1/2-way: pushed along fr 4f out and sn rdn in 4th: no imp on ldrs u.p in 6th over 1f out: kpt on into 4th nr fin* 6/4[1]

5 ½ **Luimneach Abu (IRE)**[40] 5260 6-8-11 53........................(b[1]) FMBerry 11 54
(J P Broderick, Ire) *hld up in rr of mid-div: 9th 1/2-way: tk clsr order bhd horses into st: rdn into 5th over 1f out and kpt on same pce ins fnl f: nt trble principals* 14/1

6 shd **Blue Ridge Lane (IRE)**[16] 7750 8-9-12 68........................(bt) GaryCarroll 7 69+
(John C McConnell, Ire) *v s.i.s and in rr early: 10th 1/2-way: swtchd to outer 2f out and sme late hdwy ins fnl f: nrst fin* 33/1

7 nk **That's Ours (USA)**[7] 7878 6-7-13 51........................ DavidFitzpatrick(10) 10 51
(James M Barcoe, Ire) *uns rdr bef s: hooded to load: settled in mid-div: 7th 1/2-way: rdn and no imp on ldrs under 2f out: kpt on one pce* 12/1

8 nk **Regal Warrior (IRE)**[35] 7435 11-9-9 65........................(t) RobbieDowney(5) 12 65
(J J Lambe, Ire) *settled in mid-div: 8th 1/2-way: swtchd lft over 2f out and tk clsr order: rdn in 4th 1 1/2f out and sn no ex: wknd ins fnl f* 14/1

9 2 ½ **Perfect Ten (IRE)**[23] 7679 3-8-5 53........................ NGMcCullagh 2 49
(Anthony Mulholland, Ire) *chsd ldrs: 5th 1/2-way: rdn and no ex 2f out: wknd fnl f* 10/3[2]

10 ¾ **Empresario (IRE)**[50] 4835 5-9-9 68........................(t) ConnorKing(3) 8 62
(Matthew J Smith, Ire) *s.i.s and racd in rr: last 1/2-way: rdn and tk clsr order towards rr under 2f out: one pce fnl f* 8/1

11 1 **Noble Call (IRE)**[7] 7877 6-8-1 50........................(t) IanQueally(7) 13 43
(P J Rothwell, Ire) *s.i.s: racd towards rr: 11th 1/2-way: tk clsr order u.p 2f out: sn no ex u.p: wknd fnl f* 33/1

12 22 **Montego Breeze**[22] 4165 8-8-5 47........................ LeighRoche 14 5
(John W Nicholson, Ire) *chsd ldrs and sn impr into 2nd: niggled along 4f out and wknd into st: eased under 2f out* 66/1

2m 31.8s (151.80)
**WFA** 3 from 4yo+ 6lb 12 Ran SP% 136.5
Pick Six: @3,500. Tote aggregates: 2013 @130,483.00, 2014 @125,981.00 CSF £47.45 CT £717.42 TOTE £8.10: £1.30, £1.90, £6.70; DF 32.50 Trifecta £1059.50.
**Owner** Newlands Racing Club **Bred** James Mann **Trained** Stamullen, Co Meath
■ Stewards' Enquiry : David Fitzpatrick one-day ban: used whip above shoulder height (tbn)

**FOCUS**
There's no stopping this winner on the polytrack as he earned his fourth win on this surface, defying the handicapper once more.
T/Jkpt: @2,100. T/Plt: @57.20. Pool: @44,977.80. BF

7960 - 7969a (Foreign Racing) - See Raceform Interactive

# 7948 WOLVERHAMPTON (A.W) (L-H)
Saturday, November 29

**OFFICIAL GOING: Tapeta: standard**
Wind: Light behind Weather: Overcast

## 7970 £20 RISK-FREE BET AT UNIBET MAIDEN STKS (TAPETA) 5f 20y
5:45 (5:48) (Class 5) 2-Y-O £2,911 (£866; £432; £216) Stalls Low

Form RPR

0- 1 **Middle East Pearl**[45] 7192 2-9-0 0........................ LukeMorris 7 68
(James Tate) *chsd ldr tl led over 1f out: rdn out* 12/1

406- 2 1 ¼ **Come Uppence**[52] 7029 2-9-5 68........................ JFEgan 13 68
(David Evans) *hld up: hdwy over 1f out: r.o wl ins fnl f: wnt 2nd post: nt rch wnr* 22/1

4- 3 hd **Soft Love (IRE)**[191] 2472 2-9-0 0........................ TomEaves 8 62+
(Kevin Ryan) *s.i.s: hld up: hdwy over 1f out: r.o* 12/1

4- 4 1 **Sacred Bond**[21] 7712 2-9-0 0........................ TonyHamilton 11 59
(Richard Fahey) *chsd ldrs: rdn over 1f out: styd on same pce ins fnl f* 7/2[2]

5 1 ¾ **Sir Keltic Blue** 2-9-5 0........................ DaleSwift 10 57
(Brian Ellison) *s.i.s: bhd: r.o ins fnl f: nrst fin* 66/1

423- 6 ½ **Fujiano**[41] 7308 2-9-0 66........................ DavidProbert 3 51
(Derek Haydn Jones) *led: rdn and hdd over 1f out: no ex ins fnl f* 7/1[3]

423- 7 ¾ **Winning Hunter**[16] 7755 2-9-5 73........................(tp) GeorgeBaker 9 53
(Philip Hide) *mid-div: rdn over 1f out: styd on same pce fnl f* 13/8[1]

0- 8 ½ **Tranquil Glen**[17] 7741 2-8-9 0........................ AlistairRawlinson(5) 5 46
(Michael Appleby) *mid-div: hdwy over 1f out: no ex fnl f* 66/1

220- 9 hd **Grosmont**[147] 3947 2-9-2 73........................ ConnorBeasley(3) 12 50
(James Given) *hld up: pushed along 1/2-way: nvr on terms* 17/2

04- 10 ¾ **Military Music**[23] 7685 2-8-7 0........................ CharlotteJenner(7) 6 43
(Mark Usher) *mid-div: hdwy over 1f out: rdn and wknd ins fnl f* 100/1

00- 11 nk **Equita**[7] 7881 2-9-0 0........................ LiamJones 4 42
(Robert Stephens) *prom: racd keenly: rdn over 1f out: wknd ins fnl f* 100/1

44- 12 1 **Colombia (IRE)**[119] 4919 2-9-0 0........................ PJMcDonald 1 38
(Ann Duffield) *chsd ldrs: rdn over 1f out: wknd fnl f* 50/1

13 shd **Milly Royale** 2-9-0 0........................ SteveDrowne 2 38
(Peter Makin) *hld up: rdn over 1f out: wknd fnl f* 40/1

1m 1.75s (-0.15) **Going Correction** -0.05s/f (Stan) 13 Ran SP% 116.8
Speed ratings (Par 96): **99,97,96,95,92 91,90,89,89,87 87,85,85**
CSF £251.62 TOTE £14.20: £3.70, £7.40, £5.50; EX 352.20 Trifecta £3741.60 Part won..
**Owner** Saif Ali **Bred** Biddestone Stud **Trained** Newmarket, Suffolk
■ Stewards' Enquiry : Luke Morris two-day ban: careless riding (Dec 13,15)

**FOCUS**
The opening contest was an ordinary juvenile sprint maiden in which they went a decent gallop on standard Tapeta, and the winning time was a Tapeta track record.

## 7971 LADBROKES H'CAP (TAPETA) 1m 141y
6:15 (6:18) (Class 2) (0-100,95) 3-Y-O+
£11,827 (£3,541; £1,770; £885; £442; £222) Stalls Low

Form RPR

210- 1 **Melvin The Grate (IRE)**[21] 7719 4-8-9 83........................ DavidProbert 11 94
(Andrew Balding) *hld up: hdwy over 1f out: shkn up to ld ins fnl f: r.o wl* 11/2

424- 2 2 ½ **Flow (USA)**[81] 6207 4-9-4 92........................(t) SeanLevey 8 97
(David Brown) *hld up: hdwy on outer over 1f out: r.o to go 2nd wl ins fnl f: no ch w wnr* 11/1

132- 3 hd **Earth Drummer (IRE)**[23] 7688 4-9-7 95........................ SamJames 5 100
(David O'Meara) *chsd ldrs: rdn over 1f out: styd on* 5/2[1]

044- 4 nk **Energia Flavio (BRZ)**[23] 7688 4-9-5 93........................(p) MartinHarley 10 97
(Marco Botti) *led over 7f out: rdn over 1f out: hdd and no ex ins fnl f* 9/2[3]

213- 5 hd **Ty Gwr**[25] 7641 5-9-1 89........................ DaleSwift 2 92
(Brian Ellison) *s.i.s: hld up: hdwy racd wd turning for home: styd on ins fnl f: nvr nrr* 16/1

552- 6 hd **Ingleby Angel (IRE)**[14] 7801 5-9-4 92........................ GeorgeBaker 1 95
(David O'Meara) *hld up: hdwy over 1f out: styd on same pce ins fnl f* 4/1[2]

001- 7 3 ½ **Steventon Star**[14] 7799 3-8-10 87........................(v) WilliamTwiston-Davies 6 82
(Michael Scudamore) *led 1f: chsd ldr: rdn over 2f out: wknd ins fnl f* 50/1

100- 8 4 **Ishikawa (IRE)**[9] 7852 6-8-7 84........................ JoeyHaynes(3) 9 70
(K R Burke) *chsd ldrs: rdn over 2f out: wknd fnl f* 33/1

3/0- 9 12 **Haaf A Sixpence**[315] 235 5-9-7 95........................ GrahamGibbons 3 53
(Ralph Beckett) *hld up: rdn over 2f out: wknd fnl f* 9/1

1m 47.48s (-2.62) **Going Correction** -0.05s/f (Stan)
**WFA** 3 from 4yo+ 3lb 9 Ran SP% 111.3
Speed ratings (Par 109): **109,106,106,106,106 105,102,99,88**
CSF £60.37 CT £181.33 TOTE £5.10: £1.80, £2.00, £1.40; EX 67.00 Trifecta £387.30.
**Owner** Fromthestables.com & I A Balding **Bred** Barronstown Stud **Trained** Kingsclere, Hants
■ Kosika was withdrawn. Price at time of wihdrawal 11/1. Rule 4 applies to all bets - deduction 5p in the pound.

**FOCUS**
The feature contest was a good handicap in which they went a strong gallop, and the winning time confirms the track is riding quick.

## 7972 DOWNLOAD THE LADBROKES APP H'CAP (TAPETA) 7f 32y
6:45 (6:46) (Class 6) (0-55,55) 3-Y-O+ £2,264 (£673; £336; £168) Stalls High

Form RPR

065- 1 **Baltic Prince (IRE)**[36] 7424 4-9-4 52........................ RaulDaSilva 10 68
(Tony Carroll) *mde all: rdn clr 2f out: eased nr fin* 13/2[3]

303- 2 3 ¼ **Hidden Asset**[15] 7785 4-9-6 54........................ HayleyTurner 12 61
(Michael Appleby) *s.i.s: hld up: plld hrd: hdwy and nt clr run over 1f out: r.o to go 2nd wl ins fnl f: no ch w wnr* 9/4[1]

423- 3 ¾ **Copper Cavalier**[7] 7883 3-9-2 51........................(v) MartinHarley 7 55
(Robert Cowell) *a.p: chsd wnr over 2f out: rdn over 1f out: styd on same pce fnl f* 10/3[2]

040- 4 ½ **Tableforten**[29] 7570 3-9-6 55........................(p) LiamJones 6 57
(J S Moore) *a.p: rdn over 2f out: styd on* 16/1

500- 5 1 ½ **Koharu**[30] 7556 4-9-7 55........................(p) SteveDrowne 1 54
(Peter Makin) *mid-div: rdn over 2f out: hdwy over 1f out: nt trble ldrs* 33/1

652- 6 ¾ **Hamis Al Bin (IRE)**[15] 7782 5-9-6 54........................(t) LukeMorris 4 51
(Milton Bradley) *hld up: hdwy over 1f out: hung lft and no ex ins fnl f* 9/1

025- 7 1 ¼ **Littlecote Lady**[15] 7783 5-8-12 53........................(v) CharlotteJenner(7) 2 47
(Mark Usher) *hld up: hdwy over 1f out: sn rdn: wknd ins fnl f* 28/1

000- 8 ½ **Stun Gun**[16] 7766 4-9-4 52........................ DaleSwift 3 45
(Derek Shaw) *pushed along in rr early: rdn over 1f out: n.d* 16/1

000- 9 ¾ **Officer In Command (USA)**[25] 7635 8-9-4 52........................(p) LiamKeniry 5 43
(John Butler) *s.i.s: hld up: pushed along 1/2-way: n.d* 22/1

050- 10 ½ **Bonjour Steve**[14] 7813 3-9-6 55........................(p) JoeFanning 11 44
(Richard Price) *trckd ldrs: plld hrd: rdn over 1f out: wknd fnl f* 12/1

300- 11 1 ½ **Prince Of Passion (CAN)**[15] 7782 6-9-6 54........................ TonyHamilton 8 40
(Derek Shaw) *hld up: rdn and wknd over 2f out* 50/1

001- 12 ½ **Prigsnov Dancer (IRE)**[15] 7783 9-8-13 54........................(p) DavidParkes(7) 9 38
(Deborah Sanderson) *plld hrd: trckd wnr tl over 2f out: wkng whn n.m.r over 1f out* 18/1

1m 28.46s (-0.34) **Going Correction** -0.05s/f (Stan)
**WFA** 3 from 4yo+ 1lb 12 Ran SP% 114.6
Speed ratings (Par 101): **99,95,94,93,92 91,89,89,88,87 86,85**
CSF £19.85 CT £57.41 TOTE £7.20: £2.00, £1.30, £1.50; EX 24.80 Trifecta £94.40.
**Owner** A Mills **Bred** William Pilkington **Trained** Cropthorne, Worcs

**FOCUS**
A moderate handicap.

## 7973 32RED MAIDEN STKS (TAPETA) 7f 32y
7:15 (7:18) (Class 5) 2-Y-O £2,911 (£866; £432; £216) Stalls High

Form RPR

0- 1 **Ciao Cielo (GER)**[96] 5759 2-9-5 0........................ GrahamGibbons 12 75
(David Barron) *s.i.s: hld up: hdwy over 1f out: rdn and r.o to ld post* 16/1

343- 2 shd **Rahmah (IRE)**[42] 7277 2-9-5 76........................ AdamKirby 10 75
(Robert Cowell) *w ldr: plld hrd: rdn to ld over 1f out: edgd lft ins fnl f: hdd post* 9/2[3]

0- 3 2 **Muhaafiz (IRE)**[52] 7031 2-9-5 0........................ SeanLevey 11 70
(David Brown) *hld up: hdwy over 2f out: styd on* 66/1

35- 4 1 ½ **China Club (IRE)**[19] 7731 2-9-5 0........................[1] RobertHavlin 3 66
(John Gosden) *chsd ldrs: rdn over 1f out: styd on same pce fnl f* 3/1[2]

54- 5 hd **Waaleef**[17] 7739 2-9-5 0........................ PaoloSirigu 1 66
(Marco Botti) *led: rdn and hdd over 1f out: no ex ins fnl f* 12/1

- 6 1 ¼ **Acclamate (IRE)** 2-9-5 0........................(t) MartinHarley 7 63
(Marco Botti) *hld up in tch: shkn up over 1f out: edgd lft and no ex fnl f* 15/8[1]

7 ½ **What Asham** 2-8-12 0........................ PatrickO'Donnell(7) 8 62
(Ralph Beckett) *hld up: hdwy over 2f out: rdn over 1f out: styd on same pce fnl f* 9/1

5- 8 ¾ **Royal Blessing**[49] 7113 2-9-5 0........................ LukeMorris 6 60
(George Peckham) *s.i.s: hld up: plld hrd: hdwy over 1f out: no ex ins fnl f* 40/1

00- 9 3 ¾ **Marsoomah**[33] 7495 2-9-0 0........................ TonyHamilton 5 46
(Richard Fahey) *hld up: shkn up over 2f out: nvr on terms* 100/1

10 2 ¼ **Kelloura (IRE)** 2-9-0 0........................ GeorgeChaloner 4 40
(Richard Fahey) *s.i.s: a in rr* 66/1



The Form Book, Raceform Ltd, Newbury, RG14 5SJ

632- **11** *1 1/4* **Tamarin**[39] 7363 2-9-0 66 ........ JFEgan 9 37
(David Evans) *chsd ldrs: rdn over 2f out: wknd fnl f* **14/1**

6- **12** *21* **Ace Of Marmalade (IRE)**[16] 7763 2-9-5 0 ........ TomEaves 2
(Brian Ellison) *chsd ldrs tl rdn and wknd 1/2-way* **100/1**

1m 28.57s (-0.23) **Going Correction** -0.05s/f (Stan) **12** Ran SP% **115.6**
Speed ratings (Par 96): **99,98,96,94,94 93,92,91,87,84 83,59**
CSF £84.17 TOTE £22.70: £6.70, £1.60, £7.40; EX 120.70 Trifecta £3330.30 Part won..
**Owner** Home Farm Racing Limited **Bred** *unknown **Trained** Maunby, N Yorks

**FOCUS**
An ordinary juvenile maiden in which they went a decent gallop.

## 7974 CORAL H'CAP (TAPETA) 1m 4f 50y
**7:45** (7:45) (Class 3) (0-95,92) 3-Y-O+ **£7,246** (£2,168; £1,084; £542; £270) **Stalls** Low

Form RPR

000- **1** **Personal Opinion**[97] 5720 3-9-0 **88** ........ AdamKirby 4 97
(Charlie Appleby) *a.p: rdn to ld ins fnl f: r.o* **6/4**[1]

331- **2** *1* **Cerutty (IRE)**[26] 7627 3-8-8 **82** ........ LukeMorris 8 89
(Marco Botti) *a.p: chsd ldr over 9f out tl led over 1f out: sn rdn: hdd and unable qck ins fnl f* **7/2**[3]

000- **3** *2* **Uramazin (IRE)**[23] 7688 8-9-8 **90** ........ GeorgeBaker 1 94
(Philip Hide) *hld up: rdn over 1f out: hung lft and r.o ins fnl f: nt rch ldrs* **33/1**

610/ **4** *1/2* **Aladdins Cave**[15] 7791 10-9-1 **83** ........ (vt) StevieDonohoe 6 86
(R K Watson, Ire) *hld up: hdwy u.p over 1f out: styd on same pce ins fnl f* **50/1**

453- **5** *1/2* **Art Scholar (IRE)**[15] 7784 7-8-8 **79** ........ RyanTate[(3)] 2 81
(Michael Appleby) *hld up: rdn and hdwy over 1f out: no ex ins fnl f* **11/2**

000- **6** *3 3/4* **The Lock Master (IRE)**[23] 7688 7-9-3 **90** ........ AlistairRawlinson[(5)] 5 86
(Michael Appleby) *led: hdd over 10f out: remained handy: rdn over 2f out: wknd fnl f* **40/1**

540- **7** *shd* **Esteaming**[21] 7718 4-9-10 **92** ........ GrahamGibbons 3 88
(David Barron) *hld up in tch: rdn over 3f out: wknd over 1f out* **3/1**[2]

00- **8** *1* **Vivat Rex (IRE)**[24] 7662 3-8-10 **84** ........ (b) JoeFanning 7 79
(Alan Bailey) *led at stdy pce over 10f out: qcknd over 2f out: rdn and hdd over 1f out: wknd ins fnl f* **12/1**

2m 39.81s (-0.99) **Going Correction** -0.05s/f (Stan)
**WFA** 3 from 4yo+ 6lb **8** Ran SP% **117.6**
Speed ratings (Par 107): **101,100,99,98,98 95,95,95**
CSF £7.24 CT £118.88 TOTE £2.50: £1.50, £1.60, £3.00; EX 8.00 Trifecta £86.70.
**Owner** Godolphin **Bred** Whitley Stud **Trained** Newmarket, Suffolk

**FOCUS**
A decent middle-distance handicap in which they went a steady gallop.

## 7975 BET IN PLAY AT CORAL H'CAP (TAPETA) 1m 4f 50y
**8:15** (8:15) (Class 5) (0-70,69) 3-Y-O+ **£2,911** (£866; £432; £216) **Stalls** Low

Form RPR

403- **1** **Heska (IRE)**[23] 7689 3-9-2 67 ........ (tp) LukeMorris 4 75
(Michael Appleby) *s.i.s: hld up: hdwy over 3f out: chsd ldr over 1f out: sn rdn: styd on u.p to ld wl ins fnl f: jst hld on* **5/2**[1]

444- **2** *nse* **Moccasin (FR)**[12] 7822 5-9-7 66 ........ PJMcDonald 1 73
(Geoffrey Harker) *chsd ldrs: led 2f out: rdn and hdd wl ins fnl f: styd on* **9/2**[2]

100- **3** *nk* **Thane Of Cawdor (IRE)**[17] 7744 5-9-3 62 ........ AdamKirby 3 68
(Joseph Tuite) *hld up: hdwy over 1f out: sn rdn: r.o* **14/1**[3]

**4** *1/2* **Front Run (IRE)**[82] 6202 3-9-2 67 ........ MartinHarley 7 73
(Marco Botti) *hld up: hdwy over 2f out: rdn over 1f out: r.o* **5/2**[1]

260- **5** *7* **El Bravo**[36] 7411 8-9-3 69 ........ KevinLundie[(7)] 8 63
(Shaun Harris) *hld up: hdwy over 2f out: rdn over 1f out: wknd ins fnl f* **33/1**

356- **6** *5* **Miss Crystal (IRE)**[36] 7416 3-9-4 69 ........ GeorgeBaker 9 55
(Charles Hills) *sn led: rdn and hdd 2f out: wknd fnl f* **9/2**[2]

502- **7** *15* **Anjuna Beach (USA)**[7] 7895 4-8-9 59 ........ AnnStokell[(5)] 5 21
(Ann Stokell) *hld up: plld hrd: hdwy to go 2nd over 6f out tl pushed along and wknd over 2f out* **14/1**[3]

004- **8** *6* **Ruggero**[35] 6425 4-9-4 63 ........ TomEaves 2 16
(Roy Brotherton) *chsd ldr tl over 6f out: sn rdn: wknd wl over 2f out* **66/1**

230- **9** *11* **Giant Sequoia (USA)**[42] 7290 10-8-11 56 ........ (t) ShaneKelly 6
(Des Donovan) *prom: rdn 4f out: wknd wl over 2f out* **25/1**

2m 38.63s (-2.17) **Going Correction** -0.05s/f (Stan)
**WFA** 3 from 4yo+ 6lb **9** Ran SP% **115.1**
Speed ratings (Par 103): **105,104,104,104,99 96,86,82,75**
CSF £13.80 CT £128.87 TOTE £4.10: £1.50, £1.40, £2.40; EX 14.60 Trifecta £131.00.
**Owner** Dennis & Andy Deacon **Bred** Mrs E Henry **Trained** Danethorpe, Notts

**FOCUS**
A modest middle-distance handicap in which they went an even gallop.

## 7976 DOWNLOAD THE CORAL APP H'CAP (TAPETA) (DIV I) 1m 1f 103y
**8:45** (8:45) (Class 6) (0-55,55) 3-Y-O+ **£2,264** (£673; £336; £168) **Stalls** Low

Form RPR

000- **1** **Overrider**[10] 7845 4-9-1 49 ........ (tp) LukeMorris 1 57
(Shaun Lycett) *led 1f: racd keenly and trckd ldrs: wnt 2nd over 2f out: rdn over 1f out: r.o to ld wl ins fnl f: jst hld on* **20/1**

/04- **2** *nse* **Rock Charm**[39] 7360 3-8-13 50 ........ MartinHarley 10 58
(Stuart Williams) *hld up in tch: rdn over 1f out: r.o* **6/4**[1]

160- **3** *hd* **Catching Zeds**[8] 7868 7-9-4 52 ........ (p) PJMcDonald 7 59
(Kevin Frost) *hld up: hdwy over 2f out: rdn over 1f out: r.o* **18/1**

200- **4** *3/4* **Lord Of The Storm**[79] 6267 6-8-11 50 ........ RyanWhile[(5)] 6 56
(Bill Turner) *mid-div: hmpd and lost pl over 6f out: rdn on outer over 1f out: running on whn nt clr run and swtchd lft wl ins fnl f: nt rch ldrs* **25/1**

001- **5** *shd* **Sarlat**[8] 7868 3-8-9 49 ........ AmyScott[(3)] 12 55
(Mark Brisbourne) *hld up: hdwy over 5f out: led 4f out: rdn and hdd wl ins fnl f* **9/2**[3]

**6** *3 1/4* **Moulin Rouge (DEN)**[153] 3-8-9 46 ........ StevieDonohoe 5 45
(Ian Williams) *plld hrd and prom: rdn over 1f out: no ex ins fnl f* **11/1**

260- **7** *1/2* **Indian Giver**[14] 7813 6-9-2 53 ........ (v) ConnorBeasley[(3)] 8 51
(John David Riches) *hld up: hdwy over 1f out: sn rdn: no ex ins fnl f* **10/1**

244- **8** *1/2* **Royal Mizar (SPA)**[8] 7869 4-8-11 48 ........ (p) RyanTate[(3)] 2 45
(Ralph J Smith) *prom: lost pl 4f out: hdwy over 1f out: no ex ins fnl f* **4/1**[2]

600- **9** *4 1/2* **Destiny Blue (IRE)**[25] 7643 7-9-7 55 ........ (t) RaulDaSilva 4 42
(Suzzanne France) *s.i.s: hld up: rdn over 1f out: nvr on terms* **40/1**

000- **10** *1* **Katmai River (IRE)**[92] 5893 7-8-10 51 ........ CharlotteJenner[(7)] 3 36
(Mark Usher) *trckd ldrs: led over 6f out: hdd 4f out: chsd ldr tl over 2f out: wknd fnl f* **14/1**

060- **11** *17* **Moissanite**[16] 7766 5-8-5 46 oh1 ........ (t) DanielleMooney[(7)] 13
(Sean Regan) *led over 8f out: hdd over 6f out: chsd ldrs tl pushed along and wknd over 2f out* **100/1**

2m 1.77s (0.97) **Going Correction** -0.05s/f (Stan)
**WFA** 3 from 4yo+ 3lb **11** Ran SP% **119.6**
Speed ratings (Par 101): **93,92,92,92,92 89,88,88,84,83 68**
CSF £50.06 CT £597.99 TOTE £14.50: £4.00, £1.20, £4.60; EX 72.40 Trifecta £1221.90.
**Owner** L & M Atkins **Bred** P M Cunningham **Trained** Clapton-on-the-Hill, Gloucs

**FOCUS**
The first division of a moderate handicap in which they took it in turns to set a rather muddling gallop, and the first five finished in a heap.

## 7977 DOWNLOAD THE CORAL APP H'CAP (TAPETA) (DIV II) 1m 1f 103y
**9:15** (9:15) (Class 6) (0-55,55) 3-Y-O+ **£2,264** (£673; £336; £168) **Stalls** Low

Form RPR

400- **1** **Jersey Cream (IRE)**[89] 5978 3-8-12 49 ........ MartinLane 3 63
(Andi Brown) *hld up: hdwy and nt clr run over 1f out: rdn to ld ins fnl f: r.o wl* **40/1**

401- **2** *3 1/2* **San Quentin (IRE)**[24] 7664 3-9-1 52 ........ (p) LukeMorris 13 59
(Tony Carroll) *mid-div: hdwy over 3f out: rdn over 1f out: styd on same pce ins fnl f* **9/4**[1]

430- **3** *1 1/4* **Assoluta (IRE)**[31] 7526 3-9-4 55 ........ RenatoSouza 10 59
(Sylvester Kirk) *chsd ldrs: led over 1f out: sn rdn: hdd and no ex ins fnl f* **14/1**

000- **4** *shd* **Percys Princess**[56] 6946 3-8-6 46 oh1 ........ RyanTate[(3)] 6 50
(Michael Appleby) *hld up: hdwy over 2f out: rdn over 1f out: styd on same pce ins fnl f* **5/2**[2]

403- **5** *2* **Snow Dancer (IRE)**[8] 7868 10-8-10 51 ........ (p) HarryBurns[(7)] 11 51
(John David Riches) *hld up: hdwy over 2f out: rdn over 1f out: edgd lft and wknd ins fnl f* **10/1**

005- **6** *3/4* **It's Taboo**[30] 7546 4-9-0 48 ........ LiamKeniry 12 46
(Mark Usher) *hld up: hdwy over 1f out: rdn and wknd ins fnl f* **20/1**

300- **7** *2 1/2* **My New Angel (IRE)**[79] 6267 5-8-12 46 oh1 ........ StevieDonohoe 8 39
(Daniel Mark Loughnane) *hld up: hdwy over 2f out: rdn whn n.m.r over 1f out: wknd ins fnl f* **33/1**

500- **8** *2 1/4* **Dark Phantom (IRE)**[14] 7805 3-8-10 47 ........ (b) LiamJones 5 35
(Peter Makin) *chsd ldrs: rdn over 2f out: swtchd lft over 1f out: wknd fnl f* **20/1**

036- **9** *1/2* **Flumps**[9] 7853 5-8-7 46 oh1 ........ (v[1]) EoinWalsh[(5)] 2 33
(John Stimpson) *hld up: rdn 1/2-way: n.d* **20/1**

345- **10** *1 3/4* **Yorksters Prince (IRE)**[14] 7813 7-9-6 54 ........ (p) JoeFanning 4 37
(Marjorie Fife) *led: rdn and hdd over 1f out: wknd fnl f* **10/1**

004- **11** *hd* **Caledonia Laird**[15] 7785 3-9-3 54 ........ ShaneKelly 9 37
(Jo Hughes) *hdwy to chse ldr 7f out: rdn and ev ch over 1f out: wknd fnl f* **7/1**[3]

500- **12** *5* **Buzz Law (IRE)**[3] 7924 6-8-12 49 ........ (t) ConnorBeasley[(3)] 1 21
(John Weymes) *prom: rdn over 3f out: wknd over 1f out* **33/1**

050- **13** *10* **Jessy Mae**[36] 7423 3-8-13 50 ........ RaulDaSilva 7
(Derek Haydn Jones) *broke wl: plld hrd: stdd and lost pl after 1f: hmpd over 2f out: sn wknd* **40/1**

1m 59.64s (-1.16) **Going Correction** -0.05s/f (Stan)
**WFA** 3 from 4yo+ 3lb **13** Ran SP% **121.7**
Speed ratings (Par 101): **103,99,98,98,96 96,94,92,91,90 89,85,76**
CSF £124.19 CT £1451.32 TOTE £53.60: £11.70, £1.80, £2.20; EX 227.10 Trifecta £2243.30 Part won..
**Owner** Faith Hope And Charity **Bred** Mick McGinn **Trained** Newmarket, Suffolk

**FOCUS**
The second division of a moderate handicap in which they went a decent gallop, and the winning time was significantly quicker.
T/Plt: 505.90 to a £1 stake. Pool: £148,946.38 - 214.89 winning tickets T/Qpdt: £12.40 to a £1 stake. Pool: £17,712.42 - 1,054.60 winning tickets CR

7978 - 7980a (Foreign Racing) - See Raceform Interactive

# TOKYO (L-H)
Sunday, November 30

**OFFICIAL GOING: Turf: firm**

## 7981a JAPAN CUP (GRADE 1) (3YO+) (TURF) 1m 4f
**6:55** (12:00) 3-Y-O£1,455,735 (£579,788; £364,452; £217,939; £143,381)

RPR

**1** **Epiphaneia (JPN)**[28] 4-9-0 0 ........ ChristopheSoumillon 4 126+
(Katsuhiko Sumii, Japan) *t.k.h: trckd ldr on inner: angled out to chal gng strly 2f out and sn led: rdn and qcknd clr: styd on strly fnl f: pushed out: impressive* **79/10**

**2** *4* **Just A Way (JPN)**[56] 6970 5-9-0 0 ........ YuichiFukunaga 1 120
(Naosuke Sugai, Japan) *midfield on inner: swtchd out into st: rdn 2f out: wnt 2nd over 1f out: styd on fnl f but no ch w impressive wnr* **57/10**[3]

**3** *1/2* **Spielberg (JPN)**[28] 5-9-0 0 ........ HiroshiKitamura 15 119
(Kazuo Fujisawa, Japan) *hld up towards rr: rdn over 2f out: nt clrest of runs but styd on and wnt 3rd towards fin: nvr nrr* **103/10**

**4** *3/4* **Gentildonna (JPN)**[28] 5-8-9 0 ........ RyanMoore 3 113
(Sei Ishizaka, Japan) *midfield in tch on inner: rdn and ev ch 2f out: sn readily outpcd by wnr: styd on but wl hld: lost 3rd towards fin* **13/5**[1]

**5** *nk* **Harp Star (JPN)**[56] 6970 3-8-5 0 ........ YugaKawada 6 114
(Hiroyoshi Matsuda, Japan) *hld up in midfield: rdn and fanned wd into st: styd on steadily fnl 2f but nvr able to chal* **31/10**[2]

**6** *1/2* **Ivanhowe (GER)**[29] 7603 4-9-0 0 ........ FilipMinarik 2 116
(Jean-Pierre Carvalho, Germany) *midfield on inner: rdn over 2f out: styd on steadily u.p but nvr able to chal* **71/1**

**7** *nk* **One And Only (JPN)**[35] 7484 3-8-9 0 ........ NorihiroYokoyama 10 117
(Kojiro Hashiguchi, Japan) *midfield: rdn over 2f out: styd on steadily but nvr able to chal* **133/10**

**8** *nse* **Fenomeno (JPN)**[28] 5-9-0 0 ........ YasunariIwata 16 116
(Hirofumi Toda, Japan) *hld up in midfield: rdn over 2f out: styd on steadily but nvr able to chal* **172/10**

**9** *1 1/4* **Isla Bonita (JPN)**[28] 3-8-9 0 ........ MasayoshiEbina 9 115
(Hironori Kurita, Japan) *midfield: smooth hdwy and ev ch 2f out: rdn and nt qckn over 1f out: fdd fnl f* **17/2**

**10** *1 1/4* **Tamamo Best Play (JPN)**[47] 4-9-0 0 ........ AkihideTsumura 12 112
(Katsumi Minai, Japan) *trckd ldr on outer: led 3f out: rdn and strly pressed 2f out: sn hdd: no ex and wknd fnl f* **127/1**

**11** *1 1/2* **Denim And Ruby (JPN)**[28] 4-8-9 0 ........ SuguruHamanaka 8 104
(Katsuhiko Sumii, Japan) *hld up in rr: rdn and swtchd out into st: plugged on but no real imp fnl 2f: nvr threatened* **12/1**

12 2 1/2 **Hit The Target (JPN)**[28] 6-9-0 0 ........................................ YutakaTake 5 105
(Keiji Kato, Japan) *hld up towards rr on inner: rdn and angled out 2f out: sn outpcd and btn: nvr threatened* **45/1**

13 2 1/2 **Uncoiled (FR)**[14] 5-9-0 0 ........................................ KeitaTosaki 17 101
(Yoshito Yahagi, Japan) *sn prom: rdn to chal and ev ch over 2f out: no ex and btn over 1f out: wknd* **258/1**

14 2 1/2 **Tosen Jordan (JPN)**[28] 8-9-0 0 ........................ Pierre-CharlesBoudot 11 97
(Yasutoshi Ikee, Japan) *pushed along early and sn prom in midfield: rdn over 2f out: lost pl and btn wl over 1f out: wknd* **169/1**

15 nk **Decipher (JPN)**[28] 5-9-0 0 ........................................ GregoryBenoist 13 97
(Futoshi Kojima, Japan) *midfield on outer: rdn and dropped to rr into st: sn no imp and btn* **138/1**

16 9 **Up With The Birds (CAN)**[50] 4-9-0 0 ........................(b) ERosaDaSilva 7 82
(Malcolm Pierce, Canada) *hld up in rr: rdn into st: no imp and btn fnl 2f: eased: nvr a factor* **158/1**

17 dist **Satono Shuren (JPN)**[84] 6-9-0 0 ........................................ ShinjiKawashima 14
(Akira Murayama, Japan) *led: hdd 3f out: rdn and qckly btn: wknd on rail and dropped to last: t.o* **274/1**

P **Trading Leather (IRE)**[78] 6353 4-9-0 0 ........................................ KevinManning 18
(J S Bolger, Ire) *midfield in tch: pushed along and lost pl over 4f out: broke down and t.o bef st: p.u: fatally injured* **68/1**

2m 23.1s (-2.40)
**WFA** 3 from 4yo+ 6lb **18** Ran SP% **126.4**
PARI-MUTUEL (all including 100 jpy stake): WIN 890; SHOW 320, 320, 410; DF 4120; SF 7800.
**Owner** U Carrot Farm **Bred** Northern Farm **Trained** Japan

**FOCUS**
This looked a red-hot Japan Cup beforehand despite only three overseas challengers. The home contingent included a couple who did not enjoy the run of the race in last month's Arc, while a few of these had already figured in previous Japan Cups, not least Gentildonna who was looking for a hat-trick in the race. The pace didn't look at all strong early and those that tried to come from a long way back were at a disadvantage when the leaders quickened off the home bend. As is often the case in such a situation, it paid to be handy which is exactly how the winner was ridden. The race was marred by the fatal injury incurred by Trading Leather.

# 7940 KEMPTON (A.W) (R-H)
Monday, December 1

**OFFICIAL GOING: Polytrack: standard**
Wind: virtually nil Weather: overcast, dry

## 7982 COME JUMP RACING ON BOXING DAY H'CAP — 1m 2f (P)
**2:20** (2:20) (Class 6) (0-60,60) 3-Y-O+ — **£2,264** (£673; £336; £168) **Stalls** Low

Form / RPR

045- 1 **Time Square (FR)**[12] 7846 7-9-5 58 ........................................ JimCrowley 3 66
(Tony Carroll) *t.k.h: in tch in midfield: hdwy to chse ldrs over 2f out: rdn to chse ldr jst over 1f out: kpt on u.p to ld cl home* **15/8**[1]

046- 2 nk **Understory (USA)**[33] 7527 7-9-3 56 ........................................ GeorgeBaker 14 63
(Tim McCarthy) *sn chsng ldr: led 7f out: rdn over 1f out: kpt on tl hdd and no ex cl home* **5/1**[2]

036- 3 1/2 **Estibdaad (IRE)**[69] 6636 4-9-3 56 ........................(t) WilliamTwiston-Davies 1 62
(Paddy Butler) *chsd ldrs: rdn and effrt 2f out: kpt on u.p ins fnl f* **10/1**

04- 4 2 1/4 **Runaiocht (IRE)**[27] 7632 4-8-11 50 ........................................ JimmyQuinn 7 52
(Paul Burgoyne) *taken down early: sltly hmpd leaving stalls: rdn and effrt 2f out: 5th and stl plenty to do over 1f out: styd on: nt rch ldrs* **8/1**

360- 5 1 **Lacock**[61] 6857 3-9-4 60 ........................................ AdamKirby 2 60
(Sean Curran) *led for 3f: chsd ldr tl jst over 2f out: wknd ins fnl f* **6/1**[3]

660- 6 4 1/2 **Otterbridge**[14] 7818 3-8-8 50 ow2 ........................(t) RobertHavlin 12 41
(Rod Millman) *wl in tch in midfield: lost pl and rdn over 2f out: n.d and plugged on same pce after* **50/1**

035- 7 1/2 **Claude Greenwood**[12] 7845 4-8-4 48 ........................(p) ShelleyBirkett(5) 5 38
(Linda Jewell) *chsd ldrs: rdn and over 2f out: 6th and wknd over 1f out* **12/1**

0/0- 8 hd **Astrowolf**[17] 7777 3-8-11 53 ........................................ PatCosgrave 8 42
(Mark H Tompkins) *bhd: styd on past btn horses fr over 1f out: nvr trbld ldrs* **50/1**

303- 9 1 1/2 **Travis Bickle (IRE)**[18] 7754 3-8-13 55 ........................(b) LiamKeniry 6 41
(John Flint) *towards rr: rdn 3f out: nvr trbld ldrs* **10/1**

060- 10 3/4 **Llyrical**[31] 7570 3-8-12 54 ........................................ DavidProbert 10 39
(Derek Haydn Jones) *taken down early: stdd s: hld up in rr: sme hdwy over 2f out: no prog wl over 1f out* **33/1**

600- 11 4 1/2 **Jazri**[38] 7426 3-8-13 55 ........................................ SteveDrowne 13 31
(Milton Bradley) *in tch in midfield: lost pl and u.p 4f out: bhd fnl 2f* **66/1**

000- 12 1 1/4 **Mountain Range (IRE)**[16] 7804 6-9-5 58 ........................................ ChrisCatlin 9 31
(Willie Musson) *dwlt: nvr gng wl and a in rr: bhd fnl 2f* **16/1**

000- 13 6 **Luna Sunrise**[11] 7853 3-8-7 54 ........................................ JordanVaughan(5) 4 15
(Timothy Jarvis) *in tch in midfield: hdwy 1/2-way: btn and lost pl over 2f out: bhd fnl f* **33/1**

2m 6.57s (-1.43) **Going Correction** -0.10s/f (Stan)
**WFA** 3 from 4yo+ 3lb **13** Ran SP% **119.9**
Speed ratings (Par 101): **101,100,100,98,97 94,93,93,92,91 88,87,82**
CSF £10.27 CT £76.88 TOTE £2.90: £1.20, £2.10, £3.00; EX 13.70 Trifecta £89.50.
**Owner** M S Cooke **Bred** Mme Therese Bouche & Isabelle Roussel **Trained** Cropthorne, Worcs

**FOCUS**
A modest handicap in which nothing came from too far off the pace. The winner is rated close to his best from the past two years.

## 7983 DOWNLOAD THE BETVICTOR INSTABET APP CLAIMING STKS — 7f (P)
**2:50** (2:50) (Class 5) 3-Y-O+ — **£2,911** (£866; £432) **Stalls** Low

Form / RPR

061- 1 **Monsieur Chevalier (IRE)**[9] 7894 7-9-5 82 ........................(p) AdamKirby 4 85+
(Jamie Osborne) *chsd ldr: effrt to chal over 1f out: rdn to ld 1f out: forged ahd fnl 100yds: styd on* **4/9**[1]

002- 2 1 1/4 **Doc Hay (USA)**[11] 7847 7-9-1 85 ........................................ ThomasBrown(3) 5 81
(Lee Carter) *t.k.h: led: rdn wl over 1f out: hdd 1f out: no ex and btn fnl 100yds* **2/1**[2]

500- 3 3/4 **Schottische**[44] 7288 4-8-2 57 ........................................(v) JimmyQuinn 2 63
(Derek Haydn Jones) *a 3rd: rdn 2f out: outpcd over 1f out: rallied and kpt on ins fnl f* **33/1**[3]

1m 25.26s (-0.74) **Going Correction** -0.10s/f (Stan) **3** Ran SP% **105.5**
Speed ratings (Par 103): **100,98,97**
CSF £1.55 TOTE £1.50; EX 1.40 Trifecta £1.60.
**Owner** J A Osborne **Bred** Tally-Ho Stud **Trained** Upper Lambourn, Berks

**FOCUS**
A small-field claimer and form not to get too carried away with, with the third limiting the level. The winner and second were formerly useful and are still a bit better than this, though it's not easy to pin down quite by how much.

## 7984 FOLLOW @BETVICTORRACING ON TWITTER NURSERY H'CAP — 7f (P)
**3:20** (3:21) (Class 5) (0-75,74) 2-Y-O — **£3,234** (£962; £481; £240) **Stalls** Low

Form / RPR

031- 1 **Biting Bullets (USA)**[17] 7779 2-9-7 74 ........................................ MartinDwyer 4 83+
(Jo Hughes) *t.k.h: hld up in tch: pushed along and clsd over 1f out: led 1f out: sn clr and r.o wl: readily* **11/10**[1]

121- 2 4 **Chetan**[11] 7848 2-8-12 65 ........................................ LiamKeniry 2 63
(Milton Bradley) *led: rdn 2f out: hdd 1f out: no ch w wnr but hld on for 2nd fnl f* **4/1**[2]

141- 3 nse **Mecado (IRE)**[76] 6422 2-9-2 72 ........................................ CamHardie(3) 1 72
(Richard Hannon) *chsd ldrs: rdn and effrt 2f out: nt clr run 1f out: rallied and battling for 2nd fnl f: kpt on: no ch w wnr* **4/1**[2]

535- 4 3 1/2 **Dark War (IRE)**[17] 7770 2-9-1 68 ........................................(b[1]) JimCrowley 3 56
(James Given) *chsd ldr: rdn to chal 2f out: awkward hd carriage and fnd little for press: wknd 1f out* **4/1**[2]

005- 5 17 **Invincible Zeb (IRE)**[25] 7685 2-8-9 62 ............ WilliamTwiston-Davies 5 5
(Ronald Harris) *t.k.h: hld up in tch: rdn wl over 2f out: sn struggling: lost tch 2f out* **33/1**[3]

1m 25.57s (-0.43) **Going Correction** -0.10s/f (Stan) **5** Ran SP% **110.6**
Speed ratings (Par 96): **98,93,93,89,69**
CSF £5.91 TOTE £2.00: £1.50, £2.30; EX 6.20 Trifecta £13.30.
**Owner** Merriebelle Irish Farm Limited **Bred** Daniel J Burke **Trained** Lambourn, Berks

**FOCUS**
A fair nursery in which the pace was steady.

## 7985 £25 FREE BET AT BETVICTOR.COM MAIDEN STKS (BOBIS RACE) — 1m (P)
**3:50** (3:54) (Class 4) 2-Y-O — **£4,075** (£1,212; £606; £303) **Stalls** Low

Form / RPR

2- 1 **Greatest Hits (USA)**[31] 7560 2-9-5 0 ........................................ RobertHavlin 4 83+
(John Gosden) *mde all: rdn and fnd ex over 1f out: r.o strly* **11/4**[2]

2- 2 2 **Pathway To Honour**[21] 7730 2-9-5 0 ........................................ AdamKirby 7 80+
(Charlie Appleby) *t.k.h: in tch in midfield: effrt and swtchd rt 2f out: chsd wnr over 1f out: r.o but a hld* **4/9**[1]

3 6 **Captain Koko** 2-9-5 0 ........................................ MartinHarley 2 65
(Marco Botti) *chsd ldr for 2f: 3rd and outpcd over 1f out: no ch w ldrs and one pce fnl f* **16/1**

4 2 1/2 **Sperrin (IRE)** 2-9-2 0 ........................................ CamHardie(3) 6 59
(Charlie Appleby) *chsd ldr after 2f: pushed along 1/2-way: rdn and unable qck over 2f out: no ch over 1f out: plugged on* **8/1**[3]

0- 5 nk **Goodby Inheritence**[40] 7371 2-9-5 0 ........................(t) GeorgeBaker 8 58
(Seamus Durack) *s.i.s: hld up in rr: shkn up 2f out: sn outpcd and btn: plugged on fnl f* **33/1**

6 4 **Angels Above (IRE)** 2-9-5 0 ........................................ PatCosgrave 5 49
(John Butler) *t.k.h: in tch in midfield: rdn 2f out: 4th and btn over 1f out: wknd fnl f* **66/1**

7 9 **Secret Fantasies** 2-9-0 0 ........................................ JimCrowley 1 23
(Paul Cole) *dwlt: rn green and pushed along on rr: lost tch over 2f out* **33/1**

1m 39.91s (0.11) **Going Correction** -0.10s/f (Stan) **7** Ran SP% **120.3**
Speed ratings (Par 98): **95,93,87,84,84 80,71**
CSF £4.60 TOTE £5.30: £1.90, £1.10; EX 5.30 Trifecta £18.90.
**Owner** HRH Princess Haya Of Jordan **Bred** Darley (KY) **Trained** Newmarket, Suffolk
■ Levelling was withdrawn. Price at time of withdrawal 16-1. Rule 4 does not apply.

**FOCUS**
Little depth to this maiden and the two market leaders pulled clear.

## 7986 BOOK CHRISTMAS FESTIVAL TICKETS NOW H'CAP (DIV I) — 1m (P)
**4:20** (4:24) (Class 6) (0-60,60) 3-Y-O+ — **£2,264** (£673; £336; £168) **Stalls** Low

Form / RPR

030- 1 **Dana's Present**[33] 7533 5-9-7 60 ........................................ PatCosgrave 6 69+
(George Baker) *t.k.h: chsd ldrs: pushed along to ld wl over 1f out: drvn ins fnl f: kpt on: drvn out* **1/1**[1]

050- 2 3/4 **Henry Grace (IRE)**[5] 7924 3-8-4 47 ........................(b[1]) CamHardie(3) 2 54
(Jimmy Fox) *in tch in midfield: hdwy u.p 1f out: styd on wl to go 2nd towards fin: nvr quite getting to wnr* **10/1**

050- 3 nk **Bloodsweatandtears**[27] 7633 6-9-6 59 ........................................ GeorgeBaker 9 66
(William Knight) *chsd ldr: rdn 2f out: unable qck over 1f out: rallied and styd on again ins fnl f: wnt 3rd last strides* **11/2**[2]

440- 4 nk **Eastward Ho**[66] 6715 6-8-7 51 ........................................ ShelleyBirkett(5) 11 57
(Sarah Humphrey) *led: rdn and hdd wl over 1f out: sltly outpcd over 1f out: rallied ins fnl f: kpt on but lost 2 pls towards fin* **20/1**

000- 5 2 1/2 **La Paiva (FR)**[5] 7924 3-8-1 46 oh1 ........................................ TimClark(5) 10 46
(Scott Dixon) *in tch in midfield on outer: rdn and unable qck 2f out: styd on same pce fnl f* **66/1**

060- 6 1 1/2 **Russian Ice**[11] 7853 6-9-3 56 ........................................(v[1]) AdamKirby 8 53
(Dean Ivory) *dwlt: hld up towards rr: hdwy over 2f out: rdn 2f out: no imp 1f out* **8/1**[3]

004- 7 nk **Little Indian**[11] 7854 4-9-4 57 ........................................ StevieDonohoe 5 53
(J R Jenkins) *towards rr: bhd and swtchd rt 2f out: hdwy u.p over 1f out: no imp ins fnl f* **8/1**[3]

005- 8 2 1/4 **Paradise Spectre**[11] 7853 7-9-6 59 ........................(p) LiamKeniry 1 50
(Zoe Davison) *in tch in midfield: rdn and no imp 2f out: wknd 1f out* **25/1**

/00- 9 3/4 **Crowning Star (IRE)**[11] 7854 5-9-1 54 ........................(t) JimCrowley 7 43
(Steve Woodman) *chsd ldrs: lost pl u.p over 1f out: btn whn hmpd 1f out: wknd* **16/1**

045- 10 1/2 **Skidby Mill (IRE)**[9] 7884 4-9-1 54 ........................................(v) LiamJones 4 42
(Laura Mongan) *dwlt: bustled along early: bhd: rdn and hdwy 2f out: wknd 1f out* **10/1**

610- 11 1/2 **Port Lairge**[16] 7813 4-9-3 56 ........................................(b) ChrisCatlin 3 43
(John Gallagher) *towards rr and bustled along early: hdwy u.p on inner 2f out: wknd over 1f out* **25/1**

1m 40.03s (0.23) **Going Correction** -0.10s/f (Stan)
**WFA** 3 from 4yo+ 1lb **11** Ran SP% **125.6**
Speed ratings (Par 101): **94,93,92,92,90 88,88,86,85,84 84**
CSF £12.96 CT £46.65 TOTE £2.40: £1.10, £3.60, £2.20; EX 14.70 Trifecta £86.70.
**Owner** Mrs C E S Baker **Bred** Newsells Park Stud **Trained** Manton, Wilts

**FOCUS**
A modest handicap in which the winner, off his lowest mark since he was a 3yo, landed a gamble in workmanlike fashion.

## 7987 BOOK CHRISTMAS FESTIVAL TICKETS NOW H'CAP (DIV II) 1m (P)
**4:50** (4:50) (Class 6) (0-60,59) 3-Y-O+ **£2,264** (£673; £336; £168) **Stalls** Low

Form RPR
400- **1** **Bosstime (IRE)**[18] 7765 4-9-4 56....(b[1]) RobertHavlin 7 66
(John Holt) *travelled strly: chsd ldrs: rdn to ld over 1f out: kpt on fnl f: rdn out* **12/1**
642- **2** 1 **Movie Magic**[12] 7844 3-8-8 47....(v) WilliamCarson 5 54
(John Bridger) *chsd ldr: rdn and chsd wnr over 1f out: kpt on but a hld fnl f* **10/1**
060- **3** 1 **Ambella (IRE)**[11] 7854 4-9-2 54....(v) StevieDonohoe 3 59
(Ian Williams) *hld up in rr: rdn and hdwy over 1f out: styd on ins fnl f: nt rch ldrs* **7/1[3]**
661- **4** 3/4 **Divine Rule (IRE)**[9] 7883 6-9-5 57....(p) LiamJones 1 60
(Laura Mongan) *hld up in last trio: rdn and hdwy 2f out: chsd ldrs and styd on same pce fnl f* **8/1**
612- **5** 1 **Dreaming Again**[11] 7853 4-8-10 51.... CamHardie(3) 10 52+
(Jimmy Fox) *midfield on outer: lost pl and bhd whn wd bnd 3f out: rallied and hdwy jst over 1f out: kpt on fnl f: no threat to ldrs* **11/4[1]**
220- **6** 1 1/4 **El Mirage (IRE)**[11] 7854 4-9-7 59....(p) JimCrowley 4 57
(Dean Ivory) *hld up in rr: effrt on inner 2f out: drvn and styd on same pce fnl f* **7/1[3]**
045- **7** 4 **Sebs Sensei (IRE)**[11] 7854 3-8-12 58....(b) HectorCrouch(7) 8 47
(Mark Hoad) *in tch in midfield: rdn and lost pl 3f out: n.d and plugged on same pce fnl 2f* **6/1[2]**
005- **8** 6 **Blackthorn Stick (IRE)**[21] 7735 5-9-7 59.... LiamKeniry 2 34
(John Butler) *dwlt: sn rcvrd to ld: rdn and hdd over 1f out: sn dropped out: fdd fnl f* **10/1**
306- **9** 1 **Jackpot**[11] 7854 4-8-7 45.... MartinDwyer 6 18
(Brendan Powell) *broke wl: sn settled bk to chse ldrs: rdn and struggling over 2f out: wknd over 1f out* **20/1**
6/0- **10** 1 **Ferngrove (USA)**[29] 6771 3-9-3 56....(t) MartinHarley 9 27
(Jonathan Portman) *chsd ldrs tl lost pl qckly 2f out: bhd fnl f* **12/1**

1m 39.04s (-0.76) **Going Correction** -0.10s/f (Stan)
**WFA** 3 from 4yo+ 1lb **10** Ran SP% **115.4**
Speed ratings (Par 101): **99,98,97,96,95 94,90,84,83,82**
CSF £124.46 CT £908.87 TOTE £17.50: £4.00, £3.60, £2.80; EX 163.90 Trifecta £3021.30.
**Owner** Planters (leicester) Limited **Bred** J K Dewberry **Trained** Peckleton, Leics
■ Stewards' Enquiry : Robert Havlin four-day ban: use of whip (15-18 December)

**FOCUS**
The second division of this modest handicap was run 0.99secs quicker than the first leg. The winner is rated back to his early Irish maiden form, with the runner-up confirming recent improvement.

## 7988 DOWNLOAD THE BETVICTOR APP NOW H'CAP 7f (P)
**5:20** (5:22) (Class 4) (0-85,84) 3-Y-O+ **£5,175** (£1,540; £769; £384) **Stalls** Low

Form RPR
060- **1** **Pretty Bubbles**[9] 7885 5-9-0 **77**.... PaddyAspell 7 84
(J R Jenkins) *hld up towards rr: hdwy whn nt clr run and hmpd over 1f out: str run ins fnl f to ld last strides* **50/1**
031- **2** nse **Ertikaan**[27] 7633 7-8-13 **76**.... JimCrowley 9 83
(Miss Joey Ellis) *dropped in bhd after s: hld up in tch in rr: rdn and hdwy 1f out: str run ins fnl f: wnt 2nd last strides: jst failed* **11/2[3]**
350- **3** hd **Light From Mars**[72] 6558 9-9-5 **82**....(p) WilliamTwiston-Davies 3 88
(Ronald Harris) *chsd ldrs: rdn to chse ldr 2f out: led over 1f out: kpt on u.p: hdd and lost 2 pls last strides* **33/1**
000- **4** hd **Dr Red Eye**[34] 7507 6-9-1 **78**....(p) DavidProbert 4 83
(Scott Dixon) *led: rdn 2f out: hdd over 1f out: battled and wl and ev ch after: no ex and lost 2 pls last strides* **10/1**
012- **5** 1/2 **Cool Bahamian (IRE)**[14] 7821 3-9-5 **82**....(b) JohnFahy 8 86
(Eve Johnson Houghton) *hld up in tch: clsd jst over 2f out: rdn to chse ldrs over 1f out: kpt on ins fnl f* **13/2**
/04- **6** 1 3/4 **Evening Attire**[31] 7564 3-9-4 **84**.... RyanTate(3) 6 84
(William Stone) *in tch in midfield on outer: rdn and effrt over 1f out: kpt on ins fnl f: no threat to ldrs* **16/1**
610- **7** 1 **Brigliadoro (IRE)**[30] 7601 3-9-4 **81**.... MartinHarley 10 78
(Philip McBride) *dropped in bhd after s: hld up in rr: hdwy on inner 2f out: no hdwy fnl f* **8/1**
041- **8** nse **Stonefield Flyer**[27] 7636 5-9-3 **80**....(p) GeorgeBaker 2 77
(Keith Dalgleish) *in tch in midfield: swtchd lft 2f out: pushed rt and hmpd over 1f out: np imp fnl f* **5/1[2]**
111- **9** 1 1/4 **Holiday Magic (IRE)**[21] 7729 3-9-7 **84**.... AdamKirby 5 78
(Charlie Appleby) *chsd ldrs: rdn and unable qck 2f out: btn 1f out: wknd ins fnl f* **5/4[1]**
250- **10** 3 3/4 **Piceno (IRE)**[34] 7507 6-8-8 **76**....(p) TimClark(5) 1 60
(Scott Dixon) *chsd ldr tl 2f out: sn lost pl u.p: bhd 1f out* **33/1**

1m 24.02s (-1.98) **Going Correction** -0.10s/f (Stan) **10** Ran SP% **123.8**
Speed ratings (Par 105): **107,106,106,106,105 103,102,102,101,97**
CSF £321.82 CT £9354.81 TOTE £24.50: £6.40, £1.80, £6.10; EX 443.20 Trifecta £4685.20.
**Owner** Mark Goldstein **Bred** Southill Stud **Trained** Royston, Herts

**FOCUS**
A useful and competitive handicap, in which the pace was strong, and the form should work out. The rating given to the winner is the highest she's earned away from Southwell.

## 7989 PLAY ROULETTE & BLACKJACK AT BETVICTOR.COM H'CAP 6f (P)
**5:50** (5:51) (Class 5) (0-70,70) 3-Y-O+ **£2,911** (£866; £432; £216) **Stalls** Low

Form RPR
444- **1** **Stellarta**[33] 7535 3-9-4 67.... DavidProbert 3 80+
(Michael Blanshard) *chsd ldrs: rdn to ld over 1f out: clr ins fnl f: r.o strly* **8/1[3]**
313- **2** 2 1/4 **Tychaios**[18] 7758 4-8-11 67.... AaronJones(7) 11 73+
(Stuart Williams) *in tch in midfield: swtchd lft and effrt wl over 1f out: hdwy 1f out: sn chsd clr wnr wl ins fnl f: r.o* **7/2[1]**
510- **3** 1 1/2 **Divine Call**[9] 7888 7-9-2 65....(v) LiamKeniry 8 66
(Milton Bradley) *in tch in last quartet: hdwy 2f out: rdn to chse ldrs 1f out: chsd clr wnr ins fnl f: no imp: lost 2nd wl ins fnl f* **16/1**
040- **4** 1 1/4 **Classic Pursuit**[7] 7905 3-9-5 68....(p) MartinHarley 2 65
(Ronald Harris) *chsd ldrs: rdn 2f out: drvn and unable qck over 1f out: wl hld and one pce fnl f* **7/2[1]**
200- **5** 1/2 **Noverre To Go (IRE)**[9] 7888 8-9-7 70....(p) WilliamTwiston-Davies 1 65
(Ronald Harris) *in tch in midfield: effrt towards inner 2f out: chsd ldrs but no ex over 1f out: styd on same pce fnl f* **7/1[2]**
301- **6** nse **Coiste Bodhar (IRE)**[41] 7355 3-9-4 67....(p) AdamKirby 10 62
(Scott Dixon) *taken down early: led: rdn and jnd over 1f out: sn hdd and no ex: wknd ins fnl f* **14/1**
010- **7** 3 1/2 **Half Way**[55] 7023 3-9-3 69.... ThomasBrown(3) 5 53
(Lee Carter) *dwlt: bhd: sme hdwy over 1f out: no imp fnl f* **8/1[3]**
113- **8** 1/2 **Pharoh Jake**[42] 7342 6-9-4 67.... WilliamCarson 9 49
(John Bridger) *t.k.h: chsd ldrs: rdn 2f out: sn struggling: wknd over 1f out* **20/1**
000- **9** 3/4 **Lady Phill**[17] 7776 4-9-4 67.... RobertHavlin 4 47
(Michael Attwater) *sn bustled up to chse ldr: rdn 2f out: lost 2nd over 1f out: wknd fnl f* **10/1**
020- **10** 3/4 **Another Try (IRE)**[5] 7931 9-9-2 70.... JordanVaughan(5) 6 48
(Timothy Jarvis) *in tch in midfield: rdn and unable qck 2f out: wknd over 1f out* **20/1**
330- **11** 1 1/4 **Rocket Rob (IRE)**[9] 7886 8-9-6 69.... ChrisCatlin 7 43
(Willie Musson) *a towards rr: n.d* **10/1**
000- **12** 1/2 **Sweet Talking Guy (IRE)**[5] 7931 4-9-4 70....(t) SimonPearce(3) 12 42
(Lydia Pearce) *hld up in last quartet: rdn and effrt wl over 1f out: no prog* **8/1[3]**

1m 11.16s (-1.94) **Going Correction** -0.10s/f (Stan) **12** Ran SP% **130.5**
Speed ratings (Par 103): **108,105,103,101,100 100,95,95,94,93 91,90**
CSF £39.92 CT £465.06 TOTE £8.90: £2.50, £1.60, £5.90; EX 45.70 Trifecta £575.50.
**Owner** Vincent Ward **Bred** Whitsbury Manor Stud & Pigeon House Stud **Trained** Upper Lambourn, Berks

**FOCUS**
A fair and competitive handicap, in which the pace was sound. The winner was quite impressive and the third has been rated to this year's Polytrack form.
T/Plt: £27.90 to a £1 stake. Pool: £61,108.52 - 1,593.25 winning tickets T/Qpdt: £18.00 to a £1 stake. Pool: £4,568.82 - 186.85 winning tickets SP

# 7970 WOLVERHAMPTON (A.W) (L-H)
Monday, December 1

**OFFICIAL GOING: Tapeta: standard**
Wind: Light against Weather: Overcast

## 7990 32RED CASINO H'CAP (FOR AMATEUR RIDERS) (TAPETA) 1m 5f 194y
**12:55** (12:56) (Class 6) (0-65,64) 3-Y-O+ **£2,027** (£628; £314; £157) **Stalls** Low

Form RPR
640- **1** **Indian Scout**[46] 7219 6-9-6 45....(b) MissJoannaMason(3) 4 53
(Anabel K Murphy) *mde all: rdn over 1f out: styd on wl* **20/1**
540- **2** 2 **Blue Valentino**[9] 7893 5-10-0 50.... MissSBrotherton 10 55
(Andrew Hollinshead) *hld up: hdwy over 2f out: r.o to go 2nd nr fin: nt rch wnr* **7/1**
000- **3** shd **Perennial**[14] 7822 5-10-7 64.... MrRossTurner(7) 3 69+
(Philip Kirby) *s.i.s: hld up: hdwy over 1f out: r.o: nrst fin* **20/1**
203- **4** 3/4 **Greeleys Love (USA)**[12] 7846 4-10-9 64.... MrJDoe(5) 6 68
(Luke Dace) *chsd wnr: rdn over 1f out: edgd lft and no ex wl ins fnl f* **11/4[1]**
**5** 3/4 **Toretto (IRE)**[37] 5455 6-10-2 57.... MrJPWilliams(5) 2 60
(Bernard Llewellyn) *prom: lost pl 9f out: hdwy over 1f out: styd on same pce ins fnl f* **6/1[3]**
R00- **6** 3 3/4 **Red Current**[26] 7657 10-9-2 45.... MissPBridgwater(7) 8 43
(Michael Scudamore) *plld hrd and prom: rdn over 2f out: wknd fnl f* **66/1**
300- **7** 3 **Josie's Dream (IRE)**[5] 7932 6-9-12 53 ow3.... MrJamesHughes(5) 5 46
(Jo Hughes) *hld up: hdwy 8f out: pushed along and lost pl over 3f out: n.d after* **16/1**
600- **8** 2 1/4 **Medieval Bishop (IRE)**[48] 7175 5-10-1 58.... MrTEley(7) 12 48
(Tony Forbes) *prom: rdn over 3f out: wknd over 2f out* **25/1**
246- **8** dht **Cabuchon (GER)**[5] 7932 7-10-0 57....(vt) MissKFBegley(7) 1 47
(David Evans) *plld hrd and prom: wknd over 2f out* **7/1**
550- **10** 3/4 **Candelita**[18] 6062 7-9-9 52.... MrStanSheppard(7) 13 41
(Matt Sheppard) *hld up: hdwy over 8f out: rdn over 2f out: wkng whn hmpd wl over 1f out* **16/1**
242- **11** 2 1/4 **Qibtee (FR)**[12] 7846 4-10-4 59....(b) MrAJAlonso(5) 11 45
(Les Eyre) *s.i.s: hld up: hdwy over 6f out: rdn and wknd wl over 1f out* **4/1[2]**
4/0- **12** 1 3/4 **Tram Express (FR)**[59] 6900 10-9-9 52....(t) MrJWailes(7) 9 36
(Shaun Lycett) *s.i.s: hld up: hdwy over 3f out: wknd over 2f out* **33/1**
000- **13** dist **Pepperello**[58] 6939 3-8-11 45.... MissMEdden(5) 7
(Tim Etherington) *plld hrd and prom: lost pl over 11f out: bhd fnl 8f* **125/1**

3m 7.75s (2.95) **Going Correction** -0.10s/f (Stan)
**WFA** 3 from 4yo+ 7lb **13** Ran SP% **116.3**
Speed ratings (Par 101): **87,85,85,85,84 82,81,79,79,79 78,77,**
CSF £142.62 CT £2842.80 TOTE £25.60: £4.70, £3.10, £6.10; EX 186.10 Trifecta £1901.40.
**Owner** Ridgeway Racing Club & Partner **Bred** Bearstone Stud Ltd **Trained** Wilmcote, Warwicks
■ Stewards' Enquiry : Miss Joanna Mason two-day ban: careless riding (TBC)
Miss K F Begley two-day ban: careless riding (TBC)

**FOCUS**
The winner got an easy time in front, but was on a good mark on his old Polytrack form. The second is rated close to his maiden levels, with the fourth fitting in.

## 7991 32REDPOKER.COM NURSERY H'CAP (TAPETA) (DIV I) 7f 32y
**1:25** (1:26) (Class 6) (0-60,60) 2-Y-O **£2,102** (£625; £312; £156) **Stalls** High

Form RPR
005- **1** **Lady Charlie**[55] 7014 2-8-13 52.... JoeFanning 2 57
(Jo Hughes) *broke wl: sn lost pl: hdwy over 2f out: led over 1f out: r.o: eased nr fin* **14/1**
536- **2** 1 1/2 **Clampdown**[104] 5525 2-9-5 58.... LukeMorris 5 58
(James Tate) *hld up: hdwy u.p 2f out: styd on to go 2nd nr fin: nt rch wnr* **5/1[3]**
645- **3** hd **Ya Halla (IRE)**[69] 6642 2-8-11 50.... JFEgan 1 50
(David Evans) *chsd ldrs: rdn over 1f out: styd on same pce ins fnl f* **7/2[2]**
033- **4** 4 **First Summer**[19] 7740 2-9-4 57....(p) RobertWinston 9 47+
(Shaun Harris) *prom: pushed along 3f out: carried wd and lost pl over 2f out: sn rdn: styd on same pce fnl f* **2/1[1]**
032- **5** 8 **Purple Surprise**[13] 7824 2-8-11 53.... DannyBrock(3) 3 23
(Andrew Reid) *sn led: hdd over 5f out: led again 1/2-way: rdn: edgd rt and hdd over 1f out: wknd and eased ins fnl f* **5/1[3]**
044- **6** 1 1/4 **Freeze The Secret (IRE)**[128] 4652 2-9-2 55....(p) AndrewElliott 10 22+
(David C Griffiths) *s.i.s: hdwy to ld over 5f out: hdd 1/2-way: rdn and hung rt over 2f out: hung lft and wknd over 1f out* **11/1**
006- **7** shd **Overstone Lass (IRE)**[35] 7487 2-8-1 45.... EoinWalsh(5) 4 12
(John Spearing) *sn outpcd* **66/1**

000- **8** *hd* **Misu Pete**[10] 7867 2-8-6 45 (v[1]) HayleyTurner 8 12
(Mark Usher) *chsd ldrs: rdn 3f out: wknd over 2f out* **33/1**

600- **9** *6* **Kidmeforever**[12] 7839 2-8-8 47 (p) TomEaves 6
(J S Moore) *hld up: rdn and wknd over 2f out* **25/1**

1m 28.59s (-0.21) **Going Correction** -0.10s/f (Stan) **9** Ran SP% **112.2**
Speed ratings (Par 94): **97,95,95,90,81 79,79,79,72**
CSF £78.79 CT £301.39 TOTE £8.10: £2.60, £2.20, £1.60; EX 50.50 Trifecta £359.10.
**Owner** Miss L Ormsby & J Hughes **Bred** D Curran **Trained** Lambourn, Berks

**FOCUS**
This was weak but it was won in good style by an improving sort.

## 7992 32REDPOKER.COM NURSERY H'CAP (TAPETA) (DIV II) 7f 32y
**1:55** (1:56) (Class 6) (0-60,60) 2-Y-O **£2,102** (£625; £312; £156) **Stalls** High

Form RPR

000- **1** **What Usain**[58] 6931 2-8-6 45 (v[1]) BarryMcHugh 8 51
(Geoffrey Oldroyd) *a.p: chsd ldr 2f out: sn rdn: r.o u.p to ld wl ins fnl f* **33/1**

005- **2** *1¾* **You Be Lucky (IRE)**[18] 7752 2-9-7 60 FergusSweeney 6 62
(Jo Crowley) *led: qcknd over 2f out: rdn and hdd wl ins fnl f* **7/2**[3]

343- **3** *hd* **Fast Scat (USA)**[7] 7904 2-9-2 55 (v) JFEgan 2 57
(David Evans) *plld hrd and prom: rdn over 2f out: styd on same pce ins fnl f* **3/1**[2]

000- **4** *nk* **Anniversarie**[66] 6700 2-8-6 48 ConnorBeasley[(3)] 7 49+
(John Norton) *hld up: rdn and r.o ins fnl f: nt rch ldrs* **66/1**

000- **5** *1* **Eagle Empire (IRE)**[19] 7739 2-8-12 58 JoshQuinn[(7)] 4 56+
(Richard Hannon) *s.i.s: hld up: hung lft and r.o ins fnl f: nt rch ldrs* **11/1**

000- **6** *nk* **Total Demolition (IRE)**[124] 4787 2-8-6 52 HectorCrouch[(7)] 1 50
(Olly Stevens) *hld up: hdwy and nt clr run over 1f out: swtchd rt: styd on same pce ins fnl f* **9/4**[1]

054- **7** *1¾* **Pafiya**[25] 7683 2-8-13 52 [1] GrahamGibbons 10 45
(Kristin Stubbs) *hld up in tch: rdn over 2f out: styng on same pce whne hmpd ins fnl f* **12/1**

400- **8** *hd* **Sheila Belle (IRE)**[14] 7816 2-8-6 45 (b[1]) LukeMorris 3 40
(J S Moore) *sn pushed along to chse ldr: rdn and lost 2nd over 2f out: styng on same pce whn nt clr run ins fnl f* **33/1**

601- **9** *1½* **Celestine Abbey**[7] 7904 2-9-3 56 6ex JackMitchell 9 45
(John Ryan) *chsd ldrs: rdn over 2f out: wkng whn n.m.r 1f out* **11/1**

000- **10** *hd* **Out Of Aces**[42] 7329 2-8-1 45 ShaneGray[(5)] 5 34
(Kevin Ryan) *mid-div: rdn over 2f out: wknd ins fnl f* **12/1**

1m 29.68s (0.88) **Going Correction** -0.10s/f (Stan) **10** Ran SP% **117.4**
Speed ratings (Par 94): **90,88,87,87,86 85,83,83,82,81**
CSF £145.86 CT £468.06 TOTE £20.50: £7.40, £2.10, £1.20; EX 285.40 Trifecta £1949.10.
**Owner** R C Bond **Bred** Bond Thoroughbred Corporation **Trained** Brawby, N Yorks

**FOCUS**
A lively betting heat and a suspicion that this was stronger than the first division.

## 7993 32RED.COM FILLIES' H'CAP (TAPETA) 7f 32y
**2:30** (2:31) (Class 5) (0-75,74) 3-Y-O+ **£2,911** (£866; £432; £216) **Stalls** High

Form RPR

022- **1** **Boogangoo (IRE)**[9] 7894 3-9-2 69 JoeFanning 3 78
(Grace Harris) *chsd ldr tl led over 2f out: rdn ins fnl f: styd on* **7/1**[3]

631- **2** *½* **Bint Dandy (IRE)**[31] 7575 3-9-4 74 ConnorBeasley[(3)] 8 81
(Chris Dwyer) *hld up: rdn over 1f out: r.o wl ins fnl f: nt quite rch wnr* **11/4**[2]

043- **3** *¾* **Diamond Blue**[24] 7698 6-8-11 64 TonyHamilton 4 69
(Richard Fahey) *hld up: rdn over 1f out: styd on u.p fnl f* **25/1**

350- **4** *shd* **Welsh Sunrise**[47] 7196 4-9-6 73 GrahamGibbons 6 77
(Stuart Williams) *hld up in tch: rdn and edgd lft over 1f out: styd on u.p* **16/1**

641- **5** *½* **Penny Garcia**[34] 7506 4-9-2 69 (p) DuranFentiman 5 72
(Tim Easterby) *chsd ldrs: rdn over 2f out: styd on same pce ins fnl f* **10/1**

012- **6** *nk* **Be Royale**[7] 7906 4-8-13 66 LukeMorris 1 68
(Michael Appleby) *prom: rdn to chse wnr over 1f out: no ex wl ins fnl f* **7/4**[1]

601- **7** *10* **Elusive Ellen (IRE)**[18] 7759 4-9-0 67 FergusSweeney 2 43
(Brendan Powell) *s.i.s: nt clr run over 2f out: rdn and wknd over 1f out* **20/1**

51- **8** *5* **Polly's Rose**[14] 7818 5-9-6 73 JasonHart 7 36
(Ian Semple) *led: rdn: edgd rt and hdd over 2f out: wknd fnl f* **15/2**

1m 27.17s (-1.63) **Going Correction** -0.10s/f (Stan) **8** Ran SP% **110.9**
Speed ratings (Par 100): **105,104,103,103,102 102,91,85**
CSF £24.95 CT £433.61 TOTE £6.90: £2.70, £1.60, £3.00; EX 27.40 Trifecta £611.60.
**Owner** Ronald Davies & Mrs Candida Davies **Bred** Marie & Mossy Fahy **Trained** Shirenewton, Monmouthshire

**FOCUS**
The winner seems better than ever, with the runner-up rated to form, the third to her recent best, and the fourth to her best since February peak.

## 7994 £32 FREE AT 32RED.COM NURSERY H'CAP (TAPETA) 1m 141y
**3:00** (3:01) (Class 6) (0-65,65) 2-Y-O **£2,102** (£625; £312; £156) **Stalls** Low

Form RPR

003- **1** **Splash Of Verve (IRE)**[16] 7810 2-8-10 57 JoeyHaynes[(3)] 7 63+
(Philip Kirby) *hld up: hdwy: nt clr run and swtchd rt over 1f out: led ins fnl f: r.o* **3/1**[2]

041- **2** *1¼* **More Drama (IRE)**[14] 7816 2-8-7 51 LukeMorris 8 52
(Sylvester Kirk) *a.p: rdn and ev ch ins fnl f: styd on same pce* **6/1**[3]

054- **3** *½* **As A Dream (IRE)**[18] 7762 2-9-4 62 RobertWinston 10 62
(Nikki Evans) *hld up: hmpd over 2f out: rdn: hung lft and r.o ins fnl f: nt rch ldrs* **50/1**

646- **4** *1¾* **Capsize**[19] 7739 2-9-5 63 (v[1]) JoeFanning 13 59
(Sir Michael Stoute) *chsd ldrs: rdn over 1f out: no ex ins fnl f* **11/4**[1]

005- **5** *¾* **Let Right Be Done**[17] 7779 2-9-4 62 GrahamGibbons 4 56
(Ed McMahon) *led: rdn over 1f out: hdd and no ex ins fnl f* **14/1**

000- **6** *½* **Lipstickandpowder (IRE)**[26] 7666 2-8-11 55 PaulMulrennan 5 48
(William Jarvis) *s.i.s: sn rcvrd into mid-div: hdwy over 2f out: rdn over 1f out: styd on same pce* **25/1**

000- **7** *½* **Tocororo (IRE)**[41] 7367 2-9-4 62 PhillipMakin 11 54
(Ed Dunlop) *hld up: r.o ins fnl f: nvr nrr* **8/1**

004- **8** *nk* **Smugglers Lane (IRE)**[14] 7815 2-8-4 48 ow3 JFEgan 12 39
(David Evans) *prom: chsd ldr 7f out: rdn and ev ch over 1f out: no ex ins fnl f* **10/1**

363- **9** *shd* **Simone On Time (IRE)**[12] 7839 2-9-4 62 RenatoSouza 3 53
(Sylvester Kirk) *hld up: rdn over 2f out: no ex ins fnl f* **12/1**

600- **10** *4* **Gumhrear (IRE)**[32] 7550 2-9-2 65 HarryPoulton[(5)] 2 47
(James Tate) *mid-div: hdwy 1/2-way: rdn on outer over 2f out: wknd over 1f out* **50/1**

306- **11** *1* **Yorkshire (IRE)**[40] 7378 2-9-3 61 BenCurtis 1 41
(Shaun Harris) *plld hrd: trckd ldr tl 7f out: remained handy: rdn over 1f out: wknd fnl f* **10/1**

006- **12** *4½* **Play Nicely**[46] 7228 2-9-7 65 GrahamLee 6 34
(James Given) *hld up: wknd over 2f out* **33/1**

000- **13** *hd* **Pisces**[12] 7832 2-8-1 52 RyanHolley[(7)] 9 21
(David Elsworth) *s.i.s and hmpd sn after s: a in rr* **66/1**

1m 50.19s (0.09) **Going Correction** -0.10s/f (Stan) **13** Ran SP% **121.8**
Speed ratings (Par 94): **95,93,93,91,91 90,90,90,89,86 85,81,81**
CSF £21.18 CT £766.50 TOTE £5.60: £2.20, £2.70, £9.40; EX 25.40 Trifecta £1278.40.
**Owner** The Splash Of Verve Partnership **Bred** J Donnelly **Trained** Middleham, N Yorks

**FOCUS**
Some disappointing horses on show.

## 7995 32RED H'CAP (TAPETA) 2m 119y
**3:30** (3:30) (Class 3) (0-95,87) 3-Y-O+ **£7,439** (£2,213; £1,106; £553) **Stalls** Low

Form RPR

160- **1** **Entihaa**[31] 7566 6-9-8 81 JoeFanning 3 92
(Alan Swinbank) *chsd ldr tl led over 2f out: rdn out* **8/1**

352- **2** *2¾* **Cousin Khee**[27] 7650 7-10-0 87 HayleyTurner 5 95
(Hughie Morrison) *a.p: rdn to chse ldr over 1f out: hung lft and styd on same pce ins fnl f* **7/1**

120- **3** *1¾* **Dame Lucy (IRE)**[31] 7565 4-9-9 82 LukeMorris 4 88
(Michael Appleby) *hld up: rdn over 3f out: hdwy u.p over 1f out: nt rch ldrs* **10/1**

612- **4** *1¾* **Mister Bob (GER)**[14] 7817 5-9-0 73 (p) GrahamLee 1 77
(James Bethell) *hld up: rdn over 3f out: hung lft and styd on ins fnl f: nvr on terms* **9/2**[3]

101- **5** *2¼* **Uncle Bernie (IRE)**[7] 7903 4-8-13 72 6ex RobertTart 6 73
(Andrew Hollinshead) *hld up: hdwy on outer over 2f out: rdn over 1f out: edgd lft and wknd ins fnl f* **2/1**[1]

023- **6** *1* **Hidden Justice (IRE)**[33] 7539 5-9-7 80 PhillipMakin 2 80
(John Quinn) *prom: rdn over 3f out: wknd ins fnl f* **6/1**

042- **7** *18* **Buckland (IRE)**[12] 7837 6-9-13 86 (t) PaulMulrennan 7 64
(Charlie Fellowes) *led: rdn and hdd over 2f out: wknd over 1f out* **7/2**[2]

3m 37.63s (-6.07) **Going Correction** -0.10s/f (Stan) **7** Ran SP% **120.7**
Speed ratings (Par 107): **110,108,107,107,106 105,97**
CSF £65.29 TOTE £11.50: £4.10, £5.10; EX 85.00 Trifecta £568.60.
**Owner** Elsa Crankshaw & G Allan **Bred** Wardall Bloodstock **Trained** Melsonby, N Yorks

**FOCUS**
The winner posted a small personal best on this AW debut.

## 7996 32RED ON THE APP STORE CLAIMING STKS (TAPETA) 1m 1f 103y
**4:05** (4:07) (Class 6) 2-Y-O **£2,264** (£673; £336; £168) **Stalls** Low

Form RPR

403- **1** **Auld Fyffee (IRE)**[9] 7880 2-8-0 54 LukeMorris 3 53
(John Ryan) *a.p: hmpd wl over 1f out: rdn to ld ins fnl f: styd on* **9/2**[3]

505- **2** *1* **Blue Burmese (IRE)**[62] 6842 2-8-0 51 (v[1]) HayleyTurner 5 49
(Mark Usher) *hld up: rdn: swtchd lft and r.o ins fnl f: nt rch wnr* **16/1**

544- **3** *hd* **Missandei**[12] 7834 2-8-7 62 DannyBrock[(3)] 4 59
(Marco Botti) *prom: chsd ldr over 6f out: rdn to ld over 2f out: hung rt wl over 1f out: hdd ins fnl f: styd on same pce* **11/8**[1]

300- **4** *2½* **Whisky Marmalade (IRE)**[14] 7816 2-9-0 57 SamJames 2 58
(David O'Meara) *led: hdd 8f out: chsd ldrs: rdn over 2f out: no ex ins fnl f* **25/1**

000- **5** *nse* **Beauchamp Ruby**[69] 6630 2-7-13 45 ow2 JoeyHaynes[(3)] 1 46
(Paul Fitzsimons) *hld up: hdwy and hmpd wl over 1f out: no ex ins fnl f* **50/1**

503- **6** *hd* **Politico**[14] 7816 2-8-6 53 NickyMackay 6 49
(John Gosden) *led 8f out: rdn and hdd over 2f out: hung rt wl over 1f out: no ex ins fnl f* **2/1**[2]

2m 2.32s (1.52) **Going Correction** -0.10s/f (Stan) **6** Ran SP% **105.3**
Speed ratings (Par 94): **89,88,87,85,85 85**
CSF £55.99 TOTE £4.10: £1.70, £5.00; EX 31.50 Trifecta £80.30.Auld Fyffee was claimed by Mr T. R. Gretton for £5,000. Politico was claimed by Mrs Marjorie Fife for £8,000.
**Owner** Fyffees **Bred** Tony McKiernan **Trained** Newmarket, Suffolk

**FOCUS**
This was desperately weak.

## 7997 £20 RISK-FREE BET AT UNIBET H'CAP (TAPETA) 5f 20y
**4:35** (4:36) (Class 6) (0-65,65) 3-Y-O+ **£2,264** (£673; £336; £168) **Stalls** Low

Form RPR

005- **1** **Shirley's Pride**[7] 7900 4-8-13 57 (tp) HayleyTurner 6 67
(Michael Appleby) *chsd ldrs: led over 1f out: shkn up and edgd lft ins fnl f: r.o* **3/1**[1]

314- **2** *1* **Your Gifted (IRE)**[7] 7900 7-8-9 58 (v) AlistairRawlinson[(5)] 2 64
(Lisa Williamson) *s.i.s: hdwy 1/2-way: rdn to chse wnr ins fnl f: edgd lft: r.o* **9/1**

000- **3** *nk* **Scatty Cat (IRE)**[13] 7826 4-9-1 59 (be) RobertWinston 12 64
(Daniel Mark Loughnane) *hld up: rdn and r.o ins fnl f: nrst fin* **12/1**

000- **4** *nk* **Lexington Rose**[16] 7806 3-9-7 65 (p) PaulMulrennan 5 69
(Bryan Smart) *a.p: chsd ldr over 3f out: rdn and ev ch over 1f out: styd on same pce ins fnl f* **16/1**

160- **5** *¾* **Louis Vee (IRE)**[7] 7900 6-9-2 60 (t) TomEaves 7 61
(Roy Brotherton) *hld up: r.o towards fin: nt rch ldrs* **33/1**

221- **6** *½* **Give Us A Belle (IRE)**[7] 7900 5-9-7 65 6ex (vt) LukeMorris 1 68+
(Christine Dunnett) *prom: rdn over 1f out: styng on same pce whn nt clr run ins fnl f* **11/2**[3]

004- **7** *nk* **Mr Mo Jo**[75] 6452 6-9-2 63 (b) ConnorBeasley[(3)] 3 61
(Les Eyre) *led early: chsd ldrs: rdn over 1f out: styd on same pce ins fnl f* **14/1**

102- **8** *1* **Bilash**[16] 7806 7-9-3 64 JackDuern[(3)] 8 59
(Andrew Hollinshead) *hld up: hdwy 1/2-way: rdn over 1f out: no ex ins fnl f* **10/3**[2]

000- **9** *½* **Walta (IRE)**[13] 7825 3-8-8 57 (bt) EoinWalsh[(5)] 13 50
(Roy Bowring) *dwlt: nvr on terms* **9/1**

600- **10** *¾* **Goadby**[28] 7621 3-9-2 60 GrahamGibbons 10 50
(John Holt) *sn led: rdn and hdd over 1f out: wknd ins fnl f* **11/1**

1m 1.15s (-0.75) **Going Correction** -0.10s/f (Stan) **10** Ran SP% **115.0**
Speed ratings (Par 101): **102,100,99,99,98 97,96,95,94,93**
CSF £30.14 CT £282.77 TOTE £4.20: £1.70, £2.80, £2.90; EX 36.60 Trifecta £187.10.
**Owner** M J Golding **Bred** Manor Farm Stud (rutland) **Trained** Danethorpe, Notts

**FOCUS**
The winner had been below form since her March reappearance but was down to a good mark and built on latest promise.
T/Jkpt: Not won. T/Plt: £4,199.50 to a £1 stake. Pool: £84,567.17 - 14.70 winning tickets T/Qpdt: £77.60 to a £1 stake. Pool: £9,549.40 - 90.96 winning tickets CR


The Form Book, Raceform Ltd, Newbury, RG14 5SJ

# 7990 WOLVERHAMPTON (A.W) (L-H)

Tuesday, December 2

**OFFICIAL GOING: Tapeta: standard**

Wind: Fresh against Weather: Cloudy

## 7998 DOWNLOAD THE CORAL APP AW "HANDS AND HEELS" APPRENTICE SERIES H'CAP (TAPETA) — 1m 1f 103y

**2:10** (2:10) (Class 5) (0-75,75) 3-Y-O+ **£2,911** (£866; £432; £216) **Stalls** Low

Form / RPR

1- **1** **Persona Grata**[53] 7074 3-8-9 70........................ CliffordLee(5) 1 82+
(Ed Walker) *led 1f: chsd ldrs: wnt 2nd over 1f out: shkn up to ld ins fnl f: r.o: readily* **2/1**[1]

311- **2** 3/4 **Elysian Prince**[29] 7630 3-9-4 74........................(t) GaryMahon 9 81
(Paul Cole) *chsd ldrs: wnt 2nd 4f out: led over 2f out: shkn up over 1f out: hdd ins fnl f: styd on* **4/1**[3]

635- **3** 3/4 **Lean On Pete (IRE)**[11] 7871 5-9-2 70........................ HectorCrouch 4 75
(Ollie Pears) *s.i.s: hld up: hdwy over 1f out: r.o: nt rch ldrs* **8/1**

564- **4** 3 1/4 **Evacusafe Lady**[6] 7918 3-8-11 67........................(t) CharlieBennett 6 66
(John Ryan) *hld up: pushed along and hdwy over 2f out: styd on same pce fnl f* **7/1**

130- **5** 2 1/4 **Oratorio's Joy (IRE)**[136] 4434 4-8-12 71........................ KirstenSmith(5) 5 65
(Jamie Osborne) *hld up: hdwy 5f out: styd on same pce fnl 2f* **14/1**

000- **6** 3 1/4 **Refreshestheparts (USA)**[13] 7831 5-8-12 71........................(t) AlfieDavies(5) 3 58
(George Baker) *prom tl wknd over 2f out* **25/1**

661- **7** 3 1/2 **Starfield**[14] 7829 5-9-7 75........................(v) RobHornby 8 55
(Michael Appleby) *w ldr: led over 4f out: pushed along and hdd over 2f out: wknd over 1f out* **11/4**[2]

156- **8** 4 1/2 **Tete Orange**[82] 6262 3-8-5 61........................[1] AaronJones 10 31
(Stuart Williams) *s.i.s: in rr: pushed along 1/2-way: wknd 3f out* **22/1**

650- **9** 9 **Haymarket**[46] 7251 5-8-4 61........................ MichaelKenneally(3) 2 12
(R Mike Smith) *led after 1f: hdd over 4f out: sn pushed along: wknd wl over 2f out* **33/1**

400- **10** 12 **Well Painted (IRE)**[19] 7757 5-8-12 71........................(t) PatrickVaughan(5) 7
(Andy Turnell) *s.s: hdwy 5f out: wknd wl over 2f out* **40/1**

1m 59.29s (-1.51) **Going Correction** -0.025s/f (Stan)
**WFA** 3 from 4yo+ 2lb **10** Ran SP% **123.9**
Speed ratings (Par 103): **105,104,103,100,98 95,92,88,80,70**
CSF £10.65 CT £57.22 TOTE £4.00: £1.40, £1.10, £1.90; EX 17.80 Trifecta £87.20.
**Owner** Middleham Park Racing XLI **Bred** Miss K Rausing **Trained** Newmarket, Suffolk

**FOCUS**
An ordinary apprentice handicap, but the pace was decent and it was won by the only unexposed runner in the field. The winner is rated 10lb up from her debut win, with the second in line with a better view of GB form, and the third in line with his form since break.

## 7999 32RED.COM (S) STKS (TAPETA) — 7f 32y

**2:40** (2:40) (Class 6) 2-Y-O **£2,102** (£625; £312; £156) **Stalls** High

Form / RPR

232- **1** **Red Perdita (IRE)**[28] 7631 2-8-7 69........................ MartinDwyer 3 62+
(George Baker) *trckd ldrs: shkn up to ld over 1f out: r.o: comf* **1/3**[1]

354- **2** 3 **Penelope Pitstop**[8] 7904 2-8-7 54........................ JoeFanning 2 52
(Keith Dalgleish) *disp ld tl wnt on over 4f out: rdn and hdd over 1f out: styd on same pce ins fnl f* **5/2**[2]

04- **3** 1/2 **Beau Sparkle (IRE)**[36] 7493 2-8-7 0........................ HayleyTurner 6 50
(Steph Hollinshead) *disp ld tl over 4f out: chsd ldr: rdn over 2f out: styd on same pce ins fnl f* **33/1**

0- **4** 4 **Edw Gold (IRE)**[14] 7828 2-8-12 0........................ GrahamGibbons 1 46
(David Evans) *s.i.s: hld up: rdn over 1f out: wknd fnl f* **28/1**[3]

0- **5** 33 **Snappy Mann**[141] 4260 2-8-12 0........................ ChrisCatlin 5
(Willie Musson) *s.i.s: in rr: pushed along 1/2-way: sn lost tch* **40/1**

1m 30.55s (1.75) **Going Correction** -0.025s/f (Stan) **5** Ran SP% **112.4**
Speed ratings (Par 94): **89,85,85,80,42**
CSF £1.48 TOTE £1.20: £1.10, £1.10; EX 1.50 Trifecta £4.50.Winner was bought in for 7,500gns.
**Owner** Andrew Li **Bred** Yeomanstown Stud **Trained** Manton, Wilts

**FOCUS**
A moderate and uncompetitive seller.

## 8000 32RED CASINO MEDIAN AUCTION MAIDEN STKS (TAPETA) — 7f 32y

**3:10** (3:12) (Class 6) 2-Y-O **£2,102** (£625; £312; £156) **Stalls** High

Form / RPR

6- **1** **Kaufmann**[19] 7752 2-9-5 0........................ RobertHavlin 12 79+
(John Gosden) *a.p: rdn to ld ins fnl f: r.o* **5/4**[1]

**2** 1/2 **The Dream Fast** 2-9-5 0........................ ChrisCatlin 6 78+
(Rae Guest) *s.i.s and hmpd sn after s: hld up: swtchd rt and hdwy over 1f out: sn rdn: r.o* **16/1**

423- **3** 4 **Spinaminnie (IRE)**[6] 7919 2-9-0 65........................ JoeFanning 1 63
(Mark Johnston) *led: rdn and hdd ins fnl f: no ex* **9/2**[2]

00- **4** nk **Minnie (IRE)**[32] 7573 2-9-0 0........................ StevieDonohoe 9 62
(Johnny Farrelly) *hld up: hdwy over 2f out: nt clr run ins fnl f: styd on same pce* **100/1**

433- **5** 3/4 **Vivre La Reve**[19] 7763 2-9-0 68........................ LukeMorris 3 60
(James Unett) *chsd ldr: rdn over 2f out: no ex ins fnl f* **10/1**[3]

246- **6** 1 1/4 **Bleu Astral (FR)**[32] 7573 2-9-5 76........................ TonyHamilton 2 62
(Richard Fahey) *prom: pushed along 1/2-way: wknd ins fnl f* **9/2**[2]

0- **7** nk **Thermal Column (IRE)**[11] 7867 2-9-5 0........................ GeorgeChaloner 11 64+
(Richard Fahey) *hld up: hdwy over 2f out: hmpd wl over 1f out: sn hung lft: no ex fnl f* **12/1**

0- **8** 2 **Gypsy Major**[109] 5386 2-9-5 0........................ GrahamLee 5 57
(Frederick Watson) *mid-div: lost pl 4f out: hdwy over 1f out: wknd fnl f* **200/1**

200- **9** 5 **Clever Love (FR)**[94] 5940 2-9-5 73........................ MartinDwyer 10 44
(Jo Hughes) *mid-div: hdwy to join ldrs over 4f out: rdn: hung lft and wknd over 1f out* **10/1**[3]

0- **10** nk **Strait Of Magellan (IRE)**[13] 7834 2-9-5 0........................ HayleyTurner 8 44
(Michael Bell) *s.i.s: a in rr* **33/1**

00- **11** 4 **Come Up And See Me**[55] 7037 2-9-5 0........................ PaddyAspell 4 34
(J R Jenkins) *chsd ldrs to 1/2-way* **200/1**

**12** 5 **Bold Grove** 2-9-0 0........................ EoinWalsh(5) 7 22
(Edward Bevan) *dwlt: hld up: plld hrd: wknd 1/2-way* **200/1**

1m 28.76s (-0.04) **Going Correction** -0.025s/f (Stan) **12** Ran SP% **118.0**
Speed ratings (Par 94): **99,98,93,93,92 91,90,88,82,82 77,72**
CSF £26.08 TOTE £2.70: £1.70, £5.50, £1.70; EX 29.10 Trifecta £183.70.
**Owner** Ms Rachel D S Hood **Bred** Rachel D S Hood **Trained** Newmarket, Suffolk

**FOCUS**
A modest maiden.

## 8001 32RED H'CAP (TAPETA) — 1m 5f 194y

**3:40** (3:41) (Class 4) (0-80,80) 3-Y-O+ **£4,851** (£1,443; £721; £360) **Stalls** Low

Form / RPR

213- **1** **Rowlestone Lass**[15] 7817 4-9-0 66........................ JoeFanning 4 76
(Richard Price) *a.p: chsd ldr over 2f out: led over 1f out: sn hung rt: comf* **9/1**

000- **2** 2 **Very Good Day (FR)**[11] 7870 7-9-11 77........................ TonyHamilton 8 83
(Richard Fahey) *hld up: rdn over 3f out: hdwy over 1f out: r.o: nt rch wnr* **9/2**[3]

320- **3** 1/2 **Sagesse**[138] 4351 4-9-12 78........................(p) LukeMorris 1 83
(Sir Mark Prescott Bt) *chsd ldrs: drvn over 2f out: edgd lft ins fnl f: styd on u.p* **16/1**

030/ **4** hd **Daghash**[178] 6537 5-9-4 75........................ KieranShoemark(5) 7 80
(Stuart Kittow) *hld up: rdn and hdwy over 2f out: r.o* **25/1**

322- **5** 4 1/2 **Sioux Chieftain (IRE)**[15] 7822 4-9-10 76........................ RobertWinston 3 75
(Michael Appleby) *trckd ldrs tl led 3f out: rdn and hdd over 1f out: wknd ins fnl f* **9/4**[1]

563- **6** 1/2 **Lineman**[11] 7866 4-9-4 70........................(p) ShaneKelly 6 68
(Andrew Hollinshead) *hld up: nt clr run over 2f out: sme hdwy over 1f out: nvr trbld ldrs* **8/1**

500- **7** 1 1/4 **Arashi**[15] 7817 8-9-0 66........................(v) PhillipMakin 9 62
(Derek Shaw) *hld up: rdn over 3f out: nvr on terms* **66/1**

244- **8** 15 **Arizona John (IRE)**[39] 7422 9-9-7 76........................ JoeyHaynes(3) 5 51
(John Mackie) *chsd ldr tl rdn over 3f out: wknd over 2f out* **25/1**

050- **9** 11 **Duchess Of Gazeley (IRE)**[32] 7565 4-10-0 80........................ SebSanders 2 40
(Dean Ivory) *led: rdn and hdd 3f out: wknd 2f out* **11/4**[2]

3m 1.92s (-2.88) **Going Correction** -0.025s/f (Stan) **9** Ran SP% **111.8**
Speed ratings (Par 105): **107,105,105,105,102 102,101,93,87**
CSF £46.71 CT £631.72 TOTE £5.70: £1.60, £1.90, £2.30; EX 45.70 Trifecta £253.60.
**Owner** Ocean's Five **Bred** G E Amey **Trained** Ullingswick, H'fords

**FOCUS**
A fair staying handicap, but they didn't go much of a pace. While not straightforward, this was another personal best from the winner.

## 8002 LADBROKES MAIDEN STKS (TAPETA) — 7f 32y

**4:10** (4:13) (Class 5) 3-Y-O+ **£2,911** (£866; £432; £216) **Stalls** High

Form / RPR

202- **1** **Yard Of Ale**[19] 7764 3-9-5 67........................ GrahamGibbons 2 66+
(Kristin Stubbs) *mde all: clr fr over 1f out: comf* **4/6**[1]

623- **2** 3 1/2 **Quaintrelle (IRE)**[69] 6661 3-9-0 65........................ LiamKeniry 6 49
(Ed Vaughan) *hld up in tch: chsd wnr 3f out: rdn over 1f out: styd on same pce* **6/4**[2]

605- **3** 3/4 **Patron Of Explores (USA)**[102] 5642 3-9-2 45........................(t) DeclanBates(3) 5 52
(Patrick Holmes) *a.p: rdn over 1f out: styd on same pce* **125/1**

325- **4** 1 **Llandanwg**[28] 7645 3-9-0 47........................(b[1]) PhillipMakin 7 44
(Bryan Smart) *chsd ldrs: rdn over 2f out: styd on same pce fr over 1f out* **14/1**[3]

**5** 5 **Zat Be Zat** 7-9-5 0........................ SteveDrowne 4 39
(Violet M Jordan) *s.i.s: hld up: nvr on terms* **100/1**

**6** 7 **The Fenland Man** 3-9-5 0........................ LiamJones 1 18
(James Unett) *s.s: a in rr: pushed along over 2f out: sn wknd* **33/1**

600- **7** 1 **Gifted Spirit**[45] 7285 4-9-0 45........................ ChrisCatlin 3 10
(Mark Brisbourne) *chsd wnr tl rdn 3f out: wknd 2f out* **150/1**

1m 29.14s (0.34) **Going Correction** -0.025s/f (Stan) **7** Ran SP% **112.0**
Speed ratings (Par 103): **97,93,92,91,85 77,76**
CSF £1.80 TOTE £2.00: £1.10, £1.40; EX 2.10 Trifecta £30.30.
**Owner** O J Williams **Bred** The Hon Mrs E J Wills **Trained** Norton, N Yorks

**FOCUS**
A moderate older-horse maiden and a two-horse race according to the market. The winner is not easy to pin down, with the proximity of the third and fourth suggesting he didn't need to improve.

## 8003 DOWNLOAD THE LADBROKES APP MEDIAN AUCTION MAIDEN STKS (TAPETA) — 1m 141y

**4:40** (4:40) (Class 6) 3-5-Y-O **£2,264** (£673; £336; £168) **Stalls** Low

Form / RPR

2- **1** **Rightway (IRE)**[6] 7921 3-9-5 76........................ LukeMorris 6 75
(Tony Carroll) *a.p: chsd ldr 7f out: shkn up to ld over 1f out: styd on* **4/9**[1]

2/4- **2** 1 1/2 **Miniskirt**[50] 7157 3-9-0 0........................ ChrisCatlin 5 67
(Rae Guest) *led: rdn and hdd over 1f out: styd on same pce ins fnl f* **9/4**[2]

**3** 3/4 **Laika**[27] 5-9-2 0........................ BenCurtis 3 65
(Brian Ellison) *s.i.s: hld up: hdwy 2f out: rdn over 1f out: kpt on: nt rch ldrs* **14/1**[3]

050- **4** 33 **Tilsworth Annalisa**[17] 7800 3-8-9 45........................ ShelleyBirkett(5) 1
(J R Jenkins) *chsd ldr tl 7f out: remained handy: rdn over 3f out: wknd 2f out* **80/1**

1m 49.39s (-0.71) **Going Correction** -0.025s/f (Stan)
**WFA** 3 from 5yo 2lb **4** Ran SP% **107.9**
Speed ratings (Par 101): **102,100,100,70**
CSF £1.68 TOTE £1.30; EX 1.60 Trifecta £2.20.
**Owner** B J Millen **Bred** M Valade **Trained** Cropthorne, Worcs

**FOCUS**
Another moderate maiden and basically another two-horse race. The winner is rated close to his Irish form.

## 8004 BET NOW WITH THE LADBROKES APP H'CAP (TAPETA) — 1m 141y

**5:10** (5:10) (Class 6) (0-55,55) 3-Y-O+ **£2,264** (£673; £336; £168) **Stalls** Low

Form / RPR

004- **1** **Lord Of The Storm**[3] 7976 6-8-11 50........................ RyanWhile(5) 3 62
(Bill Turner) *sn pushed along and prom: chsd ldr over 2f out: led over 1f out: rdn out* **10/1**

003- **2** 2 1/2 **Bowsers Bold**[12] 7854 3-9-5 55........................ ShaneKelly 10 61
(Marcus Tregoning) *hld up: rdn and r.o to go 2nd wl ins fnl f: no ch w wnr* **15/2**[3]

404- **3** 1 1/4 **Spokesperson (USA)**[69] 6670 6-8-12 46 oh1........................ GrahamLee 5 49
(Frederick Watson) *chsd ldr tl rdn over 2f out: styd on same pce ins fnl f* **20/1**

0/6- **4** 1 **Bryant Park (USA)**[97] 5832 5-8-13 47........................ PatCosgrave 6 48
(Jane Chapple-Hyam) *a.p: rdn over 1f out: styd on same pce ins fnl f* **16/1**

604- **5** 1/2 **Olney Lass**[10] 7884 7-8-9 46 oh1........................ SimonPearce(3) 11 46
(Lydia Pearce) *hld up: hdwy on outer over 2f out: rdn over 1f out: no ex ins fnl f* **28/1**

011- **6** *1* **Habeshia**[6] 7924 4-8-10 51 MichaelKenneally(7) 2 48+
(Michael Bell) *s.i.s: hld up: n.m.r over 6f out: nt clr run over 2f out: rdn over 1f out: nvr nrr* **7/4**[1]

/06- **7** *1 ¾* **Warden Bond**[17] 7813 6-9-7 55 (p) JoeFanning 9 48
(William Stone) *prom: forced to r wd for much of the trip: rdn over 2f out: hung lft and wknd fnl f* **11/2**[2]

060- **8** *nk* **Celestial Dawn**[54] 7057 5-8-12 46 RobertWinston 13 39
(John Weymes) *s.i.s: hld up: rdn over 1f out: nvr nrr* **40/1**

653- **9** *¾* **Focail Mear**[13] 7845 3-8-10 46 oh1 JackMitchell 4 37
(John Ryan) *led: rdn and hdd over 1f out: wknd ins fnl f* **8/1**

165- **10** *¾* **Ice Mayden**[28] 7646 3-9-0 53 ConnorBeasley(3) 7 42
(Bryan Smart) *hld up: rdn over 3f out: wknd over 1f out* **12/1**

650- **11** *2 ¼* **Classical Diva**[128] 4714 3-8-11 47 LukeMorris 12 31
(Michael Appleby) *hld up: rdn and wknd over 2f out* **9/1**

/00- **P** **Kopenhagen (IRE)**[14] 7826 3-8-12 48 ow1 (p) PhillipMakin 8
(Ed de Giles) *reluctant to s: eventually c out: p.u over 6f out* **40/1**

1m 49.66s (-0.44) **Going Correction** -0.025s/f (Stan)
**WFA** 3 from 4yo+ 2lb **12** Ran SP% **120.4**
Speed ratings (Par 101): **100,97,96,95,95 94,92,92,91,91 89,**
CSF £81.18 CT £1481.50 TOTE £14.90: £2.70, £2.70, £4.50; EX 92.60 Trifecta £1788.60.
**Owner** Mrs M S Teversham **Bred** Mrs Monica Teversham **Trained** Sigwells, Somerset

**FOCUS**
The winner is rated close to his old best.
T/Plt: £10.60 to a £1 stake. Pool: £73,471.22 - 5,038.34 winning tickets. T/Qpdt: £8.00 to a £1 stake. Pool: £6,212.79 - 570.01 winning tickets. CR

## 7437 DEAUVILLE (R-H)
### Tuesday, December 2
**OFFICIAL GOING: Polytrack: standard**

## 8005a PRIX DE PRECOLETTE (CONDITIONS) (3YO COLTS & GELDINGS) (POLYTRACK) 1m 4f 110y
**12:30** (12:00) 3-Y-O **£10,000** (£4,000; £3,000; £2,000; £1,000)

RPR

**1** **Vicquemare (FR)** 3-8-11 0 WilliamsSaraiva 12 72
(Alex Fracas, France) **83/10**

**2** *snk* **Arkadios (FR)** 3-8-11 0 YohannBourgois 7 72
(S Cerulis, France) **47/1**

**3** *¾* **Sir Medbury**[25] 3-8-11 0 CesarPasserat 14 71
(M Nigge, France) **56/10**

**4** *nse* **Tucano (IRE)**[24] 3-8-11 0 AnthonyCaramanolis 13 71
(N Clement, France) **17/5**[1]

**5** *3* **No Control (GER)**[68] 3-8-11 0 CyrilleStefan 11 66
(S Smrczek, Germany) **5/1**[3]

**6** *nse* **Maltot (FR)**[48] 3-8-11 0 EmmanuelEtienne 5 66
(S Gouyette, France) **234/10**

**7** *1 ¼* **Altaira**[176] 3-8-11 0 MlleZoePfeil 4 64
(Mme C Head-Maarek, France) **31/5**

**8** *2* **Coeur Dolois (IRE)**[18] 3-8-11 0 (b) MlleAlexandraBouvier 9 61
(A Bonin, France) **51/1**

**9** *1* **Sealed (USA)**[42] 7349 3-8-11 0 (b) NicolasBarzalona 10 59
(Gay Kelleway) *pressed ldr: pushed along bef st: rdn and lost pl over 1f out: sn no ex and btn: wknd fnl f* **37/10**[2]

**10** *snk* **Alforrocho (FR)**[156] 3-8-11 0 ThibaultSpeicher 2 59
(R Schoof, Belgium) **247/10**

**11** *6* **Queen's Hussar (GER)** 3-8-11 0 AntoineCoutier 3 49
(Frau C Brandstatter, Germany) **53/1**

**12** *8* **Goldenboy Delatour (FR)** 3-8-13 0 ow2 FrankPanicucci 6 39
(Marquise De Montaigu, France) **70/1**

**13** *1 ½* **Borneo (IRE)** 3-8-11 0 (b) RomainAuray 1 34
(Bruce Hellier, Germany) **40/1**

**14** *8* **Sydney Darnoult (FR)** 3-8-11 0 (p) ManuelZago 8 21
(B Recher, France) **99/1**

2m 40.78s (160.78) **14** Ran SP% **119.2**
WIN (incl. 1 euro stake): 9.30. PLACES: 3.30, 11.70, 2.50. DF: 200.70. SF: 358.40..
**Owner** Gerard Augustin-Normand **Bred** A Fracas & Franklin Finance S.A. **Trained** France

## 8006a PRIX LYPHARD (LISTED RACE) (3YO+) (POLYTRACK) 1m 1f 110y
**1:35** (1:35) 3-Y-O+ **£21,666** (£8,666; £6,500; £4,333; £2,166)

RPR

**1** **Vodkato (FR)**[32] 6-8-13 0 (b) TheoBachelot 14 104
(S Wattel, France) **42/10**[1]

**2** *1 ½* **Affaire Solitaire (IRE)**[33] 7559 4-9-0 0 ow1 ChristopheSoumillon 7 102
(P Khozian, France) **77/10**

**3** *1 ¼* **Bernay (IRE)**[32] 7619 3-8-11 0 AlexisBadel 1 99
(C Ferland, France) **58/10**[3]

**4** *hd* **La Banderilla (FR)**[24] 7717 4-8-9 0 CristianDemuro 12 94
(John Gosden) *bmpd and squeezed out s: hld up in rr: rdn and angled off rail 2f out: kpt on and wnt 4th post: nvr able to chal* **121/10**

**5** *hd* **Money Time (IRE)**[128] 4-8-9 0 AntoineWerle 3 93
(Henk Grewe, Germany) **52/1**

**6** *nk* **Szoff (GER)**[23] 7727 4-8-13 0 OlivierPeslier 8 97
(A Kleinkorres, Germany) **173/10**

**7** *dist* **King Rubi**[72] 3-8-11 0 EddyHardouin 5 97
(Frau Erika Mader, Germany) **53/1**

**7** *shd* **Simba (FR)**[32] 6-8-13 0 TonyPiccone 4 97
(C Lerner, France) **15/2**

**9** *snk* **Lady Wood (FR)**[18] 4-8-9 0 ThierryThulliez 16 91
(N Clement, France) **208/10**

**10** *hd* **Brindos**[90] 5-8-13 0 IoritzMendizabal 11 95
(G Arizkorreta Elosegui, Spain) **34/1**

**11** *nk* **Ciriaco (SPA)**[51] 4-8-13 0 VJanacek 13 95
(G Arizkorreta Elosegui, Spain) **269/10**

**12** *snk* **Zigzag (FR)**[185] 4-8-9 0 RonanThomas 15 91
(J E Hammond, France) **269/10**

**13** *1 ¼* **Cape Magic (IRE)**[37] 3-8-11 0 AntoineHamelin 10 93
(F-H Graffard, France) **30/1**

**14** *3* **Ocovango**[32] 4-8-13 0 MickaelBarzalona 2 86
(A Fabre, France) **11/2**[2]

**15** *2 ½* **Superplex (FR)**[13] 4-9-2 0 APietsch 6 84
(Waldemar Hickst, Germany) **114/10**

**16** *3 ½* **Honzik Chipera**[163] 3-8-11 0 FlavienPrat 9 75
(J-M Lefebvre, France) **26/1**

1m 54.91s (114.91)
**WFA** 3 from 4yo+ 2lb **16** Ran SP% **119.0**
WIN (incl. 1 euro stake): 5.20. PLACES: 2.10, 2.70, 2.30. DF: 24.80. SF: 41.90.
**Owner** Deauville Racing Club S A S **Bred** Haras D'Etreham & Vision Bloodstock Ltd **Trained** France

## 7982 KEMPTON (A.W) (R-H)
### Wednesday, December 3
**OFFICIAL GOING: Polytrack: standard**
Wind: Moderate, against Weather: Overcast, drizzly

## 8007 BETBRIGHT MOBILE APP/IRISH STALLION FARMS EBF MAIDEN FILLIES' STKS (BOBIS RACE) 6f (P)
**3:50** (3:51) (Class 4) 2-Y-O **£4,075** (£1,212; £606; £303) **Stalls** Low

Form RPR

4- **1** **Belvoir Diva**[198] 2380 2-9-0 0 TedDurcan 8 78+
(Chris Wall) *trckd ldrs: pushed along 2f out: clsd jst over 1f out: r.o to ld last 50yds: won gng away* **16/1**

**2** *1* **Time Check (USA)** 2-9-0 0 JamesDoyle 5 77+
(Saeed bin Suroor) *s.i.s and rn green early: hld up in 9th: gd prog on inner 2f out: led jst over 1f out: hung lft ins fnl f: hdd and outpcd last 50yds* **4/7**[1]

**3** *1 ¼* **Balayage (IRE)** 2-9-0 0 MartinHarley 7 72+
(Marco Botti) *dwlt: hld up in last: stl there over 2f out: gd prog over 1f out: pushed along and styd on fnl f to take 3rd last strides* **11/2**[2]

024- **4** *hd* **Dusty Blue**[7] 7920 2-9-0 0 LukeMorris 2 71
(Paul Cole) *trckd ldng pair: shkn up to ld briefly over 1f out: one pce fnl f* **10/1**

623- **5** *2* **Marilyn Mon**[18] 7808 2-9-0 68 MartinDwyer 11 65
(Jo Hughes) *racd on outer towards rr: shkn up and no prog over 2f out: sme hdwy over 1f out: kpt on same pce* **16/1**

3- **6** *½* **What Could She Be (IRE)**[25] 7712 2-9-0 0 JoeFanning 3 64
(Bryan Smart) *t.k.h early: in midfield: pushed along and cl enough over 1f out: shkn up fnl f: kpt on same pce: nvr involved* **8/1**[3]

654- **7** *¾* **Aevalon**[139] 4338 2-9-0 64 JimCrowley 4 61
(Eve Johnson Houghton) *mde most to over 2f out: steadily wknd over 1f out* **25/1**

033- **8** *¾* **Pacolita (IRE)**[20] 7752 2-9-0 68 LiamKeniry 6 59
(Sylvester Kirk) *w ldr: led over 2f out to over 1f out: wknd* **14/1**

000- **9** *7* **Exceedwell**[14] 7832 2-9-0 56 JackMitchell 10 38
(John Ryan) *chsd ldrs on outer: rdn over 2f out: wknd qckly over 1f out* **100/1**

0- **10** *5* **Lady Antonios (IRE)**[18] 7808 2-8-7 0 ThomasHemsley(7) 9 23
(Chris Dwyer) *plld hrd early: hld up in midfield: wknd qckly 2f out* **100/1**

1m 12.59s (-0.51) **Going Correction** -0.075s/f (Stan) **10** Ran SP% **123.5**
Speed ratings (Par 95): **100,98,97,96,94 93,92,91,82,75**
CSF £27.16 TOTE £22.80: £5.60, £1.10, £1.60; EX 59.00 Trifecta £338.90.
**Owner** Mrs Barry Green & Partners **Bred** Jeremy Green And Sons **Trained** Newmarket, Suffolk

**FOCUS**
This is just modest form.

## 8008 BETBRIGHT MONEYBACK OFFERS MAIDEN STKS 6f (P)
**4:20** (4:21) (Class 5) 3-Y-O+ **£2,911** (£866; £432; £216) **Stalls** Low

Form RPR

332- **1** **Silver Mirage**[12] 7865 3-9-0 63 AdamKirby 2 57
(Michael Bell) *fast away: mde all: drvn over 1f out: clr fnl f: unchal* **4/6**[1]

006- **2** *3 ¾* **Island Express (IRE)**[21] 7737 7-9-0 46 (bt) AnnStokell(5) 6 50
(Ann Stokell) *trckd ldng pair: shkn up 2f out: tk 2nd ins fnl f: kpt on but no imp on wnr* **20/1**

432- **3** *1 ½* **Two Smart (IRE)**[7] 7929 3-9-0 68 (b[1]) LukeMorris 8 40
(Daniel Kubler) *chsd wnr: rdn 1/2-way: lost 2nd over 2f out: wl btn 4th over 1f out: plugged on to take 3rd last stride* **7/4**[2]

556- **4** *shd* **Forceful Beacon**[42] 7376 4-9-0 40 [1] GeorgeDowning(5) 5 45
(Tony Carroll) *trckd ldng pair: chsd wnr over 2f out: no imp: lost 2nd and fdd ins fnl f* **11/1**[3]

00- **5** *4* **Bold Max**[34] 7548 3-9-5 42 (b) JohnFahy 3 32
(Zoe Davison) *a in 5th and nvr on terms w ldrs: rdn and no imp over 1f out* **33/1**

050- **6** *3 ¾* **Spider Bay**[106] 5518 5-9-0 41 (e[1]) HayleyTurner 7 15
(Lydia Richards) *a in 6th and wl off the pce: rdn and no prog wl over 1f out* **20/1**

6/0- **7** *3* **Queen Cee**[130] 4677 3-9-0 0 LiamJones 9 5
(Simon Hodgson) *s.i.s: wl off the pce in 7th: rdn and hd high over 2f out: no prog* **25/1**

0S6- **8** *1 ¼* **Farmshop Boy**[18] 7800 3-8-12 0 CharlieBennett(7) 4 6
(Natalie Lloyd-Beavis) *bdly outpcd in last pair: a wl bhd* **50/1**

**9** *7* **Plain Striking** 5-8-11 0 MatthewCosham(3) 1
(Dr Jeremy Naylor) *dwlt: v green and bdly outpcd: a wl bhd in last* **50/1**

1m 12.75s (-0.35) **Going Correction** -0.075s/f (Stan) **9** Ran SP% **124.9**
Speed ratings (Par 103): **99,94,92,91,86 81,77,75,66**
CSF £23.42 TOTE £1.60: £1.10, £4.50, £1.10; EX 30.80 Trifecta £55.70.
**Owner** The Queen **Bred** The Queen **Trained** Newmarket, Suffolk

**FOCUS**
This lot had raced 94 times between them without winning.

## 8009 BETBRIGHT.COM NURSERY H'CAP 1m (P)
**4:50** (4:51) (Class 5) (0-75,73) 2-Y-O **£3,234** (£962; £481; £240) **Stalls** Low

Form RPR

202- **1** **Thanksgiving Day (IRE)**[18] 7810 2-9-4 70 JamieSpencer 2 76
(Jamie Osborne) *mde all: kicked on jst over 2f out: drvn and pressed wl ins fnl f: kpt on wl* **5/2**[1]

014- **2** *¾* **Prince Of Paris**[18] 7798 2-9-5 71 RobertHavlin 7 75
(Roger Ingram) *hld up and sn in last pair: rdn and prog fr 2f out: tk 2nd ins fnl f and clsd on wnr: no imp last 50yds* **12/1**

162- **3** *3* **Barchan (USA)**[11] 7890 2-9-7 73 (t) AdamKirby 5 70
(Charlie Appleby) *dwlt: settled towards rr: prog over 2f out: rdn to chse wnr wl over 1f out: no imp: lost 2nd ins fnl f: fdd* **3/1**[2]

505- **4** *shd* **Justice First**[23] 7730 2-9-2 68 JoeFanning 3 65
(Ed Dunlop) *trckd ldrs: pushed along 3f out: nt qckn 2f out: n.d after but kpt on ins fnl f* **5/1**[3]

500- **5** *1* **Miss Minuty**[20] 7753 2-8-8 **60** LukeMorris 1 55
(Sir Mark Prescott Bt) *prom on inner: rdn to chse wnr briefly 2f out: one pce u.p over 1f out: fdd ins fnl f* **5/1**[3]

054- **6** *4* **Rum Swizzle**[14] 7835 2-8-11 **63** MartinHarley 8 49
(Harry Dunlop) *chsd wnr on outer after 1f: rdn 3f out: lost 2nd 2f out: wknd over 1f out* **16/1**

504- **7** *½* **Finton Friend (IRE)**[20] 7753 2-9-0 **66** (b) JimCrowley 6 50
(Charles Hills) *broke on terms but sn drifted bk to last: pushed along 1/2-way: rdn and no prog over 2f out* **10/1**

630- **8** *shd* **Simone On Time (IRE)**[2] 7994 2-8-10 **62** RenatoSouza 4 46
(Sylvester Kirk) *chsd wnr 1f: sn lost pl: pushed along towards rr over 3f out: struggling over 2f out* **33/1**

1m 38.66s (-1.14) **Going Correction** -0.075s/f (Stan) **8** Ran SP% **112.5**
Speed ratings (Par 96): **102,101,98,98,97 93,92,92**
CSF £32.20 CT £92.74 TOTE £3.90: £1.70, £3.80, £1.02; EX 33.90 Trifecta £105.20.
**Owner** Michael Buckley **Bred** John Burke **Trained** Upper Lambourn, Berks

**FOCUS**
An interesting, if low-grade nursery with a few of these looking capable of winning races at this level.

## 8010 BETBRIGHT CASINO H'CAP (DIV I) 1m 4f (P)
**5:20** (5:27) (Class 6) (0-55,55) 3-Y-O+ **£2,264** (£673; £336; £168) **Stalls** Centre

Form RPR

533- **1** **Thomas Blossom (IRE)**[7] 7932 4-9-0 48 (v) DavidProbert 10 59
(Patrick Chamings) *hld up in midfield: prog on outer over 3f out: clsd 2f out: rdn to ld jst over 1f out: styd on* **9/4**[1]

000- **2** *1¾* **Pahente**[11] 7895 6-8-12 46 (p) WilliamCarson 7 54
(Tony Carroll) *hld up in rr: trapped on inner over 3f out: rdn and prog over 2f out: kpt on fr over 1f out to take 2nd nr fin* **8/1**

350- **3** *nk* **Cappielow Park**[133] 4548 5-9-2 50 (p) AdamKirby 1 58
(Ali Stronge) *trckd ldrs: wnt 3rd 4f out: rdn to ld 2f out to jst over 1f out: one pce and lost 2nd nr fin* **12/1**

003- **4** *3½* **Born To Reign**[28] 7664 3-8-8 47 (v) JoeFanning 9 49
(Michael Bell) *t.k.h early: hld up in rr: pushed along over 3f out: tried to make prog over 2f out: kpt on to take 4th ins fnl f: n.d* **9/4**[1]

320- **5** *1¾* **Nellies Quest**[15] 7823 5-8-13 47 LukeMorris 6 46
(Michael Appleby) *chsd ldr: led 1/2-way: hdd u.p 2f out: steadily fdd* **6/1**[3]

665- **6** *nse* **Kingswinford (IRE)**[42] 7369 8-9-6 54 (p) PaddyAspell 8 53
(John Norton) *prom: chsd ldr 5f out to over 2f out: nt qckn u.p and lost pl over 1f out* **25/1**

/00- **7** *13* **Majnon Fajer (IRE)**[63] 6856 4-8-9 46 oh1 DannyBrock(3) 5 24
(Jane Chapple-Hyam) *prom: urged along bef 1/2-way: lost pl and btn fr 3f out* **50/1**

000- **8** *1½* **Charlies Mate**[14] 7844 3-8-7 46 oh1 MartinDwyer 3 22
(John Best) *s.s: rdn in last after 5f: nvr a factor* **66/1**

400- **9** *1* **Little Red Nell (IRE)**[210] 2069 5-8-12 46 oh1 LiamKeniry 12 20
(Martin Bosley) *in tch in midfield: pushed along over 3f out: no prog over 2f out: wknd* **66/1**

000- **10** *21* **Vexillum (IRE)**[29] 6817 5-9-1 49 (t) SteveDrowne 2
(Simon Hodgson) *wl in rr: rdn and dropped to last over 4f out: t.o* **50/1**

400- **11** *28* **Robin Hood (IRE)**[18] 7813 6-9-7 55 (b) JackMitchell 4
(Philip Mitchell) *led: rdn and hdd 1/2-way: dropped out rapidly 4f out: wl t.o* **9/2**[2]

2m 33.78s (-0.72) **Going Correction** -0.075s/f (Stan)
**WFA** 3 from 4yo+ 5lb **11** Ran SP% **123.6**
Speed ratings (Par 101): **99,97,97,95,94 94,85,84,83,69 51**
CSF £23.02 CT £186.70 TOTE £3.00: £1.10, £2.80, £2.30; EX 27.90 Trifecta £252.10.Awesome Rock was withdrawn. Price at time of withdrawal 25/1. Rule 4 does not apply.
**Owner** www.Select-Racing-Club.co.uk **Bred** Ecurie Des Monceaux **Trained** Baughurst, Hants

**FOCUS**
This has been rated slightly positively and could edge a bit higher.

## 8011 BETBRIGHT CASINO H'CAP (DIV II) 1m 4f (P)
**5:50** (5:56) (Class 6) (0-55,55) 3-Y-O+ **£2,264** (£673; £336; £168) **Stalls** Centre

Form RPR

00- **1** **Gios Last (GER)**[117] 5145 4-8-12 46 oh1 JoeFanning 8 54
(Keith Dalgleish) *trckd ldr at mod pce: led wl over 1f out: pressed and rdn ins fnl f: styd on and on top at fin* **15/8**[1]

0/3- **2** *¾* **The Yank**[203] 68 5-8-13 47 WilliamCarson 10 54
(Tony Carroll) *stdd s: t.k.h: hld up in 7th off stdy pce: rdn over 2f out: prog over 1f out: tk 2nd jst ins fnl f: kpt on but readily hld* **9/1**

036- **3** *1¼* **Golly Miss Molly**[14] 7845 3-8-9 48 (b) LukeMorris 5 53
(Jeremy Gask) *stdd s: hld up in 9th: gd prog over 2f out to chse ldrs over 1f out: drvn and kpt on same pce fnl f: gd effrt fr off the pce* **12/1**

/43- **4** *½* **Emperor Ferdinand (IRE)**[34] 7541 3-8-12 51 MartinDwyer 9 55
(Marcus Tregoning) *trckd ldng trio: rdn over 2f out: nt qckn over 1f out: styd on same pce after* **8/1**

040- **5** *1¼* **Ballyfarsoon (IRE)**[50] 7188 3-8-8 47 (vp[1]) StevieDonohoe 6 49
(Ian Williams) *chsd ldrs in 6th: drvn over 2f out: sn bdly outpcd: kpt on again fnl f* **11/2**[2]

020- **6** *1¼* **Uganda Glory (USA)**[28] 7657 4-9-7 55 FergusSweeney 7 55
(George Baker) *led at mod pce: kicked on over 3f out: hdd wl over 1f out: wknd fnl f* **12/1**

250- **7** *1* **Key To Your Heart**[60] 6946 3-8-13 52 (t) JamieSpencer 4 51
(Michael Bell) *stdd s: hld up in last off mod pce: no ch fr 3f out: sme prog u.p over 1f out* **15/2**[3]

555- **8** *hd* **Perfect Outcome**[69] 6682 3-8-13 55 RyanTate(3) 1 53
(Patrick Chamings) *trckd ldng pair: wl plcd whn dash sed over 3f out: clsd and in tch 2f out: wknd over 1f out* **8/1**

040- **9** *2¼* **Sea Tiger**[19] 7785 4-9-4 52 LiamKeniry 3 47
(Chris Gordon) *chsd ldrs in 5th: drvn and tried to cl on inner 2f out: no hdwy over 1f out: eased last 75yds* **25/1**

350- **10** *2½* **Ice Apple**[61] 6900 6-8-12 46 oh1 JimmyQuinn 2 37
(John E Long) *hld up in 8th: rdn wl over 2f out: no prog and sn wknd* **25/1**

0/0- **11** *3¾* **El Libertador (USA)**[315] 283 8-8-11 48 (b) JoeyHaynes(3) 11 33
(Eric Wheeler) *hld up in 10th: poorly plcd whn dash sed over 3f out: no prog* **33/1**

2m 38.92s (4.42) **Going Correction** -0.075s/f (Stan)
**WFA** 3 from 4yo+ 5lb **11** Ran SP% **120.2**
Speed ratings (Par 101): **82,81,80,80,79 78,78,77,76,74 72**
CSF £19.69 CT £166.51 TOTE £3.90: £1.70, £2.90, £3.20; EX 27.10 Trifecta £205.50.
**Owner** Straightline Construction Ltd **Bred** Dierk Finke **Trained** Carluke, S Lanarks

**FOCUS**
This was fully five seconds slower than the first division, so form to be wary of.

## 8012 BETBRIGHT BEST ODDS GUARANTEED H'CAP (LONDON MIDDLE DISTANCE SERIES QUALIFIER) 1m 3f (P)
**6:20** (6:23) (Class 3) (0-95,95) 3-Y-O+
**£7,158** (£2,143; £1,071; £535; £267; £134) **Stalls** Low

Form RPR

025- **1** **Bancnuanaheireann (IRE)**[18] 7803 7-9-7 **95** RyanTate(3) 2 104
(Michael Appleby) *hld up in 5th: dropped to last 5f out: prog over 2f out: drvn to chse ldr 1f out: styd on wl and edgd ahd last 50yds* **15/8**[2]

314- **2** *shd* **Anglophile**[157] 3758 3-9-1 **90** AdamKirby 4 99
(Charlie Appleby) *hld up in 4th: prog over 2f out: led wl over 1f out and sn rdn: kpt on wl but narrowly hdd last 50yds* **1/1**[1]

400- **3** *1¾* **Kings Bayonet**[25] 7718 7-9-0 **85** HayleyTurner 5 91
(Alan King) *stdd s: hld up and last tl 5f out: clsd qckly 3f out: led over 2f out gng strly but sn pressed: hdd wl over 1f out: kpt on but lost 2nd fnl f* **13/2**[3]

105- **4** *11* **Starwatch**[39] 7449 7-9-3 **88** (v) WilliamCarson 6 74
(John Bridger) *led: stdd pce after 3f tl pressed after 5f and forced to qckn: hdd and btn over 2f out: wknd and edgd lft over 1f out* **20/1**

560- **5** *½* **Stand To Reason (IRE)**[13] 7850 6-8-11 **82** ..(p) WilliamTwiston-Davies 1 67
(Tony Carroll) *trckd ldr 5f: cl up after tl hung lft and wknd over 2f out* **25/1**

500- **6** *14* **Top Diktat**[13] 7850 6-9-1 **86** ShaneKelly 3 46
(Gary Moore) *trckd ldng pair: moved up to chal 6f out: wknd over 2f out: t.o* **25/1**

2m 19.12s (-2.78) **Going Correction** -0.075s/f (Stan)
**WFA** 3 from 6yo+ 4lb **6** Ran SP% **110.6**
Speed ratings (Par 107): **107,106,105,97,97 87**
CSF £3.93 TOTE £3.00: £1.40, £1.10; EX 4.80 Trifecta £10.70.
**Owner** Dallas Racing **Bred** J S Bolger **Trained** Danethorpe, Notts

**FOCUS**
Only three of these counted and the winner and second are rated to form, with the third only a bit off his turf level.

## 8013 BETBRIGHT.COM DOWNLOAD OUR APP H'CAP 7f (P)
**6:50** (6:51) (Class 6) (0-60,66) 3-Y-O+ **£2,264** (£673; £336; £168) **Stalls** Low

Form RPR

651- **1** **Baltic Prince (IRE)**[4] 7972 4-9-5 58 6ex RaulDaSilva 2 71
(Tony Carroll) *mde all: pressed and drvn over 2f out: sn drew clr: in n.d over 1f out: pushed out fnl f* **15/8**[1]

066- **2** *4* **Indus Valley (IRE)**[11] 7883 7-9-3 56 BenCurtis 3 59
(Des Donovan) *awkward s: t.k.h in midfield: rdn over 2f out: prog over 1f out: kpt on to take 2nd nr fin* **20/1**

122- **3** *1* **Major Muscari (IRE)**[11] 7884 6-9-7 60 (p) WilliamTwiston-Davies 8 60
(Shaun Harris) *hld up in rr: rdn over 2f out: prog wl over 1f out: kpt on u.p to take 3rd nr fin* **9/2**[3]

035- **4** *½* **Applejack Lad**[11] 7883 3-9-7 60 (bt[1]) AdamKirby 11 59
(John Ryan) *chsd wnr: tried to chal over 2f out: sn btn off: lost 2nd wl ins fnl f* **15/2**

300- **5** *hd* **Happydoingnothing**[121] 4970 3-9-3 56 LukeMorris 4 55
(Christine Dunnett) *chsd ldrs: rdn over 2f out: kpt on to press for 2nd 1f out: no ex* **33/1**

301- **6** *¾* **Dana's Present**[2] 7986 5-9-13 66 6ex LiamKeniry 12 63
(George Baker) *dwlt: t.k.h: hld up wl in rr: shkn up over 2f out: no prog tl kpt on fr over 1f out: n.d* **11/4**[2]

006- **7** *1* **Morna's Glory**[63] 6862 5-8-2 46 oh1 ShelleyBirkett(5) 7 40
(Sarah Humphrey) *towards rr: shkn up over 2f out: modest hdwy over 1f out: n.d* **100/1**

566- **8** *¾* **Black Truffle (FR)**[11] 7884 4-8-4 50 (e) CharlotteJenner(7) 1 42
(Mark Usher) *prom: rdn over 2f out: fdd jst over 1f out* **25/1**

000/ **9** *¾* **Ioannou**[350] 8329 5-9-0 55 StevieDonohoe 10 43
(Ian Williams) *towards rr on outer: shkn up over 2f out: no prog over 1f out: one pce* **20/1**

6/0- **10** *½* **Malih**[13] 7853 5-8-13 55 JoeyHaynes(3) 9 44
(Eric Wheeler) *chsd ldrs: rdn over 2f out: no prog and struggling sn after: wknd jst over 1f out* **33/1**

006- **11** *1¼* **Plover**[14] 7842 4-9-7 60 RobertHavlin 13 46
(Michael Attwater) *hld up in last: shuffled along over 2f out: stl last whn hmpd and snatched up 1f out: nvr remotely involved* **12/1**

200- **12** *1¾* **Foxford**[14] 7842 3-9-7 60 DavidProbert 5 41
(Patrick Chamings) *stdd s: hld up towards rr: shkn up on inner 2f out: wknd qckly fnl f* **25/1**

1m 24.83s (-1.17) **Going Correction** -0.075s/f (Stan) **12** Ran SP% **123.2**
Speed ratings (Par 101): **103,98,97,96,96 95,94,93,92,92 90,88**
CSF £48.40 CT £163.41 TOTE £2.50: £1.10, £4.00, £2.50; EX 32.90 Trifecta £376.40.
**Owner** A Mills **Bred** William Pilkington **Trained** Cropthorne, Worcs

**FOCUS**
There's a case for rating this a little higher.

## 8014 AUNTIE VI MEMORIAL H'CAP 6f (P)
**7:20** (7:20) (Class 6) (0-60,58) 3-Y-O+ **£2,264** (£673; £336; £168) **Stalls** Low

Form RPR

032- **1** **New Rich**[11] 7887 4-9-5 58 (b) JohnFahy 11 67
(Eve Johnson Houghton) *awkward s: swtchd to inner fr wd draw and hld up in last trio: gd prog 2f out: rdn and r.o fnl f to ld last 50yds* **7/2**[2]

440- **2** *1* **Douneedahand**[43] 7364 3-8-10 56 GaryMahon(7) 2 62
(Seamus Mullins) *wl in tch: prog 2f out: clsd on ldr and led 150yds out: hdd and outpcd last 50yds* **16/1**

006- **3** *1* **Compton Prince**[11] 7887 5-9-5 58 (v) LukeMorris 8 61
(Milton Bradley) *prom: chsd clr ldr over 2f out: clsd over 1f out: kpt on but nt pce to chal fnl f* **10/1**

545- **4** *nk* **Catalinas Diamond (IRE)**[11] 7887 6-9-3 56 (t) SebSanders 3 58
(Pat Murphy) *hld up in rr: prog on inner fr 2f out: drvn and tried to cl on ldrs fnl f: kpt on same pce* **16/1**

551- **5** *¾* **Spowarticus**[12] 7864 5-9-2 55 (v) AdamKirby 6 54
(Scott Dixon) *blasted off in front and sn 4 l clr: drvn 2f out: hdd & wknd last 150yds* **5/2**[1]

044- **6** *1½* **Foie Gras**[12] 7864 4-9-2 58 ConnorBeasley(3) 1 53
(Chris Dwyer) *s.i.s: sn chsd ldrs: rdn 2f out: kpt on one pce and nvr able to threaten* **7/1**

606- **7** *2¾* **Indian Affair**[104] 5605 4-9-4 57 LiamKeniry 4 43
(Milton Bradley) *chsd clr ldr to over 2f out: wknd over 1f out* **16/1**

160- **8** *¾* **Spider Lily**[47] 7252 3-9-2 58 DeclanBates(3) 7 41
(Peter Makin) *a in rr: rdn and no prog over 2f out: n.d after* **33/1**

0/4- **9** 1 ½ **Hatta Stream (IRE)**[23] 7735 8-9-1 57 SimonPearce[(3)] 9 36
(Lydia Pearce) *prom in chsng gp tl rdn and lost pl wl over 1f out: fdd* **16/1**

020- **10** *hd* **Reginald Claude**[11] 7887 6-8-12 58 CharlotteJenner[(7)] 12 36
(Mark Usher) *hld up in last fr wd draw: detached over 2f out: nvr a factor* **25/1**

060- **11** *shd* **Swendab (IRE)**[23] 7735 6-8-12 58 (p) CiaranMckee[(7)] 10 36
(John O'Shea) *racd wd: chsd ldrs: lost grnd bnd 3f out: sn struggling: lost off-fore shoe* **33/1**

002- **12** ¾ **Time Medicean**[23] 7735 8-9-5 58 (bt[1]) RobertWinston 5 33
(Tony Carroll) *towards rr: shkn up 2f out: no imp over 1f out: wknd and eased last 100yds* **9/2[3]**

1m 12.1s (-1.00) **Going Correction** -0.075s/f (Stan) **12** Ran SP% **123.8**
Speed ratings (Par 101): **103,101,100,99,98 96,93,92,90,90 89,88**
CSF £60.37 CT £534.35 TOTE £3.70: £1.80, £5.70, £2.90; EX 81.30 Trifecta £1042.90.
**Owner** Eden Racing Club **Bred** Whitsbury Manor Stud And Mrs M E Slade **Trained** Blewbury, Oxon

**FOCUS**
A strong pace helped the winner overcome his wide draw (dropped out start) and he's rated close to his best, with the runner-up to form.
T/Plt: £6.40 to a £1 stake. Pool: £75,025.09 - 8,503.44 winning tickets T/Qpdt: £5.40 to a £1 stake. Pool: £7,754.74 - 1,053.12 winning tickets JN

## 7925 LINGFIELD (L-H)

Wednesday, December 3

**OFFICIAL GOING: Polytrack: standard**
Wind: light, half against Weather: dry, cloudy

### 8015 CORAL MOBILE "JUST THREE CLICKS TO BET" H'CAP 1m 4f (P)
**12:30** (12:30) (Class 4) (0-80,77) 3-Y-O+ **£4,690** (£1,395; £697; £348) **Stalls** Low

Form RPR

501- **1** **Mymatechris (IRE)**[43] 7350 3-9-3 75 DavidProbert 4 92
(Andrew Balding) *in tch in midfield: clsd to trck ldr over 2f out: led over 1f out: shkn up and readily qcknd clr 1f out: r.o wl: easily* **7/4[1]**

401- **2** 9 **All Talk N No Do (IRE)**[34] 7552 3-9-5 77 (tp) AdamKirby 2 80
(Seamus Durack) *led for 2f: chsd ldr tl 7f out: 3rd and rdn 2f out: kpt on to go 2nd fnl 100yds: no ch w wnr* **5/2[2]**

041- **3** *nk* **Censorius**[23] 7734 3-8-10 71 ThomasBrown[(3)] 8 74
(Lee Carter) *hld up in rr: shkn up over 2f out: hdwy on inner over 1f out: kpt on to go 3rd wl ins fnl f: no ch w wnr* **5/1[3]**

260- **4** ¾ **Investissement**[14] 7838 8-9-10 77 (p) AmirQuinn 3 78
(Lee Carter) *chsd ldrs: wnt 2nd 7f out tl rdn to ld over 2f out: clr w wnr and hdd 1f out: sn btn: plugged on same pce and lost 2 pls fnl 100yds* **12/1**

165- **5** *nk* **Mabdhool (IRE)**[41] 6143 3-9-2 74 JimCrowley 1 75
(Ali Stronge) *hld up in tch: clsd and nt clr run over 2f out: effrt and little rspnse wl over 1f out: no ch w wnr and one pce fnl f* **25/1**

426- **6** 8 **Westerly**[27] 7689 3-8-8 66 (t) LukeMorris 5 54
(Luke Dace) *in tch: rdn over 4f out: struggling and outpcd 2f out: wknd over 1f out* **20/1**

/41- **7** 1 ½ **Red Four**[26] 7343 4-9-4 71 (p) FergusSweeney 7 57
(George Baker) *chsd ldrs tl lost pl u.p 4f out: wknd 2f out* **16/1**

004- **8** 1 ¼ **Tizlove Regardless (USA)**[27] 7689 3-9-3 75 JoeFanning 6 59
(Mark Johnston) *led tl hdd and lost pl qckly over 2f out: bhd 1f out* **5/1[3]**

2m 30.96s (-2.04) **Going Correction** +0.025s/f (Slow)
**WFA** 3 from 4yo+ 5lb **8** Ran SP% **120.5**
Speed ratings (Par 105): **107,101,100,100,100 94,93,92**
CSF £6.71 CT £18.58 TOTE £2.40: £1.10, £1.30, £2.00; EX 8.30 Trifecta £29.60.
**Owner** David Brownlow **Bred** Derrick Fisher **Trained** Kingsclere, Hants

**FOCUS**
The pace was honest and the favourite finished clear of two last-time-out winners who have been rated close to form.

### 8016 32RED NURSERY H'CAP (BOBIS RACE) 1m 1y(P)
**1:00** (1:01) (Class 3) (0-95,80) 2-Y-O **£6,469** (£1,925; £962; £481) **Stalls** High

Form RPR

501- **1** **Greatest Journey**[9] 7902 2-8-8 69 6ex AlistairRawlinson[(5)] 2 79+
(Saeed bin Suroor) *hld up in tch: clsd on outer 3f out: pressed ldr 2f out: rdn to ld 1f out: sn in command and r.o wl: comf* **7/4[2]**

311- **2** 3 **Biting Bullets (USA)**[2] 7984 2-9-10 80 6ex MartinDwyer 3 83
(Jo Hughes) *hld up in tch: effrt in 3rd 2f out: drvn over 1f out: chsd clr wnr ins fnl f: r.o but no imp* **6/4[1]**

021- **3** 3 **Marmalad (IRE)**[14] 7839 2-9-7 77 JimCrowley 6 73
(Tom Dascombe) *led: rdn wl over 1f out: hdd 1f out: sn btn: lost 2nd and wknd ins fnl f* **7/2[3]**

313- **4** 6 **Mywayalways (IRE)**[32] 7595 2-9-5 75 AdamKirby 1 56
(David Evans) *chsd ldrs: rdn over 4f out: lost pl wl over 2f out: no ch fnl 2f* **16/1**

032- **5** ¾ **Perfect Orange**[20] 7756 2-8-13 74 ShaneGray[(5)] 4 53
(Marcus Tregoning) *chsd ldr tl led 5f out: rdn and hdd jst over 2f out: sn struggling: wknd over 1f out* **14/1**

1m 37.62s (-0.58) **Going Correction** +0.025s/f (Slow) **5** Ran SP% **111.1**
Speed ratings (Par 100): **103,100,97,91,90**
CSF £4.83 TOTE £2.30: £1.70, £1.30; EX 4.90 Trifecta £10.00.
**Owner** Godolphin **Bred** Meon Valley Stud **Trained** Newmarket, Suffolk

**FOCUS**
Good prize money for what effectively turned out to be a 0-80. The pace was good and the form looks reliable.

### 8017 DOWNLOAD THE LADBROKES APP H'CAP 7f 1y(P)
**1:30** (1:30) (Class 5) (0-70,72) 3-Y-O+ **£2,587** (£770; £384; £192) **Stalls** Low

Form RPR

031- **1** **Don't Be**[9] 7905 4-9-9 72 6ex LukeMorris 7 84
(Sir Mark Prescott Bt) *hld up in tch: hdwy u.p jst over 1f out: str run ins fnl f to ld fnl 75yds: gng away at fin* **2/1[1]**

004- **2** 1 ¾ **Presumido (IRE)**[19] 7776 4-9-7 70 SebSanders 2 77
(Simon Dow) *in tch in midfield: nt clr run 2f out: swtchd rt over 1f out: qcknd u.p to ld 1f out: hdd and outpcd by wnr fnl 75yds: kpt on for clr 2nd* **7/1**

050- **3** 1 ¼ **Bobby Benton (IRE)**[28] 7672 3-9-3 66 TomQueally 6 70
(Luke Dace) *hld up in detached last: clsd and in tch over 2f out: hdwy jst over 1f out: styd on ins fnl f to go 3rd towards fin: no ch w wnr* **16/1**

064- **4** ½ **Al's Memory (IRE)**[9] 7905 5-9-3 66 AdamKirby 5 68
(David Evans) *chsd ldr: rdn to chal 2f out: led over 1f out: hdd 1f out: no ex and one pce ins fnl f* **7/2[3]**

000- **5** *nk* **Clement (IRE)**[29] 7636 4-8-9 65 CiaranMckee[(7)] 3 67
(John O'Shea) *hld up in tch: swtchd lft and effrt on inner over 1f out: styd on same pce u.p ins fnl f* **33/1**

360- **6** *hd* **Hipz (IRE)**[20] 7758 3-9-2 65 (p) JimCrowley 10 66
(Laura Mongan) *in tch in midfield: clsd to chse ldrs whn nt clr run and swtchd lft jst over 1f out: rdn and styd on same pce fnl f* **25/1**

210- **7** 1 ½ **Pour La Victoire (IRE)**[20] 7758 4-9-6 69 (b) DavidProbert 4 66
(Tony Carroll) *in tch in midfield: rdn and unable qck wl over 1f out: wknd jst ins fnl f* **3/1[2]**

644- **8** 3 ½ **For Ayman**[20] 7759 3-9-5 68 SteveDrowne 8 56
(Joseph Tuite) *in tch in last trio: clsd over 2f out: rdn and no imp on outer over 1f out: bhd fnl f* **14/1**

100- **9** 1 **Ostralegus**[14] 7842 4-9-0 63 (v) BenCurtis 11 49
(John Gallagher) *led and crossed to inner: rdn 2f out: hdd over 1f out: sn btn: wknd fnl f* **25/1**

1m 24.02s (-0.78) **Going Correction** +0.025s/f (Slow) **9** Ran SP% **116.2**
Speed ratings (Par 103): **105,103,101,101,100 100,98,94,93**
CSF £16.60 CT £176.16 TOTE £3.20: £1.20, £2.10, £3.10; EX 19.10 Trifecta £181.60.
**Owner** Mrs Olivia Hoare **Bred** P E Barrett **Trained** Newmarket, Suffolk

**FOCUS**
They went a good pace. The winner was entitled to be this good on French form, and the second has been rated to form.

### 8018 CORAL APP DOWNLOAD FROM THE APP STORE CONDITIONS STKS 1m 2f (P)
**2:00** (2:00) (Class 2) 3-Y-O+ **£11,827** (£3,541; £1,770; £885) **Stalls** Low

Form RPR

141- **1** **Complicit (IRE)**[33] 7619 3-9-1 101 LukeMorris 3 109
(Paul Cole) *hld up in tch: chsng ldrs whn short of room and swtchd lft 2f out: sn rdn and qcknd to ld over 1f out: clr fnl f: r.o strly* **3/1[3]**

150- **2** 3 **Tenor (IRE)**[14] 7836 4-9-7 110 (t) AdamKirby 4 106
(John Ryan) *chsd ldr: rdn and carried rt 2f out and dropped to last over 1f out: rallied fnl f to go 2nd towards fin: no ch w wnr* **11/4[2]**

104- **3** ¾ **Energia Davos (BRZ)**[18] 7803 6-9-4 105 MartinHarley 2 102
(Marco Botti) *in tch: rdn and hdwy on outer to press ldr over 2f out: ev ch over 1f out: sn outpcd by wnr and btn 1f out: r.o same pce and lost 2nd towards fin* **7/4[1]**

1/0- **4** 5 **Prince Alzain (USA)**[300] 508 5-9-4 109 (p) JimCrowley 1 92
(Robert Cowell) *led: rdn and edgd rt bnd 2f out: sn hdd and lost pl: wknd fnl f* **4/1**

2m 4.72s (-1.88) **Going Correction** +0.025s/f (Slow)
**WFA** 3 from 4yo+ 3lb **4** Ran SP% **108.0**
Speed ratings (Par 109): **108,105,105,101**
CSF £11.04 TOTE £3.20; EX 6.80 Trifecta £18.70.
**Owner** 9.36 from Paddington **Bred** Barouche Stud Ireland Ltd **Trained** Whatcombe, Oxon

**FOCUS**
Just the four runners for this conditions race, but all boasted ratings in three figures. It was run at a muddling pace, so it's hard to be confident about the form, but the winner came right away to win impressively.

### 8019 £20 RISK-FREE BET AT UNIBET H'CAP 5f 6y(P)
**2:30** (2:30) (Class 2) (0-105,105) 3-Y-O+ **£11,971** (£3,583; £1,791; £896; £446) **Stalls** High

Form RPR

100- **1** **Dungannon**[7] 7923 7-9-1 102 (b) ThomasBrown[(3)] 3 113
(Andrew Balding) *hld up in tch: clsd and swtchd rt over 1f out: cruised upsides ldr ins fnl f: shkn up to ld fnl 100yds: sn asserted and in command: readily* **7/4[2]**

521- **2** 1 ½ **Boom The Groom (IRE)**[11] 7889 3-8-9 93 WilliamCarson 7 99
(Tony Carroll) *chsd ldr: upsides and gng best 2f out: rdn to ld over 1f out: drvn ins fnl f: hdd and one pce fnl 100yds* **5/4[1]**

010- **3** 2 **Sleepy Sioux**[11] 7889 3-8-11 95 (p) DavidProbert 6 93
(David Elsworth) *broke fast and wnt lft leaving stalls: led: rdn and jnd 2f out: drvn and hdd 1f out: outpcd fnl 100yds* **8/1**

305- **4** 3 **Picansort**[130] 4675 7-8-4 88 (b) JimmyQuinn 1 76
(Peter Crate) *in tch in 4th: effrt on inner over 1f out: drvn and no imp 1f out: wknd ins fnl f* **25/1**

P30- **5** ¾ **Ballista (IRE)**[26] 7700 6-8-4 95 PatrickVaughan[(7)] 5 80
(Tom Dascombe) *slight hmpd s: chsd ldrs: clsd on outer to join ldrs 3f out: wdst and lost pl 2f out: wknd 1f out* **9/2[3]**

58.94s (0.14) **Going Correction** +0.025s/f (Slow) **5** Ran SP% **113.9**
Speed ratings (Par 109): **99,96,93,88,87**
CSF £4.53 TOTE £3.40: £1.50, £1.10; EX 4.90 Trifecta £22.30.
**Owner** Dr E Harris **Bred** J A E Hobby **Trained** Kingsclere, Hants

**FOCUS**
A quality sprint handicap run at a good clip. This was a clear personal best from the winner, with the second rated to his Wolverhampton win.

### 8020 LADBROKES MAIDEN STKS 1m 1y(P)
**3:00** (3:02) (Class 5) 3-Y-O+ **£2,587** (£770; £384; £192) **Stalls** High

Form RPR

0- **1** **Greenside**[23] 7733 3-9-5 0 FergusSweeney 1 80+
(Henry Candy) *dwlt: sn rousted up and rcvrd to r in midfield: chsd ldrs over 2f out: nt clr run and swtchd rt over 1f out: styd on wl u.p ins fnl f to ld cl home* **5/4[1]**

642- **2** *nk* **Filosofo (IRE)**[157] 3760 3-8-12 72 TomMarquand[(7)] 3 77
(Richard Hannon) *led: sn hdd and chsd ldr: pushed into ld again over 1f out: rdn ins fnl f: kpt on but worn down and hdd cl home* **7/2[3]**

430- **3** 3 ¾ **Jacqueline Jouliac**[14] 7841 3-9-0 72 (bt[1]) RobertHavlin 2 63
(John Gosden) *racd keenly: sn led: rdn and hdd over 1f out: no ex: wknd ins fnl f* **11/4[2]**

**4** 1 **Dukes Meadow** 3-9-5 0 SteveDrowne 5 66
(Roger Ingram) *in tch in midfield: cl enough whn nt clr run and hmpd over 1f out: swtchd lft and rn green 1f out: swtchd rt and kpt on ins fnl f: no threat to wnr* **33/1**

0/5- **5** 1 **Synaesthesia (FR)**[27] 7686 3-9-0 0 WilliamTwiston-Davies 4 59
(Lady Cecil) *hld up in rr: clsd over 2f out: 5th and shkn up jst over 2f out: styd on same pce fr over 1f out* **8/1**

00/ **6** 2 ¾ **Stage Girl**[386] 7844 3-9-0 0 PaddyAspell 7 52
(Mark Hoad) *t.k.h: in tch in midfield: cl 4th and rdn 2f out: unable qck over 1f out: wknd fnl f* **100/1**

0/ **7** 3 ¼ **Kalifi (USA)**[407] 7435 3-9-0 0 TomQueally 6 45
(Stuart Kittow) *a in last pair: rdn over 4f out: struggling u.p over 2f out: no ch fnl 2f* **14/1**

00- **8** *43* **Shanghai Sunrise**[27] 7686 3-8-7 0 DavidParkes(7) 8
(Keiran Burke) *chsd ldrs tl rdn and lost pl over 2f out: lost tch 2f out: t.o*
**100/1**

1m 37.65s (-0.55) **Going Correction** +0.025s/f (Slow) 8 Ran SP% **116.0**
Speed ratings (Par 103): **103,102,98,97,96 94,90,47**
CSF £6.08 TOTE £2.10: £1.10, £2.20, £1.20; EX 7.00 Trifecta £14.50.
**Owner** Clayton, Frost, Kebell & Turner **Bred** Lordship Stud **Trained** Kingston Warren, Oxon

**FOCUS**
A modest maiden. This has been rated around the runner-up's Windsor second, which worked out well enough.

## 8021 32RED.COM AMATEUR RIDERS' H'CAP 1m 7f 169y(P)
**3:30** (3:30) (Class 6) (0-60,60) 3-Y-0+ **£1,871** (£580; £290; £145) **Stalls** Low

Form RPR

625- **1** **Crouching Harry (IRE)**[10] 7518 5-10-2 51...(p) MissJoannaMason(3) 10 61
(Anabel K Murphy) *hld up off the pce in last quartet: clsd and in tch 1/2-way: chsd ldr over 1f out: rdn to ld ins fnl f: sn in command: readily*
**8/1**[3]

664- **2** *2 3/4* **Novel Dancer**[35] 7532 6-10-2 51 (v) MrJHarding(3) 2 58
(Lydia Richards) *chsd ldrs: hdwy to ld 6f out: rdn over 1f out: hdd and one pce ins fnl f*
**12/1**

033- **3** *1* **Haines**[36] 7518 3-9-3 48 MrHHunt(5) 1 54+
(Andrew Balding) *t.k.h: led tl 10f out: chsd ldrs tl lost pl 5f out: 6th and looked hld u.p 3f out: rallied over 1f out: wnt 3rd and styd on steadily fnl f: no threat to wnr*
**10/11**[1]

404- **4** *8* **Honest Strike (USA)**[11] 7893 7-10-12 58 (bt) MissSBrotherton 11 54
(Daniel Mark Loughnane) *stdd and dropped in bhd after s: hld up wl off the pce: clsd and in tch 1/2-way: chsd ldrs 5f out tl rdn and fnd nil over 1f out: sn wknd*
**3/1**[2]

0- **5** *hd* **Green Du Ciel (FR)**[14] 7846 9-10-9 60 (t) MissHHeal(5) 6 56
(Brian Barr) *w ldr tl led 1/2-way: hdd 6f out: chsd ldr tl over 2f out: 3rd and btn over 1f out: wknd fnl f*
**50/1**

0- **6** *1* **Daidaidai (FR)**[14] 7846 4-10-9 60 MrWRussell(5) 8 54
(Gary Moore) *t.k.h: chsd ldrs: wnt 2nd over 2f out tl rdn and nil over 1f out: wknd fnl f*
**16/1**

000- **7** *7* **Vera Lou (IRE)**[36] 7518 3-9-1 46 oh1 (v1) MissPFuller(5) 7 32
(Pat Eddery) *chsd ldrs: rdn and lost pl 5f out: struggling u.p 3f out: wknd 2f out*
**33/1**

365/ **8** *11* **Mollyow (IRE)**[24] 6922 6-10-2 53 MrJPWilliams(5) 5 26
(Bernard Llewellyn) *hld up off the pce in rr: reminders over 5f out: lost tch over 3f out*
**33/1**

446- **9** *shd* **Brabazon (IRE)**[196] 2455 11-10-4 50 (bt) MrSWalker 3 23
(Emmet Michael Butterly, Ire) *racd off the pce in last quartet: clsd and in tch 1/2-way: rdn and struggling over 4f out: lost tch 3f out*
**14/1**

3m 27.79s (2.09) **Going Correction** +0.025s/f (Slow)
**WFA** 3 from 4yo+ 8lb 9 Ran SP% **116.6**
Speed ratings (Par 101): **95,93,93,89,89 88,85,79,79**
CSF £96.46 CT £169.42 TOTE £10.00: £2.10, £2.60, £1.10; EX 77.90 Trifecta £180.40.
**Owner** Ridgeway Racing Club & Partner **Bred** Moyglare Stud Farm Ltd **Trained** Wilmcote, Warwicks

**FOCUS**
A weak race that lacked pace, but the winner is rated to form.
T/Plt: £15.60 to a £1 stake. Pool: £57,874.46 - 2,701.05 winning tickets T/Qpdt: £11.40 to a £1 stake. Pool: £4,387.44 - 283.48 winning tickets SP

8022 - (Foreign Racing) - See Raceform Interactive

# 8007 KEMPTON (A.W) (R-H)
### Thursday, December 4

**OFFICIAL GOING: Polytrack: standard**
Wind: virtually nil Weather: drizzly, cold

## 8023 DOWNLOAD THE BETVICTOR INSTABET APP H'CAP (DIV I) 5f (P)
**4:15** (4:15) (Class 6) (0-60,60) 3-Y-0+ **£2,264** (£673; £336; £168) **Stalls** Low

Form RPR

530- **1** **Pearl Noir**[10] 7900 4-9-0 58 (b) TimClark(5) 8 71
(Scott Dixon) *mde all: sn clr: rdn over 1f out: styd on: unchal*
**9/2**[2]

040- **2** *3* **Warm Order**[22] 7737 3-8-7 46 LukeMorris 4 48
(Tony Carroll) *chsd wnr thrght: drvn over 1f out: no imp ins fnl f: wknd towards fin*
**7/1**[3]

040- **3** *3/4* **Imaginary Diva**[37] 7520 8-8-11 50 PaoloSirigu 2 49
(George Margarson) *chsd ldng trio: effrt in 3rd over 1f out: plugged on u.p fnl f: no threat to wnr*
**25/1**

633- **4** *1* **Nelson's Pride**[8] 7929 3-8-8 54 (b) RhiainIngram(7) 6 50
(Roger Ingram) *chsd ldng pair: rdn over 1f out: 4th and plugged on same pce fnl f*
**12/1**

533- **5** *3/4* **Quality Art (USA)**[20] 7781 6-9-0 53 LiamJones 9 46
(Simon Hodgson) *a midfield: rdn 2f out: styd on same pce after*
**9/1**

603- **6** *1/2* **Burnt Cream**[66] 6815 7-9-7 60 (t) RobertHavlin 5 51
(Martin Bosley) *s.i.s: bhd: sme hdwy u.p fnl f: nvr trbld ldrs*
**9/1**

060- **7** *1* **Trending (IRE)**[133] 4567 5-8-6 52 (bt) DavidParkes(7) 3 40
(Jeremy Gask) *a towards rr: no imp u.p over 1f out: plugged on fnl f: nvr trbld ldrs*
**16/1**

163- **8** *nse* **Bubbly Bailey**[12] 7887 4-9-7 60 (v) AdamKirby 7 47
(J R Jenkins) *dwlt: sn rdn along in midfield: edgd rt u.p and no hdwy over 1f out: nvr trbld ldrs: fin lame*
**6/5**[1]

59.91s (-0.59) **Going Correction** -0.075s/f (Stan) 8 Ran SP% **113.6**
Speed ratings (Par 101): **101,96,95,93,92 91,89,89**
CSF £35.16 CT £704.97 TOTE £5.10: £1.50, £1.70, £4.70; EX 43.70 Trifecta £631.20.
**Owner** P J Dixon & Partners **Bred** Mrs Yvette Dixon **Trained** Babworth, Notts

**FOCUS**
A weak sprint handicap. There was no hanging about and the winner burnt them all off.

## 8024 DOWNLOAD THE BETVICTOR INSTABET APP H'CAP (DIV II) 5f (P)
**4:45** (4:45) (Class 6) (0-60,60) 3-Y-0+ **£2,264** (£673; £336; £168) **Stalls** Low

Form RPR

166- **1** **Aaranyow (IRE)**[10] 7900 6-9-1 59 (t) TobyAtkinson(5) 6 68
(Clifford Lines) *mde all: rdn over 1f out: styd on*
**6/1**[3]

330- **2** *1 1/4* **First Rebellion**[10] 7900 5-9-3 56 (b) RobertTart 1 61
(Tony Carroll) *in tch in midfield: effrt u.p to chse ldr over 1f out: no imp ins fnl f*
**5/2**[2]

566- **3** *3/4* **Studfarmer**[13] 7864 4-8-8 47 oh1 ow1 (p) JohnFahy 5 49
(Polly Gundry) *bhd: last and c wd over 1f out: hdwy ins fnl f: gng on strly fin: nt rch ldrs*
**25/1**

200- **4** *1* **Ecliptic Sunrise**[12] 7887 3-9-0 53 (p) DavidProbert 9 51
(Des Donovan) *chsd ldrs tl over 1f out: kpt on same pce u.p ins fnl f* **7/1**

034- **5** *nk* **Mossgo (IRE)**[22] 7737 4-8-9 48 (t) MartinDwyer 4 45
(John Best) *dwlt: t.k.h in midfield: rdn over 1f out: kpt on same pce fnl f*
**2/1**[1]

460- **6** *1 1/4* **Purford Green**[12] 7887 5-8-7 46 (v) JimmyQuinn 8 39
(Michael Attwater) *in tch in midfield: effrt u.p on inner over 1f out: no imp fnl f*
**50/1**

200- **7** *hd* **Incomparable**[48] 7253 9-9-2 55 (v1) AdamKirby 3 47
(Scott Dixon) *chsd ldrs: struggling u.p over 1f out: wknd ins fnl f* **6/1**[3]

354- **8** *nk* **Go Charlie**[90] 6090 3-8-6 50 EoinWalsh(5) 2 41
(Lisa Williamson) *taken down early: stdd s: t.k.h in rr: swtchd lft and effrt over 1f out: no imp ins fnl f*
**20/1**

060- **9** *7* **Live Dangerously**[21] 7758 4-9-7 60 (b1) WilliamCarson 7 26
(John Bridger) *t.k.h: in tch in midfield: wknd qckly over 1f out: bhd fnl f*
**10/1**

(-0.50) **Going Correction** -0.075s/f (Stan) 9 Ran SP% **122.6**
Speed ratings (Par 101): **101,99,97,96,95 93,93,92,81**
CSF £22.44 CT £368.03 TOTE £8.40: £2.10, £1.30, £5.60; EX 26.70 Trifecta £751.80.
**Owner** Prima Racing Partnership **Bred** Jeremy Gompertz **Trained** Exning, Suffolk
■ Stewards' Enquiry : Toby Atkinson one-day ban: careless riding (Dec 18)
Martin Dwyer jockey said gelding jumped out of the stalls awkwardly
Eoin Walsh jockey said gelding hung both ways

**FOCUS**
The second division of the weak 5f handicap. The pace got more serious after a furlong or so and there was another winner from the front.

## 8025 BETVICTOR.COM H'CAP 5f (P)
**5:15** (5:15) (Class 4) (0-85,84) 3-Y-0+ **£5,175** (£1,540; £769; £384) **Stalls** Low

Form RPR

320- **1** **Diamond Charlie (IRE)**[31] 7624 6-9-6 83 SebSanders 3 91
(Simon Dow) *mde all: rdn and kicked clr over 1f out: hld on towards fin*
**16/1**

201- **2** *nk* **Salvatore Fury (IRE)**[44] 7351 4-9-0 77 (p) JimCrowley 4 84
(Keith Dalgleish) *in tch in midfield: wnt lft bnd 4f out: hdwy over 1f out: chsd wnr ins fnl f: styd on: nvr quite getting to wnr*
**5/2**[2]

010- **3** *nk* **Head Space (IRE)**[37] 7521 6-9-2 79 (v) GrahamGibbons 5 85
(Michael Attwater) *hld up in midfield: effrt 1f out: styd on strly ins fnl f* **8/1**[3]

0- **4** *1/2* **Doctor Parkes**[89] 6131 8-9-5 82 DavidProbert 9 86+
(Stuart Williams) *hld up in rr of main gp: swtchd lft over 1f out: swtchd bk rt and styd on wl ins fnl f*
**25/1**

521- **5** *shd* **Searchlight**[12] 7886 3-9-2 84 ShaneGray(5) 2 88+
(Kevin Ryan) *hld up in tch in midfield: hdwy on inner over 1f out: drvn and kpt on ins fnl f*
**11/8**[1]

006- **6** *2* **Triple Dream**[12] 7886 9-9-1 78 (tp) JimmyQuinn 10 75
(Milton Bradley) *hld up in rr of main gp: carried lft bnd after 1f out: kpt on u.p ins fnl f*
**20/1**

000- **7** *1 1/4* **Six Wives**[21] 7767 7-8-11 74 (v1) LukeMorris 7 66
(Scott Dixon) *chsd wnr: rdn and outpcd over 1f out: lost 2nd and wknd ins fnl f*
**33/1**

100- **8** *1 1/4* **Royal Bajan (USA)**[21] 7761 6-9-6 83 (v) TomQueally 8 71
(James Given) *chsd ldrs: rdn and unable qck over 1f out: wknd ins fnl f*
**33/1**

514- **9** *1/2* **Royal Acquisition**[12] 7886 4-8-11 74 (p) LiamJones 6 60
(Robert Cowell) *rdr slow removing hood: sn dropped to rr: drvn 1/2-way: nvr trbld ldrs*
**16/1**

504- **10** *3 1/2* **Baytown Kestrel**[21] 7761 3-9-3 80 (p) AdamKirby 1 53
(Jamie Osborne) *in tch in midfield: pushed along over 1f out: sn btn: bhd and eased ins fnl f*
**8/1**[3]

59.32s (-1.18) **Going Correction** -0.075s/f (Stan) 10 Ran SP% **119.2**
Speed ratings (Par 105): **106,105,105,104,104 100,98,96,96,90**
CSF £55.30 CT £357.22 TOTE £13.90: £3.40, £1.30, £2.60; EX 68.40 Trifecta £849.40.
**Owner** David & Stanley Adams **Bred** John Malone **Trained** Epsom, Surrey

**FOCUS**
This modest sprint handicap saw a third consecutive winner make all over the C&D on the card.

## 8026 £25 FREE BET AT BETVICTOR MAIDEN STKS 6f (P)
**5:45** (5:47) (Class 5) 2-Y-O **£3,234** (£962; £481; £240) **Stalls** Low

Form RPR

0- **1** **Nuno Tristan (USA)**[57] 7037 2-9-5 0 GrahamGibbons 5 81+
(William Jarvis) *chsd ldrs: rdn to ld over 1f out: r.o strly and drew clr fnl f: readily*
**15/8**[1]

46- **2** *4* **Green Tornado (IRE)**[26] 7713 2-9-5 0 AdamKirby 12 69
(Ralph Beckett) *chsd ldr: rdn and edgd lft 2f out: chsd clr wnr ins fnl f: no imp*
**11/4**[2]

65- **3** *3/4* **Stamp Of Authority (IRE)**[15] 7833 2-9-5 0 LukeMorris 7 67
(James Tate) *led: rdn and hdd over 1f out: outpcd by wnr 1f out: lost 2nd and one pce fnl f*
**9/1**

**4** *shd* **On The Huh** 2-9-5 0 TomQueally 9 67
(Michael Bell) *t.k.h: chsd ldng trio: rdn 2f out: r.o same pce* **33/1**

00- **5** *1/2* **Farendole (USA)**[42] 7398 2-9-0 0 WilliamTwiston-Davies 8 60
(Roger Charlton) *in tch in midfield: rdn and effrt wl over 1f out: kpt on ins fnl f: no threat to wnr*
**25/1**

03- **6** *nk* **Thames Knight**[15] 7840 2-9-5 0 MartinDwyer 4 64
(Marcus Tregoning) *hld up in midfield: rdn over 1f out: styd on ins fnl f: nvr trbld ldrs*
**12/1**

**7** *1* **Moving Upwards** 2-9-0 0 ShaneGray(5) 2 61+
(Kevin Ryan) *rn green in last quartet: hdwy 1f out: styd on wl fnl 150yds: nvr trbld ldrs*
**20/1**

43- **7** *dht* **Star Of The Stage**[22] 7742 2-9-5 0 TonyHamilton 10 61
(Richard Fahey) *s.i.s: sn in midfield: rdn: hung lft and fnd little 2f out: wl hld and one pce fnl f*
**11/2**[3]

0- **9** *3/4* **Step Into The Tide (IRE)**[8] 7919 2-8-12 0 NoraLooby(7) 3 59
(Joseph Tuite) *dwlt and short of room sn after s: in tch in last quartet: styd on same pce fnl 2f*
**33/1**

**10** *3/4* **Stenid** 2-9-5 0 DavidProbert 6 57
(Kevin Ryan) *rn green in rr: swtchd rt jst over 2f out: kpt on but nvr trbld ldrs*
**20/1**

0- **11** *2 1/2* **Mildmay Arms**[22] 7742 2-9-5 0 LiamJones 1 49
(Simon Hodgson) *in tch in midfield: rdn 2f out: no imp over 1f out: wknd fnl f*
**50/1**

**12** *1/2* **Spring Seraph (IRE)** 2-9-5 0 JimCrowley 11 48
(Olly Stevens) *dwlt and swtchd rt after s: a in rr* **20/1**

1m 12.92s (-0.18) **Going Correction** -0.075s/f (Stan) 12 Ran SP% **120.5**
Speed ratings (Par 96): **98,92,91,91,90 90,89,89,88,87 83,83**
CSF £6.21 TOTE £2.80: £1.10, £2.00, £2.30; EX 9.50 Trifecta £49.20.
**Owner** Clive Washbourn **Bred** Galleria Bloodstock & Samac **Trained** Newmarket, Suffolk

**FOCUS**
This 2yo maiden proved a lively betting heat there was a clear-cut winner. The third sets the level.

## 8027 BETVICTOR MAIDEN FILLIES' STKS (BOBIS RACE) 7f (P)
6:15 (6:17) (Class 5) 2-Y-O £2,587 (£770; £384; £192) Stalls Low

Form RPR
320- 1 **Rock Kristal (IRE)**[50] 7194 2-9-0 75 RobertHavlin 4 79+
(John Gosden) *sn bustled up to ld: jnd and rdn 2f out: fnd ex and asserted over 1f out: clr fnl f: r.o* 1/1[1]
05- 2 4 ½ **Farletti**[35] 7549 2-9-0 0 DavidProbert 8 67
(Andrew Balding) *chsd wnr: upsides and rdn 2f out: unable qck over 1f out: r.o same pce fnl f* 9/4[2]
0- 3 2 ¾ **Misham**[19] 7808 2-9-0 0 AdamKirby 10 59+
(Marco Botti) *hld up in tch: effrt to go 3rd 2f out: kpt on but no ch w wnr* 4/1[3]
0- 4 10 **Chester Bound**[101] 5774 2-9-0 0 MartinDwyer 2 32
(Jo Hughes) *chsd ldrs: 4th and no ex 2f out: sn wknd* 20/1
06- 5 2 ½ **Qatar Success**[8] 7920 2-9-0 0 (bt) LiamJones 1 26
(Olly Stevens) *in tch in midfield: rdn and struggling over 2f out: sn wknd* 25/1
00- 6 7 **Signs And Signals (IRE)**[13] 7867 2-9-0 0 FergusSweeney 3 7
(Ed Vaughan) *a in rr: rdn over 2f out: sn lost tch: wl bhd fnl f* 50/1
7 ¾ **Little Danielle (IRE)** 2-9-0 0 NickyMackay 5 5
(Phil McEntee) *in tch: rdn and struggling over 2f out: lost tch 2f out: wl bhd fnl f* 33/1

1m 25.9s (-0.10) **Going Correction** -0.075s/f (Stan) 7 Ran SP% **114.3**
Speed ratings (Par 93): **97,91,88,77,74 66,65**
CSF £3.35 TOTE £2.10: £1.30, £1.90; EX 4.00 Trifecta £7.60.
**Owner** Denford Stud **Bred** Stowell Park Stud **Trained** Newmarket, Suffolk

**FOCUS**
This modest 2yo fillies' maiden was run at an average pace and the two market leaders dominated.

## 8028 BOOK THE PANORAMIC FOR BOXING DAY H'CAP 1m 3f (P)
6:45 (6:45) (Class 6) (0-60,60) 3-Y-0+ £2,264 (£673; £336; £168) Stalls Low

Form RPR
556- 1 **Softly She Treads (IRE)**[37] 7517 3-8-10 53 (v) FergusSweeney 4 63
(Pat Phelan) *chsd ldrs: clsd 3f out: rdn to ld jst over 2f out: styd on wl: rdn out* 8/1
411- 2 2 ¾ **Vaguely Spanish**[20] 7785 3-8-13 56 LukeMorris 6 61
(Tony Carroll) *hld up off the pce in last trio: clsd and in tch 3f out: effrt u.p to chse wnr over 1f out: no imp ins fnl f* 1/1[1]
050- 3 3 ¼ **Kirtling**[19] 7805 3-9-3 60 AdamKirby 5 60
(Andi Brown) *hld up off the pce in rr: clsd and in tch 3f out: rdn and effrt 2f out: 3rd and no prog fnl f* 3/1[2]
500- 4 1 ¾ **Night's Watch**[24] 7734 4-9-2 55 JohnFahy 1 52
(Dai Burchell) *chsd ldr tl 1/2-way: rdn and ev ch briefly over 2f out: outpcd and btn over 1f out: plugged on same pce fnl f* 12/1
050- 5 ¾ **Keeper's Ring (USA)**[34] 7570 3-9-0 57 (b[1]) MartinHarley 3 53
(Roger Varian) *hld up off the pce in rr: clsd and in tch 3f out: 5th and no prog fnl f* 7/1[3]
004- 6 10 **Rezwaan**[30] 7635 7-9-2 55 (be) ShaneKelly 7 34
(Murty McGrath) *t.k.h: chsd ldrs: wnt 2nd 1/2-way tl led over 3f out: rdn and hdd over 2f out: sn btn: wknd over 1f out* 16/1
600- 7 2 ¾ **Run Fat Lass Run**[10] 7907 4-9-7 60 (p) HayleyTurner 8 34
(Conor Dore) *racd in midfield: rdn 4f out: wknd 2f out* 25/1
500- 8 29 **Summerling (IRE)**[20] 7777 3-9-3 60 WilliamCarson 9
(Phil McEntee) *led tl over 3f out: lost pl and bhd over 2f out: sn lost tch: t.o* 50/1

2m 20.66s (-1.24) **Going Correction** -0.075s/f (Stan)
**WFA** 3 from 4yo+ 4lb 8 Ran SP% **118.0**
Speed ratings (Par 101): **101,99,96,95,94 87,85,64**
CSF £17.03 CT £31.44 TOTE £12.10: £2.40, £1.10, £1.10; EX 24.30 Trifecta £97.50.
**Owner** Brian P Donovan **Bred** Miss Sarah Thompson **Trained** Epsom, Surrey

**FOCUS**
The field was well strung out early in this moderate handicap and finished that way.

## 8029 FOLLOW @BETVICTORRACING ON TWITTER H'CAP 1m 4f (P)
7:15 (7:16) (Class 5) (0-70,70) 3-Y-0+ £2,911 (£866; £432; £216) Stalls Centre

Form RPR
606/ 1 **Taaresh (IRE)**[27] 6280 9-9-3 70 (p) GaryMahon[(7)] 11 77
(Kevin Morgan) *chsd ldr tl 8f out: chsd ldrs tl wnt 2nd again 4f out tl led over 2f out: rdn and fnd ex 2f out: hld on wl ins fnl f: rdn out* 25/1
003- 2 nk **Thane Of Cawdor (IRE)**[5] 7975 5-9-2 62 AdamKirby 9 68+
(Joseph Tuite) *dropped in bhd after s: hld up in rr: rdn and hdwy over 2f out: chsd ldrs 1f out: wnt 2nd and pressing wnr wl ins fnl f: kpt on* 9/4[1]
005- 3 ½ **Thecornishcowboy**[34] 7562 5-9-10 70 (t) JackMitchell 2 75
(John Ryan) *chsd ldrs: rdn and effrt to chse ldrs 2f out: pressing wnr ins fnl f: kpt on* 4/1[3]
053- 4 shd **Perfect Rhythm**[22] 7744 3-8-9 63 RyanTate[(3)] 4 68
(Patrick Chamings) *in tch in midfield: rdn and hdwy to chse ldrs 3f out: wnt 2nd 2f out: pressing wnr ins fnl f: kpt on but lost 2 pls wl ins fnl f* 8/1
265- 5 1 ¾ **Chauvelin**[55] 7074 3-9-2 67 MartinHarley 3 70+
(Roger Charlton) *hld up in tch towards rr: rdn and hdwy on inner 2f out: 5th and styd on same pce ins fnl f* 7/2[2]
142/ 6 4 ½ **Dont Take Me Alive**[46] 5442 5-9-8 68 (tp) LiamKeniry 6 63
(Charlie Longsdon) *hld up in last pair: hdwy 3f out: no imp u.p over 1f out: wknd fnl f* 25/1
564/ 7 nse **Addazero**[756] 7655 5-9-4 64 SteveDrowne 8 59
(Joseph Tuite) *led tl over 4f out: lost pl over 3f out and looked wl hld over 2f out: kpt on again ins fnl f* 16/1
000- 8 4 ½ **Back Burner (IRE)**[24] 7734 6-9-5 65 (p) JohnFahy 5 53
(Dai Burchell) *t.k.h: chsd ldrs tl wnt 2nd 8f out: led over 4f out tl over 2f out: sn rdn: wknd over 1f out* 25/1
430- 9 8 **The Blue Dog (IRE)**[188] 2750 7-9-9 69 WilliamCarson 10 44
(Phil McEntee) *in tch in midfield: effrt over 2f out: sn btn: wknd wl over 1f out* 25/1
61P- 10 9 **Dalgig**[8] 7918 4-9-10 70 WilliamTwiston-Davies 1 31
(David Pipe) *in tch in midfield: rdn and btn over 2f out: sn bhd* 7/1

2m 34.22s (-0.28) **Going Correction** -0.075s/f (Stan)
**WFA** 3 from 4yo+ 5lb 10 Ran SP% **117.9**
Speed ratings (Par 103): **97,96,96,96,95 92,92,89,83,77**
CSF £79.28 CT £281.67 TOTE £13.50: £2.80, £1.30, £1.60; EX 116.60 Trifecta £1625.60.
**Owner** Roemex Ltd **Bred** Shadwell Estate Company Limited **Trained** Gazeley, Suffolk

**FOCUS**
This wasn't a bad handicap for the class but it was run at an uneven pace and resulted in a muddling finish.

## 8030 DOWNLOAD THE BETVICTOR APP APPRENTICE H'CAP 1m (P)
7:45 (7:45) (Class 6) (0-65,69) 3-Y-0+ £2,264 (£673; £336; £168) Stalls Low

Form RPR
244- 1 **India's Song**[236] 1450 4-8-13 63 (t) MillyNaseb[(7)] 7 72
(David Simcock) *in tch in midfield: hdwy between horses to ld ins fnl f: r.o wl* 33/1
003- 2 shd **Chelwood Gate (IRE)**[7] 7942 4-9-7 64 (v) RyanTate 6 72
(Patrick Chamings) *t.k.h: wl in tch in midfield: drvn and ev ch 1f out: r.o u.p: jst hld* 2/1[1]
421- 3 1 **Loraine**[10] 7907 4-9-12 69 6ex CharlesBishop 10 75
(Jamie Osborne) *stdd s: hld up in rr: hdwy on outer over 1f out: styd on wl to go 3rd wl ins fnl f: nt rch ldrs* 9/4[2]
404- 4 1 **Eastward Ho**[3] 7986 6-8-5 51 ShelleyBirkett[(3)] 1 55
(Sarah Humphrey) *chsd ldr: rdn and ev ch 2f out tl ins fnl f: r.o same pce* 10/1
002- 5 1 **Tevez**[7] 7942 9-8-11 61 (p) HollieDoyle[(7)] 9 63
(Des Donovan) *hld up in tch towards rr: rdn and hdwy over 1f out: styd on same pce ins fnl f* 10/1
324- 6 nk **Abigails Angel**[15] 7844 7-8-13 56 ThomasBrown 8 57
(Lee Carter) *led: rdn jst over 2f out: hdd ins fnl f: no ex and wknd towards fin* 10/1
560- 7 hd **Storm Runner (IRE)**[19] 7805 6-9-4 61 DannyBrock 5 62
(George Margarson) *dwlt: in tch towards rr: effrt u.p on inner 2f out: one pce and no imp ins fnl f* 14/1
001- 8 1 **Lexington Blue**[15] 7844 4-8-6 54 GaryMahon[(5)] 2 52
(Seamus Mullins) *in tch in midfield: rdn and effrt 2f out: no ex 1f out: wknd ins fnl f* 20/1
650- 9 3 ¼ **Hinton Admiral**[129] 4732 10-8-7 50 oh5 JoeyHaynes 11 41
(Pat Eddery) *broke wl: sn stdd bk into last pair: rdn and effrt on inner 2f out: no imp over 1f out: wknd fnl f* 66/1
535- 10 nse **George Baker (IRE)**[64] 6858 7-8-13 63 AlfieDavies[(7)] 4 54
(George Baker) *in tch in midfield: rdn and outpcd wl over 1f out: wknd 1f out* 25/1
621- 11 nk **Olivers Mount**[14] 7853 4-9-4 61 (t) WilliamTwiston-Davies 3 51
(Ed Vaughan) *chsd ldrs: rdn and unable qck 2f out: wknd 1f out* 8/1[3]

1m 40.14s (0.34) **Going Correction** -0.075s/f (Stan) 11 Ran SP% **122.2**
Speed ratings (Par 101): **95,94,93,92,91 91,91,90,87,87 86**
CSF £100.16 CT £227.34 TOTE £24.00: £6.00, £1.80, £1.10; EX 262.30 Trifecta £480.60.
**Owner** Mrs Julia Annable **Bred** Car Colston Hall Stud **Trained** Newmarket, Suffolk

**FOCUS**
This ordinary handicap, confined to apprentice riders, was another race run at a muddling pace. The form still looks fair for the class, though.
T/Jkpt: Not won. T/Plt: £35.20 to a £1 stake. Pool: £92,272.70 - 1908.24 winning units. T/Qpdt: £4.40 to a £1 stake. Pool: £12,993.14 - 2174.80 winning units. SP

# 8015 LINGFIELD (L-H)
Friday, December 5

**OFFICIAL GOING: Polytrack:standard**
Wind: virtually nil Weather: dry, light cloud

## 8036 32RED/IRISH STALLION FARMS EBF MAIDEN FILLIES' STKS (BOBIS RACE) 1m 1y(P)
12:30 (12:33) (Class 5) 2-Y-O £2,911 (£866; £432; £216) Stalls High

Form RPR
62- 1 **Dreamlike**[42] 7405 2-9-0 0 AdamKirby 4 82
(Luca Cumani) *chsd ldrs: rdn to chal over 1f out: kpt on wl u.p fnl 100yds to ld last stride* 5/2[1]
2 shd **Zamoura** 2-9-0 0 NickyMackay 6 82
(John Gosden) *in tch in midfield: clsd to chse ldrs over 2f out: rdn to ld over 1f out: hrd pressed but kpt on wl u.p fnl f: hdd last stride* 33/1
3 nse **Never Change (IRE)** 2-9-0 0 JamesDoyle 7 82
(Saeed bin Suroor) *hld up off the pce towards rr: hdwy 1/2-way: chsd ldrs and swtchd lft over 1f out: ev ch 1f out: kpt on wl fnl f* 5/1
2- 4 5 **Pure Line**[20] 7808 2-9-0 0 GrahamGibbons 1 70
(Ralph Beckett) *led: rdn 2f out: hdd over 1f out: sn btn and wknd qckly ins fnl f* 11/4[2]
5 ½ **Lady Of Camelot (IRE)** 2-9-0 0 RobertHavlin 12 69
(John Gosden) *chsd ldrs: carried rt bnd 2f out: no ex over 1f out: wknd jst ins fnl f* 8/1
0- 6 3 **Flighty Filia (IRE)**[51] 7194 2-9-0 0 JimCrowley 10 62
(Amanda Perrett) *hld up off the pce towards rr: hdwy into midfield 3f out: pushed along and no imp over 1f out* 66/1
3- 7 hd **Bittern (IRE)**[52] 7184 2-9-0 0 MartinLane 11 62
(Charlie Appleby) *w ldr: rn green and hung rt bnd 2f out: nt rcvr and sn btn: wknd over 1f out* 7/2[3]
8 9 **Eager Beaver** 2-9-0 0 MartinDwyer 8 41
(William Muir) *midfield tl rn green and lost pl over 4f out: lost tch 3f out* 33/1
0- 9 ½ **Onorina (IRE)**[22] 7752 2-9-0 0[1] SteveDrowne 3 40
(Jim Boyle) *in tch in midfield: rdn and lost pl over 4f out: lost tch over 2f out* 100/1
0- 10 13 **Selfrespect**[22] 7752 2-8-11 0 AmyScott[(3)] 5 10
(Henry Candy) *s.i.s: rn green in rr: rdn over 5f out: lost tch over 3f out: t.o* 100/1
0- 11 5 **Marymalade**[30] 7667 2-9-0 0 LukeMorris 9
(Harry Dunlop) *a towards rr: rdn and rn green over 4f out: lost tch 3f out: t.o* 100/1

1m 36.53s (-1.67) **Going Correction** 0.0s/f (Stan) 11 Ran SP% **115.6**
Speed ratings (Par 93): **108,107,107,102,102 99,99,90,89,76 71**
CSF £88.83 TOTE £3.00: £1.10, £8.70, £2.10; EX 72.10 Trifecta £774.60.
**Owner** Fittocks Stud & Andrew Bengough **Bred** Fittocks Stud Ltd & Arrow Farm Stud **Trained** Newmarket, Suffolk


The Form Book, Raceform Ltd, Newbury, RG14 5SJ

**FOCUS**
Even though it produced a tight finish, this didn't look a bad fillies' maiden at all and winners should come out of it.

## 8037 CORAL APP DOWNLOAD FROM THE APP STORE H'CAP 1m 4f (P)
1:00 (1:00) (Class 6) (0-65,65) 3-Y-O+ £1,940 (£577; £288; £144) Stalls Low

| Form | | | | RPR |
|---|---|---|---|---|
| 01- | 1 | | **Planetoid (IRE)**[9] 7932 6-9-8 65..........(b) WilliamTwiston-Davies 2 | 74+ |
| | | | (Jim Best) *racd in last quartet: swtchd rt and hdwy over 3f out: carried rt and hmpd over 1f out: edging lft but str run u.p ins fnl f to ld on post* 7/2[2] | |
| 330- | 2 | nse | **Maison Brillet (IRE)**[23] 7744 7-9-4 61..........(p) RobertHavlin 7 | 69 |
| | | | (Clive Drew) *racd off the pce in midfield: rdn and hdwy over 2f out: stdy on u.p to ld wl ins fnl f: hdd on post* 20/1 | |
| 232- | 3 | 2 ¼ | **Zinnobar**[21] 7777 4-9-2 62..........(p) DannyBrock(3) 5 | 66 |
| | | | (Jonathan Portman) *led for 2f: chsd clr ldr after: rdn and clsd over 2f out: led over 1f out: hdd wl ins fnl f: outpcd towards fin* 6/1 | |
| 221- | 4 | nk | **Salient**[16] 7846 10-9-3 60.......... AdamKirby 1 | 64 |
| | | | (Michael Attwater) *chsd clr ldng pair: rdn and clsd over 2f out: chsng ldrs whn carried rt and hmpd over 1f out: rallied and kpt on ins fnl f* 8/1 | |
| 000- | 5 | hd | **Snow King (USA)**[9] 7925 4-9-3 60.......... SteveDrowne 3 | 64 |
| | | | (Ted Powell) *prom in main gp: rdn and clsd over 2f out: lft chsng ldr jst over 1f out: styd on same pce fnl 100yds* 50/1 | |
| 455- | 6 | 1 ½ | **Loving Your Work**[33] 7162 3-9-3 65.......... FergusSweeney 10 | 66 |
| | | | (George Baker) *racd off the pce in last quartet: pushed along and clsd over 2f out: effrt u.p 1f out: styd on same pce ins fnl f* 8/1 | |
| 205- | 7 | 2 ¼ | **On Demand**[22] 7760 3-9-2 64..........(b[1]) DavidProbert 4 | 62 |
| | | | (Andrew Balding) *chsd ldr tl led 10f out and sn clr: 6 l ld and rdn 2f out: drifted rt and hdd over 1f out: sn btn: wknd ins fnl f* 5/1[3] | |
| /50- | 8 | ¾ | **Guards Chapel**[23] 7744 6-8-12 62..........(p) HectorCrouch(7) 8 | 58 |
| | | | (Gary Moore) *racd off the pce in last quartet: rdn over 3f out: sme prog over 2f out: kpt on ins fnl f: nvr trbld ldrs* 33/1 | |
| 506/ | 9 | hd | **Proud Times (USA)**[20] 7628 8-9-2 59..........(p) JimCrowley 6 | 55 |
| | | | (Ali Stronge) *racd off the pce in midfield: swtchd rt jst over 3f out: effrt and rdn over 2f out: one pce and no imp fr wl over 1f out* 25/1 | |
| 0- | 10 | 2 | **Leyland (IRE)**[16] 7831 5-9-1 65.......... CharlieBennett(7) 9 | 58 |
| | | | (Natalie Lloyd-Beavis) *hld up off the pce in rr: rdn over 3f out: nvr trbld ldrs* 50/1 | |
| /06- | 11 | 2 ¾ | **Takeitfromalady (IRE)**[65] 6881 5-9-4 64..........(b) ThomasBrown(3) 11 | 52 |
| | | | (Lee Carter) *racd off the pce in midfield: nt clr run and shuffled bk 3f out: bhd and rdn wl over 1f out: no prog* 9/4[1] | |

2m 31.8s (-1.20) **Going Correction** 0.0s/f (Stan)
**WFA** 3 from 4yo+ 5lb 11 Ran SP% **121.6**
Speed ratings (Par 101): **104,103,102,102,102 101,99,99,99,97 95**
CSF £77.95 CT £416.53 TOTE £4.60: £2.00, £4.80, £2.30; EX 64.10 Trifecta £275.50.
**Owner** Planetoid Partnership **Bred** Bjorn Nielsen **Trained** Lewes, E Sussex
■ Stewards' Enquiry : David Probert caution: careless riding

**FOCUS**
A modest handicap, but run at a strong pace and a dramatic finish. The runner-up has been rated to his early 2013 CD form.

## 8038 32RED.COM MAIDEN FILLIES' STKS 7f 1y(P)
1:30 (1:30) (Class 5) 3-Y-O+ £2,587 (£770; £384; £192) Stalls Low

| Form | | | | RPR |
|---|---|---|---|---|
| 224- | 1 | | **Nightlight**[18] 7818 3-9-0 68.......... JamesDoyle 2 | 66 |
| | | | (Jeremy Noseda) *mde all: rdn over 2f out: drifted rt but forged ahd u.p over 1f out: kpt on u.p fnl f: rdn out* 4/9[1] | |
| 05- | 2 | 1 ¾ | **Beggers Luck**[9] 7921 4-9-0 0.......... DavidProbert 3 | 61 |
| | | | (Eric Wheeler) *chsd ldrs: rdn and sltly outpcd 2f out: rallied 1f out: kpt on to go 2nd cl home* 100/1 | |
| 236- | 3 | nk | **Childesplay**[83] 6336 3-9-0 70.......... LukeMorris 4 | 60 |
| | | | (Heather Main) *w wnr: rdn jst over 2f out: carried rt and unable qck over 1f out: one pce u.p and hld fnl f: lost 2nd cl home* 7/4[2] | |
| | 4 | 6 | **Incantare** 4-8-11 0.......... DeclanBates(3) 1 | 44 |
| | | | (Jim Allen) *s.i.s: in tch in 4th: rdn and outpcd jst over 2f out: kpt on same pce and no imp fr over 1f out* 33/1[3] | |

1m 25.58s (0.78) **Going Correction** 0.0s/f (Stan) 4 Ran SP% **109.5**
Speed ratings (Par 100): **95,93,92,85**
CSF £23.33 TOTE £1.60; EX 15.90 Trifecta £30.20.
**Owner** Cheveley Park Stud **Bred** Cheveley Park Stud Ltd **Trained** Newmarket, Suffolk

**FOCUS**
This moderate fillies' maiden was effectively a match according to the market and the big two were soon taking each other on up front. It's been rated around the winner, with a doubt over the third.

## 8039 UNIBET OFFER DAILY JOCKEY/TRAINER SPECIALS CLASSIFIED CLAIMING STKS 5f 6y(P)
2:05 (2:05) (Class 6) 3-Y-O+ £1,940 (£577; £288; £144) Stalls High

| Form | | | | RPR |
|---|---|---|---|---|
| 606- | 1 | | **Arctic Lynx (IRE)**[15] 7847 7-8-7 68..........(p) LiamJones 2 | 72 |
| | | | (Robert Cowell) *chsd ldrs: effrt u.p over 1f out: led jst ins fnl f: r.o wl: rdn out* 7/2[3] | |
| 005- | 2 | 1 ¼ | **Noverre To Go (IRE)**[4] 7989 8-8-11 70..........(p) WilliamTwiston-Davies 5 | 72 |
| | | | (Ronald Harris) *hld up in tch in rr: clsd and nt clr run jst over 1f out: swtchd rt 1f out: hdwy u.p to chse wnr fnl 75yds: r.o but a hld* 5/2[2] | |
| 130- | 3 | 3 ¼ | **Pharoh Jake**[4] 7989 6-8-13 67.......... WilliamCarson 6 | 62 |
| | | | (John Bridger) *t.k.h: w ldrs: rdn to ld over 1f out: hdd jst ins fnl f: sn outpcd* 9/2 | |
| 054- | 4 | 1 | **Best Trip (IRE)**[18] 7819 7-8-9 69.......... MartinLane 4 | 54 |
| | | | (Brian Ellison) *led: rdn and hdd over 1f out: outpcd ins fnl f* 6/4[1] | |
| 560- | 5 | 3 ¼ | **Spic 'n Span**[21] 7781 9-8-6 46..........(b) DavidProbert 1 | 40 |
| | | | (Ronald Harris) *chsd ldrs: struggling and unbalanced bnd wl over 1f out: wknd 1f out* 33/1 | |

58.59s (-0.21) **Going Correction** 0.0s/f (Stan) 5 Ran SP% **111.9**
Speed ratings (Par 101): **101,99,93,92,87**
CSF £12.79 TOTE £4.20: £1.90, £1.90; EX 14.00 Trifecta £29.30.Arctic Lynx was claimed by Mr Conor Dore £6,000.
**Owner** Mrs J Morley & Partner **Bred** Derek Veitch And Saleh Ali Hammadi **Trained** Six Mile Bottom, Cambs

**FOCUS**
An ordinary sprint claimer. The winner has been rated a length up on his recent form.

## 8040 DAILY PRICE BOOST AT UNIBET H'CAP 6f 1y(P)
2:40 (2:40) (Class 5) (0-75,75) 3-Y-O+ £2,587 (£770; £384; £192) Stalls Low

| Form | | | | RPR |
|---|---|---|---|---|
| 063- | 1 | | **Desert Strike**[9] 7931 8-9-7 75..........(p) HayleyTurner 4 | 83 |
| | | | (Conor Dore) *taken down early: mde all: rdn over 1f out: edgd lft u.p but styd on strly ins fnl f: drvn out* 16/1 | |
| 130- | 2 | ¾ | **Thataboy (IRE)**[13] 7888 3-9-7 75.......... JamesDoyle 2 | 81 |
| | | | (Tom Dascombe) *chsd ldrs: chal over 1f out: drvn and styd on same pce ins fnl f* 6/1[3] | |
| 021- | 3 | ½ | **Suitsus**[20] 7800 3-9-2 70..........(p) JimCrowley 8 | 74 |
| | | | (Peter Makin) *t.k.h early: hld up in tch in midfield: rdn and hdwy over 1f out: r.o wl ins fnl f: swtchd rt towards fin: wnt 3rd last strides* 8/1 | |
| 044- | 4 | nk | **Temple Road (IRE)**[9] 7931 6-9-2 70..........(t) WilliamTwiston-Davies 1 | 73 |
| | | | (Milton Bradley) *dwlt: hld up in tch: hdwy to chse ldrs 2f out: drvn and pressed ldrs 1f out: no ex fnl 100yds: wknd towards fin: lost 3rd last strides* 12/1 | |
| 002- | 5 | nk | **Novellen Lad (IRE)**[21] 7776 9-9-3 71.......... RobertWinston 5 | 73 |
| | | | (Willie Musson) *hld up in last trio: hdwy over 1f out: rdn and styd on wl ins fnl f: nt rch ldrs* 4/1[2] | |
| 132- | 6 | shd | **Tychaios**[4] 7989 4-8-13 67.......... DavidProbert 10 | 69 |
| | | | (Stuart Williams) *hld up in tch: rdn jst over 2f out: swtchd lft over 1f out: styd on wl u.p ins fnl f: nt rch ldrs* 2/1[1] | |
| 230- | 7 | 1 | **Jungle Bay**[94] 6021 7-9-7 75..........(p) MartinDwyer 12 | 74 |
| | | | (Jane Chapple-Hyam) *stdd s: hld up in rr: hdwy on inner over 1f out: styd on fnl f: nt clrest of runs and swtchd rt towards fin* 25/1 | |
| 052- | 8 | 5 | **Harrogate Fair**[9] 7931 4-9-2 70..........(p) AdamKirby 11 | 53 |
| | | | (Michael Squance) *stdd s: hld up in last trio: hdwy on outer over 3f out: edgd lft and no hdwy over 1f out: styd on past btn horses ins fnl f: nvr trbld ldrs* 10/1 | |
| 200- | 9 | nse | **Black Vale (IRE)**[31] 7647 3-8-11 68.......... DannyBrock(3) 7 | 50 |
| | | | (Ralph J Smith) *chsd ldr tl over 1f out: sn struggling: wknd fnl f* 33/1 | |
| 200- | 10 | shd | **Roy's Legacy**[13] 7886 5-9-4 72.......... DuranFentiman 9 | 54 |
| | | | (Shaun Harris) *a towards rr: rdn over 2f out: no hdwy u.p over 1f out* 66/1 | |
| 020- | 11 | ¾ | **Angel Flores (IRE)**[25] 7729 3-9-7 75..........(b[1]) AmirQuinn 6 | 55 |
| | | | (Lee Carter) *chsd ldrs tl lost pl wl over 1f out: wknd 1f out* 16/1 | |
| 600- | 12 | 2 | **Saffire Song**[100] 5826 3-9-0 68.......... LiamKeniry 3 | 41 |
| | | | (Alan Bailey) *in tch in midfield: lost pl and bhd over 1f out: sn wknd* 66/1 | |

1m 11.0s (-0.90) **Going Correction** 0.0s/f (Stan) 12 Ran SP% **117.1**
Speed ratings (Par 103): **106,105,104,103,103 103,102,95,95,95 94,91**
CSF £105.53 CT £836.12 TOTE £7.10: £2.80, £2.10, £2.50; EX 79.10 Trifecta £1305.80.
**Owner** Andrew Page **Bred** Mrs Mary Rowlands **Trained** Hubbert's Bridge, Lincs

**FOCUS**
A tight sprint handicap, but they didn't go mad up front and it proved hard to make up ground from off the pace. The runner-up has been rated to form.

## 8041 LADBROKES H'CAP 1m 1y(P)
3:10 (3:11) (Class 5) (0-75,74) 3-Y-O+ £2,587 (£770; £384; £192) Stalls High

| Form | | | | RPR |
|---|---|---|---|---|
| 543- | 1 | | **Rizal Park (IRE)**[59] 7013 3-8-11 68.......... ThomasBrown(3) 2 | 76 |
| | | | (Andrew Balding) *hld up in tch in last pair: gd hdwy on inner 1f out: swtchd rt and r.o strly ins fnl f to ld nr fin* 3/1[2] | |
| 3- | 2 | nk | **Until Midnight (IRE)**[22] 7758 4-9-1 68.......... RobertTart 5 | 75 |
| | | | (Eugene Stanford) *led and set stdy gallop: rdn and qcknd jst over 2f out: r.o wl u.p tl hdd and no ex nr fin* 5/2[1] | |
| 556- | 3 | ½ | **Tommy's Secret**[79] 6466 4-9-7 74.......... MartinDwyer 6 | 80 |
| | | | (Jane Chapple-Hyam) *chsd ldr: rdn jst over 2f out: pressing wnr fnl f: unable qck fnl 100yds* 14/1 | |
| 0/3- | 4 | ½ | **Embankment**[59] 7012 5-9-3 70.......... JimCrowley 4 | 75 |
| | | | (Michael Attwater) *v.s.a: sn rcvrd and hld up in tch in rr: pushed along and clsd 2f out: styd on wl u.p ins fnl f: nt rch ldrs* 6/1[3] | |
| 000- | 5 | 1 ¼ | **Club House (IRE)**[22] 7757 4-8-12 65.......... WilliamTwiston-Davies 1 | 67 |
| | | | (Robert Mills) *t.k.h: chsd ldrs: rdn jst over 2f out: styd on same pce ins fnl f* 6/1[3] | |
| 006- | 6 | ¾ | **Tidal's Baby**[9] 7931 5-9-5 72.......... AmirQuinn 7 | 72 |
| | | | (Lee Carter) *t.k.h: hld up in tch: rdn and effrt wl over 1f out: styd on same pce u.p fnl f* 20/1 | |
| 363- | 7 | ¾ | **Dianora**[20] 7812 3-9-3 71..........(v) DavidProbert 3 | 70 |
| | | | (Sir Michael Stoute) *chsd ldrs: rdn jst over 2f out: drvn and unable qck over 1f out: hld and one pce fnl f* 7/1 | |
| 266- | 8 | 2 | **Dalaki (IRE)**[73] 6649 3-9-3 71.......... AdamKirby 8 | 65 |
| | | | (Jim Boyle) *in tch in midfield: effrt and wdst bnd 2f out: dropped to rr and btn 1f out: one pce after* 10/1 | |

1m 40.21s (2.01) **Going Correction** 0.0s/f (Stan)
**WFA** 3 from 4yo+ 1lb 8 Ran SP% **115.2**
Speed ratings (Par 103): **89,88,88,87,86 85,84,82**
CSF £11.05 CT £87.91 TOTE £4.90: £1.30, £1.30, £3.30; EX 11.80 Trifecta £93.50.
**Owner** L L Register, Martin & Valerie Slade **Bred** Irish National Stud **Trained** Kingsclere, Hants

**FOCUS**
An ordinary handicap and the early pace was moderate. The third has been rated pretty much to the balance of his form.

## 8042 CORAL MOBILE "JUST THREE CLICKS TO BET" H'CAP 1m 2f (P)
3:40 (3:40) (Class 4) (0-85,82) 3-Y-O+ £4,690 (£1,395; £697; £348) Stalls Low

| Form | | | | RPR |
|---|---|---|---|---|
| 411- | 1 | | **Gaelic Silver (FR)**[16] 7831 8-8-13 81.......... HectorCrouch(7) 2 | 93+ |
| | | | (Gary Moore) *hld up in tch: hdwy on inner over 1f out: swtchd rt and chsd clr ldr 1f out: qcknd and str run to ld towards fin* 4/1[2] | |
| 530- | 2 | ¾ | **Sheila's Buddy**[70] 6713 5-9-1 76.......... LiamKeniry 8 | 85 |
| | | | (J S Moore) *chsd ldrs: wnt 2nd over 2f out: led 2f out: rdn and qcknd clr over 1f out: r.o tl hdd and outpcd towards fin* 8/1[3] | |
| 001- | 3 | 2 ½ | **Persepolis (IRE)**[22] 7757 4-9-5 80.......... AmirQuinn 11 | 84+ |
| | | | (Lee Carter) *stdd and dropped in bhd after s: t.k.h: hld up in tch in rr: hdwy on inner over 1f out: swtchd rt and wnt 3rd fnl 75yds: r.o: nvr threatened ldrs* 5/2[1] | |
| 303- | 4 | nk | **Lu's Buddy (GR)**[16] 7831 3-8-10 74..........(t) JimCrowley 7 | 77 |
| | | | (Amanda Perrett) *hld up in tch in last quartet: hdwy and sltly hmpd over 1f out: wnt 3rd briefly fnl 100yds: kpt on: nvr threatened ldrs* 4/1[2] | |
| 460- | 5 | 2 | **Yojojo (IRE)**[16] 7838 5-9-2 77.......... AdamKirby 10 | 76 |
| | | | (Gay Kelleway) *hld up in last trio: rdn and hdwy on outer 3f out: pressed ldrs but unable qck over 1f out: wknd ins fnl f* 10/1 | |
| 000- | 6 | hd | **Coincidently**[16] 7838 4-9-2 77 ow1.......... SebSanders 3 | 76 |
| | | | (Alan Bailey) *reminders leaving stalls: sn led: rdn and hdd 2f out: 3rd and btn 1f out: wknd ins fnl f* 20/1 | |
| 12- | 7 | ½ | **Echo Brava**[80] 6439 4-9-5 80.......... FergusSweeney 9 | 78+ |
| | | | (Luke Dace) *stdd s: hld up in tch in rr: switching rt and hdwy wl over 1f out: kpt on ins fnl f: nvr trbld ldrs* 8/1[3] | |
| 233/ | 8 | ½ | **Ruban (IRE)**[801] 6570 5-9-2 77..........(t) SteveDrowne 1 | 74 |
| | | | (Stuart Williams) *t.k.h: chsd ldrs: unable qck over 1f out: wknd fnl f* 20/1 | |
| 105/ | 9 | 6 | **Lyssio (GER)**[11] 6702 7-9-7 82.......... WilliamTwiston-Davies 4 | 67 |
| | | | (Jim Best) *chsd ldr tl over 2f out: lost pl over 1f out: wknd fnl f* 25/1 | |

004/ **10** ¾ **Beedee**[399] 7656 4-9-0 82 .................................... GaryMahon(7) 5 66
(Richard Hannon) *in tch in midfield: lost pl jst over 2f out: wknd over 1f out* **20/1**

2m 5.77s (-0.83) **Going Correction** 0.0s/f (Stan)
**WFA** 3 from 4yo+ 3lb **10** Ran SP% **118.0**
Speed ratings (Par 105): **103,102,100,100,98 98,98,97,92,92**
CSF £33.82 CT £96.30 TOTE £3.60: £1.30, £3.30, £1.30; EX 35.90 Trifecta £148.50.
**Owner** The Winning Hand **Bred** Earl Haras Du Camp Bernard Et Al **Trained** Lower Beeding, W Sussex

**FOCUS**
A fair handicap, but the pace didn't look that strong. The exposed runner-up helps set the level.
T/Plt: £65.60 to a £1 stake. Pool: £62,292.77 - 692.56 winning tickets T/Qpdt: £13.80 to a £1 stake. Pool: £4,684.36 - 249.54 winning tickets SP

## 7998 WOLVERHAMPTON (A.W) (L-H)
Friday, December 5

**OFFICIAL GOING: Tapeta: standard**
Wind: Light across Weather: Overcast with the odd shower

### 8043 DOWNLOAD THE LADBROKES APP APPRENTICE H'CAP 7f 32y
**4:00** (4:03) (Class 6) (0-65,71) 3-Y-O+ **£1,940** (£577; £288; £144) **Stalls** High

Form RPR
006- **1** **Munaawib**[31] 7647 6-9-7 65 ....................(bt) DavidParkes 8 74
(Deborah Sanderson) *a.p: led over 1f out: rdn out* **25/1**
603- **2** 1 **Ambella (IRE)**[4] 7987 4-8-10 54 ....................(v) NedCurtis 3 60
(Ian Williams) *hld up: hdwy over 1f out: r.o to go 2nd wl ins fnl f: nt rch wnr* **10/1**
6/1- **3** 2 **Shotgun Start**[7] 7950 4-9-13 71 6ex .................... JordanVaughan 4 72
(Michael Wigham) *chsd ldr 2f: remained handy: wnt 2nd again 2f out: sn rdn and ev ch: styd on same pce ins fnl f* **6/5**[1]
/00- **4** nk **Grey Destiny**[171] 3344 4-8-2 51 oh1 .................... GemmaTutty(5) 7 51
(Mel Brittain) *s.i.s: rdn 3f out: hdwy over 1f out: styd on* **33/1**
005- **5** 2 **Milly's Secret (IRE)**[17] 7825 3-9-0 63 .................... JoshDoyle(5) 2 58
(David O'Meara) *hld up: hdwy over 1f out: nt trble ldrs* **16/1**
000- **6** nk **Look Here's Al**[11] 7907 3-9-0 58 .................... AdamMcLean 6 52
(Andrew Hollinshead) *prom: rdn and nt clr run over 1f out: no ex ins fnl f* **25/1**
332- **7** ¾ **Burnhope**[17] 7830 5-9-0 63 .................... RussellHarris(5) 10 55
(Scott Dixon) *sn pushed along to ld: clr over 5f out tl rdn over 2f out: hdd over 1f out: wknd ins fnl f* **3/1**[2]
140- **8** ¾ **Telegraph (IRE)**[22] 7765 3-8-12 61 .................... HarryBurns(5) 11 51
(David Evans) *prom: chsd ldr 5f out tl rdn 2f out: wknd ins fnl f* **25/1**
240- **9** 1 **Logans Lad (IRE)**[7] 7950 4-9-4 65 ....................(bt) RobHornby(3) 5 53
(Daniel Mark Loughnane) *hld up: hdwy on outer over 2f out: rdn and edgd rt fr over 1f out: wknd fnl f* **8/1**[3]
/00- **10** ½ **Omanome (IRE)**[32] 7622 3-8-11 62 ....................(p) TomMarquand(7) 1 48
(David O'Meara) *prom: lost pl after 1f: drvn along over 2f out: n.d after* **50/1**
044- **11** 13 **Myjestic Melody (IRE)**[36] 7547 6-8-2 51 oh6 ....................(t) KevinLundie(5) 9 3
(Shaun Harris) *s.i.s: a in rr: drvn along 1/2-way: wknd over 2f out* **100/1**

1m 27.99s (-0.81) **Going Correction** -0.05s/f (Stan) 11 Ran SP% **114.0**
Speed ratings (Par 101): **102,100,98,98,95 95,94,93,92,92 77**
CSF £232.60 CT £538.15 TOTE £21.60: £6.10, £2.50, £1.02; EX 215.00 Trifecta £692.10.
**Owner** Willie McKay **Bred** Shadwell Estate Company Limited **Trained** Sturton-le-Steeple, Notts

**FOCUS**
A modest handicap in which Burnhope set a fair pace in a clear lead after being driven along from the widest stall. A small pb from the winner, while the runner-up has been rated in line with her form since her early maiden runs.

### 8044 LADBROKES CLASSIFIED CLAIMING STKS 1m 141y
**4:30** (4:30) (Class 5) 3-Y-O+ **£2,587** (£770; £384; £192) **Stalls** Low

Form RPR
616- **1** **Dialogue**[21] 7774 8-8-1 70 .................... RyanTate(3) 7 65
(Andrew Reid) *trckd ldr: led 2f out: rdn over 1f out: r.o: comf* **11/10**[1]
220- **2** 2 **Les Gar Gan (IRE)**[14] 7869 3-8-2 58 .................... JimmyQuinn 5 60
(Keith Dalgleish) *a.p: rdn over 2f out: r.o to go 2nd wl ins fnl f* **14/1**
541- **3** ½ **Swift Cedar (IRE)**[39] 7489 4-9-0 67 ....................(v) JFEgan 1 69
(David Evans) *trckd ldrs: racd keenly: rdn over 2f out: styd on* **4/1**[2]
133- **4** 1 ¼ **Rainford Glory (IRE)**[129] 4749 4-8-10 60 .................... BarryMcHugh 2 62
(Tim Fitzgerald) *led: rdn and hdd 2f out: no ex ins fnl f* **33/1**
645- **5** ¾ **The Dukkerer (IRE)**[11] 7906 3-8-9 67 .................... TomMarquand(7) 4 68+
(Garry Moss) *hld up: hmpd over 7f out: hdwy over 1f out: nt trble ldrs* **12/1**
060- **6** hd **Dansili Dutch (IRE)**[14] 7871 5-8-3 69 .................... JoshDoyle(7) 3 60
(David O'Meara) *mid-div: rdn over 1f out: nt trble ldrs* **16/1**
646- **7** 1 **Conry (IRE)**[25] 7732 8-9-0 70 .................... StevieDonohoe 6 62
(Ian Williams) *s.i.s: hld up: hmpd over 7f out: rdn over 2f out: nvr on terms* **9/2**[3]
000- **8** ¾ **Prime Exhibit**[7] 7954 9-8-7 69 ....................(t) EoinWalsh(5) 9 58
(Daniel Mark Loughnane) *hld up: rdn over 1f out: n.d* **20/1**
260- **9** 12 **Juvenal (IRE)**[41] 6881 5-8-1 62 ....................(b[1]) TimClark(5) 8 24
(Paul Morgan) *s.s: a in rr: rdn and wknd 3f out* **50/1**

1m 51.38s (1.28) **Going Correction** -0.05s/f (Stan)
**WFA** 3 from 4yo+ 2lb 9 Ran SP% **115.7**
Speed ratings (Par 103): **92,90,89,88,88 87,86,86,75**
CSF £18.98 TOTE £2.10: £1.30, £3.40, £1.40; EX 20.40 Trifecta £96.50.The Dukkerer was claimed by Mr J. G. Given £12,000.
**Owner** A S Reid **Bred** Darley **Trained** Mill Hill, London NW7

**FOCUS**
An uncompetitive claimer run at a steady pace. The runner-up has been rated close to her recent level.

### 8045 £20 RISK-FREE BET AT UNIBET H'CAP 5f 216y
**5:00** (5:04) (Class 3) (0-95,92) 3-Y-O+ **£7,246** (£2,168; £1,084; £542; £270) **Stalls** Low

Form RPR
033- **1** **Secondo (FR)**[36] 7543 4-9-4 89 ....................(v) ChrisCatlin 2 99
(Robert Stephens) *s.i.s: hld up: nt clr run over 1f out: shkn up and r.o wl to ld towards fin* **12/1**
003- **2** nk **Baddilini**[16] 7843 4-9-3 88 ....................(p) MartinHarley 7 97
(Alan Bailey) *hld up in tch: rdn to chse ldr over 1f out: ev ch ins fnl f: r.o* **8/1**
410- **3** ½ **Stonefield Flyer**[4] 7988 5-8-9 80 ....................(p) GrahamLee 10 87
(Keith Dalgleish) *led 1f: remained w ldrs tl led again over 2f out: rdn over 1f out: hdd towards fin* **11/2**[3]
531- **4** 1 **Zac Brown (IRE)**[32] 7624 3-9-4 89 .................... JFEgan 3 93+
(David Barron) *stdd s: hld up: plld hrd: hdwy over 1f out: sn rdn: styd on same pce ins fnl f* **6/4**[1]
204- **5** 1 **Master Bond**[13] 7889 5-9-0 85 .................... SamJames 4 86
(David O'Meara) *prom: nt clr run and lost pl over 2f out: styd on ins fnl f* **20/1**
140- **6** 2 **Amadeus Wolfe Tone (IRE)**[16] 7843 5-9-5 90 ....................(p) TomQueally 5 85
(Jamie Osborne) *led 5f out tl rdn and hdd over 2f out: no ex ins fnl f* **5/1**[2]
000- **7** nk **Secret Asset (IRE)**[13] 7889 9-8-11 82 ....................(p) StevieDonohoe 1 76
(Jane Chapple-Hyam) *chsd ldrs: rdn over 1f out: no ex ins fnl f* **33/1**
132- **8** nse **Guishan**[65] 6872 4-8-3 81 .................... TomMarquand(7) 9 74
(Michael Appleby) *s.i.s: sn pushed along and prom: rdn over 2f out: no ex ins fnl f* **11/1**
162- **9** 2 ¼ **Smart Daisy K**[13] 7889 4-9-6 91 .................... ShaneKelly 8 77
(Andrew Hollinshead) *hld up: rdn over 1f out: nvr on terms* **11/1**
406- **10** 8 **Abi Scarlet (IRE)**[22] 7767 5-8-7 78 .................... JimmyQuinn 6 39
(Scott Dixon) *w ldrs tl rdn over 2f out: wknd fnl f* **50/1**

1m 12.88s (-1.62) **Going Correction** -0.05s/f (Stan) 10 Ran SP% **117.2**
Speed ratings (Par 107): **108,107,106,105,104 101,101,101,98,87**
CSF £102.58 CT £595.09 TOTE £14.70: £2.90, £2.50, £3.10; EX 99.40 Trifecta £638.60.
**Owner** D J Deer **Bred** John Deer **Trained** Penhow, Newport

**FOCUS**
A good, competitive sprint handicap. The runner-up has been rated as running as well as ever, while the third has been rated in line with his recent form.

### 8046 32RED NURSERY H'CAP (BOBIS RACE) 5f 216y
**5:30** (5:30) (Class 2) 2-Y-O **£9,056** (£2,695; £1,346; £673) **Stalls** Low

Form RPR
211- **1** **Anonymous John (IRE)**[27] 7714 2-9-7 85 .................... JFEgan 4 90+
(David Evans) *chsd ldrs: rdn over 2f out: led and edgd lft ins fnl f: r.o* **4/1**[3]
423- **2** 1 ¼ **Dark Side Dream**[20] 7807 2-8-2 69 .................... ConnorBeasley(3) 2 69
(Chris Dwyer) *w ldr tl led over 1f out: rdn and hdd ins fnl f: edgd lft: unable qck towards fin* **5/2**[1]
011- **3** ¾ **Anastazia**[13] 7890 2-8-12 76 .................... LukeMorris 7 74
(Paul D'Arcy) *hld up: hdwy and nt clr run over 1f out: sn rdn: styng on whn nt clr run wl ins fnl f: wnt 3rd towards fin* **3/1**[2]
055- **4** ½ **Vimy Ridge**[13] 7882 2-9-5 83 .................... MartinHarley 5 81
(Alan Bailey) *s.i.s: sn prom: rdn over 1f out: styng on same pce whn hmpd wl ins fnl f* **4/1**[3]
603- **5** 1 ½ **Lysander The Greek**[71] 6679 2-7-13 66 ....................(b) JoeyHaynes(3) 8 58
(Ralph Beckett) *hld up: pushed along 1/2-way: nvr trbld ldrs* **6/1**
562- **6** nk **Cloak And Degas (IRE)**[15] 7848 2-8-0 64 oh1 ....................(p) JimmyQuinn 1 56
(Scott Dixon) *led: rdn and hdd over 1f out: styng on same pce whn hmpd wl ins fnl f* **25/1**

1m 13.48s (-1.02) **Going Correction** -0.05s/f (Stan) 6 Ran SP% **111.7**
Speed ratings (Par 102): **104,102,101,100,98 98**
CSF £14.25 CT £32.22 TOTE £3.40: £2.30, £2.10; EX 15.90 Trifecta £29.70.
**Owner** Mrs Rachel Barnes **Bred** Tally-Ho Stud **Trained** Pandy, Monmouths

**FOCUS**
A Class 2 nursery but the top weight was only rated 85.

### 8047 BET IN PLAY AT CORAL H'CAP 1m 4f 50y
**6:00** (6:00) (Class 5) (0-70,74) 3-Y-O **£2,749** (£818; £408; £204) **Stalls** Low

Form RPR
252- **1** **Dire Straits (IRE)**[32] 7628 3-9-6 66 ....................(p) TedDurcan 4 76+
(Chris Wall) *chsd ldr: pushed along over 3f out: led wl over 1f out: sn edgd lft: rdn out* **11/10**[1]
/44- **2** 2 ½ **Captain Swift (IRE)**[119] 5132 3-9-6 66 .................... GrahamLee 2 71
(John Mackie) *hld up: pushed along over 3f out: hdwy and nt clr run over 1f out: rdn to go 2nd ins fnl f: styd on: nt trble wnr* **16/1**
415- **3** 3 ½ **Cascadia (IRE)**[13] 7895 3-8-10 56 .................... RobertHavlin 7 55
(Alison Hutchinson) *led: rdn over 2f out: hdd wl over 1f out: wknd ins fnl f* **18/1**
031- **4** nk **Heska (IRE)**[6] 7975 3-10-0 74 7ex ....................(tp) LukeMorris 1 73
(Michael Appleby) *s.i.s: sn prom: rdn and edgd lft over 1f out: wknd ins fnl f* **7/4**[2]
0- **5** ¾ **Baileys En Premier (FR)**[11] 7901 3-9-0 60 .................... BenCurtis 5 57
(Chris Dwyer) *hld up: rdn over 2f out: nvr on terms* **40/1**
443- **6** nk **Sakhra**[13] 7895 3-8-12 58 .................... GrahamGibbons 3 55
(Mark Brisbourne) *chsd ldrs: rdn over 2f out: wknd ins fnl f* **8/1**[3]

2m 38.36s (-2.44) **Going Correction** -0.05s/f (Stan) 6 Ran SP% **108.7**
Speed ratings (Par 102): **106,104,102,101,101 101**
CSF £18.31 TOTE £2.00: £1.20, £4.80; EX 21.00 Trifecta £140.80.
**Owner** D S Lee **Bred** Noel Carter **Trained** Newmarket, Suffolk

**FOCUS**
A weak race run at a modest pace. A clear pb from the winner, with the second rated as running his best race since his 2yo maiden days.

### 8048 BEST ODDS AT CORAL MAIDEN STKS 1m 1f 103y
**6:30** (6:32) (Class 5) 3-4-Y-O **£2,587** (£770; £384; £192) **Stalls** Low

Form RPR
325- **1** **L'Inganno Felice (FR)**[21] 7784 4-9-7 74 .................... GrahamLee 4 78
(Iain Jardine) *chsd ldr 8f out tl led over 2f out: shkn up over 1f out: styd on wl* **5/1**[2]
2- **2** 3 ½ **Westwood Hoe**[11] 7901 3-9-5 0 .................... RobertHavlin 2 71
(John Gosden) *led 1f: chsd ldrs: shkn up over 3f out: rdn to chse wnr over 1f out: sn edgd lft: no imp fnl f* **4/11**[1]
**3** 1 ¼ **Astral Weeks** 3-9-0 0 .................... LukeMorris 5 63
(Michael Bell) *prom: drvn along 3f out: styd on same pce fr over 1f out* **9/1**[3]
**4** ½ **Magnified** 4-9-7 0 .................... DavidNolan 6 67
(David O'Meara) *hld up: hdwy over 2f out: rdn over 1f out: no ex fnl f* **50/1**
5- **5** 2 ¾ **Lesson In Life**[52] 7176 3-9-0 0 .................... SamJames 7 56
(David O'Meara) *led after 1f: rdn and hdd over 2f out: wknd fnl f* **12/1**
**6** 9 **Strictly The One (IRE)**[31] 4-9-2 0 .................... RyanWhile(5) 1 42
(Neil Mulholland) *s.i.s: sn pushed along in rr: rdn 1/2-way: lost tch fr over 3f out* **100/1**

1m 59.47s (-1.33) **Going Correction** -0.05s/f (Stan)
**WFA** 3 from 4yo 2lb 6 Ran SP% **110.6**
Speed ratings (Par 103): **103,99,98,98,95 87**
CSF £7.02 TOTE £6.70: £2.10, £1.10; EX 10.70 Trifecta £19.70.
**Owner** A Dawson & Mrs K Campbell **Bred** E A R L Elevage Des Loges **Trained** Bonchester Bridge, Roxburgh

## 8049 CORAL.CO.UK H'CAP (DIV I) 1m 1f 103y
7:00 (7:00) (Class 6) (0-60,60) 3-Y-O £1,940 (£577; £288; £144) Stalls Low

Form RPR
6- 1 **Moulin Rouge (DEN)**[6] 7976 3-8-7 46 ........ StevieDonohoe 4 55+
(Ian Williams) *s.i.s: hld up: plld hrd: hdwy over 1f out: r.o u.p to ld post* **25/1**
301- 2 nk **Triple Star**[14] 7869 3-9-3 56 ........ HayleyTurner 9 63
(Hughie Morrison) *hld up: hdwy over 1f out: led wl ins fnl f: hdd post* **6/1**[3]
012- 3 nk **San Quentin (IRE)**[6] 7977 3-8-13 52 ........(p) LukeMorris 6 58
(Tony Carroll) *prom: pushed along 3f out: rdn and edgd lft over 1f out: r.o* **5/2**[1]
605- 4 ½ **Unbridled Joy (IRE)**[45] 7347 3-9-1 57 ........ RyanTate(3) 3 62
(Clive Cox) *led: rdn over 1f out: hdd wl ins fnl f* **15/2**
003- 5 ¾ **Sooqaan**[35] 7570 3-9-7 60 ........ GrahamLee 10 64
(Mel Brittain) *chsd ldr: rdn over 1f out: no ex towards fin* **7/2**[2]
522- 6 ½ **Company Secretary (USA)**[10] 7908 3-9-6 59 ........(p) TomQueally 2 63+
(Jo Hughes) *hld up: hdwy and hmpd over 1f out: nvr able to chal* **7/2**[2]
005- 7 ¾ **Dutch Lady Roseane**[14] 7869 3-8-7 46 oh1 ........(p) LiamJones 1 47
(James Unett) *prom: rdn over 2f out: no ex ins fnl f* **40/1**
023- 8 ½ **Yawail**[52] 7188 3-8-11 57 ........(p) KevinLundie(7) 5 57
(Brian Rothwell) *chsd ldrs: rdn over 2f out: styd on same pce fnl f* **7/2**[2]
320- P **Her Red Devil (IRE)**[35] 7570 3-9-5 58 ........ GeorgeChaloner 8
(Christopher Kellett) *hld up: rdn and wknd over 2f out: p.u fnl f* **28/1**

2m 1.96s (1.16) **Going Correction** -0.05s/f (Stan) 9 Ran SP% 113.6
Speed ratings (Par 98): **92,91,91,91,90 89,89,88,**
CSF £158.71 CT £525.49 TOTE £20.50: £4.70, £2.00, £1.10; EX 61.60 Trifecta £350.90.
**Owner** Eric Brook & Inge Knutsson **Bred** Stutteri Hjortebo **Trained** Portway, Worcs
■ Stewards' Enquiry : Ryan Tate two-day ban: careless riding (19-20 Dec)

## 8050 CORAL.CO.UK H'CAP (DIV II) 1m 1f 103y
7:30 (7:31) (Class 6) (0-60,59) 3-Y-O £1,940 (£577; £288; £144) Stalls Low

Form RPR
300- 1 **Hickster (IRE)**[14] 7868 3-8-12 55 ........(t) AlistairRawlinson(5) 9 63
(Roy Bowring) *mde all: rdn over 1f out: jst hld on* **6/1**[3]
632- 2 ½ **Crown Pleasure (IRE)**[35] 7570 3-9-7 59 ........ ChrisCatlin 2 66
(Willie Musson) *hld up: hdwy over 2f out: rdn over 1f out: r.o: wnt 2nd post* **2/1**[1]
005- 3 hd **Tohaveandtohold**[35] 7570 3-8-12 50 ........(p) LiamJones 7 57
(William Haggas) *chsd wnr: rdn over 2f out: r.o* **8/1**
300- 4 1¾ **White Rose Runner**[31] 7640 3-9-4 56 ........ GrahamLee 3 59
(Mel Brittain) *prom: rdn over 2f out: styd on same pce ins fnl f* **15/2**
024- 5 ¾ **Southern Cross**[38] 7517 3-9-5 57 ........ HayleyTurner 4 58
(Andy Turnell) *hld up: hdwy over 1f out: styd on same pce ins fnl f* **7/1**
500- 6 3 **Road Map (IRE)**[17] 7830 3-9-7 59 ........ ShaneKelly 6 54
(Daniel Mark Loughnane) *hld up: plld hrd: rdn over 1f out: nvr on terms* **28/1**
015- 7 3¼ **Sarlat**[6] 7976 3-8-8 49 ........ AmyScott(3) 8 37
(Mark Brisbourne) *s.i.s: hld up: hdwy over 6f out: rdn: edgd rt and wknd over 1f out* **7/2**[2]
030- 8 4½ **Genax (IRE)**[13] 7883 3-8-7 45 ........(p) StevieDonohoe 10 24
(Ian Williams) *chsd ldrs: rdn over 2f out: wknd over 1f out* **8/1**

2m 0.34s (-0.46) **Going Correction** -0.05s/f (Stan) 8 Ran SP% 119.8
Speed ratings (Par 98): **100,99,99,97,97 94,91,87**
CSF £19.41 CT £100.25 TOTE £6.00: £2.90, £1.40, £2.40; EX 25.10 Trifecta £249.70.
**Owner** L P Keane **Bred** Me Surrender Syndicate **Trained** Edwinstowe, Notts

**FOCUS**
The runner-up has been rated as matching her CD latest.
T/Plt: £32.40 to a £1 stake. Pool: £77,222.11 - 1,735.50 winning tickets T/Qpdt: £17.80 to a £1 stake. Pool: £8,545.24 - 353.40 winning tickets CR

8051 - 8057a (Foreign Racing) - See Raceform Interactive

# 8043 WOLVERHAMPTON (A.W) (L-H)
Saturday, December 6

**OFFICIAL GOING: Tapeta: standard**
Wind: Fresh behind Weather: Overcast

## 8058 LADBROKES H'CAP 7f 32y
6:15 (6:15) (Class 5) (0-75,75) 3-Y-O+ £2,749 (£818; £408; £204) Stalls High

Form RPR
532- 1 **Smokethatthunders (IRE)**[8] 7953 4-9-7 75 ........ AdamKirby 5 84
(James Unett) *trckd ldr tl shkn up to ld wl over 1f out: rdn out* **5/2**[2]
046- 2 1¼ **Khajaaly (IRE)**[8] 7954 7-8-13 70 ........(vt) RyanTate(3) 4 76
(Michael Appleby) *trckd ldrs: rdn to chse wnr wl ins fnl f: r.o* **9/1**
503- 3 1 **Dream Scenario**[8] 7953 4-9-4 72 ........(v) GrahamLee 2 75
(Mel Brittain) *a.p: rdn over 1f out: r.o towards fin: nt rch ldrs* **7/2**[3]
603- 4 hd **Exceeding Power**[23] 7759 3-9-3 71 ........ GeorgeBaker 8 74
(Martin Bosley) *led at stdy pce tl qcknd over 2f out: shkn up and hdd wl over 1f out: no ex wl ins fnl f* **9/1**
621- 5 1¾ **Gambino (IRE)**[15] 7871 4-8-13 70 ........ ConnorBeasley(3) 6 68
(John David Riches) *plld hrd and prom: rdn over 1f out: no ex ins fnl f* **2/1**[1]
060- 6 1½ **Naabegha**[23] 7761 7-9-7 75 ........ RobertWinston 10 69
(John Balding) *hld up: plld hrd: shkn up over 1f out: nvr on terms* **10/1**
060- 7 nse **Imaginary World (IRE)**[59] 7042 6-8-12 71 ........(e) ShaneGray(5) 7 65
(John Balding) *hld up: shkn up over 1f out: n.d* **22/1**

1m 29.0s (0.20) **Going Correction** -0.075s/f (Stan) 7 Ran SP% 117.6
Speed ratings (Par 103): **95,93,92,92,90 88,88**
CSF £25.96 CT £80.09 TOTE £3.40: £1.90, £4.30; EX 27.40 Trifecta £115.70.
**Owner** Northern Line Racing Ltd **Bred** P Doyle Bloodstock & J K Thoroughbred **Trained** Tedsmore Hall, Shropshire

**FOCUS**
A slowly run race and those held up had no chance. The winner is pretty exposed off this sort of mark but has been rated to a small pb. The runner-up has been rated close to his best.

## 8059 £20 RISK-FREE BET AT UNIBET CONDITIONS STKS (FAST TRACK QUALIFIER) (BOBIS RACE) 5f 20y
6:45 (6:45) (Class 2) 2-Y-O £9,056 (£2,695; £1,346; £673) Stalls Low

Form RPR
112- 1 **Portamento (IRE)**[42] 7439 2-9-0 100 ........ AdamKirby 3 92+
(Charlie Appleby) *prom: chsd ldr 3f out: shkn up to ld wl over 1f out: r.o: comf* **2/9**[1]
413- 2 1¾ **Apache Storm**[36] 7564 2-8-9 79 ........ RobertWinston 4 77+
(Michael Appleby) *a.p: rdn and hung lft fr over 1f out: chsd wnr ins fnl f: styd on* **4/1**[2]
231- 3 3 **Shackled N Drawn (USA)**[14] 7881 2-9-0 70 ........(t) JamieSpencer 2 71
(Olly Stevens) *s.i.s: hld up: hdwy over 1f out: sn rdn: no ex ins fnl f* **10/1**[3]
403- 4 1½ **Jimmy's Hall**[10] 7917 2-9-0 0 ........(b[1]) StevieDonohoe 1 66
(J S Moore) *chsd ldr 2f: remained handy: rdn over 1f out: no ex fnl f* **66/1**
441- 5 nse **Somedaysrdiamonds**[22] 7780 2-8-9 66 ........(p) LiamJones 5 60
(J S Moore) *sn pushed along to ld: rdn and hdd wl over 1f out: no ex fnl f* **25/1**

1m 0.5s (-1.40) **Going Correction** -0.075s/f (Stan) 2y crse rec 5 Ran SP% 116.3
Speed ratings (Par 102): **108,105,100,98,97**
CSF £1.81 TOTE £1.20: £1.02, £2.00; EX 2.00 Trifecta £3.60.
**Owner** Godolphin **Bred** Darley **Trained** Newmarket, Suffolk

**FOCUS**
There can't have been many juveniles of the winner's standard to have competed over this trip at Wolverhampton so late in the year, and the Godolphin colt quickened off a steady pace to break the 2yo course record for both the new Tapeta track (17th such contest so far) and the previous surface.

## 8060 32RED.COM IRISH STALLION FARMS EBF MAIDEN STKS 7f 32y
7:15 (7:17) (Class 5) 2-Y-O £2,911 (£866; £432; £216) Stalls High

Form RPR
3- 1 **Cilento (IRE)**[17] 7833 2-9-5 0 ........ RobertHavlin 7 72+
(John Gosden) *a.p: rdn to ld ins fnl f: edgd lft: styd on* **11/8**[1]
3- 2 ½ **Salma Gondis (IRE)**[21] 7809 2-9-0 0 ........ SamJames 8 66
(David O'Meara) *w ldr to 1/2-way: led again 2f out: sn rdn: hdd ins fnl f: styd on* **9/1**[3]
6- 3 hd **Acclamate (IRE)**[7] 7973 2-9-5 0 ........(t) PaddyAspell 12 70
(Marco Botti) *chsd ldrs: rdn and ev ch fr over 1f out: styd on* **4/1**[2]
324- 4 ¾ **Fast Charlie (IRE)**[77] 6538 2-9-5 75 ........ GrahamLee 2 68
(Ann Duffield) *hld up: hdwy over 2f out: nt clr run over 1f out: sn rdn and hung lft: r.o* **12/1**
- 5 3¼ **Silent Thunder (IRE)** 2-9-5 0 ........ JamieSpencer 4 60+
(William Haggas) *s.i.s: hld up: nt clr run over 1f out: r.o ins fnl f: nrst fin* **4/1**[2]
6 hd **Sciustree** 2-9-5 0 ........ AdamKirby 6 60+
(Marco Botti) *s.i.s and pushed along in rr early: hdwy over 2f out: rdn over 1f out: hung lft and wknd ins fnl f* **10/1**
6- 7 2 **Idle Talker (IRE)**[43] 7414 2-9-5 0 ........(t) RaulDaSilva 9 55
(Jose Santos) *hld up: hdwy u.p over 1f out: wknd ins fnl f* **50/1**
60- 8 2½ **Aruan**[46] 7367 2-9-0 0 ........ LiamKeniry 10 44
(Derek Haydn Jones) *prom: rdn and hung lft over 1f out: wknd fnl f* **66/1**
00- 9 3¼ **Mclovin Riverdance**[63] 6935 2-8-12 0 ........ RowanScott(7) 11 41
(Ann Duffield) *hld up: rdn over 1f out: n.d* **100/1**
50- 10 2 **Outlaw Kate (IRE)**[28] 7712 2-8-11 0 ........ JoeyHaynes(3) 5 31
(Michael Mullineaux) *sn pushed along in rr: sme hdwy over 1f out: wknd fnl f* **150/1**
006- 11 7 **Dazzling Display**[18] 7828 2-9-0 0 ........ JasonHart 3 14
(Richard Guest) *sn pushed along in rr: bhd fnl 4f* **150/1**
06- 12 1¾ **Spirit Of Rosanna**[10] 7917 2-9-0 0 ........ RobertWinston 1 10+
(Steph Hollinshead) *led tl rdn and hdd 2f out: eased over 1f out* **150/1**

1m 29.39s (0.59) **Going Correction** -0.075s/f (Stan) 12 Ran SP% 115.3
Speed ratings (Par 96): **93,92,92,91,87 87,85,82,78,76 68,66**
CSF £15.09 TOTE £2.30: £1.10, £2.30, £1.70; EX 15.70 Trifecta £61.60.
**Owner** HRH Princess Haya Of Jordan **Bred** Knocktoran Stud **Trained** Newmarket, Suffolk
■ Stewards' Enquiry : Jamie Spencer caution: careless riding

**FOCUS**
An ordinary maiden run at a steady pace.

## 8061 32RED CASINO H'CAP 2m 119y
7:45 (7:46) (Class 6) (0-65,65) 3-Y-O+ £2,102 (£625; £312; £156) Stalls Low

Form RPR
300- 1 **Dukes Den**[9] 7946 3-8-11 56 ........ LiamKeniry 7 65
(Sylvester Kirk) *a.p: led 3f out: rdn over 1f out: edgd rt ins fnl f: styd on* **8/1**
262- 2 1¾ **Lacey**[14] 7893 5-9-4 55 ........(p) AdamKirby 6 62
(Andrew Hollinshead) *hld up: hdwy 4f out: rdn to chse wnr over 1f out: edgd lft u.p ins fnl f: styd on same pce* **5/1**[3]
321- 3 9 **Yorkshireman (IRE)**[14] 7893 4-9-2 53 ........(b) PaddyAspell 9 49
(Lynn Siddall) *sn pushed along to chse ldr: led 5f out: rdn and hdd 3f out: wknd fnl f* **2/1**[1]
250- 4 10 **Black Iceman**[36] 7572 6-8-9 49 ........ SimonPearce(3) 1 33
(Lydia Pearce) *prom: rdn over 2f out: wknd over 1f out* **25/1**
550- 5 24 **Authentication**[32] 7643 5-8-13 50 ........ GrahamLee 2 5
(Mel Brittain) *led over 11f: rdn and wknd 3f out* **11/1**
321- 6 2¾ **Royal Trooper (IRE)**[33] 7628 8-9-7 65 ........ BeckyBrisbourne(7) 8 17
(Mark Brisbourne) *s.v.s: a wl bhd* **7/2**[2]
330- 7 22 **Jan Smuts (IRE)**[19] 7817 6-9-7 63 ........(tp) EmmaSayer(5) 5
(Wilf Storey) *hld up: drvn along 7f out: wknd over 4f out* **18/1**
204- 8 6 **Carlanda (FR)**[196] 2550 4-9-9 65 ........(p) AlistairRawlinson(5) 4
(Michael Appleby) *pushed along early in rr: hdwy over 13f out: rdn over 5f out: wknd 4f out* **13/2**

3m 34.94s (-8.76) **Going Correction** -0.075s/f (Stan) course record
**WFA** 3 from 4yo+ 8lb 8 Ran SP% 114.1
Speed ratings (Par 101): **117,116,111,107,95 94,84,81**
CSF £47.29 CT £110.60 TOTE £8.00: £2.50, £2.10, £1.40; EX 61.40 Trifecta £209.80.
**Owner** E Sharp, T Pearson & S Kirk **Bred** Aylesfield Farms Stud **Trained** Upper Lambourn, Berks

**FOCUS**
A moderate contest but a strong pace saw another track record go, the time significantly faster than the 11 previous races at this distance on the Tapeta and also a good bit quicker than any horse managed on the previous surface. This has been rated around the runner-up to his recent level.

## 8062 32RED H'CAP 1m 5f 194y
8:15 (8:20) (Class 2) (0-105,94) 3-Y-O £11,971 (£3,583; £1,791; £896; £446) Stalls Low

Form RPR
601- 1 **Entihaa**[5] 7995 6-9-7 87 6ex ........ MartinDwyer 2 96
(Alan Swinbank) *chsd ldr tl led over 2f out: rdn over 1f out: styd on wl* **3/1**[2]
001- 2 1¾ **Personal Opinion**[7] 7974 3-9-5 92 ........ AdamKirby 6 99
(Charlie Appleby) *hld up: hdwy over 2f out: rdn to chse wnr over 1f out: no imp ins fnl f* **11/8**[1]
4- 3 2 **Unanimite (FR)**[21] 721 3-9-7 94 ........ WilliamTwiston-Davies 7 98
(David Pipe) *prom: lost pl 11f out: rdn over 2f out: hdwy over 1f out: styd on same pce ins fnl f* **14/1**

/56- **4** *hd* **Cool Sky**[36] 7566 5-8-13 **79**............ StevieDonohoe 5 83
(Ian Williams) *hld up in tch: rdn over 2f out: styd on same pce ins fnl f* **10/1**

021- **5** *¾* **Gabrial's Star**[29] 7702 5-9-8 **88**............(b) GeorgeChaloner 3 91
(Richard Fahey) *sn prom: rdn over 2f out: no ex ins fnl f* **7/1**

011- **6** *8* **Street Artist (IRE)**[11] 7914 4-9-4 **84**............ RobertHavlin 1 76
(David Nicholls) *led: rdn and hdd over 2f out: wknd over 1f out* **5/1**[3]

006- **7** *19* **The Lock Master (IRE)**[7] 7974 7-9-2 **87**............ AlistairRawlinson(5) 4 52
(Michael Appleby) *s.i.s: sn prom: rdn over 5f out: wknd 3f out* **33/1**

2m 57.55s (-7.25) **Going Correction** -0.075s/f (Stan) course record
**WFA** 3 from 4yo+ 7lb **7** Ran SP% **115.0**
Speed ratings (Par 109): **117,116,114,114,114 109,98**
CSF £7.62 TOTE £4.10: £2.10, £1.40; EX 9.10 Trifecta £74.50.

**Owner** Elsa Crankshaw & G Allan **Bred** Wardall Bloodstock **Trained** Melsonby, N Yorks

**FOCUS**
Easily the quickest of 14 races run over this trip on the Tapeta so far, but the strong-staying winner, who was always well placed, got a jump on the closers rounding the final bend. The winner has been rated as running a pb.

## 8063 DOWNLOAD THE LADBROKES APP H'CAP 1m 141y
**8:45** (8:46) (Class 6) (0-60,66) 3-Y-0+ **£2,102** (£625; £312; £156) **Stalls** Low

Form RPR

050- **1** **Steel Stockholder**[36] 7568 8-9-6 59............ GrahamLee 1 67
(Mel Brittain) *chsd ldrs: nt clr run over 1f out: rdn and r.o to ld wl ins fnl f* **25/1**

511- **2** *1 ¼* **Baltic Prince (IRE)**[3] 8013 4-9-13 66 6ex............ RaulDaSilva 4 71+
(Tony Carroll) *set stdy pce tl hdd over 5f out: hmpd sn after: chsd ldrs: rdn over 2f out: led ins fnl f: sn hdd and unable qck* **13/8**[1]

260- **3** *shd* **Nelson's Bay**[32] 7639 5-8-12 56............ EmmaSayer(5) 13 61+
(Wilf Storey) *hld up: nt clr run 1f out: swtchd rt and r.o wl ins fnl f: nt rch ldrs* **20/1**

202- **4** *¾* **My Renaissance**[15] 7869 4-9-2 55............ JamieSpencer 5 58
(Ben Case) *trckd ldrs: led over 5f out: edgd lft sn after: rdn and hung rt over 1f out: hdd ins fnl f: styd on same pce* **9/2**[2]

610- **5** *shd* **Ad Vitam (IRE)**[21] 7813 6-9-7 60............(bt) AdamKirby 2 64+
(Suzzanne France) *prom: pushed along over 3f out: hmpd over 2f out: rdn and swtchd rt over 1f out: r.o towards fin* **14/1**

324- **6** *1* **Humour (IRE)**[14] 7883 3-9-3 58............ WilliamTwiston-Davies 8 59
(Christine Dunnett) *hld up: hdwy and nt clr run over 1f out: sn rdn: styd on same pce ins fnl f* **7/1**

053- **7** *1 ½* **Piccolo Express**[257] 1081 8-8-11 50............ JasonHart 6 47
(Brian Baugh) *hld up: plld hrd: hdwy on outer over 2f out: rdn over 1f out: no ex ins fnl f* **33/1**

244- **8** *hd* **Stanlow**[15] 7868 4-9-3 56............(tp) ShaneKelly 12 53
(Daniel Mark Loughnane) *hld up: hdwy over 2f out: hmpd over 1f out: styd on same pce fnl f* **11/2**[3]

000- **9** *2 ½* **Pipers Piping (IRE)**[53] 7187 8-8-11 53............ RossAtkinson(3) 10 44
(Mandy Rowland) *hld up: rdn over 2f out: nt clr run over 1f out: hung lft ins fnl f: n.d* **40/1**

061- **10** *nk* **It's All A Game**[11] 7908 3-8-13 57............(b) ThomasBrown(3) 9 47
(Richard Guest) *prom: chsd ldr over 4f out tl rdn over 3f out: hmpd over 1f out: wknd fnl f* **8/1**

446/ **11** *½* **Syrian**[243] 974 7-9-2 58............ ConnorBeasley(3) 7 47
(Richard Ford) *plld hrd: trckd ldr tl over 5f out: wnt 2nd again over 3f out: rdn over 1f out: wknd ins fnl f* **25/1**

650- **12** *2 ¾* **Roly Tricks**[9] 7942 3-8-12 53............ CharlesBishop 3 36
(Natalie Lloyd-Beavis) *s.i.s: hld up: rdn over 3f out: a in rr* **66/1**

1m 50.37s (0.27) **Going Correction** -0.075s/f (Stan)
**WFA** 3 from 4yo+ 2lb **12** Ran SP% **121.3**
Speed ratings (Par 101): **95,93,93,93,93 92,90,90,88,88 87,85**
CSF £64.28 CT £904.75 TOTE £24.40: £5.00, £1.50, £7.50; EX 102.10 Trifecta £1976.10.

**Owner** Mel Brittain **Bred** Mrs Joan M Langmead **Trained** Warthill, N Yorks

■ Stewards' Enquiry : Connor Beasley two-day ban: careless riding (20, 22 Dec)
Jamie Spencer five-day ban: careless riding (20, 22, 26-28 Dec)

**FOCUS**
A rough race. Muddling form.

## 8064 CORAL APP DOWNLOAD FROM THE APP STORE MAIDEN STKS 1m 4f 50y
**9:15** (9:15) (Class 5) 3-Y-0+ **£2,749** (£818; £408; £204) **Stalls** Low

Form RPR

4- **1** **Urban Castle (USA)**[12] 7901 3-9-0 0............ AdamKirby 4 72+
(James Tate) *chsd ldr tl rdn to ld over 1f out: styd on wl* **2/1**[2]

5/4- **2** *1 ¾* **Salmon Sushi**[17] 7841 3-9-5 74............ GeorgeBaker 2 74
(David Lanigan) *trckd ldrs: plld hrd: rdn and hung lft fr over 1f out: nt run on* **11/10**[1]

02- **3** *1 ½* **Royal Battalion**[8] 7951 3-9-5 0............ JamieSpencer 1 72
(Stuart Williams) *led: rdn over 2f out: hdd over 1f out: styd on same pce ins fnl f* **10/3**[3]

55- **4** *6* **Direct Approach (IRE)**[8] 7951 10-9-10 0............ PaddyAspell 6 62?
(Lynn Siddall) *hld up: rdn over 1f out: nvr trbld ldrs* **100/1**

43- **5** *1 ½* **Harmonical**[8] 7951 3-9-0 0............ GrahamLee 5 55
(Mel Brittain) *prom: rdn over 2f out: wknd wl over 1f out* **22/1**

**6** *½* **Claraty**[329] 4-9-5 0............ LiamKeniry 3 54?
(James Unett) *prom tl rdn and wknd fnl f* **66/1**

**7** *14* **Halling At Themoon**[24] 4-9-10 0............ ShaneKelly 7 37
(Andrew Hollinshead) *hld up: rdn and wknd over 2f out* **80/1**

2m 40.39s (-0.41) **Going Correction** -0.075s/f (Stan)
**WFA** 3 from 4yo+ 5lb **7** Ran SP% **112.1**
Speed ratings (Par 103): **98,96,95,91,90 90,81**
CSF £4.37 TOTE £3.50: £1.70, £1.10; EX 6.10 Trifecta £9.00.

**Owner** Saeed Manana **Bred** Rabbah Bloodstock Llc **Trained** Newmarket, Suffolk

**FOCUS**
The top three in the market filled the top three spots throughout in this weak and steadily run maiden.

T/Plt: £12.40 to a £1 stake. Pool: £124,294.73 - 7,300.45 winning tickets T/Qpdt: £4.70 to a £1 stake. Pool: £10,175.90 - 1,586.10 winning tickets CR

8065 - 8066a (Foreign Racing) - See Raceform Interactive

# 8023 KEMPTON (A.W) (R-H)
Monday, December 8

**OFFICIAL GOING: Polytrack: standard**

## 8067 BOOK NOW FOR BOXING DAY MAIDEN STKS 1m (P)
**2:10** (2:10) (Class 5) 2-Y-0 **£3,234** (£962; £481; £240) **Stalls** Low

Form RPR

5- **1** **Entitling (IRE)**[33] 7666 2-9-5 0............ TomQueally 12 80+
(James Fanshawe) *hld up in midfield: plenty to do and effrt 2f out: hdwy over 1f out: styd on relentlessly to ld wl ins fnl f: gng away at fin* **3/1**[1]

62- **2** *1 ½* **Putting Green**[16] 7892 2-9-5 0............ JimCrowley 13 73
(Richard Hannon) *chsd ldr: rdn over 3f out: unable qck over 1f out: no threat to wnr but rallied fnl 100yds: snatched 2nd last strides* **14/1**

4- **3** *hd* **Fiesole**[24] 7778 2-9-5 0............ AdamKirby 2 72
(Luca Cumani) *chsd ldrs: rdn and chalng over 1f out: chsd wnr wl ins fnl f: one pce and lost 2nd last strides* **7/2**[2]

2- **4** *¾* **Inexes**[23] 7811 2-9-5 0............ RobertHavlin 6 70
(John Gosden) *led: rdn and qcknd 2f out: hdd and no ex wl ins fnl f: lost 2 pls after* **3/1**[1]

0U2- **5** *¾* **Sonnolento (IRE)**[19] 7833 2-9-5 0............ LiamKeniry 4 69
(Andrew Balding) *chsd ldrs: shifting rt and effrt u.p over 1f out: kpt on same pce ins fnl f* **10/1**

00- **6** *1* **Parole (IRE)**[16] 7892 2-9-5 0............ PatCosgrave 10 66
(Hughie Morrison) *wl in tch in midfield: hdwy to chse ldrs over 3f out: outpcd u.p over 1f out: one pce fnl f* **100/1**

0- **7** *1 ½* **Mr Bissto**[45] 7413 2-9-0 0............ GeorgeDowning(5) 7 63
(Ian Williams) *hld up in midfield: pushed along 2f out: styd on steadily ins fnl f: no threat to ldrs* **100/1**

0- **8** *½* **Molten Lava (IRE)**[28] 7731 2-9-5 0............ LukeMorris 1 62
(Paul Cole) *wl in tch in midfield: rdn jst over 2f out: outpcd and btn over 1f out: plugged on same pce after* **33/1**

6- **9** *1 ¾* **Special Code (IRE)**[19] 7833 2-9-5 0............ SteveDrowne 3 58
(John Gosden) *t.k.h: hld up in midfield: rdn and unable qck wl over 1f out: wl hld and one pce fnl f* **16/1**

**10** *2 ¼* **Sumeida (USA)** 2-9-5 0............ JamieSpencer 5 53
(Jeremy Noseda) *s.i.s: rn green in rr early: hdwy 1/2-way: rdn and no hdwy over 1f out* **25/1**

**11** *2* **New Style (USA)** 2-9-0 0............ JamesDoyle 11 43
(Saeed bin Suroor) *sn dropped to rr and rn green: n.d* **7/1**[3]

6- **12** *¾* **Dexterous**[16] 7892 2-9-0 0............ WilliamTwiston-Davies 8 41
(Roger Charlton) *s.i.s: a in last quartet: n.d* **25/1**

00- **13** *2 ¼* **Copperopolis**[33] 7667 2-9-5 0............(p) FergusSweeney 9 41
(Roger Charlton) *rn green: a in rr: n.d* **100/1**

1m 39.97s (0.17) **Going Correction** -0.025s/f (Stan) **13** Ran SP% **120.0**
Speed ratings (Par 96): **98,96,96,95,94 93,92,91,90,87 85,85,82**
CSF £45.21 TOTE £5.50: £2.40, £2.80, £1.60; EX 65.00 Trifecta £259.80.

**Owner** Ben CM Wong **Bred** MCLPT Stable **Trained** Newmarket, Suffolk

**FOCUS**
Probably not a bad maiden, with the winner coming from off the pace in a race in which it paid to race handily. The level is a bit fluid behind the winner.

## 8068 £25 FREE BET AT BETVICTOR.COM H'CAP 1m (P)
**2:40** (2:41) (Class 5) (0-70,69) 3-Y-0+ **£2,911** (£866; £432; £216) **Stalls** Low

Form RPR

604- **1** **Gracious George (IRE)**[19] 7831 4-9-4 67............ JamieSpencer 8 76
(Jimmy Fox) *hld up in last trio: hdwy over 1f out: chsd clr wnr 1f out: led fnl 100yds: styd on: rdn out* **3/1**[1]

540- **2** *1* **Hardy Black (IRE)**[25] 7758 3-9-3 67............(b[1]) JamesDoyle 9 74
(Jamie Osborne) *in tch in midfield: hdwy to ld over 4f out: rdn clr 2f out: hdd and one pce fnl 100yds* **10/3**[2]

535- **3** *¾* **Sixties Love**[50] 7303 3-9-2 66............ SteveDrowne 4 71
(Simon Dow) *hld up in tch in midfield: effrt u.p 2f out: hdwy over 1f out: wnt 3rd ins fnl f: kpt on* **16/1**

000- **4** *2 ¼* **Hill Of Dreams (IRE)**[14] 7906 5-9-2 65............(b) PatCosgrave 2 65
(Dean Ivory) *in tch in midfield: rdn and hdwy over 2f out: chsd clr wnr briefly over 1f out: wknd ins fnl f* **11/1**

440- **5** *1 ¾* **World Record (IRE)**[20] 7829 4-9-6 69............ MartinDwyer 3 65
(Mick Quinn) *led for 1f: chsd ldr tl over 4f out: wnt 2nd over 2f out tl jst over 1f out: wknd ins fnl f* **20/1**

654- **6** *nk* **Evident (IRE)**[62] 7013 4-9-5 68............ WilliamCarson 6 63
(Tony Carroll) *stdd s: hld up in last trio: swtchd rt and effrt 2f out: styd on same pce and no imp ins fnl f* **12/1**

040- **7** *¾* **Pendo**[20] 7829 3-9-2 66............ LukeMorris 10 60
(Paul Cole) *in tch in midfield: unable qck u.p 2f out: wl hld and one pce fr over 1f out* **9/1**

660- **8** *3 ¾* **Stockhill Diva**[19] 7831 4-9-4 67............ LiamKeniry 5 52
(Brendan Powell) *in tch in midfield: rdn 2f out: sn btn and wknd over 1f out* **16/1**

550- **9** *39* **Guesshowmuchiloveu (IRE)**[48] 7358 3-9-3 67............[1] JimCrowley 7
(Charlie Fellowes) *a in rr and nvr gng wl: lost tch over 2f out: t.o and eased fnl f* **4/1**[3]

400- **10** *8* **Lightnin Hopkins (IRE)**[115] 5385 4-9-6 69............(v) AdamKirby 1
(John Butler) *led after 1f tl hdd over 4f out: lost 2nd and dropped out rapidly over 2f out: t.o and eased fnl f* **25/1**

1m 38.8s (-1.00) **Going Correction** -0.025s/f (Stan)
**WFA** 3 from 4yo+ 1lb **10** Ran SP% **114.5**
Speed ratings (Par 103): **104,103,102,100,98 97,97,93,54,46**
CSF £12.70 CT £136.32 TOTE £3.60: £1.40, £1.80, £3.20; EX 14.60 Trifecta £134.40.

**Owner** Mrs Barbara Fuller **Bred** D Fuller **Trained** Collingbourne Ducis, Wilts

**FOCUS**
A fair handicap run at a reasonable pace.

## 8069 VISIT AND DINE IN THE PANORAMIC NURSERY H'CAP 6f (P)
**3:10** (3:10) (Class 6) (0-65,65) 2-Y-0 **£2,264** (£673; £336; £168) **Stalls** Low

Form RPR

056- **1** **Moon River (IRE)**[26] 7742 2-9-0 **58**............ HayleyTurner 8 69+
(Brian Meehan) *in tch in midfield: effrt and wd of rivals over 1f out: led jst ins fnl f: r.o strly: readily* **10/1**

532- **2** *3* **Laura B**[14] 7904 2-9-1 **59**............ JimCrowley 3 58
(Chris Wall) *in tch in midfield: effrt on inner 2f out: pressing for placings ins fnl f: styd on to go 2nd towards fin: no threat to wnr* **5/1**[1]

000- **3** *hd* **Perfect Bounty**[26] 7741 2-8-5 **49**........................ MartinDwyer 1 47
(Clive Cox) *chsd ldr tl over 4f out: styd chsng ldrs: drvn and pressing ldrs over 1f out: kpt on same pce fnl f: wnt 3rd last strides* **9/1**

064- **4** *nk* **Beta Tauri (USA)**[48] 7345 2-9-7 **65**........................ AdamKirby 9 63
(Charlie Appleby) *led: rdn and hrd pressed wl over 1f out: hdd jst ins fnl f: styd on same pce after: lost 2 pls last strides* **5/1**[1]

640- **5** *1 ½* **Toast Of Newbury (IRE)**[126] 4967 2-9-6 **64**.................... JamesDoyle 6 57
(Jamie Osborne) *in tch in midfield: rdn and unable qck over 1f out: kpt on same pce ins fnl f* **7/1**[2]

052- **6** *shd* **You Be Lucky (IRE)**[7] 7992 2-9-2 **60**........................ FergusSweeney 7 53
(Jo Crowley) *t.k.h: chsd ldrs: hdwy to go 2nd over 4f out: drvn and ev ch 2f out: no ex 1f out: wknd fnl 100yds* **7/1**[2]

326- **7** *1* **Sky Steps (IRE)**[14] 7904 2-8-7 **51**........................(v) LukeMorris 11 41
(Philip McBride) *s.i.s: hld up in rr: sme hdwy u.p over 1f out: no imp ins fnl f* **8/1**[3]

150- **8** *nk* **Ragtime Dancer**[25] 7753 2-8-12 **61**........................(p) NedCurtis(5) 12 50
(Jonathan Portman) *in tch in midfield: unable qck u.p over 1f out: wknd ins fnl f* **12/1**

055- **9** *1 ¼* **Ifittakesforever (IRE)**[55] 7181 2-9-0 **58**....................(p) JamieSpencer 10 45+
(John Butler) *s.i.s: t.k.h: in tch on outer: rdn and effrt 2f out: no hdwy: btn and eased wl ins fnl f* **10/1**

000- **10** *shd* **Almoqatel (IRE)**[11] 7945 2-9-4 **62**........................ SteveDrowne 5 47
(Tony Newcombe) *in tch in midfield: rdn and unable qck wl over 1f out: wl hld and one pce fnl f* **33/1**

500- **11** *2 ½* **Grand Proposal**[12] 7920 2-9-5 **63**........................ PatCosgrave 2 40
(Jim Boyle) *hld up in last trio: rdn and no hdwy jst over 2f out: n.d* **14/1**

000- **12** *3* **Sparbrook (IRE)**[18] 7848 2-9-2 **60**........................ SebSanders 4 28
(Simon Dow) *bhd: rdn over 2f out: no hdwy* **25/1**

1m 13.54s (0.44) **Going Correction** -0.025s/f (Stan) **12** Ran SP% **118.8**
Speed ratings (Par 94): **96,92,91,91,89 89,87,87,85,85 82,78**
CSF £59.49 CT £482.62 TOTE £11.40: £4.30, £1.30, £4.10; EX 66.90 Trifecta £1938.00.
**Owner** Andrew Rosen & Mrs Paul Shanahan **Bred** Rockhart Trading Ltd **Trained** Manton, Wilts

**FOCUS**
A modest nursery which was soundly run. Straightforward form to rate.

## 8070 DOWNLOAD THE BETVICTOR INSTABET APP H'CAP 2m (P)
**3:40** (3:44) (Class 6) (0-65,65) 3-Y-0+ **£2,264** (£673; £336; £168) **Stalls** Low

Form RPR

223- **1** **Hazzaat (IRE)**[20] 2531 4-9-9 60........................(v) TomQueally 9 69
(Neil King) *stdd s: hld up in rr: hdwy to chse ldrs over 1f out: led ins fnl f: pushed clr: comf* **16/1**

533- **2** *2 ½* **Mighty Mambo**[33] 7657 7-9-9 60........................(tp) LukeMorris 1 66
(Lawney Hill) *in tch in midfield: rdn to chse ldr over 2f out: drvn to ld 1f out: hdd and one pce ins fnl f* **6/1**[3]

014- **3** *nk* **Shalambar (IRE)**[10] 7962 8-10-0 65........................(v) JimCrowley 8 70
(Tony Carroll) *rdn along leaving stalls: sn chsng ldrs: wnt 2nd after 3f tl led over 2f out: drvn and hdd 1f out: one pce after* **5/2**[1]

644- **4** *hd* **Golden Bird (IRE)**[24] 7777 3-9-6 65........................ SteveDrowne 2 70
(Dean Ivory) *hld up in tch: effrt u.p 2f out: 4th 1f out: kpt on but no threat to wnr* **3/1**[2]

430- **5** *2 ¾* **Noor Al Haya (IRE)**[27] 7419 4-9-8 59........................ LiamJones 3 61
(Laura Mongan) *stdd s: hld up in rr: rdn and hdwy jst over 2f out: 5th and no imp fnl f* **25/1**

U26- **6** *14* **Bowberry**[21] 7822 3-9-2 61........................ AdamKirby 6 46
(Clive Cox) *chsd ldrs: rdn 5f out: wknd over 2f out* **13/2**

340- **7** *½* **Dr Finley (IRE)**[33] 7657 7-8-9 49........................(v) SimonPearce(3) 5 34
(Lydia Pearce) *chsd ldr for 3f: styd prom: rdn 5f out: lost pl over 3f out: wknd over 2f out* **16/1**

060- **8** *1 ¼* **Superciliary**[81] 6486 5-8-13 50........................ HayleyTurner 7 33
(Chris Gordon) *led tl rdn over 2f out: sn wknd* **16/1**

3m 31.67s (1.57) **Going Correction** -0.025s/f (Stan)
**WFA** 3 from 4yo+ 8lb **8** Ran SP% **102.7**
Speed ratings (Par 101): **95,93,93,93,92 85,84,84**
CSF £85.58 CT £240.24 TOTE £9.60: £2.70, £1.30, £1.50; EX 47.00 Trifecta £94.90.
**Owner** Barry Williams & Donald Caldwell **Bred** Tribesmen Syndicate **Trained** Barbury Castle, Wiltshire

■ Delagoa Bay was withdrawn. Price at time of withdrawal 7/1. Rule 4 applies to all bets - deduction 10p in the pound.

**FOCUS**
A modest staying handicap and the pace wasn't that strong. The runner-up, third and fourth have been rated close to their marks.

## 8071 DOWNLOAD THE BETVICTOR APP NOW H'CAP (DIV I) 6f (P)
**4:10** (4:13) (Class 4) (0-80,80) 3-Y-0+ **£5,175** (£1,540; £769; £384) **Stalls** Low

Form RPR

510- **1** **Lady Brigid (IRE)**[56] 7159 3-9-4 77........................ LiamJones 6 87
(Olly Stevens) *mde all: rdn over 1f out: drifted lft but styd on wl fnl f: rdn out* **14/1**

400- **2** *1* **Strategic Force (IRE)**[134] 4697 3-9-7 80........................ AdamKirby 8 87+
(Clive Cox) *in tch in midfield: switching lft and effrt jst over 2f out: hdwy to chse ldrs 1f out: styd on to go 2nd cl home* **6/1**[3]

000- **3** *½* **Quickaswecan**[10] 7955 3-9-1 74........................ JFEgan 4 79
(Mark Johnston) *in tch in midfield: hdwy u.p wl over 1f out: chsd wnr over 1f out: kpt on but lost 2nd cl home* **25/1**

614- **4** *1* **Multitask**[24] 7775 4-9-2 75........................ LiamKeniry 9 77+
(Michael Madgwick) *stdd s: hld up in rr: effrt on outer 2f out: r.o ins fnl f: nt rch ldrs* **7/1**

040- **5** *shd* **Drive On (IRE)**[35] 7624 3-9-0 78........................(v) GeorgeDowning(5) 1 79
(Eve Johnson Houghton) *in tch in midfield: rdn and hdwy 2f out: drvn and chsd ldrs 1f out: styd on same pce fnl f* **20/1**

052- **6** *1 ¾* **Zman Awal (IRE)**[38] 7575 3-9-4 77........................ TomQueally 5 73+
(James Fanshawe) *fly-jmpd as stalls opened and slowly away: in tch towards rr: nt clr run wl over 1f out tl jst over 1f out: hdwy 1f out: kpt on ins fnl f: nvr threatened ldrs* **5/4**[1]

545- **7** *hd* **Picks Pinta**[28] 7729 3-9-0 73........................(p) MartinDwyer 3 68+
(Jo Hughes) *in tch towards rr: hdwy u.p towards inner 2f out: kpt on same pce fnl f* **11/2**[2]

023- **8** *nk* **Midnight Rider (IRE)**[18] 7847 6-9-0 80........................ PatMillman(7) 10 74
(Rod Millman) *stdd s: hld up in tch: hdwy into midfield on outer 4f out: rdn 2f out: styd on same pce* **10/1**

400- **9** *2* **Foxtrot Jubilee (IRE)**[11] 7947 4-8-13 79........................ PatrickO'Donnell(7) 7 67
(Ralph Beckett) *in tch towards rr: nt clr run over 1f out: no imp fnl f* **16/1**

550- **10** *3 ¾* **Fossa**[163] 3734 4-8-13 72........................ PatCosgrave 2 48
(Dean Ivory) *t.k.h: chsd wnr tl no ex u.p over 1f out: wknd fnl f* **33/1**

000- **11** *4 ½* **Roy's Legacy**[3] 8040 5-8-13 72........................ DuranFentiman 11 33
(Shaun Harris) *chsd ldrs tl lost pl u.p wl over 1f out: sn wknd* **66/1**

1m 12.43s (-0.67) **Going Correction** -0.025s/f (Stan) **11** Ran SP% **121.3**
Speed ratings (Par 105): **103,101,101,99,99 97,96,96,93,88 82**
CSF £95.22 CT £2112.55 TOTE £13.10: £4.00, £2.10, £4.70; EX 100.20 Trifecta £1377.80.
**Owner** M H and Mrs G Tourle **Bred** Minch Bloodstock & Brittas Stud **Trained** Chiddingfold, Surrey

**FOCUS**
A useful and competitive sprint handicap, albeit 0.43sec slower than the second division, and the pace held up. The form has been taken at face value.

## 8072 DOWNLOAD THE BETVICTOR APP NOW H'CAP (DIV II) 6f (P)
**4:40** (4:42) (Class 4) (0-80,80) 3-Y-0+ **£5,175** (£1,540; £769; £384) **Stalls** Low

Form RPR

203- **1** **Dont Have It Then**[24] 7775 3-9-2 75........................ StevieDonohoe 3 84
(Willie Musson) *hld up in last pair: clsd over 1f out: rdn and hdwy to chse wnr ins fnl f: r.o wl to ld on post* **7/1**[3]

121- **2** *nse* **Invincible Ridge (IRE)**[10] 7949 6-9-6 79........................(t) LukeMorris 10 88
(Eric Alston) *hld up in tch in last quartet: hdwy 2f out: rdn to ld 1f out: r.o: hdd on post* **7/2**[2]

512- **3** *1* **Top Offer**[24] 7775 5-8-12 71........................ ShaneKelly 4 77
(Peter Crate) *hld up in tch in midfield: rdn and effrt 1f out: kpt on same pce ins fnl f* **7/1**[3]

000- **4** *nk* **Burning Blaze**[154] 4027 4-9-0 80........................ HectorCrouch(7) 9 85
(Olly Stevens) *stdd s: hld up in rr: hdwy on inner over 1f out: chsd ldrs ins fnl f: no imp towards fin* **25/1**

003- **5** *nk* **Clear Praise (USA)**[16] 7886 7-9-4 77........................ SebSanders 7 81
(Simon Dow) *chsd ldrs: rdn jst over 2f out: kpt on same pce ins fnl f* **12/1**

441- **6** *½* **Stellarta**[7] 7989 3-9-0 73 6ex........................ SteveDrowne 5 75
(Michael Blanshard) *chsd ldrs: clsd 2f out: rdn to ld jst over 1f out: hdd 1f out: wknd towards fin* **9/4**[1]

000- **7** *½* **Clockmaker (IRE)**[11] 7947 8-9-4 77........................ HayleyTurner 2 78
(Conor Dore) *taken down early: led: wnt clr 4f out: rdn and hdd over 1f out: wknd ins fnl f* **25/1**

003- **8** *1 ¼* **Spellmaker**[50] 7307 5-8-8 72........................ EoinWalsh(5) 1 69
(Tony Newcombe) *stdd s: t.k.h: hld up in tch in rr: hdwy 2f out: chal over 1f out: wknd ins fnl f* **16/1**

001- **9** *2 ½* **Soaring Spirits (IRE)**[24] 7776 4-9-3 76........................(p) PatCosgrave 8 65
(Dean Ivory) *chsd ldr: clsd 2f out: struggling u.p over 1f out: wknd fnl f* **12/1**

000- **10** *6* **Palace Moon**[47] 7375 9-9-7 80........................(t) JimCrowley 6 50
(William Knight) *awkward as stalls opened: sn in tch in midfield: wknd qckly over 1f out* **8/1**

511- **11** *2 ¾* **Ocean Legend (IRE)**[161] 3800 9-8-13 72........................ WilliamCarson 11 33
(Tony Carroll) *in tch in midfield on outer: rdn 2f out: wknd over 1f out* **25/1**

1m 12.0s (-1.10) **Going Correction** -0.025s/f (Stan) **11** Ran SP% **121.9**
Speed ratings (Par 105): **106,105,104,104,103 103,102,100,97,89 85**
CSF £32.22 CT £182.03 TOTE £7.30: £2.40, £1.80, £2.20; EX 34.10 Trifecta £221.40.
**Owner** Laurence Mann **Bred** Charley Knoll Partnership **Trained** Newmarket, Suffolk

**FOCUS**
A bunched finish for the second division of a useful handicap, which was run 0.43sec quicker than the first leg. The hold-up horses were favoured this time.

## 8073 BETVICTOR.COM H'CAP 1m 3f (P)
**5:10** (5:11) (Class 4) (0-80,80) 3-Y-0+ **£5,175** (£1,540; £769; £384) **Stalls** Low

Form RPR

032- **1** **Past Forgetting (IRE)**[12] 7918 3-8-9 72........................ LukeMorris 8 83
(Luca Cumani) *in tch in midfield: effrt u.p 2f out: chsd ldr over 1f out: drvn to ld ins fnl f: styd on* **3/1**[2]

424- **2** *1 ¼* **Hedge End (IRE)**[18] 7850 3-9-2 79........................ JimCrowley 1 88
(Richard Hannon) *hld up in last quartet: hdwy on inner 2f out: ev ch 1f out: 2nd and one pce fnl 100yds* **9/1**

0/0- **3** *1* **Willie Wag Tail (USA)**[19] 7838 5-9-7 80........................ JamieSpencer 4 87
(Ed Walker) *led after 1f: rdn 2f out: hdd ins fnl f: no ex and btn whn short of room ins fnl f* **11/4**[1]

063- **4** *2* **Mubtadi**[48] 7350 6-9-5 78........................ MartinHarley 9 83
(Ismail Mohammed) *hld up in tch towards rr: clsd and swtchd rt 2f out: pressing ldrs whn squeezed for room and hmpd ins fnl f: one pce after* **10/1**

505- **5** *2* **Stock Hill Fair**[19] 7838 6-9-4 77........................(t) LiamKeniry 7 78
(Brendan Powell) *in tch in midfield: rdn 2f out: unable qck and btn 1f out: wknd ins fnl f* **5/1**[3]

250- **6** *¾* **Uphold**[193] 2700 7-9-5 78........................(v) AdamKirby 5 77
(Gay Kelleway) *led for 1f: chsd ldr tl over 1f out: wknd ins fnl f* **16/1**

666- **7** *2 ¾* **Karam Albaari (IRE)**[19] 7831 6-8-13 72........................ PaddyAspell 3 67
(J R Jenkins) *niggled along early: in tch in rr: rdn over 2f out: styd on same pce fr over 1f out* **16/1**

006- **8** *16* **Last Minute Lisa (IRE)**[31] 7702 4-9-0 73........................ MartinDwyer 2 40
(Sylvester Kirk) *hld up in rr: short-lived effrt over 2f out: wknd wl over 1f out* **16/1**

153- **9** *1* **Glennten**[38] 7568 5-8-13 72........................ RaulDaSilva 10 38
(Jose Santos) *chsd ldrs: rdn 2f out: unable qck and wknd over 1f out* **16/1**

505- **10** *1 ¾* **Thanks Harry**[19] 7831 3-8-7 70........................ HayleyTurner 6 33
(Andrew Balding) *in tch in midfield: rdn over 4f out: drvn and lost pl 3f out: bhd over 1f out* **10/1**

2m 18.62s (-3.28) **Going Correction** -0.025s/f (Stan)
**WFA** 3 from 4yo+ 4lb **10** Ran SP% **120.0**
Speed ratings (Par 105): **110,109,108,106,105 104,102,91,90,89**
CSF £31.49 CT £84.12 TOTE £5.10: £1.80, £2.10, £1.80; EX 24.60 Trifecta £109.40.
**Owner** S Stuckey **Bred** Grangecon Stud **Trained** Newmarket, Suffolk

**FOCUS**
A fair but competitive handicap. The runner-up has been rated as running another small pb in defeat.

## 8074 FOLLOW @BETVICTORRACING ON TWITTER H'CAP 1m 4f (P)
**5:40** (5:40) (Class 6) (0-60,60) 3-Y-0+ **£2,264** (£673; £336; £168) **Stalls** Centre

Form RPR

363- **1** **Golly Miss Molly**[5] 8011 3-8-7 48........................(b) LukeMorris 8 59+
(Jeremy Gask) *t.k.h: stdd after s: hld up in tch: smooth hdwy to join ldr on bit jst over 1f out: led fnl 100yds: nudged out* **3/1**[2]

000- **2** *¾* **Reality Show (IRE)**[12] 7932 7-9-10 60........................ DuranFentiman 7 68
(Shaun Harris) *in toouch in midfield: clsd to join ldrs 2f out: rdn to ld over 1f out: clr w cantering wnr 1f out: hdd and one pce fnl 100yds* **4/1**[3]

560- **3** 5 **Here For Good (IRE)**[12] 7925 3-9-2 57 JimCrowley 5 57
(Richard Hannon) *chsd ldrs: rdn and ev ch over 2f out: 3rd and btn 1f out: outpcd fnl f* **11/4**[1]

500- **4** 3/4 **Harrison's Cave**[16] 7895 6-9-4 57 JoeyHaynes(3) 6 56
(Sharon Watt) *hld up in tch in midfield: clsd and nt clr run 2f out: hdwy and battling for 3rd 1f out: sn outpcd* **11/2**

000- **5** 2 1/2 **Malicho**[23] 7805 5-9-7 57 (t) SebSanders 4 52
(Dean Ivory) *stdd s: t.k.h: hld up in tch in rr: effrt jst over 2f out: outpcd and btn over 1f out: wknd fnl f* **6/1**

450- **6** shd **Illegale (IRE)**[40] 7532 8-8-7 46 oh1 (bt) PhilipPrince(3) 1 41
(Nikki Evans) *t.k.h: hld up in tch in last trio: effrt on inner 2f out: wknd over 1f out* **33/1**

4/5- **7** 5 **Let's Confer**[24] 7772 5-9-3 53 JimmyQuinn 2 40
(Michael Attwater) *t.k.h: chsd ldrs: rdn over 2f out: wknd over 1f out* **20/1**

046- **8** 1 3/4 **Candesta (USA)**[51] 7290 4-9-8 58 (p) GeorgeChaloner 3 42
(Julia Feilden) *sn led: rdn and qcknd over 2f out: hdd over 1f out: sn wknd* **8/1**

2m 35.75s (1.25) **Going Correction** -0.025s/f (Stan)
**WFA** 3 from 4yo+ 5lb 8 Ran SP% **120.2**
Speed ratings (Par 101): **94,93,90,89,88 87,84,83**
CSF £16.45 CT £37.15 TOTE £4.10: £1.60, £2.30, £1.30; EX 17.90 Trifecta £48.80.
**Owner** Amelco **Bred** Brook Stud Bloodstock Ltd **Trained** Sutton Veny, Wilts

**FOCUS**
A modest handicap, in which the first two pulled clear. Muddling form.
T/Jkpt: Not won. T/Plt: £204.00 to a £1 stake. Pool: £76,798.28 - 274.81 winning tickets T/Qpdt: £70.20 to a £1 stake. Pool: £7,039.84 - 74.20 winning tickets

# 8036 LINGFIELD (L-H)
## Monday, December 8

**OFFICIAL GOING: Polytrack: standard**
Wind: Fresh, half against Weather: Fine and cold

## 8075 32RED MEDIAN AUCTION MAIDEN STKS 1m 1y(P)
12:30 (12:30) (Class 6) 2-Y-O £1,940 (£577; £288; £144) Stalls High

Form RPR

5- **1** **Noro Lim (IRE)**[19] 7834 2-9-5 0 AdamKirby 7 72
(Luca Cumani) *trckd ldr: chal fr 3f out: rdn and upsides 2f out: narrow ld over 1f out: drvn and grad asserted last 100yds* **2/1**[1]

523- **2** 1 3/4 **Toofeeg (IRE)**[20] 7827 2-9-5 76 (p) TomQueally 8 68
(William Haggas) *led: rdn and jnd 2f out: narrowly hdd over 1f out: pressed wnr tl no ex last 100yds* **3/1**[3]

005- **3** 1 1/4 **Eagle Empire (IRE)**[7] 7992 2-9-5 58 PatCosgrave 1 65
(Richard Hannon) *chsd ldng pair thrght: rdn over 2f out: nt qckn over 1f out: kpt on same pce after* **10/1**

**4** nk **Hungerford** 2-9-5 0 JimCrowley 3 64+
(Olly Stevens) *in tch: outpcd over 2f out: tk 4th over 1f out and reminder sn after: pushed along and styd on steadily fnl f* **20/1**

0- **5** 3/4 **Down To Earth**[33] 7667 2-9-5 0 LukeMorris 9 63+
(Michael Bell) *t.k.h early: racd wd in midfield: outpcd over 2f out: shkn up and styd on fr over 1f out: nrst fin* **33/1**

**6** 6 **Weald Of Kent (USA)** 2-9-5 0 NickyMackay 5 49+
(John Gosden) *slowly away: wl in rr: rdn sn after 1/2-way and struggling: nvr on terms* **5/2**[2]

**7** nk **Maid Of Kent** 2-9-0 0 HayleyTurner 4 43
(James Fanshawe) *shoved along early to chse ldng trio: lost 4th and wknd wl over 1f out* **10/1**

**8** 1 1/4 **Ever Pheasant (IRE)** 2-9-5 0 LiamJones 2 45
(J S Moore) *sn pushed along: a in rr: bhd fr 3f out* **66/1**

**9** 3 **Sarafina** 2-9-0 0 MartinDwyer 6 33
(John Best) *a towards rr: pushed along over 2f out: wknd* **50/1**

1m 39.64s (1.44) **Going Correction** +0.125s/f (Slow) 9 Ran SP% **116.2**
Speed ratings (Par 94): **97,95,94,93,92 86,86,85,82**
CSF £8.07 TOTE £2.50: £1.10, £1.40, £3.80; EX 9.50 Trifecta £38.60.
**Owner** O T I Racing **Bred** S Connolly **Trained** Newmarket, Suffolk

**FOCUS**
TurfTrax sectionals showed the time was almost 4secs slower through the first 6f than the later handicap at this trip, and unsurprisingly few got into it. It's been rated around the runner-up and the time of the race.

## 8076 32RED.COM (S) STKS 6f 1y(P)
1:00 (1:01) (Class 6) 2-Y-O £1,940 (£577; £288; £144) Stalls Low

Form RPR

115- **1** **Little**[16] 7890 2-8-8 66 DannyBrock(3) 8 67
(Jamie Osborne) *stdd s: hld up in last: nipped through on inner whn rest wd bnd 2f out: led over 1f out: rdn and pressed 100yds out: styd on wl* **3/1**[3]

062- **2** 1 1/4 **Come Uppence**[9] 7970 2-8-11 70 JFEgan 7 63
(David Evans) *in tch: pushed along fr 1/2-way: rdn 2f out: progres to go 2nd 1f out: tried to cl but no imp on wnr last 100yds* **5/4**[1]

545- **3** 1 1/2 **Tinkers Kiss (IRE)**[25] 7753 2-8-11 58 MartinHarley 2 59
(Philip McBride) *chsd ldr: rdn and carried wd bnd 2f out: nt qckn over 1f out: kpt on fnl f* **5/2**[2]

00- **4** 2 1/4 **Newton Bomb (IRE)**[47] 7377 2-8-6 0 LiamJones 6 47
(Conrad Allen) *led but hanging rt: wd bnd 2f out: hdd over 1f out: fdd* **12/1**

040- **5** 4 **Wesie's Dream**[96] 6024 2-8-6 57 HayleyTurner 5 35
(Mark Usher) *chsd ldrs: rdn over 2f out: wknd over 1f out* **25/1**

1m 14.08s (2.18) **Going Correction** +0.125s/f (Slow) 5 Ran SP% **109.6**
Speed ratings (Par 94): **90,88,86,83,78**
CSF £7.13 TOTE £3.40: £1.70, £1.10; EX 6.00 Trifecta £9.60.The winner was bought in for 7,200gns.
**Owner** A F Tait **Bred** Highclere Stud Ltd **Trained** Upper Lambourn, Berks

**FOCUS**
A modest, slowly run juvenile seller. Straightforward form to rate.

## 8077 DAILY PRICE BOOSTS AT UNIBET H'CAP 5f 6y(P)
1:30 (1:32) (Class 5) (0-70,70) 3-Y-O+ £2,587 (£770; £384; £192) Stalls High

Form RPR

231- **1** **Johnny Splash (IRE)**[76] 6631 5-9-2 65 (v) RobertWinston 4 75
(Roger Teal) *chsd ldrs: rdn over 1f out: styd on to ld last 150yds: urged along and sn clr* **4/1**[3]

200- **2** 1 3/4 **Cardinal**[24] 7776 9-9-0 63 (p) HayleyTurner 3 67
(Robert Cowell) *hld up bhd ldrs: wdst of all bnd 2f out: no prog over 1f out: rdn ins fnl f: r.o to take 2nd last stride: no ch to threaten* **6/1**

106- **3** nk **Monarch Maid**[24] 7776 3-9-2 70 ShelleyBirkett(5) 5 73
(Peter Hiatt) *prssed ldr: led 1/2-way: hrd pressed over 1f out: hdd and outpcd last 150yds: lost 2nd post* **2/1**[1]

05- **4** nk **Billy Red**[69] 6843 10-9-1 67 (bt) DannyBrock(3) 6 69
(J R Jenkins) *reluctant to enter stalls: racd wdst early: pressed ldrs: chal and upsides over 1f out: nt qckn ins fnl f* **10/1**

366- **5** 1 1/4 **Howyadoingnotsobad (IRE)**[23] 7806 6-8-9 63 RyanWhile(5) 2 60
(Bill Turner) *led to 1/2-way: styd pressing ldr: upsides on inner 1f out: fdd* **11/4**[2]

020- **6** 4 **Argent Touch**[146] 4288 3-9-1 64 GeorgeChaloner 1 47
(Derek Shaw) *awkward s: t.k.h early: hld up in last pair: rdn 2f out: wknd fnl f* **10/1**

58.68s (-0.12) **Going Correction** +0.125s/f (Slow) 6 Ran SP% **112.5**
Speed ratings (Par 103): **105,102,101,101,99 92**
CSF £27.28 TOTE £3.00: £1.80, £3.90; EX 20.30 Trifecta £59.40.
**Owner** Barry Kitcherside **Bred** J Connolly **Trained** Ashtead, Surrey

**FOCUS**
Just a modest sprint handicap.

## 8078 CORAL APP DOWNLOAD FROM THE APP STORE H'CAP 1m 2f (P)
2:00 (2:00) (Class 3) (0-95,90) 3-Y-O+ £7,439 (£2,213; £1,106; £553) Stalls Low

Form RPR

502- **1** **Swing Alone (IRE)**[171] 3424 5-9-5 88 JFEgan 5 95
(Gay Kelleway) *trckd ldng pair: rdn over 2f out: clsd on outer over 1f out: drvn ahd last 150yds: kpt on wl* **2/1**[1]

051- **2** 1/2 **Brocklebank (IRE)**[10] 7955 5-9-0 83 NickyMackay 6 89
(Simon Dow) *slowly away: hld up in last: c wdst of all bnd 2f out: rdn and prog over 1f out: styd on to take 2nd last 75yds: a hld* **6/1**

000- **3** 3/4 **Sleeper King (IRE)**[45] 7408 3-9-4 90 MartinHarley 1 94
(Luca Cumani) *t.k.h early: hld up and mostly in 5th: prog on inner and rdn over 1f out: tried to chal ins fnl f: one pce* **5/1**[3]

260- **4** 1 **Tinshu (IRE)**[23] 7803 8-9-3 86 (p) RobertWinston 4 88
(Derek Haydn Jones) *led: rdn and pressed 2f out: hdd and fdd last 150yds* **8/1**

2/0- **5** 3/4 **Teolagi (IRE)**[338] 54 4-9-2 85 ShaneKelly 2 86
(J S Moore) *chsd ldng trio: rdn 3f out: nvr able to threaten but kpt on one pce* **9/2**[2]

000- **6** 3/4 **Commissar**[65] 6943 5-8-9 78 StevieDonohoe 7 78
(Ian Williams) *trckd ldr: chal 2f out and looked to be gng strly: rdn over 1f out: wknd tamely* **5/1**[3]

2m 7.08s (0.48) **Going Correction** +0.125s/f (Slow)
**WFA** 3 from 4yo+ 3lb 6 Ran SP% **110.2**
Speed ratings (Par 107): **103,102,102,101,100 100**
CSF £13.77 TOTE £2.20: £1.50, £2.20; EX 10.30 Trifecta £46.70.
**Owner** Crook, Kelleway, Stanbrook, Brown **Bred** M Sinanan **Trained** Exning, Suffolk

**FOCUS**
A fair handicap, but they went a steady pace. Muddling form.

## 8079 LADBROKES H'CAP 7f 1y(P)
2:30 (2:30) (Class 3) (0-95,90) 3-Y-O+ £7,439 (£2,213; £1,106; £553) Stalls Low

Form RPR

312- **1** **Bint Dandy (IRE)**[7] 7993 3-8-2 74 ConnorBeasley(3) 1 82
(Chris Dwyer) *trckd ldng pair to 3f out: styd cl up: rdn over 1f out: prog to ld jst ins fnl f: styd on wl* **6/4**[1]

442- **2** 1 1/4 **First Experience**[21] 7820 3-8-9 78 MartinHarley 5 83
(Rae Guest) *t.k.h: trckd ldr: rdn to chal over 2f out: narrow ld over 1f out to jst ins fnl f: one pce* **2/1**[2]

250- **3** nk **Golden Amber (IRE)**[19] 7843 3-9-6 89 RobertWinston 6 93
(Dean Ivory) *hld up in last: prog on outer to chal 3f out: upsides and rdn 2f out: nt qckn over 1f out: fdd* **8/1**

524- **4** 1/2 **Starlight Symphony (IRE)**[16] 7885 4-8-5 74 (b) MartinLane 3 77
(Eve Johnson Houghton) *hld up in 4th: dropped to last 3f out and pce lifted sn after: rdn wl over 1f out: kpt on but n.d* **9/2**[3]

521- **5** 1 3/4 **Elhaam (IRE)**[12] 7929 3-8-2 71 oh1 PaoloSirigu 2 69
(George Margarson) *t.k.h: led at mod pce: pressed and kicked on over 2f out: hdd over 1f out: wknd ins fnl f* **8/1**

1m 25.3s (0.50) **Going Correction** +0.125s/f (Slow) 5 Ran SP% **113.7**
Speed ratings (Par 107): **102,100,100,99,97**
CSF £5.01 TOTE £2.40: £1.50, £1.10; EX 5.40 Trifecta £30.80.
**Owner** M M Foulger **Bred** Ballyhane Stud **Trained** Newmarket, Suffolk

**FOCUS**
Another steadily run race. It's been rated through the runner-up and third.

## 8080 DOWNLOAD THE LADBROKES APP H'CAP 1m 1y(P)
3:00 (3:00) (Class 4) (0-85,84) 3-Y-O+ £4,690 (£1,395; £697; £348) Stalls High

Form RPR

030- **1** **Jack Of Diamonds (IRE)**[18] 7852 5-9-4 81 RobertWinston 6 91
(Roger Teal) *s.i.s: hld up in last pair: wd bnd 2f out and prog over 1f out: cajoled along and clsd fnl f: rdn to ld last strides* **10/1**[3]

221- **2** nk **Razor Wind (IRE)**[14] 7901 3-9-1 84 ShaneGray(5) 3 94
(Charlie Appleby) *cl up: rdn over 2f out: one of several chalng over 1f out: narrow ld jst ins fnl f: styd on but hdd last strides* **11/10**[1]

321- **3** 1 1/4 **Semaral (IRE)**[16] 7885 3-9-5 83 (p) MartinLane 4 90
(Chris Wall) *hld up in midfield: prog 2f out: hd high but clsd to chal 1f out: edgd rt and nt qckn last 150yds* **3/1**[2]

030- **4** 3/4 **Cricklewood Green (USA)**[17] 7870 3-8-8 79 GaryMahon(7) 2 84
(Richard Hannon) *cl up on inner: rdn 3f out: kpt on and cl enough over 1f out: one pce fnl f* **16/1**

/30- **5** 1/2 **Wandsworth (IRE)**[94] 6100 4-8-13 76 PaddyAspell 9 80
(Roger Varian) *mostly pressed ldr: rdn to chal 2f out: nt qckn jst over 1f out: hld whn sltly impeded ins fnl f* **25/1**

000- **6** shd **Loyalty**[10] 7955 7-9-4 81 (v) GeorgeChaloner 7 85
(Derek Shaw) *t.k.h: hld up in midfield: rdn over 2f out: kpt on same pce and nvr able to chal* **33/1**

015- **7** shd **Tides Reach (IRE)**[16] 7885 3-8-13 77 (b) MartinHarley 5 80
(Roger Charlton) *led at gd pce: hrd pressed 2f out: hdd jst ins fnl f: sltly impeded and fdd* **16/1**

411- **8** 3/4 **Malaysian Boleh**[14] 7906 4-8-10 73 NickyMackay 8 75
(Simon Dow) *hld up in last pair: stl last on inner jst over 1f out: nowhere to go after and nvr able to make hdwy* **14/1**

154- **9** nk **Good Luck Charm**[28] 7729 5-9-1 78 (v) ShaneKelly 1 79
(Gary Moore) *hld up in midfield: rdn 2f out: chsd ldrs over 1f out: nt qckn and lost pl fnl f* **12/1**

1m 35.93s (-2.27) **Going Correction** +0.125s/f (Slow)
**WFA** 3 from 4yo+ 1lb 9 Ran SP% **114.6**
Speed ratings (Par 105): **116,115,114,113,113 113,113,112,111**
CSF £21.25 CT £42.98 TOTE £12.80: £2.60, £1.30, £1.40; EX 28.90 Trifecta £99.00.

**Owner** Inside Track Racing Club **Bred** Gigginstown House Stud **Trained** Ashtead, Surrey

**FOCUS**

A competitive handicap and they went a much better pace than in the opening slowly run maiden over the same trip. The runner-up has been rated as building on his maiden form and the third is also on the upgrade.

## 8081 £20 RISK-FREE BET AT UNIBET H'CAP 6f 1y(P)

3:30 (3:30) (Class 6) (0-65,65) 3-Y-O+ £1,940 (£577; £288; £144) Stalls Low

Form RPR

305- **1** **Caminel (IRE)**[35] 7621 3-9-0 58........................(b) MartinLane 3 65
(Jeremy Gask) *hld up in last pair: rdn over 2f out: prog and wdst of all over 1f out: str run to ld last 50yds* **5/1[3]**

400- **2** ½ **Dark Lane**[18] 7847 8-8-9 60........................(v) HarryBurns(7) 1 65
(David Evans) *sltly mistimed start: t.k.h: hld up in tch: progress on inner ovr 1f out: rdn to ld 100yds out: hdd & outpcd last 50yds* **12/1**

454- **3** *hd* **Ghost Train (IRE)**[19] 7842 5-9-6 64........................(p) RobertWinston 5 68
(Tim McCarthy) *led after 1f: rdn 2f out: edgd rt jst over 1f out: hdd and nt qckn last 100yds* **2/1[1]**

0/3- **4** 1 ½ **Done Dreaming (IRE)**[24] 7783 4-8-8 52........................ GeorgeChaloner 2 52
(Richard Fahey) *led 1f: chsd ldr: rdn 2f out: tried to chal and ch over 1f out: fdd last 100yds* **5/1[3]**

/62- **5** ½ **Excellent Aim**[160] 3826 7-9-4 62........................ PaoloSirigu 7 60
(George Margarson) *trckd ldng pair: rdn 2f out: hd high and nt qckn over 1f out: one pce* **16/1**

450- **6** ½ **Lujeanie**[24] 7776 8-9-7 65........................(p) ShaneKelly 4 61
(Peter Crate) *hld up in tch: gng strly 2f out: rdn and fnd nil over 1f out* **3/1[2]**

005- **7** *hd* **Wimboldsley**[39] 7547 3-8-7 51 oh1........................ NickyMackay 6 47
(Scott Dixon) *slowly away and then stdd: hld up in last: sme way off the pce 2f out: shkn up 1f out: kpt on but nvr involved* **8/1**

1m 12.4s (0.50) **Going Correction** +0.125s/f (Slow) **7 Ran SP% 116.4**

Speed ratings (Par 101): **101,100,100,98,97 96,96**

CSF £61.62 CT £158.44 TOTE £4.90: £2.50, £6.00; EX 71.50 Trifecta £353.90.

**Owner** Mark Allen **Bred** The Kathryn Stud **Trained** Sutton Veny, Wilts

**FOCUS**

A moderate race run at a steady pace. The third has been rated close to form.

T/Plt: £5.00 to a £1 stake. Pool: £58,458.70 - 8,506.37 winning tickets T/Qpdt: £3.40 to a £1 stake. Pool: £5,031.1 0 - 1,066.75 winning tickets JN

# 7908 SOUTHWELL (L-H)

Tuesday, December 9

**OFFICIAL GOING: Fibresand: standard**

Wind: Moderate across Weather: Overcast

## 8082 £20 RISK-FREE BET AT UNIBET CLASSIFIED CLAIMING STKS 6f (F)

12:00 (12:01) (Class 6) 3-Y-O+ £2,045 (£603; £302) Stalls Low

Form RPR

201- **1** **Showtime Star**[103] 5857 4-8-5 64........................[1] JFEgan 11 75
(Gay Kelleway) *trckd ldrs: hdwy over 2f out: chsd ldr wl over 1f out: sn rdn: styd on wl fnl f to ld last 75yds* **10/1**

002- **2** ½ **Speightowns Kid (USA)**[14] 7915 6-8-0 62........................(b) ConnorBeasley(3) 7 71
(Michael Herrington) *cl up towards outer: led over 2f out: pushed clr over 1f out: rdn ent fnl f: hdd and one pce last 75yds* **7/2[1]**

020- **3** 4 ½ **Bainne (IRE)**[11] 7949 4-8-9 69........................ StevieDonohoe 8 63
(James Eustace) *dwlt and bhd: swtchd lft and rdn 2f out: styd on wl appr fnl f: nrst fin* **8/1**

430- **4** ½ **Scoreline**[41] 7534 3-8-9 69........................ SamJames 3 61
(David O'Meara) *slt ld: hdd over 3f out: cl up: rdn over 2f out and grad wknd* **8/1**

530- **5** 1 ¾ **Spitfire**[35] 7647 9-8-6 68........................(t) DavidProbert 2 52
(J R Jenkins) *dwlt and towards rr: hdwy 2f out: sn rdn and kpt on fnl f: nrst fin* **14/1**

030- **6** ¾ **Lewisham**[21] 7826 4-8-2 62........................(b[1]) PatrickMathers 6 46
(David Nicholls) *s.i.s and bhd: styd alone on far rail and hdwy over 2f out: sn rdn and kpt on fnl f: nrst fin* **8/1**

316- **7** ½ **Moiety**[25] 7775 3-8-12 70........................(t) MartinHarley 12 54
(Rae Guest) *in tch on outer: hdwy to chse ldrs 1/2-way: rdn along over 2f out: sn no imp* **5/1[2]**

205- **8** 1 ¼ **Dancing Maite**[26] 7766 9-7-13 57 ow3........................ AdamMcLean(7) 4 44
(Roy Bowring) *a towards rr* **33/1**

120- **9** 1 ½ **Camanche Grey (IRE)**[42] 7505 3-8-7 68........................ AndrewElliott 1 41
(Ben Haslam) *a towards rr* **50/1**

003- **10** ½ **Gaelic Wizard (IRE)**[21] 7826 6-8-5 59........................ GemmaTutty(5) 9 42
(Karen Tutty) *a towards rr* **20/1**

405- **11** ½ **Belle Bayardo (IRE)**[11] 7959 6-8-2 68........................ LukeMorris 13 32
(Tony Carroll) *in tch on outer: wd st: rdn along over 2f out: sn wknd* **7/1[3]**

400- **12** 4 **Greenhead High**[21] 7825 6-7-13 62........................(v) JoeyHaynes(3) 5 20
(David Nicholls) *cl up: slt ld over 3f out: hdd and rdn over 2f out: sn wknd* **16/1**

065- **13** 22 **Take The Lead**[124] 5097 4-8-3 66........................(b[1]) JimmyQuinn 10
(John Weymes) *prom: rdn along 1/2-way: sn wknd* **40/1**

1m 16.18s (-0.32) **Going Correction** +0.15s/f (Slow) **13 Ran SP% 118.5**

Speed ratings (Par 101): **108,107,101,100,98 97,96,95,93,92 91,86,57**

CSF £43.07 TOTE £10.90: £3.10, £1.60, £3.30; EX 49.30 Trifecta £503.90.Speightowns Kid was claimed by A Stokell for £6000. Lewisham was claimed by L Dace for £5000.

**Owner** Gay Kelleway & Countrywide Classics **Bred** Countrywide Classics Ltd **Trained** Exning, Suffolk

**FOCUS**

Quite a competitive claimer to start. The solid runner-up has been rated close to his best since 2012.

## 8083 32RED IRISH STALLION FARMS EBF MAIDEN STKS 1m (F)

12:30 (12:30) (Class 5) 2-Y-O £2,911 (£866; £432; £216) Stalls Low

Form RPR

**1** **Weld Al Emarat** 2-9-5 0........................ GrahamLee 3 87+
(Kevin Ryan) *s.i.s and green in rr: swtchd rt to outer and smooth hdwy to join ldrs 1/2-way: led 3f out: green and edging lft throught fnl 2f: pushed out and kpt on wl towards fin* **4/1[2]**

2- **2** ½ **Reetaj**[12] 7827 2-9-5 0........................ RobertHavlin 4 84+
(Peter Chapple-Hyam) *trckd ldrs: swtchd lft to inner and pushed along over 3f out: chsd wnr over 2f out: rdn to chal over 1f out: drvn and ev ch ins fnl f: no ex towards fin* **1/1[1]**

3- **3** 9 **Captain Koko**[8] 7985 2-9-5 0........................ MartinHarley 6 63
(Marco Botti) *trckd ldrs: hdwy wl over 2f out: rdn along to chse ldng pair wl over 1f out: sn no imp* **4/1[2]**

2- **4** 5 **High Intensity**[14] 7911 2-9-5 0........................ LukeMorris 1 52
(Scott Dixon) *slt ld at stdy pce: hdd 3f out and sn pushed along: rdn over 2f out and sn outpcd* **13/2[3]**

60- **5** 6 **Celestial Dancer (FR)**[210] 2231 2-8-9 0........................ AlistairRawlinson(5) 8 33
(Michael Appleby) *prom: rdn along over 3f out: sn wknd* **40/1**

**6** 1 **Zahenda** 2-9-0 0........................ LiamKeniry 7 31
(Ismail Mohammed) *dwlt and green in rr: hdwy towards outer and cl up 1/2-way: rdn along wl over 2f out: green and sn outpcd* **16/1**

0- **7** 4 **Monsart (IRE)**[24] 7811 2-9-5 0........................ MartinDwyer 2 26
(Jo Hughes) *chsd ldrs on inner: pushed along over 4f out: sn rdn and outpcd: bhd fr wl over 2f out* **20/1**

4- **8** ½ **Sweet Midnight**[21] 7828 2-9-0 0........................ StevieDonohoe 5 20
(John Holt) *cl up: rdn along 1/2-way: wknd over 3f out* **100/1**

1m 43.72s (0.02) **Going Correction** +0.15s/f (Slow) **8 Ran SP% 117.4**

Speed ratings (Par 96): **105,104,95,90,84 83,79,79**

CSF £8.55 TOTE £6.30: £1.50, £1.10, £1.30; EX 10.00 Trifecta £35.90.

**Owner** Ahmad Abdulla Al Shaikh **Bred** Rabbah Bloodstock Limited **Trained** Hambleton, N Yorks

**FOCUS**

This was probably as good a 2yo maiden as you will ever see at Southwell. The first two came clear and the others were spread out all over Nottinghamshire. The third and those behind could support a rating a bit higher still, but this is a high enough level really for a Southwell maiden.

## 8084 LADBROKES H'CAP (DIV I) 7f (F)

1:00 (1:01) (Class 6) (0-55,55) 3-Y-O+ £1,940 (£577; £288; £144) Stalls Low

Form RPR

054- **1** **Novalist**[54] 7222 6-8-12 46 oh1........................(b) JasonHart 12 63
(Robin Bastiman) *qckly away: mde all: pushed clr over 2f out: rdn ent fnl f: kpt on strly* **16/1**

043- **2** 6 **Trust Me Boy**[35] 7645 6-8-9 46........................ SimonPearce(3) 13 47
(John E Long) *chsd ldng pair: hdwy wl over 1f out: rdn to chse wnr appr fnl f: sn drvn and no imp* **8/1**

604- **3** 1 ½ **Masked Dance (IRE)**[26] 7766 7-9-0 48........................(p) LiamKeniry 9 46
(Scott Dixon) *chsd ldrs: rdn along over 2f out: styd on fnl f: tk 3rd nr fin* **11/2[2]**

006- **4** *nk* **Sleeping Star**[25] 7782 3-9-2 50........................ PJMcDonald 7 47
(Mel Brittain) *chsd wnr: rdn over 2f out: drvn wl over 1f out: sn one pce* **14/1**

035- **5** *nse* **Lendal Bridge**[14] 7910 3-9-6 54........................(p) BarryMcHugh 2 51
(Tony Coyle) *in tch on inner: hdwy wl over 2f out: sn rdn and kpt on appr fnl f* **12/1**

323- **6** 6 **Admirable Art (IRE)**[26] 7766 4-9-7 55........................(p) LukeMorris 3 36
(Tony Carroll) *towards rr: pushed along 1/2-way: rdn over 2f out: plugged on: n.d* **6/4[1]**

300- **7** ½ **Kingsway Lad (IRE)**[40] 7548 3-8-13 47........................(t) PatrickMathers 11 27
(Derek Shaw) *dwlt: hdwy and in tch 1/2-way: wd st: rdn over 2f out: sn no imp* **10/1**

400- **8** ¾ **Meydan Style (USA)**[94] 6161 8-8-5 46 oh1........................ JordanSwarbrick(7) 10 24
(Brian Baugh) *dwlt a towards rr* **50/1**

642- **9** 6 **Sairaam (IRE)**[124] 5110 8-8-9 46 oh1........................(p) DannyBrock(3) 4 8
(Charles Smith) *n.m.r and lost pl shortly after s: sn swtchd rt to outer: a in rr* **33/1**

060- **10** 8 **Third Strike**[127] 4969 3-9-7 55........................ GeorgeBaker 8
(Gary Moore) *a towards rr* **7/1[3]**

600- **11** 1 **Tell Me When**[95] 6116 3-8-6 47........................ KevinLundie(7) 5
(Brian Rothwell) *sn outpcd and a in rr: bhd fnl 3f* **50/1**

000/ **12** 9 **Northern Champ (IRE)**[785] 7557 8-8-12 46 oh1........................ GrahamLee 1
(Rebecca Menzies) *a in rr: bhd fnl 3f* **100/1**

000- **13** *nk* **Macs Scwar**[25] 7785 7-8-7 46 oh1........................(p) TimClark(5) 14
(Paul Morgan) *dwlt: a bhd* **100/1**

000- **14** ½ **Fama Mac**[42] 7510 7-9-4 52........................ RaulDaSilva 6
(Neville Bycroft) *in tch: rdn along over 3f out: sn wknd* **66/1**

1m 30.66s (0.36) **Going Correction** +0.15s/f (Slow) **14 Ran SP% 118.7**

Speed ratings (Par 101): **103,96,94,94,94 87,86,85,78,69 68,58,57,57**

CSF £134.12 CT £805.57 TOTE £20.40: £4.70, £2.60, £2.60; EX 92.90 Trifecta £422.10.

**Owner** E N Barber **Bred** Whitsbury Manor Stud **Trained** Cowthorpe, N Yorks

**FOCUS**

A moderate handicap dominated by those that raced on or close to the pace. The winning time was 2.05sec quicker than the second division.

## 8085 LADBROKES H'CAP (DIV II) 7f (F)

1:30 (1:31) (Class 6) (0-55,55) 3-Y-O+ £1,940 (£577; £288; £144) Stalls Low

Form RPR

024- **1** **Interchoice Star**[25] 7783 9-9-6 54........................(p) GeorgeBaker 11 67
(Ray Peacock) *trckd ldrs: hdwy over 3f out: led wl over 1f out: rdn clr appr fnl f: kpt on* **4/1[1]**

566- **2** 5 **Sea Whisper**[14] 7910 3-8-12 46 oh1........................ CharlesBishop 9 46
(Ann Stokell) *prom: cl up 1/2-way: led over 2f out: rdn and hdd wl over 1f out: sn drvn and kpt on same pce* **7/1[3]**

005- **3** *hd* **La Danza**[14] 7908 4-8-5 46........................ KevinLundie(7) 12 45
(Shaun Harris) *midfield: wd st: hdwy over 2f out: sn rdn: styd on fnl f: nrst fin* **20/1**

300- **4** *nse* **Art Dzeko**[14] 7915 5-9-7 55........................ GrahamGibbons 13 54
(Brian Baugh) *led: rdn along 3f out: styd towards inner rail: hdd over 2f out: sn drvn and kpt on one pce* **8/1**

302- **5** ¾ **Little Choosey**[18] 7864 4-8-7 46........................(bt) EoinWalsh(5) 4 43
(Roy Bowring) *dwlt: swtchd rt to outer sn after s: hdwy and wd st: rdn over 2f out: kpt on u.p fnl f: nrst fin* **10/1**

633- **6** 3 ½ **Red Shadow**[62] 7036 5-9-3 51........................(p) RobertWinston 2 39
(Alan Brown) *towards rr: pushed along and wd st: hdwy 2f out: kpt on u.p fnl f: nrst fin* **8/1**

045- **7** 1 **Olney Lass**[7] 8004 7-8-9 46 oh1........................ SimonPearce(3) 1 32
(Lydia Pearce) *towards rr: sme hdwy on inner wl over 2f out: sn rdn along and n.d* **14/1**

500- **8** 1 **Classical Diva**[7] 8004 3-8-8 47........................(v[1]) AlistairRawlinson(5) 10 30
(Michael Appleby) *dwlt: hdwy on outer to chse ldrs after 2f: wd st and sn rdn along: edgd lft 2f out: sn drvn and btn* **9/2[2]**

500- **9** 5 **Rafaaf (IRE)**[118] 5303 6-9-7 55........................ StephenCraine 5 25
(Richard Phillips) *chsd ldrs: rdn along 3f out: sn drvn and outpcd* **14/1**

005- **10** 1 ¾ **Wilful Minx (FR)**[147] 4299 3-9-0 48........................ GrahamLee 7 14
(James Given) *a towards rr* **9/1**

/06- **11** 6 **Zaria**[22] 7818 3-9-1 49........................ WilliamCarson 3
(Richard Price) *a towards rr: bhd fnl 2f* **33/1**

606- **12** *nse* **Tinchy Ryder**[35] 7652 3-8-7 46 oh1 .......... AdamCarter(5) 8
(Bryan Smart) *chsd ldr: rdn along 3f out: drvn over 2f out: sn rdn and wknd: bhd and eased over 1f out* **20/1**

6/0- **13** *12* **Kaahen (USA)**[40] 7548 4-8-12 46 oh1 .......... (v) StevieDonohoe 6
(Pat Eddery) *a in rr: bhd fnl 2f* **16/1**

1m 32.71s (2.41) **Going Correction** +0.15s/f (Slow) 13 Ran SP% **123.7**
Speed ratings (Par 101): **92,86,86,86,85 81,80,78,73,71 64,64,50**
CSF £32.12 CT £517.96 TOTE £3.80: £1.50, £3.60, £6.80; EX 49.90 Trifecta £1610.80.
**Owner** John P Evitt **Bred** M Bishop **Trained** Kyre Park, Worcs

**FOCUS**
Another race where you needed to be close to the pace. The winning time was 2.05sec slower than the first division.

## 8086 LADBROKES MOBILE H'CAP 1m (F)
**2:00** (2:00) (Class 5) (0-70,70) 3-Y-0+ **£2,587** (£770; £384; £192) **Stalls** Low

Form RPR

100- **1** **Bognor (USA)**[157] 3978 3-9-6 70 .......... LukeMorris 9 84+
(Michael Appleby) *trckd ldng pair: cl up 1/2-way: led 3f out: rdn wl over 1f out: drvn ins fnl f: kpt on wl towards fin* **7/4**[1]

006- **2** *½* **Two Shades Of Grey (IRE)**[15] 7906 3-8-10 60 .......... GeorgeChaloner 12 73
(Richard Fahey) *in tch: hdwy wl over 2f out: pushed along and swtchd lft wl over 1f out: sn rdn and edgd lft over 1f out: drvn to chal ins fnl f: ev ch tl edgd lft and no ex towards fin* **11/1**

000- **3** *5* **Marciano (IRE)**[15] 7905 4-8-10 62 .......... (p) JoeyHaynes(3) 5 64
(Sue Smith) *trckd ldrs: hdwy 3f out: swtchd rt to outer 2f out and sn chal: rdn and ev ch over 1f out: drvn ent fnl f: sn one pce* **20/1**

200- **4** *5* **Hill Fort**[20] 7831 4-9-5 68 .......... (p) WilliamTwiston-Davies 6 58
(Ronald Harris) *pushed along in rr sn after s: sn swtchd rt to outer: hdwy 1/2-way: in tch 3f out: rdn and edgd lft 2f out: drvn and kpt on same pce appr fnl f* **25/1**

606- **5** *5* **Mister Marcasite**[39] 7569 4-8-13 62 .......... GrahamLee 7 41
(Mel Brittain) *slt ld: rdn along and hdd 3f out: sn drvn and grad wknd* **12/1**

100- **6** *½* **Frankthetank (IRE)**[18] 7871 3-9-5 69 .......... (p) PhillipMakin 13 46
(Keith Dalgleish) *trckd ldrs: wd st: effrt over 2f out: sn rdn and wknd* **8/1**[3]

000- **7** *3 ¼* **Amenable (IRE)**[21] 7830 7-8-11 60 .......... (p) HayleyTurner 8 30
(Conor Dore) *cl up: rdn along 3f out: drvn and wknd over 2f out* **25/1**

003- **8** *3* **I'm Super Too (IRE)**[21] 7829 7-9-2 65 .......... MartinDwyer 1 28
(Alan Swinbank) *midfield on inner: rdn along 3f out: n.d* **8/1**[3]

024- **9** *nk* **Hail Promenader (IRE)**[136] 4673 8-8-10 66 ....(tp) JoshuaBrowning(7) 11 28
(Jo Hughes) *in rr: pushed along and wd st: n.d* **16/1**

000- **10** *2 ¾* **Disclosure**[11] 7953 3-9-3 70 .......... ConnorBeasley(3) 3 26
(Les Eyre) *dwlt: a towards rr* **40/1**

600- **11** *23* **Silly Billy (IRE)**[172] 3439 6-9-4 67 .......... RobertWinston 10
(John Balding) *a towards rr: bhd fnl 3f* **16/1**

160- **12** *½* **Sam Spade (IRE)**[21] 7830 4-9-3 66 .......... (v) PatrickMathers 2
(Derek Shaw) *a in rr: bhd fnl 3f* **25/1**

021- **13** *30* **Uncle Brit**[14] 7909 8-8-10 59 .......... (p) PJMcDonald 4
(Rebecca Menzies) *a in rr: bhd and eased fnl 3f* **6/1**[2]

1m 43.67s (-0.03) **Going Correction** +0.15s/f (Slow)
**WFA** 3 from 4yo+ 1lb 13 Ran SP% **119.4**
Speed ratings (Par 103): **106,105,100,95,90 90,86,83,83,80 57,57,27**
CSF £20.16 CT £309.71 TOTE £3.00: £1.50, £3.40, £8.90; EX 21.70 Trifecta £426.50.
**Owner** 21C Telecom.co.uk **Bred** Klawervlei Stud (pty) Ltd **Trained** Danethorpe, Notts

**FOCUS**
An ordinary handicap, but the pace was sound and they finished well spread out.

## 8087 32RED CASINO NURSERY H'CAP 1m (F)
**2:30** (2:30) (Class 6) (0-65,65) 2-Y-0 **£1,940** (£577; £288; £144) **Stalls** Low

Form RPR

222- **1** **Offshore**[15] 7902 2-9-7 65 .......... (p) GrahamGibbons 6 71+
(James Tate) *pushed along sn after s: swtchd rt to outer and reminders after 1f: hdwy and cl up over 3f out: rdn to ld 1 1/2f out: sn hung rt: drvn and hung rt ins fnl f: kpt on* **9/4**[1]

506- **2** *½* **Brosnan (IRE)**[24] 7809 2-9-6 64 .......... SamJames 3 69
(Noel Quinlan) *towards rr: rdn along 3f out: hdwy 2f out: chsd wnr over 1f out: drvn and ev ch ins fnl f: no ex towards fin* **25/1**

631- **3** *7* **Pyrocumulus (IRE)**[35] 7648 2-9-2 60 .......... (p) BenCurtis 5 49
(Alan McCabe) *s.i.s: bhd and rdn along 1/2-way: swtchd rt and wd home turn: styd on u.p fnl 2f: nrst fin* **11/2**[2]

402- **4** *½* **The Olympus Man**[20] 7832 2-9-7 65 .......... (b[1]) GrahamLee 8 53
(Olly Stevens) *cl up: led 3f out: rdn and wandered 2f out: hdd 1 1/2f out and sn one pce* **6/1**[3]

355- **5** *¾* **Light Of The World (IRE)**[12] 7943 2-9-6 64 .......... GeorgeBaker 2 50
(Jamie Osborne) *chsd ldrs: rdn along 3f out: plugged on one pce fnl 2f* **6/1**[3]

240- **6** *¾* **Youonlyliveonce (IRE)**[22] 7815 2-8-9 53 .......... RaulDaSilva 4 37
(John Quinn) *slt ld: rdn along and hdd 3f out: sn drvn and grad wknd* **20/1**

026- **7** *3 ¼* **Robben**[48] 7379 2-8-12 56 .......... (p) JimmyQuinn 9 33
(John Mackie) *s.i.s: sn swtchd wd in rr: swtchd lft to inner over 3f out: sn rdn along and n.d* **12/1**

215- **8** *shd* **Excelling Oscar (IRE)**[15] 7904 2-8-10 54 .......... (b) HayleyTurner 1 30
(Conor Dore) *chsd ldrs on inner: rdn along wl over 2f out: grad wknd* **14/1**

004- **9** *15* **Magic Empress (IRE)**[80] 6537 2-7-12 45 .......... JoeyHaynes(3) 10
(Tony Coyle) *chsd ldrs: rdn along over 3f out: sn wknd* **7/1**

003- **10** *2 ½* **Naval Action**[22] 7815 2-8-1 45 .......... (p) LukeMorris 7
(Sir Mark Prescott Bt) *cl up: rdn along 3f out: drvn over 2f out: sn lost pl and bhd* **8/1**

1m 47.12s (3.42) **Going Correction** +0.15s/f (Slow) 10 Ran SP% **121.3**
Speed ratings (Par 94): **88,87,80,80,79 78,75,75,60,57**
CSF £72.70 CT £292.65 TOTE £2.70: £1.20, £9.60, £2.00; EX 79.60 Trifecta £417.80.
**Owner** Saeed Manana **Bred** S Tindall, D Ludlow & Stowell Hill Ltd **Trained** Newmarket, Suffolk

**FOCUS**
A modest nursery and this looked hard work for these juveniles. The winner has been rated as matching his latest form.

## 8088 UNIBET OFFER DAILY JOCKEY/TRAINER SPECIALS H'CAP 5f (F)
**3:00** (3:01) (Class 6) (0-60,64) 3-Y-0+ **£2,264** (£673; £336; £168) **Stalls** High

Form RPR

000- **1** **Incomparable**[5] 8024 9-9-2 55 .......... (p) DavidProbert 7 65
(Scott Dixon) *prom: led over 2f out: rdn wl over 1f out: drvn and edgd lft ins fnl f: kpt on wl towards fin* **20/1**

0/0- **2** *1 ½* **Wreningham**[25] 7781 9-9-0 53 .......... LukeMorris 10 58
(Pat Eddery) *chsd ldrs: hdwy over 2f out: rdn to chal over 1f out: drvn ins fnl f and kpt on same pce* **16/1**

500- **3** *nse* **Under Approval**[107] 5715 3-8-11 55 .......... GemmaTutty(5) 2 60
(Karen Tutty) *chsd ldrs: rdn 2f out: styng on whn edgd rt ent fnl f: kpt on towards fin* **25/1**

142- **4** *¾* **Danzoe (IRE)**[15] 7900 7-9-4 57 .......... (v) WilliamTwiston-Davies 1 59
(Christine Dunnett) *dwlt and in rr: hdwy on far rail after 2f: rdn 2f out: drvn and kpt on fnl f* **13/2**[3]

646- **5** *nk* **Meebo (IRE)**[21] 7826 3-9-7 60 .......... (vt) JFEgan 9 61
(J R Jenkins) *chsd ldrs: rdn along 2f out: kpt on same pce fnl f* **10/1**

000- **6** *nk* **College Doll**[15] 7900 5-9-2 55 .......... (t) JimmyQuinn 8 55
(Christine Dunnett) *dwlt: sn in tch: rdn along 2f out: styng on whn n.m.r and swtchd lft ent fnl f: kpt on same pce after* **22/1**

400- **7** *1 ½* **Master Of Disguise**[15] 7900 8-9-4 57 .......... GrahamGibbons 5 52
(Brian Baugh) *cl up: rdn along 2f out: drvn over 1f out: wknd fnl f* **6/1**[2]

342- **8** *1* **Lazy Sioux**[34] 7670 3-9-0 53 .......... JasonHart 11 44
(Richard Guest) *chsd ldrs: rdn along over 2f out: drvn wl over 1f out and grad wknd* **12/1**

160- **9** *nk* **Indastar**[53] 7253 4-9-5 58 .......... (t) GrahamLee 6 48
(Michael Herrington) *cl up: rdn along 2f out: sn wknd* **8/1**

500- **10** *½* **Fathom Five (IRE)**[14] 7915 10-8-10 56 .......... KevinLundie(7) 3 44
(Shaun Harris) *prom: rdn along 1/2-way: sn wknd* **50/1**

000- **11** *3* **Walta (IRE)**[8] 7997 3-8-13 57 .......... (bt) EoinWalsh(5) 14 34
(Roy Bowring) *s.i.s and bhd: reminders after 1f: rdn 1/2-way: nvr a factor* **16/1**

430- **12** *nk* **Vale Mentor (IRE)**[20] 7845 3-9-2 55 .......... LiamKeniry 12 31
(Denis Quinn) *towards rr: reminders after 1f: sn outpcd and bhd* **40/1**

301- **13** *2 ½* **Pearl Noir**[5] 8023 4-9-6 64 6ex .......... (b) TimClark(5) 4 31
(Scott Dixon) *slt ld: rdn along 1/2-way: sn hdd & wknd* **9/4**[1]

142- **14** *¾* **Your Gifted (IRE)**[8] 7997 7-9-0 58 .......... (v) AlistairRawlinson(5) 13 23
(Lisa Williamson) *in tch: rdn along over 2f out: sn drvn and wknd* **14/1**

1m 1.1s (1.40) **Going Correction** +0.325s/f (Slow) 14 Ran SP% **122.1**
Speed ratings (Par 101): **101,98,98,97,96 96,93,92,91,91 86,85,81,80**
CSF £298.18 CT £7986.80 TOTE £23.10: £6.70, £5.10, £5.70; EX 243.70 Trifecta £3945.50.
**Owner** P J Dixon & Partners **Bred** Mrs Yvette Dixon **Trained** Babworth, Notts

**FOCUS**
A moderate sprint handicap with the runners using the full width of the track. The level is a bit fluid.

## 8089 CORAL MOBILE "JUST THREE CLICKS TO BET" H'CAP 1m 6f (F)
**3:30** (3:30) (Class 5) (0-75,75) 3-Y-0+ **£2,587** (£770; £384; £192) **Stalls** Low

Form RPR

625- **1** **Royal Marskell**[14] 7914 5-9-3 69 .......... ConnorBeasley(3) 3 78
(Alison Hutchinson) *hld up towards rr: hdwy on outer 4f out: led over 2f out: rdn and edgd rt over 1f out: drvn ins fnl f: jst hld on* **10/3**[2]

263- **2** *shd* **Layline (IRE)**[14] 7914 7-9-5 68 .......... LukeMorris 6 76
(Gay Kelleway) *trckd ldrs: hdwy to chse wnr wl over 1f out: swtchd lft and drvn appr fnl f: kpt edging lft but styd on strly: jst failed* **9/2**[3]

000- **3** *2 ¼* **Bushel (USA)**[18] 7871 4-9-7 70 .......... PJMcDonald 7 75
(James Given) *led: rdn along 3f out: hdd over 2f out: sn drvn and kpt on same pce fnl f* **10/1**

221- **4** *hd* **Master Dan**[14] 7913 3-9-5 75 .......... GrahamLee 5 80
(James Given) *trckd ldr: cl up 4f out: rdn along wl over 2f out: drvn and one pce ent fnl f* **13/8**[1]

060- **5** *3 ¾* **Bold Runner**[12] 7946 3-8-12 68 .......... RaulDaSilva 2 67
(Jose Santos) *trckd ldrs on inner: rdn along over 3f out: sn drvn and one pce* **8/1**

305- **6** *6* **Gabrial The Duke (IRE)**[126] 5002 4-9-7 70 .......... GeorgeChaloner 1 61
(Richard Fahey) *hld up in rr: effrt 3f out: rdn along over 2f out: no hdwy* **16/1**

/00- **7** *15* **Danehill Flyer (IRE)**[230] 1644 4-9-1 67 .......... (e[1]) JoeyHaynes(3) 4 37
(Philip Kirby) *t.k.h: trckd ldr on inner: pushed along 4f out: rdn over 3f out: sn wknd* **16/1**

3m 16.2s (7.90) **Going Correction** +0.15s/f (Slow)
**WFA** 3 from 4yo+ 7lb 7 Ran SP% **111.3**
Speed ratings (Par 103): **83,82,81,81,79 75,67**
CSF £17.59 TOTE £4.50: £2.30, £2.60; EX 18.60 Trifecta £115.50.
**Owner** Miss Chantal Wootten **Bred** Miss V Woodward **Trained** Exning, Suffolk

**FOCUS**
They didn't go much of a pace in this modest staying handicap. A small pb from the winner.
T/Jkpt: Not won. T/Plt: £119.30 to a £1 stake. Pool of £61310.53 - 374.86 winning tickets.
T/Qpdt: £54.20 to a £1 stake. Pool of £5877.41 - 80.24 winning tickets. JR

# 8067 KEMPTON (A.W) (R-H)
Wednesday, December 10

**OFFICIAL GOING: Polytrack: standard**
Wind: light, half behind Weather: dry

## 8090 MIX BUSINESS WITH PLEASURE AT KEMPTON H'CAP 7f (P)
**3:40** (3:41) (Class 6) (0-65,65) 3-Y-0 **£2,264** (£673; £336; £168) **Stalls** Low

Form RPR

254- **1** **Rememberance Day**[61] 7078 3-9-3 61 .......... (t) RobertWinston 2 72
(Les Eyre) *t.k.h: chsd ldrs: rdn and effrt over 1f out: led ins fnl f: styd on strly* **7/1**[2]

032- **2** *1 ½* **Seven Lucky Seven**[12] 7950 3-9-5 63 .......... GrahamLee 4 70
(Michael Herrington) *t.k.h: chsd ldrs: pushed along and clsd to chal 1f out: led ins fnl f: sn hdd and outpcd fnl 100yds* **3/1**[1]

111- **3** *1 ½* **Spinning Cobblers**[18] 7884 3-9-5 63 .......... (v) SteveDrowne 5 66
(Stuart Williams) *chsd ldr: rdn to ld over 1f out: hdd ins fnl f: sn outpcd* **3/1**[1]

400- **4** *1 ½* **Kings Chapel (USA)**[37] 7622 3-8-8 59 .......... DavidParkes(7) 9 58
(Jeremy Gask) *s.i.s: hld up in last trio: effrt over 2f out: no imp tl styd on ins fnl f: nvr trbld ldrs* **25/1**

500- **5** *½* **Satellite Express (IRE)**[33] 7704 3-9-0 58 .......... JFEgan 8 56
(David Evans) *hld up in midfield: rdn and outpcd 2f out: rallied u.p 1f out: kpt on ins fnl f: no threat to ldrs* **25/1**

606- **6** *1 ½* **Hipz (IRE)**[7] 8017 3-9-2 65 .......... JordanVaughan(5) 3 59
(Laura Mongan) *chsd ldrs: rdn and outpcd 2f out: 5th and btn over 1f out: wknd fnl f* **8/1**[3]

004- **7** *nk* **Navajo Dream**[14] 7924 3-8-0 51 oh6 .......... TomMarquand(7) 7 44
(Michael Appleby) *hld up in last trio: rdn wl over 2f out: no imp* **16/1**

233- **8** *1 ¼* **Copper Cavalier**[11] 7972 3-8-7 51 .......... (v) LiamJones 1 40
(Robert Cowell) *racd freely: led tl rdn and hdd over 1f out: fdd fnl f* **8/1**[3]

005- **9** *3 ¼* **Happydoingnothing**[7] 8013 3-8-12 56 .......... MartinHarley 10 37
(Christine Dunnett) *dwlt: a in rr: rdn over 2f out: no hdwy: n.d* **16/1**



The Form Book, Raceform Ltd, Newbury, RG14 5SJ

422- **10** 2 1/4 **Movie Magic**[9] 7987 3-8-4 51 oh4..............................(v) RyanPowell(3) 11 26
(John Bridger) *dwlt: sn rcvrd: chsd ldrs 4f out tl lost pl over 2f out: wknd wl over 1f out* **25/1**

05R- **R** **Thundering Cloud (IRE)**[96] 6119 3-8-12 56.............. FergusSweeney 6
(Brendan Powell) *ref to r* **12/1**

1m 25.82s (-0.18) **Going Correction** -0.025s/f (Stan) **11** Ran SP% **115.7**
Speed ratings (Par 98): **100,98,96,94,94 92,92,90,87,84**
CSF £27.09 CT £75.63 TOTE £7.00: £2.30, £1.30, £2.00; EX 31.90 Trifecta £114.20.
**Owner** M Moulds **Bred** Bearstone Stud **Trained** Catton, North Yorkshire
■ Stewards' Enquiry : Robert Winston four-day ban: used whip in incorrect place (Dec 26-29)

**FOCUS**
An uncompetitive 3yo handicap, but the form looks fair for the class rated around the second.

## 8091 BOOK THE PANORAMIC ON 27.12.14 NURSERY H'CAP 7f (P)
**4:10** (4:11) (Class 5) (0-75,74) 2-Y-O **£2,911** (£866; £432; £216) **Stalls** Low

Form RPR

551- **1** **Gleaming Girl**[20] 7849 2-8-11 71.............................. SophieKilloran(7) 2 75
(David Simcock) *hld up in tch: effrt to chse ldrs over 1f out: str run to ld ins fnl f: r.o wl* **8/1**

354- **2** 1 **China Club (IRE)**[11] 7973 2-9-5 72.............................. RobertHavlin 1 73
(John Gosden) *chsd ldrs: swtchd rt and effrt 2f out: rdn to ld over 1f out: hdd ins fnl f: r.o same pce* **9/2**[3]

545- **3** 1/2 **Waaleef**[11] 7973 2-9-1 68.............................. MartinHarley 4 68
(Marco Botti) *in tch: pushed along and effrt over 1f out: drvn ins fnl f: styd on fnl 100yds to go 3rd towards fin: nt enough pce to rch ldrs* **2/1**[1]

035- **4** 1 **Jaganory (IRE)**[25] 7807 2-9-7 74.............................. JFEgan 3 71
(David Evans) *broke fast: led: rdn and wnt lft 2f out: drvn and hdd over 1f out: no ex ins fnl f* **14/1**

413- **5** nse **Mecado (IRE)**[9] 7984 2-9-5 72.............................. JimCrowley 7 69
(Richard Hannon) *hld up in tch in rr: rdn and effrt over 2f out: styd on u.p ins fnl f: nvr trbld ldrs* **8/1**

404- **6** 1 **Dubawi Diamond**[25] 7810 2-9-0 67.............................. LukeMorris 5 61
(James Tate) *wnt lft s: chsd ldrs: rdn and pushed lft 2f out: drvn and unable qck over 1f out: wknd ins fnl f* **7/2**[2]

304- **7** 3 **Dark Wonder (IRE)**[15] 7911 2-8-9 65..................(b[1]) ConnorBeasley(3) 6 51
(James Given) *pushed lft and hmpd s: in tch: rdn over 2f out: sn struggling: wknd over 1f out* **12/1**

1m 26.67s (0.67) **Going Correction** -0.025s/f (Stan) **7** Ran SP% **110.3**
Speed ratings (Par 96): **95,93,93,92,92 90,87**
CSF £40.34 TOTE £9.50: £4.40, £2.40; EX 44.20 Trifecta £156.10.
**Owner** Tick Tock Partnership **Bred** Rabbah Bloodstock Limited **Trained** Newmarket, Suffolk

**FOCUS**
An interesting nursery for the modest grade. There was just an ordinary pace on early, resulting in a bunched finish. Straightforward form.

## 8092 BOOK NOW FOR BOXING DAY MEDIAN AUCTION MAIDEN STKS 6f (P)
**4:40** (4:42) (Class 5) 2-Y-O **£2,587** (£770; £384; £192) **Stalls** Low

Form RPR

**1** **Gold Flash** 2-9-5 0.............................. SebSanders 4 75+
(Ralph Beckett) *in tch in midfield: rdn to ld over 1f out: hdd ins fnl f: sn led again: r.o strly* **9/2**[2]

0- **2** 1 1/4 **Lucky Leyf**[14] 7920 2-9-0 0.............................. ShaneKelly 2 66
(Gary Moore) *chsd ldrs: rdn to chal jst over 1f out: led ins fnl f: sn hdd and r.o same pce fnl 100yds* **40/1**

03- **3** 3/4 **Percella**[34] 7685 2-9-0 0..............................(t) RobertHavlin 3 64
(Hughie Morrison) *in tch in midfield: effrt u.p over 1f out: styd on ins fnl f: wnt 3rd wl ins fnl f* **12/1**

6- **4** 3/4 **Souk Al Tahab (IRE)**[21] 7840 2-9-5 0.............................. AdamKirby 5 67
(Ed Dunlop) *in tch in midfield: hdwy u.p to chse ldrs on inner over 1f out: no ex ins fnl f* **8/1**[3]

4- **5** 1 3/4 **White Dog (IRE)**[21] 7833 2-9-5 0.............................. RobertTart 6 62
(Eugene Stanford) *chsd ldr tl 2f out: unable qck and outpcd over 1f out: styd on same pce fnl f* **8/1**[3]

02- **6** 1 **Kyrenia Castle (GER)**[14] 7917 2-9-5 0.............................. JimCrowley 1 59
(Richard Hannon) *led tl rdn and hdd over 1f out: no ex and btn 1f out: fdd ins fnl f* **15/8**[1]

**6** dht **Qatar Rock (IRE)** 2-9-0 0.............................. KevinStott(5) 11 59+
(Kevin Ryan) *rn green: in tch towards rr: rdn over 2f out: no imp tl styd on steadily ins fnl f: nvr trbld ldrs* **16/1**

00- **8** shd **Step Into The Tide (IRE)**[6] 8026 2-8-12 0.............................. NoraLooby(7) 12 58
(Joseph Tuite) *racd off the pce in rr of main gp: pushed along over 1f out: styd on ins fnl f: nvr trbld ldrs* **66/1**

**9** hd **Zebead (IRE)** 2-9-5 0.............................. GrahamLee 10 58+
(William Jarvis) *towards rr of main gp: rdn and no hdwy jst over 2f out: prog 1f out: no threat to ldrs but kpt on ins fnl f* **20/1**

04- **10** 1/2 **Azamaara (IRE)**[21] 7840 2-9-0 0.............................. LukeMorris 7 51
(James Tate) *in tch in midfield: drvn and unable qck 2f out: lost pl over 1f out: wknd fnl f* **20/1**

0- **11** 1 **Avail (IRE)**[43] 7511 2-9-0 0.............................. NedCurtis(5) 8 53
(Jonathan Portman) *in tch: rdn and rn green over 2f out: hung rt and no hdwy over 1f out: nvr trbld ldrs* **66/1**

**12** 22 **Born To Be Bad (IRE)** 2-9-5 0.............................. GeorgeBaker 9
(Jamie Osborne) *s.i.s: rn green in rr: lost tch over 2f out: t.o* **8/1**[3]

1m 14.16s (1.06) **Going Correction** -0.025s/f (Stan) **12** Ran SP% **114.8**
Speed ratings (Par 96): **91,89,88,87,85 83,83,83,83,82 81,51**
CSF £181.43 TOTE £6.40: £1.90, £9.00, £2.40; EX 302.40 Trifecta £4379.90 Part won..
**Owner** Sutong Pan **Bred** C R Cawston Ltd **Trained** Kimpton, Hants

**FOCUS**
An ordinary 2yo maiden, run at a moderate early tempo, but it ought to provide some future winners during the winter.

## 8093 BETDAQ £30 FREE BET AND 3% COMM MAIDEN STKS 1m (P)
**5:15** (5:17) (Class 5) 2-Y-O **£3,234** (£962; £481; £240) **Stalls** Low

Form RPR

46- **1** **Assagher (USA)**[18] 7891 2-9-5 0.............................. NickyMackay 12 75+
(John Gosden) *chsd ldrs: wnt 2nd 5f out tl rdn to ld 1f out: r.o strly: readily* **4/1**[3]

00- **2** 3 **Cloud Seven**[26] 7778 2-9-5 0.............................. GeorgeBaker 8 68
(Chris Wall) *led after 1f: rdn and clr w wnr over 1f out: hdd 1f out: sn outpcd and btn: wkng but hld on for 2nd cl home* **12/1**

**3** 1/2 **Mr Singh** 2-9-5 0.............................. RobertHavlin 3 67+
(John Gosden) *in tch in midfield: effrt but stl plenty to do on inner 2f out: hdwy 1f out: styd on ins fnl f: wnt 3rd last strides* **11/2**

04- **4** hd **Thowar (USA)**[80] 6577 2-9-0 0.............................. ShaneGray(5) 2 66
(Kevin Ryan) *led for 1f: chsd ldr tl 5f out: 3rd and outpcd over 1f out: styd on same pce fnl f: lost 3rd last strides* **10/1**

4- **5** hd **Stay Strong (GER)**[18] 7892 2-9-5 0.............................. MartinHarley 4 66
(Saeed bin Suroor) *in tch in midfield: rdn and unable qck over 2f out: no threat to wnr but kpt on again ins fnl f* **3/1**[2]

**6** 1/2 **Solar Flair** 2-9-5 0.............................. GrahamLee 6 65+
(William Knight) *in tch in midfield: rdn and outpcd 2f out: rallied and kpt on ins fnl f: no threat to ldrs* **33/1**

**7** 3/4 **High Admiral** 2-9-5 0.............................. DavidProbert 11 63+
(Andrew Balding) *in tch towards rr: pushed along and sme hdwy over 1f out: styd on ins fnl f: nvr trbld ldrs* **10/1**

0- **8** 3/4 **Ainslie (IRE)**[77] 6660 2-9-5 0.............................. JimCrowley 1 61
(David Simcock) *in tch in midfield: rdn and unable qck 2f out: drvn and outpcd over 1f out: one pce and no threat to ldrs after* **5/2**[1]

50- **9** 3/4 **Knight Music**[14] 7927 2-9-5 0.............................. LukeMorris 9 60
(Michael Attwater) *chsd ldrs: rdn and unable qck 2f out: lost pl over 1f out: wknd fnl f* **100/1**

**10** 6 **Qatar Falcon (IRE)** 2-9-0 0.............................. KevinStott(5) 10 46
(Kevin Ryan) *s.i.s: rn green in rr: rdn and no hdwy wl over 2f out: no ch fnl 2f* **33/1**

00- **11** 5 **Casius**[13] 7941 2-9-5 0..............................(b[1]) SteveDrowne 5 34
(Harry Dunlop) *nvr travelling in rr: reminders after 2f out: lost tch over 2f out* **66/1**

00- **12** 11 **Oakling**[13] 7941 2-9-0 0.............................. LiamKeniry 13
(Sylvester Kirk) *sn niggled along in midfield: lost pl and struggling u.p over 2f out: sn lost tch* **66/1**

**13** 7 **Gharoor** 2-9-5 0.............................. FTahir 7
(John Butler) *s.i.s: hld up towards rr: rdn and lost tch over 2f out: t.o* **100/1**

1m 40.19s (0.39) **Going Correction** -0.025s/f (Stan) **13** Ran SP% **125.7**
Speed ratings (Par 96): **97,94,93,93,93 92,91,91,90,84 79,68,61**
CSF £52.62 TOTE £4.40: £1.60, £3.50, £2.40; EX 52.20 Trifecta £188.90.
**Owner** HRH Prince Faisal Bin Khaled **Bred** Barronstown Stud **Trained** Newmarket, Suffolk

**FOCUS**
There was a fair early pace on in this staying 2yo maiden. However, the leaders kicked 2f out and caught out the majority. Muddling form. The fourth has been rated as showing improved form in defeat.

## 8094 CASH OUT ON THE BETDAQ+ APP MAIDEN STKS 1m (P)
**5:50** (5:51) (Class 4) 3-Y-O+ **£4,690** (£1,395; £697; £348) **Stalls** Low

Form RPR

434- **1** **Sighora (IRE)**[215] 2118 3-9-0 78.............................. MartinHarley 3 81+
(Ismail Mohammed) *mde all: rdn and qcknd wl clr over 1f out: easily* **4/1**[2]

0/6- **2** 9 **Squire**[21] 7841 3-9-5 0.............................. JimCrowley 2 65+
(Michael Attwater) *t.k.h: hld up in tch: outpcd by wnr and drifting rt over 1f out: kpt on to go modest 2nd ins fnl f* **8/1**[3]

60- **3** 1 3/4 **Hong Kong Joe**[30] 7733 4-9-6 0..............................(e) CharlesBishop 1 61
(Lydia Richards) *chsd wnr tl 4f out: drvn and outpcd 2f out: 2nd and wl btn 1f out* **66/1**

42- **4** 2 **New Year's Night (IRE)**[83] 6482 3-9-5 0..............................[1] AdamKirby 7 56
(Charlie Appleby) *towards rr early: hdwy to chse ldrs after 2f: wnt 2nd 4f out: rdn and fnd nil 2f out: 3rd and wl btn 1f out* **2/5**[1]

/ **5** 3 **Congaree Warrior** 4-9-6 0.............................. PatCosgrave 5 50
(John Butler) *chsd ldrs tl rdn and struggling jst over 2f out: wknd 2f out* **50/1**

0/ **6** 6 **My Red Devil (IRE)**[366] 8214 3-9-0 0.............................. GeorgeChaloner 4 31
(Richard Fahey) *dwlt: t.k.h: hld up in last pair: rdn and wknd over 2f out* **25/1**

**7** 10 **Star Cloud**[31] 3-9-5 0.............................. RobertHavlin 6 13
(James Bennett) *t.k.h: hld up in last pair: rdn over 2f out: sn lost tch: t.o* **66/1**

1m 38.29s (-1.51) **Going Correction** -0.025s/f (Stan)
**WFA** 3 from 4yo+ 1lb **7** Ran SP% **111.3**
Speed ratings (Par 105): **106,97,95,93,90 84,74**
CSF £30.00 TOTE £3.50: £1.80, £2.20; EX 18.90 Trifecta £180.30.
**Owner** Sheikh Rashid Dalmook Al Maktoum **Bred** Patrick A Cassidy **Trained** Newmarket, Suffolk

**FOCUS**
An extremely uncompetitive maiden and the winner was left with a simple task. The runner-up has been rated below his pre-race mark.

## 8095 BETDAQ 50% COMMISSION REFUND H'CAP (LONDON MIDDLE DISTANCE SERIES FINAL) 1m 3f (P)
**6:20** (6:21) (Class 2) 3-Y-O+
**£37,350** (£11,184; £5,592; £2,796; £1,398; £702) **Stalls** Low

Form RPR

142- **1** **Anglophile**[7] 8012 3-8-1 90.............................. ShaneGray(5) 10 100
(Charlie Appleby) *in tch in midfield: rdn and hdwy 2f out: str chal ins fnl f: r.o wl to ld nr fin* **7/1**[3]

212- **2** nk **Grendisar (IRE)**[14] 7922 4-9-10 104..............................(p) MartinHarley 4 113
(Marco Botti) *stdd s: hld up in last quartet: clsd 2f out: switching lft and hdwy over 1f out: rdn to ld ins fnl f: r.o: hdd and no ex last strides* **8/1**

465- **3** 1 3/4 **I'm Fraam Govan**[20] 7850 6-8-11 91..............................(t) PatCosgrave 13 97
(George Baker) *chsd ldrs: rdn to chse ldr wl over 1f out: ev ch over 1f out: led ins fnl f: sn hdd: outpcd fnl 75yds* **14/1**

316- **4** 1 **Noble Gift**[21] 7837 4-8-11 91.............................. GrahamLee 2 95
(William Knight) *taken down early: led: rdn 2f out: hdd ins fnl f: no ex: wknd towards fin* **40/1**

013- **5** 1 1/4 **Rydan (IRE)**[35] 7662 3-9-3 101.............................. TomQueally 5 103
(Robert Mills) *stdd s: hld up in last quartet: rdn and hdwy on inner 2f out: no imp fnl f* **9/2**[2]

212- **6** 1 1/2 **Double Discount (IRE)**[20] 7850 4-8-13 93..................(p) JimCrowley 8 93
(Tom Dascombe) *hld up in last quartet: hdwy on outer over 1f out: styd on ins fnl f: nvr trbld ldrs* **10/1**

401- **7** 3/4 **Missed Call (IRE)**[42] 7531 4-8-5 85.............................. HayleyTurner 11 84
(James Fanshawe) *in tch in midfield: rdn and n.m.r over 2f out: no hdwy u.p over 1f out* **16/1**

004- **8** nk **Rebellious Guest**[25] 7801 5-9-1 95.............................. MartinLane 7 93
(George Margarson) *in tch in midfield: effrt jst over 2f out: no imp over 1f out: wknd fnl f* **8/1**

251- **9** 1/2 **Bancnuanaheireann (IRE)**[7] 8012 7-9-7 101 6ex.............. LukeMorris 3 98
(Michael Appleby) *in tch in midfield: rdn and effrt 2f out: drvn and no hdwy over 1f out: wknd fnl f* **16/1**

004- **10** 1 3/4 **Chapter And Verse (IRE)**[19] 7870 8-7-11 80 oh1........ JoeyHaynes(3) 9 74
(Mike Murphy) *chsd ldrs: rdn 2f out: sn struggling and lost pl over 1f out: wknd fnl f* **50/1**

103- **11** 1 1/2 **Masterpaver**[21] 7837 3-8-10 94.............................. ShaneKelly 12 86
(Alan Bailey) *in tch in midfield: rdn over 2f out: unable qck and sn lost pl: wknd over 1f out* **20/1**

054- 12 3 1/2 **Starwatch**[7] 8012 7-8-8 88....(v) WilliamCarson 6 74
(John Bridger) *chsd ldr tl 2f out: wknd u.p over 1f out* 66/1

511- 13 12 **Solidarity**[20] 7850 3-9-2 100.... AdamKirby 14 67
(Charlie Appleby) *a towards rr: rdn over 2f out: no hdwy: lost tch 2f out* 3/1[1]

2m 17.21s (-4.69) **Going Correction** -0.025s/f (Stan)
**WFA** 3 from 4yo+ 4lb 13 Ran SP% **116.1**
Speed ratings (Par 109): **116,115,114,113,112 111,111,111,110,109 108,105,97**
CSF £58.44 CT £765.16 TOTE £8.10: £2.20, £2.40, £5.50; EX 74.60 Trifecta £818.50.
**Owner** Godolphin **Bred** Darley **Trained** Newmarket, Suffolk

**FOCUS**
A strong handicap for the time of year. The solid early pace steadied at halfway, although the form is rock solid. The runner-up has posted a pb in defeat.

## 8096 BETDAQ COMMISSION FREE FOOTBALL ON SATURDAYS H'CAP 2m (P)
**6:50** (6:50) (Class 4) (0-85,85) 3-Y-O+ **£5,175** (£1,540; £769; £384) **Stalls** Low

Form RPR

013- 1 **Ridgeway Storm (IRE)**[33] 7702 4-9-8 79.... TomQueally 5 87
(Alan King) *hld up in tch in midfield: rdn and hdwy on inner 2f out: chsd clr ldr jst over 1f out: styd on wl to ld fnl 50yds* 9/4[1]

200- 2 1 **Purple Spectrum**[21] 7838 3-9-5 84.... MartinHarley 10 91
(J R Jenkins) *t.k.h: chsd ldrs: clsd to ld and travelling wl over 2f out: rdn and kicked clr over 1f out: drvn ins fnl f: hdd and no ex fnl 50yds* 25/1

6/3- 3 hd **Spiritoftomintoul**[54] 7235 5-10-0 85....(t) JimCrowley 1 92
(Tony Carroll) *t.k.h: hld up in rr: hdwy u.p 2f out: wnt 3rd and edgd rt ins fnl f: kpt on wl* 9/2[2]

432- 4 3/4 **Charlie Wells (IRE)**[13] 7946 3-8-12 77.... ShaneKelly 6 83
(Eve Johnson Houghton) *hld up in last pair: rdn and hdwy on inner but stl plenty to do over 1f out: wnt 4th ins fnl f: styd on: nt rch ldrs* 9/2[2]

054- 5 1 1/2 **Flashman**[21] 7837 5-9-5 76....(b[1]) GeorgeBaker 2 80
(Gary Moore) *in tch in midfield: n.m.r 2f out: rdn and styd on same pce fr over 1f out* 16/1

163- 6 1 **Snowy Dawn**[40] 7566 4-9-5 76.... DavidProbert 7 79
(Ben Case) *chsd ldrs: rdn and chsd clr ldr briefly over 1f out: wknd ins fnl f* 10/1

203- 7 1/2 **Sagesse**[8] 8001 4-9-7 78....(p) LukeMorris 9 81
(Sir Mark Prescott Bt) *in tch in midfield: rdn and effrt over 2f out: drvn and styd on same pce fr over 1f out* 16/1

055- 8 1/2 **Bathwick Street**[16] 7903 5-8-12 69.... JFEgan 3 71
(David Evans) *led tl over 2f out: lost 2nd u.p over 1f out: wl hld and eased towards fin* 33/1

203- 9 18 **Dame Lucy (IRE)**[9] 7995 4-9-11 82.... AdamKirby 8 62
(Michael Appleby) *t.k.h: rdn 2f out: sn btn and dropped out qckly over 1f out* 8/1

112- 10 77 **Jelly Fish**[83] 6502 3-9-6 85.... GrahamLee 11
(Brett Johnson) *taken down early: in tch in midfield: rdn 4f out: dropped out qckly over 2f out: sn lost tch: eased: t.o* 7/1[3]

3m 29.01s (-1.09) **Going Correction** -0.025s/f (Stan)
**WFA** 3 from 4yo+ 8lb 10 Ran SP% **118.4**
Speed ratings (Par 105): **101,100,100,100,99 98,98,98,89,50**
CSF £68.79 CT £243.19 TOTE £3.60: £2.20, £4.00, £1.70; EX 94.60 Trifecta £1195.10.
**Owner** W H Ponsonby **Bred** Mount Coote Stud **Trained** Barbury Castle, Wilts

**FOCUS**
Not a bad staying handicap. The fourth has been rated as posting an effort in keeping with his previous sound C&D effort.
T/Jkpt: Not won. T/Plt: £345.60 to a £1 stake. Pool: £81,319.54 - 171.73 winning tickets T/Qpdt: £77.80 to a £1 stake. Pool: £7,465.62 - 71.00 winning tickets SP

# 8075 LINGFIELD (L-H)
Wednesday, December 10

**OFFICIAL GOING: Polytrack, standard**
Wind: Fresh, across (towards stands) Weather: Fine, cold

## 8097 DOWNLOAD THE LADBROKES APP (S) STKS 7f 1y(P)
**12:30** (12:30) (Class 6) 3-Y-O+ **£1,940** (£577; £288; £144) **Stalls** Low

Form RPR

000- 1 **Lindart (ITY)**[20] 7847 3-8-5 65....(b) GaryMahon(7) 4 74
(Richard Hannon) *mde all: rdn 2f out: clr jst over 1f out: styd on strly* 12/1

245- 2 4 **Avertor**[14] 7928 8-8-12 60.... LiamJones 1 63
(Robert Stephens) *wl in tch: rdn to chse wnr 2f out: no imp over 1f out: kpt on* 7/2[2]

30B- 3 2 **Ortac Rock (IRE)**[34] 7687 5-8-12 75....(t) GeorgeChaloner 5 58
(Richard Fahey) *in tch: pushed along 1/2-way: effrt on inner 2f out and disp 2nd briefly over 1f out: one pce after* 1/1[1]

/00- 4 2 1/4 **It's Only Business**[36] 7639 4-8-7 65....(p) RyanWhile(5) 2 52
(Bill Turner) *chsd wnr to 2f out: wknd* 5/1[3]

06- 5 3 1/4 **Expensive Taste (IRE)**[14] 7928 3-9-4 72....(tp) LukeMorris 6 49
(Phil McEntee) *hld up: prog on outer 3f out: rdn 2f out: wknd qckly* 7/1

600- 6 1 1/2 **Rosie Prospects**[21] 7845 3-8-7 42....(b) JimmyQuinn 8 34
(Roger Ingram) *hld up in last: rdn over 2f out: no prog* 66/1

000- 7 13 **Crowning Star (IRE)**[9] 7986 5-8-12 54....(t) JimCrowley 7 4
(Steve Woodman) *chsd ldng pair: rdn 1/2-way: sn wknd: eased wl over 1f out: t.o* 25/1

1m 22.79s (-2.01) **Going Correction** -0.125s/f (Stan) 7 Ran SP% **114.4**
Speed ratings (Par 101): **106,101,99,96,92 91,76**
CSF £53.54 TOTE £10.00: £7.20, £1.90; EX 57.50 Trifecta £102.10.There was no bid for the winner.
**Owner** Richard Hannon **Bred** Giacinto Guglielmi Az Ag Sant'Agostino E **Trained** East Everleigh, Wilts

**FOCUS**
The opening contest was an ordinary seller in which they went a decent gallop after a level break. The runner-up has been rated near his recent level.

## 8098 CORAL MOBILE "JUST THREE CLICKS TO BET" MEDIAN AUCTION MAIDEN STKS 1m 2f (P)
**1:00** (1:00) (Class 6) 3-5-Y-O **£1,940** (£577; £288; £144) **Stalls** Low

Form RPR

45- 1 **Priors Brook**[21] 7841 3-9-5 0.... DavidProbert 2 71+
(Andrew Balding) *trckd ldr after 2f: pushed along 3f out: upsides and hanging 2f out: shkn up to take narrow ld over 1f out: drvn and fnd jst enough fnl f* 4/6[1]

505- 2 1/2 **The Gay Cavalier**[16] 7901 3-9-5 67....(t) AdamKirby 3 70
(John Ryan) *led after 1f: rdn 3f out: jnd 2f out: narrowly hdd over 1f out: kpt on but a jst hld* 5/2[2]

3 2 **Deinonychus**[117] 3-9-5 0....[1] JimCrowley 4 66+
(William Knight) *hld up in last: chsd ldng pair 3f out: rdn over 2f out: kpt on but nvr able to threaten* 5/1[3]

/00- 4 31 **Graceful Willow**[105] 5831 4-9-3 0.... JimmyQuinn 1 2
(John E Long) *led 1f: shkn up 1/2-way: wknd qckly 3f out: t.o* 66/1

2m 6.29s (-0.31) **Going Correction** -0.125s/f (Stan)
**WFA** 3 from 4yo 3lb 4 Ran SP% **106.7**
Speed ratings (Par 101): **96,95,94,69**
CSF £2.52 TOTE £1.60; EX 2.70 Trifecta £2.80.
**Owner** Mrs L Alexander **Bred** Mrs L M Alexander **Trained** Kingsclere, Hants

**FOCUS**
A modest little maiden in which they went a steady gallop. The form possibly deserves to be rated a little higher.

## 8099 CORAL.CO.UK BEST ODDS GUARANTEED ON RACING H'CAP 1m 4f (P)
**1:30** (1:30) (Class 5) (0-75,81) 3-Y-O+ **£2,587** (£770; £384; £192) **Stalls** Low

Form RPR

011- 1 **Mymatechris (IRE)**[7] 8015 3-9-11 81 6ex.... DavidProbert 6 95+
(Andrew Balding) *waited wth: trapped bhd rivals fr 3f out to wl over 1f out: quick prog to ld jst ins fnl f: rdn and r.o wl* 4/9[1]

204- 2 2 3/4 **Conserve (IRE)**[29] 3079 4-8-12 63....(b) MartinLane 7 70
(Neil King) *hld up in last pair: rdn and prog on outer fr 3f out: styd on to take 2nd ins fnl f: no ch w wnr* 33/1

222- 3 3 3/4 **Classic Mission**[28] 7744 3-8-10 69....(v[1]) DannyBrock(3) 1 70
(Jonathan Portman) *racd freely: led: kicked 3 l clr over 2f out: hdd jst ins fnl f: fnd nil* 8/1[3]

053- 4 2 1/4 **Thecornishcowboy**[6] 8029 5-9-5 70....(t) AdamKirby 9 67
(John Ryan) *hld up: prog 4f out: chsd ldr over 2f out to over 1f out: wknd* 9/2[2]

425- 5 2 1/2 **Sea Vision (IRE)**[30] 7734 4-9-9 74.... FergusSweeney 3 67
(Jo Crowley) *chsd ldr: rdn over 3f out: lost 2nd over 2f out: steadily wknd* 20/1

260- 6 3/4 **Kindlelight Storm (USA)**[50] 7366 4-8-12 68....(b) JordanVaughan(5) 2 60
(Nick Littmoden) *trckd ldrs: gng wl enough 3f out: rdn and no rspnse jst over 2f out: wknd tamely* 12/1

530- 7 11 **High Office**[29] 7452 8-9-5 70.... HayleyTurner 8 45
(Conor Dore) *hld up in last: pushed along and lost tch over 3f out: wl bhd after: nvr involved* 33/1

411- 8 12 **Sparkling Ice (IRE)**[98] 6043 3-8-5 61....(b) LukeMorris 5 16
(Zoe Davison) *chsdl ldrs: rdn 1/2-way: wkng qckly whn short of room over 2f out: t.o* 14/1

2m 30.17s (-2.83) **Going Correction** -0.125s/f (Stan)
**WFA** 3 from 4yo+ 5lb 8 Ran SP% **123.5**
Speed ratings (Par 103): **104,102,99,98,96 96,88,80**
CSF £29.69 CT £75.57 TOTE £1.30: £1.10, £9.00, £1.80; EX 27.70 Trifecta £126.50.
**Owner** David Brownlow **Bred** Derrick Fisher **Trained** Kingsclere, Hants

**FOCUS**
A fair middle-distance handicap in which they went an even gallop. The winner proved to be in a different league.

## 8100 LADBROKES H'CAP 7f 1y(P)
**2:00** (2:03) (Class 4) (0-85,84) 3-Y-O+ **£4,690** (£1,395; £697; £348) **Stalls** Low

Form RPR

110- 1 **Holiday Magic (IRE)**[9] 7988 3-9-7 84.... AdamKirby 4 93
(Charlie Appleby) *trckd ldr: shkn up to ld jst over 2f out: pressed and rdn fnl f: styd on wl and sn in command* 5/2[1]

050- 2 1 **Gigawatt**[30] 7729 4-8-9 72.... PatCosgrave 2 78
(Jim Boyle) *trckd ldng pair: rdn over 2f out: wnt 2nd jst ins fnl f and tried to chal: kpt on same pce after* 6/1

046- 3 hd **Evening Attire**[9] 7988 3-9-7 84.... GeorgeBaker 1 89
(William Stone) *t.k.h: hld up in 5th: prog on inner 2f out: tried to chal ins fnl f: styd on same pce* 6/1

004- 4 1 1/4 **Dr Red Eye**[9] 7988 6-9-1 78....(p) DavidProbert 5 80
(Scott Dixon) *led: rdn and hdd jst over 2f out: tried to rally over 1f out: lost 2nd and fdd jst ins fnl f* 3/1[2]

305- 5 hd **Corporal Maddox**[13] 7947 7-9-5 82....(p) BenCurtis 3 84
(Ronald Harris) *hld up in 6th: rdn whn v wd bnd wl over 1f out: lost grnd and n.d after: styd on ins fnl f* 12/1

252- 6 1 **Smart Salute**[30] 7729 3-8-13 76....(b) LukeMorris 6 75
(Ed Walker) *chsd ldrs in 4th: rdn wl over 2f out: nvr able to land a blow after: kpt on* 7/2[3]

400- 7 2 3/4 **Nonno Giulio (IRE)**[20] 7852 3-9-5 82.... HayleyTurner 7 73
(Simon Dow) *stdd s: t.k.h: hld up in last: pushed along an lost tch 3f out: lost little grnd after: nvr involved* 33/1

1m 23.22s (-1.58) **Going Correction** -0.125s/f (Stan) 7 Ran SP% **115.0**
Speed ratings (Par 105): **104,102,102,101,100 99,96**
CSF £18.23 TOTE £2.70: £1.30, £3.50; EX 20.70 Trifecta £97.60.
**Owner** Godolphin **Bred** Mrs Ann Fortune **Trained** Newmarket, Suffolk

**FOCUS**
A fairly decent handicap in which they went a respectable gallop and the pace held up quite well. The runner-up and third suggest this level is high enough.

## 8101 £20 RISK-FREE BET AT UNIBET H'CAP 6f 1y(P)
**2:30** (2:33) (Class 2) 3-Y-O+
**£28,012** (£8,388; £4,194; £2,097; £1,048; £526) **Stalls** Low

Form RPR

523- 1 **Lancelot Du Lac (ITY)**[14] 7923 4-9-8 103.... JimCrowley 8 112
(Dean Ivory) *trckd ldr: rdn to ld jst over 1f out: decisive move and a holding on after* 7/2[1]

212- 2 3/4 **Boom The Groom (IRE)**[7] 8019 3-8-12 93.... WilliamCarson 11 100
(Tony Carroll) *wl in rr: 10th 1/2-way: prog on inner fr 2f out: drvn to take 2nd ins fnl f: clsd on wnr fin but nvr quite able to chal* 20/1

050- 3 1 1/4 **Tarooq (USA)**[165] 3714 8-9-10 105.... GrahamGibbons 3 108
(David Barron) *towards rr: 8th 1/2-way: rdn and prog over 1f out: eased to outer fnl f: r.o to take 3rd last strides* 7/1[3]

023- 4 1/2 **Plucky Dip**[13] 7947 3-8-3 87.... DannyBrock(3) 4 88
(John Ryan) *prom in chsng gp: rdn over 2f out: nvr gng pce to chal but kpt on fnl f* 14/1

201- 5 1/2 **Diamond Charlie (IRE)**[6] 8025 6-8-8 89 6ex....(p) HayleyTurner 9 89
(Simon Dow) *led at str pce: 2 l clr over 2f out: hdd jst over 1f out: sn btn but clung on quite wl* 33/1

/14- 6 shd **Perfect Pasture**[305] 534 4-9-5 100....(v) AdamKirby 2 99
(Michael Easterby) *chsd ldrs: 3rd 2f out: shkn up and nt qckn over 1f out: pushed along and lost pls ins fnl f* 5/1[2]

550- **7** *nk* **Hasopop (IRE)**[20] 7851 4-9-5 100 (b[1]) LukeMorris 1 99
(Marco Botti) *in tch in midfield: tried to make prog on inner wl over 1f out: one pce and no real imp fnl f* **10/1**

004- **8** *nk* **Fairway To Heaven (IRE)**[21] 7843 5-8-10 91 JackMitchell 5 91
(Michael Wigham) *n.m.r s: settled in last pair: prog over 1f out: clsng on ldrs but no ch whn short of room fnl 50yds* **14/1**

001- **9** *5* **Out Do**[14] 7923 5-9-3 98 (v) SamJames 6 80
(David O'Meara) *chsd ldrs: rdn over 2f out: no imp over 1f out: wknd fnl f* **8/1**

115- **10** *2* **Steelriver (IRE)**[14] 7923 4-8-13 94 ShaneKelly 12 75
(Michael Herrington) *chsd ldrs on outer: pushed along 2f out: no hdwy over 1f out: sn heavily eased* **8/1**

311- **11** *5* **Barracuda Boy (IRE)**[21] 7843 4-9-4 99 GeorgeBaker 10 58
(Tom Dascombe) *nudged by rival s: settled in last pair: wd bnd 2f out: bhd after* **7/1**[3]

000- **12** *½* **Red Refraction (IRE)**[41] 7555 4-8-9 90 PatCosgrave 7 48
(Richard Hannon) *a in last quartet: rdn 1/2-way: wd bnd 2f out: bhd after* **33/1**

1m 9.08s (-2.82) **Going Correction** -0.125s/f (Stan) **12** Ran SP% **119.2**
Speed ratings (Par 109): **113,112,110,109,109 108,108,108,101,98 92,91**
CSF £80.05 CT £468.68 TOTE £3.60: £1.30, £4.00, £3.60; EX 69.40 Trifecta £552.50.
**Owner** M J Yarrow **Bred** Elektra Di Fausto Martellozzo & C Sas **Trained** Radlett, Herts

**FOCUS**
The feature contest was a good quality sprint handicap in which they went a strong gallop. The third has been rated close to his best off a break.

## 8102 CORAL APP DOWNLOAD FROM THE APP STORE H'CAP 1m 2f (P)
**3:00** (3:03) (Class 6) (0-65,65) 3-Y-O+ **£1,940** (£577; £288; £144) **Stalls** Low

Form RPR

000- **1** **Rakaan (IRE)**[19] 7871 7-9-7 65 StevieDonohoe 5 74
(Brendan Powell) *dwlt: towards rr: sme prog fr 2f out: rdn and str run fr over 1f out to ld ins fnl f: sn clr* **5/1**[3]

200- **2** *2* **Bridge That Gap**[14] 7925 6-9-2 60 (p) JimmyQuinn 7 65
(Roger Ingram) *in tch in midfield: waiting for room over 2f out: prog jst over 1f out: styd on wl fnl f to take 2nd last stride* **20/1**

002- **3** *shd* **Santadelacruze**[14] 7925 5-9-3 61 WilliamCarson 11 66
(Mark Hoad) *trckd ldrs: effrt on inner over 1f out: drvn to chal ins fnl f: outpcd by wnr after: lost 2nd last stride* **20/1**

606- **4** *nk* **Apache Glory (USA)**[43] 7522 6-9-1 64 (p) EoinWalsh(5) 9 68
(John Stimpson) *towards rr: rdn 3f out: prog over 1f out: styd on wl fnl f: nrst fin* **12/1**

440- **5** *½* **The Firm (IRE)**[47] 7427 5-9-6 64 GeorgeBaker 1 67
(Daniel Mark Loughnane) *led: rdn 2f out: hdd & wknd ins fnl f* **4/1**[1]

304- **6** *¾* **Day Of The Eagle (IRE)**[70] 6865 8-9-4 62 GrahamGibbons 3 64
(Michael Easterby) *settled in rr: pushed along over 2f out: sme prog and shkn up over 1f out: styd on steadily: nvr really involved* **7/1**

500- **7** *¾* **Munsarim (IRE)**[14] 7925 7-9-0 58 (b) AmirQuinn 6 58
(Lee Carter) *slowly away and urged along to get gng: wl in rr: tk fierce hold after 4f: tried to make prog fr 2f out: taken wd and styd on fnl f: no ch* **9/2**[2]

456- **8** *nk* **Kolonel Kirkup**[175] 3364 4-8-10 54 LiamKeniry 14 54
(Ali Stronge) *hld up in midfield: prog on outer over 3f out: rdn to dispute 2nd briefly 2f out: nt qckn over 1f out: fdd* **25/1**

004- **9** *nk* **Night's Watch**[6] 8028 4-8-11 55 ChrisCatlin 13 54
(Dai Burchell) *prom: rdn to dispute 2nd 2f out: wknd jst over 1f out* **20/1**

000- **10** *¾* **Dozy Joe**[21] 7846 6-9-3 61 (bt) DavidProbert 10 59
(Joseph Tuite) *dwlt: wl in rr: prog on wd outside over 3f out: disp 2nd briefly 2f out: wknd over 1f out* **16/1**

004- **11** *2¾* **Matraash (USA)**[14] 7925 8-9-2 60 (p) ShaneKelly 8 53
(Daniel Mark Loughnane) *wl in rr: sme prog on wd outside over 2f out: no ch whn nudged by rival 1f out: fdd* **5/1**[3]

440- **12** *1½* **Oyster (IRE)**[50] 7358 3-9-1 62 (b) JackMitchell 12 52
(Nick Littmoden) *chsd ldr: rdn 3f out: stl disputing 2nd over 1f out: wknd qckly* **20/1**

000/ **13** *1¼* **Corlough Mountain**[1033] 531 10-8-0 51 oh6 (p) CallumShepherd(7) 2 38
(Paddy Butler) *t.k.h: a in rr: struggling 3f out* **100/1**

406- **14** *nk* **Fair Ranger**[25] 7805 3-9-2 63 AdamKirby 4 50
(Chris Gordon) *chsd ldng pair: rdn over 3f out: lost pl over 2f out: wknd over 1f out* **16/1**

2m 5.72s (-0.88) **Going Correction** -0.125s/f (Stan)
**WFA** 3 from 4yo+ 3lb **14** Ran SP% **127.4**
Speed ratings (Par 101): **98,96,96,96,95 95,94,94,94,93 91,90,89,88**
CSF £111.97 CT £1894.45 TOTE £7.80: £2.80, £5.00, £3.10; EX 123.10 Trifecta £1751.90.
**Owner** ACC Syndicate **Bred** L Mulryan & M Fahy **Trained** Upper Lambourn, Berks
■ Stewards' Enquiry : Amir Quinn one-day ban: careless riding (Dec 26)

**FOCUS**
A modest and messy handicap in which they went an even gallop.

## 8103 LADBROKES MOBILE ALL-WEATHER "HANDS AND HEELS" APPRENTICE SERIES H'CAP (EXCELLENCE INITIATIVE) 1m 1y(P)
**3:30** (3:30) (Class 6) (0-65,65) 3-Y-O+ **£1,940** (£577; £288; £144) **Stalls** High

Form RPR

103- **1** **Meddling**[41] 7556 4-9-3 60 HectorCrouch 4 70+
(Julia Feilden) *trckd ldr 1f: styd cl up: wnt 2nd again 2f out: led on inner 1f out: styd on wl fnl f* **4/1**[2]

005- **2** *1½* **Club House (IRE)**[5] 8041 4-9-3 65 MillyNaseb(5) 5 72
(Robert Mills) *s.s: hld up in rr: stdy prog over 3f out: gng strly over 2f out: clsd over 1f out: tk 2nd ins fnl f: styd on but no imp on wnr last 75yds* **3/1**[1]

305- **3** *1¾* **Tin Pan Alley**[22] 7830 6-9-2 64 CallumShepherd(5) 1 67
(David C Griffiths) *led: urged along and hdd 1f out: outpcd* **8/1**[3]

051- **4** *¾* **Barbary (IRE)**[20] 7854 3-8-10 59 CliffordLee(5) 6 60
(Charlie Fellowes) *wl in tch: cl up 2f out: nt qckn over 1f out: one pce after* **8/1**[3]

146- **5** *1* **Zaeem**[16] 7907 5-9-4 64 (p) PaulBooth(3) 10 63
(Dean Ivory) *trckd ldrs: disp 2nd briefly 2f out: one pce over 1f out* **20/1**

304- **6** *2¼* **Choice Of Destiny**[16] 7907 3-9-5 63 GaryMahon 11 56
(Philip McBride) *towards rr: prog on inner 2f out: chsd ldrs over 1f out: fdd fnl f* **14/1**

222- **7** *hd* **Sea Soldier (IRE)**[209] 2282 6-9-0 57 RobHornby 7 50
(Andrew Balding) *nvr bttr than midfield: no prog on outer 3f out: no ch 2f out: plugged on* **8/1**[3]

010- **8** *nk* **Lexington Blue**[6] 8030 4-8-6 54 KevinLundie(5) 2 46
(Seamus Mullins) *s.s: mostly in last: pushed along 1/2-way: nvr a factor but passed sme stragglers fr 2f out* **12/1**

052- **9** *5* **Benoordenhout (IRE)**[25] 7804 3-8-12 61 ow1 (p) JackBudge(5) 8 42
(Jonathan Portman) *s.s: wl in rr: no prog over 2f out: wl btn after* **8/1**[3]

432- **10** *nk* **Sexy Secret**[25] 7799 3-9-1 64 (v) MichaelKenneally(5) 3 44
(Lydia Pearce) *wl in tch: no prog over 2f out: wknd over 1f out and edgd rt* **14/1**

000- **11** *nk* **Captain Kendall (IRE)**[18] 7887 5-8-11 59 PatrickO'Donnell(5) 12 38
(Harry Chisman) *racd wd: nvr beyond midfeld: no prog over 2f out: wknd* **33/1**

030- **12** *1½* **Harry Bosch**[40] 7569 4-9-0 64 (p) RhiainIngram(7) 9 40
(Gay Kelleway) *chsd ldr after 1f to 2f out: wknd rapidly* **25/1**

1m 37.19s (-1.01) **Going Correction** -0.125s/f (Stan)
**WFA** 3 from 4yo+ 1lb **12** Ran SP% **122.0**
Speed ratings (Par 101): **100,98,96,96,95 92,92,92,87,86 86,85**
CSF £16.51 CT £94.96 TOTE £3.90: £2.40, £2.20, £2.00; EX 19.50 Trifecta £168.50.
**Owner** Good Company Partnership **Bred** G Strawbridge & London Thoroughbred Services Ltd **Trained** Exning, Suffolk

**FOCUS**
The concluding contest was a modest handicap restricted to apprentice riders in which they went a respectable gallop. The runner-up was down in grade and is rated to win.
T/Plt: £1,416.20 to a £1 stake. Pool: £50,150.38 - 25.85 winning tickets T/Qpdt: £84.40 to a £1 stake. Pool: £5,821.00 - 51.00 winning tickets JN

8104 - 8110a (Foreign Racing) - See Raceform Interactive

# 8090 KEMPTON (A.W) (R-H)
## Thursday, December 11

**OFFICIAL GOING: Polytrack: standard**
Wind: medium, half behind Weather: dry

## 8111 BOOK NOW FOR BOXING DAY H'CAP 7f (P)
**3:50** (3:52) (Class 7) (0-50,50) 3-Y-O+ **£1,617** (£481; £240; £120) **Stalls** Low

Form RPR

465- **1** **Lewamy (IRE)**[22] 7844 4-9-3 46 TomQueally 12 57
(Michael Bell) *chsd ldr: rdn to ld over 1f out: clr ins fnl f: styd on: rdn out* **9/2**[1]

600- **2** *1¾* **Warbond**[50] 7369 6-9-4 47 (p) LiamKeniry 10 53
(Michael Madgwick) *hld up in midfield: hdwy u.p over 1f out: chsd clr wnr fnl f: styd on* **9/2**[1]

000- **3** *1* **Fire King**[15] 7924 8-9-0 50 (p) DavidParkes(7) 4 54
(Paul Burgoyne) *hld up in midfield: rdn and hdwy over 1f out: chsd wnr briefly ins fnl f: 3rd and one pce fnl 100yds* **33/1**

062- **4** *2* **Island Express (IRE)**[8] 8008 7-8-12 46 (bt) AnnStokell(5) 5 45
(Ann Stokell) *t.k.h: hld up in midfield: rdn and hdwy 2f out: kpt on ins fnl f: no threat to wnr* **20/1**

003- **5** *1* **Berwin (IRE)**[15] 7924 5-9-2 45 RenatoSouza 6 41
(Sylvester Kirk) *s.i.s and rdn along early: in rr: swtchd rt and hdwy 2f out: kpt on u.p fnl f: nvr trbld ldrs* **10/1**

060- **6** *hd* **Quantum Dot (IRE)**[14] 7940 3-9-5 48 (b) MartinHarley 1 44
(Ed de Giles) *racd keenly: led: rdn and hdd over 1f out: lost 2nd ins fnl f: fdd fnl 100yds* **7/1**[3]

005- **7** *nk* **True Spirit**[42] 7548 4-9-7 50 LukeMorris 8 45
(Paul D'Arcy) *chsd ldng pair: rdn over 2f out: unable qck and lost 3rd jst over 1f out: wknd ins fnl f* **6/1**[2]

505- **8** *½* **Khelfan**[120] 5307 3-9-7 50 SteveDrowne 7 43
(Martin Smith) *hld up towards rr: effrt 2f out: kpt on ins fnl f: nvr trbld ldrs* **14/1**

520- **9** *nk* **Sweet Piccolo**[195] 2723 4-9-3 46 WilliamTwiston-Davies 2 39
(Paddy Butler) *hld up in midfield: rdn and effrt 2f out: kpt on but no real imp* **66/1**

053- **10** *1¼* **Chez Vrony**[37] 7646 8-9-2 45 StevieDonohoe 14 34
(Dave Morris) *bhd: rdn over 2f out: sme hdwy fnl f: nvr trbld ldrs* **20/1**

605- **11** *hd* **Barwah (USA)**[68] 6940 3-9-2 45 (t) WilliamCarson 13 34
(Anthony Carson) *stdd s: hld up in rr: rdn and effrt over 2f out: sme hdwy ins fnl f: nvr trbld ldrs* **6/1**[2]

406- **12** *4½* **Princess Rose**[14] 7940 3-9-2 45 (b) LiamJones 3 22
(John Weymes) *in tch in midfield: rdn wl over 2f out: btn over 1f out: sn wknd* **25/1**

400- **13** *2¼* **Waterloo Dock**[209] 2312 9-9-2 45 CharlesBishop 9 16
(Emma Baker) *chsd ldrs: rdn 2f out: sn struggling: wknd over 1f out* **33/1**

000- **14** *10* **Stun Gun**[12] 7972 4-9-4 47 (v) GeorgeBaker 11
(Derek Shaw) *in tch in midfield: lost pl and btn over 2f out: bhd and eased wl ins fnl f* **7/1**[3]

1m 26.97s (0.97) **Going Correction** +0.05s/f (Slow) **14** Ran SP% **126.4**
Speed ratings (Par 97): **96,94,92,90,89 89,88,88,87,86 86,81,78,67**
CSF £23.05 CT £640.48 TOTE £4.70: £2.10, £2.20, £11.60; EX 31.40 Trifecta £1524.50.
**Owner** Brian Goodyear **Bred** M Wurtenberger & R Stockli **Trained** Newmarket, Suffolk

**FOCUS**
A weak contest, highlighted by the fact that coming into the race the first two had recorded one win from a combined 73 previous starts. The runner-up has been rated close to his best.

## 8112 WATCH RACING UK ANYWHERE MAIDEN AUCTION STKS 7f (P)
**4:20** (4:20) (Class 6) 2-Y-O **£2,264** (£673; £336; £168) **Stalls** Low

Form RPR

033- **1** **Chicago Bere (FR)**[20] 7867 2-8-13 69 AdamKirby 2 72
(Richard Hannon) *broke wl: sn restrained to chsd ldrs and t.k.h: swtchd lft and effrt wl over 1f out: flashed tail u.p but str run to ld ins fnl f: sn in command: pushed out* **1/1**[1]

04- **2** *1¾* **Colourfilly**[20] 7867 2-8-10 0 LukeMorris 4 62
(Ed Walker) *wnt lft s: sn led: rdn and fnd ex wl over 1f out: hdd ins fnl f: no ex* **11/8**[2]

0- **3** *8* **Pyroclastic (IRE)**[22] 7840 2-9-3 0 PatCosgrave 6 48
(Jim Boyle) *pushed lft s: sn w ldr: rdn and outpcd wl over 1f out: wknd fnl f* **33/1**

**4** *1½* **Royal Roslea** 2-8-10 0 ShaneKelly 3 37
(Marcus Tregoning) *s.i.s: rn green early: clsd and in tch 5f out: rdn and outpcd over 2f out: wl hld after* **8/1**[3]

**5** *3¼* **Lettuce Snow (IRE)** 2-8-6 0 ChrisCatlin 1 24
(Geoffrey Deacon) *s.i.s and flashing tail leaving stalls: bhd: clsd and in tch 5f out: rdn 1/2-way: wknd over 2f out* **20/1**

1m 28.26s (2.26) **Going Correction** +0.05s/f (Slow) **5** Ran SP% **110.9**
Speed ratings (Par 94): **89,87,77,76,72**
CSF £2.66 TOTE £1.80: £1.10, £1.10; EX 2.70 Trifecta £13.40.
**Owner** Middleham Park Racing LXXXI **Bred** S N C Regnier & San Gabriel Inv Inc **Trained** East Everleigh, Wilts

**FOCUS**
A modest maiden. It's been rated at face value.

## 8113 BETVICTOR SVENGALI NURSERY H'CAP (BOBIS RACE) 6f (P)
4:50 (4:50) (Class 4) (0-85,83) 2-Y-O £4,528 (£1,347; £673; £336) Stalls Low

Form RPR
251- 1 **Wentworth Falls**[15] 7920 2-9-7 83..........................(b) AdamKirby 3 99+
(Charlie Appleby) *stdd s: t.k.h: hld up in rr: pushed along and clsd over 1f out: led ins fnl f: sn clr: easily* **8/11**[1]

402- 2 4 **The Dapper Tapper (IRE)**[13] 7948 2-8-5 67..................(v) LukeMorris 6 68
(Eve Johnson Houghton) *pushed lft s: in tch in midfield: hdwy u.p 2f out: led jst over 1f out: hdd ins fnl f: no ch w wnr but kpt on to hold 2nd* **10/1**[3]

443- 3 nk **Classic Seniority**[19] 7890 2-8-9 71.......................... PatCosgrave 2 71
(Richard Hannon) *chsd ldr for 2f: rdn and ev ch over 1f out: outpcd and btn ins fnl f: r.o same pce* **12/1**

421- 4 1½ **Exceedingly**[47] 7454 2-9-0 76.......................... LiamJones 1 72
(Robert Cowell) *in tch in midfield: effrt on inner 2f out: drvn and pressing ldrs over 1f out: btn ins fnl f: wknd towards fin* **10/1**[3]

216- 5 2¼ **Lackaday**[47] 7439 2-9-1 77.......................... CharlesBishop 4 66
(William Jarvis) *led: rdn 2f out: hdd jst over 1f out: sn btn: wknd ins fnl f* **5/1**[2]

540- 6 1 **Commander Patten (IRE)**[110] 5694 2-9-6 82.................. MartinHarley 5 68
(Alan Bailey) *wnt lft s: chsd ldrs: wnt 2nd 4f out tl over 1f out: sn wknd* **10/1**[3]

1m 12.41s (-0.69) **Going Correction** +0.05s/f (Slow) **6 Ran SP% 109.5**
Speed ratings (Par 98): **106,100,100,98,95 93**
CSF £8.40 TOTE £1.70: £1.30, £2.80; EX 9.50 Trifecta £27.30.
**Owner** Godolphin **Bred** Newsells Park Stud **Trained** Newmarket, Suffolk

**FOCUS**
The favourite showed himself to be in a different class in this contest. Straightforward form.

## 8114 GET SVENS INSIDE TRACK AT BETVICTOR MEDIAN AUCTION MAIDEN STKS 1m 4f (P)
5:20 (5:20) (Class 6) 3-5-Y-O £2,264 (£673; £336; £168) Stalls Centre

Form RPR
1 **Silver Mountain**[16] 3-9-5 0.......................... GeorgeBaker 1 73
(J R Jenkins) *led tl over 10f out: chsd ldr tl 7f out: shkn up to ld over 1f out: kpt on wl fnl f: rdn out* **6/1**

004- 2 ½ **Pink And Black (IRE)**[140] 4563 3-9-0 63.......................... SteveDrowne 6 67
(William Muir) *dropped in bhd after s: hld up in rr: hdwy on inner 2f out: ev ch fnl f: kpt on but a hld* **4/1**[3]

3- 3 ¾ **Laika**[9] 8003 5-9-5 0.......................... HayleyTurner 2 66
(Brian Ellison) *in tch: rdn and effrt 2f out: drvn over 1f out: wnt 3rd ins fnl f: kpt on but nvr enough pce to chal* **11/8**[1]

55- 4 6 **Lesson In Life**[6] 8048 3-9-0 0.......................... DanielTudhope 4 56
(David O'Meara) *t.k.h: led over 10f out: rdn and hdd over 1f out: wknd ins fnl f* **3/1**[2]

5 4½ **Par Three (IRE)**[64] 7047 3-9-5 0.......................... LukeMorris 5 54
(Tony Carroll) *chsd ldrs: wnt 2nd 7f out tl wl over 1f out: wknd over 1f out* **6/1**

0- 6 1¼ **Centralized**[22] 7841 3-9-2 0..........................(b[1]) JoeyHaynes(3) 3 52?
(Eric Wheeler) *in tch in midfield: rdn and lost pl over 2f out: wl hld whn hung rt over 1f out: wknd* **66/1**

2m 38.49s (3.99) **Going Correction** +0.05s/f (Slow)
**WFA** 3 from 5yo 5lb **6 Ran SP% 117.2**
Speed ratings (Par 101): **88,87,87,83,80 79**
CSF £31.19 TOTE £4.40: £1.50, £4.20; EX 20.60 Trifecta £66.90.
**Owner** Ms Aurelija Juskaite **Bred** Mr & Mrs A E Pakenham **Trained** Royston, Herts

**FOCUS**
There was a muddling pace to this modest maiden. A small pb from the runner-up.

## 8115 BEST PRICES FOR 4 SEASON BETVICTOR NURSERY H'CAP 1m (P)
5:50 (5:50) (Class 6) (0-60,60) 2-Y-O £2,264 (£673; £336; £168) Stalls Low

Form RPR
300- 1 **Wolf Of Windlesham (IRE)**[29] 7740 2-9-5 58..........(b[1]) SteveDrowne 7 62
(Charles Hills) *mde all: drvn and fnd ex over 1f out: hld on wl fnl f: drvn out* **12/1**

153- 2 ¾ **Gavarnie Encore**[22] 7832 2-9-5 58.......................... DavidProbert 10 60
(Michael Blanshard) *in tch in midfield: hdwy u.p over 1f out: wnt 2nd and pressing wnr ins fnl f: kpt on but a hld* **7/1**

605- 3 ½ **Hana Lina**[29] 7741 2-9-7 60..........................(b) GeorgeBaker 1 61
(William Haggas) *chsd ldr for 3f: wnt 2nd again 2f out: rdn over 1f out: lost 2nd and one pce ins fnl f* **6/1**[3]

052- 4 ½ **Courier**[29] 7740 2-9-2 55.......................... AdamKirby 6 55
(Lee Carter) *in tch in midfield: effrt u.p over 1f out: chsd ldrs and one pce u.p fnl f* **4/1**[2]

006- 5 1 **Artistic Flight (IRE)**[15] 7926 2-9-7 60.......................... PatCosgrave 9 58+
(Jim Boyle) *in tch in midfield: rdn 2f out: no imp tl styd on u.p ins fnl f: no threat to ldrs* **14/1**

000- 6 hd **Jersey Bull (IRE)**[22] 7832 2-9-6 59.......................... LiamKeniry 14 56
(Michael Madgwick) *stdd after s: t.k.h: hld up in rr: clsd 2f out: swtchd rt and hdwy 1f out: keeping on same pce whn swtchd rt towards fin* **33/1**

400- 7 hd **Le Rouquin (FR)**[36] 7666 2-9-2 55..........................(vt[1]) TomQueally 3 52
(Michael Bell) *in tch in midfield: effrt u.p to chse ldrs u.p over 1f out: no ex ins fnl f* **7/2**[1]

412- 8 1¼ **More Drama (IRE)**[10] 7994 2-8-12 51.......................... LukeMorris 5 45
(Sylvester Kirk) *chsd ldrs: wnt 2nd 5f out tl 2f out: wknd 1f out* **6/1**[3]

566- 9 2¼ **Charlie's Star**[22] 7832 2-9-4 57.......................... LiamJones 12 46
(Laura Mongan) *in tch in last quartet: effrt u.p jst over 2f out: kpt on but no real imp* **20/1**

000- 10 1¼ **Epsom Poems**[57] 7198 2-9-3 56.......................... JFEgan 8 42
(Pat Phelan) *in tch: pushed along to chse ldrs 3f out: no ex and btn over 1f out: wknd fnl f* **14/1**

060- 11 1¾ **Foylesideview (IRE)**[65] 7014 2-9-2 55.......................... FergusSweeney 11 37
(Luke Dace) *towards rr: hdwy into midfield 5f out: lost pl u.p 2f out: wknd over 1f out* **20/1**

024- 12 ½ **Goolagong Girl (IRE)**[48] 7425 2-8-12 54..........(p) DannyBrock(3) 13 35
(Jane Chapple-Hyam) *hld up in tch trio: effrt u.p over 2f out: no prog* **16/1**

060- 13 36 **Arthur's Way (IRE)**[17] 7904 2-8-11 55..........(p) AlistairRawlinson(5) 4
(Lisa Williamson) *s.i.s: a in rr: lost tch 3f out: t.o* **66/1**

1m 41.53s (1.73) **Going Correction** +0.05s/f (Slow) **13 Ran SP% 124.2**
Speed ratings (Par 94): **93,92,91,91,90 90,89,88,86,85 83,82,46**
CSF £93.67 CT £586.61 TOTE £16.50: £4.80, £2.30, £1.50; EX 134.40 Trifecta £2115.90.
**Owner** Gary And Linnet Woodward **Bred** Joe And Edel Banahan **Trained** Lambourn, Berks

**FOCUS**
A moderate but competitive nursery. Straightforward form.

## 8116 DAILY SVEN-TO-1 SPECIALS AT BETVICTOR H'CAP 1m (P)
6:20 (6:20) (Class 2) (0-100,103) 3-Y-O+
£11,827 (£3,541; £1,770; £885; £442; £222) Stalls Low

Form RPR
002- 1 **Lacan (IRE)**[13] 7955 3-8-11 91.......................... MartinHarley 5 97+
(Marco Botti) *in tch in midfield: effrt u.p over 1f out: styd on and ev ch ins fnl led towards fin: drvn out* **4/1**[3]

121- 2 nk **Big Baz (IRE)**[26] 7801 4-9-2 95.......................... SteveDrowne 1 100+
(William Muir) *chsd ldrs: rdn to chal over 1f out: led 1f out: r.o u.p tl hdd and no ex towards fin* **6/4**[1]

526- 3 nk **Ingleby Angel (IRE)**[12] 7971 5-8-13 92.......................... DanielTudhope 7 96
(David O'Meara) *in tch in midfield: rdn over 2f out: hdwy u.p ins fnl f: wnt 3rd fnl 100yds: styd on wl* **10/1**

543- 4 1 **Outer Space**[21] 7852 3-8-8 88.......................... WilliamTwiston-Davies 6 90
(Jamie Osborne) *stdd s: hld up in rr: rdn over 1f out: hdwy ins fnl f: styd on to go 4th fnl 75yds: no threat to ldrs* **17/2**

020- 5 nk **Ocean Applause**[41] 7567 4-8-4 86 oh9..........................(t) DannyBrock(3) 3 87?
(John Ryan) *in tch in last pair: drvn and swtchd rt over 1f out: wnt 3rd 1f out tl fnl 100yds: r.o same pce* **50/1**

602- 6 nk **Tigers Tale (IRE)**[42] 7545 5-9-2 95..........................(v) GeorgeBaker 4 95
(Roger Teal) *led: rdn and hrd pressed 2f out: hdd over 1f out: no ex and outpcd ins fnl f* **5/2**[2]

444- 7 ½ **Energia Flavio (BRZ)**[12] 7971 4-8-13 92..........................(p) LukeMorris 8 91
(Marco Botti) *chsd ldr: rdn and ev ch 2f out: led over 1f out tl 1f out: outpcd fnl 150yds* **8/1**

300- 8 2 **Emell**[22] 7836 4-9-10 103.......................... AdamKirby 2 98
(Richard Hannon) *stdd after s: in tch in midfield: effrt on inner 2f out: chsd ldrs over 1f out: wknd ins fnl f* **25/1**

1m 38.13s (-1.67) **Going Correction** +0.05s/f (Slow)
**WFA** 3 from 4yo+ 1lb **8 Ran SP% 125.1**
Speed ratings (Par 109): **110,109,109,108,108 107,107,105**
CSF £11.55 CT £60.67 TOTE £5.50: £1.70, £1.60, £2.80; EX 16.20 Trifecta £76.00.
**Owner** Giuliano Manfredini **Bred** Sheikh Sultan Bin Khalifa Al Nahyan **Trained** Newmarket, Suffolk

**FOCUS**
A good handicap, but inconclusive form with the sixth close up from 9lb out of the handicap.

## 8117 BETVICTOR.COM H'CAP 7f (P)
6:50 (6:50) (Class 3) (0-95,95) 3-Y-O+
£7,158 (£2,143; £1,071; £535; £267; £134) Stalls Low

Form RPR
510- 1 **Related**[110] 5665 4-9-2 90..........................(b) FergusSweeney 2 100
(David Simcock) *racd keenly: chsd ldrs: rdn and fnd ex to ld over 1f out: styd on wl: drvn out* **11/1**

150- 2 ½ **Steelriver (IRE)**[1] 8101 4-9-6 94.......................... ShaneKelly 4 102
(Michael Herrington) *hld up off the pce in last pair: clsd 2f out: rdn jst over 1f out: styd on u.p to go 2nd towards fin: nvr quite getting to wnr* **9/4**[1]

056- 3 ½ **Firmdecisions (IRE)**[107] 5784 4-9-1 89.......................... TomQueally 7 96
(Dean Ivory) *hld up in midfield: rdn to chse ldr over 1f out: kpt on ins fnl f: lost 2nd towards fin* **12/1**

040- 4 ½ **Valbchek (IRE)**[49] 7437 5-9-6 94..........................(p) GeorgeBaker 1 100
(Jane Chapple-Hyam) *hld up towards rr: swtchd rt over 1f out: chsd ldrs and kpt on same pce u.p ins fnl f* **16/1**

003- 5 ¾ **Lawmans Thunder**[36] 7663 4-9-2 95.......................... TimClark(5) 9 99
(Ismail Mohammed) *off the pce in last quartet: clsd over 2f out: drvn to chse ldrs 1f out: r.o same pce ins fnl f* **7/2**[2]

406- 6 1¼ **Upavon**[15] 7923 4-9-0 88.......................... LiamKeniry 6 89
(David Elsworth) *t.k.h: midfield: clsd 2f out: rdn and chsd ldrs 1f out: no ex ins fnl f* **12/1**

112- 7 1½ **Aqua Ardens (GER)**[21] 7852 6-9-2 90..........................(t) PatCosgrave 11 87
(George Baker) *off the pce towards rr: rdn over 2f out: styd on ins fnl f: nvr trbld ldrs* **6/1**[3]

425- 8 hd **Democretes**[69] 6892 5-9-0 88.......................... MartinHarley 5 84
(Seamus Durack) *midfield: rdn to chse ldrs over 1f out: wknd ins fnl f* **10/1**

400- 9 1¾ **Forceful Appeal (USA)**[36] 7663 6-8-10 84.......................... HayleyTurner 12 76
(Simon Dow) *stdd and dropped in bhd s: wl off the pce in rr: rdn over 2f out: nvr trbld ldrs* **25/1**

540- 10 1¼ **Deauville Prince (FR)**[36] 7663 4-9-3 91..........................(p) StephenCraine 3 79
(Tom Dascombe) *chsd ldr tl 2f out: sn lost pl u.p: wknd fnl f* **20/1**

000- 11 16 **Rufford (IRE)**[58] 7168 3-9-5 93.......................... AdamKirby 10 40
(Lee Carter) *led tl over 1f out: sn dropped out: bhd and eased fnl f* **33/1**

1m 24.43s (-1.57) **Going Correction** +0.05s/f (Slow) **11 Ran SP% 117.5**
Speed ratings (Par 107): **110,109,108,108,107 106,104,104,102,100 82**
CSF £35.14 CT £318.84 TOTE £12.60: £3.20, £1.60, £3.40; EX 46.50 Trifecta £466.60.
**Owner** J Barnett & M Caine **Bred** Laundry Cottage Stud Farm **Trained** Newmarket, Suffolk

**FOCUS**
This was run at a strong pace and the form looks solid.
T/Plt: £36.90 to a £1 stake. Pool of £98332.87 - 1944.49 winning tickets. T/Qpdt: £17.90 to a £1 stake. Pool of £9352.51 - 384.50 winning tickets. SP

# 8058 WOLVERHAMPTON (A.W) (L-H)
Friday, December 12

**OFFICIAL GOING: Tapeta: standard**
Wind: Light behind Weather: Fine

## 8118 £20 RISK-FREE BET AT UNIBET NURSERY H'CAP 5f 20y
4:00 (4:02) (Class 6) (0-65,65) 2-Y-O £2,102 (£625; £312; £156) Stalls Low

Form RPR
251- 1 **True Course**[14] 7948 2-9-2 65.......................... ShaneGray(5) 4 69
(Charlie Appleby) *hld up: hdwy and nt clr run over 1f out: r.o u.p to ld wl ins fnl f* **7/4**[1]

004- 2 ½ **Mon Petit Fleur**[20] 7881 2-8-7 54.......................... ConnorBeasley(3) 2 58
(Chris Dwyer) *hmpd s: hld up: hdwy and nt clr run fr over 1f out tl wl ins fnl f: r.o* **8/1**

056- 3 ¾ **Diminutive (IRE)**[14] 7948 2-8-8 52..........................(b) StevieDonohoe 5 52
(Grace Harris) *hld up: swtchd rt and r.o wl ins fnl f: nt rch ldrs* **33/1**

054- 4 nse **Junior Ben**[37] 7665 2-8-3 47.......................... PatrickMathers 6 46
(Derek Shaw) *mid-div: hdwy 1/2-way: rdn over 1f out: ev ch ins fnl f: no ex towards fin* **25/1**

445- **5** *nk* **Bahango (IRE)**[112] 5630 2-9-1 **64**........................(p) AlistairRawlinson(5) 3 62+
(Patrick Morris) *led: rdn and edgd rt over 1f out: hdd and unable qck wl ins fnl f* **25/1**

004- **6** *3 ¾* **Lydiate Lady**[14] 7948 2-8-5 **49**........................(p) JFEgan 1 34
(Paul Green) *edgd rt s: sn pushed along to chse ldrs: rdn 1/2-way: edgd lft: wknd and eased ins fnl f* **16/1**

621- **7** *hd* **Jebediah Shine**[16] 7917 2-9-6 **64**........................ DanielTudhope 11 48+
(David O'Meara) *chsd ldrs: rdn 1/2-way: wknd ins fnl f* **6/1**[3]

550- **8** *hd* **Torridonian**[88] 6408 2-9-3 **61**........................ LukeMorris 8 44+
(James Tate) *prom: rdn over 1f out: wknd ins fnl f* **3/1**[2]

330- **9** *1* **Robin Hill**[14] 7948 2-9-4 **62**........................ GrahamLee 12 42
(William Muir) *hld up: rdn over 1f out: nt trble ldrs* **12/1**

10- **10** *3* **Toni's A Star**[14] 7948 2-8-7 **51**........................(b) RaulDaSilva 7 20
(Paul Green) *w ldr tl rdn 1/2-way: hung lft over 1f out: wknd ins fnl f* **50/1**

336- **11** *1 ½* **Strategise (IRE)**[80] 6645 2-8-6 **55**........................(p) EoinWalsh(5) 9 19
(Daniel Mark Loughnane) *hld up: rdn over 3f out: a in rr* **66/1**

1m 1.79s (-0.11) **Going Correction** -0.05s/f (Stan) **11** Ran SP% **114.4**
Speed ratings (Par 94): **98,97,96,95,95 89,89,88,87,82 80**
CSF £15.16 CT £335.52 TOTE £2.60: £1.50, £2.90, £6.90; EX 19.40 Trifecta £487.10.
**Owner** Godolphin **Bred** W A Tinkler **Trained** Newmarket, Suffolk

**FOCUS**
The time was a bit quicker than the following older-horse maiden, but they covered the final 2f around a second slower in this race and the pace had been overly strong. The standard is straightforward around the poor fourth and third.

## 8119 UNIBET OFFER DAILY JOCKEY/TRAINER SPECIALS MEDIAN AUCTION MAIDEN STKS — 5f 20y
**4:30** (4:30) (Class 6) 3-5-Y-O — **£2,102** (£625; £312; £156) **Stalls** Low

Form — RPR

402- **1** **Warm Order**[8] 8023 3-9-0 46........................ LukeMorris 6 55
(Tony Carroll) *chsd ldr tl shkn up to ld over 1f out: edgd lft: rdn out* **7/1**[3]

30- **2** *1 ½* **Silent Pursuit**[227] 1844 3-9-0 0........................ LiamKeniry 7 50
(Philip Hide) *a.p: rdn over 1f out: r.o* **11/2**[2]

504- **3** *1* **Tolly McGuiness**[27] 7800 3-9-0 45........................ ShelleyBirkett(5) 5 51
(Julia Feilden) *led: rdn and hdd over 1f out: styd on same pce ins fnl f* **33/1**

4- **4** *nk* **Summersault (IRE)**[16] 7921 3-9-5 0........................ FergusSweeney 4 50
(Jamie Osborne) *s.i.s: hld up: rdn and hung lft fr over 1f out: r.o: nt trble ldrs* **4/6**[1]

560- **5** *½* **Diamondsinthesky (IRE)**[132] 4890 3-9-0 56........................(v) PatrickMathers 3 43
(Derek Shaw) *chsd ldrs: rdn over 1f out: styd on same pce ins fnl f* **16/1**

564- **6** *1* **Forceful Beacon**[9] 8008 4-9-0 40........................(b[1]) GeorgeDowning(5) 2 45
(Tony Carroll) *prom: plld hrd early: rdn over 1f out: styd on same pce fnl f* **12/1**

0/0- **7** *3* **With A Twist**[163] 3849 3-9-0 37........................(t) DavidProbert 1 29
(Andrew Balding) *s.i.s: outpcd* **20/1**

1m 2.0s (0.10) **Going Correction** -0.05s/f (Stan) **7** Ran SP% **109.2**
Speed ratings (Par 101): **97,94,93,92,91 90,85**
CSF £40.46 TOTE £4.40: £1.30, £2.70; EX 34.30 Trifecta £313.10.
**Owner** Mrs Veronica Gilbert **Bred** Lady Whent **Trained** Cropthorne, Worcs

**FOCUS**
The winner and third came into this officially rated in the 40s. Weak form with the second and fourth disappointing.

## 8120 CORAL.CO.UK H'CAP — 1m 4f 50y
**5:00** (5:00) (Class 4) (0-85,80) 3-Y-0+ — **£4,851** (£1,443; £721; £360) **Stalls** Low

Form — RPR

103- **1** **Elbereth**[22] 7850 3-9-3 78........................ DavidProbert 5 84+
(Andrew Balding) *a.p: trckd ldr 9f out: led over 1f out: rdn and edgd lft ins fnl f: jst hld on* **1/1**[1]

065- **2** *shd* **Freewheel (IRE)**[45] 7504 4-9-10 80........................ GrahamLee 6 85
(Frederick Watson) *hld up: hdwy 8f out: rdn over 1f out: r.o* **11/2**[2]

020- **3** *nk* **Istimraar (IRE)**[24] 7008 3-8-10 74........................(p) JoeyHaynes(3) 2 79
(Philip Kirby) *chsd ldr 3f: remained handy: rdn over 2f out: ev ch ins fnl f: r.o* **10/1**

/15- **4** *2* **Amazing Star (IRE)**[42] 7578 9-9-0 70........................(tp) LiamKeniry 4 72
(John Flint) *hld up: styd on u.p ins fnl f: nt trble ldrs* **25/1**

336- **5** *1 ¼* **Mica Mika (IRE)**[153] 4204 6-9-4 79........................ SammyJoBell(5) 1 79
(Richard Fahey) *prom: racd keenly: rdn over 1f out: no ex ins fnl f* **11/2**[2]

016- **6** *hd* **Flying Power**[97] 6156 6-9-4 77........................ JacobButterfield(3) 3 76
(John Norton) *racd keenly: set stdy pce tl qcknd over 2f out: rdn and hdd over 1f out: no ex ins fnl f* **7/1**[3]

2m 42.76s (1.96) **Going Correction** -0.05s/f (Stan)
**WFA** 3 from 4yo+ 5lb **6** Ran SP% **106.2**
Speed ratings (Par 105): **91,90,90,89,88 88**
CSF £5.92 TOTE £1.80: £1.10, £2.80; EX 5.90 Trifecta £34.20.
**Owner** David Taylor **Bred** David Taylor **Trained** Kingsclere, Hants

**FOCUS**
An ordinary handicap run at a modest pace. The second and third have been rated close to their recent form.

## 8121 32RED NURSERY H'CAP — 1m 1f 103y
**5:30** (5:30) (Class 6) (0-60,59) 2-Y-0 — **£2,102** (£625; £312; £156) **Stalls** Low

Form — RPR

604- **1** **Duc De Seville (IRE)**[58] 7207 2-9-1 **53**........................ SteveDrowne 2 56+
(Clive Cox) *sn pushed along to chse ldr: led 8f out: rdn and edgd rt over 1f out: styd on gamely u.p* **14/1**

362- **2** *½* **Clampdown**[11] 7991 2-9-6 **58**........................ LukeMorris 6 60
(James Tate) *trckd ldrs: chsd wnr over 2f out: rdn and ev ch ins fnl f: styd on* **3/1**[1]

334- **3** *2 ½* **First Summer**[11] 7991 2-9-5 **57**........................(p) RobertWinston 7 54
(Shaun Harris) *hld up in tch: n.m.r over 2f out: rdn over 1f out: edgd lft and styd on same pce ins fnl f* **11/2**[3]

606- **4** *¾* **Luv U**[30] 7740 2-9-0 **52**........................ JimmyQuinn 3 48
(Ed Dunlop) *hld up: hdwy u.p over 2f out: styd on same pce ins fnl f* **8/1**

000- **5** *2 ¾* **Avenue Des Champs**[25] 7815 2-8-5 **46**........................(p) DannyBrock(3) 1 37
(Jane Chapple-Hyam) *prom: racd keenly: rdn over 1f out: no ex fnl f* **33/1**

000- **6** *1* **Celtic Ava (IRE)**[32] 7730 2-9-2 **54**........................ ShaneKelly 8 43
(Pat Phelan) *led: hdd 8f out: chsd wnr tl rdn over 2f out: hung rt and wknd ins fnl f* **12/1**

065- **7** *3 ½* **Callendula**[15] 7941 2-9-7 **59**........................ AdamKirby 11 41
(Clive Cox) *chsd ldrs: rdn over 2f out: wknd fnl f* **8/1**

500- **8** *½* **Cahar Fad (IRE)**[18] 7904 2-8-13 **51**........................ GrahamGibbons 12 32
(Steph Hollinshead) *prom: racd wd: rdn over 2f out: wknd fnl f* **66/1**

656- **9** *hd* **Diamond Runner (IRE)**[64] 7064 2-8-10 **55**........................(p) DavidParkes(7) 4 36
(Deborah Sanderson) *hld up: rdn over 3f out: nvr on terms* **25/1**

000- **10** *¾* **That Man Of Mine (IRE)**[130] 4965 2-8-7 **45**........................ WilliamCarson 9 24
(Jamie Osborne) *s.i.s: hld up: pushed along whn nt clr run and swtchd rt 3f out: nt clr run wl over 1f out: nvr on terms* **5/1**[2]

010- **11** *shd* **New Abbey Dancer (IRE)**[25] 7815 2-8-11 **49**........................(v[1]) DavidProbert 13 28
(Gay Kelleway) *s.i.s: hld up: rdn over 2f out: n.d* **16/1**

000- **12** *1* **Directional**[81] 6602 2-9-1 **58**........................(p) ShaneGray(5) 10 35
(Charlie Appleby) *hld up: rdn over 3f out: a in rr* **7/1**

006- **13** *12* **Lipstickandpowder (IRE)**[11] 7994 2-9-3 **55**........................ PaulMulrennan 5 9
(William Jarvis) *hld up: rdn over 3f out: wknd over 2f out* **25/1**

2m 1.07s (0.27) **Going Correction** -0.05s/f (Stan) **13** Ran SP% **124.1**
Speed ratings (Par 94): **96,95,93,92,90 89,86,85,85,84 84,83,73**
CSF £56.37 CT £274.62 TOTE £17.80: £4.90, £1.70, £2.00; EX 57.20 Trifecta £538.60.
**Owner** Dukes Of Beechdown **Bred** Lynch Bages & Camas Park Stud **Trained** Lambourn, Berks

**FOCUS**
They went an okay pace but few got involved in this moderate nursery. The runner-up has been rated as running right up to form.

## 8122 BET IN PLAY AT CORAL H'CAP — 1m 1f 103y
**6:00** (6:00) (Class 5) (0-70,70) 3-Y-0+ — **£2,749** (£818; £408; £204) **Stalls** Low

Form — RPR

11- **1** **Persona Grata**[10] 7998 3-9-5 70........................ DanielTudhope 8 83+
(Ed Walker) *hld up in tch: racd keenly: led over 1f out: r.o: readily* **8/13**[1]

353- **2** *1 ½* **Lean On Pete (IRE)**[10] 7998 5-9-4 70........................ JacobButterfield(3) 2 77
(Ollie Pears) *hld up: hdwy over 2f out: swtchd rt wl over 1f out: r.o* **5/1**[2]

136- **3** *½* **Coillte Cailin (IRE)**[24] 7829 4-9-3 66........................ StevieDonohoe 1 72
(Daniel Mark Loughnane) *hld up: racd wd: rdn over 1f out: styd on* **10/1**[3]

022- **4** *1 ½* **Gabrial The Terror (IRE)**[127] 5076 4-9-2 70........................ SammyJoBell(5) 6 73+
(Richard Fahey) *hld up: hmpd over 2f out: hdwy over 1f out: r.o: nt rch ldrs* **16/1**

206- **5** *nk* **Hussar Ballad (USA)**[49] 7411 5-9-1 64........................ PJMcDonald 7 66
(Mel Brittain) *plld hrd and prom: chsd ldr over 2f out: led wl over 1f out: sn hdd: no ex ins fnl f* **12/1**

600- **6** *1 ½* **Sheriff Of Nawton (IRE)**[59] 7172 3-9-5 70........................ SamJames 11 69
(David O'Meara) *hld up: edgd lft over 2f out: hdwy over 1f out: nt trble ldrs* **33/1**

600- **7** *1* **Idol Deputy (FR)**[39] 7626 8-9-2 65........................(t) RobertHavlin 12 62
(James Bennett) *hld up: r.o ins fnl f: nvr nrr* **33/1**

400- **8** *1 ½* **Subtle Knife**[16] 7918 5-9-5 68........................ WilliamCarson 4 62
(Giles Bravery) *trckd ldr tl led over 3f out: rdn and hdd wl over 1f out: wknd ins fnl f* **16/1**

400- **9** *hd* **Syncopate**[23] 7831 5-9-7 70........................ AdamKirby 10 63
(Pam Sly) *s.i.s: hld up: nvr on terms* **33/1**

424- **10** *4* **Roger Thorpe**[64] 7068 5-8-6........................ DavidParkes(7) 3 49
(Deborah Sanderson) *plld hrd and prom: rdn and wknd over 2f out* **33/1**

000- **11** *9* **Back Burner (IRE)**[8] 8029 6-9-2 65........................(p) ChrisCatlin 13 31
(Dai Burchell) *chsd ldrs: rdn over 3f out: wknd over 2f out* **50/1**

000- **12** *8* **Shady McCoy (USA)**[32] 7729 4-9-7 70........................ RobertWinston 9 19
(Ian Williams) *led: hung rt and hdd over 3f out: continued to hang rt and wknd over 2f out* **25/1**

1m 59.11s (-1.69) **Going Correction** -0.05s/f (Stan)
**WFA** 3 from 4yo+ 2lb **12** Ran SP% **124.7**
Speed ratings (Par 103): **105,103,103,101,101 100,99,98,97,94 86,79**
CSF £3.76 CT £19.86 TOTE £1.50: £1.10, £1.60, £3.60; EX 5.70 Trifecta £29.30.
**Owner** Middleham Park Racing XLI **Bred** Miss K Rausing **Trained** Newmarket, Suffolk

**FOCUS**
An above-average winner for the level. The runner-up has been rated to form, and fourth close to form on debut for Richard Fahey despite not getting the best of runs.

## 8123 LADBROKES H'CAP — 1m 141y
**6:30** (6:30) (Class 7) (0-50,56) 3-Y-0+ — **£1,940** (£577; £288; £144) **Stalls** Low

Form — RPR

150- **1** **Sarlat**[7] 8050 3-9-4 49........................ LukeMorris 7 58
(Mark Brisbourne) *hld up: hdwy over 2f out: styd on u.p to ld wl ins fnl f* **6/1**[3]

004- **2** *½* **Grey Destiny**[7] 8043 4-9-7 50........................ PJMcDonald 12 57
(Mel Brittain) *s.i.s: hdwy over 6f out: hung lft and led over 1f out: sn rdn: hdd wl ins fnl f* **7/2**[2]

041- **3** *hd* **Lord Of The Storm**[10] 8004 6-9-8 56 6ex........................ RyanWhile(5) 9 63
(Bill Turner) *prom: nt clr run and lost pl over 3f out: hdwy and nt clr run over 1f out: r.o* **7/4**[1]

306- **4** *4* **Supa Seeker (USA)**[17] 7908 8-9-1 49........................(t) GeorgeDowning(5) 11 47
(Tony Carroll) *sn pushed along in rr: hdwy over 1f out: rdn and hung lft ins fnl f: styd on same pce* **20/1**

600- **5** *1* **Celestial Dawn**[10] 8004 5-9-3 46........................ RobertWinston 1 42
(John Weymes) *dwlt: in rr: hdwy over 1f out: rdn: edgd lft and no ex ins fnl f* **25/1**

000- **6** *1 ½* **Norman's Star**[18] 7901 3-8-13 47........................ ConnorBeasley(3) 5 39
(Chris Dwyer) *chsd ldr: rdn and ev ch over 1f out: wknd ins fnl f* **16/1**

060- **7** *3* **Rio Yuma (ITY)**[86] 6454 3-8-13 49........................ ShaneGray(5) 4 34
(Kristin Stubbs) *chsd ldrs: rdn over 2f out: wknd ins fnl f* **33/1**

535- **8** *1 ½* **Bushy Glade (IRE)**[127] 5108 3-9-0 50........................ ShelleyBirkett(5) 13 32
(Julia Feilden) *chsd ldrs: rdn over 3f out: wknd fnl f* **7/1**

/64- **9** *nk* **Bryant Park (USA)**[10] 8004 5-9-4 47........................ PatCosgrave 6 28
(Jane Chapple-Hyam) *led: rdn over 2f out: hdd over 1f out: wknd ins fnl f* **6/1**[3]

005- **10** *2* **Shamiana**[28] 7785 4-9-7 50........................(b) SteveDrowne 3 26
(Daniel Kubler) *prom: rdn over 2f out: wknd fnl f* **25/1**

000- **11** *¾* **Katmai River (IRE)**[13] 7976 7-9-0 50........................ CharlotteJenner(7) 2 25
(Mark Usher) *hld up: rdn over 2f out: wknd over 1f out* **20/1**

060/ **12** *¾* **Luisa Tetrazzini (IRE)**[902] 3389 8-9-5 48........................ DavidProbert 8 21
(Bernard Llewellyn) *hld up: rdn and wknd over 2f out* **66/1**

1m 49.72s (-0.38) **Going Correction** -0.05s/f (Stan)
**WFA** 3 from 4yo+ 2lb **12** Ran SP% **127.2**
Speed ratings (Par 97): **99,98,98,94,93 92,89,88,88,86 85,85**
CSF £27.08 CT £54.82 TOTE £7.80: £2.20, £1.30, £1.30; EX 34.40 Trifecta £93.60.
**Owner** The Bourne Connection **Bred** Mr & Mrs J Laws **Trained** Great Ness, Shropshire

**FOCUS**
A moderate handicap run at a good pace. The third has been rated to his latest C&D win.

## 8124 DOWNLOAD THE LADBROKES APP H'CAP — 7f 32y
**7:00** (7:01) (Class 5) (0-75,75) 3-Y-0+ — **£2,749** (£818; £408; £204) **Stalls** High

Form — RPR

133- **1** **Rich Again (IRE)**[18] 7905 5-9-3 69........................(p) TedDurcan 4 78
(James Bethell) *hld up: hdwy over 1f out: edgd lft ins fnl f: r.o to ld nr fin* **2/1**[1]

302- **2** *nk* **Rouge Nuage (IRE)**[80] 6625 4-9-6 72 .............................. LiamJones 1 80
(Conrad Allen) *chsd ldrs: led over 1f out: rdn and edgd lft ins fnl f: hdd nr fin* **7/1**

221- **3** *1 ¾* **Boogangoo (IRE)**[11] 7993 3-9-9 75 6ex ...................... StevieDonohoe 3 78
(Grace Harris) *s.i.s: sn prom: rdn over 1f out: styd on same pce ins fnl f* **9/2**[2]

306- **4** *¾* **Tartan Trip**[207] 2400 7-8-9 68 ........................................(tp) JaneElliott[(7)] 9 69
(Michael Appleby) *hld up: rdn over 1f out: styd on ins fnl f: nt rch ldrs* **16/1**

010- **5** *1 ½* **Mount Hollow**[20] 7888 9-8-12 71 ...............................(p) RobHornby[(7)] 5 68
(Andrew Hollinshead) *s.i.s: hld up: hdwy over 1f out: no ex ins fnl f* **20/1**

005- **6** *½* **Rodrigo De Torres**[20] 7888 7-9-7 73 ................................ GrahamLee 2 69
(Frederick Watson) *led: rdn and hdd over 1f out: no ex ins fnl f* **6/1**[3]

033- **7** *1* **Dream Scenario**[6] 8058 4-9-6 72 ....................................(v) PJMcDonald 7 65
(Mel Brittain) *chsd ldrs: rdn over 1f out: no ex fnl f* **9/2**[2]

050- **8** *4* **Gilmer (IRE)**[51] 7373 3-9-1 72 ........................................ RyanWhile[(5)] 6 55
(Laura Young) *chsd ldr: wnt upsides 5f out: rdn and ev ch 2f out: wknd fnl f* **33/1**

1m 28.31s (-0.49) **Going Correction** -0.05s/f (Stan) **8** Ran SP% **110.1**
Speed ratings (Par 103): **100,99,97,96,95 94,93,88**
CSF £15.26 CT £50.97 TOTE £2.60: £1.10, £2.60, £2.20; EX 17.20 Trifecta £51.30.
**Owner** Clarendon Thoroughbred Racing **Bred** Mrs Sandra Maye **Trained** Middleham Moor, N Yorks

**FOCUS**
An ordinary handicap. The winner has been rated as running a length pb.
T/Plt: £18.50 to a £1 stake. Pool: £88,441.00 - 18.50 winning tickets T/Qpdt: £2.30 to a £1 stake. Pool: £9,916 - 3,153.68 winning tickets CR

8125 - 8131a (Foreign Racing) - See Raceform Interactive

## 8022 DEAUVILLE (R-H)

Friday, December 12

**OFFICIAL GOING: Polytrack: standard**

## 8132a PRIX PRINCELINE (CONDITIONS) (2YO FILLIES) (POLYTRACK) 7f 110y

**12:00** (12:00) 2-Y-O **£14,166** (£5,666; £4,250; £2,833; £1,416)

RPR

**1** **Burma Sea (FR)**[94] 2-8-10 0 .............................. Pierre-CharlesBoudot 4 80
(A Fabre, France) **6/5**[1]

**2** *3* **Gilded Lace**[17] 2-9-0 0 ..............................................(p) MaximeGuyon 9 77
(D Windrif, France) **36/5**

**3** *1 ¼* **Cascading Stars (IRE)**[15] 7945 2-9-0 0 .................. MickaelBarzalona 1 74
(J S Moore) *broke wl: chsd ldrs on rail: checked after 2f but sn rcvrd: cl 5th and rdn 2f out: effrt between horses over 1f out: kpt on at same pce fnl f* **18/5**[2]

**4** *nk* **Game Theory (IRE)** 2-8-7 0 .......................................... ThierryThulliez 6 66
(N Clement, France) **153/10**

**5** *½* **Dipankara (FR)**[44] 2-8-10 0 ........................................... FabriceVeron 5 68
(H-A Pantall, France) **92/10**

**6** *1* **Lily Des Indes (FR)**[28] 2-8-3 0 ..................................... LauraGrosso[(7)] 3 66
(N Clement, France) **33/1**

**7** *1 ½* **Sainte Amarante (FR)** 2-8-8 0 ow1 ........................... AntoineHamelin 8 60
(Yves de Nicolay, France) **32/1**

**8** *1* **Sleekfonteine (FR)**[35] 2-9-0 0 ............................................. AlexisBadel 2 63
(F Doumen, France) **5/1**[3]

**9** *4* **Miss Australia (FR)** 2-8-7 0 ....................................... EddyHardouin 7 47
(Marquise De Montaigu, France) **49/1**

1m 32.27s (92.27) **9** Ran SP% **120.0**
WIN (incl. 1 euro stake): 2.20. PLACES: 1.20, 1.70, 1.50. DF: 8.70. SF: 12.20.
**Owner** Gestut Ammerland **Bred** Gestut Ammerland **Trained** Chantilly, France

## 8082 SOUTHWELL (L-H)

Saturday, December 13

**OFFICIAL GOING: Fibresand: standard**
Wind: Virtually nil Weather: Fine and dry but cold

## 8133 DAILY PRICE BOOSTS AT UNIBET H'CAP 5f (F)

**12:05** (12:09) (Class 6) (0-52,52) 3-Y-O+ **£1,940** (£577; £288; £144) **Stalls** High

Form RPR

203- **1** **Very First Blade**[18] 7909 5-9-2 47 ................................(be) RobertHavlin 5 56+
(Michael Mullineaux) *cl up: rdn to ld appr fnl f: kpt on* **9/2**[2]

500- **2** *½* **Divertimenti (IRE)**[29] 7782 10-8-12 50 .......................(b) AdamMcLean[(7)] 9 57
(Roy Bowring) *cl up: slt ld over 3f: rdn and hdd appr fnl f: sn drvn and kpt on towards fin* **16/1**

434- **3** *hd* **Saved My Bacon (IRE)**[22] 7865 3-8-13 47 .............. ConnorBeasley[(3)] 6 53+
(Chris Dwyer) *trckd ldrs whn squeezed out and swtchd rt after 1f: hdwy 2f out: rdn and ev ch ent fnl f: sn drvn and kpt on same pce* **15/2**[3]

000- **4** *½* **Lucky Surprise**[21] 7887 3-9-2 47 ......................................(b) LukeMorris 1 52
(Jeremy Gask) *chsd ldrs: cl up over 2f out: sn rdn and kpt on same pce appr fnl f* **12/1**

550- **5** *¾* **Steel City Boy (IRE)**[74] 6843 11-8-10 46 oh1 ................. AnnStokell[(5)] 4 48
(Ann Stokell) *midfield: rdn along over 2f out: kpt on appr fnl f: nrst fin* **50/1**

403- **6** *½* **Imaginary Diva**[9] 8023 8-9-4 49 ........................................... PaoloSirigu 2 49
(George Margarson) *dwlt: hdwy into midfield after 1f: pushed along 2f out: sn rdn and kpt on fnl f: nrst fin* **14/1**

000- **7** *1 ¼* **Prince Of Passion (CAN)**[14] 7972 6-9-6 51 ...........(v) PatrickMathers 14 47
(Derek Shaw) *prom towards stands' rail: rdn along 2f out: grad wknd* **20/1**

315- **8** *¾* **Synonym (ITY)**[22] 7864 3-9-2 52 .............................. AlistairRawlinson[(5)] 3 45
(Michael Appleby) *s.i.s: in rr tl styd on fnl 2f: nvr nr ldrs* **15/8**[1]

/00- **9** *1* **Bond Blade**[219] 2092 6-9-1 46 oh1 ........................................ RaulDaSilva 13 35
(Suzzanne France) *in tch nr stands' rail: rdn along 2f out: sn wknd* **100/1**

000- **10** *1* **Basle**[99] 6088 7-9-1 46 oh1 .............................................(tp) GrahamLee 8 32
(Roy Brotherton) *nvr bttr than midfield* **40/1**

400- **11** *2 ½* **Nine Before Ten (IRE)**[29] 7781 6-8-8 46 oh1 ..........(tp) DavidParkes[(7)] 12 23
(Deborah Sanderson) *chsd ldrs: rdn along 1/2-way: sn wknd* **40/1**

620- **12** *5* **Redalani (IRE)**[29] 7783 4-9-7 52 ................................(b[1]) RobertWinston 11 11
(Alan Brown) *cl up: rdn along 1/2-way: sn wknd* **15/2**[3]

/00- **13** *1 ½* **Ladydolly**[46] 7520 6-9-1 46 ........................................(b) PaulMulrennan 10
(Roy Brotherton) *slt ld: hdd over 3f out: sn rdn along and wknd fr 1/2-way: bled fr nose* **50/1**

59.91s (0.21) **Going Correction** -0.05s/f (Stan) **13** Ran SP% **111.3**
Speed ratings (Par 101): **96,95,94,94,92 92,90,88,87,85 81,73,71**
CSF £63.63 CT £510.25 TOTE £3.70: £1.60, £4.40, £1.90; EX 66.80 Trifecta £367.60.
**Owner** Ogwen Valley Racing **Bred** L R Owen **Trained** Alpraham, Cheshire

■ Balinka was withdrawn. Price at time of withdrawal 14-1 - deduction of 5p in the pound applies to all bets.

**FOCUS**
A low-grade handicap but one run at a sound pace. The winner came down the centre and the winning times throughout the card suggested the surface was on the quick side. The winner has been rated close to his best.

## 8134 32RED H'CAP 1m 6f (F)

**12:40** (12:40) (Class 6) (0-60,60) 3-Y-O+ **£1,940** (£577; £288; £144) **Stalls** Low

Form RPR

504- **1** **Enzaal (USA)**[25] 7823 4-9-1 52 ........................................ JoeyHaynes[(3)] 10 62
(Philip Kirby) *trckd ldrs: hdwy and cl up over 4f out: led 3f out: jnd and rdn over 2f out: drvn over 1f out: kpt on gamely towards fin* **6/1**[3]

0/0- **2** *hd* **Generous Dream**[46] 7508 6-9-3 51 ..................................... PJMcDonald 9 60
(Mel Brittain) *hld up: stdy hdwy 5f out: chsd ldrs over 2f out: rdn to chse ldng pair over 1f out: drvn ins fnl f: kpt on wl towards fin* **25/1**

102- **3** *hd* **Adili (IRE)**[229] 1806 5-9-12 60 ........................................... LukeMorris 8 69
(Michael Appleby) *a.p: cl up 1/2-way: rdn to chal over 2f out: drvn and edgd rt jst ins fnl f: ev ch tl no ex nr fin* **7/2**[1]

636- **4** *4* **Yasir (USA)**[6] 7760 6-9-11 59 .........................................(b) HayleyTurner 2 63
(Conor Dore) *hld up in rr: hdwy over 4f out: rdn to chse ldrs 2f out: drvn and no imp appr fnl f* **12/1**

403- **5** *3* **Sawwala**[25] 7823 4-9-0 48 .................................................. DavidProbert 7 48
(J R Jenkins) *led 2f: cl up: rdn along over 3f out: sn drvn and grad wknd* **7/1**

005- **6** *nk* **Sirpertan**[24] 7643 3-8-13 54 ............................................. RobertWinston 6 53
(Marjorie Fife) *trckd ldrs: hdwy 4f out: rdn along 3f out: drvn and one pce fnl 2f* **8/1**

250- **7** *½* **Aureate**[25] 7823 10-8-7 48 .........................................(p) CharlotteJenner[(7)] 11 47
(Brian Forsey) *towards rr: sme hdwy fnl 2f: n.d* **33/1**

000- **8** *6* **Medieval Bishop (IRE)**[12] 7990 5-8-13 54 ............................. RobHornby[(7)] 12 44
(Tony Forbes) *midfield: effrt on inner over 4f out: sn rdn along and n.d* **50/1**

6/0- **9** *4 ½* **Proud Times (USA)**[8] 8037 8-9-10 58 ..................................(p) AdamKirby 5 42
(Ali Stronge) *a towards rr: bhd fnl 3f* **8/1**

530- **10** *5* **Rokeby**[47] 7500 3-8-8 49 ..................................................... AndrewElliott 4 26
(George Moore) *chsd ldrs on inner: rdn along 5f out: sn wknd and bhd fnl 3f* **33/1**

000- **11** *4* **Tight Knit (USA)**[29] 7785 4-9-2 50 .................................... GrahamLee 1 21
(John Weymes) *cl up: led after 2f: pushed along 4f out: hdd over 3f out and sn wknd* **40/1**

662- **12** *4* **Fire In Babylon (IRE)**[25] 7823 6-8-12 51 ................(b) TobyAtkinson[(5)] 3 17
(Noel Quinlan) *dwlt: swtchd to outer and hld up in rr: sme hdwy and in tch 1/2-way: sn rdn along and outpcd: bhd fnl 3f* **4/1**[2]

553- **13** *30* **Sail With Sultana**[40] 7627 3-9-1 56 .................................. PaulMulrennan 13
(Mark Rimell) *chsd ldrs on outer: pushed along 1/2-way: rdn along 5f out: sn outpcd and bhd* **25/1**

3m 7.44s (-0.86) **Going Correction** -0.125s/f (Stan)
**WFA** 3 from 4yo+ 7lb **13** Ran SP% **116.9**
Speed ratings (Par 101): **97,96,96,94,92 92,92,88,86,83 81,78,61**
CSF £154.39 CT £605.99 TOTE £7.00: £2.40, £8.70, £1.50; EX 210.20 Trifecta £1909.70.
**Owner** C B Construction (Cleveland) Limited **Bred** Shadwell Farm LLC **Trained** Middleham, N Yorks

**FOCUS**
A moderate handicap run at a reasonable gallop. The first three, who pulled clear, came down the centre. The front four are all potentially well treated on old form.

## 8135 LADBROKES H'CAP 7f (F)

**1:15** (1:16) (Class 2) (0-105,102) 3-Y-O+ **£11,971** (£3,583; £1,791; £896; £446) **Stalls** Low

Form RPR

160- **1** **Pearl Nation (USA)**[64] 7081 5-8-7 88 ................................... LukeMorris 5 104
(Michael Appleby) *chsd ldrs: rdn along on outer 1/2-way: wd st and hdwy to chse ldng pair over 2f out: rdn wl over 1f out: drvn to chal whn hung rt to stands' rail ent fnl f: sn led and kpt on strly* **15/8**[1]

400- **2** *4 ½* **Grey Mirage**[23] 7851 5-9-6 101 ..........................................(b[1]) MartinHarley 4 105
(Marco Botti) *trckd ldr: hdwy 3f out: sn cl up: rdn to ld over 1f out: drvn ent fnl f: sn hdd and kpt on same pce* **13/2**

004- **3** *3 ¾* **Frontier Fighter**[31] 7743 6-9-7 102 ................................... DanielTudhope 7 96
(David O'Meara) *trckd ldng pair: pushed along 3f out: sn rdn and outpcd: kpt on to take 3rd ins fnl f* **2/1**[2]

005- **4** *1 ½* **Repetition**[26] 7820 4-8-2 83 oh3 ......................................... HayleyTurner 6 73
(Kristin Stubbs) *led: jnd and rdn along over 2f out: drvn and hdd over 1f out: grad wknd* **8/1**

604- **5** *11* **Modern Tutor**[23] 7851 5-8-6 87 ........................................... DavidProbert 1 49
(Andrew Balding) *t.k.h: trckd ldrs: effrt 3f out: sn rdn along and outpcd fnl 2f* **11/2**[3]

035- **6** *9* **Bedloe's Island (IRE)**[21] 7889 9-8-3 84 oh2 ow1 ..................... BenCurtis 3 22
(Alan McCabe) *t.k.h: chsd ldrs: rdn along 3f out: sn drvn and outpcd* **50/1**

1m 27.17s (-3.13) **Going Correction** -0.125s/f (Stan) **6** Ran SP% **109.9**
Speed ratings (Par 109): **112,106,102,100,88 78**
CSF £13.70 TOTE £3.00: £1.70, £2.40; EX 15.80 Trifecta £27.70.
**Owner** Iddon, M&C Dixon, Taylor, Finn, O'Brien **Bred** William A Carl Estate **Trained** Danethorpe, Notts

**FOCUS**
A decent quality handicap in which an ordinary gallop picked up turning for home. The winner drifted towards the stands' rail in the closing stages. The runner-up, making his Fibresand debut, has been rated a bit off his Polytrack best.

## 8136 UNIBET OFFER DAILY JOCKEY/TRAINER SPECIALS H'CAP 5f (F)

**1:50** (1:50) (Class 3) (0-95,95) 3-Y-O+ **£7,439** (£2,213; £1,106; £553) **Stalls** High

Form RPR

000- **1** **Royal Bajan (USA)**[9] 8025 6-8-7 81 oh1 ..............................(v) PJMcDonald 2 92
(James Given) *cl up: led 1 1/2f out: sn rdn: drvn ins fnl f: edgd lft towards fin: hld on wl* **33/1**

321- **2** *nk* **Poyle Vinnie**[30] 7767 4-9-5 93 ............................................. AdamKirby 1 103
(Michael Appleby) *dwlt: hdwy to trck ldrs 1/2-way: effrt on outer over 1f out: rdn to chal ent fnl f: sn drvn and ev ch: edgd sltly rt and no ex towards fin* **7/4**[1]

566- **3** *2 ¼* **Scarborough (IRE)**[59] 7212 3-8-7 81 oh1 .............................. HayleyTurner 6 83+
(Michael Appleby) *trckd ldrs: hdwy 2f out: sn rdn and hung lft ent fnl f: kpt on same pce* **6/1**[3]

300- **4** *1 ½* **Woolfall Sovereign (IRE)**[287] 802 8-9-3 91 ............................... TomQueally 4 87
(George Margarson) *chsd ldrs: rdn along 2f out: kpt on same pce u.p fnl f* **16/1**

215- **5** *hd* **Searchlight**[9] 8025 3-8-5 84 ShaneGray(5) 10 80
(Kevin Ryan) *racd nr stands' rail: prom: rdn along over 2f out: grad wknd* **12/1**

000- **6** *1/2* **Viva Verglas (IRE)**[21] 7889 3-8-10 84 (b) GrahamGibbons 8 78
(David Barron) *slt ld: rdn 2f out: hdd 1 1/2f out: hld whn n.m.r and eased jst ins fnl f* **9/1**

433- **7** *1 1/2* **Even Stevens**[21] 7889 6-9-7 95 (p) LukeMorris 3 84
(Scott Dixon) *cl up: rdn along 2f out: wknd appr fnl f* **5/2**[2]

500- **8** *1* **Oriental Relation (IRE)**[16] 7947 3-8-4 81 oh1 (b) ConnorBeasley(3) 9 66
(James Given) *cl up: rdn along 2f out: sn drvn and wknd* **33/1**

504- **9** *3 3/4* **Dangerous Age**[16] 7947 4-8-7 81 oh1 LiamJones 5 52
(J S Moore) *a towards rr: rdn along and outpcd fr 1/2-way* **28/1**

/11- **10** *9* **Dutiful Son (IRE)**[257] 1212 4-9-0 88 PaulMulrennan 7 27
(David C Griffiths) *dwlt and swtchd rt to stands' rail after s: in rr: wnt markedly lft towards far rail 1/2-way: a bhd* **20/1**

57.91s (-1.79) **Going Correction** -0.05s/f (Stan) **10** Ran SP% **116.9**
Speed ratings (Par 107): **112,111,107,105,105 104,102,100,94,80**
CSF £88.72 CT £417.14 TOTE £36.70: £6.00, £1.30, £2.20; EX 162.60 Trifecta £861.40.
**Owner** The Cool Silk Partnership **Bred** West Wind Farm **Trained** Willoughton, Lincs
■ Stewards' Enquiry : P J McDonald caution: careless riding

**FOCUS**
A very useful sprint and one run at a good gallop. The first two, who pulled clear in the closing stages, came down the centre.

## 8137 BET NOW WITH THE LADBROKES APP H'CAP — 1m (F)
**2:25** (2:25) (Class 6) (0-60,60) 3-Y-O+ **£1,940** (£577; £288; £144) **Stalls** Low

Form RPR

604- **1** **Major Rowan**[18] 7910 3-8-3 46 ConnorBeasley(3) 1 59+
(Bryan Smart) *dwlt and in rr: hdwy over 3f out: chsd ldrs 2f out: rdn wl over 1f out: styd on wl fnl f to ld last 75yds* **17/2**

653- **2** *1 1/4* **Pat's Legacy (USA)**[65] 7061 8-9-6 59 (p) RobertWinston 7 68
(Marjorie Fife) *trckd ldrs: cl up 1/2-way: led 3f out: pushed clr over 2f out: rdn over 1f out: jnd and drvn ins fnl f: hdd and no ex last 75yds* **11/4**[1]

005- **3** *4* **Falcon's Reign (FR)**[30] 7765 5-9-7 60 (p) LukeMorris 4 60
(Michael Appleby) *cl up: rdn along 3f out: drvn and kpt on same pce fnl 2f* **3/1**[2]

001- **4** *1 1/2* **Hickster (IRE)**[8] 8050 3-8-12 57 (t) AlistairRawlinson(5) 8 53
(Roy Bowring) *sn led: rdn along and hdd 3f out: drvn over 2f out and sn one pce* **5/1**[3]

230- **5** *3/4* **Yawail**[8] 8049 3-8-9 56 (p) KevinLundie(7) 10 51
(Brian Rothwell) *dwlt and in rr: reminders after 2f: rdn along over 3f out: styd on fr wl over 1f out: nrst fin* **20/1**

650- **6** *nk* **Quite Sparky**[83] 5331 7-9-0 53 PJMcDonald 5 47
(Geoffrey Harker) *towards rr: hdwy 3f out: rdn to chse ldrs 2f out: sn drvn and no imp appr fnl f* **20/1**

520- **7** *1 1/2* **Cyflymder (IRE)**[86] 6481 8-9-2 55 AndrewElliott 6 45
(David C Griffiths) *prom: chsd wnr over 2f out: sn rdn and wknd wl over 1f out* **20/1**

610- **8** *3* **It's All A Game**[7] 8063 3-9-2 56 (b) JasonHart 9 40
(Richard Guest) *chsd ldrs on outer: rdn along and wd st: sn hung rt: drvn 2f out and sn btn* **8/1**

302- **9** *21* **Mitchum**[39] 7639 5-8-13 52 (v) GrahamLee 3
(Ron Barr) *a in rr* **12/1**

000- **10** *72* **Pepperello**[12] 7990 3-8-6 46 oh1 (p[1]) RaulDaSilva 2
(Tim Etherington) *prom on inner: pushed along after 2f: rdn and awkward over 4f out: sn lost pl and bhd fnl 3f* **100/1**

1m 43.88s (0.18) **Going Correction** -0.125s/f (Stan)
**WFA** 3 from 5yo+ 1lb **10** Ran SP% **112.9**
Speed ratings (Par 101): **94,92,88,87,86 86,84,81,60,**
CSF £29.63 CT £86.65 TOTE £9.80: £2.20, £1.70, £1.60; EX 48.50 Trifecta £230.40.
**Owner** David H Cox **Bred** David H Cox **Trained** Hambleton, N Yorks

**FOCUS**
An ordinary handicap in which the front two (who came down the centre) did well to pull clear. The gallop was reasonable. It's been rated around the well-supported runner-up.

## 8138 CORAL APP DOWNLOAD FROM THE APP STORE MAIDEN STKS — 1m 4f (F)
**3:00** (3:00) (Class 5) 3-4-Y-O **£2,587** (£770; £384; £192) **Stalls** Low

Form RPR

40- **1** **Stonecutter (IRE)**[24] 7841 3-9-5 0 MartinHarley 5 84+
(Marco Botti) *trckd ldng pair: smooth hdwy and cl up over 3f out: led wl over 2f out: green and sn pushed along: clr ins fnl f: eased nr fin* **10/11**[1]

004- **2** *1* **Percys Princess**[14] 7977 3-8-9 45 AlistairRawlinson(5) 3 74
(Michael Appleby) *cl up: led 5f out: rdn along and hdd wl over 2f out: drvn and kpt on same pce fnl f* **33/1**

350- **3** *11* **New Tarabela**[88] 6432 3-9-5 77 LukeMorris 2 61
(Tony Carroll) *trckd ldng pair: hdwy 4f out: rdn along 3f out: sn one pce* **6/1**[3]

024- **4** *12* **By Jupiter**[29] 7772 3-9-0 74 TomQueally 1 37
(Michael Bell) *slt ld: pushed along and hdd 5f out: sn rdn and outpcd fnl 3f* **2/1**[2]

4- **5** *22* **Magnified**[8] 8048 4-9-10 0 DanielTudhope 4
(David O'Meara) *hld up in rr: hdwy on outer 4f out: chsd ldng pair over 3f out: sn rdn and wknd* **16/1**

2m 37.11s (-3.89) **Going Correction** -0.125s/f (Stan)
**WFA** 3 from 4yo 5lb **5** Ran SP% **108.8**
Speed ratings (Par 103): **107,106,99,91,76**
CSF £26.07 TOTE £2.30: £3.40, £6.00; EX 21.80 Trifecta £85.20.
**Owner** Mrs J Magnier, D Smith & M Tabor **Bred** Gigginstown House Stud **Trained** Newmarket, Suffolk

**FOCUS**
An uncompetitive event in which the market leader and 45-rated runner-up pulled clear in the straight. The gallop was an ordinary one to the home turn. There are doubts over the third and fourth so the winner has been rated close to his debut effort.

## 8139 DOWNLOAD THE LADBROKES APP H'CAP — 7f (F)
**3:35** (3:36) (Class 6) (0-55,55) 3-Y-O+ **£1,940** (£577; £288; £144) **Stalls** Low

Form RPR

541- **1** **Novalist**[4] 8084 6-9-3 51 6ex (b) JasonHart 4 64
(Robin Bastiman) *slt ld: rdn along 2f out: hdd narrowly over 1f out: sn drvn and rallied wl to ld again ins fnl f: styd on wl towards fin* **11/10**[1]

443- **2** *2* **Sleet (IRE)**[177] 3407 3-9-2 50 (b) AdamKirby 6 58
(Michael Appleby) *cl up: chal over 2f out: sn rdn: led over 1f out: drvn and hdd ins fnl f: kpt on same pce* **4/1**[2]

030- **3** *1* **Eium Mac**[22] 7869 5-8-12 46 oh1 (b) RaulDaSilva 8 51
(Neville Bycroft) *towards rr: hdwy 3f out: rdn along on outer over 2f out: styd on u.p appr fnl f: nrst fin* **40/1**

236- **4** *1 1/4* **Admirable Art (IRE)**[4] 8084 4-9-7 55 (p) WilliamCarson 5 57
(Tony Carroll) *midfield: hdwy over 2f out: rdn to chse ldrs wl over 1f out: swtchd rt and drvn appr fnl f: one pce* **5/1**[3]

404- **5** *nk* **Tableforten**[14] 7972 3-9-6 54 (p) StevieDonohoe 2 55
(J S Moore) *chsd ldrs: rdn along wl over 2f out: drvn over 1f out: one pce* **12/1**

043- **6** *6* **Masked Dance (IRE)**[4] 8084 7-9-0 48 (p) LiamKeniry 1 33
(Scott Dixon) *chsd ldng pair on inner: rdn along 3f out: grad wknd* **12/1**

000- **7** *1/2* **Classical Diva**[4] 8085 3-8-12 46 [1] HayleyTurner 12 30
(Michael Appleby) *chsd ldrs on outer: wd st: sn rdn and wknd 2f out* **14/1**

046- **8** *2 3/4* **Flying Applause**[22] 7868 9-8-5 46 oh1 (b) AdamMcLean(7) 11 23
(Roy Bowring) *dwlt: a in rr* **33/1**

605- **9** *8* **Templar Boy**[39] 7652 3-9-0 48 BenCurtis 3 4
(J R Jenkins) *chsd ldrs on inner: rdn along 3f out: sn wknd* **33/1**

500- **10** *15* **Only For You**[57] 7250 4-8-12 46 oh1 RobertWinston 7
(Alan Brown) *chsd ldrs: rdn along 1/2-way: sn wknd* **50/1**

1m 29.19s (-1.11) **Going Correction** -0.125s/f (Stan) **10** Ran SP% **116.6**
Speed ratings (Par 101): **101,98,97,96,95 88,88,85,76,58**
CSF £5.30 CT £107.00 TOTE £2.20: £1.30, £1.30, £6.20; EX 6.60 Trifecta £151.40.
**Owner** E N Barber **Bred** Whitsbury Manor Stud **Trained** Cowthorpe, N Yorks

**FOCUS**
A moderate handicap in which the gallop was sound throughout. The winner came down the centre. The winner has been rated pretty much back to his best, with the second running a small pb.
T/Plt: £94.30 to a £1 stake. Pool: £61,451.83 - 475.27 winning tickets T/Qpdt: £10.20 to a £1 stake. Pool: £4,662.06 - 337.7 winning tickets JR

# 8118 WOLVERHAMPTON (A.W) (L-H)
### Saturday, December 13

**OFFICIAL GOING: Tapeta: standard**
Wind: Light behind Weather: Fine

## 8140 DAILY PRICE BOOSTS AT UNIBET MAIDEN STKS — 5f 20y
**5:45** (5:45) (Class 5) 2-Y-O **£2,911** (£866; £432; £216) **Stalls** Low

Form RPR

04- **1** **Mo Henry**[54] 7329 2-9-5 0 GeorgeChaloner 6 73+
(Richard Whitaker) *chsd ldrs: pushed along 1/2-way: rdn to ld ins fnl f: r.o* **20/1**

3- **2** *3/4* **Lamps Of Heaven (IRE)**[21] 7881 2-9-0 0 LiamJones 2 65
(Olly Stevens) *plld hrd and prom: rdn and ev ch ins fnl f: r.o* **5/1**[2]

222- **3** *1/2* **Secret Glance**[17] 7920 2-9-5 76 GrahamGibbons 4 69
(Ed McMahon) *s.i.s: swtchd rt and hdwy 4f out: led 1/2-way: rdn and hdd ins fnl f: styd on same pce* **4/6**[1]

43- **4** *5* **Soft Love (IRE)**[14] 7970 2-9-0 0 GrahamLee 5 46
(Kevin Ryan) *led to 1/2-way: wknd ins fnl f* **6/1**[3]

5- **5** *1 1/4* **Optimystic (IRE)**[17] 7919 2-9-0 0 DavidProbert 3 41
(Andrew Balding) *plld hrd and prom: rdn over 1f out: wknd fnl f* **10/1**

55- **6** *1 1/2* **Kodiac Lady (IRE)**[29] 7771 2-9-0 0 LukeMorris 7 38
(James Tate) *prom: hmpd and lost pl 4f out: rdn 1/2-way: hung lft over 1f out: sn wknd* **14/1**

320- **7** *1* **Tamarin**[14] 7973 2-9-0 65 JFEgan 8 35
(David Evans) *prom: hmpd and lost pl 4f out: hdwy u.p 1/2-way: wknd over 1f out* **25/1**

00- **8** *nk* **Lady Antonios (IRE)**[10] 8007 2-8-11 0 ConnorBeasley(3) 1 31
(Chris Dwyer) *sn pushed along in rr: bhd fr 1/2-way* **125/1**

1m 1.1s (-0.80) **Going Correction** -0.10s/f (Stan) **8** Ran SP% **116.1**
Speed ratings (Par 96): **102,100,100,92,90 87,86,85**
CSF £116.43 TOTE £25.90: £4.40, £2.30, £1.10; EX 81.60 Trifecta £394.20.
**Owner** Shevlin Whelan Syndicate **Bred** Shevlin-Whelan Syndicate **Trained** Scarcroft, W Yorks

**FOCUS**
A relatively uncompetitive juvenile sprint maiden and just fair form. The first three came down the centre of the straight. The form might be worth a few lengths better than it's been rated.

## 8141 UNIBET OFFER DAILY JOCKEY/TRAINER SPECIALS H'CAP — 5f 216y
**6:15** (6:15) (Class 3) (0-90,89) 3-Y-O+ **£7,246** (£2,168; £813; £813; £270) **Stalls** Low

Form RPR

061- **1** **Trojan Rocket (IRE)**[23] 7847 6-9-5 87 (p) GeorgeBaker 9 97
(Michael Wigham) *mde all: qcknd over 2f out: rdn over 1f out: styd on* **3/1**[2]

503- **2** *1* **Light From Mars**[12] 7988 9-9-1 83 (p) WilliamTwiston-Davies 4 90
(Ronald Harris) *prom: chsd wnr 5f out: rdn and ev ch over 1f out: styd on same pce wl ins fnl f* **14/1**

406- **3** *1 1/2* **Amadeus Wolfe Tone (IRE)**[8] 8045 5-9-7 89 (p) AdamKirby 2 91
(Jamie Osborne) *hld up in tch: rdn over 1f out: styd on u.p* **7/2**[3]

430- **3** *dht* **Money Team (IRE)**[44] 7543 3-9-5 87 GrahamGibbons 8 89
(David Barron) *chsd wnr 1f: remained handy: rdn over 2f out: styd on* **17/2**

310- **5** *1/2* **Ambitious Boy**[26] 7821 5-9-1 83 LiamKeniry 1 83
(Andrew Hollinshead) *hld up: hdwy over 1f out: sn rdn: r.o* **20/1**

331- **6** *3/4* **Good Authority (IRE)**[21] 7888 7-8-7 80 JordanVaughan(5) 3 78
(Victor Dartnall) *prom: rdn over 1f out: styd on* **7/1**

000- **7** *nk* **Secret Witness**[16] 7947 8-8-11 79 (b) LukeMorris 5 76
(Ronald Harris) *hmpd sn after s: hld up: hdwy over 1f out: styd on same pce fnl f* **18/1**

/65- **8** *1/2* **Bond Fastrac**[197] 2732 7-8-10 78 BarryMcHugh 6 73
(Geoffrey Oldroyd) *s.i.s: hld up: rdn over 1f out: nt trble ldrs* **40/1**

101- **9** *7* **Realize**[37] 7687 4-8-7 80 ShaneGray(5) 7 53
(Kevin Ryan) *chsd ldrs: rdn over 2f out: wknd over 1f out* **5/2**[1]

1m 13.37s (-1.13) **Going Correction** -0.10s/f (Stan) **9** Ran SP% **118.0**
Speed ratings (Par 107): **103,101,99,99,99 98,97,96,87**
WIN: £4.70; PL: Light From Mars £3.00, Trojan Rocket £1.60, Amadeus Wolfe Tone £0.70, Money Team £1.40; EX: £47.80; CSF: £45.30; TC: TR/LFM/AWT £77.79, TR/LFM/MT £164.09; TF: TR/LFM/AWT £140.40, TR/LFM/MT £294.30.
**Owner** G Linder, D Hassan, R Warner **Bred** Mrs G F Fox **Trained** Newmarket, Suffolk
■ Stewards' Enquiry : Shane Gray three-day ban: careless riding (Dec 27-29)

**FOCUS**
It paid to be up with the pace and few got into it. The form can be rated as useful.

## 8142 DAILY PRICE BOOSTS AT UNIBET H'CAP (DIV I) — 5f 216y
**6:45** (6:45) (Class 6) (0-65,65) 3-Y-O+ **£2,264** (£673; £336; £168) **Stalls** Low

Form RPR

600- **1** **Point North (IRE)**[71] 6898 7-9-7 65 (b) DanielTudhope 11 73
(John Balding) *hld up: hdwy on outer over 2f out: rdn and r.o to ld post* **12/1**

112- **2** *shd* **Sewn Up**[19] 7905 4-9-6 64.....................(p) PhillipMakin 10 72
(Keith Dalgleish) *chsd ldrs: pushed along over 2f out: rdn over 1f out: led nr fin: hdd post* **13/8**[1]

526- **3** *nk* **Hamis Al Bin (IRE)**[14] 7972 5-8-8 52.....................(t) LukeMorris 2 59
(Milton Bradley) *hld up: hdwy over 2f out: led ins fnl f: sn rdn and edgd lft: hdd nr fin* **10/1**

013- **4** *½* **Insolenceofoffice (IRE)**[22] 7864 6-9-3 64..........(p) ConnorBeasley(3) 8 69
(Richard Ford) *chsd ldrs: rdn over 1f out: ev ch ins fnl f: unable qck towards fin* **15/2**[3]

210- **5** *¾* **Wedgewood Estates**[44] 7547 3-8-13 57..................... LiamKeniry 3 60
(Tony Carroll) *s.i.s: hld up: hdwy over 1f out: sn rdn: r.o* **16/1**

405- **6** *4* **Kodafine (IRE)**[23] 7847 3-9-1 59.....................(v[1]) JFEgan 5 49
(David Evans) *s.i.s: sn pushed along in rr: styd on ins fnl f: nvr nrr* **14/1**

452- **7** *1* **Deftera Fantutte (IRE)**[28] 7800 3-9-2 60..................... AdamKirby 12 47
(Natalie Lloyd-Beavis) *chsd ldrs: rdn 1/2-way: wknd fnl f* **8/1**

036- **8** *½* **Senator Bong**[129] 5045 4-9-4 62..................... GrahamLee 6 47
(Peter Grayson) *hld up: nvr on terms* **33/1**

051- **9** *nk* **Shirley's Pride**[12] 7997 4-9-4 62.....................(tp) HayleyTurner 4 46
(Michael Appleby) *w ldr 2f: led 1/2-way: rdn over 1f out: wknd and hdd ins fnl f* **9/2**[2]

060- **10** *2½* **Senora Lobo (IRE)**[46] 7510 4-8-0 51 oh6..........(p) RobHornby(7) 1 27
(Lisa Williamson) *prom: rdn over 2f out: wknd over 1f out* **125/1**

000- **11** *2½* **Fathom Five (IRE)**[4] 8088 10-8-5 56..................... KevinLundie(7) 9 24
(Shaun Harris) *sn led: hdd 1/2-way: rdn over 2f out: wknd over 1f out* **50/1**

1m 13.83s (-0.67) **Going Correction** -0.10s/f (Stan) **11** Ran SP% **114.2**
Speed ratings (Par 101): **100,99,99,98,97 92,91,90,90,86 83**
CSF £30.70 CT £209.57 TOTE £12.50: £2.90, £1.20, £2.40; EX 71.90 Trifecta £1309.30.
**Owner** Billy Herring **Bred** Barronstown Stud **Trained** Scrooby, S Yorks

**FOCUS**
There was no hanging about in the first division of the modest sprint handicap and the front three came from off the pace.

## 8143 DAILY PRICE BOOSTS AT UNIBET H'CAP (DIV II) 5f 216y
**7:15** (7:16) (Class 6) (0-65,64) 3-Y-0+ **£2,264** (£673; £336; £168) **Stalls** Low

Form RPR

446- **1** **Foie Gras**[10] 8014 4-8-11 57..................... ConnorBeasley(3) 3 66
(Chris Dwyer) *hld up in tch: rdn and swtchd rt ins fnl f: r.o to ld nr fin* **12/1**

515- **2** *nk* **Spowarticus**[10] 8014 5-8-11 54.....................(v) LukeMorris 1 62
(Scott Dixon) *sn led: rdn over 1f out: edgd rt ins fnl f: hdd nr fin* **9/2**[2]

002- **3** *½* **Dark Lane**[5] 8081 8-9-3 60.....................(v) GrahamGibbons 2 66
(David Evans) *plld hrd and prom: chsd ldr 2f out: rdn and ev ch ins fnl f: styd on* **9/1**

200- **4** *½* **Black Dave (IRE)**[15] 7950 4-9-5 62..................... JFEgan 6 67
(David Evans) *hld up: hdwy over 1f out: sn rdn: r.o: nt rch ldrs* **6/1**[3]

322- **5** *1¾* **Seven Lucky Seven**[3] 8090 3-9-6 63..................... GrahamLee 5 62
(Michael Herrington) *s.i.s: hld up: nt clr run over 1f out: r.o ins fnl f: nt rch ldrs* **6/4**[1]

103- **6** *2* **Divine Call**[12] 7989 7-9-7 64.....................(v) LiamKeniry 4 57
(Milton Bradley) *hld up: hmpd over 1f out: styd on ins fnl f: nvr trbld ldrs* **12/1**

000- **7** *¾* **Bertie Blu Boy**[19] 7906 6-9-3 60.....................(p) AdamKirby 9 50
(Lisa Williamson) *chsd ldr tl rdn 2f out: wknd ins fnl f* **20/1**

500- **8** *½* **Bonjour Steve**[14] 7972 3-8-5 53.....................(p) ShaneGray(5) 7 42
(Richard Price) *s.i.s: hdwy over 4f out: rdn over 2f out: wknd ins fnl f* **33/1**

504- **9** *½* **Imperator Augustus (IRE)**[15] 7950 6-9-4 64.......... DeclanBates(3) 10 51
(Patrick Holmes) *s.i.s: hld up: hdwy on outer 2f out: rdn over 1f out: wknd fnl f* **14/1**

520- **10** *1½* **Mey Blossom**[36] 7697 9-9-1 58.....................(p) GeorgeChaloner 8 40
(Richard Whitaker) *led early: chsd ldrs: rdn over 2f out: wknd fnl f* **33/1**

650- **11** *3* **Clapperboard**[44] 7556 3-9-5 62.....................(b) WilliamCarson 11 35
(Paul Fitzsimons) *s.i.s: a in rr: wknd over 2f out* **66/1**

1m 13.34s (-1.16) **Going Correction** -0.10s/f (Stan) **11** Ran SP% **116.7**
Speed ratings (Par 101): **103,102,101,101,98 96,95,94,93,91 87**
CSF £62.76 CT £518.63 TOTE £11.70: £3.40, £2.00, £3.30; EX 73.10 Trifecta £660.90.
**Owner** Mrs Shelley Dwyer **Bred** Sir Eric Parker **Trained** Newmarket, Suffolk

**FOCUS**
Division two of a modest sprint handicap and the pace was true.

## 8144 CORAL H'CAP 1m 1f 103y
**7:45** (7:45) (Class 2) 3-Y-0+
**£28,012** (£8,388; £4,194; £2,097; £1,048; £526) **Stalls** Low

Form RPR

323- **1** **Earth Drummer (IRE)**[14] 7971 4-9-1 95..................... DanielTudhope 6 104
(David O'Meara) *hld up: hdwy over 1f out: r.o u.p to ld nr fin* **9/2**[3]

100- **2** *½* **Spes Nostra**[15] 7955 6-8-8 88.....................(b) GrahamGibbons 1 96
(David Barron) *led: clr over 5f out tl over 3f out: rdn over 1f out: edgd lft ins fnl f: hdd nr fin* **8/1**

445- **3** *½* **Solar Deity (IRE)**[37] 7688 5-9-10 104..................... MartinHarley 8 111
(Marco Botti) *broke wl: sn stdd and lost pl: hld up: pushed along and hdwy over 1f out: rdn and edgd lft ins fnl f: r.o* **5/2**[2]

242- **4** *1½* **Flow (USA)**[14] 7971 4-8-12 92.....................(t) PJMcDonald 5 96
(David Brown) *s.i.s: sn prom: rdn over 2f out: nt clr run ins fnl f: styd on same pce* **10/1**

403- **5** *1* **Patriotic (IRE)**[22] 7870 6-8-0 83 ow3.....................(p) ConnorBeasley(3) 4 85
(Chris Dwyer) *hld up: hdwy 3f out: rdn over 1f out: styd on same pce ins fnl f* **22/1**

231- **6** *1¼* **Maverick Wave (USA)**[17] 7930 3-9-6 102..................... RobertHavlin 2 101
(John Gosden) *trckd ldr: rdn over 2f out: no ex ins fnl f* **2/1**[1]

005- **7** *6* **Streets Of Newyork**[97] 6171 7-7-11 80 oh2..................... JoeyHaynes(3) 7 66
(Brian Ellison) *s.i.s: hld up: rdn over 3f out: wknd over 2f out* **33/1**

105- **8** *21* **Star Links (USA)**[273] 977 8-8-11 91.....................(b) LukeMorris 3 33
(S Donohoe, Ire) *plld hrd: trckd ldrs tl rdn over 3f out: wknd over 2f out* **25/1**

1m 57.57s (-3.23) **Going Correction** -0.10s/f (Stan)
**WFA** 3 from 4yo+ 2lb **8** Ran SP% **111.4**
Speed ratings (Par 109): **110,109,109,107,106 105,100,81**
CSF £36.94 CT £105.19 TOTE £5.20: £2.00, £1.80, £1.50; EX 31.70 Trifecta £90.50.
**Owner** Middleham Park Racing LXV & Partner **Bred** M Ryan **Trained** Nawton, N Yorks

**FOCUS**
Some smart handicappers on view and there was an honest pace for a decent prize.

## 8145 BET IN PLAY AT CORAL H'CAP 1m 4f 50y
**8:15** (8:15) (Class 6) (0-60,59) 3-Y-0+ **£2,264** (£673; £336; £168) **Stalls** Low

Form RPR

206- **1** **Uganda Glory (USA)**[10] 8011 4-9-5 54.....................(v) PatCosgrave 7 62
(George Baker) *hld up: hdwy over 7f out: lost pl over 2f out: rallied over 1f out: r.o u.p to ld wl ins fnl f* **28/1**

506- **2** *1* **Dancing Primo**[21] 7895 8-9-1 57 ow1..................... BeckyBrisbourne(7) 3 63
(Mark Brisbourne) *hld up: hdwy 5f out: rdn to ld over 1f out: edgd rt and hdd wl ins fnl f* **14/1**

460- **3** *¾* **Cabuchon (GER)**[12] 7990 7-9-6 55.....................(vt) JFEgan 8 60
(David Evans) *hld up: hdwy u.p 2f out: r.o* **16/1**

541- **4** *½* **Well Owd Mon**[21] 7895 4-9-3 52.....................(p) GeorgeBaker 5 56
(Andrew Hollinshead) *s.i.s: hld up: rdn over 1f out: r.o ins fnl f: nt rch ldrs* **4/1**[2]

153- **5** *½* **Cascadia (IRE)**[8] 8047 3-8-12 55..................... ConnorBeasley(3) 12 59
(Alison Hutchinson) *led: rdn and hdd over 1f out: styd on same pce ins fnl f* **11/1**

024- **6** *1¼* **Mazij**[17] 7932 6-9-2 51..................... WilliamCarson 6 53
(Peter Hiatt) *chsd ldrs: rdn over 2f out: no ex wl ins fnl f* **12/1**

000- **7** *1* **Merchant Of Medici**[22] 7869 7-9-8 57.....................(p) PJMcDonald 11 57
(Micky Hammond) *plld hrd and prom: rdn over 1f out: styd on same pce fnl f* **25/1**

050/ **8** *nk* **Etaad (USA)**[185] 3129 3-8-6 53.....................(p) GaryMahon(7) 9 53
(S Donohoe, Ire) *prom: rdn over 2f out: no ex fnl f* **9/2**[3]

123- **9** *nk* **San Quentin (IRE)**[8] 8049 3-8-13 53.....................(p) LukeMorris 2 52
(Tony Carroll) *hld up: hdwy u.p over 1f out: no ex ins fnl f* **11/4**[1]

020- **10** *nk* **Anjuna Beach (USA)**[14] 7975 4-9-5 59.....................[1] AnnStokell(5) 1 58
(Ann Stokell) *s.i.s: hld up: plld hrd: nvr on terms* **33/1**

300- **11** *½* **Goldmadchen (GER)**[25] 7823 6-9-4 53..................... GrahamLee 4 51
(James Given) *prom: pushed along over 6f out: rdn and lost pl over 3f out: n.d after* **14/1**

060- **12** *1* **Musikhani**[28] 7006 4-9-4 53.....................(b[1]) AdamKirby 10 49
(Philip Kirby) *chsd ldr: drvn along over 2f out: wknd fnl f* **20/1**

2m 39.76s (-1.04) **Going Correction** -0.10s/f (Stan)
**WFA** 3 from 4yo+ 5lb **12** Ran SP% **115.1**
Speed ratings (Par 101): **99,98,97,97,97 96,95,95,95,95 94,94**
CSF £353.23 CT £6337.52 TOTE £15.20: £6.00, £3.90, £4.60; EX 370.60 Trifecta £2318.60 Part won..
**Owner** George Baker & Partners **Bred** Walmac Farm Llc **Trained** Manton, Wilts

**FOCUS**
Modest fare and the pace was muddling. It turned into a sprint and the form should not be taken at face value.

## 8146 32RED CONDITIONS STKS (FAST TRACK QUALIFIER) 2m 119y
**8:45** (8:45) (Class 2) 3-Y-0+ **£12,291** (£3,657; £1,827; £913) **Stalls** Low

Form RPR

111- **1** **Hidden Gold (IRE)**[44] 7554 3-8-9 98..................... GrahamLee 7 98+
(Saeed bin Suroor) *hld up: hdwy over 2f out: shkn up to ld 1f out: r.o: comf* **1/2**[1]

010- **2** *2* **Ted Spread**[19] 7107 7-9-5 90.....................(t) LukeMorris 2 98
(Suzy Smith) *hld up: hdwy 1/2-way: rdn over 2f out: styd on same pce ins fnl f* **16/1**

520- **3** *nse* **Harris Tweed**[17] 7922 7-9-5 105.....................(p) GeorgeBaker 3 98
(William Haggas) *led after 1f: rdn 3f out: hdd 1f out: styd on same pce* **7/1**[3]

011- **4** *1¾* **Entihaa**[7] 8062 6-9-5 92..................... RobertWinston 5 96
(Alan Swinbank) *s.i.s: sn pushed along: hdwy to chse ldr 14f out: rdn and ev ch over 1f out: no ex ins fnl f* **5/1**[2]

00- **5** *9* **Snowmane (IRE)**[17] 7922 3-8-11 94.....................(p) PaulMulrennan 1 85
(James Given) *led 1f: remained handy: rdn over 1f out: wknd ins fnl f* **16/1**

005- **6** *10* **Mister Fizz**[30] 7539 6-9-5 83..................... StevieDonohoe 6 73
(Miss Imogen Pickard) *chsd ldrs tl rdn and wknd 4f out* **66/1**

020- **7** *34* **Regal Park (IRE)**[39] 7643 7-9-5 60..................... TimClark 4 32
(Miss Imogen Pickard) *hld up: rdn over 5f out: wknd over 4f out* **150/1**

3m 36.77s (-6.93) **Going Correction** -0.10s/f (Stan)
**WFA** 3 from 6yo+ 8lb **7** Ran SP% **109.8**
Speed ratings (Par 109): **112,111,111,110,105 101,85**
CSF £9.66 TOTE £1.50: £1.20, £4.50; EX 8.50 Trifecta £27.40.
**Owner** Godolphin **Bred** Darley **Trained** Newmarket, Suffolk

**FOCUS**
The pace was honest enough for this high-quality conditions event, which featured a couple of Group 3 winners and a Listed scorer and it was the latter who produced an eyecatching victory.

## 8147 LADBROKES MAIDEN STKS 7f 32y
**9:15** (9:17) (Class 5) 3-Y-0+ **£2,911** (£866; £432; £216) **Stalls** High

Form RPR

60- **1** **Undulate**[26] 7818 3-9-0 0..................... GrahamLee 4 67
(Peter Niven) *a.p: rdn over 1f out: r.o to ld wl ins fnl f* **4/1**[2]

652- **2** *¾* **Sir Billy Wright (IRE)**[36] 7699 3-9-5 68..................... JFEgan 1 70
(David Evans) *led: rdn over 1f out: hdd wl ins fnl f* **2/11**[1]

5- **3** *13* **Zat Be Zat**[11] 8002 7-9-5 0..................... SteveDrowne 3 36
(Violet M Jordan) *hld up: hdwy over 2f out: wknd over 1f out* **33/1**

0/0- **4** *½* **Disco Dale (IRE)**[18] 7910 3-9-5 0..................... DavidNolan 5 35
(Richard Fahey) *chsd ldr tl rdn 3f out: wknd over 1f out* **14/1**[3]

50- **5** *7* **Brian The Lion**[109] 5796 3-8-12 0..................... KevinLundie(7) 6 17
(Shaun Harris) *chsd ldrs: rdn over 4f out: wknd over 2f out* **66/1**

6- **6** *3* **The Fenland Man**[11] 8002 3-9-5 0..................... StevieDonohoe 2 9
(James Unett) *s.i.s: outpcd* **50/1**

1m 27.93s (-0.87) **Going Correction** -0.10s/f (Stan) **6** Ran SP% **117.7**
Speed ratings (Par 103): **100,99,84,83,75 72**
CSF £5.48 TOTE £6.00: £1.90, £1.02; EX 7.40 Trifecta £33.10.
**Owner** G C Wragg **Bred** Juddmonte Farms Ltd **Trained** Barton-le-Street, N Yorks

**FOCUS**
A weak maiden and the early pace was strong. The front two drew well clear.

T/Plt: £238.60 to a £1 stake. Pool: £122,959.02 - 376.08 winning units. T/Qpdt: £73.00 to a £1 stake. Pool: £10,795.98 - 109.29 winning units. CR

# 8132 DEAUVILLE (R-H)

Saturday, December 13

**OFFICIAL GOING: Polytrack: standard**

## 8148a PRIX DE MONDEVILLE (MAIDEN) (2YO COLTS & GELDINGS) (POLYTRACK) 6f 110y

**10:45** (12:00) 2-Y-O **£10,416** (£4,166; £3,125; £2,083; £1,041)

RPR

1 **Borsakov (IRE)**[29] 2-9-2 0 MickaelBarzalona 4 80
(Mme Pia Brandt, France) **3/5[1]**

2 1 **Taryn** 2-9-2 0 VJanacek 8 77
(M Delcher Sanchez, France) **184/10**

3 2 1/2 **Super Nothing (IRE)**[29] 2-9-2 0 DavidBreux 3 70
(G Botti, France) **122/10**

4 1 1/4 **Angel Royal (FR)**[37] 2-9-2 0 FabriceVeron 9 67
(H-A Pantall, France) **74/10[2]**

5 shd **Spectacle Attendu (FR)** 2-8-11 0 ThierryThulliez 5 61
(Y Gourraud, France) **25/1**

6 1/2 **Charlton Heights (IRE)**[22] 7867 2-9-2 0 IoritzMendizabal 10 65
(J S Moore) *chsd ldng gp on outer: 5th and scrubbed along 2 1/2f out: outpcd over 1 1/2f out: kpt on ins fnl f: nt pce to get involved* **196/10**

7 nk **Dawn Prayer**[54] 7344 2-9-2 0 AntoineWerle 7 64
(H-A Pantall, France) **269/10**

8 3/4 **Avocat (FR)** 2-8-11 0 StephanePasquier 6 57
(Y Barberot, France) **107/10**

9 2 1/2 **Bounty Pursuit** 2-8-11 0 AntoineHamelin 1 50
(E J O'Neill, France) **28/1**

10 1/2 **Chuck A Luck (FR)**[51] 2-9-2 0 AntoineCoutier 2 54
(F Chappet, France) **17/2[3]**

1m 18.18s (78.18) **10** Ran SP% **121.9**
PARI-MUTUEL (all including 1 euro stake): WIN 1.60; PLACE 1.20, 3.30, 2.20; DF 16.70; SF 28.90.
**Owner** Alain Jathiere **Bred** Niarchos Family **Trained** France

## 8149a PRIX DE MAROLLES (CLAIMER) (2YO) (POLYTRACK) 7f 110y

**12:15** (12:00) 2-Y-O **£8,333** (£3,333; £2,500; £1,666; £833)

RPR

1 **Oui Monsieur (FR)**[10] 2-8-11 0 (b) StevanBourgois 6 67
(Robert Collet, France) **33/1**

2 nse **One Way (FR)**[10] 2-9-2 0 (p) FrankPanicucci 13 72
(Y Gourraud, France) **43/5**

3 nk **Kunst Basel (FR)**[46] 2-9-2 0 FabriceNicoleau 15 71
(H-A Pantall, France) **28/1**

4 1 1/4 **Speed Machine (IRE)**[118] 5478 2-9-4 0 JulienGrosjean 3 70
(Paul Cole) *t.k.h: hld up bhd ldng pair: cl 5th and pushed along over 2f out: sn nt clr run and swtchd outside: in clr ent fnl f: styng on whn sltly hmpd and jockey stopped riding 100yds out: nt rcvr* **8/5[1]**

5 3/4 **Really Tonic (FR)**[36] 2-8-8 0 (p) NJeanpierre 14 58
(F Doumen, France) **234/10**

6 snk **Sourdeval**[134] 4883 2-8-8 0 YohannBourgois 10 58
(C Lerner, France) **16/1**

7 3/4 **Racy Rules (IRE)**[36] 2-8-11 0 (p) NicolasBarzalona 4 59
(Mario Hofer, Germany) **76/10[3]**

8 1/2 **Sparkling Frost (FR)**[30] 2-8-8 0 (b) AntoineCoutier 2 55
(S Wattel, France) **103/10**

9 snk **Zephir (FR)**[36] 2-9-1 0 (p) PaulineProd'homme 7 62
(D Prod'Homme, France) **163/10**

10 1/2 **Snow Guest (FR)**[67] 7027 2-8-11 0 (b) CyrilleStefan 9 57
(Y Barberot, France) **39/1**

11 1 1/4 **First Company (FR)**[29] 2-9-2 0 RomainAuray 8 59
(S Wattel, France) **58/10[2]**

12 hd **Claudia Eria (FR)**[36] 2-9-2 0 MarcNobili 5 58
(P Van De Poele, France) **137/10**

13 3 **Cheyenne Bellevue (FR)**[12] 2-8-11 0 EmmanuelEtienne 16 46
(P Leblanc, France) **121/1**

14 5 **Oro Negro (FR)**[273] 2-8-11 0 (p) GuillaumeFourrier 1 34
(E Nicoleau, France) **82/1**

15 1 3/4 **French Plaisir (FR)**[36] 2-8-11 0 (p) AlexisAchard 12 30
(A Bonin, France) **73/1**

16 1 1/2 **Style D'Ouilly (FR)**[36] 2-8-8 0 AnthonyCaramanolis 11 24
(H De Nicolay, France) **83/1**

1m 31.31s (91.31) **16** Ran SP% **120.1**
PARI-MUTUEL (all including 1 euro stake): WIN 34.20; PLACE 8.00, 2.90, 7.50; DF 120.50; SF 377.60.
**Owner** Mme Didier Ricard **Bred** Mlle L Collet Vidal & Mlle C Collet Vidal **Trained** Chantilly, France

## 8150a PRIX LUTHIER (LISTED RACE) (3YO+) (POLYTRACK) 7f 110y

**12:45** (12:00) 3-Y-0+ **£21,666** (£8,666; £6,500; £4,333; £2,166)

RPR

1 **Majestic Mount**[51] 7437 4-8-11 0 StephanePasquier 7 102
(Rod Collet, France) **17/5[1]**

2 1 **Dylar (FR)**[18] 7-8-11 0 VincentVion 3 99
(L Nyffels, France) **132/10**

3 3 **Bluefire**[18] 4-8-8 0 MickaelBarzalona 1 89
(H-A Pantall, France) *broke wl: chsd ldrs on inner: cl 4th and rdn 1 1/2f out: kpt on u.p fnl f but nt pce of first two* **43/5**

4 nk **Mogadishio (FR)**[57] 7242 7-8-11 0 DelphineSantiago 12 91
(S Smrczek, Germany) **159/10**

5 1/2 **Moohaarib (IRE)**[38] 7668 3-8-11 0 IoritzMendizabal 14 91
(Marco Botti) *sn chsng ldrs towards outer: sltly outpcd and dropped into midfield 3f out: rdn and kpt on u.p fr 1 1/2f out: nt pce to trble ldrs* **81/10**

6 nse **Dastarhon (IRE)**[51] 7437 4-8-11 0 (p) AntoineHamelin 10 89
(Mme Pia Brandt, France) **32/5[3]**

7 hd **Stillman (FR)**[34] 3-8-11 0 (p) NicolasPerret 4 90
(P Khozian, France) **26/5[2]**

8 1/2 **Lazzaz (FR)**[16] 5-8-11 0 ThomasHenderson 6 88
(D De Watrigant, France) **26/1**

9 1/2 **Cubalibre (FR)**[21] 4-8-11 0 (b) Roberto-CarlosMontenegro 13 86
(P Sogorb, France) **148/10**

10 shd **Guinnevre (IRE)**[23] 7856 4-8-8 0 AlexisBadel 11 83
(G Botti, France) **94/10**

11 shd **Pont Neuilly (FR)**[18] 7916 4-8-13 0 ow2 (p) Pierre-CharlesBoudot 8 88
(Yves de Nicolay, France) **185/10**

12 1 **Alice's Dancer (IRE)**[40] 7629 5-8-8 0 MickaelForest 2 80
(Mme G Rarick, France) **56/1**

13 8 **Si Luna (GER)**[40] 7629 5-8-8 0 TheoBachelot 15 60
(W Mongil, Germany) **33/1**

14 1 3/4 **Kolonel (GER)**[23] 7856 5-8-11 0 EddyHardouin 9 59
(Mario Hofer, Germany) **207/10**

1m 27.63s (87.63) **14** Ran SP% **120.8**
PARI-MUTUEL (all including 1 euro stake): WIN 4.40; PLACE 1.70, 3.20, 2.80; DF 32.60; SF 63.00.
**Owner** Graham Robinson **Bred** G Robinson & Mme G Robinson **Trained** France

# 7897 SHA TIN (R-H)

Sunday, December 14

**OFFICIAL GOING: Turf: good to firm**

## 8151a LONGINES HONG KONG VASE (GROUP 1) (3YO+) (TURF) 1m 4f

**6:00** (12:00) 3-Y-0+
**£732,476** (£282,710; £128,504; £73,247; £42,406; £25,700)

RPR

1 **Flintshire**[43] 7611 4-9-0 0 MaximeGuyon 4 115+
(A Fabre, France) *hld up in midfield: pushed along into st: rdn and hdwy on outer over 1f out: edgd rt and chal ent fnl f: led 120yds out: styd on wl and a doing enough: shade cosily* **11/8[1]**

2 1/2 **Willie Cazals (IRE)**[21] 7899 6-9-0 0 (p) DouglasWhyte 3 114
(A S Cruz, Hong Kong) *hld up towards rr: pushed along into st: rdn and hdwy on outer ent fnl f: styd on wl and wnt 2nd towards fin: nt quite pce of wnr* **6/1[2]**

3 1 1/4 **Khaya (NZ)**[14] 5-9-0 0 (t) MircoDemuro 11 112
(J Size, Hong Kong) *worked across fr wd draw and sn led: set stdy pce: pushed along to qckn whn strly pressed into st: rdn over 1f out: styd on but hdd 120yds out: dropped to 3rd and hld* **33/1**

4 nk **Dominant (IRE)**[21] 7899 6-9-0 0 JoaoMoreira 2 111
(J Moore, Hong Kong) *stdd and hld up in midfield on inner: rdn and hdwy to chal on rail ent fnl f: kpt on same pce and sn hld* **8/1**

5 3/4 **Curren Mirotic (JPN)**[168] 3771 6-9-0 0 (t) KenichiIkezoe 6 110
(Osamu Hirata, Japan) *midfield in tch: clsd to press ldr on outer over 3f out: rdn and effrt 2f out: styd on same pce fr over 1f out: jst hld on for 5th* **9/1**

6 nse **Red Cadeaux**[40] 7653 8-9-0 0 GeraldMosse 7 110
(Ed Dunlop) *midfield: pushed along into st: rdn and outpcd over 1f out: styd on wl towards fin and almost snatched 5th post but nvr able to chal* **13/2[3]**

7 2 **Snow Sky**[92] 6329 3-8-9 0 RyanMoore 5 107
(Sir Michael Stoute) *midfield on inner: angled out into st: rdn and effrt over 1f out: nt qckn: no ex and btn fnl f* **7/1**

8 2 **Empoli (GER)**[77] 6806 4-9-0 0 AdriedeVries 11 103
(P Schiergen, Germany) *slow to s: hld up in last: rdn and stl in rr 2f out: no real imp on ldrs and nvr on terms* **25/1**

9 1 3/4 **Bubble Chic (FR)**[21] 7899 6-9-0 0 KTeetan 8 101
(D J Hall, Hong Kong) *led early and crossed to rail: sn hdd and trckd ldr: rdn and effrt into st: no ex and btn ent fnl f: wknd* **25/1**

10 nk **Parish Hall (IRE)**[71] 6919 5-9-0 0 (t) KevinManning 9 100
(J S Bolger, Ire) *dwlt: hld up and a towards rr: rdn over 2f out: outpcd and no imp in st: sn btn: nvr a factor* **33/1**

11 19 1/2 **Rainbow Chic (IRE)**[21] 7898 5-9-0 0 (bt) BrettPrebble 1 69
(C Fownes, Hong Kong) *t.k.h: sn trcking ldr on inner: rdn and effrt on rail early in st: no ex and btn over 1f out: wknd and eased fnl f: t.o* **25/1**

2m 29.83s (1.63)
**WFA** 3 from 4yo+ 5lb **11** Ran SP% **120.8**
PARI-MUTUEL (all including 10 hkd stake): WIN 21.00; PLACE 10.10, 18.50, 38.00; DF 82.00.
**Owner** K Abdullah **Bred** Juddmonte Farms Ltd **Trained** Chantilly, France

**FOCUS**
They went steady early on before the pace picked up rounding the turn into the straight. Tactical pace won the day for the favourite. The front-running third limits the form.

## 8152a LONGINES HONG KONG SPRINT (GROUP 1) (3YO+) (TURF) 6f

**6:40** (12:00) 3-Y-0+
**£821,261** (£316,978; £144,081; £82,126; £47,546; £28,816)

RPR

1 **Aerovelocity (NZ)**[21] 7897 6-9-0 0 (bt) ZacPurton 7 120
(P O'Sullivan, Hong Kong) *broke wl and mde virtually all: jnd briefly into st: rdn and qcknd over 1f out: r.o against rail fnl f: drvn out and hld on wl* **9/2[2]**

2 nk **Peniaphobia (IRE)**[21] 7897 3-9-0 0 (tp) DouglasWhyte 6 119
(A S Cruz, Hong Kong) *trckd ldrs: rdn 2f out: wnt 2nd ent fnl f: r.o wl but nt quite pce of wnr* **4/1[1]**

3 3/4 **Straight Girl (JPN)**[70] 5-8-10 0 YasunariIwata 13 112
(Hideaki Fujiwara, Japan) *midfield in tch: rdn into st: r.o and wnt 3rd ins fnl f: nt quite pce to chal* **16/1**

4 1/2 **Gordon Lord Byron (IRE)**[57] 7272 6-9-0 0 WayneLordan 2 115
(T Hogan, Ire) *midfield in tch on inner: rdn into st: r.o and wnt 4th ins fnl f: nt quite pce to chal* **11/1**

5 1 3/4 **Golden Harvest (AUS)**[21] 7897 6-9-0 0 (t) RyanMoore 14 109
(A T Millard, Hong Kong) *hld up in rr: fanned wd into st: rdn over 1f out: kpt on steadily and wnt 5th towards fin: nvr nrr* **33/1**

6 1/2 **Buffering (AUS)**[36] 7724 7-9-0 0 (b) DamianBrowne 8 108
(Robert Heathcote, Australia) *pressed wnr on outer: effrt and disp ld briefly into st: rdn and outpcd ent fnl f: sn no ex and btn: fdd: jst hld on for 6th* **16/1**

7 nse **Smart Volatility (AUS)**[21] 7897 6-9-0 0 GeraldMosse 12 108
(K W Lui, Hong Kong) *hld up in rr: rdn 2f out: kpt on wl towards fin and almost snatched 6th post but nvr able to chal* **16/1**

8 3/4 **Snow Dragon (JPN)**[70] 6-9-0 0 (t) TakuyaOno 10 105
(Noboru Takagi, Japan) *hld up in last: fanned wd into st: rdn 2f out: kpt on wl towards fin and wnt 8th fnl stride but nvr able to chal* **20/1**

9 nk **Sole Power**[70] 6966 7-9-0 0 RichardHughes 5 104
(Edward Lynam, Ire) *sn midfield: pushed wd into st and sn rdn: kpt on same pce and nvr able to chal: dropped to 9th fnl stride* **8/1**

10 ¾ **Sterling City (AUS)**[21] 7897 6-9-0 0..............................(t) JoaoMoreira 3 102
(J Moore, Hong Kong) *midfield: rdn and angled out into st: kpt on same pce and wl hld fnl f* **10/1**

11 *nse* **Lucky Nine (IRE)**[21] 7897 7-9-0 0..............................(b) BrettPrebble 4 102
(C Fownes, Hong Kong) *trckd ldrs on inner: rdn into st: kpt on same pce against rail tl btn ins fnl f: wknd* **5/1**[3]

12 1 ¾ **Spalato (NZ)**[21] 7897 5-9-0 0.............................. MNunes 11 96
(John F O'Hara, Singapore) *trckd ldrs on outer: rdn and brief effrt into st: outpcd and btn over 1f out: wknd* **25/1**

13 1 ½ **Flagship Shine (AUS)**[21] 7897 5-9-0 0..............................(p) NashRawiller 9 91
(J Moore, Hong Kong) *hld up: rdn and no imp fnl 2f: nvr a factor* **25/1**

14 5 **Little Gerda (USA)**[91] 5-8-10 0..............................(t) MircoDemuro 1 71
(Ippo Sameshima, Japan) *hld up on inner: rdn and angled out 2f out: outpcd but keeping on whn eased qckly as if smething amiss ent fnl f: sn dropped to last* **16/1**

1m 8.57s (68.57) **14 Ran SP% 122.3**
PARI-MUTUEL (all including 10 hkd stake): WIN 39.50; PLACE 15.00, 14.50, 131.50; DF 55.50.
**Owner** Daniel Yeung Ngai **Bred** N E Schick & S J Till **Trained** Hong Kong

**FOCUS**
This looked pretty open, with the key domestic trial having produced several hard-luck stories.

## 8153a LONGINES HONG KONG MILE (GROUP 1) (3YO+) (TURF) 1m
7:50 (12:00) 3-Y-0+

**£1,021,028** (£394,081; £179,127; £102,102; £59,112; £35,825)

RPR

1 **Able Friend (AUS)**[21] 7898 5-9-0 0..............................(p) JoaoMoreira 11 127+
(J Moore, Hong Kong) *stdd s and hld up in rr: pushed along to cl and angled out 2f out: chal ent fnl f and sn led: qcknd smartly under hand ride and sn clr: coasted home: impressive* **4/6**[1]

2 4 ¼ **Gold-Fun (IRE)**[21] 7898 5-9-0 0..............................(v[1]) DouglasWhyte 6 117
(R Gibson, Hong Kong) *sn led: set solid pce: narrowly hdd over 2f out: rdn to ld again over 1f out: hdd by wnr ins fnl f and readily outpcd: kpt on and jst hld on for 2nd* **9/2**[2]

3 *nk* **Grand Prix Boss (JPN)**[21] 6-9-0 0.............................. YasunariIwata 10 116
(Yoshito Yahagi, Japan) *midfield: clsd 3f out: rdn 2f out: kpt on wl fnl 150yds and wnt 3rd cl home: almost snatched 2nd post but no ch w wnr* **16/1**

4 ½ **World Ace (JPN)**[21] 5-9-0 0.............................. ZacPurton 4 115
(Yasutoshi Ikee, Japan) *in rr early: sn midfield on inner: rdn and clsd into st: kpt on wl towards fin and wnt 4th fnl strides: no ch w wnr* **12/1**

5 *nse* **Glorious Days (AUS)**[189] 7-9-0 0..............................(b) MircoDemuro 7 115
(J Size, Hong Kong) *chsd clr ldng pair: clsd 3f out and w ldrs into st: rdn and stl ev ch ent fnl f: sn readily outpcd by wnr: kpt on but lost two pls cl home* **12/1**

6 *nk* **Fiero (JPN)**[21] 5-9-0 0.............................. YuichiFukunaga 1 114
(Hideaki Fujiwara, Japan) *t.k.h: midfield: rdn 2f out: kpt on wl towards fin but nvr able to chal* **9/1**[3]

7 ¾ **Trade Storm**[43] 7613 6-9-0 0.............................. JamieSpencer 5 113
(David Simcock) *hld up: rdn into st: sn outpcd: styd on fnl 2f but n.d* **16/1**

8 *nk* **Hana's Goal (JPN)**[21] 7898 5-8-10 0.............................. NashRawiller 3 108
(Kazuhiro Kato, Japan) *midfield: rdn 2f out: outpcd fr over 1f out: kpt on but wl hld* **66/1**

9 2 ¾ **Secret Sham (AUS)**[21] 7898 5-9-0 0.............................. NeilCallan 2 105
(J Moore, Hong Kong) *led early: sn trcking ldr: led again narrowly over 2f out: rdn and hdd over 1f out: no ex and btn fnl f: wknd* **66/1**

10 1 ¼ **Captain Cat (IRE)**[25] 7836 5-9-0 0..............................(p) JamesDoyle 8 103
(Roger Charlton) *stdd and hld up: sn last: rdn into st: no imp and btn ent fnl f: nvr a factor* **20/1**

1m 33.49s (-1.21) **10 Ran SP% 123.1**
PARI-MUTUEL (all including 10 hkd stake): WIN 13.50; PLACE 10.50, 12.50, 86.00; DF 21.50.
**Owner** Dr & Mrs Cornel Li Fook Kwan **Bred** Ramsey Pastoral Co Pty Ltd **Trained** Hong Kong

**FOCUS**
Perhaps not the deepest field ever for this race, but it was hard not to be taken with how easily the favourite won. A pb from the winner, while the fifth and seventh help set the level.

## 8154a LONGINES HONG KONG CUP (GROUP 1) (3YO+) (TURF) 1m 2f
8:30 (12:00) 3-Y-0+

**£1,109,813** (£428,348; £194,704; £110,981; £64,252; £38,940)

1 **Designs On Rome (IRE)**[21] 7899 4-9-0 0.............................. JoaoMoreira 3 118
(J Moore, Hong Kong) *stdd and hld up: sn in rr: last and nudged along 4f out: rdn and fanned wd into st: styd on steadily and chal wl ins fnl f: led cl home: a jst getting there* **7/4**[1]

2 *shd* **Military Attack (IRE)**[21] 7899 6-9-0 0.............................. ZacPurton 8 118
(C Fownes, Hong Kong) *hld up in midfield: rdn 2f out: styd on steadily and chal wl ins fnl f: led narrowly and briefly towards fin: hdd cl home: jst hld* **9/2**[2]

3 1 **Criterion (NZ)**[43] 7602 4-9-0 0..............................(b) HughBowman 9 116
(David A Hayes & Tom Dabernig, Australia) *trckd ldr: chal gng strly 2f out: rdn to ld over 1f out: styd on wl but steadily reeled in fnl f and hdd towards fin: dropped to 3rd and hld* **14/1**

4 ½ **Cirrus Des Aigles (FR)**[57] 7275 8-9-0 0.............. ChristopheSoumillon 4 115
(Mme C Barande-Barbe, France) *midfield: rdn into st: styd on wl for 4th but nt quite pce to chal* **10/1**

5 ½ **Helene Super Star (USA)**[21] 7899 4-9-0 0..............................(t) MircoDemuro 7 114
(A S Cruz, Hong Kong) *dwlt: hld up in midfield: rdn into st: styd on steadily and wnt 5th towards fin: nvr able to chal* **66/1**

6 1 **Farraaj (IRE)**[43] 7602 5-9-0 0.............................. AndreaAtzeni 6 112
(Roger Varian) *midfield in tch: rdn into st: kpt on same pce fnl 2f and nvr quite able to chal: dropped to 6th towards fin* **6/1**[3]

7 ½ **Archimedes (JPN)**[287] 5-9-0 0.............................. YasunariIwata 2 111
(Hideaki Fujiwara, Japan) *midfield on inner: travelled wl into st: rdn over 1f out: kpt on same pce and nvr able to chal* **10/1**

8 ½ **California Memory (USA)**[21] 7899 8-9-0 0.............. MatthewChadwick 11 110
(A S Cruz, Hong Kong) *dwlt sltly and hld up in last: rdn 2f out: styd on u.p fnl f but nvr gng pce to chal and wl hld* **20/1**

9 1 ¼ **Same World**[21] 7898 6-9-0 0.............................. NashRawiller 5 108
(J Moore, Hong Kong) *led: strly pressed 2f out: rdn and hdd over 1f out: no ex fnl f: steadily fdd* **100/1**

10 *nk* **Pleasure Gains**[14] 5-9-0 0.............................. GeraldMosse 1 107
(K L Man, Hong Kong) *prom on inner: rdn and effrt into st: kpt on same pce tl no ex whn sltly squeezed out fnl f: btn and fdd* **33/1**

11 *nk* **Endowing (IRE)**[21] 7899 5-9-0 0..............................(e) BrettPrebble 10 107
(J Size, Hong Kong) *hld up and sn towards rr: rdn in last into st: outpcd and no imp fnl 2f: n.d* **20/1**

12 ½ **Blazing Speed**[21] 7899 5-9-0 0..............................(t) NeilCallan 12 106
(A S Cruz, Hong Kong) *in tch on outer: rdn and brief effrt into st: no ex and btn over 1f out: wknd: dropped to last fnl f* **6/1**[3]

2m 1.96s (0.56) **12 Ran SP% 122.9**
PARI-MUTUEL (all including 10 hkd stake): WIN 19.50; PLACE 11.00, 16.00, 79.00; DF 45.50.
**Owner** Cheng Keung Fai **Bred** Moyglare Stud Farm Ltd **Trained** Hong Kong

**FOCUS**
The early pace was steady and gradually increased, and the first two came from behind. The third was always handy and helps set the standard.

8155 - 8160a (Foreign Racing) - See Raceform Interactive

# 8140 WOLVERHAMPTON (A.W) (L-H)
Monday, December 15

**OFFICIAL GOING: Tapeta: standard**
Wind: Light behind Weather: Cloudy

## 8161 BET IN PLAY AT CORAL AMATEUR RIDERS' H'CAP (DIV I) (TAPETA) 1m 1f 103y
1:55 (1:56) (Class 5) (0-75,73) 3-Y-0+ **£2,807** (£870; £435; £217) **Stalls** Low

Form RPR

012- 1 **Pivotman**[24] 7871 6-10-13 72..............................(bt) MrHAABannister 8 84+
(Michael Easterby) *s.i.s: rcvrd to ld at stdy pce after 1f: qcknd 2f out: rdn out* **8/11**[1]

010- 2 2 ¼ **Automotive**[19] 7925 6-10-5 64.............................. MrRBirkett 3 69
(Julia Feilden) *s.i.s: hld up: hdwy 3f out: chsd wnr 2f out: rdn over 1f out: styd on same pce ins fnl f* **10/1**

/05- 3 1 ¼ **Breakheart (IRE)**[224] 2012 7-10-9 73.............................. MrHHunt[(5)] 2 75+
(Andrew Balding) *prom: lost pl 4f out: hdwy over 1f out: edgd lft and r.o ins fnl f: nt rch ldrs* **16/1**

231- 4 3 **Warfare**[125] 5269 5-10-2 66.............................. MissHDukes[(5)] 4 62
(Tim Fitzgerald) *hld up: effrt on outer over 2f out: rdn and edgd lft over 1f out: styd on same pce* **8/1**[3]

064- 5 2 ¼ **Gabrial The Thug (FR)**[41] 7642 4-9-11 59 oh2.........(t) MrTHamilton[(3)] 9 50
(Richard Fahey) *chsd ldrs: rdn over 2f out: wknd fnl f* **16/1**

462- 6 2 ½ **Tilstarr (IRE)**[93] 6338 4-10-2 68.............................. MrHTeal[(7)] 7 54
(Roger Teal) *prom: chsd wnr over 5f out tl rdn 2f out: wknd fnl f* **9/2**[2]

500- 7 ½ **Medal Of Valour (JPN)**[26] 7846 6-9-9 61..............................(tp) MrTGillard[(7)] 1 46
(Mark Gillard) *led 1f: chsd wnr tl over 5f out: rdn 4f out: wknd wl over 1f out* **25/1**

460- 8 1 ¼ **Power Up**[26] 7846 3-9-5 59 oh5.............................. MissGFriswell[(7)] 6 41
(Jane Chapple-Hyam) *hld up: hdwy over 3f out: rdn and wknd over 1f out* **33/1**

2m 0.52s (-0.28) **Going Correction** -0.025s/f (Stan)
**WFA** 3 from 4yo+ 2lb **8 Ran SP% 114.8**
Speed ratings (Par 103): **100,98,96,94,92 90,89,88**
CSF £9.37 CT £67.09 TOTE £1.60: £1.10, £2.20, £3.50; EX 12.20 Trifecta £64.20.
**Owner** K Wreglesworth **Bred** Cheveley Park Stud Ltd **Trained** Sheriff Hutton, N Yorks

**FOCUS**
Not too many in-form types and a steady gallop to the home turn means this bare form isn't entirely reliable. The winner raced against the inside rail throughout. The winner was better than this in the past.

## 8162 BET IN PLAY AT CORAL AMATEUR RIDERS' H'CAP (DIV II) (TAPETA) 1m 1f 103y
2:30 (2:30) (Class 5) (0-75,72) 3-Y-0+ **£2,807** (£870; £435; £217) **Stalls** Low

Form RPR

000- 1 **Fujin Dancer (FR)**[61] 5678 9-10-12 70.............................. MissHBethell 9 80+
(Brian Ellison) *hld up: hdwy 2f out: rdn to ld 1f out: r.o wl* **3/1**[2]

6/0- 2 2 ½ **Syrian**[9] 8063 7-9-7 58 oh4.............................. MissEChaston[(7)] 7 62
(Richard Ford) *s.i.s: hld up: hdwy over 2f out: styd on same pce ins fnl f* **50/1**

530- 3 ½ **Glennten**[7] 8073 5-11-0 72.............................. MrSWalker 2 75
(Jose Santos) *a.p: chsd ldr over 2f out: led wl over 1f out: rdn and hdd 1f out: styd on same pce* **9/4**[1]

006- 4 ¾ **Tight Lipped (IRE)**[68] 7044 5-10-9 67..............................(p) MrRBirkett 1 68
(Julia Feilden) *led: rdn over 2f out: hung rt and hdd wl over 1f out: styd on same pce fnl f* **7/2**[3]

363- 5 1 ½ **Estibdaad (IRE)**[14] 7982 4-9-10 59 oh1 ow1.............(t) MissMBryant[(5)] 6 57
(Paddy Butler) *chsd ldr tl rdn over 2f out: hung rt wl over 1f out: styd on same pce* **11/1**

100- 6 1 ½ **John Potts**[197] 2806 9-10-5 63.............................. MissSBrotherton 5 58
(Brian Baugh) *hld up: pushed along over 3f out: hdwy over 1f out: no ex ins fnl f* **8/1**

240- 7 2 ¾ **Hail Promenader (IRE)**[6] 8086 8-10-3 66.........(tp) MrJamesHughes[(5)] 4 55
(Jo Hughes) *hld up: rdn over 2f out: wknd over 1f out* **16/1**

334- 8 ½ **Rainford Glory (IRE)**[10] 8044 4-9-11 60.............................. MissHDukes[(5)] 8 48
(Tim Fitzgerald) *chsd ldrs tl rdn and wknd over 1f out* **14/1**

005- 9 8 **La Paiva (FR)**[14] 7986 3-9-7 58 oh13.............................. MrKLocking[(5)] 3 29
(Scott Dixon) *prom: rdn over 2f out: wknd over 1f out* **100/1**

2m 0.67s (-0.13) **Going Correction** -0.025s/f (Stan)
**WFA** 3 from 4yo+ 2lb **9 Ran SP% 112.9**
Speed ratings (Par 103): **99,96,96,95,94 93,90,90,83**
CSF £124.74 CT £394.29 TOTE £4.50: £1.80, £5.90, £1.40; EX 84.90 Trifecta £514.40.
**Owner** W A Bethell **Bred** Loughtown Stud Ltd **Trained** Norton, N Yorks

**FOCUS**
Division two of a fair handicap, and a length slower than division one. The gallop was an ordinary one and the winner raced just off the inside rail in the straight. He ran to 86 when winning this last year.

## 8163 CORAL CONNECT (S) STKS (TAPETA) 1m 4f 50y
3:05 (3:05) (Class 6) 3-Y-0+ **£1,940** (£577; £288; £144) **Stalls** Low

Form RPR

/11- 1 **La Estrella (USA)**[334] 186 11-9-8 83.............................. GrahamLee 4 69
(Don Cantillon) *a.p: pushed along 5f out: chsd ldr over 3f out: led ins fnl f: styd on* **8/11**[1]

336- 2 1 ¼ **Noguchi (IRE)**[186] 3134 9-9-5 70..............................(p) AshleyMorgan[(3)] 6 67
(Chris Dwyer) *led at stdy pce tl qcknd over 2f out: rdn and edgd lft over 1f out: hdd ins fnl f: styd on same pce* **14/1**

604- 3 *shd* **Investissement**[12] 8015 8-9-8 76..............................(p) AmirQuinn 1 67
(Lee Carter) *chsd ldrs: rdn over 2f out: nt clr run over 1f out: swtchd rt ins fnl f: styd on* **2/1**[2]

040- 4 ¾ **Matraash (USA)**[5] 8102 8-9-8 60..............................(be) ShaneKelly 3 66
(Daniel Mark Loughnane) *hld up: hdwy over 2f out: shkn up over 1f out: styd on* **11/1**[3]

00- **5** *5* **Leyland (IRE)**[10] 8037 5-8-11 60..............................(b) CharlieBennett(7) 5 54
(Natalie Lloyd-Beavis) *hld up: rdn over 5f out: sn outpcd* **66/1**

400- **6** *8* **Love Tangle (IRE)**[30] 4951 3-8-13 70..............................(p) LiamKeniry 2 41
(Anthony Middleton) *chsd ldr tl rdn over 3f out: wknd over 2f out* **50/1**

2m 39.31s (-1.49) **Going Correction** -0.025s/f (Stan)
**WFA** 3 from 5yo+ 5lb **6** Ran SP% **109.7**
Speed ratings (Par 101): **103,102,102,101,98 92**
CSF £12.24 TOTE £1.70: £1.10, £4.50; EX 10.50 Trifecta £18.80.There was no bid for the winner.
**Owner** Don Cantillon **Bred** Five Horses Ltd And Theatrical Syndicate **Trained** Newmarket, Suffolk

**FOCUS**
A fair claimer, but an ordinary gallop to the home turn means this bare form may prove a bit misleading. The winner raced centre-to-far side in the straight and was some way off his best.

## 8164 32RED H'CAP (TAPETA) 1m 5f 194y
**3:40** (3:41) (Class 5) (0-75,75) 3-Y-O+ **£3,234** (£962; £481; £240) **Stalls** Low

Form RPR

311- **1** **Topaling**[24] 7866 3-8-7 61.............................. JimmyQuinn 1 72
(Mark H Tompkins) *hld up in tch: rdn and swtchd lft over 1f out: styd on u.p to ld wl ins fnl f* **7/1**[3]

521- **2** *hd* **Dire Straits (IRE)**[10] 8047 3-9-6 74..............................(p) TedDurcan 5 84
(Chris Wall) *chsd ldr tl led wl over 1f out: rdn and hdd wl ins fnl f: styd on* **5/2**[1]

131- **3** *1 1/4* **Rowlestone Lass**[13] 8001 4-9-12 73.............................. GeorgeBaker 3 81
(Richard Price) *chsd ldrs: rdn over 1f out: styd on same pce towards fin* **7/1**[3]

413- **4** *1 1/4* **Censorius**[12] 8015 3-9-3 71..............................(v) AmirQuinn 8 77
(Lee Carter) *s.i.s: hld up: pushed along over 3f out: hdwy over 1f out: styd on: nt rch ldrs* **16/1**

442- **5** *1/2* **Moccasin (FR)**[16] 7975 5-9-7 68.............................. PJMcDonald 4 73
(Geoffrey Harker) *chsd ldrs: rdn over 1f out: edgd lft: styd on* **10/1**

011- **6** *6* **Star Anise (FR)**[58] 7290 3-9-2 70.............................. GrahamLee 2 67
(Harry Dunlop) *hld up: rdn and hdwy over 1f out: wknd ins fnl f* **15/2**

3/ **7** *1/2* **Ted Dolly (IRE)**[62] 5451 10-9-3 64..............................(p) StevieDonohoe 9 60
(Tom Symonds) *sn led: rdn and hdd wl over 1f out: wknd ins fnl f* **80/1**

4- **8** *16* **Front Run (IRE)**[16] 7975 3-9-0 68.............................. AdamKirby 7 42
(Marco Botti) *hld up: rdn over 3f out: wknd over 2f out* **3/1**[2]

0/4- **9** *4 1/2* **Daghash**[13] 8001 5-10-0 75.............................. PatCosgrave 6 43
(Stuart Kittow) *prom: rdn over 3f out: wknd over 2f out* **16/1**

3m 2.24s (-2.56) **Going Correction** -0.025s/f (Stan)
**WFA** 3 from 4yo+ 7lb **9** Ran SP% **112.4**
Speed ratings (Par 103): **106,105,105,104,104 100,100,91,88**
CSF £24.03 CT £126.31 TOTE £6.30: £2.10, £1.40, £1.70; EX 24.60 Trifecta £97.50.
**Owner** M P Bowring **Bred** Dullingham Park Stud & M P Bowring **Trained** Newmarket, Suffolk

**FOCUS**
A fair handicap for the grade in which several previous winners came to the fore in the closing stages. The gallop was on the steady side and the winner raced towards the far rail in the straight. The form is rated slightly positively around the fifth.

## 8165 32RED.COM CLAIMING STKS (TAPETA) 1m 141y
**4:10** (4:10) (Class 5) 2-Y-O **£2,264** (£673; £336; £168) **Stalls** Low

Form RPR

323- **1** **Spindle (IRE)**[20] 7911 2-9-5 70.............................. LiamKeniry 4 69
(Mark Usher) *chsd ldrs: rdn to ld wl ins fnl f: styd on* **11/8**[2]

443- **2** *shd* **Missandei**[14] 7996 2-8-6 61.............................. DannyBrock(3) 6 59
(Marco Botti) *s.i.s: hld up: hdwy and shkn up 2f out: rdn to ld ins fnl f: sn hdd: styd on* **11/10**[1]

004- **3** *1 1/2* **Whisky Marmalade (IRE)**[14] 7996 2-8-11 58.............................. SamJames 5 58
(David O'Meara) *chsd ldr tl rdn to ld and edgd lft over 1f out: hdd and no ex ins fnl f* **9/1**[3]

404- **4** *2 3/4* **Reet Petite (IRE)**[20] 7912 2-8-1 40..............................(b[1]) RaulDaSilva 2 43
(James Evans) *hld up: rdn over 1f out: styd on ins fnl f: nvr nrr* **25/1**

043- **5** *2 1/2* **Beau Sparkle (IRE)**[13] 7999 2-8-7 53.............................. HayleyTurner 3 44
(Steph Hollinshead) *led: rdn over 2f out: hdd over 1f out: wknd ins fnl f* **14/1**

1m 53.78s (3.68) **Going Correction** -0.025s/f (Stan) **5** Ran SP% **110.2**
Speed ratings (Par 96): **82,81,80,78,76**
CSF £3.22 TOTE £3.10: £1.40, £1.10; EX 3.40 Trifecta £9.80.Missandei was claimed by Miss S Hollinshead for £7000.
**Owner** Saxon House Racing **Bred** M Vsetecka **Trained** Upper Lambourn, Berks

**FOCUS**
An ordinary claimer featuring only fillies and a race in which the market leaders asserted in the closing stages. The gallop was on the steady side and the winner raced centre-to-far side in the straight. Straightforward form.

## 8166 32RED CASINO MEDIAN AUCTION MAIDEN STKS (TAPETA) 1m 1f 103y
**4:40** (4:41) (Class 6) 2-Y-O **£2,264** (£673; £336; £168) **Stalls** Low

Form RPR

03- **1** **Counterproof (IRE)**[30] 7811 2-9-5 0.............................. NickyMackay 10 75+
(John Gosden) *chsd ldrs: led 6f out: rdn out* **5/4**[1]

46- **2** *3* **Amadeity (IRE)**[31] 7778 2-9-5 0.............................. PatCosgrave 2 69
(Jo Hughes) *a.p: rdn over 1f out: styd on same pce ins fnl f* **8/1**

03- **3** *nk* **Whitchurch**[18] 7941 2-9-5 0..............................(t) DavidProbert 8 68
(Andrew Balding) *a.p: rdn over 1f out: styd on same pce ins fnl f* **10/3**[2]

60- **4** *1 1/4* **Little Lord Nelson**[54] 7382 2-9-5 0..............................(t) WilliamTwiston-Davies 5 66
(Stuart Williams) *hld up: hdwy over 1f out: sn rdn and hung lft: styd on same pce ins fnl f* **12/1**

63- **5** *hd* **Sweet Selection**[26] 7835 2-9-0 0.............................. HayleyTurner 3 61
(Hughie Morrison) *disp ld over 3f: chsd wnr: rdn and edgd rt over 2f out: no ex ins fnl f* **4/1**[3]

**6** *3/4* **Quill Art** 2-9-5 0.............................. GeorgeChaloner 11 64+
(Richard Fahey) *s.i.s: hld up: rdn over 3f out: styd on fr over 1f out: nt trble ldrs* **25/1**

50- **7** *1/2* **Candella**[18] 7941 2-8-11 0.............................. RossAtkinson(3) 6 58
(Roger Varian) *mid-div: rdn over 2f out: no imp fnl f* **33/1**

**8** *1/2* **Tom Paine** 2-9-5 0.............................. JasonHart 9 62
(Garry Moss) *hld up: hdwy over 3f out: rdn and hung lft over 2f out: styd on same pce fr over 1f out* **100/1**

**9** *hd* **Chorlton House** 2-9-5 0.............................. StevieDonohoe 7 62+
(Johnny Farrelly) *s.i.s: hld up: pushed along over 3f out: hung lft fr over 1f out: nvr on terms* **66/1**

00- **10** *3 3/4* **Bangers (IRE)**[45] 7573 2-9-5 0.............................. GeorgeBaker 4 55
(Tom Dascombe) *disp ld tl over 3f: remained handy: rdn over 2f out: wknd over 1f out* **100/1**

0- **11** *63* **Sunfyre (IRE)**[27] 7827 2-9-5 0.............................. RaulDaSilva 1
(James Evans) *s.i.s: outpcd* **200/1**

2m 1.55s (0.75) **Going Correction** -0.025s/f (Stan) **11** Ran SP% **117.1**
Speed ratings (Par 94): **95,92,92,90,90 90,89,89,89,85 29**
CSF £12.29 TOTE £2.90: £1.60, £2.50, £1.30; EX 14.00 Trifecta £50.00.
**Owner** HRH Princess Haya Of Jordan **Bred** Ellasha Partnership **Trained** Newmarket, Suffolk

**FOCUS**
Not much strength in depth but fair form from the winner, who won with a bit in hand. The gallop was no more than fair and the winner came down the centre. They finished in a heap behind the winner but the form makes plenty of sense.

## 8167 LADBROKES MAIDEN STKS (TAPETA) 1m 141y
**5:10** (5:13) (Class 5) 3-Y-O+ **£2,911** (£866; £432; £216) **Stalls** Low

Form RPR

424- **1** **New Year's Night (IRE)**[5] 8094 3-9-5 0.............................. AdamKirby 4 76+
(Charlie Appleby) *trckd ldr tl led over 2f out: clr fr over 1f out: easily* **2/9**[1]

6- **2** *8* **Mustafiz (USA)**[21] 7901 3-9-5 0.............................. SamJames 3 57
(Noel Quinlan) *chsd ldrs: rdn to go 2nd 2f out: sn outpcd* **7/2**[2]

050- **3** *2 3/4* **Dutch Lady Roseane**[10] 8049 3-9-0 42..............................(p) LiamJones 5 46
(James Unett) *led: rdn and hdd over 2f out: styd on same pce* **14/1**[3]

0- **4** *1 1/2* **Roxy Madam**[21] 7901 5-8-13 0.............................. RossAtkinson(3) 2 43
(Mandy Rowland) *s.i.s: hld up: effrt over 2f out: sn outpcd* **50/1**

00/ **5** *24* **Tundridge**[1129] 7398 5-9-7 0.............................. WilliamTwiston-Davies 1
(John Spearing) *hld up: pushed along 1/2-way: wknd over 2f out* **28/1**

1m 49.68s (-0.42) **Going Correction** -0.025s/f (Stan)
**WFA** 3 from 5yo 2lb **5** Ran SP% **116.1**
Speed ratings (Par 103): **100,92,90,89,67**
CSF £1.62 TOTE £1.30: £1.10, £1.20; EX 1.70 Trifecta £3.60.
**Owner** Godolphin **Bred** Mrs C L Weld **Trained** Newmarket, Suffolk

**FOCUS**
A most uncompetitive event and one in which the gallop was on the steady side. The easy winner came down the centre-to-far side in the straight. and didn't need to match his best.

## 8168 DOWNLOAD THE LADBROKES APP H'CAP (TAPETA) 1m 141y
**5:40** (5:40) (Class 5) (0-75,75) 3-Y-O+ **£2,911** (£866; £432; £216) **Stalls** Low

Form RPR

405- **1** **Miss Lillie**[46] 7552 3-8-13 69.............................. RobertWinston 6 79
(Roger Teal) *hld up: nt clr run over 2f out: hdwy over 1f out: rdn to ld and hung lft wl ins fnl f* **16/1**

/30- **2** *nk* **Leonard Thomas**[26] 7831 4-9-6 74.............................. GeorgeBaker 3 83
(David Lanigan) *hld up: hdwy over 2f out: rdn to ld ins fnl f: sn edgd lft and hdd: styd on* **5/2**[1]

300- **3** *1 3/4* **Comrade Bond**[21] 7905 6-8-13 67.............................. JimmyQuinn 1 72
(Mark H Tompkins) *plld hrd and prom: rdn and ev ch ins fnl f: styd on same pce* **50/1**

133- **4** *1/2* **Almanack**[17] 7955 4-9-7 75.............................. StevieDonohoe 11 79
(Ian Williams) *hld up: rdn over 1f out: r.o wl ins fnl f: nt rch ldrs* **6/1**[3]

035- **5** *nk* **Reggie Bond**[45] 7569 4-8-13 67..............................(b) BarryMcHugh 7 70+
(Geoffrey Oldroyd) *trckd ldrs: plld hrd: rdn to ld over 1f out: hdd and no ex ins fnl f* **15/2**

564- **6** *1/2* **Shamaheart (IRE)**[21] 7906 4-9-2 70..............................(p) DavidAllan 9 72
(Geoffrey Harker) *hld up: hdwy over 2f out: nt clr run over 1f out: styd on same pce ins fnl f* **9/1**

000- **7** *2* **Prime Exhibit**[10] 8044 9-8-7 66..............................(t) EoinWalsh(5) 4 64
(Daniel Mark Loughnane) *hld up: rdn over 2f out: styd on ins fnl f: nvr nrr* **66/1**

214- **8** *1 1/2* **Memoria**[24] 7871 3-9-5 75.............................. ChrisCatlin 12 69
(Rae Guest) *chsd ldr tl hung lft over 3f out: sn rdn: wknd fnl f* **13/2**

215- **9** *nk* **Gambino (IRE)**[9] 8058 4-8-13 70.............................. ConnorBeasley(3) 2 64
(John David Riches) *plld hrd and prom: chsd ldr over 3f out: led 2f out: rdn and hdd over 1f out: wknd ins fnl f* **9/1**

213- **10** *3 3/4* **Loraine**[11] 8030 4-9-3 71.............................. FergusSweeney 10 56
(Jamie Osborne) *hld up: rdn over 1f out: n.d* **5/1**[2]

200- **11** *1/2* **Venutius**[45] 7569 7-8-13 67.............................. GrahamGibbons 8 51
(Ed McMahon) *led: rdn and hdd 2f out: wknd fnl f* **33/1**

233/ **12** *1/2* **Dha Chara (IRE)**[597] 1829 4-9-4 72.............................. LiamKeniry 5 55
(Andrew Hollinshead) *hld up in tch: racd keenly: rdn over 2f out: sn wknd* **66/1**

1m 48.07s (-2.03) **Going Correction** -0.025s/f (Stan)
**WFA** 3 from 4yo+ 2lb **12** Ran SP% **118.4**
Speed ratings (Par 103): **108,107,106,105,105 105,103,101,101,98 97,97**
CSF £55.38 CT £2015.96 TOTE £14.80: £4.50, £1.60, £10.50; EX 73.00 Trifecta £4542.40.
**Owner** The Rat Racers **Bred** Newsells Park Stud & Cannon Bloodstock **Trained** Ashtead, Surrey

**FOCUS**
A fair handicap run at a decent gallop and this form should prove reliable. The winner came down the centre in the straight and is rated closer to her early best.
T/Jkpt: £377.60 to a £1 stake. Pool of £8361.80- 18.80 winning tickets. T/Plt: £5.40 to a £1 stake. Pool of £89869.82 - 12081.46 winning tickets. T/Qpdt: £2.80 to a £1 stake. Pool of £6956.50 - 1828.52 winning tickets. CR

# 8111 KEMPTON (A.W) (R-H)
### Tuesday, December 16

**OFFICIAL GOING: Polytrack: standard**
Wind: virtually nil Weather: dry

## 8169 FOLLOW @BETVICTORRACING ON TWITTER H'CAP 1m 2f (P)
**2:20** (2:20) (Class 5) (0-70,70) 3-Y-O+ **£3,234** (£962; £481; £240) **Stalls** Low

Form RPR

041- **1** **What A Dandy (IRE)**[19] 7942 3-8-12 64..............................(p) PatCosgrave 3 72
(Jim Boyle) *chsd ldrs: rdn to ld over 1f out: jst hld on* **8/1**

305- **2** *nse* **Oratorio's Joy (IRE)**[14] 7998 4-9-7 70.............................. AdamKirby 2 78
(Jamie Osborne) *s.i.s: rdn along at times: towards rr: hdwy into midfield 1/2-way: rdn 3f out: swtchd lft and drvn over 1f out: chsd wnr fnl f: grad clsd: jst failed* **3/1**[1]

001- **3** *nk* **Young Dottie**[20] 7925 8-9-4 67.............................. RichardHughes 6 74
(Pat Phelan) *hld up in last pair: hdwy over 2f out: rdn to chse ldrs 1f out: kpt on wl ins fnl f: nt quite rch ldrs* **14/1**

005- **4** *1 1/4* **Nelson Quay (IRE)**[122] 5426 4-9-6 69.............................. MartinLane 11 74
(Jeremy Gask) *s.i.s: bhd and bustled along early: hdwy over 1f out: nt clr run 1f out: styd on wl ins fnl f: nt rch ldrs* **7/1**

120- **5** *shd* **Ana Shababiya (IRE)**[49] 7522 4-9-7 70.............................. TomQueally 4 74
(Ismail Mohammed) *in tch in midfield: effrt and sltly hmpd over 1f out: kpt on same pce ins fnl f* **14/1**

002- **6** *nk* **Bridge That Gap**[6] 8102 6-8-11 60................................(p) JimmyQuinn 7 64
(Roger Ingram) *hld up towards rr: hdwy on inner over 1f out: styd on same pce ins fnl f* **8/1**

13- **7** *1* **Dream Ruler**[125] 5304 3-9-4 70.................................. FergusSweeney 10 72
(Jo Crowley) *chsd ldrs: effrt whn hmpd over 1f out: nt rcvr and one pce ins fnl f* **9/2[2]**

451- **8** *6* **Time Square (FR)**[15] 7982 7-8-12 61............................... JimCrowley 1 51
(Tony Carroll) *w ldr tl led 6f out: rdn and hdd over 1f out: losing pl whn squeezed for room and hmpd 1f out: wknd fnl f* **6/1[3]**

000- **9** *6* **Notebook**[33] 7757 3-8-3 62......................................... SophieKilloran(7) 9 40
(Martin Smith) *in tch in midfield: rdn over 2f out: wd and lost pl bnd 2f out: sn wknd* **40/1**

305- **10** *3/4* **Byrd In Hand (IRE)**[19] 7942 7-8-13 62......................... WilliamCarson 8 38
(John Bridger) *led tl 6f out: lost pl u.p over 2f out: wknd wl over 1f out* **50/1**

210- **11** *11* **Olivers Mount**[12] 8030 4-8-12 61.......................................(t) LiamKeniry 5 15
(Ed Vaughan) *t.k.h: hld up in tch in midfield: rdn and wd bnd 2f out: sn btn and wknd* **16/1**

2m 5.91s (-2.09) **Going Correction** -0.10s/f (Stan)
**WFA** 3 from 4yo+ 3lb **11** Ran SP% **115.8**
Speed ratings (Par 103): **104,103,103,102,102 102,101,96,92,91 82**
CSF £31.64 CT £335.55 TOTE £10.20: £3.40, £1.40, £4.10; EX 32.80 Trifecta £343.50.

**Owner** Inside Track Racing Club **Bred** Pat Beirne **Trained** Epsom, Surrey

■ Stewards' Enquiry : Adam Kirby one-day ban; careless riding (30th Dec)

**FOCUS**
They went a decent pace for this open handicap and the form looks sound. The winner has improved recently.

## 8170 BETVICTOR SVENGALI NURSERY H'CAP 5f (P)
**2:50** (2:52) (Class 5) (0-75,70) 2-Y-O £3,234 (£962; £481) **Stalls** Low

Form RPR

313- **1** **Shackled N Drawn (USA)**[10] 8059 2-9-7 70...............(tp) JimCrowley 5 75
(Olly Stevens) *stdd s: t.k.h: hld up in 3rd: swtchd lft and effrt 1f out: qckly u.p to ld wl ins fnl f: r.o wl* **10/11[1]**

01- **2** *1 1/4* **Middle East Pearl**[17] 7970 2-9-6 69.................................... AdamKirby 4 69
(James Tate) *t.k.h: pressed ldr: rdn and ev ch over 1f out: led ins fnl f: hdd and styd on same pce wl ins fnl f* **13/8[2]**

344- **3** *3/4* **One Moment**[42] 7649 2-8-7 61......................................... ShaneGray(5) 2 58
(Robert Cowell) *sn led: rdn over 1f out: hdd and r.o same pce ins fnl f* **13/2[3]**

1m 0.59s (0.09) **Going Correction** -0.10s/f (Stan) **3** Ran SP% **103.8**
Speed ratings (Par 96): **95,93,91**
CSF £2.52 TOTE £1.90; EX 2.40.

**Owner** Clipper Logistics **Bred** Pam & Martin Wygod **Trained** Chiddingfold, Surrey

**FOCUS**
Two withdrawals took much of the interest out of this handicap which was run at an honest pace. Not form to place too much faith in.

## 8171 GET SVENS INSIDE TRACK AT BETVICTOR H'CAP 5f (P)
**3:20** (3:20) (Class 4) (0-85,85) 3-Y-O+ £5,175 (£1,540; £769; £384) **Stalls** Low

Form RPR

460- **1** **Fair Value (IRE)**[24] 7886 6-9-0 78....................................... HayleyTurner 7 87
(Simon Dow) *mde all: 4 l clr and pushed along over 1f out: jst hld on* **8/1**

04- **2** *shd* **Doctor Parkes**[12] 8025 8-9-4 82....................................... DavidProbert 1 90
(Stuart Williams) *racd in midfield: effrt on inner over 1f out: chsd clr wnr ins fnl f: styd on wl: jst failed* **3/1[2]**

520- **3** *1* **Harrogate Fair**[11] 8040 4-8-8 72.....................................(p) ChrisCatlin 3 76
(Michael Squance) *off the pce in last trio: swtchd lft and hdwy over 1f out: styd on wl ins fnl f: wnt 3rd towards fin: nt rch ldrs* **25/1**

012- **4** *nk* **Salvatore Fury (IRE)**[12] 8025 4-9-0 78............................(p) JimCrowley 5 81
(Keith Dalgleish) *hld up in midfield: hdwy over 1f out: pressing for 2nd 1f out: kpt on same pce fnl 100yds* **7/4[1]**

066- **5** *nk* **Triple Dream**[12] 8025 9-8-13 77.....................................(tp) JimmyQuinn 4 79
(Milton Bradley) *t.k.h: chsd wnr tl over 3f out: rdn over 1f out: chsd clr wnr 1f out tl ins fnl f: one pce* **12/1**

022- **6** *1 1/2* **Doc Hay (USA)**[15] 7983 7-9-4 82......................................... AmirQuinn 6 79
(Lee Carter) *taken down early: bustled along leaving stalls: chsd wnr over 3f out tl 1f out: btn whn nt clr run wl ins fnl f* **7/1[3]**

252- **7** *2 1/2* **Secret Millionaire (IRE)**[91] 6441 7-9-0 78...............[1] FergusSweeney 2 66
(Luke Dace) *dwlt: sn outpcd in rr: sme hdwy fnl f: n.d* **12/1**

054- **8** *1 1/2* **Picansort**[13] 8019 7-9-7 85.......................................(b) GeorgeBaker 9 67
(Peter Crate) *stdd s: hld up off the pce in rr: n.d* **12/1**

58.96s (-1.54) **Going Correction** -0.10s/f (Stan) **8** Ran SP% **111.9**
Speed ratings (Par 105): **108,107,106,105,105 102,98,96**
CSF £30.86 CT £574.64 TOTE £10.10: £2.50, £1.30, £4.70; EX 41.80 Trifecta £1443.90.

**Owner** Don & Val Churston **Bred** Edward Hyde **Trained** Epsom, Surrey

**FOCUS**
The pace was sound for this fair sprint handicap. The winner is rated to her best in the past year.

## 8172 BOOK NOW FOR BOXING DAY MEDIAN AUCTION MAIDEN STKS 1m 3f (P)
**3:50** (3:51) (Class 6) 3-5-Y-O £2,264 (£673; £336; £168) **Stalls** Low

Form RPR

640- **1** **Elysian Fields (GR)**[27] 7841 3-9-0 65.................................. AdamKirby 4 63
(Amanda Perrett) *pressed ldr tl reminders to ld wl over 1f out: clr 1f out: comf* **1/5[1]**

035- **2** *6* **Sawwala**[3] 8134 4-9-4 48............................................ DavidProbert 3 53
(J R Jenkins) *led tl rdn over 2f out: hdd wl over 1f out: sn outpcd and btn: hld on for 2nd* **9/2[2]**

6- **3** *nk* **Strictly The One (IRE)**[11] 8048 4-9-4 0.............................. RyanWhile(5) 2 57
(Neil Mulholland) *t.k.h: hld up in tch: rdn wl over 2f out: no ch w wnr but battling for 2nd fnl f: kpt on* **40/1[3]**

6- **4** *6* **Claraty**[10] 8064 4-9-4 0.............................................. LiamKeniry 1 42
(James Unett) *chsd ldrs: rdn over 2f out: no imp: wknd fnl f* **50/1**

2m 23.34s (1.44) **Going Correction** -0.10s/f (Stan)
**WFA** 3 from 4yo 4lb **4** Ran SP% **105.9**
Speed ratings (Par 101): **90,85,85,81**
CSF £1.33 TOTE £1.10; EX 1.40 Trifecta £3.20.

**Owner** Mrs Alexandra J Chandris **Bred** Queensway S A **Trained** Pulborough, W Sussex

**FOCUS**
A desperately weak maiden run at a steady pace. The runner-up sets the standard.

## 8173 DAILY SVEN-TO-1 SPECIALS AT BETVICTOR MAIDEN FILLIES' STKS (BOBIS RACE) 1m (P)
**4:20** (4:22) (Class 4) 2-Y-O £4,075 (£1,212; £606; £303) **Stalls** Low

Form RPR

33- **1** **Cartier (IRE)**[105] 6001 2-9-0 0.......................................... JimCrowley 2 78+
(David Simcock) *in tch in midfield: clsd 2f out: rdn to ld jst over 1f out: r.o wl fnl f: rdn out* **7/2[2]**

30- **2** *2 3/4* **Bittern (IRE)**[11] 8036 2-9-0 0............................................. AdamKirby 10 70
(Charlie Appleby) *hld up in midfield: clsd 2f out: rdn to chse wnr 1f out: r.o same pce fnl f* **7/1**

**3** *3/4* **Zamzama (IRE)** 2-9-0 0.................................................. PhillipMakin 12 68+
(Saeed bin Suroor) *s.i.s: off the pce towards rr: rdn and hdwy 2f out: styd on wl ins fnl f: nvr trbld ldrs* **5/1[3]**

53- **4** *3/4* **Vanishing**[24] 7891 2-9-0 0............................................. AntonioFresu 4 66
(Ed Walker) *in tch in midfield: rdn and effrt 2f out: kpt on u.p ins fnl f* **12/1**

06- **5** *shd* **Flighty Filia (IRE)**[11] 8036 2-9-0 0.................................. LiamKeniry 1 66
(Amanda Perrett) *chsd ldrs: wnt 2nd over 3f out: ev ch u.p over 1f out tl jst over 1f out: one pce fnl f* **100/1**

**6** *1* **Lemoncetta (USA)** 2-9-0 0............................................ SteveDrowne 13 64+
(John Gosden) *sn wl off the pce in last quartet: clsd but stl plenty to do over 1f out: styd on wl ins fnl f: nt rch ldrs* **25/1**

0- **7** *hd* **Desert Morning (IRE)**[53] 7405 2-9-0 0......................... FergusSweeney 7 63
(David Simcock) *in tch in midfield: clsd 2f out: sn rdn and unable qck: kpt on same pce fnl f* **33/1**

**7** *dht* **Vereri Senes** 2-9-0 0.................................................. TomQueally 5 63+
(Ed Dunlop) *awkward leaving stalls and s.i.s: sn rcvrd into midfield but stl off the pce: clsd and swtchd rt 2f out: chsd ldrs 1f out: no ex fnl f* **100/1**

4- **9** *3 3/4* **Lahayeb**[19] 7943 2-9-0 0............................................. RichardHughes 11 55
(Richard Hannon) *chsd ldr tl over 3f out: rdn and unable qck 2f out: btn over 1f out: wknd fnl f* **7/1**

222- **10** *1 1/4* **Waldnah**[41] 7658 2-9-0 75.................................................. NickyMackay 3 52
(John Gosden) *racd keenly: led: rdn and hdd over 1f out: sn btn and wknd fnl f* **11/4[1]**

5- **11** *1 1/4* **Crystalin (IRE)**[31] 7809 2-9-0 0........................................ PaoloSirigu 6 49
(Marco Botti) *chsd ldrs: no ex u.p 2f out: wknd over 1f out* **66/1**

5- **12** *2 1/2* **Rustique**[19] 7944 2-8-7 0............................................. CliffordLee(7) 14 43
(Ed Walker) *stdd to rr after s: n.d* **100/1**

**13** *22* **Emirates Holidays (USA)** 2-9-0 0......................................... MartinLane 9
(Charlie Appleby) *s.i.s: rdn along in rr thrght: wl bhd over 2f out: t.o* **16/1**

00- **14** *3 1/2* **Beccabuddyblues (GR)**[33] 7756 2-9-0 0................................ PatCosgrave 8
(Amanda Perrett) *chsd ldrs: hung lft and lost pl over 3f out: wl bhd fnl f: t.o* **100/1**

1m 38.73s (-1.07) **Going Correction** -0.10s/f (Stan) **14** Ran SP% **116.4**
Speed ratings (Par 95): **101,98,97,96,96 95,95,95,91,90 89,86,64,61**
CSF £26.53 TOTE £4.90: £1.80, £2.80, £2.70; EX 27.70 Trifecta £188.00.

**Owner** Al Asayl Bloodstock Ltd **Bred** Sheikh Sultan Bin Khalifa Al Nahyan **Trained** Newmarket, Suffolk

**FOCUS**
Some big stables lined up for this fillies' maiden which was run at a sound pace. The principals came from the rear and the winner can rate a good deal higher.

## 8174 BETVICTOR.COM NURSERY H'CAP 1m (P)
**4:50** (4:52) (Class 5) (0-75,75) 2-Y-O £3,234 (£962; £481; £240) **Stalls** Low

Form RPR

056- **1** **Tempus Temporis (USA)**[20] 7927 2-9-6 74...............(b[1]) NickyMackay 5 86+
(John Gosden) *hld up in last pair: gd hdwy 3f out: rdn to ld 2f out: wnt clr 1f out: r.o strly: readily* **3/1[1]**

532- **2** *6* **Cape Cay**[25] 7867 2-9-1 69.............................................. GrahamGibbons 6 67
(Ralph Beckett) *t.k.h: chsd ldrs: rdn and effrt 2f out: no ch w wnr but kpt on to go 2nd wl ins fnl f* **3/1[1]**

105- **3** *1/2* **What A Party (IRE)**[91] 6436 2-9-1 74........................... ShelleyBirkett(5) 3 71
(Gay Kelleway) *chsd ldrs: rdn and ev ch over 1f out: btn jst over 1f out: wknd and lost 2nd wl ins fnl f* **33/1**

300- **4** *1* **Imperial Link**[19] 7943 2-8-11 65.................................(b[1]) JimCrowley 7 60
(Paul Cole) *stdd after s: hld up in rr: effrt over 2f out: 4th and no ch w wnr over 1f out: kpt on* **25/1**

040- **5** *6* **Wally's Wisdom**[20] 7927 2-9-5 73.......................................... AmirQuinn 1 54
(Lee Carter) *sn bustled along to ld: rdn and hdd 2f out: sn btn: wknd over 1f out* **12/1[2]**

213- **6** *1* **Gleneely Girl (IRE)**[116] 5626 2-9-3 71................................... ChrisCatlin 4 49
(Rae Guest) *chsd ldr tl over 2f out: short of room and sn dropped to rr: wknd over 1f out* **14/1[3]**

1m 39.32s (-0.48) **Going Correction** -0.10s/f (Stan) **6** Ran SP% **71.1**
Speed ratings (Par 96): **98,92,91,90,84 83**
CSF £4.28 TOTE £3.00: £1.10, £1.40; EX 5.70 Trifecta £50.70.

**Owner** HRH Princess Haya Of Jordan **Bred** Briland Farm & Robert & Stacy Mitchell **Trained** Newmarket, Suffolk

■ Mountainside was withdrawn. Price at time of withdrawal 11-8. Rule 4 applies to all bets - deduction 40p in the pound.

**FOCUS**
An interesting handicap, despite the withdrawal of the short-price favourite, who refused to enter the stalls. The winner showed useful form but this lacked depth.

## 8175 RACING UK ANYWHERE ALL WEATHER "HANDS AND HEELS" APPRENTICE SERIES H'CAP (EXCELLENCE INITIATIVE) 1m (P)
**5:20** (5:20) (Class 6) (0-60,60) 4-Y-O+ £2,264 (£673; £336; £168) **Stalls** Low

Form RPR

001- **1** **Bosstime (IRE)**[15] 7987 4-9-7 60....................................(b) RobHornby 5 77+
(John Holt) *sn led and t.k.h: allowed to go clr 1/2-way: 6 l clr 3f out: rdn along hands and heels over 1f out: kpt on* **5/2[1]**

060- **2** *3 1/4* **Youm Jamil (USA)**[54] 6267 7-8-2 46.......................(t) TomMarquand(5) 11 52
(Tony Carroll) *s.i.s: hld up in rr: rdn and hdwy over 1f out: chsd clr wnr fnl 150yds: kpt on but nvr a threat* **9/1**

510- **3** *1 3/4* **Delightful Sleep**[33] 7766 6-9-2 58.......................................... HarryBurns(3) 4 60
(David Evans) *hld up in last trio: rdn and hdwy over 1f out: kpt on to go 3rd wl ins fnl f: nvr trbld ldrs* **14/1**

600- **4** *1/2* **Strategic Action (IRE)**[27] 7844 5-8-4 46 oh1....(tp) CallumShepherd(3) 2 47
(Linda Jewell) *broke fast: sn restrained to chse wnr: rdn and tried to cl over 2f out: no real imp: lost 2 pls ins fnl f* **20/1**

242- **5** *3/4* **Litmus (USA)**[155] 4264 5-8-13 55...............................(b) TomasHarrigan(3) 1 54
(Simon Dow) *hld up in midfield: rdn and effrt 2f out: styd on same pce fnl f: no threat to wnr* **8/1[3]**



The Form Book, Raceform Ltd, Newbury, RG14 5SJ

606- **6** 1/2 **Russian Ice**[15] 7986 6-8-12 54..............................(p) PaulBooth(3) 6 52
(Dean Ivory) *dwlt: hld up in last trio: swtchd lft and rdn 2f out: kpt on: nvr trbld wnr* **16/1**

645- **7** 4 **Roy Rocket (FR)**[20] 7924 4-8-7 46 oh1.................. HectorCrouch 10 35
(John Berry) *in tch in midfield: rdn to go prom in chsng gp 3f out: no imp: wknd 1f out* **6/1**[2]

000- **8** nk **Gladsome**[76] 6863 6-8-12 51........................................ GaryMahon 3 39
(Sarah Humphrey) *t.k.h: in tch in midfield: rdn and no hdwy over 2f out: wknd 1f out* **66/1**

116- **9** 1 **Habeshia**[14] 8004 4-8-11 53.............................. MichaelKenneally(3) 7 39
(Michael Bell) *chsd ldrs: rdn 3f out: no imp: lost pl over 1f out: bhd fnl f* **5/2**[1]

1m 40.13s (0.33) **Going Correction** -0.10s/f (Stan) **9** Ran SP% **111.3**
Speed ratings (Par 101): **94,90,89,88,87 87,83,82,81**
CSF £25.40 CT £252.10 TOTE £3.50: £1.30, £2.90, £3.20; EX 24.90 Trifecta £281.10.
**Owner** Planters (leicester) Limited **Bred** J K Dewberry **Trained** Peckleton, Leics

**FOCUS**
A modest handicap, confined to apprentice riders, run at a steady pace. The winner stole it from the front and the form should be treated with caution.
T/Plt: £28.10 to a £1 stake. Pool: £65,812.16 - 1704.67 winning units. T/Qpdt: £8.60 to a £1 stake. Pool: £6229.34 - 535.70 winning units. SP

# 8133 SOUTHWELL (L-H)

## Tuesday, December 16

**OFFICIAL GOING: Fibresand: standard**
Wind: Light across Weather: Overcast

### 8176 LADBROKES H'CAP — 7f (F)
**12:25** (12:25) (Class 6) (0-65,65) 3-Y-0+ **£1,940** (£577; £288; £144) **Stalls** Low

Form RPR

320- **1** **Burnhope**[11] 8043 5-9-5 63........................................ LukeMorris 7 76
(Scott Dixon) *trckd ldrs: hdwy to ld 2f out: rdn clr appr fnl f: styd on* **3/1**[2]

113- **2** 5 **Best Tamayuz**[21] 7915 3-9-2 65.................................. TimClark(5) 1 65
(Scott Dixon) *chsd ldrs on inner: pushed along 3f out: rdn to dispute ld over 2f out: chsd wnr fr wl over 1f out: no imp fnl f* **2/1**[1]

043- **3** 5 **Arabian Flight**[28] 7830 5-9-1 64..........................(p) AlistairRawlinson(5) 2 51
(Michael Appleby) *cl up: led 4f out: rdn along 3f out: hdd 2f out: sn drvn and kpt on one pce* **5/1**[3]

030- **4** 1 1/2 **Gaelic Wizard (IRE)**[7] 8082 6-8-10 59..................... GemmaTutty(5) 8 42
(Karen Tutty) *dwlt and towards rr: hdwy 1/2-way: wd st: sn rdn and no imp* **8/1**

055- **5** 3 3/4 **Milly's Secret (IRE)**[11] 8043 3-9-2 60..........................[1] DanielTudhope 5 33
(David O'Meara) *chsd ldrs: rdn along and outpcd after 3f: sn swtchd rt to outer and wd st: drvn and plugged on: n.d* **9/1**

500- **6** 2 1/2 **Clapperboard**[3] 8143 3-9-4 62..........................(p) GrahamLee 4 29
(Paul Fitzsimons) *slt ld: hdd 4f out: rdn along 3f out: sn drvn and wknd* **33/1**

242- **7** 1 **Wotalad**[24] 7883 4-9-1 59..........................(p) GeorgeChaloner 6 23
(Richard Whitaker) *prom on outer: rdn along 3f out: wknd over 2f out* **8/1**

660- **8** 6 **Howz The Family (IRE)**[265] 1101 3-8-11 60.................. EoinWalsh(5) 3 9
(John Spearing) *sn rdn along and outpcd in rr: bhd fr 1/2-way* **66/1**

1m 28.82s (-1.48) **Going Correction** -0.15s/f (Stan) **8** Ran SP% **111.7**
Speed ratings (Par 101): **102,96,90,88,84 81,80,73**
CSF £8.92 CT £26.44 TOTE £4.50: £1.40, £1.30, £1.90; EX 8.90 Trifecta £30.30.
**Owner** P J Dixon & Partners **Bred** Mrs S M Roy **Trained** Babworth, Notts

**FOCUS**
A moderate handicap, but the pace was good with a contested lead and it resulted in a 1-2 for trainer Scott Dixon. The winner found a bit on recent form.

### 8177 32RED CASINO FILLIES' H'CAP — 1m (F)
**12:55** (12:55) (Class 5) (0-75,75) 3-Y-0+ **£2,587** (£770; £384; £192) **Stalls** Low

Form RPR

224- **1** **Queen Of Skies (IRE)**[292] 767 5-8-9 63.......................... LiamJones 8 70
(Michael Appleby) *cl up: led over 3f out: rdn 2f out: drvn ent fnl f: kpt on wl towards fin* **11/4**[1]

540- **2** 1/2 **Heavens Eyes (IRE)**[64] 7162 3-8-10 65........................ MartinDwyer 6 70
(Jo Hughes) *sn slt ld: pushed along and hdd over 3f out: rdn over 2f out: drvn ent fnl f: kpt on wl towards fin* **16/1**

464- **3** hd **Artistic Queen**[18] 7954 3-9-5 74.............................. LukeMorris 4 78
(James Tate) *trckd ldrs: effrt on inner 3f out: rdn along over 2f out: drvn and kpt on wl fnl f* **9/2**[2]

321- **4** 1 1/4 **Wu Zetian**[21] 7910 3-9-1 70.................................. ShaneKelly 7 72
(Pam Sly) *trckd ldrs: hdwy 3f out: rdn 2f out: edgd lft wl over 1f out: drvn and ev ch whn edgd lft again jst ins fnl f: kpt on same pce* **11/4**[1]

644- **5** 6 **Evacusafe Lady**[14] 7998 3-8-9 67..........................(t) RyanPowell(3) 5 55
(John Ryan) *a towards rr* **10/1**

455- **6** 3/4 **The Dukkerer (IRE)**[11] 8044 3-8-12 67........................ GrahamLee 2 53
(James Given) *prom early: pushed along and lost pl after 3f: swtchd rt and wd st: n.d* **8/1**[3]

600- **7** 3/4 **Imaginary World (IRE)**[10] 8058 6-9-1 69.................(p) DanielTudhope 1 54
(John Balding) *dwlt: hdwy over 3f out: wd st: in tch and rdn over 2f out: n.d* **9/1**

0/0- **8** 14 **Atlantic Affair (IRE)**[59] 7282 3-9-6 75........................ JFEgan 3 27
(Mark Johnston) *cl up: pushed along and lost pl bef 1/2-way: in rr after* **14/1**

1m 42.64s (-1.06) **Going Correction** -0.15s/f (Stan)
**WFA** 3 from 5yo+ 1lb **8** Ran SP% **114.3**
Speed ratings (Par 100): **99,98,98,97,91 90,89,75**
CSF £49.09 CT £192.11 TOTE £4.00: £1.30, £3.70, £1.60; EX 46.80 Trifecta £434.50.
**Owner** Ferrybank Properties Limited **Bred** Sheikh Sultan Bin Khalifa Al Nayhan **Trained** Danethorpe, Notts

**FOCUS**
An ordinary fillies' handicap in which the first four pulled well clear. The winner is only rated to form.

### 8178 CORAL APP DOWNLOAD FROM THE APP STORE CLAIMING STKS — 1m 3f (F)
**1:25** (1:25) (Class 6) 3-Y-0+ **£1,940** (£577; £288; £144) **Stalls** Low

Form RPR

141- **1** **Reve De Nuit (USA)**[42] 7651 8-9-2 92........................ JoeyHaynes(3) 1 94
(K R Burke) *sn slt ld on inner: pushed clr over 2f out: wandered and shkn up ent fnl f: easily* **1/6**[1]

064- **2** 9 **Sofias Number One (USA)**[42] 7651 6-8-4 65 ow2(b) AdamMcLean(7) 4 71
(Roy Bowring) *cl up: rdn along 3f out: chsd wnr and drvn thrght fnl 2f: kpt on: no ch w wnr* **10/1**[3]

000- **3** 9 **Energia Eros (BRZ)**[32] 7784 5-9-5 84..........................(b) JFEgan 3 64
(John Berry) *hld up in tch: hdwy to chse ldng pair 4f out: rdn 3f out: sn drvn and one pce* **14/1**

060- **4** 8 **King's Warrior (FR)**[26] 7850 7-9-3 85........................ PaulMulrennan 5 48
(Peter Chapple-Hyam) *trckd ldng pair on inner: rdn along 5f out: sn outpcd and bhd* **5/1**[2]

0/4- **5** 4 1/2 **Worcharlie'slass**[47] 7541 3-8-0 42 ow3.................(p) ConnorBeasley(3) 6 30
(Michael Herrington) *cl up on outer: rdn along 6f out: sn outpcd and bhd* **80/1**

2m 23.73s (-4.27) **Going Correction** -0.15s/f (Stan)
**WFA** 3 from 5yo+ 4lb **5** Ran SP% **119.3**
Speed ratings (Par 101): **109,102,95,90,86**
CSF £3.91 TOTE £1.20: £1.10, £3.00; EX 3.40 Trifecta £13.80.
**Owner** Mrs Z Wentworth **Bred** Ecurie Du Haras De Meautry **Trained** Middleham Moor, N Yorks

**FOCUS**
As uncompetitive a claimer as you are ever likely to see. The runner-up is a key to the form.

### 8179 UNIBET RACING APP NURSERY H'CAP — 6f (F)
**1:55** (1:56) (Class 6) (0-60,59) 2-Y-0 **£2,264** (£673; £336; £168) **Stalls** Low

Form RPR

423- **1** **Pancake Day**[18] 7948 2-8-12 50................................ AndrewElliott 1 53
(Jason Ward) *trckd ldr on inner: hdwy 2f out: rdn to ld over 1f out: hung rt ent fnl f: sn drvn and kpt on* **10/1**

550- **2** nk **Ifittakesforever (IRE)**[8] 8069 2-9-6 58..........................(e[1]) GrahamLee 6 60
(John Butler) *trckd ldrs: hdwy over 2f out: chsd ldrs and rdn over 1f out: drvn and kpt on wl fnl f* **14/1**

605- **3** 1 **Bannister Bell (IRE)**[28] 7824 2-9-0 52........................ JFEgan 8 51
(David Evans) *led: rdn along over 2f out: hdd over 1f out and sn drvn: no ex wl ins fnl f* **10/1**

600- **4** 5 **Kyllach Me (IRE)**[38] 7712 2-8-4 45.......................... ConnorBeasley(3) 5 29
(Bryan Smart) *in rr: hdwy and wd st: rdn over 2f out: kpt on fnl f: nrst fin* **9/1**

550- **5** 1/2 **Freedom Rose (IRE)**[83] 6663 2-8-7 45........................ PatrickMathers 3 28
(Derek Shaw) *towards rr: hdwy on inner 3f out: sn rdn and kpt on appr fnl f: nrst fin* **66/1**

446- **6** hd **Freeze The Secret (IRE)**[15] 7991 2-9-3 55.................. FergalLynch 11 37
(David C Griffiths) *chsd ldrs: rdn along over 2f out: grad wknd* **25/1**

001- **7** 3/4 **Milady Eileen (IRE)**[28] 7824 2-8-9 52...................... SammyJoBell(5) 7 32
(Richard Fahey) *in tch: wd st: rdn along over 2f out: sn drvn and n.d* **9/4**[1]

060- **8** 2 1/2 **Yorkshire (IRE)**[15] 7994 2-9-7 59.............................. RobertWinston 10 31
(Shaun Harris) *prom: effrt and cl up 3f out: rdn over 2f out: sn drvn and wknd* **9/2**[2]

325- **9** 2 1/2 **Purple Surprise**[15] 7991 2-8-7 52........................ AlfieWarwick(7) 12 17
(Andrew Reid) *a towards rr* **8/1**[3]

053- **10** 6 **Striking Stone**[21] 7912 2-8-9 47..........................(p) MartinDwyer 4
(Jo Hughes) *chsd ldrs: rdn along bef 1/2-way: sn wknd* **16/1**

006- **11** 4 1/2 **Vejovis**[61] 7223 2-9-7 59..........................(p) LukeMorris 13
(Sir Mark Prescott Bt) *s.i.s: a bhd* **9/1**

1m 16.31s (-0.19) **Going Correction** -0.15s/f (Stan) **11** Ran SP% **116.1**
Speed ratings (Par 94): **95,94,93,86,85 85,84,81,78,70 64**
CSF £139.63 CT £1436.45 TOTE £7.80: £2.70, £4.20, £3.00; EX 114.80 Trifecta £967.10.
**Owner** Stuart Matheson & Jill Ward **Bred** Stuart Matheson **Trained** Middleham, N Yorks

**FOCUS**
A moderate nursery in which only one of the 11 remaining runners had previously been successful. Not form to be with.

### 8180 UNIBET OFFER DAILY JOCKEY/TRAINER SPECIALS H'CAP — 5f (F)
**2:30** (2:31) (Class 5) (0-75,75) 3-Y-0+ **£2,911** (£866; £432; £216) **Stalls** High

Form RPR

005- **1** **Sleepy Blue Ocean**[33] 7767 8-9-7 75..........................(p) RobertWinston 4 85
(John Balding) *cl up: slt ld 1/2-way: rdn over 1f out: drvn ins fnl f: kpt on wl towards fin* **11/2**[3]

410- **2** 3/4 **Alpha Tauri (USA)**[154] 4288 8-9-1 72........................ JoeyHaynes(3) 3 79
(Charles Smith) *in tch: hdwy wl over 1f out: rdn to chse ldng pair ins fnl f: kpt on* **20/1**

000- **3** 1/2 **Shawkantango**[18] 7949 7-8-12 66..........................(v) PatrickMathers 1 72
(Derek Shaw) *s.i.s and bhd: rdn along and hdwy on far side 1/2-way: styd on u.p appr fnl f: nrst fin* **16/1**

304- **4** 1 **Scoreline**[7] 8082 3-9-1 69........................................ DanielTudhope 5 71
(David O'Meara) *prom: rdn along 2f out: drvn ent fnl f and kpt on same pce* **11/4**[1]

061- **5** shd **Rambo Will**[41] 7670 6-9-4 72.................................. FergalLynch 8 74
(J R Jenkins) *towards rr: hdwy 2f out: sn rdn and kpt on wl fnl f: nrst fin* **8/1**

606- **6** 1/2 **Sir Geoffrey (IRE)**[33] 7761 8-8-9 68..........................(p) TimClark(5) 7 68
(Scott Dixon) *chsd ldrs: rdn along 2f out: drvn and kpt on fnl f* **10/1**

200- **7** 1 1/4 **Bapak Bangsawan**[18] 7949 4-8-11 70........................ AnnStokell(5) 11 65
(Ann Stokell) *cl up: rdn along 1/2-way: sn drvn and grad wknd* **66/1**

000- **8** nk **First In Command (IRE)**[24] 7888 9-9-5 73....................(t) ShaneKelly 2 82
(Daniel Mark Loughnane) *prom: effrt to chal over 1f out: sn rdn to dispute ld and ev ch whn broke down last 100yds: fatally injured* **14/1**

016- **9** 1/2 **Coiste Bodhar (IRE)**[15] 7989 3-8-11 65..........................(p) LukeMorris 10 57
(Scott Dixon) *slt ld to 1/2-way: sn rdn and wknd wl over 1f out* **14/1**

000- **10** 3/4 **Six Wives**[12] 8025 7-9-4 72..........................(p) PaulMulrennan 12 62
(Scott Dixon) *chsd ldrs: rdn along wl over 1f out: sn btn* **33/1**

035- **11** 1/2 **Mops Angel**[28] 7826 3-8-2 63.............................. JaneElliott(7) 13 51
(Michael Appleby) *a towards rr* **14/1**

332- **12** 1 3/4 **Indian Tinker**[33] 7761 5-9-6 74..........................(v) LiamJones 9 56
(Robert Cowell) *dwlt: a in rr* **5/1**[2]

50- **13** 1/2 **Rock On Candy**[48] 7534 5-9-1 69.............................. GrahamLee 6 49
(John Spearing) *chsd ldrs: rdn along over 2f out: sn wknd* **33/1**

59.58s (-0.12) **Going Correction** +0.075s/f (Slow) **13** Ran SP% **116.9**
Speed ratings (Par 103): **103,101,101,99,99 98,96,95,95,93 93,90,89**
CSF £114.75 CT £1115.59 TOTE £7.20: £2.70, £7.30, £5.50; EX 132.50 Trifecta £1447.50.
**Owner** Billy Herring **Bred** Exors Of The Late N Ahamad & P C Scott **Trained** Scrooby, S Yorks

**FOCUS**
An ordinary sprint handicap in which eight of the 13 runners had been successful at least once over this CD. Those drawn low dominated, but the race was marred by the fatal injury incurred by First In Command.

## 8181 DAILY PRICE BOOSTS AT UNIBET MEDIAN AUCTION MAIDEN STKS 6f (F)
**3:00** (3:00) (Class 6) 3-5-Y-O **£1,940** (£577; £288; £144) **Stalls** Low

Form RPR
005- **1** **Satellite Express (IRE)**[6] 8090 3-9-0 58..............................(v[1]) JFEgan 3 57
(David Evans) *cl up: chsd ldr 1/2-way: chal 2f out and sn rdn: drvn over 1f out: kpt on to ld last 110yds* **9/4**[1]
420- **2** 2 **Lazy Sioux**[7] 8088 3-9-0 53.............................. JasonHart 5 51
(Richard Guest) *led: jnd and rdn 2f out: drvn over 1f out: edgd rt ent fnl f: hdd and kpt on same pce last 110yds* **11/4**[2]
005- **3** 1 3/4 **Bold Max**[13] 8008 3-9-5 42..............................(b) LukeMorris 4 50
(Zoe Davison) *chsd ldrs: rdn along over 2f out: drvn and kpt on same pce appr fnl f* **14/1**
**4** 4 1/2 **Cookie Ring (IRE)**[45] 5838 3-9-2 51.............................. DeclanBates(3) 2 36
(Patrick Holmes) *chsd ldng pair on inner: cl up wl over 2f out: sn rdn: drvn wl over 1f out and sn wknd* **7/1**[3]
003- **5** 2 1/2 **Knockamany Bends (IRE)**[32] 7782 4-9-5 52.............. RobertWinston 7 28
(John Wainwright) *in rr: hdwy on outer 1/2-way: rdn along over 2f out: sn no imp* **9/4**[1]
1m 16.5s **Going Correction** -0.15s/f (Stan) **5 Ran SP% 107.4**
Speed ratings (Par 101): **94,91,89,83,79**
CSF £8.24 TOTE £2.80: £2.30, £1.60; EX 8.50 Trifecta £42.70.
**Owner** Keith M Pinfield **Bred** Razza Del Pian Del Lago **Trained** Pandy, Monmouths
**FOCUS**
A desperately weak maiden in which the two fillies (the highest rated pair in the field) dominated throughout. Unconvincing form.

## 8182 DAILY PRICE BOOSTS AT UNIBET H'CAP 6f (F)
**3:30** (3:30) (Class 5) (0-75,75) 3-Y-O+ **£2,587** (£770; £384; £192) **Stalls** Low

Form RPR
15- **1** **Razin' Hell**[95] 6297 3-8-13 67..............................(v) BenCurtis 10 80
(Alan McCabe) *qckly away and cl up: led after 2f: rdn over 1f out: drvn and edgd lft ins fnl f: kpt on wl towards fin* **6/1**
030- **2** 1 **Shades Of Silk**[22] 7906 3-8-10 67.............................. ConnorBeasley(3) 8 77
(James Given) *qckly away: slt ld 2f: cl up: rdn to chal over 1f out and ev ch: drvn and edgd sltly lft ins fnl f: kpt on same pce* **9/1**
242- **3** 3/4 **Thorpe Bay**[18] 7949 5-9-0 73.............................. AlistairRawlinson(5) 1 81+
(Michael Appleby) *towards rr: swtchd rt to outer and wd st: hdwy over 2f out: sn rdn and styd on wl fnl f: nrst fin* **9/2**[2]
022- **4** 3 1/4 **Speightowns Kid (USA)**[7] 8082 6-8-5 64 ow2..........(b) AnnStokell(5) 4 61
(Ann Stokell) *in tch: hdwy on outer to join ldrs 1/2-way: wd st: rdn over 2f out: no imp appr fnl f* **8/1**
003- **5** 1/2 **Quickaswecan**[8] 8071 3-9-6 74.............................. JFEgan 9 70
(Mark Johnston) *dwlt: hdwy to chse ldng pair after 2f: rdn over 2f out: swtchd lft wl over 1f out: wknd* **5/1**[3]
060- **6** 1/2 **Abi Scarlet (IRE)**[11] 8045 5-9-7 75.............................. LukeMorris 5 69
(Scott Dixon) *chsd ldrs: rdn along wl over 2f out: grad wknd* **8/1**
360- **7** 5 **Amosite**[32] 7775 8-9-2 70..............................(v) FergalLynch 2 48
(J R Jenkins) *in tch on inner: rdn along wl over 2f out: sn wknd* **50/1**
030- **8** 6 **Pennine Warrior**[49] 7505 3-9-7 75..............................(p) PaulMulrennan 3 34
(Scott Dixon) *dwlt and sn swtchd wd to outer: sn outpcd and bhd fr 1/2-way* **9/4**[1]
056- **9** 5 **Flighty Clarets (IRE)**[18] 7949 4-8-11 65.............................. GeorgeChaloner 6 8
(Richard Fahey) *chsd ldrs: rdn along wl over 2f out: sn wknd* **25/1**
1m 15.17s (-1.33) **Going Correction** -0.15s/f (Stan) **9 Ran SP% 117.9**
Speed ratings (Par 103): **102,100,99,95,94 94,87,79,72**
CSF £59.83 CT £268.41 TOTE £7.40: £2.60, £3.50, £1.90; EX 70.70 Trifecta £430.40.
**Owner** Timms, Timms, McCabe & Warke **Bred** Alan J McCabe **Trained** Averham Park, Notts
**FOCUS**
An ordinary sprint handicap, but an interesting race for the grade and a bit of a touch was landed. The form is rated on the positive side.
T/Plt: £144.70 to a £1 stake. Pool: £70,925.35 - 357.68 winning units. T/Qpdt: £40.20 to a £1 stake. Pool: £5807.84 - 106.80 winning units. JR

# 8169 KEMPTON (A.W) (R-H)
Wednesday, December 17
**OFFICIAL GOING: Polytrack: standard**
Wind: Moderate, across (away from stands) Weather: Overcast with showers

## 8183 WATCH RACING UK ON 3 DEVICES (S) STKS 7f (P)
**4:05** (4:07) (Class 6) 2-Y-O **£2,264** (£673; £336; £168) **Stalls** Low

Form RPR
135- **1** **Mecado (IRE)**[7] 8091 2-8-9 72.............................. TomMarquand(7) 1 64
(Richard Hannon) *mde virtually all: shkn up whn pressed over 1f out: rdn and kpt on wl fnl f* **13/8**[2]
244- **2** 3/4 **Dusty Blue**[14] 8007 2-8-6 74.............................. LukeMorris 4 54
(Tony Carroll) *t.k.h: hld up in tch: wnt 2nd 2f out: sn shkn up to chal: nt qckn 1f out: kpt on but hld after* **8/13**[1]
300- **3** 2 1/2 **Aqlette**[54] 7421 2-8-6 61..............................(v[1]) JFEgan 3 54
(David Evans) *t.k.h: w wnr: lost 2nd and nt qckn 2f out: one pce after* **25/1**[3]
04- **4** 3 1/4 **Edw Gold (IRE)**[15] 7999 2-8-8 0.............................. DeclanBates(3) 2 59
(David Evans) *pushed along in last bef 1/2-way: struggling to stay in tch after: n.d* **50/1**
1m 27.36s (1.36) **Going Correction** +0.025s/f (Slow) **4 Ran SP% 105.8**
Speed ratings (Par 94): **93,92,89,85**
CSF £2.85 TOTE £4.10; EX 3.10 Trifecta £5.50.The winner was bought in for £4,800.
**Owner** Potensis Bloodstock Ltd & J Palmer Brown **Bred** J F Tuthill **Trained** East Everleigh, Wilts
■ The first winner for 16yo Tom Marquand.
**FOCUS**
A small turnout and obviously uncompetitive, but this wouldn't be the weakest seller that will be run here over the winter. However it's not hard to have reservations.

## 8184 DINE IN THE PANORAMIC MEDIAN AUCTION MAIDEN STKS 6f (P)
**4:40** (4:40) (Class 6) 2-Y-O **£2,264** (£673; £336; £168) **Stalls** Low

Form
**1** **Volunteer Point (IRE)** 2-9-0 0.............................. CharlesBishop 8 72+
(Mick Channon) *wl in tch: prog 2f out: edgd rt but rdn to ld jst over 1f out: kpt on wl and asserted last 100yds* **9/4**[2]
**2** 3/4 **Dutch Golden Age (IRE)** 2-9-5 0.............................. GeorgeBaker 2 75+
(Gary Moore) *trckd ldng pair: chsd ldr 2f out and sn chalng: nrly upsides 1f out: kpt on but hld by wnr last 100yds* **6/1**[3]
432- **3** 1 **Rahmah (IRE)**[18] 7973 2-9-5 76.............................. AdamKirby 4 72
(Robert Cowell) *led: drvn and hdd jst over 1f out: nt qckn and hld in 3rd whn sltly short of room ins fnl f* **11/10**[1]
0- **4** 2 1/2 **Born To Be Bad (IRE)**[7] 8092 2-9-5 0............ WilliamTwiston-Davies 7 65+
(Jamie Osborne) *dwlt: settled in last: rdn over 2f out: prog to take 4th fnl f: n.d but kpt on* **50/1**
00- **5** 2 **Thermal Column (IRE)**[15] 8000 2-9-5 0.............................. GeorgeChaloner 1 59
(Richard Fahey) *sn in 6th: tried to make prog over 2f out: no hdwy over 1f out* **25/1**
06- **6** 3 1/2 **Dippinganddiving (IRE)**[25] 7881 2-9-0 0.............................. RaulDaSilva 3 43
(Jose Santos) *chsd ldrs: wd bnd 3f out and sn rdn: wknd over 1f out* **100/1**
4- **7** 8 **On The Huh**[13] 8026 2-9-5 0.............................. TomQueally 9 24
(Michael Bell) *chsd ldr to over 2f out: wknd qckly* **8/1**
1m 12.96s (-0.14) **Going Correction** +0.025s/f (Slow) **7 Ran SP% 110.6**
Speed ratings (Par 94): **101,100,98,95,92 88,77**
CSF £14.67 TOTE £3.30: £1.80, £2.40; EX 16.00 Trifecta £35.10.
**Owner** Box 41 **Bred** G Strawbridge & London Thoroughbred Services Ltd **Trained** West Ilsley, Berks
**FOCUS**
No more than a fair maiden, but good performances from the front two on their debuts. The form could be rated a length higher.

## 8185 BETDAQ £50 FREE BET FILLIES' H'CAP 7f (P)
**5:10** (5:10) (Class 5) (0-75,74) 3-Y-O+ **£3,234** (£962; £481; £240) **Stalls** Low

Form RPR
004- **1** **Hill Of Dreams (IRE)**[9] 8068 5-8-12 65..............................(b) PatCosgrave 3 75+
(Dean Ivory) *chsd ldrs: rdn to go 3rd wl over 1f out: clsd to ld jst ins fnl f: styd on strly* **13/2**
363- **2** 2 1/2 **Childesplay**[12] 8038 3-8-9 62.............................. MartinLane 2 65
(Heather Main) *trckd ldr: rdn 2f out: led jst over 1f out to jst ins fnl f: outpcd* **25/1**
046- **3** 1/2 **A Legacy Of Love (IRE)**[37] 7729 3-9-7 74.............................. GeorgeBaker 4 76
(Amanda Perrett) *led: rdn 2f out: hdd and one pce jst over 1f out* **5/1**[2]
034- **4** 3/4 **Flamborough Breeze**[20] 7942 5-8-9 62..............................(bt) LiamKeniry 5 62
(Ed Vaughan) *hld up towards rr: cajoled along to make sme prog fr 2f out: rdn and kpt on same pce fnl f* **17/2**
206- **5** nk **Oasis Spirit**[34] 7758 4-9-3 70..............................(v) DavidProbert 7 69
(Andrew Balding) *in tch in midfield: sme prog 2f out: no imp on ldrs fnl f: one pce* **5/1**[2]
435- **6** 1/2 **Nimble Kimble**[167] 3890 3-9-6 73.............................. LukeMorris 10 71
(James Eustace) *hld up in last pair: shkn up 2f out: rdn and kpt on fr over 1f out: nrst fin* **10/1**
060- **7** 2 3/4 **Plover**[14] 8013 4-8-7 60 oh1.............................. JimmyQuinn 6 50
(Michael Attwater) *t.k.h early: chsd ldrs: lost pl and pushed along 1/2-way: struggling over 2f out* **25/1**
504- **8** nk **Welsh Sunrise**[16] 7993 4-9-6 73.............................. GrahamGibbons 8 65
(Stuart Williams) *chsd ldng pair: rdn over 2f out: lost 3rd and wknd wl over 1f out: eased* **9/2**[1]
/50- **9** 1/2 **Boadicee**[179] 3476 3-9-4 71.............................. NickyMackay 1 59
(John Gosden) *slowly away and pushed along in last early: rdn and no real prog 2f out* **6/1**[3]
030- **10** 1 1/4 **Shaunas Spirit (IRE)**[49] 7530 6-8-10 70.............................. PaulBooth(7) 9 55
(Dean Ivory) *t.k.h in midfield: rdn over 2f out: sn wknd* **25/1**
660- **11** 7 **Honeymoon Express (IRE)**[25] 7888 4-8-11 69...(p) ShelleyBirkett(5) 12 35
(Julia Feilden) *racd on outer: towards rr: wd bnd 3f out: sn wknd and bhd* **50/1**
1m 25.48s (-0.52) **Going Correction** +0.025s/f (Slow) **11 Ran SP% 112.3**
Speed ratings (Par 100): **103,100,99,98,98 97,94,94,93,92 84**
CSF £157.08 CT £660.86 TOTE £7.70: £2.20, £4.90, £2.00; EX 107.60 Trifecta £745.40.
**Owner** I Gethin & R Gethin **Bred** Miss Breda Wright **Trained** Radlett, Herts
**FOCUS**
Just a modest level, but a number of these looked fairly handicapped and a case could be made for the majority of the field, so competitive enough for the grade. The third looks the best guide.

## 8186 WIN £10,000,000 ON THE BETDAQ COLOSSUS H'CAP 6f (P)
**5:40** (5:42) (Class 5) (0-70,69) 3-Y-O+ **£3,234** (£962; £481; £240) **Stalls** Low

Form RPR
605- **1** **Welease Bwian (IRE)**[33] 7775 5-8-10 65.............................. AaronJones(7) 2 74
(Stuart Williams) *restless stalls: in tch in midfield: prog 2f out: cajoled along to chal fnl f: styd on wl to ld narrowly last 50yds* **14/1**
100- **2** hd **Pour La Victoire (IRE)**[14] 8017 4-9-6 68..............................(b) LukeMorris 3 76
(Tony Carroll) *t.k.h: trckd ldng pair: gng easily over 2f out: rdn to ld 1f out: sn pressed: kpt on wl but narrowly hdd last 50yds* **2/1**[1]
340- **3** 2 1/4 **Bookmaker**[37] 7735 4-8-10 58.............................. WilliamCarson 11 60
(John Bridger) *wl in rr: rdn over 2f out: prog wl over 1f out: sustained effrt to take 3rd nr fin: no ch to threaten* **33/1**
444- **4** 3/4 **Temple Road (IRE)**[12] 8040 6-9-7 69..............................(t) LiamKeniry 7 68
(Milton Bradley) *trckd ldrs: poised to chal gng easily 2f out: asked to deliver jst over 1f out: no rspnse and qckly btn* **7/1**[3]
014- **5** 1/2 **Misstemper (IRE)**[147] 4544 3-9-4 66..............................(p) RaulDaSilva 8 64
(Jose Santos) *mde most fr wd draw but pestered: hdd and fdd 1f out* **20/1**
000- **6** 1/2 **Rigolleto (IRE)**[97] 6249 6-9-6 68.............................. AdamKirby 9 64
(Anabel K Murphy) *gd spd fr wd draw and pressed ldr: stl chalng jst over 1f out: fdd* **12/1**
300- **7** nk **Aye Aye Skipper (IRE)**[107] 5987 4-8-4 59.............................. PaulBooth(7) 5 55
(Dean Ivory) *sn chsd ldrs: rdn over 2f out: lost pl and struggling for pce after* **33/1**
600- **8** 1/2 **Archibald Thorburn (IRE)**[34] 7759 3-9-6 68..........(v[1]) CharlesBishop 6 62
(Peter Hedger) *dwlt: mostly in last tl prog on inner jst over 2f out: no imp on ldrs 1f out: fdd* **8/1**
404- **9** nk **Classic Pursuit**[16] 7989 3-9-5 67..............................(p) TomQueally 4 60
(Ronald Harris) *t.k.h: hld up in midfield: rdn and no prog over 2f out: n.d over 1f out* **7/2**[2]
400- **10** 4 **Italian Tom (IRE)**[19] 7950 7-9-0 62.............................. RobertWinston 10 43
(Ronald Harris) *dwlt: a wl in rr: bhd over 1f out* **20/1**
630- **11** 1/2 **Costa Filey**[21] 7931 3-9-7 69.............................. GeorgeBaker 1 49
(Ed Vaughan) *blindfold off late and slowly away: plld hrd in rr: no prog over 2f out: sn bhd* **9/1**
1m 12.5s (-0.60) **Going Correction** +0.025s/f (Slow) **11 Ran SP% 118.9**
Speed ratings (Par 103): **105,104,101,100,100 99,99,98,97,92 91**
CSF £40.97 CT £956.84 TOTE £12.10: £3.20, £1.60, £9.90; EX 57.50 Trifecta £1598.70.
**Owner** W E Enticknap **Bred** Nils Koop **Trained** Newmarket, Suffolk

**FOCUS**
A moderate, run of the mill sprint handicap. There wasn't much pace on and they went half a second slower than the earlier 2yo maiden.

## 8187 BETDAQ - NO PREMIUM CHARGE MAIDEN AUCTION STKS 1m (P)
6:10 (6:10) (Class 5) 2-Y-O £3,234 (£962; £481; £240) Stalls Low

Form RPR
22- **1** **Quest For Wonder**[20] 7941 2-8-12 0 LukeMorris 2 72
(James Tate) *trckd ldng pair: wnt 2nd 3f out: led over 2f out but immediately jnd and rdn: drvn over 1f out: kpt on to assert ins fnl f* **2/7**[1]

0- **2** *1 1/4* **Faith Matters (IRE)**[20] 7941 2-8-11 0 JFEgan 5 68+
(Marco Botti) *dwlt but sn chsd ldrs: wd bnd 3f out but prog to chal sn after: nt qckn 2f out but pressed wnr after: no ex last 100yds* **4/1**[2]

35- **3** *5* **Little Miss Mighty**[147] 4541 2-8-7 0 JackMitchell 4 53
(Nick Littmoden) *t.k.h: led to over 2f out: steadily wknd over 1f out* **14/1**[3]

**4** *3* **Deftera Lad (IRE)** 2-8-12 0 ShaneKelly 3 51
(Pat Phelan) *slowly away: hld up in last pair: shkn up over 2f out: sn lft bhd: rn green but plugged on* **66/1**

0- **5** *2* **Mr Sundowner (USA)**[32] 7811 2-9-3 0 AdamKirby 6 51
(Noel Quinlan) *t.k.h: pressed ldr: jinked 6f out: lost 2nd 3f out: sn btn* **16/1**

00- **6** *1* **Sporting Bob**[28] 7835 2-8-12 0 JimmyQuinn 1 44
(Robert Eddery) *hld up in last pair: pushed along and lft bhd fr over 2f out* **100/1**

1m 41.66s (1.86) **Going Correction** +0.025s/f (Slow) **6** Ran SP% **112.8**
Speed ratings (Par 96): **91,89,84,81,79 78**
CSF £1.87 TOTE £1.10: £1.02, £1.90; EX 2.20 Trifecta £4.60.
**Owner** Saif Ali **Bred** Card Bloodstock **Trained** Newmarket, Suffolk

**FOCUS**
No depth to this maiden, but not exactly a penalty kick for the winner.

## 8188 BETDAQ 50% REFUND FIRST 3 MONTHS H'CAP 1m (P)
6:40 (6:41) (Class 4) (0-85,85) 3-Y-O+ £5,175 (£1,540; £769; £384) Stalls Low

Form RPR
431- **1** **Rizal Park (IRE)**[12] 8041 3-8-6 71 DavidProbert 5 80
(Andrew Balding) *trckd ldrs: wnt 3rd 3f out gng wl: shkn up to cl fr 2f out: drvn to ld jst ins fnl f: styd on wl* **9/2**[2]

611- **2** *1 1/4* **Nigel's Destiny (USA)**[37] 7732 3-9-2 81 ShaneKelly 3 87
(Jeremy Noseda) *pressed ldr: led 1/2-way: rdn over 2f out: hdd jst ins fnl f: kpt on but readily hld last 100yds* **11/10**[1]

313- **3** *1/2* **Miss Buckshot (IRE)**[25] 7885 3-9-0 79 TomQueally 7 84
(Rae Guest) *settled in last trio: pushed along 3f out: rdn and prog fr 2f out to take 3rd ins fnl f: styd on* **5/1**[3]

10- **4** *2 1/4* **Sensible Way (USA)**[179] 3476 3-9-0 79 MartinDwyer 1 79
(Richard Hannon) *led to 1/2-way: pressed ldr to over 1f out: wknd ins fnl f* **20/1**

266- **5** *nk* **Extraterrestrial**[26] 7870 10-8-13 77 GeorgeChaloner 9 77
(Richard Fahey) *hld up in last trio: rdn over 2f out: hanging and hd high after: styd on ins fnl f whn r was over* **20/1**

010- **6** *2 3/4* **Steventon Star**[18] 7971 3-9-6 85 (t) WilliamTwiston-Davies 4 78
(Michael Scudamore) *v awkward s: hld up in last trio: rdn over 2f out: no great prog over 1f out: wl btn after* **10/1**

513- **7** *7* **Barnmore**[76] 6886 6-8-13 77 CharlesBishop 8 69
(Peter Hedger) *chsd ldrs: rdn over 2f out: wkng whn heavily eased fnl f w jockey looking down* **6/1**

006- **8** *6* **Top Diktat**[14] 8012 6-8-13 84 HectorCrouch(7) 6 48
(Gary Moore) *racd wd: chsd ldng pair: rdn 1/2-way: wknd rapidly 3f out* **33/1**

1m 38.66s (-1.14) **Going Correction** +0.025s/f (Slow)
**WFA** 3 from 6yo+ 1lb **8** Ran SP% **112.2**
Speed ratings (Par 105): **106,104,104,102,101 98,91,85**
CSF £9.23 CT £24.09 TOTE £6.00: £1.30, £1.20, £1.70; EX 10.90 Trifecta £47.90.
**Owner** L L Register, Martin & Valerie Slade **Bred** Irish National Stud **Trained** Kingsclere, Hants

**FOCUS**
A decent race for this time of year and they went three seconds quicker than the preceding juvenile maiden.

## 8189 WATCH RACING UK ANYWHERE H'CAP 2m (P)
7:10 (7:10) (Class 6) (0-60,66) 3-Y-O+ £2,264 (£673; £336; £168) Stalls Low

Form RPR
333- **1** **Haines**[14] 8021 3-8-7 49 DavidProbert 9 63+
(Andrew Balding) *mde all: won early skirmish for ld then set stdy pce: stretched on 5f out: sent for home 3f out: wl clr 2f out: rdn out* **2/1**[1]

231- **2** *9* **Hazzaat (IRE)**[9] 8070 4-10-4 66 6ex (v) TomQueally 1 69
(Neil King) *hld up in last pair: plenty to do once pce lifted 5f out: rdn and prog over 2f out: kpt on to take remote 2nd last stride* **7/2**[2]

15P- **3** *shd* **Graylyn Ruby (FR)**[42] 7657 9-9-9 57 AdamKirby 4 60
(Robert Eddery) *hld up in midfield: gng bttr than most over 3f out: rdn over 2f out and sn chsd clr wnr: no imp after: lost 2nd post* **8/1**

000- **4** *2 3/4* **Danglydontask**[50] 7517 3-8-1 46 DannyBrock(3) 6 46
(David Arbuthnot) *hld up in tch: plenty to do once pce lifted 5f out: rdn wl over 2f out: plugged on but no ch* **12/1**

034- **5** *1* **Born To Reign**[14] 8010 3-8-5 47 (v) LukeMorris 7 45
(Michael Bell) *prom: chsd wnr 9f out: rdn 4f out: wl outpcd fr 3f out: lost 2nd and fdd 2f out* **13/2**[3]

305- **6** *4 1/2* **Noor Al Haya (IRE)**[9] 8070 4-9-4 59 CharlotteJenner(7) 5 52
(Laura Mongan) *slowly away: hld up in last pair: plenty to do once pce lifted 5f out: sme prog on inner over 2f out: wknd over 1f out* **14/1**

550- **7** *2* **Perfect Outcome**[14] 8011 3-8-11 53 LiamKeniry 3 44
(Patrick Chamings) *wl in tch: rdn and no prog over 2f out whn already outpcd: wknd* **33/1**

401- **8** *15* **Indian Scout**[16] 7990 6-9-1 49 (b) RobertWinston 8 22
(Anabel K Murphy) *chsd wnr to 9f out: styd prom tl wknd rapidly over 2f out: t.o* **10/1**

560- **9** *8* **Magicalmysterytour (IRE)**[29] 7823 11-9-3 51 ChrisCatlin 2 14
(Willie Musson) *t.k.h: in midfield tl wknd 5f out: sn last and t.o* **20/1**

3m 31.78s (1.68) **Going Correction** +0.025s/f (Slow)
**WFA** 3 from 4yo+ 8lb **9** Ran SP% **111.2**
Speed ratings (Par 101): **96,91,91,90,89 87,86,78,74**
CSF £8.18 CT £41.59 TOTE £2.40: £1.10, £1.40, £2.90; EX 9.60 Trifecta £32.60.
**Owner** Bow River Racing **Bred** Spring Bloodstock Ltd **Trained** Kingsclere, Hants

**FOCUS**
A weak staying race which was turned into a procession.
T/Plt: £46.80 to a £1 stake. Pool: £68,440.72 - 1,066.49 winning tickets. T/Qpdt: £8.30 to a £1 stake. Pool: £10,549.72 - 935.01 winning tickets. JN

# 8097 LINGFIELD (L-H)
Wednesday, December 17

**OFFICIAL GOING: Polytrack: standard to slow**
Wind: light, across Weather: OVERCAST

## 8190 CORAL APP DOWNLOAD FROM THE APP STORE CLASSIFIED (S) STKS 1m 2f (P)
12:30 (12:31) (Class 6) 3-Y-O+ £1,940 (£577; £288; £144) Stalls Low

Form RPR
100- **1** **Classic Colori (IRE)**[22] 7914 7-9-9 70 (b) WilliamTwiston-Davies 7 74
(Martin Keighley) *in tch in midfield: rdn over 4f out: drvn to ld over 1f out: styd on* **8/1**[3]

314- **2** *3 1/2* **Pearl Ransom (IRE)**[272] 1023 4-9-9 60 (v) RobertWinston 2 67
(Alan Bailey) *t.k.h: chsd ldr for 2f: chsd ldrs after: rdn over 2f out: sltly outpcd over 1f out: styd on u.p fnl f to go 3rd towards fin* **7/2**[1]

006- **3** *1/2* **Refreshestheparts (USA)**[15] 7998 5-9-3 68 (t) PatCosgrave 4 60
(George Baker) *in tch in midfield: rdn over 2f out: ev ch over 1f out: outpcd by wnr and btn jst ins fnl f: lost 2nd towards fin* **9/2**[2]

300- **4** *6* **Incendo**[74] 6942 8-9-9 65 (v) HayleyTurner 1 55
(Conor Dore) *v.s.a: clsd to bk of field 7f out: rdn 3f out: sn struggling: wl hld over 1f out: plugged on* **10/1**

000- **5** *7* **Well Painted (IRE)**[15] 7998 5-9-9 68 (bt) AdamKirby 10 41
(Andy Turnell) *wnt lft and awkward leaving stalls: sn bustled up and rcvrd to chse ldr 8f out: drvn to ld over 2f out: hdd over 1f out: sn btn and fdd fnl f* **7/2**[1]

105- **6** *1 3/4* **King Olav (UAE)**[190] 3078 9-9-9 70 LukeMorris 5 38
(Tony Carroll) *in tch in midfield: rdn over 4f out: outpcd and btn 2f out: eased towards fin* **8/1**[3]

004- **7** *1 1/2* **It's Only Business**[7] 8097 4-8-12 65 (p) RyanWhile(5) 8 29+
(Bill Turner) *racd keenly: led tl hdd and rdn over 2f out: sn btn: wknd over 1f out* **9/2**[2]

5/6- **8** *38* **Al Guwair (IRE)**[30] 7401 4-9-3 60 (p) WilliamCarson 3
(Mark Hoad) *niggled along in last pair: dropped to last 5f out: lost tch over 3f out: t.o* **33/1**

2m 7.79s (1.19) **Going Correction** +0.125s/f (Slow)
**WFA** 3 from 4yo+ 3lb **8** Ran SP% **115.1**
Speed ratings (Par 101): **100,97,96,92,86 85,83,53**
CSF £36.39 TOTE £13.10: £3.50, £1.10, £1.50; EX 53.00 Trifecta £445.90.The winner was bought in for 6,000gns.
**Owner** Mrs L M Ponting **Bred** Frank Dunne **Trained** Condicote, Gloucs

**FOCUS**
The opening contest was a modest seller, in which they went a decent gallop on standard to slow Polytrack, but the winning time was slow. The winner was fully entitled to win on these terms on earlier 2014 form.

## 8191 32RED.COM/IRISH STALLION FARMS EBF MAIDEN FILLIES' STKS (BOBIS RACE) 7f 1y(P)
1:00 (1:01) (Class 5) 2-Y-O £3,067 (£905; £453) Stalls Low

Form RPR
3- **1** **Falling Petals (IRE)**[222] 2107 2-9-0 0 NickyMackay 7 75+
(John Gosden) *mde all: shkn up and fnd ex over 1f out: in command and r.o wl fnl f: readily* **5/4**[1]

02- **2** *2* **Nancy Astor**[48] 7549 2-9-0 0 SteveDrowne 6 70+
(John Gosden) *bmpd s: t.k.h: chsd ldrs: wnt 2nd and pressing wnr jst over 2f out: pushed along and styd on same pce fr over 1f out* **5/1**[2]

**3** *1/2* **Middle England (IRE)** 2-9-0 0 AdamKirby 4 68+
(Charlie Appleby) *t.k.h: hld up in tch in midfield: hdwy to chse ldng pair and rdn over 1f out: r.o same pce fnl f* **5/1**[2]

4- **4** *5* **Omotenashi (USA)**[20] 7944 2-9-0 0 JackMitchell 9 55
(Roger Varian) *chsd ldr tl jst over 2f out: rdn and outpcd over 1f out: wknd ins fnl f* **8/1**

0- **5** *hd* **Packed House**[28] 7833 2-9-0 0 SebSanders 3 54
(Ralph Beckett) *hld up in last quartet: rdn and outpcd over 2f out: no ch w ldrs but kpt on ins fnl f* **10/1**

600- **6** *3/4* **Fleetwood Poppy**[105] 6032 2-9-0 50 JimmyQuinn 11 52
(Michael Attwater) *t.k.h: hld up in tch in midfield: rdn and outpcd over 2f out: no threat to ldrs fr over 1f out* **100/1**

**7** *1 1/4* **Moon Eyes** 2-9-0 0 ShaneKelly 5 49
(William Haggas) *broke wl: in tch in midfield: shkn up and unable qck over 2f out: rdn over 1f out: sn wknd* **7/1**[3]

**8** *3 1/2* **Dutchess Of Art** 2-9-0 0 LiamJones 10 39
(Olly Stevens) *dwlt: in tch in last quartet: rdn and struggling over 2f out: n.d fnl 2f* **50/1**

00- **9** *12* **Solveig's Song**[34] 7756 2-9-0 0 HayleyTurner 8 7
(Steve Woodman) *a towards rr: rdn 4f out: wknd over 2f out* **100/1**

**10** *22* **Gold Leaf** 2-9-0 0 LiamKeniry 1
(John E Long) *sn dropped to rr and rdn along: lost tch 3f out: t.o* **100/1**

1m 26.17s (1.37) **Going Correction** +0.125s/f (Slow) **10** Ran SP% **115.4**
Speed ratings (Par 93): **97,94,94,88,88 87,85,81,68,43**
CSF £7.64 TOTE £2.50: £1.20, £1.70, £1.10; EX 7.30 Trifecta £22.30.
**Owner** HRH Princess Haya Of Jordan **Bred** Darley **Trained** Newmarket, Suffolk
■ Kelloura was withdrawn. Price at the time of withdrawal 100-1. Rule 4 does not apply.

**FOCUS**
A fair juvenile fillies' maiden in which they went a proper gallop, but the first four were always prominent. The first two represent the same owner and trainer.

## 8192 32RED/IRISH STALLION FARMS EBF MAIDEN STKS 7f 1y(P)
1:30 (1:31) (Class 5) 2-Y-O £3,067 (£905; £453) Stalls Low

Form RPR
**1** **Master Of Irony (IRE)** 2-9-0 0 JamieSpencer 7 73+
(Ralph Beckett) *dwlt: in tch in last quartet: rdn and effrt whn wd bnd wl over 1f out: hdwy to ld fnl 100yds: r.o wl* **11/4**[2]

**2** *1 1/4* **Rockfast** 2-9-0 0 ShaneKelly 3 69+
(Gary Moore) *rn green: in tch in last quartet: hdwy but stl showing greenness over 1f out: pressing ldrs ins fnl f: kpt on* **16/1**

5- **3** *1/2* **Illusive Force (IRE)**[144] 4676 2-9-0 0 SteveDrowne 1 68
(Charles Hills) *led: rdn wl over 1f out: wandered u.p and hdd fnl 100yds: no ex* **9/4**[1]

503- **4** *3/4* **Ertidaad (IRE)**[21] 7920 2-9-0 70 AdamKirby 9 66
(Pat Eddery) *chsd ldrs: rdn over 1f out: ev ch and carried lft ins fnl f: one pce fnl 75yds* **7/2**[3]

56- **5** *1* **Woofie (IRE)**[33] 7779 2-9-0 0.................................. GeorgeChaloner 4 65+
(Richard Fahey) *chsd ldrs: short of room and swtchd rt over 1f out: styd on u.p fnl 100yds* **25/1**

024- **6** *3/4* **The Olympus Man**[8] 8087 2-9-0 65...........................(b) LukeMorris 5 61
(Olly Stevens) *w ldr: rdn and ev ch 2f out tl wknd ins fnl f* **10/1**

00- **7** *hd* **Peterhouse (USA)**[21] 7926 2-9-0 0.................................. NickyMackay 8 61
(John Gosden) *s.i.s: bhd: outpcd over 2f out: rallied and styd on ins fnl f: nvr trbld ldrs* **8/1**

6- **8** *2* **Angels Above (IRE)**[16] 7985 2-9-0 0.................................. TomQueally 2 55
(John Butler) *chsd ldrs: rdn and unable qck over 1f out: wknd ins fnl f* **20/1**

00- **9** *36* **Sir Veillance**[97] 6268 2-9-0 0.................................................. FTahir 6
(John Butler) *a towards rr: last and lost tch over 2f out: t.o* **100/1**

1m 26.47s (1.67) **Going Correction** +0.125s/f (Slow) **9** Ran SP% **115.3**
Speed ratings (Par 96): **95,93,93,92,91 90,89,87,46**
CSF £43.87 TOTE £3.20: £1.20, £7.60, £1.10; EX 53.30 Trifecta £289.20.
**Owner** Qatar Racing Limited **Bred** Tinnakill Bloodstock **Trained** Kimpton, Hants
■ A winner for Jamie Spencer, his first since changing his mind about retiring.

**FOCUS**
A fair juvenile maiden in which they went an honest enough gallop. Ordinary form, rated around the time and some of those down the field.

## 8193 32RED CASINO H'CAP — 1m 7f 169y(P)
**2:00** (2:00) (Class 5) (0-70,70) 3-Y-O+ **£2,587** (£770; £384; £192) **Stalls** Low

Form RPR

011- **1** **Planetoid (IRE)**[12] 8037 6-9-13 69.................(b) WilliamTwiston-Davies 5 78
(Jim Best) *in tch in midfield: rdn and hdwy over 1f out: chal 1f out: drvn to ld ins fnl f: r.o wl* **6/1**[3]

005- **2** *1 1/2* **Keep Kicking (IRE)**[21] 7932 7-9-1 64...................... TomasHarrigan(7) 2 71
(Simon Dow) *dwlt: hld up in tch in rr: rdn and hdwy bnd 2f out: chal 1f out: r.o same pce fnl 100yds* **7/1**

640- **3** *3/4* **Opera Buff**[54] 7419 5-10-0 70...........................................(p) SebSanders 4 76
(Jose Santos) *led: rdn over 2f out: drvn and hrd pressed 1f out: hdd and no ex ins fnl f* **9/2**[2]

041- **4** *1 1/4* **Fennann**[45] 5556 3-9-4 68.................................................(b) GeorgeBaker 1 73
(Gary Moore) *hld up in tch in last trio: nt clr run over 2f out: hdwy towards inner 1f out: no imp fnl 100yds* **6/1**[3]

251- **5** *1/2* **Crouching Harry (IRE)**[14] 8021 5-9-0 56.......................(p) AdamKirby 8 60
(Anabel K Murphy) *in tch in last trio: swtchd rt and wd bnd wl over 1f out: hdwy and edging lft 1f out: styd on* **7/1**

001- **6** *3 1/2* **Dukes Den**[11] 8061 3-8-12 62................................................ LiamKeniry 9 62
(Sylvester Kirk) *chsd ldr tl lost pl wl over 1f out: wknd fnl f* **3/1**[1]

242/ **7** *1/2* **Four Nations (USA)**[399] 7863 6-9-11 67.............................. PatCosgrave 7 66
(George Baker) *in tch: rdn and effrt over 2f out: unable qck and short of room jst over 1f out: wknd ins fnl f* **16/1**

324- **8** *3 1/4* **Wintour Leap**[30] 7817 3-9-2 66............................................. ChrisCatlin 3 62
(Robert Stephens) *taken down early: chsd ldrs: rdn and unable qck over 1f out: sn btn: wknd ins fnl f* **12/1**

010- **9** *1 3/4* **My Lord**[8] 7539 6-9-13 69...................................................... LukeMorris 6 62
(Luke Dace) *in tch in midfield: rdn and chsd ldrs over 2f out: lost pl and bhd wl over 1f out: wknd over 1f out* **33/1**

3m 28.1s (2.40) **Going Correction** +0.125s/f (Slow)
**WFA** 3 from 5yo+ 8lb **9** Ran SP% **113.3**
Speed ratings (Par 103): **99,98,97,97,97 95,95,93,92**
CSF £46.45 CT £205.36 TOTE £7.60: £1.90, £3.70, £2.00; EX 36.80 Trifecta £336.80.
**Owner** Planetoid Partnership **Bred** Bjorn Nielsen **Trained** Lewes, E Sussex

**FOCUS**
A modest staying handicap in which they went quite steadily in the formative stages. The third to fifth help with the level.

## 8194 CORAL MOBILE "JUST THREE CLICKS TO BET" H'CAP — 1m 2f (P)
**2:35** (2:35) (Class 4) (0-85,84) 3-Y-O+ **£5,175** (£1,540; £769; £384) **Stalls** Low

Form RPR

212- **1** **Razor Wind (IRE)**[9] 8080 3-9-4 **84**.................................... AdamKirby 4 95+
(Charlie Appleby) *in tch: shkn up to chse ldrs 2f out: led over 1f out: r.o wl and drew clr fnl f: rdn out* **4/9**[1]

/10- **2** *2 1/2* **Cayuga**[317] 457 5-9-7 **84**..................................................... TomQueally 8 90
(Brett Johnson) *dwlt: hld up in tch in last trio: rdn and hdwy over 1f out: chsd wnr wl ins fnl f: no imp* **20/1**

100- **3** *1* **Moonvoy**[27] 7857 3-9-4 **84**................................................. ShaneKelly 5 88
(Jeremy Noseda) *chsd ldr: clsd and upsides 3f out: rdn to ld 2f out: hdd over 1f out: r.o same pce and lost 2nd wl ins fnl f* **8/1**[3]

302- **4** *1 1/4* **Sheila's Buddy**[12] 8042 5-9-2 **79**......................................... LiamKeniry 1 81
(J S Moore) *dwlt: t.k.h in midfield: rdn and effrt jst over 1f out: kpt on same pce ins fnl f* **8/1**[3]

013- **5** *hd* **Persepolis (IRE)**[12] 8042 4-9-3 **80**...................................... AmirQuinn 2 81
(Lee Carter) *t.k.h: chsd ldrs: swtchd rt and effrt over 1f out: drvn and no ex 1f out: styd on same pce fnl f* **6/1**[2]

120- **6** *3 1/2* **Echo Brava**[12] 8042 4-9-2 **79**............................................. LukeMorris 7 74
(Luke Dace) *dwlt: in tch in rr: rdn over 3f out: nvr trbld ldrs* **33/1**

043- **7** *2 1/2* **Investissement**[2] 8163 8-8-10 **78** ow2......................(p) HarryPoulton(5) 3 70
(Lee Carter) *sn led: rdn over 2f out: hdd 2f out: btn 1f out: wknd and eased ins fnl f* **25/1**

154- **8** *5* **Tee It Up Tommo (IRE)**[25] 7894 5-9-3 **80**......................... GeorgeBaker 6 60
(Michael Wigham) *chsd ldrs on outer: rdn 2f out: btn and lost pl over 1f out: wknd fnl f* **8/1**[3]

2m 5.33s (-1.27) **Going Correction** +0.125s/f (Slow)
**WFA** 3 from 4yo+ 3lb **8** Ran SP% **128.4**
Speed ratings (Par 105): **110,108,107,106,106 103,101,97**
CSF £18.21 CT £53.30 TOTE £1.30: £1.10, £5.10, £2.20; EX 25.30 Trifecta £156.90.
**Owner** Godolphin **Bred** Stone Ridge Farm **Trained** Newmarket, Suffolk

**FOCUS**
The feature contest was a decent handicap in which they went a true gallop. The winenr built on recent good runs.

## 8195 UNIBET H'CAP — 6f 1y(P)
**3:10** (3:10) (Class 6) (0-65,64) 3-Y-O+ **£1,940** (£577; £288; £144) **Stalls** Low

Form RPR

662- **1** **Indus Valley (IRE)**[14] 8013 7-9-0 57.................................... ShaneKelly 3 65
(Des Donovan) *chsd ldrs: rdn and effrt over 1f out: led fnl 100yds: r.o wl* **5/1**[2]

063- **2** *3/4* **Compton Prince**[14] 8014 5-9-1 58.................................(v) LiamKeniry 2 64
(Milton Bradley) *hld up in tch in midfield: rdn and hdwy jst over 1f out: ev ch ins fnl f: chsd wnr and r.o same pce fnl 100yds* **5/1**[2]

543- **3** *nk* **Ghost Train (IRE)**[9] 8081 5-9-7 64.............................(p) HayleyTurner 6 69
(Tim McCarthy) *led: rdn wl over 1f out: hdd and one pce fnl 100yds* **9/2**[1]

004- **4** *1* **Saskia's Dream**[25] 7887 6-9-0 57...............................(v) PatCosgrave 11 59
(Jane Chapple-Hyam) *chsd ldr: rdn and ev ch over 1f out tl ins fnl f: wknd towards fin* **14/1**

206- **5** *1 1/4* **Assertive Agent**[57] 7364 4-9-2 59.................................... WilliamCarson 7 57
(Tony Carroll) *in tch in midfield: effrt u.p over 1f out: kpt on ins fnl f* **12/1**

651- **6** *1/2* **Chevise (IRE)**[25] 7887 6-9-7 64......................................(b) AdamKirby 1 61
(Steve Woodman) *chsd ldrs: rdn 2f out: no ex u.p over 1f out: wknd ins fnl f* **5/1**[2]

000- **7** *2 3/4* **Volito**[19] 7950 8-9-2 59............................................................. RobertWinston 5 47
(Anabel K Murphy) *hld up in tch in last trio: rdn and hdwy on inner over 1f out: wknd ins fnl f* **20/1**

054/ **8** *nk* **Tom Hall**[747] 7930 4-9-3 60.............................................. GrahamGibbons 9 47
(David Menuisier) *t.k.h: in tch in midfield: unable qck u.p over 1f out: wknd ins fnl f* **25/1**

000- **9** *1 1/2* **Ostralegus**[14] 8017 4-9-5 62................................................. BenCurtis 4 45
(John Gallagher) *t.k.h: hld up in tch in midfield: n.m.r and shuffled bk 4f out: effrt u.p over 1f out: no imp* **10/1**

400- **10** *nse* **Logans Lad (IRE)**[12] 8043 4-9-6 63..........................(vt) StevieDonohoe 8 46
(Daniel Mark Loughnane) *bhd: detached last and drvn over 2f out: n.d* **7/1**[3]

600- **11** *12* **Kuanyao (IRE)**[123] 5423 8-9-5 62...........................(b) FergusSweeney 10 9
(Conor Dore) *dwlt: hdwy into midfield but stuck wd after 1f: rdn and struggling over 2f out: wknd 2f out* **16/1**

1m 12.95s (1.05) **Going Correction** +0.125s/f (Slow) **11** Ran SP% **118.6**
Speed ratings (Par 101): **98,97,96,95,93 92,89,88,86,86 70**
CSF £30.54 CT £122.31 TOTE £6.40: £2.00, £2.70, £1.80; EX 35.60 Trifecta £262.80.
**Owner** W P Flynn **Bred** P Morris & B McKenna **Trained** Newmarket, Suffolk

**FOCUS**
A modest sprint handicap in which they went an even gallop after a level break. The second and third set a solid standard.

## 8196 CORAL.CO.UK BEST ODDS GUARANTEED ON RACING APPRENTICE H'CAP — 1m 4f (P)
**3:40** (3:40) (Class 5) (0-70,70) 3-Y-O+ **£2,587** (£770; £384; £192) **Stalls** Low

Form RPR

052- **1** **Celestial Bay**[21] 7932 5-8-13 64.................................... DavidParkes(5) 2 75
(Sylvester Kirk) *hld up in rr: clsd to trck ldrs over 2f out: rdn to ld over 1f out: sn drew clr: readily* **8/1**

605- **2** *7* **Bold Runner**[8] 8089 3-9-3 68.........................................(p) RossAtkinson 6 68
(Jose Santos) *t.k.h: chsd ldrs: wnt 2nd 9f out tl rdn to ld 2f out: hdd over 1f out: sn outpcd: no ch w wnr but hld on to 2nd fnl f* **7/1**[3]

403- **3** *1/2* **Ruzeiz (USA)**[21] 7918 5-9-4 69..................................... RobHornby(5) 4 68
(Peter Hedger) *t.k.h: in tch: rdn and outpcd 2f out: no ch w wnr but plugged on fnl f* **5/4**[1]

216- **4** *2 1/2* **Rowan Ridge**[270] 1065 6-9-3 70................................ CallumShepherd(7) 7 65
(William Knight) *chsd ldrs: niggled along 6f out: chsng ldrs and unable qck whn n.m.r over 1f out: wknd fnl f* **12/1**

214- **5** *7* **Salient**[12] 8037 10-8-11 60....................................... AlistairRawlinson(3) 1 44
(Michael Attwater) *chsd ldrs: rdn and lost pl over 4f out: wknd 2f out: sn bhd* **7/1**[3]

432- **6** *1 3/4* **Darting**[22] 7913 3-9-1 66................................................. ThomasBrown 3 47
(Andrew Balding) *t.k.h: led: rdn and hdd 2f out: btn over 1f out: sn wknd* **3/1**[2]

2m 33.0s **Going Correction** +0.125s/f (Slow)
**WFA** 3 from 4yo+ 5lb **6** Ran SP% **113.2**
Speed ratings (Par 103): **105,100,100,98,93 92**
CSF £60.11 TOTE £7.10: £3.40, £3.10; EX 57.80 Trifecta £237.00.
**Owner** Homebred Racing **Bred** Chris Wall **Trained** Upper Lambourn, Berks

**FOCUS**
The concluding contest was a modest middle-distance handicap for apprentice riders. The gallop was a perfectly respectable one. Not the deepest race but the winner ran to his career best.
T/Plt: £10.00 to a £1 stake. Pool: £63,500.54 - 4,615.71 winning tickets. T/Qpdt: £5.00 to a £1 stake. Pool: £5,949.08 - 873.82 winning tickets. SP

# 8183 KEMPTON (A.W) (R-H)
Thursday, December 18

**OFFICIAL GOING: Polytrack: standard**

## 8197 BETVICTOR SVENGALI CLAIMING STKS — 1m (P)
**4:15** (4:15) (Class 6) 3-Y-O **£2,264** (£673; £336; £168) **Stalls** Low

Form RPR

114- **1** **Geordan Murphy**[28] 7852 3-9-7 79.................................... DavidProbert 3 89
(Andrew Balding) *chsd ldr for 3f: chsd ldrs tl cruised upside ldr and carried lft fr 2f out: pushed into ld 1f out: r.o strly: readily* **8/13**[1]

001- **2** *4 1/2* **Lindart (ITY)**[8] 8097 3-8-6 65................................(b) JoshQuinn(7) 1 71
(Richard Hannon) *led: jnd and hung lft 2f out: hdd 1f out: sn btn but kpt on for clr 2nd* **7/1**[3]

040- **3** *3 1/2* **Ghosting (IRE)**[22] 7918 3-9-4 69..............................(tp) GeorgeBaker 5 68
(Tom Dascombe) *dwlt: hld up in rr: rdn and effrt 2f out: wnt modest 3rd 1f out: no imp* **9/2**[2]

660- **4** *1 1/2* **Dalaki (IRE)**[13] 8041 3-9-2 69.......................................... PatCosgrave 2 62
(Jim Boyle) *hld up in last pair: effrt 2f out: sn btn: wknd over 1f out* **20/1**

460- **5** *1/2* **Bush Beauty (IRE)**[35] 7759 3-8-0 68 ow1...................... GaryMahon(7) 4 52
(Philip McBride) *t.k.h: chsd ldrs: wnt 2nd 5f out tl 2f out: sn hrd drvn and btn over 1f out: wknd fnl f* **10/1**

1m 39.08s (-0.72) **Going Correction** +0.075s/f (Slow) **5** Ran SP% **106.5**
Speed ratings (Par 98): **106,101,98,96,96**
CSF £4.95 TOTE £1.30: £1.02, £3.60; EX 3.60 Trifecta £11.50.Geordan Murphy was clamied by P. Kirby for £18000.
**Owner** B P McGuire **Bred** M A L Evans **Trained** Kingsclere, Hants
■ Stewards' Enquiry : Josh Quinn one-day ban: careless riding (Jan 1)

**FOCUS**
Just a fair claimer but it produced an easy winner. He rates a personal best even with doubts over the field.

## 8198 GET SVENS INSIDE TRACK AT BETVICTOR H'CAP (DIV I) — 1m (P)
**4:45** (4:47) (Class 6) (0-55,55) 3-Y-O+ **£2,264** (£673; £336; £168) **Stalls** Low

Form RPR

050- **1** **Barwah (USA)**[7] 8111 3-8-11 46 oh1...............................(t) WilliamCarson 2 55
(Anthony Carson) *dwlt: hdwy into midfield after 2f: drvn to chse ldr over 1f out: led ins fnl f: styd on: rdn out* **7/1**[3]

002- **2** 1 1/2 **Warbond**[7] 8111 6-8-13 47....................(p) LiamKeniry 3 54
(Michael Madgwick) *in tch in midfield: drvn and hdwy to chse ldng pair 1f out: kpt on to snatch 2nd last stride: no threat to wnr* **11/4**[1]

600- **3** *shd* **Benandonner (USA)**[33] 7813 11-9-6 54.................... ShaneKelly 8 61
(Mike Murphy) *chsd ldrs: rdn to ld 2f out: drvn 1f out: hdd and one pce ins fnl f: lost 2nd last stride* **16/1**

125- **4** 1 1/2 **Dreaming Again**[17] 7987 4-9-3 51.................... KieranO'Neill 9 54
(Jimmy Fox) *sn pushed along in last quartet: drvn over 2f out: hdwy over 1f out: styd on: nvr trbld ldrs* **7/2**[2]

046- **5** 3 **Rezwaan**[14] 8028 7-8-12 53....................(be) HectorCrouch(7) 4 49
(Murty McGrath) *hld up in midfield: rdn and no hdwy jst over 2f out: hdwy over 1f out: styd on ins fnl f: nvr threatened ldrs* **11/4**[1]

400- **6** 6 **Sea Tiger**[15] 8011 4-9-1 49.................... AdamKirby 11 32
(Chris Gordon) *sn bhd and bustled along in rr: styd on past btn horses fnl f: nvr trbld ldrs* **8/1**

000- **7** *shd* **Jazri**[17] 7982 3-9-2 51....................(b1) WilliamTwiston-Davies 7 32
(Milton Bradley) *w ldr tl led 3f out: rdn and hdd 2f out: btn over 1f out: wknd fnl f* **16/1**

000- **8** 2 1/4 **Stan Nineteen (IRE)**[191] 3087 3-9-6 55.................... SteveDrowne 1 31
(Simon Hodgson) *stdd after s: hld up in last quartet: swtchd rt and sme hdwy over 1f out but nvr on terms w ldrs: wknd fnl f* **33/1**

000- **9** 2 **Cuthbert (IRE)**[49] 7546 7-8-5 46 oh1....................(v) GaryMahon(7) 5 19
(Michael Attwater) *chsd ldrs: unable qck u.p 2f out: wknd over 1f out* **66/1**

006- **10** 10 **Praise N Glory**[129] 5249 3-8-11 46 oh1.................... CharlesBishop 10
(Linda Jewell) *led tl 3f out: sn u.p and lost pl: bhd fnl f* **100/1**

0/0- **11** 3 **Echoes Of War**[248] 1491 5-8-12 46 oh1.................... FergusSweeney 6
(John Bridger) *t.k.h: hld up in midfield: rdn and no hdwy jst over 2f out: sn wknd: bhd and eased wl ins fnl f* **66/1**

1m 40.64s (0.84) **Going Correction** +0.075s/f (Slow)
**WFA** 3 from 4yo+ 1lb **11** Ran SP% **117.8**
Speed ratings (Par 101): **98,96,96,94,91 85,85,83,81,71 68**
CSF £26.44 CT £307.78 TOTE £11.80: £2.40, £1.40, £3.30; EX 32.50 Trifecta £317.70.
**Owner** Hugh & Mindi Byrne **Bred** Shadwell Farm LLC **Trained** Newmarket, Suffolk

**FOCUS**
A moderate handicap run 1.56secs slower than the preceding claimer. The winner was unexposed and the next two were close to form.

## 8199 GET SVENS INSIDE TRACK AT BETVICTOR H'CAP (DIV II) 1m (P)
**5:15** (5:16) (Class 6) (0-55,54) 3-Y-O+ **£2,264** (£673; £336; £168) **Stalls** Low

Form RPR

030- **1** **Tsarglas**[49] 7546 3-8-8 45....................(v1) DannyBrock(3) 7 54+
(Stuart Williams) *dwlt: sn rcvrd to chse ldr over 6f out: led over 3f out: drvn and wnt clr over 1f out: kpt up to work and a holding rivals fnl f* **3/1**[2]

502- **2** 1 1/4 **Henry Grace (IRE)**[17] 7986 3-8-13 47....................(b) KieranO'Neill 5 53
(Jimmy Fox) *stdd s: hld up in last quartet: rdn and hdwy 3f out: chsd clr wnr 1f out: steadily clsd but nvr gng to rch wnr* **9/4**[1]

040- **3** 1 **Caledonia Laird**[19] 7977 3-9-5 53....................(p) MartinDwyer 3 57
(Jo Hughes) *s.i.s: t.k.h: hld up in last: hdwy 2f out: wnt 3rd ins fnl f: kpt on but nvr gng to rch wnr* **13/2**

060- **4** 1 3/4 **Warden Bond**[16] 8004 6-9-6 53....................(p) GeorgeBaker 2 54
(William Stone) *racd in midfield: effrt over 2f out: chsd clr wnr over 1f out tl 1f out: kpt on same pce ins fnl f* **7/2**[3]

345- **5** 1 **Black Widow**[33] 7800 3-8-11 45.................... StevieDonohoe 1 42
(Pat Eddery) *dwlt: racd in last pair: effrt on inner over 2f out: no imp and swtchd lft over 1f out: styd on fnl f: nvr trbld ldrs* **25/1**

/00- **6** 1 1/2 **Malih**[15] 8013 5-9-6 53.................... AdamKirby 6 48
(Eric Wheeler) *chsd ldrs: rdn to chse wnr 3f out: sn drvn and no imp: lost 2nd over 1f out: wknd ins fnl f* **14/1**

220- **7** *nk* **Movie Magic**[8] 8090 3-9-1 49....................(v) WilliamCarson 8 42
(John Bridger) *led for 1f: chsd ldrs after: rdn and outpcd over 2f out: no imp over 1f out* **8/1**

000- **8** 59 **Zand Man**[28] 7853 4-8-12 45....................(b) WilliamTwiston-Davies 11
(Milton Bradley) *led after 1f tl hdd over 3f out: dropped to rr qckly over 2f out: sn t.o and virtually p.u over 1f out* **66/1**

1m 41.07s (1.27) **Going Correction** +0.075s/f (Slow)
**WFA** 3 from 4yo+ 1lb **8** Ran SP% **114.4**
Speed ratings (Par 101): **96,94,93,92,91 89,89,30**
CSF £10.20 CT £39.06 TOTE £4.80: £1.70, £1.30, £2.30; EX 11.30 Trifecta £61.30.
**Owner** Essex Racing Club et al **Bred** Redland Bloodstock Limited **Trained** Newmarket, Suffolk
■ Stewards' Enquiry : Danny Brock two-day ban: used whip above permitted level (Jan 1-2)

**FOCUS**
The second leg of this handicap was run 0.43secs slower than the first division. The always well-placed winner is unexposed and looks capable of better.

## 8200 COME RACING ON BOXING DAY H'CAP 6f (P)
**5:45** (5:47) (Class 7) (0-50,50) 3-Y-O+ **£1,940** (£577; £288; £144) **Stalls** Low

Form RPR

660- **1** **Black Truffle (FR)**[15] 8013 4-9-2 47....................(v) LiamKeniry 8 57
(Mark Usher) *stdd and dropped in bhd after s: hld up in rr: hdwy and nt clr run over 1f out: squeezed through to chse ldrs 1f out: led ins fnl f: r.o wl* **7/1**

400- **2** 1 **Lucky Royale**[27] 7864 6-9-4 49.................... MartinLane 2 56
(Jeremy Gask) *chsd ldrs: effrt u.p and ev ch over 1f out: r.o same pce ins fnl f* **8/1**

302- **3** 1/2 **Encapsulated**[21] 7940 4-8-11 49....................(p) RhiainIngram(7) 9 54
(Roger Ingram) *t.k.h: pressed ldrs: led 2f but hanging rt: hdd and one pce ins fnl f* **13/2**[3]

600- **4** 3/4 **Doctor Hilary**[187] 3230 12-9-4 49....................(v) WilliamCarson 3 53
(Mark Hoad) *hld up in midfield: hdwy and nt clr run jst over 1f out tl ins fnl f: styd on wl u.p towards fin* **33/1**

606- **5** 1 **Quantum Dot (IRE)**[7] 8111 3-9-3 48....................(b) DavidProbert 6 47
(Ed de Giles) *chsd ldrs: effrt u.p and pressing ldrs over 1f out: no ex ins fnl f: wknd towards fin* **9/4**[1]

000- **6** 2 **The Boss Of Me**[143] 4732 3-8-10 48....................(bt1) ChrisMeehan(7) 10 41
(Sean Curran) *in tch in midfield on outer: rdn and no imp over 1f out tl styd on u.p fnl 100yds: nvr threatened ldrs* **20/1**

000- **7** 1 1/2 **Kingsway Lad (IRE)**[9] 8084 3-9-2 47....................(v1) CharlesBishop 1 35
(Derek Shaw) *towards rr: rdn over 2f out: swtchd ins and sme hdwy u.p wl over 1f out: no imp fnl f* **6/1**[2]

501- **8** 3/4 **River Dreamer (IRE)**[233] 1855 3-9-5 50....................(t) ChrisCatlin 11 36
(Robert Stephens) *in tch in midfield but stuck wd: rdn and lost pl over 2f out: no threat to ldrs but kpt on fnl f* **25/1**

540- **9** *hd* **Twilight Angel**[143] 4733 6-9-5 50.................... StevieDonohoe 4 35
(Pat Eddery) *led tl 2f out: no ex and btn over 1f out: wknd fnl f* **25/1**

624- **10** 1 3/4 **Island Express (IRE)**[7] 8111 7-9-0 50....................(bt) AnnStokell(5) 5 30
(Ann Stokell) *w ldrs tl unable qck u.p over 2f out: btn over 1f out: wknd fnl f* **12/1**

050- **11** 1 1/4 **Night Trade (IRE)**[30] 7826 7-9-3 48....................(p) AdamKirby 7 24
(Ronald Harris) *s.i.s: a in rr* **14/1**

1m 13.67s (0.57) **Going Correction** +0.075s/f (Slow) **11** Ran SP% **111.8**
Speed ratings (Par 97): **99,97,97,96,94 92,90,89,88,86 84**
CSF £55.33 CT £383.38 TOTE £8.10: £2.20, £2.30, £3.00; EX 56.30 Trifecta £299.00.
**Owner** Ushers Court **Bred** Peter Harris **Trained** Upper Lambourn, Berks

**FOCUS**
A rock-bottom handicap that produced a good finish. The winner was below the mark he won off over C&D in April, while the runner-up showed first real form since missing last year.

## 8201 DAILY SVEN-TO-1 SPECIALS AT BETVICTOR MEDIAN AUCTION MAIDEN STKS 7f (P)
**6:15** (6:15) (Class 5) 2-Y-O **£3,234** (£962; £481; £240) **Stalls** Low

Form RPR

5- **1** **Showtime Blues**[22] 7920 2-9-5 0.................... GeorgeBaker 7 82+
(Amanda Perrett) *chsd ldng trio: rdn to ld over 1f out: styd on wl and drew clr ins fnl f: eased towards fin* **8/1**[3]

3- **2** 2 3/4 **Plaisir (IRE)**[21] 7944 2-9-0 0.................... AdamKirby 6 67
(Marco Botti) *chsd ldrs: effrt u.p and ev ch over 1f out: outpcd and btn ins fnl f: kpt on same pce after* **4/5**[1]

0- **3** *nk* **Glorious Asset**[36] 7742 2-9-5 0.................... AntonioFresu 1 71
(Ed Walker) *chsd ldng pair: rdn and effrt 2f out: drvn and pressed ldrs over 1f out: sn outpcd: 3rd and one pce fnl f* **8/1**[3]

452- **4** 6 **Lady Pinnacle**[35] 7752 2-9-0 68.................... DavidProbert 3 50
(Andrew Balding) *led: rdn and hrd pressed 2f out: drvn and hdd over 1f out: wknd fnl f* **11/4**[2]

00- **5** 3 **Alfie The Pug**[21] 7941 2-9-5 0.................... FergusSweeney 4 47
(Pat Phelan) *racd off the pce in midfield: rdn and no hdwy 2f out: nvr trbld ldrs* **50/1**

0- **6** 1/2 **Sample (FR)**[22] 7919 2-9-0 0....................[1] WilliamTwiston-Davies 2 41+
(Roger Charlton) *v.s.a: bhd: clsd onto bk of field but nt on terms 1/2-way: rdn and wknd over 2f out* **12/1**

**7** 1 1/2 **Ohsosecret** 2-9-0 0.................... SteveDrowne 8 36
(Stuart Williams) *s.i.s: off pce in last pair: sme hdwy into midfield 1/2-way: 5th and no imp 2f out: wknd over 1f out* **66/1**

**8** 18 **Golden Beryl** 2-9-0 0.................... ShaneKelly 5
(Mike Murphy) *sn pushed along in last trio: dropped to last 1/2-way: lost tch over 2f out: t.o* **100/1**

1m 27.2s (1.20) **Going Correction** +0.075s/f (Slow) **8** Ran SP% **116.6**
Speed ratings (Par 96): **96,92,92,85,82 81,79,59**
CSF £15.27 TOTE £9.20: £2.00, £1.10, £2.60; EX 20.20 Trifecta £122.90.
**Owner** A D Spence **Bred** R J & S A Carter **Trained** Pulborough, W Sussex

**FOCUS**
This juvenile contest involved only the first four throughout. The winner did it really well and the runner-up is rated close to his debut form.

## 8202 BETVICTOR.COM FILLIES' H'CAP 1m 4f (P)
**6:45** (6:46) (Class 5) (0-75,74) 3-Y-O+ **£3,234** (£962; £481; £240) **Stalls** Centre

Form RPR

624- **1** **Quenelle**[27] 7866 3-9-3 72.................... GeorgeBaker 1 83
(Ed Dunlop) *hld up off the pce in last quartet: clsd and in tch 1/2-way: rdn and effrt 2f out: chsd wnr over 1f out: styd on wl to ld wl ins fnl f* **10/3**[2]

660- **2** 1 **Asia Minor (IRE)**[22] 7922 5-9-10 74.................... AdamKirby 3 83+
(Dr Jon Scargill) *stdd s: hld up off the pce in last pair: clsd and in tch 1/2-way: quick move on outer 3f out: led and kicked clr over 2f out: drvn over 1f out: hdd and no ex wl ins fnl f* **5/2**[1]

521- **3** 3 **Celestial Bay**[1] 8196 5-9-0 64.................... LiamKeniry 7 69
(Sylvester Kirk) *hld up off the pce in last quartet: clsd and in tch 1/2-way: hdwy to press ldrs 3f out: rdn and chsd ldr over 2f out tl over 1f out: styd on same pce fnl f* **5/1**[3]

042- **4** 1 **Conserve (IRE)**[8] 8099 4-8-13 63....................(b) MartinLane 2 66
(Neil King) *dwlt and bustled along leaving stalls: hld up off the pce in last pair: clsd and in tch 1/2-way: drvn over 2f out: 4th and styd on same pce fr over 1f out* **8/1**

361- **5** 3 1/4 **Cataria Girl (USA)**[36] 7744 5-9-5 69....................(t) MartinDwyer 6 67
(Marcus Tregoning) *racd in midfield: clsd 1/2-way: rdn over 3f out: outpcd and btn over 2f out: n.d after* **12/1**

534- **6** 1/2 **Perfect Rhythm**[14] 8029 3-8-6 64.................... RyanTate(3) 4 61
(Patrick Chamings) *led for 2f: chsd ldrs tl over 2f out: sn struggling u.p: wknd over 1f out* **6/1**

455- **7** 1 1/4 **Lady Of Yue**[27] 7866 4-8-12 62.................... RobertTart 8 57
(Eugene Stanford) *chsd ldrs tl hdwy to ld after 2f: slowed pce 1/2-way: hdd and rdn over 2f out: wknd over 1f out* **12/1**

300- **8** 14 **The Blue Dog (IRE)**[14] 8029 7-9-2 66.................... WilliamCarson 5 39
(Phil McEntee) *mostly chsd ldr tl 3f out: sn wknd: bhd fnl f* **66/1**

2m 34.94s (0.44) **Going Correction** +0.075s/f (Slow)
**WFA** 3 from 4yo+ 5lb **8** Ran SP% **110.6**
Speed ratings (Par 100): **101,100,98,97,95 95,94,85**
CSF £11.24 CT £36.94 TOTE £4.10: £1.40, £1.20, £1.60; EX 13.10 Trifecta £44.40.
**Owner** Miss Julia Delves Broughton **Bred** Stanley Estate And Stud Co **Trained** Newmarket, Suffolk

**FOCUS**
A modest fillies' handicap, with no great depth, in which the market leaders fought out the finish. The winner came off the good pace set by the leaders early.

## 8203 BEST PRICES FOR 4 SEASONS BETVICTOR CONDITIONS STKS 7f (P)
**7:15** (7:15) (Class 2) 3-Y-O+
**£11,827** (£3,541; £1,770; £885; £442; £222) **Stalls** Low

Form RPR

011- **1** **Unforgiving Minute**[28] 7852 3-9-4 94.................... AdamKirby 4 113
(Clive Cox) *hld up in rr: effrt over 1f out: qcknd smartly under hands and heels riding to ld fnl 150yds: r.o strly: impressive* **10/11**[1]

043- **2** 3 **Frontier Fighter**[5] 8135 6-9-4 102.................... SamJames 1 105
(David O'Meara) *led: rdn and kicked clr 2f out: hdd and r.o same pce fnl 150yds* **11/1**

004- **3** 1 3/4 **Linton (AUS)**[47] 7599 8-9-4 107....................(b) LukeMorris 3 100
(Marco Botti) *hld up in tch: drvn to chse clr ldr 2f out: no imp: 3rd and r.o same pce fr over 1f out* **11/4**[2]

500- **4** 2 1/2 **Hasopop (IRE)**[8] 8101 4-9-4 100....................(p) MartinLane 6 94
(Marco Botti) *t.k.h: hld up in tch: effrt u.p wl over 1f out: 4th and no imp over 1f out* **10/1**

404- **5** *6* **Valbchek (IRE)**[7] 8117 5-9-4 94....................................(p) PatCosgrave 2 78
(Jane Chapple-Hyam) *chsd ldrs: wnt 2nd 1/2-way tl 2f out: wknd over 1f out* **9/1**[3]

0/ **6** *10* **Rain God (USA)**[490] 5454 4-9-4 90...................................... GeorgeBaker 5 52
(Gary Moore) *chsd ldr tl 1/2-way: rdn and lost pl over 2f out: wknd 2f out* **40/1**

1m 24.84s (-1.16) **Going Correction** +0.075s/f (Slow) **6** Ran SP% **108.9**
Speed ratings (Par 109): **109,105,103,100,93 82**
CSF £11.39 TOTE £1.60: £1.10, £2.80; EX 7.30 Trifecta £19.50.
**Owner** P W Harris **Bred** Equine Breeding Ltd **Trained** Lambourn, Berks

**FOCUS**
This feature race attracted some smart performers, but most had doubts surrounding them and the time was ordinary. That said, the winner looks a Group performer in the making on this surface.

## 8204 CONSTANTINE, ENA FETTEL, LINDA EMERY MEMORIAL H'CAP 7f (P)
**7:45** (7:45) (Class 5) (0-75,75) 3-Y-O+ **£3,234** (£962; £481; £240) **Stalls** Low

Form RPR

300- **1** **Jungle Bay**[13] 8040 7-9-6 74....................................(p) MartinDwyer 2 85
(Jane Chapple-Hyam) *hld up in midfield: clsd 2f out: rdn to ld ins fnl f: r.o strly* **20/1**

211- **2** *1 3/4* **Varsovian**[22] 7931 4-9-4 72.................................... JimmyQuinn 9 78
(Dean Ivory) *in tch in midfield: rdn and qcknd between horses to ld over 1f out: hdd and r.o same pce ins fnl f* **7/2**[1]

501- **3** *1* **Franco's Secret**[22] 7921 3-9-4 72.................................(p) CharlesBishop 1 76
(Peter Hedger) *chsd ldrs: rdn and ev ch over 1f out tl ins fnl f: r.o same pce* **8/1**

034- **4** *3/4* **Exceeding Power**[12] 8058 3-9-2 70.................................(t) LukeMorris 6 72
(Martin Bosley) *in tch in midfield: effrt 2f out: chsd ldrs and r.o same pce fnl f* **25/1**

144- **5** *1/2* **Multitask**[10] 8071 4-9-7 75.................................... LiamKeniry 14 76
(Michael Madgwick) *stdd s: t.k.h: hld up in rr: hdwy on inner 2f out: swtchd lft and kpt on ins fnl f: nvr trbld ldrs* **8/1**

500- **6** *1* **Lord Ofthe Shadows (IRE)**[50] 7530 5-9-0 75............ GaryMahon(7) 13 73
(Richard Hannon) *chsd ldr: rdn to ld 2f out: hdd over 1f out: wknd ins fnl f* **25/1**

502- **7** *3/4* **Gigawatt**[8] 8100 4-9-4 72.................................(p) PatCosgrave 8 68
(Jim Boyle) *chsd ldrs: drvn and unable qck 2f out: styd on same pce fr over 1f out* **9/2**[2]

/61- **8** *nse* **Mukaynis (IRE)**[27] 7865 3-8-10 69.................................... ShaneGray(5) 11 65
(Kevin Ryan) *in tch in midfield: rdn 2f out: outpcd and btn over 1f out: one pce after* **5/1**[3]

022- **9** *nse* **Rouge Nuage (IRE)**[6] 8124 4-9-4 72.................................... LiamJones 12 68
(Conrad Allen) *led: rdn over 2f out: hdd 2f out and sn no ex: wknd fnl f* **14/1**

110- **10** *1 1/2* **Malaysian Boleh**[10] 8080 4-9-5 73.................................... AdamKirby 3 65
(Simon Dow) *hld up in last quartet: effrt 2f out: no real imp: nvr trbld ldrs* **8/1**

160- **11** *7* **Penny's Boy**[51] 7513 3-9-4 72.................................(t) SteveDrowne 4 46
(Simon Hodgson) *a towards rr: rdn and no hdwy 2f out: sn wknd* **66/1**

004- **12** *1 1/4* **Big Whiskey (IRE)**[34] 7774 4-9-7 75.........................(t) FergusSweeney 5 45
(John Best) *a towards rr: rdn over 2f out: sn btn* **9/1**

1m 25.46s (-0.54) **Going Correction** +0.075s/f (Slow) **12** Ran SP% **121.0**
Speed ratings (Par 103): **106,104,102,102,101 100,99,99,99,97 89,88**
CSF £88.07 CT £643.10 TOTE £18.10: £4.20, £2.00, £4.10; EX 135.40 Trifecta £1727.70.
**Owner** Brewster/Harding & Essex Racing Club **Bred** Stowell Hill Ltd & Major & Mrs R B Kennard **Trained** Dalham, Suffolk

**FOCUS**
A fair and competitive contest run 0.42secs slower than the preceding conditions race, but it was soundly run. The winner is rated to his best in this country.
T/Plt: £8.00 to a £1 stake. Pool of £93735.33- 8453.11 winning tickets. T/Qpdt: £3.30 to a £1 stake. Pool of £10898.56 - 2423.32 winning tickets. SP

# 8176 SOUTHWELL (L-H)
Thursday, December 18

**OFFICIAL GOING: Fibresand: standard**
Wind: strong across Weather: Overcast

## 8205 32RED IRISH STALLION FARMS EBF MAIDEN STKS 7f (F)
**12:30** (12:32) (Class 5) 2-Y-O **£2,911** (£866; £432; £216) **Stalls** Low

Form RPR

5- **1** **Danseur Noble**[63] 7223 2-9-5 0.................................... LukeMorris 9 80+
(James Tate) *trckd ldrs: hdwy 3f out: led 1 1/2f out: sn rdn clr: kpt on* **3/1**[2]

36- **2** *3 1/4* **What Could She Be (IRE)**[15] 8007 2-9-0 0................ PaulMulrennan 7 64
(Bryan Smart) *trckd ldrs: hdwy 3f out: rdn and green whn sltly outpcd 2f out: styd on u.p fnl f* **7/1**

244- **3** *1 3/4* **Fast Charlie (IRE)**[12] 8060 2-9-5 73.................................... PJMcDonald 2 64
(Ann Duffield) *in tch on inner: pushed along 3f out: rdn 2f out: hdwy on inner rail over 1f out: kpt on fnl f* **9/2**[3]

4- **4** *2 1/4* **Crusading (USA)**[30] 7827 2-9-5 0.................................... JFEgan 4 58
(Mark Johnston) *sn slt ld: green and pushed along after 3f: rdn wl over 2f out: wandered and hdd 1 1/2f out: sn wknd* **9/4**[1]

**5** *1 1/4* **Cool Beans**[123] 5472 2-8-12 0.................................... AdamMcLean(7) 5 57
(Roy Bowring) *in tch: rdn along 3f out: kpt on one pce fnl 2f* **33/1**

**6** *6* **Exclusive Diamond** 2-9-0 0.................................... PhillipMakin 1 33+
(Bryan Smart) *s.i.s and bhd tl sme late hdwy* **25/1**

00- **7** *20* **Forest Missile (IRE)**[40] 7713 2-9-5 0.................................... BarryMcHugh 6
(John Wainwright) *a towards rr: outpcd and bhd fr 1/2-way* **150/1**

60- **8** *2* **Idle Talker (IRE)**[12] 8060 2-9-5 0.................................(t) RaulDaSilva 3
(Jose Santos) *cl up: pushed after 3f: rdn over 3f out and sn wknd* **66/1**

0- **9** *3/4* **Moving Upwards**[14] 8026 2-9-0 0.................................... ShaneGray(5) 8 +
(Kevin Ryan) *cl up: hung rt home turn: sn rdn and wknd* **9/2**[3]

1m 30.0s (-0.30) **Going Correction** -0.125s/f (Stan) **9** Ran SP% **113.6**
Speed ratings (Par 96): **96,92,90,87,86 79,56,54,53**
CSF £23.03 TOTE £4.20: £1.50, £2.30, £1.30; EX 26.30 Trifecta £86.40.
**Owner** Saeed Manana **Bred** J W Parry **Trained** Newmarket, Suffolk

**FOCUS**
An ordinary maiden with only one runner having raced on Fibresand previously. The gallop was a modest one and the majority headed down the centre of the home straight. The winner was in command for the final 2f and the runner-up helps set the level.

## 8206 £10 FREE BET AT 32REDSPORT.COM (S) STKS 1m (F)
**1:00** (1:01) (Class 6) 2-Y-O **£2,045** (£603; £302) **Stalls** Low

Form RPR

040- **1** **Magic Empress (IRE)**[9] 8087 2-8-6 40.................................... BarryMcHugh 5 50
(Tony Coyle) *trckd ldrs on outer: hdwy 3f out: led 2f out: rdn wl over 1f out: drvn ins fnl f: hld on wl* **33/1**

052- **2** *nk* **Blue Burmese (IRE)**[17] 7996 2-8-6 52.........................(be[1]) HayleyTurner 4 49
(Mark Usher) *hld up: hdwy wl over 2f out: rdn to chse ldrs over 1f out: drvn and styd on fnl f* **16/1**

303- **3** *1/2* **Activation**[30] 7828 2-8-4 50.................................... CharlieBennett(7) 6 53
(Hughie Morrison) *trckd ldr: hdwy over 2f out: rdn wl over 1f out: sn drvn and ev ch tl no ex last 75yds* **2/1**[2]

014- **4** *1 1/4* **Pat Mustard**[29] 7832 2-9-2 65.................................... TomQueally 2 55
(Jamie Osborne) *hld up in rr: hdwy 3f out: chsd ldrs 2f out: rdn over 1f out: kpt on one pce* **1/1**[1]

043- **5** *13* **Whisky Marmalade (IRE)**[3] 8165 2-8-6 58.................................... SamJames 1 15
(David O'Meara) *led 1f: cl up: rdn along over 3f out: sn wknd* **11/2**[3]

005- **6** *4* **Beauchamp Ruby**[17] 7996 2-8-6 46.................................... LiamJones 3 6
(Paul Fitzsimons) *cl up: led after 1f: rdn along and edgd lft over 2f out: sn hdd: hung lft and hit inner rail: wknd qckly* **28/1**

1m 44.58s (0.88) **Going Correction** -0.125s/f (Stan) **6** Ran SP% **111.0**
Speed ratings (Par 94): **90,89,89,87,74 70**
CSF £396.59 TOTE £37.60: £17.60, £3.40; EX 306.80 Trifecta £1465.30.There was no bid for the winner. Pat Mustard was subject to a friendly claim.
**Owner** Tony Coyle **Bred** Tally-Ho Stud **Trained** Norton, N Yorks

**FOCUS**
A shock result for this poor seller, in which the two market leaders both disappointed. There was a sound pace, and the first four, who all held chances a furlong out, came well clear. More negatives than positives and not much to take forward.

## 8207 ALL NEW 32REDSPORT.COM MAIDEN FILLIES STKS 1m (F)
**1:30** (1:30) (Class 5) 3-Y-O+ **£2,587** (£770; £384; £192) **Stalls** Low

Form RPR

/42- **1** **Miniskirt**[16] 8003 3-9-0 70.................................... ChrisCatlin 1 78
(Rae Guest) *mde all: pushed clr wl over 1f out: easily* **4/6**[1]

33- **2** *8* **Laika**[7] 8114 5-9-1 0.................................... HayleyTurner 4 61
(Brian Ellison) *trckd ldrs: hdwy 3f out: chsd wnr over 2f out: sn rdn and no imp* **13/8**[2]

006- **3** *15* **Bay Street Belle**[35] 7764 3-9-0 49.................................... PhillipMakin 3 26
(Alison Hutchinson) *cl up: rdn along over 3f out: plugged on one pce fr over 2f out* **66/1**

050- **4** *3 1/2* **Roxy Hart**[70] 7068 3-9-0 60.................................(e[1]) LiamJones 6 17
(Robert Cowell) *prom: sn pushed along: rdn over 3f out: sn wknd* **14/1**[3]

**5** *9* **Bow Belle**[108] 4-9-1 0.................................... FergalLynch 5
(J R Jenkins) *dwlt: green and sn outpcd: a bhd* **25/1**

000- **6** *2 1/2* **Tell Me When**[9] 8084 3-9-0 47.................................(e[1]) BarryMcHugh 7
(Brian Rothwell) *chsd ldrs on outer: rdn along bef 1/2-way: sn outpcd and bhd* **80/1**

1m 42.13s (-1.57) **Going Correction** -0.125s/f (Stan)
**WFA** 3 from 4yo+ 1lb **6** Ran SP% **111.3**
Speed ratings (Par 103): **102,94,79,75,66 64**
CSF £1.92 TOTE £1.70: £1.10, £1.50; EX 2.40 Trifecta £25.10.
**Owner** C J Mills **Bred** C J Mills **Trained** Newmarket, Suffolk

**FOCUS**
An uncompetitive, moderate fillies' maiden in which the well backed favourite made all. She gave the runner-up a bigger beating compared with Wolverhampton latest.

## 8208 RACING SPECIALS AT 32REDSPORT.COM H'CAP 1m 6f (F)
**2:00** (2:01) (Class 6) (0-65,63) 3-Y-O+ **£1,940** (£577; £288; £144) **Stalls** Low

Form RPR

00- **1** **Canadian Diamond (IRE)**[14] 3856 7-9-4 53..........(p) StevieDonohoe 11 67+
(Brendan Powell) *prom: hdwy and cl up over 4f out: led 3f out: rdn along 2f out: drvn and kpt on wl fnl f* **14/1**

600- **2** *1 1/4* **Rock Of Ages**[86] 6632 5-9-6 55.................................(b) LiamJones 13 64
(Neil King) *pushed along after s and hdwy on outer to ld after 2f: rdn along and hdd 5f out: drvn along over 3f out: kpt on wl u.p fnl 2f* **6/1**

/65- **3** *1 3/4* **Shirls Son Sam**[30] 7823 6-8-10 45.................................... DuranFentiman 10 52
(Chris Fairhurst) *hld up: hdwy and in tch over 5f out: rdn along to chse ldrs 3f out: drvn and kpt on appr fnl f: nrst fin* **20/1**

/02- **4** *3 3/4* **Generous Dream**[5] 8134 6-9-2 51.................................... PJMcDonald 2 52
(Mel Brittain) *trckd ldrs: pushed along and outpcd over 3f out: rdn and hdwy to chse ldrs over 2f out: sn drvn and no imp* **7/2**[1]

303- **5** *5* **Sheila's Heart**[35] 7760 4-9-9 63.................................... ShelleyBirkett(5) 3 57
(John E Long) *trckd ldrs on inner: pushed along and lost pl 5f out: plugged on u.p fnl 2f: n.d* **7/2**[1]

0/0- **6** *2 1/2* **Mazovian (USA)**[23] 7908 6-8-12 50.................................... DeclanBates(3) 7 41
(Michael Chapman) *towards rr: rdn along 7f out: drvn 5f out and bhd: plugged on fnl 2f: n.d* **66/1**

040- **7** *shd* **Carlanda (FR)**[12] 8061 4-9-12 61.................................(p) LukeMorris 12 52
(Michael Appleby) *prom: cl up 1/2-way: led 5f out: rdn along over 3f out: drvn and hdd wl over 2f out: sn wknd* **9/2**[2]

044- **8** *1 1/2* **Honest Strike (USA)**[15] 8021 7-9-8 57.........................(bt) RobertWinston 4 46
(Daniel Mark Loughnane) *hld up towards rr: stdy hdwy 1/2-way: chsd ldrs over 3f out: rdn over 2f out: sn wknd* **14/1**

364- **9** *hd* **Yasir (USA)**[5] 8134 6-9-10 59.................................(b) HayleyTurner 9 47
(Conor Dore) *hld up in rr: hdwy on outer 1/2-way: chsd ldrs 4f out: rdn along 3f out: drvn and wknd over 2f out* **11/2**[3]

000- **10** *nk* **Rajeh (IRE)**[84] 6682 11-8-7 45.................................... JacobButterfield(3) 6 33
(Peter Grayson) *a bhd* **66/1**

200- **11** *1 1/4* **Regal Park (IRE)**[5] 8146 7-9-6 60.................................... TimClark(5) 8 46
(Miss Imogen Pickard) *in tch: rdn along 1/2-way: sn lost pl and bhd* **25/1**

3m 7.42s (-0.88) **Going Correction** -0.125s/f (Stan)
**WFA** 3 from 4yo+ 7lb **11** Ran SP% **117.2**
Speed ratings (Par 96): **97,96,95,93,90 88,88,87,87,87 86**
CSF £92.50 CT £1688.84 TOTE £19.50: £6.10, £3.60, £6.90; EX 163.70 Trifecta £3337.80.
**Owner** Nicholls Family **Bred** J S Bolger **Trained** Upper Lambourn, Berks


The Form Book, Raceform Ltd, Newbury, RG14 5SJ

**FOCUS**
This wasn't a strong contest, even allowing for the grade, and there was a lack of good recent form, but it was competitive enough. The winner rates a bit better than the bare form. They went a sedate pace and it paid to race prominently.

## 8209 LADBROKES H'CAP 7f (F)
2:30 (2:32) (Class 4) (0-85,82) 3-Y-O+ £4,690 (£1,395; £697; £348) Stalls Low

Form RPR
035- **1** **Patriotic (IRE)**$^{5}$ 8144 6-9-5 80..........(p) BenCurtis 6 92
(Chris Dwyer) *reminders sn after s and towards rr: gd hdwy on outer over 3f out: chal over 2f out: rdn to ld 1 1/2f out: drvn out* 8/1

505- **2** 3/4 **Westminster (IRE)**$^{20}$ 7955 3-9-0 75.......... HayleyTurner 13 85
(Michael Appleby) *prom: cl up over 3f out: rdn to ld 2f out: hdd and drvn 1 1/2f out: sn edgd lft: kpt on same pce fnl f* 2/1$^{1}$

601- **3** 2 **Pretty Bubbles**$^{17}$ 7988 5-9-4 79.......... FergalLynch 11 84
(J R Jenkins) *dwlt and towards rr: hdwy 1/2-way: chsd ldrs over 2f out: sn rdn: kpt on same pce appr fnl f* 5/1$^{2}$

500- **4** 3/4 **Kung Hei Fat Choy (USA)**$^{27}$ 7870 5-9-1 76..........(b) PJMcDonald 3 79
(James Given) *trckd ldrs on inner: hdwy and cl up 3f out: sn led: rdn and hdd 2f out: ev ch tl drvn and kpt on same pce appr fnl f* 10/1

125- **5** hd **Toto Skyllachy**$^{26}$ 7894 9-8-13 74.......... DanielTudhope 10 76+
(David O'Meara) *chsd ldrs: rdn along over 2f out: drvn and kpt on same pce fr over 1f out* 11/2$^{3}$

100- **6** 6 **Red Primo (IRE)**$^{71}$ 7035 3-9-2 77.......... BarryMcHugh 1 64
(Tony Coyle) *towards rr: hdwy 3f out: rdn 2f out and nvr nr ldrs* 16/1

014- **7** 2 3/4 **My Son Max**$^{22}$ 7928 6-8-13 77..........(v) MatthewCosham$^{(3)}$ 2 57
(Nikki Evans) *s.i.s: a towards rr* 50/1

000- **8** 1/2 **Ready (IRE)**$^{31}$ 7821 4-9-5 80.......... LiamJones 4 58
(Garry Moss) *a towards rr* 50/1

500- **9** 1 1/2 **Piceno (IRE)**$^{17}$ 7988 6-8-7 73..........(p) TimClark$^{(5)}$ 12 47
(Scott Dixon) *chsd ldrs: rdn along 3f out: sn wknd* 14/1

240- **10** 1/2 **Kingscroft (IRE)**$^{20}$ 7955 6-9-4 79..........(b) PaulMulrennan 5 52
(Michael Herrington) *trckd ldrs: hdwy 1/2-way: rdn along wl over 2f out: sn wknd* 25/1

044- **11** 5 **Dr Red Eye**$^{8}$ 8100 6-9-3 78..........(p) LukeMorris 7 38
(Scott Dixon) *led: rdn along and hdd 3f out: sn wknd* 7/1

000- **12** 6 **Ishikawa (IRE)**$^{19}$ 7971 6-9-2 82.......... JordanVaughan$^{(5)}$ 9 26
(K R Burke) *cl up: slt ld 3f out: sn rdn and hdd over 2f out: wknd qckly* 25/1

1m 28.11s (-2.19) **Going Correction** -0.125s/f (Stan) **12** Ran SP% **122.2**
Speed ratings (Par 105): **107,106,103,103,102 95,92,92,90,89 84,77**
CSF £24.40 CT £92.68 TOTE £6.80: £1.80, £1.90, £2.00; EX 38.40 Trifecta £188.50.
**Owner** M M Foulger **Bred** Darley **Trained** Newmarket, Suffolk

**FOCUS**
A decent 7f handicap, featuring nine course winners, and those with the best recent form came to the fore, giving it a solid look. They went a good gallop and came down the middle in the home straight. The winning time was 1.89sec quicker than the opening maiden over the same trip. Several of these were potentially well-treated on form round here.

## 8210 DAILY PRICE BOOSTS AT UNIBET H'CAP 5f (F)
3:00 (3:01) (Class 6) (0-65,65) 3-Y-O+ £1,940 (£577; £288; £144) Stalls High

Form RPR
/31- **1** **Extreme Supreme**$^{44}$ 7652 3-9-7 65..........(v$^{1}$) PatrickMathers 6 77
(Derek Shaw) *cl up: rdn over 1f out: led jst ins fnl f: kpt on* 5/1$^{2}$

006- **2** 1 1/4 **College Doll**$^{9}$ 8088 5-8-11 55..........(t) JimmyQuinn 4 62
(Christine Dunnett) *led: rdn over 1f out: hdd jst ins fnl f: kpt on same pce* 16/1

002- **3** 1/2 **Divertimenti (IRE)**$^{5}$ 8133 10-8-0 51 oh1..........(b) AdamMcLean$^{(7)}$ 3 56
(Roy Bowring) *prom: rdn along and edgd lft to far rail over 1f out: drvn and kpt on fnl f* 15/2$^{3}$

001- **4** 1 1/2 **Incomparable**$^{9}$ 8088 9-8-9 58 6ex..........(p) ShaneGray$^{(5)}$ 7 58
(Scott Dixon) *trckd ldrs: pushed along 1/2-way: rdn over 1f out: kpt on same pce fnl f* 10/1

000- **5** 3/4 **Saffire Song**$^{13}$ 8040 3-9-1 64.......... TimClark$^{(5)}$ 2 61
(Alan Bailey) *towards rr: rdn along over 2f out: kpt on fnl f* 8/1

021- **6** nk **Lucky Mark (IRE)**$^{23}$ 7915 5-9-2 60..........(p) DanielTudhope 8 56
(John Balding) *trckd ldrs: cl up 1/2-way: rdn 2f out and grad wknd* 11/4$^{1}$

055- **6** dht **Laughing Rock (IRE)**$^{23}$ 7915 4-8-9 53..........(v) LukeMorris 1 49
(Michael Appleby) *dwlt and towards rr: hdwy 1/2-way: sn rdn and kpt on fnl f* 5/1$^{2}$

000- **8** 2 1/2 **Lupo D'Oro (IRE)**$^{35}$ 7758 5-9-4 62.......... RobertWinston 10 49
(John Best) *towards rr: pushed along after 2f: rdn over 2f out: kpt on fnl f* 14/1

465- **9** 1 3/4 **Meebo (IRE)**$^{9}$ 8088 3-9-2 60..........(vt) JFEgan 9 41
(J R Jenkins) *chsd ldrs: cl up 1/2-way: rdn 2f out and sn wknd* 9/1

000- **10** 13 **Fama Mac**$^{9}$ 8084 7-8-8 52.......... RaulDaSilva 11
(Neville Bycroft) *dwlt: a bhd: eased fnl f* 66/1

58.83s (-0.87) **Going Correction** -0.125s/f (Stan) **10** Ran SP% **116.0**
Speed ratings (Par 101): **101,99,98,95,94 94,94,90,87,66**
CSF £80.84 CT £596.67 TOTE £5.20: £2.00, £6.10, £2.40; EX 110.50 Trifecta £998.80.
**Owner** Mrs Lyndsey Shaw **Bred** Derek Shaw **Trained** Sproxton, Leics

**FOCUS**
Quite a good race for the class, featuring a scattering of C&D victors and last-time-out winners. Those up with the decent pace dominated. The winner built on his maiden form.

## 8211 CORAL MOBILE JUST THREE CLICKS TO BET H'CAP 1m 4f (F)
3:30 (3:30) (Class 4) (0-85,81) 3-Y-O+ £4,690 (£1,395; £697; £348) Stalls Low

Form RPR
251- **1** **Royal Marskell**$^{9}$ 8089 5-8-13 75 6ex.......... TobyAtkinson$^{(5)}$ 6 88
(Alison Hutchinson) *trckd ldng pair: cl up 1/2-way: led over 4f out: rdn clr wl over 1f out: styd on strly* 9/2

160- **2** 5 **Jacobs Son**$^{24}$ 7903 6-9-6 77.......... LukeMorris 2 82
(Michael Appleby) *trckd ldrs: pushed along over 4f out: rdn and outpcd over 3f out: swtchd lft to inner rail and drvn over 1f out: styd on to take modest 2nd nr fin* 5/2$^{1}$

**3** nk **Brassbound (USA)**$^{63}$ 7391 6-8-13 70.......... HayleyTurner 5 75
(Michael Appleby) *cl up: led after 5f: pushed along and hdd over 4f out: chsd wnr and rdn 3f out: drvn fnl 2f: kpt on same pce and lost modest 2nd nr fin* 3/1$^{2}$

632- **4** 1 1/4 **Layline (IRE)**$^{9}$ 8089 7-8-11 68.......... JFEgan 4 71
(Gay Kelleway) *trckd ldrs: hdwy 4f out: effrt 3f out: rdn over 2f out: drvn wl over 1f out and no imp* 7/2$^{3}$

354- **5** 10 **Mishrif (USA)**$^{121}$ 5533 8-9-3 74..........(v) FergalLynch 3 61
(J R Jenkins) *sn led: hdd after 5f: rdn along over 5f out: sn lost pl and bhd* 25/1

300- **6** 8 **Puzzle Time**$^{28}$ 7850 4-9-10 81.......... RobertWinston 1 55
(Giles Bravery) *hld up: hdwy on outer 1/2-way: cl up over 4f: rdn along 3f out: drvn over 2f out and sn wknd* 6/1

2m 37.23s (-3.77) **Going Correction** -0.125s/f (Stan) **6** Ran SP% **112.1**
Speed ratings (Par 105): **107,103,103,102,95 90**
CSF £16.10 TOTE £4.80: £1.90, £1.40; EX 15.90 Trifecta £75.20.
**Owner** Miss Chantal Wootten **Bred** Miss V Woodward **Trained** Exning, Suffolk

**FOCUS**
A fair handicap run at a decent gallop, though it was turned into a procession by the winner, who came well clear of the remainder. This rates a clear personal best.
T/Jkpt: Not won. T/Plt: £2,677.90 to a £1 stake. Pool of £65445.03 - 17.84 winning tickets. T/Qpdt: £84.40 to a £1 stake. Pool of £7454.49 - 65.30 winning tickets. JR

# 8148 DEAUVILLE (R-H)
Thursday, December 18

**OFFICIAL GOING: Polytrack: standard**

## 8212a PRIX DE PUTANGES (CLAIMER) (2YO COLTS & GELDINGS) (POLYTRACK) 1m 1f 110y
12:00 (12:00) 2-Y-O £8,333 (£3,333; £2,500; £1,666; £833)

RPR
**1** **Good Deal (FR)** 2-8-10 0 ow1..........(p) YoannRousset 13
(J Merienne, France) 42/1

**2** 1/2 **Oui Monsieur (FR)**$^{5}$ 8149 2-9-0 0..........(b) StevanBourgois 12
(Robert Collet, France) 63/10

**3** 3 **Rivolochop (FR)**$^{62}$ 2-8-9 0..........(p) FreddyDiFede 8
(C Boutin, France) 78/10

**4** 2 **Helmsman (IRE)**$^{41}$ 7723 2-8-13 0..........(b$^{1}$) JosephineGordon 1
(J S Moore) *pushed along early: sn midfield in tch on inner: rdn 2f out: angled out ent fnl f: kpt on but nt pce to chal* 23/10$^{1}$

**5** 3 1/2 **Atilla (FR)**$^{64}$ 2-8-9 0..........(p) ValentinGambart 10
(M Boutin, France) 59/10$^{3}$

**6** 3 1/2 **Johnchop (FR)** 2-8-13 0..........(p) MarcNobili 5
(J-M Lefebvre, France) 30/1

**7** 1 **Hartwood (FR)**$^{178}$ 2-8-13 0..........(p) CyrilleStefan 11
(F-X De Chevigny, France) 55/1

**8** 3 1/2 **Giant Swing (FR)**$^{35}$ 2-8-9 0..........(b$^{1}$) AdrienMoreau 3
(M Boutin, France) 85/1

**9** 1/2 **Atlas Royal (FR)**$^{119}$ 5618 2-8-9 0.......... NicolasBarzalona 4
(Mario Hofer, Germany) 74/10

**10** 6 **Mille Of Journey (FR)** 2-8-9 0.......... ThibaultSpeicher 7
(S Kobayashi, France) 28/1

**11** hd **Orion Des Charps (FR)** 2-9-2 0.......... YohannBourgois 9
(G Collet, France) 53/1

**P** **Ruby's Teddy Bear (IRE)**$^{49}$ 2-8-9 0..........(b) AntoineCoutier 2
(S Wattel, France) 16/5$^{2}$

1m 58.87s (118.87) **12** Ran SP% **119.4**
WIN (incl. 1 euro stake): 43.20. PLACES: 12.00, 2.80, 2.90. DF: 136.40. SF: 484.00.
**Owner** Ecurie Des Anges Earl **Bred** R Baudouin & Mme L Hiver **Trained** France

8213 - 8217a (Foreign Racing) - See Raceform Interactive

# 8205 SOUTHWELL (L-H)
Friday, December 19

**OFFICIAL GOING: Fibresand: standard**
Wind: Strong half behind Weather: Fine and dry

## 8218 LADBROKES H'CAP 1m (F)
12:00 (12:00) (Class 6) (0-60,60) 3-Y-O+ £2,264 (£673; £336; £168) Stalls Low

Form RPR
035- **1** **Sooqaan**$^{14}$ 8049 3-9-6 60.......... PJMcDonald 5 71
(Mel Brittain) *trckd ldrs: cl up over 3f out: led wl over 2f out: rdn over 1f out: kpt on wl u.p towards fin* 10/1

062- **2** nk **Two Shades Of Grey (IRE)**$^{10}$ 8086 3-9-6 60..........(p) GeorgeChaloner 1 70
(Richard Fahey) *in tch: pushed along 3f out: hdwy 2f out: rdn to chal ins fnl f: ev ch tl drvn and edgd lft last 100yds: no ex nr fin* 9/4$^{1}$

050- **3** 2 3/4 **General Tufto**$^{62}$ 7290 9-8-9 51..........(b) JoeyHaynes$^{(3)}$ 8 56
(Charles Smith) *in tch on outer: hdwy and wd st: rdn to chse ldng pair wl over 1f out: sn drvn and kpt on same pce* 16/1

053- **4** 3 1/4 **Falcon's Reign (FR)**$^{6}$ 8137 5-9-7 60..........(v$^{1}$) LukeMorris 3 58
(Michael Appleby) *prom: rdn along wl over 2f out: sn one pce* 5/1

226- **5** 1 **Company Secretary (USA)**$^{14}$ 8049 3-9-5 59..........(p) MartinDwyer 7 53
(Jo Hughes) *cl up: led after 1 1/2f: jnd over 3f out: sn rdn and hdd wl over 2f out: sn drvn: edgd lft and wknd over 1f out* 7/2$^{2}$

411- **6** 11 **Novalist**$^{6}$ 8139 6-9-4 57 12ex.......... JasonHart 4 27
(Robin Bastiman) *slt ld: pushed along and hdd after 1 1/2f: rdn along after 3f: sn lost pl and bhd* 9/2$^{3}$

103- **7** 19 **Delightful Sleep**$^{3}$ 8175 6-9-5 58.......... JFEgan 6
(David Evans) *a towards rr* 16/1

050- **8** 2 1/4 **Blackthorn Stick (IRE)**$^{18}$ 7987 5-9-4 57.......... LiamKeniry 2
(John Butler) *cl up: pushed along after 3f: sn rdn and lost pl 1/2-way: sn bhd* 50/1

1m 43.66s (-0.04) **Going Correction** -0.075s/f (Stan)
**WFA** 3 from 5yo+ 1lb **8** Ran SP% **110.7**
Speed ratings (Par 101): **97,96,93,90,89 78,59,57**
CSF £30.75 CT £343.81 TOTE £12.20: £3.50, £1.10, £3.10; EX 39.40 Trifecta £904.80.
**Owner** Mel Brittain **Bred** J A And Mrs Duffy **Trained** Warthill, N Yorks

**FOCUS**
A moderate handicap to start.

## 8219 LADBROKES CLASSIFIED STKS 7f (F)
12:30 (12:30) (Class 6) 3-Y-O+ £1,940 (£577; £288; £144) Stalls Low

Form RPR
050- **1** **Wimboldsley**$^{11}$ 8081 3-9-0 50.......... LukeMorris 8 58
(Scott Dixon) *t.k.h: trckd ldrs: led after 2f: rdn over 2f out: drvn and edgd lft ent fnl f: kpt on u.p towards fin* 7/2$^{2}$

045- **2** nk **Tableforten**$^{6}$ 8139 3-9-0 54..........(v$^{1}$) LiamJones 7 57
(J S Moore) *trckd ldrs: hdwy 1/2-way: chsd wnr wl over 2f out: rdn over 1f out: drvn ins fnl f: kpt on towards fin* 2/1$^{1}$

355- **3** 3 3/4 **Lendal Bridge**[10] 8084 3-8-9 54..............................(p) ShaneGray(5) 2 47+
(Tony Coyle) *prom on inner: pushed along: n.m.r and lost pl after 2 1/2f: in rr whn n.m.r 1/2-way: swtchd rt and hdwy 3f out: chsd ldrs over 1f out: kpt on ins fnl f: nrst fin* **4/1**[3]

000- **4** 1 **Classical Diva**[6] 8139 3-8-9 46..........................(be) AlistairRawlinson(5) 6 45
(Michael Appleby) *in tch whn n.m.r and hmpd after 2f: sn swtchd rt: hdwy to chse ldng pair 1/2-way: rdn over 2f out: sn drvn and one pce* **20/1**

254- **5** 3/4 **Llandanwg**[17] 8002 3-9-0 47..........................(b) PaulMulrennan 9 43
(Bryan Smart) *chsd ldrs on outer: rdn along wl over 2f out: drvn wl over 1f out and sn one pce* **8/1**

053- **6** 11 **La Danza**[10] 8085 4-8-7 46.................................... KevinLundie(7) 5 14
(Shaun Harris) *led 2f: sn pushed along and lost pl: bhd fr 1/2-way* **16/1**

300- **7** nse **Vale Mentor (IRE)**[10] 8088 3-9-0 55..........................(p) LiamKeniry 4 14
(Denis Quinn) *cl up: pushed along: n.m.r and lost pl after 2 1/2f: bhd fr 1/2-way* **20/1**

053- **8** 4 **Patron Of Explores (USA)**[17] 8002 3-8-11 48..........(t) DeclanBates(3) 3 4
(Patrick Holmes) *cl up: n.m.r and lost pl after 2 1/2f: sn swtchd rt: wd st and bhd* **7/1**

030/ **9** 9 **Rich Harvest (USA)**[1196] 5917 9-9-0 37........................ MartinDwyer 10
(Ray Peacock) *chsd ldrs on inner: rdn along 3f out: sn wknd* **100/1**

1m 30.77s (0.47) **Going Correction** -0.075s/f (Stan) **9** Ran SP% **115.6**
Speed ratings (Par 101): **94,93,89,88,87 74,74,70,59**
CSF £10.68 TOTE £3.40: £1.30, £1.70, £1.60; EX 13.40 Trifecta £84.40.
**Owner** Paul J Dixon And The Chrystal Maze Ptn **Bred** Paul Dixon & Crystal Maze Partnership **Trained** Babworth, Notts

**FOCUS**
A moderate 0-55 classified event and this lot had a combined record of 4-119 coming into the race.

## 8220 32RED FILLIES' MAIDEN STKS (BOBIS RACE) 1m (F)
**1:00** (1:01) (Class 5) 2-Y-O **£2,587** (£770; £384; £192) **Stalls** Low

Form RPR

**1** **Nadder** 2-9-0 0.......................................... DavidProbert 5 77+
(Andrew Balding) *cl up: led wl over 2f out: rdn appr fnl f: kpt on strly* **12/1**

22- **2** 2 1/2 **Pin Up (IRE)**[35] 7778 2-9-0 0.............................. GeorgeChaloner 7 71
(Richard Fahey) *dwlt and sn pushed along in rr: hdwy to trck ldrs after 2f: effrt 3f out: rdn along to chse wnr over 1f out: sn no imp* **1/2**[1]

042- **3** 8 **Sylvette**[34] 7809 2-9-0 70.................................... JackMitchell 4 53
(Roger Varian) *led: rdn along 3f out: sn rdn and one pce fnl 2f* **11/2**[2]

062- **4** 1 1/4 **Brosnan (IRE)**[10] 8087 2-9-0 64.............................. SamJames 6 50
(Noel Quinlan) *chsd ldrs on outer: wd st: rdn along over 2f out: drvn wl over 1f out: sn one pce* **17/2**[3]

00- **5** 22 **Shamazing**[22] 7944 2-9-0 0..............................(b[1]) PaulMulrennan 1
(Kevin Ryan) *chsd ldrs on inner: pushed along and lost pl after 2f: rdn along bef 1/2-way: sn outpcd and bhd* **50/1**

**6** 10 **Perle Express** 2-9-0 0..............................................[1] LukeMorris 2
(Michael Appleby) *chsd ldrs: rdn along bef 1/2-way: sn outpcd and bhd* **20/1**

**U** **Serenade** 2-8-9 0.......................................... KevinStott(5) 3
(Kevin Ryan) *s.i.s: green: bucking and uns rdr sn after s* **10/1**

1m 44.65s (0.95) **Going Correction** -0.075s/f (Stan) **7** Ran SP% **116.1**
Speed ratings (Par 93): **92,89,81,80,58 48,**
CSF £19.20 TOTE £14.90: £4.90, £1.10; EX 27.80 Trifecta £96.10.
**Owner** Mrs James Wigan **Bred** Mrs James Wigan **Trained** Kingsclere, Hants

**FOCUS**
They finished well spread out in this maiden. The third and fourth were both officially rated 70, which gives an indication of what the impressive winner has achieved.

## 8221 ALL NEW 32REDSPORT.COM NURSERY H'CAP 7f (F)
**1:35** (1:36) (Class 6) (0-60,60) 2-Y-O **£2,264** (£673; £336; £168) **Stalls** Low

Form RPR

150- **1** **Excelling Oscar (IRE)**[10] 8087 2-9-1 54..........................(b) LiamKeniry 4 61
(Conor Dore) *trckd ldrs: hdwy 1/2-way: effrt and cl up on outer 2f out: rdn to ld jst ins fnl f: sn edgd lft and styd on wl* **4/1**[2]

000- **2** 2 1/2 **Never Easy (IRE)**[58] 7378 2-9-6 59.......................... PatrickMathers 3 59
(Richard Fahey) *led: rdn along 2f out: drvn and edgd lft ent fnl f: sn hdd and kpt on same pce* **17/2**[3]

053- **3** 1 3/4 **Hana Lina**[8] 8115 2-9-7 60..................................(b) GeorgeBaker 1 56
(William Haggas) *trckd ldrs on inner: effrt 2f out: sn rdn: drvn and hld whn n.m.r ins fnl f: one pce* **7/2**[1]

630- **4** nk **Theydon Thunder**[137] 4965 2-8-10 52........................ RosieJessop(3) 5 47
(Peter Charalambous) *prom: cl up 1/2-way: rdn along and ev ch 2f out: kpt on same pce appr fnl f* **33/1**

005- **5** 1 **Miss Minuty**[16] 8009 2-9-6 59.................................... LukeMorris 6 51
(Sir Mark Prescott Bt) *chsd ldrs: pushed along after 3f: rdn along 3f out: kpt on one pce fnl 2f* **4/1**[2]

050/ **6** 1/2 **Josie Joe**[206] 2642 2-9-5 58.................................... PaulMulrennan 8 49
(David Evans) *racd wd: towards rr: rdn along and hdwy on outer 2f out: kpt on fnl f: nrst fin* **14/1**

000- **7** 1 **Marsoomah**[20] 7973 2-8-13 52..........................[1] GeorgeChaloner 7 40
(Richard Fahey) *dwlt and in rr: hdwy and in tch 1/2-way: rdn along over 2f out: sn no imp* **9/1**

000- **8** 28 **Come Up And See Me**[17] 8000 2-8-6 45........................ DavidProbert 2
(J R Jenkins) *chsd ldrs on inner: rdn along and lost pl after 3f: sn bhd* **33/1**

1m 31.1s (0.80) **Going Correction** -0.075s/f (Stan) **8** Ran SP% **95.3**
Speed ratings (Par 94): **92,89,87,86,85 85,83,51**
CSF £25.27 CT £70.70 TOTE £4.20: £1.40, £3.40, £1.10; EX 29.90 Trifecta £158.60.
**Owner** Mrs Jennifer Marsh **Bred** Miss Hilary McLoughlin **Trained** Hubbert's Bridge, Lincs
■ Let Right Be Done was withdrawn. Price at time of withdrawal 5/1. Rule 4 applies to all bets - deduction 15p in the pound.

**FOCUS**
Only one of these had been successful before and that was in a seller, but he remained the only winner in the field afterwards. The field was reduced by one when Let Right Be Done was withdrawn after getting under his stall.

## 8222 DAILY ENHANCED "MAGIC MULTIPLES" AT UNIBET NURSERY H'CAP 6f (F)
**2:10** (2:10) (Class 5) (0-75,75) 2-Y-O **£2,587** (£770; £384; £192) **Stalls** Low

Form RPR

233- **1** **Spinaminnie (IRE)**[17] 8000 2-8-11 65.......................... PaulMulrennan 2 68
(Mark Johnston) *led: rdn along wl over 1f out: hdd appr fnl f: drvn on inner and rallied ins fnl f to ld again nr fin* **11/4**[3]

164- **2** nse **Rita's Boy (IRE)**[63] 7231 2-9-2 75.......................... JordanVaughan(5) 1 78
(K R Burke) *trckd ldrs on inner: swtchd rt and hdwy over 2f out: rdn to chal over 1f out: led appr fnl f: hdd and nt qckn nr fin* **7/4**[1]

332- **3** 3 **Seychelloise**[30] 7840 2-8-12 66.................................... LukeMorris 3 59
(Sir Mark Prescott Bt) *cl up: rdn along wl over 2f out: drvn and kpt on same pce appr fnl f* **5/2**[2]

200- **4** 1 1/4 **Grosmont**[20] 7970 2-9-2 70.......................................... PJMcDonald 4 59
(James Given) *trckd ldng pair on outer: effrt over 2f out: sn rdn and cl up: tl drvn and one pce fr over 1f out* **11/2**

1m 15.58s (-0.92) **Going Correction** -0.075s/f (Stan) **4** Ran SP% **107.0**
Speed ratings (Par 96): **103,102,98,97**
CSF £7.77 TOTE £3.00; EX 9.20 Trifecta £22.90.
**Owner** Mrs Lisa Kelly **Bred** Mrs Lisa Kelly **Trained** Middleham Moor, N Yorks

**FOCUS**
Just the four runners, but they seemed to go a solid pace in this nursery.

## 8223 UNIBET OFFER DAILY JOCKEY/TRAINER SPECIALS CLAIMING STKS 6f (F)
**2:45** (2:45) (Class 6) 3-Y-O+ **£1,940** (£577; £288; £144) **Stalls** Low

Form RPR

606- **1** **Abi Scarlet (IRE)**[3] 8182 5-8-5 75.......................... DavidParkes(7) 2 77
(Scott Dixon) *cl up: led wl over 2f out: rdn along over 1f out: edgd rt ins fnl f: hld on wl towards fin* **15/2**[3]

011- **2** 1/2 **Showtime Star**[10] 8082 4-9-0 64.............................. DavidProbert 5 77
(Gay Kelleway) *dwlt sltly and hld up in rr: hdwy 1/2-way: chsd wnr 2f out: rdn and edgd rt ent fnl f: drvn and kpt on towards fin* **7/4**[2]

050- **3** 6 **Pearl Blue (IRE)**[41] 7716 6-8-12 94.............................. LukeMorris 4 56
(Jamie Osborne) *trckd ldrs: hdwy 3f out: chsd ldng pair and rdn 2f out: sn drvn and kpt on same pce* **5/4**[1]

160- **4** 1 **Moiety**[10] 8082 3-8-4 70..........................................(t) RyanTate(3) 6 48
(Rae Guest) *trckd ldrs: pushed along 3f out: rdn over 2f out: sn one pce* **10/1**

000- **5** 1 1/2 **Prince Of Passion (CAN)**[6] 8133 6-8-8 51..............(v) PatrickMathers 1 44
(Derek Shaw) *slt ld: rdn along 1/2-way: sn hdd and drvn: grad wknd* **66/1**

663- **6** 12 **Foxy Music**[172] 3793 10-8-7 77..........................(b) BarryMcHugh 3 5
(Tony Coyle) *t.k.h: cl up on outer: pushed along and wd st: sn rdn and wknd* **16/1**

1m 15.13s (-1.37) **Going Correction** -0.075s/f (Stan) **6** Ran SP% **109.0**
Speed ratings (Par 101): **106,105,97,96,94 78**
CSF £19.93 TOTE £8.20: £3.30, £1.80; EX 24.90 Trifecta £40.00.
**Owner** Ontoawinner 4 & Homecroft Wealth Racing **Bred** Henry O'Callaghan **Trained** Babworth, Notts

**FOCUS**
A wide range of abilities in this claimer and being able to handle the surface meant everything. Official ratings went out of the window.

## 8224 DOWNLOAD THE LADBROKES APP H'CAP 7f (F)
**3:20** (3:20) (Class 5) (0-70,76) 3-Y-O+ **£2,587** (£770; £384; £192) **Stalls** Low

Form RPR

001- **1** **Bognor (USA)**[10] 8086 3-9-13 76 6ex.......................... LukeMorris 8 87+
(Michael Appleby) *trckd ldrs: hdwy 3f out: rdn to chal wl over 1f out: edgd lft and slt ld ent fnl f: drvn out* **10/11**[1]

061- **2** 1 **Munaawib**[14] 8043 6-8-12 68..........................(bt) DavidParkes(7) 6 76
(Deborah Sanderson) *cl up: led 3f out: jnd and rdn 2f out: hdd ent fnl f: kpt on* **9/1**[3]

203- **3** 1 **Bainne (IRE)**[10] 8082 4-9-6 69.............................. StevieDonohoe 7 74
(James Eustace) *dwlt and in rr: hdwy and wd st: sn rdn: styd on wl appr fnl f: nrst fin* **10/1**

201- **4** 1 1/4 **Burnhope**[3] 8176 5-9-1 69 6ex.............................. TimClark(5) 1 71
(Scott Dixon) *slt ld: pushed along 1/2-way: hdd 3f out: rdn wl over 2f out: drvn over 1f out: one pce* **3/1**[2]

345- **5** 1/2 **Piccadilly Jim (IRE)**[34] 7812 3-9-3 66.......................... PatrickMathers 3 67
(Richard Fahey) *towards rr and sn rdn along: hdwy on inner wl over 2f out: rdn to chse ldrs wl over 1f: drvn and no imp fnl f* **25/1**

501- **6** 3 3/4 **Brooke's Bounty**[45] 7639 4-9-1 64.......................... GeorgeChaloner 5 55
(Richard Fahey) *a towards rr* **16/1**

000- **7** 5 **Silly Billy (IRE)**[10] 8086 6-9-4 67..........................(p) BarryMcHugh 2 45
(John Balding) *chsd ldrs: rdn along 3f out: sn wknd* **25/1**

600- **8** 5 **Madame Mirasol (IRE)**[21] 7954 3-9-1 69..........(p) KevinStott(5) 4 34
(Kevin Ryan) *sn rdn along in rr: a outpcd and a bhd* **12/1**

1m 28.65s (-1.65) **Going Correction** -0.075s/f (Stan) **8** Ran SP% **117.7**
Speed ratings (Par 103): **106,104,103,102,101 97,91,86**
CSF £10.97 CT £51.29 TOTE £2.30: £1.10, £2.30, £3.10; EX 10.70 Trifecta £75.10.
**Owner** 21C Telecom.co.uk **Bred** Klawervlei Stud (pty) Ltd **Trained** Danethorpe, Notts

**FOCUS**
A fair handicap for the grade with half the field last-time-out winners.
T/Plt: £46.00 to a £1 stake. Pool: £59,000.04 - 935.03 winning tickets T/Qpdt: £12.60 to a £1 stake. Pool: £3,918.92 - 230.00 winning tickets JR

# 8161 WOLVERHAMPTON (A.W) (L-H)
Friday, December 19

**OFFICIAL GOING: Tapeta: standard**
Wind: Strong behind Weather: Cloudy

## 8225 32RED CASINO MAIDEN AUCTION STKS (TAPETA) 7f 32y
**3:50** (3:51) (Class 6) 2-Y-O **£2,102** (£625; £312; £156) **Stalls** High

Form RPR

66- **1** **Charlton Heights (IRE)**[6] 8148 2-8-12 0..........................(p) LiamJones 5 68
(J S Moore) *sn led: rdn over 1f out: sn hung rt: r.o* **5/2**[2]

622- **2** 1 1/4 **Come Uppence**[11] 8076 2-9-0 70.................................... JFEgan 2 67
(David Evans) *led early: stdd to chse wnr: rdn over 2f out: edgd rt fnl f: styd on* **13/8**[1]

**3** 1 1/2 **Virtual Reality** 2-9-2 0.......................................... JackMitchell 3 65+
(Philip McBride) *dwlt: hld up: pushed along 1/2-way: hdwy over 1f out: hung lft and r.o ins fnl f: nt rch ldrs* **4/1**[3]

5- **4** 5 **Wisteria**[41] 7712 2-8-6 0.......................................... NickyMackay 1 41
(David C Griffiths) *chsd ldrs: rdn over 2f out: wknd fnl f* **11/2**

060- **5** 7 **Spirit Of Rosanna**[13] 8060 2-8-10 0 ow1.......................... RobertHavlin 6 27
(Steph Hollinshead) *chsd ldrs: rdn over 2f out: wknd over 1f out* **100/1**

1m 30.67s (1.87) **Going Correction** -0.075s/f (Stan) **5** Ran SP% **103.0**
Speed ratings (Par 94): **86,84,82,77,69**
CSF £6.01 TOTE £3.30: £2.10, £1.10; EX 6.50 Trifecta £16.50.
**Owner** Kieron Badger & J S Moore **Bred** Padraic Connolly **Trained** Upper Lambourn, Berks


The Form Book, Raceform Ltd, Newbury, RG14 5SJ

**FOCUS**
A desperately weak maiden in which the winner was allowed to set a modest pace.

## 8226 32RED NURSERY H'CAP (BOBIS RACE) (TAPETA) 7f 32y
4:20 (4:20) (Class 4) (0-85,81) 2-Y-O £3,881 (£1,155; £577; £288) Stalls High

Form RPR
61- 1 **Kaufmann**[17] 8000 2-9-7 81 .......... RobertHavlin 3 84
(John Gosden) *sn trcking ldr: rdn to ld over 1f out: r.o* 5/4[1]
01- 2 ½ **Victory Megastar**[44] 7660 2-9-4 78 .......... SteveDrowne 4 80
(Clive Cox) *hld up in tch: shkn up over 2f out: ev ch ins fnl f: styd on* 11/8[2]
561- 3 nse **Just Marion (IRE)**[30] 7832 2-8-4 64 .......... JFEgan 2 66
(David Evans) *chsd ldrs: rdn and ev ch whn edgd rt ins fnl f: styd on* 20/1
13- 4 7 **Gabrial The Tiger (IRE)**[81] 6820 2-8-6 71 .......... SammyJoBell(5) 1 54
(Richard Fahey) *led: shkn up over 2f out: rdr dropped rein and hdd over 1f out: wknd ins fnl f* 15/2[3]
1m 30.3s (1.50) **Going Correction** -0.075s/f (Stan) 4 Ran SP% **103.1**
Speed ratings (Par 98): **88,87,87,79**
CSF £2.92 TOTE £1.90; EX 3.10 Trifecta £7.70.
**Owner** Ms Rachel D S Hood **Bred** Rachel D S Hood **Trained** Newmarket, Suffolk

**FOCUS**
The early pace was steady and they covered the last 2f around a second quicker than the preceding juvenile maiden. The final time was 0.37secs faster.

## 8227 32RED.COM MAIDEN STKS (TAPETA) 5f 216y
4:50 (4:51) (Class 5) 2-Y-O £2,749 (£818; £408; £204) Stalls Low

Form RPR
1 **Luis Vaz De Torres (IRE)** 2-9-5 0 .......... DavidNolan 6 73+
(Richard Fahey) *a.p: chsd ldr over 2f out: rdn to ld and edgd lft 1f out: r.o* 66/1
3- 2 ¾ **Balayage (IRE)**[16] 8007 2-9-0 0 .......... MartinLane 5 66+
(Marco Botti) *s.s: hld up: hdwy over 1f out: r.o to go 2nd nr fin: nt rch wnr* 4/5[1]
2- 3 nk **Ershaad (IRE)**[23] 7919 2-9-5 0 .......... JackMitchell 10 70
(Roger Varian) *chsd ldrs: rdn over 1f out: edgd lft ins fnl f: styd on* 7/4[2]
5- 4 nk **Sir Keltic Blue**[20] 7970 2-9-5 0 .......... PaulPickard 1 69
(Brian Ellison) *led: rdn over 2f out: hung lft and hdd 1f out: kpt on* 14/1
64- 5 nk **Souk Al Tahab (IRE)**[9] 8092 2-9-5 0 .......... GeorgeBaker 7 68
(Ed Dunlop) *hld up: hdwy over 1f out: rdn and hung lft ins fnl f: styd on* 8/1[3]
6 2 **Chasing Rubies (IRE)** 2-9-0 0 .......... WilliamTwiston-Davies 2 57+
(Michael Bell) *prom: rdn over 1f out: nt clr run ins fnl f: styd on same pce* 50/1
7 1¾ **Houdini** 2-9-5 0 .......... TomQueally 8 56+
(Jamie Osborne) *s.i.s: in rr: pushed along 1/2-way: styd on ins fnl f: nvr nrr* 14/1
020- 8 7 **Jubilee Spirit**[87] 6642 2-9-5 60 .......... CharlesBishop 12 34
(Geoffrey Oldroyd) *s.s: a in rr* 33/1
00- 9 1 **Mildmay Arms**[15] 8026 2-9-5 0 .......... LiamJones 3 31
(Simon Hodgson) *drvn along 1/2-way: a in rr* 100/1
0- 10 ½ **Brean Golf Birdie**[22] 7943 2-8-9 0 .......... RyanWhile(5) 9 24
(Bill Turner) *chsd ldr tl rdn over 2f out: wknd over 1f out* 100/1
00- 11 15 **Lady Vellyn**[44] 7666 2-9-0 0 .......... LiamKeniry 11
(Derek Haydn Jones) *prom: racd keenly: rdn and wknd over 2f out* 100/1
1m 14.65s (0.15) **Going Correction** -0.075s/f (Stan) 11 Ran SP% **125.7**
Speed ratings (Par 96): **96,95,94,94,93 91,88,79,78,77 57**
CSF £130.61 TOTE £26.30: £9.20, £1.10, £1.10; EX 174.80 Trifecta £691.60.
**Owner** Lets Go Racing 1 **Bred** Peter Molony **Trained** Musley Bank, N Yorks

**FOCUS**
They went a fair pace but there was a bunched finish.

## 8228 DAILY ENHANCED "MAGIC MULTIPLES" AT UNIBET H'CAP (TAPETA) 5f 216y
5:20 (5:21) (Class 2) (0-105,105) 3-Y-O+ £11,971 (£3,583; £1,791; £896; £446) Stalls Low

Form RPR
/04- 1 **Pretend (IRE)**[55] 7455 3-8-6 **95** .......... ShaneGray(5) 2 107
(Charlie Appleby) *s.i.s: sn prom: rdn to ld wl ins fnl f: r.o* 5/2[1]
122- 2 ½ **Boom The Groom (IRE)**[9] 8101 3-8-9 **93** .......... WilliamCarson 1 103
(Tony Carroll) *chsd ldrs: led over 1f out: rdn and hdd wl ins fnl f* 4/1[2]
331- 3 1¼ **Secondo (FR)**[14] 8045 4-8-8 **92** .......... (v) ChrisCatlin 10 98
(Robert Stephens) *hld up: swtchd rt and hdwy over 1f out: r.o wl ins fnl f: nt rch ldrs* 8/1
023- 4 ¾ **Badr Al Badoor (IRE)**[21] 7952 4-8-11 **95** ow1 .......... TomQueally 9 99
(James Fanshawe) *hld up: hdwy and n.m.r 2f out: rdn over 1f out: styd on same pce ins fnl f* 4/1[2]
305- 5 1¾ **Ballista (IRE)**[16] 8019 6-8-9 **93** .......... LiamKeniry 5 91
(Tom Dascombe) *chsd ldr tl rdn over 1f out: no ex wl ins fnl f* 33/1
016- 6 1½ **Caspian Prince (IRE)**[96] 6378 5-9-2 **105** .......... (t) GeorgeDowning(5) 8 98
(Tony Carroll) *led 5f out: hdd over 1f out: wknd wl ins fnl f* 25/1
211- 7 3¼ **Saint Pois (FR)**[90] 3-8-5 **89** .......... LiamJones 4 72
(Tony Carroll) *chsd ldrs: rdn over 2f out: wknd over 1f out* 20/1
503- 8 shd **Tarooq (USA)**[9] 8101 8-9-7 **105** .......... GrahamGibbons 3 87
(David Barron) *prom: rdn over 2f out: wknd over 1f out* 11/2[3]
040- 9 ½ **Fairway To Heaven (IRE)**[9] 8101 5-8-7 **91** .......... DavidProbert 6 72
(Michael Wigham) *sn pushed along in rr: nvr on terms* 8/1
650- 10 1¼ **Bond Fastrac**[6] 8141 7-7-9 **86** oh8 .......... AaronJones(7) 7 63
(Geoffrey Oldroyd) *a in rr* 100/1
1m 11.84s (-2.66) **Going Correction** -0.075s/f (Stan) course record 10 Ran SP% **118.7**
Speed ratings (Par 109): **114,113,111,110,108 106,102,101,101,99**
CSF £12.28 CT £70.65 TOTE £3.30: £1.20, £1.60, £2.10; EX 13.10 Trifecta £66.10.
**Owner** Godolphin **Bred** Azienda Agricola Loreto Luciani **Trained** Newmarket, Suffolk

**FOCUS**
A decent sprint handicap run at a strong pace. The time was easily the quickest of 67 races to be over this trip on the Tapeta here.

## 8229 UNIBET OFFER DAILY JOCKEY/TRAINER SPECIALS H'CAP (DIV I) (TAPETA) 5f 20y
5:50 (5:50) (Class 6) (0-55,55) 3-Y-O+ £2,102 (£625; £312; £156) Stalls Low

Form RPR
004- 1 **Spray Tan**[35] 7781 4-9-7 55 .......... LukeMorris 6 63
(Tony Carroll) *chsd ldr: rdn over 1f out: r.o to ld wl ins fnl f* 11/2[3]
000- 2 ¾ **Salvado (IRE)**[28] 7864 4-9-1 54 .......... GeorgeDowning(5) 3 59+
(Tony Carroll) *mid-div: hmpd 4f out: hdwy over 1f out: r.o to go 2nd nr fin: nt rch wnr* 7/1
604- 3 ½ **Qatar Princess (IRE)**[23] 7929 3-9-5 53 .......... (v[1]) JFEgan 7 57
(J R Jenkins) *led: rdn over 1f out: hdd and unable qck wl ins fnl f* 10/1
106- 4 ¾ **Gypsy Rider**[35] 7781 5-8-11 50 .......... EoinWalsh(5) 5 51+
(Henry Tett) *pushed along in rr early: nt clr run 2f out: hdwy u.p over 1f out: styd on* 13/2
000- 5 ¾ **Two Turtle Doves (IRE)**[44] 7671 8-9-7 55 .......... RobertHavlin 2 53
(Michael Mullineaux) *chsd ldrs: rdn over 1f out: no ex ins fnl f* 12/1
/34- 6 ½ **Done Dreaming (IRE)**[11] 8081 4-9-4 52 .......... DavidNolan 8 48
(Richard Fahey) *prom: rdn 1/2-way: styd on same pce fnl f* 6/1
522- 7 3½ **China Excels**[95] 6409 7-8-13 50 .......... RossAtkinson(3) 9 34
(Mandy Rowland) *s.i.s: hld up: shkn up over 1f out: nvr on terms* 3/1[1]
540- 8 ¾ **Go Charlie**[15] 8024 3-8-9 48 .......... AlistairRawlinson(5) 1 29
(Lisa Williamson) *s.i.s: sn pushed along and a in rr* 25/1
600- 9 1 **Straight Gin**[35] 7781 3-8-13 47 .......... (p) PJMcDonald 10 24
(Alan Berry) *chsd ldrs tl rdn and wknd over 1f out* 40/1
345- 10 6 **Mossgo (IRE)**[15] 8024 4-8-13 47 .......... MartinDwyer 4 3
(John Best) *mid-div: hmpd 4f out: pushed along over 2f out: wknd over 1f out* 5/1[2]
1m 1.23s (-0.67) **Going Correction** -0.075s/f (Stan) 10 Ran SP% **120.2**
Speed ratings (Par 101): **102,100,100,98,97 96,91,90,88,78**
CSF £45.28 CT £382.52 TOTE £5.50: £1.80, £2.00, £3.70; EX 46.30 Trifecta £313.10.
**Owner** Silks Racing Partnership **Bred** Lady Whent **Trained** Cropthorne, Worcs

**FOCUS**
Not many got into this and there was a one-two for Tony Carroll, who is enjoying his best year to date on the Flat in Britain both in terms of winners and prize money.

## 8230 UNIBET OFFER DAILY JOCKEY/TRAINER SPECIALS H'CAP (DIV II) (TAPETA) 5f 20y
6:20 (6:21) (Class 6) (0-55,55) 3-Y-O+ £2,102 (£625; £312; £156) Stalls Low

Form RPR
004- 1 **Shaft Of Light**[114] 5820 3-9-7 55 .......... (v[1]) PatrickMathers 3 64
(Derek Shaw) *chsd ldrs: pushed along 1/2-way: r.o u.p to ld nr fin* 20/1
004- 2 ½ **Ecliptic Sunrise**[15] 8024 3-9-4 52 .......... (b[1]) ShaneKelly 1 59
(Des Donovan) *led: rdn over 1f out: hdd nr fin* 4/1[2]
335- 3 1 **Quality Art (USA)**[15] 8023 6-9-2 50 .......... SteveDrowne 9 54
(Simon Hodgson) *hld up: hdwy over 1f out: r.o* 12/1
552- 4 ¾ **Rat Catcher (IRE)**[35] 7781 4-8-6 47 .......... (b) RobHornby(7) 2 48
(Lisa Williamson) *prom: nt clr run 2f out: swtchd lft over 1f out: sn rdn: styd on* 9/2[3]
343- 5 shd **Rightcar**[312] 556 7-8-12 46 .......... LiamKeniry 10 47
(Peter Grayson) *s.s: hld up: r.o ins fnl f: nvr nrr* 28/1
021- 6 1¼ **Warm Order**[7] 8119 3-9-4 52 6ex .......... LukeMorris 4 48
(Tony Carroll) *chsd ldr: rdn over 1f out: no ex ins fnl f* 5/2[1]
245- 7 1 **Artemis (IRE)**[149] 4546 3-9-7 55 .......... LiamJones 6 47
(Conrad Allen) *s.i.s: hdwy over 3f out: rdn over 1f out: no ex fnl f* 11/1
/02- 8 3 **Wreningham**[10] 8088 9-9-5 53 .......... TomQueally 8 35
(Pat Eddery) *chsd ldrs: rdn over 1f out: wknd fnl f* 10/1
200- 9 1 **Dear Ben**[235] 1804 5-9-2 50 .......... JasonHart 7 28
(Brian Baugh) *broke wl: lost pl after 1f: n.d after* 33/1
455- 10 nk **Minty Jones**[35] 7781 5-8-13 47 .......... (b) RobertHavlin 5 24
(Michael Mullineaux) *chsd ldrs tl rdn and wknd over 1f out* 7/1
1m 1.81s (-0.09) **Going Correction** -0.075s/f (Stan) 10 Ran SP% **115.5**
Speed ratings (Par 101): **97,96,94,93,93 91,89,84,83,82**
CSF £95.90 CT £1023.83 TOTE £26.80: £7.90, £1.50, £3.80; EX 166.60 Trifecta £2333.90.
**Owner** Derek Shaw **Bred** Mrs C R Philipson & Mrs H G Lascelles **Trained** Sproxton, Leics

**FOCUS**
The time was 0.58secs slower than the first leg.

## 8231 BET IN PLAY AT CORAL H'CAP (TAPETA) 1m 4f 50y
6:50 (6:50) (Class 6) (0-65,65) 3-Y-O+ £2,102 (£625; £312; £156) Stalls Low

Form RPR
526- 1 **Angus Glens**[28] 7866 4-9-6 61 .......... (p) MartinLane 9 73
(David Dennis) *chsd ldr tl led over 8f out: pushed clr fr over 2f out: eased towards fin* 7/2[1]
3/0- 2 5 **Ted Dolly (IRE)**[4] 8164 10-9-9 64 .......... StevieDonohoe 2 68
(Tom Symonds) *mid-div: hdwy over 3f out: rdn to chse wnr over 1f out: styd on same pce* 16/1
062- 3 1½ **Dancing Primo**[6] 8145 8-8-10 56 .......... EoinWalsh(5) 8 58
(Mark Brisbourne) *hld up: hdwy over 2f out: sn rdn: styd on same pce fr over 1f out: wnt 3rd wl ins fnl f* 9/2[3]
603- 4 3½ **Cabuchon (GER)**[6] 8145 7-9-0 55 .......... (vt) JFEgan 4 51
(David Evans) *chsd ldrs: rdn to chse wnr over 2f out tl over 1f out: wknd fnl f* 9/2[3]
065- 5 1 **Mister Marcasite**[10] 8086 4-9-7 62 .......... PJMcDonald 10 56
(Mel Brittain) *hld up: nt clr run over 3f out: rdn over 2f out: nvr on terms* 10/1
004- 6 ¾ **Harrison's Cave**[11] 8074 6-8-13 57 .......... JoeyHaynes(3) 5 50
(Sharon Watt) *led over 3f: chsd wnr tl rdn over 2f out: wknd over 1f out* 11/1
554- 7 hd **Direct Approach (IRE)**[13] 8064 10-9-4 59 .......... GeorgeBaker 6 52
(Lynn Siddall) *hld up: effrt over 2f out: n.d* 16/1
300- 8 10 **Giant Sequoia (USA)**[20] 7975 10-8-13 54 .......... (t) ShaneKelly 1 31
(Des Donovan) *mid-div: rdn over 3f out: sn wknd* 20/1
/00- 9 26 **The Bunny Catcher**[16] 7645 3-8-5 51 oh6 .......... PatrickMathers 7
(Sharon Watt) *s.i.s: drvn along over 5f out: wknd wl over 2f out* 66/1
216- R **Royal Trooper (IRE)**[13] 8061 8-9-3 65 .......... BeckyBrisbourne(7) 3
(Mark Brisbourne) *ref to r* 4/1[2]
2m 38.12s (-2.68) **Going Correction** -0.075s/f (Stan)
**WFA** 3 from 4yo+ 5lb 10 Ran SP% **114.0**
Speed ratings (Par 101): **105,101,100,98,97 97,97,90,73,**
CSF £59.36 CT £255.04 TOTE £5.30: £1.80, £3.40, £1.90; EX 67.10 Trifecta £356.20.
**Owner** Corbett Stud **Bred** Lady Bamford **Trained** Hanley Swan, Worcestershire

**FOCUS**
Modest form.

## 8232 DOWNLOAD THE CORAL APP H'CAP (TAPETA) 1m 1f 103y
7:20 (7:20) (Class 6) (0-65,65) 3-Y-O £2,102 (£625; £312; £156) Stalls Low

Form RPR
630- 1 **Archipeligo**[56] 7411 3-9-7 65 .......... DavidNolan 6 78
(Iain Jardine) *a.p: chsd ldr over 1f out: rdn to ld ins fnl f: r.o wl* 9/2[3]
540- 2 3½ **Lynngale**[36] 7765 3-9-0 63 .......... ShaneGray(5) 7 69
(Kristin Stubbs) *led: pushed clr over 2f out: rdn over 1f out: hdd and no ex ins fnl f* 10/1
032- 3 1½ **Bowsers Bold**[17] 8004 3-8-12 56 .......... ShaneKelly 3 59
(Marcus Tregoning) *hld up: hdwy over 1f out: styd on to go 3rd post: nt trble ldrs* 6/1

320- 4 shd **Sexy Secret**[9] 8103 3-9-6 64 (v) RobertHavlin 1 67
(Lydia Pearce) *sn pushed along to chse ldrs: wnt 2nd 3f out tl rdn over 1f out: no ex fnl f* **16/1**
210- 5 1 1/2 **Mary Le Bow**[37] 7744 3-9-5 63 (p) GeorgeBaker 4 62
(Victor Dartnall) *hld up: hdwy over 2f out: rdn over 1f out: wknd fnl f* **11/4**[1]
013- 6 2 3/4 **Saturation Point**[34] 7804 3-9-5 63 TomQueally 5 57
(James Toller) *hld up: rdn over 3f out: wknd fnl f* **3/1**[2]
054- 7 8 **Unbridled Joy (IRE)**[14] 8049 3-8-10 57 RyanTate(3) 2 34
(Clive Cox) *chsd ldr tl pushed along 3f out: wknd over 1f out* **15/2**

1m 58.72s (-2.08) **Going Correction** -0.075s/f (Stan) 7 Ran SP% **110.9**
Speed ratings (Par 98): **106,102,101,101,100 97,90**
CSF £43.92 CT £258.74 TOTE £6.30: £2.30, £7.90; EX 62.30 Trifecta £282.90.
**Owner** Tapas Partnership **Bred** Dachel Stud **Trained** Bonchester Bridge, Roxburgh

**FOCUS**
The runner-up set a decent pace, but few got involved with the front in the market disappointing.
T/Plt: £72.50 to a £1 stake. Pool: £86,234.66 - 867.40 winning tickets T/Qpdt: £27.10 to a £1 stake. Pool: £11,839.10 - 323.21 winning tickets CR

8233 - 8239a (Foreign Racing) - See Raceform Interactive

# 8190 LINGFIELD (L-H)
## Saturday, December 20

**OFFICIAL GOING: Polytrack: standard to slow**
Wind: LIGHT, ACROSS Weather: DRY AND BRIGHT

## 8240 32RED.COM CLAIMING STKS 6f 1y(P)
**12:25** (12:25) (Class 6) 2-Y-O **£1,940** (£577; £288; £144) **Stalls** Low

Form RPR
433- 1 **Classic Seniority**[9] 8113 2-9-6 72 GeorgeBaker 2 73
(Richard Hannon) *chsd ldrs: clsd over 2f out: rdn to ld over 1f out: in command and r.o wl fnl f* **5/4**[1]
151- 2 1 3/4 **Little**[12] 8076 2-8-8 70 JennyPowell(5) 9 60
(Jamie Osborne) *stdd s: hld up off the pce in rr: clsd over 2f out: effrt and rdn to chse wnr 1f out: r.o but no imp fnl f* **7/4**[2]
563- 3 1/2 **Diminutive (IRE)**[8] 8118 2-8-7 52 (b) StevieDonohoe 4 52
(Grace Harris) *chsd ldrs: rdn and clsd over 2f out: kpt on same pce u.p fnl f* **16/1**
453- 4 5 **Tinkers Kiss (IRE)**[12] 8076 2-8-0 62 GaryMahon(7) 5 36
(Philip McBride) *off the pce in last pair: clsd over 2f out: swtchd ins and effrt u.p over 1f out: wknd ins fnl f* **5/1**[3]
000- 5 1 1/4 **Sparbrook (IRE)**[12] 8069 2-8-6 58 HayleyTurner 1 31
(Simon Dow) *led: rdn 2f out: hdd over 1f out: btn and lost 2nd 1f out: wknd ins fnl f* **33/1**
600- 6 2 1/4 **Foylesideview (IRE)**[9] 8115 2-9-2 52 (b[1]) FergusSweeney 6 34
(Luke Dace) *pressed ldr: rdn 2f out: lost pl and btn over 1f out: sn wknd* **33/1**

1m 12.36s (0.46) **Going Correction** +0.125s/f (Slow) 6 Ran SP% **109.2**
Speed ratings (Par 94): **101,98,98,91,89 86**
CSF £3.42 TOTE £2.20: £1.10, £1.70; EX 3.60 Trifecta £17.00.
**Owner** Middleham Park Racing LXIII & R Hannon **Bred** E Cantillon, D Cantillon & A Driver **Trained** East Everleigh, Wilts

**FOCUS**
The going was officially described as standard to slow. An ordinary juvenile claimer to start in which the pace looked fair thanks to a contested lead.

## 8241 32RED NOVICE STKS 1m 1y(P)
**12:55** (12:55) (Class 5) 2-Y-O **£2,587** (£770; £384; £192) **Stalls** High

Form RPR
142- 1 **Prince Of Paris**[17] 8009 2-9-4 75 MartinLane 3 79
(Roger Ingram) *chsd ldrs: rdn 5f out: cl enough in 3rd and drvn 2f out: styd on to ld fnl 100yds: rdn out* **6/1**[3]
552- 2 1 **Percy Alleline**[69] 7131 2-9-7 88 (v) SebSanders 4 80
(Ralph Beckett) *chsd ldr tl led 6f out: shkn up over 2f out: drvn and hdd over 1f out: ev ch after tl no ex fnl 100yds* **4/6**[1]
63- 3 nk **Acclamate (IRE)**[14] 8060 2-9-0 0 (t) AdamKirby 6 72
(Marco Botti) *led for 2f: chsd ldr: rdn to chal and hung lft over 1f out: stl hanging and led 1f out: fnd little and hdd fnl 100yds: sn dropped to 3rd and btn* **5/2**[2]
P00- 4 14 **Lady Spangles (IRE)**[23] 7944 2-8-9 0 StevieDonohoe 1 35
(J S Moore) *s.i.s: in tch in midfield tl rdn and lost pl 4f out: lost tch 3f out* **100/1**
5 3/4 **Soqotra** 2-8-9 0 LukeMorris 5 33
(Peter Chapple-Hyam) *s.i.s: in tch in last pair: rdn and btn 2f out: sn wknd* **20/1**
6 2 3/4 **Ballroom Angel** 2-8-9 0 LiamKeniry 2 27
(Philip Hide) *s.i.s: hld up in last pair: rdn over 2f out: wknd 2f out* **66/1**

1m 38.38s (0.18) **Going Correction** +0.125s/f (Slow) 6 Ran SP% **110.1**
Speed ratings (Par 96): **104,103,102,88,87 85**
CSF £10.24 TOTE £6.90: £2.60, £1.10; EX 10.70 Trifecta £21.80.
**Owner** G E Ley **Bred** T G Roddick **Trained** Epsom, Surrey

**FOCUS**
A modest novice event in which only three truly mattered and the trio were the only ones ever in it.

## 8242 LADBROKES CONDITIONS STKS 1m 1y(P)
**1:25** (1:25) (Class 3) 3-Y-O+ **£7,439** (£2,213; £1,106; £553) **Stalls** High

Form RPR
606- 1 **Edu Querido (BRZ)**[146] 4711 5-8-12 96 [1] LukeMorris 4 101+
(Marco Botti) *sn led and styd wd early: shkn up and qcknd 2f out: drvn and in command 1f out: r.o wl* **5/4**[1]
301- 2 3 3/4 **Jack Of Diamonds (IRE)**[12] 8080 5-8-12 85 RobertWinston 3 91
(Roger Teal) *chsd ldrs: wnt 2nd over 4f out: rdn over 2f out: unable qck over 1f out: wl hld and one pce fnl f* **7/4**[2]
000- 3 1 1/2 **Emell**[9] 8116 4-8-12 100 KieranO'Neill 1 88
(Richard Hannon) *t.k.h: chsd ldr tl over 4f out: rdn 2f out: drvn and styd on same pce fnl f* **11/4**[3]
4 23 **Nelson's Hill** 4-8-12 0 RobertHavlin 2 35
(W De Best-Turner) *s.i.s: sn rcvrd and in tch in rr: shkn up 3f out: sn outpcd and lost tch* **100/1**

1m 37.12s (-1.08) **Going Correction** +0.125s/f (Slow) 4 Ran SP% **108.5**
Speed ratings (Par 107): **110,106,104,81**
CSF £3.77 TOTE £2.30; EX 3.90 Trifecta £4.90.
**Owner** Stefan Friborg **Bred** Stud Eternamente Rio **Trained** Newmarket, Suffolk

**FOCUS**
Only three of the four remaining runners mattered in this conditions event. The early pace was slow with sectional times suggesting they covered the first half of the contest 1.51sec slower than the 2yos in the previous race, but things certainly quickened up in the second half.

## 8243 CORAL MOBILE "JUST THREE CLICKS TO BET" H'CAP 1m 4f (P)
**2:00** (2:00) (Class 2) (0-100,96) 3-Y-O+ **£12,938** (£3,850; £1,924; £962) **Stalls** Low

Form RPR
421- 1 **Anglophile**[10] 8095 3-8-13 95 ShaneGray(5) 2 103+
(Charlie Appleby) *in tch in midfield: swtchd lft and wnt between horses to 1f out: led ins fnl f: r.o wl* **3/1**[2]
111- 2 shd **Mymatechris (IRE)**[10] 8099 3-8-13 90 DavidProbert 9 98+
(Andrew Balding) *in tch in midfield: clsd to chse ldrs and widish bnd 2f out: ev ch ins fnl f: r.o wl: jst hld* **11/4**[1]
144- 3 1 **Castilo Del Diablo (IRE)**[24] 7930 5-9-10 96 (p) AdamKirby 4 102+
(David Simcock) *hld up in tch in last trio: swtchd rt and effrt on outer over 1f out: styd on strly ins fnl f: nt rch ldrs* **3/1**[2]
003- 4 1/2 **Uramazin (IRE)**[21] 7974 8-9-4 90 LiamKeniry 7 96
(Philip Hide) *stdd s: hld up in tch in rr: swtchd lft and hdwy jst over 1f out: ev ch ins fnl f: r.o same pce fnl 100yds* **33/1**
524- 5 hd **Pintrada**[31] 7838 6-8-10 82 TedDurcan 5 87
(James Bethell) *chsd ldr: rdn wl over 1f out: ev ch 1f out: led ins fnl f: sn hdd and lost 3 pls towards fin* **8/1**
021- 6 1/2 **Swing Alone (IRE)**[12] 8078 5-9-4 90 JFEgan 8 94
(Gay Kelleway) *t.k.h early: in tch in midfield: rdn 2f out: ev ch ins fnl f: no ex fnl 100yds* **16/1**
005- 7 1 1/2 **Viewpoint (IRE)**[24] 7930 5-9-9 95 GeorgeBaker 1 97
(Richard Hannon) *chsd ldrs: effrt on inner over 1f out: ev ch 1f out: wknd fnl 100yds* **16/1**
653- 8 shd **I'm Fraam Govan**[10] 8095 6-9-7 93 (t) PatCosgrave 6 95
(George Baker) *led: rdn 2f out: hdd ins fnl f: wknd fnl 100yds* **7/1**[3]
544/ 9 1 **Purple Sage (IRE)**[1751] 823 8-9-1 87 StevieDonohoe 3 87
(Brendan Powell) *bmpd leaving stalls: hld up in tch: effrt on inner and pressing ldrs 1f out: wknd ins fnl f* **66/1**

2m 34.6s (1.60) **Going Correction** +0.125s/f (Slow)
**WFA** 3 from 5yo+ 5lb 9 Ran SP% **116.5**
Speed ratings (Par 109): **99,98,98,97,97 97,96,96,95**
CSF £11.82 CT £26.22 TOTE £3.80: £1.40, £1.20, £1.70; EX 13.50 Trifecta £55.70.
**Owner** Godolphin **Bred** Darley **Trained** Newmarket, Suffolk

**FOCUS**
A decent middle-distance handicap featuring a couple of improvers and they fought out the finish, but the race was run at a very steady pace and it took them over 55sec to cover the first half-mile. All nine runners were still within a length or two of each other passing the furlong pole.

## 8244 CORAL APP DOWNLOAD FROM THE APP STORE QUEBEC STKS (LISTED RACE) 1m 2f (P)
**2:35** (2:35) (Class 1) 3-Y-O+
**£22,684** (£8,600; £4,304; £2,144; £1,076; £540) **Stalls** Low

Form RPR
122- 1 **Grendisar (IRE)**[10] 8095 4-9-5 104 (p) AdamKirby 4 99+
(Marco Botti) *dwlt: in tch in midfield: effrt to chse ldrs and rdn wl over 1f out: led 1f out: in command after: rdn out* **11/10**[1]
043- 2 3/4 **Energia Davos (BRZ)**[17] 8018 6-9-3 104 (p) LukeMorris 6 93
(Marco Botti) *in tch in midfield: rdn over 2f out: styd on wl u.p fnl f: wnt 2nd cl home: nvr a real threat to wnr* **6/1**[3]
512- 3 hd **Brocklebank (IRE)**[12] 8078 5-9-3 84 WilliamTwiston-Davies 3 93
(Simon Dow) *stdd s: hld up in rr: clsd 2f out: nt clr run 1f out: hdwy u.p ins fnl f: chsd wnr wl ins fnl f: r.o: lost 2nd last strides* **33/1**
604- 4 1 1/4 **Tinshu (IRE)**[12] 8078 8-8-12 84 (p) RobertWinston 7 86
(Derek Haydn Jones) *chsd ldrs: rdn and pressing ldr 2f out tl outpcd by wnr 1f out: styd on same pce fnl f* **33/1**
053- 5 hd **Dominandros (FR)**[24] 7930 3-9-0 92 DavidProbert 5 90
(Gay Kelleway) *led: rdn 2f out: drvn and hdd 1f out: one pce after: lost 3 pls wl ins fnl f: sddle slipped* **16/1**
515- 6 2 **Baltic Knight (IRE)**[31] 7836 4-9-3 110 GeorgeBaker 1 86
(Richard Hannon) *in tch in midfield: rdn and unable qck 2f out: trying to switch rt over 1f out: no imp fnl f* **6/4**[2]
221- 7 2 3/4 **Heho**[36] 7773 3-8-9 73 MartinDwyer 2 76
(William Knight) *in tch in midfield: effrt u.p 2f out: wknd fnl f* **33/1**

2m 7.29s (0.69) **Going Correction** +0.125s/f (Slow)
**WFA** 3 from 4yo+ 3lb 7 Ran SP% **116.6**
Speed ratings: **102,101,101,100,100 98,96**
CSF £8.75 TOTE £2.10: £1.10, £4.00; EX 6.70 Trifecta £66.40.
**Owner** Mohamed Albousi Alghufli **Bred** Old Carhue & Graeng Bloodstock **Trained** Newmarket, Suffolk

**FOCUS**
Probably not the strongest Listed contest ever run around here and again the early pace was visually steady (backed up by the sectional times) before developing into a 3f sprint. It resulted in a 1-2 for trainer Marco Botti.

## 8245 UNIBET OFFER DAILY JOCKEY/TRAINER SPECIALS H'CAP 5f 6y(P)
**3:10** (3:10) (Class 5) (0-70,70) 3-Y-O+ **£2,587** (£770; £384; £192) **Stalls** High

Form RPR
200- 1 **Dreams Of Glory**[62] 7307 6-9-3 66 (b) LukeMorris 8 77
(Ron Hodges) *chsd ldr: rdn 2f out: drvn to ld and edgd rt 1f out: styd on: drvn out and a holding on* **16/1**
165- 2 1/2 **Birdie Queen**[65] 7215 4-9-7 70 GeorgeBaker 6 79
(Gary Moore) *t.k.h: hld up in midfield: swtchd rt and effrt u.p over 1f out: styd on strly u.p ins fnl f: wnt 2nd cl home: nvr quite getting to wnr* **3/1**[1]
311- 3 1/2 **Johnny Splash (IRE)**[12] 8077 5-9-7 70 (v) RobertWinston 9 77
(Roger Teal) *chsd ldrs: effrt u.p over 1f out: chsd wnr fnl 75yds: styd on but lost 2nd cl home* **7/2**[2]
303- 4 1 3/4 **Pharoh Jake**[15] 8039 6-9-2 65 WilliamCarson 2 66
(John Bridger) *racd in midfield: rdn and effrt over 1f out: kpt on fnl f: nvr threatened ldrs* **16/1**
036- 5 1/2 **Burnt Cream**[16] 8023 7-8-10 59 (t) RobertHavlin 4 58
(Martin Bosley) *hld up in rr: hdwy over 1f out: kpt on u.p ins fnl f: nvr trbld ldrs* **20/1**
661- 6 1 **Aaranyow (IRE)**[16] 8024 6-8-9 63 (t) TobyAtkinson(5) 3 59
(Clifford Lines) *led: rdn over 1f out: hdd 1f out: lost 2nd fnl 75yds: wknd towards fin* **8/1**[3]
061- 7 nk **Arctic Lynx (IRE)**[15] 8039 7-9-5 68 (p) HayleyTurner 5 63
(Conor Dore) *a towards rr: rdn over 1f out: kpt on ins fnl f: nvr trbld ldrs* **7/2**[2]

054- **8** 1 3/4 **Billy Red**[12] 8077 10-9-3 66......(bt) FergusSweeney 1 54
(J R Jenkins) *chsd ldrs: rdn 2f out: no ex over 1f out: wknd ins fnl f* **10/1**

002- **9** 1 1/4 **Cardinal**[12] 8077 9-9-0 63......(p) AdamKirby 7 47
(Robert Cowell) *a towards rr and wd: n.d* **8/1**[3]

58.61s (-0.19) **Going Correction** +0.125s/f (Slow) **9** Ran SP% **117.3**
Speed ratings (Par 103): **106,105,104,101,100 99,98,95,93**
CSF £64.85 CT £213.97 TOTE £17.50: £4.20, £1.90, £1.80; EX 85.10 Trifecta £501.60.
**Owner** P E Axon **Bred** P E Axon **Trained** Charlton Mackrell, Somerset

**FOCUS**
A few old favourites took part in this modest sprint handicap.

## 8246 CORAL.CO.UK BEST ODDS GUARANTEED ON RACING H'CAP — 1m 4f (P)
3:40 (3:40) (Class 6) (0-65,64) 3-Y-O — £1,940 (£577; £288; £144) Stalls Low

Form — RPR

631- **1** **Golly Miss Molly**[12] 8074 3-8-13 56......(b) LukeMorris 1 64+
(Jeremy Gask) *in tch in midfield: rdn to ld over 1f out: drvn ins fnl f: styd on and asserted fnl 75yds* **3/1**[1]

104- **2** 1 **Rockie Road (IRE)**[46] 7645 3-8-8 51...... WilliamCarson 3 57
(Mick Quinn) *in tch in midfield: clsd to join ldrs over 3f out: rdn to ld 2f out: hdd over 1f out: kpt and ev ch tl no ex fnl 75yds* **16/1**

556- **3** 1/2 **Loving Your Work**[15] 8037 3-9-7 64......(v[1]) PatCosgrave 5 69
(George Baker) *hld up in tch: hdwy 3f out: chsd ldrs and drvn over 1f out: styd on same pce fnl f* **3/1**[1]

0- **4** 1 1/2 **Highsalvia Cosmos**[22] 7526 3-9-3 60......(bt) RobertHavlin 8 63
(Mark Hoad) *stdd s: hld up in rr: hdwy over 1f out: drvn over 1f out: kpt on ins fnl f: no threat to ldrs* **66/1**

434- **5** 3/4 **Emperor Ferdinand (IRE)**[17] 8011 3-8-8 51...... BenCurtis 7 53
(Marcus Tregoning) *chsd ldrs: wnt 2nd 10f out tl led over 2f out: hdd 2f out and rdn: unable qck and drifted rt 1f out: r.o same pce fnl f* **8/1**[3]

053- **6** 4 1/2 **Tohaveandtohold**[15] 8050 3-8-8 51......(p) LiamJones 2 45
(William Haggas) *led for 2f: chsd ldrs tl rdn and lost pl over 2f out: wknd over 1f out* **8/1**[3]

042- **7** 1 1/4 **Pink And Black (IRE)**[9] 8114 3-9-6 63...... MartinDwyer 4 55
(William Muir) *t.k.h: chsd ldrs tl hdd to ld over 4f out: hdd over 2f out: btn over 1f out: wknd fnl f* **6/1**[2]

60F- **8** 6 **Dark Tsarina (IRE)**[45] 7664 3-8-2 50......[1] TimClark(5) 10 33
(Michael Madgwick) *in tch in midfield: rdn 3f out: no prog: wknd wl over 1f out* **50/1**

012- **9** 1/2 **Triple Star**[15] 8049 3-9-0 57...... HayleyTurner 6 39
(Hughie Morrison) *t.k.h: hld up in rr: rdn over 2f out: sn btn: wknd 2f out* **6/1**[2]

006- **10** 10 **Norman's Star**[8] 8123 3-8-2 45...... NickyMackay 9 11
(Chris Dwyer) *t.k.h: chsd ldrs tl hdd led after 2f out: hdd over 4f out: lost pl over 3f out: bhd over 1f out* **16/1**

2m 36.61s (3.61) **Going Correction** +0.125s/f (Slow) **10** Ran SP% **116.0**
Speed ratings (Par 98): **92,91,91,90,89 86,85,81,81,74**
CSF £56.99 CT £156.51 TOTE £2.80: £1.10, £4.40, £1.60; EX 43.80 Trifecta £229.80.
**Owner** Amelco **Bred** Brook Stud Bloodstock Ltd **Trained** Sutton Veny, Wilts

**FOCUS**
A moderate middle-distance handicap for 3yos and another race where they dawdled early.
T/Plt: £7.30 to a £1 stake. Pool: £65,767.81 - 6,500.52 winning tickets T/Qpdt: £5.10 to a £1 stake. Pool: £4,261.83 - 607.17 winning tickets SP

8197
# KEMPTON (A.W) (R-H)
### Monday, December 22

**OFFICIAL GOING: Polytrack: standard**

## 8247 BETBRIGHT BEST ODDS GUARANTEED MAIDEN AUCTION FILLIES' STKS (BOBIS RACE) — 7f (P)
1:15 (1:16) (Class 5) 2-Y-O — £3,234 (£962; £481; £240) Stalls Low

Form — RPR

**1** **My Mistress (IRE)** 2-8-10 0...... WilliamCarson 7 80+
(Anthony Carson) *in tch in midfield: swtchd lft and hdwy over 1f out: led ins fnl f: r.o strly* **4/1**[2]

**2** 1/2 **Dat Il Do** 2-8-8 0...... GeorgeChaloner 8 76+
(Noel Quinlan) *t.k.h: chsd ldrs tl led and travelling strly 2f out: rdn over 1f out: hdd ins fnl f: r.o but a hld* **8/1**[3]

- **3** 6 **Trikasana** 2-8-4 0...... RyanTate(3) 6 59
(Clive Cox) *chsd ldr: ev ch and rdn 2f out: 3rd and wknd ins fnl f* **11/1**

034- **4** 3 **Azure Amour (IRE)**[172] 3875 2-8-12 64...... GrahamGibbons 3 56
(Ralph Beckett) *led: hdd and rdn 2f out: 4th and wknd fnl f* **11/10**[1]

4- **5** 1 **Royal Roslea**[11] 8112 2-8-10 0...... ShaneKelly 5 51
(Marcus Tregoning) *dwlt and pushed along in rr: rdn over 3f out: no threat to ldrs but kpt on fnl f* **20/1**

**6** shd **Dutch Fredie G** 2-8-7 0...... DavidProbert 2 48
(Gary Moore) *chsd ldrs: rdn and no ex 2f out: wknd over 1f out* **10/1**

**7** 3/4 **Suffolk Sky** 2-8-7 0......(b[1]) LukeMorris 4 46
(Ed Vaughan) *chsd ldrs: rdn and unable qck 2f out: wknd over 1f out* **14/1**

5- **8** 6 **Lettuce Snow (IRE)**[11] 8112 2-8-6 0...... ChrisCatlin 9 29
(Geoffrey Deacon) *in tch in midfield: rdn and struggling over 3f out: wl bhd over 1f out* **66/1**

**9** shd **Surelookit (IRE)** 2-8-9 0 ow1...... StevieDonohoe 1 32
(John Butler) *dwlt and bustled along early: sme hdwy into midfield after 2f: rdn and wknd over 2f out* **50/1**

- **10** 1/2 **Bollywood Dream** 2-8-4 0...... DannyBrock(3) 10 28
(Jonathan Portman) *bucking leaving stalls: a in rr: lost tch over 2f out* **50/1**

**11** 3 1/4 **Beach Plaza (IRE)** 2-8-8 0...... RobertHavlin 11 20
(Robert Mills) *a in rr: lost tch over 2f out* **25/1**

1m 27.47s (1.47) **Going Correction** +0.05s/f (Slow) **11** Ran SP% **116.8**
Speed ratings (Par 93): **93,92,85,82,81 80,80,73,73,72 68**
CSF £33.72 TOTE £5.70: £1.50, £2.50, £3.20; EX 31.20 Trifecta £282.10.
**Owner** David J Newman & Ross Bennett **Bred** Helen Smith & Sally Mullen **Trained** Newmarket, Suffolk

**FOCUS**
Not much strength in depth but fair form from the first two, who pulled clear (in the centre) in the closing stages. The gallop was an ordinary one to the intersection.

## 8248 BETBRIGHT MONEYBACK OFFERS H'CAP — 1m (P)
1:45 (1:45) (Class 5) (0-75,74) 3-Y-O+ — £3,234 (£962; £481; £240) Stalls Low

Form — RPR

042- **1** **Presumido (IRE)**[19] 8017 4-9-3 70...... SebSanders 10 79
(Simon Dow) *hld up in midfield: rdn and hdwy over 1f out: qcknd to ld ins fnl f: r.o wl* **14/1**

32- **2** 1 **Until Midnight (IRE)**[17] 8041 4-9-2 69...... RobertTart 13 76
(Eugene Stanford) *in tch in midfield: rdn and hdwy to chal 2f out: ev ch over 1f out: wnt 2nd and one pce fnl 75yds* **8/1**[3]

503- **3** 1 **Bobby Benton (IRE)**[19] 8017 3-8-11 65...... LukeMorris 12 68
(Luke Dace) *dwlt: hld up towards rr: hdwy u.p over 1f out: styd on u.p ins fnl f: wnt 3rd towards fin* **8/1**[3]

222- **4** 1/2 **Freddy With A Y (IRE)**[39] 7758 4-9-6 73......(v) GeorgeBaker 14 76
(Gary Moore) *in tch in midfield: hdwy to chse ldrs 1/2-way: rdn to ld wl over 1f out: hdd and r.o same pce ins fnl f* **7/1**[2]

102- **5** nse **Woodbridge**[24] 7954 3-9-0 68...... ShaneKelly 7 70
(Richard Fahey) *led: hdd and rdn wl over 1f out: no ex and outpcd ins fnl f* **10/1**

300- **6** 1 **Kuwait Star**[82] 6865 5-8-6 64...... ShelleyBirkett(5) 1 65
(Sarah Humphrey) *w ldrs: rdn and unable qck wl over 1f out: wknd ins fnl f* **66/1**

026- **7** 1 1/2 **Gannicus**[26] 7918 3-9-1 69......(p) StevieDonohoe 6 65
(Brendan Powell) *in tch in midfield: rdn 2f out: no imp fr over 1f out* **9/1**

041- **8** nse **Gracious George (IRE)**[14] 8068 4-9-0 70...... DannyBrock(3) 8 67
(Jimmy Fox) *hld up in rr: swtchd rt and hdwy over 1f out: styd on fnl f: nvr trbld ldrs* **4/1**[1]

/34- **9** 1/2 **Embankment**[17] 8041 5-9-3 70...... RobertHavlin 5 66
(Michael Attwater) *dwlt: hdwy into midfield after 2f: unable qck over 1f out: wknd ins fnl f* **10/1**

563- **10** 1 1/4 **Tommy's Secret**[17] 8041 4-9-7 74...... MartinDwyer 9 67
(Jane Chapple-Hyam) *in tch in midfield: rdn and unable qck over 1f out: wknd ins fnl f* **14/1**

244- **11** 3/4 **Starlight Symphony (IRE)**[14] 8079 4-9-6 73......(b) AdamKirby 2 65
(Eve Johnson Houghton) *in tch in midfield: wknd u.p over 1f out* **8/1**[3]

465- **12** 1/2 **Next Stop**[26] 7918 3-9-0 68...... GrahamGibbons 3 57
(David Nicholls) *in tch in midfield: struggling u.p over 2f out: wknd over 1f out* **12/1**

546- **13** 7 **Evident (IRE)**[14] 8068 4-8-12 65...... WilliamCarson 11 39
(Tony Carroll) *stdd bk to rr after s: swtchd to inner and effrt 2f out: no hdwy* **33/1**

010- **14** 20 **Elusive Ellen (IRE)**[21] 7993 4-8-13 66......[1] FergusSweeney 4
(Brendan Powell) *a in rr: last and rdn 1/2-way: t.o* **33/1**

1m 38.87s (-0.93) **Going Correction** +0.05s/f (Slow)
**WFA** 3 from 4yo+ 1lb **14** Ran SP% **122.4**
Speed ratings (Par 103): **106,105,104,103,103 102,100,100,100,99 98,97,90,70**
CSF £122.64 CT £679.47 TOTE £22.80: £7.60, £2.90, £2.60; EX 133.30 Trifecta £2595.30.
**Owner** R Moss & J Page **Bred** Lynn Lodge Stud **Trained** Epsom, Surrey

**FOCUS**
Mainly exposed sorts but a fair handicap run at an ordinary gallop. The winner came down the centre in the straight.

## 8249 BETBRIGHT.COM MAIDEN STKS — 1m (P)
2:20 (2:21) (Class 4) 3-Y-O+ — £4,851 (£1,443; £721; £360) Stalls Low

Form — RPR

22- **1** **Made With Love**[184] 3477 3-9-5 0...... RobertHavlin 8 77+
(John Gosden) *mde all: rdn 2f out: asserted u.p 1f out: drew clr fnl f: rdn out* **1/7**[1]

**2** 5 **Belahodood** 3-9-5 0...... AdamKirby 1 65+
(William Haggas) *chsd ldrs: wnt 2nd 6f out: rdn and effrt 2f out: btn 1f out: wknd ins fnl f* **4/1**[2]

**3** 2 3/4 **Silver Secret** 3-9-0 0...... ShelleyBirkett(5) 2 58
(Miss Joey Ellis) *s.i.s: hld up in last pair: rdn and sme hdwy over 1f out: wnt modest 3rd 1f out: no threat to wnr* **50/1**

50- **4** 5 **Tiger Stone**[95] 6485 3-9-0 0...... DavidProbert 7 41
(Michael Blanshard) *t.k.h: chsd wnr for 2f: 3rd and outpcd over 1f out: wknd fnl f* **50/1**

**5** 1/2 **Senator Matt** 4-9-6 0...... RobertTart 3 46
(John Berry) *in tch in midfield: rdn and outpcd 2f out: n.d after* **25/1**[3]

- **6** 3/4 **Ladyhawk (IRE)** 10-8-10 0......(v[1]) TimClark(5) 5 39
(Polly Gundry) *in tch in midfield: rdn 2f out: sn outpcd and btn* **50/1**

63- **7** 2 **Strictly The One (IRE)**[6] 8172 4-8-13 0...... ChrisMeehan(7) 4 39
(Neil Mulholland) *s.i.s: a in last pair: outpcd over 2f out: no ch after* **33/1**

1m 42.0s (2.20) **Going Correction** +0.05s/f (Slow)
**WFA** 3 from 4yo+ 1lb **7** Ran SP% **120.2**
Speed ratings (Par 105): **91,86,83,78,77 77,75**
CSF £1.28 TOTE £1.10: £1.10, £1.60; EX 1.40 Trifecta £11.60.
**Owner** Normandie Stud Ltd **Bred** Normandie Stud Ltd **Trained** Newmarket, Suffolk

**FOCUS**
A most uncompetitive maiden and one in which the gallop was on the steady side. The winner came down the centre in the straight.

## 8250 COME JUMP RACING ON BOXING DAY H'CAP — 1m 3f (P)
2:50 (2:51) (Class 6) (0-65,64) 3-Y-O+ — £2,264 (£673; £336; £168) Stalls Low

Form — RPR

561- **1** **Softly She Treads (IRE)**[18] 8028 3-9-3 61......(v) FergusSweeney 7 69
(Pat Phelan) *chsd ldrs: shkn up to ld 2f out: hld on wl u.p fnl f* **11/2**[2]

323- **2** nk **Bowsers Bold**[3] 8232 3-8-12 56...... ShaneKelly 2 63
(Marcus Tregoning) *t.k.h: hld up in tch in midfield: nt clr run 2f out: gap opened and rdn to chal ins fnl f: fnd less than looked likely and hld towards fin* **6/1**[3]

663- **3** shd **Fair Comment**[26] 7925 4-9-6 60...... DavidProbert 5 67
(Michael Blanshard) *in tch in midfield: effrt and drvn to chal over 1f out: ev ch after: no ex cl home* **20/1**

060- **4** 1 1/2 **Takeitfromalady (IRE)**[17] 8037 5-9-8 62......(b) StevieDonohoe 9 66
(Lee Carter) *s.i.s: bustled along early: towards rr: hdwy over 2f out: styd on u.p fnl f* **10/1**

046- **5** nk **Day Of The Eagle (IRE)**[12] 8102 8-9-7 61...... GrahamGibbons 12 65
(Michael Easterby) *in tch in midfield: hdwy and ev ch u.p 2f out: outpcd ins fnl f* **10/1**

246- **6** nk **Mcbirney (USA)**[26] 7925 7-9-8 62...... LukeMorris 11 65
(Paul D'Arcy) *hld up in rr: hdwy on outer over 1f out: kpt on u.p ins fnl f* **7/1**

032- **7** ¾ **Thane Of Cawdor (IRE)**[18] 8029 5-9-10 64 .................... AdamKirby 10 66
(Joseph Tuite) *hld up in last quartet: effrt u.p and edging rt over 1f out: kpt on: nvr gng to rch ldrs* **7/2**[1]

302- **8** ½ **Maison Brillet (IRE)**[17] 8037 7-9-10 64 ....................(p) RobertHavlin 1 65
(Clive Drew) *in tch in midfield: rdn 2f out: no imp: styd on same pce fnl f* **16/1**

012- **9** 3 **Gracefilly**[38] 7785 3-9-3 61 .................................. AntonioFresu 3 57
(Ed Walker) *in tch in midfield: effrt on inner wl over 1f out: no prog: wknd ins fnl f* **8/1**

044- **10** nk **Eastward Ho**[18] 8030 6-8-5 50 ....................(p) ShelleyBirkett(5) 4 46
(Sarah Humphrey) *chsd ldr tl over 2f out: wknd over 1f out* **33/1**

000- **11** nk **Idol Deputy (FR)**[10] 8122 8-9-6 63 ....................(tp) AshleyMorgan(3) 14 58
(James Bennett) *s.i.s: a towards rr: n.d* **20/1**

360- **12** 11 **Bennelong**[90] 6636 8-9-3 62 ....................(b) HarryPoulton(5) 13 38
(Lee Carter) *racd keenly: led tl 2f out: sn dropped out* **33/1**

000- **13** 9 **Munsarim (IRE)**[12] 8102 7-9-2 56 ....................(p) AmirQuinn 6 17
(Lee Carter) *in tch in midfield on outer: v wd bnd 4f out: sn lost pl: wknd over 2f out* **20/1**

2m 21.01s (-0.89) **Going Correction** +0.05s/f (Slow)
**WFA** 3 from 4yo+ 4lb **13** Ran SP% **119.7**
Speed ratings (Par 101): **105,104,104,103,103 103,102,102,100,99 99,91,85**
CSF £35.42 CT £617.31 TOTE £6.40: £2.30, £2.70, £4.30; EX 40.20 Trifecta £970.50.
**Owner** Brian P Donovan **Bred** Miss Sarah Thompson **Trained** Epsom, Surrey

**FOCUS**
A modest handicap run at a reasonable gallop. The gutsy winner raced centre-to-far side in the straight.

## 8251 BETBRIGHT CASINO H'CAP 7f (P)
**3:20** (3:22) (Class 4) (0-80,80) 3-Y-O+ **£5,175** (£1,540; £769; £384) **Stalls** Low

Form RPR

311- **1** **Don't Be**[19] 8017 4-9-3 76 .................................. LukeMorris 9 88
(Sir Mark Prescott Bt) *chsd ldrs: rdn to chal over 1f out: clr w ldr ins fnl f: styd on to ld last stride* **2/1**[1]

100- **2** shd **Brigliadoro (IRE)**[21] 7988 3-9-3 79 .................... DannyBrock(3) 3 90
(Philip McBride) *chsd ldrs: rdn to ld over 1f out: hrd pressed and drew clr w wnr ins fnl f: styd on: hdd last stride* **6/1**[3]

323- **3** 2¾ **Footstepsintherain (IRE)**[31] 7871 4-9-3 76 ........... FergusSweeney 2 80
(David Dennis) *t.k.h: hld up in tch in midfield: rdn and hdwy over 1f out: 3rd and r.o same pce fnl f* **5/1**[2]

312- **4** hd **Ertikaan**[21] 7988 7-8-13 77 .................... ShelleyBirkett(5) 5 80
(Miss Joey Ellis) *hld up in tch: effrt towards inner over 1f out: battling for 3rd and kpt on fnl f: no threat to ldrs* **6/1**[3]

230- **5** 1¾ **Midnight Rider (IRE)**[14] 8071 6-8-13 79 .................... PatMillman(7) 4 78
(Rod Millman) *chsd ldrs: rdn 2f out: unable qck and sltly hmpd over 1f out: wl hld and one pce fnl f* **20/1**

000- **6** nk **Polar Kite (IRE)**[48] 7636 6-8-12 71 .................... KierenFox 1 69
(Roger Ingram) *hld up in rr: hdwy towards inner over 1f out: styd on ins fnl f: no threat to ldrs* **33/1**

004- **7** ½ **Burning Blaze**[14] 8072 4-9-7 80 .................... AdamKirby 11 76
(Olly Stevens) *in tch in midfield: shkn up 2f out: sn rdn and no imp: wl hld and one pce fnl f* **16/1**

000- **8** ¾ **Sheikh The Reins (IRE)**[39] 7759 5-8-8 67 .................... MartinDwyer 10 61
(John Best) *led: rdn 2f out: sn hdd and btn: wknd fnl f* **66/1**

000- **9** nse **Palace Moon**[14] 8072 9-9-4 77 ....................(t) RobertHavlin 7 71
(William Knight) *in tch in midfield: rdn and no hdwy over 1f out: one pce and wl hld fnl f* **33/1**

540- **10** nse **Good Luck Charm**[14] 8080 5-9-4 77 ....................(v) GeorgeBaker 6 71
(Gary Moore) *t.k.h: hld up towards rr: effrt towards inner over 1f out: rdn and no hdwy 1f out* **7/1**

460- **11** 2½ **Conry (IRE)**[17] 8044 8-8-9 68 .................... StevieDonohoe 13 56
(Ian Williams) *hld up in rr: no imp u.p over 1f out: n.d* **33/1**

140- **12** 3¾ **Toga Tiger (IRE)**[31] 7870 7-9-3 76 .................... WilliamCarson 8 54
(Kevin Frost) *dwlt and short of room leaving stalls: a towards rr: n.d* **20/1**

000- **13** 2¼ **Trader Jack**[100] 6313 5-9-7 80 .................... StephenCraine 12 52
(David Flood) *in tch in midfield: rdn and lost pl over 2f out: wknd over 1f out* **33/1**

1m 26.07s (0.07) **Going Correction** +0.05s/f (Slow) **13** Ran SP% **119.7**
Speed ratings (Par 105): **101,100,97,97,95 95,94,93,93,93 90,86,83**
CSF £12.58 CT £56.37 TOTE £2.70: £1.70, £1.90, £1.80; EX 15.70 Trifecta £67.10.
**Owner** Mrs Olivia Hoare **Bred** P E Barrett **Trained** Newmarket, Suffolk

**FOCUS**
A fair handicap but a steady early gallop saw those held up at a disadvantage. The first two, who came down the centre, pulled clear in the closing stages.

## 8252 BETBRIGHT.COM DOWNLOAD OUR APP H'CAP 6f (P)
**3:50** (3:51) (Class 4) (0-85,85) 3-Y-O+ **£5,175** (£1,540; £769; £384) **Stalls** Low

Form RPR

002- **1** **Strategic Force (IRE)**[14] 8071 3-9-3 81 .................... AdamKirby 6 92
(Clive Cox) *chsd ldrs: rdn to chal and hung lft 1f out: sn led: hdd wl ins fnl f: sn led again: drvn out* **11/4**[1]

03P- **2** nk **Time And Place**[191] 3256 4-9-0 78 .................... ShaneKelly 9 88
(Richard Fahey) *in tch in midfield: effrt u.p to chse ldrs over 1f out: drvn to ld wl ins fnl f: sn hdd and ex* **12/1**

000- **3** 1 **Secret Asset (IRE)**[17] 8045 9-9-2 80 ....................(b[1]) MartinDwyer 7 87
(Jane Chapple-Hyam) *hld up in midfield: rdn and effrt over 1f out: hdwy 1f out: styd on wl ins fnl f: nt rch ldrs* **15/2**

103- **4** 1¼ **Head Space (IRE)**[18] 8025 6-9-1 79 ....................(v) GrahamGibbons 5 82
(Michael Attwater) *in tch in midfield: rdn and unable qck 2f out: rallied and styd on ins fnl f* **4/1**[2]

100- **5** ½ **Whaleweigh Station**[32] 7852 3-9-7 85 ....................(v[1]) GeorgeBaker 2 86
(J R Jenkins) *led: rdn over 1f out: hdd ins fnl f: wknd towards fin* **11/2**[3]

405- **6** 1½ **Drive On (IRE)**[14] 8071 3-8-8 77 ....................(v) GeorgeDowning(5) 8 73
(Eve Johnson Houghton) *stdd s: t.k.h: hld up in rr: swtchd rt and hdwy over 1f out: kpt on fnl f: nvr trbld ldrs* **12/1**

520- **7** ½ **Secret Millionaire (IRE)**[6] 8171 7-9-0 78 .................... LukeMorris 3 73
(Luke Dace) *in tch in midfield: rdn and no hdwy 2f out: styd on same pce after* **25/1**

101- **8** ¾ **Lady Brigid (IRE)**[14] 8071 3-9-3 81 .................... LiamJones 11 73
(Olly Stevens) *chsd ldr tl 2f out: hung lft u.p after: btn 1f out: wknd fnl f* **7/1**

000- **9** 1½ **Clockmaker (IRE)**[14] 8072 8-8-12 76 .................... FergusSweeney 1 64
(Conor Dore) *taken down early: chsd ldrs tl jst over 2f out: wknd over 1f out* **16/1**

000- **10** 3½ **Nonno Giulio (IRE)**[12] 8100 3-9-1 79 .................... DavidProbert 4 55
(Simon Dow) *taken down early: hmpd leaving stalls: hld up in rr: wknd over 1f out* **25/1**

1m 12.0s (-1.10) **Going Correction** +0.05s/f (Slow) **10** Ran SP% **115.3**
Speed ratings (Par 105): **109,108,107,105,104 102,102,101,99,94**
CSF £37.07 CT £218.70 TOTE £3.10: £1.20, £3.20, £3.30; EX 27.70 Trifecta £230.30.
**Owner** Peter Ridgers **Bred** D J Sweeney **Trained** Lambourn, Berks

**FOCUS**
A useful handicap in which the gallop was sound throughout. The winner came down the centre.

## 8253 VISIT AND DINE IN THE PANORAMIC H'CAP 2m (P)
**4:20** (4:20) (Class 6) (0-65,67) 3-Y-O+ **£2,264** (£673; £336; £168) **Stalls** Low

Form RPR

331- **1** **Haines**[5] 8189 3-8-10 55 6ex .................... DavidProbert 4 66+
(Andrew Balding) *mde all: rdn and wnt clr over 2f out: in command after: styd on* **4/9**[1]

4/0- **2** 5 **Addazero**[18] 8029 5-9-10 61 .................... AdamKirby 12 66
(Joseph Tuite) *t.k.h: chsd ldr thrght: rdn and outpcd by wnr over 2f out: wl hld but kpt on for clr 2nd* **12/1**

005- **3** 3 **Leyland (IRE)**[7] 8163 5-9-2 60 ....................(b) CharlieBennett(7) 6 61
(Natalie Lloyd-Beavis) *chsd ldrs: rdn 5f out: lost pl and wd bnd 3f out: rallied to go 3rd 1f out: no ch w ldrs* **66/1**

060- **4** 1¼ **Artisan**[30] 7893 6-9-6 57 ....................(t) LukeMorris 1 57
(Shaun Lycett) *hld up in midfield: effrt over 2f out: battling for 3rd but no ch w ldrs over 1f out: kpt on* **16/1**

444- **5** 1¾ **Golden Bird (IRE)**[14] 8070 3-9-6 65 ....................(p) ChrisCatlin 10 62
(Dean Ivory) *wl in tch in midfield: rdn 5f out: outpcd by ldng pair over 2f out: wl hld and battling for 3rd over 1f out: wknd ins fnl f* **10/1**[3]

000- **6** ½ **Arashi**[20] 8001 8-9-12 63 ....................(v) GeorgeBaker 11 60
(Derek Shaw) *hld up in last trio: travelling wl but nt clr run over 3f out: hdwy to battle for 3rd but no ch w ldrs over 1f out: wknd ins fnl f* **9/1**[2]

2/6- **7** 5 **Dont Take Me Alive**[18] 8029 5-10-0 65 ........(tp) WilliamTwiston-Davies 5 56
(Charlie Longsdon) *in tch in midfield: rdn and outpcd over 2f out: battling for wl hld 3rd 2f out: wknd 1f out* **25/1**

500- **8** 8 **Guards Chapel**[17] 8037 6-9-3 61 ....................(be) JasonNuttall(7) 8 42
(Gary Moore) *in tch in midfield: rdn and lost pl whn bmpd bnd 3f out: sn wknd* **33/1**

060- **9** 3¼ **Montaff**[26] 7760 8-9-10 61 ....................(e) MartinDwyer 9 38
(Richard Guest) *hld up in last pair: nvr on terms: wknd over 2f out* **16/1**

300- **10** 4 **Rookery (IRE)**[80] 6899 3-9-0 59 .................... RobertHavlin 3 32
(Roger Ingram) *chsd ldrs tl over 2f out: sn wknd* **50/1**

034- **11** 2½ **Greeleys Love (USA)**[21] 7990 4-9-13 64 .................... CharlesBishop 13 34
(Luke Dace) *stdd s: hld up in rr: wknd over 2f out: t.o* **16/1**

3m 31.25s (1.15) **Going Correction** +0.05s/f (Slow)
**WFA** 3 from 4yo+ 8lb **11** Ran SP% **123.9**
Speed ratings (Par 101): **99,96,95,94,93 93,90,86,85,83 81**
CSF £7.73 CT £210.38 TOTE £1.40: £1.10, £3.20, £6.00; EX 10.40 Trifecta £461.60.
**Owner** Bow River Racing **Bred** Spring Bloodstock Ltd **Trained** Kingsclere, Hants

**FOCUS**
A modest handicap in which the gallop was an ordinary one and very few figured. The well-handicapped winner raced towards the far side in the straight.
T/Jkpt: Not won. T/Plt: £134.40 to a £1 stake. Pool: £82,096.23 - 445.64 winning tickets T/Qpdt: £9.40 to a £1 stake. Pool: £8,136.08 - 639.70 winning tickets SP

# 8225 WOLVERHAMPTON (A.W) (L-H)
Monday, December 22

**OFFICIAL GOING: Tapeta: standard**
Wind: Strong behind Weather: Overcast

## 8254 DAILY ENHANCED "MAGICAL MULTIPLES" AT UNIBET MEDIAN AUCTION MAIDEN STKS (TAPETA) 5f 20y
**1:40** (1:40) (Class 5) 2-Y-O **£2,911** (£866; £432; £216) **Stalls** Low

Form RPR

455- **1** **Bahango (IRE)**[10] 8118 2-9-0 62 .................... ShaneGray(5) 4 71
(Patrick Morris) *mde all: rdn and edgd rt over 1f out: r.o* **7/2**[3]

026- **2** 1½ **Kyrenia Castle (GER)**[12] 8092 2-9-5 70 .................... KieranO'Neill 3 66
(Richard Hannon) *sn outpcd: hdwy u.p over 1f out: r.o to go 2nd wl ins fnl f: nt rch wnr* **11/8**[1]

335- **3** 1¼ **Vivre La Reve**[20] 8000 2-9-0 65 .................... PaulMulrennan 1 56
(James Unett) *a.p: chsd wnr 2f out: rdn over 1f out: styd on same pce and lost 2nd wl ins fnl f* **5/2**[2]

65- **4** 2¾ **Desert Apostle (IRE)**[26] 7917 2-9-0 0 .................... PatrickMathers 5 46
(Derek Shaw) *chsd wnr tl rdn 2f out: hung lft and no ex fnl f* **25/1**

6- **5** 10 **Bahama Blue**[62] 7345 2-9-0 0 ....................(b[1]) HayleyTurner 2 10
(James Eustace) *prom: pushed along over 3f out: rdn and wknd 2f out* **15/2**

1m 1.61s (-0.29) **Going Correction** -0.025s/f (Stan) **5** Ran SP% **108.5**
Speed ratings (Par 96): **101,98,96,92,76**
CSF £8.52 TOTE £4.80: £2.90, £1.10; EX 9.10 Trifecta £17.90.
**Owner** Chester Racing Club Ltd **Bred** Corduff Stud Ltd **Trained** Prescot, Merseyside

**FOCUS**
An ordinary maiden in which the winner was having his tenth race.

## 8255 DAILY PRICE BOOSTS AT UNIBET H'CAP (TAPETA) 5f 20y
**2:10** (2:10) (Class 5) (0-75,75) 3-Y-O+ **£2,911** (£866; £432; £216) **Stalls** Low

Form RPR

044- **1** **Scoreline**[6] 8180 3-8-7 68 .................... JoshDoyle(7) 1 77
(David O'Meara) *a.p: shkn up to ld ins fnl f: rdn out* **15/2**[3]

004- **2** nk **Black Dave (IRE)**[9] 8143 4-8-8 62 .................... JFEgan 6 70
(David Evans) *hld up in tch: racd keenly: rdn and ev ch ins fnl f: edgd lft: r.o* **4/1**[2]

400- **3** ½ **Captain Whoosh (IRE)**[188] 3331 3-9-1 69 .................... PhillipMakin 2 75
(John Quinn) *hld up: hdwy and nt clr run over 1f out: r.o* **10/1**

0- **4** ¾ **Pensax Lad (IRE)**[30] 7888 3-9-3 71 .................... RobertWinston 10 75
(Ronald Harris) *s.s: hld up: hmpd wl over 2f out: swtchd lft and r.o ins fnl f: nt rch ldrs* **10/1**

020- **5** nse **Bilash**[21] 7997 7-8-10 64 .................... BenCurtis 7 67
(Andrew Hollinshead) *hmpd sn after s: in rr: hdwy u.p over 1f out: r.o* **14/1**

000- **6** 1 **West Coast Dream**[24] 7949 7-8-13 67 .................... PaulMulrennan 5 67
(Roy Brotherton) *chsd ldr: hmpd wl over 3f out: led 1/2-way: rdn and hdd ins fnl f: styd on same pce* **8/1**

302- **7** 2½ **Thataboy (IRE)**[17] 8040 3-9-7 75 .................... LiamKeniry 4 66
(Tom Dascombe) *chsd ldrs: rdn over 1f out: no ex fnl f* **9/4**[1]

040- **8** 2 **Mr Mo Jo**[21] 7997 6-8-5 62 (b) JacobButterfield(3) 3 46
(Les Eyre) *led to 1/2-way: wknd fnl f* **14/1**
206- **9** 3 1/2 **Argent Touch**[14] 8077 3-8-8 62 PatrickMathers 8 33
(Derek Shaw) *hmpd sn after s: hld up: plld hrd: rdn and wknd 2f out* **28/1**
060- **U** **Profile Star (IRE)**[49] 7623 5-8-11 65 SteveDrowne 9
(Violet M Jordan) *uns rdr leaving stalls* **33/1**
1m 1.95s (0.05) **Going Correction** -0.025s/f (Stan) **10** Ran SP% **111.5**
Speed ratings (Par 103): **98,97,96,95,95 93,89,86,81,**
CSF £35.84 CT £295.21 TOTE £6.40: £2.50, £1.90, £2.70; EX 32.70 Trifecta £261.50.
**Owner** K Nicholson & Partners **Bred** Mickley Stud **Trained** Nawton, N Yorks
**FOCUS**
A middling handicap in which there were a few hard-luck stories despite a good gallop.

## 8256 UNIBET OFFER DAILY JOCKEY/TRAINER SPECIALS MAIDEN STKS (TAPETA) 5f 216y
**2:40** (2:42) (Class 5) 3-Y-0+ **£2,911** (£866; £432; £216) **Stalls** Low

Form RPR
44- **1** **Summersault (IRE)**[10] 8119 3-9-5 0 HayleyTurner 3 73
(Jamie Osborne) *mde virtually all: rdn and hung rt ins fnl f: styd on* **4/1**[2]
522- **2** 3/4 **Sir Billy Wright (IRE)**[9] 8147 3-9-5 68 JFEgan 7 70
(David Evans) *sn trcking wnr: racd keenly: rdn over 2f out: hung rt ins fnl f: kpt on* **2/7**[1]
240- **3** 7 **Island Express (IRE)**[4] 8200 7-9-0 48 (bt) AnnStokell(5) 4 48
(Ann Stokell) *hld up: racd keenly: hdwy over 1f out: rdn and hung rt fnl f: no ex* **40/1**
060- **4** nk **Zaria**[13] 8085 3-8-9 47 ShaneGray(5) 5 42
(Richard Price) *prom: rdn 1/2-way: no ex fnl f* **66/1**
334- **5** 5 **Nelson's Pride**[18] 8023 3-8-7 52 (b) RhiainIngram(7) 2 26
(Roger Ingram) *led early: chsd ldrs: shkn up over 1f out: wknd fnl f* **16/1**[3]
53- **6** 1/2 **Zat Be Zat**[9] 8147 7-9-5 0 LiamKeniry 6 29
(Violet M Jordan) *hld up: rdn over 1f out: nvr on terms* **50/1**
060- **7** 19 **Princess Rose**[11] 8111 3-9-0 42 RobertWinston 8
(John Weymes) *chsd ldrs: rdn 1/2-way: wknd over 2f out* **40/1**
1m 13.96s (-0.54) **Going Correction** -0.025s/f (Stan) **7** Ran SP% **112.0**
Speed ratings (Par 103): **102,101,91,91,84 83,58**
CSF £5.35 TOTE £5.70: £1.60, £1.10; EX 7.00 Trifecta £23.10.
**Owner** Mrs F Walwyn A Taylor D Christian **Bred** Dr Dean Harron & Mr Kemal Kurt **Trained** Upper Lambourn, Berks
**FOCUS**
Two runners predictably dominated some moderate rivals.

## 8257 LADBROKES H'CAP (TAPETA) 7f 32y
**3:10** (3:11) (Class 4) (0-85,85) 3-Y-0+ **£5,175** (£1,540; £769; £384) **Stalls** High

Form RPR
331- **1** **Rich Again (IRE)**[10] 8124 5-8-7 71 (p) PJMcDonald 9 80
(James Bethell) *hld up: hdwy over 1f out: shkn up to ld wl ins fnl f: edgd lft: r.o* **8/1**[3]
161- **2** nk **Shyron**[35] 7820 3-9-7 85 BarryMcHugh 6 93
(George Margarson) *mid-div: hdwy over 2f out: nt clr run over 1f out tl wl ins fnl f: sn rdn: r.o* **4/1**[2]
161- **3** 1 1/4 **Mr Bossy Boots (IRE)**[123] 5603 3-9-3 81 PatCosgrave 3 86
(Ralph Beckett) *a.p: rdn and ev ch fr over 1f out tl styd on same pce wl ins fnl f* **6/4**[1]
611- **4** hd **Order Of Service**[35] 7821 4-9-0 78 (t) GaryBartley 8 82
(Jim Goldie) *s.i.s: hld up: hdwy over 1f out: nt clr run and rdr dropped whip ins fnl f: r.o* **17/2**
000- **5** 1/2 **Silverware (USA)**[24] 7955 6-9-0 83 ShaneGray(5) 5 86
(Kristin Stubbs) *prom: rdn and ev ch fr over 1f out tl no ex wl ins fnl f* **22/1**
310- **6** nk **Ace Master**[146] 4752 6-8-7 78 AdamMcLean(7) 12 80
(Roy Bowring) *led: rdn over 1f out: hdd and no ex wl ins fnl f* **100/1**
321- **7** 2 **Smokethatthunders (IRE)**[16] 8058 4-9-0 78 PaulMulrennan 2 75
(James Unett) *chsd ldrs: wnt 2nd 1/2-way: rdn and ev ch over 1f out: no ex ins fnl f* **11/1**
055- **8** nse **Corporal Maddox**[12] 8100 7-9-4 82 (p) BenCurtis 11 79
(Ronald Harris) *hld up: rdn over 1f out: nt trble ldrs* **20/1**
006- **9** hd **Loyalty**[14] 8080 7-9-1 79 (v) PatrickMathers 7 75
(Derek Shaw) *hld up: pushed along 4f out: rdn over 2f out: hung lft ins fnl f: nt trble ldrs* **14/1**
4/0- **10** 5 **Beedee**[17] 8042 4-8-5 76 JoshQuinn(7) 10 59
(Richard Hannon) *hld up: rdn 1/2-way: a in rr* **40/1**
005- **11** 2 3/4 **Monsea (IRE)**[97] 6424 3-9-7 85 DavidNolan 4 61
(Brian Ellison) *mid-div: rdn 1/2-way: wknd wl over 1f out* **14/1**
003- **12** 3/4 **Rasaman (IRE)**[35] 7820 10-8-10 77 RyanPowell(3) 1 51
(Jim Goldie) *chsd ldr to 1/2-way: rdn over 1f out: cl up whn hmpd ins fnl f: eased* **33/1**
1m 28.49s (-0.31) **Going Correction** -0.025s/f (Stan) **12** Ran SP% **118.8**
Speed ratings (Par 105): **100,99,98,98,97 97,94,94,94,88 85,84**
CSF £38.08 CT £75.25 TOTE £8.60: £2.40, £1.60, £1.60; EX 42.20 Trifecta £121.40.
**Owner** Clarendon Thoroughbred Racing **Bred** Mrs Sandra Maye **Trained** Middleham Moor, N Yorks
**FOCUS**
This was a decent handicap with some progressive types in the first three. It was run at a good gallop and the form should work out.

## 8258 DOWNLOAD THE LADBROKES APP H'CAP (DIV I) (TAPETA) 1m 141y
**3:40** (3:40) (Class 6) (0-55,55) 3-Y-0+ **£2,264** (£673; £336; £168) **Stalls** Low

Form RPR
043- **1** **Spokesperson (USA)**[20] 8004 6-8-12 46 oh1 JFEgan 9 54
(Frederick Watson) *hld up in tch: chsd ldr 3f out: sn rdn: led ins fnl f: jst hld on* **7/2**[1]
040- **2** nse **Navajo Dream**[12] 8090 3-8-10 46 oh1 RobertWinston 5 54
(Michael Appleby) *hld up: hdwy over 3f out: rdn over 2f out: r.o* **9/2**[2]
000- **3** 1 1/2 **Pipers Piping (IRE)**[16] 8063 8-9-3 51 JimmyQuinn 2 55
(Mandy Rowland) *hld up: hdwy over 1f out: rdn and swtchd lft ins fnl f: r.o* **18/1**
500- **4** 3/4 **Key To Your Heart**[19] 8011 3-8-9 50 (t) ShaneGray(5) 3 53
(Michael Bell) *mid-div: hdwy over 2f out: rdn over 1f out: styd on* **7/1**
000- **5** 1 **Katmai River (IRE)**[10] 8123 7-8-6 47 (v) CharlotteJenner(7) 11 47
(Mark Usher) *led over 7f out: rdn over 1f out: hdd and unable qck ins fnl f* **12/1**
050- **6** 1 **Tukitinyasok (IRE)**[31] 7868 7-9-6 54 BarryMcHugh 4 52
(Clive Mulhall) *led 1f: chsd ldrs: rdn over 2f out: styd on same pce ins fnl f* **11/1**
603- **7** 3/4 **Catching Zeds**[23] 7976 7-9-5 53 (p) PJMcDonald 7 49
(Kevin Frost) *s.i.s: hld up: hdwy over 1f out: styd on same pce ins fnl f* **9/2**[2]
040- **8** 10 **Ruggero**[23] 7975 4-9-7 55 PaulMulrennan 1 28
(Roy Brotherton) *hld up: rdn over 2f out: wknd wl over 1f out* **20/1**
505- **9** 3/4 **Keeper's Ring (USA)**[18] 8028 3-9-5 55 (b) HayleyTurner 10 27
(Roger Varian) *chsd ldrs: wnt 2nd 5f out tl rdn 3f out: wknd wl over 1f out* **11/2**[3]
/00- **10** 17 **Courtezan**[26] 7921 3-8-10 46 oh1 (p) LiamKeniry 8
(Jamie Osborne) *hld up: racd keenly: hdwy to chse ldr over 6f out tl 5f out: wknd over 3f out* **28/1**
1m 49.91s (-0.19) **Going Correction** -0.025s/f (Stan)
**WFA** 3 from 4yo+ 2lb **10** Ran SP% **116.0**
Speed ratings (Par 101): **99,98,97,96,96 95,94,85,84,69**
CSF £18.87 CT £247.48 TOTE £5.60: £1.50, £1.90, £5.80; EX 22.40 Trifecta £328.40.
**Owner** F Watson **Bred** Stone Farm **Trained** Sedgefield, Co Durham
**FOCUS**
A solid pace down the back straight in this low-grade handicap set it up for the hold-up runners.

## 8259 DOWNLOAD THE LADBROKES APP H'CAP (DIV II) (TAPETA) 1m 141y
**4:10** (4:10) (Class 6) (0-55,55) 3-Y-0+ **£2,264** (£673; £336; £168) **Stalls** Low

Form RPR
006- **1** **Cherry Tiger**[34] 7823 4-9-0 48 LiamKeniry 9 56
(Graeme McPherson) *pushed along early: led over 7f out: rdn over 1f out: edgd rt inside fnl f: styd on* **7/1**[3]
501- **2** 1 **Sarlat**[10] 8123 3-9-4 54 PaulMulrennan 1 60
(Mark Brisbourne) *hld up in tch: rdn over 1f out: edgd rt ins fnl f: styd on* **15/2**
032- **3** 1/2 **Ambella (IRE)**[17] 8043 4-9-2 55 (v) ShaneGray(5) 3 60
(Ian Williams) *chsd ldr tl over 5f out: wnt 2nd again over 2f out: rdn and edgd rt ins fnl f: styd on same pce* **7/4**[1]
006- **4** 2 3/4 **Look Here's Al**[17] 8043 3-8-10 53 (p) RobHornby(7) 2 52
(Andrew Hollinshead) *hld up: nt clr run over 2f out: hdwy over 1f out: rdn and no imp ins fnl f* **9/1**
000- **5** hd **Boboli Gardens**[32] 7853 4-9-5 53 SamJames 4 51
(Noel Quinlan) *s.i.s: hld up: hdwy over 1f out: styd on same pce ins fnl f* **3/1**[2]
005- **6** 5 **Celestial Dawn**[10] 8123 5-8-12 46 oh1 RobertWinston 7 33
(John Weymes) *hld up: rdn over 1f out: nvr on terms* **25/1**
066- **7** nk **Russian Ice**[6] 8175 6-9-6 54 (tp) PatCosgrave 8 40
(Dean Ivory) *chsd ldrs: wnt 2nd over 5f out tl rdn over 2f out: over 1f out* **14/1**
0- **8** 3/4 **Postillion (IRE)**[38] 7792 6-9-1 49 PJMcDonald 6 33
(Richard Ford) *led 1f: chsd ldrs: rdn over 2f out: wknd over 1f out* **8/1**
553- **9** 1 **Previous Acclaim (IRE)**[98] 6394 3-8-3 46 oh1 (p) AdamMcLean(7) 5 28
(Julia Feilden) *hld up: a in rr* **50/1**
503- **10** nse **Dutch Lady Roseane**[7] 8167 3-8-10 46 oh1 (p) PatrickMathers 10 28
(James Unett) *hld up: hdwy over 6f out: rdn over 3f out: wknd wl over 1f out* **33/1**
1m 50.32s (0.22) **Going Correction** -0.025s/f (Stan)
**WFA** 3 from 4yo+ 2lb **10** Ran SP% **122.2**
Speed ratings (Par 101): **98,97,96,94,94 89,89,88,87,87**
CSF £60.40 CT £134.46 TOTE £6.60: £2.30, £1.90, £1.20; EX 44.80 Trifecta £98.80.
**Owner** Mrs S M McPherson **Bred** Elsdon Farms **Trained** Upper Oddington, Gloucs
**FOCUS**
The winner set a modest gallop that left him with a bit to offer when challenged in the straight.

## 8260 CORAL CONNECT H'CAP (TAPETA) 1m 1f 103y
**4:40** (4:43) (Class 5) (0-75,75) 3-Y-0+ **£2,911** (£866; £432; £216) **Stalls** Low

Form RPR
006- **1** **Sheriff Of Nawton (IRE)**[10] 8122 3-8-12 68 SamJames 11 77
(David O'Meara) *hld up: hdwy over 2f out: rdn to ld wl ins fnl f: r.o* **6/1**[3]
413- **2** nk **Swift Cedar (IRE)**[17] 8044 4-8-13 67 JFEgan 12 75
(David Evans) *a.p: rdn and ev ch ins fnl f: r.o* **8/1**
251- **3** nk **L'Inganno Felice (FR)**[17] 8048 4-9-7 75 DavidNolan 8 83
(Iain Jardine) *chsd ldrs: led over 2f out: rdn: edgd rt and hdd wl ins fnl f: styd on* **2/1**[1]
161- **4** shd **Dialogue**[17] 8044 8-8-11 68 RyanTate(3) 10 76
(Andrew Reid) *led 1f: chsd ldrs: rdn and ev ch ins fnl f: styd on* **9/2**[2]
056- **5** 2 1/2 **Gabrial The Duke (IRE)**[13] 8089 4-8-8 67 SammyJoBell(5) 9 69
(Richard Fahey) *hld up: hdwy over 1f out: rdn and edgd rt ins fnl f: styd on same pce* **14/1**
/00- **6** shd **Take Two**[45] 7702 5-9-7 75 JimmyQuinn 4 77
(Alex Hales) *hld up: hdwy over 1f out: rdn and edgd lft ins fnl f: styd on same pce* **20/1**
400- **7** 6 **A Little Bit Dusty**[22] 7822 6-9-4 72 (p) HayleyTurner 3 61
(Conor Dore) *chsd ldr: rdn and ev ch over 2f out: wknd ins fnl f* **25/1**
606- **8** 3/4 **Dansili Dutch (IRE)**[17] 8044 5-8-5 66 JoshDoyle(7) 5 54
(David O'Meara) *mid-div: rdn over 2f out: wknd fnl f* **16/1**
154- **9** hd **Amazing Star (IRE)**[10] 8120 9-9-1 69 (tp) LiamKeniry 2 56
(John Flint) *chsd ldrs: nt clr run over 2f out: rdn whn n.m.r over 1f out: wknd fnl f* **15/2**
500- **10** 10 **Gilmer (IRE)**[10] 8124 3-8-7 68 RyanWhile(5) 1 34
(Laura Young) *led over 8f out: rdn and hdd over 2f out: wknd fnl f* **66/1**
010- **11** 23 **Menelik (IRE)**[111] 6019 5-8-13 67 (p) PatCosgrave 6
(Des Donovan) *hld up: a in rr: drvn along over 3f out: sn lost tch* **33/1**
1m 59.14s (-1.66) **Going Correction** -0.025s/f (Stan)
**WFA** 3 from 4yo+ 2lb **11** Ran SP% **114.3**
Speed ratings (Par 103): **106,105,105,105,103 103,97,97,96,88 67**
CSF £49.40 CT £128.57 TOTE £8.10: £2.40, £2.70, £1.10; EX 69.50 Trifecta £304.50.
**Owner** Direct Racing **Bred** Lawman Syndicate & Pipe View Stud **Trained** Nawton, N Yorks
**FOCUS**
A fair handicap run at a decent gallop which made it essential to get the trip.

## 8261 BEST ODDS GUARANTEED AT CORAL H'CAP (TAPETA) 1m 4f 50y
**5:10** (5:11) (Class 6) (0-65,65) 3-Y-0+ **£2,264** (£673; £336; £168) **Stalls** Low

Form RPR
042- **1** **Percys Princess**[9] 8138 3-8-11 61 AlistairRawlinson(5) 2 79
(Michael Appleby) *led 1f: chsd ldr tl led again over 4f out: pushed clr fnl 2f: easily* **11/4**[1]
244- **2** 9 **Pim Street (USA)**[34] 7829 4-9-8 62 SamJames 4 66
(David O'Meara) *hld up: swtchd rt over 4f out: hdwy over 3f out: chsd wnr wl over 1f out: styd on same pce* **13/2**
200- **3** 2 **Dhaular Dhar (IRE)**[30] 7895 12-9-5 59 GaryBartley 11 60
(Jim Goldie) *hld up: racd keenly: hdwy over 1f out: wnt 3rd wl ins fnl f: nt trble ldrs* **28/1**
034- **4** 1 1/2 **Cabuchon (GER)**[3] 8231 7-8-9 56 (vt) HollieDoyle(7) 6 54
(David Evans) *hld up: nt clr run over 2f out: hdwy over 1f out: wnt 4th nr fin: nt trble ldrs* **14/1**

513- **5** *nk* **Helmsley Flyer (IRE)**[286] 915 4-9-10 64................(b[1]) HayleyTurner 10 62
(Trevor Wall) *chsd ldrs: rdn over 2f out: wknd fnl f* **12/1**

420- **6** *6* **Qibtee (FR)**[21] 7990 4-9-5 59.................................. RobertWinston 9 47
(Les Eyre) *hld up: nt clr run over 2f out: n.d* **6/1**[3]

002/ **7** *2 ½* **Taroum (IRE)**[52] 6821 7-9-10 64....................................(t) LiamKeniry 7 48
(John Flint) *prom: rdn over 3f out: wknd over 2f out* **33/1**

644- **8** *2 ½* **Cropley (IRE)**[24] 7951 5-9-2 61..............................(b) AnnStokell(5) 12 41
(Ann Stokell) *mid-div: hdwy over 8f out: lost pl over 6f out: wknd over 3f out* **66/1**

061- **9** *2 ½* **Uganda Glory (USA)**[9] 8145 4-9-4 58..............................(v) PatCosgrave 3 34
(George Baker) *mid-div: rdn over 2f out: wknd over 1f out* **6/1**[3]

002- **10** *6* **Reality Show (IRE)**[14] 8074 7-9-8 62.............................. DuranFentiman 1 29
(Shaun Harris) *chsd ldrs: rdn over 3f out: wknd 2f out* **5/1**[2]

411- **11** *2* **Master Of Song**[34] 7823 7-8-10 57.........................(p) AdamMcLean(7) 8 21
(Roy Bowring) *led after 1f: hdd over 4f out: wknd 2f out* **10/1**

16R- **R** **Royal Trooper (IRE)**[3] 8231 8-9-4 65...................(p) BeckyBrisbourne(7) 5
(Mark Brisbourne) *ref to r* **16/1**

2m 38.24s (-2.56) **Going Correction** -0.025s/f (Stan)
**WFA** 3 from 4yo+ 5lb **12 Ran SP% 122.5**
Speed ratings (Par 101): **107,101,99,98,98 92,92,91,89,85 84,**
CSF £21.06 CT £428.87 TOTE £3.70: £1.30, £2.00, £8.30; EX 24.00 Trifecta £755.70.
**Owner** Exors of the Late N A Blyth **Bred** Norman A Blyth **Trained** Danethorpe, Notts

**FOCUS**
The pace was solid for the trip, adding credibility to the performance of the always-prominent winner.
T/Plt: £13.90 to a £1 stake. Pool: £90,054.97 - 4,699.92 winning tickets T/Qpdt: £3.50 to a £1 stake. Pool: £9,103.48 - 1,915.45 winning tickets CR

## 8254 WOLVERHAMPTON (A.W) (L-H)
### Friday, December 26

**OFFICIAL GOING: Tapeta: standard**
Wind: Light, behind Weather: Overcast, snow after race 5

## 8262 DAILY PRICE BOOSTS AT UNIBET EBF IRISH STALLIONS MAIDEN STKS (TAPETA) 5f 20y
**1:10** (1:10) (Class 5) 2-Y-O **£2,911** (£866; £432; £216) **Stalls Low**

Form RPR

262- **1** **Kyrenia Castle (GER)**[4] 8254 2-9-5 70........................(p) KieranO'Neill 4 70
(Richard Hannon) *mde all: pressed 3f out: rdn 2f out: kpt on wl: a jst holding on* **8/1**

323- **2** *hd* **Rahmah (IRE)**[9] 8184 2-9-5 77.....................................(p) AdamKirby 2 69
(Robert Cowell) *trckd ldr: pressed ldr 3f out: rdn 2f out: kpt on but a jst hld* **9/4**[2]

223- **3** *1* **Secret Glance**[13] 8140 2-9-5 78................................... StevieDonohoe 3 66
(Ed McMahon) *dwlt: in tch: rdn 2f out: one pce and nvr quite rch ldng pair* **5/4**[1]

**4** *2 ¼* **Tavener** 2-9-5 0.................................................... GrahamGibbons 1 58
(William Jarvis) *s.i.s: hld up in tch: pushed along 2f out: no ex ins fnl f* **3/1**[3]

1m 2.39s (0.49) **Going Correction** 0.0s/f (Stan) **4 Ran SP% 111.3**
Speed ratings (Par 96): **96,95,94,90**
CSF £25.69 TOTE £5.40; EX 12.70 Trifecta £13.20.
**Owner** Middleham Park Racing Lxxxv **Bred** Frau Cl Loseken **Trained** East Everleigh, Wilts

**FOCUS**
The first three had between them been beaten favourites seven times prior to this, so it's hardly form to be positive about.

## 8263 DAILY ENHANCED "MAGIC MULTIPLES" AT UNIBET CONDITIONS STKS (TAPETA) 5f 216y
**1:45** (1:45) (Class 2) 3-Y-O+ **£11,827** (£3,541; £1,770; £885; £442) **Stalls Low**

Form RPR

041- **1** **Pretend (IRE)**[7] 8228 3-9-4 95.................................... AdamKirby 6 102+
(Charlie Appleby) *trckd ldr: led appr fnl f: pushed clr: easily* **1/4**[1]

210- **2** *5* **Smokethatthunders (IRE)**[4] 8257 4-9-4 78.......................... RobHornby 3 86
(James Unett) *led: rdn whn hdd appr fnl f: one pce and no ch w wnr* **28/1**

032- **3** *1* **Baddilini**[21] 8045 4-9-4 89.......................................(p) ChrisCatlin 2 83
(Alan Bailey) *hld up in tch: rdn 2f out: one pce* **5/1**[2]

000- **4** *2* **Red Refraction (IRE)**[16] 8101 4-9-4 87........................ KieranO'Neill 4 76
(Richard Hannon) *hld up: rdn 2f out: neveer threatened* **14/1**

004- **5** *1* **Woolfall Sovereign (IRE)**[13] 8136 8-9-4 90...................... BarryMcHugh 1 73
(George Margarson) *trckd ldr: rdn and outpcd 2f out: sn btn* **10/1**[3]

1m 14.21s (-0.29) **Going Correction** 0.0s/f (Stan) **5 Ran SP% 115.9**
Speed ratings (Par 109): **101,94,93,90,89**
CSF £11.75 TOTE £1.20: £1.02, £9.70; EX 10.90 Trifecta £23.20.
**Owner** Godolphin **Bred** Azienda Agricola Loreto Luciani **Trained** Newmarket, Suffolk

**FOCUS**
The runner-up limits the level in this steadily run conditions event. The level revolves around the runner-up.

## 8264 CORAL CASINO H'CAP (TAPETA) 1m 4f 50y
**2:25** (2:25) (Class 5) (0-75,75) 3-Y-O+ **£3,234** (£962; £481; £240) **Stalls Low**

Form RPR

052- **1** **Oratorio's Joy (IRE)**[10] 8169 4-9-2 70............................ ShaneGray(3) 4 80
(Jamie Osborne) *hld up: rdn and hdwy on outer 2f out: jnd ldr ins fnl f: styd on to ld towards fin* **11/4**[1]

41- **2** *nk* **Urban Castle (USA)**[20] 8064 3-9-2 72.............................. AdamKirby 8 81
(James Tate) *trckd ldng pair: rdn to ld 2f out: edgd rt ins fnl f: sn jnd: kpt on but hdd towards fin* **11/4**[1]

411- **3** *2 ¼* **Final Countdown**[30] 5108 3-9-3 73................................ RaulDaSilva 2 79
(John Quinn) *midfield: rdn 2f out: chsd ldr appr fnl f: briefly n.m.r in between ldng pair ins fnl f: no ex and hld in 3rd fnl 75yds* **8/1**

442- **4** *2 ½* **Captain Swift (IRE)**[21] 8047 3-8-12 68............................ JimmyQuinn 1 69
(John Mackie) *trckd ldng pair: rdn and outpcd over 1f out: no ex ins fnl f* **6/1**[3]

355- **5** *nse* **All The Winds (GER)**[39] 7822 9-9-3 68............... WilliamTwiston-Davies 6 69
(Shaun Lycett) *hld up in rr: sme hdwy 2f out: sn rdn: no further imp* **12/1**

166- **6** *2 ¾* **Flying Power**[14] 8120 6-9-7 75............................. JacobButterfield(3) 3 72
(John Norton) *midfield on outer: hdwy 3f out: rdn 2f out: wknd ins fnl f* **10/1**

261- **7** *1 ½* **Angus Glens**[7] 8231 4-9-2 67 6ex.............................(p) FergusSweeney 7 61
(David Dennis) *trckd ldr: led 10f out: rdn whn hdd 2f out: wknd* **4/1**[2]

605- **8** *6* **El Bravo**[27] 7975 8-8-9 67........................................(p) KevinLundie(7) 5 52
(Shaun Harris) *led: hdd 10f out: remained prom tl wknd wl over 1f out* **33/1**

2m 38.94s (-1.86) **Going Correction** 0.0s/f (Stan)
**WFA** 3 from 4yo+ 5lb **8 Ran SP% 118.5**
Speed ratings (Par 103): **106,105,104,102,102 100,99,95**
CSF £10.71 CT £53.91 TOTE £4.00: £1.30, £1.20, £2.20; EX 17.30 Trifecta £78.70.
**Owner** A F Tait **Bred** R Mahon & J Reilly **Trained** Upper Lambourn, Berks

**FOCUS**
A modest handicap run at an ordinary pace. The fourth has been rated close to his CD latest.

## 8265 BET IN PLAY AT CORAL H'CAP (TAPETA) 1m 1f 103y
**3:05** (3:05) (Class 6) (0-60,60) 3-Y-O+ **£2,264** (£673; £336; £168) **Stalls Low**

Form RPR

050- **1** **Stamp Duty (IRE)**[112] 6119 6-8-7 46 oh1.......................... RaulDaSilva 2 55
(Suzzanne France) *in tch: rdn over 2f out: led ins fnl f: hld on all out* **33/1**

61- **2** *nk* **Moulin Rouge (DEN)**[21] 8049 3-8-7 48........................ StevieDonohoe 11 56
(Ian Williams) *hld up in midfield: rdn 2f out: r.o strly on wd outside fr appr fnl f: jst failed* **4/1**[1]

440- **3** *1* **Stanlow**[20] 8063 4-9-2 55..........................(p) WilliamTwiston-Davies 5 61
(Daniel Mark Loughnane) *trckd ldr: rdn and ev ch ins fnl f: kpt on* **13/2**

546- **4** *hd* **Spirit Of Gondree (IRE)**[29] 7942 6-9-7 60.........................(b) AdamKirby 6 65
(Milton Bradley) *dwlt: hld up: rdn 2f out: kpt on fnl f* **6/1**[3]

154/ **5** *½* **Poppy Bond**[385] 8184 4-9-4 57................................... GrahamGibbons 3 61
(Alan Bailey) *racd keenly: led: rdn over 1f out: hdd ins fnl f: no ex* **8/1**

006- **6** *1* **Yourinthewill (USA)**[35] 7869 6-8-11 55......................... EoinWalsh(5) 4 57
(Daniel Mark Loughnane) *midfield: rdn over 1f out: one pce* **5/1**[2]

024- **7** *¾* **My Renaissance**[20] 8063 4-8-11 55.......................... AlistairRawlinson(5) 9 56
(Ben Case) *midfield: rdn and hdwy to chse ldr on outer over 2f out: wknd ins fnl f* **4/1**[1]

/02- **8** *2 ¾* **Syrian**[11] 8162 7-9-1 54.............................................. HayleyTurner 7 49
(Richard Ford) *v.s.a: hld up in rr: rdn over 2f out: nvr threatened* **6/1**[3]

045- **9** *6* **Poor Duke (IRE)**[35] 7868 4-9-1 57.........................(be) JoeyHaynes(3) 1 39
(Michael Mullineaux) *hld up: rdn over 2f out: wknd over 1f out* **12/1**

/00- **10** *14* **Mick Dundee (IRE)**[321] 538 4-9-0 60........................(t) NicolaGrundy(7) 10 13
(Richard Ford) *trckd ldr: wknd 2f out: eased* **33/1**

2m 1.22s (0.42) **Going Correction** 0.0s/f (Stan)
**WFA** 3 from 4yo+ 2lb **10 Ran SP% 123.3**
Speed ratings (Par 101): **98,97,96,96,96 95,94,92,86,74**
CSF £170.05 CT £1002.42 TOTE £28.00: £7.50, £2.00, £3.10; EX 213.60 Trifecta £1615.70 Pool of £2064.63 carried over to Saturday 27th December..
**Owner** Newstart Partnership **Bred** Windymains Farm Ltd **Trained** Norton, N Yorks

**FOCUS**
A moderate race run at a fair pace. The third and fourth have been rated close to their recent marks.

## 8266 BET IN PLAY AT CORAL H'CAP (TAPETA) 1m 1f 103y
**3:40** (3:40) (Class 2) (0-105,105) 3-Y-O+ **£11,971** (£3,583; £1,791; £896; £446) **Stalls Low**

Form RPR

123- **1** **Brocklebank (IRE)**[6] 8244 5-8-5 86 oh2.......................... NickyMackay 6 96
(Simon Dow) *hld up in tch: hdwy over 2f out: rdn to ld 1f out: kpt on* **9/1**

453- **2** *1 ¾* **Solar Deity (IRE)**[13] 8144 5-9-3 105...........................(p) RobHornby(7) 3 111
(Marco Botti) *hld up in rr: rdn over 1f out: kpt on: wnt 2nd towards fin* **3/1**[2]

440- **3** *½* **Energia Flavio (BRZ)**[15] 8116 4-8-7 91..........................(p) RyanTate(3) 2 96
(Marco Botti) *led: rdn 2f out: hdd 1f out: no ex: lost 2nd towards fin* **8/1**

002- **4** *1 ¼* **Spes Nostra**[13] 8144 6-8-9 90...............................(b) GrahamGibbons 1 93
(David Barron) *trckd ldr: rdn over 2f out: no ex ins fnl f* **13/2**

302- **5** *nk* **Gold Trail (IRE)**[160] 4448 3-8-2 88................................ ShaneGray(3) 5 90+
(Charlie Appleby) *in tch: rdn 2f out: sn one pce and btn whn briefly n.m.r ins fnl f* **13/8**[1]

040- **6** *3 ¼* **Rebellious Guest**[16] 8095 5-8-13 94............................... BarryMcHugh 4 89
(George Margarson) *hld up in tch: rdn 2f out: sn struggling* **9/2**[3]

1m 58.81s (-1.99) **Going Correction** 0.0s/f (Stan)
**WFA** 3 from 4yo+ 2lb **6 Ran SP% 115.7**
Speed ratings (Par 109): **108,106,106,104,104 101**
CSF £37.23 TOTE £7.90: £2.70, £1.90; EX 32.50 Trifecta £141.00.
**Owner** J C G Chua **Bred** Vincent Reen **Trained** Epsom, Surrey

**FOCUS**
A good handicap. The runner-up has been rated to his latest form.

## 8267 32RED NURSERY H'CAP (BOBIS RACE) (TAPETA) 1m 141y
**4:15** (4:15) (Class 3) (0-95,79) 2-Y-O **£6,301** (£1,886; £943; £472) **Stalls Low**

Form RPR

011- **1** **Greatest Journey**[23] 8016 2-9-2 79...................... AlistairRawlinson(5) 4 87+
(Saeed bin Suroor) *trckd ldr: upsides on bit over 2f out: led wl over 1f out: pushed clr: comf* **1/2**[1]

331- **2** *2 ¾* **Chicago Bere (FR)**[15] 8112 2-8-12 70.............................. KieranO'Neill 1 72
(Richard Hannon) *hld up: rdn 2f out: wnt 2nd appr fnl f: kpt on but no ch w wnr* **7/1**[3]

021- **3** *4* **Thanksgiving Day (IRE)**[23] 8009 2-9-4 76............................ AdamKirby 3 70
(Jamie Osborne) *led: rdn over 2f out: hdd wl over 1f out: wknd* **3/1**[2]

223- **4** *14* **Red Stripes (USA)**[32] 7902 2-8-0 58.............................(b) HayleyTurner 2 22
(Brian Meehan) *trckd ldr: rdn 3f out: wknd* **14/1**

1m 48.4s (-1.70) **Going Correction** 0.0s/f (Stan) **4 Ran SP% 110.8**
Speed ratings (Par 100): **107,104,101,88**
CSF £4.77 TOTE £1.40; EX 4.20 Trifecta £8.30.
**Owner** Godolphin **Bred** Meon Valley Stud **Trained** Newmarket, Suffolk

**FOCUS**
A disappointing turnout - just four runners and the top weight was rated 16lb below the race ceiling. The race was run in heavy snow. The runner-up has been rated to the bare form of his latest effort.

## 8268 LADBROKES H'CAP (TAPETA) 7f 32y
**4:45** (4:47) (Class 5) (0-75,75) 3-Y-O+ **£3,234** (£962; £481; £240) **Stalls High**

Form RPR

220- **1** **Rouge Nuage (IRE)**[8] 8204 4-9-5 73................................ JimmyQuinn 5 83
(Conrad Allen) *chsd ldrs: rdn over 2f out: led jst ins fnl f: edgd lft: kpt on* **10/1**

134- **2** *1* **Queen Aggie (IRE)**[28] 7959 4-8-11 70.................... GeorgeDowning(5) 4 77
(Tony Carroll) *hld up: rdn 2f out: kpt on fnl f: wnt 2nd post* **6/1**[3]

531- **3** *nk* **Know Your Name**[28] 7953 3-8-10 67...........................(v) ShaneGray(3) 6 74
(David Evans) *in tch: smooth hdwy 2f out: rdn and ev ch over 1f out: one pce: lost 2nd post* **2/1**[1]

213- **4** *1* **Boogangoo (IRE)**[14] 8124 3-9-4 72............................... StevieDonohoe 1 76
(Grace Harris) *led: rdn whn hdd jst ins fnl f: no ex* **7/1**

0B3- 5 1 **Ortac Rock (IRE)**16 8097 5-9-2 70 (t) DavidNolan 3 71
(Richard Fahey) *chsd ldrs: rdn over 2f out: one pce* 9/1
021- 6 1/2 **Yard Of Ale**24 8002 3-8-13 67 GrahamGibbons 2 67
(Kristin Stubbs) *s.i.s: hld up: rdn 2f out: keeping on whn n.m.r 110yds out* 9/2[2]
134- 7 4 **For Shia And Lula (IRE)**73 7183 5-9-2 75 EoinWalsh(5) 7 65
(Daniel Mark Loughnane) *prom: rdn over 2f out: wknd over 1f out* 9/1
000- 8 3 1/4 **Mowhoob**73 7178 4-8-13 67 (t) GaryBartley 10 48
(Jim Goldie) *hld up: rdn over 2f out: sn btn* 16/1
110- 9 11 **Ocean Legend (IRE)**18 8072 9-9-2 70 AdamKirby 8 23
(Tony Carroll) *prom on outer: wknd 2f out: eased* 10/1
1m 28.26s (-0.54) **Going Correction** 0.0s/f (Stan) **9** Ran SP% **122.4**
Speed ratings (Par 103): **103,101,101,100,99 98,94,90,77**
CSF £72.79 CT £172.89 TOTE £14.00: £3.40, £2.20, £1.40; EX 92.30 Trifecta £398.80.
**Owner** sportsdays.co.uk **Bred** Dermot Farrington **Trained** Newmarket, Suffolk
**FOCUS**
A modest race run at a decent pace, and in the snow. A small pb from the winner.
T/Plt: £144.50 to a £1 stake. Pool of £34,120.47- 172.28 winning tickets. T/Qpdt: £15.20 to a £1 stake. Pool of £2,833.71 - 137.30 winning tickets. AS

## 8212 DEAUVILLE (R-H)
### Friday, December 26

**OFFICIAL GOING: Polytrack: standard**

**8276a PRIX DU HOME (CONDITIONS) (2YO) (POLYTRACK) 1m 1f 110y**
10:55 (12:00) 2-Y-0 £12,083 (£4,833; £3,625; £2,416; £1,208)

RPR
1 **Princess Charm (IRE)**196 2-8-10 0 AntoineHamelin 4
(C Lerner, France) 41/10[2]
2 1 1/4 **Hot Hot Very Hot (FR)** 2-8-3 0 MlleMarylineEon(7) 2
(J Boisnard, France) 122/10
3 3/4 **Lucky Team (FR)**25 2-9-0 0 AdrienFouassier 5
(J Boisnard, France) 11/2[3]
4 1/2 **What A Party (IRE)**10 8174 2-9-1 0 FabriceVeron 9
(Gay Kelleway) *dwlt sltly and edgd lft s: w.w in tch: 5th and pushed along 2 1/2f out: rdn to chse ldrs last 300yds: kpt on u.p fnl f: nt pce to chal* 81/10
5 1 1/2 **Winter Magic (FR)**8 2-8-8 0 AlexisBadel 8
(T Castanheira, France) 116/10
6 2 1/2 **Vaargas (IRE)**77 2-8-11 0 MaximeGuyon 10
(Mme Pia Brandt, France) 8/5[1]
7 snk **Wild Wild West (FR)**49 2-8-10 0 (b) EddyHardouin 3
(Yannick Fouin, France) 113/10
8 hd **Sleekfonteine (FR)**14 8132 2-8-10 0 TonyPiccone 6
(F Doumen, France) 36/5
1m 58.28s (118.28) **8** Ran SP% **120.3**
WIN (incl. 1 euro stake): 5.10. PLACES: 1.90, 3.50, 2.00. DF: 37.50. SF: 54.30.
**Owner** Gerard Tocze **Bred** M Parrish **Trained** France

## 8218 SOUTHWELL (L-H)
### Saturday, December 27

**OFFICIAL GOING: Fibresand: standard**
Wind: Light behind Weather: Fine and dry but cold

**8277 CORAL.CO.UK H'CAP 1m 4f (F)**
12:10 (12:10) (Class 6) (0-60,59) 3-Y-0+ £2,264 (£673; £336; £168) Stalls Low

Form RPR
603- 1 **Here For Good (IRE)**19 8074 3-8-9 56 GaryMahon(7) 3 67
(Richard Hannon) *a.p: cl up after 4f: led over 3f out: rdn 2f out: drvn and edgd rt ins fnl f: kpt on* 9/2[3]
000- 2 2 1/4 **Banreenahreenkah (IRE)**30 5596 4-8-10 45 (t) WilliamCarson 8 52
(Paul Fitzsimons) *midfield: hdwy and in tch over 5f out: effrt to chse ldrs 3f out: rdn 2f out: kpt on u.p fnl f* 28/1
000- 3 5 **Blue Talisman (IRE)**39 6480 3-9-1 55 (e) DuranFentiman 10 54
(Tim Easterby) *trckd ldrs: hdwy 4f out: cl up 3f out: rdn to chal over 2f out: drvn and one pce appr fnl f* 9/1
000- 4 2 1/4 **Rajeh (IRE)**9 8208 11-8-10 45 FergusSweeney 5 41
(Peter Grayson) *in rr: hdwy over 3f out: rdn over 2f out: kpt on u.p: nrst fin* 33/1
/06- 5 6 **Mazovian (USA)**9 8208 6-8-10 48 (p) JacobButterfield(3) 7 34
(Michael Chapman) *chsd ldrs: rdn along and sltly outpcd 5f out: plugged on u.p fnl 2f* 16/1
620- 6 shd **Fire In Babylon (IRE)**14 8134 6-9-2 51 (b) PatCosgrave 1 37
(Noel Quinlan) *hld up towards rr: pushed along over 4f out: hdwy and wd st: rdn over 2f out and sn no imp* 10/3[2]
436- 7 2 1/2 **Sakhra**22 8047 3-9-3 57 GrahamGibbons 4 39
(Mark Brisbourne) *prom: pushed along 4f out: rdn 3f out: sn wknd* 11/4[1]
340- 8 2 1/4 **Rainford Glory (IRE)**12 8162 4-9-10 59 BarryMcHugh 2 37
(Tim Fitzgerald) *led: rdn along 4f out: hdd over 3f out and wknd 2f out* 12/1
500- 9 nk **Aureate**14 8134 10-8-6 48 ow1 (p) CharlotteJenner(7) 6 26
(Brian Forsey) *sn pushed along in rr: rdn 1/2-way: a bhd* 10/1
460- 10 1 1/4 **Flying Applause**14 8139 9-8-3 45 (b) AdamMcLean(7) 9 21
(Roy Bowring) *dwlt and sn pushed along: sme hdwy on outer 1/2-way: rdn over 4f out: sn outpcd and bhd* 25/1
2m 39.63s (-1.37) **Going Correction** -0.15s/f (Stan)
**WFA** 3 from 4yo+ 5lb **10** Ran SP% **110.8**
Speed ratings (Par 101): **98,96,93,91,87 87,85,84,84,83**
CSF £119.89 CT £1035.42 TOTE £5.50: £1.30, £8.00, £3.90; EX 166.50 Trifecta £1515.00 Part won..
**Owner** Middleham Park Racing LXXII **Bred** Thurso Limited **Trained** East Everleigh, Wilts

**FOCUS**
A moderate handicap in which the gallop was an ordinary one. The winner came down the centre in the straight. The runner-up has been rated a bit off her May turf seller form.

**8278 DAILY PRICE BOOSTS AT UNIBET NURSERY H'CAP 5f (F)**
12:45 (12:50) (Class 5) (0-75,78) 2-Y-0 £2,587 (£770; £384) Stalls High

Form RPR
642- 1 **Rita's Boy (IRE)**8 8222 2-9-10 78 DanielTudhope 4 79
(K R Burke) *cl up: effrt 2f out: rdn over 1f out: kpt on ins fnl f: led nr fin* 2/9[1]
603- 2 nk **Zebs Lad (IRE)**44 7762 2-8-11 65 (p) WilliamTwiston-Davies 2 65
(Ronald Harris) *cl up on outer: rdn to take slt ld over 1f out: drvn and edgd rt ins fnl f: hdd nr fin* 8/1[3]
210- 3 2 3/4 **Jebediah Shine**15 8118 2-8-10 64 SamJames 3 54
(David O'Meara) *led: rdn along 2f out: hdd appr fnl f: sn one pce* 5/1[2]
1m 0.14s (0.44) **Going Correction** 0.0s/f (Stan) **3** Ran SP% **109.6**
Speed ratings (Par 96): **96,95,91**
CSF £2.71 TOTE £1.20; EX 2.50 Trifecta £3.50.
**Owner** Middleham Park Racing CVI & Mrs E Burke **Bred** A M F Persse **Trained** Middleham Moor, N Yorks
**FOCUS**
A disappointing turnout. The gallop was only fair and the winner raced against the stands' rail throughout. The form is anything but solid.

**8279 UNIBET OFFER DAILY JOCKEY/TRAINER SPECIALS H'CAP 6f (F)**
1:15 (1:19) (Class 3) (0-90,89) 3-Y-0+ £7,762 (£2,310; £1,154; £577) Stalls Low

Form RPR
320- 1 **Guishan**22 8045 4-8-8 81 AlistairRawlinson(5) 6 89
(Michael Appleby) *cl up: led over 2f out: rdn over 1f out: drvn ins fnl f: edgd lft and hld on wl towards fin* 9/4[1]
006- 2 shd **Viva Verglas (IRE)**14 8136 3-8-13 81 GrahamGibbons 3 88
(David Barron) *chsd ldrs: hdwy 2f out: rdn over 1f out: drvn and styd on ins fnl f: jst failed* 7/2[2]
000- 3 nk **Canyari (IRE)**155 4636 3-8-11 79 PatrickMathers 7 85
(Richard Fahey) *chsd ldrs: wd st: hdwy 2f out: rdn over 1f out: drvn and edgd lft ins fnl f: kpt on wl towards fin* 16/1
005- 4 nk **Whaleweigh Station**5 8252 3-9-3 85 (v) GeorgeBaker 1 90
(J R Jenkins) *slt ld on inner: pushed along 3f out: hdd over 2f out: cl up and ev ch tl drvn and one pce ins fnl f* 5/1[3]
2/0- 5 2 1/2 **Claim The Roses (USA)**255 1518 3-9-7 89 FergusSweeney 4 86
(Ed Vaughan) *towards rr: hdwy over 2f out: rdn to chse ldrs over 1f out: sn hung lft and no imp fnl f* 5/1[3]
300- 6 1 **Pennine Warrior**11 8182 3-8-7 75 oh1 (p) BarryMcHugh 8 69
(Scott Dixon) *cl up 2f: sn rdn along and lost pl: outpcd and bhd fr 1/2-way* 8/1
110- 7 2 **Saint Pois (FR)**8 8228 3-9-5 87 WilliamCarson 5 74
(Tony Carroll) *prom: cl up 1/2-way: rdn over 2f out: grad wknd* 16/1
300- 8 6 **Clubland (IRE)**52 7669 5-8-3 78 AdamMcLean(7) 2 46
(Roy Bowring) *cl up: rdn along whn n.m.r and lost pl 1/2-way: sn bhd* 9/1
1m 14.38s (-2.12) **Going Correction** -0.15s/f (Stan) **8** Ran SP% **119.2**
Speed ratings (Par 107): **108,107,107,107,103 102,99,91**
CSF £10.73 CT £102.42 TOTE £3.30: £1.30, £1.60, £4.50; EX 11.90 Trifecta £144.50.
**Owner** Brian D Cantle **Bred** B D Cantle **Trained** Danethorpe, Notts
■ Stewards' Enquiry : Patrick Mathers two-day ban: use of whip (10-11 Jan)
**FOCUS**
A useful handicap run at a reasonable pace. The winner came down the centre and the first four finished in a heap. The winner has been rated as running a pb on her return here.

**8280 DAILY PRICE BOOSTS AT UNIBET MAIDEN STKS 6f (F)**
1:45 (1:49) (Class 5) 3-Y-0+ £3,234 (£962; £481; £240) Stalls Low

Form RPR
0- 1 **Minister Of Fun**44 7764 3-9-5 0 BarryMcHugh 1 73
(Scott Dixon) *t.k.h: prom on inner: n.m.r and stdd over 3f out: swtchd rt and hdwy over 2f out: chal wl over 1f out: rdn to ld and rn green appr fnl f: kpt on* 20/1
520- 2 1 1/2 **Deftera Fantutte (IRE)**14 8142 3-8-7 59 CharlieBennett(7) 3 62
(Natalie Lloyd-Beavis) *sn led: jnd and rdn over 2f out: drvn and hdd appr fnl f: kpt on same pce* 9/4[2]
662- 3 6 **Sea Whisper**18 8085 3-9-0 45 CharlesBishop 6 43
(Ann Stokell) *cl up: chal over 2f out: ev ch: sn rdn and edgd lft over 1f out: one pce* 4/1[3]
232- 4 2 1/4 **Quaintrelle (IRE)**25 8002 3-9-0 62 (b1) FergusSweeney 5 36
(Ed Vaughan) *dwlt: hdwy on outer to trck ldrs over 3f out: wd st: rdn over 2f out: sn drvn and btn* 11/8[1]
0/0- 5 2 3/4 **Ri Na Si**33 7907 4-9-0 48 (p) AlistairRawlinson(5) 4 32
(Michael Appleby) *prom: rdn along bef 1/2-way: sn outpcd and bhd fnl 2f* 8/1
000- 6 13 **L'Es Fremantle (FR)**53 7646 3-9-2 28 (p) JacobButterfield(3) 2
(Michael Chapman) *cl up: pushed along and lost pl after 2f: bhd fr 1/2-way* 66/1
1m 15.11s (-1.39) **Going Correction** -0.15s/f (Stan) **6** Ran SP% **110.2**
Speed ratings (Par 103): **103,101,93,90,86 69**
CSF £62.67 TOTE £17.10: £8.00, £1.40; EX 78.10 Trifecta £135.20.
**Owner** P J Dixon & Partners **Bred** Mrs Y E Mullin & B McGarrigle **Trained** Babworth, Notts
**FOCUS**
A low-grade maiden in which the pace was fair. The winner came down the centre and the first two pulled clear. The runner-up has been rated to form.

**8281 LADBROKES H'CAP 1m (F)**
2:25 (2:25) (Class 4) (0-85,80) 3-Y-0+ £5,175 (£1,540; £769; £384) Stalls Low

Form RPR
610- 1 **Starfield**25 7998 5-8-10 74 (v) AlistairRawlinson(5) 3 89
(Michael Appleby) *cl up: led after 2f: pushed clr wl over 2f out: rdn and wandered fr over 1f out: kpt on strly* 2/1[1]
255- 2 5 **Toto Skyllachy**9 8209 9-9-1 74 DanielTudhope 6 77
(David O'Meara) *in tch: hdwy on outer 3f out: rdn over 2f out: chsd wnr appr fnl f: no imp* 11/4[2]
004- 3 2 1/2 **Kung Hei Fat Choy (USA)**9 8209 5-9-1 74 (b) GrahamGibbons 1 71
(James Given) *slt ld on inner 2f: cl up: pushed along over 3f out: rdn to chse wnr over 2f out: drvn over 1f out and kpt on same pce* 13/2
210- 4 1 1/2 **Royal Holiday (IRE)**39 7829 7-8-12 71 (b) BarryMcHugh 7 64
(Marjorie Fife) *cl up on outer: rdn along wl over 2f out: sn drvn and wknd* 13/2
113- 5 3 1/2 **Naoise (IRE)**35 7894 6-9-0 76 (t) JacobButterfield(3) 5 61
(Ollie Pears) *trckd ldrs: pushed along wl over 2f out: sn rdn and n.d* 6/1[3]

000- **6** ¾ **Piceno (IRE)**[9] 8209 6-8-6 70..........................................(p) TimClark(5) 4 54
(Scott Dixon) *cl up: rdn along 3f out: wknd over 2f out* **20/1**

605- **7** 1½ **Stand To Reason (IRE)**[24] 8012 6-9-7 80..(b[1]) WilliamTwiston-Davies 2 60
(Tony Carroll) *in tch: rdn along 3f out: sn btn* **14/1**

1m 40.24s (-3.46) **Going Correction** -0.15s/f (Stan) **7** Ran SP% **112.4**
Speed ratings (Par 105): **111,106,103,102,98 97,96**
CSF £7.35 TOTE £3.20: £1.50, £2.80; EX 8.60 Trifecta £26.60.
**Owner** Dallas Racing **Bred** Dunchurch Lodge Stud Co **Trained** Danethorpe, Notts

**FOCUS**
A fair handicap in which an ordinary gallop increased turning for home. The winner edged towards the far side in the straight. The winner has been rated close to his best.

## 8282 DOWNLOAD THE LADBROKES APP H'CAP 1m (F)
**3:00** (3:05) (Class 6) (0-65,70) 3-Y-O+ **£2,264** (£673; £336; £168) **Stalls** Low

Form RPR

132- **1** **Best Tamayuz**[11] 8176 3-9-1 65.......................................... TimClark(5) 1 78
(Scott Dixon) *trckd ldrs on inner: hdwy 3f out: chal 2f out: rdn to ld jst over 1f out: drvn and edgd rt ins fnl f: kpt on strly* **5/1**[2]

/54- **2** 2¼ **Walk Like A Giant**[193] 3332 3-9-1 63........................................ RyanTate(3) 9 71
(Michael Appleby) *hld up: hdwy over 3f out: rdn to chse ldrs wl over 1f out: drvn and edgd lft ent fnl f: no imp* **9/4**[1]

240- **3** 1 **Roger Thorpe**[15] 8122 5-9-1 62.............................. JacobButterfield(3) 7 69
(Deborah Sanderson) *cl up: wd st: rdn over 2f out: drvn and sltly outpcd over 1f out: kpt on fnl f* **6/1**[3]

042- **4** 1 **Putin (IRE)**[39] 7829 6-9-0 63..............................(tp) AlistairRawlinson(5) 6 67
(Phil McEntee) *cl up: led 3f out: jnd and rdn 2f out: drvn and hdd over 1f out: wknd ins fnl f* **7/1**

004- **5** 6 **Hill Fort**[18] 8086 4-9-6 64..................................(p) WilliamTwiston-Davies 4 55
(Ronald Harris) *trckd ldrs: hdwy 3f out: rdn over 2f out: sn drvn and wknd* **8/1**

050- **6** ½ **On Demand**[22] 8037 3-9-4 63.................................................... TomEaves 2 51
(Simon Hodgson) *towards rr: sme hdwy over 2f out: sn rdn and n.d* **20/1**

014- **7** nk **Burnhope**[8] 8224 5-9-12 70............................................... BarryMcHugh 8 59
(Scott Dixon) *chsd ldrs on outer: rdn along 3f out: wknd 2f out* **5/1**[2]

650- **8** 3¼ **Rio Cobolo (IRE)**[120] 5895 8-9-3 64.................... NataliaGemelova(3) 3 45
(Keith Reveley) *led: rdn along and hdd 3f out: wknd 2f out* **28/1**

300- **9** 4 **Surround Sound**[75] 6627 4-9-0 58............................ DuranFentiman 10 30
(Tim Easterby) *in tch on wd outside: rdn along over 3f out: sn outpcd* **16/1**

600- **10** 3¾ **Sam Spade (IRE)**[18] 8086 4-9-6 64..........................(v) PatrickMathers 5 27
(Derek Shaw) *dwlt: sn rdn along and a in rr: bhd fnl 3f* **25/1**

1m 41.89s (-1.81) **Going Correction** -0.15s/f (Stan)
**WFA** 3 from 4yo+ 1lb **10** Ran SP% **119.9**
Speed ratings (Par 101): **103,100,99,98,92 92,91,88,84,80**
CSF £16.75 CT £71.03 TOTE £4.90: £1.50, £1.10, £2.60; EX 18.40 Trifecta £193.20.
**Owner** Paul J Dixon **Bred** Rabbah Bloodstock Limited **Trained** Babworth, Notts

**FOCUS**
A modest handicap run at an ordinary gallop to the home turn. The winner came down the centre in the straight. The race has been rated slightly positively, with the third to form and the fourth close to his CD latest.

## 8283 DOWNLOAD THE CORAL APP H'CAP 1m 3f (F)
**3:35** (3:36) (Class 5) (0-75,75) 3-Y-O+ **£2,587** (£770; £384; £192) **Stalls** Low

Form RPR

065- **1** **Hussar Ballad (USA)**[15] 8122 5-8-11 62.......................... DuranFentiman 5 71
(Mel Brittain) *set stdy pce: qcknd 4f out: rdn clr over 2f out: styd on strly* **10/3**[2]

062- **2** 3 **Luv U Whatever**[32] 7914 4-9-7 75.............................................. RyanTate(3) 3 79
(Michael Appleby) *trckd ldrs: hdwy 3f out: swtchd rt and rdn to chse wnr wl over 1f out: drvn and no imp fnl f* **11/10**[1]

660- **3** 1½ **Karam Albaari (IRE)**[19] 8073 6-9-5 70...................... FergusSweeney 1 71
(J R Jenkins) *hld up in rr: tk clsr order 5f out: wd st and hdwy wl over 2f out: rdn wl over 1f out: kpt on same pce fnl f* **16/1**

532- **4** 2 **Lean On Pete (IRE)**[15] 8122 5-9-2 70.................... JacobButterfield(3) 4 68
(Ollie Pears) *hld up in tch: wd st: effrt wl over 2f out: sn rdn along and kpt on same pce* **7/2**[3]

214- **5** 3¾ **Master Dan**[18] 8089 3-9-6 75...........................................(p) TomEaves 2 67
(James Given) *chsd wnr: pushed along over 4f out: rdn along over 3f out: drvn wl over 2f out: sn wknd* **9/1**

2m 26.95s (-1.05) **Going Correction** -0.15s/f (Stan)
**WFA** 3 from 4yo+ 4lb **5** Ran SP% **108.8**
Speed ratings (Par 103): **97,94,93,92,89**
CSF £7.29 TOTE £4.70: £1.30, £1.20; EX 7.80 Trifecta £58.80.
**Owner** Mel Brittain **Bred** Darley **Trained** Warthill, N Yorks

**FOCUS**
A fair handicap but one in which the slow gallop played into the hands of the front-runner, who came down the centre in the straight. The third has been rated to his recent Polytrack level.
T/Plt: £131.60 to a £1 stake. Pool: £46,658.09 - 258.63 winning units. T/Qpdt: £21.10 to a £1 stake. Pool: £4721.50 - 164.85 winning units. JR

# 8262 WOLVERHAMPTON (A.W) (L-H)
Saturday, December 27

**OFFICIAL GOING: Tapeta: standard**
Wind: Fresh across Weather: Raining

## 8284 DAILY ENHANCED "MAGIC MULTIPLES" AT UNIBET H'CAP (TAPETA) 5f 20y
**4:05** (4:06) (Class 6) (0-60,60) 3-Y-O+ **£2,264** (£673; £336; £168) **Stalls** Low

Form RPR

420- **1** **Your Gifted (IRE)**[18] 8088 7-8-13 59..........................(v) GaryMahon(7) 6 67
(Lisa Williamson) *hld up: hdwy over 1f out: rdn to ld wl ins fnl f: r.o* **12/1**

524- **2** nk **Rat Catcher (IRE)**[8] 8230 4-8-1 47..............................(b) RobHornby(7) 8 54
(Lisa Williamson) *chsd ldrs: shkn up over 1f out: rdn and edgd rt ins fnl f: r.o* **5/1**[3]

500- **3** ½ **De Repente (IRE)**[77] 7111 3-9-4 57.......................................... HayleyTurner 7 62
(Michael Appleby) *led: pushed along 1/2-way: rdn and hdd wl ins fnl f: styd on* **5/1**[3]

400- **4** 2 **Telegraph (IRE)**[22] 8043 3-9-7 60................................................ JFEgan 1 62+
(David Evans) *chsd ldrs: hmpd 1/2-way: rdn over 1f out: styd on same pce ins fnl f* **11/4**[1]

202- **5** hd **Lazy Sioux**[11] 8181 3-8-8 50...........................................(v[1]) NeilFarley(3) 11 47
(Richard Guest) *chsd ldrs: rdn over 1f out: styd on same pce ins fnl f* **10/1**

605- **6** 2½ **Louis Vee (IRE)**[26] 7997 6-9-5 58......................................(t) ShaneKelly 9 46
(Roy Brotherton) *s.i.s: hdwy to join ldr over 3f out: rdn over 1f out: wknd ins fnl f* **4/1**[2]

005- **7** 1½ **Two Turtle Doves (IRE)**[8] 8229 8-9-0 53........................ RobertHavlin 2 36
(Michael Mullineaux) *prom tl rdn and wknd wl over 1f out* **12/1**

603- **8** 2½ **My Meteor**[33] 7900 7-9-5 58...................................................... SteveDrowne 3 32
(Tony Newcombe) *bhd fnl 4f* **4/1**[2]

1m 1.19s (-0.71) **Going Correction** -0.075s/f (Stan) **8** Ran SP% **124.5**
Speed ratings (Par 101): **102,101,100,97,97 93,90,86**
CSF £76.79 CT £352.63 TOTE £6.00: £2.00, £1.80, £2.20; EX 49.50 Trifecta £611.70.
**Owner** Anthony Thomas Sykes **Bred** Rathasker Stud **Trained** Saighton, Cheshire

**FOCUS**
A strongly run if only moderate sprint handicap. The winner has been rated as running her best race since her 2011 peak.

## 8285 UNIBET OFFER DAILY JOCKEY/TRAINER SPECIALS H'CAP (TAPETA) (DIV I) 5f 216y
**4:40** (4:40) (Class 6) (0-55,56) 3-Y-O+ **£2,264** (£673; £336; £168) **Stalls** Low

Form RPR

263- **1** **Hamis Al Bin (IRE)**[14] 8142 5-9-4 52..........................(t) PatCosgrave 11 61
(Milton Bradley) *hld up: hdwy over 1f out: rdn to ld and edgd lft wl ins fnl f: r.o* **5/1**[3]

600- **2** nk **Trending (IRE)**[23] 8023 5-8-8 49..................................(bt) DavidParkes(7) 6 57
(Jeremy Gask) *hld up in tch: plld hrd: led ins fnl f: sn rdn and hdd: edgd lft: r.o* **9/1**

601- **3** 1½ **Black Truffle (FR)**[9] 8200 4-9-3 51...........................................(v) LiamKeniry 7 57+
(Mark Usher) *hld up: hdwy and hmpd over 1f out: nt clr run ins fnl f: running on whn hmpd and eased nr fin* **13/2**

002- **4** nse **Salvado (IRE)**[8] 8229 4-9-3 56................................. GeorgeDowning(5) 8 59
(Tony Carroll) *a.p: chsd ldr over 3f out: rdn and hung lft over 1f out: ev ch ins fnl f: styng on same pce whn nt clr run towards fin* **3/1**[1]

000- **5** ½ **Master Of Disguise**[18] 8088 8-9-7 55.............................. GeorgeBaker 4 58+
(Brian Baugh) *led 1f: remained handy: hmpd over 1f out: swtchd rt ins fnl f: styd on* **15/2**

663- **6** 1½ **Studfarmer**[23] 8024 4-8-12 46 oh1...................................(p) HayleyTurner 5 43+
(Polly Gundry) *led 5f out: sn hdd: remained handy: rdn whn hmpd over 1f out: styd on same pce ins fnl f* **9/2**[2]

400- **7** ¾ **Seraphima**[78] 7074 4-8-5 46 oh1..........................................(v) RobHornby(7) 2 40
(Lisa Williamson) *hld up: swtchd rt over 2f out: rdn over 1f out: hung lft ins fnl f: nt trble ldrs* **66/1**

500- **8** hd **Night Trade (IRE)**[9] 8200 7-8-12 46...................................(b) DavidProbert 1 40
(Ronald Harris) *mid-div: hmpd and lost pl 4f out: rdn over 2f out: one pce fnl f* **28/1**

010- **9** ½ **Prigsnov Dancer (IRE)**[28] 7972 9-8-13 54..............(p) KevinLundie(7) 10 46
(Deborah Sanderson) *prom: led over 4f out: pushed clr 2f out: rdn over 1f out: hdd & wknd ins fnl f* **20/1**

031- **10** 4 **Very First Blade**[14] 8133 5-9-2 50.................................(be) RobertHavlin 9 29
(Michael Mullineaux) *prom: rdn over 2f out: wknd wl over 1f out* **15/2**

1m 13.95s (-0.55) **Going Correction** -0.075s/f (Stan) **10** Ran SP% **116.4**
Speed ratings (Par 101): **100,99,97,97,96 94,93,93,92,87**
CSF £48.14 CT £296.91 TOTE £5.80: £1.70, £3.40, £2.30; EX 55.40 Trifecta £451.30.
**Owner** Philip Banfield **Bred** Mrs H Owen **Trained** Sedbury, Gloucs
■ Stewards' Enquiry : George Baker two-day ban: careless riding (10 -11 Jan)

**FOCUS**
A rough race with plenty of traffic problems in behind the principals. The winner has been rated to form.

## 8286 UNIBET OFFER DAILY JOCKEY/TRAINER SPECIALS H'CAP (TAPETA) (DIV II) 5f 216y
**5:10** (5:12) (Class 6) (0-55,55) 3-Y-O+ **£2,264** (£673; £336; £168) **Stalls** Low

Form RPR

330- **1** **Copper Cavalier**[17] 8090 3-9-2 50..........................................(v) AdamKirby 2 60
(Robert Cowell) *mde all: rdn over 1f out: edgd lft ins fnl f: styd on* **10/3**[2]

060- **2** 1¼ **Indian Affair**[24] 8014 4-9-7 55.................................................(t) LiamKeniry 3 61
(Milton Bradley) *a.p: chsd wnr 2f out: rdn and nt clr run ins fnl f: kpt on* **9/1**[3]

400- **3** 1¼ **Diamond Vine (IRE)**[72] 7222 6-8-12 46 oh1..............(p) DavidProbert 11 48
(Ronald Harris) *mid-div: hdwy over 1f out: styd on: nt rch ldrs* **40/1**

600- **4** ½ **Swendab (IRE)**[24] 8014 6-8-13 54..............................(b) CiaranMckee(7) 9 54
(John O'Shea) *a.p: chsd wnr over 3f out tl 2f out: styd on same pce ins fnl f* **25/1**

250- **5** ½ **Littlecote Lady**[28] 7972 5-8-10 51..........................(v) CharlotteJenner(7) 5 50
(Mark Usher) *s.s: hld up: rdn over 1f out: r.o ins fnl f: nt rch ldrs* **20/1**

032- **6** nk **Hidden Asset**[28] 7972 4-9-6 54............................................ HayleyTurner 6 52
(Michael Appleby) *chsd ldrs: rdn over 1f out: styd on same pce ins fnl f* **10/11**[1]

064- **7** 1 **Gypsy Rider**[8] 8229 5-8-11 50.......................................... EoinWalsh(5) 10 45
(Henry Tett) *stmbld sn after s: sn pushed along in rr: styd on ins fnl f: nvr trbld ldrs* **10/1**

000- **8** ½ **Daneglow (IRE)**[35] 7884 4-8-9 46 oh1......................(e) JoeyHaynes(3) 12 39
(Mike Murphy) *hld up: hdwy over 1f out: sn rdn: no imp fnl f* **40/1**

500- **9** 7 **Jessy Mae**[28] 7977 3-8-13 47..............................................(v[1]) PatCosgrave 13 18
(Derek Haydn Jones) *prom: rdn over 2f out: wknd over 1f out* **28/1**

000- **10** 1¾ **Basle**[14] 8133 7-8-12 46 oh1...........................................(tp) JimmyQuinn 7 11
(Roy Brotherton) *mid-div: drvn along over 2f out: wknd over 1f out* **80/1**

400- **11** hd **Go Charlie**[8] 8229 3-8-5 46 oh1...................................... RobHornby(7) 8 10
(Lisa Williamson) *chsd ldrs: rdn over 2f out: wknd over 1f out* **50/1**

1m 14.14s (-0.36) **Going Correction** -0.075s/f (Stan) **11** Ran SP% **114.7**
Speed ratings (Par 101): **99,97,95,95,94 93,92,91,82,80 80**
CSF £29.39 CT £1022.12 TOTE £4.60: £1.30, £2.70, £6.00; EX 24.40 Trifecta £350.70.
**Owner** Mrs D Rix, J Partridge & Partner **Bred** Shadwell Estate Company Limited **Trained** Six Mile Bottom, Cambs

**FOCUS**
This was a deal more competitive than the market suggested. A length pb from the winner, with the third in line with his form since the spring.

## 8287 32RED.COM MAIDEN AUCTION STKS (TAPETA) 5f 216y
**5:40** (5:41) (Class 6) 2-Y-O **£2,264** (£673; £336; £168) **Stalls** Low

Form RPR

034- **1** **Jimmy's Hall**[21] 8059 2-8-13 65..................................(b) StevieDonohoe 2 67
(J S Moore) *chsd ldr: rdn 2f out: styd on u.p to ld nr fin* **11/2**[3]

222- **2** nk **Come Uppence**[8] 8225 2-9-0 70...............................................(v[1]) JFEgan 6 67
(David Evans) *sn led: clr 2f out: rdn over 1f out: hung lft and hdd nr fin* **11/10**[1]

035- **3** 10 **Galago (IRE)**[115] 6024 2-9-0 69...................................(p) LiamKeniry 5 37
(Sylvester Kirk) *s.i.s: hdwy over 3f out: rdn and wknd over 2f out* **2/1**[2]

600- **4** 4 1/2 **Aruan**[21] 8060 2-8-7 55 ........ DavidProbert 1 17
(Derek Haydn Jones) *chsd ldrs: rdn over 3f out: wknd wl over 2f out* **9/1**
405- **5** 7 **Wesie's Dream**[19] 8076 2-8-7 57 ........ (v[1]) HayleyTurner 3
(Mark Usher) *dwlt: sn outpcd* **28/1**
1m 14.08s (-0.42) **Going Correction** -0.075s/f (Stan) **5** Ran SP% **109.8**
Speed ratings (Par 94): **99,98,85,79,69**
CSF £12.09 TOTE £6.00: £2.70, £1.50; EX 10.70 Trifecta £22.60.
**Owner** J S Moore **Bred** Newsells Park Stud **Trained** Upper Lambourn, Berks
**FOCUS**
A weak affair.

## 8288 32RED MAIDEN STKS (TAPETA) 1m 141y
**6:10** (6:11) (Class 5) 2-Y-O **£2,911** (£866; £432; £216) **Stalls** Low

Form RPR
**1** **Jack Hobbs** 2-9-5 0 ........ RobertHavlin 10 78+
(John Gosden) *s.s: hdwy over 6f out: shkn up to ld over 1f out: edgd lft ins fnl f: r.o* **1/1**[1]
06- **2** 3 **Dutch Uncle**[47] 7731 2-9-5 0 ........ GeorgeBaker 6 72
(Ed Dunlop) *hld up: hdwy over 2f out: rdn and hung lft fr over 1f out: styd on same pce ins fnl f* **6/1**[3]
622- **3** hd **Royal Albert Hall**[31] 7926 2-9-5 73 ........ PatCosgrave 11 71
(Olly Stevens) *a.p: chsd ldr over 3f out: led over 2f out: rdn and hdd over 1f out: styd on same pce ins fnl f* **5/1**[2]
**4** 5 **Beau Knight** 2-9-5 0 ........ SteveDrowne 8 61+
(William Jarvis) *s.i.s: hld up: hdwy over 1f out: edgd lft ins fnl f: styd on to go 4th nr fin: nt trble ldrs* **20/1**
32- **5** nk **Salma Gondis (IRE)**[21] 8060 2-9-0 0 ........ DanielTudhope 4 55
(David O'Meara) *led: hdd over 6f out: chsd ldr tl over 3f out: sn rdn: wknd fnl f* **12/1**
4- **6** 1 1/2 **Sperrin (IRE)**[26] 7985 2-9-0 0 ........ KevinStott(5) 12 57
(Charlie Appleby) *hld up: rdn over 3f out: nvr on terms* **10/1**
00- **7** 1/2 **Mr Bissto**[19] 8067 2-9-0 0 ........ GeorgeDowning(5) 1 56
(Ian Williams) *prom: rdn over 2f out: wknd over 1f out* **40/1**
**8** 7 **Hubertas** 2-9-5 0 ........ PhillipMakin 3 41
(John Quinn) *s.i.s: sn pushed along in rr: nvr on terms* **66/1**
6- **9** shd **Inflexiball**[64] 7425 2-9-0 0 ........ JimmyQuinn 2 36
(John Mackie) *prom: rdn over 3f out: wknd over 2f out* **125/1**
33- **10** 4 1/2 **Captain Koko**[18] 8083 2-9-5 0 ........ AdamKirby 13 32
(Marco Botti) *chsd ldr tl led over 6f out: rdn and hdd over 2f out: wknd over 1f out* **10/1**
50- **11** 4 1/2 **Crystalin (IRE)**[11] 8173 2-8-9 0 ........ AlistairRawlinson(5) 7 17
(Marco Botti) *hld up: a in rr: wknd 3f out* **50/1**
0- **12** nk **Chorlton House**[12] 8166 2-9-5 0 ........ StevieDonohoe 9 22
(Johnny Farrelly) *hld up: rdn over 3f out: sn wknd* **28/1**
1m 47.38s (-2.72) **Going Correction** -0.075s/f (Stan) 2y crse rec **12** Ran SP% **121.7**
Speed ratings (Par 96): **109,106,106,101,101 100,99,93,93,89 85,85**
CSF £7.09 TOTE £2.20: £1.10, £2.80, £2.00; EX 10.40 Trifecta £34.50.
**Owner** Bailey, Hall & Hood **Bred** Minster Stud **Trained** Newmarket, Suffolk
**FOCUS**
An informative maiden and a big performance from the well backed winner.

## 8289 32RED CASINO H'CAP (TAPETA) 1m 5f 194y
**6:40** (6:43) (Class 6) (0-60,58) 3-Y-O+ **£2,264** (£673; £336; £168) **Stalls** Low

Form RPR
405- **1** **Ballyfarsoon (IRE)**[24] 8011 3-8-7 46 ........ (v) StevieDonohoe 7 55
(Ian Williams) *a.p: chsd ldr 3f out: led over 1f out: rdn and edgd lft ins fnl f: styd on* **4/1**[3]
414- **2** 3/4 **Well Owd Mon**[14] 8145 4-9-6 52 ........ (p) GeorgeBaker 8 59
(Andrew Hollinshead) *s.i.s: hld up: hdwy over 1f out: sn rdn: r.o to go 2nd wl ins fnl f: nt rch wnr* **5/2**[1]
545- **3** 1 **Nolecce**[30] 6899 7-9-4 57 ........ RobHornby(7) 5 63
(Tony Forbes) *chsd ldr tl led 4f out: rdn and hdd over 1f out: edgd lft and styd on same pce ins fnl f* **22/1**
5- **4** 1 **Toretto (IRE)**[26] 7990 6-9-10 56 ........ DavidProbert 1 60
(Bernard Llewellyn) *prom: lost pl over 3f out: styd on u.p fr over 1f out* **9/2**
622- **5** 1 3/4 **Lacey**[21] 8061 5-9-12 58 ........ (p) AdamKirby 4 60
(Andrew Hollinshead) *chsd ldrs: rdn over 3f out: styd on same pce fr over 1f out* **11/4**[2]
440- **6** 5 **Honest Strike (USA)**[9] 8208 7-9-9 55 ........ (tp) ShaneKelly 9 50
(Daniel Mark Loughnane) *hld up: hdwy over 2f out: wknd over 1f out* **10/1**
505- **7** 6 **Brian The Lion**[14] 8147 3-8-2 48 ow3 ........ KevinLundie(7) 3 34
(Shaun Harris) *hld up: rdn over 3f out: wknd over 1f out* **33/1**
465- **8** 3 3/4 **Tactical Strike**[95] 6637 3-9-3 56 ........ JimmyQuinn 2 37
(Shaun Harris) *led 10f: rdn over 2f out: wknd wl over 1f out* **20/1**
3m 4.7s (-0.10) **Going Correction** -0.075s/f (Stan)
**WFA** 3 from 4yo+ 7lb **8** Ran SP% **114.6**
Speed ratings (Par 101): **97,96,96,95,94 91,88,86**
CSF £14.10 CT £191.26 TOTE £5.10: £1.50, £1.40, £5.00; EX 16.10 Trifecta £199.80.
**Owner** Patrick Kelly **Bred** A O'Sullivan **Trained** Portway, Worcs
**FOCUS**
A moderate staying handicap. Muddling form rated around the well-placed third.

## 8290 DOWNLOAD THE CORAL APP H'CAP (TAPETA) 1m 1f 103y
**7:10** (7:11) (Class 4) (0-85,84) 3-Y-O+ **£5,175** (£1,540; £769; £384) **Stalls** Low

Form RPR
141- **1** **Dream Child (IRE)**[36] 7870 3-9-0 84 ........ KevinStott(5) 1 93+
(Charlie Appleby) *hld up: hdwy over 1f out: shkn up to ld ins fnl f: edgd lft: jst hld on* **5/2**[2]
111- **2** shd **Persona Grata**[15] 8122 3-8-12 77 ........ DanielTudhope 2 86+
(Ed Walker) *hld up in tch: chsd ldr over 1f out: rdn and ev ch ins fnl f: r.o* **5/4**[1]
000- **3** 1 3/4 **Vivat Rex (IRE)**[28] 7974 3-9-2 81 ........ (v[1]) ShaneKelly 4 86
(Alan Bailey) *led: qcknd over 2f out: rdn and hdd ins fnl f: styd on same pce* **33/1**
500- **4** 1/2 **Off The Pulse**[59] 7538 4-9-1 78 ........ JimmyQuinn 7 82
(John Mackie) *hld up: hdwy over 1f out: sn rdn: styd on* **25/1**
321- **5** 1 3/4 **Park Place**[42] 7812 4-8-13 76 ........ PhillipMakin 5 76
(John Quinn) *prom: nt clr run over 2f out: rdn over 1f out: styd on same pce* **14/1**
454- **6** 1 1/4 **Berlusca (IRE)**[29] 7955 5-9-6 83 ........ SamJames 6 81
(David O'Meara) *plld hrd: led 1f: trckd ldr tl 3f out: rdn over 1f out: no ex fnl f* **11/1**
406- **7** 1/2 **Gworn**[124] 5749 4-9-6 83 ........ GeorgeBaker 3 80
(Ed Dunlop) *chsd ldrs: wnt 2nd 3f out tl over 1f out: wknd ins fnl f* **3/1**[3]
1m 59.6s (-1.20) **Going Correction** -0.075s/f (Stan)
**WFA** 3 from 4yo+ 2lb **7** Ran SP% **119.8**
Speed ratings (Par 105): **102,101,100,99,98 97,96**
CSF £6.46 TOTE £3.40: £1.50, £1.40; EX 7.20 Trifecta £74.70.
**Owner** Godolphin **Bred** Darley **Trained** Newmarket, Suffolk
**FOCUS**
A competitive affair featuring some progressive individuals. The race is potentially a bit better than it's been rated if the third can confirm this improvement.

## 8291 LADBROKES H'CAP (TAPETA) 7f 32y
**7:40** (7:42) (Class 7) (0-50,50) 3-Y-O+ **£1,940** (£577; £288; £144) **Stalls** High

Form RPR
060- **1** **Spoken Words**[79] 7057 5-9-2 45 ........ (b) ConnorBeasley 2 53
(John David Riches) *s.i.s: hld up: hmpd over 2f out: swtchd rt and hdwy over 1f out: sn rdn: edgd lft and r.o to ld post* **28/1**
501- **2** nk **Barwah (USA)**[9] 8198 3-9-7 50 ........ (t) WilliamCarson 4 57+
(Anthony Carson) *hld up: pushed along and hdwy 2f out: rdn to ld over 1f out: sn hung lft: hdd post* **5/4**[1]
530- **3** 2 1/4 **Piccolo Express**[21] 8063 8-9-6 49 ........ JasonHart 5 50
(Brian Baugh) *trckd ldrs: hung rt: led wl over 1f out: sn hdd: styd on same pce ins fnl f* **5/1**[3]
400- **4** 3/4 **Natalia**[43] 7783 5-9-4 47 ........ (p) AdamKirby 8 46
(Andrew Hollinshead) *hld up: hdwy over 2f out: rdn and edgd lft over 1f out: styd on same pce ins fnl f* **9/2**[2]
004- **5** nk **Compton Silver**[30] 7940 4-8-11 45 ........ (p) ShelleyBirkett(5) 11 43
(Miss Joey Ellis) *chsd ldrs: wnt 2nd 1/2-way tl rdn over 2f out: no ex wl ins fnl f* **9/2**[2]
000- **6** hd **Forzarzi (IRE)**[36] 7864 10-9-2 45 ........ PhillipMakin 1 43
(John David Riches) *hld up: hdwy over 1f out: no ex wl ins fnl f* **25/1**
420- **7** 1 1/4 **Sairaam (IRE)**[18] 8084 8-8-13 45 ........ (p) JoeyHaynes(3) 6 40
(Charles Smith) *chsd ldr to 1/2-way: sn rdn: wknd wl ins fnl f* **28/1**
550- **8** nk **Minty Jones**[8] 8230 5-9-2 45 ........ (be) RobertHavlin 12 39
(Michael Mullineaux) *sn led: rdn and hdd wl over 1f out: wknd ins fnl f* **12/1**
0/0- **9** 21 **Luisa Tetrazzini (IRE)**[15] 8123 8-9-2 45 ........ (p) DavidProbert 7
(Bernard Llewellyn) *s.i.s: rdn 1/2-way: wknd over 2f out* **50/1**
1m 28.79s (-0.01) **Going Correction** -0.075s/f (Stan) **9** Ran SP% **117.9**
Speed ratings (Par 97): **97,96,94,93,92 92,91,90,66**
CSF £63.68 CT £225.49 TOTE £16.30: £4.60, £1.10, £2.30; EX 109.70 Trifecta £727.30.
**Owner** Mrs L Wohlers **Bred** Mark Johnston Racing Ltd **Trained** Pilling, Lancashire
**FOCUS**
A poor finale and weak form.
T/Plt: £111.30 to a £1 stake. Pool: £115,949.88 - 760.32 winning units. T/Qpdt: £9.80 to a £1 stake. Pool: £14,371.30 - 1082.00 winning units. CR

# 8240 LINGFIELD (L-H)
Sunday, December 28

**OFFICIAL GOING: Polytrack: standard**
Wind: Moderate, against Weather: Fine, cold

## 8292 32RED.COM / BRITISH STALLION STUDS EBF MAIDEN STKS 7f 1y(P)
**11:45** (11:46) (Class 5) 2-Y-O **£2,911** (£866; £432; £216) **Stalls** Low

Form RPR
6- **1** **Solar Flair**[18] 8093 2-9-5 0 ........ AdamKirby 3 72
(William Knight) *trckd ldng pair: wnt 2nd over 1f out: drvn to ld last 150yds: styd on* **12/1**
542- **2** 1 **China Club (IRE)**[18] 8091 2-9-5 74 ........ RobertHavlin 12 69
(John Gosden) *led and crossed fr wd draw to inner: rdn over 1f out: hdd and one pce last 150yds* **7/1**
5- **3** 1 1/2 **Silent Thunder (IRE)**[22] 8060 2-9-5 0 ........ DanielTudhope 2 65
(William Haggas) *awkward s: in tch in 7th: rdn over 2f out: no prog tl styd on wl fnl f to take 3rd last strides* **7/4**[1]
0- **4** nk **Arkansas Slim (IRE)**[46] 7741 2-9-5 0 ........ WilliamTwiston-Davies 1 64
(Charles Hills) *trckd ldrs in 6th: pushed along and prog on inner wl over 1f out: tk 3rd briefly nr fin: kpt on* **100/1**
**5** hd **Double Heaven** 2-9-5 0 ........ GeorgeBaker 9 64
(Ed Walker) *t.k.h and rn green: sn in last pair: pushed along 2f out: stdy prog jst over 1f out: styd on in encouraging fashion nr fin* **25/1**
4- **6** hd **Must Have (FR)**[155] 4684 2-9-5 0 ........ SteveDrowne 8 63
(William Jarvis) *chsd ldr: shkn up and lost 2nd over 1f out: fdd ins fnl f* **3/1**[2]
**7** hd **Never Miss** 2-9-0 0 ........ ShaneKelly 4 58
(Saeed bin Suroor) *slowly away: towards rr: shkn up 2f out: sme prog jst over 1f out: kpt on but nvr gng pce to threaten* **6/1**[3]
60- **8** 3/4 **Special Code (IRE)**[20] 8067 2-9-5 0 ........ (t) NickyMackay 7 60
(John Gosden) *trckd ldng quartet: pushed along 2f out: no imp whn shkn up briefly 1f out: kpt on tl lost pl and eased nr fin* **33/1**
0- **9** 1 1/4 **What Asham**[29] 7973 2-9-5 0 ........ SebSanders 11 57
(Ralph Beckett) *dwlt: sn chsd ldng trio: lost pl and fdd over 1f out* **12/1**
45- **10** shd **White Dog (IRE)**[18] 8092 2-9-5 0 ........ RobertTart 6 57
(Eugene Stanford) *t.k.h: hld up in rr: shkn up 2f out: hd at awkward angle and no prog over 1f out* **33/1**
**11** 1 1/2 **Tango Turner (IRE)** 2-9-0 0 ........ HarryPoulton(5) 10 53
(Jamie Poulton) *slowly away: settled in last: rdn and tried to make grnd over 1f out: sn no prog* **100/1**
650- **12** 4 **Convicted (FR)**[69] 7344 2-9-5 0 ........ StevieDonohoe 5 42
(Ian Williams) *a in rr: rdn 3f out: sn btn* **100/1**
1m 26.03s (1.23) **Going Correction** +0.05s/f (Slow) **12** Ran SP% **116.2**
Speed ratings (Par 96): **94,92,91,90,90 90,90,89,87,87 86,81**
CSF £87.92 TOTE £13.30: £3.60, £2.10, £1.10; EX 74.20 Trifecta £286.90.
**Owner** Circuit Racing & The Kimber Family **Bred** Farmers Hill Stud **Trained** Patching, W Sussex
**FOCUS**
A maiden with some interesting lightly raced types, run at a medium pace.

## 8293 32RED CASINO NURSERY H'CAP (BOBIS RACE) 7f 1y(P)
**12:15** (12:15) (Class 2) 2-Y-O **£8,821** (£2,640; £1,320; £660; £329) **Stalls** Low

Form RPR
312- **1** **Chicago Bere (FR)**[2] 8267 2-8-0 70 ........ JimmyQuinn 4 74
(Richard Hannon) *hld up in last: shkn up and prog on outer wl over 1f out: led jst ins fnl f: urged along and styd on wl* **3/1**[3]

111- **2** *1* **Anonymous John (IRE)**[23] 8046 2-9-7 91 JFEgan 2 92
(David Evans) *t.k.h: n.m.r after 2f: trckd ldrs: rdn to take 2nd and chal 1f out: wnr sn wnt by: kpt on* 11/4[2]

414- **3** *½* **Rockaroundtheclock (IRE)**[34] 7902 2-8-1 74 RyanTate(3) 5 74
(Paul Cole) *pressed ldr: shkn up to ld over 2f out: hdd and one pce jst ins fnl f* 8/1

331- **4** *1 ¼* **Classic Seniority**[8] 8240 2-8-5 75 HayleyTurner 1 72
(Richard Hannon) *t.k.h early: trckd ldrs: pushed along in 4th 2f out: reminder jst over 1f out: kpt on same pce* 12/1

611- **5** *2 ¼* **Kaufmann**[9] 8226 2-8-13 83 RobertHavlin 3 74
(John Gosden) *led: rdn and hdd over 2f out: wknd fnl f* 5/4[1]

1m 25.92s (1.12) **Going Correction** +0.05s/f (Slow) **5** Ran SP% **114.9**
Speed ratings (Par 102): **95,93,93,91,89**
CSF £12.12 TOTE £4.80: £1.90, £1.40; EX 11.90 Trifecta £60.10.
**Owner** Middleham Park Racing LXXXI **Bred** S N C Regnier & San Gabriel Inv Inc **Trained** East Everleigh, Wilts

**FOCUS**
Solid form despite the small field and a disappointing run by the favourite.

## 8294 DOWNLOAD THE LADBROKES APP MAIDEN STKS 1m 1y(P)
**12:45** (12:47) (Class 5) 3-Y-O+ **£2,587** (£770; £384; £192) **Stalls** High

Form RPR

22- **1** **Westwood Hoe**[23] 8048 3-9-5 0 RobertHavlin 3 72+
(John Gosden) *mde all: rdn and 2 l clr 2f out: kpt on u.p* 1/1[1]

4- **2** *1 ¾* **Dukes Meadow**[25] 8020 3-9-5 0 SteveDrowne 7 68
(Roger Ingram) *chsd wnr over 6f out: rdn over 2f out: kpt on but nvr able to throw down a chal* 5/1[3]

4- **3** *2 ¼* **Incantare**[23] 8038 4-8-12 0 DeclanBates(3) 4 58
(Jim Allen) *trckd ldng pair after 2f: tried to chal for 2nd on inner over 1f out: one pce after* 50/1

**4** *2 ½* **Clovelly Bay (IRE)** 3-9-5 0 ShaneKelly 5 56+
(Marcus Tregoning) *slowly away: hld up in last trio: pushed along and sme prog wl over 1f out: reminders and styd on same pce fnl f* 10/1

0/6- **5** *1 ¼* **Stage Girl**[25] 8020 3-9-0 52 HayleyTurner 2 48
(Mark Hoad) *t.k.h: hld up in last trio: pushed along and sme prog 2f out: no hdwy 1f out* 50/1

422- **6** *½* **Filosofo (IRE)**[25] 8020 3-8-12 73 TomMarquand(7) 1 52
(Richard Hannon) *t.k.h: trckd wnr tl hit rail over 6f out: lost pl over 4f out: brushed rail twice more and struggling over 2f out* 2/1[2]

**7** *7* **Stardanse** 3-9-0 0 WilliamCarson 6 30
(John Bridger) *v.s.a: t.k.h and prom after 2f: wknd rapidly 2f out* 33/1

/5- **8** *4* **Congaree Warrior**[18] 8094 4-9-6 0 PatCosgrave 8 27
(John Butler) *heavily restrained s t.k.h and hld up in last trio: v wd bnd 2f out and lost grnd: sn eased* 25/1

1m 38.5s (0.30) **Going Correction** +0.05s/f (Slow)
**WFA** 3 from 4yo 1lb **8** Ran SP% **119.8**
Speed ratings (Par 103): **100,98,96,93,92 91,84,80**
CSF £6.99 TOTE £2.10: £1.10, £1.80, £6.40; EX 6.10 Trifecta £128.40.
**Owner** A E Oppenheimer **Bred** Hascombe And Valiant Studs **Trained** Newmarket, Suffolk

**FOCUS**
A decent maiden which should produce winners. The form isn't solid though, with the first two 1-2 throughout.

## 8295 LADBROKES H'CAP 1m 1y(P)
**1:15** (1:16) (Class 2) (0-105,103) 3-Y-O+ **£11,971** (£3,583; £1,791; £896; £446) **Stalls** High

Form RPR

101- **1** **Melvin The Grate (IRE)**[29] 7971 4-8-9 88 DavidProbert 10 101
(Andrew Balding) *hld up in last: gd prog fr 2f out to ld jst ins fnl f: drvn clr: decisively* 9/4[1]

026- **2** *2* **Tigers Tale (IRE)**[17] 8116 5-8-13 95 (v) DannyBrock(3) 6 103
(Roger Teal) *t.k.h: trckd ldrs: rdn and nt qckn over 1f out: styd on to take 2nd ins fnl f: no ch w wnr* 8/1

210- **3** *2 ¼* **Silverheels (IRE)**[59] 7545 5-8-2 84 (b) RyanTate(3) 8 87
(Paul Cole) *hld up in rr: effrt and wdst of all bnd 2f out: rdn and nt qckn wl over 1f out: styd on fnl f to take 3rd last strides* 12/1

006- **4** *nk* **Alfred Hutchinson**[43] 7801 6-9-5 98 DanielTudhope 2 100
(Geoffrey Oldroyd) *hld up in tch: gng wl whn waiting for room 2f out: clsd over 1f out: easily outpcd fnl f* 9/2[3]

002- **5** *¾* **Grey Mirage**[15] 8135 5-9-7 100 (b) AdamKirby 9 100
(Marco Botti) *t.k.h: racd wd early and prog to ld after 1f: drvn more than 2 l clr over 2f out: hdd & wknd jst ins fnl f* 11/4[2]

/00- **6** *2 ½* **Haaf A Sixpence**[29] 7971 5-9-0 93 StevieDonohoe 7 88
(Ralph Beckett) *wl in tch: prog to dispute 2nd 2f out: wknd tamely jst over 1f out* 20/1

0/6- **7** *5* **Rain God (USA)**[10] 8203 4-8-1 87 HectorCrouch(7) 5 70
(Gary Moore) *a towards rr: dropped to last and struggling over 2f out: no ch after* 66/1

500- **8** *shd* **Santefisio**[53] 7663 8-9-0 93 (b) JFEgan 3 76
(Keith Dalgleish) *towards rr: urged along over 3f out: trying to make grnd whn no room over 2f out: wknd* 10/1

000- **9** *nk* **George Guru**[43] 7801 7-9-0 93 (p) RobertHavlin 1 75
(John Bridger) *v awkward to load into stall: led 1f out: chsd ldr: wknd qckly over 1f out* 20/1

1m 35.49s (-2.71) **Going Correction** +0.05s/f (Slow) **9** Ran SP% **114.5**
Speed ratings (Par 109): **115,113,110,110,109 107,102,102,101**
CSF £20.28 CT £176.30 TOTE £3.40: £1.80, £2.60, £3.00; EX 17.50 Trifecta £128.00.
**Owner** Fromthestables.com & I A Balding **Bred** Barronstown Stud **Trained** Kingsclere, Hants

**FOCUS**
They went a sound gallop for this ordinary handicap. Another pb from the winner, with the runner-up running as well as ever to beat the rest.

## 8296 32RED H'CAP 1m 7f 169y(P)
**1:45** (1:47) (Class 2) (0-105,94) 3-Y-O+ **£11,971** (£3,583; £1,791; £896; £446) **Stalls** Low

Form RPR

034- **1** **Uramazin (IRE)**[8] 8243 8-9-10 90 LiamKeniry 6 98
(Philip Hide) *hld up in last: stl only 5th 2f out but gng easily: prog and pushed into the ld 1f out: drvn and kpt on last 150yds* 6/1[2]

111- **2** *½* **Planetoid (IRE)**[11] 8193 6-8-9 75 oh2 (b) WilliamTwiston-Davies 5 82
(Jim Best) *trckd ldrs after 6f: shkn up 2f out: rdn to chal 1f out: kpt on fnl f but hld by wnr* 6/1[2]

522- **3** *¾* **Cousin Khee**[27] 7995 7-9-7 87 DanielTudhope 2 93
(Hughie Morrison) *trckd ldr 6f and again over 3f out: drvn to chal and upsides 1f out: nt qckn* 2/1[1]

102- **4** *3 ¼* **Ted Spread**[15] 8146 7-9-12 92 (t) AdamKirby 4 94
(Suzy Smith) *trckd ldr after 6f: led 5f out: drvn over 2f out: hdd & wknd 1f out* 2/1[1]

120- **5** *2 ½* **Jelly Fish**[18] 8096 3-8-9 83 (t) PatCosgrave 1 82
(Brett Johnson) *in tch: urged along over 3f out: effrt u.p over 2f out: wknd over 1f out* 20/1

/05- **6** *14* **Chiberta King**[39] 7837 8-10-0 94 (p) DavidProbert 3 76
(Andrew Balding) *led at mod pce: hdd and rdn 5f out: dropped to last 3f out: t.o* 8/1[3]

3m 23.77s (-1.93) **Going Correction** +0.05s/f (Slow)
**WFA** 3 from 6yo+ 8lb **6** Ran SP% **111.1**
Speed ratings (Par 109): **106,105,105,103,102 95**
CSF £39.20 TOTE £8.40: £4.30, £2.40; EX 42.20.
**Owner** S P C Woods **Bred** Davin Investments Ltd **Trained** Findon, W Sussex

**FOCUS**
Some decent stayers contested this, but the pace was nothing special and that probably helped the winner, who normally races at 1m2f-1m4f. The third has been rated close to form.

## 8297 UNIBET H'CAP 6f 1y(P)
**2:15** (2:20) (Class 4) (0-80,80) 3-Y-O+ **£4,568** (£1,367; £683; £342; £170) **Stalls** Low

Form RPR

010- **1** **Soaring Spirits (IRE)**[20] 8072 4-9-3 76 (p) PatCosgrave 3 85
(Dean Ivory) *trckd ldng pair: rdn to chal 1f out: drvn ahd last 75yds: hld on* 8/1

124- **2** *shd* **Salvatore Fury (IRE)**[12] 8171 4-9-5 78 (p) JFEgan 2 86
(Keith Dalgleish) *trckd ldrs: rdn and clsd to ld 1f out: hdd 75yds out: styd on: jst hld* 4/1[2]

525- **3** *nk* **Diamond Lady**[39] 7843 3-9-4 80 RyanTate(3) 11 87+
(William Stone) *hld up towards rr: clsd over 1f out and waiting for room: gap appeared and drvn to chal ins fnl f: styd on: jst hld* 5/1[3]

444- **4** *1 ¼* **Temple Road (IRE)**[11] 8186 6-8-10 69 ow1 (tp) LiamKeniry 7 72
(Milton Bradley) *stdd s: hld up in last quartet: prog 2f out: waiting for room over 1f out: tried to chal fnl f: one pce last 100yds* 12/1

034- **5** *nk* **Head Space (IRE)**[6] 8252 6-9-6 79 (v) GeorgeBaker 6 81
(Michael Attwater) *w.w in midfield: clsd over 1f out: rdn and kpt on same pce fnl f* 7/2[1]

203- **6** *½* **Harrogate Fair**[12] 8171 4-8-13 72 (p) ChrisCatlin 4 72
(Michael Squance) *v reluctant to enter stalls: chsd ldrs: cl up over 1f out: sn rdn and nt qckn: one pce after* 12/1

631- **7** *¾* **Desert Strike**[23] 8040 8-9-5 78 (p) HayleyTurner 10 76
(Conor Dore) *pressed ldr: led wl over 1f out to 1f out: fdd last 125yds* 14/1

035- **8** *½* **Clear Praise (USA)**[20] 8072 7-8-11 77 TomasHarrigan(7) 1 73
(Simon Dow) *stdd s: hld up in last quartet: pushed along and sme prog over 1f out: nvr on terms* 8/1

300- **9** *1 ½* **Rocket Rob (IRE)**[27] 7989 8-8-8 67 JimmyQuinn 12 59
(Willie Musson) *stdd s: hld up in last: pushed along on inner over 1f out: nt clr run jst ins fnl f: pushed along again nr fin: nvr involved* 25/1

560- **10** *nse* **Flighty Clarets (IRE)**[12] 8182 4-7-13 63 SammyJoBell(5) 5 54
(Richard Fahey) *nvr beyond midfield: urged along and no imp on ldrs over 1f out: fdd* 25/1

150- **11** *1 ¾* **Ask The Guru**[68] 7357 4-9-0 73 (v) RobertHavlin 8 59
(Michael Attwater) *led: rdn and hdd wl over 1f out: sn wknd* 33/1

000- **12** *1 ¼* **Vincentti (IRE)**[117] 6006 4-9-2 75 DavidProbert 9 57
(Ronald Harris) *stdd s: hld up in last quartet: wdst of all bnd 2f out: shkn up and no prog: nvr involved* 8/1

1m 11.7s (-0.20) **Going Correction** +0.05s/f (Slow) **12** Ran SP% **124.9**
Speed ratings (Par 105): **103,102,102,100,100 99,98,98,96,96 93,92**
CSF £41.46 CT £184.58 TOTE £11.00: £3.70, £2.40, £1.80; EX 58.30 Trifecta £390.80.
**Owner** Mrs Doreen Carter **Bred** Kevin & Meta Cullen **Trained** Radlett, Herts

**FOCUS**
A middle-rank but competitive handicap, run at a good tempo, so the form should make sense in similar events. The winner has been rated pretty much back to his best.

## 8298 BET NOW WITH THE LADBROKES APP H'CAP (DIV I) 7f 1y(P)
**2:50** (2:50) (Class 6) (0-65,65) 3-Y-O+ **£1,940** (£577; £288; £144) **Stalls** Low

Form RPR

142- **1** **Pearl Ransom (IRE)**[11] 8190 4-9-4 62 (v) JFEgan 8 70
(Alan Bailey) *trckd ldr: rdn over 2f out: led over 1f out: drvn and hld on wl* 3/1[1]

364- **2** *¾* **West Leake (IRE)**[215] 2648 8-8-12 56 LiamKeniry 2 62
(Paul Burgoyne) *awkward s: hld up in rr: prog gng easily fr 3f out: pushed along over 1f out: wnt 2nd ins fnl f: rdn and nt qckn: hld after* 33/1

632- **3** *½* **Childesplay**[11] 8185 3-9-4 62 MartinLane 9 67
(Heather Main) *trckd ldrs: rdn wl over 1f out: styd on fnl f to take 3rd last stride* 10/1

614- **4** *shd* **Divine Rule (IRE)**[27] 7987 6-8-13 57 (p) LiamJones 4 62
(Laura Mongan) *hld up in midfield: rdn and prog 2f out: wnt 2nd briefly 1f out: nt qckn and kpt on same pce after* 10/1

220- **5** *1 ¼* **Sea Soldier (IRE)**[18] 8103 6-8-10 57 ThomasBrown(3) 5 58
(Andrew Balding) *in rr: rdn bef 1/2-way and struggling: kpt on fr over 1f out: nrst fin* 6/1[3]

000- **6** *1* **Bertie Blu Boy**[15] 8143 6-9-1 59 (b) RobertHavlin 1 58
(Lisa Williamson) *led: drvn 2 l clr over 2f out: hdd and fdd over 1f out* 5/1[2]

500- **7** *2* **Hellbender (IRE)**[40] 7830 8-9-6 64 DavidProbert 11 58
(Shaun Harris) *towards rr: rdn 3f out: no real prog* 16/1

365- **8** *1* **Shifting Star (IRE)**[39] 7842 9-9-6 64 (vt) WilliamCarson 3 55
(John Bridger) *trckd ldrs on inner: rdn over 2f out: no prog over 1f out: fdd* 12/1

505- **9** *hd* **The Happy Hammer (IRE)**[45] 7759 8-9-3 61 (b) RobertTart 6 52
(Eugene Stanford) *dwlt: a in rr: nt gng wl after 2f* 16/1

433- **10** *5* **Ghost Train (IRE)**[11] 8195 5-9-7 65 (p) HayleyTurner 10 43
(Tim McCarthy) *prom tl nudged along and dropped away qckly fr 3f out* 7/1

1m 24.36s (-0.44) **Going Correction** +0.05s/f (Slow) **10** Ran SP% **119.8**
Speed ratings (Par 101): **104,103,102,102,101 99,97,96,96,90**
CSF £115.13 CT £904.38 TOTE £3.80: £1.60, £5.30, £2.50; EX 101.50 Trifecta £1177.00.
**Owner** T & Z Racing Club **Bred** J Erhardt **Trained** Newmarket, Suffolk

**FOCUS**
A strong pace favoured the hold-up runners in this routine handicap, so the always-prominent winner did particularly well. The runner-up has been rated to his spring CD form.

## 8299 BET NOW WITH THE LADBROKES APP H'CAP (DIV II) 7f 1y(P)
**3:20** (3:20) (Class 6) (0-65,64) 3-Y-O+ **£1,940** (£577; £288; £144) **Stalls** Low

Form RPR

005- **1** **Clement (IRE)**[25] 8017 4-8-13 63 CiaranMckee(7) 5 73
(John O'Shea) *hld up in midfield: gng wl 3f out: prog 2f out to chse ldr over 1f out: drvn and styd on wl fnl f to ld last 75yds* 10/1

644- **2** 1 1/4 **Al's Memory (IRE)**[25] 8017 5-9-7 64 ........ JFEgan 2 70
(David Evans) *fast away: led: rdn over 2f out: stl 2 l up 1f out: worn down last 75yds* **7/4**[1]

403- **3** shd **Bookmaker**[11] 8186 4-9-0 57 ........ WilliamCarson 10 63
(John Bridger) *stdd s: hld up in detached last: prog towards inner 2f out: drvn and r.o fnl f: nrly snatched 2nd but no ch to chal* **12/1**

621- **4** 1/2 **Indus Valley (IRE)**[11] 8195 7-9-4 61 ........ ShaneKelly 7 66
(Des Donovan) *hld up in rr: promising prog on outer over 1f out to cl on ldrs fnl f: effrt flattened out last 100yds* **7/1**[3]

604- **5** 3 **Jonnie Skull (IRE)**[33] 7908 8-8-6 56 ........(vt) PatrickO'Donnell(7) 3 53
(Phil McEntee) *t.k.h early: chsd ldr after 2f: rdn over 2f out: lost 2nd over 1f out: fdd* **25/1**

046- **6** 3/4 **Choice Of Destiny**[18] 8103 3-9-2 62 ........ DannyBrock(3) 6 57
(Philip McBride) *trckd ldr 2f: styd handy: rdn over 2f out: nt qckn wl over 1f out: fdd* **7/1**[3]

603- **7** 1 1/4 **Hong Kong Joe**[18] 8094 4-9-7 64 ........(e) CharlesBishop 4 56
(Lydia Richards) *hld up towards rr: rdn over 2f out and sn struggling: no real prog after* **6/1**[2]

600- **8** hd **Kakapuka**[34] 7905 7-9-5 62 ........ GeorgeBaker 9 53
(Anabel K Murphy) *in tch on outer: rdn over 2f out: one pce and no real danger whn hmpd jst ins fnl f* **12/1**

350- **9** 1 **Teen Ager (FR)**[227] 2282 10-9-1 58 ........ JimmyQuinn 8 47
(Paul Burgoyne) *hld up towards rr: pushed along and yet to be asked serious question whn nt clr run 1f out and snatched up: nt rcvr* **25/1**

001- **10** 2 1/4 **Oak Bluffs (IRE)**[43] 7813 3-8-9 57 ........ SammyJoBell(5) 1 40
(Richard Fahey) *prom: rdn and sed to lose pl on inner whn hmpd over 1f out: no ch after* **8/1**

1m 24.62s (-0.18) **Going Correction** +0.05s/f (Slow) **10** Ran SP% **118.9**
Speed ratings (Par 101): **103,101,101,100,97 96,95,94,93,91**
CSF £28.41 CT £218.98 TOTE £15.20: £3.40, £1.30, £2.50; EX 37.20 Trifecta £500.00.
**Owner** K W Bell **Bred** P Kelly **Trained** Elton, Gloucs

**FOCUS**
The runner-up set a good pace in this modest handicap. The third has been rated to his AW best despite the race not panning out ideally for him from a wide draw.
T/Plt: £74.10 to a £1 stake. £74,478.81 - 733.62 winning tickets. T/Qpdt: £24.60 to a £1 stake. £8,804.09 - 264.56 winning tickets. JN

## 8276 DEAUVILLE (R-H)
Sunday, December 28

**OFFICIAL GOING: Polytrack: standard**

### 8300a PRIX MISS SATAMIXA (FAST TRACK QUALIFIER) (LISTED RACE) (3YO+ FILLIES & MARES) (POLYTRACK) 7f 110y
1:45 (12:00) 3-Y-O+ £21,666 (£8,666; £6,500; £4,333; £2,166)

RPR

**1** **Fresles (IRE)**[43] 7802 3-8-11 0 ........ AlexisBadel 16 101
(Mme Pia Brandt, France) **17/2**

**2** nse **Caointiorn (FR)**[49] 3-8-11 0 ........ TheoBachelot 6 101
(S Wattel, France) **116/10**

**3** 1 1/4 **Plaisanciere (FR)**[58] 7619 3-8-11 0 ........ EddyHardouin 8 98
(F Rohaut, France) **43/10**[1]

**4** 3/4 **Lamar (IRE)**[59] 7553 3-8-11 0 ........ DavyBonilla 2 96
(James Tate) *prom: ev ch whn short of room and shuffled bk into st: rdn over 1f out: rallied and kpt on wl fnl f but nvr bk on terms w ldrs* **108/10**

**5** nk **Sosia (GER)**[25] 8022 3-8-11 0 ........ MaximeGuyon 5 95
(C Laffon-Parias, France) **105/10**

**6** hd **Hasturianita (IRE)**[44] 3-8-11 0 ........ JulienAuge 9 95
(Mme Pia Brandt, France) **39/1**

**7** 1/2 **Slippers Best**[91] 4-8-11 0 ........ FabienLefebvre 13 93
(J E Hammond, France) **96/10**

**8** hd **Stereo Love (FR)**[39] 7836 3-8-11 0 ........ RonanThomas 4 93
(Clive Cox) *midfield on inner: rdn and effrt 2f out: kpt on same pce and hld fnl f: lost multiple pls towards fin* **49/1**

**9** 1 1/4 **Lady Wood (FR)**[26] 8006 4-8-11 0 ........ TonyPiccone 10 90
(N Clement, France) **34/1**

**10** hd **Stosur (IRE)**[30] 7952 3-8-11 0 ........(b) AntoineHamelin 11 89
(Gay Kelleway) *midfield: rdn to hold position bef st: nt clr run and swtchd rt over 1f out: kpt on same pce fnl f and n.d* **36/1**

**11** 3/4 **Si Luna (GER)**[15] 8150 5-8-11 0 ........ AntoineWerle 3 87
(W Mongil, Germany) **65/1**

**12** hd **Akemi (IRE)**[31] 4-8-11 0 ........ ValentinSeguy 14 87
(X Thomas-Demeaulte, France) **53/1**

**13** 1 1/4 **Bluefire**[15] 8150 4-8-11 0 ........ FabriceVeron 7 84
(H-A Pantall, France) *rrd s: hld up in last: pushed along 3f out: rdn and swtchd rt over 1f out: keeping on but wl hld whn sltly short of room towards fin: eased* **53/10**[3]

**14** 1 **Paola Lisa (FR)**[38] 7857 3-8-11 0 ........ ThierryThulliez 12 81
(N Clement, France) **48/10**[2]

**15** nse **Guinnevre (IRE)**[15] 8150 4-8-11 0 ........ AurelienLemaitre 1 81
(G Botti, France) **42/1**

**16** 8 **Winshine (FR)**[38] 7857 3-8-11 0 ........ DelphineSantiago 15 61
(S Smrczek, Germany) **152/10**

1m 26.85s (86.85) **16** Ran SP% **119.0**
WIN (incl. 1 euro stake): 9.50. PLACES: 3.00, 3.60, 2.30. DF: 62.20. SF: 176.40.
**Owner** Gerard Augustin-Normand **Bred** E Puerari, F Mc Nulty, Oceanic B'Stock **Trained** France

## 8277 SOUTHWELL (L-H)
Monday, December 29

**8301 Meeting Abandoned** - frozen track

## 8292 LINGFIELD (L-H)
Tuesday, December 30

**OFFICIAL GOING: Polytrack: standard**
Wind: Light, across Weather: Cloudy, cold

### 8308 32RED NURSERY H'CAP (BOBIS RACE) 6f 1y(P)
12:20 (12:20) (Class 4) (0-85,83) 2-Y-O £3,752 (£1,116; £557; £278) Stalls Low

Form RPR

165- **1** **Lackaday**[19] 8113 2-9-1 77 ........ CharlesBishop 1 79
(William Jarvis) *trckd ldrs gng wl: wnt 2nd wl over 1f out: drvn and styd on fnl f to ld last 75yds* **12/1**

314- **2** 1/2 **Classic Seniority**[2] 8293 2-8-6 75 ........ TomMarquand(7) 7 75
(Richard Hannon) *pressed ldng pair on outer: rdn 2f out: styd on wl last 100yds to take 2nd fnl strides* **6/1**

341- **3** nk **Jimmy's Hall**[3] 8287 2-8-9 71 6ex ........(b) StevieDonohoe 2 70
(J S Moore) *mde most: sent for home over 2f out: drvn over 1f out: hdd and fdd last 75yds* **10/1**

113- **4** hd **Anastazia**[25] 8046 2-9-0 76 ........ JFEgan 6 75
(Paul D'Arcy) *hld up in last: effrt on outer 2f out: rdn over 1f out: styd on ins fnl f: nvr rchd ldrs* **11/4**[2]

041- **5** 2 1/4 **Mo Henry**[17] 8140 2-9-2 78 ........ GeorgeChaloner 3 70
(Richard Whitaker) *chsd ldrs: rdn 2f out: nt qckn on inner over 1f out: one pce after* **9/4**[1]

406- **6** 3 3/4 **Commander Patten (IRE)**[19] 8113 2-8-12 79 ........[1] TimClark(5) 4 60
(Alan Bailey) *w ldr: pushed along 1/2-way: lost 2nd wl over 1f out: hanging and wknd* **14/1**

520- **7** 16 **Arabian Bride (IRE)**[114] 6165 2-9-7 83 ........ AdamKirby 5 16
(Robert Cowell) *pushed along after 1f: sn struggling: t.o* **5/1**[3]

1m 11.58s (-0.32) **Going Correction** 0.0s/f (Stan) **7** Ran SP% **111.8**
Speed ratings (Par 98): **102,101,100,100,97 92,71**
CSF £76.82 TOTE £12.80: £4.60, £2.40; EX 108.60 Trifecta £957.50.
**Owner** Ms E L Banks **Bred** Andrew Parrish **Trained** Newmarket, Suffolk

**FOCUS**
A fair nursery and a good pace thanks to a disputed lead.

### 8309 DOWNLOAD THE LADBROKES APP H'CAP 1m 1y(P)
12:50 (12:50) (Class 6) (0-65,65) 3-Y-O £1,940 (£577; £288; £144) Stalls High

Form RPR

033- **1** **Bobby Benton (IRE)**[8] 8248 3-9-7 65 ........ CharlesBishop 6 74
(Luke Dace) *dwlt: t.k.h and hld up in rr: prog on outer 3f out: rdn to ld wl over 1f out: hrd pressed fnl f: hld on wl* **6/4**[1]

402- **2** nk **Lynngale**[11] 8232 3-9-2 63 ........ ShaneGray(3) 5 71
(Kristin Stubbs) *chsd ldrs: rdn 3f out: struggling in 6th over 2f out: styd towards inner and prog to chse wnr jst over 1f out: str chal fnl f: jst hld* **7/1**

353- **3** 2 1/2 **Sixties Love**[22] 8068 3-9-7 65 ........ SteveDrowne 2 68
(Simon Dow) *t.k.h early: hld up: effrt over 2f out but swtchd v wd bnd sn after: kpt on fr over 1f out to take 3rd ins fnl f: no ch* **7/2**[2]

326- **4** 1 1/4 **Darting**[13] 8196 3-9-7 65 ........ DavidProbert 4 65
(Andrew Balding) *chsd ldr: pushed along 3f out: lost 2nd 2f out: steadily fdd* **5/1**[3]

536- **5** 1 1/4 **Tohaveandtohold**[10] 8246 3-8-7 51 oh1 ........(b[1]) LiamJones 3 48
(William Haggas) *led at str pce: rdn and hdd wl over 1f out: wknd fnl f* **10/1**

220- **6** 3 1/2 **Turnbury**[36] 7907 3-9-5 63 ........(tp) JackMitchell 7 52
(Robert Mills) *chsd ldng pair: rdn whn n.m.r 2f out: sn lost pl and btn* **8/1**

065- **7** nk **Expensive Taste (IRE)**[20] 8097 3-9-7 65 ........(vt[1]) AdamKirby 1 53
(Phil McEntee) *dwlt: a in last pair: struggling fr 1/2-way: no prog* **20/1**

1m 37.28s (-0.92) **Going Correction** 0.0s/f (Stan) **7** Ran SP% **116.4**
Speed ratings (Par 98): **104,103,101,99,98 95,94**
CSF £13.34 TOTE £2.40: £1.30, £4.10; EX 11.60 Trifecta £49.40.
**Owner** Mark Benton **Bred** Old Carhue & Graeng Bloodstock **Trained** Okehurst Lane, W Sussex

**FOCUS**
A moderate handicap, but they went a strong pace. The winner has been rated up slightly on his recent form, with the runner-up being rated as running a small pb.

### 8310 CORAL MOBILE "JUST THREE CLICKS TO BET" MAIDEN STKS 1m 2f (P)
1:20 (1:20) (Class 5) 3-Y-O £2,587 (£770; £384; £192) Stalls Low

Form RPR

/42- **1** **Salmon Sushi**[24] 8064 3-9-5 74 ........ GeorgeBaker 2 81
(David Lanigan) *stdd s: hld up in last: prog on outer 3f out: wd bnd 2f out: hd at awkward angle whn rdn over 1f out: drvn and styd on wl fnl f to ld last 50yds* **5/1**[3]

**2** nk **Shorana (IRE)**[65] 7478 3-9-0 0 ........ JamieSpencer 1 76
(C F Swan, Ire) *trckd ldng pair: rdn to chal over 1f out: led ins fnl f: hdd and one pce u.p last 50yds* **5/6**[1]

33- **3** 1 1/4 **Ocean Boulevard**[46] 7772 3-9-0 0 ........ AdamKirby 8 73
(Luca Cumani) *trckd ldr: shkn up to chal 3f out: drvn to ld wl over 1f out: hdd and one pce ins fnl f* **4/1**[2]

/55- **4** 3 3/4 **Synaesthesia (FR)**[27] 8020 3-9-0 0 ........ TedDurcan 5 66
(Lady Cecil) *hld up in last trio: pushed along over 2f out: swtchd towards inner over 1f out: no imp after* **33/1**

0- **5** 1 1/2 **Millionaires Row (USA)**[249] 1701 3-9-0 0 ........ NickyMackay 4 63
(John Gosden) *hld up in last trio: pushed along and last 3f out: pushed along again 2f out: no real prog* **6/1**

**6** 1 3/4 **Procurement**[129] 3-9-0 0 ........ HayleyTurner 6 59
(Simon Dow) *led: pressed 3f out: shkn up and hdd wl over 1f out: fdd* **33/1**

0/0- **7** 2 **Kalifi (USA)**[27] 8020 3-9-0 0 ........ PatCosgrave 3 55
(Stuart Kittow) *trckd ldng pair: pushed along 3f out: no prog on inner over 1f out: fdd* **100/1**

2m 8.86s (2.26) **Going Correction** 0.0s/f (Stan) **7** Ran SP% **112.4**
Speed ratings (Par 102): **90,89,88,85,84 83,81**
CSF £9.30 TOTE £5.50: £2.10, £1.20; EX 12.30 Trifecta £28.50.
**Owner** Ben & Sir Martyn Arbib **Bred** Arbib Bloodstock Partnership **Trained** Upper Lambourn, Berks

**FOCUS**
An interesting maiden, though the pace didn't look that strong. The second and third have been rated close to their pre-race marks.

## 8311 LADBROKES MOBILE H'CAP 7f 1y(P)
**1:50** (1:53) (Class 6) (0-55,55) 3-Y-O+ **£1,940** (£577; £288; £144) **Stalls** Low

Form RPR

364- **1** **Admirable Art (IRE)**[17] 8139 4-9-5 **53**..........................(p) AdamKirby 10 63
(Tony Carroll) *dwlt: hld up in last pair: gd prog over 1f out: burst through fnl f to ld last 120yds: sn clr* **6/1**[3]

000- **2** 1 ½ **Aye Aye Skipper (IRE)**[13] 8186 4-9-0 **55**.................... PaulBooth(7) 12 61
(Dean Ivory) *trckd ldrs: short of room briefly over 1f out: clsd jst ins fnl f: rdr in a tangle but kpt on to take 2nd last 75yds* **16/1**

050- **3** nk **Soul Instinct**[34] 7928 3-8-11 **52**.............................. TomasHarrigan(7) 6 57
(Simon Dow) *hld up in midfield: prog on outer over 1f out: styd on fnl f to take 3rd last strides* **33/1**

450- **4** ¾ **Skidby Mill (IRE)**[29] 7986 4-9-4 **52**................................ LiamJones 8 55
(Laura Mongan) *trckd ldng pair: rdn to ld jst over 1f out: hdd and fdd last 120yds* **12/1**

451- **5** nk **Dream And Hope**[61] 7548 3-9-3 **54**............................ DannyBrock(3) 7 57
(Philip McBride) *dwlt: hld up in last pair: tried to make grnd on inner fr 2f out: limited prog tl styd on ins fnl f: unable to threaten* **11/4**[1]

323- **6** ¾ **Ambella (IRE)**[8] 8259 4-9-7 **55**..........................(v) StevieDonohoe 2 56+
(Ian Williams) *hld up in last quartet: urged along and no prog over 1f out: drvn and styd on fnl f: nrst fin* **5/1**[2]

454- **7** ½ **Catalinas Diamond (IRE)**[27] 8014 6-9-7 **55**..................(t) SebSanders 5 54
(Pat Murphy) *blindfold off v late but sed on terms: hld up in last quartet: rdn and wdst of all bnd 2f out: prog over 1f out: effrt flattened out last 100yds* **8/1**

506- **8** 1 **Spider Bay**[27] 8008 5-8-12 **46** oh1................................(e) HayleyTurner 1 43
(Lydia Richards) *settled in midfield: pushed along and cl enough jst over 1f out: fdd last 150yds* **100/1**

233- **9** ¾ **Rocky's Pride (IRE)**[38] 7884 8-9-5 **53**....................... GeorgeChaloner 4 48
(Richard Whitaker) *trckd ldrs: pushed along over 2f out: trying to chal on inner whn nowhere to go 1f out: no ch after* **6/1**[3]

504- **10** hd **Dancing Sal (IRE)**[125] 5832 3-9-7 **55**.........................(b) GeorgeBaker 13 49
(Gary Moore) *prom tl wknd over 1f out* **20/1**

200- **11** 1 ½ **Cyflymder (IRE)**[17] 8137 8-9-5 **53**............................................ JFEgan 9 43
(David C Griffiths) *rdn to ld: hdd & wknd jst over 1f out* **10/1**

540- **12** ¾ **One Last Dream**[214] 2722 5-9-2 **55**............................(b) RyanWhile(5) 11 43
(Ron Hodges) *pressed ldr to over 1f out: wknd qckly* **33/1**

060- **13** hd **Jackpot**[29] 7987 4-8-12 **46** oh1.......................................... PatCosgrave 3 34
(Brendan Powell) *a towards rr: rdn on outer and no prog 2f out* **25/1**

1m 24.51s (-0.29) **Going Correction** 0.0s/f (Stan) **13** Ran SP% **121.2**
Speed ratings (Par 101): **101,99,98,98,97 96,96,95,94,94 92,91,91**
CSF £93.13 CT £2932.12 TOTE £6.40: £2.40, £5.80, £9.00; EX 136.80 Trifecta £3907.80 Part won..
**Owner** D Morgan **Bred** Longview Stud & Bloodstock Ltd **Trained** Cropthorne, Worcs

**FOCUS**
A moderate handicap and something of a typical Lingfield finish, with horses appearing late from all over the place. Plenty of these are on potentially good marks, but the form is not solid.

## 8312 LADBROKES H'CAP 1m 1y(P)
**2:20** (2:20) (Class 3) (0-95,96) 3-Y-O **£7,246** (£2,168; £1,084; £542; £270) **Stalls** High

Form RPR

**1** **Tournament**[75] 3-8-13 **87**.................................................. JamieSpencer 2 93+
(Seamus Durack) *hld up in 4th: hanging whn asked for effrt over 1f out: cajoled along hands and heels and r.o fnl f to ld post* **4/1**[2]

216- **2** shd **Beach Bar (IRE)**[123] 5882 3-9-1 **89**..................................... AdamKirby 5 94+
(William Knight) *sn led: rdn and pressed 2f out and edgd sltly rt: drvn and kpt on fr over 1f out: hdd post* **7/4**[1]

406- **3** ½ **Rebellious Guest**[4] 8266 5-9-7 **94**................................ GeorgeBaker 3 99
(George Margarson) *trckd ldr after 3f: rdn to chal and hung sltly rt bnd 2f out: nt qckn fnl f: lost 2nd nr fin* **7/4**[1]

231- **4** ½ **Brocklebank (IRE)**[4] 8266 5-9-2 **96** 6ex................. TomasHarrigan(7) 6 100
(Simon Dow) *hld up in last: shkn up to cl on ldrs over 1f out: nt qckn ins fnl f* **6/1**[3]

04- **5** 1 ¾ **Sensible Way (USA)**[13] 8188 3-8-6 **80** oh2....................... JimmyQuinn 1 79
(Richard Hannon) *chsd ldr 3f: urged along fr 1/2-way: styd in tch tl fdd fnl f* **16/1**

1m 38.42s (0.22) **Going Correction** 0.0s/f (Stan)
**WFA** 3 from 5yo+ 1lb **5** Ran SP% **112.9**
Speed ratings (Par 107): **98,97,97,96,95**
CSF £11.79 TOTE £3.90: £2.20, £1.30; EX 9.10 Trifecta £20.60.
**Owner** Stephen Tucker **Bred** Juddmonte Farms Ltd **Trained** Upper Lambourn, Berkshire

**FOCUS**
A decent handicap, but they went no pace early. The form is a bit muddling.

## 8313 CORAL.CO.UK BEST ODDS GUARANTEED ON RACING H'CAP 1m 4f (P)
**2:50** (2:50) (Class 5) (0-70,68) 3-Y-O+ **£2,587** (£770; £384; £192) **Stalls** Low

Form RPR

143- **1** **Zambeasy**[72] 7309 3-9-5 **68**.................................................. GeorgeBaker 9 79
(Philip Hide) *t.k.h: prog to ld after 2f: mde rest: sent for home 2f out: drvn and wl in command fnl f: readily* **9/4**[1]

**2** 2 ¼ **Pirate Cove (IRE)**[66] 7466 4-9-6 **64**........................................ JFEgan 3 71
(Mark Johnston) *trckd ldrs: rdn over 2f out: tk 2nd over 1f out: styd on but no imp on wnr* **5/1**[3]

655- **3** ¾ **Chauvelin**[26] 8029 3-9-3 **66**.............................. WilliamTwiston-Davies 7 72+
(Roger Charlton) *hld up in midfield: shkn up and effrt whn short of room over 2f out: wd bnd sn after: hanging over 1f out: styd on fnl f to take 3rd nr fin* **4/1**[2]

005- **4** 1 **Snow King (USA)**[25] 8037 4-9-2 **60**.............................. SteveDrowne 2 64
(Ted Powell) *hld up towards rr: rdn over 2f out: kpt on same pce fr over 1f out: n.d* **20/1**

346- **5** nse **Perfect Rhythm**[12] 8202 3-8-11 **63**.................................. RyanTate(3) 6 67
(Patrick Chamings) *cl up: rdn to chse wnr over 2f out to over 1f out: one pce after* **12/1**

3- **6** 1 **Deinonychus**[20] 8098 3-9-3 **66**.......................................... AdamKirby 5 69
(William Knight) *t.k.h: hld up in rr: rdn and prog to chse ldrs over 2f out: wknd jst over 1f out* **7/1**

323- **7** ¾ **Zinnobar**[25] 8037 4-9-1 **62**.......................................(p) DannyBrock(3) 8 63
(Jonathan Portman) *led 2f: chsd wnr to over 2f out: styd cl up on inner tl wknd qckly fnl f* **6/1**

004- **8** 9 **Incendo**[13] 8190 8-9-3 **61**.........................................(v) HayleyTurner 4 48
(Conor Dore) *stdd s: t.k.h: hld up in last: brief effrt 3f out: wknd over 2f out: sn bhd* **20/1**

000- **9** 166 **The Blue Dog (IRE)**[12] 8202 7-9-6 **64**............................ WilliamCarson 1
(Phil McEntee) *in tch: wknd rapidly over 3f out: sn t.o and virtually p.u* **33/1**

2m 32.68s (-0.32) **Going Correction** 0.0s/f (Stan)
**WFA** 3 from 4yo+ 5lb **9** Ran SP% **114.4**
Speed ratings (Par 103): **101,99,99,98,98 97,97,91,**
CSF £13.01 CT £41.71 TOTE £2.90: £1.30, £2.20, £1.60; EX 17.30 Trifecta £91.60.
**Owner** Heart Of The South Racing **Bred** Frank Brady **Trained** Findon, W Sussex

**FOCUS**
An ordinary handicap and eventually a fair pace thanks to the winner. The runner-up has been rated to the best of her Irish form on her debut for Mark Johnston, with the fourth to his CD latest.

## 8314 CORAL.CO.UK H'CAP (DIV I) 1m 2f (P)
**3:20** (3:22) (Class 6) (0-55,55) 3-Y-O+ **£1,940** (£577; £288; £144) **Stalls** Low

Form RPR

612- **1** **Moulin Rouge (DEN)**[4] 8265 3-8-11 **48**........................ StevieDonohoe 7 57
(Ian Williams) *hld up in 5th: rdn wl over 2f out: prog and wdst of all over 1f out: drvn to ld last 150yds: hld on wl* **7/4**[1]

030- **2** nk **Top Set (IRE)**[34] 7924 4-9-2 **50**..................................(p) HayleyTurner 4 58
(Simon Dow) *stdd s: hld up in last: urged along 3f out: rdn and prog on inner wl over 1f out: drvn to chal ins fnl f: styd on but a jst hld* **4/1**[2]

006- **3** shd **Rosie Prospects**[20] 8097 3-8-9 **46** oh1..........................(b) JimmyQuinn 10 54
(Roger Ingram) *hld up in 7th: shkn up and gd prog over 1f out: chal ins fnl f: nt qckn last 50yds* **66/1**

460- **4** 4 ½ **Candesta (USA)**[22] 8074 4-9-2 **55**..........................(b) ShelleyBirkett(5) 12 54
(Julia Feilden) *trckd ldr: led wl over 2f out and sent for home: 3 l clr over 1f out: hdd & wknd qckly last 150yds* **25/1**

600- **5** ¾ **Third Strike**[21] 8084 3-9-1 **52**.......................... WilliamTwiston-Davies 11 49
(Gary Moore) *chsd ldng trio: rdn over 2f out: wknd over 1f out* **20/1**

/00- **6** ½ **Fen Flyer**[42] 7823 5-8-12 **46** oh1.................................................. JFEgan 6 42
(John Berry) *hld up in 6th: rdn 3f out: no imp on ldrs over 1f out: no ch after* **10/1**

600- **7** 1 **Nifty Kier**[35] 7909 5-9-0 **48**................................................ NickyMackay 2 42
(Phil McEntee) *chsd ldng pair: wnt 2nd briefly over 1f out: wknd qckly fnl f* **33/1**

0/6- **8** 2 ½ **Young Jackie**[35] 7909 6-9-5 **53**............................................ PaoloSirigu 5 42
(George Margarson) *hld up in last pair: rdn over 3f out: no prog and struggling 2f out* **10/1**

005- **9** 1 **Malicho**[22] 8074 5-9-7 **55**......................................................(t) PatCosgrave 8 42
(Dean Ivory) *led at str pce: hdd wl over 2f out: wknd rapidly over 1f out* **6/1**[3]

2/0- **10** 14 **Angelena Ballerina (IRE)**[35] 7908 7-9-5 **53**...................(v) AdamKirby 1 12
(Andy Turnell) *a towards rr: wknd over 3f out: t.o* **16/1**

2m 5.99s (-0.61) **Going Correction** 0.0s/f (Stan)
**WFA** 3 from 4yo+ 3lb **10** Ran SP% **107.8**
Speed ratings (Par 101): **102,101,101,98,97 97,96,94,93,82**
CSF £6.70 CT £230.75 TOTE £2.30: £1.20, £2.20, £8.90; EX 8.20 Trifecta £519.90.
**Owner** Eric Brook & Inge Knutsson **Bred** Stutteri Hjortebo **Trained** Portway, Worcs
■ Rule 4 of 10p in the pound applies to all bets; Withdrawn: Youm Jamil

**FOCUS**
A moderate handicap reduced by one when Youm Jamil was withdrawn after bursting out of his stall. There are grounds for rating the race higher with the second and third well treated.

## 8315 CORAL.CO.UK H'CAP (DIV II) 1m 2f (P)
**3:50** (3:50) (Class 6) (0-55,55) 3-Y-O+ **£1,940** (£577; £288; £144) **Stalls** Low

Form RPR

431- **1** **Sabre Rock**[45] 7805 4-9-0 **53**..................................(t) ShelleyBirkett(5) 5 66+
(Julia Feilden) *prom in chsng gp: wnt 2nd 1/2-way: clsd to ld jst over 2f out: rdn clr over 1f out: kpt on* **6/4**[1]

030- **2** 2 ¾ **Catching Zeds**[8] 8258 7-9-2 **53**.....................................(p) ShaneGray(3) 7 59
(Kevin Frost) *hld up in rr: pushed along and prog on inner 2f out: rdn and styd on to take 2nd last 75yds: no ch to threaten wnr* **20/1**

042- **3** ¾ **Rock Charm**[31] 7976 3-9-0 **51**................................................ PatCosgrave 6 56
(Stuart Williams) *hld up in midfield: rdn to chse ldrs over 2f out: drvn into 2nd briefly fnl f: one pce after* **9/4**[2]

465- **4** ½ **Rezwaan**[12] 8198 7-9-2 **50**....................................................(v) ShaneKelly 8 54
(Murty McGrath) *hld up in midfield: trckd ldrs over 2f out: sn rdn: chsd wnr briefly over 1f out: one pce* **8/1**[3]

026- **5** 2 ½ **Nouvelle Ere**[34] 7924 3-8-7 **47**.......................................... JoeyHaynes(3) 4 46
(Tony Carroll) *chsd clr ldr to 1/2-way: rdn over 3f out: styd chsng ldrs: fdd over 1f out* **10/1**

440- **6** ½ **Royal Mizar (SPA)**[31] 7976 4-8-13 **47**............ WilliamTwiston-Davies 3 45
(Ralph J Smith) *hld up in midfield: rdn and no imp on ldrs over 2f out: one pce after* **25/1**

100- **7** hd **Lexington Blue**[20] 8103 4-9-5 **53**...................................... SteveDrowne 9 50
(Seamus Mullins) *hld up in rr: rdn wl over 2f out: no prog and wl btn over 1f out: plugged on* **16/1**

425- **8** 4 ½ **Litmus (USA)**[14] 8175 5-9-7 **55**....................................(b) HayleyTurner 10 43
(Simon Dow) *dwlt: hld up in last: pushed along and wl off the pce over 2f out: no ch after* **12/1**

500- **9** 6 **Chandrayaan**[245] 1836 7-8-12 **46** oh1...............................(v) LiamKeniry 2 22
(John E Long) *led and sn clr at str pce: hdd & wknd rapidly jst over 2f out* **66/1**

605- **10** 8 **Permitted**[251] 1654 3-9-1 **52**........................................... StevieDonohoe 1 12
(Lee Carter) *dwlt: hld up in rr: pushed along over 3f out: sn wknd and wl bhd* **33/1**

245- **11** 27 **Southern Cross**[15] 8050 3-9-4 **55**...................................... AdamKirby 11
(Andy Turnell) *hld up in last pair: wknd over 4f out: t.o* **16/1**

2m 5.56s (-1.04) **Going Correction** 0.0s/f (Stan)
**WFA** 3 from 4yo+ 3lb **11** Ran SP% **123.5**
Speed ratings (Par 101): **104,101,101,100,98 98,98,94,89,83 61**
CSF £41.56 CT £73.52 TOTE £3.20: £1.40, £3.60, £1.50; EX 34.80 Trifecta £103.00.
**Owner** Miss J Feilden **Bred** J H Mayne **Trained** Exning, Suffolk

**FOCUS**
They went a decent pace in this with Chandrayaan soon bolting off into a clear lead. The winning time was 0.43sec quicker than the first division. The runner-up has been rated as matching her penultimate Wolverhampton run.

T/Plt: £754.10 to a £1 stake. Pool: £107,682.23 - 104.23 winning units. T/Qpdt: £52.00 to a £1 stake. Pool: £13,618.69 - 193.70 winning units. JN



The Form Book, Raceform Ltd, Newbury, RG14 5SJ

# 8308 LINGFIELD (L-H)

Wednesday, December 31

**OFFICIAL GOING: Polytrack: standard**

Wind: light, half behind Weather: overcast, dry

## 8316 BET NOW WITH THE LADBROKES APP APPRENTICE (S) STKS 1m 1y(P)

12:40 (12:40) (Class 6) 3-Y-O+ **£1,940** (£577; £288; £144) **Stalls** High

Form RPR

000- **1** **Prime Exhibit**[16] 8168 9-9-7 63 (t) NedCurtis 6 68
(Daniel Mark Loughnane) *hld up in tch: rdn and effrt to ld 1f out: led ins fnl f: r.o wl: rdn out* **7/1**[3]

040- **2** 3/4 **It's Only Business**[14] 8190 4-9-1 55 (v[1]) AdamMcLean 2 60
(Bill Turner) *t.k.h: chsd ldrs: rdn and ev ch over 1f out: r.o but a hld fnl 100yds* **9/2**[2]

100- **3** nk **Elusive Ellen (IRE)**[9] 8248 4-8-13 65 (t) RobHornby(3) 4 61
(Brendan Powell) *in tch in midfield: effrt over 1f out: kpt on wl u.p fnl 100yds* **7/1**[3]

430- **4** 1 **Investissement**[14] 8194 8-9-7 75 (p) LukeRowe 3 63
(Lee Carter) *dwlt: sn pushed up to ld: shkn up over 1f out: hdd ins fnl f: styng on same pce whn short of room ins fnl f* **10/11**[1]

600- **5** 8 **Bennelong**[9] 8250 8-9-7 62 (b) CharlotteJenner 1 45
(Lee Carter) *t.k.h: w ldr tl hung rt and lost pl bnd 2f out: wknd 1f out* **10/1**

350- **6** 2 **Sutton Sid**[42] 7846 4-9-2 56 (v) TomMarquand(5) 5 40
(Paddy Butler) *v.s.a: rdn along in rr: clsd 1/2-way: lost tch over 2f out* **33/1**

100/ **7** 3 1/2 **Mister Green (FR)**[548] 3906 8-8-12 63 ow2 (bt) JackBudge(5) 7 28
(David Flood) *hld up in tch: btn over 2f out: wknd over 1f out* **25/1**

1m 38.64s (0.44) **Going Correction** +0.075s/f (Slow) **7** Ran SP% **111.4**
Speed ratings (Par 101): **100,99,98,97,89 87,84**
CSF £36.15 TOTE £8.40: £4.40, £2.70; EX 47.80 Trifecta £269.10.There was no bid for the winner. It's Only Business was claimed by Mr Carl Chapman for £6,000.
**Owner** R M Brilley **Bred** Matthews Breeding And Racing Ltd **Trained** Baldwin's Gate, Staffs

**FOCUS**
Not a strong race, and a bit of a bunched finish. Not an easy race to assess, and it's been rated cautiously.

## 8317 32RED NURSERY H'CAP 7f 1y(P)

1:10 (1:13) (Class 5) (0-75,75) 2-Y-O **£2,587** (£770; £384; £192) **Stalls** Low

Form RPR

430- **1** **Star Of The Stage**[27] 8026 2-8-13 **67** ShaneKelly 8 73
(Richard Fahey) *t.k.h: mde all: set stdy gallop: rdn and qcknd 2f out: in command fnl f: rdn out* **6/1**[3]

005- **2** 1 3/4 **Glorious Dancer**[42] 7840 2-8-10 **64** AntonioFresu 14 65
(Ed Walker) *dwlt: in tch in midfield: effrt to chse wnr 2f out: kpt on u.p ins fnl f: nvr a threat to wnr* **8/1**

645- **3** hd **Souk Al Tahab (IRE)**[12] 8227 2-9-3 **71** GeorgeBaker 2 72
(Ed Dunlop) *in tch in midfield: effrt u.p over 1f out: kpt on wl fnl f: no threat to wnr* **5/1**[2]

623- **4** 1 3/4 **Barchan (USA)**[28] 8009 2-9-5 **73** (t) AdamKirby 1 69
(Charlie Appleby) *hld up towards rr: sme hdwy but nt clr run 2f out: swtchd lft over 1f out: styd on wl u.p fnl f: nvr trbld ldrs* **6/4**[1]

004- **5** 2 **Minnie (IRE)**[29] 8000 2-8-11 **65** StevieDonohoe 3 56
(Johnny Farrelly) *chsd ldrs: effrt on inner over 1f out: no imp fnl f* **20/1**

033- **6** 1 1/2 **Percella**[21] 8092 2-8-7 **68** (t) CharlieBennett(7) 5 55
(Hughie Morrison) *chsd ldrs: rdn and unable qck 2f out: wknd fnl f* **14/1**

006- **7** hd **Fleetwood Poppy**[14] 8191 2-8-5 **59** JimmyQuinn 6 45
(Michael Attwater) *in tch in midfield: r.o same pce u.p fr over 1f out* **100/1**

321- **8** 1/2 **Red Perdita (IRE)**[29] 7999 2-9-1 **69** PatCosgrave 4 54
(George Baker) *in tch in midfield: drvn and no hdwy over 1f out* **8/1**

000- **9** nk **Grand Proposal**[23] 8069 2-8-6 **60** WilliamCarson 13 44
(Jim Boyle) *stdd and dropped in bhd s: rdn over 2f out: sme hdwy fnl f: nvr trbld ldrs* **66/1**

405- **10** 7 **Toast Of Newbury (IRE)**[23] 8069 2-8-5 **62** ShaneGray(3) 11 27
(Jamie Osborne) *a in rr: rdn and outpcd over 2f out: n.d after* **12/1**

646- **11** 3/4 **Beauchamp Ace**[119] 6039 2-9-1 **69** FergusSweeney 9 32
(Paul Fitzsimons) *chsd ldr tl over 2f out: sn wknd* **33/1**

000- **12** 1 1/4 **Almoqatel (IRE)**[23] 8069 2-7-11 **58** PaddyPilley(7) 7 18
(Tony Newcombe) *a in rr: bhd fnl 2f* **66/1**

1m 25.21s (0.41) **Going Correction** +0.075s/f (Slow) **12** Ran SP% **119.2**
Speed ratings (Par 96): **100,98,97,95,93 91,91,90,90,82 81,80**
CSF £51.74 CT £261.56 TOTE £9.30: £2.70, £2.60, £2.20; EX 65.90 Trifecta £377.40.
**Owner** Cheveley Park Stud **Bred** Cheveley Park Stud Ltd **Trained** Musley Bank, N Yorks

**FOCUS**
They went steady here and the winner had the run of things out in front.

## 8318 32RED.COM MEDIAN AUCTION MAIDEN STKS 7f 1y(P)

1:40 (1:43) (Class 6) 2-Y-O **£1,940** (£577; £288; £144) **Stalls** Low

Form RPR

**1** **Evo Campo (IRE)** 2-9-0 0 LiamKeniry 2 70
(Mark Usher) *broke fast: stdd bk to chse ldng pair: effrt to chal on inner 1f out: led wl ins fnl f: r.o wl* **66/1**

32- **2** 3/4 **Plaisir (IRE)**[13] 8201 2-9-0 0 AdamKirby 8 68
(Marco Botti) *chsd ldr: rdn and sltly outpcd over 1f out: rallied ins fnl f: styd on to go 2nd nr fin* **5/4**[1]

25- **3** hd **Free One (IRE)**[49] 7739 2-9-5 0 GeorgeBaker 3 72
(Jeremy Noseda) *sn led: rdn over 1f out: hdd and one pce wl ins fnl f: lost 2nd nr fin* **7/4**[2]

02- **4** 1 1/2 **Lucky Leyf**[21] 8092 2-9-0 0 ShaneKelly 5 63
(Gary Moore) *chsd ldrs: rdn over 1f out: drvn and styd on same pce fnl f* **8/1**

0- **5** 1 1/4 **Vale Of Iron (IRE)**[100] 6603 2-9-5 0 SteveDrowne 10 65
(John Best) *racd in midfield: modest 7th and sme hdwy over 1f out: styd on wl ins fnl f: nvr trbld ldrs* **66/1**

03- **6** 1 **Pyroclastic (IRE)**[20] 8112 2-9-5 0 PatCosgrave 1 62
(Jim Boyle) *in tch in midfield: rdn and outpcd 2f out: n.d but kpt on steadily ins fnl f* **50/1**

**7** 5 **Limerick Lord (IRE)** 2-9-5 0 JamieSpencer 7 49
(Stuart Williams) *stdd s: hld up in rr: outpcd over 2f out: n.d after* **5/1**[3]

00- **8** 1/2 **Strait Of Magellan (IRE)**[29] 8000 2-9-5 0 HayleyTurner 11 47
(Michael Bell) *a towards rr: rdn 5f out: wknd over 2f out* **66/1**

0- **9** 3 1/2 **Gold Leaf**[14] 8191 2-8-9 0 ShelleyBirkett(5) 6 33
(John E Long) *racd in midfield: 6th and no hdwy over 1f out: wknd fnl f* **100/1**

**10** 1 1/2 **Benjamin Disraeli (IRE)** 2-9-5 0 MartinDwyer 9 34
(John Best) *s.i.s: rn green in rr thrght* **14/1**

**11** 23 **Caramba (IRE)** 2-9-0 0 StevieDonohoe 12
(Brendan Powell) *s.i.s: sn bustled along and rcvrd to r in midfield: lost pl 3f out: wl bhd fnl f* **66/1**

1m 26.34s (1.54) **Going Correction** +0.075s/f (Slow) **11** Ran SP% **124.2**
Speed ratings (Par 94): **94,93,92,91,89 88,82,82,78,76 50**
CSF £159.95 TOTE £58.30: £11.40, £1.10, £1.40; EX 364.70 Trifecta £1416.30.
**Owner** Saxon House Racing **Bred** Richard O'Hara **Trained** Upper Lambourn, Berks

**FOCUS**
Few got into this and there was a shock result.

## 8319 DAILY ENHANCED "MAGIC MULTIPLES" AT UNIBET H'CAP 6f 1y(P)

2:10 (2:12) (Class 6) (0-65,65) 3-Y-O+ **£1,940** (£577; £288; £144) **Stalls** Low

Form RPR

200- **1** **Reginald Claude**[28] 8014 6-8-6 **57** CharlotteJenner(7) 3 65
(Mark Usher) *hld up in tch in midfield: effrt 1f out: r.o wl fnl 100yds to ld last stride* **12/1**

026- **2** shd **Gabrial's Wawa**[274] 1215 4-9-2 **60** AdamKirby 7 67
(Michael Squance) *hld up in tch: hdwy on outer 1f out: rdn to ld ins fnl f: r.o: hdd last stride* **11/4**[1]

506- **3** 1 3/4 **Lujeanie**[23] 8081 8-9-5 **63** (v) ShaneKelly 5 64
(Peter Crate) *t.k.h: chsd ldr: rdn over 1f out: drvn and ev ch briefly ins fnl f: sltly hmpd and outpcd fnl 75yds* **5/1**

632- **4** shd **Compton Prince**[14] 8195 5-9-2 **60** (v) LiamKeniry 8 61
(Milton Bradley) *t.k.h: hld up in tch: rdn and effrt to chal ins fnl f: fnd little and outpcd fnl 75yds* **5/1**

540- **5** 1 3/4 **Billy Red**[11] 8245 10-9-4 **65** (bt) DannyBrock(3) 2 60
(J R Jenkins) *led: rdn over 1f out: drvn and hdd ins fnl f: wknd towards fin* **10/1**

410- **6** 1 3/4 **Random**[37] 7906 3-9-7 **65** StevieDonohoe 4 55
(Daniel Mark Loughnane) *chsd ldrs: rdn and unable qck over 1f out: wknd ins fnl f* **4/1**[3]

606- **7** nk **Purford Green**[27] 8024 5-8-7 **51** oh6 (v) JimmyQuinn 6 40
(Michael Attwater) *in tch: no hdwy u.p over 1f out: wknd ins fnl f* **66/1**

452- **8** 1 **Tableforten**[12] 8219 3-8-10 **54** (v) LiamJones 1 39
(J S Moore) *v.s.a: clsd and in tch 1/2-way: nt clr run over 2f out: keeping on same pce and btn whn nt clr run wl ins fnl f* **7/2**[2]

1m 12.2s (0.30) **Going Correction** +0.075s/f (Slow) **8** Ran SP% **120.5**
Speed ratings (Par 101): **101,100,98,98,96 93,93,92**
CSF £47.69 CT £195.61 TOTE £11.80: £3.20, £1.40, £1.80; EX 56.80 Trifecta £329.40.
**Owner** High Five Racing **Bred** Whitsbury Manor Stud **Trained** Upper Lambourn, Berks
■ Stewards' Enquiry : Stevie Donohoe one-day ban; careless riding (14th Jan)

**FOCUS**
A tight little race in which the pace collapsed inside the last. Modest form rated around the winner.

## 8320 LADBROKES H'CAP 7f 1y(P)

2:40 (2:40) (Class 4) (0-85,85) 3-Y-O+ **£4,568** (£1,367; £683; £342; £170) **Stalls** Low

Form RPR

612- **1** **Shyron**[9] 8257 3-9-7 **85** MartinLane 3 95
(George Margarson) *chsd ldrs: effrt on inner over 1f out: rdn to ld ins fnl f: r.o: rdn out* **5/4**[1]

463- **2** 3/4 **Evening Attire**[21] 8100 3-9-6 **84** GeorgeBaker 5 92
(William Stone) *led: rdn and fnd ex over 1f out: hdd and one pce ins fnl f* **5/1**[3]

526- **3** 2 1/4 **Zman Awal (IRE)**[23] 8071 3-8-13 **77** HayleyTurner 9 79
(James Fanshawe) *chsd ldrs: 3rd and r.o same pce fnl 150yds* **9/2**[2]

233- **4** 2 1/2 **Footstepsintherain (IRE)**[9] 8251 4-8-12 **76** FergusSweeney 7 72
(David Dennis) *chsd ldrs: upsides ldrs 3f out tl outpcd and btn over 1f out: wknd fnl f* **9/2**[2]

000- **5** 3/4 **Ready (IRE)**[13] 8209 4-8-13 **77** (p) LiamJones 8 71
(Garry Moss) *in tch in midfield: rdn and unable qck over 1f out: wl hld and one pce fnl f* **25/1**

005- **6** 1 1/2 **Glastonberry**[189] 3581 6-8-13 **77** ChrisCatlin 1 67
(Geoffrey Deacon) *hld up in last trio: rdn over 1f out: no prog: nvr trbld ldrs* **25/1**

200- **7** 1/2 **Secret Millionaire (IRE)**[9] 8252 7-8-13 **77** CharlesBishop 6 66
(Luke Dace) *stdd s: t.k.h: hld up in rr: rdn over 1f out: no hdwy: wl hld fnl f* **33/1**

000- **8** 2 3/4 **Trader Jack**[9] 8251 5-9-2 **80** AdamKirby 4 61
(David Flood) *t.k.h: hld up in last trio: rdn over 1f out: sn btn: wknd fnl f* **20/1**

1m 24.16s (-0.64) **Going Correction** +0.075s/f (Slow) **8** Ran SP% **112.9**
Speed ratings (Par 105): **106,105,102,99,98 97,96,93**
CSF £7.18 CT £20.64 TOTE £2.20: £1.10, £1.50, £1.80; EX 8.50 Trifecta £21.60.
**Owner** F Butler **Bred** F Butler **Trained** Newmarket, Suffolk

**FOCUS**
This looks pretty sound form for the grade. Sound form, with the winner rated similar to his Wolverhampton win last time out.

## 8321 DOWNLOAD THE LADBROKES APP H'CAP 1m 1y(P)

3:10 (3:10) (Class 5) (0-75,72) 3-Y-O+ **£1,678** (£1,678; £384; £192) **Stalls** High

Form RPR

013- **1** **Franco's Secret**[13] 8204 3-9-6 **72** (p) CharlesBishop 9 78+
(Peter Hedger) *stdd s: hld up in last trio: effrt over 1f out: str burst wl ins fnl f to join ldr on post* **5/1**[3]

011- **1** dht **Bosstime (IRE)**[15] 8175 4-9-2 **67** (b) AdamKirby 6 74
(John Holt) *t.k.h: chsd ldrs: chal over 1f out: led 1f out: drvn ins fnl f: jnd on post* **4/1**[2]

100- **3** 1/2 **Malaysian Boleh**[13] 8204 4-9-7 **72** WilliamTwiston-Davies 7 78
(Simon Dow) *hld up in tch in rr: swtchd rt and effrt over 1f out: r.o strly u.p ins fnl f: wnt 3rd nr fin* **12/1**

411- **4** shd **What A Dandy (IRE)**[15] 8169 3-9-1 **67** (p) PatCosgrave 1 72
(Jim Boyle) *chsd ldrs: rdn 2f out: drvn and ev ch 1f out: no ex wl ins fnl f* **7/1**

403- **5** 1 1/2 **Stormbound (IRE)**[57] 7633 5-9-5 **70** MartinLane 2 73
(Paul Cole) *led tl over 6f out: chsd ldr tl over 1f out: stl pressing ldrs u.p 1f out: wknd ins fnl f* **9/4**[1]

260- **6** nse **Gannicus**[9] 8248 3-9-3 **69** (p) LiamKeniry 5 70
(Brendan Powell) *dwlt: rcvrd to ld over 6f out: rdn over 1f out: hdd ins fnl f: outpcd and btn fnl 75yds* **7/1**

356- **7** 1 **Nimble Kimble**[14] 8185 3-9-3 **72** RyanTate(3) 8 71
(James Eustace) *hld up in tch in rr: effrt over 1f out: kpt on: nvr able to chal* **8/1**

510- **8** *1 ¼* **Fearless Lad (IRE)**[209] 2930 4-9-1 **66**.......................... MartinDwyer 4 63
(John Best) *in tch in midfield: rdn and unable qck 2f out: wknd ins fnl f* **25/1**

600- **9** *3 ½* **Penny's Boy**[13] 8204 3-9-2 **68**..............................(t) SteveDrowne 3 56
(Simon Hodgson) *in tch in midfield: rdn 2f out: sn outpcd: wknd fnl f* **50/1**

1m 38.89s (0.69) **Going Correction** +0.075s/f (Slow)
**WFA** 3 from 4yo+ 1lb **9** Ran SP% **117.0**
Speed ratings (Par 103): **99,99,98,98,96 96,95,94,91**WIN: Franco's Secret 3.30, Bosstime 2.10; PL: Malaysian Boleh 3.60 , Franco's Secret 2.10, Bosstime 1.80; EX: FS&BT: 14.10, BT&FS: 10.90; CSF: FS&BT: 12.86, BT&FS: 12.37; TC: FS&BT&MB: 114.75, FS&BT&MB: 110.94; TF: FS&BT&MB: 151.70, FS&BT&MB: 104.00, £27, £OwnerP C F Racing Ltd Bred Trifecta £J J Whelan Trained Eastergate, W Sussex.
**Owner** Planters (leicester) Limited **Bred** J K Dewberry **Trained** Peckleton, Leics

**FOCUS**

A bunched finish and the judge couldn't split the first two in the photo. A small pb from Franco's Secret, with the third and fourth close to their marks.

## 8322 DAILY PRICE BOOSTS AT UNIBET H'CAP 5f 6y(P)

**3:40** (3:40) (Class 6) (0-65,65) 3-Y-0+ **£1,940** (£577; £288; £144) **Stalls** High

Form RPR

034- **1** **Pharoh Jake**[11] 8245 6-9-5 **63**.......................... WilliamCarson 6 72+
(John Bridger) *in tch: clsd 2f out: nt clr run over 1f out: gap opened and squeezed between horses ins fnl f: str run to ld last stride* **3/1**[2]

450- **2** *shd* **Artemis (IRE)**[12] 8230 3-8-9 **53**.............................. LiamJones 1 60
(Conrad Allen) *in tch: hdwy to chse ldrs 2f out: drvn to ld ins fnl f: r.o: hdd last stride* **10/1**

423- **3** *nk* **Bush Warrior (IRE)**[235] 2158 3-9-7 **65**..........................(p) JimmyQuinn 3 71
(Robert Eddery) *taken down early: dwlt: in tch in rr: effrt on inner over 1f out: r.o wl u.p fnl 100yds: nt quite rch ldrs* **5/2**[1]

216- **4** *½* **Give Us A Belle (IRE)**[30] 7997 5-9-4 **62**......................(vt) AdamKirby 2 66
(Christine Dunnett) *led: rdn over 1f out: hdd ins fnl f: no ex towards fin* **9/2**[3]

60U- **5** *¾* **Profile Star (IRE)**[9] 8255 5-9-7 **65**.............................. SteveDrowne 7 66
(Violet M Jordan) *chsd ldrs: outpcd over 1f out: swtchd lft and rallied ins fnl f: nt clr run and no imp fnl 50yds* **16/1**

043- **6** *1 ¼* **Qatar Princess (IRE)**[12] 8229 3-8-6 **53**......................(v) DannyBrock(3) 5 50
(J R Jenkins) *racd keenly: pressed ldr: rdn and ev ch over 1f out: wknd ins fnl f* **6/1**

115- **7** *3* **Imjin River (IRE)**[335] 383 7-8-10 **57**..............................(t) RyanTate(3) 4 43
(William Stone) *in tch: effrt over 1f out: wknd ins fnl f* **10/1**

625- **8** *1 ¼* **Excellent Aim**[23] 8081 7-9-2 **60**.............................. PaoloSirigu 8 41
(George Margarson) *in tch in midfieldbut stuck wd: rdn over 1f out: wknd fnl f* **8/1**

59.24s (0.44) **Going Correction** +0.075s/f (Slow) **8** Ran SP% **121.2**
Speed ratings (Par 101): **99,98,98,97,96 94,89,87**
CSF £34.98 CT £87.84 TOTE £4.90: £1.50, £2.70, £1.50; EX 34.30 Trifecta £289.60.
**Owner** The Hair & Haberdasher Partnership **Bred** J J Bridger **Trained** Liphook, Hants

**FOCUS**

There was a contested lead here and the race was set up for a closer. The winner has been rated to his best and the runner-up to her best mark since Jan/Feb.
T/Jkpt: Not won. T/Plt: £94.70 to a £1 stake. Pool: £160,225.84 - 1,234.65 winning tickets
T/Qpdt: £6.50 to a £1 stake. Pool: £25,480.78 - 2,888.00 winning tickets SP

# INDEX TO FLAT RACING

Horses are shown in alphabetical order; the trainer's name follows the name of the horse. The figures to the right are current master ratings for all-weather and turf; the all-weather rating is preceded by the letter 'a'. Underneath the horse's name is its age, colour and sex in abbreviated format e.g. 6 b g indicates the horse is six-years-old, bay in colour, and a gelding. The descriptive details are followed by the race numbers of the races in which it has taken part in chronological order; a superscript figure indicates its finishing position in that race (brackets indicate it was the winner of the race).


**Aabir (IRE)** *Marco Botti* a75
2 b c Invincible Spirit(IRE) Phillippa (IRE) (Galileo (IRE))
(7891) ◆

**Aaranyow (IRE)** *Clifford Lines* a68 54
6 ch g Compton Place Cutpurse Moll (Green Desert (USA))
3630[5] 4306[7] 4546[3] 4833[8] 5423[7] 5801[4] 6561[6] 7117[5] (7285) 7670[6] 7900[6] (8024) 8245[6]

**Aazif (IRE)** *Ian Williams* a65 72
5 ch g Nayef(USA) Ayun (USA) (Swain (IRE))
2142[6] 3249[7] 3424[7]

**Abaco (USA)** *Claude McGaughey III* 106
6 ch m Giant's Causeway(USA) Cat Cay (USA) (Pleasant Colony (USA))
7607a[7]

**Abaq** *Richard Hannon* a78 74
2 b f Oasis Dream Indian Ink (IRE) (Indian Ridge)
3558[2] (4075)

**Abatis (USA)** *Charles Hills* 46
3 bb f Aptitude(USA) Rouwaki (USA) (Miswaki (USA))
3229[7]

**Abbakova (IRE)** *Paul Cole* 89
3 ch f Dandy Man(IRE) Over Rating (Desert King (IRE))
3245[10]

**Abba Zabba (IRE)** *David Evans* 39
2 b g Bushranger(IRE) Tipperary Boutique (IRE) (Danehill Dancer (IRE))
2666[5] 2944[12] 3847[9]

**Abbey Angel (IRE)** *Richard Fahey* 89
2 b f Arcano(IRE) Sanna Bay (IRE) (Refuse To Bend (IRE))
2697[5] 3267[4] 4626[2] (5335) 6151[2] (6691)

**Abbey Village (IRE)** *Richard Fahey* 86
3 ch g Aqlaam Balladonia (Primo Dominie)
2236[3] (2733) 3378[19]

**Abbotsfield (IRE)** *Ben Haslam* a32 71
4 ch f Sakhee's Secret May Day Queen (IRE) (Danetime (IRE))
76[7] 4791[3] (5642) 6863[9]

**Abby Cadabby (IRE)** *A Oliver* a41 84
3 b f Jeremy(USA) Yaqoot (Pivotal)
3491a[9]

**Abdel (FR)** *J-M Osorio* a100 106
6 b h Dyhim Diamond(IRE) Leonor De Guzman (SPA) (Glauco (SPA))
202a[4] 394a[7]

**Abdication** *Gary Moore* a59 7
3 b g Royal Applause Bowled Out (GER) (Dansili)
468[9] 664[4] 1208[9] 1808[11] 2694[13]

**Abendwind (GER)** *Waldemar Hickst* 103
3 b c Wiesenpfad(FR) Adela (GER) (Tannenkonig (IRE))
3028a[5] 4247a[10] 7727a[8]

**Abigails Angel** *Lee Carter* a66 55
7 br m Olden Times Make Ready (Beveled (USA))
467[6] 755[10] 1016[3] 1236[3] 1836[2] 2465[6] 2723[4] 2923[8] 3554[2] 4046[3] 4738[4] 5978[2] 6396[4] 6715[3] 7347[2] 7844[8] 8030[6]

**Abilene** *F-H Graffard* a90 98
4 ch f Samum(GER) Altamira (Peintre Celebre (USA))
5369a[4] 6162a[4] 7070a[9]

**Ability N Delivery** *Michael J Browne* a65 67
9 gr g Kyllachy Tryptonic (FR) (Baryshnikov (AUS))
788a[5]

**Abi Scarlet (IRE)** *Scott Dixon* a77 78
5 b m Baltic King Petarga (Petong)
20[4] (297) (479) 552[3] 909[5] 1497[2] (2398) 2905[5] (3793) 7159[4] 7506[7] 7767[6] 8045[10] 8182[6] (8223)

**Able Dash** *Michael Blake* a75 53
4 ch g Dutch Art Evasive Quality (FR) (Highest Honor (FR))
(590) (1100) 2300[7]

**Able Friend (AUS)** *J Moore* 127
5 ch g Shamardal(USA) Ponte Piccolo (NZ) (Volksraad)
2004a[2] (7898a) (8153a)

**Able Mate** *Clive Cox* 58
2 ch c Shamardal(USA) Anse Victorin (USA) (Mt. Livermore (USA))
2964[6] 4270[11] 5201[9]

**Able Spirit** *Brian Meehan* a65 69
2 b g Invincible Spirit(IRE) Sierra (Dr Fong (USA))
4800[4] 5655[14] 6058[5] 6629[10] 6867[6] 7454[4]

**Aboody** *Sir Mark Prescott Bt* a42
3 b g Dutch Art Rabshih (IRE) (Green Desert (USA))
355[9] 614[5] 741[8]

**About Turn** *Charlie Appleby*
3 ch c Pivotal Doctor's Glory (USA) (Elmaamul (USA))
4404[7]

**Above Standard (IRE)** *Michael Easterby* a86 96
6 ch g Shamardal(USA) Prealpina (IRE) (Indian Ridge)
3239[17] 3714[12]

**Above The Law (IRE)** *A Oliver* a74 72
5 b g Lawman(FR) Pearl Of The Sea (IRE) (Fusaichi Pegasus (USA))
128a[9] 4556a[4] 6078a[6]

**Above The Rest (IRE)** *Timothy Jarvis* a84 91
3 b c Excellent Art Aspasias Tizzy (USA) (Tiznow (USA))
2733[5] 3804[2] ◆ 5039[3] (5400) 6149[5] (6552) 6895[6]

**Above The Stars** *Conor Dore* a71 70
6 b m Piccolo Swindling (Bahamian Bounty)
114[5] 258[10]

**Abraham Monro** *Ruth Carr* 59
4 gr g Kyllachy Pendulum (Pursuit Of Love)
2955[9] 3530[3] 4069[8] 4571[10] 5287[6] 5683[3] 6120[7] 7056[8]

**Abraxa (IRE)** *C Ferland* a65 98
3 gr f Verglas(IRE) Dancing Flower (IRE) (Compton Place)
599a[2] 7482a[3]

**Abscent Friends** *Bill Turner* a71 85
2 b g Showcasing Lucky Dip (Tirol)
(1363) 1512[2] 1866[3] 2258[2] 2845[6]

**Abseil (USA)** *Sir Michael Stoute* a84 102
4 b g First Defence(USA) Intercontinental (Danehill (USA))
1216[3] ◆ (1612) 2113[2] (2959) 3356[8] 4200[13] 4648[19] 6532[4] 7276[23]

**Absent Amy (IRE)** *Amy Weaver* a80 79
5 b m Redback Twitcher's Delight (Polar Falcon (USA))
32[5] 265[5]

**Absolute (IRE)** *Marco Botti* 37
3 b g Danehill Dancer(IRE) Beyond Belief (IRE) (Sadler's Wells (USA))
4407[11] 5388[8]

**Absolute Bearing (IRE)** *Tim Etherington* a44 54
5 b g Majestic Missile(IRE) Garnock Academy (USA) (Royal Academy (USA))
575[6] 676[5] 799[5] (2658) 3000[9] 3530[12] 4358[5] 5244[6]

**Absolute Champion (USA)** *Jamie Osborne* a74
2 b g Henrythenavigator(USA) Alegendinmyownmind (Cape Cross (IRE))
6660[6] 7542[2] (7742)

**Absolutely So (IRE)** *Andrew Balding* a98 113
4 b g Acclamation Week End (Selkirk (USA))
294[2] ◆ 534[3] ◆ 715[7] 1172[2] (1943) ◆ 3452[15] 4200[2] (5653) 6522[8] 7272[8]

**Absolute Sway** *Charlie Appleby* a46 82
3 b c New Approach(IRE) Parisian Elegance (Zilzal (USA))
3434[4] 4325[9]

**Abstraction (IRE)** *R K Watson* a105 106
4 b c Majestic Missile(IRE) Bronze Queen (IRE) (Invincible Spirit (IRE))
393a[4] 680a[8] 5154a[2] 7433a[2]

**Abushamah (IRE)** *Kevin Prendergast* 84
3 b g Nayef(USA) Adaala (USA) (Sahm (USA))
3491a[4]

**Abu Sidra (FR)** *G E Mikhalides* a103 107
5 gr h Shirocco(GER) Mary Doun (FR) (Smadoun (FR))
769a[8] 898a[13] 3030a[5] 3746a[5] 7437a[10]

**Abyaat (IRE)** *Richard Hannon* a62 3
3 b g Halling(USA) Why Dubai (USA) (Kris S (USA))
642[7] 1797[8] 2081[9] 2491[10]

**Abys (FR)** *Mme Pia Brandt* 101
4 gr f Montjeu(IRE) Dibenoise (FR) (Kendor (FR))
5369a[5] 6956a[6] 7558a[9]

**Acantos (FR)** *J Heloury* 65
2 b f Alexandros Famatina (SWI) (Zieten (USA))
1094a[3]

**Acapulco Bay** *Dai Burchell* a44 56
10 b g Pursuit Of Love Lapu-Lapu (Prince Sabo)
2834[3] 3853[6] 5277[4] 5343[3]

**Acaster Malbis (FR)** *Richard Hannon* 95
2 ch c Arcano(IRE) Acatama (USA) (Efisio)
5149[2] 5655[11] 6256[7] 6520[2]

**Accepted (IRE)** *T Stack* 104
2 ch g Approve(IRE) Birthday Present (Cadeaux Genereux)
5692[5] 6286[3]

**Accession (IRE)** *Charlie Fellowes* a88 95
5 b g Acclamation Pivotal's Princess (IRE) (Pivotal)
1275[4] 1796[4] (2684) 4783[4] (5433) 6320[6] (6755) 7715[14]

**Accipiter** *Chris Wall* a94 94
2 ch f Showcasing Mexican Hawk (USA) (Silver Hawk (USA))
(2918) ◆ 3721[5] (4150) 4646[7] 5380[4] 6142[5] (6513) 7238[9]

**Acclamate (IRE)** *Marco Botti* a72
2 b c Acclamation Rouge Noir (USA) (Saint Ballado (CAN))
7973[6] 8060[3] 8241[3]

**Acclio (IRE)** *Clive Brittain* a77 87
3 b f Acclamation Hovering (IRE) (In The Wings)
1579[3] 7384[8] (7640) 7717[11]

**Accra Beach (USA)** *Roger Charlton* 77
2 ch g Speightstown(USA) Didina (Nashwan (USA))
4270[2] ◆ 4943[2]

**Accra Girl** *Marjorie Fife*
2 b f Captain Gerrard(IRE) Ela D'Argent (IRE) (Ela-Mana-Mou)
4626[12]

**Ace Chop (FR)** *P Marion* a64
5 b g Night Tango(GER) Scotch Mockery (FR) (Persifleur (USA))
178a[7]

**Ace Master** *Roy Bowring* a86 78
6 ch g Ballet Master(USA) Ace Maite (Komaite (USA))
(255) 552[8] 1446[13] 1803[3] (4571) 4752[7] 8257[6]

**Ace Of Marmalade (IRE)** *Brian Ellison*
2 b g Duke Of Marmalade(IRE) Pharapache (USA) (Lyphard (USA))
7763[6] 7973[12]

**Acer Diamonds (IRE)** *Luke Dace* a58 68
5 b g Red Clubs(IRE) Tree House (USA) (Woodman (USA))
293[6]

**Aces (IRE)** *Charles Hills* 109
2 b c Dark Angel(IRE) Cute Ass (IRE) (Fath (USA))
(5500) ◆ 6326[3]

**Ach Alannah (IRE)** *James Unett* 14
3 gr f Marju(IRE) Cidaris (IRE) (Persian Bold)
2384[7] 2759[5]

**Achnaha (IRE)** *P D Deegan* 93
3 b f Haatef(USA) Sanna Bay (IRE) (Refuse To Bend (IRE))
1076a[3] 2263a[8] 4276a[9]

**Achtung** *Luke Comer* a41 60
4 b c Montjeu(IRE) Funsie (FR) (Saumarez)
4951a[9] 6374a[11]

**Achtung (SPA)** *J Lopez Sanchez* 95
6 ch h Sulamani(IRE) Aurea (GER) (Silvano (GER))
4722a[9] 6392a[3]

**Ach Was (GER)** *W Figge*
6 b g Desert Prince(IRE) Al Qahira (GER) (Big Shuffle (USA))
728a[F]

**A Colorier (FR)** *J-P Bourdin* a56
3 ch g Paint The Cat(USA) Suave Miss (FR) (Suave Dancer (USA))
751a[7]

**Acolyte (IRE)** *Roger Charlton* a77 77
2 b g Acclamation Obsara (Observatory (USA))
5377[3] (6103) 7079[7]

**Acquaint (IRE)** *John Wainwright* a61 57
3 gr f Verglas(IRE) Azia (IRE) (Desert Story (IRE))
2354[8] 2616[9] 3950[4] 4261[8] 4497[9] 5717[6] 5917[4] 6627[6]

**Acquittal** *James Fanshawe* a62
2 b f Lawman(FR) Zamid (FR) (Namid)
5821[7] 6606[6]

**Across The Cape** *Michael Bell* a17 43
3 ch f Manduro(GER) Cape Marien (IRE) (Cape Cross (IRE))
4052[9]

**Across The Rhine (USA)** *S Seemar* a86 99
8 ch g Cuvee(USA) Seductive Smile (USA) (Silver Hawk (USA))
112a[14]

**Acting Talent (USA)** *M C Grassick* a66 71
4 b f Bernstein(USA) Soaring Emotions (USA) (Kingmambo (USA))
787[4]

**Action Front (USA)** *Derek Shaw* a52 71
6 bb g Aptitude(USA) Palisade (USA) (Gone West (USA))
7[7]

**Action Master** *J J Lambe* 70
8 b g Domedriver(IRE) All Is Fair (Selkirk (USA))
4255[7]

**Activation** *Hughie Morrison* a53 49
2 b g Stimulation(IRE) Patteresa Girl (Auction House (USA))
4025[13] 4338[8] 4846[5] 5489[11] 6040[11] 6205[4] 6811[6] 7064[3] 7740[9] 7828[3] 8206[3]

**Active Spirit (IRE)** *Saeed bin Suroor* 87
3 ch g Pivotal Local Spirit (USA) (Lion Cavern (USA))
(1486) 2148[8]

**Act Of Charity (IRE)** *Gay Kelleway* a89 88
3 b g Royal Applause Kay Es Jay (FR) (Xaar)
436a[3] 553a[8] 1979[8] 3719[3] 4323[9] 4679[2]

**Actonetaketwo** *Ron Hodges* a51 52
4 b f Act One Temple Dancer (Magic Ring (IRE))
4279[8] 5071[7] 5751[3] 6087[2] 6407[3] 7303[7]

**Acton Gold** *Brian Baugh* a50 49
5 b m And Beyond(IRE) Antonia Bertolini (Bertolini (USA))
13[5] 941[7] 1138[9] 1745[5] 4797[2] 5512[10] 6086[7]

**Act Your Shoe Size** *Keith Dalgleish* a64 66
5 b m Librettist(USA) Howards Heroine (IRE) (Danehill Dancer (IRE))
1190[12] 1598[10] 2293[7] 3572[9] 3608[6] 4517[7] 5142[10] 7813[3] ◆ 7907[3]

**Adaay (IRE)** *William Haggas* 101
2 b c Kodiac Lady Lucia (IRE) (Royal Applause)
(2298) (2873) 3318[8] 4398[3]

**Ada Lovelace** *John Gallagher* a64 76
4 b f Byron Satin Braid (Diktat)
1896[4] 2435[3] (3125) 3422[4] 4401[4] (5070) 5355[7] 6025[8]

**Adam Forever** *Michael Wigham* a43
3 b g Myboycharlie(IRE) Dust (Green Desert (USA))
1008[8] 1107[8] 1296[5]

**Adam's Ale** *Mark Walford* 92
5 b g Ishiguru(USA) Aqua (Mister Baileys)
1447[5] 1538[3] 2136[3] 2364[3] (3399) 3948[10] 4418[6] 5016[2] 5888[11] 6235[4] ◆ 6763[2] 7330[9]

**Adam's Peak (IRE)** *D Sepulchre* a70 70
3 b c Zamindar(USA) Altamira (Peintre Celebre (USA))
3745a[2]

**Adaptability** *Brian Meehan* 67
3 ch f Mastercraftsman(IRE) Sierra (Dr Fong (USA))
1722[9] 2279[12] 2804[5] 3380[P]

**Addazero** *Joseph Tuite* a66 63
5 b g Putra Sas(IRE) Poker Queen (Karinga Bay)
8029[7] 8253[2]

**Addictive Dream (IRE)** *John Murray* a110 109
7 ch g Kheleyf(USA) Nottambula (IRE) (Thatching)
644[5] (802) 1066[4] 1557[12] 2076[4] 2989[3] 3241[14] 5160[6] 6327[14] 6918[9]

**Addictive Nature (IRE)** *John Gallagher* a58 54
4 b g Acclamation Movie Queen (Danehill (USA))
1141[7] 1790[2] 2174[9] 3093[5] 3896[6]

**Addikt (IRE)** *John Spearing* a63 68
9 b h Diktat Frond (Alzao (USA))
(484) 838[8] 1138[11] 6031[6]

**Adechop (FR)** *A De Watrigant* 70
2 bb g Soave(GER) Black Smith (FR) (Indian Rocket)
5706a[7]

**Adelaide (IRE)** *A P O'Brien* 114
3 b c Galileo(IRE) Elletelle (IRE) (Elnadim (USA))
2194a[2] (2579a) 3417[2] 3994a[2] (5458a) 6379a[3] (7467a)

**Adelasia (IRE)** *Charlie Appleby* 82
2 ch f Iffraaj Flaming Song (IRE) (Darshaan)
3267[5] (4346) 5436[11] 6691[2]

**Adele (GER)** *Mark Johnston* 73
2 b f Intikhab(USA) Adalawa (IRE) (Barathea (IRE))
5494[2] 5910[5] 6950a[9]

**Adeste Fideles (USA)** *A P O'Brien* a84 71
3 b f Giant's Causeway(USA) Imagine (IRE) (Sadler's Wells (USA))
6585a[6] 7579a[10]

**Adhwaa** *B W Hills* 94
3 br f Oasis Dream Hammiya (IRE) (Darshaan)
(1868) 2316[10] 3357[18] 4147[10]

**Adiator** *Neville Bycroft* 72
6 b m Needwood Blade Retaliator (Rudimentary (USA))
(2421) 3092[2] 3338[6] 4471[11] 5333[9]

**Adili (IRE)** *Michael Appleby* a69 51
5 ch g Dubai Destination(USA) Adirika (IRE) (Miswaki (USA))
361[5] 567[4] 1092[2] (1248) 1605[9] 1806[2] 8134[3]

**Adimendis (IRE)** *Michael Dods* a52 50
3 b g Elnadim(USA) Endis (IRE) (Distant Relative)
3849[6] 4653[5] 5427[4] 5893[6] 7424[9]

**Adiynara (IRE)** *Neil Mulholland* a74 64
6 b m Halling(USA) Adirika (IRE) (Miswaki (USA))
612[3] (857) 1210[5] 2947[6]

**Adjudant Chef (FR)** *D Rabhi* a75 71
4 b g Vita Rosa(JPN) Puggy (IRE) (Mark Of Esteem (IRE))
266a[6]

**Admirable Art (IRE)** *Tony Carroll* a63 49
4 b g Excellent Art Demi Voix (Halling (USA))
181[8] 589[11] 750[10] 2021[5] 2669[2] 3242[5] (6087) 7167[3] 7645[2] 7766[3] 8084[6] 8139[4] (8311)

**Admirable Duque (IRE)** *Dominic Ffrench Davis* a78 75
8 b g Selkirk(USA) Stunning (USA) (Nureyev (USA))
158[4] 1941[12] 2305[8] 2774[6] 4322[4] 4985[2] 5047[4] 5800[5] 6252[4] 6721[4] 7072[5] 7343[6]

**Admiral Kitten (USA)** *Michael J Maker* 112
4 b c Kitten's Joy(USA) Reachinforthestars (USA) (Grand Slam (USA))
5457a[6]

**Admirals Braid (SAF)** *Ismail Mohammed* a51
6 b g Captain Al(SAF) Astral Emblem (SAF) (National Emblem (SAF))
238a[14]

**Admiral's Gold (IRE)** *Edward Creighton* a49
2 ch c Mount Nelson Lolita's Gold (USA) (Royal Academy (USA))
6604[11] 7731[10]

**Admirals Walk (IRE)** *Barry Brennan* a46 63
4 b g Tagula(IRE) Very Racy (USA) (Sri Pekan (USA))
511[12] 603[13] 846[9] 1015[9] 1386[7] 1666[4] 2609[4]

**Admire Flight (JPN)** *Mitsuru Hashida* 109
5 b h Manhattan Cafe(JPN) Admire Kiseki (JPN) (Tony Bin)
2002a[11]

**Admire Rakti (JPN)** *Tomoyuki Umeda* 119
6 b h Heart's Cry(JPN) Admire Teresa (JPN) (Helissio (FR))
2002a[13] (7301a) 7653a[22]

**Adore** *Sir Michael Stoute* a68 71
3 b f Oasis Dream Fantasize (Groom Dancer (USA))
2063[7] 2504[6] (3614) 3946[8] 4329[11]

**Adriana (GER)** *M Rulec* 108
6 b m Poliglote An Angel (GER) (Trempolino (USA))
1827a[13] 2815a[8] 7558a[12]

**Adroitly (AUS)** *Saeed bin Suroor* a87 91
7 br g Octagonal(NZ) Easy Out (AUS) (Anabaa (USA))
598a[9] 773a[9]

**Adulation (IRE)** *William Haggas* 81
2 b f Acclamation Petite Spectre (Spectrum (IRE))
2866[3] 3353[11] (3841) 4603a[5] 5770[6]

**Aduvee** *Ronald Harris* 2
4 b f Avonbridge Emma Peel (Emarati (USA))
6073[8] 6421[10] 6988[11]

**Advance (FR)** *Ruth Carr* a64 65
3 b g Aqlaam Rabeera (Beat Hollow)
739[2] 6862[2] 7250[2] ◆ 7640[3]

**Adventurer (FR)** *F-H Graffard* a70 48
3 ch c Falco(USA) Avezia (FR) (Night Shift (USA))
1620a[5]

**Adventure Seeker (IRE)** *Ed Vaughan* a78 105
3 gr c Dalakhani(IRE) Adventure (USA) (Unbridled's Song (USA))
1509[5] (2319) 4893[6] 5691[2] 6287[6] 7106[2]

**Ad Vitam (IRE)** *Suzzanne France* a64 65
6 ch g Ad Valorem(USA) Love Sonnet (Singspiel (IRE))
65[6] 913[4] 1105[8] 1309[5] (1606) 2215[11] 3485[5] 3549[8] 3915[4] 5376[13] 5683[2] 6120[2] 6674[6] (7644) 7813[10] 8063[5]

**Aeolian Blue** *William Knight* a69
4 ch f Bahamian Bounty Blue Mistral (IRE) (Spinning World (USA))
275[6] (1405) 1896[3] 2459[2] 2887[4]

**Aeolus** *Ed McMahon* 109
3 b g Araafa(IRE) Bright Moll (Mind Games)
1514[3] 2343[6] (2767) 3352[23] 5963a[4] 6920[6]

**Aerialist (IRE)** *J S Bolger* a93 73
3 ch c Sea The Stars(IRE) Maoineach (USA) (Congaree (USA))
7433a[4]

**Aeronautical (AUS)** *Lionel Cohen* 107
6 b g Encosta De Lago(AUS) Moon Fever (AUS) (Fusaichi Pegasus (USA))
1468a[15]

**Aerovelocity (NZ)** *P O'Sullivan* 120
6 b g Pins(AUS) Exodus (NZ) (Kaapstad (NZ))
7897a[14] (8152a)

**Aertex (IRE)** *Richard Hannon* a87 93
3 b f Exceed And Excel(AUS) Gingham (Barathea (IRE))
(1897) ◆ (2340) 3247[7] 4436[11] 7802[7]

**Aetna** *Michael Easterby* 111
4 b f Indesatchel(IRE) On The Brink (Mind Games)
(1305) 1506[10] (2254) ◆ 6689[3] 7122[10] (7716)

**Aevalon** *Eve Johnson Houghton* a61 68
2 b f Avonbridge Blaina (Compton Place)
2007[2] 2493[6] 3933[5] 4338[4] 8007[7]

**A Fari Spenti (IRE)** *P L Giannotti* 80
2 b f Excellent Art Sun Moon And Stars (IRE) (Galileo (IRE))
7321a[6]

**Affaire De Coeur** *David Simcock* a61 74
3 b f Dalakhani(IRE) Divergence (USA) (Red Ransom (USA))
1616[4] 2082[5] 3277[3] 4211[6] 5340[6]

**Affaire Solitaire (IRE)** *P Khozian* a102 111
4 b c Danehill Dancer(IRE) Arlesienne (IRE) (Alzao (USA))
6955a[5] 7559a[9] 8006a[2]

**Affectionate Lady (IRE)** *W McCreery* a52 57
3 b f Dandy Man(IRE) Agouti (Pennekamp (USA))
7959a[8]

**Affiche (USA)** *N Clement* a71 68
3 b f Northern Afleet(USA) Eternity (Suave Dancer (USA))
7164a[6]

**Affinia Fifty (IRE)** *Patrick Martin* a47 42
4 b f Refuse To Bend(IRE) Newgate Lodge (IRE) (Namid)
128a[7]

**Aficionado** *Keith Dalgleish* a67 75
4 ch g Halling(USA) Prithee (Barathea (IRE))
1197[2] 1307[5]

**Afjaan (IRE)** *William Haggas* 66
2 b c Henrythenavigator(USA) Elusive Galaxy (IRE) (Elusive City (USA))
7382[4]

**Afkar (IRE)** *Clive Brittain* a79 77
6 b g Invincible Spirit(IRE) Indienne (IRE) (Indian Ridge)
245[3] 314[7] 825[5] 2527[2] 2876[7] 5346[9] 5727[5] 6466[9] 7556[9]

**Afonso De Sousa (USA)** *A P O'Brien* a106 93
4 br c Henrythenavigator(USA) Mien (USA) (Nureyev (USA))
1078a[19] 6909a[6]

**Afortable (USA)** *Chris Block* 96
3 rg c Fort Prado(USA) Taxable Deduction (USA) (Prized (USA))
4230a[5]

**African Art (USA)** *Mlle B Renk* a83 83
8 ch g Johannesburg(USA) Perovskia (USA) (Stravinsky (USA))
729a[3]

**African Plains** *Mme C Head-Maarek* a80 78
3 b f Oasis Dream African Rose (Observatory (USA))
5294a[4]

**African Story** *Saeed bin Suroor* a124 115
7 ch g Pivotal Blixen (USA) (Gone West (USA))
508a[2] 901a[8] (1183a)

**Afro** *Peter Hedger* a72 74
4 b f Araafa(IRE) Largo (IRE) (Selkirk (USA))
(64) ◆ 253[2] 1355[7] 1496[2] 1941[4] (2774) 3151[7]

**After Math (FR)** *C Gourdain* a63 75
3 b c Sunday Break(JPN) Ducere (IRE) (Lando (GER))
4952a[14]

**Afternoon Sunlight (IRE)** *D K Weld* 103
3 ch f Sea The Stars(IRE) Lady Luck (IRE) (Kris)
(2186a) 4477a[2]

**After The Goldrush** *Richard Hannon* 79
3 b g Kyllachy Fine Lady (Selkirk (USA))
1654[3] 2307[3] 2624[3] (2847) 3144[7] 4028[4] 4982[6] 5629[11] 7417[11]

**After The Storm** *John O'Shea* a69 66
5 b g Dylan Thomas(IRE) Inchiri (Sadler's Wells (USA))
115[2] 343[2] 581[4] 776[4] 1003[7]

**Agadoo** *Shaun Harris* a50 61
2 b f Multiplex Agooda (Rainbow Quest (USA))
1712[3] 2071[8] 2979[4] 4494[6] 5798[9] 6400[3] 6643[12] 7055[4] (7487)

**Against Rules (FR)** *Robert Collet* a61 61
2 b f Aussie Rules(USA) Around Me (IRE) (Johannesburg (USA))
5619a[11] 7027a[3]

**Against The Tide (IRE)** *Richard Hannon* a59
4 ch f Teofilo(IRE) Hundred Year Flood (USA) (Giant's Causeway (USA))
189[4] 343[5]

**Agama (GER)** *F Kurz* 95
4 ch f Sholokhov(IRE) Ariana (GER) (Dashing Blade)
7483a[10]

**Agapanthus (GER)** *Neil Mulholland* a37 50
9 b g Tiger Hill(IRE) Astilbe (GER) (Monsun (GER))
68[8] 2942[11] 4107[6] (4718a)

**Ageless (USA)** *Arnaud Delacour* a102 109
5 b m Successful Appeal(USA) Special One (USA) (Point Given (USA))
7609a[4]

**Agena (IRE)** *A P O'Brien* 97
3 b c Galileo(IRE) Dietrich (USA) (Storm Cat (USA))
3765a[5]

**Agent Allison** *Peter Chapple-Hyam* a76 103
4 b f Dutch Art Loquacity (Diktat)
394a[10] 683a[8] 4782[11] 6464[6] 6708[11]

**Agent Murphy** *Brian Meehan* 103
3 b c Cape Cross(IRE) Raskutani (Dansili)
(2690) ◆ (3243) 4698[2] 6127[3]

**Age Of Elegance (IRE)** *Olly Stevens* 57
2 b f Makfi Elegant Pride (Beat Hollow)
7405[6]

**Age Of Innocence** *A Fabre* a94 95
3 b c Invincible Spirit(IRE) Elusive Legend (USA) (Elusive Quality (USA))
4930a[7]

**Agerzam** *Roger Varian* a97 75
4 b g Holy Roman Emperor(IRE) Epiphany (Zafonic (USA))
234[2] 3275[8] 5677[11]

**Aglaophonos** *Ian Williams* a78 79
4 ch g Dutch Art Lasting Image (Zilzal (USA))
200[9]

**Agnes Seice (IRE)** *V Luka Jr* 51
2 b f Strategic Prince Colomone Cross (IRE) (Xaar)
6385a[5]

**Agnes Stewart (IRE)** *Edward Lynam* 110
2 gr f Lawman(FR) Anice Stellato (IRE) (Dalakhani (IRE))
4598a[2] (6289) 7240[2]

**Agrapart (FR)** *Nick Williams* 83
3 b g Martaline Afragha (IRE) (Darshaan)
2003a[9] 7164a[2] (7681a)

**Agreeable Lady (IRE)** *Tim Easterby* 29
2 b f Approve(IRE) Spirit of Hope (IRE) (Danehill Dancer (IRE))
6757[12] 7246[8]

**Agreement (IRE)** *John Quinn* a60 79
4 b g Galileo(IRE) Cozzene's Angel (USA) (Cozzene (USA))
3321[15] 3717[16] 4217[12] 5334[7] 5890[12] 6622[3]

**Ahlan Emarati (IRE)** *Peter Chapple-Hyam* 107
2 b c Holy Roman Emperor(IRE) Indaba (IRE) (Indian Ridge)
(1571) 3374[3] 3738a[2] 4780[4] 5692[3] 6286[13]

**Ahoy There (IRE)** *Tom Tate* 70
3 ch g Captain Rio Festivite (IRE) (Fasliyev (USA))
5245[2] 7340[4]

**Ahtoug** *Charlie Appleby* a103 118
6 b h Byron Cherokee Rose (IRE) (Dancing Brave (USA))
(107a) 393a[8] 680a[2] 897a[2] 1179a[2] 3319[5] 3981[7] 4438[9]

**Ahzeemah (IRE)** *Saeed bin Suroor* a84 117
5 b g Dubawi(IRE) Swiss Roll (IRE) (Entrepreneur)
2315[6] 3377[9] 4823[2]

**Aimee (IRE)** *Mlle B Renk* a22 78
2 gr f Alfred Nobel(IRE) Silverdreammachine (IRE) (Marju (IRE))
6591a[9]

**Ainippe (IRE)** *G M Lyons* 101
2 b f Captain Rio Imitation (Darshaan)
6286[5] 6530[3]

**Ainslie (IRE)** *David Simcock* a61
2 rg c Mastercraftsman(IRE) Capriole (Noverre (USA))
6660[9] 8093[8]

**Aint Got A Scooby (IRE)** *Clive Cox* a77 80
4 br g Red Clubs(IRE) La Bataille (USA) (Out Of Place (USA))
1351[6] 1899[5] 2270[3] ◆ 2862[8]

**Ain't No Surprise (IRE)** *Jennie Candlish* a32 63
3 b f Kheleyf(USA) Harmonist (USA) (Hennessy (USA))
19[2] 187[2] 311[2] (464) 499[3] 541[3] 6155[7] 6615[6]

**Air Chief** *Andrew Crook* a17 56
9 ch g Dr Fong(USA) Fly For Fame (Shaadi (USA))
385[6]

**Air Of Mystery** *Marcus Tregoning* 89
2 ch f Sakhee's Secret Belle Des Airs (IRE) (Dr Fong (USA))
(6361) 7238[8]

**Air Of York (IRE)** *Ronald Harris* a60 51
2 b c Vale Of York(IRE) State Secret (Green Desert (USA))
1349[8] 2007[10] 3847[4] 5180[9] 5525[8] 6248[3] 6422[7] 7190[7] 7453[9] 7701[2] 7824[4] 7948[9]

**Air Pilot** *Ralph Beckett* 115
5 b g Zamindar(USA) Countess Sybil (IRE) (Dr Devious (IRE))
1691[2] (2354) 2957[2] (6548) ◆ 7243[3] (7598)

**Air Squadron** *Ralph Beckett* a69 71
4 b g Rail Link Countess Sybil (IRE) (Dr Devious (IRE))
3796[4] (4678) 5466[3] 6107[3] 6881[2]

**Aiyana** *Hughie Morrison* a75 82
4 ch f Indian Haven Coventina (IRE) (Daylami (IRE))
1501[4] 3078[2] 4322[6] 5878[4] 6493[2] (6632) (7129) 7419[2]

**Ajaadat** *Roger Varian* a71 77
2 b f Shamardal(USA) Taarkod (IRE) (Singspiel (IRE))
3563[2] 5037[4] 6041[2] (6448)

**Ajalo (FR)** *Waldemar Hickst* 82
2 b c King's Best(USA) Wings Of Glory (GER) (Monsun (GER))
7726a[7]

**Ajasam** *M Weiss* 88
3 b c King's Best(USA) Funseeker (UAE) (Halling (USA))
3512a[7]

**Ajaxana (GER)** *Waldemar Hickst* 109
3 b f Rock Of Gibraltar(IRE) Arlekinada (Lycius (USA))
1619a[2] (2584a) 4247a[2] 4955a[9] 5965a[4]

**A J Cook (IRE)** *Ron Barr* a64 64
4 b g Mujadil(USA) Undertone (IRE) (Noverre (USA))
2726[3] 3338[12] 4005[5] 4314[5] 4532[3] 4796[7] 4960[12] 5375[3] 5499[6] 5683[5] 6671[3] 7009[5]

**Ajig** *Eve Johnson Houghton* a71 75
3 ch f Bahamian Bounty Atwirl (Pivotal)
2063[10] 2433[8] 4329[3] 4789[2] (5006) 5492[5] 5980[2] 6304[3] (6459) 7186[9] 7397[7]

**Ajjaadd (USA)** *Ted Powell* a95 106
8 b g Elusive Quality(USA) Millstream (USA) (Dayjur (USA))
1944[6] 2503[7] 3927[2] 4700[12] 5925[15] (6209) 6549[3] 6918[8] 7441[2]

**Ajmal Ihsaas** *Marco Botti* 79
2 b f Acclamation Secret History (USA) (Bahri (USA))
2107[2]

**Ajman Bridge** *Luca Cumani* a82 99
4 ch g Dubawi(IRE) Rice Mother (IRE) (Indian Ridge)
2154[6] 3730[8] 4400[2] 4756[2] 5695[5]

**Ajmany (IRE)** *Luca Cumani* a94 106
4 b g Kheleyf(USA) Passarelle (USA) (In The Wings)
1948[2] 2618[12] 4667[2] 5928[8] (6878)

**Akalmia (FR)** *J-M Lefebvre* a71 77
3 b f Enrique Alligoria (FR) (Gold Away (IRE))
(1139a)

**Akavit (IRE)** *Ed de Giles* a41 45
2 b c Vale Of York(IRE) Along Came Molly (Dr Fong (USA))
3536[6] 4025[14] 5201[8] 5823[8]

**Akavoroun (AUS)** *Ciaron Maher* 103
5 bb g Lacryma Cristi(IRE) Salquetta (AUS) (Salieri (USA))
7128a[4]

**Akbabend** *Chris Gordon* a20 21
8 b g Refuse To Bend(IRE) Akdariya (IRE) (Shirley Heights)
3179[8]

**Akdam (IRE)** *Tony Carroll* a68 71
4 br g Dubai Destination(USA) Akdara (IRE) (Sadler's Wells (USA))
801[9]

**Akeed Champion** *Richard Fahey* 85
2 b c Dubawi(IRE) Shy Lady (FR) (Kaldoun (FR))
6125[2] 7123[4]

**Akeed Mofeed** *R Gibson* a109 120
5 b h Dubawi(IRE) Wonder Why (GER) (Tiger Hill (IRE))
1183a[5]

**Akemi (IRE)** *X Thomas-Demeaulte* a87 103
4 b f Footstepsinthesand Hitra (USA) (Langfuhr (CAN))
3291a[7] 5369a[11] 8300a[12]

**Akinspirit (IRE)** *Michael Butler* a61 61
10 b g Invincible Spirit(IRE) Akebia (USA) (Trempolino (USA))
794a[5]

**Akira (IRE)** *J R Barry* 103
4 b f Acclamation Saik (USA) (Riverman (USA))
1076a[9] 5955a[5] 6585a[4]

**Aksil (FR)** *M Boutin* a77 105
4 b f Spirit One(FR) Nera Zilzal (IRE) (Zilzal (USA))
836a[9] 1207a[6] 2799a[7] 3746a[9] 5963a[5] 6994a[11] 7327a[3] 7656a[8] 7856a[11]

**Aktabantay** *Hugo Palmer* 108
2 b c Oasis Dream Splashdown (Falbrav (IRE))
1977[2] 2428[2] (3619) 4199[2] (5926) 6968a[6]

**Akton City (FR)** *J-P Delaporte* a74 67
7 b g Sagacity(FR) Tanea (FR) (Exit To Nowhere (USA))
3373a[14]

**Al** *Luca Cumani* a67 59
2 b c Halling(USA) Incarnation (IRE) (Samum (GER))
6103[3] 7537[4]

**Aladdins Cave** *R K Watson* a86 90
10 b g Rainbow Quest(USA) Flight Of Fancy (Sadler's Wells (USA))
7974[4]

**Alakhtal (IRE)** *Charles Hills* a68 70
2 br g Lord Shanakill(USA) Definite Opinion (IRE) (Kheleyf (USA))
2777[5] 3330[7] 5799[7]

**Alandil (FR)** *M Boutin* a58
2 ch c Muhaymin(USA) Alanna (FR) (Bering)
5618a[6]

**Alanna Bheag (IRE)** *M C Grassick* a36 48
3 b f Kodiac Strina (IRE) (Indian Ridge)
786[7]

**Alanos (IRE)** *James Ewart* a64 71
5 b g Choisir(AUS) Pickwick Papers (Singspiel (IRE))
1760[5] 2215[8] 2477[2] 3299[11] 7494[12]

**Alans Pride (IRE)** *Michael Dods* 79
2 ch g Footstepsinthesand True Crystal (IRE) (Sadler's Wells (USA))
3297[2] (3945) (5141) 6151[3] 6529[3] 7041[3]

**Al Aqabah (IRE)** *Brian Gubby* a75 70
9 ch m Redback Snow Eagle (IRE) (Polar Falcon (USA))
245[11]

**Alara (FR)** *P Monfort* a65 79
4 ch g Kendargent(FR) Bida (FR) (Lone Bid (FR))
6569a[3]

**Alasdair (FR)** *Matthieu Palussiere* a62 77
2 b c Alexandros Zarazienne (FR) (Zieten (USA))
6244a[4]

**Alaskakonigin (GER)** *Markus Klug* 97
3 rg f Sternkonigin(GER) Annouche (GER) (Unfuwain (USA))
7482a[9]

**Alaskan Bullet (IRE)** *Brian Ellison* a85 82
5 b g Kodiac Czars Princess (IRE) (Soviet Star (USA))
2350[6] 2825[8] 3458[3] 3659[3] 4488[7] 4859[4]

**Alaskan Wing (IRE)** *Tony Coyle* a49 63
2 br g Kodiac Canary Bird (IRE) (Catrail (USA))
1732[4] 2051[8] 6158[6] (7003) 7497[2]

**Albadorata (IRE)** *Gianluca Bietolini* 69
3 b f Intikhab(USA) Capriccioli (FR) (Jeune Homme (USA))
3513a[6]

**Al Bandar (IRE)** *Richard Hannon* 81
2 b c Monsieur Bond(IRE) Midnight Mystique (IRE) (Noverre (USA))
4129[3] 4429[2] ◆ 4935[2] (5519) 6499[2]

**Albaqaa** *P J O'Gorman* a87 91
9 ch g Medicean Basbousate Nadia (Wolfhound (USA))
4169[4] 4442[6] 4786[5]

**Albasharah (USA)** *Saeed bin Suroor* a89 114
5 b m Arch(USA) Desert Gold (USA) (Seeking The Gold (USA))
6464[2] (7105) ◆ 7273[7]

**Alba Verde** *Sir Mark Prescott Bt* a73 39
3 gr f Verglas(IRE) Algarade (Green Desert (USA))
3781[7] 4562[3] 5005[10] 5864[5] (6339) ◆ (6768) (7204) 7903[8]

**Albayan (IRE)** *A Al Raihe* a76 72
5 b h Street Cry(IRE) Ama (USA) (Storm Cat (USA))
238a[11]

**Albecq** *David Evans* 57
2 b g Paco Boy(IRE) Helen Sharp (Pivotal)
5377[6] 6204[9] 6517[12] 7131[8]

**Albegna (GER)** *H Blume* a75 73
4 ch f Sabiango(GER) Anzasca (GER) (Green Tune (USA))
2192a[6]

**Alben Star (IRE)** *Richard Fahey* a110 113
6 b g Clodovil(IRE) Secret Circle (Magic Ring (IRE))
271[8] (348) 534[2] 886[5] (1557) ◆ 1975[4] 2786[13] 3452[4] 3737a[4] ◆ 4895[3] 5674[2] 6533[26] 7272[13]

**Albert Bridge** *Ralph Beckett* a77 95
6 gr g Hernando(FR) Alvarita (Selkirk (USA))
1981[3] 2289[12] 5924[8] 7476a[3]

**Albert Herring** *Jonathan Portman* a46
2 b g Tobougg(IRE) Balsamita (FR) (Midyan (USA))
7941[12]

**Alberto** *Jo Hughes* a47 36
4 b g Bertolini(USA) Al Awaalah (Mukaddamah (USA))
1819[6] 2723[5] 3123[6] 3527[8] 3820[5] 4534[11] 5978[10]

**Albertochop (FR)** *X Betron* a78 82
2 ch c Deportivo Perle De Star (FR) (Indian Rocket)
5329a[6]

**Albonetti (AUS)** *Sue Jaensch* 100
5 b m Ustinov(AUS) Command Performer (AUS) (Royal Academy (USA))
7126a[6]

**Albonny (IRE)** *Timothy Jarvis* a76 76
5 b g Aussie Rules(USA) Silk Law (IRE) (Barathea (IRE))
1418[13] 1692[5] 2108[4] 2482[6] 2739[6] (4076) 5083[3] 5890[10] 6514[6] 7124[15] 7946[6]

**Alborz (IRE)** *Tim Vaughan* a70 74
5 b g Dubai Destination(USA) Mount Elbrus (Barathea (IRE))
64[4] 1000[5]

**Al Busayyir (IRE)** *Marco Botti* a73 93
3 b g Amadeus Wolf Helen Wells (IRE) (Sadler's Wells (USA))
(1509) (2617) 2986[9] 3965[2] ◆

**Alcaeus** *Sir Mark Prescott Bt* a82 103
4 b c Hernando(FR) Alvarita (Selkirk (USA))
4144[2]

**Alcando (IRE)** *Denis Coakley* a71 77
4 ch g Alhaarth(IRE) Cantando (IRE) (Hamas (IRE))
1789[6] 2414[10] 2884[4] 3555[2] 4050[2]

**Alcohuaz (CHI)** *Lennart Reuterskiold Jr* a97 98
9 b g Merchant Of Venice(USA) Giverny (CHI) (Hussonet (USA))
2244a[5] 3996a[6] 5966a[3]

**Aldabra (FR)** *D Prod'Homme* a86 93
3 gr f Sinndar(IRE) Atlantic Light (Linamix (FR))
237a[3]

**Aldar (FR)** *A Savujev* a66 78
2 b c New Approach(IRE) Birmanie (USA) (Aldebaran (USA))
7317a[8]

**Aldborough (IRE)** *Ralph Beckett* a75 79
4 b g Danehill Dancer(IRE) Kitty O'Shea (Sadler's Wells (USA))
1216[5] 1809[6] (2670) 3860[8] 4423[10] 7125[12]

**Aldeburgh** *Claire Dyson* a71 71
5 b g Oasis Dream Orford Ness (Selkirk (USA))
119[4] 582[2] 990[3] 1281[5] 1899[4] 7626[12]

**Alderaan (IRE)** *Tony Coyle* 68
2 gr f Zebedee Rublevka Star (USA) (Elusive Quality (USA))
2386[5] 2725[2] 3188[4] 3648[9] 3947[8] 4172[7]

**Alderley** *Martyn Meade* a66 62
3 b f Three Valleys(USA) Doctor's Note (Pursuit Of Love)
3733[8] 4411[3] 5057[3]

**Al Destoor** *Anthony Middleton* a78 78
4 ch g Teofilo(IRE) In A Silent Way (IRE) (Desert Prince (IRE))
7772[2] ◆

**Aldo** *Sean Curran* a64 64
7 b g Lucky Owners(NZ) Chaperone (Shaamit (IRE))
7182[11] 7895[4]

**Aldous Snow (CAN)** *Malcolm Pierce* a92 105
5 b g Theatrical(IRE) Brave Destiny (USA) (Quiet American (USA))
6390a[6]

**Aldreth** *Michael Easterby* a56 63
3 b g Champs Elysees Rowan Flower (IRE) (Ashkalani (IRE))
1632[4] 1904[2] 2237[5] 2867[2] 3135[10] 3789[12] 5512[13]

**Aldwick Bay (IRE)** *Tom Dascombe* a68 81
6 b g Danehill Dancer(IRE) Josie Doocey (IRE) (Sadler's Wells (USA))
1724[6] (2701) 2963[5] 4985[3] 5371[3] 5678[11]

**Alea Iacta** *A Fabre* 104
2 b f Invincible Spirit(IRE) Almiranta (Galileo (IRE))
(7069a) 7557a[5]

**Aledaid (IRE)** *Richard Hannon* 81
2 b g Acclamation Lanark Belle (Selkirk (USA))
2298[5] 2964[3] 6496[3] 6998[5]

**A Legacy Of Love (IRE)** *Amanda Perrett* a78 69
3 b f Sea The Stars(IRE) Nashmiah (IRE) (Elusive City (USA))
2044[2] *(2929)* 3280[5] 3936[8] 4282[4] *7729[6] 8185[3]*

**Alegro (ITY)** *Stefano Botti* 88
3 b c Montalegre(IRE) La Sultana (IRE) (Spectrum (IRE))
2376a[13]

**Alejandro (IRE)** *David O'Meara* a102 105
5 b g Dark Angel(IRE) Carallia (IRE) (Common Grounds)
2202[4] 2548[4] (3202) 3964[3] (4681) 5919[5] 6290[5] *7555[4] 7851[3]*

**Aleksandar** *Jim Goldie* a74 78
5 ch g Medicean Alexander Celebre (IRE) (Peintre Celebre (USA))
1929[4] 2213[3] (2515) 3240[4] (3829) 4361[3] 5083[4] 5564[4] 6404[4] 6579[4] 6794[7] 7508[12] *7817[12]*

**Al Enbess (IRE)** *Ruth Carr* a72 50
4 b g Kyllachy Taghreed (IRE) (Zamindar (USA))
*1003[6] 1222[5]* 1673[7] *1854[2]*

**Alert** *Jonathan Portman* 36
2 b f Zamindar(USA) Tereshkina (IRE) (Sadler's Wells (USA))
7450[13]

**Alexandra Dancer (FR)** *J-P Delaporte* 41
2 ch f Martillo(GER) Funambula Dancer (FR) (Funambule (USA))
2755a[9]

**Alexandrakollontai (IRE)** *Alistair Whillans* a55 89
4 b f Amadeus Wolf Story (Observatory (USA))
1376[14] 1566[7] 1967[5] 2332[6] (2677) 3359[8] 3575[5] 4194[6] (4515) 4902[2] 5396[2] 6013[5] (6598) 6824[3] 7060[13] 7384[7]

**Alexandra Palace (SAF)** *M F De Kock* a108 63
5 b g Jet Master(SAF) Alexander Bi (IRE) (Darshaan)
*(306a) 681a[8] 773a[3] 901a[13]*

**Alexanor (IRE)** *Marco Botti* a70 60
3 b c Pivotal Butterfly Cove (USA) (Storm Cat (USA))
1400[5]

**Alexi (IRE)** *Harry Dunlop* 42
2 b f Amadeus Wolf Alexander Wonder (IRE) (Redback)
4906[7] 6393[4] 7217[5] 7536[8]

**Alex My Boy (IRE)** *Mark Johnston* 110
3 b c Dalakhani(IRE) Alexandrova (IRE) (Sadler's Wells (USA))
(1600) 2347[2] ◆ 3003[7] 3379[8] (3884) (5144) ◆ 5668[2] ◆ 6329[8]

**Alex Vino (IRE)** *Sir Michael Stoute* a97 94
3 b c High Chaparral(IRE) Rare Ransom (Oasis Dream)
1279[4] (4586) 5465[4] *(6044)* 6438[3] 6878[4]

**Alfaayza (IRE)** *K R Burke* a70 57
3 b f Dansili Ayun (USA) (Swain (IRE))
*51[4] 166[3]*

**Al Fahidi (IRE)** *A Oliver* a67 72
4 b f Singspiel(IRE) Bastakiya (IRE) (Dubai Destination (USA))
4805a[5]

**Alfajer** *Marco Botti* a75 74
2 b f Mount Nelson Sakhee's Song (IRE) (Sakhee (USA))
6754[2] *(7550)*

**Al Farahidi (USA)** *A bin Huzaim* a81 79
7 b g Seeking The Gold(USA) Banksia (Marju (IRE))
*241a[13]*

**Al Fareej (IRE)** *James Tate* a79 97
2 b f Iffraaj Shining Hour (USA) (Red Ransom (USA))
2402[2] ◆ 2866[2] 3353[14] *(5042)* 5380[2] 5694[3] 6513[10] 7238[7]

**Alfie Bond** *Brian Rothwell* 38
2 ch g Monsieur Bond(IRE) Assuage (Wolfhound (USA))
2014[8] 3947[13]

**Alfie Lunete (IRE)** *J S Moore* a65 68
3 b f Footstepsinthesand La Lunete (Halling (USA))
*338[5] 401[4] 429[4]*

**Alfie The Pug** *Pat Phelan* a59
2 b g Pastoral Pursuits Kapsiliat (IRE) (Cape Cross (IRE))
*6101[9] 7941[7] 8201[5]*

**Alfkona (GER)** *Jozef Roszival* 90
6 b m Areion(GER) Ariana (GER) (Dashing Blade)
1477a[5]

**Alforrocho (FR)** *R Schoof* a59 58
3 b c King's Best(USA) Pomposa (IRE) (Barathea (IRE))
*8005a[10]*

**Alfred Hutchinson** *Geoffrey Oldroyd* a107 101
6 ch g Monsieur Bond(IRE) Chez Cherie (Wolfhound (USA))
*144[3] (314) 715[5] 887[5] 1558[3]* 2286[5] 2784[5] 4212[4] 4681[2] 5653[7] 6124[10] *7801[6]* 8295[4]

**Alfresco** *Martin Bosley* a60 62
10 b g Mtoto Maureena (IRE) (Grand Lodge (USA))
*428[6] 846[2] 1105[10]* 2843[3] *4056[3] (4732)*

**Al Furat (USA)** *Ron Barr* a28 63
6 b g El Prado(IRE) No Frills (IRE) (Darshaan)
1644[2] 2055[9] 2654[6] 3205[12] 3623[5] 4000[9] 4319[5] 4470[4] 4797[4] 5678[3] 6541[9]

**Algaith (USA)** *B W Hills* a85 62
2 b c Dubawi(IRE) Atayeb (USA) (Rahy (USA))
6712[8] *(7030) (7574)*

**Algar Lad** *David O'Meara* 104
4 ch g Kheleyf(USA) Winding (USA) (Irish River (FR))
3191[2] (3386) 3666[5] 4016[3] 4174[3] (4859) (6130) 6327[12] 6745[13]

**Al Ghuwariyah (IRE)** *Kevin Ryan* 86
2 b f Acclamation Church Melody (Oasis Dream)
1528[2] 1924[2] 3353[21] (4185) (4869) 6513[7]

**Al Gomry** *Richard Fahey* 83
2 b g Exceed And Excel(AUS) Welsh Cake (Fantastic Light (USA))
3199[4] (3713) 5286[5] 6256[20]

**Al Guwair (IRE)** *Mark Hoad* a69
4 b g Shirocco(GER) Katariya (IRE) (Barathea (IRE))
*7401[6] 8190[8]*

**Alhaarth Beauty (IRE)** *Phil McEntee* a66 74
4 b f Alhaarth(IRE) Endis (IRE) (Distant Relative)
*1104[5] 1238[9] 1388[7]*

**Alhaban (IRE)** *Ronald Harris* a66 52
8 gr g Verglas(IRE) Anne Tudor (IRE) (Anabaa (USA))
*445[8] 922[5] 1040[6] (2937)* 3209[9] *4073[12]*

**Alhamareer (IRE)** *Richard Hannon* a52 33
2 ch g Teofilo(IRE) Ribot's Guest (IRE) (Be My Guest (USA))
7039[8] *7730[12]*

**Alhania (USA)** *Saeed bin Suroor* a67
2 bb f Medaglia d'Oro(USA) Dessert (USA) (Storm Cat (USA))
*7658[3]*

**Al Hanyora** *Richard Hannon* a46
3 b f Teofilo(IRE) Chrysalis (Soviet Star (USA))
*748[8]*

**Alhavolle (IRE)** *J-M Capitte* a74
4 b f Alhaarth(IRE) Virevolle (FR) (Kahyasi)
*266a[7]*

**Alhebayeb (IRE)** *M F De Kock* a90 109
4 gr c Dark Angel(IRE) Miss Indigo (Indian Ridge)
107a[12] *396a[9]* 509a[10]

**Alhella** *Kevin Ryan* 70
2 b f Kyllachy Maid In The Shade (Forzando)
4499[7] 5232[5] 6434[2]

**Alhellal (IRE)** *M Phelan* a65 60
8 b g Kalanisi(IRE) Zafayana (IRE) (Mark Of Esteem (IRE))
4746a[19] 7142a[20]

**Ali Bin Nayef** *Charles Hills* a70 49
2 b g Nayef(USA) Maimoona (IRE) (Pivotal)
*6101[5] 6565[5]* 6859[7]

**Alice's Dancer (IRE)** *Mme G Rarick* a80 94
5 b m Clodovil(IRE) Islandagore (IRE) (Indian Ridge)
*364[3] 627[6] 767[6] 927[5]* 1375[3] (1873) 2318[3] 2861[3] (3425) 5965a[9] 6620a[3] 7095a[4] 7629a[14] *8150a[12]*

**Alisios (GR)** *Luca Cumani* a80 78
3 b c Ialysos(GR) Macanuda (IRE) (Slickly (FR))
*1897[3]* 2968[9] 4021[4]

**A Little Bit Dusty** *Conor Dore* a83 74
6 ch g Needwood Blade Dusty Dazzler (IRE) (Titus Livius (FR))
*21[6] (209) 471[7] (641) (911) 1003[3] 1140[5] 1628[6]* 3226[6] 3556[5] 4058[7] (5495) 6062[4] 6699[13] 7822[10] 8260[7]

**Alive Alive Oh** *T Stack* 105
4 b f Duke Of Marmalade(IRE) Higher Love (IRE) (Sadler's Wells (USA))
2572a[6] 5955a[3] 6585a[8]

**Ali Vital (NZ)** *Robbie Laing* 93
5 b g Yamanin Vital(NZ) Ali Rosa (NZ) (Personal Escort (USA))
7395a[10]

**Alizari (IRE)** *Barry Brennan* a43 76
5 b g Oratorio(IRE) Alaya (IRE) (Ela-Mana-Mou)
*41[4] 695[6]*

**Aljamaaheer (IRE)** *Roger Varian* 117
5 ch h Dubawi(IRE) Kelly Nicole (IRE) (Rainbow Quest (USA))
1531[3] 3451[3] 4201[9] 6328[2] 6971a[12]

**Al Jamal** *Jeremy Gask* a87 63
4 b f Authorized(IRE) Kydd Gloves (USA) (Dubai Millennium)
*2922[13]* 3802[7] *5040[10]*

**Alkasser (IRE)** *D K Weld* 107
3 b g Shamardal(USA) Alexander Queen (IRE) (King's Best (USA))
3737a[16] 6353a[7]

**Al Kazeem** *Roger Charlton* 126
6 b h Dubawi(IRE) Kazeem (Darshaan)
4437[4] (5687) 6353a[5] 6970a[10] 7275[2]

**Alketios (GR)** *Luca Cumani* 82
3 b g Kavafi(IRE) Mazea (IRE) (Montjeu (IRE))
2432[4] (3465) 4549[6] 5196[11]

**Al Khan (IRE)** *Ollie Pears* a80 91
5 b g Elnadim(USA) Popolo (IRE) (Fasliyev (USA))
*549[6] 1020[7]* 1275[7] *1497[3]* 2677[11] *3402[2]* (3599) 3952[4] 4421[3] (4707) 5143[6] 5810[3] (5986) 6285[11] 6824[11]

**Alkhayyam (IRE)** *Brian Meehan* 53
2 b c Oasis Dream Tariysha (IRE) (Daylami (IRE))
5646[12]

**Al Khisa (IRE)** *G E Mikhalides* a60 63
4 b f Diamond Green(FR) Rectify (IRE) (Mujadil (USA))
*805a[12]*

**All Ablaze (IRE)** *Damian Joseph English* a82 65
4 b g Antonius Pius(USA) Strawberry Sands (Lugana Beach)
*788a[9]*

**All About Time** *David O'Meara* 74
2 b f Azamour(IRE) Up And About (Barathea (IRE))
5655[8] 6148[2] (6641)

**Alla Breve** *Sir Michael Stoute* a61
2 b f Dansili Allegretto (IRE) (Galileo (IRE))
*7011[5]*

**All At Sea** *A Fabre* 104
2 b f Sea The Stars(IRE) Albanova (Alzao (USA))
6956a[5] 7558a[7]

**All Blues (FR)** *M Boutin* a52 48
2 bb f Lord Shanakill(USA) Sepia (Dansili)
*3872a[7] 5026a[9]*

**Allegation (FR)** *David Lanigan* a83 79
3 b f Lawman(FR) Anja (IRE) (Indian Ridge)
4413[2] *4966[2] 5822[5] 6634[10]*

**Allegra Tak (ITY)** *H Rogers* a46 92
8 b m Invincible Spirit(IRE) No Tiktak (IRE) (Diktat)
1824a[10] 5958a[17]

**Allegrezza** *D Smaga* 89
3 b f Sir Percy Allegro Viva (USA) (Distant View (USA))
4249a[6]

**Allegria (IRE)** *John Gosden* a76 88
3 gr f Dalakhani(IRE) Drifting (IRE) (Sadler's Wells (USA))
1701[5] ◆ *2650[4]* (3106) 3918[3] 4887[4] 7020[7]

**Allergic Reaction (IRE)** *William Knight* a73 68
3 b g Kyllachy Wood Chorus (Singspiel (IRE))
*1794[4]* (2643) 3316[3] 4120[4] 4942[4] *5795[3] (6635)* 7172[11]

**All Gone (IRE)** *S Donohoe* a14 45
5 b g Kayrawan(USA) Atuf (USA) (Danzig (USA))
4728[8]

**All In (GER)** *Claudia Erni* 77
6 br g Auenadler(GER) Akademica (IRE) (Royal Academy (USA))
7618a[7]

**All Include (FR)** *N Milliere* a11 69
3 ch g High Rock(IRE) Ardalina (FR) (Sillery (USA))
2003a[8] 5227a[10]

**Allinornothing (IRE)** *Cathrine Witso Slettemark* 71
2 ch f Kyllachy Minshar (Noverre (USA))
6386a[6]

**All My Love (IRE)** *Richard Hannon* a58 68
2 b f Lord Shanakill(USA) Afilla (Dansili)
*2918[6]* 3558[8] 4403[9] *5279[7]* 5875[6] (7165)

**Allnecessaryforce (FR)** *Alex Hales* a71 82
4 gr g Verglas(IRE) Kosmic View (USA) (Distant View (USA))
2016[5] 2700[2] 2787[3] 7409[16] *7734[8]*

**All Or Nothin (IRE)** *Paddy Butler* a61 78
5 b g Majestic Missile(IRE) Lady Peculiar (CAN) (Sunshine Forever (USA))
2124[6] *2648[5] 3393[9]* 5422[3]

**All Reddy** *Tom Dascombe* a70 71
3 ch g Compton Place Raphaela (FR) (Octagonal (NZ))
*941[4] 1287[2]* 1738[4] 2506[5] *2998[7]* 3880[6]

**All Right Now** *Tony Newcombe* a60 59
7 b g Night Shift(USA) Cookie Cutter (IRE) (Fasliyev (USA))
*59[7] (833) 1017[8] 1365[7] 1892[5]* 2250[7]

**All Rounder (USA)** *John Gosden* a54 73
2 gr f Mizzen Mast(USA) Summer Shower (Sadler's Wells (USA))
3558[3] 4403[10] *5037[7] 5554[10]*

**All Set To Go (IRE)** *A Oliver* 105
3 gr g Verglas(IRE) Firecrest (IRE) (Darshaan)
1200a[6] 1458a[3]

**All Talk N No Do (IRE)** *Seamus Durack* a83 82
3 b c Kodiac Woodren (USA) (Woodman (USA))
(2307) 2781[6] 5203[3] 5884[10] 6460[4] 7161[7] *(7552) 8015[2]*

**All That Remains (IRE)** *Brian Ellison* a42 36
9 b g King's Theatre(IRE) Morning Breeze (IRE) (Bigstone (IRE))
1359[8] *3404[10]*

**All The News (USA)** *J-C Rouget* 76
2 b c Bernardini(USA) Black Speck (USA) (Arch (USA))
5706a[5]

**All The Winds (GER)** *Shaun Lycett* a84 71
9 ch g Samum(GER) All Our Luck (GER) (Spectrum (IRE))
*125[3] 293[9] 544[2] 732[5] 999[5] (1628)* 2162[7] 2966[2] *5259[6]* 5984[6] *6942[3]* 7366[5] 7822[5] 8264[5]

**Alluring Star** *Michael Easterby* a67 72
6 b m Gentleman's Deal(IRE) Alustar (Emarati (USA))
1309[6] (1649) (1930) (2164) 2293[4] 2605[2] 3096[4] 3575[3] 4108[13]

**All Valentine (FR)** *S Wattel* 71
3 bl f Elusive City(USA) All Speedy (FR) (Pyramus (USA))
1907a[10]

**Almaardiyah (IRE)** *Richard Hannon* a60 69
2 b f High Chaparral(IRE) Danehill's Dream (IRE) (Danehill (USA))
4914[8] 5416[6] 7450[15] *7832[8]*

**Almaas (USA)** *Saeed bin Suroor* a48 48
5 ch g Hard Spun(USA) Summer Dream Girl (USA) (Unbridled (USA))
4673[2]

**Almadaa** *David Marnane* a96 74
7 b g Exceed And Excel(AUS) Masaader (USA) (Wild Again (USA))
(4556a)

**Almagest** *David O'Meara* 93
6 br g Galileo(IRE) Arabesque (Zafonic (USA))
3341[6] 4068[5] 4289[2] 4685[4] (5017) 7409[17]

**Almalad (AUS)** *Gai Waterhouse* 110
3 bb g Al Maher(AUS) Ilhaam (AUS) (Secret Savings (USA))
7467a[13]

**Almalyk (FR)** *X Nakkachdji* a94 103
5 gr g Oratorio(IRE) Alnamara (FR) (Linamix (FR))
*669a[5]*

**Al Manaal** *Mick Channon* a83 87
4 b f Echo Of Light Mall Queen (USA) (Sheikh Albadou)
1716[4] (2121) 2861[5] 3212[5] 3727[8] 4271[8] 4680[8] 4982[3] 5629[4] *(6269)* 6736[3]

**Almanaar** *F Head* a85 79
2 ch g Dubawi(IRE) Baqah (IRE) (Bahhare (USA))
5706a[2]

**Almanack** *Ian Williams* a81 73
4 b g Haatef(USA) Openness (Grand Lodge (USA))
*1049[7]* 1446[11] 2955[11] *(3854) 4078[8]* 4795[4] 5536[2] 5887[2] 6334[6] 6478[3] *(7185) 7774[3] 7955[3]* 8168[4]

**Almandin (GER)** *Jean-Pierre Carvalho* 112
4 b g Monsun(GER) Anatola (GER) (Tiger Hill (IRE))
(2815a)

**Almargo (IRE)** *Mark Johnston* a88 106
3 b c Invincible Spirit(IRE) Alexander Youth (IRE) (Exceed And Excel (AUS))
*(923) (1146) (1315)* 1563[4] 1696[7] 2088[6] (2962) 3253[17] 3378[10] (3716) 4166[13] 4826[3] (5665) ◆ 6124[15] 6354a[2] 7276[27]

**Almashooqa (USA)** *Roger Varian* a66 93
3 bb f Dubawi(IRE) Almoutezah (USA) (Storm Cat (USA))
1424[6] 2365[2] 3423[2] 4211[2] 5634[2] (6282) 6756[3]

**Almax** *Michael Bell* 53
3 b g Rock Of Gibraltar(IRE) Inya Lake (Whittingham (IRE))
2877[7] 3074[10] 5000[4] 6088[4] *6567[9]*

**Almerzem (USA)** *Saeed bin Suroor* a87 79
3 bb g Medaglia d'Oro(USA) Tashawak (IRE) (Night Shift (USA))
3248[5] *3856[5]* 4359[8] *(6487)* 6685[9] *7033[5]*

**Almoonqith (USA)** *M F De Kock* a88 92
4 br c Dynaformer(USA) Bohemian Lady (USA) (Carson City (USA))
*243a[5] 681a[13]*

**Almoqatel (IRE)** *Tony Newcombe* a63 59
2 b c Clodovil(IRE) Majestic Night (IRE) (Mujadil (USA))
*5488[9]* 5874[10] *(6676)* 7379[7] *7525[9] 7945[7] 8069[10] 8317[12]*

**Almosthaditall (USA)** *Patrick J Flynn* a79 67
3 b f Henrythenavigator(USA) Steady Cat (USA) (Storm Cat (USA))
4950a[4]

**Almost Nowhere (IRE)** *Michael Appleby* a29 44
2 br f Erewhon(USA) Lianda (USA) (Danzig (USA))
6448[7] 6694[8] 6976[7] *7648[11] 7815[13]*

**Almuhalab** *Charles Hills* 78
3 bb g Dansili Ghanaati (USA) (Giant's Causeway (USA))
4621[2] 6298[2] ◆ 7210[6]

**Al Muheer (IRE)** *Tom Dascombe* a76 79
9 b g Diktat Dominion Rose (USA) (Spinning World (USA))
1345[10] 1646[9] 1957[10] 2234[3] 2351[11] 2603[6] 3094[2] 3400[2] 3572[8] 3955[6] 4291[4] 4703[4] 5295[3] 5793[8] *6341[11]* 6822[4] 7098[5] 7249[3] ◆ 7456[4] 7601[2] 7819[2] 7953[8]

**Almuheet** *Brian Ellison* a94 94
3 b g Dansili Arwaah (IRE) (Dalakhani (IRE))
1714[5] 3480[6] 4826[6] 5385[3] 5656[3] 6214[2] 6476[3] 6936[4] *7227[2]*

**Al Mukhdam** *Ed de Giles* a83 83
4 b g Exceed And Excel(AUS) Sakhya (IRE) (Barathea (IRE))
1275[5] ◆ 1564[11] 2562[13] 2953[9] 3400[3] 4190[2] 4810[3] 5413[8] 5903[2] 6304[4] *(6841) 7185[9]*

**Al Naamah (IRE)** *A Fabre* 94
2 b f Galileo(IRE) Alluring Park (IRE) (Green Desert (USA))
6219a[6]

**Alnashama** *Charles Hills* 78
2 bb c Dubawi(IRE) Ghanaati (USA) (Giant's Causeway (USA))
6203[5] 6860[2] 7380[2]

**Alnashmy (FR)** *J Peromingo* a99 86
6 br h Shamardal(USA) Legendary (FR) (Fabulous Dancer (USA))
*207a[2] 504a[5] 808a[11]*

**Al Nejmaa (IRE)** *N Sauer* a77 82
7 ch g Theatrical(IRE) Mark My Words (USA) (Aptitude (USA))
(3089a)

**Al Nofor (IRE)** *Richard Hannon* 65
2 b f Shamardal(IRE) First Fleet (USA) (Woodman (USA))
6553[4]

**Alnoomaas (IRE)** *Luke Dace* a82 82
5 b g Oasis Dream Remarkable Story (Mark Of Esteem (IRE))
*91[6] 312[2] 470[3] 587[6] 841[3] 1017[2] 1388[2] 1921[5] 2471[4]* 5629[5] (5951) (6398) 6680[4] 7017[4]

**Aloft (IRE)** *A P O'Brien* 112
2 b c Galileo(IRE) Dietrich (USA) (Storm Cat (USA))
(6928) 7442[2]

**Along Again (IRE)** *Sir Michael Stoute* a33 98
3 b f Elusive City(USA) American Adventure (USA) (Miswaki (USA))
1515[15] 3724[8] 5467[10]

**Alonsoa (IRE)** *Henry Candy* 96
2 ch f Raven's Pass(USA) Alasha (IRE) (Barathea (IRE))
(3558) ◆ (4585) 5190[4] 6289[8]

**A Lovable Rogue** *Ian Semple* 54
2 b c Dutch Art Dance Card (Cape Cross (IRE))
4382[8] 5013[5] 5759[5]

**Alpha (GER)** *R Werning* 88
5 b m Electric Beat Adela (GER) (Tannenkonig (IRE))
5966a[10] 7483a[5]

**Alphabetique** *Peter Chapple-Hyam* a68 70
3 b f Zamindar(USA) Almamia (Hernando (FR))
*1427[5]* 2310[4] 3154[6] 4092[4] 4863[6] 5975[5] 7000[4] *7704[11]*

**Alpha Bravo** *Mme C Head-Maarek* 94
2 b c Oasis Dream Kilo Alpha (King's Best (USA))
7069a[2]

**Alpha Delphini** *Bryan Smart*
3 b g Captain Gerrard(IRE) Easy To Imagine (USA) (Cozzene (USA))
7501[14]

**Alpha Delta Whisky** *John Gallagher* a73 77
6 ch g Intikhab(USA) Chispa (Imperial Frontier (USA))
*1019[7]* 2070[5] 3033[5] 3939[2] ◆ 4553[2] 5535[5] 6455[14] 6872[16] *7806[3]*

**Alpha Spirit** *Mick Channon* a66 63
2 b f Sixties Icon Queen Of Narnia (Hunting Lion (IRE))
1726[6] 2128[4] *2460[4]* 3063[6] 5285[9] *6016[7]* 6735[4]

**Alpha Tauri (USA)** *Charles Smith* a79 72
8 b g Aldebaran(USA) Seven Moons (JPN) (Sunday Silence (USA))
347[6] 565[2] 651[4] 766[2] 862[4] (1127) 4288[13] 8180[2]

**Alpine Affair** *Brian Meehan* a60 77
2 b c Invincible Spirit(IRE) Demi Voix (Halling (USA))
1977[13] 2298[10] 3136[7] (4410) 4605[3] 5129[5] 6135[4] 7116[10]

**Alpine Flower (IRE)** *Tim Easterby* 66
3 b f Intense Focus(USA) Wine House (IRE) (Sadler's Wells (USA))
1713[4] 2985[4] 3486[3] 4067[4] 5055[6]

**Alpine Mist** *Peter Makin* a75 44
4 b f Elusive Quality(USA) Snowtime (IRE) (Galileo (IRE))
456[8] 800[3] 2012[8] 2471[7] 3235[8]

**Alpine Storm (IRE)** *Mark Johnston* a74 77
3 b f Raven's Pass(USA) Lurina (IRE) (Lure (USA))
1427[6] 3643[3] 3923[4] (4516) 4832[4] 5235[2] 5566[2] 5758[5] 6129[5] 6316[4] 6616[7] 6793[5] 7185[3] 7829[8]

**Al Queena (GER)** *Frau C Barsig* 91
3 ch f Lord Of England(GER) Al Qahira (GER) (Big Shuffle (USA))
7483a[4]

**Alquimia (IRE)** *Richard Fahey* a52 82
3 gr f Medicean Cleide Da Silva (USA) (Monarchos (USA))
1346[3] (1723) 2274[2] 3200[8] 3663[3] 4300[2] 4782[10] 5446[7] 5999[4] (7445)

**Al Quintana (GER)** *S Richter* 98
5 b m Sholokhov(IRE) Al Qahira (GER) (Big Shuffle (USA))
5965a[3] 7483a[14]

**Alraihjan (KSA)** *B Al Shaibani* a90
4 gr g Official Flame(USA) Wadood (KSA) (Mizzen Mast (USA))
304a[9] 504a[13]

**Al Raqeeb (IRE)** *Gary Harrison* a81 78
4 b g Lawman(FR) Caerlina (IRE) (Caerleon (USA))
587[5] 843[8]

**Al Rayyan (IRE)** *Kevin Ryan* 78
2 ch c Danehill Dancer(IRE) Inca Trail (USA) (Royal Academy (USA))
2450[4] 4467[3] (5078) 5762[7] 6684[4]

**Alsaaeqah (KSA)** *B Al Shaibani* 107
7 b m Dynever(USA) Forante (USA) (Forty Niner (USA))
(393a) 897a[9]

**Al Saham** *Saeed bin Suroor* a94 106
5 b g Authorized(IRE) Local Spirit (USA) (Lion Cavern (USA))
(2142) (3730) 4213[8]

**Al Senad** *Peter Chapple-Hyam* 82
3 ch c Exceed And Excel(AUS) Waafiah (Anabaa (USA))
1486[3] 2384[3] 3156[3] (3951) 4328[8] 5677[10] 6814[6]

**Alshaahraman (USA)** *Brian Meehan* 57
2 b c Daaher(CAN) Bashoosha (USA) (Distorted Humor (USA))
6259[12]

**Al Shoogh** *David Simcock* a66 24
3 b f Nayef(USA) Bakhoor (IRE) (Royal Applause)
323[6]

**Al's Memory (IRE)** *David Evans* a87 78
5 b g Red Clubs(IRE) Consensus (IRE) (Common Grounds)
38[7] 153[2] 234[7] 472[6] 689[7] 1020[8] 1630[9] 4262[2] 4907[3] 5281[9] 5750[9] 6639[6] 7071[11] 7759[6] 7905[4] 8017[4] 8299[2]

**Altaayil (IRE)** *Sir Michael Stoute* a91 97
3 br g Sea The Stars(IRE) Alleluia (Caerleon (USA))
1587[8] 2485[2] 3270[2] 3884[2] 6344[2] 7102[2]

**Altaira** *Mme C Head-Maarek* a68 73
3 b c Dubawi(IRE) Peach Pearl (Invincible Spirit (IRE))
8005a[7]

**Alta Lilea (IRE)** *Mark Johnston* 103
4 b f Galileo(IRE) In My Life (IRE) (Rainbow Quest (USA))
2294[10] 2785[10]

**Altano (GER)** *A Wohler* 116
8 b g Galileo(IRE) Alanda (GER) (Lando (GER))
(2229a) 3377[6] 5743a[3] 7486a[8]

**Alterite (FR)** *Chad C Brown* 113
4 b f Literato(FR) Ana Luna (Dream Well (FR))
5459a[11]

**Altesse** *J S Bolger* 101
3 ch f Hernando(FR) Alvarita (Selkirk (USA))
7144a[3]

**Al Thakhira** *Marco Botti* 110
3 b f Dubawi(IRE) Dahama (Green Desert (USA))
1435[2] 2195a[8] 2581a[11] 6254[3] (6922) 7242[5]

**Althania (USA)** *John Gosden* a74
2 ch f Street Cry(IRE) Gabriellina Giof (Ashkalani (IRE))
5305[3] ◆ 7944[2]

**Altharoos (IRE)** *Sally Hall* 97
4 br g Sakhee(USA) Thamara (USA) (Street Cry (IRE))
4922[14] 5446[9] 5771[10] 6491[7]

**Althon (IRE)** *John Gosden* 54
2 b c Dansili Mountain Chain (USA) (Royal Academy (USA))
3929[8]

**Altjira** *Scott Dixon* 36
3 ch g Piccolo The City Kid (IRE) (Danetime (IRE))
4539[4]

**Alto Adige (FR)** *F Chappet* 85
2 ch c Vespone(IRE) Tempola (FR) (Anabaa (USA))
6618a[3]

**Altroquando (IRE)** *Stefano Botti* 94
2 b c Aussie Rules(USA) Altezza Reale (King's Best (USA))
7479a[4]

**Altruism (IRE)** *Charlie Appleby* 97
4 b g Authorized(IRE) Bold Assumption (Observatory (USA))
2154[5] ◆

**Altruistic (IRE)** *J P Murtagh* 104
3 ch c Galileo(IRE) Altesse Imperiale (IRE) (Rock Of Gibraltar (IRE))
2187a[6]

**Aluette (FR)** *S Smrczek* 61
2 ch f Sabiango(GER) Al Qahira (GER) (Big Shuffle (USA))
6950a[5]

**Alumina (IRE)** *Andrew Balding* a88 73
3 b f Invincible Spirit(IRE) La Reine Mambo (USA) (High Yield (USA))
86[3] (374) (547) (613) ◆ (1006) (1093) (1225) 3357[15] 3724[9] 4323[10]

**Alumna (USA)** *A Fabre* a75 109
4 b f Mr Greeley(USA) Alma Mater (Sadler's Wells (USA))
1827a[10] 7070a[6]

**Alutiq (IRE)** *Olly Stevens* a86 99
3 b f Kodiac Marasem (Cadeaux Genereux)
(183) 1067[7] 1555[6] 2343[7] 3357[21] 3788[8] 5176[8]

**Alvar (USA)** *M Halford* a75 20
6 ch g Forest Danger(USA) Diameter (USA) (Boundary (USA))
(7961a)

**Al Waab (IRE)** *Doug Watson* 111
4 ch c Danehill Dancer(IRE) Aunt Julia (In The Wings)
595a[14] 812a[5] 902a[12]

**Always Be Ready** *Lady Cecil* a65 19
2 b c Equiano(FR) Broughtons Flight (IRE) (Hawk Wing (USA))
5248[8] 6603[8] 7113[2]

**Always Ready (FR)** *C Bresson* a81 80
3 b c Orpen(USA) Always Pretty (FR) (El Prado (IRE))
2630a[4]

**Always Resolute** *Timothy Jarvis* a64 71
3 b g Refuse To Bend(IRE) Mad Annie (USA) (Anabaa (USA))
1847[12] 4356[5] (5077) 6480[13] 7526[5]

**Always Smile (IRE)** *Saeed bin Suroor* a75
2 b f Cape Cross(IRE) Eastern Joy (Dubai Destination (USA))
(7345) ◆

**Always True (GER)** *N Milliere* a59 33
4 ch f Martillo(GER) All An Star (Galileo (IRE))
178a[8]

**Alwilda** *Sir Mark Prescott Bt* a98 95
4 gr f Hernando(FR) Albanova (Alzao (USA))
(3932) 4945[6] 5668[8] 6288[9] 6979[2] 7554[3] 7769a[5]

**Alys Love** *William Muir* 87
3 b f New Approach(IRE) Porthcawl (Singspiel (IRE))
1435[9] 2384[4] 3276[4] 3755[2] 4271[10]

**Alzammaar (USA)** *Charles Hills* a71 77
3 b g Birdstone(USA) Alma Mater (Sadler's Wells (USA))
1218[3] 1627[2] 2494[3] 3655[8]

**Alzanti (USA)** *Amanda Perrett* a77 87
3 b f Arch(USA) Proud Fact (USA) (Known Fact (USA))
(3890) 4679[6] 6129[9]

**Alzarica (IRE)** *Malcolm Saunders*
3 b g Amadeus Wolf Allegorica (IRE) (Alzao (USA))
5504[14] 6087[11]

**Amabelle (GER)** *Waldemar Hickst* 95
2 ch f Danehill Dancer(IRE) Antonym (USA) (Bahri (USA))
6778a[3] 7315a[4]

**Amadea (GER)** *P Schiergen* 73
3 bb f Lauro(GER) Amore (GER) (Lando (GER))
4064a[7]

**Amadeity (IRE)** *Jo Hughes* a69 52
2 b g Amadeus Wolf Magadar (USA) (Lujain (USA))
4429[4] 7778[6] 8166[2]

**Amadeus Dream (IRE)** *Milton Bradley*
2 b c Amadeus Wolf Spring Glory (Dr Fong (USA))
3934[12] 6903[8]

**Amadeus Wolfe Tone (IRE)** *Jamie Osborne* a96 90
5 b g Amadeus Wolf Slieve (Selkirk (USA))
2833[6] (3313) 3702[9] 4121[5] 4355[6] 4983[7] 5650[7] (6089) (6423) 6872[7] (7365) 7700[4] 7843[10] 8045[6] ◆ 8141[3]

**Amadiva (IRE)** *Dean Ivory* a22 32
3 b f Amadeus Wolf Divine Quest (Kris)
3229[9]

**Amahoro** *Mick Channon* a84 84
3 b f Sixties Icon Evanesce (Lujain (USA))
487[2] 613[5] 1570[2] 2122[7] 2508[3] 2626[2] 3068[3] 3565[2] 4133[2] 4328[2]

**Amandichope (FR)** *S Wattel* a54 71
2 b f Soave(GER) Thimea (FR) (Nombre Premier)
6591a[4]

**Amantius** *Johnny Farrelly* a77 50
5 b g Multiplex Ghana (GER) (Bigstone (IRE))
2207[3]

**Amanto (GER)** *Paul Nicholls* 74
4 b g Medicean Amore (GER) (Lando (GER))
5435[2]

**A Ma Reine (FR)** *S Wattel* a55 35
2 gr f King's Best(USA) Apparence (IRE) (Sinndar (IRE))
4883a[8] 5619a[8]

**Amarillo (IRE)** *P Schiergen* 115
5 b h Holy Roman Emperor(IRE) Alte Kunst (IRE) (Royal Academy (USA))
(2006a) 2765[9] 4758[5] 5966a[7] 7242[8]

**Amaron** *Andreas Lowe* 117
5 ch h Shamardal(USA) Amandalini (Bertolini (USA))
(1478a) 1908a[7] (3511a) 4247a[3] 6054a[2] 6808a[5]

**Amaseena (IRE)** *Roger Varian* a70 76
3 gr f Shamardal(USA) Indian Belle (IRE) (Indian Ridge)
2130[2]

**Amative (FR)** *S Wattel* a73 70
3 ch f Green Tune(USA) Alamagna (FR) (Anabaa (USA))
3745a[3]

**Amaze** *Brian Ellison* 90
6 ch g Pivotal Dazzle (Gone West (USA))
1164[20] 1306[4] 2137[6] 2790[4] 3055[2] 3718[2]

**Amaze Me** *Nick Littmoden* 80
2 ch f Aqlaam Princess Miletrian (IRE) (Danehill (USA))
5429[4] ◆ 6067[13] 6751[8]

**Amazing Blue Sky** *Ruth Carr* a42 65
8 b g Barathea(IRE) Azure Lake (USA) (Lac Ouimet (USA))
1675[12] 2476[8] 2738[4] 2872[4] 3052[4] (3535) 3912[4] 4293[4] 4709[5] 5145[5] 5495[4] 5765[6] 6627[3] 6825[5]

**Amazing Maria (IRE)** *Ed Dunlop* 106
3 gr f Mastercraftsman(IRE) Messias Da Silva (USA) (Tale Of The Cat (USA))
2960[17] 5407a[11] 6254[10]

**Amazing Star (IRE)** *John Flint* a74 76
9 b g Soviet Star(USA) Sadika (IRE) (Bahhare (USA))
(562) 790a[5] 8120[4] 8260[9]

**Amazonit (GER)** *Waldemar Hickst* 94
3 bb c Kamsin(GER) Arpista (GER) (Chief Singer)
4007a[18] 6806a[11] 7316a[7]

**Amazour (IRE)** *Ismail Mohammed* a74 76
2 b c Azamour(IRE) Choose Me (IRE) (Choisir (AUS))
4424[8] 5488[3] ◆ 6270[2] 7037[2]

**Ambella (IRE)** *Ian Williams* a69 59
4 gr f Dark Angel(IRE) Showmesomething (IRE) (Mujadil (USA))
456[6] (660) 748[4] 1510[5] 1846[8] 6767[9] 7303[6] 7854[7] 7987[3] 8043[2] 8259[3] 8311[6]

**Amber Crystal** *John Gallagher* a45 73
2 b f Multiplex Glitz (IRE) (Hawk Wing (USA))
1764[6] 2276[3] 2716[2] 3211[3] 4338[2] 5028[2] 5620[5] (5779) 6322[7] 6629[8]

**Amber Isle (USA)** *Roger Charlton* a78 78
3 b f First Defence(USA) Family (USA) (Danzig (USA))
2682[2] (3469) 4078[9]

**Amberjam (IRE)** *Martin Smith* a43 23
4 b g Duke Of Marmalade(IRE) Makarova (IRE) (Sadler's Wells (USA))
915[5] 1574[6]

**Amberley (FR)** *E Moullec* a76 69
5 b g Anabaa(USA) Desert Jewel (USA) (Caerleon (USA))
836a[10]

**Amber Mile** *Ralph Beckett* 66
2 b f Rip Van Winkle(IRE) Rose Street (IRE) (Noverre (USA))
6208[7] 6868[5] 7405[7]

**Amber Moon** *Ann Stokell* a47 30
9 ch m Singspiel(IRE) Merewood (USA) (Woodman (USA))
78[6] 268[3] 352[2] 530[5] 869[5] 964[7] 1036[5] 1386[9] 1503[7]

**Amber Sky (AUS)** *P F Yiu* 120
5 b g Exceed And Excel(AUS) Truly Wicked (AUS) (Rubiton (AUS))
(1179a) 7897a[8]

**Ambiance (IRE)** *Katharina Stenefeldt* 93
3 b c Camacho Thawrah (IRE) (Green Desert (USA))
2287[5] 3245[9] 3478[9] 6387a[4]

**Ambitious Boy** *Andrew Hollinshead* a87 78
5 bl g Striking Ambition Cherished Love (IRE) (Tomba)
5081[7] 6095[4] 6313[3] 6736[4] 7071[3] 7183[3] (7521) 7821[7] 8141[5]

**Ambitious Brew (USA)** *Martin F Jones* a98 105
4 bb g Tizbud(USA) Kathwen (USA) (Forest Wildcat (USA))
7609a[7]

**Ambitious Dragon (NZ)** *A T Millard* 114
8 b g Pins(AUS) Golden Gamble (NZ) (Oregon (USA))
7898a[3]

**Ambitious Icarus** *Richard Guest* a60 86
5 b g Striking Ambition Nesting Box (Grand Lodge (USA))
2136[9] 2350[10] 2727[3] 2803[8] 3399[5] 3831[7] 5170[8] 5298[2] 5913[8] 6235[8] (6452) 6511[16] 6758[6] 7103[6] 7215[4] 7505[2] 7534[8]

**Ambleside** *Michael Easterby* a65 85
4 b g Cape Cross(IRE) Zarara (USA) (Manila (USA))
5792[5] 6171[9] 6761[3] 7281[12] 7409[10]

**Ambonnay Rouge (IRE)** *Michael Appleby* a20
2 ch f Arakan(USA) Ambonnay (Ashkalani (IRE))
7406[10] 7649[7]

**Ambrass (GER)** *W Mongil* a43
3 ch c Konigstiger(GER) Alphabetique (FR) (Zieten (USA))
5027a[8]

**Ameenah (FR)** *F Rossi* 105
2 b f American Post Miximaa (Anabaa (USA))
(7654a)

**Amelia George** *Julia Feilden* a13
4 b f Avonbridge Tamara (Marju (IRE))
422[8] 1024[10]

**Amelia Jay** *Danielle McCormick* a54 55
4 b f Avonbridge Rainbow Spectrum (FR) (Spectrum (IRE))
318[5]

**Amenable (IRE)** *Conor Dore* a75 79
7 b g Bertolini(USA) Graceful Air (IRE) (Danzero (AUS))
8[7] 258[9] 1017[10] 1689[3] 1966[4] (2232) 2486[7] 2677[4] (2907) 3246[2] (3359) 4050[3] 4494[12] 5601[10] 5951[7] 6455[11] 6821[7] 7830[8] 8086[7]

**American Artist (IRE)** *Roger Varian* 85
2 ch c Danehill Dancer(IRE) American Adventure (USA) (Miswaki (USA))
6058[4] (6652)

**American Devil (FR)** *E Libaud* 112
5 b h American Post Alcestes Selection (Selkirk (USA))
(2799a) 3451[5] 3997a[2] 6182a[3]

**American Hope (USA)** *Mike Murphy* a103 109
3 b c Lemon Drop Kid(USA) Cedrat (FR) (Enrique)
778[2] 1067[2] 1300[3] 1555[4] 3378[6] 4647[2] 5665[12]

**Amethyst Dawn (IRE)** *Tim Easterby* a38 67
8 gr m Act One A L'Aube (IRE) (Selkirk (USA))
548[5] 718[9] 3099[6] 3885[6]

**Ametrine (IRE)** *William Jarvis* 62
3 b f Fastnet Rock(AUS) Amethyst (IRE) (Sadler's Wells (USA))
2404[14] 2927[3] 3326[3] 4092[6]

**Am Fae Govan Tae (IRE)** *Seamus Durack* a40
3 b c Acclamation Lysandra (IRE) (Danehill (USA))
605[8]

**Amira's Prince (IRE)** *William Mott* 114
5 b h Teofilo(IRE) Twice The Ease (Green Desert (USA))
2228a[6]

**Amirli (IRE)** *A De Royer-Dupre* a69 83
3 ch g Medicean Amenapinga (FR) (Spinning World (USA))
3869a[5]

**Amir Pasha (UAE)** *Micky Hammond* a42 58
9 br g Halling(USA) Clarinda (IRE) (Lomond (USA))
2620[5] 3398[5] 3532[7] 5200[8]

**Amis Reunis** *Alan Berry* a56 59
5 b m Bahamian Bounty Spring Clean (FR) (Danehill (USA))
9[5] 58[8] 196[6] 353[10] 466[9] 692[8] 1270[7] 1497[5] 1972[10] 2219[4] 2479[5] 3099[2] (3530) 3833[2] 4005[6] 4194[7] 4511[4] 4629[7] 4961[2] 5265[3] 5499[8] 6495[8] 6595[6] 6758[5] 6834[7] 7644[13] 7783[8]

**Amistades (IRE)** *F-X De Chevigny* a77 72
3 b f Iffraaj Rose's Destination (IRE) (Dubai Destination (USA))
795a[5] 4464a[12]

**Amona (IRE)** *Andreas Lowe* 44
2 rg f Aussie Rules(USA) Abbasharjah (GER) (Tiger Hill (IRE))
7315a[12]

**Among Angels** *Richard Hannon* 81
2 b g Acclamation Love Action (IRE) (Motivator)
2298[4] (2623) 3322[9] 3751[5] 5929[6]

**Amonit (FR)** *J Hirschberger* 87
4 b c Kentucky Dynamite(USA) Seduisante (FR) (Anabaa (USA))
5461a[6] 6180a[10]

**Amontillado (IRE)** *Richard Hannon* a60 45
3 b f Pastoral Pursuits Almost Amber (USA) (Mt. Livermore (USA))
157[4] 236[6] 1029[7]

**Amood (IRE)** *Simon West* a85 81
3 ch c Elnadim(USA) Amanah (USA) (Mr Prospector (USA))
(2883) 3719[4] 5649[4] 6886[4] 7185[5] 7530[2]

**Amorous Adventure (GER)** *K Demme* 98
3 ch c Poseidon Adventure(IRE) Auenprincess (GER) (Kornado)
4007a[8]

**Amosite** *J R Jenkins* a78 76
8 b m Central Park(IRE) Waterline Dancer (IRE) (Danehill Dancer (IRE))
362[2] 757[9] 1080[5] 1224[3] 1739[3] 2096[3] 2398[2] 3125[5] 4408[6] (4768) 5097[3] 5535[6] 7775[9] 8182[7]

**Amour A Papa (FR)** *J-Y Artu* 111
3 gr f Montmartre(FR) Prudence Royale (FR) (Loup Solitaire (USA))
2267a[2] 3289a[2]

**Amour De Nuit (IRE)** *Sir Mark Prescott Bt* a61 48
2 b g Azamour(IRE) Umthoulah (IRE) (Unfuwain (USA))
6985[8] 7228[5] ◆ 7631[12]

**Amourita (IRE)** *Jonathan Portman* a61 24
3 b f Azamour(IRE) Akarita (IRE) (Akarad (FR))
1011[2] 1380[6] 2613[7] 6426[12] 6856[9] 7229[6]

**Ampleforth** *Ian Williams* a67 75
6 ch g Pivotal Anna Amalia (IRE) (In The Wings)
1140[3]

**Amralah (IRE)** *Robert Hickmott* 115
4 b c Teofilo(IRE) Sharp Mode (USA) (Diesis)
1973[3] 2314[6] 3930[2] (4437) (5175) 7602a[14]

**Amtired** *Marjorie Fife* a63 64
8 gr g Beauchamp King Rising Talisker (Primitive Rising (USA))
269[2] 366[7] 1129[3] 1674[9] 2806[4] 3155[8]

**Amulet** *Eve Johnson Houghton* a72 102
4 gr f Ishiguru(USA) Loveofmylife (Dr Fong (USA))
1437[11] 1945[6] (2144) 2956[9] 3244[11] 4060[4] 4607[6] 6458[4] 6707[7] 7095a[2] 7629a[2] 7916a[5]

**Amy Eria (IRE)** *F Rohaut* a85 107
3 b f Shamardal(USA) Berroscoberro (FR) (Octagonal (NZ))
(4009a) 5407a[5] 6182a[9]

**Amygdala (USA)** *Stuart Williams* a83 84
3 ch f Van Nistelrooy(USA) Sabreen (USA) (Foolish Pleasure (USA))
4811[3] ◆ 5211[4] 6021[8] 7017[3] 7365[10]

**Anaconda (FR)** *Tom Dascombe* a108 83
5 b g Anabaa(USA) Porretta (IRE) (Indian Ridge)
716[3] 1068[10] 1558[9] ◆ 2085[11] (3064) 3645[2]

**Anaerobio (ARG)** *M F De Kock* a81 113
7 b h Catcher In The Rye(IRE) Potra Anala (ARG) (Potrillon (ARG))
(112a) (308a) 678a[5] 902a[3] 1181a[5]

**Ana Ettihady (ITY)** *Kevin Ryan* a29
3 b g Red Rocks(IRE) American Beauty (GER) (Goofalik (USA))
930[6] 1126[5]

**Anahita (FR)** *J-C Rouget* 104
3 b f Turtle Bowl(IRE) Nazlia (FR) (Polish Precedent (USA))
3808a[6] 4840a[2]

**Ana Musica (FR)** *P Demercastel* a47 61
4 b f Green Tune(USA) Ana Marie (FR) (Anabaa (USA))
935a[4]

**Anaphortuna (FR)** *A Clement* a35
3 b f Soldier Of Fortune(IRE) Anaphora (IRE) (Goofalik (USA))
599a[9]

**Ana Shababiya (IRE)** *Ismail Mohammed* a74 74
4 ch f Teofilo(IRE) Call Later (USA) (Gone West (USA))
1348[3] 1617[10] 2199[4] 3080[3] 4092[5] 5036[9] (5975) 6813[2] 7522[10] 8169[5]

**Anastazia** *Paul D'Arcy* a75 71
2 br f Kyllachy Meddle (Diktat)
2918[5] 3563[4] 4126[5] 4605[2] 5285[7] 6008[4] 6555[8] 6924[7] (7728) (7890) 8046[3] 8308[4]

**Anaxis (FR)** *Rod Collet* a84 72
7 ch g Muhtathir Monadis (USA) (Miswaki (USA))
5964a[10]

**An Cat Dubh (IRE)** *Ian Williams* a74 76
5 b g One Cool Cat(USA) Bella Estella (GER) (Sternkoenig (IRE))
5895[9] 6346[6] 6767[4] (7098) 7435a[5]

**An Chulainn (IRE)** *Mark Johnston* a71 74
3 ch f Tamayuz Livius Lady (IRE) (Titus Livius (FR))
2274[8] 2639[5] 4515[3] 4903[2] 5046[2] 5768[2] 5999[3] 6365[4] 6870[9]

**Ancient Cross** *Michael Easterby* a56 106
10 b g Machiavellian(USA) Magna Graecia (IRE) (Warning)
1484[12] 1734[16] 2283[12] 2786[8] 4683[11] 7080[8] 7441[16]

**Ancient Greece** *George Baker* a77 83
7 b g Pivotal Classicism (USA) (A.P. Indy (USA))
56[9] 376[7] 638a[10] 729a[7] 843[3] 1281[8] (1624a) (2592a) 5721[10] (6251) 6714[11]

**Ancient King (IRE)** *Peter G Moody* 100
4 b g Ramonti(FR) Queen Of Rap (IRE) (Alhaarth (IRE))
7126a[10]

**Ancil (USA)** *Mrs Joan Scott* a61 104
5 ch g City Zip(USA) Le Grand Belle (USA) (With Approval (CAN))
3319[14] 6391a[11]

**Anderiego (IRE)** *David O'Meara* 101
6 b g Invincible Spirit(IRE) Anna Frid (GER) (Big Shuffle (USA))
1733[6] ◆ 1958[11] 2699[4] 3254[14] 3383[2] 3667[3] (4635) 4922[12] 5681[3] 6214[3] (6476) 6936[8] 7081[11]

**Andoyas (GER)** *J Hirschberger* 100
3 bb c Lando(GER) Auengunst (GER) (Waky Nao)
1781a[3] 2377a[4]

**Andreas (GER)** *Markus Klug* 102
5 ch h Dr Fong(USA) Annouche (GER) (Unfuwain (USA))
729a[5]

**Andretti** *Roger Varian* a74
2 b c Oasis Dream Anna Amalia (IRE) (In The Wings)
3474[9] 4301[8] 6103[5] (6662) (6944)

**Android (IRE)** *Clive Cox* a78 73
3 ch g Dandy Man(IRE) Noble View (USA) (Distant View (USA))
284[2] 605[3] (1379) 2083[8] 2945[8] 3225[4] 3790[7]

**Andry Brusselles** *C Delcher-Sanchez* a77 96
4 b f Hurricane Run(IRE) Dont Dili Dali (Dansili)
6392a[2] (6917a) 7486a[13]

**Aneedh** *Clive Mulhall* a66 71
4 b g Lucky Story(USA) Seed Al Maha (USA) (Seeking The Gold (USA))
1659[6] 3205[14] 4710[12] 5788[2] (6622) 7866 [7]

**Aneto Peak** *Nigel Tinkler* 53
2 b g Sleeping Indian Spanish Gold (Vettori (IRE))
4493[5] 5086[7] 5297[8] 5885[9] 6447[13]

**Anfield** *Mick Quinn* a56 46
3 b f Captain Gerrard(IRE) Billie Holiday (Fairy King (USA))
15[5] 213[6] 481[4] 1860[6] 3433[7] 3679[8] 6340[7]

**Angela Renee (USA)** *Todd Pletcher* a107
2 b f Bernardini(USA) Pilfer (USA) (Deputy Minister (CAN))
7606a[10]

**Angel Cake (IRE)** *Michael Appleby* a72 48
5 b m Dark Angel(IRE) Royal Jelly (King's Best (USA))
589[6] 718[5] 736[8] 3334[6] 3971[12]

**Angelena Ballerina (IRE)** *Andy Turnell* a13 22
7 ch m Indian Haven Nom Francais (First Trump)
7908[8] 8314[10]

**Angel Flores (IRE)** *Lee Carter* a76 80
3 b f Art Connoisseur(IRE) Emmas Princess (IRE) (Bahhare (USA))
3575[6] (4297) 4898[11] 5675[2] 7729[11] 8040[11]

**Angel Gabrial (IRE)** *Richard Fahey* a94 111
5 b g Hurricane Run(IRE) Causeway Song (USA) (Giant's Causeway (USA))
956[4] 1562[4] (1735) ◆ 2073[2] (3717) 4823[5] 5652[5] 6288[7]

**Angelic Air** *John Gosden* a85 80
3 b f Oasis Dream Innocent Air (Galileo (IRE))
(1767) ◆ 2340[11]

**Angelic Lord (IRE)** *Tom Dascombe* 104
2 b c Dark Angel(IRE) Divine Design (IRE) (Barathea (IRE))
(2866) 3318[6] 4123[5] (6230)

**Angelic Upstart (IRE)** *Andrew Balding* a85 92
6 b g Singspiel(IRE) Rada (IRE) (Danehill (USA))
(1267) 2311[3] 2959[8] 4118[3] (4827) 5669[2] 6257[7] 6713[10]

**Angelito** *Ed McMahon* a80 83
5 ch g Primo Valentino(IRE) Supreme Angel (Beveled (USA))
2945[5] 3213[2] 3948[4] 5677[2] 6096[5] 6324[5] 7073[6]

**Angel Light (SWE)** *Tommy Gustafsson* a77 94
6 b m Most Welcome Maudie (SWE) (Diaghlyphard (USA))
(6388a)

**Angel Of Joy (IRE)** *G M Lyons* 83
3 gr g Dark Angel(IRE) Moy Joy (IRE) (Orpen (USA))
5958a[15]

**Angelo Poliziano** *Jo Hughes* a73 74
8 ch g Medicean Helen Sharp (Pivotal)
208[3] 272[3] 478[2] 845[4] 889[5] 1448[8]

**Angelot Du Berlais (FR)** *Dr Richard Newland* a67 86
5 b g Poliglote Afragha (IRE) (Darshaan)
463[4] 558[2]

**Angel Royal (FR)** *H-A Pantall* a75
2 b c Astronomer Royal(USA) Lady Angele (FR) (Ski Chief (USA))
8148a[4]

**Angels Above (IRE)** *John Butler* a55
2 b c Dark Angel(IRE) Fag End (IRE) (Treasure Kay)
7985[6] 8192[8]

**Angels Calling** *K R Burke* a38 64
4 b f Multiplex Angel Voices (IRE) (Tagula (IRE))
2166[7] 2454[4] 2726[4] 5000[6] 5636[6] 5889[5]

**Angel's Pursuit (IRE)** *Robert Cowell* a92 91
7 ch g Pastoral Pursuits Midnight Angel (Machiavellian (USA))
36[2] ◆ 294[5]

**Angels Wings (IRE)** *Charles Hills* a79 68
2 b f Dark Angel(IRE) Startarette (USA) (Dixieland Band (USA))
3648[7] 4396[5] (5255) 6253[12]

**Angel Terrace (USA)** *Jonathan E Sheppard* a94 102
5 ch m Ghostzapper(USA) Another Storm (USA) (Gone West (USA))
7326a[6]

**Angel Vision (IRE)** *Sir Michael Stoute* 63
2 b f Oasis Dream Islington (IRE) (Sadler's Wells (USA))
6066[4]

**Angel Way (IRE)** *Mike Murphy* a80 80
5 br m Trans Island Zilayah (USA) (Zilzal (USA))
2275[4] 3275[2] 3462[3] 4078[11] 5830[2] 7669[8]

**Anginola (IRE)** *David Dennis* a56 62
5 b m Kodiac Lady Montekin (Montekin)
1664[12] 2212[8] 3390[4] 4080[5] 4341[3] 4808[4] 5280[3] 5832[5] 5978[3] 6195[4] (6394) 6771[11]

**Anglo Irish** *John Gosden* a92 85
3 b c Dansili Tebee (Selkirk (USA))
51[2] (316) (1407) 2077[10] 3419[9] 4651[4] (5552) (6036) 7203[6]

**Anglophile** *Charlie Appleby* a103 98
3 ch g Dubawi(IRE) Anna Palariva (IRE) (Caerleon (USA))
2685[3] (2839) 3758[4] 8012[2] (8095) (8243)

**Angus Glens** *David Dennis* a73 67
4 gr g Dalakhani(IRE) Clara Bow (IRE) (Sadler's Wells (USA))
1108[5] 1354[6] 1791[4] 2248[6] 3032[3] 3818[9] (4088) 4552[4] 4942[5] 5721[7] 6252[5] 6395[6] 7251[3] 7452[6] 7628[5] 7777[2] 7866 [6] (8231) 8264[7]

**Angus Og** *K R Burke* a83 92
4 b g Pastoral Pursuits Winter Moon (Mujadil (USA))
1305[10] 1566[4] (2136) 2898[6] 6260[17] 6531[26]

**Anipa** *Roger Varian* a76 96
3 ch f Sea The Stars(IRE) Anna Amalia (IRE) (In The Wings)
(888) (1494) (2072) 2960[15] 4443[11] 6882a[8]

**Anjaal** *Richard Hannon* 111
3 ch c Bahamian Bounty Ballymore Celebre (IRE) (Peintre Celebre (USA))
1532[5] 3352[12] 4758[3] 5354[5] 6710[7]

**Anjin (IRE)** *Sir Mark Prescott Bt* a67 53
3 b g Danehill Dancer(IRE) Twyla Tharp (IRE) (Sadler's Wells (USA))
70[7] 230[4] ◆ 3683[4] 4579[7] 5185[3] 5426[4] 6037[4] 6632[5] 7118[7]

**Anjuna Beach (USA)** *Ann Stokell* a66 62
4 b g Artie Schiller(USA) Hidden Temper (USA) (Miswaki (USA))
821[11] (1023) 1215[4] (1874) 2084[7] 3553[5] 4433[6] 7651[5] 7765[10] 7895[2] 7975[7] 8145[10]

**Annaboda (IRE)** *Soren Jensen* 85
4 b f Duke Of Marmalade(IRE) Moonbi Ridge (IRE) (Definite Article)
6388a[7]

**Anna Dolce (FR)** *Harry Dunlop* a40
2 b f Areion(GER) Anna Spectra (IRE) (Spectrum (IRE))
4054[8]

**Annaluna (IRE)** *David Evans* a62 74
5 b m Whipper(USA) Annaletta (Belmez (USA))
349[7] 1242[2] 1574[3] 1895[5] (3179) (3851) 4322[3] 4818[2] 4843[3] (5924) 6360[5] 6640[6] 7065[3] 7572[4]

**Anna's Vision (IRE)** *Jeremy Noseda* a65 76
3 b f Invincible Spirit(IRE) House In Wood (FR) (Woodman (USA))
3729[2] 4590[2] 5181[2] 5417[4] 6988[4]

**Annawi** *Henry Candy* 87
4 b f Dubawi(IRE) Anna Of Brunswick (Rainbow Quest (USA))
1956[3] 2772[5] 3502[4] 4112[5]

**Anneani (IRE)** *Paul Green* 27
2 b f Bushranger(IRE) Hazium (IRE) (In The Wings)
4973[10] 5807[12] 7638[6]

**Annecdote** *Jonathan Portman* 107
4 b f Lucky Story(USA) May Fox (Zilzal (USA))
2155[3] ◆ 3355[10]

**Annes Rocket (IRE)** *Jimmy Fox* a63 78
9 b g Fasliyev(USA) Aguilas Perla (IRE) (Indian Ridge)
92[5] 288[4] 467[10] 740[6] 3825[4] 4206[4] 4564[2] 5314[7]

**Anne's Valentino** *Malcolm Jefferson* a4 62
4 b f Primo Valentino(IRE) Annie's Gift (IRE) (Presenting)
1374[5] (2213) (2620) 3269[2] 3845[5] 4115[3] 5240[2] 5794[6]

**Annie's Rose** *Bryan Smart* 55
3 b f Captain Gerrard(IRE) Annie Harvey (Fleetwood (IRE))
4998[12]

**Annina (IRE)** *Henry Candy* 86
4 b f Singspiel(IRE) Lysandra (IRE) (Danehill (USA))
2157[7] 3890[3]

**Anniversarie** *John Norton* a49 39
2 ch f Major Cadeaux Razzle (IRE) (Green Desert (USA))
4346[12] 5982[8] 6700[10] 7992[4]

**Announcement** *Ian Williams* a75 73
3 ch f Proclamation(IRE) Anapola (GER) (Polish Precedent (USA))
1013[5] 2330[4]

**Annunciation** *Richard Hannon* a100 107
4 b c Proclamation(IRE) Rockburst (Xaar)
1172[4] 1484[2] 2149[2] 3452[23] 3960[8] 4889[6] 5160[9] 5623[6]

**Anodin (IRE)** *F Head* 119
4 b c Anabaa(USA) Born Gold (USA) (Blushing Groom (FR))
1908a[5] 2587a[2] 3317[3] 5480a[2] 6971a[5] 7613a[2]

**Anonymous John (IRE)** *David Evans* a92 89
2 b g Baltic King Helibel (IRE) (Pivotal)
2756[5] 3215[3] 3524[2] 4185[4] 4939[3] 5799[3] 7254[2] (7336) (7714) (8046) 8293[2]

**Another Citizen (IRE)** *Tim Easterby* a73 82
6 b g Byron Royal Rival (IRE) (Marju (IRE))
2136[10]

**Another Cocktail** *Hughie Morrison* a81 100
4 b g Dalakhani(IRE) Yummy Mummy (Montjeu (IRE))
1651[6] 3321[2]

**Another For Joe** *Jim Goldie* 85
6 b g Lomitas Anna Kalinka (GER) (Lion Cavern (USA))
1598[9] 1970[2] (2477) 2912[7] 3050[3] (3572) 3955[5] 4491[7] 4963[6] 6476[14] 6836[13] 7567[10]

**Another Journey** *Lisa Williamson* a39 32
5 b g Rail Link Singasongosixpence (Singspiel (IRE))
150[5] 352[5] 515[3] 672[8] 2609[5] 3134[7] 3521[8] 3780[9] 7309[15]

**Another Lincolnday** *David Barron* 76
3 ch g Desideratum Another Paris (Paris House)
1969[3] 2422[9] (4360) 5449[3]

**Another Party (FR)** *Matthieu Palussiere* a107 108
3 ch c Pomellato(GER) Jummana (FR) (Cadeaux Genereux)
1207a[3] 5223a[6] 6182a[2]

**Another Royal** *Tim Easterby* 71
3 b f Byron Royal Punch (Royal Applause)
1611[3] 2165[7] 2828[6] 3440[3] 4071[2] 4512[4] 5089[2] 5715[2] 6215[3] 6674[3] (7250) (7502)

**Another Try (IRE)** *Timothy Jarvis* a76 71
9 b g Spinning World(USA) Mad Annie (USA) (Anabaa (USA))
(2124) 2684[8] 3227[9] 4156[7] 5861[4] 6477[8] 7636[2] 7931[8] 7989[10]

**Another Wise Kid (IRE)** *Paul Midgley* a89 105
6 b g Whipper(USA) Romancing (Dr Devious (IRE))
991[5] ◆ 1193[7] 1305[7] 1695[3] (2390) 3666[2] 4174[9] (4418) 4976[2] 5445[6] 6576[2] 7122[3] 7408[10]

**Anoubis (FR)** *K Borgel* 18
3 b c Elusive City(USA) Aspolina (IRE) (Trempolino (USA))
630a[7]

**Ansaab** *Alan McCabe* a91 93
6 b g Cape Cross(IRE) Dawn Raid (IRE) (Docksider (USA))
457[2] 840[13] 1164[6] (1483) 1715[8] 2253[15] 2699[3] 3271[4] 3917[3] 4447[2] 4661[2] 5418[9] 6531[12] 6713[13]

**An Saighdiur (IRE)** *Andrew Slattery* a93 111
7 b g Acclamation Brief Sentiment (IRE) (Brief Truce (USA))
(1333a) ◆ 1824a[8] 2570a[3] 3284a[8] 5219a[6] 5699a[7] 6533[7] 7140a[3] 7272[14]

**Ansgar (IRE)** *Sabrina J Harty* a99 117
6 b g Celtic Swing Jemmy's Girl (IRE) (Pennekamp (USA))
3317[10] (4459a) 5361a[7] (5722) (6328) 6971a[6]

**Answered** *J S Bolger* 105
3 b c Authorized(IRE) Dublino (USA) (Lear Fan (USA))
1458a[2] 2187a[4]

**Antalya (GER)** *Markus Klug* 23
3 b f Areion(GER) Annina (GER) (Diktat)
7483a[15]

**Antequera (FR)** *C Lecrivain* a44
3 b f Carlotamix(FR) Winter Brook (FR) (Al Nasr (FR))
599a[8]

**Anthem Alexander (IRE)** *Edward Lynam* 115
2 ch f Starspangledbanner(AUS) Lady Alexander (IRE) (Night Shift (USA))
(3353) 5608[3] 6751[2]

**Antigua (SWE)** *Tommy Gustafsson* 79
2 ch f Archipenko(USA) On Light (SWE) (Midyan (USA))
6386a[4]

**Antinori (IRE)** *S Seemar* a94 94
8 b g Fasliyev(USA) Albavilla (Spectrum (IRE))
242a[3]

**Antioch (IRE)** *Jennie Candlish*
3 b g Papal Bull Sharadja (IRE) (Doyoun)
167[8]

**Antiquus (IRE)** *Ms Joanna Morgan* a87 87
5 bb m Footstepsinthesand Antiguan Wells (IRE) (Sadler's Wells (USA))
3737a[13] 7873a[5]

**Anton Chigurh** *Philip McBride* a73 80
5 b g Oasis Dream Barathiki (Barathea (IRE))
1128[5] 1439[10] 1811[5] 2034[8] 5320[4] 6035[7] 6713[15] 6841[4]

**Anton Dolin (IRE)** *Michael Mullineaux* a34 36
6 ch g Danehill Dancer(IRE) Ski For Gold (Shirley Heights)
5371[11] 5600[11] 6062[12]

**Anwar Dubai** *M Al Muhairi* a42
3 ch f Aqlaam Ha'Penny Beacon (Erhaab (USA))
203a[10]

**Anya** *Henry Candy* a87 82
5 b m Monsieur Bond(IRE) Dyanita (Singspiel (IRE))
2121[6] 3066[3] 4271[7] 4968[2] (5505) 6681[2]

**Any Given Day (IRE)** *Donald McCain* a45 67
9 gr g Clodovil(IRE) Five Of Wands (Caerleon (USA))
5572[6]

**Any Given Time (IRE)** *David Simcock* a34
2 ch c Fast Company(IRE) Five Of Wands (Caerleon (USA))
6660[11] 7739[13]

**Anymore (FR)** *J-Y Artu* a64 60
3 ch f My Risk(FR) Mont Doree (FR) (Mansonnien (FR))
1139a[9]

**Anytimeatall (IRE)** *Alan Bailey* a19 63
3 b f Kodiac Under My Skin (IRE) (Mark Of Esteem (IRE))
4307[4] 5061[5] 5860[10] 6815[11]

**Aomen Rock** *James Fanshawe* a78 65
4 b g Rock Of Gibraltar(IRE) Siren Sound (Singspiel (IRE))
1281[9] 1799[4] 2687[8] 3123[4] (4073) 5040[7] 6035[4] 6904[9]

**Apache (IRE)** *Jane Chapple-Hyam* a94 93
6 b g Galileo(IRE) Charroux (IRE) (Darshaan)
2461[11]

**Apache Glory (USA)** *John Stimpson* a80 86
6 bb m Cherokee Run(USA) Jumeirah Glory (USA) (Deputy Minister (CAN))
146[2] 369[4] 849[8] 1022[7] 2270[14] 5284[6] 6341[8] 7522[6] 8102[4]

**Apache Gold (IRE)** *John J Walsh* a56 66
6 b g Golden Snake(USA) Lady Sarelle (IRE) (Tagula (IRE))
5958a[13]

**Apache Spirit** *A Fabre* 107
3 b c Invincible Spirit(IRE) Agathe Rare (IRE) (Sadler's Wells (USA))
1481a[8]

**Apache Storm** *Michael Appleby* a87 76
2 ch f Pivotal Best Side (IRE) (King's Best (USA))
6453[4] ◆ 6700[4] (7192) 7564[3] 8059[2]

**Aphrilis (IRE)** *Brian Ellison* a37 61
3 b f Tagula(IRE) Gutter Press (IRE) (Raise A Grand (IRE))
2217[7] 4873[5] 5246[2] 5642[4] 6765[6] 7420[11]

**Apollo Eleven (IRE)** *Donald McCain* 58
5 b g Manduro(GER) Arlesienne (IRE) (Alzao (USA))
7008[10]

**Apophenia** *Richard Fahey* a54
3 b f Virtual Quadrophenia (College Chapel)
5[4] 622[7]

**Aposcalivic (FR)** *P Lenogue* a54 61
3 ch f Falco(USA) Exaltante (Cape Cross (IRE))
5227a[5]

**Apostle (IRE)** *David Simcock* a97 97
5 gr g Dark Angel(IRE) Rosy Dudley (IRE) (Grand Lodge (USA))
(38) 426[3] 566[2] 715[11] 2113[5] 2758[2] 3244[5] 3716[5] 4169[3] 4347[3] (4938) 5919[4] 6281[3]

**Apparatchika** *M F De Kock* 56
3 b f Archipenko(USA) Kesara (Sadler's Wells (USA))
4590[4]

**Appease** *John Butler* a83 58
5 b g Oasis Dream Penchee (Grand Lodge (USA))
560[3] ◆ 698[5] 1014[2] 1241[2] 2033[7] 2462[9] 3670[7] 7687[7] 7819[3]

**Appellez Baileys (FR)** *Chris Dwyer* a50 44
3 b g Halling(USA) Bitza Baileys (IRE) (Zamindar (USA))
142[5] 254[7] 473[7] 1634[6] 1684[7] 2526[11] 3121[5] 3326[9] 3673[8] 5122[3] 5534[5]

**Appiano (FR)** *Y Barberot* a68 79
3 b c Orpen(USA) Appearance (GER) (Monsun (GER))
1907a[5] 4465a[8]

**Appleberry (IRE)** *Michael Appleby* 86
2 b f Approve(IRE) Passage To India (IRE) (Indian Ridge)
1482[6] (2051) 2313[4] 3415[10]

**Applejack Lad** *John Ryan* a78 70
3 ch g Three Valleys(USA) Fittonia (FR) (Ashkalani (IRE))
3480[12] 4074[14] 4654[7] 4868[4] 5008[9] 5492[6] 6567[3] 7259[9] 7424[3] 7883[5] 8013[4]

**Application** *Bryan Smart* a34 44
3 ch g Major Cadeaux Choisette (Choisir (AUS))
127[7] 267[6] 480[9] 2392[9]

**Approaching (IRE)** *Amanda Perrett* a69 51
3 ch c New Approach(IRE) Dust Dancer (Suave Dancer (USA))
7024[7] 7528[10] 7733[6]

**Approaching Star (FR)** *Ismail Mohammed* a63 70
3 ch f New Approach(IRE) Madame Arcati (IRE) (Sinndar (IRE))
1424[7] 2082[4] 3568[4] 4657[6]

**Approach The West (IRE)** *James Tate* 73
3 b f New Approach(IRE) Damsel (Danzero (AUS))
1723[7] 6262[9]

**Approbare (IRE)** *T M Walsh* a80 96
2 b g Approve(IRE) Tabrina (IRE) (Fasliyev (USA))
5954a[5] 6348a[7]

**Appyjack** *Tony Carroll* a63 63
6 b g Royal Applause Petrikov (IRE) (In The Wings)
88[12] 377[7] 484[4] (1015) 1387[8] 2443[3] 3115[5] 3576[2] 4798[5] (5005) 5291[4] 5908[4] 6715[6] 6883[3]

**Apricot Sky** *Henry Candy* a70 92
4 ch g Pastoral Pursuits Miss Apricot (Indian Ridge)
(1678) 2352[9] 3313[9] 3927[7] 4762[8] 5350[3] (6096) 6744[11]

**April Ciel** *Ronald Harris* a63 74
5 b g Septieme Ciel(USA) By Definition (IRE) (Definite Article)
2248[7] 2693[4] 2947[3] 3175[2] 3585[8] (3853) 4209[7] 4948[14] 6007[11] 6091[8] 6426[10]

**Aprovado (IRE)** *Michael Dods* 63
2 b g Approve(IRE) Aldburgh (Bluebird (USA))
3620[6] 5013[6] 5759[9] 7055[2]

**Apsis Dream (FR)** *T Castanheira* a78 76
3 b g Apsis Vestale Bleue (Anabaa (USA))
720a[10]

**Aqdaar** *Mark Johnston* a31
2 b c Shamardal(USA) Ayun (USA) (Swain (IRE))
7400[11]

**Aqlette** *David Evans* a66 62
2 ch f Aqlaam Violette (Observatory (USA))
2979$^8$ 4784$^4$ 5255$^3$ 6678$^{10}$ 7421$^7$ 8183$^3$

**Aqua Ardens (GER)** *George Baker* a95 93
6 b g Nayef(USA) Arduinna (GER) (Winged Love (IRE))
172$^2$ 300$^3$ 1667$^2$ 2068$^3$ 2772$^9$ 3438$^3$ (4352) (5629) (6263) (6789) 7852$^2$ 8117$^7$

**Aquatinta (GER)** *Clive Cox* 87
4 b f Samum(GER) Arpista (GER) (Chief Singer)
1945$^8$

**Aqueous (IRE)** *James Tate*
3 ch f Art Connoisseur(IRE) Aquatint (Dansili)
2551$^6$

**Aquilleus** *G Henrot* 42
3 b g Peintre Celebre(USA) Arlesienne (IRE) (Alzao (USA))
2003a$^{11}$

**Arab Dawn** *Hughie Morrison* a98 95
3 gr g Dalakhani(IRE) Victoire Celebre (USA) (Stravinsky (USA))
(1947) ◆ (2303) (2685) 3379$^5$ 6257$^3$ 6548$^4$ 7203$^2$

**Arabian Beauty (IRE)** *Saeed bin Suroor* 86
3 b f Shamardal(USA) Express Way (ARG) (Ahmad (ARG))
3750$^6$ 4472$^4$ (5371) (5948) 6315$^3$

**Arabian Bride (IRE)** *Robert Cowell* a16 84
2 ch f Raven's Pass(USA) Rasana (Royal Academy (USA))
3296$^2$ (3606) 4157$^5$ 5085$^2$ 6165$^{13}$ 8308$^7$

**Arabian Comet (IRE)** *William Haggas* a78 105
3 b f Dubawi(IRE) Aviacion (BRZ) (Know Heights (IRE))
(1858) (2827) 3200$^3$ (4145) 4824$^2$ 5611$^2$ 6255$^5$

**Arabian Flight** *Michael Appleby* a71 44
5 b m Exceed And Excel(AUS) Emirates First (IRE) (In The Wings)
75$^6$ 320$^2$ (387) (565) 907$^3$ 1125$^6$ 1247$^3$ 1450$^6$ 5573$^{10}$ 6195$^7$ (6716) 6858$^4$ 7078$^{10}$ 7647$^4$ 7830$^3$ 8176$^3$

**Arabian Gold (AUS)** *David Vandyke* 108
4 gr f Dubawi(IRE) Coablo (AUS) (Vettori (IRE))
7128a$^{14}$

**Arabian Heights** *Ian Williams* a75 86
6 gr g Araafa(IRE) Makhsusah (IRE) (Darshaan)
61$^5$ 256$^5$ 643$^4$ 849$^5$ (922) 1000$^4$

**Arabian Illusion (FR)** *Andrew Balding* a71
2 ch c Makfi Arabian Spell (IRE) (Desert Prince (IRE))
7730$^3$

**Arabian Music (IRE)** *David Simcock* a75
3 b f Kheleyf(USA) Areyaam (USA) (Elusive Quality (USA))
275$^2$ (645) 854$^5$

**Arabian Oasis** *Charlie Appleby* 84
2 b c Oasis Dream Love Divine (Diesis)
5393$^2$ 6056$^7$

**Arabian Queen (IRE)** *David Elsworth* 100
2 b f Dubawi(IRE) Barshiba (IRE) (Barathea (IRE))
2107$^{10}$ (2402) 3353$^6$ (4164) 5190$^5$ 6751$^6$

**Arabian Revolution** *Saeed bin Suroor* a71 93
3 gr g Dalakhani(IRE) Mont Etoile (IRE) (Montjeu (IRE))
(2924) 3892$^2$ 4819$^5$ 7135$^8$ 7650$^4$

**Arabian Sunset (IRE)** *Simon Waugh* 48
3 b f Dubawi(IRE) Summer Sunset (IRE) (Grand Lodge (USA))
2355$^{16}$ 3828$^{10}$ 4495$^{12}$ 6119$^{10}$

**Arable** *Charles Hills* a76 87
3 ch c Three Valleys(USA) Cut Corn (King's Theatre (IRE))
1208$^2$ 1911$^6$ 2432$^3$ (4426) 4821$^{11}$ 6292$^7$

**Arab Spring (IRE)** *Sir Michael Stoute* a83 115
4 b c Monsun(GER) Spring Symphony (IRE) (Darshaan)
(1208) (1715) (2314) (3449) 4124$^4$

**Aragosta** *James Fanshawe* a84 67
4 ch f Pivotal Langoustine (AUS) (Danehill (USA))
2511$^3$ (5548) 6269$^2$ 6890$^2$

**Araldo** *Michael Moroney* 107
6 b h High Chaparral(IRE) Alanda (GER) (Lando (GER))
7301a$^5$ 7653a$^7$

**Aramadyh** *James Tate* a74 34
3 gr f Authorized(IRE) Swift Dispersal (Shareef Dancer (USA))
357$^2$ 473$^5$ 1135$^5$

**Aramist (IRE)** *Alan Swinbank* 95
4 gr g Aussie Rules(USA) Mistic Sun (Dashing Blade)
(2168) (2520) 3574$^5$ 4160$^9$ (5465) 6133$^9$ ◆ 6747$^3$ 7083$^3$ 7718$^2$

**Aran Sky (IRE)** *K R Burke* a68 72
3 b g Arakan(USA) Fayr Sky (IRE) (Fayruz)
1192$^8$ 1858$^3$ 2163$^2$ 2805$^7$ 3360$^4$ 6515$^4$ 7225$^4$ 7417$^6$

**Arantes** *Mick Channon* a82 88
3 b g Sixties Icon Black Opal (Machiavellian (USA))
(734) 1279$^2$ 1652$^6$ 2337$^7$ 2761$^3$ 3183$^4$ 4453$^6$ 4855$^6$ 5302$^3$ 5812$^4$ 6460$^7$

**Arashi** *Derek Shaw* a76 69
8 b g Fantastic Light(USA) Arriving (Most Welcome)
253$^7$ 476$^6$ 656$^3$ 842$^2$ 992$^3$ 1043$^4$ 1374$^9$ (2683) (2885) 3151$^6$ 4076$^5$ 7539$^{12}$ 7817$^9$ 8001$^7$ 8253$^6$

**Aratika (FR)** *W Walton* a70 64
2 b f Air Chief Marshal(IRE) Nostalchia (FR) (Genereux Genie)
5590a$^7$

**Arbaab** *Sir Michael Stoute* 73
3 br c Dynaformer(USA) Kaseema (USA) (Storm Cat (USA))
1357$^7$ 5038$^P$

**Arbitrageur (IRE)** *Donal Kinsella* a83 67
5 b g Elusive City(USA) Mother's Hope (IRE) (Idris (IRE))
3737a$^{17}$ 6082a$^7$

**Arcamante (ITY)** *K R Burke* a60 80
3 b g High Chaparral(IRE) Caractere (IRE) (Indian Ridge)
1035$^3$ 1587$^7$ 2221$^5$ 3064$^3$ 4332$^7$ 4803$^4$ 5628$^3$ 5815$^3$ 6461$^2$ 6864$^4$ 7177$^2$ 7566$^{11}$

**Arcanman (IRE)** *Ronald Harris*
2 b c Arcano(IRE) Rose Bourbon (USA) (Woodman (USA))
6652$^{10}$ 7827$^8$

**Arcano Gold (IRE)** *Richard Fahey* 80
2 ch c Arcano(IRE) Azia (IRE) (Desert Story (IRE))
4216$^6$ 4633$^7$ 5386$^3$ ◆ 7169$^3$ 7443$^2$ (7666)

**Arcas (IRE)** *Alan Jones* a65 7
5 br g Shamardal(USA) Callisto (IRE) (Darshaan)
4738$^{12}$

**Arc Cara (ITY)** *Ralph Beckett* 73
2 b g Arcano(IRE) Folcara (IRE) (Brief Truce (USA))
2776$^5$ 3279$^6$

**Archandel Michael (CZE)** *Christina Bucher* a42 86
3 bb g Tiger Cafe(JPN) Abba (CZE) (Sectori (USA))
3512a$^8$

**Archange (FR)** *H-A Pantall* a72 75
2 b f Arcano(IRE) Carinae (USA) (Nureyev (USA))
3170a$^4$

**Archduchess** *Rae Guest* a79 71
3 b f Archipenko(USA) Eminencia (Sadler's Wells (USA))
2432$^{12}$ 2924$^{10}$ 3471$^2$ (4292) 4616$^3$

**Archelao (IRE)** *Lee Carter* a63 33
6 br g Cape Cross(IRE) Brindisi (Dr Fong (USA))
88$^2$ 289$^8$

**Arch Enemy** *Michael Easterby* 63
2 b c Archipenko(USA) All A Dream (Desert Story (IRE))
2200$^4$ 2788$^3$ 5443$^P$

**Archery Peak** *Luca Cumani* 81
2 b c Arch(USA) Come Touch The Sun (IRE) (Fusaichi Pegasus (USA))
6259$^3$ 6928$^6$

**Archibald Thorburn (IRE)** *Peter Hedger* a74 58
3 br g Duke Of Marmalade(IRE) Winged Harriet (IRE) (Hawk Wing (USA))
6890$^6$ 7351$^8$ 7759$^{10}$ 8186$^8$

**Archie (IRE)** *Tom Dascombe* 83
2 b c Fast Company(IRE) Winnifred (Green Desert (USA))
(3136) ◆

**Archiebeau** *Jonathan Portman* a64 46
3 gr g Archipenko(USA) Si Belle (IRE) (Dalakhani (IRE))
717$^5$ 951$^{10}$ 5719$^6$ 6486$^{11}$ 7229$^8$

**Archie Rice (USA)** *Tom Keddy* a78 52
8 b g Arch(USA) Gold Bowl (USA) (Seeking The Gold (USA))
(146) 250$^9$ 1899$^9$ 3064$^6$ 3475$^6$ 4402$^7$

**Archie's Advice** *Keith Dalgleish* a76 67
3 b g Archipenko(USA) Flylowflylong (IRE) (Danetime (IRE))
2292$^7$ 2952$^5$ 3103$^3$ 4363$^7$ 4490$^3$ (4706) 5269$^3$ (7527) (7918)

**Archimedes (JPN)** *Hideaki Fujiwara* 115
5 b h Admire Moon(JPN) Archeology (USA) (Seeking The Gold (USA))
8154a$^7$

**Archipeligo** *Iain Jardine* a78 73
3 b g Archipenko(USA) Red Slew (Red Ransom (USA))
4830$^4$ 6599$^6$ 6982$^3$ 7411$^{16}$ (8232)

**Archive** *Rae Guest* a69 74
4 b f Dansili Modesta (IRE) (Sadler's Wells (USA))
(558)

**Arch Villain (IRE)** *Amanda Perrett* a103 96
5 b g Arch(USA) Barzah (IRE) (Darshaan)
(285) 1556$^2$

**Arch Walker (IRE)** *John Weymes* a31 53
7 ch g Choisir(AUS) Clunie (Inchinor)
1843$^9$ 2514$^{12}$ 3092$^6$ 4101$^9$ 4567$^9$ 4664$^6$ 5316$^2$ 5594$^3$ 6023$^5$ 6866$^{10}$

**Arc Lighter (USA)** *Seamus Durack* a77 65
5 b g Street Cry(IRE) Flamelet (USA) (Theatrical (IRE))
6332$^{10}$ 6943$^9$

**Ar Colleen Aine** *Mick Channon* a67 68
2 b f Paco Boy(IRE) Stan's Smarty Girl (USA) (Smarty Jones (USA))
1482$^4$ 1764$^2$ 2064$^3$ 3922$^2$ 4057$^8$ 4815$^3$ 5129$^3$ 5779$^3$ 6104$^8$ (6563) (6941) 7112$^4$ 7362$^5$ 7571$^5$

**Arcossi** *Ann Duffield* 40
2 ch f Arcano(IRE) Ossiana (IRE) (Polish Precedent (USA))
1732$^9$ 5372$^4$ 5910$^7$ 6205$^{10}$ 6428$^6$

**Arctic (IRE)** *Tracey Collins* 105
7 gr g Shamardal(USA) Shawanni (Shareef Dancer (USA))
1333a$^5$ 3737a$^{23}$ (Dead)

**Arctic Feeling (IRE)** *Richard Fahey* a89 99
6 ch g Camacho Polar Lady (Polar Falcon (USA))
1506$^7$ 1961$^{14}$ 2352$^5$ 2732$^3$ 2992$^{12}$ 3599$^4$ 4128$^6$ (4632) 5081$^2$ (5784) 6369a$^4$ 6531$^7$ 6872$^{14}$ (7080) 7280$^4$

**Arctic Lynx (IRE)** *Conor Dore* a88 72
7 b g One Cool Cat(USA) Baldemara (FR) (Sanglamore (USA))
1489$^2$ 2123$^2$ 2446$^3$ 3386$^5$ 4284$^7$ 4765$^4$ 5281$^7$ 5830$^3$ 6236$^3$ 6441$^7$ 6898$^6$ 7775$^7$ 7847$^6$ (8039) 8245$^7$

**Arctic Moon (USA)** *Charlie Appleby* a81 41
3 bb f Raven's Pass(USA) Golden Sphinx (USA) (Storm Cat (USA))
1233$^2$ 1767$^2$

**Ardeola (GER)** *Jean-Pierre Carvalho* 95
3 ch f Manduro(GER) Anatola (GER) (Tiger Hill (IRE))
3046a$^5$

**Ardingly (IRE)** *Paul Cole* a77 69
4 b f Danehill Dancer(IRE) Asnieres (USA) (Spend A Buck (USA))
6357$^6$ 6681$^9$

**Ardlui (IRE)** *Tim Easterby* 98
6 b g Galileo(IRE) Epping (Charnwood Forest (IRE))
1735$^9$ 2314$^{10}$ 3717$^5$ 7083$^5$ 7409$^3$ 7718$^6$

**Ardmay (IRE)** *Kevin Ryan* a62 96
5 b g Strategic Prince Right After Moyne (IRE) (Imperial Ballet (IRE))
1196$^5$ 1539$^6$ 2137$^3$ 2699$^5$ 3094$^6$ 3368$^4$ (5413) 6937$^7$ 7334$^3$

**A Ready Dream (FR)** *Rod Collet* a97 95
5 ch g More Than Ready(USA) Mary Montagu (IRE) (Danehill Dancer (IRE))
177a$^4$ 669a$^8$

**Area Fifty One** *Nicky Henderson* a87 108
6 b g Green Desert(USA) Secret History (USA) (Bahri (USA))
(1194) 2143$^9$

**Areion (IRE)** *J S Moore* a67 63
2 gr f Zebedee Grecian Glory (IRE) (Zafonic (USA))
1788$^{10}$ 2328$^8$ (2680) 3211$^5$ 4143$^8$ 5119a$^7$ 5619a$^5$ 5844a$^5$

**Arethusa** *Ed Dunlop* a66 82
2 b f Rip Van Winkle(IRE) Acquifer (Oasis Dream)
3858$^2$ (4444) (5626)

**Argaki (IRE)** *Keith Dalgleish* a73 82
4 ch g Strategic Prince Amathusia (Selkirk (USA))
1724$^{15}$ 2603$^7$ 3361$^2$ 3457$^3$ 3999$^6$ 4359$^6$ 4761$^{13}$ 4827$^{11}$ 5810$^2$ 6476$^{13}$ 6937$^9$ 7185$^6$ 7350$^{10}$ 7829$^{11}$

**Argent Knight** *William Jarvis* a86 94
4 gr g Sir Percy Tussah (Daylami (IRE))
1383$^6$ 2108$^6$ 2561$^8$ 3453$^6$ 4685$^7$ 5017$^7$ 6557$^4$ 7107$^{22}$

**Argent Touch** *Derek Shaw* a50 61
3 gr g Elnadim(USA) The Manx Touch (IRE) (Petardia)
15$^2$ (98) 216$^2$ 481$^2$ 650$^2$ 762$^2$ 1005$^4$ 2802$^8$ 3433$^5$ 3650$^7$ 4059$^2$ 4288$^9$ 8077$^6$ 8255$^9$

**Argot** *Anthony Carson* 73
3 b g Three Valleys(USA) Tarot Card (Fasliyev (USA))
1725$^3$ 2749$^5$ 3430$^3$ 3978$^8$ 5206$^5$

**Aria Di Primavera** *Stefano Botti* 94
2 b f Selkirk(USA) Aria Di Festa (IRE) (Orpen (USA))
7321a$^4$

**Arianrhod (IRE)** *Donald McCain* a71 53
3 b f Duke Of Marmalade(IRE) Risera (IRE) (Royal Academy (USA))
828$^4$ 988$^4$ 1817$^5$ 3644$^8$ 4316$^6$ 4789$^4$ 5256$^5$

**Aristocracy** *Mick Channon* a64 74
3 b g Royal Applause Pure Speculation (Salse (USA))
404$^4$ 3986$^5$ 4388$^6$ 4817$^2$ 5108$^2$ (5338)

**Aristocratic Duty** *Sylvester Kirk* a66 65
3 b f Zamindar(USA) Duty Paid (IRE) (Barathea (IRE))
1920$^5$ 2470$^7$ 2775$^{10}$ 3144$^5$ 4047$^2$ 4152$^5$ 4654$^5$ 6022$^2$ 6567$^7$ 7000$^7$

**Aristote** *P Van De Poele* a84 93
8 ch h Domedriver(IRE) Abime (USA) (Woodman (USA))
1828a$^{11}$

**Arizona John (IRE)** *John Mackie* a79 86
9 b g Rahy(USA) Preseli (IRE) (Caerleon (USA))
870$^9$ 1133$^4$ (1659) 2168$^3$ 2520$^2$ 3341$^4$ 6206$^5$ 6579$^2$ 6761$^4$ 7422$^4$ 8001$^8$

**Arizona Snow** *Ronald Harris* a59 61
2 b c Phoenix Reach(IRE) Calgary (Pivotal)
1741$^4$ 2007$^6$ 3847$^5$ 5120$^4$ (5517) 6237$^{11}$

**Arkadios (FR)** *S Cerulis* a72
3 b g Elusive City(USA) Blue Card (FR) (Trempolino (USA))
8005a$^2$

**Arkansas Slim (IRE)** *Charles Hills* a64
2 b g Montjeu(IRE) Janoubi (Dansili)
7741$^{11}$ 8292$^4$

**Arlecchino (IRE)** *Ed McMahon* a77 78
4 b g Hernando(FR) Trullitti (IRE) (Bahri (USA))
265$^2$ 498$^2$ 782$^2$ 1051$^3$ 1454$^3$ 1724$^4$ 2382$^4$ 3334$^3$ 3919$^3$ 4568$^4$ 5077$^6$ 5521$^5$ 5899$^6$

**Arlecchino's Leap** *Mark Usher* a66 73
2 br c Kheleyf(USA) Donna Giovanna (Mozart (IRE))
1417$^{10}$ 1807$^3$ 2413$^2$ 2993$^2$ 3210$^5$ 4143$^5$ 4605$^5$ 5028$^5$ (5506) 6016$^5$ 6629$^7$

**Arluno (FR)** *J-Y Artu* a60 53
5 gr g Chichicastenango(FR) Ambrosianella (FR) (Take Risks (FR))
3089a$^9$

**Armada Bay (IRE)** *Bryan Smart* a53 51
4 b g Tamayuz Yara (IRE) (Sri Pekan (USA))
71$^1$ 435$^7$

**Armed Guard (IRE)** *Edward Lynam* a61 61
5 b h Medicean Fairest Of All (IRE) (Sadler's Wells (USA))
794a$^2$

**Armelle (FR)** *Scott Dixon* a55 67
3 b f Milk It Mick Park Ave Princess (IRE) (Titus Livius (FR))
86$^4$ 378$^2$ 753$^5$ 1048$^5$ 2020$^9$ 4998$^3$ (5390) (5683) 7502$^2$ 7644$^4$ 7825$^6$

**Armistice Day (IRE)** *David Brown*
2 b f Azamour(IRE) Announcing Peace (Danehill (USA))
7406$^8$

**Armourer (IRE)** *William Muir* a64 68
3 b g Azamour(IRE) Engraving (Sadler's Wells (USA))
2417$^2$ 2735$^{10}$ 3541$^3$ 4303$^6$ 4948$^6$ 5520$^5$ 6193$^9$ 7188$^6$ 7427$^{10}$

**Arms Around Me (IRE)** *Bryan Smart* 55
2 ch g Lope De Vega(IRE) Mexican Milly (IRE) (Noverre (USA))
5852$^8$ 6860$^4$

**Army Bulletin (IRE)** *A Fabre* 108
3 b c Invincible Spirit(IRE) Alessandria (Sunday Silence (USA))
2242a$^2$ 3028a$^3$ 3807a$^5$ 4483a$^2$ 5406a$^6$

**Arnold Lane (IRE)** *Mick Channon* a92 111
5 b h Footstepsinthesand Capriole (Noverre (USA))
112a$^{13}$ 304a$^{10}$ 3452$^{19}$ 3732$^3$ 4188$^5$ 4895$^{11}$ 5778$^4$ 7122$^7$ 7408$^5$

**Arod (IRE)** *Peter Chapple-Hyam* a75 113
3 b c Teofilo(IRE) My Personal Space (USA) (Rahy (USA))
(1491) 2285$^2$ 2990$^4$ (4366) 5578$^5$

**Arousal** *Michael Bell* a34 46
2 b f Stimulation(IRE) Midnight Mover (IRE) (Bahamian Bounty)
1488$^{11}$ 1633$^5$ 2173$^7$ 6237$^7$ 7014$^8$

**Arpegio (FR)** *S Wattel* a79 60
3 b c King's Best(USA) Fongagain (IRE) (Dr Fong (USA))
4465a$^5$

**Ar Poulgwenn (IRE)** *J-C Rouget* a76 83
3 b g Nayef(USA) Ballerina Blue (IRE) (High Chaparral (IRE))
194a$^6$ (630a) 4838a$^5$ (5959a)

**Arquimedes (IRE)** *Charles Hills* a61 57
3 b g Montjeu(IRE) Piste Noire (USA) (Diesis)
4587$^6$ 7015$^7$

**Arracourt** *Tim Easterby* 64
2 b g Multiplex Retaliator (Rudimentary (USA))
5241$^7$ 5712$^4$ 6146$^4$ 6648$^{11}$

**Arranger (IRE)** *Martyn Meade* 76
3 gr f Bushranger(IRE) El Morocco (USA) (El Prado (IRE))
2340$^9$ 2745$^3$ ◆ 3067$^9$

**Arrayan** *Alexandra Dunn* a56 66
9 b g Catcher In The Rye(IRE) Ganga (IRE) (Generous (IRE))
7733$^{10}$

**Arr' Kid (USA)** *Keith Dalgleish* a91 82
4 b c Medaglia d'Oro(USA) Viaduct (USA) (Thunder Gulch (USA))
350$^5$ (567) ◆ 961$^3$ (1091) 1556$^{13}$ 2108$^5$ 2739$^8$ 5564$^8$ 7333$^P$

**Arrowtown** *Roger Charlton* a58
2 b f Rail Link Protectress (Hector Protector (USA))
6605$^7$

**Arrowzone** *Garry Moss* a74 91
3 b g Iffraaj Donna Giovanna (Mozart (IRE))
(976) (1346) 2510$^{10}$ 2827$^3$ (5206) 5713$^2$ 6936$^5$ 7417$^4$

**Arryzona** *Christine Dunnett* a23
3 b g Phoenix Reach(IRE) Southwarknewsflash (Danetime (IRE))
2877$^{11}$ 3796$^5$ 4265$^{10}$ 5321$^8$ 6015$^{10}$ 6632$^8$

**Arsenale (GER)** *Michael Appleby* a57 55
3 b f Nicaron(GER) Alte Rose (GER) (Monsun (GER))
6494$^3$ 7210$^4$ 7686$^7$

**Art Charter (FR)** *K R Burke* 67
2 b f Artiste Royal(IRE) Lady Sylvester (USA) (Elusive Quality (USA))
6056$^{13}$ 6742$^3$ 7230$^7$

**Art Contemporain (USA)** *P Bary* a67 107
4 rg c Smart Strike(CAN) Super Lina (FR) (Linamix (FR))
6917a$^9$

**Art Dzeko** *Brian Baugh* a71 60
5 b g Acclamation Delitme (IRE) (Val Royal (FR))
126$^{11}$ (563) 766$^{13}$ 934$^3$ 1573$^9$ 7915$^9$ 8085$^4$

**Arte Del Calcio** *Tony Carroll* a49 49
5 b g Manduro(GER) Movie Queen (Danehill (USA))
40$^5$ 117$^8$ 737$^8$ 959$^6$

**Artemis (IRE)** *Conrad Allen* a63 46
3 b f Marju(IRE) Silver Arrow (USA) (Shadeed (USA))
(373) 485$^3$ 573$^4$ 926$^5$ 1039$^5$ 1264$^3$ 2686$^6$ 3228$^5$ 3522$^2$ 3679$^4$ 4546$^5$ 8230$^7$ 8322$^2$

**Artemis Agrotera (USA)** *Michael Hushion* a118
3 b f Roman Ruler(USA) Indy Glory (USA) (A.P. Indy (USA))
7608a$^7$

**Artesa** *M Augelli* 60
4 ch f Medecis Pas Le Temps (FR) (Be My Guest (USA))
6392a$^6$

**Artesana** *William Knight* a50 55
2 ch f Mastercraftsman(IRE) Koniya (IRE) (Doyoun)
4054$^{10}$ 5881$^9$ 7353$^7$

**Arte Volante** *B Grizzetti* 92
2 b f Dutch Art Aline's Wings (ITY) (In The Wings)
3775a$^3$

**Artfilly (IRE)** *Ed Walker* a56 68
2 b f Art Connoisseur(IRE) Tallassee (Indian Ridge)
1528$^{12}$ 3232$^2$ 4269$^7$ 4610$^3$ 5253$^5$ 5974$^7$ 6610$^9$

**Artful Artist (IRE)** *A J Martin* a38 90
5 b g Excellent Art Silly Goose (IRE) (Sadler's Wells (USA))
7476a$^9$

**Artful Lady (IRE)** *George Margarson* a53 68
5 br m Excellent Art Fear And Greed (IRE) (Brief Truce (USA))
339$^8$ 603$^9$ 2435$^8$

**Artful Prince** *James Given* 84
4 ch g Dutch Art Royal Nashkova (Mujahid (USA))
1607$^{15}$ 2162$^9$ 2540$^4$ 3254$^2$ 3977$^3$ 4427$^3$ 5203$^6$ 5792$^6$ 6166$^6$ 6672$^{13}$ 6870$^4$ 7042$^3$ 7538$^2$

**Artful Rogue (IRE)** *Amanda Perrett* a89 87
3 b g Excellent Art Szabo (IRE) (Anabaa (USA))
50$^2$ 2418$^3$ 3183$^5$ 4077$^2$ 4855$^2$ 5135$^3$ 5670$^2$ (6485) 7203$^4$

**Arthenus** *James Fanshawe* a60
2 b c Dutch Art Lady Hen (Efisio)
7731$^8$

**Arthur MartinLeake (IRE)** *K R Burke* 78
2 b c Alfred Nobel(IRE) Golden Shine (Royal Applause)
3367$^3$ 3536$^2$ (5104) 5607$^{13}$ 6322$^5$ 6977$^3$ 7232$^3$

**Arthurs Secret** *John Quinn* a74 78
4 ch g Sakhee's Secret Angry Bark (USA) (Woodman (USA))
(1197) 2520$^5$ 3205$^6$ 5639$^6$

**Arthur's Way (IRE)** *Lisa Williamson* a55 63
2 b g Royal Applause Chantilly Pearl (USA) (Smart Strike (CAN))
3889$^7$ 4270$^8$ 4885$^6$ 5072$^3$ 5875$^{13}$ 7396$^9$ 7536$^6$ 7904$^9$ 8115$^{13}$

**Arthur The King (IRE)** *N Bertran De Balanda* 83
4 ch c Medicean Applauded (IRE) (Royal Applause)
2192a[5]

**Artic Promise** *Brian Meehan*
2 gr g Verglas(IRE) Artistry (Night Shift (USA))
2903[6] 3312[12]

**Artigiano (USA)** *Charlie Appleby* a52 109
4 ch g Distorted Humor(USA) Angel Craft (USA) (A.P. Indy (USA))
110a[3] 508a[15] 2891[2] 3356[12] 4711[4]

**Artisan** *Shaun Lycett* a59 53
6 ch g Medicean Artisia (IRE) (Peintre Celebre (USA))
6274[7] 6670[7] 7251[8] 7657[6] 7893[9] 8253[4]

**Artist Cry** *Richard Fahey* a50 9
2 ch c Dutch Art Twenty Seven (IRE) (Efisio)
7082[9] 7741[7]

**Artiste Lady (FR)** *Mme C Head-Maarek* a72 76
3 b f Artiste Royal(IRE) Fantasy Lady (USA) (Grand Slam (USA))
2411a[4]

**Artistical (IRE)** *Lee Carter* a78 67
4 b c Excellent Art Royale Figurine (IRE) (Dominion Royale)
(250)

**Artistic Charm** *David Simcock* a85 88
3 b f Dutch Art Greenfly (Green Desert (USA))
1515[14] 3674[6] 4445[2] 5612[U] 7196[6]

**Artistic Flare** *John Quinn* 38
2 ch f Dutch Art Pantile (Pivotal)
6641[11] 7498[7]

**Artistic Flight (IRE)** *Jim Boyle* a58 4
2 b c Art Connoisseur(IRE) Robin (Slip Anchor)
7512[12] 7739[10] 7926[6] 8115[5]

**Artistic Jewel (IRE)** *Ed McMahon* a94 110
5 ch m Excellent Art Danish Gem (Danehill (USA))
2161[6] 3278[5] 4171[7] 6167[4] ◆ 6929[9]

**Artistic Muse (IRE)** *Charles Hills* 81
3 b f Excellent Art Course De Diamante (IRE) (Galileo (IRE))
2404[13] 3184[4] 3537[7] 4574[2] (5003) 5723[3] 6137[10] 6741[4]

**Artistic Queen** *James Tate* a78 77
3 b f Dutch Art Ellway Queen (USA) (Bahri (USA))
(5181) 5726[4] 6902[6] 7954[4] 8177[3]

**Art Obsession (IRE)** *David Barron* a81 88
3 b g Excellent Art Ghana (IRE) (Lahib (USA))
6345[2] (6792)

**Art Of Dreams (FR)** *B Grizzetti* 98
5 b h Dutch Art Giant Dream (Giant's Causeway (USA))
2375a[7]

**Art Official (IRE)** *Richard Hannon* a83 88
3 b c Excellent Art Dama'A (IRE) (Green Desert (USA))
1696[6] 2567[6] 2962[9] 4679[4] 5550[4] 6552[4]

**Art Of War (IRE)** *Tom Dascombe* 91
3 b g Invincible Spirit(IRE) Chica Roca (USA) (Woodman (USA))
1394[3] (2365) 3379[18] 4855[10]

**Art Of Zapping (FR)** *C Escuder* a80 84
3 b g Desert Style(IRE) Any Colour (Anshan)
(3745a)

**Artplace (IRE)** *S Smrczek* a90 93
4 b g Teofilo(IRE) Ginostra (Oasis Dream)
805a[2] 7026a[7]

**Art Scene (IRE)** *Patrick J Flynn* a54 53
4 b f Excellent Art Scenaria (IRE) (Scenic (IRE))
7959a[10]

**Art Scholar (IRE)** *Michael Appleby* a83 86
7 b g Pyrus(USA) Marigold (FR) (Marju (IRE))
2783[6] 3161[4] 3860[6] 5238[3] 5639[7] 6664[4] 7211[4] 7516[5] 7784[3] ◆ 7974[5]

**Art Show** *Noel C Kelly* a14 5
5 b m Dutch Art Regina (Green Desert (USA))
692[11]

**Artwork Genie (IRE)** *Jean-Pierre Carvalho* 100
3 b f Excellent Art Brief Escapade (IRE) (Brief Truce (USA))
2584a[6] 3873a[3] 6384a[6] 7629a[9]

**Arty Campbell (IRE)** *Bernard Llewellyn* a79 81
4 b g Dylan Thomas(IRE) Kincob (USA) (Kingmambo (USA))
292[3] (992) 1418[3] 2011[2] 2482[8] 3424[4] 4606[7] 5341[6] 6283[3]

**Aruan** *Derek Haydn Jones* a52
2 b f Equiano(FR) Chantress (Peintre Celebre (USA))
6718[6] 7367[10] 8060[8] 8287[4]

**Aruaru (GER)** *Christina Bucher* 57
5 ch h Lomitas Aruba (GER) (Big Shuffle (USA))
729a[P]

**Aryal** *Mark Johnston* a88 85
4 gr g Singspiel(IRE) Majoune (FR) (Take Risks (FR))
870[2] 961[2] 1171[6] 1553[4] 1651[10] 1971[7] 3004[5] 3371[4] (3544) 3815[3]

**Aryizad (IRE)** *Alan Swinbank* a41 76
5 b m Hurricane Run(IRE) Daziyra (IRE) (Doyoun)
5101[4] 5716[6] 6062[3] 6433[3] 7411[3]

**Arystyn Gouli (FR)** *X Thomas-Demeaulte* a53 81
2 ch f Compton Place Flam (Singspiel (IRE))
5617a[7] 7468a[9]

**As A Dream (IRE)** *Nikki Evans* a62 68
2 b f Azamour(IRE) Wedding Dream (Oasis Dream)
1349[4] 1571[13] 2436[5] 3312[9] (4999) 5279[4] 6610[11] 7515[5] 7762[4] 7994[3]

**Asantasana (FR)** *C Ferland* a78 84
2 gr f Youmzain(IRE) La Fleur D'Arthus (FR) (Nombre Premier)
6958a[14]

**Asbaab (USA)** *Brian Meehan* 101
4 ch g Jazil(USA) Alsaabeqa (USA) (Sakhee (USA))
1973[12] 3321[18]

**Asbury Boss (IRE)** *M Halford* 93
3 gr g Dalakhani(IRE) Nick's Nikita (IRE) (Pivotal)
7142a[4]

**Ascendant** *Andrew Reid* a76 61
8 ch g Medicean Ascendancy (Sadler's Wells (USA))
1383[7] 2034[6] 3859[7] 5137[6] 7866[10]

**Ascending Angel (IRE)** *Richard Hannon* a51
3 b f Sea The Stars(IRE) Maskaya (IRE) (Machiavellian (USA))
1768[9] 2061[13]

**Ascot Memory (IRE)** *S Wattel* a54 92
3 b f Iffraaj Flash And Dazzle (IRE) (Bertolini (USA))
193a[10]

**As D'Artois (FR)** *C Boutin* a65 78
4 bb g Medecis Vallabelle (FR) (Valanour (IRE))
722a[8]

**Aseela (IRE)** *George Moore* a51 61
4 b f Teofilo(IRE) Valse Mystique (IRE) (Grand Lodge (USA))
1673[9] (2135) 5448[7] 5788[4] 6119[9] 7499[3]

**Asgardella (IRE)** *W McCreery* 92
4 b f Duke Of Marmalade(IRE) Peaceful Kingdom (USA) (King Of Kings (IRE))
1076a[7]

**As Good As Gold (IRE)** *A P O'Brien* 86
2 b f Oasis Dream You'll Be Mine (USA) (Kingmambo (USA))
3763a[8] 4598a[6]

**Asha** *David C Griffiths* a48 63
3 ch f Dutch Art Golden Asha (Danehill Dancer (IRE))
4022[10] 4569[7] 5417[3] 5997[2] 7250[4] 7704[10]

**Ashapurna (IRE)** *William Knight*
2 ch f Tamayuz Bond Deal (IRE) (Pivotal)
7206[7]

**Ashbina** *Madeleine Smith* a69 71
5 b m Royal Applause Crystal Power (USA) (Pleasant Colony (USA))
6388a[13]

**Ash Cloud (FR)** *P Azzopardi* 61
5 b m Slickly(FR) Tramonto (Sri Pekan (USA))
178a[0]

**Ashdown Lad** *Tom Symonds* a70 83
5 ch g Sir Percy Antibes (IRE) (Grand Lodge (USA))
1849[2] 2108[7] 3034[9] 3851[6]

**Ashford (IRE)** *Martyn Meade* a53
2 br f Yeats(IRE) Little Empress (IRE) (Holy Roman Emperor (IRE))
7399[6] 7941[10]

**Ashkalara** *Stuart Howe* a53 63
7 b m Footstepsinthesand Asheyana (IRE) (Soviet Star (USA))
382[8] 1910[6] 2689[6] 3390[3] 3853[2] 4799[2] 5421[9]

**Ashkannd (FR)** *A De Royer-Dupre* a75 101
3 b c Sinndar(IRE) Ashalanda (FR) (Linamix (FR))
4483a[6]

**Ashkari (IRE)** *Clive Cox* a80 82
3 ch g Dutch Art Frivolity (Pivotal)
(1569) 2122[8] 2611[6] 3936[10] 6025[4] 6562[2] 7071[5] 7352[2]

**Ashpan Sam** *John Spearing* a78 111
5 b g Firebreak Sweet Patoopie (Indian Ridge)
1975[7] 2283[4] 2503[2] (2992) 3732[8] 4895[14] 5575[5] 6533[23] 7122[17] 7408[12]

**Ashridge Lad** *Brian Meehan* 73
2 b g Invincible Spirit(IRE) Leavingonajetplane (IRE) (Danehill (USA))
6125[5] 6545[5]

**Asia Minor (IRE)** *Dr Jon Scargill* a89 62
5 ch m Pivotal Anka Britannia (USA) (Irish River (FR))
(450) 1553[6] 6664[6] 7565[6] 7922[10] 8202[2]

**Asian Trader** *William Haggas* a67 95
5 b g Acclamation Tiger Waltz (Pivotal)
2275[9] (2803) 3666[8] 5925[10] 7080[16]

**Asima (IRE)** *Charles Hills* a58 65
2 ch f Halling(USA) Sospira (Cape Cross (IRE))
6553[7] 6868[6] 7194[7]

**Askaud (IRE)** *Scott Dixon* a79 99
6 b m Iffraaj Tarabaya (IRE) (Warning)
832[4] ◆ 1164[21] 1442[2] 1728[2] 1945[4] 2286[6] 2840[4] 4851[16] 5418[10] 5612[8] 6207[9] 6688[10] 7085[14] 7276[18]

**Ask Dad** *Damian Joseph English* a81 79
4 b g Intikhab(USA) Don't Tell Mum (IRE) (Dansili)
2147[15] 6078a[7] 7873a[10]

**Asker (IRE)** *Zoe Davison* 58
6 b g High Chaparral(IRE) Pay The Bank (High Top)
2966[5] 7452[4]

**Ask Me Nicely (IRE)** *A P O'Brien* 81
2 b f Fastnet Rock(AUS) Queen Titi (IRE) (Sadler's Wells (USA))
6798a[5]

**Ask The Guru** *Michael Attwater* a77 77
4 b g Ishiguru(USA) Tharwa (IRE) (Last Tycoon)
470[4] 532[2] 1019[3] 1109[3] 1489[8] 2645[4] (4102) 4399[5] 7357[7] 8297[11]

**Asmar (IRE)** *Fawzi Abdulla Nass* a110
3 b c Cape Cross(IRE) Zaneton (FR) (Mtoto)
594a[5] (896a) 1178a[2]

**A Soldier's Life (IRE)** *A Fabre* 107
3 b c Authorized(IRE) Aynthia (USA) (Zafonic (USA))
1621a[4] 7769a[6]

**A Southside Boy (GER)** *Jim Goldie* 69
6 b g Samum(GER) Anthurium (GER) (Hector Protector (USA))
(1763) 2678[3] 3240[5] 4361[4] 4962[4] 5812[5] 6480[4] ◆ 6832[8] 7100[8]

**Aspasius (GER)** *K Demme* a55 80
2 b g Desert Prince(IRE) Aspasia Lunata (GER) (Tiger Hill (IRE))
4524a[4]

**Asperites (IRE)** *D Prod'Homme* a76 56
4 b f Danehill Dancer(IRE) Olimpic Girl (IRE) (Darshaan)
722a[3]

**Aspirant** *Marjorie Fife* a78 68
3 b g Rail Link Affluent (Oasis Dream)
232[2] 1225[2] ◆ 1358[12] 1818[7] 2429[12] 2936[7] 3460[6] 3908[14] 6866[13] 7644[19]

**Assagher (USA)** *John Gosden* a75
2 b c Giant's Causeway(USA) Imagine (IRE) (Sadler's Wells (USA))
7371[4] 7891[6] (8093)

**Assault On Rome (IRE)** *Mark Johnston* a72 86
2 b f Holy Roman Emperor(IRE) Naomh Geileis (USA) (Grand Slam (USA))
2744[9] (2979) 3580[4] 4178[2] 4524a[3] 5672[3] 5929[3] 6253[15] 6749[4] 7131[7]

**Assembly** *Mark Rimell* a41 73
4 ch g Kyllachy Constitute (USA) (Gone West (USA))
2048[5] 2718[9] 3848[14] 4415[8] 4678[8] 5202[3]

**Assertive Agent** *Tony Carroll* a63 66
4 b f Assertive Agent Kensington (Mujahid (USA))
296[3] 687[5] 3231[2] 3734[3] 4431[2] 4908[2] 6666[9] 7364[6] 8195[5]

**Assez Clair (USA)** *Mme C Head-Maarek* a102 61
4 b c Pleasant Tap(USA) Pretty Clear (USA) (Mr Prospector (USA))
6163a[4]

**Assoluta (IRE)** *Sylvester Kirk* a59 58
3 ch f Danehill Dancer(IRE) A P Easy (USA) (A.P. Indy (USA))
1098[5] 1793[7] 2491[6] 2927[6] 3146[9] 3567[3] 3819[3] 4210[3] (4563) 4844[3] 5491[5] 6193[4] 7426[3] 7526[7] 7977[3]

**Astaire (IRE)** *Kevin Ryan* 113
3 b c Intense Focus(USA) Runway Dancer (Dansili)
1436[5] 2256[2] ◆ 3451[6] 4201[11] 5654[10] 6134[11]

**A Star In My Eye (IRE)** *Kevin Ryan* a42 87
4 b f Authorized(IRE) Vyatka (Lion Cavern (USA))
1444[10] 1882[3] 3205[16] 4663[3] (5639) 6206[3] 7289[11]

**Asteroidea** *Pam Sly* 89
3 b f Sea The Stars(IRE) Speciosa (IRE) (Danehill Dancer (IRE))
1880[2] 3270[3] (4020) 5465[2]

**Aster's Approval** *Mrs Ilka Gansera-Leveque* a46 57
4 b g With Approval(CAN) Aster (IRE) (Danehill (USA))
3332[7] 3677[5] 6042[7] 6272[7]

**Astonishing (IRE)** *Sir Michael Stoute* a94 110
4 b f Galileo(IRE) Amazing Krisken (USA) (Kris S (USA))
1434[4] 2764[6] 3961[7] 4443[5]

**Astorya (TUR)** *U Bilik* 105
5 b h Sri Pekan(USA) Melita (IRE) (Tagula (IRE))
6185a[7]

**Astra Hall** *Ralph Beckett* a49 90
5 ch m Halling(USA) Star Precision (Shavian)
1934[2] 2259[3] 2760[5] 4113[6] 5003[5] 7305[2]

**Astral Rose** *Jonathan Portman* a44 49
3 b f Pastoral Pursuits Rosapenna (IRE) (Spectrum (IRE))
2023[4] 2505[9] 3679[3] 4337[7] 5136[5] 5905[2] 6613[7] 7355[8]

**Astral Weeks** *Michael Bell* a63
3 b f Sea The Stars(IRE) Miss Universe (IRE) (Warning)
8048[3]

**Astrea** *Nigel Tinkler* 47
2 b f Assertive All Business (Entrepreneur)
1656[6] 2615[8] 3091[3] 3967[4] 4449[3] 5885[7] 6428[9]

**Astrelle (IRE)** *Marco Botti* a31 98
2 br f Makfi Miss Mariduff (USA) (Hussonet (USA))
2918[8] 3267[3] 4346[2] (4884) (5436) 5664[4] 6289[7] 6926[2] 7448[4]

**Astrocat** *Mark H Tompkins*
3 b f Zamindar(USA) Mega (IRE) (Petardia)
6982[9]

**Astrodiamond** *Mark H Tompkins* a20
3 b f Black Sam Bellamy(IRE) Astromancer (USA) (Silver Hawk (USA))
6901[8] 7349[8]

**Astrologo (SPA)** *M Delzangles* a65 72
4 ch g King's Best(USA) Caldas (IRE) (Sadler's Wells (USA))
5961a[13]

**Astronereus (IRE)** *Amanda Perrett* 98
3 ch c Sea The Stars(IRE) Marie Rheinberg (GER) (Surako (GER))
2334[9] 3031[2] (4168) 4821[8] ◆ 5164[2] 6127[4]

**Astrophysics** *David Elsworth* 106
2 ch c Paco Boy(IRE) Jodrell Bank (IRE) (Observatory (USA))
4618[4] 5091[2] (5671) 6286[2] 6879[2]

**Astrovirtue** *Mark H Tompkins* a53
3 b g Virtual Astrolove (IRE) (Bigstone (IRE))
50[8] 1793[6] 2926[14]

**Astrowolf** *Mark H Tompkins* a42 64
3 b g Halling(USA) Optimistic (Reprimand)
7777[10] 7982[8]

**Asuka Kurichan (JPN)** *Naosuke Sugai* a82 111
7 b h Sterling Rose(JPN) Laurel Waltz (JPN) (Dyna Letter (JPN))
2002a[18]

**Asulaman (GER)** *S Cerulis* a92 58
7 b g Sulamani(IRE) Andrelhina (Tirol)
806a[8] 7026a[14]

**Asyad (IRE)** *Sir Michael Stoute* 92
3 b f New Approach(IRE) Elle Danzig (GER) (Roi Danzig (USA))
3560[2] (3968) 6559[8]

**Atab (IRE)** *Charles Hills* 73
2 b f New Approach(IRE) Moon's Whisper (USA) (Storm Cat (USA))
6065[5] (7169)

**Atalan** *Hughie Morrison* 57
2 b c Azamour(IRE) Capriolla (In The Wings)
6653[6] 7134[10] 7666[10]

**Atalanta Bay (IRE)** *Marcus Tregoning* a77 67
4 b f Strategic Prince Wood Sprite (Mister Baileys)
64[3] (1919) 3472[4] 4369[4] 5551[3] (6338) (7072)

**Athania (IRE)** *Mrs A Corson* a35 28
8 ch m Fath(USA) Xania (Mujtahid (USA))
1625a[5] 2594a[8] 4040a[2] 5229a[5]

**Ath Cliath (IRE)** *C Boutin* a49 52
2 b f Intense Focus(USA) Rain Dancer (IRE) (Sadler's Wells (USA))
7027a[8]

**Athenian (IRE)** *Sir Mark Prescott Bt* a97 100
5 b m Acclamation Ziria (IRE) (Danehill Dancer (IRE))
(4445) 4668[9] 5467[6] (5965a) 6689[6] 7483a[8]

**Athletic** *Andrew Reid* a100 103
5 b g Doyen(IRE) Gentle Irony (Mazilier (USA))
(817) 1102[3] 1297[2] (1668) 2059[3] 4078[4] (4408) 4620[2] 4866[3] 6145[3] (6281) 6535[2] 6740[3] 7168[2] 7555[6] 7715[4]

**Athwaab** *Simon Hodgson* a38 42
7 b m Cadeaux Genereux Ahdaaf (USA) (Bahri (USA))
449[9] 693[7] 858[12] 972[4]

**Atilla (FR)** *M Boutin* a58 61
2 b g Agnes Kamikaze(JPN) Atlantique (IRE) (Alzao (USA))
3871a[3] 5618a[5] 5900a[4] 8212a[5]

**Atlante (AUS)** *Michael, Wayne & John Hawkes* 107
4 b c Fastnet Rock(AUS) Readyforcatherine (AUS) (More Than Ready (USA))
7128a[15]

**Atlantic Affair (IRE)** *Mark Johnston* a27 80
3 gr f Clodovil(IRE) Adultress (IRE) (Ela-Mana-Mou)
7282[14] 8177[8]

**Atlantis Crossing (IRE)** *Jim Boyle* a96 75
5 b g Elusive City(USA) Back At De Front (IRE) (Cape Cross (IRE))
804[2] ◆ 1070[4] 1834[6] 2500[6] 2772[6] 3180[6] 3734[2] 4024[6] 4406[2] 4609[3] 4918[4] 5422[4] 5650[6] 6872[15]

**Atlas Royal (FR)** *Mario Hofer* a47 55
2 ch g Astronomer Royal(USA) Aerdee (FR) (Highest Honor (FR))
4881a[5] 5618a[10] 8212a[9]

**Atletico (IRE)** *Roger Varian* 80
2 b c Kodiac Queenofthefairies (Pivotal)
4025[2] ◆ 4618[2] ◆

**Atreus** *Michael Easterby* 63
2 b g Indesatchel(IRE) Devassa (Reel Buddy (USA))
2051[6] 2949[3] 3201[3] 3529[3] 5285[5] 5373[4] 6008[3] 6643[8]

**Attain** *Julia Feilden* a65 62
5 b g Dansili Achieve (Rainbow Quest (USA))
116[4] 345[10] (537) 643[7] 958[2] 1450[5] 1875[4] 2721[7]

**Attention Seaker** *Tim Easterby* 75
4 b f Bollin Eric Pay Attention (Revoque (IRE))
6640[8] 7177[14]

**Attenzione (IRE)** *Marco Botti* a75 66
3 b g Shamardal(USA) Fig Tree Drive (USA) (Miswaki (USA))
2881[5] 3977[9] 4574[6] 5038[8]

**Attique (FR)** *F-X De Chevigny* a38 25
2 b f Fairly Ransom(USA) Gente Au Loup (FR) (Arctic Tern (USA))
5901a[9]

**Attraction (GER)** *J D Hillis* 81
2 b f Soldier Hollow Attention Please (GER) (Sternkoenig (IRE))
(6950a)

**Auction (IRE)** *Ed Dunlop* a96 97
4 b f Mr Greeley(USA) Exhibit One (USA) (Silver Hawk (USA))
1577[6] 2554[5] 3307[7] 3665[4] 4782[5] 5369a[10] 6129[4] 6793[4] 7384[3] 7553[5]

**Audacia (IRE)** *Hugo Palmer* a68 102
4 b f Sixties Icon Indiannie Moon (Fraam)
2318[6] 2956[8] (4060) 5927[5] 7243[11] 7717[7]

**Audacious** *Charles Pogson* a9 52
6 b g Motivator Flash Of Gold (Darshaan)
1689[8] 2270[10] 3155[9] 4415[11]

**Auden (USA)** *J R Jenkins* a62 72
6 b g Librettist(USA) Moyesii (USA) (Diesis)
67[6] 366[6] 458[9] 685[7] 821[10] 1087[2] 1129[2] (2720) 3553[4] 4116[6]

**Auditor (USA)** *C Ferland* a99 102
4 ch c Kingmambo(USA) Queen Of Money (USA) (Corporate Report (USA))
309a[7] 593a[14]

**Auf Wiedersehen** *James Fanshawe* a40 48
3 b g Byron Buena Notte (IRE) (Halling (USA))
3525[7] 4089[4]

**Augusta (GER)** *Waldemar Hickst* 26
2 b f Tertullian(USA) Acerba (GER) (Monsun (GER))
6950a[10]

**Augusta Ada** *Ollie Pears* 89
3 b f Byron Preference (Efisio)
2361[4] 3300[3] 3788[7] 4902[5] (6492) 6689[4] 7330[13]

**Auld Fyffee (IRE)** *John Ryan* a64 66
2 b f Haatef(USA) Lucky Fountain (IRE) (Lafontaine (USA))
3933[8] 4202[7] 4403[11] 5279[3] 5798[8] 6250[7] 6473[4] 6830[4] 7075[12] 7880[3] (7996)

**Auntie Dif** *Derek Shaw* a36
2 b f Equiano(FR) Meditation (Inchinor)
5255[8] 5569[6] 6158[11] 7190[5]

**Auntie Mildred (IRE)** *David O'Meara* a45 58
4 b f Elnadim(USA) Nahrayn (USA) (Elusive Quality (USA))
351[6] 556[6] 676[9] 2473[10]

**Aureate** *Brian Forsey* a56 45
10 ch g Jade Robbery(USA) Anne D'Autriche (IRE) (Rainbow Quest (USA))
400[6] 546[3] (912) 1248[2] 1501[5] 7823[12] 8134[7] 8277[9]

**Aurelia Cotta (IRE)** *Charles Hills* a57 77
3 b f Holy Roman Emperor(IRE) Art Work (Zafonic (USA))
(1684) (2417) ◆ 3135[11] (3814)

**Au Renoir** *Kevin Ryan* a2
4 ch f Peintre Celebre(USA) Goodbye (Efisio)
434[4] 649[9] 833[8]

**Aureolin Gulf** *Andrew Hollinshead* a52 61
5 b g Proclamation(IRE) Vermilion Creek (Makbul)
17[2] 321[4] 676[10] 4415[12] 6160[7]

**Au Revoir (IRE)** *A Fabre* 113
4 b c Singspiel(IRE) First (Highest Honor (FR))
984a[4] 2106a[6] 6381a[4] 7653a[8]
**Aurora Borealis (IRE)** *Ed Dunlop* a62 58
3 b f Montjeu(IRE) Elafaak (USA) (Gulch (USA))
2649[7] 4500[7] 5520[7] 7309[6] 7458[7]
**Auspicion** *William Haggas* 78
2 bb c Dansili Superstar Leo (IRE) (College Chapel)
4695[2] ◆ 6125[6]
**Aussi Celebre (IRE)** *E Lellouche* a66 112
5 gr h Aussie Rules(USA) Femme Celebre (IRE) (Peintre Celebre (USA))
723a[4] 984a[9] 1784a[9]
**Aussie Andre** *Jeremy Noseda* 69
3 b g High Chaparral(IRE) Hana Dee (Cadeaux Genereux)
2271[9]
**Aussie Reigns (IRE)** *William Knight* a109 106
4 b g Aussie Rules(USA) Rohain (IRE) (Singspiel (IRE))
205a[2] 398a[5] 598a[7] 812a[5] 1068[3] 1559[6] ◆ 2957[5] 3449[8] 4849[4] 5693[12] 6069[2]
**Aussie Ruler (IRE)** *Ronald Harris* 73
2 br g Aussie Rules(USA) Experiment (IRE) (Whipper (USA))
3779[2] 4025[3] 4760[2] 5242[3] 6038[4] 6363[3] 7038[10]
**Aussie Sky (IRE)** *Daniel Mark Loughnane* a45 32
3 b f Aussie Rules(USA) Skyscape (Zafonic (USA))
261[7] 411[4] 1449[3] 1648[8] 1855[6] 5801[6] 6340[6] 7865[5] 7940[8]
**Aussie Valentine (IRE)** *P D Deegan* a80 90
3 b g Aussie Rules(USA) Love Valentine (IRE) (Fruits Of Love (USA))
2337[8]
**Austerian** *Gay Kelleway* 40
3 ro c Mastercraftsman(IRE) Singed (Zamindar (USA))
1517[11]
**Austin Friars** *Charlie Appleby* 67
2 b g New Approach(IRE) My Luigia (IRE) (High Estate)
3720[7] 4750[4] 6694[4]
**Australia** *A P O'Brien* 129
3 ch c Galileo(IRE) Ouija Board (Cape Cross (IRE))
1951[3] ◆ (2990) (3739a) (5578) 6353a[2]
**Australia Day (IRE)** *Paul Webber* a84 92
11 gr g Key Of Luck(USA) Atalina (FR) (Linamix (FR))
1493[9] 3274[5] 5812[6]
**Authentication** *Mel Brittain* a32 57
5 b g Authorized(IRE) Valley Of Gold (FR) (Shirley Heights)
1605[10] 2424[5] 2738[12] 5090[2] 5200[5] 7509[5] 7643[9] 8061[5]
**Authorized Spirit** *Stuart Williams* 25
2 b f Authorized(IRE) World Spirit (Agnes World (USA))
7377[13]
**Authorized Too** *William Haggas* a75 87
3 b g Authorized(IRE) Audaz (Oasis Dream)
4089[3] (5318) 6075[4] 7305[9]
**Autignac (FR)** *Mlle S-V Tarrou* 76
3 b f Solon(GER) Recambe (IRE) (Cape Cross (IRE))
2411a[5]
**Automated** *Clive Brittain* 94
3 b g Authorized(IRE) Red Blooded Woman (USA) (Red Ransom (USA))
1438[2] 1699[5] 2087[6] 4435[5] 5094[3] 6098[10] 6465[7]
**Automotive** *Julia Feilden* a72 70
6 b g Beat Hollow Bina Ridge (Indian Ridge)
1385[5] 1864[3] 2963[9] (3147) 3616[3] 4548[10] 4942[9] ◆ 5721[2] 7044[12] (7804) 7925[8] 8161[2]
**Autopilot** *Anabel K Murphy* a51 70
3 b g Kyllachy Khyber Knight (IRE) (Night Shift (USA))
823[4] 1389[7] 1786[6] 2013[6] 2688[9] 3554[7] 4210[6]
**Autre Qualite (IRE)** *Stefano Botti* 108
3 b c Intikhab(USA) Swinging Secret (IRE) (Classic Secret (USA))
2376a[2]
**Autumn Lily (USA)** *Charlie Appleby* a82 101
3 b f Street Cry(IRE) Arlette (IRE) (King Of Kings (IRE))
203a[5] 505a[8]
**Autumn Revue** *Tim Easterby* 42
2 b f Monsieur Bond(IRE) Revue Princess (IRE) (Mull Of Kintyre (USA))
2014[6] 2736[7] 3091[5] 3435[5] 4449[4]
**Autumns Blush (IRE)** *Jeremy Noseda* a85 75
3 b f Kheleyf(USA) Park Romance (IRE) (Dr Fong (USA))
3068[8] 4328[5] 4697[4] 4862[4] 6314[4] (7286)
**Autumn Tide (IRE)** *Adrian Paul Keatley* a62 65
3 b f Jeremy(USA) September Tide (IRE) (Thatching)
(5169) 5237[8] 5631[6] 6172a[5] 6475[3]
**Autumn Tonic (IRE)** *Simon Dow* 24
2 b c Approve(IRE) Trempjane (Lujain (USA))
6038[9]
**Autun (USA)** *Brian Ellison* a55 85
4 b g Empire Maker(USA) Sense Of Joy (Dansili)
2699[10]
**Auvray (FR)** *E Lellouche* a78 109
3 b c Le Havre(IRE) Ameyrah (IRE) (In The Wings)
3290a[5] 4251a[11] 5481a[3] (6183a) (6954a)
**Avabin (IRE)** *M Gonnelli* 93
2 b c Amadeus Wolf Azorina Vidalii (GER) (Linamix (FR))
7655a[6]
**Avail (IRE)** *Jonathan Portman* a53
2 b g Moss Vale(IRE) Mistress Bailey (IRE) (Mister Baileys)
7511[7] 8092[11]
**Available (IRE)** *John Mackie* a68 85
5 b m Moss Vale(IRE) Divert (IRE) (Averti (IRE))
69[4] 3227[2] 3483[4] 4132[3] 4537[3] 5766[6] 5986[3] 6692[4]
**Ava's Secret (IRE)** *David Peter Nagle* a50 18
3 b f Indian Haven Kashra (IRE) (Dancing Dissident (USA))
416a[7]
**Ave Cesare** *M Delcher Sanchez* a71 57
3 b c Holy Roman Emperor(IRE) Nessa (FR) (Marchand De Sable (USA))
194a[12]
**Avenir Certain (FR)** *J-C Rouget* a104 118
3 b f Le Havre(IRE) Puggy (IRE) (Mark Of Esteem (IRE))
(2195a) (3289a) (5545a) 6970a[11]
**Aventador (FR)** *T Castanheira* 111
3 b r Zafeen(FR) Day Of Dream (IRE) (Rainbows For Life (CAN))
1621a[2] 2194a[5] 2818a[7]
**Avenue Des Champs** *Jane Chapple-Hyam* a40 52
2 b g Champs Elysees Penang Cry (Barathea (IRE))
4618[12] 5104[6] 6102[9] 6646[8] 7075[8] 7815[7] 8121[5]
**Avenue Du Monde (FR)** *Richard Hannon* 55
2 ch f Champs Elysees Marla (GER) (Pentire)
4781[9] 5344[8] 6361[6] 6811[3]
**Avenue Gabriel** *P D Deegan* 104
3 b f Champs Elysees Vas Y Carla (USA) (Gone West (USA))
1201a[3] 2581a[4] 3766a[7]
**Avenue Montaigne (IRE)** *John Joseph Murphy* a86 92
2 bb f Showcasing Dialing Tone (USA) (Distant View (USA))
3763a[6] 7563[5]
**Avertor** *Robert Stephens* a63 68
8 b g Oasis Dream Avessia (Averti (IRE))
4370[3] 5275[3] 5751[5] 7202[2] 7847[4] 7928[5] 8097[2]
**Aviator (GER)** *James Eustace* a77 70
6 br g Motivator Amore (GER) (Lando (GER))
1444[11] 2289[15] 2981[6] 4077[9] 5035[3] 6141[10]
**Avidly** *Julia Feilden* a72 63
4 b f Beat Hollow Balmy (Zafonic (USA))
276[3] 849[12] 1143[6] 1568[6] 2270[7] 3123[3] 3427[6] 5731[6] 6636[5] 7291[9] 7632[6] 7785[6]
**Avocadeau (IRE)** *William Muir* a69 72
3 b g Lawman(FR) Christmas Cracker (FR) (Alhaarth (IRE))
2013[5] 2385[5] (2948) 3683[2] 4272[5] 4817[3] 5318[4] 6110[7] (6813)
**Avocat (FR)** *Y Barberot* a57
2 b c Muhtathir Anyaar (IRE) (Green Desert (USA))
8148a[8]
**Avon Breeze** *Richard Whitaker* a71 90
5 b m Avonbridge African Breeze (Atraf)
2136[8] 2390[2] 2656[2] 3342[3] 3571[5] 4317[7] (5199) 5444[5] 5677[4] 6760[9]
**Avondream** *Milton Bradley* a59 11
5 b g Avonbridge Amazing Dream (IRE) (Thatching)
159[3] 291[5] 346[5] 688[3] 1282[12] 1573[14] 3178[8]
**Avonmore Star** *Alan McCabe* a70 72
6 b g Avonbridge Pooka's Daughter (IRE) (Eagle Eyed (USA))
248[7] 540[8] 646[4] 835[9] 1584[5] ◆ 2127[4] ◆ (3150) (3329) 3549[3] 4471[10] 4571[11] 5602[13] 5766[12] 6495[9] (7622)
**Avon Pearl** *Rune Haugen* a105 105
5 ch h Avonbridge Warden Rose (Compton Place)
509a[4] (679a) 899a[6] (2245a) 4247a[4] 4957a[7] 6054a[9]
**Avon Scent** *Christopher Mason* 50
4 b f Avonbridge Ferrybridge (IRE) (Mister Baileys)
2667[6] 3849[5] 5272[4] 6088[6]
**Avonvalley** *Peter Grayson* a70 42
7 b m Avonbridge Piper's Ash (USA) (Royal Academy (USA))
1814[4] 5130[7] 5602[11] 6077[5] 6273[7] 6561[9]
**Avra (FR)** *T Larriviere* 93
3 b c Soviet Star(USA) Casmine (FR) (Tot Ou Tard (IRE))
630a[9]
**Awake My Soul (IRE)** *Gianluca Bietolini* a68 105
5 ch g Teofilo(IRE) Field Of Hope (IRE) (Selkirk (USA))
1171[12] 1736[4] 2253[3] 3047a[5] 4212[8] 4667[3] ◆ (5238) 6590a[5] 7617a[10]
**Award (IRE)** *John Gosden* a77 82
3 b f Tamayuz Fantastic Account (Fantastic Light (USA))
2061[2] 2404[3] 3154[4] (3652)
**Awattan** *Ed Vaughan* a69
4 b f Singspiel(IRE) Mureefa (USA) (Bahri (USA))
422[5] 697[5]
**Awesome Power** *William Haggas* a73 65
2 b c Dubawi(IRE) Fairy Godmother (Fairy King (USA))
7560[7] (7926) ◆
**Awesome Rock (IRE)** *Roger Ingram* a50 38
5 ch g Rock Of Gibraltar(IRE) Dangerous Diva (IRE) (Royal Academy (USA))
5864[4] 7532[6]
**Awjab (IRE)** *Brian Meehan* a46 78
2 b g Bahamian Bounty Applause (IRE) (Danehill Dancer (IRE))
5309[9] 5752[6] 6517[4] 6931[2] 7374[9]
**Axa Reim (IRE)** *F Boccardelli* 83
5 b g Cape Cross(IRE) My Personal Space (USA) (Rahy (USA))
2375a[10]
**Ayaar (IRE)** *Luca Cumani* a100 104
4 bb c Rock Of Gibraltar(IRE) Teide Lady (Nashwan (USA))
1576[3] 2145[4] 3356[5] 4648[12] 6185a[5]
**Aya's Gift** *Ed Walker* a64 48
3 ch g Compton Place Ringarooma (Erhaab (USA))
4193[5] 4788[10] 5207[6] 5423[5] 6647[9]
**Aye Aye Digby (IRE)** *Patrick Chamings* a85 83
9 b g Captain Rio Jane Digby (IRE) (Magical Strike (USA))
(1893) 2559[5] 3749[5] 4553[5] (5182) 5951[6]
**Aye Aye Skipper (IRE)** *Dean Ivory* a67 82
4 b g Captain Marvelous(IRE) Queenfisher (Scottish Reel)
3088[14] 4131[9] 5059[3] 5602[12] 5987[8] 8186[7] 8311[2]
**Ayrad (IRE)** *Roger Varian* 110
3 ch c Dalakhani(IRE) Sweet Firebird (IRE) (Sadler's Wells (USA))
1517[5] (1969) 2818a[11] 5755[2] 6711[3] 7275[8]
**Azabitmour (FR)** *John Best* a68 66
4 b g Azamour(IRE) Brixa (FR) (Linamix (FR))
68[4] 283[6] 380[2] 454[9]
**Azagal (IRE)** *Tim Easterby* 98
3 b f Azamour(IRE) Brave Madam (IRE) (Invincible Spirit (IRE))
1515[9] (1937) 2316[13] 2983[3] 3455[6] 4176[3] 4661[4] ◆ 5612[9] 6112[6] 6234[6] ◆ 6895[8] 7168[3] 7451[7]
**Azamaara (IRE)** *James Tate* a57 13
2 b f Azamour(IRE) Causeway Queen (IRE) (Giant's Causeway (USA))
3267[12] 7840[4] 8092[10]
**Azari** *B Grizzetti* 96
2 b c Azamour(IRE) Atasari (IRE) (Whipper (USA))
7147a[3]
**Azilian** *Paul Cole* a70 67
2 b c Azamour(IRE) Zietory (Zieten (USA))
6545[6] 7730[4] 7927[3]
**Azmaam (IRE)** *Richard Hannon* 92
2 gr c Dark Angel(IRE) Miss Indigo (Indian Ridge)
3474[2] ◆ 4550[7] 5078[2] (5922) 6684[6] 6925[4]
**Azraff (IRE)** *Marco Botti* 94
2 b c Paco Boy(IRE) Gee Kel (IRE) (Danehill Dancer (IRE))
2642[4] 3381[3] 3924[2] (5147) (5762) 6686[4]
**Azrag (USA)** *Michael Attwater* a90 75
6 rg g Mizzen Mast(USA) Call Account (USA) (Private Account (USA))
2461[9] 3249[8] 3859[8] 4144[8] 4552[5] 5137[7] 5600[5] 5863[7] 6343[5] 7065[8]
**Azrur (IRE)** *David Brown* a63 92
4 b g Sir Percy Tiger Spice (Royal Applause)
1070[9] 1564[2] 2425[4] 4146[8] 4866[6] (5378)
**Azucardel (FR)** *T Lallie* a64 74
3 b g Della Francesca(USA) Azucar (IRE) (Desert Prince (IRE))
4775a[4]
**Azure Amour (IRE)** *Ralph Beckett* a56 62
2 b f Azamour(IRE) Al Euro (FR) (Mujtahid (USA))
2771[13] 3467[3] 3875[4] 8247[4]
**Azurite (IRE)** *G M Lyons* a88 94
3 b g Azamour(IRE) High Lite (Observatory (USA))
3491a[3]
**Azzir (IRE)** *Timothy Jarvis* a59 63
2 gr c Echo Of Light Lady Georgina (Linamix (FR))
5131[4] 6125[11] 6743[6] 7835[6]
**Baan (USA)** *James Eustace* a55 64
11 ch g Diesis Madaen (USA) (Nureyev (USA))
405[U] 842[9] 1197[8] 3632[4]
**Baarez (USA)** *Roger Varian* 87
3 ch g Hard Spun(USA) Sortita (GER) (Monsun (GER))
3108[5] 4147[9]
**Baars Causeway (IRE)** *Timothy Jarvis* a69 61
3 ch f Intense Focus(USA) Barbera (GER) (Night Shift (USA))
1404[6] 2049[2] 2686[3] 3225[5] 3588[6] 4972[6] 5820[5] 6883[8] 7632[10]
**Babala (FR)** *A Fabre* 15
2 b f Great Journey(JPN) Babyla (Linamix (FR))
5590a[15]
**Baba O'Riley (IRE)** *R Le Dren Doleuze* a81 96
4 b c Whipper(USA) Speckled Hen (IRE) (Titus Livius (FR))
7916a[8]
**Baby Bush (IRE)** *Richard Hannon* 84
3 b f Holy Roman Emperor(IRE) Mainstream Opinion (IRE) (Indian Ridge)
1420[9] 2340[8] (2745) 3425[5] 4445[5] 4697[10] 7159[15] 7451[6]
**Baby Foot (IRE)** *F Rossi* a103 104
3 b c Footstepsinthesand Baby Houseman (Oasis Dream)
(193a) (553a)
**Babylona (FR)** *Philippe Le Geay* a43 43
7 b m Equerry(USA) Branigann (FR) (Septieme Ciel (USA))
57a[12]
**Baby Queen (IRE)** *Brian Baugh* a20 65
8 b m Royal Applause Kissing Time (Lugana Beach)
3222[9] 3954[6] 4285[5] 4848[4] 5399[4] 5780[3] 6273[8]
**Baby Strange** *Derek Shaw* a58 93
10 gr g Superior Premium The Manx Touch (IRE) (Petardia)
1193[6] 1484[8] 1938[9] 2562[11] 2992[9] 5437[2] 6094[6] 6736[9] 7071[9] 7535[5]
**Bacall** *Kevin Ryan* 20
2 b f Paco Boy(IRE) Xtrasensory (Royal Applause)
2348[9]
**Baccalaureate (FR)** *Sue Smith* a65 67
8 b g High Chaparral(IRE) Rose D'Or (IRE) (Polish Precedent (USA))
1377[8] 2139[6]
**Baccarat (IRE)** *Richard Fahey* a74 116
5 ch g Dutch Art Zut Alors (IRE) (Pivotal)
1443[2] 2254[2] (3452) 6134[8] 6576[4] 7272[11]
**Bachotheque (IRE)** *Tim Easterby* 83
4 b g Chineur(FR) Bacchanalia (IRE) (Blues Traveller (IRE))
1903[4] 2332[15] (2602) 3256[12] 4471[9] 4925[7] 5411[5] 6094[8] (6477) ◆ 7060[8]
**Back Burner (IRE)** *Dai Burchell* a89 83
6 br g Big Bad Bob(IRE) Marl (Lycius (USA))
3[7] (407) 674[5] 870[4] 1268[3] (1495) 1816[3] 2670[3] 3582[7] 5035[4] 6156[8] 6566[8] 7422[9] 7734[12] 8029[8] 8122[11]
**Back In The Frame** *David O'Meara* a60 64
4 b f Dutch Art Ile Deserte (Green Desert (USA))
69[6]
**Back On Baileys** *John Ryan* a42 42
3 b f Kyllachy Baileys Gleam (Compton Place)
216[5] 315[7] 481[5] 739[4] 1211[8] 2023[7] 2388[7] 2931[7] 3323[3] 3549[10] 3679[6] 4101[8] 4337[6]
**Back On The Trail** *Michael Blake* a55 53
4 b g Singspiel(IRE) Boleyna (USA) (Officer (USA))
1097[7] 1385[9] 1664[13]
**Backstage Gossip** *Hughie Morrison* a74 71
3 b f Sakhee's Secret Theatre Royal (Royal Applause)
1677[4] 2125[2] (2489) 3581[8] 4741[4] 5290[4] (7252)
**Back To Base (IRE)** *David Wachman* 88
2 ch f Lope De Vega(IRE) Indian Express (Indian Ridge)
3763a[5]
**Baddilini** *Alan Bailey* a97 92
4 b g Bertolini(USA) Baddi Heights (FR) (Shirley Heights)
779[6] (890) 991[2] 1172[7] 1975[21] 7843[3] 8045[2] 8263[3]
**Badet (FR)** *L A Urbano-Grajales* 73
2 b c Monsun(GER) Bahama Love (USA) (Hennessy (USA))
5940a[5]
**Badger Daly (IRE)** *J R Hagan* a62 67
8 b g Celtic Swing Brittas Blues (IRE) (Blues Traveller (IRE))
790a[4] 4805a[7]
**Badr Al Badoor (IRE)** *James Fanshawe* a99 103
4 b f Acclamation Dani Ridge (IRE) (Indian Ridge)
4347[4] 5418[2] (6290) 6920[10] 7743[2] 7952[3] 8228[4]
**Baha** *John Gosden* 75
3 b c Dubawi(IRE) Anamato (AUS) (Redoute's Choice (AUS))
3804[4] ◆
**Bahama Bay** *Stuart Williams* a46
4 b f Bahamian Bounty Green Bonnet (IRE) (Green Desert (USA))
449[8]
**Bahama Blue** *James Eustace* a37
2 ch f Bahamian Bounty Blue Siren (Bluebird (USA))
7345[6] 8254[5]
**Bahama Dancer** *Jason Ward* a39
3 ch f Bahamian Bounty Arlene Phillips (Groom Dancer (USA))
5018[8] 6344[8] 7210[10] 7686[10]
**Bahamian Art** *Mark Johnston* 53
2 ch f Bahamian Bounty Astrodonna (Carnival Dancer)
1504[5] 1837[5] 2513[5]
**Bahamian C** *Richard Fahey* 83
3 b g Bahamian Bounty Amandian (IRE) (Indian Ridge)
1486[6] 2020[8] 3360[5] (3662) (4387) 5496[2] 5810[4] 6649[4] 6836[3] 7538[4]
**Bahamian Desert** *David O'Meara* a28 55
2 b g Bahamian Bounty Noble Desert (FR) (Green Desert (USA))
5167[7] 5807[7] 6270[9]
**Bahamian Heights** *Clive Brittain* a89 97
3 b g Bahamian Bounty Tahirah (Green Desert (USA))
2767[6] 4281[4] 4669[17] 5675[11] 6094[2] 6260[4]
**Bahamian Sunrise** *Richard Fahey* 74
2 ch g Bahamian Bounty Tagula Sunrise (IRE) (Tagula (IRE))
1732[7] 2328[2] 3570[2] 4218[3] 5679[3]
**Bahango (IRE)** *Patrick Morris* a71 64
2 b g Bahamian Bounty Last Tango (IRE) (Lion Cavern (USA))
1504[9] 1670[7] 2615[3] 3049[4] 4011[3] 4702[4] 5266[4] 5630[5] 8118[5] ◆ (8254)
**Baiadera (GER)** *R Dzubasz* a81 104
7 ch m Tertullian(USA) Belinga (GER) (Tannenkonig (IRE))
2006a[6] 4841a[7]
**Baiafa (ITY)** *G Botti* a68 63
2 b c Blu Air Force(IRE) Tofa (IRE) (Alhaarth (IRE))
3691a[5]
**Baie Fleurie (FR)** *J Rossi* 64
2 b f Diamond Green(FR) Baie Des Fleurs (FR) (Chelsea Manor)
3744a[7]
**Baile Atha Cliath (IRE)** *Declan Carroll* a55 34
5 b g Barathea(IRE) Danielli (IRE) (Danehill (USA))
269[7]
**Baileys En Premier (FR)** *Chris Dwyer* a57
3 b g Exceed And Excel(AUS) Numberonedance (USA) (Trempolino (USA))
7901[7] 8047[5]
**Baileys Forever** *James Given* a43 69
3 ch f Mount Nelson Forever Fine (USA) (Sunshine Forever (USA))
2130[8] 2657[10]
**Baileys Partytime** *Mark Johnston* 47
3 b f Aqlaam Third Party (Terimon)
6862[3]
**Baileys Pursuit** *Christine Dunnett* a23 60
2 ch f Pastoral Pursuits Royal Mistress (Fasliyev (USA))
1169[7] 1528[15] 1859[4] 3157[3] (3894) 4410[3] 6040[6]
**Bailiwick** *Daniel Kubler* a67
3 b g Oratorio(IRE) Imperial Bailiwick (IRE) (Imperial Frontier (USA))
6765[2] (7117)
**Bailley (FR)** *A Wohler* 91
2 b f Galileo(IRE) Beyond The Dream (USA) (Fusaichi Pegasus (USA))
6778a[4]
**Baillonette (FR)** *S Kobayashi* 73
3 b f Crossharbour Shanghai Queen (Exit To Nowhere (USA))
(5592a)
**Bainne (IRE)** *James Eustace* a74 84
4 b f Strategic Prince Laemeen (IRE) (Danehill Dancer (IRE))
294[10] 1041[8] 1145[10] 1489[10] 1789[8] 2691[4] ◆ 7220[9] 7767[2] 7949[10] 8082[3] 8224[3]
**Baino Hope (FR)** *J-C Rouget* 105
3 b f Jeremy(USA) Baino Ridge (FR) (Highest Honor (FR))
(5481a) 6954a[3]
**Baitha Alga (IRE)** *Richard Hannon* 106
2 b c Fast Company(IRE) Tawaafur (Fantastic Light (USA))
2507[2] (2756) (2987) (3374) 5692[9] 6547[6]
**Bajan Bear** *David Nicholls* a75 87
6 ch g Compton Place Bajan Rose (Dashing Blade)
91[4] 248[3] 451[5] 746[8] 3668[5] ◆ (4131) 4421[2] 4609[6] (4961) 5888[2] 6260[12] 6511[10] 6824[4]

**Bajan Beauty (IRE)** *Charles Hills* a50 76
3 b f Footstepsinthesand Blue Crystal (IRE) (Lure (USA))
1498[4] 2385[4] (3385) 4020[5]
**Bajan Rebel** *Michael Easterby* a50 61
3 ch f Bahamian Bounty Silca Key (Inchinor)
1601[6] (2205) 2828[3] 3300[6] 3950[9] 5497[8] 5640[13] 7291[12] 7645[7]
**Bajan Story** *Michael Blanshard* a59 54
5 b g Lucky Story(USA) Bajan Rose (Dashing Blade)
1105[4] 1771[8] 2669[4] (3178) 4564[3] 4908[10] 5000[7] 5751[6] 6715[11] 7547[9] 7844[10]
**Bajan Tryst (USA)** *J-V Toux* a72 94
8 bb g Speightstown(USA) Garden Secrets (USA) (Time For A Change (USA))
3030a[4]
**Baker Man (IRE)** *Sylvester Kirk* a63 70
3 b g Dandy Man(IRE) Anne Bonney (Jade Robbery (USA))
1101[8] 1425[3]
**Bakht A Rawan (IRE)** *Mark Usher* a34 61
2 b g Rip Van Winkle(IRE) Foolish Ambition (GER) (Danehill Dancer (IRE))
2623[7] 3082[6] 3728[9] 5828[7] 6294[5]
**Bakken (USA)** *Chad C Brown* a109
4 b c Distorted Humor(USA) General Jeanne (USA) (Honour And Glory (USA))
7612a[8]
**Balady (IRE)** *Dominic Ffrench Davis* a78 80
5 b m Zamindar(USA) Faydah (USA) (Bahri (USA))
2141[0]
**Balansiya (IRE)** *D K Weld* 102
3 b f Shamardal(USA) Baliyana (IRE) (Dalakhani (IRE))
1201a[2]
**Balashkova (FR)** *Chad C Brown* 98
4 b f Montjeu(IRE) Ecume Du Jour (FR) (Hawk Wing (USA))
2227a[6]
**Balatina** *Chris Dwyer* a59 51
4 ch f Byron Primavera (Anshan)
1141[0] 483[4]
**Balayage (IRE)** *Marco Botti* a72
2 b f Invincible Spirit(IRE) Shamwari Lodge (IRE) (Hawk Wing (USA))
8007[3] 8227[2]
**Balaythous (FR)** *Mlle B Renk* a101 101
8 ch g Bahhare(USA) Silirisa (FR) (Sillery (USA))
5961a[8]
**Balbec (FR)** *C Boutin* a55
2 b f Approve(IRE) Red Bravo (USA) (Red Ransom (USA))
6698a[11]
**Balboni (IRE)** *Mark Michael McNiff* 27
6 b g Winged Love(IRE) Hamari Gold (IRE) (Priolo (USA))
7509[10]
**Bal De France (FR)** *S Kobayashi* 90
3 b c Della Francesca(USA) Baldoranic (FR) (Panoramic)
1621a[5]
**Bal D'Or (FR)** *J Boisnard* a84 65
3 b g Creachadoir(IRE) Queen's Ball (King's Theatre (IRE))
2003a[3]
**Balducci** *David O'Meara* a74 105
7 b g Dansili Miss Meltemi (IRE) (Miswaki Tern (USA))
2453[4] (3306) 3573[3] (3886) 4442[7] 5609[3] 6748[10] 7081[15]
**Balfour (FR)** *P Nicot* a66 76
3 b c Myboycharlie(IRE) Phone The Diva (USA) (Phone Trick (USA))
4465a[3] 4838a[4]
**Balinka** *Mel Brittain* a38 70
4 b f Bahamian Bounty Eurolinka (IRE) (Tirol)
1343[7] 1694[6] 1843[11] 2233[4] 2421[4] 2724[11] 5390[12] 7783[11]
**Balios (IRE)** *David Simcock* a83
2 ch c Shamardal(USA) Elle Galante (GER) (Galileo (IRE))
(7730)
**Balladry (USA)** *S Seemar* a94 89
6 gr h Unbridled's Song(USA) Storm Song (USA) (Summer Squall (USA))
202a[5] 507a[12]
**Ballarina** *Eric Alston* a57 66
8 b m Compton Place Miss Uluwatu (IRE) (Night Shift (USA))
1604[6] 2675[6]
**Ball Dancing (USA)** *Mme Pia Brandt* a83 110
3 bb f Exchange Rate(USA) Ball Gown (USA) (Silver Hawk (USA))
2816a[2] 3289a[5]
**Ballesteros** *Richard Fahey* a78 101
5 ch g Tomba Flamenco Dancer (Mark Of Esteem (IRE))
1421[5] 2283[11] 2989[16] 3241[17] 5160[3] 5918[3] 6533[10] 6745[10] 7280[3] 7441[12] 7700[12]
**Ballet Of Doha (IRE)** *Richard Hannon* 48
2 b f Zebedee Night Of Joy (IRE) (King's Best (USA))
5643[8]
**Ballinderry Boy** *Andrew Balding* a86 103
4 b g Kayf Tara Spring Dream (IRE) (Kalanisi (IRE))
2405[6] 3321[11] 4777[11]
**Ballista (IRE)** *Tom Dascombe* a106 102
6 b g Majestic Missile(IRE) Ancient Secret (Warrshan (USA))
249[3] 713[8] 802[3] 1557[6] 2074[3] 3278[6] 4188[10] 4937[4] 5918P 7034[3] 7700[7] 8019[5] 8228[5]
**Ballroom Angel** *Philip Hide* a27
2 gr f Dark Angel(IRE) Ballroom Dancer (IRE) (Danehill Dancer (IRE))
8241[6]
**Ballyadam Brook (IRE)** *Terence O'Brien* a78 81
10 b g Alderbrook Luna Fleur (IRE) (Shardari)
7476a[13]

**Ballybacka Queen (IRE)** *P A Fahy* 99
3 b f Hurricane Run(IRE) Zankara (FR) (Linamix (FR))
2186a[3] 2581a[10] 4461a[9]
**Bally Broadwell** *Michael Madgwick* a58
4 b f Kayf Tara Ballyhoo (IRE) (Supreme Leader)
4966[10] 5490[6] 6043[3]
**Ballyfarsoon (IRE)** *Ian Williams* a55 44
3 ch g Medicean Amzara (IRE) (Montjeu (IRE))
1681[9] 2026[8] 3153[10] 7118[4] 7188[11] 8011[5] (8289)
**Ballyheigue (IRE)** *Liam Corcoran* a61 65
5 b g High Chaparral(IRE) Lypharden (IRE) (Lyphard's Special (USA))
209[4] 1117[2] (1567) 2595a[2] 2512[2] 4041a[6] 4856[7]
**Ballyhurst (IRE)** *Richard Fahey*
3 b g High Chaparral(IRE) Billet (IRE) (Danehill (USA))
1841[5] 6011[9]
**Ballymore Castle (IRE)** *Richard Fahey* 90
2 br g Invincible Spirit(IRE) Ballymore Lady (USA) (War Chant (USA))
1417[3] ◆ (2089) 2987[2] 6556[3] 6925[5]
**Ballyshonagh** *Chris Wall* a67 61
4 b f Tiger Hill(IRE) Shamara (IRE) (Spectrum (IRE))
2498[6] 3235[5] 3473[3]
**Balmont Mast (IRE)** *Edward Lynam* a102 73
6 b g Balmont(USA) Corn Futures (Nomination)
206a[4] 597a[5] 898a[5] 1180a[8] 2378a[9]
**Balmoral Castle** *Jonathan Portman* a61 88
5 b g Royal Applause Mimiteh (USA) (Maria's Mon (USA))
1209[4] (2021) 2300[2] (2963) (4501) (5669) 6523[5]
**Balofilo** *P A Fahy* a36 32
4 b f Teofilo(IRE) Baladewa (GER) (Monsun (GER))
7877a[8]
**Balouba (FR)** *C Scandella* a61 77
3 ch f Ragmar(FR) Multipolaire (FR) (Gold Away (IRE))
391a[5]
**Baltic Baroness (GER)** *A Fabre* a74 113
4 b f Shamardal(USA) Born Wild (GER) (Sadler's Wells (USA))
1341a[4] 1783a[6] 2631a[5] (6380a)
**Baltic Brave (IRE)** *Hughie Morrison* a77 91
3 b g Baltic King Negria (IRE) (Al Hareb (USA))
1669[4] 2208[2] 2647[2] ◆ (2879) 3480[2] ◆ (4404) 4647[9] 5649[3] 6895[13]
**Baltic Comtesse (FR)** *A Fabre* 103
2 b f Lope De Vega(IRE) Born Wild (GER) (Sadler's Wells (USA))
7393a[2]
**Baltic Fire (IRE)** *K R Burke* a67 66
3 b g Baltic King Teutonic (IRE) (Revoque (IRE))
753[3] 1214[2] 1657[6] 2165[2] 3430[4] 4300[3] 4871[3] 5522[3] 5891[3] 6516[7] 7346[2]
**Baltic Gin (IRE)** *Malcolm Saunders* a54 63
4 b f Baltic King Dehy Deeday Bay (IRE) (Brave Act)
1147[2] 1282[11] 1573[15]
**Baltic Knight (IRE)** *Richard Hannon* a105 114
4 b c Baltic King Night Of Joy (IRE) (King's Best (USA))
1870[9] 2223[4] 2554[4] 3731[2] 4437[8] (6060) 6955a[12] 7599[5] (7668) 7836[5] 8244[6]
**Baltic Prince (IRE)** *Tony Carroll* a72 40
4 b g Baltic King Brunswick (Warning)
95[8] 319[8] 503[2] 7661[0] 918[2] 940[2] 1227[4] 1288[3] 1610[10] 2293[5] 2914[10] 3604[6] 4707[6] 5797[2] 6227[9] 6720[7] 6766[6] 7424[5] (7972) (8013) 8063[2]
**Baltic Spirit (IRE)** *Keith Dalgleish* 65
3 b f Baltic King Beau Petite (Kyllachy)
1642[4] ◆ 1758[7] 2296[10] 2951[8] 3359[6] 3609[7] 4193[2] 4257[11] 4519[7] 4725[9]
**Baltic Storm (IRE)** *J D Hillis* 91
3 b c Kandahar Run Born Wild (GER) (Sadler's Wells (USA))
4007a[14]
**Balty Boys (IRE)** *Brian Ellison* 108
5 b g Cape Cross(IRE) Chatham Islands (USA) (Elusive Quality (USA))
1165[12] 1719[5] 2113[8] 2784[7] (2891) 3456[5] 3962[11] (4442) 4771a[15] 5928[7] 6132[2] 6752[17]
**Balu** *Mme J Romich* 66
4 gr g With Approval(CAN) Hermanita (Hernando (FR))
7769a[8]
**Bamboccianti** *Richard Fahey* a64 82
2 ch g Dutch Art Brooklyn's Sky (Septieme Ciel (USA))
5397[5] ◆ (6168) ◆ 7807[4]
**Bamiyan (FR)** *T Lemer* 109
4 gr c Kouroun(FR) Baenia (FR) (Verglas (IRE))
2799a[3] 3997a[6] (6182a) 7656a[6]
**Banaadeer (IRE)** *Richard Hannon* a88 82
3 ch c Tamayuz Loose Julie (IRE) (Cape Cross (IRE))
(2083) 3247[8]
**Banana Split** *P Harley* 85
2 b f Kyllachy Chicita Banana (Danehill Dancer (IRE))
4524a[5] 6053a[4] 7485a[5]
**Bancnuanaheireann (IRE)** *Michael Appleby* a104 101
7 b g Chevalier(IRE) Alamanta (IRE) (Ali-Royal (IRE))
840[4] 1559[5] 1973[8] 5163[5] 5695[8] 6752[20] 7597[2] 7803[5] (8012) 8095[9]
**Bandanetta (FR)** *A Bonin* 85
2 b f Soldier Of Fortune(IRE) Bandaneira (GER) (Tertullian (USA))
(5590a)
**Banditry (IRE)** *Michael Bell* 77
2 b c Iffraaj Badalona (Cape Cross (IRE))
5149[5] (5494)
**Bane (IRE)** *Ronald O'Leary* a49 56
3 ch g Tamayuz Hidden Heart (USA) (Kingmambo (USA))
6157[9]

**Bangers (IRE)** *Tom Dascombe* a55
2 b g Alfred Nobel(IRE) Sandbox Two (IRE) (Foxhound (USA))
7076[8] 7573[10] 8166[10]
**Bang In Trouble (IRE)** *Des Donovan*
2 b g Papal Bull Shinkoh Rose (FR) (Warning)
5104[7]
**Bank Of Burden (USA)** *Niels Petersen* a99 108
7 ch g Hawk Wing(USA) Wewantitall (Pivotal)
305a[6] 598a[12] 812a[7] (3090a) 3772a[2] 4956a[5] (5744a) (6389a) 6914a[3]
**Bank Of Gibraltar** *Peter Chapple-Hyam* 51
2 ch g Rock Of Gibraltar(IRE) Banksia (Marju (IRE))
7667[6]
**Banna Boirche (IRE)** *M Halford* a100 94
8 b g Lucky Owners(NZ) Ziet D'Alsace (FR) (Zieten (USA))
509a[9] 679a[12] 808a[7]
**Bannister Bell (IRE)** *David Evans* a51 44
2 b c Holy Roman Emperor(IRE) Bells Of Ireland (UAE) (Machiavellian (USA))
3779[4] 4260[2] 4541[7] 5120[5] 6642[9] 6941[6] 7112[9] 7824[5] 8179[3]
**Bannock (IRE)** *Charlie Appleby* a101 105
5 b g Bertolini(USA) Laoub (USA) (Red Ransom (USA))
808a[13]
**Bannock Town** *Linda Perratt* 13
3 b g Denounce Miss Pigalle (Good Times (ITY))
2292[8] 3103[9] 4900[6] 5233[9] 5566[6] 5857[3] 6516[9] 6834[9]
**Banoffee (IRE)** *Hughie Morrison* a99 104
4 b f Hurricane Run(IRE) Nanabanana (IRE) (Anabaa (USA))
307a[6] 682a[6] 2115[3]
**Banovallum** *Michael Easterby* a68 81
4 b g Invincible Spirit(IRE) Sinduda (Anabaa (USA))
1190[13] 1376[10] 2019[8] ◆ (2233) 2552[6] 3256[17] 6451[6] 7179[10] 7505[9]
**Banreenahreenkah (IRE)** *Paul Fitzsimons* a52 58
4 b f Steppe Dancer(IRE) Carmencita (Rock Of Gibraltar (IRE))
2135[4] 2381[3] 2609[2] 3224[5] 3798[10] 5030[7] 5596[11] 8277[2]
**Bantam (IRE)** *Ed Dunlop* a91 97
4 b f Teofilo(IRE) Firecrest (IRE) (Darshaan)
2783[8] 5162[4] 5579[16] 6061[11] 7110[6] 7565[2]
**Banzari** *Michael Bell* 94
2 b f Motivator Bantu (Cape Cross (IRE))
6065[2] 6289[5] (7209)
**Baojun (FR)** *R Rohne* a26 71
3 b c Astronomer Royal(USA) Singapore City (FR) (Sagacity (FR))
7630a[9]
**Bapak Asmara (IRE)** *Kevin Ryan* a64 72
2 ro g Zebedee Sheba Five (USA) (Five Star Day (USA))
5852[6] 7361[5] 7712[2]
**Bapak Bangsawan** *Ann Stokell* a79 73
4 b g Pastoral Pursuits Nsx (Roi Danzig (USA))
80[2] 175[3] 299[4] 432[5] (730) 1283[2] 2167[13] 2606[3] 3138[2] ◆ 7761[10] 7949[12] 8180[7]
**Bapak Chinta (USA)** *Kevin Ryan* a78 78
5 rg g Speightstown(USA) Suena Cay (USA) (Maria's Mon (USA))
1049[5] 1261[9] 1429[4] 1967[11]
**Bapak Muda (USA)** *Kevin Ryan* a72 80
4 ch g Distorted Humor(USA) Shiva (JPN) (Hector Protector (USA))
2331[1] 359[9] 1447[4] 1717[9] 2171[9] 2605[4] 3359[10] 4195[9] 4358[4] 5390[5] 5510[10]
**Bapak Pesta (IRE)** *Kevin Ryan* a59 63
4 b g Haatef(USA) Penny Fan (Nomination)
7[8] 171[6] 317[2] (368) 590[13] 1087[3] 1596[10]
**Baracoa** *H-F Devin* a67 79
3 b f Royal Applause Digger Girl (USA) (Black Minnaloushe (USA))
4464a[2]
**Baraka (GER)** *P Schiergen* a74 81
3 ch f Lomitas Bless You (USA) (Dynaformer (USA))
7270a[4]
**Baratom (FR)** *F-X De Chevigny* a58 49
8 ch g Beaudelaire(USA) Belga Wood (USA) (Woodman (USA))
57a[13]
**Baraweez (IRE)** *Brian Ellison* 103
4 b g Cape Cross(IRE) Aquarelle Bleue (Sadler's Wells (USA))
1191[5] (1762) 2234[2] (3190) 3621[2] 4771a[3] (4949a) (6354a) 7276[17]
**Barbados Bob (USA)** *Michael Wigham* a66 63
4 b g Speightstown(USA) Lemon Lady (USA) (Lemon Drop Kid (USA))
75[3]
**Barbancourt (FR)** *J-L Dubord* a69
8 b g Solon(GER) Neasham Little Star (FR) (Diamond Shoal)
437a[8]
**Barbara Elizabeth** *Tony Coyle* 51
3 b f Sir Percy Fair View (GER) (Dashing Blade)
1840[4] 2655[4] 3098[11] 3498[6] 3950[12] 4468[13] 4749[5] 6622[4]
**Barbarous (IRE)** *David Barron* 67
2 ch c Lope De Vega(IRE) Dehbanu (IRE) (King's Best (USA))
6577[2]
**Barbary (IRE)** *Charlie Fellowes* a63 55
3 b g Rock Of Gibraltar(IRE) Silver Cache (USA) (Silver Hawk (USA))
(665) ◆ 774[4] 1403[7] 2998[8] 3971[10] 6243[5] (7854) 8103[4]
**Barbecue Eddie (USA)** *Doug Watson* a113 96
10 br g Stormy Atlantic(USA) The Green Owl (USA) (Carson City (USA))
111a[9] 306a[13] 768a[5]
**Barbs Princess** *Charles Hills* a77 75
4 ch f Bahamian Bounty Halland Park Girl (IRE) (Primo Dominie)
69[2] 196[2] 453[3] 2542[2] 3305[7]

**Barchan (USA)** *Charlie Appleby* a72 63
2 b g War Front(USA) Malamado (USA) (Broken Vow (USA))
1977[8] 2859[5] 3119[7] (5828) 6679[6] 7890[2] 8009[3] 8317[4]
**Baricella (FR)** *N Sauer* a53 54
3 b f Falco(USA) Bakufu (IRE) (King's Best (USA))
2290a[9]
**Barista (IRE)** *Brian Forsey* a46 70
6 b g Titus Livius(FR) Cappuccino (IRE) (Mujadil (USA))
1800[5] 2177[3]
**Barkston Ash** *Eric Alston* a55 104
6 b g Kyllachy Ae Kae Ae (USA) (King Of Kings (IRE))
909[8] 1193[3] (1537) 1734[2] (2352) 2562[3] 3737a[18] 3960[3] 4384[13] 6354a[17] 6760[8]
**Barleycorn Lady (IRE)** *Mark Walford* 67
3 b f Nayef(USA) Partly Sunny (Alhaarth (IRE))
(1303) 2235[2] 7251[10]
**Barley Mow (IRE)** *Richard Hannon* a107 109
3 b g Zamindar(USA) Harvest Queen (IRE) (Spinning World (USA))
1300[2] 1516[4] (1953) 2502[4] 3375[5]
**Barnaby Brook (CAN)** *Nick Littmoden* a66 48
4 b g North Light(IRE) Mascara (USA) (Milwaukee Brew (USA))
2443[5]
**Barnet Fair** *David Nicholls* a85 103
6 br g Iceman Pavement Gates (Bishop Of Cashel)
991[9] 2123[4] 2989[6] 3666[6] ◆ 4179[6] 4700[2] (4892) 6131[5] ◆ 6533[14]
**Barney McGrew (IRE)** *Michael Dods* a71 83
11 b g Mark Of Esteem(IRE) Success Story (Sharrood (USA))
4471[13] 5088[6] 5766[2] 6213[15]
**Barnmore** *Peter Hedger* a82 38
6 b g Royal Applause Veronica Franco (Darshaan)
1799[6] 2079[6] (2687) (3112) 3861[5] 4968[4] 5487[5] ◆ (6035) 6886[3] 8188[7]
**Baronessa (IRE)** *Richard Hannon* 44
2 b f Royal Applause All Embracing (IRE) (Night Shift (USA))
2771[6] 3557[13]
**Baroness Daniela** *H-A Pantall* a61 97
4 b f Tiger Hill(IRE) Bedara (Barathea (IRE))
4824[10] 7769a[10]
**Barongo (IRE)** *Mme B Suter* a84 93
9 ch g Distant Music(USA) Blazing Soul (IRE) (Common Grounds)
1828a[9]
**Baron Run** *K R Burke* a71 84
4 ch g Bertolini(USA) Bhima (Polar Falcon (USA))
1191[11] 1447[10] 2677[8] 3102[3] (4383) 5236[11] (6013) 6511[23] (6824)
**Baron Spikey (IRE)** *Ann Duffield* 70
2 ch g Lord Shanakill(USA) Sharp Diversion (USA) (Diesis)
4467[7] 4723[2] 5464[8]
**Baroot** *M F De Kock* 39
2 ch c Dubawi(IRE) Time Honoured (Sadler's Wells (USA))
6462[10] 6683[9]
**Barqeyya (IRE)** *John Gosden* a62
2 b f Shamardal(USA) Almass (IRE) (Elnadim (USA))
7011[4]
**Barracuda Boy (IRE)** *Tom Dascombe* a106 99
4 b g Bahamian Bounty Madame Boulangere (Royal Applause)
(1313) 3452[20] 4412[9] 4895[20] 6159[12] 6467[3] (6744) (7843) 8101[11]
**Barren Brook** *Michael Easterby* 85
7 b g Beat Hollow Carinthia (IRE) (Tirol)
1356[8] 1842[2] (2162) 3254[4] 3573[5] 4175[7] 4635[4] 5196[6] 6476[9] 6936[6] 7335[3]
**Barri Gotic (FR)** *M Boutin* a64 76
4 gr g Soave(GER) Lunix (FR) (Linamix (FR))
796a[5]
**Bar Shy** *Tim Easterby* 35
3 b g Dutch Art Notable Lady (IRE) (Victory Note (USA))
2867[11]
**Bartack (IRE)** *David O'Meara* a87 100
4 b g Acclamation Bentley's Bush (IRE) (Barathea (IRE))
1483[14] 2054[4] 2603[3] (3005) 3397[3] 4212[2] 4635[5] 4922[4] (5446) (5771) 6226[3] 6752[25] 7211[5]
**Bartel (IRE)** *Ed Vaughan* 84
2 b c Aussie Rules(USA) Kirunavaara (IRE) (Galileo (IRE))
5149[3] 5760[2] (6462)
**Bartholomew Fair** *Luca Cumani* 92
2 b c Dansili Rebecca Sharp (Machiavellian (USA))
5315[2] ◆ (6497) 7104[7]
**Barton Bounty** *Peter Niven* a65 61
7 b g Bahamian Bounty Tenebrae (IRE) (In The Wings)
1428[8]
**Barwah (USA)** *Anthony Carson* a57 29
3 b f Discreet Cat(USA) Enfiraaj (USA) (Kingmambo (USA))
6437[6] 6661[7] 6940[5] 8111[11] (8198) 8291[2]
**Barwick** *Lady Herries* a83 90
6 b g Beat Hollow Tenpence (Bob Back (USA))
1354[5] 1636[5] (2305) 3274[3] 4119[2] 4736[3] (5073) (5756) 6685[10]
**Barye** *David Simcock* a79 79
3 b g Archipenko(USA) Oblige (Robellino (USA))
316[5] (607) 2748[7] 3421[3] 4272[2] 5038[4] 6044[8] 6722[2]
**Basateen (IRE)** *Richard Hannon* 103
2 ch c Teofilo(IRE) Tasha's Dream (USA) (Woodman (USA))
4167[3] ◆ (4570) 5576[3]
**Basem** *Saeed bin Suroor* 98
3 b c Pivotal Gonbarda (GER) (Lando (GER))
(1529) ◆ 2544[2] (5882) 6878[6]
**Bashiba (IRE)** *Nigel Tinkler* 76
3 ch g Iffraaj Nightswimmer (IRE) (Noverre (USA))
1611[9] 2023[8] 2387[3] (3228) 3487[2] 3972[10] (4469) 5169[6] (5715) (6029) 6451[5]

**Basil Berry** *Chris Dwyer* a80 94
3 b g Tobougg(IRE) Dolly Coughdrop (IRE) (Titus Livius (FR))
*(311) 401$^{2}$* ◆ *604$^{2}$ (659) 854$^{3}$ 1013$^{3}$ 1390$^{4}$* (1714) 2112$^{7}$ (2333) 3273$^{5}$ 3694$^{2}$ 4176$^{2}$ (5204) 5675$^{3}$ 6234$^{9}$
**Basil The Great** *Tom Dascombe* a64 49
2 ch g Panis(USA) Teia Tephi (Elnadim (USA))
*1363$^{3}$* 1505$^{6}$ *2680$^{3}$ 2928$^{7}$* 3312$^{10}$
**Basingstoke (IRE)** *Simon Hodgson* a79 33
5 b g Elusive City(USA) Ryninch (IRE) (Dr Devious (IRE))
*(170) (268) 767$^{7}$ 1026$^{8}$ 1217$^{8}$ 1886$^{5}$ 2399$^{11}$ 2884$^{12}$ 5833$^{9}$*
**Basle** *Roy Brotherton* a48 52
7 b m Trade Fair Gibaltarik (IRE) (Jareer (USA))
*963$^{9}$* 3848$^{15}$ 6088$^{13}$ *8133$^{10}$ 8286$^{10}$*
**Basoco** *Harry Dunlop* 61
2 b g Paco Boy(IRE) Tart And A Half (Distant Relative)
6203$^{9}$ 6984$^{7}$ 7512$^{13}$
**Bathrat Amal (JPN)** *Charlie Appleby* 62
4 ch f New Approach(IRE) Zameyla (IRE) (Cape Cross (IRE))
3315$^{9}$ 3653$^{9}$
**Bathwick Street** *David Evans* a71 47
5 ch g Compton Place Bahawir Pour (USA) (Green Dancer (USA))
5276$^{9}$ *7650$^{5}$ 7903$^{5}$ 8096$^{8}$*
**Bathyrhon (GER)** *Mme Pia Brandt* a100 112
4 b c Monsun(GER) Be My Lady (GER) (Be My Guest (USA))
2819a$^{5}$ 5743a$^{4}$ (6383a) 6972a$^{2}$
**Batrana** *M F De Kock* 86
3 br f Cape Cross(IRE) Sesmen (Inchinor)
4867$^{2}$ ◆ (5648) ◆ 6707$^{8}$
**Battalion (IRE)** *William Haggas* a109 112
4 b g Authorized(IRE) Zigarra (Halling (USA))
(1736) ◆ 2335$^{7}$ 3722$^{5}$ *6139$^{3}$* 7447$^{3}$ *(7803)* ◆
**Battersea** *Roger Varian* 103
3 b c Galileo(IRE) Gino's Spirits (Perugino (USA))
1587$^{5}$ 3673$^{2}$ (4183) (6127) 7106$^{19}$
**Battle Command (USA)** *Peter Chapple-Hyam* 83
3 bb c Stormy Atlantic(USA) Charmsil (USA) (Silver Charm (USA))
(1680) 2510$^{9}$ 3672$^{3}$ 4404$^{8}$ *7035$^{11}$*
**Battle Group** *Johnny Farrelly* a10
9 b g Beat Hollow Cantanta (Top Ville)
*4543$^{13}$ 5490$^{8}$*
**Battle Of Marathon (USA)** *A P O'Brien* 103
2 b c War Front(USA) Sayedah (IRE) (Darshaan)
3738a$^{6}$ 6800a$^{3}$
**Battle Of Marengo (IRE)** *David Simcock* a26 118
4 b c Galileo(IRE) Anna Karenina (IRE) (Green Desert (USA))
*508a$^{16}$* 900a$^{12}$ 4437$^{9}$ 4849$^{7}$ 6288$^{11}$
**Battleranger (IRE)** *Keith Dalgleish* a61 72
2 b c Bushranger(IRE) La Bataille (USA) (Out Of Place (USA))
3186$^{5}$ 3827$^{2}$ 4382$^{4}$ 4723$^{4}$ 7054$^{7}$ *7362$^{3}$ 7525$^{7}$*
**Battleoftheboyne (IRE)** *Michael Mulvany* a33 71
5 b g Majestic Missile(IRE) Khaytada (IRE) (Doyoun)
5958a$^{12}$
**Bavarian Nordic (USA)** *Richard Whitaker* a63 61
9 b g Barathea(IRE) Dubai Diamond (Octagonal (NZ))
*303$^{6}$* 1362$^{10}$ 1674$^{12}$
**Bawina (IRE)** *C Laffon-Parias* a61 113
3 b f Dubawi(IRE) Esneh (IRE) (Sadler's Wells (USA))
2195a$^{4}$ 3289a$^{7}$ (4721a) (5407a) 6382a$^{5}$
**Bayan (IRE)** *Gordon Elliott* a68 92
5 b g Danehill Dancer(IRE) Kindling (Dr Fong (USA))
1735$^{8}$ 6349a$^{4}$
**Bayan Kasirga (IRE)** *Richard Fahey* a55 88
4 b f Aussie Rules(USA) Gwyllion (USA) (Red Ransom (USA))
1444$^{14}$ 1651$^{8}$ 2259$^{14}$ 2760$^{9}$ 3341$^{9}$ 3787$^{2}$ 4417$^{5}$ 4921$^{7}$ (5414) 6099$^{3}$ 6480$^{3}$ 6761$^{8}$
**Bayern (USA)** *Bob Baffert* a124
3 bb c Offlee Wild(USA) Alittlebitearly (USA) (Thunder Gulch (USA))
*2357a$^{9}$ (7614a)*
**Bay Knight (IRE)** *Ann Stokell* a60 89
8 b g Johannesburg(USA) Sabeline (IRE) (Caerleon (USA))
*399$^{7}$ 552$^{4}$ 777$^{9}$* 7534$^{16}$
**Bayleyf (IRE)** *Lee Carter* a78 84
5 b g Kheleyf(USA) Hi Katriona (IRE) (Second Empire (IRE))
*1799$^{2}$ 2059$^{5}$ 3118$^{3}$* 3422$^{7}$ 3879$^{3}$ 4352$^{3}$ 4810$^{6}$ 5252$^{2}$ 5758$^{4}$ (5979) (6191) 6398$^{3}$ 6789$^{6}$
**Baynunah (USA)** *James Fanshawe* a74 78
3 br f Medaglia d'Oro(USA) Damaniyat Girl (USA) (Elusive Quality (USA))
*2061$^{3}$* 2433$^{6}$ (3430) 4397$^{7}$ 5685$^{4}$ *7035$^{7}$*
**Bayran (FR)** *G Doleuze* 37
4 b c Super Celebre(FR) Bone China (IRE) (Sadler's Wells (USA))
5225a$^{12}$
**Bayrir (FR)** *Marco Botti* a106 112
5 b h Medicean Balankiya (IRE) (Darshaan)
5687$^{5}$ 6233$^{3}$ *6909a$^{3}$*
**Bay Street Belle** *Alison Hutchinson* a26 58
3 ch f Bahamian Bounty Donna Anna (Be My Chief (USA))
3664$^{5}$ 3916$^{7}$ 4455$^{7}$ 5499$^{12}$ *7424$^{12}$ 7764$^{6}$ 8207$^{3}$*
**Baytown Bertie** *Lydia Richards* a40 7
5 b g Orientor Baytown Flyer (Whittingham (IRE))
*1110$^{11}$ 1387$^{11}$*
**Baytown Kestrel** *Jamie Osborne* a85 61
3 b f Captain Gerrard(IRE) Litewska (IRE) (Mujadil (USA))
*788a$^{10}$* 1445$^{8}$ *(2933)* 3484$^{7}$ 3571$^{7}$ 4282$^{5}$ *7365$^{13}$ 7761$^{4}$ 8025$^{10}$*
**Bazzana** *Martyn Meade* 83
2 b f Zebedee Bazelle (Ashkalani (IRE))
2269$^{3}$ (2622) 3415$^{13}$

**Beach Action (FR)** *Charles Hills* 39
2 bb g Footstepsinthesand Shagadellic (USA) (Devil's Bag (USA))
6299$^{7}$
**Beach Bar (IRE)** *William Knight* a94 91
3 b g Azamour(IRE) Toasted Special (USA) (Johannesburg (USA))
1655$^{2}$ ◆ (3108) 5882$^{6}$ *8312$^{2}$*
**Beach Belle** *Kevin Prendergast* 103
2 b f Invincible Spirit(IRE) Beach Bunny (IRE) (High Chaparral (IRE))
(2856a) 5218a$^{4}$ 5734a$^{6}$ 6372a$^{7}$
**Beach Plaza (IRE)** *Robert Mills* a20
2 b f Moss Vale(IRE) Uhud (IRE) (Mujtahid (USA))
*8247$^{11}$*
**Beach Rhythm (USA)** *Jim Allen* a62 75
7 ch g Footstepsinthesand Queen's Music (USA) (Dixieland Band (USA))
(2008) 3033$^{8}$ (3939) 5880$^{7}$
**Beach Samba (IRE)** *Ed Dunlop* a71 72
2 ch c Lope De Vega(IRE) Braziliz (USA) (Kingmambo (USA))
5149$^{4}$ 5655$^{13}$ 6115$^{4}$ 6668$^{2}$ 6996$^{7}$ *7374$^{4}$*
**Beach Walker** *Brian Meehan* 64
2 b f Footstepsinthesand Danemere (IRE) (Danehill (USA))
6066$^{10}$ 6554$^{4}$ 7377$^{8}$
**Beachwood Bay** *Jo Hughes* a67 49
6 b g Tobougg(IRE) The Terrier (Foxhound (USA))
*273$^{4}$ 934$^{10}$ 1448$^{10}$*
**Beacon** *Richard Hannon* 107
2 b c Paco Boy(IRE) Key Light (IRE) (Acclamation)
1712$^{4}$ (2276) (3211) (3928) 4757$^{3}$ 5692$^{6}$ (6286)
**Beacon Lady** *William Knight* a29 102
5 ch m Haafhd Oriental Lady (IRE) (King's Best (USA))
(1651) 2988$^{6}$ 3449$^{15}$ 4824$^{7}$ (5755) 6546$^{7}$
**Beacon Lodge (IRE)** *T Stack* 102
9 b g Clodovil(IRE) Royal House (FR) (Royal Academy (USA))
1078a$^{20}$
**Beacon Tarn** *Eric Alston* a78 58
4 b f Shamardal(USA) Baize (Efisio)
*175$^{9}$ 299$^{3}$ 1127$^{3}$* 1694$^{5}$ 2159$^{9}$
**Beakers N Num Nums (IRE)** *William Jarvis* a51 78
3 b c Iffraaj Ivy League Star (IRE) (Sadler's Wells (USA))
2346$^{7}$ 2850$^{8}$ 3316$^{4}$ ◆ (3898) 4332$^{3}$ 4651$^{10}$ 5884$^{6}$ 6460$^{2}$ 6870$^{7}$
**Bear Behind (IRE)** *Tom Dascombe* a91 102
5 b g Kodiac Gerobies Girl (USA) (Deposit Ticket (USA))
1305$^{11}$ 1442$^{11}$ (2166) (2562) 2898$^{2}$ 3458$^{2}$ 3960$^{7}$ 4895$^{21}$ 6131$^{11}$
**Beardwood** *Richard Fahey* 75
2 ch c Dutch Art Valentina Guest (IRE) (Be My Guest (USA))
7713$^{2}$
**Be A Rebel** *John E Long* a40
4 b f Cockney Rebel(IRE) Star Apple (Barathea (IRE))
*282$^{6}$ 657$^{11}$* 1574$^{8}$
**Bearing Kisses (IRE)** *Shaun Harris* a11 37
3 gr f Clodovil(IRE) Masakira (IRE) (Royal Academy (USA))
*232$^{6}$*
**Bearskin (IRE)** *Ann Duffield* 68
3 br g Kodiac Dark Arts (USA) (Royal Anthem (USA))
1611$^{5}$ 1906$^{7}$ 3344$^{7}$ 3534$^{4}$ 3846$^{3}$ (4455) 5089$^{6}$ (5631) 5808$^{2}$ 6575$^{4}$ 7057$^{13}$
**Beastfromtheeast** *Ed Walker* a52
3 b g Oratorio(IRE) Bronze Star (Mark Of Esteem (IRE))
*254$^{6}$ 480$^{2}$ 1029$^{5}$ 1239$^{5}$*
**Beatabout (IRE)** *Paul Green* a9
2 b c Bushranger(IRE) Dress Up (IRE) (Noverre (USA))
6058$^{9}$ 6931$^{P}$ *7254$^{9}$* 7637$^{11}$
**Beatabout The Bush (IRE)** *Charles Hills* a52 56
3 bb g Bushranger(IRE) Queen Of Fibres (IRE) (Scenic (IRE))
*284$^{5}$ 477$^{8}$*
**Beat Baby (IRE)** *Niels Petersen* a99 111
7 ch g Johannesburg(USA) Najiya (Nashwan (USA))
393a$^{2}$ 897a$^{10}$ 1179a$^{12}$ *2244a$^{6}$* 6387a$^{3}$
**Beat The Ballot (IRE)** *Tracey Collins* a76 74
5 br g Big Bad Bob(IRE) Cosmic Speed Queen (USA) (On To Glory (USA))
*6082a$^{3}$*
**Beat The Shower** *Peter Niven* a27 66
8 b g Beat Hollow Crimson Shower (Dowsing (USA))
2055$^{5}$ 2620$^{4}$ 3532$^{4}$ 4474$^{3}$ 5240$^{3}$ (5466) 6864$^{12}$ 7333$^{7}$
**Beat The Tide** *Michael Dods* 83
4 b g Black Sam Bellamy(IRE) Sablonne (USA) (Silver Hawk (USA))
1934$^{5}$ 2424$^{3}$ 3532$^{2}$ 4874$^{2}$ 5334$^{5}$ 5890$^{8}$ 6651$^{7}$
**Beaubec (FR)** *M Boutin* a63 70
2 b c Air Chief Marshal(IRE) Uvana Bere (FR) (Della Francesca (USA))
4881a$^{3}$
**Beauchamp Ace** *Paul Fitzsimons* a32 70
2 b g Compton Admiral Aquarelle (Kenmare (FR))
2777$^{6}$ 5029$^{4}$ 6039$^{6}$ *8317$^{11}$*
**Beauchamp Bella** *Paul Fitzsimons* a22
4 b f Manduro(GER) Baharah (USA) (Elusive Quality (USA))
*642$^{8}$* 2442$^{14}$
**Beauchamp Diamond** *Paul Fitzsimons*
2 b f Compton Admiral Orange Sunset (IRE) (Roanoke (USA))
7511$^{8}$ *7778$^{10}$*
**Beauchamp Fire** *Paul Fitzsimons*
2 b c Compton Admiral Bestemor (Selkirk (USA))
4395$^{13}$

**Beauchamp Kite** *Paul Fitzsimons* a17 3
3 b g Compton Admiral Orange Sunset (IRE) (Roanoke (USA))
*2881$^{10}$* 4435$^{11}$ 4785$^{7}$
**Beauchamp Melba** *Paul Fitzsimons* a49 17
3 b f Compton Admiral Ashford Castle (USA) (Bates Motel (USA))
1808$^{10}$ 2280$^{11}$ 2690$^{12}$ *2997$^{3}$ 3471$^{5}$ 5283$^{7}$* 5747$^{4}$ 6714$^{9}$ *7664$^{8}$*
**Beauchamp Ruby** *Paul Fitzsimons* a46 33
2 b f Cockney Rebel(IRE) Beauchamp Utopia (Compton Admiral)
5973$^{11}$ 6246$^{11}$ *6630$^{8}$ 7996$^{5}$ 8206$^{6}$*
**Beauchamp Sunset** *Paul Fitzsimons* a51
4 b g Tiger Hill(IRE) Orange Sunset (IRE) (Roanoke (USA))
*368$^{4}$ 570$^{6}$ 759$^{10}$*
**Beau Eile (IRE)** *David Barron* 74
2 b f Arcano(IRE) Mona Em (IRE) (Catrail (USA))
5332$^{2}$ 6168$^{2}$ ◆ (7004)
**Beau Knight** *William Jarvis* a61
2 b c Sir Percy Nicola Bella (IRE) (Sadler's Wells (USA))
*8288$^{4}$*
**Beaulie** *Keith Reveley* 15
4 ch f Black Sam Bellamy(IRE) Fairlie (Halling (USA))
2392$^{8}$ 2653$^{9}$ 3485$^{8}$
**Beau Mistral (IRE)** *Paul Green* a76 79
5 ch m Windsor Knot(IRE) Carpet Lover (IRE) (Fayruz)
*1224$^{6}$ 1266$^{2}$* 1604$^{4}$ 2056$^{7}$ 2297$^{4}$ 2602$^{5}$ 3921$^{4}$ 4391$^{8}$
**Beaumont Cooper** *Anabel K Murphy* a43 36
5 b g Invincible Spirit(IRE) Atlantide (USA) (Southern Halo (USA))
*575$^{8}$ 754$^{8}$* 3178$^{6}$
**Beaumont's Party (IRE)** *Brian Ellison* a71 101
7 b g High Chaparral(IRE) Miss Champagne (FR) (Bering)
2891$^{5}$ 3457$^{7}$ 4922$^{9}$ 5238$^{7}$ 5633$^{10}$ 6098$^{12}$
**Beau Nash (IRE)** *Richard Hannon* a88 96
3 b c Dandy Man(IRE) Dathuil (IRE) (Royal Academy (USA))
1278$^{3}$ 1937$^{2}$ 2556$^{3}$ 3378$^{22}$ 5919$^{3}$ 6281$^{6}$
**Beausant** *George Baker* 30
2 ch c Orientor Hanella (IRE) (Galileo (IRE))
7512$^{10}$
**Beau Satchel** *Adrian McGuinness* a78 77
4 b g Indesatchel(IRE) Sweet Patoopie (Indian Ridge)
(4950a)
**Beau Sparkle (IRE)** *Steph Hollinshead* a50 38
2 b f Baltic King Cabopino (IRE) (Captain Rio)
*7113$^{10}$* 7493$^{4}$ *7999$^{3}$ 8165$^{5}$*
**Beautiful Ending** *Saeed bin Suroor* a73 69
2 ch f Exceed And Excel(AUS) Pearl Kite (USA) (Silver Hawk (USA))
6517$^{5}$ *(7367)*
**Beautiful Heroine (IRE)** *F-H Graffard* 96
3 b f High Chaparral(IRE) Blue Sail (USA) (Kingmambo (USA))
7736a$^{4}$
**Beautifull Mind (IRE)** *Alan Bailey* a36
2 gr f Zebedee Alexander Family (IRE) (Danetime (IRE))
*1169$^{5}$*
**Beautiful Romance** *Saeed bin Suroor* 90
2 b f New Approach(IRE) Mazuna (IRE) (Cape Cross (IRE))
(7406) ◆
**Beautiful Stranger (IRE)** *Keith Dalgleish* a78 79
3 b g Iffraaj Monarchy (IRE) (Common Grounds)
*(568) 892$^{2}$ 1149$^{3}$* 2218$^{3}$ 2517$^{2}$ 2828$^{4}$ 3002$^{5}$ 5891$^{6}$ 6477$^{3}$ (6515) 6792$^{2}$ 6822$^{6}$ *7373$^{10}$* 7640$^{5}$ *7954$^{3}$*
**Beautiful View** *Richard Hannon* 86
4 ch f Dubawi(IRE) Flamenco Dancer (Mark Of Esteem (IRE))
2032$^{4}$ 2318$^{11}$ 2757$^{8}$
**Beautifulwildthing** *Richard Fahey* 6
4 b f Mount Nelson Euro Empire (USA) (Bartok (IRE))
6454$^{15}$
**Beauty Of The Sea** *Roger Varian* a60 60
2 b f Elusive Quality(USA) Raymi Coya (CAN) (Van Nistelrooy (USA))
3888$^{8}$ 5667$^{5}$ 6420$^{5}$ *7753$^{7}$ 7902$^{6}$*
**Beauty Prince** *Clive Cox* a67 34
2 b g Arcano(IRE) Singed (Zamindar (USA))
6517$^{18}$ *7779$^{2}$*
**Beauty Traou Land (FR)** *B De Montzey* a62
2 b f Hurricane Cat(USA) Anablue (FR) (Anabaa (USA))
*5026a$^{5}$ 5619a$^{6}$*
**Beaver Creek** *Ralph J Smith* a5 31
3 ch c Three Valleys(USA) Delta (Zafonic (USA))
2334$^{16}$ 3248$^{13}$ 5648$^{5}$ 6298$^{7}$ *6661$^{10}$*
**Be Bold** *Richard Hannon* a83 82
2 ch g Assertive Marysienka (Primo Dominie)
1417$^{5}$ *1575$^{2}$* (2246) 4205$^{2}$ 4439$^{23}$ 4605$^{6}$ *6854$^{2}$* 7131$^{4}$ *7661$^{2}$ 7755$^{4}$*
**Beccabuddyblues (GR)** *Amanda Perrett* a38
2 ch f Reel Buddy(USA) Second Of May (Lion Cavern (USA))
*7658$^{9}$ 7756$^{9}$ 8173$^{14}$*
**Bechir (FR)** *P Van De Poele* a66
3 ch c Bernebeau(FR) Oja (FR) (Lahint (USA))
4465a$^{10}$
**Beckermet (IRE)** *Ruth Carr* a46 78
12 b g Second Empire(IRE) Razida (IRE) (Last Tycoon)
1376$^{4}$ 1610$^{4}$ 1905$^{4}$ 2166$^{4}$ 2549$^{3}$ 3053$^{3}$ 3660$^{7}$
**Beck's Bolero (IRE)** *Mrs A Corson* a12 52
8 ch g Haafhd Prealpina (IRE) (Indian Ridge)
1624a$^{4}$ 2596a$^{3}$ 4040a$^{6}$ 4717a$^{5}$ 5970a$^{3}$ 6187a$^{7}$
**Become Aware** *Tim Etherington*
2 b g Sakhee(USA) Sainte Gig (FR) (Saint Cyrien (FR))
*7891$^{10}$*
**Becquanaille (FR)** *P Van De Poele* 71
2 b c Slickly(FR) Berangele (FR) (Medaaly)
7027a$^{2}$ 7344a$^{5}$

**Bed Bed** *Michael Bell* a42 43
3 b f Nayef(USA) Bedara (Barathea (IRE))
*1032$^{5}$* 2028$^{7}$
**Bedloe's Island (IRE)** *Alan McCabe* a91 69
9 b g Statue Of Liberty(USA) Scenaria (IRE) (Scenic (IRE))
*271$^{4}$* 1193$^{12}$ *1313$^{3}$* 1506$^{12}$ *7767$^{3}$ 7889$^{5}$ 8135$^{6}$*
**Beedee** *Richard Hannon* a66 70
4 b g Beat Hollow Dawnus (IRE) (Night Shift (USA))
*8042$^{10}$ 8257$^{10}$*
**Beep** *Lydia Richards* a55 71
4 b f Beat Hollow Dialing Tone (USA) (Distant View (USA))
2498$^{5}$ 3032$^{4}$ 3540$^{4}$ 4548$^{6}$ 5383$^{3}$ 5873$^{4}$ 6007$^{4}$ *6856$^{7}$* 7343$^{10}$
**Befortyfour** *Muredach Kelly* a55 48
9 b g Kyllachy Ivania (First Trump)
*6851$^{2}$ 6897$^{12}$*
**Beggers Belief** *Zoe Davison* a60 41
6 ch g Bertolini(USA) Dropitlikeit's Hot (IRE) (Tagula (IRE))
*185$^{6}$ 247$^{4}$ 759$^{4}$ 959$^{9}$*
**Beggers Luck** *Eric Wheeler* a61
4 b f Lucky Story(USA) Dropitlikeit's Hot (IRE) (Tagula (IRE))
*341$^{8}$ 7921$^{5}$ 8038$^{2}$*
**Beijing Star** *Charles Hills* a48 15
2 ch c Dylan Thomas(IRE) Signella (Selkirk (USA))
4395$^{12}$ *7354$^{10}$*
**Belahodood** *William Haggas* a65
3 b c New Approach(IRE) Broken Peace (USA) (Devil's Bag (USA))
*8249$^{2}$*
**Belango (GER)** *R Dzubasz* 102
8 ch g Tertullian(USA) Brighella (GER) (Lomitas)
6914a$^{11}$
**Belardo (IRE)** *Roger Varian* 119
2 b c Lope De Vega(IRE) Danaskaya (IRE) (Danehill (USA))
(3626) 4123$^{4}$ ◆ (5431) 6326$^{4}$ (7241) ◆
**Belayer (IRE)** *Kevin Ryan* 77
3 b g Whipper(USA) Stella Del Mattino (USA) (Golden Gear (USA))
1658$^{6}$ 2257$^{18}$ 2638$^{6}$
**Beldale Memory (IRE)** *Clive Cox* 91
3 b f Camacho Hartstown House (IRE) (Primo Dominie)
1435$^{11}$
**Belfilo (IRE)** *Andrew Balding* a84 77
3 ch g Teofilo(IRE) Belsay (Belmez (USA))
*717$^{2}$ (951)* 1419$^{6}$ 2319$^{10}$ 4584$^{3}$ *6143$^{2}$*
**Belgian Bill** *George Baker* a110 109
6 b h Exceed And Excel(AUS) Gay Romance (Singspiel (IRE))
2145$^{3}$ 3356$^{7}$ ◆ 4648$^{17}$ 4851$^{5}$ 5666$^{7}$ 6185a$^{6}$ 7276$^{14}$
**Belgrade** *Richard Hannon* a77 61
2 b c Rock Of Gibraltar(IRE) Powder Blue (Daylami (IRE))
4666$^{9}$ *6102$^{2}$ (6565)*
**Belinsky (IRE)** *Dean Ivory* a52 49
7 b g Compton Place Westwood (FR) (Anabaa (USA))
*296$^{10}$ 424$^{8}$* 2029$^{7}$ *2459$^{4}$*
**Bella Alamoto** *John Bridger*
2 b f Almaty(IRE) Mtoto Girl (Mtoto)
3076$^{12}$ *3387$^{8}$*
**Bella Duchessa (GER)** *P Schiergen* 87
4 ch f Duke Of Marmalade(IRE) Bora Blues (Peintre Celebre (USA))
7768a$^{10}$
**Bellajeu** *Ralph Beckett* 79
2 b f Montjeu(IRE) Arbella (Primo Dominie)
3888$^{9}$ 5078$^{4}$ 7450$^{2}$
**Bella Lulu** *Roger Varian* 60
2 b f Iffraaj Loulwa (IRE) (Montjeu (IRE))
6753$^{6}$
**Bella Nostalgia (IRE)** *Hugo Palmer* 52
2 ch f Raven's Pass(USA) Fafinta (IRE) (Indian Ridge)
7405$^{10}$
**Bella Nouf** *William Haggas* 71
2 b f Dansili Majestic Sakeena (IRE) (King's Best (USA))
7108$^{6}$
**Bell'Arte (IRE)** *Laura Mongan* a55 61
4 b f Zamindar(USA) Art Eyes (USA) (Halling (USA))
*454$^{6}$ 580$^{6}$ 657$^{9}$ 842$^{10}$* 2465$^{7}$
**Bella Varenna (IRE)** *Marco Botti* a71 67
3 b f Lawman(FR) Sarawati (IRE) (Haafhd)
3653$^{4}$ *(4081) 5036$^{6}$ 6338$^{4}$* 7162$^{3}$
**Belle Bayardo (IRE)** *Tony Carroll* a69 76
6 b g Le Vie Dei Colori Heres The Plan (IRE) (Revoque (IRE))
*273$^{7}$ 452$^{3}$ 511$^{7}$ 798$^{5}$ 1010$^{3}$ 1104$^{3}$* 1639$^{3}$ 2008$^{4}$ 2435$^{2}$ (2722) 3237$^{6}$ 3549$^{5}$ (4428) 4905$^{8}$ (6088) 6657$^{13}$ 7337$^{4}$ 7759$^{11}$ 7959a$^{5}$ 8082$^{11}$
**Belle Caroline (USA)** *Tim Pitt* 20
3 b f Street Sense(USA) Ebaraya (IRE) (Sadler's Wells (USA))
1303$^{11}$
**Belle De Crecy (IRE)** *Mme C Head-Maarek* 112
5 b m Rock Of Gibraltar(IRE) Bloemfontain (IRE) (Cape Cross (IRE))
1783a$^{8}$ 3171a$^{6}$ 5369a$^{2}$
**Belle De Lawers** *James Bethell* 96
3 b f Black Sam Bellamy(IRE) Scotland The Brave (Zilzal (USA))
(1722) 2316$^{5}$ 3143$^{8}$
**Belle D'Or (USA)** *John Gosden* 106
3 b f Medaglia d'Oro(USA) Glatisant (Rainbow Quest (USA))
2780$^{2}$ (3276) ◆ (3983) 6707$^{2}$
**Belle Dormant (IRE)** *Seamus Durack* 61
2 b f Rip Van Winkle(IRE) Lady Rockfield (IRE) (Rock Of Gibraltar (IRE))
4396$^{8}$ 6246$^{5}$
**Belle Du Jour (FR)** *M Boutin* 74
2 b f Dyhim Diamond(IRE) Decatur (Deploy)
(1271a) 3029a$^{5}$ 6698a$^{10}$

**Belle Et Bete (IRE)** *G M Lyons* 91
2 b f Big Bad Bob(IRE) Petite Cherie (IRE) (Fasliyev (USA))
3763a[11]

**Belle Fille** *David Brown* 74
2 ch f Makfi Belle Allemande (CAN) (Royal Academy (USA))
1528[5] 2107[7] 3461[3]

**Belle Gallantey (USA)** *Rudy Rodriguez* a112
5 ch m After Market(USA) Revealed (USA) (Old Trieste (USA))
*7593a[9]*

**Belle Intrigue** *Marjorie Fife*
4 ch f Sakhee's Secret Belle Bellino (FR) (Robellino (USA))
*1125[8]*

**Belle Miss (FR)** *E Caroux* 52
3 b f Laverock(IRE) Miss Hernando (Hernando (FR))
*194a[11]*

**Belle Nellie (IRE)** *Nigel Tinkler* 55
2 b f Kodiac Mildmay (USA) (Elusive Quality (USA))
3909[5] 6453[6] 6867[5] 7497[3]

**Belle Park** *Victor Dartnall* a61 75
7 b m Hamairi(IRE) Cape Siren (Warning)
(2672) 3175[3] 3853[5] 5338[3] (6086) (7340)

**Belle Peinture (FR)** *Alan Lockwood* a47 50
3 ch f Peintre Celebre(USA) Grosgrain (USA) (Diesis)
*71[5] 198[2]* 2237[7] 2616[10] 3534[5] 3973[2] 4292[6] 6454[3] 6628[10] 7283[5]

**Belle Star** *Noel Quinlan*
3 b f Royal Applause Dixie Belle (Diktat)
3677[7]

**Belle Travers** *Richard Fahey* 73
2 ch f Bahamian Bounty Forthefirstime (Dr Fong (USA))
(6931)

**Belletriste (FR)** *Sylvester Kirk* 82
3 gr f Literato(FR) Mulled Wine (FR) (Night Shift (USA))
2489[4] 2946[3] 3801[2] (5226a) 6446a[7] 7026a[6] 7722a[8]

**Belliciosa (FR)** *Christian Le Galliard* a25 27
2 ch f Dr Fong(USA) Like Afleet (USA) (Afleet Alex (USA))
5590a[14]

**Bello (AUS)** *Charlie Appleby* a102 109
6 b g Exceed And Excel(AUS) Cara Bella (Seeking The Gold (USA))
*597a[4] 898a[8] 1180a[13]*

**Bell Weir** *Dianne Sayer* 76
6 gr g Tobougg(IRE) Belly Dancer (IRE) (Danehill Dancer (IRE))
5456a[4] 6228[4] 6640[7]

**Belrog** *Ralph Beckett* a79 74
3 ch g New Approach(IRE) Millennium Dash (Nashwan (USA))
*1391[2]*

**Belshazzar (JPN)** *Kunihide Matsuda* a119 110
6 br h King Kamehameha(JPN) Maruka Candy (JPN) (Sunday Silence (USA))
*1183a[11]*

**Bel Sprinter (AUS)** *Jason Warren* 115
7 b g Bel Esprit(AUS) Gavroche (AUS) (Snippets (AUS))
1468a[14]

**Beltor** *Sir Mark Prescott Bt* 80
3 b g Authorized(IRE) Carahill (AUS) (Danehill (USA))
(6672) 7043[3]

**Be Lucky** *Michael Easterby* a67 80
4 ch f Kyllachy Spritzeria (Bigstone (IRE))
1604[2] 1967[9] 3256[15] 3612[6] 6475[8]

**Belvoir Diva** *Chris Wall* a78 66
2 br f Exceed And Excel(AUS) Merry Diva (Bahamian Bounty)
2380[4] *(8007)*

**Be Mine (FR)** *S Jeddari* a49 43
2 gr f Great Journey(JPN) Belle Oubava (FR) (Linamix (FR))
4882a[14]

**Be My Gal** *Roger Charlton* a74 107
3 b f Galileo(IRE) Longing To Dance (Danehill Dancer (IRE))
1423[2] ◆ (1945) 3808a[3] (4840a) 5545a[7] 6655[4]

**Benandonner (USA)** *Mike Murphy* a62 60
11 ch g Giant's Causeway(USA) Cape Verdi (IRE) (Caerleon (USA))
*152[2] (321)* ◆ *672[2] (780) 1036[2] 1917[5]* 2689[2] 3334[7] 5096[5] *7288[7] 7813[13]* 8198[3]

**Benbecula** *Richard Mitchell* a61 82
5 b g Motivator Isle Of Flame (Shirley Heights)
*427[7]* 3274[4] 4678[3] 5878[3]

**Ben Bulben Pace (IRE)** *Mark Johnston* 57
3 b g Fastnet Rock(AUS) Littlepacepaddocks (IRE) (Accordion)
3302[5]

**Ben Hall (IRE)** *Mike Murphy* a100 98
3 b g Bushranger(IRE) Sassy Gal (IRE) (King's Best (USA))
*(778)* 2767[7] 3253[18] 3969[5] 4712[8] 5675[9] 6170[13] *6764[7]*

**Benidorm** *Richard Guest* a53 51
6 b g Bahamian Bounty Famcred (Inchinor)
*869[10]* 3363[6] *3798[3] 5103[4]* 5244[2] 5376[4] 5854[3] *5893[8]* 6544[7] 6833[9] 7056[4] 7222[5] *7646[8]*

**Benjamin Disraeli (IRE)** *John Best* a34
2 b c Champs Elysees Strike Lightly (Rainbow Quest (USA))
*8318[10]*

**Ben Muir** *Stuart Williams* 26
2 b g Observatory(USA) Chapel Corner (IRE) (Alhaarth (IRE))
7380[10] 7713[10]

**Bennelong** *Lee Carter* a68 63
8 b g Bahamian Bounty Bundle Up (USA) (Miner's Mark (USA))
*247[6] 490[6] 601[3] (661) (754) 1023[2] 1097[3] 1232[3] 1406[7]* 1771[2] 2282[4] 2464[4] 2651[4] 2862[5] (3235) 3473[5] 3878[6] 4273[5] 4582[3] (5041) 5428[4] 5975[3] 6243[6] 6636[8] 8250[12] 8316[5]

**Benoordenhout (IRE)** *Jonathan Portman* a68 59
3 br g Footstepsinthesand Tara Too (IRE) (Danetime (IRE))
*1918[4]* 2416[7] 2694[6] *(4084) 4738[7] 5428[3] (5865)* 6696[12] 7517[4] *7804[2] 8103[9]*

**Benouville (FR)** *C Baillet* 54
2 b f Siyouni(FR) Bellifiore (FR) (Verglas (IRE))
1402a[8]

**Bentons Lad** *George Moore* 53
3 br g Bollin Eric Spirit Of Ecstacy (Val Royal (FR))
1372[3] 1840[5] 2237[4] 2616[7] 4497[2] 5682[3] 7500[8]

**Benvenue (IRE)** *R Biondi* 109
5 ch h Iffraaj Guest Harbour (IRE) (Be My Guest (USA))
(3047a)

**Be Perfect (USA)** *David Nicholls* a97 90
5 b g Street Cry(IRE) Binya (GER) (Royal Solo (IRE))
*(462) 803[9]* 1562[11] 1735[12] 4685[6] 5144[4] 5334[2] 6133[13] 6514[10] 7124[16]

**Berbice (IRE)** *Linda Perratt* a39 60
9 gr g Acclamation Pearl Bright (FR) (Kaldoun (FR))
4254[6] 4523[6] 4727[2] 5640[6] 5854[7] 6114[9] 6405[9] 6478[7] 6595[2] 6833[4] 7056[10]

**Be Ready (IRE)** *Saeed bin Suroor* 108
3 ch c New Approach(IRE) Call Later (USA) (Gone West (USA))
1532[6]

**Bereka** *Richard Fahey* a64 66
3 b f Firebreak Alexander Ballet (Mind Games)
*855[3] 1045[2]* 3821[2] *5257[9]* 6575[5]

**Bereni Ka (FR)** *L Tassart* a57 102
3 b f Vadasin(IRE) Ile Aux Moines (IRE) (Bering)
1502a[5] 2586a[2] 3289a[11] 7319a[6] 7720a[11]

**Bergan (GER)** *Mick Channon* a65 53
3 ch g Halling(USA) Baltic Gift (Cadeaux Genereux)
*1011[4]* 1438[13] *2917[8]* 3818[7]

**Berkeley Street (USA)** *Jane Chapple-Hyam* a65 58
4 b g Street Cry(IRE) Dream Ticket (USA) (Danzig (USA))
*67[9] 910[7] 1836[5]* 2609[7] 2843[6] 3632[6] *4326[7]* 5076[7]

**Berkeley Vale** *Roger Teal* a63 67
3 b g Three Valleys(USA) Intriguing Glimpse (Piccolo)
4654[4] *6022[4]* 6397[14] *7556[8]*

**Berkshire (IRE)** *Paul Cole* 117
3 b c Mount Nelson Kinnaird (IRE) (Dr Devious (IRE))
1436[9] (7243)

**Berkshire Beauty** *Andrew Balding* 64
2 b f Aqlaam Salim Toto (Mtoto)
3557[11] 4330[5] 5351[9] 7207[8]

**Berland (IRE)** *Michael Bell* 80
2 br c Cape Cross(IRE) Ballantrae (IRE) (Diktat)
4301[2] (4993) 5762[4]

**Berlin Berlin** *Markus Klug* 105
5 b m Dubai Destination(USA) Bombazine (IRE) (Generous (IRE))
3770a[7] 5231a[2] 6180a[6] 6956a[10]

**Berling (IRE)** *Jessica Long* a92 104
7 gr g Montjeu(IRE) Danaskaya (IRE) (Danehill (USA))
*2245a[6]* 3090a[5] 3772a[8] 5744a[13] 7243[10]

**Berlino Di Tiger (BRZ)** *Eduardo Caramori* a28 105
6 ch h Tiger Heart(USA) Rainha Da Bateria (BRZ) (Torrential (USA))
1179a[11]

**Berlusca (IRE)** *David O'Meara* a88 89
5 b g Holy Roman Emperor(IRE) Shemanikha (FR) (Sendawar (IRE))
*200[10] 560[6]* 3463[6] 3910[2] 4453[5] 4635[3] 4753[6] 5446[8] (6057) 6704[12] *7784[4] 7870[5] 7955[4] 8290[6]*

**Bermuda Reef (IRE)** *P Schiergen* 110
4 b c Oasis Dream Borgia (GER) (Acatenango (GER))
(4006a) 4720a[11] 5938a[7] 7316a[4] 7727a[9]

**Bernay (IRE)** *C Ferland* a99 100
3 b g King's Best(USA) Beringold (Bering)
*7619a[3] 8006a[3]*

**Bernhard (IRE)** *Sir Michael Stoute* a45
2 b c Bernardini(USA) Nasheej (USA) (Swain (IRE))
*7927[10]*

**Bernisdale** *John Flint* a56 67
6 ch m Bertolini(USA) Carradale (Pursuit Of Love)
2419[3] 5208[3]

**Be Royale** *Michael Appleby* a76 73
4 b f Byron Sofia Royale (Royal Applause)
2282[5] 2775[4] (3160) 3547[5] 4108[6] *6160[5] 6766[4]* 7494[10] *(7830) 7906[2] 7993[6]*

**Berrahri (IRE)** *John Best* a75 83
3 b g Bahri(USA) Band Of Colour (IRE) (Spectrum (IRE))
1907a[6] 2112[11] 2962[13] 3643[9] 4620[8] *5304[7] 6022[8] 6342[7] 6883[6] 7197[8] 7369[8]*

**Bertha Burnett (IRE)** *Brian Rothwell* a11 58
3 gr f Verglas(IRE) Starsazi (Observatory (USA))
2355[7] 3950[7] 4292[3] 4871[2] 5245[3] 5891[8]

**Bertie Baby** *Gay Kelleway* 13
3 br f Bertolini(USA) Los Organos (IRE) (Turtle Island (IRE))
*579[7]*

**Bertie Blu Boy** *Lisa Williamson* a67 58
6 b g Central Park(IRE) Shaymee's Girl (Wizard King)
*17[12] 92[2] (288) (428) (603) 740[3] 846[3] 1017[4] 1297[4]* 4578[9] (5138) 5605[5] 6122[15] 7556[11] 7906[11] 8143[7] 8298[6]

**Bertie Le Belge (IRE)** *G M Lyons* a77 97
2 b g Big Bad Bob(IRE) Ski For Gold (Shirley Heights)
6348a[4]

**Bertie Moon** *Geoffrey Deacon* a70 83
4 b g Bertolini(USA) Fleeting Moon (Fleetwood (IRE))
3805[6] (4030) 4273[2] (4743) 4985[6] 5345[4] 7516[3]

**Bertiewhittle** *David Barron* a110 108
6 ch g Bahamian Bounty Minette (Bishop Of Cashel)
*109a[3] 306a[11] 715[3] 886[3]* 1719[6] 2145[19] 2784[6]

**Bertinoro (IRE)** *Stefano Botti* 101
3 b c Aussie Rules(USA) Swirling (IRE) (Galileo (IRE))
2376a[6]

**Bert The Alert** *Laura Mongan* a68 53
6 b g Proclamation(IRE) Megalex (Karinga Bay)
*(400) 606[3] 818[4] 1065[3] 1140[4] 1242[3] 1895[2]* 2468[P]

**Berwin (IRE)** *Sylvester Kirk* a59 53
5 b m Lawman(FR) Topiary (IRE) (Selkirk (USA))
*4433[8] 4737[7] 5036[8] 5547[7]* 6028[5] 6195[3] *6481[10] 7360[10] 7924[3] 8111[5]*

**Be Seeing You** *Roger Charlton* a69 71
3 ch g Medicean Oshiponga (Barathea (IRE))
2222[4] *4074[13]* 5903[4] 7309[4]

**Best Be Careful (IRE)** *John James Feane* a66 69
6 b m Exceed And Excel(AUS) Precautionary (Green Desert (USA))
5154a[7] 6815[6]

**Best Boy** *David C Griffiths* 24
2 b c Myboycharlie(IRE) Best Dancer (King's Best (USA))
7713[9]

**Best Dressed** *David Brown* 76
2 b g Pastoral Pursuits All The Nines (IRE) (Elusive City (USA))
4570[3] 5050[5] 5922[6] (6574)

**Best Endeavour** *William Muir* a79 72
2 b c Medicean Striving (IRE) (Danehill Dancer (IRE))
2964[8] 4550[8] 5201[6] 5684[2] 6115[3] *(6678) 7224[4]*

**Best Example (USA)** *Saeed bin Suroor* 74
2 ch g King's Best(USA) Born Something (IRE) (Caerleon (USA))
4216[4] 6190[5] (6790) 7404[4]

**Best Fouad (FR)** *M Le Forestier* 103
3 bb g King's Best(USA) Raheefa (USA) (Riverman (USA))
6589a[7]

**Best Kept** *Amanda Perrett* a82 80
3 ch g Sakhee's Secret Ashlinn (IRE) (Ashkalani (IRE))
*2063[5]* 2481[5] 2968[5] 3197[5] 3986[3] 4332[5] *5008[7] 5557[9] 7358[4]*

**Best Love Royal (FR)** *F-X De Chevigny* a46 62
3 b c Kingsalsa(USA) Queen Love Royale (FR) (Enrique)
*194a[10]* 630a[5]

**Best Of Order (IRE)** *David O'Meara* a84 103
7 ch h Pivotal Groom Order (Groom Dancer (USA))
(2202) 2784[4] 3189[7] 4200[11] 5178[8] 5711[8]

**Best Of Times** *Saeed bin Suroor* 95
2 b c Dubawi(IRE) Nabati (USA) (Rahy (USA))
4167[6] (5625) (6876)

**Best Regards (IRE)** *P Harley* a77 103
4 bb f Tamayuz Neverletme Go (IRE) (Green Desert (USA))
4841a[8]

**Best Tamayuz** *Scott Dixon* a78 49
3 ch g Tamayuz Pink Ivory (Sakhee (USA))
*1126[4]* 1939[9] 5390[6] 5715[9] *(7766) (7826) 7915[3] 8176[2] (8282)*

**Best Trip (IRE)** *Brian Ellison* a70 92
7 b g Whipper(USA) Tereed Elhawa (Cadeaux Genereux)
1734[6] ◆ 2283[10] 2992[16] 3221[14] 5444[13] 5650[2] *6155[5]* 6872[6] 7330[12] *7687[5] 7819[4] 8039[4]*

**Beta Tauri (USA)** *Charlie Appleby* a63 61
2 bb f Oasis Dream Beta (Selkirk (USA))
6641[8] 7019[6] *7345[4] 8069[4]*

**Bethan** *Julia Feilden* a62 61
5 b m Nayef(USA) Elizabethan Age (FR) (King's Best (USA))
*1[3] 912[2] 1117[5]* 2874[3] 3682[3] 4092[3] 4592[3] *5551[8]*

**Bethany Bay (IRE)** *John Patrick Shanahan* a26 84
4 b f Dylan Thomas(IRE) Spinney (Unfuwain (USA))
6736[5]

**Betimes** *John Gosden* a86 95
3 ch f New Approach(IRE) See You Later (Emarati (USA))
1976[15] 2767[2] 3253[10]

**Better Chance (IRE)** *Saeed bin Suroor* a34 75
3 b f Shamardal(USA) Victoria Star (IRE) (Danehill (USA))
3916[2] *5044[6]*

**Better Lucky (USA)** *Thomas Albertrani* a115 113
5 b m Ghostzapper(USA) Sahara Gold (USA) (Seeking The Gold (USA))
*7608a[2]*

**Better Value (IRE)** *Noel Quinlan* a65 54
4 b g Ad Valorem(USA) Varmint Lady (IRE) (Orpen (USA))
*366[10]*

**Bettolle (ITY)** *Silvia Casati* 100
5 b m Blu Air Force(IRE) Happy Sue (IRE) (City On A Hill (USA))
1477a[4] 2375a[5]

**Betty Bere (FR)** *K R Burke* a69 71
3 b f Peer Gynt(JPN) Monatora (FR) (Hector Protector (USA))
*1233[5]* (3332) 3978[7] 4623[4] 5685[9]

**Betty Boo (IRE)** *Shaun Harris* a27 67
4 ch f Thousand Words Poker Dice (Primo Dominie)
1503[5] 1905[3] (2726) 2955[3] 3846[7] 4891[7] 7502[18] 7671[7]

**Betty The Thief (IRE)** *Tom Dascombe* 60
3 b f Teofilo(IRE) Siphon Melody (USA) (Siphon (BRZ))
6429[4]

**Between Wickets** *Marcus Tregoning* 91
3 b g Compton Place Intermission (IRE) (Royal Applause)
1511[2] 1946[2] 2339[3] 3229[2] (3695) 4647[7] (5311) 6301[4] 6785[3]

**Beyeh (IRE)** *Michael Appleby* a19 68
6 b m King's Best(USA) Cradle Rock (IRE) (Desert Sun)
7508[10]

**Beylerbey (USA)** *Mark Johnston* a72 35
4 bb f Street Cry(IRE) Connie Belle (USA) (Storm Cat (USA))
*456[3] 660[8] 824[6] 962[2] 1080[7]* 1510[6] 1863[5]

**Beyond Brilliance (IRE)** *A P O'Brien* a90 101
3 b f Holy Roman Emperor(IRE) Charroux (IRE) (Darshaan)
2042a[8] 4276a[3] 4461a[4] 5024a[12] 5955a[6] 6370a[7] *7579a[7]*

**Beyond Henry (USA)** *J E Pease* a84 84
2 b c Henrythenavigator(USA) Beyond The Waves (USA) (Ocean Crest (USA))
*7723a[2]*

**B Fifty Two (IRE)** *Charles Hills* a101 109
5 br g Dark Angel(IRE) Petite Maxine (Sharpo)
2110[14] 2849[2] (3693) 4179[17] 5575[3] (5918) 6231[10] 6994a[4] 7441[19]

**Bhaktapur (FR)** *F Rohaut* a93 92
3 b f Naaqoos Queen Maeve (Selkirk (USA))
*194a[7] (545a)*

**Bickershaw** *Richard Fahey* 41
2 b c Equiano(FR) Ring Of Love (Magic Ring (IRE))
4109[10]

**Bifocal** *Ian Semple* 62
3 b g Footstepsinthesand Clear Vision (Observatory (USA))
3832[2]

**Big Bad Jack** *David Brown* 48
2 b g Kheleyf(USA) Spate Rise (Speightstown (USA))
6976[11]

**Big Bad Lily (IRE)** *K J Condon* a74 70
6 br m Big Bad Bob(IRE) Ginger Lily (IRE) (Lucky Guest)
3686a[7]

**Big Bane Theory (USA)** *Carla Gaines* a101 107
5 b h Artie Schiller(USA) Shebane (USA) (Alysheba (USA))
*7591a[5]*

**Big Baz (IRE)** *William Muir* a101 96
4 b g Pivotal Gracefully (IRE) (Orpen (USA))
*(101) 559[3]* 1948[14] ◆ 2309[5] 2772[11] 5849[2] 6304[2] (6748) 7236[2] ◆ *(7801)* ◆ *8116[2]*

**Big Bear (FR)** *George Peckham* 56
2 b g Thewayyouare(USA) Alivera (FR) (Danehill (USA))
4109[8]

**Big Blue** *A Fabre* 107
2 ch c Galileo(IRE) Board Meeting (IRE) (Anabaa (USA))
7317a[2] 7721a[3]

**Big Blue Kitten (USA)** *Chad C Brown* a99 114
6 b h Kitten's Joy(USA) Spent Gold (USA) (Unaccounted For (USA))
7324a[2]

**Big Blue Spirit** *Darrin Miller* a73 101
5 b h Invincible Spirit(IRE) Blue Sail (USA) (Kingmambo (USA))
7325a[7]

**Big Boned (USA)** *Ed Dunlop* a68 45
3 b f Street Sense(USA) Lizzy Cool (USA) (Saint Ballado (CAN))
*1315[6]* 3518[7] 3966[9]

**Big Bradon (IRE)** *Agostino Affe'* 87
3 b c Diamond Green(FR) Kakatiya (IRE) (Barathea (IRE))
1779a[10]

**Big Break** *D K Weld* 107
4 br f Dansili Fame At Last (USA) (Quest For Fame)
2572a[4] 3412a[4] (6963a)

**Big Chill (IRE)** *Charles Hills* a74 79
2 b c Acclamation Royal Consort (IRE) (Green Desert (USA))
1936[6] *3524[3]* ◆ 4207[2] 4809[3] 5310[4] *6854[5]* 7041[6]

**Big City Boy (IRE)** *Phil McEntee* a55 52
6 b g Tamarisk(IRE) Cuddles (IRE) (Taufan (USA))
*639[10] 1263[10] 2394[7] 4056[2]* 4341[2] 4655[9] 5105[3] 5977[3] 6195[8] *7652[2] 7825[11]*

**Big Easy (GER)** *Philip Hobbs* 97
7 b g Ransom O'War(USA) Basilea Gold (GER) (Monsun (GER))
6557[2] (7107)

**Big Fortune** *David C Griffiths*
4 b g Motivator Small Fortune (Anabaa (USA))
*3796[6]* 4978[7]

**Bigindie (IRE)** *John Weymes* 42
4 ch g Indian Haven Graceful Air (IRE) (Danzero (AUS))
4066[5]

**Big John B (USA)** *Philip D'Amato* 110
5 bb g Hard Spun(USA) Baldomera (USA) (Doneraile Court (USA))
7611a[9]

**Big Johnny D (IRE)** *David Barron* 103
5 ch g Alhaarth(IRE) Bakiya (USA) (Trempolino (USA))
1719[13] 2113[10] (3645) 4872[3] 5919[11] (6226) ◆ 6752[7] 7081[14]

**Big Kenny** *Neil King* a63 59
3 b g Multiplex Jezadil (IRE) (Mujadil (USA))
*99[2] 198[3] 473[3] 561[6] (664) (1257)* 4088[2] *4657[4]*

**Big Kick (CAN)** *Michael Machowsky* 104
5 b g Tiznow(USA) Diamant Lady (USA) (Mr Greeley (USA))
5457a[10]

**Big Macher (USA)** *Richard Baltas* a118
4 b g Beau Genius(CAN) Insight (USA) (Kris S (USA))
*7612a[9]*

**Big McIntosh (IRE)** *John Ryan* 62
2 b c Bushranger(IRE) Three Decades (IRE) (Invincible Spirit (IRE))
1512[6] 3049[3] 3429[5] 4203[4]

**Big Memory (FR)** *Tony McEvoy* 107
4 b g Duke Of Marmalade(IRE) Nicara (GER) (Nebos (GER))
(7126a) 7301a[10]

**Big Orange** *Michael Bell* a82 112
3 b g Duke Of Marmalade(IRE) Miss Brown To You (IRE) (Fasliyev (USA))
*1380[2] (1830)* 3419[4] (5920) (6894) 7271[5]

**Big Red** *Robin Bastiman* 50
2 ch f Sakhee's Secret Hickleton Lady (IRE) (Kala Shikari)
67577 732910

**Big Storm Coming** *Ruth Carr* a75 85
4 b g Indesatchel(IRE) Amber Valley (Foxhound (USA))
30004 (3667) 43943 46359 (5088) 59154 62145 66393 69362

**Big Thunder** *Sir Mark Prescott Bt* a80 102
4 gr g Dalakhani(IRE) Charlotte O Fraise (IRE) (Beat Hollow)
371717 47597 51616 557911 62878

**Big Time (IRE)** *John Joseph Murphy* 113
3 br c Kheleyf(USA) Beguine (USA) (Green Dancer (USA))
2571a5 335219 5966a13

**Big Time Billy (IRE)** *Alan Phillips* a49 82
8 b m Definite Article Zaratu (IRE) (Key Of Luck (USA))
53413 58903 616910 73336

**Big Tom Prado (USA)** *Christine K Janks* 91
3 rg g Fort Prado(USA) Lil Minnlet (USA) (Black Minnaloushe (USA))
4230a6

**Big Whiskey (IRE)** *John Best* a91 75
4 ch g Ad Valorem(USA) El Opera (IRE) (Sadler's Wells (USA))
13013 ◆ 15787 187112 66094 68868 76368 77744 820412

**Bikini Club** *Paul D'Arcy* a19 49
3 br f Pastoral Pursuits Black Sea Pearl (Diktat)
5796 66013 12808 16329

**Bikini Island (USA)** *Andrew Balding* 79
3 bb f Dynaformer(USA) Another Par Three (USA) (Spinning World (USA))
37508 62823 67382 73056 75168

**Biladi (FR)** *X Thomas-Demeaulte* 102
5 b g Authorized(IRE) Serpenta (GER) (Protektor (GER))
4722a3 6383a10

**Bilash** *Andrew Hollinshead* a70 65
7 gr g Choisir(AUS) Goldeva (Makbul)
2592 24147 31499 41023 48335 560210 (6273) 681510 78062 79978 82555

**Bilidn** *Ben De Haan* a71 80
6 b m Tiger Hill(IRE) Brightest Star (Unfuwain (USA))
44417 48184

**Bilimbi (IRE)** *William Haggas* 95
3 b g Duke Of Marmalade(IRE) Starship (IRE) (Galileo (IRE))
(1563) 25656 33784 ◆

**Billabong (MOR)** *P Bary* a102
5 gr h Gentlewave(IRE) Lunattori (Vettori (IRE))
79223

**Billingsgate (IRE)** *Charlie Appleby* a104 101
3 b g Exceed And Excel(AUS) Island Babe (USA) (Kingmambo (USA))
16905 20633 (3273) (4331) 46476 58242 66885 (7545)

**Bill Jem (FR)** *D Sepulchre* a61
3 b g King's Best(USA) Hill Of Grace (Desert Prince (IRE))
1620a8

**Billowing (IRE)** *John Gosden* a73
3 ch f Candy Ride(ARG) Cloudspin (USA) (Storm Cat (USA))
174DSQ

**Billy Blue (IRE)** *John Gosden* a81 80
3 b g High Chaparral(IRE) Silk Dress (IRE) (Gulch (USA))
31978 45012 50382 54305 62396 73508

**Billy Bond** *Richard Fahey* 56
2 b g Monsieur Bond(IRE) Princess Cocoa (IRE) (Desert Sun)
19557 662311 72463

**Billyford (IRE)** *Liam Roche* a82 93
9 b g Lil's Boy(USA) Alamanta (IRE) (Ali-Royal (IRE))
5957a13

**Billyoakes (IRE)** *Mick Channon* a84 81
2 b g Kodiac Reality Check (IRE) (Sri Pekan (USA))
19776 (2291) 42188 43484 46867 53733 60034 63128 66782 72242 (7415) (7571)

**Billy Red** *J R Jenkins* a76 52
10 ch g Dr Fong(USA) Liberty Bound (Primo Dominie)
9110 1915 4707 11095 18787 28657 (3393) 38263 45462 50452 586111 68435 80774 82458 83195

**Billy Redpath** *Frederick Watson* 20
6 b g Distant Music(USA) Shardda (Barathea (IRE))
28996

**Billy Slater** *Richard Fahey* 74
2 br c Pastoral Pursuits Procession (Zafonic (USA))
20897 27564 31363

**Bimbo** *Richard Fahey* 80
2 b f Iffraaj Birthday Suit (IRE) (Daylami (IRE))
(3497) 40573 56088 625310 72377

**Binky Blue (IRE)** *Brian Ellison* 69
2 b f Approve(IRE) Sabander Bay (USA) (Lear Fan (USA))
13424 15059 19004 32018 (3435) 51412 61653 66916

**Bin Singspiel** *James Tate* a96 85
4 br g Singspiel(IRE) Mexican Hawk (USA) (Silver Hawk (USA))
32049

**Bint Alzain (IRE)** *Pat Phelan* a78 56
5 b m Marju(IRE) Barconey (IRE) (Danehill Dancer (IRE))
4026

**Bint Dandy (IRE)** *Chris Dwyer* a82 74
3 b f Dandy Man(IRE) Ceol Loch Aoidh (IRE) (Medecis)
62697 66336 68633 (7575) 79932 (8079)

**Bint Malyana (IRE)** *Paul D'Arcy* a69 73
3 b f Bahamian Bounty Malyana (Mtoto)
1032 48744 52563 58612 61545 702314 75755 795010

**Biographer** *David Lanigan* a91 114
5 b g Montjeu(IRE) Reflective (USA) (Seeking The Gold (USA))
13988 270411 56685 62885 72712

**Biography** *Richard Hannon* a83 81
3 ch g Assertive Dahshah (Mujtahid (USA))
20833 34807 39369

**Bionic Indian** *Michael Easterby* 52
2 b g Acclamation Strawberry Moon (IRE) (Alhaarth (IRE))
565516

**Biotic** *Rod Millman* a76 73
3 b g Aqlaam Bramaputra (IRE) (Choisir (AUS))
(1211) 13792 30873 38552 (4329) 48014 59866 70132

**Bipartisan (IRE)** *Michael Bell* 64
2 b f Bahamian Bounty Bijou A Moi (Rainbow Quest (USA))
64347 670110

**Biraaj (IRE)** *Matthieu Palussiere* 98
2 ch c Iffraaj Annie The Doc (Nayef (USA))
7468a3 (7855a)

**Birdie Must Fly** *Jimmy Fox* a37 30
2 ch f Major Cadeaux Musical Day (Singspiel (IRE))
27717 311310 385810 62949 701412

**Birdie Queen** *Gary Moore* a79 76
4 b f Pastoral Pursuits Silver Miss (FR) (Numerous (USA))
2443 4486 32313 (3820) 41012 45647 58602 (6189 ) 70236 72155 82452

**Birdman (IRE)** *David Simcock* a74 78
4 b g Danehill Dancer(IRE) Gilded Vanity (IRE) (Indian Ridge)
(235) 4655 62511 398212 43317 50409 63348 67899 71362 753011 77325 79283

**Birdy Dream (FR)** *Y Durepaire*
3 gr f Astronomer Royal(USA) Gulch Affair (USA) (Gulch (USA))
599a12

**Birikyno** *Mark Usher* a54 55
3 b g Piccolo Alvarinho Lady (Royal Applause)
8610 4117

**Birkdale Boy (IRE)** *Richard Fahey* 53
2 br g Alfred Nobel(IRE) Yaky Romani (IRE) (Victory Note (USA))
23866 32559 421612

**Birthday Guest (GER)** *Philip Kirby* 34
5 ch g Areion(GER) Birthday Spectrum (GER) (Spectrum (IRE))
764314

**Birthday Prince (GER)** *Christian Sprengel* a90 102
6 ch g Areion(GER) Birthday Spectrum (GER) (Spectrum (IRE))
2006a10 5966a5 7437a9 7604a4

**Birthday Treat (FR)** *Yannick Fouin* 52
3 gr f Martaline Ealore (FR) (Kendor (FR))
5592a6

**Biscuiteer** *Scott Dixon* a59 59
3 ch f Byron Ginger Cookie (Bold Edge)
865 3744 6083 7863 (1039) 14256 (1626) 23885 26758 32283 44699 489010 581911

**Bishan Bedi (IRE)** *William Jarvis* a57 66
3 b g Intikhab(USA) Knockatotaun (Spectrum (IRE))
1423 24427 31584 (4365) 48135 57293

**Bishara (USA)** *Sir Michael Stoute* 61
2 ch f Dubawi(IRE) Kaseema (USA) (Storm Cat (USA))
75947

**Bishop Of Ruscombe** *Andrew Balding* a80 68
3 b c Mount Nelson Pain Perdu (IRE) (Waajib (IRE))
5882 (839) 50385 60449 70163

**Bishop's Castle (USA)** *Brian Ellison* a84 87
5 b g Distorted Humor(USA) Miss Caerleona (FR) (Caerleon (USA))
117110 16076 32547 37032 (4175) 54876

**Bishop Wulstan (IRE)** *Richard Hannon* a51 65
3 b g Oratorio(IRE) Laurentine (USA) (Private Account (USA))
24164 28604 33262 35672 (3819) 41063 48637 55204 57192 619311

**Bison Grass** *Giles Bravery* a64 69
4 b g Halling(USA) Secret Blend (Pivotal)
12168 227015 29308 49117 53437

**Bispham Green** *David O'Meara* a70 89
4 b g Green Desert(USA) Royal Grace (Royal Applause)
26568 (3138) 34589 44183 46098 48597 676310

**Bitaphon (IRE)** *Michael Appleby* a67 63
5 br g Acclamation Pitrizzia (Lando (GER))
303 12273 16068 18007 76459

**Biting Bullets (USA)** *Jo Hughes* a83 74
2 b c Bluegrass Cat(USA) Mary Ellise (USA) (In Excess)
332220 41032 45708 62703 (7779) (7984) 80162

**Bitter Lake (USA)** *Charlie Appleby* 85
2 bb f Halling(USA) Suez (Green Desert (USA))
(2744) 34157 75966

**Bittern (IRE)** *Charlie Appleby* a70
2 ch f New Approach(IRE) Oiseau Rare (FR) (King's Best (USA))
71843 ◆ 80367 81732

**Bitusa (USA)** *Karen Tutty* a41 63
4 b g Roman Ruler(USA) Richen (USA) (Well Decorated (USA))
12497 16082 24269 44687 45307

**Bivouac (UAE)** *Alan Swinbank* a56 42
10 b g Jade Robbery(USA) Tentpole (USA) (Rainbow Quest (USA))
11112 12265

**Bix (IRE)** *Alan Berry* a47 58
4 b g Holy Roman Emperor(IRE) Belle Rebelle (IRE) (In The Wings)
25 633 1994 2204 3632 21357 309910 38305 41956 43586 58068 65765

**Biz The Nurse (IRE)** *Stefano Botti* 111
4 b c Oratorio(IRE) Biz Bar (Tobougg (IRE))
2191a2 3047a3 6590a2 7323a3

**Bizzario** *Mark Johnston* 79
2 b g Raven's Pass(USA) All's Forgotten (USA) (Darshaan)
45183 48844 (5408) 62803 67595

**Bizzy Nizzy (FR)** *P Lenogue* a44 76
4 b f Great Journey(JPN) Risky Nizzy (Cape Cross (IRE))
5546a6

**Blackadder** *Pat Phelan* a51 49
2 b g Myboycharlie(IRE) Famcred (Inchinor)
62619 66756 73365 774014

**Blackasyourhat (IRE)** *Roger Ingram* a53 12
2 b c Le Cadre Noir(IRE) Mattrah (USA) (Machiavellian (USA))
35367 45426 75425 77717

**Black Bird Runs (FR)** *F-H Graffard* a64 67
2 ch f Evasive Moon Tree (FR) (Groom Dancer (USA))
4839a9

**Blackbriar** *T Stack* a85 92
2 br f Kyllachy Starry Sky (Oasis Dream)
2569a5 5954a6 65306

**Black Caesar (IRE)** *Philip Hide* a64 55
3 b g Bushranger(IRE) Evictress (IRE) (Sharp Victor (USA))
13903 20639 22817 30678 684312 722012 784211

**Black Cherry** *Richard Hannon* 76
2 b f Mount Nelson Arctic Char (Polar Falcon (USA))
36715 43963 60662

**Black Dave (IRE)** *David Evans* a72 73
4 b g Excellent Art Miss Latina (IRE) (Mozart (IRE))
28846 41542 44145 49687 58494 62495 66166 70002 70783 72882 764710 79508 81434 82552

**Black Douglas** *Jim Goldie* a44 61
5 b g Kyllachy Penmayne (Inchinor)
183814 24527 24797 29097 40052 42575 45194 49607 52374 53904 55656 (5636) 58977 62138 667411 68669 70576

**Blacke Forest** *William Muir* a62
3 b f Manduro(GER) Welsh Cake (Fantastic Light (USA))
4472 5123 10244 247011 308713

**Blackfoot Brave (IRE)** *Michael Dods* 62
2 ch g Iffraaj Beatrix Potter (IRE) (Cadeaux Genereux)
30492 538610 61158

**Black Geronimo** *Roy Bowring* a62 44
3 b c Sleeping Indian Voice (Zamindar (USA))
5686 7625 9313 11304 18903

**Black Granite (IRE)** *Jeremy Noseda* a91 86
2 b g Dark Angel(IRE) Glisten (Oasis Dream)
23086 31196 44096 (6294) (6684) (7226)

**Black Hornet (CAN)** *Pat Parente* a107 107
4 bb g Pioneering(USA) Start Stinging (USA) (Siphon (BRZ))
7325a2

**Black Iceman** *Lydia Pearce* a58 39
6 gr g Iceman Slite (Mind Games)
36828 47372 55583 63395 66324 70652 72875 75727 80614

**Black Label** *Harry Dunlop* a75 66
3 b g Medicean Black Belt Shopper (IRE) (Desert Prince (IRE))
20814 28503 31839 37122 45406 60453 64853 70324

**Black Minstrel (IRE)** *Amanda Perrett* a69 66
5 b g Dylan Thomas(IRE) Overlook (Generous (IRE))
(1835) ◆ 40518 454813

**Black Night (IRE)** *Stuart Williams* 65
2 b c Excellent Art Starfish (IRE) (Galileo (IRE))
70394

**Black Pudding (IRE)** *Ollie Pears* 58
2 b g Baltic King Top Of The Ridge (IRE) (Celtic Swing)
35694 39474 44166 48995 51943 (5767) 64287

**Black Rider (IRE)** *Julie Camacho* a57 74
4 b g Elnadim(USA) Barracade (IRE) (Barathea (IRE))
30968 343910

**Black Rose (GER)** *Frau Marion Rotering* 39
2 bb f Sholokhov(IRE) Bali's Dream (FR) (Big Shuffle (USA))
6385a7 6950a8

**Black Schnapps (IRE)** *William Muir* a80 96
3 b g Manduro(GER) Ornellaia (IRE) (Mujadil (USA))
13524 (1690) (1983) 25663 337912 51796

**Black Shadow** *Amanda Perrett* a75 98
3 b g New Approach(IRE) Shadow Dancing (Unfuwain (USA))
18092 (2485) 29862 489310 57204 654814 71355

**Blacksmiths Arms** *Michael Easterby* a19
4 b g Multiplex Kingsfold Blaze (Mazilier (USA))
5155

**Black Snowflake (USA)** *S Seemar* a79 67
7 b g Elusive Quality(USA) Black Escort (USA) (Southern Halo (USA))
241a14

**Blackstone Vegas** *Derek Shaw* a56 61
8 ch g Nayef(USA) Waqood (USA) (Riverman (USA))
1066 4547

**Blackthorn Stick (IRE)** *John Butler* a67 63
5 b g Elusive City(USA) Hi Lyla (IRE) (Lahib (USA))
(126) 2194 3195 9585 11213 70129 734712 77355 79878 82188

**Black Tie Dancer (IRE)** *B Duchemin* 8
3 gr g Mastercraftsman(IRE) Opera Star (IRE) (Sadler's Wells (USA))
34717 7681a9

**Black Truffle (FR)** *Mark Usher* a63 45
4 b g Kyllachy Some Diva (Dr Fong (USA))
4284 603010 8464 11109 13864 (1766) 20299 26483 315016 66667 72595 75486 78846 80138 (8200) 82853

**Blacktype (FR)** *Christophe Clement* a85 101
3 b c Dunkerque(FR) Theorie (FR) (Anabaa (USA))
169a2 6949a5

**Black Vale (IRE)** *Ralph J Smith* a72 27
3 b g Moss Vale(IRE) Limit (IRE) (Barathea (IRE))
5415 7745 (823) 10932 12255 16697 18292 29062 (3388) 35232 663312 76477 80409

**Black Widow** *Pat Eddery* a45
3 b f Bertolini(USA) Malvadilla (IRE) (Doyoun)
40864 55683 76524 78005 81995

**Blades Lad** *Peter Niven* a76 74
5 ch g Haafhd Blades Girl (Bertolini (USA))
2533 (476) 7635

**Bladewood Girl** *J R Jenkins* a62 61
6 b m Needwood Blade Willmar (IRE) (Zafonic (USA))
784 1794 3774 6618 (858) 11312 13654 18632 27223 47323 51103 64814

**Blaine** *Kevin Ryan* 108
4 ch g Avonbridge Lauren Louise (Tagula (IRE))
15065 22543 342017 4188U (4384) 489523 (5575) 65333 69215

**Blame Love (USA)** *Mark Johnston* a65
2 b c Blame(USA) Twisted Tale (USA) (Tale Of The Cat (USA))
35245

**Blanche Des Clos (FR)** *J Heloury* a28
3 ch f Naaqoos Sarabande (Nashwan (USA))
482a13

**Blarney Stone (IRE)** *A De Royer-Dupre* a96 84
3 ch f Peintre Celebre(USA) Bastet (IRE) (Giant's Causeway (USA))
5843a11

**Blaze It** *Brian Ellison* 47
3 b f Captain Gerrard(IRE) Hillside Heather (IRE) (Tagula (IRE))
35313 39515 ◆

**Blazeofenchantment (USA)** *John Wainwright* a82 51
4 b g Officer(USA) Willow Rush (USA) (Wild Rush (USA))
64610 9295 10826 29017 354711 51002 (5571) 60356 68417

**Blazing Chilli** *Bill Turner* a25
3 b g Firebreak Janet Girl (Polar Falcon (USA))
34718

**Blazing Desert** *William Kinsey* a64 69
10 b g Beat All(USA) Kingsfold Blaze (Mazilier (USA))
213 2214 3494 ◆ 6092 9152 411510

**Blazing Knight (IRE)** *Chris Gordon* a80 69
4 b g Red Clubs(IRE) Johar Jamal (IRE) (Chevalier (IRE))
9257 11449 16675 20655 24864 288411 33296 40244 457810

**Blazing Rose (IRE)** *David O'Meara* 51
2 ch f Intikhab(USA) Radhwa (FR) (Shining Steel)
21347 238610 26736 40183 45298 48706 51946

**Blazing Speed** *A S Cruz* 121
5 b g Dylan Thomas(IRE) Leukippids (IRE) (Sadler's Wells (USA))
1181a10 2004a6 (7899a) 8154a12

**Blazon (FR)** *Mlle C Gryson* a90 100
7 gr g Verglas(IRE) Hidden Silver (Anabaa (USA))
3907a4

**Blencathra** *Jo Hughes* 33
2 rg g Hellvelyn Frontline In Focus (IRE) (Daggers Drawn (USA))
294414 36066

**Blessington (IRE)** *John Gosden* a90 102
4 b g Kheleyf(USA) Madam Ninette (Mark Of Esteem (IRE))
803 14925 (2110) 342015

**Bletchley Park** *Richard Fahey* 58
2 ch c Mastercraftsman(IRE) Puzzling (Peintre Celebre (USA))
70849

**Bleu Astral (FR)** *Richard Fahey* a63 80
2 b g Astronomer Royal(USA) Passion Bleue (In The Wings)
61462 68614 75736 80006

**Bleu Azur (FR)** *Mario Hofer* 85
2 ch c Soldier Of Fortune(IRE) Black Dalhia (FR) (Sanglamore (USA))
7145a7

**Blighty (IRE)** *Lady Cecil* a82 85
4 ch g Beat Hollow Brisk Breeze (GER) (Monsun (GER))
17627 235114 53192 57302 64656

**Bling King** *Geoffrey Harker* a76 80
5 b g Haafhd Bling Bling (IRE) (Indian Ridge)
12816 16072 16608 26542 36242 40014

**Bling Ring (USA)** *Charles Hills* a8 66
2 bb f Arch(USA) Youcan'ttakeme (USA) (He's Tops (USA))
49149 56436 67355 69962 725811

**Blithe Spirit** *Eric Alston* a62 97
3 b f Byron Damalis (IRE) (Mukaddamah (USA))
14452 (2116) 25649 34599 41584 569611 61599

**Blizzard Blues (USA)** *Aytach Sadik*
8 ch g Mr Greeley(USA) Blush Damask (USA) (Green Dancer (USA))
5259P

**Blockade (IRE)** *James Tate* a73 70
3 br f Kheleyf(USA) Barracade (IRE) (Barathea (IRE))
151512 615910

**Bloodsweatandtears** *William Knight* a72 53
6 b g Barathea(IRE) Celestial Princess (Observatory (USA))
2868 5892 84310 10402 12157 16657 69995 763311 79863

**Blossom Lane** *John Gosden* a61 50
3 ch f New Approach(IRE) Monturani (IRE) (Indian Ridge)
712 2367 4888

**Blue Aegean** *Charlie Appleby* 85
2 b f Invincible Spirit(IRE) Blue Azure (USA) (American Chance (USA))
24933 (2888) 335320 53806 59216

**Blue Amazon (IRE)** *Lee Carter* 15
2 b f Acclamation Amazon Beauty (IRE) (Wolfhound (USA))
372812 45776

**Blue Army** *Saeed bin Suroor* a64 68
3 b g Exceed And Excel(AUS) La Presse (USA) (Gone West (USA))
2996[7] 4130[5] 4791[5] 7012[4] 7427[9]

**Blue Atlantic (USA)** *Mark Johnston* 78
3 b g Stormy Atlantic(USA) Bluemamba (USA) (Kingmambo (USA))
(1508) 3003[5] 3491a[7] 3797[6]

**Blue Bere (FR)** *J Boisnard* a80 83
3 b f Hold That Tiger(USA) Miss Fine (FR) (Kaldoun (FR))
4252a[2] 6913a[5]

**Blue Bounty** *Mark H Tompkins* a71 67
3 ch g Bahamian Bounty Laheen (IRE) (Bluebird (USA))
2526[2] 3037[2] 4495[3] 5930[5] 6240[2] 6488[4] 7776[3] 7865[3]

**Blue Bullet (IRE)** *Brian Ellison* a66 70
4 b g Red Clubs(IRE) Blue Holly (IRE) (Blues Traveller (IRE))
790a[10] 2350[9] 2727[4] 4531[9] 6938[9]

**Blue Burmese (IRE)** *Mark Usher* a49 66
2 ch f Camacho Love City (IRE) (Spectrum (IRE))
2022[7] 2173[2] 2771[9] 3173[7] 5569[5] 6072[5] 6563[10] 6842[5] 7996[2] 8206[2]

**Blue Clumber** *Shaun Harris* a55 49
4 b f Sleeping Indian Blue Nile (IRE) (Bluebird (USA))
2838[5] 3099[5] 3828[4] 4046[7] (4733) 5138[6] 5573[8] 5797[6] 6161[5] 6407[13] 6423[6]

**Blue Dancer (USA)** *Greg Tracy* a92
2 bb c Bluegrass Cat(USA) Two Halos (USA) (Saint Ballado (CAN))
7610a[10]

**Blue Deer (IRE)** *Lee Carter* a69 58
6 b g Bahamian Bounty Jaywick (UAE) (Jade Robbery (USA))
229[5] 377[12]

**Blue Eyed Boy** *Roy Brotherton*
2 b g Stimulation(IRE) Lilly Blue (IRE) (Hawk Wing (USA))
3461[7] 4103[5] 4943[9] 5593[8]

**Bluefire** *H-A Pantall* a89 60
4 gr f Distorted Humor(USA) Filarmonia (ARG) (Slew Gin Fizz (USA))
5965a[11] 8150a[3] 8300a[13]

**Bluegrass Blues (IRE)** *Paul Cole* a94 93
4 gr g Dark Angel(IRE) Dear Catch (IRE) (Bluebird (USA))
1437[22] 1576[4] 4783[13] 5346[4] (6334) 7455[7] 7663[5]

**Blue Hussar (IRE)** *A P O'Brien* 101
3 b g Montjeu(IRE) Metaphor (USA) (Woodman (USA))
2153[4] ◆ 2579a[5] 6349a[8] 7144a[4] 7476a[16]

**Blue Jack** *Zoe Davison* a58 73
9 b g Cadeaux Genereux Fairy Flight (IRE) (Fairy King (USA))
6020[9] 7352[8]

**Blue Jacket (USA)** *Dianne Sayer* 36
3 ro f Mizzen Mast(USA) Complex (USA) (Unbridled's Song (USA))
2553[5] 3302[9] 3362[9]

**Blue Maisey** *Edwin Tuer* a69 75
6 b m Monsieur Bond(IRE) Blue Nile (IRE) (Bluebird (USA))
1356[7] 5640[11] 6217[2] (6626) 6863[10] 7411[17]

**Blue Noodles** *John Wainwright* a59 55
8 b g Reset(AUS) Gleam Of Light (IRE) (Danehill (USA))
81[11] 201[8]

**Blue Oyster** *Philip McBride* a67
3 b f Medicean Bluebelle (Generous (IRE))
70[6] 316[8] (434) 561[3] 1124[2] 1239[3]

**Blue Rambler** *Charlie Appleby* 108
4 b g Monsun(GER) La Nuit Rose (FR) (Rainbow Quest (USA))
7492[3]

**Blue Ridge Lane (IRE)** *John C McConnell* a69 70
8 ch g Indian Ridge Upperville (IRE) (Selkirk (USA))
7962a[6]

**Blues Dancer** *Sylvester Kirk* 63
2 b g Norse Dancer(IRE) Indiana Blues (Indian Ridge)
5212[3] 5745[6]

**Blue Sea (IRE)** *A Al Raihe* a83 79
5 b h Singspiel(IRE) Height Of Vanity (IRE) (Erhaab (USA))
243a[9]

**Blue Soave (FR)** *F Chappet* a94 108
6 ch g Soave(GER) Rhapsody In Blue (FR) (Bering)
6182a[4]

**Blue Sonic** *Jim Goldie* 62
4 gr f Proclamation(IRE) Big Mystery (IRE) (Grand Lodge (USA))
3607[4] 4299[4] 4728[2] 5168[5] 5234[6] 6122[2] 6601[7] 7061[7]

**Blue Surf** *Amanda Perrett* 104
5 ch g Excellent Art Wavy Up (IRE) (Brustolon)
2154[2] 2555[4] 2991[3] 3962[9] 4756[6] 5668[6] 6005[2] 6656[3] 7142a[8]

**Blue Talisman (IRE)** *Tim Easterby* a54 63
3 ch g Alhaarth(IRE) Amaniy (USA) (Dayjur (USA))
1372[5] 2198[5] (2616) 2893[4] 4134[11] 6216[10] 6480[15] 8277[3]

**Blue Tiger's Eye (IRE)** *A bin Harmash* a80 72
6 br g Motivator Bush Cat (USA) (Kingmambo (USA))
243a[4]

**Blue Top** *Mark Walford* a56 65
5 b g Millkom Pompey Blue (Abou Zouz (USA))
2327[12] 2620[6] 3269[4] 3535[4] 4474[4] 6117[7] 6410[10] 7283[8]

**Blue Valentino** *Andrew Hollinshead* a58 52
5 b g Primo Valentino(IRE) Blue Water (Shaamit (IRE))
6344[7] 6738[5] 7067[4] 7893[11] 7990[2]

**Blue Waltz** *Luca Cumani* 99
3 b f Pivotal Blue Symphony (Darshaan)
3277[2] 4699[2] (5382) (6258) 7105[11]

**Blue Wave (IRE)** *Mark Johnston* a107 103
4 b g Raven's Pass(USA) Million Waves (IRE) (Mull Of Kintyre (USA))
(160) ◆ (270) 427[3] (611) (784) 956[5] 1556[8] 1736[8] 2342[2] 2991[P]

**Blurred Vision** *William Jarvis* 88
3 b c Royal Applause Sparkling Eyes (Lujain (USA))
(2789)

**Blushing Bere (FR)** *E Leenders* a75 98
3 b g Hurricane Cat(USA) Niska (USA) (Smart Strike (CAN))
3290a[9]

**Blythe Prince** *Danielle McCormick*
2 b c Dutch Art Arculinge (Paris House)
5128[9]

**Blythe Star (IRE)** *Danielle McCormick* 53
2 b g Thewayyouare(USA) Run To Jane (IRE) (Doyoun)
4884[7] 5408[6] 6056[10] 6669[7] 7230[8]

**Bnedel (IRE)** *Richard Hannon* a73
2 b c Teofilo(IRE) Dance Club (IRE) (Fasliyev (USA))
5184[3] (6630)

**Boadicee** *John Gosden* a59 42
3 b f Aqlaam Fen Guest (Woodborough (USA))
2892[5] 3476[8] 8185[9]

**Boann (IRE)** *J S Moore* a51 57
2 b f Vale Of York(IRE) Ma Vie En Rose (IRE) (Red Ransom (USA))
2666[3] 3322[23] 3872a[11] 4882a[5] 5544a[14] 5662a[7] 5844a[14]

**Boarding Party (USA)** *Charlie Fellowes* a62 56
2 ch g More Than Ready(USA) Oceans Apart (Desert Prince (IRE))
6551[12] 7030[5]

**Bob** *Les Eyre* a76 80
4 b g Assertive Celestial Harmony (Polish Precedent (USA))
1483[16] 2017[7] 2763[3] 3094[5] (6232) 6639[2] 7403[5]

**Boban (AUS)** *Chris Waller* 117
5 br g Bernardini(USA) Kenbelle (AUS) (Kenmare (FR))
1186a[7]

**Bobbie's Girl (IRE)** *William Haggas* a67 64
2 b f Big Bad Bob(IRE) Lamanka Lass (USA) (Woodman (USA))
4784[11] 5821[4] 6224[3] 6996[6]

**Bobby Benton (IRE)** *Luke Dace* a78 70
3 b g Invincible Spirit(IRE) Remarkable Story (Mark Of Esteem (IRE))
230[6] 468[2] 748[2] 954[2] (1090) 3197[10] 4077[5] 7672[10] 8017[3] 8248[3] ◆ (8309)

**Bobbyscot (IRE)** *Mark Hoad* a56 82
7 b g Alhaarth(IRE) Sogno Verde (IRE) (Green Desert (USA))
2033[2] (2248) 3065[3]

**Bobby's Flyer (IRE)** *Tim Easterby* 52
2 b c Bushranger(IRE) Emma Dora (IRE) (Medaglia d'Oro (USA))
1879[5] 2359[7] 3569[6]

**Bobby's Kitten (USA)** *Chad C Brown* a57 112
3 b c Kitten's Joy(USA) Celestial Woods (USA) (Forestry (USA))
3994a[8] 6391a[3] (7609a)

**Bob Masnicken** *Tom Dascombe* a46 61
3 b g Dandy Man(IRE) Twilight Belle (IRE) (Fasliyev (USA))
919[5]

**Boboli Gardens** *Noel Quinlan* a56 75
4 b g Medicean Park Crystal (IRE) (Danehill (USA))
2877[4] 4090[5] 5834[7] 7042[14] 7427[12] 7626[11] 7853[10] 8259[5]

**Bobs Her Uncle** *James Bethell* a73 69
5 b m Fair Mix(IRE) Shazana (Key Of Luck (USA))
250[8]

**Bob's World** *Jennie Candlish* a79 84
5 b g Multiplex Vocation (IRE) (Royal Academy (USA))
(1418) 1692[2] 2289[7]

**Bocaiuva (IRE)** *F Chappet* 110
3 ch f Teofilo(IRE) Breath Of Love (USA) (Mutakddim (USA))
1480a[4] 2267a[4] 3289a[8] 4840a[5] (6882a) 7558a[2]

**Boccalino (GER)** *P Schaerer* a83 86
6 b g Iron Mask(USA) Bella Monica (GER) (Big Shuffle (USA))
555a[4] 638a[3] 728a[2]

**Bodegas (FR)** *M Figge* 66
3 gr g Sinndar(IRE) Bocarosa (IRE) (Linamix (FR))
7164a[4]

**Bodhi (FR)** *J-F Bernard* a103 114
3 b c Hurricane Cat(USA) Kentucky Beauty (FR) (Orpen (USA))
(2242a) 3807a[6] 6571a[2] 7318a[3]

**Body And Soul (IRE)** *Tim Easterby* 108
4 b f Captain Rio Goodwood March (Foxhound (USA))
1734[9] 2161[3] ◆ 2256[11] 2786[2] 3241[4] 3715[4] 4937[6]

**Body Beautiful (IRE)** *G M Lyons* 83
3 b f Big Bad Bob(IRE) Forever Phoenix (Shareef Dancer (USA))
3167a[7]

**Body Language (IRE)** *Ian Williams* a82 99
6 b m Beat Hollow Banco Suivi (IRE) (Nashwan (USA))
2073[14] 2294[4] 3321[14] 3985[4]

**Boetie's Dream (IRE)** *P Bary* a77 88
3 b c Oasis Dream Source Of Life (IRE) (Fasliyev (USA))
1907a[4]

**Bofalco (IRE)** *C Lotoux* a75 79
3 b g Falco(USA) Lonesome Me (FR) (Zafonic (USA))
2003a[5]

**Bogart** *Kevin Ryan* 109
5 ch g Bahamian Bounty Lauren Louise (Tagula (IRE))
2283[17] 4179[13] 4683[10] 5575[6] 6327[2] 6531[3] 7080[U] 7408[4]

**Bogey Hole (IRE)** *Nikki Evans* a59 44
5 gr m Aussie Rules(USA) Sticky Green (Lion Cavern (USA))
3780[8] 5342[5] 6486[14]

**Bogha Baisti (IRE)** *Mrs Y Dunleavy* a48
4 b f Footstepsinthesand Osireion (Pivotal)
7877a[13]

**Bognor (USA)** *Michael Appleby* a87 59
3 b g Hard Spun(USA) Ms Blue Blood (USA) (A.P. Indy (USA))
1588[6] 1947[8] (2936) 3135[12] 3978[9] (8086) (8224)

**Bogsnog (IRE)** *Kristin Stubbs* a81 72
4 b g Moss Vale(IRE) Lovers Kiss (Night Shift (USA))
20[3] 1031[3] (1152) 1429[6] 1630[8] 2054[6] 2549[12] 3227[8] 3668[12] 6074[10] 6544[3] 6767[3] 7077[10] 7906[12]

**Bohemian Rhapsody (IRE)** *Sean Curran* a66 91
5 b g Galileo(IRE) Quiet Mouse (USA) (Quiet American (USA))
784[11] 2160[2] 3204[10] 4441[6] 7305[8]

**Boisterous (USA)** *Todd Pletcher* a115 111
7 bb h Distorted Humor(USA) Emanating (USA) (Cox's Ridge (USA))
3025a[7] 4231a[4]

**Boite (IRE)** *Peter Chapple-Hyam* 99
4 b g Authorized(IRE) Albiatra (USA) (Dixieland Band (USA))
3717[13] 4606[8] 4759[5] 5673[9] 6283[5] 7306[5]

**Boker Mazal (FR)** *D Chenu* a72
3 b g Daramsar(FR) Killdora (FR) (Kendor (FR))
751a[3]

**Bold** *Roger Charlton* 69
2 b c Oasis Dream Minority (Generous (IRE))
5847[2] 7040[3]

**Bold Adventure** *Willie Musson* a65 54
10 ch g Arkadian Hero(USA) Impatiente (USA) (Vaguely Noble)
380[5] 3579[3]

**Bold And Free** *David Thompson* a66 54
4 b g Bertolini(USA) Lady Broughton (IRE) (Grand Lodge (USA))
476[5] 831[5] 2738[7] 3095[4] 3535[6] 3958[4] 4665[7] 4792[7] 6122[12] 6673[3] 7283[9] 7499[4] 7895[9]

**Bold Appeal** *Ralph Beckett* a71 61
2 b g Nayef(USA) Shy Appeal (IRE) (Barathea (IRE))
6085[4] (6903) 7404[5]

**Bold Arial** *Eve Johnson Houghton* 64
3 b f Authorized(IRE) No Frills (IRE) (Darshaan)
2497[6]

**Boldbob (IRE)** *Micky Hammond* 56
2 gr c Verglas(IRE) Special Park (USA) (Trempolino (USA))
4633[11] 5494[4] 6146[6]

**Bold Captain (IRE)** *John Quinn* 77
3 ch g Captain Rio Indianaca (IRE) (Indian Danehill (IRE))
(4022) 5015[4] 5713[5] 7445[4] 7640[8]

**Bold Cross (IRE)** *Edward Bevan* a44 73
11 b g Cape Cross(IRE) Machikane Akaiito (IRE) (Persian Bold)
2947[12] 3226[8] 3515[4] 4105[7] 4948[13] 5596[8] 6028[6] 6210[2] 6426[4]

**Bold Duke** *Edward Bevan* a41 80
6 b g Sulamani(IRE) Dominant Duchess (Old Vic)
2382[5] 2670[5] 2981[5] 3175[5] 6706[14] 7309[11]

**Bold Grove** *Edward Bevan* a22
2 b g Proclamation(IRE) Trysting Grove (IRE) (Cape Cross (IRE))
8000[12]

**Bold Lass (IRE)** *David Lanigan* a72 97
3 b f Sea The Stars(IRE) My Branch (Distant Relative)
2383[2] 3117[7] (4537) 5505[2] (6129)

**Bold Max** *Zoe Davison* a50 43
3 b g Assertive Jane's Payoff (IRE) (Danetime (IRE))
98[3] 302[2] 374[7] 753[6] 865[4] 1007[6] 1802[3] 2044[5] 2397[7] 2860[3] 7222[9] 7548[8] 8008[5] 8181[3]

**Bold Prediction (IRE)** *K R Burke* a89 98
4 b g Kodiac Alexander Eliott (IRE) (Night Shift (USA))
1103[5] 1637[3] (1744) 1958[3] 2362[2] 2869[2] 3397[2] 3621[5] 5771[2] 6226[2] 6748[3] 7022[7]

**Bold Ring** *Edward Creighton* a72 63
8 ch m Bold Edge Floppie Disk (Magic Ring (IRE))
154[4] 428[7] 718[6] 1023[10] (1110) 1554[13] 2121[5] 2646[11] 3233[3] 3390[7] 4055[4] 4266[8] 4905[4] 5425[4] 5977[4] 7346[6]

**Bold Runner** *Jose Santos* a81 75
3 ch g Mount Nelson Music In Exile (USA) (Diesis)
1382[2] 1792[2] 2247[2] (2491) 3673[6] 4322[2] 5276[5] 6143[3] 6461[4] 7366[10] 7539[6] 7946[8] 8089[5] 8196[2]

**Bold Sniper** *Sir Michael Stoute* 110
4 b g New Approach(IRE) Daring Aim (Daylami (IRE))
1948[3] ◆ 3416[2] 4214[3] 5693[17] 6330[3]

**Bold Spirit** *Richard Hannon* a64 76
3 b g Invincible Spirit(IRE) Far Shores (USA) (Distant View (USA))
1980[3] 2846[2] 3114[5] 4569[3] 5205[2]

**Bold Thady Quill (IRE)** *K J Condon* a93 108
7 ch g Tale Of The Cat(USA) Jazzie (FR) (Zilzal (USA))
1078a[4] 1252a[5] 1333a[4] 1473a[8] 4771a[11] 5957a[20] 6354a[3] 6458[6] 7276[11]

**Bolero D'Azur (FR)** *D Prod'Homme* a49 58
3 gr f Verglas(IRE) Snake Dancer (IRE) (Golden Snake (USA))
194a[14] 391a[11]

**Bolingbroke (IRE)** *Saeed bin Suroor* a21 102
5 b g King's Best(USA) Noble Rose (IRE) (Caerleon (USA))
2294[9]

**Bolivia Sport (FR)** *P Chevillard* a55 47
3 bb f High Rock(IRE) Shy Mail (ARG) (Shy Tom (USA))
2978a[10]

**Bollihope** *John Gosden* 74
2 ch c Medicean Hazy Dancer (Oasis Dream)
4550[4] 7380[5]

**Bollin Fergus** *Mrs A Corson* 13
10 br g Vettori(IRE) Bollin Harriet (Lochnager)
1622a[7] 3048a[4]

**Bollin Judith** *Jim Best* a50 44
8 br m Bollin Eric Bollin Nellie (Rock Hopper)
186[3] 379[7] 606[7]

**Bollywood Dream** *Jonathan Portman* a28
2 b f Sleeping Indian Act Three (Beat Hollow)
8247[10]

**Boltcity (FR)** *Braem Horse Racing Sprl* a71 63
7 b g Elusive City(USA) Combloux (USA) (Southern Halo (USA))
57a[6]

**Bombalurina (IRE)** *George Peckham* a26
2 ch f Rip Van Winkle(IRE) Real Cat (USA) (Storm Cat (USA))
7193[13]

**Bombardment (USA)** *Charlie Appleby* a86 84
3 gr c War Front(USA) Niceling (USA) (Maria's Mon (USA))
2881[3] (4130) (5040) 5349[3] 6609[8]

**Bombay Mix** *Charlie Fellowes* a40 57
2 gr f Sleeping Indian Mix It Up (Linamix (FR))
2928[9] 4126[10] 4527[5] 5285[6] 6678[11]

**Bombelli (USA)** *Mme A Fabre* a79 50
3 b g Thewayyouare(USA) Bailonguera (ARG) (Southern Halo (USA))
169a[9] 6221a[4]

**Bomber (ITY)** *Stefano Botti* a67
4 b g King Charlemagne(USA) Agapeline (ITY) (Coral Reef (ITY))
266a[2]

**Bombineta (FR)** *P Adda* a69 72
3 gr f Martaline Hopamare (FR) (Muhtathir)
1907a[7] 2290a[8]

**Bonanza Creek (IRE)** *Luca Cumani* 84
4 b f Anabaa(USA) Bright Moon (USA) (Alysheba (USA))
1942[8] 2821a[10]

**Bon Chance** *Michael Easterby* 49
3 b g Byron Stolen Melody (Robellino (USA))
3370[4] 3914[9] 4318[6] 7056[14]

**Bond Artist (IRE)** *Geoffrey Oldroyd* a60 44
5 b m Excellent Art Pitrizza (IRE) (Machiavellian (USA))
(672) 964[2] 2019[11] 3075[10]

**Bond Blade** *Suzzanne France* a35 36
6 ch g Needwood Blade Bond Cat (IRE) (Raise A Grand (IRE))
910[8] 2092[7] 8133[9]

**Bond Club** *Geoffrey Oldroyd* a58 70
4 b g Misu Bond(IRE) Bond Platinum Club (Pivotal)
464[5] 1343[4] 2166[2] 2653[5] (2838) 3093[6] 5265[4] 7180[14] 7502[7]

**Bond Empire** *Geoffrey Oldroyd* 66
4 b g Misu Bond(IRE) At Amal (IRE) (Astronef)
3700[8] 4569[4] 5195[4] 6042[5]

**Bondesire** *David O'Meara* 103
4 b f Misu Bond(IRE) Lawless Bridget (Alnasr Alwasheek)
(1506) 2361[2] (2757) 2992[6] 3203[2] 4683[15] 5160[4] 5445[13] 5754 6760[5] 7280[12]

**Bond Fastrac** *Geoffrey Oldroyd* a73 76
7 b g Monsieur Bond(IRE) Kanisfluh (Pivotal)
1305[6] 2732[5] 8141[8] 8228[10]

**Bondi (GER)** *Frau J Mayer* 89
3 rg f It's Gino(GER) Bear Nora (GER) (Highest Honor (FR))
1502a[8]

**Bondi Beach Babe** *James Turner* a57 57
4 b f Misu Bond(IRE) Nice One (Almaty (IRE))
2093[4] 2329[4] 2985[6] 3548[4] 4070[9] 6409[5] 6866[6] 7253[2] 7364[7] 7644[11]

**Bondi Beach Boy** *James Turner* 89
5 b g Misu Bond(IRE) Nice One (Almaty (IRE))
2390[10] 2656[5] 3138[3] 3571[4] 3948[6] 4174[8] 6235[12] (6451) (6695) 6763[5] 7330[14]

**Bondi Mist (IRE)** *Jonathan Geake* a53 65
5 gr m Aussie Rules(USA) Akoya (IRE) (Anabaa (USA))
1355[9] 2942[10] 3853[8] 4568[3] 7419[6]

**Bond Mystery** *Richard Whitaker* 51
2 b g Monsieur Bond(IRE) Scooby Dooby Do (Atraf)
6935[9] 7495[6]

**Bonds Choice** *Richard Fahey* 71
2 ch f Monsieur Bond(IRE) Collette's Choice (Royal Applause)
2288[5] 2788[6] 3255[3]

**Bond's Gift** *Geoffrey Oldroyd* 63
4 ch f Monsieur Bond(IRE) Bond Shakira (Daggers Drawn (USA))
3700[7] 3916[6] 4791[12] 6716[12]

**Bond's Girl** *Richard Fahey* 95
2 ch f Monsieur Bond(IRE) Blades Girl (Bertolini (USA))
(1656) (2521) 3415[11] 4439[4] (6256) 7121[2]

**Bond Starprincess** *George Moore* 35
2 ch f Monsieur Bond(IRE) Presidium Star (Presidium)
6861[7] 7174[8]

**Bonfire** *Gai Waterhouse* 106
5 b g Manduro(GER) Night Frolic (Night Shift (USA))
7126a[7]

**Bonfire Heart** *Daniel Mark Loughnane* a67
2 b f Exceed And Excel(AUS) Marisa (GER) (Desert Sun)
6271[5] 7062[4] 7361[6] 7684[2] (7840)

**Bongo Beat** *Michael Attwater* a67
3 ch c Beat Hollow Steppin Out (First Trump)
231[7] 1044[6] 1258[6] 1898[8] 3116[7]

**Bonita Brown Eyes (IRE)** *J S Moore* a22 27
2 b f Fast Company(IRE) Fiddle Player (IRE) (Trans Island)
3311[8] 4079[7] 6205[U] 6563[11]

**Bonjour Steve** *Richard Price* a62 65
3 b g Bahamian Bounty Anthea (Tobougg (IRE))
166[2] 187[3] 1278[5] 1851[7] 2249[2] 2668[2] 3380[3] 3936[5] 5987[10] 7339[5] 7813[8] 7972[10] 8143[8]

**Bonnie Charlie** *David Nicholls* a38 83
8 ch g Intikhab(USA) Scottish Exile (IRE) (Ashkalani (IRE))
1538$^6$ 1967$^6$ 2456$^9$ 2951$^6$ 3610$^4$ 3668$^6$ ◆ 4131$^6$ 4383$^6$ 4796$^U$ 5636$^{RR}$

**Bonnie Fairy** *Michael Appleby* a50 29
3 b f Notnowcato Cheviot Heights (Intikhab (USA))
28$^5$ 5598$^5$ 5820$^8$

**Bonnie Grey** *Rod Millman* 98
2 gr f Hellvelyn Crofters Ceilidh (Scottish Reel)
(2172) ◆ 2703$^4$ 3721$^6$ 4585$^3$ 5664$^2$ 6289$^6$

**Bon Port** *Hughie Morrison* a70 59
3 b f Major Cadeaux Miss Poppy (Averti (IRE))
103$^3$ 2027$^5$ (4613) 5280$^2$ 6722$^4$ 7068$^6$

**Bon Voyage** *Richard Hannon* 95
3 b c Kyllachy Coming Home (Vettori (IRE))
1513$^7$ 2025$^2$ 2339$^4$ 2690$^5$ 3804$^{11}$ 3914$^2$

**Boogangoo (IRE)** *Grace Harris* a78 75
3 b f Acclamation Spice World (IRE) (Spinning World (USA))
(356) (499) 785$^5$ 955$^3$ 1135$^6$ 1400$^2$ 1913$^4$ 2130$^3$ 2624$^4$ 3144$^8$ 3850$^8$ 4613$^4$ 4968$^9$ 6633$^7$ 7044$^8$ 7303$^2$ 7894$^2$ (7993) 8124$^3$ 8268$^4$

**Boogy Man (ITY)** *C Boutin* a100 93
3 b c Orpen(USA) Little Lodge (IRE) (Grand Lodge (USA))
4465a$^7$

**Booker** *David Wachman* 97
3 gr f Mastercraftsman(IRE) Reflected Image (IRE) (Refuse To Bend (IRE))
2186a$^5$ 6963a$^6$

**Bookmaker** *John Bridger* a63 61
4 b g Byron Cankara (IRE) (Daggers Drawn (USA))
5272$^5$ 5504$^{11}$ (5972) 6666$^4$ 6995$^3$ 7556$^4$ 7735$^7$ 8186$^3$ 8299$^3$

**Bookrunner (USA)** *M Delzangles* a85 112
3 b c Tiznow(USA) Take The Ribbon (USA) (Chester House (USA))
1272a$^4$ 1951$^{11}$

**Booktheband (IRE)** *Clive Brittain* a55 43
4 ch g Dubawi(IRE) Songbook (Singspiel (IRE))
252$^6$ 989$^4$ 2465$^8$ 2875$^8$ 3115$^6$ 3682$^6$ 3824$^{10}$ 5832$^9$

**Booloo (IRE)** *Garry Moss* a49 46
3 b g Bushranger(IRE) Ink Pot (USA) (Green Dancer (USA))
1801$^3$

**Boom And Bust (IRE)** *Marcus Tregoning* a62 111
7 b g Footstepsinthesand Forest Call (Wolfhound (USA))
1533$^9$ 4187$^6$ 4758$^7$ 5609$^{12}$ 6358$^4$ 7022$^5$ 7599$^8$

**Boomerang Bob (IRE)** *Charles Hills* a66 105
5 b h Aussie Rules(USA) Cozzene's Pride (USA) (Cozzene (USA))
2256$^9$ 2848$^{12}$ 3452$^5$ 4188$^3$ 4937$^7$ 6920$^{14}$

**Boomshackerlacker (IRE)** *George Baker* a43 108
4 gr g Dark Angel(IRE) Allegrina (IRE) (Barathea (IRE))
1870$^5$ 3416$^8$ 4644a$^2$ 4851$^{14}$ 6965a$^2$ (7618a) 7916a$^4$

**Boom The Groom (IRE)** *Tony Carroll* a104 79
3 b g Kodiac Ecco Mi (IRE) (Priolo (USA))
6893$^{12}$ 7564$^5$ 7738$^2$ (7889) ◆ 8019$^2$ 8101$^2$ 8228$^2$

**Boom To Bust (IRE)** *Barry Brennan* a84 48
6 br g Big Bad Bob(IRE) Forever Phoenix (Shareef Dancer (USA))
126$^4$ 262$^2$ 367$^7$

**Boonga Roogeta** *Peter Charalambous* a71 99
5 b m Tobougg(IRE) Aberlady Bay (IRE) (Selkirk (USA))
(2047) 2331$^5$ 4060$^5$ 4442$^5$ 5162$^9$ 7384$^5$ 7565$^9$

**Boots And Spurs** *Stuart Williams* a78 97
5 b g Oasis Dream Arctic Char (Polar Falcon (USA))
1164$^{16}$ 2145$^7$ 2984$^4$ 3251$^7$

**Bo Peep (IRE)** *Seamus Mullins*
4 ch f Captain Rio Estacado (IRE) (Dolphin Street (FR))
4543$^{12}$

**Bop It** *David O'Meara* a75 94
5 b g Misu Bond(IRE) Forever Bond (Danetime (IRE))
2352$^4$ 3342$^7$ ◆ 3702$^{10}$ 4317$^5$ 5081$^4$ (5766) 6150$^5$ 6744$^9$ 7330$^8$ 7507$^{12}$

**Boqa (IRE)** *T Stack* 103
3 b c Danehill Dancer(IRE) Mowaadah (IRE) (Alzao (USA))
2579a$^3$

**Borak (IRE)** *Marco Botti* a69 69
2 b g Kodiac Right After Moyne (IRE) (Imperial Ballet (IRE))
7040$^4$ 7560$^8$ 7892$^3$

**Border Bandit (USA)** *Tracy Waggott* 89
6 b g Selkirk(USA) Coretta (IRE) (Caerleon (USA))
(2519) 3190$^3$ (3400) 3572$^6$ (4290) (4451) 5196$^U$ 5446$^6$ 5681$^2$ 6226$^6$ 6713$^{17}$ 6936$^{14}$

**Border Guard** *Milton Bradley* 20
3 b g Selkirk(USA) Argent Du Bois (USA) (Silver Hawk (USA))
1569$^9$ 1790$^3$ 3074$^4$ 3518$^{10}$ 5257$^8$

**Border Legend** *Roger Charlton* a89 103
5 ch g Selkirk(USA) Bonnie Doon (IRE) (Grand Lodge (USA))
2154$^3$ ◆ 2783$^3$ 3730$^4$ (4400) 4888$^4$ 5676$^2$ 6548$^7$

**Borderlescott** *Robin Bastiman* a85 105
12 b g Compton Place Jeewan (Touching Wood (USA))
1561$^2$ 2076$^7$ 3241$^{15}$ 4174$^5$ 4895$^{18}$ 6131$^4$ 6467$^5$ 7101$^2$

**Boris Grigoriev (IRE)** *Michael Easterby* a55 77
5 bb g Excellent Art Strategy (Machiavellian (USA))
4494$^9$ 5912$^6$ 6512$^{14}$ 7178$^5$ 7506$^6$

**Borneo (IRE)** *Bruce Hellier* a34
3 ch g Danehill Dancer(IRE) Borghesa (GER) (Galileo (IRE))
8005a$^{13}$

**Born In Bombay** *Andrew Balding* a89 95
3 b c Shamardal(USA) Pearl Dance (USA) (Nureyev (USA))
579$^3$ (748) 1954$^2$ (3378) ◆

**Bornonville** *J E Pease* 76
2 b c Nayef(USA) Norfolk Broads (IRE) (Noverre (USA))
5706a$^6$

**Born To Be Alive (FR)** *Robert Collet* a72 54
3 b g Dylan Thomas(IRE) Wait And See (FR) (Montjeu (IRE))
7681a$^{12}$

**Born To Be Bad (IRE)** *Jamie Osborne* a65
2 b c Arcano(IRE) Lady Of Kildare (IRE) (Mujadil (USA))
8092$^{12}$ 8184$^4$

**Born To Fly (IRE)** *Nick Littmoden* a59 66
3 b f Kodiac Cayambe (IRE) (Selkirk (USA))
3158$^5$ (4048) 4654$^8$ 4998$^{10}$ 5427$^2$ 6022$^{11}$ 7288$^6$

**Born To Reign** *Michael Bell* a52 51
3 b g Sir Percy Oat Cuisine (Mujahid (USA))
1002$^5$ 4265$^9$ 4830$^6$ 5402$^8$ 6193$^7$ 7229$^7$ 7664$^3$ 8010$^4$ 8189$^5$

**Born To Run (GER)** *R Dzubasz* 102
3 b c Shirocco(GER) Bravo Gorl (GER) (Tauchsport (GER))
3073a$^4$ 7603a$^{14}$

**Born To Shine (USA)** *Tracy Waggott* 3
6 b g Suave(USA) Sentimental Keep (USA) (Behrens (USA))
2950$^3$

**Born To Surprise** *Lee Carter* a89 101
5 b g Exceed And Excel(AUS) Dubai Surprise (IRE) (King's Best (USA))
840$^9$ 1164$^{13}$ 1301$^4$ (2157) ◆ 2849$^5$ 4323$^7$ 4650$^2$ 5728$^5$

**Boronia (IRE)** *Charles O'Brien* a58 57
4 gr f Dalakhani(IRE) Mount Eliza (IRE) (Danehill (USA))
794a$^4$ (Dead)

**Borough Belle** *Henry Candy* a55 49
3 ch f Bertolini(USA) Sheesha (USA) (Shadeed (USA))
1767$^8$ 2688$^6$ 3087$^{11}$ 3527$^5$ 6421$^5$ 6717$^4$ 7218$^5$

**Borough Boy (IRE)** *Derek Shaw* a68 70
4 b g Jeremy(USA) Ostrusa (AUT) (Rustan (HUN))
59$^3$ ◆ 121$^2$ 3150$^8$ 3854$^6$ 3935$^3$ (5082) 5287$^4$ 5602$^7$ 5777$^2$ 5987$^6$ 6346$^{10}$ 6858$^2$ 7180$^3$ 7533$^5$ 7830$^6$ 7915$^4$

**Borsakov (IRE)** *Mme Pia Brandt* a80
2 b c Dylan Thomas(IRE) Million Wishes (Darshaan)
(8148a)

**Bosham** *Michael Easterby* a64 75
4 b g Shamardal(USA) Awwal Malika (USA) (Kingmambo (USA))
2167$^5$ 3948$^9$ ◆ 4511$^2$ 4632$^7$ 5298$^5$ 6150$^{10}$ 6452$^7$ 6671$^{11}$

**Bossa Nova Baby (IRE)** *Peter Chapple-Hyam* a64 69
4 b f High Chaparral(IRE) Attilia (GER) (Tiger Hill (IRE))
3371$^5$ 3803$^7$

**Bosstime (IRE)** *John Holt* a77 44
4 b g Clodovil(IRE) Smoken Rosa (USA) (Smoke Glacken (USA))
5395$^6$ 6715$^4$ 7077$^8$ 7765$^{12}$ (7987) (8175) (8321)

**Bossy Guest (IRE)** *Mick Channon* 97
2 b c Medicean Ros The Boss (IRE) (Danehill (USA))
(2288) 3318$^{10}$ 4199$^7$ (4670) 5770$^2$ ◆ 6556$^2$ 6925$^3$

**Boston Blue** *Tony Carroll* a58 50
7 b g Halling(USA) City Of Gold (IRE) (Sadler's Wells (USA))
380$^4$ 657$^7$ 6019$^{11}$ 6486$^{12}$ 7133$^9$

**Boston Rocker (IRE)** *Hughie Morrison* 102
4 b f Acclamation Rocking (Oasis Dream)
6209$^5$ 6929$^{10}$

**Boston Two Step** *Mark Johnston* a38
2 b c Pivotal Danse Arabe (IRE) (Seeking The Gold (USA))
7660$^{14}$ 7920$^8$

**Bosun Breese** *Paul Midgley* a41 91
9 b g Bahamian Bounty Nellie Melba (Hurricane Sky (AUS))
1695$^9$ 1961$^{18}$ 2727$^6$ 3138$^6$ 3395$^3$ 3954$^4$ 4114$^{13}$ 4714$^7$ 6580$^7$

**Botanique (FR)** *M Pimbonnet* a68 82
8 ch g Panis(USA) Dhaunasing (FR) (Sin Kiang (FR))
752a$^7$

**Botanist** *Shaun Harris* a54 65
7 b g Selkirk(USA) Red Camellia (Polar Falcon (USA))
78$^5$ 352$^P$ 1800$^4$ 2381$^5$ (2844) 3075$^3$ 3791$^6$ (3971) ◆ 4408$^2$ 4620$^5$ 5075$^7$ 5530$^6$ 6086$^5$ 6628$^2$

**Bothy** *Brian Ellison* a18 28
8 ch g Pivotal Villa Carlotta (Rainbow Quest (USA))
7235$^9$

**Bottoms Up (IRE)** *Robert Collet* a52 73
4 b c Whipper(USA) Graten (IRE) (Zieten (USA))
805a$^9$

**Bouclier (IRE)** *Luca Cumani* a68 94
4 ch c Zamindar(USA) Bastet (IRE) (Giant's Causeway (USA))
2922$^9$ 3917$^6$

**Bouggatti** *Lady Herries* a58 62
6 b g Tobougg(IRE) Western Sal (Salse (USA))
2305$^{10}$ 2683$^6$ 3680$^4$

**Bouncing Czech** *Amanda Perrett* 42
2 b g Dandy Man(IRE) Correlandie (USA) (El Corredor (USA))
4103$^4$ 4760$^{13}$ 5091$^9$

**Bountiful Forest** *Kevin Frost* a25 59
3 ch f Bahamian Bounty Through The Forest (USA) (Forestry (USA))
6272$^{11}$ 6720$^{10}$

**Bountiful Sin** *George Margarson* a64 49
3 ch g Sinndar(IRE) Tropical Barth (IRE) (Peintre Celebre (USA))
236$^2$ 488$^4$

**Bounty Bah** *Mark Usher* a45 20
2 ch g Bahamian Bounty Eternity Ring (Alzao (USA))
5210$^{10}$ 5555$^8$ 6039$^9$

**Bountybeamadam** *George Baker* a48 83
4 b f Bahamian Bounty Madamoiselle Jones (Emperor Jones (USA))
1026$^6$ 1873$^5$ 2669$^3$ (3177) (3850) 4761$^{15}$ 5505$^5$ 6657$^{11}$

**Bounty Pursuit** *E J O'Neill* a50
2 b g Pastoral Pursuits Poyle Dee Dee (Oasis Dream)
8148a$^9$

**Bourbon Courage (USA)** *Kellyn Gorder* a114
5 b h Lion Heart(USA) Shine Forth (USA) (Carson City (USA))
7612a$^4$

**Bourbon Prince** *Michael Bell* a54 54
3 ch g Aqlaam Good Enough (FR) (Mukaddamah (USA))
1394$^9$ 1683$^2$ 1852$^3$ 2742$^6$ 4085$^4$ 4738$^9$ 5106$^6$

**Bourree (GER)** *Andreas Lowe* 100
2 b f Siyouni(FR) Bearlita (GER) (Lomitas)
(7315a)

**Bousatet (FR)** *Kevin Ryan* a60 77
4 b f Muhtathir Miss Mission (IRE) (Second Empire (IRE))
1275$^2$ 1607$^{10}$ 2024$^4$

**Bousfield** *Declan Carroll* a70 24
3 b g Duke Of Marmalade(IRE) Exodia (Dr Fong (USA))
2163$^7$

**Bow And Arrow** *Charlie Appleby* a82
2 b c Iffraaj Isobel Archer (Oasis Dream)
4301$^7$ (5009)

**Bow Belle** *J R Jenkins*
4 ch f Cockney Rebel(IRE) Miss Ippolita (Diktat)
8207$^5$

**Bowberry** *Clive Cox* a66 58
3 b f Cockney Rebel(IRE) Blaeberry (Kirkwall)
2418$^8$ ◆ 3142$^7$ 4368$^6$ 5048$^6$ 6818$^U$ 7458$^2$ ◆ 7822$^6$ 8070$^6$

**Bow Creek (IRE)** *Mark Johnston* a108 118
3 b c Shamardal(USA) Beneventa (Most Welcome)
1067$^9$ (1300) 1563$^5$ 2114$^2$ 3378$^2$ 4850$^3$ (5666) (6352a)

**Bowdler's Magic** *David Thompson* a73 86
7 b g Hernando(FR) Slew The Moon (ARG) (Kitwood (USA))
3204$^{11}$ 3501$^4$ 4068$^6$ 4662$^3$ 5334$^4$ 5890$^{14}$ 6493$^6$ 6864$^6$ 7177$^6$ 7643$^2$

**Bowie Boy (IRE)** *Ralph Beckett* a81 84
3 b c Intikhab(USA) Catatonic (Zafonic (USA))
188$^2$ (588) 2921$^7$ 4074$^6$ 4801$^2$ 5311$^4$

**Bowmans Well (IRE)** *Peter Purdy* a10
9 b m Cadeaux Genereux Guignol (IRE) (Anita's Prince)
215$^8$

**Bowmore (SPA)** *J Heloury* 93
2 b c Caradak(IRE) Famous Angel (FR) (In The Wings)
3029a$^4$

**Bowsers Bold** *Marcus Tregoning* a63 57
3 gr g Firebreak Cristal Clear (IRE) (Clodovil (IRE))
1669$^5$ 2647$^{10}$ 3144$^{14}$ 7527$^7$ 7854$^3$ 8004$^2$ 8232$^3$ 8250$^2$

**Bowson Fred** *Michael Easterby* 78
2 b c Monsieur Bond(IRE) Bow Bridge (Bertolini (USA))
1560$^4$ 2231$^7$ 3713$^5$ 4172$^5$ (4857) (5409) 5998$^2$ 6128$^5$

**Bowstar** *Michael Attwater* a83 23
5 b m Oasis Dream Bold Empress (USA) (Diesis)
118$^3$ 287$^8$ (372) 574$^6$ 1020$^9$ 1102$^2$ 4182$^6$ 4971$^5$

**Boxer Beat (IRE)** *Paul W Flynn* a51 56
7 b g Xaar Pantoufle (Bering)
794a$^7$

**Boxing Shadows** *Les Eyre* a68 77
4 b g Camacho Prima Ballerina (Pivotal)
1244$^{10}$ 1487$^5$ (1643) 2056$^2$ 2364$^7$ 3399$^3$ 3571$^2$ 3948$^{14}$ 4494$^7$ 4714$^3$ 5053$^3$ 5912$^8$ 6406$^2$ ◆ 6695$^2$ 7534$^2$ 7697$^6$

**Boy In The Bar** *David Barron* 96
3 ch g Dutch Art Lipsia (IRE) (Dubai Destination (USA))
2158$^2$ (2524) 2897$^4$ (3790) 4712$^2$ 5438$^3$

**Boy The Bell** *Ollie Pears* a62 60
7 b g Choisir(AUS) Bella Beguine (Komaite (USA))
126$^{10}$ 498$^6$

**Boy Wonder** *Mick Channon* 68
3 ch g Compton Place Kindallachan (Magic Ring (IRE))
(1860) 6758$^9$ 7023$^{13}$

**Brabazon (IRE)** *Emmet Michael Butterly* a62 70
11 b g In The Wings Azure Lake (USA) (Lac Ouimet (USA))
1150$^4$ 1242$^4$ 2455$^6$ 8021$^9$

**Bracelet (IRE)** *A P O'Brien* 112
3 b f Montjeu(IRE) Cherry Hinton (Green Desert (USA))
(1201a) 1976$^{14}$ (3376) (4461a)

**Bracka Legend (IRE)** *David Barron* 63
2 ch g Approve(IRE) Glyndebourne (USA) (Rahy (USA))
6453$^{13}$ 7246$^7$ 7495$^4$

**Bracken Brae** *Mark H Tompkins* 32
2 b f Champs Elysees Azure Mist (Bahamian Bounty)
6754$^9$

**Bradbury (IRE)** *Eric Alston* a72 72
6 ch g Redback Simonaventura (IRE) (Dr Devious (IRE))
4575$^{10}$ 6099$^6$

**Brae Hill (IRE)** *Richard Fahey* a74 104
8 b g Fath(USA) Auriga (Belmez (USA))
(1164) 1721$^{12}$ 2784$^3$ 3420$^{21}$ 3645$^3$ 4648$^{28}$

**Braes Of Lochalsh** *Jim Goldie* 67
3 b g Tiger Hill(IRE) Gargoyle Girl (Be My Chief (USA))
3998$^4$ 4978$^4$ 5388$^4$ ◆ 6011$^5$

**Bragging (USA)** *Sir Michael Stoute* a70 113
3 bb f Exchange Rate(USA) Boasting (USA) (Kris S (USA))
1920$^3$ ◆ (2404) 2892$^2$ (4668) ◆ (5612) ◆ 6254$^2$

**Braidley (IRE)** *James Bethell* 94
3 b g Dylan Thomas(IRE) All Our Hope (USA) (Gulch (USA))
2565$^7$ 2983$^2$ 3455$^2$ 4212$^6$ 4821$^4$ 5695$^6$ 5914$^7$ 7119$^3$

**Brambles (NZ)** *Peter G Moody* 112
6 b g Savabeel(AUS) Prickle (NZ) (Pins (AUS))
7301a$^4$ 7602a$^9$ 7653a$^{15}$

**Bramshill Lass** *Amanda Perrett* a78 63
5 ch m Notnowcato Disco Ball (Fantastic Light (USA))
471$^2$ 758$^6$ 992$^7$ 1941$^{11}$ 2683$^8$ 3078$^4$

**Brando** *Kevin Ryan* 81
2 ch c Pivotal Argent Du Bois (USA) (Silver Hawk (USA))
2698$^4$ 5655$^{10}$ 6168$^3$ 7082$^2$ 7503$^2$

**Brandon Castle** *Andrew Balding* 72
2 b g Dylan Thomas(IRE) Chelsey Jayne (IRE) (Galileo (IRE))
6317$^3$ 6874$^7$ 7217$^3$

**Brandywell Boy (IRE)** *Dominic Ffrench Davis* a44 47
11 b g Danetime(IRE) Alexander Eliott (IRE) (Night Shift (USA))
192$^9$ 313$^7$ 483$^3$ 586$^{10}$ 2459$^7$ 3077$^4$

**Branston De Soto** *Mark Johnston* a63 70
3 b g Hernando(FR) Julatten (IRE) (Alhaarth (IRE))
761$^5$ 3303$^4$ 3818$^{10}$

**Brasilia Sport (FR)** *P Chevillard* a63
3 gr f High Rock(IRE) Pipsila (FR) (Linamix (FR))
599a$^6$

**Brasingaman Eric** *George Moore* 72
7 b g Bollin Eric Serene Pearl (IRE) (Night Shift (USA))
7509$^{12}$

**Brassbound (USA)** *Michael Appleby* a75 65
6 b g Redoute's Choice(AUS) In A Bound (AUS) (Ashkalani (IRE))
8211$^3$

**Brass Ring** *John Gosden* a102 111
4 b g Rail Link Moraine (Rainbow Quest (USA))
(1299) 1950$^5$ 2335$^5$ 3453$^3$ 4823$^4$ 6288$^6$ 7107$^4$

**Brave Decision** *Suzy Smith* a68 48
7 gr g With Approval(CAN) Brave Vanessa (USA) (Private Account (USA))
210$^2$ 6007$^7$ 6856$^5$ 7526$^2$ 7804$^4$

**Brave Helios** *Jonathan Portman* a62 60
4 b g High Chaparral(IRE) Renowned (IRE) (Darshaan)
580$^2$ 656$^4$

**Brave Imp** *Kevin Ryan* a50 67
3 b g Sleeping Indian Impetuous (Inchinor)
3124$^{10}$ 3792$^8$ 3938$^6$

**Bravo Echo** *Michael Attwater* a100 88
8 b g Oasis Dream Bold Empress (USA) (Diesis)
314$^{12}$ 713$^{12}$ 836a$^4$ 1042$^5$ (1174) 1576$^4$ (3180) 4181$^{10}$ 5092$^3$ 5824$^7$ 6140$^{11}$ 6657$^3$ 7437a$^8$

**Bravo Ragazzo (IRE)** *A Al Raihe* a70 45
4 b c Pivotal Kitza (IRE) (Danehill (USA))
239a$^2$

**Bravo Zolo (IRE)** *Marco Botti* a87 75
2 b c Rip Van Winkle(IRE) Set Fire (IRE) (Bertolini (USA))
5760$^4$ (6138) (6854)

**Brazen** *Ernst Oertel* a75 75
4 b c Kyllachy Molly Brown (Rudimentary (USA))
240a$^5$

**Brazen Spirit** *Clive Cox* a75 75
2 gr c Zebedee Never Say Deya (Dansili)
1276$^8$ 1977$^4$ 2487$^4$ 3584$^2$ 4439$^{12}$ 4853$^{10}$ 6312$^6$ 7771$^4$ (7919)

**Brazos (IRE)** *Clive Brittain* a99 109
3 gr c Clodovil(IRE) Shambodia (IRE) (Petardia)
1067$^8$ 1420$^3$ (2111) 3352$^6$ 3982$^{13}$ 4648$^{18}$ 5434$^3$ 6921$^8$ 7242$^{10}$ 7555$^8$

**Bread** *Garry Moss* 65
2 b g Alfred Nobel(IRE) Sweet Power (Pivotal)
4467$^5$ 5680$^5$

**Breakable** *Tim Easterby* 79
3 ch f Firebreak Magic Myth (IRE) (Revoque (IRE))
6516$^3$ (6863) 7445$^2$ 7640$^2$

**Breakheart (IRE)** *Andrew Balding* a77 69
7 b g Sakhee(USA) Exorcet (FR) (Selkirk (USA))
1796$^8$ 2012$^5$ 8161$^3$ ◆

**Brean Golf Birdie** *Bill Turner* a48
2 br f Striking Ambition Straight As A Die (Pyramus (USA))
7943$^9$ 8227$^{10}$

**Brean Splash Susie** *Bill Turner* a42 52
3 b f Tobougg(IRE) Straight As A Die (Pyramus (USA))
919$^6$ 1104$^6$ 1277$^4$ 1626$^4$ 2023$^6$ 2625$^2$ 3214$^9$ 7221$^3$ 7420$^8$ 7671$^{12}$

**Breccbennach** *Seamus Durack* a85 87
4 b g Oasis Dream Next (In The Wings)
(1041) (1490) 3313$^{12}$ 3676$^6$ 4983$^4$ 5677$^{12}$ 7521$^7$

**Breenainthemycra (IRE)** *Eoin Doyle* a55
3 b c Jeremy(USA) Crystal Theatre (IRE) (King's Theatre (IRE))
416a$^4$

**Breezealong Riley** *Zoe Davison* 24
5 b m Arkadian Hero(USA) Mountain Magic (Magic Ring (IRE))
800$^6$ 1767$^{10}$ 2864$^{10}$

**Breezolini** *Muredach Kelly* a67 71
6 b m Bertolini(USA) African Breeze (Atraf)
128a$^4$

**Breitling Flyer (USA)** *Leo Azpurua Jr* a41 95
3 ch c Ghostzapper(USA) Starbuster (USA) (Housebuster (USA))
813a$^6$

**Bremner** *Hugo Palmer* 91
3 b g Manduro(GER) Maggie Lou (IRE) (Red Ransom (USA))
1953$^8$ 2748$^5$ 3379$^{16}$

**Brendan Brackan (IRE)** *G M Lyons* a108 114
5 b g Big Bad Bob(IRE) Abeyr (Unfuwain (USA))
111a[3] 397a[12] 899a[15] 2185a[2] 3412a[3] 5361a[2] 6350a[9] 6963a[2] 7274[9]

**Bretherton** *Richard Fahey* a87 91
3 ch g Exceed And Excel(AUS) Cliche (IRE) (Diktat)
159[2] (477) 573[3] 850[5] 1013[6] 1614[2] 2257[7] (2567) 2962[12]

**Breton Rock (IRE)** *David Simcock* 116
4 b g Bahamian Bounty Anna's Rock (IRE) (Rock Of Gibraltar (IRE))
(1443) ◆ 1728[3] (2150) 2765[2] (5434) 7242[3]

**Brex Drago (ITY)** *Stefano Botti* 98
2 b c Mujahid(USA) Shibuni's Thea (IRE) (Barathea (IRE))
7147a[4]

**Brian Noble** *Richard Fahey* 81
3 b c Royal Applause Little Greenbird (Ardkinglass)
2088[7]

**Brian The Lion** *Shaun Harris* a34 28
3 b g Byron Molly Pitcher (IRE) (Halling (USA))
5202[5] 5796[12] 8147[5] 8289[7]

**Bridge Arabrab (IRE)** *Pierpaolo Sbariggia* 83
3 br f Erewhon(USA) Lianda (USA) (Danzig (USA))
7480a[10]

**Bridge Builder** *Peter Hedger* 48
4 b g Avonbridge Amazing Dream (IRE) (Thatching)
2689[13] 3824[6]

**Bridgekeeper** *James Eustace* 63
2 ch c Avonbridge Rosy Outlook (USA) (Trempolino (USA))
4829[3] 5500[7] 6261[8] 6869[6] 7165[8]

**Bridge Of Avon** *Mel Brittain* 26
3 b f Avonbridge Out Like Magic (Magic Ring (IRE))
1906[9]

**Bridget Gem** *Nigel Tinkler* 31
2 br f Avonbridge Diamond Surprise (Mark Of Esteem (IRE))
7637[9]

**Bridge That Gap** *Roger Ingram* a67 47
6 b h Avonbridge Figura (Rudimentary (USA))
2916[8] 3556[9] 4273[12] 4658[4] 4911[6] 7359[10] 7426[2] 7744[7] 7925[12] 8102[2] 8169[6]

**Bridge Valley** *Alan McCabe* a34 57
7 ch g Avonbridge Go Between (Daggers Drawn (USA))
100[10] 2937[6] 4732[11]

**Bridie ffrench** *Mick Channon* a75 78
3 b f Bahamian Bounty Wansdyke Lass (Josr Algarhoud (IRE))
(456) 1723[3] 2130[6] 2340[6] (2639) 3273[12] 4176[5]

**Brigadoon** *Michael Appleby* a82 90
7 b g Compton Place Briggsmaid (Elegant Air)
163[9] 514[9] (1377) 1659[3] 2160[4] 3926[2] 5052[5] 6433[2] (6761) 7440[8]

**Brigand Chief** *Luke Dace* a41 29
2 ch g Aqlaam Soundwave (Prince Sabo)
5625[9] 6630[7]

**Bright Abbey** *Dianne Sayer* a75 82
6 ch g Halling(USA) Bright Hope (IRE) (Danehill (USA))
(868) 1599[2]

**Bright Acclaim** *Jo Hughes* a27
3 b g Acclamation Bright Vision (Indian Ridge)
564[7] 6298[8]

**Bright Applause** *Tracy Waggott* a53 78
6 b g Royal Applause Sadaka (USA) (Kingmambo (USA))
3371[2] 3699[7] 4454[5] 4979[5]

**Bright Approach (IRE)** *John Gosden* 93
3 ch f New Approach(IRE) Zam Zoom (IRE) (Dalakhani (IRE))
(1423) ◆ 2072[3] 3376[11]

**Bright Beacon** *Charlie Appleby* a61 76
3 b f Manduro(GER) Waldmark (GER) (Mark Of Esteem (IRE))
4413[4] 5382[2] 6238[5]

**Bright Cecily (IRE)** *Clive Cox* 86
3 b f Excellent Art Roman Love (IRE) (Perugino (USA))
1868[7] 3195[6] 3968[5] 4947[2] 6026[2] (6365) 6746[3] ◆

**Bright Flash** *David Brown* 76
2 ch f Dutch Art Quadri (Polish Precedent (USA))
4781[4] 5655[4] (6224)

**Brightline (JPN)** *Ippo Sameshima* a112 111
5 bl h Fuji Kiseki(JPN) Cherie's Smile (USA) (King Of Kings (IRE))
1176a[5]

**Brightside** *Tracy Waggott* 30
2 b g Indesatchel(IRE) Romantic Destiny (Dubai Destination (USA))
3481[12] 5386[7] 7173[6]

**Bright Society (IRE)** *Sean Curran* a39 41
3 b g Diamond Green(FR) Soul Society (IRE) (Inchinor)
3567[8] 4734[6]

**Brigliadoro (IRE)** *Philip McBride* a90 78
3 ch g Excellent Art Milady's Pride (Machiavellian (USA))
847[2] ◆ 1861[3] 3145[3] 3430[6] (7035) 7601[10] 7988[7] 8251[2]

**Brindle** *Richard Fahey* 64
2 b f Iffraaj Anglezarke (IRE) (Acclamation)
4389[4] 5332[4] 6093[9] 7497[6]

**Brindos** *G Arizkorreta Elosegui* a95 87
5 b h Singspiel(IRE) Ribbons And Bows (IRE) (Dr Devious (IRE))
8006a[10]

**Brioniya** *A De Royer-Dupre* 101
3 ch f Pivotal Bahia Breeze (Mister Baileys)
7319a[2] 7629a[5]

**Brisanto** *M G Mintchev* 107
2 b c Dansili Briseida (Pivotal)
(7145a)

**Brisk** *David Evans* a76 74
3 ch f Nayef(USA) Dance Dress (USA) (Nureyev (USA))
5622[4] 6298[3] (6638) 6945[8]

**Britain (IRE)** *David C Griffiths* a59 51
3 b f Manduro(GER) Unreal (Dansili)
762[6] 933[5] 1343[2] 1642[7] 1905[7]

**British Art** *Paul Cole* a77 74
2 b g Iffraaj Bush Cat (USA) (Kingmambo (USA))
1879[7] 3429[2] 7400[2] 7542[3] 7770[4]

**British Embassy (IRE)** *Eve Johnson Houghton* a70 66
2 b g Clodovil(IRE) Embassy Belle (IRE) (Marju (IRE))
2151[4] 2487[3] 3193[5] 4057[2] 4364[7] 6104[4] 6294[7] (7363)

**Brittleton** *Harry Dunlop* a56 47
2 b g Aqlaam Fairy Dance (IRE) (Zafonic (USA))
6874[9] 7354[9] 7631[8]

**Broadway Boogie (IRE)** *J-C Rouget* 43
2 b c Distorted Humor(USA) Grande Melody (IRE) (Grand Lodge (USA))
5588a[9]

**Broadway Duchess (IRE)** *Richard Hannon* a96 99
4 ch f New Approach(IRE) Annee Lumiere (IRE) (Giant's Causeway (USA))
1577[3] 2155[5]

**Broadway Ranger (IRE)** *Charles Hills* a53 72
3 b c Bushranger(IRE) Broadways Millie (IRE) (Imperial Ballet (IRE))
1569[3] 2035[5] 2329[2] 2759[3] 3519[4]

**Brockfield** *Mel Brittain* a73 67
8 ch g Falbrav(IRE) Irish Light (USA) (Irish River (FR))
1003[5] 2540[5] 2806[11] 5300[4] (6628) 7044[9]

**Brocklebank (IRE)** *Simon Dow* a100 78
5 b g Diamond Green(FR) La Stellina (IRE) (Marju (IRE))
314[2] 574[5] 715[9] 1020[2] 1070[2] 1437[21] 1834[8] 2959[12] 3221[9] 3753[9] 4355[8] 5785[7] ◆ 6263[5] 6789[11] 7375[10] 7774[5] ◆ (7955) 8078[2] 8244[3] (8266) 8312[4]

**Brockwell** *Tom Dascombe* 97
5 b g Singspiel(IRE) Noble Plum (IRE) (King's Best (USA))
2073[8] 2561[4] 3321[9] 4217[3] 4777[4]

**Broctune Papa Gio** *Keith Reveley* 76
7 b g Tobougg(IRE) Fairlie (Halling (USA))
1609[5] 3439[4] 4108[14] 5088[7] (5640) (6217) 6490[4] 6865[10] 7249[4]

**Brokopondo (IRE)** *Miss Evanna McCutcheon* 59
2 b g Bushranger(IRE) Saramacca (IRE) (Kahyasi)
3945[8]

**Bronze Angel (IRE)** *Marcus Tregoning* a97 116
5 b g Dark Angel(IRE) Rihana (IRE) (Priolo (USA))
1437[7] 2336[5] 3420[4] (4212) 4648[13] 4851[7] 5609[4] 6332[2] (6752) (7276) 7599[3]

**Bronze Beau** *Kristin Stubbs* a59 86
7 ch g Compton Place Bella Cantata (Singspiel (IRE))
1566[2] 1961[4] 2350[2] 2656[6] 2727[9] 3239[13] 3611[9] 4114[5] 4494[5] 4833[6] 5498[11] 5912[11] 6406[7] 6819[2] 6938[2] 7103[4] 7342[5]

**Bronze Maquette (IRE)** *Gary Moore* a75 103
2 b f Dark Angel(IRE) Precious Citizen (USA) (Proud Citizen (USA))
(1663) ◆ 2308[4] 2403[3] 3580[3] 4143[2] (4605) (5380) 6286[12] 6933[6]

**Bronzo (CHI)** *Jorge Andres Inda* a108
5 b g Fusaichi Pegasus(USA) Bateria Blindada (CHI) (Memo (CHI))
7591a[4]

**Brooch (USA)** *D K Weld* 105
3 b f Empire Maker(USA) Daring Diva (Dansili)
(6585a) ◆

**Brooke's Bounty** *Richard Fahey* a55 67
4 ch g Bahamian Bounty Choysia (Pivotal)
4729[2] 5295[2] 6477[5] 7098[7] (7639) 8224[6]

**Brookes Boy (IRE)** *Michael Dods*
3 b g Tagula(IRE) Satan's Sister (Tout Ensemble)
2354[14]

**Brooklyn Bowl (USA)** *F Rohaut* a71 98
4 b g Henrythenavigator(USA) Turtle Bow (FR) (Turtle Island (IRE))
4644a[5]

**Brosnan (IRE)** *Noel Quinlan* a69 60
2 ch f Champs Elysees Clytha (Mark Of Esteem (IRE))
7084[5] 7425[7] 7809[6] 8087[2] 8220[4]

**Brotherly Company (IRE)** *Richard Fahey* 72
2 b c Fast Company(IRE) Good Lady (IRE) (Barathea (IRE))
7637[2]

**Brothersofthetime (USA)** *Antonio Sano* a93
3 bb c Bob And John(USA) Hostility (USA) (Devil His Due (USA))
813a[3]

**Brother Tiger** *David C Griffiths* a84 83
5 b g Singspiel(IRE) Three Secrets (IRE) (Danehill (USA))
3882[9] 4581[2] (5830) 6324[3] 6763[11]

**Broughtonian** *Marco Botti*
2 b g Invincible Spirit(IRE) Quan Yin (IRE) (Sadler's Wells (USA))
6702[12]

**Broughtons Charm (IRE)** *Willie Musson* a81 81
4 b f Invincible Spirit(IRE) Parisian Elegance (Zilzal (USA))
924[3] (1247) 2024[3] 2318[4] 2608[3] 3125[2]

**Broughtons Secret** *Willie Musson* a56 82
3 b f Aqlaam Hidden Meaning (Cadeaux Genereux)
5796[6]

**Brown Diamond (IRE)** *Charles Hills* 78
3 b f Fastnet Rock(AUS) Adjalisa (IRE) (Darshaan)
1433[3] ◆ 2072[9] 4699[4] (5883) 6129[8] 7417[8]

**Brown Eyed Honey** *William Haggas* a87 96
3 b f Elusive City(USA) Tiger Mist (IRE) (Galileo (IRE))
(1381) 2277[6] (4074) (4794)

**Brown Glaze (USA)** *Richard Hannon*
3 b f War Front(USA) Easy To Cope (USA) (Copelan (USA))
1422[19]

**Brown Panther** *Tom Dascombe* a74 119
6 b h Shirocco(GER) Treble Heights (IRE) (Unfuwain (USA))
(2115) (2704) 3377[3] 4250a[2] 4823[3] (6374a) 7611a[11]

**Brown Pete (IRE)** *Ann Stokell* a56 52
6 bb g Aussie Rules(USA) Banba (IRE) (Docksider (USA))
152[6] 1288[4] 1865[2] 2396[3] 2674[5] 2874[5] 7546[4] 7635[3] 7869[3] 7924[2]

**Brownsea Brink** *Richard Hannon* a98 101
4 b c Cadeaux Genereux Valiantly (Anabaa (USA))
1042[2] ◆ 1437[3] 2145[13]

**Brown Sugar (IRE)** *Richard Hannon* a110 108
3 b c Tamayuz Lady Livius (IRE) (Titus Livius (FR))
4852[14] 5674[6] 6522[3] 6920[7]

**Brownsville (USA)** *Mark Johnston* a74 74
3 b g Bernstein(USA) Net Worth (USA) (Forty Niner (USA))
614[3] 731[10] 1006[2] 1101[7] 1817[2] 2211[5] 2617[6] 3146[11] 4020[3]

**Brown Velvet** *Hugo Palmer* a63 68
2 b f Kodiac Silkenveil (IRE) (Indian Ridge)
1633[2] 2064[2] (2413) 3751[6] 5028[3] 6104[6] 6610[6]

**Brunello** *Philip Kirby* a65 63
6 b g Leporello(IRE) Lydia Maria (Dancing Brave (USA))
361[3] 513[4] 831[4]

**Brutus (FR)** *Richard Hannon* a79 68
2 b c Desert Style(IRE) Belle Alicia (FR) (Smadoun (FR))
6259[10] 6876[3] 7199[2]

**Bryant Park (USA)** *Jane Chapple-Hyam* a53
5 ch g Street Cry(IRE) Cala (FR) (Desert Prince (IRE))
5832[6] 8004[4] 8123[9]

**Bryce Canyon (IRE)** *F-H Graffard* 71
3 b f Galileo(IRE) Bright Sky (IRE) (Wolfhound (USA))
7681a[2]

**Brycewise** *Michael Wigham* a17
3 b g Firebreak Jan Mayen (Halling (USA))
684[7] 855[8] 906[6]

**Buaiteoir (FR)** *Nikki Evans* a67 48
8 b g Mineshaft(USA) Witching Hour (FR) (Fairy King (USA))
184[3] 290[11] 858[8] 2592a[6] 4039a[6] 6155[6]

**Bubble Chic (FR)** *D J Hall* 117
6 bb g Chichicastenango(FR) Bubble Back (FR) (Grand Lodge (USA))
7899a[6] 8151a[9]

**Bubbles In Paris** *Lennart Reuterskiold Jr* 76
2 ch f Nayef(USA) Sospel (Kendor (FR))
6386a[5]

**Bubbly Bailey** *J R Jenkins* a64 58
4 b g Byron Night Gypsy (Mind Games)
76[3] 281[8] 592[3] (760) 1010[2] ◆ 1369[6] 2459[3] 2830[4] 3323[2] 3896[3] 5126[4] 5316[4] 5801[8] (7191) 7735[6] 7887[3] 8023[8]

**Bubbly Bellini (IRE)** *Adrian McGuinness* a93 95
7 b g Mull Of Kintyre(USA) Gwapa (IRE) (Imperial Frontier (USA))
1333a[6] 1473a[6] 3420[20] 4480a[7] 6369a[9]

**Buccaneer Bob (IRE)** *Miss Susan A Finn* a64 45
6 br g Big Bad Bob(IRE) Cosmic Speed Queen (USA) (On To Glory (USA))
7877a[12]

**Buccaneers Vault (IRE)** *Michael Dods* 84
2 gr g Aussie Rules(USA) Heaven's Vault (IRE) (Hernando (FR))
(1504) 2521[3] 4157[2] 5085[3] 5680[3] 6375a[17] 6933[18]

**Buckland (IRE)** *Charlie Fellowes* a94 91
6 b g Oratorio(IRE) Dollar Bird (IRE) (Kris)
1973[14] 3111[5] 3860[3] 4622[7] 5161[2] 6287[13] 6896[4] 7837[2] 7995[7]

**Buckland Beau** *Charlie Fellowes* a72 62
3 b g Rock Of Gibraltar(IRE) Heavenly Whisper (IRE) (Halling (USA))
1395[7] 1680[6] 2205[8] 2647[11] 3389[6] 4830[3] 5304[5] (6858)

**Buckleberry** *Jonathan Portman* 72
2 ch g Sakhee's Secret Smart Hostess (Most Welcome)
2173[4] 2622[2] 3081[5] (3467) 4944[4] 6064[6] 7156[6]

**Buckstay (IRE)** *Peter Chapple-Hyam* a95 98
4 b g Lawman(FR) Stella Del Mattino (USA) (Golden Gear (USA))
2091[7] 2772[2] (3577) 4761[2] 6140[3] 6752[4] 7276[9]

**Buckwheat** *Charlie Appleby* 111
4 b g Manduro(GER) Russian Snows (IRE) (Sadler's Wells (USA))
598a[6] 811a[9] 2143[8]

**Buffering (AUS)** *Robert Heathcote* 120
7 b g Mossman(AUS) Action Annie (AUS) (Anabaa (USA))
1468a[3] 7724a[4] 8152a[6]

**Bukhari (FR)** *J-C Rouget* 90
2 gr c Dalakhani(IRE) Brofalya (FR) (Fasliyev (USA))
(5292a)

**Bulas Belle** *Edwin Tuer* 65
4 b f Rob Roy(USA) Bula Rose (IRE) (Alphabatim (USA))
5374[7] 6118[5] 6494[2] (7284) 7508[4]

**Bull Market (IRE)** *Alan Jones*
11 b g Danehill(USA) Paper Moon (IRE) (Lake Coniston (IRE))
2916[10]

**Bull Point (AUS)** *Chris Waller* 109
4 b c Fastnet Rock(AUS) Rose Of Cimmaron (AUS) (Bite The Bullet (USA))
7128a[6]

**Bullseye Babe** *Mark Usher* a51 37
4 ch f Notnowcato Mary Sea (FR) (Selkirk (USA))
2396[7] 2885[11] 3404[11]

**Bunce (IRE)** *Linda Perratt* a86 83
6 b g Good Reward(USA) Bold Desire (Cadeaux Genereux)
1606[9] (1905) 2297[2] 2473[2] 2677[6] 2914[4] (3191) 3610[5] 3659[5] 3831[5] 4004[6] 4383[5] (4488) 4859[2] 4901[5] 5563[5] 5632[6] 6013[9] 6512[12] 7103[5]

**Bundle Of Joy (AUS)** *D J Hall* 113
5 ch g Magic Albert(AUS) Lady Starstruck (AUS) (Mr Henrysee (USA))
7897a[10]

**Bungle Inthejungle** *Mick Channon* 108
4 b c Exceed And Excel(AUS) Licence To Thrill (Wolfhound (USA))
107a[14]

**Bunker (IRE)** *Richard Hannon* 107
3 br c Hurricane Run(IRE) Endure (IRE) (Green Desert (USA))
2285[5] 3417[5]

**Buonarroti (IRE)** *A P O'Brien* 102
3 b g Galileo(IRE) Beauty Is Truth (IRE) (Pivotal)
1200a[5] 7144a[9]

**Burano (IRE)** *Brian Meehan* a66 105
5 ch h Dalakhani(IRE) Kalimanta (IRE) (Lake Coniston (IRE))
110a[10] 202a[10] 398a[3] 683a[6] 812a[10] 1437[8] 1948[7] 3356[13] 3982[9] 4400[5] 6226[4] 6688[6] (7449)

**Burauq** *William Muir* a52 63
2 b c Kyllachy Riccoche (IRE) (Oasis Dream)
5248[4] 5684[4] 6190[4] 7112[5] 7257[7]

**Bureau (IRE)** *Mark Johnston* a85 91
3 ch f Halling(USA) Embassy (Cadeaux Genereux)
1655[5] 2431[2] 3182[3] (3502) 3725[3] 3968[2] 4162[3] (4453) 4667[7] 4915[3] 5401[3] 5720[9] 6127[18] 6465[4] 6930[5] 7334[5] 7702[5]

**Buredyma** *William Haggas* 87
3 ch f Dutch Art Petong's Pet (Petong)
(2560) (3647) 4112[6] (5107) 6129[12] 7384[2]

**Burggraf** *J D Hillis* 90
4 ch c Medicean Borghesa (GER) (Galileo (IRE))
4722a[12]

**Burj Alzain (IRE)** *Fawzi Abdulla Nass* a72 74
6 b h Marju(IRE) Bahareeya (USA) (Riverman (USA))
240a[13]

**Burma Bridge** *Richard Hannon* a46 64
2 ro g Avonbridge Mandalay Lady (Environment Friend)
6545[14] 6997[2] 7217[2] 7625[8]

**Burma Sea (FR)** *A Fabre* a80 80
2 ch f Lope De Vega(IRE) Bougainvillea (GER) (Acatenango (GER))
(8132a)

**Burmese Breeze** *Chris Wall* a39 41
3 b g Shirocco(GER) Crimson Topaz (Hernando (FR))
1357[9] 2081[11] 3471[6]

**Burneston** *James Bethell* 52
2 b c Rock Of Gibraltar(IRE) Grain Of Gold (Mr Prospector (USA))
5494[5]

**Burnham** *Hughie Morrison* a86 85
5 b g Nayef(USA) Salim Toto (Mtoto)
1493[2] 2490[5] 2920[8] 3574[10]

**Burnhope** *Scott Dixon* a76 57
5 b g Choisir(AUS) Isengard (USA) (Cobra King (USA))
8[8] 489[6] 587[10] 826[7] 2127[3] 3149[11] 4534[3] 6397[3] 7025[3] 7830[2] 8043[7] (8176) 8224[4] 8282[7]

**Burning Blaze** *Olly Stevens* a86 56
4 b g Danroad(AUS) Demeter (USA) (Diesis)
314[9] 804[10] 1190[17] 4027[8] 8072[4] 8251[7]

**Burning Desire (IRE)** *M F De Kock* 25
3 b c Galileo(IRE) Flames (Blushing Flame (USA))
7210[7]

**Burning The Clocks (IRE)** *Peter Chapple-Hyam* a74 77
2 b c Tagula(IRE) Precipitous (IRE) (Indian Ridge)
2612[3] 3119[5] 4338[3] 4757[8] 6158[3] 7216[2] 7439[7]

**Burning Thread (IRE)** *Tim Etherington* a46 99
7 b g Captain Rio Desert Rose (Green Desert (USA))
3241[13] (3458) 3666[10] 4179[12] 4889[5] 5419[10] 6130[15] 6624[3] 7101[7]

**Burnt Cream** *Martin Bosley* a58 67
7 b m Exceed And Excel(AUS) Basbousate Nadia (Wolfhound (USA))
2008[11] 3323[8] (3896) 4285[2] 4848[2] 5399[2] 5594[6] 6455[7] 6815[3] 8023[6] 8245[5]

**Burnt Fingers (IRE)** *Rod Millman* a70 74
4 b f Kheleyf(USA) Play With Fire (FR) (Priolo (USA))
(1215) 1716[3] 2282[8] 2775[3] 3885[5]

**Burn The Boats (IRE)** *G M Lyons* a100 97
5 br g Big Bad Bob(IRE) Forever Phoenix (Shareef Dancer (USA))
2145[20] 3737a[19] 5957a[7] 6354a[15] 6533[24]

**Burnt Sugar (IRE)** *Richard Hannon* a110 111
2 b c Lope De Vega(IRE) Lady Livius (IRE) (Titus Livius (FR))
2777[2] 4110[2] (4909) 5580[5] (6142) 6968a[4] 7557a[8]

**Burren View Lady (IRE)** *Denis Gerard Hogan* a90 78
4 br f Dansili Westerly Gale (USA) (Gone West (USA))
(36) 348[5] 1554[14] 2361[7] 2953[5] 3342[9] 3920[3] 4344[3] (4629) 5199[3] 5398[5] 7873a[12] 7959a[9]

**Burtonwood** *Richard Fahey* 82
2 b g Acclamation Green Poppy (Green Desert (USA))
1276[2] (1583) 2308[4] 2987[4] 4203[5] 5580[11] 6165[8] 6256[21] 7131[9]

**Burwaaz** *Ed Dunlop* a66 100
5 b h Exceed And Excel(AUS) Nidhaal (IRE) (Observatory (USA))
2778[11]

**Busatto (USA)** *Mark Johnston* a80 98
4 bb c Bernardini(USA) Lyphard's Delta (USA) (Lyphard (USA))
744[7] 942[5] 1811[6] (2234) (2382) 2478[7] 2959[10] 3251[2] 3397[4] 3726[2] 3982[10] 4442[8] 4756[4] 5174[9] 5695[11] 5928[16] 6548[9] 6987[7]

**Bush Beauty (IRE)** *Philip McBride* a73 70
3 b f Bushranger(IRE) Scottendale (Zilzal (USA))
5427[7] (7253) 7457[4] 7698[6] 7759[7] 8197[5]

**Bushel (USA)** *James Given* a77 89
4 b g Street Cry(IRE) Melhor Ainda (USA) (Pulpit (USA))
6664[7] 7043[9] 7871[9] 8089[3]

**Bushido (FR)** *P Bary* a78 76
3 ro c Bernebeau(FR) Belga Wood (USA) (Woodman (USA))
4952a[6]

**Bushranger Bay (IRE)** *Tim Easterby* a36 53
2 b g Bushranger(IRE) Zafaraya (IRE) (Ashkalani (IRE))
2386[11] 5443[9] 5679[6] 6412[7] 7208[9]

**Bushtiger (IRE)** *David Barron* 30
2 b g Bushranger(IRE) Emma's Surprise (Tobougg (IRE))
5297[12] 5813[6] 6453[10]

**Bushtown Boy (IRE)** *Mark Johnston* a51 60
2 b c Bushranger(IRE) Cakestown Lady (IRE) (Petorius)
3199[7] 3626[5] 7113[4] 7362[10] 7487[5]

**Bush Warrior (IRE)** *Robert Eddery* a71 67
3 b g Bushranger(IRE) Lady Corduff (IRE) (Titus Livius (FR))
824[4] 1018[2] 2158[3] 8322[3]

**Bushy Glade (IRE)** *Julia Feilden* a32 54
3 b f Bushranger(IRE) Cladantom (IRE) (High Estate)
3477[5] 4304[3] ◆ 5108[5] 8123[8]

**Business Bay (USA)** *Patrick Clinton*
7 bb g Salt Lake(USA) Jeweled Lady (USA) (General Meeting (USA))
5529[13] 6062[13] 6628[13]

**Busker (USA)** *A bin Harmash* a100 104
6 ch h Street Cry(IRE) Adonesque (IRE) (Sadler's Wells (USA))
(108a) 398a[4] 593a[10] 807a[5]

**Bussa** *David Evans* a76 71
6 b g Iceman Maid To Dance (Pyramus (USA))
53[9] 592[6]

**Buster Brown (IRE)** *Gary Moore* a72 68
5 ch g Singspiel(IRE) Gold Dodger (USA) (Slew O'Gold (USA))
1302[8] 7925[5]

**Bustopher (USA)** *Charlie Appleby* a93 88
4 bb g Elusive Quality(USA) Catstar (USA) (Storm Cat (USA))
(1216) 1834[3] 2062[7]

**Busy Bimbo (IRE)** *Alan Berry* a48 58
5 b m Red Clubs(IRE) Unfortunate (Komaite (USA))
195[5] 346[6] 353[7] 610[4] 1147[5] 1887[6] (1972) 2296[5] 2514[5] 2909[4] 3104[6] 3913[9] 4287[10] 4362[2] 4725[7] 5130[2] 5565[11] 6796[9] (7009)

**Bute Hall** *David Thompson* a87 88
5 ch g Halling(USA) Les Hurlants (IRE) (Barathea (IRE))
(197) 514[3] 784[3] 1444[3] 1935[4] 2314[4] 2787[5]

**Bute Street** *Chris Gordon* a65 67
9 b g Superior Premium Hard To Follow (Dilum (USA))
1916[2] 2531[6]

**Buthelezi (USA)** *Brian Ellison* a89 92
6 bb g Dynaformer(USA) Ntombi (USA) (Quiet American (USA))
3717[15] 3962[8] 4622[5] 4888[6] 5299[7] 5673[2] (6536) 6794[2]

**Butler (IRE)** *Braem Horse Racing Sprl* a67 62
7 ch g Noverre(USA) True Fantasy (USA) (Seeking The Gold (USA))
3089a[8]

**Butterfly McQueen (USA)** *Andrew Balding* 100
4 b f Curlin(USA) Distant Roar (CAN) (Storm Cat (USA))
1162[7] 2956[6] 4060[7] 5695[12]

**Button Down** *Lady Cecil* a83 86
3 b f Oasis Dream Modesta (IRE) (Sadler's Wells (USA))
2279[2] 3106[2] 4020[2] 4543[2] 5356[5] 6344[4]

**Buxton** *Roger Ingram* a51 48
10 b g Auction House(USA) Dam Certain (IRE) (Damister (USA))
4341[9] 4732[4] 5138[4] 5523[7] 7819[5] 7884[8]

**Buy Out Boy** *Michael Appleby* a62 62
3 gr g Medicean Tiger's Gene (GER) (Perugino (USA))
988[5] 1124[7] 3405[5] 4063[8] 4420[8] 4540[7] 5102[6]

**Buzz Law (IRE)** *John Weymes* a60 58
6 b g Fasliyev(USA) Buzz Two (IRE) (Case Law)
49[7] 677[8] 1596[9] 2823[3] 3162[4] 3427[5] 4116[5] 4381[5] 5537[5] 6481[9] 7924[11] 7977[12]

**Bwana (IRE)** *P J Prendergast* 87
2 b c Footstepsinthesand Lovely Blossom (FR) (Spinning World (USA))
2855a[6] 3322[24]

**Bwindi (IRE)** *J P Murtagh* a64 61
3 b g High Chaparral(IRE) Caona (USA) (Miswaki (USA))
5102[2]

**By Jupiter** *Michael Bell* a78 75
3 ch f Sea The Stars(IRE) Maid Of Killeen (IRE) (Darshaan)
3141[4] 3502[5] 4081[2] 5003[3] 6239[8] 7182[2] 7772[4] 8138[4]

**Byrae** *Polly Gundry* a60 40
4 ch f Byron Proud Mary (IRE) (Acclamation)
1767[6] 2489[7] 2690[13] 5138[9] 6426[13]

**Byrd In Hand (IRE)** *John Bridger* a64 68
7 b g Fasliyev(USA) Military Tune (IRE) (Nashwan (USA))
281[3] 446[2] 754[5] 844[2] 1015[7] 1986[3] 2723[2] ◆ 3075[2] 3230[2] 3825[2] (4046) 4428[2] 4798[6] 5075[4] 5425[3] 5950[7] (7000) 7219[6] 7513[3] 7759[9] 7942[5] 8169[10]

**By Rights** *Tony Carroll* a54 76
3 b f Byron Legend House (FR) (Grand Lodge (USA))
2035[6] 2397[6] (2802) 3228[4] 5290[2] (5923) ◆ 7215[10]

**Byronaissance** *Neville Bycroft* a44 55
5 ch g Byron Renaissance Lady (IRE) (Imp Society (USA))
4791[13] 5568[6] 5916[4] 7010[6] 7501[12]

**Byronegetonefree** *John E Long* a54
3 b g Byron Lefty's Dollbaby (USA) (Brocco (USA))
2996[10] 4265[6] 5186[8] 6015[5] 6856[6]

**Byroness** *Heather Main* a73 64
4 b f Byron Parting Gift (Cadeaux Genereux)
84[9] 853[7] 1121[4] 1454[9]

**Byron Gala** *Marco Botti* a62 44
3 b g Byron Tenuta Di Gala (IRE) (Nashwan (USA))
753[2] 1033[3] 1214[5] 1403[2]

**Byron's Dream** *Jedd O'Keeffe* a54 65
4 b g Byron Fresher (Fabulous Dancer (USA))
1689[9] 2426[2] 3299[5]

**Byron's Gold** *Ben De Haan* a65 75
3 ch f Byron Dance To The Blues (IRE) (Danehill Dancer (IRE))
1677[2] (2384) 4741[5] 6189 [5] 7575[11]

**By The Moon (USA)** *Michelle Nevin* a109
2 bb f Indian Charlie(USA) By The Light (USA) (Malibu Moon (USA))
7606a[8]

**Cabal** *Andrew Crook* a50 63
7 br m Kyllachy Secret Flame (Machiavellian (USA))
88[6] 697[4] 1761[7] 3398[9] 4381[6] 7540[5]

**Cabaretune (FR)** *F Doumen* 92
9 b g Green Tune(USA) Cabaret Club (FR) (Top Ville)
1828a[4]

**Cabbies Lou** *Noel Wilson* 68
2 b f Sakhee's Secret Regal Run (USA) (Deputy Minister (CAN))
1837[2] (2134) 2521[5] 4313[6] 5630[9] 6222[7] 6510[12]

**Cabelo (IRE)** *Brian Ellison* 73
2 b f Azamour(IRE) Fringe (In The Wings)
5297[4] ◆ 6168[5] 6641[3] 7084[3]

**Cabidochop (FR)** *A De Watrigant* a61 93
5 b g Indian Rocket Very Sol (FR) (Solicitor I (FR))
(3373a)

**Cabin Fever** *Ralph Beckett* 76
3 ch f Medicean Folly Lodge (Grand Lodge (USA))
2109[5] 3315[7] 4435[7] 5884[11] 6986[5]

**Cable Bay (IRE)** *Charles Hills* 115
3 b c Invincible Spirit(IRE) Rose De France (IRE) (Diktat)
5653[10] 6328[6] 6710[6] 7242[2]

**Cabral (USA)** *C Ferland* a105 100
3 b c Henrythenavigator(USA) Gamely Girl (USA) (Arch (USA))
6949a[9]

**Cabuchon (GER)** *David Evans* a60 66
7 b g Fantastic Light(USA) Catella (GER) (Generous (IRE))
283[2] 382[2] (490) 742[4] 801[5] 1574[10] (2599a) 2327[9] 2465[3] 3310[7] 3521[5] 4107[4] 4264[3] 4568[2] 5121[5] 5338[6] 5599[4] 6210[6] 6818[2] 7846[4] 7932[6] 7990[8] 8145[3] 8231[4] 8261[4]

**Cactus Valley (IRE)** *Roger Charlton* a71 95
5 b g Lawman(FR) Beech Gardens (Sadler's Wells (USA))
1653[9] 3499[3] 3931[7]

**Cadeau Magnifique** *Richard Fahey* 69
2 b g Dutch Art Cadeau Speciale (Cadeaux Genereux)
6115[7] 6667[4] 7123[5]

**Cadeaux Pearl** *Scott Dixon* a69 69
6 b g Acclamation Anneliina (Cadeaux Genereux)
8[5] 147[6] 383[8] 1378[9] 1887[2] (2955) 3366[2] 3668[11] (3913) 4494[4] 4997[7] 5298[7] 6758[11]

**Cadeaux Power** *Clive Brittain* a70 78
3 b f Major Cadeaux Right Answer (Lujain (USA))
1530[8] 2061[7]

**Cadmium** *Harry Dunlop* a64 52
3 b f Major Cadeaux Miss Mirasol (Sheikh Albadou)
1832[7] 2278[15] 4055[8] 4562[5] 5005[11] 5314[2] 6070[6] 7197[2] (7376) (7546) 7942[7]

**Cadmium Loch** *Andrew Hollinshead* a63 24
6 b g Needwood Blade Vermilion Creek (Makbul)
692[4] (973) (1148) 1311[7] 1573[12]

**Cadore (IRE)** *Lucy Normile* 53
6 b g Hurricane Run(IRE) Mansiya (Vettori (IRE))
3238[3]

**Caelica (IRE)** *Charles Hills* 65
2 b f Sea The Stars(IRE) Vital Statistics (Indian Ridge)
7108[8] 7406[9]

**Caerwyn** *Tony Carroll* a68 65
4 ch g Pastoral Pursuits Preference (Efisio)
90[5] 229[6]

**Caesars Gift (IRE)** *Derek Shaw* a62 62
3 b g Holy Roman Emperor(IRE) Jazz Up (Cadeaux Genereux)
4614[5]

**Caeser The Gaeser (IRE)** *Richard Guest* 6
2 b g Captain Rio Alchimie (IRE) (Sri Pekan (USA))
3529[10]

**Cafe Cortado (IRE)** *Claes Bjorling* 56
2 b f Fast Company(IRE) Gold Blended (IRE) (Goldmark (USA))
2725[7] (3157) 4364[3] 4870[2] 6386a[11]

**Cafe Society (FR)** *David Simcock* a98 107
4 b g Motivator Mishina (FR) (Highest Honor (FR))
1973[6] (2405) 3416[3] 4849[3] 5432[7]

**Cafetiere** *Paul Cole* a76 73
3 b f Iffraaj Coffee Cream (Common Grounds)
3117[13] 3388[6]

**Caffeine** *William Muir* 98
3 b g Sakhee's Secret Coffee Time (IRE) (Efisio)
(5775) (6170) ◆

**Cagoule** *David O'Meara* a52 84
3 b g Oasis Dream Pretty Face (Rainbow Quest (USA))
4900[2] 5568[2] 5916[3]

**Cahal (IRE)** *David Nicholls* a23 63
3 b g Bushranger(IRE) Cabopino (IRE) (Captain Rio)
(1648) 2218[4] 2517[5] 3647[5] 4019[4] 4532[9] 4998[5] 5499[2] 5853[6] 7057[7]

**Cahala Dancer (IRE)** *Roger Teal* a37 38
6 ch m Elnadim(USA) Ranma (In The Wings)
4266[9]

**Cahar Fad (IRE)** *Steph Hollinshead* a49 50
2 b g Bushranger(IRE) Tarbiyah (Singspiel (IRE))
4054[6] 4541[8] 5056[5] 7740[11] 7904[7] 8121[8]

**Cahill (IRE)** *Alan King* a70 73
2 b g Lawman(FR) Malaspina (IRE) (Whipper (USA))
3929[7] 4550[3] 5745[3] 6101[6] 6648[9]

**Caigemdar (IRE)** *David Barron* 75
2 b f Tagula(IRE) Honey Feather (IRE) (Intikhab (USA))
3933[3] 4357[5] (7278)

**Cairdiuil (IRE)** *I Madden* a45 78
8 b g Bachelor Duke(USA) Lilabelle (IRE) (Lil's Boy (USA))
(4805a) 4950a[3]

**Cai Shen (IRE)** *Jamie Osborne* a105 103
6 ch g Iffraaj Collada (IRE) (Desert Prince (IRE))
(1268)

**Caius College Girl (IRE)** *David Barron* 78
2 b f Royal Applause Galeaza (Galileo (IRE))
3497[4] (5493)

**Caja (FR)** *H-A Pantall* a83 79
3 ch f Touch Down(GER) Centinela (Caerleon (USA))
5482a[8]

**Cajoling (IRE)** *Jonathan Portman* 80
2 br f Intense Focus(USA) Acquiesced (IRE) (Refuse To Bend (IRE))
1788[9] (2220) 2703[7] 3721[9] 4345[2] 4913[12] 5626[7] 6253[13]

**Cajun (FR)** *F Rossi* a83 96
3 gr c Stormy River(FR) Glittering Star (FR) (Lomitas)
545a[2]

**Calaf** *Jonjo O'Neill* a77 89
6 b g Dubai Destination(USA) Tarandot (IRE) (Singspiel (IRE))
513[8]

**Calamari (FR)** *X Thomas-Demeaulte* a90 87
4 b c Turtle Bowl(IRE) Gold Mine (FR) (Gold Away (IRE))
(796a)

**Calamity Jane** *Ralph Beckett* a54 35
3 b f Lawman(FR) Yesteryear (Green Desert (USA))
1920[10] 2560[7] 3523[6]

**Calamity Kate (USA)** *Kelly Breen* a86
2 b f Yes It's True(USA) Justmeandmyshadow (USA) (Tiznow (USA))
6915a[9]

**Calculated Risk** *John Quinn* a61 81
5 ch g Motivator Glen Rosie (IRE) (Mujtahid (USA))
1359[3] 2289[8] 7333[5]

**Caldercruix (USA)** *James Evans* a86 79
7 ch g Rahy(USA) Al Theraab (USA) (Roberto (USA))
11[8]

**Caledonia** *Jim Goldie* 78
7 b g Sulamani(IRE) Vanessa Bell (IRE) (Lahib (USA))
1599[8] (3240) 5890[11] 6640[5] 7124[4] 7566[10]

**Caledonia Lady** *Mme M Bollack-Badel* 105
5 b m Firebreak Granuaile O'Malley (IRE) (Mark Of Esteem (IRE))
1572[3] (2161) 4841a[3] 6378a[3] 6994a[6] 7656a[2]

**Caledonia Laird** *Jo Hughes* a57 62
3 b g Firebreak Granuaile O'Malley (IRE) (Mark Of Esteem (IRE))
1048[4] 1223[8] (2416) 2695[3] 3618[3] 4415[5] 5530[7] 6568[9] 7785[4] 7977[11] 8199[3]

**Caledonia Prince** *Jo Hughes* a81 55
6 b g Needwood Blade Granuaile O'Malley (IRE) (Mark Of Esteem (IRE))
1113[5] 1886[6]

**Calgary Cat (CAN)** *Kevin Attard* a113 108
4 ch g Cowtown Cat(USA) Big Sink Star (USA) (A.P. Indy (USA))
7325a[3]

**Califante** *T Hogan* a79 98
4 b f Kyllachy Call Mariah (USA) (Dixie Union (USA))
2757[5] 2823[5] 3167a[5] 3864a[3] 4276a[4]

**California Chrome (USA)** *Art Sherman* a125 116
3 ch c Lucky Pulpit(USA) Love The Chase (USA) (Not For Love (USA))
(1964a) (2357a) 3026a[4] 7614a[3]

**California Memory (USA)** *A S Cruz* 119
8 gr g Highest Honor(FR) Kalpita (USA) (Spinning World (USA))
2004a[11] 7899a[4] 8154a[8]

**Calima Breeze** *Charles Hills* 45
2 b f Oasis Dream Paris Winds (IRE) (Galileo (IRE))
7412[5] ◆

**Callendula** *Clive Cox* a59
2 ch f Halling(USA) Oatey (Master Willie)
7184[8] 7625[6] 7941[5] 8121[7]

**Calling Out (FR)** *J-P Gauvin* 112
3 b c Martaline Exit The Straight (IRE) (Exit To Nowhere (USA))
2242a[3] 3807a[2] 4278a[6] 6571a[3] 6957a[3]

**Calling You (IRE)** *S Donohoe* a65 64
5 b g Erewhon(USA) Lianda (USA) (Danzig (USA))
676[2] 4724[2] 5897[3]

**Callisto Light** *Michael Squance* a65 44
7 ch m Medicean Luminda (IRE) (Danehill (USA))
(281) 589[2] 815[10]

**Call Me Crockett (IRE)** *Richard Guest* a52 61
2 ch g Intense Focus(USA) Forest Storm (USA) (Woodman (USA))
4129[10] 4659[3] 5099[5] 5630[7] 6669[6] 6830[7] 7257[3]

**Call Me Pj (IRE)** *Oliver McKiernan* a73 70
7 b g Fath(USA) Sally Anne (ITY) (Scenic (IRE))
7903[3]

**Call Of Duty (IRE)** *Dianne Sayer* a64 67
9 br g Storming Home Blushing Barada (USA) (Blushing Groom (FR))
783[7] 1249[9] 1596[3] (1761) 2475[3] 2913[2] 3134[5] 4000[2] 4387[2] 4858[3] 4959[2] 5268[4] 6000[2] 6223[5] 7098[3]

**Call Out Loud** *Sir Michael Stoute* 46
2 b c Aqlaam Winner's Call (Indian Ridge)
4395[9]

**Calm Attitude (IRE)** *Rae Guest* 89
4 ch f Dutch Art Turban Heights (IRE) (Golan (IRE))
(1910) 2670[4] 4453[2] 5928[2] 7341[5]

**Calm Bay (IRE)** *H Rogers* a75 82
8 b g Medecis Queen Sigi (IRE) (Fairy King (USA))
4480a[8]

**Calrissian (GER)** *F Foresi* a84 101
10 ch g Efisio Centaine (Royal Academy (USA))
392a[3] 7026a[2]

**Calrissian (IRE)** *Timothy Jarvis* a65 77
3 ch g Lando(GER) Dallaah (Green Desert (USA))
1725[15] 2647[13] 5006[7] 6019[8] 7456[7]

**Caltra Colleen** *Mick Channon* 75
2 b f Sixties Icon Mistic Magic (IRE) (Orpen (USA))
2652[4] (3267) 4178[5]

**Calvin Williams (FR)** *M Nigge* a105 110
4 gr c Carlotamix(FR) Quellaffaire (FR) (Charge D'Affaires)
3171a[5] 5960a[9] 6592a[5]

**Calypso Beat (USA)** *Kevin Ryan* a35 103
2 b f Speightstown(USA) African Skies (Johannesburg (USA))
2460[7] (3223) (3721) 5190[2] 5707a[2] 6709[9]

**Calyxa** *Ferdinand J Leve* 110
4 b f Pivotal Chantra (GER) (Lando (GER))
2715a[4] (3873a) 4720a[3] 5742a[7] 6808a[3] 7480a[3]

**Camache Queen (IRE)** *Joseph Tuite* a60 57
6 b m Camacho Alinda (IRE) (Revoque (IRE))
934[9] 1010[6] 1804[7] 1986[10]

**Camachoice (IRE)** *Marco Botti* a82 68
4 b g Camacho Nouvelle Reve (GER) (Acatenango (GER))
56[8] 181[3] 300[4] 698[6] 843[4] (1083)

**Camagueyana** *Ralph Beckett* a75 67
2 b f Archipenko(USA) Caribana (Hernando (FR))
4499[6] ◆ 5644[4] (7739)

**Camanche Grey (IRE)** *Ben Haslam* a63 40
3 gr g Camacho Sense Of Greeting (IRE) (Key Of Luck (USA))
765[3] 1676[6] 2015[13] (3938) 4974[2] 7505[12] 8082[9]

**Cambio De Planes** *C Delcher-Sanchez* 98
5 b g Dutch Art Barreda (IRE) (Linamix (FR))
6378a[8] 6994a[10]

**Camborne** *John Gosden* a92 116
6 b g Doyen(IRE) Dumnoni (Titus Livius (FR))
2315[7] 2704[10] 3450[8] 5432[8] 6546[6]

**Cambridge** *Charles Hills* 86
3 b f Rail Link Alumni (Selkirk (USA))
2255[7]

**Camden Market (FR)** *F Vermeulen* a28 25
2 ch c Creachadoir(IRE) Appearance (GER) (Monsun (GER))
3871a[9] 4881a[9]

**Camdora (IRE)** *Jamie Osborne* a50 37
2 b f Arcano(IRE) Crimphill (IRE) (Sadler's Wells (USA))
4075[7] 6701[8] 7037[11]

**Cameley Dawn** *Malcolm Saunders* 63
3 b f Alhaarth(IRE) Apply Dapply (Pursuit Of Love)
1403[14] 1792[7] 3518[5] 5005[5] (5122) 5520[3] 5908[2] 6193[6]

**Camelopardalis** *Philip McBride* a41 70
5 b m Tobougg(IRE) Bonne Etoile (Diesis)
1453[6] (1865) (2531) 2894[3] 3475[4]

**Cameo Tiara (IRE)** *Richard Hannon* a80 85
3 b f High Chaparral(IRE) Cuilaphuca (IRE) (Danetime (IRE))
(1233) 2504[4] 3560[4] 4145[4] 4855[8] 5877[11]

**Cameron Highland (IRE)** *Roger Varian* 108
5 b h Galileo(IRE) Landmark (USA) (Arch (USA))
3722[6] 4756[11] 5688[7]

**Camerooney** *Marjorie Fife* a69 81
11 b g Sugarfoot Enkindle (Relkino)
406[7] 1609[4] 2518[3] (2911) 3301[5] 3572[7] 4387[3] (4858) 5562[3] 6214[11] (6836)

**Caminel (IRE)** *Jeremy Gask* a68 65
3 b f Kyllachy Jalissa (Mister Baileys)
756[3] 1039[4] 1379[8] 2470[6] (3231) 3709[6] 4908[9] 6297[3] 6889[7] 7621[5] (8081)

**Camondo (IRE)** *Y-M Porzier* a75 80
3 ch g Champs Elysees Brooklyn Academy (USA) (Royal Academy (USA))
7681a[5]

**Canadian Diamond (IRE)** *Brendan Powell* a67 67
7 ch g Halling(USA) Six Nations (USA) (Danzig (USA))
2917[9] 3856[11] (8208)

**Canadian Run (IRE)** *Robert Mills* a89 79
4 ch g Hurricane Run(IRE) Vale View (FR) (Anabaa (USA))
56[7] 342[3] 840[12]

**Canary Lad (IRE)** *Timothy Jarvis* 54
3 ch c Iffraaj Sweet Myrtle (USA) (Mutakddim (USA))
5352[5] 5862[6] 7021[8]

**Canary Row (IRE)** *P J Prendergast* 99
4 b g Holy Roman Emperor(IRE) Fresh Mint (IRE) (Sadler's Wells (USA))
1078a[3] 5957a[5]

**Canary Wharf (IRE)** *M Al Muhairi* a81 74
5 b h Danehill Dancer(IRE) Wedding Morn (IRE) (Sadler's Wells (USA))
239a[6]

**Candelita** *Matt Sheppard* a41 54
7 b m Trade Fair Gramada (IRE) (Cape Cross (IRE))
2595a[4] 2770[4] 4115[8] 4673[5] 5403[5] 6062[10] 7990[10]

**Candella** *Roger Varian* a58 57
2 b f Stimulation(IRE) Wolumla (IRE) (Royal Applause)
6742[5] 7941[8] 8166[7]

**Candesta (USA)** *Julia Feilden* a65 21
4 b g First Defence(USA) Wandesta (Nashwan (USA))
282[4] 581[3] 1197[11] 1919[10] 3899[4] 7290[6] 8074[8] 8314[4]

**Candlelight (IRE)** *Charles Hills* a64 53
2 b f Zebedee Masai Queen (IRE) (Mujadil (USA))
4269[9] ◆ 4577[2] ◆ 5042[3] 5985[6] 6408[5]

**Candle Of The Sea (IRE)** *Ed Vaughan* a53 56
2 br f Makfi Playwithmyheart (Diktat)
2979[5] 5037[8] 5973[6] 6412[3]

**Candy Boy (USA)** *John W Sadler* a116
3 b c Candy Ride(ARG) She's An Eleven (USA) (In Excess)
*1964a[13] 7614a[6]*

**Candy Kendall (FR)** *T Lemer* a50 52
2 ch f Evasive Riberalta (FR) (Muhtathir)
1271a[7]

**Candy Kitten** *Paul Cole* a72 50
4 b f Assertive Birthday Venture (Soviet Star (USA))
*410[2] 691[3] 1209[5]* 2021[11] *6716[8]*

**Candyman Can (IRE)** *Dominic Ffrench Davis* a73 76
4 b g Holy Roman Emperor(IRE) Palwina (FR) (Unfuwain (USA))
*(115) 476[2]*

**Cane Cat (IRE)** *Tony Carroll* a58 64
7 bb m One Cool Cat(USA) Seven Wonders (USA) (Rahy (USA))
*105[4] 317[4] 571[4]*

**Cannock Chase (USA)** *Sir Michael Stoute* a72 111
3 b c Lemon Drop Kid(USA) Lynnwood Chase (USA) (Horse Chestnut (SAF))
(1353) (2337) (3375)

**Canny Kool** *Brian Ellison* 84
2 b g Kheleyf(USA) Kool Acclaim (Royal Applause)
4659[8] 5464[2] (6453) 7099[5]

**Canon Law (IRE)** *David O'Meara* a81 56
4 b g Holy Roman Emperor(IRE) Delisha (Salse (USA))
*101[2] 539[3] 995[3] 1267[7]*

**Canova (IRE)** *Roger Charlton* a74 72
3 ch g Art Connoisseur(IRE) Rain Dancer (IRE) (Sadler's Wells (USA))
1586[10] 1913[6] 3516[3] 4329[8] 4742[3] 5313[2] 5621[3]

**Can't Change It (IRE)** *David Simcock* a86 80
3 gr g Verglas(IRE) All Tied Up (IRE) (Desert Prince (IRE))
*(231)* ◆ *404[5] 850[7]* 1913[3] 2111[8] (2833) *5603[2]* 7445[6]

**Cantor** *Paul Morgan* a67 63
6 b g Iceman Choir Mistress (Chief Singer)
*320[4] 537[5] 571[10] 1428[7]*

**Can't Stop The Kid (USA)** *Donna Green* a47
3 bb c Montbrook(USA) Halo Reality (USA) (Prospector's Halo (USA))
*813a[5]*

**Canwinn (IRE)** *D Selvaratnam* a101 89
8 b g Refuse To Bend(IRE) Born To Glamour (Ajdal (USA))
242a[12]

**Canyari (IRE)** *Richard Fahey* a85 86
3 b g Dandy Man(IRE) Morna's Fan (FR) (Lear Fan (USA))
1278[4] 2317[16] 3704[7] 4636[11] *8279[3]* ◆

**Can You Conga** *Michael Easterby* a64 93
4 b g Piccolo Takes Two To Tango (Groom Dancer (USA))
1193[11] 1484[10] 4712[10] 5419[12] 5888[8] 6094[7]

**Caointiorn (FR)** *S Wattel* a101 95
3 b f Stormy River(FR) Champagnepouryoyo (USA) (Bering)
7268a[8] *8300a[2]*

**Capaill Liath (IRE)** *Kevin Ryan* a88 94
6 gr g Iffraaj Bethesda (Distant Relative)
*162[2] 399[4] 602[4]* 1191[3] 1345[5] 1957[2] 2351[3] *2469[5]* 3221[10] 3645[4]

**Cape Arrow** *Paul Cole* a68 68
3 b g Cape Cross(IRE) Aiming (Highest Honor (FR))
1792[3] *(2098)* 2719[3] *2934[5]* 4134[9]

**Cape Breton** *Patrick Chamings* a52
8 b g Cape Cross(IRE) Red Bouquet (Reference Point)
*686[7]*

**Cape Caster (IRE)** *Ralph Beckett* a74 94
3 br g Cape Cross(IRE) Playboy Mansion (IRE) (Grand Lodge (USA))
1166[2] ◆ 1730[2] 2347[4] (2850) 3587[3] 3892[4] 4855[5] (5877) 6685[3] 7410[2]

**Cape Castle (IRE)** *Clive Brittain* 14
3 b f Cape Cross(IRE) Kaabari (USA) (Seeking The Gold (USA))
*5007[13]*

**Cape Cay** *Ralph Beckett* a70 62
2 gr f Cape Cross(IRE) White Cay (Dalakhani (IRE))
2623[5] 3082[3] *7867[2] 8174[2]*

**Cape Explorer** *Brian Ellison* 60
5 b g Cape Cross(IRE) Eve (Rainbow Quest (USA))
5496[13]

**Cape Factor (IRE)** *Rae Guest* a68 100
3 b f Oratorio(IRE) Crossanza (IRE) (Cape Cross (IRE))
2195a[16] 5965a[2] 7242[9] 7629a[15]

**Cape Good Hope** *Clive Brittain* 19
3 b f Cape Cross(IRE) Fann (USA) (Diesis)
6247[4]

**Cape Hideaway** *Mark Walford* 73
2 b g Mount Nelson Amiata (Pennekamp (USA))
5050[6] 5493[8] (6147) 6759[6]

**Cape Ice (IRE)** *F Head* a71 57
3 b f Cape Cross(IRE) Soft Ice (IRE) (Kingmambo (USA))
2290a[3]

**Cape Icon** *Clive Cox* 85
3 b c Mount Nelson Cape Merino (Clantime)
(1844) 2495[2] 2983[5]

**Cape Karli (IRE)** *Kevin Ryan* a44 66
3 br f Cape Cross(IRE) Karliysha (IRE) (Kalanisi (IRE))
1280[5] 1959[6] 3568[6] 5018[4] 5534[7] 6461[6] 6981[3] 7500[10] *7760[7]*

**Capelita** *Clive Brittain* a76 83
3 b f Cape Cross(IRE) Zamhrear (Singspiel (IRE))
4590[3] 6922[8] *7285[2] 7663[8]*

**Capellanus (IRE)** *Brian Ellison* a82 81
8 b g Montjeu(IRE) Secret Dream (IRE) (Zafonic (USA))
*961[4]*

**Capel Path (USA)** *Sir Michael Stoute* 78
2 bb c Street Cry(IRE) Miss Lucifer (FR) (Noverre (USA))
5646[8] 6300[3] (6861)

**Cape Magic (IRE)** *F-H Graffard* a93 95
3 b f Cape Cross(IRE) Galley (Zamindar (USA))
*8006a[13]*

**Cape Mystery** *Peter Chapple-Hyam* a63 68
3 bb f Cape Cross(IRE) Maramba (Rainbow Quest (USA))
2129[6] 2511[5] 3142[2] 4617[6] 4947[5] *6337[6]*

**Cape Of Approval (IRE)** *T Stack* 110
5 b g Cape Cross(IRE) Wyola (USA) (Sadler's Wells (USA))
3284a[5]

**Cape Of Hope (IRE)** *Tom Dascombe* a80 80
4 b g Cape Cross(IRE) Bright Hope (IRE) (Danehill (USA))
*255[7] 862[6] 917[6] 1152[2]* 1375[7] 1609[6] 2166[6] 2653[4] 2726[6] 3366[4] 3609[2] (4530) 4875[3] (5202) 6095[7] *6898[2]* 7167[5] 7687[8]

**Cape Point** *Michael Blanshard* a36 57
2 b g Showcasing Queensgate (Compton Place)
3584[8] *4577[4]* 5593[4] *6888[10]*

**Capers Royal Star (FR)** *Paul Cole* a69 61
3 b g What A Caper(IRE) Arundhati (IRE) (Royal Academy (USA))
2224[10] 2948[3] 3538[7] 3805[5] *4911[5]*

**Cape Safari (IRE)** *Tim Vaughan* a84 44
5 b m Cape Cross(IRE) Finnmark (Halling (USA))
*73[9] 831[12] 974[5] 1248[4]*

**Cape Samba** *Ismail Mohammed* a83 79
5 b g Cape Cross(IRE) Dancing Feather (Suave Dancer (USA))
2131[7] 3272[14] 3463[7]

**Cape Spirit (IRE)** *Andrew Balding* 54
2 b f Cape Cross(IRE) Fearless Spirit (USA) (Spinning World (USA))
6735[6]

**Cape Summit** *Ed Dunlop* a79 66
3 ch g Tamayuz Peace Summit (Cape Cross (IRE))
*2998[5]* 3421[6] 4420[5] *5304[2] 6034[2] 6483[2]* 6999[6] *7373[3]*

**Cape Town (GER)** *M Weiss* a27
9 bb g Diktat Conga (Robellino (USA))
*555a[8]*

**Capetown Kid** *Sylvester Kirk* a62 55
4 gr g Cape Town(IRE) Doris Souter (IRE) (Desert Story (IRE))
*1232[9] 1835[6]* 2923[12] *3115[8]*

**Cape Tribulation** *Malcolm Jefferson* 77
10 b g Hernando(FR) Gay Fantastic (Ela-Mana-Mou)
2289[14] 2739[5] 7124[13]

**Cape Victoria** *Andrew Balding* 64
3 b f Mount Nelson Victoria Montoya (High Chaparral (IRE))
3514[3]

**Cape Wrath** *Richard Hannon* 80
3 rg c Verglas(IRE) Capades Dancer (USA) (Gate Dancer (USA))
1983[5] 2495[4]

**Cape Xenia** *Henry Candy* 65
2 b f Cape Cross(IRE) Xaphania (Sakhee (USA))
5351[3] ◆ (5982) 6499[7]

**Cap la Nna** *David C Griffiths* a21
2 ch f Captain Gerrard(IRE) Lady Duxyana (Most Welcome)
2173[8] *5253[8] 5507[4] 5896[8]*

**Capitaine** *Seamus Mullins*
2 b c Captain Gerrard(IRE) Ruffie (IRE) (Medicean)
*3794[5]*

**Capital Attraction (USA)** *Ernst Oertel* a114 91
7 ch g Speightstown(USA) Cecilia's Crown (USA) (Chief's Crown (USA))
*111a[10] 306a[3] 596a[4] (810a) 899a[3] 1176a[15]*

**Capitol Gain (IRE)** *George Baker* a59 77
5 b g Bahamian Bounty Emmas Princess (IRE) (Bahhare (USA))
*14[5] 4326[5]*

**Capmonde (IRE)** *William Knight* a54 66
3 b f Cape Cross(IRE) Esclarmonde (IRE) (In The Wings)
*2061[10]* 2780[10] 3537[5] 4356[3]

**Capo Maximo** *Yves de Nicolay* 98
2 b c Cape Cross(IRE) Quezon Sun (GER) (Monsun (GER))
5706a[3] 7317a[3] 7721a[5]

**Capone (IRE)** *Michael Attwater* a106 67
9 b g Daggers Drawn(USA) Order Of The Day (USA) (Dayjur (USA))
*55[9] 249[6] 452[4]*

**Capo Rosso (IRE)** *Tom Dascombe* a105 100
4 b g Red Clubs(IRE) Satin Cape (IRE) (Cape Cross (IRE))
*(1316)* (2362) 3456[6] 4212[15] 4851[13] *6411[2] 6943[5] (7455)* ◆ *7801[7]*

**Cap O'Rushes** *Charlie Appleby* a69 113
4 b g New Approach(IRE) Valley Of Gold (FR) (Shirley Heights)
2143[5] 2785[12] 6233[6]

**Cappella Sansevero** *G M Lyons* a89 112
2 b c Showcasing Madam President (Royal Applause)
(2569a) 3318[2] 3738a[5] 5218a[3] (5954a) 7239[4]

**Cappielow Park** *Ali Stronge* a58 55
5 b g Exceed And Excel(AUS) Barakat (Bustino)
2836[3] 3336[5] 4548[7] *8010[3]*

**Caprior Bere (FR)** *K R Burke* 91
2 b g Peer Gynt(JPN) Hush Hush (USA) (Horse Chestnut (SAF))
2386[2] 3448[8] 4416[2] (5329a) 5740a[5] 6136[5]

**Capsize** *Sir Michael Stoute* a62
2 b c Showcasing Change Course (Sadler's Wells (USA))
*6103[6] 6718[4] 7739[6] 7994[4]*

**Cap Sizun (FR)** *P Schaerer* 95
5 b g Gold Away(IRE) Texaloula (FR) (Kendor (FR))
*729a[U]*

**Captain Bob (IRE)** *Charles Hills* 92
3 b g Dark Angel(IRE) Birthday Present (Cadeaux Genereux)
(1681) 2088[2] (3247) 3980[4] 5348[3] 6744[10]

**Captain Carey** *Malcolm Saunders* a51 52
8 b g Fraam Brigadiers Bird (IRE) (Mujadil (USA))
3152[7]

**Captain Cat (IRE)** *Roger Charlton* a111 117
5 bb g Dylan Thomas(IRE) Mother Of Pearl (IRE) (Sadler's Wells (USA))
*344[2] (1558)* ◆ (5354) ◆ 5666[3] ◆ (6132) 6710[2] 7274[5] *7836[4]* 8153a[10]

**Captain Colby (USA)** *Kevin Ryan* 87
2 b g Bernstein(USA) Escape To Victory (Salse (USA))
(1955) 2258[4] 4439[20] (6322)

**Captain Cullen (IRE)** *Gerard Keane* a88 96
5 b g Strategic Prince Missouri (Charnwood Forest (IRE))
1078a[9] (5958a)

**Captain Dunne (IRE)** *Tim Easterby* a56 83
9 b g Captain Rio Queen Bodicea (IRE) (Revoque (IRE))
1695[12] 1961[16] 3006[8] (3921) 4114[8] (4630) 5016[9] 5498[12] 6096[11] 6324[8] 6763[3] *7767[7]*

**Captain Felix** *Jane Chapple-Hyam* a47 47
2 b c Captain Gerrard(IRE) Sweet Applause (IRE) (Acclamation)
7380[8] *7542[7]*

**Captain Future** *Bryan Smart* a52 30
2 b g Captain Gerrard(IRE) Saorocain (IRE) (Kheleyf (USA))
5813[5] 7277[6] 7713[8]

**Captain Gee** *John Quinn* a47 58
3 b c Captain Gerrard(IRE) Gagajulu (Al Hareb (USA))
5389[9] 5631[7]

**Captain George (IRE)** *James Fanshawe* a75 73
3 b g Bushranger(IRE) High Society Girl (IRE) (Key Of Luck (USA))
1681[7] 2442[8] 3914[4] ◆ 4830[2] *5557[5]* 6192[5] *6633[11]*

**Captain Joy (IRE)** *Tracey Collins* a106 100
5 gr g Dark Angel(IRE) Ardea Brave (IRE) (Chester House (USA))
*306a[6]* 595a[13] *810a[7]* 5957a[8] 6354a[14]

**Captain Kendall (IRE)** *Harry Chisman* a91 60
5 b g Clodovil(IRE) Queen's Lace (IRE) (King's Best (USA))
*294[8] 1799[9]* 2488[4] 2890[4] 5082[8] *6240[12] 6889[11] 7887[8] 8103[11]*

**Captain Koko** *Marco Botti* a65
2 b c Selkirk(USA) Lady Artemisia (IRE) (Montjeu (IRE))
*7985[3] 8083[3] 8288[10]*

**Captain Marmalade (IRE)** *Roger Charlton* a68 69
2 gr g Duke Of Marmalade(IRE) Elisium (Proclamation (IRE))
2298[8] 3842[3] *6675[4]* 7379[3] *7755[5]*

**Captain Midnight (IRE)** *David Brown* a86 86
3 b g Bushranger(IRE) Beverley Macca (Piccolo)
*1136[5]* 1952[7] 2333[3] 3137[3] 4176[8] 4679[5] 5051[4]

**Captain Mo** *Marco Botti* a66
3 b c Captain Gerrard(IRE) Plum Blossom (Beat All (USA))
*37[7] 422[3] (668)* ◆ *1220[6]*

**Captain Morley** *David Simcock* a81 97
3 b g Hernando(FR) Oval Office (Pursuit Of Love)
*(167)* ◆ 2077[2] (2761) 3379[3] 5691[9] 6756[4]

**Captain My Captain (IRE)** *John Joseph Murphy* 97
2 ch c Captain Rio Indiana Annie (IRE) (Indian Ridge)
6375a[5]

**Captain Myles (IRE)** *Tim Pitt* a78 90
3 ch g Captain Rio Untimely (Inchinor)
*(19) 183[5] 613[4] 785[4] 1897[9]* (2429) 3219[4] 3959[3] (4390) 4898[4] 5923[5]

**Captain Navarre** *Lydia Pearce* 83
2 b g Excellent Art Quantum (IRE) (Alhaarth (IRE))
6683[5] 7383[2]

**Captain Oats (IRE)** *Pam Ford* a46 63
11 b g Bahhare(USA) Adarika (Kings Lake (USA))
2836[2] (3209) 3852[4] 4279[7] 5343[2] *6900[6]*

**Captain Obvious (AUS)** *Hai Wang Tan* a104 102
9 gr g Verglas(IRE) Shathor (AUS) (Tirol)
2378a[4]

**Captain Ramius (IRE)** *Kevin Ryan* a94 109
8 b g Kheleyf(USA) Princess Mood (GER) (Muhtarram (USA))
1163[2] 1443[4] 1734[5] 2145[24] 3960[6] 5445[18] 6124[13] 6533[16]

**Captain Revelation** *Tom Dascombe* a75 75
2 ch g Captain Rio Agony Aunt (Formidable (USA))
4185[7] *5099[2]* ◆ *5799[2]* (6690) 7055[6]

**Captain Rhyric** *James Moffatt* 52
5 ch g Dylan Thomas(IRE) Nuts In May (USA) (A.P. Indy (USA))
2053[6] 2738[8] 2913[3] 3623[4] 4259[6]

**Captain Royale (IRE)** *Tracy Waggott* a58 83
9 ch g Captain Rio Paix Royale (Royal Academy (USA))
1843[7] 1905[2] (2364) 2606[5] 3191[10] 3399[2] 3659[8] 4114[9] 4901[2] 5498[6] 5913[2] 6695[8] 7506[2]

**Captain Ryan** *Peter Makin* a61 68
3 b g Captain Gerrard(IRE) Ryan's Quest (IRE) (Mukaddamah (USA))
3323[6] 3426[5] 3784[5] 4567[3] 4847[3] 5518[2] (5905) 6399[4] (6816) *7253[7]*

**Captain Scooby** *Richard Guest* a70 74
8 b g Captain Rio Scooby Dooby Do (Atraf)
*9[7] 59[4] 258[11] 1009[7] 1089[4] 1282[5]* 1972[4] 2233[3] 2296[4] 2473[6] 2830[2] 3104[2] 3366[3] 3530[11] 3913[5] 4288[5] 4960[3] 6014[5] 5858[4] 6595[3] 6866[4] 7009[2] 7057[5] 7222[7] 7520[2] 7644[12] (7671) 7737[3]

**Captain Secret** *Marco Botti* a97 75
3 ch f Captain Gerrard(IRE) Obsessive Secret (IRE) (Grand Lodge (USA))
*(62) (1136) 1555[8]* 2161[7] *6607[10] 7738[8]*

**Captain Sharpe** *Bernard Llewellyn* a59 69
6 ch g Tobougg(IRE) Helen Sharp (Pivotal)
(1915) 2252[5] 3179[4] 3780[3] 4818[6] 5240[6]

**Captain Starlight (IRE)** *Jo Crowley* a76
4 b g Captain Marvelous(IRE) Jewell In The Sky (IRE) (Sinndar (IRE))
*181[4] 627[10] 4968[10] 6035[3] 7012[7] 7633[5]*

**Captain Sun (FR)** *Y-M Porzier* a60 76
3 b g Monsun(GER) Capitale (FR) (Pivotal)
*6221a[7]*

**Captain Swift (IRE)** *John Mackie* a74 62
3 br g Captain Rio Grannys Reluctance (IRE) (Anita's Prince)
*551[4]* 5132[4] *8047[2]* ◆ *8264[4]*

**Captain T** *Richard Ford* a37 29
3 b g Captain Gerrard(IRE) Royaltea (Desert King (IRE))
*500[4] 1147[4]* 1343[6] *2209[10]* 2388[11]

**Captain Whoosh (IRE)** *John Quinn* a75 48
3 gr g Dandy Man(IRE) Caerella (IRE) (Alzao (USA))
1585[2] 2035[4] 3068[7] 3331[8] *8255[3]*

**Caramack** *David Evans* a80 78
4 ch g Danehill Dancer(IRE) Oshiponga (Barathea (IRE))
*(147) (319) (540) 1152[3]* 1630[4] 3177[2] 3646[4] 3782[2] 4414[4] 4961[RR] 5750[RR] 5986[9] *6414[RR] 7729[RR]*

**Caramba (IRE)** *Brendan Powell*
2 b f Lord Shanakill(USA) Known Class (USA) (Known Fact (USA))
*8318[11]*

**Caramelita** *J R Jenkins* a72 66
7 b m Deportivo Apple Of My Eye (Fraam)
*95[5] 362[3] 835[5] (908) (1001)*

**Cara's Request (AUS)** *Michael Dods* a68 81
9 gr g Urgent Request(IRE) Carahill (AUS) (Danehill (USA))
2171[2] (3000) 3533[4] 4156[2] 4861[6] 5385[13] 5887[4] 6477[4] *7183[8] 7830[4]*

**Caratterina (IRE)** *C De Ferrari & N Ferrucci* a69
6 ch m Captain Rio Brioney (IRE) (Barathea (IRE))
*392a[8]*

**Caravan Rolls On** *Danny O'Brien* a84 105
6 b h Hernando(FR) Grain Only (Machiavellian (USA))
(7395a)

**Carazam (IRE)** *Bernard Llewellyn* a42 80
7 b g Azamour(IRE) Carallia (IRE) (Common Grounds)
2381[7] 4534[8] 5049[5]

**Card High (IRE)** *Wilf Storey* 62
4 b g Red Clubs(IRE) Think (FR) (Marchand De Sable (USA))
2135[5] 2427[7] 2724[10] 3604[8] 4532[7] 5269[5] 6122[13] (6823) (7540)

**Cardinal** *Robert Cowell* a67 72
9 ch h Pivotal Fictitious (Machiavellian (USA))
2159[2] 2637[3] 5060[5] 5861[9] 7213[12] 7342[2] 7534[11] *7776[7] 8077[2] 8245[9]*

**Cardinal Palace (IRE)** *John Joseph Murphy* a100 101
4 b g Papal Bull Heat (King's Best (USA))
7492[6]

**Cards** *Kevin Ryan* a41 54
4 b f Tobougg(IRE) Card Games (First Trump)
*1112[5]* 1713[3] 2296[14]

**Carentan (FR)** *P Chatelain* a65 79
3 ch f Literato(FR) Birdy Namnam (USA) (Langfuhr (CAN))
5368a[4]

**Caridadi (IRE)** *Charlie Appleby* 76
3 b g Invincible Spirit(IRE) Charity Belle (USA) (Empire Maker (USA))
1346[9]

**Caritas (GER)** *M Nigge* 42
2 bb f Shirocco(GER) Codera (GER) (Zilzal (USA))
1094a[12] 5941a[8]

**Carla Bianca (IRE)** *D K Weld* a72 108
3 gr f Dansili Majestic Silver (IRE) (Linamix (FR))
(5955a)

**Carlanda (FR)** *Michael Appleby* a73 68
4 ch f Lando(GER) Carousel Girl (USA) (Gulch (USA))
*548[4] 829[2]* ◆ *932[2]* 1091[7] 2550[4] *8061[8] 8208[7]*

**Carlo Bay (FR)** *J-C Rouget* 74
2 b c Diktat Lady Cree (IRE) (Medicean)
5292a[3]

**Carlo Bugatti (IRE)** *A P O'Brien* 105
3 b c Montjeu(IRE) Marquesa (USA) (Kingmambo (USA))
1458a[4] 2087[8] 3379[7]

**Carlos Moheba (GER)** *R Storp* a65 75
8 b g Next Desert(IRE) Cadisha (GER) (Platini (GER))
*806a[11]*

**Carnamoney** *David Barron* 61
3 ch g Monsieur Bond(IRE) House Of Frills (Paris House)
1671[6] 2420[2]

**Carnevale** *Ralph Beckett* a91 89
3 ch f New Approach(IRE) Festivale (IRE) (Invincible Spirit (IRE))
*2649[4]* (3142) 3968[3] 4680[7] (5647) *6665[2] 7662[4]*

**Carnival King (IRE)** *Brian Meehan* a62 67
2 b c Arcano(IRE) Validate (Alhaarth (IRE))
4270[3] *6268[8]*

**Carnt Cash Sorry** *Ed Vaughan* 32
3 b g Authorized(IRE) Eternity Ring (Alzao (USA))
*1044[7]* 2271[13] 2925[6]

**Caroline Norton (USA)** *John Gosden* a40
2 bb f Henrythenavigator(USA) Fifth Avenue Doll (USA) (Marquetry (USA))
*7659[9]*

**Caroline's Beach (IRE)** *J S Moore* a48 43
3 ch f Footstepsinthesand Rohain (IRE) (Singspiel (IRE))
*86[11] 665[9]*

**Caroz (FR)** *M Boutin* a83
7 b g Sevres Rose(IRE) Calling Grace (FR) (General Assembly (USA))
*3907a[5] 5964a[15]*

**Carpe Diem (USA)** *Todd Pletcher* a116
2 ch c Giant's Causeway(USA) Rebridled Dreams (USA) (Unbridled's Song (USA))
*7610a[2]*

**Carragold** *Mel Brittain* a48 75
8 b g Diktat Shadow Roll (IRE) (Mark Of Esteem (IRE))
1362[9] (3095) 7672[4]

**Carraig Rock** *Hughie Morrison* a73 71
4 b g Beat Hollow Riverine (Risk Me (FR))
3106$^{6}$ 3401$^{4}$ 3856$^{6}$ 4501$^{5}$ 5426$^{3}$ 6107$^{4}$ 6699$^{5}$ 7133$^{10}$

**Carraroe Flyer (IRE)** *Adrian Paul Keatley* a72 67
4 b f Sintarajan(IRE) Liffeydale (IRE) (Ajraas (USA))
(3056) 3363$^{5}$ (5171) 6514$^{7}$

**Carrera** *Michael Blanshard* a61 64
4 b g Sixties Icon Aileen's Gift (IRE) (Rainbow Quest (USA))
211$^{2}$ 467$^{4}$ 1917$^{4}$ 2689$^{5}$ (3075) 3562$^{5}$ 4073$^{10}$ 4655$^{8}$ 4905$^{3}$ 5425$^{6}$ 5797$^{3}$ 6407$^{2}$ 7632$^{2}$ 7854$^{2}$

**Carron Valley** *Keith Dalgleish* a52
2 b c Royal Applause Clear Impression (IRE) (Danehill (USA))
7400$^{10}$ 7660$^{10}$ 7827$^{5}$

**Carrot Top** *Ralph Beckett* 61
2 ch f Assertive Opopmil (IRE) (Pips Pride)
2557$^{4}$ 4269$^{F}$

**Carrowbeg (IRE)** *Lawney Hill* a42 53
6 b g Cape Cross(IRE) Love And Affection (USA) (Exclusive Era (USA))
3064$^{7}$ 4744$^{7}$ 5208$^{6}$ 5567$^{8}$ 6394$^{8}$

**Carry On Deryck** *Sylvester Kirk* 93
2 b c Halling(USA) Mullein (Oasis Dream)
(4943) ◆ 5431$^{4}$ 6291$^{6}$ 7331$^{4}$

**Carry Out (FR)** *H-A Pantall*
2 bb c Air Chief Marshal(IRE) Respite (Pivotal)
7468a$^{8}$

**Carthage (IRE)** *Richard Hannon* 82
3 b g Mastercraftsman(IRE) Pitrizzia (Lando (GER))
1690$^{3}$ 1984$^{6}$ 3031$^{3}$ 3750$^{5}$ 4801$^{5}$

**Carthaginian (IRE)** *Martin Todhunter* a21 81
5 b g Azamour(IRE) Khayrat (IRE) (Polar Falcon (USA))
3438$^{5}$ 4296$^{9}$ 5495$^{13}$

**Cartier (IRE)** *David Simcock* a78 76
2 b f Montjeu(IRE) Rosamixa (FR) (Linamix (FR))
5416$^{3}$ ◆ 6001$^{3}$ (8173)

**Cartmell Cleave** *Stuart Kittow* a67 53
2 b g Pastoral Pursuits There's Two (IRE) (Ashkalani (IRE))
3584$^{7}$ 4260$^{3}$ 5874$^{7}$ (7112)

**Carve (USA)** *Brad H Cox* a113
4 bb g First Samurai(USA) Apt (USA) (A.P. Indy (USA))
7591a$^{6}$

**Casar (IRE)** *M Delcher Sanchez* 94
6 ch g Hurricane Run(IRE) Thoroughly (IRE) (Woodman (USA))
4722a$^{10}$ 6917a$^{7}$

**Cascades (IRE)** *David Elsworth* a63 64
2 b f Montjeu(IRE) Seattle Ribbon (USA) (Seattle Dancer (USA))
5187$^{7}$ 5821$^{8}$ 6554$^{5}$ 7398$^{5}$

**Cascadia (IRE)** *Alison Hutchinson* a61 41
3 br f Mujadil(USA) Tucum (IRE) (Diktat)
190$^{5}$ 543$^{2}$ 653$^{3}$ (865) 931$^{2}$ ◆ 2805$^{10}$ 3407$^{8}$ 4970$^{11}$ 5321$^{6}$ 6939$^{4}$ (7458) 7895$^{5}$ 8047$^{3}$ 8145$^{5}$

**Cascading** *Hughie Morrison* a84 99
3 b f Teofilo(IRE) Angel Falls (Kingmambo (USA))
1424$^{2}$ 2280$^{4}$ 3085$^{5}$ (3877) 4945$^{3}$ 6255$^{8}$ 7554$^{9}$

**Cascading Stars (IRE)** *J S Moore* a74 60
2 b f Tagula(IRE) Subtle Affair (IRE) (Barathea (IRE))
4980$^{5}$ 6246$^{8}$ 6838$^{6}$ 7396$^{2}$ 7770$^{2}$ 7839$^{2}$ (7945) 8132a$^{3}$

**Case Statement** *M D O'Callaghan* 80
2 b c Showcasing La Gessa (Largesse)
3318$^{P}$

**Cash In Mind (FR)** *E J O'Neill* a68 76
3 b c Creachadoir(IRE) Dynamic Dream (USA) (Dynaformer (USA))
169a$^{5}$

**Cash Is King** *Robert Johnson* a45 75
4 b g Bahamian Bounty Age Of Chivalry (IRE) (Invincible Spirit (IRE))
19$^{3}$ 2469$^{6}$ 5642$^{2}$ 6674$^{18}$ 7502$^{13}$

**Cash Or Casualty (IRE)** *Damian Joseph English* a83 77
6 b g Footstepsinthesand La Quinta (IRE) (Indian Ridge)
790a$^{8}$ 1499$^{6}$

**Cashpoint** *Ian Williams* a82 94
9 b g Fantastic Light(USA) Cashew (Sharrood (USA))
2253$^{9}$ (2618) 2991$^{8}$ (3907a) 5162$^{8}$ 5964a$^{4}$

**Casila (IRE)** *Mark Johnston* 61
2 b f High Chaparral(IRE) Miletrian (IRE) (Marju (IRE))
7170$^{4}$ 7667$^{5}$

**Casius** *Harry Dunlop* a51
2 b c Teofilo(IRE) Mary Pekan (IRE) (Sri Pekan (USA))
7631$^{13}$ 7941$^{11}$ 8093$^{11}$

**Caspar Netscher** *David Simcock* 112
5 b h Dutch Art Bella Cantata (Singspiel (IRE))
5223a$^{13}$ 5674$^{7}$ 6134$^{7}$ 6920$^{5}$ (7325a) 7609a$^{8}$

**Casper Lee (IRE)** *Michael Herrington* a53 48
3 b g Kheleyf(USA) Shallop (Salse (USA))
173$^{11}$ 664$^{3}$ 1661$^{6}$ 2237$^{6}$ 2393$^{7}$ 2638$^{3}$ 2931$^{3}$ 3407$^{10}$ 3793$^{5}$ 4314$^{11}$

**Caspian Prince (IRE)** *Tony Carroll* a100 107
5 ch g Dylan Thomas(IRE) Crystal Gaze (IRE) (Rainbow Quest (USA))
36$^{5}$ (80) (148) 644$^{10}$ 788a$^{6}$ 1313$^{4}$ (1650) 1742$^{3}$ 2074$^{2}$ (2989) 3241$^{6}$ 4480a$^{2}$ 4852$^{15}$ (6172a) 6378a$^{5}$ 8228$^{6}$

**Cassandane (IRE)** *Mark Johnston* 52
2 br f Jeremy(USA) Princess Atoosa (USA) (Gone West (USA))
4825$^{7}$ 5718$^{9}$ 5981$^{6}$ 6830$^{6}$

**Cassells Rock (IRE)** *A J Martin* a81 92
4 br g Rock Of Gibraltar(IRE) Se La Vie (FR) (Highest Honor (FR))
6349a$^{2}$

**Cassie Jem** *David C Griffiths* a48 11
4 ch f Dubai Destination(USA) Generous Jem (Generous (IRE))
2655$^{8}$ 5894$^{4}$

**Cassini (FR)** *Mme Pia Brandt* a83 74
4 b g Astronomer Royal(USA) Mulled Wine (FR) (Night Shift (USA))
796a$^{8}$

**Castagna Girl** *Denis Coakley* 64
3 ch f Major Cadeaux Ewenny (Warrshan (USA))
1832$^{11}$

**Castagnou (IRE)** *P Bary* a34 94
3 b g Lawman(FR) Around Me (IRE) (Johannesburg (USA))
(2630a)

**Casterbridge** *Eric Alston* 79
2 b g Pastoral Pursuits Damalis (IRE) (Mukaddamah (USA))
1560$^{5}$ 2071$^{4}$ (2472) 3322$^{18}$ 4159$^{5}$

**Castilo Del Diablo (IRE)** *David Simcock* a103 89
5 br g Teofilo(IRE) Hundred Year Flood (USA) (Giant's Causeway (USA))
(54) 212$^{2}$ 803$^{5}$ (1213) 1556$^{4}$ 7930$^{4}$ 8243$^{3}$

**Castlebay (FR)** *N Bertran De Balanda* a70 73
3 ch f Green Tune(USA) Castilly (Inchinor)
5959a$^{4}$

**Castle Combe (IRE)** *Marcus Tregoning* a79 77
3 b g Dylan Thomas(IRE) Mundus Novus (USA) (Unbridled's Song (USA))
1220$^{2}$ 1727$^{5}$ 3421$^{4}$ 3814$^{3}$ 4812$^{4}$ 5468$^{6}$ 6044$^{10}$ 6487$^{2}$ 7016$^{2}$

**Castle Guest (IRE)** *M Halford* a69 100
5 b g Rock Of Gibraltar(IRE) Castelletto (Komaite (USA))
4379a$^{9}$

**Castlemorris King** *Brian Barr* a46 70
6 br g And Beyond(IRE) Brookshield Baby (IRE) (Sadler's Wells (USA))
6367$^{3}$ 7016$^{8}$

**Castle Talbot (IRE)** *Charles Hills* a57 65
2 b g Rock Of Gibraltar(IRE) Louve Sacree (USA) (Seeking The Gold (USA))
6861$^{3}$ 7200$^{5}$

**Castorienta** *George Baker* a67 79
3 ch f Orientor The Lady Caster (City On A Hill (USA))
(605) 936$^{6}$ 3821$^{4}$ 4297$^{2}$ 4788$^{2}$ (5205) ◆ 5753$^{4}$ 6189$^{7}$

**Casual Mover (IRE)** *John Best* a81 66
6 b g Diamond Green(FR) Baileys On Line (Shareef Dancer (USA))
3226$^{11}$ 4273$^{6}$

**Casual Smile** *Andrew Balding* 92
3 ch f Sea The Stars(IRE) Casual Look (USA) (Red Ransom (USA))
2152$^{7}$ 3423$^{3}$

**Catadupa** *Roger Charlton* a9 64
3 ch f Selkirk(USA) Caribana (Hernando (FR))
1438$^{9}$ 1984$^{4}$ 2279$^{6}$ 3711$^{12}$ 4134$^{4}$

**Catakanta** *Denis Coakley* 28
2 b g Notnowcato Akanta (GER) (Wolfhound (USA))
6675$^{12}$ 7155$^{9}$ 7511$^{6}$

**Catalinas Diamond (IRE)** *Pat Murphy* a62 65
6 b m One Cool Cat(USA) Diamondiferous (USA) (Danzig (USA))
192$^{5}$ 339$^{5}$ 603$^{8}$ (798) 1110$^{4}$ 1405$^{4}$ 1573$^{6}$ (2029) 2250$^{2}$ 3088$^{5}$ 3734$^{4}$ 4049$^{5}$ 4282$^{3}$ 4564$^{5}$ 5355$^{8}$ (5907) 6272$^{6}$ 6666$^{5}$ 7364$^{4}$ 7887$^{5}$ 8014$^{4}$ 8311$^{7}$

**Catalyze** *Paddy Butler* a61 62
6 b g Tumblebrutus(USA) Clarita Dear (CHI) (Hussonet (USA))
(215) 274$^{3}$ 864$^{7}$ (972) 1009$^{3}$ 1312$^{3}$ 1573$^{2}$ 1668$^{11}$ 1986$^{7}$ 3231$^{8}$ 3393$^{6}$ 4049$^{9}$ 5422$^{6}$ 6631$^{9}$

**Cataria Girl (USA)** *Marcus Tregoning* a72 69
5 b m Discreet Cat(USA) Elaflaak (USA) (Gulch (USA))
92$^{4}$ (822) (1097) 1232$^{11}$ 2720$^{3}$ (4105) 4799$^{4}$ 5599$^{3}$ 6426$^{3}$ 7358$^{6}$ (7744) 8202$^{5}$

**Cat Bere (FR)** *C Lerner* a66 57
2 bb c Hold That Tiger(USA) Help From Heaven (IRE) (Titus Livius (FR))
5618a$^{3}$

**Catcall (FR)** *P Sogorb* 117
5 b g One Cool Cat(USA) Jurata (IRE) (Polish Precedent (USA))
680a$^{5}$ 897a$^{5}$ 1179a$^{5}$ (2197a) ◆ 2820a$^{2}$ 6378a$^{6}$ 6966a$^{10}$ 7656a$^{3}$ 7856a$^{9}$

**Catch Dream (FR)** *L Baudron* 66
2 b g Alex The Winner(USA) Super Nana (FR) (Anabaa (USA))
7344a$^{4}$

**Catching Zeds** *Kevin Frost* a59 52
7 b m Lucky Story(USA) Perfect Poppy (Shareef Dancer (USA))
368$^{7}$ 671$^{5}$ (783) (1050) 1428$^{6}$ 7868$^{7}$ 7976$^{3}$ 8258$^{7}$ 8315$^{2}$

**Categorical** *Keith Reveley* a74 78
11 b g Diktat Zibet (Kris)
1567$^{2}$ 1971$^{3}$ 2515$^{8}$ 2739$^{9}$ 7247$^{6}$

**Catflap (IRE)** *Derek Haydn Jones* a62 64
5 b m One Cool Cat(USA) Consignia (IRE) (Definite Article)
141$^{6}$ 383$^{6}$

**Catharina** *Richard Hannon* a29 43
2 ch f Dutch Art Lambadora (Suave Dancer (USA))
4396$^{14}$ 4980$^{9}$ 5305$^{9}$

**Cathedral** *Philip Kirby* a70 67
5 b g Invincible Spirit(IRE) Capades Dancer (USA) (Gate Dancer (USA))
181$^{5}$ 583$^{3}$ 690$^{3}$ 849$^{3}$ 1022$^{4}$ (1209) 1362$^{2}$ 2702$^{6}$ 3112$^{6}$ 3582$^{8}$ 7702$^{11}$

**Caties Do Dah** *Alan Berry* 23
2 b f Misu Bond(IRE) Mitchelland (Namaqualand (USA))
4357$^{8}$ 5264$^{9}$ 5767$^{6}$

**Cat Melody (FR)** *P Marion* a77 76
6 ch m Hurricane Cat(USA) Sabmalody (FR) (Riche Mare (FR))
392a$^{4}$

**Cat O'Mountain (USA)** *Charlie Appleby* a114 96
4 bb g Street Cry(IRE) Thunder Kitten (USA) (Storm Cat (USA))
(202a) ◆ 681a$^{10}$ 901a$^{4}$ 1183a$^{3}$ 6139$^{5}$ (6909a)

**Catushaba (IRE)** *C Lerner* a83 83
4 gr f Aussie Rules(USA) Allegro Vivace (FR) (Muhtathir)
5964a$^{13}$

**Catwilldo (IRE)** *Garvan Donnelly* a69 71
4 b f One Cool Cat(USA) Hypocrisy (Bertolini (USA))
(128a) 7873a$^{13}$

**Caught On The Bid (IRE)** *Ed de Giles* a69
2 b c Footstepsinthesand Peps (IRE) (Val Royal (FR))
6675$^{2}$ 7031$^{4}$

**Cavaleiro (IRE)** *Marcus Tregoning* a72 100
5 ch g Sir Percy Khibraat (Alhaarth (IRE))
1578$^{11}$

**Cavalieri (IRE)** *Philip Kirby* a72 75
4 b g Oratorio(IRE) Always Attractive (IRE) (King's Best (USA))
1197$^{7}$ (1644) ◆ 1929$^{6}$ 2728$^{9}$ 3134$^{4}$ 3699$^{5}$ 4726$^{4}$ 5414$^{5}$

**Cavallo Bella** *David Barron* 13
3 gr f Bertolini(USA) Crosby Millie (Linamix (FR))
1441$^{9}$ 2389$^{8}$

**Cavalry Guard (USA)** *Tim McCarthy* a34 57
10 ch g Officer(USA) Leeward City (USA) (Carson City (USA))
290$^{10}$

**Cavalryman** *Saeed bin Suroor* a108 118
8 b h Halling(USA) Silversword (FR) (Highest Honor (FR))
(811a) 1177a$^{2}$ (4124) (4823) 5652$^{4}$

**Cay Dancer** *Richard Hannon* 96
3 gr f Danehill Dancer(IRE) White Cay (Dalakhani (IRE))
(1711) 1985$^{5}$ 2340$^{4}$ (3195) 3758$^{3}$ (4397) 5401$^{2}$

**Cayjo** *Mark Johnston* 52
3 b g Josr Algarhoud(IRE) Caysue (Cayman Kai (IRE))
1662$^{4}$ 3097$^{10}$ 4299$^{6}$ 5101$^{7}$ 5495$^{14}$

**Cayman Cry (USA)** *Brian Meehan* 65
3 ch f Street Cry(IRE) On A Cloud (USA) (Silver Hawk (USA))
3276$^{6}$ 3755$^{10}$

**Cayuga** *Brett Johnson* a90 87
5 b g Montjeu(IRE) Ithaca (USA) (Distant View (USA))
(89) 457$^{9}$ 8194$^{2}$

**Cazador (IRE)** *A Wohler* 89
3 b c Samum(GER) Concetta (GER) (Winged Love (IRE))
3512a$^{5}$

**Cease (USA)** *David Jacobson* a99 94
7 b g War Chant(USA) Limit (USA) (Cox's Ridge (USA))
2005a$^{3}$

**Ceaseless (IRE)** *James Tate* 76
2 b f Iffraaj Sheer Bliss (IRE) (Sadler's Wells (USA))
4828$^{3}$ 5644$^{2}$

**Ceelo** *Lydia Pearce* a69 78
4 b g Green Desert(USA) Mindsharp (USA) (Gone West (USA))
746$^{6}$ 993$^{7}$ 1238$^{5}$ 1613$^{8}$ 1893$^{4}$ 2488$^{5}$ 2887$^{7}$ 3222$^{7}$ 4042$^{5}$

**Ceevee** *Tim Vaughan* a58
4 ch g Vita Rosa(JPN) Calonnog (IRE) (Peintre Celebre (USA))
343$^{4}$ 558$^{6}$ 581$^{6}$ 1242$^{5}$

**Celebre (FR)** *F Rossi* 62
3 ch f Peintre Celebre(USA) Al Ribh (USA) (A.P. Indy (USA))
7268a$^{10}$

**Celebrian** *Alex Hales* a52 29
7 b m Fasliyev(USA) Triplemoon (USA) (Trempolino (USA))
73$^{5}$ 640$^{3}$ 974$^{2}$

**Celesteen (IRE)** *C Lerner* a64 59
3 b f Azamour(IRE) Lunaska (FR) (Ashkalani (IRE))
2978a$^{11}$

**Celestial Bay** *Sylvester Kirk* a75 67
5 b m Septieme Ciel(USA) Snowy Mantle (Siberian Express (USA))
3887$^{6}$ 4271$^{11}$ 4798$^{4}$ 5383$^{2}$ 6086$^{4}$ 6617$^{7}$ (6856) 7133$^{7}$ 7744$^{5}$ 7932$^{2}$ (8196) 8202$^{3}$

**Celestial Dancer (FR)** *Michael Appleby* a33 38
2 bb f Dr Fong(USA) Rabeera (Beat Hollow)
1837$^{6}$ 2231$^{11}$ 8083$^{5}$

**Celestial Dawn** *John Weymes* a61 41
5 b m Echo Of Light Celestial Welcome (Most Welcome)
121$^{9}$ 244$^{6}$ 1009$^{9}$ 1369$^{5}$ 1838$^{11}$ 2094$^{8}$ 2451$^{6}$ 7057$^{10}$ 8004$^{8}$ 8123$^{5}$ 8259$^{6}$

**Celestial House** *N Clement* a49 70
2 b c Acclamation Mystic Spirit (IRE) (Invincible Spirit (IRE))
2755a$^{6}$ 6385a$^{2}$

**Celestial Knight** *James Fanshawe* a74 38
3 b g Compton Place Garter Star (Mark Of Esteem (IRE))
2846$^{7}$ 3700$^{6}$ 4306$^{10}$ 4970$^{2}$ 5832$^{2}$ (6243) 6857$^{5}$ (7533)

**Celestial Magic** *Jonathan Portman* 44
2 b g Black Sam Bellamy(IRE) Mighty Merlin (Royal Applause)
6085$^{6}$ 6646$^{9}$

**Celestial Path (IRE)** *Sir Mark Prescott Bt* 111
2 br c Footstepsinthesand Miss Kittyhawk (IRE) (Hawk Wing (USA))
(4633) ◆ (6136) ◆ 7442$^{3}$

**Celestial Ray** *Linda Jewell* a72 65
5 ch g Pivotal Heavenly Ray (USA) (Rahy (USA))
2079$^{4}$ 2463$^{7}$ 2864$^{4}$ 3233$^{2}$ 3805$^{2}$ 4579$^{2}$ 5303$^{12}$

**Celestial Vision (USA)** *Tom Dascombe* a38 72
2 b g Henrythenavigator(USA) Damini (USA) (Seeking The Gold (USA))
1583$^{3}$ 2269$^{4}$ 3210$^{4}$ 3922$^{4}$ 4410$^{8}$ 7780$^{7}$ 7880$^{5}$

**Celestine Abbey** *John Ryan* a54 49
2 b f Authorized(IRE) Billie Jean (Bertolini (USA))
2306$^{9}$ 3194$^{11}$ 4499$^{13}$ 5279$^{6}$ 5489$^{9}$ (7904) 7992$^{9}$

**Cellalando (FR)** *S Cerulis* a67 83
4 b g Lando(GER) Cellamare (FR) (Alhaarth (IRE))
2821a$^{7}$ 5546a$^{3}$ 5961a$^{12}$

**Celtic Ava (IRE)** *Pat Phelan* a51
2 b f Peintre Celebre(USA) Denices Desert (Green Desert (USA))
6675$^{9}$ 7353$^{8}$ 7730$^{9}$ 8121$^{6}$

**Celtic Charlie (FR)** *Pat Phelan* a61 43
9 ch g Until Sundown(USA) India Regalona (USA) (Dehere (USA))
120$^{6}$

**Celtic Monarch (IRE)** *Mark Michael McNiff* a52 53
5 b g Celtic Swing Trim (IRE) (Ela-Mana-Mou)
695$^{5}$

**Celtic Rock** *J C Fernandez* 110
5 ch h Rock Of Gibraltar(IRE) Luna Celtica (IRE) (Celtic Swing)
3171a$^{4}$

**Celtic Sixpence (IRE)** *Nick Kent* a75 82
6 b m Celtic Swing Penny Ha'Penny (Bishop Of Cashel)
(1845) 2351$^{13}$ 2549$^{8}$ 2954$^{3}$ 3220$^{2}$ 4161$^{3}$ 4831$^{2}$ 5496$^{11}$ 6285$^{5}$ 6841$^{6}$

**Celtic Sunlight** *Pat Phelan* a50
4 ch g Sakhee(USA) For Love (USA) (Sultry Song (USA))
282$^{5}$ 403$^{7}$ 581$^{9}$

**Celtic Tune (FR)** *L Viel* 42
3 b g Green Tune(USA) Kerry Rose (FR) (Tel Quel (FR))
2003a$^{12}$

**Censorius** *Lee Carter* a77 71
3 b g Notnowcato Meredith (Medicean)
1529$^{11}$ 1844$^{6}$ 2221$^{10}$ 3146$^{10}$ 3711$^{3}$ (4658) 5038$^{6}$ 6019$^{3}$ 6864$^{9}$ 7500$^{4}$ (7734) 8015$^{3}$ 8164$^{4}$

**Centralized** *Eric Wheeler* a52
3 ch g Central Park(IRE) Millie The Filly (Erhaab (USA))
7841$^{11}$ 8114$^{6}$

**Centre Haafhd** *David Barron* 78
3 b g Haafhd Deira Dubai (Green Desert (USA))
1693$^{8}$ 2295$^{6}$ 3663$^{4}$ (4512) 5055$^{5}$ 5769$^{5}$

**Centrifugal (IRE)** *Doug Watson* a82 81
5 ch g Pivotal Tempting Fate (IRE) (Persian Bold)
239a$^{3}$

**Centurius** *Marco Botti* a100 101
4 ch g New Approach(IRE) Questina (FR) (Rainbow Quest (USA))
977$^{3}$ 1360$^{7}$ 1973$^{10}$ 2461$^{6}$

**Century (IRE)** *A P O'Brien* 104
3 b c Montjeu(IRE) Mixed Blessing (Lujain (USA))
2114$^{4}$ 3419$^{2}$

**Cerise Firth** *Steph Hollinshead* a30 53
2 b f Pastoral Pursuits Vermilion Creek (Makbul)
2172$^{7}$ 2652$^{6}$ 3842$^{5}$ 5593$^{7}$ 7488$^{6}$ 7816$^{6}$ 7912$^{5}$

**Certavi (IRE)** *Brendan Powell* a86 92
5 b g Antonius Pius(USA) The Quiet Woman (IRE) (Barathea (IRE))
1175$^{2}$ (2272)

**Certerach (IRE)** *M Halford* a95 113
6 b g Halling(USA) Chartres (IRE) (Danehill (USA))
(305a) 507a$^{3}$ 811a$^{3}$ (1177a) 3764a$^{2}$ 5652$^{7}$ 6374a$^{9}$ 7144a$^{8}$

**Certificate** *Roger Varian* 94
3 ch g Pivotal Graduation (Lomitas)
3083$^{3}$ (3537) 5686$^{2}$ 6466$^{2}$

**Certify (USA)** *Charlie Appleby* 113
4 b f Elusive Quality(USA) Please Sign In (USA) (Doc's Leader (USA))
(395a) 682a$^{4}$ 3355$^{12}$ 4165$^{7}$

**Cerutty (IRE)** *Marco Botti* a89 51
3 b c Shamardal(USA) Mouriyana (IRE) (Akarad (FR))
5831$^{6}$ 6298$^{5}$ 6634$^{3}$ 7195$^{3}$ (7627) 7974$^{2}$

**Chachkova (USA)** *D B Bagceci* 105
4 ch f Tapit(USA) Lisa M (USA) (Banker's Gold (USA))
6164a$^{6}$

**Chadic** *Mark Johnston* a62 95
2 b c Echo Of Light Hawsa (USA) (Rahy (USA))
3136$^{9}$ 3875$^{2}$ (4253) 4780$^{6}$ 5576$^{8}$ 6136$^{4}$ 6529$^{9}$ 6853$^{6}$

**Chain Of Daisies** *Henry Candy* 67
2 b f Rail Link Puya (Kris)
6065$^{10}$ 6420$^{3}$ 7018$^{6}$

**Chain Of Events** *Michael Wigham* a77 88
7 ch g Nayef(USA) Ermine (IRE) (Cadeaux Genereux)
655$^{3}$ 859$^{4}$ 1120$^{2}$ 1636$^{7}$ (2270) (2702) (3196) 3931$^{5}$ 6713$^{14}$ 7125$^{14}$ 7562$^{8}$

**Chalnetta (FR)** *C Ferland* a87 110
4 gr f Oratorio(IRE) Aifa (Johann Quatz (FR))
2819a$^{4}$ 5462a$^{2}$ 6380a$^{9}$

**Chamberlain** *John Murray* a26 44
3 b g Indesatchel(IRE) Citron (Reel Buddy (USA))
5497$^{9}$ 6009$^{9}$ 6405$^{11}$ 6674$^{14}$ 6866$^{12}$

**Chambois (FR)** *M Delzangles* 86
2 gr c Whipper(USA) Carmel (FR) (Highest Honor (FR))
4932a$^{7}$

**Chameur (FR)** *Mme M Bollack-Badel* a84 108
3 ch c Shirocco(GER) Crystals Sky (FR) (Hernando (FR))
795a$^{4}$ 3028a$^{4}$ 4930a$^{2}$

**Chamois (USA)** *Christophe Clement* 110
4 ch c Smart Strike(CAN) Meridiana (GER) (Lomitas)
3025a$^{10}$

**Chamonix (IRE)** *A P O'Brien* 93
5 b g Galileo(IRE) L'Ancresse (IRE) (Darshaan)
6349a$^{10}$

**Champagne Bob** *Tom Dascombe* a73 67
2 gr g Big Bad Bob(IRE) Exclusive Approval (USA) (With Approval (CAN))
6718$^{2}$ 7537$^{3}$ 7778$^{5}$

**Champagne Charley** *Des Donovan* a61 64
3 b f Myboycharlie(IRE) Crossed Wire (Lycius (USA))
1713$^{5}$ 2125$^{5}$ 2625$^{3}$ 3228$^{2}$ 3707$^{9}$ 4307$^{2}$ 4546$^{6}$ 5105$^{8}$

**Champagne Royale** *Sharon Watt*
2 b f Royal Applause Choysia (Pivotal)
5767[8]

**Champagne Rules** *Sharon Watt* 83
3 gr g Aussie Rules(USA) Garabelle (IRE) (Galileo (IRE))
(1357) 1883[6] 2839[2] 4359[7]

**Champagne Sydney (IRE)** *Richard Hannon* a86 83
3 ch g Iffraaj Special Touch (IRE) (Spinning World (USA))
1540[5] 2112[8] 5092[2] 5410[5] 6044[12] 6552[2] 7035[4]

**Championship (IRE)** *Richard Hannon* a90 104
3 ch g Exceed And Excel(AUS) Aljafliyah (Halling (USA))
1580[6] 2921[3] ◆ 3651[2] 4826[8] 5177[3] (6332) ◆

**Champs D'Or** *Marco Botti* a51 56
3 b f Champs Elysees Shemriyna (IRE) (King Of Kings (IRE))
2404[8] 2967[8] 5186[6]

**Chancelier (FR)** *J-C Rouget* a92 93
4 b g Peer Gynt(JPN) Particuliere (Spectrum (IRE))
2821a[5]

**Chancery (USA)** *David O'Meara* a85 103
6 bb g Street Cry(IRE) Follow That Dream (Darshaan)
1194[3] 1736[2] ◆ 2314[8] 3722[3] 4214[5] 4696[7] 5174[8] 5651[8] 6133[14] 6752[18] 7083[9]

**Chances Are (IRE)** *Keith Dalgleish* 74
2 ch f Dandy Man(IRE) Incendio (Siberian Express (USA))
4510[2] (4919) 5714[8] 6574[6]

**Chance To Dance (IRE)** *J S Bolger* a107 108
4 b g Teofilo(IRE) Crystal Ballet (USA) (Royal Academy (USA))
(4379a) 5115a[4] 6350a[3] 7144a[2]

**Chanceuse** *Gary Moore* a56 62
3 b f Lucky Story(USA) Miss Madame (IRE) (Cape Cross (IRE))
745[9] (931) 1257[2] 1793[8] 2609[3] 3614[6] 4088[4] 4536[4] 4785[2] 5106[3] (5977) 6396[9]

**Chandrayaan** *John E Long* a54 51
7 ch g Bertolini(USA) Muffled (USA) (Mizaaya)
81[7] 179[3] 377[10] 844[5] 1387[7] 1836[8] 8315[9]

**Chanson De Marins (FR)** *John Holt* 46
2 b f Le Havre(IRE) Easy To Sing (Johannesburg (USA))
4346[9]

**Chant (IRE)** *Ann Duffield* a68 80
4 b g Oratorio(IRE) Akarita (IRE) (Akarad (FR))
3205[8] 4296[2] 4704[2] 5716[2] 6169[4] 6579[3] 7008[4] 7281[9] 7504[9]

**Chantecler** *Hughie Morrison* a73 64
3 br g Authorized(IRE) Snow Goose (Polar Falcon (USA))
2031[3] 2682[9] 3315[10] 4134[10] 5139[8] 5864[6] (6410)

**Chantrea (IRE)** *Lady Cecil* a77
3 br f Dansili Celestial Lagoon (JPN) (Sunday Silence (USA))
(741) ◆ 957[2] 1389[2] 2024[7] 4263[2] 4612[4]

**Chaparella (IRE)** *Mark Johnston* a32 40
4 b f High Chaparral(IRE) Carakiysa (IRE) (Docksider (USA))
1919[9] 2216[11] 2550[6] 2915[6] 3535[12]

**Chapel Choir** *Sir Michael Stoute* a54 66
2 b f Dalakhani(IRE) Chorist (Pivotal)
6868[4] 7367[7]

**Chapellerie (IRE)** *Brendan Powell* a72 70
5 b m Acclamation Castellane (FR) (Danehill (USA))
402[2] 1227[2] ◆ 1369[8] 4733[2] (5136) 5602[2] (6077) 6562[7] 7697[4]

**Chapter And Verse (IRE)** *Mike Murphy* a91 72
8 gr g One Cool Cat(USA) Beautiful Hill (IRE) (Danehill (USA))
89[3] 533[5] 1175[3] 2270[9] 3335[6] 4273[9] (4786) 6166[12] 7531[8] 7870[4] 8095[10]

**Chapter Five** *Ian Williams* a58 72
7 b m Grape Tree Road Northern Shadows (Rock Hopper)
3269[3] 3976[2]

**Chapter Seven** *G M Lyons* a74 111
5 ch g Excellent Art My First Romance (Danehill (USA))
205a[8] 398a[9] 593a[15] 1078a[7] 7144a[7]

**Character Onesie (IRE)** *Richard Fahey* 67
2 b g Dark Angel(IRE) Flame Keeper (IRE) (Pivotal)
6319[3] 6757[4]

**Charava (IRE)** *W McCreery* 67
2 br g Captain Marvelous(IRE) Sweet Compliance (Safawan)
6375a[27]

**Charay (FR)** *F Rossi* a86
3 b c Footstepsinthesand Colca (IRE) (Desert Style (IRE))
237a[5]

**Charedal** *Iain Jardine* 31
6 gr m Polar Impact Paris Mist (Paris House)
2910[6] 3302[10] 3664[8] 4014[10]

**Charity Line (IRE)** *Marco Botti* 107
4 ch f Manduro(GER) Holy Moon (IRE) (Hernando (FR))
3961[9]

**Charlemagne Diva** *Richard Guest* a56 67
4 b f Holy Roman Emperor(IRE) Opera Ridge (FR) (Indian Ridge)
2542[7] 3530[8] 4131[8] 4629[6] 4875[8]

**Charles Camoin (IRE)** *Sylvester Kirk* a80 98
6 b g Peintre Celebre(USA) Birthday (IRE) (Singspiel (IRE))
1437[6] 1653[7] 2957[7] (4184) 4608[6] 4756[5] 5162[7]

**Charles De Mille** *George Moore* 68
6 b g Tiger Hill(IRE) Apple Town (Warning)
1376[11] (1673) 2519[8] 3400[6] 3919[7] 4533[2] 5127[5] 5793[2] 6672[14]

**Charles Messier** *Bryan Smart* 58
2 b g Acclamation Praesepe (Pivotal)
2513[4] 3296[7] 5464[6] 7497[13]

**Charles Molson** *Henry Candy* a87 94
3 b g Monsieur Bond(IRE) Arculinge (Paris House)
1700[4] 2344[5] 3253[8] 4166[15] 5204[6] 5675[8] 6144[4] ◆ 6424[3] 6789[8] 7445[3]

**Charles The Great (IRE)** *J Moore* 118
5 b g Holy Roman Emperor(IRE) Jojeema (Barathea (IRE))
7897a[9]

**Charleys Angel** *Pat Phelan* a34
3 b f Myboycharlie(IRE) Muwasim (USA) (Meadowlake (USA))
374[5] 1104[7] 1211[6]

**Charlie Croker (IRE)** *Kevin Ryan* 88
2 b c Fast Company(IRE) Officious Madam (USA) (Officer (USA))
4708[2] ◆ (5807) 6612[3] 7079[8]

**Charlie Lad** *Ollie Pears* 72
2 b g Myboycharlie(IRE) Night Owl (Night Shift (USA))
3199[8] 5464[4] 5813[3] 6642[2] (7038)

**Charlie's Angel (FR)** *H-F Devin* 82
3 b f Myboycharlie(IRE) Classic Actress (USA) (Lear Fan (USA))
(1907a)

**Charlie's Approval (IRE)** *Ben Haslam* 35
2 b f Approve(IRE) Authenticate (Dansili)
6489[9] 7496[5]

**Charlies Mate** *John Best* a54
3 br g Myboycharlie(IRE) Retainage (USA) (Polish Numbers (USA))
311[10] 1794[12] 2927[11] 5138[13] 5558[10] 7347[10] 7844[9] 8010[8]

**Charlie's Star** *Laura Mongan* a57 65
2 b f Hellvelyn Sweet Sorrow (IRE) (Lahib (USA))
1169[2] 1417[2] (1633) 2071[3] 4150[5] 4439[15] 4939[4] 5620[4] 5845[4] 6676[3] 7363[5] 7753[6] 7832[6] 8115[9]

**Charlie Wells (IRE)** *Eve Johnson Houghton* a83 76
3 b g High Chaparral(IRE) Numbers Game (Rainbow Quest (USA))
1765[6] 2847[6] 3516[DSQ] 3850[2] 4350[3] 4817[4] 4941[4] (5395) 5647[3] 6303[4] 7531[3] 7946[2] 8096[4]

**Charlotte Rhodes** *Marco Botti* a62
4 br f Halling(USA) Kunda (IRE) (Intikhab (USA))
13[3] 210[6]

**Charlotte's Day** *Sir Mark Prescott Bt* a87 71
3 b f Dalakhani(IRE) Charlotte O Fraise (IRE) (Beat Hollow)
(6075) 6283[6]

**Charlotte's Secret** *Richard Fahey* a61 63
2 ch g Sakhee's Secret Charlotte Point (USA) (Distorted Humor (USA))
3358[6] 4216[7] 5086[4] 5798[2] 6211[4] 6669[9]

**Charlton Heights (IRE)** *J S Moore* a68
2 b g Strategic Prince Personal Design (IRE) (Traditionally (USA))
7867[6] 8148a[6] (8225)

**Charly Chop (FR)** *Matthieu Palussiere* 63
2 ch c Soave(GER) Valse Bluette (FR) (Goldneyev (USA))
7027a[12]

**Charme Du Reverdy (FR)** *Alex Fracas* 34
2 ch f Vision D'Etat(FR) Parcel (Beat Hollow)
5662a[9]

**Charming Kitten (USA)** *Todd Pletcher* a96 108
4 bb c Kitten's Joy(USA) Iteration (USA) (Wild Again (USA))
4010a[7]

**Charming Thought** *Charlie Appleby* 117
2 b c Oasis Dream Annabelle's Charm (IRE) (Indian Ridge)
5397[2] ◆ (6038) (6612) (7239)

**Charm Spirit (IRE)** *F Head* 124
3 b c Invincible Spirit(IRE) L'Enjoleuse (IRE) (Montjeu (IRE))
(1272a) 1951[5] (3028a) (4278a) (6382a) (7274)

**Charmy Dukesse (IRE)** *Marco Botti* a66 53
3 b f Duke Of Marmalade(IRE) Nashatara (USA) (Nashwan (USA))
1423[11] 1846[11] 3970[5]

**Charpoy (USA)** *Lee Smyth* a50 50
6 b g Street Cry(IRE) Honolua Bay (USA) (Storm Bird (CAN))
794a[11]

**Chartbreaker (FR)** *A Wohler* 92
3 b c Shirocco(GER) Caucasienne (FR) (Galileo (IRE))
3293a[4]

**Charter (IRE)** *Michael Wigham* a80 92
4 b g Elusive City(USA) Lucky Norwegian (IRE) (Almutawakel)
5308[4] 5834[3] (6558) ◆ (6891)

**Chasing Halos (USA)** *M Al Muhairi* a105 94
7 b h Elusive Quality(USA) Ballado's Halo (USA) (Saint Ballado (CAN))
240a[3]

**Chasing Rubies (IRE)** *Michael Bell* a57
2 b f Tamayuz Laureldean Lady (IRE) (Statue Of Liberty (USA))
8227[6]

**Chasse Maree (FR)** *Alain Couetil* 101
3 ch f Muhtathir Street Kendra (FR) (Kendor (FR))
7768a[3]

**Chatalong (IRE)** *Richard Fahey* a47
3 b f Invincible Spirit(IRE) Chatline (IRE) (One Cool Cat (USA))
94[4] 298[7]

**Chateau Lola** *Derek Shaw* a56 20
5 b m Byron Glensara (Petoski)
58[7] 164[8] 556[9] 610[6]

**Chatez (IRE)** *Alan King* 102
3 b g Dandy Man(IRE) Glory Days (GER) (Tiger Hill (IRE))
(1655) ◆ 2148[2] ◆ (2565) 3378[12] 4448[3] 7276[12]

**Chatham House Rule** *Michael Bell* a79 76
3 gr c Authorized(IRE) Cozy Maria (USA) (Cozzene (USA))
1960[4] 2422[8] 3385[3] 7401[2]

**Chatsworth Express** *Richard Whitaker* a54
3 b g Redoubtable(USA) Teo Torriate (IRE) (Daggers Drawn (USA))
70[11] 302[7]

**Chattanooga Line** *George Baker* a65
4 b f Rail Link Gay Romance (Singspiel (IRE))
1380[4]

**Chatty Man (IRE)** *David C Griffiths*
2 b g Approve(IRE) Grenouillere (USA) (Alysheba (USA))
6259[17] 6757[13] 7244[13]

**Chaudhary (SWI)** *M Boutin* a76 49
4 b g Zamindar(USA) Chelsea (SWI) (Danehill Dancer (IRE))
796a[12]

**Chautauqua (AUS)** *Michael, Wayne & John Hawkes* 125
4 gb g Encosta De Lago(AUS) Lovely Jubly (AUS) (Lion Hunter (AUS))
7724a[2]

**Chauvelin** *Roger Charlton* a72 67
3 b g Sir Percy Enforce (USA) (Kalanisi (IRE))
2031[2] 6738[6] 7074[5] 8029[5] 8313[3]

**Chebsey Beau** *John Quinn* 36
4 b g Multiplex Chebsey Belle (IRE) (Karinga Bay)
4062[5]

**Checkpoint** *Tony Coyle* a63 71
5 ch g Zamindar(USA) Kalima (Kahyasi)
1710[7] 2215[10] 3791[2] 4156[6] 4498[7]

**Cheeco** *Ruth Carr* a40
2 ch g Shami Mandarin Lady (Timeless Times (USA))
2903[4] 3435[8]

**Cheeky Chapman** *Clive Mulhall* 56
2 ch g Stimulation(IRE) Athboy Auction (Auction House (USA))
2866[7] 3947[6] 4467[9] 5297[9] 6212[12]

**Cheeky Lady (FR)** *F Rohaut* 80
2 b f Siyouni(FR) La Fresca (Peintre Celebre (USA))
5329a[4] 6958a[4]

**Cheeky Peta'S** *James Given* a49 60
3 b f Compton Place Cheeky Girl (College Chapel)
213[3] 346[7] 3440[6]

**Cheeky Wee Red** *Alistair Whillans* a26 43
6 ch m Pastoral Pursuits Swynford Elegance (Charmer)
1310[9] 1673[14] 2457[4] 2676[7] 3363[7] 3623[11]

**Cheerio Sweetie (IRE)** *David Evans* a84 77
2 b f Captain Rio Curve (IRE) (Desert Style (IRE))
(1259) ◆ 1560[2] 2071[7] 3211[6]

**Cheers Buddy (IRE)** *Lee Smyth* a72 62
6 b g Acclamation Victorian Dancer (IRE) (Groom Dancer (USA))
790a[3]

**Chefchaouen (IRE)** *J S Moore* a64 31
2 b f Dylan Thomas(IRE) Love Thirty (Mister Baileys)
3557[15] 5026a[2] 5544a[10] 5901a[12] 7631[4] 7867[5] 7941[6]

**Cheik Bere (FR)** *M Figge* 86
2 b c Hold That Tiger(USA) Kunoichi (USA) (Vindication (USA))
3806a[4] 5405a[10] 7485a[6]

**Chellalla** *Ian Williams* a43 72
5 b m Elnadim(USA) Cheloca (Selkirk (USA))
3935[10] (5425) 5573[5] 6843[11]

**Chella Thriller (SPA)** *Alastair Lidderdale* a61 58
5 b m Chevalier(IRE) Arundhati (IRE) (Royal Academy (USA))
1100[5] 1354[13] 2863[6] 3308[9]

**Chelwood Gate (IRE)** *Patrick Chamings* a80 74
4 gb g Aussie Rules(USA) Jusoor (USA) (El Prado (IRE))
3861[10] 4352[4] 5378[5] 6236[7] 6658[9] 7339[10] 7942[3] 8030[2]

**Chemical Charge (IRE)** *Ralph Beckett* a93 80
2 ch c Sea The Stars(IRE) Jakonda (USA) (Kingmambo (USA))
(6875) (7798)

**Chene Boppe (FR)** *F-X De Chevigny* a79 82
4 ch g Turtle Bowl(IRE) Beggars Belief (IRE) (Common Grounds)
5961a[6]

**Cherek (FR)** *J-C Rouget* 104
2 b c Paco Boy(IRE) Cherryxma (FR) (Linamix (FR))
(5940a) 6570a[3] 7557a[4]

**Cherry Empress (IRE)** *Jo Hughes* a56 56
2 b f Holy Roman Emperor(IRE) Cherry Creek (IRE) (Montjeu (IRE))
5774[9] 6246[10] 6361[5] 6888[4] 7824[8]

**Cherry Princess** *Stuart Williams* a60 62
4 ch f Act One Francia (Legend Of France (USA))
2066[3] 2923[10] 3553[2] 3824[2] 4343[4] 4763[3] (4808) 5096[2] 5787[4] 6396[7] 7853[4]

**Cherry Street** *Denis Quinn* a73 73
5 b g Alhaarth(IRE) Weqaar (USA) (Red Ransom (USA))
6141[9] 7359[6] 7569[2] 7831[10]

**Cherry Tiger** *Graeme McPherson* a63 61
4 b g Tiger Hill(IRE) Lolla's Spirit (IRE) (Montjeu (IRE))
4473[3] 6252[7] 7115[7] 7518[8] 7823[6] (8259)

**Chesieres (FR)** *A Le Duff* a49 29
3 b f Kingsalsa(USA) Kiss Me Goodknight (First Trump)
795a[13] 5370a[11]

**Chesil Beach** *Andrew Balding* a71 92
3 b f Phoenix Reach(IRE) Seaflower Reef (IRE) (Robellino (USA))
2211[6] (2997) 3391[6] 3567[5] 4261[3] 4615[3] 4834[2] (5520) (6325) ◆ (6741) (7102)

**Chess Valley** *Willie Musson* a34 73
3 b f Shamardal(USA) Grecian Air (FR) (King's Best (USA))
2879[5] 3421[7] 4152[3] 4365[2] 5008[8] 5980[6] 6647[10] 7339[2] ◆ 7513[2]

**Chester Aristocrat** *Eric Alston* a14 81
5 ch g Sakhee(USA) New Light (Generous (IRE))
6095[8] 6511[20] 6736[13] 7183[11]

**Chester Bound** *Jo Hughes* a32 5
2 gr f Equiano(FR) Varanasi (High Chaparral (IRE))
5774[11] 8027[4]

**Chester Deal** *Jo Hughes* a82 85
2 b g Multiplex Elusive Deal (USA) (Elusive Quality (USA))
1276[8] 1571[5] 1872[6] 4529[2] 4967[3] (5618a) (5900a) 6245a[4] 6958a[11]

**Chester Deelyte (IRE)** *Lisa Williamson* a52 42
6 b m Desert Style(IRE) Bakewell Tart (IRE) (Tagula (IRE))
100[8] 370[10] 586[6] 688[9] 858[5] 4788[9] 5422[5] 6023[4] 7253[5]

**Chester'slittlegem (IRE)** *Mrs A Corson* a51 57
5 b m Atraf Ceylon Round (FR) (Royal Applause)
1573[11] 1787[10] 2598a[7] 3496a[5] 4038a[3] 4715a[2] 5228a[2] 6186a[2]

**Chesturo (IRE)** *A Wohler* 88
3 ch f Manduro(GER) Joyfullness (USA) (Dixieland Band (USA))
7483a[7]

**Chetan** *Milton Bradley* a64 59
2 b c Alfred Nobel(IRE) Island Music (IRE) (Mujahid (USA))
1872[4] 2173[6] 2246[3] 3081[6] 3934[7] 4967[5] 6040[8] 6422[2] (7529) 7753[2] (7848) 7984[2]

**Chevalgris** *Alan Swinbank* 82
4 gr g Verglas(IRE) Danzelline (Danzero (AUS))
4290[10] 5465[6] 5890[7] 6152[4] 6493[3] 6864[3] 7177[12]

**Chevallier** *Richard Hannon* a70 76
2 b g Invincible Spirit(IRE) Magical Romance (IRE) (Barathea (IRE))
4142[6] 4943[4] 5439[2] 6039[2] 6659[2] 7155[6] 7728[4]

**Cheval Rouge (IRE)** *H Rogers* a53 87
7 ch m Tagula(IRE) Izibi (FR) (Saint Cyrien (FR))
1078a[10]

**Cheveton** *Richard Price* a52 88
10 ch g Most Welcome Attribute (Warning)
4946[5] 5623[9] 7212[8]

**Chevise (IRE)** *Steve Woodman* a68 68
6 b m Holy Roman Emperor(IRE) Lipica (IRE) (Night Shift (USA))
(53) 339[3] 714[8] 1017[9] 1110[5] 1405[3] 1896[5] 2486[9] (3422) 4401[2] 5624[6] 7556[5] (7887) 8195[6]

**Cheworee** *Tom Dascombe* a81 89
5 b m Milk It Mick Jodrell Bank (IRE) (Observatory (USA))
1850[6] (3697) 4188[6] 4762[2] 6096[10] 7330[15]

**Cheyenne Bellevue (FR)** *P Leblanc* a48
2 b g Iron Mask(USA) Baiona (FR) (Lujain (USA))
8149a[13]

**Cheyenne Home (USA)** *P Bary* a88 103
4 b g Empire Maker(USA) Cheyenne Dream (Dancing Brave (USA))
2821a[2]

**Cheyenne Red (IRE)** *Michael Herrington* a38 53
8 br g Namid Red Leggings (Shareef Dancer (USA))
215[4] 563[6]

**Cheyne Walk (SWI)** *Mme B Suter* a15 61
3 b f Vespone(IRE) Chelsea (SWI) (Danehill Dancer (IRE))
2978a[17]

**Chez Vrony** *Dave Morris* a56 59
8 b g Lujain(USA) Polish Abbey (Polish Precedent (USA))
18[2] 201[2] 281[9] 1015[3] 1631[7] 2092[5] 7646[3] 8111[10]

**Chiara Wells (IRE)** *A Floris* 95
5 gr m Refuse To Bend(IRE) Docklands Grace (USA) (Honour And Glory (USA))
1477a[3] 2375a[14]

**Chiberta King** *Andrew Balding* a80 111
8 b g King's Best(USA) Glam Rock (Nashwan (USA))
7662[8] 7837[5] 8296[6]

**Chicago (IRE)** *John Patrick Shanahan* 102
5 b g Montjeu(IRE) Lady Karr (Mark Of Esteem (IRE))
1562[7] 3764a[6]

**Chicago Bere (FR)** *Richard Hannon* a74 68
2 b c Peer Gynt(JPN) Fitness Queen (USA) (Gilded Time (USA))
6456[3] 6660[3] 6958a[16] 7200[3] 7867[3] (8112) 8267[2] (8293)

**Chicago Girl (IRE)** *J P Murtagh* a47 92
3 b f Azamour(IRE) Angelic Sounds (IRE) (The Noble Player (USA))
2042a[6]

**Chicquita (IRE)** *A P O'Brien* 114
4 b f Montjeu(IRE) Prudenzia (IRE) (Dansili)
6370a[2] 6970a[15] 7273[3] 7611a[5]

**Chief Barker (IRE)** *Larry Rivelli* 104
3 b c Azamour(IRE) Millay (Polish Precedent (USA))
4230a[P]

**Chief Executive (IRE)** *Mandy Rowland* a62 35
4 gr g Dalakhani(IRE) Lucky (IRE) (Sadler's Wells (USA))
171[9] 1269[5] 1675[13] 2252[9] 6768[11]

**Chief Hawkeye (IRE)** *J-V Toux* a71 89
5 b g Hawk Wing(USA) Pacy's Ridge (IRE) (Indian Ridge)
(7026a) 7856a[16]

**Chief Spirit** *James Eustace* 69
2 b c Norse Dancer(IRE) Indian Angel (Indian Ridge)
6497[6] 6875[3]

**Childesplay** *Heather Main* a67 75
3 ch f Byron Parting Gift (Cadeaux Genereux)
1422[2] 5044[2] 5883[3] 6336[6] 8038[3] 8185[2] 8298[3]

**Chillie Billie** *J Larkin* a76 75
5 ch g Piccolo Chilly Cracker (Largesse)
5958a[7] 7873a[3]

**Chilly Miss** *Malcolm Jefferson* 60
5 b m Iceman Fairlie (Halling (USA))
3953[5] 4705[5] 5388[3] 6000[4]

**Chiltern Secret** *Dean Ivory* a35 46
4 ch f Sakhee's Secret Regal Curtsy (Royal Applause)
81[9] 251[11]

**Chil The Kite** *Hughie Morrison* a98 117
5 b g Notnowcato Copy-Cat (Lion Cavern (USA))
306a[12] 509a[8] 812a[9] 1068[9] (2336) 3356[2] 5434[5] 5666[6] 6921[12] 7276[6]

**Chilworth Bells** *David Barron* a48 60
2 ch g Sixties Icon Five Bells (IRE) (Rock Of Gibraltar (IRE))
2964[10] 3481[6] 3875[5] *4967[8]* 5372[2] *5823[13]* 6205[5] (6428) 7165[4] 7536[2] *7816[5]* *7912[2]*

**Chilworth Icon** *Mick Channon* a98 103
4 b g Sixties Icon Tamara Moon (IRE) (Acclamation)
*207a[8]* *1042[3]* 1442[7] *1576[6]* 1862[7] 3483[3] 3876[2] 3964[4] 4146[11] 4918[6] 5433[5] (5925) 6327[5] ◆ 6745[7] 7122[12]

**China Club (IRE)** *John Gosden* a73
2 b c Shamardal(USA) Twyla Tharp (IRE) (Sadler's Wells (USA))
*7372[3]* *7731[5]* *7973[4]* *8091[2]* *8292[2]*

**China Excels** *Mandy Rowland* a54 46
7 b g Exceed And Excel(AUS) China Beauty (Slip Anchor)
*694[7]* *864[5]* *1001[4]* *1089[5]* 1584[6] *1887[5]* *5801[2]* *6409[2]* *8229[7]*

**China In My Hands** *James Bethell* a52 65
3 gr f Dark Angel(IRE) Cheap Thrills (Bertolini (USA))
1611[10] 2020[6] 2517[7] 3333[4] 3828[5] 4046[6]

**Chinanigans (IRE)** *D T Kelly* a52
4 b g Chineur(FR) Vinesgrove (IRE) (Danetime (IRE))
*7961a[10]*

**Chindeni** *Ed Vaughan* a45 54
3 b f Teofilo(IRE) Choysia (Pivotal)
*914[5]* 2967[9] 3568[5] 3877[6]

**Chinese Jade** *Sir Mark Prescott Bt* a52 90
3 gr g Cape Cross(IRE) Chinese White (IRE) (Dalakhani (IRE))
4280[4] 4845[2] (5810) 6111[2] 6892[8]

**Chinotto (IRE)** *Andrew Balding* a85 33
3 b g Duke Of Marmalade(IRE) Muskoka Dawn (USA) (Miswaki (USA))
*659[2]* *785[2]* 2222[U]

**Chipie Royale (FR)** *Mme C Barande-Barbe* a25 5
2 b f Great Journey(JPN) Tofu (Anabaa (USA))
6619a[8]

**Chiquito (FR)** *J-L Pelletan* a74 49
2 bb c Air Chief Marshal(IRE) Dudu (SPA) (Mdudu)
*5618a[8]* *5900a[2]*

**Chiswick Bey (IRE)** *Richard Fahey* a72 74
6 b g Elusive City(USA) Victoria Lodge (IRE) (Grand Lodge (USA))
5197[12] 6232[13] (6674) 7179[4] 7600[3] *7830[9]*

**Chitu (USA)** *Bob Baffert* a114
3 ch c Henny Hughes(USA) Sea Gift (USA) (A.P. Indy (USA))
*1964a[9]*

**Chivers (IRE)** *Tim Easterby* 74
3 b g Duke Of Marmalade(IRE) Thara (USA) (Hennessy (USA))
2621[2] (3098) 3655[5] 4316[3] (5200) 6169[8] 6637[3] 6981[5]

**Chloe's Dream (IRE)** *Linda Perratt* a47 68
4 gr f Clodovil(IRE) Extravagance (IRE) (King's Best (USA))
1759[7] 1966[5] 2514[10] 2675[5] 3191[9] 3609[10] 3833[4] 4005[7] 4195[7] 4257[8] 4362[6] 4519[3] 4725[4] 4960[11] 5237[7] 5565[4] 5858[8] 6406[12]

**Chocala (IRE)** *Alan King* a80 94
4 b g Rock Of Gibraltar(IRE) Arbella (Primo Dominie)
1735[3] (2108)

**Choc'A'Moca (IRE)** *Paul Midgley* a25 69
7 b g Camacho Dear Catch (IRE) (Bluebird (USA))
1643[9] 2233[5] 2606[9] 3093[8] 3338[3] (3548) 3913[2] 4288[11] (4795) 5806[7] 6114[2] 6452[3] 6674[15]

**Chocolatier (FR)** *M Delzangles* a81 100
3 b f Lawman(FR) Sweet Shop (Grand Lodge (USA))
1782a[4] 2586a[5] 6882a[9]

**Choice Of Destiny** *Philip McBride* a68 69
3 ch f Haafhd Lumpini Park (Halling (USA))
*71[4]* *919[2]* *1101[5]* *1449[8]* (2878) 3144[11] 4063[3] 4742[6] 5522[4] *6342[4]* *7456[3]* *7556[7]* 7907[4] 8103[6] 8299[6]

**Choisan (IRE)** *Tim Easterby* 82
5 b g Choisir(AUS) Attanagh (IRE) (Darnay)
1197[4] (1929) 2139[4] 2900[4] 3240[8] 4454[4] 5083[5] 5301[3] 6171[7] 6480[2] 7247[3]

**Chollima** *Tim Easterby* 48
2 ch c Monsieur Bond(IRE) Magic Myth (IRE) (Revoque (IRE))
2358[10] 3481[8] 4216[11] 5335[10] 6211[6]

**Chookie Royale** *Keith Dalgleish* a113 93
6 ch g Monsieur Bond(IRE) Lady Of Windsor (IRE) (Woods Of Windsor (USA))
*144[2]* *(465)* *716[8]* *(886)* 1165[17] *1558[8]*

**Chookie's Lass** *Keith Dalgleish* a72 71
3 ch f Compton Place Lady Of Windsor (IRE) (Woods Of Windsor (USA))
*573[9]* *1149[2]* 4383[8] 4861[8] 5631[3] (5808) 5994[4] 6478[13] 6575[3] 6835[9] *7697[5]* *7950[5]*

**Chooseday (IRE)** *Kevin Ryan* 96
5 b g Choisir(AUS) Break Of Day (USA) (Favorite Trick (USA))
1193[15] 1506[2] 2352[11] 2992[13] 3239[12] 4061[9] 5016[10] 5444[3] 5888[14] 6512[17] (Dead)

**Chopin (GER)** *A Wohler* 116
4 b c Santiago(GER) Caucasienne (FR) (Galileo (IRE))
1478a[2] 2338[4]

**Choppy Water (IRE)** *Tim Easterby* 53
2 b g Zebedee Brewing Storm (IRE) (King Charlemagne (USA))
5264[8] 6115[6]

**Chopsoave (FR)** *N Caullery* a88 95
6 ch h Soave(GER) Moon Serenade (Key Of Luck (USA))
*6992a[12]*

**Choral Clan (IRE)** *Philip Mitchell* a64 45
3 b g Oratorio(IRE) Campbellite (Desert Prince (IRE))
*1384[2]* *2078[3]* 2417[6] *3389[2]* *4969[2]* *5865[5]*

**Choral Festival** *John Bridger* a65 80
8 b m Pivotal Choirgirl (Unfuwain (USA))
*1021[7]* 1354[4] (1875) (2300) 2628[6] 3325[3] 3803[6] 4501[3] 4743[2] (5214) 5948[4] 6303[9] *7033[9]* 7160[5] 7516[10]

**Choral Rhythm (IRE)** *Tony Carroll* a44 48
4 b f Oratorio(IRE) Sierra (Dr Fong (USA))
*81[10]* *251[5]* *737[10]*

**Chord Chart (IRE)** *S Seemar* a80 94
3 b g Acclamation Musical Bar (IRE) (Barathea (IRE))
*204a[10]* 770a[4] *896a[7]*

**Chorlton House** *Johnny Farrelly* a62
2 ch g Compton Place Really Ransom (Red Ransom (USA))
*8166[9]* *8288[12]*

**Chorlton Manor (IRE)** *Tim Pitt* a65 70
3 b g Kheleyf(USA) Pearl Of The Sea (IRE) (Fusaichi Pegasus (USA))
2090[7] 3068[6] 3790[6]

**Chortle** *Charlie Appleby* a61 65
3 b f Dubawi(IRE) Portmanteau (Barathea (IRE))
2523[7]

**Chorus of Lies** *Charlie Appleby* 70
2 b c Teofilo(IRE) Cherry Orchard (IRE) (King's Best (USA))
6683[10] 7039[3] 7498[3]

**Chosen Character (IRE)** *Tom Dascombe* 101
6 b g Choisir(AUS) Out Of Thanks (IRE) (Sadler's Wells (USA))
1193[16] 1442[14] 1721[10] 2699[2] (3109) 3886[3] 4187[7] 4938[8] 5919[8] 6281[7] 6704[9]

**Chosen Forever** *Lee James* a54 44
9 b g Choisir(AUS) Forever Bond (Danetime (IRE))
*2901[9]* 4797[5]

**Chosen One (IRE)** *Ruth Carr* a57 67
9 ch g Choisir(AUS) Copious (IRE) (Generous (IRE))
1378[10] 1643[5] 2056[11] 2724[5] 3338[4] (4005) 4257[12] 4714[6] 5375[12] 5819[6] 6866[14]

**Chrissycross (IRE)** *Roger Teal* a83 58
5 b m Cape Cross(IRE) Penang (IRE) (Xaar)
*118[5]* *300[7]* 2498[7] *2935[6]*

**Christmas Hamper (IRE)** *Sir Michael Stoute*
2 b c Dubawi(IRE) Gift Range (IRE) (Spectrum (IRE))
*7811[10]*

**Christmas Light** *Brian Ellison* a65 85
7 b m Zafeen(FR) Arabian Dancer (Dansili)
2790[7] 3205[11] 3544[8]

**Christopher Chua (IRE)** *Michael Scudamore* a52 54
5 gr g Clodovil(IRE) Pearls Of Wisdom (Kyllachy)
*100[9]* *402[7]* *586[4]* *760[2]* 2008[3] 2831[2] 3231[11]

**Christophermarlowe (USA)** *John Gosden* 97
2 b c Tapit(USA) Dress Rehearsal (IRE) (Galileo (IRE))
(6300) ◆ (6784) ◆

**Christopher Wren (USA)** *Nick Gifford* a58 95
7 ch g D'Wildcat(USA) Ashley's Coy (USA) (Country Pine (USA))
(1493) 2558[4] 2991[5] 6987[8]

**Chuck A Luck (FR)** *F Chappet* a54 68
2 ch g Trempolino(USA) Rouvraie (FR) (Anabaa (USA))
*8148a[10]*

**Chuckamental** *Bryan Smart* a57 63
3 b g Captain Marvelous(IRE) Stoneacre Sarah (Cadeaux Genereux)
*346[2]* *608[6]* 2551[3] 2870[8] 3228[7] 4193[7] 4974[5] 5715[12]

**Chuck Hatch** *Ed Walker* 9
3 b g Sakhee(USA) Forest Fire (SWE) (Never So Bold)
3248[14]

**Chufft** *Hughie Morrison* a23
3 b f Sleeping Indian Relkida (Bertolini (USA))
*2125[9]*

**Chunghua (USA)** *Ed Walker* a75
3 ch g Elusive Quality(USA) Mananiyya (IRE) (Ashkalani (IRE))
*495[2]* *(739)*

**Churada (IRE)** *J-M Lefebvre* a66 59
4 b f Green Tune(USA) Agiel (FR) (Bering)
935a[9]

**Chutney (IRE)** *Richard Hannon* a57 74
3 b f Exceed And Excel(AUS) Crackle (Anshan)
1985[8] 3067[4] 3708[2] 4329[6] *5046[5]*

**Ciao Cielo (GER)** *David Barron* a75 40
2 b g Lord Of England(GER) Celebration Night (IRE) (Hawk Wing (USA))
5759[7] *(7973)*

**Ciaras Cookie (IRE)** *David Evans* a43 63
2 b f Approve(IRE) Preach (IRE) (Danehill Dancer (IRE))
*1169[8]* *1741[7]* 2623[6] 3312[7] 3967[2] (4302) 5148[4] *5554[11]* 6205[3] 6610[10] (6996) 7488[7]

**Cigar Street (USA)** *William Mott* a107
5 bb h Street Sense(USA) Arcadiana (USA) (Deputy Minister (CAN))
*7614a[7]*

**Cilento (IRE)** *John Gosden* a73
2 rg c Raven's Pass(USA) Kapria (FR) (Simon Du Desert (FR))
*7833[3]* *(8060)*

**Cincinnati Girl (IRE)** *Denis Coakley* a71 72
3 b f Dylan Thomas(IRE) Diamond Circle (Halling (USA))
*1894[3]* ◆ 2404[6] 2850[2] 3631[3] 4947[6] *6341[3]* 7162[6] *7359[5]*

**Cincinnati Kit** *Stuart Williams* a66 86
5 br m Cape Cross(IRE) Princess Georgina (Royal Applause)
1572[11] 2275[6] 3459[11]

**Cincuenta Pasos (IRE)** *Joseph Tuite* a76 73
3 ch g Footstepsinthesand Sweet Nicole (Okawango (USA))
2429[11] *2886[6]* 3198[4] (5314) *5492[3]* 6616[5]

**Cinnamon Spice** *Harry Dunlop* a39 65
3 bb g High Chaparral(IRE) Hot And Spicy (Grand Lodge (USA))
2773[9] 3248[12] 5313[10] *6856[12]*

**Cinnilla** *Ralph Beckett* 94
3 b f Authorized(IRE) Caesarea (GER) (Generous (IRE))
1438[8] 2279[5] 2735[3] 3673[5] 4134[5] 4948[3] (5878) (6091) ◆ 7106[3] 7768a[8]

**Cinquante Nuances (IRE)** *Mme Pia Brandt* a83
3 b g Peintre Celebre(USA) Danish Mermaid (Danehill Dancer (IRE))
*795a[2]*

**Ciocco Sam (GER)** *C Von Der Recke* a69
6 bb g Samum(GER) Cioccolata (GER) (Winged Love (IRE))
*638a[4]*

**Circling (IRE)** *David Wachman* a82 100
3 ch f Galileo(IRE) Chanting (USA) (Danehill (USA))
3285a[3] 5024a[5]

**Circuitous** *Keith Dalgleish* a55 86
6 b g Fasliyev(USA) Seren Devious (Dr Devious (IRE))
2602[2] 2825[7] 3573[16] 4258[5] 5143[8] 5444[18] 6217[13] 6477[12]

**Circumvent** *Paul Cole* a104 92
7 ch g Tobougg(IRE) Seren Devious (Dr Devious (IRE))
*1068[6]* 1439[6] *1578[4]* 1948[6] 3306[3] (3383) *3907a[9]*

**Ciriaco (SPA)** *G Arizkorreta Elosegui* a95 86
4 b c Caradak(IRE) Fallopio (USA) (El Prado (IRE))
*8006a[11]*

**Cirrus Des Aigles (FR)** *Mme C Barande-Barbe* a109 126
8 b g Even Top(IRE) Taille De Guepe (FR) (Septieme Ciel (USA))
1182a[2] (1783a) (2587a) (2988) 6957a[5] 7275[5] 8154a[4]

**Cirtee** *Tim Etherington*
2 b f Monsieur Bond(IRE) Slip Star (Slip Anchor)
5332[9] 5910[10]

**Cisca Bere (FR)** *M Pimbonnet* 74
2 bb f Hold That Tiger(USA) Niska (USA) (Smart Strike (CAN))
4603a[7]

**Cisco Boy** *Tim Easterby* 59
2 b g Paco Boy(IRE) Miss Wells (IRE) (Sadler's Wells (USA))
2288[7] 2895[3] 4416[9] 5335[8] 6669[14]

**Citisonsmith (IRE)** *Paul Green* a38 33
2 b g Amadeus Wolf Ink Pot (USA) (Green Dancer (USA))
6059[8] 6935[10] *7254[7]*

**Citizen Kaine (IRE)** *Jo Hughes* a68 63
3 ch g Manduro(GER) Precious Citizen (USA) (Proud Citizen (USA))
*839[2]* *1220[5]* 2596a[5] 3850[9] *5011[3]* *5556[5]* *6037[7]* *6410[11]*

**Citron Spirit (IRE)** *Matthieu Palussiere* 108
2 b c Invincible Spirit(IRE) Citron Presse (USA) (Lemon Drop Kid (USA))
(6123a) 6968a[7]

**City Ground (USA)** *Michael Easterby* a70 74
7 bb g Orientate(USA) Magnet (USA) (Seeking The Gold (USA))
1168[9] *1450[3]* 2963[2] 4293[2] 4755[2] (5076) (6187a) 6626[10] 7044[7]

**City Lad (NZ)** *D Koh* 99
6 b g Elusive City(USA) Snuff (NZ) (Deputy Governor (USA))
2379a[10]

**City Money (IRE)** *M Delcher Sanchez* 105
2 b c Elusive City(USA) Peachmelba (USA) (Theatrical (IRE))
4953a[2] 6220a[2] 7655a[8]

**City Of Angkor Wat (IRE)** *Jo Hughes* a70 53
4 b g Elusive City(USA) Kathleen Rafferty (IRE) (Marju (IRE))
*3473[6]* 4673[8] *5512[2]* *5893[3]* *(6771)* *7868[2]* *7909[2]*

**City Of Culture (IRE)** *W McCreery* a70 73
6 b m Elusive City(USA) Danestar (Danehill (USA))
*6078a[3]*

**City Zip** *Alan McCabe*
4 ch f Lucky Story(USA) Urban Calm (Cadeaux Genereux)
2389[14] *2902[5]*

**Civil War (IRE)** *Gary Moore* a80 86
5 b g Scorpion(IRE) Silvestre (ITY) (Unfuwain (USA))
(1355) (1941) 7539[9]

**Clabare** *Ian Semple* a59 56
3 b g Proclamation(IRE) Choral Singer (Daylami (IRE))
3486[7] 4022[13] 5857[2] 6405[5] 6834[2] 7250[7] *7699[4]*

**Cladocera (GER)** *A De Royer-Dupre* a105 104
3 b f Oasis Dream Caesarine (FR) (Pivotal)
3808a[10] 5407a[10] *7836[2]*

**Claim The Roses (USA)** *Ed Vaughan* a93 46
3 bb c Speightstown(USA) Reboot (USA) (Rubiano (USA))
1518[11] *8279[5]*

**Clampdown** *James Tate* a60 55
2 ch g Kheleyf(USA) Miss McGuire (Averti (IRE))
2007[8] 2541[5] 3304[3] 5525[6] *7991[2]* *8121[2]*

**Clapperboard** *Paul Fitzsimons* a63 47
3 b f Royal Applause Roseum (Lahib (USA))
*1738* *3543* *5414* *10483* *12573* 1666[2] *(1918)* *2209[2]* *2469[2]* (2860) *3389[4]* (5071) 5522[6] 7078[5] 7556[12] 8143[11] 8176[6]

**Clara De Lune (FR)** *R Le Gal* a71 94
5 b m Bleu D'Altair(FR) Lidawar (FR) (Sendawar (IRE))
6569a[11]

**Claraty** *James Unett* a54
4 b f Firebreak Claradotnet (Sri Pekan (USA))
*8064[6]* *8172[4]*

**Clarence Beeks (IRE)** *Brian Ellison*
4 gr g Verglas(IRE) Dazzling Dancer (Nashwan (USA))
*409[6]*

**Clary (IRE)** *James Unett* a65 45
4 b f Clodovil(IRE) Kibarague (Barathea (IRE))
*1631[4]* 2021[7] 4156[10] *7548[3]*

**Classical Art (IRE)** *Roger Varian* a57 82
3 ch g Excellent Art Ask Carol (IRE) (Foxhound (USA))
*1795[12]* 2769[3] (3541) 5276[4] 5877[8] 6741[3]

**Classical Diva** *Michael Appleby* a48 48
3 b f Amadeus Wolf America Lontana (FR) (King's Theatre (IRE))
1373[8] 2387[7] 3228[6] 3534[9] *3792[3]* 4071[6] 4287[5] 4714[8] *8004[11]* *8085[8]* *8139[7]* *8219[4]*

**Classical Duet (USA)** *Mark Johnston* a82 77
3 b c Teofilo(IRE) Mialuna (Zafonic (USA))
4705[6] 5018[2] *(5490)* 6137[9] 6433[6]

**Classical Rose** *Charlie Fellowes* 62
2 b f Amadeus Wolf Monaazalah (IRE) (Green Desert (USA))
7377[7]

**Classic Collection** *Saeed bin Suroor* a89 77
2 b c Cape Cross(IRE) Local Spirit (USA) (Lion Cavern (USA))
2642[2] *(7200)* ◆ *7574[4]*

**Classic Colori (IRE)** *Martin Keighley* a74 84
7 b g Le Vie Dei Colori Beryl (Bering)
(3915) *5258[8]* *7914[7]* *(8190)*

**Classic Devotion (USA)** *Charlie Appleby* a79
3 b g Street Cry(IRE) Serenading (USA) (A.P. Indy (USA))
*1258[3]* *1797[2]* *2685[9]* 3675[P]

**Classic Flyer** *David O'Meara* 71
2 b g Stimulation(IRE) Tranquil Flight (Oasis Dream)
3454[7] 3713[4] 3947[5] 5014[2] ◆ 5637[6] 5985[5] (6643) 6791[3] 7055[7]

**Classic Image** *Rae Guest* 17
2 b f Exceed And Excel(AUS) Reflected Image (IRE) (Refuse To Bend (IRE))
5774[10] 6453[12]

**Classic Mission** *Jonathan Portman* a73 67
3 ch g Bahamian Bounty Triple Cee (IRE) (Cape Cross (IRE))
1786[7] 2417[7] 3559[5] *5006[6]* 5719[4] *6037[2]* *6267[2]* *7068[2]* *7527[2]* *7744[2]* *8099[3]*

**Classic Orange** *Simon Waugh* 11
4 ch f Assertive Classical Song (IRE) (Fayruz)
1600[6]

**Classic Pursuit** *Ronald Harris* a73 73
3 b c Pastoral Pursuits Snake's Head (Golden Snake (USA))
1350[9] 1570[7] 2278[5] *2886[5]* *(3855)* 4890[3] 5381[5] 6552[7] *7698[4]* *7905[8]* *7989[4]* *8186[9]*

**Classic Seniority** *Richard Hannon* a75 69
2 b c Kyllachy Dramatic Solo (Nayef (USA))
4025[11] 4270[7] (4846) *5306[5]* 5974[6] *7029[2]* 7378[4] *7849[4]* *7890[3]* *8113[3]* *(8240)* *8293[4]* *8308[2]*

**Classic Villager** *Philip Hide* a70 75
2 b c Authorized(IRE) Sablonne (USA) (Silver Hawk (USA))
3194[6] ◆ 3748[5] 5712[2] *6565[4]* *6602[3]* *7425[2]*

**Classy Anne** *Jim Goldie* 86
4 ch f Orientor Class Wan (Safawan)
1758[13] 1972[2] (2473) (2909) (3104) 3191[4] 4257[2] 4725[2] (4901) 5170[6] 6013[4] 6512[5] 6824[2] 7103[2] 7669[2]

**Classy Lassy (IRE)** *Brian Ellison* a44 81
3 b f Tagula(IRE) Classic Style (IRE) (Desert Style (IRE))
2421[9] 2870[9] 3237[9] 3487[9] 3913[14] 4294[8] *5512[9]* 6454[16] 6796[8]

**Classy Trick (USA)** *Patrick Morris* a59 31
4 b g Hat Trick(JPN) Classiest Gem (CAN) (Dehere (USA))
*152[3]* *351[4]* *676[8]*

**Claude Carter** *Alistair Whillans* 50
10 b g Elmaamul(USA) Cruz Santa (Lord Bud)
3103[6] 3302[8] 4522[3] 5146[6] 6117[6]

**Claude Greenwood** *Linda Jewell* a62 56
4 b g Lucky Story(USA) Greenmeadow (Sure Blade (USA))
*92[7]* *467[5]* *755[8]* *1016[10]* 2069[5] 2722[5] 3035[4] 3230[6] *4433[9]* 5033[5] 5291[5] (5978) 6396[2] 7000[9] 7369[3] 7845[5] 7982[7]

**Claude Monet (BRZ)** *Simon Dow* a55 60
5 ch g Vettori(IRE) Femme Fatale (BRZ) (Clackson (BRZ))
*210[11]* *446[3]* *661[5]* *1015[5]* *1236[4]* *1386[3]* *1836[4]* 2722[8]

**Claudia Eria (FR)** *P Van De Poele* a62 78
2 b f Hold That Tiger(USA) Sa Premiere (FR) (Nombre Premier)
5543a[3] *5844a[8]* 6591a[15] *8149a[12]*

**Clayton** *Kevin Ryan* a87 110
5 b g Peintre Celebre(USA) Blossom (Warning)
(1360) 1653[2] 2294[8]

**Clear Focus (IRE)** *Brendan Powell* a44 56
3 ch f Intense Focus(USA) Sofistication (IRE) (Dayjur (USA))
*1626[2]* 2023[5] 2526[5] 2668[6] 3214[3] (3564) 4102[2] 4715a[5] 5518[3] 6023[6] 6297[10] *7420[12]*

**Clearing** *Jim Boyle* a86 54
4 br f Sleeping Indian Spring Clean (FR) (Danehill (USA))
*(2648)* 2965[8] *3581[6]* *(4614)* *7073[2]* *7521[2]* *7886[2]*

**Clear Loch** *John Spearing* a50 50
4 gr g Proclamation(IRE) Loch Shiel (IRE) (Selkirk (USA))
*319[11]* 3230[4]

**Clear Mind** *John Gosden* a84 76
3 b f Rail Link Comma (USA) (Kingmambo (USA))
2310[3] ◆ *(4325)* *7033[6]* 7565[7]

**Clear Praise (USA)** *Simon Dow* a84 81
7 b g Songandaprayer(USA) Pretty Clear (USA) (Mr Prospector (USA))
*444[4]* *658[5]* *820[10]* *991[6]* *1261[4]* (2065) 2718[10] 3551[4] 3876[5] 4121[9] *7073[11]* *7365[9]* 7886[3] 8072[5] 8297[8]

**Clear Spell (IRE)** *Alistair Whillans* a73 80
3 b g Tamayuz Beat The Rain (Beat Hollow)
*119[3]* *341[2]* *423[4]* 2292[3] 2769[4] 3303[6] (4904) 5387[3] 6012[2] 6637[2] 7100[2]

**Clear Spring (IRE)** *John Spearing* a69 103
6 b h Chineur(FR) Holly Springs (Efisio)
1734[4] ◆ 2110[12] (2849) 3714[10] 4895[15] 5445[8] 5778[2] 6327[10] 6440[2] 6760[6]

**Clement (IRE)** *John O'Shea* a73 65
4 b g Clodovil(IRE) Winnifred (Green Desert (USA))
6455[13] 7307[7] 7636[9] 8017[5] (8299)

**Cleo Fan (ITY)** *Stefano Botti* 106
3 b c Mujahid(USA) Cuprea (IRE) (Best Of The Bests (IRE))
7617a[2]

**Clergyman** *Martyn Meade* a76 77
2 b c Pastoral Pursuits Doctor's Note (Pursuit Of Love)
5555[4] 6024[2] 6489[3] 6623[3] 6887[2] (7254)

**Clerk's Choice (IRE)** *William Jarvis* a85 90
8 b g Bachelor Duke(USA) Credit Crunch (IRE) (Caerleon (USA))
591[2] 3859[6]

**Clever Cookie** *Peter Niven* 110
6 b g Primo Valentino(IRE) Mystic Memory (Ela-Mana-Mou)
(1691) (2253) ◆ (2785) 4214[9] 5693[6] 6288[4]

**Clever Love (FR)** *Jo Hughes* a44 74
2 gr g Silver Frost(IRE) Sharp's Love (IRE) (Fasliyev (USA))
1094a[13] 1571[6] 2944[10] 4330[2] 5588a[7] 5940a[7] 8000[9]

**Clever Miss** *Alan McCabe* a61 74
3 b f Mount Nelson Clever Millie (USA) (Cape Canaveral (USA))
761[4] 1507[7] 1832[9] 2447[2] 2929[7] 3300[11] 4047[5] 5205[4] 5763[6]

**Cliff (IRE)** *Nigel Tinkler* 75
4 b g Bachelor Duke(USA) Silesian (IRE) (Singspiel (IRE))
3097[4] 3601[6] 4022[5] 4713[3] 5195[3] 5415[2] 6232[5] 6490[7]

**Cliff House (IRE)** *John J Walsh* 85
4 b g Mustameet(USA) Babble On (IRE) (Anita's Prince)
7142a[7] 7476a[7]

**Climaxfortackle (IRE)** *Derek Shaw* a68 71
6 b m Refuse To Bend(IRE) Miss Asia Quest (Rainbow Quest (USA))
60[4] 259[7] 511[2] 576[7] 993[10] 1080[6] 2174[8] (2435) 3149[2] 5601[8] 5776[4] 7023[12] 7213[7] 7622[8]

**Cloak And Degas (IRE)** *Scott Dixon* a62 59
2 b g Sakhee's Secret Coup De Torchon (FR) (Namid)
5297[7] 6115[11] 6887[5] 7257[6] 7848[2] 8046[6]

**Clockmaker (IRE)** *Conor Dore* a89 89
8 b g Danetime(IRE) Lady Ingabelle (IRE) (Catrail (USA))
38[5] 314[13] 534[10] 890[7] 1041[4] 1943[8] 2548[8] (3036) 3716[11] 4188[7] 4648[29] 4938[9] 5665[14] 6144[9] 6320[11] 7947[10] 8072[7] 8252[9]

**Clock On Tom** *Michael Easterby* a47 67
4 b g Trade Fair Night Owl (Night Shift (USA))
2171[11] 3439[11] 5075[6]

**Clock Opera (IRE)** *William Stone* a70 65
4 b f Excellent Art Moving Diamonds (Lomitas)
340[3] 453[5] (1896) 2312[4] 3384[9] 3966[4] 4788[8] 5287[11]

**Clodoaldo (IRE)** *Brian Meehan* 61
3 b g Clodovil(IRE) Salonga (IRE) (Shinko Forest (IRE))
3229[6] 3978[6] 4268[3]

**Clodovil Doll (IRE)** *James Tate* a44 64
2 gr f Clodovil(IRE) Titus Wood (IRE) (Titus Livius (FR))
2022[5] 2348[3] 2666[2] 4576[6] 6643[9]

**Clonard Street** *A J Martin* 105
2 b c Archipenko(USA) Moi Aussi (USA) (Mt. Livermore (USA))
6800a[2] 7721a[6]

**Clon Brulee (IRE)** *Saeed bin Suroor* a99 112
5 ch g Modigliani(USA) Cloneden (IRE) (Definite Article)
108a[6] 394a[4] 681a[4] 2957[3] (5188) ◆ 5928[3] (6233) 7243[4]

**Clondaw Warrior (IRE)** *W P Mullins* a54 90
7 br g Overbury(IRE) Thespian (IRE) (Tiraaz (USA))
7142a[18] (7476a)

**Clorofilla (IRE)** *Marco Gasparini* 105
4 b f Refuse To Bend(IRE) Crudelia (IRE) (Great Commotion (USA))
(1477a) 2375a[6] 7320a[7] 7725a[10]

**Close Hatches (USA)** *William Mott* a121
4 bb f First Defence(USA) Rising Tornado (USA) (Storm Cat (USA))
6973a[4] 7593a[11]

**Closing** *Nick Littmoden* a57 43
2 ch f Compton Place Rosewood Belle (USA) (Woodman (USA))
3975[5] 6675[3]

**Cloud Line** *William Haggas* 83
3 b f Danehill Dancer(IRE) Superstar Leo (IRE) (College Chapel)
3664[2] ◆ 4446[2] (4867)

**Cloud Monkey (IRE)** *Martin Todhunter* a62 88
4 bb g Marju(IRE) Sweet Clover (Rainbow Quest (USA))
1724[14] 2168[7] 2728[3] 3371[3] 4423[5] 4921[8] 5639[2] 6223[7] 6699[16]

**Cloudscape (IRE)** *John Gosden* a81 109
3 b c Dansili Set The Scene (IRE) (Sadler's Wells (USA))
(1535) ◆ 1953[5] 2748[2] 3375[4] 4778[4]

**Cloud Seven** *Chris Wall* a68
2 br c New Approach(IRE) Regrette Rien (USA) (Unbridled's Song (USA))
7382[16] 7778[7] 8093[2]

**Clouds Rest** *Richard Fahey* 88
2 b f Showcasing Ahwahnee (Compton Place)
1583[2] ◆ (2014) ◆ (2302) 3353[15] 4159[4] 4686[9] (5714) 5998[3] 6703[4]

**Cloudy Spirit** *Andrew Hollinshead* a69 84
9 gr m Silver Patriarch(IRE) Miss Lacroix (Picea)
3501[8] 4217[8]

**Clovelly Bay (IRE)** *Marcus Tregoning* a56
3 b g Bushranger(IRE) Crystalline Stream (FR) (Polish Precedent (USA))
8294[4]

**Cloverdale** *Mark Johnston* a86 53
4 ch f Pivotal Lane County (USA) (Rahy (USA))
(1112) 1345[16] 1564[12] 1733[11]

**Clowance Estate (IRE)** *Roger Charlton* a103 101
5 b g Teofilo(IRE) Whirly Bird (Nashwan (USA))
1213[3] 1581[2] 2073[13]

**Clown (FR)** *Mme M Bollack-Badel* 47
2 b c Kouroun(FR) Cleanaway (FR) (Kahyasi)
5544a[9]

**Club House (IRE)** *Robert Mills* a77 72
4 b g Marju(IRE) Idesia (IRE) (Green Desert (USA))
155[3] 286[4] (493) (583) 627[3] (690) 825[4] 1142[4] 1234[6] 2471[9] 7205[11] 7533[9] 7757[8] 8041[5] 8103[2]

**Clubhouse Ride (USA)** *Craig A Lewis* a114 82
6 ch h Candy Ride(ARG) Seeking Results (USA) (Seeking The Gold (USA))
5781a[10]

**Clubland (IRE)** *Roy Bowring* a85 81
5 b g Red Clubs(IRE) Racjilanemm (Kyllachy)
36[6] 175[8] 299[6] 552[7] 1440[2] 1678[2] (1892) 2890[5] 3227[10] 3702[6] 4131[5] 4571[2] (4875) 5766[3] 6346[3] 7212[13] 7669[7] 8279[8]

**Clumber Place** *Shaun Harris* a42 72
8 ch m Compton Place Inquirendo (USA) (Roberto (USA))
1310[3] 1930[2] 2219[6] 4108[9] 4489[3] (5168) (5233) 5415[4] 6232[10] 6863[8] 7180[15] 7494[11]

**Cluster (AUS)** *Peter & Paul Snowden* 107
4 b c Fastnet Rock(AUS) Tarcoola Diamond (AUS) (Last Tycoon)
7724a[13]

**Coach Bombay (IRE)** *Adrian Brendan Joyce* a58 42
6 b g Ad Valorem(USA) Molly-O (IRE) (Dolphin Street (FR))
2455[7]

**Coach Montana (IRE)** *Christine Dunnett* a53 53
5 b g Proud Citizen(USA) Market Day (Tobougg (IRE))
281[12] 370[12] 676[11] 754[4] 846[11] 996[2] 2907[6] 3160[12] 3527[4] 4055[9]

**Coastal Passage** *Gordon Elliott* a60 51
6 b g Ishiguru(USA) Ellcon (IRE) (Royal Applause)
219[7] 783[8]

**Coastal Storm** *Jennie Candlish* a58 42
3 b f Manduro(GER) Ruff Shod (USA) (Storm Boot (USA))
1382[5] ◆ 2926[10] 7115[11]

**Cobham's Circus (IRE)** *Marcus Tregoning* 64
3 ch g Hernando(FR) Protectorate (Hector Protector (USA))
2026[7] 2339[9] 2996[6] 4332[9]

**Cocker** *Tom Dascombe* a56 23
2 b g Shirocco(GER) Treble Heights (IRE) (Unfuwain (USA))
7425[5] 7667[13]

**Cockney Belle** *Marco Botti* a69 53
3 br f Cockney Rebel(IRE) Fustaan (IRE) (Royal Applause)
4535[6] 5304[6] 6154[6] 6568[5]

**Cockney Bob** *J Parize* a96 90
3 b g Cockney Rebel(IRE) Wizby (Wizard King)
237a[2] 436a[2] 553a[5] 721a[2] 1340a[8] 7269a[3]

**Cockney Class (USA)** *Dave Roberts* a78 90
7 rg g Speightstown(USA) Snappy Little Cat (USA) (Tactical Cat (USA))
163[8] 408[6] 698[9] 1744[3]

**Cockney Island** *Philip McBride* 87
2 b f Cockney Rebel(IRE) Island Rhapsody (Bahamian Bounty)
5344[2] 5725[2] 6256[4] 6933[22]

**Cock Of The North** *Scott Dixon* 102
2 ch c Cockney Rebel(IRE) Camp Fire (IRE) (Lahib (USA))
(1161) 2703[2] 3318[11] 4199[3] 5926[4] 7442[8]

**Cocktail Queen (IRE)** *Mme M Bollack-Badel* a81 111
4 b f Motivator Premier Prize (Selkirk (USA))
1434[6] 1869[5] (5461a) (5962a)

**Cocoa's Princess** *Richard Fahey* a49
3 b f Kyllachy Princess Cocoa (IRE) (Desert Sun)
174[4] 824[5]

**Coconell** *Peter Hiatt* a75
4 b f Rock Of Gibraltar(IRE) Marula (IRE) (Sadler's Wells (USA))
1226[3]

**Cocoon (IRE)** *A P O'Brien* a73 92
2 b f Galileo(IRE) Mystical Lady (IRE) (Halling (USA))
4598a[8] 7462a[3]

**Coco Sun (FR)** *W Mongil* a53 107
4 b f Marchand De Sable(USA) Carola (POL) (Gairloch)
(7629a)

**Code Of Honor** *Saeed bin Suroor* a87 112
4 b g Zafeen(FR) Verbal Intrigue (USA) (Dahar (USA))
205a[7] 595a[2] (6519) 7243[9]

**Code Red** *William Muir* 100
2 ch c Bahamian Bounty Just Devine (IRE) (Montjeu (IRE))
5271[6] 6363[5] (7037) (7439) ◆

**Codger's Gift (IRE)** *Richard Fahey* a51 53
2 b f Footstepsinthesand Moonbi Ridge (IRE) (Definite Article)
5255[4] 5807[6] 7228[7]

**Coeur Dolois (IRE)** *A Bonin* a66 36
3 b g High Chaparral(IRE) Tallulah Bell (USA) (Gone West (USA))
8005a[8]

**Coillte Cailin (IRE)** *Daniel Mark Loughnane* a72 71
4 b f Oratorio(IRE) Forest Walk (IRE) (Shinko Forest (IRE))
37[2] 127[4] 542[3] 642[2] 735[4] 2509[3] 2806[8] 3705[5] 4579[5] 7068[3] (7522) 7626[3] 7829[6] 8122[3]

**Coin Broker (IRE)** *David O'Meara* 66
3 b f Montjeu(IRE) Cash Run (USA) (Seeking The Gold (USA))
2236[2] 2740[6] 3534[3] 3950[5] 4316[5]

**Coincidently** *Alan Bailey* a76 88
4 b f Acclamation Miss Chaussini (IRE) (Rossini (USA))
1014[10] 1568[4] 1762[4] 2318[8] 3476[4] 3644[2] 5413[2] (5787) 5855[5] 6476[2] 6534[8] 6713[11] 7110[12] 7838[8] 8042[6]

**Coin Of The Realm (IRE)** *Miss Imogen Pickard* a71 97
9 b g Galileo(IRE) Common Knowledge (Rainbow Quest (USA))
514[8] 641[6] 848[7]

**Coiste Bodhar (IRE)** *Scott Dixon* a71 60
3 b g Camacho Nortolixa (FR) (Linamix (FR))
195[4] 401[9] 622[3] 745[2] 867[6] (1277) 1611[4] (1914) 2049[5] 2281[6] 3388[3] 3523[4] 4155[3] 4535[4] 5987[7] 6889[3] 7057[8] (7355) 7989[6] 8180[9]

**Colinca's Lad (IRE)** *Peter Charalambous* a49 84
12 b g Lahib(USA) Real Flame (Cyrano De Bergerac)
2445[7] 2980[2] 3681[4] 3874[4]

**Collaboration** *Andrew Balding* a84 89
3 b g Halling(USA) Red Shareef (Marju (IRE))
(1135) ◆ 1702[2] 2337[5] 3003[12] 4821[14] 5884[5] 6855[7]

**Collani (IRE)** *M Nigge* a75 77
3 b c Aussie Rules(USA) Les Planches (Tropular)
4952a[13] 5370a[4]

**Collateral Risk (IRE)** *Stefano Botti* 99
3 b c Duke Of Marmalade(IRE) Paint In Green (IRE) (Invincible Spirit (IRE))
1779a[6] 2376a[9]

**College Doll** *Christine Dunnett* a62 56
5 ch m Piccolo Southwarknewsflash (Danetime (IRE))
114[4] 797[9] 908[4] 1270[2] (1500) 3896[7] 4546[4] 5399[5] 5780[2] 6631[5] 6897[6] 7534[12] 7671[11] 7900[12] 8088[6] 8210[2]

**Collodi (GER)** *David Bridgwater* a55 81
5 b g Konigstiger(GER) Codera (GER) (Zilzal (USA))
376[3] 7411[5]

**Collosium (IRE)** *Michael Dods* 77
2 b g Showcasing Ragsta (IRE) (Key Of Luck (USA))
1536[3]

**Colmar Kid (IRE)** *M Al Muhairi* a107 81
4 b c Choisir(AUS) Roselyn (Efisio)
596a[9]

**Colombia (IRE)** *Ann Duffield* a38 49
2 b f Art Connoisseur(IRE) Credibility (Komaite (USA))
4624[4] 4919[4] 7970[12]

**Colonel Mak** *David Barron* a77 104
7 br g Makbul Colonel's Daughter (Colonel Collins (USA))
1484[11] 1734[8] 2254[15] (2898) 5445[17] 7280[10] 7408[13]

**Colonialiste (IRE)** *F Head* 98
2 ch f Lord Of England(GER) Sahel (GER) (Monsun (GER))
6219a[5] 7393a[9]

**Colorada** *William Knight* a67 71
2 ch f Lope De Vega(IRE) Isabella Glyn (IRE) (Sadler's Wells (USA))
6754[3] 7108[5] 7549[4]

**Color Code (FR)** *M Boutin* a59 78
3 ch c Desert Prince(IRE) Chatcat (SWI) (Brief Truce (USA))
3809a[5] 4465a[2]

**Colourbearer (IRE)** *Milton Bradley* a79 48
7 ch g Pivotal Centifolia (FR) (Kendor (FR))
8[3] 248[8] (347) 913[3] 938[4] 1311[4] 3848[11] 5601[6] 6346[7]

**Colour Blue (IRE)** *W McCreery* a81 93
3 b f Holy Roman Emperor(IRE) Catch The Blues (IRE) (Bluebird (USA))
4276a[11] 6354a[7]

**Colour Catcher** *Charlie Appleby* a76 58
2 b g Dubawi(IRE) Many Colours (Green Desert (USA))
1575[3] 2057[2] 3387[3] 6363[6]

**Colourfilly** *Ed Walker* a62 23
2 ch f Compton Place Where's Broughton (Cadeaux Genereux)
7407[14] 7867[4] 8112[2]

**Colourful** *Lady Cecil* a80 68
3 b f Champs Elysees Rainbow Lake (Rainbow Quest (USA))
2061[4] 2649[2] 3653[3] 4504[9]

**Colour Guard** *M Al Muhairi* a83 88
6 b g Shamardal(USA) Colorvista (Shirley Heights)
241a[8]

**Colour My World** *Ed McMahon* a67 68
4 gr g With Approval(CAN) Nadeszhda (Nashwan (USA))
264[2] 643[6] 1036[3] 1288[2] 1717[4] 2463[13] (2843)

**Colour Party (IRE)** *John Gosden* a77 74
2 b f Invincible Spirit(IRE) Dress Uniform (USA) (Red Ransom (USA))
7108[13] 7594[2] (7808) 7945[3]

**Colours Of Glory (IRE)** *Charles Hills* a47 61
2 ch f Mastercraftsman(IRE) Valentine Hill (IRE) (Mujadil (USA))
4444[16] 4809[5] 5982[3] 6261[7] 7064[8]

**Colours Of Victory** *Kevin Ryan* 22
2 b c Holy Roman Emperor(IRE) Purple Vision (Rainbow Quest (USA))
5386[9] 6146[9] 6462[12]

**Columbian Roulette (IRE)** *Charles Hills* a62 42
3 b g Bushranger(IRE) Rainbow Lyrics (IRE) (Rainbow Quest (USA))
28[U] 267[2] 3326[14] 3798[2] ◆

**Comanche Chieftain (CAN)** *Michael Appleby* 66
2 b c Broken Vow(USA) Platinum Preferred (CAN) (Vindication (USA))
4884[6] 5982[4] 7084[6]

**Comanchero (IRE)** *Andrew Balding* a75 76
3 b g Camacho Trempjane (Lujain (USA))
(2249) 3198[7] 3518[3] (4191) 4356[4] 4613[2] 5206[3] 6232[9] 6616[3] 7220[5]

**Combat Zone (IRE)** *Mario Hofer* a88 111
8 b g Refuse To Bend(IRE) Zeiting (IRE) (Zieten (USA))
1478a[3]

**Combustible (IRE)** *Daniel Mark Loughnane* a78 81
4 b f Halling(USA) Jazz Baby (IRE) (Fasliyev (USA))
689[8]

**Comedy Club (IRE)** *Charles O'Brien* a72 66
3 b g Iffraaj Love In The Mist (USA) (Silver Hawk (USA))
7435a[13]

**Comedy House** *Michael Madgwick* a70 53
6 b g Auction House(USA) Kyle Akin (Vettori (IRE))
848[2] 1100[2] 6007[5] 6635[9] (7777)

**Comedy King (IRE)** *Luca Cumani* 85
3 bb g Dansili Comic (IRE) (Be My Chief (USA))
1730[7] (2422) 3499[6] 5094[6]

**Comedy Queen (USA)** *Charlie Appleby* a74
2 bb f Distorted Humor(USA) Miss Caerleona (FR) (Caerleon (USA))
(6606)

**Come On Blue Chip (IRE)** *Paul D'Arcy* a100 95
5 b g Holy Roman Emperor(IRE) Rapid Action (USA) (Quest For Fame)
220[3]

**Come On Dave (IRE)** *John Butler* a87 80
5 b g Red Clubs(IRE) Desert Sprite (IRE) (Tagula (IRE))
662[2] (889) (1814) 2364[8] 2933[8] 3693[5] 4128[3] (4981) (5045) 5754 6096[8] 7212[5] 7330[4] 7669[10] 7886[5]

**Come On Galey** *Kristin Stubbs* 13
2 b g Arabian Gleam Magical Flute (Piccolo)
3236[5]

**Come On Lulu** *Shaun Harris* 27
3 ch f Calcutta Flashing Floozie (Muhtarram (USA))
1303[9] 1597[4]

**Come On Sunshine** *Brian Ellison* 68
3 b g Authorized(IRE) Tagula Sunrise (IRE) (Tagula (IRE))
1508[8] 2198[4] 7509[4]

**Come Up And See Me** *J R Jenkins* a37 10
2 b g Cockney Rebel(IRE) Sakhacity (Sakhee (USA))
6660[10] 7037[12] 8000[11] 8221[8]

**Come Uppence** *David Evans* a67 72
2 b g Captain Gerrard(IRE) Waterline Twenty (IRE) (Indian Danehill (IRE))
1276[4] ◆ 2089[5] 2499[4] 4083[5] 5408[4] 6375a[14] 7029[6] 7970[2] 8076[2] 8225[2] 8287[2]

**Comfort And Joy (IRE)** *Lee Carter* a19
4 b f Byron Dodona (Lahib (USA))
276[6]

**Comical** *George Moore* a18 45
5 b g Dubai Destination(USA) Amusing Time (IRE) (Sadler's Wells (USA))
1675[8] 2738[10]

**Comino (IRE)** *Kevin Ryan* 91
3 b g Tagula(IRE) Malta (USA) (Gone West (USA))
1540[4] 2257[11] 4191[4] 4572[7] (5497) (6430) 6895[4] (7282) 7507[2] 7719[20]

**Commanche** *Chris Dwyer* a79 79
5 ch g Sleeping Indian Happy Memories (IRE) (Thatching)
1190[9] 1618[2] 1678[6] 2147[7] 2332[2] 3256[6] ◆ 4128[5] 4406[8] 4765[8] 5060[4] 5726[2] 6235[11] 6558[3] 7337[7] 7687[4] 7847[8]

**Commandable (AUS)** *Ian Semple* a62 56
10 b g Commands(AUS) Achievable (AUS) (Waajib (IRE))
34[5] 258[2] 1602[6] 1758[9] 2473[5] 3609[9]

**Commandaria (USA)** *Jeremy Noseda* a77 70
2 ch f Smart Strike(CAN) Cassis (USA) (Red Ransom (USA))
3076[3] ◆ 5821[2] 6032[2]

**Commander Kirk (IRE)** *Markus Klug* 64
4 b g Holy Roman Emperor(IRE) Kestrel Quest (USA) (Silver Hawk (USA))
7618a[10]

**Commander Patten (IRE)** *Alan Bailey* a83 83
2 ro g Clodovil(IRE) Idle Rich (USA) (Sky Classic (CAN))
2269[2] 2776[2] 3322[10] (4079) 4348[5] 5409[4] 5694[9] 8113[6] 8308[6]

**Commanding Curve (USA)** *Dallas Stewart* a118
3 b r Master Command(USA) Mother (USA) (Lion Hearted (USA))
1964a[2] 3026a[9]

**Commanding Force** *John Bridger* a17
3 b g Authorized(IRE) Ghazal (USA) (Gone West (USA))
6015[P]

**Commanding Jewel (AUS)** *Leon & Troy Corstens* 108
5 br m Commands(AUS) Regard (AUS) (Zabeel (NZ))
7128a[10]

**Commandingpresence (USA)** *John Bridger* a63 73
8 bb m Thunder Gulch(USA) Sehra (USA) (Silver Hawk (USA))
1221[8] 1405[7] 1766[2] 1878[5] 2486[3] 2994[8] 3393[10] 4049[10] 4431[6] 4908[8] 5423[4] 5972[4] 6397[8]

**Commemorative** *Charles Hills* 105
2 ch c Zamindar(USA) Revered (Oasis Dream)
5881[4] (6259) (7104) 7590a[7]

**Commissar** *Ian Williams* a87 80
5 b g Soviet Star(USA) Sari (Faustus (USA))
(627) 655[2] 977[4] (1175) 1299[6] 1553[7] 2405[5] 2851[4] 3172a[7] 3802[6] 4184[4] 4761[14] 5196[9] 6943[10] 8078[6]

**Commissioner (USA)** *Todd Pletcher* a119
3 b c A.P. Indy(USA) Flaming Heart (USA) (Touch Gold (USA))
3026a[2]

**Commodore (IRE)** *George Baker* 74
2 b c Kodiac Deportment (Barathea (IRE))
4270[13] 6517[6] (7308)

**Common Cents** *Ian Williams* a30 35
5 ch g Pivotal Small Change (IRE) (Danzig (USA))
2147[17]

**Common Touch (IRE)** *Willie Musson* a101 96
6 ch g Compton Place Flying Finish (FR) (Priolo (USA))
2707[9] 4442[10] 5189[6] 5665[15] 6097[7]

**Communicator** *Andrew Balding* a98 100
6 b g Motivator Goodie Twosues (Fraam)
285[2] 462[3] 803[4] 1556[3] 2073[3] 5162[3] 5651[16] 6133[3] 7107[9] 7718[4]

**Commute** *D Smaga* 100
4 b f Rail Link Zorleni (Zafonic (USA))
(2821a) 6218a[4]

**Company Secretary (USA)** *Jo Hughes* a67 59
3 gr g Awesome Again(CAN) Maria Elena (USA) (El Prado (IRE))
1173[7] 1632[3] 1852[2] 2679[2] 4426[5] 5027a[5] 7813[2] ◆ 7908[2] 8049[6] 8218[5]

**Competent** *Kristin Stubbs* 34
2 b g Compton Place Pantita (Polish Precedent (USA))
6831[3]

**Complicate (AUS)** *Saeed bin Suroor* a108 108
5 b g Commands(AUS) Chaparra (AUS) (Canny Lad (AUS))
112a[8] 597a[3] 898a[3] 1180a[9] 3960[4] 4438[10] (5778)

**Complicit (IRE)** *Paul Cole* a109 101
3 b c Captain Rio Molomo (Barathea (IRE))
1555[11] 2343[5] 3378[21] 4930a[3] 5687[3] (7066) 7449[4] (7619a) (8018)

**Complimentor (IRE)** *X Thomas-Demeaulte* a104 104
4 ch c Acclamation Lovely Blossom (FR) (Spinning World (USA))
836a[2] 2799a[4] 3997a[7]

**Compton** *Stuart Williams* a93 91
5 ch g Compton Place Look So (Efisio)
(161) ◆ 287[3] 1190[19] 3969[2] 4355[4] 4447[3] (6144) 6892[6]

**Compton Albion (IRE)** *Jeremy Gask* a57 48
4 ch f Compton Place Yomalo (IRE) (Woodborough (USA))
2648[7] 3231[10] 5126[3] 5801[9]

**Compton Bird** *Paul Fitzsimons* a85 83
5 b m Motivator Noble Peregrine (Lomond (USA))
(589) (853) 1577[5] 3968[4] (4354) 5073[9] 6141[11] 6523[7] 6714[10]

**Compton Mill** *Hughie Morrison* a67 75
2 b c Compton Place Classic Millennium (Midyan (USA))
6545[4] ◆ 7353[6]

**Compton Park** *Les Eyre* a94 103
7 ch h Compton Place Corps De Ballet (IRE) (Fasliyev (USA))
1190[4] 1538[8] (4712) (5081) 5444[7] (5888) 6327[15] 6531[23] 7122[11] 7408[11] 7700[6] 7843[9]

**Compton Prince** *Milton Bradley* a69 60
5 ch g Compton Place Malelane (IRE) (Prince Sabo)
192[4] (424) 628[9] 993[3] 1878[8] 2887[10] 3393[5] 6889[9] 7364[10] 7887[6] 8014[3] 8195[2] 8319[4]

**Compton River** *Bryan Smart* a25 68
2 b c Compton Place Inagh River (Fasliyev (USA))
1342[6] 1900[3] 2824[7] 5813[2] 6212[2] 7004[3] 7649[6]

**Compton Silver** *Miss Joey Ellis* a57
4 ch g Haafhd Anna Oleanda (IRE) (Old Vic)
263[3] ◆ 321[2] 661[3] 781[5] 1015[10] 7547[8] 7940[4] 8291[5]

**Comptonspirit** *Brian Baugh* a49 76
10 ch m Compton Place Croeso Cynnes (Most Welcome)
2414[13] 3222[6] 3817[5] 4102[4] 4564[4] 4960[8]

**Compton Viking (IRE)** *Paul Fitzsimons* a47
2 ch c Equiano(FR) Feather Boa (IRE) (Sri Pekan (USA))
6158[8]

**Computer (USA)** *Charles Hills* 77
3 ch c Mizzen Mast(USA) Tolerance (USA) (Seeking The Gold (USA))
1529[7] 2075[9]

**Comrade Bond** *Mark H Tompkins* a77 77
6 ch g Monsieur Bond(IRE) Eurolink Cafe (Grand Lodge (USA))
1616[6] (2527) 2905[8] 5320[9] 7220[3] 7601[7] 7905[7] 8168[3]

**Conceptuelle (FR)** *C Lotoux* a83 79
4 gr f Stormy River(FR) Intellectuelle (Caerleon (USA))
(2192a)

**Concoct (IRE)** *Tom Dascombe* a11
3 b f Aqlaam Jinskys Gift (IRE) (Cadeaux Genereux)
189[10]

**Concrete Mac** *Hughie Morrison* a62 73
3 b g Mastercraftsman(IRE) Merry Diva (Bahamian Bounty)
1570[4] 2278[7] 3518[4] (4674) 6251[5] 7202[6]

**Conducting** *Gay Kelleway* a71 67
6 b g Oratorio(IRE) Aiming (Highest Honor (FR))
(685) 830[2]

**Confessional** *Tim Easterby* a99 99
7 b g Dubawi(IRE) Golden Nun (Bishop Of Cashel)
2074[8] 2353[4] 2766[5] 3241[11] 3666[4] 4188[2] 4892[7] 5445[3] 6131[8] 6760[7] 7280[2] 7441[4] 7700[3]

**Confidential Creek** *Ollie Pears* a67 62
4 b g Sakhee's Secret Upstream (Prince Sabo)
9[4] 258[13] 1602[7] 2907[9]

**Confiture** *Michael Blanshard* a57
3 b f Duke Of Marmalade(IRE) Sandtime (IRE) (Green Desert (USA))
456[5] 1214[6] 1403[10] 2688[12] 4084[9] 4732[10]

**Conflicting** *Charlie Fellowes* a31 76
3 b g Kyllachy Piper's Ash (USA) (Royal Academy (USA))
187[6] 6552[6] 7172[9]

**Conflicting Advice (USA)** *Sir Michael Stoute* a61 72
2 b c Iffraaj Assertive Lass (AUS) (Zeditave (AUS))
7166[2] 7779[4]

**Confucius Legend (IRE)** *Jim Boyle* a58 17
3 b g Oratorio(IRE) Midnight Partner (IRE) (Marju (IRE))
51[6] 488[5] 1812[7] 2694[12]

**Congaree Warrior** *John Butler* a50
4 ch g Congaree(USA) Peace And Love (IRE) (Fantastic Light (USA))
8094[5] 8294[8]

**Conjuring (IRE)** *Mike Murphy* a60 70
2 b f Showcasing Trick (IRE) (Shirley Heights)
2460[8] 5509[3] (6024) 6749[3] ◆ 7237[4]

**Conjuror's Bluff** *Frederick Watson* 31
6 b g Tiger Hill(IRE) Portmeirion (Polish Precedent (USA))
2518[7] 4730[7] 6227[10] 6670[9]

**Connacht Council (IRE)** *W McCreery* a78 71
4 ch g Haatef(USA) Asfurah's Dream (IRE) (Nayef (USA))
790a[2] 4805a[10] 6078a[4]

**Connaught Water (IRE)** *Jonathan Portman* a25 62
3 b g Aussie Rules(USA) Chingford (IRE) (Redback)
1914[7] (3214) 3564[4] 4820[4] 5905[3] 6297[13] 6858[9]

**Connected (FR)** *E Lellouche* 86
2 ch f Linngari(IRE) Syllable (Halling (USA))
6991a[3] 7654a[6]

**Connecticut** *Luca Cumani* 110
3 b c New Approach(IRE) Craigmill (Slip Anchor)
1517[3] ◆ (2334) (3200) ◆ (4622) ◆ 5691[3] 7106[9]

**Connexion Francais** *Tim Etherington* a29 40
3 b f Lucarno(USA) Sainte Gig (FR) (Saint Cyrien (FR))
2517[10] 3653[10] 4875[7] 5598[6] 6627[11] 7225[7]

**Cono Zur (FR)** *Ruth Carr* a60 76
7 b g Anabaa(USA) Alaskan Idol (USA) (Carson City (USA))
1356[10] 1718[8] 2518[6] 3056[5] 3604[2] (4014)

**Conquerant** *Charlie Appleby* a75 84
3 ch g Dubawi(IRE) The World (Dubai Destination (USA))
2466[3] 2696[6] 4368[2] 4587[3] 5400[2] (5814) 6345[6]

**Conquestadim** *Hughie Morrison* a76 66
4 b g Elnadim(USA) Conquestadora (Hernando (FR))
(1798) 2670[6] 3556[7] 4656[2] 6043[2]

**Conquest Eclipse (USA)** *Mark Casse* a104
2 b f Malibu Moon(USA) Grand Traverse Bay (USA) (Repriced (USA))
7606a[7]

**Conquest Harlanate (CAN)** *Mark Casse* a103 100
2 b f Harlan's Holiday(USA) Allison's Pride (USA) (Dixieland Band (USA))
7592a[11]

**Conquest Typhoon (CAN)** *Mark Casse* a92 104
2 b c Stormy Atlantic(USA) Swanky Bubbles (CAN) (Ascot Knight (CAN))
7590a[4]

**Conquete (FR)** *P Bary* a63 81
3 ch f Kyllachy Chesnut Bird (IRE) (Storm Bird (CAN))
3372a[12] 4464a[6]

**Conry (IRE)** *Ian Williams* a79 77
8 ch g Captain Rio Altizaf (Zafonic (USA))
57a[2] 181[7] 646[2] (647) 750[3] 1267[4] 1316[3] 1710[9] (2054) (2548) 3645[5] 4352[2] 4650[7] 4922[15] 4959[3] 5711[5] 5761[5] (6155) 6411[6] 7282[4] 7732[6] 8044[7] 8251[11]

**Conserve (IRE)** *Neil King* a76 70
4 b f Duke Of Marmalade(IRE) Minor Point (Selkirk (USA))
276[2] 581[2] 776[5] 935a[2] 2199[10] 3079[4] 8099[2] 8202[4]

**Consign** *Jeremy Noseda* a97 102
4 b g Dutch Art Maid To Dance (Pyramus (USA))
625[6] 1165[13] 1719[10] 6332[8] (6688) 6892[2] ◆

**Consistant** *Brian Baugh* a64 65
6 b g Reel Buddy(USA) Compact Disc (IRE) (Royal Academy (USA))
121[4] (353) 511[3] ◆ 688[8] 1148[5] 1448[4] 2127[2] 3298[3] 3848[3] (4370) 5897[8]

**Consort (IRE)** *Sir Michael Stoute* 86
2 gr c Lope De Vega(IRE) Mundus Novus (USA) (Unbridled's Song (USA))
(6712) ◆

**Consortium (IRE)** *David Simcock* a54 60
2 b g Teofilo(IRE) Wish List (IRE) (Mujadil (USA))
5947[4] 6652[6] 7372[6]

**Constable Buckley** *Mick Channon* 80
2 b c Naaqoos Naadrah (Muhtathir)
5377[2] 6653[4]

**Constant Applause** *Mrs Ilka Gansera-Leveque* 36
2 b c Showcasing Never Away (Royal Applause)
5874[11] 6212[7]

**Constantine** *Richard Hannon* a72 85
3 b g Holy Roman Emperor(IRE) Whatami (Daylami (IRE))
2921[8] 3538[5] 3882[2] 4404[5] 5081[9] 5603[7] 6891[11] 7337[2]

**Constanzina (FR)** *Mrs A Malzard* a32 32
5 b m Samum(GER) Madame Constanze (IRE) (Mozart (IRE))
1624a[5] 2599a[5] 3048a[5] 4718a[7]

**Contesurmoi (FR)** *P Adda* a74 63
4 b g One Cool Cat(USA) Ymlaen (IRE) (Desert Prince (IRE))
796a[2] 6569a[9]

**Continental Drift (USA)** *Roger Charlton* a76 53
3 bb f Smart Strike(CAN) Intercontinental (Danehill (USA))
2383[7]

**Continuum** *Peter Hedger* 104
5 bb g Dansili Clepsydra (Sadler's Wells (USA))
1398[4] 2143[4] 3449[3] (4213) 4759[6]

**Contributer (IRE)** *Ed Dunlop* a108 115
4 b c High Chaparral(IRE) Serisia (FR) (Exit To Nowhere (USA))
(1170) 1697[3] (3416)

**Convergence (IRE)** *G M Lyons* 103
2 b c Cape Cross(IRE) Zahoo (IRE) (Nayef (USA))
4599a[3] 5735a[5] 6800a[4]

**Conversational (IRE)** *Mick Channon* a80 71
4 b f Thousand Words Alpine Flair (IRE) (Tirol)
(118) 457[8] 674[8]

**Converti** *Carroll Gray* a33 32
10 b g Averti(IRE) Conquestadora (Hernando (FR))
475[6] 537[7] 640[7]

**Convey** *Sir Michael Stoute* a90
2 b c Dansili Insinuate (USA) (Mr Prospector (USA))
(7031)

**Conveyance (USA)** *S Seemar* a100
7 gr h Indian Charlie(USA) Emptythetill (USA) (Holy Bull (USA))
769a[3]

**Conveyor Belt (IRE)** *David O'Meara* 55
3 br f Pivotal Gift Range (IRE) (Spectrum (IRE))
1303[3] 1645[6]

**Convicted (FR)** *Ian Williams* a42 62
2 b c Lawman(FR) Passiflore I (FR) (Sillery (USA))
5494[6] 6743[5] 7344a[10] 8292[12]

**Cookie Ring (IRE)** *Patrick Holmes* a36 46
3 b g Moss Vale(IRE) Talah (Danehill (USA))
8181[4]

**Cool Athlete (IRE)** *David Marnane* a72 70
8 b g Bahri(USA) Perfect Fun (Marju (IRE))
4805a[U]

**Cool Bahamian (IRE)** *Eve Johnson Houghton* a88 85
3 b g Bahamian Bounty Keritana (FR) (One Cool Cat (USA))
1563[9] 2111[9] 2921[5] 3538[3] 4147[6] 4761[7] 5031[6] 6895[9] (7530) 7821[2] 7988[5]

**Cool Baranca (GER)** *Dianne Sayer* 59
8 b m Beat Hollow Cool Storm (IRE) (Rainbow Quest (USA))
1929[7] 2455[2] 2550[2] 5171[7] 6542[5] 7006[6] (7283) 7508[11]

**Cool Beans** *Roy Bowring* a57 60
2 b g Kyllachy Stellar Brilliant (USA) (Kris S (USA))
8205[5]

**Coolcalmcollected (IRE)** *Chris Wall* a61 61
2 b f Acclamation Jalissa (Mister Baileys)
3671[9] 7407[5] 7808[5] ◆

**Cool Choice** *Nick Littmoden* 2
2 b g Pastoral Pursuits Ridotto (Salse (USA))
2612[8] 4541[9]

**Coolfighter (GER)** *N Dooly* a76 85
6 ch g Black Sam Bellamy(IRE) Cool Storm (IRE) (Rainbow Quest (USA))
7476a[8]

**Coolibah (IRE)** *Charles O'Brien* 95
4 b f Peintre Celebre(USA) Honour Bright (IRE) (Danehill (USA))
5024a[10]

**Cool Music (IRE)** *Mel Brittain* a52 74
4 b f One Cool Cat(USA) Musicology (USA) (Singspiel (IRE))
(2389) 3254[18] 5496[7] 7575[10]

**Cool Reception** *Ollie Pears* a7
3 b f Royal Applause Winter Ice (Wolfhound (USA))
645[8] 2389[11] 3097[11] 3601[7] 4974[10]

**Cool Sky** *Ian Williams* a83 78
5 b g Millkom Intersky High (USA) (Royal Anthem (USA))
4940[5] 7566[6] 8062[4]

**Cool Star (FR)** *A Bonin* a73 85
9 ch g Starborough Valverda (USA) (Irish River (FR))
3373a[10]

**Cool Strutter (IRE)** *David O'Meara* 93
2 b c Kodiac Cassava (IRE) (Vettori (IRE))
4109[3] 4409[2] (5091) 5694[5] 6513[11] 7121[5] 7485a[4]

**Cooper** *Kevin Ryan* 31
2 b c Sir Percy Blossom (Warning)
7713[7]

**Cooptado (ARG)** *Doug Watson* a109 102
4 b c Equal Stripes(ARG) Coordinada (ARG) (Ride The Rails (USA))
1178a[5]

**Coorg (IRE)** *Sir Michael Stoute* 56
2 ch c Teofilo(IRE) Creese (Halling (USA))
6551[11]

**Copleys Walk (IRE)** *John Joseph Murphy* a64 90
2 b g Excellent Art Silk Slippers (Oasis Dream)
4814[3] 6053a[2]

**Copperbelt** *Mark Johnston* a69 70
3 b c Royal Applause Luanshya (First Trump)
5570[5] 6421[3] 7063[3]

**Copper Canyon** *Vanja Sandrup* a86 88
6 ch g Haafhd Deep Ravine (USA) (Gulch (USA))
2245a[8]

**Copper Cavalier** *Robert Cowell* a60
3 ch g Haafhd Elle Crystal (Mozart (IRE))
165[6] 280[4] (411) 7376[4] 7548[2] 7883[3] 7972[3] 8090[8] (8286)

**Copper Dock (IRE)** *T G McCourt* a59 53
10 b g Docksider(USA) Sundown (Polish Precedent (USA))
503[4] 511[8] 4556a[6]

**Copper Ern** *Jimmy Fox*
5 ch g Young Ern Croeso Cynnes (Most Welcome)
7733[13]

**Copper Falls** *Mrs A Malzard* a42 50
5 b m Trade Fair Strat's Quest (Nicholas (USA))
(1623a) 4038a[9] 4715a[8]

**Copperopolis** *Roger Charlton* a41 23
2 b c Authorized(IRE) Azeema (IRE) (Averti (IRE))
7414[9] 7667[16] 8067[13]

**Copper To Gold** *Robin Bastiman* a4 51
5 ch m Avonbridge Faithful Beauty (IRE) (Last Tycoon)
2094[11] 2479[8] 3630[2] 4341[U] 5233[6] 6833[8]

**Copperwood** *Lee Carter* a61 84
9 ch g Bahamian Bounty Sophielu (Rudimentary (USA))
49[2] 180[5] 379[8] 685[6] 775[5] 822[7] 953[5] 1302[7] 1923[5] 4738[3] 5425[8] 6394[7]

**Coprah** *Cathrine Erichsen* a57 96
6 b g Bertolini(USA) Oatcake (Selkirk (USA))
3090a[7] 5744a[3]

**Coral Mist** *Charles Hills* 98
3 ch f Bahamian Bounty Treasure Trove (USA) (The Minstrel (CAN))
1435[7] 3357[24]

**Cordero (IRE)** *Wesley A Ward* 87
2 b c Giant's Causeway(USA) Half Queen (USA) (Deputy Minister (CAN))
3448[6]

**Cordial** *Stuart Williams* a72 88
3 b f Oasis Dream Mirabilis (USA) (Lear Fan (USA))
3916[5] (4539) 5204[4] 5501[2] 6153[2] (6468) 6689[8] 7716[10]

**Cordite (IRE)** *Michael Appleby* 107
3 ch c Footstepsinthesand Marion Haste (IRE) (Ali-Royal (IRE))
1516[7] 2377a[5] 3252[5] 6458[8] 7022[3] 7168[8] 7668[4]

**Corlough Mountain** *Paddy Butler* a38 38
10 ch g Inchinor Two Step (Mujtahid (USA))
8102[13]

**Cornborough** *Mark Walford* 75
3 ch g Sir Percy Emirates First (IRE) (In The Wings)
(1344) 1714[4] 7438[3] ◆ 7640[6]

**Corncockle** *David O'Meara* a82 81
3 b f Invincible Spirit(IRE) Alovera (IRE) (King's Best (USA))
149[6] 2390[9] 3386[2] 4488[6] 4977[9] 5912[10]

**Cornish Path** *Henry Candy* a62 80
3 b f Champs Elysees Quintrell (Royal Applause)
1586[7] 2274[4] 3198[2] 4074[8] 4623[2] 5685[3] 6316[2] 7160[8]

**Corn Maiden** *Phil McEntee* a58 67
5 b m Refuse To Bend(IRE) Namat (IRE) (Daylami (IRE))
1874[3] 2614[3] (2874) 3475[7] 3899[2] 4303[3] 4591[2] 5786[2]

**Cornrow** *John Gosden* a94 102
4 ch c New Approach(IRE) Needlecraft (IRE) (Mark Of Esteem (IRE))
(5178) 6124[3] 6752[13] 7276[13]

**Cornwallville (IRE)** *F-H Graffard* a87 96
2 ch c Makfi Morinqua (IRE) (Cadeaux Genereux)
1161[11] 2246[2] 2755a[5] (3029a) 3691a[4] (5118a) 5405a[7] 7317a[7]

**Corporal Maddox** *Ronald Harris* a93 88
7 b g Royal Applause Noble View (USA) (Distant View (USA))
234[4] 372[7] (472) 804[7] 991[3] 1042[4] 1193[13] 1492[10] (1667) 1938[2] 2202[6] 3483[5] 3876[8] 4347[7] 4783[6] 5081[8] 5750[4] 6089[3] 6558[10] 7947[5] 8100[5] 8257[8]

**Correggio** *Micky Hammond* 81
4 ch g Bertolini(USA) Arian Da (Superlative)
(1881) 2234[8] 3254[6] 3499[5] 4349[5] 4710[5] 5299[5] 5999[5] 6491[6]

**Correggio (NZ)** *Murray Johnson* 79
5 b g Excellent Art Magical Moment (Sadler's Wells (USA))
7395a[12]

**Corton Lad** *Keith Dalgleish* a87 89
4 b g Refuse To Bend(IRE) Kelucia (IRE) (Grand Lodge (USA))
1599[7] 2216[3] 3004[3] (3624) 3829[4] (4704) 4827[7] 5633[6] 6479[4] 7402[6] 7702[4]

**Cosette (IRE)** *Henry Candy* 86
3 b f Champs Elysees Luanas Pearl (IRE) (Bahri (USA))
(1812) 2273[3] 3541[5] 4209[2] 4803[2] 5353[4] 6099[2] 6705[7]

**Cosima (FR)** *G Doleuze* a87 84
3 b f Iffraaj My Sara (Mujahid (USA))
5843a[5] 7722a[3]

**Cosmic Cannonball (IRE)** *J S Bolger* 103
4 b g Holy Roman Emperor(IRE) Uimhir A Haon (IRE) (Montjeu (IRE))
6370a[4] 7476a[22]

**Cosmic Chatter** *David Barron* 102
4 b g Paris House Paradise Eve (Bahamian Bounty)
1734[7] 2353[8] 2898[3] 3716[8] 4384[9] 4976[9] 6531[25]

**Cosmic Halo** *Richard Fahey* a78 83
5 ch m Halling(USA) Cosmic Case (Casteddu)
1716[5] 2091[9] 2826[5] 3457[5] 3999[5] 4680[2] 5757[6] (6166) 6491[4] 6870[3] 7350[5]

**Cosmic Ray** *Andrew Balding* a62 76
2 b g Phoenix Reach(IRE) Beat Seven (Beat Hollow)
4731[5] 5519[2] 6279[3] 6719[5] (7156)

**Cosmic Statesman** *Richard Fahey* 59
2 ch g Halling(USA) Cosmic Case (Casteddu)
4659[5] 5167[5] 6146[5] ◆ 6648[5]

**Cosquillas (IRE)** *Mark Johnston* a65 40
3 b f Selkirk(USA) Crystany (IRE) (Green Desert (USA))
50[6] (355) 613[3] 6009[8]

**Cosseted** *James Fanshawe* 97
4 b f Pivotal Fondled (Selkirk (USA))
1716[2] (2331) 2783[2] (3644) 4945[7] ◆ 6257[10] 7105[14]

**Costa Del Fortune (IRE)** *Paul Morgan*
5 ch m Heliostatic(IRE) Midris (IRE) (Namid)
320[7]

**Costa Filey** *Ed Vaughan* a72 75
3 b g Pastoral Pursuits Cosmic Destiny (IRE) (Soviet Star (USA))
(82) 2122[3] 4043[6] 4862[3] 7931[9] 8186[11]

**Costume (NZ)** *Graeme & Debbie Rogerson* 106
5 b m Savabeel(AUS) Disguised (NZ) (O'Reilly (NZ))
7602a[12]

**Cotai Glory** *Charles Hills* 111
2 ch c Exceed And Excel(AUS) Continua (USA) (Elusive Quality (USA))
2428[7] 3322[6] ◆ (4103) 4398[2] (4757) 6286[U] 6966a[16]

**Cotil Red (FR)** *J-V Toux* a38
2 ch c Redback Cotil Lady (FR) (Northern Crystal)
7027a[10]

**Coto (IRE)** *M J Tynan* a62 81
2 b f Fast Company(IRE) Let Me Shine (USA) (Dixie Union (USA))
2569a[4] 3353[13]

**Cottam Maybel** *Michael Easterby* a45 33
5 b m Doyen(IRE) Northern Bird (Interrex (CAN))
642[6] 861[6] 1428[9]

**Cotton Club (IRE)** *Rod Millman* a74 82
3 b g Amadeus Wolf Slow Jazz (USA) (Chief's Crown (USA))
954[5] 1214[4] (1588) 1947[2] 2506[2] 3197[4] 3587[4] 4332[4] 5094[7] 5877[2] 6608[8] 7135[7]

**Cougar Mountain (IRE)** *A P O'Brien* 112
3 b c Fastnet Rock(AUS) Descant (USA) (Nureyev (USA))
4201[5] 5654[9] 6134[12]

**Couleur Du Large (FR)** *C Lerner* a54 29
2 gr f Silver Frost(IRE) Eugenia Montez (FR) (Beaudelaire (USA))
7163a[7]

**Couloir Extreme (IRE)** *Gary Moore* a76 83
4 gr g Verglas(IRE) Chica Roca (USA) (Woodman (USA))
2627[8] 3472[7] 3874[6] 4501[8] (4985) 5435[5]

**Coulsty (IRE)** *Richard Hannon* 110
3 b c Kodiac Hazium (IRE) (In The Wings)
(2343) 3352[7] 4127[7] 4937[2] 5410[2] (5963a)

**Counterfeiter** *Saeed bin Suroor* a73 84
4 b g Singspiel(IRE) Grain Of Truth (Gulch (USA))
681a[15]

**Counterglow (IRE)** *Charlie Appleby* a91 69
5 b g Echo Of Light Quintellina (Robellino (USA))
207a[11]

**Countermand** *Andrew Balding* 56
2 b g Authorized(IRE) Answered Prayer (Green Desert (USA))
7537[7]

**Counterproof (IRE)** *John Gosden* a75 47
2 br c Authorized(IRE) Ellasha (Shamardal (USA))
7666[12] 7811[3] (8166)

**Counter Ridge (SAF)** *Marco Botti* a90 95
5 b m Tiger Ridge(USA) Counterpoise (SAF) (Counter Action (SAF))
5728[7] 6260[2] 7543[4] 7802[9] 7923[11]

**Countess Lovelace** *Pat Phelan* a60
4 b f Byron Muwasim (USA) (Meadowlake (USA))
491[4]

**Countess Lupus (IRE)** *Lisa Williamson*
3 b f Amadeus Wolf Papaha (FR) (Green Desert (USA))
15[4] 165[3] 216[4] 374[6] 608[8] 666[3] 855[6] 994[6] 1047[5] 5853[11] 6030[6] 6816[5] 7355[U]

**Count Montecristo (FR)** *Kevin Ryan* 68
2 b c Siyouni(FR) Blackberry Pie (USA) (Gulch (USA))
6509[6] 7123[8]

**Count Paris (USA)** *A bin Huzaim* a79 72
8 ch h Pivotal Dearly (Rahy (USA))
239a[14]

**Country Blue (FR)** *Mrs A Malzard* 46
5 bl h Country Reel(USA) Exica (FR) (Exit To Nowhere (USA))
1623a[8] 2598a[5] 2591a[2] 3496a[2] 4038a[7] 4715a[4] 5228a[7] 6186a[3]

**Country Drive (USA)** *Ed Dunlop* 71
3 ch f Shirocco(GER) Call Mariah (USA) (Dixie Union (USA))
4569[6]

**Country Gorl (FR)** *P Sogorb* 80
2 bb f Country Reel(USA) Gorl D'Ouilly (FR) (Man O West (FR))
3027a[7] 4603a[3]

**Coup De Grace (IRE)** *Pat Phelan* a74 74
5 b g Elusive City(USA) No Way (IRE) (Rainbows For Life (CAN))
(292) ◆ 758[5] 1418[4] 7129[7]

**Coup De Theatre (FR)** *P Van De Poele* a106 107
5 ch h Gold Away(IRE) Storma (FR) (Starborough)
1371a[7]

**Courageous Rock (USA)** *Ed Vaughan* a82 82
3 bb g Rock Hard Ten(USA) To The Brim (CAN) (Ascot Knight (CAN))
1394[5] 3432[4] 4325[2]

**Courcy (FR)** *G Botti* a82 79
4 b g Mizzen Mast(USA) Insan Mala (IRE) (Bahhare (USA))
6992a[6]

**Courier** *Lee Carter* a56 48
2 b f Equiano(FR) Pivotal Drive (IRE) (Pivotal)
5344[11] 6408[6] 6852[9] 7165[5] 7740[2] 8115[4]

**Coursing** *Sir Mark Prescott Bt* a56 20
2 bb f Kyllachy Granuaile O'Malley (IRE) (Mark Of Esteem (IRE))
7004[8] 7192[11] 7454[6] 7780[6] 7948[7]

**Courtesy Call (IRE)** *Nicky Henderson* a92 68
5 br g Manduro(GER) Three Wrens (IRE) (Second Empire (IRE))
2920[3]

**Courtezan** *Jamie Osborne* a18
3 gr f Captain Gerrard(IRE) Ultimate Court (IRE) (Kendor (FR))
7818[10] 7921[7] 8258[10]

**Courtofversailles (USA)** *A Fabre* 93
2 b c Giant's Causeway(USA) Measure (USA) (Seeking The Gold (USA))
4953a[7] 6570a[7]

**Court Room (IRE)** *John Gosden* a79 79
3 b c Cape Cross(IRE) Reform Act (USA) (Lemon Drop Kid (USA))
1069[4] 1258[2] (7418)

**Cousin Khee** *Hughie Morrison* a95 41
7 b g Sakhee(USA) Cugina (Distant Relative)
3574[13] 4077[7] 4736[8] 5259[2] (5572) 6156[3] 6664[5] 7650[2] 7995[2] 8296[3]

**Covert Desire** *Ismail Mohammed* a79 75
6 ch h Pivotal Secret Flame (Machiavellian (USA))
238a[3]

**Covert Love (IRE)** *Hugo Palmer* a60
2 b f Azamour(IRE) Wing Stealth (IRE) (Hawk Wing (USA))
7354[5]

**Cowslip** *George Moore* a8 61
5 b m Tobougg(IRE) Forsythia (Most Welcome)
1359[9] 1605[5] 2139[10] 2900[3] 5200[7] 5794[4] 7007[6] 7508[7]

**Coyled Spring (IRE)** *Tony Coyle* 47
2 b f Baltic King Abbey Park (USA) (Known Fact (USA))
5086[5] 5443[11]

**Crackentorp** *Tim Easterby* a53 94
9 b g Generous(IRE) Raspberry Sauce (Niniski (USA))
2259[10] 2787[14] 3250[8] 3622[4]

**Cracker** *Ralph Beckett* a54
2 b f Smart Strike(CAN) Tottie (Fantastic Light (USA))
7659[4]

**Crackerjack King (IRE)** *David A Hayes & Tom Dabernig* 110
6 rg h Shamardal(USA) Claba Di San Jore (IRE) (Barathea (IRE))
7127a[12]

**Crack Shot (IRE)** *Clive Brittain* 75
2 ch c Lope De Vega(IRE) Slap Shot (IRE) (Lycius (USA))
3474[7] 4885[2] 7561[5]

**Crack The Whip (IRE)** *J-V Toux* a56
3 b f Whipper(USA) Curve (IRE) (Desert Style (IRE))
5959a[7]

**Cradle Of Life (IRE)** *Ed Dunlop* 66
3 ch f Notnowcato Pursuit Of Life (Pursuit Of Love)
1423[12]

**Crafted (IRE)** *Mark Johnston* a70 78
3 b g Shamardal(USA) Designed (Zamindar (USA))
1805[3] (3389) ◆ 3647[3] (3846) ◆ 4017[2]

**Craftsmanship (FR)** *Robert Eddery* a67 82
3 ch c Mastercraftsman(IRE) Jennie Jerome (IRE) (Pivotal)
1620a[7] 2027[4] (2805) 3144[3] 4982[4] 6990[6] (7514) 7732[9]

**Craftybird** *Gary Moore* 27
3 ch f Mastercraftsman(IRE) Tobaranama (IRE) (Sadler's Wells (USA))
7002[7]

**Crafty Business (IRE)** *Gary Moore* a63 21
3 b g Bushranger(IRE) Champion Tipster (Pursuit Of Love)
1831[5] 2126[6] 2682[8] 3114[9] 4263[8] 4545[9] 6022[5] 6995[10]

**Crafty Choice** *Richard Hannon* 103
2 b c Intikhab(USA) Song Of Passion (IRE) (Orpen (USA))
4270[6] 4676[4] (5029) (5645) ◆ (7041) (7383) 7721a[4]

**Crafty Exit** *William Knight* a55 64
3 gr g Mastercraftsman(IRE) Demerger (USA) (Distant View (USA))
1680[5] 2996[9] 4074[10]

**Crafty Roberto** *Alex Hales* a40 41
6 ch g Intikhab(USA) Mowazana (IRE) (Galileo (IRE))
6274[9]

**Crafty Spell** *Mark Johnston* a28 37
3 ro f Mastercraftsman(IRE) Isle Of Flame (Shirley Heights)
1269[4] 1840[8]

**Craggaknock** *Mark Walford* 76
3 b g Authorized(IRE) Goodie Twosues (Fraam)
1542[11] 2735[7] (3789) 4921[4] 5465[8]

**Crakehall Lad (IRE)** *Alan Swinbank* a76 72
3 ch g Manduro(GER) My Uptown Girl (Dubai Destination (USA))
2506[8] 3303[8] 5682[2] (6216) 6539[3] 6832[5] (7247) 7500[12]

**Cravat** *Ed de Giles* a73 80
5 b g Dubai Destination(USA) Crinolette (IRE) (Sadler's Wells (USA))
655[12] (1040) 1121[5] (1717) 2519[9] 2862[2] 3190[7] 3878[4]

**Crawford Avenue** *Clive Cox* 71
2 b f Equiano(FR) Miss Meggy (Pivotal)
2107[6] 3215[2] 3799[3]

**Crazee Diamond** *Mick Channon* a70 49
3 b f Rock Of Gibraltar(IRE) Final Dynasty (Komaite (USA))
731[2] (994) 1379[7] 2943[7]

**Crazy Chic (IRE)** *Marco Botti* a83 81
3 gr g Exceed And Excel(AUS) Martines (FR) (Linamix (FR))
(5417) 6020[3] 7159[8]

**Crazy Train** *Keiran Burke* 29
5 ch m Sir Harry Lewis(USA) Vent D'Aout (IRE) (Imp Society (USA))
2667[5] 2846[10] 3315[16] 4738[13] 4911[13]

**Createur (IRE)** *Alain Couetil* 91
3 b g Muhtathir Cracovie (Caerleon (USA))
3810a[6]

**Creative Genius** *Ed Walker* 42
2 b c Acclamation Divine Power (Kyllachy)
3706[5] 4787[8]

**Crepusculedesdieux (FR)** *M Delcher Sanchez* a82 78
3 b g Honours List(IRE) Pousselea (IRE) (Docksider (USA))
3372a[15]

**Cresselia (FR)** *S Smrczek* 78
3 b f Sinndar(IRE) Honorable Love (Highest Honor (FR))
2978a[2]

**Crew Cut (IRE)** *Stuart Williams* a77 91
6 gr g Acclamation Carabine (USA) (Dehere (USA))
1975[17] 2503[6] 2992[7] 4447[6] 5437[4] 7600[4]

**Cricklewood Green (USA)** *Richard Hannon* a84 87
3 ch g Bob And John(USA) B Berry Brandy (USA) (Event Of The Year (USA))
1696[4] 2112[3] 2496[6] 4104[3] 6301[7] 7634[3] 7870[9] 8080[4]

**Crikey (IRE)** *Kevin Ryan* a45 65
2 b c Kodiac Callanish (Inchinor)
4790[5] 5922[5] 6319[4] 6629[6] 7258[10]

**Crisis Averted (IRE)** *Richard Fahey* a79 74
3 ch g Compton Place Luxuria (IRE) (Kheleyf (USA))
(195) ◆ 501[3] (936) 3271[10] 3484[5] 4660[5] 6898[9]

**Crisolles (FR)** *J-C Rouget* a97 110
3 b f Le Havre(IRE) Sandsnow (IRE) (Verglas (IRE))
1782a[3] 5545a[2] 6969a[11]

**Crisscrossed** *Amanda Perrett* a61
2 b c Oasis Dream Double Crossed (Caerleon (USA))
7926[3] ◆

**Cristal Fashion (IRE)** *G M Lyons* a70 96
3 b f Jeremy(USA) Mango Groove (IRE) (Unfuwain (USA))
2263a[6] 3285a[7]

**Cristina's Journey (USA)** *Dale Romans* a105
2 b f Any Given Saturday(USA) Toss The Feather (USA) (Dixie Union (USA))
7606a[11]

**Cristoforo Colombo (USA)** *A P O'Brien* a100 107
4 b c Henrythenavigator(USA) La Traviata (USA) (Johannesburg (USA))
1473a[4]

**Cristy's Call (IRE)** *Gavin Cromwell* a66 62
5 ch g Danroad(AUS) Absolute Glee (USA) (Kenmare (FR))
7961a[8]

**Criteria (IRE)** *John Gosden* a76 105
3 b f Galileo(IRE) Aleagueoftheirown (IRE) (Danehill Dancer (IRE))
1424[3] (1797) 2152[2] 3376[3] 4443[2] 5479a[4] 6255[3] 6708[4]

**Criterion (NZ)** *David A Hayes & Tom Dabernig* 116
4 ch c Sebring(AUS) Mica's Pride (AUS) (Bite The Bullet (USA))
7127a[2] 7467a[7] 7602a[5] 8154a[3]

**Critical Risk (IRE)** *Brian Meehan* 77
2 ch g Pivotal High Reserve (Dr Fong (USA))
2837[3] ◆ 3381[2] 4424[6]

**Crius (IRE)** *Daniel Kubler* a88 100
5 b h Heliostatic(IRE) Fearless Flyer (IRE) (Brave Act)
145[7]

**Croi An Or (IRE)** *T Stack* a96 102
5 b g Windsor Knot(IRE) Exponent (USA) (Exbourne (USA))
4771a[12]

**Crooked Arrow (IRE)** *Marjorie Fife* a55
6 b g Galileo(IRE) Mythologie (FR) (Bering)
649[4] 1035[5] 1495[5]

**Cropley (IRE)** *Ann Stokell* a52 65
5 gr g Galileo(IRE) Niyla (IRE) (Darshaan)
1167[9] 1915[2] 2055[2] 7650[6] 7913[4] 7951[4] 8261[8]

**Croquembouche (IRE)** *Ed de Giles* a52 92
5 b g Acclamation Wedding Cake (IRE) (Groom Dancer (USA))
1399[6] 3217[8] 3574[12] 4104[4] 4710[3] (5095) 6098[9] (6357) 7289[10]

**Crosse Fire** *Scott Dixon* a70 71
2 b g Monsieur Bond(IRE) Watersilk (IRE) (Fasliyev (USA))
2612[4] 4790[7] 5242[2] 5714[6] 7649[2] 7714[4] 7917[4]

**Crossley** *Geoffrey Oldroyd* a58 67
5 ch g Monsieur Bond(IRE) Dispol Diamond (Sharpo)
2843[4] 6122[9] 6454[6] 7188[5] 7248[13]

**Crouching Harry (IRE)** *Anabel K Murphy* a61 58
5 b g Tiger Hill(IRE) Catwalk Dreamer (IRE) (Acatenango (GER))
1874[6] 2614[4] 2836[5] (3852) 5076[6] 5121[2] 7518[5] (8021) 8193[5]

**Crowded** *Charlie Appleby* 72
3 ch g Pivotal Bustling (Danehill (USA))
3925[7] 4368[5] 4984[4] 5647[5]

**Crowdmania** *Mark Johnston* a92 91
3 ch g Shamardal(USA) Riotous Applause (Royal Applause)
157[2] (217) (955) (1013) 1513[10] 1861[2] 2111[4] (2544) 3378[29] 4447[5] 4671[3] 4922[16] 5258[2] 5348[2] 5649[2] 6145[7] 6411[3] 6792[3] 7081[7] 7438[8]

**Crow Down (IRE)** *Simon Waugh* 68
5 b g Oratorio(IRE) Louve Sereine (FR) (Sadler's Wells (USA))
4454[9]

**Crowley's Law** *Tom Dascombe* a79 104
3 b f Dubawi(IRE) Logic (Slip Anchor)
1956[2] (2510) (2840) ◆ 3357[11] 3983[3] 5312[8] 6164a[2] 7553[9]

**Crown Choice** *Jedd O'Keeffe* a76 50
9 b g King's Best(USA) Belle Allemande (CAN) (Royal Academy (USA))
102[8] 319[9] 562[7]

**Crown Command (IRE)** *William Muir* 78
2 ch c Lope De Vega(IRE) Pivotal Role (Pivotal)
7234[2] 7561[4]

**Crown Green** *Karen Tutty* 24
2 b f Royal Applause Grasshoppergreen (IRE) (Barathea (IRE))
6115[13] 6860[9] 7245[12]

**Crowning Star (IRE)** *Steve Woodman* a55 56
5 b g Royal Applause Dossier (Octagonal (NZ))
7347[8] 7854[8] 7986[9] 8097[7]

**Crown Of Aragon** *A Oliver* a74 80
3 b g Archipenko(USA) Midnight Allure (Aragon)
2883[4] (3712) 7435a[8]

**Crown Pleasure (IRE)** *Willie Musson* a66 68
3 b f Royal Applause Tarbiyah (Singspiel (IRE))
2431[7] 4623[6] 5394[8] 6613[6] 7187[3] 7570[2] 8050[2]

**Crown The Kitten (USA)** *Wesley A Ward* 90
2 b g Kitten's Joy(USA) Queen Stephanie (USA) (Proud Citizen (USA))
3448[10]

**Crucible** *Daniel Kubler* 20
3 b g Danehill Dancer(IRE) Baize (Efisio)
1680[9]

**Cruck Realta** *Mick Channon* 97
4 b f Sixties Icon Wansdyke Lass (Josr Algarhoud (IRE))
5669[7] 6098[7]

**Cruise Tothelimit (IRE)** *Ian Williams* a72 92
6 b g Le Vie Dei Colori Kiva (Indian Ridge)
2110[13] 2562[7] 2732[2] 2849[3] 3216[7] 3749[3] 4391[2] 4531[2] 4925[5] 5199[4] 5411[4] 5888[3] (6094) (6150) 6511[19] 6744[8] 7233[11] 7669[6]

**Crusading (USA)** *Mark Johnston* a58
2 b c Street Cry(IRE) Danelagh (AUS) (Danehill (USA))
7827[4] 8205[4]

**Cry Fury** *Gary Moore* a88 96
6 b g Beat Hollow Cantanta (Top Ville)
160[6]

**Cry Joy (USA)** *Charlie Appleby* a85
3 b c Street Cry(IRE) Blushing Ogygian (USA) (Ogygian (USA))
5831[11] 6677[6]

**Crysdal** *David Lanigan* 57
3 b f Dalakhani(IRE) Crystal Music (USA) (Nureyev (USA))
4446[7] 5772[5]

**Crystal Diamond** *F Head* a73 105
3 b f Teofilo(IRE) Diamond Dance (FR) (Dancehall (USA))
6917a[2] (7768a)

**Crystalin (IRE)** *Marco Botti* a62
2 b f Arcano(IRE) Loose Julie (IRE) (Cape Cross (IRE))
7809[5] 8173[11] 8288[11]

**Crystalized (IRE)** *Dean Ivory* a54 57
3 ch f Rock Of Gibraltar(IRE) Magnificent Bell (IRE) (Octagonal (NZ))
401[7] 745[5] 1211[4] 1833[3] (2045) 3214[2] 3564[7] 4055[6]

**Crystal Lake (IRE)** *Ralph Beckett* a89 95
3 gr c Verglas(IRE) Entail (USA) (Riverman (USA))
(1173) (1540) (2063) 2781[3] 4198[5] 4551[4] (4982) 5274[9]

**Crystal Malt (IRE)** *Richard Hannon* 74
2 b f Intikhab(USA) Elegantly (IRE) (Rock Of Gibraltar (IRE))
2557[3] 3267[2] 3888[2] 4604[10] 6749[10] 7406[6]

**Crystal Nymph (IRE)** *Richard Hannon* a72 81
3 ch f Rock Of Gibraltar(IRE) Flower Of Kent (USA) (Diesis)
1846[3] (2277) 3085[4] 4504[8] 5430[4] 6608[7]

**Crystal Pearl** *Mark H Tompkins* a73 73
3 b f Beat Hollow Missouri (Charnwood Forest (IRE))
1635[7] 2273[4] 4051[4] 6239[9] 6981[9] 7359[3]

**Crystal Wish** *Kevin Ryan* 59
2 b f Exceed And Excel(AUS) Crystal Mountain (USA) (Monashee Mountain (USA))
3107[9] 3841[3] 4510[4] 5014[6]

**Crystal Zvezda** *Sir Michael Stoute* a77 69
2 ch f Dubawi(IRE) Crystal Star (Mark Of Esteem (IRE))
6521[3] ◆ (7549) ◆

**Ctappers** *Michael Madgwick* a46 63
5 b g Imperial Dancer Stride Home (Absalom)
246[10] 656[9] 2923[13]

**Cubalibre (FR)** *P Sogorb* a86 102
4 bb g Early March Shereda (IRE) (Indian Ridge)
8150a[9]

**Cubanita** *Ralph Beckett* 111
5 b m Selkirk(USA) Caribana (Hernando (FR))
(1434) 2315[11] 2764[7] 6546[3] 7273[6] 7603a[2]

**Cueca (FR)** *Jonathan Portman* a54 51
3 b f Country Reel(USA) Costa Packet (IRE) (Hussonet (USA))
1832[4] 3087[14] 3588[8] 4732[7] 4970[10] 6194[4] 6613[4] 7021[6] 7632[3]

**Cumbrianna** *Bryan Smart* a64 64
2 b f Hellvelyn Positivity (Monsieur Bond (IRE))
2652[2] 5264[3] 6489[6] (7685)

**Cunning Act** *Jonathan Portman*
6 ch g Act One Saffron Fox (Safawan)
1981[P]

**Cunning Plan (IRE)** *Raymond York* a31 37
7 ch g Bachelor Duke(USA) Madamaa (IRE) (Alzao (USA))
4327[7]

**Cupulation** *Amy Weaver* a54 40
2 b g Stimulation(IRE) Coffee Cup (IRE) (Royal Academy (USA))
2642[8] 3570[6] 3658[5] 5507[2] 6040[9] 6563[6] 7014[13]

**Curbyourenthusiasm (IRE)** *David Simcock* a70 81
3 gr g Mastercraftsman(IRE) Mohican Princess (Shirley Heights)
1808[3] 2492[2] ◆ 3673[3] 5276[6]

**Curious Mind** *Sir Mark Prescott Bt* a76 28
4 b f Dansili Intrigued (Darshaan)
7416[14]

**Curlew (IRE)** *Chris Down* a26 16
8 b g Cape Cross(IRE) Billbill (USA) (Storm Cat (USA))
754[9] 1100[7]

**Curren Mirotic (JPN)** *Osamu Hirata* 118
6 ch g Heart's Cry(JPN) Star Mie (USA) (A.P. Indy (USA))
8151a[5]

**Cursory Glance (USA)** *Roger Varian* a76 113
2 b f Distorted Humor(USA) Time Control (Sadler's Wells (USA))
(2460) (3415) 5608[2] (6372a)

**Curved** *Lady Cecil* a68 3
3 br f Oasis Dream Passage Of Time (Dansili)
3174[8] 4966[5] 6238[6] 7044[10] (Dead)

**Custom Cut (IRE)** *David O'Meara* a104 120
5 b g Notnowcato Polished Gem (IRE) (Danehill (USA))
1162[3] 1473a[2] 2150[2] 2765[8] 3252[3] (3731) (4711) (5361a) (5690) (6710) 7274[8]

**Custom House (IRE)** *John E Long* a57 52
6 b g Tale Of The Cat(USA) L'Acajou (CAN) (Gulch (USA))
81[6] 184[7] 290[9] 858[11]

**Cuthbert (IRE)** *Michael Attwater* a46 35
7 ch g Bertolini(USA) Tequise (IRE) (Victory Note (USA))
211[9] 288[10] 851[7] 1386[11] 1668[12] 5138[12] 7546[9] 8198[9]

**Cyclone** *Jonjo O'Neill* a13 88
4 b g Teofilo(IRE) Ascot Cyclone (USA) (Rahy (USA))
5379[8]

**Cyflymder (IRE)** *David C Griffiths* a60 60
8 b g Mujadil(USA) Nashwan Star (IRE) (Nashwan (USA))
288[5] 310[4] 421[5] 537[4] 671[8] 1596[5] 2219[2] 3233[4] 3528[3] 3645[6] 4055[2] (4266) 4578[6] 5139[5] 5833[2] 6481[7] 8137[7] 8311[11]

**Cygnet** *Peter Bowen* a19 90
8 b g Dansili Ballet Princess (Muhtarram (USA))
85[8]

**Cymro (IRE)** *Tom Dascombe* 77
2 gr c Dark Angel(IRE) Dictatrice (FR) (Anabaa (USA))
2756[2] 6420[4] 6694[2] 7328[2]

**Cypress Point (FR)** *Ed Vaughan* a42 38
3 gr f Oratorio(IRE) Miss Sazanica (FR) (Zafonic (USA))
1024[8] 2109[10] 3074[7]

**Cyril** *Kevin Ryan* a70 70
2 b g Rail Link Nurse Gladys (Dr Fong (USA))
6268[5] ◆ 6668[3] 7097[5]

**Czech It Out (IRE)** *Amanda Perrett* 91
4 b g Oratorio(IRE) Naval Affair (IRE) (Last Tycoon)
1943[4] 2500[2] 2747[8]

**Daaree (IRE)** *Saeed bin Suroor* a89 72
4 b c Teofilo(IRE) Mawaakeb (USA) (Diesis)
5150[3] 5730[4] (6274) (6855) (7402) 7703[P]

**Daar Rashid (USA)** *M Al Muhairi* a73
4 b c Exceed And Excel(AUS) Sayyedati Symphony (USA) (Gone West (USA))
239a[12]

**Dabadiyan (IRE)** *M Halford* a107 108
4 b g Zamindar(USA) Dabista (IRE) (Highest Honor (FR))
205a[5] 598a[4] 900a[5] 1177a[6] 3764a[4] 5736a[5]

**Dabayin (FR)** *M Boutin* a53 69
3 b f Great Journey(JPN) Mandaley (FR) (Goldneyev (USA))
2978a[12]

**Dabuki (FR)** *Geoffrey Harker* a64 59
4 b g Desert Style(IRE) Semenova (FR) (Green Tune (USA))
2520[9] 3301[6] (3843) 4296[10] 4979[6] 5716[9] 6597[12] 7279[7] 7628[6] 7895[12]

**Daddy D T (USA)** *John W Sadler* a93 105
2 ch r Scat Daddy(USA) Issues (USA) (Awesome Again (CAN))
7590a[3]

**Daddy Long Legs (USA)** *M F De Kock* a109 105
5 ch h Scat Daddy(USA) Dreamy Maiden (USA) (Meadowlake (USA))
111a[6] 307a[10] 398a[12]

**Daddy's Kid (USA)** *Reid Nagle* 104
3 b g Scat Daddy(USA) Snow Kid (USA) (Lemon Drop Kid (USA))
6949a[2]

**Da Do Run Run** *Brian Meehan* 84
4 b g Sixties Icon Fascinatin Rhythm (Fantastic Light (USA))
1651[2]

**Dad's Girl** *Ollie Pears* 65
2 ch f Sakhee's Secret China Cherub (Inchinor)
2615[7] 4286[2] (5561) 7038[9]

**Dafeef** *Doug Watson* a99 101
7 b g Medicean Almahab (USA) (Danzig (USA))
112a[3] 308a[12] 396a[6]

**Daghash** *Stuart Kittow* a80 81
5 b g Tiger Hill(IRE) Zibet (Kris)
8001[4] 8164[9]

**Dagher** *Peter Chapple-Hyam* 79
2 b c New Approach(IRE) Sakhya (IRE) (Barathea (IRE))
6125[8] (6860)

**Daidaidai (FR)** *Gary Moore* a54
4 b g Lando(GER) Noble World (GER) (Winged Love (IRE))
7846[15] 8021[6]

**Daily Advertiser (USA)** *Tony Carroll* a48
6 b g Street Cry(IRE) Silabteni (USA) (Nureyev (USA))
1034[4] 1268[6]

**Daisie Cutter** *Graeme McPherson* a34 21
4 b f Tobougg(IRE) Bowled Out (GER) (Dansili)
1288[5] 1865[7]

**Daisy Boy (IRE)** *Stuart Williams* 76
3 b g Cape Cross(IRE) Muluk (IRE) (Rainbow Quest (USA))
2927[2] (4789) 5336[2] (6649) 7309[7]

**Daisy's Secret** *George Baker* a59 59
3 ch f Sakhee's Secret Darling Daisy (Komaite (USA))
2681[6] 4029[6] 6247[6]

**Dakar Style (FR)** *E Lellouche* a78 79
4 b c Desert Style(IRE) Winter Ice (USA) (Kingmambo (USA))
6992a[11]

**Dakota Canyon (IRE)** *Richard Fahey* a71 77
5 b g Rock Of Gibraltar(IRE) Dakota Sioux (IRE) (College Chapel)
410[5] 1881[2] 2234[7] 2607[2] 2912[2] 3254[11] 3718[4]

**Dakota City** *P Bary* a62 86
3 b c Three Valleys(USA) West Dakota (USA) (Gone West (USA))
5027a[4]

**Daksha (FR)** *Waldemar Hickst* 107
4 b f Authorized(IRE) Dareen (IRE) (Rahy (USA))
(1827a) 2631a[3] 3873a[6] 6914a[2] 7482a[5] 7736a[7]

**Dalaki (IRE)** *Jim Boyle* a65 76
3 b g Dalakhani(IRE) Lunda (IRE) (Soviet Star (USA))
(1657) 2363[4] 4887[5] 5521[2] 6034[6] 6649[6] 8041[8] 8197[4]

**Dalarosso** *Ed Dunlop* a63 65
3 b g Dalakhani(IRE) Jamboretta (IRE) (Danehill (USA))
1401[6] 1635[6]

**Dalasi (IRE)** *Henry Candy* 62
3 b f Dalakhani(IRE) Holly's Kid (USA) (Pulpit (USA))
3804[5] 4500[5] 4984[6] 5980[8] 7309[12]

**Dalasiri (IRE)** *Sabrina J Harty* a60 84
5 gr g Dylan Thomas(IRE) Dalataya (IRE) (Sadler's Wells (USA))
4746a[18] 6349a[15]

**Dalayna (FR)** *A De Royer-Dupre* 109
4 b f Anabaa(USA) Daltaiyma (IRE) (Doyoun)
2155[7] 7070a[2] 7559a[8] 7916a[2]

**Dalgig** *David Pipe* a75 81
4 b g New Approach(IRE) Bright Halo (IRE) (Bigstone (IRE))
2924[3] 3472[3] 4116[2] 4354[2] 5259[3] 5898[6] (6986) 7516[6] (7754) 7918[P] 8029[10]

**Daliance (IRE)** *Lucy Wadham* a86 67
5 ch g Dalakhani(IRE) Everlasting Love (Pursuit Of Love)
652[3]

**Dalkova** *J P Murtagh* a32 100
5 b m Galileo(IRE) Dalasyla (IRE) (Marju (IRE))
4276a[2] 6354a[16]

**Dalmarella Dancer (IRE)** *K R Burke* a76 75
3 gr f Mastercraftsman(IRE) Ting A Greeley (Mr Greeley (USA))
1427[2] (1888) 2274[6] 2740[5] 3885[3] ◆ 4472[6] 4802[3] 5505[4] 6945[5] 7416[13]

**Dalmatia (IRE)** *Sir Michael Stoute* a81 79
3 gr f Cape Cross(IRE) Dalataya (IRE) (Sadler's Wells (USA))
2881[2] 3750[2] 4434[6] 6238[3] 7210[2] 7734[3]

**Damascene** *Marco Botti* a74 83
3 b c Oasis Dream Acts Of Grace (USA) (Bahri (USA))
1353[6] 1861[4] 2506[4] (3897) ◆

**Dame Des Lys (FR)** *J Heloury* a68 70
2 b f Layman(USA) Dame Oceane (FR) (Ocean Of Wisdom (USA))
1402a[3] 4603a[8] 5619a[2]

**Dame Liberty (IRE)** *Richard Hannon* 78
2 ch f Tamayuz Elizabeth Swann (Bahamian Bounty)
(2493)

**Dame Lucy (IRE)** *Michael Appleby* a88 88
4 b f Refuse To Bend(IRE) Sheer Glamour (IRE) (Peintre Celebre (USA))
4443[13] 5319[7] (7043) 7416[2] ◆ 7565[10] 7995[3] 8096[9]

**Dame Nellie Melba** *Mark Johnston* a84 78
4 gr f Aussie Rules(USA) Scandalette (Niniski (USA))
146[10]

**Damour (GER)** *Markus Klug* 84
2 b f Azamour(IRE) Desabina (GER) (Big Shuffle (USA))
7481a[3]

**Danadana (IRE)** *Luca Cumani* a110 117
6 b h Dubawi(IRE) Zeeba (IRE) (Barathea (IRE))
1533[6] 2086[3] 4682[6] 5175[5] 6163a[3] 6655[2]

**Dana's Present** *George Baker* a76 67
5 ch g Osorio(GER) Euro Empire (USA) (Bartok (IRE))
2079[3] 3112[3] 3861[8] 4968[6] 5629[7] 6035[10] 6337[7] 7000[3] 7533[8] (7986) 8013[6]

**Dance** *Rod Millman* a51 36
5 b m Erhaab(USA) Shi Shi (Alnasr Alwasheek)
247[2] 454[3] 759[2] 989[5]

**Dancealot** *Clive Brittain* a68 83
3 b f Lawman(FR) Dance Of Light (USA) (Sadler's Wells (USA))
1530[14] 2063[8] 3117[10] (3936) 4971[8] 6254[15]

**Dance And Dance (IRE)** *Ed Vaughan* a95 103
8 b g Royal Applause Caldy Dancer (IRE) (Soviet Star (USA))
235[3] 1164[10] 2311[2] 2959[6] (3621) 4648[24] 6752[14]

**Dance Bid** *Clive Brittain* a62 77
3 b f Authorized(IRE) Dancing Fire (USA) (Dayjur (USA))
1655[10] 2120[3]

**Dance For Georgie** *Ben Haslam* a76 73
5 ch m Motivator Chetwynd (IRE) (Exit To Nowhere (USA))
(65) 359[6] 461[5]

**Danceintothelight** *Micky Hammond* a51 62
7 gr g Dansili Kali (Linamix (FR))
3482[3] 3845[4] 4962[8] 5815[6]

**Dance King** *Tim Easterby* 88
4 ch g Danehill Dancer(IRE) One So Wonderful (Nashwan (USA))
1539[8] (3004) 3574[9] 4144[5] (4710) 5633[8] 6098[6] 6479[3] 6937[3]

**Dance Of Fire** *Andrew Balding* 85
2 b c Norse Dancer(IRE) Strictly Dancing (IRE) (Danehill Dancer (IRE))
4550[5] 4896[4] (5783) (6331) 7104[9]

**Dance Of Heroes** *Jeremy Noseda* a80 87
3 b c Danehill Dancer(IRE) Helena Molony (IRE) (Sadler's Wells (USA))
(827) 5884[3] ◆ 6685[5]

**Dancequest (IRE)** *F Head* a88 98
3 b f Dansili Featherquest (Rainbow Quest (USA))
6882a[10]

**Dancethenightaway (IRE)** *William Jarvis* 41
2 b f Holy Roman Emperor(IRE) Dolce Dovo (Medicean)
5725[11] 6041[10]

**Dancetrack (USA)** *Charles Hills* 84
2 b c First Defence(USA) Jazz Drummer (USA) (Dixieland Band (USA))
5646[5] ◆ (6204) 6686[5]

**Dance With Another (IRE)** *A P O'Brien* 87
3 b f Danehill Dancer(IRE) Quarter Moon (IRE) (Sadler's Wells (USA))
1076a[10] 5024a[11]

**Dancewithastranger (IRE)** *Cathrine Witso Slettemark* 70
2 b f Fast Company(IRE) Bulrushes (Byron)
6386a[7]

**Dance With Fate (USA)** *Peter Eurton* a111
3 bb c Two Step Salsa(USA) Flirting With Fate (USA) (Saint Ballado (CAN))
1964a[6]

**Dancin Alpha** *Alan Swinbank* 70
3 ch g Bahamian Bounty Phoebe Woodstock (IRE) (Grand Lodge (USA))
2737[4] 3302[2] 5018[6] 5469[3]

**Dancing Angel** *James Eustace* a47 57
3 ch f Norse Dancer(IRE) Indian Angel (Indian Ridge)
2329[3] 2846[6] 3156[4] 4049[4] 4972[9] 5425[7] 7218[8]

**Dancing Bride (IRE)** *John C McConnell* a47 14
2 b f Vale Of York(IRE) Look Who's Dancing (Observatory (USA))
6375a[25]

**Dancing Cosmos (IRE)** *John Patrick Shanahan* a79 87
4 b f Holy Roman Emperor(IRE) The Real Thing (IRE) (Traditionally (USA))
1598[2] 2117[4] 3361[7] 4359[5]

**Dancing Freddy (IRE)** *Ann Stokell* a64 78
7 b g Chineur(FR) Majesty's Dancer (IRE) (Danehill Dancer (IRE))
383[4] 835[8] 908[3] 1001[2] 1089[2] 1369[7] 1487[2] 1618[P]

**Dancing Juice** *Brian Ellison* a55 59
3 b g Major Cadeaux Mancunian Way (Green Desert (USA))
1039[8] 1246[4] (3487) 3972[5] 4193[3] 5061[2] 7900[13]

**Dancing Maite** *Roy Bowring* a58 60
9 ch g Ballet Master(USA) Ace Maite (Komaite (USA))
29[9] 273[8] 1584[2] 2127[12] 3149[4] 4131[3] 4344[2] 7622[10] 7766[5] 8082[8]

**Dancing Moon (IRE)** *Mick Channon* a52 58
2 b f Danehill Dancer(IRE) Moon Dazzle (USA) (Kingmambo (USA))
2436[3] 2888[7] 4626[13] 5845[5] 6413[5] 6842[6]

**Dancing Primo** *Mark Brisbourne* a63 64
8 b m Primo Valentino(IRE) Tycoon's Last (Nalchik (USA))
2701[4] 6699[5] 7175[8] 7452[5] 7628[9] 7895[6] 8145[2] 8231[3]

**Dancing Sal (IRE)** *Gary Moore* a66 56
3 b f Azamour(IRE) Miss Tango Hotel (Green Desert (USA))
187[5] 311[9] 2860[7] 3754[4] 4048[4] 4341[5] 4428[9] 5832[4] 8311[10]

**Dancing Sands (IRE)** *H-A Pantall* a101 106
3 b f Dubawi(IRE) Past The Post (USA) (Danzig (USA))
553a[4] 1273a[3] 4009a[8] 4721a[4] 6164a[3] 7616a[3] 7916a[11]

**Dancing Springs (IRE)** *Bill Turner*
2 b f Bushranger(IRE) Deep Springs (USA) (Storm Cat (USA))
6024[10] 6205[11]

**Dancing Welcome** *Milton Bradley* a77 63
8 b m Kyllachy Highland Gait (Most Welcome)
1312[7]

**Dancruise (IRE)** *Kristin Stubbs*
2 b g Dandy Man(IRE) Crua Mna (Bahamian Bounty)
5679[10]

**Dandarrell** *Julie Camacho* a69 56
7 b g Makbul Dress Design (IRE) (Brief Truce (USA))
96[3] 366[8] 647[4] (910) 4468[4] 5899[13] 7829[5]

**Dandino** *Marco Botti* a103 117
7 br h Dansili Generous Diana (Generous (IRE))
3450[6] 4124[6] 5457a[2] 6139[4]

**Dandy (GER)** *Andrew Balding* a79 83
5 b g Nayef(USA) Diacada (GER) (Cadeaux Genereux)
1899[2] 2270[13] 2882[4] (3175) (4104) 4586[4] 5413[7] 5757[5] ◆ 6357[5]

**Dandy Boy (ITY)** *David Marnane* a88 103
8 b h Danetime(IRE) Fleet Of Light (Spectrum (IRE))
3452[22]

**Dandyleekie (IRE)** *G M Lyons* a93 91
2 b g Dandy Man(IRE) Cockaleekie (USA) (Alphabet Soup (USA))
6375a[29]

**Dandys Perier (IRE)** *Ronald Harris* a61 42
3 br g Dandy Man(IRE) Casual Remark (IRE) (Trans Island)
(86) 401[5] 547[3] 1264[2] 2281[4] 3087[8] 4785[5] 5820[9]

**Danegeld** *Paul Cole*
2 b c Danehill Dancer(IRE) Kirkinola (Selkirk (USA))
6602[11]

**Daneglow (IRE)** *Mike Murphy* a56 18
4 ch f Thousand Words Valluga (IRE) (Ashkalani (IRE))
164[2] 466[3] 973[7] 1282[7] 7420[13] 7884[7] 8286[8]

**Danehill Flyer (IRE)** *Philip Kirby* a37 46
4 b g Danehill Dancer(IRE) Zagreb Flyer (Old Vic)
1307[9] 1644[9] 8089[7]

**Danehill Revival** *William Haggas* 93
3 b f Pivotal Danehill Destiny (Danehill Dancer (IRE))
(1361) 1867[4] 2840[3] 6929[8] 7451[4]

**Dan Emmett (USA)** *John Wainwright* a67 79
4 ch g Flower Alley(USA) Singing Dixie (USA) (Dixieland Band (USA))
1960[7] 2424[8] 4319[13] (5240) 7177[3] 7333[2]

**Danequest (IRE)** *Rodger Sweeney* a40 57
5 b g Stardan(IRE) Tinquest (Rainbow Quest (USA))
794a[13]

**Daneside (IRE)** *Simon West* a53 71
7 b g Danehill Dancer(IRE) Sidecar (IRE) (Spectrum (IRE))
92[12] 192[2] 339[7] 425[7] 2426[11] 2907[8] 2937[4] 3242[8] 3535[13] 3798[9]

**Danette (USA)** *J Keith Desormeaux* a105
2 b f Curlin(USA) Sugar Britches (USA) (Dixieland Band (USA))
7606a[5]

**Dan Excel (IRE)** *J Moore* 119
6 b g Shamardal(USA) Love Excelling (FR) (Polish Precedent (USA))
2004a[3] (2379a)

**Danfazi (IRE)** *Kristin Stubbs* a72 74
3 ch g Dandy Man(IRE) Distant Shore (IRE) (Jareer (USA))
354[4] 1585[7] 1676[5] 2015[10] 3600[9] 4974[4] 5565[8]

**Dangerous Age** *J S Moore* a87 82
4 br f Sleeping Indian Rye (IRE) (Charnwood Forest (IRE))
444[2] ◆ 644[3] 1049[2] 1145[9] 1742[8] 4282[2] 5595[2] 6235[17] 7017[5] 7843[7] 7947[4] 8136[9]

**Dangerous Moonlite (IRE)** *Richard Hannon* 89
2 b f Acclamation Light It Up (IRE) (Elusive City (USA))
(2107) 3353[10] (3757) 5380[8] 6067[12]

**Danglydontask** *David Arbuthnot* a59 53
3 b g Lucky Story(USA) Strat's Quest (Nicholas (USA))
2682[11] 3525[4] 4658[10] 5908[5] 6193[10] 6946[10] 7517[7] 8189[4]

**Daniel Thomas (IRE)** *Ann Stokell* a65 55
12 b g Dansili Last Look (Rainbow Quest (USA))
(40) 88[5] 281[7] 435[3] 1016[8] 1138[7] 1819[2] 1923[2] 2212[7]

**Danisa** *David Bridgwater* a57 86
5 b m Shamardal(USA) Divisa (GER) (Lomitas)
567[6]

**Danish Design (FR)** *J E Pease* a23
2 b f American Post Asque (Dansili)
3640a[8]

**Dani Wallon (FR)** *C Delcher-Sanchez* 98
3 gr c Martaline Camille's Secret (FR) (Oasis Dream)
6446a[6] 7327a[2] 7856a[3]

**Dank** *Sir Michael Stoute* a86 116
5 b m Dansili Masskana (IRE) (Darshaan)
1181a[3] 3354[5] 7607a[4]

**Danny Boy (USA)** *Dale Romans* a94 102
2 rg c Harlan's Holiday(USA) Unbridled Beauty (USA) (Unbridled's Song (USA))
7590a[8]

**Dannyday** *Sir Michael Stoute* 71
2 b c Dansili Dayrose (Daylami (IRE))
6259[7] 6985[4]

**Danny O'Ruairc (IRE)** *James Moffatt* 72
2 b c Fast Company(IRE) Tawoos (FR) (Rainbow Quest (USA))
2736[3] ◆ 3620[5] 4253[5] 5576[9] 6331[9]

**Danot (IRE)** *Keith Dalgleish* 75
2 ch g Zebedee Hapipi (Bertolini (USA))
2214[6] 3570[4] 4065[2] 4357[6] (4493) 5266[5] 5998[4] (6400) 6510[2]

**Dansante** *Amanda Perrett* a45 44
3 b f Champs Elysees Danseuse Du Soir (IRE) (Thatching)
140[5] 231[6] 5977[5] 6568[6]

**Danseur De Feu (IRE)** *Kevin Prendergast* a76 69
4 ch f Danehill Dancer(IRE) Ugo Fire (IRE) (Bluebird (USA))
4805a[12]

**Danseur Noble** *James Tate* a80
2 b c Kheleyf(USA) Posy Fossil (USA) (Malibu Moon (USA))
7223[5] (8205)

**Danseuse De Reve (IRE)** *J E Hammond* 57
3 b f Invincible Spirit(IRE) Reve D'Iman (FR) (Highest Honor (FR))
2290a[6]

**Dansili Dutch (IRE)** *David O'Meara* a69 79
5 gr m Dutch Art Joyful Leap (Dansili)
152[5] (497) 612[7] 697[6] 910[5] 1510[4] 2199[3] 2426[3] 2676[4] 2911[4] 3604[5] (4381) 5166[2] 5640[2] 6232[3] (6706) 7008[9] 7459[6] 7871[7] 8044[6] 8260[8]

**Danza (USA)** *Todd Pletcher* a116
3 ch c Street Boss(USA) Champagne Royale (USA) (French Deputy (USA))
1964a[3] ◆

**Danza Classica (GER)** *M Nigge* a58 86
3 b f Peintre Celebre(USA) Dynamica (GER) (Dashing Blade)
3046a[9] 5959a[5]

**Danzella** *Chris Fairhurst* 6
2 b f Desideratum Danzatrice (Tamure (IRE))
7278[7]

**Danzeno** *Michael Appleby* 117
3 b g Denounce Danzanora (Groom Dancer (USA))
(1518) ◆ 3253[9] (3715) 6290[2] 6920[2]

**Danzig In The Dark (IRE)** *Tim Easterby* 51
3 b f Mastercraftsman(IRE) Cape Jasmine (IRE) (Danehill (USA))
1645[5] 2235[5]

**Danzing Girl (IRE)** *David O'Meara* 13
2 b f Bushranger(IRE) Prime Time Girl (Primo Dominie)
5712[8]

**Danzki (IRE)** *Gay Kelleway* a54 62
3 b g Bushranger(IRE) Miniver (IRE) (Mujtahid (USA))
2053[2] 2516[5] 7501[11] 7764[5] 7910[8]

**Danzoe (IRE)** *Christine Dunnett* a71 62
7 br g Kheleyf(USA) Fiaba (Precocious)
777[8] 1238[3] 1584[4] 2070[4] 3392[5] 4049[11] 4595[4] 5059[5] 5316[5] (5574) 5860[9] 6561[7] 6897[3] 7191[2] (7519) 7670[4] 7900[2] 8088[4]

**Danz Star (IRE)** *Malcolm Saunders* 64
3 ch g Ad Valorem(USA) Await (IRE) (Peintre Celebre (USA))
1911[7] 2832[2]

**Da'Quonde (IRE)** *Bryan Smart* a69 95
6 br m Pivotal Bobcat Greeley (USA) (Mr Greeley (USA))
1305[5] ◆ 2076[6] 2353[3] 2766[3] 6745[14]

**Daramakfi (FR)** *F Head* 79
2 b f Makfi Darakiyla (IRE) (Last Tycoon)
(5941a)

**Dara Tango (FR)** *A J Martin* a43 68
7 b g Lando(GER) Dara Dancer (Batshoof)
(7509)

**Daraybi (FR)** *A De Royer-Dupre* 114
3 b c Street Cry(IRE) Daryaba (IRE) (Night Shift (USA))
1481a[5] 3746a[4]

**D'Arcy Indiana** *Amy Weaver* a41 49
3 b g Royal Applause Prowse (USA) (King Of Kings (IRE))
1684[8] 3281[9] 3603[8]

**Daredevil (USA)** *Todd Pletcher* a120
2 ch c More Than Ready(USA) Chasethewildwind (USA) (Forty Niner (USA))
7610a[11]

**Dare To Achieve** *William Haggas* 104
4 b g Galileo(IRE) Mussoorie (FR) (Linamix (FR))
(2294) 2991[7] 5693[10] 6501[6]

**Daring Dragon** *Derek Shaw* a79 58
4 gr g Intikhab(USA) The Manx Touch (IRE) (Petardia)
102[7] 249[5] 489[2] 746[3] 1191[17] 1739[6] 2687[9] 3227[5] 5437[10]

**Daring Indian** *Tom Dascombe* a73 71
6 ch g Zamindar(USA) Anasazi (IRE) (Sadler's Wells (USA))
292[4] ◆ 430[3] 1140[2] 1359[11] 1743[2] 1941[6]

**Daring Life (IRE)** *Gabriele Miliani* 68
3 b f Cape Cross(IRE) Flying Flag (IRE) (Entrepreneur)
2590a[11]

**Daring Match (GER)** *J Hirschberger* a88 98
3 ch c Call Me Big(GER) Daring Action (Arazi (USA))
5966a[4]

**Daring Pursuit** *K R Burke* a23
4 b f Pastoral Pursuits Daring Destiny (Daring March)
31[4] 174[7] 1347[8]

**Daring Storm (GER)** *S Wattel* a86 86
4 b g Big Shuffle(USA) Daring Action (Arazi (USA))
1478a[7] 7026a[3]

**Dark Amber** *Brendan Powell* a61 72
4 b f Sakhee(USA) Donna Vita (Vettori (IRE))
1354[10] 2415[3] 2750[4] 3803[2] 4417[3] 5353[5] ◆ 5878[5] 6367[4] 6881[8] 7628[11]

**Dark Ambition (IRE)** *N Minner* a46 49
5 b h Dark Angel(IRE) Date Mate (USA) (Thorn Dance (USA))
3089a[10]

**Dark And Dangerous (IRE)** *Brendan Powell* a45 61
6 b g Cacique(IRE) Gilah (IRE) (Saddlers' Hall (IRE))
2046[4] 2465[5] 2614[2] 2770[8] 7895[10]

**Dark Black Diamond (FR)** *Mlle S-V Tarrou* 64
3 b f Green Tune(USA) Diamond White (Robellino (USA))
2411a[6]

**Dark Castle** *Micky Hammond* a89 91
5 b g Dark Angel(IRE) True Magic (Magic Ring (IRE))
1537[9] 1938[6] 2732[4] ◆ 3256[2] 3702[4] 4317[3] 4712[9] 5888[9] 6260[8] 6692[7]

**Dark Crusader (IRE)** *A J Martin* a57 101
4 bb f Cape Cross(IRE) Monty's Girl (IRE) (High Chaparral (IRE))
3717[10] 5024a[2] 5611[9] 6255[11]

**Dark Crystal** *Linda Perratt* a58 68
3 b f Multiplex Glitz (IRE) (Hawk Wing (USA))
1601[7] 3100[4] (4017) 4194[4] (4254) 4363[6] 5168[6] 5235[8] 5566[3] 6515[3] 6601[3] 7180[13]

**Dark Days** *Paul Cole* a72 58
3 b c Black Sam Bellamy(IRE) Darwinia (GER) (Acatenango (GER))
1438[11] 1984[9] 2221[11] 2926[5] 3567[6] 4134[7] 5949[2] 6856[2] 7229[3] (7572)

**Dark Deed** *Sir Michael Stoute* a70
2 b c Dansili High Heeled (IRE) (High Chaparral (IRE))
7731[3]

**Dark Diamond (IRE)** *Robert Cowell* a54
4 b g Dark Angel(IRE) Moon Diamond (Unfuwain (USA))
7910[3]

**Dark Dream (FR)** *N Caullery* a75 78
3 ch g Maille Pistol(FR) Anse Crawen (FR) (Muhtathir)
7630a[3]

**Dark Emerald (IRE)** *Brendan Powell* a75 106
4 gr g Dark Angel(IRE) Xema (Danehill (USA))
(2156) 3036[3] (3431) 3964[2] 5163[4] 5665[7] 6335[2] (6560) 7022[2]

**Darkening (IRE)** *Ismail Mohammed* a78 92
4 b g Shamardal(USA) Dama'A (IRE) (Green Desert (USA))
241a[9]

**Darkening Night** *James Tate* 46
2 b c Cape Cross(IRE) Garanciere (FR) (Anabaa (USA))
7667[10]

**Dark Kingdom (IRE)** *Ed Walker* 80
2 bl g Lord Shanakill(USA) Roskeen (IRE) (Grand Lodge (USA))
(6420) (7378)

**Dark Lane** *David Evans* a71 69
8 b g Namid Corps De Ballet (IRE) (Fasliyev (USA))
(35) 141[4] 208[5] 339[6] 938[5] 1148[3] 1487[10] 1573[10] 1639[2] 1912[4] 2174[6] 3088[3] 3561[4] 3784[4] 4151[2] (4267) 4981[3] 5247[5] 5595[7] 6764[4] 7252[4] 7758[11] 7847[7] 8081[2] 8143[3]

**Dark Leopard** *Roger Charlton* a77 75
3 b g Dubawi(IRE) Clouded Leopard (USA) (Danehill (USA))
1298[2] 1725[11] 2083[9]

**Dark Noir (FR)** *B Dutruel* a64 78
3 b g Redback Guerrera Noire (FR) (Enrique)
3869a[7]

**Dark Ocean (IRE)** *Jedd O'Keeffe* a77 77
4 b g Dylan Thomas(IRE) Neutral (Beat Hollow)
(1356) 1881[9] 2293[2] 5172[4] 5855[8] 6841[2] 7012[5] 7567[5]

**Dark Opal (IRE)** *John Weymes* a12 74
4 b f Camacho Dark Albatross (USA) (Sheikh Albadou)
1843[5] 2096[5] 2232[4] 2421[7] 5130[5] 5333[5] 7056[13] 7510[13]

**Dark Phantom (IRE)** *Peter Makin* a52 40
3 b g Dark Angel(IRE) Stoneware (Bigstone (IRE))
1980[7] 3084[4] 3754[3] 4341[6] 5183[4] 5833[5] 6647[12] 7805[7] 7977[8]

**Dark Profit (IRE)** *Charles Hills* 78
2 gr c Dark Angel(IRE) Goldthroat (IRE) (Zafonic (USA))
2776[9] 4389[3] 4760[3] 5580[7]

**Dark Ranger** *Tim Pitt* a88 84
8 br g Where Or When(IRE) Dark Raider (IRE) (Definite Article)
1770[2] ◆ 2342[5] 2920[6] 3453[P]

**Dark Ray (IRE)** *L Riccardi* 99
5 b m Dark Angel(IRE) Magiustrina (IRE) (Indian Ridge)
7480a[11]

**Dark Reality (IRE)** *Ralph Beckett* a33 62
3 b f Intikhab(USA) Sunny Slope (Mujtahid (USA))
3083[9] 4969[7] 6086[14]

**Dark Reckoning** *Ann Duffield* 100
2 b f Equiano(FR) Impressible (Oasis Dream)
3656[4] 4357[3] (4708) (5447) 5770[5] (6530)

**Dark Ruler (IRE)** *Alan Swinbank* a69 94
5 b g Dark Angel(IRE) Gino Lady (IRE) (Perugino (USA))
(1196) 1444[2] 1651[3] 5144[2] 5633[7] 6061[5] 6536[3] 6794[3] (7334) 7718[5]

**Dark Sea (IRE)** *E Botti* a81 104
3 b c Sea The Stars(IRE) Drifa (ITY) (Hamas (IRE))
2376a[5] 7617a[11]

**Dark Side Dream** *Chris Dwyer* a69 22
2 b g Equiano(FR) Dream Day (Oasis Dream)
4167[11] 5099[3] 6271[4] 7224[3] 7807[3] 8046[2]

**Dark Skies (IRE)** *David Wachman* a83 90
3 b f Invincible Spirit(IRE) Royal Devotion (IRE) (Sadler's Wells (USA))
4557a[8] 6963a[5]

**Dark Swan (IRE)** *Sir Mark Prescott Bt* a52
2 b f Zamindar(USA) Brooklyn's Storm (USA) (Storm Cat (USA))
6630[5]

**Dark Symphony (IRE)** *Mark Usher* a32
2 b f Amadeus Wolf Vampire Blues (IRE) (Azamour (IRE))
4260[7] 4542[5] 5604[8] 6072[7] 6676[8]

**Dark Tsarina (IRE)** *Michael Madgwick* a59 22
3 b f Soviet Star(USA) Dark Raider (IRE) (Definite Article)
50[4] 316[6] 827[6] 1124[6] 1588[11] 2078[12] 2621[8] 3819[8] 4261[5] 5048[3] 5491[6] 6986[7] 7664[F] 8246[8]

**Dark War (IRE)** *James Given* a71 53
2 b g Dark Angel(IRE) Waroonga (IRE) (Brief Truce (USA))
6115[9] 7037[5] 7223[3] 7770[5] 7984[4]

**Dark Wave** *Ed Walker* a72 80
2 ch g Zebedee Rule Britannia (Night Shift (USA))
4829[7] 5752[3] 6204[8] (6669) (6884) (7328) 7595[4]

**Dark Wonder (IRE)** *James Given* a55 68
2 b g Dark Angel(IRE) Wondrous Story (USA) (Royal Academy (USA))
3881[6] 4829[4] 5995[3] 7379[8] 7911[4] 8091[7]

**Darling Boyz** *John Quinn* 58
3 ch g Auction House(USA) Summertime Parkes (Silver Patriarch (IRE))
3362[8] 4292[4]

**Darma (IRE)** *Martyn Meade* a71
2 b f Acclamation Dark Dancer (FR) (Danehill (USA))
6660[4] (7361)

**Darnathean** *Paul D'Arcy* a76 72
5 b g Librettist(USA) Meddle (Diktat)
65[5] 295[8] 603[4] 815[6] (996) 1613[6] (2069) 2463[12] 2721[6] 3227[3] 3328[4] 4578[2] ◆ (5125) (5303) 5729[6] 6890[5] 7202[8]

**Darrell Rivers** *Giles Bravery* a52
2 b f Hellvelyn First Term (Acclamation)
7192[9]

**Darrington** *Richard Fahey* 74
2 b g Archipenko(USA) Rosablanca (IRE) (Sinndar (IRE))
5386[4] 6056[3] (6694)

**Darroun (IRE)** *Shaun Lycett* 47
6 gr g Dalakhani(IRE) Darayka (FR) (Dr Fong (USA))
322[7]

**Darselect** *F Vermeulen* a89 68
3 b c Bertolini(USA) Pygmalion (IRE) (Dr Devious (IRE))
6221a[2]

**Darshini** *Sir Michael Stoute* 80
2 b c Sir Percy Fairy Flight (USA) (Fusaichi Pegasus (USA))
3929[2] (4550) 5310[5]

**Dartagnan D'Azur (FR)** *W Hefter* 110
5 gr h Slickly(FR) Dinner Bell (FR) (Highest Honor (FR))
5330a[4] (7189a) 7617a[3]

**Darting** *Andrew Balding* a71 72
3 b f Shamardal(USA) Dararita (IRE) (Halo (USA))
1768[4] 2404[4] 3195[7] 3978[4] 5975[4] 7358[3] 7913[2] 8196[6] 8309[4]

**Dartmouth** *Sir Michael Stoute* 78
2 b c Dubawi(IRE) Galatee (FR) (Galileo (IRE))
5625[6] (6456)

**Dartrix** *Michael Dods* a44 75
5 b m Dutch Art Shrink (Mind Games)
1440[14] 2421[6] 2677[7] 4629[4] ◆ 5089[4] 5390[8] 5635[7]

**Darwin (USA)** *A P O'Brien* a90 119
4 b c Big Brown(USA) Cool Ghoul (USA) (Silver Ghost (USA))
2570a[6] 3451[10] 4459a[2] 4779[3] 6352a[7] 6971a[13]

**Dasaateer (IRE)** *Roger Varian* 46
2 b c Mount Nelson Trishuli (Indian Ridge)
7039[7]

**Dashing Home (GER)** *Waldemar Hickst* 84
2 b c Dashing Blade Deinum (GER) (Sholokhov (IRE))
6123a[6]

**Dashing Star** *David Elsworth* 106
4 b g Teofilo(IRE) Dashiba (Dashing Blade)
2779[4] 3449[5] 3962[4] 4759[4] 6747[5] 7440[2] 7718[3]

**Dashing Storm** *Jeremy Gask* a48
4 b f Milk It Mick Salalah (Lion Cavern (USA))
402[9]

**Dashwood** *J F Levins* a81 87
7 b g Pivotal Most Charming (FR) (Darshaan)
(1758) 3737a[5]

**Dastarhon (IRE)** *Mme Pia Brandt* a95 111
4 b c Dansili Top Toss (IRE) (Linamix (FR))
397a[4] 683a[5] 899a[8] 5960a[6] 7437a[4] 8150a[6]

**Dat Il Do** *Noel Quinlan* a76
2 b f Bahamian Bounty Broughtons Revival (Pivotal)
8247[2] ◆

**Dauphine De France (FR)** *Y Barberot* 58
2 b f Air Chief Marshal(IRE) Un Petit Tour (FR) (Double Bed (FR))
5662a[6]

**Dauran (IRE)** *A De Royer-Dupre* 90
3 b c Manduro(GER) Dawera (IRE) (Spinning World (USA))
4775a[3]

**David Livingston (IRE)** *M F De Kock* 115
5 b h Galileo(IRE) Mora Bai (IRE) (Indian Ridge)
110a[12]

**Davids Park** *John Joseph Murphy* 101
3 b g Lucky Story(USA) Dijital Power (Pivotal)
1200a[4] 1458a[7] 2571a[9]

**David's Secret** *Roy Brotherton* a51 41
4 ch g Sakhee's Secret Mozie Cat (IRE) (Mozart (IRE))
126[6] 263[10] 516[6] 1081[9]

**D'Avignon (USA)** *John Gosden* a72 79
3 bb c Smart Strike(CAN) No Matter What (USA) (Nureyev (USA))
1654[4] 2307[2] 3159[5] 3974[2]

**Dawn Catcher** *Geoffrey Deacon* a62 84
4 ch f Bertolini(USA) First Dawn (Dr Fong (USA))
654[6] 777[7] 845[3] (1584) 2434[4] 2994[5] (3707) (3887) 4762[14] 6650[5] (7534)

**Dawnfromthepast (IRE)** *Luke Dace* a30 35
3 b g Tagula(IRE) Ball Cat (FR) (Cricket Ball (USA))
86[9] 280[6] 378[10]

**Dawn Prayer** *H-A Pantall* a64 59
2 b c Acclamation Nice Matin (USA) (Tiznow (USA))
7344a[7] 8148a[7]

**Dawn Rock** *Simon Dow* a47 55
4 b f Rock Of Gibraltar(IRE) Ommadawn (IRE) (Montjeu (IRE))
737[9] 1012[12] 1835[7]

**Dawn Salute (FR)** *H-A Pantall* a62 50
4 b c Royal Applause Nice Matin (USA) (Tiznow (USA))
392a[5]

**Dayaday (FR)** *C Boutin* 69
2 b f Sunday Break(JPN) Debby (USA) (Woodman (USA))
3744a[9] (4882a) 5543a[4] 6244a[10] 7027a[7]

**Dayatthespa (USA)** *Chad C Brown* 114
5 ch m City Zip(USA) M'Lady Doc (USA) (Doc's Leader (USA))
(7607a)

**Daydreamer** *William Haggas* a84 64
3 b g Duke Of Marmalade(IRE) Storyland (USA) (Menifee (USA))
1612[10] 2221[9] 2735[6] (3391) ◆ 3797[2] (4657) 4863[5] 6608[9] 7672[9]

**Daylight** *Andrew Balding* a78 90
2 ch g Firebreak Dayville (USA) (Dayjur (USA))
(2718) (2995) 4762[5] 4892[9] 5623[11] 6089[7] 6558[9] 6880[6] 7017[8] 7307[5]

**Day Of Conquest** *Richard Hannon* a95 105
3 ch c Major Cadeaux Dayville (USA) (Dayjur (USA))
4826[2] ◆ 5192[4] 6124[8] 7022[8]

**Day Of The Eagle (IRE)** *Michael Easterby* a65 73
8 b g Danehill Dancer(IRE) Puck's Castle (Shirley Heights)
1446[8] 2019[3] 2549[9] 3949[6] 4394[4] 5530[3] 6543[7] 6865[4] 8102[6] 8250[5]

**Day Star Lad** *Derek Shaw* a70 31
3 b g Footstepsinthesand Eurolink Mayfly (Night Shift (USA))
6[3] 173[3] 267[3] (480) 753[7] (1007) 1116[3] 7178[15] 7647[11]

**Daytona Bay** *Ferdinand J Leve* 102
4 b f Motivator Daytona (GER) (Lando (GER))
2001a[5] 7316a[3] 7603a[10]

**Dazeen** *Michael Herrington* a72 77
7 b g Zafeen(FR) Bond Finesse (IRE) (Danehill Dancer (IRE))
1689[11] (7078) 7259[4] 7697[7]

**Dazza** *Gary Moore* a53 72
3 ch f Bertolini(USA) Another Secret (Efisio)
338[3] 573[6] 5861[10] 6716[10] (7337) 7535[12] 7847[10] 7928[7]

**Dazzling (IRE)** *A P O'Brien* 101
3 b f Galileo(IRE) Secret Garden (IRE) (Danehill (USA))
2263a[3] 2960[14] 3285a[2]

**Dazzling Display** *Richard Guest* a14 10
2 ch f Stimulation(IRE) Dazzling Quintet (Superlative)
7637[10] 7712[9] 7828[6] 8060[11]

**Dazzling Valentine** *Alan Bailey* a66 75
6 b m Oratorio(IRE) Bedazzling (IRE) (Darshaan)
21[5] 385[4] 612[5] 737[7] (1210) 1729[11] 1816[4] 2046[5] 2693[8]

**Deadline Day (IRE)** *Roger Varian* a62 48
3 b g Montjeu(IRE) Madame Cerito (USA) (Diesis)
1808[8] 2201[8] 2842[4] 6682[9] 7229[2]

**Dean Deifir (IRE)** *David Peter Nagle* a46 65
3 ch f Fracas(IRE) Rajani (IRE) (Johannesburg (USA))
4950a[12]

**Deano's Devil (IRE)** *Richard Fahey* a52
3 b f Medicean Peninsula Girl (IRE) (Cape Cross (IRE))
142[6] 291[7] 480[10] 1032[4]

**Dear Ben** *Brian Baugh* a53 35
5 b g Echo Of Light Miss Up N Go (Gorytus (USA))
693[2] 937[2] 1270[11] 1804[8] 8230[9]

**Dear Bruin (IRE)** *John Spearing* 66
2 b f Kodiac Namu (Mujahid (USA))
3933[4] 4787[4] 6361[4] 7155[4]

**Dear Demi (AUS)** *Clarry Conners* 111
5 b m Dehere(USA) Shirley (AUS) (Zabeel (NZ))
7127a[7]

**Dear Maurice** *Tobias B P Coles* a68 76
10 b g Indian Ridge Shamaiel (IRE) (Lycius (USA))
288[7] 340[8]

**Deauville Dancer (IRE)** *Sir Mark Prescott Bt* a59 88
3 b g Tamayuz Mathool (IRE) (Alhaarth (IRE))
2080[4] 3818[3] (4134) (5341) (5890) ◆

**Deauville Prince (FR)** *Tom Dascombe* a98 99
4 b g Holy Roman Emperor(IRE) Queen Of Deauville (FR) (Diableneyev (USA))
2113[6] 2758[11] 3420[10] 4938[7] 6097[2] 6535[5] 7227[4] 7663[9] 8117[10]

**Deavin** *Nick Littmoden* a31
3 b c Mind Games So Discreet (Tragic Role (USA))
622[6] 731[8] 1084[5]

**Debdebdeb** *Andrew Balding* a70 98
4 b f Teofilo(IRE) Windmill (Ezzoud (IRE))
(2010) 2558[2] 3424[5] 4213[5] 5161[4] 5673[4] 6255[12] 7107[30]

**Debit** *Clive Cox* 79
3 b g Pivotal Silver Kestrel (USA) (Silver Hawk (USA))
2667[2] 3083[5] 5775[2] 6249[3] 6552[8] 7438[2]

**Debt Free Dame** *Michael Easterby* 39
2 ch f Arcano(IRE) Runkerry Point (USA) (Giant's Causeway (USA))
1656[7] 4750[7] 5241[6]

**Debt Settler (IRE)** *Luke Dace* a62 62
3 b g Art Connoisseur(IRE) Musical Dancer (Monsieur Bond (IRE))
149[5] 2035[2] 2208[4]

**Debutante (FR)** *A De Royer-Dupre* 96
3 b f Gold Away(IRE) Danedrop (IRE) (Danehill (USA))
7916a[3]

**Debutante Blues (USA)** *Mark Johnston*
3 rg f Dubawi(IRE) Filarmonia (ARG) (Slew Gin Fizz (USA))
6265[5]

**Decathlete (USA)** *A Fabre* 111
3 b c Medaglia d'Oro(USA) Rahiyah (USA) (Rahy (USA))
6382a[9] 6955a[9]

**Decent Fella (IRE)** *Ann Stokell* a69 78
8 b g Marju(IRE) Mac Melody (IRE) (Entrepreneur)
432[6] 572[6] 779[7] 1021[8] 1224[5] 1839[4] 2718[8] 3096[11] (4594) 4961[8] 5124[7] 5470[3] 5602[3] 5979[6] 6821[9]

**Deceptive Vision (CAN)** *Malcolm Pierce* 112
4 b f A.P. Indy(USA) Eye Of The Sphynx (CAN) (Smart Strike (CAN))
7326a[3]

**Decibelle** *Jane Chapple-Hyam* a48 50
2 b f Indesatchel(IRE) Buffy Boo (Agnes World (USA))
3671[12] 4403[8] 5549[6] 6237[5] 7014[7]

**Decipher (JPN)** *Futoshi Kojima* 112
5 b h Deep Impact(JPN) Mizna (USA) (Dubai Millennium)
7981a[15]

**Decision By One** *S J Mahon* a66 84
5 ch g Bahamian Bounty Intellibet One (Compton Place)
87[8] 233[9] 425[8] 562[10] 2669[10] 3093[2] 3392[2] (3783) 3848[8] 6078a[8]

**Decisive Rebel** *Jo Hughes* a35 51
2 b g Cockney Rebel(IRE) Be Decisive (Diesis)
2172[5] 2673[5] 3658[3] 4065[6] 5662a[10] 6941[7]

**Declamation (IRE)** *Alistair Whillans* a53 76
4 ch g Shamardal(USA) Dignify (IRE) (Rainbow Quest (USA))
3050[7] 4001[7] 4517[6] 5172[6] 5797[5] 6600[8]

**Decorated Knight** *Roger Varian* 82
2 ch c Galileo(IRE) Pearling (USA) (Storm Cat (USA))
6259[2]

**Deebaj (IRE)** *Mark Johnston* 72
2 br c Authorized(IRE) Athreyaa (Singspiel (IRE))
6743[7] 7134[3]

**Deeds Not Words (IRE)** *Mick Channon* 98
3 b g Royal Applause Wars (IRE) (Green Desert (USA))
1445[3] 2344[8] 3253[20] 3478[7] (4166) 4669[8] 5165[7] 5623[10] 6170[11] 6760[10] 6893[8] 7132[11]

**Deep Blue Diamond** *Ollie Pears* 39
2 b f Sir Percy Apple Blossom (IRE) (Danehill Dancer (IRE))
6623[7] 7004[5]

**Deep Blue Sea** *Anthony Carson* 71
2 b f Rip Van Winkle(IRE) Semaphore (Zamindar (USA))
5725[3] (6434) 7237[10] ◆

**Deeper Magic (IRE)** *J S Moore* a55 38
2 b g Clodovil(IRE) White Queen (IRE) (Spectrum (IRE))
5148[7] 6085[10] 6602[7] 7064[11]

**Deep Resolve (IRE)** *Alan Swinbank* a67 72
3 b g Intense Focus(USA) I'Ll Be Waiting (Vettori (IRE))
(1364) 1904[3] 2198[2] 2934[4] 7411[13]

**Deepsand (IRE)** *Tim Easterby* 82
5 br g Footstepsinthesand Sinamay (USA) (Saint Ballado (CAN))
1724[11] 2259[5] ◆ 2728[2] 3341[3] 4113[5] 4575[2] 5017[4] 6099[4] (6404) 7124[6] 7539[7]

**Deerfield** *Charlie Appleby* a76 79
2 b c New Approach(IRE) Sandtime (IRE) (Green Desert (USA))
4666[8] 5184[2] (5886)

**Defence Council (IRE)** *Ollie Pears* 85
6 b g Kheleyf(USA) Miss Gally (IRE) (Galileo (IRE))
1191[RR] 4314[RR]

**Defence Event (USA)** *John Gosden* a58
2 b c First Defence(USA) Rio Carnival (USA) (Storm Cat (USA))
7199[5]

**Deficit (IRE)** *Steve Gollings* a87 88
4 gr g Dalakhani(IRE) Venturi (Danehill Dancer (IRE))
5288[7] (5825) 7566[9]

**Defining Year (IRE)** *D K Weld* a78 98
6 b g Hawk Wing(USA) Tajaathub (USA) (Aljabr (USA))
1078a[6] 4379a[6] 4771a[4] 5957a[21]

**Definite Secret** *James Tate* a60
3 ch f Sakhee's Secret Jasmick (IRE) (Definite Article)
173[5] 547[6] 865[6]

**Defrost My Heart (IRE)** *A De Royer-Dupre* 102
3 b f Fastnet Rock(AUS) Perfect Hedge (Unfuwain (USA))
3808a[5]

**Deftera Fantutte (IRE)** *Natalie Lloyd-Beavis* a62
3 b f Amadeus Wolf Carranza (IRE) (Lead On Time (USA))
4265[8] 7355[4] 7682[5] 7800[2] 8142[7] 8280[2]

**Deftera Lad (IRE)** *Pat Phelan* a51
2 b g Fast Company(IRE) Speedbird (USA) (Sky Classic (CAN))
8187[4]

**Deia Sunrise (IRE)** *Paul Webber* a81 76
5 gr g Clodovil(IRE) Hedera (USA) (Woodman (USA))
145[8] 623[11]

**Deinonychus** *William Knight* a69
3 b c Authorized(IRE) Sharp Dresser (USA) (Diesis)
8098[3] 8313[6]

**Deja Bougg** *David Evans* a55 53
3 b f Tobougg(IRE) La Riveraine (USA) (Riverman (USA))
2946[12] 4268[4] 4543[9] 5102[3] 5556[7]

**Delagoa Bay (IRE)** *Sylvester Kirk* a53 45
6 b m Encosta De Lago(AUS) Amory (GER) (Goofalik (USA))
4737[12] 6900[3] 7524[2] (7657) 7893[3]

**Delaire** *Roger Varian* 74
2 b g Sakhee's Secret Moody Margaret (Bahamian Bounty)
6261[3] 6997[3]

**De Lesseps (USA)** *James Moffatt* a55 53
6 ch g Selkirk(USA) Suez (Green Desert (USA))
(12) 367[4] 833[5] 1819[5] 4961[7] 5636[4] 7056[12]

**Delhi** *P Bary* a98 99
3 b f High Chaparral(IRE) Dream Day (Oasis Dream)
3808a[9]

**Delicious Patrica** *Ed McMahon* a33 33
5 b m Multiplex Cerulean Rose (Bluegrass Prince (IRE))
565[8]

**Delightful Sleep** *David Evans* a67 64
6 b g Sulamani(IRE) Naemi (GER) (Tannenkonig (IRE))
39[4] 156[5] 467[11] 736[3] 998[7] 2689[8] 2844[3] 3576[8] 3781[3] 4105[4] 4153[7] 4905[7] 5273[3] 5751[8] 6771[12] 7115[8] 7187[2] 7426[5] (7646) 7766[12] 8175[3] 8218[7]

**Delivery** *A Fabre* 104
3 b f Rail Link Deliberate (King's Best (USA))
2816a[4] 3808a[2] 5407a[12]

**Della Star (FR)** *A Lyon* a52 43
4 gr g Della Francesca(USA) Ma Bonne Etoile (FR) (Medaaly)
935a[6]

**Dellbuoy** *Pat Phelan* a73 62
5 b g Acclamation Ruthie (Pursuit Of Love)
405[6] 2702[5] 3874[7]

**Delores Rocket** *Kevin Ryan* a68 72
4 b f Firebreak Artistic (IRE) (Noverre (USA))
1376[15] 1440[11] 1846[10] 2427[4] 2676[2]

**Delusional** *Roger Charlton* 73
2 b c Oasis Dream Take The Hint (Montjeu (IRE))
4142[9] 6456[2]

**Deluxe** *Richard Hannon* 79
2 b c Acclamation Ainia (Alhaarth (IRE))
4760[5] 5093[2] 6300[6]

**Delysdream** *Christine Dunnett*
2 br c Dutch Art Goodbye Cash (IRE) (Danetime (IRE))
6039[10] 6462[13]

**Demeteor (ITY)** *R Menichetti* 102
4 b c Mujahid(USA) Eros Love (ITY) (Love The Groom (USA))
2191a[7] 2374a[8] 3047a[6] 3776a[7]

**Democretes** *Seamus Durack* a96 97
5 ch g Cadeaux Genereux Petite Epaulette (Night Shift (USA))
3036[4] 6097[4] 6498[2] 6892[5] 8117[8]

**Demoiselle (IRE)** *P Bary* a79 74
3 gr f Dalakhani(IRE) Amonita (Anabaa (USA))
7164a[7]

**Demoiselle Bond** *Lydia Richards* a67 10
6 ch m Monsieur Bond(IRE) Baytown Flyer (Whittingham (IRE))
402[5] 798[8]

**Demora** *Michael Appleby* a90 109
5 b m Deportivo Danzanora (Groom Dancer (USA))
(3241) 4179[4] 4852[11] 6231[4] 6918[10] 7441[3]

**Denbigh Raur (IRE)** *T G McCourt* a44 48
4 bb f Footstepsinthesand Gate Lodge (IRE) (Grand Lodge (USA))
502[10]

**Denim And Ruby (JPN)** *Katsuhiko Sumii* 114
4 b f Deep Impact(JPN) Venenciador (JPN) (King Kamehameha (JPN))
1182a[10] 7981a[11]

**Denison Flyer** *Lawrence Mullaney* a29 40
7 b g Tobougg(IRE) Bollin Victoria (Jalmood (USA))
5240[7]

**Dennis** *Tim Easterby* a56 71
4 b g Mind Games Hetti Lewis (Sir Harry Lewis (USA))
2169[16] 4291[7] 5088[9] 5602[8] 6122[7]

**Denton Carnival (IRE)** *Michael Dods* 48
2 ch g Captain Rio Be My Lover (Pursuit Of Love)
2615[6]

**Denton Dawn (IRE)** *Michael Dods* a52 72
2 b f Fast Company(IRE) Rectify (IRE) (Mujadil (USA))
1955[2] 2472[2] 3403[4]

**Denusa (IRE)** *Laura Grizzetti* a79 91
3 b f Aussie Rules(USA) Ardent Lady (Alhaarth (IRE))
193a[7] 720a[4]

**Denzille Lane (IRE)** *Mark Johnston* a80 85
2 ch g Iffraaj Alexander Youth (IRE) (Exceed And Excel (AUS))
2291[2] 2543[6] (2903) 3322[11] 4218[2] 4625[4] 5580[13] 6128[9] 6510[9]

**Depden (IRE)** *John Butler* a50 46
6 ch g Captain Rio Attribute (Warning)
1877[8] 2907[10]

**Derbaas (USA)** *A Al Raihe* a103 101
8 b h Seeking The Gold(USA) Sultana (USA) (Storm Cat (USA))
110a[9] 207a[5] 306a[8] 509a[6] 679a[6] 808a[9]

**Derbyshire (IRE)** *Kevin Ryan* a82 76
3 b g Green Tune(USA) Statia (FR) (Anabaa (USA))
(3158) 3897[2] 4350[4] 5420[5] 5795[5] (6154) 6478[4] 6902[2]

**De Repente (IRE)** *Michael Appleby* a62 52
3 b f Captain Rio Suddenly (Puissance)
1396[11] 1737[5] 2295[9] 3921[6] 4315[5] 4994[7] 7111[13] 8284[3]

**Derfenna Art (IRE)** *Seamus Durack* a72 58
5 b g Excellent Art Cordelia (Green Desert (USA))
67[3] 469[3]

**De Rigueur** *Marco Botti* a90 110
6 b g Montjeu(IRE) Exclusive (Polar Falcon (USA))
1736[9] 2342[7] (2779) (3962) 5693[16] 5920[3] 7107[2]

**Der Meister (IRE)** *Andrew Balding* 89
3 ro g Mastercraftsman(IRE) Agnetha (GER) (Big Shuffle (USA))
(1616) (2225) 5877[7] (6685)

**Dernier Chichi (FR)** *D Allard* a57
5 gr g Chichicastenango(FR) Garantie Bio (FR) (Take Risks (FR))
57a[14]

**Dernier Empereur (FR)** *C Ferland* a82 80
3 b c Holy Roman Emperor(IRE) Dix Huit (USA) (Gone West (USA))
169a[6]

**Descaro (USA)** *John O'Shea* a56 58
8 gr g Dr Fong(USA) Miarixa (FR) (Linamix (FR))
454[4] 580[3] 2836[7] 3179[5]

**Desert Ace (IRE)** *Michael Dods* a73 99
3 ch g Kheleyf(USA) Champion Place (Compton Place)
1350[3] 1700[8] 2626[7] (3331) (3565) 4898[6] 5696[14] 6893[6] (7132) 7889[11]

**Desert Apostle (IRE)** *Derek Shaw* a46
2 b f Tagula(IRE) Cambara (Dancing Brave (USA))
7701[6] 7917[5] 8254[4]

**Desert Blanc** *C Baillet* a97 104
6 b h Desert Style(IRE) Lumiere Rouge (FR) (Indian Ridge)
2799a[9] 3997a[5] 6182a[6] 7437a[3]

**Desert Blossom (IRE)** *Charlie Appleby* 96
4 ch f Shamardal(USA) Elshamms (Zafonic (USA))
2840[5] 4668[6] ◆

**Desert Chief** *Richard Whitaker* 22
2 b g Kheleyf(USA) African Breeze (Atraf)
7496[7]

**Desert Colours** *Kevin Ryan* a69 85
3 b g Exceed And Excel(AUS) Awwal Malika (USA) (Kingmambo (USA))
311[11] 786[4] (919) (1048) (1101) (1403) (1601) 3187[2] 3719[6]

**Desert Command** *Andrew Balding* a90 88
4 b g Oasis Dream Speed Cop (Cadeaux Genereux)
(1789) 2503[4] 2992[5] 4121[2] 4983[5]

**Desert Creek (IRE)** *David Nicholls* a68 79
8 ch g Refuse To Bend(IRE) Flagship (Rainbow Quest (USA))
1376[8] 1710[4] 3910[7]

**Desert Encounter (IRE)** *David Simcock* 76
2 b c Halling(USA) La Chicana (IRE) (Invincible Spirit (IRE))
6998[4] 7666[2]

**Desert Force** *Richard Hannon* 84
2 b c Equiano(FR) Mail The Desert (IRE) (Desert Prince (IRE))
4695[4] 5309[2] (6517) 7131[10]

**Desert Island Dusk** *John Bridger* a32 16
3 b g Superior Premium Desert Island Disc (Turtle Island (IRE))
5491[8] 5829[7] 6194[10] 6986[8]

**Desert Jeuney (AUS)** *Nigel Blackiston* 109
5 br g Desert King(IRE) Preps (AUS) (Jeune)
7128a[3]

**Desert Law (IRE)** *Saeed bin Suroor* a82 101
6 b g Oasis Dream Speed Cop (Cadeaux Genereux)
107a[3] 680a[4] 2283[18] 3732[4] 6159[6] 6740[13]

**Desert Morning (IRE)** *David Simcock* a63 45
2 b f Pivotal Arabian Mirage (Oasis Dream)
7405[12] 8173[7]

**Desert Ranger (IRE)** *James Tate* a78 83
3 b c Bushranger(IRE) Maleha (IRE) (Cape Cross (IRE))
(731) (1149) 1518[10] 3225[6] (3895) 4628[4] (5727) 6466[8] 6713[21] 7183[6]

**Desert Recluse (IRE)** *Ian Williams* a76 81
7 ch g Redback Desert Design (Desert King (IRE))
1418[6] 1849[5] 3151[5] 3851[5] 4441[8] 5435[6] 6651[5]

**Desert Snow** *Saeed bin Suroor* a99 94
3 rg f Teofilo(IRE) Requesting (Rainbow Quest (USA))
2280[2] 2917[2] (3857) 4452[4] 6559[2] 7020[4] (7289) (7837)

**Desert Society (IRE)** *Richard Hannon* a70 85
3 b c Kheleyf(USA) Sensasse (IRE) (Imperial Ballet (IRE))
3464[8] 3672[2] 4650[13] 5031[11] 6423[3] 6986[3]

**Desert Strike** *Conor Dore* a86 79
8 b g Bertolini(USA) Mary Jane (Tina's Pet)
(87) 233[8] 312[4] 432[4] 572[2] 654[5] 777[5] ◆ (866) 1019[4] 1109[2] 1283[3] (1739) (1921) 2645[7] 2919[2] 6020[4] (6764) 7017[9] 7365[12] 7687[6] 7931[3] (8040) 8297[7]

**Desert Wings (IRE)** *Charlie Appleby* a93 84
4 ch g Raven's Pass(USA) Rise And Fall (USA) (Quiet American (USA))
241a[12]

**Designate (IRE)** *Ralph Beckett* a70 71
2 b g Approve(IRE) Rihana (IRE) (Priolo (USA))
1259[3] 1575[5] 2007[4] 4430[4] 5285[8] 5506[2] (5885) 6447[6] 7029[3]

**Designs On Rome (IRE)** *J Moore* 123
4 b g Holy Roman Emperor(IRE) Summer Trysting (USA) (Alleged (USA))
7899a[5] (8154a)

**Desire** *Richard Fahey* 36
2 ch f Kyllachy Colonel's Daughter (Colonel Collins (USA))
7004[6] 7496[6]

**Desiree Clary (GER)** *Waldemar Hickst* 100
2 b f Sholokhov(IRE) Dynamica (GER) (Dashing Blade)
7315a[2]

**Desmios (FR)** *C Laffon-Parias* 80
2 b c Hold That Tiger(USA) Sapfo (FR) (Peintre Celebre (USA))
4932a[2]

**Desperado (JPN)** *Akio Adachi* a107 118
6 b h Neo Universe(JPN) Meine Noel (JPN) (Tony Bin)
2002a[17]

**Desperado Dancer** *Natalie Lloyd-Beavis* 23
3 b g Iffraaj Madam Ninette (Mark Of Esteem (IRE))
5272[6] 5775[10]

**Despot (IRE)** *Charles Hills* a89 92
3 gr c Verglas(IRE) Ms Bossy Boots (USA) (Grand Slam (USA))
(1769) ◆ (2058) 3137[5] 4181[5] (4679)

**Destination Aim** *Frederick Watson* 74
7 b g Dubai Destination(USA) Tessa Reef (IRE) (Mark Of Esteem (IRE))
3344[4] 3668[9] 5887[9] 7180[7]

**Destin Blue (FR)** *P Marion* a82 81
6 b h Anabaa Blue Noble Presence (FR) (Fasliyev (USA))
(178a) 584a[5]

**Destiny Blue (IRE)** *Suzzanne France* a42 64
7 b g Danehill Dancer(IRE) Arpege (IRE) (Sadler's Wells (USA))
1345[9] 1607[13] 2162[10] 3035[5] 4792[4] 5331[6] 6490[10] 7643[15] 7976[9]

**Destiny Highway (FR)** *Mlle M Henry* a73 72
4 b g Sir Percy Grace Bankes (Efisio)
2192a[2]

**Destiny's Kitten (IRE)** *Tom Dascombe* 83
3 b f Naaqoos Safqa (Singspiel (IRE))
(2118) 2567[5] 3247[6]

**Destiny's Shadow (IRE)** *George Baker* a47
2 b g Dark Angel(IRE) Lunar Love (IRE) (In The Wings)
5351[11] 6101[10]

**Destor (GER)** *U Stech* 106
4 rg c Sternkoenig(IRE) Desimona (GER) (Monsun (GER))
2001a[3]

**Detmann (FR)** *Y Durepaire* 80
2 bb c Lawman(FR) Incoming (Selkirk (USA))
5940a[2]

**De Treville** *A Fabre* 104
2 b c Oasis Dream Dar Re Mi (Singspiel (IRE))
6570a[2]

**Deuce Again** *John Gosden* a79 79
3 b f Dubawi(IRE) Match Point (Unfuwain (USA))
3141[5] 4435[3]

**Devilment** *Charlie Appleby* a102 95
3 b g Cape Cross(IRE) Mischief Making (USA) (Lemon Drop Kid (USA))
(2060) 2748[4] 4584[2] 5179[5] 6156[2] 6665[3] 6943[6]

**Devils In My Head** *Keiran Burke* a12
4 b f Kheleyf(USA) Alexandra S (IRE) (Sadler's Wells (USA))
7921[8]

**Devilution (IRE)** *Derek Shaw* a40 22
2 b g Bluegrass Cat(USA) Meniatarra (USA) (Zilzal (USA))
5009[10] 5296[8] 5799[10]

**Devious Spirit (IRE)** *Richard Fahey* 62
2 br g Intikhab(USA) Unintentional (Dr Devious (IRE))
5241[2] 6375a[19] 7329[3]

**Devon Drum** *Paul Webber* a81
6 b g Beat Hollow West Devon (USA) (Gone West (USA))
(686) 1219[3] 7531[9] 7866[8]

**Devonshire Place (IRE)** *Roger Charlton* a60 54
2 b f Rip Van Winkle(IRE) Councilofconstance (IRE) (Footstepsinthesand)
7594[10] 7891[7]

**Devote Myself (IRE)** *John Flint* a52 35
5 b m Kodiac Hazarama (IRE) (Kahyasi)
118[7] 289[12] 435[8] 1050[4] 1138[5] ◆ 1288[6] 1819[3] 2689[10] 3208[10] 3781[9]

**Dewala** *Michael Appleby* a84 76
5 b m Deportivo Fuwala (Unfuwain (USA))
270[2] 386[3] 764[6]

**Dew Pond** *Tim Easterby* a48 47
2 b g Motivator Rutland Water (IRE) (Hawk Wing (USA))
4467[6] 5098[4] 6668[10]

**Dexterous** *Roger Charlton* a58
2 b f Mastercraftsman(IRE) Daring Aim (Daylami (IRE))
7892[6] 8067[12]

**Dha Chara (IRE)** *Andrew Hollinshead* a55 51
4 b g Ramonti(FR) Campiglia (IRE) (Fairy King (USA))
8168[12]

**Dhaular Dhar (IRE)** *Jim Goldie* a60 66
12 b g Indian Ridge Pescara (IRE) (Common Grounds)
2215[5] 2475[7] 2674[3] 2911[3] 3190[5] 3361[6] 3828[3] 4014[5] 4254[2] 4520[2] 4858[5] 5421[8] 5815[2] 6597[3] 6825[2] 7100[9] 7895[7] 8261[3]

**Diaghan (FR)** *M Delzangles* 105
3 gr c Lawman(FR) Diamilina (FR) (Linamix (FR))
1340a[4] 2194a[7]

**Dialogue** *Andrew Reid* a76 57
8 b g Singspiel(IRE) Zonda (Fabulous Dancer (USA))
1606[4] 3344[2] 3908[4] 5711[4] 6402[6] (7456) 7774[6] (8044) 8260[4]

**Diamant (GER)** *Wido Neuroth* a55 103
4 b c Zamindar(USA) Diamantgottin (GER) (Fantastic Light (USA))
4956a[6]

**Diamant De Vati (FR)** *S Wattel* a85 78
3 b c Kingsalsa(USA) Reine De Vati (FR) (Take Risks (FR))
169a[7] 795a[8] 1551a[5]

**Diamond Back (IRE)** *Denis Quinn* a37
3 b c Diamond Green(FR) Raqiqah (Unbridled's Song (USA))
626[6] 823[6] 988[7]

**Diamond Blue** *Richard Fahey* a69 71
6 ch m Namid Petra Nova (First Trump)
1447[8] 1758[2] 2602[12] 3384[2] 3668[2] 4421[5] 4891[2] 5641[3] 6475[13] 6758[4] 7698[3] 7993[3]

**Diamond Charlie (IRE)** *Simon Dow* a92 76
6 br g Diamond Green(FR) Rosy Lydgate (Last Tycoon)
55[4] 148[3] 534[12] 719[3] 802[4] 1041[7] 1650[5] 2050[6] 2718[7] 5182[3] 5559[2] 7624[10] (8025) 8101[5]

**Diamond Creek (IRE)** *Richard Fahey* 83
2 b f Kodiac Boudica (IRE) (Alhaarth (IRE))
(2541) 3001[6] (3188) 4164[5] 4439[9] 4920[5] 5791[4] 6256[18] 6933[17] 7231[6]

**Diamond Dame (IRE)** *John Joseph Hanlon* a52 53
5 b m King's Best(USA) Arabian Treasure (USA) (Danzig (USA))
7877a[6]

**Diamond Dove (GER)** *Andreas Lowe* 106
3 ch f Dr Fong(USA) Dyveke (GER) (Lando (GER))
2584a[3] 3873a[2] 4955a[2] 5927[6] 7727a[4]

**Diamondhead (IRE)** *Ed de Giles* a75 82
5 b g Kyllachy Hammrah (Danehill (USA))
1144[5] 1447[12] 1921[6] (2414) 3213[3] 3533[9] 3783[5]

**Diamond Joel** *Mick Channon* a60 50
2 b c Youmzain(IRE) Miss Lacroix (Picea)
7666[9] 7834[3]

**Diamond Kathi (GER)** *Mario Hofer* a70 72
4 ch f Toylsome Diamond Sun (Primo Dominie)
722a[6]

**Diamond Lady** *William Stone* a87 87
3 b f Multiplex Ellen Mooney (Efisio)
1614[10] 1952[10] (3305) 4406[5] 4918[2] 5675[12] 6336[2] 6872[5] 7564[2] 7843[5] 8297[3]

**Diamond Lucy (IRE)** *John Butler* 54
3 b f Diamond Green(FR) Hi Lyla (IRE) (Lahib (USA))
28[6]

**Diamond Pro (IRE)** *Christopher Kellett* a17 59
5 b g Diamond Green(FR) Speedbird (USA) (Sky Classic (CAN))
361[8] 3309[10]

**Diamond River (FR)** *P Monfort* a58 58
3 gr f Stormy River(FR) Pierre De L'Une (FR) (Dyhim Diamond (IRE))
4252a[9]

**Diamond Runner (IRE)** *Deborah Sanderson* a49 60
2 b g Amadeus Wolf Hawk Eyed Lady (IRE) (Hawk Wing (USA))
4330[8] 5072[2] 5519[6] 6811[5] 7064[6] 8121[9]

**Diamonds A Dancing** *Brian Gubby* a74 56
4 ch g Delta Dancer Zing (Zilzal (USA))
1980[5] 2401[7] 2884[8] 3576[6] (6857) (7036) (7259) 7759[13]

**Diamond Sam** *Sylvester Kirk* a33 30
2 ch c Compton Place Kurtanella (Pastoral Pursuits)
1417[11] 6603[12]

**Diamondsinthesky (IRE)** *Derek Shaw* a57 49
3 b f Dandy Man(IRE) Colourpoint (USA) (Forest Wildcat (USA))
174[2] 302[3] 745[8] 933[2] 1039[3] 1585[5] 3972[6] 4890[8] 8119[5]

**Diamond Solitaire (IRE)** *Timothy Jarvis* a53 51
3 br f Diamond Green(FR) Eastern Blue (IRE) (Be My Guest (USA))
2125[8] 3801[6] 4337[8] 5080[10] 7520[4] 7781[12] 7940[10]

**Diamond Vine (IRE)** *Ronald Harris* a48 50
6 b g Diamond Green(FR) Glasnas Giant (Giant's Causeway (USA))
34[10] 586[4] 799[2] 972[2] 1148[7] 1312[6] 2008[5] 2831[4] 3848[5] 5000[2] 5624[4] 6023[8] 7222[10] 8286[3]

**Diana D'Aumont (FR)** *Mme C Rondele* a64 74
3 ch f Linngari(IRE) Moscowa (FR) (Alamo Bay (USA))
7722a[5]

**Dianora** *Sir Michael Stoute* a70 78
3 b f New Approach(IRE) Nannina (Medicean)
2339[7] 3423[4] 4802[2] 5448[6] 6192[3] 7195[6] 7812[3] 8041[7]

**Diatomic (IRE)** *Tom Dascombe* a55 65
2 b g Bushranger(IRE) Gilded Truffle (IRE) (Peintre Celebre (USA))
1342[10] 2051[5] 2673[3] 3297[3] 3620[4] 5285[4] 5798[5] 6648[6] 6869[5]

**Diaz (IRE)** *Mark Johnston* 95
2 b g Azamour(IRE) New Girlfriend (IRE) (Diesis)
3194[4] ◆ (3474) 3883[2] 4645[4] 5431[3] 6375a[11]

**Dibajj (FR)** *A De Royer-Dupre* a91 108
4 ch f Iffraaj Goleta (IRE) (Royal Applause)
2197a[4] 2820a[3] 3746a[7]

**Dick Doughtywylie** *John Gosden* a107 108
6 b g Oasis Dream Sugar Mill (FR) (Polar Falcon (USA))
1068[4] 1559[2] 3416[7]

**Dick Whittington (IRE)** *A P O'Brien* 114
2 b c Rip Van Winkle(IRE) Sahara Sky (IRE) (Danehill (USA))
3448[3] (4460a) (5218a)

**Diddy Eric** *Micky Hammond* 59
4 b g Oratorio(IRE) Amber Queen (IRE) (Cadeaux Genereux)
2135[6] 2674[4] 3363[3] 4958[4] (5084) (5268) 5495[9]

**Diescentric (USA)** *Julie Camacho* a95 111
7 b g Diesis Hawzah (Green Desert (USA))
4425[5]

**Diesel Ten (IRE)** *Patrick O Brady* a40 89
4 b g Refuse To Bend(IRE) Zoudie (Ezzoud (IRE))
1078a[U]

**Different** *Bryan Smart* a74 71
4 ch f Bahamian Bounty Hill Welcome (Most Welcome)
87[6]

**Different Scenario** *Mel Brittain* a27 53
3 b f Araafa(IRE) Racina (Bluebird (USA))
3343[8] 4495[10] 5331[2] 5495[11] 7006[7]

**Digeanta (IRE)** *W P Mullins* 94
7 b g Helissio(FR) Scolboa Gold (IRE) (Accordion)
4746a[8] 6349a[7] 7107[5] 7476a[12]

**Digital Rebellion (IRE)** *Charlie Appleby* a66 75
2 ch c Dubawi(IRE) Rebelline (IRE) (Robellino (USA))
3474[6] 4570[9] 5315[3] 5782[6] 7902[5]

**Dikta Del Mar (SPA)** *T Martins* 98
2 b f Diktat Marmaria (SPA) (Limpid)
3027a[4] 4603a[2] 6220a[4] (7485a)

**Diktari (FR)** *F Chappet* 67
2 bb f Diktat Rubies (Inchinor)
6591a[14]

**Dildar (IRE)** *Paul Nicholls*
6 b g Red Ransom(USA) Diamond Tango (FR) (Acatenango (GER))
2558[P]

**Diletta Tommasa (IRE)** *John Stimpson* a69 75
4 ch f Dylan Thomas(IRE) Chronicle (Observatory (USA))
151[4] 345[11] 697[3] 1097[5] 1729[5] 3080[8] 3308[5] (4473) 4658[3] (4763) 6192[7] 6672[5] 7459[9]

**Dime Dancer (IRE)** *Werner Glanz* a72 75
3 b f Azamour(IRE) Happy Land (IRE) (Refuse To Bend (IRE))
7270a[6] 7630a[4]

**Dimension** *Conor Murphy* a105 111
6 bb g Medicean Palatial (Green Desert (USA))
7609a[12]

**Diminutive (IRE)** *Grace Harris* a58 48
2 ch f Fast Company(IRE) Take It Easee (IRE) (Noverre (USA))
1889[4] 2206[3] 2395[6] 3312[6] (3967) 4283[5] 4542[2] 5133[6] 5525[7] 6017[4] 6563[5] 6842[8] 7064[10] 7684[5] 7948[6] 8118[3] 8240[3]

**Dimitar (USA)** *Johnny Farrelly* a74 48
5 b g Mizzen Mast(USA) Peace And Love (IRE) (Fantastic Light (USA))
359[7] 540[7] (646) 817[4] 1152[4] 1799[8] 2669[7] 4073[8] 6088[11] 6342[3] 7077[6]

**Dingari (FR)** *Mario Hofer* a53 61
2 b f Linngari(IRE) Diamantwelle (IRE) (Xaar)
7163a[6]

**Ding Ding** *Mick Channon* a51 56
3 ch f Winker Watson Five Bells (IRE) (Rock Of Gibraltar (IRE))
5071[5] 5719[3] 6194[2]

**Dinkum Diamond (IRE)** *Henry Candy* 112
6 b h Aussie Rules(USA) Moving Diamonds (Lomitas)
(1163) 1531[4] 1949[7] 2766[6] 3241[3] 3981[3] 4937[5] 6134[9] 6549[7]

**Dinneratmidnight** *Ralph Beckett* a88 84
3 b g Kyllachy The Terrier (Foxhound (USA))
(1677) 2317[14] (4262) 5204[7] ◆ 5650[11] 7365[11]

**Dino Mite** *Peter Chapple-Hyam* a83 77
3 b f Doctor Dino(FR) Compose (Anabaa (USA))
1701[12] (3796) 5288[5] 5800[7]

**Diodoros (FR)** *F Chappet* a81 100
8 ch g High Chaparral(IRE) Light Quest (USA) (Quest For Fame)
178a[3]

**Dipankara (FR)** *H-A Pantall* a68 71
2 gr f Aqlaam La Barquera (Nayef (USA))
8132a[5]

**Diplomatic (IRE)** *Michael Squance* a80 58
9 b g Cape Cross(IRE) Embassy (Cadeaux Genereux)
(181) 457[7] 587[3] 843[7] 927[3]

**Dippinganddiving (IRE)** *Jose Santos* a46 14
2 ch f Captain Rio Arabis (Arazi (USA))
7573[9] 7881[6] 8184[6]

**Diracan (IRE)** *Nick Littmoden* 60
2 b f Alfred Nobel(IRE) Ikan (IRE) (Sri Pekan (USA))
2652[5] 3557[10] 3933[6] 5180[3] 5436[8] 6040[3] 6610[13]

**Direct Approach (IRE)** *Lynn Siddall* a62
10 b g Tel Quel(FR) Miss Telimar (IRE) (Montelimar (USA))
7627[5] 7951[5] 8064[4] 8231[7]

**Directional** *Charlie Appleby* a47
2 b g Raven's Pass(USA) Rose Street (USA) (Street Cry (IRE))
5009[8] 6102[8] 6602[8] 8121[12]

**Director (IRE)** *William Haggas* 35
2 b g Danehill Dancer(IRE) Toolentidhaar (USA) (Swain (IRE))
7413[8]

**Directorship** *Patrick Chamings* a82 95
8 br g Diktat Away To Me (Exit To Nowhere (USA))
1948[8] 3244[7] 3753[6] 4331[4] 4761[6] 5213[5] 7852[7]

**Direct Times (IRE)** *Peter Chapple-Hyam* 65
3 b g Acclamation Elegant Times (IRE) (Dansili)
(6862)

**Direct Trade** *Mark Usher* a48 26
4 ch f Trade Fair Bold Love (Bold Edge)
18[5] 184[11]

**Dire Straits (IRE)** *Chris Wall* a84 66
3 b c Teofilo(IRE) Kalagold (IRE) (Magical Strike (USA))
3074[12] 3537[8] 3804[10] 5011[6] 5829[2] 6461[5] 7628[2] (8047) 8164[2] ◆

**Disa Leader (SAF)** *M F De Kock* a106 105
9 b g Parade Leader(USA) Plumosa (SAF) (Sapieha (IRE))
112a[9] 306a[4] 509a[3] 679a[8] 810a[2]

**Disavow** *Mark Johnston* 77
2 b f Shamardal(USA) Dunnes River (USA) (Danzig (USA))
3358[5] (3642) (4012) 4203[6] 5147[5] 7005[7]

**Disclosure** *Les Eyre* a51 76
3 b g Indesatchel(IRE) Gemini Gold (IRE) (King's Best (USA))
2333[11] 2768[6] 3342[2] 3650[5] 4019[12] 4297[3] 5080[6] 5470[10] (5892) 6431[8] 6822[10] 7953[9] 8086[10]

**Disco Dale (IRE)** *Richard Fahey* a35
3 gr g Verglas(IRE) Artisia (IRE) (Peintre Celebre (USA))
7910[7] 8147[4]

**Disco Dave (IRE)** *Daniel Mark Loughnane* a66 45
6 ch g Dalakhani(IRE) Amoureux (USA) (Deputy Minister (CAN))
(39) 116[2] 410[4] 433[3] 497[6]

**Discoverer (IRE)** *M Al Muhairi* a87 56
5 b h Bernardini(USA) Danuta (USA) (Sunday Silence (USA))
241a[7]

**Discovery Bay** *Brian Ellison* a76 76
6 b g Dansili Rainbow's Edge (Rainbow Quest (USA))
2305[3] 2515[3] 3466[5] 4704[5]

**Discreetly** *Hughie Morrison* 71
3 b f Sakhee's Secret Aqaba (Lake Coniston (IRE))
1844[4] ◆ 2392[2] 2967[10]

**Discrete (FR)** *H-F Devin* a78 95
3 b f Doctor Dino(FR) Calling All Angels (FR) (Ange Gabriel (FR))
4249a[4] 6218a[7]

**Discussiontofollow (IRE)** *Mike Murphy* a92 103
4 b g Elusive City(USA) Tranquil Sky (Intikhab (USA))
(294) ◆ 1492[3] 3737a[3] (4179) 4895[6] 6369a[5]

**Disegno (IRE)** *Sir Michael Stoute* a88 102
2 b c Fastnet Rock(AUS) Seven Magicians (USA) (Silver Hawk (USA))
2777[3] (3578) 4645[2]

**Di's Gift** *Richard Guest* 77
5 b g Generous(IRE) Di's Dilemma (Teenoso (USA))
3385[6] 4062[2] 4978[3] 5527[5] 5984[8]

**Dishy Guru** *Michael Blanshard* a77 74
5 ch g Ishiguru(USA) Pick A Nice Name (Polar Falcon (USA))
53[7] 244[5] 449[4] (797) 987[4] (1238) 1787[5] 2174[11] 3392[3] ◆ 3707[7] (4546) 5281[5] 6455[5] (6658) 6873[13] 7357[10]

**Dispour (IRE)** *Donald McCain* a11 81
4 ch g Monsun(GER) Dalataya (IRE) (Sadler's Wells (USA))
2091[10]

**Disprove (IRE)** *Hugo Palmer* a79 85
2 b f Approve(IRE) Deraaya (IRE) (Mujahid (USA))
3671[4] 4269[2] ◆ (5555) 6053a[3] 6530[9] 7448[8]

**Dissent (IRE)** *James Given* a85 82
5 b g Dansili Centifolia (FR) (Kendor (FR))
272[4] 478[5] 797[2] 908[6] (1270) ◆ 3793[4] (4049) 4581[6] (5281) 5830[4] 6511[4] 7624[2]

**Dissident (AUS)** *Peter G Moody* 120
4 bb c Sebring(AUS) Diana's Secret (AUS) (Anabaa (USA))
7127a[6]

**Dissolution** *Sir Michael Stoute* 83
2 b c New Approach(IRE) Portodora (USA) (Kingmambo (USA))
4395[5] 5655[5] 6056[2] (6653)

**Distant High** *Richard Price* 63
3 b f High Chaparral(IRE) Distant Dreamer (USA) (Rahy (USA))
2442[5] 3121[2] 3695[2] 4191[6] 4817[6] 5004[4] 5685[8] 5980[5] 6426[7] 7025[5] ◆ 7303[4]

**Distant Past** *Kevin Ryan* a77 82
3 b g Pastoral Pursuits Faraway Lass (Distant Relative)
1445[5] 2015[4] 3331[6] 3959[2] 5087[3] 5601[7] (6153) 6512[9] 7073[10]

**Distant Shadow** *Chris Wall* a38 40
3 gr f Rock Of Gibraltar(IRE) Daheeya (Daylami (IRE))
1395[9] 2339[13] 2682[14] 3214[12]

**District Attorney (IRE)** *Chris Fairhurst* a56 57
5 b g Lawman(FR) Mood Indigo (IRE) (Indian Ridge)
2738[6] 3535[5] 3843[8] 4755[6] 5200[2] 6216[3]

**Disushe Star** *Keith Dalgleish* 9
2 ch g Kheleyf(USA) Canis Star (Wolfhound (USA))
4486[5] 6108[6] 6509[10]

**Dittander** *Richard Hannon* a74 80
2 b f Exceed And Excel(AUS) Penny's Gift (Tobougg (IRE))
(1764) ◆ (4283) 4913[10] 5409[3] 5879[5] 7201[7]

**Divea** *Anthony Carson* a70 48
5 b m Dylan Thomas(IRE) Cumin (USA) (Fusaichi Pegasus (USA))
(974) 1046[2] 2097[5] 2980[6]

**Divertimenti (IRE)** *Roy Bowring* a57 58
10 b g Green Desert(USA) Ballet Shoes (IRE) (Ela-Mana-Mou)
34[2] 3150[10] 4131[10] 4370[4] 4788[6] (5287) 5777[3] 5987[4] 6120[5] 6495[10] 7782[7] 8133[2] 8210[3]

**Dividend Dan (IRE)** *Mike Murphy* a60 55
4 ch g Danroad(AUS) Pip'n Judy (IRE) (Pips Pride)
736[5] (916) 1121[6] 1450[8] 1813[4] 2469[3] 3527[7] 4432[5]

**Divina Comedia (FR)** *N Clement* a88 96
3 gr f Footstepsinthesand Divine Promesse (FR) (Verglas (IRE))
5843a[2] 7268a[3] 7857a[5]

**Divine (IRE)** *Mick Channon* a74 97
3 b f Dark Angel(IRE) Carallia (IRE) (Common Grounds)
(447) 1711[3] (2295) 2965[2] 3459[7] 4166[14]

**Divine Bay** *Gary Moore* a40 36
3 b f Dutch Art Inchcoonan (Emperor Jones (USA))
2694[15] 3527[10]

**Divine Call** *Milton Bradley* a72 73
7 b g Pivotal Pious (Bishop Of Cashel)
83[3] (295) 576[2] 841[7] 1766[8] 2174[5] 2887[8] 3149[7] 3848[2] 4908[3] 5602[4] 5897[2] 6889[4] 7252[5] (7307) 7888[9] 7989[3] 8143[6]

**Divine Davis (FR)** *L A Urbano-Grajales* a59
4 b f Whipper(USA) Aldovea (Nashwan (USA))
392a[11]

**Divine Law** *Richard Hannon* 76
2 ch c Major Cadeaux Yanomami (USA) (Slew O'Gold (USA))
2007[9] 2622[3] 3081[3] (3963) 5250[4] 6529[9] 7156[8]

**Divine Oath (USA)** *Todd Pletcher* a100 103
3 b c Broken Vow(USA) Rejoicing (USA) (Forestry (USA))
(4230a) 5458a[6]

**Divine Rule (IRE)** *Laura Mongan* a64 47
6 br g Cacique(IRE) Island Destiny (Kris)
289[3] 445[7] 578[4] 780[3] 815[3] 1023[3] (1141) 1385[6] 1771[6] 2646[8] 2864[8] 3576[10] 4266[6] 4658[8] 4808[6] 6481[12] 6771[3] 7036[4] 7546[6] 7844[6] (7883) 7987[4] 8298[4]

**Divine Warrior (IRE)** *Timothy Jarvis* a63 35
3 b c High Chaparral(IRE) Lady Of Talent (USA) (Siphon (BRZ))
3925[9] 7528[9] 7733[9] 7925[13]

**Divin Leon (FR)** *M Boutin* a85 90
6 b h Divine Light(JPN) Nera Zilzal (IRE) (Zilzal (USA))
584a[4]

**Division Belle** *William Muir* a64 64
3 gr f Dalakhani(IRE) Multiplication (Marju (IRE))
2224[3] 2695[5] 3968[7] 5284[8] 5865[4] 6682[6] 7197[9]

**Dixie Gwalia** *Michael Attwater* a62 39
6 b m Tobougg(IRE) Dixieanna (Night Shift (USA))
244[12] 452[6] 556[7]

**Dixie's Dream (IRE)** *William Jarvis* a96 85
5 b g Hawk Wing(USA) Hams (USA) (Dixie Union (USA))
163[4] (457) 804[6] ◆ 1164[14] 1437[15]

**Diyoudar (FR)** *Rod Collet* a75 65
3 b c Elusive City(USA) Diasilixa (FR) (Linamix (FR))
2003a[2] 3869a[3] 5027a[3] 5705a[5]

**Dizzey Heights (IRE)** *Stuart Kittow* a52
2 b f Halling(USA) Extreme Pleasure (IRE) (High Chaparral (IRE))
7198[8]

**Dizzy River (IRE)** *Brian Ellison* 40
9 ch g Flemensfirth(USA) Dizzy Dealer (IRE) (Le Bavard (FR))
3385[8]

**Dj Gerry** *Nick Kent* 1
3 b g Cockney Rebel(IRE) Lady Trish (Red Ransom (USA))
7332[7]

**Djinni (IRE)** *Richard Hannon* a67 82
3 ro f Invincible Spirit(IRE) La Persiana (Daylami (IRE))
2122[6] 2749[6] 3280[3] 3890[6] 4329[5] 4611[5] 5096[4] 5751[11] 6647[8]

**Doc Charm** *Keith Dalgleish* a46 80
2 b g Hellvelyn Songsheet (Dominion)
2450[2] (3049) 4822[8] 6510[5] 6820[4] 7226[10]

**Doc Hay (USA)** *Lee Carter* a89 97
7 b g Elusive Quality(USA) Coherent (USA) (Danzig (USA))
1397[3] 1734[13] 2283[16] 2353[10] 2992[11] 3241[8] 3666[11] 4384[8] 5444[20] (5711) 6260[14] 7101[4] (7330) 7441[12] 7715[7] 7847[2] 7983[2] 8171[6]

**Docofthebay (IRE)** *Scott Dixon* a80 89
10 ch g Docksider(USA) Baize (Efisio)
552[5] 911[4] 1167[11] 1717[2] 2131[5] 2546[11]

**Docs Legacy (IRE)** *Richard Fahey* a94 91
5 b g Ad Valorem(USA) Lunamixa (GER) (Linamix (FR))
5174[13] 6098[4] ◆ 6566[7] 6937[2] 7334[2] 7641[7] (7688)

**Docteur Vigousse (FR)** *J Parize* a67 53
3 gr g Dr Fong(USA) Loulane (FR) (Commands (AUS))
360a[9] 482a[5] 585a[9]

**Doctor De L'Aube (FR)** *C Plisson* 67
3 b c Doctor Dino(FR) Eclat De Lune (FR) (Sinndar (IRE))
2003a[10]

**Doctor Hilary** *Mark Hoad* a56 38
12 b g Mujahid(USA) Agony Aunt (Formidable (USA))
34[4] 274[9] 563[2] 864[3] (1369) 1804[2] 2094[6] 2907[7] 3230[11] 8200[4]

**Doctor Kehoe** *Richard Fahey* 68
2 b g Cockney Rebel(IRE) Ogre (USA) (Tale Of The Cat (USA))
2731[4] 3728[13] 6319[7]

**Doctor Parkes** *Stuart Williams* a90 92
8 b g Diktat Lucky Parkes (Full Extent (USA))
55[8] 271[5] 644[11] 1193[10] (3033) 3458[4] 3693[6] 3927[6] 4412[5] 6131[9] 8025[4] 8171[2]

**Doctor Sardonicus** *David Simcock* a84 84
3 ch g Medicean Never A Doubt (Night Shift (USA))
1946[6] 2681[2] (3229) 4671[4] 6345[5] 7530[4]

**Doctor Sim (IRE)** *D De Waele* a83 69
5 b g King's Best(USA) Mas A Fuera (IRE) (Alzao (USA))
3089a[12]

**Doctors Papers** *David Brown* a24 41
2 ch g Stimulation(IRE) Inya Lake (Whittingham (IRE))
6831[5] 7244[8] 7752[10]

**Doctor Watson** *Tom Tate* 39
2 ch g Winker Watson Cibenze (Owington)
2386[12] 7234[8] 7495[10]

**Dodina (IRE)** *Brian Ellison* a74 74
4 b f Acclamation Etica (IRE) (Barathea (IRE))
69[3] 196[4] (1343) 1843[12] 2542[4] 3338[10] 3571[6] 4314[7] 4752[8]

**Doesyourdogbite (IRE)** *Andrew Hollinshead* 65
2 b g Notnowcato Gilah (IRE) (Saddlers' Hall (IRE))
6279[6] 7169[6] 7666[16]

**Doggy Tail (IRE)** *Stefano Botti* a70
4 b f Elusive City(USA) Penfection (IRE) (Orpen (USA))
392a[12]

**Do It All (USA)** *Saeed bin Suroor* a98 100
7 b h Distorted Humor(USA) Stupendous Miss (USA) (Dynaformer (USA))
110a[6] 309a[11]

**Dolce N Karama (IRE)** *John Patrick Shanahan* a87 86
3 b g The Carbon Unit(USA) Janna's Jewel (IRE) (Traditionally (USA))
204a[8] 770a[8] 2571a[8] 3998[3] 4360[3] 5851[2] 6738[3]

**Doldrums (USA)** *Mark Johnston* a81 27
4 b f Bernardini(USA) Appealing Storm (USA) (Valid Appeal (USA))
21[4] 200[7] (358) 494[6] 641[2] 732[4] 891[5] 1003[2] 1108[7] 1355[11] 1724[13]

**Dollar Bill** *Nick Gifford* a60 66
5 ch g Medicean Jardin (Sinndar (IRE))
1941[9] 3453[11] 4149[3]

**Dolly Colman (IRE)** *Zoe Davison* a52 42
6 bg m Diamond Green(FR) Absolutely Cool (IRE) (Indian Ridge)
116[7] 246[11]

**Dolniya (FR)** *A De Royer-Dupre* a91 117
3 b f Azamour(IRE) Daltama (IRE) (Indian Ridge)
(3773a) 6380a[3] 6970a[5]

**Dolorous** *John Gosden* a57 70
2 b f Vale Of York(IRE) High Days (IRE) (Hennessy (USA))
3888[3] ◆ 4784[6] 5253[3] 6629[9]

**Dolphin Rock** *Brian Ellison* a71 84
7 b g Mark Of Esteem(IRE) Lark In The Park (IRE) (Grand Lodge (USA))
1483[15] 2762[4] 3368[5] 4402[5] 5413[4] 6166[9] 6626[4] 7251[6]

**Dolphin Village (IRE)** *Richard Fahey* a81 92
4 b g Cape Cross(IRE) Reform Act (USA) (Lemon Drop Kid (USA))
1934[7] (3341) (4538) 5651[3] 6005[6] 6786[9] 7083[11]

**Domeside** *M Delcher Sanchez* 103
8 b h Domedriver(IRE) Buck's Fizz (Kris)
6383a[8] 7486a[10]

**Dominada (IRE)** *Brian Ellison* 89
2 b c Mastercraftsman(IRE) Red Blossom (USA) (Silver Hawk (USA))
3619[5] 4633[3] 5576[6] 6225[2]

**Dominandros (FR)** *Gay Kelleway* a96 92
3 b g Teofilo(IRE) Afya (Oasis Dream)
2630a[6] (3869a) (4775a) 5591a[9] 7619a[5] 7930[3] 8244[5]

**Dominant (IRE)** *J Moore* 119
6 bl h Cacique(IRE) Es Que (Inchinor)
1182a[5] 7899a[11] 8151a[4]

**Dominate** *Richard Hannon* a76 89
4 b c Assertive Blue Goddess (IRE) (Blues Traveller (IRE))
1492[9] 2030[6] 2778[6] 3313[5] 3876[6] 5559[4] (5750) 6089[2] 7132[7] 7669[9] 7947[7]

**Domination** *C Byrnes* a82 105
7 b g Motivator Soliza (IRE) (Intikhab (USA))
(3321) 3985[3]

**Dominic Cork** *Kevin Ryan* a64 69
2 gr g Zebedee Giusina Mia (USA) (Diesis)
2214[3] 2513[3] 3304[4] 4172[6] 4853[11] 5506[5] 6211[2] 6574[4] (6830) 7374[5]

**Dominike (ITY)** *Marco Botti* a60 52
2 b f Duke Of Marmalade(IRE) Donoma (IRE) (Beat Hollow)
6041[7] 7367[5]

**Dominium (USA)** *Jeremy Gask* a83 76
7 b g E Dubai(USA) Sudenlylastsummer (USA) (Rinka Das (USA))
1731[9] 2312[6] 3118[6] 4024[5] 4545[2] 5182[2] 5422[2] (6346) 7071[2] 7521[8]

**Do More Business (IRE)** *Liam Corcoran* a62 55
7 b g Dubai Destination(USA) Tokyo Song (USA) (Stravinsky (USA))
317[3] 435[2] 538[3] 736[7] 822[3] 964[5] 998[5] 1745[4] 2596a[4]

**Donavista (FR)** *F-H Graffard* a85 72
3 b f Soldier Of Fortune(IRE) La Boisserie (FR) (Dansili)
1139a[2] 5404a[4]

**Don Bosco (FR)** *D Smaga* a113 113
7 ch h Barathea(IRE) Perfidie (IRE) (Monsun (GER))
1371a[9]

**Done Dreaming (IRE)** *Richard Fahey* a57 63
4 b g Diamond Green(FR) Wishing Chair (USA) (Giant's Causeway (USA))
7783[3] 8081[4] 8229[6]

**Donna Bella (FR)** *S Smrczek* a73 73
3 b f Desert Style(IRE) Diamantwelle (IRE) (Xaar)
(5227a)

**Donna Graciosa (GER)** *Mark Johnston* 58
2 b f Samum(GER) Donna Alicia (GER) (Highland Chieftain)
6497[3] 6742[6]

**Donna Prassede (ITY)** *Stefano Botti* 97
3 b f Manduro(GER) Everarda (GER) (Singspiel (IRE))
1780a[11] 2590a[7] 3513a[4]

**Donncha (IRE)** *Robert Eddery* a80 93
3 br c Captain Marvelous(IRE) Seasonal Style (IRE) (Generous (IRE))
2112[2] ◆ (6990) 7597[6]

**Donnerschlag** *Andreas Lowe* 103
4 ch g Bahamian Bounty Dame Hester (IRE) (Diktat)
5966a[12]

**Donn Halling (IRE)** *V Luka Jr* 107
6 b g Halling(USA) Papering (IRE) (Shaadi (USA))
7469a[6]

**Donny Rover (IRE)** *Michael Appleby* a39 97
3 b g Excellent Art My Lass (Elmaamul (USA))
(1586) 1979[4] 2481[6] 3200[2] 4147[4] 4821[12] (5345) (6870)

**Don Padeja** *Jonjo O'Neill* a54 80
4 br g Dansili La Leuze (IRE) (Caerleon (USA))
5414[7]

**Don Ricardo (IRE)** *Richard Fahey* a46 36
2 b c Acclamation City Dancer (IRE) (Elusive City (USA))
2601[6] 6271[8] 6831[6] 7453[7] 7683[8]

**Don Sigfredo (IRE)** *Tom Dascombe* a73 84
2 b g Majestic Missile(IRE) Harvest Joy (IRE) (Daggers Drawn (USA))
1259[5] 1741[2] 2944[4] 3937[2] 4185[2] (4939) 6135[8] 6739[6] 7224[8]

**Don't** *Julia Feilden* a74 64
3 b f Invincible Spirit(IRE) Frigid (Indian Ridge)
1381[7] 2383[8] 5107[4] 5492[7] 7633[8] 7842[8]

**Don't Be** *Sir Mark Prescott Bt* a88 72
4 b f Cape Cross(IRE) Faslen (USA) (Fasliyev (USA))
3628[3] 4593[7] 7575[3] (7905) (8017) (8251) ◆

**Dont Bother Me (IRE)** *Marco Botti* a101 106
4 br c Dark Angel(IRE) Faleh (USA) (Silver Hawk (USA))
1719[4] 2145[9] 2778[3] 3452[7] 4648[2] 5418[7]

**Don't Call Me (IRE)** *David Nicholls* a101 111
7 ch g Haafhd Just Call Me (NZ) (Blues Traveller (IRE))
465[4] 749[2] 1721[15] 2145[8] 4212[7] 4648[5] (5163) 6124[12] 6534[2] 7081[6]

**Dont Have It Then** *Willie Musson* a84 83
3 b g Myboycharlie(IRE) Mondovi (Kyllachy)
86[8] (401) (573) 1260[3] 2015[6] 2886[2] (3426) 3936[3] 5675[6] 6468[2] 6872[12] 7775[3] (8072)

**Dontpaytheferryman (USA)** *Peter Hiatt* a57 36
9 ch g Wiseman's Ferry(USA) Expletive Deleted (USA) (Dr Blum (USA))
176[7] 252[4] 303[4] 433[5] 546[5] 567[7] 639[8] 831[9] 912[5] 959[7] 1004[4]

**Don't Stare** *James Fanshawe* a87 102
4 b g Zamindar(USA) Joshua's Princess (Danehill (USA))
2062[3] 2922[4] 4091[3] 5203[5] 6036[4] (6292) 6919[4]

**Dont Take Me Alive** *Charlie Longsdon* a63 63
5 b g Araafa(IRE) Up At Dawn (Inchinor)
8029[6] 8253[7]

**Don't Tell** *George Moore* 43
4 ch f Sakhee's Secret Starry Sky (Oasis Dream)
2135[9]

**Don't Tell Annie** *Tim Easterby* 86
2 b f Royal Applause Oasis Breeze (Oasis Dream)
(1482) 2313[5] 3001[2] (3337)

**Don't Tell Bertie** *Tom Tate* 29
2 b f Bertolini(USA) Rockburst (Xaar)
2014[9] 2358[6]

**Dont Tell Chris (FR)** *John Quinn* 47
2 b g Lawman(FR) Enigma (GER) (Sharp Victor (USA))
6976[9] 7244[6]

**Don't Tell Louise** *William Muir* 20
2 b f Medicean Lyra's Daemon (Singspiel (IRE))
7018[10]

**Dont Tell Nan** *Derek Shaw* a51 39
3 b f Major Cadeaux Charlie Girl (Puissance)
3972[9] 4891[9] 5333[11] 5574[2] 6851[5]

**Don't Tell Sophia (USA)** *Philip A Sims* a115 103
6 b m Congaree(USA) Lost Expectations (USA) (Valid Expectations (USA))
(6973a) 7593a[2]

**Doomah (IRE)** *Richard Hannon* 80
2 b f Holy Roman Emperor(IRE) Sweet Namibia (IRE) (Namid)
1788[2] (2173) 2845[5] 3649[3] 4205[4]

**Doonard Prince (IRE)** *Ross O'Sullivan* a70 70
5 b g Footstepsinthesand Fly Haia (!RE) (Flying Spur (AUS))
4556a[3] 6078a[2]

**Doppler Effect** *Ann Duffield* a25 73
2 ch g Monsieur Bond(IRE) Scarlet Oak (Zamindar (USA))
4708[3] 5561[3] 5995[2] 6537[3] 6757[10]

**Dorado (GER)** *Markus Klug* 95
4 b g Silvano(GER) Desca (GER) (Cadeaux Genereux)
7727a[12]

**Dora's Gift** *Edwin Tuer*
5 b m Cadeaux Genereux Conquestadora (Hernando (FR))
7281[13]

**Dorback** *Tony Newcombe* a70 88
7 ch g Kyllachy Pink Supreme (Night Shift (USA))
60[3] 259[10] 489[8] 1238[7] 2865[6]

**Dormello (IRE)** *D Selvaratnam* a104 104
6 b h Dansili Field Of Hope (IRE) (Selkirk (USA))
112a[7] 305a[8] 598a[10]

**Dorothy B (IRE)** *John Gosden* a63 104
3 b f Fastnet Rock(AUS) Slow Sand (USA) (Dixieland Band (USA))
1515[13] 2343[10]

**Dorraar (IRE)** *Roger Varian* a71 78
3 b f Shamardal(USA) Dorrati (USA) (Dubai Millennium)
1534[13] 1920[2] 2404[7] (3280) 3708[3] 4573[4]

**Dorry K (IRE)** *Jim Best* a48 37
5 b m Ad Valorem(USA) Ashtaroute (USA) (Holy Bull (USA))
1263[4] 1874[9]

**Dorset Cream** *Lady Cecil* a69 62
3 b f Dansili Blend (Zafonic (USA))
1424[5] 2133[6] 3655[7]

**Dorset Gift** *Michael Bell* a21 22
3 b f Royal Applause Cefira (USA) (Distant View (USA))
1298[5] 1713[8] 2125[10] 5321[10]

**Dorsett (USA)** *Brian A Lynch* 104
4 b c Artie Schiller(USA) Dontgetinmyway (USA) (Machiavellian (USA))
6391a[7]

**Dotties Boy** *Pat Phelan* a33
2 ch g Kheleyf(USA) Auntie Dot Com (Tagula (IRE))
5555[9] 6852[10]

**Double Bluff (IRE)** *Mark Johnston* 110
3 b c Azamour(IRE) Damask Rose (IRE) (Dr Devious (IRE))
1419[3] 2153[8] 2986[11] 4385[2] 4696[2] (4893) 5179[8]

**Double Bronze** *Milton Bradley*
2 gr c Verglas(IRE) Rhapsodize (Halling (USA))
4965[10] 5604[11]

**Double Czech (IRE)** *Patrick Chamings* a55 75
3 b g Bushranger(IRE) Night Of Joy (IRE) (King's Best (USA))
1389[8] 1786[2] 2013[4] 2624[6] 3145[9] (4155) 5381[6] 5753[3] 6657[14] 7202[10] 7337[6]

**Double Dealites** *Jamie Poulton* a59 53
4 b f Double Trigger(IRE) Linden Grace (USA) (Mister Baileys)
1143[5] 2280[9] 3385[7] 4082[4] ◆ 4678[5] 6007[10]

**Double Diamond (FR)** *C Ferland* 95
3 ch f Muhtathir Diamond Light (USA) (Fantastic Light (USA))
4721a[5]

**Double Discount (IRE)** *Tom Dascombe* a99 91
4 b g Invincible Spirit(IRE) Bryanstown Girl (IRE) (Kalanisi (IRE))
2309[3] 3341[5] 4184[3] 5695[9] 6106[3] 6664[2] (7033) 7850[2] 8095[6]

**Double First** *Kevin Frost*
3 ch f Avonbridge Amicella (Laroche (GER))
7818[11]

**Double Heaven** *Ed Walker* a64
2 b g Dutch Art Popocatepetl (FR) (Nashwan (USA))
8292[5]

**Double K** *Paul Midgley* 47
2 b g Kodiac Kelucia (IRE) (Grand Lodge (USA))
4450[10] 4624[P] 6447[7] 7245[4]

**Double Look (IRE)** *D Guillemin* 100
3 gr c Mastercraftsman(IRE) Paper Profits (Kendor (FR))
1340a[7]

**Double Up** *Roger Varian* a82 84
3 b g Exceed And Excel(AUS) My Love Thomas (IRE) (Cadeaux Genereux)
(824) 2122[2] ◆ 3114[2] 4390[3] 5438[10]

**Doubly Clever (IRE)** *Charles Hills* a69 67
2 ch g Iffraaj Smartest (IRE) (Exceed And Excel (AUS))
4666[6] 6268[4] 6556[8]

**Dougal (IRE)** *Richard Hannon* 93
2 b c Zebedee Liscoa (IRE) (Foxhound (USA))
1807[2] (2064) (2308) 4123[9] 4757[7] 6256[5] 7171[2]

**Dougal Philps** *Dr Richard Newland* a68 68
5 b g Echo Of Light Bella Bertolini (Bertolini (USA))
2684[9] 3177[7] 4369[6] 4792[5]

**Douglas Bank (IRE)** *Richard Fahey* 28
2 b g Dandy Man(IRE) Balance The Books (Elmaamul (USA))
2358[7] 2837[7] 4382[9]

**Douglas Pasha (IRE)** *Martin Smith* a59
4 b g Compton Place Lake Nayasa (Nayef (USA))
2843[8] 3576[14]

**Doumaran (FR)** *A De Royer-Dupre* 106
3 b g Authorized(IRE) Diamond Tango (FR) (Acatenango (GER))
5481a[2] 6183a[4] 6954a[5]

**Douneedahand** *Seamus Mullins* a66 54
3 b f Royal Applause Our Sheila (Bahamian Bounty)
98[4] 315[6] 745[4] 1047[2] 1425[2] (1449) 4285[7] 5307[4] 5624[8] 6897[4] 7111[4] 7364[12] 8014[2]

**Doux Douce (IRE)** *S M Duffy* a59 54
7 ch g Galileo(IRE) Captivating (IRE) (Wolfhound (USA))
7877a[3]

**Dove Mountain (IRE)** *Gary Brown* a62 75
3 b c Danehill Dancer(IRE) Virginia Waters (USA) (Kingmambo (USA))
70[5] 213[5] 536[3] 3114[10] 3522[6] 4972[12]

**Dover The Moon (IRE)** *Tom Gretton* a59 23
3 b g Bushranger(IRE) Gold Script (FR) (Script Ohio (USA))
1403[11] 1632[7] 1918[6] 2281[10] 2860[6] 3214[6] 4042[8] 7118[8]

**Dovils Date** *Tim Vaughan* a64 82
5 gr g Clodovil(IRE) Lucky Date (IRE) (Halling (USA))
(2468)

**Dovil's Duel (IRE)** *Rod Millman* a71 74
3 b g Clodovil(IRE) Duelling (Diesis)
1122[4] 1390[7]

**Do Wah Diddy Diddy** *Clive Cox* a73 75
3 b g Teofilo(IRE) Quite Elusive (USA) (Elusive Quality (USA))
1587[9] 2497[5] 2773[11] 5313[5] 5689[3] 6091[4] 7182[3]

**Down To Earth** *Michael Bell* a63 21
2 gr c Aussie Rules(USA) May Fox (Zilzal (USA))
7667[15] 8075[5]

**Downtown Boy (IRE)** *Ray Craggs* a49 46
6 br g Kheleyf(USA) Uptown (IRE) (Be My Guest (USA))
3238[4] 3535[8]

**Dozy Joe** *Joseph Tuite* a60 53
6 b g Sleeping Indian Surrey Down (USA) (Forest Wildcat (USA))
52[7] 161[8] 445[2] ◆ 583[4] 589[10] 852[4] 910[3] (1034) (1086) 1454[6] 1875[6] 7358[13] 7633[13] 7846[7] 8102[10]

**Dragline** *Tim Easterby* 57
2 b g Stimulation(IRE) Dane Dancing (IRE) (Danehill (USA))
1342[7] 1955[6] 3394[5] 3963[2] 4529[4] 5129[6] 6830[2]

**Dragon Falls (IRE)** *Charlie Appleby* a101 105
5 b g Distorted Humor(USA) Tizdubai (USA) (Cee's Tizzy (USA))
504a[6] 679a[11] 808a[2] 7066[6]

**Dragon Fei (IRE)** *Dermot Anthony McLoughlin* a11 85
4 b f Jeremy(USA) Wallonia (IRE) (Barathea (IRE))
612[8] 7144a[11]

**Dragon King (IRE)** *Michael Dods* 72
2 ch g Dylan Thomas(IRE) Alexander Queen (IRE) (King's Best (USA))
(2736) 6211[5]

**Dragonnade (FR)** *P Hern* a82 82
7 b m Victory Note(USA) Gaily Zest (USA) (St Jovite (USA))
5964a[7]

**Dragonstone (FR)** *D De Watrigant* a63
3 b c Muhtathir Solar Crystal (IRE) (Alzao (USA))
482a[4]

**Dragoon Guard (IRE)** *Marco Botti* a74 84
3 b c Jeremy(USA) Elouges (IRE) (Dalakhani (IRE))
1279[3]

**Drastic Art** *Michael Bell*
2 ch f Dutch Art Drastic Measure (Pivotal)
6408[12]

**Drawnfromthepast (IRE)** *Ed Walker* a63 75
9 ch g Tagula(IRE) Ball Cat (FR) (Cricket Ball (USA))
87[2] 208[8] 662[4] (1104) (1388) 2312[8]

**Dream Ally (IRE)** *Micky Hammond* a55 73
4 b g Oasis Dream Alexander Alliance (IRE) (Danetime (IRE))
1440[8] 1643[8] 2171[8] 3530[15] (4195) 4421[7] 4632[13] 4997[6] 5470[9] 6213[12] 6595[8]

**Dream And Hope** *Philip McBride* a60 48
3 b f Royal Applause Senta's Dream (Danehill (USA))
3822[4] 5267[7] 6939[5] 7197[4] 7256[5] (7548) 8311[5]

**Dream And Search (GER)** *Anthony Honeyball* a66 56
3 b c Raven's Pass(USA) Diamond Eyes (GER) (Winged Love (IRE))
2506[7] 3268[9] 6367[6] 6883[13]

**Dream Approval (IRE)** *Daniel Kubler* a68 74
2 gr f Approve(IRE) Courting Shinney (King's Theatre (IRE))
3181[7] (3550) 4157[6] 5554[3] 5974[2] (6222) 6574[5] 7374[6]

**Dream Big (IRE)** *Jo Crowley* a68 38
3 b f Echo Of Light Lovely Dream (IRE) (Elnadim (USA))
988[3] 1380[5] 2650[7] 3146[13] 3559[9]

**Dream Catcher (FR)** *Henry Candy* a72 72
6 gr g Della Francesca(USA) Gallopade (FR) (Kendor (FR))
1678[3] 2250[10] 3088[11] 3935[6] 4545[4] 5247[6] (5602) 6266[8] 6843[6] 7213[10]

**Dream Child (IRE)** *Charlie Appleby* a93 86
3 ch f Pivotal Poseidon's Bride (USA) (Seeking The Gold (USA))
2650[3] 3652[3] 4052[3] (6839) 7416[4] (7870) (8290)

**Dream Impossible (IRE)** *Peter Makin* a56 67
3 b f Iffraaj Romea (Muhtarram (USA))
2647[6] 3087[2] (3781) 4426[U] 4742[2] 5252[6] 6484[9]

**Dreaming Again** *Jimmy Fox* a55 23
4 b g Young Ern Maedance (Groom Dancer (USA))
92[6] 377[8] 737[6] 1016[5] 1141[3] 5139[6] 5560[6] (7347) 7853[2] 7987[5] 8198[4]

**Dreaming Beauty** *Jeremy Noseda* a86 73
3 b f Oasis Dream Independence (Selkirk (USA))
3184[2] ◆ 4407[6] 5388[2] 6265[4] (6904)

**Dreaming Brave** *Amanda Perrett* a65 64
3 b g Sleeping Indian Beechnut (IRE) (Mujadil (USA))
588[4] 2339[10] 2883[F] 6717[7]

**Dream Job** *Saeed bin Suroor* 53
2 b f Dubawi(IRE) Coretta (IRE) (Caerleon (USA))
7594[11]

**Dreamlike** *Luca Cumani* a82 68
2 b f Oasis Dream So Silk (Rainbow Quest (USA))
6553[6] 7405[2] ◆ (8036)

**Dream Ruler** *Jo Crowley* a75
3 b g Holy Roman Emperor(IRE) Whatcameoverme (USA) (Aldebaran (USA))
(816) 5304[3] 8169[7]

**Dream Scenario** *Mel Brittain* a79 63
4 b f Araafa(IRE) Notjustaprettyface (USA) (Red Ransom (USA))
3339[6] 4108[10] 4294[5] 4629[8] 7953[3] 8058[3] 8124[7]

**Dreamsgonewild (USA)** *Bruce F Alexander* 108
5 bb g Freud(USA) Twin Stroller (CAN) (Strolling Along (USA))
7325a[8]

**Dream Sika (IRE)** *Ruth Carr* a59 54
3 b g Elnadim(USA) Enchantment (Compton Place)
1373[6] 1642[8] 1925[2] 2388[10] 5715[3] 6114[3] 6340[3] (6561) 6897[8] 7519[6]

**Dreams Of Glory** *Ron Hodges* a77 74
6 ch h Resplendent Glory(IRE) Pip's Dream (Glint Of Gold)
(2070) 2414[3] 2718[6] 3213[7] 4284[4] 5070[5] 5595[5] 5724[3] 6455[2] 6658[7] 7307[15] (8245)

**Dreams Of Reality** *Tom Dascombe* a80 68
3 b f Bushranger(IRE) No Nightmare (USA) (Lion Heart (USA))
1137[2] (1430) (2470) 3882[5] 4186[6] 4971[6] 7073[4]

**Dream Spirit (IRE)** *William Haggas* 102
3 b g Invincible Spirit(IRE) Dream Valley (IRE) (Sadler's Wells (USA))
(3477) (5192) ◆ 6560[5] 6978[3]

**Dream Tune** *Ernst Oertel* a97 73
5 b g Oasis Dream Play Bouzouki (Halling (USA))
242a[9]

**Dream Walker (FR)** *Brian Ellison* a54 97
5 gr g Gold Away(IRE) Minnie's Mystery (FR) (Highest Honor (FR))
1164[12] 1637[2] 1903[5] 2336[3] 2707[2] 3716[9] 5446[2] 6354a[9] 6934[4] 7276[21] (7597) 7715[9]

**Dreamy Ciara** *Raymond York* a56
4 b f Multiplex Billie Holiday (Fairy King (USA))
2963[10] 4326[10]

**Dream Youn (FR)** *Mlle C Cardenne* a44 47
9 b g Dream Well(FR) Ghayouna (FR) (Doyoun)
920a[13]

**Dreese (IRE)** *James Tate* a86 71
3 b c Dandy Man(IRE) Lucky Flirt (USA) (Gulch (USA))
(1147) (1818) 3122[7] 7820[8]

**Dress Down (USA)** *M Al Muhairi* a66
4 gr c Raven's Pass(USA) Bare Necessities (USA) (Silver Deputy (CAN))
238a[10]

**Dress Drive (IRE)** *M Arienti* 94
3 b c Yeats(IRE) Diagon Alley (FR) (Cadeaux Genereux)
1779a[4]

**Dr Faustus (IRE)** *Doug Watson* a84 91
9 gr g Sadler's Wells(USA) Requesting (Rainbow Quest (USA))
243a[6]

**Dr Finley (IRE)** *Lydia Pearce* a61 59
7 ch g Dr Fong(USA) Farrfesheena (USA) (Rahy (USA))
214[5] 454[2] 842[4] (1242) 1895[7] 2531[4] 3269[3] 3632[2] 4082[7] 4769[5] 5547[3] 6216[6] 6486[3] 7204[4] 7657[8] 8070[7]

**Driefontein (AUS)** *Gai Waterhouse* 114
5 b m Fastnet Rock(AUS) Follow Gold (AUS) (Export Price (FR))
7724a[10]

**Drifter (IRE)** *Tom Dascombe* a63 67
3 b g Footstepsinthesand Bright Bank (IRE) (Sadler's Wells (USA))
976[2] 1269[7] 1830[6] 2671[4] 3120[3] 4333[8]

**Drifting Mist** *M Halford* a93 96
4 gr f Muhtathir Fenella's Link (Linamix (FR))
3285a[5]

**Drinks For Losers (IRE)** *Ian Semple* 48
3 b g Mastercraftsman(IRE) Heart's Desire (IRE) (Royal Applause)
2422[11] 3103[5] 3607[5]

**Drinkuptrig (IRE)** *Stuart Williams* a64 60
3 b c Bushranger(IRE) Maybe In May (USA) (Miswaki (USA))
338[4] 665[P]

**Dr Irv** *Philip Kirby* 83
5 ch g Dr Fong(USA) Grateful (Generous (IRE))
1599[6] 2289[5] 3204[6] 3845[2] 4068[2] ◆ 5017[5] 5890[4] 6169[2] 6640[2] 7124[7]

**Drive On (IRE)** *Eve Johnson Houghton* a85 79
3 b g Tagula(IRE) Thelma Louise (IRE) (Desert Style (IRE))
279[3] 624[2] 667[2] 1013[4] 4262[6] 5012[2] 5381[8] 6355[4] 7624[9] 8071[5] 8252[6]

**Dr King (ITY)** *J-C Rouget* a90 84
2 b c Dr Fong(USA) Sommerflora (GER) (Pivotal)
6991a[6]

**Dr No** *Richard Hannon* a96 101
2 gr g Aussie Rules(USA) Annalina (USA) (Cozzene (USA))
1583[5] (2428) 3318[7] ◆ 4780[8] 5131[3] 6142[6]

**Drole De Mek (FR)** *W Walton* a62 86
3 ch g Chineur(FR) Inassouvie (FR) (Lord Of Men)
5404a[7]

**Dropzone (USA)** *Richard Lee* a28 21
5 b g Smart Strike(CAN) Dalisay (IRE) (Sadler's Wells (USA))
3973[8]

**Dr Red Eye** *Scott Dixon* a91 88
6 ch g Dr Fong(USA) Camp Fire (IRE) (Lahib (USA))
715[8] 886[10] 1042[9] 1114[5] 2117[6] 2548[10] (4355) 4938[6] 5444[10] 6281[4] 6789[10] 7282[8] 7507[7] 7988[4] 8100[4] 8209[11]

**Drumkilbo** *Lady Cecil* a71 73
2 b c Shamardal(USA) Rex Regina (IRE) (King's Best (USA))
3387[4] ◆ 3893[3] 4740[3] 7244[9]

**Drummer (GER)** *P Schiergen* 72
2 b c Duke Of Marmalade(IRE) Douala (Dubawi (IRE))
6053a[8]

**Drummers Drumming (USA)** *Alan Berry*
8 b g Stroll(USA) Afleet Summer (USA) (Afleet (CAN))
1083[6]

**Drummond** *Bernard Llewellyn* a52 64
5 b g Zamindar(USA) Alrisha (IRE) (Persian Bold)
475[5] 640[9]

**Drummore Road (IRE)** *John Patrick Shanahan* 73
3 b c The Carbon Unit(USA) Eliza Berry (IRE) (Montjeu (IRE))
2114[7] 6741[5] (Dead)

**Druot** *Peter Makin* 67
2 b c Champs Elysees Trick Of Ace (USA) (Clever Trick (USA))
7560[4]

**Dr Victoria** *John Norton* a35 35
5 ch m Three Valleys(USA) Spielbound (Singspiel (IRE))
3916[11] 4571[12]

**Dry Your Eyes (IRE)** *Mark Johnston* a61 73
3 b f Shamardal(USA) Kindling (Dr Fong (USA))
(2237) 2491[4] 2761[8]

**Dual Mac** *Neville Bycroft* 79
7 br g Paris House Carol Again (Kind Of Hush)
2425[8] 3097[6] (5196) 6936[13] 7334[7]

**Dubai Breeze (IRE)** *Clive Brittain* a62 76
2 b f Lope De Vega(IRE) Expectation (IRE) (Night Shift (USA))
2306[6] 3557[3] ◆ 4126[8] 4605[4] 5043[4]

**Dubai Celebration** *Julie Camacho* a75 63
6 b g Dubai Destination(USA) Pretty Poppy (Song)
406[2] (733) (1134) 2540[9] 3699[12]

**Dubai Dynamo** *Ruth Carr* a84 94
9 b g Kyllachy Miss Mercy (IRE) (Law Society (USA))
1191[6] 1451[4] 1762[5] (2017) 2362[3] 2478[3] 2869[4] (3221) 3456[2] 3621[3] 4002[3] 4491[4] 5446[4] 5771[7] 5919[12] 6688[4] 6740[6] 7227[7]

**Dubai Hadeia** *Charlie Appleby* a60 79
3 b f Dubawi(IRE) Blaise Castle (USA) (Irish River (FR))
2061[9] 3276[5] 3755[5] (4617) 6026[3] 6365[5]

**Dubai Hills** *David O'Meara* a71 96
8 b g Dubai Destination(USA) Hill Welcome (Most Welcome)
1114[4] 1903[6] (2763) 3202[4] 3703[5] 4491[3] 4922[10] 5178[7] 6704[7] 7085[19]

**Dubai Kiss** *Harry Whittington*
5 b g Dubai Destination(USA) Smooch (Inchinor)
*1011[6]*

**Dubai Skyline (USA)** *Clive Brittain* a28 7
3 b f Medaglia d'Oro(USA) Love Of Dubai (USA) (More Than Ready (USA))
*6483[9]* 7304[11]

**Dubai Star (IRE)** *John Gosden* 91
3 b g Dubawi(IRE) Tango Tonic (IRE) (Trans Island)
(6982) 7538[16]

**Dubara Reef (IRE)** *Paul Green* a52 59
7 ch g Dubawi(IRE) Mamara Reef (Salse (USA))
*915[8]* (1605) 2055[4] 2801[11] 3336[7] *4474[6]* 5794[5] *6768[9]*

**Dubawi Coast** *James Tate* 57
3 b f Dubawi(IRE) Portmeirion (Polish Precedent (USA))
1569[5] 2625[5] 3677[6]

**Dubawi Diamond** *James Tate* a69 61
2 b c Dubawi(IRE) Darrfonah (IRE) (Singspiel (IRE))
5296[5] 5745[4] *7551[7]* *7810[4]* *8091[6]*

**Dubawi Fun** *Ismail Mohammed* a84 88
3 b c Dubawi(IRE) Arabian Treasure (USA) (Danzig (USA))
*204a[14]* 505a[10] 770a[5] 3378[30] *4323[11]* *5012[5]* *6145[6]* 6424[4] *7035[3]* 7334[8]

**Dubawi Light** *James Tate* a72 64
3 b g Dubawi(IRE) Shesadelight (Shirley Heights)
*341[3]* ◆ *(468)* 1279[7] 2391[5]

**Dubawi Sound** *Hugo Palmer* a96 101
6 b g Dubawi(IRE) Hannah's Music (Music Boy)
1437[13] 1728[6] 2145[25] 3122[9] 3969[8]

**Dubday** *Jassim Al Ghazali* a95 100
4 ch c Dubawi(IRE) Dayrose (Daylami (IRE))
1182a[14]

**Ducab (IRE)** *A bin Harmash* a97 88
4 b g Dansili Twyla Tharp (IRE) (Sadler's Wells (USA))
*(243a)*

**Duca Di Mantova** *R Biondi* 108
5 ch g Manduro(GER) Vale Mantovani (Wolfhound (USA))
1603a[7] 7323a[2] 7617a[8]

**Duca Valentinois (IRE)** *J P Murtagh* a73 75
2 b c Holy Roman Emperor(IRE) Love Valentine (IRE) (Fruits Of Love (USA))
6375a[10]

**Duc De Seville (IRE)** *Clive Cox* a56 53
2 b g Duke Of Marmalade(IRE) Splendid (IRE) (Mujtahid (USA))
3381[6] 4800[6] 5351[10] 7207[4] *(8121)* ◆

**Duchess Of Gazeley (IRE)** *Dean Ivory* a92 94
4 ch f Halling(USA) Flying Finish (FR) (Priolo (USA))
*803[3]* ◆ *956[3]* *1213[9]* *1556[7]* 1981[5] 7565[8] *8001[9]*

**Duchess Of Ripon (IRE)** *Bryan Smart* 7
2 br f Lord Shanakill(USA) Rakiza (IRE) (Elnadim (USA))
6449[12]

**Due Diligence (USA)** *A P O'Brien* a95 116
3 b c War Front(USA) Bema (USA) (Pulpit (USA))
3451[2]

**Duelling Dragon (USA)** *Stuart Kittow* a57 81
3 b g Henrythenavigator(USA) Ometsz (IRE) (Singspiel (IRE))
*605[5]* 3914[5] 4791[2] (5195) 7567[2]

**Duke Cosimo** *David Barron* a87 92
4 ch g Pivotal Nannina (Medicean)
1537[4] (2332) 4471[5] 5081[3] (5444)

**Duke Derby (IRE)** *Niels Petersen* a92 99
3 b c Duke Of Marmalade(IRE) Tocopilla (FR) (Medaaly)
*896a[4]*

**Duke Of Aricabeau (IRE)** *Lydia Pearce* a43 47
5 ch g Modigliani(USA) Essential Fear (IRE) (Pivotal)
*4578[11]* *5510[11]*

**Duke Of Clarence (IRE)** *Richard Fahey* a74 106
5 gr g Verglas(IRE) Special Lady (FR) (Kaldoun (FR))
2073[7] 2314[2] 2779[2]

**Duke Of Destiny (IRE)** *Ed Walker* a81 76
5 br g Bachelor Duke(USA) Marghelan (FR) (Soviet Star (USA))
1845[8] 2341[9] *2930[7]* 3427[7] 4273[11] 5110[4]

**Duke Of Dunton (IRE)** *Tony Carroll* a44 47
3 b g Duke Of Marmalade(IRE) Southern Migration (USA) (Kingmambo (USA))
*6482[8]* 7024[8] *7370[4]*

**Duke Of Ellington (FR)** *M Figge* a71 80
2 b g Duke Of Marmalade(IRE) Abime (USA) (Woodman (USA))
5292a[5]

**Duke Of Firenze** *Robert Cowell* 105
5 ch g Pivotal Nannina (Medicean)
5289[7] 6209[3] 6533[22] 6923[6] ◆ 7132[5] (7280)

**Duke Of Grazeon (IRE)** *Mrs Ilka Gansera-Leveque* a76 70
4 b g Duke Of Marmalade(IRE) Rambler (Selkirk (USA))
1446[7] 1881[8] 4408[5] *4613[6]* 5711[P]

**Duke Of North (IRE)** *James Fanshawe* 70
2 b g Danehill Dancer(IRE) Althea Rose (IRE) (Green Desert (USA))
3429[8] 4109[4] 4829[6]

**Duke Of Romance** *John Ryan*
2 ch g Duke Of Marmalade(IRE) Chance For Romance (Entrepreneur)
3893[6]

**Duke Of Sonning** *Alan King* 65
2 ch g Duke Of Marmalade(IRE) Moonshadow (Diesis)
7170[5] 7512[6] 7667[12]

**Duke Of Yorkshire** *Tim Easterby* 75
4 b g Duke Of Marmalade(IRE) Dame Edith (FR) (Top Ville)
1935[8] 2801[6] 2980[5] 4498[2] 4856[8] 5300[2] 6166[2] 6323[6] 6937[5] 7281[4]

**Dukes Delight (IRE)** *David Lanigan* a79 57
4 b f Duke Of Marmalade(IRE) Fashion Model (Rainbow Quest (USA))
*(6942)*

**Dukes Den** *Sylvester Kirk* a65
3 b g Duke Of Marmalade(IRE) Green Room (FR) (In The Wings)
2773[14] *6677[5]* *7067[3]* *7777[9]* *7946[7]* *(8061)* *8193[6]*

**Dukes Meadow** *Roger Ingram* a68
3 b g Pastoral Pursuits Figura (Rudimentary (USA))
*8020[4]* *8294[2]*

**Dulciadargent (FR)** *N Clement* a75 74
2 b f Kendargent(FR) Dulce De Leche (FR) (Victory Note (USA))
4839a[6] (6244a) 6958a[2]

**Dullingham** *Charlie Appleby* a83 89
3 b g Dubawi(IRE) Dixey (Diktat)
1883[4] 2617[5] 3273[8] ◆ 3538[6] *4580[4]*

**Duly Acclaimed (IRE)** *J S Moore* a58 45
3 b f Acclamation Cloonkeary (In The Wings)
*231[4]* *665[5]* *(743)* *1239[4]* 2381[6]

**Dumbfounded (FR)** *Lady Herries* a74 71
6 bb g Vettori(IRE) Take The Light (FR) (Take Risks (FR))
*2916[2]* (3632) *4076[2]* *5137[3]*

**Dunaden (FR)** *M Delzangles* a102 124
8 b h Nicobar La Marlia (FR) (Kaldounevees (FR))
*508a[6]* 1182a[9]

**Duncan (GER)** *F Chappet* 75
3 b g Nayef(USA) Diacada (GER) (Cadeaux Genereux)
7681a[4]

**Dungannon** *Andrew Balding* a113 106
7 b g Monsieur Bond(IRE) May Light (Midyan (USA))
393a[11] 680a[10] 3452[21] 4179[15] 5289[4] 5918[2] (6923) (7441) ◆ 7716[7] *7923[10]* *(8019)*

**Dunhoy (IRE)** *Tony Newcombe* a74 84
6 ch g Goodricke Belle Of The Blues (IRE) (Blues Traveller (IRE))
*350[P]*

**Dunnington** *Mel Brittain* 49
5 b g Gentleman's Deal(IRE) First Harmony (First Trump)
3153[9]

**Dunnscotia** *Paul Webber* 61
2 b g Showcasing Black And Amber (Weldnaas (USA))
4270[5] 5091[8] 5593[3]

**Dunn's River (FR)** *Jamie Osborne* 52
3 gr g Mastercraftsman(IRE) Prairie Moon (Halling (USA))
2832[3]

**Duquesa Penguin** *Jo Hughes* 89
2 ch g Winker Watson Quaker Parrot (Compton Place)
1161[15] 1271a[3]

**Durch Den Monsun (FR)** *Mme M-C Chaalon* 45
6 b g Malinas(GER) Bywaldor (FR) (Magwal (FR))
5225a[9]

**Duretto** *Andrew Balding* a80 80
2 ch g Manduro(GER) Landinium (ITY) (Lando (GER))
7413[2] ◆ *(7834)*

**Durham Express (IRE)** *Colin Teague* a43 54
7 b g Acclamation Edwina (IRE) (Caerleon (USA))
*563[8]* *864[4]* *934[6]* *1089[7]* *1365[10]* *2094[9]*

**Dursey Island (USA)** *Richard Hannon* a79 83
3 b c Elusive Quality(USA) Incircle Miss (USA) (Dayjur (USA))
1433[14] 2075[2] 2773[8] (3184)

**Dusky Queen (IRE)** *Richard Fahey* 97
4 b f Shamardal(USA) Sanna Bay (IRE) (Refuse To Bend (IRE))
1442[5] (2318) 3202[3] 4212[16] 4573[3] 5612[4] 6320[3] 6534[12] 7451[2]

**Dusty Blue** *Tony Carroll* a71 44
2 ch f Medicean Jazz Jam (Pivotal)
3888[7] *7192[2]* *7920[4]* *8007[4]* *8183[2]*

**Dusty Storm (IRE)** *Ed McMahon* a73 86
4 ch f Kyllachy Halliwell House (Selkirk (USA))
1961[13] 3138[5] 4630[5] 5333[7] (6399) 6873[9]

**Dusty Trail (IRE)** *John Butler* a45 41
10 b g Indian Danehill(IRE) Lingering Melody (IRE) (Nordico (USA))
*7182[10]*

**Dutchartcollector** *Gary Moore* a66 42
3 b g Dutch Art Censored (Pivotal)
*236[5]* ◆ 1947[10] 2695[8] 3781[12]

**Dutch Art Dealer** *Paul Cole* a96 86
3 b g Dutch Art Lawyers Choice (Namid)
3480[5] 4147[3] 4404[2] 5441[2] *(6145)* *(7227)*

**Dutch Breeze** *Tim Easterby* 84
3 ch g Dutch Art Oasis Breeze (Oasis Dream)
1959[2] 2317[6] 2789[2] (3370) 4021[3] 4636[3] 4977[4] 5696[16] 6736[15]

**Dutch Connection** *Charles Hills* 108
2 ch c Dutch Art Endless Love (IRE) (Dubai Destination (USA))
3279[3] 3881[2] (4896) (5576) 6373a[3]

**Dutch Courage** *Richard Fahey* 98
3 b f Dutch Art Poldhu (Cape Cross (IRE))
1435[6] 2316[4] 3357[10] 3724[6] 5612[12] 6068[5] 7451[5]

**Dutch Descent (IRE)** *David Barron* 66
3 b g Royal Applause Wagtail (Cape Cross (IRE))
1959[4] 3343[4] 3601[4] 5088[10]

**Dutchess Of Art** *Olly Stevens* a39
2 br f Dutch Art Kind Of Light (Primo Dominie)
*8191[8]*

**Dutch Falcon** *William Muir* 47
2 ch g Pivotal Luminance (IRE) (Danehill Dancer (IRE))
3728[11] 4740[9]

**Dutch Fredie G** *Gary Moore* a48
2 ch f Dutch Art Flawless Diamond (IRE) (Indian Haven)
*8247[6]*

**Dutch Garden** *David Brown* 67
2 b c Fastnet Rock(AUS) Swan Wings (Bahamian Bounty)
4864[6]

**Dutch Golden Age (IRE)** *Gary Moore* a75
2 b c Kodiac Magic Melody (Petong)
*8184[2]*

**Dutch Interior** *Gary Moore* a84 82
3 ch g Dutch Art Rotunda (Pivotal)
3247[9] 3783[3] *4078[3]* 4697[9] 5945[6] *(6680)* *7017[6]*

**Dutch Lady** *John Holt* a54 62
3 ch f Dutch Art Tattling (Warning)
1647[5] (2355) 2741[3] 3828[7] 4415[3] 4871[5] 5892[2] 6647[6] *7187[5]*

**Dutch Lady Roseane** *James Unett* a47 21
3 b f Dutch Art Lady Rose Anne (IRE) (Red Ransom (USA))
*962[4]* 3925[11] *5796[9]* *7256[7]* *7635[7]* *7785[10]* *7869[5]* *8049[7]* *8167[3]* *8259[10]*

**Dutch Law** *Hughie Morrison* a71
2 b c Dutch Art Lawyers Choice (Namid)
*6604[8]* *7223[2]* ◆

**Dutch Masterpiece** *Gary Moore* a80 113
4 b g Dutch Art The Terrier (Foxhound (USA))
1421[8]

**Dutch Mistress** *James Unett* a65 73
5 b m Dutch Art Royal Mistress (Fasliyev (USA))
2608[6] 3220[7]

**Dutch Party** *Richard Fahey* 73
2 b f Dutch Art Third Party (Terimon)
2306[2] ◆ 6065[7]

**Dutch Portrait** *Paul Cole* a76 73
2 b g Dutch Art Silken Promise (USA) (Pulpit (USA))
2298[14] *5009[2]* 5625[4] 6064[4] *6884[2]* *7374[7]*

**Dutch Rifle** *James Tate* a85 76
3 b f Dutch Art Vodka Shot (USA) (Holy Bull (USA))
2510[6] *5100[4]* *(5795)* 6026[4] 6500[4] *6839[7]*

**Dutch Robin (IRE)** *Mick Channon* 69
2 b f Fast Company(IRE) Autumn Star (IRE) (Mujadil (USA))
6361[3] 6652[5] 6875[10]

**Dutch Romance** *Charles Hills* 94
3 ch f Dutch Art Endless Love (IRE) (Dubai Destination (USA))
1435[10] 2316[12]

**Dutch Rose (IRE)** *David O'Meara* a91 105
5 ch m Dutch Art Eloquent Rose (IRE) (Elnadim (USA))
2144[7] (2784) 3252[6] 4060[2] 4681[6] 5612[5] 6060[2] 6254[14] 6922[4] ◆ *7553[6]*

**Dutch S** *Clive Cox* a69 81
3 ch f Dutch Art Park Law (IRE) (Fasliyev (USA))
2340[5] *3117[8]* 3615[5]

**Dutch Uncle** *Ed Dunlop* a72 59
2 b c Dutch Art Evasive Quality (FR) (Highest Honor (FR))
7380[7] *7731[6]* *8288[2]*

**Dutiful Son (IRE)** *David C Griffiths* a92 26
4 b g Invincible Spirit(IRE) Grecian Dancer (Dansili)
*(746)* *(1212)* *8136[10]*

**Dux Scholar** *Doug Watson* a98 115
6 b h Oasis Dream Alumni (Selkirk (USA))
110a[7] 308a[7] 509a[14] 809a[2] 897a[3] 1179a[8]

**Dye Fore (USA)** *J-C Rouget* a88
3 bb c Giant's Causeway(USA) Homebound (USA) (Dixie Union (USA))
*(482a)* *721a[6]*

**Dylan Mouth (IRE)** *Stefano Botti* 116
3 b c Dylan Thomas(IRE) Cottonmouth (IRE) (Noverre (USA))
(2376a) 3417[8] (6590a) (7323a)

**Dylan's Centenary** *Rod Millman* a65 59
3 b g Kyllachy Sheka (Ishiguru (USA))
*1069[6]* *1389[10]* *1918[2]* 3281[4] 3754[U] *4969[6]* *5820[7]* 6030[2] *6488[7]* 6816[4] *7376[8]*

**Dylan's Storm (IRE)** *David Dennis* a64 64
2 b g Zebedee Storm Lady (IRE) (Alhaarth (IRE))
4389[9] 5271[5] 5847[5] *6678[3]* ◆

**Dylar (FR)** *L Nyffels* a99 105
7 ch g Subsidy Balarama (FR) (Saint Cyrien (FR))
3291a[11] 7559a[13] *8150a[2]*

**Dynaglow (USA)** *John Gosden* a70 79
3 b f Dynaformer(USA) Lantern Glow (USA) (Mineshaft (USA))
2504[5] 3195[8] 3615[3] 4623[5] *5308[10]*

**Dynamic Impact (USA)** *Mark Casse* a113
3 b c Tiznow(USA) Featherbed (USA) (Smart Strike (CAN))
*2357a[7]*

**Dynamic Ranger (USA)** *Gary Moore* a73 46
3 b g US Ranger(USA) Dynamous (USA) (Dynaformer (USA))
*316[2]* *839[3]* 2418[10] 4356[6] *5795[8]*

**Dynamic Sky (CAN)** *Mark Casse* a105 111
4 bb c Sky Mesa(USA) Murani (USA) (Distorted Humor (USA))
6390a[2] 7324a[3]

**Dynamic Vision (IRE)** *Roger Varian* a71 71
3 b c Shamardal(USA) Mazaaya (USA) (Cozzene (USA))
1511[9] *1831[3]* 2236[7] *3116[6]* (3683)

**Dynamite Dixie (IRE)** *Phil McEntee* a74 83
5 b g Dylan Thomas(IRE) Lavender Blue (Galileo (IRE))
5958a[16] *7732[7]* *7953[10]*

**Dynamite Inventor (IRE)** *Kevin Ryan* a67 72
2 b g Alfred Nobel(IRE) Lintera (GER) (Night Shift (USA))
5241[8] 5982[5] 6449[2] *7353[5]*

**Dynamoon (FR)** *H-A Pantall* a61 61
4 b f Kentucky Dynamite(USA) Moon Gorge (Pursuit Of Love)
*178a[10]*

**Dynamo Walt (IRE)** *Derek Shaw* a79 68
3 b g Acclamation Cambara (Dancing Brave (USA))
*(1425)* 1851[3] 2889[5] *3855[3]* *5012[9]* *5601[4]* *6562[6]* 7213[5] *7457[2]* 7670[10] *(7806)* ◆ *7949[3]*

**Dynastic** *Tony Coyle* a78 60
5 b g Dynaformer(USA) Demure (Machiavellian (USA))
1197[9] *1501[3]* *(1806)* 2055[7] *(2394)* *2904[2]* *5572[7]*

**Eager Beaver** *William Muir* a41
2 b f Duke Of Marmalade(IRE) Kahlua Kiss (Mister Baileys)
*8036[8]*

**Eager To Bow (IRE)** *Patrick Chamings* a74 61
8 b g Acclamation Tullawadgeen (IRE) (Sinndar (IRE))
*1297[8]* 2048[4] 3328[5] 4428[6] (5423) *6858[3]*

**Eagle Empire (IRE)** *Richard Hannon* a65 44
2 b c Jeremy(USA) Red Eagle (IRE) (Eagle Eyed (USA))
6420[7] 7040[9] *7739[7]* *7992[5]* *8075[3]*

**Eagle Rock (IRE)** *Tom Tate* 93
6 b g High Chaparral(IRE) Silk Fan (IRE) (Unfuwain (USA))
1562[9] 2289[2] 2782[3] 3204[2] (3654) 4217[6] 5579[7] 6133[10]

**Eagle Top** *John Gosden* 120
3 ch c Pivotal Gull Wing (IRE) (In The Wings)
(1438) ◆ 1727[4] (3417) ◆ 4649[4]

**Ealain Aibrean (IRE)** *David Evans* a69 75
3 b f Excellent Art April (IRE) (Rock Of Gibraltar (IRE))
*98[2]* *232[3]* *(512)* *650[3]* *762[4]* *936[8]* 1642[6] 1851[6]

**Ear D'Rhythm (USA)** *Rudy Rodriguez* 76
4 bb f Medaglia d'Oro(USA) Tropic Rhythm (USA) (Dynaformer (USA))
2227a[5]

**Earl Of Fire (GER)** *C Boutin* a48 81
9 ch g Areion(GER) Evry (GER) (Torgos)
*57a[11]*

**Earl Of Menteith (IRE)** *Mark Johnston* 81
3 b c Shamardal(USA) Inchmahome (Galileo (IRE))
(3998) ◆ 4448[4] ◆

**Earl Of Tinsdal (GER)** *A Wohler* 111
6 b h Black Sam Bellamy(IRE) Earthly Paradise (GER) (Dashing Blade)
5231a[4] 6806a[2] 7603a[3]

**Earl's Bridge** *Bill Turner* 55
3 b g Avonbridge Regal Quest (IRE) (Marju (IRE))
5321[5] 5596[12]

**Earls Quarter (IRE)** *Ian Williams* a70 77
8 b g Shantou(USA) Par Street (IRE) (Dolphin Street (FR))
*1218[2]* 6881[4]

**Early Morning (GER)** *Dr A Bolte* 95
5 b m Mamool(IRE) Evening Danzig (GER) (Danzig Connection (USA))
7482a[11]

**Early Morning (IRE)** *Harry Dunlop* 84
3 gr g New Approach(IRE) Summer's Eve (Singspiel (IRE))
1730[4] 2769[2]

**Early Ouest (FR)** *P Leray* a87
4 b g Early March Belle De L'Ouest (FR) (Quai Voltaire (USA))
*836a[7]*

**Early Prime (FR)** *H-A Pantall* a82 97
3 b f Early March Valprime (FR) (Nombre Premier)
1273a[8]

**Early Run Run (FR)** *M Le Forestier* a72 51
4 b g Early March Allez La Classe (FR) (Mujadil (USA))
*796a[3]*

**Earnshaw (USA)** *A Fabre* 112
3 gr c Medaglia d'Oro(USA) Emily Bronte (Machiavellian (USA))
1272a[5] 1965a[2] 2818a[13] 5591a[2]

**Earth Amber** *Nicky Henderson* 103
5 ch m Hurricane Run(IRE) Too Marvelous (FR) (Dansili)
1398[2] 1869[2] 5161[9] 7107[29]

**Earth Drummer (IRE)** *David O'Meara* a104 103
4 b g Dylan Thomas(IRE) In Dubai (USA) (Giant's Causeway (USA))
3737a[9] 4923[7] 5915[3] ◆ (6535) *7455[3]* *7688[2]* *7971[3]* *(8144)*

**East Coast Lady (IRE)** *Robert Eddery* 89
2 b f Kodiac Alexander Anapolis (IRE) (Spectrum (IRE))
3671[3] (4126) 4913[15] 6253[2] 6709[7] 7237[5]

**Eastern Belle** *John Gosden* 106
3 b f Champs Elysees Fleche D'Or I (Bay Express)
1534[2] ◆ 2484[2] (3143) 4894[4]

**Eastern Dragon (IRE)** *Michael Scudamore* a77 83
4 b g Elnadim(USA) Shulammite Woman (IRE) (Desert Sun)
*265[4]* *540[4]* *757[8]* 2048[2] (2486) (2669) 3180[5] 4121[3] 4588[4] 6249[7] 6789[5] (7220) 7567[3]

**Eastern Impact (IRE)** *Richard Fahey* 109
3 b g Bahamian Bounty Kate The Great (Xaar)
1445[6] 1952[4] (2344) 3253[5] 4669[2] (5438) 6533[27] 6921[9]

**Eastern Magic** *Andrew Hollinshead* a56 62
7 b g Observatory(USA) Inchtina (Inchinor)
1574[4] (3269) *4082[5]* 5909[2] 7007[2] *7893[6]*

**Eastern Promise (FR)** *D Sepulchre* a68
2 b f Air Chief Marshal(IRE) Krestena (FR) (Kendor (FR))
*(5619a)*

**Eastern Racer (IRE)** *Brian Ellison* 76
2 b g Bushranger(IRE) Queen Cobra (IRE) (Indian Rocket)
3713[3] 4185[3] 4439[22] 5714[4] 6427[2]

**Eastern Romance** *William Haggas* a64 64
2 b f Duke Of Marmalade(IRE) Dance East (Shamardal (USA))
6553[5] *7194[4]*

**Eastern Rules (IRE)** *M Halford* a108 109
6 b g Golden Snake(USA) Eastern Ember (Indian King (USA))
*396a[3]* *(504a)* (678a) *899a[12]* *1176a[9]* 3412a[2] 4459a[3]

**Easter Sky (IRE)** *David O'Meara* a69 94
4 b g Authorized(IRE) Suedoise (Kris)
1608[2] (2016) ◆

**East India** *A P O'Brien* 92
2 ch c Galileo(IRE) Field Of Hope (IRE) (Selkirk (USA))
6348a[6]

**Eastlands Lad (IRE)** *Micky Hammond* a22 53
5 bb g Strategic Prince Uisce Tine (IRE) (Bluebird (USA))
1673[10] 2219[3] 3344[3] 4023[9] 4534[5] 7078[11]

**Eastside Gallery** *S Smrczek* a66
5 b m Avonbridge Eastern Lyric (Petong)
57a[4]

**East Texas Red (IRE)** *Mick Quinn* a56 69
4 ch c Danehill Dancer(IRE) Evangeline (Sadler's Wells (USA))
209[5]

**Eastward Ho** *Sarah Humphrey* a57 59
6 ch g Resplendent Glory(IRE) Mofeyda (IRE) (Mtoto)
1673[13] 2911[5] 3301[8] 4014[8] 5893[4] 6076[4] 6715[8] 7986[4] 8030[4] 8250[10]

**Easydoesit (IRE)** *Tony Carroll* a74 66
6 b g Iffraaj Fawaayid (USA) (Vaguely Noble)
104[2] 168[4] 1743[4]

**Easy Feeling (USA)** *J-C Rouget* 63
2 b f Elusive Quality(USA) Wonder Woman (USA) (Storm Cat (USA))
4839a[5] 5293a[8]

**Easy Risk (FR)** *Yannick Fouin* 89
3 b f My Risk(FR) Entre Deux Mers (FR) (Saint Estephe (FR))
4464a[5]

**Easy Road** *Cathrine Erichsen* a85 93
4 b g Compton Place Broughtons Revival (Pivotal)
4957a[4]

**Easy Terms** *Edwin Tuer* 97
7 b m Trade Fair Effie (Royal Academy (USA))
1360[9]

**Easy Tiger** *William Muir* a73
2 b g Refuse To Bend(IRE) Extremely Rare (IRE) (Mark Of Esteem (IRE))
(7353) (7770) ◆

**Eatsleepracerepeat** *Lady Cecil* a71 62
2 b c Myboycharlie(IRE) Highland Jewel (IRE) (Azamour (IRE))
5391[5] 6838[3] 7353[2] 7523[2] 7839[5]

**Ebanoran (IRE)** *John M Oxx* 110
3 b c Oasis Dream Ebadiyla (IRE) (Sadler's Wells (USA))
1200a[3] 2187a[2] 2990[9] 3765a[3]

**Ebasani (IRE)** *John M Oxx* 95
3 ch c Manduro(GER) Ebatana (IRE) (Rainbow Quest (USA))
1458a[6]

**Ebazziyr (IRE)** *James Leavy* 101
6 b g Cape Cross(IRE) Ebadiyla (IRE) (Sadler's Wells (USA))
1750a[5]

**Ebeltoft (IRE)** *P Schiergen* 99
2 b c Lawman(FR) Estefania (GER) (Acatenango (GER))
6377a[4] 7145a[5] 7726a[3]

**Eben Dubai (IRE)** *Sir Michael Stoute* a48 42
2 b g New Approach(IRE) Eldalil (Singspiel (IRE))
3578[7] 4570[7]

**Ebiyza (IRE)** *A De Royer-Dupre* 110
4 ch f Rock Of Gibraltar(IRE) Ebalista (IRE) (Selkirk (USA))
1784a[7] 2588a[5]

**Ebony Clarets** *Linda Perratt* a38 50
5 b m Kyllachy Pachanga (Inchinor)
1930[8] 2219[11] 2454[3] 2676[10] 2911[6] 3056[2] 3363[4] 4000[7] 6837[9]

**Ebony Express** *Alan Swinbank* a35 91
5 bl g Superior Premium Coffee Ice (Primo Dominie)
1306[2] 1653[11] 2259[6] 2787[15] 4289[3] 4995[3] 5890[5] (6228) (7281)

**Eccleston** *David O'Meara* 99
3 b g Acclamation Miss Meggy (Pivotal)
(1700) 1968[2] 2287[3] 3253[13] 5925[4] 7080[12] 7408[7]

**Echo Brava** *Luke Dace* a86 87
4 gr g Proclamation(IRE) Snake Skin (Golden Snake (USA))
(85) ◆ 160[2] 494[2] 784[6] 2034[3] 2482[12] 3196[5] 4104[2] 4351[2] 5073[3] (5800) 6439[2] 8042[7] ◆ 8194[6]

**Echoes Of War** *John Bridger* a40
5 b g Echo Of Light Waraqa (USA) (Red Ransom (USA))
1491[12] 8198[11]

**Echologic** *Brian Baugh* a38 35
4 b g Echo Of Light Crown City (USA) (Coronado's Quest (USA))
37[10] 673[7] 3465[6] 4797[7] 5751[9] 6088[12] 6834[5] 7117[8]

**Echo Of Lightning** *Brian Ellison* 67
4 b g Echo Of Light Classic Lass (Dr Fong (USA))
1310[2] (1596) 1930[4] 2215[6] 3604[4] 5166[3] 5233[5] (7494)

**Echua (IRE)** *Emmet Michael Butterly* a76 73
8 b g King's Best(USA) Canouan (IRE) (Sadler's Wells (USA))
214[3] (260)

**Ecliptic Sunrise** *Des Donovan* a59 59
3 b f Compton Place Winter Moon (Mujadil (USA))
3156[5] 3677[3] 4111[8] 4972[8] 5205[5] 5801[10] 6297[4] 6815[5] 6995[2] 7644[7] 7887[7] 8024[4] 8230[2]

**Economic Crisis (IRE)** *Alan Berry* a63 77
5 ch m Excellent Art Try The Air (IRE) (Foxhound (USA))
1565[6] 1758[6] (1966) (2297) 2677[3] 3102[5] 3359[5] 3611[8] 3831[3] 4531[8] 4902[6] 5130[4] 5298[4] 6406[9] 6580[5] 6595[11]

**Economy** *Sir Michael Stoute* a89 89
4 gr g Dalakhani(IRE) Quiff (Sadler's Wells (USA))
(1218) 2461[3] 3932[2]

**Eco Warrior** *J W Hills* a73 78
4 b g Echo Of Light Kryssa (Kris)
67[10] (282) 382[3] (1791) 2270[12]

**Ectot** *E Lellouche* 118
3 b c Hurricane Run(IRE) Tonnara (IRE) (Linamix (FR))
(1481a) (6379a) 6970a[17]

**Edas** *Thomas Cuthbert* a44 59
12 b g Celtic Swing Eden (IRE) (Polish Precedent (USA))
2427[10] 2701[5] 3605[5] 4958[3] 5337[7] 6628[4] 6795[4]

**Eddiemaurice (IRE)** *John Flint* a71 78
3 ch g Captain Rio Annals (Lujain (USA))
74[4] 301[5] 561[5] 1346[8] 1847[8] 2235[4] 2805[9] 3360[6] (3534) (3911) 4063[4] 5245[4] 5566[4] 6161[2] 6342[5] 6431[5] (6615) 7161[4]

**Edelmira (IRE)** *D K Weld* 106
3 ch f Peintre Celebre(USA) Elbasana (IRE) (Indian Ridge)
3285a[6] (5024a) ◆

**Ederan (IRE)** *Rod Collet* 107
4 ch c Peintre Celebre(USA) Ebareva (IRE) (Machiavellian (USA))
4722a[4] 6383a[6]

**Ede's The Business** *Pat Phelan* a55 30
3 ch f Halling(USA) My Amalie (IRE) (Galileo (IRE))
236[8] 2926[9] 4085[3] 4658[6] 5491[7]

**Edgar Balthazar** *Keith Dalgleish* 73
2 b c Pastoral Pursuits Assistacat (IRE) (Lend A Hand)
(4192)

**Edge (IRE)** *Bernard Llewellyn* a52 80
3 b c Acclamation Chanter (Lomitas)
2088[8] 2833[8] 5719[5] 6284[6] 6615[5] 7494[3]

**Edged Out** *Christopher Mason* 77
4 b f Piccolo Edge Of Light (Xaar)
1789[5] 2414[6] 3561[9] (4151) 4399[4] 4833[7] 5275[4] 6025[5] 6314[7]

**Edge Of Heaven** *Jonathan Portman* a65 66
2 b f Pastoral Pursuits Halfwaytoparadise (Observatory (USA))
4541[2] 5604[2] 5981[4] 6769[6] 7353[3] 7625[3]

**Edge Of Love** *Ed Walker* 59
2 b f Kyllachy Upskittled (Diktat)
6435[4]

**Edge Of Sanity (IRE)** *Brian Ellison* a85 105
5 b h Invincible Spirit(IRE) Saor Sinn (IRE) (Galileo (IRE))
5161[8] (5579)

**Edgeworth (IRE)** *David Bridgwater* a64 63
8 b g Pyrus(USA) Credibility (Komaite (USA))
3521[2] 4107[3]

**Edgware Road** *Andy Turnell* a68 65
6 ch g Selkirk(USA) Bayswater (Caerleon (USA))
117[10] 317[8] 783[3] 869[9] 1835[4] (3973) (4327) 4755[8] 5721[4]

**Edie White** *Lawrence Mullaney* 32
2 b f Bahamian Bounty Croeso Bach (Bertolini (USA))
3947[10] 5050[7] 5443[7] 6453[8] 6642[10]

**Edith Anne** *Paul Midgley* a26 50
4 b f Sakhee's Secret Accusation (IRE) (Barathea (IRE))
9[11] 549[7]

**Ed Led Jed (IRE)** *John C McConnell* a52 54
3 b f Baltic King Winning Note (IRE) (Victory Note (USA))
6010[3]

**Edmund Halley (FR)** *Harry Dunlop* a16 11
2 b g Astronomer Royal(USA) Lazy Afternoon (IRE) (Hawk Wing (USA))
1807[5] 3082[10] 3578[9]

**Educate** *Ismail Mohammed* a110 113
5 b g Echo Of Light Pasithea (IRE) (Celtic Swing)
397a[6] 901a[5] 1181a[13] 3930[4] 4214[4] 5175[4] 6752[9] 7120[3] 7243[5] 7598[4] 7803[2]

**Edu Querido (BRZ)** *Marco Botti* a101 106
5 ch h Holzmeister(USA) Kournikova (BRZ) (Irish Fighter (USA))
509a[7] ◆ 772a[4] 902a[6] 2086[6] 2958[6] 3416[11] 4711[6] (8242)

**Edward Elgar** *Natalie Lloyd-Beavis* 54
3 ch g Avonbridge Scooby Dooby Do (Atraf)
1441[7] 2020[11] 3343[5] 4063[5] 4300[5] 5717[10] 6121[14] (6673) 7360[12]

**Edw Gold (IRE)** *David Evans* a59
2 ch g Fast Company(IRE) Hams (USA) (Dixie Union (USA))
7828[8] 7999[4] 8183[4]

**Eeny Mac (IRE)** *Neville Bycroft* a45 80
7 ch g Redback Sally Green (IRE) (Common Grounds)
(3094) 3544[4] 3910[5] 4290[3] 4453[7] 4753[7] 4975[3] 5299[6] 5711[3] 6166[15] 6626[6] 6937[10]

**Effect (IRE)** *Jo Hughes* a40
3 b c Bahri(USA) Wana Doo (USA) (Grand Slam (USA))
1258[7]

**Effectual** *Roger Varian* 70
2 b f Exceed And Excel(AUS) Our Faye (College Chapel)
4269[3] ◆

**Efflorescence (USA)** *Charlie Appleby* 90
2 b f Exceed And Excel(AUS) Floristry (Fasliyev (USA))
(4403) 5664[6] 6067[7]

**Effusive** *William Haggas* a74 80
2 ch f Starspangledbanner(AUS) Thrill (Pivotal)
(2824) 3415[8] 6530[10] 7255[6]

**Egmont** *George Moore* 32
2 b c Notnowcato Salutare (IRE) (Sadler's Wells (USA))
5078[8] 5886[9] 6976[8]

**Egotist (IRE)** *Milton Bradley* a72 58
6 ch g Halling(USA) Devil's Imp (IRE) (Cadeaux Genereux)
940[6]

**Egyptian Warrior (IRE)** *A P O'Brien* a87 92
5 bb g Galileo(IRE) Beltisaal (FR) (Belmez (USA))
6349a[11]

**Ehtifaal (IRE)** *William Haggas* 74
3 b g Teofilo(IRE) Kashoof (Green Desert (USA))
2201[7] 3607[2]

**Eighteen Summers (USA)** *Edward Lynam* a63 89
7 ch g Lion Heart(USA) Azarina (IRE) (Kenmare (FR))
4379a[7]

**Eilean Mor** *R Mike Smith* a58 61
6 ch g Ishiguru(USA) Cheviot Heights (Intikhab (USA))
1761[2] 2476[3] 3056[3] (3657) 4000[5] 4014[4] (4259) 4520[4] 4856[6] 5171[5] 5567[4] 6113[4] 6402[4] (6597) 6825[6]

**Eileen Celio (FR)** *B Legros*
2 ch c Monsieur Bond(IRE) Irish Folklore (IRE) (Traditionally (USA))
5292a[10]

**Eileen Gray (IRE)** *Charles Hills* a37 43
2 b f Mastercraftsman(IRE) Fact (American Post)
2276[9] 3267[11] 5037[10] 6359[5] 7450[11]

**Einsteins Folly (IRE)** *J S Bolger* a73 102
4 b c Whipper(USA) Azra (IRE) (Danehill (USA))
1078a[15] 2580a[4]

**Eium Mac** *Neville Bycroft* a54 50
5 b g Presidium Efipetite (Efisio)
2426[8] 2658[5] 3339[7] 4468[10] 7639[3] 7869[11] 8139[3]

**Ejadah (IRE)** *Roger Varian* 87
3 b f Clodovil(IRE) Bintalreef (USA) (Diesis)
3154[5] (3885) 5074[5]

**Ektihaam (IRE)** *Roger Varian* 118
5 b g Invincible Spirit(IRE) Liscune (IRE) (King's Best (USA))
2086[5] 3450[10]

**Elabela (IRE)** *J E Hammond* a73 82
4 ch f Tamayuz Benalmadena (FR) (Nashwan (USA))
7026a[8]

**Ela Goog La Mou** *Peter Charalambous* a47 71
5 b m Tobougg(IRE) Real Flame (Cyrano De Bergerac)
(1617) 1864[2] 2444[7] 3705[2] 5058[3] 5533[2] (5731) 6076[9] 6210[4]

**Eland Ally** *Tom Tate* 78
6 b g Striking Ambition Dream Rose (IRE) (Anabaa (USA))
2332[16] 3138[4] 3702[2] 3882[7] 4471[8] 4632[4] 5766[7] 6213[11] 6671[14] 6873[2]

**Elassi (FR)** *Mme L Audon*
3 b g Enrique Amouage (IRE) (Groom Dancer (USA))
7164a[9]

**El Beau (IRE)** *John Quinn* 81
3 ch g Camacho River Beau (IRE) (Galileo (IRE))
3464[3] 4419[3] 5051[3] 6284[3] 7125[6]

**Elbereth** *Andrew Balding* a84
3 b f Mount Nelson Masandra (IRE) (Desert Prince (IRE))
3856[3] (5010) 6487[8] 7850[3] (8120)

**El Bravo** *Shaun Harris* a63 75
8 ch g Falbrav(IRE) Alessandra (Generous (IRE))
2327[15] 2762[6] 3192[4] (3785) (4709) 5073[10] 5716[7] 6012[6] 6403[2] ◆ 7133[6] 7411[7] 7975[5] 8264[8]

**El Campeon** *Simon Dow* a52 35
2 bb g Multiplex Villabella (FR) (Hernando (FR))
2276[7] 2622[8] 4079[6] 5554[7] 5823[6] 7740[13]

**El Che** *Mick Channon* a59 77
2 gr f Winker Watson Rose Cheval (USA) (Johannesburg (USA))
1528[3] 1837[3]

**El Conquerador (TUR)** *Onur Dogan* 108
4 ch c Okawango(USA) Adhaaba (USA) (Dayjur (USA))
6185a[4]

**Eldarion (IRE)** *A Lyon* a68 65
6 ch h Aragorn(IRE) Madame Cerito (USA) (Diesis)
3089a[11]

**Eldo River (IRE)** *Luigi Biagetti* 100
5 ch h Le Vie Dei Colori In Deira (IRE) (Ashkalani (IRE))
2375a[12] 7320a[3]

**El Draque (USA)** *Sir Mark Prescott Bt* a51
2 b g Henrythenavigator(USA) Miss Fanny (USA) (Theatrical (IRE))
6931[10] 7371[6]

**El Duque** *Bill Turner* a59 52
3 b g Byron Royal Tavira Girl (IRE) (Orpen (USA))
165[4] 261[4] 374[2] (541) 665[2] 867[5] 1606[10] 2230[4] 3388[4] 3523[7] 4042[4] 4365[4] 7355[7] 7735[10]

**Election Night** *Tim Easterby* 73
3 b f Mount Nelson Psychic (IRE) (Alhaarth (IRE))
1192[10] (1902) 2295[3] 2870[3] 3300[8] 4660[4] 6758[2] 7023[7] 7337[5]

**Elector Of Saxony (USA)** *Z Hegedus* a86 87
3 b c Henrythenavigator(USA) Apert (USA) (Valiant Nature (USA))
4952a[3]

**Electric (IRE)** *Jo Hughes* 47
2 ch g Fast Company(IRE) Triple Wood (USA) (Woodman (USA))
3542[6]

**Electric Qatar** *Alan McCabe* a84 74
5 b g Pastoral Pursuits Valandraud (IRE) (College Chapel)
20[8] 318[2] (478) (549) 834[3] 909[10] 1487[11] 2933[10] 3338[14] 7806[10]

**Elegante (FR)** *E Lellouche* a68 76
2 b f On Est Bien(IRE) Almadina (FR) (Pistolet Bleu (IRE))
5941a[3]

**Elegant Ophelia** *Dean Ivory* a72 61
5 ch m Osorio(GER) Ela's Giant (Giant's Causeway (USA))
120[7] 278[4] 490[5] 821[2] 989[2] 1232[5] 1729[14] 2916[4] 3155[3] (4264) (4734) 5036[4] 5551[2] 6338[8] 7366[6] 7628[12]

**Elegant Peace (IRE)** *D K Weld* a75 96
3 ch f Intense Focus(USA) Magical Peace (IRE) (Magical Wonder (USA))
7579a[12]

**Elektrum (IRE)** *G Botti* a95 95
3 b f High Chaparral(IRE) Carolines Secret (Inchinor)
2590a[5] 4249a[3]

**El Estruendoso (ARG)** *M F De Kock* a98 106
5 ch g Giant's Causeway(USA) Estricta (ARG) (Roy (USA))
108a[5] 309a[2] 509a[2] 595a[6]

**Elettrotreno (IRE)** *A Giorgi* 101
4 b c Modigliani(USA) Alycus (USA) (Atticus (USA))
2375a[4]

**Eleusis** *Chris Wall* 84
3 b f Elnadim(USA) Demeter (USA) (Diesis)
1634[3] 3938[2] (5531) 6468[4]

**Elevato (TUR)** *Z Guneli* 99
4 b f Kaneko(TUR) Zeynep Hanim (TUR) (Distant Relative)
6164a[7]

**Elevator Action (IRE)** *Richard Fahey* a19 45
2 b f Lord Shanakill(USA) Miss Gibraltar (Rock Of Gibraltar (IRE))
2134[6] 4527[7] 4973[9] 6237[10]

**El Fenix (IRE)** *Gary Moore* a55 60
2 b c Lope De Vega(IRE) Woodmaven (USA) (Woodman (USA))
5500[8] 6299[6] 6604[5]

**Elhaam (IRE)** *George Margarson* a69 56
3 b f Shamardal(USA) Loulwa (IRE) (Montjeu (IRE))
5548[8] 6988[5] 7501[2] (7929) 8079[5]

**Elhaame (IRE)** *Luca Cumani* a29 102
4 b g Acclamation Gold Hush (USA) (Seeking The Gold (USA))
1973[9] 3449[6] 5174[3] (5676) 6257[6]

**Elidor** *Mick Channon* 106
4 br g Cape Cross(IRE) Honorine (IRE) (Mark Of Esteem (IRE))
(1444) 2143[3] 3449[4] 4606[4] 5693[3] 6287[4]

**Eliminator (FR)** *J-C Rouget* 26
2 b c Desert Style(IRE) Gallopade (FR) (Kendor (FR))
3691a[9]

**Elis Eliz (IRE)** *Michael Wigham* a77 45
2 b f Lord Shanakill(USA) Suailce (IRE) (Singspiel (IRE))
5973[8] 6271[3] ◆ 6719[2] (7181)

**Elis Gury** *M G Mintchev* 78
4 ch g Refuse To Bend(IRE) Nizza (GER) (Acatenango (GER))
3770a[9]

**Elite Army** *Saeed bin Suroor* a83 109
3 b c Authorized(IRE) White Rose (GER) (Platini (GER))
1702[3] (2496) (3379)

**Elite Force (IRE)** *Roger Charlton* a65 73
3 ch g Medicean Amber Queen (IRE) (Cadeaux Genereux)
1433[6] ◆ 1795[10] 4130[4] 5214[4] 5980[3]

**Elite Freedom (IRE)** *Brian Baugh* a49 56
3 b f Acclamation Jebel Musa (IRE) (Rock Of Gibraltar (IRE))
3149[12] 3564[3] 3966[8] 4101[7] 4567[6] 4891[12] 5605[3] 6160[9]

**Elite Gardens (USA)** *Saeed bin Suroor* 103
2 ch f Speightstown(USA) Flagrant (USA) (Rahy (USA))
(1977) 3415[18] (6295)

**Elizabeth Coffee (IRE)** *John Weymes* a59 66
6 b m Byron Queens Wharf (IRE) (Ela-Mana-Mou)
1761[4] (2875) 3208[2] (3705) 3973[6] 4533[3] 4663[5] 5678[7] 6644[10]

**Elizabeth Ernest** *Richard Fahey* 55
2 b f Exceed And Excel(AUS) Elusive Sue (USA) (Elusive Quality (USA))
2349[4] 3297[9] 3606[3] 4410[7]

**Elizabeth Flynn (IRE)** *K R Burke* a61 72
2 b f Strategic Prince Criss Eria (FR) (Diableneyev (USA))
1536[4] (1741) 2071[5] 2302[6] 4057[9] 4493[2] 4920[8] 5254[2] 5637[9] 5896[2]

**Elizabeth March (IRE)** *E J O'Neill* a4 56
2 b f Bushranger(IRE) Beth (Deportivo)
1094a[11]

**Elizona** *James Fanshawe* a85 79
3 b f Pastoral Pursuits Morning After (Emperor Jones (USA))
2442[2] 3586[2] (4653) 5986[8] 7035[2]

**Elkaayed (USA)** *Roger Varian* 111
4 ch g Distorted Humor(USA) Habibti (USA) (Tabasco Cat (USA))
1533[8] 2335[4] 3354[8]

**Ellaal** *Ruth Carr* a69 79
5 b g Oasis Dream Capistrano Day (USA) (Diesis)
39[2] 105[7] 269[6] 1036[4] 1168[5] (1288) 1454[2] 1675[6] 2019[4] 2293[3] (2546) 2912[5] (3301) 3791[7] 4290[5] 4517[2] 4858[2] (5142) 5268[3] 5496[4] 6111[4] 6323[9] 6626[3] 6822[2] 7042[9]

**Ella Motiva (IRE)** *Mark Brisbourne* a42 53
4 b f Motivator Stormy View (USA) (Cozzene (USA))
1453[9] 1875[7]

**Ella's Delight (IRE)** *Martin Todhunter* 81
4 b f Camacho Swift Alchemist (Fleetwood (IRE))
(2329) 4925[10] 5641[6] 7178[9]

**Elle Dorado** *Tom Dascombe* a70 70
2 ch f Paco Boy(IRE) Clever Millie (USA) (Cape Canaveral (USA))
3642[4] (6868) 7226[6]

**Ellen May** *Nick Littmoden* a58 38
4 b f Rock Of Gibraltar(IRE) Triskel (Hawk Wing (USA))
2442[13] 2994[9] 4092[8] 4732[12]

**Elle Rebelle** *Mark Brisbourne* a63 58
4 b f Cockney Rebel(IRE) Lille Ida (Hawk Wing (USA))
1877[3] 2479[9] (3327) 3554[4] 5075[3] 5950[4] 5977[2] (6407) 7187[6] 7427[5] 7813[11] 7869[8]

**Ellerina** *Chris Fairhurst* 38
2 b f Stimulation(IRE) Dream Quest (Rainbow Quest (USA))
4018[7] 5494[8]

**Elleval (IRE)** *David Marnane* a112 108
4 b g Kodiac Penny Rouge (IRE) (Pennekamp (USA))
309a[6] 595a[8] (681a) 901a[12] 1176a[7] 3765a[4] 4711[5] 5690[6] 6350a[2]

**Elle West** *Michael Easterby* 57
3 ch f Elnadim(USA) Leominda (Lion Cavern (USA))
1375[5] 1647[9] 1906[5] 2204[5] 3150[14] 3946[12] 4069[11]

**El Libertador (USA)** *Eric Wheeler* a60 44
8 bb g Giant's Causeway(USA) Istikbal (USA) (Kingmambo (USA))
283[9] 8011[11]

**Ellies Girl (IRE)** *Ronald Harris*
6 b m Clodovil(IRE) Miss Toto (Mtoto)
*474$^9$*

**Ellies Image** *Richard Ford* a43 58
7 b m Lucky Story(USA) Crown City (USA) (Coronado's Quest (USA))
*18$^8$ 263$^9$ 321$^5$ 673$^4$ 869$^4$ 1138$^8$* (2479) 3053$^4$ 4069$^7$

**Ellingham (IRE)** *Christine Dunnett* a56 52
3 b f Bushranger(IRE) No Way (IRE) (Rainbows For Life (CAN))
*1920$^9$ 2397$^9$ 3522$^5$* 3896$^8$ 4590$^5$ *4972$^{10}$ 7376$^9$ 7865$^7$*

**Ellinis (FR)** *P Marion* a77 75
6 b m Pythios(IRE) Ipeiros (GR) (Pivotal)
*584a$^{14}$*

**Elliptique (IRE)** *A Fabre* a90 113
3 br c New Approach(IRE) Uryale (FR) (Kendor (FR))
1340a$^5$ 2194a$^6$ 6379a$^4$

**El Massivo (IRE)** *Brian Ellison* a53 63
4 b g Authorized(IRE) Umthoulah (IRE) (Unfuwain (USA))
1307$^6$ 2055$^8$ 2327$^{11}$

**Elmer J** *Declan Carroll* 19
2 b g Hellvelyn Mis Chicaf (IRE) (Prince Sabo)
7246$^{11}$

**El Mirage (IRE)** *Dean Ivory* a66 63
4 b f Elusive Quality(USA) Hucking Hot (Desert Prince (IRE))
*91$^8$ 489$^7$ 628$^{10}$ 993$^{12}$ 1766$^4$* ◆ 2029$^5$ 2994$^6$ 3231$^7$ *5041$^3$* 5425$^2$ *5833$^7$ 6883$^2$* 7188$^2$ 7424$^2$ 7704$^2$ 7854$^{10}$ 7987$^6$

**Elm Park** *Andrew Balding* 118
2 b c Phoenix Reach(IRE) Lady Brora (Dashing Blade)
4800$^3$ (5377) (5876) (6750) (7442) ◆

**El Najmm (IRE)** *Roger Varian* a74 77
3 ch g Sea The Stars(IRE) My Dubai (IRE) (Dubai Millennium)
*1044$^2$* 1727$^6$

**Eloquence** *Tom Dascombe* a47 48
3 b f Oratorio(IRE) Noble Plum (IRE) (King's Best (USA))
2804$^8$ *4052$^5$* 4830$^5$

**Elora Princess (GER)** *Markus Klug* 95
3 ch f Desert Prince(IRE) Elora (GER) (Alkalde (GER))
1619a$^9$

**El Padrino (NZ)** *Hai Wang Tan* a114 101
6 b g Mr Nancho(ARG) Crownie (AUS) (Luskin Star (AUS))
2378a$^6$

**Elpida (USA)** *David Simcock* a75 60
3 b f Giant's Causeway(USA) Swan Nebula (USA) (Seeking The Gold (USA))
*1143$^2$ 2649$^5$* 3877$^5$ *5036$^3$ 5898$^3$ (7772)*

**El Roca (AUS)** *Trent Busuttin & Natalie Young* 113
4 b c Fastnet Rock(AUS) Rubimill (AUS) (Rubiton (AUS))
1186a$^3$

**El Salvador (IRE)** *A P O'Brien* a97 109
5 ch h Galileo(IRE) Balisada (Kris)
1750a$^2$ 2704$^8$ 3453$^2$ 3764a$^7$ 5115a$^5$ (7142a)

**Elshaadin** *Roger Varian* 70
3 gr f Dalakhani(IRE) Distinctive Look (IRE) (Danehill (USA))
1722$^5$ 3141$^6$

**Elsie Bay** *Gary Moore* a59 69
5 b m Sakhee(USA) Mary Sea (FR) (Selkirk (USA))
3308$^6$ 3803$^{12}$ (4343)

**Elsiniaar** *Roger Varian* 87
4 bl g New Approach(IRE) Comic (IRE) (Be My Chief (USA))
(4393) 5178$^4$

**Elspeth's Boy (USA)** *Philip Kirby* a78 64
7 bb g Tiznow(USA) Miss Waki Club (USA) (Miswaki (USA))
*498$^5$* 1168$^{11}$

**El Suizo (FR)** *H-A Pantall* 102
2 b c Meshaheer(USA) Belle Suisse (FR) (Hamas (IRE))
(1402a) (3027a) 4953a$^3$

**Eltheeb** *Michael Dods* a70 88
7 gr g Red Ransom(USA) Snowdrops (Gulch (USA))
2168$^9$ 3205$^5$ 3574$^3$ 4710$^4$ 5052$^4$ 7008$^2$

**Elualla (IRE)** *Nigel Tinkler* a39 58
3 b f Elusive City(USA) Cote Quest (USA) (Green Desert (USA))
*165$^9$ 786$^6$* 1277$^{10}$

**Elusive** *Ann Stokell* a19
8 b m Reel Buddy(USA) Love Is All (IRE) (Second Empire (IRE))
*1243$^6$ 1430$^9$*

**Elusive Award (USA)** *T J O'Mara* a55 53
7 b g Elusive Quality(USA) Victoria Cross (IRE) (Mark Of Esteem (IRE))
*7961a$^5$*

**Elusive Band (USA)** *Bernard Llewellyn* a38 69
4 b g Elusive Quality(USA) Dancing Band (USA) (Dixieland Band (USA))
2135$^8$ 2672$^{12}$ 3208$^7$ 3778$^6$ 4149$^6$

**Elusive Ellen (IRE)** *Brendan Powell* a71 68
4 b f Elusive City(USA) Ellen's Girl (IRE) (Desert Prince (IRE))
3755$^6$ *7397$^{13}$ (7759) 7993$^7$ 8248$^{14}$ 8316$^3$*

**Elusive Epona (USA)** *Richard Fahey* 72
2 b f Elusive Quality(USA) Genuine Charm (USA) (Dixie Union (USA))
(2513)

**Elusive Gent (IRE)** *Adrian Paul Keatley* a58 59
7 b g Elusive City(USA) Satin Cape (IRE) (Cape Cross (IRE))
5166$^9$ 5234$^3$ 5635$^8$

**Elusive George (IRE)** *John Quinn* a77 85
3 b c Elusive City(USA) Sur Ma Vie (USA) (Fusaichi Pegasus (USA))
*787$^2$ 923$^2$* (1347) 1884$^4$ 1940$^8$ 3225$^2$ 4390$^4$ (4572) 6170$^4$

**Elusive Guest (FR)** *George Margarson* 85
3 b g Elusive City(USA) Mansoura (IRE) (Kalanisi (IRE))
1353$^{12}$ 3153$^3$ (3804) ◆ 4419$^5$

**Elusive Hawk (IRE)** *David Evans* a94 84
10 b g Noverre(USA) Two Clubs (First Trump)
*262$^3$ (651)*

**Elusive In Paris (IRE)** *M C Grassick* a80 82
5 b g Elusive City(USA) Bradwell (IRE) (Taufan (USA))
*6078a$^9$*

**Elusive Laurence (IRE)** *Mrs John Harrington* a74 65
3 b f Lawman(FR) Super Supreme (IND) (Zafonic (USA))
*7435a$^6$*

**Elusive Lily** *Robert Collet* a25 61
2 b f Elusive City(USA) Painting (IRE) (Peintre Celebre (USA))
5617a$^9$ *5844a$^{16}$*

**Elusive Pearl (FR)** *F Rossi* 102
3 b f Elusive City(USA) Spirit Of Pearl (IRE) (Invincible Spirit (IRE))
2226a$^6$

**Elusive Prince** *T Hogan* a50 79
6 b g Storming Home Ewenny (Warrshan (USA))
4950a$^6$

**Elusive Time (IRE)** *Takashi Kodama* a93 99
6 b g Elusive City(USA) Brosna Time (IRE) (Danetime (IRE))
6354a$^8$

**Elusive Warrior (USA)** *Alan McCabe* a59 49
11 b g Elusive Quality(USA) Love To Fight (CAN) (Fit To Fight (USA))
*126$^7$ 387$^3$ 565$^3$ 833$^7$ 1087$^6$*

**Elusivity (IRE)** *Peter Crate* a91 95
6 b g Elusive City(USA) Tough Chic (IRE) (Indian Ridge)
*55$^{11}$ 348$^3$* 1650$^2$ 1944$^7$ 2283$^2$ 2989$^{14}$ 5925$^8$ 6745$^6$ 7132$^3$ 7441$^{15}$ *7738$^5$ 7843$^6$ 7923$^9$*

**El Valle (FR)** *Mlle V Dissaux* 97
2 b c Dobby Road(FR) Dohibane (FR) (Danehill (USA))
4932a$^6$ 7094a$^6$ 7855a$^2$

**El Viento (FR)** *Richard Fahey* a87 103
6 ch g Compton Place Blue Sirocco (Bluebird (USA))
1421$^4$ ◆ 1734$^{11}$ 2254$^{16}$ 2786$^6$ 3732$^5$ 4892$^{13}$ 6260$^{18}$ 6744$^{13}$

**Elysian Fields (GR)** *Amanda Perrett* a65 64
3 ch f Champs Elysees Second Of May (Lion Cavern (USA))
2967$^6$ *7528$^4$ 7841$^7$ (8172)*

**Elysian Flyer (IRE)** *Richard Hannon* 97
2 b c Majestic Missile(IRE) Starisa (IRE) (College Chapel)
(5271) (5906) (6879)

**Elysian Prince** *Paul Cole* a84 75
3 b c Champs Elysees Trinkila (USA) (Cat Thief (USA))
*2060$^4$* 2303$^7$ *2936$^6$* 3974$^7$ *6633$^3$* 6877$^3$ *(7225) (7630a) 7998$^2$*

**Ely Valley** *Ron Barr*
4 b f Haafhd Welsh Valley (USA) (Irish River (FR))
4533$^8$ 4791$^{14}$

**Emaad (USA)** *Mark Johnston* a70 74
3 b c Arch(USA) Red Dot (USA) (Diesis)
1509$^7$ *2998$^3$* 3466$^2$

**Emaratiya Ana (IRE)** *Roger Varian* a71 94
3 b f Excellent Art Tina Heights (Shirley Heights)
*(1024)* 1530$^4$ 2484$^4$ 3376$^9$ 4249a$^5$

**Embankment** *Michael Attwater* a76 72
5 b g Zamindar(USA) Esplanade (Danehill (USA))
*7012$^3$ 8041$^4$ 8248$^9$*

**Emblaze** *Bryan Smart* a54 64
2 b f Showcasing Chushka (Pivotal)
5128$^4$ 6701$^4$ *7228$^4$*

**Embsay Crag** *Philip Kirby* a58 81
8 b g Elmaamul(USA) Wigman Lady (IRE) (Tenby)
2520$^3$ 3501$^3$ 7333$^4$

**Emef Diamond** *Mick Channon* 82
3 b g Firebreak On The Brink (Mind Games)
1586$^3$ 2481$^9$ 3464$^7$ 3897$^5$ 5051$^2$ 5713$^3$ 6431$^2$ 6871$^4$ 7445$^5$

**Emef Rock (IRE)** *Mick Channon* a67 69
2 b g Acclamation Sveva (IRE) (Danehill Dancer (IRE))
2480$^5$ 2944$^5$ 3311$^3$ 3779$^3$ 4410$^6$ (5974) 6574$^3$ 6739$^5$ *7201$^5$ 7363$^3$* 7515$^3$

**Emell** *Richard Hannon* a99 109
4 ch c Medicean Londonnetdotcom (IRE) (Night Shift (USA))
*749$^5$* 1162$^6$ 3731$^7$ 5666$^2$ 6132$^4$ 6458$^3$ 7599$^7$ *7836$^{12}$ 8116$^8$ 8242$^3$*

**Emerahldz (IRE)** *Richard Fahey* a69 92
3 b f Excellent Art Sancia (IRE) (Docksider (USA))
1401$^3$ (2235) 2735$^2$ (3303) 5132$^3$ (5442) 7083$^2$ 7440$^7$

**Emerald Breeze (IRE)** *Tim Pitt* a74 39
3 b f Tagula(IRE) Rebel Aclaim (IRE) (Acclamation)
*480$^3$ (786) (867) (1047) 1130$^5$ 3388$^7$*

**Emerald Gg (IRE)** *J S Moore* a44 8
3 b g Diamond Green(FR) Florista Gg (URU) (Gulpha Gorge (USA))
*187$^8$*

**Emerald Sea** *Chris Wall* a66 70
4 b f Green Desert(USA) Wind Surf (USA) (Lil's Lad (USA))
*1896$^8$ 2887$^6$* 3630$^6$

**Emerald Star** *P Schiergen* 102
3 b f Mount Nelson Ares Vallis (IRE) (Caerleon (USA))
1619a$^3$ (2155) 4171$^{11}$ 5965a$^5$

**Emerald Swell (IRE)** *Brian Meehan* a37 59
3 gr f Dalakhani(IRE) Dance Of The Sea (IRE) (Sinndar (IRE))
3142$^5$ *4052$^7$*

**Emerald Wilderness (IRE)** *Mark Rimmer* a95 59
10 b g Green Desert(USA) Simla Bibi (Indian Ridge)
*144$^4$ 235$^9$ 426$^{10}$ 840$^5$* 1196$^7$

**Emerging** *David Elsworth* a10 90
4 b g Mount Nelson Pan Galactic (USA) (Lear Fan (USA))
6987$^6$

**Emerita (IRE)** *D K Weld* 96
3 gr f Mizzen Mast(USA) Ebaza (IRE) (Sinndar (IRE))
7144a$^5$

**Emily Davison (IRE)** *Ann Stokell* a56 59
3 gr f Moss Vale(IRE) Carabine (USA) (Dehere (USA))
1347$^7$ 1647$^7$ 2729$^5$ *2906$^6$* (3395) (3609) 4257$^6$ 4796$^3$ 5375$^9$ 5889$^3$ 5994$^6$ 6671$^7$ 6821$^3$ 7644$^{15}$ *7735$^3$ 7825$^7$*

**Emily Of Tinsdal (GER)** *P Harley* 105
5 b m Librettist(USA) Earthly Paradise (GER) (Dashing Blade)
5231a$^7$ 5938a$^{11}$ 7482a$^6$ 7727a$^{11}$

**Emilys Girl (IRE)** *Ronald Harris* 27
2 b f Camacho Lamassu (IRE) (Entrepreneur)
2692$^6$ 3933$^{14}$ 4999$^7$ 5746$^6$ 6248$^7$ 6645$^8$

**Emily Yeats** *Paul Webber* a42 61
3 b f Yeats(IRE) Lasso (Indian Ridge)
3142$^4$ 4413$^6$ *7032$^7$*

**Emirates Airline** *Saeed bin Suroor* 60
2 b g Dubawi(IRE) Moonlife (IRE) (Invincible Spirit (IRE))
4142$^4$ 5439$^6$

**Emirates Challenge (IRE)** *Saeed bin Suroor* a44 60
2 b f Cape Cross(IRE) Sand Vixen (Dubawi (IRE))
2800$^6$ 4269$^6$ 5104$^4$ 6791$^9$ *7362$^7$ 7648$^7$*

**Emirates Flyer** *Saeed bin Suroor* a107 104
3 b g Acclamation Galapagar (USA) (Miswaki (USA))
*(204a) 594a$^2$ 896a$^2$ 1178a$^3$ 7066$^2$*

**Emirates Galloper (IRE)** *Saeed bin Suroor* 82
3 b g Dalakhani(IRE) Emmy Award (IRE) (Sadler's Wells (USA))
3182$^6$ 4361$^7$

**Emirate's Girl (ARG)** *Takashi Kodama* a46 108
4 b f Lizard Island(USA) Embrasable (ARG) (Equalize (USA))
6955a$^{14}$

**Emirates Holidays (USA)** *Charlie Appleby*
2 b f Dubawi(IRE) New Morning (IRE) (Sadler's Wells (USA))
*8173$^{13}$*

**Emirates Joy (USA)** *Charlie Appleby* a78
3 b f Street Cry(IRE) Zofzig (USA) (Danzig (USA))
*5007$^3$* ◆ *6033$^2$ 6940$^3$ 7196$^{13}$*

**Emirates Skycargo (IRE)** *Charlie Appleby* 30
2 b c Iffraaj Catchline (USA) (Bertolini (USA))
5149$^{11}$

**Emirates Skywards (IRE)** *Charlie Appleby* 81
2 b c Dubawi(IRE) Mont Etoile (IRE) (Montjeu (IRE))
6362$^2$ 6743$^2$ 7230$^2$

**Emirati Spirit** *Roger Varian* 75
3 b c New Approach(IRE) Dance Lively (USA) (Kingmambo (USA))
1511$^6$ 2026$^5$

**Emjayem** *Ed McMahon* a84 81
4 ch g Needwood Blade Distant Stars (IRE) (Distant Music (USA))
2434$^5$ 4114$^4$ 4752$^3$ *(5601)* 6324$^4$ 6650$^8$

**Emkanaat** *Amy Weaver* a84 76
6 b g Green Desert(USA) Miss Anabaa (Anabaa (USA))
*342$^2$* ◆ *372$^4$ 574$^7$ 2005a$^4$*

**Emma Bovary** *John Norton* a13
2 ch f Monsieur Bond(IRE) Rapturous (Zafonic (USA))
*5507$^5$ 7062$^{12}$*

**Emma Dilemma (FR)** *T Doumen*
3 gr f Smadoun(FR) Deglet Nour (FR) (Fly To The Stars)
5227a$^{11}$

**Emman Bee (IRE)** *Luke Dace* a66 80
5 gr m Dark Angel(IRE) Two Sets To Love (IRE) (Cadeaux Genereux)
*376$^2$ 491$^5$ 747$^6$* 3032$^2$ 3556$^2$ 4045$^6$ 4273$^8$ 4942$^3$ (5075) 5425$^5$ (5950)

**Emmessess (IRE)** *Christine Dunnett*
3 b g Desert Millennium(IRE) Azira (Arazi (USA))
3156$^9$ 3914$^{13}$

**Emollient (USA)** *William Mott* a113 113
4 b f Empire Maker(USA) Soothing Touch (USA) (Touch Gold (USA))
5459a$^9$ 7607a$^9$

**Emotional Kitten (USA)** *Wesley A Ward* a12 107
4 ch f Kitten's Joy(USA) Silent Emotion (USA) (Ghazi (USA))
7615a$^4$

**Emperatriz** *John Holt* a74 69
4 b f Holy Roman Emperor(IRE) Fairmont (IRE) (Kingmambo (USA))
*388$^4$ 548$^3$ 647$^7$* 4153$^6$ 4620$^3$ 4963$^4$ 5394$^3$

**Emperor Ferdinand (IRE)** *Marcus Tregoning* a55 30
3 b g Holy Roman Emperor(IRE) Moon Flower (IRE) (Sadler's Wells (USA))
7167$^4$ *7541$^3$ 8011$^4$ 8246$^5$*

**Emperor Julius (IRE)** *Jo Crowley* a70 66
4 b g Antonius Pius(USA) Queen's Victory (Mujadil (USA))
*587$^{11}$ 817$^{10}$* 4655$^4$ 6088$^2$ 7167$^6$

**Emperor Max (AUS)** *S Gray* 113
5 b g Holy Roman Emperor(IRE) Maxerelle (AUS) (Strategic (AUS))
2378a$^2$

**Emperors Warrior (IRE)** *Richard Hannon* a62 62
2 ch g Thewayyouare(USA) World Sprint (GER) (Waky Nao)
3429$^{12}$ 4330$^{10}$ 5519$^3$ 6085$^5$ *6663$^4$ 6884$^{13}$ 7396$^{14}$*

**Empire Storm (GER)** *Michael Attwater* a108 113
7 b h Storming Home Emy Coasting (USA) (El Gran Senor (USA))
*111a$^2$ 508a$^{11}$ 596a$^3$ 899a$^{10}$* 1697$^5$ 2338$^5$ 2765$^6$ 3291a$^8$ 3731$^3$ 4180$^9$ 5263a$^6$ 6458$^5$ 6921$^2$ 7276$^3$

**Empoli (GER)** *P Schiergen* 116
4 ch c Halling(USA) Estefania (GER) (Acatenango (GER))
683a$^2$ 1182a$^4$ 2988$^4$ 3774a$^6$ 5962a$^5$ (6806a) 8151a$^8$

**Emporium** *Nick Littmoden* a35 38
3 b f Exceed And Excel(AUS) Australian Dreams (Magic Ring (IRE))
1534$^{18}$ *5427$^8$*

**Empresario (IRE)** *Matthew J Smith* a65 84
5 ch g Hurricane Run(IRE) La Stravaganza (USA) (Rainbow Quest (USA))
*7962a$^{10}$*

**Empress Adelaide** *William Haggas* 93
4 ch f Pivotal Emperice (USA) (Empire Maker (USA))
2762$^9$ 3725$^6$

**Empress Ali (IRE)** *Tom Tate* 91
3 b f Holy Roman Emperor(IRE) Almansa (IRE) (Dr Devious (IRE))
2422$^7$ (2899) 3643$^2$ 4941$^2$ ◆ (6737) 7119$^5$

**Emulating (IRE)** *James Fanshawe* a83 78
4 ch g Duke Of Marmalade(IRE) Ascendancy (Sadler's Wells (USA))
*(1231)* 1724$^5$ 2445$^5$ 3371$^6$ *(4077)*

**Encapsulated** *Roger Ingram* a58 64
4 b g Zamindar(USA) Star Cluster (Observatory (USA))
*1221$^7$* (1573) 1639$^4$ 2029$^2$ 2488$^7$ 3088$^{15}$ 3470$^9$ 4428$^8$ 4908$^5$ 5518$^4$ 5977$^8$ *7420$^3$ 7782$^9$ 7940$^2$ 8200$^3$*

**Enchanted Garden** *Malcolm Jefferson* a45 74
6 ch g Sulamani(IRE) Calachuchi (Martinmas)
3240$^2$ 5334$^6$ 6864$^{10}$

**Encipher (USA)** *A Al Raihe* a104 91
5 b h Elusive Quality(USA) Secret Charm (IRE) (Green Desert (USA))
*504a$^{11}$*

**En Civil (IRE)** *D Guillemin* a87
3 b g Elusive City(USA) En Vitesse (Peintre Celebre (USA))
*237a$^4$*

**Encke (USA)** *Charlie Appleby* 110
5 b h Kingmambo(USA) Shawanda (IRE) (Sinndar (IRE))
4849$^2$ 6374a$^3$ 6919$^3$ (Dead)

**Encore D'Or** *Ralph Beckett* a88 76
2 b c Oasis Dream Entente Cordiale (IRE) (Ela-Mana-Mou)
5671$^2$ 6517$^{11}$ *(7113)*

**Encore Encore (FR)** *Harry Dunlop* a53 61
3 b f Royal Applause Angel Rose (IRE) (Definite Article)
*1220$^8$* 1786$^4$ 4329$^9$ *5256$^6$* 6087$^5$ 6613$^5$

**Encore L'Amour** *David Simcock* 100
2 b f Azamour(IRE) Centime (Royal Applause)
3648$^3$ 4626$^4$ (5746) 7393a$^6$ 7596$^8$

**Encore Un Fois** *Ruth Carr* a60 67
6 br g Val Royal(FR) Factice (USA) (Known Fact (USA))
*565$^5$ 830$^4$ 1249$^2$* ◆ *1496$^4$*

**Encountering (IRE)** *James Fanshawe* 70
3 b g Duke Of Marmalade(IRE) Naval Affair (IRE) (Last Tycoon)
5018$^5$

**Endeavor** *Dianne Sayer* 54
9 ch g Selkirk(USA) Midnight Mambo (USA) (Kingmambo (USA))
2915$^7$

**Enderby Spirit (GR)** *Bryan Smart* a82 88
8 gr g Invincible Spirit(IRE) Arctic Ice (IRE) (Zafonic (USA))
1672$^{11}$ 2332$^{14}$ 4471$^{16}$ 5265$^2$ 6213$^2$ 6824$^{13}$

**Endislie (IRE)** *J S Moore* 50
2 b g Amadeus Wolf Endis (IRE) (Distant Relative)
1161$^{14}$ 2622$^6$ 2976a$^5$ 3201$^{11}$ 5148$^8$

**Endless Credit (IRE)** *Luca Cumani* 89
4 bb g High Chaparral(IRE) Pay The Bank (High Top)
2787$^{13}$ 3574$^7$ 4349$^4$ 4832$^2$ 5528$^6$ 6465$^3$ 7335$^5$

**Endless Seas** *Michael Appleby* 43
3 ch f Refuse To Bend(IRE) Ocean Ballad (Bering)
3925$^{10}$ 4413$^7$ 4713$^6$

**Endless Time (IRE)** *Charlie Appleby* a77 74
2 b f Sea The Stars(IRE) Mamonta (Fantastic Light (USA))
4914$^5$ *(5549)*

**End Of Line** *Andrew Balding* 100
3 b g Pastoral Pursuits Just Devine (IRE) (Montjeu (IRE))
1696$^2$ ◆ 2196a$^9$ 2706$^3$ 5749$^3$ 6332$^9$ 7119$^6$

**Endowing (IRE)** *J Size* 117
5 b g Danehill Dancer(IRE) Brazilian Samba (IRE) (Sadler's Wells (USA))
7899a$^3$ 8154a$^{11}$

**Energia Davos (BRZ)** *Marco Botti* a105 108
6 gr g Torrential(USA) Star Brisingamen (USA) (Maria's Mon (USA))
*202a$^3$ 593a$^3$ 773a$^5$ 1170$^6$* 3217$^4$ (5174) 6548$^{11}$ *7803$^4$ 8018$^3$ 8244$^2$*

**Energia Dust (BRZ)** *Fabricio Borges* a97 90
6 ch h Amigoni(IRE) Key Largo (BRZ) (Roi Normand (USA))
*2245a$^3$ 3996a$^5$* 4957a$^5$

**Energia El Gigante (BRZ)** *Fabricio Borges* a98 98
5 br g Point Given(USA) Lira Da Guanabara (BRZ) (Pitu Da Guanabara (BRZ))
3090a$^{10}$ 4956a$^2$ 5744a$^8$ 6389a$^2$

**Energia Eros (BRZ)** *John Berry* a78 73
5 b g Point Given(USA) Super Eletric (BRZ) (Choctaw Ridge (USA))
*54$^{13}$ 398a$^{14}$ 3722$^8$ 7066$^7$ 7784$^8$ 8178$^3$*

**Energia Flavio (BRZ)** *Marco Botti* a97 95
4 gr c Agnes Gold(JPN) Lira Da Guanabara (BRZ) (Pitu Da Guanabara (BRZ))
5163$^9$ 6748$^4$ *7688$^4$ 7971$^4$ 8116$^7$ 8266$^3$*

**Energia Fox (BRZ)** *Marco Botti* a100 94
4 ch f Agnes Gold(JPN) Super Eletric (BRZ) (Choctaw Ridge (USA))
5688$^3$ 6255$^{13}$ *7803$^3$* ◆ *7930$^6$*

**Energia Fribby (BRZ)** *Marco Botti* 108
4 b f Agnes Gold(JPN) Karla Dora (BRZ) (Nugget Point (IRE))
(6321) 6919$^{5}$

**Energizer (GER)** *Charlie Appleby* a99 104
5 b h Monsun(GER) Erytheis (USA) (Theatrical (IRE))
205a$^{6}$ 810a$^{5}$ 3416$^{6}$ 5609$^{13}$ 6560$^{6}$

**Enfys Hud** *David Evans* 63
3 b f Multiplex Kyllachy Magic (Kyllachy)
3643$^{8}$ 4536$^{7}$ 5747$^{3}$ 5846$^{8}$

**Engaging Smile** *Ralph Beckett* a77
2 b f Exceed And Excel(AUS) Bronze Star (Mark Of Esteem (IRE))
7192$^{4}$ (7943)

**Engai (GER)** *David Bridgwater* a49 67
8 b g Noroit(GER) Enigma (GER) (Sharp Victor (USA))
6627$^{2}$ 7251$^{4}$ 7846$^{13}$

**Englishman** *Charles Hills* 99
4 b c Royal Applause Tesary (Danehill (USA))
1442$^{12}$ 1938$^{7}$ 2629$^{2}$ 3431$^{2}$ 5189$^{3}$ 5444$^{12}$ (7233) 7408$^{8}$

**English Summer** *Richard Fahey* a83 89
7 b g Montjeu(IRE) Hunt The Sun (Rainbow Quest (USA))
2950$^{2}$ 3249$^{2}$ (3696) 4160$^{3}$ 4423$^{2}$ (4940) 5924$^{6}$ 6349a$^{12}$ 6747$^{8}$ (7279) (7504)

**Engrossing** *Peter Niven* a79 75
5 b g Tiger Hill(IRE) Pan Galactic (USA) (Lear Fan (USA))
1607$^{18}$ 2017$^{9}$ 2654$^{3}$ 3139$^{2}$ 3999$^{7}$ 4427$^{5}$ 7281$^{7}$ 7504$^{4}$

**Enjeu (IRE)** *A Fabre* 79
2 b c Montjeu(IRE) Wingspan (USA) (Silver Hawk (USA))
6916a$^{4}$

**Enlace** *Mark Johnston* 91
2 b f Shamardal(USA) Crossover (Cape Cross (IRE))
(4357) 4913$^{2}$ 5286$^{3}$ 5921$^{4}$ 6510$^{11}$ 7237$^{14}$

**Enliven** *Andrew Balding* a79 78
3 b f Dansili Aurore (IRE) (Fasliyev (USA))
1422$^{7}$ 3601$^{2}$ (5412) 6263$^{6}$ 6890$^{4}$

**Enniscorthy Myles (USA)** *Tim Pitt* a9
3 b g Forestry(USA) Sans Reward (IRE) (Barathea (IRE))
1166$^{10}$ 1817$^{6}$ 2075$^{11}$ 4834$^{8}$

**Ennistown** *Charlie Appleby* 108
4 b g Authorized(IRE) Saoirse Abu (USA) (Mr Greeley (USA))
2154$^{4}$ 2618$^{9}$ (6693) 7449$^{6}$ 7718$^{21}$

**Enobled** *Sir Michael Stoute* a79 93
4 b c Dansili Peeress (Pivotal)
1437$^{16}$ 3244$^{4}$ ◆ 4400$^{3}$ 5188$^{5}$ 6098$^{2}$ 6292$^{2}$ 7110$^{9}$

**Enough Paint (IRE)** *J Heloury* 89
2 ch f New Approach(IRE) Ginostra (Oasis Dream)
(5617a) 6991a$^{5}$

**Enquiring** *Mark Johnston* a64 64
3 b c Cape Cross(IRE) Questina (FR) (Rainbow Quest (USA))
(960) (1098) 1382$^{3}$ 1588$^{10}$ 1792$^{5}$ 2198$^{7}$ 3098$^{10}$ (3567) 3819$^{2}$ 3912$^{6}$

**Enraptured (IRE)** *John Gosden* a64 85
3 b f Oasis Dream Arty Crafty (USA) (Arch (USA))
4436$^{4}$ ◆ 5612$^{7}$

**En Reve** *Seamus Durack* 54
3 b f Shirocco(GER) Night Symphonie (Cloudings (IRE))
1423$^{10}$ 4052$^{11}$ 4435$^{10}$ 5904$^{4}$ 6818$^{7}$

**Enriching (USA)** *Nick Littmoden* a70 77
6 ch g Lemon Drop Kid(USA) Popozinha (USA) (Rahy (USA))
583$^{6}$ 801$^{6}$ 2444$^{3}$ 3162$^{3}$ 3427$^{13}$ 3898$^{2}$ 4548$^{5}$ 4763$^{6}$ 5537$^{3}$ 5950$^{5}$

**Entente** *Peter Makin* a62 66
2 b c Mawatheeq(USA) Amarullah (FR) (Daylami (IRE))
4054$^{5}$ 5351$^{5}$ 5874$^{13}$ 7181$^{3}$ 7728$^{8}$

**Entertainment** *John Gosden* 82
2 ch f Halling(USA) Opera Comique (FR) (Singspiel (IRE))
6753$^{7}$ 7377$^{2}$

**Enthusiastic** *George Margarson* a91 86
6 b g Galileo(IRE) Que Puntual (ARG) (Contested Bid (USA))
2272$^{5}$ 2700$^{7}$

**Entifaadha** *M Al Muhairi* a88 92
5 b g Dansili Model Queen (USA) (Kingmambo (USA))
242a$^{4}$

**Entihaa** *Alan Swinbank* a96 89
6 b g Tiger Hill(IRE) Magic Tree (UAE) (Timber Country (USA))
1307$^{3}$ 1848$^{2}$ 2289$^{3}$ 2561$^{3}$ 3240$^{6}$ 3622$^{2}$ 4606$^{6}$ 5564$^{2}$ (6169) 6557$^{6}$ 7566$^{8}$ (7995) (8062) 8146$^{4}$

**Entitling (IRE)** *James Fanshawe* a80 70
2 b c Mastercraftsman(IRE) Splash Mountain (IRE) (Peintre Celebre (USA))
7666$^{5}$ (8067)

**Entity** *Sir Michael Stoute* a49
2 ch f Shamardal(USA) Echelon (Danehill (USA))
6606$^{7}$

**Entrapping** *John E Long* a61 61
4 b g Tiger Hill(IRE) Meddle (Diktat)
252$^{5}$ 459$^{4}$ 838$^{10}$ 1012$^{4}$ 1232$^{7}$ 2875$^{7}$ 3115$^{3}$

**Entree** *P Bary* a97 109
4 b f Halling(USA) West Dakota (USA) (Gone West (USA))
1827a$^{2}$ 2631a$^{6}$ 7095a$^{3}$

**Entree Parfaite (FR)** *Yannick Fouin* a59 65
2 b f Enrique Entre Deux Mers (FR) (Saint Estephe (FR))
5293a$^{6}$ 5941a$^{6}$

**Enville (IRE)** *William Haggas* 70
2 b c Aussie Rules(USA) La Sibilla (Fantastic Light (USA))
5752$^{4}$ 6108$^{3}$ 6694$^{3}$

**Envisioning (IRE)** *Richard Hannon* a56 58
2 b g Dylan Thomas(IRE) Lady Taufan (IRE) (Taufan (USA))
6101$^{8}$ 6317$^{5}$ 6984$^{8}$ 7488$^{8}$

**Enzaal (USA)** *Philip Kirby* a62 56
4 b g Invasor(ARG) Ekleel (IRE) (Danehill (USA))
3544$^{10}$ 4175$^{10}$ 4793$^{8}$ 5421$^{11}$ 5899$^{9}$ 6341$^{9}$ 6542$^{7}$ 7290$^{5}$ 7628$^{8}$ 7823$^{4}$ (8134)

**Ephraim** *Markus Klug* 29
3 b g Rail Link Enrica (Niniski (USA))
6589a$^{10}$

**Epic Battle (IRE)** *George Margarson* a76 89
4 b g Acclamation Wrong Key (IRE) (Key Of Luck (USA))
560$^{2}$ 840$^{11}$ (3499) 4184$^{8}$ 4586$^{3}$ 6156$^{7}$ 6693$^{5}$

**Epic Find (USA)** *Charles Hills* 44
2 b f Henrythenavigator(USA) Madamascus (USA) (Sheikh Albadou)
3888$^{12}$ 4129$^{8}$ 5667$^{10}$

**Epic Storm (IRE)** *Martin Keighley* a65 52
6 b g Montjeu(IRE) Jaya (USA) (Ela-Mana-Mou)
2430$^{4}$

**Epicuris** *Mme C Head-Maarek* 112
2 b c Rail Link Argumentative (Observatory (USA))
(7317a) (7721a)

**Epic Voyage (USA)** *Brian Ellison* a85 77
3 b g Empire Maker(USA) Costume (Danehill (USA))
2932$^{2}$ (3832) 4390$^{7}$ 5196$^{12}$ 5571$^{4}$

**Epiphaneia (JPN)** *Katsuhiko Sumii* 126
4 b c Symboli Kris S(USA) Cesario (JPN) (Special Week (JPN))
(7981a)

**Epithet (IRE)** *Charlie Appleby* 86
2 b g Shamardal(USA) Epic Similie (Lomitas)
2776$^{3}$ ◆ (3429) ◆ 3883$^{4}$ 4218$^{5}$ 6128$^{10}$

**Epsom Flyer** *Pat Phelan* a38 40
4 ch g Haafhd River Cara (USA) (Irish River (FR))
7002$^{6}$ 7518$^{7}$

**Epsom Hill (SWE)** *Charlie Fellowes* 104
3 b c Homme D'Honneur(FR) Energiya Sacc (SWE) (Exceller (USA))
2201$^{3}$ 2899$^{3}$ 3541$^{6}$ 4058$^{2}$ (4921) (5379) 6133$^{2}$ 7106$^{12}$

**Epsom Poems** *Pat Phelan* a51 33
2 b g Pastoral Pursuits My Amalie (IRE) (Galileo (IRE))
3467$^{9}$ 6852$^{7}$ 7198$^{9}$ 8115$^{10}$

**Epsom Salts** *Pat Phelan* a68 65
9 b g Josr Algarhoud(IRE) Captive Heart (Conquistador Cielo (USA))
214$^{7}$ 382$^{9}$ 4082$^{2}$ 4615$^{5}$

**Equally Fast** *William Muir* a80 71
2 b c Equiano(FR) Fabulously Fast (USA) (Deputy Minister (CAN))
3311$^{5}$ 4583$^{2}$ (6158) 7255$^{8}$

**Equiaire** *John Weymes* 31
2 b f Equiano(FR) Forest Prize (Charnwood Forest (IRE))
3529$^{9}$ 4192$^{6}$ 5885$^{10}$

**Equilicious** *Charles Hills* a35
2 b f Equiano(FR) Fabine (Danehill Dancer (IRE))
7345$^{8}$ 7550$^{11}$

**Equita** *Robert Stephens* a47
2 b f Equiano(FR) Oasis Jade (Oasis Dream)
6659$^{10}$ 7881$^{7}$ 7970$^{11}$

**Equitable** *Lady Cecil* a77 64
3 b g Dansili Honest Quality (USA) (Elusive Quality (USA))
(954) 1861$^{8}$ 2781$^{11}$ 4427$^{8}$ 5550$^{9}$

**Equitania** *Alan Bailey* a99 92
4 b f Pastoral Pursuits Clarice Orsini (Common Grounds)
4$^{7}$ 271$^{U}$

**Equitanus (IRE)** *Andrew Balding* a64 83
2 b c Shamardal(USA) Wedding Gift (FR) (Always Fair (USA))
5009$^{4}$ 6063$^{2}$

**Equity Risk (USA)** *Kevin Ryan* a72 98
4 b g Henrythenavigator(USA) Moon's Tune (USA) (Dixieland Band (USA))
2483$^{7}$ 3431$^{9}$ 4635$^{10}$ 5446$^{12}$ 6891$^{3}$ ◆

**Equleus** *Jeremy Gask* a60
2 b c Equiano(FR) Merle (Selkirk (USA))
6852$^{6}$ 7400$^{8}$

**Eragons Dream (IRE)** *F Sanchez* a64 56
7 b h Arakan(USA) Embraceable (IRE) (Mull Of Kintyre (USA))
4776a$^{5}$

**Erelight (IRE)** *S Donohoe* a48 52
6 bb m Erewhon(USA) Caradene (IRE) (Ballad Rock)
673$^{3}$ 4727$^{4}$ 7959a$^{3}$

**Eretara (IRE)** *S Donohoe* a46 49
5 b m Erewhon(USA) Hi Fasliyev (IRE) (Fasliyev (USA))
672$^{7}$ 869$^{8}$ 4730$^{4}$

**Eric (GER)** *C Von Der Recke* 107
3 ch c Tertullian(USA) Ericarrow (IRE) (Bollin Eric)
1781a$^{7}$ 4007a$^{4}$ (5484a) 6914a$^{6}$ 7603a$^{6}$

**Eric The Viking** *Richard Guest*
2 b g Monsieur Bond(IRE) Whatdo You Want (IRE) (Spectrum (IRE))
7638$^{10}$ 7763$^{5}$ 7827$^{6}$

**Erik The Red (FR)** *Kevin Ryan* 75
2 b c Kendargent(FR) Norwegian Princess (IRE) (Fairy King (USA))
5655$^{7}$ 6259$^{6}$

**Erkis De La Vis (FR)** *Mme C Barande-Barbe* a70 68
3 b g Redback Buckwood (Saumarez)
7630a$^{7}$

**Erlkonig (GER)** *Anthony Mullins* 90
4 gr g Sternkoenig(IRE) Elora (GER) (Alkalde (GER))
6349a$^{14}$

**Ermine Ruby** *Charles Hills* a62 43
3 b f Cape Cross(IRE) Ruby Rocket (IRE) (Indian Rocket)
741$^{4}$ 1534$^{15}$ 3343$^{7}$ (4056) 5057$^{5}$

**Ermyn Lodge** *Pat Phelan* a70 64
8 br g Singspiel(IRE) Rosewood Belle (USA) (Woodman (USA))
2490$^{7}$ 3249$^{10}$ 5547$^{6}$ 6632$^{2}$ 7946$^{9}$

**Ermyntrude** *Pat Phelan* a61 61
7 bb m Rock Of Gibraltar(IRE) Ruthie (Pursuit Of Love)
179$^{9}$

**Ernest Hemingway (IRE)** *A P O'Brien* a98 116
5 br h Galileo(IRE) Cassydora (Darshaan)
1177a$^{8}$ (3764a)

**Errigal Lad** *Garry Woodward* a57 53
9 ch g Bertolini(USA) La Belle Vie (Indian King (USA))
58$^{4}$ ◆ 1282$^{10}$ 1584$^{9}$ 3150$^{13}$

**Erroneous (IRE)** *David Simcock* a85 92
3 br g Footstepsinthesand Atir Love (USA) (Green Dancer (USA))
2088$^{5}$ 3247$^{5}$ 3719$^{2}$ 4821$^{9}$ (5730) 6284$^{4}$ 7203$^{7}$

**Ershaad (IRE)** *Roger Varian* a71
2 b g Acclamation Emerald Peace (IRE) (Green Desert (USA))
7919$^{2}$ 8227$^{3}$

**Ershaadaat (IRE)** *Saeed bin Suroor* a73 46
2 b f Cape Cross(IRE) Almansoora (USA) (Bahri (USA))
7194$^{2}$ 7638$^{4}$

**Ertidaad (IRE)** *Pat Eddery* a69 46
2 b c Kodiac Little Scotland (Acclamation)
7491$^{5}$ 7742$^{8}$ 7920$^{3}$ 8192$^{4}$

**Ertijaal (IRE)** *William Haggas* a105 108
3 b g Oasis Dream Shabiba (USA) (Seeking The Gold (USA))
(1067) (1555) ◆ 1951$^{13}$ 4200$^{5}$ 4937$^{3}$ 5653$^{8}$

**Ertikaan** *Miss Joey Ellis* a83 55
7 b g Oasis Dream Aunty Mary (Common Grounds)
4650$^{10}$ 6240$^{3}$ (7633) 7988$^{2}$ 8251$^{4}$ ◆

**Ervedya (FR)** *J-C Rouget* 109
2 b f Siyouni(FR) Elva (IRE) (King's Best (USA))
(4953a) 5741a$^{3}$ 6967a$^{2}$

**Erwhons Gift (IRE)** *S Donohoe* a52 53
3 bb f Erewhon(USA) Agnes Gift (Agnes World (USA))
675$^{8}$ 4730$^{8}$

**Escado (AUS)** *Matt Laurie* 101
5 b g Casino Prince(AUS) Secret Cause (AUS) (Giant's Causeway (USA))
7128a$^{7}$

**Escalating** *Pat Eddery* a88 89
2 ch c Three Valleys(USA) Pure Joy (Zamindar (USA))
1161$^{7}$ (1575) (1866) 2703$^{6}$ 6142$^{9}$ ◆ 7224$^{7}$

**Escape To Glory (USA)** *Michael Dods* a80 90
6 b g Bernstein(USA) Escape To Victory (Salse (USA))
(1610) 2351$^{2}$ 3202$^{8}$ 3573$^{11}$ (4258) 4923$^{3}$ 5385$^{7}$ 6097$^{6}$ 6476$^{5}$ 7060$^{12}$ 7335$^{6}$

**Escaping Midge (IRE)** *Tim Easterby* a32 51
3 b f Acclamation Queen Margrethe (Grand Lodge (USA))
2389$^{12}$ 2871$^{6}$ 3531$^{2}$

**Escarlata Rossa** *J S Moore* a36 46
3 b f Multiplex Ella Y Rossa (Bertolini (USA))
3121$^{7}$ 4088$^{5}$ 5048$^{7}$ 6394$^{6}$

**Escrick (IRE)** *David Simcock* 72
2 b f Vale Of York(IRE) Dubai Power (Cadeaux Genereux)
4396$^{13}$ 4999$^{2}$ 5332$^{3}$ (5859) 6253$^{6}$ 7237$^{3}$

**Eseej (USA)** *Geoffrey Deacon* a35 53
9 ch g Aljabr(USA) Jinaan (USA) (Mr Prospector (USA))
3179$^{7}$ 4942$^{10}$

**Eshtiaal (USA)** *Brian Meehan* 100
4 b g Dynaformer(USA) Enfiraaj (USA) (Kingmambo (USA))
2558$^{5}$ 3449$^{12}$ 4606$^{10}$ 5379$^{6}$

**Eshtyaaq** *David Evans* a79 76
7 b g Mark Of Esteem(IRE) Fleet Hill (IRE) (Warrshan (USA))
16$^{5}$ 471$^{6}$ 1848$^{9}$ 2175$^{4}$ 2482$^{11}$

**Eskadi (FR)** *C Boutin* a61 67
6 gr g Verglas(IRE) Partageuse (FR) (Green Tune (USA))
178a$^{9}$

**Esk Valley Lady** *Philip Kirby* 14
2 b f Three Valleys(USA) Glory Oatway (IRE) (Desert Prince (IRE))
1342$^{9}$ 1504$^{12}$ 1656$^{10}$ 4528$^{9}$ 6211$^{14}$

**Esles (FR)** *C Laffon-Parias* 98
6 b g Motivator Resquilleuse (USA) (Dehere (USA))
(3172a)

**Esoterique (IRE)** *A Fabre* 118
4 b f Danehill Dancer(IRE) Dievotchka (Dancing Brave (USA))
1371a$^{4}$ (1974) 3355$^{9}$ (4954a) 6382a$^{4}$ 6927$^{4}$

**Especial** *Bryan Smart* 74
2 b c Misu Bond(IRE) Lady In The Bath (Forzando)
6058$^{3}$ 6757$^{2}$ 7496$^{3}$

**Espoir En Tete (FR)** *P Adda* a87 79
3 b c Dr Fong(USA) Egypt Moon (Zieten (USA))
169a$^{12}$ 6221a$^{5}$

**Esprit De Midas** *K Kukk* 17
8 b g Namid Spritzeria (Bigstone (IRE))
1623a$^{9}$ 2592a$^{7}$

**Esprit Des Temps (GER)** *W Mongil* a67 67
7 ch g Tertullian(USA) Eshaya (GER) (Platini (GER))
3373a$^{11}$

**Es Que Love (IRE)** *Clive Cox* a105 116
5 br h Clodovil(IRE) Es Que (Inchinor)
1531$^{2}$ 2256$^{3}$ 3319$^{9}$ 3451$^{11}$ 4438$^{3}$ (4758) 6134$^{6}$ 6328$^{4}$ 6971a$^{9}$

**Essaka (IRE)** *Mick Channon* a54 65
2 b c Equiano(FR) Dream Vision (USA) (Distant View (USA))
3584$^{4}$ 3889$^{3}$ 4216$^{8}$ 5929$^{9}$ 6422$^{8}$ (6645) 7378$^{11}$ 7529$^{7}$

**Essanar** *Andrew Hollinshead* a41 59
3 br g Notnowcato Spirito Libro (USA) (Lear Fan (USA))
3695$^{3}$ 4130$^{13}$ 4789$^{7}$ 5402$^{2}$ 6157$^{11}$ 6699$^{9}$ 7304$^{5}$ 7517$^{11}$

**Esteaming** *David Barron* a88 99
4 b g Sir Percy Night Over Day (Most Welcome)
(1306) 1735$^{5}$ ◆ 2561$^{6}$ 3111$^{2}$ 5673$^{5}$ 7083$^{4}$ 7718$^{14}$ 7974$^{7}$

**Esteban** *Marco Botti* a71 71
3 b g Cape Cross(IRE) Young And Daring (USA) (Woodman (USA))
3925$^{4}$ 4587$^{4}$ 5039$^{6}$

**Estemaala (IRE)** *David O'Meara* a45 76
5 b m Cape Cross(IRE) Elutrah (Darshaan)
868$^{5}$

**Estibdaad (IRE)** *Paddy Butler* a66 44
4 b g Haatef(USA) Star Of Siligo (USA) (Saratoga Six (USA))
2066$^{7}$ 2212$^{5}$ 4326$^{3}$ (4738) 5428$^{2}$ 5721$^{9}$ 6031$^{3}$ 6636$^{6}$ 7982$^{3}$ 8162$^{5}$

**Estidhkaar (IRE)** *Richard Hannon* 116
2 b c Dark Angel(IRE) Danetime Out (IRE) (Danetime (IRE))
2480$^{2}$ (3140) (4199) (6326) 7241$^{4}$

**Estikhraaj** *Roger Varian* a71
2 b c Dansili Shimah (USA) (Storm Cat (USA))
7660$^{5}$ 7891$^{5}$

**Estimate (IRE)** *Sir Michael Stoute* 115
5 b m Monsun(GER) Ebaziya (IRE) (Darshaan)
3377$^{DSQ}$ 4823$^{8}$ 5652$^{2}$ (6288) 7271$^{9}$

**Estournel** *Harry Dunlop* 38
2 b f Danehill Dancer(IRE) Estephe (IRE) (Sadler's Wells (USA))
7450$^{12}$

**Etaab (USA)** *William Haggas* a77 107
3 b f Street Cry(IRE) Ethaara (Green Desert (USA))
1534$^{6}$ ◆ (1920) ◆ (3159) (4573) 5151$^{4}$ (6707) 6927$^{7}$

**Etaad (USA)** *S Donohoe* a53 58
3 b c Intidab(USA) Red's Lucky Lady (USA) (Lucky Lionel (USA))
8145$^{8}$

**Etalondes (FR)** *J-C Rouget* a86 103
4 b c Royal Applause Fancy Dance (Rainbow Quest (USA))
6620a$^{4}$

**Eternitys Gate** *Peter Chapple-Hyam* a87 78
3 b g Dutch Art Regency Rose (Danehill (USA))
2524$^{2}$ 2846$^{3}$ 3370$^{3}$ 5249$^{3}$ (6356) 6873$^{4}$ (7073)

**Ethics Girl (IRE)** *John Berry* a79 85
8 b m Hernando(FR) Palinisa (FR) (Night Shift (USA))
2052$^{3}$ 2547$^{4}$ 3161$^{2}$ (4119) 5073$^{5}$

**Etibaar (USA)** *Brian Meehan* 51
2 b c Kitten's Joy(USA) Oh Deanne O (USA) (Dynaformer (USA))
7382$^{8}$

**Etienne Gerard** *Nigel Tinkler* 67
2 b g Captain Gerrard(IRE) Alucica (Celtic Swing)
6489$^{7}$ 6757$^{3}$ 7082$^{11}$ 7496$^{8}$

**Eton Dorney (USA)** *Kevin Tork* a77 14
5 b g Medaglia d'Oro(USA) Sweet And Firm (USA) (Peteski (CAN))
6304$^{8}$ 6482$^{9}$ 6677$^{8}$

**Eton Forever (IRE)** *Roger Varian* a104 113
7 b g Oratorio(IRE) True Joy (IRE) (Zilzal (USA))
(1728) 2765$^{3}$ 3723$^{3}$ 7272$^{6}$ 7836$^{6}$

**Eton Rambler (USA)** *George Baker* a58 78
4 bb g Hard Spun(USA) Brightbraveandgood (USA) (Smart Strike (CAN))
1909$^{6}$ 2693$^{3}$ 3310$^{2}$ 3556$^{DSQ}$ 4209$^{3}$ (6264) 6787$^{9}$ 7247$^{5}$

**Eton Rifles (IRE)** *Stuart Williams* 112
9 b g Pivotal Maritsa (IRE) (Danehill (USA))
(1207a) 2256$^{8}$ 2766$^{2}$ 3284a$^{4}$ (Dead)

**Eugenic** *Rod Millman* a62 61
3 br g Piccolo Craic Sa Ceili (IRE) (Danehill Dancer (IRE))
1008$^{7}$ 1384$^{7}$ 2668$^{4}$ 3214$^{8}$ (3754) 4085$^{6}$ 4210$^{2}$ 4817$^{7}$ 6070$^{7}$ 6883$^{4}$ 7346$^{3}$

**Euphrasia (IRE)** *Joseph G Murphy* a47 106
5 b m Windsor Knot(IRE) Bishop's Lake (Lake Coniston (IRE))
1076a$^{8}$ 2263a$^{7}$ 2580a$^{3}$ 5742a$^{5}$ 6956a$^{7}$

**Eurato (FR)** *John Spearing* a64 57
4 ch g Medicean Double Green (IRE) (Green Tune (USA))
1351$^{11}$ 1715$^{10}$ 2311$^{9}$ 2699$^{8}$ 5274$^{8}$ 7343$^{4}$ 7734$^{7}$ 7932$^{10}$

**Euro Charline** *Marco Botti* a99 112
3 b f Myboycharlie(IRE) Eurolink Artemis (Common Grounds)
(892) 1515$^{2}$ 1976$^{5}$ 3418$^{3}$ (4607) (5459a)

**Euro Mac** *Neville Bycroft* 36
2 ch f Sir Percy Oomph (Shareef Dancer (USA))
5679$^{8}$ 6668$^{8}$

**Euroquip Boy (IRE)** *Michael Scudamore* a40 67
7 b g Antonius Pius(USA) La Shalak (IRE) (Shalford (IRE))
(2174) 2435$^{10}$ 3149$^{10}$ (3848) 4788$^{5}$ 5751$^{2}$ 6088$^{7}$

**Euroquip Susie** *Michael Scudamore* a35
6 b m Monsieur Bond(IRE) Fizzy Lady (Efisio)
5039$^{14}$ 5622$^{6}$ 6033$^{9}$

**Eurozone (AUS)** *Bart & James Cummings* 112
4 ch c Northern Meteor(AUS) Miss Vandal (AUS) (Don't Say Halo (USA))
1186a$^{15}$

**Eurystheus (IRE)** *Michael Appleby* a85 93
5 b g Acclamation Dust Flicker (Suave Dancer (USA))
1607$^{8}$ 2162$^{5}$ 2763$^{4}$ (3254) 4184$^{6}$ 6292$^{4}$ 6713$^{8}$ (7567) 7718$^{12}$

**Euston Square** *Alistair Whillans* a70 73
8 b g Oasis Dream Krisia (Kris)
1675$^{10}$ 2476$^{9}$ 3535$^{7}$ 4000$^{11}$

**Euthenia** *Mick Channon* a61 68
2 b f Winker Watson Funny Girl (IRE) (Darshaan)
2928$^{5}$ ◆ 3232$^{9}$ 3642$^{2}$ 4178$^{3}$ 4626$^{8}$ 5250$^{3}$ 5875$^{3}$ 6359$^{6}$ 6884$^{11}$

**Eutropius (IRE)** *Alan Swinbank* a45 84
5 b g Ad Valorem(USA) Peps (IRE) (Val Royal (FR))
1362$^{7}$ (1598) (2169) 2351$^{7}$ 3005$^{2}$ 3572$^{P}$

**Eva Clare (IRE)** *K R Burke* a69 56
3 b f Majestic Missile(IRE) College Of Arms (Lujain (USA))
*500[2] (765) 1005[3]* 1615[3] 7103[9]

**Evacusafe Lady** *John Ryan* a73 66
3 ch f Avonbridge Snow Shoes (Sri Pekan (USA))
*1575 401[11] 563[3] 1007[3] 1093[4] 1384[3] 1794[7] 1918[3]* 5534[4] *6407[4]* (6715) (6939) (7068) 7459[4] 7773[5] 7885[6] 7918[4] 7998[4] 8177[5]

**Evanescent (IRE)** *John Quinn* a40 90
5 b g Elusive City(USA) Itsanothergirl (Reprimand)
1191[15] 1646[10] 2548[12] 3483[6] 4661[7] 5196[10] (6478) 6692[2] 7060[2] 7282[3] (7507) 7719[5]

**Evasion Des Mottes (FR)** *Mme A-M Poirier* 58
2 ch f Evasive Faery Eria (FR) (Trempolino (USA))
4883a[6] (5662a) 6591a[13]

**Evasive's First (FR)** *F Rossi* 107
2 ch c Evasive Zalia (FR) (Oasis Dream)
(6570a)

**Evening Attire** *William Stone* a92 81
3 b g Pastoral Pursuits Markova's Dance (Mark Of Esteem (IRE))
6234[11] 7564[4] *7988[6] 8100[3] 8320[2]*

**Evening Rain (USA)** *Saeed bin Suroor* a90 83
2 ch f Raven's Pass(USA) Danuta (USA) (Sunday Silence (USA))
4396[4] 5429[2] ◆ 5921[2] 6783[2] *(7201) 7661[4]*

**Evens And Odds (IRE)** *Peter Grayson* a63 74
10 ch g Johannesburg(USA) Coeur De La Mer (IRE) (Caerleon (USA))
*1270[6] 2094[7]* 2914[9]

**Even Stevens** *Scott Dixon* a106 81
6 br g Ishiguru(USA) Promised (IRE) (Petardia)
*(4) 148[4] 271[2] (644) 1066[3]* 1193[14] *1557[11]* 2786[10] 2989[17] 5419[8] 5925[16] 6235[19] 7212[4] *7738[3]* 7889[3] 8136[7]

**Ever Fortune (USA)** *Brian Ellison* 80
5 ch g El Corredor(USA) Beyond Price (USA) (King Of Kings (IRE))
(1885) 2016[3] 2547[2] 3004[4]

**Evergreen Forest (IRE)** *Natalie Lloyd-Beavis* a55 56
6 ch g Haafhd Inaaq (Lammtarra (USA))
*2464[7] 2916[3] 3521[4]* 4041a[2] 5121[4] 6027[4] 6818[8]

**Everlasting Light** *Tim Walford* a71 65
4 b f Authorized(IRE) Blue Rocket (IRE) (Rock Of Gibraltar (IRE))
*33[6]*

**Everlasting Spring (IRE)** *David Peter Nagle* a78 65
6 b g High Chaparral(IRE) Lady Marshall (FR) (Octagonal (NZ))
*6344[5]*

**Ever One (FR)** *A Bonin* 74
2 gr c Slickly(FR) Evergrey (FR) (Verglas (IRE))
5544a[3] 6244a[3]

**Ever Pheasant (IRE)** *J S Moore* a45
2 b g Alfred Nobel(IRE) Indian Bounty (Indian Ridge)
*8075[8]*

**Ever Strong (GER)** *Dr A Bolte* 102
6 b g Lomitas Emy Coasting (USA) (El Gran Senor (USA))
5938a[5] (7316a) 7727a[13]

**Evervescent (IRE)** *Graeme McPherson* a54 76
5 b g Elnadim(USA) Purepleasureseeker (IRE) (Grand Lodge (USA))
2300[3] 2862[3] 3226[5] 3880[4] (4427) 5127[3] 6251[3]

**Everyday (IRE)** *George Baker* a64 62
2 b g Alfred Nobel(IRE) Profound Emotion (Mark Of Esteem (IRE))
5056[4] *5604[3]*

**Every Honour** *Mark Johnston*
3 ch g Duke Of Marmalade(IRE) Time Honoured (Sadler's Wells (USA))
*551[7]*

**Ever Yours (IRE)** *John Joseph Murphy* a57 60
3 br f Tagula(IRE) Quiet Please (IRE) (Rock Of Gibraltar (IRE))
2387[4] 4820[5]

**Every Time** *Andrew Balding* a76 82
3 b f Pivotal Time Away (IRE) (Darshaan)
1517[7] *2082[3]* 2497[7] 3154[3] 3977[4]

**Evident (IRE)** *Tony Carroll* a82 66
4 b g Excellent Art Vestavia (IRE) (Alhaarth (IRE))
2341[6] 2876[5] 5213[6] 5346[6] *5834[5] 7013[4] 8068[6] 8248[13]*

**Evie Jay (IRE)** *Paul Green* a10 66
3 ch f Windsor Knot(IRE) Carpet Lover (IRE) (Fayruz)
2606[15] 3534[11]

**Evita Peron** *Ralph Beckett* 105
3 ch f Pivotal Entente Cordiale (IRE) (Ela-Mana-Mou)
(1422) ◆ 1868[2] 2584a[4] (3724) 5407a[6] 6254[5]

**Evo Campo (IRE)** *Mark Usher* a70
2 b f Approve(IRE) Billie Bailey (USA) (Mister Baileys)
*(8318)*

**Evviva (ITY)** *Stefano Botti* 87
2 b f Ramonti(FR) Everarda (GER) (Singspiel (IRE))
7321a[5]

**Ewell Place (IRE)** *Richard Fahey* a72 73
5 br g Namid Miss Gibraltar (Rock Of Gibraltar (IRE))
*52[11] 102[5] 320[5] 910[4]* 1717[3] 2546[2] 2823[2] 3242[3] 4254[3] 4903[8] (5166) 5793[7] *6074[9]* 6836[8] *7427[6]*

**Exactement (IRE)** *Sabrina J Harty* a96 96
4 ch f Speightstown(USA) Rakiza (IRE) (Elnadim (USA))
3864a[8] 4276a[7] 4459a[8]

**Exact Science (IRE)** *David Brown* 4
2 ch g Kyllachy Alchemy (IRE) (Sadler's Wells (USA))
6462[11] 6690[8]

**Examiner (IRE)** *William Haggas* a89 95
3 ch g Excellent Art Therry Girl (IRE) (Lahib (USA))
*(143) (375) 659[4]* 3243[4] ◆ 4198[3] 4821[10] 5720[3] ◆ 6737[11] 7119[2]

**Excaper (USA)** *Ian Black* a90 107
5 rg h Exchange Rate(USA) Ada Ruckus (CAN) (Bold Ruckus (USA))
7325a[4]

**Excedo Praecedo** *Amanda Perrett* a60 54
3 b g Exceed And Excel(AUS) Merle (Selkirk (USA))
2688[10] 2927[9] *3389[7]* 4046[4]

**Exceed And Exceed** *George Margarson* a47 58
3 b c Exceed And Excel(AUS) Gandini (Night Shift (USA))
*338[8]*

**Exceeder** *Marco Botti* a81 73
3 b c Exceed And Excel(AUS) Norfolk Broads (IRE) (Noverre (USA))
*926[4]* 2090[4] 3539[9] 4766[4] *5603[3]*

**Exceedexpectations (IRE)** *Lee Carter* a81 69
5 b g Intikhab(USA) Jazan (IRE) (Danehill (USA))
*30[5] 126[9] 497[5] (963) (1312) 2463[6] 2887[9] 3527[2] (4055)* (4544) 5834[2] 6035[8] 6263[8] 7636[6] 7928[2]

**Exceedingly** *Robert Cowell* a72 75
2 b f Exceed And Excel(AUS) Miss Rochester (IRE) (Montjeu (IRE))
3671[2] 4126[5] 5667[4] 6435[2] *(7454) 8113[4]*

**Exceeding Power** *Martin Bosley* a75 68
3 b g Exceed And Excel(AUS) Extreme Beauty (USA) (Rahy (USA))
*(6) 62[4] 279[4]* 2429[4] *3114[3]* 4206[6] *7351[7] 7759[3] 8058[4] 8204[4]*

**Exceed Policy** *David Dennis* a33 47
3 ch g Exceed And Excel(AUS) Policy Setter (USA) (Deputy Minister (CAN))
3248[11] *3528[8] 4970[8]* 5530[10] 5908[7] 6193[12] 7021[4]

**Exceedwell** *John Ryan* a43 56
2 b f Exceed And Excel(AUS) Muja Farewell (Mujtahid (USA))
6434[11] 6867[9] 7594[8] *7832[10] 8007[9]*

**Excel Best** *James Tate* a39
3 b g Exceed And Excel(AUS) Hannah's Dream (IRE) (King's Best (USA))
*74[3]*

**Excellent Aim** *George Margarson* a65 63
7 b g Exceed And Excel(AUS) Snugfit Annie (Midyan (USA))
*663[6]* 3826[2] *8081[5] 8322[8]*

**Excellent George** *Stuart Williams* 66
2 b c Exceed And Excel(AUS) Princess Georgina (Royal Applause)
5091[3] 6168[7] 6556[6]

**Excellent Guest** *George Margarson* 104
7 b g Exceed And Excel(AUS) Princess Speedfit (FR) (Desert Prince (IRE))
2145[18] 3420[24] 4916[3] 5189[7] (6892) 7597[8]

**Excellent News (IRE)** *Tony Forbes* a49 40
5 ch m Excellent Art Subito (Darshaan)
*68[5] 106[4] 460[5] 609[7] 915[6] 997[4] 1453[4] 1891[2] 2396[8]* 2937[3] 6076[7] 6564[9]

**Excellent Puck (IRE)** *Shaun Lycett* a88 83
4 b g Excellent Art Puck's Castle (Shirley Heights)
*200[3]* ◆ *220[2] 698[4] 870[3]* (4402) 5345[3] 6323[3] ◆ 6870[8] 7562[7]

**Excellent Result (IRE)** *Saeed bin Suroor* 112
4 b g Shamardal(USA) Line Ahead (IRE) (Sadler's Wells (USA))
305a[4] (507a) (900a) 1182a[11] 4124[5] 4823[6] 6184a[5]

**Excellent Royale (IRE)** *Charles Hills* a76 69
3 b c Excellent Art Farbenspiel (IRE) (Desert Prince (IRE))
*70[2] (188)* 1586[11] 2734[5]

**Excellent Team** *Saeed bin Suroor* 53
2 b c Teofilo(IRE) Seradim (Elnadim (USA))
7666[8]

**Excellent View** *H-A Pantall* 77
3 b f Shamardal(USA) Pearl Grey (Gone West (USA))
7722a[6]

**Excelling Oscar (IRE)** *Conor Dore* a61
2 b g Excellent Art Three Pennies (Pennekamp (USA))
*5507[6]* 5982[11] *6563[9] 7014[9] 7648[2] (7828) 7904[5] 8087[8] (8221)*

**Excel's Beauty** *James Tate* 98
3 b f Exceed And Excel(AUS) Continua (USA) (Elusive Quality (USA))
1572[10] 3219[8] 4412[10]

**Exceptionelle** *Roger Varian* a90 93
4 br f Exceed And Excel(AUS) Turning Leaf (IRE) (Last Tycoon)
1572[8] 2123[5] 3458[8] 4946[8]

**Exchange** *Frau M Muller* a70 73
6 b g Kheleyf(USA) Quantum Lady (Mujadil (USA))
*638a[6]*

**Exchequer (IRE)** *Richard Hannon* a89 92
3 ch g Exceed And Excel(AUS) Tara's Force (IRE) (Acclamation)
*(1296)* 1420[10] 6688[2] *7375[6]* 7597[5]

**Excilly** *Tom Dascombe* a67 82
2 br f Excellent Art Afra Tsitsi (FR) (Belong To Me (USA))
4389[2] 6700[2] *7076[3]*

**Exciting Dream** *J Moore* 108
4 b g Bertolini(USA) Riva Royale (Royal Applause)
7897a[7]

**Exclusive Contract (IRE)** *Ollie Pears* a59 65
3 br f High Chaparral(IRE) Birthday (IRE) (Singspiel (IRE))
2466[7] *3712[8]* 4026[3] (4268) 5145[2] 5449[6] 6539[6] 6932[4] 7021[5]

**Exclusive Dancer** *George Moore* a15 68
5 gr m Notnowcato Exclusive Approval (USA) (With Approval (CAN))
*7068[11]*

**Exclusive Diamond** *Bryan Smart* a33
2 b f Iffraaj Poppets Sweetlove (Foxhound (USA))
*8205[6]*

**Exclusive Strike (USA)** *Jason Servis* 106
7 ch g Smart Strike(CAN) Glaire (BRZ) (Roi Normand (USA))
4010a[8]

**Exclusive Waters (IRE)** *Tracy Waggott* a79 69
4 b g Elusive City(USA) Pelican Waters (IRE) (Key Of Luck (USA))
*49[4] 445[3] 578[2] 767[2] (928)* 1682[4] 1845[6] 2301[5] 4394[5] 5252[3] 5758[6] 6672[3] (6865) 7251[5] 7829[9]

**Executrix** *Sir Michael Stoute* a54 64
3 b f Oasis Dream Exclusive (Polar Falcon (USA))
1534[14] 3822[3] *5007[9]* 5598[3] *6242[7]*

**Exemplary** *Alexandra Dunn* a72 68
7 b g Sulamani(IRE) Epitome (IRE) (Nashwan (USA))
*285[7] 462[5]*

**Exentricity** *Mick Channon* 79
2 b f Paco Boy(IRE) Wansdyke Lass (Josr Algarhoud (IRE))
1982[2] 2313[7] ◆ 2557[2] 2987[8] 3563[8]

**Ex Ex** *Nick Littmoden* a87 89
4 b g Exceed And Excel(AUS) Temple Of Thebes (IRE) (Bahri (USA))
*(159) (489) 628[6] 2919[5]* (3479)

**Exit Europe** *Andrew Reid* a26
2 ch g Bahamian Bounty Depressed (Most Welcome)
*7030[10]*

**Exkaliber** *Richard Ford* a56 1
5 b g Exceed And Excel(AUS) Kalindi (Efisio)
*693[4] 937[6]* 3366[9]

**Exoplanet Blue** *Henry Candy* a63 41
2 b f Exceed And Excel(AUS) Tut (IRE) (Intikhab (USA))
5429[9] *7062[7]*

**Ex Oriente (IRE)** *Stuart Williams* a82 83
5 b g Azamour(IRE) Little Whisper (IRE) (Be My Guest (USA))
1196[14] 2259[15] 3475[3] (3681) ◆ 3932[3] 4685[5] 5144[7] 5442[4] 5639[5] *5863[2]* 6169[9] 6501[3] 6557[7] 6896[7] *7366[3]*

**Exotic Guest** *Ruth Carr* a52 77
4 ch g Bahamian Bounty Mamoura (IRE) (Lomond (USA))
*1244[8]* 1487[7] 1843[4] 2159[5] 2473[7] (3668) 4003[3] 5089[5] 5390[3] 5636[3] 6213[3] 6674[2] 6835[5] ◆

**Expect** *Jeremy Noseda* a86 76
3 b f Invincible Spirit(IRE) Expressive (Falbrav (IRE))
*149[2] 650[5]*

**Expense Claim (IRE)** *S Seemar* a25 97
5 b g Intikhab(USA) Indolente (IRE) (Diesis)
398a[13]

**Expensive Date** *Paul Cole* a83 85
2 ch f Monsieur Bond(IRE) Cheap Thrills (Bertolini (USA))
2302[4] (2716) 3415[19] *(4083) 5134[3]* 5906[3] *7255[3]* 7563[3]

**Expensive Taste (IRE)** *Phil McEntee* a69 76
3 b g Moss Vale(IRE) Priceoflove (IRE) (Inchinor)
5958a[11] *7928[6] 8097[5] 8309[7]*

**Experimentalist** *Tim Vaughan* a62 68
6 b g Monsieur Bond(IRE) Floppie (FR) (Law Society (USA))
*282[3]*

**Expert (IRE)** *Richard Hannon* a94 104
3 gr g Mastercraftsman(IRE) Raphimix (FR) (Linamix (FR))
*1067[5]* 1518[2] 1867[5] 2344[6] 4895[15] 5348[4] 6234[4] ◆ 6893[11]

**Expert Fighter (USA)** *Saeed bin Suroor* a102 96
5 ch g Dubai Destination(USA) Porto Roca (AUS) (Barathea (IRE))
2342[8] *(3860)* 4696[5]

**Explain** *Martyn Meade* 77
2 ch c Kyllachy Descriptive (IRE) (Desert King (IRE))
4109[9] 5625[5] 6462[3] (7055)

**Exploratory (USA)** *A bin Harmash* a80
4 ch g New Approach(IRE) Arlette (IRE) (King Of Kings (IRE))
*(238a)*

**Explosive Lady (IRE)** *K R Burke* 91
2 gr f Alfred Nobel(IRE) My Girl Lisa (USA) (With Approval (CAN))
(3975) 4646[3] 5770[3] 6375a[2]

**Expose** *Shaun Harris* a89 93
6 ch g Compton Place Show Off (Efisio)
*80[6] (412) 719[8]* 1541[3] 2332[10] *5830[5]* (6235) (6511) 6744[7] *7455[9] 7624[4] 7843[8]*

**Express Himself (IRE)** *Ed McMahon* 87
3 b g Dylan Thomas(IRE) Lightwood Lady (IRE) (Anabaa (USA))
1880[3] 3153[4] (3925) 4810[2] 5528[4] 6214[8] (6871)

**Exton** *Shaun Harris* a28 44
5 ch g Selkirk(USA) Woodnook (Cadeaux Genereux)
3153[12] 5851[5] 6429[6] 6837[8] *7256[11]*

**Extortionist (IRE)** *Olly Stevens* 115
3 b c Dandy Man(IRE) Dream Date (IRE) (Oasis Dream)
1949[10] 3245[11] (3478) 3736a[2] (3981) 4852[2] 5654[3] 6134[15] 6371a[7]

**Extra Noble** *Ralph Beckett* a92 105
3 b g Sir Percy La Peinture (GER) (Peintre Celebre (USA))
1563[2] 2337[3]

**Extrasolar** *Amanda Perrett* a91 93
4 b g Exceed And Excel(AUS) Amicable Terms (Royal Applause)
1731[6] 2110[10] 2992[15] (3275) 3927[5] (4284) 6130[13] 6260[7] 6614[3] 6923[12]

**Extraterrestrial** *Richard Fahey* a79 84
10 b g Mind Games Expectation (IRE) (Night Shift (USA))
2763[2] (3703) 4290[4] 5178[9] 6476[8] 7136[2] 7538[6] *7870[6] 8188[5]*

**Extreme Supreme** *Derek Shaw* a77 71
3 b g Piccolo Kitty Kitty Cancan (Warrshan (USA))
*7285[3] (7652) (8210)*

**Extremity (IRE)** *Hugo Palmer* a89 106
3 ch g Exceed And Excel(AUS) Chanterelle (IRE) (Indian Ridge)
1420[7] (2383) *2921[2]* 3980[3] (4761) 5656[2] (6149) 6752[26]

**Extroverted** *Doug Watson* a52 57
6 ch g Exceed And Excel(AUS) Star Profile (IRE) (Sadler's Wells (USA))
*238a[8]*

**Exzachary** *Jo Hughes* a84 79
4 b g Multiplex Icky Woo (Mark Of Esteem (IRE))
(2177) ◆ 2763[7] 2833[7] *3402[4]* 4156[12] 7341[9]

**Eyasi (IRE)** *P Harley* a79 79
3 ch c Areion(GER) Estefania (GER) (Acatenango (GER))
5661a[4]

**Eye Contact** *Sir Michael Stoute* a79 81
3 br g Dansili Modern Look (Zamindar (USA))
1517[12] 4130[3] 4845[4] *5550[2]* (6429)

**Eyeful** *A Fabre* 101
3 b f Muhtathir Beautifix (GER) (Bering)
4009a[5] 7326a[5]

**Eye Glass (IRE)** *Tim Easterby* 66
2 b f Intense Focus(USA) Petite Arvine (USA) (Gulch (USA))
2615[2] 4286[3]

**Eye In The Sky (IRE)** *Niels Petersen* a92 102
3 gr c Sinndar(IRE) Saudade (GER) (Linamix (FR))
505a[4] 770a[9] *896a[10]*

**Eye Of The Storm (IRE)** *A P O'Brien* 114
4 ch c Galileo(IRE) Mohican Princess (Shirley Heights)
3450[9] (5115a) 5457a[5] 6374a[10]

**Eye Of The Tiger (GER)** *J P Murtagh* a82 84
9 ch g Tiger Hill(IRE) Evening Breeze (GER) (Surumu (GER))
*(283)* 5276[3] 7142a[13] 7476a[19]

**Fabled City (USA)** *Keith Dalgleish* a52 76
5 ch g Johannesburg(USA) Fabulous Fairy (USA) (Alydar (USA))
2296[9] 3000[7] 3660[6]

**Fab Lolly (IRE)** *James Bethell* a83 66
4 b f Rock Of Gibraltar(IRE) Violet Ballerina (IRE) (Namid)
*245[2] (587) (718) 924[2] 1102[4] 1554[7]*

**Fade To Grey (IRE)** *Shaun Lycett* a55 28
10 gr g Aljabr(USA) Aly McBear (USA) (Alydeed (CAN))
*915[4] 1151[3]* 1485[5] *7287[7]*

**Fadhaa (IRE)** *M Al Muhairi* a81 69
6 b g Bahri(USA) Weqaar (USA) (Red Ransom (USA))
*243a[7]*

**Fadhayyil (IRE)** *B W Hills* 108
2 b f Tamayuz Ziria (IRE) (Danehill Dancer (IRE))
5187[2] ◆ (6066) 6709[2] ◆

**Faery Song (IRE)** *David Lanigan* a66
2 b f Lawman(FR) Chervil (Dansili)
*7193[4] 7550[4]*

**Faintly (USA)** *Amanda Perrett* a80 83
3 b c Kitten's Joy(USA) Tinge (USA) (Kingmambo (USA))
*6885[4]*

**Fair Boss (IRE)** *F Chappet* a76 86
6 ch h Mamool(IRE) Fair Dream (GER) (Dashing Blade)
*178a[6]* 920a[4]

**Fair Breeze** *Richard Phillips* a58 53
7 b m Trade Fair Soft Touch (IRE) (Petorius)
*68[6] 460[2] (639) 781[3] 997[5]*

**Fair Bunny** *Alan Brown* a23 21
7 b m Trade Fair Coney Hills (Beverley Boy)
3093[9] 4532[10] 5300[6] *7645[11]*

**Fair Comment** *Michael Blanshard* a67 65
4 b f Tamayuz Cliche (IRE) (Diktat)
*2468 1141[2] 1387[4] 1835[5]* 2672[6] 2923[3] 3309[3] 3818[4] 4279[3] 5343[5] (5848) 6086[6] 7001[6] *7925[3]* 8250[3]

**Fair Dubawi (IRE)** *B Grizzetti* 93
3 b f Dubawi(IRE) Fair Nashwan (Nashwan (USA))
1780a[6]

**Fair Flutter (IRE)** *Richard Fahey* 70
3 b g Manduro(GER) Polish Affair (IRE) (Polish Patriot (USA))
2018[4]

**Fair Loch** *K R Burke* a76 79
6 gr g Fair Mix(IRE) Ardentinny (Ardross)
2728[4]

**Fair Moon (FR)** *D Smaga* a82 74
4 b f Gold Away(IRE) La Fee De Breizh (FR) (Verglas (IRE))
*796a[9]*

**Fair Ranger** *Chris Gordon* a74 74
3 b g Bushranger(IRE) Fairmont (IRE) (Kingmambo (USA))
3519[3] 4043[5] 4572[5] 5314[4] 5624[5] *7202[4] 7533[10] 7805[6] 8102[14]*

**Fair Share** *Lady Cecil* a91
3 b c Rail Link Quota (Rainbow Quest (USA))
*(7032) 7402[4]*

**Fair Trade** *Alan Swinbank* a22 85
7 ch g Trade Fair Ballet (Sharrood (USA))
*32[6]*

**Fair Value (IRE)** *Simon Dow* a88 86
6 b m Compton Place Intriguing Glimpse (Piccolo)
*532[3] 1145[3]* 1650[3] 1944[10] 3033[4] 3551[6] *7886[7] (8171)*

**Fair Venture (IRE)** *Michael Dods* 38
2 b g Intikhab(USA) Aqua Vitae (IRE) (Camacho)
6115[10] 6668[11]

**Fairway To Heaven (IRE)** *Michael Wigham* a94 102
5 b g Jeremy(USA) Luggala (IRE) (Kahyasi)
2110[9] 3271[13] (3732) 5445[11] 7122[15] *7543[9] 7843[4] 8101[8] 8228[9]*

**Fairweather Trader (IRE)** *Paul Midgley* 53
2 br g Amadeus Wolf Royal Superlative (King's Best (USA))
1901[4] 2134[5] 2824[8] (3091) 3435[6] 4065[4] 6447[9]

**Fairyinthewind (IRE)** *Brendan Powell* a79 71
5 ch m Indian Haven Blue Daze (Danzero (AUS))
*1241[7]*

**Fairy Mist (IRE)** *John Bridger* a44 60
7 b g Oratorio(IRE) Prealpina (IRE) (Indian Ridge)
*117[6] 179[7] 377[11] 844[7] 1141[6]* 1668[7] 2722[2] 3327[4] (3554) (4042) 4655[10] 5071[3] 5523[6]

**Fairy Wing (IRE)** *Ann Stokell* a55 66
7 b g Hawk Wing(USA) Mintaka (IRE) (Fairy King (USA))
170[7] 383[10] 1021[9] 1245[8] 1804[5] 2094[4] ◆ 2723[9] 7940[2]

**Faithful Creek (IRE)** *Brian Meehan* 104
2 b c Bushranger(IRE) Open Verse (USA) (Black Minnaloushe (USA))
2776[8] 3474[4] (4353) 4780[7] 5740a[2] 6348a[3] 7590a[5]

**Faith In You** *R Chotard* a57 69
3 ch f Zamindar(USA) Spiritual Healing (IRE) (Invincible Spirit (IRE))
3809a[9]

**Faith Jicaro (IRE)** *John Groucott* a38 46
7 b m One Cool Cat(USA) Wings To Soar (USA) (Woodman (USA))
2885[9]

**Faith Matters (IRE)** *Marco Botti* a68
2 ch f Arcano(IRE) Luanas Pearl (IRE) (Bahri (USA))
7941[9] 8187[2]

**Fa'Iz (IRE)** *E Charpy* a67 68
5 br g Dansili Carisolo (Dubai Millennium)
238a[2]

**Fajry (USA)** *Saeed bin Suroor* a91 87
3 bb c Dixie Union(USA) Tahfeez (USA) (Aljabr (USA))
(3343) 4208[3] 4753[5] 5258[3]

**Falasteen (IRE)** *Milton Bradley* a73 67
7 ch g Titus Livius(FR) Law Review (IRE) (Case Law)
313[6] 466[8]

**Falbo (IRE)** *Laura Grizzetti* a48 60
3 b c Duke Of Marmalade(IRE) Sheer Elegance (IRE) (Pivotal)
360a[12]

**Falcolina (IRE)** *Yannick Fouin* a75 76
4 b f Falco(USA) Flamenba (USA) (Kingmambo (USA))
5964a[8]

**Falconet (DEN)** *Bent Olsen* 91
4 b c Falco(USA) Seattle's Wood (USA) (Woodman (USA))
5744a[7]

**Falconize (IRE)** *Charles Hills* 65
2 b f Henrythenavigator(USA) Crystal Crossing (IRE) (Royal Academy (USA))
7019[4]

**Falcon's Reign (FR)** *Michael Appleby* a63 65
5 ch g Haafhd Al Badeya (IRE) (Pivotal)
2251[6] 2772[10] 5235[5] 6904[11] 7538[14] 7765[5] 8137[3] 8218[4]

**Falest (IRE)** *D Crisanti* 102
5 ch h Refuse To Bend(IRE) Mandolin (IRE) (Sabrehill (USA))
7604a[2]

**Falkhair (FR)** *C Boutin* a79 50
3 b c Falco(USA) Life Is Beautiful (IRE) (Septieme Ciel (USA))
629a[4]

**Fallen In Line (IRE)** *John Gosden* a42 77
3 b c Pivotal Fallen Star (Brief Truce (USA))
1529[14] 2201[2] 5039[12] 6982[8]

**Falling Petals (IRE)** *John Gosden* a75 73
2 ch f Raven's Pass(USA) Infinite Spirit (USA) (Maria's Mon (USA))
2107[3] (8191)

**Falmouth Harbour** *Paul Cole*
2 b g Champs Elysees Divina Mia (Dowsing (USA))
7835[11] 7941[14]

**False Witness (IRE)** *David Nicholls* 69
3 b g Amadeus Wolf Ten Commandments (IRE) (Key Of Luck (USA))
1347[2] 1543[11] 2474[6] 3650[13] 4297[6] 4411[12]

**Fama Mac** *Neville Bycroft* a51 9
7 b g Fraam Umbrian Gold (IRE) (Perugino (USA))
5912[12] 6627[12] 7510[12] 8084[14] 8210[10]

**Fame Again** *Michael Easterby* a78 76
6 b g Gentleman's Deal(IRE) Ballet Fame (USA) (Quest For Fame)
102[3]

**Fame Game (JPN)** *Yoshitada Munakata* 119
4 bb c Heart's Cry(JPN) Hall Of Fame (JPN) (Allez Milord (USA))
2002a[6]

**Familliarity** *Roger Varian* a57 87
4 ch f Nayef(USA) Millistar (Galileo (IRE))
2047[3] 3500[3] 4160[5] 6708[10]

**Famous Kid (USA)** *Saeed bin Suroor* a97 104
3 ch c Street Cry(IRE) Moyesii (USA) (Diesis)
1529[4] (2170) 2748[6] (6106) (6756) 7106[17]

**Famous Poet (IRE)** *Saeed bin Suroor* a95 102
5 b g Exceed And Excel(AUS) Asfurah (USA) (Dayjur (USA))
242a[13]

**Famous Seamus (NZ)** *Noel Mayfield-Smith* 116
6 b g Elusive City(USA) Clinique (NZ) (Dance Floor (USA))
1468a[11] 7724a[6]

**Famous Tales** *Edward Creighton* a45
4 b f Zamindar(USA) Fame Game (IRE) (Fasliyev (USA))
5548[10] 6482[7] 7733[12]

**Famous Warrior (IRE)** *Doug Watson* a90 79
7 b g Alhaarth(IRE) Oriental Fashion (IRE) (Marju (IRE))
207a[14]

**Fanciful Angel (IRE)** *Marco Botti* a100 93
2 gr c Dark Angel(IRE) Fanciful Dancer (Groom Dancer (USA))
3429[3] (3893) ◆ 4670[5] 6142[4] 7121[3]

**Fannaan (USA)** *John Gosden* 100
2 ch c Speightstown(USA) Titian Time (USA) (Red Ransom (USA))
(6702) ◆ (7381)

**Fanny (FR)** *F Rossi* 92
4 b f Panis(USA) Sea Life (FR) (Anabaa (USA))
7856a[5]

**Fanny Again** *Denis Coakley* a58
2 b f Nayef(USA) Sweet Wilhelmina (Indian Ridge)
7193[10] 7752[9] 7943[6]

**Fanoos** *Mme G Rarick* a86 90
5 b m Dutch Art Miss Otis (Danetime (IRE))
587[2] 825[7] (1026) 1554[6] (2608) 3731[9] 4644a[8] 6994a[12] 7656a[12] 7856a[15]

**Fantastic Moon** *Jeremy Noseda* 106
4 ch c Dalakhani(IRE) Rhadegunda (Pivotal)
309a[10]

**Fantasy Gladiator** *John Quinn* a84 61
8 b g Ishiguru(USA) Fancier Bit (Lion Cavern (USA))
38[4] 153[8] 457[6] 677[3] 3628[5] 5320[7] 6035[9] 6890[3] 7530[6] 7821[4]

**Fantasy Invader (IRE)** *Gary Moore* a50 43
4 b g Captain Marvelous(IRE) Fields Of Joy (GER) (Waky Nao)
402[8] 760[8]

**Fantasy Justifier (IRE)** *Ronald Harris* a40 75
3 b g Arakan(USA) Grandel (Owington)
1914[2] 2870[2] 3518[8] 4155[4] (5080) 6025[10] 6657[12] 7830[11]

**Fantasy King** *James Moffatt* a76 79
8 b g Acclamation Fantasy Ridge (Indian Ridge)
732[3] 7247[4]

**Fanzine** *M D O'Callaghan* a73 78
4 ch f Medicean Dash To The Front (Diktat)
2301[2] 3086[2] 7435a[3]

**Faraajh (IRE)** *James Tate* a84 66
2 ch f Iffraaj Neshla (Singspiel (IRE))
3324[3] 3947[3] 4973[3] (5798) 6064[7] (7116) 7882[7]

**Far Afield** *J-P Gallorini* a70 100
4 b g Rail Link Posteritas (USA) (Lear Fan (USA))
4644a[7]

**Farang Jai Dee (IRE)** *Declan Carroll* 32
2 b g Approve(IRE) Fruit O'The Forest (IRE) (Shinko Forest (IRE))
4170[7] 4286[10]

**Faraway Run (IRE)** *P Khozian* a102 102
5 b h Hurricane Run(IRE) Melatonina (IRE) (King Charlemagne (USA))
177a[2]

**Farendole (USA)** *Roger Charlton* a60 17
2 b f First Defence(USA) Quick To Please (USA) (Danzig (USA))
6874[10] 7398[7] 8026[5]

**Farham (USA)** *Richard Fahey* 75
2 b c Smart Strike(CAN) Diamondrella (Rock Of Gibraltar (IRE))
4550[2] 6473[3]

**Farinacci** *Stefano Botti* 62
2 b c Sleeping Indian Lola Sapola (IRE) (Benny The Dip (USA))
7147a[5]

**Farletti** *Andrew Balding* a67 57
2 b f Royal Applause Le Badie (IRE) (Spectrum (IRE))
7108[10] 7549[5] 8027[2]

**Farlow (IRE)** *Richard Fahey* a81 96
6 ch g Exceed And Excel(AUS) Emly Express (IRE) (High Estate)
1164[4] (1442) 1958[9] 2425[3] 2959[5] 3716[4] 4922[8] 5433[4] 6531[13] 7060[3] 7276[15] 7715[6]

**Farmah (USA)** *F Rohaut* a98 115
3 b f Speightstown(USA) Torrestrella (IRE) (Orpen (USA))
629a[2] 2226a[4] 6446a[2] (6994a) (7725a)

**Farmers Dream (IRE)** *John Spearing* a29 36
7 b m Antonius Pius(USA) Beucaire (IRE) (Entrepreneur)
18[9] 858[10]

**Farmleigh House (IRE)** *W J Martin* a111 66
7 ch g Medecis Tabessa (USA) (Shahrastani (USA))
206a[8] 597a[13] 6369a[20]

**Farmshop Boy** *Natalie Lloyd-Beavis* a19 30
3 b g Sagamix(FR) Littleton Zephir (USA) (Sandpit (BRZ))
6421[9] 7157[S] 7800[6] 8008[8]

**Farquhar (IRE)** *Peter Chapple-Hyam* 100
3 ch c Archipenko(USA) Pointed Arch (IRE) (Rock Of Gibraltar (IRE))
1702[7] 2303[5] (2769) 3200[6] 5179[4] 6287[12] (7106) 7718[16]

**Farraaj (IRE)** *Roger Varian* a105 120
5 b g Dubai Destination(USA) Pastorale (Nureyev (USA))
1068[5] 1948[5] (2957) (4214) 5690[4] 7602a[3] 8154a[6]

**Far Ranging (USA)** *Julie Camacho* 62
3 b f US Ranger(USA) Hutchinson (USA) (Gregorian (USA))
2392[4] 3097[7] 3543[2] 4574[5]

**Farrier (USA)** *S Seemar* a106
6 b g Tapit(USA) Wild Vision (USA) (Wild Again (USA))
773a[2]

**Fascinating Rock (IRE)** *D K Weld* 110
3 b c Fastnet Rock(AUS) Miss Polaris (Polar Falcon (USA))
(1458a) ◆ (2187a) 2990[8] 3739a[5]

**Fashion Alert (USA)** *Todd Pletcher* a102
2 b f Old Fashioned(USA) Titan Queen (USA) (Tiznow (USA))
6915a[6]

**Fashion Line (IRE)** *Michael Bell* a93 96
4 b f Cape Cross(IRE) Shadow Roll (IRE) (Mark Of Esteem (IRE))
(323) (674) 887[4] 1554[4] 2032[2] 2144[8] 3055[3] 4323[6]

**Fast Act (IRE)** *Kevin Ryan* 105
2 ch c Fast Company(IRE) Nullarbor (Green Desert (USA))
1276[5] ◆ (3570) 4439[3] 4757[2] 5607[12] 6286[4]

**Fast Anna (USA)** *Kathy Ritvo* a111
3 bb c Medaglia d'Oro(USA) Dreaming Of Anna (USA) (Rahy (USA))
7612a[5]

**Fast Charlie (IRE)** *Ann Duffield* a68 73
2 b c Fast Company(IRE) Where's Charlotte (Sure Blade (USA))
3620[9] 5296[3] 5922[2] 6538[4] 8060[4] 8205[3]

**Fast Dancer (IRE)** *Joseph Tuite* 83
2 b g Fast Company(IRE) Tereed Elhawa (Cadeaux Genereux)
4270[14] 5443[2] 5874[2] 6363[2]

**Fast Delivery** *Saeed bin Suroor* a81 90
3 b g Authorized(IRE) Rosenreihe (IRE) (Catcher In The Rye (IRE))
1394[2] (1853) 2481[10] 6044[6]

**Fast Finian (IRE)** *Ann Stokell* a54 94
5 gr g Clodovil(IRE) Delphie Queen (IRE) (Desert Sun)
3122[11] 3795[7] (4358) 4963[9]

**Fast Freddie** *Mrs A Corson* a30 21
10 b g Agnes World(USA) Bella Chica (IRE) (Bigstone (IRE))
1623a[5] 2597a[3] 2592a[5] 4038a[8] 4717a[8] 5971a[4] 6187a[8]

**Fast Green (FR)** *Rod Millman* a17
3 b g Green Tune(USA) La Bahamienne (IRE) (Fasliyev (USA))
6682[11]

**Fastidious** *M D O'Callaghan* a88 93
5 b g Exceed And Excel(AUS) Felicitous (King's Best (USA))
4949a[5]

**Fast Lola** *Olly Stevens* a11 58
2 b f Equiano(FR) Tembladora (IRE) (Docksider (USA))
3199[6] 5255[7]

**Fast Magic (IRE)** *Kevin Ryan* 64
2 b c Fast Company(IRE) Nofa's Magic (IRE) (Rainbow Quest (USA))
3330[6] 4389[5] 4919[5]

**Fastnet Mist (IRE)** *David Wachman* a96 95
3 b f Fastnet Rock(AUS) Masseera (IRE) (Alzao (USA))
5024a[7] 7579a[5]

**Fastnet Red** *John Gosden* 82
3 b g Fastnet Rock(AUS) Gyroscope (Spinning World (USA))
1353[5] 2773[5] 3248[6] ◆ 3892[3] ◆ 5095[3]

**Fast On (IRE)** *Seamus Fahey* a56 62
5 gr g Verglas(IRE) Dream State (IRE) (Machiavellian (USA))
833[6]

**Fast Romance (USA)** *Paul Cole* 69
2 b f Fastnet Rock(AUS) Satulagi (USA) (Officer (USA))
3888[10] 4398[5] 4825[5]

**Fast Scat (USA)** *David Evans* a57 56
2 ch f Scat Daddy(USA) Furusato (USA) (Sendawar (IRE))
3215[7] 3550[3] 4079[3] 4846[3] 7763[4] 7904[3] 7992[3]

**Fast Shot** *Tim Easterby* a51 103
6 b g Fasliyev(USA) Final Pursuit (Pursuit Of Love)
1305[9] (1484) (1734) 2254[4] 3452[18] 5445[10] 6533[5] 7122[9] 7408[9]

**Fast Track** *David Barron* 97
3 b g Rail Link Silca Boo (Efisio)
3478[4] ◆ 4390[2] (4669) ◆ 6170[14]

**Fat Al (AUS)** *Peter G Moody* 107
6 b g Al Maher(AUS) Fatoon (AUS) (Snaadee (USA))
1186a[12]

**Fate (FR)** *A De Royer-Dupre* 108
5 b m Teofilo(IRE) Specificity (USA) (Alleged (USA))
2631a[12] 7070a[3] (7558a)

**Fat Gary** *Tom Dascombe* a93 89
4 ch g Dutch Art Suzuki (IRE) (Barathea (IRE))
36[3] 122[5] 294[4] 431[4]

**Father Bertie** *Tim Easterby* 74
2 b g Firebreak Magical Music (Fraam)
6757[6] 7084[8] 7496[2] 7638[5]

**Father Shine (IRE)** *Shaun Harris* a47 58
11 bb g Supreme Leader Shean Hill (IRE) (Bar Dexter (USA))
14[6] 1197[5] (2455) 3336[6] 4115[5] 4492[5]

**Father Stone** *David Elsworth* a69 53
2 ch c Winker Watson Peintre D'Argent (IRE) (Peintre Celebre (USA))
3113[7] 3474[8] 4618[7] 5148[5] 5823[2] (6237) 6662[4] 6884[3]

**Fathom Five (IRE)** *Shaun Harris* a66 65
10 b g Fath(USA) Ambria (ITY) (Final Straw)
59[8] 478[6] 651[10] 766[7] 934[5] 1001[6] 1081[7] 1365[6] (1639) 2451[3] (2724) (2830) (3366) 3530[19] 4288[6] 4344[5] 7670[13] 7915[8] 8088[10] 8142[11]

**Fattsota** *David O'Meara* a90 107
6 b g Oasis Dream Gift Of The Night (USA) (Slewpy (USA))
3962[12] 5174[4] (5440) 5755[3] 7120[2] 7492[5]

**Faufiler (IRE)** *P Bary* 111
3 b f Galileo(IRE) Six Perfections (FR) (Celtic Swing)
(7319a)

**Faure Island** *Henry Candy* a82 85
3 b g Myboycharlie(IRE) Free Offer (Generous (IRE))
1725[13] 3037[4] 3426[2] 3936[4] 4535[2] 5055[3] 5526[3] 5903[3] 6337[2] ◆ (6616) 6871[6] 7136[7]

**Favorite Girl (GER)** *Michael Appleby* a71 66
6 b m Shirocco(GER) Favorite (GER) (Montjeu (IRE))
1729[4] 5984[3] 6942[2]

**Favourite Treat (USA)** *Ruth Carr* a74 93
4 b g Hard Spun(USA) Truart (USA) (Yes It's True (USA))
235[7] 472[5] 689[6] 5681[4] 6214[7]

**Fawkner (AUS)** *Robert Hickmott* 118
7 bb g Reset(AUS) Dane Belltar (AUS) (Danewin (AUS))
(7127a) 7467a[2] 7653a[10]

**Fawn** *William Haggas* 35
3 ch f Selkirk(USA) Blue Dream (IRE) (Cadeaux Genereux)
7418[5]

**Faydhan (USA)** *John Gosden* 100
2 bb c War Front(USA) Agreeable Miss (USA) (Speightstown (USA))
(3881)

**Fayreway (IRE)** *Martyn Meade* 55
2 b f Strategic Prince Leopard Creek (Weldnaas (USA))
3082[4] ◆ 6997[7]

**Fazenda's Girl** *Michael Easterby* a47 53
2 b f Stimulation(IRE) Goes A Treat (IRE) (Common Grounds)
2349[6] 2541[8] 3201[5] 3435[3] 4870[4] 5335[3] 6211[12] 6563[7] 7245[5]

**Fazza** *Edwin Tuer* a66 83
7 ch g Sulamani(IRE) Markievicz (IRE) (Doyoun)
1345[4] 1733[8] 2519[3] 3254[5] 3572[11] 4451[3] 4922[7] 5054[5] 5793[4] 6490[8] 7125[16]

**Fearless Hunter (GER)** *Rune Haugen* 93
4 b g Alhaarth(IRE) Firedance (GER) (Lomitas)
3090a[4] 3772a[10] 4956a[3] 5744a[5]

**Fearless Lad (IRE)** *John Best* a70 24
4 b g Excellent Art Souffle (Zafonic (USA))
(90) 289[6] (458) 747[5] 1120[5] 1798[5] (2646) 2930[9] 8321[8]

**Fear Or Favour (IRE)** *Clive Cox* 93
3 b g Haatef(USA) Insaaf (Averti (IRE))
(1570) 2344[2] ◆

**Feathered (USA)** *Todd Pletcher* a106
2 b f Indian Charlie(USA) Receipt (USA) (Dynaformer (USA))
7606a[4]

**Featsdontfailmenow** *Lisa Williamson* a7 34
2 b f Misu Bond(IRE) Gunalt Joy (Blue Dakota (IRE))
1788[8] 2348[6] 3215[9] 3692[4] 7190[10] 7453[11]

**Febrayer Star (IRE)** *Robert Cowell* a51
3 br c Majestic Missile(IRE) Ginger Not Blonde (USA) (Atticus (USA))
1211[3] 1449[7] 1833[2] 2397[8]

**Fed Biz (USA)** *Bob Baffert* a119 111
5 b h Giant's Causeway(USA) Spunoutacontrol (USA) (Wild Again (USA))
7591a[7]

**Federal Blue (USA)** *Milton Bradley* a4 85
4 b g Elusive Quality(USA) Blue Duster (USA) (Danzig (USA))
1789[10] 2251[10] 2947[13] 3177[8]

**Feedyah (USA)** *Charlie Appleby* a95 98
3 b f Street Cry(IRE) Red Dune (IRE) (Red Ransom (USA))
506a[3] 771a[2] 3357[6] 4436[7]

**Feeling Easy (IRE)** *Robert Eddery* a49 86
2 b f Bushranger(IRE) Easy Feeling (IRE) (Night Shift (USA))
2928[8] (3557) (4205) 4913[14] (5983) 6253[4] 6749[6] 6926[8]

**Feel The Heat** *Bryan Smart* 78
7 ch g Firebreak Spindara (IRE) (Spinning World (USA))
1967[8] 2522[9] 4194[8] (6821) 7669[13]

**Feen Melody (FR)** *P Demercastel* a65 56
3 b f Zafeen(FR) Desert Melody (FR) (Green Desert (USA))
4464a[9]

**Fehaydi** *D Selvaratnam* a62 74
4 b g Nayef(USA) Red Camellia (Polar Falcon (USA))
243a[16]

**Feisty Dragon (IRE)** *Jamie Osborne* a44 38
3 b f Camacho Ejder (IRE) (Indian Ridge)
188[10] 787[5] 923[3] 1684[6] 2209[9]

**Felcine (IRE)** *G Botti* a90 103
3 b f Duke Of Marmalade(IRE) Red Rosie (USA) (Red Ransom (USA))
1780a[3] 3808a[4] 6882a[5]

**Felice (IRE)** *Scott Dixon* a37 27
4 b f Papal Bull Tarabaya (IRE) (Warning)
13[4] 1132[8]

**Felician (GER)** *Ferdinand J Leve* 109
6 b g Motivator Felicity (GER) (Inchinor)
3291a[4] 4247a[7] 6054a[4] 6384a[3] 6965a[4] 7322a[2]

**Felitsia (BUL)** *Gerald Geisler*
2 b f Kartun(GER) Flawia (FR) (Cadeaux Genereux)
6053a[10]

**Felix De Vega (IRE)** *Richard Hannon* a79 80
2 b c Lope De Vega(IRE) Lafite (Robellino (USA))
5881[6] 6279[5] 7040[2] 7348[2]

**Felix Leiter** *K R Burke* 89
2 ch g Monsieur Bond(IRE) Spiralling (Pivotal)
4192[2] (4589) (5285) (5580) 6135[7]

**Felwah** *William Haggas* 99
3 ch f Aqlaam Efisio's Star (Efisio)
2560[5] ◆ (3074) (3615) 4182[2] (5396) (6068) 6922[5]

**Female Strategy (IRE)** *Mark Brisbourne* a52 28
3 br f Holy Roman Emperor(IRE) Strategy (Machiavellian (USA))
218[4] 373[4] 645[5] 3326[13]

**Femme De Menage** *Andrew Balding* a30 35
3 ch f Bahamian Bounty Duena (Grand Lodge (USA))
1980[10] 2681[14] 3537[12] 4326[9]

**Fencing (USA)** *John Gosden* 115
5 ch g Street Cry(IRE) Latice (IRE) (Inchinor)
1162[2] 1533[3] 1870[4] 2223[2] 3252[2] 7243[7] 7444[3]

**Fendale** *Bryan Smart* 97
2 b c Exceed And Excel(AUS) Adorn (Kyllachy)
(3947) ◆ (5140) ◆ 5692[7] 6513[5] 7238[11]

**Fenella Foghorn** *Jonathan Portman* a50 45
3 b f Elnadim(USA) Bundle Up (USA) (Miner's Mark (USA))
1829[5]

**Fen Flyer** *John Berry* a50 32
5 ch g Piccolo Maraffi (IRE) (Halling (USA))
7291[7] 7823[8] 8314[6]

**Feng Shui** *Jamie Osborne* a78
2 b g Iffraaj Whazzis (Desert Prince (IRE))
7660[2]

**Fennann** *Gary Moore* a73 16
3 b g Dutch Art Embraced (Pursuit Of Love)
2850[P] 4407[12] 5135[4] (5556) 8193[4]

**Fenomeno (JPN)** *Hirofumi Toda* 116
5 bb h Stay Gold(JPN) De Laroche (IRE) (Danehill (USA))
(2002a) 7981a[8]

**Feodora (GER)** *A Wohler* 111
3 ch f Lord Of England(GER) Forever Nice (GER) (Greinton)
2584a[7] 3289a[10] (4955a) 6969a[5] 7603a[4]

**Ferayha (IRE)** *Roger Varian*
3 b f Cape Cross(IRE) Albahja (Sinndar (IRE))
6002[P]

**Ferdy (IRE)** *Paul Green* a56 74
5 b h Antonius Pius(USA) Trinity Fair (Polish Precedent (USA))
*95[4] 367[8] 766[6] 918[4] 1138[4]* 1310[6] 2296[8] 3134[3] 3535[2] 3845[3] 4427[6] 5127[6] 5811[2] 6223[4] 6699[11]

**Ferevia (IRE)** *C Laffon-Parias* 110
4 b f Motivator Frynia (USA) (Cat Thief (USA))
2631a[10]

**Fergand (FR)** *M Drean* a60 45
5 b g Great Journey(JPN) Queen Elodie (FR) (Cardoun (FR))
*57a[8]*

**Ferngrove (USA)** *Jonathan Portman* a49 57
3 gr g Rockport Harbor(USA) Lucky Pipit (Key Of Luck (USA))
*6771[7] 7987[10]*

**Ferryview Place** *Ian Williams* a55 56
5 b g Compton Place Songsheet (Dominion)
*1086[5] 1288[7]* (3308) 3880[2] 3973[3] 4744[3] *5428[5] 6031[2] 6856[10] 7292[5] 7347[3]*

**Fervent Prince** *A bin Huzaim* a86 91
9 b g Averti(IRE) Maria Theresa (Primo Dominie)
110a[11] 242a[11]

**Festival Theatre (IRE)** *Sir Michael Stoute* a86 84
3 ch g Danehill Dancer(IRE) Scottish Stage (IRE) (Selkirk (USA))
*1407[4]* 2087[7] 4855[7] ◆ *6036[5]* 6987[4]

**Festive Cheer (FR)** *A P O'Brien* a73 78
4 b c Montjeu(IRE) Bold Classic (USA) (Pembroke (USA))
1182a[13] 4477a[4]

**Fetan Joa (FR)** *J Heloury* 99
3 b f Enrique Grape Tree Hills (FR) (Grape Tree Road)
1273a[10] 4009a[9]

**Feuerblitz (GER)** *M Figge* 113
5 b h Big Shuffle(USA) Flamingo Island (GER) (Acatenango (GER))
2815a[9] 6592a[4] 7603a[7]

**Fever Few** *Chris Wall* a73 82
5 b m Pastoral Pursuits Prairie Oyster (Emperor Jones (USA))
1613[11] 3160[4] (3708) 4108[5] (4891) 5776[5] 6463[2]

**Fey** *Charlie Appleby* a75
2 b f New Approach(IRE) Persinette (USA) (Kingmambo (USA))
*(7658)*

**Fibre Optic** *Luca Cumani* 72
2 b g Rip Van Winkle(IRE) Wind Surf (USA) (Lil's Lad (USA))
6712[9] 7169[2] 7666[7]

**Ficelle (IRE)** *Nikki Evans* a33 58
5 b m Chineur(FR) Petite Boulangere (IRE) (Namid)
*179[11] 844[8]* 1787[6] 2250[8] 2838[7] 5273[6] 5751[12] 7222[6]

**Fickle Feelings (IRE)** *David Barron* a53 53
3 b f Nayef(USA) Caravan Of Dreams (IRE) (Anabaa (USA))
1960[9] 2354[11] 2899[4] 3545[5] 4304[7] 7284[3] *7664[4]*

**Fidelity** *Jonathan Geake* 35
2 b c Halling(USA) Sir Kyffin's Folly (Dansili)
7414[7]

**Fidelma Moon (IRE)** *K R Burke* a76 68
2 b f Dylan Thomas(IRE) Ridiforza (FR) (Starborough)
5056[2] *(6071)* 7237[11]

**Fiducia** *Simon Dow* a69 69
4 b f Lawman(FR) Silca Key (Inchinor)
*493[6] 853[9] 3526[4]* 4352[5] *(5832) 6337[4]*

**Field Force** *Sophie Leech* a70 50
3 b g Champs Elysees Fairy Steps (Rainbow Quest (USA))
1946[7] *2681[4]* 3849[8] *7032[8] 7202[12]*

**Field Game** *Hughie Morrison* a87 90
2 b c Pastoral Pursuits Tarqua (IRE) (King Charlemagne (USA))
3536[4] *5569[2] 6158[2] (6659) 7255[2]* (7503)

**Fieldgunner Kirkup (GER)** *David Barron* a77 87
6 b g Acclamation Fire Finch (Halling (USA))
1190[15] 1564[10] 1957[6] 2425[6] 2841[2] ◆ 4923[5] (5197) 6207[6] 6430[5] 6535[9] 7085[12] 7507[4] 7719[21] *7820[6]*

**Fieldmouse** *Eve Johnson Houghton* a55 44
2 b f Champs Elysees Intervene (Zafonic (USA))
7450[9] *7756[5]*

**Field Of Dream** *Jamie Osborne* a99 112
7 b g Oasis Dream Field Of Hope (IRE) (Selkirk (USA))
(3356) 4648[26]

**Fieldsman (USA)** *Ed Dunlop* a83 94
2 b c Hard Spun(USA) R Charlie's Angel (USA) (Indian Charlie (USA))
4395[6] 4896[3] 5391[2] (6190) (6783) *7882[4]*

**Fiero (JPN)** *Hideaki Fujiwara* 118
5 bb h Deep Impact(JPN) Ruby (IRE) (Danehill (USA))
8153a[6]

**Fiery Sunset** *Michael Bell* a85 80
3 b f Galileo(IRE) Five Fields (USA) (Chester House (USA))
1423[5] 1738[5] 3174[2] 3918[4] *(4543)* 5691[12] 6741[6]

**Fiesolana (IRE)** *W McCreery* 116
5 b m Aussie Rules(USA) Tidal Reach (USA) (Kris S (USA))
1908a[6] 2572a[2] 3355[4] 5223a[3] (6351a) 6971a[7] 7607a[8]

**Fiesole** *Luca Cumani* a72
2 b c Montjeu(IRE) Forgotten Dreams (IRE) (Olden Times)
*7778[4]* ◆ *8067[3]*

**Fife Jo** *Jim Goldie* 53
4 b g Misu Bond(IRE) Musical Refrain (IRE) (Dancing Dissident (USA))
1758[12] 2219[9] 2452[5] 2479[10] 2909[8] 4004[7] 4257[10] 4725[10] 5565[7] 6796[7]

**Fiftyshadesdarker (IRE)** *George Baker* a64 22
3 gr g Invincible Spirit(IRE) Poetry In Motion (IRE) (Ballad Rock)
*2682[7]* 3315[15] *4579[8] 5006[8] 6243[2] 6567[4] 6771[6]*

**Fiftyshadesfreed (IRE)** *George Baker* a97 64
3 gr g Verglas(IRE) Vasilia (Dansili)
*2058[6] 2647[4]* 3144[6] 3709[3] *4613[3] 5139[4] (5899) (6160) (6770) 7066[5]*

**Fiftyshadesofgrey (IRE)** *George Baker* a92 85
3 gr g Dark Angel(IRE) Wohaida (IRE) (Kheleyf (USA))
*854[4]* 1350[4] 2090[6] 3539[8] 4679[3] 5311[5] ◆ 5785[3] 6191[6] *(7205) 7373[2] (7403)* 7564[6]

**Figaro** *Tim Vaughan* 59
6 ch g Medicean Chorist (Pivotal)
2482[13] 4552[6]

**Fighting Back** *Amanda Perrett* a76 77
3 b g Galileo(IRE) Maroochydore (IRE) (Danehill (USA))
*2881[6] 3857[4]* 4168[6] *5185[5]* 5527[2] 5878[10] *6239[7]*

**Figment** *John Gosden* 73
2 b f Acclamation First Exhibit (Machiavellian (USA))
6641[4] 7406[3]

**Fig Roll** *Daniel Mark Loughnane* a37 99
3 b f Bahamian Bounty Cake (IRE) (Acclamation)
3278[7]

**Figure Of Speech (IRE)** *Charlie Appleby* a107 107
3 b g Invincible Spirit(IRE) Epic Similie (Lomitas)
*204a[6]* 505a[6]

**Filaga (FR)** *M Figge* 90
3 b f Soldier Hollow Finessa (GER) (Law Society (USA))
2584a[10]

**Filament Of Gold (USA)** *Mark Johnston* a82 60
3 b g Street Cry(IRE) Raw Silk (USA) (Malibu Moon (USA))
*(561) 670[2]* 1883[5] *2685[10] (4051)*

**Filimbi (USA)** *William Mott* a95 110
4 rg f Mizzen Mast(USA) Flute (USA) (Seattle Slew (USA))
(7615a)

**Fillydelphia (IRE)** *Patrick Holmes* 53
3 b f Strategic Prince Lady Fonic (Zafonic (USA))
3543[4] 4022[6] 4513[5] 5239[5]

**Filly Green (FR)** *F Chappet* 79
2 b f Diamond Green(FR) Green Grass (FR) (Verglas (IRE))
5740a[8]

**Filly Medi (FR)** *C Delcher-Sanchez* a74 96
4 gr f Medecis Anais Filly (FR) (Verglas (IRE))
2821a[4]

**Filosofo (IRE)** *Richard Hannon* a77 75
3 b c Teofilo(IRE) Think (FR) (Marchand De Sable (USA))
1491[5] *1795[11]* 2222[6] 3064[4] 3760[2] *8020[2] 8294[6]*

**Filou (SWI)** *P Schaerer* 90
3 b c Lord Of England(GER) Fujairah (SWI) (Sri Pekan (USA))
3512a[4]

**Final Button (SAF)** *M F De Kock* a84 97
6 ch g Tiger Ridge(USA) Red Buttons (SAF) (Shoe Danzig (USA))
242a[14]

**Final Countdown** *John Quinn* a79 78
3 ch g Selkirk(USA) Culture Queen (King's Best (USA))
*230[3] 357[5]* 3760[4] (4540) (5108) *8264[3]*

**Final Decision** *Saeed bin Suroor* 70
2 b c Dubawi(IRE) Silkwood (Singspiel (IRE))
2428[4] (Dead)

**Final Delivery** *Jim Boyle* a67 60
5 b g Three Valleys(USA) Bowled Out (GER) (Dansili)
*67[11] 210[4] 590[12] 916[2] 1428[3]*

**Final Score (IRE)** *Stefano Botti* 107
3 ch f Dylan Thomas(IRE) Holy Moon (IRE) (Hernando (FR))
(2590a) 3376[5] (7480a)

**Findhorn Magic** *Peter Makin* a71 61
3 b f Kyllachy Enchanted Princess (Royal Applause)
2946[6] 5249[4] *(6488) 7356[10]*

**Findog** *Linda Perratt* 74
4 b g Pastoral Pursuits Night Home (ITY) (Night Shift (USA))
1566[6] 1966[7] 2514[9] 2675[9] 3831[8] 4257[4] 4519[5] 4664[3] 4725[5] 5236[9] 6796[3] 6835[4] 7061[11]

**Fine Cut (IRE)** *T Stack* a88 82
3 gr g Dark Angel(IRE) Non Dimenticar Me (IRE) (Don't Forget Me)
*416a[5]* 2116[5]

**Fine Judgment** *William Muir* a56 47
2 b f Compton Place Blue Lyric (Refuse To Bend (IRE))
3076[11] 3799[6] *4909[3]* 5985[11]

**Fine 'n Dandy (IRE)** *Tom Dascombe* a54 93
3 ch g Dandy Man(IRE) Pearly Brooks (Efisio)
1397[5] 2116[6] 3219[9] 3927[15]

**Fine Prince (IRE)** *Robert Mills* 82
2 ch g Strategic Prince Theebah (Bahamian Bounty)
1349[2] 2276[2] 2987[7] 3374[7] (3934)

**Fine Tune (IRE)** *Linda Jewell* a55 57
3 b g Medicean Phillippa (IRE) (Galileo (IRE))
1529[12] *2881[8] 6483[11]*

**Fine View (USA)** *Saeed bin Suroor* a69
2 b f Arch(USA) Nesselrode (USA) (Lemon Drop Kid (USA))
*7549[3]* ◆

**Fine Vintage (FR)** *Mark Johnston* a71 71
3 b g Montjeu(IRE) Viking's Cove (USA) (Miswaki (USA))
2696[4] 3396[6] 4058[3]

**Finflash (IRE)** *Mick Channon* a48 80
3 b g Jeremy(USA) Sinegronto (IRE) (Kheleyf (USA))
1615[5] 2406[5] 4186[4] 4862[8] 5381[4] 5777[7] 6297[8] 7213[13]

**Fingal's Cave (IRE)** *Mick Channon* 79
2 ch c Fast Company(IRE) Indiannie Moon (Fraam)
3613[3] 4142[2] 4684[2] 5271[2] 5408[2] (5981) 6977[5]

**Fingers Crossed (USA)** *Kiaran McLaughlin* 76
3 bb f Elusive Quality(USA) Ruth E (USA) (A.P. Indy (USA))
2227a[7]

**Finglass (IRE)** *Y Gourraud* a77 66
3 b f Elusive City(USA) Samya (Invincible Spirit (IRE))
(2978a) *7630a[6]*

**Finial** *Clive Cox* 78
2 ch f Dutch Art Rotunda (Pivotal)
3223[4] 4396[6] (6246) 7131[5]

**Finidaprest (IRE)** *B Grizzetti* 95
3 bb f Dylan Thomas(IRE) Sunsemperchi (Montjeu (IRE))
1780a[5] 2590a[4] 3513a[5]

**Finlodex** *Murty McGrath* a61 58
7 ch g Pastoral Pursuits Ela Aphrodite (Halling (USA))
*368[11]*

**Finn Class (IRE)** *Michael Dods* a84 82
3 b g Exceed And Excel(AUS) Finnmark (Halling (USA))
1563[3] 2333[4] 3002[4] 3480[9] 6792[6] *7732[11]*

**Finnegans Wake (USA)** *Peter Miller* a107 109
5 b h Powerscourt Boat's Ghost (USA) (Silver Ghost (USA))
5460a[5] 7611a[10]

**Finn Mac** *John Norton* 57
4 ch g Norse Dancer(IRE) Strictly Elsie (IRE) (No Excuse Needed)
2658[8] 3439[15] 4534[12]

**Finsbury Square (IRE)** *F Chappet* a78 91
2 b c Siyouni(FR) Diamond Square (FR) (Dyhim Diamond (IRE))
6991a[4] 7855a[3]

**Finton Friend (IRE)** *Charles Hills* a64 66
2 b c Fast Company(IRE) Right Ted (IRE) (Mujadil (USA))
4943[6] 5684[6] 6038[5] *7257[10] 7753[4] 8009[7]*

**Fintry (IRE)** *A Fabre* 116
3 b f Shamardal(USA) Campsie Fells (UAE) (Indian Ridge)
(2817a) (5927) 6927[3]

**Fire Blaze (IRE)** *Charlie Appleby* 81
3 gr f Dubawi(IRE) Nahoodh (IRE) (Clodovil (IRE))
2965[9]

**Fire Eyes** *David Brown* 84
4 b c Exceed And Excel(AUS) Wunders Dream (IRE) (Averti (IRE))
1561[6] 3241[16]

**Fire Fighter (IRE)** *Alan King* a95 86
6 b g Tiger Hill(IRE) Firecrest (IRE) (Darshaan)
4746a[3] 6896[2]

**Fire Fighting (IRE)** *Mark Johnston* a105 111
3 b g Soldier Of Fortune(IRE) Savoie (FR) (Anabaa (USA))
2566[4] 2982[4] 3379[17] 3965[5] 4452[3] 4855[3] (5123) 5430[2] *5552[3]* 5914[2] (6315) (6479) 6737[6] 6930[2] 7106[10] *7662[2] 7803[6] 7922[6]*

**Firefoot (ITY)** *G Botti* a52 37
2 b c Bold Fact(USA) Wassy (ITY) (Astronef)
*5618a[9]*

**Fire In Babylon (IRE)** *Noel Quinlan* a68 40
6 b g Montjeu(IRE) Three Owls (IRE) (Warning)
*(123) 246[5] (303) (349) (569) 648[7] 829[6] 4322[7] 4910[5] 5259[8]* 5864[11] 6410[6] 6768[6] 7823[2] 8134[12] 8277[6]

**Fire King** *Paul Burgoyne* a55 57
8 b g Falbrav(IRE) Dancing Fire (USA) (Dayjur (USA))
*575[4] (844) 1023[9] 1215[8] 7924[13] 8111[3]*

**Fire Ship** *William Knight* a56 111
5 b g Firebreak Mays Dream (Josr Algarhoud (IRE))
1698[6] 2223[3] 3291a[10] 3731[4] 5960a[3] 6620a[7] 7022[4] 7599[2]

**Fire Spinner (IRE)** *Ed Dunlop* 43
3 ch f Galileo(IRE) Mubkera (IRE) (Nashwan (USA))
1701[11]

**Firestorm (GER)** *P Schiergen* 100
3 b c Dylan Thomas(IRE) Fitness (IRE) (Monsun (GER))
3512a[2] 5484a[3] 6589a[6]

**Firfol (FR)** *Mme Pia Brandt* a75 77
3 b c Rail Link Mappa (FR) (Linamix (FR))
*600a[2]* 5368a[15]

**Firgrove Bridge (IRE)** *Kevin Ryan* a55 77
2 ch g Dandy Man(IRE) Over Rating (Desert King (IRE))
(1879) 2543[5] 3337[3] 4218[7] 5790[3] 6427[6] *7362[8]*

**Firmament** *Jeremy Noseda* 82
2 b c Cape Cross(IRE) Heaven Sent (Pivotal)
6462[4] 6985[2] (7413)

**Firmdecisions (IRE)** *Dean Ivory* a96 84
4 b g Captain Rio Luna Crescente (IRE) (Danehill (USA))
*372[2] 658[2] (1020)* 2110[15] 3879[7] 4866[5] 5784[6] *8117[3]*

**First Avenue** *Laura Mongan* a82 90
9 b g Montjeu(IRE) Marciala (IRE) (Machiavellian (USA))
*591[5] 1770[6]* 3453[7]

**First Battalion (IRE)** *Ian Williams*
6 b g Sadler's Wells(USA) Mubkera (IRE) (Nashwan (USA))
*6632[9] 7360[11]*

**First Cat** *K Kukk* a32 58
7 b g One Cool Cat(USA) Zina La Belle (Mark Of Esteem (IRE))
1623a[3] 2592a[2] (4717a) 6187a[6]

**First Class** *Rae Guest* a68 68
6 b g Oasis Dream Break Point (Reference Point)
*245[7] 451[7] 587[4] 750[5] 1217[3]* 1613[7]

**First Class Mail** *Mick Channon* 63
2 ch g Winker Watson Hairspray (Bahamian Bounty)
3728[6] 4338[5] 4618[5] 5525[10] 6250[12]

**First Commandment** *Tim Easterby* 44
3 b g Major Cadeaux Golden Nun (Bishop Of Cashel)
1906[11]

**First Company (FR)** *S Wattel* a84 81
2 b c Elusive City(USA) Amnesia (USA) (Septieme Ciel (USA))
*3640a[2] (5739a) 8149a[11]*

**First Dream (IRE)** *Richard Hannon* a45
2 b c Oasis Dream First (Highest Honor (FR))
6300[8] *7371[9]*

**First Embrace (IRE)** *William Jarvis* 53
3 b f Dubawi(IRE) Bronwen (IRE) (King's Best (USA))
2560[6]

**First Experience** *Rae Guest* a83 81
3 b f Tamayuz Lolla's Spirit (IRE) (Montjeu (IRE))
*(103) 487[3] (957)* 1543[5] 3936[6] (4535) 4811[2] 5398[2] 6112[4] *7196[4] 7820[2] 8079[2]*

**First Flight (IRE)** *Saeed bin Suroor* 104
3 b g Invincible Spirit(IRE) First Of Many (Darshaan)
1696[3] 2565[3] 3378[9] (4667) ◆ 5720[5] 6548[2] ◆ 7120[4] ◆

**First Glance** *Michael Appleby* a46 42
5 br g Passing Glance Lady Santana (IRE) (Doyoun)
5596[7]

**First In Command (IRE)** *Daniel Mark Loughnane* a86 80
9 b g Captain Rio Queen Sigi (IRE) (Fairy King (USA))
1541[10] 1789[4] 2350[12] *2933[11] 3793[2]* 3921[2] 4267[7] 4630[3] (5275) 6096[12] 7159[13] *7888[13] 8180[8]*

**First Mohican** *Alan King* 113
6 ch g Tobougg(IRE) Mohican Girl (Dancing Brave (USA))
1533[7] 2335[3] 2785[8] 3416[12] 7718[7]

**First Move** *Mark Johnston* a73 72
4 b c New Approach(IRE) Loving Kindness (USA) (Seattle Slew (USA))
*1627[3]* 1960[11] 3607[3] 3958[9]

**First Post (IRE)** *Derek Haydn Jones* a85 87
7 b g Celtic Swing Consignia (IRE) (Definite Article)
*61[4] 342[7] 457[5] 744[3] 1175[6]* 1439[3] 1871[8] 2248[2] 2772[3] 3196[9] 5251[3] 5931[6] (6304) 7136[4] 7538[5]

**First Rebellion** *Tony Carroll* a61 59
5 ch g Cockney Rebel(IRE) First Dawn (Dr Fong (USA))
1787[8] 2830[5] 3561[11] *4733[7]* 5000[5] *6409[4] 6561[5] 6720[3] (6851)* 6983[3] 7671[3] *7900[8] 8024[2]*

**First Sargeant** *Michael Appleby* a67 65
4 gr g Dutch Art Princess Raya (Act One)
*1454[11]* 1613[9] *2092[10]* 2806[3] 5599[2] *6015[7]* 7284[7] (7518)

**First Summer** *Shaun Harris* a59 55
2 b g Cockney Rebel(IRE) Silken Dalliance (Rambo Dancer (CAN))
*6270[7] 6719[6] 7076[9]* 7536[3] *7740[3] 7991[4] 8121[3]*

**First Warning** *Tim Pitt* a80 38
4 b g Rail Link Tricked (Beat Hollow)
*182[4] 1128[2]* 2119[8] *3078[3]*

**Fisher** *John Quinn* a60 63
5 br g Jeremy(USA) Elfin Laughter (Alzao (USA))
1885[3] 2327[10] 7175[5]

**Fishlake Rebel** *David C Griffiths* a39 51
4 b g Cockney Rebel(IRE) Fishlake Flyer (IRE) (Desert Style (IRE))
*1110[13] 1223[5]*

**Fit The Bill (IRE)** *James Tate* a55 51
2 b c Iffraaj Najam (Singspiel (IRE))
1977[10] 6147[5] *7779[7]*

**Fityaan** *M Al Muhairi* a105 85
6 b g Haafhd Welsh Diva (Selkirk (USA))
107a[9] 393a[14]

**Fitz Flyer (IRE)** *David Nicholls* a84 88
8 b g Acclamation Starry Night (Sheikh Albadou)
1650[10] 2074[11] 3666[3] ◆ 4174[6] 4418[4] 4762[17] 5766[9] 6150[8] 6511[24] *6764[3] (6898) 7623[3] 7687[F]*

**Fitzgerald (IRE)** *Marco Botti* a71 61
3 b c Duke Of Marmalade(USA) La Vida Loca (IRE) (Caerleon (USA))
*355[5] (735) (975) 2060[5]* 4388[5]

**Fitzwilliam** *Mick Channon* 52
2 ch g Sixties Icon Canadian Capers (Ballacashtal (CAN))
3140[7]

**Fitzwilly** *Mick Channon* a39 74
4 b g Sixties Icon Canadian Capers (Ballacashtal (CAN))
1359[2] 1574[2]

**Five Iron (USA)** *Brian A Lynch* a100 110
4 ch c Sharp Humor(USA) Tee Off (USA) (Thunder Gulch (USA))
3025a[5]

**Fix It (IRE)** *J P Murtagh* a71 78
3 b c Excellent Art Precipice (Observatory (USA))
*416a[3]*

**Fizzolo** *Karen Tutty* a26 43
3 b f Piccolo Fizzy Treat (Efisio)
*1223[6] 1364[5]* 1634[9] 1860[5] 4994[4] 5375[13] 5889[6]

**Flag Of Glory** *Peter Hiatt* a65 69
7 b g Trade Fair Rainbow Sky (Rainbow Quest (USA))
*85[10] 250[13] 405[8]* 2701[7] 3398[U] 3785[2] 3973[5] *4326[2]* 4755[7] 5076[4] 5338[4] 5773[3] (6210) *6636[9]* 7251[12]

**Flagship Shine (AUS)** *J Moore* 113
5 bb g Tale Of The Cat(USA) Dixie Paradise (USA) (Dixie Union (USA))
7897a[3] 8152a[13]

**Flag War (GER)** *Saeed bin Suroor* a94 94
3 ch g Dubawi(IRE) Fantastic Flame (IRE) (Generous (IRE))
*(6344)* 7106[15]

**Flamborough Breeze** *Ed Vaughan* a81 66
5 ro m Ad Valorem(USA) Lothian Lass (IRE) (Daylami (IRE))
118[2] 493[7] 843[9] 3733[6] 4271[9] 4905[5] 6035[12] 6635[11] 7533[3] 7942[4] 8185[4]

**Flamboyant (FR)** *Patrick Gallagher* a82 104
3 b c Peer Gynt(JPN) Relicia Bere (FR) (Until Sundown (USA))
193a[2] 3994a[3]

**Flame Hero (NZ)** *L Ho* 102
5 b g Savabeel(AUS) Rhysess (NZ) (Pins (AUS))
2004a[9]

**Flamenco Flyer** *Edward Bevan* a26 35
5 b g Fantastic Spain(USA) Magical Gift (Groom Dancer (USA))
558[7] 941[10] 1111[4] 1911[5]

**Flamingo Beat** *Christine Dunnett* a37 71
4 ch g Beat Hollow Flamingo Flower (USA) (Diesis)
911[5] 1222[4] 1374[10] 4769[7]

**Flamingo Star (GER)** *Waldemar Hickst* 117
4 b c Areion(GER) Flamingo Island (GER) (Acatenango (GER))
(6965a) (7559a)

**Flaming Spear (IRE)** *Kevin Ryan* 94
2 ch c Lope De Vega(IRE) Elshamms (Zafonic (USA))
(4216)

**Flaming Star** *John Holt* 43
3 b f Firebreak Day Star (Dayjur (USA))
3832[4]

**Flamme Fantastique (GER)** *William Haggas* 27
2 b f Nayef(USA) Flames To Dust (GER) (Oasis Dream)
6208[8] 6554[9]

**Flash City (ITY)** *Ruth Carr* a65 87
6 b g Elusive City(USA) Furnish (Green Desert (USA))
191[4] 347[7] 1127[7] 4114[2] 4391[3] 4521[2] 4752[2] (4833) 6109[4] 6451[3] 6695[4] (7103)

**Flash Crash** *Anthony Carson* a79 71
5 b g Val Royal(FR) Tessara (GER) (Big Shuffle (USA))
(14) (104) 322[2]

**Flash Fire (IRE)** *Mark Johnston* 90
2 b c Shamardal(USA) Flamelet (USA) (Theatrical (IRE))
4695[3] 5050[2] (5397) 6003[2] (6538)

**Flashheart (IRE)** *Marcus Tregoning* 81
4 b g Nayef(USA) Emerald Peace (IRE) (Green Desert (USA))
3065[7] 3977[6] 4501[6] 6813[3]

**Flashman** *Gary Moore* a83 88
5 ch g Doyen(IRE) Si Si Si (Lomitas)
1175[8] 1581[5] 7837[4] 8096[5]

**Flashy Diva** *Henry Candy* a69 75
2 ch f Showcasing Dazzling View (USA) (Distant View (USA))
3557[12] 5210[3] (5667) 6312[7] 7255[4]

**Flashy Memories** *Richard Fahey* 75
2 ch c Dubawi(IRE) Flashy Wings (Zafonic (USA))
(7638)

**Flashy Queen (IRE)** *Joseph Tuite* a59 80
3 ch f Bahamian Bounty Somersault (Pivotal)
1146[5] 1669[3] (2035) 2406[7] (2889) 3959[7]

**Flashy Star** *Paul Henderson* a49 62
5 ch m Mr Greeley(USA) Galileo's Star (IRE) (Galileo (IRE))
6486[5]

**Flatcapper (IRE)** *Richard Fahey* a46 61
2 b f Captain Marvelous(IRE) Wicked Maria (IRE) (Daylami (IRE))
2652[3] 3542[3] 3945[5] 4529[5] 5085[7] 6412[4]

**Flawless Pink** *Jeremy Noseda* a56 67
3 br f More Than Ready(USA) High Heel Sneakers (Dansili)
3074[2] 3916[4] 5469[2] 5796[7] 6037[9] 6647[13]

**Fleckerl (IRE)** *William Muir* a82 82
4 b g Danehill Dancer(IRE) Spinola (FR) (Spinning World (USA))
560[5] 1351[5] 2068[2] 3212[2] 3468[2] ◆ 4280[3] 4761[16]

**Fleeting Indian (IRE)** *Linda Jewell* a49 56
5 b g Sleeping Indian Glebe Garden (Soviet Star (USA))
1877[9] 2401[6] 2723[7] 3323[7] 3800[3] 4653[4] 5423[3]

**Fleetwood Bella** *Michael Attwater*
3 ch f Byron Royal Ivy (Mujtahid (USA))
1296[6] 3525[9]

**Fleetwood Nix** *Pat Phelan* a40
4 b f Acclamation Antediluvian (Air Express (IRE))
276[5] 403[8] 1119[5] 1874[12]

**Fleetwood Poppy** *Michael Attwater* a52 20
2 b f Kheleyf(USA) Steppin Out (First Trump)
4320[6] 5429[11] 6032[8] 8191[6] 8317[7]

**Fleetwoodsands (IRE)** *David Evans* a59 43
7 b g Footstepsinthesand Litchfield Hills (USA) (Relaunch (USA))
192[11] 370[3] 377[5] 676[6] (755) 1023[5] 1215[3] 1387[9]

**Flemish School** *David Elsworth* a91 95
4 ch f Dutch Art Rosewood Belle (USA) (Woodman (USA))
1219[2] 1770[4] (2034) 2272[6] 2779[10] 3930[6] 4443[6] 6098[4] 6714[8] 7662[5] 7850[6]

**Fleur De Printemps** *F Vermeulen* 70
2 b f Silver Frost(IRE) Lemon Twist (IRE) (Marju (IRE))
4312a[3] 5293a[2] 5941a[7]

**Fleurtille** *Ray Craggs* a33 80
5 b m Tillerman Miss Fleurie (Alzao (USA))
1376[12] 1643[4] ◆ (1843) 2056[3] 2421[3] 2552[3] 3237[8] 6863[2] 7179[2] 7506[4]

**Flexible Flyer** *Mark Walford* a86 82
5 b g Exceed And Excel(AUS) Windermere Island (Cadeaux Genereux)
(1446) 2169[9] 3533[7] 4108[7]

**Flic Flac (IRE)** *D K Weld* a92 92
6 ch m Bahamian Bounty Polite Reply (IRE) (Be My Guest (USA))
4557a[6]

**Flicka's Boy** *Tony Coyle* 73
2 b g Paco Boy(IRE) Selkirk Sky (Selkirk (USA))
2866[4] 4624[3] 5013[3] 5637[2] 6115[2] 6322[6] (6623) 7038[5]

**Flicksta (USA)** *John Ryan* a71 70
3 b g Hard Spun(USA) Sindy Jacobson (USA) (More Than Ready (USA))
7071[7] 7569[3] 7759[2] 7954[5]

**Fligaz (FR)** *Martyn Meade* a56 87
2 ch f Panis(USA) Fligane (FR) (Bering)
6659[3] (7130) 7563[2] 7855a[7]

**Flight Fight** *Chris Wall* a56 64
3 b g Raven's Pass(USA) Sunspear (IRE) (Montjeu (IRE))
1208[7] 1491[11] 2271[11] 6635[13]

**Flight Officer** *Saeed bin Suroor* 94
3 b c New Approach(IRE) Danuta (USA) (Sunday Silence (USA))
(7210)

**Flight Risk (IRE)** *J S Bolger* a78 103
3 ch c Teofilo(IRE) Raghida (IRE) (Nordico (USA))
5219a[4] 6172a[2] 7140a[5]

**Flighty Clarets (IRE)** *Richard Fahey* a64 73
4 ch f Bahamian Bounty Flying Clarets (IRE) (Titus Livius (FR))
2421[2] 2914[11] 3462[5] 7949[6] 8182[9] 8297[10]

**Flighty Filia (IRE)** *Amanda Perrett* a66
2 gr f Raven's Pass(USA) Coventina (IRE) (Daylami (IRE))
7194[10] 8036[6] 8173[5]

**Flintshire** *A Fabre* 125
4 bb c Dansili Dance Routine (Sadler's Wells (USA))
2988[2] 3774a[4] 6381a[2] 6970a[2] 7611a[2] (8151a)

**Flippant (IRE)** *William Haggas* 91
3 ch f Pivotal Moon Dazzle (USA) (Kingmambo (USA))
(1913) 2986[8] (5430) 6258[5]

**Flipping** *Stuart Kittow* a66 65
7 br g Kheleyf(USA) Felona (Caerleon (USA))
3781[5] 5005[2] (5512) 6160[2] 7187[4] 7340[2]

**Flirtinaskirt** *Ed McMahon* a76 73
4 b f Avonbridge Talampaya (USA) (Elusive Quality (USA))
383[3] 3092[8]

**Floating Along (IRE)** *G M Lyons* a72 89
4 b f Oasis Dream Politesse (USA) (Barathea (IRE))
4557a[5]

**Flora Medici** *Sir Mark Prescott Bt* a47 75
3 b f Sir Percy Florentia (Medicean)
4191[7] 4842[3]

**Flotilla (FR)** *M Delzangles* a110 115
4 b f Mizzen Mast(USA) Louvain (IRE) (Sinndar (IRE))
395a[4] 682a[2] 1176a[3]

**Flow (USA)** *David Brown* a97 99
4 bb c Medaglia d'Oro(USA) Enthused (USA) (Seeking The Gold (USA))
(2137) 2783[4] 3251[4] 5728[2] 6207[4] 7971[2] 8144[4]

**Flow Chart (IRE)** *Peter Grayson* a55 45
7 b g Acclamation Free Flow (Mujahid (USA))
215[2] 370[9] 502[4] 610[3] 693[5] 760[5] 973[2] 1282[9] 1804[3] 2907[4] 3104[4]

**Floweret (USA)** *Charlie Appleby* a29
2 ch f Street Cry(IRE) Nawaiet (USA) (Zilzal (USA))
7184[12]

**Flowing Air (IRE)** *Richard Brabazon* a73 67
4 b f Authorized(IRE) Al Kamah (USA) (Kingmambo (USA))
5426[6]

**Flumps** *John Stimpson* a47 28
5 ch m Auction House(USA) Demolition Jo (Petong)
6195[6] 7188[9] 7546[3] 7853[6] 7977[9]

**Fly A Kite** *Jonathan Portman* 47
3 b g Assertive High Bird (IRE) (Polar Falcon (USA))
1984[11] 3537[13] 5504[10]

**Flyball** *Richard Hannon* 77
2 b g Proclamation(IRE) Bella Bertolini (Bertolini (USA))
1161[3] (1276) 1512[4] 3322[22] 5607[14]

**Flycatcher (IRE)** *Richard Fahey* 86
3 ro f Medicean Night Haven (Night Shift (USA))
(1507) 1956[4] 2749[2] (3340) 3608[2] 4634[6] 5468[4]

**Fly Grazer (IRE)** *J S Moore* a47 54
2 b f Moss Vale(IRE) Graze On Too (IRE) (Rainbow Quest (USA))
2246[5] 3201[7] 3435[2] 4882a[4] 5119a[10] 5619a[14] 5901a[6]

**Flying Applause** *Roy Bowring* a43 40
9 b g Royal Applause Mrs Gray (Red Sunset)
7[6] 4415[10] 4749[9] 5291[7] 5761[11] 7646[4] 7868[6] 8139[8] 8277[10]

**Flying Author (IRE)** *Phil McEntee* a49 49
3 b g Authorized(IRE) Fly Free (Halling (USA))
488[6] 577[4] 1002[3] 1088[4] 1239[2] 2694[10] 3391[7] 4261[9] 7664[7] 7777[7] 7932[11]

**Flying Bear (IRE)** *Jeremy Gask* a75 84
3 b g Kodiac Marinebird (IRE) (Bad As I Wanna Be (IRE))
1396[7] 1700[6] 2317[13] 3185[2] 4121[6] (4399) 4898[2] ◆ 5438[8] 6020[6] 6355[5]

**Flying By** *Rae Guest* a52
3 b f Byron Flyfisher (USA) (Riverman (USA))
1024[9] 1364[3] 1844[12] 2209[4] 6932[6]

**Flying Cape (IRE)** *Andrew Hollinshead* a84 75
3 b g Cape Cross(IRE) Reine Zao (FR) (Alzao (USA))
193a[5] 390a[7] 482a[2] 585a[4] 721a[7] 751a[4] 1279[6] 1856[3] 2319[7] 3146[14] 4316[2] 4709[3] 5527[4] 5716[3] 6325[5] 6541[4] 7182[9] 7628[3] 7866 [11]

**Flying Fantasy** *William Haggas* a49 67
2 b g Oasis Dream Disco Volante (Sadler's Wells (USA))
5646[11] 6603[7] 7166[3]

**Flying Giant (IRE)** *Jo Hughes* a58 39
4 ch g Danroad(AUS) Our Emmy Lou (Mark Of Esteem (IRE))
31[2] 269[8] 1819[7] 2597a[5] 5103[11]

**Flying Grange** *Tim Easterby* 36
2 b c Hellvelyn Flying Highest (Spectrum (IRE))
2895[7] 3296[9] 4884[9] 5241[9]

**Flying Hammer** *William Haggas* 74
2 b c Acclamation Ruse (Diktat)
7561[3]

**Flying Jib** *D K Weld* a88 104
3 ro f Oasis Dream Jibboom (USA) (Mizzen Mast (USA))
(2042a) 3995a[8] 6351a[8]

**Flying Kyte** *Pat Phelan* a41 41
3 bb g Pastoral Pursuits Red Kyte (Hawk Wing (USA))
280[3] 378[4]

**Flying Light (IRE)** *Graeme McPherson* a65 75
8 b g Chevalier(IRE) Light-Flight (IRE) (Brief Truce (USA))
7129[2]

**Flying Machine (IRE)** *Richard Fahey* a84 87
2 b g Kodiac Dancing Prize (IRE) (Sadler's Wells (USA))
1936[2] 2359[2] 3140[5] (4157) ◆ 5672[2] 6854[4]

**Flying Officer (USA)** *John Gosden* 111
4 b g Dynaformer(USA) Vignette (USA) (Diesis)
(1398) 6687[2] 7271[6]

**Flying Power** *John Norton* a89 81
6 b g Dubai Destination(USA) Rah Wa (USA) (Rahy (USA))
386[6] 611[3] 870[5] 1133[2] 2520[6] (3226) 3699[9] 4662[7] (5127) 6156[6] 8120[6] 8264[6]

**Flying The Flag (IRE)** *M F De Kock* 112
4 ch c Galileo(IRE) Halfway To Heaven (IRE) (Pivotal)
5690[5] 6711[5]

**Flyman** *Richard Fahey* 104
4 b g Pastoral Pursuits Satin Bell (Midyan (USA))
(1193) 2145[22] 4895[17] 5445[19]

**Fly Solo** *Alan Swinbank* a77 82
5 b g Soviet Star(USA) Vino (Efisio)
21[2] 514[5] 1377[2] 2216[4] (2728)

**Fly To The Moon (IRE)** *David Wachman* 94
3 b f Holy Roman Emperor(IRE) Royal Ballerina (IRE) (Sadler's Wells (USA))
3737a[12]

**Fly With Me (FR)** *E Libaud* a81 116
4 gr c Beat Hollow Bird Of Paradise (FR) (Highest Honor (FR))
1784a[3] (2588a) 4250a[5] 5743a[2] 6972a[8] 7486a[9]

**Focail Mear** *John Ryan* a48 48
3 b f Oratorio(IRE) Glittering Image (IRE) (Sadler's Wells (USA))
3631[7] 4867[5] 5400[5] 5832[8] 6454[5] 6946[7] 7002[2] 7360[6] 7664[5] 7845[3] 8004[9]

**Focus On Venice (IRE)** *J S Bolger* 105
3 b c Intense Focus(USA) Marina Of Venice (IRE) (Galileo (IRE))
2570a[5]

**Foie Gras** *Chris Dwyer* a68 54
4 b g Kyllachy Bint Zamayem (IRE) (Rainbow Quest (USA))
339[4] 428[10] 576[5] 740[10] (993) ◆ 1221[4] 1766[10] 2029[6] 2463[10] 2901[4] 3402[10] 4050[4] 7864[4] 8014[6] (8143)

**Foiled** *Nikki Evans*
4 b g Dutch Art Isengard (USA) (Cobra King (USA))
1691[10] 3781[11] 5280[8]

**Fol Hollow (IRE)** *Stuart Coltherd* a53 67
9 b g Monashee Mountain(USA) Constance Do (Risk Me (FR))
2909[10] 3099[14] 3954[8] 4362[7] 5237[12] 5858[7]

**Folklo (FR)** *M Mace* a60
3 ch g Falco(USA) Floride (IRE) (Sadler's Wells (USA))
360a[10]

**Folk Melody (IRE)** *Charlie Appleby* 93
3 b f Street Cry(IRE) Folk Opera (IRE) (Singspiel (IRE))
1515[8] 2316[8] 3727[7] 4436[6]

**Follow The Faith** *Mick Channon* a36 59
2 b f Piccolo Keeping The Faith (IRE) (Ajraas (USA))
4781[10] 5667[8] 6032[9] 6420[6] 6830[5] (7217)

**Fontanelice (IRE)** *Stefano Botti* 102
2 b f Vale Of York(IRE) Choose Me Please (IRE) (Choisir (AUS))
(3775a) (7321a)

**Fonterutoli (IRE)** *Roger Ingram* a65 61
7 gr g Verglas(IRE) Goldendale (IRE) (Ali-Royal (IRE))
92[8] 210[7]

**Footbridge (USA)** *Eoin Harty* a114
4 b c Street Cry(IRE) Thousand Islands (Dubai Millennium)
7614a[10]

**Footsieonehundred (IRE)** *Patrick Gilligan* a53
3 b f Footstepsinthesand Zapping (IRE) (Lycius (USA))
2883[6] 3712[7] 4074[7] 4611[9]

**Foot Soldier (IRE)** *C F Swan* a63 69
5 b g Danehill Dancer(IRE) West Brooklyn (USA) (Gone West (USA))
5456a[6]

**Footstepsintherain (IRE)** *David Dennis* a89 79
4 b g Footstepsinthesand Champagne Toni (IRE) (Second Empire (IRE))
2156[8] 3036[11] 3479[6] 4537[5] 5638[6] 5986[4] 6191[4] 6767[2] 7183[7] 7530[3] 7757[2] 7871[3] 8251[3] 8320[4]

**For Ayman** *Joseph Tuite* a72 61
3 b g Bertolini(USA) Saharan Song (IRE) (Singspiel (IRE))
(2158) 2886[10] 3519[6] 7356[4] 7759[4] 8017[8]

**Forbidden Love** *Richard Hannon* 47
2 b f Dubawi(IRE) Indian Love Bird (Efisio)
5429[8] 6065[9]

**Forced Family Fun** *John Quinn* a62 87
4 b g Refuse To Bend(IRE) Juniper Girl (IRE) (Revoque (IRE))
(1307) 7504[3]

**Forceful Appeal (USA)** *Simon Dow* a91 82
6 bb g Successful Appeal(USA) Kinetic Force (USA) (Holy Bull (USA))
(153) ◆ 314[8] (689) 1042[6] 1301[8] 3036[8] 3879[4] 4447[8] 7663[10] 8117[9]

**Forceful Beacon** *Tony Carroll* a45 37
4 ch g Assertive Shore Light (USA) (Gulch (USA))
3332[6] 3517[5] 3800[5] 7376[6] 8008[4] 8119[6]

**Forcible** *David Brown* 68
2 b g Stimulation(IRE) Least Said (USA) (Trempolino (USA))
1977[9] 2269[5] 3701[8] 7208[8]

**Foreign Diplomat** *William Haggas* a77 81
2 b c Oasis Dream Longing To Dance (Danehill Dancer (IRE))
5655[3] 6517[2] 7199[3]

**Foreign Rhythm (IRE)** *Ron Barr* a61 68
9 ch m Distant Music(USA) Happy Talk (IRE) (Hamas (IRE))
1500[3] (1604) 2542[6] 3395[5] 4471[15] 4629[3] 5089[10] 6671[9] 6866[11] 7502[14]

**Forest Edge (IRE)** *David Evans* a108 102
5 b g Amadeus Wolf Compass Light (USA) (Lear Fan (USA))
(249) 644[7] 713[11] 1066[10] 1172[8] 1484[9] 2758[13] 3693[4] (3969) 4412[3] 4700[9] (5152) (5623) 5918[5] 6369a[3]

**Forester (IRE)** *Mlle P Peelman* 98
4 gr c Danehill Dancer(IRE) Amenixa (FR) (Linamix (FR))
3373a[12]

**Forest Glen (IRE)** *Sylvester Kirk* a50 58
3 b f Camacho Lisfannon (Bahamian Bounty)
4545[8] 4820[3] ◆ 5034[5] 5846[9] 6666[8] 7036[12]

**Forest Maiden (IRE)** *Charlie Appleby* a76
2 b f Invincible Spirit(IRE) Lady Marian (GER) (Nayef (USA))
(6605)

**Forest Missile (IRE)** *John Wainwright*
2 b g Majestic Missile(IRE) Garnock Academy (USA) (Royal Academy (USA))
7082[10] 7713[13] 8205[7]

**Foreteller** *Chris Waller* 115
7 b g Dansili Prophecy (IRE) (Warning)
7127a[8] 7467a[5] 7602a[13]

**Forever Beauty (GER)** *Frau R Weissmeier* 99
4 ch f Dashing Blade Forever Nice (GER) (Greinton)
3873a[4]

**Forever Now** *John Gosden* a63 111
3 b c Galileo(IRE) All's Forgotten (USA) (Darshaan)
2746[2] ◆ (3270) 4122[3] (5668) ◆ 6329[6]

**Forever Snow (USA)** *Fabricio Borges* a46 92
5 rg m Lion Heart(USA) Bullagio (USA) (Holy Bull (USA))
6388a[2]

**Forevertheoptimist (IRE)** *Doug Watson* a89 92
5 gr g Verglas(IRE) Hankering (IRE) (Missed Flight)
241a[4]

**Forgiving Glance** *Philip Kirby* a24 57
2 gr f Passing Glance Giving (Generous (IRE))
3186[3] 3794[4] 4467[8] 5141[6]

**Forgotten Hero (IRE)** *Charles Hills* a91 101
5 bb g High Chaparral(IRE) Sundown (Polish Precedent (USA))
3962[7] (4608) 5928[6] 6330[2] 6752[16] 7440[9]

**Forgotten Rules (IRE)** *D K Weld* 117
4 b g Nayef(USA) Utterly Heaven (IRE) (Danehill (USA))
(7271)

**Forgotten Voice (IRE)** *Nicky Henderson* a115 114
9 b g Danehill Dancer(IRE) Asnieres (USA) (Spend A Buck (USA))
2335[2] 3450[4] 4823[7] 5652[6]

**Forjatt (IRE)** *D Selvaratnam* a112 114
6 b g Iffraaj Graceful Air (IRE) (Danzero (AUS))
595a[3] 899a[4]

**Forres (IRE)** *Richard Hannon* a54 64
2 b f Fastnet Rock(AUS) Slieve (Selkirk (USA))
7018[5] 7399[5]

**Forrest Flyer (IRE)** *Jim Goldie* a37 70
10 b g Daylami(IRE) Gerante (USA) (Private Account (USA))
1763[5] ◆ 2455[3] 3051[P]

**For Shia And Lula (IRE)** *Daniel Mark Loughnane* a80 70
5 b g Majestic Missile(IRE) Jack-N-Jilly (IRE) (Anita's Prince)
102[9] 464[4] 503[5] 690[8] 1083[4] 1297[3] 1606[7] 2069[3] 2864[7] (3233) 3526[2] (4578) 5523[5] (6074) (6414) 6841[3] 7183[4] 8268[7]

**Fort Bastion (IRE)** *David O'Meara* 103
5 b g Lawman(FR) French Fern (IRE) (Royal Applause)
1442[6] ◆ 1719[7] (1958) 2286[2] 2891[4] 3356[22] 3621[6] 4200[4] 4648[8] 4851[6] 5609[11] 6124[4] 6752[15] 6921[10] 7276[16]

**Fort Belvedere** *Keith Dalgleish* a28 94
6 ch g King's Best(USA) Sweet Folly (IRE) (Singspiel (IRE))
763[6] 1345[14]

**Fort Berkeley (IRE)** *Paul Cole* a85 51
3 b g Fastnet Rock(AUS) Verbania (IRE) (In The Wings)
1438[12] 2917[4] ◆ 3856[2] 4547[2] (5404a)

**Forte** *Ralph Beckett* a77 99
2 ch f New Approach(IRE) Prowess (IRE) (Peintre Celebre (USA))
5821[3] ◆ (7011) 7240[6]

**Forte Dei Marmi** *Roger L Attfield* a57 114
8 b g Selkirk(USA) Frangy (Sadler's Wells (USA))
6390a[9]

**Fortinbrass (IRE)** *John Balding* a85 89
4 b g Baltic King Greta D'Argent (IRE) (Great Commotion (USA))
36[4] 257[4] 479[5]

**Fort Knox** *Charlie Appleby* a42 111
4 b g Dubawi(IRE) Savannah Belle (Green Desert (USA))
2336[2] 3420[27]

**Fortrose Academy (IRE)** *Chris Gordon* a51 67
5 b g Iceman Auspicious (Shirley Heights)
1221[9] 1448[6] 3848[16]
**Fortuna Glas (IRE)** *Donald McCain* 62
2 gr c Verglas(IRE) Fortuna Limit (Linamix (FR))
5852[7] 6577[3] 7054[4]
**Forward March** *Johnny Farrelly* a70 53
4 b g Beat Hollow Cantanta (Top Ville)
2444[6] 2907[7] 5898[5]
**Forza Blacky** *Philip McBride* a72 46
2 br g Manduro(GER) Rightside (High Chaparral (IRE))
5149[10] 6101[4] 6602[6] 7525[5]
**Forzarzi (IRE)** *John David Riches* a46 46
10 b g Forzando Zarzi (IRE) (Suave Dancer (USA))
3056[9] 5605[7] 6077[7] 7864[7] 8291[6]
**Fossa** *Dean Ivory* a79 63
4 b g Dubai Destination(USA) Gayanula (USA) (Yonaguska (USA))
1678[8] 2312[5] 2687[5] 3734[7] 8071[10]
**Fosters Cross (IRE)** *Thomas Mullins* a69 81
12 b g Dr Massini(IRE) Francie's Treble (Quayside)
4746a[10]
**Found (IRE)** *A P O'Brien* 115
2 b f Galileo(IRE) Red Evie (IRE) (Intikhab (USA))
6372a[3] (6967a)
**Fountain Of Youth (IRE)** *A P O'Brien* 108
3 b c Oasis Dream Attraction (Efisio)
2571a[10] 3412a[7] (3736a) 6371a[6]
**Four Cheers (IRE)** *Clive Brittain* a60 63
3 b c Exceed And Excel(AUS) O Fourlunda (Halling (USA))
3477[4] 3804[6] 5044[3] 6889[10] 7704[4]
**Four Nations (USA)** *George Baker* a77 77
6 ch g Langfuhr(CAN) Kiswahili (Selkirk (USA))
8193[7]
**Four Seasons (IRE)** *Charlie Appleby* a99 86
2 b c Dubawi(IRE) Please Sing (Royal Applause)
2308[8] (2642) 3322[16] 7079[3] 7443[4] (7661) (7882)
**Foxcover (IRE)** *Richard Fahey* a62 79
3 ch g Raven's Pass(USA) Cover Girl (IRE) (Common Grounds)
1962[2] 5814[3] 7117[4]
**Foxford** *Patrick Chamings* a61 67
3 b f Clodovil(IRE) Pulau Pinang (IRE) (Dolphin Street (FR))
1296[4] 1946[4] 3144[12] 3849[2] 7533[7] 7842[9] 8013[12]
**Foxhaven** *Patrick Chamings* a39 71
12 ch g Unfuwain(USA) Dancing Mirage (IRE) (Machiavellian (USA))
85[9] 2947[5] 6007[3]
**Foxie Girl** *John Best* a36
3 b f Virtual Santiburi Girl (Casteddu)
230[8] 951[8]
**Foxtrot Jubilee (IRE)** *Ralph Beckett* a90 79
4 b g Captain Marvelous(IRE) Cool Cousin (IRE) (Distant Relative)
381[4] 1678[10] 7947[11] 8071[9]
**Foxtrot Knight** *Olly Stevens* a56 63
2 b g Kyllachy Rustam (Dansili)
2057[5] 2499[7] 3119[4] 3937[6] 4313[4] 6941[4]
**Foxtrot Pearl (IRE)** *John Holt* a63 68
3 b f Bahamian Bounty Nina Blini (Bertolini (USA))
3469[4] 4186[5] 4795[13] (6215) 6674[19] 7286[4] 7622[12] 7950[6]
**Foxtrot Romeo (IRE)** *Marco Botti* a109 101
5 b g Danehill Dancer(IRE) Hawala (IRE) (Warning)
1437[10] 1721[6] 2202[5] 3202[2] ◆ 3716[3] ◆ 4683[19] 5433[2] 5919[7] 6159[2] 6531[4] (7700)
**Fox Trotter (IRE)** *Brian Meehan* 100
2 br c Bushranger(IRE) Miss Brief (IRE) (Brief Truce (USA))
(4110) ◆ 4822[4] 6256[17] 6612[4] 6933[5] 7446[2]
**Foxy Boris (FR)** *Paul Cole* a60
2 bb g Aussie Rules(USA) Why Worry (FR) (Cadeaux Genereux)
5377[13] 6718[5] 7372[4] 7839[7]
**Foxy Clarets (IRE)** *Richard Fahey* 89
3 ch g Camacho Muscari (Indian Ridge)
1358[11] 1884[5] 2474[2] (3503) (3882) 4669[10] 5204[5] 5444[15] 6013[12]
**Foxy Forever (IRE)** *Michael Wigham* a88 92
4 b g Kodiac Northern Tara (IRE) (Fayruz)
2275[3] ◆ 3122[5] 6130[14] 6923[13] 7365[3]
**Foxy Music** *Tony Coyle* a89 12
10 b g Foxhound(USA) Primum Tempus (Primo Dominie)
(1244) 2076[9] 2390[8] 2732[6] 2933[6] 3793[3] 8223[6]
**Foylesideview (IRE)** *Luke Dace* a59 66
2 b g Dark Angel(IRE) Showerproof (Peintre Celebre (USA))
2964[12] 3194[8] 3524[6] 5306[7] 5554[8] 6884[6] 7014[10] 8115[11] 8240[6]
**Frac Daddy (USA)** *Kenneth McPeek* a112 105
4 rg c Scat Daddy(USA) Skipper's Mate (USA) (Skip Away (USA))
2228a[4]
**Fractal** *David Simcock* a74 101
3 b g High Chaparral(IRE) Clincher Club (Polish Patriot (USA))
(51) ◆ (5984) (6425)
**Fractional (IRE)** *A Fabre* a92 113
5 b g Manduro(GER) Sharp Point (IRE) (Royal Academy (USA))
(6592a) (6957a)
**Fragile Earth (IRE)** *John Patrick Shanahan* 66
2 b f The Carbon Unit(USA) Mad Madam Mym (Hernando (FR))
6735[2]
**Framed Masterpiece** *Paul Fitzsimons* a80 64
3 ch g Dutch Art Photographie (USA) (Trempolino (USA))
(1116)
**Framley Garth (IRE)** *David Elsworth* a69 73
2 b g Clodovil(IRE) Two Marks (USA) (Woodman (USA))
1512[7] 2269[8] 2776[10] 3720[6] 4364[4] 4764[4] 5148[3] 5823[3] 6237[2] 6602[4] 6663[5] 6887[3] 7064[2] (7230) 7404[2]
**Francine (IRE)** *Stefano Botti* 76
3 b f Dylan Thomas(IRE) Dixie Schic (USA) (Dixieland Band (USA))
1780a[17] 3513a[3]
**Francisco** *Richard Hannon* a64
2 b c Paco Boy(IRE) Blue Goddess (IRE) (Blues Traveller (IRE))
6852[4]
**Francis Scott Key (IRE)** *Brian Meehan* a44 66
2 ch c Starspangledbanner(AUS) Breezeway (IRE) (Grand Lodge (USA))
3584[6] 4109[7] 4906[5] 5554[9] 5974[9]
**Franco Is My Name** *Peter Hedger* a91 73
8 b g Namid Veronica Franco (Darshaan)
89[10]
**Franco's Secret** *Peter Hedger* a78 56
3 b g Sakhee's Secret Veronica Franco (Darshaan)
2681[7] 7158[5] 7528[8] (7921) 8204[3] (8321)
**Frangipanni (IRE)** *Roger Charlton* a69 78
3 bb f Dansili Frizzante (Efisio)
(1833) ◆ 2470[5] (3518) 3890[7]
**Frankenstein** *B Grizzetti* 103
7 b g Dubawi(IRE) Lifting (IRE) (Nordance (USA))
2374a[6]
**Frankie** *Jimmy Fox* a51 44
3 ch g Firebreak Winterbourne (Cadeaux Genereux)
3083[8] 5039[10] 6018[13] 7346[10]
**Frankie M (JER)** *Mrs A Corson*
4 b g Denounce Natacha Rostow (Pursuit Of Love)
2594a[9] 4039a[4]
**Franklin D (USA)** *Michael Bell* 86
2 b c Medaglia d'Oro(USA) Kissed By A Star (USA) (Kingmambo (USA))
3448[7]
**Franklin Nights** *Polly Gundry* 29
4 ch g Franklins Gardens Springtime Lady (Desert Dirham (USA))
2381[9] 3083[11]
**Frank's Folly (IRE)** *Mark Walford* 67
5 b g Tiger Hill(IRE) Pocket Book (IRE) (Reference Point)
2327[16] 2738[14]
**Frank The Barber (IRE)** *Steph Hollinshead* 60
2 gr g Zebedee Red Rosanna (Bertolini (USA))
3461[6] 3813[2] 4652[6] 5014[4] 5985[8] 6212[8]
**Frankthetank (IRE)** *Keith Dalgleish* a75 69
3 ch g Captain Gerrard(IRE) Mi Amor (IRE) (Alzao (USA))
165[5] (173) 267[5] (653) (761) 975[4] 1116[2] 1723[8] 1927[3] 2218[8] (2906) 7636[11] 7871[12] 8086[6]
**Frankyfourfingers (FR)** *C Delcher-Sanchez* 105
4 bb c Sunday Break(JPN) Texaloula (FR) (Kendor (FR))
5263a[4] 6620a[5]
**Frantical** *Luke Dace* a70 63
2 b g Observatory(USA) Quest For Freedom (Falbrav (IRE))
5555[2] (6646)
**Frascata (FR)** *Yves de Nicolay* a89 101
5 gr g Kaldounevees(FR) Loyal Lass (USA) (Cadeaux Genereux)
4841a[6] 6994a[7] 7656a[13]
**Frasers Hill** *Roger Varian* a91 48
5 ch g Selkirk(USA) Shemriyna (IRE) (King Of Kings (IRE))
1578[8] ◆
**Fratellino** *Alan McCabe* a94 81
7 ch h Auction House(USA) Vida (IRE) (Wolfhound (USA))
4[8] 271[6] 479[7] 719[7] 1584[8]
**Fray** *Roger Charlton* 90
3 b f Champs Elysees Short Dance (USA) (Hennessy (USA))
(4623) 5151[2] 6129[13]
**Freaky Girl (FR)** *Robert Collet* a53 68
2 b f Sandwaki(USA) Yippee (IRE) (Orpen (USA))
3691a[7] 5119a[6] 5617a[10] 5844a[12] 6591a[11]
**Freddie Bolt** *Frederick Watson* 43
8 b g Diktat Birjand (Green Desert (USA))
4755[9]
**Freddy Q (IRE)** *Tony Newcombe* a53 74
5 ch g Iffraaj Barnabas (ITY) (Slip Anchor)
1262[4] 1919[8] 2947[9] 3585[5] (4568) 4964[3]
**Freddy With A Y (IRE)** *Gary Moore* a76 79
4 b g Amadeus Wolf Mataji (IRE) (Desert Prince (IRE))
1492[14] 2157[6] 2462[6] 3088[7] 3468[3] 4156[9] 4674[2] 5624[3] 5979[2] 7220[2] 7494[2] 7758[2] 8248[4]
**Frederic** *Luca Cumani* a80 68
3 b g Zamindar(USA) Frangy (Sadler's Wells (USA))
4407[9] 5648[3] 6018[3] 6484[10] 7349[3]
**Frederic Chopin** *Stuart Williams* a66 70
3 ch g Tamayuz Eliza Gilbert (Noverre (USA))
236[3] ◆ 473[2] 577[3] 960[2] 2028[6] 2926[7] (3120) 3823[5] 4333[2] 4803[6] (5628)
**Frederick Engels** *J Moore* a100 115
5 b g Iceman Colonel's Daughter (Colonel Collins (USA))
7897a[10]
**Fredricka** *Garry Moss* a64 78
3 ch f Assertive Vintage Steps (IRE) (Bahamian Bounty)
765[4] 1425[4] 1642[2] 2802[6] 3487[6] (4295) (4725) 6671[4] (7058) 7535[7] 7767[4]
**Free Code (IRE)** *James Tate* a90 96
3 b g Kodiac Gerobies Girl (USA) (Deposit Ticket (USA))
1614[6] 2330[2] 3378[11] 4125[7] 6411[5]
**Freedom Flying** *Lee James* a31 30
11 b m Kalanisi(IRE) Free Spirit (IRE) (Caerleon (USA))
1004[3] 3404[6] 4115[9] 5240[8]
**Freedom Rose (IRE)** *Derek Shaw* a45
2 br f Alfred Nobel(IRE) Colourpoint (USA) (Forest Wildcat (USA))
4075[9] 4610[5] 5255[5] 6663[10] 8179[5]
**Freedom's Light** *John Gosden* a81 107
4 b f Galileo(IRE) Aricia (IRE) (Nashwan (USA))
1636[2] 1942[3] 2764[2] (3500)
**Freedom Tales (FR)** *M Boutin* a79 79
3 b g Tertullian(USA) Fridas World (Agnes World (USA))
4465a[6]
**Free Eagle (IRE)** *D K Weld* 120
3 b c High Chaparral(IRE) Polished Gem (IRE) (Danehill (USA))
(6350a) 7275[3]
**Free Entry (IRE)** *James Tate* a77 79
2 b f Approve(IRE) Dear Catch (IRE) (Bluebird (USA))
2014[2] ◆ 2824[2] 5255[2] 5593[2] (6489)
**Free House** *Jessica Long* 95
5 ch g Sir Percy Coming Home (Vettori (IRE))
3772a[4] 6389a[6]
**Freemason** *Sir Michael Stoute* a82 70
3 b g Cape Cross(IRE) Candy Mountain (Selkirk (USA))
5347[3] 5796[2] 6608[10] 7304[7]
**Free One (IRE)** *Jeremy Noseda* a72
2 b c Fast Company(IRE) Tatamagouche (IRE) (Sadler's Wells (USA))
7200[2] 7739[5] 8318[3]
**Free Port Lux** *F Head* 114
3 b c Oasis Dream Royal Highness (GER) (Monsun (GER))
1340a[2] (2194a) 2818a[14] 4251a[4] 5406a[2] (6571a) 6970a[19]
**Free Radical** *Noel Quinlan* 66
2 b c Iffraaj La Jwaab (Alhaarth (IRE))
7495[3]
**Free Rein** *Ralph Beckett* 80
3 b f Dansili Sant Elena (Efisio)
2780[4] (3664) ◆ 4163[7] 5776[2] 6095[5]
**Free To Love** *Charles Hills* 75
2 br f Equiano(FR) All Quiet (Piccolo)
2771[2] 4828[4]
**Freewheel (IRE)** *Frederick Watson* a88 84
4 br g Galileo(IRE) La Chunga (USA) (More Than Ready (USA))
1164[15] 1444[6] 7504[5] 8120[2]
**Free Wheeling (AUS)** *Saeed bin Suroor* a109 104
6 b g Ad Valorem(USA) Miss Carefree (AUS) (Last Tycoon)
112a[6] 306a[2] 678a[6] (808a) 3731[8] 4872[2] 6124[9]
**Freeze The Secret (IRE)** *David C Griffiths* a37 52
2 b f Kodiac Campiglia (IRE) (Fairy King (USA))
2328[7] 3975[4] 4652[4] 7991[6] 8179[6]
**Free Zone** *Robert Cowell* 109
5 b g Kyllachy Aldora (Magic Ring (IRE))
2074[12] 2989[19] 4700[10] 5289[3] 5925[17] 7080[2] 7280[11]
**Freida** *Karen Tutty*
2 b f Mullionmileanhour(IRE) La Corujera (Case Law)
1482[8]
**Freight Train (IRE)** *Mark Johnston* 82
2 b c Manduro(GER) Sigonella (IRE) (Priolo (USA))
3136[6] (3701)
**Fremont (IRE)** *Hugo Palmer* a50 69
7 b g Marju(IRE) Snow Peak (Arazi (USA))
6714[3]
**French Accent** *John Best* a42 38
3 ch f Elnadim(USA) Saralea (FR) (Sillery (USA))
188[9] 588[7] 753[8] 2078[11] 2694[5] 4321[6]
**French Flirt** *Timothy Jarvis* a60 48
3 ch f Peintre Celebre(USA) Cream Tease (Pursuit Of Love)
3664[4] 4393[6] 5007[5] 6515[9] 7459[11]
**French Navy** *Charlie Appleby* 118
6 b h Shamardal(USA) First Fleet (USA) (Woodman (USA))
1533[2] 1870[3] (2554) (2958) (7599)
**French Plaisir (FR)** *A Bonin* a30
2 ch c Linngari(IRE) Rose Bewitched (FR) (My Risk (FR))
8149a[15]
**Frenzified** *Luca Cumani* 71
2 b f Yeats(IRE) Librettista (AUS) (Elusive Quality (USA))
7108[15] 7594[3]
**Fresh Kingdom (IRE)** *James Fanshawe* a81 58
3 ch g Dubawi(IRE) Polyquest (IRE) (Poliglote)
1612[9] 2842[3] 3315[12] (4911) 5899[3] (6239)
**Fresles (IRE)** *Mme Pia Brandt* a101 100
3 b f Royal Applause Luna Celtica (IRE) (Celtic Swing)
1273a[9] 4009a[3] 5963a[9] 6994a[13] 7802[2] (8300a)
**Fret** *Henry Candy* 62
2 b f Fastnet Rock(AUS) Her Grace (IRE) (Spectrum (IRE))
4396[7] 5305[P] (Dead)
**Fridge Kid** *Dr Jon Scargill* 61
2 b f Kheleyf(USA) Snow Shoes (Sri Pekan (USA))
5643[9] 6261[5] 6753[11]
**Frine (IRE)** *C Laffon-Parias* 110
4 b f High Chaparral(IRE) Castalia (Cardoun (FR))
5462a[5] (6956a) 7486a[6]
**Frog Hollow** *David O'Meara* a88 78
5 gr g Intikhab(USA) The Manx Touch (IRE) (Petardia)
1721[11] 6535[7] 7545[9]
**Frognal (IRE)** *Ann Stokell* a79 45
8 b g Kheleyf(USA) Shannon Dore (IRE) (Turtle Island (IRE))
1689[7] 2901[8]
**Frognal Bear (IRE)** *Richard Hannon* a73 73
2 b c Kodiac Lily In The Pond (Kyllachy)
6103[2] 6299[5] 6652[3] (7223)
**From Frost** *Andrew Balding* a96 86
3 b g Nayef(USA) Salutare (IRE) (Sadler's Wells (USA))
(1088) ◆ (3797) ◆ 4113[7] 5164[6] 5691[14] 6656[4] 7020[3]
**Frontier Fighter** *David O'Meara* a108 58
6 b g Invincible Spirit(IRE) Rawabi (Sadler's Wells (USA))
(61) 163[6] 314[6] (566) 764[2] (1114) 1558[10] 2113[7] 7743[4] 8135[3] 8203[2]
**Frontline Phantom (IRE)** *K R Burke* a40 75
7 b g Noverre(USA) Daisy Hill (Indian Ridge)
1167[6] 1617[7] 2476[5] 2875[3] (3334) ◆ 3363[2] 3623[6] 4593[2] 5077[4] (5421) (5533) 6223[3] 6706[9]
**Front Page News** *Robert Eddery* a83 82
4 ch f Assertive Branston Berry (IRE) (Mukaddamah (USA))
1275[8] (2341) 3036[13] 3674[4] 4053[7] 4866[8] 5650[4] (6021) 6558[8] 6872[9] 7530[8]
**Front Run (IRE)** *Marco Botti* a73 63
3 b c Amadeus Wolf Prima Volta (Primo Dominie)
7975[4] 8164[8]
**Frosted Off** *John Spearing* a47 49
4 gr g Verglas(IRE) Dispol Veleta (Makbul)
844[4] 1668[4] 3149[13] 7221[8]
**Frost Fire (USA)** *Mark Johnston* a78 39
4 b f Medaglia d'Oro(USA) Alta Love (USA) (Gone West (USA))
(151)
**Frostman (FR)** *Jo Hughes* a70 64
2 gr g Silver Frost(IRE) Santa Marina (FR) (Kendor (FR))
1402a[10] 3113[3] 5292a[9] 5588a[5]
**Frosty Berry** *Paul Midgley* a67 70
5 gr m Proclamation(IRE) Star Entry (In The Wings)
(1674) 2213[5] 4427[4] 4942[2] 6062[9]
**Frosty Flyer (FR)** *Richard Fahey* 54
2 gr g Silver Frost(IRE) Perruche Grise (FR) (Mark Of Esteem (IRE))
6058[7] 6790[4]
**Frosty Friday** *J R Jenkins* a59 51
6 b m Storming Home Seasonal Blossom (IRE) (Fairy King (USA))
7[4]
**Frosty The Snowman (IRE)** *Ruth Carr* a61 64
3 gr g Mastercraftsman(IRE) Sleeveless (USA) (Fusaichi Pegasus (USA))
1608[3] 2098[5] 3545[8] 3978[2] 4420[3] 4574[4] 5132[6]
**Frosty Times (FR)** *Richard Fahey* a38 54
2 b g Silver Frost(IRE) Ego (Green Desert (USA))
1936[8] 2386[9] 2837[5] 5141[3] (5372) 6072[6] 7156[7]
**Frozen Over** *Chris Down* a64 81
6 b g Iceman Pearly River (Elegant Air)
3175[4]
**Frozen Princess** *Jamie Osborne* a64 63
2 b f Showcasing Super Midge (Royal Applause)
1488[8] 4652[3] 5120[2] 7003[9] (7701) 7948[5]
**Fruit Pastille** *Hughie Morrison* a85 89
3 b f Pastoral Pursuits Classic Millennium (Midyan (USA))
140[3] ◆ 311[6] 568[2] ◆ 1846[4] 2624[9] 3281[2] 3614[3] (4579) 5521[4] 6034[9] (6337) (6945) (7384) 7553[10]
**Fruity (IRE)** *Clive Cox* 81
2 b f Camacho Belle Of The Blues (IRE) (Blues Traveller (IRE))
2697[4] (3648) 6375a[4]
**Fruity Bun** *Keiran Burke* a26 52
4 b f Dr Fong(USA) Little Conker (Red Ransom (USA))
581[10]
**Fuel Injection** *Paul Midgley* a71 66
3 gr g Pastoral Pursuits Smart Hostess (Most Welcome)
481[3] (650) 1005[2] 1737[6] 2406[4] 2889[3] 3959[8] 4315[3] 4636[8] 4977[6] 5389[7]
**Fugleman (IRE)** *Ben Haslam* 80
2 b c Fast Company(IRE) Quinzey (JPN) (Carnegie (IRE))
(3296)
**Fujiano** *Derek Haydn Jones* a51 68
2 b f Equiano(FR) The Fugative (Nicholas (USA))
1788[4] 2220[6] 2888[4] 3415[21] 4815[4] 5985[2] 7308[3] 7970[6]
**Fujin** *Shaun Harris* a44 57
3 b g Oasis Dream Phantom Wind (USA) (Storm Cat (USA))
1671[10] 1939[4] 2217[3] 2802[11] 4873[8] 5389[4] 5715[11] 6866[3] 7222[2] 7420[6] 7670[12]
**Fujin Dancer (FR)** *Brian Ellison* a86 65
9 ch g Storming Home Badaayer (USA) (Silver Hawk (USA))
85[4] 744[6] 1659[4] 2168[8] 2981[7] 5678[8] (8162)
**Fulbright** *Charlie Appleby* a113 115
5 b h Exceed And Excel(AUS) Lindfield Belle (IRE) (Fairy King (USA))
(109a) 308a[6] 596a[5]
**Fulki (FR)** *J Heloury* 50
2 b f King's Best(USA) Filzeta (IRE) (Fasliyev (USA))
2755a[12] 6698a[8]
**Fullaah (IRE)** *Saeed bin Suroor* 79
3 b f Shamardal(USA) Zahrat Dubai (Unfuwain (USA))
2422[2]
**Full Combat (SAF)** *M F De Kock* a96 92
4 b c Go Deputy(USA) Full Card (SAF) (Western Winter (USA))
204a[5] 594a[10] 896a[8]
**Full Day** *Brian Ellison* a69 79
3 ch f Champs Elysees Capistrano Day (USA) (Diesis)
1192[7] 1509[8] (2018) 3003[4] 3396[2] 4189[3]
**Full In Have (FR)** *N Leenders* a42 71
3 b f Great Journey(JPN) Antilles (IRE) (Danehill (USA))
599a[11] 5226a[3]
**Full Mast (USA)** *Mme C Head-Maarek* a80 112
2 b c Mizzen Mast(USA) Yashmak (USA) (Danzig (USA))
(6181a) (6968a)
**Full Moon Fever (IRE)** *Ed Walker* a71 83
3 b f Azamour(IRE) Hasaiyda (IRE) (Hector Protector (USA))
1118[3] (1452) 2072[6] 2685[8] 4249a[7] 4947[4] (7305) 7504[6] 7838[13]
**Full Of Speed (USA)** *James Fanshawe* a61 26
2 ch g Raven's Pass(USA) Knock Twice (USA) (Two Punch (USA))
4570[12] 7031[6] 7551[8]

**Fullon Clarets** *Richard Fahey* 79
2 ch g Equiano(FR) Palinisa (FR) (Night Shift (USA))
2949[2] 5013[4] 6474[2]

**Full Steam Ahead (IRE)** *David Marnane* 87
3 b g Rock Of Gibraltar(IRE) Star Studded (Cadeaux Genereux)
5696[6]

**Fundao (SWI)** *Carmen Bocskai* a92 94
5 ch g Blue Canari(FR) Farinha (SWI) (Wolfhound (USA))
177a[6] 729a[6]

**Funding Deficit (IRE)** *Jim Goldie* a51 71
4 ch g Rakti Bukat Timah (Inchinor)
1447[14] 1758[4] 1930[5] 2518[4] 3610[2] 3833[6] 4004[5] 4861[4] 5237[9] 5565[10] 6121[4] (6600) 6836[11] 7180[2] 7249[2]

**Funinthesand (IRE)** *Wido Neuroth* a98 96
5 b g Footstepsinthesand Funny Legend (NOR) (Funambule (USA))
2245a[4] 3090a[8] 3772a[9]

**Funky Cold Medina** *Tom Keddy* a76 72
4 b f Cockney Rebel(IRE) Monica Campbell (Sakhee (USA))
84[4] 359[2] 461[6] 1864[7]

**Funky Munky** *Alistair Whillans* a57 57
9 b g Talaash(IRE) Chilibang Bang (Chilibang)
123[4] 433[2] 640[6] 2455[4] 7284[2] 7508[13]

**Fun Mac (GER)** *Hughie Morrison* a86 89
3 ch g Shirocco(GER) Favorite (GER) (Montjeu (IRE))
(1727) 2566[5] 3892[8] 4893[5] 5691[16] 6608[2] 7135[2]

**Funtime Barry (IRE)** *Richard Hannon* a28
2 ch c Lord Shanakill(USA) No Greater Love (USA) (Stravinsky (USA))
6565[8] 7354[12] 7880[6]

**Furas (IRE)** *Saeed bin Suroor* a85
3 br g Shamardal(USA) Albaraari (Green Desert (USA))
3577[8] 5012[6] 5553[5]

**Furiously Fast (IRE)** *Clive Brittain* a63
2 b c Fast Company(IRE) Agouti (Pennekamp (USA))
5098[3] ◆

**Furnace (IRE)** *E Charpy* a67 84
10 b g Green Desert(USA) Lyrical Dance (USA) (Lear Fan (USA))
239a[5]

**Fury** *William Haggas* 103
6 gr g Invincible Spirit(IRE) Courting (Pursuit Of Love)
2286[10] 2959[4] 3251[9] 4442[4] (5749)

**Fuscetta (GER)** *Waldemar Hickst* 92
2 b f Tiger Hill(IRE) Fusca (GER) (Lando (GER))
(7481a)

**Future Empire** *Saeed bin Suroor* 104
2 ch c New Approach(IRE) Fann (USA) (Diesis)
(4666) ◆ 5926[2] 7104[3]

**Future Security (IRE)** *Anthony Middleton* a85 46
5 ch g Dalakhani(IRE) Schust Madame (IRE) (Second Set (IRE))
(729a) 870[6] 2119[6]

**Futuro Anteriore (IRE)** *L la Strina* 102
4 b c Diamond Green(FR) Lost Icon (IRE) (Intikhab (USA))
2374a[9]

**Fuwairt (IRE)** *Richard Hannon* 90
2 b g Arcano(IRE) Safiya Song (IRE) (Intikhab (USA))
2380[3] (2829) 3322[8] 4150[2] (4430) 5173[3] 6230[3] 6739[9] 6933[23]

**Fuzzy Logic (IRE)** *Bernard Llewellyn* a44 48
5 b g Dylan Thomas(IRE) Gates Of Eden (USA) (Kingmambo (USA))
1915[3] 3179[3] 3780[5] 5342[2] 5909[4]

**Fyrecracker (IRE)** *Marcus Tregoning* 85
3 ch g Kheleyf(USA) Spirit of Hope (IRE) (Danehill Dancer (IRE))
3083[2] (3816) (4697) 5675[10]

**Gabbiano** *Jeremy Gask* a71 94
5 b g Zafeen(FR) Hollybell (Beveled (USA))
2110[6] 3271[6] 4146[5] 4609[4] 5623[7] 6130[8] 7017[10]

**Gabrial (IRE)** *Richard Fahey* a104 111
5 b g Dark Angel(IRE) Guajira (FR) (Mtoto)
110a[2] (309a) 595a[4] 772a[5] 899a[9] 1176a[11] 5693[18] 5920[6] 6321[4] 6532[3] 7120[6] (7490)

**Gabrial's Bounty (IRE)** *Richard Fahey* a44 55
5 ch g Bahamian Bounty Social Storm (USA) (Future Storm (USA))
2117[7] 3221[13] 4161[7] 5632[8] 6077[9]

**Gabrial's Gift (IRE)** *Scott Dixon* a84 77
5 gr g Verglas(IRE) Sahara Lady (IRE) (Lomitas)
11[10] 381[3] 909[11]

**Gabrial's Hope (FR)** *Tracy Waggott* a42 70
5 b g Teofilo(IRE) Wedding Night (FR) (Valanour (IRE))
49[8] 209[2] 379[2] 1129[4] 1675[5] 2607[10] (3436) 3623[2] 4470[6] 5640[10] 6119[2] 6672[6] 7175[11]

**Gabrial's Kaka (IRE)** *Richard Fahey* 109
4 b g Jeremy(USA) Love In May (IRE) (City On A Hill (USA))
1165[6] (1437) 1721[2] 2086[4] 3356[17] 3982[3] 5609[5] 6752[27] 7276[7] ◆

**Gabrial's King (IRE)** *David Simcock* a96 98
5 b g Hurricane Run(IRE) Danella (IRE) (Platini (GER))
125[6] 1398[6] 2073[9] 2760[2] 3034[4] 3321[13] (4217) 6557[8] 7107[16] 7409[7] 7703[2]

**Gabrial's Lady (IRE)** *Richard Fahey* 42
3 b f Authorized(IRE) Prinquet (USA) (Marquetry (USA))
6073[9] 6282[5] 6738[8]

**Gabrial's Star** *Richard Fahey* a94 93
5 b g Hernando(FR) Grain Only (Machiavellian (USA))
623[2] 784[7] 1377[4] (2119) 2259[11] 2760[8] 6283[4] 6747[4] 7107[21] 7422[2] (7702) 8062[5]

**Gabrial's Wawa** *Michael Squance* a73 67
4 b g Dubai Destination(USA) Celestial Welcome (Most Welcome)
255[5] 388[7] 690[7] 815[2] ◆ 1215[6] 8319[2]

**Gabrial The Boss (USA)** *Michael Mullineaux* a78 57
4 ch g Street Boss(USA) Bacinella (USA) (El Gran Senor (USA))
(180) 410[6] 582[3] 732[2]

**Gabrial The Duke (IRE)** *Richard Fahey* a75 76
4 ch g Duke Of Marmalade(IRE) Literacy (USA) (Diesis)
1628[4] 2445[6] 2762[7] (3224) (3585) 3898[3] 4470[7] 5002[5] 8089[6] 8260[5]

**Gabrial The Great (IRE)** *Donald McCain* 101
5 b g Montjeu(IRE) Bayourida (USA) (Slew O'Gold (USA))
2085[7]

**Gabrial The Hero (USA)** *David Simcock* a69 92
5 b g War Front(USA) Ball Gown (USA) (Silver Hawk (USA))
(4349) (4917) 5651[13]

**Gabrial The Terror (IRE)** *Richard Fahey* a73 74
4 b g Kheleyf(USA) Simla Bibi (Indian Ridge)
558[3] 686[6] 871[5] 1617[6] 2444[5] 3226[10] (3553) 3853[3] 4190[7] 4340[2] 5076[2] 8122[4]

**Gabrial The Thug (FR)** *Richard Fahey* a63 48
4 b g Azamour(IRE) Baliyna (USA) (Woodman (USA))
1864[4] 2457[6] 3208[3] (3623) 4058[13] 4190[6] 5529[2] 5899[4] 7098[8] 7426[6] 7642[4] 8161[5]

**Gabrial The Tiger (IRE)** *Richard Fahey* a54 71
2 b g Kodiac Invincible (Slip Anchor)
(6319) 6820[3] 8226[4]

**Gabrial The Viking (IRE)** *Richard Fahey* 77
2 b g Approve(IRE) Xarzee (IRE) (Xaar)
5922[3] (6279) 6529[5]

**Gabriel's Lad (IRE)** *Denis Coakley* a95 114
5 b g Dark Angel(IRE) Catherine Wheel (Primo Dominie)
886[7] 1728[5] (2145) 3723[7] 4648[14] 5653[4]

**Gadobout Dancer** *Keith Dalgleish* a44 51
7 b m Tobougg(IRE) Delta Tempo (IRE) (Bluebird (USA))
1761[10] 2457[2] 2475[11] 3056[4] 3364[2] 4381[8] 5084[10] 5166[10]

**Gaelic Ice** *Martin Hill* a58 64
5 b m Iceman Gaelic Lime (Lomitas)
(5748)

**Gaelic O'Reagan** *Robert Eddery* a55
3 b g Refuse To Bend(IRE) Gaelic Roulette (IRE) (Turtle Island (IRE))
1008[4] 1730[9] 2346[11] 4830[8] 6022[12]

**Gaelic Silver (FR)** *Gary Moore* a93 80
8 b g Lando(GER) Galatza (FR) (Johann Quatz (FR))
(421) 953[2] 1142[3] (1236) 1665[2] 2702[7] 2862[4] (7516) (7831) (8042)

**Gaelic Way (FR)** *J Merienne* a67 83
3 ch g Creachadoir(IRE) Green Way (FR) (Green Tune (USA))
3745a[8]

**Gaelic Wizard (IRE)** *Karen Tutty* a68 58
6 b g Fasliyev(USA) Fife (IRE) (Lomond (USA))
425[9] 2029[8] (3795) 4069[3] 5376[7] 5711[2] (5996) 6674[9] 7180[9] 7826[3] 8082[10] 8176[4]

**Gaelique Show (FR)** *P Khozian* a63 68
8 b g Anabaa(USA) Gaelic Dream (FR) (Shining Steel)
752a[5]

**Gaga A (URU)** *D Smaga* a100 106
5 rg m T. H. Approval(USA) Yin (BRZ) (Quinze Quilates (BRZ))
1827a[5] 2631a[8] 4561a[4] (5369a) 5742a[9] 6592a[6] 7189a[3] 7558a[5] (7736a)

**Gaiete (FR)** *A Bonin* a79 87
4 ch f Kentucky Dynamite(USA) Grenade (FR) (Bering)
796a[7]

**Gailo Chop (FR)** *A De Watrigant* 115
3 ch g Deportivo Grenoble (FR) (Marignan (USA))
(1340a) (1621a) 3994a[4] (5406a)

**Gaily Game** *J-C Rouget* a67 102
6 b g Montjeu(IRE) Gaily Tiara (USA) (Caerleon (USA))
3907a[7]

**Gainsborough's Art (IRE)** *Harry Chisman* a63 22
9 ch g Desert Prince(IRE) Cathy Garcia (IRE) (Be My Guest (USA))
247[10]

**Gala Award (USA)** *Todd Pletcher* a88 105
3 b c Bernardini(USA) Wilshewed (USA) (Carson City (USA))
3994a[10]

**Gala Casino Star (IRE)** *Lawrence Mullaney* a67 87
9 ch g Dr Fong(USA) Abir (Soviet Star (USA))
2519[6] 3436[4] 4470[8] 6706[6] 7044[2] 7175[7]

**Galactic Halo** *Lady Cecil* a64
3 b f Rail Link Star Cluster (Observatory (USA))
7074[4] 7401[3]

**Galactic Heroine** *James Given* 86
3 b f Galileo(IRE) Thermopylae (Tenby)
2422[6] (3653) 4298[2] 4893[11] 6152[3] 6937[8]

**Galago (IRE)** *Sylvester Kirk* a37 74
2 b g Bushranger(IRE) She's A Softie (IRE) (Invincible Spirit (IRE))
3889[6] 4943[3] 6024[5] 8287[3]

**Galatian** *Rod Millman* a76 53
7 ch g Traditionally(USA) Easy To Imagine (USA) (Cozzene (USA))
2884[7] 3227[7] 4073[2] 4673[6] (5308) 6240[7] 6766[8]

**Galaxe (FR)** *Rod Collet* 100
3 b f High Chaparral(IRE) Galaxie Des Sables (FR) (Marchand De Sable (USA))
4721a[7] 7268a[9]

**Galaxy (IRE)** *Alan McCabe* a70 63
3 b g Oratorio(IRE) Gravitation (Galileo (IRE))
143[4] 861[3] 1166[6] 1635[9] 2132[6] 2616[5]

**Gale Force** *James Fanshawe* a74 68
3 b f Shirocco(GER) Hannda (IRE) (Dr Devious (IRE))
3652[5] 4966[4] 6485[4] 7176[2]

**Gale Force Ten** *M F De Kock* a108 115
4 b c Oasis Dream Ronaldsay (Kirkwall)
308a[13] 595a[7] 772a[7] 898a[12]

**Galesburg (FR)** *P Decouz* a71 55
3 b f Sageburg(IRE) Galaxia (FR) (Alamo Bay (USA))
391a[2]

**Galician** *Mark Johnston* a106 106
5 gr m Redoute's Choice(AUS) Gweneira (Machiavellian (USA))
144[5]

**Galileano (IRE)** *Marco Botti* a59 58
2 ch f Galileo(IRE) Flamingo Sea (USA) (Woodman (USA))
5827[4] 6742[4] 7230[9]

**Galilee Chapel (IRE)** *Alistair Whillans* a55 52
5 b g Baltic King Triple Zero (IRE) (Raise A Grand (IRE))
2674[7] 3054[8] 4014[2]

**Galiotto (IRE)** *Noel Williams* a63 65
8 b g Galileo(IRE) Welsh Motto (USA) (Mtoto)
400[3] (454) 657[3] 842[5] 4615[7]

**Galiway** *A Fabre* 110
3 b c Galileo(IRE) Danzigaway (USA) (Danehill (USA))
1481a[3] 2196a[5] 2818a[9]

**Galizzi (USA)** *Michael Bell* a89 94
3 b g Dansili Dancing Abbie (USA) (Theatrical (IRE))
(1269) ◆ 1856[2] 2986[7] 4183[8] 5442[2] (5818) 6127[6] 6705[5] 7106[16]

**Gallante (IRE)** *A Fabre* 118
3 b c Montjeu(IRE) Crazy Volume (IRE) (Machiavellian (USA))
1621a[3] 2194a[3] (4251a) 6379a[6]

**Gallena** *James M Barrett* a67 54
4 b f Invincible Spirit(IRE) Emily Blake (IRE) (Lend A Hand)
128a[6]

**Gallic Destiny (IRE)** *Andrew Balding* a76 78
3 b g Champs Elysees Cross Your Fingers (USA) (Woodman (USA))
1118[5] 1452[2] (2081) 2530[3] 4392[2] 5356[4]

**Galuppi** *J R Jenkins* a72 80
3 b g Galileo(IRE) La Leuze (IRE) (Caerleon (USA))
1357[2] 1720[2] 7015[3] 7332[2] 7913[3]

**Galvanize** *Kevin Ryan* 85
3 b g Bahamian Bounty Xtrasensory (Royal Applause)
1757[2] (2138) 3247[11] 4021[5] 4912[5] 5177[6]

**Gambino (IRE)** *John David Riches* a76 73
4 b c Red Clubs(IRE) Temptation Island (IRE) (Spectrum (IRE))
3530[9] 3601[3] 4195[3] (4489) 4730[2] 5142[2] (5562) 6232[12] 6836[10] 7042[6] 7568[2] (7871) 8058[5] 8168[9]

**Gambler's Roll (USA)** *Philip D'Amato* a51
2 ch c Eskendereya(USA) Edgewise (USA) (Yes It's True (USA))
7605a[5]

**Gambling Girl (IRE)** *Mrs John Harrington* 80
5 ch m Hawk Wing(USA) Gambling Spirit (Mister Baileys)
4746a[13]

**Gambol (FR)** *B W Hills* a70 87
4 ch g New Approach(IRE) Guardia (GER) (Monsun (GER))
1730[8] 2025[8] 3546[3] (3919) 4552[2] 4995[2] 5579[6] 6169[12]

**Game Mascot** *Peter Hiatt* a86 64
4 ch g Kheleyf(USA) Tolzey (USA) (Rahy (USA))
3759[7] 4868[5] 5686[9] 6251[6] 6904[8] 7647[3] 7830[10]

**Game On Dude (USA)** *Bob Baffert* a126
7 bb g Awesome Again(CAN) Worldly Pleasure (USA) (Devil His Due (USA))
5781a[4]

**Game Pie (IRE)** *Hugo Palmer* 81
2 b c Tamayuz Princess Nala (IRE) (In The Wings)
6259[4] 6683[2] 7173[2]

**Games Day (FR)** *E Lellouche* a73 73
3 b g Super Celebre(FR) Goldance (FR) (Goldneyev (USA))
585a[5]

**Game Show** *Charlie Appleby* a76 62
2 b c Dubawi(IRE) Dream Play (IRE) (In The Wings)
5494[7] 5886[4] (6602)

**Gamesome (FR)** *Olly Stevens* 106
3 b c Rock Of Gibraltar(IRE) Hot Coal (USA) (Red Ransom (USA))
2343[9] 3253[4] ◆ 3732[2]

**Gamesters Lad** *Tom Dascombe* a27 59
2 b g Firebreak Gamesters Lady (Almushtarak (IRE))
1732[5] 2829[5] 3181[4] 4012[5] 7112[7] 7684[6]

**Game Theory (IRE)** *N Clement* a66
2 b f Aussie Rules(USA) Atullia (GER) (Tertullian (USA))
8132a[4]

**Game Zone (IRE)** *F Rohaut* 105
3 b f Hurricane Run(IRE) Go Lovely Rose (IRE) (Pivotal)
5479a[2] 6882a[7] 7768a[6]

**Gammarth (FR)** *H-A Pantall* a98 110
6 ch h Layman(USA) Emouna Queen (IRE) (Indian Ridge)
3746a[6] 5223a[11] 5963a[2] 6971a[8] (7656a)

**Gangbuster** *Richard Hannon* 33
2 b c Whipper(USA) Teresa Balbi (Master Willie)
3311[7]

**Ganges (IRE)** *James Toller* a58 82
3 b c Shamardal(USA) Quantum (IRE) (Alhaarth (IRE))
1511[5] 1979[3] 3428[4] 4272[4] 4886[3] 5347[P]

**Gangster Squad (FR)** *Martyn Meade* a81 79
3 b f Astronomer Royal(USA) Cobblestone Road (USA) (Grindstone (USA))
3897[4] 5038[3]

**Gang Warfare** *Olly Stevens* a77 77
3 b g Medicean Light Impact (IRE) (Fantastic Light (USA))
1582[11] 2871[2] 3332[2] 4077[6] 4501[4] 7205[5]

**Gannicus** *Brendan Powell* a75 74
3 b g Phoenix Reach(IRE) Rasmani (Medicean)
1400[7] (2013) 2307[7] 3197[7] 3655[4] 5670[8] 6303[8] 6981[10] 7633[2] 7918[6] 8248[7] 8321[6]

**Ganny (FR)** *E Lellouche* a75 72
3 ch f Footstepsinthesand Twelve Bar Blues (Nashwan (USA))
1139a[6]

**Ganymede** *Eve Johnson Houghton* a73 81
3 b g Oasis Dream Gaze (Galileo (IRE))
119[5] 1258[5] 1530[13] 4948[9] 5521[6] (6022) (6297) 6657[2] 7403[11]

**Gap Year (USA)** *Kiaran McLaughlin* a89
2 b f Bernardini(USA) Dubai Escapade (USA) (Awesome Again (CAN))
6915a[7]

**Garlin Blues (FR)** *J Phelippon* a50 76
6 b g Anabaa Blue Garlinote (FR) (Poliglote)
3089a[3] 6569a[5]

**Garlingari (FR)** *Mme C Barande-Barbe* a79 108
3 b g Linngari(IRE) Garlinote (FR) (Poliglote)
585a[3] 5591a[7] 7318a[4]

**Garraun (IRE)** *Jeremy Noseda* a62 57
3 b f Tamayuz French Fern (IRE) (Royal Applause)
1677[5] 2126[7] 3316[10]

**Garswood** *Richard Fahey* 117
4 b c Dutch Art Penchant (Kyllachy)
1698[5] 2765[4] 3723[2] 4758[4] (5223a)

**Garvie Bay** *Michael Blanshard*
4 ch g Trade Fair Silver Gyre (IRE) (Silver Hawk (USA))
5822[RR]

**Gas Total (BRZ)** *D Smaga* a75 97
5 b m Sulamani(IRE) Club Med (BRZ) (Reve Dore (USA))
5263a[7]

**Gatepost (IRE)** *Richard Fahey* a71 88
5 br g Footstepsinthesand Mandama (IRE) (Warning)
3221[6] 3646[3] 4258[4] 4783[10] 5385[2] ◆ 6281[2] 6511[15] 6740[8] 7085[5] 7236[4]

**Gatewood** *John Gosden* a106 111
6 b h Galileo(IRE) Felicity (IRE) (Selkirk (USA))
1194[2] (2143) (2555) 3722[2] (5224a) 5962a[2] 7653a[12]

**Gathering Power (IRE)** *Edward Lynam* a73 109
4 b f Kyllachy Nutkin (Act One)
2564[2] 3167a[6] 4557a[3] 5699a[5] 7140a[2] 7272[7]

**Gauchita** *K R Burke* a51 38
3 b f Invincible Spirit(IRE) Rex Regina (IRE) (King's Best (USA))
1855[7] 5819[9] 6409[7] 7252[9]

**Gaudy (IRE)** *Kevin Ryan* 92
2 b c Dandy Man(IRE) Red Beach (IRE) (Turtle Island (IRE))
2288[4] 3394[3] 4253[4] (4659) 5607[4] 6256[14]

**Gavarnie Encore** *Michael Blanshard* a60 47
2 b c Intikhab(USA) Greeley Bright (USA) (Mr Greeley (USA))
2622[7] 3082[7] 4079[4] (6663) 7257[5] 7832[3] 8115[2]

**Gavlar** *William Knight* a76 73
3 b g Gentlewave(IRE) Shawhill (Dr Fong (USA))
1847[2] 2492[3] 3146[5] 3789[6] (4547) 4657[3] 5877[5] 6608[5] 7133[8]

**Gay Marriage (IRE)** *John Gosden* a73 79
3 b f New Approach(IRE) Doctrine (Barathea (IRE))
2498[2] 3560[5] 4504[7] 5557[8] 6034[10]

**Gea And Tea** *Robert Eddery* 96
2 b c Captain Gerrard(IRE) Lilac Dreams (Second Set (IRE))
3429[10] 4207[4] 4864[5] 6108[5] 6499[4] 6648[3]

**Geanie Mac (IRE)** *Linda Perratt* a50 63
5 ch m Needwood Blade Dixie Evans (Efisio)
1763[3] 2515[5] 3238[5] 3829[2] 4015[2] 4520[5] 4726[3] 4856[2] 5146[2] 5567[2] (5856)

**Gebayl** *Roger Ingram* a63
4 b f Compton Place Glimpse (Night Shift (USA))
384[5] 563[F]

**Geeaitch** *Peter Hiatt* a73 65
5 ch g Cockney Rebel(IRE) Grand Rebecca (IRE) (Namid)
106[2] 283[3] 590[9] (1249) (1496) 1909[4]

**Gee Sharp** *Julie Camacho* a58 45
3 b g Captain Gerrard(IRE) Cumbrian Concerto (Petong)
411[3] 753[9] 2393[10] 2741[5]

**Genax (IRE)** *Ian Williams* a47 53
3 b f Green Desert(USA) Steam Cuisine (Mark Of Esteem (IRE))
3528[7] 4294[3] 5103[8] 6121[11] 7547[3] 7883[9] 8050[8]

**General (FR)** *S Kobayashi* a78 66
3 gr c Great Journey(JPN) Generalite (FR) (Kendor (FR))
360a[6] 482a[3]

**General A Rod (USA)** *Michael J Maker* a113
3 bb c Roman Ruler(USA) Dynamite Eyes (USA) (Dynaformer (USA))
1964a[11] 2357a[4] 3026a[7]

**General Brook (IRE)** *David Wachman* a82 90
4 b g Westerner Danse Grecque (IRE) (Sadler's Wells (USA))
4771a[7]

**General Bunching (USA)** *Thomas Cleary* a63 52
6 br g Vindication(USA) Listen (USA) (Chester House (USA))
794a[8] 7877a[10] 7961a[4]

**Generalissime (FR)** *A De Royer-Dupre* a96 97
4 gr g Literato(FR) Rotina (FR) (Crystal Glitters (USA))
5263a[5]

**General Jack (USA)** *Michael J Maker* a84 101
3 ch c Giant's Causeway(USA) J'Ray (USA) (Distant View (USA))
5458a[7]

**General Tufto** *Charles Smith* a62 43
9 b g Fantastic Light(USA) Miss Pinkerton (Danehill (USA))
(7) 78[3] 171[7] 317[9] 537[3] 640[2] 831[7] 998[3] 1086[2] 1228[2] 1428[2] 1800[2] 2092[2] 2399[2] 2937[2] 3798[6] 5731[3] 6407[11] 6627[5] 7290[10] 8218[3]

**Generalyse** *Ben De Haan* a82 82
5 b g Cadeaux Genereux Dance To The Blues (IRE) (Danehill Dancer (IRE))
2147[13] 2995[3] 3313[11] 3882[10] 4401[3] 5182[5] 5595[3] (5987) 6872[13] *7351[3]*
**Generosidade (URU)** *D Smaga* 106
5 b m Nedawi Xiang-Vi (BRZ) (Quinze Quilates (BRZ))
5462a[7]
**Generous Dream** *Mel Brittain* a60 43
6 ch m Generous(IRE) First Harmony (First Trump)
7508[8] *8134[2]* ◆ *8208[4]*
**Gengis (FR)** *G Doleuze* a90 100
4 gr c King's Best(USA) Ashiyna (IRE) (Green Desert (USA))
*7437a[7]*
**Gen I Am** *Richard Hannon* a46 64
2 ch f Aqlaam Gennie Bond (Pivotal)
3888[11] 4269[10] 4980[4] 5525[2] *6237[8]*
**Genius Beast (USA)** *Charlie Appleby* 88
6 b g Kingmambo(USA) Shawanda (IRE) (Sinndar (IRE))
305a[12]
**Genius Boy** *James Tate* a76 98
4 ch c New Approach(IRE) One So Marvellous (Nashwan (USA))
*(941)* 1660[2] 2168[4] 2540[3] (2876) (3162) (3437) (4091) 5354[7] 5749[7] 6752[28]
**Gentildonna (JPN)** *Sei Ishizaka* 117
5 b m Deep Impact(JPN) Donna Blini (Bertolini (USA))
(1182a) 7981a[4]
**Gentle Breeze (IRE)** *H-A Pantall* a73 85
3 b f Dubawi(IRE) Laureldean Gale (USA) (Grand Slam (USA))
2226a[9]
**Gentledor (FR)** *Y Barberot* a65 66
2 bb c Gentlewave(IRE) Sariyra (FR) (Sinndar (IRE))
2976a[2] 3691a[10]
**Gentleman Duke (IRE)** *A L T Moore* a60 74
6 b g Bachelor Duke(USA) Housekeeping (Dansili)
7476a[15]
**Gentlemax (FR)** *Jim Boyle* a69 61
4 b g Gentlewave(IRE) Marcela Howard (IRE) (Fasliyev (USA))
*(343)* *848[6]* 1941[13] 5208[8] *5547[8]* *6564[4]* *(7526)* *7804[6]*
**Gentlemen** *Phil McEntee* a49
3 ch g Ad Valorem(USA) Stoney Cove (IRE) (Needwood Blade)
2442[RR] 2525[9]
**Gentlemusic (FR)** *Marco Botti* a68 60
2 b f Gentlewave(IRE) Makhalina (IRE) (Red Ransom (USA))
6066[6] 6641[5] *(7076)*
**Gentle Persuasion** *Amanda Perrett* a27 46
2 b f Rock Of Gibraltar(IRE) Play Bouzouki (Halling (USA))
6652[8] *7194[14]*
**Gentora (FR)** *H-A Pantall* 91
2 b f Gentlewave(IRE) Oranor (FR) (Starborough)
7317a[6]
**Geoffrey Chaucer (USA)** *A P O'Brien* 112
3 b c Montjeu(IRE) Helsinki (Machiavellian (USA))
2187a[3] 2990[16] 4007a[17]
**Geological (IRE)** *Richard Hannon* a84 80
2 b c Rock Of Gibraltar(IRE) Bean Uasal (IRE) (Oasis Dream)
2964[4] (3324) 4143[6] 5409[2] 6128[6] 6312[3] *(7224)*
**Geology** *Kevin Ryan* 17
2 b g Rock Of Gibraltar(IRE) Baralinka (IRE) (Barathea (IRE))
5264[10]
**Geonpi (IRE)** *F Rossi* a69
3 b c Footstepsinthesand Maria Gabriella (IRE) (Rock Of Gibraltar (IRE))
*4952a[11]*
**Geordan Murphy** *Andrew Balding* a89 82
3 b g Firebreak Sukuma (IRE) (Highest Honor (FR))
*6018[12]* *6661[2]* (7158) (7513) *7852[4]* *(8197)*
**Geordie George (IRE)** *John Quinn* 95
2 b g Kodiac Trika (First Trump)
(2895) 3619[2] 4348[3] 5580[3] 6510[4] 7079[5]
**George Bailey (IRE)** *Bryan Smart* a43 63
2 b g Zebedee Zuzu (IRE) (Acclamation)
4192[5] 6623[4] 7246[4] *7701[5]*
**George Baker (IRE)** *George Baker* a76 76
7 b g Camacho Petite Maxine (Sharpo)
*1026[5]* 1623a[2] *2471[2]* 3088[13] 3468[5] *4072[6]* 4717a[3] 5873[5] 6070[3] *6858[5]* *8030[10]*
**George Benjamin** *Michael Appleby* a69 64
7 b g Trade Fair Unchain My Heart (Pursuit Of Love)
*170[3]* *300[6]* *(367)* 2021[3] 2164[4]
**George Bowen (IRE)** *Richard Fahey* 84
2 gr g Dark Angel(IRE) Midnight Oasis (Oasis Dream)
(3569) 4123[10] 4853[5] 6003[5] 6510[3] 7079[2]
**George Cinq** *Michael Bell* a92 95
4 b g Pastoral Pursuits Fairnilee (Selkirk (USA))
*1578[6]* ◆ 2156[4] 2707[3] 3050[4] (4148) 4331[2] 4827[3] *6140[6]* 6560[3] *7227[9]* ◆ *7455[2]*
**George Dryden (IRE)** *Ann Duffield* 98
2 b c Zebedee Key To Fortune (GER) (Big Shuffle (USA))
(4416) 5286[2] 6286[6] 6933[14]
**George Fenton** *Conor Dore* a65 62
5 ch g Piccolo Mashmoum (Lycius (USA))
*20[2]* *122[6]* *255[4]* *389[3]* *1497[4]*
**George Guru** *John Bridger* a104 96
7 b g Ishiguru(USA) Waraqa (USA) (Red Ransom (USA))
*235[5]* *314[5]* *(625)* *715[2]* *(1070)* *1558[5]* 1943[3] 2483[2] 3244[6] 4851[17] 6688[11] *7555[9]* 7801[8] 8295[9]
**George Rooke (IRE)** *Keith Dalgleish* a80 90
4 b g Rock Of Gibraltar(IRE) Double Fantasy (GER) (Indian Ridge)
2453[2] (3102) 3572[3] 3955[3] 4783[3] 5446[5] 6535[3] *7365[6]*
**Georgetown** *A bin Harmash* 90
4 ch c Manduro(GER) Summertime Legacy (Darshaan)
242a[6]
**Georgian Bay (IRE)** *K R Burke* a105 103
4 b g Oratorio(IRE) Jazzie (FR) (Zilzal (USA))
*38[2]* ◆ *314[11]* *749[4]* *(1576)* 2145[12] 3420[8] 4200[6] 4648[21] 6335[3] 7276[10] *7743[5]*
**Georgian Firebird** *Alan Swinbank* 56
4 b f Firebreak Skovshoved (IRE) (Danetime (IRE))
5374[6] 6092[12] 6432[7] 7177[13]
**Georgia's Gamble (IRE)** *Lee Carter* a23 52
2 b g Strategic Prince My Sweet Georgia (IRE) (Royal Applause)
6551[14] *7660[13]* *7834[10]*
**Gereon (GER)** *C Zschache* 108
6 b g Next Desert(IRE) Golden Time (GER) (Surumu (GER))
2715a[3] 4247a[5] 6054a[8] 6914a[8] 7618a[2]
**German Rules** *Yasmin Almenrader* a68 78
3 gr c Aussie Rules(USA) Bonnie Belle (Imperial Ballet (IRE))
*7630a[10]*
**Gerrard's Slip** *Bryan Smart*
2 b g Captain Gerrard(IRE) Park's Girl (Averti (IRE))
7713[11]
**Gerry The Glover (IRE)** *Brian Ellison* 80
2 b g Approve(IRE) Umlani (IRE) (Great Commotion (USA))
3713[2] (4286) 5607[8] 6256[16] 6529[6]
**Get Knotted (IRE)** *Michael Dods* 78
2 ch g Windsor Knot(IRE) Genuinely (IRE) (Entrepreneur)
5086[U] 5679[2] (6474)
**Get Lucky (FR)** *C Lerner* a83 70
3 b c Elusive City(USA) Leila (FR) (Lahint (USA))
*5482a[9]* *6221a[9]*
**G Force (IRE)** *David O'Meara* 121
3 b c Tamayuz Flanders (IRE) (Common Grounds)
(1671) (2317) ◆ 3245[3] 4215[2] 4852[5] 5654[6] ◆ (6134) 7272[15]
**Ghaamer (USA)** *A Al Raihe* a96 87
4 b g Hard Spun(USA) Teeba (USA) (Seeking The Gold (USA))
242a[5]
**Ghaawy** *Sir Michael Stoute* 91
3 b g Teofilo(IRE) Asawer (IRE) (Darshaan)
5676[5]
**Ghalib (IRE)** *Marco Botti* a67 62
2 ch c Lope De Vega(IRE) Gorband (USA) (Woodman (USA))
3148[9] 4025[8] *5009[3]* *5554[4]* *6884[4]*
**Ghany (IRE)** *William Haggas* a76 77
3 b f Lawman(FR) Broken Spectre (Rainbow Quest (USA))
4168[3] 6788[2] ◆ *7195[5]* *7686[2]* *7841[3]*
**Gharaaneej (IRE)** *John Gosden* a65 71
3 br f Pivotal Neverletme Go (IRE) (Green Desert (USA))
4446[8] *5044[4]* 6638[2] 7024[2] 7303[3] *(7682)*
**Gharoor** *John Butler*
2 b c Thewayyouare(USA) Connessa (IRE) (Invincible Spirit (IRE))
*8093[13]*
**Ghazi (IRE)** *Saeed bin Suroor* a89 63
3 b g Exceed And Excel(AUS) Concordia (Pivotal)
7410[8] *7634[5]* *7870[2]*
**Ghinia (IRE)** *Pam Sly* 79
3 b f Mastercraftsman(IRE) Jorghinia (FR) (Seattle Slew (USA))
1723[2] (2274) 3195[9] 3968[6]
**Ghor (FR)** *M Boutin* a81 99
6 ch g Gold Away(IRE) Pragmatica (Inchinor)
7026a[4]
**Ghost Cat** *Brian Meehan* a75 75
2 ch c Equiano(FR) Lomapamar (Nashwan (USA))
3279[5] 4117[4] 4740[2] *(5099)*
**Ghosting (IRE)** *Tom Dascombe* a76 75
3 ro g Invincible Spirit(IRE) Exclusive Approval (USA) (With Approval (CAN))
2075[8] 4393[4] 5004[3] 5430[6] *5895[5]* *6484[2]* *6722[3]* *7185[7]* *7757[4]* *7918[7]* *8197[3]*
**Ghostly Arc (IRE)** *Noel Wilson* 45
2 b g Arcano(IRE) Cheyenne's Spirit (IRE) (Sadler's Wells (USA))
7084[13] 7498[10]
**Ghostly Wonder (USA)** *Andrew Hansen* 71
3 rg c Corinthian(USA) Another Wonder (USA) (Wild Again (USA))
4230a[9]
**Ghost Of A Girl (IRE)** *T G McCourt* a49 52
4 gr f Verglas(IRE) Donnelly's Hollow (IRE) (Dockside (USA))
*516[7]*
**Ghost Train (IRE)** *Tim McCarthy* a69 66
5 b g Holy Roman Emperor(IRE) Adrastea (IRE) (Monsun (GER))
*295[4]* *603[2]* *688[2]* *(846)* *1221[2]* *3393[4]* *6889[5]* *7842[4]* *8081[3]* 8195[3] 8298[10]
**Ghostwing** *Ralph J Smith* a40 72
7 gr g Kheleyf(USA) Someone's Angel (USA) (Runaway Groom (CAN))
*114[6]* ◆ *258[3]* *489[9]* *587[12]* *799[7]* 2722[7] 3230[12] *3521[7]* 3824[8]
**Ghufa (IRE)** *Lydia Pearce* a52 41
10 b g Sakhee(USA) Hawriyah (USA) (Dayjur (USA))
*5283[3]* *5864[9]*
**Ghurair (USA)** *Chad C Brown* 108
4 bb c Elusive Quality(USA) Alta Moda (Sadler's Wells (USA))
4010a[6]
**Giacallure (USA)** *Richard Scherer* 87
3 rg c Giacomo(USA) Seductiva (USA) (Lure (USA))
4230a[7]
**Giannizzero (IRE)** *Marco Botti* a38 64
2 b c Royal Applause Baileys Gleam (Compton Place)
4301[5] 4829[2] 5397[3] 6294[8] *7029[7]*
**Giantouch (USA)** *Marco Botti* a79 59
2 b c Giant's Causeway(USA) Beauty O' Gwaun (IRE) (Rainbow Quest (USA))
3720[5] 4570[5] *6603[2]* *7226[2]* ◆
**Giant Samurai (USA)** *John Quinn* a74 58
3 ch g First Samurai(USA) Willow Point (USA) (Fusaichi Pegasus (USA))
3002[8] 3625[8] *4263[3]*
**Giant Sandman (IRE)** *Rune Haugen* a87 109
7 b h Footstepsinthesand Sharamana (IRE) (Darshaan)
*597a[12]*
**Giant's Cauldron (GER)** *P Schiergen* 107
3 ch c Peintre Celebre(USA) Golden Time (GER) (Surumu (GER))
3293a[7] 4007a[16] 6180a[4]
**Giant Sequoia (USA)** *Des Donovan* a64 42
10 ch g Giant's Causeway(USA) Beware Of The Cat (USA) (Caveat (USA))
*4582[4]* 5033[7] *5508[4]* *(5558)* *5864[2]* *6339[3]* *7290[9]* *7975[9]* *8231[8]*
**Giantstepsahead (IRE)** *Denis Quinn* a62 85
5 br g Footstepsinthesand Salty Air (IRE) (Singspiel (IRE))
*1923[3]* (2443) 3308[2] (4303) (5150) 7125[10]
**Giant Swing (FR)** *M Boutin*
2 b c Air Chief Marshal(IRE) Raflebery (Hernando (FR))
*8212a[8]*
**Gibeon (IRE)** *Richard Hannon* a85 85
2 b c Cape Cross(IRE) Gravitation (Galileo (IRE))
(5149) 6520[5] *6853[3]*
**Gideon Jukes** *Richard Fahey* a46 67
2 ch g Cockney Rebel(IRE) Polish Sprite (Danzig Connection (USA))
2428[5] 5013[7] *5799[8]*
**Gifted Girl (IRE)** *Paul Cole* a90 106
5 b m Azamour(IRE) Hoodwink (IRE) (Selkirk (USA))
1974[3] 2284[8] 3355[14] 4607[4] 5312[2] ◆ 5687[7] 6464[7] 6707[6] *7553[7]*
**Gifted Heir (IRE)** *Ray Peacock* a24 14
10 b g Princely Heir(IRE) Inzar Lady (IRE) (Inzar (USA))
*321[10]* *783[9]* 4534[10] 4797[11] 5338[8]
**Gifted Leader (USA)** *Ian Williams* 35
9 b g Diesis Zaghruta (USA) (Gone West (USA))
2782[7]
**Gifted Spirit** *Mark Brisbourne* a11
4 b f Indesatchel(IRE) Dispol Verity (Averti (IRE))
3695[6] *7117[9]* *7285[9]* *8002[7]*
**Gift Of Rain (IRE)** *Ed Dunlop* a61 73
3 b f Galileo(IRE) La Sylvia (IRE) (Oasis Dream)
*1858[4]* 2643[2] 2948[5] *4547[9]*
**Gift Of Silence** *Bernard Llewellyn* a68 86
5 gr m Cadeaux Genereux Not A Word (Batshoof)
1863[3] 2448[6] 3160[3] 3678[3] *4433[2]* 4763[2] 4996[3] 5502[2] (6062) (6285) 6746[8] (7411)
**Giftorm (USA)** *Fredrik Reuterskiold* a95 95
4 b g War Pass(USA) High Cholesterol (USA) (Until Sundown (USA))
4957a[2] 5744a[9]
**Gigawatt** *Jim Boyle* a79 79
4 b g Piccolo Concubine (IRE) (Danehill (USA))
*5308[8]* *6414[2]* 6789[4] 7220[7] *7351[5]* *7729[7]* *8100[2]* *8204[7]*
**Gilbey's Mate** *John Gosden* a79 83
3 b g Medicean Al Joudha (FR) (Green Desert (USA))
1586[4] 2203[2] 3273[3] *4074[5]* *6044[7]*
**Gilded Frame** *J S Moore* a62 66
4 b g I Was Framed(USA) Glint (Pivotal)
*3235[6]* 3818[8]
**Gilded Lace** *D Windrif* a78 78
2 b f Virtual Regal Gallery (IRE) (Royal Academy (USA))
2771[4] 3415[14] *4054[7]* 6064[11] 6400[2] 6698a[2] 7027a[4] *8132a[2]*
**Gilded Lili (IRE)** *Charles Hills* 72
2 b f Big Bad Bob(IRE) City Vaults Girl (IRE) (Oratorio (IRE))
7108[17] 7450[3]
**Gild Master** *Alan King* a73 71
2 b c Excellent Art Nirvana (Marju (IRE))
*4731[3]* 6874[2] *7730[7]*
**Gilmer (IRE)** *Laura Young* a78 71
3 b g Exceed And Excel(AUS) Cherokee Rose (IRE) (Dancing Brave (USA))
3484[9] *6770[5]* *7373[12]* *8124[8]* *8260[10]*
**Gimme Five** *Alan King* a67 64
3 b g Champs Elysees Waitingonacloud (In The Wings)
(1792) 2247[3] 2735[4] *(7229)* ◆
**Ginger Jack** *Keith Dalgleish* a76 90
7 ch g Refuse To Bend(IRE) Coretta (IRE) (Caerleon (USA))
1733[2] 2618[5] 3109[6] 3573[6] 4453[8] 7125[2] 7597[3] *7688[6]*
**Gingka (FR)** *Mme P Butel* a51 81
4 b g One Cool Cat(USA) Top Sauce (Hector Protector (USA))
2192a[8]
**Gin Trap (USA)** *Olly Stevens* a50 40
2 b c Distorted Humor(USA) Ticket To Seattle (USA) (Capote (USA))
5091[6] *6270[6]*
**Ginwar (ITY)** *Stefano Botti* 104
2 b c Martino Alonso(IRE) Rosemary Girl (IRE) (Celtic Swing)
(3775a) 7147a[2]
**Giny Queen (FR)** *Mlle V Dissaux* a58 58
3 bb f King's Best(USA) Lady Weasley (FR) (Zieten (USA))
1907a[9]
**Ginzan** *Malcolm Saunders* a67 82
6 b m Desert Style(IRE) Zyzania (Zafonic (USA))
*1286[4]* 1789[7] 1912[6] 2414[4] 2945[3] 3275[3] 3561[4] 3749[4] (4339) 4741[2] 5124[2] 5411[2] 5776[3] 6189[3] 6313[4] 7215[7]
**Gioia Di Vita** *David Thompson* a80 80
4 b g Sakhee(USA) Dhuyoof (IRE) (Sinndar (IRE))
*168[2]* *544[4]* *784[10]* 1307[4] 1724[12] 3436[5] 3919[6] 4427[10] 5090[3] 5765[3] (6119) 6542[11] 7175[9]
**Giorgio's Dragon (IRE)** *Robert Stephens* a32 51
5 b g Le Vie Dei Colori Broadways Millie (IRE) (Imperial Ballet (IRE))
*126[8]*
**Gios Last (GER)** *Keith Dalgleish* a79
4 rg g Paolini(GER) Giovanella (IRE) (Common Grounds)
4319[12] 5145[7] *(8011)*
**Giovanni Boldini (USA)** *A P O'Brien* a107 115
3 b c War Front(USA) Dancing Trieste (USA) (Old Trieste (USA))
*1178a[4]* 2196a[7] 3352[3]
**Giovanni Di Bicci** *Lady Cecil* a54 44
2 b g Medicean Marula (IRE) (Sadler's Wells (USA))
*6604[9]* *7372[7]* 7561[7]
**Giovanni Jack** *Alan Swinbank* 73
4 ch g Three Valleys(USA) Marching West (USA) (Gone West (USA))
3434[6] 4022[11] 4066[3] (4856) 4964[4] (5567) 5815[4] 6113[6] 7100[5]
**Gipsy Doll** *Paul Cole* a34 48
2 b f Dansili Gipsy Moth (Efisio)
4126[11] 4499[12] 5120[3] *5823[11]*
**Girl At The Sands (IRE)** *Edward Creighton* a69 55
4 gr f Clodovil(IRE) Invincible Woman (IRE) (Invincible Spirit (IRE))
*424[9]* *651[11]*
**Girl Of The Rain (IRE)** *Stefano Botti* 68
4 b f Refuse To Bend(IRE) Bagnolese (ITY) (Cape Cross (IRE))
1477a[10]
**Girolamo (GER)** *P Schiergen* 114
5 ch h Dai Jin Golden Time (GER) (Surumu (GER))
2001a[7] 2704[4] 5432[10] 6806a[4] 7603a[13]
**Give It A Whirl** *Christine Dunnett*
3 br f Pastoral Pursuits Life's A Whirl (Machiavellian (USA))
3916[13]
**Give Us A Belle (IRE)** *Christine Dunnett* a72 63
5 b g Kheleyf(USA) Bajan Belle (IRE) (Efisio)
*259[5]* *694[4]* ◆ *845[6]* 1378[3] 1584[7] 2724[6] *3392[8]* 3896[5] 5316[7] 5780[5] 5860[6] *6273[2]* ◆ *6897[2]* (7900) 7997[6] 8322[4]
**Give Us A Reason** *James Toller* a64 27
4 b f Motivator Ela's Giant (Giant's Causeway (USA))
*2081[10]* 2924[8] *4081[3]* *4734[2]* *5508[3]* *6157[3]* *7290[4]*
**Glace (IRE)** *Mark Johnston* a69 50
3 gr f Verglas(IRE) Swynford Lady (IRE) (Invincible Spirit (IRE))
*(422)* *604[4]* *1093[3]*
**Gladiatrix** *Rod Millman* a88 95
5 b m Compton Place Lady Dominatrix (IRE) (Danehill Dancer (IRE))
1572[13] 2161[4] 2564[7] 2965[7] (4027) 4412[8] 5419[13] 6231[8] 6923[5] 7080[13] 7441[8]
**Gladsome** *Sarah Humphrey* a39 58
6 b m Resplendent Glory(IRE) Christening (IRE) (Lahib (USA))
*1813[7]* 2954[2] 3575[8] 3956[3] 4294[4] 4515[7] *5573[9]* 6863[11] *8175[8]*
**Gladstone (FR)** *J-C Rouget* a83 78
3 b g Mizzen Mast(USA) Bahia Gold (USA) (Woodman (USA))
*(585a)*
**Gladstone (IRE)** *Jeremy Gask* a50 33
6 b g Dansili Rockerlong (Deploy)
*6682[8]* *7360[14]*
**Glanely (IRE)** *Martyn Meade* a82 78
4 b g Exceed And Excel(AUS) Bon Ton Roulet (Hawk Wing (USA))
*372[6]* *2059[2]* 5536[5]
**Glan Lady (IRE)** *Ian Williams* a45 45
8 b m Court Cave(IRE) Vanished (IRE) (Fayruz)
*1745[6]*
**Glaring** *A Fabre* 106
3 b c Champs Elysees Brightest (Rainbow Quest (USA))
3290a[4] 6183a[2] 6954a[6]
**Glasgon** *Declan Carroll* a35 50
4 gr g Verglas(IRE) Miss St Tropez (Danehill Dancer (IRE))
2021[8] *6715[10]*
**Glasgow Central** *Charles Hills* 78
3 b g Rail Link Musical Key (Key Of Luck (USA))
1582[6] 2075[3] 2418[4] 4168[7] 6714[6]
**Glasgow Gailes (USA)** *K R Burke* 74
2 b c Exchange Rate(USA) Copper Beauty (USA) (Deputy Commander (USA))
4740[7] (5212)
**Glasgow Kiss (IRE)** *John Patrick Shanahan* 58
3 b f The Carbon Unit(USA) Green Glen (IRE) (Hawk Wing (USA))
4299[3] (Dead)
**Glass Office** *David Simcock* a81 110
4 gr c Verglas(IRE) Oval Office (Pursuit Of Love)
809a[6]
**Glastonberry** *Geoffrey Deacon* a85 52
6 gr m Piccolo Elderberry (Bin Ajwaad (IRE))
*233[2]* *714[12]* *(820)* *1554[10]* 2435[8] *3581[5]* *8320[6]*
**Gleaming Girl** *David Simcock* a75 44
2 b f Arabian Gleam Desert Liaison (Dansili)
5344[9] *5821[5]* *6605[5]* *(7849)* *(8091)*
**Gleaming Princess** *Milton Bradley* a13 2
2 b f Arabian Gleam Hansomis (IRE) (Titus Livius (FR))
*5896[7]* 6363[7] *7421[11]*
**Glebe Spirit (IRE)** *Richard Hannon* a67 78
3 b c Invincible Spirit(IRE) Starry Messenger (Galileo (IRE))
*1769[3]* 3037[8] 3316[2] (3559)
**Glee (GER)** *Jean-Pierre Carvalho* 97
4 b f Dansili Guadalupe (GER) (Monsun (GER))
6162a[8]
**Gleese The Devil (IRE)** *Richard Fahey* a79 83
3 br g Manduro(GER) Causeway Song (USA) (Giant's Causeway (USA))
4130[12] 4705[2] 6118[3] 7162[2] *7689[5]*

**Glenalmond (IRE)** *K R Burke* 107
2 b c Iffraaj Balladonia (Primo Dominie)
(4486) ◆ 5692$^4$ ◆ 6326$^6$

**Glenard** *Charles Hills* a94 100
4 b g Arch(USA) Olaya (USA) (Theatrical (IRE))
1213$^6$ 2073$^5$ 2561$^9$ 3717$^8$ 4144$^3$ 4696$^3$ (5651) 6133$^5$ 6747$^7$

**Glenbuck Lass (IRE)** *Alan Bailey* a53
2 gr f Dandy Man(IRE) Certainlei (IRE) (Definite Article)
6158$^7$ 7062$^{10}$ 7881$^5$

**Gleneagles (IRE)** *A P O'Brien* 116
2 b c Galileo(IRE) You'resothrilling (USA) (Storm Cat (USA))
(4599a) (5735a) ◆ (6373a) 6968a$^3$

**Gleneely Girl (IRE)** *Rae Guest* a49 72
2 b f Intense Focus(USA) Timber Tops (UAE) (Timber Country (USA))
3304$^2$ 4018$^2$ (4701) 5626$^3$ 8174$^6$

**Glenleven (USA)** *S Seemar* a93
6 br g Forest Wildcat(USA) Miss Adorable (USA) (Mr Prospector (USA))
241a$^{11}$

**Glenlini** *Jim Goldie* a28 62
8 b m Bertolini(USA) Glenhurich (IRE) (Sri Pekan (USA))
688$^{10}$

**Glen Moss (IRE)** *David Brown* a103 107
5 b h Moss Vale(IRE) Sail With The Wind (Saddlers' Hall (IRE))
1576$^2$ (1719) 2145$^2$ 3452$^9$ ◆ 4200$^8$ 5653$^3$ 6522$^7$

**Glennten** *Jose Santos* a78 68
5 b g Ishiguru(USA) Uplifting (Magic Ring (IRE))
121$^8$ 251$^4$ 274$^8$ 370$^6$ 1386$^6$ (1836) 2212$^2$ (3115) (4326) 4582$^2$ 5560$^4$ 5756$^6$ (6161) 6341$^5$ 7001$^3$ (7219) 7358$^5$ 7568$^3$ 8073$^9$ 8162$^3$

**Glenridding** *James Given* a68 66
10 b g Averti(IRE) Appelone (Emperor Jones (USA))
562$^9$ 996$^9$

**Glen's Diamond** *Richard Fahey* 114
6 b g Intikhab(USA) Posta Vecchia (USA) (Rainbow Quest (USA))
2315$^8$

**Glens Wobbly** *Jonathan Geake* a52 61
6 ch g Kier Park(IRE) Wobbly (Atraf)
2252$^7$ 2923$^4$ (2942) 3852$^7$ 4107$^5$ 4568$^5$ (5597) 5904$^6$ (6027) 7419$^7$

**Global City (IRE)** *S Seemar* a90 71
8 b h Exceed And Excel(AUS) Victory Peak (Shirley Heights)
240a$^7$

**Global Explorer (USA)** *Stuart Williams* a69 48
3 b g Henrythenavigator(USA) Trulips (USA) (Elusive Quality (USA))
(15) 315$^3$ 401$^3$ ◆ 429$^2$ 667$^3$ (745) 957$^4$

**Global Force (IRE)** *Saeed bin Suroor* a47 82
2 b g Shamardal(USA) Pioneer Bride (USA) (Gone West (USA))
7371$^7$ 7667$^2$

**Global Leader (IRE)** *Paul D'Arcy* a74 84
4 b g Dark Angel(IRE) Headborough Lass (IRE) (Invincible Spirit (IRE))
40$^6$ (1631) (1813) 1930$^3$ 2884$^2$ 3160$^2$ (4090) (4588)

**Global Thrill** *Bernard Llewellyn* a87 107
5 b g Big Shuffle(USA) Goonda (Darshaan)
1478a$^6$ 2245a$^7$ 2715a$^9$ 5755$^6$ 6748$^8$

**Global View (USA)** *Thomas F Proctor* a69 106
3 bb c Galileo(IRE) Egyptian Queen (USA) (Storm Cat (USA))
3994a$^7$ 5458a$^4$

**Global Village (IRE)** *Brian Ellison* a69 104
9 b g Dubai Destination(USA) Zelding (IRE) (Warning)
887$^{11}$ 1164$^9$ 1715$^4$ 2253$^{13}$

**Glorious Asset** *Ed Walker* a71
2 b c Aqlaam Regal Asset (USA) (Regal Classic (CAN))
7742$^7$ 8201$^3$

**Glorious Dancer** *Ed Walker* a65 14
2 br c Royal Applause Provence (Averti (IRE))
7329$^9$ 7712$^{12}$ 7840$^5$ 8317$^2$

**Glorious Days (AUS)** *J Size* 122
7 br g Hussonet(USA) San Century (NZ) (Centaine (AUS))
2004a$^4$ 8153a$^5$

**Glorious Dubai (IRE)** *Saeed bin Suroor*
2 ch c Monsun(GER) Mandellicht (IRE) (Be My Guest (USA))
6630$^P$ (Dead)

**Glorious Empire (IRE)** *Ed Walker* a89 106
3 br g Holy Roman Emperor(IRE) Humble And Proud (IRE) (Pivotal)
(1390) 3352$^{16}$ (4169) 4647$^4$ (5348)

**Glorious Magic (IRE)** *Olly Stevens* a64
2 bb c Zebedee Sharplaw Destiny (IRE) (Petardia)
5278$^2$ 6190$^6$ 6268$^{11}$

**Glorious Protector (IRE)** *Ed Walker* a96 109
4 b g Azamour(IRE) Hasaiyda (IRE) (Hector Protector (USA))
1299$^3$ ◆ 2142$^9$ (4204) (5688) 6546$^4$ 7447$^5$

**Glorious Star (IRE)** *Ed Walker* a73 78
4 ch g Soviet Star(USA) Caerlonore (IRE) (Traditionally (USA))
1498$^3$ (2095) 2527$^3$ 3272$^7$

**Glorious Sun** *Ed Walker* a87 78
3 b g Medicean Sweet Cando (IRE) (Royal Applause)
4407$^3$ 5195$^2$ 5831$^5$ (6661) 7634$^2$ 7852$^5$

**Glory Awaits (IRE)** *Kevin Ryan* a101 112
4 ch c Choisir(AUS) Sandbox Two (IRE) (Foxhound (USA))
1176a$^{13}$ 3317$^7$ (4187) 4758$^6$ 5653$^2$ (6185a)

**Gm Hopkins** *John Gosden* 108
3 b g Dubawi(IRE) Varsity (Lomitas)
(1395) (6301) (6713) ◆ 7081$^4$ 7668$^3$

**Goadby** *John Holt* a57 66
3 gr f Kodiac Gone Sailing (Mizzen Mast (USA))
1449$^6$ 2553$^2$ 3231$^4$ 3966$^2$ (4532) 4891$^6$ 5777$^9$ 7621$^9$ 7997$^{10}$

**Goal (IRE)** *Charles Smith* a76 68
6 b g Mujadil(USA) Classic Lin (FR) (Linamix (FR))
23$^7$ 29$^7$

**Goal Keeper (AUS)** *T Kieser* a101 101
6 b g Untouchable(AUS) My Cousin Rachel (AUS) (Kampala)
2378a$^8$

**Go Amwell** *J R Jenkins* a45 33
11 b g Kayf Tara Daarat Alayaam (IRE) (Reference Point)
455$^7$ 657$^6$ 1284$^4$

**Goathland (IRE)** *Peter Chapple-Hyam* 66
2 b c Teofilo(IRE) Royals Special (IRE) (Caerleon (USA))
7560$^6$

**Go Charlie** *Lisa Williamson* a41 51
3 b g Myboycharlie(IRE) Branston Gem (So Factual (USA))
923$^5$ 1569$^8$ 2838$^6$ 2932$^5$ 3214$^5$ 3564$^2$ 3816$^2$ 4101$^4$ 4816$^2$ 5034$^3$ 5905$^5$ 6090$^4$ 8024$^8$ 8229$^8$ 8286$^{11}$

**Go Complain** *Alan McCabe*
2 b f Mount Nelson Trounce (Barathea (IRE))
5416$^{14}$

**Go Dan Go (IRE)** *Keith Dalgleish* 62
2 b c Dandy Man(IRE) Without Words (Lion Cavern (USA))
5852$^3$ 6509$^8$ 7054$^3$

**Goddess Of Gloom** *Peter Chapple-Hyam* 57
3 br f Firebreak Charcoal (Primo Valentino (IRE))
2489$^9$ 2780$^{14}$ 3229$^4$ 4047$^6$

**Godric** *Tom Dascombe* a68 30
2 ch c Winker Watson Bea Menace (USA) (Mizzen Mast (USA))
2928$^4$ 3394$^8$ 3847$^8$

**God's Speed (IRE)** *Rae Guest* a91 83
3 b g Oratorio(IRE) Guilia (Galileo (IRE))
127$^2$ (515) 721a$^3$ 1419$^5$ 1883$^3$ 3419$^{10}$ 6106$^8$ 6566$^4$ 6839$^3$

**God Willing** *Ed Dunlop* a102 101
3 b c Arch(USA) Bourbon Ball (USA) (Peintre Celebre (USA))
1580$^4$ 4127$^5$ 5656$^{11}$ 6519$^2$ 6752$^{31}$ 7119$^4$ 7490$^2$ 7801$^3$

**Godwit** *Eugene Stanford* a36
6 b m Noverre(USA) Hen Harrier (Polar Falcon (USA))
6076$^8$

**Go Far** *Alan Bailey* a106 103
4 b g Dutch Art Carranita (IRE) (Anita's Prince)
161$^3$ 286$^6$ 389$^2$ 496$^5$ (913) 925$^2$ (1031) 1212$^5$ 1742$^7$ 1975$^8$ 2562$^9$ 2919$^3$ 3479$^4$ 4128$^4$ 4317$^2$ (4765) (5419) (6159) 6327$^6$ 6533$^{18}$ 7700$^5$

**Go For Broke** *Richard Hannon* a78 73
3 ch c Assertive Level Pegging (IRE) (Common Grounds)
2278$^{11}$ 3037$^{10}$ 3145$^4$ (3516) 4654$^3$ 5314$^3$ 6070$^{11}$ (7013)

**Go For Goal (IRE)** *D K Weld* 109
3 gr g Verglas(IRE) Triple Try (IRE) (Sadler's Wells (USA))
(1200a)

**Go Gently (IRE)** *George Baker* a48 53
2 ch g Zebedee Playful (Piccolo)
1349$^9$ 2151$^6$ 5278$^4$ 6248$^2$ 6888$^7$

**Gogeo (IRE)** *Alan Swinbank* a86 87
7 b g Val Royal(FR) Steal 'Em (Efisio)
(385) (763)

**Gogglebox** *Tom Dascombe*
2 ch f Nayef(USA) Looby Loo (Kyllachy)
4499$^{14}$

**Go Glamorous (IRE)** *Ronald Harris* a71 71
3 b f Elnadim(USA) Glamorous Air (IRE) (Air Express (IRE))
3484$^4$ 3817$^6$ 4891$^{10}$ 5724$^4$ 6029$^7$

**Go Go Green (IRE)** *Jim Goldie* a64 78
8 b g Acclamation Preponderance (IRE) (Cyrano De Bergerac)
1440$^6$ 1695$^7$ 2350$^{14}$ 2456$^5$ (2732) 3006$^4$ 3239$^4$ 3952$^6$ 4256$^6$ 5081$^5$ 5170$^4$ 5236$^3$ (5498) 6013$^{11}$ 6512$^8$ 7103$^7$ 7535$^{11}$

**Go Grazeon** *John Quinn* a49 49
2 ch f Monsieur Bond(IRE) Graze On And On (Elmaamul (USA))
7278$^F$ 7713$^4$ 7911$^5$

**Goiania** *P Schiergen* 98
3 b f Oasis Dream Goathemala (GER) (Black Sam Bellamy (IRE))
1619a$^7$ (7483a)

**Going French (IRE)** *Grace Harris* a76 51
7 ch g Frenchmans Bay(FR) Easy Going (Hamas (IRE))
2890$^7$ 3393$^{11}$ 5602$^6$ 5897$^4$ 6368$^4$

**Going Somewhere (BRZ)** *D Smaga* 116
5 ch h Sulamani(IRE) Angel Star (BRZ) (Special Nash (IRE))
1784a$^{10}$ 2819a$^P$ 4250a$^3$ 5224a$^3$ 5962a$^3$ 6383a$^7$ 6972a$^7$

**Goken (FR)** *H-A Pantall* 108
2 b c Kendargent(FR) Gooseley Chope (FR) (Indian Rocket)
1094a$^2$ (3806a) 4482a$^4$ 5741a$^4$ 6966a$^{11}$ 7655a$^3$

**Golan Guy (IRE)** *Sean Curran* 57
9 b g Golan(IRE) Countess Marengo (IRE) (Revoque (IRE))
7452$^{10}$

**Goldan Jess (IRE)** *Philip Kirby* a60 72
10 b g Golan(IRE) Bendis (GER) (Danehill (USA))
4076$^7$ 4962$^{13}$

**Gold Approach** *William Haggas* a70 83
3 ch f New Approach(IRE) Samira Gold (FR) (Gold Away (IRE))
1427$^3$ (2466) 3419$^7$ 4452$^5$

**Gold Beau (FR)** *Kristin Stubbs* a78 83
4 b g Gold Away(IRE) Theorie (FR) (Anabaa (USA))
925$^4$ 1217$^2$ 1610$^9$ 2059$^7$ 2602$^7$ 3359$^3$ 3599$^5$ (4194) 4383$^4$ (4724) 5766$^8$ 6263$^{12}$ 6511$^{21}$ 6824$^6$

**Gold Chain (IRE)** *Dianne Sayer* a39 70
4 b f Authorized(IRE) Mountain Chain (USA) (Royal Academy (USA))
1247$^4$ 1510$^7$ 2872$^6$ 3301$^7$ 3958$^6$ (4015) 4726$^6$ 4962$^5$ 6113$^7$ 7100$^3$

**Gold City (IRE)** *S Seemar* a112 82
5 b g Pivotal Storm Lily (USA) (Storm Cat (USA))
112a$^{12}$ 396a$^2$ (768a) 899a$^5$ 1176a$^4$

**Gold Class** *Ed McMahon* a62 56
3 ch g Firebreak Silken Dalliance (Rambo Dancer (CAN))
1683$^9$ 2028$^5$ 2393$^{13}$ (3407) 5267$^4$

**Gold Club** *Ed McMahon* a50 69
3 b g Multiplex Oceana Blue (Reel Buddy (USA))
2015$^3$ ◆ 2429$^5$ 3225$^7$ 4059$^4$ 4565$^3$ 6029$^4$

**Goldcrest** *Henry Candy* 88
2 ch f Assertive Level Pegging (IRE) (Common Grounds)
3076$^7$ (3888) 4646$^8$ 5879$^4$ (6989)

**Golden Amber (IRE)** *Dean Ivory* a93 93
3 b f Holy Roman Emperor(IRE) Time Of Gold (USA) (Banker's Gold (USA))
183$^4$ 624$^3$ 778$^5$ 1555$^{12}$ 1693$^2$ 2161$^5$ 7843$^{11}$ 8079$^3$

**Golden Beryl** *Mike Murphy*
2 b f Tobougg(IRE) Precise Lady (IRE) (Azamour (IRE))
8201$^8$

**Golden Bird (IRE)** *Dean Ivory* a70
3 b g Sinndar(IRE) Khamsin (USA) (Mr Prospector (USA))
5010$^7$ 5822$^4$ 6485$^6$ 7401$^4$ 7777$^4$ 8070$^4$ 8253$^5$

**Golden Bowl (FR)** *Ian Williams* 106
4 b g Turtle Bowl(IRE) Maid Of Dawkins (IRE) (Kendor (FR))
1736$^7$ 2073$^{16}$

**Goldenboy Delatour (FR)** *Marquise De Montaigu* a60
3 ch g Full Of Gold(FR) Palenka (FR) (Mister Sicy (FR))
8005a$^{12}$

**Goldencents (USA)** *Leandro Mora* a123
4 b c Into Mischief(USA) Golden Works (CAN) (Banker's Gold (USA))
(7591a)

**Golden Club (FR)** *N Caullery* a62 66
5 b g One Cool Cat(USA) Life On The Road (IRE) (Persian Heights)
5546a$^8$

**Golden Desert (IRE)** *Simon Dow* a75 77
10 b g Desert Prince(IRE) Jules (IRE) (Danehill (USA))
52$^5$ 310$^6$ 451$^6$ 603$^5$

**Golden Emerald** *Mike Murphy* a81 74
3 b g Peintre Celebre(USA) Flying Finish (FR) (Priolo (USA))
5039$^4$ 5504$^4$ 7157$^5$ 7733$^3$

**Golden Future** *Peter Niven* a48 65
11 b g Muhtarram(USA) Nazca (Zilzal (USA))
1605$^{13}$ 2512$^6$ 3482$^9$ 4856$^4$ 5146$^7$ 6117$^{10}$

**Golden Groom** *Patrick Holmes* a6 50
11 b g Groom Dancer(USA) Reine De Thebes (FR) (Darshaan)
7591$^2$

**Golden Guepard (IRE)** *A Fabre* 108
3 b c Hurricane Run(IRE) Grey Lilas (IRE) (Danehill (USA))
1965a$^4$ 4251a$^7$

**Golden Harvest (AUS)** *A T Millard* 112
6 b g Al Maher(AUS) Marzipan (NZ) (Gold Brose (AUS))
7897a$^4$ 8152a$^5$

**Golden Horn** *John Gosden* 83
2 b c Cape Cross(IRE) Fleche D'Or (Dubai Destination (USA))
(7537) ◆

**Golden Journey (IRE)** *Clive Cox* a79 78
3 ch c Nayef(USA) Beatrix Potter (IRE) (Cadeaux Genereux)
1655$^9$ (3421) 4332$^6$ 5552$^4$ 6239$^5$ 6654$^6$

**Golden Jubilee (USA)** *Nigel Twiston-Davies* a79 76
5 bb g Zavata(USA) Love Play (USA) (Friendly Lover (USA))
641$^3$ 782$^4$ 1355$^6$ 2300$^9$ 3617$^2$ (5002) 5621$^2$ 6264$^3$ 6367$^2$

**Goldenrod** *Ralph Beckett* 79
3 b g Pivotal Prairie Flower (IRE) (Zieten (USA))
1984$^7$ 2773$^{13}$ 4168$^4$

**Golden Spear** *Noel Quinlan* 83
3 ch c Kyllachy Penmayne (Inchinor)
1400$^6$ ◆ 1725$^7$ (2391) 2968$^4$ 5849$^3$ 7043$^4$

**Golden Spun (USA)** *Bryan Smart* 78
2 bb g Hard Spun(USA) Scarlet's Tara (USA) (Goodbye Doeny (USA))
3827$^4$ 5655$^{15}$ (5995) 6427$^3$ (6977)

**Golden Steps (FR)** *Marco Botti* a98 102
3 b g Footstepsinthesand Kocooning (IRE) (King's Best (USA))
(1634) 2611$^2$ (3271) 4166$^3$ 4669$^6$ 5165$^2$ 6893$^4$ 7441$^6$ 7802$^4$

**Golden Ticket (USA)** *Kenneth McPeek* a118 88
5 bb h Speightstown(USA) Business Plan (USA) (Deputy Minister (CAN))
7591a$^8$

**Golden Town (IRE)** *Saeed bin Suroor* 107
3 b g Invincible Spirit(IRE) Princesse Dansante (IRE) (King's Best (USA))
1436$^8$ 1954$^5$ (4198) 4916$^2$

**Golden Wedding (IRE)** *Eve Johnson Houghton* a71 61
2 b g Archipenko(USA) Peace Lily (Dansili)
2928$^3$ ◆ 4207$^5$ 4731$^4$ 6064$^9$

**Golden Zephyr (IRE)** *B W Hills* a67 70
2 ch f Tamayuz Anyaas (IRE) (Green Desert (USA))
2107$^4$ 2918$^3$ 3706$^3$ 4686$^6$

**Goldfellow** *Peter Chapple-Hyam* 30
3 b g Winker Watson Nedwa (In The Wings)
1634$^7$ 2655$^9$

**Gold Flash** *Ralph Beckett* a75
2 b g Kheleyf(USA) My Golly (Mozart (IRE))
(8092)

**Gold-Fun (IRE)** *R Gibson* 120
5 ch g Le Vie Dei Colori Goodwood March (Foxhound (USA))
2004a$^5$ 7898a$^2$ 8153a$^2$

**Gold Leaf** *John E Long* a33
2 ch f Kheleyf(USA) Lefty's Dollbaby (USA) (Brocco (USA))
8191$^{10}$ 8318$^9$

**Goldmadchen (GER)** *James Given* a61 56
6 b m Ivan Denisovich(IRE) Goldkatze (GER) (Czaravich (USA))
303$^5$ 474$^3$ (640) (959) 1132$^2$ 1249$^3$ 1453$^3$ 1740$^3$ 2199$^{11}$ 7823$^9$ 8145$^{11}$

**Gold Pearl (USA)** *S Seemar* a102 62
6 br h Henny Hughes(USA) Gold Pattern (USA) (Slew O'Gold (USA))
509a$^{16}$

**Gold Prince (IRE)** *Sylvester Kirk* 81
2 b c Nayef(USA) Premier Prize (Selkirk (USA))
5093$^4$ 5847$^4$ (6293)

**Gold Pursuit** *Alan Swinbank* 78
2 br g Pastoral Pursuits Goldeva (Makbul)
1955$^4$ 6489$^2$ 7004$^4$

**Goldream** *Robert Cowell* a85 109
5 br g Oasis Dream Clizia (IRE) (Machiavellian (USA))
(1975) 2778$^4$ 3927$^3$ 4683$^2$ (5160) 6327$^4$ 6745$^2$

**Gold Run** *Olly Stevens* 66
3 b g Hurricane Run(IRE) Trick (IRE) (Shirley Heights)
4407$^8$ 6611$^3$ 7304$^8$

**Gold Sands (IRE)** *James Tate* a76
2 b f Cape Cross(IRE) Lil's Jessy (IRE) (Kris)
7399$^3$

**Gold Ship (JPN)** *Naosuke Sugai* 125
5 gr h Stay Gold(JPN) Point Flag (JPN) (Mejiro McQueen (JPN))
2002a$^7$ 6970a$^{14}$

**Gold Show** *Edwin Tuer* 75
5 gr m Sir Percy Pearl Bright (FR) (Kaldoun (FR))
1362$^3$

**Goldslinger (FR)** *Dean Ivory* 26
2 b g Gold Away(IRE) Singaporette (FR) (Sagacity (FR))
3193$^7$ 3536$^8$

**Goldstorm** *Brian Baugh* a73 86
6 ch m Storming Home Antonia Bertolini (Bertolini (USA))
1744$^4$ 2117$^{10}$ 3272$^{12}$ 5176$^9$ 5528$^9$ 6057$^{11}$

**Gold Struck** *John Gosden* 75
3 br c Raven's Pass(USA) Love The Rain (Rainbow Quest (USA))
3432$^6$

**Goldtara (FR)** *A Lyon* a86 111
6 ch m Gold Away(IRE) Diatara (FR) (Sillery (USA))
1784a$^4$ 2588a$^2$ 4250a$^6$ 6383a$^9$

**Gold Trail (IRE)** *Charlie Appleby* a90 93
3 ch c Teofilo(IRE) Goldthroat (IRE) (Zafonic (USA))
2496$^2$ 2982$^3$ 3379$^9$ 4448$^2$ 8266$^5$

**Gold Waltz** *Ralph Beckett* a71 63
2 b f Acclamation Corps De Ballet (IRE) (Fasliyev (USA))
1528$^{11}$ (2436) 3415$^{20}$ 4345$^6$ (5043) 6104$^2$ 7201$^4$

**Gold Weight** *Michael Madgwick* a42
4 ch g Denounce Jewel (IRE) (Cyrano De Bergerac)
251$^{12}$

**Gold Will (IRE)** *Ralph Beckett* a73
2 b c Invincible Spirit(IRE) Ermine And Velvet (Nayef (USA))
6604$^2$ ◆ 7030$^2$

**Goldy Espony (FR)** *Chad C Brown* a85 108
3 rg f Vespone(IRE) Goldy Honor (FR) (Highest Honor (FR))
721a$^5$ (1502a) 2586a$^6$ 3995a$^6$

**Goleador (USA)** *Marco Botti* a21 17
3 b g English Channel(USA) Stormin' Home (USA) (Storm Cat (USA))
670$^3$ 1588$^{13}$ 1858$^2$ 2998$^{10}$

**Golfa (SPA)** *R Avial Lopez* 28
2 b f Hannouma(IRE) Gold Classic (FR) (Mizzen Mast (USA))
4882a$^{12}$

**Golly Miss Molly** *Jeremy Gask* a64 45
3 b f Exceed And Excel(AUS) Amicable Terms (Royal Applause)
1833$^4$ 2931$^5$ 3528$^2$ 4611$^6$ 4969$^{10}$ 5832$^3$ 6267$^7$ 6939$^8$ 7292$^3$ 7845$^6$ 8011$^3$ (8074) (8246)

**Gomati** *Matthieu Palussiere* 100
2 b c Oasis Dream Gracefully (IRE) (Orpen (USA))
5740a$^9$ 7069a$^4$

**Go Nani Go** *Ed de Giles* a86 91
8 b g Kyllachy Go Between (Daggers Drawn (USA))
1145$^2$ (1566) 2074$^5$ 3239$^{16}$ 4128$^9$ 4609$^9$ 5350$^5$ 6235$^{14}$

**Gone Dutch** *James Fanshawe* a94 90
4 ch g Dutch Art Ice Palace (Polar Falcon (USA))
1439$^2$ ◆ 2309$^7$ 3196$^7$ (3582) 5440$^6$ 6106$^2$ 7289$^8$

**Goneinaminute** *Tony Coyle* 58
2 b f Bushranger(IRE) Nevada Princess (IRE) (Desert Prince (IRE))
6694$^5$ 7174$^{12}$

**Gone With The Wind (GER)** *Jeremy Noseda* a77 61
3 b c Dutch Art Gallivant (Danehill (USA))
(284) (926) 1350$^7$ 6020$^7$ 6680$^3$ ◆ 7403$^7$

**Goninodaethat** *Jim Goldie* 72
6 b g Proclamation(IRE) Big Mystery (IRE) (Grand Lodge (USA))
1758$^5$ (2451) 2914$^8$ (3054) 3102$^7$ 4003$^6$ (4256) 4487$^5$ 5236$^5$ 6477$^{11}$ 6835$^{11}$ 7057$^{12}$

**Gonna Run (FR)** *J-C Rouget* a99 111
3 b c Hurricane Cat(USA) Realdad (ARG) (Victory Speech (USA))
2818a$^5$

**Good Authority (IRE)** *Victor Dartnall* a86 89
7 b g Chineur(FR) Lady Alexander (IRE) (Night Shift (USA))
1492[6] 2156[5] 2684[4] 3180[3] 3753[4] 4181[6] 5308[2] 6144[3] 6424[2] 6891[8] 7403[3] 7601[3] (7888) 8141[6]
**Good Boy Alex** *Alan Berry*
2 gr c Arabian Gleam Animal Cracker (Primo Dominie)
7503[6]
**Good Boy Jackson** *R Mike Smith* a5 71
6 b g Firebreak Fisher Island (IRE) (Sri Pekan (USA))
1760[6] 2477[8]
**Goodby Inheritence** *Seamus Durack* a58
2 b c Medicean Chili Dip (Alhaarth (IRE))
7371[11] 7985[5]
**Good Contact (USA)** *Saeed bin Suroor* 93
2 b c Teofilo(IRE) Mayoress (Machiavellian (USA))
4167[2] (5201) 6004[2] 6784[2]
**Good Deal (FR)** *J Merienne*
2 bb g Kingsalsa(USA) Good To Win (FR) (Hurricane Run (IRE))
(8212a)
**Good Donna (GER)** *J Hirschberger* 104
3 b f Doyen(IRE) Good Harmony (King's Best (USA))
(7482a)
**Good Hope** *Michael Bell* 78
3 b f Cape Cross(IRE) Fairy Godmother (Fairy King (USA))
3277[6] (4092)
**Good Judge (USA)** *Saeed bin Suroor* 28
2 rg c Cape Cross(IRE) Summer Fete (IRE) (Pivotal)
6702[10]
**Good Luck Charm** *Gary Moore* a82 85
5 b g Doyen(IRE) Lucky Dice (Perugino (USA))
1871[6] 2500[4] 3036[10] 3314[4] 3879[5] 5031[4] 5986[7] (6657) 7375[5] 7729[4] 8080[9] 8251[10]
**Goodlukin Lucy** *Keith Dalgleish* a59 56
7 ch m Supreme Sound Suka Ramai (Nashwan (USA))
176[6] 1117[4] 1567[6]
**Good Move (IRE)** *Brian Rothwell* 36
2 b f Aussie Rules(USA) Lady Lafitte (USA) (Stravinsky (USA))
5813[7] 7084[12] 7495[12]
**Goodnightsuzy (IRE)** *Ed Walker* 79
2 b f Azamour(IRE) Suzy Bliss (Spinning World (USA))
6093[4] (6701) ◆
**Good Of Luck** *Warren Greatrex* a41 71
5 b g Authorized(IRE) Oops Pettie (Machiavellian (USA))
322[6]
**Good Place (USA)** *Saeed bin Suroor* 94
2 ch f Street Cry(IRE) Causeway Lass (AUS) (Giant's Causeway (USA))
4403[2] (5424) (6126) 7240[7]
**Good Speech (IRE)** *Tom Tate* a63 80
4 ch f Haatef(USA) Privileged Speech (USA) (General Assembly (USA))
2259[9] 3699[8] 4710[7] 4979[4] 6062[8] 6672[8]
**Good To Remember** *Ruth Carr*
3 ch f Shami Mandarin Lady (Timeless Times (USA))
4365[5] 5198[7]
**Good Value** *Sir Michael Stoute* a86 87
3 ch g Champs Elysees Change Course (Sadler's Wells (USA))
1353[7] (1765) ◆ 2009[2] 2685[2] 4183[6] 4698[4] 5720[8]
**Goodwood Mirage (IRE)** *Jonjo O'Neill* 103
4 b g Jeremy(USA) Phantom Waters (Pharly (FR))
6133[15]
**Goodwood Moonlight** *William Knight* a59
2 b g Azamour(IRE) Corrine (IRE) (Spectrum (IRE))
7730[10] 7926[4]
**Goodwood Storm** *William Knight* a73 76
3 ch f Shamardal(USA) Artifice (Green Desert (USA))
1832[5] ◆ 2647[3] 4329[10] 4654[2] 5181[3] (6437) 7352[5]
**Goodyearforroses (IRE)** *Rae Guest* 79
2 b f Azamour(IRE) Guilia (Galileo (IRE))
(7018) ◆
**Goolagong Girl (IRE)** *Jane Chapple-Hyam* a55 58
2 b f Avonbridge Lady Berta (Bertolini (USA))
2918[9] 3381[4] 4301[6] 5489[5] 5823[7] 6842[2] 7425[4] 8115[12]
**Go On Chas** *Ian Semple* 49
2 b g Myboycharlie(IRE) Dead Womans Pass (IRE) (High Chaparral (IRE))
3049[5] 4253[7] 4723[5]
**Gordol Du Mes (USA)** *Gianluca Bietolini* 91
4 ch c Exchange Rate(USA) Twinkle Twinkle (USA) (Arazi (USA))
2375a[8]
**Gordon Lord Byron (IRE)** *T Hogan* a110 121
6 b g Byron Boa Estrela (IRE) (Intikhab (USA))
(1186a) 1468a[6] 2004a[7] 3451[8] 5699a[2] 6134[2] 6352a[3] 6971a[2] (7272) 8152a[4]
**Goring (GER)** *Eve Johnson Houghton* a75 75
2 b c Areion(GER) Globuli (GER) (Surako (GER))
2298[6] 2642[3] 3322[19] 5271[3] 6229[2] 6925[10] (7573)
**Go Sakhee** *Roger Varian* a67 86
3 br g Sakhee's Secret Bling Bling (IRE) (Indian Ridge)
2805[4] (3316) 4120[5] 5108[3] (5768) 6303[2]
**Gosh (IRE)** *Mme Pia Brandt* a76 104
4 ch f Peintre Celebre(USA) Ragazza Mio (IRE) (Generous (IRE))
2106a[4]
**Gospel Choir** *Sir Michael Stoute* 116
5 ch g Galileo(IRE) Chorist (Pivotal)
1533[4] ◆ (1950) (2315)
**Got Breizh (FR)** *J Heloury* a73 74
3 b g Footstepsinthesand Hideaway Girl (Fasliyev (USA))
751a[10] 4838a[7]
**Gotcha** *James Bethell* 69
3 bl f Fair Mix(IRE) Shazana (Key Of Luck (USA))
2389[2] 3664[7] 4513[4]
**Got Fly (FR)** *C Ferland* a103 103
3 b c Early March Gotdream (FR) (Loup Solitaire (USA))
(169a)
**Gothic** *Sir Michael Stoute* 95
3 b g Danehill Dancer(IRE) Riberac (Efisio)
1702[4] 2481[2] 3243[9] 3986[4] (5203) 6127[5] 6756[5]
**Gothic Dance (IRE)** *B Grizzetti* 99
5 ch m Dalakhani(IRE) Future Flight (Polar Falcon (USA))
(7604a)
**Got Lucky (USA)** *Todd Pletcher* a102
3 bb f A.P. Indy(USA) Malka (USA) (Deputy Minister (CAN))
6973a[5]
**Gottcher** *Ian Semple* a53 79
6 b g Fasliyev(USA) Danalia (IRE) (Danehill (USA))
3191[12] 3611[10] 4521[6] 5601[9] 6109[9]
**Got To Dance** *Ralph Beckett* a73 72
3 b f Selkirk(USA) Mullein (Oasis Dream)
1381[3] 2278[4] 2717[5] 3790[4]
**Got To Dream** *Mark Johnston* a75 85
3 b f Duke Of Marmalade(IRE) Lady Of Everest (IRE) (Montjeu (IRE))
(5301) ◆ 5552[8] 5914[6] 6321[7]
**Govinda (USA)** *Hans-Inge Larsen* a70 102
7 bb g Pulpit(USA) Garden In The Rain (FR) (Dolphin Street (FR))
3996a[10] 4957a[8]
**Gowanharry (IRE)** *Michael Dods* 85
5 ch m Choisir(AUS) Aahgowangowan (IRE) (Tagula (IRE))
1850[DSQ] 2456[3] 3006[2] 4488[3] 5170[2] 5498[10] 6763[12]
**Gower Princess** *Ronald Harris* a66 63
3 ch f Footstepsinthesand Hollow Quaill (IRE) (Entrepreneur)
2943[5] 3588[7] 6029[5] 6297[6]
**Go White Lightning (IRE)** *Malcolm Saunders* a43 55
2 br f Lord Shanakill(USA) Ghurra (USA) (War Chant (USA))
2246[4] 3173[5] 3558[10] 4364[6] 6413[9] 6676[6]
**Gown (IRE)** *Charles Hills* a83 83
3 b f Excellent Art Chehalis Sunset (Danehill Dancer (IRE))
3890[2] 4163[2] 4436[9] 5826[2] 6302[4]
**Grace And Favour** *Andrew Balding* a70 74
3 b f Montjeu(IRE) Gryada (Shirley Heights)
1701[4] 2299[8] 3174[4] 4051[5]
**Gracefilly** *Ed Walker* a68 44
3 b f Invincible Spirit(IRE) Marula (IRE) (Sadler's Wells (USA))
4446[10] 5548[2] 6243[8] 6716[6] 7219[7] (7632) 7785[2] 8250[9]
**Graceful Act** *Ron Barr* a56 62
6 b m Royal Applause Minnina (IRE) (In The Wings)
(1309) 1673[5] 2219[8] 2427[3] 2954[4] 3846[6] 4294[10] 4795[11] 5337[9] (5773) 6628[6] 6863[7]
**Graceful Grit (IRE)** *F-H Graffard* 98
3 b f Holy Roman Emperor(IRE) Liu (IRE) (Top Ville)
3357[4] 4721a[6] 7319a[3] 7720a[4] 7857a[8]
**Graceful Willow** *John E Long* a2 17
4 b f Phoenix Reach(IRE) Opera Belle (Dr Fong (USA))
3074[9] 5831[13] 8098[4]
**Grace Hull** *Garry Moss* a71 73
4 gr f Piccolo Smart Hostess (Most Welcome)
59[2] 95[2] 273[2] (511) 766[5] 913[2] (1082) 4294[2] 5640[5] 6221[6] 6716[7]
**Graceland (FR)** *Michael Bell* 69
2 bb f Mastercraftsman(IRE) Jeunesse Lulu (IRE) (Montjeu (IRE))
5643[5] 6333[2] 7163a[4]
**Grace Of Love (IRE)** *J-C Rouget* a81
3 b f Lawman(FR) Rampoldina (Montjeu (IRE))
4952a[4]
**Gracia Directa (GER)** *D Moser* 105
6 b m Kyllachy Glyceria (IRE) (Common Grounds)
2006a[3] 2564[10]
**Gracie Hart** *Jo Hughes* a57 67
3 b f Sakhee's Secret Dictatrix (Diktat)
1767[4] 2316[14]
**Gracie's Games** *John Spearing* a49 59
8 b m Mind Games Little Kenny (Warning)
2831[5] 3935[8] (5000) 5247[2] 5777[6] 6272[5]
**Gracious George (IRE)** *Jimmy Fox* a78 76
4 b g Oratorio(IRE) Little Miss Gracie (Efisio)
286[3] 376[4] 825[3] 1142[5] 1682[3] 2012[6] 2684[5] 3180[7] 4549[3] 5096[3] 6303[3] 6523[6] 7552[6] 7831[4] (8068) 8248[8]
**Graciously** *A De Royer-Dupre* 90
3 b f Shamardal(USA) Gracefully (IRE) (Orpen (USA))
(7722a) 7857a[17]
**Graffiti Art** *Brendan Powell* a68 48
5 b m Kayf Tara Art Affair (GER) (Germany (USA))
4653[3] 5822[3] 6344[6]
**Grain De Beaute (IRE)** *Marco Gasparini* 85
3 b f Lawman(FR) Compradore (Mujtahid (USA))
1477a[7]
**Gramercy (IRE)** *David Simcock* a71 99
7 b g Whipper(USA) Topiary (IRE) (Selkirk (USA))
1719[12] 2145[5] 2503[5] 2758[10] 2984[3] 3212[4] 4212[13] 5189[4] 5623[8] 5750[2] 6089[4]
**Gran Canaria Queen** *Tim Easterby* a65 86
5 bb m Compton Place Ex Mill Lady (Bishop Of Cashel)
2297[6] 3191[5] 3659[2] (3952) 4471[2] 4902[3] 5444[8] 6013[3] 6511[11] 7085[8] 7505[4]
**Grandad Mac** *Alan Coogan* a69 68
6 b g Invincible Spirit(IRE) No Rehearsal (FR) (Baillamont (USA))
(33) 1174 (176) (252) 303[7] 476[3] 569[3]
**Grandad's World (IRE)** *Richard Fahey* 87
2 b c Kodiac Nose One's Way (IRE) (Revoque (IRE))
(5464) 6256[9]
**Grand Arch (USA)** *Brian A Lynch* 112
5 b g Arch(USA) Bacinella (USA) (El Gran Senor (USA))
6391a[5] 7613a[11]
**Grand Argentier (FR)** *Matthieu Palussiere* 69
2 b c Palace Episode(USA) Ashkadima (IRE) (Ashkalani (IRE))
3691a[6]
**Grand Beauty (IRE)** *Richard Fahey* 76
2 ch f Kheleyf(USA) Grand Zafeen (Zafeen (FR))
3394[2] 3909[2]
**Grand Canyon (IRE)** *Ralph Beckett* 71
2 b g High Chaparral(IRE) Cleide Da Silva (USA) (Monarchos (USA))
5745[2]
**Grand Depart** *James Bethell* 19
2 b f Royal Applause Path Of Peace (Rock Of Gibraltar (IRE))
6935[12]
**Grand Diamond (IRE)** *Jim Goldie* a53 66
10 b g Grand Lodge(USA) Winona (IRE) (Alzao (USA))
1763[6] 2216[10] 2512[4] 3051[3] 3657[4] 4015[3] 4259[5] 4492[3] 4856[3] 5171[2] 5567[3] 6113[5] 6480[9] 6832[9] 7059[8]
**Granddukeoftuscany (IRE)** *A P O'Brien* 100
3 b c Galileo(IRE) Crystal Valkyrie (IRE) (Danehill (USA))
5577[5] 6329[11]
**Grandest** *John Gosden* a82 84
3 b g Dansili Angara (Alzao (USA))
1390[6] 1861[7] 2936[4] 3428[3]
**Grandeur (IRE)** *Jeremy Noseda* a115 118
5 rg g Verglas(IRE) Misskinta (IRE) (Desert Sun)
(716) 1068[8] (1559) 2228a[3] 3025a[4] 4231a[2] (6655) 7243[12]
**Grandezza (GER)** *K Borgel* a61 74
4 b f Samum(GER) Grouper (USA) (Gone West (USA))
5546a[2]
**Grand Gold** *Seamus Durack* a63 76
5 b g Librettist(USA) Night Symphonie (Cloudings (IRE))
606[6] 747[4]
**Grandiloquent** *Brian Ellison* a70 69
5 b g Rail Link High Praise (USA) (Quest For Fame)
433[4] 609[6] (781) 872[4]
**Grand Jipeck (IRE)** *Brian Ellison* a21 20
4 b g Soviet Star(USA) Inourthoughts (IRE) (Desert Style (IRE))
1309[7] 1838[15]
**Grand Liaison** *James Given* a59 64
5 b m Sir Percy Dancinginthedark (IRE) (Fasliyev (USA))
2199[9] 2610[4] 4081[7] 4979[2] ◆ 5495[6] 6651[6] 6699[7]
**Grandma Dotty (IRE)** *C F Swan* a64 69
5 b m Hurricane Run(IRE) High Reef (FR) (Shareef Dancer (USA))
7435a[9]
**Grand Meister** *Michael Bell* a81 77
3 gr g Mastercraftsman(IRE) Wait It Out (USA) (Swain (IRE))
2221[3] 2685[4] 3396[4] 4547[8] (5302) 5552[6] 6665[5]
**Grand Oriente (ITY)** *Luciano Vitabile* 86
3 b c Blu Air Force(IRE) Iberian Dancer (CAN) (El Gran Senor (USA))
7604a[7]
**Grandorio (IRE)** *David O'Meara* a70 96
4 b g Oratorio(IRE) Grand Splendour (Shirley Heights)
2253[18] 2787[6] 3204[4] 4173[8] 4685[3] 5162[P]
**Grand Prix Boss (JPN)** *Yoshito Yahagi* a96 120
6 b h Sakura Bakushin O(JPN) Rosy Mist (JPN) (Sunday Silence (USA))
8153a[3]
**Grand Proposal** *Jim Boyle* a61 70
2 gr g Exceed And Excel(AUS) Si Belle (IRE) (Dalakhani (IRE))
3297[5] 3606[4] 3945[3] 4897[3] 5335[4] 6165[7] 6449[3] 6884[5] 7328[9] 7920[7] 8069[11] 8317[9]
**Grand Spirit (IRE)** *Luca Cumani* 86
2 b c Lord Shanakill(USA) Spirit Watch (IRE) (Invincible Spirit (IRE))
4129[7] 5029[2] (5947)
**Grand Vintage (FR)** *W Mongil* a102 97
5 b h Marchand De Sable(USA) Fifty Niner (FR) (Fijar Tango (FR))
6382a[8] 7437a[2]
**Granell (IRE)** *Brian Meehan* a72 82
4 ch g Excellent Art Granny Kelly (USA) (Irish River (FR))
1845[7] 2251[3] 2610[2] 2966[4] (3874)
**Gran Maestro (USA)** *Ruth Carr* a73 82
5 ch g Medicean Red Slippers (USA) (Nureyev (USA))
1377[7] 1644[6] 2168[2] ◆ 2327[3] 2547[3] (2730) 2947[4]
**Granny Alice** *Noel Quinlan* 70
2 b f Intikhab(USA) Tell Mum (Marju (IRE))
1528[7] (1900) 2313[8]
**Granola** *David Brown* a35 55
2 b f Makfi Common Knowledge (Rainbow Quest (USA))
5789[5] 6271[7] 7082[5] 7278[6] 7515[2] 7714[3]
**Graphene** *Rod Millman* a53 61
3 b g Nayef(USA) Annapurna (IRE) (Brief Truce (USA))
954[6] 1208[8] 1793[10] (2694) 3146[6] 4106[6] 4948[10] 5748[5]
**Graphic (IRE)** *William Haggas* a112 114
5 ch g Excellent Art Follow My Lead (Night Shift (USA))
(1162) 1870[2] 2958[2] (4008a) 5690[7] 7274[11] 7559a[4] 7836[3] ◆
**Graphic Guest** *Robert Cowell* 97
4 ch f Dutch Art Makara (Lion Cavern (USA))
1397[2] ◆ 2197a[8] 2564[4] 6549[9] 7080[17] 7280[6]
**Grasped** *Lady Cecil* a89 70
4 ch f Zamindar(USA) Imroz (USA) (Nureyev (USA))
(1392) 2016[8] (4434) 5035[2] 5487[2] 6036[6]
**Grass Roots** *Charles Hills* 48
2 bb c Pastoral Pursuits Southern Psychic (USA) (Alwasmi (USA))
6545[10]
**Gratzie** *Mick Channon* a71 88
3 b f Three Valleys(USA) La Gazzetta (IRE) (Rossini (USA))
675[4] 914[3] 1346[4] 1655[3] 2211[4] 2671[5] 3159[4] (3618) 3946[5] (5598) (6262) (6785)
**Gravitate** *Paul Webber* a70 55
5 ch g Pivotal Spacecraft (USA) (Distant View (USA))
655[6] 1100[4] 2916[6] 5338[9]
**Gravitational (IRE)** *Chris Wall* a87 85
4 b g Invincible Spirit(IRE) Flower Of Kent (USA) (Diesis)
1731[10] 2147[11] 2522[3] (3118) 3861[6] 4783[5] 6145[4] 6736[11] 6891[13]
**Graylyn Ruby (FR)** *Robert Eddery* a62 60
9 b g Limnos(JPN) Nandi (IRE) (Mujadil (USA))
185[2] (459) 590[5] 992[4] 1242[U] (1895) 3309[4] 5240[4] 5909[3] (6486) 7204[5] 7657[P] 8189[3]
**Grayswood** *William Muir* a77 69
4 gr g Dalakhani(IRE) Argent Du Bois (USA) (Silver Hawk (USA))
1644[5] 2651[6] 3151[4] 3680[3] 4093[4] (5001) 5597[5] 6542[6] 7072[4]
**Grazed Knees (IRE)** *David Brown* 72
2 b g Majestic Missile(IRE) Carpet Lover (IRE) (Fayruz)
1726[7] 2800[3] 3215[4]
**Grazie Mille (FR)** *Yannick Fouin* 56
3 b g Chichi Creasy(FR) Angesse (FR) (Indian River (FR))
7681a[6]
**Great Conquest (USA)** *Jamie Osborne* a61
4 b c First Samurai(USA) Conquestress (USA) (Cherokee Run (USA))
289[7] 469[6] 571[U]
**Greatday Allweek (IRE)** *Seamus Mullins* 39
5 ch m Kutub(IRE) Correct And Right (IRE) (Great Commotion (USA))
2404[12] 2924[6] 4543[11]
**Great Demeanor (USA)** *Dianne Sayer* a60 60
4 b g Bernstein(USA) Hangin Withmy Buds (USA) (Roar (USA))
782[8] 1245[7] 1609[9] 1760[4] 2452[9] 3298[12]
**Greatest (FR)** *Mme G Rarick* a66 52
5 b g Anabaa(USA) Golden Life (USA) (Coronado's Quest (USA))
752a[3]
**Greatest Hits (USA)** *John Gosden* a83 74
2 b c Cape Cross(IRE) Northern Melody (IRE) (Singspiel (IRE))
7560[2] (7985)
**Greatest Journey** *Saeed bin Suroor* a87 53
2 ch g Raven's Pass(USA) Sensationally (Montjeu (IRE))
5947[5] 6603[5] 6925[15] (7902) (8016) (8267)
**Great Expectations** *J R Jenkins* a68 81
6 b g Storming Home Fresh Fruit Daily (Reprimand)
389[4] 1275[6] 1667[4] 1873[2] 2157[2] 2833[4] 4537[6] 5346[3] 5785[4] 6424[6] 7220[6] 7513[5]
**Great Fighter** *Saeed bin Suroor* a91 90
4 b g Street Cry(IRE) Evil Empire (GER) (Acatenango (GER))
2787[12] 3424[3] 4217[11]
**Great Glen** *Ralph Beckett* 80
2 b c High Chaparral(IRE) Grand Opening (IRE) (Desert King (IRE))
6928[4]
**Great Hall** *John Quinn* a93 104
4 b g Halling(USA) L'Affaire Monique (Machiavellian (USA))
202a[9] 507a[5] 4213[3] 5693[19] 6287[5] 6747[2]
**Great Link** *Tony Carroll* a82 99
5 b g Rail Link The Strand (Gone West (USA))
(41)
**Greatolo (FR)** *T Larriviere* a56 93
3 b c Great Journey(JPN) Volosella (FR) (Volochine (IRE))
237a[11]
**Great Park (IRE)** *Martyn Meade* 81
2 bb c Vale Of York(IRE) Telesina (ITY) (Marju (IRE))
(3620) 4853[7] 5929[5] 6499[3] (7379)
**Great Silence (FR)** *F Doumen* a63 63
3 gr g Great Journey(JPN) Henrietta (FR) (Hernando (FR))
5370a[13]
**Great Storm** *Gary Moore* a39 37
3 b f Proclamation(IRE) Night Storm (Night Shift (USA))
6988[8] 7157[8] 7528[12]
**Great Virtues (IRE)** *A Fabre* a78 100
3 b f Teofilo(IRE) Gold's Dance (FR) (Goldneyev (USA))
2816a[6] 7720a[3]
**Great Wave (IRE)** *David Simcock* a56 74
3 gr f Duke Of Marmalade(IRE) Rosamixa (FR) (Linamix (FR))
2210[8] 5532[2] 5997[4]
**Great White Eagle (USA)** *A P O'Brien* 107
3 b c Elusive Quality(USA) Gender Dance (USA) (Miesque's Son (USA))
2571a[6] 3352[21] 5361a[9]
**Grecian (IRE)** *Paul Cole* a76 81
3 gr g Dark Angel(IRE) Law Review (IRE) (Case Law)
2317[8] 2626[3] 3068[2]
**Grecian Tiger (IRE)** *D K Weld* 84
5 b g Tiger Hill(IRE) Allexina (Barathea (IRE))
4746a[2] 7142a[5]

**Greeb** *Charles Hills* 92
3 bb c Oasis Dream Shamtari (IRE) (Alhaarth (IRE))
1518[3] 2611[5] (3702) 4669[9] 5675[4]

**Greek Canyon (IRE)** *G M Lyons* a84 97
5 gr g Moss Vale(IRE) Lazaretta (IRE) (Dalakhani (IRE))
3737a[22]

**Greek Islands (IRE)** *Edward Creighton* a63 59
6 b g Oasis Dream Serisia (FR) (Exit To Nowhere (USA))
12[4] (156) 281[4] 421[2] 467[8] 939[5] 1105[6] 1386[2] 1836[3] 2722[9] 3528[4] 3576[3] 4056[4] 4266[4] 4616[6] 5978[6] 6481[5] 6851[3] 6983[2] 7191[5]

**Greek Spirit (IRE)** *Alan McCabe* a69 40
4 b f Invincible Spirit(IRE) Greek Symphony (IRE) (Mozart (IRE))
4546[8] 4891[13] 6240[8] 6716[11]

**Greeleys Love (USA)** *Luke Dace* a68 89
4 ch g Mr Greeley(USA) Aunt Winnie (IRE) (Deputy Minister (CAN))
3802[8] 4204[8] 5267[5] 5788[5] 6155[2] 7359[7] 7846[3] 7990[4] 8253[11]

**Greenbury (IRE)** *Ann Duffield* 51
3 b g Jeremy(USA) Truly Genuine (IRE) (Hernando (FR))
1308[10] 1647[3] 3833[10] 4314[3] 4725[6] 4974[7]

**Green Byron (FR)** *Mme Pia Brandt* a68 108
4 b c Green Tune(USA) Heritiere (AUS) (Anabaa (USA))
1784a[6] 7769a[7]

**Green Door (IRE)** *Olly Stevens* a91 109
3 b c Camacho Inourhearts (IRE) (Pips Pride)
3319[12] 3981[8] 4158[2] 4480a[14] 5289[2] 6209[2] 6624[2] 6920[12]

**Green Du Ciel (FR)** *Brian Barr* a60 81
9 gr g Smadoun(FR) Sucre Blanc (FR) (Green Tune (USA))
7846[10] 8021[5]

**Green Earth (IRE)** *Pat Phelan* a60 67
7 b g Cape Cross(IRE) Inchyre (Shirley Heights)
2916[7] 3553[6] 4264[4]

**Greengage Summer** *Mick Channon* 65
3 b f Sixties Icon Linda Green (Victory Note (USA))
1946[5] 2339[8] 2773[10] 3144[13]

**Greenhead High** *David Nicholls* a48 42
6 b g Statue Of Liberty(USA) Artistry (Night Shift (USA))
60[5] 272[5] 297[4] 651[3] 663[7] (938) 1115[7] 1378[2] 1602[3] 1838[6] 2166[5] 2724[3] 2909[5] 3609[4] 4960[12] 7825[10] 8082[12]

**Green Howard** *Robin Bastiman* a87 96
6 ch g Bahamian Bounty Dash Of Lime (Bold Edge)
1538[4] 2136[5] 2548[3] 3202[5] 3917[7] 4635[2] 5196[5] (5887) (6111) 6531[10] 6936[11] 7060[4] 7455[6] 7719[11]

**Green Light (FR)** *J E Hammond* 52
3 b g Way Of Light(USA) Soma Bay (FR) (Bahri (USA))
5227a[12]

**Green Light** *Ralph Beckett* 87
3 b g Authorized(IRE) May Light (Midyan (USA))
2497[2] 3031[5] 3750[4] 5276[10] 5884[2] 6737[8] 7211[3] 7641[4]

**Green Millionaire** *Jeremy Gask* a63 33
4 b g Green Desert(USA) Millyant (Primo Dominie)
192[6] 449[10] 797[7] 937[4] 1010[11]

**Green Monkey** *James Fanshawe* a80 86
4 b g Green Desert(USA) Firenze (Efisio)
1922[5] 2275[11] 2446[2] (3122) 3702[12] 4305[5] 5498[14] 6021[4] 6441[6]

**Green Moon (IRE)** *Robert Hickmott* 115
7 b h Montjeu(IRE) Green Noon (FR) (Green Tune (USA))
7301a[9]

**Green Paradise** *G E Mikhalides* a37 74
3 b g Marju(IRE) Asfurah's Dream (IRE) (Nayef (USA))
6221a[12]

**Greenside** *Henry Candy* a80
3 b c Dubawi(IRE) Katrina (IRE) (Ela-Mana-Mou)
7733[7] (8020)

**Green Special (ITY)** *Dave Roberts* a72 52
4 ch g Denon(USA) Groove (ITY) (Dashing Blade)
410[3]

**Green Speed (FR)** *Mme M Bollack-Badel* a70 103
3 ch f Green Tune(USA) Speed Of Sound (Zafonic (USA))
1502a[4] 2586a[7] 7720a[9]

**Greensward** *Conor Dore* a81 53
8 b g Green Desert(USA) Frizzante (Efisio)
113[4] 181[2] 286[2] 376[6] 690[4] 843[11] 1021[5] 1354[12] 2463[5] 2930[4] 3327[7] 4266[11]

**Green Sweet (USA)** *F Head* 91
2 ch c Smart Strike(CAN) Only Green (IRE) (Green Desert (USA))
5940a[3]

**Green Tornado (IRE)** *Ralph Beckett* a69 50
2 b c Equiano(FR) Loch Verdi (Green Desert (USA))
7412[4] 7713[6] 8026[2]

**Green Zone (IRE)** *Nigel Tinkler* 79
3 b g Bushranger(IRE) Incense (Unfuwain (USA))
1346[14] 1657[9] 2355[8] 2742[2] 3333[2] 3534[2] (4063) (4300) 4631[7] (5349) 5930[7] 6871[8]

**Gregori (IRE)** *Brian Meehan* a87 56
4 b c Invincible Spirit(IRE) Three Wrens (IRE) (Second Empire (IRE))
191[3] (532) (1261) 1922[6] 7669[14] 7889[12]

**Gregoria (IRE)** *William Haggas* 79
2 b f Holy Roman Emperor(IRE) Queen Padme (IRE) (Halling (USA))
2128[6] 2716[3] (4885) 5436[3] 6253[5] 6749[9]

**Gregorian (IRE)** *John Gosden* 118
5 b h Clodovil(IRE) Three Days In May (Cadeaux Genereux)
2958[5] (3723) 4201[3] 5223a[10] 5434[2] 6328[3]

**Grenade** *Richard Hannon* a56 71
2 b g Paco Boy(IRE) Amira (Efisio)
3082[9] 5148[2] 5408[3] 5874[4] 6887[6] 7415[7]

**Grendisar (IRE)** *Marco Botti* a113 59
4 b c Invincible Spirit(IRE) Remarkable Story (Mark Of Esteem (IRE))
54[4] ◆ 285[5] (427) ◆ 956[2] 1171[2] 1553[2] (7662) 7922[2] 8095[2] (8244)

**Grethel (IRE)** *Alan Berry* a11 41
10 b m Fruits Of Love(USA) Stay Sharpe (USA) (Sharpen Up)
2213[6] 3605[7]

**Gretzky** *Matthew J Smith* a90 86
7 b g King's Best(USA) Estabilizada (ARG) (Halo Sunshine (USA))
784[8]

**Greve Generale** *C Boutin* 45
3 b f Manduro(GER) Alaskan Way (USA) (Giant's Causeway (USA))
2978a[15]

**Grevillea (IRE)** *Mick Channon* 86
3 b f Admiralofthefleet(USA) Louve Heureuse (IRE) (Peintre Celebre (USA))
(1352) 1540[3] 2112[9] 2565[5] 2892[4] 3538[4] 4162[4] 5311[3] 5882[2] 6871[3] 7160[3] 7417[10]

**Grey Bet (IRE)** *S Lanteri* 80
3 br f Camacho Tennessee Valley (USA) (Quiet American (USA))
1780a[8]

**Grey Blue (IRE)** *Nicky Henderson* a75 70
4 gr g Verglas(IRE) Zut Alors (IRE) (Pivotal)
(1027) 1798[7] 2610[6]

**Grey Danube (IRE)** *D J Bunyan* a88 52
5 gr g Verglas(IRE) Redrightreturning (Diktat)
788a[3] 3737a[21] 7873a[7]

**Grey Destiny** *Mel Brittain* a57 46
4 gr g Desideratum Mother Corrigan (IRE) (Paris House)
1310[8] 3344[8] 8043[4] ◆ 8123[2]

**Greyemkay** *Richard Price* a57 63
6 gr g Fair Mix(IRE) Magic Orb (Primo Dominie)
1232[8] 1453[7] 1865[8] 2834[4] 3208[8] 3781[2] 4105[3] 4415[2] 5005[4] (5273) (5621) 6086[11] 6706[12]

**Greyfriarschorista** *Tom Keddy* a93 78
7 ch g King's Best(USA) Misty Heights (Fasliyev (USA))
61[3] 550[3] 832[2] 1114[3] 1803[4] 2922[7]

**Grey Frost (FR)** *G Lassaussaye* a71 51
3 gr g Verglas(IRE) Ego (Green Desert (USA))
169a[8] 4465a[12]

**Grey Greezly (FR)** *B Grizzetti* 101
3 b c Red Rocks(IRE) Dan Grey (IRE) (Danehill (USA))
1779a[8] 2376a[10]

**Greylami (IRE)** *Clive Cox* a86 82
9 gr g Daylami(IRE) Silent Crystal (USA) (Diesis)
744[12] 3032[6]

**Grey Mirage** *Marco Botti* a110 61
5 b g Oasis Dream Grey Way (USA) (Cozzene (USA))
(144) (715) 1558[4] 6921[14] 7851[8] 8135[2] 8295[5]

**Grey Odyssey** *Dean Ivory* a8 50
3 gr g Verglas(IRE) Reading Habit (USA) (Half A Year (USA))
4984[7] 5648[4]

**Grey Panel (FR)** *T Le Brocq* 43
6 gr g Largesse Minnie's Mystery (FR) (Highest Honor (FR))
1625a[2] 2594a[2] (4040a) 4717a[9]

**Grey Sensation (IRE)** *K R Burke* 79
2 gr c Aussie Rules(USA) Sensasse (IRE) (Imperial Ballet (IRE))
4701[7] 4993[3] (5759) 6229[4] ◆ 6759[4]

**Grey Star** *Daniel Mark Loughnane*
3 gr f Paris House Floods Of Tears (Lucky Story (USA))
6073[10]

**Grey Zeb (IRE)** *Keith Dalgleish* a67 78
2 gr g Zebedee Tomintoul Singer (IRE) (Johannesburg (USA))
2949[6] 3188[2] 4439[19] (4624) 5511[3] 6933[13] 7224[6]

**Grigolo** *Mark Johnston* 85
2 b c Shamardal(USA) Dubai Opera (USA) (Dubai Millennium)
2698[3] 3140[8] 4167[10] (4897) ◆ (5310) 6151[5]

**Griraz (FR)** *P Sogorb* a81 111
9 gr g Nombre Premier Niraz (FR) (Nikos)
723a[5]

**Grise De Gris (FR)** *J-L Pelletan* 54
2 gr f Gris De Gris(IRE) Passy Auteuil (IRE) (Sholokhov (IRE))
1402a[7]

**Gris Noir (FR)** *Y Durepaire* a87 87
5 b g Green Tune(USA) Petite Ourse (Green Desert (USA))
5961a[2]

**Grissom (IRE)** *Tim Easterby* 90
8 b g Desert Prince(IRE) Misty Peak (IRE) (Sri Pekan (USA))
1442[4] ◆ 1928[4] 2117[2] 2562[4] 3202[7] 3714[5]

**Groor** *James Tate* 95
2 b c Archipenko(USA) Alta Moda (Sadler's Wells (USA))
2386[7] 3194[7] ◆ 3448[12] 4364[2] (4750) 5310[3] 5876[2] 6377a[2] 7468a[6]

**Groovejet** *Peter Chapple-Hyam* a84 103
3 b f Cockney Rebel(IRE) Vino Veritas (USA) (Chief's Crown (USA))
(99) 1240[2] 2072[8] 3143[5] 4443[3] 4824[5] 6255[2] 7107[15]

**Grosmont** *James Given* a71 29
2 br g Hellvelyn Aimee's Delight (Robellino (USA))
2395[3] 2903[2] 3403[2] 3947[12] 7970[9] 8222[4]

**Groundbreaking** *Charlie Appleby* 106
4 b g New Approach(IRE) Ladeena (IRE) (Dubai Millennium)
(2309) 3449[11] 5174[14]

**Ground Ginger** *James Bethell* a46 40
4 ch g Byron Hoh Hedsor (Singspiel (IRE))
497[4] 590[6]

**Groundworker (IRE)** *Sylvester Kirk* a65 82
3 b g Tagula(IRE) Notepad (King's Best (USA))
1569[4] 2035[3] 2406[2] (2505) 3433[2] (3756) 4328[7] 5204[8]

**Growl** *Brian Meehan* 95
2 b c Oasis Dream Desert Tigress (USA) (Storm Cat (USA))
(4695) ◆ 5576[7] 6547[2] 7439[8]

**Grumpy Angel** *Richard Fahey* a40
2 b f Exceed And Excel(AUS) Eye To Eye (Exit To Nowhere (USA))
5511[4] 6158[9] 7113[6]

**Guaracha** *Clive Brittain* a71 74
3 ch g Halling(USA) Pachanga (Inchinor)
888[3] 1044[4] 3923[5] 4593[6] (5096) 5647[6]

**Guardi (IRE)** *Dean Ivory* a50 41
5 gr g Dalakhani(IRE) Grizel (Lion Cavern (USA))
368[9] 484[8]

**Guardini (FR)** *Jean-Pierre Carvalho* 105
3 gr c Dalakhani(IRE) Guantana (GER) (Dynaformer (USA))
(3290a) 4251a[10] 6379a[5] 6806a[7]

**Guard of Honour (IRE)** *Rebecca Curtis* a66 70
3 b g Galileo(IRE) Queen Of France (USA) (Danehill (USA))
3891[7] 5135[5] 5851[4]

**Guards Chapel** *Gary Moore* a72 63
6 b g Motivator Intaaj (IRE) (Machiavellian (USA))
818[5] 7744[13] 8037[8] 8253[8]

**Guavia (GER)** *P Schiergen* 58
2 b f Invincible Spirit(IRE) Goathemala (GER) (Black Sam Bellamy (IRE))
7481a[9]

**Guerre (USA)** *A P O'Brien* 108
3 bb c War Front(USA) Golden Toast (USA) (Hennessy (USA))
(1824a) ◆ 3319[16] 6371a[8] 6966a[13]

**Guesshowmuchiloveu (IRE)** *Charlie Fellowes* a68 73
3 b c Cape Cross(IRE) Overruled (IRE) (Last Tycoon)
4924[5] 5504[5] 6018[5] 6982[5] 7358[9] 8068[9]

**Guest Of Honour (IRE)** *Marco Botti* a102 117
5 b h Cape Cross(IRE) Risera (IRE) (Royal Academy (USA))
1162[4] (3252) ◆ (4180) 7128a[9] 7467a[P]

**Guiding Light (IRE)** *Andrew Balding* 76
2 b g Acclamation Venus Rising (Observatory (USA))
3429[7] (3847) 4897[8] 5782[5] 6783[3]

**Guilded Spirit** *Stuart Kittow* a54 75
4 b g Ishiguru(USA) Soft Touch (IRE) (Petorius)
1355[5] 3556[6] 4369[5] 5313[7] 6086[8] 6426[11]

**Guiliani (IRE)** *Jean-Pierre Carvalho* 105
3 b c Tertullian(USA) Guadalupe (GER) (Monsun (GER))
3807a[8]

**Guilty (IRE)** *Richard Hannon* 81
2 b c Fast Company(IRE) Red Titian (IRE) (Titus Livius (FR))
2944[6] 3536[3] 4044[3] (4619) 5147[3] (6280)

**Guinnevre (IRE)** *G Botti* a83 100
4 ch f Duke Of Marmalade(IRE) Galistic (IRE) (Galileo (IRE))
2006a[2] 5966a[6] 6620a[8] 7320a[5] 7725a[2] 7856a[2] 8150a[10] 8300a[15]

**Guishan** *Michael Appleby* a89 86
4 b f Ishiguru(USA) Fareham (Komaite (USA))
8[4] (174) 273[3] 383[7] 2127[5] 2398[4] 3237[2] (4132) (5097) (5398) 6492[3] 6872[2] 8045[8] ◆ (8279)

**Guising** *David Brown* a79 92
5 ch g Manduro(GER) Trick Or Treat (Lomitas)
3196[10] 4710[8] 5800[6] 6487[7] 6942[7]

**Guizzo Vincente** *F Saggiomo* 86
3 ch c Footstepsinthesand New Design (IRE) (Bluebird (USA))
1779a[12]

**Gulfstream Kitten (USA)** *Gianluca Bietolini* a84 71
3 b c Kitten's Joy(USA) Mambo With G (USA) (Old Trieste (USA))
1779a[9] 4952a[10] 5370a[6]

**Gulland Rock** *William Muir* a59 70
3 b g Exceed And Excel(AUS) Sacre Coeur (Compton Place)
(1642) 2505[2] 3084[2] 3756[2] 4307[3] 5486[3] 6029[6] 6814[4]

**Gumhrear (IRE)** *James Tate* a55 45
2 b f Kodiac Tip the Scale (USA) (Valiant Nature (USA))
3563[6] 4320[8] 7550[7] 7994[10]

**Gun Case** *Ed Walker* 78
2 b c Showcasing Bassinet (USA) (Stravinsky (USA))
(5439) 6135[6]

**Gung Ho (FR)** *Tony Newcombe* a54 63
5 bb h Marju(IRE) Moonlit Water (Rainbow Quest (USA))
446[10] 1012[11] 2084[8] (2863)

**Gung Ho Jack** *John Best* a68 59
5 b g Moss Vale(IRE) Bijan (IRE) (Mukaddamah (USA))
841[8] 993[11] 1221[12] 2887[3] 3422[5] 4049[7] 4595[3] 5303[9]

**Gunner Lindley (IRE)** *Stuart Coltherd* a56 91
7 ch g Medicean Lasso (Indian Ridge)
559[8] 1360[5]

**Gunning For Glory** *Dean Ivory* a59
4 b g Indesatchel(IRE) Today's The Day (Alhaarth (IRE))
211[10] 428[12]

**Gurkha Friend** *Karen McLintock* 79
2 b c Showcasing Parabola (Galileo (IRE))
4357[2] 4684[3]

**Gwafa (IRE)** *Marco Botti* 97
3 gr c Tamayuz Atalina (FR) (Linamix (FR))
2271[5] 3891[2] (4621) 5179[2] ◆ 6127[2]

**Gwel Stad (FR)** *E Libaud* 18
2 b c Vision D'Etat(FR) Magic Sarah (IRE) (Alhaarth (IRE))
5588a[11]

**Gworn** *Ed Dunlop* a93 86
4 b g Aussie Rules(USA) Crochet (IRE) (Mark Of Esteem (IRE))
1164[17] 1316[2] 1733[9] 2957[4] 4756[16] 5749[6] 8290[7]

**Gypsy Jazz (IRE)** *Ann Stokell* a12 29
7 b m Antonius Pius(USA) Dawn's Folly (IRE) (Bluebird (USA))
272[9] 362[5]

**Gypsy Major** *Frederick Watson* a57
2 ch g Major Cadeaux Romany Gypsy (Indesatchel (IRE))
5386[12] 8000[8]

**Gypsy Rider** *Henry Tett* a61 41
5 b g Ishiguru(USA) Spaniola (IRE) (Desert King (IRE))
428[5] 846[6] 2864[9] 5510[5] 5978[9] 6666[10] (7520) 7737[8] 7781[6] 8229[4] 8286[7]

**Haadeeth** *David Evans* a69 68
7 b g Oasis Dream Musical Key (Key Of Luck (USA))
20[7] 141[7] 233[10] 347[2] 424[4] 535[3] 557[2] 628[8] 714[10] 841[9] 889[2] 1030[3] 1221[3] 1311[3] 1388[6] 2598a[2] 2435[9] 2887[5] 3549[6] 4151[4] 4370[2] 4567[2] 4848[3] 5000[10] 5594[2] (6815)

**Haafaguinea** *Saeed bin Suroor* a107 108
4 ch g Haafhd Ha'Penny Beacon (Erhaab (USA))
202a[2] 398a[2] 5755[4]

**Haaf A Sixpence** *Ralph Beckett* a98 99
5 b g Haafhd Melody Maker (Diktat)
235[12] 7971[9] 8295[6]

**Haaffa Sovereign** *George Margarson* a37 39
3 ch g Haafhd Royal Nashkova (Mujahid (USA))
341[9] 607[7] 2643[7] 4304[14]

**Haajes** *Paul Midgley* a48 84
10 ch g Indian Ridge Imelda (USA) (Manila (USA))
863[6] 1961[10] 2297[3] 2364[6] 3191[3] 3611[4] 4114[6] 4494[6] 5498[2] 5913[6] 6451[7] (6938) 7534[13]

**Haalan** *Clive Brittain* 74
2 b f Sir Percy Fin (Groom Dancer (USA))
5644[7] 7563[4]

**Haames (IRE)** *Kevin Morgan* a57 63
7 b g Kheleyf(USA) Jumilla (USA) (El Gran Senor (USA))
1600[5] 2126[9] 2733[8] 3361[9] 7346[5] 7632[8]

**Haarib** *Ed Walker* a66 64
2 b c Bushranger(IRE) Munaawashat (IRE) (Marju (IRE))
4906[6] 5519[4] 6103[4] 6996[5]

**Haatheq (USA)** *A Al Raihe* a114 101
7 b h Seeking The Gold(USA) Alshadiyah (USA) (Danzig (USA))
596a[2] 899a[13] 1176a[10]

**Habdab** *Richard Hannon* a64 69
3 ch f Halling(USA) Dawnus (IRE) (Night Shift (USA))
51[3] 167[6] 311[8] 4029[4] 4563[5]

**Habeshia** *Michael Bell* a72 54
4 ch g Muhtathir Lumiere Rouge (FR) (Indian Ridge)
815[8] 1023[8] 2399[4] 2689[11] 3798[11] 5105[6] 5532[7] 6121[12] (7845) (7924) 8004[6] 8175[9]

**Habibah (IRE)** *Hugo Palmer* 1
2 b f Bushranger(IRE) Sheila Blige (Zamindar (USA))
1349[12]

**Hab Reeh** *Ruth Carr* a53 70
6 gr g Diktat Asian Love (Petong)
934[7] 1115[4] 1311[5] (1838) 2296[2] 2452[2] 2914[2] (3099) 3359[4] 4194[5] 5082[7] 5806[6] 6014[8] 6217[10] 6674[10] 7061[10]

**Hadaatha (IRE)** *Roger Varian* 113
3 gr f Sea The Stars(IRE) Hathrah (IRE) (Linamix (FR))
(1534) 2299[3] (6464) 6969a[3] 7273[9]

**Hadaj** *Michael Herrington* a75 69
5 b g Green Desert(USA) My Amalie (IRE) (Galileo (IRE))
1193[5] 1506[6] 1975[5] 2136[2] 2548[7] 2778[5] 3221[5] 3571[3] 3948[3] 4061[8] 4471[4] 4650[8] 5888[16] 6155[3] 6430[11] 6736[12] 7071[4] 7506[11] 7949[9]

**Hadya (IRE)** *James Tate* a70
3 b f Teofilo(IRE) Lafleur (IRE) (Grand Lodge (USA))
4052[6]

**Hafina** *Michael Easterby* 39
2 b f Multiplex Danifah (IRE) (Perugino (USA))
3107[10] 3394[9] 4528[4] 4993[7]

**Hagree (IRE)** *Declan Carroll* a88 79
3 b g Haatef(USA) Zuniga's Date (USA) (Diesis)
(1287) 1580[3] 2111[5] 2921[10] 3577[7] 5378[4] 7355[2] 7954[7]

**Haidees Reflection** *Lucy Normile* 53
4 b f Byron Exchanging Glances (Diktat)
1757[4] 2053[5] 3664[3] 5166[7] 5634[4]

**Hail Bold Chief (USA)** *Alan Swinbank* a36 59
7 b g Dynaformer(USA) Yanaseeni (USA) (Trempolino (USA))
4958[2]

**Hail Clodius (IRE)** *Richard Hannon* 87
2 b c Clodovil(IRE) Dhairkana (IRE) (Soviet Star (USA))
4570[4] 4885[3] (5391)

**Hail Promenader (IRE)** *Jo Hughes* a70 72
8 b g Acclamation Tribal Rite (Be My Native (USA))
39[5] 211[8] 537[2] 910[2] (1087) (2597a) 2770[10] 3589[2] 4673[4] 8086[9] 8162[7]

**Hail Tiberius** *Martin Keighley* a70 76
7 b g Iktibas Untidy Daughter (Sabrehill (USA))
88[3] 400[2] 606[4] 652[2]

**Hail To Princess** *Patrick Chamings* a46 32
4 ch f Dr Fong(USA) Bob's Princess (Bob's Return (IRE))
1664[9] 4268[6]

**Haines** *Andrew Balding* a66 51
3 ch g Shirocco(GER) Spring Dream (IRE) (Kalanisi (IRE))
2491[5] 2926[11] 7360[3] 7518[3] 8021[3] (8189) (8253) ◆

**Hajoum (IRE)** *A Al Raihe* a80 91
8 b h Exceed And Excel(AUS) Blue Iris (Petong)
240a[11]

**Hajras (IRE)** *Mark Johnston* a103 105
5 b g Dubai Destination(USA) Nufoos (Zafonic (USA))
716[5]

**Hakeem (USA)** *En B Ogullari* a108
3 b c Harlan's Holiday(USA) Michigan Bluff (USA) (Skywalker (USA))
6163a[2]

**Hakuna Matata** *Michael Dods* a81 85
7 b g Dubai Destination(USA) Green Song (FR) (Green Tune (USA))
1356[11] (1842) 2603[4] 3437[3] 5196[7] 5496[8] 6214[4] 6490[5] 6936[16]

**Hala Hala (IRE)** *Michael Bell* a72 79
3 b f Invincible Spirit(IRE) Galistic (IRE) (Galileo (IRE))
1225[6] 2892[3] 3608[7] 4623[3] 5107[2] 5763[2] 6057[6] 7397[10]

**Hala Madrid** *Andrew Balding* 45
2 ch f Nayef(USA) Ermine (IRE) (Cadeaux Genereux)
6652[9]

**Halarath (IRE)** *C Moore* a62 44
5 b m Alhaarth(IRE) Galante V (FR) (Vorias (USA))
7877a[11] 7961a[12]

**Halation (IRE)** *David Simcock* a90 94
3 b g Azamour(IRE) Ghenwah (FR) (Selkirk (USA))
1612[5] 1894[2] (2392) 3159[2] (3719) (4801) 5656[8] 6566[5]

**Haleo** *William Muir* a38 68
3 ch g Halling(USA) Oatey (Master Willie)
2418[5] 2850[9] 3814[8] 4080[3] 4268[5]

**Half A Billion (IRE)** *Michael Dods* a77 87
5 b g Acclamation Amankila (IRE) (Revoque (IRE))
1938[10] 4925[2] 7159[12] 7506[8]

**Halfsin (IRE)** *Marco Botti* a93 88
6 b g Haafhd Firesteed (IRE) (Common Grounds)
541[2] 344[10] (560) 764[7] 2091[11] 2762[11]

**Half Way** *Lee Carter* a74 59
3 b g Haafhd Amhooj (Green Desert (USA))
2058[5] 3518[2] 4263[5] (5044) 5629[10] 6155[8] (6613) 7023[9] 7989[7]

**Hallbeck** *Henry Candy* a67 75
3 ch f Halling(USA) Goslar (In The Wings)
1730[5] 2280[7] 3146[8] 3789[4] 4333[4] 5036[5] (5949) 6252[6] 6699[10]

**Hallelujah** *James Fanshawe* a106 98
6 b m Avonbridge My Golly (Mozart (IRE))
2564[5] 4438[7] 4895[9] 6167[6] (7034) 7700[8] 7923[2]

**Halling At Themoon** *Andrew Hollinshead* a37
4 ch g Halling(USA) Opera De Luna (Singspiel (IRE))
8064[7]

**Hallingham** *Jonathan Portman* a73 73
4 b g Halling(USA) In Luck (In The Wings)
2084[3] 2672[9] 3147[6] 3853[4] (4548) 5139[2] 6007[9] 6706[3] 7044[5]

**Halling's Wish** *Gary Moore* a57 62
4 br g Halling(USA) Fair View (GER) (Dashing Blade)
2923[2] 3780[4] (5904)

**Halljoy (IRE)** *Clive Brittain* a72 91
3 b f Halling(USA) Tithcar (Cadeaux Genereux)
800[2]

**Hall Of Fame (IRE)** *J S Bolger* 102
2 ch c Teofilo(IRE) Halla Siamsa (IRE) (Montjeu (IRE))
5735a[3] 6373a[4]

**Hall Of Mirrors (IRE)** *A P O'Brien* 112
4 ch g Duke Of Marmalade(IRE) Apache Dream (IRE) (Indian Ridge)
2040a[3] 2580a[5] 3416[5] (5733a) 6350a[6]

**Hallouella** *David Elsworth* a63 63
3 ch f Halling(USA) Louella (USA) (El Gran Senor (USA))
515[2] 871[3] 1032[2] 2098[3] 2621[3] 3120[5] 3796[3] 6193[2] 6818[4] 7532[3] 7893[7]

**Halloween Moon** *James Bethell* a41 32
3 b g Halling(USA) Mamounia (IRE) (Green Desert (USA))
1632[5] 2742[4]

**Hallstatt (IRE)** *John Mackie* a73 79
8 ch g Halling(USA) Last Resort (Lahib (USA))
(2430) (3151) 3654[2] 4068[4] 4874[3] 5764[7] 6651[8]

**Halul** *A Oliver* a53 62
4 b g Dutch Art Bella Bertolini (Bertolini (USA))
4805a[15]

**Hamble** *Giles Bravery* a58 63
5 b g Librettist(USA) Time For Tea (IRE) (Imperial Frontier (USA))
2443[2] (2923) 3552[7] 5011[5] 5208[4] 5864[7]

**Hambletts (IRE)** *Robert Mills* a65 60
2 b g Alfred Nobel(IRE) Lady Of The Inn (IRE) (Hamas (IRE))
6603[11] 7134[7] 7348[3]

**Hamelin (IRE)** *Lady Cecil* a83 104
4 b c Cape Cross(IRE) Love Divine (Diesis)
2142[2] 3449[13]

**Hamilton Hill** *Bernard Llewellyn* a3 28
7 b g Groom Dancer(USA) Loriner's Lass (Saddlers' Hall (IRE))
5621[8]

**Hamis Al Bin (IRE)** *Milton Bradley* a62 62
5 b g Acclamation Paimpolaise (IRE) (Priolo (USA))
121[3] 244[2] 448[3] ◆ 687[6] 1573[2] 2127[8] 2414[5] 3848[10] 6272[4] 6666[6] 7364[5] 7782[2] 7972[6] 8142[3] (8285)

**Hammered Silver (IRE)** *Mike Murphy* a53 51
4 gr g Dalakhani(IRE) Desert Ease (IRE) (Green Desert (USA))
686[10] 1627[4] 3315[13] 4737[11] 6028[13]

**Hamoody (USA)** *Joseph Tuite* a82 81
10 ch g Johannesburg(USA) Northern Gulch (USA) (Gulch (USA))
35[4] 208[7] 1104[2] (1368) 1431[5] 1803[6] (2050) (2401) 2793[3] 3213[6] 6025[3] 6236[4] 6313[8] 6898[3] 7357[2] 7521[6] 7623[4]

**Hamza (IRE)** *Kevin Ryan* 114
5 b g Amadeus Wolf Lady Shanghai (IRE) (Alhaarth (IRE))
1179a[6] (1531) 2197a[7] 3452[14] 4852[6] 5219a[3] 5699a[3] 6533[17] 6966a[18]

**Hanalei Bay (IRE)** *Keith Dalgleish* a80 85
4 b c Tamayuz Genial Jenny (IRE) (Danehill (USA))
3361[5] (4001) 4707[3] (4903) 5413[6] (6009) 6476[10] 6836[2] 7634[6] 7955[8]

**Hana Lina** *William Haggas* a61 60
2 b f Oasis Dream Queen's Logic (IRE) (Grand Lodge (USA))
6754[6] ◆ 7193[11] 7741[5] 8115[3] 8221[3]

**Hana's Goal (JPN)** *Kazuhiro Kato* 114
5 ch m Orewa Matteruze(JPN) Shanghai Jell (JPN) (Shanghai (USA))
7898a[9] 8153a[8]

**Handasy** *F Rohaut* a82
3 b g Hard Spun(USA) Atayeb (USA) (Rahy (USA))
390a[4]

**Handeli (FR)** *Y Durepaire* a72 81
3 ch f Doctor Dino(FR) High Definition (IRE) (Starborough)
5404a[3]

**Handheld** *Julia Feilden* a65 83
7 ch g Observatory(USA) Kid Gloves (In The Wings)
1196[3] 1810[4] 2162[8] 2876[4] (5058) 7043[5] 7562[2] 7870[7]

**Handiwork** *Steve Gollings* a68 78
4 ch g Motivator Spinning Top (Alzao (USA))
7182[4] (7508)

**Hand Puppet (IRE)** *A Fabre* a77 98
3 b f Manduro(GER) Grecian Slipper (Sadler's Wells (USA))
5479a[7] 6419a[5]

**Handsome Dude** *David Barron* 85
2 b c Showcasing Dee Dee Girl (IRE) (Primo Dominie)
4450[5] (7082)

**Handsome Maestro (IRE)** *J Phelippon* a80 80
3 b g Dansili Graceful Bering (USA) (Bering)
806a[6]

**Handsome Man (IRE)** *Saeed bin Suroor* 104
5 ch g Nayef(USA) Danceabout (Shareef Dancer (USA))
305a[9]

**Handsome Ransom** *David O'Meara* a77 88
5 b g Red Ransom(USA) Maid For The Hills (Indian Ridge)
3341[8] 3654[3]

**Handsome Stranger (IRE)** *Alan Bailey* a70 64
4 ch g Tamayuz Just Special (Cadeaux Genereux)
(571) 849[11] (859) 922[2] 1027[4] 1354[7] 1638[6] 3224[4] 4080[4]

**Handwoven (IRE)** *Mark Johnston* a74 72
3 b g Shamardal(USA) Seamstress (IRE) (Barathea (IRE))
906[2] 1126[3] 1507[3] 1657[5] 2013[2] 2236[4] 2516[3] 3158[2] 3360[3] 3627[3] 3821[7] (4043)

**Hangon Harriet** *Pam Sly* 56
2 b f Sir Percy Black Salix (USA) (More Than Ready (USA))
2979[6] 3701[9]

**Hangover Kid (USA)** *Jason Servis* 112
6 b h Lemon Drop Kid(USA) Absolute Patience (USA) (Rakeen (USA))
(4231a) 7611a[6]

**Hannah Louise (IRE)** *Roger Ingram* a41
3 b f Iffraaj Answer Do (Groom Dancer (USA))
423[7] 564[8] 823[7]

**Hannahs Turn** *Chris Dwyer* a93 84
4 b f Dubai Destination(USA) Fontaine House (Pyramus (USA))
(60) ◆ 175[2] 479[3] 566[3] 1247[2] 1554[12] 1975[19] 2608[5] 2757[4] (3462) 4027[5] 4741[6] 5776[7] 6314[8]

**Hannington** *Andrew Balding* a78 67
3 ch g Firebreak Manderina (Mind Games)
3525[8] (4830) 5795[4] 6100[5]

**Hanno (USA)** *Ed Dunlop* a72 78
3 b g Henrythenavigator(USA) Archstone (USA) (Arch (USA))
1433[4] 2842[2] 3184[3] 4713[2] 5412[2] 5772[2]

**Hanoverian Baron** *Tony Newcombe* a93 99
9 b g Green Desert(USA) Josh's Pearl (IRE) (Sadler's Wells (USA))
386[P]

**Hansinger (IRE)** *Cathrine Erichsen* a82 96
9 b g Namid Whistfilly (First Trump)
6387a[6]

**Happy As Harry** *Bryan Smart* 7
2 b c Monsieur Bond(IRE) The Washerwoman (Classic Cliche (IRE))
6667[10] 7173[7]

**Happydoingnothing** *Christine Dunnett* a62 51
3 b g Avonbridge Neferura (Mister Baileys)
605[7] 739[3] 1229[2] 1634[5] 2879[6] 3389[3] 4266[10] 4970[7] 8013[5] 8090[9]

**Happy Families** *Heather Main* a67 73
4 b f Singspiel(IRE) One Of The Family (Alzao (USA))
1393[3] (2419) 3249[5] 3752[4] 5597[2] 6338[7]

**Happy Jack (IRE)** *Michael Wigham* 38
3 b g Elusive City(USA) Miss Pelling (IRE) (Danehill Dancer (IRE))
1634[8] 2525[6] 3156[8]

**Happy Monster (FR)** *M Boutin* a77 63
6 b g Xaar Armama (Linamix (FR))
752a[6]

**Happy Pursuit** *Stuart Williams* 49
2 b f Pastoral Pursuits Carollan (IRE) (Marju (IRE))
2612[7] 4444[14] 4666[10]

**Happy Trails (AUS)** *Paul Beshara* 117
7 ch g Good Journey(USA) Madame Flurry (AUS) (Perugino (USA))
7127a[5] 7467a[6] (7602a)

**Harasiya (IRE)** *John M Oxx* 109
4 br f Pivotal Hazariya (IRE) (Xaar)
3766a[8] 5361a[5]

**Harboured (USA)** *Jim Boyle* a64 38
3 b f Rockport Harbor(USA) Gulch Girl (USA) (Gulch (USA))
371[5] 512[5] 675[3] 4472[7] 5109[6] 5865[6] 6037[8]

**Harbour Patrol (IRE)** *Richard Hannon* a60 77
2 b c Acclamation Traou Mad (IRE) (Barathea (IRE))
4760[10] 6038[3] 6545[3] 6984[3] 7741[4]

**Hard Baby (TUR)** *En B Ogullari* 73
3 b f Unaccounted For(USA) Uni Baby (IRE) (Flying Spur (AUS))
6164a[8]

**Hard Core Debt** *Brian Ellison* 79
4 b g Muhtathir Al Durrah (USA) (Darshaan)
1196[16] 1483[6] 1710[12] 2653[8] 3005[4] 3439[3] 3844[3] (4197) 4359[4] 4514[6]

**Hardest Core (USA)** *Edward Graham* 118
4 bb g Hard Spun(USA) Lillybuster (USA) (Housebuster (USA))
(5460a) 7611a[8]

**Hard Man (FR)** *P Schaerer* 85
3 b c Elusive City(USA) La Hernanda (IRE) (Hernando (FR))
3512a[9]

**Hard N Sharp (IRE)** *Kevin Ryan* 81
2 b c Approve(IRE) Paix Royale (Royal Academy (USA))
5852[2] (6594)

**Hard Run (USA)** *Robert Cowell* a38 48
4 b g Cherokee Run(USA) Meniatarra (USA) (Zilzal (USA))
6073[5] 6437[4]

**Hard To Find (IRE)** *David Evans* 20
2 b g Fast Company(IRE) Mrs Seek (Unfuwain (USA))
1276[12] 1901[5]

**Hard To Handel** *Ralph Beckett* a76 56
2 b g Stimulation(IRE) Melody Maker (Diktat)
5874[5] 6271[6] (6719) 7374[8]

**Hardy Black (IRE)** *Jamie Osborne* a74
3 b g Pastoral Pursuits Wondrous Story (USA) (Royal Academy (USA))
37[3] (218) 6154[7] 6633[5] 7533[4] 7758[9] 8068[2]

**Hardy Pink (IRE)** *Jamie Osborne* 45
3 b f Clodovil(IRE) Secret Circle (Magic Ring (IRE))
3801[8]

**Hardy Plume** *Denis Coakley* a42 56
5 ch g Manduro(GER) Macleya (GER) (Winged Love (IRE))
570[7] 1012[8] 1835[8]

**Hares Grove (IRE)** *Richard Price* 21
5 ch g Kheleyf(USA) Attribute (Warning)
3695[7] 3938[7] 4567[10] 5000[9]

**Harlem Shake (IRE)** *Marco Gasparini* 105
3 b g Moss Vale(IRE) Ladylishandra (IRE) (Mujadil (USA))
2226a[3] (7320a) 7725a[4]

**Harlequin Jinks** *Mark Usher* a34 20
3 b f Lucky Story(USA) Crofters Ceilidh (Scottish Reel)
447[4] 675[6] 855[7] 2667[8] 3407[9] 4261[7] 4562[8]

**Harlequin Striker (IRE)** *Mick Channon* 81
2 b g Bahamian Bounty Air Maze (Dansili)
2964[5] 3748[2] 4207[3] 4676[2] 5309[7] (6261) (6550) 6783[4]

**Harley Rebel** *Neil Mulholland* a27 47
2 br g Cockney Rebel(IRE) Al Kahina (Mark Of Esteem (IRE))
7308[10] 7511[5] 7919[9]

**Harmonical** *Mel Brittain* a55 41
3 ch f Desideratum First Harmony (First Trump)
7332[4] 7951[3] 8064[5]

**Harmonic Lady** *Mel Brittain* 62
4 ch f Trade Fair First Harmony (First Trump)
(2655) 7335[7]

**Harmony Bowl (IRE)** *Gary Moore*
2 b f Kodiac Millay (Polish Precedent (USA))
7511[P]

**Harold Lloyd** *Henry Candy* a43
2 b c Cape Cross(IRE) Silent Act (USA) (Theatrical (IRE))
7731[11]

**Harpers Ruby** *Neville Bycroft* a27 1
4 b f Byron La Belle Katherine (USA) (Lyphard (USA))
1270[10] 3366[8]

**Harpist (IRE)** *David Wachman* a90 90
4 b f Danehill Dancer(IRE) Moon Seeker (IRE) (Desert King (IRE))
7579a[9]

**Harps Of Bretagne** *Lisa Williamson* 33
2 b f Monsieur Bond(IRE) Lavernock Lady (Don't Forget Me)
3945[11] 5078[7] 6085[9]

**Harp Star (JPN)** *Hiroyoshi Matsuda* 123
3 b f Deep Impact(JPN) Historic Star (JPN) (Falbrav (IRE))
6970a[6] 7981a[5]

**Harrison's Cave** *Sharon Watt* a61 78
6 b g Galileo(IRE) Sitara (Salse (USA))
3240[11] 3605[2] 4492[6] 4856[5] 5146[3] 5856[3] 6000[6] (6480) 6825[4] 7059[2] 7279[5] 7628[7] 7895[8] 8074[4] 8231[6]

**Harris Tweed** *William Haggas* a98 109
7 b g Hernando(FR) Frog (Akarad (FR))
1869[7] 2143[7] 3500[5] 7492[2] 7922[7] 8146[3]

**Harrogate Fair** *Michael Squance* a78 74
4 b g Trade Fair Starbeck (IRE) (Spectrum (IRE))
746[9] 993[8] 1283[6] 1618[4] 1843[3] 2159[3] (2637) (2743) 4128[11] 7761[5] 7931[2] 8040[8] 8171[3] 8297[6]

**Harry Bosch** *Gay Kelleway* a69 73
4 b g Kyllachy Fen Guest (Woodborough (USA))
(2012) 2772[12] 3306[5] 4118[6] 4432[3] 5394[6] 5834[6] 6232[15] 6617[3] 7569[8] 8103[12]

**Harry Hunt** *Graeme McPherson* a85 91
7 b g Bertolini(USA) Qasirah (IRE) (Machiavellian (USA))
7566[13]

**Harry Hurricane** *George Baker* a77 80
2 b c Kodiac Eolith (Pastoral Pursuits)
1276[3] ◆ 1512[3] 2458[2] 3322[13] 4439[13]

**Harry's Dancer (IRE)** *John Quinn* 88
2 b f Kodiac Dance On (Caerleon (USA))
(2348) 3353[8] 4439[8] 4869[2] 6703[7]

**Harry's Holiday (USA)** *Michael J Maker* a105
3 b c Harlan's Holiday(USA) Daisy Mason (USA) (Orientate (USA))
1964a[16]

**Harry's Princess (IRE)** *John M Oxx* a85 101
3 b f Strategic Prince Harry's Irish Rose (USA) (Sir Harry Lewis (USA))
1201a[4] 2186a[6] 5869a[7] 7579a[11]

**Harry's Summer (USA)** *Nick Littmoden* a59
3 bb g Roman Ruler(USA) Magnificent Lady (USA) (Cherokee Run (USA))
188[6] 1403[6] 1794[10]

**Harry Trotter (IRE)** *David Marnane* a89 92
5 b g Kodiac Defined Feature (IRE) (Nabeel Dancer (USA))
788a[8] 3737a[8] 4480a[16] 7873a[11]

**Hartlebury** *James Bethell* a44 51
4 ch g Sakhee's Secret Marakabei (Hernando (FR))
73[8]

**Hartnell** *Mark Johnston* 111
3 b g Authorized(IRE) Debonnaire (Anabaa (USA))
1652[5] 2153[2] (3419) (4122) 5577[6] 6329[7]

**Hartwood (FR)** *F-X De Chevigny*
2 b g King's Best(USA) Calyx (FR) (Irish River (FR))
8212a[7]

**Harvest Mist (IRE)** *Shaun Lycett* a63 53
6 ch m Captain Rio Thaw (Cadeaux Genereux)
219[6] 453[2] 663[3] 819[4] 1125[4]

**Harwoods Star (IRE)** *Amanda Perrett* a71 67
4 b g Danehill Dancer(IRE) Showbiz (IRE) (Sadler's Wells (USA))
2251[2] 3589[3] 3805[8] 4579[3] 5041[8] 6070[10] 6426[8] 7197[6]

**Harwoods Volante (IRE)** *Amanda Perrett* a95 77
3 ch g Kheleyf(USA) Semiquaver (IRE) (Mark Of Esteem (IRE))
279[2] (624) 850[2] 1555[9] 2556[10] 4281[5] 4912[7] 6006[9] 6607[4] 6880[13]

**Hasanour (USA)** *M Halford* 90
4 b g Giant's Causeway(USA) Hasanka (IRE) (Kalanisi (IRE))
5957a[3]

**Hasopop (IRE)** *Marco Botti* a108 89
4 b g Haatef(USA) Convenience (IRE) (Ela-Mana-Mou)
715[6] 886[2] 1174[2] 1557[7] 1728[7] 7034[5] 7555[5] 7851[9] 8101[7] 8203[4]

**Hassle (IRE)** *Clive Cox* 101
5 b g Montjeu(IRE) Canterbury Lace (USA) (Danehill (USA))
(1848) (2160) 2760[6] (4144) 4606[2] 5161[3] 6133[6] 7142a[14]

**Hasturianita (IRE)** *Mme Pia Brandt* a95 74
3 b f Dubawi(IRE) Habilea (FR) (Grand Lodge (USA))
7722a[7] 8300a[6]

**Haswell (SPA)** *M Delcher Sanchez* 72
3 b f Caradak(IRE) Malinche (Hernando (FR))
7722a[16]

**Hatari (FR)** *Matthieu Palussiere* a86 74
3 b g My Risk(FR) Mehany (FR) (Danehill (USA))
553a[6]

**Hatchet Harry (IRE)** *David Evans* a66 77
2 br c Footstepsinthesand Deryshicca (IRE) (Danehill Dancer (IRE))
4409[4] (4739) 5134[4] 6739[2] 7415[5]

**Hatha Hooh** *Ismail Mohammed* 81
3 b c Exceed And Excel(AUS) Mystery Ocean (Dr Fong (USA))
1513[12] 2317[15] 3331[9]

**Hathal (USA)** *William Haggas* 79
2 ch c Speightstown(USA) Sleepytime (IRE) (Royal Academy (USA))
6712[2] ◆

**Hatsaway (IRE)** *Clive Brittain* 87
3 b c Dubawi(IRE) Scotch Bonnet (IRE) (Montjeu (IRE))
2271[3] 2746[4] 3419[6] 4886[4] 5882[5] 6301[6]

**Hattaash** *M Al Muhairi* a91 87
5 b g Oasis Dream Cattiva Generosa (Cadeaux Genereux)
240a[2]

**Hatta Stream (IRE)** *Lydia Pearce* a56 46
8 b g Oasis Dream Rubies From Burma (USA) (Forty Niner (USA))
7735[4] 8014[9]

**Hatton Cross (IRE)** *T J O'Mara* a73 67
5 b g Moss Vale(IRE) Last Gasp (Barathea (IRE))
5958a[2]

**Hatton Springs (IRE)** *Stuart Coltherd* a31 49
3 b f Jeremy(USA) Oopsadaisy (IRE) (High Chaparral (IRE))
3103[4] 3953[6] 4360[4] 7291[11] 7501[15]

**Haut De L'Affiche (FR)** *F Vermeulen* a64
3 b f Elusive City(USA) Elle S'Voyait Deja (USA) (Carson City (USA))
795a[11]

**Havana Beat (IRE)** *Andrew Balding* 106
4 b g Teofilo(IRE) Sweet Home Alabama (IRE) (Desert Prince (IRE))
1950[6] 2779[5] 3377[7] (3985) 5457a[3]

**Havana Cooler (IRE)** *Luca Cumani* 106
4 ch c Hurricane Run(IRE) Unquenchable (USA) (Kingmambo (USA))
3449[3] 3962[6] 4759[2] 6133[U]

**Havana Girl (IRE)** *Harry Dunlop* a57 47
3 ch f Teofilo(IRE) Future Flight (Polar Falcon (USA))
2025[9] 6238[7] 6901[4] 7204[9]

**Have A Nice Day** *Sabrina J Harty* a75 78
4 b g Oratorio(IRE) Centrepiece (Pivotal)
4949a[4]

**Havelovewilltravel (IRE)** *Jeremy Noseda* a83 80
4 b f Holy Roman Emperor(IRE) Strategy (Machiavellian (USA))
146[3] 782[3] (1022) 1393[2] 4271[5] 5505[7]

**Having A Ball** *Geoffrey Deacon* a73 54
10 b g Mark Of Esteem(IRE) All Smiles (Halling (USA))
3973[9] 5338[5] 5873[7]

**Having A Blast (USA)** *M Delzangles* a89 100
3 gr f Exchange Rate(USA) Blasted (USA) (Dynaformer (USA))
5407a[9] 7629a[8]

**Hawaiian Freeze** *J Moon* a22 28
5 b m Avonbridge Autumn Affair (Lugana Beach)
$671^{10}$ $5228a^{8}$ $6187a^{4}$

**Hawkesbury** *Charlie Appleby* a83 102
2 gr g Shamardal(USA) Nahoodh (IRE) (Clodovil (IRE))
$3113^{2}$ (3649) $5431^{2}$ $7381^{2}$

**Hawkeyethenoo (IRE)** *Jim Goldie* a108 114
8 b g Hawk Wing(USA) Stardance (USA) (Rahy (USA))
$314^{4}$ $713^{7}$ $1557^{4}$ $2149^{3}$ $2256^{5}$ $2563^{8}$ $3241^{7}$ $3451^{14}$ $4648^{9}$ $6124^{6}$ $6533^{11}$ $7276^{20}$

**Hawkin (IRE)** *Ralph Beckett* a68 80
2 b f Big Bad Bob(IRE) Margaux Magique (IRE) (Xaar)
$3223^{11}$ $3728^{4}$ $6065^{4}$ $6749^{2}$ $7398^{4}$

**Hawkmeister (IRE)** *Richard Hannon* a67 72
2 gr g Mastercraftsman(IRE) Lake Ladoga (Green Desert (USA))
$3140^{6}$ $3748^{4}$ $4054^{3}$ $5072^{5}$ $5718^{4}$

**Hawk Moth (IRE)** *John Spearing* a69 66
6 b g Hawk Wing(USA) Sasimoto (USA) (Saratoga Six (USA))
$1664^{10}$ $2021^{10}$ $3075^{6}$ $3554^{3}$ $4046^{2}$ (4655) $5075^{2}$ (5523) $5950^{2}$ $6397^{7}$ $7368^{3}$ $7704^{3}$

**Hawkspur (AUS)** *Chris Waller* 116
5 ch g Purrealist(AUS) Mollyhawk (AUS) (Catbird (AUS))
$7301a^{8}$ $7602a^{11}$

**Haxby (IRE)** *Roger Varian* 90
2 b g Vale Of York(IRE) Endless Peace (IRE) (Russian Revival (USA))
$1726^{2}$ (2328) $2845^{3}$ $3322^{5}$ $4439^{2}$

**Hayba** *Marco Botti* 56
2 b f Invincible Spirit(IRE) Loch Jipp (USA) (Belong To Me (USA))
$7019^{9}$

**Hay Chewed (IRE)** *Conrad Allen* 102
3 b f Camacho Titian Saga (IRE) (Titus Livius (FR))
$1700^{2}$ $2287^{6}$ $3245^{2}$ (3459) $3981^{9}$ $4852^{9}$ $6549^{8}$

**Haydn's Lass** *Marcus Tregoning* a59 72
3 b f Sir Percy String Quartet (IRE) (Sadler's Wells (USA))
$4368^{4}$ ◆ $4978^{2}$ $5976^{5}$ $7734^{9}$

**Hayed** *Edward Creighton* a28
2 b f Azamour(IRE) Galileo's Star (IRE) (Galileo (IRE))
$6606^{10}$ $7371^{12}$

**Hayek** *Tim Easterby* a56 71
7 b g Royal Applause Salagama (IRE) (Alzao (USA))
$1309^{4}$ $2021^{9}$ $2427^{5}$ (3798) $4381^{7}$ $5268^{5}$ $5571^{7}$ $5854^{9}$

**Hayley** *Jim Goldie* 17
4 b f Halling(USA) Gargoyle Girl (Be My Chief (USA))
$2476^{10}$ $3661^{9}$

**Haymarket** *R Mike Smith* a12 66
5 b g Singspiel(IRE) Quickstyx (Night Shift (USA))
$6477^{6}$ $6795^{5}$ $7251^{9}$ $7998^{9}$

**Hazard Warning (IRE)** *James Given* a66 62
4 b g Haatef(USA) Hazardous (Night Shift (USA))
$913^{5}$ $1030^{4}$ $1892^{4}$ $2127^{9}$ $3913^{4}$ $4287^{3}$ $4532^{8}$ $6077^{P}$

**Hazel Brook** *Mary Hambro* a54 58
5 b m High Chaparral(IRE) Didbrook (Alzao (USA))
$1691^{7}$ $2279^{9}$ $2613^{5}$ $3179^{6}$ $3579^{7}$

**Hazelrigg (IRE)** *Tim Easterby* a57 83
9 b g Namid Emma's Star (ITY) (Darshaan)
$3138^{7}$ $4488^{5}$ $4901^{7}$ $5298^{8}$ $5498^{4}$ $6150^{9}$ $6235^{7}$ ◆ $6475^{9}$ $6938^{8}$ $7213^{3}$ $7534^{5}$ $7671^{8}$

**Hazzaat (IRE)** *Neil King* a69 65
4 ch g Iffraaj Hurricane Irene (IRE) (Green Desert (USA))
$590^{8}$ $776^{7}$ $1426^{2}$ $1740^{2}$ $2531^{3}$ (8070) $8189^{2}$

**Hazza The Jazza** *Richard Guest* a50 67
4 br g Jeremy(USA) Zagaleta (Sri Pekan (USA))
$2844^{6}$ $4306^{8}$ $4727^{3}$ $6122^{11}$ $6272^{10}$ $6834^{8}$

**Heading Home (FR)** *John Quinn* 59
2 b g Dutch Art Nelly Dean (Pivotal)
$3481^{10}$ $5493^{6}$ $5760^{7}$ $7055^{8}$

**Heading To First** *Paddy Butler* a15 45
7 b g Sulamani(IRE) Bahirah (Ashkalani (IRE))
$475^{7}$ $570^{8}$ $3521^{9}$ $4327^{6}$

**Headline News (IRE)** *Rae Guest* a71 94
5 ch m Peintre Celebre(USA) Donnelly's Hollow (IRE) (Docksider (USA))
$3065^{4}$ $4184^{11}$ $5203^{4}$ ◆ $6061^{2}$ $6559^{3}$ $7305^{4}$ (7565) $7718^{10}$

**Headlong (IRE)** *Brian Meehan* a63 68
3 gr g Aussie Rules(USA) Trois Graces (USA) (Alysheba (USA))
$2307^{5}$ $2624^{8}$ $3145^{8}$ $3670^{3}$ $3971^{4}$

**Head Of Steam (USA)** *Micky Hammond* a95 96
7 ch g Mizzen Mast(USA) Summer Mist (USA) (Miswaki (USA))
$1733^{7}$

**Head Space (IRE)** *Michael Attwater* a85 85
6 b g Invincible Spirit(IRE) Danzelline (Danzero (AUS))
$1672^{8}$ $2136^{7}$ $2522^{7}$ $2825^{5}$ $3342^{4}$ $3702^{5}$ (4114) $4471^{14}$ $4925^{8}$ $5199^{5}$ $5498^{3}$ $5766^{5}$ $5888^{6}$ $6150^{7}$ $6898^{7}$ (7352) ◆ $7521^{11}$ $8025^{3}$ $8252^{4}$ $8297^{5}$

**Heart Beat Song** *James Moffatt* a43 42
6 b g Cape Cross(IRE) Polly Perkins (IRE) (Pivotal)
$851^{6}$ $1813^{6}$ $4958^{9}$

**Heartbreak Hero** *William Haggas* 105
2 b c Exceed And Excel(AUS) Artistic Blue (USA) (Diesis)
$2777^{9}$ $3626^{2}$ (4270) (5620) $6256^{2}$ $6556^{4}$ $6925^{11}$

**Heart Focus (IRE)** *J S Bolger* 99
3 br f Intense Focus(USA) Have A Heart (IRE) (Daggers Drawn (USA))
$2581a^{8}$

**Heartily (IRE)** *H-A Pantall* 105
3 b f Dubawi(IRE) Heart's Content (IRE) (Daylami (IRE))
$1139a^{8}$ $6162a^{2}$ $7482a^{4}$ $7736a^{3}$

**Heart Locket** *Roger Charlton* 33
2 b f Champs Elysees Zante (Zafonic (USA))
$6875^{11}$

**Heart Of Africa** *Charlie Appleby* a75 69
2 b f Cape Cross(IRE) Carisolo (Dubai Millennium)
$4626^{10}$ $5549^{4}$ $6041^{4}$ $6448^{6}$ (6840)

**Hearts And Minds (IRE)** *Braem Horse Racing Sprl* a71 74
5 b g Clodovil(IRE) Heart's Desire (IRE) (Royal Applause)
$806a^{15}$

**Heartsong (IRE)** *John Gallagher* a64 77
5 b m Kheleyf(USA) Semiquaver (IRE) (Mark Of Esteem (IRE))
$272^{2}$ $478^{3}$ $908^{2}$ $1001^{3}$ $1405^{5}$ (1694) $2486^{2}$ (2890) $7307^{11}$ $7506^{3}$ $7906^{10}$

**Heartstrings** *Mick Channon* a16 75
3 b f Invincible Spirit(IRE) Strings (Unfuwain (USA))
$2404^{9}$ $3268^{5}$ $3950^{8}$ $4386^{7}$ $4742^{4}$ $5252^{5}$ $5522^{8}$ $5846^{3}$ $6454^{7}$ $7197^{13}$ $7517^{3}$ $7642^{5}$

**Heatstroke (IRE)** *Charles Hills* a84 38
2 b c Galileo(IRE) Walklikeanegyptian (IRE) (Danehill (USA))
$4896^{10}$ (7371) ◆

**Heavenlyfriendship** *Brendan Powell* a52 41
2 b f Multiplex Nut (IRE) (Fasliyev (USA))
$2888^{8}$ $3563^{7}$ $3858^{7}$ $6888^{11}$ $7529^{10}$

**Heavenly River (FR)** *K R Burke* a59 59
3 b f Stormy River(FR) Aaliyah (GER) (Anabaa (USA))
$914^{F}$ $1303^{6}$ $4791^{4}$ $5246^{3}$ $6822^{9}$ $7427^{11}$

**Heavens Above (IRE)** *Ed Dunlop* a50 51
2 b f Montjeu(IRE) Sharplaw Star (Xaar)
$7019^{10}$ $7193^{8}$ $7406^{7}$ $7815^{12}$

**Heavens Edge** *Christopher Mason* 81
3 b f Royal Applause Elidore (Danetime (IRE))
$2340^{13}$ $4133^{7}$

**Heavens Eyes (IRE)** *Jo Hughes* a70 14
3 b f Oasis Dream Snowtime (IRE) (Galileo (IRE))
$5548^{5}$ $6238^{4}$ $7162^{7}$ $8177^{2}$

**Heaven's Guest (IRE)** *Richard Fahey* 111
4 b g Dark Angel(IRE) Bakewell Tart (IRE) (Tagula (IRE))
$1163^{6}$ $1531^{6}$ $2145^{14}$ $3420^{22}$ (4200) $4648^{4}$ $4851^{10}$ $5653^{9}$ $6533^{4}$ $6921^{3}$

**Heaven's Secret (IRE)** *Richard Fahey* a76 70
2 gr g Clodovil(IRE) Secret Circle (Magic Ring (IRE))
$2824^{4}$ $3613^{5}$ (5799) $6510^{6}$ $7116^{8}$

**Heavy Metal** *Mark Johnston* a80 106
4 b g Exceed And Excel(AUS) Rock Opera (SAF) (Lecture (USA))
$1042^{8}$ $1682^{5}$ (2068) $2309^{9}$ $2762^{10}$ $3189^{2}$ (3483) $3621^{8}$ (3964) (4648) $4851^{2}$ $5665^{9}$ $5919^{10}$ $6124^{14}$ $6921^{7}$ $7276^{5}$

**Heavy Metal (SAF)** *S G Tarry* a96 113
6 b g Silvano(GER) Percussion (SAF) (Baroon)
$308a^{10}$ $508a^{10}$ $900a^{14}$

**Hecton Lad (USA)** *Mme L De Blende* a68 58
7 b g Posse(USA) Foxy Queen (USA) (Fit To Fight (USA))
$3373a^{16}$

**Hector's Chance** *Heather Main* a79 72
5 ch g Byron Fleur A Lay (USA) (Mr Greeley (USA))
$1167^{3}$ $3147^{2}$ $3556^{8}$ $6007^{8}$ $6487^{10}$

**Hector's House** *Nikki Evans* 35
8 b g Tobougg(IRE) Thrasher (Hector Protector (USA))
$1915^{5}$ $2252^{13}$

**Hedge End (IRE)** *Richard Hannon* a88 84
3 gr f Verglas(IRE) Trilemma (Slip Anchor)
$1240^{5}$ $1913^{5}$ $2277^{5}$ $2968^{3}$ $3421^{2}$ $4074^{3}$ $4271^{3}$ $4782^{2}$ $5094^{2}$ $6106^{5}$ $6315^{4}$ $7350^{2}$ $7850^{4}$ $8073^{2}$

**Heeraat (IRE)** *William Haggas* a86 114
5 b h Dark Angel(IRE) Thawrah (IRE) (Green Desert (USA))
$1561^{5}$ $2256^{7}$ $4438^{2}$

**Heezararity** *Jonathan Geake* a71 75
6 b g Librettist(USA) Extremely Rare (IRE) (Mark Of Esteem (IRE))
(1354) $3815^{4}$

**Heho** *William Knight* a79 66
3 b f Dansili Nitya (FR) (Indian Ridge)
$1582^{5}$ $2129^{2}$ ◆ $2431^{4}$ $3159^{6}$ $5046^{4}$ $5570^{2}$ $7157^{2}$ (7773) $8244^{7}$

**Heidi's Delight (IRE)** *Ann Duffield* a56 47
5 b m Red Clubs(IRE) Alexander Confranc (IRE) (Magical Wonder (USA))
$7^{5}$ (77) $4070^{6}$ $4515^{4}$ $5573^{6}$ $5797^{7}$

**Heige (ITY)** *Pietro Sbariggia* 83
2 b c Colossus(IRE) Moonjoy (USA) (Miswaki (USA))
$7725a^{8}$

**Heights Of Glory (FR)** *C Lerner* 52
3 ch f King's Best(USA) Volcania (FR) (Neustrien (FR))
$1139a^{10}$

**Heinrich (USA)** *Sylvester Kirk* a63 52
3 rg g Henrythenavigator(USA) C'Est La Cat (USA) (Mountain Cat (USA))
$5044^{7}$ $5606^{6}$ $6018^{10}$ $6568^{3}$ $6858^{8}$ $7259^{7}$ $7517^{8}$ $7845^{7}$

**Heisman (IRE)** *Olly Stevens* a95
3 b c Teofilo(IRE) Luminata (IRE) (Indian Ridge)
$1216^{2}$ (1795) $7545^{3}$ (7774) ◆

**Hejaz (IRE)** *John Butler* a53 69
4 ch g Manduro(GER) Halawanda (IRE) (Ashkalani (IRE))
$168^{5}$ $410^{9}$ $646^{12}$ $1284^{6}$ $1819^{8}$ $5075^{9}$ $6273^{10}$

**Helamis** *Denis Quinn* a53 42
4 b f Shirocco(GER) Alnoor (USA) (Danzig (USA))
$3682^{5}$ $4737^{10}$

**Helene Spirit (IRE)** *C Fownes* a89 119
7 ch g Footstepsinthesand Arazena (USA) (Woodman (USA))
$2004a^{13}$

**Helene Super Star (USA)** *A S Cruz* a111 114
4 bb g War Front(USA) Black Speck (USA) (Arch (USA))
$7899a^{9}$ $8154a^{5}$

**Helen's Armada (IRE)** *John Patrick Shanahan* a64 64
3 b f Oratorio(IRE) The Real Thing (IRE) (Traditionally (USA))
$3360^{7}$ $4363^{5}$ $5166^{6}$ $5235^{4}$ $5848^{6}$

**Hellain (FR)** *E Lellouche* a71 80
3 b c Le Havre(IRE) Maria Perle (FR) (Poliglote)
$3869a^{4}$

**Hellbender (IRE)** *Shaun Harris* a78 56
8 ch g Exceed And Excel(AUS) Desert Rose (Green Desert (USA))
$11^{4}$ $102^{2}$ (310) $451^{12}$ $627^{9}$ $1082^{4}$ $1499^{3}$ $2479^{2}$ $3000^{2}$ $3339^{5}$ $4072^{8}$ $7830^{7}$ $8298^{7}$

**He'llberemembered (IRE)** *P G Fahey* a72 81
11 ch g Blue Ocean(USA) Remember Rob (IRE) (Deep Society)
$7142a^{6}$

**Hell For Leather** *Bill Turner* 50
2 gr g Hellvelyn Bengers Lass (USA) (Orientate (USA))
$1900^{6}$ $2360^{3}$ $2944^{8}$ $3658^{6}$ $4283^{6}$

**Hell Hath No Fury** *Michael Appleby* a70 73
5 b m Oratorio(IRE) Sagamartha (Rainbow Quest (USA))
$3632^{5}$ (4737) $5137^{4}$ (6493) $6979^{4}$ $7333^{3}$ (7817)

**Hello Beautiful (IRE)** *Brian Ellison* 67
3 ch f Captain Rio Tekhania (IRE) (Dalakhani (IRE))
$5411^{6}$ $5913^{9}$ $6938^{5}$

**Hell Of A Lord** *Bill Turner* a38 79
2 br c Hellvelyn Miss Brookie (The West (USA))
$1259^{4}$ $1726^{3}$ $2089^{3}$ $2507^{9}$ $3656^{5}$

**Hellolini** *Robin Bastiman* a38 48
4 b f Bertolini(USA) Smiddy Hill (Factual (USA))
$2514^{8}$ $3104^{3}$ $4005^{8}$ $5237^{10}$ $7520^{6}$

**Hello Paris** *Lucy Normile*
3 b f Art Connoisseur(IRE) Latin Beauty (IRE) (Sadler's Wells (USA))
$6599^{7}$

**Hello Sweetness** *Jason Ward* a36 52
3 b f Aqlaam Atnab (USA) (Riverman (USA))
$1503^{3}$ $1852^{4}$ $2135^{2}$ $2393^{12}$ $3098^{9}$ $3950^{14}$ $5198^{4}$ $5788^{6}$

**Helmsley Flyer (IRE)** *Trevor Wall* a62 51
4 b g Baltic King Dorn Hill (Lujain (USA))
(433) $609^{5}$ (872) $915^{3}$ $8261^{5}$

**Helmsman (IRE)** *J S Moore* a72
2 b g Alhaarth(IRE) La Cuvee (Mark Of Esteem (IRE))
$7198^{5}$ $7723a^{4}$ $8212a^{4}$

**He Loves Me (FR)** *E Lellouche* a91 91
3 b c Enrique She Hates Me (IRE) (Hawk Wing (USA))
$390a^{6}$ $630a^{2}$

**Helwan (FR)** *J-F Bernard* a92 109
3 b c Bernstein(USA) I'm Right (USA) (Rahy (USA))
(1551a) (6446a)

**Hemi Bossena** *Bill Turner*
2 ch f Aqlaam Millsini (Rossini (USA))
$1901^{6}$

**Hendry Trigger** *Bernard Llewellyn* 59
5 ch g Double Trigger(IRE) Denise Best (IRE) (Goldmark (USA))
$1916^{8}$ $2836^{6}$ $3209^{8}$

**Henke (IRE)** *Nigel Tinkler* 63
3 b g Elnadim(USA) Miss Frangipane (IRE) (Acclamation)
$1657^{11}$ $2524^{4}$ $3124^{5}$ $3380^{5}$ $4019^{8}$ $4627^{6}$ (4785) $5202^{4}$ $5889^{4}$

**Henley** *William Jarvis* 76
2 b c Royal Applause Making Waves (IRE) (Danehill (USA))
$3148^{5}$ $4170^{3}$ $4739^{2}$ $5671^{7}$

**Hennythelovepenny (USA)** *Peter Miller* a98
2 ch f Henny Hughes(USA) Amaretta (USA) (Woodman (USA))
$7606a^{12}$

**Henpecked** *Alistair Whillans* a50 67
4 b f Footstepsinthesand Poule De Luxe (IRE) (Cadeaux Genereux)
$1167^{7}$ $1970^{7}$ (2475) $3052^{9}$ $5855^{3}$ $6597^{4}$ $6942^{9}$ $7175^{6}$ $7643^{11}$

**Henrietta Dancer** *Malcolm Saunders* 21
2 ch f Sakhee's Secret Craic Sa Ceili (IRE) (Danehill Dancer (IRE))
$3584^{9}$ $3934^{10}$

**Henry Grace (IRE)** *Jimmy Fox* a58
3 b c Oratorio(IRE) Little Miss Gracie (Efisio)
$378^{7}$ $665^{8}$ $6858^{7}$ $7527^{5}$ $7924^{8}$ $7986^{2}$ $8199^{2}$

**Henryhudsonbridge (USA)** *Brian Meehan* 72
2 b c Henrythenavigator(USA) Harlan Ash (USA) (Harlan (USA))
$6784^{4}$ $7171^{3}$ $7381^{3}$

**Henry Morgan** *David Brown* 45
7 ch g Bahamian Bounty Hill Welcome (Most Welcome)
$6796^{5}$ $7025^{15}$

**Henrytheaeroplane (USA)** *Richard Fahey* 82
2 b c Henrythenavigator(USA) April Pride (Falbrav (IRE))
$3883^{3}$ $4518^{2}$ $4935^{4}$ $6509^{2}$ (7097)

**Henry The Aviator (USA)** *Mark Johnston* a42 93
4 b g Henrythenavigator(USA) Fashion Star (USA) (Chief's Crown (USA))
$2202^{7}$ $2959^{16}$ $3383^{6}$ $5528^{3}$ $5810^{8}$ $6214^{6}$ $6566^{10}$ $6986^{2}$

**Hepijeu (FR)** *J Heloury* a68
3 b g Palace Episode(USA) Helenjeu (Montjeu (IRE))
$751a^{8}$

**Herbalist** *K Kukk* a56 66
4 ch g Haafhd Puya (Kris)
$88^{11}$ $379^{3}$ $571^{5}$ $1453^{2}$ $1874^{4}$ $2720^{4}$ (3208) $4717a^{2}$ $5230a^{3}$ $5970a^{2}$

**Herecomestheband** *George Baker* 64
2 b c Bertolini(USA) Green Supreme (Primo Dominie)
$5500^{9}$ $6261^{6}$ $7155^{8}$

**Here Comes When (IRE)** *Andrew Balding* 118
4 b g Danehill Dancer(IRE) Quad's Melody (IRE) (Spinning World (USA))
(2113) $2765^{5}$ $3356^{25}$ (6054a) (7242)

**Here For Good (IRE)** *Richard Hannon* a67 50
3 b g Aqlaam North East Bay (USA) (Prospect Bay (CAN))
$230^{5}$ $7340^{6}$ $7626^{5}$ $7777^{6}$ $7925^{9}$ $8074^{3}$ (8277) ◆

**Here Now** *Charlie Appleby* a72 78
2 b g Dubawi(IRE) Hall Hee (IRE) (Invincible Spirit (IRE))
$3924^{3}$ $4424^{5}$ $5783^{2}$ (6364) $7226^{5}$

**Here Now And Why (IRE)** *Ian Semple* a44 50
7 br g Pastoral Pursuits Why Now (Dansili)
$1378^{7}$ $1602^{9}$ $2514^{6}$ $3530^{17}$ $4257^{9}$ $4796^{5}$ $5565^{9}$ $6114^{4}$ $6580^{4}$ $6821^{8}$ $7520^{8}$

**Her Honour (IRE)** *John Gosden* a69
3 b f Shamardal(USA) Hazarayna (Polish Precedent (USA))
$660^{4}$ $914^{2}$

**Hermosa Vaquera (IRE)** *Anna Newton-Smith* a19 65
4 b f High Chaparral(IRE) Sundown (Polish Precedent (USA))
$5503^{8}$

**Hernandoshideaway** *Michael Dods* 81
2 b c Hernando(FR) Alba Stella (Nashwan (USA))
(5167) ◆

**Hernando Torres** *Michael Easterby* a66 67
6 b g Iffraaj Espana (Hernando (FR))
$2124^{3}$ $2770^{7}$ $3785^{3}$ $7522^{3}$

**Heroique (IRE)** *Tim Easterby* a53 77
3 b f Acclamation Gay Heroine (Caerleon (USA))
$1884^{6}$ $2897^{2}$ $3460^{3}$ $3788^{5}$ $4496^{2}$ $4628^{3}$ $5097^{6}$ $5497^{4}$ $5769^{4}$ $7179^{12}$

**Hero Look (IRE)** *Stefano Botti* 108
2 b c Lope De Vega(IRE) Roscoff (IRE) (Daylami (IRE))
(7147a)

**Hero's Story** *Jim Goldie* a42 64
4 b g Mount Nelson Red Roses Story (FR) (Pink I (FR))
$3004^{7}$ $3661^{7}$ $5495^{12}$ $5856^{5}$ $6825^{8}$

**Herostatus** *Jason Ward* a94 91
7 ch g Dalakhani(IRE) Desired (Rainbow Quest (USA))
$1444^{8}$ $1735^{13}$ $2289^{11}$ $3501^{6}$

**Her Red Devil (IRE)** *Christopher Kellett* a67 63
3 b f Jeremy(USA) All Began (IRE) (Fasliyev (USA))
$486^{12}$ $735^{2}$ $941^{3}$ $1308^{5}$ $1588^{8}$ $2165^{10}$ $3828^{2}$ (4363) $4706^{3}$ $5239^{2}$ $5809^{2}$ $6267^{4}$ $6823^{3}$ $7225^{2}$ $7570^{12}$ $8049^{P}$

**He's A Striker (IRE)** *Michael Blake* a49 78
4 br g Footstepsinthesand Aiming Upwards (Blushing Flame (USA))
$1003^{4}$ $1354^{3}$

**Hesat (FR)** *M Boutin* a54 83
2 b f Country Reel(USA) Divinatrice (FR) (Numerous (USA))
(1094a) $3027a^{9}$ $3744a^{3}$ $5844a^{10}$

**Hesbaan (IRE)** *Marcus Tregoning* a80 86
3 b g Acclamation Celestial Dream (IRE) (Oasis Dream)
$2996^{4}$ $3517^{2}$ $4022^{2}$ $4587^{2}$ (5469) $6192^{2}$ $6649^{2}$ $7185^{8}$

**He's Got Rhythm (IRE)** *David Marnane* a79 76
9 b g Invincible Spirit(IRE) Kathy Jet (USA) (Singspiel (IRE))
$6082a^{9}$

**Hesinfront (USA)** *Dale Romans* a71 89
3 bb c War Front(USA) Classy Marlin (USA) (Sky Classic (CAN))
$4230a^{8}$

**Heska (IRE)** *Michael Appleby* a75 71
3 b g Rock Of Gibraltar(IRE) Sweet Sioux (Halling (USA))
$3970^{4}$ (4495) $5108^{F}$ $5795^{6}$ $6075^{3}$ $6608^{4}$ $6981^{7}$ $7689^{3}$ (7975) $8047^{4}$

**Hesketh Bank** *Richard Fahey* 87
3 b g Aqlaam Wendylina (IRE) (In The Wings)
$1192^{6}$ $1738^{3}$ $2292^{2}$ (3003) $4183^{10}$ $7106^{20}$

**He's My Boy (IRE)** *James Fanshawe* a69 69
3 gr g Dark Angel(IRE) Rose Of Battle (Averti (IRE))
$2329^{8}$ $2686^{5}$ $3433^{12}$ $3972^{7}$ $4411^{4}$ (4862) $5492^{2}$ $6213^{6}$

**He's No Angel (IRE)** *Clive Cox* a57 62
5 ch g Excellent Art Gentle Night (Zafonic (USA))
$1168^{7}$

**He's No Saint** *David Marnane* a89 101
3 b g Dutch Art Stellar Brilliant (USA) (Kris S (USA))
(505a) $896a^{5}$

**Hestia (FR)** *A Fabre* a87 100
3 gr f High Chaparral(IRE) Perruche Grise (FR) (Mark Of Esteem (IRE))
$5843a^{4}$ $7629a^{4}$

**He's Your Man (FR)** *Chris Waller* 116
5 bb g Cape Cross(IRE) Via Saleria (IRE) (Arazi (USA))
$7602a^{2}$

**Heureuse (FR)** *D Prod'Homme* a78 46
3 b f Raven's Pass(USA) Hometown (Storming Home)
$391a^{3}$

**Hey Bob (IRE)** *Keith Dalgleish* 8
2 br c Big Bad Bob(IRE) Bounty Star (IRE) (Fasliyev (USA))
$4701^{8}$ $5807^{11}$

**Hey Joe (FR)** *Mario Hofer* 55
2 b c Redback Manon (Alzao (USA))
$5706a^{8}$ $6958a^{13}$

**Hey Leroy (USA)** *Manuel J Azpurua* 106
4 b g Any Given Saturday(USA) Galashey (USA) (Gulch (USA))
$3025a^{9}$

**Hey Little Gorl (GER)** *Markus Klug* 101
4 ch f Sternkoenig(IRE) Homing Instinct (Arctic Tern (USA))
$3770a^{10}$ $5231a^{5}$ $6806a^{10}$

**Hey You (IRE)** *Richard Hannon* a63 34
2 b f Whipper(USA) Selkis (FR) (Darshaan)
$4499^{11}$ $7345^{3}$ $7542^{4}$ ◆ $7832^{5}$

**Hickster (IRE)** *Roy Bowring* a63 52
3 br g Intense Focus(USA) Surrender To Me (USA) (Royal Anthem (USA))
1400$^{13}$ 1725$^{8}$ 2889$^{7}$ 3405$^{8}$ 4411$^{11}$ 7021$^{3}$ 7704$^{8}$ 7868$^{8}$ (8050) ◆ 8137$^{4}$

**Hidden Agenda** *Michael Blanshard* a41 39
2 b f Avonbridge Night Kiss (FR) (Night Shift (USA))
3081$^{8}$ 3467$^{7}$ 4054$^{9}$ 5489$^{7}$ 5823$^{9}$ 6250$^{6}$ 6662$^{6}$

**Hidden Ambition** *Steph Hollinshead* a13
5 b m Striking Ambition Orchard Bay (Formidable I (USA))
7074$^{12}$ 7686$^{11}$

**Hidden Asset** *Michael Appleby* a61 49
4 ch g Sakhee's Secret Petite Epaulette (Night Shift (USA))
5103$^{10}$ 5529$^{4}$ (6076) ◆ 6771$^{5}$ 7256$^{3}$ 7369$^{7}$ 7785$^{3}$ 7972$^{2}$ 8286$^{6}$

**Hidden Cove (IRE)** *A De Royer-Dupre* 104
4 b f Nayef(USA) Pas D'Heure (IRE) (Arazi (USA))
6383a$^{4}$ 6917a$^{3}$ 7768a$^{2}$

**Hidden Gold (IRE)** *Saeed bin Suroor* a101 95
3 b f Shamardal(USA) Melikah (IRE) (Lammtarra (USA))
(2279) 3085$^{8}$ (3918) 5052$^{2}$ 6127$^{9}$ (6794) (7203) ◆ (7554) ◆ (8146) ◆

**Hidden Justice (IRE)** *John Quinn* a80 85
5 b g Lawman(FR) Uncharted Haven (Turtle Island (IRE))
2289$^{10}$ 7124$^{2}$ 7539$^{3}$ ◆ 7995$^{6}$

**Hidden Oasis (IRE)** *David Wachman* 104
3 b g Lawman(FR) Spesialta (Indian Ridge)
4949a$^{8}$

**Hidden Power** *Jo Hughes* a62 39
3 b g Elusive Quality(USA) Northern Mischief (USA) (Yankee Victor (USA))
5400$^{6}$ 6298$^{6}$ 7015$^{6}$

**Hidden Rebel** *Alistair Whillans* 55
2 b f Cockney Rebel(IRE) Medicea Sidera (Medicean)
5679$^{4}$ 6861$^{5}$ 7174$^{7}$

**Hidden Talent** *Steph Hollinshead* a27 69
4 b g Kyllachy Creative Mind (IRE) (Danehill Dancer (IRE))
320$^{6}$ 3149$^{15}$ 3576$^{13}$ 4072$^{10}$ 5273$^{7}$ 7489$^{7}$

**Hidden Universe (IRE)** *D K Weld* 89
8 gr g Linamix(FR) Hint Of Humour (USA) (Woodman (USA))
7142a$^{2}$ 7476a$^{5}$

**Hierarch (IRE)** *David Simcock* a74 70
7 b g Dansili Danse Classique (IRE) (Night Shift (USA))
376$^{5}$ 583$^{5}$ 780$^{2}$ 852$^{2}$ (979) 1082$^{2}$ 3112$^{4}$ 3427$^{9}$ 4072$^{2}$ 5523$^{4}$ 5950$^{8}$ 7953$^{5}$

**Hier Encore (FR)** *David Menuisier* a29
2 ch g Kentucky Dynamite(USA) Hierarchie (FR) (Sillery (USA))
4207$^{13}$ 6565$^{7}$

**High Admiral** *Andrew Balding* a63
2 ch c New Approach(IRE) Wosaita (Generous (IRE))
8093$^{7}$

**Highball (USA)** *Wayne Catalano* 100
3 b c Lemon Drop Kid(USA) Cayuga's Waters (USA) (Langfuhr (CAN))
4230a$^{3}$ 5458a$^{5}$

**High Celebrity (FR)** *A Fabre* 111
2 b f Invincible Spirit(IRE) High Surf (USA) (Storm Cat (USA))
4164$^{2}$ (6220a) 6751$^{3}$

**High Church (IRE)** *Roger Charlton* 98
3 b g High Chaparral(IRE) Tamso (USA) (Seeking The Gold (USA))
1582$^{7}$ 2221$^{4}$ 3750$^{3}$ (4332) 5877$^{6}$ ◆ (6206) 6756$^{2}$

**High Drama (IRE)** *Andrew Balding* a68 71
3 b f High Chaparral(IRE) Highland Shot (Selkirk (USA))
1920$^{7}$ 2690$^{6}$ 3277$^{7}$ 7397$^{11}$ 7757$^{5}$

**High Duty** *P Schiergen* 108
3 b c Oratorio(IRE) Heart Of Ice (IRE) (Montjeu (IRE))
2006a$^{9}$ 2799a$^{6}$ 3807a$^{7}$ 6965a$^{6}$

**Higher Power** *James Fanshawe* 63
2 b c Rip Van Winkle(IRE) Lady Stardust (Spinning World (USA))
7667$^{4}$

**Highest Level (IRE)** *Saeed bin Suroor* 71
2 b g Invincible Spirit(IRE) Halle Bop (Dubai Millennium)
7495$^{2}$ ◆

**Highfield Lass** *Chris Fairhurst* 49
3 b f Cayman Kai(IRE) Jendorcet (Grey Ghost)
4791$^{9}$ 5400$^{4}$ 6494$^{4}$

**Highfields Dancer** *Gary Moore* a67
6 b g Silver Patriarch(IRE) Linguistic Dancer (Aragon)
(776) 1231$^{P}$

**High Intensity** *Scott Dixon* a63
2 b c Sir Percy Woodbeck (Terimon)
7911$^{2}$ 8083$^{4}$

**High Jinx (IRE)** *James Fanshawe* 113
6 b g High Chaparral(IRE) Leonara (GER) (Surumu (GER))
1398$^{3}$ 2315$^{5}$ 2704$^{2}$ (4722a) 6383a$^{3}$ (6972a) 7486a$^{2}$

**Highland Acclaim (IRE)** *David O'Meara* a74 107
3 b g Acclamation Emma's Star (ITY) (Darshaan)
1304$^{5}$ 1513$^{4}$ 1939$^{7}$ 2138$^{3}$ (3256) ◆ 3480$^{8}$ 4146$^{3}$ 4660$^{3}$ (4918) (5165) 6124$^{5}$ 6533$^{9}$ 6921$^{6}$ 7122$^{2}$

**Highland Castle** *David Elsworth* a30 100
6 b g Halling(USA) Reciprocal (IRE) (Night Shift (USA))
1770$^{8}$ 2342$^{4}$ 5673$^{11}$ 6061$^{3}$ 6330$^{7}$ 6714$^{4}$

**Highland Colori (IRE)** *Andrew Balding* a69 116
6 b g Le Vie Dei Colori Emma's Star (ITY) (Darshaan)
2150$^{4}$ 2848$^{5}$ 3723$^{4}$ 4438$^{12}$ 5354$^{6}$ 5653$^{5}$ 7122$^{5}$ 7242$^{7}$ 7444$^{7}$

**Highland Duke (IRE)** *Clive Cox* 95
5 b g Dansili House In Wood (FR) (Woodman (USA))
1437$^{9}$ 1948$^{10}$

**Highland Knight (IRE)** *Andrew Balding* a108 114
7 b g Night Shift(USA) Highland Shot (Selkirk (USA))
886$^{8}$ 1070$^{6}$ 1558$^{2}$ 2958$^{4}$ 4180$^{6}$ 4711$^{7}$ 6519$^{3}$

**Highland Princess (IRE)** *Paul Midgley* a38 41
3 b f Amadeus Wolf Ten Spot (IRE) (Intikhab (USA))
5$^{6}$ 302$^{6}$

**Highland Rebel (IRE)** *Richard Fahey* a60 56
3 b g Dandy Man(IRE) Dancing Tempo (Vettori (IRE))
1853$^{3}$ 3486$^{5}$

**Highland Reel (IRE)** *A P O'Brien* 110
2 b c Galileo(IRE) Hveger (AUS) (Danehill (USA))
(4780)

**Highland Stardust** *Clive Cox* a36 57
3 b f Sakhee(USA) Highland Starlight (USA) (Dixieland Band (USA))
3423$^{6}$ 4210$^{7}$ 5283$^{10}$

**Highlife Dancer** *Mick Channon* a32 74
6 br g Imperial Dancer Wrong Bride (Reprimand)
2067$^{2}$ 2305$^{4}$ (2614) 2874$^{2}$ 2942$^{7}$ 3310$^{4}$ 3617$^{4}$ 4273$^{3}$ 4548$^{3}$ 4948$^{4}$ 5277$^{5}$ (5599) 5899$^{12}$ 6395$^{5}$ 6787$^{6}$ 7001$^{5}$ 7343$^{8}$

**High Love (IRE)** *Tom Dascombe* 67
3 b f High Chaparral(IRE) All Embracing (IRE) (Night Shift (USA))
1357$^{11}$ 1960$^{6}$ 2310$^{7}$ 3803$^{4}$ 4504$^{2}$ 4834$^{5}$

**Highly Excited (USA)** *Roger Varian* a46 15
3 ch g Exchange Rate(USA) Miss Delta Dawn (USA) (Thirty Six Red (USA))
3074$^{11}$

**Highly Likely (IRE)** *Steve Woodman* a61 48
5 b g Elnadim(USA) Height Of Fantasy (IRE) (Shirley Heights)
283$^{8}$ 838$^{3}$ 1406$^{5}$ 2066$^{4}$ 2863$^{7}$ 3473$^{8}$ 5558$^{5}$ 6031$^{5}$ 7369$^{2}$ 7632$^{5}$ 7844$^{11}$

**Highly Toxic (IRE)** *Patrick J Flynn* 95
3 gr g Dalakhani(IRE) Chiang Mai (IRE) (Sadler's Wells (USA))
1200a$^{7}$ 2187a$^{5}$

**High Master (IRE)** *Richard Hannon* a77 70
3 b c High Chaparral(IRE) Enchant (Lion Cavern (USA))
1765$^{2}$ 1947$^{5}$ 2433$^{4}$ (3116) 4651$^{9}$

**High Meadow Jenny** *James Turner*
3 b f Boogie Street High Meadow Rose (Emperor Fountain)
6540$^{7}$

**High Office** *Conor Dore* a45 79
8 b g High Chaparral(IRE) White House (Pursuit Of Love)
1196$^{2}$ 1362$^{4}$ 1599$^{3}$ 2272$^{3}$ 2787$^{2}$ 3205$^{3}$ 3574$^{14}$ 4361$^{6}$ 6794$^{5}$ 7124$^{5}$ 7279$^{3}$ 7452$^{9}$ 8099$^{7}$

**High On Life** *Jamie Osborne* a72 108
3 b g Invincible Spirit(IRE) Lovely Thought (Dubai Destination (USA))
(2625) (3068) (3470) (3704) 4166$^{10}$ 5696$^{3}$ 6327$^{7}$ (6745)

**High On The Hog (IRE)** *Mark Brisbourne* a48 50
6 b g Clodovil(IRE) Maraami (Selkirk (USA))
516$^{10}$ 676$^{4}$ 858$^{9}$ 963$^{8}$ 2479$^{6}$ 2844$^{2}$ 3328$^{6}$ 3935$^{7}$ 4042$^{6}$ 4341$^{7}$ 4534$^{2}$ 5071$^{8}$ 6397$^{10}$

**Highplains Drifter (IRE)** *David Lanigan*
3 b g High Chaparral(IRE) Qhazeenah (Marju (IRE))
2881$^{11}$

**Highsalvia Cosmos** *Mark Hoad* a71 52
3 b g High Chaparral(IRE) Salvia (Pivotal)
7526$^{9}$ 8246$^{4}$

**High Secret (IRE)** *Sir Mark Prescott Bt* a85 73
3 b g High Chaparral(IRE) Secret Question (USA) (Rahy (USA))
(6644) (6817) (6900) 7072$^{3}$

**High Spirit (IRE)** *Mme Pia Brandt* 106
4 b g Danehill Dancer(IRE) Sina Cova (IRE) (Barathea (IRE))
6955a$^{6}$

**High Stand** *Daniel Mark Loughnane* a52 52
3 b g Kyllachy Maugwenna (Danehill (USA))
416a$^{8}$ 731$^{9}$ 1285$^{8}$

**High Star (FR)** *J-C Rouget* a93 92
7 ch g High Yield(USA) Etoile D'Or (FR) (Midyan (USA))
(5222a) (5964a)

**High Time Too (IRE)** *Hugo Palmer* a89 68
4 b f High Chaparral(IRE) Dane Thyme (IRE) (Danetime (IRE))
200$^{5}$ 493$^{5}$ (843) (1234) 1554$^{2}$ ◆ 2062$^{2}$ 3573$^{10}$ 4323$^{5}$ 5040$^{4}$ 6140$^{15}$

**High Tone** *Dean Ivory* a56 56
4 b f Bertolini(USA) High Finale (Sure Blade (USA))
3323$^{5}$ 3820$^{7}$ 4595$^{2}$ 5105$^{11}$ 6272$^{2}$ 6666$^{11}$ 7036$^{10}$ 7420$^{4}$ 7737$^{2}$ 7782$^{4}$

**High Valley** *Charlie Appleby* 50
2 ch g New Approach(IRE) Bathilde (IRE) (Generous (IRE))
6497$^{7}$

**Highway Code (USA)** *Richard Lee* a65 78
8 b g Street Cry(IRE) Fairy Heights (IRE) (Fairy King (USA))
3699$^{3}$ ◆ 4423$^{7}$ 5127$^{2}$ 6099$^{5}$ 6942$^{6}$

**Highway Pursuit** *George Moore* 50
3 b g Pastoral Pursuits Extreme Pleasure (IRE) (High Chaparral (IRE))
1344$^{5}$ 2355$^{13}$ 2867$^{10}$ 5374$^{8}$

**Highway United (IRE)** *Sean Curran* a24 8
4 ch f Arakan(USA) Luscinia (Bluebird (USA))
37$^{9}$ 159$^{5}$

**Hija** *Rod Millman* a46 29
3 b f Avonbridge Pantita (Polish Precedent (USA))
7632$^{9}$ 7854$^{11}$

**Hikayati (IRE)** *William Haggas* 56
2 b f Iffraaj Diam Queen (GER) (Lando (GER))
2107$^{8}$

**Hiking (USA)** *Roger Charlton* a85 91
3 b f First Defence(USA) Trekking (USA) (Gone West (USA))
3273$^{9}$ (4208) 4782$^{7}$ 5627$^{2}$ 6785$^{5}$

**Hilali (IRE)** *Gary Brown* a48 44
5 b g Sakhee(USA) Mufradat (IRE) (Desert Prince (IRE))
101$^{4}$ 2687$^{10}$ 3118$^{9}$ 3526$^{9}$ 7291$^{8}$

**Hillbilly Boy (IRE)** *Martin Smith* a81 103
4 b g Haafhd Erreur (IRE) (Desert King (IRE))
(113) 540$^{2}$ (825) (1191) 1734$^{3}$ 2110$^{2}$ (2747) 3420$^{12}$

**Hill Fort** *Ronald Harris* a78 70
4 ch g Pivotal Cairns (UAE) (Cadeaux Genereux)
(403) 698$^{8}$ 849$^{9}$ 1196$^{11}$ 3515$^{5}$ 4942$^{6}$ 6086$^{2}$ 7001$^{7}$ 7831$^{11}$ 8086$^{4}$ 8282$^{5}$

**Hillgrove Angel (IRE)** *David Evans* a69 71
2 gr g Dark Angel(IRE) Theben (GER) (Monsun (GER))
4270$^{10}$ 4809$^{6}$ 5351$^{6}$ 5875$^{9}$ 6205$^{2}$ 6648$^{2}$ 6869$^{2}$ 7338$^{4}$ 7839$^{4}$

**Hill Of Dreams (IRE)** *Dean Ivory* a75 63
5 b m Indian Danehill(IRE) Shaunas Vision (IRE) (Dolphin Street (FR))
181$^{9}$ 589$^{4}$ 750$^{7}$ 852$^{3}$ (1121) 1215$^{5}$ 6414$^{7}$ 7013$^{7}$ 7906$^{8}$ 8068$^{4}$ (8185)

**Hills And Dales (IRE)** *Charlie Appleby* a74 76
2 b g Acclamation Soul Mountain (IRE) (Rock Of Gibraltar (IRE))
5149$^{8}$ 6204$^{2}$ ◆ 6667$^{12}$ 7551$^{2}$ 7741$^{3}$

**Hillstar** *Sir Michael Stoute* a91 119
4 b c Danehill Dancer(IRE) Crystal Star (Mark Of Esteem (IRE))
1183a$^{14}$ 2115$^{2}$ 3450$^{2}$ 4124$^{2}$ 5175$^{2}$ (6546) (7324a)

**Hilton Jelois (FR)** *J-L Pelletan* a45 41
2 b g Hannouma(IRE) Jenne Jelois (FR) (My Risk (FR))
4881a$^{7}$ 5900a$^{6}$

**Hi Note** *Sheena West* a66 86
6 b m Acclamation Top Tune (Victory Note (USA))
3249$^{3}$ 3932$^{5}$ 4045$^{3}$ 4351$^{5}$ 5073$^{8}$ 6360$^{6}$ 7452$^{7}$

**Hint Of A Tint (IRE)** *David Wachman* a92 101
4 b f Danehill Dancer(IRE) Mine Excavation (FR) (Galileo (IRE))
4771a$^{6}$ 5957a$^{17}$

**Hinton Admiral** *Pat Eddery* a61 46
10 b g Spectrum(IRE) Shawanni (Shareef Dancer (USA))
449$^{7}$ 687$^{2}$ 799$^{3}$ 918$^{6}$ 1110$^{10}$ 1312$^{5}$ 1388$^{5}$ 1631$^{6}$ 1986$^{6}$ 2435$^{6}$ 3527$^{6}$ 4055$^{5}$ 4732$^{8}$ 8030$^{9}$

**Hiorne Tower (FR)** *John Best* a52 64
3 b c Poliglote Hierarchie (Sillery (USA))
2466$^{6}$ 2924$^{5}$ 4333$^{10}$ 5011$^{10}$ 5829$^{8}$

**Hippy (FR)** *E Libaud* a81 107
6 b m Muhtathir Peace And Love (FR) (Highest Honor (FR))
(4561a) 5742a$^{8}$ 6957a$^{2}$ 7559a$^{7}$

**Hipz (IRE)** *Laura Mongan* a71 70
3 br f Intense Focus(USA) Radha (Bishop Of Cashel)
1277$^{3}$ 3800$^{2}$ 4813$^{3}$ ◆ 5307$^{2}$ 6266$^{4}$ 6766$^{3}$ 7356$^{6}$ 7758$^{8}$ 8017$^{6}$ 8090$^{6}$

**Hisaabaat (IRE)** *D K Weld* 88
6 b g Dubawi(IRE) Phariseek (IRE) (Rainbow Quest (USA))
7476a$^{4}$

**Hispania (IRE)** *John Mackie* a42 51
4 b f Teofilo(IRE) Badalona (Cape Cross (IRE))
317$^{6}$ 516$^{11}$

**His Race To Win (CAN)** *Malcolm Pierce* a104 93
4 b c Stormy Atlantic(USA) Fleet Of Foot (CAN) (Gone West (USA))
6391a$^{8}$

**History Book (IRE)** *Charlie Appleby* a89 89
4 b f Raven's Pass(USA) Pure Illusion (IRE) (Danehill (USA))
3066$^{4}$ 4112$^{2}$ 5505$^{3}$ 6681$^{7}$ 6945$^{3}$ 7885$^{2}$

**Hitchens (IRE)** *David Barron* a108 113
9 b g Acclamation Royal Fizz (IRE) (Royal Academy (USA))
206a$^{9}$ 393a$^{16}$ 713$^{10}$ 890$^{3}$ 1531$^{7}$ 2848$^{11}$ 3715$^{5}$ 4188$^{9}$ 4384$^{5}$ 4683$^{12}$ 5445$^{12}$ 6290$^{4}$ 6531$^{24}$

**Hi There (IRE)** *Richard Fahey* a50 104
5 b g Dark Angel(IRE) Ornellaia (IRE) (Mujadil (USA))
1165$^{10}$ 1653$^{4}$ 2253$^{12}$ 2957$^{6}$ 4756$^{15}$ 6479$^{10}$ 7083$^{10}$ 7449$^{3}$ 7641$^{10}$

**Hit The Jackpot (IRE)** *David O'Meara* a59 102
5 ch g Pivotal Token Gesture (IRE) (Alzao (USA))
(1660) (1926) ◆ 2869$^{3}$ (3397) 3499$^{4}$ 4212$^{5}$ 4608$^{2}$ 5163$^{6}$ 5695$^{4}$ 6693$^{4}$

**Hit The Lights (IRE)** *Patrick Chamings* a48 60
4 b g Lawman(FR) Dawn Chorus (IRE) (Mukaddamah (USA))
2070$^{3}$ 3392$^{7}$ 4431$^{8}$ 4908$^{4}$ 6077$^{6}$ 7111$^{12}$ 7347$^{11}$

**Hit The Target (JPN)** *Keiji Kato* 115
6 ch h King Kamehameha(JPN) Latir (JPN) (Tamamo Cross (JPN))
2002a$^{15}$ 7981a$^{12}$

**Hoist The Colours (IRE)** *David Lanigan* a89 83
3 b g Sea The Stars(IRE) Multicolour Wave (IRE) (Rainbow Quest (USA))
3315$^{6}$ 4621$^{3}$ (5135) 6502$^{4}$ 7020$^{8}$

**Hokko Brave (JPN)** *Yasutoshi Matsunaga* 115
6 b h Marvelous Sunday(JPN) Hokko Memory (JPN) (Dancing Brave (USA))
2002a$^{3}$

**Hokko Tarumae (JPN)** *Katsuichi Nishiura* a120
5 b h King Kamehameha(JPN) Madam Cherokee (JPN) (Cherokee Run (USA))
1183a$^{16}$

**Hoku (IRE)** *Bent Olsen* a56 89
3 b f Holy Roman Emperor(IRE) Scylla Cadeaux (IRE) (Cadeaux Genereux)
6388a$^{12}$

**Holberg Suite** *John Gosden* a76 76
3 b f Azamour(IRE) Humouresque (Pivotal)
1491$^{6}$ 2081$^{3}$ 2924$^{2}$ (3401)

**Hold Firm** *Mark H Tompkins* a43 43
2 b c Refuse To Bend(IRE) Four Miracles (Vettori (IRE))
3626$^{8}$ 3875$^{7}$ 5098$^{6}$ 5823$^{4}$ 6669$^{4}$

**Hold The Line (IRE)** *John Patrick Shanahan* a93 93
4 b g Ivan Denisovich(IRE) Janna's Jewel (IRE) (Traditionally (USA))
243a$^{14}$ (3999) 5238$^{9}$

**Hold The Star** *Ann Stokell* a44 9
8 b m Red Ransom(USA) Sydney Star (Machiavellian (USA))
77$^{7}$ 321$^{6}$ 358$^{5}$ 996$^{4}$ 1631$^{8}$ 2024$^{6}$

**Holiday Magic (IRE)** *Charlie Appleby* a93 40
3 gr g Dark Angel(IRE) Win Cash (IRE) (Alhaarth (IRE))
4130$^{9}$ 5796$^{3}$ (6018) (6484) (7729) 7988$^{9}$ (8100)

**Holland Park** *Richard Hannon* 77
2 b c More Than Ready(USA) B Berry Brandy (USA) (Event Of The Year (USA))
3720$^{3}$

**Holley Shiftwell** *Stuart Williams* a87 89
4 ch f Bahamian Bounty Persario (Bishop Of Cashel)
3246$^{6}$ 3676$^{2}$ 4445$^{8}$ 5152$^{6}$ (5677) 6130$^{12}$ 6614$^{U}$ 6918$^{5}$ 7738$^{4}$

**Holli Deya** *Andi Brown* a51 30
4 b f Halling(USA) Never Say Deya (Dansili)
17$^{7}$ 1105$^{11}$ 5071$^{11}$

**Hollie Point** *Charlie Appleby* 78
2 b f Dubawi(IRE) Camlet (Green Desert (USA))
3076$^{5}$ 3648$^{6}$ 4626$^{3}$ 5910$^{2}$ 6641$^{2}$ 7278$^{2}$

**Hollowina** *David Brown* 84
4 ch f Beat Hollow Trick Or Treat (Lomitas)
2764$^{11}$ 3665$^{7}$

**Hollydanfaye** *Paul Green* 34
4 b f Avonbridge Canina (Foxhound (USA))
2511$^{7}$ 2909$^{9}$ 5130$^{8}$

**Holly Filly (IRE)** *F Vermeulen* a81 98
4 b f Holy Roman Emperor(IRE) Casmine (FR) (Tot Ou Tard (IRE))
(266a) 7070a$^{8}$ 7629a$^{12}$

**Hollywood All Star (IRE)** *Graeme McPherson* a41 45
5 b g Kheleyf(USA) Camassina (IRE) (Taufan (USA))
3852$^{6}$

**Holy Angel (IRE)** *Tim Easterby* a79 79
5 b g Dark Angel(IRE) Bakewell Tart (IRE) (Tagula (IRE))
1440$^{13}$ 1961$^{9}$ 2364$^{9}$ 2953$^{4}$ 3399$^{8}$ 3599$^{2}$ 3882$^{6}$

**Holy Cesar** *C Gourdain* a52 73
4 b c Holy Roman Emperor(IRE) Janet (Emperor Jones (USA))
796a$^{15}$

**Homage (IRE)** *William Haggas* a92 104
4 b g Acclamation Night Sphere (IRE) (Night Shift (USA))
(3759) 5824$^{6}$ 6752$^{10}$ (7081)

**Homeboy (IRE)** *David Evans* a44 53
6 b g Camacho Berenica (IRE) (College Chapel)
208$^{4}$ 339$^{9}$ 353$^{8}$ 563$^{10}$ 688$^{6}$ 760$^{7}$ 864$^{9}$ 1877$^{7}$ 2598a$^{6}$ 2830$^{9}$ 3549$^{2}$ 3784$^{6}$ 4101$^{10}$ 4306$^{12}$ 4534$^{9}$

**Home Cummins (IRE)** *Richard Fahey* 91
2 b f Rip Van Winkle(IRE) Alava (IRE) (Anabaa (USA))
2788$^{2}$ (3481) 5436$^{4}$ (6253) 6709$^{8}$

**Home Flyer (IRE)** *Mark Walford* a69
3 b g Tagula(IRE) Lady Flyer (IRE) (Eagle Eyed (USA))
7210$^{8}$ 7812$^{4}$

**Home Of The Brave (IRE)** *Hugo Palmer* a101 94
2 ch c Starspangledbanner(AUS) Blissful Beat (Beat Hollow)
3728$^{2}$ (4618) ◆ 6142$^{3}$

**Home Run Kitten (USA)** *David Hofmans* a94 104
3 ch c Kitten's Joy(USA) Grand Slam Girl (USA) (Grand Slam (USA))
7609a$^{11}$

**Homestretch** *Mick Channon* 85
3 b c Holy Roman Emperor(IRE) Sharp Mode (USA) (Diesis)
2112$^{6}$ 2383$^{3}$ 2968$^{2}$ 3455$^{5}$ 3957$^{6}$

**Honcho (IRE)** *David Elsworth* a58 76
2 gr g Dark Angel(IRE) Disco Lights (Spectrum (IRE))
3113$^{5}$ 4109$^{6}$ 4666$^{4}$ (5128) 5672$^{8}$ 6135$^{9}$ 7038$^{12}$

**Honest Bob'S** *Brian Ellison* a79 75
2 b c Winker Watson Vilnius (Imperial Dancer)
2172$^{6}$ (2360) (3658) 4218$^{6}$ 4920$^{6}$ 5511$^{2}$ 6447$^{3}$ 7255$^{7}$ 7503$^{4}$

**Honest Strike (USA)** *Daniel Mark Loughnane* a65 56
7 b g Smart Strike(CAN) Honest Lady (USA) (Seattle Slew (USA))
104$^{3}$ 214$^{4}$ 361$^{2}$ 742$^{3}$ 860$^{2}$ 1117$^{3}$ 1262$^{2}$ 1605$^{14}$ 1806$^{5}$ 6768$^{2}$ 7065$^{5}$ 7524$^{4}$ 7657$^{10}$ 7893$^{4}$ 8021$^{4}$ 8208$^{8}$ 8289$^{6}$

**Honey Badger** *Alison Hutchinson* a40
3 bb g Pastoral Pursuits Taminoula (IRE) (Tagula (IRE))
7074$^{9}$

**Honey Meadow** *Robert Eddery* a71 71
3 ch f Avonbridge All The Nines (IRE) (Elusive City (USA))
1350$^{5}$ 1940$^{4}$ 2657$^{4}$ 3145$^{6}$ 3855$^{4}$ 4262$^{7}$ 4972$^{4}$ 5897$^{5}$ 6488$^{6}$ 6872$^{10}$ 7111$^{7}$ 7346$^{7}$

**Honeymoon Cocktail (FR)** *J-C Rouget* 98
3 gr c Martaline Caipirinia (FR) (Hawk Wing (USA))
6913a$^{4}$

**Honeymoon Express (IRE)** *Julia Feilden* a59 80
4 br f Mujadil(USA) Royal Jelly (King's Best (USA))
2312$^{2}$ 3125$^{4}$ 3708$^{5}$ 4594$^{3}$ 4765$^{6}$ 6463$^{6}$ 7888$^{11}$ 8185$^{11}$

**Honey Of A Kitten (USA)** *David Evans* a77 77
6 b g Kitten's Joy(USA) Sweet Baby Jane (USA) (Kingmambo (USA))
49$^{5}$ 151$^{3}$ 643$^{2}$ 733$^{4}$

**Honey Required** *Alan Bailey* a57 62
2 b f Makfi Tiger Mist (IRE) (Galileo (IRE))
4075$^{5}$ (5148) 5929$^{7}$ 6499$^{5}$ 7208$^{3}$ 7396$^{11}$ 7828$^{5}$

**Honeysuckle Lil (IRE)** *Tim Easterby* 76
2 b f Alfred Nobel(IRE) Twinberry (IRE) (Tagula (IRE))
4633$^{6}$ 4973$^{4}$ (6115) 6510$^{7}$ 6977$^{8}$

**Honeysuckle Rose (FR)** *F Chappet* a82 90
3 ch f Turtle Bowl(IRE) Valleyrose (IRE) (Royal Academy (USA))
7558a[11]
**Hong Kong Joe** *Lydia Richards* a61 38
4 b g Oasis Dream Singed (Zamindar (USA))
7418[6] 7733[11] 8094[3] 8299[7]
**Honiton Lace** *Phil McEntee* a60 45
3 ch f Tobougg(IRE) Mellifluous (IRE) (Noverre (USA))
409[4] 684[5] 976[4] 1683[6] 2281[3] 2695[6] 3559[6] 4026[4] 4304[8] (5106) 5846[7] 7766[9] 7883[8]
**Honor Bound** *Ralph Beckett* 97
3 b f Authorized(IRE) Honorine (IRE) (Mark Of Esteem (IRE))
(1809) (2152) 2960[16] 4122[4] 4824[8] 5479a[8]
**Honourable Knight (IRE)** *Mark Usher* a75 69
6 b g Celtic Swing Deemeh (IRE) (Brief Truce (USA))
182[5] 471[8] 818[9] 1231[2] 1849[8] 1941[10] 2468[3] 2885[7] 3086[3] 3761[4] 4149[7] (4582) (4744) 5689[6] 6632[10]
**Honoured (IRE)** *Michael Appleby* a88 72
7 ch g Mark Of Esteem(IRE) Traou Mad (IRE) (Barathea (IRE))
32[2] 763[2] (1111) 1366[4] 1553[8] 4710[6]
**Honour Promise (IRE)** *William Muir* a45 52
2 b f Jeremy(USA) Karenaragon (Aragon)
6868[9] 7198[11] 7835[8]
**Honzik Chipera** *J-M Lefebvre* a75
3 b c Archipenko(USA) Kong Moon (FR) (Hernando (FR))
8006a[16]
**Hooded (USA)** *Roger Charlton* a78 85
3 b c Empire Maker(USA) Yashmak (USA) (Danzig (USA))
2303[8] 4651[3] ◆ 5670[4] 6318[5]
**Hoodna (IRE)** *Saeed bin Suroor* a103 107
4 b f Invincible Spirit(IRE) Heaven's Cause (USA) (Giant's Causeway (USA))
2778[2] 3674[2] 4200[3] 4895[12] 5467[5]
**Hoofalong** *Michael Easterby* a27 89
4 b g Pastoral Pursuits Baymist (Mind Games)
1938[12] 2350[15] 6095[9] 7330[5]
**Hoof It** *Michael Easterby* a109 103
7 b g Monsieur Bond(IRE) Forever Bond (Danetime (IRE))
713[3] 1172[3] 3452[17] ◆ 4683[14] 7923[7]
**Hoofithully** *Michael Easterby* 45
2 ch g Stimulation(IRE) Splicing (Sharpo)
1161[13] 4633[13] 4919[6] 5242[7]
**Hoof's So Lucky** *Michael Easterby* a12 49
3 ch f Compton Place Lucky Dip (Tirol)
2931[6] 3407[12]
**Hookergate Grammar** *Keith Reveley* 38
2 b g Yeats(IRE) Oulianovsk (IRE) (Peintre Celebre (USA))
7244[11] 7498[9]
**Hooke's Law (IRE)** *Brian Meehan* 76
3 b g Lawman(FR) Woodland Orchid (IRE) (Woodman (USA))
2025[7] ◆ (2511)
**Hoon (IRE)** *Rae Guest* 73
3 b g Camacho Luggala (IRE) (Kahyasi)
2447[3] 3198[3]
**Hoop Of Colour (USA)** *Lady Cecil* 91
3 b f Distorted Humor(USA) Surya (USA) (Unbridled (USA))
2404[2] (3141) (4417) 5094[4]
**Hoorayforhollywood** *Sir Michael Stoute* 75
2 b f Oasis Dream Dalisay (IRE) (Sadler's Wells (USA))
2744[5] 4346[3] 4825[4] 6359[2]
**Hootenanny (USA)** *Wesley A Ward* a70 116
2 b c Quality Road(USA) More Hennessy (USA) (Hennessy (USA))
(3322) 5741a[2] (7590a)
**Hoovergetthekeys (USA)** *M Narduzzi* 98
3 b g Henrythenavigator(USA) Honeypenny (USA) (Royal Academy (USA))
1779a[3] 2376a[8]
**Hope And Fortune (IRE)** *John Butler* 22
3 b f High Chaparral(IRE) Vantive (USA) (Mr Prospector (USA))
7158[6] 7501[8]
**Hopefilly (IRE)** *Ed Walker* 80
3 b f Compton Place Kondakova (IRE) (Soviet Star (USA))
2626[3] 3331[10]
**Hope For Glory** *Jason Ward* a40 60
5 b g Proclamation(IRE) Aissa (Dr Devious (IRE))
4062[6] 4978[5] 5267[2] 6342[9] 6673[2]
**Hopeigetlucky** *Stuart Kittow* 49
3 br g Lucky Story(USA) Maxilla (IRE) (Lahib (USA))
3750[9] 4543[14] 5628[6]
**Hopes N Dreams (IRE)** *Kevin Ryan* a88 95
6 b m Elusive City(USA) Hope Of Pekan (IRE) (Sri Pekan (USA))
1734[10] 2353[5] 2989[18] (3830) 4384[10] 4892[12] 5444[16] 5784[3] 6467[6] 6576[3] 6929[6]
**Hope You Dance (FR)** *David Simcock* 51
2 ch f Mastercraftsman(IRE) Anna Of Dubai (GER) (Dubai Destination (USA))
7206[4]
**Hors De Combat** *James Fanshawe* a88 113
3 ch g Mount Nelson Maid For Winning (USA) (Gone West (USA))
1420[5] (1954) 3378[3] ◆ 4850[2] 5666[5] ◆ 6710[3]
**Horseshoe Bay (IRE)** *Sir Michael Stoute* a69
2 b c Arch(USA) Sweepstake (IRE) (Acclamation)
7551[4] ◆
**Horsetracker** *Ian Williams* a62 63
2 b f Multiplex Miss Lesley (Needwood Blade)
3881[8] 4626[7] 4935[3] 5798[3] 6364[4] 6648[10] 6769[4] 6944[6] 7165[6] 7396[10]
**Horsewithnoname (IRE)** *T G McCourt* a66 55
7 b g Daylami(IRE) City Zone (IRE) (Zafonic (USA))
794a[10] 7961a[9]
**Horsforth** *Tony Coyle* 79
2 b f Kyllachy Lady McBeth (IRE) (Avonbridge)
1161[5] 1482[2] 1955[3] 4057[5] (4751) 5694[8] 6322[3]
**Horsted Keynes (FR)** *Roger Varian* a103 108
4 ch g Giant's Causeway(USA) Viking's Cove (USA) (Miswaki (USA))
(1862) 3420[2] ◆ 4648[15] 4851[15] 5722[5]
**Hortensia Diamond (FR)** *K R Burke* 35
3 b f Falco(USA) Diamond Life (FR) (Montjeu (IRE))
5589a[5] 7270a[13]
**Horvat Clan (USA)** *David Cannizzo* 95
5 bb g Purim(USA) Sanibel Breeze (USA) (Exploit (USA))
4231a[6]
**Hostile Fire (IRE)** *Ed de Giles* a50 83
3 b g Iffraaj Royal Esteem (Mark Of Esteem (IRE))
1214[8] (1683) (4415) (4742) 5647[2] 6057[7] (6431) 6737[9] 6990[3] 7417[7]
**Host The Band** *Tony Newcombe* a23 15
10 b m Bandmaster(USA) Hosting (Thatching)
1891[4] 2252[11]
**Hot Amber (USA)** *Robert Cowell* a41 46
3 ch f Langfuhr(CAN) Tres Chaud (USA) (French Deputy (USA))
3124[8] 3406[7] 3627[2]
**Hot Chilli Kiss (FR)** *K Demme* 60
2 bb f Elusive City(USA) Santinama (FR) (Linamix (FR))
7481a[8]
**Hot Coffee (IRE)** *Tom Dascombe* 93
3 b f Haatef(USA) Cafe Creme (IRE) (Catrail (USA))
2088[3] 2565[4] 3357[16] 4163[5] 4782[6] 6258[4] 6746[6] 7416[11]
**Hot Hot Very Hot (FR)** *J Boisnard*
2 b f Youmzain(IRE) Quelle Chaleur (FR) (Double Bed (FR))
8276a[2]
**Hot Mustard** *Michael Bell* a53 68
4 b g Pastoral Pursuits Lihou Island (Beveled (USA))
1638[5] (2529) 3056[7] 3629[2] 4090[2] 4593[4] 5109[2] 5394[7] 6086[12]
**Hototo** *Fawzi Abdulla Nass* 105
4 ch g Sleeping Indian Harlem Dancer (Dr Devious (IRE))
107a[2] 680a[3] 897a[6]
**Hot Right Now** *K R Burke* a74 6
4 ch f Sleeping Indian American Rouge (IRE) (Grand Lodge (USA))
(366) 548[2] (1131)
**Hot Shot (IRE)** *P Harley* a61 71
2 ch f Strategic Prince Nurama (Daylami (IRE))
6950a[4]
**Hot Spice** *Michael Easterby* 81
6 b g Kodiac Harlestone Lady (Shaamit (IRE))
1644[4] (3482) (3845) 4217[7] (4874) 5764[2] 7124[14] 7539[8]
**Hot Stock (FR)** *Jo Hughes* a64 47
3 b g Elusive City(USA) Hermance (Enrique)
311[5] 477[5]
**Hot Streak (IRE)** *Kevin Ryan* a91 116
3 ch c Iffraaj Ashirah (USA) (Housebuster (USA))
1949[3] ◆ (2563) 3319[3] 4201[7] 5654[5] 6134[16] 6966a[15]
**Hot Sugar (USA)** *Michael Appleby* a72 58
5 b g Lemon Drop Kid(USA) Plaisir Des Yeux (FR) (Funambule (USA))
511[11] 549[4] 736[6]
**Houdini** *Jamie Osborne* a56
2 b c Pivotal Regina (Green Desert (USA))
8227[7] ◆
**Hound Music** *Jonathan Portman* 71
2 ch f Ashkalani(IRE) Saffron Fox (Safawan)
2744[4] ◆ 3558[7] 5309[5] 6610[3] 7237[12]
**House Captain** *Richard Hannon* a56 75
3 ch c Captain Gerrard(IRE) Dalmunzie (IRE) (Choisir (AUS))
3537[9] 4886[6] 5378[3] 5861[3] 6236[9] 7205[10]
**House Limit (IRE)** *J Larkin* a55 54
5 br g Red Clubs(IRE) Fritillary (Vettori (IRE))
794a[12] 7877a[2]
**Housemaker** *K R Burke* 76
2 b f Nayef(USA) Blaenavon (Cadeaux Genereux)
5643[2] ◆ 6208[2]
**Housewives Choice** *James Bethell* a57 49
3 ch f Black Sam Bellamy(IRE) Maid Of Perth (Mark Of Esteem (IRE))
2082[6] 2899[5] 7074[8]
**Houteville** *P Sogorb* a76 67
2 b f Arcano(IRE) Holy Moly (USA) (Rock Of Gibraltar (IRE))
6698a[4]
**Howlin'For You** *David Brown* a60 46
2 ch f Kheleyf(USA) Angry Bark (USA) (Woodman (USA))
1764[3] 2206[5] 3297[8] 3894[3]
**How Rude** *Mel Brittain*
3 b f Virtual My Golly (Mozart (IRE))
1303[14] 1608[13]
**Howyadoingnotsobad (IRE)** *Bill Turner* a67 65
6 b g Kodiac Beau Petite (Kyllachy)
2414[8] 2645[8] 3470[6] 6399[3] 6658[6] 7806[6] 8077[5]
**Howz The Family (IRE)** *John Spearing* a21 22
3 b g Myboycharlie(IRE) Lady Raj (USA) (El Prado (IRE))
103[4] 357[6] 670[6] 1101[9] 8176[8]
**Ho Yam Lay** *Nick Littmoden* a21 60
2 ch f Sakhee's Secret Winterbourne (Cadeaux Genereux)
2269[6] 2622[4] 3894[2] 4619[6] 5489[10]
**Hoy Hoy (IRE)** *Mick Channon* a66 74
3 b g Iffraaj Luxie (IRE) (Acclamation)
1433[5] 1894[5] 2667[3] 3486[2] (3849)
**Hualapai (IRE)** *G Botti* a68 77
3 b f High Chaparral(IRE) Haleyev (IRE) (Fasliyev (USA))
3745a[6] 4840a[7]
**Hubertas** *John Quinn* a41
2 b g Lord Of England(GER) Western Eyes (IRE) (Rock Of Gibraltar (IRE))
8288[8]
**Huff And Puff** *Venetia Williams* a89 86
7 b g Azamour(IRE) Coyote (Indian Ridge)
1735[7] 2561[5]
**Hug And A Kiss (USA)** *A Fabre* 107
3 rg f Thewayyouare(USA) Primrose Hill (USA) (Giant's Causeway (USA))
1502a[2] 2267a[3] 3773a[5] 4840a[6]
**Hughies Bay (IRE)** *Garvan Donnelly* a28 50
4 b g Jeremy(USA) Mrs Pankhurst (Selkirk (USA))
4805a[16]
**Hugie Boy (IRE)** *Scott Dixon* 11
2 ch c Art Connoisseur(IRE) Piece Unique (Barathea (IRE))
4633[12]
**Hulcolt (IRE)** *Garry Moss* a75 77
3 b g Acclamation Fusili (IRE) (Silvano (GER))
5197[8] 5638[8] (6625) 7403[6] 7757[13]
**Hully Gully (GER)** *C Ferland* a66
3 gr f Verglas(IRE) High Will (FR) (High Chaparral (IRE))
(599a)
**Humidor (IRE)** *George Baker* a81 101
7 b g Camacho Miss Indigo (Indian Ridge)
2503[7] 3732[6] 4892[5] 5419[5] 5754 6327[3] 7132[4] 7272[10]
**Humour (IRE)** *Christine Dunnett* a65 52
3 b g Invincible Spirit(IRE) Hucking Hot (Desert Prince (IRE))
2384[6] 3343[6] 7259[3] 7423[2] 7883[4] 8063[6]
**Humphry Repton** *Mark H Tompkins* 25
2 b g Virtual Qilin (IRE) (Second Set (IRE))
6690[6]
**Hundi (IRE)** *Charles Hills* 85
2 b f Fastnet Rock(AUS) Hawala (IRE) (Warning)
3671[8] 4781[2] 5429[3] 6555[2]
**Hungerford** *Olly Stevens* a64
2 b c Pastoral Pursuits Truly Pink (Mr Greeley (USA))
8075[4]
**Hunters Belt (IRE)** *George Bewley* a66 64
10 b g Intikhab(USA) Three Stars (Star Appeal)
2213[4] 2512[3]
**Hunters Creek (IRE)** *John Gosden* a79 97
3 b g Cape Cross(IRE) Cinnamon Rose (USA) (Trempolino (USA))
1530[7] 2345[4] 3378[28] 3886[4] 4198[8]
**Hunter's Light (IRE)** *Saeed bin Suroor* a116 114
6 ch h Dubawi(IRE) Portmanteau (Barathea (IRE))
508a[4] 1181a[8]
**Hunting Ground (USA)** *Mark Johnston* a105 68
4 b g Street Cry(IRE) Panty Raid (USA) (Include (USA))
(322) 386[2] 1299[4] 1556[12] 1735[11] 2289[17] 2640[2] 2760[10] 3532[8] 4015[7] 4520[3] (6156) 7289[9]
**Hunting Tower** *J J Lambe* a63 66
10 b g Sadler's Wells(USA) Fictitious (Machiavellian (USA))
3605[4] 4259[4]
**Huntsmans Close** *Roger Charlton* 98
4 b g Elusive Quality(USA) Badminton (Zieten (USA))
(1492) 2849[6] 3271[12] 3876[3] 4892[6] 5784[2] 6290[3] (6531)
**Hurricancrys (FR)** *J Boisnard* 74
3 b g Hurricane Cat(USA) Crystivoli (FR) (Northern Crystal)
4252a[5]
**Hurricane Alert** *Ralph Beckett* a71
2 b c Showcasing Raggle Taggle (IRE) (Tagula (IRE))
7400[6] 7771[2] 7881[9]
**Hurricane Harry** *William Knight* a64 61
3 b g Royal Applause Stormy Weather (Nashwan (USA))
468[5] 748[3] 3031[7] 4077[10] 4658[9] 5899[8]
**Hurricane Red (IRE)** *Lennart Reuterskiold Jr* a101 103
4 ch c Hurricane Run(IRE) Bounce (FR) (Trempolino (USA))
2245a[2] 3090a[2] 3772a[3] 5231a[6] 6389a[4]
**Hurrimera (ITY)** *R Menichetti* 65
3 b f Hurricane Run(IRE) Calimera (ARG) (Luhuk (USA))
1780a[16] 2590a[12]
**Hurry Home Poppa (IRE)** *John Mackie* a59 70
4 b g Holy Roman Emperor(IRE) My Renee (USA) (Kris S (USA))
1660[7] 2327[17] 2872[3] 3226[4] (3976) 4575[5] 6651[3] 6864[2] (7643)
**Hurryupharriet (IRE)** *W McCreery* 98
3 b f Camacho Nova Tor (IRE) (Trans Island)
1572[12]
**Hussar Ballad (USA)** *Mel Brittain* a71 68
5 b g Hard Spun(USA) Country Melody (USA) (Gone West (USA))
(1675) 2509[2] 2654[7] 7411[6] 8122[5] ◆ (8283)
**Hustle Bustle (IRE)** *David Brown* a69 53
3 b f Elusive City(USA) Coachhouse Lady (USA) (Rahy (USA))
786[2] 1048[2] (1264) ◆ 1449[2] 2470[2] 3433[11] 3855[6]
**Huzzah (IRE)** *Michael Appleby* a65 81
9 b g Acclamation Borders Belle (IRE) (Pursuit Of Love)
17[3] 78[2] 179[6] (516) (671) 781[6] 939[2]
**Hyakuman (FR)** *M Boutin* 48
2 gr c Stormy River(FR) Orzie (FR) (Solicitor I (FR))
1402a[9]
**Hydrant** *Richard Guest* a48 86
8 b g Haafhd Spring (Sadler's Wells (USA))
560[8] 1113[6] 2162[4] 2423[4] 2762[2] ◆ 3139[4] 3335[3] 3977[5] 4290[9] 5172[3] 5319[4] 6323[7] 6870[11] 7251[7]
**Hydrogen** *Peter Chapple-Hyam* 76
3 b c Galileo(IRE) Funsie (FR) (Saumarez)
2746[6]
**Hymenaios (IRE)** *Richard Hannon* 90
3 ch c Danehill Dancer(IRE) Wedding Morn (IRE) (Sadler's Wells (USA))
(1166) 1702[5] 2986[3] 3587[7] 5251[2]
**Hymn Of Hope (IRE)** *Noel Quinlan* a46 54
2 b c Acclamation Musical Treat (IRE) (Royal Academy (USA))
7039[6] 7371[8]
**Hypatia (IRE)** *John Joseph Murphy* a50 63
4 b f Holy Roman Emperor(IRE) Kahira (IRE) (King's Best (USA))
570[4]
**Hyperlink (IRE)** *Michael Bell* a76 77
5 b g Cape Cross(IRE) Surf The Web (IRE) (Ela-Mana-Mou)
2963[8] (4319) 5756[7]
**Hyphaema (IRE)** *Clive Cox* a69 55
2 b f Rock Of Gibraltar(IRE) Kotdiji (Mtoto)
6868[10] 7405[9] 7943[3]
**Hypnotism** *Ronald Harris* a39 41
4 ch g Pivotal Hypnotize (Machiavellian (USA))
1664[8] 1916[7]
**Hypothese (IRE)** *Matthieu Palussiere* 59
2 b f Dutch Art Hieroglyph (Green Desert (USA))
4883a[5]
**I Am Beautiful (IRE)** *A P O'Brien* 98
2 b f Rip Van Winkle(IRE) Monevassia (USA) (Mr Prospector (USA))
(3763a) 5218a[6] 5734a[7] 6372a[9]
**Iambertie** *J S Moore* 2
2 b g Bertolini(USA) Iamfine (IRE) (Whipper (USA))
1271a[12] 1505[11]
**I Am Not Here (IRE)** *Timothy Jarvis* a59 62
3 b c Amadeus Wolf Newgate Lodge (IRE) (Namid)
1433[10] 2201[5] 3804[8] 4420[11] 5313[11] 5949[5] (7256)
**I Am Who I Am** *Iain Jardine* a41 36
4 b f Notnowcato Elusive Kitty (USA) (Elusive Quality (USA))
13[6] 434[5] 6117[9] 7059[6]
**Ian's Memory (USA)** *Jeremy Noseda* a68 50
3 bb c Smart Strike(CAN) Rite Moment (USA) (Vicar (USA))
1795[8] 5647[7]
**Icanboogie** *Anthony Middleton* a49 44
4 b g Tobougg(IRE) Dubai Marina (Polish Precedent (USA))
92[11]
**Icandi** *Alan Berry* a34 51
2 b f Indesatchel(IRE) Some Diva (Dr Fong (USA))
2993[4] 3232[6] 4018[6] 6888[9] 7701[7] 7828[7]
**Icarium (FR)** *C Laffon-Parias* a86 92
3 ch c Medicean Delfinia (FR) (Drastikos (GR))
5368a[16]
**Ice Apple** *John E Long* a52 53
6 b m Iceman Star Apple (Barathea (IRE))
185[3] 455[3] 759[7] 2531[2] 2942[4] 4082[6] 4737[3] 5547[5] 6900[7] 8011[10]
**Iceberg (IRE)** *C Ferland* 99
2 b c Shamardal(USA) Soft Ice (IRE) (Kingmambo (USA))
5478a[3] 6570a[6]
**Iceblast** *Michael Easterby* a72 69
6 b g Iceman Medici Princess (Medicean)
52[2] 161[4] 248[4] 3099[8] 3530[U] 3952[8] (4070) ◆ 4961[6] ◆ 5337[4] 5887[10] 6014[4] 7180[8] 7502[17]
**Icebuster** *Rod Millman* a92 92
6 ch g Iceman Radiate (Sadler's Wells (USA))
182[2] 386[5] 1553[11] 2033[4] 2309[8] 3274[2] 3752[2] 4349[8]
**Ice Cream Truck (USA)** *A C Avila* a89
4 b g Pleasantly Perfect(USA) Coconut Popsicle (USA) (Smart Strike (CAN))
5781a[7]
**Ice Falcon (IRE)** *James Tate* a38 31
3 gr f Verglas(IRE) Katimont (IRE) (Montjeu (IRE))
1616[8]
**Ice Lord (IRE)** *Clive Cox* 80
2 gr c Verglas(IRE) Special Lady (FR) (Kaldoun (FR))
7407[2]
**Ice Love (FR)** *T Castanheira* a102 101
3 b f Three Valleys(USA) Xcape To Victory (IRE) (Cape Cross (IRE))
237a[6] 1273a[7] 2195a[13] 3746a[8] 4171[5] 5963a[7] 7629a[11]
**Iceman George** *Denis Quinn* a35 36
10 b g Beat Hollow Diebiedale (Dominion)
3309[9] 4264[11]
**Ice Mayden** *Bryan Smart* a50 57
3 b f Major Cadeaux Reel Cool (Reel Buddy (USA))
2896[3] 3362[3] 3946[3] 4495[5] (6454) 7423[6] 7646[5] 8004[10]
**Ice Slice (IRE)** *James Eustace* a79 85
3 b g Dark Angel(IRE) Ice Rock (IRE) (Rock Of Gibraltar (IRE))
1390[5] (2163) 2781[8] 3428[6] 4074[4] 5038[7] 6990[7] (7417)
**Ice Tres** *Rod Millman* a59 59
5 br m Iceman Tup Tim (Emperor Jones (USA))
68[2] 210[10] 609[8] 959[2] 1249[8] 1919[6] 3115[4] 3585[4] 4264[6]
**Ichimoku** *Bryan Smart* a34 56
4 b g Indesatchel(IRE) Mythicism (Oasis Dream)
12[7] 1972[7] 2724[8] (3092) 3548[10] 4288[3] 5390[10] 7519[7]
**Ickymasho** *Jonathan Portman* a66 69
2 b f Multiplex Icky Woo (Mark Of Esteem (IRE))
4444[8] 5210[2] 5874[6] 6422[6] 7257[2]
**I Confess** *Geoffrey Harker* a81 57
9 br g Fantastic Light(USA) Vadsagreya (FR) (Linamix (FR))
66[4] 445[4] 643[8]
**Icy Blue** *Richard Whitaker* a68 69
6 b g Iceman Bridal Path (Groom Dancer (USA))
(289) 1446[2] 1881[6] 2171[4] 2546[7] 3096[5] 3533[3] 4023[6] 5054[4] 5496[5] 6217[P]
**Idamante** *Kristin Stubbs* 36
3 b g Amadeus Wolf Gower Valentine (Primo Valentino (IRE))
1211[P]
**Idarose (IRE)** *John David Riches* a7 24
5 b m Scorpion(IRE) Garra Princess (IRE) (Golan (IRE))
3880[9] 4387[9] 5145[6]
**Idder (IRE)** *Roger Varian* 85
3 br c Authorized(IRE) Epiphany (Zafonic (USA))
1279[5] 3273[4] 4388[2] 5132[7]

**Idea (USA)** *Sir Michael Stoute* a93 83
3 gr g Mizzen Mast(USA) Discuss (USA) (Danzig (USA))
2257$^{9}$ *(2921)* ◆ 3378$^{16}$ 4198$^{11}$ 5410$^{10}$

**Ideal (GER)** *Ferdinand J Leve* 103
4 b c Areion(GER) Intschu Tschuna (GER) (Lando (GER))
5938a$^{13}$

**Ideal Approach (IRE)** *M Delcher Sanchez* 76
2 br c Bushranger(IRE) Faleh (USA) (Silver Hawk (USA))
(6958a)

**Idee Libre (FR)** *Yannick Fouin* a47 78
4 b f Librettist(USA) Tiptonia (USA) (Kendor (FR))
3172a$^{6}$ 5225a$^{3}$

**Idle Curiosity (IRE)** *Jim Boyle* a64 64
4 b f Red Clubs(IRE) Idle Fancy (Mujtahid (USA))
*53$^{4}$* ◆ *340$^{7}$ 603$^{11}$ 819$^{5}$ 1010$^{8}$ 1123$^{6}$ 1386$^{10}$*
1668$^{13}$

**Idle Talker (IRE)** *Jose Santos* a55 48
2 b c Dandy Man(IRE) Special Pearl (IRE) (Alhaarth (IRE))
7414$^{6}$ *8060$^{7}$ 8205$^{8}$*

**I Do Know (IRE)** *S Donohoe* a58
4 gr f Posse(USA) I Don't Know (USA) (Star De Naskra (USA))
*5894$^{3}$*

**Idol Deputy (FR)** *James Bennett* a74 60
8 gr g Silver Deputy(CAN) Runaway Venus (USA) (Runaway Groom (CAN))
*1014$^{11}$ 1267$^{6}$ 1899$^{10}$* 2162$^{12}$ *3235$^{3}$ 3472$^{6}$*
*7522$^{8}$ 7626$^{9}$ 8122$^{7}$ 8250$^{11}$*

**Idyllic Star (IRE)** *Jim Goldie* a57 61
5 ch m Choisir(AUS) Idolize (Polish Precedent (USA))
7639$^{5}$ *7894$^{6}$*

**Ifan (IRE)** *Tim Vaughan* a80 84
6 b g Ivan Denisovich(IRE) Montana Miss (IRE) (Earl Of Barking (IRE))
*690$^{2}$ (1454)* (2862) 3681$^{2}$ *4736$^{6}$* 6264$^{10}$

**Iffranesia (FR)** *Robert Cowell* a77 93
4 ch f Iffraaj Farnesina (FR) (Anabaa (USA))
*383$^{2}$ (510) (654) 834$^{4}$* (1850) 2361$^{3}$ (3920)
(4609) 5419$^{10}$ 5925$^{6}$ 6923$^{8}$

**If I Do (FR)** *P Bary* 74
2 gr f Iffraaj Doriana (FR) (Kendor (FR))
4839a$^{3}$

**Ifittakesforever (IRE)** *John Butler* a60 52
2 bb g Kodiac Bobby Jane (Diktat)
3297$^{7}$ 3934$^{5}$ *7181$^{5}$ 8069$^{9}$ 8179$^{2}$*

**If I Were A Boy (IRE)** *Dominic Ffrench Davis* a64 74
7 b m Invincible Spirit(IRE) Attymon Lill (IRE) (Marju (IRE))
*382$^{5}$ 857$^{6}$ 1232$^{6}$ 2084$^{5}$* ◆ *3080$^{2}$* 3540$^{2}$
4105$^{2}$ (4273) (5503) 6523$^{12}$

**Ifrika** *Clive Brittain* a71 69
3 ch f Iffraaj Poyle Caitlin (IRE) (Bachir (IRE))
*955$^{2}$ 1240$^{6}$*

**Iftaar (IRE)** *D Grilli* 81
3 b g Bushranger(IRE) Kheleyf's Silver (IRE) (Kheleyf (USA))
(2044) 2508$^{2}$ 3225$^{8}$ 3672$^{8}$ 7320a$^{9}$

**Iftikaar (IRE)** *Philip Kirby* a52 69
4 b g Cape Cross(IRE) Anbella (FR) (Common Grounds)
4299$^{2}$ 4924$^{4}$ 5772$^{6}$ 6405$^{7}$ 7098$^{12}$ (7642)

**Ifwecan** *Mark Johnston* a96 98
3 b g Exceed And Excel(AUS) Kirk (Selkirk (USA))
1954$^{6}$ 2295$^{8}$ (3002) 3378$^{26}$ 3982$^{2}$ 4491$^{8}$ 4826$^{4}$
5410$^{8}$ 5771$^{8}$ 6748$^{5}$ *7227$^{3}$ 7555$^{7}$ 7801$^{5}$*

**Iggy** *Michael Easterby* a74 62
4 ch g Lucarno(USA) Fujakka (IRE) (Vettori (IRE))
*1448$^{3}$* 1602$^{4}$ 2219$^{7}$ 3092$^{7}$ 3298$^{11}$ 6674$^{4}$ 7025$^{7}$

**Igider (IRE)** *Roger Varian* 86
3 b c Teofilo(IRE) Changeable (Dansili)
2271$^{4}$ 2773$^{2}$ (3315)

**Ignight** *Mark Usher* a43 47
3 ch c Compton Place Time Clash (Timeless Times (USA))
3426$^{7}$ 4820$^{2}$ 5399$^{9}$ 5905$^{4}$ *6488$^{5}$*

**Ignis Away (FR)** *Mme Pia Brandt* a73 55
4 b f Gold Away(IRE) Danedrop (IRE) (Danehill (USA))
935a$^{12}$

**Iguacu** *Richard Price* a37 47
10 b g Desert Prince(IRE) Gay Gallanta (USA) (Woodman (USA))
5748$^{3}$ *7572$^{5}$*

**Iguazu Falls (USA)** *A bin Harmash* a88 108
9 ch g Pivotal Anna Palariva (IRE) (Caerleon (USA))
112a$^{2}$ 308a$^{4}$

**Ihtikar (USA)** *Lucy Normile* a69 43
4 b g Invasor(ARG) Ranin (Unfuwain (USA))
2216$^{12}$

**Ihtimal (IRE)** *Saeed bin Suroor* a113 110
3 b f Shamardal(USA) Eastern Joy (Dubai Destination (USA))
*(506a) (771a)* 1976$^{3}$ 2960$^{5}$

**Ikc Dragon Heart (USA)** *Johan Reutersköld* a80 65
4 b g Lion Heart(USA) Champaigne Amelia (USA) (Cure The Blues (USA))
*2244a$^{4}$ 3996a$^{7}$*

**Iktiview** *Philip Kirby* 62
6 ch g Iktibas Eastview Princess (J B Quick)
*260$^{6}$* 1359$^{7}$

**Ile De Re (FR)** *Kevin Frost* 101
8 gr g Linamix(FR) Ile Mamou (IRE) (Ela-Mana-Mou)
6747$^{10}$ 7409$^{11}$

**Iletaitunefois (FR)** *G Pannier* a68 67
3 ch f Sandwaki(USA) Unepetitehistoire (FR) (Sagacity (FR))
*599a$^{3}$*

**Il Gran Capo (IRE)** *Roger Ingram* 40
3 b g Cape Cross(IRE) Rambler (Selkirk (USA))
3537$^{11}$ 3804$^{9}$ *4325$^{12}$*

**I'll Be Good** *Alan Berry* a72 66
5 b g Red Clubs(IRE) Willisa (Polar Falcon (USA))
*(259)* ◆ *347$^{4}$ 412$^{4}$ 694$^{10}$* 1378$^{11}$ 2473$^{4}$ 2629$^{8}$
2951$^{2}$ 3338$^{13}$ 4860$^{6}$ 4994$^{6}$ 5237$^{11}$

**Illegal Action (USA)** *Olly Stevens* a55 51
3 b c Smart Strike(CAN) Polar Circle (USA) (Royal Academy (USA))
*173$^{4}$*

**Illegale (IRE)** *Nikki Evans* a55 45
8 b m Poliglote Pinkai (IRE) (Caerleon (USA))
*185$^{4}$ 454$^{8}$ 759$^{9}$ 1836$^{7}$* 2596a$^{6}$ 2836$^{12}$ *3710$^{2}$*
*4264$^{5}$* 5001$^{7}$ *5283$^{8}$ 5864$^{8}$* 6817$^{4}$ 7360$^{5}$ 7532$^{7}$
8074$^{6}$

**Illogical** *Ed Dunlop* a73 77
2 b f Paco Boy(IRE) Logic (Slip Anchor)
5643$^{4}$ ◆ 6435$^{3}$ 6701$^{2}$ *(7114)*

**Illuminating Dream (IRE)** *David Brown* a74 78
3 b f High Chaparral(IRE) Massada (Most Welcome)
*506a$^{10}$ 771a$^{8}$* 1658$^{5}$

**Illusive Force (IRE)** *Charles Hills* a68 68
2 ch c Iffraaj Geesala (IRE) (Barathea (IRE))
4676$^{5}$ *8192$^{3}$*

**Illustrious Prince (IRE)** *Julie Camacho* a70 85
7 b g Acclamation Sacred Love (IRE) (Barathea (IRE))
*540$^{6}$ 757$^{7}$ 929$^{7}$ 1082$^{5}$* 1710$^{3}$ 2341$^{12}$ 2841$^{4}$
(3227) 3485$^{2}$ 5197$^{6}$ 5385$^{6}$ 6639$^{4}$

**Illya Kuryakin** *Peter Chapple-Hyam* 56
2 b g Cockney Rebel(IRE) Vino Veritas (USA) (Chief's Crown (USA))
6259$^{16}$ 6812$^{2}$ 7040$^{8}$

**Il Penna (FR)** *Laura Grizzetti* a59 53
4 b c Orpen(USA) Santenay (IRE) (Alzao (USA))
*266a$^{12}$*

**Il Pittore (FR)** *G Botti* a93 66
3 b c Mr Greeley(USA) Spira (IRE) (Sadler's Wells (USA))
1779a$^{7}$

**Il Presuntuoso (FR)** *M Boutin* a80 65
3 b c Orpen(USA) Torrian (IRE) (Intikhab (USA))
*629a$^{6}$*

**Illumination** *Michael Easterby* a46 25
2 b f Indesatchel(IRE) Jan Mayen (Halling (USA))
6447$^{11}$ *6563$^{8}$* 7329$^{11}$ *7523$^{6}$*

**I'm A Butterfly (IRE)** *Eve Johnson Houghton* 62
2 b f Teofilo(IRE) Am I (USA) (Thunder Gulch (USA))
5187$^{5}$ 6065$^{6}$

**Imaginary Diva** *George Margarson* a65 55
8 b m Lend A Hand Distant Diva (Distant Relative)
*313$^{2}$ 466$^{6}$ 662$^{3}$ 1089$^{3}$* 1639$^{7}$ 4768$^{3}$ 5316$^{8}$
6399$^{7}$ *7191$^{4}$ 7520$^{9}$ 8023$^{3}$* 8133$^{6}$

**Imaginary World (IRE)** *John Balding* a80 77
6 b m Exceed And Excel(AUS) Plutonia (Sadler's Wells (USA))
*461$^{2}$ (548) 862$^{3}$ 929$^{4}$* 1510$^{3}$ *1857$^{2}$* 3096$^{2}$
*3402$^{3}$* 4112$^{8}$ *(5256)* 6057$^{10}$ *6269$^{6}$* 7042$^{15}$
*8058$^{7}$* 8177$^{7}$

**Imagining (USA)** *Claude McGaughey III* 115
6 ch h Giant's Causeway(USA) Daydreaming (USA) (A.P. Indy (USA))
(2228a) 3025a$^{6}$ 7611a$^{7}$

**I'm Already Sexy (USA)** *Wayne Catalano* 106
4 bb f Ready's Image(USA) Klohho (USA) (Trempolino (USA))
5459a$^{6}$ 7615a$^{5}$

**I'm Back (IRE)** *Saeed bin Suroor* a102 97
4 b c Exceed And Excel(AUS) Paracel (USA) (Gone West (USA))
240a$^{12}$ 5749$^{8}$ *6943$^{2}$*

**Im Dapper Too** *John Davies* a58 52
3 b g Dapper Lonely One (Perryston View)
1542$^{13}$ 5469$^{5}$ 6118$^{6}$ 6544$^{6}$ *7646$^{2}$ 7764$^{4}$*

**I'm Fraam Govan** *George Baker* a99 99
6 ch g Fraam Urban Dancer (IRE) (Generous (IRE))
4756$^{12}$ 5695$^{3}$ ◆ 6330$^{4}$ *7703$^{6}$ 7850$^{5}$ 8095$^{3}$*
*8243$^{8}$*

**I'm Harry** *George Baker* a66 76
5 b g Haafhd First Approval (Royal Applause)
*(1012)* ◆ (1622a) 2599a$^{2}$ (2593a) (3155) 3919$^{2}$
4030$^{2}$ 4716a$^{3}$

**Imjin River (IRE)** *William Stone* a64 60
7 b g Namid Lady Nasrana (FR) (Al Nasr (FR))
*(58) (258) 383$^{5}$ 8322$^{7}$*

**I'm Lucy (IRE)** *Linda Jewell* a7
3 b f Papal Bull Melaaya (USA) (Aljabr (USA))
2466$^{8}$ *2917$^{12}$*

**Immediate** *D Smaga* 85
2 b f Oasis Dream Emergency (Dr Fong (USA))
(6619a) 7094a$^{8}$

**Impatiente (FR)** *A Lyon* a86 83
4 b f Gold Away(IRE) Good To Dance (IRE) (Groom Dancer (USA))
*5961a$^{3}$*

**Impeccability** *John Mackie* a51 53
4 b f Lucky Story(USA) Impeccable Guest (IRE) (Orpen (USA))
*68$^{9}$ 1132$^{5}$ 1453$^{5}$* 3309$^{5}$ 4749$^{2}$ 5331$^{3}$ ◆ 5748$^{6}$
*6157$^{10}$* 6542$^{3}$ 7006$^{5}$ *7524$^{3}$*

**Impedimanta (IRE)** *M Delzangles* 67
2 b f Aussie Rules(USA) Fontcia (FR) (Enrique)
5590a$^{5}$

**Imperative (USA)** *George Papaprodromou* a117
4 b g Bernardini(USA) Call Her (USA) (Caller I.D. (USA))
*5781a$^{3}$ 7614a$^{9}$*

**Imperator Augustus (IRE)** *Patrick Holmes* a69 71
6 b g Holy Roman Emperor(IRE) Coralita (IRE) (Night Shift (USA))
*79$^{7}$ 589$^{7}$ 757$^{4}$ 817$^{6}$* 2019$^{9}$ (2219) 2605$^{6}$
3000$^{5}$ 3237$^{3}$ 3572$^{12}$ (4069) 4707$^{5}$ 5415$^{7}$ *7950$^{4}$*
*8143$^{9}$*

**Imperia (USA)** *Kiaran McLaughlin* a112 100
2 bb c Medaglia d'Oro(USA) Cocoa Beach (CHI) (Doneraile Court (USA))
7590a$^{10}$

**Imperial Glance** *Andrew Balding* a56 74
4 br g Passing Glance Juno Mint (Sula Bula)
1281$^{7}$ 2721$^{2}$ 3850$^{7}$ 4673$^{7}$

**Imperial Legend (IRE)** *David Nicholls* 93
5 b g Mujadil(USA) Titian Saga (IRE) (Titus Livius (FR))
1650$^{6}$ 2350$^{3}$ 2456$^{10}$ 4174$^{4}$ 4488$^{8}$ 4859$^{5}$ 5563$^{8}$
6235$^{6}$ 6512$^{6}$

**Imperial Link** *Paul Cole* a60 67
2 b f Rail Link Imperia (GER) (Tertullian (USA))
4943$^{7}$ 6434$^{4}$ 6868$^{3}$ 7378$^{8}$ *7943$^{8}$ 8174$^{4}$*

**Imperial March (IRE)** *Clive Cox* 50
2 b g Arch(USA) Sneak Preview (Monsieur Bond (IRE))
7407$^{6}$

**Imperial Spirit** *Jo Hughes* a64 57
4 b g Imperial Dancer Country Spirit (Sayf El Arab (USA))
*9$^{8}$ 192$^{12}$ 478$^{7}$*

**Imperial War (IRE)** *Richard Hannon* a9 52
2 b c Lawman(FR) Halicardia (Halling (USA))
6317$^{6}$ 6812$^{3}$ *7372$^{9}$*

**Imperiator** *P Decouz* a106 112
3 b g Footstepsinthesand Jarhes (IRE) (Green Desert (USA))
1272a$^{3}$ 2799a$^{10}$

**Impertinent** *Anthony Carson* a53 27
4 b f Halling(USA) Incarnation (IRE) (Samum (GER))
2875$^{9}$ *7292$^{12}$*

**Impressive Victory (USA)** *Saeed bin Suroor* a80
2 bb f Street Cry(IRE) Long Lashes (USA) (Rock Hard Ten (USA))
*4075$^{3}$ 5305$^{2}$*

**Improvized** *William Muir* a53 63
3 b f Authorized(IRE) Rhapsodize (Halling (USA))
1494$^{8}$ *2080$^{5}$* 2643$^{5}$ *3711$^{11}$* 5277$^{6}$ (5846) (6999)
7218$^{7}$

**Impulsive Moment (IRE)** *Andrew Balding* a76 105
3 ch g Galileo(IRE) Luas Line (IRE) (Danehill (USA))
1699$^{2}$ ◆ 2990$^{11}$ 4385$^{3}$

**Imshivalla (IRE)** *Richard Fahey* 91
3 b f Acclamation Subtle Affair (IRE) (Barathea (IRE))
1601$^{5}$ 1711$^{5}$ 2218$^{7}$ 3300$^{4}$ 3885$^{2}$ (4419) (5051)
(5468) 5882$^{7}$ 6476$^{11}$ (7119)

**I'm Super Too (IRE)** *Alan Swinbank* a71 79
7 b g Fasliyev(USA) Congress (IRE) (Dancing Brave (USA))
*1245$^{3}$* 1675$^{7}$ 1970$^{3}$ (2293) 2519$^{4}$ 2790$^{2}$ 3361$^{8}$
3785$^{4}$ 5172$^{5}$ 5855$^{7}$ 6822$^{7}$ *7829$^{3}$ 8086$^{8}$*

**Imtiyaaz (IRE)** *Roger Varian* 62
2 b f Starspangledbanner(AUS) Endure (IRE) (Green Desert (USA))
6434$^{8}$

**I'Mwaitingforyou** *Peter Bowen*
5 ch m Needwood Blade Elegant Lady (Selkirk (USA))
6738$^{9}$ *7067$^{5}$*

**Inauguration (IRE)** *Charles Hills* a61 42
2 b f Acclamation Carraigoona (IRE) (Rock Of Gibraltar (IRE))
4781$^{8}$ *6032$^{4}$*

**Inca Drum (USA)** *Pat Eddery* a60 23
3 b c Empire Maker(USA) Around (Danehill (USA))
1166$^{9}$ *1797$^{9}$*

**Incantare** *Jim Allen* a58
4 gr f Proclamation(IRE) Mythical Charm (Charnwood Forest (IRE))
*8038$^{4}$ 8294$^{3}$*

**Ince Moss** *Richard Fahey* 40
2 br f Invincible Spirit(IRE) Royal Grace (Royal Applause)
6700$^{7}$ 7503$^{P}$

**Incendo** *Conor Dore* a81 44
8 ch g King's Best(USA) Kindle (Selkirk (USA))
*250$^{2}$ 450$^{6}$* 920a$^{5}$ *(1140)* 1828a$^{6}$ *2394$^{3}$* (2547)
3064$^{2}$ (3438) *3860$^{4}$* 4538$^{5}$ (4996) 5502$^{3}$ *6274$^{10}$*
*6942$^{12}$ 8190$^{4}$* 8313$^{8}$

**Inchila** *Peter Chapple-Hyam* 112
3 b f Dylan Thomas(IRE) Inchiri (Sadler's Wells (USA))
(1424) ◆ 2299$^{4}$ 2960$^{4}$ 3376$^{P}$

**Inciting Incident (IRE)** *Ed McMahon* a66 88
3 b g Camacho Halliwell House (Selkirk (USA))
*936$^{5}$ 1146$^{3}$* 1851$^{4}$ *2886$^{7}$* 3669$^{7}$ (4411) (5753)
(6006)

**Included** *Amanda Perrett* a49
2 b f Champs Elysees Cordoba (Oasis Dream)
*7659$^{6}$*

**Incomparable** *Scott Dixon* a68 60
9 ch g Compton Place Indian Silk (IRE) (Dolphin Street (FR))
*908$^{7}$* 2675$^{3}$ (3093) 3548$^{5}$ 4494$^{10}$ 5207$^{2}$ 7057$^{9}$
*7253$^{9}$ 8024$^{7}$ (8088) 8210$^{4}$*

**Incredible Fresh (IRE)** *James Fanshawe* a67 74
3 b g Bushranger(IRE) Red Fox (IRE) (Spectrum (IRE))
*1795$^{9}$* 2432$^{6}$ 3343$^{2}$ *5550$^{7}$ 7063$^{4}$*

**Incurs Four Faults** *Keith Dalgleish* a65 69
3 b g Halling(USA) Rapsgate (IRE) (Mozart (IRE))
*477$^{9}$ 765$^{7}$ 906$^{3}$ 1223$^{2}$* 1684$^{4}$ 2674$^{6}$ 3053$^{6}$
(3603) 4196$^{P}$ (4359) 4516$^{2}$ 5414$^{4}$ 5811$^{5}$

**Indaria** *Rod Millman* 82
2 b f Sleeping Indian Azharia (Oasis Dream)
2692$^{4}$ (3583) (4815) 5714$^{7}$ 6128$^{7}$

**Indastar** *Michael Herrington* a65 42
4 b g Indesatchel(IRE) Charcoal (Primo Valentino (IRE))
*5103$^{6}$ (6409)* 6720$^{6}$ *7253$^{10}$ 8088$^{9}$*

**Indego Blues** *David Nicholls* 83
5 b g Indesatchel(IRE) Yanomami (USA) (Slew O'Gold (USA))
6824$^{12}$ 7179$^{5}$ 7505$^{10}$

**Indelible Ink (IRE)** *Sir Michael Stoute* a75 75
2 b g Invincible Spirit(IRE) Serres (IRE) (Daylami (IRE))
3429$^{6}$ 4467$^{2}$ *6565$^{2}$*

**Indepub** *Martin Todhunter* 60
5 b g Indesatchel(IRE) Champenoise (Forzando)
3661$^{6}$ 4296$^{8}$ 4962$^{11}$

**Indescribable (IRE)** *Mark Johnston* 83
2 b g Invincible Spirit(IRE) Subtle Charm (Machiavellian (USA))
2146$^{8}$ 2756$^{6}$ (3119) 3692$^{3}$ 4172$^{4}$ (4686) 4920$^{7}$
5998$^{5}$ 6312$^{2}$

**Indian Affair** *Milton Bradley* a72 67
4 b c Sleeping Indian Rare Fling (USA) (Kris S (USA))
*83$^{2}$ 295$^{5}$ 576$^{3}$ 841$^{6}$ 938$^{2}$ 1115$^{2}$ 1766$^{7}$*
3150$^{4}$ 3519$^{5}$ 4908$^{6}$ 5287$^{9}$ 5605$^{6}$ 8014$^{7}$ 8286$^{2}$

**Indianapolis (USA)** *Bob Baffert* a108
3 bb c Medaglia d'Oro(USA) Pretty N Smart (USA) (Beau Genius (CAN))
*7612a$^{10}$*

**Indianaughty (USA)** *Marco Botti* a77
2 b c Indian Charlie(USA) Be Fair (USA) (Exchange Rate (USA))
*3578$^{3}$* ◆ *(5278)*

**Indian Champ** *Kevin Ryan* a22 67
2 b g Sleeping Indian Bebe De Cham (Tragic Role (USA))
*2395$^{8}$* 4192$^{3}$ 4701$^{4}$ 4993$^{4}$ 5285$^{2}$ 5630$^{3}$

**Indian Chief (IRE)** *David Nicholls* 110
4 b g Montjeu(IRE) Buck Aspen (USA) (Seeking The Gold (USA))
6752$^{22}$ 7120$^{8}$

**Indian Giver** *John David Riches* a58 62
6 b m Indesatchel(IRE) Bint Baddi (FR) (Shareef Dancer (USA))
3052$^{8}$ 3604$^{3}$ (3828) 4197$^{4}$ 4381$^{3}$ *5512$^{3}$* 5809$^{3}$
6600$^{7}$ 6837$^{2}$ 7061$^{6}$ *7813$^{7}$ 7976$^{7}$*

**Indian Jack (IRE)** *Ed Walker* a98 95
6 ch g Indian Haven Almaviva (IRE) (Grand Lodge (USA))
*(56)* ◆ *(533) 840$^{6}$*

**Indian Joe** *J S Moore* a41 47
2 b c Sleeping Indian Belle De Nuit (IRE) (Statoblest)
2829$^{6}$ 4760$^{12}$ *5799$^{9}$ 7529$^{12}$*

**Indian Keys** *Kevin Ryan* 67
2 ch f Sleeping Indian Newkeylets (Diktat)
1837$^{4}$ 2328$^{3}$ 2673$^{2}$ 3620$^{2}$ 4913$^{9}$ 5885$^{8}$

**Indian Maharaja (IRE)** *A P O'Brien* a73 85
3 b c Galileo(IRE) Again (IRE) (Danehill Dancer (IRE))
1200a$^{8}$ 5577$^{9}$ 6350a$^{10}$ *6909a$^{8}$*

**Indian Rainbow (IRE)** *Andreas Lowe* 112
3 ch f Indian Haven Pent House (IRE) (Titus Livius (FR))
2584a$^{2}$ 3873a$^{5}$ 5407a$^{2}$

**Indian Scout** *Anabel K Murphy* a53 51
6 b g Indesatchel(IRE) Manderina (Mind Games)
1875$^{5}$ 2894$^{6}$ 3209$^{2}$ 3553$^{3}$ 3973$^{4}$ 4343$^{6}$ 7002$^{4}$
7219$^{8}$ *(7990) 8189$^{8}$*

**Indian Tim** *Milton Bradley*
2 b c Sleeping Indian River City Moon (USA) (Riverman (USA))
4150$^{6}$

**Indian Tinker** *Robert Cowell* a79 79
5 b g Sleeping Indian Breakfast Creek (Hallgate)
1618$^{3}$ 1878$^{4}$ 2364$^{2}$ 3707$^{4}$ (5060) 5880$^{2}$ 7215$^{3}$
7535$^{3}$ *7761$^{2}$ 8180$^{12}$*

**Indian Trifone (IRE)** *Ed Walker* a71 75
4 ch c Indian Haven Almaviva (IRE) (Grand Lodge (USA))
*(1084)* ◆ 1845$^{9}$ 2702$^{8}$ 3254$^{8}$ 4402$^{2}$ 5150$^{7}$
*6141$^{8}$ 7358$^{8}$*

**Indian Violet (IRE)** *Zoe Davison* a61 66
8 b g Indian Ridge Violet Spring (IRE) (Exactly Sharp (USA))
*211$^{5}$ 575$^{7}$ 737$^{4}$ 822$^{5}$ 1016$^{6}$ 1105$^{2}$ (1386)*
*1917$^{8}$* 2069$^{8}$ *3233$^{11}$*

**India's Song** *David Simcock* a72
4 b f Zamindar(USA) Sea Chorus (Singspiel (IRE))
*382$^{4}$ (578) 733$^{2}$ 822$^{4}$ 998$^{2}$ 1051$^{4}$ 1450$^{4}$*
*(8030)*

**Indignant** *Richard Hannon* a83 106
4 ch f Gold Away(IRE) Moiava (FR) (Bering)
2336$^{10}$ (3278) 4171$^{3}$ 4854$^{3}$ 5722$^{4}$ 6254$^{12}$ 6929$^{4}$

**Indigo (FR)** *Hanne Bechmann* a36 82
4 b f Falco(USA) Blanche (FR) (Loup Solitaire (USA))
6388a$^{9}$

**Indigo Lady** *W McCreery* 94
4 b f Sir Percy Seal Indigo (IRE) (Glenstal (USA))
1076a$^{11}$ 4478a$^{7}$

**Indira** *John Berry* a67 84
3 ch f Sleeping Indian Forever Loved (Deploy)
*37$^{4}$ 127$^{3}$ 434$^{3}$ 665$^{6}$ 1007$^{4}$ 1098$^{3}$* 2688$^{3}$
3316$^{7}$ (4316) 4863$^{2}$ (5449) 5818$^{2}$ 6541$^{2}$ 7102$^{5}$

**Indomitable Spirit** *Martin Smith* a58 22
2 b g Zebedee Gayala (IRE) (Iron Mask (USA))
5056$^{8}$ *6101$^{7}$* 6683$^{11}$ *7014$^{6}$*

**Indomito (GER)** *W Mongil* a99 102
8 b h Areion(GER) Insola (GER) (Royal Solo (IRE))
*(669a)*

**Indonesienne (IRE)** *C Ferland* 111
3 b f Muhtathir Mydarshaan (Darshaan)
1480a$^{3}$ 2195a$^{10}$ 3773a$^{4}$ 5479a$^{5}$

**Induna (AUS)** *Saeed bin Suroor* a69 69
6 b g Elusive Quality(USA) Camarena (NZ) (Danehill (USA))
*243a$^{12}$*

**Indus Valley (IRE)** *Des Donovan* a68 63
7 ch g Indian Ridge Gloriously Bright (USA) (Nureyev (USA))
*(274) 449$^{6}$ (740) 851$^{4}$* 1613$^{4}$ 2164$^{7}$ *2646$^{7}$*
3160$^{6}$ *(3527) 4072$^{5}$ 5605$^{11}$ 6035$^{13}$* 6715$^{9}$
7259$^{6}$ 7883$^{6}$ 8013$^{2}$ (8195) 8299$^{4}$

**Indy (IRE)** *David Barron* 98
3 b c Indian Haven Maddie's Pearl (IRE) (Clodovil (IRE))
2706$^{2}$ 7119$^{8}$ 7410$^{3}$

**Inevitable** *Mark Johnston* a46 78
3 b g Dubawi(IRE) Come What May (Selkirk (USA))
*2060$^{7}$* 3789$^{2}$ (3978)

**Inexes** *John Gosden* a72
2 bg c Exceed And Excel(AUS) Likeable (Dalakhani (IRE))
*7811$^{2}$ 8067$^{4}$*

**Infinite Magic (USA)** *Wayne Catalano* a83 104
4 b r More Than Ready(USA) Truly Enchanting (IRE) (Danehill Dancer (IRE))
5457a[8]

**Inflection (IRE)** *Hugo Palmer* a69 74
3 b f Rock Of Gibraltar(IRE) Rubileo (Galileo (IRE))
2682[4] 4569[2] 5007[4] 5763[3] 7438[9]

**Inflexiball** *John Mackie* a50
2 b f Refuse To Bend(IRE) Sphere (IRE) (Daylami (IRE))
7425[6] 8288[9]

**In Focus (IRE)** *Alan Swinbank* a62 78
3 ch c Intense Focus(USA) Reine De Neige (Kris)
2524[5] 3187[5] (3946) (4067) ◆ 4300[6] (5566) 6345[4] 6792[5]

**In For A Pound (FR)** *P Monfort* a69
3 ch f Soldier Of Fortune(IRE) Tchikala (Inchinor)
3745a[5]

**In For Dinner (FR)** *P Monfort* a71 65
3 b c My Risk(FR) Illoughane (FR) (Slickly (FR))
360a[8] 585a[7] 1620a[4]

**Informality (IRE)** *J Moon*
3 b f Haafhd Casual Glance (Sinndar (IRE))
5970a[6] 6188a[P]

**Ingenti** *Christopher Wilson* 75
6 ch m Blue Dakota(IRE) Kungfu Kerry (Celtic Swing)
1843[6] 2542[5] 3831[6] 3954[5] 4901[8] 5375[6] 5635[4] 5819[4] 5912[7] 6213[14] 6580[3] 6671[8] (7510) 7671[10]

**Ingleby Angel (IRE)** *David O'Meara* a97 103
5 br g Dark Angel(IRE) Mistress Twister (Pivotal)
1721[5] 1958[2] 2286[9] 3356[27] 4214[13] 4491[2] 5163[7] 5771[5] 6332[7] 6752[12] 7236[5] 7490[5] 7801[2] ◆ 7971[6] 8116[3]

**Ingleby Hollow** *David O'Meara* 52
2 ch g Beat Hollow Mistress Twister (Pivotal)
6931[7] 7173[3] 7637[6]

**Ingleby Spring (IRE)** *Richard Fahey* 63
2 br f Zebedee Jouel (FR) (Machiavellian (USA))
1900[5] 2615[4] 3529[2] 4012[3] 4899[6]

**Ingleby Symphony (IRE)** *Richard Fahey* a59 89
4 b f Oratorio(IRE) Alizaya (IRE) (Highest Honor (FR))
1762[2] 2017[3] 2477[5] 3254[10] 3502[2] (5172) (5235) 6479[9] 7125[15]

**Inheritance** *Sir Michael Stoute* a57 59
3 b f Oasis Dream Peeress (Pivotal)
1767[5] 2681[12] 3433[10]

**Iniciar (GER)** *Jean-Pierre Carvalho* 106
4 b c Galileo(IRE) Iota (GER) (Tiger Hill (IRE))
2001a[4] 5231a[8] 6180a[8]

**Inis Airc (IRE)** *Sylvester Kirk* a62 65
3 b f Footstepsinthesand Inis Boffin (Danehill Dancer (IRE))
2489[2] 3729[3] 4677[6] 5307[3]

**Inishmot Duchess (IRE)** *T G McCourt* a67 75
6 bl m Medecis Inishmot Lady (IRE) (Great Commotion (USA))
128a[10]

**Inis Meain (USA)** *Denis Gerard Hogan* a40 112
7 b g Bernstein(USA) Runaway Fields (USA) (Runaway Groom (CAN))
1750a[3] 7144a[14]

**Initial (FR)** *C Boutin* a86 90
3 b c Sageburg(IRE) Isarnixe (GER) (Banyumanik (IRE))
436a[4]

**Injaz** *Kevin Ryan* a62 64
3 ch g Compton Place Belle's Edge (Danehill Dancer (IRE))
1543[4] 2397[2] 2870[4] 3405[4] 4019[5] 5080[4] 5492[9] 6477[7]

**Injun Sands** *Jane Chapple-Hyam* 73
3 b g Halling(USA) Serriera (FR) (Highest Honor (FR))
1529[13] 2201[9] 2746[7] 3655[2] 4672[3]

**Inke (IRE)** *Jim Boyle* a64 63
2 br f Intikhab(USA) Chifney Rush (IRE) (Grand Lodge (USA))
6261[4] 6652[4] 6997[4] 7396[3]

**Inkerman (IRE)** *Jamie Osborne* a77 79
4 b g Duke Of Marmalade(IRE) Lady Taufan (IRE) (Taufan (USA))
2126[3] 2902[2] 3227[6] 3850[6] 4432[2] 4674[5] 5202[2] 6087[3] 6397[12]

**Inniscastle Boy** *Jim Goldie* a33 41
5 b g Sir Percy Galapagar (USA) (Miswaki (USA))
2457[5] 3052[5] 4259[12] 5144[9]

**Inniscastle Lad** *William Muir* 83
2 b c Kyllachy Glencal (Compton Place)
3728[5] (4409) 4853[4] 5672[5] 6135[2] 7415[4]

**Innocently (IRE)** *David O'Meara* 90
3 ch g Kheleyf(USA) Innocency (USA) (Diesis)
3399[4] 3756[3] (4315) 4636[6] (4977) 5696[9]

**Innocent Touch (IRE)** *Richard Fahey* 88
3 bl g Intense Focus(USA) Guajira (FR) (Mtoto)
1509[4] (1904) 2319[5] 3003[3] (3655) 4189[2] 4887[2] 5691[10]

**Innoko (FR)** *Tony Carroll* a72 60
4 gr g Carlotamix(FR) Chalana (Ashkalani (IRE))
293[10] 458[4] 801[7] 958[4] 1097[6] 2301[8] 2672[4] 3336[2] 3852[9] 5001[10] 6410[9] 7256[2] (7426) (7635) 7805[5] ◆ (7877a)

**Innovative Idea (USA)** *Eoin Harty* a88
2 b f Bernardini(USA) Golden Velvet (USA) (Seeking The Gold (USA))
6915a[11]

**Innsbruck** *John Quinn* 87
4 b g Tiger Hill(IRE) Lille Hammer (Sadler's Wells (USA))
2119[3] 2981[4] 3654[4] 4175[2] 6292[8] (6932)

**Inordinate (USA)** *P Bary* 98
2 b c Harlan's Holiday(USA) Out Of Reach (Warning)
(6245a)

**Insaany** *Mark Johnston* 89
3 b c Shamardal(USA) Mother Of Pearl (IRE) (Sadler's Wells (USA))
1597[2] (2133) (2506) 3055[5] (3675) 4400[6] 4821[5] 5669[6]

**In Seine** *John Best* a59 45
3 b g Champs Elysees Fancy Rose (USA) (Joyeux Danseur (USA))
142[9] 607[5] 839[5] 5689[7] 6339[8] 6682[12] 7518[RR]

**Inshaa** *Sir Michael Stoute* 46
2 b c Dansili Hidden Brief (Barathea (IRE))
5149[9]

**Inside Knowledge (USA)** *Garry Woodward* a42 48
8 rg g Mizzen Mast(USA) Kithira (Danehill (USA))
2[4] 1284[5]

**Insight (IRE)** *John Spearing* 61
3 b f Bushranger(IRE) Ribbon Glade (UAE) (Zafonic (USA))
1280[7] 1681[7] 2129[8] 2775[9]

**Insolenceofoffice (IRE)** *Richard Ford* a69 60
6 b g Kodiac Sharp Diversion (USA) (Diesis)
(83) 147[4] 295[3] 576[10] 841[5] 6897[11] 7111[10] 7364[13] (7782) 7864[3] 8142[4]

**Inspector Norse** *Sylvester Kirk* a70 84
3 b g Norse Dancer(IRE) Indiana Blues (Indian Ridge)
1433[9] 1894[4] 3315[8] (4356) 5008[6] 5311[6] 6262[2] 6516[2] (6714) 7161[8]

**Inspire** *Mark Usher*
2 gr f Hellvelyn Time Clash (Timeless Times (USA))
4269[11]

**Inspiriter** *H-A Pantall* a74 101
3 b f Invincible Spirit(IRE) Floristry (Fasliyev (USA))
6994a[8] (7856a)

**Instant Attraction (IRE)** *Jedd O'Keeffe* a89 88
3 b g Tagula(IRE) Coup De Coeur (IRE) (Kahyasi)
1358[5] 1725[2] 2257[6] 2781[4] 3273[6] 4074[11] 5197[3] 5496[3] (6345) 6770[6] 7085[3] 7438[4] 7719[7]

**Instant Karma (IRE)** *Michael Bell* a69 84
3 b g Peintre Celebre(USA) Kotdiji (Mtoto)
6485[5] (7332)

**Integral** *Sir Michael Stoute* 119
4 b f Dalakhani(IRE) Echelon (Danehill (USA))
1974[2] (3355) (4165) 4954a[3] (6927) 7274[7]

**Integrity (USA)** *Chad C Brown* a110
4 bb c Hard Spun(USA) Generosity (USA) (Unbridled's Song (USA))
(2005a)

**Intense Feeling (IRE)** *Lee Carter* a58 75
3 br f Intense Focus(USA) Titania (Fairy King (USA))
217[4] 354[2] 568[7] 1277[2] 1570[6] 1914[3] (2209) (2281) 2647[7] 3388[5] 3523[5] 4969[5] 5427[6] 5753[5] 5972[6]

**Intense Holiday (USA)** *Todd Pletcher* a110
3 bb c Harlan's Holiday(USA) Intensify (USA) (Unbridled's Song (USA))
1964a[12]

**Intense Pride (IRE)** *T Hogan* 77
2 ch c Intense Focus(USA) Greannmhar (USA) (Distorted Humor (USA))
6375a[6]

**Intense Style (IRE)** *J S Bolger* a100 89
2 ch c Intense Focus(USA) Style Queen (IRE) (Galileo (IRE))
2855a[7]

**Intense Tango** *K R Burke* 85
3 b f Mastercraftsman(IRE) Cover Look (SAF) (Fort Wood (USA))
1423[7] 2109[6] 4392[4] (5132) 6137[2] 6637[4] 7409[15]

**Intensical (IRE)** *J S Bolger* 103
3 b c Intense Focus(USA) Christinas Letter (IRE) (Galileo (IRE))
3737a[6] 4459a[4] 4771a[9] 5957a[19] 6354a[12]

**Intensive (IRE)** *Jamie Osborne* a50
3 ch f Intense Focus(USA) Alinea (USA) (Kingmambo (USA))
37[8] 189[6] 316[12] 653[7]

**Interakt** *Joseph Tuite* a55 59
7 b m Rakti Amelie Pouliche (FR) (Desert Prince (IRE))
1877[4] 1986[U] 2174[4] 2722[6] 3327[5] 3589[8] 4337[5]

**Interception (IRE)** *David Lanigan* a92 99
4 ch f Raven's Pass(USA) Badee'A (IRE) (Marju (IRE))
1554[5] ◆ 2157[3] ◆ 2861[2] 5826[4] ◆ (6336) ◆ 6922[3]

**Interchoice Star** *Ray Peacock* a67 55
9 b g Josr Algarhoud(IRE) Blakeshall Girl (Piccolo)
(18) (100) 511[5] (694) 866[5] 1892[7] 2174[3] 2435[7] 5897[9] 6897[7] 7111[8] 7519[2] 7783[4] (8085)

**Interconnection** *Ed Vaughan* a65 77
3 ch g Mount Nelson Lacework (Pivotal)
1817[3] 2095[2] 3135[3] 3789[3] 4350[2] 5534[3] 6091[6] (7176)

**Interior Minister** *Jonjo O'Neill* a61 88
4 b g Nayef(USA) Sister Maria (USA) (Kingmambo (USA))
2034[7]

**Interject (USA)** *Charles Hills* a55 68
3 bb f Empire Maker(USA) Introducing (USA) (Deputy Minister (CAN))
1423[8] 4022[3]

**Intermath (IRE)** *David Evans* a73 84
3 br g Camacho Royal Interlude (IRE) (King's Theatre (IRE))
624[8] 892[5] 1352[2] 1586[8] 2333[8] 2839[6]

**Intermedium** *Charlie Appleby* a83 84
3 ro g Exceed And Excel(AUS) Gweneira (Machiavellian (USA))
1296[3] 2083[4] 3156[2] (3677)

**International Name** *Saeed bin Suroor* a75 57
2 ch g Iffraaj Dove (IRE) (Sadler's Wells (USA))
5881[11] 6565[3]

**International Star (USA)** *Michael J Maker* a99 102
2 b c Fusaichi Pegasus(USA) Parlez (USA) (French Deputy (USA))
7590a[9]

**Interpret (USA)** *M Al Muhairi* a108 36
6 b g Distorted Humor(USA) Quendom (ARG) (Interprete (ARG))
508a[14] 900a[15]

**Inthar (USA)** *S Seemar* a89 96
5 ch g Medicean Mont Etoile (IRE) (Montjeu (IRE))
305a[7]

**Intibaah** *Brian Meehan* a87 114
4 b g Elnadim(USA) Mawaared (Machiavellian (USA))
(2149) 6920[8] 7272[5]

**Intilaaq (USA)** *Roger Varian* 79
2 b c Dynaformer(USA) Torrestrella (IRE) (Orpen (USA))
6125[3]

**Intimation** *Sir Michael Stoute* 50
2 b f Dubawi(IRE) Infallible (Pivotal)
7018[9]

**Intimhir (IRE)** *F Head* 105
4 ch f Muhtathir Sahel (GER) (Monsun (GER))
1827a[11] 5369a[9]

**Intimidator (IRE)** *Clive Brittain* a62
3 b c Intikhab(USA) Zither (Zafonic (USA))
7682[7]

**Intiwin (IRE)** *Richard Fahey* 83
2 b g Intikhab(USA) Muluk (IRE) (Rainbow Quest (USA))
2698[2] 3255[3] 4253[3] 4633[2] (5760) 6256[15] 7443[5]

**Intomist (IRE)** *Jim Boyle* a77 78
5 ch g Strategic Prince Fast Temper (USA) (In The Wings)
161[2] 472[4] 627[7] 817[5] 2282[3] 2486[6] 3088[2] (3734) 3879[2] 4355[3] 4588[5] 5785[2] 6263[7] 6789[P]

**Intransigent** *Andrew Balding* a112 115
5 b g Trans Island Mara River (Efisio)
304a[11] 597a[14] 678a[7] 886[6] 1174[3] 3420[7] 4187[4] (4937) 5665[8] (6921) 7555[3] (7802)

**Intrepid (IRE)** *Ian Williams* a81 74
4 b g Invincible Spirit(IRE) Imiloa (USA) (Kingmambo (USA))
1283[4] 1429[5] 1739[8] 2905[4] 3795[5]

**Intrigo** *Charlie Appleby* a99 103
4 b g Medicean A Thousand Smiles (IRE) (Sadler's Wells (USA))
207a[3] 394a[5] 679a[5]

**Intrinsic** *Robert Cowell* a61 106
4 b c Oasis Dream Infallible (Pivotal)
(2147) (2503) (4895) 5674[8] 6327[18]

**Intrude** *David Simcock* 56
2 b g Intikhab(USA) Don't Tell Mum (IRE) (Dansili)
6985[7] 7637[5]

**Intruder** *Richard Fahey* a61 71
2 ch c Major Cadeaux Intrusion (Indesatchel (IRE))
4192[4] 4701[5] 5253[4] 5714[2] 6222[2] 6690[4] 7130[5]

**Intuitif (FR)** *H-F Devin* 34
2 b c Makfi Gold Harvest (FR) (Kaldounevees (FR))
1402a[11]

**Invador** *Jean-Pierre Carvalho* 98
3 b c Tertullian(USA) Iora (GER) (Konigsstuhl (GER))
3073a[8] 5484a[5]

**Invasor Luck (USA)** *James Fanshawe* a86 68
3 b c Invasor(ARG) Lonely Ahead (USA) (Rahy (USA))
1380[3] 1830[3] 3428[7] 4051[2] 5010[2] 5552[7] (6045) 6608[3] 7203[8]

**Invectus Hero** *Derek Shaw* 18
2 b g Paco Boy(IRE) Blur (Oasis Dream)
7712[8]

**Investissement** *Lee Carter* a84 80
8 b g Singspiel(IRE) Underwater (USA) (Theatrical (IRE))
(3521) 4080[2] 6721[2] 6930[6] 7838[12] 8015[4] 8163[3] 8194[7] 8316[4]

**Invigilator** *Derek Shaw* a71 45
6 b g Motivator Midpoint (USA) (Point Given (USA))
147[5] 248[5] 576[6] (841) 1031[5] 1739[5] 2127[11] 6843[9] 7252[8] 7621[11] 7671[6] 7825[3] 7915[6]

**Invincible Diamond (IRE)** *Mrs A M O'Shea* 82
2 ch g Arakan(USA) Invincible Woman (IRE) (Invincible Spirit (IRE))
5954a[7]

**Invincible Fresh (IRE)** *James Fanshawe* 96
3 b g Footstepsinthesand Princess Serena (USA) (Unbridled's Song (USA))
(2996) (3917) 5192[3]

**Invincible Gold (IRE)** *Ed Walker* a81 90
2 b c Invincible Spirit(IRE) Urgele (FR) (Zafonic (USA))
2380[6] 4666[2] (5488) (6165) 6925[8]

**Invincible Hero (IRE)** *Declan Carroll* a55 89
7 b g Invincible Spirit(IRE) Bridelina (FR) (Linamix (FR))
1191[16]

**Invincible Lad (IRE)** *Ed McMahon* a73 68
10 b g Invincible Spirit(IRE) Lady Ellen (Horage)
2159[7] 2890[9] 6866[2] 7213[14]

**Invincible Ridge (IRE)** *Eric Alston* a88 80
6 b g Invincible Spirit(IRE) Dani Ridge (IRE) (Indian Ridge)
5958a[6] (7623) 7888[2] (7949) 8072[2]

**Invincible Strike (IRE)** *James Tate* a95 95
3 gr c Invincible Spirit(IRE) Lazaretta (IRE) (Dalakhani (IRE))
3253[19] 4872[4] 6159[4] 6467[9]

**Invincible Wish (IRE)** *Brian Ellison* a65 49
2 b g Vale Of York(IRE) Moonlight Wish (IRE) (Peintre Celebre (USA))
3570[7] 4510[5] 4919[8] 5525[5] (6413) 6944[2] 7075[5] 7648[6] 7828[2] (7912)

**Invincible Zeb (IRE)** *Ronald Harris* a57 69
2 br g Zebedee Cruise Line (Rainbow Quest (USA))
2200[5] 2413[6] 2829[4] 3875[6] 4967[10] 6064[13] 7685[5] 7984[5]

**In Vino Veritas (IRE)** *Ann Duffield* 71
3 b g Art Connoisseur(IRE) Robin (Slip Anchor)
1357[8] 1661[4] 2319[12] 4386[4] 4709[6] 4754[6] 5495[3] 5856[2] 6480[6] 6832[7] 7175[2]

**Invisible Eye** *Mick Channon* 66
2 br g Winker Watson Fading Away (Fraam)
4740[12] 4943[5] 5767[P] 7336[3] 7511[4]

**Invisible Touch** *Martin Smith*
4 gr f Act One Zarma (FR) (Machiavellian (USA))
5648[6]

**Invoke (IRE)** *Michael Bell* a75 77
3 b f Kodiac Tides (Bahamian Bounty)
1409[3] 1818[4] 2278[8] 2943[6] 3588[2] 3966[3] 4611[2] 5046[3] 5638[3] 6302[5] 7196[8]

**Inxile (IRE)** *David Nicholls* a86 102
9 b g Fayruz Grandel (Owington)
1163[8] 1397[4] 1561[3] 2076[8] 2283[9] 2786[18] 3395[2] 4412[4] (4762) 5016[8] 5918[6] 6131[6] 6531[19] 7280[9]

**Inyordreams** *James Given* a59 105
3 b f Teofilo(IRE) Wunders Dream (IRE) (Averti (IRE))
(1940) 2257[3] ◆ 3459[2] 4171[9] 6254[13] (6929) 7716[6]

**Ioannou** *Ian Williams* a43
5 b g Excellent Art Sandtime (IRE) (Green Desert (USA))
8013[9]

**Iotapa (USA)** *John W Sadler* a116 99
4 bb f Afleet Alex(USA) Concinnous (USA) (El Corredor (USA))
7593a[3]

**Ipswich (IRE)** *A De Royer-Dupre* a93 106
4 ch f Danehill Dancer(IRE) Imperial Beauty (USA) (Imperial Ballet (IRE))
1827a[4] 2631a[9] 3171a[2] 4561a[2] 5742a[10]

**Iptisam** *James Tate* a106 88
5 ch g Rahy(USA) Grain Of Truth (Gulch (USA))
534[5] 713[4] 1066[2] ◆ 1949[11] 6624[P]

**Irene Hull (IRE)** *Garry Moss* a59 43
3 b f Excellent Art Wing Diva (IRE) (Hawk Wing (USA))
2209[5] 2878[9] 3407[2] 4495[9]

**Irish Belle (IRE)** *Tony Carroll* 8
2 ch f Duke Of Marmalade(IRE) Flower Of Kent (USA) (Diesis)
7491[6] 7752[13]

**Irish Boy (IRE)** *Christine Dunnett* a48 39
6 b g Desert Millennium(IRE) Shone Island (IRE) (Desert Sun)
2434[8] 3222[10] 3612[6] 4595[6] 4848[6] 6273[9]

**Irish Girls Spirit (IRE)** *Paul Midgley* 75
5 b m Desert Millennium(IRE) Shone Island (IRE) (Desert Sun)
1604[8] 4630[4] 4994[2] 5819[2] (6796) (6819)

**Irish Mission (CAN)** *Christophe Clement* a97 102
5 ch m Giant's Causeway(USA) Misty Mission (CAN) (Miswaki (USA))
7607a[11]

**Irish Rookie (IRE)** *Martyn Meade* 95
2 b f Azamour(IRE) Bold Assumption (Observatory (USA))
(7108) (7596)

**Irish Surf (USA)** *Dan L Hendricks* a107 101
4 b c Giant's Causeway(USA) Surfside (USA) (Seattle Slew (USA))
5781a[5]

**Irish Sweetheart (IRE)** *Christine Dunnett*
3 b f Desert Millennium(IRE) Run Sweetheart (USA) (Bold Run (FR))
7528[14] 7818[12]

**Irish Tears** *John Gosden* a72 70
3 b c Compton Place Deora De (Night Shift (USA))
409[3]

**Iron Butterfly** *James Eustace* a45 67
5 b m Shirocco(GER) Coh Sho No (Old Vic)
1359[4] 7508[5]

**Irondale Express** *Tony Coyle* 71
3 b f Myboycharlie(IRE) Olindera (GER) (Lomitas)
1348[6] 2205[2] 2740[3] 4023[3] 4318[3] 6540[5] 7494[15] 7642[6]

**Ironstone (IRE)** *M Cheno* a47 70
5 b g Holy Roman Emperor(IRE) Lettre De Cachet (USA) (Secreto (USA))
5225a[7]

**Irradiance (IRE)** *H-A Pantall* a70 81
3 b f Raven's Pass(USA) Pure Illusion (IRE) (Danehill (USA))
7722a[2]

**Isabella Beeton** *Pat Phelan* a71 44
3 b f Archipenko(USA) Famcred (Inchinor)
1655[8] 2152[9] 2498[8] 4120[7] 4613[7] 4970[5]

**Isabella Bird** *Mick Channon* a61 84
3 b f Invincible Spirit(IRE) Meetyouthere (IRE) (Sadler's Wells (USA))
1433[8] 1722[2] (7157)

**Isabella Liberty (FR)** *Robert Eddery* a67 81
3 b f Soldier Of Fortune(IRE) Samsa (FR) (Zafonic (USA))
599a[4] 1139a[3] (2411a) 5368a[11] 6685[12]

**Isabella Sings (USA)** *Todd Pletcher* 99
2 ch f Eskendereya(USA) Isobel Baillie (Lomitas)
7592a[12]

**Isdaal** *Kevin Morgan* a62 68
7 ch m Dubawi(IRE) Faydah (USA) (Bahri (USA))
380[8] 1919[3] 2199[6] 2678[5] 3365[2] 4081[4] 4734[7]

**Iseemist (IRE)** *John Gallagher* a70 91
3 gr f Verglas(IRE) Krasivaya (IRE) (Soviet Star (USA))
957[3] 1389[4] (1669) (2278) 2965[4] 3539[2] (4121) 4339[4] 5675[5] 6511[2] 7233[6]

**I See You (FR)** *Mlle A Voraz* 55
2 ch c Air Chief Marshal(IRE) Dalmara (FR) (Halling (USA))
5940a[6]

**Ishetoo** *Peter Grayson* a54 45
10 b g Ishiguru(USA) Ticcatoo (IRE) (Dolphin Street (FR))
164[3] (483) 610[2] 693[3] 797[10] 937[9] 972[5] 1081[2] 3104[5] 3609[8] 4362[9] 4848[5] 5138[7] 5390[13]

**Ishiamber** *George Baker* a92 93
4 ch f Ishiguru(USA) Black And Amber (Weldnaas (USA))
275[3] 486[4] 588[3] (1123) (1230) (2048) (2945) 3788[9] (5826) 6492[4] 6922[10]

**Ishiamiracle** *Phil McEntee* a59 55
5 ch m Ishiguru(USA) Sukuma (IRE) (Highest Honor (FR))
268[4]

**Ishi Honest** *Mark Usher* a63 59
4 b f Ishiguru(USA) Honesty Pays (Dr Fong (USA))
2127[13] 2838[2] 3149[6] (3528) 4056[5] 4578[7] 5071[10] 5510[6] 6030[5] 6409[8]

**Ishikawa (IRE)** *K R Burke* a90 91
6 b g Chineur(FR) Nautical Light (Slip Anchor)
56[6] 638a[9] 744[2] 942[3] 1451[2] (1871) 2131[4] (2707) 3244[8] 7852[12] 7971[8] 8209[12]

**Ishisoba** *Mark Hoad* a23 60
4 ch f Ishiguru(USA) Bundle Up (USA) (Miner's Mark (USA))
174[3] 371[6] 448[11] 844[10] 1223[7] 2069[9] 5075[10] 7222[8]

**Isla Bonita (JPN)** *Hironori Kurita* 119
3 bb c Fuji Kiseki(JPN) Isla Cozzene (USA) (Cozzene (USA))
7981a[9]

**Island Express (IRE)** *Ann Stokell* a50 53
7 b g Chineur(FR) Cayman Expresso (IRE) (Fayruz)
76[2] 269[10] 495[4] 531[3] 1035[6] 1486[9] 1677[8] 5568[5] 5916[5] 6116[3] 6437[8] 6631[10] 7652[7] 7737[6] 8008[2] 8111[4] 8200[10] 8256[3]

**Island Legend (IRE)** *Milton Bradley* a78 55
8 b g Trans Island Legand Of Tara (USA) (Gold Legend (USA))
191[2] 412[7] 572[5] 730[5] 987[2] 1787[11] 3077[3] 3520[9] 5486[5]

**Island Remede** *Ed Dunlop* a71 100
3 b f Medicean Island Odyssey (Dansili)
2152[5] 2960[11] 5611[4] 6708[7] 7447[2] 7768a[4]

**Isntshesomething** *Richard Guest* 25
2 br f Assertive Princess Almora (Pivotal)
7407[13] 7713[12]

**Is She Any Good (IRE)** *David Evans* a43 16
2 b f Kodiac Meaon (IRE) (Oratorio (IRE))
1482[7] 1741[6] 2944[9] (Dead)

**Istikshaf (IRE)** *Saeed bin Suroor* a54 82
3 b c Exceed And Excel(AUS) Shinko Hermes (IRE) (Sadler's Wells (USA))
239a[15]

**Istimraar (IRE)** *Philip Kirby* a79 78
3 b g Dansili Manayer (IRE) (Sadler's Wells (USA))
2077[7] 2769[8] 6539[2] 7008[7] 8120[3]

**Istinfaar (USA)** *Roger Varian* 66
2 b c Street Cry(IRE) Yaqeen (Green Desert (USA))
6874[5]

**Isyalia (FR)** *A Fabre* a59 69
3 b f Elusive City(USA) Pretty Soon (FR) (Zafonic (USA))
3372a[7]

**Italian Beauty (IRE)** *Timothy Jarvis* a54 25
2 b f Thewayyouare(USA) Edelfa (IRE) (Fasliyev (USA))
5210[9] 6093[11] 7631[6] 7832[7]

**Italian Lady (USA)** *Ollie Pears* a51 65
5 bb m Medaglia d'Oro(USA) Way Beyond (USA) (Ordway (USA))
321[8]

**Italian Symphony (IRE)** *Brendan Powell*
4 b f Galileo(IRE) Tea Break (Daylami (IRE))
3174[7] 3891[9]

**Italian Tom (IRE)** *Ronald Harris* a75 69
7 b h Le Vie Dei Colori Brave Cat (IRE) (Catrail (USA))
1912[5] 2559[3] (2887) 3313[10] 4151[3] 4206[5] 5082[4] 5777[4] 7023[10] 7950[11] 8186[10]

**Itlaaq** *Michael Easterby* a82 97
8 b g Alhaarth(IRE) Hathrah (IRE) (Linamix (FR))
1562[6] (1935) 2314[3] 2787[8] 4173[5] (4685) 5579[8] 6169[7] 6761[5] 7235[12]

**It Must Be Faith** *Michael Appleby* a81 89
4 b g Mount Nelson Purple Rain (IRE) (Celtic Swing)
2444[4] 3272[5] 3306[6] 4061[10] 4571[7] 5060[2] 5535[2] (6495) 6695[6] (7535) (7669) 7889[6]

**Itoobeboss (IRE)** *Rod Collet* a80 82
3 gr g Lawman(FR) Dookus (IRE) (Linamix (FR))
1551a[4] 2196a[10]

**Itorio (IRE)** *Ms Sheila Lavery* 100
2 b c Oratorio(IRE) Image Of (IRE) (Close Conflict (USA))
4460a[4] 5735a[4]

**It's All A Game** *Richard Guest* a65 62
3 ch g Sleeping Indian St Edith (IRE) (Desert King (IRE))
(28) 267[4] 1285[2] 1648[6] (1890) 2165[3] 2355[5] (2742) 3054[3] 3662[5] 4292[9] 4612[6] 5233[3] 5891[2] 6121[5] 6543[5] 7647[9] 7766[6] (7908) 8063[10] 8137[8]

**It's A Mans World** *Brian Ellison* a52 68
8 b g Kyllachy Exhibitor (USA) (Royal Academy (USA))
3718[6] 4498[8] 5235[7] 5639[4]

**It's A Yes From Me** *James Fanshawe* a53 56
3 b g Bahamian Bounty Valjarv (IRE) (Bluebird (USA))
3370[5] 4111[5] 5195[5] 5820[6] 7025[10] 7346[9]

**Its Gonna Be Me (IRE)** *William Haggas* 74
2 b g Zebedee Dorn Hill (Lujain (USA))
5439[8] 6039[5] 6690[3] 7131[3]

**Itsindebag** *J S Moore* a53 51
2 b f Indesatchel(IRE) Darling Buds (Reel Buddy (USA))
1488[6] 2499[6] 2716[4] 3550[4] 4542[3] 5133[2] 6563[2] 7258[9]

**Itsinthepost (FR)** *Matthieu Palussiere* 73
2 b c American Post Sakkara Star (IRE) (Mozart (IRE))
5292a[6]

**Its Lady Mary** *Paul Cole* a66 22
2 ch f Exceed And Excel(AUS) Sentimental Value (USA) (Diesis)
3888[14] 4320[3] 4610[2] 7398[6]

**Its My Story (FR)** *J Reynier* a62 85
2 b c Vatori(FR) Family Story (FR) (Gold Away (IRE))
5739a[3]

**It's Not It (IRE)** *S Wattel* a79 84
3 ch c Tamayuz Its On The Air (IRE) (King's Theatre (IRE))
5368a[2] 7681a[3]

**Its Not Me Its You** *Brendan Powell* a64 30
3 b g Pastoral Pursuits Maystock (Magic Ring (IRE))
2221[15] 2418[11] 2682[6] 3116[9] 3711[13] 5795[10] 6043[P]

**Itsnowcato** *Ed Walker* a78 79
3 b g Notnowcato Blaenavon (Cadeaux Genereux)
3675[2] 4196[2] 4651[6] 6487[4]

**It's Only Business** *Bill Turner* a60 41
4 ch g Haafhd Noble Plum (IRE) (King's Best (USA))
7373[13] 7639[7] 8097[4] 8190[7] 8316[2]

**It's Taboo** *Mark Usher* a51 63
4 b f Tobougg(IRE) Faraway Moon (Distant Relative)
2775[7] 3280[7] 3733[5] 4273[13] 5252[7] 5751[10] 6397[13] 7188[8] ◆ 7546[5] 7977[6]

**It's Time For Bed** *Linda Perratt* 8
2 gr f Zebedee Mystical Ayr (IRE) (Namid)
6474[6]

**Ivanhoe** *Michael Blanshard* a70 76
4 b g Haafhd Marysienka (Primo Dominie)
1909[2] (2175) 2490[2] 4441[3] 5341[5] 5878[9]

**Ivanhowe (GER)** *Jean-Pierre Carvalho* 118
4 b c Soldier Hollow Indigo Girl (GER) (Sternkoenig (IRE))
(2001a) 2819a[6] (6180a) 6970a[18] (7603a) 7981a[6]

**Ivawood (IRE)** *Richard Hannon* 117
2 b c Zebedee Keenes Royale (Red Ransom (USA))
(3193) ◆ (4123) ◆ (4822) 7239[2]

**Iveagh Gardens (IRE)** *Charles O'Brien* 97
3 b f Mastercraftsman(IRE) Woodland Chant (USA) (War Chant (USA))
7483a[2] 7857a[11]

**Ivestar (IRE)** *Michael Easterby* a63 54
9 b g Fraam Hazardous (Night Shift (USA))
59[5] 258[7] 511[4] 1010[4] 1270[3] 1282[8] 1804[6] 1838[8]

**Ivor's Princess** *Rod Millman* a70 74
5 b m Atraf Rosina May (IRE) (Danehill Dancer (IRE))
84[2] 750[4] 924[6] 1099[2] 1791[3] (2693) 3086[6] 3803[5]

**Ivors Rebel** *David Elsworth* a82 78
2 b c Cockney Rebel(IRE) Sopran Cross (ITY) (Cape Cross (IRE))
1575[6] ◆ (2007) 5209[3] 5906[4] 6375a[7] (6629)

**Ivy Port** *Michael Appleby* a73 66
4 b f Deportivo Ivy Bridge (IRE) (Namid)
(269) 388[6] 3979[10] 4472[3] 5234[5] 5571[8]

**I Will Excel (IRE)** *M D O'Callaghan* 96
2 b c Exceed And Excel(AUS) Da's Wish (IRE) (Sadler's Wells (USA))
2855a[5] 3738a[7]

**Iwilsayzisonlyonce** *Joseph Tuite* a61 49
4 ch g Kyllachy Resistance Heroine (Dr Fong (USA))
592[12]

**Ixelles Diamond (IRE)** *Richard Fahey* 80
3 br f Diamond Green(FR) Silk Point (IRE) (Barathea (IRE))
(2024) 2433[5] 3956[4] 4523[3] 4912[3] (5785) ◆ 6112[5] 6789[12] 7600[7]

**Izaaj (USA)** *A bin Harmash* a95 94
7 ch g Giant's Causeway(USA) Miss Coronado (USA) (Coronado's Quest (USA))
108a[7] 307a[9] 398a[7]

**Izbushka (IRE)** *Ian Williams* a65 61
3 b g Bushranger(IRE) Zaynaba (IRE) (Traditionally (USA))
50[5] 190[4] 198[4] 488[3] 828[6] 2132[3] ◆ 2385[6] 2735[9] 4134[8]

**I Zingari** *Sir Michael Stoute* a66 65
2 b c Dansili Hi Calypso (IRE) (In The Wings)
7169[7] 7730[6]

**Izola** *Miss Evanna McCutcheon* 99
4 ch f Beat Hollow Pivka (Pivotal)
2572a[14]

**Izzthatright (IRE)** *Richard Fahey* 98
2 b g Moss Vale(IRE) Miss Adelaide (IRE) (Alzao (USA))
2231[4] 2541[4] 3201[2] (4313) 4939[2] (5373) (5770)

**Izzy Boy (USA)** *Mark Johnston* a63 57
4 b g Elusive Quality(USA) Michele Royale (USA) (Groovy (USA))
102[4] 835[6] 996[6]

**Izzy Piccolina (IRE)** *Geoffrey Deacon*
6 b m Morozov(USA) Chloara (IRE) (Flemensfirth (USA))
3856[10]

**Jaahiez (USA)** *Roger Varian* a79 73
3 b c More Than Ready(USA) Nasmatt (Danehill (USA))
218[3] 423[3] (626) 975[2] 1352[3] 1897[7] 3464[6]

**Jacbequick** *Ollie Pears* 82
3 b g Calcutta Toking N' Joken (IRE) (Mukaddamah (USA))
(2236) (3547) 3946[2] 4290[6] (4496) 4794[3] 5915[8] 6431[6]

**Jack Barker** *Robin Bastiman* 57
5 b g Danbird(AUS) Smiddy Hill (Factual (USA))
1486[10] 1649[9] 2658[9] 3630[3] 4101[11] 4727[5]

**Jack Bear** *Jonathan Portman* a55 34
3 b g Joe Bear(IRE) Colins Lady (FR) (Colonel Collins (USA))
3712[9] 5039[9] 6002[4]

**Jack Daddy** *Joseph G Murphy* 85
5 b g Monsun(GER) Snow Princess (IRE) (Ela-Mana-Mou)
5456a[3]

**Jack Dexter** *Jim Goldie* 118
5 bb g Orientor Glenhurich (IRE) (Sri Pekan (USA))
1163[3] 2256[6] 2563[5] 3319[7] 3451[7] 4201[10] 6533[8] 7272[3] 7716[4]

**Jack Firefly** *Michael Murphy*
5 b g Echo Of Light Charlottebutterfly (Millkom)
3123[10] 4326[11]

**Jack Hobbs** *John Gosden* a78
2 b c Halling(USA) Swain's Gold (USA) (Swain (IRE))
(8288)

**Jackie Ellis (IRE)** *Paul W Flynn* a65 69
3 b f Excellent Art Dancing With Stars (IRE) (Where Or When (IRE))
6722[8]

**Jackie Love (IRE)** *Roger Ingram* a57 57
6 b m Tobougg(IRE) Gutter Press (IRE) (Raise A Grand (IRE))
251[13] 602[7] 754[11] 851[8] 1387[12] 1877[10]

**Jack Luey** *Lawrence Mullaney* a63 93
7 b g Danbird(AUS) Icenaslice (IRE) (Fayruz)
2390[4] 2656[3] 3239[3] 3714[6] 4471[3] 4925[6] 5419[6] 6511[18] 7330[11]

**Jack Milton (USA)** *Todd Pletcher* 110
4 bb c War Front(USA) Preserver (USA) (Forty Niner (USA))
6391a[9]

**Jack Muscolo (USA)** *C Cardaioli* a59 56
4 b c Pomeroy(USA) Promenade Road (CAN) (Dance Brightly (CAN))
266a[8]

**Jack Naylor** *Mrs John Harrington* 106
2 b f Champs Elysees Fashionable (Nashwan (USA))
(4598a) 6967a[3]

**Jack Of Diamonds (IRE)** *Roger Teal* a91 78
5 b g Red Clubs(IRE) Sakkara Star (IRE) (Mozart (IRE))
1042[7] 1834[4] 2341[5] 2922[3] 3468[4] 4549[2] 5040[8] 5931[8] 7732[3] 7852[10] (8080) 8242[2]

**Jackpot** *Brendan Powell* a47 34
4 b f Avonbridge Strat's Quest (Nicholas (USA))
(1625a) 2594a[7] 4039a[3] 4717a[6] 5229a[2] 5971a[3] 6188a[3] 7456[8] 7854[6] 7987[9] 8311[13]

**Jacksonfire** *Michael Mullineaux* a11
2 ch c Firebreak Fitolini (Bertolini (USA))
7254[8]

**Jack Sparrow (GER)** *Frau C Brandstatter* a48 81
5 b g Noroit(GER) Jeanine (GER) (Neshad (USA))
5222a[3]

**Jack's Revenge (IRE)** *George Baker* a77 104
6 br g Footstepsinthesand Spirit Of Age (IRE) (Indian Ridge)
1165[7] 1943[2] 3420[5] 4771a[5] 4949a[2] 5749[4] 6755[2] 7276[26]

**Jacob Black** *Keith Dalgleish* 91
3 b c Amadeus Wolf First Eclipse (IRE) (Fayruz)
(3362) (4514) 5816[4] (5999) 6534[6]

**Jacob Cats** *William Knight* a85 86
5 b g Dutch Art Ballet (Sharrood (USA))
1437[19] 1834[5] 2309[6] 2959[14] (3515) 3815[2] 4354[5] 4827[5] 6141[2] 6656[2] 7402[5]

**Jacobean (IRE)** *A P O'Brien* 100
2 b c High Chaparral(IRE) Civility Cat (USA) (Tale Of The Cat (USA))
7442[4]

**Jacob's Pillow** *William Haggas* a75 88
3 b g Oasis Dream Enticing (IRE) (Pivotal)
(3156) 4281[2] 5501[4] 6170[9]

**Jacobs Son** *Michael Appleby* a84 68
6 ch g Refuse To Bend(IRE) Woodwin (IRE) (Woodman (USA))
859[2] 911[2] (1222) 1729[6] 2097[4] (2935) 3624[6] 7903[7] 8211[2]

**Jacqueline Jouliac** *John Gosden* a75
3 b f Oasis Dream Sugar Mill (FR) (Polar Falcon (USA))
6033[4] 7686[3] 7841[8] 8020[3]

**Jacquotte Delahaye** *David Brown* a85 83
3 ch f Kyllachy Mary Read (Bahamian Bounty)
2929[2] ◆ (3300) 3957[7] 5649[7] 6345[3] 6792[8] 7196[10]

**Jadel** *D Camuffo* 89
3 b f Mount Nelson Cuppacocoa (Bertolini (USA))
1477a[6] 1780a[12]

**Jaeger Connoisseur (IRE)** *K R Burke* a43 45
3 b f Art Connoisseur(IRE) Nilassiba (Daylami (IRE))
1855[4] 3380[11] 4071[7]

**Jaeger Train (IRE)** *K R Burke* a74 74
3 b g Captain Rio Marigold (FR) (Marju (IRE))
70[3] 477[2] (906) 1940[3] 3790[3]

**Jaganory (IRE)** *David Evans* a74 73
2 b c Dylan Thomas(IRE) Jacquelin Jag (IRE) (Fayruz)
2829[2] (3082) 3448[13] 4205[3] 6679[2] ◆ 7116[11] 7661[3] 7807[5] 8091[4]

**Jaguar Mail (JPN)** *Noriyuki Hori* 112
10 b h Jungle Pocket(JPN) Haya Beni Komachi (JPN) (Sunday Silence (USA))
2002a[16]

**Jailawi (IRE)** *Ismail Mohammed* 93
3 b g Iffraaj Tortue (IRE) (Turtle Island (IRE))
2339[11] 2996[2] (3914) 4794[2] (5686)

**Jaiyana** *James Tate* a52
2 b f Dansili Jira (Medicean)
7944[6]

**Jakey (IRE)** *Pat Phelan* a85 88
4 b g Cape Cross(IRE) Off Message (IRE) (In The Wings)
(1219) ◆ 1651[5] 2405[4] (3878) 6786[6]

**Jakkalberry (IRE)** *Marco Botti* a101 119
8 b h Storming Home Claba Di San Jore (IRE) (Barathea (IRE))
(220)

**Jakodima (IRE)** *Richard Hannon* 61
2 b c Kodiac Jasmina (GER) (Monsun (GER))
6497[8] 7512[8]

**Jaladee** *Roger Varian* a78 82
4 b g Cape Cross(IRE) Atamana (IRE) (Lahib (USA))
1281[4] 2048[3] (3468)

**Jalebi** *Jim Boyle* a58
3 ch f Sleeping Indian Sweet Pickle (Piccolo)
5[3] 94[6] 1039[6] 1211[2] 1449[5]

**Jalingo (IRE)** *Mark Johnston* a88 88
3 b g Cape Cross(IRE) Just Special (Cadeaux Genereux)
143[2] 375[3] 854[6] (5855) 6166[4] 6357[3] 6786[4] 7203[3]

**Jallota** *Charles Hills* a90 111
3 b g Rock Of Gibraltar(IRE) Lady Lahar (Fraam)
594a[9] 770a[2] 1178a[11] 4826[13] 6522[2] 7444[6]

**Jalusive (IRE)** *Christine Dunnett* a50 32
5 br g Elusive City(USA) Jaldini (IRE) (Darshaan)
468[10] 816[6] 1612[11] 2525[8] 5105[10] 5574[7]

**Jamaica (IRE)** *A P O'Brien* 101
2 gr c Galileo(IRE) Dialafara (FR) (Anabaa (USA))
5576[4]

**Jamaica Grande** *Dave Morris* a68 57
6 ch g Doyen(IRE) Mary Sea (FR) (Selkirk (USA))
221[2] 277[2]

**Jamaican Bolt (IRE)** *Geoffrey Oldroyd* a79 100
6 b g Pivotal Chiming (IRE) (Danehill (USA))
1305[3] 2254[6] 2786[12] 3239[5] 5016[6] 5419[3] 5925[5] 6744[3] 7080[4] 7233[3] (7408) 7715[11]

**Jambobo** *Chris Down* a46
5 b g Acclamation Hovering (IRE) (In The Wings)
452[5] 815[9] 1025[5]

**Jamboree Girl** *Tim Easterby* a67 76
3 b f Bahamian Bounty Danehurst (Danehill (USA))
2015[15] 2317[9] 3462[2] 3959[6] 4890[2] 5769[3] 6153[3]

**Jamesbo's Girl** *David Barron* 87
4 ch f Refuse To Bend(IRE) Donna Anna (Be My Chief (USA))
2167[10] 3384[4] 3952[2] (4421) (4902) 5612[6] ◆ 6492[6] 7506[9]

**Jamesie (IRE)** *David Marnane* a107 109
6 b g Kodiac Pretty Woman (IRE) (Night Shift (USA))
109a[7] (304a) 597a[2] 898a[4] 1180a[11] 3284a[2] 3736a[4] 5154a[4] 5219a[2] (5699a) 6371a[5]

**James Pollard (IRE)** *Bernard Llewellyn* a61 70
9 ch g Indian Ridge Manuetti (IRE) (Sadler's Wells (USA))
277[9] 490[8] 639[3] 838[7] 989[7]

**Jamhoori** *Jeremy Gask* a79 77
6 b h Tiger Hill(IRE) Tanasie (Cadeaux Genereux)
241a[3] 5824[11] 7567[6] 7634[8]

**Jamie Lee's Girl** *David Flood* a20
3 br f Pastoral Pursuits Cape Wood (Cape Cross (IRE))
1918[9] 2418[12] 3523[8] 4101[12]

**Jammy Guest (IRE)** *George Margarson* a83 94
4 b g Duke Of Marmalade(IRE) Ardbrae Lady (Overbury (IRE))
3420[26] 4347[2] 5665[10] 6097[11] 6891[14] 7375[4] 7600[9]

**Jammy Moment** *Linda Perratt* a70 71
3 ch f Duke Of Marmalade(IRE) Special Moment (IRE) (Sadler's Wells (USA))
188[7] 684[3] 4052[4] 6622[2] 6832[4] 7102[7] 7500[3]

**Jamr** *A bin Harmash* a107 109
6 br g Singspiel(IRE) Never Enough (GER) (Monsun (GER))
683a[4] 900a[8] 1177a[14]

**Janaab (IRE)** *Tim Easterby* a60 76
4 ch g Nayef(USA) Mood Indigo (IRE) (Indian Ridge)
1718[7] 2605[5] 3400[5] 3791[3] 4394[2] 4858[4] 5077[9] (5793) 6232[2] 6285[4]

**Jan De Heem** *Tina Jackson* a45 72
4 ch g Dutch Art Shasta (Shareef Dancer (USA))
4058[12] 4454[6] 4793[7] 6628[7] 7247[7]

**Jane's Memory (IRE)** *Rae Guest* 97
2 ch f Captain Rio Dancing Jest (IRE) (Averti (IRE))
(2612) 3027a[2] 3806a[2] 6513[12]

**Janie Runaway (IRE)** *Brian Meehan* a56 65
4 b f Antonius Pius(USA) Await (IRE) (Peintre Celebre (USA))
1891[7]

**Janna's Jingle (IRE)** *S Seemar* a73 85
4 b f Oratorio(IRE) Bonnie Bluebell (IRE) (Montjeu (IRE))
239a[13]

**Jan Smuts (IRE)** *Wilf Storey* a59 71
6 b g Johannesburg(USA) Choice House (USA) (Chester House (USA))
1374[7] 1605[2] 2139[7] (2424) 3532[6] 4662[2] 4962[3] 5815[5] 6404[5] 6864[7] 7177[5] 7509[3] 7643[3] 7817[8] 8061[7]

**Jan Van Hoof (IRE)** *Richard Fahey* a74 58
3 b g Dutch Art Cosenza (Bahri (USA))
994[2] 6116[2] (7699)

**Jardim (BRZ)** *M Kettle* a102 57
8 gr h Ski Champ(USA) Copacabana Beach (BRZ) (Midnight Tiger (USA))
202a[12]

**Jargon (FR)** *Michael Bell* a82 89
2 b g Naaqoos Cobblestone Road (USA) (Grindstone (USA))
3536[5] (4338) (4731) 6331[8] 6916a[2]

**Jarlath** *Seamus Mullins* a79 81
3 b g Norse Dancer(IRE) Blue Lullaby (IRE) (Fasliyev (USA))
(1029) (1382) 1812[3] (2385) 2893[7] 3391[3] 4333[7] (4948) 5552[5] 7016[5]

**Jasmine Blue (IRE)** *Paul Cole* 67
2 b f Galileo(IRE) Impressionist Art (USA) (Giant's Causeway (USA))
7108[7]

**Jason Bournes (FR)** *E Lellouche* a75 75
7 b g Westerner Doucelisa (FR) (Cardoun (FR))
7620a[2]

**J'Aspire** *Stuart Williams* 52
2 b f Zamindar(USA) Ipsa Loquitur (Unfuwain (USA))
7377[9]

**Jathabah (IRE)** *Clive Brittain* a81 104
4 b f Singspiel(IRE) Zibet (Kris)
2115[4] 2779[12]

**Jaunty Dove** *Miss Imogen Pickard* a38
12 b m Atraf Flossy Dove (Le Moss)
652[4]

**Java Rose** *Charlie Longsdon* a83 62
5 b m Ishiguru(USA) Mighty Splash (Cape Cross (IRE))
(293) 450[8] 758[2] 1418[9] 5083[7] 6107[2] 7946[4]

**Jawaab (IRE)** *Philip Kirby* a61 57
10 ch g King's Best(USA) Canis Star (Wolfhound (USA))
14[2] 73[3] 1485[3] 4115[4] 5466[6]

**Jawhar (IRE)** *Doug Watson* a82 100
6 ch g Halling(USA) Kawn (Cadeaux Genereux)
(242a) 398a[10]

**Jawinski (IRE)** *David Evans* a58 49
4 b g Jeremy(USA) Karinski (USA) (Palace Music (USA))
3778[4] 5001[6] 5283[9]

**Jawking** *James Unett* a66
5 b g Compton Place Just Down The Road (IRE) (Night Shift (USA))
3921[7] 5136[7]

**Jay Bee Blue** *Sean Curran* a83 79
5 b g Kyllachy Czarna Roza (Polish Precedent (USA))
38[6] 294[7] 574[2] 658[4] 779[4] 1014[8] 1234[5] 1490[6] 1873[4] 2414[2] 2691[3] 4024[8] 4406[10]

**Jayeff Herring (IRE)** *Michael Bell* a57
3 b g Excellent Art Biasca (Erhaab (USA))
71[3] 2878[12] 3407[6] 5893[5] 6939[10]

**Jay Gee Speedfit (IRE)** *George Margarson* a50 25
3 b c Bushranger(IRE) Prodigal Daughter (Alhaarth (IRE))
1612[12] 2329[9] 2682[12] 3121[6]

**Jay Kay** *K R Burke* a47 68
5 b g Librettist(USA) Turn Back (Pivotal)
5005[3] (5234) (5530) 5640[12] 7180[6] 7765[8]

**Jaywalker (IRE)** *Mick Channon* a79
3 b g Footstepsinthesand Nipping (IRE) (Night Shift (USA))
(1106)

**Jazri** *Milton Bradley* a58 59
3 b g Myboycharlie(IRE) Read Federica (Fusaichi Pegasus (USA))
378[5] 670[5] 1235[6] 1683[3] (2028) 2643[3] 3135[2] 3643[4] 4209[6] 5747[6] 7292[11] 7426[9] 7982[11] 8198[7]

**Jazz (IRE)** *Charles Hills* a87 88
3 b c Danehill Dancer(IRE) Jazz Baby (IRE) (Fasliyev (USA))
1358[7] 1693[5] 2090[3] 2626[4] 3704[4] 4013[2] 4918[3]

**Jazz Bay** *John Bridger* a46 54
3 ch g Refuse To Bend(IRE) Shasta (Shareef Dancer (USA))
291[9] 684[8] 738[5] 855[5] 1106[4] 1626[3] 2045[3] 2505[4] 3084[5] 3820[6] 4341[8]

**Jazz Girl (IRE)** *A Oliver* a91 97
6 ch m Johar(USA) Madame Boulangere (Royal Applause)
2040a[5] 2263a[9]

**Jazzi Top** *John Gosden* a73 70
2 b f Danehill Dancer(IRE) Zee Zee Top (Zafonic (USA))
6753[3] 7193[3]

**Jazz Master** *Luca Cumani* a93 92
4 b c Singspiel(IRE) Turn Of A Century (Halling (USA))
1715[2] 2461[2] 3111[3] 6106[7] 7033[2]

**Jazzy Lady (IRE)** *David Evans* a78 54
3 b f Intikhab(USA) Lock's Heath (CAN) (Topsider (USA))
(190) 357[4] 404[2] 499[2]

**Jeanne Girl (IRE)** *Mrs John Harrington* 100
2 b f Rip Van Winkle(IRE) Sister Golightly (Mtoto)
3763a[2] 5734a[4] 6372a[8]

**Jebediah Shine** *David O'Meara* a64 64
2 ch f Kyllachy Ardessie (Bahamian Bounty)
3367[5] 3841[6] 5297[2] (7917) 8118[7] 8278[3]

**Jebel Tara** *Alan Brown* a72 79
9 b g Diktat Chantilly (FR) (Sanglamore (USA))
1930[6] 2215[12] 2399[8] 3054[7] 3299[10] 3828[8] 5233[4] 5571[5] 5761[4] 6121[6]

**Jebril (FR)** *Jonathan Portman* 82
4 b g Astronomer Royal(USA) Happy Clapper (Royal Applause)
2192a[4] (2770) 3515[2] 5756[3]

**Jebulani** *Barry Murtagh* a43 60
4 b g Jelani(IRE) Susan's Dowry (Efisio)
460[7] 695[9] 3605[6] 4259[9] 4522[7] 5331[8] 6117[11] 6542[12]

**Jedi** *A bin Huzaim* a73 82
8 ch g Pivotal Threefold (USA) (Gulch (USA))
305a[11] 507a[14]

**Jed Water (FR)** *C Boutin* a72 67
3 ro f Stormy River(FR) Scottish Diva (Selkirk (USA))
3745a[4]

**Jeer (IRE)** *Michael Easterby* a70 73
10 ch g Selkirk(USA) Purring (USA) (Mountain Cat (USA))
247[9]

**Jellicle Ball (IRE)** *John Gosden* a82
2 b f Invincible Spirit(IRE) Dance Troupe (Rainbow Quest (USA))
(7399) ◆

**Jellwa (IRE)** *Mick Channon* a41 65
2 b f Iffraaj Chatifa (IRE) (Titus Livius (FR))
4444[11] 6093[7] 6659[6]

**Jelly Fish** *Brett Johnson* a90 91
3 ch g Observatory(USA) Grand Coral (Grand Lodge (USA))
2719[7] 3814[4] (4209) (6143) ◆ 6502[2] 8096[10] 8296[5]

**Jelly Monger (IRE)** *Dominic Ffrench Davis* 87
2 b f Strategic Prince Royal Jelly (King's Best (USA))
(6065) 6926[7]

**Jembatt (IRE)** *Michael Mulvany* a63 76
7 ch g Captain Rio Silly Imp (IRE) (Imperial Frontier (USA))
4556a[5]

**Jemimaville (IRE)** *Giles Bravery* a34 47
7 b m Fasliyev(USA) Sparkling Isle (Inchinor)
483[5] 937[8] 1089[6] 1369[9]

**Jen Jos Enigma (IRE)** *Noel Quinlan* 73
2 b f Kodiac Taraba (IRE) (Inchinor)
4764[3] (6085)

**Jenny Sparks** *Mick Channon* a50 48
3 b f Winker Watson Stephanie's Mind (Mind Games)
82[5] 232[5] 541[6] 1211[P] 1384[5] 1648[12] 4627[3] 5106[4] 5321[11] 7546[10]

**Jenny Twigg** *Chris Fairhurst* a11 31
4 b f Paris House Yorke's Folly (USA) (Stravinsky (USA))
2985[7] 3700[4] 4629[9] 5333[12]

**Jeremos (IRE)** *Richard Hannon* a71 69
3 b c Jeremy(USA) Bon Ton Roulet (Hawk Wing (USA))
(1008) 2307[8]

**Jeremy Road (FR)** *D Darlix* a73 73
4 bl c Jeremy(USA) Roadaniya (FR) (Grape Tree Road)
796a[13]

**Jeremy's Jet (IRE)** *Andrew Balding* a68 76
3 b g Jeremy(USA) Double Vie (IRE) (Tagula (IRE))
6045[4] 7032[6] 7418[2]

**Jersey Belle** *Mick Channon* a60 59
2 b f Piccolo Stephanie's Mind (Mind Games)
1764[4] 2057[4] 2458[6] 2928[6] 4345[4] 5180[4] 5875[12] 6428[4]

**Jersey Brown (IRE)** *Mick Channon* a54 73
3 br f Marju(IRE) Daniysha (IRE) (Doyoun)
2224[2] 2624[2] ◆ 2847[3] 3037[11] 4329[7] 4813[4] 5355[9] 6070[2] 6316[3] 6647[2] (6837) 7160[7] 7302[3]

**Jersey Bull (IRE)** *Michael Madgwick* a56 54
2 b g Clodovil(IRE) Chaguaramas (IRE) (Mujadil (USA))
1349[5] 1571[3] 2007[3] (2359) 2543[7] 3963[4] 6679[8] 7515[8] 7832[9] 8115[6]

**Jersey Cream (IRE)** *Andi Brown* a63 53
3 ch f Iffraaj Unicamp (Royal Academy (USA))
2416[9] 3326[7] 3554[6] 4733[4] 5280[7] 5978[8] (7977)

**Jersey Jewel (FR)** *Richard Hannon* a78 70
2 bb f Naaqoos Nikolenka (IRE) (Indian Ridge)
5746[2] 6105[2] 7011[3]

**Jessy Mae** *Derek Haydn Jones* a52 53
3 b f Oratorio(IRE) Welsh Valley (USA) (Irish River (FR))
142[4] 254[3] 1684[9] 5272[3] 6088[8] 6717[5] 7423[8] 7977[13] 8286[9]

**Je T'Aime Encore** *Gay Kelleway* 57
2 b c Acclamation Mimisel (Selkirk (USA))
5439[7] 5981[8] 6497[5]

**Jethou Island** *Henry Candy* a61 67
3 ch f Virtual Lihou Island (Beveled (USA))
5007[10] 5504[6] ◆ 6661[4] 7303[8] 7804[5]

**Jet Mate (IRE)** *William Muir* a59 57
2 ch g Fast Company(IRE) Anazah (USA) (Diesis)
1259[8] 1872[5] 2380[7] 4967[4] ◆ 5823[5] 6072[2] 6413[4] 6884[8] (7064) 7396[7]

**Jewelled** *Ralph J Smith* a74 78
8 b m Fantastic Light(USA) Danemere (IRE) (Danehill (USA))
376[9] 627[8] 801[3] 857[3] 2770[2] (3079) 3874[5] (4045) 4351[6]

**Jewelled Dagger (IRE)** *Sharon Watt* a35 60
10 b g Daggers Drawn(USA) Cappadoce (IRE) (General Monash (USA))
959[8] 1674[11] 4797[12] 5240[12] 5371[10] 5773[9]

**Jewelled Prince** *Richard Fahey* 71
2 ch c Zamindar(USA) Diamond Lass (IRE) (Rock Of Gibraltar (IRE))
5264[2] 6509[7] 7166[4] 7443[8]

**Jezza** *Victor Dartnall* a71 71
8 br g Pentire Lara (GER) (Sharpo)
1418[7] 2683[2] 3851[3] 4076[6] 5547[4] 6343[8] 6881[7] (7419) 7946[5]

**Jialing River (FR)** *R Chotard* 62
2 b f King's Best(USA) Lady Of Akita (USA) (Fantastic Light (USA))
5590a[11] 6958a[12]

**Jiayuguan (IRE)** *N Clement* a88 99
3 ch f Teofilo(IRE) Ponte Vechio (FR) (American Post)
6882a[3]

**Jillanar (IRE)** *George Margarson* 69
2 b f Lawman(FR) Lunduv (IRE) (Pivotal)
4126[3] ◆ 4604[5] 6434[5] 7378[3]

**Jillnextdoor (IRE)** *Mick Channon* 96
4 b f Henrythenavigator(USA) Royal Shyness (Royal Academy (USA))
1572[7] 2123[3] 2564[8] 2757[6] 3693[2] 4445[7] 4762[15] 6068[6] 6314[2]

**Jim (GER)** *Christina Bucher* a83 80
3 b c Doyen(IRE) Joliesse (USA) (Red Ransom (USA))
721a[10] 3512a[10]

**Jiminy** *Alan Berry* a58 37
4 b g Acclamation Grasshoppergreen (IRE) (Barathea (IRE))
258[4] 298[3] 478[4] 549[5] 693[6] 1243[5] 1343[5] 2093[6] 2658[11] 3531[5]

**Jimmy Crackle (IRE)** *Brian Ellison* a30 62
3 b g Intense Focus(USA) Slieve (Selkirk (USA))
1304[3] 3534[7] 5239[6] 5717[3] 5917[2] 6515[6]

**Jimmy Sewell (IRE)** *Michael Appleby* a75 46
5 b g Catcher In The Rye(IRE) Starway To Heaven (ITY) (Nordance (USA))
4736[12]

**Jimmy's Girl (IRE)** *Chris Dwyer* a58 60
2 ch f Equiano(FR) Scottish Exile (IRE) (Ashkalani (IRE))
2402[6] 2692[2] 3210[2] 4652[7] (5133) 5506[6] 6017[5] 6645[9] 7190[4] 7453[12]

**Jimmy's Hall** *J S Moore* a70 69
2 b g Kyllachy Up At Dawn (Inchinor)
3550[6] 3871a[6] 4883a[2] 5118a[6] 5616a[6] 5739a[4] 6212[4] 6591a[12] 7917[3] 8059[4] (8287) 8308[3]

**Jimmy Styles** *Clive Cox* a101 111
10 ch g Inchinor Inya Lake (Whittingham (IRE))
1163[4] 1421[2] 1975[14] 3452[25] 6533[21]

**Jim Tango (FR)** *Karen McLintock* 41
10 bb g Jimble(FR) Fitanga (FR) (Fijar Tango (FR))
4522[4] 7007[8]

**Jinky** *Linda Perratt* a64 82
6 b g Noverre(USA) Aries (GER) (Big Shuffle (USA))
1565[3] 1759[4] 2456[8] 2677[10] 3102[6] (4003) 4016[2] 4256[2] 4487[3] 4724[4] 5170[3] 5236[6] 6013[6] 6475[6] 6835[3] 7103[3]

**Jiroft (ITY)** *Ann Stokell* a92 79
7 b g Blu Air Force(IRE) Dexia (ITY) (Indian Ridge)
4[3] 271[10] 431[5] 644[12] 1944[5] 2390[5] 3122[8] 3676[7] 4027[9] 4553[3] 5945[7] 6324[7] 6695[11] 7623[6]

**Jive** *Richard Hannon* a63 73
3 b f Major Cadeaux Lindy Hop (IRE) (Danehill Dancer (IRE))
1381[6] 1570[3] 1832[8] 2429[3] 2745[2] 3300[5] 3650[8]

**Jjs Pride (IRE)** *Denis Quinn* a27 66
5 b g One Cool Cat(USA) Yaselda (Green Desert (USA))
81[12] 215[6]

**Jo Bibidia** *Jonathan Portman* a59
2 ch f Joe Bear(IRE) Veni Bidi Vici (Horse Chestnut (SAF))
6606[8] 7198[4] 7523[3]

**Jo De Vati (FR)** *S Wattel* a101 101
4 b c Vatori(FR) Etoile De Vati (FR) (Kingsalsa (USA))
836a[5] 7026a[10]

**Jodies Jem** *William Jarvis* a90 91
4 br g Kheleyf(USA) First Approval (Royal Applause)
2311[7] 2707[4] 3931[4] 4453[3] 4827[2] 5446[3] 6713[7] 7545[5] 7852[6]

**Joe Eile (IRE)** *John Quinn* a92 99
6 b g Iffraaj Encouragement (Royal Applause)
566[5] 890[6] 1193[18] 1646[6] 1958[5] 2362[6] 2548[5] 3202[11] 4661[11]

**Joe Packet** *Jonathan Portman* a71 100
7 ch g Joe Bear(IRE) Costa Packet (IRE) (Hussonet (USA))
2254[18] 2503[9] 2849[4] 2992[8] 3479[5] 4918[5] 5392[2] 5750[8] 6558[5] 6880[5] 7307[8]

**Joey Black** *Susan Corbett* 16
2 b g Kheleyf(USA) Black Moma (IRE) (Averti (IRE))
7496[9] 7638[9]

**Joey's Destiny (IRE)** *George Baker* 101
4 ch g Kheleyf(USA) Maid Of Ailsa (USA) (Pivotal)
1193[2] 1492[2] 2110[11] (3152) 4895[8] 5623[5] 6755[5] 7168[4] 7272[12]

**Jofranka** *David Barron* a48 85
4 b f Paris House Gypsy Fair (Compton Place)
1850[5] 3006[5] 3659[6] 3920[5] 4630[2] 4859[6] 6512[4] 6763[6]

**Johann Bach (IRE)** *Patrick G Harney* a77 62
5 b g Oratorio(IRE) Belleinga (IRE) (Orpen (USA))
(7435a)

**Johann Strauss** *A P O'Brien* a89 110
3 b c High Chaparral(IRE) Inchmina (Cape Cross (IRE))
1530[6] 2571a[4]

**Johara (IRE)** *Chris Wall* a100 88
3 b f Iffraaj Hurricane Irene (IRE) (Green Desert (USA))
(2525) (3114) 3704[2] (4971)

**John Caesar (IRE)** *Jeremy Noseda* a77 54
3 b c Bushranger(IRE) Polish Belle (Polish Precedent (USA))
4111[6] 5181[6] 6018[6] 7012[2]

**Johnchop (FR)** *J-M Lefebvre*
2 b c Deportivo Water Bells (IRE) (Val Royal (FR))
8212a[6]

**John Coffey (IRE)** *Michael Appleby* a59 71
5 b g Acclamation Appleblossom Pearl (IRE) (Peintre Celebre (USA))
7950[9]

**John F Kennedy (IRE)** *A P O'Brien* 113
2 b c Galileo(IRE) Rumplestiltskin (IRE) (Danehill (USA))
(6348a)

**John Joiner** *Peter Makin* a48 57
2 b g Captain Gerrard(IRE) Nigella (Band On The Run)
4846[4] 6024[4] 6659[7] 7308[7] 7771[6]

**Johnno** *David Nicholls* a85 98
5 br g Excellent Art Vert Val (USA) (Septieme Ciel (USA))
1191[13] 1483[8] (2603) ◆ 3221[3] ◆ (3573) 4169[2] 4442[2] 5919[14]

**Johnny Barnes (IRE)** *John Gosden* 106
2 b c Acclamation Mahalia (IRE) (Danehill (USA))
(5315) 6004[3] (7171) 7557a[2]

**Johnny B Goode (IRE)** *Richard Fahey* a70 79
2 b g Approve(IRE) Musica E Magia (IRE) (King's Theatre (IRE))
1505[7] 1726[9] 3613[4] 4625[2] (5242) (6003) 6510[8] 7571[3] 7714[2]

**Johnny Cavagin** *Richard Guest* a66 91
5 b g Superior Premium Beyond The Rainbow (Mind Games)
1190[2] 1903[2] (2549) 3202[14] 4347[U] 5385[4] 6260[11] 7507[5]

**Johnny Guitar (ARG)** *Patrick Shaw* a48 112
5 b g Lode(USA) Jolie Caresse (USA) (Septieme Ciel (USA))
2379a[9]

**Johnny Sorrento** *Tim Pitt* a54
2 b g Zamindar(USA) Glorious Dreams (USA) (Honour And Glory (USA))
1161[17] 1259[2] 1741[5] 3201[12] 5254[3] 5506[7] 6248[10] 6676[7] 6941[8]

**Johnny Splash (IRE)** *Roger Teal* a77 61
5 b g Dark Angel(IRE) Ja Ganhou (Midyan (USA))
192[8] 313[5] 340[9] (799) 921[3] 1238[2] 2648[2] 3393[12] 3707[6] 3820[2] (4337) 4614[2] 5045[3] 5126[2] 5860[3] (6631) (8077) 8245[3]

**John Potts** *Brian Baugh* a67 41
9 b g Josr Algarhoud(IRE) Crown City (USA) (Coronado's Quest (USA))
263[2] (538) (736) 1385[7] 2806[12] 8162[6]

**John Reel (FR)** *David Evans* a89
5 b g Country Reel(USA) John Quatz (FR) (Johann Quatz (FR))
7733[4] 7812[2] (7951)

**Joie De Reve (IRE)** *David Simcock* a78 68
3 b f Footstepsinthesand La Caprice (USA) (Housebuster (USA))
486[2] ◆ (962) 1579[4] 3581[4] 4367[5]

**Join Up (FR)** *J-C Rouget* 84
2 b f Palace Episode(USA) Country Jane (FR) (Country Reel (USA))
3744a[2] 5119a[3]

**Jolie Blonde** *Sir Mark Prescott Bt* a54 79
3 ch f Sir Percy Affaire D'Amour (Hernando (FR))
(6818) (7006) ◆ 7509[2]

**Jolie De Vivre (IRE)** *Sylvester Kirk* a58 66
2 b c Thewayyouare(USA) Jolie Clara (FR) (Kahyasi)
4896[9] 5718[6] 6602[5] 7134[11] 7815[6]

**Jolievitesse (FR)** *K R Burke* 94
2 b c Elusive City(USA) Volvoreta (Suave Dancer (USA))
4389[6] 5386[2] ◆ (6225) 7104[6]

**Jolly Good Kitten (USA)** *Gianluca Bietolini* 100
2 b c Kitten's Joy(USA) Ballade's Girl (USA) (Saint Ballado (CAN))
(7468a)

**Jolly Old Chap (FR)** *M Nigge* a88 40
4 b c Acclamation Compulsive Quality (USA) (Elusive Quality (USA))
805a[4]

**Jolly Red Jeanz (IRE)** *Tom Dascombe* a71 68
3 ch f Intense Focus(USA) Sovienne (IRE) (Soviet Star (USA))
512[2] 675[2] (855) 1851[8] 2208[5] 4186[DSQ] 5923[8] 6902[7] 7286[3] 7621[2] 7950[3]

**Jonh Jonh (FR)** *W Walton* a85 86
3 b c Chineur(FR) Flower (Zamindar (USA))
237a[9]

**Jonnie Skull (IRE)** *Phil McEntee* a62 70
8 b g Pyrus(USA) Sovereign Touch (IRE) (Pennine Walk)
1637[6] 2270[6] 2876[8] 3427[4] 3895[4] 4342[5] 4593[5] 4767[2] 5058[2] (5110) 5319[5] 5537[6] 5727[6] 7013[6] 7883[7] 7908[4] 8299[5]

**Jonny Delta** *Jim Goldie* 87
7 ch g Sulamani(IRE) Send Me An Angel (IRE) (Lycius (USA))
(1562) 1971[5] 2561[7] 3240[9] 5144[8] 6514[2] 7107[10]

**Jonny Rae** *Andrew Balding* a77 76
3 b g Shirocco(GER) Lady Brora (Dashing Blade)
2773[6] 4543[4]

**Jontleman (IRE)** *Mick Channon* a66 81
4 b g Whipper(USA) Gandia (IRE) (Danehill (USA))
1710[10] 2124[2] 3088[4] 3612[3] 4024[7] 4401[7] 4907[5] 5523[2] 5951[4] (6249) 6558[6]

**Joohaina (IRE)** *Marco Botti* a88 72
3 b f New Approach(IRE) Rouge Noir (USA) (Saint Ballado (CAN))
613[2] 850[6]

**Jordan Princess** *Luca Cumani* a63 104
3 b f Cape Cross(IRE) Princess Nada (Barathea (IRE))
1978[2] 2484[7] 3143[7] 4436[5] (5723) 6708[2]

**Jordaura** *Alan Berry* a37 78
8 br g Primo Valentino(IRE) Christina's Dream (Spectrum (IRE))
1885[7] 2701[8] 2913[4] 7251[13]

**Josefa** *Noel Quinlan* 33
2 bb f Equiano(FR) Jenny Lake (USA) (Danzig (USA))
3933[9]

**Joshua Potman (IRE)** *Tom Dascombe* 68
2 gr g Zebedee Road To Reality (IRE) (Indian Danehill (IRE))
3883[5] 4935[5] 5494[3]

**Joshua The First** *Ian Semple* a63 68
5 br g Kheleyf(USA) Newkeylets (Diktat)
1596[7] 2475[12] 2911[8] 3105[7]

**Joshua Tree (IRE)** *Ed Dunlop* a109 114
7 b h Montjeu(IRE) Madeira Mist (IRE) (Grand Lodge (USA))
901a[6] 1177a[11] 1783a[5] 2988[7] 3450[7]

**Josie Joe** *David Evans* a49 45
2 ch f Stimulation(IRE) Minette (Bishop Of Cashel)
1276[9] 1363[5] 2642[7] 8221[6]

**Josie's Dream (IRE)** *Jo Hughes* a55 58
6 b g Tau Ceti Gallery Breeze (Zamindar (USA))
475[3] 640[10] 7932[7] 7990[7]

**Journey** *John Gosden* 60
2 b f Dubawi(IRE) Montare (IRE) (Montjeu (IRE))
6041[5]

**Journeyman (SAF)** *M F De Kock* a89 95
4 b c Trippi(USA) Rambo's Love (SAF) (Rambo Dancer (CAN))
204a[9] 505a[5] 594a[11]

**Joy And Fun (NZ)** *D Cruz* 120
11 b g Cullen(AUS) Gin Player (NZ) (Defensive Play (USA))
1179a[9]

**Joyeuse** *Lady Cecil* 109
3 b f Oasis Dream Kind (IRE) (Danehill (USA))
1435[3] 1976[11] (2564) 3167a[2] 4171[2] 5223a[9] 6254[9] 7242[6]

**Joyful Friend** *John Gosden* a79
3 b f Dubawi(IRE) Cheerleader (Singspiel (IRE))
(50) ◆

**Joyful Motive** *Michael Chapman* a55 55
5 ch g Motivator Triple Joy (Most Welcome)
1092[3] (1117) 1248[3] 1359[5] 1485[8] 1806[6] 2394[6] 3310[5] 3404[4] 3682[7] 5240[10]

**Joyful Risk (IRE)** *Martin Bosley* a67
4 ch f Kheleyf(USA) Joyfullness (USA) (Dixieland Band (USA))
456[4] 660[3] 1024[5] 7633[9]

**Joyful Sound (IRE)** *Brian Ellison* 65
6 b g Acclamation Eman's Joy (Lion Cavern (USA))
2546[3] 3660[3] (4730) 5640[9]

**Joyful Star** *Frederick Watson*
4 b g Teofilo(IRE) Extreme Beauty (USA) (Rahy (USA))
3998[5] 5018[7]

**Joy Of Being (USA)** *Charlie Appleby* a20
2 bb f Street Cry(IRE) Any For Love (ARG) (Southern Halo (USA))
5305[10]

**Joyous** *Dean Ivory* a69 71
4 b f Assertive Ivory's Joy (Tina's Pet)
53[3] 4267[4] (4675) 4981[6] 6463[5] 7286[11] 7623[5] 7806[12]

**Joys Of Spring (IRE)** *Luca Cumani* 94
3 b f Invincible Spirit(IRE) Sonachan (IRE) (Darshaan)
1612[2] 2967[2] 3560[6] 4271[2] (4631) ◆ 5107[3] 6129[2]

**Juara (IRE)** *Anthony Mulholland* a68 68
4 b f Iffraaj Aquiform (Cadeaux Genereux)
794a[6]

**Jubilance (IRE)** *Bent Olsen* a87 96
5 b g Oratorio(IRE) Literacy (USA) (Diesis)
3090a[3] 3772a[7] 5744a[4] 6389a[8]

**Jubilee Brig** *Andy Turnell* a88 85
4 b g Kheleyf(USA) Voile (IRE) (Barathea (IRE))
399[2] (452) 602[2] (805a) (1038) 1261[2] (1429) 2117[5] 2919[7] 3122[4] 4650[5] 4963[7]

**Jubilee Spirit** *Geoffrey Oldroyd* a34 60
2 b g Misu Bond(IRE) Bond Babe (Forzando)
2541[9] 3842[6] 4110[7] 6040[2] 6642[7] *8227[8]*

**Judge 'n Jury** *Ronald Harris* a93 105
10 ch g Pivotal Cyclone Connie (Dr Devious (IRE))
2123[7] 2283[15] 2803[2] 2989[10] 3927[9] (5289) 5575[15] 5925[6] 6745[9] 7080[18]

**Judicial (IRE)** *Roger Charlton* a83 83
2 b g Iffraaj Marlinka (Marju (IRE))
(3889) (4814) ◆ *(5511)*

**Judicious** *Geoffrey Harker* 73
7 ch g Pivotal Virtuous (Exit To Nowhere (USA))
1660[6]

**Judy The Beauty (CAN)** *Wesley A Ward* a116 98
5 ch m Ghostzapper(USA) Holy Blitz (USA) (Holy Bull (USA))
*(7608a)*

**Julia Stardust** *Alan Coogan*
2 b f Early March Subtilty (With Approval (CAN))
1528[16] *1764[7]* 4618[13] *5569[7]*

**Jullundar (IRE)** *Jo Hughes* a70 70
4 b g Refuse To Bend(IRE) Announcing Peace (Danehill (USA))
*10[3] 221[7]*

**Jumbo Prado (USA)** *John Stimpson* a69 56
5 rg g El Prado(IRE) Sant Elena (Efisio)
*406[10] 1745[2]* 2457[7] *3233[6]* 4279[6] *4433[5]* 5109[4] *5512[4] (5893) 6161[3] (6342) 7533[13]* 7907[2]

**Jumbo Steps (IRE)** *Jim Goldie* a54 72
7 b g Footstepsinthesand Night Delight (IRE) (Night Shift (USA))
1760[3] 2677[12] 3006[6] 3668[7] 3954[2] 4003[4] 4521[5] 4961[4] 5236[4] 6405[2] 7056[7]

**Jumeirah Glory (IRE)** *Richard Fahey* 78
2 b g Fast Company(IRE) Lady Dettoria (FR) (Vettori (IRE))
(3186) 3649[4] (5782) 6529[4]

**Juncart** *Kevin Ryan* 88
2 b c Dutch Art Juncea (Elnadim (USA))
5013[8] 6059[6] 6537[2] (6831) (7231)

**June's Moon** *Jonathan Portman* 63
2 b f Hellvelyn Rioliina (IRE) (Captain Rio)
1488[5] 3557[7] 3975[2] 4751[5] 5524[3] 6422[9]

**Jungle Bay** *Jane Chapple-Hyam* a85 81
7 b g Oasis Dream Dominica (Alhaarth (IRE))
*1261[5]* 1731[5] *2645[6]* 3313[6] *3854[5]* 4594[2] 5536[3] *6021[7] 8040[7] (8204)*

**Jungle Cat (IRE)** *Mark Johnston* 109
2 b c Iffraaj Mike's Wildcat (USA) (Forest Wildcat (USA))
2450[3] (2964) 3318[3] ◆ 4123[2] 4822[3] 5692[2] 6547[5]

**Junior Ben** *Derek Shaw* a46 22
2 b g Equiano(FR) Pretty Girl (IRE) (Polish Precedent (USA))
*3580[6] 6158[10] 6659[8] 7453[5]* 7665[4] *8118[4]* ◆

**Junoob** *Chris Waller* a102 113
6 ch g Haafhd Faydah (USA) (Bahri (USA))
7301a[7] 7653a[18]

**Jupiter Storm** *Gary Moore* a81 88
5 ch g Galileo(IRE) Exciting Times (FR) (Jeune Homme (USA))
1493[6] 2034[2] (2851) 3065[9] 6425[2] *7838[14]*

**Jusquiame Noire (IRE)** *Y Gourraud* a62 86
3 b f Holy Roman Emperor(IRE) Black Crystal (USA) (Elusive Quality (USA))
7857a[9]

**Just A Pound (IRE)** *Jo Hughes* a62 63
4 b g Ad Valorem(USA) Gallery Breeze (Zamindar (USA))
*30[6] 538[6]*

**Just A Way (JPN)** *Naosuke Sugai* 130
5 b h Heart's Cry(JPN) Sibyl (JPN) (Wild Again (USA))
(1181a) 6970a[8] 7981a[2]

**Just Because** *Edward Creighton* a59 26
2 b g Mawatheeq(USA) Muwakaba (USA) (Elusive Quality (USA))
2499[8] *3113[6] 3387[5] 6629[5] 7728[9]*

**Justcallhimbilly** *Shaun Harris* 53
4 ch g Phoenix Reach(IRE) Rainbows Guest (IRE) (Indian Lodge (IRE))
4713[5] 5374[10] 6011[7]

**Justcallmehandsome** *Dominic Ffrench Davis* a54 32
12 ch g Handsome Ridge Pearl Dawn (IRE) (Jareer (USA))
*17[5] 263[8]*

**Just Charlie** *Henry Candy* a64 65
4 b g Piccolo Siryena (Oasis Dream)
1695[11] 3152[6]

**Just Duchess** *Michael Blanshard* a47 50
4 b f Avonbridge Red Countess (Pivotal)
2720[5] 3209[4] 4107[7] 5001[5] 5850[2] 6818[3] *7065[4]* 7518[4] *7657[5]*

**Just Five (IRE)** *John Weymes* a53 48
8 b g Olmodavor(USA) Wildsplash (USA) (Deputy Minister (CAN))
*1015[2] (1138)* 1228[8] *1745[3] 3798[8] 5893[9]*

**Just Gorgeous (IRE)** *A P O'Brien* 85
3 b f Galileo(IRE) Halfway To Heaven (IRE) (Pivotal)
5024a[6]

**Justice Belle (IRE)** *Ed Walker* a66 66
2 b f Montjeu(IRE) Metaphor (USA) (Woodman (USA))
6753[8] 7512[2] *7927[2]*

**Justice Day (IRE)** *David Elsworth* 111
3 b c Acclamation Rock Exhibition (Rock Of Gibraltar (IRE))
2287[4] 2563[4] 2848[4] 3319[13] (3960) 4201[12] 5674[5] 6549[2] (6918) 7656a[7]

**Justice First** *Ed Dunlop* a68 45
2 b c Zebedee Nelly's Glen (Efisio)
7166[5] 7407[9] *7730[5] 8009[4]*

**Justice Good (IRE)** *David Elsworth* 104
2 b c Acclamation Qui Moi (CAN) (Swain (IRE))
1417[6] (1807) (2308) (2845) 3318[4]

**Justice Well** *David Elsworth* 90
2 b c Halling(USA) Porthcawl (Singspiel (IRE))
(2777) 3448[5]

**Justify** *Roger Varian* a68 68
2 b f Dalakhani(IRE) Purity (Pivotal)
*5549[3]* 6148[3] *7184[10]*

**Justineo** *Roger Varian* a93 110
5 b h Oasis Dream Loulwa (IRE) (Montjeu (IRE))
1949[6] 2563[6] 2820a[6] (4889) 6167[3] 6966a[17]

**Just Isla** *Peter Makin* a55 67
4 ch f Halling(USA) Island Rapture (Royal Applause)
3177[6] 3555[3] 4342[4] 5125[2] 5314[5] 5972[2] 6397[2] *7202[7]*

**Just Marion (IRE)** *David Evans* a66 65
2 b f Bushranger(IRE) Dolphin Stamp (IRE) (Dolphin Street (FR))
*1169[3]* 1872[2] 2089[6] 2359[9] 3091[2] (3312) 4157[P] 5525[3] *5798[12] (6072)* 6375a[15] *6662[11] 7075[9] 7258[5]* 7396[6] (7832) 8226[3]

**Just No Rules** *Tony Coyle* 35
2 gr f Aussie Rules(USA) Grand Lucre (Grand Slam (USA))
2652[7] 3529[8] 3842[7] 6669[13] 7488[9]

**Justonefortheroad** *Richard Fahey* a54 101
8 b g Domedriver(IRE) Lavinia's Grace (USA) (Green Desert (USA))
1191[10] 1345[15] (1503) 2351[6] 2763[5] 3035[6] 3382[4]

**Just One Kiss** *Lady Cecil* a84 78
4 b f Cape Cross(IRE) Kissing (Grand Lodge (USA))
*(189) (376) 493[3]*

**Just Paul (IRE)** *Philip Kirby* 86
4 b g Clodovil(IRE) Tatamagouche (IRE) (Sadler's Wells (USA))
1191[14] 1607[3] (1928) ◆ 2548[13] 3189[5] 3573[7] 4661[6] 5143[4] 5915[5] 6430[9]

**Just Poppy (IRE)** *Iain Jardine* 49
5 ch m Ad Valorem(USA) Nebulae (IRE) (Unfuwain (USA))
*264[3]*

**Just Rubie** *Michael Blanshard* a63 11
3 b f Refuse To Bend(IRE) Island Rapture (Royal Applause)
*7845[12]*

**Just Silca** *Mick Channon* 63
2 ch f Teofilo(IRE) Silca Chiave (Pivotal)
6521[4]

**Just Soldier (FR)** *F Chappet* a35 31
3 gr c Soldier Of Fortune(IRE) Just Aerdee (FR) (Kahyasi)
*3869a[11]*

**Just The Judge (IRE)** *Charles Hills* 111
4 bb f Lawman(FR) Faraday Light (IRE) (Rainbow Quest (USA))
1533[5] 2956[3] 3766a[3] 5459a[3] (7326a) 7607a[3]

**Just The Tip (IRE)** *Keith Dalgleish* a73 76
2 b f Kodiac Annus Iucundus (IRE) (Desert King (IRE))
2291[7] (3236) 3619[6] (4702) 5014[5] 5140[3] 6427[4] 6513[14] *(7029)*

**Just The Tonic** *Marjorie Fife* a65 81
7 ch m Medicean Goodwood Blizzard (Inchinor)
1672[9] 2602[8] 3340[4] 3844[6] 4294[9] 5088[12]

**Just Us Two (IRE)** *Robert Cowell* 77
2 b c Royal Applause Sarah's First (Cadeaux Genereux)
5091[5] ◆ 6299[2] (6867)

**Jutland** *Doug Watson* a107 105
7 b g Halling(USA) Dramatique (Darshaan)
305a[5] 507a[8] 811a[4]

**Juvenal (IRE)** *Paul Morgan* a68 66
5 b g Holy Roman Emperor(IRE) Final Opinion (IRE) (King's Theatre (IRE))
1503[8] 2019[2] 2546[8] 4470[5] 4996[2] 5621[6] 6881[10] *8044[9]*

**Juventas** *Mick Channon* 77
2 ch f Sixties Icon The Screamer (IRE) (Insan (USA))
1879[4] (2306) 3448[9] 3721[8] 4178[7]

**J Wonder (USA)** *Brian Meehan* 110
3 b f Footstepsinthesand Canterbury Lace (USA) (Danehill (USA))
(1435) 2195a[7] 3418[7] (4854) 6254[7]

**Kaab (IRE)** *Ed Dunlop* 83
3 b g Kheleyf(USA) Ms Victoria (IRE) (Fasliyev (USA))
1518[12] 3704[8] 4594[4]

**Kaabamix (FR)** *D Windrif* a69 74
4 gr f Carlotamix(FR) Sindella (IRE) (Sendawar (IRE))
2192a[7]

**Kaaber (USA)** *Roy Brotherton*
3 b g Daaher(CAN) Taseel (USA) (Danzig (USA))
*7901[11]*

**Kaahen (USA)** *Pat Eddery* a41 10
4 bb g Jazil(USA) Khassah (Green Desert (USA))
*7548[9] 8085[13]*

**Kadla (FR)** *C Laffon-Parias* a63 63
2 bb f Falco(USA) Kalisia (King's Best (USA))
6698a[3]

**Kafeel (USA)** *Roger Varian* a83 91
3 b g First Samurai(USA) Ishraak (USA) (Sahm (USA))
*2063[4]* 2962[2] (3782) 4647[11]

**Kagami** *Simon Dow* a54 73
3 ch g Teofilo(IRE) Sky Wonder (Observatory (USA))
2271[6] ◆ 2924[4] 3270[5] *6043[4] 7533[14] 7799[6]*

**Kahouanne (FR)** *T Lemer* 95
2 ch c Cockney Rebel(IRE) Bramaputra (IRE) (Choisir (AUS))
(6916a)

**Kahruman (USA)** *E Charpy* a84 90
5 br g Mr Greeley(USA) Jaleela (USA) (Kingmambo (USA))
*239a[4]*

**Kai** *Alan McCabe* a64 42
5 b g Kyllachy Belle Ile (USA) (Diesis)
*33[5] 171[10] 269[9] 288[9]*

**Kaigun (CAN)** *Mark Casse* a89 114
4 ch g Northern Afleet(USA) Cruising Kris (CAN) (Kris S (USA))
3025a[2] 4010a[5] 6391a[2] 7613a[10]

**Kailong (FR)** *E Leenders* 74
2 b f Great Journey(JPN) Delticia (FR) (Della Francesca (USA))
4312a[4] 6958a[6]

**Kaine Keira** *Paul Midgley* 35
2 ch g Archipenko(USA) Mme De Stael (Selkirk (USA))
6931[8] 7123[10]

**Kais (FR)** *F Monnier* a67 91
3 b g Redback Polychrome (FR) (Bering)
*3745a[7]*

**Kaiss (USA)** *S Seemar* a100 97
7 ch g Seeking The Gold(USA) November Snow (USA) (Storm Cat (USA))
*808a[5]*

**Kaiulani (IRE)** *Mick Channon* 94
3 b f Danehill Dancer(IRE) Royal Shyness (Royal Academy (USA))
5438[11]

**Kaizen Factor** *Micky Hammond* a48 64
3 b g Azamour(IRE) Best Side (IRE) (King's Best (USA))
*1124[3]* 1792[9] 2247[5] 4497[7] 4834[6] 5466[5]

**Kakapuka** *Anabel K Murphy* a76 74
7 br g Shinko Forest(IRE) No Rehearsal (FR) (Baillamont (USA))
*245[12] (451) 646[8] 757[3] 1297[9]* 3177[3] (3555) 4156[4] *4544[3]* 5125[6] *7758[12] 7905[9]* 8299[8]

**Kakatosi** *Mike Murphy* a88 91
7 br g Pastoral Pursuits Ladywell Blaise (IRE) (Turtle Island (IRE))
1862[3] 2311[4] 3109[4] 4181[3] 4783[14] (5346) 6207[7] 6891[9] 7601[8]

**Kalaatah (USA)** *Saeed bin Suroor* a97
3 b f Dynaformer(USA) Teeba (USA) (Seeking The Gold (USA))
*(7195) (7689) 7922[4]*

**Kalahari (IRE)** *Lucy Wadham* 72
5 b g Halling(USA) Semaphore (Zamindar (USA))
(2806)

**Kalahari Kingdom (IRE)** *Richard Fahey* 65
3 b g Footstepsinthesand Visite Royale (USA) (Danehill Dancer (IRE))
1657[4] 2165[4] 2355[4] 2879[4] (3333) 3911[5]

**Kalamill (IRE)** *Shaun Lycett* a75 54
7 b g Kalanisi(IRE) Desert Pageant (IRE) (Desert King (IRE))
*591[6]*

**Kalani's Diamond** *David O'Meara* 42
4 ch f Kalani Bay(IRE) Cryptonite Diamond (USA) (Hennessy (USA))
1486[11] 2389[13] 3951[6] 4873[6] 6114[10] 7010[4]

**Kalann (IRE)** *Sabrina J Harty* a77 109
7 b g Barathea(IRE) Karkiyla (IRE) (Darshaan)
4746a[9] 6288[3]

**Kaldera (GER)** *P Harley* 108
3 ch f Sinndar(IRE) Konigstochter (GER) (Dai Jin)
4064a[4] (6589a) 6954a[7]

**Kalendar Girl (IRE)** *Maria Sandh* a56 85
6 b m Motivator Kalanda (Desert King (IRE))
6389a[9]

**Kalidjar (FR)** *M Delzangles* 78
3 b g Dylan Thomas(IRE) Kadiana (IRE) (Grand Lodge (USA))
2630a[5]

**Kalifi (USA)** *Stuart Kittow* a55
3 bb f First Defence(USA) Out Of Reach (Warning)
*8020[7] 8310[7]*

**Kalispell (IRE)** *Charlie Appleby* 93
4 b f Singspiel(IRE) Genovefa (USA) (Woodman (USA))
2010[3] 2501[6]

**Kalithea** *Julie Camacho* a60 51
4 b f Kheleyf(USA) Baralinka (IRE) (Barathea (IRE))
*1365[8]* 2653[3] 3344[9]

**Kalk Bay (IRE)** *Michael Easterby* a91 89
7 b g Hawk Wing(USA) Politesse (USA) (Barathea (IRE))
1483[3] 1564[6] 3202[6] 3483[8] 5681[7] 7125[11] 7507[8]

**Kallisha** *Ralph Beckett* 87
3 b f Whipper(USA) Shallika (IRE) (Alhaarth (IRE))
(1701) 2152[4] ◆ 4443[10] 7105[13] 7717[8]

**Kallisima** *Ed McMahon* a25 30
2 b f Arcano(IRE) Kallithea (IRE) (Dr Fong (USA))
6742[7] *7367[12]*

**Kalon Brama (IRE)** *Peter Charalambous* a61 67
3 b f Kodiac Gilded Truffle (IRE) (Peintre Celebre (USA))
1615[4] 2049[6] 2274[9] 3433[9] (4536) 4789[3] 4868[2] 5349[5]

**Kalsa (IRE)** *Robert Collet* 102
3 b f Whipper(USA) Sovana (IRE) (Desert King (IRE))
7268a[7] (7857a)

**Kamalaya** *Richard Hannon* 64
3 b c Teofilo(IRE) Saint Ann (USA) (Geiger Counter (USA))
2334[13]

**Kamaran (IRE)** *Mario Hofer* 57
2 b c Manduro(GER) Kristin's Charm (USA) (Swain (IRE))
5292a[7]

**Kamellata (FR)** *H-A Pantall* 101
3 b f Pomellato(GER) Kamakura (GER) (Exit To Nowhere (USA))
3046a[3] 5407a[6]

**Kanaf (IRE)** *M Al Muhairi* a103 101
7 b g Elnadim(USA) Catcher Applause (Royal Applause)
*768a[4]*

**Kanes Pass (IRE)** *W McCreery* a51 105
5 br m Clodovil(IRE) Pagan Game (IRE) (Montjeu (IRE))
4950a[5]

**Kaniza (FR)** *Y Barberot* a68 55
3 b f Myboycharlie(IRE) Lizzy's Township (USA) (Delaware Township (USA))
2290a[12]

**Kanotier (FR)** *Mme M Bollack-Badel* a74 88
6 b h Daliapour(IRE) Knout (FR) (Kendor (FR))
5222a[2]

**Kansai** *David Simcock* 55
2 b f Bahamian Bounty Xeralda (IRE) (Xaar)
3107[7] 3799[4]

**Kantara Castle (IRE)** *John Mackie* a56 72
3 b g Baltic King Arbitration (IRE) (Bigstone (IRE))
*(187) 356[2]* 1690[6] 3273[11] 4574[3] 5420[4] *6722[10]* 7411[15]

**Karadargent (FR)** *M Boutin* a78 81
4 b g Kendargent(FR) Tishkara (FR) (Xaar)
*796a[16]*

**Karaka Jack** *Jim Goldie* a85 91
7 ch g Pivotal Mauri Moon (Green Desert (USA))
*832[6]* 1190[7] 1598[3] 1724[3] 2790[6] 3190[4] 4650[4] 5235[3] (5681) (6936) 7641[13]

**Karakontie (JPN)** *J E Pease* 120
3 b c Bernstein(USA) Sun Is Up (JPN) (Sunday Silence (USA))
1481a[2] (2196a) 2818a[8] 6971a[11] (7613a)

**Karaktar (IRE)** *A De Royer-Dupre* 92
2 b c High Chaparral(IRE) Karawana (IRE) (King's Best (USA))
7069a[3]

**Karam Albaari (IRE)** *J R Jenkins* a90 79
6 b h King's Best(USA) Lilakiya (IRE) (Dr Fong (USA))
*89[8] 533[6] 744[4] 1175[7]* 3802[5] 4349[10] *4736[7]* 5251[4] (6303) 6649[3] *7016[6] 7734[6]* 7831[6] 8073[7] 8283[3]

**Karate Queen** *Ron Barr* a56 52
9 b m King's Best(USA) Black Belt Shopper (IRE) (Desert Prince (IRE))
2658[7]

**Karens Legacy (IRE)** *Jim Goldie* a19 18
6 ch m Exceed And Excel(AUS) Stardance (USA) (Rahy (USA))
1758[14]

**Karezak (IRE)** *Alan King* a81 92
3 b g Azamour(IRE) Karawana (IRE) (King's Best (USA))
6092[2] *6677[2]*

**Karibu Gardens (USA)** *Josie Carroll* 109
4 bb c Flower Alley(USA) Flower Forest (USA) (Kris S (USA))
6390a[8]

**Karl Marx (IRE)** *Mark Gillard* a24 50
4 b g Red Clubs(IRE) Brillano (FR) (Desert King (IRE))
2252[6] 2836[10]

**Karltheodor (GER)** *R Dzubasz* 101
3 bb c Desert Prince(IRE) Kaprella (GER) (Lomitas)
4007a[11]

**Karluk (IRE)** *Eve Johnson Houghton* 48
2 b f Kodiac Danccalli (IRE) (Traditionally (USA))
1488[9] 2022[8] 3210[6] 3550[5]

**Karma Chameleon** *Doug Watson* a83 49
5 b g Haafhd Mrs Snaffles (IRE) (Indian Danehill (IRE))
*239a[9]*

**Karraar** *Richard Hannon* 89
3 b g Dubawi(IRE) Maghya (IRE) (Mujahid (USA))
1582[3] 1911[3] 2334[4] 2746[3] 3248[3] 3931[6] 4893[8] (6432)

**Kasb (IRE)** *John Gosden* 94
2 ch g Arcano(IRE) Cape Columbine (Diktat)
(1417) ◆ 2521[2] 3318[13] (5672) 6256[6] 6933[4]

**Kasbah (IRE)** *J P Murtagh* 91
2 b c Acclamation Dance Hall Girl (IRE) (Dansili)
2855a[4] 5218a[5] 5607[5]

**Kasbhom** *Anthony Carson* a69 74
4 b g Refuse To Bend(IRE) Summerstrand (IRE) (Cape Cross (IRE))
*(121) 425[3] 996[3] (1227)* (1613) 2529[4] 3427[10]

**Kashgar** *Bernard Llewellyn* a67 93
5 b g Hernando(FR) Miss Katmandu (IRE) (Rainbow Quest (USA))
1418[12] 2175[2] 2482[2] 3034[2] (3698) 4606[3] 5161[7] (6005) 6283[2]

**Kashmiri Star** *Mick Quinn* 61
5 b m Barathea(IRE) Biriyani (IRE) (Danehill (USA))
1613[10]

**Kashmiri Sunset** *Ed de Giles* 93
3 b g Tiger Hill(IRE) Sagamartha (Rainbow Quest (USA))
1395[5] ◆ 1847[3] (2247) 2491[2] ◆ 5276[2] 5691[4] 6137[4] ◆ 6705[4] (7124)

**Kashmir Peak (IRE)** *John Quinn* a97 94
5 b g Tiger Hill(IRE) Elhareer (IRE) (Selkirk (USA))
*547 125[2] 462[2] 611[2] 784[9]* 2314[9] 4349[9] 7083[7] 7440[5]

**Kashstaree** *David Barron* 53
3 b f Sakhee(USA) Celestial Welcome (Most Welcome)
1588[12] 2237[3] 2616[8] 3098[5] 3303[7] 7283[2] 7500[11]

**Kaskarau (FR)** *X Thomas-Demeaulte* 85
3 b c Zamindar(USA) Synergy (FR) (Victory Note (USA))
(4252a)

**Kaspersky (IRE)** *E Botti* 101
3 b c Footstepsinthesand Croanda (IRE) (Grand Lodge (USA))
6808a[7] 7616a[4]

**Kassbaan** *Marco Botti* 66
2 br g Kodiac Town And Gown (Oasis Dream)
1977[11] 2413[3] 4110[3]

**Kassiodor (GER)** *Sophie Leech* a14
7 b g Tiger Hill(IRE) Kitcat (GER) (Monsun (GER))
*446[11]*

**Kastela Stari** *Tim Fitzgerald* a44 54
7 b m Beat Hollow Campaspe (Dominion)
*463[6] 558[4] 649[5]* 3336[4] 4296[3] 4962[9] 7006[10]

**Kastini** *Denis Coakley* a78 84
4 b g Halling(USA) Toucantini (Inchinor)
1729[2] (2301) 2702[2] 3196[11] 4400[7] 5345[5] *6487[5] 6855[5]*

**Katawi** *Chris Wall* a61 99
3 b f Dubawi(IRE) Purring (USA) (Mountain Cat (USA))
*2125[4]* 3124[2] (3650) 4131[7] (5381) ◆ 6994a[5] 7716[8]

**Kate Kelly (IRE)** *Jo Hughes* a16
3 b f Bushranger(IRE) Tranquil Sky (Intikhab (USA))
930$^9$ 1045$^4$

**Kathinka (GER)** *M Munch* a94 94
4 b f Speedmaster(GER) Karsawina (GER) (Lando (GER))
5369a$^7$

**Kathlatino** *Micky Hammond* 64
7 b m Danbird(AUS) Silver Rhythm (Silver Patriarch (IRE))
1374$^8$ 1674$^2$ (2738) 3269$^7$ 4964$^{10}$ 5240$^5$

**Kathleen Frances** *Ali Stronge* a57 69
7 b m Sakhee(USA) Trew Class (Inchinor)
544$^5$ 655$^{13}$ 857$^5$

**Katie Gale** *Michael Appleby* a68 39
4 b f Shirocco(GER) Karla June (Unfuwain (USA))
(3404)

**Katie Hall (IRE)** *C W J Farrell* a50 45
3 b f Rock Of Gibraltar(IRE) Wakel Star (IRE) (Almutawakel)
4556a$^7$

**Katies Joy (IRE)** *Ian Semple* 16
3 b f Art Connoisseur(IRE) Jinxy Jill (Royal Applause)
4900$^7$ 5642$^6$ 6116$^9$

**Katie Taylor (IRE)** *Rae Guest* a52 60
4 b f Acclamation Monaazalah (IRE) (Green Desert (USA))
4569$^5$ 5246$^4$ 7682$^9$ 7884$^9$

**Katja** *B W Hills* a64 61
3 b f Sleeping Indian Toffee Vodka (IRE) (Danehill Dancer (IRE))
371$^4$ 622$^2$ 1039$^2$ ◆ 1430$^2$ 2505$^8$ 3561$^6$ 3972$^3$

**Katmai River (IRE)** *Mark Usher* a58 57
7 b g Choisir(AUS) Katavi (USA) (Stravinsky (USA))
(17) 263$^7$ 497$^2$ 671$^7$ 964$^3$ 1138$^2$ 1385$^{10}$ (1819) 2720$^7$ 3576$^4$ 3781$^8$ 5071$^9$ 5512$^8$ 5893$^7$ 7976$^{10}$ 8123$^{11}$ 8258$^5$

**Katniss (IRE)** *Stuart Williams* 28
2 ch f Champs Elysees Nicene (USA) (Pulpit (USA))
5149$^{12}$ 5391$^7$ 5644$^8$

**Katsumi (FR)** *E Caroux*
3 b f Red Rocks(IRE) Sumiko (Fantastic Light (USA))
194a$^{15}$

**Katy Spirit (IRE)** *Michael Blanshard* a65 58
4 b f Invincible Spirit(IRE) Katy Guest (IRE) (Be My Guest (USA))
83$^8$ 296$^9$

**Kaufmann** *John Gosden* a84
2 b c Showcasing Mini Mosa (Indian Ridge)
7752$^6$ (8000) (8226) 8293$^5$

**Kavanagh (SAF)** *M F De Kock* a113 119
7 b g Tiger Ridge(USA) Quaestio (USA) (Seeking The Gold (USA))
206a$^5$ 308a$^5$ 678a$^8$ (809a)

**Kawaii** *Philip McBride*
2 b f Myboycharlie(IRE) Aliena (IRE) (Grand Lodge (USA))
6753$^{12}$

**Kayaan** *Pam Sly* a60 63
7 br g Marju(IRE) Raheefa (USA) (Riverman (USA))
1848$^6$

**Kayalar (IRE)** *Evan Williams* a58 74
6 b g Noverre(USA) Katiykha (IRE) (Darshaan)
513$^6$

**Kay Gee Be (IRE)** *Alan Berry* a67 82
10 b g Fasliyev(USA) Pursuit Of Truth (USA) (Irish River (FR))
539$^5$ 1268$^4$ 2021$^6$ 2509$^5$ 2911$^7$ 4394$^6$ 4958$^6$ 5773$^7$

**Kaylan's Rose** *Barry Murtagh*
4 b f Kayf Tara Ostfanni (IRE) (Spectrum (IRE))
4066$^7$

**Kaylee** *Kevin Tork* a57 41
5 b m Selkirk(USA) Mrs Brown (Royal Applause)
185$^{12}$ 370$^{13}$ 483$^6$ 662$^6$ 760$^9$ 858$^{13}$

**Kayo Koko (IRE)** *Ann Duffield* 71
2 b f Zebedee Negria (IRE) (Al Hareb (USA))
(4527) 5373$^6$

**Kaytom** *John Wainwright* a16 50
3 b f Misu Bond(IRE) Morristown Music (IRE) (Distant Music (USA))
2389$^{10}$ 3486$^8$ 3951$^8$ 4469$^{10}$ 4627$^{10}$ 7639$^P$ 7783$^{12}$

**Kazak** *Robert Stephens* 32
4 b g Royal Applause Kazeem (Darshaan)
3616$^P$ 4154$^7$

**Keble (IRE)** *John Gosden* 73
2 b c Teofilo(IRE) Vadazing (FR) (Spinning World (USA))
6859$^3$

**Keena (FR)** *J-C Rouget* a93 77
3 b f Acclamation Kerasha (FR) (Daylami (IRE))
5294a$^2$

**Keene** *Philip McBride* a79 62
4 b g Cockney Rebel(IRE) Lumpini Park (Halling (USA))
120$^2$ 250$^{11}$ (345)

**Keene's Pointe** *Kristin Stubbs* a75 64
4 br g Avonbridge Belle's Edge (Danehill Dancer (IRE))
451$^{13}$ 690$^{11}$ 1665$^5$ 2646$^9$ 4072$^7$ 4503$^3$ 5303$^3$ 7025$^2$ (7368) 7704$^7$ 7905$^5$

**Keen Move** *Ismail Mohammed* a63 63
2 b g Aussie Rules(USA) Kekova (Montjeu (IRE))
3381$^7$ 4527$^4$ 5098$^2$ 6420$^8$ 7396$^{13}$ 7815$^5$

**Keep Calm** *John Mackie* a67 67
4 b g War Chant(USA) Mayaar (USA) (Grand Slam (USA))
1134$^3$ 1729$^9$ 2327$^8$ 2801$^4$ 3151$^3$ 4575$^9$ 6900$^8$ 7283$^P$

**Keeper's Ring (USA)** *Roger Varian* a54 60
3 b f Street Cry(IRE) Liffey Dancer (IRE) (Sadler's Wells (USA))
5007$^{11}$ 5504$^8$ 6483$^5$ 7570$^8$ 8028$^5$ 8258$^9$

**Keep In Line (GER)** *Saeed bin Suroor* a55
2 b c Soldier Hollow Kastila (GER) (Sternkoenig (IRE))
7660$^9$

**Keep It Dark** *Tony Coyle* a74 87
5 b g Invincible Spirit(IRE) Tarneem (USA) (Zilzal (USA))
1127$^2$ 1244$^9$ 1447$^7$ 1695$^5$ 1843$^2$ (2056) 2350$^{11}$ 2390$^6$ (2656) 2727$^8$ 5925$^{11}$ 7212$^{10}$ 7330$^6$ 7669$^4$ 7761$^9$

**Keep Kicking (IRE)** *Simon Dow* a74 71
7 b g Tiger Hill(IRE) Dalannda (IRE) (Hernando (FR))
(214) 283$^7$ (580) 742$^2$ 1043$^3$ 2468$^4$ 3034$^{12}$ 3234$^4$ 7366$^{11}$ 7777$^8$ 7932$^5$ 8193$^2$

**Keep 'r Lit** *Miss Imogen Pickard* a28
2 b f Multiplex Cashel Dancer (Bishop Of Cashel)
1169$^6$ 1349$^7$ 1663$^6$ 1901$^3$ 2928$^{12}$ 7809$^8$

**Keep The Dream** *N Caullery* a65 41
4 b g Oasis Dream Mimisel (Selkirk (USA))
722a$^2$ 796a$^6$

**Keep The Secret** *William Knight* a68 64
4 ch f Sakhee's Secret Starfleet (Inchinor)
1385$^4$ ◆ 1771$^5$ 2529$^5$

**Keep To The Beat** *Kevin Ryan* a63 66
3 b f Beat Hollow Cadeau Speciale (Cadeaux Genereux)
165$^7$ 261$^2$ ◆ 411$^6$ 2526$^{10}$ 3380$^8$ 3950$^3$ 4386$^2$ 4793$^3$ 5534$^6$ 5980$^7$

**Keep Up (GER)** *Saeed bin Suroor* 57
2 b g Monsun(GER) Katy Carr (Machiavellian (USA))
5646$^{10}$ 6497$^9$

**Kelamita (IRE)** *Hughie Morrison* a79 43
3 ch f Pivotal Keladora (USA) (Crafty Prospector (USA))
1792$^6$ 3567$^9$ 5491$^2$ (6157) 6900$^2$ (7182) 7422$^3$ 7817$^{10}$

**Kelinni (IRE)** *Marco Botti* a100 103
6 b g Refuse To Bend(IRE) Orinoco (IRE) (Darshaan)
2143$^6$ 2555$^3$ 2991$^{10}$ 3730$^5$ 4759$^8$ 5673$^6$ 6257$^4$ 6693$^3$ 7289$^2$

**Kelloura (IRE)** *Richard Fahey* a40
2 ch f Mastercraftsman(IRE) Ocean Talent (USA) (Aptitude (USA))
7973$^{10}$

**Kellys Eye (IRE)** *Ian Williams* a75 79
7 b g Noverre(USA) Limit (IRE) (Barathea (IRE))
60$^2$ 257$^U$

**Kelly's Finest (IRE)** *James Bethell* 74
2 ch f Intense Focus(USA) Priory Rock (IRE) (Rock Of Gibraltar (IRE))
5443$^6$ 5910$^3$ ◆ 6448$^5$ 7005$^3$ ◆ 7404$^3$

**Kelpie Blitz (IRE)** *Paul Morgan* a69 82
5 gr g Verglas(IRE) Summer Spice (IRE) (Key Of Luck (USA))
369$^6$ 655$^9$ 940$^7$ 3235$^7$ 3778$^2$ 4568$^6$

**Kemosabe (IRE)** *M Delzangles* a69 66
3 ch c Champs Elysees Selouma (FR) (Grape Tree Road)
5592a$^5$

**Kenbella (FR)** *H-A Pantall* 105
4 gr f Kendargent(FR) Nebela (FR) (Bernebeau (FR))
5369a$^3$ 7095a$^6$

**Kenbest (FR)** *H-A Pantall* a83 97
3 gr c Kendargent(FR) Maybe (GER) (Dashing Blade)
1481a$^6$ 2242a$^6$ (3810a) 4930a$^6$

**Kenfreeze (FR)** *H-A Pantall* 103
2 b c Kendargent(FR) Damdam Freeze (FR) (Indian Rocket)
6181a$^5$ 6570a$^5$ 7557a$^7$

**Kenhope (FR)** *H-A Pantall* 112
4 b f Kendargent(FR) Bedford Hope (GER) (Chato (USA))
1371a$^8$ 1908a$^9$ 3355a$^8$ 6351a$^4$ 6955a$^4$ 7559a$^{12}$

**Kenny Powers** *Tom Dascombe* a80 92
5 b g Vital Equine(IRE) Alexander Ballet (Mind Games)
886$^9$ 1443$^6$ 1719$^9$ 2336$^P$

**Kenny's Girl (IRE)** *William Muir* a65 68
4 b f Manduro(GER) Tanz (IRE) (Sadler's Wells (USA))
1210$^2$ 1496$^5$ 1848$^4$ 2175$^6$ 2628$^{10}$

**Kenny The Captain (IRE)** *Tim Easterby* 88
3 ch g Captain Rio Kelso Magic (USA) (Distant View (USA))
1358$^8$ 1937$^5$ 3704$^6$ 6763$^{14}$ 7212$^7$ 7505$^7$

**Kenouska (FR)** *H-A Pantall* 99
2 ch f Kendargent(FR) Dame Anouska (IRE) (Exceed And Excel (AUS))
(2755a) (4603a) 4953a$^8$ 6220a$^5$ 7094a$^5$ 7654a$^3$

**Kent Ragstone (USA)** *Murty McGrath* a79
5 ch g Stonesider(USA) Sweet Charity (USA) (A.P. Indy (USA))
4076$^P$ 4656$^7$

**Kenzadargent (FR)** *J-C Rouget* a85 108
3 bl f Kendargent(FR) Quiza Bere (FR) (Epistolaire (IRE))
1096a$^4$ 1782a$^2$ 2817a$^3$

**Kepple's Best (IRE)** *Alan Berry*
2 b c Moss Vale(IRE) Mrs Kepple (King's Best (USA))
1560$^6$ 5167$^9$ 6400$^4$

**Kept** *Ronald Harris* a64 73
5 ch g Pivotal Possessed (Desert Prince (IRE))
7$^{10}$

**Keravnos (FR)** *C Gourdain* a94 92
4 b g Elusive City(USA) Kypriano's Angel (FR) (Kendor (FR))
7437a$^5$

**Kerbaaj (USA)** *Ruth Carr* 70
4 bb g Dixie Union(USA) Mabaahej (USA) (Belong To Me (USA))
2054$^{11}$ 6625$^9$ 7248$^9$

**Kerdelan (IRE)** *P Monfort* a71 71
3 b c Archipenko(USA) Scarlett's Pride (FR) (Singspiel (IRE))
600a$^3$ 2003a$^4$

**Kerlogot (FR)** *T Castanheira* 23
2 ch c Medecis Honey Gem (FR) (Gold Away (IRE))
7027a$^{15}$

**Kerman (FR)** *J-C Rouget* 98
2 b c Invincible Spirit(IRE) Kerasha (FR) (Daylami (IRE))
(5616a)

**Kernoff (IRE)** *M Halford* a105 100
3 b g Excellent Art Daganya (IRE) (Danehill Dancer (IRE))
(3686a) 4480a$^9$ 6369a$^6$

**Kerosin (GER)** *Jean-Pierre Carvalho* 102
3 b c Tertullian(USA) Karavel (GER) (Monsun (GER))
1781a$^4$ 2377a$^6$ 7727a$^2$

**Kerrymerry (IRE)** *Ismail Mohammed* a57 49
2 b c Vale Of York(IRE) Reasonably Devout (CAN) (St Jovite (USA))
5604$^9$ 6462$^5$ 7076$^7$ 7648$^4$

**Kersivay** *Mrs A Malzard* a58 52
8 b g Royal Applause Lochmaddy (Selkirk (USA))
2598a$^3$ (3496a) 4038a$^6$ 5228a$^3$ 6186a$^6$

**Keshiro (GER)** *Stefano Botti* 101
4 ch c Shirocco(GER) Kesh Kumay (IRE) (Danehill (USA))
2374a$^2$

**Ketchikan (IRE)** *S Cerulis* a83 98
4 b c Dansili Bayberry (UAE) (Bering)
437a$^2$

**Kettlewell** *Warren Greatrex* a75
5 ch g Auction House(USA) Angel Chimes (Most Welcome)
(150) 471$^4$

**Key Code** *E J O'Neill* 53
2 b c Kheleyf(USA) Passkey (Medicean)
4883a$^9$ 5118a$^7$ 5662a$^5$

**Key To Your Heart** *Michael Bell* a56 21
3 b f Sakhee(USA) You Too (Monsun (GER))
2883$^9$ 3401$^5$ 5893$^2$ 6407$^5$ 6946$^{12}$ 8011$^7$ 8258$^4$

**Khafayya (IRE)** *Mark Johnston* 50
2 b g Mawatheeq(USA) Tamazug (Machiavellian (USA))
6861$^6$

**Khajaaly (IRE)** *Michael Appleby* a79 47
7 b g Kheleyf(USA) Joyfullness (USA) (Dixieland Band (USA))
10$^2$ (102) 540$^3$ 587$^7$ (677) (862) 979$^2$ 2844$^5$ 3402$^7$ 4415$^6$ 7521$^9$ 7820$^4$ 7954$^6$ 8058$^2$

**Khalaas** *William Haggas* 77
2 b g Iffraaj Bahia Breeze (Mister Baileys)
7380$^3$

**Khalice** *James Given* 81
3 b f Bahamian Bounty Siena Gold (Key Of Luck (USA))
1358$^{10}$ 1693$^9$ 2361$^6$ 3704$^9$ 4071$^5$ 4469$^8$

**Khatiba (IRE)** *Roger Varian* a97 84
3 b f Kheleyf(USA) Tempete (Dubai Millennium)
(486) 1013$^2$ 3425$^4$ 4132$^2$ 4572$^3$ 5032$^3$ 6302$^2$ (7196) 7663$^2$ (7952)

**Khawaater** *Roger Varian* a69 69
2 ch f Haatef(USA) Balaagha (USA) (Mr Greeley (USA))
2306$^8$ 2644$^2$ 3232$^3$ 4450$^2$ 4999$^4$ 5974$^3$ 6422$^3$ (6852)

**Khawatim** *Richard Guest* a95 91
6 b g Intikhab(USA) Don't Tell Mum (IRE) (Dansili)
4$^9$

**Khaya (NZ)** *J Size* 112
5 b g Librettist(USA) Miss Cosimo (AUS) (Giant's Causeway (USA))
8151a$^3$

**Khee Society** *David Evans* a64 76
3 b g Sakhee(USA) Society Rose (Saddlers' Hall (IRE))
734$^5$ 761$^2$ 1032$^3$ 1588$^2$ 1847$^5$ (2688) 3316$^5$ 3516$^4$ 4208$^4$ 4817$^5$ 5274$^2$

**Khelac** *Micky Hammond* a5 71
4 b g Kheleyf(USA) Miss Lacey (IRE) (Diktat)
1644$^{10}$ 2164$^{10}$ 6672$^{15}$

**Khelfan** *Martin Smith* a51 33
3 b f Kheleyf(USA) Fanny's Fancy (Groom Dancer (USA))
1860$^7$ 2158$^5$ 2525$^7$ 3522$^4$ ◆ 4545$^5$ 4972$^7$ 5307$^5$ 8111$^8$

**Khelman (IRE)** *Richard Fahey* 93
4 b g Kheleyf(USA) Mandolin (IRE) (Sabrehill (USA))
1191$^2$ 1710$^2$ (1967) 2549$^4$ 3102$^2$ (3610) 4384$^{12}$ (5143) 6535$^{10}$ 7233$^{12}$

**Kheskianto (IRE)** *Michael Chapman* a30 54
8 b m Kheleyf(USA) Gently (IRE) (Darshaan)
252$^9$ 3155$^5$ 3546$^6$ 4293$^5$ 4617$^7$ 4755$^3$ 5337$^8$ 5529$^9$ 6628$^5$

**Khione** *Luca Cumani* 104
5 b m Dalakhani(IRE) Sularina (IRE) (Alhaarth (IRE))
1434$^5$ 2315$^9$ 2764$^9$ 4443$^7$ 4945$^9$

**Khloe** *Michael Blanshard* a12 40
3 gr f Clodovil(IRE) Owdbetts (IRE) (High Estate)
1833$^6$

**Khubala (IRE)** *Hugo Palmer* a69 105
5 b g Acclamation Raghida (IRE) (Nordico (USA))
5674$^9$ 6440$^6$ 6923$^2$ ◆ 7132$^6$ 7408$^3$

**Khusoosy (USA)** *Saeed bin Suroor* a85 83
2 b g Hard Spun(USA) Elmaleeha (Galileo (IRE))
5393$^3$ (6317) 7041$^5$ (7544)

**Khutze (GER)** *Eve Johnson Houghton* a58
3 b g Duke Of Marmalade(IRE) Kalahari Dancer (Dalakhani (IRE))
626$^5$ 816$^5$

**Kiama Bay (IRE)** *Richard Fahey* a92 97
8 b g Fraam La Panthere (USA) (Pine Bluff (USA))
54$^9$ 124$^2$

**Kibaar** *B W Hills* 98
2 b c Pastoral Pursuits Ashes (IRE) (General Monash (USA))
1417$^8$ 1866$^2$ 2413$^4$ (3779) (4218) 4936$^2$ 5580$^2$ 6256$^{13}$ 6547$^3$

**Kickboxer (IRE)** *Mick Channon* 106
3 gr g Clodovil(IRE) Ajig Dancer (Niniski (USA))
1358$^6$ 1700$^5$ 2090$^2$ 2317$^3$ (2611) 3253$^3$ (3369) 3694$^4$ 4166$^{12}$ 5438$^6$ (6131) 6918$^2$ 7101$^3$ 7441$^9$

**Kicking Leaves (IRE)** *J S Moore* a50 46
2 b g Fast Company(IRE) Show Me The Money (IRE) (Mujadil (USA))
6205$^9$ 6676$^5$ 7536$^9$

**Kicking The Can (IRE)** *Peter Chapple-Hyam* a76 62
3 gr c Aussie Rules(USA) Silk Meadow (IRE) (Barathea (IRE))
3525$^3$ 4265$^3$ 5186$^4$ 5976$^4$ 7074$^2$

**Kickingthelilly** *Rae Guest* a90 82
5 ch m Byron Teller (ARG) (Southern Halo (USA))
2871$^{11}$ 674$^9$

**Kicky Blue (GER)** *T Clout* a63 107
4 b f Dashing Blade Karina Du Commeaux (FR) (Law Society (USA))
4250a$^7$ 5462a$^6$ 6383a$^2$ 6972a$^5$

**Kid Cruz (USA)** *Linda Rice* a112
3 b c Lemon Drop Kid(USA) Layreebelle (USA) (Tale Of The Cat (USA))
2357a$^8$

**Kidmeforever** *J S Moore* a52 52
2 ch f Piccolo Shore Light (USA) (Gulch (USA))
1488$^{12}$ 1788$^3$ 2172$^4$ 2360$^2$ 2771$^5$ 3967$^3$ 5133$^3$ 5180$^7$ 5885$^6$ 6842$^9$ 7839$^8$ 7991$^9$

**Kidnapped (AUS)** *S Seemar* a31 67
8 br g Viscount(AUS) Youthful Presence (AUS) (Dehere (USA))
242a$^{15}$

**Kielty's Folly** *Brian Baugh* a61 65
10 gr g Weet-A-Minute(IRE) Three Sweeties (Cruise Missile)
7$^3$ 171$^P$

**Kifaaya** *Mark Johnston* 73
2 b c Intikhab(USA) Juniper Girl (IRE) (Revoque (IRE))
3924$^5$ 4633$^{10}$ 5167$^3$ 5782$^3$ 6225$^3$ (6811)

**Kikonga** *Luca Cumani* a90 97
4 b f Danehill Dancer(IRE) Kibara (Sadler's Wells (USA))
3725$^5$ 4145$^2$ 6061$^7$ 6559$^5$ 7110$^4$ 7554$^{11}$

**Kilava (FR)** *T Clout* a84 93
3 b f Invincible Spirit(IRE) Agiel (FR) (Bering)
7856a$^{12}$

**Kilburn** *Alastair Lidderdale* a47 68
10 b g Grand Lodge(USA) Lady Lahar (Fraam)
156$^6$ 281$^{11}$ 2770$^9$

**Kilfinichen Bay (IRE)** *Violet M Jordan* a57
6 b g Westerner Cailin Deas (IRE) (Pistolet Bleu (IRE))
776$^6$

**Kilimandjaro (FR)** *C Gourdain* a73 51
4 b g Elusive City(USA) Relais D'Aumale (Rainbow Quest (USA))
5222a$^8$

**Kilk** *Stuart Kittow* a19 54
6 b m Striking Ambition Bathwick Alice (Mark Of Esteem (IRE))
754$^{10}$

**Killing Time (IRE)** *Ralph Beckett* a85 78
3 b g Oratorio(IRE) Enchanting Muse (USA) (Fusaichi Pegasus (USA))
1195$^5$ 1655$^7$ 5040$^5$ 5758$^8$ (6609) 6990$^9$

**Kill Or Cure (IRE)** *Charles Hills* a58 65
2 b g Acclamation Welsh Mist (Damister (USA))
6103$^7$ 6517$^7$ 6867$^4$

**Kilruane Shea (IRE)** *S Curling* a51 62
3 br g Captain Rio Smart Starprincess (IRE) (Soviet Star (USA))
7877a$^9$

**Kilt Rock (IRE)** *Doug Watson* a98 99
7 ch g Giant's Causeway(USA) Eliza (USA) (Mt. Livermore (USA))
240a$^4$

**Kimbali (IRE)** *Declan Carroll* a63 79
5 b g Clodovil(IRE) Winnifred (Green Desert (USA))
1739$^7$ 2177$^5$ 2381$^2$ 2469$^8$ (3382) (3908) (4291) 4753$^3$ 4922$^{11}$ 6217$^7$ 6430$^6$ 6626$^2$ 7456$^6$ 7538$^{12}$

**Kimbay (IRE)** *Noel Lawlor* a80 71
4 ch f Windsor Knot(IRE) Gilda Lilly (USA) (War Chant (USA))
4556a$^2$ 7873a$^2$

**Kimberella** *David Nicholls* a84 102
4 b g Kyllachy Gleam Of Light (IRE) (Danehill (USA))
1193$^9$ (1538) 1975$^{10}$ 2353$^6$ 3714$^3$ (4188) 4683$^7$ 5445$^7$ 5575$^{14}$ 6281$^8$ 6760$^3$ 7408$^{18}$

**Kindia (IRE)** *Michael Attwater* a78 29
6 b m Cape Cross(IRE) Susu (Machiavellian (USA))
185$^8$ 281$^{10}$ 484$^3$

**Kind Invitation** *Charlie Appleby* a76 83
3 b f New Approach(IRE) French Bid (AUS) (Anabaa (USA))
1868$^8$ 2431$^3$ 3560$^8$

**Kindlelight Storm (USA)** *Nick Littmoden* a76 59
4 b g Stormy Atlantic(USA) Rose Of Zollern (IRE) (Seattle Dancer (USA))
117$^2$ 283$^5$ (406) (643) (958) (1051) 3977$^8$ 4743$^6$ 5426$^2$ 6904$^6$ 7366$^7$ 8099$^6$

**Kindly Dismiss (FR)** *H-A Pantall* 98
2 b f Excellent Art Dianaba (FR) (Diktat)
5707a$^4$ 6219a$^7$ 7094a$^7$ 7855a$^4$

**Kinema (IRE)** *Ed Walker* a79 75
3 b g Galileo(IRE) Bon Nuit (IRE) (Night Shift (USA))
1582$^8$ 2735$^5$ 3135$^4$ 4420$^2$ 5108$^4$ 5534$^2$ 6239$^{11}$ (7359)

**Kinematic** *Andrew Balding* 83
2 b f Kyllachy Spinning Top (Alzao (USA))
2107$^9$ 2744$^2$ 3193$^3$ 6038$^2$ (6739) 7231$^3$

**King Air (FR)** *Rod Collet* a88 100
7 b g Kingsalsa(USA) Haine Amour (FR) (Mtoto)
1371a$^{10}$

**Kingaroo (IRE)** *Garry Woodward* a58 45
8 b g King Charlemagne(USA) Lady Naomi (USA) (Distant View (USA))
475$^4$ 648$^5$ 759$^{11}$ (2396) 2801$^{12}$ 3404$^9$

**King Bertie (IRE)** *Michael Wigham* a92 69
4 b g Clodovil(IRE) Jouel (FR) (Machiavellian (USA))
(909)

**King Bolete (IRE)** *Luca Cumani* 81
2 b c Cape Cross(IRE) Chanterelle (FR) (Trempolino (USA))
6204[6] (7040)

**King Calypso** *Denis Coakley* a81 76
3 ch g Sir Percy Rosa De Mi Corazon (USA) (Cozzene (USA))
2028[4] 2694[3] 3326[4] ◆ (4085) 4562[2] 4844[2] (5491) (6037) 6654[3] (7016) 7402[2]

**King Couture (IRE)** *Michael Easterby* 16
3 br g Erewhon(USA) Hi Fasliyev (IRE) (Fasliyev (USA))
2899[8] 3434[8] 4062[8] 4318[7]

**King Crimson** *Mick Channon* a71 81
2 ch c Captain Gerrard(IRE) Elegant Lady (Selkirk (USA))
1417[12] 1575[4] 1859[2] 2151[2] 5409[7] (5593) (5998)

**Kingdom (IRE)** *Gary Moore* a9 27
4 b g Montjeu(IRE) Shadow Song (IRE) (Pennekamp (USA))
6656[7]

**Kingfisher (IRE)** *A P O'Brien* 113
3 b c Galileo(IRE) Mystical Lady (IRE) (Halling (USA))
1458a[5] (2114) 2990[10] 3739a[2] 5578[6] 6353a[6]

**King Jerry (IRE)** *Ralph Beckett* 73
2 b g Intikhab(USA) Lady Docker (IRE) (Docksider (USA))
4740[4] 5874[3] 6420[2]

**King Kenny** *Mrs A Corson* a49 50
9 ch g Lomitas Salanka (IRE) (Persian Heights)
1624a[2] 2593a[3] 3495a[3] (4041a) 4716a[5] (5230a) 5969a[2] 6188a[4]

**Kingkevi (FR)** *N Leenders* a47
2 bb g Khalkevi(IRE) Kingsa Al Mare (FR) (Kingsalsa (USA))
5900a[8]

**Kinglami** *Brian Gubby* a85 86
5 b g Kingsalsa(USA) Red Japonica (Daylami (IRE))
2030[2] 2147[8] 2919[8] 4262[5] 4650[3] 4892[7] 5433[7] 6144[7] (7159)

**Kingman** *John Gosden* 128
3 b c Invincible Spirit(IRE) Zenda (Zamindar (USA))
(1436) ◆ 1951[2] (2571a) (3320) ◆ (4779) (5480a)

**King Of Arnor** *S Cerulis*
6 b g Monsun(GER) Luce (IRE) (Sadler's Wells (USA))
723a[11]

**King Of Eden (IRE)** *Eric Alston* a77 89
8 b g Royal Applause Moonlight Paradise (USA) (Irish River (FR))
1190[6] 1672[3] 2117[3] 2425[9] 2763[6] 3221[12] 3359[2] ◆ 3610[3] 4061[5] 4161[8] 6824[9] 7403[4] 7729[3] 7954[9]

**King Of Macedon (IRE)** *Mark Johnston* a81 84
3 b g Invincible Spirit(IRE) Allexina (Barathea (IRE))
1350[10] 2257[10] 2734[4] ◆ 3002[2] 3108[4] 3464[4] 3910[4] 4258[6] 4628[2] 4810[5] 5143[3] 5349[4] 5713[6] 6263[9] 6704[8]

**King Of Normandy (FR)** *Richard Hannon* 96
2 ch c Soldier Of Fortune(IRE) Innocent Affair (IRE) (Night Shift (USA))
5706a[4] 6259[9] 7446[3]

**King Of Paradise (IRE)** *Eric Alston* a48 72
5 b g Hurricane Run(IRE) Silly Game (IRE) (Bigstone (IRE))
1306[3] 1562[10] 2119[4] 2423[5] 2868[4] 3829[8] 4454[7] 5077[10] 5856[6] 6597[2] 6706[2] ◆ 7044[3] 7522[9] 7628[10]

**King Of The Celts (IRE)** *Tim Easterby* 75
6 b g Celtic Swing Flamands (IRE) (Sadler's Wells (USA))
1167[4] 1660[4] 2868[2] 3254[16] 3544[6] 4498[9] 4975[4] 6672[12] 7411[8]

**King Of The Danes** *Mark Johnston* a70 96
4 b g Dansili Our Queen Of Kings (Arazi (USA))
1539[7] 2017[4] 2362[5] (2912)

**King Of The Picts (IRE)** *John Patrick Shanahan* 78
5 ch g Rock Of Gibraltar(IRE) Belle Rebelle (IRE) (In The Wings)
1599[5]

**King Olav (UAE)** *Tony Carroll* a80 63
9 ch g Halling(USA) Karamzin (USA) (Nureyev (USA))
79[5] 292[2] 758[7] (1120) 2305[9] 3078[5] 8190[6]

**King Pin** *Tracy Waggott* a62 74
9 b g Pivotal Danehurst (Danehill (USA))
1607[5] 3439[9] 4108[4] 4703[3] 5197[10] 5761[3] 7249[6]

**King Rubi** *Frau Erika Mader* a97 100
3 ch c Green Tune(USA) King's Doll (IRE) (King's Best (USA))
1178a[9] 8006a[7]

**Kingsbarns (IRE)** *A P O'Brien* 118
4 b c Galileo(IRE) Beltisaal (FR) (Belmez (USA))
1252a[3] 5733a[2] 6381a[5] 7274[6]

**Kings Bayonet** *Alan King* a91 94
7 ch g Needwood Blade Retaliator (Rudimentary (USA))
1941[3] (2640) 3250[5] (4160) ◆ 4759[12] 6061[4] 7083[8] 7718[22] 8012[3]

**King's Bond** *Ronald Harris* a44 36
2 b c Monsieur Bond(IRE) Oke Bay (Tobougg (IRE))
3813[5] 4965[7] 5593[5] 6250[13]

**Kingsbridge** *Rod Millman* 80
2 b c Avonbridge Wild Academy (IRE) (Royal Academy (USA))
2964[7] (3304) 4143[7] 5580[8] 6064[3] 7131[11]

**Kings Canyon (FR)** *S Kobayashi* a88 60
7 b h Kingsalsa(USA) Always Pretty (FR) (El Prado (IRE))
806a[9]

**Kings Chapel (USA)** *Jeremy Gask* a58 58
3 b g Elusive Quality(USA) Ladyecho (USA) (Alphabet Soup (USA))
5775[6] 6356[4] 6988[9] 7622[9] 8090[4]

**Kingscombe (USA)** *Linda Jewell* a83 55
5 rg g Mizzen Mast(USA) Gombeen (USA) (Private Account (USA))
(648) (829) (932) (1226) 1848[7] 6107[5] 6721[8] (7650)

**King's Concerto (IRE)** *Dean Ivory* 41
2 ch c Thewayyouare(USA) Major Minor (IRE) (Desert Prince (IRE))
5519[5] 5947[8]

**Kingscroft (IRE)** *Michael Herrington* a85 86
6 b g Antonius Pius(USA) Handsome Anna (IRE) (Bigstone (IRE))
1483[13] 1957[11] 2234[6] 3254[13] (3463) 3703[6] 3955[2] 4349[2] 4608[4] 4922[3] 5054[3] 5413[5] 6430[4] 7185[2] 7636[4] 7955[9] 8209[10]

**Kings Fete** *Sir Michael Stoute* 108
3 b c King's Best(USA) Village Fete (Singspiel (IRE))
2773[4] (3248) (4173) 4893[2] 5668[3] ◆ 6329[9]

**Kingsgate Choice (IRE)** *Ed de Giles* a97 113
7 b g Choisir(AUS) Kenema (IRE) (Petardia)
1066[6] 2197a[6] 5160[7]

**Kingsgate Native (IRE)** *Robert Cowell* a77 117
9 b g Mujadil(USA) Native Force (IRE) (Indian Ridge)
1949[2] 2563[3] 3981[2] 4215[4] 4852[8] 5911[4] 6231[9] (6624)

**King's Hall** *M Figge* a91 98
6 ch g Halling(USA) Konigin Turf (GER) (Turfkonig (GER))
2715a[8] 3511a[7]

**King's Prospect** *Tracy Waggott* 60
3 b g Authorized(IRE) Sovereign's Honour (USA) (Kingmambo (USA))
1960[13] 2422[10] 3953[3] 4574[8] 4706[6]

**King's Request (IRE)** *Laura Mongan* a80 64
4 ch g New Approach(IRE) Palace Weekend (USA) (Seattle Dancer (USA))
(471) (742) (1043) 1556[11] 6264[9] 7946[10]

**King's Road** *Anabel K Murphy* a27 39
9 ch g King's Best(USA) Saphire (College Chapel)
1874[10] 2614[8] 7002[3] 7518[12]

**Kingston Eucalypt** *David Elsworth* a76 73
4 b f Halling(USA) Derartu (AUS) (Last Tycoon)
1393[4] 2628[8] 3064[5]

**Kingston Hill** *Roger Varian* 123
3 rg c Mastercraftsman(IRE) Audacieuse (Rainbow Quest (USA))
1951[8] 2990[2] 3984[4] (6329) 6970a[4]

**Kingston Sassafras** *Ed Walker* a47 56
2 b c Halling(USA) Kingston Acacia (King Of Roses (AUS))
5500[6] 6261[10] 7030[9] 7815[11]

**King's Warrior (FR)** *Peter Chapple-Hyam* a77 86
7 b g King's Best(USA) Save Me The Waltz (FR) (Halling (USA))
1653[6] 2253[16] 7641[6] 7850[8] 8178[4]

**Kingsway Lad (IRE)** *Derek Shaw* a49 49
3 b g New Approach(IRE) Obsessive (USA) (Seeking The Gold (USA))
865[3] 7420[10] 7548[10] 8084[7] 8200[7]

**Kingswinford (IRE)** *John Norton* a56 62
8 b g Noverre(USA) Berenica (IRE) (College Chapel)
3915[3] 4537[7] 5041[6] 6161[6] 7369[5] 8010[6]

**King To Be (IRE)** *Richard Hannon* a74 48
2 b c Myboycharlie(IRE) Becuille (IRE) (Redback)
7031[2] 7412[6]

**King Torus (IRE)** *David O'Meara* a90 98
6 b g Oratorio(IRE) Dipterous (IRE) (Mujadil (USA))
(2425) (2869) (4347) 4648[6] 5418[5] 5771[4] 5919[13] 6226[5] 6755[11] 7715[3]

**King Zeal (IRE)** *Barry Leavy* a51 71
10 b g King's Best(USA) Manureva (USA) (Nureyev (USA))
2835[2]

**Kinkohyo** *Bryan Smart* a55 39
3 b f Indesatchel(IRE) Mythicism (Oasis Dream)
481[7] 1373[7] 1611[6] 2387[11]

**Kinloch Pride** *Noel Wilson* 24
2 ch f Kyllachy Pride Of Kinloch (Dr Devious (IRE))
6168[10] 7082[12]

**Kinloss** *Richard Hannon* a64 67
3 ch f Kheleyf(USA) Celtic Cross (Selkirk (USA))
1389[9] 2224[12]

**Kinnara** *Sylvester Kirk* a57
2 b f Kyllachy Tinnarinka (Observatory (USA))
7808[6] 7867[10]

**Kinshasa** *Luca Cumani* a83 96
3 b c Pivotal Kibara (Sadler's Wells (USA))
1491[4] 2346[4] ◆ (2881) (3587) 4183[7] 6438[2] 6930[8]

**Kip** *Sir Michael Stoute* 60
2 b f Rip Van Winkle(IRE) Catopuma (USA) (Elusive Quality (USA))
6754[7]

**Kipuka** *Paul Cole* 61
2 b f Authorized(IRE) Rakata (USA) (Quiet American (USA))
4396[9] ◆ 6001[5]

**Kiram (FR)** *J-C Rouget* 113
3 b c Elusive City(USA) King Luna (FR) (King's Best (USA))
1272a[2] 2196a[6]

**Kirikkale (FR)** *P Demercastel* a81 82
3 gr c Vatori(FR) Sekara (FR) (Grey Risk (FR))
169a[11]

**Kirkman (IRE)** *James Bethell* a55 74
3 ch g Virtual Validate (Alhaarth (IRE))
1738[6] 2616[2] 3796[2] (4497) 5334[3] 5890[9]

**Kirkstall Abbey (IRE)** *Simon Hodgson*
3 b f Bushranger(IRE) Spanish Falls (Belmez (USA))
1606[5] 3121[8] 4046[8]

**Kirramosa (NZ)** *John Sargent* 106
4 b f Alamosa(NZ) Freyja (NZ) (Danske (NZ))
7127a[11]

**Kirtling** *Andi Brown* a62
3 ro g Araafa(IRE) Cape Maya (Cape Cross (IRE))
5347[8] 6018[9] 7074[7] 7458[5] 7805[8] ◆ 8028[3]

**Kirtling Belle** *Keith Dalgleish* 74
3 br f Pastoral Pursuits Twenty Seven (IRE) (Efisio)
3298[6] 3600[2] 3669[2] 4383[3] 4511[6] 5808[3] 6475[5] 6671[10]

**Kisanji** *Alan McCabe* 72
3 b g Teofilo(IRE) Al Kamah (USA) (Kingmambo (USA))
1166[4] 1438[10] 2492[5] 2805[8] (3121) 3430[2] 3946[9] 4300[9] 4871[6] 5415[13]

**Kisgreen (FR)** *C Baillet* 20
2 b f Desert Style(IRE) Atabaska (FR) (Ashkalani (IRE))
2976a[9]

**Kissavos** *Y Barberot* a82 70
8 b g Montjeu(IRE) Loxandra (Last Tycoon)
920a[9]

**Kissed By Fire** *Jim Boyle* a47
4 ch f Sleeping Indian Desert Cristal (IRE) (Desert King (IRE))
82[3] 486[9]

**Kiss From A Rose** *Rae Guest* a63 63
3 ch f Compton Place Daytrose (Daylami (IRE))
1851[5] 2387[6] 3124[3] 3935[5] 5287[3] 5715[4] 6029[9]

**Kiss Of Spring (IRE)** *David O'Meara* a58 67
3 br f Dansili In The Light (Inchinor)
626[4] 5772[3] 6118[2] 6540[2] 6837[5]

**Kiss The Stars (IRE)** *T G McCourt* a80 82
4 b f Thousand Words Lady Piste (IRE) (Ali-Royal (IRE))
3686a[6]

**Kissy Suzuki** *Hughie Morrison* a30
2 b f Sakhee's Secret Yonder (And Beyond (IRE))
7834[7]

**Kisumu** *Sir Michael Stoute* 71
2 b c High Chaparral(IRE) Arum Lily (USA) (Woodman (USA))
6203[2] 6874[4]

**Kitten's Lady (USA)** *Gianluca Bietolini* 82
3 ch f Kitten's Joy(USA) Personal Odyssey (USA) (Lemon Drop Kid (USA))
1780a[10] 7604a[8]

**Kitten's Red (USA)** *Ed Dunlop* 67
2 ch c Kitten's Joy(USA) Arbor (USA) (Forestry (USA))
6259[14] 6683[6] 7134[8]

**Kitty Bequick** *Peter Hedger* a34 24
3 ch f Piccolo Cat Patrol (One Cool Cat (USA))
5352[6] 5775[8] 6356[7] 7929[5]

**Kiwayu** *Philip Kirby* a88 93
5 b g Medicean Kibara (Sadler's Wells (USA))
3204[3] ◆ 4173[9] 4995[4] 6169[6]

**Kiwi Bay** *Michael Dods* a80 92
9 b g Mujahid(USA) Bay Of Plenty (FR) (Octagonal (NZ))
(1345) 1607[9] 2603[2] 3272[9] 3437[4] 4002[2] 4922[2] (5054) 5681[5] 5915[2] 6534[5] 6936[7] 7719[4]

**Kiyoshi** *Charles Hills* 111
3 b f Dubawi(IRE) Mocca (IRE) (Sri Pekan (USA))
3418[10] 4165[6] 4607[2] 5407a[4] (6254) 6927[5]

**Kizingo (IRE)** *Charles Hills* 66
2 b f Oasis Dream Enora (GER) (Noverre (USA))
4980[7] 6093[6]

**Kizuna (JPN)** *Shozo Sasaki* 122
4 bb c Deep Impact(JPN) Catequil (CAN) (Storm Cat (USA))
2002a[4]

**Kleitomachos (IRE)** *Stuart Kittow* 80
6 b g Barathea(IRE) Theben (GER) (Monsun (GER))
1493[5] 1848[3] 4423[6] 5924[4] 7566[5]

**Kleo (GR)** *Luca Cumani* a90 103
3 b f Kavafi(IRE) Selfish (Bluebird (USA))
2026[3] 2404[5] 3315[2] ◆ (4052) (4680) 5312[10] 6464[4] (7410)

**K Lightning (IRE)** *Sarah Humphrey* a59 56
4 ch g Danehill Dancer(IRE) Arosa (IRE) (Sadler's Wells (USA))
741[9] 1387[5] 1761[3] 2396[2] 2836[9] 3208[P]

**Kloud Gate (FR)** *J Heloury* 88
2 ch c Astronomer Royal(USA) Talkata (IRE) (Suave Dancer (USA))
5740a[6] 7147a[7]

**Klynch** *Ruth Carr* a85 97
8 b g Kyllachy Inchcoonan (Emperor Jones (USA))
(1224) ◆ 1440[9] 1538[7] 1967[3] 2332[13] 2602[4] 2825[6] 4013[6] 4487[4] 4961[5] (5236) 5632[2] 6013[7] 6824[8]

**Knavery (USA)** *Roger Varian* a95 91
3 bb c Candy Ride(ARG) Tight Spin (USA) (Favorite Trick (USA))
(2682) 3651[3] 4323[4] 6943[4]

**Kneesy Earsy Nosey** *Ann Stokell* a21
8 ch m Compton Place Evie Hone (IRE) (Royal Academy (USA))
63[4] 199[5] 353[12] 474[8] 7645[P]

**Knife Point (GER)** *Hugo Palmer* a41 93
3 b g High Chaparral(IRE) Knightsbridge (BRZ) (Yagli (USA))
4325[11] (5374) 6152[2] 6685[2] 7020[2] 7106[4]

**Knight Charm** *Gay Kelleway* a66 50
4 b g Haafhd Enchanted Princess (Royal Applause)
266a[3] 392a[14] 722a[7] 796a[11] 1408[8] 1666[3] 1854[4] 2066[9]

**Knightly Escapade** *Brian Ellison* a74 84
6 ch g Sakhee(USA) Queen Of Iceni (Erhaab (USA))
868[3] 1692[7] (3622) 4217[2] 5579[15] 6169[3]

**Knight Music** *Michael Attwater* a60 40
2 b c Sir Percy Lyric Art (USA) (Red Ransom (USA))
7414[5] 7927[8] 8093[9]

**Knight Of Glin** *David Barron* 39
3 b g Strategic Prince Shamrock Lady (IRE) (Orpen (USA))
1969[4] 2392[7]

**Knight Owl** *James Fanshawe* a92 94
4 b g Rock Of Gibraltar(IRE) Miss Ivanhoe (IRE) (Selkirk (USA))
1345[3] (2131) 2772[4] 4938[10] 5528[5] (6214) 6936[10] 7545[4] 7852[8]

**Knight's Parade (IRE)** *Gordon Elliott* a76 74
4 b g Dark Angel(IRE) Toy Show (IRE) (Danehill (USA))
(5456a)

**Knights Templar (IRE)** *Patrick J Flynn* a52 70
7 b g Trade Fair Step Aloft (Shirley Heights)
4949a[9]

**Knockamany Bends (IRE)** *John Wainwright* a55 59
4 b g Majestic Missile(IRE) Sweet Compliance (Safawan)
502[2] 3093[10] 3440[2] 4288[8] 5105[2] 5683[7] 6120[9] 7782[3] 8181[5]

**Knockgraffon Lad (USA)** *Brendan Powell* a85 49
7 b g Forestry(USA) Miss Dahlia (USA) (Strawberry Road (AUS))
623[7] 956[7]

**Knockroon** *Andrew Balding* a73 67
3 b g Royal Applause Spring Touch (USA) (Elusive Quality (USA))
1173[3] 1511[8] 2122[5] 7117[6] 7352[10]

**Knock Stars (IRE)** *Patrick Martin* a85 85
6 b m Soviet Star(USA) Knockatotaun (Spectrum (IRE))
788a[4]

**Know No Fear** *Alastair Lidderdale* a49 61
9 b g Primo Valentino(IRE) Alustar (Emarati (USA))
3576[11]

**Know Your Name** *David Evans* a74 79
3 ch g Halling(USA) Lady Agnes (Singspiel (IRE))
613[6] 1723[4] 2383[4] (3144) 3782[3] 4161[9] 4426[6] 5903[6] 6871[5] 7757[3] (7953) 8268[3]

**Koala Bear** *James Fanshawe* a65 64
4 b f Oasis Dream Birthday Suit (IRE) (Daylami (IRE))
2681[5] 2985[3] ◆ 3384[8] 4891[3] 5355[10]

**Koben Sky** *Bernard Llewellyn*
6 br m Kahyasi Santana Lady (IRE) (Blakeney)
3568[7]

**Ko Cache (IRE)** *Keith Dalgleish* a45 85
2 b f Kodiac Silver Cache (USA) (Silver Hawk (USA))
1363[6] (1670) 2313[9] (3001) 3353[12]

**Kodafine (IRE)** *David Evans* a68 67
3 br f Kodiac Zafine (Zafonic (USA))
103[5] 1570[8] 2208[3] 2278[6] 2638[4] 2886[8] 3388[2] (3523) 3966[5] (4186) 4324[3] 4847[4] 6297[14] 7355[3] 7622[4] 7806[9] 7847[5] 8142[6]

**Kodestiny (IRE)** *Ismail Mohammed* a47 43
2 b f Kodiac Singingintherain (IRE) (Kyllachy)
1528[13] 1764[5] 2436[6] 2725[9]

**Kodiac Krossing** *Jamie Osborne* a41
2 b f Kodiac Special Destiny (Tobougg (IRE))
6393[6] 6887[7] 7181[6]

**Kodiac Lady (IRE)** *James Tate* a59
2 b f Kodiac Weeping Willow (IRE) (Kheleyf (USA))
7454[5] 7771[5] 8140[6]

**Kodi Bear (IRE)** *Clive Cox* 114
2 br c Kodiac Hawattef (IRE) (Mujtahid (USA))
2298[2] 3318[5] ◆ (4645) 7241[2]

**Kodicil (IRE)** *Mark Walford* 74
6 b g Kodiac Miss Caoimhe (IRE) (Barathea (IRE))
4874[4] 5466[4] (5794)

**Kodiva (IRE)** *Charles Hills* 92
2 b f Kodiac Operissimo (Singspiel (IRE))
4825[2] ◆ 5232[2] 7596[3]

**Koharu** *Peter Makin* a62 66
4 rg f Ishiguru(USA) Vellena (Lucky Story (USA))
1896[6] 2486[10] 3088[9] 3329[2] 5082[5] 6266[5] 6995[8] 7556[10] 7972[5]

**Kokaltash (FR)** *M Delzangles* 113
4 ch c Haafhd Kozaka (FR) (Mark Of Esteem (IRE))
1371a[2] 1908a[3]

**Kokovoko (IRE)** *Andrew Balding* a65
3 br g Trans Island Khazaria (FR) (Sinndar (IRE))
7370[3] 7921[3]

**Koliakhova (FR)** *John Flint* 81
3 b f Literato(FR) Lia Waltz (FR) (Linamix (FR))
3154[8] (4026) 5340[2] 5877[3] 6894[6]

**Kolonel (GER)** *Mario Hofer* a59 109
5 b g Manduro(GER) Kristin's Charm (USA) (Swain (IRE))
5966a[9] 7656a[5] 7856a[7] 8150a[14]

**Kolonel Kirkup** *Ali Stronge* a54 45
4 b g Dr Fong(USA) Strawberry Lolly (Lomitas)
1675[4] 2475[4] 2915[5] 3364[6] 8102[8]

**Kommander Kirkup** *Michael Dods* 87
3 ch g Assertive Bikini (Trans Island)
1939[3] 4111[3] (4873) 5243[6] 5769[2] 6094[9]

**Komtess Ka (FR)** *A Junk* a25 29
2 bl f Persian Combat(USA) Kriska (FR) (Kaldou Star)
4882a[11] 5901a[11] 7027a[14]

**Konig Concorde (GER)** *Christian Sprengel* a90 85
9 b g Big Shuffle(USA) Kaiserin (GER) (Ile De Bourbon (USA))
(728a) 2006a[5] 4247a[11]

**Konigin Ricke (GER)** *M Figge* 30
2 b f Goodricke Konigin Shuffle (GER) (Big Shuffle (USA))
4312a[5] 5293a[12]

**Konkan (IRE)** *L Riccardi* 92
3 gr f Aussie Rules(USA) Cheloca (Selkirk (USA))
1780a[9] 7320a[6] 7725a[9]

**Konnos Bay** *Shaun Harris*
2 b c Phoenix Reach(IRE) Rasmalai (Sadler's Wells (USA))
7666[17]

**Konzert (ITY)** *Ian Williams* a66 66
4 b g Hurricane Cat(USA) Known Alibi (USA) (Known Fact (USA))
5313[8] 5599[5]

**Kool And The Gang (IRE)** *J Albrecht* a79
4 b c Elusive City(USA) Knightsbridge (BRZ) (Yagli (USA))
7437a[11]

**Koolgreycat (IRE)** *Noel Wilson* 31
5 gr m One Cool Cat(USA) Brooks Masquerade (Absalom)
2724[13] 3846[9] 4070[7]

**Kool Kompany (IRE)** *Richard Hannon* 112
2 br c Jeremy(USA) Absolutely Cool (IRE) (Indian Ridge)
(1726) (2403) (2855a) 3318[12] (3738a) (4482a) 5218a[2] 5607[6] 7239[5]

**Kopassus (IRE)** *Peter Chapple-Hyam* a18 54
2 b g Holy Roman Emperor(IRE) Couverture (USA) (Lear Fan (USA))
4167[9] 4750[8] 5315[6] 6669[5] 7075[11]

**Kopenhagen (IRE)** *Ed de Giles* a54 6
3 ch c Captain Rio Quizzical Lady (Mind Games)
6720[8] 7826[10] 8004[P]

**Koptoon** *Tom Dascombe* a84 72
2 b g Rip Van Winkle(IRE) Mania (IRE) (Danehill (USA))
4760[4] 5493[3] (6660) 7201[2] 7571[6]

**Korbous (IRE)** *Richard Brabazon* a78 78
5 ch g Choisir(AUS) Puppet Play (IRE) (Broken Hearted)
6082a[2]

**Koreen (IRE)** *A Fabre* 96
3 b c Samum(GER) Pony Girl (IRE) (Darshaan)
7164a[3]

**Korngold** *Barry Leavy* a48 59
6 b g Dansili Eve (Rainbow Quest (USA))
2052[5] 2396[6] 2836[13]

**Kosika (USA)** *Mark Johnston* a85 101
4 b f Hard Spun(USA) Song Of Africa (USA) (Alzao (USA))
1667[3] ◆ 2054[5] ◆ 2121[3] (2415) ◆ 2608[4] 3220[4] (3575) (3879) (4436) 4668[10] 5609[8] 6164a[5] 7168[5] 7490[10] 7851[6]

**Kovolini** *Geoffrey Deacon* a57
4 ch f Bertolini(USA) Petrikov (IRE) (In The Wings)
748[7] 1024[7] 1233[8]

**Kozideh (FR)** *J-C Rouget* 96
3 ch f Gold Away(IRE) Kozaka (FR) (Mark Of Esteem (IRE))
7319a[9]

**Kozmina Bay** *Bernard Llewellyn* a49 45
5 b m Notnowcato Kozmina (IRE) (Sadler's Wells (USA))
474[4] 640[4] 2836[8]

**Krackerjill (IRE)** *Mark Usher* a61 39
3 b f Kheleyf(USA) Knockenduff (Oratorio (IRE))
165[8] 374[9] 665[10] 786[9] 1048[6]

**Krafty One** *John Gosden* a54
2 ch f Mastercraftsman(IRE) Wonderful Desert (Green Desert (USA))
7550[6]

**Kraka Gym (IRE)** *Michael Easterby* a65 62
3 b g Clodovil(IRE) Accounting (Sillery (USA))
568[4] (753) 960[5] 1308[4] 1657[3] 2165[8] 3545[7] 3911[8] 4300[8] 5891[9] 6568[2] (7423)

**Kramulkie (IRE)** *A Marcialis* 104
4 b g Aussie Rules(USA) Intricate Design (Zafonic (USA))
3776a[3] 7616a[2]

**Krazy Paving** *Mick Channon* 73
2 b g Kyllachy Critical Path (IRE) (Noverre (USA))
6517[8] 6867[2] (7155)

**Kristal Hart** *Neil Mulholland* a47 58
5 b m Lucky Story(USA) Moly (FR) (Anabaa (USA))
275[8] 486[11] 660[7] 998[6] 1835[9] 3208[5] 4105[6] (5596) (5971a) 6187a[3]

**Kroaz (FR)** *J Heloury* 26
2 gr f Silver Frost(IRE) Equibeauta (Nashwan (USA))
3029a[9]

**Krypton Factor** *George Peckham* a109 106
6 br g Kyllachy Cool Question (Polar Falcon (USA))
206a[6] 597a[7] 898a[11] 1180a[10] 6060[4] 6440[3] (6576) 7034[2]

**Kuala Queen (IRE)** *Denis Coakley* 70
3 b f Kodiac See Nuala (IRE) (Kyllachy)
1569[2] 1980[6]

**Kuanyao (IRE)** *Conor Dore* a84 83
8 b g American Post Nullarbor (Green Desert (USA))
113[2] (208) 312[7] 399[6] 602[5] (662) 1038[2] 1261[8] 1489[3] 1678[5] 1893[2] 2401[5] 2933[4] 3033[7] 3854[9] 4344[6] 5100[8] 5423[8] 8195[11]

**Kubeba (IRE)** *Paul Cole* a73
3 b g Kodiac Brillano (FR) (Desert King (IRE))
5039[7] 5427[3] 6018[4] 6484[4] 6717[3] 7074[3] 7918[8]

**Kuda Huraa (IRE)** *Alan King* a92 93
6 b g Montjeu(IRE) Healing Music (FR) (Bering)
2405[3] 2991[14] 4538[3] 5379[5]

**Kudu Country (IRE)** *Tom Tate* 71
8 gr g Captain Rio Nirvavita (FR) (Highest Honor (FR))
3139[3] 4427[9] 5049[2] 5678[5] 6706[10] 7343[2]

**Kune Kune** *Rae Guest* a91 94
5 b m Sir Percy Katy O'Hara (Komaite (USA))
1572[5] 3459[8]

**Kung Hei Fat Choy (USA)** *James Given* a92 67
5 b g Elusive Quality(USA) Lady Succeed (JPN) (Brian's Time (USA))
(75) 909[3] 1499[5] (1630) 1803[2] 3844[7] 4580[6] 5088[5] 5258[6] 6144[5] 6477[9] 7494[16] 7636[5] 7729[9] 7870[11] 8209[4] 8281[3]

**Kunst Basel (FR)** *H-A Pantall* a71 56
2 bb f Naaqoos Marisa Merz (IRE) (Lend A Hand) (5026a) 5844a[6] 6958a[9] 8149a[3]

**Kuwait Star** *Sarah Humphrey* a65 76
5 ch g Resplendent Glory(IRE) Mofeyda (IRE) (Mtoto)
1718[9] 2546[6] 3299[4] (3958) (4394) 4963[3] 6232[7] 6865[9] 8248[6]

**Kylach Me If U Can** *Kevin Ryan* 77
2 b c Kyllachy Raskutani (Dansili)
1505[2] 1732[3] 2358[3] (4259) 5085[5] 6165[6] 7005[5]

**Kyleakin Lass** *Jonathan Portman* a84 102
5 b m Kyllachy Local Fancy (Bahamian Bounty)
1421[6] 1944[3] 2283[19] 2803[6] 4445[P]

**Kyle Of Bute** *Richard Ford* a58 55
8 ch g Kyllachy Blinding Mission (IRE) (Marju (IRE))
40[3] (317) 368[2] 671[6] 838[4] 2475[8]

**Kylies Wild Card** *Simon Hodgson* a40 43
2 b f Aussie Rules(USA) Jemiliah (Dubai Destination (USA))
5519[8] 5859[5] 7113[8] 7453[6] 7684[7] 7848[4]

**Kyllach Me (IRE)** *Bryan Smart* a29 29
2 b c Kyllachy Good For Her (Rock Of Gibraltar (IRE))
6537[6] 7638[7] 7712[10] 8179[4]

**Kyllachykov (IRE)** *Robin Bastiman* a61 56
6 ch g Kyllachy Dance On (Caerleon (USA))
33[4] 252[2] 460[6] 912[6] 1249[4] 1891[5] 7540[9] 7823[11]

**Kyllachy Rise** *Richard Hannon* a94 96
4 b c Kyllachy Up And About (Barathea (IRE))
55[3]

**Kyllachy Star** *Richard Fahey* a76 75
8 b g Kyllachy Jaljuli (Jalmood (USA))
(52) 153[3] 255[3] 496[7] 646[11] 979[3] 1356[2] 1718[3] 1970[6] 2841[7] 3237[5] 5168[2] (5638) 6057[5] 6323[5]

**Kylladdie** *Steve Gollings* a78 78
7 ch g Kyllachy Chance For Romance (Entrepreneur)
1440[10] 1905[6] (2312)

**Kyllarney** *Charles Hills* 53
2 b f Kyllachy Hurricane Harriet (Bertolini (USA))
4980[8] 6039[7] 6551[10]

**Kyrenia Castle (GER)** *Richard Hannon* a70
2 b c Dashing Blade Key To Win (FR) (Halling (USA))
7867[12] 7917[2] 8092[6] 8254[2] (8262)

**Kyurem (IRE)** *T Clout* a79 100
4 gr f Verglas(IRE) Epistoliere (IRE) (Alzao (USA))
6218a[5] 7070a[7] 7768a[9]

**La Bacouetteuse (FR)** *Iain Jardine* a27 77
9 b g Miesque's Son(USA) Toryka (Vettori (IRE))
1929[5] 3829[6] (4522) 4769[3] (5146) 5564[6] 5812[3] 6493[4] 6832[3] 7124[9] 7509[9]

**Labaik (FR)** *J E Hammond* a77 71
3 b g Montmartre(FR) Avanguardia (GER) (Choisir (AUS))
3869a[2] 5027a[7]

**La Banderilla (FR)** *John Gosden* a94 98
4 b f Muhtathir La Bandera (Bahhare (USA))
7105[4] 7717[6] 8006a[4]

**La Berma (IRE)** *F Chappet* a80 103
2 b f Lawman(FR) Full Snow Moon (USA) (Vindication (USA))
7094a[2]

**Labise (IRE)** *Ralph Beckett* a72 77
3 b f Azamour(IRE) What A Picture (FR) (Peintre Celebre (USA))
486[3] 1233[3] 5504[2] (6265)

**La Brana** *Derek Shaw*
2 b g Exceed And Excel(AUS) Oatcake (Selkirk (USA))
3148[10]

**La Brava** *Lisa Williamson*
4 ch f Kheleyf(USA) La Belga (ARG) (Roy (USA))
1790[4] 2389[15]

**Labyrinthine (IRE)** *James Unett* a59
4 ch f Pivotal Madame Cerito (USA) (Diesis)
1143[4]

**Lacan (IRE)** *Marco Botti* a98 89
3 b c New Approach(IRE) Invincible Isle (IRE) (Invincible Spirit (IRE))
1395[2] 2432[2] (3153) 6713[12] 7119[7] 7955[2] (8116)

**La Canaada (IRE)** *H Rogers* a43 63
6 b m Antonius Pius(USA) Dame Rochelle (IRE) (Danehill Dancer (IRE))
128a[11] 4556a[12]

**Lacerta** *Micky Hammond* 58
3 b g Astronomer Royal(USA) Rubber (IRE) (Namid)
2365[7] 4022[8] 4713[4]

**Lacey** *Andrew Hollinshead* a62 52
5 b g Rail Link Shamana (USA) (Woodman (USA))
513[3] 1046[5] 1265[3] 3404[7] 5508[6] 6768[3] 7065[6] 7287[2] 7524[6] 7893[2] 8061[2] 8289[5]

**Lacing** *Richard Fahey* 91
2 b f Equiano(FR) Lacework (Pivotal)
1528[8] 3497[3] 4126[2] 4913[7] (6555) 6924[2] 7448[6]

**Lackaday** *William Jarvis* a79 76
2 gr c Kyllachy Day Creek (Daylami (IRE))
4760[8] 5248[2] 5500[3] 5874[9] 6690[2] (7216) 7439[6] 8113[5] (8308)

**Lac Leman (GER)** *R Dzubasz* 82
3 bb c Doyen(IRE) Learned Lady (JPN) (Fuji Kiseki (JPN))
3073a[7]

**Lacock** *Sean Curran* a71 68
3 b g Compton Place Puya (Kris)
3145[7] 3760[5] 4613[5] 5214[3] 6567[6] 6857[8] 7982[5]

**Lacocodanza** *George Moore* 41
5 b m Tamure(IRE) Miss Petronella (Petoski)
1960[12] 2354[9] 2952[4] 3482[11]

**Lac Sacre (FR)** *John Flint* a57 57
5 b g Bering Lady Glorieuse (FR) (Le Glorieux)
106[3] 400[5] (1916) 2252[3] 2942[3]

**La Cuesta (IRE)** *Jamie Osborne* a87 85
2 b f Showcasing Dowager (Groom Dancer (USA))
2944[2] 3353[7] ◆ 6168[4] (6408) 6703[3] 6989[4]

**Lacy (GER)** *Waldemar Hickst* 107
3 b f Authorized(IRE) La Vinchina (GER) (Oasis Dream)
4064a[2] 4955a[4] (6162a) 7480a[2]

**Ladalco (FR)** *Waldemar Hickst* 82
4 b g Lando(GER) Little Memories (IRE) (Montjeu (IRE))
935a[3]

**La Danza** *Shaun Harris* a52 43
4 b f Country Reel(USA) Freedom Song (Singspiel (IRE))
1297[7] 1718[5] 2454[5] 3220[5] 3971[13] 5079[8] 5510[3] 6543[10] 7424[11] 7908[5] 8085[3] 8219[6]

**L'Addition** *William Jarvis* a71 65
2 b f Exceed And Excel(AUS) La Adelita (IRE) (Anabaa (USA))
(4320) 4913[6] 5974[5] 7201[8]

**Laderia (FR)** *Mlle T Puitg* 84
3 b f Linda's Lad Numeria (FR) (Numerous (USA))
1139a[4]

**Ladies Are Forever** *Geoffrey Oldroyd* a105 111
6 b m Monsieur Bond(IRE) Forever Bond (Danetime (IRE))
7136 1066[5] ◆ (1572) 2256[10] ◆ (4171) 4852[10] 5467[4] 6167[2] 6918[6]

**Ladies Dancing** *Chris Down* a57 32
8 b g Royal Applause Queen Of Dance (IRE) (Sadler's Wells (USA))
590[2] 821[4]

**La Donacella** *Daniel Kubler* 45
2 b f Sir Percy Tessie (Tiger Hill (IRE))
4604[8]

**Ladweb** *John Gallagher* a58 93
4 ch g Bertolini(USA) Adweb (Muhtarram (USA))
987[6] 1244[6] (1878) (2434) (2691) 3386[4] 4892[16] 5925[2] 6512[2] 7132[2]

**Lady Amakhala** *George Moore* a19 41
6 b m Val Royal(FR) Isla Negra (IRE) (Last Tycoon)
1366[5] 2097[8]

**Lady Ampthill (IRE)** *John Spearing* 14
2 b f Strategic Prince Pixie's Blue (IRE) (Hawk Wing (USA))
6393[5]

**Lady Antonios (IRE)** *Chris Dwyer* a31
2 b f Bushranger(IRE) Rahika Rose (Unfuwain (USA))
7808[8] 8007[10] 8140[8]

**Lady Armada** *Jo Hughes* a21
2 b f Arabian Gleam Gramada (IRE) (Cape Cross (IRE))
1314[10] 1741[8]

**Lady Artiste (IRE)** *Alan Swinbank* 78
4 ch f Excellent Art Elauyun (IRE) (Muhtarram (USA))
1348[10] 1716[6] (2171) (2604) 3000[8] 5385[9] 6009[4]

**Lady Atlas** *David Brown* a55 57
2 ch f Dutch Art Paqueretta (FR) (Dr Fong (USA))
4829[9] 5464[5] 5725[7] 6237[4] 6643[2] 7529[6]

**Lady Ballantrae (IRE)** *Simon Dow* a31 16
2 b f Henrythenavigator(USA) Marseille Express (USA) (Caerleon (USA))
2859[9] 4117[6] 4610[7] 7816[9]

**Lady Bayside** *Malcolm Saunders* a73 79
6 ch m Ishiguru(USA) Seldemosa (Selkirk (USA))
2669[11] 3176[2] 3733[7] 3850[4] 4153[4] 5340[4] 5503[5] 6070[5] 6251[2] (7303)

**Lady Bee (IRE)** *George Baker*
2 b f Lawman(FR) Rainbow Lyrics (IRE) (Rainbow Quest (USA))
7412[11]

**Lady Bingo (IRE)** *Sir Mark Prescott Bt* a74 67
3 b f Galileo(IRE) Sharp Lisa (USA) (Dixieland Band (USA))
4513[3] 5007[6] 5606[7] 6338[3] 6899[2] 7177[7] 7817[11]

**Lady Bling** *Bill Turner* 40
2 b f Showcasing Bling Bling (IRE) (Indian Ridge)
1276[10] 1571[14]

**Lady Brigid (IRE)** *Olly Stevens* a87 78
3 b f Holy Roman Emperor(IRE) Brigids Cross (IRE) (Sadler's Wells (USA))
2061[8] 2560[2] 2967[5] (6988) 7159[7] (8071) 8252[8]

**Lady Bubbles** *Michael Easterby* a40 51
3 b f Distant Peak(IRE) Mount Hillaby (IRE) (Mujadil (USA))
4871[4] 5084[4] 5717[9] 5917[3] 6564[11] 7187[7]

**Lady Calantha** *Alan Berry* a26 49
4 b f Byron Brooklyn's Sky (Septieme Ciel (USA))
5857[5] 7250[10] 7825[12]

**Lady Charlie** *Jo Hughes* a57 54
2 b f Myboycharlie(IRE) Fancy Rose (USA) (Joyeux Danseur (USA))
2944[11] 3606[2] 4338[8] 6040[7] 7014[5] (7991)

**Lady Cooper** *Willie Musson* a58
4 b f Ishiguru(USA) Mistress Cooper (Kyllachy)
4086[3] 4735[7] 7376[10]

**Lady Cordie** *Jim Goldie* 26
2 b f Monsieur Bond(IRE) Lady Benjamin (Spinning World (USA))
5493[11] 7246[9]

**Lady Correspondent (USA)** *John Gosden* 78
2 b f War Front(USA) Fanzine (USA) (Cozzene (USA))
(6754)

**Lady Crossmar (IRE)** *Richard Hannon* a83 82
3 b f Duke Of Marmalade(IRE) Rekindled Cross (IRE) (Cape Cross (IRE))
3198[8] 3566[3] 4155[2] 4428[4] 4655[2] (4811) 5308[5] 5873[2] 6240[4] (6617) (6766)

**Lady Dam's (FR)** *C Boutin* a70 73
3 ch f Turtle Bowl(IRE) Chalouchi (USA) (Mt. Livermore (USA))
720a[8] 4464a[13]

**Lady Dancer (IRE)** *George Moore* 30
3 b f Captain Rio Anessia (Fantastic Light (USA))
1373[5] 1647[13] 2553[4] 2726[5] 3366[10] 4530[8]

**Lady Day** *Richard Hannon*
3 b f Selkirk(USA) Lady Links (Bahamian Bounty)
1424[10]

**Lady Desire (IRE)** *Keith Dalgleish* 89
2 b f Lookin At Lucky(USA) Princess Desire (IRE) (Danehill (USA))
2601[4] (3358) (5129) 6530[12] 6933[20] 7443[9]

**Ladydolly** *Roy Brotherton* a26 18
6 b m Kyllachy Lady Pekan (Sri Pekan (USA))
6851[8] 7520[10] 8133[13]

**Lady D's Rock (IRE)** *Clive Cox* a48 34
2 gr f Aussie Rules(USA) Za Za (Barathea (IRE))
4346[10] 7194[11] 7658[6]

**Lady Dutch** *B Grizzetti* 99
3 b f Dutch Art Monjouet (IRE) (Montjeu (IRE))
1780a[2] 2590a[9] 6807a[3] 7146a[3] 7480a[8]

**Lady Eli (USA)** *Chad C Brown* 113
2 bb f Divine Park(USA) Sacre Coeur (USA) (Saint Ballado (CAN))
(7592a)

**Lady Estella (IRE)** *Marco Botti* a67 65
2 b f Equiano(FR) Lady Scarlett (Woodman (USA))
6701[3] 7194[3]

**Lady Frances** *Mark Johnston* a93 93
3 b f Exceed And Excel(AUS) Lady Catherine (Bering)
(501) 778[6] 1555[7] 1937[3] 2111[10] 2556[7] 3342[8] 3694[5] 4053[3] (4317) 4669[7] (5032) 5438[9] 5612[10] 6112[2] 6281[5] 6598[3] 6755[4] 7451[9] 7923[12]

**Lady Gemini** *Jo Hughes* 79
2 b f Myboycharlie(IRE) Gemini Gold (IRE) (King's Best (USA))
3353[18] 3563[3] 4216[2] 4913[5] 5608[9] 6299[4]

**Lady Gibraltar** *Timothy Jarvis* a60 97
5 b m Rock Of Gibraltar(IRE) Lady Adnil (IRE) (Stravinsky (USA))
2283[6] 2989[13] 3927[13] 5211[5] 5754 5945[5]

**Lady Guinevere** *Stuart Williams* a66 73
4 b f Pivotal Birdie (Alhaarth (IRE))
1846[2] 2498[4] 3176[6] 5848[3] 7042[2] 7157[8]

**Lady Hare (IRE)** *David Simcock* a60
2 b f Approve(IRE) Peaceful Kingdom (USA) (King Of Kings (IRE))
7193[6] 7549[9]

**Ladyhawk (IRE)** *Polly Gundry* a39
10 b m Turtle Island(IRE) Love You Madly (IRE) (Bob Back (USA))
8249[6]

**Lady Heidi** *Philip Kirby* 97
3 b f High Chaparral(IRE) Water Feature (Dansili)
2255[9]

**Lady Horatia** *William Muir* a86 88
3 gr f Mount Nelson Lady Xara (IRE) (Xaar)
1534[8] (2049) ◆ 2611[3] 3305[2] 3788[2] 4445[3] 4971[3] 5437[5] 6112[3] 6336[5] 7365[5]

**Lady Ibrox** *Alan Brown* a81 91
4 b f Ishiguru(USA) Last Impression (Imp Society (USA))
1145[6] 1565[8] 1967[7] 2398[3] 4752[5] 5199[11]

**Lady In Blue (IRE)** *David O'Meara* a69 69
3 ch f Iffraaj Compton Girl (Compton Place)
573[7] 936[3] 1543[10] 1814[5]

**Lady In White (IRE)** *Roger Varian* 48
2 gr f Zebedee Alexander Phantom (IRE) (Soviet Star (USA))
3193[6] 3583[5]

**Lady Jade** *Nigel Tinkler* 46
2 ch f Compton Place Chilly Cracker (Largesse)
3947[11] 4286[12] 5194[2] 5525[9] 5767[7] 6428[10]

**Lady Jamesway (IRE)** *Ann Duffield* 25
3 b f Acclamation Baltic Dip (IRE) (Benny The Dip (USA))
1888[6] 3908[9] 5761[9]

**Lady John John (FR)** *S Wattel* a81 74
3 b f Shirocco(GER) Lady Glitters (FR) (Homme De Loi (IRE))
5404a[5]

**Lady Kashaan (IRE)** *Alan Swinbank* a40 96
5 b m Manduro(GER) Lady's Secret (IRE) (Alzao (USA))
1562[8] 5144[3] 5579[3] 6133[7] 6501[2] 7107[20] 7409[8]

**Lady Kathian (IRE)** *Joseph Tuite* a62
3 gr f Verglas(IRE) Nurama (Daylami (IRE))
275[5] 588[5] 1786[9]

**Lady Knight (IRE)** *J S Moore* a66 20
3 b f Champs Elysees Knight's Place (IRE) (Hamas (IRE))
166[4] 190[6] 1847[13] 2978a[16] 3754[9] 4026[5]

**Lady Kyllar** *George Margarson* a65 57
2 b f Kyllachy Miss Otis (Danetime (IRE))
2220[4] 4269[8] 7881[2]

**Lady Lara (IRE)** *Timothy Jarvis* 108
3 b f Excellent Art Shanty (Selkirk (USA))
1435[4] 1976[13] 2316[3] 3357[5] 5176[2] ◆ 5690[3] (6522)

**Lady Liberty (IRE)** *Andreas Lowe* 99
4 b f Shirocco(GER) Love And Laughter (IRE) (Theatrical (IRE))
6162a[5] 7070a[5] 7482a[10]

**Lady Liz** *George Moore* 50
3 b f Byron Sister Rose (FR) (One Cool Cat (USA))
1344[6] 1902[6] 2355[14] 2729[3] 4063[7] 5195[6] 5793[9] 7501[4] 7639[8]

**Lady Lovelace** *Ed Vaughan* 25
3 b f Byron Grain Of Salt (Montjeu (IRE))
4089[5]

**Lady Lunchalot (USA)** *Laura Mongan* a80 78
4 b f More Than Ready(USA) Betty Johanne (USA) (Johannesburg (USA))
79[11] 146[5] 345[2] 450[2] 849[6] 1022[5] (1108) 1493[4] 1553[5] 1899[7] 2862[6] 3079[3] 7366[8]

**Lady Lydia (IRE)** *Conrad Allen* 78
3 b f Kheleyf(USA) Piece Unique (Barathea (IRE))
2122[4] 2745[4] 3198[5] 3433[6]

**Lady Maesmor** *Martyn Meade* a64 68
2 b f Kyllachy Pulsate (Inchinor)
4260[5] 4589[3] (5056) 6678[8]

**Lady Mai (IRE)** *Richard Fahey* 58
3 b f Camacho Evelyn One (Alhaarth (IRE))
1373[3] 1611[8] 2388[4] 2802[7] 3399[9] 3896[4] 4974[3] 5169[3]

**Lady Marita (IRE)** *David Evans* a59 59
2 b f Dandy Man(IRE) Straight Miss (IRE) (In The Wings)
2557[5] 3353[19] 3757[3] 4576[4] 6422[4] 7497[10] 7848[6]

**Lady Marl** *Gary Moore* a63 72
3 b f Duke Of Marmalade(IRE) Empress Anna (IRE) (Imperial Ballet (IRE))
(2224) 6484[8] 7160[4] 7514[8]

**Lady Marmelo (IRE)** *Philip Kirby* a62 67
4 b f Duke Of Marmalade(IRE) Mooretown Lady (IRE) (Montjeu (IRE))
7175[3] 7643[8]

**Lady Mascot (IRE)** *Richard Hannon* 65
2 ch f Zebedee Tradmagic (IRE) (Traditionally (USA))
3076[9] 3557[8] 4444[5] 5626[5]

**Lady Mega (IRE)** *Edward Lynam* a72 91
3 br f Kodiac Naias (IRE) (Namid)
3686a[2] 4480a[4] 6369a[12]

**Lady Montenegro** *Ann Duffield* a40 49
3 b f Milk It Mick Floral Spark (Forzando)
1373[4] 1648[7] 1855[5] 3366[6] 3548[9] 4314[10] 4627[9]

**Lady Moscou (IRE)** *James Tate* a80 85
2 b f Sir Percy Place De Moscou (IRE) (Rock Of Gibraltar (IRE))
3063[2] 3497[2] (4129) 4585[5] *6071[2]* 6436[2] 6691[3]

**Lady Of Camelot (IRE)** *John Gosden* a69
2 b f Montjeu(IRE) Marquesa (USA) (Kingmambo (USA))
*8036[5]*

**Lady Of Dubai** *Luca Cumani* 94
2 b f Dubawi(IRE) Lady Of Everest (IRE) (Montjeu (IRE))
4126[7] 5644[3] ◆ (6554) 7596[2]

**Lady Of Illusion** *Mark Usher* 37
2 b f Compton Place Doric Lady (Kyllachy)
2993[6] 3975[7] 5209[5]

**Lady Of The Vine (USA)** *Andrew Balding* 52
4 b f Master Command(USA) Silverbulletlover (USA) (Gulch (USA))
*31[6]*

**Lady Of Yue** *Eugene Stanford* a66 76
4 b f Manduro(GER) Desert Royalty (IRE) (Alhaarth (IRE))
2270[17] (2628) 3218[7] 4119[4] 4622[8] 5756[5] 6787[4] *7182[5] 7866[5] 8202[7]*

**Lady Penko (FR)** *C Delcher-Sanchez* 101
3 b f Archipenko(USA) Hespera (Danehill (USA))
2586a[3]

**Lady Percy (IRE)** *Mark Usher* a49 60
5 b m Sir Percy Genuinely (IRE) (Entrepreneur)
(2836) 3778[3] 5748[4] *6031[4] 6768[10]* 7518[10]

**Lady Petrus** *K Kukk* a19 20
9 b m Oasis Dream Odalisque (IRE) (Machiavellian (USA))
1622a[8] 2594a[5] 4718a[2] (5229a) 5969a[4] 6188a[5]

**Lady Phill** *Michael Attwater* a66 71
4 ch f Avonbridge Lady Filly (Atraf)
*1261[10]* 1789[9] 3280[4] 3734[8] 4206[3] *4545[6]* 4811[5] 5355[4] (5861) 6658[2] 7215[8] 7342[7] *7776[9] 7989[9]*

**Lady Pimpernel** *Henry Candy* 103
4 ch f Sir Percy Angeleno (IRE) (Belong To Me (USA))
3196[3] 4145[5] (4915) (5312)

**Lady Pinnacle** *Andrew Balding* a68
2 b f Zamindar(USA) Lady Donatella (Last Tycoon)
*6605[4] 7193[5] 7752[2] 8201[4]*

**Lady Poppy** *George Moore* a44 69
4 b f Kyllachy Poppets Sweetlove (Foxhound (USA))
*69[5] 259[9]* 1604[3] 1643[10] (3338) 3920[9] 4531[6] 5130[6] 5819[12] 6671[13]

**Lady Rain** *Ronald Harris* a31 39
5 b m Resplendent Glory(IRE) Devils Desire (Superior Premium)
*483[7] 610[5]* 2667[7] 3520[6] 4101[6] 4341[10]

**Lady Ranger (IRE)** *Adrian Paul Keatley* a52 56
3 b f Bushranger(IRE) Annus Iucundus (IRE) (Desert King (IRE))
(2668) 3100[U] 4556a[11] 5236[2]

**Lady Red Oak** *Tom Dascombe* 69
3 ch f Medicean Nuit Sans Fin (FR) (Lead On Time (USA))
1846[6] 2740[9] 3121[3]

**Lady's Day (GER)** *Werner Glanz* 93
5 b m Librettist(USA) Lady Annina (FR) (Dashing Blade)
7146a[6]

**Lady Simpatico** *Frau S Weis*
2 b f Monsieur Bond(IRE) Willow Burn Wisp (Fruits Of Love (USA))
4524a[9]

**Lady Sorento** *Tim Pitt* a36
3 b f Tobougg(IRE) Maidenhair (IRE) (Darshaan)
*5010[8]* 6092[14] 6613[10]

**Lady Spangles (IRE)** *J S Moore* a49
2 b f Starspangledbanner(AUS) Lady Of Garmoran (USA) (Mr Greeley (USA))
*6105[P] 7660[12] 7944[7] 8241[4]*

**Lady Sparkler (IRE)** *Roger Varian* a74 77
3 b f Tamayuz Capote West (USA) (Capote (USA))
3469[3] 3801[3] (4654) 6262[8] *7397[6]*

**Lady Sybil (FR)** *Y Barberot* 102
2 b f Siyouni(FR) Arsila (IRE) (Tirol)
5617a[2] 7393a[4]

**Lady Sylvia** *Joseph Tuite* a82 77
5 ch m Haafhd Abide (FR) (Pivotal)
*4513 690[6] 853[5] 1230[5]* 2963[6] 3427[2] 3678[7] 4798[2] 5685[5] (6070) *(6242) 7397[2] 7757[6]*

**Lady Tiana** *Lucy Wadham* a70 107
3 b f Sir Percy Cartoon (Danehill Dancer (IRE))
(1846) (2498) 3195[2] 4182[4] 4782[8] 6746[2] (7211) *(7717)*

**Lady Tyne** *Roger Charlton* a57 93
3 ch f Halling(USA) Susun Kelapa (USA) (St Jovite (USA))
2072[7] 4945[8] 6061[14] *6665[6]* 7416[9]

**Lady Ultra (IRE)** *Ms Sheila Lavery* a82 86
3 ch f Dandy Man(IRE) Non Ultra (USA) (Peintre Celebre (USA))
7140a[8]

**Lady Vellyn** *Derek Haydn Jones* 14
2 gr f Hellvelyn Alvarinho Lady (Royal Applause)
4676[10] 7666[15] *8227[11]*

**Lady Who** *William Muir* a68
4 b f Sir Percy Herminoe (Rainbow Quest (USA))
*445[6]*

**Lady Wood (FR)** *N Clement* a91 73
4 b f Vespone(IRE) Princesse Bilbao (FR) (Highest Honor (FR))
*8006a[9] 8300a[9]*

**Lady Yeats** *George Moore* 81
3 b f Yeats(IRE) Oblique (IRE) (Giant's Causeway (USA))
(1348) 2077[8] 3110[5] 5449[4] (7177)

**Lady Zodiac (IRE)** *Andrew Balding* a52 57
2 b f Kodiac Treacle Noir (IRE) (Raise A Grand (IRE))
2436[7] *2680[4]* 3215[6] 3937[4] 4410[2] 5180[2] 5517[2] *5828[6] 6016[8]*

**La Estatua** *James Tate* a32 69
2 b f Lope De Vega(IRE) Statua (IRE) (Statoblest)
3847[2] 4409[5] 4993[2] 6364[3] *6769[8]*

**La Estrella (USA)** *Don Cantillon* a90 66
11 b g Theatrical(IRE) Princess Ellen (Tirol)
*(63) (186) (8163)*

**Laeyos (GER)** *P Harley* a95 91
5 b g Soldier Hollow Laeya Star (GER) (Royal Dragon (USA))
7618a[3]

**La Favorita (IRE)** *Phil McEntee* a55 43
2 b f Acclamation Favoritely (USA) (Favorite Trick (USA))
4126[12] 5667[9] 6700[9] *7740[5] 7816[4] 7880[2]*

**La Femme Fatale (GER)** *M Munch* 91
3 gr f Dai Jin Linamox (FR) (Linamix (FR))
7769a[9]

**Laffan (IRE)** *Tim Easterby* a96 102
5 b g Dark Angel(IRE) Lady Corduff (IRE) (Titus Livius (FR))
2113[4] 2548[2] 2758[5] 3189[6] 3964[5] (4661) 5609[14] 5919[9] 6534[9]

**Laftah (IRE)** *Roger Varian* 87
3 b f Invincible Spirit(IRE) Liscune (IRE) (King's Best (USA))
2511[4] 3097[2] (3586) (4367) 4668[5] 6129[11]

**Lager Time (IRE)** *David Evans* a74 74
4 b g Tagula(IRE) Polish Belle (Polish Precedent (USA))
*(2459)* 3686a[9] 4556a[10]

**La Giovanella (FR)** *Alex Fracas* a60 68
2 b f Le Havre(IRE) Gaelic Music (FR) (Poliglote)
5590a[6] 5941a[9]

**La Gohanniere (FR)** *F Rohaut* a95 95
3 b f Le Havre(IRE) Landskia (FR) (Lando (GER))
7720a[5]

**La Goutte D'Or (FR)** *M Seror* a51 63
3 ch f Soave(GER) Vocatine (IRE) (Royal Applause)
3809a[3]

**Laguna Belle** *Pat Phelan* a42 45
4 ro f Dutch Art Slite (Mind Games)
*189[8] 486[10] 1119[6]* 2069[4] 3327[9] *3526[7]*

**Laguna Boy (FR)** *Y Barberot* a81 83
3 ch c Adlerflug(GER) Loving Away (FR) (Gold Away (IRE))
*600a[5]* 4252a[3]

**Laguna Drive (IRE)** *Stefano Botti* 94
3 b c Aussie Rules(USA) Love Parade (IRE) (Zieten (USA))
1779a[11]

**Lahaag** *John Gosden* 106
5 b g Marju(IRE) Chater (Alhaarth (IRE))
2253[11] 2779[13] 3449[9] 5174[6] 5651[7] 6287[11]

**La Havrese (FR)** *Ann Duffield* 71
3 ch f Le Havre(IRE) La Buena (IRE) (Big Shuffle (USA))
3664[6] 4512[3] (4998) 5376[3] 5809[4]

**Lahayeb** *Richard Hannon* a64
2 b f High Chaparral(IRE) Tea Break (Daylami (IRE))
*7943[4] 8173[9]*

**Lahent** *Charlie Fellowes* a46
2 b c Makfi Misty Waters (IRE) (Caerleon (USA))
*7199[7]*

**Lahinch Classics (IRE)** *David Wachman* a81 104
3 b f Galileo(IRE) Lahinch (IRE) (Danehill Dancer (IRE))
2299[2] 4478a[2]

**La Hoguette (FR)** *J-C Rouget* a97 111
3 b f Le Havre(IRE) Isanous (FR) (Zamindar (USA))
2817a[2] 4278a[3] 6955a[8]

**La Hoofon** *Michael Dods* 43
2 b f Mastercraftsman(IRE) Polish Lake (Polish Precedent (USA))
6641[9] 7174[10]

**Lahqa (IRE)** *F Head* a87 86
3 b f Tamayuz Mahaatheer (IRE) (Daylami (IRE))
(5589a)

**Laia Chope (FR)** *X Nakkachdji* 93
3 b f Soave(GER) Chopinette (FR) (Sin Kiang (FR))
6446a[4]

**Laidback Romeo (IRE)** *Clive Cox* 81
2 b c Kodiac Belmora (USA) (Scrimshaw (USA))
3140[3] 3613[7] 4884[5] 5929[2] (6759)

**Laika** *Brian Ellison* a66
5 b m Rail Link Space Quest (Rainbow Quest (USA))
*8003[3] 8114[3] 8207[2]*

**Lake Alfred (USA)** *Lady Cecil* a75 14
3 gr g Mizzen Mast(USA) Brief Look (Sadler's Wells (USA))
*951[3]* 5347[6]

**Lake George (IRE)** *James M Barrett* a67 76
6 b g Alkaadhem Ballyronan Girl (IRE) (Elbio)
4950a[7] 5958a[9]

**Lake Hawk (IRE)** *A Al Raihe* a58
5 b h Hawk Wing(USA) Princess Electra (IRE) (Lake Coniston (IRE))
*238a[4]*

**La Khaleesi (FR)** *Y Gourraud* 101
2 ch f Alexandros Ciel Bleu (Septieme Ciel (USA))
5707a[4] 7393a[5]

**Lakmee (FR)** *A Clement* 68
3 bb f Le Havre(IRE) Chenoa (Red Ransom (USA))
5226a[5]

**Lakritze (FR)** *E Libaud* a77 86
4 b f Orpen(USA) Laita (IRE) (Kenmare (FR))
*796a[14]*

**Laleh (GER)** *Mario Hofer* 79
2 ch f Toylsome Lomitas Dream (Lomitas)
4524a[7] 6053a[6] 6591a[3]

**Lamar (IRE)** *James Tate* a98 98
3 b f Cape Cross(IRE) Deveron (USA) (Cozzene (USA))
1515[4] 1976[10] 2299[5] 3357[7] *7553[2] 8300a[4]*

**Lambert Pen (USA)** *Peter Hiatt* a56 62
4 ch g Johannesburg(USA) Whiletheiron'shot (USA) (Smart Strike (CAN))
*1268[5] 1428[5]* 1874[7] *2212[4]* 2614[5] *3115[10]*

**La Mer (FR)** *Mme G Rarick* a56
3 ch f Green Tune(USA) Mermaids Quay (IRE) (Key Of Luck (USA))
*482a[7]*

**La Messalina (FR)** *Alex Fracas* a80 79
4 b f Apsis Mariyati (FR) (Marignan (USA))
6569a[2]

**La Mezcla (FR)** *Rod Collet* a77 75
2 gr f Aussie Rules(USA) Histoire (IRE) (Whipper (USA))
*(3872a)* 5119a[2] *(5844a)* 6916a[5]

**L'Ami Fernand (FR)** *D De Waele* a66 71
3 ch g Layman(USA) Baby Chope (FR) (Indian Rocket)
*720a[9]*

**L'Ami Louis (IRE)** *Ian Semple* 88
6 b g Elusive City(USA) Princess Electra (IRE) (Lake Coniston (IRE))
1565[9] 2456[7] 3256[9] 3458[7] 4004[4] 4256[10] 4724[6] 5766[11]

**Lamorak (FR)** *Hugo Palmer* a80 79
3 b g King's Best(USA) Indian Jewel (GER) (Local Suitor (USA))
2221[2] 2655[2] *3401[2]*

**L'Amour De Ma Vie (USA)** *Mme Pia Brandt* a106 116
5 rg m Dansili Cuaba (USA) (Smoke Glacken (USA))
395a[2] (682a) 902a[11] 3355[2] 4954a[4] 6808a[9] *7593a[10]*

**Lamps Of Heaven (IRE)** *Olly Stevens* a65
2 b f Invincible Spirit(IRE) Star Studded (Cadeaux Genereux)
*7881[3] 8140[2]*

**Lamsa (IRE)** *Ed Dunlop* 49
2 b f Invincible Spirit(IRE) Golden Flyer (FR) (Machiavellian (USA))
6041[8]

**Lamubaaly (IRE)** *Alexandra Dunn* a65 69
3 b g Le Havre(IRE) Seracina (Nashwan (USA))
6877[6] *7229[4] 7524[9]*

**Lamyaa** *Charles Hills* a45
2 ch f Arcano(IRE) Divine Grace (IRE) (Definite Article)
*7809[7]*

**Lanai (IRE)** *David Barron* 69
2 b f Camacho Stately Princess (Robellino (USA))
2128[3] 2513[2]

**La Napoule** *Richard Hannon* a68 45
3 ch f Piccolo Peggy Spencer (Formidable (USA))
*142[2] 284[3] 486[5]* 1914[8] 2274[11] 3087[7] 3754[5] 4789[5] *5820[2] (6765)*

**Lanark (IRE)** *Mark Johnston* 94
3 b c Cape Cross(IRE) Amenixa (FR) (Linamix (FR))
1530[12] 2330[5]

**Lancelot Du Lac (ITY)** *Dean Ivory* a112 108
4 b g Shamardal(USA) Dodie Mae (USA) (Capote (USA))
*1172[5] 1557[8]* 2254[14] 2848[8] 3452[12] ◆ 4179[9] 7441[5] ◆ 7716[2] *7923[3] (8101)*

**Landau (IRE)** *Gordon Elliott* a79 77
4 gr g Aussie Rules(USA) Before The Storm (Sadler's Wells (USA))
4951a[4] *6082a[8]*

**Landesherr (GER)** *Thomas Cuthbert* a26 60
7 b g Black Sam Bellamy(IRE) Lutte Marie (GER) (Frontal (FR))
4293[12] 4964[15] 6627[9]

**Landing Night (IRE)** *Ann Duffield* 70
2 b c Kodiac Night Delight (IRE) (Night Shift (USA))
6319[2] 6594[4]

**Lando Blue (IRE)** *C Lerner* a85 85
4 b c Lando(GER) Freezing (USA) (Bering)
*5961a[9]*

**Landolino (FR)** *Mrs C Gilbert* a60 62
9 b g Trempolino(USA) Champagne Sorbet (FR) (Kaldounevees (FR))
3048a[2]

**Landwade Lad** *James Fanshawe* a78 79
2 b g Dansili Sell Out (Act One)
3720[4] 4550[6] 5886[2] 6684[3] *7544[2]*

**Langavat (IRE)** *Nigel Tinkler* 97
3 b c Bushranger(IRE) Bishop's Lake (Lake Coniston (IRE))
2304[9] 3245[12] 3960[9] 4889[4] 5378[2] 6149[6] 6468[7]

**Langham Lily (USA)** *Sarah Humphrey* a69 49
5 bb m Badge Of Silver(USA) Silver Frau (USA) (Silver Charm (USA))
*293[8] 405[9]*

**Langley Vale** *Roger Teal* a82 84
5 b g Piccolo Running Glimpse (IRE) (Runnett)
*658[11] 1144[3] 1921[9]* 3313[4] 3879[6] *(4581)* 5124[4] 6006[2] 6398[4] 6880[10]

**Langstaff (CAN)** *Scott H Fairlie* a96 97
4 bb g Saffir(USA) Chick (USA) (Sky Classic (CAN))
7325a[9]

**Lankan Rupee (AUS)** *Mick Price* 125
5 b g Redoute's Choice(AUS) Estelle Collection (NZ) (Stravinsky (USA))
(1468a) 7724a[3]

**La Paiva (FR)** *Scott Dixon* a46 33
3 b f Milk It Mick Cora Pearl (IRE) (Montjeu (IRE))
*174[5] 753[10] 919[4]* 1611[7] 2387[9] *7766[8] 7924[9] 7986[5] 8162[9]*

**La Petite Maison (FR)** *D Prod'Homme* 96
3 b f Enrique Tora Tune (FR) (Green Tune (USA))
7857a[13]

**Lapis Blue (IRE)** *David Evans* a77 63
4 b f Invincible Spirit(IRE) Triple Try (IRE) (Sadler's Wells (USA))
*(69) 196[5]*

**Lap Of Luxury (IRE)** *John Gosden* 80
2 ch f Galileo(IRE) Halland Park Lass (IRE) (Spectrum (IRE))
(6700) ◆

**La Pyle (FR)** *Mme Pia Brandt* 84
3 b f Le Havre(IRE) Lidana (IRE) (King's Best (USA))
(7270a)

**Larabesque (IRE)** *A Fabre* 63
3 br f Monsun(GER) La Peregrina (FR) (Shirley Heights)
1139a[13]

**Lara Lipton (IRE)** *Jane Chapple-Hyam* a45
3 b f Excellent Art Dyness (USA) (Dynaformer (USA))
1517[13] *2917[10]* 3385[12] *5283[12] 5556[8]*

**Larch (IRE)** *Richard Hannon* a23 44
2 b f Acclamation Shady Nook (IRE) (Key Of Luck (USA))
*2460[9]* 3223[8]

**La Regence (FR)** *S Wattel* a82 78
5 gr m Slickly(FR) Reine Breeze (FR) (Phantom Breeze)
*5964a[9]*

**Larghetto (USA)** *Ian Williams* a69 55
6 b m Giant's Causeway(USA) Marquetessa (USA) (Marquetry (USA))
*445[5] 6160[10] 6716[5] 7077[3] 7368[6] 7423[3] 7698[2] (7735) 7825[4]*

**Larra Chope (FR)** *C Boutin* a59 67
3 b f Deportivo Deauville Royale (Royal Applause)
3809a[6]

**L'Artiste (IRE)** *John Quinn* 70
3 gr f Mastercraftsman(IRE) Sepia (Dansili)
2740[7] 3300[7] 3946[11] 5336[7]

**Lascaux** *Luke Dace* a64 75
5 ch m Pivotal Tora Bora (Grand Lodge (USA))
*209[3]*

**Laseen (IRE)** *N Clement* a87 81
3 b f Dylan Thomas(IRE) La Seine (USA) (Rahy (USA))
7720a[8]

**Laser Blazer** *Alan King* a75 80
6 b g Zafeen(FR) Sashay (Bishop Of Cashel)
2774[8] 5073[2] ◆ 5878[12]

**Lashkaal** *John Gosden* 76
2 b f Teofilo(IRE) Mudaaraah (Cape Cross (IRE))
2744[6] 4346[4] 7108[4] 7378[2]

**Lastchancelucas** *Declan Carroll* a58 80
4 b g Ishiguru(USA) Light Of Aragon (Aragon)
1193[17] 1305[4] 1506[9] (1961) 2350[5] 2732[7] 3216[8] 3948[8] 4174[10] 4925[4] 6235[16] 6695[5] *7071[10]*

**Last Chance Ranch** *Derek Shaw* a41
4 b g Manduro(GER) Rakata (USA) (Quiet American (USA))
*246[7] 459[11]*

**Last Destination (IRE)** *Nigel Tinkler* a37 58
6 b g Dubai Destination(USA) Maimana (IRE) (Desert King (IRE))
2546[10] 3096[12] 3547[2] 3949[7] 5295[6] 5854[8] 6601[6]

**Last Echo (IRE)** *Ralph Beckett* a57 79
3 b f Whipper(USA) Priory Rock (IRE) (Rock Of Gibraltar (IRE))
*422[4]* ◆ *660[5] 1220[7] 3711[10]* 4678[4] (5343) (5786) 7133[4] 7409[9]

**Last Honours (FR)** *C Boutin* a47 56
2 b c Honours List(IRE) Une Autre Aventure (FR) (Diableneyev (USA))
*3871a[7]*

**Last Impact (JPN)** *Hiroyoshi Matsuda* 119
4 bb c Deep Impact(JPN) Superior Pearl (JPN) (Timber Country (USA))
2002a[9]

**Lastkingofscotland (IRE)** *Conor Dore* a85 81
8 b g Danehill Dancer(IRE) Arcade (Rousillon (USA))
*20[6] 65[4] 126[5] 248[6]*

**Last Minute Lisa (IRE)** *Sylvester Kirk* a89 76
4 b f Strategic Prince Bradwell (IRE) (Taufan (USA))
*295[7] 718[4] 846[12] 993[9] 1297[6]* 1668[3] 2164[3] 2689[3] (2864) 3075[4] (3824) (4116) 4351[3] 4808[3] 5435[3] (6007) 6264[4] 6500[2] 7422[10] 7554[7] 7702[6] 8073[8]

**Last Supper** *James Bethell* a50 52
5 b m Echo Of Light Scotland The Brave (Zilzal (USA))
5269[7] 6122[14]

**Las Verglas Star (IRE)** *Richard Fahey* a78 92
6 gr g Verglas(IRE) Magnificent Bell (IRE) (Octagonal (NZ))
1360[8] 1715[6] 2137[7] (2762) 3217[5] 4175[6] 4827[9] 5238[2] 5792[4]

**Latch Onto Blue** *Charles Hills* a62 74
2 b c Kyllachy Something Blue (Petong)
1936[4] 3311[2] (4011) 4430[3] *5043[6]* (Dead)

**Late Charge (AUS)** *Wendy Kelly* 104
4 br c Hard Spun(USA) Fantagonal (AUS) (Octagonal (NZ))
7128a[11]

**Late Night Mark (IRE)** *Charles Hills* a70 81
3 b c Marju(IRE) Khatela (IRE) (Shernazar)
*341[5]* ◆ *607[2]* 1353[2] 2690[4]

**Latenightrequest** *Richard Fahey* 100
3 b f Major Cadeaux Love Quest (Pursuit Of Love)
1195[3] (1883) 2255[6] 3143[9] (6061) 6737[12] 7106[23] (7440) 7718[11]

**Lateral Thinking (IRE)** *James Evans* a31 72
4 b g Excellent Art Sumingasefa (Danehill (USA))
1168[12]

**Late Shipment** *Mark Johnston* a79 89
3 b g Authorized(IRE) Time Over (Mark Of Esteem (IRE))
*(1239)* 1372[2] 2761[5] 3110[6] 3932[6] (4672) 5288[3] 5812[2] 6325[3]

**Latharnach (USA)** *Charlie Appleby* 97
2 b c Iffraaj Firth Of Lorne (IRE) (Danehill (USA))
4167[4] (4800) (6457)

**Lat Hawill (IRE)** *Marco Botti* 102
3 b c Invincible Spirit(IRE) Arbella (Primo Dominie)
1436[4] 2196a[12] 2983[6]

**La Tia (USA)** *Armando de la Cerda* a107 107
5 bb m City Place(USA) La Adelita (USA) (Sky Classic (CAN))
5459a[4]

**Latin Charm (IRE)** *Marco Botti* a93 90
3 b g Cape Cross(IRE) Di Moi Oui (Warning)
1690[2] 2319[3] 3003[13] 5132[2] 5877[4] 6438[5] (7161) *(7838)*

**Latin Rebel (IRE)** *Jim Goldie* 64
7 b g Spartacus(IRE) Dance To The Beat (Batshoof)
1761[6] 2216[6] 2455[5] 2915[2] 3101[2] 3365[7] 4492[4] 4904[2] 4964[5] 5856[4] 6480[5] 7059[4] 7100[6]

**La Tinta Bay** *Richard Hannon* a73 78
3 b f Compton Place Cumana Bay (Dansili)
3117[11] 4053[8] 4502[2] 5032[4] 5381[7] 6552[3] 7017[11] 7489[6] 7847[11]

**Laugharne** *Roger Charlton* a73 87
3 b g Authorized(IRE) Corsican Sunset (USA) (Thunder Gulch (USA))
1535[8] 2060[6] 5877[10] 7161[5]

**Laughing Jack** *George Baker* a80 85
6 b g Beat Hollow Bronzewing (Beldale Flutter (USA))
1636[10] 2270[5] (2966) 3574[6] 5276[7] (5812)

**Laughing Rock (IRE)** *Michael Appleby* a60 50
4 b f Rock Of Gibraltar(IRE) The Last Laugh (Kyllachy)
196[7] 362[4] 651[5] 835[3] 934[2] 1080[3] 7259[10] 7671[5] 7915[5] 8210[6]

**Laura (GER)** *Waldemar Hickst* 72
3 b f Montjeu(IRE) Laurencia (Shirley Heights)
7681a[7]

**Laura B** *Chris Wall* a59
2 b f Acclamation New Design (IRE) (Bluebird (USA))
4202[10] 5604[7] 6071[5] 6662[5] 7014[3] 7904[2] 8069[2]

**Laura Green** *F Trappolini* a52
8 bb m Kheleyf(USA) Laura's Show (Polar Falcon (USA))
392a[13]

**Laura Secord (CAN)** *Heather Main* a74 74
4 b f Henny Hughes(USA) Heart Lake (CAN) (Unbridled (USA))
1910[2] 2305[7] 6091[7] 7744[10]

**Laurelita (IRE)** *George Baker* 83
3 b f High Chaparral(IRE) Chervil (Dansili)
1096a[6] 2277[7] 3195[5] 5123[4] 5884[9] 7161[10]

**Laurence** *Luca Cumani* 63
2 b c Dubawi(IRE) Victoire Celebre (USA) (Stravinsky (USA))
7206[3] 7667[3]

**Lavallo (GER)** *Waldemar Hickst* a69 80
7 b g Konigstiger(GER) Lavender Blue (GER) (Law Society (USA))
57a[5]

**Lavender Lane (IRE)** *J E Hammond* 111
3 ch f Shamardal(USA) Alix Road (FR) (Linamix (FR))
3289a[9] 3773a[3] 5545a[3] 6969a[6]

**L'Avenue (IRE)** *James Tate* a71 64
3 b f Champs Elysees Mrs Seek (Unfuwain (USA))
167[2] (1153) 1509[11] 4948[12]

**La Vetus (SPA)** *M Delcher Sanchez* a55 56
3 b f Pyrus(USA) La Catedral (Rock Of Gibraltar (IRE))
720a[11]

**La Vien Zen (IRE)** *Ann Duffield* 53
2 b f Dylan Thomas(IRE) Se La Vie (FR) (Highest Honor (FR))
5494[11] 5712[6] 6976[10]

**Law Appeal** *Brian Meehan* 66
3 b g Lawman(FR) Demi Voix (Halling (USA))
3074[3]

**Law Keeper (IRE)** *James Tate* a68 79
3 b f Lawman(FR) Lisieux Orchid (IRE) (Sadler's Wells (USA))
3602[2] (4705) 5527[3] 6192[4] 6841[5] 7459[10]

**Lawmans Thunder** *Ismail Mohammed* a102 94
4 b g Lawman(FR) Rhapsodize (Halling (USA))
1173[5] (1771) ◆ (2079) (2462) 3456[7] 6140[12] 6688[8] 7663[3] 8117[5]

**Lawn Ranger (USA)** *Kenneth McPeek* 104
2 b c US Ranger(USA) Lalka (CAN) (Dynaformer (USA))
7590a[6]

**Lawsong (IRE)** *Jamie Osborne* a67
3 b g Lawman(FR) Flaming Song (IRE) (Darshaan)
468[4]

**Lawyer (IRE)** *Luca Cumani* a71 91
3 b g Acclamation Charaig (Rainbow Quest (USA))
1614[4] 3243[7] (4028) 4671[5] 5258[5] 6214[U] 6688[3] 6895[11]

**Layali Al Andalus** *S Seemar* a97 95
7 b g Halling(USA) Lafite (Robellino (USA))
108a[2] 307a[2] 593a[9] 681a[11]

**Laybach (IRE)** *Jim Goldie* 40
10 br g Bach(IRE) River Breeze (IRE) (Sharifabad (IRE))
3051[5]

**Layerthorpe (IRE)** *David Brown* a54 41
2 b c Vale Of York(IRE) Strobinia (IRE) (Soviet Star (USA))
6931[6] 7407[16] 7739[8]

**Layl (USA)** *Mark Johnston* a96 77
4 bb c Street Cry(IRE) Cymbal (IRE) (Singspiel (IRE))
3[2]

**Layla's Boy** *Simon West* a63 48
7 ch g Sakhee(USA) Gay Romance (Singspiel (IRE))
68[11] 546[10] 959[5] 2935[5] 3404[3] 5508[9]

**Layla's Hero (IRE)** *David Nicholls* a69 85
7 b g One Cool Cat(USA) Capua (USA) (Private Terms (USA))
219[3] (273) 384[3] 1224[7] 2167[2] 2296[3] 2914[7] 4383[2] (4487) 4571[3] (5817) 6013[2] 6511[13] 7282[15] 7506[5]

**Layla's Oasis** *Richard Fahey* a76 73
4 b f Oasis Dream Kirk (Selkirk (USA))
69[7] (196) 299[5]

**Layla's Red Devil (IRE)** *Richard Fahey* a65 67
3 b f Dalakhani(IRE) Brazilian Samba (IRE) (Sadler's Wells (USA))
1240[7] 1508[4] 4189[6] 6325[6]

**Layline (IRE)** *Gay Kelleway* a78 72
7 b g King's Best(USA) Belle Reine (King Of Kings (IRE))
16[4] 182[3] 322[3] 494[4] 1743[3] 2067[5] 2394[2] 2651[5] (3899) 4093[5] 4744[5] 7651[2] 7817[6] 7914[3] 8089[2] 8211[4]

**Lazarus Bell** *Alan Brown* a64 89
4 ch g Bahamian Bounty Snake's Head (Golden Snake (USA))
1345[2] 1564[5] 1733[5] 2425[10] 2699[6] 3202[12] 3437[5] 5197[7] 5681[9]

**Lazy Days In Loule (IRE)** *Noel Wilson* 62
2 b f Approve(IRE) Lazy Lady (Selkirk (USA))
1342[8] (1505) 2313[10] 3188[3] 3909[4] 5637[8] 6211[11] 6642[6]

**Lazy Sioux** *Richard Guest* a53 58
3 b f Sleeping Indian Aimee's Delight (Robellino (USA))
1713[7] 2828[10] 3366[5] 6866[5] 7010[3] 7457[3] 7519[4] 7670[2] 8088[8] 8181[2] 8284[5]

**Lazzaz (FR)** *D De Watrigant* a88 99
5 b g Bahri(USA) Rosalita (FR) (Nashamaa)
8150a[0]

**Lead A Merry Dance** *Sylvester Kirk* a67 67
3 b f Bertolini(USA) Green Supreme (Primo Dominie)
2489[5] 2946[2] 3586[4] 4324[4] 4972[3] 6297[2] 7023[5] 7842[3]

**Leaderene** *Mark Johnston* a77 82
3 b f Selkirk(USA) La Felicita (Shareef Dancer (USA))
4084[2] (4321) (4591) 4921[5] (5185) (6450) ◆ 6794[4] 7565[12]

**Leader Writer (FR)** *H-A Pantall* 99
2 b c Pivotal Miss Emma May (IRE) (Hawk Wing (USA))
6618a[4] 7468a[2]

**Leading Actress (IRE)** *W McCreery* a73 81
2 b f Makfi Emmy Award (IRE) (Sadler's Wells (USA))
3763a[7]

**Leading Light (IRE)** *A P O'Brien* 121
4 b c Montjeu(IRE) Dance Parade (USA) (Gone West (USA))
(2370a) ◆ (3377) (5736a) 6374a[2] 7271[7]

**Lead My Way (FR)** *J-L Guillochon* a64
3 gr g Al Namix(FR) Marie Du Lys (FR) (Polish Summer)
600a[4]

**Leaf (IRE)** *David Wachman* 86
3 b f Montjeu(IRE) Tree Chopper (USA) (Woodman (USA))
5024a[8]

**Leah Claire (IRE)** *W McCreery* a60 97
8 ch m Tomba Kate Emily (IRE) (Priolo (USA))
2370a[5]

**Lean And Keen (IRE)** *Sean Byrne* a74 83
4 b g Antonius Pius(USA) Fury Dance (USA) (Cryptoclearance (USA))
4771a[14]

**Lean On Pete (IRE)** *Ollie Pears* a82 56
5 b g Oasis Dream Superfonic (FR) (Zafonic (USA))
265[3] 498[3] 782[6] (1003) 1222[2] 1495[3] 7186[6] 7651[3] 7871[5] 7998[3] 8122[2] 8283[4]

**Lear's Rock (IRE)** *Ralph Beckett* a65 76
2 b g Rock Of Gibraltar(IRE) Cordelia (Green Desert (USA))
4330[4] 5072[4] 5604[4] 6064[2] 6759[2] 7228[3]

**Le Bambou (FR)** *P Demercastel* 67
2 b c Siyouni(FR) My Fantasy (IRE) (Desert King (IRE))
6916a[6]

**Le Bandit (FR)** *J Rossi* a87
3 b g Archange D'Or(IRE) Galop Du Bouffey (FR) (Cardoun (FR))
4952a[5]

**Le Big (GER)** *P Schaerer* a73 83
10 b g Big Shuffle(USA) La Luganese (IRE) (Surumu (GER))
728a[4]

**Le Bosphore (FR)** *M Pimbonnet* a52 64
7 b g Kingsalsa(USA) Queen Of Colours (Royal Academy (USA))
437a[3] 584a[16]

**Le Bouscot (FR)** *Mme P Butel* a44 37
2 b c Great Pretender(IRE) Carla Song (FR) (Nikos)
5900a[7]

**Le Chat D'Or** *Michael Dods* 95
6 b g One Cool Cat(USA) Oh So Well (IRE) (Sadler's Wells (USA))
2478[2] (3050) 4491[6] 6748[7] 7236[7] 7490[4]

**Le Cheile (IRE)** *Brendan W Duke* a69 65
3 b f Intense Focus(USA) Faoileoir (USA) (Dehere (USA))
4950a[P]

**Le Deluge (FR)** *Ann Stokell* a72 73
4 b g Oratorio(IRE) Princess Sofia (UAE) (Pennekamp (USA))
1196[15] 1598[7] 1957[8] 2169[12] (4470) 4710[10] 5421[7] 5721[5] 5950[6] (6696) 7522[7] 7754[2]

**Le Drakkar (AUS)** *A bin Huzaim* a85 108
9 gr g Anabaa(USA) My Mo Rally (NZ) (Mi Preferido (USA))
308a[14] 509a[5] 768a[8]

**Lees Anthem** *Mel Brittain* a50 67
7 b g Mujahid(USA) Lady Rock (Mistertopogigo (IRE))
1838[9] 2232[2] 2743[3] 3092[4] 3150[2] 3530[2]

**Le Falgoux (FR)** *C Boutin* a49 54
7 b h Ocean Of Wisdom(USA) Kiss Me Goodknight (First Trump)
3373a[15]

**Leftrightleftright (IRE)** *Luke Dace* a14
3 b g Tagula(IRE) Henrietta Mews (Compton Place)
1433[15] 2469[7]

**Legacy (USA)** *John W Sadler* a100 72
4 bb f Sightseeing(USA) Royal Flush (USA) (Smart Strike (CAN))
7615a[8]

**Legal Advisor** *Philip Kirby* 47
3 b g Proclamation(IRE) Mafatin (IRE) (Sadler's Wells (USA))
3602[5] 4299[7] 4713[7] 6825[9] 7256[12]

**Legal Legacy** *Lee Carter* a66 60
8 ch g Beat Hollow Dans Delight (Machiavellian (USA))
469[4] 822[6] 1105[9] 1263[9]

**Legal Trip (IRE)** *Stefano Botti*
3 ch f Rock Of Gibraltar(IRE) Double Fantasy (GER) (Indian Ridge)
3513a[7]

**Legal Waves (IRE)** *Alan Swinbank* 91
4 b g Lawman(FR) Surf The Web (IRE) (Ela-Mana-Mou)
1608[5] 3499[2] 3998[2] 4360[2] 5052[3] (6011) (6491)

**Legendary** *Ed Vaughan* a93 111
5 b g Exceed And Excel(AUS) Red Carnation (IRE) (Polar Falcon (USA))
200[2] 457[3]

**Legend Rising (IRE)** *Martyn Meade* a72 97
3 ch c Tamayuz Encouragement (Royal Applause)
1614[5] (2088) 3378[8] ◆ 4198[7]

**Legend's Gate (IRE)** *Charlie Appleby* a79 80
2 b c New Approach(IRE) Arthur's Girl (Hernando (FR))
6928[3] 7372[2]

**Legerity (IRE)** *Charlie Appleby* 17
2 b f Dubawi(IRE) Much Faster (IRE) (Fasliyev (USA))
5416[13]

**Lehaaf (ARG)** *M F De Kock* a97 97
5 b g Excellent Art Sarkha (AUS) (Danehill (USA))
207a[4] 769a[10]

**Lehaim (FR)** *M Nigge* 108
2 b c Siyouni(FR) El Cuerpo E L'Alma (USA) (Harlan's Holiday (USA))
3806a[3] 4482a[3] 5741a[7]

**Lehena (FR)** *Matthieu Palussiere* a56
3 b f Bushranger(IRE) Mousseline (USA) (Barathea (IRE))
482a[12]

**Leigh Court (USA)** *Josie Carroll* a113 102
4 bb f Grand Slam(USA) Padmore (USA) (French Deputy (USA))
7608a[5]

**Leisure Time Bowl** *Rod Collet* a81 92
3 b c Elusive Quality(USA) Turtle Bow (FR) (Turtle Island (IRE))
6913a[2]

**Leitir Mor (IRE)** *J S Bolger* a74 109
4 b c Holy Roman Emperor(IRE) Christinas Letter (IRE) (Galileo (IRE))
1824a[6] 2185a[8] 3412a[5] 4649[8] 5361a[8] 5699a[9] 6352a[5] 6963a[8]

**Leitrim Pass (USA)** *William Haggas* a80 83
4 ch g Raven's Pass(USA) Santolina (USA) (Boundary (USA))
250[3] 293[4]

**Le Laitier (FR)** *Scott Dixon* a63 75
3 b g Milk It Mick La Brigitte (Tobougg (IRE))
(1611) 2015[8] 2429[10] 4131[2] 4411[9] (5055) 5470[6] 6285[10] 7356[9]

**Le Maitre Chat (USA)** *Clive Cox* 97
3 b g Tale Of The Cat(USA) Bedside Story (Mtoto)
1438[3] 4984[5] (5851) 6366[2] 6896[3] ◆ 7306[2]

**Lemoncetta (USA)** *John Gosden* a64
2 ch f Lemon Drop Kid(USA) Excelente (IRE) (Exceed And Excel (AUS))
8173[6]

**Lemon Pearl** *Mme C Head-Maarek* a69 89
4 ch f Singspiel(IRE) Basemah (FR) (Lemon Drop Kid (USA))
2821a[9]

**Lena Player (SWE)** *Linda Jewell*
3 ch f Honeysuckle Player(SWE) Russian Rhapsody (SWE) (Sonnen Gold)
447[5] 717[8]

**Lendal Bridge** *Tony Coyle* a58 55
3 ch g Avonbridge Dunloe (IRE) (Shaadi (USA))
1223[3] 2204[4] 2657[3] 3503[3] 5089[9] 7644[17] 7764[3] 7910[5] 8084[5] 8219[3]

**Lenderking (IRE)** *Michael Chapman* a6 16
6 b g Sleeping Indian Roses From Ridey (IRE) (Petorius)
268[5] 1805[4] 2092[6]

**Leo Luna** *Gary Moore* a61 56
5 b g Galileo(IRE) Eva Luna (USA) (Alleged (USA))
1418[10]

**Leonard (GER)** *Frau S Weis* 69
5 b h Echo Of Light Laronja (GER) (Areion (GER))
7618a[9]

**Leonardo (GER)** *James Fanshawe* a32 57
2 ch g Areion(GER) Lolli Pop (GER) (Cagliostro (GER))
7537[6] 7739[14]

**Leonard Thomas** *David Lanigan* a83
4 b g Singspiel(IRE) Monawara (IRE) (Namaqualand (USA))
7552[3] ◆ 7831[7] 8168[2]

**Leoncavallo (IRE)** *Charlie Appleby* 52
2 b g Cape Cross(IRE) Nafura (Dubawi (IRE))
7382[7] 7667[7]

**Leonida (FR)** *J-M Beguigne* 76
2 b c Lawman(FR) Avventura (USA) (Johannesburg (USA))
5292a[2]

**Leonido** *M G Mintchev* 79
2 b c Rip Van Winkle(IRE) Lukrecia (IRE) (Exceed And Excel (AUS))
7145a[8]

**Le Prelat (FR)** *J-M Capitte* a77
3 gr g Falco(USA) Andriana (IRE) (Second Empire (IRE))
(360a) 545a[5]

**Le Reverend (FR)** *D Windrif* a68 83
5 gr h Keltos(FR) Revolera (FR) (Bering)
1828a[3]

**Le Ring (FR)** *F Rossi* a86 110
4 b c Slickly(FR) Joha (FR) (Johann Quatz (FR))
7189a[2]

**Le Roumois (FR)** *E Libaud* a81 81
8 b g Muhtathir Blanchelande (IRE) (Subotica (FR))
(1828a)

**Le Rouquin (FR)** *Michael Bell* a52 67
2 ch g Siyouni(FR) Tenue D'Amour (FR) (Pursuit Of Love)
5391[4] 5922[9] 7666[11] 8115[7]

**Leroy Parker (IRE)** *Barry Murtagh* 70
6 ch g Titus Livius(FR) Jameela (IRE) (Danehill (USA))
1567[4] 2055[13] 2915[8]

**Les Andelys** *Michael Murphy* a20
8 b g Zieten(USA) Oasis Song (IRE) (Selkirk (USA))
692[9] 1365[9]

**Les Beaufs (FR)** *Mme V Seignoux* 118
5 b g Apsis Yeomanry (FR) (Saumarez)
1784a[8] 2588a[8] 6383a[11]

**Le Scribe (FR)** *G Botti* a57 85
3 b g Orpen(USA) Rhodagna (IRE) (Mark Of Esteem (IRE))
(5368a)

**L'Es Fremantle (FR)** *Michael Chapman* a23
3 b g Orpen(USA) Grand Design (Danzero (AUS))
543[4] 4536[8] 4996[5] 7229[9] 7499[7] 7646[9] 8280[6]

**Les Gar Gan (IRE)** *Keith Dalgleish* a60 75
3 b f Iffraaj Story (Observatory (USA))
3114[7] 3359[7] 3650[4] 3956[2] 4294[6] 4515[6] 5142[8] 5717[5] 6110[3] 6480[8] (7021) 7499[2] 7541[2] 7869[10] 8044[2]

**Lesha (IRE)** *Kevin Ryan* a71 98
3 b g Amadeus Wolf Dane Blue (IRE) (Danehill Dancer (IRE))
99[4] 357[3] 1346[2] 1655[4] (2203) 3108[2] (3464) 4198[4] 4761[9] 5177[2] 5656[12] 6149[2] 6535[4] 6737[5]

**Lesson In Life** *David O'Meara* a56 62
3 b f Duke Of Marmalade(IRE) Vanity (IRE) (Thatching)
7176[5] 8048[5] 8114[4]

**Lesstalk In Paris (IRE)** *J-C Rouget* 111
3 b f Cape Cross(IRE) Top Toss (IRE) (Linamix (FR))
(1480a) 2195a[12] 3418[2]

**L'Etacq** *Richard Hannon* a72 75
2 b c Royal Applause Miss Sophisticat (Alhaarth (IRE))
2276[5] 3181[2] (3524) ◆ 4439[24] (5028) 5620[3] 6064[10] 6550[4] 7201[6]

**Lethal Legacy (IRE)** *Richard Hannon* a69 82
2 b c Alfred Nobel(IRE) Cafe Creme (IRE) (Catrail (USA))
4395[4] 4896[8] 7031[3]

**Le Tiger Still (GER)** *P Vovcenko* 92
2 b c Tiger Hill(IRE) La Candela (GER) (Alzao (USA))
6123a[3] 7726a[9]

**Let Me In (IRE)** *Bernard Llewellyn* a23 57
4 ch g Pivotal I Hearyou Knocking (IRE) (Danehill Dancer (IRE))
2248[9] 2672[13]

**Le Torrent** *Henry Candy* a59 56
2 ch g Sir Percy Cinnas Ransom (Red Ransom (USA))
5212[5] 5625[8] 6743[8] 7396[4] 7815[9]

**Let Right Be Done** *Ed McMahon* a60 39
2 gr g Lawman(FR) Cheerfully (Sadler's Wells (USA))
6668[9] 7200[7] 7779[5] 7994[5]

**Let's Confer** *Michael Attwater* a40
5 ch m Doyen(IRE) Vrennan (Suave Dancer (USA))
7772[5] 8074[7]

**Let'sgoforit (IRE)** *Bodil Hallencreutz* a103 88
6 gr g Verglas(IRE) Slewcie (USA) (Seattle Slew (USA))
(2244a) (3996a)

**Let's Go Live** *Tony Coyle* 53
4 b g Firebreak Enchantment (USA) (Cozzene (USA))
3908[11] 4749[7]

**Let's Make Adeal (AUS)** *Nigel Blackiston* 106
5 b m Red Ransom(USA) Let's Get Famous (AUS) (Danehill (USA))
7126a[3]

**Letterfromamerica (USA)** *S Seemar* a85 79
3 b f Ghostzapper(USA) Kindness (Indian Ridge)
203a[3] 506a[9] 771a[7] 896a[9]

**Letthemusictakeus (IRE)** *Y Durepaire* a79 85
3 b f Holy Roman Emperor(IRE) Side Of Paradise (IRE) (Sadler's Wells (USA))
553a[9]

**Lettuce Snow (IRE)** *Geoffrey Deacon* a29
2 b f Clodovil(IRE) Lola Rosa (IRE) (Peintre Celebre (USA))
8112[5] 8247[8]

**Le Valentin (FR)** *Mlle C Nicot* a80 97
8 b g Slickly(FR) Vallabelle (FR) (Valanour (IRE))
7026a[12]

**Le Vie Infinite (IRE)** *R Brogi* 92
7 b h Le Vie Dei Colori Looking Back (IRE) (Stravinsky (USA))
2375a[9]

**Levitate** *John Quinn* a83 110
6 ch g Pivotal Soar (Danzero (AUS))
1165[15] 1870[7] 2286[11] 3356[16] 6332[5] ◆ 7081[5] 7276[4] (7715)

**Levoila (FR)** *L Larrigade* 76
3 b c Deportivo Rastella (FR) (Funambule (USA))
1551a[6]

**Lewamy (IRE)** *Michael Bell* a57 44
4 b g Amadeus Wolf Thai Dye (UAE) (Jade Robbery (USA))
846[8] 1040[7] 1917[6] 3075[8] 4056[8] 4733[6] 5138[2] 5280[5] 5537[4] 6122[6] 7844[5] (8111)

**Lewisham** *David Nicholls* a83 85
4 b g Sleeping Indian Almunia (IRE) (Mujadil (USA))
2352[3] 2992[10] 3714[9] 4146[12] 5199[10] 5887[12] 6478[12] 7178[12] 7687[3] 7826[8] 8082[6]

**Lewis Valentine (IRE)** *Bryan Smart* 71
2 b c Rip Van Winkle(IRE) Full Of Love (IRE) (Hawk Wing (USA))
6668[4] 7637[3]

**Lexa King's (FR)** *C Lerner* a70 54
3 ch g King's Best(USA) Lexa (FR) (Sanglamore (USA))
2290a[11]

**Lexi Grady Alice** *Mark H Tompkins* a44 43
2 b f Royal Applause Missoula (IRE) (Kalanisi (IRE))
5187[8] 6205[7] 7064[7]

**Lexington Abbey** *Kevin Ryan* 95
3 b g Sleeping Indian Silvereine (FR) (Bering)
1693[4] 2295[5] 2768[4] 3219[7] (4133) 4636[4] 4977[2] 5696[2] 6170[2] 6531[5] 6893[5]

**Lexington Bay (IRE)** *Richard Fahey* a81 81
6 b g High Chaparral(IRE) Schust Madame (IRE) (Second Set (IRE))
16[3] 270[3] 350[4] 5421[2] 6152[5] 6536[4] 7281[6]

**Lexington Blue** *Seamus Mullins* a69 60
4 b g Bertolini(USA) Jasmine Breeze (Saddlers' Hall (IRE))
5975[8] 6883[9] 7369[10] (7844) 8030[8] 8103[8] 8315[7]

**Lexington Place** *Ruth Carr* a66 88
4 ch g Compton Place Elidore (Danetime (IRE))
3006[3] 3239[7] 6096[6] 6512[16] 6763[9]

**Lexington Rose** *Bryan Smart* a69 76
3 b f Captain Gerrard(IRE) Silca Destination (Dubai Destination (USA))
1585[9] (3600) 4315[6] 5087[5] 6109[8] 6452[9] 7286[7] 7806[11] ◆ 7997[4]

**Lexington Times (IRE)** *Richard Hannon* 103
2 b c Paco Boy(IRE) Fuaigh Mor (IRE) (Dubai Destination (USA))
3720[2] (4167) 4865[3] 5447[3] 5926[3] 6256[8] 7446[4]

**Lexi's Beauty (IRE)** *Brian Baugh* a42 53
4 br f Kheleyf(USA) Voyage Of Dreams (USA) (Riverman (USA))
34[6] 273[10] 556[5] 692[7] 1887[8] 2658[2] 3099[7] 3938[4] 4455[5] 4875[6]

**Lexi's Hero (IRE)** *Richard Fahey* a91 98
6 b g Invincible Spirit(IRE) Christel Flame (Darshaan)
8[2] (122) (312) 412[2] 644[9] 3216[2] 4188[4] 4762[16] (5411) 5665[13] 5918[7] 6531[21] 6745[5] 7132[10] 7233[15]

**Lexi's Red Devil (IRE)** *Marco Botti* a71 66
2 b f Danehill Dancer(IRE) Challow Hills (USA) (Woodman (USA))
4914[11] 5416[5] 5827[2] 6769[3] 7207[5]

**Leyland (IRE)** *Natalie Lloyd-Beavis* a61 77
5 b g Peintre Celebre(USA) Lasting Chance (USA) (American Chance (USA))
7831[9] 8037[10] 8163[5] 8253[3]

**L Ge R** *Peter Charalambous* a40 60
3 b f Pastoral Pursuits Cashbar (Bishop Of Cashel)
1616[5] 3428[10] 5395[8] 6939[6] 7664[9] 7854[9]

**L'Hirondelle (IRE)** *Michael Attwater* a53 50
10 b g Anabaa(USA) Auratum (USA) (Carson City (USA))
1302[9] 3080[10] 3576[12]

**Libbard** *Roger Charlton* 61
2 ch f Galileo(IRE) Clouded Leopard (USA) (Danehill (USA))
7405[4]

**Libeccio (FR)** *Andrew Balding* a74 79
3 b g Shirocco(GER) Francais (Mark Of Esteem (IRE))
1028[2] 1367[2] 1984[5] 2934[3] (3823)

**Liber** *Bent Olsen* 100
4 b c Ishiguru(USA) Startori (Vettori (IRE))
2244a[8] 4957a[3] 6387a[2]

**Liberal Angel (FR)** *K R Burke* a49 67
2 b f Librettist(USA) Angel Voices (IRE) (Tagula (IRE))
2697[6] 5590a[4] 6700[3] 7574[3]

**Liberal Lady** *Robert Johnson*
6 b m Statue Of Liberty(USA) Noble Story (Last Tycoon)
4664[9] 5089[12] 5683[15]

**Liberry Gold (GER)** *P Harley* 100
2 ch c Adlerflug(GER) Laey Diamond (GER) (Dai Jin)
7726a[2]

**Liberte Mon Amour (FR)** *J Heloury* 47
2 b f Enrique Liberte De Penser (FR) (Pennekamp (USA))
1094a[9]

**Liberty Jack (IRE)** *Jim Boyle* a82 92
4 b g Sakhee(USA) Azeema (IRE) (Averti (IRE))
312[5] 493[4] 655[5] 927[2] (1021) 1103[2] 1234[3] 3314[6] 4118[4] (4447) 4783[7] 5623[2] 5888[4] 6369a[7]

**Liberty Red (GER)** *Ed Dunlop* a70 88
3 b g Dubawi(IRE) Late Night (GER) (Groom Dancer (USA))
(1119) 1509[3] ◆

**Liberty Rules (IRE)** *Malcolm Saunders*
2 b c Aussie Rules(USA) Polynesian Queen (IRE) (Statue Of Liberty (USA))
7308[11]

**Liberty Sky (IRE)** *Richard Fahey* 62
2 b f Rip Van Winkle(IRE) High Spot (Shirley Heights)
2979[3] ◆

**Libido (FR)** *C Boutin* a64 93
3 b g Librettist(USA) Lady Hawk (GER) (Grand Lodge (USA))
7269a[12]

**Libran (IRE)** *Alan Swinbank* 89
3 b g Lawman(FR) True Crystal (IRE) (Sadler's Wells (USA))
(1597) (2120) ◆ 2617[2] 3003[8] 3965[4] 6978[5]

**Libra Romana (IRE)** *Sir Mark Prescott Bt* a46 56
3 b f Holy Roman Emperor(IRE) Sliding Scale (Sadler's Wells (USA))
280[5] 3627[5] 4048[5] 4495[6] 4905[2] 5183[6] 5978[5] 6396[3] 6823[5] 6939[11]

**Librettista (FR)** *Frau S Weis* 80
4 b f Librettist(USA) Pilgrim Of Grace (FR) (Bering)
7483a[12] 7618a[11]

**Licence To Till (USA)** *Alan Berry* a87 84
7 b g War Chant(USA) With A Wink (USA) (Clever Trick (USA))
1495[4] (1816) 2119[5] (3035) 3382[2] 3718[5] 4156[13] 4959[6]

**Lichen Angel** *Richard Whitaker* a47 42
4 gr f Dark Angel(IRE) Moss Likely (IRE) (Clodovil (IRE))
290[8] 516[5]

**Lidari (FR)** *Peter G Moody* 114
5 b h Acclamation Laxlova (FR) (Linamix (FR))
1186a[9] 7301a[6] 7653a[19]

**Liebling** *Niels Petersen* 90
3 b f Touch Down(GER) Lupinie (GER) (Platini (GER))
6388a[3]

**Lie To Me (FR)** *Mme G Rarick* a60 79
4 b g Slickly(FR) Lady Carole (FR) (Subotica (FR))
5546a[11]

**Lieutenant Dan (IRE)** *Michael Appleby* a73 57
7 b g Danroad(AUS) Dakhira (Emperor Jones (USA))
96[8] 319[6] 562[8]

**Lieutenant Kaffee (USA)** *Richard Fahey* 91
2 b c First Defence(USA) Major Allie (USA) (Officer (USA))
(3330) ◆ (3883) 4199[6] 5680[2]

**Lieutenant Miller** *Nicky Henderson* 98
8 b g Beat All(USA) Still Runs Deep (Karinga Bay)
3321[7] 4777[P]

**Life And Times (USA)** *Mark Johnston* a93 79
6 bb g Medaglia d'Oro(USA) Sur Ma Vie (USA) (Fusaichi Pegasus (USA))
(1085) (1317) 1356[13] 1578[9] 2868[6] 3217[6] 3499[7] 4091[4] 4549[4] 4975[6] 5811[3] 6210[5] 6770[2] 6885[8]

**Lifeisforliving (FR)** *Matthieu Palussiere* a71 75
2 b f Hold That Tiger(USA) Azucar (IRE) (Desert Prince (IRE))
3027a[8] 5844a[2]

**Lifejacket (IRE)** *Ed Dunlop* a62 60
3 ch g Notnowcato My American Beauty (Wolfhound (USA))
1616[6] 1844[9] 2927[4] 3389[9] 4084[3] 4763[5] (5833) 6242[4] 6635[5]

**Life Knowledge (IRE)** *Patrick Holmes* 47
2 ch g Thewayyouare(USA) Rosa Bellini (IRE) (Rossini (USA))
6577[6] 6859[8] 7173[4]

**Life Less Ordinary (IRE)** *Jamie Osborne* a72
2 b g Thewayyouare(USA) Dont Cross Tina (IRE) (Cape Cross (IRE))
6903[5] (7425)

**Life Partner (IRE)** *Charlie Appleby* a83 96
4 b g Cape Cross(IRE) Miss Intimate (USA) (War Chant (USA))
2202[3] 2747[2] 3431[3] 3886[6]

**Ligeia** *Richard Hannon* a77 82
3 b f Rail Link Elegant Beauty (Olden Times)
3117[9] 3727[6] 4436[10] 5008[4] 5398[3] (5685) 6459[5] 7416[8]

**Light And Shade** *James Tate* a76
2 b f Aqlaam Tara Moon (Pivotal)
(7756)

**Light Breaks (IRE)** *Sir Mark Prescott Bt* a36 57
2 b g Dylan Thomas(IRE) Anywaysmile (IRE) (Indian Ridge)
5009[9] 6859[6] 7217[6]

**Light Burst (USA)** *Ismail Mohammed* a89 60
5 b h Hard Spun(USA) Kew Garden (USA) (Seattle Slew (USA))
241a[6]

**Lightening Stricks (IRE)** *M J Tynan* a73 76
7 b g King's Best(USA) Opera Comique (FR) (Singspiel (IRE))
790a[13]

**Light Fantastic** *Ed Dunlop* a81 71
2 b f Acclamation Blue Beacon (Fantastic Light (USA))
5187[3] (5821) 6105[3] 6924[9]

**Light From Mars** *Ronald Harris* a90 88
9 gr g Fantastic Light(USA) Hylandra (USA) (Bering)
122[2] 348[6] 381[2] ◆ 574[4] 820[5] (1102) 1190[14] 1731[8] 2919[6] 3783[2] 4154[3] (4406) 5437[3] 6020[5] 6558[11] 7988[3] 8141[2]

**Light Glass (IRE)** *Richard Hannon* 53
2 b f Lope De Vega(IRE) Truth Beauty (IRE) (Dubai Destination (USA))
6753[9]

**Light Heavy (IRE)** *J S Bolger* a78 105
5 ch h Teofilo(IRE) Siamsa (USA) (Quest For Fame)
1252a[4]

**Light In Paris (IRE)** *J-C Rouget* 97
2 b f Aussie Rules(USA) Grande Rousse (FR) (Act One)
5740a[3] 6967a[8]

**Lightning Charlie** *Amanda Perrett* a81 84
2 b g Myboycharlie(IRE) Lighted Way (Kris)
6517[3] ◆ 7130[2] (7400)

**Lightning Moon (IRE)** *Ed Walker* 114
3 b c Shamardal(USA) Catch The Moon (IRE) (Peintre Celebre (USA))
(1980) (2768) ◆ (6920)

**Lightning Shower (USA)** *Marco Botti* a69 66
3 b c Mr Greeley(USA) Lightning Show (USA) (Storm Cat (USA))
1401[4] ◆ 1812[4] 2198[6]

**Lightning Spear** *Olly Stevens* a88 94
3 ch c Pivotal Atlantic Destiny (IRE) (Royal Academy (USA))
(7538) ◆

**Lightning Spree (IRE)** *Kevin Ryan* 42
2 gr g Jeremy(USA) Spree (IRE) (Dansili)
7407[8]

**Lightning Stride** *Brian Meehan* a75 83
2 ch c Equiano(FR) Fame Is The Spur (Motivator)
1977[12] (2380) 2987[5] 3580[5] 4123[11] 4430[2] 5620[2]

**Lightning Thunder** *Olly Stevens* 111
3 b f Dutch Art Sweet Coincidence (Mujahid (USA))
1976[2] 2581a[2] 3418[9] 5176[4]

**Lightnin Hopkins (IRE)** *John Butler* a82 74
4 b g Kodiac Bundle Of Joy (IRE) (Golan (IRE))
1938[8] 2425[7] 2953[6] 3844[4] 4487[9] 5385[10] 8068[10]

**Light Of Asia (IRE)** *Ed Dunlop* a56 79
3 b c Oratorio(IRE) Lucy Cavendish (USA) (Elusive Quality (USA))
1394[6] 1817[4] 2847[2] 3360[2] 5002[3] 5975[6] (6699) 7020[5] 7281[5]

**Light Of Love** *Henry Candy* a48
2 b f Dylan Thomas(IRE) May Light (Midyan (USA))
7739[9]

**Light Of The World (IRE)** *Jamie Osborne* a67
2 b f Fastnet Rock(AUS) Gassal (Oasis Dream)
6605[3] 7184[5] 7943[5] 8087[5]

**Light Rose (IRE)** *Jeremy Gask* a77 79
4 b f Cape Cross(IRE) Laureldean Lady (IRE) (Statue Of Liberty (USA))
1026[4] 1731[11] 2884[5] 3581[7] 4181[11] 5308[6]

**Lightscameraction (IRE)** *Gay Kelleway* a89 95
2 ch c Pastoral Pursuits Silca Boo (Efisio)
(4652) 5405a[4] 5694[4] 6513[8] 6991a[2] 7099[2] 7571[2]

**Light The City (IRE)** *Ruth Carr* a62 72
7 b g Fantastic Light(USA) Marine City (JPN) (Carnegie (IRE))
(474) 569[2] 609[4]

**Light Weight (IRE)** *Kevin Ryan* 73
3 b f Danehill Dancer(IRE) Foofaraw (USA) (Cherokee Run (USA))
3195[11] 3978[11]

**Like A Carousel (AUS)** *Ken Keys* 106
5 ch g Helike(USA) Carnival Ride (AUS) (Spinning World (USA))
7395a[3]

**Like A Diamond (IRE)** *Ann Stokell* a87 55
4 b g Antonius Pius(USA) Silk Law (IRE) (Barathea (IRE))
(127) 408[2] (514) 611[6] 5487[9] 7870[P]

**Like A Prayer** *Ralph Beckett* a74 66
3 b g Compton Place Floating (Oasis Dream)
(378) ◆ (492) 2307[6] 2847[5] 6034[5] 6484[5] 7186[5]

**Like Clockwork** *Mark H Tompkins* a54 59
5 b g Rail Link Tenpence (Bob Back (USA))
185[9]

**Likelihood (USA)** *John Gosden* a81 87
3 gr f Mizzen Mast(USA) Light Jig (Danehill (USA))
2299[7] 2685[5] 3085[3] 3502[6]

**Likely (GER)** *David Barron* 93
2 ch f Exceed And Excel(AUS) La Pilaya (GER) (Pivotal)
(2601) ◆

**Like Me (IRE)** *N Clement* a81 76
3 b f Duke Of Marmalade(IRE) Queen Of Tara (IRE) (Sadler's Wells (USA))
7270a[7] 7630a[2]

**Lilac Lace (IRE)** *Tim Easterby* a74 90
4 b f Captain Marvelous(IRE) Lilac Mist (Spectrum (IRE))
1442[9] 1733[10] 1956[6] 2318[9] 2954[5] 4451[6] 4925[3] 5197[9] 5887[8] 6716[4] 7248[2] (7451)

**Lilac Tree** *Mark Johnston* a84 85
4 b g Dubawi(IRE) Kalidasa (USA) (Nureyev (USA))
(350) 623[6] 3878[2] 3999[4]

**Lilac Vale (IRE)** *Tim Easterby* 41
2 b f Moss Vale(IRE) Lilac Mist (Spectrum (IRE))
6212[10] 6623[8] 7245[7]

**Lila De Viette (FR)** *C Plisson* 77
3 b f Sinndar(IRE) Innamorata (FR) (True Brave (USA))
5592a[3]

**Lilbourne Lass** *K R Burke* a52 93
3 ch f Pastoral Pursuits Talampaya (USA) (Elusive Quality (USA))
1067[13] 1572[14]

**Lilian Baylis (IRE)** *Luca Cumani* a38
2 b f Shamardal(USA) Kiyra Wells (IRE) (Sadler's Wells (USA))
7194[13]

**Liliargh (IRE)** *Ben Haslam* 68
5 b m Acclamation Discover Roma (IRE) (Rock Of Gibraltar (IRE))
1310[7] 2427[6] 2911[9] (5499) 7644[5]

**Lilienthal (IRE)** *S Kobayashi* 87
7 b h Montjeu(IRE) Anna Monda (GER) (Monsun (GER))
5330a[6]

**Lili Moon (GER)** *Werner Glanz* 97
5 bb m Desert Prince(IRE) Lisibila (GER) (Acatenango (GER))
7146a[4] 7558a[10]

**Lille Prinsesse** *Bent Olsen* 48
2 ch f Dutch Art Sallysaysso (IRE) (Danehill Dancer (IRE))
6386a[12]

**Lilliofttheballet (IRE)** *Jim Goldie* a39 18
7 b m Rakti Lillibits (USA) (Kingmambo (USA))
686[11]

**Lilly Junior** *Brian Ellison* a72 75
3 b f Cape Cross(IRE) Sweet Lilly (Tobougg (IRE))
2061[5] 2422[5] 3276[3] 4090[3] 4516[U] 5198[3] (5772) 6269[8] 6793[6]

**Lil Rockerfeller (USA)** *Richard Hannon* a63 82
3 ch g Hard Spun(USA) Layounne (USA) (Mt. Livermore (USA))
403[4] 3537[4] (4350) (5435)

**Lil Sophella (IRE)** *Patrick Holmes* a70 64
5 ch m Indian Haven Discotheque (USA) (Not For Love (USA))
2518[5] 2911[2] 3242[2] 3949[4] 4023[5] 4665[3] 5291[3] 5773[6] 6223[9] (6601) 6836[9] 7427[2] 7575[6]

**Lily Des Indes (FR)** *N Clement* a66
2 b f American Post Fleur Des Indes (FR) (Ganges (USA))
8132a[6]

**Lily Edge** *John Bridger* a67 60
5 b m Byron Flaming Spirt (Blushing Flame (USA))
589[13] 685[4] 815[12] 989[9] 1120[3] 1210[3] 1406[3] 1835[3] (2084) 2693[5] (3080) 3473[4] 4081[5] 4658[5] (5428) 6019[6] 6635[6]

**Lily Moreton (IRE)** *Noel Wilson* 71
2 b f Kodiac Hollow Haze (USA) (Woodman (USA))
2349[2] 2725[3] 3236[3] 4869[6] 5561[2]

**Lily Rules (IRE)** *Tony Coyle* 99
3 br f Aussie Rules(USA) Causeway Charm (USA) (Giant's Causeway (USA))
1515[6] 2255[2] 2960[9] 3665[6] 5927[8] 7119[11]

**Liman (IRE)** *Mme Pia Brandt* a91 93
4 ch c Trade Fair Lady Of The Inn (IRE) (Hamas (IRE))
6992a[9]

**Limario (GER)** *A Savujev* a111 105
4 bb c Areion(GER) Limaga (Lagunas)
901a[9] 1176a[6] 2379a[8] 6955a[10]

**Limato (IRE)** *Henry Candy* a97 116
2 b g Tagula(IRE) Come April (Singspiel (IRE))
(3113) (3580) (4398) (6933)

**Limegrove** *David Evans* a78 78
3 b f Captain Gerrard(IRE) Cherry Belle (IRE) (Red Ransom (USA))
374[8] 608[11] 786[8] 919[7]

**Limerick Lord (IRE)** *Stuart Williams*
2 b c
8318[7]

**Limon Squeezy** *Mike Murphy* a44
5 b m Royal Applause Limonia (GER) (Perugino (USA))
76[6] 964[8] 2092[8]

**Limousine** *Charles Hills* a79 78
3 ch f Beat Hollow Market Forces (Lomitas)
1438[7] 3270[4] 5186[2] (5822) 6258[7]

**L'Importante** *Marco Botti* a75 74
3 b g New Approach(IRE) L'Indiscreta (Desert Prince (IRE))
1069[2] ◆ 2733[6]

**Linarda (DEN)** *Carmen Bocskai* 61
4 bb f Rock Of Gibraltar(IRE) Miss Skycat (USA) (Tale Of The Cat (USA))
5965a[8]

**Lince Suertudo (FR)** *Brian Ellison* a26 74
3 ch g Astronomer Royal(USA) La Cibeles (FR) (Cardoun (FR))
1002[4] 1959[3] 2737[3]

**Lincoln (IRE)** *Mick Channon* a84 101
3 b c Clodovil(IRE) Gilt Linked (Compton Place)
1136[3] 1420[6] 1658[2] 2176[2] 2567[2] 2962[8] 3539[3] 4021[2] 4660[2] 5410[4] (6234) (6740)

**Lincolnrose (IRE)** *Michael Appleby* a44 54
4 gr f Verglas(IRE) Imelda (USA) (Manila (USA))
2443[6] 2806[7]

**Linda Garota (FR)** *Mlle V Bougeard* a68
3 ch f Linngari(IRE) Xaliska (BRZ) (Special Nash (IRE))
795a[10]

**Lindaro (GER)** *P Schiergen* 88
3 bb c Sinndar(IRE) Larella (GER) (Anabaa (USA))
3073a[6]

**Lindart (ITY)** *Richard Hannon* a74 78
3 ch g Dutch Art Linda Surena (ARG) (Southern Halo (USA))
739[5] 2339[14] 3382[6] 4268[2] 5247[3] (5624) 6236[10] 7757[7] 7847[9] (8097) 8197[2]

**Linda's Sister** *John Quinn* 55
4 ch f Piccolo Pompey Blue (Abou Zouz (USA))
2985[5] 3486[4] 3951[2]

**Linden Rose** *Steph Hollinshead*
5 b m Striking Ambition Inchtina (Inchinor)
463[8]

**Lindenthaler (GER)** *Fredrik Reuterskiold* a85 108
6 b h Azamour(IRE) Lasira (GER) (Vettori (IRE))
3772a[6] 4956a[4]

**L'Indiscrete (FR)** *J Bertran De Balanda* 69
3 b f Enrique L'Exploratrice (FR) (Trempolino (USA))
5370a[3]

**Lindsay's Dream** *Zoe Davison* a42 51
8 b m Montjeu(IRE) Lady Lindsay (IRE) (Danehill Dancer (IRE))
1664[5] 1875[3] 2923[9] 3308[8] 7219[4]

**Line Drummer (FR)** *J Reynier* 106
4 b c Galileo(IRE) Miss Bio (FR) (River Mist (USA))
4008a[3] 6592a[8] 7322a[3]

**Lineman** *Andrew Hollinshead* a79 75
4 b g Rail Link Shamana (USA) (Woodman (USA))
544[3] (732) 999[3] 1133[3] 1849[3] 2160[6] 3151[2] 3976[3] 4423[8] 5800[2] 6099[9] 6721[5] 7072[6] 7866 [3] 8001[6]

**Line Of Reason (IRE)** *Paul Midgley* a66 105
4 br g Kheleyf(USA) Miss Party Line (USA) (Phone Trick (USA))
1212[9] 1672[5] 2522[2] 3256[8] (3342) (3737a) (4174) 4683[8] 5575[7] 5911[3] 6167[5]

**L'Inganno Felice (FR)** *Iain Jardine* a83 78
4 br g Librettist(USA) Final Overture (FR) (Rossini (USA))
6011[3] 6599[3] 7335[2] 7784[5] (8048) 8260[3]

**L'Ingenue** *Ralph Beckett* 70
2 b f New Approach(IRE) Green Room (FR) (In The Wings)
7450[4] ◆

**Lingfield Lupus (IRE)** *John Best* a46 44
3 b g Amadeus Wolf Clytha (Mark Of Esteem (IRE))
2926[13] 4084[4] 4911[8] 5048[4] 5864[10] 6339[9] 7517[6] 7635[5]

**Lingreville (FR)** *J-M Lefebvre* a63 85
3 b f Le Havre(IRE) Lady Calido (USA) (El Prado (IRE))
436a[7] 2978a[6]

**Linguine (FR)** *Seamus Durack* 95
4 ch c Linngari(IRE) Amerissage (USA) (Rahy (USA))
1444[12] 1971[6] (2981) 4173[10] 4622[3] 5633[3] 6330[8] 7409[6]

**Linkable** *Brendan Powell* a72 67
5 b g Rail Link Fashionable (Nashwan (USA))
405[3]

**Links Drive Lady** *Dean Ivory* a78 94
6 br m Striking Ambition Miskina (Mark Of Esteem (IRE))
1492[15] (2030) (2629) 2965[6] 3788[10] 5152[2] 5784[4] 6689[5] 7233[4] 7543[7] 7716[P]

**Linton (AUS)** *Marco Botti* a100 100
8 gr g Galileo(IRE) Heather (NZ) (Centaine (AUS))
902a[10] 6934[3] 7599[4] 8203[3]

**Lion Beacon** *Amanda Perrett* a89 91
4 ch g Beat Hollow Second Of May (Lion Cavern (USA))
1935[2] 2482[3] 2782[6] (3424) 4777[10] 5825[5] (Dead)

**Lion Court (IRE)** *Dai Burchell* a20 34
6 ch g Iffraaj Spanish Falls (Belmez (USA))
5273[4]

**Lionel Joseph** *George Baker* a15
2 b g Compton Place Floppie (FR) (Law Society (USA))
*6604[12]* 6874[11]
**Lionheart** *Peter Crate* a80 64
4 ch g Zamindar(USA) Victoire Celebre (USA) (Stravinsky (USA))
*3426 1102[5]* 1667[6] 2147[12] 3879[9] 4339[5] 4673[9] 6266[10] 6397[11] 6995[7]
**Lion On The Prowl (IRE)** *Alexandra Dunn* a27
10 b g Sadler's Wells(USA) Ballerina (IRE) (Dancing Brave (USA))
*3521[6]*
**Lions Arch (IRE)** *Richard Hannon* a89 85
4 b g Rock Of Gibraltar(IRE) Swynford Lady (IRE) (Invincible Spirit (IRE))
*163[7]*
**Lipocco** *J D Hillis* a83 95
10 br g Piccolo Magical Dancer (IRE) (Magical Wonder (USA))
*(555a)*
**Lips Dancer (IRE)** *Andreas Lowe* a90
5 ch g Big Shuffle(USA) Lips Plane (IRE) (Ashkalani (IRE))
*6992a[3]*
**Lipstickandpowder (IRE)** *William Jarvis* a48 53
2 gr f Mastercraftsman(IRE) Raphimix (FR) (Linamix (FR))
5643[7] 6753[10] 7666[14] *7994[6] 8121[13]*
**Lisahane Bog** *Peter Hedger* a56 39
7 b g Royal Applause Veronica Franco (Darshaan)
*247[3] 459[2] 530[3] 747[8] 1012[7]* 5229a[6]
**Lisamour (IRE)** *Paul Cole* a72 82
3 b f Azamour(IRE) Lisa De La Condra (IRE) (Galileo (IRE))
*1795[3] 2081[5]* (2492) (3154)
**Lisanor** *John Gosden* 49
3 b f Raven's Pass(USA) Arthur's Girl (Hernando (FR))
1280[9] 2925[3]
**Lisnavagh (FR)** *H-F Devin* a77 83
2 ch f Doctor Dino(FR) Sweet Lady Jane (FR) (Kaldounevees (FR))
*5844a[3]*
**Literally On Fire (IRE)** *Brendan Powell* a43
3 ch g Rock Of Gibraltar(IRE) Toolentidhaar (USA) (Swain (IRE))
*231[8] 423[6] 748[9] 923[6] 1285[6] 1449[4] 1626[6]*
**Litigant** *Seamus Durack* a104 90
6 b g Sinndar(IRE) Jomana (IRE) (Darshaan)
*(803)* ◆ *(1556)* ◆
**Litmus (USA)** *Simon Dow* a61 57
5 ch m Latent Heat(USA) Fairy Glade (USA) (Gone West (USA))
*(469) 691[4] 821[7] 1016[2] 1302[11]* 1664[7] 1875[2] *2212[6]* 2720[2] 2863[2] 3552[2] 3824[4] *4264[2]* 8175[5] 8315[8]
**Little** *Jamie Osborne* a67 67
2 b f Paco Boy(IRE) Wafeira (Dansili)
5524[2] 6024[3] (6393) *6884[10] 7258[6] (7421) (7762) 7890[5] (8076) 8240[2]*
**Little Alexis (USA)** *Carlo Vaccarezza* a100
3 b f Mr Greeley(USA) Dream Child (USA) (Giant's Causeway (USA))
*7608a[9]*
**Little Arrows (IRE)** *K J Condon* a70 69
8 b g Danehill Dancer(IRE) Lovers Walk (USA) (Diesis)
*7435a[14]*
**Little Belter (IRE)** *Tom Dascombe* a54 70
2 gr c Dandy Man(IRE) On Thin Ice (IRE) (Verglas (IRE))
2800[4] 3215[10] 3881[4] ◆ 5790[4] *7363[6]*
**Little Big Man** *Sylvester Kirk* a71 41
3 b g Sleeping Indian Doris Souter (IRE) (Desert Story (IRE))
*6[2] 338[6] (354) 573[5] (1829)*
**Little Big Shot (IRE)** *F-H Graffard* 98
3 b g Whipper(USA) Gravieres (FR) (Saint Estephe (FR))
3997a[8] (4465a)
**Little Briar Rose** *John Spearing* a34 46
3 ch f Sleeping Indian Penrice Castle (Averti (IRE))
1851[9] 2802[9] 3939[5] 5780[4] *6561[11] 7519[9]*
**Little Bruv** *Tim Easterby* 49
3 b g Observatory(USA) Ailincala (IRE) (Pursuit Of Love)
3098[8] 4134[6] 4497[3] *5102[7]* 5682[5]
**Little Buxted (USA)** *Robert Mills* a83 81
4 bb g Mr Greeley(USA) Mo Cheoil Thu (IRE) (In The Wings)
*2882[7] 3472[5] 4077[4]* 4402[4] *4736[2]* 5442[6] 5931[2] *6487[6]* 7341[4] *7552[2] 7831[2]*
**Little Choosey** *Roy Bowring* a64 54
4 ch f Cadeaux Genereux Little Nymph (Emperor Fountain)
*510[5] 688[5] 819[6] 1009[6]* 1573[8] 2008[6] 3549[4] 4042[3] 5071[12] *7864[2] 8085[5]*
**Littlecote Lady** *Mark Usher* a59 55
5 b m Byron Barefooted Flyer (USA) (Fly So Free (USA))
*296[2] 740[11] 1009[2] 7783[5] 7972[7] 8286[5]*
**Little Danielle (IRE)** *Phil McEntee* a5
2 b f Dansant Sacha Wild (Kheleyf (USA))
*8027[7]*
**Littledean Jimmy (IRE)** *John O'Shea* a49
9 br g Indian Danehill(IRE) Gold Stamp (Golden Act (USA))
*686[8]*
**Little Eli** *Eric Alston* a69 72
4 b g Green Desert(USA) Princess Ellis (Compton Place)
(1602) 3138[9] 3697[8] 4257[7] 4391[4] (6671) 6938[11] 7534[3] *7698[5]*
**Little Flo** *Brendan Powell* a56 56
3 ch f Midnight Legend Sweet Robinia (IRE) (Bob Back (USA))
1984[8] 2310[9] 2773[12] 3819[4] 4844[4] 6193[5] *6946[3]*
**Little Garcon (USA)** *S Cerulis* a74 56
7 b g Bernstein(USA) Demure (Machiavellian (USA))
*392a[10]*

**Little Gerda (USA)** *Ippo Sameshima* 115
5 rg m Closing Argument(USA) Bijoux Miss (USA) (Buddha (USA))
8152a[14]
**Little Herbert** *John Bridger*
3 ch g Avonbridge Filemot (Largesse)
*1296[7]*
**Little Houidini** *Keith Dalgleish* a21 45
2 b g Arabian Gleam Milli Can Can (Supreme Sound)
4518[4] 4993[6] 5386[6] 6642[4] 6830[8] *7648[10]*
**Little Indian** *J R Jenkins* a67 68
4 b g Sleeping Indian Once Removed (Distant Relative)
*154[3] 583[6] 1385[8]* 1613[5] (1876) 3327[8] 4655[7] *5280[6] 7346[8] 7765[11] 7854[4] 7986[7]*
**Little Lady Katie (IRE)** *K R Burke* 86
2 b f Lord Shanakill(USA) Akarita (IRE) (Akarad (FR))
2824[9] (4973) 5436[5] 6253[3] 6749[7] (7237)
**Little Lord Nelson** *Stuart Williams* a71 57
2 b g Mount Nelson Cactus Curtsey (Royal Applause)
5210[6] 7382[10] *8166[4]*
**Little Mask (FR)** *M Boutin* 73
2 bl f Iron Mask(USA) Little Anchor (FR) (Kendor (FR))
1271a[2] 3029a[6] 3744a[6]
**Little Miss Becky** *Giles Bravery* a3
3 b f Piccolo Boojum (Mujtahid (USA))
5400[7] 5978[11]
**Littlemissblakeney** *Hugo Palmer* a85 95
2 b f Sir Percy Littlemisssunshine (IRE) (Oasis Dream)
1670[2] *2057[3] (2458)* 3353[5] ◆ 3721[7] 5694[7]
**Little Miss Mighty** *Nick Littmoden* a53 49
2 b f Mighty Spia (USA) (Diesis)
3934[3] *4541[5] 8187[3]*
**Littlemissparton** *Ollie Pears* 27
2 b f Sir Percy Miss Prism (Niniski (USA))
7174[9]
**Littlemisspositive** *Martin Smith* a55 39
2 b f Pastoral Pursuits Spirito Libro (USA) (Lear Fan (USA))
*7198[6]* 7512[9]
**Little Palaver** *Clive Cox* a70 74
2 b g Showcasing Little Nymph (Emperor Fountain)
2499[2] 3081[2] 5271[4] 5981[3] 6550[3] *(6887)* 7515[6]
**Little Polyanna** *Alan Berry*
2 b f Indesatchel(IRE) Simianna (Bluegrass Prince (IRE))
5813[8] 6212[13] 7004[10]
**Little Rainbow (FR)** *V Luka Jr* a53 67
3 b c Orpen(USA) Princess Giulia (IRE) (Rock Of Gibraltar (IRE))
1551a[8]
**Little Red Nell (IRE)** *Martin Bosley* a46 26
5 b m Red Clubs(IRE) Naughty Nell (Danehill Dancer (IRE))
*251[10] 592[11] 855[4] 1110[8]* 2069[7] *8010[9]*
**Little Riggs** *Ed Walker* a63 68
2 b c Cape Cross(IRE) Craighall (Dubawi (IRE))
4740[5] ◆ 5309[8] 6203[4] 7156[2] *7544[5]*
**Little Shambles** *Mark Johnston* a79 94
3 ch f Shamardal(USA) Meiosis (USA) (Danzig (USA))
1486[8] (1645) 2745[11] 3122[3] 3305[6] (3844) 4163[6] 4783[8] 5410[12] 5612[2] (5816) 6320[7] 6498[5] 6893[9] *7700[10]*
**Little Sista** *Bryan Smart* 57
2 ch f Equiano(FR) Clifton Dancer (Fraam)
1482[9] 3841[4] 4790[8] 6401[8] 6791[8]
**Live Dangerously** *John Bridger* a68 66
4 b g Zamindar(USA) Desert Lynx (IRE) (Green Desert (USA))
2215[2] 3299[3] 3660[5] 3908[5] 4254[4] 4523[4] 5089[7] (5635) 5889[2] 5996[2] 6406[10] 6475[11] 6821[4] 7057[3] *7368[11]* 7502[6] *7758[14] 8024[9]*
**Live Grace (IRE)** *Mlle B Renk* a67 57
3 ch f Archipenko(USA) Sadinga (IRE) (Sadler's Wells (USA))
3372a[11]
**Lively Little Lady** *Mrs A Corson*
4 b f Beat All(USA) Ever So Lonely (Headin' Up)
1623a[7] 2591a[4] 3496a[6] 4039a[5] 4715a[7] 5971a[5] 6187a[9]
**Livia Drusilla (IRE)** *Brian Ellison*
3 b f Holy Roman Emperor(IRE) Shaiyadima (IRE) (Zamindar (USA))
6862[8] *7652[9]*
**Livia's Dream (IRE)** *Ed Walker* a99 99
5 b m Teofilo(IRE) Brindisi (Dr Fong (USA))
1942[6] 5920[7] 6321[2] 6708[6] *7554[4] (7922)*
**Living Desert** *H-A Pantall* a74 73
4 gr g Oasis Dream Sell Out (Act One)
*722a[4]*
**Living It Large (FR)** *Ed de Giles* a63 67
7 ch g Bertolini(USA) Dilag (IRE) (Almutawakel)
3749[6] 4391[10] 5070[6] 6025[12] 6399[8]
**Living Leader** *Grace Harris* a75 74
5 b g Oasis Dream Royal Jade (Last Tycoon)
*120[3] 293[5] 410[8]* 2021[2] 2806[9] 2963[4] 3427[3] 3971[5] 4153[2] 4415[4] (4673) 4798[7] 5721[3] 6070[4] 6657[4] *7373[8]* 7758[5] (7928)
**Living The Life (IRE)** *Gary Mandella* a107 83
4 b f Footstepsinthesand Colour And Spice (IRE) (Machiavellian (USA))
*287[7] 689[2] (779) 1020[3] (1554) 7608a[10]*
**Lizalia (FR)** *Jo Hughes* a50 38
3 b f Panis(USA) Leave of Absence (FR) (Exit To Nowhere (USA))
*1920[11]* 3372a[14] 3567[10]
**Lizzie Tudor** *Andrew Balding* a79 86
4 ch f Tamayuz Silca Destination (Dubai Destination (USA))
5092[5] 5686[6] 6292[5] 6746[5] *7531[7]*
**Lizzy's Dream** *Robin Bastiman* a31 56
6 ch g Choisir(AUS) Flyingit (USA) (Lear Fan (USA))
1602[8] 2232[9] 4287[9] 6580[8] *7519[8]*

**Llanarmon Lad (IRE)** *Brian Ellison* 103
5 b g Red Clubs(IRE) Blue Crystal (IRE) (Lure (USA))
1724[10] (2351) 2959[2] (3726) 4442[3] 5174[2] 5695[7]
**Llandanwg** *Bryan Smart* a44 51
3 b f Lawman(FR) New Light (Generous (IRE))
2524[7] 4900[4] 5642[3] 6833[2] *7645[5] 8002[4] 8219[5]*
**Llewellyn** *Declan Carroll* a61 70
6 b g Shamardal(USA) Ffestiniog (IRE) (Efisio)
(1375) 1610[2] 2177[4] 2602[13] 3227[4] 3955[8] 4291[9] *6767[8] 7077[11] 7368[8]*
**Llyrical** *Derek Haydn Jones* a59 65
3 b g Firebreak One Of The Family (Alzao (USA))
*1725[9]* 2224[6] 3145[2] 3518[9] 4907[9] 5530[9] *6077[8] 7291[6] 7570[11] 7982[10]*
**Loafer** *Zoe Davison*
4 b g Beat Hollow Cartuccia (IRE) (Doyoun)
*7772[7]*
**Loaves And Fishes** *Clive Cox* 81
2 b f Oasis Dream Miracle Seeker (Rainbow Quest (USA))
(6742)
**Lobster Pot** *Hugo Palmer* a52 71
3 b f Dylan Thomas(IRE) Classical Flair (Distant Music (USA))
(5388) 7172[12] *7918[11]*
**Local Flier** *T G McCourt* a56 87
3 b f Byron Local Fancy (Bahamian Bounty)
6369a[19]
**Local Hero (FR)** *Y Durepaire* 93
3 b f Zamindar(USA) L'Etoile De Mer (FR) (Caerleon (USA))
3289a[12] 4721a[10] 7319a[11]
**Local Hero (GER)** *Steve Gollings* 86
7 b g Lomitas Lolli Pop (GER) (Cagliostro (GER))
2160[3] 2787[4] 3204[5] 4995[5] 5633[9]
**Local Time** *Saeed bin Suroor* a92 98
2 b f Invincible Spirit(IRE) Marie De Medici (USA) (Medicean)
*4320[4] (5037) (6241)* (6926)
**Lochalsh (IRE)** *William Knight* a56 73
3 ch g Duke Of Marmalade(IRE) Kylemore (IRE) (Sadler's Wells (USA))
*1830[7]* 2491[3] 2926[3] *3711[14] 4321[5]* (5277) 5949[6] 6699[3]
**Loch Ma Naire (IRE)** *Ed Dunlop* a73 86
3 gr f Galileo(IRE) Hotelgenie Dot Com (Selkirk (USA))
1508[6] *1898[3]* 2671[2] 3396[3] 4354[3] 4812[3] (5340) 5948[7] 7161[3] 7416[12]
**Lockedoutaheaven (IRE)** *Marco Botti* a70
3 ch g Rock Of Gibraltar(IRE) Second Burst (IRE) (Sadler's Wells (USA))
*218[5] 734[3] 941[2]*
**Lockhart (IRE)** *Mark Johnston* 90
3 b c Acclamation Coeur De La Mer (IRE) (Caerleon (USA))
4022[4] 4446[5] (4713) 5177[5] 5468[2] 5656[10] 6111[5] (6466) 6785[6]
**Lockout (USA)** *Mark Casse* a98 109
5 bb h Limehouse(USA) Non Sibi (USA) (Wild Deputy (USA))
6391a[6] 7325a[6]
**Lockwood** *Saeed bin Suroor* a94 116
5 gr g Invincible Spirit(IRE) Emily Bronte (Machiavellian (USA))
2150[3] 3252[4]
**Locky Taylor (IRE)** *Kevin Ryan* a56 63
3 b g Bushranger(IRE) Hawk Eyed Lady (IRE) (Hawk Wing (USA))
1486[7] 2870[10] 3530[16] 3833[3] 4489[9] 4900[3]
**Locommotion** *Jo Hughes* 48
2 gr g Proclamation(IRE) Miss Madame (IRE) (Cape Cross (IRE))
7413[7]
**Lodovico Il Moro (IRE)** *L Riccardi* 104
4 b c Shamardal(USA) Kykuit (IRE) (Green Desert (USA))
2191a[4] 3047a[10] 7617a[7]
**Logans Lad (IRE)** *Daniel Mark Loughnane* a72 50
4 b g Baltic King Lulu Island (Zafonic (USA))
2488[6] 3178[2] 3848[13] (4314) *5602[5] (5897)* 6674[13] *6843[3] 7252[2] 7621[4] 7950[7] 8043[9] 8195[10]*
**Logorrheic** *Ralph Beckett* a78
2 b g Thewayyouare(USA) Thousandkissesdeep (IRE) (Night Shift (USA))
*7752[7] (7941)*
**Logotype (JPN)** *Tsuyoshi Tanaka* 120
4 bb c Lohengrin(JPN) Stereotype (JPN) (Sunday Silence (USA))
1181a[6]
**Lola Beaux** *Mrs John Harrington* a87 97
2 b f Equiano(FR) Polly Perkins (IRE) (Pivotal)
6798a[2]
**Lola Montez (IRE)** *David Lanigan* a65 47
3 b f Duke Of Marmalade(IRE) Fille De Joie (IRE) (Royal Academy (USA))
*2649[6]* 3141[10] 3750[10] *4734[4] 5283[4] 6015[3] 6636[3] (7115) 7426[11] 7869[7]*
**Lolita** *J R Jenkins* 65
2 ch f Sir Percy Miss Ippolita (Diktat)
4980[3] 5667[7] 6435[9]
**Loma Mor** *Alan McCabe* a64 48
3 b f Auction House(USA) Dancing Loma (FR) (Danehill Dancer (IRE))
*216[6] 315[8] 786[12]* 1642[10] 4595[5] *5574[10]*
**Lomond Lassie** *Keith Dalgleish* 57
3 ch f Sakhee's Secret Numanthia (IRE) (Barathea (IRE))
2387[12] 2517[4] 3054[4] 3360[8] 3625[6] 4195[8]
**Londonia** *Paul Cole* a61
2 gr g Paco Boy(IRE) Snowdrops (Gulch (USA))
*6102[6] 6604[7] 6852[5]*
**London Life (IRE)** *Tom Dascombe* 79
2 b f Approve(IRE) Bellacoola (GER) (Lomitas)
1276[7] 1528[4] 2089[2] (2641) 3353[16] 4150[3] 5405a[9] 5921[3]
**London Mayor (IRE)** *Roger Varian* a57 46
2 b c High Chaparral(IRE) Sri Kandi (Pivotal)
*6102[7]* 7382[13] *7778[8]*

**Lonely Ranger (USA)** *Amy Weaver* a58
2 b c US Ranger(USA) Gypsy Swap (USA) (Woodman (USA))
*5555[10] 6270[10] 7076[6] 7396[12]*
**Lone Ranger (FR)** *Y Gourraud* 94
6 b h Muhtathir L'Etoile De Mer (FR) (Caerleon (USA))
3172a[5]
**Lone Star Boy (IRE)** *Tom Dascombe* 65
2 b c Starspangledbanner(AUS) Pascali (Compton Place)
6935[6] 7234[7]
**Lone Warrior (IRE)** *David Evans* a81 97
3 b g Oratorio(IRE) Warrior Wings (Indian Ridge)
*624[7] 975[5]*
**Long Awaited (IRE)** *David Barron* 97
6 b g Pivotal Desertion (IRE) (Danehill (USA))
1944[4] 2283[7] 2786[15] 5419[2] 5754 6131[2] 6467[8] 6745[4] 7080[6] 7280[5]
**Long Cross** *John Gosden* 98
3 b c Cape Cross(IRE) Majestic Roi (USA) (Street Cry (IRE))
4435[4] ◆ (5347) 6257[8]
**Longfield Lad (IRE)** *John J Walsh* a75 66
4 b g Amadeus Wolf Michaels Pride (IRE) (Distant View (USA))
4805a[6]
**Longina (GER)** *P Schiergen* 107
3 ch f Monsun(GER) Love Academy (GER) (Medicean)
(3046a) 4955a[3] 6384a[2] 6914a[4]
**Long John (AUS)** *Charlie Appleby* a115 115
4 b g Street Cry(IRE) Hosiery (AUS) (Night Shift (USA))
*(594a) 1178a[6]* 4180[3] 4682[7]
**Long Journey Home (IRE)** *Daniel William O'Sullivan* a91 92
6 b g Dansili Quest For Eternity (IRE) (Sadler's Wells (USA))
2091[6] 4379a[8]
**Longshadow** *Jason Ward* 83
4 ch g Monsun(GER) La Felicita (Shareef Dancer (USA))
*1003[8]* 1197[12] 1485[2] 1605[3] (3532) (3661) 4289[4] (4662) 4777[3] 5564[3] 5890[2] 6514[9]
**Longside** *Charles Hills* a73 48
2 b c Oasis Dream Hypoteneuse (IRE) (Sadler's Wells (USA))
4864[8] *6852[2] 7361[3] 7551[5]*
**Long View (IRE)** *Sir Michael Stoute* a80 86
3 b f Galileo(IRE) Highland Gift (IRE) (Generous (IRE))
4413[3] ◆ *4966[3]* (5976) 6708[13]
**Lookbeforeyouleap** *David O'Meara* a75 69
4 ch f Teofilo(IRE) One Giant Leap (IRE) (Pivotal)
*150[4]*
**Look Here's Al** *Andrew Hollinshead* a72 66
3 gr g Alhaarth(IRE) Look Here's Dee (Dansili)
1940[5] 2429[14] 3225[3] 3650[11] 4411[8] 5080[8] 7213[17] *7621[10] 7697[9] 7907[8] 8043[6] 8259[4]*
**Looking** *P Cottier* a70 75
5 ch h Gold Away(IRE) Gold Round (IRE) (Caerleon (USA))
*752a[2]*
**Looking Good** *David Brown* 70
2 b f Makfi Primo Heights (Primo Valentino (IRE))
2493[5] 2744[3] 5493[4] 5929[4] 6550[2] 7018[4]
**Look On By** *Ruth Carr* a52 62
4 gr g Byron Where's Carol (Anfield I)
*1227[6]* 1673[12] 2215[7] 2426[10] (3105) 3828[6] 4197[6] 4730[9] *6407[10]* 6543[9] 6833[7] *7291[5] 7646[7]*
**Loom Of Life (IRE)** *Richard Fahey* 71
2 b g Rip Van Winkle(IRE) Feeling Wonderful (IRE) (Fruits Of Love (USA))
3701[4] ◆ 4424[9] 5886[6]
**Loose Cannon (FR)** *D Windrif* a66 87
2 b f Palace Episode(USA) Electricity (Elusive City (USA))
2976a[8] (3744a) 4603a[6] 5119a[9] 5405a[6] *5844a[9]* 6991a[7]
**Loot** *Bill Turner* 56
3 b g Bahamian Bounty Amira (Efisio)
2846[5] 3469[6] 3816[3] *4324[9]* 7337[9]
**Lopito De Vega (IRE)** *James Given* 48
2 ch g Lope De Vega(IRE) Athenian Way (IRE) (Barathea (IRE))
4409[7] 4787[6] 5397[6]
**Loraine** *Jamie Osborne* a75 41
4 b f Sir Percy Emirates First (IRE) (In The Wings)
*5280[4]* 5908[8] *6243[4] 6635[2] (7907) 8030[3] 8168[10]*
**Lord Aeryn (IRE)** *Richard Fahey* 94
7 b g Antonius Pius(USA) White Paper (IRE) (Marignan (USA))
1078a[5] 1399[3] 1733[3] 2351[10] 2699[9]
**Lord Avonbrook** *Andrew Crook* 46
4 b g Avonbridge Miss Brook (The West (USA))
7248[14]
**Lord Ben Stack (IRE)** *K R Burke* 91
2 b c Dylan Thomas(IRE) Beringold (Bering)
4424[4] (6056) 6750[5]
**Lord Brantwood** *Mick Channon* a65 67
3 b g Sir Percy Diddymu (IRE) (Revoque (IRE))
*1216[7]* 1491[9] 1947[4] 2385[7] 2948[4] 3281[8]
**Lord Buffhead** *Richard Guest* a54 64
5 br g Iceman Royal Pardon (Royal Applause)
*58[10] 100[5] 274[11] (556) 692[3] 937[3] 1270[5]* 1378[6] *1804[4] 1887[7]* 2232[5] 2296[6] 2473[8] 2514[7] 2724[9] 2831[8] 4287[7] (5237) 5375[5] 5635[6] 6014[2] 6120[10] 6409[9] (7056) 7221[9] 7502[12] 7644[2] 7670[14]
**Lord Clyde** *Richard Fahey* a58 74
3 ch g Sakhee's Secret Sabina (Prince Sabo)
1671[7] 2524[6] *2932[3]*
**Lord Emery (GER)** *M Figge* a75 66
6 b h Mamool(IRE) Latley (GER) (Sillery (USA))
1828a[8]
**Lord Empire (IRE)** *David Simcock* a73 65
3 b g Invincible Spirit(IRE) Miss Ghena (USA) (Gone West (USA))
4407[5] *5039[8] 5606[2]*

**Lord Franklin** *Eric Alston* a59 82
5 ch g Iceman Zell (IRE) (Lend A Hand)
1356[4] 1598[6] 1970[4] (2509) 2730[2] 2912[4] 4058[4] 4359[2] 4793[S] 5855[2] 6166[11] (6578) (7042) 7334[4]

**Lord Golan** *Ann Stokell* a60 53
6 b g Singspiel(IRE) Lady Golan (IRE) (Golan (IRE))
*68[7]*

**Lord Of The Dance (IRE)** *Michael Mullineaux* a66 83
8 ch g Indian Haven Maine Lobster (USA) (Woodman (USA))
*977[7]* 2117[8] 2699[7] 3573[14] 4650[12] 4963[5] 5810[6] *6414[9] 6857[4] 7288[9]*

**Lord Of The Land (IRE)** *A Fabre* 102
3 b c Shamardal(USA) Lady Vettori (Vettori (IRE))
7559a[11]

**Lord Of The Nile (IRE)** *David O'Meara* a60 81
3 ch c Galileo(IRE) Magic Carpet (IRE) (Danehill (USA))
1542[2] (2053) 2363[3] 3002[6] 7282[13]

**Lord Of The Rock (IRE)** *Michael Dods* 79
2 b c Rock Of Gibraltar(IRE) La Sylphide (Rudimentary (USA))
6509[3]

**Lord Ofthe Shadows (IRE)** *Richard Hannon* a81 89
5 ch g Kyllachy Golden Shadow (IRE) (Selkirk (USA))
2500[5] *2922[5]* 3314[2] 3759[2] 4148[7] 4761[10] 5686[5] 6304[7] *7530[7] 8204[6]*

**Lord Of The Storm** *Bill Turner* a63 57
6 b g Avonbridge Just Run (IRE) (Runnett)
*4326[4]* 5291[2] *5558[8] 6267[10] 7976[4] (8004) 8123[3]*

**Lord Of Words (IRE)** *Brian Ellison* 58
2 b g Thousand Words Dame Laura (IRE) (Royal Academy (USA))
3481[7] 3945[4] 4659[4] 5241[3] 5645[7] 7245[3]

**Lord Sinclair (USA)** *S Woods* a101 102
5 gr g Mizzen Mast(USA) Great Connection (USA) (Dayjur (USA))
7898a[7]

**Lord Van Percy** *Andrew Balding* a95 107
4 b g Sir Percy Enforce (USA) (Kalanisi (IRE))
*(1071)* 1973[5] (2342) ◆ 3717[9] (4759) 5693[2] ◆ 7126a[5]

**Lorenza Chope (FR)** *C Boutin* 51
2 bb f Deportivo Amour Parfait (IRE) (Spinning World (USA))
1271a[9]

**Loretta Martin** *Mick Channon* 63
2 gr f Sixties Icon Easy Red (IRE) (Hunting Lion (IRE))
(1872) 3448[14]

**L'Orfeo** *Saeed bin Suroor* a68 89
4 ch g Singspiel(IRE) Limeira (Bertolini (USA))
5251[5] 6466[5]

**Lorimer's Lot (IRE)** *Mark Walford* 74
3 ch f Camacho Alwiyda (USA) (Trempolino (USA))
1543[3] (1737) 2015[14] 2727[7] 3399[10] 4114[14] 4315[7] 6671[12] 7179[14]

**Los Cerritos (SWI)** *K Demme* 104
2 ch c Dr Fong(USA) La Coruna (SWI) (Arazi (USA))
(7726a)

**Lostinparadise** *Matthieu Palussiere* 81
2 ch f Exceed And Excel(AUS) Paradise Way (Elusive Quality (USA))
3027a[5] 3806a[7]

**Lost In Paris (IRE)** *Tony Coyle* a63 84
8 b g Elusive City(USA) Brazilia (Forzando)
*834[8] 1224[4] 1244[7]* 1447[13] 2056[10] 3948[11] 4752[9] 5819[8] 6671[16]

**Lostintheclouds** *Mike Murphy* a57 68
3 b f Firebreak Day By Day (Kyllachy)
*5007[12]* 5862[3] *6482[5]* 7160[9]

**Lostock Hall (IRE)** *K R Burke* 84
2 b c Lord Shanakill(USA) Cannikin (IRE) (Lahib (USA))
4659[6] 5760[3] (6509) 7404[7]

**Lotara** *Michael Appleby* 50
2 b f Monsieur Bond(IRE) Cheviot Heights (Intikhab (USA))
1482[5]

**Lothair (IRE)** *Alan Swinbank* a41 78
5 b g Holy Roman Emperor(IRE) Crafty Example (USA) (Crafty Prospector (USA))
1446[9] 1710[6] 1966[3] (2167) 2522[6] 2677[5] 4194[3] 4961[9] 5470[4] 5632[4] 7179[8]

**Lottie Dod (IRE)** *Charles O'Brien* a85 88
4 b f Invincible Spirit(IRE) Sharapova (IRE) (Elusive Quality (USA))
1824a[9] 2042a[9]

**Lotus Garden (FR)** *F Chappet* a85 68
3 gr c Dark Angel(IRE) Lili St Cyr (IRE) (Rock Of Gibraltar (IRE))
*390a[2] 553a[7]*

**Louarn (IRE)** *J Heloury* a66 82
3 b f Elusive City(USA) Lil's Jessy (IRE) (Kris)
*237a[10]*

**Loucal** *Noel Quinlan* a41 64
4 b g Lucky Story(USA) Penny Ha'Penny (Bishop Of Cashel)
*1302[12]* 1876[3] 2864[6] 3155[4] 3678[5] 4592[6]

**Loud** *Amy Weaver* a78 74
4 ch g Dutch Art Applauding (IRE) (Royal Applause)
*757[6] (929) 1031[6] 1286[6] 1499[4] 1744[5]* 2293[6] 3180[9] 3660[2] 3910[6] 5125[5] *6240[5]* 6562[5] 7339[6] 7647[2]

**Loudly (USA)** *Jeremy Noseda* a53
2 gr f War Front(USA) T.K.O. Lady (USA) (Two Punch (USA))
*6660[8]*

**Louie De Palma** *Clive Cox* 101
2 b c Pastoral Pursuits Tahirah (Green Desert (USA))
(3536) (4143) 4822[2]

**Louis The Pious** *David O'Meara* 114
6 bb g Holy Roman Emperor(IRE) Whole Grain (Polish Precedent (USA))
1484[7] 1719[2] 2145[21] (3420) 4200[7] 4648[11] 6124[7] (6533) 6920[3] 7444[5]

**Louis Vee (IRE)** *Roy Brotherton* a64 60
6 bb g Captain Rio Mrs Evans (IRE) (College Chapel)
*18[7] 201[6] (502) (610)* ◆ *(693)* ◆ 2174[10] 3520[8] 3939[6] (5780) *6273[6] 7900[9] 7997[5]* 8284[6]

**Louisville Lip (IRE)** *Patrick J Flynn* a70 77
7 b g Orpen(USA) Former Drama (USA) (Dynaformer (USA))
4951a[7]

**Loulou Vuitton** *Steph Hollinshead* a61 43
4 ch f Needwood Blade Shepherds Warning (IRE) (Vettori (IRE))
*63[2] 176[5] 475[6] 570[5]*

**Loumarin (IRE)** *Martyn Meade* a71 65
2 b f Bushranger(IRE) Masela (IRE) (Medicean)
3557[4] ◆ (4087) *4576[3] (6016)*

**Loussia (FR)** *Yannick Fouin* a86 98
5 b m Footstepsinthesand Obsidianne (FR) (Machiavellian (USA))
5369a[8]

**Louvain (FR)** *P Demercastel* a84 92
5 b g Vatori(FR) Loupy Glitters (FR) (Loup Solitaire (USA))
*6992a[8]*

**Louve Indienne (FR)** *N Bertran De Balanda* 54
2 b f Early March Indiena (Indian Ridge)
5119a[11]

**Lovable (CAN)** *J-C Rouget*
3 b f Survivalist(USA) Zawaahy (USA) (El Gran Senor (USA))
*194a[9]*

**Lovato (GER)** *P Schiergen* 86
2 b c Lauro(GER) Larella (GER) (Anabaa (USA))
7726a[6]

**Love D'Oro (USA)** *Mark Johnston*
3 b f Medaglia d'Oro(USA) Unbridled Belle (USA) (Broken Vow (USA))
2613[8]

**Love Excel** *Charles Hills* a84
4 b c Exceed And Excel(AUS) Navajo Love Song (IRE) (Dancing Brave (USA))
*1234[4] 1630[3]*

**Love Happens** *Ferdinand J Leve* 101
5 b m Motivator Lavorna (GER) (Acatenango (GER))
6807a[2] 7616a[8]

**Love Island** *Richard Whitaker* a98 103
5 b m Acclamation Sally Traffic (River Falls)
1734[12] (2361) 2757[3] 3203[3] 3666[9] 5918[4] 6327[11] 6598[5] 7408[17]

**Lovelocks (IRE)** *Charles Hills* a7 76
3 b f High Chaparral(IRE) Civility Cat (USA) (Tale Of The Cat (USA))
1509[6] 2077[6] 6092[3] 6461[8] *7366[12]*

**Lovely Jee Pee (IRE)** *Mme Pia Brandt* a56 60
4 ch f Peintre Celebre(USA) Lovely Sea (FR) (Bering)
935a[5]

**Lovely Memory (IRE)** *Saeed bin Suroor* a78 45
2 b f Shamardal(USA) Folk Opera (IRE) (Singspiel (IRE))
6435[8] *7399[2]*

**Lovely Surprise (IRE)** *Ismail Mohammed* a67
2 ch f Shamardal(USA) Dubai Surprise (IRE) (King's Best (USA))
*7756[4]*

**Love Marmalade (IRE)** *Alistair Whillans* a70 88
4 ch g Duke Of Marmalade(IRE) Green Castle (IRE) (Indian Ridge)
1562[5] (2216) 3004[6] 3457[6] 4160[8] 4704[3] 5144[6] 5639[8] 6536[9]

**Lover Man (IRE)** *Keith Dalgleish* a45 104
5 b g Lawman(FR) Seltitude (IRE) (Fairy King (USA))
2353[9] 3666[13]

**Love's Secret** *Marco Gasparini* 86
3 b f Pivotal L'Affaire Monique (Machiavellian (USA))
6807a[7]

**Love Tangle (IRE)** *Anthony Middleton* a41 75
3 b g Azamour(IRE) Dragnet (IRE) (Rainbow Quest (USA))
1494[3] 1983[6] 2719[4] 3110[8] 4951a[10] *8163[6]*

**Loving Home** *John Gosden* a76 90
3 b c Shamardal(USA) Fallen In Love (Galileo (IRE))
1353[3] 1730[3] 2481[3] 3432[2] 4332[2] *(5282)* 6292[3]

**Loving Spirit** *James Toller* a103 106
6 b g Azamour(IRE) Lolla's Spirit (IRE) (Montjeu (IRE))
*1578[5]* 2145[23] 3356[19] 4200[10] *6140[7]* 6522[5] (7022) 7168[7] 7490[6]

**Loving Your Work** *George Baker* a69 74
3 b g Royal Applause Time Crystal (IRE) (Sadler's Wells (USA))
*1898[2]* 2225[3] (3146) 3419[8] 4591[4] 6091[5] 7162[5] *8037[6] 8246[3]*

**Low Cut Affair (IRE)** *Gay Kelleway* a72 72
2 b f Fast Company(IRE) Sunlit Silence (IRE) (Green Desert (USA))
*1169[4]* (1488) 1670[6] 1982[5] 4422[3] 4815[2] ◆ *5043[3] (5254)* 5409[5] *(5507) 7780[3] 7890[6]*

**Lowengang** *Carmen Bocskai* a70 65
9 ch g Lomitas Euro Empire (USA) (Bartok (IRE))
*752a[4]*

**Lowenthal (GER)** *S Smrczek* a58 80
4 bb c Mamool(IRE) Linara (GER) (Windwurf (GER))
2192a[11]

**Lower East Side** *S Wattel* a94 77
4 ch g Teofilo(IRE) Uryale (FR) (Kendor (FR))
3373a[5] *5964a[2]*

**Lower Lake (FR)** *Mark Brisbourne* a42 62
4 b g Medecis Black Dalhia (FR) (Sanglamore (USA))
*1452[7] 1816[5]*

**Low Key (IRE)** *David Pipe* a66 89
7 b g Pentire La Capilla (Machiavellian (USA))
*(278)* (7452)

**Lowther** *Lee Carter* a97 82
9 b g Beat All(USA) Ever So Lonely (Headin' Up)
*3448 5338 62510*

**Loyal N Trusted** *Karen Tutty* a67 57
6 b g Motivator Baby Don't Cry (USA) (Street Cry (IRE))
1446[14] *1800[6]*

**Loyal Royal (IRE)** *Milton Bradley* a66 88
11 b g King Charlemagne(USA) Supportive (IRE) (Nashamaa)
*296[8] 466[4]*

**Loyalty** *Derek Shaw* a91 45
7 b g Medicean Ecoutila (USA) (Rahy (USA))
*235[8] 344[7] 887[13] 1071[8] 1578[10] 2062[5] 2462[2] 2922[10] 7820[7]* 7955[11] 8080[6] 8257[9]

**Luannan (IRE)** *J-C Rouget* a84 105
3 b c Zamindar(USA) Laxlova (FR) (Linamix (FR)) (4930a)

**Lucarelli (GER)** *Ferdinand J Leve* 104
8 b h High Chaparral(IRE) Lavorna (GER) (Acatenango (GER))
2229a[5]

**Lucia Valentina (NZ)** *Kris Lees* 113
4 br f Savabeel(AUS) Staryn Glenn (NZ) (Montjeu (IRE))
7301a[3] 7653a[13]

**Lucida (IRE)** *J S Bolger* 111
2 b f Shamardal(USA) Lura (USA) (Street Cry (IRE))
5734a[2] 6372a[2] (6709) 7240[5]

**Lucifers Shadow (IRE)** *Mrs C Gilbert* a62 50
5 gr g Dark Angel(IRE) Marianne's Dancer (IRE) (Bold Fact (USA))
1625a[6] 4039a[2] 4717a[4] 5971a[2] 6187a[2]

**Lucilla** *Michael Squance* a60 48
4 b f Holy Roman Emperor(IRE) Lady In Waiting (Kylian (USA))
*1631[3]*

**Lucilla Aurelius (IRE)** *Tony Coyle* a7 42
2 b f Holy Roman Emperor(IRE) Spiritual Air (Royal Applause)
2359[5] 3529[4] 3945[10] *5099[7]* 5372[3] 5767[5]

**Lucilo (FR)** *N Leenders* 56
3 b g Lauro(GER) Lucia (FR) (April Night (FR))
2003a[6]

**Luck Of The Game (USA)** *David Simcock* a76 84
3 b c Thewayyouare(USA) Luck Be A Lady (IRE) (Alhaarth (IRE))
*(1817)* 2273[2] 2506[3] 3675[5]

**Luck Of The Kitten (USA)** *Wesley A Ward* 108
2 ch c Kitten's Joy(USA) Anura (IRE) (Giant's Causeway (USA))
7590a[2]

**Luckster** *David Evans* a59 60
4 b g Lucky Story(USA) Bisaat (USA) (Bahri (USA))
*104[4] 292[6] 361[6] 656[8]*

**Lucky Beggar (IRE)** *Charles Hills* 110
4 gr c Verglas(IRE) Lucky Clio (IRE) (Key Of Luck (USA))
(1421) 2076[5] 2820a[5] 4215[8]

**Lucky Bridle (IRE)** *W P Mullins* 98
5 b g Dylan Thomas(IRE) Auction Room (USA) (Chester House (USA))
3717[12] 4771a[18]

**Lucky Clover** *Malcolm Saunders* 46
3 ch f Lucky Story(USA) Willisa (Polar Falcon (USA))
*1147[6]* 1569[7] 2667[4] 3938[3] 5000[8] 6090[3] 6816[3]

**Lucky Dan (IRE)** *Paul Green* a66 69
8 b g Danetime(IRE) Katherine Gorge (USA) (Hansel (USA))
*432[7] 677[7] 913[7] 938[6]* 1584[3] 2167[6] 3138[12] 4394[P] 4997[8]

**Lucky Di** *Peter Hedger* a76 75
4 br f Araafa(IRE) Lucky Date (IRE) (Halling (USA))
*52[6] 2884[13]* 3422[3] *3854[2]* 4788[4] 5355[3] 5624[2] 6006[6] *6680[5] (7202) 7758[10]*

**Lucky Diva** *Bill Turner* a52 63
7 ch m Lucky Story(USA) Cosmic Countess (IRE) (Lahib (USA))
3209[6] (3780) 4107[2] 4769[2] 5909[6] *6486[6]*

**Lucky Dottie** *Pat Phelan* a48 40
3 bb f Lucky Story(USA) Auntie Dot Com (Tagula (IRE))
*(738) 1029[4] 1235[7]* 2416[10] 7517[10]

**Lucky Jim** *Chris Wall* a75 71
3 b g Lucky Story(USA) Lateralle (IRE) (Unfuwain (USA))
1401[10] *1898[4]* 2893[5] *(6564)* 6981[6]

**Lucky Kristale** *George Margarson* 110
3 b f Lucky Story(USA) Pikaboo (Pivotal)
1976[16] 3418[11] 6254[8]

**Lucky Leopardsfoot** *John Spearing* a54
4 b c Echo Of Light Je Suis Belle (Efisio)
*558[5]* ◆

**Lucky Leyf** *Gary Moore* a66
2 b f Kheleyf(USA) Lucky Dice (Perugino (USA))
*7920[9] 8092[2] 8318[4]*

**Lucky Lion** *Andreas Lowe* 117
3 b c High Chaparral(IRE) Lips Arrow (GER) (Big Shuffle (USA))
(1781a) (2377a) 4007a[2] (4720a) 6180a[7]

**Lucky Lodge** *Mel Brittain* a71 70
4 b g Lucky Story(USA) Melandre (Lujain (USA))
1440[4] 1610[3] 2171[7] 3149[3] 4421[4] 4632[10] 5089[3] 6213[10] (7179) *(7954)*

**Lucky Look (FR)** *D Smaga* 107
4 b f Teofilo(IRE) Victoria College (FR) (Rock Of Gibraltar (IRE))
4722a[5]

**Lucky Mark (IRE)** *John Balding* a70 60
5 b g Moss Vale(IRE) Vracca (Vettori (IRE))
*58[5] 121[5] 449[5] (692) 1001[5] 1282[2]* 2127[6] 4287[2] ◆ 4994[3] *5574[3] 6273[3]* 6561[2] 7111[9] 7826[2] (7915) 8210[6]

**Lucky Mellor** *Barry Murtagh* a34 21
7 b g Lucky Story(USA) Lady Natilda (First Trump)
*58[9] 466[7] 556[8]*

**Lucky Mountain** *Scott Dixon* a67 35
4 ch c Mount Nelson Wild Clover (Lomitas)
*269[5] 661[11]*

**Lucky Nine (IRE)** *C Fownes* a109 121
7 b g Dubawi(IRE) Birjand (Green Desert (USA))
(2378a) 7897a[5] 8152a[11]

**Lucky North** *Mel Brittain* 30
4 ch g Lucky Story(USA) Eurolink Cafe (Grand Lodge (USA))
6494[6] 7642[7]

**Lucky Player (USA)** *Steven Asmussen* a101
2 b c Lookin At Lucky(USA) Janetstickettocats (USA) (Storm Cat (USA))
*7610a[8]*

**Lucky Royale** *Jeremy Gask* a56 53
6 b m Lucky Story(USA) Bella Bertolini (Bertolini (USA))
*6631[4] 7191[7] 7864[9] 8200[2]*

**Lucky Serena (IRE)** *Agostino Affe'* 101
4 b f Bertolini(USA) Singora Lady (IRE) (Intikhab (USA))
7480a[9] 7616a[5]

**Lucky Speed (IRE)** *P Schiergen* 113
4 b c Silvano(GER) Lysuna (GER) (Monsun (GER))
2815a[3] 3770a[4] 5231a[3] 6180a[9]

**Lucky Stars** *Gay Kelleway* a16 7
4 ch f Lucky Story(USA) Cosmic Countess (IRE) (Lahib (USA))
*2211[9]* 4590[7]

**Lucky Surprise** *Jeremy Gask* a52 58
3 b f Lucky Story(USA) Bella Bertolini (Bertolini (USA))
2505[7] 3149[16] *4056[10]* 4564[6] 5907[4] 6399[2] *6631[2] 7191[10]* 7644[10] *7887[11] 8133[4]*

**Lucky Team (FR)** *J Boisnard* a73 56
2 gr c Namid Kestria (IRE) (Keltos (FR))
*8276a[3]*

**Lucky Times** *Mel Brittain* a70 66
3 b f Lucky Story(USA) Paradise Eve (Bahamian Bounty)
1902[5] 2420[3] 2551[2] 2802[3] 4019[13] (5389) 5715[6] 7510[9]

**Lucky Visione** *Gay Kelleway* a71 47
3 b g Lucky Story(USA) Maid For Running (Namaqualand (USA))
1635[5] 2120[5] 2719[6] 3683[6] 5108[6]

**Lucky Windmill** *Tracy Waggott* 41
7 b g Lucky Story(USA) Windmill Princess (Gorytus (USA))
4454[8] 4792[9]

**Luctor Emergo (IRE)** *Keith Dalgleish* a71 42
5 b g Amadeus Wolf Batilde (IRE) (Victory Piper (USA))
*(361) 476[4]*

**Lucy Bee** *Michael Appleby* a59 65
4 ch f Haafhd Procession (Zafonic (USA))
*199[3]*

**Lucy The Painter (IRE)** *Peter Makin* a64 55
2 b f Excellent Art Royal Bounty (IRE) (Generous (IRE))
6517[14] 6701[7] *7345[5] (7683)*

**Luhaif** *Julia Feilden* a103 96
4 b g Cape Cross(IRE) Hot And Spicy (Grand Lodge (USA))
*235[2]* ◆ *465[3] 625[7] 1070[8]* 1351[12] 2154[7] 3306[2] (3629) 4148[6] 5031[5] 5319[6] 6285[8] 6498[4]

**Luimneach Abu (IRE)** *J P Broderick* a54 51
6 b g High Chaparral(IRE) Mamlakah (IRE) (Unfuwain (USA))
*7962a[5]*

**Lui Rei (ITY)** *Fawzi Abdulla Nass* a95 107
8 b g Reinaldo(FR) My Luigia (IRE) (High Estate)
*109a[8] 304a[8]*

**Luisa Tetrazzini (IRE)** *Bernard Llewellyn* a21 17
8 b m Hawk Wing(USA) Break Of Day (USA) (Favorite Trick (USA))
*8123[12] 8291[9]*

**Luis Vaz De Torres (IRE)** *Richard Fahey* a73
2 b c Tagula(IRE) Tekhania (IRE) (Dalakhani (IRE))
*(8227)*

**Lujeanie** *Peter Crate* a79 62
8 br g Lujain(USA) Ivory's Joy (Tina's Pet)
*(141) 233[6] 535[4] 714[6] 1388[4] (1448) 1893[5]* 4553[6] 5124[8] 5423[2] *6236[6]* 6815[4] *7202[5]* 7776[8] 8081[6] 8319[3]

**Lulani (IRE)** *Harry Dunlop* 79
2 b f Royal Applause Louverissa (IRE) (Verglas (IRE))
6066[5] (7450)

**Lulu The Zulu (IRE)** *Michael Appleby* 103
6 ch m Danroad(AUS) Timbervati (USA) (Woodman (USA))
1537[5] 2024[5] 2448[2] (3220) ◆ 4181[2] 4783[2] 6129[7] 6891[2] (7444) 7715[2]

**Lumpaz (FR)** *F Foresi* a75 80
7 b g Okawango(USA) Laita (IRE) (Kenmare (FR))
*584a[10]*

**Luna Mission (IRE)** *Marco Botti* a74 67
2 b f Acclamation Bowness (Efisio)
*6032[3]* 6434[3] *(7062)*

**Luna Moon** *Jeremy Noseda* 72
2 b f Equiano(FR) Luanshya (First Trump)
(5344)

**Lunar Deity** *Stuart Williams* a89 78
5 b g Medicean Luminda (IRE) (Danehill (USA))
1351[8] 1948[12] 3036[5] 4866[11] 5346[7] 5758[3] 6285[7] *(6885)*

**Lunarian** *Mick Channon* 68
3 ch f Bahamian Bounty One Giant Leap (IRE) (Pivotal)
2489[3] 2946[9] 3801[7] (5034) (5316) 5715[10]

**Lunar Knot** *Alan McCabe* a51 54
2 b f Stimulation(IRE) Moon Bird (Primo Dominie)
*1363[8]* 1633[3] 2128[7] *2903[5] 6413[7]* 6996[8] *7683[9]*

**Lunar Spirit** *Ralph Beckett* a70 78
3 b f Invincible Spirit(IRE) Kitty O'Shea (Sadler's Wells (USA))
1661[2] (2523) 5768[3] 7341[3]

**Lunasea (IRE)** *Luca Cumani* a85 73
3 b c Sea The Stars(IRE) Musical Treat (IRE) (Royal Academy (USA))
7418$^{4}$ *(7841)*
**Luna Sunrise** *Timothy Jarvis* a50 59
3 b f Virtual Moon Crystal (Fasliyev (USA))
3755$^{7}$ 4329$^{14}$ *7853$^{8}$ 7982$^{13}$*
**Lunesdale Buddy** *Alan Berry* 42
3 b c Indesatchel(IRE) Darling Buds (Reel Buddy (USA))
2138$^{4}$ 2551$^{4}$ 3486$^{9}$ 4974$^{8}$ 5819$^{13}$ 7010$^{7}$
**Lunette (IRE)** *Ralph Beckett* a77 75
4 b f Teofilo(IRE) Princess Luna (GER) (Grand Lodge (USA))
3476$^{5}$ 4408$^{4}$ 5629$^{8}$
**Lungarno Palace (USA)** *John Gallagher* a83 92
3 b g Henrythenavigator(USA) Good Time Sally (USA) (Forestry (USA))
*(696)* 1979$^{5}$ (3428) 4698$^{5}$ 6786$^{3}$ ◆ 7125$^{4}$ 7562$^{3}$
**Lupin Violet (IRE)** *J E Pease* 80
3 gr f Dalakhani(IRE) Fearless Spirit (USA) (Spinning World (USA))
2411a$^{2}$
**Lupo D'Oro (IRE)** *John Best* a69 79
5 b g Amadeus Wolf Vital Laser (USA) (Seeking The Gold (USA))
1490$^{5}$ 2147$^{10}$ 2629$^{7}$ 3246$^{8}$ 4128$^{8}$ 4609$^{7}$ *6021$^{6}$*
6872$^{11}$ 7535$^{8}$ *7758$^{13}$ 8210$^{8}$*
**Lu's Buddy (GR)** *Amanda Perrett* a78 76
3 b g Reel Buddy(USA) Papality (Giant's Causeway (USA))
3248$^{10}$ 4984$^{3}$ 5504$^{7}$ *7831$^{3}$ 8042$^{4}$*
**Luso's Way (IRE)** *John Joseph Hanlon* a56 51
6 b m Stowaway Coccinella (IRE) (Luso)
*6768$^{4}$*
**Lustrous** *Richard Hannon* 106
3 b f Champs Elysees Tamzin (Hernando (FR))
1868$^{5}$ (2316) 3376$^{2}$ 4461a$^{7}$ 4894$^{5}$ 5610$^{4}$
**Lutindi (GER)** *P Schiergen* 94
3 ch f Adlerflug(GER) Lasira (GER) (Vettori (IRE))
4064a$^{5}$ 6162a$^{6}$ 7482a$^{8}$
**Lutine Charlie (IRE)** *Pat Eddery* a66 60
7 b g Kheleyf(USA) Silvery Halo (USA) (Silver Ghost (USA))
*30$^{2}$ 170$^{6}$ 353$^{4}$ 446$^{6}$ 562$^{2}$ 740$^{4}$ 916$^{3}$ 963$^{2}$*
1668$^{8}$ *1771$^{7}$* 2864$^{2}$ 3075$^{7}$ 3562$^{8}$ 3825$^{5}$ 5897$^{6}$
(6396)
**Luvlylynnthomas** *Micky Hammond* 29
2 gr f Equiano(FR) Dansa Queen (Dansili)
1879$^{8}$ 2725$^{8}$ 7329$^{13}$
**Luv U** *Ed Dunlop* a52 48
2 b f Royal Applause Love Roi (ITY) (Roi Danzig (USA))
6066$^{11}$ 6462$^{6}$ 6754$^{8}$ *7740$^{6}$ 8121$^{4}$*
**Luv U Honey** *Brian Baugh* a31 7
3 b f Captain Gerrard(IRE) Lady Suesanne (IRE) (Cape Cross (IRE))
*765$^{5}$ 906$^{4}$ 1264$^{5}$* 1647$^{11}$ 2023$^{9}$ 3849$^{10}$
**Luv U Whatever** *Michael Appleby* a88 59
4 b g Needwood Blade Lady Suesanne (IRE) (Cape Cross (IRE))
*(32) 270$^{6}$ 698$^{3}$ 891$^{6}$* 1493$^{7}$ 7334$^{6}$ *7702$^{7}$*
*7784$^{6}$ 7914$^{2}$ 8283$^{2}$*
**Lwah (IRE)** *Richard Hannon* 67
2 b c Lawman(FR) On My Kness (FR) (Fasliyev (USA))
3063$^{7}$ 3875$^{3}$ 4440$^{4}$
**Lyavenita (FR)** *J-V Toux* a58
2 b f Execute(FR) Yaven (FR) (Marchand De Sable (USA))
*5026a$^{7}$*
**Lydiate Lady** *Paul Green* a49 47
2 b f Piccolo Hiraeth (Petong)
4973$^{14}$ 5789$^{7}$ ◆ 6093$^{10}$ *7453$^{13}$ 7948$^{4}$ 8118$^{6}$*
**Lydie Chope (FR)** *A De Watrigant* 57
2 b f Deportivo Very Astair (FR) (Astair (FR))
5617a$^{11}$
**Lyfka** *Paul Cole* a90 50
2 ch f Kheleyf(USA) Tarkamara (IRE) (Medicean)
1726$^{8}$ 2220$^{5}$ 3330$^{5}$ *4576$^{2}$* ◆ 4815$^{5}$ *6016$^{2}$*
*7112$^{2}$ (7362) 7525$^{6}$ (7755) 7849$^{3}$*
**Lynngale** *Kristin Stubbs* a71 66
3 b f Myboycharlie(IRE) Belle Annie (USA) (Aptitude (USA))
*564$^{3}$* 1308$^{6}$ 2020$^{3}$ 2355$^{10}$ 3362$^{4}$ 4304$^{2}$ (4562)
5109$^{3}$ *6076$^{2}$ 6267$^{5}$ 7288$^{4}$ 7765$^{13}$ 8232$^{2}$* 8309$^{2}$
**Lyn Valley** *Mark Johnston* a101 100
3 b g Shamardal(USA) Demisemiquaver (Singspiel (IRE))
1530$^{5}$ 1954$^{3}$ 2565$^{8}$ 2986$^{5}$ 3378$^{15}$ 3982$^{8}$ 4448$^{7}$
(4821) 5695$^{15}$ 6257$^{12}$ *7930$^{2}$* ◆
**Lyric Ballad** *Hughie Morrison* a77 83
4 b f Byron Skies Are Blue (Unfuwain (USA))
1882$^{4}$ 2628$^{4}$ *3582$^{4}$* 4434$^{7}$ 5414$^{3}$ 6699$^{15}$
**Lyric Street (IRE)** *Donald McCain* a80 83
6 b g Hurricane Run(IRE) Elle Danzig (GER) (Roi Danzig (USA))
*1091$^{5}$*
**Lysander The Greek** *Ralph Beckett* a59 70
2 b g Exceed And Excel(AUS) Hector's Girl (Hector Protector (USA))
4142$^{7}$ 4676$^{3}$ 5309$^{6}$ 6165$^{12}$ *6679$^{3}$ 8046$^{5}$*
**Lys Des Aigles (FR)** *Mme C Barande-Barbe* a71 73
3 b f Blue Bresil(FR) Emystone (FR) (L'Emigrant (USA))
7722a$^{9}$
**Lysino (GER)** *Keith Dalgleish* 83
5 ch g Medicean Lysuna (GER) (Monsun (GER))
(3051) (3238)
**Lyssio (GER)** *Jim Best* a67 70
7 b g Motivator Lysuna (GER) (Monsun (GER))
*8042$^{9}$*
**Maahir** *Marco Botti* a76 80
3 b c Cape Cross(IRE) Trick Or Treat (Lomitas)
*614$^{U}$ 816$^{4}$ (1035)* 2120$^{2}$
**Maakirr (IRE)** *Roy Bowring* a79 31
5 b g Street Cry(IRE) Zayn Zen (Singspiel (IRE))
*(8) (95) 257$^{P}$*
**Maarek** *Miss Evanna McCutcheon* a61 118
7 b g Pivotal Ruby Rocket (IRE) (Indian Rocket)
1333a$^{7}$ 1824a$^{2}$ (2256) 2570a$^{2}$ 5219a$^{5}$ 5699a$^{8}$
6134$^{10}$ 6966a$^{11}$ 7272$^{4}$ 7656a$^{11}$

**Mabait** *David Simcock* a72 99
8 b g Kyllachy Czarna Roza (Polish Precedent (USA))
1862$^{4}$ 2483$^{5}$ 3251$^{10}$ 3420$^{18}$ 4212$^{12}$ 4827$^{6}$
6320$^{10}$ 6560$^{7}$
**Mabdhool (IRE)** *Ali Stronge* a75 76
3 b g Mount Nelson Berry Baby (IRE) (Rainbow Quest (USA))
1947$^{7}$ 2417$^{3}$ *2998$^{4}$* (3514) 4020$^{6}$ *6143$^{5}$ 8015$^{5}$*
**Macarthurs Park (IRE)** *Alan Berry* a49 40
2 b f Equiano(FR) La Tintoretta (IRE) (Desert Prince (IRE))
*1314$^{4}$* 1663$^{2}$ 2089$^{8}$ 4422$^{4}$ 5517$^{5}$ *5896$^{6}$* 6791$^{5}$
7232$^{4}$ *7453$^{10}$ 7824$^{6}$*
**Macbeth (IRE)** *Michael Appleby* 99
5 b g Acclamation Filandre (Cadeaux Genereux)
2779$^{8}$ 3449$^{14}$ 5440$^{3}$ 6589a$^{8}$
**Maccabees** *Roger Curtis* a52 57
5 b g Motivator Takarna (IRE) (Mark Of Esteem (IRE))
*454$^{5}$*
**Macdillon** *Stuart Kittow* a74 78
8 b g Acclamation Dilys (Efisio)
(5880) 6455$^{12}$ 7534$^{9}$ *7888$^{6}$*
**Machiavelian Storm (IRE)** *Ed Dunlop* a53 47
2 gr f Dark Angel(IRE) Terri's Charmer (USA) (Silver Charm (USA))
6434$^{9}$ *6675$^{8}$ 7193$^{7}$* 7487$^{3}$
**Machica (FR)** *D Guillemin* a72
2 b f Elusive City(USA) Sara Moon (IRE) (Barathea (IRE))
*5844a$^{13}$*
**Machucambo (FR)** *C Ferland* 109
3 ch c Anabaa Blue Materialiste (IRE) (Zafonic (USA))
4251a$^{9}$
**Mack's Sister** *Michael Madgwick* a44 33
7 ch m Pastoral Pursuits Linda's Schoolgirl (IRE) (Grand Lodge (USA))
*1766$^{11}$ 5138$^{10}$ 5833$^{8}$ 6851$^{7}$ 7854$^{12}$ 7940$^{5}$*
**Macnamara** *Harry Dunlop* a21 7
3 ch f Dylan Thomas(IRE) Portrait Of A Lady (IRE) (Peintre Celebre (USA))
*1380$^{7}$* 2927$^{13}$ 3754$^{7}$
**Mac's Power (IRE)** *Willie Musson* a85 64
8 b g Exceed And Excel(AUS) Easter Girl (Efisio)
*208$^{2}$ 535$^{2}$ 820$^{2}$ 1212$^{7}$* 2849$^{9}$
**Macs Scwar** *Paul Morgan* a32
7 b g Dinar(USA) Quakeress (IRE) (Brief Truce (USA))
*6677$^{9}$ 7349$^{9}$ 7528$^{13}$ 7785$^{12}$ 8084$^{13}$*
**Mac's Superstar (FR)** *James Fanshawe* a83 81
4 b g Elusive City(USA) Diamond Light (USA) (Fantastic Light (USA))
*(2059) 2684$^{6}$ 3118$^{2}$* 3703$^{4}$ 4447$^{9}$ 5496$^{6}$
**Mad About Harry (IRE)** *Linda Jewell* a71 22
4 b g Mujadil(USA) Caro Mio (IRE) (Danehill Dancer (IRE))
4548$^{12}$ *6485$^{8}$ 6856$^{8}$ 7204$^{10}$*
**Madagascar Moll (IRE)** *David O'Meara* a55 64
3 bb f Captain Gerrard(IRE) Fontanally Springs (IRE) (Namid)
2421$^{5}$ 2870$^{5}$ 2951$^{4}$ 3600$^{6}$ 4469$^{7}$ 4891$^{11}$ 5333$^{3}$
5994$^{2}$ *6340$^{5}$* 6821$^{6}$ *7355$^{5}$*
**Madame Ascension** *David Evans* a32 43
2 ch f Captain Gerrard(IRE) Madame Jones (IRE) (Lycius (USA))
3173$^{8}$ 3967$^{5}$ 5148$^{6}$ *5489$^{12}$ 7648$^{8}$*
**Madame Cecile (ITY)** *G Botti* a77 86
3 b f Blu Air Force(IRE) Lamiore (IRE) (Alhaarth (IRE))
2978a$^{3}$
**Madame Chiang** *David Simcock* 115
3 b f Archipenko(USA) Robe Chinoise (Robellino (USA))
(2255) 2960$^{10}$ 6380a$^{6}$ (7273)
**Madame Defarge (IRE)** *J E Hammond* 100
4 b f Motivator Friendlier (Zafonic (USA))
1974$^{6}$ 2764$^{10}$ 3307$^{6}$ 7916a$^{7}$
**Madame Kintyre** *Rod Millman* a49 54
6 b m Trade Fair Chorus (Bandmaster (USA))
*59$^{9}$*
**Madame Mime Artist** *Alastair Lidderdale* a55
3 b f Dutch Art Silent Waters (Polish Precedent (USA))
*486$^{7}$ 741$^{7}$ 1235$^{9}$*
**Madame Mirasol (IRE)** *Kevin Ryan* a76 68
3 b f Sleeping Indian Confidentiality (IRE) (Desert Style (IRE))
1507$^{6}$ 2218$^{9}$ 2828$^{5}$ 3344$^{6}$ *(5257) 5605$^{2}$*
*6269$^{5}$ 6484$^{6}$ 7871$^{11}$ 7954$^{8}$ 8224$^{8}$*
**Madame Rouge** *David Evans* a15 78
3 ch f Major Cadeaux Crocolat (Croco Rouge (IRE))
*4966$^{8}$* (5339) 6425$^{3}$
**Madam Lilibet (IRE)** *Sharon Watt* 74
5 b m Authorized(IRE) Foxilla (IRE) (Foxhound (USA))
1359$^{6}$ 1605$^{7}$ 6493$^{5}$ 7177$^{10}$ (7333)
**Madam Mai Tai** *Robin Bastiman* 13
2 ch f Compton Place Dash Of Lime (Bold Edge)
6757$^{11}$
**Madam Midnight** *David Simcock* a69
2 ch f Shamardal(IRE) Miss Marvellous (USA) (Diesis)
*5827$^{3}$ 6840$^{3}$*
**Madamoiselle Bond** *William Jarvis* a69 70
2 b f Monsieur Bond(IRE) Katy O'Hara (Komaite (USA))
1633$^{4}$ *(2206)* 2403$^{4}$ 4313$^{2}$ 4913$^{11}$ 5373$^{2}$ *6104$^{5}$*
6538$^{3}$
**Madeed** *Brian Meehan* 99
3 b g Nayef(USA) Danehill Dreamer (USA) (Danehill (USA))
1516$^{6}$ 3378$^{7}$ ◆ 4821$^{3}$ ◆ 5720$^{2}$ ◆ 6098$^{3}$
**Mad Endeavour** *Stuart Kittow* a44 62
3 b g Muhtathir Capefly (Cape Cross (IRE))
1808$^{7}$ 3849$^{3}$ 4569$^{8}$ 5402$^{6}$ 6421$^{4}$ 7025$^{9}$ *7423$^{7}$*
**Made With Love** *John Gosden* a77 88
3 b c Exceed And Excel(AUS) Maid To Perfection (Sadler's Wells (USA))
1529$^{2}$ ◆ 3477$^{2}$ *(8249)* ◆

**Madrasa (IRE)** *Keith Reveley* a61 75
6 b g High Chaparral(IRE) Shir Dar (FR) (Lead On Time (USA))
1644$^{7}$ 2216$^{7}$ 2550$^{5}$ 3482$^{4}$ (4474) 4662$^{4}$ 5090$^{4}$
5639$^{10}$ 6216$^{2}$ 7247$^{8}$
**Madrinas Prince (IRE)** *Paddy Butler*
5 b g Prince Arch(USA) Madrina (Waajib (IRE))
*341$^{10}$ 686$^{12}$ 1069$^{9}$* 5423$^{9}$
**Madurai (GER)** *Waldemar Hickst* 103
3 b c Marju(IRE) Moonlight Danceuse (IRE) (Bering)
4007a$^{7}$ 7316a$^{2}$
**Maesmor Magic (IRE)** *Martyn Meade* 54
2 ch f Thousand Words Ide Say (IRE) (Grand Lodge (USA))
2692$^{3}$ 3613$^{10}$
**Mafeteng** *David Thompson* a33 65
6 b m Nayef(USA) Marakabei (Hernando (FR))
3918$^{6}$ 4423$^{9}$ 5090$^{7}$
**Mafi (IRE)** *Mark Hoad* a72 75
6 b g Modigliani(USA) Yulara (IRE) (Night Shift (USA))
*154$^{8}$*
**Maftool (USA)** *Saeed bin Suroor* a103 110
2 bb c Hard Spun(USA) With Intention (USA) (Mr Greeley (USA))
4117$^{2}$ (5050) *6142$^{2}$* (6686) 7241$^{5}$
**Maftoon (IRE)** *Richard Hannon* 79
2 b c Dark Angel(IRE) Chincoteague (IRE) (Daylami (IRE))
3429$^{4}$ ◆ 4424$^{3}$ 4896$^{5}$ 6064$^{5}$ (6648)
**Maggie Aron** *Tim Vaughan* a45 47
8 gr m Generous(IRE) Pems Gift (Environment Friend)
3780$^{7}$
**Maggie Dalton (IRE)** *J S Bolger* 96
5 b m Mr Greeley(USA) Bowstring (IRE) (Sadler's Wells (USA))
5957a$^{4}$ 6585a$^{7}$
**Maggie Pink** *Michael Appleby* a88 96
5 b m Beat All(USA) Top Notch (Alderbrook)
*11$^{3}$ 372$^{5}$ (461) 917$^{2}$ 1554$^{3}$ 6681$^{5}$ 7196$^{3}$*
(7600) 7719$^{8}$ *7952$^{6}$*
**Maggie's Diamond** *Richard Fahey* 60
3 b f Authorized(IRE) Parsonagehotelyork (IRE) (Danehill (USA))
3097$^{3}$ ◆ 4791$^{7}$ 5768$^{4}$
**Magh Meall** *David Nicholls* 67
2 b f Monsieur Bond(IRE) Tibesti (Machiavellian (USA))
1536$^{10}$ 4624$^{5}$ 5332$^{8}$ 6643$^{5}$ 7003$^{2}$ (7277)
**Magical Daze** *Sylvester Kirk* 70
2 b f Showcasing Poulaine Bleue (Bertolini (USA))
7130$^{3}$ 7308$^{2}$
**Magical Effect (IRE)** *Charlie Appleby* a76
2 ch c New Approach(IRE) Purple Glow (IRE) (Orientate (USA))
*7114$^{2}$*
**Magical Macey (USA)** *David Barron* a68 107
7 ch g Rossini(USA) Spring's Glory (USA) (Honour And Glory (USA))
2283$^{14}$ 2786$^{14}$ 3241$^{10}$ 5918$^{8}$ 6327$^{16}$ 7080$^{10}$
7280$^{7}$ 7441$^{14}$
**Magical Memory (IRE)** *Charles Hills* 84
2 gr c Zebedee Marasem (Cadeaux Genereux)
1417$^{7}$ 2071$^{6}$ 3193$^{2}$ (3613) 4439$^{16}$ 4853$^{6}$
**Magical Mischief** *Chris Fairhurst* 62
4 b f Rob Roy(USA) Magical Flute (Piccolo)
1303$^{12}$ 2389$^{6}$ 3908$^{15}$ 4797$^{6}$ 6638$^{3}$ 7248$^{5}$ 7501$^{3}$
**Magicalmysterytour (IRE)** *Willie Musson* a60 61
11 b g Sadler's Wells(USA) Jude (Darshaan)
*283$^{4}$ 455$^{2}$ 656$^{5}$ 1263$^{2}$ 2212$^{3}$* 2614$^{6}$ (2801)
*6339$^{10}$ 6900$^{5}$* 7518$^{6}$ *7823$^{10}$ 8189$^{9}$*
**Magical Peak** *Eric Alston* a21
2 gr f Hellvelyn Enjoy The Magic (Namaqualand (USA))
*7701$^{8}$*
**Magical Rose (IRE)** *Conrad Allen* a69 75
4 b f Elusive City(USA) Xarzee (IRE) (Xaar)
*845 319$^{4}$ 496$^{9}$* 2029$^{3}$ 2448$^{4}$ 2843$^{7}$ 4306$^{11}$
**Magical Roundabout (IRE)** *Richard Hannon* 77
2 gr g Zebedee Chimere (FR) (Soviet Lad (USA))
(1349) 1866$^{4}$ 2258$^{5}$ 3922$^{5}$ 5645$^{8}$
**Magical Speedfit (IRE)** *George Margarson* a39 45
9 ch g Bold Fact(USA) Magical Peace (IRE) (Magical Wonder (USA))
2070$^{6}$ 3612$^{8}$
**Magical Thomas** *Marcus Tregoning* a58 58
2 ch c Dylan Thomas(IRE) Magical Cliche (USA) (Affirmed (USA))
5351$^{8}$ 6085$^{3}$ *7198$^{7}$*
**Magic Art (IRE)** *Marco Botti* a78 88
4 b f Nayef(USA) Artisti (Cape Cross (IRE))
1942$^{9}$ 2331$^{4}$ 3218$^{5}$ 4663$^{2}$ *6156$^{4}$* 7105$^{15}$
**Magic Artist (IRE)** *W Figge* 108
3 br c Iffraaj Artisti (Cape Cross (IRE))
(3073a) 4007a$^{9}$ 4720a$^{4}$ 6054a$^{2}$ 6808a$^{4}$
**Magic Beat** *Pat Phelan* a28 31
4 ch f Byron Marah (Machiavellian (USA))
*661$^{9}$*
**Magic Circle (IRE)** *Ralph Beckett* 54
2 b g Makfi Minkova (IRE) (Sadler's Wells (USA))
6259$^{15}$ 6874$^{8}$ 7413$^{6}$
**Magic City (IRE)** *Richard Hannon* a107 106
5 b g Elusive City(USA) Annmarie's Magic (IRE) (Flying Spur (AUS))
1437$^{14}$ 1943$^{7}$ 2483$^{4}$ 3753$^{2}$ 4851$^{3}$ 5163$^{3}$ 5665$^{3}$
◆ *(7743)*
**Magic Dancer** *Ralph Beckett* 79
2 b c Norse Dancer(IRE) King's Siren (IRE) (King's Best (USA))
6984$^{2}$ (7512)
**Magic Empress (IRE)** *Tony Coyle* a50 33
2 b f Baltic King Red Trance (IRE) (Soviet Star (USA))
3296$^{8}$ 5443$^{8}$ 6537$^{4}$ *8087$^{9}$ (8206)*
**Magic Florence (IRE)** *James Given* a68 72
2 ch f Zebedee Lady Shanghai (IRE) (Alhaarth (IRE))
1161$^{4}$ 1560$^{3}$ 2313$^{11}$ 3841$^{2}$ *(4577)* 5380$^{9}$
5791$^{5}$ *6016$^{6}$*

**Magic Frost (FR)** *Y Gourraud* a68 68
2 gr c Silver Frost(IRE) Flinch (Zafonic (USA))
5292a$^{8}$ 6618a$^{6}$
**Magic Hurricane (IRE)** *James Fanshawe* a94 103
4 b g Hurricane Run(IRE) Close Regards (IRE) (Danehill (USA))
1715$^{5}$ *(2461)* (3111) 3962$^{3}$ 4756$^{9}$ 6233$^{5}$ 7120$^{5}$
**Magician (IRE)** *A P O'Brien* a83 125
4 b c Galileo(IRE) Absolutelyfabulous (IRE) (Mozart (IRE))
1182a$^{6}$ (2040a) 2580a$^{2}$ 3354$^{2}$ 4649$^{6}$ 5460a$^{2}$
**Magic Ice** *John Berry* a32 38
4 b f Royal Applause Winter Ice (Wolfhound (USA))
4306$^{5}$ *7924$^{10}$*
**Magic Mac** *Hughie Morrison* a58 58
2 b f Stimulation(IRE) Supatov (USA) (Johannesburg (USA))
2771$^{14}$ 3181$^{8}$ 3557$^{6}$ *5279$^{5}$ 5828$^{2}$* (6248) 6610$^{5}$
*7258$^{2}$*
**Magic Magnolia (IRE)** *Mark Gillard* 50
3 b f Azamour(IRE) Royal Aly (USA) (Royal Academy (USA))
3514$^{4}$
**Magic Maisie** *Alistair Whillans* 39
3 b f Tiger Hill(IRE) Silcasue (Selkirk (USA))
6282$^{6}$ 7176$^{11}$
**Magic Movies (FR)** *X Thomas-Demeaulte* a91
3 b g Kentucky Dynamite(USA) Highborne (FR) (Anabaa (USA))
*721a$^{13}$*
**Magic Music Man** *K R Burke* 77
3 b g Authorized(IRE) Magic Music (IRE) (Magic Ring (IRE))
5018$^{3}$ ◆ 5374$^{2}$ 6092$^{10}$ 7281$^{8}$
**Magic Of Reality (FR)** *Lady Cecil* a96 98
4 ch f Galileo(IRE) Breathe (FR) (Ocean Of Wisdom (USA))
*1577$^{2}$* 3109$^{3}$ 3665$^{3}$
**Magic Round (IRE)** *Bill Turner* a44 15
2 gr g Zebedee Street Kitty (IRE) (Tiger Hill (IRE))
2276$^{8}$ 3210$^{7}$ *7685$^{6}$ 7824$^{9}$*
**Magic Shoes (IRE)** *Susan Corbett* a44 52
3 b f Manduro(GER) Ammo (IRE) (Sadler's Wells (USA))
1424$^{9}$ *2061$^{14}$* 2491$^{7}$ 5388$^{6}$ 5765$^{10}$ 6010$^{8}$
**Magic Skyline (IRE)** *Brian Ellison* 66
4 b f Refuse To Bend(IRE) Grecian Air (FR) (King's Best (USA))
1348$^{5}$ 2016$^{9}$ 2213$^{9}$
**Magic Time (IRE)** *Ann Duffield* a32 72
2 b f Zebedee Louvolite (IRE) (Fayruz)
1656$^{3}$ 2051$^{7}$ 4450$^{3}$ 4869$^{5}$ *5896$^{5}$* 6447$^{12}$
**Magika** *Marco Botti* a92 77
4 b f Dubawi(IRE) Aline's Wings (ITY) (In The Wings)
*3$^{5}$ (125) 611$^{4}$ 784$^{4}$*
**Magique (IRE)** *Jeremy Noseda* a81 88
4 b f Jeremy(USA) Misskinta (IRE) (Desert Sun)
2750$^{2}$ 3314$^{3}$ 3727$^{5}$ (4782)
**Magistrat (IRE)** *Alain Couetil* a94 91
3 ch c Medicean Lumiere Noire (FR) (Dashing Blade)
2630a$^{2}$
**Magnified** *David O'Meara* a67
4 b g Passing Glance Scrutinize (IRE) (Selkirk (USA))
*8048$^{4}$ 8138$^{5}$*
**Magnolia Beach (IRE)** *G M Lyons* a106 104
3 b c Footstepsinthesand Misskinta (IRE) (Desert Sun)
3491a$^{2}$ 4379a$^{2}$ 5733a$^{4}$ *6909a$^{4}$*
**Magnolia Ridge (IRE)** *Kristin Stubbs* a78 80
4 b g Galileo(IRE) Treasure The Lady (IRE) (Indian Ridge)
*250$^{10}$ 582$^{7}$* (1167) 1307$^{10}$ 1660$^{3}$ 2216$^{5}$ 2509$^{7}$
2872$^{8}$ 3436$^{2}$ 3919$^{4}$ 4303$^{5}$ 4964$^{13}$ 6062$^{5}$ 6210$^{3}$
7175$^{13}$
**Magnus Maximus** *Richard Hannon* a92 88
3 b c Holy Roman Emperor(IRE) Chanrossa (IRE) (Galileo (IRE))
(1513) 3378$^{17}$ 4826$^{11}$ 6522$^{11}$
**Magnus Romeo** *Marco Botti* a71 48
3 b g Manduro(GER) Chili Dip (Alhaarth (IRE))
*1258$^{4}$* 1940$^{10}$ 2805$^{12}$
**Magrooma (AUS)** *M F De Kock* a95 93
4 br f Dubawi(IRE) Cavallina (USA) (Theatrical (IRE))
*203a$^{2}$ 506a$^{5}$ 771a$^{4}$*
**Magroora (AUS)** *M F De Kock* a93 81
4 br f Dubawi(IRE) Tilly's Place (AUS) (Puissance)
*203a$^{6}$ 506a$^{7}$*
**Mahadee (IRE)** *Tom Dascombe* a78 80
9 br g Cape Cross(IRE) Rafiya (Halling (USA))
*180$^{2}$ (445) 582$^{6}$ (601) 685$^{3}$ 953$^{3}$ (1065)*
*(1151)*
**Maha Kumari (GER)** *Markus Klug* 74
2 b f Soldier Hollow Muriel (IRE) (Fath (USA))
7315a$^{9}$
**Mahlah (IRE)** *John Butler*
3 b f Acclamation Somerset Falls (UAE) (Red Ransom (USA))
*7729$^{12}$*
**Mahon Falls** *David Evans* a51 51
3 ch f Dandy Man(IRE) Saphire (College Chapel)
*216$^{3}$ 346$^{3}$ 373$^{3}$ 608$^{7}$ 765$^{8}$*
**Mahsoob** *John Gosden* a91
3 b c Dansili Mooakada (IRE) (Montjeu (IRE))
*(7733)*
**Mahsooba (USA)** *Ed Dunlop* 79
2 b f Hard Spun(USA) Ishraak (USA) (Sahm (USA))
4346$^{5}$ (4914) 5436$^{10}$ 6359$^{4}$
**Maid A Million** *David Elsworth* a72 97
4 b f Kyllachy Poldhu (Cape Cross (IRE))
3203$^{9}$ 3431$^{6}$ 3674$^{5}$
**Maiden Approach** *Richard Fahey* a68 81
3 b f New Approach(IRE) Ivowen (USA) (Theatrical (IRE))
2130$^{5}$ 2740$^{2}$ 3268$^{2}$ 3974$^{5}$ (4472) 5079$^{2}$ 5681$^{10}$

**Maid In Rio (IRE)** *Mark Johnston* a66 106
3 ch f Captain Rio Silver Whale (FR) (Highest Honor (FR))
1540[8] *2210[5]* (2735) (3396) (3673) 4183[3] (4392) (4606) 4777[7] 5481a[7] 6069[4]

**Maid In Rome (IRE)** *Tim Easterby* 54
2 b f Holy Roman Emperor(IRE) Kashra (IRE) (Dancing Dissident (USA))
3570[8] 3947[7] ◆ 4286[4] 6222[6] 6623[6] 7497[5]

**Maid Of Kent** *James Fanshawe* a43
2 br f Halling(USA) First Fantasy (Be My Chief (USA))
*8075[7]*

**Maid Of Silk (IRE)** *Neil Mulholland* a50 54
8 b m Blueprint(IRE) Silk Style (Polish Precedent (USA))
*997[6] 1111[3]*

**Maid Of The Glens (IRE)** *John Patrick Shanahan* 101
3 b f The Carbon Unit(USA) There's A Light (IRE) (Fantastic Light (USA))
1597[3] 2804[2] (3607) 4461a[6] 5545a[6] 6350a[7] 6737[13]

**Maid Of Tuscany (IRE)** *Neil Mulholland* a62 58
3 b f Manduro(GER) Tuscania (USA) (Woodman (USA))
2416[8] 2926[2] 3567[4] *4261[4] 4616[5] 5048[5]* 5747[2] *6037[6]* 6394[2] *6946[11]*

**Maillot Jaune (IRE)** *Patrick Holmes* a48 44
4 b f Ramonti(FR) Roclette (USA) (Rock Of Gibraltar (IRE))
2729[8] 3364[7] 3843[5] 4533[4] 5084[7] 6210[7] 6454[8] 6837[7] 7499[5] *7646[10]*

**Main De Fer** *A Fabre* a63 70
3 b g Pyrus(USA) Kydd Gloves (USA) (Dubai Millennium)
*3869a[8]*

**Main Sequence (USA)** *H Graham Motion* a113 118
5 ch g Aldebaran(USA) Ikat (IRE) (Pivotal)
(4010a) (7611a)

**Maintop (FR)** *N Milliere* a82 82
8 b h Royal Academy(USA) Madeleine's Blush (USA) (Rahy (USA))
*584a[7]*

**Mairise** *Sir Michael Stoute* a67 73
3 b g Authorized(IRE) Maigold Lass (Mark Of Esteem (IRE))
1635[4] 2319[6] 3428[5] *4547[5]*

**Maisie's Minion** *F-H Graffard* a53
2 b c Librettist(USA) Annabelle Ja (FR) (Singspiel (IRE))
*3640a[6]*

**Maison Brillet (IRE)** *Clive Drew* a69 64
7 b g Pyrus(USA) Stormchaser (IRE) (Titus Livius (FR))
*606[2] 747[3] 989[6] (1232) 1919[7]* 2468[2] *2885[3] 3234[3] 7744[11] 8037[2]* 8250[8]

**Maison De Ville (GER)** *Brian Ellison* 52
6 b m Sholokhov(IRE) Morbidezza (GER) (Lecroix (GER))
6432[6]

**Majenski (IRE)** *Jamie Osborne* 27
2 b g Camacho D'Addario (IRE) (Galileo (IRE))
1571[11] 1872[7] 2622[10] 4739[4]

**Majenta (IRE)** *Kevin Prendergast* a91 99
4 b f Marju(IRE) What A Picture (FR) (Peintre Celebre (USA))
1076a[12] 7142a[19] 7476a[21]

**Majestic Dream (IRE)** *Michael Easterby* a60 78
6 b g Exceed And Excel(AUS) Tallassee (Indian Ridge)
1610[11] 3299[8] 3979[4] 4291[11] 4632[11] *5605[9]* 5761[2] 5987[9] 7248[12]

**Majestic Harbor (USA)** *Sean McCarthy* a119
6 b h Rockport Harbor(USA) Champagne Royale (USA) (French Deputy (USA))
*5781a[6] 7614a[13]*

**Majestic Hero (IRE)** *Ronald Harris* 82
2 b g Majestic Missile(IRE) Xena (IRE) (Mull Of Kintyre (USA))
1726[4] (2666) 3322[14] 5580[6] (5879) 6128[8] 6989[5]

**Majestic Hope (GER)** *A Wohler* 85
2 b f Holy Roman Emperor(IRE) Milana (GER) (Highest Honor (FR))
6123a[4] 7481a[5]

**Majestic Jasmine (IRE)** *A Wohler* a94 99
4 ch f New Approach(IRE) Majestic Roi (USA) (Street Cry (IRE))
4006a[5]

**Majestic Manannan (IRE)** *David Nicholls* a61 80
5 b g Majestic Missile(IRE) Miraculous (IRE) (Marju (IRE))
*8[6] 412[6]* 1541[6] 2167[7] 3611[6] 3952[5] (4714) 5913[10] 6475[7] 6938[12]

**Majestic Manner** *William Haggas* 75
2 ch f Dubawi(IRE) Majestic Roi (USA) (Street Cry (IRE))
4499[3] (6041) ◆ 7237[8] ◆

**Majestic Moon (IRE)** *Richard Fahey* 103
4 b g Majestic Missile(IRE) Gala Style (IRE) (Elnadim (USA))
1564[9] 1928[2] 2747[3] (3189) 4648[10] 5445[16] 5666[5] 6531[16]

**Majestic Mount** *Rod Collet* a102 102
4 b c Exceed And Excel(AUS) Our Poppet (IRE) (Warning)
*(7437a) (8150a)*

**Majestic Myles (IRE)** *Richard Fahey* a80 109
6 b g Majestic Missile(IRE) Gala Style (IRE) (Elnadim (USA))
1484[4]

**Majestic Presence (USA)** *Jerry Hollendorfer* a98
2 ch f Majestic Warrior(USA) Shining Victory (USA) (Victory Gallop (CAN))
*7606a[9]*

**Majestic Queen (IRE)** *Tracey Collins* a97 103
4 b f Kheleyf(USA) Night Fairy (IRE) (Danehill (USA))
2144[3] (3167a) 3864a[2] 5699a[4] 6369a[15]

**Majestic Song** *James Toller* a77 55
3 b f Royal Applause Sakhee's Song (IRE) (Sakhee (USA))
*2125[6]* 2384[5] *(4324) 4971[4]* 5650[12] *7286[6] 7697[2] 7931[5]*

**Majestic Sun (IRE)** *Peter Chapple-Hyam* a73 76
3 b g King's Best(USA) Shining Vale (USA) (Twilight Agenda (USA))
*1403[9]* 1847[4] 3316[8] *3711[4]* 3912[2] 4333[6] *6564[2]* (6787) *6942[4]*

**Majeyda (USA)** *Charlie Appleby* a97 103
3 bb f Street Cry(IRE) Alzerra (UAE) (Pivotal)
1515[3] 1976[6] 3357[17] *7952[2]*

**Majik Charly (FR)** *T Castanheira* a49 66
2 ch c Soave(GER) Kapi Creek (FR) (Sicyos (USA))
6618a[5]

**Majnon Fajer (IRE)** *Jane Chapple-Hyam* a36 27
4 b g Captain Marvelous(IRE) Noble View (USA) (Distant View (USA))
*6483[10] 6856[11] 8010[7]*

**Major Attitude** *Clive Cox* a38 56
2 b c Major Cadeaux Alexander Ballet (Mind Games)
5906[5] 7037[15] *7542[9]*

**Major Crispies** *James Eustace* a97 103
3 b g Pastoral Pursuits Nellie Melba (Hurricane Sky (AUS))
*(667)* ◆ *778[3] 1067[3] 1555[10]* 2304[3] 3352[22] 4166[11] 5165[8] 6170[7] 6614[4] 6923[9]

**Majorities** *Brian Meehan* 81
3 b g Major Cadeaux Mania (IRE) (Danehill (USA))
1844[5] 2510[3] (3187)

**Major Jack** *Roger Charlton* a94 85
3 b g Kheleyf(USA) Azeema (IRE) (Averti (IRE))
2384[2] *(4086)* 4669[5] 5204[3] *(6020)* 7843[2] *7923[4]*

**Major Mac** *Hughie Morrison* a53 70
2 ch g Shirocco(GER) Spring Fashion (IRE) (Galileo (IRE))
6293[11] 7134[9] 7414[3] *7730[11]*

**Major Maximus** *Mrs C Gilbert* a51 10
7 br g Domedriver(IRE) Madame Maxine (USA) (Dayjur (USA))
1622a[9]

**Major Muscari (IRE)** *Shaun Harris* a65 60
6 ch g Exceed And Excel(AUS) Muscari (Indian Ridge)
*58[2] 121[6] 2094[3]* 2233[8] 2724[2] 2909[3] *3393[7]* 3548[7] *4055[3]* 4287[11] *6409[6] (6720) 7111[2]* 7884[2] 8013[3]

**Major Pusey** *John Gallagher* 49
2 ch c Major Cadeaux Pusey Street Lady (Averti (IRE))
6702[9]

**Major Rowan** *Bryan Smart* a59 48
3 b g Captain Gerrard(IRE) Julie's Gift (Presidium)
2236[8] 4066[4] 4497[4] 5682[6] 7176[9] *7910[4] (8137)* ◆

**Majraa (FR)** *J-C Rouget* a95 82
3 b f Invincible Spirit(IRE) Santa Louisia (Highest Honor (FR))
5226a[2]

**Makafeh** *Luca Cumani* 96
4 br g Elusive Quality(USA) Demisemiquaver (Singspiel (IRE))
2085[9]

**Make A Fuss** *Gerry Enright* a2
5 gr m Proclamation(IRE) Fustaan (IRE) (Royal Applause)
*760[11] 1232[13]* 3554[8]

**Make It Reel (FR)** *Doug Watson* a87 81
3 b c Country Reel(USA) Maka (FR) (Slickly (FR))
*204a[13]* 505a[2] 770a[7] 897a[13]

**Make It Up** *Andrew Balding* 97
2 b c Halling(USA) American Spirit (IRE) (Rock Of Gibraltar (IRE))
(4809) 5424[2] (6004) 6686[7]

**Make On Madam (IRE)** *Brian Ellison* a66 76
2 b f Captain Rio Rye (IRE) (Charnwood Forest (IRE))
1656[4] ◆ 2051[2] 2541[2] *(3403)* 6375a[24] *7116[9]*

**Makhfar (IRE)** *John Gosden* 83
3 b g Bushranger(IRE) Let Me Shine (USA) (Dixie Union (USA))
3469[2] (3700)

**Makin A Statement (IRE)** *John Quinn* 77
2 b g Bahamian Bounty Star Now (Librettist (USA))
1583[6] 1670[3] 7277[4]

**Making Shapes** *Peter Chapple-Hyam* 74
2 b c Makfi Danceabout (Shareef Dancer (USA))
7666[4]

**Makin The Rules (IRE)** *John Quinn* 79
3 b g Lawman(FR) Shinto Duchess (IRE) (Bachelor Duke (USA))
2257[12] 3369[3] 3503[2] (4071) 4421[8] 5411[7]

**Makin Trouble (IRE)** *John Quinn* 41
2 b g Lawman(FR) Crafty Notion (IRE) (Viking Ruler (AUS))
7246[6] 7496[10]

**Makramah (USA)** *Richard Hannon* a61
2 ch f Elusive Quality(USA) What A Treasure (IRE) (Cadeaux Genereux)
*7193[12] 7549[8]*

**Makruma** *B W Hills* 80
3 b f Dubawi(IRE) Qelaan (USA) (Dynaformer (USA))
1423[6] 2365[3] 3276[2]

**Makweti** *F Doumen* 102
2 b f Makfi Hometown (Storming Home)
6967a[7] 7393a[7]

**Makzon (USA)** *Sir Michael Stoute* 37
2 b c Henrythenavigator(USA) Fab's Melody (USA) (Devil's Bag (USA))
7407[10]

**Malabar** *Mick Channon* 108
2 b f Raven's Pass(USA) Whirly Bird (Nashwan (USA))
2697[2] 3415[4] (4604) (5664) ◆ 6372a[4] 6967a[4]

**Malachim Mist (IRE)** *Oliver Sherwood* 88
3 gr g Dark Angel(IRE) Sixfields Flyer (IRE) (Desert Style (IRE))
1279[8] 2112[5] 3243[12] 3917[8] 4208[6] 4501[9] 7167[9]

**Malaf (USA)** *John Gosden* a76
2 b c Elusive Quality(USA) Holy Wish (USA) (Lord At War (ARG))
*(7892)* ◆

**Malandrino (FR)** *B Goudot* 84
2 b c Zanzibari(USA) Vireli (FR) (Miesque's Son (USA))
5329a[2]

**Malanos (IRE)** *Tony Carroll* a32 36
6 bb g Lord Of England(GER) Majorata (GER) (Acatenango (GER))
7343[7]

**Malarkey (IRE)** *John Gosden*
2 ch f Raven's Pass(USA) Laughing Owl (IRE) (Dubai Destination (USA))
*4320[9]*

**Malaysian Boleh** *Simon Dow* a80 59
4 ch g Compton Place Orlena (USA) (Gone West (USA))
*472[3] 677[6] 1102[6]* 1876[7] *2471[6]* 3246[10] 3734[5] *4072[9] 6074[2]* ◆ 6617[9] *7078[6] 7202[3]* 7368[4] (7842) (7906) 8080[8] 8204[10] 8321[3]

**Malice** *Peter Chapple-Hyam* 50
2 b f Makfi Shemriyna (IRE) (King Of Kings (IRE))
7108[16] 7405[11] ◆

**Malicho** *Dean Ivory* a66 59
5 ch g Manduro(GER) Shane (GER) (Kornado)
1399[7] *1796[9]* 6304[6] 6990[12] *7533[12] 7805[10] 8074[5] 8314[9]*

**Malicieuse (IRE)** *J E Pease* 92
2 b f Galileo(IRE) Moonlight's Box (USA) (Nureyev (USA))
4931a[3] 5741a[8] 7094a[4] 7485a[3]

**Malih** *Eric Wheeler* a64 58
5 b g Echo Of Light Sultry Lass (USA) (Private Account (USA))
*7853[9] 8013[10] 8199[6]*

**Malimbi (IRE)** *Mark Johnston*
2 b c Cape Cross(IRE) Mirina (FR) (Pursuit Of Love)
4550[10]

**Maljaa** *Roger Varian* 84
2 ch g Paco Boy(IRE) Kerry's Dream (Tobougg (IRE))
2731[2] ◆ (4170)

**Malka (FR)** *Frau Erika Mader* 98
3 ch f Green Tune(USA) Quadrupa (GER) (Big Shuffle (USA))
3810a[3] 7483a[3]

**Mallory Heights (IRE)** *Luca Cumani* a84 76
4 gr g Dalakhani(IRE) My Dark Rosaleen (Sadler's Wells (USA))
2272[8] 3205[10] 4209[5] *4736[11] 6141[12]*

**Mallymkun** *K R Burke* 74
2 b f Kheleyf(USA) Harriet's Girl (Choisir (AUS))
5332[5] 6093[3] 6701[5] 7278[3]

**Malory Towers** *James Fanshawe* a67 58
3 b f Giant's Causeway(USA) Dalisay (IRE) (Sadler's Wells (USA))
1491[8] *1797[6] 3116[4]* ◆ 3655[9]

**Malossol (USA)** *G Botti* a101 96
5 b h Rahy(USA) Mambo Queen (USA) (Kingmambo (USA))
*806a[10]*

**Malraaj** *Richard Fahey* 63
3 b g Iffraaj Lafontaine Bleu (Piccolo)
2733[7] 3302[7]

**Maltease Ah** *Andrew Reid* a63 38
5 br m Librettist(USA) Manic (Polar Falcon (USA))
*1405[8]* 2008[7] *7781[11]*

**Maltot (FR)** *S Gouyette* a66 70
3 b c Le Havre(IRE) Yezidis (FR) (Ski Chief (USA))
*8005a[6]*

**Malvasia (FR)** *J-C Rouget* a67 68
2 b f Hannouma(IRE) Charmer Sweet (USA) (Afternoon Deelites (USA))
5293a[4]

**Malvia** *Michael Bell* 40
2 b c Exceed And Excel(AUS) Always On My Mind (Distant Relative)
5439[9]

**Ma Marie (FR)** *S Smrczek* 83
2 ch f Champs Elysees Medinella (GER) (Pivotal)
7315a[7]

**Mambo Fever** *David C Griffiths* a61 44
3 b f Footstepsinthesand Mambo's Melody (Kingmambo (USA))
7501[6] *(7764)* ◆

**Mambomiss (FR)** *D De Watrigant* 104
3 ch f Mastercraftsman(IRE) Mambo Mistress (USA) (Kingmambo (USA))
5479a[3]

**Mambo Paradise** *Mark Johnston* 75
2 b f Makfi Mambo Halo (USA) (Southern Halo (USA))
(1924) 2302[5] 2987[6]

**Mambo Rhythm** *Mark Johnston* a59 79
3 b f Authorized(IRE) Mambo Halo (USA) (Southern Halo (USA))
*1391[5]* 1880[6] 2385[3] 2616[3] 3498[3] 3829[5] 4189[5] 4726[5] 5270[2] 5520[6] (6110) (6284) 6539[5] 6761[6]

**Mambo Spirit (IRE)** *Tony Newcombe* a67 71
10 b g Invincible Spirit(IRE) Mambodorga (USA) (Kingmambo (USA))
*95[7] 249[9] 1009[10]* 1573[5] 3328[3] (4564) 4961[12] 6266[9] *6562[3]* 6815[2] *7364[2] 7698[10]*

**Mamourg (FR)** *Mlle C Chenu* 59
2 b c Crossharbour Marmuhta (FR) (Muhtathir)
6619a[6]

**Manalapan (IRE)** *P J Prendergast* a107 107
4 b g Six Sense(JPN) Mia Mambo (USA) (Affirmed (USA))
*307a[5]* 507a[7] *773a[4]*

**Man Amongst Men (IRE)** *Brian Meehan* a84 83
3 b g Holy Roman Emperor(IRE) Bankeress (IRE) (Barathea (IRE))
*204a[12]* 505a[11] 770a[6]

**Manatee** *A Fabre* 115
3 b c Monsun(GER) Galatee (FR) (Galileo (IRE))
(7318a)

**Manatee Bay** *David Nicholls* 74
4 b g Royal Applause Dash Of Lime (Bold Edge)
1487[8] 1966[2] 2297[5] 2606[7] 2955[5] 3548[U] 3913[3] 4511[7] 5298[3] 5565[5] (6213) 6451[4] ◆ 6835[2] 7023[2] 7248[4]

**Manchestar** *Richard Fahey* a52 90
4 b g Elusive City(USA) Grande Terre (IRE) (Grand Lodge (USA))
(1190) (1607) 2362[9]

**Manchester (FR)** *Niels Petersen* a98 91
6 ch g Domedriver(IRE) Metaline (FR) (Dr Fong (USA))
*593a[12] 773a[8]* 5744a[14]

**Manchu (FR)** *F Chappet* a77 77
3 bb g Great Journey(JPN) Marishaan (IRE) (Darshaan)
*720a[2]* 4465a[9]

**Manchurian High (USA)** *Lilli Kurtinecz* a54 104
6 ch g The Daddy(USA) Corredor's Wind (USA) (El Corredor (USA))
4010a[9]

**Mancora (FR)** *J-C Rouget* a83 80
2 ch f Iffraaj Mantadive (FR) (Okawango (USA))
(5293a)

**Mandalaya (USA)** *A De Royer-Dupre* a84 92
3 b f Elusive Quality(USA) Mandesha (FR) (Desert Style (IRE))
7720a[7]

**Mandalay King (IRE)** *Marjorie Fife* a42 75
9 b g King's Best(USA) Mahamuni (IRE) (Sadler's Wells (USA))
(2914) 3599[7] 4383[7] 6013[10] 6758[6] 7178[14]

**Mandamus (IRE)** *Ms Sheila Lavery* 89
2 b g Lawman(FR) Stefanella (IRE) (Alzao (USA))
7462a[4]

**Mandarin Girl** *Richard Hannon* 44
2 b f Paco Boy(IRE) Cake (IRE) (Acclamation)
1536[9] 1663[3]

**Manderley (IRE)** *Richard Hannon* a64 107
3 gr f Clodovil(IRE) Three Days In May (Cadeaux Genereux)
1435[5] 1976[4] (2804) 3724[7] 4854[9] 5176[3]

**Mandria (IRE)** *Daniel Kubler* a57 47
2 b f Duke Of Marmalade(IRE) Albertine Rose (Namid)
*4999[6]* 5774[6] *7398[8] 7683[6]*

**Mandy Layla (IRE)** *Bryan Smart* a53 68
4 ch f Excellent Art Chervil (Dansili)
*1500[4]* (4362) 4860[4] 6580[9]

**Mandy's Boy (IRE)** *Ian Williams* a63 75
4 b g Kyllachy African Queen (IRE) (Cadeaux Genereux)
3147[5]

**Mandy The Nag (USA)** *Nikki Evans* a82 66
4 bb f Proud Citizen(USA) Storm To Glory (USA) (Storm Bird (CAN))
3220[6] 4255[6] *5100[7] 5573[4]* 6822[5] 7167[2] *7765[7] 7907[5]*

**Mange All** *William Haggas* 102
3 b g Zamindar(USA) Blancmange (Montjeu (IRE))
2334[3] (3543) 4125[5] (4647) ◆ 6257[2] 6713[4]

**Mango Diva** *Sir Michael Stoute* a91 105
4 b f Holy Roman Emperor(IRE) Mango Mischief (IRE) (Desert King (IRE))
2284[4] 2956[5] (4478a) 4894[6] 6370a[5]

**Manhattan Swing (IRE)** *Brian Ellison* a79 96
4 b g Invincible Spirit(IRE) Bluebell Park (USA) (Gulch (USA))
7718[15]

**Maningrey (GER)** *Waldemar Hickst* a101 104
5 b g Soldier Hollow Mandrella (GER) (Surumu (GER))
5263a[2] (6620a) 7618a[5]

**Man In The Arena** *Dr Jon Scargill* a42 40
4 b g Bertolini(USA) Torver (Lake Coniston (IRE))
*377[9]*

**Maninthemirror (FR)** *Mme Pia Brandt* a64
3 ch g Le Havre(IRE) Kota Kinabalu (Ashkalani (IRE))
*3869a[6]*

**Man Look** *Andrew Balding* a46
2 b c Nayef(USA) Charlecote (IRE) (Caerleon (USA))
*7739[11]*

**Mannaro (IRE)** *Marco Botti* 81
3 b g Manduro(GER) Donoma (IRE) (Beat Hollow)
1702[8] 2303[6]

**Man Of Erin (IRE)** *J F Levins* a41 85
6 b g Invincible Spirit(IRE) Dark Rosaleen (IRE) (Darshaan)
1078a[17]

**Man Of Harlech** *Andrew Balding* 89
3 b c Dansili Ffestiniog (IRE) (Efisio)
(1808) 2330[3] 5882[3]

**Manofmanytalents** *Michael Squance* 91
2 b g Bertolini(USA) Starbeck (IRE) (Spectrum (IRE))
5091[4] 6299[3] 7121[4] 7439[4]

**Man Of Music** *Tony Carroll* a40 37
3 b c Piccolo Blue Goddess (IRE) (Blues Traveller (IRE))
6421[6] 6988[10] *7370[6]*

**Man Of Plenty** *Ed Dunlop* 89
5 ch g Manduro(GER) Credit-A-Plenty (Generous (IRE))
1935[3] 2289[16] 2739[10] 3240[7]

**Manolito** *Hughie Morrison* a68 69
2 b g High Chaparral(IRE) Break Time (Dansili)
5377[5] ◆ 6203[3] 6702[4] *7525[3]*

**Manomine** *Clive Brittain* a77 81
5 b g Manduro(GER) Fascinating Hill (FR) (Danehill (USA))
*849[2] 990[4]* (2467) (3032) 4441[4] 5379[7] *5800[4] 6274[3] 6487[3]* 6930[7]

**Manorov** *T G McCourt* a61 50
4 b g Sholokhov(IRE) Mandel Set (GER) (Second Set (IRE))
*7961a[2]*

**Manor Way (IRE)** *Richard Hannon* a62 60
3 b g Holy Roman Emperor(IRE) Cannikin (IRE) (Lahib (USA))
*1214[7] 2078[7]* 2224[9] 2416[13]

**Manshaa (IRE)** *Mark Johnston* a40 78
2 ch c Dubawi(IRE) Ghizlaan (USA) (Seeking The Gold (USA))
4750[2] ◆ 5393[4] 6279[2] 6790[2] 7661[6]

**Mantoba** *Doug Watson* a96 92
6 b h Noverre(USA) Coming Home (Vettori (IRE))
243a[13]

**Mantonize (USA)** *Brian Meehan* 71
3 ch c Smart Strike(CAN) L'Ile Aux Loups (IRE) (Rock Of Gibraltar (IRE))
1582[9] 2511[2]

**Mantou (IRE)** *Michael Bell* 88
3 ch g Teofilo(IRE) Shadow Roll (IRE) (Mark Of Esteem (IRE))
2877[9] 3153[6] 3914[3] 4698[6] (5387) 5691[U] ◆ 6137[11] 6502[3]

**Many Levels** *John Quinn* a57 37
4 br g Nayef(USA) Polygueza (FR) (Be My Guest (USA))
642[4] 783[4]

**Maoi Chinn Tire (IRE)** *Jennie Candlish* a55 82
7 b g Mull Of Kintyre(USA) Primrose And Rose (Primo Dominie)
(3309) (3336) ◆ 3482[2] (4296) 4522[2] (5564) 5764[3] 6514[8]

**Maontri (IRE)** *M J Tynan* a95 56
7 b m Catcher In The Rye(IRE) Arabian Dream (IRE) (Royal Academy (USA))
7579a[13] 7873a[6]

**Maply (FR)** *Y Barberot* a74
2 b c Slickly(FR) Mapow (FR) (Kendor (FR))
3640a[5]

**Mappin Time (IRE)** *Tim Easterby* a95 88
6 b g Orientate(USA) Different Story (USA) (Stravinsky (USA))
122[3] (257) 479[4] 909[2] 1313[2] 1429[2] (1742) 4683[16] 4976[10]

**Ma Ptite Sarah (FR)** *E Caroux* a69 82
2 b f Siyouni(FR) Holiday Maker (Dubai Destination (USA))
1094a[6] 5329a[7] 5844a[7]

**Maputo** *Charlie Appleby* 116
4 b g Cape Cross(IRE) Insijaam (USA) (Secretariat (USA))
397a[3]

**Maraakib (IRE)** *Brian Meehan* 83
2 b g Dark Angel(IRE) Mrs Cee (IRE) (Orpen (USA))
2964[9] 3924[4] 6551[2] (7166)

**Maraayill (IRE)** *Marco Botti* a77 82
3 b c Sea The Stars(IRE) Navajo Moon (IRE) (Danehill (USA))
1586[9] 1897[5] 2879[2] (3145) 4572[6] 5603[6] 6891[6]

**Marabea** *R Rohne* 99
2 ch f Archipenko(USA) Violin Time (USA) (Theatrical (IRE))
7321a[2]

**Marabout (IRE)** *Mel Brittain* a44 60
4 b g Haafhd Nirvana (Marju (IRE))
1843[13]

**Maracuja** *Mark Johnston* 83
3 b f Medicean Blinking (Marju (IRE))
1582[2] 1738[2] 2292[4] 3103[2] 3644[3] (4255) 4680[5] 5238[10] 6746[11]

**Maraheb** *A Al Raihe* a94 78
6 b h Redoute's Choice(AUS) Hureya (USA) (Woodman (USA))
109a[5] ◆ 504a[8]

**Marangu (IRE)** *F Pedrono* a61 51
8 b g Intikhab(USA) Massada (Most Welcome)
806a[12]

**Marasim** *Roger Varian* a51
2 ch c Exceed And Excel(AUS) Muffled (USA) (Mizaaya)
7400[9]

**Marble Statuette (USA)** *A J Martin* a76
4 gr f Mizzen Mast(USA) Offbeat Fashion (IRE) (Rock Of Gibraltar (IRE))
323[4] 542[4] 718[7] (7959a)

**Marbre Rose (IRE)** *F Head* 100
3 b f Smart Strike(CAN) Manerbe (USA) (Unbridled's Song (USA))
1273a[5]

**Marcano (IRE)** *Rod Millman* 82
2 b c Arcano(IRE) Aquatint (Dansili)
2298[3] (3748) 5607[18]

**Marcelli (GER)** *W Figge* 102
5 bb g Sholokhov(IRE) Mandel Set (GER) (Second Set (IRE))
6384a[4]

**March** *Robert Cowell* a59 103
4 b f Dutch Art Royal Pardon (Royal Applause)
1572[6] 2848[14] 3674[7]

**Marchese Marconi (IRE)** *A P O'Brien* a72 92
5 b h Galileo(IRE) Charroux (IRE) (Darshaan)
4746a[15] 7142a[3]

**Marching Time** *Doug Watson* a91 98
8 b g Sadler's Wells(USA) Marching West (USA) (Gone West (USA))
242a[10]

**Marchman (USA)** *J Keith Desormeaux* a96 118
4 b c Sharp Humor(USA) Sookie Sookie (USA) (Indian Charlie (USA))
7609a[13]

**March On (USA)** *William Haggas* 75
2 b f War Front(USA) Stroll By (USA) (Stroll (USA))
4828[2] 5725[5]

**Marciano (IRE)** *Sue Smith* a81 62
4 b g Pivotal Kitty Matcham (IRE) (Rock Of Gibraltar (IRE))
75[5] 7178[8] 7506[10] 7905[10] 8086[3]

**Marcret (ITY)** *Ruth Carr* a83 103
7 b g Martino Alonso(IRE) Love Secret (USA) (Secreto (USA))
1539[3] 2085[10] 2478[5] 2758[3] 3217[7] 3621[4] 4212[11] 6097[9] (6320) 6740[5] 7236[3]

**Marcus Antonius** *Jim Boyle* a71 62
7 b g Mark Of Esteem(IRE) Star Of The Course (USA) (Theatrical (IRE))
1027[7]

**Marcus Caesar (IRE)** *Ruth Carr* 69
4 b g Antonius Pius(USA) Skyscape (Zafonic (USA))
1125[7] 1446[15] 1606[12] 1649[11] 2171[10] 2451[7]

**Mareef (IRE)** *Kevin Morgan* 31
4 b g Oasis Dream Katayeb (IRE) (Machiavellian (USA))
6437[7]

**Maremmadiavola (IRE)** *Edward Lynam* a96 93
3 b f Kheleyf(USA) Naked Poser (IRE) (Night Shift (USA))
6354a[5]

**Marengo** *Ed de Giles* a59 74
3 gr g Verglas(IRE) Cloudchaser (IRE) (Red Ransom (USA))
5303[6] (5751) 6034[8] 6706[5] 7162[4] 7309[5] 7514[2]

**Margaret's Mission (IRE)** *Jeremy Noseda* 65
3 b f Shamardal(USA) Wimple (USA) (Kingmambo (USA))
1534[9] 2346[8] 2877[5]

**Margot Rose** *Harry Dunlop* a51 57
2 b f Kheleyf(USA) Sanjuna (Tiger Hill (IRE))
4396[10] 4846[2] 5859[4] 6248[9] 7529[8]

**Margrets Gift** *Tim Easterby* 74
3 ch f Major Cadeaux Its Another Gift (Primo Dominie)
1543[6] 2217[2] 2657[2] 2910[2] 4455[2] 5080[3] (5333) 7058[2]

**Maria Bella (IRE)** *Charlie Appleby* a88 87
3 ch f Raven's Pass(USA) Infinite Spirit (USA) (Maria's Mon (USA))
(3117) 3615[2] 5826[3] 7196[14]

**Maria Montez** *Charles Hills* a75 77
5 b m Piccolo Easy Feeling (IRE) (Night Shift (USA))
4206[8] (4908) 5182[6] 6189[8] 6680[6] 7286[2] 7357[5] 7949[11]

**Maria's Choice (IRE)** *Alan McCabe* a84 86
5 b g Oratorio(IRE) Amathusia (Selkirk (USA))
89[7]

**Marie D'o (FR)** *J Van Handenhove* a73 92
3 b f Librettist(USA) Suave Marie (IRE) (Suave Dancer (USA))
5482a[11]

**Mariele (IRE)** *W Hefter* a78 88
3 b f Shirocco(GER) Mureefa (USA) (Bahri (USA))
1619a[8]

**Mariet** *Suzy Smith* a61 43
5 ch m Dr Fong(USA) Medway (IRE) (Shernazar)
459[7] 580[8]

**Marigot Bay** *Gay Kelleway* 79
2 b f Paco Boy(IRE) Mamma Morton (IRE) (Elnadim (USA))
5209[2] (5524) 5921[5] 6989[2] 7232[2] 7503[5]

**Marilyn Mon** *Jo Hughes* a65
2 b f Multiplex Future Regime (IRE) (Xaar)
3157[6] 7345[2] 7808[3] 8007[5]

**Marina Ballerina** *Roy Bowring* a68 44
6 bb m Ballet Master(USA) Marinaite (Komaite (USA))
7[9] (13) 252[3] 648[2] 831[10] (1129) 1501[2] 1806[4] 2097[3]

**Mariners Moon (IRE)** *David O'Meara* 79
3 ch g Mount Nelson Dusty Moon (Dr Fong (USA))
1308[9] 1657[2] (2020) ◆ 2204[9] 2827[5] 3464[10] 3911[4] 4298[3] 4754[2] 5768[5] 6166[7] 6596[3] 6672[10]

**Marishi Ten (IRE)** *Jo Davis* a62 65
4 b f Invincible Spirit(IRE) Scripture (IRE) (Sadler's Wells (USA))
853[6] 5006[9]

**Marjong** *Simon Dow* a82 82
4 b f Mount Nelson Vermilliann (IRE) (Mujadil (USA))
746[2] 1212[6] 2030[5] ◆ 2965[5] 3305[3] 3876[7] 4971[2] 5281[3] 5834[4] 6336[3]

**Markami (FR)** *Johnny Farrelly* a78 63
4 ch g Medicean Marque Royale (Royal Academy (USA))
(2207) 2920[11] 4076[8] 5898[P] 6274[8] 6651[9]

**Markaz (IRE)** *B W Hills* 103
2 gr c Dark Angel(IRE) Folga (Atraf)
2507[6] 3279[4] (4142) 4853[2] 6230[2] 6686[2]

**Market Puzzle (IRE)** *Mark Brisbourne* a38 54
7 ch g Bahamian Bounty Trempjane (Lujain (USA))
1865[9] 2212[9] 4808[7] 5033[2] 6028[11] 6394[5] 6706[8]

**Market Share** *P Bary* a100 111
4 b g Zamindar(USA) Winter Solstice (Unfuwain (USA))
3291a[5] 4008a[5]

**Market Storm (FR)** *Brian Meehan* a68 53
3 b g After Market(USA) Minted (USA) (Mineshaft (USA))
1720[4] 3695[5] 4191[8] 6633[10]

**Marksmanship (IRE)** *Ciaron Maher* 104
6 b h Galileo(IRE) Maroochydore (IRE) (Danehill (USA))
7395a[2]

**Mark's Whisper (IRE)** *Bill Turner* a46
2 b f Kodiac Coral Dawn (IRE) (Trempolino (USA))
1314[5] 1575[7]

**Marlborough House** *Keith Dalgleish* a59 25
4 b g Dylan Thomas(IRE) Eurolink Raindance (IRE) (Alzao (USA))
5508[10]

**Marlinda (FR)** *C Boutin* a49 64
2 ch f Linda's Lad Marola (FR) (Kendor (FR))
2976a[6] 3872a[8]

**Marlismamma (FR)** *David O'Meara* a37 55
3 ch f Turtle Bowl(IRE) Karawan (Kris)
267[7] 865[5] 1648[3] 2165[9] 2545[4] 2741[4] 3946[10] 4495[7] 4627[2] 4998[8]

**Marlot** *Jim Boyle* a34 19
2 ch g Mount Nelson Photographie (USA) (Trempolino (USA))
5881[13] 7031[12]

**Marmala (FR)** *Niels Petersen* 88
4 b f Astronomer Royal(USA) Misty Daylight (USA) (Seeking Daylight (USA))
6388a[6]

**Marmalad (IRE)** *Tom Dascombe* a77 67
2 b c Duke Of Marmalade(IRE) Primissima (GER) (Second Set (IRE))
2507[4] 2895[2] 6743[9] 7525[2] (7839) 8016[3]

**Marmalady (IRE)** *Gary Moore* a86 95
4 ch f Duke Of Marmalade(IRE) Grecian Glory (IRE) (Zafonic (USA))
1490[3] 2147[3] 2645[5] 5559[3] 6130[2] (6313) 7543[6]

**Marmande (IRE)** *Daniel Kubler* a55 44
3 ch f Duke Of Marmalade(IRE) Roselyn (Efisio)
70[10] 341[7] 486[8] 5183[5]

**Mar Mar (IRE)** *Saeed bin Suroor* a97 100
4 b f Invincible Spirit(IRE) Queen Of Tara (IRE) (Sadler's Wells (USA))
1679[2] 2149[5] 3203[7] 4445[4] 4895[13]

**Marmarus** *Clive Cox* a81 63
3 b g Duke Of Marmalade(IRE) Polly Perkins (IRE) (Pivotal)
1681[4] 3144[9] 3709[5] (4263) 4612[2] 5303[5] (6567) (6902)

**Marma's Boy** *Ralph Beckett* 78
2 ch g Duke Of Marmalade(IRE) Graduation (Lomitas)
4395[10] 5625[2] 6293[2]

**Marmoom** *Charles Hills* 92
3 ch g Dutch Art Cosmic Song (Cosmonaut)
1192[3] 4111[2] (4446) 4912[4] (5649) 6234[10]

**Marmot** *Roger Charlton* a67 66
2 b c Champs Elysees Winter Bloom (USA) (Aptitude (USA))
6293[5] 7573[4]

**Marmot Bay (IRE)** *Philip Kirby* a63
4 b f Kodiac Tides (Bahamian Bounty)
164[6] 502[11] 511[9]

**Maro** *Derek Shaw* a37 27
3 b g Royal Applause Meditation (Inchinor)
355[12] 500[5] 731[7] 933[3] 1246[5] 1373[10] 1626[7] 2526[6] 2878[8]

**Marphilly (IRE)** *John Best* a53 44
3 b f Amadeus Wolf Pilda (IRE) (Princely Heir (IRE))
189[5] 588[6] 1124[4] 1794[11] 2393[9] 2878[6] 4304[4] 4592[7]

**Mars (IRE)** *M F De Kock* a104 121
4 ch c Galileo(IRE) Massarra (Danehill (USA))
596a[7] 902a[7] 1182a[P]

**Marsali (USA)** *D K Weld* 87
2 bb f More Than Ready(USA) Milago (USA) (Danzig (USA))
4598a[7]

**Marshall Jennings (IRE)** *Richard Hannon* 88
2 b g Lawman(FR) Zuniga's Date (USA) (Diesis)
3194[2] ◆ 4395[2] 5128[3] (5752) 6331[2] 6784[3]

**Marsh Daisy** *Hughie Morrison* 105
3 ch f Pivotal Bella Lambada (Lammtarra (USA))
1423[4] ◆ (2109) (2484) 2960[13] 5479a[6] 6655[3] 7105[8]

**Marshgate Lane (USA)** *Mark Johnston* a107 100
5 b h Medaglia d'Oro(USA) Louvain (IRE) (Sinndar (IRE))
1559[10]

**Marsh Hawk** *Richard Hannon* 106
2 b f Invincible Spirit(IRE) Asaawir (Royal Applause)
(5187) ◆ 6067[2] (6521) ◆ 7240[4]

**Marsh Pride** *Ann Duffield* a76 80
2 b f Stimulation(IRE) Peneia (USA) (Nureyev (USA))
(5443) 6071[3] 6530[8]

**Marsoomah** *Richard Fahey* a46 37
2 b f Aqlaam Bukhoor (IRE) (Danehill (USA))
6641[12] 7495[7] 7973[9] 8221[7]

**Martha's Stand (FR)** *E Libaud* 65
3 b g King's Best(USA) Achtal (IRE) (Sadler's Wells (USA))
2003a[13] 5370a[5]

**Marti Ella** *J S Moore* 41
2 b f Major Cadeaux Reel Cool (Reel Buddy (USA))
2064[4] 3157[4] 3435[7] 3967[6] 4302[5]

**Martinas Delight (USA)** *Timothy Jarvis* a72 79
4 b f Johannesburg(USA) Lerici (USA) (Woodman (USA))
1118[6] 1729[7] (2199) (3139) 3926[3] 5203[7] 5503[3] 5948[6] 7043[7] 7416[10]

**Martinette (USA)** *Charles Hills* a63
3 bb f Mizzen Mast(USA) Faraway Flower (USA) (Distant View (USA))
1143[3] 1424[11]

**Marti's Boy** *J S Moore* a24
3 ch g Bertolini(USA) Rock Art (IRE) (Rock Of Gibraltar (IRE))
187[U] 541[7]

**Martlet** *John Gosden* 76
2 b f Dansili Marywell (Selkirk (USA))
6208[3] ◆

**Maruschka (IRE)** *V Luka Jr* a58 64
3 ch f Medicean Mac Rhapsody (Night Shift (USA))
4464a[4]

**Marvellous (IRE)** *A P O'Brien* 117
3 b f Galileo(IRE) You'resothrilling (USA) (Storm Cat (USA))
1201a[6] (2581a) 2960[6] 4461a[8]

**Marvo** *Bernard Llewellyn* a61 56
10 b g Bahamian Bounty Mega (IRE) (Petardia)
179[10] 281[5] 474[6] 673[6]

**Marweena (IRE)** *Martin Smith* a61 53
3 b f Cape Cross(IRE) Dunes Queen (USA) (Elusive Quality (USA))
70[4] 1768[6] 2126[8] 3627[7] 6857[6]

**Mary Ann Bugg (IRE)** *Phil McEntee* a43 42
2 b f Bushranger(IRE) Shobobb (Shamardal (USA))
1859[6] 3232[7] 3304[5] 3967[7] 4302[6] 7881[8]

**Marydale** *Henry Candy* a75 73
3 ch f Aqlaam Mary Goodnight (King's Best (USA))
2339[12] 3083[4] 3801[4] 4611[3] (5492) ◆ 6304[5]

**Mary Is Back (FR)** *C Boutin* a62 62
3 ch f Redback Coup De Marie (IRE) (Mujadil (USA))
2978a[8]

**Mary Le Bow** *Victor Dartnall* a71 60
3 b f Sir Percy Bermondsey Girl (Bertolini (USA))
236[4] 488[2] 668[5] 1220[4] 2621[9] 3116[5] 3803[9] 4563[2] 5302[4] 6087[4] 6426[2] (7570) 7744[8] 8232[5]

**Marymalade** *Harry Dunlop*
2 ch f Duke Of Marmalade(IRE) Fastback (IRE) (Singspiel (IRE))
7667[17] 8036[11]

**Mary McPhee** *Charles Hills* 77
2 ch f Makfi Aunty Mary (Common Grounds)
1528[10] 2436[2] (3933) 4585[7] 6253[16]

**Mary's Prayer** *John Holt* a44 46
3 b f Champs Elysees Phi Phi (IRE) (Fasliyev (USA))
323[8] 642[5] 871[7] 2655[5] 4473[13] 6076[11] 6454[10] 7021[7]

**Mary's Secret** *Tom Dascombe* a67 40
2 b f Exceed And Excel(AUS) Don't Tell Mary (IRE) (Starcraft (NZ))
5789[9] 6408[4] 7062[3]

**Marzante (USA)** *Roger Charlton* a72 77
6 gr g Maria's Mon(USA) Danzante (USA) (Danzig (USA))
4808[2] 6855[6]

**Marzocco (USA)** *John Gosden* a81 112
3 bb g Kitten's Joy(USA) Dynamia (USA) (Dynaformer (USA))
1652[2] ◆ 2502[2] 3419[3] 4251a[5] 5577[4] 6329[5] 6894[2] 7271[8]

**Masai (IRE)** *A P O'Brien* a95 96
3 b c Oasis Dream I'm In Love (USA) (Zafonic (USA))
4480a[12] 6369a[13]

**Masai Moon** *Rod Millman* a73 64
10 b g Lujain(USA) Easy To Imagine (USA) (Cozzene (USA))
11[5] 245[10] 589[9] (835) (934) 1115[3] 1689[10] 2300[8] 3088[6] 3795[4] 4072[4] 4673[3] 5247[7]

**Masamah (IRE)** *Marco Botti* a105 111
8 gr g Exceed And Excel(AUS) Bethesda (Distant Relative)
304a[3] 393a[6] 769a[9] 2076[2] 2786[17] 3241[2] 4179[5] 4700[5] ◆ 5160[10]

**Masarah (IRE)** *Clive Brittain* a99 100
4 b f Cape Cross(IRE) Fragrancy (IRE) (Singspiel (IRE))
2144[4] 2956[4] 3355[13] 4060[10] 5467[8]

**Mash Potato (IRE)** *Michael Dods* 80
4 b g Whipper(USA) Salva (Grand Lodge (USA))
1362[5] 2607[6] 7411[2] 7672[5]

**Masipa (IRE)** *Rae Guest* a60
2 b f Lawman(FR) Barconey (IRE) (Danehill Dancer (IRE))
5555[5]

**Masiyann (FR)** *A Bonin* a78 90
4 b g Anabaa(USA) Marasima (IRE) (Barathea (IRE))
3172a[8]

**Masked Dance (IRE)** *Scott Dixon* a60 59
7 gr g Captain Rio Brooks Masquerade (Absalom)
353[3] 766[4] 835[2] 973[6] 1309[8] 2094[5] 5287[5] 7056[6] 7644[16] 7766[4] 8084[3] 8139[6]

**Masked Marvel** *Robert Hickmott* 108
6 b h Montjeu(IRE) Waldmark (GER) (Mark Of Esteem (IRE))
7126a[13]

**Maskoon** *Kevin Prendergast* 97
3 ch g Aqlaam Tamazug (Machiavellian (USA))
4771a[8] 5957a[16]

**Mason Hindmarsh** *Karen McLintock* a72 73
7 ch g Dr Fong(USA) Sierra Virgen (USA) (Stack (USA))
1929[3] 2424[4] 3661[2] 4296[6] 5017[3] 5764[5] 6640[9]

**Masquerading (IRE)** *Jonjo O'Neill* a95 91
4 b g Singspiel(IRE) Moonlight Dance (USA) (Alysheba (USA))
1383[2] ◆ 2561[10]

**Massini's Trap (IRE)** *J A Nash* a64 79
5 b g Dr Massini(IRE) Sparrow's Trap (IRE) (Magical Wonder (USA))
4746a[11] 7142a[9] 7476a[14]

**Massiyn (IRE)** *Robert Hickmott* 105
5 ch h Zamindar(USA) Masilia (IRE) (Kahyasi)
7127a[10]

**Mass Rally (IRE)** *Michael Dods* a91 113
7 b g Kheleyf(USA) Reunion (IRE) (Be My Guest (USA))
1163[9] 2149[6] 2256[4] 5575[9] ◆ 6167[7] 6533[20] 7122[16] 7408[6]

**Master Apprentice (IRE)** *Andrew Balding* 98
2 gr c Mastercraftsman(IRE) Lady Hawkfield (IRE) (Hawk Wing (USA))
5881[3] 6300[2] (6985) 7557a[9]

**Master Bond** *David O'Meara* a86 92
5 b g Misu Bond(IRE) Bond Royale (Piccolo)
2167[3] 3256[5] (3831) (5170) 5563[2] 6096[2] ◆ 7233[10] 7889[4] 8045[5]

**Master Carpenter (IRE)** *Rod Millman* 106
3 ch c Mastercraftsman(IRE) Fringe (In The Wings)
1436[3] 1699[3] 2345[2] (2706) (3807a) 4483a[3] 6382a[10] 6710[12]

**Master Choice (IRE)** *William Haggas* a45 37
2 b g Mastercraftsman(IRE) No Quest (IRE) (Rainbow Quest (USA))
6203[7] 6604[10] 7031[9] 7328[6]

**Master Clockmaker (IRE)** *Ann Duffield* 70
3 gr g Mastercraftsman(IRE) Mairead Anne (USA) (Elusive Quality (USA))
1542[3] 1880[5] 3789[9] 7501[9]

**Master Dan** *James Given* a81 52
3 b g Mastercraftsman(IRE) Danella (IRE) (Platini (GER))
1400[9] 1847[11] 2098[2] 2621[6] 3797[5] 5101[2] 5343[6] 6075[2] 7627[2] (7913) 8089[4] 8283[5]

**Master Dancer** *Philip Hide* a73 77
3 gr g Mastercraftsman(IRE) Isabella Glyn (IRE) (Sadler's Wells (USA))
2496[4] 3197[6] 3974[3] 5550[5] 6044[5] 6722[6] 7359[11]

**Mastered (IRE)** *John Best* a43 35
4 ch g Refuse To Bend(IRE) Woodmaven (USA) (Woodman (USA))
1105[12] 2443[7] 2874[6]

**Masterful Act (USA)** *Alan McCabe* a106 58
7 ch g Pleasantly Perfect(USA) Catnip (USA) (Flying Paster (USA))
(3) (386) 764[4] 1556[14] 6169[11] 7703[8]

**Master Of Disguise** *Brian Baugh* a68 88
8 b g Kyllachy St James's Antigua (IRE) (Law Society (USA))
9[3] 259[3] 510[2] 694[8] 889[4] 1082[7] 7900[7] 8088[7] 8285[5]

**Master Of Finance (IRE)** *Mark Johnston* a79 94
3 ch g Mastercraftsman(IRE) Cheal Rose (IRE) (Dr Devious (IRE))
(1927) 2337[6] 3003[2] 3512a[3] 4893[9] 5188[2] 5792[7] 6737[2] 7119[10] 7410[7] 7688[7]

**Master Of Irony (IRE)** *Ralph Beckett* a73
2 b g Makfi Mother Of Pearl (IRE) (Sadler's Wells (USA))
(8192)

**Master Of Song** *Roy Bowring* a71 49
7 ch g Ballet Master(USA) Ocean Song (Savahra Sound)
1227[5] 2935[2] 3226[7] 3971[11] 4415[7] 5103[3] 5530[4] (7645) (7823) 8261[11]

**Master Of Speed (IRE)** *Roger Varian* 57
2 ch g Mastercraftsman(IRE) Mango Groove (IRE) (Unfuwain (USA))
7537[5]

**Master Of Suspense** *Peter Chapple-Hyam* 79
3 ch g Exceed And Excel(AUS) Ridotto (Salse (USA))
1511[4] 1677[3] 2344[9] (5916)

**Master Of Time (IRE)** *P D Deegan* a85 64
3 br g Amadeus Wolf Lady Causeway (USA) (Giant's Causeway (USA))
(416a)

**Master Of War** *D Selvaratnam* a99 106
4 ch c Compton Place Mamma Morton (IRE) (Elnadim (USA))
304a[13] 504a[4] 679a[9]

**Masterpaver** *Alan Bailey* a100 64
3 gr g Mastercraftsman(IRE) Most-Saucy (Most Welcome)
(71) (236) ◆ (488) 668[3] 1033[4] 1220[3] 1635[8] 2998[6] 3391[2] 3643[6] (5038) 5185[4] 5552[2] 6855[2] 7033[3] 7545[12] (7703) 7803[7] 7837[3] 8095[11]

**Master Plan (SAF)** *M F De Kock* 110
6 b g Jet Master(SAF) Princess Polly (SAF) (Royal Chalice (SAF))
398a[6]

**Master Rooney (IRE)** *Geoffrey Harker* 72
8 bb g Cape Cross(IRE) Wimple (USA) (Kingmambo (USA))
3338[16]

**Master Speaker (IRE)** *Martin Hassett* a93 99
4 b g Danehill Dancer(IRE) First Breeze (USA) (Woodman (USA))
3284a[3] 4480a[10] 6371a[9] 7433a[7]

**Master's Spirit (IRE)** *P Demercastel* 99
3 gr c Mastercraftsman(IRE) Lavayssiere (FR) (Sicyos (USA))
2818a[12] 5591a[3]

**Master The World (IRE)** *David Elsworth* 100
3 gr g Mastercraftsman(IRE) Zadalla (Zaha (CAN))
1516[9] 1951[12] 3965[3] 4198[6] 4801[3] (5656) 6149[3] 6560[2] 6688[7] 7410[5]

**Master Zephyr** *Roger Charlton* a69 61
2 b g Shirocco(GER) Missy Dancer (Shareef Dancer (USA))
4800[5] 5874[8] 6545[11] (7075)

**Mataajir (USA)** *Derek Shaw* a69 30
6 b g Redoute's Choice(AUS) Hamasah (USA) (Irish River (FR))
17[8] (78) 171[2] 252[7] 366[9]

**Matalleb (USA)** *John Gosden* 87
3 b g Elusive Quality(USA) Our Rite Of Spring (USA) (Stravinsky (USA))
(1433) ◆ 2148[6]

**Mata Utu (IRE)** *C Escuder* 70
3 b c Slickly(FR) Efisia (FR) (Efisio)
7269a[4]

**Mateka** *Roger Charlton*
3 ch f Nayef(USA) Marakabei (Hernando (FR))
6298[9]

**Matorio (FR)** *H-A Pantall* a88 110
4 b f Oratorio(IRE) Matwan (FR) (Indian Rocket)
1908a[2] 2587a[6] 4008a[4] 6955a[7] 7559a[6] 7916a[12]

**Matraash (USA)** *Daniel Mark Loughnane* a82 76
8 b h Elusive Quality(USA) Min Alhawa (USA) (Riverman (USA))
66[3] (199) 407[4] 685[5] 1034[3] 3064[8] 3438[2] 4080[DSQ] 4470[3] 4792[2] 5521[8] 7288[10] 7626[10] 7925[4] ◆ 8102[11] 8163[4]

**Matravers** *Sir Michael Stoute* a86 73
3 b c Oasis Dream Maakrah (Dubai Destination (USA))
2877[6] 3153[8] (3970) 4549[5] (6034) 6609[2]

**Matreas (FR)** *J Phelippon* a54 71
7 b g Peintre Celebre(USA) Tritonia (GR) (Saddlers' Hall (IRE))
920a[8]

**Matron** *James Fanshawe* a52 57
2 ch f Bahamian Bounty Prescription (Pivotal)
5344[7] 6270[5]

**Matterhorn (USA)** *Todd Pletcher* a103
3 b c Tapit(USA) Winter Garden (USA) (Roy (USA))
3026a[8]

**Mattmu** *Tim Easterby* 112
2 b c Indesatchel(IRE) Katie Boo (IRE) (Namid)
1712[2] 2231[2] 2601[2] (4389) (4936) 6256[3] 6933[2] (7121) (7655a)

**Mattydillon** *Kevin Prendergast* a73 76
2 ch g Elnadim(USA) Almurooj (Zafonic (USA))
6375a[8]

**Matuszak (USA)** *William Mott* a96
3 bb c Bernardini(USA) Golden Sonata (USA) (Mr Prospector (USA))
3026a[10]

**Maui (FR)** *Mlle V Dissaux* a58 73
2 ch f Doctor Dino(FR) Iza Bere (FR) (Shining Steel)
2755a[7] 4312a[6] 5617a[6] 6245a[6] 6619a[5]

**Mauny (FR)** *Mlle A Voraz* a75 83
3 ch f Montmartre(FR) Rafale Pearl (FR) (Verbier (FR))
1139a[5] 2411a[3]

**Maupiti Express (FR)** *David O'Meara* a58 39
3 b g Chineur(FR) Azucar (FR) (Marathon (USA))
543[3]

**Maureb (IRE)** *Tony Coyle* 64
2 br f Excellent Art Almost Blue (USA) (Mr Greeley (USA))
5241[4] 5680[4] 6375a[18]

**Maureen (IRE)** *Richard Hannon* 89
4 b f Holy Roman Emperor(IRE) Exotic Mix (FR) (Linamix (FR))
1163[5] ◆ 1945[7]

**Maven** *Tim Easterby* a77 93
6 b m Doyen(IRE) Bollin Jeannie (Royal Applause)
1196[6] 1539[2] (1882) 2253[10] 2618[7] 2826[2] 3251[11] 3644[4] 4680[3] 5695[10] 6258[3] 6479[2] 6746[10] 6870[6] 7641[2]

**Maverick Wave (USA)** *John Gosden* a106 104
3 ch c Elusive Quality(USA) Misty Ocean (USA) (Stormy Atlantic (USA))
(4580) ◆ 5192[2] 6332[4] 6752[23] 7276[2] 7688[3] (7930) ◆ 8144[6]

**Maverik** *William Knight* a95 93
6 ch g Iceman Nouvelle Lune (Fantastic Light (USA))
4331[5] 4761[18] (5528) 5895[4] 6320[2] 6740[12] 7227[8]

**Mavree (IRE)** *Tim Easterby* a35 38
3 b f Captain Marvelous(IRE) Hemasree (IRE) (Exceed And Excel (AUS))
261[6] 480[6]

**Mawaakef (IRE)** *J R Jenkins* a95 95
6 b g Azamour(IRE) Al Euro (FR) (Mujtahid (USA))
85[3] 427[4] 623[9]

**Mawaqeet (USA)** *Donald McCain* 99
5 b g Dynaformer(USA) Lady Ilsley (USA) (Trempolino (USA))
2073[11] 3717[18]

**Mawaseel** *B W Hills* a66 71
3 ch g Sea The Stars(IRE) Kareemah (IRE) (Peintre Celebre (USA))
1529[10] 2497[3] 3248[7] 4325[5] 5191[3] 6611[4]

**Mawfoor (IRE)** *Brian Meehan* 93
3 b g Iffraaj Miss Odlum (IRE) (Mtoto)
2111[6] 2565[13] 3378[27] 3980[7] 4404[4]

**Mawhub** *S Seemar* a101 89
5 b g Singspiel(IRE) Native Blue (Seeking The Gold (USA))
243a[8]

**Max Attack (FR)** *A Junk* a42 62
2 bb g Persian Combat(USA) Marabounta (FR) (Zieten (USA))
4932a[10] 5588a[6] 6591a[10]

**Max Beauty (FR)** *A Al Raihe* a77
3 ch f American Post Nebraska I (FR) (Octagonal (NZ))
203a[8]

**Maxie T** *Mark Johnston* a71 79
3 b g Dalakhani(IRE) Ballet Ballon (USA) (Rahy (USA))
668[4] (1033) (1372) 1530[10] 2077[4] 2494[4] 3183[6]

**Maximus Dream (TUR)** *C Turan* a96
5 b h Oasis Dream Sweet Mischief (IRE) (Sadler's Wells (USA))
6163a[5]

**Max La Fripouille (FR)** *Rod Collet* 93
2 b c Panis(USA) Codicille (FR) (Mendocino (USA))
6181a[6]

**Max The Machine** *Derek Shaw* a66 64
4 b g Intikhab(USA) Digamist Girl (IRE) (Digamist (USA))
9[9] 921[5]

**Maxwell (IRE)** *Ralph Beckett* a77 63
2 b c Big Bad Bob(IRE) Gladiole (GER) (Platini (GER))
6293[7] 7371[2]

**Maya Desnuda (IRE)** *J Heloury* 65
2 b f Intense Focus(USA) Duchess Ravel (IRE) (Bachelor Duke (USA))
5662a[4]

**Mayan Flight (IRE)** *Tony Carroll* a39 42
6 b g Hawk Wing(USA) Balimaya (IRE) (Barathea (IRE))
246[9] 459[9] 1263[8]

**Maybe I Wont** *James Moffatt* a21 23
9 b g Kyllachy Surprise Surprise (Robellino (USA))
4962[10]

**Maybeme** *Neville Bycroft* a39 80
8 b m Lujain(USA) Malvadilla (IRE) (Doyoun)
1660[5] (2540) 2868[3] (3368) 4454[3] 4680[6] 5448[4] 5716[8] 6166[5]

**Maybe Now Baby (IRE)** *David Simcock* 68
2 b f Kodiac Slow Jazz (USA) (Chief's Crown (USA))
3223[6] 3888[15] 5344[3] 6749[8] 7237[6] 7487[8]

**Maybe Tomorrow** *David Simcock* 66
2 b f Zamindar(USA) Appointed One (USA) (Danzig (USA))
6553[10] 7377[5]

**Mayfield Boy** *Mel Brittain* 79
3 b c Authorized(IRE) Big Pink (IRE) (Bigstone (IRE))
2203[4] (2749) 3273[10] 4419[2] 4631[6] 4794[4] 5420[6] 6490[11]

**Mayfield Girl (IRE)** *Mel Brittain* a70 82
4 br f One Cool Cat(USA) Rose Of Mooncoin (IRE) (Brief Truce (USA))
1850[2] 1961[8] 2361[5] 3256[16] 4632[8] 5333[10] 5498[13] 7949[4]

**Maygo's Joy** *Ralph J Smith* a46 42
4 b g Josr Algarhoud(IRE) Nikki Bea (IRE) (Titus Livius (FR))
90[6] 179[14]

**May Hay** *Anthony Carson* a74 65
4 b f Dubai Destination(USA) Trounce (Barathea (IRE))
3174[5] 4966[7] 5490[7] 6682[4] 7006[2] 7287[4] 7657[4]

**Mayhem (IRE)** *P Sogorb* 111
3 bb f Whipper(USA) Hit The Sky (IRE) (Cozzene (USA))
(6419a) 6956a[2] 7480a[4]

**May Hill Rebel** *Richard Guest* 46
2 b f Cockney Rebel(IRE) Hill Tribe (Tiger Hill (IRE))
5910[9] 6148[7] 6449[11] 7003[6]

**Maymyo (IRE)** *Sylvester Kirk* a69 69
3 b c Invincible Spirit(IRE) Lady Windermere (IRE) (Lake Coniston (IRE))
2846[4] 3083[6] 4535[5] (5820) 6488[10] 7023[3] 7670[7]

**May One** *Mick Channon* 28
2 b f Winker Watson Excellent Day (IRE) (Invincible Spirit (IRE))
1571[10] 1901[7] 3894[5]

**May Queen** *Chris Wall* a68 58
3 ch f Shamardal(USA) Mango Lady (Dalakhani (IRE))
3142[6] 3652[7] 4052[12] 6037[3] 6682[3] (7291)

**May's Boy** *James Moffatt* a62 58
6 gr h Proclamation(IRE) Sweet Portia (IRE) (Pennekamp (USA))
6597[11]

**Maysville (IRE)** *Tony Coyle* a56 56
3 b f Lawman(FR) Morality (Elusive Quality (USA))
1647[4] 2020[10] 2906[5]

**Mayumi (IRE)** *A Fabre* a96 93
3 b f Rock Of Gibraltar(IRE) Majura (GER) (Samum (GER))
6419a[6]

**Mazaaher** *B W Hills* a83 74
4 b g Elnadim(USA) Elutrah (Darshaan)
2772[8] 3272[4] (5258) 5895[3] 6523[10] 6839[4]

**Mazeppa** *Keith Dalgleish* 77
4 b c Byron Howards Heroine (IRE) (Danehill Dancer (IRE))
2477[9] 3054[5] (3242)

**Mazij** *Peter Hiatt* a55 46
6 b m Haafhd Salim Toto (Mtoto)
120[8] 278[6] 458[8] 612[4] 648[4] 781[7] 1000[2] 1132[7] 1453[8] 2396[5] 2923[7] 3115[11] 4343[5] (4749) 5331[4] 6028[8] 7360[2] 7932[4] 8145[6]

**Mazoula (IRE)** *Hugo Palmer* a60 59
2 b f Camacho Molaaf (Shareef Dancer (USA))
3799[5] 4652[5] 5210[4] 5828[5] (6412) 7258[8]

**Mazovian (USA)** *Michael Chapman* a41 33
6 b g E Dubai(USA) Polish Style (USA) (Danzig (USA))
7908[7] 8208[6] 8277[5]

**Mbhali (IRE)** *Mark Johnston* a77 74
3 b c Cape Cross(IRE) Ma Paloma (FR) (Highest Honor (FR))
230[2] 403[2] 536[2] 717[3] 3385[5] 3822[2] 3974[8]

**Mcbirney (USA)** *Paul D'Arcy* a72 71
7 b g Danehill Dancer(IRE) Dear Girl (IRE) (Fairy King (USA))
655[7] 1617[2] 1815[3] 2464[6] 2963[7] 3398[6] 5395[9] 7068[9] 7635[2] 7744[4] 7925[6] 8250[6]

**McCarthy Mor (IRE)** *Richard Fahey* a50 61
3 b g Bushranger(IRE) Alexander Anapolis (IRE) (Spectrum (IRE))
1890[5] 2205[3] 2878[11] 3380[2] 3650[3] 4455[4] 4997[4] 6516[8] 7644[3]

**McCartney (GER)** *S Seemar* a53 99
9 b g In The Wings Messina (GER) (Dashing Blade)
112a[15]

**McCool Bannanas** *James Unett* a61 67
6 b g Firebreak Dances With Angels (IRE) (Mukaddamah (USA))
65[3] 319[10] 1717[5] 2843[5]

**McCreery** *Roger Charlton* 78
2 b c Big Bad Bob(IRE) Dolma (FR) (Marchand De Sable (USA))
(6551) ◆

**Mclovin Riverdance** *Ann Duffield* a41 50
2 b g Lawman(FR) Electric Dream (Royal Applause)
6449[8] 6935[13] 8060[9]

**Mcmonagle (USA)** *Alan Brown* a72 62
6 ch g Mizzen Mast(USA) Dippers (USA) (Polish Numbers (USA))
96[7] 1673[11] 3436[7] 3908[13] 4468[6] 4792[3] 5529[10] 5893[10]

**Mcvicar** *John Davies* a38 66
5 b g Tobougg(IRE) Aries (GER) (Big Shuffle (USA))
7175[14]

**Meadow Cross (IRE)** *Tim Easterby* 28
2 b f Cape Cross(IRE) Hovering (IRE) (In The Wings)
4346[11]

**Meadway** *Bryan Smart* a94 92
3 b g Captain Gerrard(IRE) Tibesti (Machiavellian (USA))
1445[7] 1737[3] ◆ 1968[3] 2317[11] 2897[5] 3484[3] (4636) 5243[4] 5923[4] (6763) 7330[10] (7761)

**Meandmyshadow** *Alan Brown* a52 88
6 ch m Tobougg(IRE) Queen Jean (Pivotal)
1446[16] 1694[3] 2332[8] 2955[6] (3298) 3384[6] 3882[3] 4132[5] 4632[3] 5398[6] (5641) 5817[3] 6558[12] 6736[7] 7506[12]

**Meandra (IRE)** *N Clement* 73
3 b f Dubawi(IRE) Mystic Spirit (IRE) (Invincible Spirit (IRE))
5368a[9]

**Meandre (FR)** *Doug Watson* a92 116
6 gr h Slickly(FR) Penne (FR) (Sevres Rose (IRE))
598a[2] 900a[4] 1182a[7]

**Meaning Of Life (IRE)** *Stefano Botti* a64 68
3 b c Exceed And Excel(AUS) Emirates Hills (Dubawi (IRE))
892[4] 7604a[10]

**Mecado (IRE)** *Richard Hannon* a72 73
2 ch c Compton Place Corryvreckan (IRE) (Night Shift (USA))
5009[5] (5120) 5782[4] (6422) 7984[3] 8091[5] (8183)

**Mecca's Angel (IRE)** *Michael Dods* a97 115
3 gr f Dark Angel(IRE) Folga (Atraf)
(1445) ◆ (1968) 2226a[5] (6231) (6549)

**Mecca's Mirage (IRE)** *Michael Dods* a70 68
2 ch f Footstepsinthesand Dangle (IRE) (Desert Style (IRE))
1656[2] (2395) 3922[6] 4345[7] 5014[3] 5506[4] (6447)

**Medaillon (FR)** *Mario Hofer* a76 76
3 b c Medicean Raisonnable (Common Grounds)
3869a[10] 5705a[3]

**Medal Count (USA)** *Dale Romans* a117 104
3 b c Dynaformer(USA) Brisquette (USA) (Unbridled's Song (USA))
1964a[8] 3026a[3]

**Medallero (USA)** *Clive Brittain* 15
3 b c Medaglia d'Oro(USA) Rajeem (Diktat)
2346[10] 5347[7]

**Medal Of Valour (JPN)** *Mark Gillard* a59 67
6 b g Medaglia d'Oro(USA) Tres Tres Joli (USA) (Gone West (USA))
2401[8] 3035[2] 4911[10] 5596[5] (6028) 6813[5] 7309[9] 7846[9] 8161[7]

**Medam** *Shaun Harris* a71 62
5 b m Medicean Mamounia (IRE) (Green Desert (USA))
65[7] 147[3] (251) (351) 562[3] 718[2] 853[4] 952[6] 1123[3] 2479[4] (3149) 3575[7] (4611) 5256[2] 5415[12] 5763[4] 6074[8] 7286[10] 7622[2]

**Medburn Cutler** *Paul Henderson* a61 60
4 ch g Zafeen(FR) Tiegs (IRE) (Desert Prince (IRE))
1119[4] 1911[8] 2497[8] 2923[5] 3208[11] 3824[7] 5001[4] (5342) 6264[7] 7419[3] 7657[2]

**Meddling** *Julia Feilden* a70 67
4 ch f Halling(USA) Piffling (Pivotal)
461[7] 691[2] 922[6] 1131[3] (1917) 3390[8] 7556[3] (8103)

**Medecis Mountain** *John Wainwright* a55 48
5 b g Medecis Moon Cat (IRE) (Desert Story (IRE))
(201) 428[8] ◆ 3485[7] 3908[10] 4473[14] 4727[6]

**Media Hype** *K R Burke* a77 90
7 b h Tiger Hill(IRE) Hyperspectra (Rainbow Quest (USA))
54[14] 1171[11] 1736[6] 2314[7]

**Mediate** *Mark Johnston* 62
3 ch c New Approach(IRE) Miss Prim (Case Law)
3602[3]

**Medicean Bliss (IRE)** *Jeremy Gask* a69 57
2 b f Medicean So Blissful (IRE) (Cape Cross (IRE))
5042[5] 5667[6] 6408[2] 7113[3]

**Medicean Man** *Jeremy Gask* a111 113
8 ch g Medicean Kalindi (Efisio)
393a[3] (680a) (769a) 1179a[4] 3319[4] 3451[13] 7802[5]

**Medicean Melody** *David Simcock* a42 34
2 br f Royal Applause Meredith (Medicean)
5821[11] 6606[9] 7405[13]

**Medicean Queen (IRE)** *Clive Brittain* 49
3 b f Medicean Qui Moi (CAN) (Swain (IRE))
3142[8]

**Medicine Hat** *George Moore* 62
3 b g Multiplex Blushing Heart (Observatory (USA))
4924[3] 5388[5]

**Medici Time** *Tim Easterby* 80
9 gr g Medicean Pendulum (Pursuit Of Love)
1541[8] 2602[11] 2914[5] 3399[6] 3702[11] 3831[4] 4494[2] 4901[4] 5437[9] 5913[3]

**Medieval Bishop (IRE)** *Tony Forbes* a53 64
5 b g Bachelor Duke(USA) On The Backfoot (IRE) (Bob Back (USA))
1307[8] 1929[2] 2515[4] 3532[5] 5200[6] 6564[7] 7175[10] 7990[8] 8134[8]

**Mediteranea (FR)** *F-M Cottin* a55 40
3 b f Smart Strike(CAN) Mare Nostrum (Caerleon (USA))
1139a[12]

**Mediterranean Sea (IRE)** *J R Jenkins* a81 79
8 b m Medecis High Glider (High Top)
361[4]

**Medley Chic (IRE)** *F Head* 103
2 ch c Medicean Sorciere (IRE) (Orpen (USA))
(4932a) (5740a)

**Medrano** *David Brown* 97
2 b c Archipenko(USA) Trick Or Treat (Lomitas)
2507[8] 3136[2] ◆ (4424) 6136[2] 6750[6]

**Meebo (IRE)** *J R Jenkins* a69 58
3 b f Captain Rio Abbeyleix Lady (IRE) (Montjeu (IRE))
94[3] 302[4] 547[2] 651[2] 1223[4] 1384[8] 1860[4] 2397[3] 2526[7] 2931[2] 3406[2] 3792[2] 4324[8] (5568) 6340[4] 7457[6] 7671[4] 7826[6] 8088[5] 8210[9]

**Meerjungfrau (GER)** *A Wohler* 102
3 br f Manduro(GER) Meergottin (GER) (Dashing Blade)
(1619a)

**Meeska Moska (FR)** *C Plisson* a45 54
3 ch g Lando(GER) Red Valentine (IRE) (Bad As I Wanna Be (IRE))
2003a[7]

**Meeson** *Violet M Jordan*
3 gr g Fair Mix(IRE) Premiere Foulee (FR) (Sillery (USA))
2733[9]

**Meetha Achar** *Jim Boyle* a47
4 b f Sakhee(USA) Sweet Pickle (Piccolo)
844[3]

**Meetings Man (IRE)** *Ali Stronge* a84 87
7 gr g Footstepsinthesand Missella (IRE) (Danehill (USA))
2034[4] (2651) 2835[3] (3475) (4552) 5047[3] (6439) 7539[11] 7838[10]

**Meeting Waters** *William Haggas* a88 99
3 ch f Aqlaam Paradise Isle (Bahamian Bounty)
2639[2] 4053[2] 5032[2] (6112) 6922[2]

**Meet Me Halfway** *Chris Wall* a76 90
4 b f Exceed And Excel(AUS) Pivotal Drive (IRE) (Pivotal)
1230[2] (1863) (2448) 3879[8] (4866) 6892[11]

**Megalala (IRE)** *John Bridger* a66 67
13 b g Petardia Avionne (Derrylin)
(1664) (2046) 2464[3] 4273[4] 5076[3] 5383[4] 5787[2] 6395[7] 7001[10]

**Megaleka** *Alan Bailey* a90 95
4 b f Misu Bond(IRE) Peyto Princess (Bold Arrangement)
(466) 694[3] (777) 866[4] 1080[4] (1378) (1618) (1759) 2096[4] 2456[6] 2803[7] 4128[2] 4412[2] 4531[7] 4762[4] 5016[4] 5419[17] 6512[18] (7212) 7441[10] 7738[6] 7889[10]

**Megamunch (IRE)** *Kristin Stubbs* a78 63
4 b g Camacho Liscoa (IRE) (Foxhound (USA))
5235[9] 5761[10] 7098[6] 7639[4]

**Mehdi (IRE)** *Richard Fahey* a100 95
5 b g Holy Roman Emperor(IRE) College Fund Girl (IRE) (Kahyasi)
5888[5] 6320[8] 6531[2] 6740[9]

**Mehronissa** *Ed Vaughan* 80
2 ch f Iffraaj Miss University (USA) (Beau Genius (CAN))
(5643) ◆

**Meiner Lacrima (JPN)** *Hiroyuki Uehara* 119
6 ch h Chief Bearhart(CAN) Teardrops (JPN) (Sunday Silence (USA))
2004a[10]

**Mejaen (FR)** *P Decouz* 72
2 b g Shirocco(GER) Huaca (USA) (Thunder Gulch (USA))
5588a[3]

**Mekong River (IRE)** *A P O'Brien* 110
3 b c Galileo(IRE) Simply Perfect (Danehill (USA))
2153[9] 2579a[2] (3765a)

**Melbourne Shuffle (USA)** *John Gosden* a71
2 bb f Street Cry(IRE) Liffey Dancer (IRE) (Sadler's Wells (USA))
7184[9] 7659[2]

**Melchope (FR)** *E J O'Neill* a59 64
2 ch f Deportivo Parmelie (FR) (Pivotal)
2976a[3] 5026a[6] 5544a[13]

**Meleagros (IRE)** *Alain Couetil* a86 114
5 b h King's Best(USA) Viola Royale (IRE) (Royal Academy (USA))
2106a[2] 3774a[5] 5224a[4] 6381a[6]

**Melodica** *Roger Charlton* a64 53
2 b f Dansili Maganda (IRE) (Sadler's Wells (USA))
7450[8] 7927[4]

**Melodious** *David Elsworth* a74 45
2 b f Cape Cross(IRE) Gower Song (Singspiel (IRE))
6924[8] 7398[2]

**Melody Of Love** *Brian Meehan* 95
4 b f Haafhd Tamzin (Hernando (FR))
2155[6] 2956[10] 3674[8]

**Melrose Abbey (IRE)** *Ralph Beckett* 95
3 ch f Selkirk(USA) Villa Carlotta (Rainbow Quest (USA))
(1911) 2277[2] (3725) 6255[9] 7717[5]

**Melvin The Grate (IRE)** *Andrew Balding* a101 90
4 b g Danehill Dancer(IRE) Hawala (IRE) (Warning)
6990[2] (7236) ◆ 7719[12] (7971) (8295)

**Memoria** *Rae Guest* a80 61
3 b f Teofilo(IRE) Midnight Shift (IRE) (Night Shift (USA))
7158[2] (7686) 7871[4] ◆ 8168[8]

**Memorial Day (IRE)** *Saeed bin Suroor* a67
3 b c Cape Cross(IRE) Reunite (IRE) (Kingmambo (USA))
7682[3]

**Memories Galore (IRE)** *Harry Dunlop* 50
2 b g Invincible Spirit(IRE) Persian Memories (IRE) (Indian Ridge)
4800[8]

**Memory Cloth** *Brian Ellison* a76 96
7 b g Cape Cross(IRE) Gossamer (Sadler's Wells (USA))
(1168) (1281) (1724) 2091[4] 2423[2] 3574[4] 5633[11] 6098[11]

**Memory Lane (FR)** *J-M Beguigne* a63 76
3 b f Orpen(USA) Belle Esprit (Warning)
5589a[3]

**Menardais (FR)** *P Bary* a98 111
5 b g Canyon Creek(IRE) Madeleine's Blush (USA) (Rahy (USA))
(7916a)

**Mendacious Harpy (IRE)** *George Baker* a54 73
3 b f Dark Angel(IRE) Idesia (IRE) (Green Desert (USA))
1352[6] 1725[6] 2224[5] 3037[7] 3559[4] 5057[2] 5598[2] 6154[4] (6540) 7302[2] 7339[3] 7494[4]

**Mendelita** *Richard Fahey* 67
3 ch f Archipenko(USA) Dame De Noche (Lion Cavern (USA))
1542[9] 1959[5] 2365[4] 3396[5] 4420[7] (5270) 5818[3] 6541[8]

**Men Don't Cry (IRE)** *Ed de Giles* a82 80
5 b g Street Cry(IRE) Naissance Royale (IRE) (Giant's Causeway (USA))
(2465) 3086[4] (3552) (3778) 4709[4] 4910[2] 5073[11] 5863[4] 6274[2] 6696[3] 7016[7]

**Menelik (IRE)** *Des Donovan* a73 67
5 b g Oasis Dream Chica Roca (USA) (Woodman (USA))
310[7] 359[4] (775) 1027[3] 1108[2] 2207[6] 2646[12] 4080[6] (5560) 6019[7] 8260[11]

**Menorah (IRE)** *Philip Hobbs* 107
9 b g King's Theatre(IRE) Maid For Adventure (IRE) (Strong Gale)
2704[9]

**Mensoora (SAF)** *M F De Kock* a102 90
4 b f Jet Master(SAF) Mansoor (AUS) (Giant's Causeway (USA))
395a[5] 506a[2] 771a[3]

**Meqlaam (GER)** *K Demme* 52
2 b c Aqlaam Melody Fair (IRE) (Montjeu (IRE))
4524a[8] 6123a[9]

**Mercers Row** *Karen Tutty* a62 78
7 b g Bahamian Bounty Invincible (Slip Anchor)
1447[6] 1643[7] 2171[3] (2605) 3299[2] 3547[8] 4471[6] 4961[10] 5605[8] 6227[8] 6758[3] 7179[7] 7502[10]

**Merchant Of Dubai** *Jim Goldie* a74 82
9 b g Dubai Destination(USA) Chameleon (Green Desert (USA))
2515[2] 3192[2] 4204[3] 4575[3] 5564[7] (6403) 6536[5] 6794[6]

**Merchant Of Medici** *Micky Hammond* a57 70
7 b g Medicean Regal Rose (Danehill (USA))
1356[6] 1675[3] 2216[2] 2701[3] 3134[2] 3398[7] 4175[3] 4319[2] 4709[7] 5371[2] 5678[4] 6062[7] 6597[10] 7869[9] 8145[7]

**Mercury** *Kevin Ryan* 60
2 ch g Showcasing Miss Rimex (IRE) (Ezzoud (IRE))
4684[8] 5264[4] 6059[9]

**Mercury Magic** *David Menuisier* a57 62
3 b g Oratorio(IRE) Lochridge (Indian Ridge)
284[6] 1980[9] 2158[4] 2643[4] 3754[2] 4969[4] 5529[7] 6037[12] 6426[5] 6939[2] 7369[4] 7785[7]

**Mercy Me** *Julia Feilden* 8
2 b f Mawatheeq(USA) Fantastic Santanyi (Fantastic Light (USA))
7209[7]

**Merdon Castle (IRE)** *David Elsworth* a79 92
2 b c Acclamation Siren's Gift (Cadeaux Genereux)
(2057) 2403[2] 3322[17]

**Merhee (AUS)** *M F De Kock* a106 105
6 b h Elusive Quality(USA) Dizzy De Lago (AUS) (Encosta De Lago (AUS))
304a[2] 393a[12] 769a[5]

**Merhoob (IRE)** *Marco Botti* a68
2 b c Cape Cross(IRE) Lady Slippers (IRE) (Royal Academy (USA))
7574[2]

**Meridius (IRE)** *Nick Littmoden* a74 72
4 b g Invincible Spirit(IRE) Eliza Acton (Shirley Heights)
628[5] 741[6] 1430[3] 1766[6] 2463[4] 2887[12] (3088) 4620[7] 5422[7] 5951[8] 6889[6]

**Meri Shika (FR)** *Roger L Attfield* 97
4 bl f Spirit One(FR) Folle Biche (FR) (Take Risks (FR))
7326a[8]

**Meritocracy (IRE)** *Paul Cole* a90 86
3 br g Kheleyf(USA) Chiosina (IRE) (Danehill Dancer (IRE))
1518[5] 1952[6] 2344[11] 3185[3] 3539[6] 3809a[4] 4697[7] 5012[3] 5482a[4] 6021[2] 6296[4] 6607[7]

**Merletta** *Jeremy Noseda* a75 100
3 b f Raven's Pass(USA) Light Hearted (Green Desert (USA))
3245[13]

**Merritt Island** *Sir Mark Prescott Bt* a61 50
2 b f Exceed And Excel(AUS) Moon Crystal (Fasliyev (USA))
7018[8] 7194[7] 7399[7]

**Merry Dancer (IRE)** *Paul Webber* 60
2 ch f Duke Of Marmalade(IRE) Starlit Sky (Galileo (IRE))
7450[5]

**Merry Me (IRE)** *Andrew Balding* a79 101
3 b f Invincible Spirit(IRE) Thought Is Free (Cadeaux Genereux)
1765[4] (2210) (5849) 6301[3] 6785[4] 7717[3]

**Mersad (IRE)** *James Tate* a75 61
3 ch g Shamardal(USA) Fortress (Generous (IRE))
217[2]

**Merton Place (USA)** *Charlie Appleby* a55
2 b c Street Cry(IRE) Lakabi (USA) (Nureyev (USA))
7778[11]

**Meshaheera (FR)** *F Sanchez* a58 72
4 b f Meshaheer(USA) Odienne Jem (FR) (Cadeaux Genereux)
5222a[6]

**Meshardal (GER)** *Ruth Carr* a73 76
4 b g Shamardal(USA) Melody Fair (IRE) (Montjeu (IRE))
1369[2] (1804) (2094) 2552[2] 2677[2]

**Meshavita (FR)** *M Pimbonnet* a58 33
2 b f Meshaheer(USA) Evita (ITY) (Shantou (USA))
2976a[7] 3872a[6]

**Messi (GER)** *P Harley* 96
4 ch g New Approach(IRE) Messina (GER) (Dashing Blade)
5938a[8]

**Messila Star** *Jeremy Noseda* a85 55
4 ch c Pivotal Jamboretta (IRE) (Danehill (USA))
1873[6] 3118[4] 3577[3] 3861[2] (4968) ◆ 6609[9] 6885[9]

**Metaboss (USA)** *Jeff Bonde* a78
2 ch c Street Boss(USA) Spinning Yarns (USA) (Free House (USA))
7605a[4]

**Meteoroid (USA)** *Lady Cecil* a77 80
3 bb g Dynaformer(USA) Enthused (USA) (Seeking The Gold (USA))
1586[5] 2222[3] 3383[3] 7186[7] 7350[4]

**Methaaly (IRE)** *Michael Mullineaux* a64 62
11 b g Red Ransom(USA) Santorini (USA) (Spinning World (USA))
353[5] 466[5] 692[5] 937[DSQ] 2830[8] 3099[9] 4961[11] 5082[2] (6023) 6272[8] 7056[9] 7111[5] 7253[4] (7364) 7622[6] 7864[11]

**Metropolitan Chief** *Paul Burgoyne* a59 56
10 b g Compton Place Miss Up N Go (Gorytus (USA))
114[7] 402[3] 687[4] 799[4]

**Mey Blossom** *Richard Whitaker* a63 63
9 ch m Captain Rio Petra Nova (First Trump)
69[8] 296[6] 1487[9] 1604[5] 3338[8] 3530[5] 3548[8] 4069[5] (4287) 4494[3] 4714[4] 4752[4] 5913[5] 6077[2] ◆ 7697[8] 8143[10]

**Meydan Style (USA)** *Brian Baugh* a24 36
8 b g Essence Of Dubai(USA) Polish Ruby (USA) (Polish Pro (USA))
4381[4] 5291[8] 6161[7] 8084[8]

**Mezajy (IRE)** *Michael Bell* 67
2 b c Makfi Maidin Maith (IRE) (Montjeu (IRE))
6204[4] 6859[4]

**Mezel** *B W Hills* a77 84
3 b g Tamayuz Mumayeza (Indian Ridge)
1897[4] 2333[9] 4551[2]

**Mezmaar** *Kevin Morgan* 95
5 b g Teofilo(IRE) Bay Tree (IRE) (Daylami (IRE))
2984[7] 3886[7] 4982[5] 5727[7]

**Mezzotint (IRE)** *Stuart Williams* a84 104
5 b g Diamond Green(FR) Aquatint (Dansili)
1165[16] 2254[20] 3420[25] 4200[9] 4681[7] 5189[5] 5418[4] ◆ 5728[6] 5919[2] 6320[9] 6531[15]

**Mfiftythreedotcom (IRE)** *Richard Fahey* 74
3 ch g Tamayuz Pearl Trader (IRE) (Dubai Destination (USA))
1507[2] 2027[3] 3137[4] 3647[2] 4191[5] 5088[2] 6515[2] 7494[13]

**Miako (USA)** *Michael Appleby* a74
4 ch g Speightstown(USA) Bond Queen (USA) (Stormy Atlantic (USA))
93[2] 272[7]

**Miakora** *Mick Quinn* a44 54
6 ch m Compton Place Hickleton Lady (IRE) (Kala Shikari)
3125[6] 3630[7] 3966[11] 5316[6]

**Miami Carousel (IRE)** *John Quinn* 87
2 ch c Zebedee Florida City (IRE) (Pennekamp (USA))
2231[3] 2824[3] 3358[3] (4057) 4313[3] 4625[6] (7079)

**Miami Gator (IRE)** *K R Burke* a60 56
7 ch g Titus Livius(FR) Lovere (St Jovite (USA))
10[5] 156[3] (377) 673[2] 755[4] ◆ 7766[10] 7909[4]

**Miaplacidus (IRE)** *Richard Fahey* 66
3 b f Shamardal(USA) Nandy's Cavern (Lion Cavern (USA))
1400[12] 2204[6] (2729) 3300[2] 3575[4] 4067[3] 4628[5] 5441[5]

**Mia San Triple** *Jeremy Noseda* a75 92
3 b f Invincible Spirit(IRE) Atlantide (USA) (Southern Halo (USA))
2126[2] (3801) (4741) 5211[2] 6468[3] 7947[12]

**Mia's Boy** *Chris Dwyer* a97 95
10 b g Pivotal Bint Zamayem (IRE) (Rainbow Quest (USA))
145[5] 235[6] 426[4] 625[5] 804[9] 1014[6] 1241[5] 1834[7] 7186[4] 7784[7] 7955[6]

**Mica Mika (IRE)** *Richard Fahey* a83 87
6 ch g Needwood Blade Happy Talk (IRE) (Hamas (IRE))
3[6] 160[7] 408[3] (544) 763[4] 891[2] 999[2] 1196[4] 1553[3] 2259[4] 2790[5] 3250[3] 3730[3] 4204[6] 8120[5]

**Michachope (FR)** *A De Watrigant* 34
2 ch f Muhaymin(USA) Halloween Star (FR) (Wagon Master (FR))
1094a[14]

**Michaela** *Paul Webber* a59
2 ch f Sholokhov(IRE) La Capilla (Machiavellian (USA))
7658[4]

**Michaelmas (USA)** *A P O'Brien* a97 104
3 b c Elusive Quality(USA) Christmas Kid (USA) (Lemon Drop Kid (USA))
2571a[7] 3352[13] 4459a[6] 6352a[8] 6909a[5]

**Michael's Nook** *Alastair Lidderdale* a58 54
7 b g Intikhab(USA) Mysterious Plans (IRE) (Last Tycoon)
201[9] 370[14] 516[9]

**Mickdaam (IRE)** *M F De Kock* a92 104
5 b h Dubawi(IRE) Ribot's Guest (IRE) (Be My Guest (USA))
595a[10] 807a[6]

**Mick Duggan** *Ralph Beckett* a87 70
4 ch g Pivotal Poppy Carew (IRE) (Danehill (USA))
(4322) (5137) 6501[5]

**Mick Dundee (IRE)** *Richard Ford* a66
4 b g Aussie Rules(USA) Lucky Oakwood (USA) (Elmaamul (USA))
12[9] 538[8] 8265[10]

**Mickey Haller (IRE)** *Brian Meehan* 67
2 b c Approve(IRE) Miss Assertive (Zafonic (USA))
4395[7]

**Mick Slates (IRE)** *Declan Carroll* 66
5 b g Moss Vale(IRE) Sonic Night (IRE) (Night Shift (USA))
1309[10]

**Mick's Yer Man** *Bill Turner* a81 106
3 b g Bahamian Bounty Sheer Indulgence (FR) (Pivotal)
926[3] 1122[7] (1278) 1518[4] (1867) 2556[8]

**Mico Margarita (USA)** *Steven Asmussen* a112 87
4 ch c Run Away And Hide(USA) Wide Range (USA) (Mineshaft (USA))
7612a[12]

**Micras** *Andrew Balding* a65 88
3 b f Medicean Purple Heather (USA) (Rahy (USA))
1809[5] 2466[4] 3655[3] 5003[4] 5490[5] (6026) 6714[2] 7341[6]

**Microlight** *John E Long* a51 45
6 b g Sleeping Indian Skytrial (USA) (Sky Classic (CAN))
274[4] 448[8] 687[9] 798[4] 5136[3]

**Midas Haze** *Michael Bell* 61
2 ch f Pivotal Eva's Request (IRE) (Soviet Star (USA))
5644[6]

**Midaz** *Hughie Morrison* a76 46
4 br g Zamindar(USA) Schlague (FR) (Pulpit (USA))
1245[2] 1886[2] 2669[8] 3795[6] 4579[10] 5571[3]

**Middle East Pearl** *James Tate* a69
2 b f Equiano(FR) Zia (GER) (Grand Lodge (USA))
7192[7] (7970) 8170[2]

**Middle England (IRE)** *Charlie Appleby* a68
2 b f Dubawi(IRE) Mannington (AUS) (Danehill (USA))
8191[3]

**Midlander (IRE)** *Mark Johnston* a77 78
2 b c Shamardal(USA) Mille (Dubai Millennium)
3387[2] ◆ 3893[2] 4185[6] 4529[7] 5790[2] 5995[4] (6537)

**Midnight Bahia (IRE)** *Dean Ivory* a58 27
5 b m Refuse To Bend(IRE) Midnight Partner (IRE) (Marju (IRE))
68[10] 185[11]

**Midnight Chorister** *Alex Hales* a68
6 b g Midnight Legend Royal Musical (Royal Abjar (USA))
581[5] 686[3] 776[3] 1120[4] 1798[9]

**Midnight Dance (IRE)** *Ralph Beckett* a58 44
2 b f Danehill Dancer(IRE) Dark Missile (Night Shift (USA))
6660[5] 7308[6]

**Midnight Destiny (IRE)** *Derek Shaw* a48 57
2 ro f Dark Angel(IRE) Cappella (IRE) (College Chapel)
2302[7] 2641[3] 3107[6] 4083[3] 4422[2] 5384[3] 5779[5] 5985[3]

**Midnight Dream (FR)** *Kristin Stubbs* a80 49
4 b g Country Reel(USA) Tatante (IRE) (Highest Honor (FR))
93[7] 295[10]

**Midnight Dynamo** *Jim Goldie* 83
7 b m Lujain(USA) Miss Hermione (Bahamian Bounty)
3239[10] 3459[10] 3659[4] 4003[5] 4488[2] ◆ 4902[7] (5563) 5641[4] 5911[7] 6109[7] 6511[6]

**Midnight Feast** *Lee Carter* a74 62
6 b g Ishiguru(USA) Prince's Feather (IRE) (Cadeaux Genereux)
154[6] 583[2] 780[4] 852[6] 3233[10] 5303[8] 5833[6]

**Midnight Rider (IRE)** *Rod Millman* a86 87
6 b g Red Ransom(USA) Foreplay (IRE) (Lujain (USA))
1492[13] 2030[3] 2629[5] 4146[15] 5650[10] 7159[2] 7847[3] 8071[8] 8251[5]

**Midnight Sequel** *Neil Mulholland* a60 60
5 b m Midnight Legend Silver Sequel (Silver Patriarch (IRE))
(185) 277[7] 459[8] 1622a[2] (2594a) 4716a[2] 5230a[2] (5969a) 6188a[2]

**Midnight Warrior** *Ron Barr* a57 63
4 b g Teofilo(IRE) Mauri Moon (Green Desert (USA))
1596[6] 2426[7] 2658[4] 3439[12] 3846[10] 4069[10] 4473[6] 4755[4] (4958) 5495[2] 6119[3] (6542) 7283[6]

**Midnite Angel (IRE)** *Richard Hannon* a89 101
3 gr f Dark Angel(IRE) Two Sets To Love (IRE) (Cadeaux Genereux)
1579[2] 2316[7] 3357[14] (3727) 4009a[7]

**Midnite Ride (IRE)** *Richard Fahey* 66
2 b f Footstepsinthesand Takaliyda (IRE) (Azamour (IRE))
5807[4] 6224[2] 6735[8]

**Midtech Star (IRE)** *Ian Williams* a78 46
2 b g Kodiac Royal Rival (IRE) (Marju (IRE))
5241[5] (6838) 7171[4]

**Midterm Break (IRE)** *David Barron* a77 89
2 ch g Intense Focus(USA) Kayak (Singspiel (IRE))
1536[2] (1889) (2543) 3322[12] 4439[14] 5672[6] (6375a)

**Mid Yorkshire Golf** *Peter Grayson* a53
5 b m Doyen(IRE) Jodeeka (Fraam)
121[7] 1430[8]

**Mieuquebien (FR)** *R Limayrac*
6 b h Osorio(GER) Revtanea (FR) (Revoque (IRE))
806a[16]

**Mighty Bond** *Tracy Waggott*
2 b g Misu Bond(IRE) Mighty Flyer (IRE) (Mujtahid (USA))
7498[15]

**Mighty Force (IRE)** *Nick Littmoden* a56 39
3 b g Acclamation Ikan (IRE) (Sri Pekan (USA))
187[7] 338[7] 429[5] 608[5]

**Mighty Mambo** *Lawney Hill* a66 67
7 b g Fantastic Light(USA) Mambo's Melody (Kingmambo (USA))
458[7] (657) 818[3] 992[5] 7204[3] 7657[3] 8070[2]

**Mighty Missile (IRE)** *Tom Tate* 70
3 ch g Majestic Missile(IRE) Magdalene (FR) (College Chapel)
2896[2] 4793[6] 5449[2] 5794[2] 6539[4] 7235[4]

**Mighty Warrior** *Richard Fahey* 76
2 ch c Bahamian Bounty Just Dreams (Salse (USA))
3337[2] 3893[4] 5128[7] (6642) 7055[10]

**Mighty Yar (IRE)** *Lady Cecil* a75 105
4 gr c Teofilo(IRE) Karaliyfa (IRE) (Kahyasi)
1398[7] (1973) 2779[7] 4173[2] 5693[13] 6330[6]

**Mighty Zip (USA)** *Kevin Ryan* 47
2 ch c City Zip(USA) Incredulous (FR) (Indian Ridge)
4624[6]

**Mignolino (IRE)** *David Barron* 83
2 b g Kodiac Caterina Di Cesi (Cape Town (IRE))
1670[5] (2258) 3001[5] 3374[8] 5580[12]

**Miguela McGuire** *Eric Alston* a46 58
3 b f Sir Percy Miss McGuire (Averti (IRE))
1308[8] 2828[9] 3362[5] 4292[10] 6599[4] 6738[4] 7570[6]

**Miguel Grau (USA)** *Roger Varian* a83 83
4 b g City Zip(USA) Zuri Ridge (USA) (Cox's Ridge (USA))
89[2] 744[11] 4975[2] 5730[3] 6713[19]

**Miisele (FR)** *P Munsch*
2 b f Fuisse(FR) Mirageleve (FR) (Tobougg (IRE))
6385a[10]

**Mikandy (IRE)** *Clive Cox* a73 60
2 b f Arcano(IRE) Belle De Cadix (IRE) (Law Society (USA))
3558[12] 4346[6] 5305[8] 5798[4] 6250[4] 6811[4] 7075[4] (7740) (7815)

**Mikey Miss Daisy** *Martin Hill* a15 57
3 ch f Champs Elysees Savoy Street (Vettori (IRE))
2279[7] 3174[6] 4966[9]

**Milady Eileen (IRE)** *Richard Fahey* a50 44
2 ch f Footstepsinthesand Arazena (USA) (Woodman (USA))
4216[9] 4570[6] 6147[7] 6643[7] (7824) 8179[7]

**Mildmay Arms** *Simon Hodgson* a50
2 b g Kheleyf(USA) Akathea (Barathea (IRE))
7742[9] 8026[11] 8227[9]

**Milehigh Butterfly (USA)** *William R Connelly* a95
2 bb f Sky Mesa(USA) Hummingbird Kiss (CAN) (Smart Strike (CAN))
6915a[4]

**Miles Magician (GER)** *B Recher*
5 b g Platini(GER) Mille Espoir (FR) (Mille Balles (FR))
752a[10]

**Miles Of Sunshine** *Ron Hodges* a55 56
9 b g Thowra(FR) Rainbow Nation (Rainbow Quest (USA))
530[2] 639[2]

**Military Attack (IRE)** *C Fownes* a96 123
6 b g Oratorio(IRE) Almaaseh (IRE) (Dancing Brave (USA))
1183a[10] 2379a[3] 7899a[2] 8154a[2]

**Military Music** *Mark Usher* a48
2 b f Captain Gerrard(IRE) Cumbrian Concerto (Petong)
7181[8] 7685[4] 7970[10]
**Milky Way (IRE)** *Gary Moore* 75
2 b c Galileo(IRE) Beauty Bright (IRE) (Danehill (USA))
(7414) ◆
**Millar Rose (IRE)** *K R Burke* a61 67
2 b f Vale Of York(IRE) Barbera (GER) (Night Shift (USA))
1656[5] 2051[3] 2725[6] (4065) 4702[6] 6447[2] 6941[3] 7421[6]
**Mille Of Journey (FR)** *S Kobayashi*
2 bl g Great Journey(JPN) Mille Flora (IRE) (Be My Guest (USA))
8212a[10]
**Millgate** *Richard Fahey* 52
2 b c Equiano(FR) Milly-M (Cadeaux Genereux)
2291[6] 3881[10]
**Mill I Am (USA)** *Stuart Williams* a66 61
4 b f Henny Hughes(USA) Courageous (USA) (Kingmambo (USA))
(81) 446[8] (592) 819[2] ◆ 1123[5] 1230[4] 3384[10] 4341[4] 5057[6] 5071[2]
**Millies Quest** *Martin Smith* a54 67
5 b m Generous(IRE) Alexander Star (IRE) (Inzar (USA))
592[10] 760[6] 1010[10]
**Millionaires Row (USA)** *John Gosden* a63 49
3 bb f Dynaformer(USA) Ladue (USA) (Demons Begone (USA))
1701[9] 8310[5]
**Millkwood** *John Davies* a59 81
4 b g Millkom Wedgewood Star (Bishop Of Cashel)
1191[8] 1376[2] 1610[5] 2169[3] 2549[6] 3272[3] 3572[13] 4924[2] 5887[5] 6166[14] 6429[2] (7501)
**Milly Royale** *Peter Makin* a38
2 b f Royal Applause Milly Fleur (Primo Dominie)
7970[13]
**Milly's Gift** *Clive Cox* a91 103
4 b f Trade Fair Milly's Lass (Mind Games)
2110[4] 2757[7] (3927) 4179[2] 4700[11] (6614) 6918[3]
**Milly's Secret (IRE)** *David O'Meara* a62 79
3 ch f Sakhee's Secret Swan Sea (USA) (Sea Hero (USA))
1358[9] 4358[3] 4902[4] 5470[5] 5763[5] 6613[8] 7286[8] 7575[9] 7825[5] 8043[5] 8176[5]
**Mime Dance** *Andrew Balding* a72 88
3 b g Notnowcato Encore My Love (Royal Applause)
1655[6] 2962[6] 3247[4] 3455[4] 4810[4] (5031) 5410[6] 6285[6] 6789[2]
**Mimi Luke (USA)** *Alan Bailey* a67 67
3 b f US Ranger(USA) Hard As Nails (USA) (Holy Bull (USA))
756[2] 1106[2] 1404[7] 1570[9] 3114[8] 3679[2] 4324[2] 4972[2] 5105[4] (5532)
**Mimulus (FR)** *J E Pease* 67
2 b c Evasive Nabella (Rock Of Gibraltar (IRE))
5616a[8]
**Min Alemarat (IRE)** *Marco Botti* 99
3 ch c Galileo(IRE) Baraka (IRE) (Danehill (USA))
1517[6] 1984[2] (2696) 5481a[5] 7106[24]
**Minalisa** *Rae Guest* a69 103
5 b m Oasis Dream Mina (Selkirk (USA))
2848[9] 3278[4] (4557a) 6533[2]
**Mind Of Madness (IRE)** *David Brown* 103
2 b c Azamour(IRE) Siodull (IRE) (Oasis Dream)
(1512) 2873[2] 3322[15] 3374[2] ◆ 4123[7] (5694) 6286[9] 6513[2] 6933[8]
**Mindsforgemanacles (IRE)** *C Boutin* a65 59
3 b f Oratorio(IRE) Medicean Star (IRE) (Galileo (IRE))
720a[13]
**Mindsomer (FR)** *F Chappet* 100
2 b c Diamond Green(FR) Mindset (IRE) (Vettori (IRE))
4953a[5] 5740a[7] 6570a[4]
**Mindurownbusiness (IRE)** *David Simcock* a97 95
3 b c Cape Cross(IRE) Whos Mindin Who (IRE) (Danehill Dancer (IRE))
(847) ◆ 1580[5] (1861) 3378[23] (4118) 4915[4] 6411[4] 7066[4] ◆
**Miner's Lamp (IRE)** *Charlie Appleby* 109
3 b g Shamardal(USA) Truly Mine (IRE) (Rock Of Gibraltar (IRE))
1979[2] (2347) 3417[6] 4183[9] 7106[22] 7449[7]
**Minestrone (IRE)** *Tom Dascombe* 63
2 b f Holy Roman Emperor(IRE) Campbellite (Desert Prince (IRE))
4202[6]
**Ming Zhi Cosmos (FR)** *N Clement* a98 102
3 b f Duke Of Marmalade(IRE) The Wise Lady (FR) (Ganges (USA))
3808a[8] (6807a) 7656a[9]
**Minimee** *Phil McEntee* a63 72
4 b g Dubai Destination(USA) Malaaq (Green Desert (USA))
65[2] (184) 219[5] 288[6] 340[5] 424[7] 1668[9] 1876[2]
**Mini Minstrel** *Alan McCabe*
2 br f Pastoral Pursuits Bruma (IRE) (Footstepsinthesand)
1656[11]
**Minionette (IRE)** *Alan Swinbank* 54
3 b f Manduro(GER) La Vita E Bella (IRE) (Definite Article)
1542[7] 1713[6] 2165[6] 2679[4]
**Mini's Destination** *John Holt* a40 57
6 b m Dubai Destination(USA) Heather Mix (Linamix (FR))
3334[4] 3614[5] 6086[10]
**Miniskirt** *Rae Guest* a78 56
3 b f Naaqoos Minnola (Royal Applause)
7157[4] 8003[2] (8207)
**Minister Of Fun** *Scott Dixon* a73
3 b g Pastoral Pursuits Diane's Choice (Komaite (USA))
7764[9] (8280)
**Minister Of Mayhem** *Nick Mitchell* 78
4 ch g Sakhee's Secret First Fantasy (Be My Chief (USA))
1439[13]
**Mink Coat** *Rae Guest*
3 b f Amadeus Wolf Grand Slam Maria (FR) (Anabaa (USA))
1084[6]
**Minley** *Charlie Fellowes* a75 72
3 b g Acclamation Fatal Attraction (Oasis Dream)
667[6] 1146[2] 1818[5] 2717[4] (3522)
**Minnie (IRE)** *Johnny Farrelly* a62 45
2 b f Sakhee's Secret Numerus Clausus (FR) (Numerous (USA))
6735[9] 7573[7] 8000[4] 8317[5]
**Minnie Miracle** *Mark Usher*
3 ch f Compton Place Splicing (Sharpo)
159[7]
**Minnyvinny** *James Unett* a22
3 b f Multiplex Bounty Reef (Bahamian Bounty)
15[7]
**Minorette (USA)** *Chad C Brown* 108
3 ch f Smart Strike(CAN) Silk And Scarlet (Sadler's Wells (USA))
(3995a)
**Minot Street (CAN)** *John C McConnell* a78 43
4 b g Van Nistelrooy(USA) Just Outta Here (USA) (Rahy (USA))
7877a[4] (7962a)
**Minstrel Lad** *Lydia Pearce* a65 73
6 ch g Where Or When(IRE) Teal Flower (Pivotal)
67[4] 406[3] 571[6] 1302[2] 1617[9] 2300[4] (2610) 2875[2] 4273[10] 4402[6] 5139[7] 5395[4] 5575[7] 7172[2] 7822[8]
**Minstrels Gallery (IRE)** *Lucy Wadham* a66 63
5 ch g Refuse To Bend(IRE) Lilakiya (IRE) (Dr Fong (USA))
755[2] (1016) 1209[2] 1617[5] 2046[3]
**Mintaka (FR)** *A De Royer-Dupre* 89
3 gr f Zamindar(USA) Minatlya (FR) (Linamix (FR))
2195a[15] 3773a[6]
**Minty Jones** *Michael Mullineaux* a45 55
5 b h Primo Valentino(IRE) Reveur (Rossini (USA))
(2667) 3099[13] 3882[8] 4370[6] 4788[3] 5207[4] 7057[14] 7510[4] 7670[5] 7781[5] 8230[10] 8291[8]
**Miracle Ninetynine (IRE)** *Richard Hannon* 67
2 b c Big Bad Bob(IRE) Scrumptious (Sakhee (USA))
6551[5] 7413[4]
**Miracle Of Medinah** *Mark Usher* a79 105
3 ch c Milk It Mick Smart Ass (IRE) (Shinko Forest (IRE))
1514[6] 2343[8] 2961[4] 3352[15] 4187[2] 6335[5] 6522[9]
**Mirandola (FR)** *Yves de Nicolay* a73 86
5 ch m Anabaa Blue Connaissance (IRE) (Choisir (AUS))
3373a[8]
**Mireille (IRE)** *Mme Pia Brandt* a80 99
3 b f Dalakhani(IRE) Australie (IRE) (Sadler's Wells (USA))
(7268a)
**Mirsaale** *Keith Dalgleish* a80 109
4 ch g Sir Percy String Quartet (IRE) (Sadler's Wells (USA))
1068[14] 2555[2] 2991[12] 3500[4] 4759[9] 6532[6]
**Mirza** *Rae Guest* a68 113
7 b g Oasis Dream Millyant (Primo Dominie)
2197a[5] 2563[7] 3030a[2] (4841a) 5911[2] (6378a) 6966a[5]
**Misha (FR)** *D Darlix* a48
3 gr f Sinndar(IRE) Mary Read (FR) (Medicean)
5294a[7]
**Mishaal (IRE)** *Michael Herrington* a94 88
4 ch g Kheleyf(USA) My Dubai (IRE) (Dubai Millennium)
1447[9] 2054[9] 2825[4] 3660[9] 4291[2] (4703) 4938[2] 5197[2] 6095[3] ◆ 6511[5] 7719[14] 7821[3] (7947)
**Misham** *Marco Botti* a59
2 ch f Shamardal(USA) Mi Anna (GER) (Lake Coniston (IRE))
7808[7] 8027[3]
**Mishko (IRE)** *Steve Gollings* a46 76
3 b c Amadeus Wolf Miss Shangri La (Rainbow Quest (USA))
3268[4] 3631[4] 4863[3] 6239[10]
**Mishrif (USA)** *J R Jenkins* a83 79
8 bb g Arch(USA) Peppy Priscilla (USA) (Latin American (USA))
300[2] 929[6] 1222[3] (1886) 3629[3] 5100[5] 5533[4] 8211[5]
**Misleading** *Peter Chapple-Hyam* a80 78
2 ch g Footstepsinthesand Danny's Choice (Compton Place)
(4760) 6142[8]
**Misleading Promise (IRE)** *John Butler* a69
4 b g Refuse To Bend(IRE) Farthing (IRE) (Mujadil (USA))
10[6] 199[2] 320[3]
**Misplaced Fortune** *Nigel Tinkler* a39 97
9 b m Compton Place Tide Of Fortune (Soviet Star (USA))
1734[14] 2318[5] 3203[4] 3788[3] 4061[3] 5612[11] 6095[6] 6492[2] 6692[8]
**Miss Acclaimed (IRE)** *Brian Ellison* a53 68
3 gr f Acclamation Miss Shaan (FR) (Darshaan)
1246[3] 1902[4] 2517[6] 3405[7] 3662[6] 4067[6]
**Miss Alicia (IRE)** *Bodil Hallencreutz* 69
3 b f Haatef(USA) Maria Luisa (IRE) (King's Best (USA))
6386a[8]
**Missandei** *Marco Botti* a61 47
2 b f Red Rocks(IRE) Onda Chiara (ITY) (Dane Friendly)
7209[5] 7625[4] 7834[4] 7996[3] 8165[2]
**Miss Atomic Bomb** *Jeremy Noseda* a87 91
3 b f Intikhab(USA) Green Bonnet (IRE) (Green Desert (USA))
1818[2] 2745[8] 3117[4] 3615[4] 5686[4] 6301[2] ◆
**Miss Australia (FR)** *Marquise De Montaigu* a47
2 gr f Mr. Sidney(USA) Dedicace (USA) (El Prado (IRE))
8132a[9]
**Miss Bella Rose** *Richard Guest* a26 17
7 gr m Silver Patriarch(IRE) City Rose (Tragic Role (USA))
463[7] 649[8] 1608[9] 2213[11]
**Miss Blakeney** *Marcus Tregoning* a80 73
5 b m Sir Percy Misplace (IRE) (Green Desert (USA))
3585[2] 5002[4]
**Miss Brazil (IRE)** *Richard Hannon* a73 79
3 ch f Exceed And Excel(AUS) Amazon Beauty (IRE) (Wolfhound (USA))
1400[10] 1669[2] 3067[2] 3586[3] (4590) 5182[4] 5753[2] 6189[4] 7352[3]
**Miss Buckshot (IRE)** *Rae Guest* a84 76
3 b f Tamayuz Miss Bellbird (IRE) (Danehill (USA))
1563[10] 2968[7] 3428[8] 7205[3] ◆ (7634) 7885[3] 8188[3]
**Miss Crystal (IRE)** *Charles Hills* a55 74
3 b f Montjeu(IRE) Crystal Curling (IRE) (Peintre Celebre (USA))
316[3] ◆ 1960[3] 5374[3] 6026[5] 7416[6] 7975[6]
**Miss Doina (FR)** *E Nicoleau* 18
2 bb f Prince Kirk(FR) Miss Oversea (FR) (Royal Academy (USA))
1271a[11]
**Missed Call (IRE)** *James Fanshawe* a90 88
4 b f Authorized(IRE) Incoming Call (USA) (Red Ransom (USA))
2331[3] 3218[2] 4622[4] 6685[4] 7211[7] (7531) 8095[7]
**Miss Ella Jade** *Richard Whitaker* a34 59
5 b m Danbird(AUS) Keen Melody (USA) (Sharpen Up)
546[7] 6076[10] 6932[5]
**Missfire** *Brian Baugh*
4 b f Firebreak Gary's Indian (IRE) (Indian Danehill (IRE))
6429[8]
**Miss France (IRE)** *A Fabre* 117
3 b f Dansili Miss Tahiti (IRE) (Tirol)
1273a[6] (1976) 3289a[5] 4954a[2] 6927[2]
**Miss Giler** *John Gosden* a50
2 b f High Chaparral(IRE) Funday (Daylami (IRE))
7756[6]
**Miss Glorioso** *Alexandra Dunn* a9
5 b m Helissio(FR) Miss Glory Be (Glory Of Dancer)
159[6]
**Missile Command (IRE)** *Jane M Foley* a63 51
6 b g Majestic Missile(IRE) Blusienka (IRE) (Blues Traveller (IRE))
790a[12]
**Miss Inga Sock (IRE)** *Eve Johnson Houghton* a60 53
2 ch f Tagula(IRE) Support Fund (IRE) (Intikhab (USA))
5209[4] 5555[3] 5982[7]
**Mission Approved** *Luca Cumani* a90 96
4 b g Dansili Moon Search (Rainbow Quest (USA))
3122[2] 3702[3] 4502[3] 4892[2] 6260[5] 6531[6] 6923[3] 7543[5]
**Mission Impossible** *Tracy Waggott* a41 72
9 gr g Kyllachy Eastern Lyric (Petong)
1838[7] 2166[3] 2552[4] 2955[2] 3298[5] 4664[2] 4796[2] (5089) 5265[9] 5996[4] 7502[11]
**Missisipi Baileys (FR)** *Mark Johnston* 41
2 b f Aqlaam Missisipi Star (IRE) (Mujahid (USA))
6594[5] 6831[4]
**Mississippi** *David Barron* a84 94
5 b g Exceed And Excel(AUS) Ruby Rocket (IRE) (Indian Rocket)
3271[5] 3714[4] 4305[3] 5199[8] 5888[10] 6260[6] 6511[7]
**Mississippi Queen (USA)** *Michael Bell* a59 24
3 b f Artie Schiller(USA) Siempre Asi (USA) (Silver Hawk (USA))
4699[5] 5796[8] 6483[8] 7682[6] 7907[10]
**Miss Jonh (FR)** *Martyn Meade* a54
2 ch f Deportivo Flower (Zamindar (USA))
2206[4] 7701[3] 7917[7]
**Miss Laroc (IRE)** *Jeremy Gask* a30
2 b f Zebedee Madame Boulangere (Royal Applause)
6408[11]
**Miss Lillie** *Roger Teal* a79 81
3 b f Exceed And Excel(AUS) Never Lose (Diktat)
1515[10] 2639[7] 3539[4] 4053[6] 4436[8] 5826[6] 6336[4] 6633[4] 7397[9] 7552[5] (8168)
**Miss Lucy Jane** *Richard Fahey* a67 81
3 ch f Aqlaam Ocean View (USA) (Gone West (USA))
1888[2] 2523[4] (3545) (3950) 4397[2] 5401[6]
**Miss Macnamara (IRE)** *Martin Todhunter* a54 78
5 b m Dylan Thomas(IRE) Kincob (USA) (Kingmambo (USA))
1605[4] (2055) ◆ (2550) 3698[3] 4068[3] 4662[5] 4964[6] (5815) 6228[6] (6832) 7124[8]
**Miss Marjurie (IRE)** *Denis Coakley* a98 98
4 b f Marju(IRE) Kazatzka (Groom Dancer (USA))
1973[2] (2991) 5668[7] 6708[9] 7554[2]
**Miss Matiz** *Tracy Waggott* 46
7 b m Rock City Doodle Wood (Nomination)
3439[14] 3846[12]
**Miss Minuty** *Sir Mark Prescott Bt* a58 48
2 gr f Verglas(IRE) Miss Provence (Hernando (FR))
5973[7] 7254[5] 7550[8] 7753[8] 8009[5] 8221[5]
**Miss Mohawk (IRE)** *Alan Brown* a46 44
5 ch m Hawk Wing(USA) Karmafair (IRE) (Always Fair (USA))
14[4] 73[4]
**Miss Moppet** *Hughie Morrison* a64 50
3 b f Nayef(USA) So Blissful (IRE) (Cape Cross (IRE))
1768[5] ◆ 2681[9] 3074[5] 4063[9] 6567[8]
**Miss Mullberry** *David O'Meara* 88
2 b f Kodiac Chaenomeles (USA) (Fusaichi Pegasus (USA))
2601[7] 3215[8] 3656[2] 4686[2] (4920) (5791) 6513[6]
**Miss Phone Girl** *Bent Olsen*
2 br f Pastoral Pursuits Willows World (Agnes World (USA))
6386a[14]
**Miss Rafael (FR)** *S Wattel* a58 79
3 gr f Rock Of Gibraltar(IRE) Miss Salvador (FR) (Smadoun (FR))
2978a[9]
**Miss Rebero** *Tim Fitzgerald* a44 37
4 b f Cockney Rebel(IRE) One Zero (USA) (Theatrical (IRE))
5233[7] 5376[14] 6015[6]
**Miss Ruby Royale** *Paul Midgley*
2 ch f Monsieur Bond(IRE) Amoureuse (Needwood Blade)
7004[9]
**Miss Sophisticated** *David Barron* 66
3 b f Bahamian Bounty Miss Sophisticat (Alhaarth (IRE))
1400[11] 1657[10] 2729[7]
**Misstemper (IRE)** *Jose Santos* a69
3 b f Diamond Green(FR) Legnani (Fasliyev (USA))
1404[2] 2125[3] 2802[10] (3792) 4544[4] 8186[5]
**Miss Tiger Lily** *Harry Dunlop* a78 78
4 b f Tiger Hill(IRE) Waitingonacloud (In The Wings)
1043[6] 1629[3] 2207[2] 2419[5]
**Miss Tree** *John Quinn* a54 78
3 b f Literato(FR) Tunguska (Silver Patriarch (IRE))
1841[3] 2354[3] 2952[2] 4020[4] 7176[3] 7500[2]
**Miss Tweedy** *Rod Millman* a50 59
3 b f Sleeping Indian Ile Royale (Royal Applause)
847[5] 1007[5] 1235[5] 1914[4] 2281[8]
**Miss Understood (IRE)** *David Simcock* a72 57
2 b f Excellent Art Puck's Castle (Shirley Heights)
7209[4] 7512[7] (7835)
**Missunited (IRE)** *Michael Winters* 115
7 bb m Golan(IRE) Lets Clic Together (IRE) (Don't Forget Me)
1869[4] 3377[2] (4824)
**Miss Van Gogh** *Richard Fahey* 58
2 b f Dutch Art Accede (Acclamation)
2173[5] 3296[5] 3841[5] 5141[5] 6830[3] (7488)
**Miss Verdoyante** *Sir Mark Prescott Bt* a33
3 b f Montjeu(IRE) Miss Provence (Hernando (FR))
51[8] 198[5]
**Missy Wells** *Mark Walford* a48 66
4 b f Misu Bond(IRE) Aqua (Mister Baileys)
1303[2] 1805[2] 2199[2] 2523[2] 2872[10] 4058[11] 5421[3] 6062[11]
**Mistamel (IRE)** *Eve Johnson Houghton* a71 70
2 b g Rip Van Winkle(IRE) Without Precedent (FR) (Polish Precedent (USA))
3063[4] 3929[6] 7353[4]
**Mister Archie** *Alistair Whillans* 43
2 b g Archipenko(USA) Zooming (IRE) (Indian Ridge)
6225[5] 6577[5] 6860[8] 7208[4]
**Mister Arden (FR)** *Harry Dunlop* a56 56
2 b c Desert Style(IRE) Katie Arden (IRE) (Barathea (IRE))
2276[6] 2680[7] 2993[5] 5739a[2] 6619a[7] 7029[8] 7336[6] 7536[7]
**Mister Bawi (FR)** *H-A Pantall* 96
4 ch g Dubawi(IRE) Miss Sissy (FR) (Sicyos (USA))
723a[6]
**Mister Big Shuffle (GER)** *Niels Petersen* a66 98
4 br g Big Shuffle(USA) Marmorea (IRE) (Tiger Hill (IRE))
679a[16] 808a[12]
**Mister Bob (GER)** *James Bethell* a79 33
5 ch g Black Sam Bellamy(IRE) Mosquera (GER) (Acatenango (GER))
2084[6] 2476[7] 2935[3] 3404[2] (4656) (5547) 6632[6] (7065) 7817[2] 7995[4]
**Mister Brightside (IRE)** *Jeremy Noseda* a67 78
2 b c Lord Shanakill(USA) Lamh Eile (IRE) (Lend A Hand)
6457[3] 7030[4]
**Mister Carrot** *George Baker* a66
4 b g Elusive City(USA) It's Twilight Time (Royal Applause)
686[2]
**Mister Chop (FR)** *W Walton* a60 87
9 b g Panis(USA) Ducie (Distant Relative)
392a[2]
**Mister Dancer (IRE)** *C Lerner* 86
2 b c Danehill Dancer(IRE) Mary's Precedent (FR) (Storming Home)
6916a[3]
**Mister Fantastic** *Dai Burchell* a22 35
8 ch g Green Tune(USA) Lomapamar (Nashwan (USA))
474[5] 640[11]
**Mister Fizz** *Miss Imogen Pickard* a88 93
6 b g Sulamani(IRE) Court Champagne (Batshoof)
3205[4] ◆ (3926) 4119[5] 5379[2] 5633[4] 6061[9] 6536[7] 7539[5] 8146[6]
**Mister Frosty (IRE)** *Michael Squance* a56 54
8 gr g Verglas(IRE) La Chinampina (FR) (Darshaan)
474[2]
**Mister Green (FR)** *David Flood* a28 13
8 b g Green Desert(USA) Summertime Legacy (Darshaan)
8316[7]
**Misterioso (IRE)** *Richard Hannon* 95
2 b c Iffraaj Roystonea (Polish Precedent (USA))
3748[3] (4207) 6750[4] 6925[6]
**Misterious Boy (IRE)** *Stefano Botti* 100
2 ch c Arcano(IRE) Biz Bar (Tobougg (IRE))
(7479a)
**Mister Manannan (IRE)** *David Nicholls* a7 96
7 b g Desert Style(IRE) Cover Girl (IRE) (Common Grounds)
36[7] 299[8] 1541[9] 2056[9] 3399[11] 3659[7] 4114[3] (4494) (4752) 5053[5] 6096[16] 6512[19] 6763[15]
**Mister Marcasite** *Mel Brittain* a70 70
4 gr g Verglas(IRE) No Rehearsal (FR) (Baillamont (USA))
1845[2] 2019[6] 5415[10] 7569[6] 8086[5] 8231[5] ◆
**Mister Mayday (IRE)** *George Baker* a61 74
3 br g Kheleyf(USA) Soxy Doxy (IRE) (Hawk Wing (USA))
1403[5] 1765[5] 2688[2] 3559[2] 4544[7] (5252) 6088[3] 6617[6] (7001) 7172[7] 7309[13]

**Mister Music** *Brian Meehan* a86 105
5 b g Singspiel(IRE) Sierra (Dr Fong (USA))
1870[8] 6748[9] 7236[9]

**Mister Musicmaster** *Ron Hodges* a82 85
5 b g Amadeus Wolf Misty Eyed (IRE) (Paris House)
*1617[7] 6026[6]* (4153) *4580[3]* 5785[5] 6249[2] 6789[7] 7159[10] *7456[9]*

**Mister Pagan** *Keith Dalgleish* 87
6 b g Sulamani(IRE) Gunner Marc (Gunner B)
7124[3] 7566[12]

**Mister Papy (FR)** *C Plisson* a33 44
2 b c Domedriver(IRE) Miss Sylvaine (FR) (Mister Tullio (FR))
*3871a[8]* 7344a[8]

**Mister Rockandroll** *Mark Johnston* a70 66
2 b c Rock Of Gibraltar(IRE) Cruel Sea (USA) (Mizzen Mast (USA))
6056[9] 6317[4] *6602[2]* 7230[5]

**Mister Romaldo (ITY)** *Gianluca Bietolini* 71
4 b c Romaldo(GER) Sweet Didi (IRE) (High Chaparral (IRE))
6569a[8]

**Mister Segway (IRE)** *Robert Collet* a66 65
6 b h Dansili Aplysia (USA) (Storm Cat (USA))
*806a[5]*

**Mister Smart (FR)** *D Darlix* a86 86
4 b g Smadoun(FR) Miss Canon (FR) (Cadoudal (FR))
2821a[8]

**Mister Universe** *Mark Johnston* 92
2 br c Cape Cross(IRE) Miss Ivanhoe (IRE) (Selkirk (USA))
2288[2] (2788) 4199[5] 5876[3]

**Mister Uno (IRE)** *Ann Duffield* a26 70
3 b c Tamayuz Starlight Smile (USA) (Green Dancer (USA))
1372[4] 2028[2] 3303[2] (4386) 4726[2] 5449[5] 6110[4] 6596[2] 6981[11]

**Mister York** *Mel Brittain* 55
2 b g Monsieur Bond(IRE) Knavesmire (IRE) (One Cool Cat (USA))
1505[8] 2358[5] 4286[5] 4684[7] 7329[12]

**Misti River (FR)** *J C Napoli* a63 50
3 gr f Stormy River(FR) Mist (FR) (Numerous (USA))
*391a[4]*

**Mistiroc** *Jim Goldie* 93
3 br g Rocamadour Mistinguett (IRE) (Doyoun)
4886[5] (5634) (6098) ◆ 6479[5] 7106[6] ◆

**Mistral** *Steph Hollinshead* 55
2 b f Multiplex Song Of The Desert (Desert Sun)
2771[10] 3542[4] 4330[7] 5712[5] 6742[8]

**Mistress And Maid** *Joseph Tuite* a33 22
3 ch f Dutch Art Passing Fancy (Grand Lodge (USA))
*140[7] 373[6]*

**Mistress Makfi (IRE)** *Mark Johnston* 40
2 ch f Makfi Rapid Ransom (USA) (Red Ransom (USA))
1536[8] 3497[6]

**Mistress Shy** *Peter Hiatt* a55 2
7 b m Zafeen(FR) Nicholas Mistress (Beveled (USA))
*179[13] 563[11] 783[10]*

**Mistrusting (IRE)** *Charlie Appleby* 86
2 b f Shamardal(USA) Misheer (Oasis Dream)
4604[2] ◆ (6093)

**Mists Of Time (IRE)** *Pat Eddery* a53 60
4 b f Excellent Art Capriole (Noverre (USA))
*456[9] 718[8] 838[9] 1087[8]* 1664[11] *3528[9] 4326[6] 6031[7]*

**Misty Eyes** *Geoffrey Harker* a54
5 b m Byron Wax Eloquent (Zaha (CAN))
*18[11] 592[7] 7819[6]*

**Misty Pearl** *Michael Appleby* 31
4 b f Royal Applause Pearl Valley (Indian Rocket)
1639[6] 2164[6]

**Misty Sparkler** *Jamie Osborne* a73 65
3 ch f Mount Nelson Statua (IRE) (Statoblest)
*284[4] (346)*

**Misu Mac** *Neville Bycroft* 17
4 b f Misu Bond(IRE) Umbrian Gold (IRE) (Perugino (USA))
7250[9] 7501[10]

**Misu Pete** *Mark Usher* a37
2 b c Misu Bond(IRE) Smart Ass (IRE) (Shinko Forest (IRE))
*4079[8] 7685[7] 7867[9] 7991[8]*

**Mitcd (IRE)** *Martin Todhunter* 61
3 gr f Mastercraftsman(IRE) Halicardia (Halling (USA))
2517[8] 2867[5] 3603[5] 6000[8]

**Mitchell** *K R Burke* a39 68
4 ch g Haafhd Maid To Matter (Pivotal)
1309[2] 1838[3] (2653) 3096[9] 3485[U] 4798[9] 5110[5] 5376[9] 5854[10]

**Mitchelton (FR)** *Mark Johnston* 79
3 b f High Chaparral(IRE) Fortunately (Forzando)
2826[3] 3340[5] 3911[3]

**Mitchum** *Ron Barr* a59 57
5 b g Elnadim(USA) Maid To Matter (Pivotal)
*565[6] 651[9] 910[6]* 1606[2] 2019[12] 2653[2] 5376[12] 6122[16] 6217[9] 6670[3] 7249[9] 7639[2] *8137[9]*

**Mitlaa (FR)** *P Monfort* a65 74
3 b f Naaqoos Djayapura (FR) (Fabulous Dancer (USA))
*720a[12]*

**Mitzi Blue (IRE)** *D Darlix* a66 84
5 b m Anabaa Blue Moonlight Melody (GER) (Law Society (USA))
6917a[8]

**Mixed Message (IRE)** *Brian Ellison* a76 72
4 b f Kodiac Berenica (IRE) (College Chapel)
*859[5]* 1356[12] 4470[2] (4792) (5788) 6232[6] 6672[11] 6932[2] 7411[9] (7499) *7914[8]*

**Miyachiku** *Ed Dunlop* a72 73
3 ch g Pivotal First Bloom (USA) (Fusaichi Pegasus (USA))
*1208[4]* 2871[3]

**Mizyen (IRE)** *D T Hughes* a54 76
4 b g Teofilo(IRE) Housekeeper (IRE) (Common Grounds)
4805a[8]

**Mizzava (IRE)** *M Halford* a59 104
4 bb f Cape Cross(IRE) Flamanda (Niniski (USA))
2572a[7] 5955a[7] 6585a[5]

**Mizzeni (FR)** *Gay Kelleway* a35 29
3 gr g Verglas(IRE) Bashful (IRE) (Brief Truce (USA))
5227a[7]

**Mizzou (IRE)** *Luca Cumani* 109
3 b c Galileo(IRE) Moments Of Joy (Darshaan)
3106[4] (4062) (4887) (6137) 6894[3]

**M J Woodward** *Paul Green* a66 65
5 b g Needwood Blade Canina (Foxhound (USA))
2296[11] (2606)

**M'Lady Ermyn** *Pat Phelan* a55 49
3 b f Pastoral Pursuits Penelope Tree (IRE) (Desert Prince (IRE))
*488[7]*

**Mlle Agapee (IRE)** *J Rossi* a48 78
4 b f Whipper(USA) Ziria (IRE) (Danehill Dancer (IRE))
*805a[11]*

**Moaning Butcher** *Dave Roberts* a29 53
4 b g Lucarno(USA) Musical Chimes (Josr Algarhoud (IRE))
*430[4] 6410[12]*

**Mobhirr** *Marco Botti* a67 60
3 br c Sea The Stars(IRE) Silent Heir (AUS) (Sunday Silence (USA))
*6677[7] 6901[5] 7015[4]* 7500[9]

**Mobley Chaos** *Ronald Harris* a46 27
4 b g Darnay Emmarander (Bob's Return (IRE))
*365[4] 731[5] 833[9] 1081[10]*

**Mobsta (IRE)** *Mick Channon* 86
2 b c Bushranger(IRE) Sweet Nicole (Okawango (USA))
7412[2] ◆ (7713)

**Moccasin (FR)** *Geoffrey Harker* a76 76
5 b g Green Tune(USA) Museum Piece (Rainbow Quest (USA))
*1451[3]* 2016[6] 2423[7] 2868[5] 4175[11] 5268[2] 7335[4] *7626[4] 7822[4] 7975[2] 8164[5]*

**Mocklershill (FR)** *F Chappet* 96
2 b c Siyouni(FR) Irish Vintage (FR) (Loup Solitaire (USA))
4953a[6] 6220a[6] 7094a[9]

**Mocky Glaz (FR)** *D Windrif* a45 60
2 b c Cockney Rebel(IRE) Mini Penny (FR) (Pennekamp (USA))
1271a[5] *5900a[9]*

**Model Pupil** *A Mishreff* a109 109
5 b h Sinndar(IRE) Modesta (IRE) (Sadler's Wells (USA))
811a[6] 900a[10]

**Modem** *Rod Millman* a75 76
4 b g Motivator Alashaan (Darshaan)
*450[3]* ◆ *848[4]* 1355[4] 1909[5] 2670[2]

**Moderah** *James Fanshawe* 58
2 b f Makfi Meetyouthere (IRE) (Sadler's Wells (USA))
7019[7]

**Modern Family (FR)** *Y Barberot* a79 90
2 ch f Excellent Art Ascot Family (IRE) (Desert Style (IRE))
(4883a)

**Modern History (IRE)** *Charlie Appleby* a103 93
6 b g Shamardal(USA) Fatefully (USA) (Private Account (USA))
*109a[2] 768a[6]*

**Modernism** *David Simcock* a84 94
5 b g Monsun(GER) La Nuit Rose (FR) (Rainbow Quest (USA))
*89[6] (200) (408) 533[4] 611[5]* 2405[2] 2779[3] 3217[10] 3730[7] 4160[6] 5651[15] *6156[5]* 6664[3] 6839[2]

**Modernstone** *William Knight* a106 91
4 b f Duke Of Marmalade(IRE) Post Modern (USA) (Nureyev (USA))
*54[2]* ◆ *(212) 716[2] 1170[2]*

**Modern Tutor** *Andrew Balding* a84 82
5 b g Selkirk(USA) Magical Romance (IRE) (Barathea (IRE))
2984[6] 7168[6] 7715[12] *7851[4] 8135[5]*

**Modify** *David O'Meara* a46 57
3 ch f New Approach(IRE) Hill Welcome (Most Welcome)
2742[8] *3407[11]* 4386[3] 5402[3] (5682) 6216[7]

**Mogadishio (FR)** *S Smrczek* a91 106
7 b h American Post Nebraska I (FR) (Octagonal (NZ))
*806a[4]* 6382a[7] 7242[12] *8150a[4]*

**Mohair** *Tony Carroll* a70 33
5 b m Motivator Cashmere (Barathea (IRE))
*185[7] 469[5]*

**Mohatem (USA)** *B W Hills* 83
2 ch c Distorted Humor(USA) Soul Search (USA) (A.P. Indy (USA))
6259[5] (6683)

**Moheebb (IRE)** *Robert Johnson* a42 66
10 b g Machiavellian(USA) Rockerlong (Deploy)
1374[11]

**Moheet (IRE)** *Richard Hannon* 88
2 b c High Chaparral(IRE) Abunai (Pivotal)
(6874)

**Mo Henry** *Richard Whitaker* a73 56
2 b c Monsieur Bond(IRE) Mo Mhuirnin (IRE) (Danetime (IRE))
6757[8] 7329[4] *(8140) 8308[5]*

**Moholoholo (IRE)** *Hugo Palmer* 76
3 b c High Chaparral(IRE) Pray (IRE) (Priolo (USA))
2432[5]

**Moidore** *John Quinn* a79 92
5 b g Galileo(IRE) Flash Of Gold (Darshaan)
1562[12] 1735[10] 2289[9] (2739) 5161[5] 6514[3] ◆ 7107[18] *7650[3]*

**Moiety** *Rae Guest* a72
3 b f Myboycharlie(IRE) Millinsky (USA) (Stravinsky (USA))
*7117[3] (7370) 7775[6] 8082[7] 8223[4]*

**Moissanite** *Sean Regan* a4 4
5 b m Danbird(AUS) Nikita Sunrise (IRE) (Namid)
*497[10] 1086[6] 7766[11] 7976[11]*

**Mojawiz** *Charlie Appleby* a73 67
2 b g Dubawi(IRE) Zayn Zen (Singspiel (IRE))
7666[6] *7778[3]* ◆ *7927[5]*

**Mojo Bear** *Sylvester Kirk* a65 63
4 b f Indesatchel(IRE) Four Legs Good (IRE) (Be My Guest (USA))
*88[4] 156[4]*

**Mojolika** *Patrick Holmes* a54 77
6 ch g Motivator Kalandika (Diesis)
4754[4] 5764[6] 7175[4]

**Mokka (FR)** *F Foresi* a61
3 ch f Astronomer Royal(USA) Fulcrum (Pivotal)
*193a[9]*

**Molesne Chop (FR)** *Mlle C Cardenne* a41 73
3 ch g Deportivo Amour Parfait (IRE) (Spinning World (USA))
(3809a)

**Molko Jack (FR)** *Michael Mullineaux* a31
10 bb g Lavirco(GER) Line As (FR) (Cadoudal (FR))
*6901[7]*

**Mollasses** *Jonathan Portman* a71 73
3 b f Authorized(IRE) Muscovado (USA) (Mr Greeley (USA))
*1240[3]* 2277[4] 3146[7]

**Molly Ahoy** *Alan McCabe* a64 47
3 b f Captain Gerrard(IRE) Demolition Molly (Rudimentary (USA))
*1112[2] 1364[4]* 2129[10] *2902[4]* 3380[4] *4049[8]* 4627[8]

**Molly Approve (IRE)** *Tony Coyle* 51
2 b f Approve(IRE) Kathleen Rafferty (IRE) (Marju (IRE))
2979[9] 5386[8] 6667[6]

**Molly Cat** *Alan Swinbank* 71
4 ch f Dylan Thomas(IRE) Pentatonic (Giant's Causeway (USA))
1600[3] 1969[2] 6432[5] 7008[8] 7176[4]

**Molly Jones** *Derek Haydn Jones* a61 70
5 b m Three Valleys(USA) And Toto Too (Averti (IRE))
*59[6] 258[8] 384[6]* 2008[2] 2830[6] (4101) 4285[3] (4567) (4848) 5595[6]

**Molly Le Clou (GER)** *J Hirschberger* 95
2 rg c Doyen(IRE) Molly Maxima (GER) (Big Shuffle (USA))
(6377a) 7145a[3] 7726a[4]

**Molly Morgan (USA)** *Dale Romans* a110
5 b m Ghostzapper(USA) Capitulation (USA) (Distorted Humor (USA))
*6973a[3]*

**Molly On The Shore** *Ralph Beckett* 62
3 b f Halling(USA) Zahrtee (IRE) (Alhaarth (IRE))
2334[11]

**Mollyow (IRE)** *Bernard Llewellyn* a26 29
6 ch m Iceman Corryvreckan (IRE) (Night Shift (USA))
*8021[8]*

**Molten Lava (IRE)** *Paul Cole* a66
2 b c Rock Of Gibraltar(IRE) Skehana (IRE) (Mukaddamah (USA))
*7731[7] 8067[8]*

**Momayyaz (IRE)** *Saeed bin Suroor* a99 97
3 b f Elusive Quality(USA) Surrealism (Pivotal)
4407[2] *(5007)* 5627[5] *(6411)* 6978[4] *7545[5]*

**Mombasa** *Harry Dunlop* 81
4 b g Dubawi(IRE) Limuru (Salse (USA))
1418[11] 2248[8]

**Mombasa (GER)** *P Schiergen* a41 85
7 b m Black Sam Bellamy(IRE) Murnau (IRE) (Rudimentary (USA))
7769a[11]

**Moment In Time (IRE)** *David Simcock* a74 109
5 b m Tiger Hill(IRE) Horatia (IRE) (Machiavellian (USA))
*682a[5]* 811a[7] 1177a[4] 2764[8] 3307[8] 3961[6] 4213[4] 4945[2] 5457a[4] 6255[6]

**Moment Of Change (AUS)** *Peter G Moody* 117
6 b g Barely A Moment(AUS) Europium (AUS) (Metal Storm (FR))
7724a[5]

**Momentus (IRE)** *David Simcock* 100
3 b f Montjeu(IRE) Race For The Stars (USA) (Fusaichi Pegasus (USA))
2152[3] ◆ 2960[8] (4413) 5611[5]

**Momkinzain (USA)** *Lucinda Russell* a31 41
7 b g Rahy(USA) Fait Accompli (USA) (Louis Quatorze (USA))
2678[7]

**Momo No Sekku (FR)** *S Kobayashi* a80 98
3 b f Leroidesanimaux(BRZ) Academic Angel (USA) (Royal Academy (USA))
1782a[5] 6882a[6]

**Monakova (IRE)** *David O'Meara* a73 96
4 b f Diamond Green(FR) Koukalova (IRE) (Desert Prince (IRE))
3305[5] 4112[7]

**Monarch Maid** *Peter Hiatt* a74 75
3 b f Captain Gerrard(IRE) Orange Lily (Royal Applause)
2994[3] 3561[7] 4469[2] 4890[5] 5724[6] 6029[2] (6758) *7352[7] 7776[6] 8077[3]*

**Monashka Bay (IRE)** *Michael Blanshard* a60
3 b g Kodiac River Style (IRE) (Desert Style (IRE))
*(666) 1146[4] 1379[6]* 2278[13] *2647[9] 4324[6] 5820[10]*

**Monatorio (FR)** *H-A Pantall* 70
3 b c Vespone(IRE) Midyanila (FR) (Midyan (USA))
(2003a)

**Mon Brav** *Brian Ellison* a73 88
7 b g Sampower Star Danehill Princess (IRE) (Danehill (USA))
1190[11] 1541[5] 1938[5] 2332[4] 2559[2] (2953) 3256[3] 3702[7] 4632[2] 5197[4] 5444[6] 5650[8] 6511[9] (6872) 7085[17]

**Mon Cadeaux** *A bin Huzaim* a43 86
7 b g Cadeaux Genereux Ushindi (IRE) (Montjeu (IRE))
240a[14]

**Mon Cigar (IRE)** *Denis Coakley* a72 61
3 b g Bushranger(IRE) Practicallyperfect (IRE) (King Charlemagne (USA))
4677[5] 5249[5] 5775[5] *6857[11] 7556[2]* ◆ *7842[2]*

**Moncucay (FR)** *F Foresi*
2 b g Way Of Light(USA) Montmarie (FR) (Montjeu (IRE))
7027a[9]

**Mondlicht (USA)** *Mark Johnston* a90
4 b g Malibu Moon(USA) Moonlight Cruise (USA) (Silver Deputy (CAN))
*(564)* ◆ *(832)* ◆

**Monel** *Jim Goldie* 71
6 ch g Cadeaux Genereux Kelucia (IRE) (Grand Lodge (USA))
1310[5] 1758[8] 1838[4] (2452) 2479[3] (3053) 3102[4] 4004[3] 5415[6] 6478[11] 7056[2]

**Money Drop (ITY)** *Stefano Botti* 97
2 b f Martino Alonso(IRE) Khanstan (IRE) (Barathea (IRE))
7321a[3]

**Moneypennie** *Marcus Tregoning* a52 53
3 b f Captain Gerrard(IRE) Snoozy (Cadeaux Genereux)
*2078[10]* 2416[11] 3281[5] 4048[2] 4654[6]

**Money Spider (IRE)** *J F Levins* 77
5 b m Danehill Dancer(IRE) Regal Darcey (IRE) (Darshaan)
5193[4]

**Money Talks** *Michael Madgwick* a70 67
4 br g Motivator Movie Mogul (Sakhee (USA))
*2683[3] 3579[5]*

**Money Team (IRE)** *David Barron* a89 95
3 b g Kodiac Coral Dawn (IRE) (Trempolino (USA))
(2015) (3484) 4898[9] 5696[4] 6170[3] *7543[8] 8141[3]*

**Money Time (IRE)** *Henk Grewe* a93 87
4 b f Arch(USA) Green Girl (FR) (Lord Of Men)
3873a[8] *8006a[5]*

**Mon Gris (IRE)** *Kristin Stubbs* 46
2 gr g Falco Turpitude (Caerleon (USA))
7054[6] 7498[8]

**Monika Jem (FR)** *S Jesus* a76 89
3 ch f Redback Beauty Jem (FR) (Red Ransom (USA))
*436a[6] 721a[9]*

**Monksford Lady** *Donald McCain* a25 56
2 b f Lope De Vega(IRE) Viennese Whirl (Montjeu (IRE))
3296[5] 4011[5] *5099[4]* 6222[5]

**Monna Valley** *Stuart Williams* 40
2 ch g Exceed And Excel(AUS) Monnavanna (IRE) (Machiavellian (USA))
7166[6]

**Monnoyer** *Scott Dixon* a73 46
5 ch g Dutch Art Ellebanna (Tina's Pet)
*9[6] 297[5] 766[3] 1115[6] 1892[6]*

**Monoceros (USA)** *P Bary* a87 103
3 b c Giant's Causeway(USA) Divine Proportions (USA) (Kingmambo (USA))
2242a[4] *(5705a)*

**Monolite (FR)** *J Hirschberger* 55
5 ch m Monos(GER) Opportunistic (IRE) (Mukaddamah (USA))
6569a[6]

**Monopoli** *Shaun Harris* a60 63
5 ch m Cadeaux Genereux Jump Ship (Night Shift (USA))
1910[4] (2609) 2863[5] 3155[11] 6706[7] 7219[3] 7540[3]

**Mon Petit Fleur** *Chris Dwyer* a58
2 b f Arabian Gleam Mon Petit Diamant (Hector Protector (USA))
*7454[7] 7649[8] 7881[4] 8118[2]*

**Mon Petit Secret** *Kevin Ryan* a67 15
3 b f Sakhee's Secret Crabapple (Alhaarth (IRE))
*(675) 892[8]* 1507[10] 1884[8]

**Mon P'Tit Lu (FR)** *J-L Foursans-Bourdette* a78
4 gr g Nombre Premier Lucy Toto (Mtoto)
*722a[9]*

**Monsart (IRE)** *Jo Hughes* a52
2 b g Echo Of Light Monet's Lady (IRE) (Daylami (IRE))
*7811[8] 8083[7]*

**Monsea (IRE)** *Brian Ellison* a92 71
3 gr c Manduro(GER) Sea Drift (FR) (Warning)
1954[7] 2983[4] 4551[7] 5311[9] 6424[5] *8257[11]*

**Monsieur Chabal** *Jamie Osborne* a54 3
3 b g Avonbridge Coup De Torchon (FR) (Namid)
*1830[5] 2126[10] 2211[8]* 2927[12] *3471[3] 4433[10] 5048[8]*

**Monsieur Chevalier (IRE)** *Jamie Osborne*a95 70
7 b g Chevalier(IRE) Blue Holly (IRE) (Blues Traveller (IRE))
1492[7] ◆ 2336[4] 3152[4] *4323[2] 5824[9] 6140[8]* 6548[10] 7136[6] *(7894) (7983)*

**Monsieur Jamie** *J R Jenkins* a85 83
6 b g Monsieur Bond(IRE) Primula Bairn (Bairn (USA))
*175[7] 549[3]* 1618[5] 1912[3] 2159[10] 5880[6] 7307[4] 7535[6] *7767[8]*

**Monsieur Jimmy** *Declan Carroll* 54
2 ch g Monsieur Bond(IRE) Artistic License (IRE) (Chevalier (IRE))
1161[16] 2014[7] 2231[5]

**Monsieur Joe (IRE)** *Paul Midgley* a89 111
7 b g Choisir(AUS) Pascali (Compton Place)
107a[6] 393a[7] 680a[6] *1066[9]* (2283) 2786[7] 2989[7] 3736a[3] 4215[3] 4700[7] 4852[13] 5654[11] 6231[7]

**Monsieur Lavene (IRE)** *Robert Mills* a71
3 b g Kodiac Sign Of Luck (IRE) (Daylami (IRE))
*(622) 762[3]*

**Monsieur Pontaven** *Robin Bastiman* a52 55
7 b g Avonbridge Take Heart (Electric)
*317[5] 516[8]*

**Monsieur Rieussec** *Jonathan Portman* 87
4 bl g Halling(USA) Muscovado (USA) (Mr Greeley (USA))
2311[8] 3065[5] 4538[2]

**Monsieur Rouge (IRE)** *Alan McCabe* a14
2 b g Monsieur Bond(IRE) Brosna Time (IRE) (Danetime (IRE))
*5604[10]*

**Monsieur Royal (FR)** *C Plisson* a63 71
2 b c Domedriver(IRE) Royalrique (FR) (Enrique)
2755a[8] 3871a[4] (4881a)

**Monsieur Royale** *Geoffrey Oldroyd* a73 55
4 ch g Monsieur Bond(IRE) Bond Royale (Piccolo)
141[5] 3530[7] 3913[8] 4195[2] 4571[5] 5683[4] 6405[6] 7078[9]

**Monsieur Valentine** *Tony Carroll* a34 39
2 ch c Monsieur Bond(IRE) Minnina (IRE) (In The Wings)
7216[3] 7542[10] 7713[5]

**Monsynn (FR)** *C Lerner* a80 84
5 b h Rail Link Breath Of Love (USA) (Mutakddim (USA))
1828a[10]

**Montaff** *Richard Guest* a42 66
8 b g Montjeu(IRE) Meshhed (USA) (Gulch (USA))
6433[8] 7124[10] 7509[6] 7760[8] 8253[9]

**Montaigne** *Ralph Beckett* a82 85
3 b c Exceed And Excel(AUS) Autumn Pearl (Orpen (USA))
1350[2] 1700[3] ◆

**Montalban (FR)** *D De Waele* a93 80
7 b g Elusive City(USA) Realy Queen (USA) (Thunder Gulch (USA))
3373a[4]

**Montalcino (IRE)** *Brian Meehan* 93
2 b f Big Bad Bob(IRE) Fair Sailing (IRE) (Docksider (USA))
4396[12] (5416) 6126[2]

**Montaly** *Andrew Balding* a73 100
3 b g Yeats(IRE) Le Badie (IRE) (Spectrum (IRE))
(1279) 1727[2] 2566[2] 3419[5] (5179) 6127[8]

**Montaser (IRE)** *David Simcock* 107
5 b g Rail Link For Example (USA) (Northern Baby (CAN))
2073[17] 3217[12]

**Mont Athos (FR)** *J Van Handenhove* a84 72
5 ch g My Risk(FR) Sea Goddess (FR) (Crystal Glitters (USA))
5546a[10]

**Montbazon (FR)** *Alan King* a80 80
7 bb g Alberto Giacometti(IRE) Duchesse Pierji (FR) (Cadoudal (FR))
3106[3] 3857[3]

**Montclair (IRE)** *A Fabre* 112
4 b c Montjeu(IRE) Minaccia (GER) (Platini (GER))
(1784a) 2588a[4] 4250a[9]

**Monte Cassino (IRE)** *Bryan Smart* a64 64
9 ch g Choisir(AUS) Saucy Maid (IRE) (Sure Blade (USA))
918[3] 996[7] 3833[8] 5510[7] 7424[10]

**Montefalcon (IRE)** *Richard Fahey* 63
2 b g Footstepsinthesand Gwyllion (USA) (Red Ransom (USA))
1879[6] 6668[6] 7123[7]

**Monte Fanum (ITY)** *C Felaco* 77
4 ch c Blu Air Force(IRE) Arsulvela (IRE) (Wixim (USA))
7616a[10]

**Montego Breeze** *John W Nicholson* a5 13
8 b m Tipsy Creek(USA) Mofeyda (IRE) (Mtoto)
7962a[12]

**Montesquieu (FR)** *C Boutin* a73 69
4 b g Silvano(GER) Beiramar (IRE) (Monsun (GER))
5546a[7]

**Monte Viso** *Stuart Kittow* a44 64
3 b g Piccolo Mrs Snaffles (IRE) (Indian Danehill (IRE))
3709[7] 4370[9] 5522[5] 6194[7]

**Monthly Medal** *Wilf Storey* a43 59
11 b g Danehill Dancer(IRE) Sovereign Abbey (IRE) (Royal Academy (USA))
1675[14] 2426[6] 3623[3] 4319[6] 4665[6]

**Montiridge (IRE)** *Richard Hannon* 110
4 b c Ramonti(FR) Elegant Ridge (IRE) (Indian Ridge)
1698[2] 2338[8] 2848[10] 3451[12]

**Montjen (IRE)** *Karen Tutty* a37
4 b f Montjeu(IRE) Nuriva (USA) (Woodman (USA))
542[6] 776[8]

**Montjess (IRE)** *Laura Mongan* a79 42
4 b f Montjeu(IRE) Wing Stealth (IRE) (Hawk Wing (USA))
260[5] 992[2] 2683[4] 3078[8] 3874[8] 4656[6]

**Montone (IRE)** *Sir Michael Stoute*
3 ch g Danehill Dancer(IRE) Leocorno (IRE) (Pivotal)
1880[7]

**Mont Pelato (USA)** *M Weiss* a76
6 rg h Forest Danger(USA) Zada Rae (USA) (Unbridled's Song (USA))
638a[2]

**Mont Ras (IRE)** *David O'Meara* a104 107
7 ch g Indian Ridge Khayrat (IRE) (Polar Falcon (USA))
109a[4] 306a[9] (509a)

**Mont Signal** *Daniel Kubler* a63 47
4 ch g Pivotal Anse Victorin (USA) (Mt. Livermore (USA))
(1081) 1228[5] 1813[5]

**Montviron (FR)** *E Lellouche* 101
3 b c Le Havre(IRE) Manita (IRE) (Peintre Celebre (USA))
6970a[20]

**Monty Fay (IRE)** *Derek Haydn Jones* a47 44
5 bb g Iffraaj Blast (USA) (Roar (USA))
3178[5] 3520[5] 4151[5] 5423[6] 6088[10] 6764[5]

**Monumental Man** *James Unett* a80 86
5 b g Vital Equine(IRE) Spark Up (Lahib (USA))
1145[7] 1695[8] (2275) 3216[5] 3676[3] 4284[2] 4762[10] 5677[6] 6096[14] 6324[2] 6650[2]

**Monzino (USA)** *Michael Chapman* a73 50
6 bb g More Than Ready(USA) Tasso's Magic Roo (USA) (Tasso (USA))
72[4] 253[6] 385[5] 569[4] 652[6] 831[6] 1117[6] 3843[2] 4115[6] 4319[4] 4749[6] 4996[4] 7540[8]

**Moodrick (FR)** *Olly Stevens* 54
2 gr c Dark Angel(IRE) Flying Plover (IRE) (Danehill Dancer (IRE))
4760[11]

**Moohaarib (IRE)** *Marco Botti* a91 103
3 b c Oasis Dream Evita (Selkirk (USA))
1587[3] ◆ 2334[6] (2871) (3651) 4647[3] ◆ 5656[9] (6978) 7668[2] 8150a[5]

**Moojaned (IRE)** *Dai Burchell* a52 32
3 b g Raven's Pass(USA) Mufradat (IRE) (Desert Prince (IRE))
4500[10] 5039[13] 5606[8] 6568[8]

**Moonadee (IRE)** *B W Hills* 63
2 gr g Haatef(USA) Again Royale (IRE) (Royal Academy (USA))
3194[9] 4207[10] 4429[7]

**Moon Arc (IRE)** *Keith Dalgleish* 50
2 b g Arcano(IRE) Moon Unit (IRE) (Intikhab (USA))
4450[9] 4659[9] 5242[4] 6008[6]

**Moonbi Creek (IRE)** *D K Weld* a50 67
7 b g Fasliyev(USA) Moonbi Range (IRE) (Nordico (USA))
4805a[13] 4950a[10]

**Moonday Sun (USA)** *Andy Turnell* a100 94
5 gr h Mizzen Mast(USA) Storm Dove (USA) (Storm Bird (CAN))
426[2] 533[3] 840[3] 1437[18] 1558[11] 4761[5] 5669[4] 5928[13] 6560[4] 7136[3] 7341[7] 7955[12]

**Moon Dice (IRE)** *Paul W Flynn* a68 76
9 b g Norwich Ella Come Back (IRE) (Bob Back (USA))
4746a[6]

**Moonee Valley (FR)** *Mario Hofer* 104
2 ch f Aqlaam Moon Romance (FR) (Nayef (USA))
6219a[4] (7393a)

**Moon Eyes** *William Haggas* a49
2 b f Oasis Dream Enticing (IRE) (Pivotal)
8191[7]

**Moonfaarid** *M F De Kock* a76 81
3 b g Dubawi(IRE) Manoeuvre (IRE) (Galileo (IRE))
6483[3] 6885[7] 7035[10]

**Moonlight Dash** *S Seemar* a89 97
6 b g Monsun(GER) Kind Regards (IRE) (Unfuwain (USA))
398a[11]

**Moonlightnavigator (USA)** *John Quinn* 88
2 bb c Henrythenavigator(USA) Victorica (USA) (Exbourne (USA))
4216[5] (4518) 5762[2] 6165[5] (6473)

**Moonlight Sonata** *Sir Michael Stoute* 74
2 b f Galileo(IRE) Blue Rhapsody (Cape Cross (IRE))
6041[3] ◆ 6553[2]

**Moonlight Swing (FR)** *P Bary* 77
2 b f Palace Episode(USA) Moonlight Sail (USA) (Irish River (FR))
5293a[5]

**Moonlight Venture** *Kevin Ryan* a79 74
3 ch g Tobougg(IRE) Evening (Mark Of Esteem (IRE))
551[2] (861) 1714[3] 4496[5] 5550[8] 6633[2]

**Moonlit Sky** *James Tate* a68
3 b c Myboycharlie(IRE) Calico Moon (USA) (Seeking The Gold (USA))
684[6] 1002[2] 1153[4]

**Moon Over Rio (IRE)** *Ben Haslam* 63
3 b f Captain Rio Moonchild (GER) (Acatenango (GER))
1303[10] (5331) 6000[3]

**Moonraker** *Mick Channon* 103
2 ch c Starspangledbanner(AUS) Licence To Thrill (Wolfhound (USA))
(2146) 4822[7] 5694[2] ◆ 6286[7] 7238[10]

**Moonrise Landing (IRE)** *Ralph Beckett* a73 81
3 gr f Dalakhani(IRE) Celtic Slipper (IRE) (Anabaa (USA))
(1044) ◆ 2152[8]

**Moon River (IRE)** *Brian Meehan* a69 57
2 b f Exceed And Excel(AUS) Dame Blanche (IRE) (Be My Guest (USA))
3888[5] 4499[8] 4781[5] 7742[6] (8069)

**Moonspring (IRE)** *Robert Cowell* a78 77
3 gr f Aussie Rules(USA) Unintentional (Dr Devious (IRE))
(1045) 1832[6] (2208) (2686) (2886) 3581[3] 4132[7] 4862[5] (5437) 6680[9] 7220[11]

**Moontime** *Charlie Appleby* a89 84
3 b g Sea The Stars(IRE) Time On (Sadler's Wells (USA))
1652[8] 2060[3] 2566[6] 7409[12]

**Moontown** *Charles Hills* a76 69
3 ch g Sea The Stars(IRE) Eva's Request (IRE) (Soviet Star (USA))
827[2] 951[4] 3248[9] 4368[3] 4948[7] 7552[10]

**Moon Trip** *Geoffrey Deacon* a51 69
5 b g Cape Cross(IRE) Fading Light (King's Best (USA))
1418[14] 2011[6] 2683[7]

**Moonvoy** *Jeremy Noseda* a88 85
3 b f Cape Cross(IRE) Needles And Pins (IRE) (Fasliyev (USA))
1529[3] 2389[4] 5007[2] 5352[3] (5862) 6922[7] 7857a[18] 8194[3]

**Moonwood** *Ollie Pears* a15 52
3 ch f Three Valleys(USA) Woodcock Moon (Kyllachy)
1888[5] 2201[10] 2871[5] 4017[4] 4304[10]

**Moonyr (FR)** *Mlle H Mennessier* a31 71
6 b g Hernando(FR) Mydarshaan (Darshaan)
5225a[5] 5961a[16] 6569a[7]

**Moorhouse Lad** *Garry Moss* a86 91
11 b g Bertolini(USA) Record Time (Clantime)
175[5] 444[3] 863[2] 1565[5] 1695[10] 2434[2] 3033[10] 4114[7] 4833[9]

**Moorsholm (IRE)** *Alan Swinbank* 26
3 b g High Chaparral(IRE) Arctic Freedom (USA) (War Chant (USA))
6429[9] 7332[6]

**Mops Angel** *Michael Appleby* a60 70
3 b f Piccolo Tanning (Atraf)
7213[9] 7670[3] 7826[5] 8180[11]

**Morache Music** *Peter Makin* a99 111
6 b g Sleeping Indian Enchanted Princess (Royal Applause)
2149[4] 2848[7] 3732[9] 3960[2] 4425[4] (5418) 6060[3] 6921[5] 7668[5] 7851[4]

**Morawij** *Roger Varian* a93 84
4 ch g Exceed And Excel(AUS) Sister Moonshine (FR) (Piccolo)
1561[7] 4179[14] 4683[18] 5289[6]

**Mord (ITY)** *E Botti* 73
3 b c Giovane Imperatore Fagiudizi (Nashwan (USA))
2375a[11]

**More Aspen (USA)** *S Seemar* a86 59
3 ch f More Than Ready(USA) Jade Aspen (USA) (Jade Hunter (USA))
203a[4] 506a[8] 771a[5] 896a[6]

**More Beau (USA)** *Ed Dunlop* a57 73
3 bb c More Than Ready(USA) Frontier Beauty (USA) (Gone West (USA))
1173[6] 1486[4] 1939[6] (2657) 3855[8]

**More Drama (IRE)** *Sylvester Kirk* a52 45
2 b f Thewayyouare(USA) Our Drama Queen (IRE) (Danehill Dancer (IRE))
4676[8] 4980[10] 5488[6] 6237[6] 6842[7] 7064[4] (7816) 7994[2] 8115[8]

**Moreno (USA)** *Eric J Guillot* a118
4 b g Ghostzapper(USA) Danceinthesunlight (CAN) (A.P. Indy (USA))
7614a[14]

**More Questions (IRE)** *Edward Lynam* a71 96
4 b g Moss Vale(IRE) Twenty Questions (Kyllachy)
4480a[15] (Dead)

**Morera (IRE)** *P Schiergen* 78
2 b f Echo Of Light Mary Martins (IRE) (Orpen (USA))
5293a[9] 6385a[3]

**More Spice (IRE)** *Robert Cowell* a52
2 b c Exceed And Excel(AUS) High Spice (USA) (Songandaprayer (USA))
7454[9]

**More Than Sacred (AUS)** *Robert Smerdon* 103
5 b m More Than Ready(USA) Danalaga (AUS) (Danehill (USA))
7395a[4]

**More Than Sotka (FR)** *Matthieu Palussiere* a90 101
4 ch f Dutch Art King's Doll (IRE) (King's Best (USA))
2715a[5] 5369a[6] 6620a[2] 7629a[7]

**Morga (IRE)** *Desmond McDonogh* a69 96
4 b f Whipper(USA) Langfuhrina (USA) (Langfuhr (CAN))
1076a[5] 2263a[4] 3285a[4] 7142a[17]

**Morgana** *Simon Hodgson*
6 b m Norse Dancer(IRE) En Vacances (IRE) (Old Vic)
1218[5]

**Morgans Bluff** *Pat Phelan* a38 42
3 ch f Bahamian Bounty River Cara (USA) (Irish River (FR))
1211[7] 2860[5]

**Moriarty (IRE)** *Chris Waller* 112
6 b g Clodovil(IRE) Justice System (USA) (Criminal Type (USA))
7301a[14] 7602a[8]

**Moriond (USA)** *David Simcock* a57
3 ch g Street Cry(IRE) Modesty Blaise (USA) (A.P. Indy (USA))
951[7] 1119[3] 1452[5] 2997[6]

**Morna's Glory** *Sarah Humphrey* a40 62
5 b m Resplendent Glory(IRE) Tipsy Cake (Tipsy Creek (USA))
1649[10] 3334[8] 6862[6] 8013[7]

**Morning (GER)** *M Delcher Sanchez* a43 43
2 ch f Footstepsinthesand Mamourina (IRE) (Barathea (IRE))
5026a[8]

**Morning Frost (IRE)** *M Halford* a99 106
4 gr f Duke Of Marmalade(IRE) Evening Time (IRE) (Keltos (FR))
1333a[10] 2042a[7] 3167a[8]

**Mornin' Gorgeous** *Micky Hammond* a35 64
4 ch f Motivator Sentimental Value (USA) (Diesis)
2523[3]

**Morning Watch (IRE)** *Lady Cecil* a83 71
3 b g Azamour(IRE) Lady Of Kildare (IRE) (Mujadil (USA))
(1391) 3110[7] 4672[5] 6141[3] ◆ 7016[4]

**Mornin Mr Norris** *John Quinn* a49 49
3 b g Byron Fractured Foxy (Foxhound (USA))
568[8] 1130[2] 1285[3] 1647[6] 3105[9] 3407[5]

**Moro Tap (USA)** *Michael J Maker* 102
4 rg c Tapit(USA) Ghost Dancing (USA) (Silver Ghost (USA))
5457a[7]

**Morrocoy (IRE)** *G Botti* a77 80
6 b g Redback Silence (IRE) (Alzao (USA))
(57a)

**Moruadh (IRE)** *Sir Michael Stoute* 54
2 b f Fastnet Rock(AUS) Olympienne (IRE) (Sadler's Wells (USA))
7108[12]

**Moscato** *Sir Mark Prescott Bt* a54 91
3 gr g Hernando(FR) Alba Stella (Nashwan (USA))
4106[5] (4834) 5628[2] (6502) (6640) (6864)

**Moscow Eight (IRE)** *E J O'Neill* a70 80
8 b g Elusive City(USA) Hurricane Lily (IRE) (Ali-Royal (IRE))
7026a[15]

**Moshe (IRE)** *Hughie Morrison* a78 86
3 b g Dansili Rosinka (IRE) (Soviet Star (USA))
1654[2] 2334[15] 5557[6] 5984[2] (6611) 6714[5] 7539[2]

**Mosman** *Dean Ivory* a69 21
4 b g Haafhd Last Dream (IRE) (Alzao (USA))
105[5] 406[4] 578[6]

**Mossgo (IRE)** *John Best* a68 52
4 b g Moss Vale(IRE) Perovskia (USA) (Stravinsky (USA))
87[4] 470[6] 572[4] 687[7] 777[6] 3323[4] 4285[4] 4546[7] 5860[7] 6631[8] 7191[3] 7737[4] 8024[5] 8229[10]

**Moss Hill** *Jason Ward* a25 58
5 b g Moss Vale(IRE) Borders Belle (IRE) (Pursuit Of Love)
77[6] 2658[10] 5103[12]

**Moss Quito (IRE)** *David O'Meara* a63 61
4 b g Moss Vale(IRE) Gold Majesty (Josr Algarhoud (IRE))
5[5]

**Mossy Marie (IRE)** *Eric Alston* 48
3 b f Moss Vale(IRE) Molly Marie (IRE) (Fasliyev (USA))
1671[8] 2389[7] 2910[3] 4193[4] 6819[7] 7250[6]

**Mostaneer (IRE)** *N Clement* 99
2 ch c Dutch Art King's Doll (IRE) (King's Best (USA))
(5706a)

**Most Tempting** *Robert Cowell* a60 29
2 ch f Showcasing La Carot (Motivator)
5509[6] 6032[5] 6435[10] 7190[3] 7453[2] 7780[2]

**Motamayezah** *Alan McCabe* a33 8
3 ch f Tamayuz Classical Dancer (Dr Fong (USA))
1852[5] 3333[11]

**Moulin Rouge (DEN)** *Ian Williams* a57
3 ch f Zambezi Sun Embattle (FR) (Dernier Empereur (USA))
7976[6] (8049) 8265[2] (8314)

**Mountain Dew** *Ralph Beckett* a61 46
3 b f Tiger Hill(IRE) Ecstasy (Pursuit Of Love)
1233[7] 1582[12] 2418[9] 3116[8] 3567[11]

**Mountain Kingdom (IRE)** *Sir Mark Prescott Bt* a73 81
3 b g Montjeu(IRE) Althea Rose (IRE) (Green Desert (USA))
3537[6] 3953[2] 4657[2] 5062[2] 5356[7] 6274[12] 6696[5]

**Mountain Lion (IRE)** *Saeed bin Suroor* a72 70
3 b c Invincible Spirit(IRE) Tuzla (FR) (Panoramic)
239a[8]

**Mountain Man** *Michael Easterby* 64
2 b g Hellvelyn Jane Jubilee (IRE) (Mister Baileys)
1161[10] 1712[5] 2231[6] 4057[7] 4529[3]

**Mountain Range (IRE)** *Willie Musson* a78 46
6 b g High Chaparral(IRE) Tuscany Lady (IRE) (Danetime (IRE))
79[9] ◆ 458[3] 6341[12] 6904[10] 7358[12] 7804[9] 7982[12]

**Mountain Rescue (IRE)** *Roger Charlton* a82
2 b g High Chaparral(IRE) Amber Queen (IRE) (Cadeaux Genereux)
(6675) 7374[2] ◆

**Mountain River (IRE)** *J S Moore* a34
3 br g Footstepsinthesand Animalu (IRE) (Dalakhani (IRE))
3712[12] 4325[13] 5427[9] 6015[9]

**Mountainside** *Charlie Appleby* a74 69
2 ch g Dubawi(IRE) Maids Causeway (IRE) (Giant's Causeway (USA))
3578[5] 4301[3] 7891[2]

**Mount Athos (IRE)** *Marco Botti* a97 120
7 b g Montjeu(IRE) Ionian Sea (Slip Anchor)
900a[3] 1182a[8] (2335)

**Mount Cheiron (USA)** *Dianne Sayer* a62 61
3 b g Henrythenavigator(USA) Chalamont (IRE) (Kris)
2474[5] 2828[8] 3364[8] 4014[7] 4530[3] 4706[4] 4998[2] 5811[7] 6227[3] 6544[5] 7098[10]

**Mount Glenn** *Mark Johnston* a53
3 b c Mount Nelson Glen Rosie (IRE) (Mujtahid (USA))
409[5] 642[3] 735[5]

**Mount Hollow** *Andrew Hollinshead* a78 48
9 b g Beat Hollow Lady Lindsay (IRE) (Danehill Dancer (IRE))
7307[10] (7698) 7888[10] 8124[5]

**Mount Isa (IRE)** *Mme Pia Brandt* a78 74
2 b g Bushranger(IRE) Fee Eria (FR) (Always Fair (USA))
1259[6] 2395[5] 2623[4] 4881a[2] 5118a[2] (5544a) 7723a[3]

**Mount Logan (IRE)** *Luca Cumani* 108
3 ch c New Approach(IRE) Vistaria (USA) (Distant View (USA))
(3182) ◆ 4125[3] 5179[3] (6330) 7718[13]

**Mount Macedon** *Luca Cumani* a73 70
4 b g Hernando(FR) White Palace (Shirley Heights)
1849[7]

**Mount Shamsan** *William Haggas* a75 87
4 b g Danehill Dancer(IRE) Shamaiel (IRE) (Lycius (USA))
1069[5] 2354[6] 2733[2] ◆ (5018) ◆ 5928[14]

**Mount Tahan (IRE)** *Kevin Ryan* 75
2 b c Lope De Vega(IRE) Sorpresa (USA) (Pleasant Tap (USA))
5655[6] 6667[3]

**Mourinho (AUS)** *Peter Gelagotis* 106
7 b g Oratorio(IRE) Benevolent (NZ) (Generous (IRE))
7602a[7]

**Move In Time** *David O'Meara* a75 115
6 ch g Monsieur Bond(IRE) Tibesti (Machiavellian (USA))
2766[4] 3241[12] 4215[6] (4405) 5160[2] 5575[2] 6378a[2] (6966a)

**Movementneverlies** *Richard Phillips* a68 67
4 ch f Medicean Frabjous (Pivotal)
1099[5]

**Moves Like Jagger (IRE)** *Phil McEntee* a47 23
4 b g Danehill Dancer(IRE) Lucky Spin (Pivotal)
672[5] 869[6]

**Move To Strike (IRE)** *J S Bolger* 89
4 b c Lawman(FR) Alamanta (IRE) (Ali-Royal (IRE))
5957a[12]

**Move Your Vision (IRE)** *Zuzana Kubovicova* 92
5 b h Galileo(IRE) Cash Run (USA) (Seeking The Gold (USA))
4720a[10]

**Movie Magic** *John Bridger* a54 38
3 b f Multiplex Alucica (Celtic Swing)
1769[5] 2078[8] 2688[8] 6661[8] 6986[6] 7360[7] 7518[11] 7664[6] 7799[4] 7844[2] 7987[2] 8090[10] 8199[7]

**Moviesta (USA)** *Bryan Smart* a85 115
4 b g Hard Spun(USA) Miss Brickyard (USA) (A.P. Indy (USA))
1949[5] 2256[12] 4201[8] 4852[3] 5654[4] 6134[17] 6966a[3]

**Moving Melody** *Richard Fahey* 71
2 ch f Equiano(FR) Luxuria (IRE) (Kheleyf (USA))
(1837)

**Moving Upwards** *Kevin Ryan* a61
2 ch g Bahamian Bounty Rainbow End (Botanic (USA))
8026[7] 8205[9]

**Moving Waves (IRE)** *Ollie Pears* a61 58
3 b f Intense Focus(USA) Kimola (IRE) (King's Theatre (IRE))
2393[5] 2867[6] 3098[2] 3912[3] 4292[7] (5102)

**Mowhoob** *Jim Goldie* a48 76
4 b g Medicean Pappas Ruby (USA) (Red Ransom (USA))
1446[12] 1596[2] 1930[7] (2516) 3000[3] (3237) 4013[4] 4861[5] 5143[9] 6477[10] 7178[10] 8268[8]

**Moxey** *Danielle McCormick* a49 48
3 ch g Nayef(USA) Emily Blake (IRE) (Lend A Hand)
1588[14] 2020[7] 2742[9] 4495[8] 5402[7] 5717[12] 7908[3]

**Moydin** *Mick Channon* a59
2 b c Motivator Yding (IRE) (Danehill (USA))
7425[3]

**Mr Bissto** *Ian Williams* a63
2 b c High Chaparral(IRE) Senta's Dream (Danehill (USA))
7413[9] 8067[7] 8288[7]

**Mr Bossy Boots (IRE)** *Ralph Beckett* a86 58
3 b c Teofilo(IRE) Zelding (IRE) (Warning)
(423) ◆ 4912[6] (5603) 8257[3]

**Mr Bounty** *M D O'Callaghan* a63 58
4 b g Bahamian Bounty Zamindari (Zamindar (USA))
(1009) 5234[4]

**Mr Bright Eyes (FR)** *D Windrif* a52 51
2 b c Approve(IRE) Age Of Refinement (IRE) (Pivotal)
3871a[5] 4881a[6]

**Mr Burbidge** *Neil Mulholland* a95 37
6 b g Midnight Legend Twin Time (Syrtos)
(72) 285[8] 803[8] (1004) 1383[3] 1556[10] 7107[31]

**Mr Chocolate Drop (IRE)** *Mandy Rowland* a54 51
10 b g Danetime(IRE) Forest Blade (IRE) (Charnwood Forest (IRE))
17[4] (179) 377[6] 446[5] 755[5] 1596[8] 2164[9] 2806[5] 3678[8] 4592[5]

**Mr Christopher (IRE)** *Noel Wilson* 48
2 b g Bahamian Bounty Embassy Pearl (IRE) (Invincible Spirit (IRE))
2359[8] 6509[9] 7084[11]

**Mr Churchill (IRE)** *Ismail Mohammed* a60 65
5 b h Invincible Spirit(IRE) Mayoress (Machiavellian (USA))
238a[13]

**Mr Cool Cash** *Ann Duffield* 47
2 b c Firebreak Cashleen (USA) (Lemon Drop Kid (USA))
5852[5] 7097[6] 7329[6]

**Mr Dandy Man (IRE)** *Ronald Harris* 77
3 ch g Dandy Man(IRE) Boudica (IRE) (Alhaarth (IRE))
2035[7] 2406[6] (3084) 4133[6] 4328[3] 4636[5] 5501[6] 6296[7] 6455[9]

**Mr David (USA)** *Claes Bjorling* a78 96
7 b g Sky Mesa(USA) Dancewiththebride (USA) (Belong To Me (USA))
162[3] 287[4] (399) 3996a[9] 6387a[8]

**Mr Fickle (IRE)** *Gary Moore* a60 64
5 b g Jeremy(USA) Mamara Reef (Salse (USA))
7526[6]

**Mr Fitzroy (IRE)** *Jo Davis* a46 77
4 ch g Kyllachy Reputable (Medicean)
5276[8]

**Mr Frankie** *Ed de Giles* a70
3 b g Sleeping Indian Shes Minnie (Bertolini (USA))
6073[3] ◆ 6717[2] 7528[5]

**Mr Gallivanter (IRE)** *John Quinn* 87
3 ch g Heliostatic(IRE) Purepleasureseeker (IRE) (Grand Lodge (USA))
1195[2] 1883[2] 3003[6] 4113[2] 4392[3] 5164[7] 6450[4]

**Mr Gatsby** *Mark Walford* 68
3 b g Lucky Story(USA) Otylia (Wolfhound (USA))
5195[9] 5469[8] 6118[4] 6626[11]

**Mr Gnocchi (AUS)** *C S Shum* 110
5 b g Hard Spun(USA) Sunflower Street (AUS) (Fantastic Light (USA))
7899a[8]

**Mr Gotham** *C Impelluso* a65 98
5 b g Stormy River(FR) Raphaela (FR) (Octagonal (NZ))
2191a[10]

**Mr Greenspan (USA)** *Richard Hannon* a73 77
3 b g Mr Greeley(USA) In Escrow (USA) (Vindication (USA))
1208[3] 2346[3] 4500[9]

**Mr Hawk (FR)** *Yannick Fouin* 69
3 b g Mr. Sidney(USA) Miss Alabama (FR) (Anabaa (USA))
1551a[7]

**Mr Hichens** *Karen George* a25 26
9 b g Makbul Lake Melody (Sizzling Melody)
6342[10]

**Mr Lando** *Tony Carroll* a71 65
5 b g Shirocco(GER) Capitana (GER) (Lando (GER))
503[3] 539[6] 646[6] 922[4] 1664[4] 2084[2] 2464[2] 4734[5] 5502[4] 6771[10] 6942[10] (7369) 7527[8] 7961a[13]

**Mr Man In The Moon (IRE)** *Mandy Rowland* a33 48
6 gr g Verglas(IRE) Dancing Drop (Green Desert (USA))
760[10]

**Mr Matthews (IRE)** *K R Burke* a37 82
3 b g Diamond Green(FR) Five Sisters (Mujahid (USA))
1358[3] 1693[7] 2111[3] 2567[4] 3243[10] 3455[7] 5468[5] 6334[5] 7373[11]

**Mr McLaren** *David O'Meara* 87
3 b g Royal Applause Mamma Morton (IRE) (Elnadim (USA))
2737[7] (2910) 3663[2] 4496[3] (4628) ◆ 5385[11] 5816[2] 6431[3] 6792[4] 6980[3]

**Mr Mo Jo** *Les Eyre* a61 67
6 b g Danbird(AUS) Nampara Bay (Emarati (USA))
3093[7] 3338[2] (3611) 3948[12] 4714[10] 5298[9] 5819[10] 6452[4] 7997[7] 8255[8]

**Mr Morocco** *Noel Quinlan* 53
2 b c Shirocco(GER) Moxby (Efisio)
5646[13] 7040[7] 7382[15]

**Mr Muzzare (USA)** *M Massimi Jr* 98
5 b h Langfuhr(CAN) Clefairy (IRE) (Sri Pekan (USA))
6808a[12] 7604a[9]

**Mr O'Ceirin (NZ)** *Ciaron Maher* 109
7 b g Postponed(USA) Cadell (NZ) (Yachtie (AUS))
7653a[21]

**Mr Opulence** *T Le Brocq* a40 52
5 ch g Generous(IRE) Miss Opulence (IRE) (Kylian (USA))
1622a[5] 2592a[4] 4718a[3]

**Mr Plod** *Andrew Reid* a52 38
9 ch g Silver Patriarch(IRE) Emily-Mou (IRE) (Cadeaux Genereux)
2801[9] 4082[P]

**Mr Pommeroy (FR)** *H-A Pantall* a100 108
3 ch c Linngari(IRE) Amerissage (USA) (Rahy (USA))
193a[3] (436a) (721a) 1340a[3] 2818a[6] 3807a[3] 4720a[7] 6571a[4]

**Mr Quicksilver** *Andrew Balding* a51
2 gr c Dansili Last Second (IRE) (Alzao (USA))
6241[5]

**Mr Red Clubs (IRE)** *Michael Appleby* a81 83
5 b g Red Clubs(IRE) Queen Cobra (IRE) (Indian Rocket)
79[8] (410) 674[4] 733[3] 843[2] (940) 1021[2] 1637[5] 2016[2]

**Mrs Biggs** *Declan Carroll* 65
2 ch f Paco Boy(IRE) Hoh Chi Min (Efisio)
3296[3] (3529)

**Mrs Burbidge** *Neil Mulholland* a41
4 b f Pasternak Twin Time (Syrtos)
486[13] 660[10] 800[5]

**Mrs Eve (IRE)** *Alan Bailey* a47 65
2 ch f Bahamian Bounty Catbells (IRE) (Rakti)
6093[12] 6754[5] 7108[11] 7728[10]

**Mrs Gorsky** *Patrick Holmes* a37 13
4 b f Duke Of Marmalade(IRE) Dowager (Groom Dancer (USA))
2170[9] 2389[9] 2738[15] 4664[8] 5234[7]

**Mr Shekells** *Philip McBride* 67
2 b g Three Valleys(USA) Quip (Green Desert (USA))
1859[5] 2359[6] 3429[9] (4364) 4619[3] 5335[9] (6211) 6436[3]

**Mr Singh** *John Gosden* a67
2 b c High Chaparral(IRE) Sundari (IRE) (Danehill (USA))
8093[3]

**Mrs Medley** *Ann Stokell* a30 21
8 b m Rambling Bear Animal Cracker (Primo Dominie)
58[11] 94[7] 298[8] 645[7] 994[7]

**Mr Smith** *John Gosden* a34 68
3 gr c Galileo(IRE) Intrigued (Darshaan)
2271[10] 2746[9] 4333[5] 4834[4]

**Mr Snoozy** *Mark Walford* 86
5 b g Pursuit Of Love Hard To Follow (Dilum (USA))
1306[5] 1692[3] 2289[4] 2739[4] 3204[8] 7235[11]

**Mr Soprano** *Stuart Williams* a59 59
3 ch g Halling(USA) Rima Baciata (Fantastic Light (USA))
748[5] 2432[11] 3537[10] 6194[3]

**Mr Speaker (USA)** *Claude McGaughey III* a111 112
3 bb c Pulpit(USA) Salute (USA) (Unbridled (USA))
(3994a) 6949a[6]

**Mr Sundowner (USA)** *Noel Quinlan* a51
2 bb g Scat Daddy(USA) Bold Answer (USA) (Dynaformer (USA))
7811[9] 8187[5]

**Mrs Warren** *George Baker* a68 78
4 b f Kyllachy Bold Bunny (Piccolo)
114[9] 1668[2] 2463[2] (3328) 4515[5] (5777) 6346[12] 7220[10] 7403[10]

**Mr Vendman (IRE)** *Ian Williams* a44 52
4 b g Whipper(USA) So Precious (IRE) (Batshoof)
1265[4]

**Mr Wickfield** *John Best* a64 57
3 b c Champs Elysees First Approval (Royal Applause)
3146[12] 4743[5] 5062[5] 5628[7] 6343[2] 7006[4] 7333[9]

**Mr Win (IRE)** *Chris Wall* a56 97
3 b g Intikhab(USA) Midnight Oasis (Oasis Dream)
2524[3] ◆ 3037[6] ◆ (3709) 4766[2] (5675) 6893[3]

**Mr. Z (USA)** *D Wayne Lukas* a107
2 ch c Malibu Moon(USA) Stormy Bear (USA) (Storm Cat (USA))
7610a[5]

**Ms Eboracum (IRE)** *Edward Creighton* a54
2 b f Vale Of York(IRE) Ms Victoria (IRE) (Fasliyev (USA))
2680[5] 4909[4] 5509[8] 7190[6] 7631[11] 7770[3]

**Mshawish (USA)** *M Delzangles* a65 119
4 bb c Medaglia d'Oro(USA) Thunder Bayou (USA) (Thunder Gulch (USA))
308a[2] (772a) 1181a[4] 2004a[8]

**Mu'Ajiza** *Paul Midgley* a49 101
4 ch f Pivotal Siyasa (USA) (Rahy (USA))
2047[4] 2790[10] (3097) (3608) 4060[8] 4923[4] 5467[3] 6929[5] 7408[16]

**Mubaraza (IRE)** *Ed Dunlop* a92 106
5 ch g Dalakhani(IRE) Mokaraba (Unfuwain (USA))
1735[2] ◆ 2073[4] 6557[10] 7107[24]

**Mubtaahij (IRE)** *M F De Kock* a89 72
2 b c Dubawi(IRE) Pennegale (IRE) (Pennekamp (USA))
6712[5] 6928[7]

**Mubtadi** *Ismail Mohammed* a89 88
6 b g Dr Fong(USA) Noble Peregrine (Lomond (USA))
942[2] 1439[14] 5895[7] 6839[6] 7350[3] 8073[4]

**Mubtaghaa (IRE)** *William Haggas* 101
2 b c Acclamation Mabalane (IRE) (Danehill (USA))
2146[2] (2800) 3322[3] ◆ 4123[8] (5607) 6686[3]

**Much Promise** *John Gosden* a81 68
3 b f Invincible Spirit(IRE) Prowess (IRE) (Peintre Celebre (USA))
2745[10]

**Muck 'N' Brass (IRE)** *J Larkin* a63 43
5 bb g Aussie Rules(USA) Crystal Springs (IRE) (Kahyasi)
7961a[3]

**Mucky Molly** *Alison Hutchinson* a62 50
6 ch m Bahamian Bounty Indian Flag (IRE) (Indian Ridge)
12[3] 77[3] 251[2] 370[11] 563[3] 833[4] 1081[P]

**Mufarrh (IRE)** *A Al Raihe* a113 98
7 b g Marju(IRE) What A Picture (FR) (Peintre Celebre (USA))
111a[8] 396a[4] 509a[13] 596a[6] 810a[8]

**Muffarreh (USA)** *B W Hills* 72
2 b c First Samurai(USA) Sarayir (USA) (Mr Prospector (USA))
5655[9]

**Muffin McLeay (IRE)** *David Barron* 94
6 b g Hawk Wing(USA) Youngus (USA) (Atticus (USA))
2137[8] 2423[9] 2981[8] 3368[2] 4453[4] 4975[5]

**Muffri'Ha (IRE)** *William Haggas* 84
2 b f Iffraaj Grecian Dancer (Dansili)
6435[5] (6735) 7448[5]

**Mu Gamara** *Rod Collet* a69 71
3 b f Muhtathir Mooteeah (IRE) (Sakhee (USA))
6913a[7]

**Mugharred (USA)** *B W Hills* 15
2 rg c Bernardini(USA) Wid (USA) (Elusive Quality (USA))
7412[9]

**Muhaafiz (IRE)** *David Brown* a70
2 br g Lord Shanakill(USA) Yasmin Satine (IRE) (Key Of Luck (USA))
7031[10] 7973[3]

**Muhaarar** *Charles Hills* 113
2 b c Oasis Dream Tahrir (IRE) (Linamix (FR))
(2200) ◆ 4123[3] 4645[3] (5692) 7239[3]

**Muhaarib Al Emarat (IRE)** *Richard Fahey* a18 70
2 b c Approve(IRE) Appletreemagic (IRE) (Indian Danehill (IRE))
4170[6] 4527[2] 5264[6] 6008[7] 6867[7] (7515) 7770[6]

**Muharaaj (IRE)** *Matthieu Palussiere* a100 77
3 b c Iffraaj Desert Sprite (IRE) (Tagula (IRE))
7619a[6]

**Muharrer** *Michael Dods* a84 99
5 b g Shamardal(USA) Shawahid (USA) (A.P. Indy (USA))
(2423) 3457[4] (4491) ◆ 4922[6] 5957a[11] 6534[4] 6713[3]

**Muhawalah (IRE)** *Roger Varian* a83 88
3 ch f Nayef(USA) Al Ishq (FR) (Nureyev (USA))
2967[4] 3652[2] 4052[2] (4513) 5123[2]

**Muhdiq (USA)** *Mike Murphy* a87 82
5 b g Hard Spun(USA) Enfiraaj (USA) (Kingmambo (USA))
122[4] 431[2] 644[6] (1049) 1489[4] 1742[5] 2933[5]

**Muhtadim (IRE)** *William Haggas* 47
2 b c Dubawi(IRE) Dhelaal (Green Desert (USA))
6935[7]

**Muir Lodge** *George Baker* a89 92
3 ch g Exceed And Excel(AUS) Miss Chaussini (IRE) (Rossini (USA))
1136[4] 1513[9] 3876[4] 6159[7] 6744[5] 6895[3]

**Mujaarib (AUS)** *M F De Kock* 117
6 br h Nadeem(AUS) Mihnah (IRE) (Lahib (USA))
(397a) 683a[3] 900a[13]

**Mujaazef** *A Al Raihe* a101 88
7 b g Dubawi(IRE) Khubza (Green Desert (USA))
304a[4] 769a[7]

**Mujas** *F Turner* 91
3 b c Mujahid(USA) Vitta's Touch (USA) (Touch Gold (USA))
1779a[5] 7322a[6]

**Mujassam** *Roger Varian* 79
2 ch c Kyllachy Naizak (Medicean)
6702[6] 7037[3] (7412)

**Mujazif (IRE)** *David Nicholls* 97
4 br g Shamardal(USA) Red Bandanna (IRE) (Montjeu (IRE))
2548[6] 3109[7] 3917[4] 4212[3] 5771[P] 6476[12] 6891[5] 7085[11] 7507[3] (7719)

**Mukaynis (IRE)** *Kevin Ryan* a74 72
3 b c Tamayuz Wild Ways (Green Desert (USA))
6221a[6] (7865) 8204[8]

**Mukhadram** *William Haggas* a119 123
5 b h Shamardal(USA) Magic Tree (UAE) (Timber Country (USA))
1183a[2] 3354[4] (3984) 4649[3] 5578[4] 6353a[4]

**Mukhayyam** *Sir Michael Stoute* 93
2 b g Dark Angel(IRE) Caster Sugar (USA) (Cozzene (USA))
4670[6] (5386) (6151) ◆ 7104[8] 7446[5]

**Mukhmal (IRE)** *Mark Johnston* 99
2 ch c Bahamian Bounty May Day Queen (IRE) (Danetime (IRE))
(1560) (2071) 3374[6] 3928[2] 4757[4] 5607[9] 6286[11]

**Mullion Cove** *John Best* a33 31
2 b f Mullionmileanhour(IRE) Beechnut (IRE) (Mujadil (USA))
5684[11] 6434[10] 7523[5]

**Mullionheir** *John Best* a40 61
2 b g Mullionmileanhour(IRE) Peyto Princess (Bold Arrangement)
2680[8] 3081[9] 5210[5] 6016[9] 7003[4]

**Mull Of Killough (IRE)** *Jane Chapple-Hyam* a104 117
8 b g Mull Of Kintyre(USA) Sun Shower (IRE) (Indian Ridge)
1176a[12] (1533) 2379a[7] 3317[8] 4180[2]

**Multellie** *Tim Easterby* 61
2 b g Multiplex Bollin Nellie (Rock Hopper)
5494[9] 6147[3] 6667[7] 7328[3]

**Multi Bene** *Ed McMahon* a88 100
5 b g Multiplex Attlongglast (Groom Dancer (USA))
1399[5] 1958[6] 3109[2] 3886[2] 5178[2] 5771[6]

**Multi Grain** *Brian Ellison* 70
2 b f Sir Percy Grain Only (Machiavellian (USA))
3497[5] 4444[4] ◆ 5232[4] 5762[3] (6449)

**Multiplier** *Kristin Stubbs* 70
2 b g Multiplex Best Bidder (USA) (Mr Greeley (USA))
1505[3] 2014[5] (2673) 4012[4] 5085[6] 7208[6]

**Multi Quest** *Jo Hughes* a52 61
2 b f Multiplex Ryan's Quest (IRE) (Mukaddamah (USA))
1314[6] 1571[7] 2128[9] (3813) 4283[2] 5119a[8] 7421[4] 7780[5]

**Multistar** *Chris Wall* a53 65
2 b f Multiplex Express Logic (Air Express (IRE))
5604[6] ◆ 5982[2] 6646[6] 7378[10]

**Multitask** *Michael Madgwick* a81 64
4 b g Multiplex Attlongglast (Groom Dancer (USA))
289[2] (425) ◆ 628[7] (714) ◆ (1144) 2147[9] 2414[14] 2684[3] 2995[7] 4581[8] 5834[8] 6145[5] 7514[6] (7758) 7775[4] 8071[4] 8204[5]

**Mulzamm (IRE)** *Charlie Appleby* a77 77
2 b c Cape Cross(IRE) Vine Street (IRE) (Singspiel (IRE))
4570[2] (6604)

**Mumarasaat (USA)** *Phil McEntee* a42 39
3 b f Elusive Quality(USA) Reefaljamal (USA) (Dixieland Band (USA))
2126[12] 2442[10] 2681[13]

**Mumford** *Richard Hannon* 74
2 b c Stimulation(IRE) Noble Nova (Fraam)
2837[4] 3461[2] 4025[6]

**Mumm Mumm De Mumm (SWE)** *Tommy Gustafsson* 61
2 b f Gloria De Campeao(BRZ) The Fast Lane (SWE) (Songline (SWE))
6386a[9]

**Mumtaza** *Richard Hannon* a45 53
3 b f Nayef(USA) Natagora (FR) (Divine Light (JPN))
2967[7]

**Munaaser** *Sir Michael Stoute* 105
3 b g New Approach(IRE) Safwa (IRE) (Green Desert (USA))
1357[5] (2026) 2496[3] 2781[9] (4671) 5656[5] 6713[2]

**Munaawib** *Deborah Sanderson* a76 51
6 b g Haafhd Mouwadh (USA) (Nureyev (USA))
(30) 126[3] 170[4] 366[4] (503) 646[7] 7249[7] 7647[6] (8043) 8224[2]

**Munatas** *Roger Varian* 77
3 b c Sea The Stars(IRE) Dashing (IRE) (Sadler's Wells (USA))
1357[3] 1691[3]

**Mundahesh (IRE)** *A Al Raihe* a91 98
4 ch g Tamayuz Kawn (Cadeaux Genereux)
(241a) 683a[11] 897a[12]

**Munfallet (IRE)** *David Brown* a78 83
3 b g Royal Applause Princess Mood (GER) (Muhtarram (USA))
1107[2] 1298[3] 1530[9] 2203[3] 2510[7] 3704[3] 4572[4] (4677) 5381[3] (6575) 6893[7]

**Mungo Park** *Gay Kelleway* a82 84
6 b g Selkirk(USA) Key Academy (Royal Academy (USA))
2097[2] ◆

**Munjally** *Patrick Holmes* a72 79
3 b g Acclamation Parabola (Galileo (IRE))
1795[6] 2611[4] 5417[7] 6431[9] 6835[12]

**Munjaz** *John Gosden* 97
3 ch c Sea The Stars(IRE) Qurrah (IRE) (Zafonic (USA))
(1517) 2153[7]

**Munsarim (IRE)** *Lee Carter* a80 50
7 b g Shamardal(USA) Etizaaz (USA) (Diesis)
89[4] 180[3] 286[5] (849) (953) 1065[4] 1108[3] 2651[2] 3078[7] 3472[8] 3878[7] 4354[7] 4968[8] 5560[5] 6019[10] 7925[11] 8102[7] 8250[13]

**Munstead Pride** *Andrew Balding* a76 67
2 ch g Sir Percy Memsahib (Alzao (USA))
6875[6] 7169[5] (7827)

**Muntadab (IRE)** *Sir Michael Stoute* a52
2 b c Invincible Spirit(IRE) Chibola (ARG) (Roy (USA))
5009[6]

**Muqaawel (USA)** *Mark Johnston* a82 80
2 b c Daaher(CAN) Ekleel (IRE) (Danehill (USA))
(3381) ◆ 3963[3] 4897[6] ◆ 6165[15] 7116[2]

**Muqarred (USA)** *Saeed bin Suroor* a76
2 bb g Speightstown(USA) Bawaara (FR) (Quiet American (USA))
3113[9] 7400[3] 7660[3]

**Muqtaser (USA)** *Roger Varian* 86
2 b c Distorted Humor(USA) Life Well Lived (USA) (Tiznow (USA))
6125[4] (7173)

**Muraaqaba** *Mark Johnston* 104
2 b f Dubawi(IRE) Nufoos (Zafonic (USA))
(3671) 4646[4] (5190) ◆ 6289[2]

**Muradif (IRE)** *William Haggas* a81 66
2 b g Zebedee Romany Princess (IRE) (Viking Ruler (AUS))
2788[5] 3330[4] 4044[4] (4967) 5306[2] 7226[3] 7544[4] 7945[6]

**Muraweg (IRE)** *Fawzi Abdulla Nass* a81 95
8 b g Kheleyf(USA) Lady Moranbon (USA) (Trempolino (USA))
109a[14] 509a[15]

**Murbeh (IRE)** *A Al Raihe* a89 90
6 b g Elusive City(USA) My Funny Valentine (IRE) (Mukaddamah (USA))
769a[11]

**Murcar** *Liam Corcoran* a87 75
9 ch g Medicean In Luck (In The Wings)
322[5]

**Murcielago (GER)** *M Keller* a85 99
7 ch g Areion(GER) My Angel (GER) (Luigi (GER))
2197a[11] 7856a[13]

**Murgan** *Peter Chapple-Hyam* 78
2 b c Galileo(IRE) Approach (Darshaan)
6859[5] 7383[3]

**Musaafer (IRE)** *M Al Muhairi* a81 89
7 b g Marju(IRE) Alexander Icequeen (IRE) (Soviet Star (USA))
242a[16]

**Musaddas** *Saeed bin Suroor* a94 89
4 b g Exceed And Excel(AUS) Zuleika Dobson (Cadeaux Genereux)
241a[2] 3153[2] 3577[2] (4299) 5040[2] 5824[3] 6140[14] (7663)

**Musalaha (IRE)** *Ed Dunlop* a59 55
3 b f Nayef(USA) Gilded (IRE) (Redback)
1382[4] 1793[9] 3711[5]

**Muscadelle** *Eve Johnson Houghton*
2 b f Azamour(IRE) Sauterne (Rainbow Quest (USA))
6985[9]

**Mushaakis (IRE)** *A Al Raihe* a69 91
4 b g Shamardal(USA) Shamayel (Pivotal)
243a[10]

**Mushir** *Roger Varian* a68 104
3 b c Oasis Dream Shimah (USA) (Storm Cat (USA))
1514[2] 2304[6] 4187[3] (4872) 5653[13]

**Mushreq (AUS)** *M F De Kock* a101 116
6 b g Flying Spur(AUS) Alharir (AUS) (Jeune)
(110a) 397a[2] 772a[3] 902a[5]

**Musical Comedy** *Richard Hannon* 106
3 b g Royal Applause Spinning Top (Alzao (USA))
1867[2] (2304) 3352[18] 6920[15]

**Musical Molly (IRE)** *Brian Ellison* a75 64
3 gr f Mastercraftsman(IRE) Park Approach (IRE) (Indian Ridge)
(3406) 3669[8] 5097[2] ◆ 5573[2] 6516[5] 7825[2] 7915[7]

**Musical Moon** *Lady Herries* a60 67
4 b g Piccolo Lunasa (IRE) (Don't Forget Me)
5135[6] 5822[6] 6274[11] 6881[3] 7419[9]

**Musical Theme** *Willie Musson* a55 55
3 b f Mount Nelson Motif (Observatory (USA))
839[4] 1616[7] 2025[6] ◆ 2805[11]

**Music And Dance** *Sir Michael Stoute* a76 65
2 b f Galileo(IRE) Jamboretta (IRE) (Danehill (USA))
6041[6] ◆ 6434[6] (7193)

**Musicante Di Breme (FR)** *M Amerio* 92
4 b g Mujahid(USA) Elendil (IRE) (Celtic Swing)
7322a[5] 7616a[9]

**Music In The Rain (IRE)** *David O'Meara* 83
6 b g Invincible Spirit(IRE) Greek Symphony (IRE) (Mozart (IRE))
(1646) ◆ 1957[4] 7236[12] 7490[8] 7719[16]

**Music Man (IRE)** *Jo Crowley* a85
4 b g Oratorio(IRE) Chanter (Lomitas)
623[4]

**Music Master** *Henry Candy* 115
4 b c Piccolo Twilight Mistress (Bin Ajwaad (IRE))
(1679) 2848[6] 3451[4] (4438) 6134[3]

**Musicora** *Richard Hannon* a90 94
3 b f Acclamation Belladera (IRE) (Alzao (USA))
1985[2] 2840[2] 3724[5] 4668[8] 5627[6] 6068[7] (6880)

**Music Theory (IRE)** *Charlie Appleby* a110 103
3 b g Acclamation Key Girl (IRE) (Key Of Luck (USA))
4442[11] 7555[2] ◆

**Musikhani** *Philip Kirby* a49 61
4 b f Dalakhani(IRE) Musicanna (Cape Cross (IRE))
1848[8] 2216[9] 2801[10] 3482[10] 5090[6] 7006[9] 8145[12]

**Mustadaam (IRE)** *Brian Meehan* 84
3 br g Dansili Sundus (USA) (Sadler's Wells (USA))
1517[4] 3385[2] 3923[3] (4368) 6206[4]

**Mustadeem (IRE)** *Brian Meehan* 89
2 b c Arcano(IRE) Hureya (USA) (Woodman (USA))
2298[7] 3140[2] (3929)

**Mustadrik (USA)** *J W Hills* a60 63
3 b c Jazil(USA) Uroobah (USA) (Dynaformer (USA))
1401[5] 2363[6] 2688[5]

**Mustafiz (USA)** *Noel Quinlan* a62
3 ch g Distorted Humor(USA) Somethinaboutbetty (USA) (Forestry (USA))
7901[6] 8167[2]

**Mustaheel (IRE)** *A Al Raihe* a104 108
5 b g Lawman(FR) Lidanski (IRE) (Soviet Star (USA))
308a[8] 504a[2] 679a[4] ◆ 772a[6]

**Mustajeeb** *D K Weld* 121
3 ch c Nayef(USA) Rifqah (USA) (Elusive Quality (USA))
(2185a) 2571a[3] (3352) 6352a[2] 7613a[6]

**Mustajjid** *Roger Varian* a70
3 b c Byron Skara Brae (Inchinor)
(787) 955[4] 1725[14]

**Mustamir (IRE)** *James Tate* 84
3 b g Medicean Perfect Plum (IRE) (Darshaan)
1517[9] 3466[6] (4812) 5670[6] 6640[3] 7306[6]

**Mustaqbal (IRE)** *Mark Johnston* a41 63
2 b c Invincible Spirit(IRE) Alshamatry (USA) (Seeking The Gold (USA))
6757[5] 7114[7]

**Mustard** *Sir Michael Stoute* a68 82
2 b c Motivator Flash Of Gold (Darshaan)
6102[3] (6743)

**Must Be Me** *Marco Gasparini* a59 92
4 b f Trade Fair Roodeye (Inchinor)
6807a[5]

**Must Have (FR)** *William Jarvis* a63 74
2 ch g Le Havre(IRE) Belle Et Brave (FR) (Falbrav (IRE))
4684[4] 8292[6]

**Mustique Dancer (IRE)** *Richard Fahey* 46
2 b f Rip Van Winkle(IRE) Cilium (IRE) (War Chant (USA))
5416[10] 6148[8] 7244[12]

**Mutafaakir (IRE)** *Ruth Carr* a69 90
5 b g Oasis Dream Moon's Whisper (USA) (Storm Cat (USA))
(1731) 1938[3] 2136[4] 2352[6] 2898[7] 3342[5] (4016) 4531[3] 5016[5] 5563[7] 6235[9] (6650) 7212[2] 7330[7]

**Mutafarrej** *Mark Johnston* a51 70
2 b c Paco Boy(IRE) Crinkle (IRE) (Distant Relative)
3394[7] 4142[5] 4760[6] 5373[7] 6211[10] 7363[7]

**Mutajare (IRE)** *A Al Raihe* a109 103
6 b g Cadeaux Genereux Bona Dea (IRE) (Danehill (USA))
307a[3] 508a[12] 681a[5] ◆ 812a[11] 901a[14]

**Mutakayyef** *William Haggas* 116
3 ch c Sea The Stars(IRE) Infallible (Pivotal)
1433[2] 1953[2] (2497) 3375[2] 7243[2] ◆ 7598[3]

**Mutamakkin (USA)** *Sir Michael Stoute* 88
2 bb c War Front(USA) La Laja (USA) (El Prado (IRE))
6712[4] ◆ (7123)

**Mutamid** *Ismail Mohammed* a65 37
2 b c Medicean Inchberry (Barathea (IRE))
3748[8] 6604[3] 7166[7]

**Mutaraadif (USA)** *Roger Varian* a70 68
3 b c Dynaformer(USA) Dawla (Alhaarth (IRE))
2881[7] 3432[7]

**Mutarakez (IRE)** *Brian Meehan* 80
2 ch c Fast Company(IRE) Nightswimmer (IRE) (Noverre (USA))
7037[4] (7407)

**Mutarjim (USA)** *M Al Muhairi* a47 60
5 b g Dynaformer(USA) Thunder Kitten (USA) (Storm Cat (USA))
238a[12]

**Mutasayyid** *Richard Hannon* 86
2 ch c Bahamian Bounty Clear Voice (USA) (Cryptoclearance (USA))
5201[3] ◆ (6125)

**Mutashaded (USA)** *Roger Varian* 110
4 b g Raven's Pass(USA) Sortita (GER) (Monsun (GER))
1434[8]

**Mutatis Mutandis (IRE)** *Ed Walker* 98
3 gr f Mastercraftsman(IRE) Amathia (IRE) (Darshaan)
1690[4] 2152[6] 3143[4] 5312[9] 6532[2] 7105[6]

**Mutawathea** *Richard Hannon* a85 88
3 b g Exceed And Excel(AUS) Esteemed Lady (IRE) (Mark Of Esteem (IRE))
(1298) ◆ 3980[2] 4198[9] 6431[7]

**Muteela** *Mark Johnston* a75 109
3 b f Dansili Nufoos (Zafonic (USA))
(1658) ◆ (2781) (3357) 4854[2] 5722[2] 6254[6] (6934) 7242[11]

**Muthmir (IRE)** *William Haggas* 115
4 b g Invincible Spirit(IRE) Fairy Of The Night (IRE) (Danehill (USA))
3714[2] ◆ (4683) 4895[5] (6327) ◆

**Mutin (FR)** *M F De Kock* a85 70
4 b c Kentucky Dynamite(USA) Mytographie (FR) (Anabaa (USA))
109a[10] 202a[11]

**Mutual Force (USA)** *A Al Raihe* a80 83
6 b h Arch(USA) Freeroll (USA) (Touch Gold (USA))
239a[7]

**Mutual Regard (IRE)** *J P Murtagh* a100 116
5 b g Hernando(FR) Hidden Charm (IRE) (Big Shuffle (USA))
(5693) ◆ 7653a[14]

**Muwaary** *John Gosden* 115
3 bb c Oasis Dream Wissal (USA) (Woodman (USA))
(1420) ◆ 2196a[4] 3352[2] 4278a[5]

**Muwalla** *Chris Grant* a51 53
7 b g Bahri(USA) Easy Sunshine (IRE) (Sadler's Wells (USA))
4964[11]

**Muzaahim (IRE)** *Kevin Morgan* a54 81
3 ch g Tamayuz Elizabeth Swann (Bahamian Bounty)
2630a[3] 6540[3] 7799[7]

**Muzarkash** *B W Hills* 68
2 b g Kyllachy Quinzey's Best (IRE) (King's Best (USA))
1583[7] 4676[6] 5128[6] 5779[2] 6312[9]

**Muzey's Princess** *Michael Mullineaux*
8 b m Grape Tree Road Premier Princess (Hard Fought)
580[9] 974[7]

**My Ambivalent (IRE)** *Roger Varian* a69 114
5 b m Authorized(IRE) Darrery (Darshaan)
1182a[3] (2284) 2988[3] 3766a[4] 7653a[17]

**Myasun (FR)** *C Baillet* a107 113
7 ch g Panis(USA) Spain (FR) (Bering)
836a[3] 1207a[2] 3746a[10] 4841a[5] 5963a[6] 6994a[9]

**Myboyalfie (USA)** *J R Jenkins* a80 91
7 b g Johannesburg(USA) Scotchbonnetpepper (USA) (El Gran Senor (USA))
1014[9] 1351[4] (1682) 1871[7] 2707[8] 5213[8] 6609[11]

**My Boy Bob** *Richard Fahey* 43
3 b g Myboycharlie(IRE) Empress Jain (Lujain (USA))
2551[5] 3097[8]

**Myboydaniel** *Brian Ellison* 26
2 b g Myboycharlie(IRE) Priti Fabulous (IRE) (Invincible Spirit (IRE))
4919[10]

**My Bubba** *Brian Meehan* 55
2 b c Dutch Art Moyoko (IRE) (Mozart (IRE))
6517[13]

**My Catch (IRE)** *A Savujev* a78 102
3 b c Camacho Catch The Sea (IRE) (Barathea (IRE))
204a[3] 594a[6] (770a) 897a[7] 1180a[12] 6182a[11]

**My Destination (IRE)** *Declan Carroll* a68 75
5 b g Dubai Destination(USA) Gossamer (Sadler's Wells (USA))
1167[12] 1374[3] 1605[8] 2055[3] 2175[5] 2738[2] 3269[5] 3532[3] (4115) 4296[4]

**My Dream Boat (IRE)** *Donald McCain* 78
2 b c Lord Shanakill(USA) Betty Burke (Choisir (AUS))
3358[2] 4486[2] 7234[4]

**My Escapade (IRE)** *Simon Waugh* 52
3 ch f Tamayuz Highly Respected (IRE) (High Estate)
1361[4] 1542[6] 2292[6] 4497[6] 6117[4] 6864[13] 7283[3] 7643[10]

**My Freedom (IRE)** *Saeed bin Suroor* a110 103
6 b g Invincible Spirit(IRE) Priere (Machiavellian (USA))
109a[6] 504a[3] 768a[2] 3716[7] 4648[25] 5609[15]

**Mygameanyours (IRE)** *Tony Carroll* 50
6 b m Bahamian Bounty Plausabelle (Royal Applause)
3916[9]

**My Gigi** *Laura Mongan* a65 45
4 b f Medicean Choirgirl (Unfuwain (USA))
295[9] 2864[11] 4578[RR] 5303[10] 6015[11]

**My Girl Jo (FR)** *David O'Meara* 47
2 gr f Whipper(USA) Prairie Moon (Halling (USA))
4751[8] 4973[5] 5781[10]

**My Good Brother (IRE)** *T G McCourt* a105 101
5 b g Elusive City(USA) Final Favour (IRE) (Unblest)
3284a[7] 4480a[3] 5154a[6] 6172a[3] 6369a[16] 7433a[5]

**My Guardian Angel** *Mark H Tompkins* a56 72
5 b g Araafa(IRE) Angels Guard You (Bahamian Bounty)
852[5] 3678[4] 5395[2] 6672[9]

**My History (IRE)** *Mark Johnston* a72 79
4 b c Dubawi(IRE) Reine Zao (FR) (Alzao (USA))
32[4]

**My Inspiration (IRE)** *Amy Weaver* a77 81
3 b f Invincible Spirit(IRE) Lulua (USA) (Bahri (USA))
2389[3] 2759[2] 3503[5] (5249) 5501[5] 6236[5] 6880[7] 7307[2] ◆ 7669[12]

**Myjestic Melody (IRE)** *Shaun Harris* a47 52
6 b m Majestic Missile(IRE) Bucaramanga (IRE) (Distinctly North (USA))
3609[11] 4042[9] 6796[4] 7547[4] 8043[11]

**My Jolie (IRE)** *A Fabre* 100
3 b f Oratorio(IRE) Sixty Secrets (USA) (Louis Quatorze (USA))
1502a[7] 2267a[6]

**My Kingdom (IRE)** *Stuart Williams* a80 87
8 b g King's Best(USA) Nebraas (Green Desert (USA))
56[5] 310[3] (535) 714[11] (1275) (1710)

**My Kingdom Of Fife** *Chris Waller* 104
9 b g Kingmambo(USA) Fairy Godmother (Fairy King (USA))
1186a[14]

**Mylaporyours (IRE)** *Rod Millman* a60 71
2 b f Jeremy(USA) Kuwinda (Hunting Lion (IRE))
1488[7] (1788) 1982[3] 2521[4] 4364[5] 5043[5] 5620[6] 7029[4] 7201[9]

**My Learned Friend (IRE)** *Andrew Balding* a58 63
10 b g Marju(IRE) Stately Princess (Robellino (USA))
251[9] 661[10]

**Mylenachope (FR)** *C Boutin* a46 59
2 b f Deportivo Chopinette (FR) (Sin Kiang (FR))
1094a[4] 3872a[10] 7027a[13]

**Mylenis (FR)** *P Cathelin*
3 b f Bleu D'Altair(FR) Qualine Du Chenet (FR) (River Bay (USA))
5589a[6]

**My Lord** *Luke Dace* a73 76
6 br g Ishiguru(USA) Lady Smith (Greensmith)
(168) 379[6] 801[2] 1027[2] 1108[6] 2774[3] 4985[9] (7133) 7539[10] 8193[9]

**My Manekineko** *J R Jenkins* a65 68
5 b g Authorized(IRE) Echo River (USA) (Irish River (FR))
33[7] 277[4] 571[11] 1596[11] (1638) 2529[6] 3805[4] 4107[3] 4428[3] 4655[3] 5041[12] 6242[8]

**My Mate (IRE)** *Clive Brittain* 73
2 ch c Approve(IRE) Date Mate (USA) (Thorn Dance (USA))
2308[7] 3194[10] 4301[4] 4897[7] 5875[2] 6165[14]

**Mymatechris (IRE)** *Andrew Balding* a98 75
3 br g High Chaparral(IRE) Splendeur (FR) (Desert King (IRE))
316[7] (3568) 4672[4] 5259[5] 5670[9] (7350) (8015) (8099) 8243[2]

**My Meteor** *Tony Newcombe* a64 69
7 b g Bahamian Bounty Emerald Peace (IRE) (Green Desert (USA))
3749[8] 4102[7] 4675[4] (4960) (5594) 6025[7] 6815[9] 7307[6] 7697[10] 7900[3] 8284[8]

**My Mistress (IRE)** *Anthony Carson* a80
2 ch f Mastercraftsman(IRE) Majestic Eviction (IRE) (King's Theatre (IRE))
(8247) ◆

**My Mo (FR)** *David Dennis* a55 44
2 b g Silver Frost(IRE) Anna Ivanovna (FR) (Fasliyev (USA))
5128[8] 5593[6] 5982[9] 6662[2] 6888[2] 7258[4]

**My My My Diliza** *J S Moore* a57 53
3 br f Sakhee's Secret Diliza (Dilum (USA))
165[2] (216) 315[9]

**My Name Is Rio (IRE)** *Michael Dods* a68 93
4 ch g Captain Rio Walk In My Shadow (IRE) (Orpen (USA))
(1440) (1672) 2352[8] (4061) 4976[4] 5888[7] 6511[3] 6744[2]

**My New Angel (IRE)** *Daniel Mark Loughnane* a54 53
5 gr m Dark Angel(IRE) Mynu Girl (IRE) (Charnwood Forest (IRE))
3233[7] 3781[6] 4473[8] 5075[5] 5596[3] 6028[7] 6267[13] 7977[7]

**My Propeller (IRE)** *Peter Chapple-Hyam* a81 106
5 b m Holy Roman Emperor(IRE) Incise (Dr Fong (USA))
107a[11] 393a[15] 680a[9]

**My Pupite (FR)** *G Botti* a37 70
2 gr f Aussie Rules(USA) Feltzer (FR) (Indian Rocket)
5619a[15]

**My Red Devil (IRE)** *Richard Fahey* a48
3 b f Duke Of Marmalade(IRE) Square Pants (USA) (King Of Kings (IRE))
8094[6]

**My Renaissance** *Ben Case* a62 55
4 bb g Medicean Lebenstanz (Singspiel (IRE))
263[6] (570) 838[2] 1232[12] 1836[9] 5529[12] 6157[6] 6771[2] 7256[8] 7869[2] 8063[4] 8265[7]

**My Reward** *Charles Hills* a90 93
2 b c Rail Link Tarot Card (Fasliyev (USA))
(6362) (6853) 7331[3]

**My Scat Daddy (USA)** *Zoe Davison* a56 47
5 b g Scat Daddy(USA) Will Be A Bates (USA) (Bates Motel (USA))
251[7] 428[9] 575[5] 755[7] 858[3] 963[6] 1015[4]

**My Sebastian** *Philip McBride* 85
2 b c Myboycharlie(IRE) Native Ring (FR) (Bering)
4764[2] (5393)

**My Secret Dream (FR)** *Ron Hodges* a40 58
3 b f Stormy River(FR) Aventure Secrete (FR) (Polish Precedent (USA))
2066[2] 2491[9] 3037[9] 3316[9]

**My Single Malt (IRE)** *Julie Camacho* a79 86
6 b g Danehill Dancer(IRE) Slip Dance (IRE) (Celtic Swing)
29[4] 410[7] 539[2] 782[5] (1036) 1085[2] 1267[3] 1744[2] 2169[10] (4156) 4938[3] 6285[2] 7085[16]

**My Son Max** *Nikki Evans* a87 75
6 b g Avonbridge Pendulum (Pursuit Of Love)
431[6] 820[9] (907) 1113[2] 1351[7] 1710[5] 2012[4] 2841[3] 3795[3] 4588[3] (5295) 6082a[4] 7179[11] (7819) 7928[4] 8209[7]

**My Sonny Boy** *Lisa Williamson*
3 b g Imperial Dancer Lily Of Tagula (IRE) (Tagula (IRE))
5606[10]

**My Specialbru** *Tracy Waggott* 62
2 b g Arabian Gleam Carati (Selkirk (USA))
4527[8] 6115[5] 6537[5]

**My Spirit (IRE)** *William Haggas* 102
3 b f Invincible Spirit(IRE) My Renee (USA) (Kris S (USA))
(2129) (2826) (3560) 5312[3] ◆ 6419a[2] 6708[5]

**Mysterial** *Declan Carroll* a57 48
4 b g Invincible Spirit(IRE) Diamond Dilemma (IRE) (Sinndar (IRE))
909[12] 1190[10] 1537[8] 1839[5] 2215[4] 2351[8] 2607[5] 3096[7] 3547[4] 3949[9] 4523[7] 4530[4] 5244[5] 7568[7]

**Mysterious Star (FR)** *Martyn Meade* a60 45
2 b c Iron Mask(USA) Red Star (IRE) (Lure (USA))
6085[8] 6646[10] 7076[5]

**Mysterious Wonder** *Philip Kirby* a60 64
4 b g Oasis Dream Raskutani (Dansili)
1649[3] 2427[8] 3339[4] 4069[6] 6014[13] 6454[2] 7025[16]

**Mystery Bet (IRE)** *Richard Fahey* a83 84
4 b f Kheleyf(USA) Dancing Prize (IRE) (Sadler's Wells (USA))
32[3] 6770[7] 7125[8] 7459[7]

**Mystery Code** *Alan King* 64
2 b f Tobougg(IRE) Mystery Lot (IRE) (Revoque (IRE))
7019[5] ◆

**Mystery Drama** *Alan King* a81 85
4 b f Hernando(FR) Mystery Lot (IRE) (Revoque (IRE))
2305[2] 2700[3] 3085[6] 4736[4] 5353[2] 6141[5]

**Mystery Train (ARG)** *Darrell Vienna* a108
4 bb r Not For Sale(ARG) American Whisper (USA) (Quiet American (USA))
5781a[9]

**Mystical King** *Linda Perratt* 31
4 b g Notnowcato Mystical Ayr (IRE) (Namid)
1969[8] 3103[8] 4259[10] 4489[7] 4728[6]

**Mystical Maze** *Mark Brisbourne* 44
3 b f Multiplex Musical Maze (Distant Music (USA))
1722[10] 2237[9] 3326[6] 3950[10] 4562[6] 5122[5] 5846[5]

**Mystical Moment** *Edwin Tuer* a66 77
4 ch f Dutch Art Tinnarinka (Observatory (USA))
1376[3] 1607[17] 2169[14] 2549[11] 2954[6]

**Mystical Sapphire** *Jo Crowley* a95 91
4 b f Sakhee's Secret Nadyma (IRE) (Daylami (IRE))
5213[4] 5824[8] 6207[11] 7196[12]

**Mystic And Artist** *K R Burke* 76
2 b f Excellent Art Mystical Spirit (IRE) (Xaar)
2348[4] 4499[2] (5232) 5664[8]

**Mystic Angel (IRE)** *William Muir* a34 53
3 gr f Dark Angel(IRE) Tintern (Diktat)
2129[9] 2804[6] 3277[8] 4084[6] 5030[6]

**Mystic Driver (FR)** *F-X De Chevigny* a64
2 b c Alberto Giacometti(IRE) Nibbling Lady (Dolphin Street (FR))
5618a[4]

**Mystic Jade** *Richard Hannon* a76 80
2 ch f Raven's Pass(USA) Mauri Moon (Green Desert (USA))
5667[3] ◆ 6001[2] 6605[2] 7237[13]

**Mystic Miraaj** *Tim Easterby* 65
2 ch g Iffraaj Salsa Brava (IRE) (Almutawakel)
6931[4] 7244[5] 7495[5]

**Mystified (IRE)** *Alan Berry* a37 35
11 b g Raise A Grand(IRE) Sunrise (IRE) (Sri Pekan (USA))
2213[10]

**Mystify Me** *Ed McMahon* a56
2 b c Firebreak She Mystifies (Indesatchel (IRE))
6660[7] 7254[6]

**My Stone (FR)** *Mme C Barande-Barbe* a87 105
6 b g Vatori(FR) Emystone (FR) (L'Emigrant (USA))
5263a[3] 5960a[7]

**My Strategy (IRE)** *Michael Bell* a62 60
2 b g Strategic Prince Mythie (FR) (Octagonal (NZ))
6683[8] 7217[4] 7660[6]

**My Stroppy Poppy** *Alan Phillips* a24 27
5 b m Multiplex Aspen Ridge (IRE) (Namid)
2177[6] 6073[7] 6421[8] 6717[8]

**My Sweet Lord** *Mark Usher* a59 59
4 b g Byron Sweetest Revenge (IRE) (Daggers Drawn (USA))
244[4] 448[2] 603[6]

**My Target (IRE)** *Saeed bin Suroor* a88 66
3 b c Cape Cross(IRE) Chercheuse (USA) (Seeking The Gold (USA))
3383[4] 3861[3] 4580[2]

**Mythical City (IRE)** *Mark Johnston* a44 66
2 b f Rock Of Gibraltar(IRE) Rainbow City (IRE) (Rainbow Quest (USA))
6509[5] ◆ 6976[2] ◆ 7382[6] 7659[8]

**Mythical Madness** *Charlie Appleby* a85 89
3 b c Dubawi(IRE) Miss Delila (USA) (Malibu Moon (USA))
3434[2] (4500) 5094[5] 5430[3] ◆ 6036[7]

**Mythical Maid (IRE)** *Seamus Mullins*
2 ch f Arakan(USA) Bonne (Namid)
5973[12]

**Mythical Moment** *William Haggas* 56
2 b f Authorized(IRE) Dancing Fire (USA) (Dayjur (USA))
7084[10] 7405[8] ◆

**Mythmaker** *Bryan Smart* 79
2 b c Major Cadeaux Mythicism (Oasis Dream)
4701[3] 5086[2] ◆ (5679) 6280[2] 6933[10]

**My Time** *Michael Mullineaux* a58 58
5 b g Mind Games Tick Tock (Timeless Times (USA))
1478[8] 1584[11] 4005[10] 4614[6] 5287[10] 6897[10]

**My Titania (IRE)** *John M Oxx* 108
3 b f Sea The Stars(IRE) Fairy Of The Night (IRE) (Danehill (USA))
3418[4] 4478a[3]

**Mywayalways (IRE)** *David Evans* a56 75
2 b g Baltic King Goose Island (IRE) (Kahyasi)
4079[5] 4424[7] 4676[7] 5147[4] 6294[3] (7207) 7595[3] 8016[4]

**My Year Is A Day (FR)** *J-C Rouget* 94
2 b f King's Best(USA) Aliyeska (IRE) (Fasliyev (USA))
4931a[2]

**Mzuri (IRE)** *Ms Sheila Lavery* 74
2 b f Tagula(IRE) Meadow (Green Desert (USA))
6375a[13]

**Naabaha (FR)** *F Head* 66
2 ch c Naaqoos La Bahamienne (IRE) (Fasliyev (USA))
5588a[4]

**Naabegha** *John Balding* a94 74
7 ch g Muhtathir Hawafiz (Nashwan (USA))
55[7] 234[8] 314[10] 566[6] 820[7] 1164[11] 1537[7] 1731[4] 2718[2] 2995[5] 3702[8] 4061[6] 7761[7] 8058[6] ◆

**Naadirr (IRE)** *Marco Botti* a81 112
3 b c Oasis Dream Beach Bunny (IRE) (High Chaparral (IRE))
1513[3] 2304[2] 3253[2] ◆ 4438[4] 5674[4] (6167) ◆

**Naady** *Ed Dunlop* a60
2 bb f Mawatheeq(USA) Al Tamooh (IRE) (Dalakhani (IRE))
7354[4] 7834[6]

**Naaz (IRE)** *Ed Dunlop* a90 87
4 ch c Tamayuz Naazeq (Nashwan (USA))
56[2]

**Nabatean (IRE)** *Andrew Balding* 97
3 b g Rock Of Gibraltar(IRE) Landinium (ITY) (Lando (GER))
1911[2] (2925) ◆ 4183[5] 7106[5] ◆ (7539) ◆

**Nabbaash** *J-C Rouget* a95 104
3 b c Aqlaam Poppo's Song (CAN) (Polish Navy (USA))
1340a[6] 5591a[5]

**Nabeel (IRE)** *Saeed bin Suroor* 78
3 b g Invincible Spirit(IRE) Screen Star (IRE) (Tobougg (IRE))
3695[4] 4130[2] 4767[4]

**Nabhan** *A Wohler* 90
2 b c Youmzain(IRE) Danidh Dubai (IRE) (Noverre (USA))
4524a[6] 6377a[3] 7726a[5]

**Nabucco** *John Gosden* 113
5 b h Dansili Cape Verdi (IRE) (Caerleon (USA))
2554[3] ◆ 4437[3] 5175[6] 5461a[4] 6233[4] (6711)

**Nabucco (GER)** *R Rohne* 101
4 b c Areion(GER) Numero Uno (GER) (Lavirco (GER))
1603a[5] 2589a[8]

**Nabulio (FR)** *F Chappet* a46 79
3 b g Whipper(USA) Gone For Dixie (USA) (Gone West (USA))
3809a[8]

**Naburn** *Alan Swinbank* a50 75
6 b g Cape Cross(IRE) Allespagne (USA) (Trempolino (USA))
911[3] (1374) 1567[3] 2139[3]

**Nadder** *Andrew Balding* a77
2 ch f Notnowcato Tavy (Pivotal)
(8220)

**Nadelwald** *P Schiergen* 97
3 b c Shamardal(USA) Nobilissima (GER) (Bluebird (USA))
1781a[5] 2377a[10] 3511a[8]

**Nadema Rose (IRE)** *Keith Dalgleish* a61 53
5 b m Elnadim(USA) Noctilucent (JPN) (Lammtarra (USA))
978[3] 1092[4]

**Nafa (IRE)** *Daniel Mark Loughnane* a89 88
6 br m Shamardal(USA) Champs Elysees (USA) (Distant Relative)
148[6] 1145[8]

**Nafaath (IRE)** *Donald McCain* a71 83
8 ch g Nayef(USA) Alshakr (Bahri (USA))
2739[7] 3501[5] 4423[4] 5341[2] 5924[2] 6514[5]

**Nafaqa (IRE)** *B W Hills* 109
2 b c Sir Percy Maghya (IRE) (Mujahid (USA))
3448[4] ◆ (4395) (6291) 6750[2]

**Nafar (GER)** *C Boutin* a79 84
6 b g Singspiel(IRE) Nouvelle Princesse (GER) (Bluebird (USA))
752a[9]

**Nagambie (IRE)** *Mark Johnston* 49
3 b f Duke Of Marmalade(IRE) Sina Cova (IRE) (Barathea (IRE))
1166[8] 5374[5]

**Naggers (IRE)** *Paul Midgley* 80
3 ch g Excellent Art Trika (First Trump)
1347[U] 1486[2] 1939[2] (2619) 3790[2] 4176[7]

**Nahual (FR)** *J Bertran De Balanda* a81 92
3 b c American Post Nahuala (FR) (Chichicastenango (FR))
5368a[7]

**Naivasha** *Robert Cowell* a69 81
3 b f Captain Gerrard(IRE) Netta (IRE) (Barathea (IRE))
2093[2] (2551) (2943) 3331[2]

**Naizah (IRE)** *Ed Dunlop* a58
2 b f Tamayuz Etizaaz (USA) (Diesis)
7194[6]

**Najm Suhail** *A Al Raihe* a95 95
3 b g Proclamation(IRE) Najoom Zaman (IRE) (Green Desert (USA))
204a[4] 505a[3] 770a[3] 896a[3]

**Nakeeta** *Iain Jardine* 82
3 b g Sixties Icon Easy Red (IRE) (Hunting Lion (IRE))
3603[4] (4420) 4941[3] (6012) 6450[3]

**Nakkado (FR)** *R Chotard* 64
2 b c Naaqoos Multimedia (FR) (Exit To Nowhere (USA))
6618a[7]

**Nakuti (IRE)** *Sylvester Kirk* a97 95
3 b f Mastercraftsman(IRE) Sheba Five (USA) (Five Star Day (USA))
1260[2] ◆ (1725) 1985[4] 2556[4] 2962[5] 3357[12] (4163) 4826[7] 6234[7] 6740[4] 6922[6] 7553[4] 7857a[4]

**Nalon** *J-M Lefebvre* 65
3 b g Holy Roman Emperor(IRE) Drama Playout (Kendor (FR))
5227a[4]

**Named Asset** *Jedd O'Keeffe* 61
2 b c Invincible Spirit(IRE) Sabria (USA) (Miswaki (USA))
5242[5] 5807[3] 6453[5] 7055[3]

**Nameitwhatyoulike** *Bryan Smart* 97
5 b g Trade Fair Emma Peel (Emarati (USA))
1164[19] 3714[11] 4317[8] 4923[8] 6430[2] 6891[10] 7601[9]

**Namely (IRE)** *Sir Mark Prescott Bt* a48 41
3 b f Rock Of Gibraltar(IRE) Viz (IRE) (Darshaan)
7256[10] 7632[11]

**Namera (GER)** *P Harley* 99
5 b m Areion(GER) Najinskaja (GER) (Tannenkonig (IRE))
5966a[11] 7320a[2] 7725a[6]

**Nam Hai (IRE)** *Michael Bell* a73 74
3 b g Fastnet Rock(AUS) Bowstring (IRE) (Sadler's Wells (USA))
1353[9] (1627) 2077[9] 3110[4] 7020[6] 7343[3]

**Namhroodah (IRE)** *James Tate* a72
2 bg f Sea The Stars(IRE) Independant (Medicean)
(7659)

**Nam June Paik (FR)** *J Parize* a66 78
4 b g Orpen(USA) Marisa Merz (IRE) (Lend A Hand)
5964a[14]

**Nam Ma Prow** *Simon West* a34 55
3 ch g Bahamian Bounty Charlotte Vale (Pivotal)
1269[3] 1840[6] 2393[3] 2867[3] 3098[3] 4420[4] 5917[5] 7007[7]

**Nancy** *Mark H Tompkins* a9 24
3 b f Rail Link Feabhas (IRE) (Spectrum (IRE))
2924[9] 3385[11] 4052[10]

**Nancy Astor** *John Gosden* a70 62
2 b f Shamardal(USA) Summer's Lease (Pivotal)
2744[8] 7549[2] 8191[2]

**Nancy From Nairobi** *Mick Channon* 97
3 b f Sixties Icon Madame Hoi (IRE) (Hawk Wing (USA))
1424[4] ◆ 1701[2] 2255[4] 3376[8] 4385[6] (4984) 6127[15] 6655[5]

**Nanton (USA)** *Jim Goldie* a77 90
12 rg g Spinning World(USA) Grab The Green (USA) (Cozzene (USA))
3250[7] 4113[4] (4575) 5421[4] (5678) 6713[6] 7110[7]

**Naoise (IRE)** *Ollie Pears* a83 73
6 ch g Stormy Atlantic(USA) Machinale (USA) (Kingmambo (USA))
4514[3] 4703[2] 5054[7] 6232[11] 6625[7] 7042[11] (7427) (7569) 7894[3] 8281[5]

**Napoleon Solo** *Peter Chapple-Hyam* 59
2 b c Cockney Rebel(IRE) Trump Street (First Trump)
6551[9]

**Narborough** *Mick Channon* a61 62
3 b g Winker Watson Solmorin (Fraam)
666[2] 1018[3] 1277[8] 1642[3] 2023[3] 2505[5] 2802[2] 4735[2] 5399[3] 6029[3]

**Narcissist (IRE)** *Michael Easterby* 75
5 b g Dylan Thomas(IRE) Gabare (FR) (Galileo (IRE))
7335[8]

**Narniyn (IRE)** *A De Royer-Dupre* 113
4 b f Dubawi(IRE) Narmina (IRE) (Alhaarth (IRE))
(3171a) 3774a[3] 4894[2] 5742a[4] 6969a[8]

**Narrow Hill (GER)** *P Sogorb* 113
6 b g Tiger Hill(IRE) Naroona (GER) (Silver Hawk (USA))
(723a) 1784a[5] 7486a[3]

**Nashmi** *George Peckham* a61 64
3 b g Compton Place Black Tribal (IRE) (Mukaddamah (USA))
3145[13] 3430[7] 7077[4] 7423[11]

**Nashville (IRE)** *Richard Fahey* a74 86
5 b g Galileo(IRE) Brown Eyes (Danehill (USA))
2289[13] 2739[2] 3240[3] 3698[2] 4217[5] 5193[3] 5924[3] (6514) 7124[12] 7235[6]

**Nasijah** *James Tate* a76 48
4 b f Authorized(IRE) Nasij (USA) (Elusive Quality (USA))
323[2] 3953[4]

**Nassau Storm** *William Knight* a90 89
5 b g Bahamian Bounty Got To Go (Shareef Dancer (USA))
(287) 472[2] 715[4] 1020[4] 1301[2] 2062[4] 5686[3] 6100[4] 6334[7] 6886[6] 7375[3]

**Natalia** *Andrew Hollinshead* a54 52
5 ch m Dutch Art Pintle (Pivotal)
3230[6] 5079[9] 5683[6] 6940[4] 7424[7] 7783[7] 8291[4]

**Nathr (USA)** *Charles Hills* a76 80
3 bb c Dixie Union(USA) Sweet Rider (USA) (Seeking The Gold (USA))
3914[8] 4677[4] 5412[3] 6073[2] (7024) 7373[4]

**National Service (USA)** *Stuart Williams* a75 72
3 b g War Chant(USA) Cotton Club Ballet (USA) (Street Cry (IRE))
485[2] 624[4] ◆ 1005[5] 1146[6] 3138[10] 3433[4] ◆ 4328[4] 4636[12] 6355[6] 6455[4] 6843[7] 7357[8]

**Native Charmer** *Ed McMahon* a13 50
2 b c Pastoral Pursuits Oceana Blue (Reel Buddy (USA))
2612[5] 3330[8] 5099[6]

**Native Falls (IRE)** *Alan Swinbank* a69 79
3 ch g Elnadim(USA) Sagrada (GER) (Primo Dominie)
1543[8] 2166[8] (3485) 3625[2] 4003[2] 4297[5] 5638[7] (5889) 6213[4] 6346[4] (6835)

**Native Heart** *Phil McEntee* a60 85
3 gr f Clodovil(IRE) She's My Outsider (Docksider (USA))
1422[9] 1831[4] 2281[2] (2638) (2892)

**Natural Charm (IRE)** *Roger Varian* a55 83
2 ch f City Zip(USA) Natural Flair (USA) (Giant's Causeway (USA))
4075[6] 5029[3] (5910) (6359) 7331[8]

**Natural Choice** *Saeed bin Suroor* a80 70
3 b f Teofilo(IRE) Oiseau Rare (FR) (King's Best (USA))
1690[7]

**Natural Nine (IRE)** *Roger Varian* a77 77
2 b c Shamardal(USA) Source Of Life (IRE) (Fasliyev (USA))
6204[3] 6621[2] 7371[3] 7798[2]

**Natural Order (USA)** *K R Burke* a86 93
2 ch c Munnings(USA) Allure D'Amour (USA) (Giant's Causeway (USA))
(1936) 2873[3] 3580[2] 4199[4] 6256[10] 6686[6] 7331[7]

**Natures Law (IRE)** *Keith Dalgleish* a43 66
4 b f Lawman(FR) Misaayef (USA) (Swain (IRE))
2454[6] 2676[9] 3237[7] 3668[10] 4195[4] 4256[9] 4489[8]

**Naughtybychoice** *Ollie Pears* a52 47
4 gr g Dubai Destination(USA) Gracia (Linamix (FR))
474[7]

**Nauka (GER)** *Markus Klug* 81
3 bb f Kallisto(GER) Nagoya (GER) (Goofalik (USA))
2590a[10]

**Nausica Time (GER)** *S Smrczek* 111
4 bb f Dubawi(IRE) Namat (IRE) (Daylami (IRE))
1827a[12] 4006a[3] 4720a[6] (5938a)

**Nautilus** *John Gosden* a100 108
4 b g Medicean Fickle (Danehill (USA))
784[2] 1071[7] (5673) (6133)

**Navajo Chief** *Timothy Jarvis* a64 110
7 b g King's Best(USA) Navajo Rainbow (Rainbow Quest (USA))
(2286) 4212[18] 5163[10] 5609[18] 6748[6] 7081[12]

**Navajo Dream** *Michael Appleby* a54 43
3 ch f Selkirk(USA) Rubies From Burma (USA) (Forty Niner (USA))
914[6] 2053[4] 2432[10] 3333[10] 7924[4] 8090[7] 8258[2]

**Naval Action** *Sir Mark Prescott Bt* a44 24
2 b g Lawman(FR) Dance Of The Sea (IRE) (Sinndar (IRE))
6718[7] 6935[11] 7200[8] 7815[3] 8087[10]

**Naval Command (USA)** *William Kaplan* a93
2 ch f Midshipman(USA) Lucky Flyer (USA) (Fusaichi Pegasus (USA))
6915a[5]

**Navarra (SPA)** *G Arizkorreta Elosegui* 92
4 b f Caradak(IRE) Lady Cree (IRE) (Medicean)
7736a[6]

**Nave (USA)** *David Simcock* a85 83
7 b g Pulpit(USA) Lakabi (USA) (Nureyev (USA))
158[3] 450[5] 2627[6] 3086[5] 3874[2] 4119[3] (4351) 4812[2]

**Navigate (IRE)** *Martyn Meade* 80
2 b c Iffraaj Dorothy Dene (Red Ransom (USA))
5881[5] 6712[6] 7123[3] (7511)

**Nawaasy (USA)** *Charles Hills* a69
2 b f Distorted Humor(USA) Stormin Maggy (USA) (Storm Cat (USA))
7367[3] ◆

**Nawwaar (USA)** *A Al Raihe* a105 113
5 ch h Distorted Humor(USA) Mostaqeleh (USA) (Rahy (USA))
112a[10] 809a[5] 898a[7] 1180a[5]

**Naxos Beach (IRE)** *A Di Dio* 93
5 ch m Act One Alimony (IRE) (Groom Dancer (USA))
1477a[9]

**Nayel (IRE)** *Richard Hannon* 75
2 b c Acclamation Soliza (IRE) (Intikhab (USA))
7380[4]

**Nay Secret** *Jim Goldie* a51 53
6 b g Nayef(USA) Nouveau Cheval (Picea)
6480[10] 7059[3] 7643[6] 7893[5]

**Nearly Caught (IRE)** *Hughie Morrison* a92 106
4 b g New Approach(IRE) Katch Me Katie (Danehill (USA))
1434[9] 2561[2] 5693[8] 7107[6]

**Nearly Not Mine** *Giada Ligas* 92
3 b f Pastoral Pursuits The Lady Mandarin (Groom Dancer (USA))
1780a[4]

**Neath Abbey** *William Muir*
2 ch f Notnowcato Ewenny (Warrshan (USA))
7756[12]

**Neatico (GER)** *P Schiergen* 113
7 b h Medicean Nicola Bella (IRE) (Sadler's Wells (USA))
1478a[4] 2587a[5] 3511a[6] 4006a[4] 5461a[5] 6054a[5]

**Nebula Storm (IRE)** *Gary Moore* 73
7 b g Galileo(IRE) Epping (Charnwood Forest (IRE))
(5502)

**Nebulla** *Noel Quinlan* 83
2 ch c Iffraaj Kelowna (IRE) (Pivotal)
7123[2] (7667)

**Ned's Indian (IRE)** *Sabrina J Harty* a86 86
6 bb g Sleeping Indian Zanella (IRE) (Nordico (USA))
4379a[3]

**Needless Shouting (IRE)** *Mick Channon* a68 82
3 b g Footstepsinthesand Ring The Relatives (Bering)
561[2] 670[4] 1214[3] 1403[3] 1616[3] 2998[9] 3316[6] 3818[6] (4333) (5062) 5318[2] 6325[2] 6705[6]

**Needs The Run** *David Evans* a56 32
3 b g Ivan Denisovich(IRE) Maydew (Pursuit Of Love)
142[7] 188[8] 218[6] 743[3] 865[2] 1029[3] 1235[8] 1632[6] 1906[6]

**Needwood Park** *Ray Craggs* a25 25
6 br g Needwood Blade Waterpark (Namaqualand (USA))
3535[9]

**Neighbother** *Richard Fahey* 72
3 b g Invincible Spirit(IRE) Aravonian (Night Shift (USA))
2295[7] 2657[12]

**Nellies Quest** *Michael Appleby* a52 52
5 b m Rainbow High Dream Seeker (IRE) (Kahyasi)
551[5] 888[4] 941[6] 1086[3] 1228[4] 7197[3] 7540[2] 7823[7] 8010[5]

**Nellie The Elegant** *Tim Vaughan* a67 44
3 b f Mount Nelson Mexican Hawk (USA) (Silver Hawk (USA))
(542) 1116[4] 4763[7]

**Nelson Of The Nile** *Jonathan Portman* a65 63
3 b g Mount Nelson Appleby (Anabaa (USA))
1809[10] 3031[6] 3712[6] 5011[4] 5628[4] 7204[6]

**Nelson Quay (IRE)** *Jeremy Gask* a76 60
4 b g Holy Roman Emperor(IRE) Frippet (IRE) (Ela-Mana-Mou)
489[5] 817[7] (1302) 1664[2] (2464) 2720[9] 4548[11] 5426[5] 8169[4]

**Nelson's Bay** *Wilf Storey* a61 64
5 b g Needwood Blade In Good Faith (USA) (Dynaformer (USA))
1673[4] 2518[2] 3439[6] 3958[7] 4023[11] 4473[11] 5562[2] 5811[8] 6121[7] 6544[2] 6600[6] 7639[9] 8063[3] ◆

**Nelson's Hill** *W De Best-Turner* a35
4 b g Mount Nelson Regal Step (Royal Applause)
8242[4]

**Nelson's Pride** *Roger Ingram* a57 62
3 b f Mount Nelson Bandanna (Bandmaster (USA))
1611[12] 2470[9] 3149[5] 3530[4] 4288[2] 4535[3] 5333[6] 5853[5] 7370[2] 7699[6] 7800[3] 7929[3] 8023[4] 8256[5]

**Nelsons Trick** *Rod Millman* a56 64
2 b f Mount Nelson Mild Deception (IRE) (Glow (USA))
3858[6] 4825[10] 5746[4] 6294[6]

**Nenge Mboko** *George Baker* a90 87
4 b g Compton Place Floppie (FR) (Law Society (USA))
1212[3]

**Nerfair Premier (FR)** *T Castanheira* a56 73
3 bb g Sumitas(GER) Nerfairchichi (FR) (Chichicastenango (FR))
7681a[8]

**Nero Emperor (IRE)** *T Stack* a98 103
5 b g Holy Roman Emperor(IRE) Blue Iris (Petong)
107a[P]

**Nesterenko (GER)** *Nicky Henderson*
5 b g Doyen(IRE) Nordwahl (GER) (Waajib (IRE))
2067[6]

**Neston Grace** *Simon Hodgson* a64 67
6 b m Kayf Tara Politely (Tragic Role (USA))
776[2] 1218[DSQ] 1491[7] 2419[4] 5551[6]

**Netsuke (IRE)** *F Vermeulen* a68 81
3 b f Aragorn(IRE) Notting Hill (BRZ) (Jules (USA))
1907a[2]

**Network Perfection** *Michael Easterby* a43 50
3 ch g Distant Peak(IRE) Word Perfect (Diktat)
5402[5] 5765[7] 6157[7]

**Neuf Des Coeurs** *Keith Dalgleish* a36 65
3 b f Champs Elysees Intervene (Zafonic (USA))
2676[6] 3303[9] 3662[7] 6010[2] 6516[6] 6823[6] 7426[8]

**Neuilly** *Gary Moore* a72 66
7 b m Nayef(USA) Narasimha (USA) (Nureyev (USA))
1622a[6] 2465[2]

**Neve (GER)** *Mario Hofer* 80
2 b f Tertullian(USA) Navalde (GER) (Alkalde (GER))
6053a[5]

**Never A Quarrel (IRE)** *Jeremy Gask* a72 61
4 b f Acclamation Welsh Mist (Damister (USA))
128a[5]

**Never Change (IRE)** *Saeed bin Suroor* a82
2 b f New Approach(IRE) Auspicious (Shirley Heights)
8036[3] ◆

**Never Easy (IRE)** *Richard Fahey* a59 63
2 gr c Zebedee Silk Point (IRE) (Barathea (IRE))
4708[4] 5493[7] 6453[7] 7378[9] 8221[2]

**Never Forever** *Jim Goldie* 83
5 ch g Sir Percy Codename (Sadler's Wells (USA))
1970[5] 2477[3] 2912[3] 3190[2] 3999[2] (4196)

**Never Miss** *Saeed bin Suroor* a58
2 b f Shamardal(USA) Pictavia (IRE) (Sinndar (IRE))
8292[7]

**Never To Be (USA)** *John Gosden* a87 82
3 b g Thewayyouare(USA) Kitty Foille (USA) (Black Minnaloushe (USA))
854[2] 6466[5] 6886[5] 7375[2]

**Never Up (GER)** *David O'Meara* 81
3 b g Danehill Dancer(IRE) Never Green (IRE) (Halling (USA))
6011[4] 6432[3] (6762) 7125[18] 7504[8]

**New Abbey Dancer (IRE)** *Gay Kelleway* a50 46
2 b f Thewayyouare(USA) Brave Cat (IRE) (Catrail (USA))
2089[10] 4541[6] 5056[6] 6646[7] (6842) 7815[10] 8121[11]

**New Alliance (IRE)** *J S Bolger* 89
2 b f New Approach(IRE) Dochas Is Gra (IRE) (High Chaparral (IRE))
4598a[5] (Dead)

**New Bidder** *Jedd O'Keeffe* 88
3 bb g Auction House(USA) Noble Nova (Fraam)
(1358) (1693) 2257[13] 6744[15] 7233[16]

**New Brunswick (GER)** *John Gosden* a58 65
2 b c Shamardal(USA) Nianga (GER) (Lomitas)
3929[5] 4429[5] *5009[7]* *6884[7]* 7207[6] 7379[9]

**Newbury Street** *Patrick Holmes* a36 24
7 b g Namid Cautious Joe (First Trump)
*754[7]* *1010[7]* 1309[8] 1606[11] 2724[7]

**New Colours** *Marcus Tregoning* a67 72
3 gr g Verglas(IRE) Briery (IRE) (Salse (USA))
1401[9] *1898[7]* 2222[2] 2671[3] 3541[4] 4120[3] 4498[4] 7309[10] *(7541)*

**New Decade** *Milton Bradley* a71 60
5 ch g Pivotal Irresistible (Cadeaux Genereux)
*259[11]* *913[8]* *1448[11]* 2250[3] 2488[2] 2691[2] 2865[4] 3213[8] 3935[9] 7213[16] 7307[12] *7621[12]*

**Newera** *Tom Dascombe* 53
2 ch c Makfi Coming Home (Vettori (IRE))
5078[6] 6056[8]

**New Fforest** *Andrew Balding* a72 100
4 b f Oasis Dream Ffestiniog (IRE) (Efisio)
2989[9] 3458[6] 3927[11] 4700[14] 6130[18]

**Newforge House (IRE)** *Dai Burchell*
6 b g High-Rise(IRE) Treasure Island (Rainbow Quest (USA))
*7894[7]*

**Newgate Princess** *Tony Coyle* 55
2 b f Bahri(USA) Arctic Queen (Linamix (FR))
5886[7] 6148[5] 6448[8] 7328[13]

**Newgate Queen** *Tony Coyle* 64
3 gr f Phoenix Reach(IRE) Arctic Queen (Linamix (FR))
1348[8] 1840[3] (2198)

**New Identity (IRE)** *Denis Coakley* a62 82
3 b c Rock Of Gibraltar(IRE) Zaafran (Singspiel (IRE))
2690[3] ◆ 3517[3] 5862[2] 7024[3] *7733[8]*

**New Lease Of Life** *Jim Goldie* 68
5 b g Orientor Primo Heights (Primo Valentino (IRE))
1758[3] 2451[4] 2675[7] 3191[7] 3952[7] 4489[5] 4730[5] 5499[3] (5858) 6114[5] 6475[9] (7057) 7502[16]

**New Leyf (IRE)** *Jeremy Gask* a76 69
8 bb g Kheleyf(USA) Society Fair (FR) (Always Fair (USA))
*925[3]* *1212[4]* 1731[13] *2059[4]* 2401[3] *2684[7]* *3118[5]* 4431[9] *5308[3]* *6021[3]* *6240[6]* *7202[9]*

**New Outlook (USA)** *F Chappet* a100 99
6 b g Awesome Again(CAN) Tikkanita (USA) (Cozzene (USA))
*6992a[10]*

**New Providence** *Hugo Palmer* 103
2 ch f Bahamian Bounty Bayja (IRE) (Giant's Causeway (USA))
(3706) (4345) 4913[3] 5607[2] (6067) 6709[3]

**New Reaction** *Amanda Perrett* a70
3 b g New Approach(IRE) Intaaj (IRE) (Machiavellian (USA))
*2917[6]* *3856[9]* *5282[3]*

**New Rich** *Eve Johnson Houghton* a69 57
4 b g Bahamian Bounty Bling Bling (IRE) (Indian Ridge)
*83[5]* *489[3]* *(576)* *993[5]* *1221[11]* 2691[7] *2887[11]* 3848[7] 4370[7] 4908[7] *6666[3]* *7887[2]* (8014)

**New Row** *William Jarvis* a72 51
3 b f Teofilo(IRE) Memo (Groom Dancer (USA))
*2058[4]* 2624[10] *3117[12]*

**Newsletter (IRE)** *K J Condon* 102
2 b f Sir Percy Payphone (Anabaa (USA))
2856a[5] 3353[3] 4460a[5]

**Newspeak (IRE)** *Charlie Appleby* 30
2 b c New Approach(IRE) Horatia (IRE) (Machiavellian (USA))
6743[10]

**Newstead Abbey** *David Barron* a93 101
4 b g Byron Oatcake (Selkirk (USA))
*715[14]* 1484[5] 1719[3] 1943[6] 2758[4] 3189[4] 6531[18] 6740[2]

**New Story** *Ismail Mohammed* 102
3 b c New Approach(IRE) Al Hasnaa (Zafonic (USA))
2334[7] 3248[4] (3750) (4388)

**New Strategy (IRE)** *Saeed bin Suroor* 77
2 b g Lawman(FR) Kate The Great (Xaar)
7244[2] (7560)

**New Stream (IRE)** *Clive Brittain* a34
3 b c New Approach(IRE) Shimna (Mr Prospector (USA))
*5796[10]*

**New Street (IRE)** *Richard Fahey* 88
3 gr c Acclamation New Deal (Rainbow Quest (USA))
1861[5] 2363[2] 2617[3] (3466)

**New Style (USA)** *Saeed bin Suroor* a43
2 b f Street Cry(IRE) Land Of Dreams (Cadeaux Genereux)
*8067[11]*

**New Tarabela** *Tony Carroll* a80 84
3 ch g New Approach(IRE) Tarabela (CHI) (Hussonet (USA))
*403[5]* *717[4]* *951[2]* *1269[2]* 1600[2] 2494[2] 3110[3] 4289[5] 6432[8] *8138[3]*

**Newton Bomb (IRE)** *Conrad Allen* a47 71
2 b f Fast Company(IRE) Athlumney Dancer (Shareef Dancer (USA))
6375a[28] 7377[12] *8076[4]*

**Newton's Law (IRE)** *Brian Meehan* a79 82
3 b g Lawman(FR) Royal Alchemist (Kingsinger (IRE))
2026[2] ◆ 2346[2] 2996[3] 3709[2] 4043[3] 4697[3] 5249[2] (5501) 6096[4] *7073[7]*

**Newtown Cross (IRE)** *Jimmy Fox* a62 49
4 ch c Kheleyf(USA) Sacred Pearl (IRE) (Daylami (IRE))
*(380)* *657[8]* *(842)* *(1262)* 1915[7] *2683[5]* 4678[7] *5137[5]* *6486[7]*

**New Year's Night (IRE)** *Charlie Appleby* a87
3 ch g Raven's Pass(USA) Nightime (IRE) (Galileo (IRE))
*5796[4]* *6482[2]* *8094[4]* *(8167)*

**New Youmzain (FR)** *Michael Appleby* 86
5 b g Sinndar(IRE) Luna Sacra (FR) (Sadler's Wells (USA))
(1485) 1692[8] 2482[10] 3501[9]

**Next Door (IRE)** *David Barron* a46 74
4 b f Elusive City(USA) Lamh Eile (IRE) (Lend A Hand)
1694[4] 2726[2] 3660[8]

**Next Edition (IRE)** *Philip Kirby* a67 88
6 b g Antonius Pius(USA) Starfish (IRE) (Galileo (IRE))
2790[9] 4921[2] 6171[2]

**Next Generation (IRE)** *Olly Stevens* a41 35
2 b f Royal Applause Gazebo (Cadeaux Genereux)
2151[7] *3113[8]*

**Next Stop** *David Nicholls* a71 70
3 b f Rail Link Reaching Ahead (USA) (Mizzen Mast (USA))
*748[6]* *(1235)* *2080[2]* 4490[4] 6152[6] *7918[5]* *8248[12]*

**Nezar (IRE)** *George Margarson* a85 97
3 ch g Mastercraftsman(IRE) Teddy Bears Picnic (Oasis Dream)
*204a[11]* *594a[8]* 3378[24] 4765[7] 5649[5] 6234[3] 6895[7]

**Nibbling (IRE)** *Paul Cole* a66 89
3 b f Invincible Spirit(IRE) Albarouche (Sadler's Wells (USA))
2560[U] *5294a[6]*

**Niblawi (IRE)** *Michael Bell* a74
2 b c Vale Of York(IRE) Finnmark (Halling (USA))
*7835[2]* *7941[4]*

**Nice Chief (FR)** *J-Y Artu* a43 64
5 ch m Ski Chief(USA) Nice Donna (FR) (Nice Havrais (USA))
3089a[4]

**Niceofyoutotellme** *Ralph Beckett* a97 103
5 b g Hernando(FR) Swain's Gold (USA) (Swain (IRE))
(1948) 3356[9] 4756[10] 6752[2] *7803[10]*

**Niceonemyson** *Christopher Wilson* 67
5 b g Misu Bond(IRE) Kungfu Kerry (Celtic Swing)
1838[2] 2233[2] 2606[8] 3150[3] 4571[7] 5817[5] 6122[3] 6405[4] 6674[7] 7248[11] 7502[15]

**Nice Story (IRE)** *R Storp* 80
4 ch f Suave(USA) Royal Aly (USA) (Royal Academy (USA))
2599a[3]

**Nicholascopernicus (IRE)** *Ed Walker* a76 98
5 ch g Medicean Ascendancy (Sadler's Wells (USA))
1981[7] 2787[9] 3730[2] 4173[6] 5188[4] (5251) 6061[12] 6548[5]

**Nick The Odds (IRE)** *Jo Hughes* a68 65
3 b g Diamond Green(FR) Impressive Act (IRE) (Brave Act)
*(254)* *(543)* *568[5]* *907[2]* *931[4]*

**Nicky's Brown Miss (USA)** *Savino A Capilupi* 92
2 b f Big Brown(USA) Nicksappealinglady (USA) (Successful Appeal (USA))
7592a[13]

**Nicolosio (IRE)** *Waldemar Hickst* 113
4 b c Peintre Celebre(USA) Nicolaia (GER) (Alkalde (GER))
5461a[2] 5938a[10] 6914a[12] 7727a[5]

**Nifty Kier** *Phil McEntee* a64 59
5 b g Kier Park(IRE) Yeldham Lady (Mujahid (USA))
*126[7]* *467[7]* *592[4]* *846[10]* *1105[5]* *1386[5]* 1639[8] 1666[6] 2689[4] 2923[11] *3526[5]* 3971[6] (4592) 4738[10] (5109) 5533[5] 5731[5] 7645[6] 7844[7] 7909[7] 8314[7]

**Nigel's Destiny (USA)** *Jeremy Noseda* a87
3 b c Giant's Causeway(USA) Ticket To Seattle (USA) (Capote (USA))
*1795[5]* 7157[6] *(7528)* *(7732)* *8188[2]*

**Niger (IRE)** *Ronald Harris* a56
5 ch h Pivotal Tithcar (Cadeaux Genereux)
*399[P]*

**Night Fever (IRE)** *John Gosden* 72
3 b f Galileo(IRE) Ask For The Moon (FR) (Dr Fong (USA))
1978[5]

**Night Generation (GER)** *Sir Mark Prescott Bt* a50 48
2 ch g Sholokhov(IRE) Night Woman (GER) (Monsun (GER))
6860[6] *7076[10]* *7573[8]*

**Nightlight** *Jeremy Noseda* a66
3 b f Pivotal Floodlit (Fantastic Light (USA))
*6482[3]* *6940[2]* *7682[2]* *7818[4]* *(8038)*

**Night Melody (IRE)** *P Schiergen* 74
2 gr f Dalakhani(IRE) Norderney (GER) (Dai Jin)
6950a[2]

**Night Of Light (IRE)** *P Bary* 102
2 b f Sea The Stars(IRE) Celestial Lagoon (JPN) (Sunday Silence (USA))
6219a[2] 6967a[6] 7654a[2]

**Night Of Thunder (IRE)** *Richard Hannon* 124
3 ch c Dubawi(IRE) Forest Storm (Galileo (IRE))
1436[2] (1951) 3320[2] 3984[8] 6382a[3] 7274[2]

**Night Party (IRE)** *Saeed bin Suroor* a89 85
3 b f Dansili La Salina (GER) (Singspiel (IRE))
(1662) *6566[6]* 7110[8]

**Night's Watch** *Dai Burchell* a54 41
4 b c Authorized(IRE) Nachtigall (GER) (Danehill (USA))
*(116)* *345[3]* *458[5]* *7426[12]* *7734[11]* *8028[4]* *8102[9]*

**Night Trade (IRE)** *Ronald Harris* a59 54
7 b m Trade Fair Compton Girl (Compton Place)
*34[8]* *121[10]* (2831) 3088[8] 3848[9] 4024[9] 4431[5] 5000[3] 5355[6] 5624[9] 6030[3] 6995[4] 7221[7] *7782[5]* *7826[7]* 8200[11] 8285[8]

**Night Wish (GER)** *W Figge* 109
4 rg c Sholokhov(IRE) Night Woman (GER) (Monsun (GER))
2001a[2] 2815a[5] 4720a[9] 6180a[3] 6806a[3] 7603a[8]

**Nijinsky Blood (FR)** *C Bruno* a79 64
7 b g Fantastic Light(USA) Daraydala (IRE) (Royal Academy (USA))
920a[11]

**Nimble (IRE)** *D Smaga* a59 44
2 b f Excellent Art Deira (USA) (Green Desert (USA))
1349[11] 1872[3] *3872a[5]* 5590a[12]

**Nimble Kimble** *James Eustace* a76 77
3 ch f Kirkwall Lovely Lyca (Night Shift (USA))
*(1389)* 1711[2] 2130[4] *2929[3]* 3890[5] *8185[6]* *8321[7]*

**Ninas Terz (GER)** *P Schiergen* 103
3 ch f Tertullian(USA) Nina Celebre (IRE) (Peintre Celebre (USA))
2584a[5] 4955a[12]

**Nine Before Ten (IRE)** *Deborah Sanderson* a26 41
6 ch m Captain Rio Sagaing (Machiavellian (USA))
2724[4] 2955[12] *7781[8]* *8133[11]*

**Nine Iron (IRE)** *Tim Vaughan* a68 55
4 gr g Verglas(IRE) Sevi's Choice (USA) (Sir Ivor (USA))
*6942[11]*

**Ninepins (IRE)** *Richard Hannon* a63 48
2 b f Rip Van Winkle(IRE) Cland Di San Jore (IRE) (Lando (GER))
6065[8] *7194[12]* *7659[3]*

**Ninepointsixthree** *John O'Shea* a36 53
4 b g Bertolini(USA) Armada Grove (Fleetwood (IRE))
*115[7]* 2836[4] 3852[8]

**Nine Realms** *Charlie Appleby* a96 103
5 b g Green Desert(USA) Bourbonella (Rainbow Quest (USA))
*207a[15]*

**Ninety Minutes (IRE)** *John Best* a73 71
3 b g Oratorio(IRE) Fleeting Mirage (USA) (Afleet Alex (USA))
1725[4] 2307[4] 3144[10]

**Ninfea (GER)** *A Wohler* 93
3 ch f Selkirk(USA) Night Lagoon (GER) (Lagunas)
4955a[11]

**Ninfea (IRE)** *Neil King* a66 65
6 b m Le Vie Dei Colori Attymon Lill (IRE) (Marju (IRE))
*(3710)* 4093[2] (4769) 4843[2] 5317[3] *6632[3]*

**Ninjago** *Richard Hannon* a92 111
4 b c Mount Nelson Fidelio's Miracle (USA) (Mountain Cat (USA))
1975[3] 3452[13] 4895[2]

**Ninny Noodle** *Miss Imogen Pickard*
4 b f Proclamation(IRE) Court Champagne (Batshoof)
*1888[7]* 2696[7] 3224[8]

**Ninth Legion (AUS)** *Michael, Wayne & John Hawkes* 109
5 b g Fastnet Rock(AUS) Xaar's Jewel (AUS) (Xaar)
1186a[8]

**Nirva (IRE)** *Ralph Beckett* a43 80
3 gr f Verglas(IRE) Nirvana (Marju (IRE))
(1280) 2316[11] 2639[4] 3672[6] 5151[3]

**Nissaki Kasta** *Hughie Morrison* a51 61
3 ch f Sakhee's Secret Casterossa (Rossini (USA))
1684[3] *2078[5]* 2695[4] *3711[6]*

**Niva (IRE)** *M Weiss* a46
5 gr m Tagula(IRE) Memphis Belle (Linamix (FR))
*555a[7]*

**Nixyba** *Tim Vaughan* a63
3 b f Cockney Rebel(IRE) Hisaronu (IRE) (Stravinsky (USA))
*254[4]* *614[2]* *914[4]* *4579[12]*

**Niyama (GER)** *Mario Hofer* 91
2 b f Tertullian(USA) Noble Lady (GER) (Sholokhov (IRE))
6123a[2] 7654a[4]

**No Backchat (IRE)** *Kevin Ryan* a39
2 b c Dutch Art Brilliana (Danehill Dancer (IRE))
*7926[9]*

**Nobbly Bobbly (IRE)** *James Bethell* 66
2 br c High Chaparral(IRE) Rock Queen (IRE) (Rock Of Gibraltar (IRE))
4885[4]

**Noble Alan (GER)** *Nicky Richards* a88 95
11 gr g King's Theatre(IRE) Nirvavita (FR) (Highest Honor (FR))
2168[5] 2760[4] (3574) 5238[5] 6433[4] 7125[9] 7641[8]

**Noble Asset** *John Quinn* 86
3 ch g Compton Place Chance For Romance (Entrepreneur)
1676[3] (2217) 3219[3] 3669[3] 4315[2] 4977[7] 5913[7] (6109) (6512)

**Noble Call (IRE)** *P J Rothwell* a60 60
6 b g King's Best(USA) Really (IRE) (Entrepreneur)
*7877a[7]* *7962a[11]*

**Noble Cause** *Luke Dace* a28 25
2 b f Showcasing Noble Peregrine (Lomond (USA))
3799[8] *4577[5]* *5042[7]* 6248[6]

**Noble Citizen (USA)** *David Simcock* a102 99
9 b g Proud Citizen(USA) Serene Nobility (USA) (His Majesty (USA))
*(172)* ◆ *(256)* *(550)* *887[6]* *1114[2]* *1558[6]* *2245a[10]* (4916) 6335[4]

**Noble Deed** *Michael Attwater* a93 76
4 ch g Kyllachy Noble One (Primo Dominie)
*55[6]* *234[3]* ◆ *534[6]* 3152[5] 4892[18] *7017[7]*

**Noble Descent** *Sir Michael Stoute* a70
3 ch f Pivotal Noble Lady (Primo Dominie)
*4052[8]* *5548[6]* *6033[3]* *6722[9]*

**Noble Gift** *William Knight* a96 93
4 ch g Cadeaux Genereux Noble Penny (Pennekamp (USA))
1439[8] 1871[3] *2461[5]* 4204[5] 5203[2] *6036[3]* (6656) *7837[6]* *8095[4]*

**Noble Master** *Sylvester Kirk* a42 50
2 b g Sir Percy Eurolinka (IRE) (Tirol)
3140[11] 3748[9] 5947[6] *6412[5]* *6842[10]*

**Noble Mission** *Lady Cecil* 123
5 b h Galileo(IRE) Kind (IRE) (Danehill (USA))
1434[2] (1697) (2086) (2580a) (3774a) 4720a[2] (7275)

**Noble Protector** *Stuart Kittow* a87 108
4 b f Haafhd All Glory (Alzao (USA))
*1175[5]* (1568) 1942[2] (4443) 5611[3]

**Noble Raven (FR)** *Mme A-M Poirier* 96
3 ch f Raven's Pass(USA) Noble Ginger (FR) (Generous (IRE))
5481a[4] 6183a[6]

**Noble Reach** *Lawrence Mullaney* a51 53
3 b f Phoenix Reach(IRE) Comtesse Noire (CAN) (Woodman (USA))
3916[10] 4370[8] 5683[13] 6122[10] 6454[4] *6946[4]* *7291[13]* 7642[2]

**Noble Silk** *Lucy Wadham* a99 101
5 gr g Sir Percy Tussah (Daylami (IRE))
*803[2]* *1213[2]* *1581[4]* (2561) 3717[4] 4759[3] 5920[5] 7107[28] *7703[4]*

**Noblesse Anime (IRE)** *L Riccardi* 88
3 b f Aussie Rules(USA) Noble Hero (IRE) (Daggers Drawn (USA))
1780a[7]

**Noblest** *William Haggas* a60
2 ch f Pivotal Noble One (Primo Dominie)
*7192[5]*

**Noble Storm (USA)** *Ed McMahon* a108 109
8 b g Yankee Gentleman(USA) Changed Tune (USA) (Tunerup (USA))
2074[7] (2353) 2766[8] 6231[11] 6624[5]

**Noble Vision (IRE)** *John Gosden* a48
2 b f Teofilo(IRE) Rafting (IRE) (Darshaan)
*7756[7]*

**No Compromise** *Richard Phillips* a36 35
5 b m Avonbridge Highly Liquid (Entrepreneur)
*872[6]* 4343[7]

**No Control (GER)** *S Smrczek* a77 67
3 b g Dashing Blade Namat (IRE) (Daylami (IRE))
*8005a[5]*

**Noctuelle (FR)** *N Caullery* a73 76
3 ch f Green Tune(USA) Karalka (IRE) (Brief Truce (USA))
2978a[7] 7270a[10]

**Nocturn** *Jeremy Noseda* a94 107
5 b g Oasis Dream Pizzicato (Statoblest)
*534[9]* *713[9]*

**Nocturnal Affair (SAF)** *Frau Erika Mader* a90 105
8 b g Victory Moon(SAF) Aretha (SAF) (Centenary (USA))
1824a[3] 3452[27] 5966a[8]

**No Delusion (USA)** *Charlie Appleby* a71 27
2 b f Street Cry(IRE) Dream Empress (USA) (Bernstein (USA))
1528[14] *2460[2]*

**No Dominion (IRE)** *A Oliver* a83 87
5 b g Dylan Thomas(IRE) Boast (Most Welcome)
1607[4] 2131[6] 2762[8] 3272[6] 3979[3] 5957a[6]

**Noel's Hope** *Simon Dow* a43
4 b g Anabaa(USA) Sourire (Domedriver (IRE))
*816[7]* *1216[11]*

**No Fear (IRE)** *W McCreery* 65
2 b g Camacho Know Doubt (IRE) (King's Best (USA))
6375a[20]

**Noguchi (IRE)** *Chris Dwyer* a72 69
9 ch g Pivotal Tuscania (USA) (Woodman (USA))
*350[6]* *(652)* *1091[2]* *1366[6]* 2327[4] 2467[3] *2904[3]* 3134[6] *8163[2]*

**No Indication (IRE)** *John Butler* 41
3 b g Tagula(IRE) Cape Sydney (IRE) (Cape Cross (IRE))
1959[9] 2996[F]

**No Leaf Clover (IRE)** *Ollie Pears* 103
3 b c Kodiac Rajmahal (UAE) (Indian Ridge)
1436[8] 2304[5] 2767[5] 3369[2] 4166[8] 5165[6]

**Nolecce** *Tony Forbes* a63 60
7 ch g Reset(AUS) Ghassanah (Pas De Seul)
*1740[4]* 2175[3] 2801[2] (3134) 3976[4] *5508[7]* *5898[2]* *6157[5]* *6343[4]* *6899[5]* *8289[3]*

**Nolohay (IRE)** *C Laffon-Parias* 108
3 ch c Dubawi(IRE) Antioquia (Singspiel (IRE))
1965a[3] 2818a[15] 5406a[7]

**Nomad Arrow (IRE)** *X Thomas-Demeaulte* a68 89
3 gr c Footstepsinthesand Aseena (IRE) (Verglas (IRE))
3810a[5]

**No Mood** *C Laffon-Parias* a84 97
3 ch c Monsun(GER) Impressionnante (Danehill (USA))
2242a[5] 4930a[8]

**Nomos (FR)** *N Sauer* 70
2 b c Dai Jin Nova Scotia (GER) (Sholokhov (IRE))
1094a[8]

**Nona Blu** *Harry Dunlop* a75 41
2 b g Diktat Shivering (Royal Applause)
2666[4] *(6101)* *6853[5]*

**Nonagon** *Wilf Storey* 33
3 b g Pastoral Pursuits Nine Red (Royal Applause)
6118[7] 6862[7] 7501[7] 7639[10]

**No Nay Never (USA)** *Wesley A Ward* a107 117
3 bb c Scat Daddy(USA) Cat's Eye Witness (USA) (Elusive Quality (USA))
*813a[2]* 7609a[2]

**No News (FR)** *X Nakkachdji* 104
4 ch f Gentlewave(IRE) Nickelle (FR) (Sagamix (FR))
1827a[8] 2631a[11] 7558a[8] 7736a[5]

**Nonno Giulio (IRE)** *Simon Dow* a73 90
3 ch g Halling(USA) Contrary (IRE) (Mark Of Esteem (IRE))
1652[9] 2706[4] 3108[3] 3651[4] 4447[7] *7852[11]* *8100[7]* *8252[10]*

**No Not Yet** *Michael Dods* 21
2 b f Notnowcato True Vision (IRE) (Pulpit (USA))
7407[15]

**Noodles Blue Boy** *Ollie Pears* a68 87
8 b g Makbul Dee Dee Girl (IRE) (Primo Dominie)
1695[14] 2167[8] ◆ 2364[10] 3222[2] 3612[2] 3948[7] 4494[8] 5053[2] (5298) 5563[6] 6235[18] 6763[7] 7103[8]

**No One Knows** *Charles Hills* 75
2 br f Pastoral Pursuits Toffee Vodka (IRE) (Danehill Dancer (IRE))
1488[3] ◆ 1670[4] 2402[4] (3922) 4619[5] 7131[6]

**Noor Al Haya (IRE)** *Laura Mongan* a61 65
4 b f Tamayuz Hariya (IRE) (Shernazar)
1916[3] 2252[2] (5909) 6360[4] 6817[3] 7419[8] *8070[5]* *8189[6]*

**Noosa Sound** *John Davies* 55
4 ch f Halling(USA) Crimson Topaz (Hernando (FR))
1674[8] 2674[10] 3535[3] 5200[10]

**Nooshi (GER)** *J Hirschberger* 60
3 rg f Shirocco(GER) Noosham (IRE) (Daylami (IRE))
5227a[3]

**Noozhoh Canarias (SPA)** *C Laffon-Parias* 116
3 b c Caradak(IRE) Noozhah (Singspiel (IRE))
1951[6] 4201[6] 6182a[8] 6971a[3]

**No Poppy (IRE)** *Tim Easterby* 91
6 b m Chineur(FR) Capetown Girl (Danzero (AUS))
1345[7] 1926[4] 2331[6] 2604[4] 3094[8] 3340[3] 4112[10] 4472[5] (5079) 5196[3] 6057[2] (6704) 6936[9] 7081[3] 7384[4] 7641[12]

**No Quarter (IRE)** *Tracy Waggott* 68
7 b g Refuse To Bend(IRE) Moonlight Wish (IRE) (Peintre Celebre (USA))
1606[6] 3339[3] 3844[5] 4070[4] ◆ 5088[3] (5244) 6217[12] 6543[6] 7180[10]

**Norab (GER)** *Marco Botti* a90 81
3 b g Galileo(IRE) Night Woman (GER) (Monsun (GER))
1438[5] 1720[3] 2494[6] 5878[11] (6461) (7422) 7703[3]

**Nora Batty** *Bill Turner* a37 44
3 b f Zamindar(USA) Soolaimon (IRE) (Shareef Dancer (USA))
2946[5] 3801[9] 4735[6] 7191[8]

**Nordican Sea (FR)** *N Leenders* a34
2 b f Diamond Green(FR) Inchica (FR) (King's Best (USA))
5901a[10]

**Nordico (GER)** *Mario Hofer* 106
3 ch c Medicean Norwegian Pride (FR) (Diktat)
1781a[2] 2377a[2] 3073a[3] 4247a[9] 5484a[4] (6384a) 7322a[4]

**Nordic Quest (IRE)** *Nicky Henderson* a77 80
5 b g Montjeu(IRE) Nordtanzerin (GER) (Danehill Dancer (IRE))
2702[3] 3823[4]

**Nordic Truce (USA)** *P Monfort* a96 97
7 b h Yes It's True(USA) Nyramba (Night Shift (USA))
5222a[7]

**No Refund (IRE)** *Martin Smith* a64 61
3 b g Invincible Spirit(IRE) Evangeline (Sadler's Wells (USA))
341[6] 468[6] 823[2] 1794[6] 2997[7] 4495[11] 4789[6] 5138[11] 5510[9] (7025) 7218[6]

**Norfolk Sky** *Laura Mongan* a83 75
5 ch m Haafhd Cayman Sound (Turtle Island (IRE))
(182)

**Norfolk Sound** *Chris Wall* a62 63
3 b f Pastoral Pursuits Cayman Sound (Turtle Island (IRE))
3332[5] 4569[9] 5400[3] 5891[4] 6647[7] 7292[2] 7635[6]

**Norfolk Sunset** *Ed Vaughan* 19
2 b f Pastoral Pursuits Cayman Sound (Turtle Island (IRE))
5056[7]

**Normal Equilibrium** *Robert Cowell* 96
4 b g Elnadim(USA) Acicula (IRE) (Night Shift (USA))
1506[11] (2123) 2283[8] 2786[4] 2992[4] 3927[10] 4418[2] 5016[3] 5419[9] 5925[3] 6131[3] 6467[2] 6745[15] 7132[9]

**Normandy Barriere (IRE)** *Nigel Tinkler* 50
2 b c Rock Of Gibraltar(IRE) Ma Paloma (FR) (Highest Honor (FR))
6058[6] 6690[5] 7123[9]

**Normandy Knight** *Richard Fahey* 70
2 b g Acclamation Prayer (IRE) (Rainbow Quest (USA))
4624[8] 5439[3] 6168[9] 7079[6]

**Normanna (IRE)** *Marco Botti* a59 32
3 b f Elusive City(USA) Nantes (GER) (Night Shift (USA))
5531[3] 6116[7]

**Norman's Star** *Chris Dwyer* a45
3 b g Tiger Hill(IRE) Canis Star (Wolfhound (USA))
422[9] 649[7] 7901[10] 8123[6] 8246[10]

**Noro Lim (IRE)** *Luca Cumani* a72
2 b g Thewayyouare(USA) Rohain (IRE) (Singspiel (IRE))
7834[5] (8075)

**Norphin** *Simon Hodgson* a41 59
4 b g Norse Dancer(IRE) Orphina (IRE) (Orpen (USA))
570[10]

**Norse Blues** *David Barron* a79 88
6 ch g Norse Dancer(IRE) Indiana Blues (Indian Ridge)
1442[8] 1958[10] 2362[8] 2758[7] 3456[4] 3621[7] 5771[9] 6320[5] 6476[4] ◆ 6534[7] 7085[18] 7236[13] 7538[8] 7719[19]

**Norse King (FR)** *Mme M Bollack-Badel* a74 117
5 ch g Norse Dancer(IRE) Angel Wing (Barathea (IRE))
(984a) 1341a[2] 1783a[3] 2819a[3] 7318a[2]

**Norse Legend** *Daniel Kubler* 47
3 b g Norse Dancer(IRE) Methodical (Lujain (USA))
1792[4] 2926[6]

**Norse Light** *Ralph Beckett* a75 78
3 ch g Norse Dancer(IRE) Dimelight (Fantastic Light (USA))
2221[12] 2773[3] 3514[2] 4189[4] 4985[7] 6274[4] 6762[2] (7304)

**Norse Prize (FR)** *Mme M Bollack-Badel* a68 107
3 ch c Norse Dancer(IRE) Cinder's Prize (Sinndar (IRE))
1965a[5] 3290a[3] 4483a[5]

**Norse Star (IRE)** *Sylvester Kirk* a76 78
3 b g Norse Dancer(IRE) Spot Prize (USA) (Seattle Dancer (USA))
1118[2] ◆ 1494[2] (2132) 2494[7] 3587[4] 4584[5] 4893[13] 5356[6] 6239[12]

**North America** *Charlie Appleby* 8
2 b c Dubawi(IRE) Northern Mischief (USA) (Yankee Victor (USA))
4666[12]

**North Bay Lady (IRE)** *John Wainwright* 49
2 b f Fast Company(IRE) Straight Sets (IRE) (Pivotal)
3255[8] 3648[10] 4750[6] 6211[9] 6669[3] 6869[4] 7209[6] 7328[10]

**North Cape (USA)** *Alastair Lidderdale*
8 b g Action This Day(USA) Cape (USA) (Mr Prospector (USA))
2966[6]

**Northern Champ (IRE)** *Rebecca Menzies*
8 b g Mull Of Kintyre(USA) Comprehension (USA) (Diesis)
8084[12]

**Northern Rocked (IRE)** *D K Weld* a65 91
8 b g Refuse To Bend(IRE) Gifts Galore (IRE) (Darshaan)
4949a[7]

**Northern Star (IRE)** *John Mackie* 85
4 b f Montjeu(IRE) Slow Sand (USA) (Dixieland Band (USA))
1439[12] 5792[8] 6649[5]

**Northern Surprise (IRE)** *Timothy Doyle* 70
3 b g Azamour(IRE) Surprise Treat (IRE) (Shalford (IRE))
4950a[8]

**Northgate Lad (IRE)** *Brian Ellison* 81
2 gr g Dark Angel(IRE) Canosa (IRE) (Catrail (USA))
(2231) 2543[4]

**Northside Prince (IRE)** *Alan Swinbank* a72 92
8 b g Desert Prince(IRE) Spartan Girl (IRE) (Ela-Mana-Mou)
2678[2] 3004[2] (3192) 3475[2] 4196[3] 5371[7] 5764[4] 6171[3]

**Nortron (IRE)** *Andrew Balding* 75
2 b c Makfi Nessa (FR) (Marchand De Sable (USA))
7123[6] 7511[2]

**Norville (IRE)** *Lee Smyth* a71 73
7 b g Elusive City(USA) Saraposa (IRE) (Ahonoora)
7959a[7]

**Norway Cross** *Luca Cumani* 91
4 b f Cape Cross(IRE) Queen Of Norway (USA) (Woodman (USA))
2010[2] 2700[6] 5931[3] (6987) 7409[4] 7768a[11]

**Norwegian Reward (IRE)** *Conrad Allen* a45 50
6 ch g Hernando(FR) Stay Behind (Elmaamul (USA))
1917[7] 3427[12]

**No Second Thoughts (IRE)** *Michael Squance* a22 29
3 b f Oratorio(IRE) Margot (Sadler's Wells (USA))
2526[8] 2927[10] 3120[6]

**No Such Number** *Sandy Forster* a68 76
6 b g King's Best(USA) Return (USA) (Sadler's Wells (USA))
85[6] 829[3] 1226[2] 1501[6] 3632[3] 4115[2] 4769[4] 5547[2] 5863[5] 7177[16]

**Nota Cambiata (USA)** *John Gosden* a66 58
2 b c Elusive Quality(USA) Mo Cheoil Thu (IRE) (In The Wings)
6456[6] 6712[10] 7200[4] 7525[4]

**Not Again** *Tim Easterby* 34
2 b g Notnowcato Royal Bloom (IRE) (Royal Applause)
7084[15] 7498[11]

**Not A Given (USA)** *Charlie Appleby* a93
5 b h Any Given Saturday(USA) Any For Love (ARG) (Southern Halo (USA))
306a[14]

**Not Another Bill** *Chris Wall* a60
3 ch g Notnowcato Composing (IRE) (Noverre (USA))
2081[8]

**Notaprayer** *Tim Easterby* 32
3 b g Notnowcato Punch Drunk (Beat Hollow)
1344[8] 2354[13]

**Notarised** *Mark Johnston* 90
3 b c Authorized(IRE) Caribbean Dancer (USA) (Theatrical (IRE))
1195[4] 2303[3] (2530) 3003[9] 3491a[8] 4452[2] 4651[5] 4940[2] 5073[4] 5414[2] 5691[15] 6127[13] (6438)

**Notebook** *Martin Smith* a74 55
3 b g Invincible Spirit(IRE) Love Everlasting (Pursuit Of Love)
167[3] 1662[2] 2363[8] 6902[12] 7513[8] 7757[11] 8169[9]

**Not Enough Eddie (USA)** *Leandro Mora* a20
2 ch g Square Eddie(CAN) Too Much Excess (USA) (Inexcess (IRE))
7605a[7]

**Notgordonitsrodger (IRE)** *Phil McEntee* a58
4 b g Footstepsinthesand Caribbean Breeze (IRE) (Barathea (IRE))
1853[4] 2126[13] 2682[10] 4595[7]

**Nothing Special** *Tom Dascombe* a63 63
3 gr f Verglas(IRE) Barathiki (Barathea (IRE))
1084[3] 1357[10] 1542[4] 2210[3] 2676[8] 3105[3] 4432[4]

**Notion (IRE)** *F Chappet* a81 86
6 gr h Sadler's Wells(USA) Reina Blanca (Darshaan)
584a[13]

**Not Never** *Hugo Palmer* 76
2 ch g Notnowcato Watchoverme (Haafhd)
7134[5] (7498)

**Notnowdear** *Ann Duffield* 50
2 ch g Notnowcato Cup Of Love (USA) (Behrens (USA))
5712[7] 5995[6] 6577[7]

**Notnow Penny** *Milton Bradley* a49 45
3 ch f Notnowcato Tuppenny (Salse (USA))
608[4] 1264[4] 3214[11] 3564[11] 6368[3]

**Notre Archange (FR)** *F Lemercier* 42
2 b c Archange D'Or(IRE) Sharp Note (FR) (Victory Note (USA))
7344a[9]

**Not Rigg (USA)** *Nick Littmoden* a70 66
4 b g Henrythenavigator(USA) St Helens Shadow (USA) (Septieme Ciel (USA))
589[12] 780[5] 3160[5] 3562[2] 3979[8] 4655[5] 5075[11] 5512[5]

**Not So Sleepy** *Hughie Morrison* 90
2 ch g Beat Hollow Papillon De Bronze (IRE) (Marju (IRE))
(7206) 7446[6]

**Notts So Blue** *Shaun Harris* a33 55
3 b f Pastoral Pursuits Blue Nile (IRE) (Bluebird (USA))
1801[4] 2742[5] 3407[4] 4490[5] 5166[5] (5239) 6010[5]

**Nouveau Foret** *Ed Walker* a72 11
2 b f Myboycharlie(IRE) Forest Express (AUS) (Kaaptive Edition (NZ))
6434[12] 7194[5] (7752)

**Nouvelle Ere** *Tony Carroll* a55 54
3 b g Archipenko(USA) Sinister Ruckus (USA) (Trippi (USA))
1681[6] 2026[10] 2329[7] 4742[8] 6661[6] 7036[11] 7369[13] 7845[2] 7924[6] 8315[5]

**Novabridge** *Neil Mulholland* a73 69
6 ch g Avonbridge Petrovna (IRE) (Petardia)
654[2] (921) 2598a[4] 3496a[4] (4038a) 5228a[6] 6186a[5]

**Nova Champ (IRE)** *Stuart Williams* a73 84
3 ch g Intikhab(USA) Baby Bunting (Wolfhound (USA))
1396[10] 1615[2] (1952) 2344[7] 2962[10] (3539) 4669[18] 5012[8] 6558[4]

**Novalist** *Robin Bastiman* a64 48
6 ch g Avonbridge Malelane (IRE) (Prince Sabo)
34[9] 258[6] 502[5] 563[9] 864[2] 1148[8] 2094[2] 2452[4] 2907[2] 3099[11] 4288[10] 5636[5] 7222[4] (8084) (8139) 8218[6]

**Nova Princesse (GER)** *Marco Botti* a77 53
3 b f Desert Prince(IRE) Nova Scotia (GER) (Sholokhov (IRE))
279[5] 667[5] 936[7] (1260) 3114[4] 4053[4] 4971[7]

**Nova Valorem (IRE)** *C Boutin* a81 94
6 ch h Ad Valorem(USA) Utr (USA) (Mr Prospector (USA))
806a[2] 3373a[6] 3907a[6]

**Novel Dancer** *Lydia Richards* a61 72
6 b g Dansili Fictitious (Machiavellian (USA))
368[8] 530[4] 656[7] (1263) 1895[3] (2212) (2916) 3552[6] 4737[6] 5558[6] 7532[4] 8021[2]

**Novellen Lad (IRE)** *Willie Musson* a90 70
9 b g Noverre(USA) Lady Ellen (Horage)
234[5] 658[6] 991[10] 1492[11] 2919[4] 4078[10] 6020[8] 6680[10] 7351[9] 7776[2] 8040[5]

**Noverre To Go (IRE)** *Ronald Harris* a76 83
8 ch g Noverre(USA) Ukraine Venture (Slip Anchor)
1893[3] 2718[4] 2919[10] 3213[5] 3749[2] 4339[2] 5124[6] 5559[5] 6236[2] 6898[8] 7888[8] 7989[5] 8039[2]

**Novirak (IRE)** *James Fanshawe* a48 97
6 gr g Noverre(USA) Manchaca (FR) (Highest Honor (FR))
5379[3] 6133[4] 6687[3] 7409[2]

**No Wind No Rain** *Yves de Nicolay* 98
3 ch f Green Tune(USA) Queseraisjesanstoi (FR) (Rainbow Quest (USA))
4840a[4] 7319a[5] 7720a[10]

**No Win No Fee** *Michael Appleby* a75 86
4 b g Firebreak Milliscent (Primo Dominie)
29[2] 172[6] 406[6] 2519[2] 3335[2] (3977) 4148[3] (4832) 5676[4] 6870[5] (7172) 7562[6]

**Now Say Boooom** *Luke Dace* a34 34
2 b f Proclamation(IRE) Grezie (Mark Of Esteem (IRE))
1417[9] 2057[7] 2402[10] 5180[8] 5489[13] 7199[8]

**Now Spun (USA)** *A Al Raihe* a76 97
4 b c Hard Spun(USA) Campionessa (USA) (A.P. Indy (USA))
112a[16] 504a[14] 683a[13]

**Now We Can** *N Clement* a112 113
5 b h Martillo(GER) Notre Dame (GER) (Acatenango (GER))
1177a[12] 2819a[2]

**Now What** *Jonathan Portman* a65 67
7 ch m Where Or When(IRE) Vallauris (Faustus (USA))
2614[7] (4149) (6252) 7343[12]

**Nubar Boy** *Ian Williams* a74 74
7 ch g Compton Place Out Like Magic (Magic Ring (IRE))
(92) 211[4] 421[3] 565[7] (852) 1121[2] 1503[2] 1717[6] 2471[3] 3585[7] 3616[2] 4340[4] 4501[7]

**Nucifera (USA)** *J E Pease* 106
2 b c More Than Ready(USA) Lotus Sutra (USA) (Kingmambo (USA))
(4312a) (5478a) 6181a[2] 6968a[8]

**Nufooth (IRE)** *Richard Hannon* 69
2 b f Elnadim(USA) Sahaayeb (IRE) (Indian Haven)
3267[6] 4202[4] 4906[2] 5947[3]

**Nu Form Fire (IRE)** *Nigel Tinkler* 51
3 b g Footstepsinthesand Maimana (IRE) (Desert King (IRE))
1648[9] 1906[10] 2230[2] 2387[5]

**Nullarbor Sky (IRE)** *Lucy Wadham* a62 92
4 gr f Aussie Rules(USA) Grenouillere (USA) (Alysheba (USA))
(2445) (3161) 4917[3] 5673[10] 6465[2] 7105[17]

**Number One London (IRE)** *Brian Meehan* a77 91
4 b g Invincible Spirit(IRE) Vadorga (Grand Lodge (USA))
1810[3] 2627[4] (3034) 3453[6] 4441[11] 5288[4] 5579[13] 6228[2] 6747[9] 7129[12]

**Number Winner (FR)** *M Gentile* a70 75
4 b c Orpen(USA) Amonita (GER) (Medaaly)
266a[4]

**Numrood** *George Peckham* a58 26
3 b g Mount Nelson Hms Pinafore (IRE) (Singspiel (IRE))
4265[4] 5010[6] 5282[2] 7219[9] 7359[9]

**Nuno Tristan (USA)** *William Jarvis* a81 40
2 b c Henrythenavigator(USA) Saintly Speech (USA) (Southern Halo (USA))
7037[7] (8026)

**Nuntius (GER)** *A Wohler* 107
4 rg c Dalakhani(IRE) Night Lagoon (GER) (Lagunas)
5938a[2]

**Nur Jahan (IRE)** *David Lanigan* a67 72
4 b f Selkirk(USA) Have Faith (IRE) (Machiavellian (USA))
(5570) 5927[9]

**Nurpur (IRE)** *David O'Meara* a17 88
4 b f Dark Angel(IRE) The Good Life (IRE) (Rainbow Quest (USA))
1345[11] 1762[3] ◆ 2144[5] 6704[10] 7538[10] 7784[10]

**Nusantara** *Paul Cole* a66 50
3 b f New Approach(IRE) Pentatonic (Giant's Causeway (USA))
1797[4] 2310[6]

**Nutbush** *Mick Channon* a40 51
3 b f Sixties Icon Hairy Night (IRE) (Night Shift (USA))
1422[17] 1645[4] 1918[7] 2209[8] 2668[5] 3087[5] 3214[7] 3564[9] 4048[8]

**Nyanza (GER)** *Alan King* a82 76
3 b f Dai Jin Nouvelle Fortune (IRE) (Alzao (USA))
(1793) (2080) 3146[3] 4504[3] 7072[2]

**Nymeria (GER)** *Waldemar Hickst* 91
2 b f Soldier Hollow Naroома (GER) (Silver Hawk (USA))
7315a[6]

**Nymphea (IRE)** *P Schiergen* 116
5 ch m Dylan Thomas(IRE) Neele (IRE) (Peintre Celebre (USA))
2631a[3] 3770a[5] 4824[9] 6184a[4] 6969a[9]

**Oakbank (USA)** *Brett Johnson* a56 50
3 b g Empire Maker(USA) Summer Shower (Sadler's Wells (USA))
1391[8] 1797[10] 3712[11] 4321[4] 4615[4] 5556[3] 5628[5] 6486[2] 7229[5]

**Oak Bluffs (IRE)** *Richard Fahey* a64 60
3 b g Royal Applause Key Stage (IRE) (King's Best (USA))
1939[5] 2296[12] 2955[8] 3359[9] 4108[11] (7813) 8299[10]

**Oakham** *A bin Huzaim* a56 61
4 ch c Shirocco(GER) Lady Catherine (Bering)
238a[9]

**Oak Harbour** *A De Royer-Dupre* 100
3 b c Sinndar(IRE) Onega Lake (IRE) (Peintre Celebre (USA))
(3512a)

**Oakley Dancer** *Tony Carroll* a26 21
3 ch f Assertive My Dancer (IRE) (Alhaarth (IRE))
786[11] 1264[6] 1914[6] 2023[10]

**Oakley Girl** *Stuart Williams* 31
2 b f Sir Percy Pivotting (Pivotal)
5391[6]

**Oakley Star** *Gay Kelleway* a33 45
2 b f Multiplex Star Welcome (Most Welcome)
7594[14] 7739[12]

**Oakling** *Sylvester Kirk* a30
2 b f High Chaparral(IRE) Lambroza (IRE) (Grand Lodge (USA))
7756[11] 7941[13] 8093[12]

**Oasis Dancer** *Doug Watson* a94 95
7 b g Oasis Dream Good Enough (FR) (Mukaddamah (USA))
242a[2]

**Oasis Fantasy (IRE)** *Ed Dunlop* 92
3 br g Oasis Dream Cara Fantasy (IRE) (Sadler's Wells (USA))
1702[6] 2719[2] ◆ (3183) 4183[2] 4893[4] 6685[6] 7440[3]

**Oasis Mirage** *Robert Cowell* a71 65
3 b f Oasis Dream Canda (USA) (Storm Cat (USA))
3156[7] 3677[2] 4295[2] (4735) 5061[3]

**Oasis Spirit** *Andrew Balding* a77 72
4 b f Oasis Dream Fearless Spirit (USA) (Spinning World (USA))
1080[2] 1554[11] 7758[6] 8185[5]

**Obboorr** *John Wainwright* a71 70
5 b g Cape Cross(IRE) Felawnah (USA) (Mr Prospector (USA))
(277) 405[4] 4058[5] 5049[3] 5899[5]

**Obliterator (IRE)** *G M Lyons* a108 106
3 br g Oratorio(IRE) Faraday Light (IRE) (Rainbow Quest (USA))
1516[2] ◆ 2571a[11] 3375[8]

**Obliteright (IRE)** *William Knight* a90 83
5 ch g Bertolini(USA) Doctrine (Barathea (IRE))
3036[6] 4181[9] 4783[12] 5346[2] 6145[9] 6885[6]

**Observational** *Roger Charlton* 105
3 ch c Galileo(IRE) Party (IRE) (Cadeaux Genereux)
1530[2] ◆ (2502) 4778[6] 5577[7]

**Obsidian (USA)** *John Gosden* 93
3 b c Street Cry(IRE) Latice (IRE) (Inchinor)
2334[5] ◆ 3248[2] 4168[5]

**Obsidian Rock (USA)** *J S Moore* a37
2 bb g More Than Ready(USA) Balletomaine (IRE) (Sadler's Wells (USA))
7926[10]

**Obstacle** *Paul Webber* 84
4 ch g Observatory(USA) Stage Left (Nashwan (USA))
1493[8]

**Obstinate (IRE)** *Andrew Balding* a76 77
3 b g Fastnet Rock(AUS) Sangita (Royal Academy (USA))
954[4] 2075[4] 2881[4] 7304[9]

**Obviously (IRE)** *Philip D'Amato* a95 121
6 b g Choisir(AUS) Leala (IRE) (Montjeu (IRE))
7613a[5]

**Occhio Della Mente (IRE)** *E Botti* 104
7 b h Le Vie Dei Colori Croanda (IRE) (Grand Lodge (USA))
1603a[2] 2191a[3] 3047a[9] 7617a[9]

**Ocean Applause** *John Ryan* a87 84
4 b g Royal Applause Aldora (Magic Ring (IRE))
(49) 146[7] (369) 623[3] 698[10] 744[10] 1175[4] 1354[11] 1637[7] 2270[8] 2444[2] 3162[2] 3544[2] 3878[3] 4190[4] 4498[3] (4593) 4620[4] 5040[6] 5487[8] 6141[4] 6264[8] 6870[2] 7567[8] 8116[5]

**Ocean Bentley (IRE)** *Tony Carroll* a26
2 b g Amadeus Wolf Bentley's Bush (IRE) (Barathea (IRE))
4270[16] 7217[7] 7542[11]

**Ocean Blue (JPN)** *Yasutoshi Ikee* 114
6 b h Stay Gold(JPN) Peu A Peu (GER) (Dashing Blade)
2002a[12]

**Ocean Boulevard** *Luca Cumani* a73 70
3 b f Danehill Dancer(IRE) Ventura Highway (Machiavellian (USA))
7418[3] 7772[3] 8310[3]

**Ocean Crystal** *John Ryan* a51 61
2 b f Stimulation(IRE) Crystal Gale (IRE) (Verglas (IRE))
2993[3] 3232[8] 4202[8] 4403[7] 4913[17] 5436[7] 5823[12] 6412[12] 6903[4]

**Ocean Legend (IRE)** *Tony Carroll* a85 70
9 b g Night Shift(USA) Rose Of Mooncoin (IRE) (Brief Truce (USA))
113[3] 310[2] 464[2] 790a[6] 1026[3] 2401[2] (2721) 3112[5] 3555[DSQ] (3800) 8072[11] 8268[9]

**Oceanographer** *Charlie Appleby* 76
2 b c Sea The Stars(IRE) Que Puntual (ARG) (Contested Bid (USA))
6300[4] (6976)

**Ocean Power (IRE)** *Richard Phillips* a49 51
4 b g Papal Bull Petticoat Power (IRE) (Tomba)
247[5] 380[3] 656[6] 759[5] 842[6] 959[10]

**Ocean Sheridan (IRE)** *Michael Dods* 70
2 b g Starspangledbanner(AUS) Endless Night (GER) (Tiger Hill (IRE))
2601[3] 3296[4] 3947[2] 4702[3] 5443[4] 6623[2] (7329)

**Ocean Storm (IRE)** *James Tate* a62 85
3 b c Royal Applause Cedar Sea (IRE) (Persian Bold)
3383[5] 5528[7]

**Ocean Tempest** *John Ryan* a100 121
5 gr g Act One Ipsa Loquitur (Unfuwain (USA))
109a[11] 306a[10] 509a[11] 679a[3] 808a[6] 899a[11] (1165) 1437[4] (1870) (2223) 2715a[7] 3356[14] 3731[10] (5919) 6132[3] 6710[9] 7243[8] 7599[6] 7836[9]

**Ocho Ocho Ocho (USA)** *James Cassidy* a109
2 bb c Street Sense(USA) Winner (USA) (Horse Chestnut (SAF))
(7605a)

**Ocovango** *A Fabre* a107 106
4 br c Monsun(GER) Crystal Maze (Gone West (USA))
3171a[3] 4561a[7] 8006a[14]

**Odd Ball (IRE)** *Lisa Williamson* a48 10
7 b g Redback Luceball (IRE) (Bluebird (USA))
964[6] 1138[10] 1631[9]

**Oddysey (IRE)** *Michael Dods* a84 92
5 b m Acclamation Darling Smile (IRE) (Darshaan)
1956[7] 2351[4] 3066[2] 3340[2] 4112[4] 4832[5] 5681[6] 6057[8] 6490[2] 6945[4] 7538[11]

**Odeliz (IRE)** *K R Burke* 108
4 ch f Falco(USA) Acatama (USA) (Efisio)
1076a[2] 1974[5] 2284[3] 2956[2] 4478a[4] 5927[2] 6585a[3] 7326a[2]

**Odeon** *James Given* 106
3 b g Galileo(IRE) Kite Mark (Mark Of Esteem (IRE))
(1608) 2285[4] 3417[7] 4385[4] 5577[3] 6894[4] 7718[17]

**Odin (IRE)** *Don Cantillon* a89 86
6 b g Norse Dancer(IRE) Dimelight (Fantastic Light (USA))
85[5] 4349[3] 4917[5] 6036[9]

**Odisseia (IRE)** *Edward Lynam* 92
3 bb f Clodovil(IRE) Bent Al Fala (IRE) (Green Desert (USA))
3357[9]

**Odyssee (FR)** *Marco Botti* a88 79
4 ch f Teofilo(IRE) Uruk (Efisio)
426[9] 674[7]

**Oeil De Tigre (FR)** *Tony Carroll* a60 99
3 b g Footstepsinthesand Suerte (Halling (USA))
2226a[7] 4669[19] 5438[12] 6923[11] 7233[8]

**Oetzi** *Timothy Jarvis* a63 74
6 ch g Iceman Mad Annie (USA) (Anabaa (USA))
1439[4] ◆ 1848[5] 2464[U] 7419[4] 7760[4]

**Ofelia (IRE)** *Brian Ellison* 49
3 b f Teofilo(IRE) Rose Bourbon (USA) (Woodman (USA))
2236[6] 2741[7] 3534[8] 3950[6] ◆ 4350[5] 4749[4] 5102[5]

**Off Art** *Tim Easterby* 99
4 ch g Dutch Art Off Camera (Efisio)
1165[5] ◆ 1958[12]

**Offbeat Safaris (IRE)** *Ronald Harris* a63 63
6 b g Le Vie Dei Colori Baywood (Emarati (USA))
30[4] 77[2] 446[9]

**Offering Plan (USA)** *Chad C Brown* 98
2 bb c Spring At Last(USA) Rosalie Road (USA) (Street Cry (IRE))
7590a[13]

**Offherocker** *Claire Dyson* a29
7 b m Generosity Houston Heiress (USA) (Houston (USA))
35[6] 124[3] 197[6]

**Officer Drivel (IRE)** *Luke Dace* a73 71
3 b g Captain Rio Spiritville (IRE) (Invincible Spirit (IRE))
316[9] 473[4] 668[2] 785[3] (1011) 1407[3] 1856[4] 2481[7]

**Officer In Command (USA)** *John Butler* a55 47
8 bb g Officer(USA) Luv To Stay N Chat (USA) (Candi's Gold (USA))
407[2] 685[2] 775[3] 953[4] 1083[3] 1236[2] 2079[8] 2464[9] 2901[6] 3795[9] 4578[8] 6160[8] 6857[7] 7635[8] 7972[9]

**Officer Sydney (IRE)** *Brian Meehan* 47
2 b g Lawman(FR) Morena Park (Pivotal)
6545[12]

**Offshore** *James Tate* a71 65
2 gr c Iffraaj Ronaldsay (Kirkwall)
2380[5] 2859[4] 3584[5] 6250[5] 6811[2] 7815[2] 7902[2] (8087)

**Offshore Bond** *Jedd O'Keeffe* 66
3 b g Bahamian Bounty Miss Rimex (IRE) (Ezzoud (IRE))
2015[11]

**Off The Pulse** *John Mackie* a88 87
4 b g Araafa(IRE) Off By Heart (Royal Applause)
200[4] 2137[4] (2699) 3050[2] 6839[5] 7236[8] 7538[9] 8290[4]

**Ogaritmo** *Alex Hales* a72 57
5 ch m Manduro(GER) Querida (Rainbow Quest (USA))
210[8] 469[2] 590[4] 656[2] 842[8] 1574[5] 2084[4] 2419[2] 4737[5] 5403[6] 5600[10]

**Ogbourne Downs** *Charles Hills* a93 88
4 b g Royal Applause Helen Sharp (Pivotal)
1351[10] 2382[2] (3212) 4028[5] (4549) 4761[8] 5669[8] 6609[5] (6886) 7136[10] 7545[10]

**O'Gorman** *Gary Brown* a86 87
5 b g Sleeping Indian Harryana (Efisio)
658[10] 863[3] 909[6] 1145[4] 1490[4] 2629[3] 3313[3] 5281[8] 5830[8]

**Ohio (IRE)** *Nick Littmoden* a59 53
3 b f Teofilo(IRE) Royals Special (IRE) (Caerleon (USA))
4304[9] 5491[3] (5829) 6193[8] 6899[8]

**Oh So Sassy** *Chris Wall* a97 91
4 b f Pastoral Pursuits Almasi (IRE) (Petorius)
2645[2] (3581) 4128[7] 5419[4] 6130[16]

**Ohsosecret** *Stuart Williams* a36
2 ch f Sakhee's Secret Warden Rose (Compton Place)
8201[7]

**Oh Star (USA)** *John Gosden* a76 103
3 b f Tale Of The Cat(USA) Sleepytime (IRE) (Royal Academy (USA))
2681[3] 3141[2] 3653[2] (4089) 4721a[2]

**Oil Of England (GER)** *Werner Glanz* 104
3 bb c Lord Of England(GER) Oligarchica (GER) (Desert King (IRE))
2376a[3] 3073a[5] 6590a[3] 7617a[5]

**Oil Strike** *Michael Easterby* a71 57
7 b g Lucky Story(USA) Willisa (Polar Falcon (USA))
8[9] 7806[8] ◆

**Okiel Des Mottes (FR)** *E Lellouche* a86 103
5 b g Ange Gabriel(FR) Oktodez (GER) (Java Gold (USA))
(584a)

**Old Fashion** *Ed Dunlop* a65 50
2 b f Shirocco(GER) Oriental Dance (Fantastic Light (USA))
3076[10] 3858[5] 4626[6] 5279[2] 5798[7] 6669[12]

**Old Guard** *Roger Charlton* a78 85
3 b g Notnowcato Dolma (FR) (Marchand De Sable (USA))
1680[3] 3537[2] (4265)

**Oldjoesaid** *Paul Midgley* a41 84
10 b g Royal Applause Border Minstral (IRE) (Sri Pekan (USA))
863[7] 1961[3] 2350[8] 2656[4] 3138[11] 3697[2] 4418[8] 5016[7] 5498[7] (5912) 6235[13] 6873[6] 7535[10]

**Old Man Clegg** *Michael Easterby* 73
4 b g Pastoral Pursuits Stolen Melody (Robellino (USA))
1376[7] 1839[6] 5499[4] (6121) 6477[2] 7180[11] 7494[9]

**Old Pal (FR)** *Niels Petersen* a27 96
5 b h Soldier Hollow Syllable (Halling (USA))
3090a[9] 5744a[6]

**Old Town Boy** *Philip McBride* a69 99
3 b c Myboycharlie(IRE) Native Ring (FR) (Bering)
409[2] 607[4] (1401) 1979[7] (2363) 2761[2] 6685[11] (7083) 7718[9]

**Old Way (IRE)** *Venetia Williams* a67 88
8 b g Gold Away(IRE) Brooklyn's Dance (FR) (Shirley Heights)
260[3] 322[4]

**Oliandra (FR)** *M Figge* 68
5 b m Lando(GER) Oligarchica (GER) (Desert King (IRE))
920a[6]

**Oliver's Gold** *Mark Walford* a45 47
6 b g Danehill Dancer(IRE) Gemini Gold (IRE) (King's Best (USA))
959[4] 5495[7]

**Olivers Mount** *Ed Vaughan* a65 37
4 ch g Mount Nelson Phoebe Woodstock (IRE) (Grand Lodge (USA))
92[3] 117[3] 281[2] 446[4] 838[6] (1387) 1917[2] 2646[6] 4327[2] (7853) 8030[11] 8169[11]

**Olivia Fallow (IRE)** *Paul Midgley* 70
2 b f Vale Of York(IRE) Spinning Maid (USA) (Forestry (USA))
2051[4] ◆ (3367) 3786[5] 4686[3] 4869[3] 5637[4]

**Ol' Man River (IRE)** *A P O'Brien* 114
2 b c Montjeu(IRE) Finsceal Beo (IRE) (Mr Greeley (USA))
(6800a)

**Olney Lass** *Lydia Pearce* a49 72
7 b m Lucky Story(USA) Zalebe (Bahamian Bounty)
2448[5] 2718[3] 3125[7] 4047[4] 5650[5] 5979[3] 6189[6] 7220[8] 7884[4] 8004[5] 8085[7]

**Olymnia** *Robert Eddery* a58 62
3 b f Teofilo(IRE) Diotima (High Estate)
1139a[11] 1691[4] 2616[4] 3120[7] 5011[7] 6110[5] 6339[7]

**Olympic Charm** *Derek Shaw* a13 62
2 b g Invincible Spirit(IRE) Super Sleuth (IRE) (Selkirk (USA))
3578[11] 4109[5] 5242[6]

**Olympic Glory (IRE)** *Richard Hannon* 127
4 b c Choisir(AUS) Acidanthera (Alzao (USA))
(2338) 2587a[4] 5480a[3] (6971a)

**Olynard (IRE)** *Michael Mullineaux* a50 61
8 b g Exceed And Excel(AUS) Reddening (Blushing Flame (USA))
639[12]

**Oly'Roccs (IRE)** *Philip Kirby* a55 44
3 b g Tagula(IRE) Orpendonna (IRE) (Orpen (USA))
355[7] (1852) 3534[6] 4911[4] 5512[11] 5600[2]

**Omaha Gold (IRE)** *Bryan Smart* 73
3 b f Kodiac Naraina (IRE) (Desert Story (IRE))
4977[8] 6695[10]

**O Ma Lad (IRE)** *John Quinn* a80 96
6 ch g Redback Raydaniya (IRE) (In The Wings)
1444[7] 1971[2] 2259[8] 4361[5] 5083[2] 6228[5] 7281[10]

**Omanome (IRE)** *David O'Meara* a48 70
3 b f Acclamation Dance Set (Selkirk (USA))
7249[11] 7622[11] 8043[10]

**Omaticaya (IRE)** *V Fazio* 105
3 br f Bernstein(USA) Pronghorn (USA) (Gulch (USA))
1477a[11] (2375a) 3746a[11] 7320a[8]

**Omega Omega** *Liam Corcoran* a51 50
5 b m Halling(USA) In Luck (In The Wings)
176[3] 303[8] 831[8] (2595a) 4082[8]

**Omid** *Dianne Sayer* a55 48
6 b g Dubawi(IRE) Mille Couleurs (FR) (Spectrum (IRE))
7284[4]

**Ominous** *Nigel Blackiston* 68
5 b g Oasis Dream Merle (Selkirk (USA))
7395a[P]

**Omnipresent** *David O'Meara* a84 80
4 b g Rail Link Protectress (Hector Protector (USA))
1659[5] 1934[8] (2904)

**Omotenashi (USA)** *Roger Varian* a55
2 b f Henrythenavigator(USA) Million Gift (JPN) (Sunday Silence (USA))
7944[4] 8191[4]

**Omotesando** *Mark Brisbourne* a51 44
4 b g Street Cry(IRE) Punctilious (Danehill (USA))
1153[5] 1452[4] 1865[5] 2207[4] 2475[9] 3208[6] 3554[5]

**On And On (IRE)** *Richard Fahey* a52
4 br f Rock Of Gibraltar(IRE) Dapple Dawn (IRE) (Celtic Swing)
19[5] 291[6] 645[6]

**On Appro** *Tim Easterby* a48 42
2 b f Approve(IRE) No Nightmare (USA) (Lion Heart (USA))
1504[11] 1900[8] 2395[4] 3367[4] 4065[3] 4857[7]

**On Call Now** *X Thomas-Demeaulte* 101
5 b h Acclamation Cumbrian Princess (Mtoto)
7189a[4]

**On Demand** *Simon Hodgson* a69 70
3 ch f Teofilo(IRE) Mimisel (Selkirk (USA))
551[3] 930[2] 1112[3] 5004[6] 5848[5] 7001[2] 7309[8] 7760[5] 8037[7] 8282[6]

**One And Only (FR)** *P Decouz* a77 77
4 ch f Muhtathir Alaskan Way (USA) (Giant's Causeway (USA))
(722a)

**One And Only (JPN)** *Kojiro Hashiguchi* 118
3 bb c Heart's Cry(JPN) Virtue (JPN) (Taiki Shuttle (USA))
7981a[7]

**One Boy (IRE)** *Michael Dods* 86
3 ch g Captain Gerrard(IRE) Paris Song (IRE) (Peintre Celebre (USA))
1396[3] (1676) 2317[7] 2897[6] 3484[6] 3948[2] 5243[2] 6153[4]

**One Chance (IRE)** *John Butler* 95
3 b f Invincible Spirit(IRE) Towards (USA) (Fusaichi Pegasus (USA))
1513[5] 1867[6] 2287[2] 3245[4] 5154a[5] 5925[13] 6549[6] (7101)

**Onedargent (FR)** *J-P Gallorini* 102
4 gr g Kendargent(FR) One Day (FR) (Act One)
4561a[5]

**Oneeightofamile (IRE)** *N Dooly* 77
9 b g Catcher In The Rye(IRE) Punta Gorda (IRE) (Roi Danzig (USA))
5456a[5]

**One Kool Dude** *Micky Hammond* a45 60
5 ch g Iceman Hiraeth (Petong)
1643[12] 2233[9] 2677[9] 3339[8] 4070[8] 5390[9] 5806[3] 6120[12]

**One Last Dream** *Ron Hodges* a64 56
5 ch g Resplendent Glory(IRE) Pip's Dream (Glint Of Gold)
92[9] 289[9] 428[2] 603[7] 1787[3] 1986[5] 2250[4] 2722[10] 8311[12]

**Onelastfling** *Sylvester Kirk* a54 36
2 b f Paco Boy(IRE) Goodie Twosues (Fraam)
4610[6] 5210[8] 6838[5]

**One Lucky Dane (USA)** *Bob Baffert* a99
2 b c Lookin At Lucky(USA) Echo Harbor (USA) (Boston Harbor (USA))
7610a[6]

**One Moment** *Robert Cowell* a69 70
2 ch f Notnowcato Two Step (Mujtahid (USA))
2460[3] 2800[2] 3211[2] 3583[7] 4576[5] 5859[2] 6408[3] 7336[4] 7649[4] 8170[3]

**One Pekan (IRE)** *Roger Varian* a87 90
4 b g Hard Spun(USA) Stormy Blessing (USA) (Storm Cat (USA))
2033[5] 2876[2] 3457[2] 4091[2] (5757) 7718[20]

**One Pursuit (IRE)** *Brendan Powell* a49 98
6 br g Pastoral Pursuits Karinski (USA) (Palace Music (USA))
(1909) 2272[4] (2700) 2981[3] 3449[17]

**One Scoop Or Two** *Andrew Hollinshead* a78 77
8 b g Needwood Blade Rebel County (IRE) (Maelstrom Lake)
539[4] 646[5] 1085[4] 1450[2] 1718[4]

**One Spirit (IRE)** *F Dunne* 100
6 b m Invincible Spirit(IRE) Recite (JPN) (Forty Niner (USA))
2185a[3] 2572a[13] 3412a[6]

**One Way (FR)** *Y Gourraud* a74 75
2 ch c Hold That Tiger(USA) Bali Boom (FR) (Jeune Homme (USA))
8149a[2]

**One Way Or Another (AUS)** *David Evans* a73 62
11 b g Carnegie(IRE) True Blonde (AUS) (Naturalism (NZ))
53[5] 141[9] 340[6] 424[5] 562[4] 603[3] 939[3] 1311[8] (2596a) 2864[5] 3233[9] 3527[9]

**One Word More (IRE)** *Charles Hills* a100 104
4 b g Thousand Words Somoushe (IRE) (Black Minnaloushe (USA))
1437[12] 3420[19] 6207[8] 6755[6]

**On High** *Richard Hannon* a63 68
2 b f Exceed And Excel(AUS) Kirk (Selkirk (USA))
3671[6] 4403[5] 5305[6] 6294[2]

**Onirique (IRE)** *X Nakkachdji* 77
3 b f Teofilo(IRE) Blue Blue Sky (IRE) (Anabaa (USA))
7857a[10]

**Online Alexander (IRE)** *Kevin Ryan* 107
3 b f Acclamation Dance Club (IRE) (Fasliyev (USA))
3068[4] 3484[2] (4898) ◆ (5696) 6231[6] 6918[4]

**Only For You** *Alan Brown* a25 27
4 b f Elusive City(USA) Enlisted (IRE) (Sadler's Wells (USA))
5412[5] 5814[5] 6120[11] 7250[8] 8139[10]

**Only Joking** *Hugo Palmer* a62 78
2 b f Aussie Rules(USA) Cliche (IRE) (Diktat)
2173[3] 2460[5] (5241) 6229[7] 7237[9]

**Only One Galileo (IRE)** *J J Lambe* a21 20
4 b f Mujadil(USA) Galileo's Way (IRE) (Galileo (IRE))
794a[3]

**Only Orsenfoolsies** *Micky Hammond* 87
5 b g Trade Fair Desert Gold (IRE) (Desert Prince (IRE))
2790[8] 3205[2] ◆ (3787) (4454) 5465[7] 7125[17]

**Only Ten Per Cent (IRE)** *J R Jenkins* a82 78
6 b g Kheleyf(USA) Cory Everson (IRE) (Brief Truce (USA))
9[2] 87[3] (272) 470[5] 572[7] 834[6] (1115) 1921[7] 2312[7] 2933[2] 3561[12] 4431[4] 4675[3] (5207) 5724[5] (6455) 6873[11] 7534[6] 7761[3]

**Onlyyouknowme (IRE)** *F Rossi* a100 64
6 b m Martino Alonso(IRE) Sopran New (USA) (Cozzene (USA))
836a[8]

**Onorina (IRE)** *Jim Boyle* a40
2 b f Arcano(IRE) Miss Honorine (IRE) (Highest Honor (FR))
7752 [11] 8036[9]

**On Stage** *Brendan Powell* 62
5 ch m Act One In The Stocks (Reprimand)
1574[7] 3852[3] 4744[4]

**On The Cusp (IRE)** *Ann Stokell* a69 65
7 b g Footstepsinthesand Roman Love (IRE) (Perugino (USA))
96[5] 546[2] (831) 912[3] 1496[6] 2399[9]

**On The High Tops (IRE)** *Colin Teague* a7 41
6 b g Kheleyf(USA) Diplomats Daughter (Unfuwain (USA))
6120[8] 6796[6] 6866[7] 7009[6] 7519[10]

**On The Hoof** *Michael Easterby* a69 63
5 gr g Monsieur Bond(IRE) Smart Hostess (Most Welcome)
4963[8] 5421[12] 5678[6] 6670[6] 7259[2]

**On The Huh** *Michael Bell* a67
2 b g Avonbridge Red Sovereign (Danzig Connection (USA))
8026[4] 8184[7]

**On The Rocks (FR)** *T Clout* a63 49
4 gr f Verglas(IRE) Princess D'Orange (FR) (Anabaa (USA))
935a[7]

**On The Tiles** *David Brown* a45 59
2 gr c Royal Applause Secret Night (Dansili)
3148[8] 3881[7] 7113[7] 7753[10]

**Oor Jock (IRE)** *Adrian McGuinness* a62 87
6 ch g Shamardal(USA) Katdogawn (Bahhare (USA))
4949a[6] 5958a[3] 6369a[17]

**Ooty Hill** *Roger Charlton* 84
2 gr c Dubawi(IRE) Mussoorie (FR) (Linamix (FR))
(7380)

**Open Eagle (IRE)** *David O'Meara* a93 106
5 b g Montjeu(IRE) Princesse De Viane (FR) (Kaldoun (FR))
2073[10] 2991[9] 3962[15] 5465[5] (7125) 7440[4] (7641) (7718)

**Open The Red** *Amanda Perrett* a43 70
2 b g Lawman(FR) Acquainted (Shamardal (USA))
6874[3] 7134[12] 7371[10]

**Open Your Heart (GER)** *R Dzubasz* 98
3 ch c Samum(GER) Dramraire Mist (Darshaan)
3293a[5] 4007a[3] 5231a[9] 7323a[6]

**Opera Box** *Marcus Tregoning* a95 92
6 b m Singspiel(IRE) Annex (Anabaa (USA))
1299[7] ◆ 2010[4] 6106[4] 6855[3] 7531[4]

**Opera Buff** *Jose Santos* a83 78
5 b g Oratorio(IRE) Opera Glass (Barathea (IRE))
1811[3] 2490[4] 2920[2] 5083[6] 5825[6] 6721[6] 7129[4] 7419[11] 8193[3]

**Opera Fan (FR)** *Mark Johnston* a69 83
3 b f Cape Cross(IRE) Persian Belle (Machiavellian (USA))
(1661) 2009[3] 2719[5] 3116[3] 3391[5] 4540[4] (4979) 5353[3] 5670[5] 6206[2]

**Operateur (IRE)** *Ben Haslam* a64 74
6 b g Oratorio(IRE) Kassariya (IRE) (Be My Guest (USA))
1674[7] (2913) (3101) (3365) (3605) 3657[3] 4196[5]

**Ophir** *William Muir* a56 64
3 b g Nayef(USA) Ermine (IRE) (Cadeaux Genereux)
1809[8] 2221[6] 2690[7] 3711[9] 5011[9]

**Opinion (IRE)** *Chris Waller* 108
5 b g Oasis Dream Kiltubber (IRE) (Sadler's Wells (USA))
7653a[11]

**Opium Bullet** *Jozef Roszival* 79
3 b c Royal Applause Our Poppet (IRE) (Warning)
2006a[8]

**Opportuna** *Tom Dascombe* a47 70
2 b f Rock Hard Ten(USA) Veiled Beauty (USA) (Royal Academy (USA))
5128[2] 7278[4] 7658[7]

**O'Prado Ole (USA)** *Dale Romans* 102
4 ch c English Channel(USA) Mexican Moonlight (USA) (El Prado (IRE))
7324a[9]

**Optimystic (IRE)** *Andrew Balding* a51
2 ch f Exceed And Excel(AUS) Psychic (IRE) (Alhaarth (IRE))
7919[5] 8140[5] ◆

**Opt Out** *Alistair Whillans* a66 72
4 ch g Pivotal Easy Option (IRE) (Prince Sabo)
1565[7] 1759[6] 2167[9] 2473[9] 2514[11] (4004) 4256[4] 4487[2] 4861[3] 5168[7] 6013[14] 6478[9] 6836[6] 7248[10]

**Opus (IRE)** *Lucy Wadham* a59 50
5 br g Danehill Dancer(IRE) Mixed Blessing (Lujain (USA))
73$^{2}$ 657$^{4}$ 831$^{2}$ 1117$^{7}$ 1226$^{4}$

**Opus Dei** *John Murray* a55 49
7 b g Oasis Dream Grail (USA) (Quest For Fame)
6014$^{11}$ 6495$^{4}$ 7025$^{14}$

**Opus Too (IRE)** *Julia Feilden* a52 38
3 b g Lawman(FR) Jerez (IRE) (Lake Coniston (IRE))
2842$^{5}$ 4500$^{8}$ 5282$^{4}$ 5829$^{6}$

**Oracle Boy** *William Muir* a72 64
3 b g Mount Nelson Snow Princess (IRE) (Ela-Mana-Mou)
1353$^{11}$ 1793$^{11}$ 3326$^{5}$ 3819$^{7}$ (5402) 5596$^{6}$ 6119$^{4}$ (6899)

**Oracolo (IRE)** *David Simcock* a75 63
2 b g Cape Cross(IRE) Illuminise (IRE) (Grand Lodge (USA))
6838$^{8}$ 7638$^{3}$ (7867)

**Orage Noir (FR)** *H-A Pantall* a77 82
3 b c Astronomer Royal(USA) Atlantic Crossing (GER) (Observatory (USA))
600a$^{9}$

**O'Raghallaigh (IRE)** *Richard Fahey* a27
3 b f Papal Bull Kahyasi Moll (IRE) (Brief Truce (USA))
824$^{7}$ 1084$^{4}$ 1372$^{6}$

**Orangefield (FR)** *H-A Pantall* a50 84
3 b g Soave(GER) Moon Serenade (Key Of Luck (USA))
3809a$^{11}$

**Orator (IRE)** *F-H Graffard* a81 102
4 b c Galileo(IRE) Airwave (Air Express (IRE))
4561a$^{DSQ}$

**Oratorio's Joy (IRE)** *Jamie Osborne* a82 76
4 b f Oratorio(IRE) Seeking The Fun (USA) (Alhaarth (IRE))
160$^{4}$ 350$^{2}$ 514$^{7}$ 2012$^{7}$ 2750$^{5}$ 3176$^{3}$ (3616) 4030$^{3}$ 4434$^{9}$ 7998$^{5}$ 8169$^{2}$ (8264)

**Orbec (FR)** *J-C Rouget* 109
3 b c Le Havre(IRE) Langrune (IRE) (Fasliyev (USA))
2194a$^{4}$

**Orbit The Moon (IRE)** *Michael Dods* a54 83
6 b g Oratorio(IRE) Catch The Moon (IRE) (Peintre Celebre (USA))
1447$^{3}$ ◆ 1672$^{2}$ 1839$^{2}$ 2332$^{7}$ 2602$^{9}$ 3483$^{7}$ 4108$^{12}$ 5088$^{11}$

**Orchestra (IRE)** *A P O'Brien* 112
3 b c Galileo(IRE) Bywayofthestars (Danehill (USA))
(2087) 2990$^{12}$ 3739a$^{3}$

**Ordensritter (GER)** *Chris Down* a93 79
6 ch g Samum(GER) Dramraire Mist (Darshaan)
(818) 1043$^{2}$ 1213$^{7}$ 2011$^{4}$ 2482$^{7}$

**Order Of Service** *Jim Goldie* a85 77
4 ch g Medicean Choir Gallery (Pivotal)
1762$^{6}$ 2453$^{6}$ 3050$^{5}$ (3660) 4001$^{2}$ 4258$^{7}$ 4729$^{4}$ 5562$^{5}$ 5895$^{6}$ 6478$^{5}$ 6795$^{6}$ (7248) (7821) 8257$^{4}$

**Order Of St George (IRE)** *A P O'Brien* 102
2 b c Galileo(IRE) Another Storm (USA) (Gone West (USA))
7104$^{5}$

**Orders From Rome (IRE)** *Charlie Fellowes* a66 43
5 b g Holy Roman Emperor(IRE) Fatat Alarab (USA) (Capote (USA))
1799$^{3}$ 2721$^{8}$ 3160$^{7}$ 4266$^{3}$ 4911$^{2}$ 5560$^{7}$

**Oregon Gift** *Mark Johnston* a78 68
2 b g Major Cadeaux Dayville (USA) (Dayjur (USA))
2214$^{4}$ 4044$^{2}$ 4416$^{4}$ 4885$^{5}$ 6976$^{3}$ 7739$^{2}$ 7834$^{2}$ (7927)

**Orgilgo Bay (IRE)** *John C McConnell* 96
4 b g Lawman(FR) Third Dimension (FR) (Suave Dancer (USA))
7476a$^{20}$

**Oricano** *Karen Tutty* 48
2 ch f Arcano(IRE) Dhuyoof (IRE) (Sinndar (IRE))
3529$^{7}$ 4790$^{6}$ 5679$^{5}$ 6224$^{5}$ 7277$^{7}$

**Oriental Cavalier** *Mark Buckley* a40 47
8 ch g Ishiguru(USA) Gurleigh (IRE) (Pivotal)
40$^{7}$ 252$^{8}$

**Oriental Dream (IRE)** *Nigel Tinkler* 29
3 b c Shamardal(USA) Oriental Melody (IRE) (Sakhee (USA))
1608$^{12}$ 2204$^{7}$ 2741$^{6}$ 5321$^{12}$

**Oriental Fox (GER)** *Mark Johnston* 111
6 ch g Lomitas Oriental Pearl (GER) (Big Shuffle (USA))
1869$^{3}$ 2704$^{7}$ 3377$^{5}$ 3717$^{6}$

**Oriental Heights** *Jim Goldie* 44
3 b f Orientor Harrken Heights (IRE) (Belmez (USA))
4111$^{11}$ 5417$^{5}$ 5857$^{4}$ 6116$^{5}$ 6595$^{14}$

**Oriental Magic (GER)** *C Ferland* a92 94
3 bb f Doyen(IRE) Oriental Pearl (GER) (Big Shuffle (USA))
2584a$^{11}$ 4064a$^{3}$ 4955a$^{6}$ 6162a$^{7}$ 7736a$^{8}$

**Oriental Maid** *Brian Ellison* a22 50
3 b f Sakhee's Secret Julia Domna (Dominion)
346$^{8}$ 906$^{5}$ 1304$^{4}$ 1647$^{8}$

**Oriental Relation (IRE)** *James Given* a92 76
3 gr g Tagula(IRE) Rofan (USA) (Cozzene (USA))
183$^{2}$ (279) 1067$^{11}$ 1555$^{13}$ 1968$^{4}$ 2317$^{18}$ 3331$^{5}$ 4133$^{4}$ 4636$^{7}$ 5243$^{3}$ 6153$^{5}$ 6607$^{8}$ 7947$^{9}$ 8136$^{8}$

**Oriental Splendour (IRE)** *Roger Charlton* a70 74
2 br c Strategic Prince Asian Lady (Kyllachy)
4025$^{7}$ 5309$^{4}$ ◆ 5684$^{5}$ 6629$^{3}$ 7728$^{2}$

**Orient Class** *Paul Midgley* 79
3 ch g Orientor Killer Class (Kyllachy)
(1373) 1676$^{2}$ (1925) 4059$^{6}$ 4469$^{3}$ (6475) 6671$^{6}$

**Orienteer** *A Fabre* 98
3 b c Dansili Take The Hint (Montjeu (IRE))
6571a$^{5}$

**Orient Sky** *Paul Midgley* 58
3 b g Orientor Sister Eugenie (IRE) (Indian Lodge (IRE))
1192$^{9}$ 3935$^{4}$ ◆ 4019$^{11}$

**Orife (IRE)** *C Ferland* a88 98
7 b h Marchand De Sable(USA) Entente Cordiale (IRE) (Ela-Mana-Mou)
5222a$^{9}$

**Orion Des Charps (FR)** *G Collet*
2 b c Dobby Road(FR) Aurane De Ples (FR) (Marignan (USA))
8212a$^{11}$

**Orion Love** *H-A Pantall* 109
4 ch f Zamindar(USA) Okocha (GER) (Platini (GER))
2819a$^{7}$

**Orion's Bow** *John Gosden* a83 71
3 ch c Pivotal Heavenly Ray (USA) (Rahy (USA))
1795$^{7}$ 4130$^{8}$ (4612) 5258$^{4}$ 5930$^{6}$ 6609$^{10}$

**Orkney Island** *Charlie Appleby* 77
3 gr g Dubawi(IRE) Ronaldsay (Kirkwall)
3432$^{5}$

**Orlando Rogue (IRE)** *George Baker* a35 76
2 b c Bushranger(IRE) Boston Ivy (USA) (Mark Of Esteem (IRE))
2298$^{9}$ 3063$^{4}$ (4301) 6684$^{7}$ 7374$^{10}$

**Orlando Star (CAN)** *Roger Teal* a46 58
3 b g Henrythenavigator(USA) Clayton's Lass (USA) (Forest Camp (USA))
2058$^{7}$ 2847$^{8}$ 3329$^{3}$ 3821$^{5}$ 4324$^{7}$ 5183$^{8}$ 7355$^{9}$

**Ormer** *David Evans* a43 40
3 b f Kyllachy Authoritative (Diktat)
753$^{4}$ 960$^{8}$ 1098$^{6}$ 2694$^{14}$

**Orobas (IRE)** *Harry Whittington* a44 49
2 b g Dark Angel(IRE) Miss Mujadil (IRE) (Mujadil (USA))
2622$^{5}$ 4943$^{8}$ 5248$^{6}$ 5823$^{10}$ 6413$^{8}$ 7904$^{8}$

**Oromo (FR)** *J Phelippon* a93 96
3 b g Elusive City(USA) Hamida (USA) (Johannesburg (USA))
5482a$^{6}$

**Oro Negro (FR)** *E Nicoleau* a34 12
2 ch g Naaqoos Impudica (URU) (Mo Rum (USA))
8149a$^{14}$

**Orpello (IRE)** *Stefano Botti* 107
5 b h Orpen(USA) Princess Angelina (IRE) (Almutawakel)
(1603a) 2191a$^{6}$ 3047a$^{8}$ 6590a$^{7}$

**Orpen'Arry (IRE)** *Paul Burgoyne* a65 66
6 b g Orpen(USA) Closing Time (IRE) (Topanoora)
737$^{2}$ 989$^{3}$ 1232$^{2}$ 1771$^{12}$

**Orpsie Boy (IRE)** *Ruth Carr* a69 73
11 b g Orpen(USA) Nordicolini (IRE) (Nordico (USA))
2171$^{5}$ 3000$^{6}$ (3339) 4156$^{5}$ 5168$^{3}$ 5887$^{6}$ 6767$^{6}$

**Orsino (GER)** *R Rohne* 109
7 b h Mamool(IRE) Orosole (GER) (Platini (GER))
(2374a) 3047a$^{2}$ 6590a$^{4}$

**Ortac Rock (IRE)** *Richard Fahey* a78 81
5 b g Aussie Rules(USA) Fashion Guide (IRE) (Bluebird (USA))
5913$^{4}$ ◆ 6789$^{3}$ ◆ 7282$^{10}$ 7687$^{8}$ 8097$^{3}$ 8268$^{5}$

**Orwellian** *Bryan Smart* a55 75
5 b g Bahamian Bounty Trinny (Rainbow Quest (USA))
34$^{3}$ ◆ 273$^{6}$ 384$^{2}$ (864) 934$^{8}$ (2296) 2914$^{3}$ 4523$^{2}$ 4707$^{4}$ 6405$^{3}$ 6543$^{2}$ 7077$^{5}$ ◆ (7180) 7647$^{5}$

**Oryetta (USA)** *G Botti* a74 87
3 b f Henrythenavigator(USA) Storm The Church (USA) (Pulpit (USA))
3513a$^{2}$

**Osaila (IRE)** *Richard Hannon* 108
2 b f Danehill Dancer(IRE) Mennetou (IRE) (Entrepreneur)
2888$^{2}$ 3415$^{5}$ (4348) (4646) 6372a$^{5}$ (6924) 7592a$^{3}$

**Osaruveetil (IRE)** *William Haggas* a84
3 b g Teofilo(IRE) Caraiyma (IRE) (Shahrastani (USA))
(7349) ◆

**Oscars Journey** *J R Jenkins* a62 72
4 ch g Dubai Destination(USA) Fruit Of Glory (Glory Of Dancer)
2159$^{4}$ 2951$^{5}$ 4981$^{4}$ 5290$^{3}$ 5860$^{4}$ 6983$^{4}$ (7213)

**Oscuro** *Tim Easterby* 52
3 b g Manduro(GER) Jabbara (IRE) (Kingmambo (USA))
2236$^{5}$ 2899$^{7}$ 3789$^{13}$

**Osgood** *Gary Moore* a48 55
7 b g Danehill Dancer(IRE) Sabreon (Caerleon (USA))
405$^{10}$ 2916$^{11}$ 3521$^{3}$ 6768$^{8}$

**Oskar Denarius (IRE)** *Marcus Tregoning* a62 57
3 b g Authorized(IRE) Elizabethan Age (FR) (King's Best (USA))
2031$^{5}$ 5044$^{5}$ 6018$^{8}$

**Osmior (IRE)** *G Botti* a70
3 b c Excellent Art Sersoura (FR) (Dalakhani (IRE))
194a$^{8}$ 390a$^{9}$

**Osorios Trial** *Kevin Frost* a49 49
7 ch g Osorio(GER) Skytrial (USA) (Sky Classic (CAN))
7290$^{8}$ 7369$^{11}$

**Osteopathic Remedy (IRE)** *Michael Dods* a81 100
10 ch g Inchinor Dolce Vita (IRE) (Ela-Mana-Mou)
1442$^{15}$ 1958$^{4}$ 2362$^{12}$ 2869$^{7}$ 3437$^{6}$ 4212$^{10}$ (4922) 5771$^{3}$ 6534$^{11}$ 7081$^{8}$ 7490$^{3}$

**Ostinato (GER)** *Andreas Lowe* a98 100
6 b h Ransom O'War(USA) Oxotica (GER) (Subotica (FR))
6589a$^{5}$

**Ostralegus** *John Gallagher* a70 68
4 b g Choisir(AUS) Midnight Pearl (USA) (Woodman (USA))
(119) 255$^{6}$ 1021$^{6}$ 1297$^{5}$ 1689$^{2}$ 2250$^{5}$ 2841$^{5}$ 6617$^{10}$ (7346) 7633$^{12}$ 7842$^{7}$ 8017$^{9}$ 8195$^{9}$

**Ottavino (IRE)** *Jane Chapple-Hyam* a24 15
5 b g Piccolo Indian's Feather (IRE) (Indian Ridge)
5731$^{7}$

**Otterbridge** *Rod Millman* a41 48
3 ch f Avonbridge Amazing Dream (IRE) (Thatching)
6482$^{6}$ 7024$^{6}$ 7818$^{8}$ 7982$^{6}$

**Ottoman Empire (FR)** *S Seemar* a105 104
8 ch g Pivotal Chesnut Bird (IRE) (Storm Bird (CAN))
108a$^{3}$ (394a) 807a$^{4}$ 901a$^{11}$

**Oud Malakiy (IRE)** *Richard Fahey* 46
2 b f Iffraaj Majestic Desert (Fraam)
2200$^{6}$ 3223$^{7}$

**Oui Monsieur (FR)** *Robert Collet* a67 78
2 b c Whipper(USA) Calasetta (IRE) (Montjeu (IRE))
3029a$^{3}$ 6958a$^{10}$ (8149a) 8212a$^{2}$

**Our Boy Jack (IRE)** *Richard Fahey* a60 95
5 b g Camacho Jina (IRE) (Petardia)
1451$^{6}$ 1646$^{2}$ 1957$^{9}$ 2548$^{P}$ 4156$^{11}$ 4923$^{2}$ 5915$^{6}$ (7060) 7236$^{10}$ 7490$^{7}$ 7719$^{18}$

**Our Channel (USA)** *William Haggas* 107
3 ch c English Channel(USA) Raw Gold (USA) (Rahy (USA))
(1652) 2990$^{13}$ 4230a$^{2}$ 4851$^{8}$ 6185a$^{2}$

**Our Folly** *Stuart Kittow* a46 79
6 b g Sakhee(USA) Regent's Folly (IRE) (Touching Wood (USA))
1418$^{2}$ 2482$^{5}$ 3851$^{2}$ 4818$^{3}$ 5341$^{4}$ 6360$^{3}$ 7129$^{9}$ 7566$^{4}$

**Our Gabrial (IRE)** *Richard Fahey* a86 95
3 b g Rock Of Gibraltar(IRE) Jojeema (Barathea (IRE))
(166) 301$^{2}$ 2088$^{4}$ 2839$^{5}$ 3243$^{13}$ (3643) 4162$^{2}$ 4651$^{2}$ (5164) 5691$^{8}$ 6127$^{12}$ 6737$^{15}$ 7106$^{11}$ 7703$^{5}$

**Our Golden Girl** *Shaun Lycett* a61 51
4 ch f Dutch Art Nemorosa (Pivotal)
278$^{2}$ 590$^{7}$ 821$^{9}$ 2916$^{5}$ 3404$^{5}$ 4107$^{8}$

**Our Grey Lady** *Bill Turner* a16 56
3 gr f Proclamation(IRE) Just Run (IRE) (Runnett)
4873$^{2}$ 5775$^{7}$ 6356$^{3}$ 6815$^{7}$ 7285$^{8}$

**Our Ivor** *Michael Appleby* a87 81
5 gr g Cape Town(IRE) Caprice (Mystiko (USA))
172$^{8}$ 550$^{6}$ 1886$^{4}$ 2251$^{9}$

**Our Kylie (IRE)** *Tony Coyle* 68
2 b f Jeremy(USA) Prakara (IRE) (Indian Ridge)
2736$^{4}$ 3267$^{8}$ 3542$^{2}$ 4467$^{12}$ 6691$^{5}$ (6869)

**Our Phylli Vera (IRE)** *Alan King* a45 80
5 b m Motivator With Colour (Rainbow Quest (USA))
1910$^{5}$ 7452$^{3}$

**Our Queenie (IRE)** *Richard Hannon* a78 93
3 ch f Strategic Prince Matibibi (ITY) (Barathea (IRE))
2965$^{3}$ 3674$^{3}$ 4163$^{4}$ 4669$^{4}$ 5152$^{5}$ 5675$^{7}$ 6607$^{9}$ 7196$^{9}$ 7451$^{3}$

**Our Red Devil (IRE)** *David Simcock* a44
3 ch g Dandy Man(IRE) Candela Bay (IRE) (Captain Rio)
354$^{5}$

**Our Time Will Come (IRE)** *John Quinn* 53
2 b f Rock Of Gibraltar(IRE) Signorina Cattiva (USA) (El Gran Senor (USA))
4389$^{7}$

**Outback (FR)** *D Sepulchre* 8
3 b g Muhtathir Olympic Skater (IRE) (Loup Solitaire (USA))
5370a$^{12}$

**Outbacker (IRE)** *Mark Johnston* a80 67
3 b f Aussie Rules(USA) Naomh Geileis (USA) (Grand Slam (USA))
(140) 850$^{4}$ 1136$^{2}$ 1225$^{3}$ 1614$^{11}$ 2090$^{10}$ 2474$^{7}$ 2929$^{9}$ 3405$^{2}$ 3581$^{2}$ 3956$^{5}$ 4262$^{8}$ 4997$^{5}$ 6223$^{2}$ 6578$^{5}$ 6945$^{9}$ 7459$^{3}$

**Outback Ruler (IRE)** *Clive Cox* 75
2 gr c Aussie Rules(USA) My American Beauty (Wolfhound (USA))
2146$^{7}$ 2623$^{3}$ 4129$^{5}$ 4944$^{3}$ 5782$^{2}$ 6375a$^{9}$ 7379$^{5}$

**Outback Traveller (IRE)** *Jeremy Noseda* a87 110
3 b c Bushranger(IRE) Blue Holly (IRE) (Blues Traveller (IRE))
1390$^{2}$ (3480) 3917$^{5}$ (4912) 5728$^{3}$ 6207$^{5}$ (6895)

**Outback Warrior (IRE)** *Kevin Ryan* a65 51
3 b c Bushranger(IRE) Choice House (USA) (Chester House (USA))
316$^{10}$ 1090$^{2}$

**Outbid** *Tony Carroll* a57 56
4 ch f Auction House(USA) Thicket (Wolfhound (USA))
244$^{10}$ 448$^{10}$ 797$^{4}$ (937) 972$^{3}$ 1270$^{9}$ 2008$^{9}$ 2831$^{6}$ (3784) 4101$^{5}$

**Out Do** *David O'Meara* a103 104
5 ch g Exceed And Excel(AUS) Ludynosa (USA) (Cadeaux Genereux)
1975$^{11}$ 2254$^{9}$ ◆ 2562$^{8}$ 3271$^{2}$ 3483$^{2}$ 4384$^{3}$ 4683$^{5}$ 4976$^{3}$ (5445) 6327$^{9}$ 7122$^{8}$ 7700$^{11}$ (7923) 8101$^{9}$

**Outer Space** *Jamie Osborne* a92 86
3 b g Acclamation Venoge (IRE) (Green Desert (USA))
1518$^{7}$ 1952$^{5}$ 2317$^{17}$ 4146$^{14}$ 4609$^{5}$ 4898$^{7}$ (5553) 6607$^{3}$ 6895$^{6}$ 7663$^{4}$ 7852$^{3}$ 8116$^{4}$

**Outlaw Country (IRE)** *Charlie Appleby* 93
2 br c Teofilo(IRE) Neverletme Go (IRE) (Green Desert (USA))
2308$^{3}$ (6203) 6925$^{2}$

**Outlawed** *Ed Walker* a83 87
3 b c Kyllachy Regent's Park (Green Desert (USA))
2733$^{3}$ (3083) (3672)

**Outlaw Kate (IRE)** *Michael Mullineaux* a31 31
2 b f Bushranger(IRE) Diosper (USA) (Diesis)
7493$^{5}$ 7712$^{11}$ 8060$^{10}$

**Outlaw Torn (IRE)** *Richard Guest* a69 66
5 ch g Iffraaj Touch And Love (IRE) (Green Desert (USA))
(67) 171$^{4}$ 406$^{8}$ 643$^{5}$ 733$^{6}$ 1085$^{5}$ 1167$^{2}$ 1673$^{2}$ 2215$^{3}$ (2518) 3190$^{8}$ 3333$^{5}$ 3463$^{2}$ 3718$^{9}$ 4197$^{2}$ 4293$^{9}$ 4661$^{10}$ 4858$^{7}$ 4903$^{4}$ 5640$^{4}$ 6160$^{4}$ 6601$^{2}$ 6795$^{3}$ 6865$^{6}$ 7288$^{3}$ 7522$^{5}$

**Out Of Aces** *Kevin Ryan* a34 10
2 ch c Piccolo Subtle Move (USA) (Known Fact (USA))
5799$^{11}$ 6474$^{7}$ 7329$^{8}$ 7992$^{10}$

**Out Of Bounds (USA)** *Saeed bin Suroor* a110 110
5 ch h Discreet Cat(USA) Unbridled Elaine (USA) (Unbridled's Song (USA))
2223$^{5}$ 4437$^{5}$ 6257$^{5}$

**Out Of Orbit** *Mark Gillard* 2
3 b f Manipulator(IRE) Into Orbit (Safawan)
4677$^{10}$ 6087$^{10}$

**Outrageous Request** *William Stone* a77 74
8 ch g Rainbow Quest(USA) La Sorrela (IRE) (Cadeaux Genereux)
567$^{3}$ 1043$^{5}$ 1418$^{8}$ 1849$^{4}$ 2272$^{9}$

**Outstrip** *Charlie Appleby* 119
3 rg c Exceed And Excel(AUS) Asi Siempre (USA) (El Prado (IRE))
1951$^{14}$ 3320$^{3}$ 4779$^{4}$ 6710$^{8}$

**Overlord** *Sir Mark Prescott Bt* a56 48
2 b g Lawman(FR) Hip (Pivotal)
4885$^{7}$ 5184$^{4}$ 5874$^{12}$ 7258$^{7}$

**Overrider** *Shaun Lycett* a62 50
4 b g Cockney Rebel(IRE) Fustaan (IRE) (Royal Applause)
(964) 1923$^{6}$ 4798$^{8}$ 5797$^{11}$ 5977$^{9}$ 7188$^{12}$ 7845$^{10}$ (7976)

**Overrule (USA)** *Chris Bealby* a51 52
10 b g Diesis Her Own Way (USA) (Danzig (USA))
1248$^{6}$

**Overstone Lass (IRE)** *John Spearing* a12 22
2 b f Excellent Art Clinging Vine (USA) (Fusaichi Pegasus (USA))
1732$^{8}$ 2622$^{9}$ 3467$^{10}$ 7487$^{6}$ 7991$^{7}$

**Over The Ocean (USA)** *Niels Petersen* a102 91
4 rg c Rockport Harbor(USA) Endless Sea (CAN) (Mt. Livermore (USA))
(2244a) 3996a$^{2}$ 4957a$^{6}$ 6387a$^{5}$

**Oxsana** *William Haggas* a91 94
3 b f Dubawi(IRE) Turning Leaf (IRE) (Last Tycoon)
203a$^{7}$ 506a$^{6}$ 3357$^{22}$ 4436$^{3}$ 5468$^{3}$ 6892$^{10}$

**Oyster (IRE)** *Nick Littmoden* a66 66
3 br f Diamond Green(FR) Lost Icon (IRE) (Intikhab (USA))
2417$^{8}$ 2998$^{2}$ 3978$^{3}$ 4547$^{3}$ 4863$^{4}$ 6636$^{4}$ 7358$^{11}$ 8102$^{12}$

**Ozz** *James Unett* 66
5 gr m Aussie Rules(USA) Spicey (Mizoram (USA))
2174$^{12}$

**Pablo Del Monte (USA)** *Wesley A Ward* a103 93
3 ch c Giant's Causeway(USA) One Hot Wish (USA) (Bring The Heat (USA))
2357a$^{6}$

**Pabusar** *Ann Stokell* a91 101
6 b g Oasis Dream Autumn Pearl (Orpen (USA))
80$^{4}$ 381$^{5}$ 452$^{2}$ 658$^{9}$ 863$^{5}$ 1020$^{10}$ 1244$^{5}$ 1630$^{6}$ 2400$^{7}$ 2905$^{6}$ 3402$^{9}$ 4545$^{3}$ 4714$^{2}$

**Pachadargent (FR)** *F Rossi* 103
3 b g Kendargent(FR) Sabasha (FR) (Xaar)
5591a$^{4}$ 7189a$^{6}$

**Pacific Heights (IRE)** *Brian Ellison* a73 106
5 b g Galileo(IRE) Song To Remember (USA) (Storm Cat (USA))
2113$^{3}$ (2758) 3356$^{11}$ 4214$^{8}$ 4648$^{7}$ 4949a$^{3}$ 6124$^{11}$ 6752$^{11}$

**Pacific Trip** *Andrew Balding* a50 37
3 b g Tagula(IRE) Marajuana (Robellino (USA))
2883$^{7}$ 3754$^{6}$ 4733$^{10}$ 5005$^{6}$ 6087$^{7}$

**Pacify** *Ralph Beckett* a71
2 b g Paco Boy(IRE) Supereva (IRE) (Sadler's Wells (USA))
(7731)

**Packed House** *Ralph Beckett* a54
2 b f Azamour(IRE) Riotous Applause (Royal Applause)
7833$^{8}$ 8191$^{5}$

**Packing Whiz (IRE)** *C Fownes* 119
6 ch g Trade Fair Swizzle (Efisio)
7898a$^{10}$

**Pack Leader (IRE)** *Amanda Perrett* 92
3 b g Hurricane Run(IRE) Bright Enough (Fantastic Light (USA))
2466$^{2}$ (3031) 3587$^{2}$ 4893$^{12}$ 5164$^{8}$ 5757$^{3}$ 6656$^{5}$ 7135$^{4}$

**Pack Together** *Richard Hannon* 94
2 b f Paco Boy(IRE) New Assembly (IRE) (Machiavellian (USA))
(3076) ◆ 4585$^{2}$

**Pacngo** *Tim Easterby* 60
2 b f Paco Boy(IRE) Orange Pip (Bold Edge)
4450$^{4}$ 4919$^{3}$ 5789$^{3}$ 6427$^{7}$

**Paco Keed (FR)** *Y Gourraud* a63 87
3 b c Lawman(FR) Freezing (USA) (Bering)
5370a$^{7}$

**Pacolita (IRE)** *Sylvester Kirk* a65 67
2 ch f Paco Boy(IRE) Clara (IRE) (In The Wings)
7192$^{10}$ 7511$^{3}$ 7752$^{3}$ 8007$^{8}$

**Paco Royale** *Agostino Affe'* 59
2 b c Paco Boy(IRE) Ile Royale (Royal Applause)
7147a$^{6}$

**Paco's Dream** *Harry Dunlop* 55
2 b f Paco Boy(IRE) Isle Of Flame (Shirley Heights)
2771$^{11}$ 3467$^{5}$ 3934$^{9}$ 4178$^{6}$ 5180$^{5}$ 6040$^{12}$ 6250$^{8}$

**Paco's Sunshine (IRE)** *Brian Ellison* 64
2 b f Paco Boy(IRE) Nuage Irise (Rainbow Quest (USA))
4751$^{2}$ ◆ 6375a$^{23}$

**Pacquita** *Mark Johnston* a60 50
3 b f Dubawi(IRE) Pryka (ARG) (Southern Halo (USA))
(267) 473$^{6}$

**Pact** *Lee Carter*
2 b f Paco Boy(IRE) Jade Pet (Petong)
6603$^{14}$

**Pactolus (IRE)** *Stuart Williams* a75 76
3 b g Footstepsinthesand Gold Marie (IRE) (Green Desert (USA))
(291) ◆ 3067$^{3}$ 3672$^{5}$ 4404$^{3}$ 5727$^{4}$ 6263$^{4}$ ◆

**Paddy Again (IRE)** *Bill Turner* a42 74
2 b f Moss Vale(IRE) Belle Watling (IRE) (Street Cry (IRE))
1161$^{2}$ (1342) 1982$^{4}$ 2403$^{5}$ 6739$^{7}$ 7038$^{8}$ 7255$^{9}$

**Paddys Motorbike (IRE)** *David Evans* 78
2 ch c Fast Company(IRE) Saffa Garden (IRE) (King's Best (USA))
3173$^{2}$ 3751$^{4}$ 4906$^{4}$ (5745) 6520$^{4}$ 7041$^{2}$

**Paddy's Rock (IRE)** *Ann Duffield* 70
3 b g Whipper(USA) Hedera (USA) (Woodman (USA))
3298[8] 3846[5] 4363[3] 5166[4] (5717) (5854) 6822[8]
**Paddys Runner** *Alan King* 26
2 gr g Sir Percy Frosty Welcome (USA) (With Approval (CAN))
5377[10]
**Paddy's Saltantes (IRE)** *J S Moore* a73 65
4 b g Redback Shall We Tell (Intikhab (USA))
*49[3] (229) 345[7] 578[5]*
**Padlock (IRE)** *David Simcock* a78
2 br c Key Of Luck(USA) Rumuz (IRE) (Marju (IRE))
*7076[4] (7911)*
**Paene Magnus (IRE)** *J S Bolger* a106 106
5 ch g Teofilo(IRE) Luminaria (IRE) (Danehill (USA))
2040a[4] *6909a[7]*
**Pafiya** *Kristin Stubbs* a51 52
2 b g Paco Boy(IRE) Tafiya (Bahri (USA))
5264[7] 6279[7] 6790[5] *7683[4] 7992[7]*
**Pageant Belle** *Roger Charlton* a85 80
3 ch f Bahamian Bounty Procession (Zafonic (USA))
(3916) 4551[6] *6145[2] 6681[6]* 7417[5]
**Pahente** *Tony Carroll* a54 42
6 bg g Silver Patriarch(IRE) Miss Tehente (FR) (Tehente (FR))
2770[11] 3556[10] *4737[9]* 5898[7] *7895[11] 8010[2]*
**Paid (SWE)** *Henrik Engblom* 81
4 ch f Eishin Dunkirk(USA) Lalla Top Top (SWE) (Mr Eubanks (USA))
6388a[10]
**Paige (USA)** *Donnie K Von Hemel* a97
2 ch f Sky Mesa(USA) Perfect Story (USA) (Tale Of The Cat (USA))
*6915a[3]*
**Painted Black** *Jane Chapple-Hyam*
3 br g Manduro(GER) Openness (Grand Lodge (USA))
7210[9] *7841[P]*
**Painted Tail (IRE)** *Andrew Crook* a24 62
7 b m Mark Of Esteem(IRE) Bronwen (IRE) (King's Best (USA))
3624[4] 5270[8] 6223[8] *6899[6]*
**Paint It Red (IRE)** *Richard Guest*
3 ch f Papal Bull Skerries (IRE) (Dr Fong (USA))
*7909[9]*
**Paint The Star (IRE)** *Richard Hannon* 72
2 b f Acclamation Art Work (Zafonic (USA))
2402[3]
**Paiza (IRE)** *H-A Pantall* a93 93
4 b c Zamindar(USA) Tobermory (IRE) (Green Desert (USA))
1207a[5]
**Palabre (USA)** *F Head* a76 82
3 ch f Giant's Causeway(USA) Quiet Royal (USA) (Royal Academy (USA))
*5294a[3]* 7722a[10]
**Palace (IRE)** *A P O'Brien* 104
3 b f Fastnet Rock(AUS) Lady Icarus (Rainbow Quest (USA))
2186a[2] 2581a[5] 2960[7] (4276a) 4461a[10] 5361a[4] 5955a[8] 6351a[10]
**Palace (USA)** *Linda Rice* a119
5 b h City Zip(USA) Receivership (USA) (End Sweep (USA))
*7612a[6]*
**Palace Art (IRE)** *Peter Casey* a59 63
4 b f Excellent Art Palace Star (IRE) (Desert Style (IRE))
*794a[9]*
**Palace Dragon (IRE)** *Sir Mark Prescott Bt* a68 63
3 b g Lawman(FR) Mayonga (IRE) (Dr Fong (USA))
*4085[5] 4970[3] (5280)*
**Palace Moon** *William Knight* a90 60
9 b g Fantastic Light(USA) Palace Street (USA) (Secreto (USA))
*294[3] 658[3] 1041[2]* 1492[12] 6891[17] *7375[9] 8072[10] 8251[9]*
**Palace Prince (GER)** *Andreas Lowe* 95
2 bb c Areion(GER) Palace Princess (GER) (Tiger Hill (IRE))
(4524a) 6123a[8]
**Palace Princess (FR)** *Ed Dunlop* a63 64
3 ch f Dubawi(IRE) Queen Of Norway (USA) (Woodman (USA))
1507[8] 1847[14] *2647[12]* 3124[6] 3627[4] *6716[3] 7078[8]* (7302)
**Palang (USA)** *Andreas Lowe* 107
2 bb c Hat Trick(JPN) Pavlova (USA) (Stravinsky (USA))
7721a[2]
**Palazzo Bianco** *Brian Ellison* a94 91
6 b g Shirocco(GER) White Palace (Shirley Heights)
2119[9] 2342[6] 3034[8] 3501[11]
**Pal Ella** *Keith Dalgleish* 24
3 ch f Byron Bridge Pal (First Trump)
3302[11] 4360[5] 7176[10] *7646[11]*
**Pale Mimosa (IRE)** *D K Weld* 112
5 b m Singspiel(IRE) Katch Me Katie (Danehill (USA))
2370a[3] (5652) 6374a[5] 6972a[3] 7486a[4]
**Palerma** *Mick Channon* 82
3 b f Shamardal(USA) West Lorne (USA) (Gone West (USA))
1422[8] 2560[3] (3277) 4782[9] 5401[5] 6459[2] 7416[5]
**Palladius** *M D O'Callaghan* a36 26
4 ch f Sakhee's Secret With Distinction (Zafonic (USA))
*1015[8]*
**Pallasator** *Sir Mark Prescott Bt* a96 115
5 b g Motivator Ela Athena (Ezzoud (IRE))
3962[2] (4696) ◆ 5693[4] ◆ 6374a[7] (6687) 7271[3]
**Pallister** *Mark Johnston* 95
2 b c Pivotal Punctilious (Danehill (USA))
2731[3] ◆ (3255) ◆ (3786) 4780[5] 5926[5] 7383[4]
**Palma Sola (FR)** *D Guillemin* a50
2 gr f Showcasing Finest Cape (Anabaa (USA))
*5844a[11]*
**Palm Frond** *Mlle L-L Rohn-Pelvin* a83 86
6 ch g Shirocco(GER) Palmeira (GER) (Lomitas)
*584a[6]*
**Pal Of The Cat** *Brian Gubby* a69 86
4 ch g Choisir(AUS) Evenstorm (USA) (Stephen Got Even (USA))
(1489) 1944[8] 3275[4]
**Paloma Dancer** *Harry Dunlop* a45 67
2 b f Refuse To Bend(IRE) Anapola (GER) (Polish Precedent (USA))
*5555[6] 6675[7]* 7493[2]
**Palus San Marco (IRE)** *Tony Carroll* a65 83
5 b g Holy Roman Emperor(IRE) Kylemore (IRE) (Sadler's Wells (USA))
*200[8] 450[10] 1022[8]* 1354[2] 1811[4] 2305[6] 3310[3] 3761[6] 7343[11]
**Pamona (IRE)** *Luca Cumani* 90
2 b f Duke Of Marmalade(IRE) Palanca (Inchinor)
6753[2] (7377)
**Pam Pam (FR)** *S Wattel* a81 78
3 b f King's Best(USA) Ponte Tresa (FR) (Sicyos (USA))
*5843a[10]*
**Pamushana (IRE)** *Richard Fahey* 69
2 b f Teofilo(IRE) Singitta (Singspiel (IRE))
4202[5] 5296[2]
**Panatella** *James Fanshawe* a77 69
3 b f Medicean Panna (Polish Precedent (USA))
5382[7] 6092[4] *6677[3] 7032[2] 7349[2] 7734[4] 7901[3]*
**Pancake Day** *Jason Ward* a55 50
2 b c Mullionmileanhour(IRE) Fangfoss Girls (Monsieur Bond (IRE))
5013[9] 5297[10] 5679[6] 6212[9] 6645[4] 7497[4] *7762[2] 7948[3] (8179)*
**Pandar** *Milton Bradley* a90 86
5 b g Zamindar(USA) Pagnottella (IRE) (Dansili)
*890[4] 1313[5]* 1489[9] (1944) 2283[13] 2992[14] 3697[4] 5350[4] 5444[14] 6089[6] 6736[2] 7132[8] 7507[13] *7687[8]*
**Panda Spirit (USA)** *Sir Michael Stoute* a80 85
2 b f Invincible Spirit(IRE) Towanda (USA) (Dynaformer (USA))
*2918[2] (3858)* 4619[2] 4913[8] (6499)
**Pan Di Stelle (FR)** *C Lerner* a76 76
3 b f Panis(USA) Orion Queen (FR) (Speedmaster (GER))
4464a[3]
**Pandora's Pyx** *Philip Hide* 17
2 b f Indesatchel(IRE) Hope Chest (Kris)
7377[14]
**Pandorica** *Bernard Llewellyn* a69 74
6 b m Indesatchel(IRE) Hope Chest (Kris)
2672[3] (2834) 3218[6] 3644[6] 4985[8] 7133[5] 7343[5]
**Panettone (IRE)** *Roger Varian* a63 71
5 b m Montjeu(IRE) Tea Break (Daylami (IRE))
(3540) 4045[4] 4617[8] 6787[8] *7527[4] 7932[8]*
**Pantella (IRE)** *R Storp* 30
6 b m Fasliyev(USA) Double Fantasy (GER) (Indian Ridge)
4038a[5]
**Panther Cat (ITY)** *Gianluca Bietolini* 98
2 b c Tale Of The Cat(USA) Committed Actress (USA) (Theatrical (IRE))
7479a[2]
**Panthero (FR)** *J Antoniello* 47
2 gr c Gentlewave(IRE) Panthesilea (FR) (Kendor (FR))
6385a[6]
**Panther Patrol (IRE)** *Eve Johnson Houghton* a85 82
4 b g Tagula(IRE) Quivala (USA) (Thunder Gulch (USA))
*91[9]* 1678[4] 2414[9] ◆ 3216[4] 3887[4] (4401) *(4545)* (5124) *(5559)* 6398[2] 6880[11] *7947[6]*
**Pantoloni** *Charlie Appleby* 49
3 b g Dansili Short Skirt (Diktat)
3465[4]
**Pants On Fire (USA)** *Kelly Breen* a109
6 bb h Jump Start(USA) Cabo De Noche (USA) (Cape Town (USA))
*7591a[3]*
**Panzi Potter Too** *Michael Dods* 34
3 gr f Winker Watson Toy Top (USA) (Tactical Cat (USA))
2420[4] 3343[9]
**Paola Lisa (FR)** *N Clement* a96 102
3 b f Pomellato(GER) Lost Ring (FR) (Bering)
7857a[2] *8300a[14]*
**Papagena Star (IRE)** *Markus Klug* 102
3 b f Amadeus Wolf Penelope Star (GER) (Acatenango (GER))
1619a[5] 3046a[4] (4064a) 4955a[8] 6806a[6] 7603a[12]
**Paparima (IRE)** *Paul Green*
3 b f Elnadim(USA) Daily Double (FR) (Unfuwain (USA))
2802[13] 3534[10]
**Papier** *Richard Hannon* a50 46
2 b f Paco Boy(IRE) Angus Newz (Compton Place)
2402[7] *3858[8]* 4499[10]
**Paple Blessing (IRE)** *David Bridgwater* a38 49
4 b f Papal Bull Pareesa (Dalakhani (IRE))
5904[8] *6486[8]* 6622[5]
**Paradise Child** *Bill Turner* a29 53
3 ch f Compton Place Halfwaytoparadise (Observatory (USA))
2045[5] 2802[12] 3087[12] 3564[12] 5034[7]
**Paradise Spectre** *Zoe Davison* a68 72
7 b g Firebreak Amber's Bluff (Mind Games)
2065[4] 2124[7] *2887[2]* 3077[2] *3854[8] 4050[8] 7202[11] 7735[9] 7853[5] 7986[8]*
**Parbold (IRE)** *Richard Fahey* 109
3 b g Dandy Man(IRE) Gala Style (IRE) (Elnadim (USA))
1514[5] 2343[4] ◆ 2767[3] 2961[2] 3352[17] 4127[3] 5609[10]
**Parfum De Roi (FR)** *Y-M Porzier* 64
3 b g King's Best(USA) Mieux Mieux (IRE) (Mark Of Esteem (IRE))
1620a[6] 3372a[9]
**Paris Carver (FR)** *Jonathan Portman* a56
2 b f Monsieur Bond(IRE) Rose Of Coma (IRE) (Kheleyf (USA))
*4542[4] 5133[5] 6017[3] 6412[2] 6676[4]*
**Parish (IRE)** *Roger Varian* 65
2 b g Dark Angel(IRE) Penicuik (Hernando (FR))
6875[9] 7414[4]
**Parish Hall (IRE)** *J S Bolger* a103 113
5 b h Teofilo(IRE) Halla Siamsa (IRE) (Montjeu (IRE))
1750a[6] 2040a[2] 3354[6] 3765a[2] (4477a) 5733a[3] 6352a[6] 6919[2] 8151a[10]
**Parisian Melody** *Mel Brittain* 35
3 b f Paris House Melandre (Lujain (USA))
3531[4] 3951[9]
**Parisian Pyramid (IRE)** *Lee Carter* a71 80
8 gr g Verglas(IRE) Sharadja (IRE) (Doyoun)
*53[2]* ◆ *147[2] 296[4] 347[5] 535[6] 714[5] 826[2] 4050[5] 4578[3]* 5138[3] (5247) (5422) 5726[5] 5951[2] 6263[2] 6657[6] 7159[14]
**Paris Snow** *Ian Williams* a61 88
4 b g Montjeu(IRE) Snow Key (USA) (Cozzene (USA))
*5961a[15] 7072[7]* 7508[9] *7822[12]*
**Park Dancer** *Martin Bosley* a48
7 b m Kier Park(IRE) Kerry Dancer (Ballet Royal (USA))
*660[9] 1025[6]*
**Park Glen (IRE)** *Noel Quinlan* 80
2 b f Tagula(IRE) Notley Park (Wolfhound (USA))
4589[6] (5086) (5845) 7121[6] 7503[3]
**Parkhill Star** *Tom Dascombe* a64 37
3 b f Araafa(IRE) Runaway Star (Superlative)
*127[6] 355[4] 512[4] 787[3] 1147[3]* 1611[11]
**Park Place** *John Quinn* a76 81
4 b g Beat Hollow Blend (Zafonic (USA))
2170[3] 5299[4] ◆ 6265[3] 6599[2] *(7812) 8290[5]*
**Parliament (IRE)** *Ann Duffield* 47
2 b g Fast Company(IRE) Yaselda (Green Desert (USA))
6146[7] 6449[10] 6859[F]
**Parole (IRE)** *Hughie Morrison* a66
2 ch c Mastercraftsman(IRE) Leniency (IRE) (Cape Cross (IRE))
*7660[8] 7892[7] 8067[6]*
**Parranda (USA)** *Jerry Hollendorfer* a108 107
5 ch m English Channel(USA) Dynamic Feature (USA) (Rahy (USA))
7607a[6]
**Parsley (IRE)** *Richard Hannon* 100
2 br f Zebedee Montefino (IRE) (Shamardal (USA))
2128[2] (2499) 3721[2] 4164[4] 4439[6] (5209) 5380[3] 6530[2] (7109) 7655a[10]
**Parsons Green** *Michael Attwater* a44
5 b m Sakhee(USA) Anastasia Venture (Lion Cavern (USA))
*185[10] 282[7] 580[7]*
**Par Three (IRE)** *Tony Carroll* a54 56
3 bb g Azamour(IRE) Little Whisper (IRE) (Be My Guest (USA))
*8114[5]*
**Partisan Politics (USA)** *Chad C Brown* 98
2 ch f More Than Ready(USA) Bluegrass Princess (USA) (Dynaformer (USA))
7592a[6]
**Partner's Gold (IRE)** *Alan Berry* a49 52
4 b c Red Clubs(IRE) Unfortunate (Komaite (USA))
*12[2] 171[12] 201[3] 351[3] 367[6] 1081[8] 2094[10]*
**Party Line** *Mark Johnston* 97
5 b m Montjeu(IRE) Party (IRE) (Cadeaux Genereux)
2294[6] 2785[11] 3204[7] 3424[6]
**Party Palace** *Stuart Howe* a40 57
10 b m Auction House(USA) Lady-Love (Pursuit Of Love)
*1232[10] 2084[9]* 5904[5]
**Party Royal** *Ruth Carr* a91 83
4 b g Royal Applause Voliere (Zafonic (USA))
*887[3] 1070[7] 1316[5] 1559[11]* 2085[8] 2362[10] 3463[3] 3573[4] 3955[7] 5999[2] 6490[3] *6770[3] 7186[8]*
**Parzival (IRE)** *G Botti* 76
2 b c Myboycharlie(IRE) Slyta (FR) (Slickly (FR))
5588a[2]
**Pasaka Boy** *Jonathan Portman* 98
4 ch g Haafhd Shesha Bear (Tobougg (IRE))
1653[8] 2253[4] 2991[4] 3730[9] 4400[4] 4917[4] 5757[2] 6786[2] (7110)
**Paschendale** *M Al Muhairi* a91 78
7 b h Refuse To Bend(IRE) Fading Light (King's Best (USA))
*243a[3]*
**Pas D'Action** *Mrs A Malzard* 60
6 ch g Noverre(USA) Bright Vision (Indian Ridge)
1623a[4] 2597a[4] 2594a[3] (4715a) 6187a[5]
**Pas De Cheval (IRE)** *Sir Michael Stoute* a70 69
3 ch g Pivotal Olympienne (IRE) (Sadler's Wells (USA))
2271[8] 4062[3] 4886[7] *5490[4] 6143[4]*
**Pas De Deux (GER)** *Yasmin Almenrader* 103
4 b g Saddex Palucca (GER) (Big Shuffle (USA))
7727a[10]
**Pashan Garh** *Pat Eddery* a55 73
5 b g Anabaa(USA) Mimisel (Selkirk (USA))
1190[5] 1980[4] 2669[6] 2833[2] 3646[5] *4580[8]* 5412[4] 5750[5] *7013[5]* 7157[3] 7339[7] 7494[5] 7600[10]
**Paso Doble (USA)** *Mark Fournier* a100 89
8 ch g Bold n'Flashy(CAN) Dance Lessons (USA) (Foxhound (USA))
7325a[5]
**Passaggio (ITY)** *A Cascio* 100
6 b h Exceed And Excel(AUS) Copious (IRE) (Generous (IRE))
2589a[3] 6808a[11]
**Passato (GER)** *Jo Davis* a39 49
10 b g Lando(GER) Passata (FR) (Polar Falcon (USA))
5435[4]
**Passiflore (FR)** *Mme Pia Brandt* 78
2 b f Siyouni(FR) Liwana (IRE) (Rainbow Quest (USA))
(7163a)
**Passing By** *Richard Hannon* a75 71
3 b f Raven's Pass(USA) Miss Anabaa (Anabaa (USA))
*(1107)* 2431[5] 3085[7] 4211[8] *4544[5]*
**Passing Star** *Charles Hills* a103 105
3 b c Royal Applause Passing Hour (USA) (Red Ransom (USA))
*(579) (854) (1122)* ◆ *1555[2]* ◆ 3352[14] 4826[5] 5609[17] *7555[13]*
**Passionada** *Ed McMahon* a73 65
5 bb m Avonbridge Lark In The Park (IRE) (Grand Lodge (USA))
*259[8]* 3222[5] 3921[3] 4511[3] 5375[8] *6273[4] 6897[9]*
**Passionate Affair (IRE)** *Jamie Osborne* a72 65
3 ch g Broken Vow(USA) Charmgoer (USA) (Nureyev (USA))
*1153[2] 1391[7]* 2363[7] *2997[2] (3471) 3711[8]* 4106[4] *4616[4]* 5121[3] *5556[4] 5829[4] 6043[5]*
**Passionate Appeal** *Ann Duffield* 55
2 b g Lawman(FR) Amaryllis (IRE) (Sadler's Wells (USA))
6147[6] 6449[6] 6976[4]
**Passionateshepherd (ITY)** *C Impelluso* 39
3 b f Blu Air Force(IRE) Palombella Rossa (IRE) (Fayruz)
1780a[14]
**Passion Blanche** *J-C Rouget* a93 96
3 b f Dutch Art Siren Sound (Singspiel (IRE))
*553a[3]* 6446a[5]
**Passion Du Tango (FR)** *T Larriviere*
5 ch m Vespone(IRE) Miss Lagoda (FR) (Sicyos (USA))
*178a[0]*
**Passion Play** *Bill Turner* a57 60
6 gr m Act One Addicted To Love (Touching Wood (USA))
*3472[9] 4051[7] 5011[8]* 5317[4] *6343[9]*
**Pass Muster** *Philip Kirby* a78 83
7 b g Theatrical(IRE) Morning Pride (IRE) (Machiavellian (USA))
(1599) 3240[10] 6404[3]
**Pass The Time** *Neil Mulholland* a59 57
5 b m Passing Glance Twin Time (Syrtos)
*(73) 278[7]*
**Past Forgetting (IRE)** *Luca Cumani* a83 73
3 b f Pivotal Brigitta (IRE) (Sadler's Wells (USA))
3755[4] 4984[2] *5831[4]* 6672[7] 7304[3] *7918[2] (8073)*
**Pasticcio** *Charlie Appleby* 77
2 ch c New Approach(IRE) Passe Passe (USA) (Lear Fan (USA))
4044[7] (4429) 5645[5] 6783[6]
**Pastoral Dancer** *Richard Rowe* a50 17
5 b g Pastoral Pursuits Dancing Flame (Groom Dancer (USA))
*81[2] 290[12] 592[9] 858[6]* 3422[10] *7887[12]*
**Pastoral Girl** *James Given* 95
2 b f Pastoral Pursuits Talampaya (USA) (Elusive Quality (USA))
2348[5] 3353[9] 3933[2] 4646[2] 6067[11] 6530[13] (7493)
**Pastoral Jet** *Richard Rowe* a65 25
6 bb h Pastoral Pursuits Genteel (IRE) (Titus Livius (FR))
*88[13] 852[7] 1387[10] 3233[5]*
**Pastoral Player** *Hughie Morrison* a67 114
7 b g Pastoral Pursuits Copy-Cat (Lion Cavern (USA))
2145[6] 3420[9] 4648[23] 4851[12] 5433[3] 6207[10] 6755[9] 7597[4] 7719[15]
**Pastoral Witness** *Clive Brittain* a54 66
3 b f Pastoral Pursuits Witness (Efisio)
*1404[5]* 2447[5]
**Pastureyes** *Scott Dixon* a54 74
4 ch f Milk It Mick Veils Of Salome (Arkadian Hero (USA))
1447[2] 2167[11] 2677[14] (4344) (5819) 6399[6] 6763[16] *7698[7]*
**Patavium (IRE)** *Edwin Tuer* a31 57
11 b g Titus Livius(FR) Arcevia (IRE) (Archway (IRE))
1374[4] 2055[11] 2620[9] 3398[2] 3843[4]
**Patavium Prince (IRE)** *Jo Crowley* a65 66
11 ch g Titus Livius(FR) Hoyland Common (IRE) (Common Grounds)
*603[12]*
**Patentar (FR)** *Marco Botti* a107 111
3 b c Teofilo(IRE) Poppets Sweetlove (Foxhound (USA))
1532[4] 2706[5] (6335) ◆ 6934[3] *7743[3]*
**Pathway To Honour** *Charlie Appleby* a80
2 ch c New Approach(IRE) Cheerleader (Singspiel (IRE))
*7730[2] 7985[2]*
**Patience Alexander (IRE)** *David Evans* a87 98
2 b f Kodiac Star Profile (IRE) (Sadler's Wells (USA))
*(1314)* (2313) 3415[3] 5173[4] 5608[6]
**Pat Mustard** *Jamie Osborne* a64 37
2 b g Royal Applause Umniya (IRE) (Bluebird (USA))
7037[8] 7155[7] *7400[7] (7753) 7832[4] 8206[4]*
**Patong (FR)** *Y Gourraud* a82 84
2 b c American Post Souraya (FR) (Kaldounevees (FR))
4932a[4] 6958a[8]
**Patriotic (IRE)** *Chris Dwyer* a92 74
6 b g Pivotal Pescara (IRE) (Common Grounds)
*342[5] 533[7] (767)* 3254[17] 4090[4] *5100[6]* 5533[6] 6232[8] 6865[3] 7339[4] 7567[9] *7870[3] 8144[5]* (8209)
**Patrona Ciana (FR)** *David O'Meara* a69 82
4 b f Falco(USA) Bavaria Patrona (FR) (Kahyasi)
(1760) ◆ 2318[7] *2398[5]* 3139[6] 3608[4] 4530[2] 5079[10] 5562[7] 6217[4] 6478[8]
**Patronella (IRE)** *David Simcock* a57 60
3 b f High Chaparral(IRE) English Ballet (IRE) (Danehill Dancer (IRE))
*542[5] 717[7] 1069[7]* 3230[8] 4152[4] 5522[2] *5833[4] 6939[9]*
**Patron Of Explores (USA)** *Patrick Holmes* a52 33
3 b g Henrythenavigator(USA) India Halo (ARG) (Halo Sunshine (USA))
2420[5] 2737[9] 3951[4] 4455[6] 4795[10] 5642[5] *8002[3] 8219[8]*

**Pat's Legacy (USA)** *Marjorie Fife* a68 68
8 ch g Yankee Gentleman(USA) Sugars For Nanny (USA) (Brocco (USA))
2607[3] 3299[6] 4058[6] 5142[5] 7061[3] 8137[2] ◆

**Pattaya (ITY)** *Stefano Botti* 107
6 b h Philomatheia(USA) Tirsa (Benny The Dip (USA))
2191a[9] 2374a[4] 3776a[2]

**Patterned** *Luca Cumani* 85
3 b f Dansili Paisley (Pivotal)
3153[5] (4029) 4782[3] 5448[5] 6746[9]

**Patty Fingers (IRE)** *Declan Carroll* a49 52
4 b f Ramonti(FR) Residual (IRE) (Trempolino (USA))
1348[4]

**Pavers Bounty** *Noel Wilson* a36 48
3 ch g Bahamian Bounty Pride Of Kinloch (Dr Devious (IRE))
2474[4] 3440[7] 7900[11]

**Pavers Star** *Noel Wilson* a61 66
5 ch g Pastoral Pursuits Pride Of Kinloch (Dr Devious (IRE))
1602[12] 1972[6] 2473[11] 3530[14] 3913[12] 4519[2] 4860[3] 5819[3] (6114) 6406[3] (6866) 7510[2]

**Pavlosk (USA)** *Sir Michael Stoute* 103
4 b f Arch(USA) Tsar's Pride (Sadler's Wells (USA))
1728[8] 2155[4] 4060[6]

**Paximadia (AUS)** *Saeed bin Suroor* a95 105
4 br c Commands(AUS) Latona (Fantastic Light (USA))
594a[7] 1178a[7]

**Pay Day Kitten (USA)** *D K Weld* 92
4 b f Kitten's Joy(USA) Annual Dues (USA) (Devil His Due (USA))
4746a[20]

**Pay The Greek** *Noel Quinlan* 38
3 b c Sleeping Indian To Grace (IRE) (Barathea (IRE))
374[10]

**Peace Accord** *Michael Wigham* a85 83
4 ch g Pivotal Embassy (Cadeaux Genereux)
(5797) (6120) (6240) 6495[2] (6890)

**Peace And War (USA)** *Olly Stevens* a102 85
2 b f War Front(USA) More Oats Please (USA) (Smart Strike (CAN))
(2644) ◆ 3415[6] 5131[2] (6915a)

**Peace At Last (IRE)** *H-A Pantall* a103 110
4 b c Oasis Dream National Day (IRE) (Barathea (IRE))
1371a[6] 2715a[2] 3511a[4] 4247a[6] 6054a[7] 6965a[3] (7327a)

**Peace Burg (FR)** *A P O'Brien* 113
4 b f Sageburg(IRE) Peace Talk (FR) (Sadler's Wells (USA))
2042a[2] 2572a[10] 3355[7] 3766a[5] 4165[3] 4478a[5]

**Peacemaker (IRE)** *Eve Johnson Houghton* a54 69
3 b f High Chaparral(IRE) Sauterne (Rainbow Quest (USA))
1352[8] 2013[3] 2936[8] 3559[7] 3978[5] 4333[3] 4834[7] 6461[7] 7162[9]

**Peace Mine (CAN)** *M Mace* 71
3 gr f Mineshaft(USA) Peace Dream (FR) (Linamix (FR))
1139a[7] 5368a[13]

**Peacenluvpeacenluv (USA)** *George Papaprodromou* a87 87
2 b r Artie Schiller(USA) No Serenading (USA) (Cure The Blues (USA))
7605a[2]

**Peace Palace** *Harry Dunlop*
3 b f Archipenko(USA) Mennetou (IRE) (Entrepreneur)
2883[11]

**Peace Seeker** *Anthony Carson* a94 94
6 b g Oasis Dream Mina (Selkirk (USA))
820[3] 1490[2] 1650[7] (2446) 2803[4] 4305[2] 4765[3] 5623[4] 6467[10] 6764[2] (7017)

**Peace Society (USA)** *A Wohler* 87
2 bb f Iffraaj Peace Royale (GER) (Sholokhov (IRE))
(6053a) 7315a[8]

**Peachez** *Seamus Durack* a72 49
6 ch m Observatory(USA) Streccia (Old Vic)
158[5] 742[6] 848[8] 4107[9]

**Peacock** *Richard Hannon* 101
2 b c Paco Boy(IRE) Rainbow's Edge (Rainbow Quest (USA))
(2776) 4645[5] 6291[3]

**Peadar Miguel** *Michael Mullineaux* a55 30
7 b g Danroad(AUS) La Corujera (Case Law)
7287[6]

**Peak Royale** *Richard Hannon* 81
3 b g Royal Applause Mountain Law (USA) (Mountain Cat (USA))
2383[5] 3185[6]

**Peak Storm** *John O'Shea* a45 76
5 b g Sleeping Indian Jitterbug (IRE) (Marju (IRE))
493[8] 2251[5] 2833[5] 3177[4] 3850[5] 4153[5] 5058[4] 5721[6] 6423[4] 7339[9]

**Pearl Acclaim (IRE)** *David Nicholls* a80 96
4 b g Acclamation With Colour (Rainbow Quest (USA))
1975[13] 2353[2] 5918[11] 6327[19] 7080[7] 7280[13]

**Pearl Bell (IRE)** *Olly Stevens* a53 50
4 b f Camacho Magnificent Bell (IRE) (Octagonal (NZ))
5181[5] 6215[6] 7117[7]

**Pearl Blue (IRE)** *Jamie Osborne* a56 100
6 b m Exceed And Excel(AUS) Sanfrancullinan (IRE) (Bluebird (USA))
1650[4] ◆ 2123[6] 2803[5] (4128) 5925[9] 7080[5] 7716[9] 8223[3]

**Pearl Castle (IRE)** *John Quinn* 99
4 b g Montjeu(IRE) Ghurra (USA) (War Chant (USA))
(3250) 4173[4] 5651[4] 6287[7]

**Pearl Diamond (GER)** *Waldemar Hickst* 92
2 b f Areion(GER) Pretty Su (IRE) (Surumu (GER))
7315a[5]

**Pearl Flute (IRE)** *F-H Graffard* a87 109
4 b g Piccolo Secret Melody (FR) (Inchinor)
308a[3] 597a[11]

**Pearl Ice** *Charlie Fellowes* a82 100
6 b g Iffraaj Jezebel (Owington)
1172[6] 1734[15] 2747[5]

**Pearlise (FR)** *Scott Dixon*
2 b f Milk It Mick Cora Pearl (IRE) (Montjeu (IRE))
1889[6] 2128[10] 2949[5]

**Pearl Nation (USA)** *Michael Appleby* a104 95
5 b g Speightstown(USA) Happy Nation (USA) (Lear Fan (USA))
153[5] 479[2] 689[5] 917[3] 1267[5] 1630[5] 2054[7] (3628) 4537[4] (5100) ◆ (6097) 6704[6] 7081[10] (8135) ◆

**Pearl Noir** *Scott Dixon* a73 62
4 b g Milk It Mick Cora Pearl (IRE) (Montjeu (IRE))
58[6] 95[3] 934[4] 1001[9] 1448[2] 2127[7] 2232[6] 2907[3] 3793[6] 3913[7] (4288) 4714[9] 6399[5] (6897) 7111[6] 7356[5] 7622[3] 7900[10] (8023) 8088[13]

**Pearl Of Africa (IRE)** *Edward Lynam* a99 108
4 b f Jeremy(USA) Kournikova (SAF) (Sportsworld (USA))
395a[3] 682a[3] 2185a[5] 2572a[5] 3766a[6] 5955a[2]

**Pearlofthequarter** *Jonathan Portman* a64 6
3 b f Rock Of Gibraltar(IRE) Run For Lassie (USA) (Fappiano (USA))
4434[11] 5512[12]

**Pearl Princess (FR)** *Olly Stevens* a71
3 b f Astronomer Royal(USA) Tambura (FR) (Kaldoun (FR))
930[4] 1107[3] 1498[2] (1805)

**Pearl Ransom (IRE)** *Alan Bailey* a70 67
4 b g Intikhab(USA) Massada (Most Welcome)
90[3] (467) 1023[4] 8190[2] (8298)

**Pearlred (FR)** *M Boutin* 76
2 b f Redback Cat's Pearl (FR) (Enrique)
3744a[5]

**Pearl's Azinger (IRE)** *David Barron* 70
2 gr f Zebedee Pearly Brooks (Efisio)
2725[4] (2949) 7231[7]

**Pearl Secret** *David Barron* 117
5 ch h Compton Place Our Little Secret (IRE) (Rossini (USA))
(1397) 1949[8] 2563[2] 3319[10] (5911) 6134[5] 6966a[14]

**Pearlside (FR)** *M Delcher Sanchez* 108
4 b f Alhaarth(IRE) Prickly Pearl (IRE) (Lahib (USA))
7916a[9]

**Pearl Spice (IRE)** *Tim Pitt* a81 83
4 ch g Dalakhani(IRE) Cinnamon Rose (USA) (Trempolino (USA))
1849[6] 2430[3]

**Pea Shooter** *David Nicholls* a81 87
5 b g Piccolo Sparkling Eyes (Lujain (USA))
5199[9] 5444[9] 5912[2] ◆ 6235[2] ◆ 6512[11] 7505[5] ◆

**Pedregalejo (IRE)** *P Van De Poele* a78 67
6 b g High Chaparral(IRE) Highphar (FR) (Highest Honor (FR))
3089a[5]

**Peeps** *Mark H Tompkins* 57
2 ch f Halling(USA) Twelfth Night (IRE) (Namid)
5187[6] 6694[7]

**Peewave (FR)** *W Hefter* 84
2 b c Gentlewave(IRE) Prairie Scilla (GER) (Dashing Blade)
5329a[3]

**Pegasus Bridge (FR)** *K Borgel* a53 73
4 gr c Slickly(FR) Tarkwa (Doyoun)
2192a[3]

**Peintre Setois (FR)** *F Foresi* a66
3 b c Archange D'Or(IRE) Genuine Lauren (USA) (Elusive Quality (USA))
482a[6]

**Pelagian (USA)** *Michael Attwater* a52 58
3 b g Henrythenavigator(USA) Japon (Alzao (USA))
2686[4] 3426[6] 5183[3] (6194) 7036[6] 7197[5]

**Pelerin (IRE)** *Marco Botti* a107 100
3 ch f Shamardal(USA) Fragrancy (IRE) (Singspiel (IRE))
1515[11] (1956) 2316[6] 3143[2] 3665[5] 5312[5] 6707[4] (7579a)

**Pelmanism** *Gay Kelleway* a71 76
7 b g Piccolo Card Games (First Trump)
364[2] 560[7] 698[7] 1167[10] 1711[11] 2124[8] 2164[5]

**Pembroke Pride** *Philip Hide* a51
4 b f Indesatchel(IRE) Elegia Prima (Mon Tresor)
189[9] 403[6] 660[11] 1012[5] 1210[4] 2419[6]

**Penalty Scorer** *Richard Guest* a49 51
2 ch f Captain Gerrard(IRE) Mindfulness (Primo Dominie)
1161[9] 1342[3] 1504[4] 1656[8] 3236[4] 3937[8] 4302[2] 4702[5] 4857[3] 4899[2] 5384[4] 5630[6] 5985[7] 6645[2] 6791[6] 7453[4] 7497[7]

**Penang Paparaja (IRE)** *Michael Bell* a59 49
2 b c Dansili Penang Pearl (FR) (Bering)
7407[7] 7660[7]

**Penara** *Philip Hide* a53 38
3 b f Archipenko(USA) Takegawa (Giant's Causeway (USA))
823[5]

**Penbryn (USA)** *Nick Littmoden* a65 25
7 b g Pivotal Brocatelle (Green Desert (USA))
156[2] 288[8] 464[7]

**Pencaitland** *Noel Wilson* 35
2 b f Champs Elysees Anthea (Tobougg (IRE))
2386[14] 3481[11] 3945[9] 6669[15]

**Pencil** *James Eustace* 58
2 b f Excellent Art Penelewey (Groom Dancer (USA))
5104[3] 5725[6]

**Pencil Hill (IRE)** *Tracey Collins* a64 82
9 b g Acclamation Como (USA) (Cozzene (USA))
3686a[4] 5958a[5]

**Pendley Legacy** *Clive Cox* a36 59
3 b f Leporello(IRE) Albavilla (Spectrum (IRE))
2418[6] ◆ 3141[9] 3652[8] 4970[9]

**Pendo** *Paul Cole* a74 75
3 b g Denounce Abundant (Zafonic (USA))
1008[9] 1404[4] 1769[6] 2429[13] 4579[4] (5873) 6242[2] 6616[2] 7358[7] 7633[4] 7829[12] 8068[7]

**Penelope Pitstop** *Keith Dalgleish* a53 57
2 b f Captain Gerrard(IRE) Obsessive Secret (IRE) (Grand Lodge (USA))
6790[3] 7097[7] 7421[3] 7648[5] 7904[4] 7999[2]

**Peng (ITY)** *Stefano Botti* 99
4 b c Docksider(USA) Pietrasanta (Singspiel (IRE))
3776a[9]

**Penglai Pavilion (USA)** *Charlie Appleby* 106
4 bb g Monsun(GER) Maiden Tower (Groom Dancer (USA))
900a[7] 1950[8] 2315[12] 6711[6] 7447[7]

**Penhill** *James Bethell* 96
3 b g Mount Nelson Serrenia (IRE) (High Chaparral (IRE))
1509[9] (1847) 2319[2] 3200[4] (4298) (4452) 5691[6] 6127[11] 7106[14]

**Peniaphobia (IRE)** *A S Cruz* 119
3 b g Dandy Man(IRE) Umlani (IRE) (Great Commotion (USA))
(7897a) 8152a[2]

**Penina (IRE)** *Brian Ellison* a27 70
3 b f Lawman(FR) Poussiere d'Or (IRE) (Grape Tree Road)
2218[5] 2545[2] 3575[9] 3668[3] 4370[5] 4795[9] 7178[7]

**Penitent** *David O'Meara* a96 117
8 b g Kyllachy Pious (Bishop Of Cashel)
1176a[14] 1698[3] 2185a[6] (2765) 2958[7] 3723[8] 4187[5] 5653[12] 6132[5] ◆ 6328[7] ◆ 6934[5]

**Penmaen (IRE)** *J E Hammond* 100
4 b f Pivotal Lady Grace (IRE) (Orpen (USA))
6378a[7] 6994a[3] 7656a[10]

**Pennine Panther** *Henry Candy* 78
3 b g Notnowcato Kozmina (IRE) (Sadler's Wells (USA))
2485[5] 3891[4] (5191) 5877[9]

**Pennine Warrior** *Scott Dixon* a73 82
3 b g Lucky Story(USA) Discoed (Distinctly North (USA))
1940[7] 2768[2] 3067[5] 4404[6] 5199[2] (5769) 6260[13] 7179[3] 7505[8] 8182[8] 8279[6]

**Penny Dreadful** *Scott Dixon* 57
2 b f Piccolo Trina's Pet (Efisio)
6496[6]

**Penny Drops** *William Haggas* a85 98
3 b f Invincible Spirit(IRE) Penny Cross (Efisio)
1713[2] (2125) 2556[2] 2961[3] 3724[2] 5438[4] 6929[3] 7268a[2] 7952[5]

**Penny Garcia** *Tim Easterby* a72 75
4 b f Indesatchel(IRE) Katie Boo (IRE) (Namid)
1247[5] 1903[10] 2890[6] 4132[6] 6150[6] 7178[4] (7506) 7993[5]

**Pennyking (FR)** *Frau Marion Rotering* 50
2 b c Sinndar(IRE) Pepperjuice (GER) (Big Shuffle (USA))
6385a[4]

**Penny Pepper (IRE)** *Eve Johnson Houghton* 74
2 b f Fast Company(IRE) Evening Time (IRE) (Keltos (FR))
4980[2] 5667[2]

**Penny Pursuits** *Alan Berry* 57
3 b f Pastoral Pursuits Sattelight (Fraam)
2553[3] 3054[9] 7501[13]

**Penny Royale** *Tim Easterby* 68
2 b f Monsieur Bond(IRE) Royal Punch (Royal Applause)
2014[10] 2788[7] 3394[4] 5266[2] 5714[3] 6253[11]

**Penny's Boy** *Simon Hodgson* a72 76
3 ch g Firebreak Sunderland Echo (IRE) (Tagula (IRE))
892[3] 1122[5] 1389[5] 1786[5] 2058[2] 2647[5] 3037[3] 3145[12] 3821[3] 4329[4] (4817) 5123[6] 6192[6] 6615[2] (6877) 7172[6] 7513[7] 8204[11] 8321[9]

**Penny Stock (IRE)** *Mark Johnston* a56 51
4 b f Dansili Beta (Selkirk (USA))
221[3] 303[9] 459[12]

**Pensax Boy** *Ian Williams* 73
2 b g Rail Link Cyclone Connie (Dr Devious (IRE))
3701[2] 4467[10] 5377[4]

**Pensax Lad (IRE)** *Ronald Harris* a75 74
3 gr g Verglas(IRE) Betelgeuse (Kalaglow)
2122[9] 2717[6] 3972[4] ◆ 4411[7] 5080[7] (5526) 7888[12] 8255[4]

**Pensierieparole** *B Grizzetti* 80
2 ch c Exceed And Excel(AUS) Pursuit Of Charge (Pursuit Of Love)
3775a[4]

**Pensionnat (IRE)** *Ralph Beckett* a54
2 b f Cape Cross(IRE) Surval (IRE) (Sadler's Wells (USA))
7658[5]

**Pentameter** *John Butler* a68 56
5 br g Dansili Tuning (Rainbow Quest (USA))
1119[2] 1491[10] 1899[11] 2270[18] 3308[10]

**Pepe Mi Amor (IRE)** *H-A Namur* a54
4 gr g Verglas(IRE) Miss Bali Dancer (IRE) (Mister Baileys)
722a[12]

**Pepito Grillo** *L A Urbano-Grajales* a77 84
6 b g Kheleyf(USA) Dena (Deploy)
5964a[6]

**Pepperello** *Tim Etherington* 43
3 b g Lucky Story(USA) Rhuby River (IRE) (Bahhare (USA))
2871[7] 3543[5] 5195[8] 6564[12] 6939[12] 7990[13] 8137[10]

**Per (FR)** *J-P Gauvin* a59
3 b c Elusive City(USA) Escolhida (IRE) (Montjeu (IRE))
720a[3]

**Perardua** *Richard Fahey* a61 79
2 ch f Cockney Rebel(IRE) Quiquillo (USA) (Cape Canaveral (USA))
1741[3] 2172[3] (2725) 3922[3] 4625[3] (5014) 5879[2] 6322[9] 7253[11]

**Perceived** *Henry Candy* 68
2 ch f Sir Percy New Light (Generous (IRE))
5351[7] ◆ 5981[5] 6646[4] (7208)

**Percella** *Hughie Morrison* a64 53
2 b f Sir Percy Temple Of Thebes (IRE) (Bahri (USA))
7018[7] 7685[3] 8092[3] 8317[6]

**Perceus** *Marcus Tregoning* a71 80
2 b c Sir Percy Lady Hestia (USA) (Belong To Me (USA))
6520[3] 7354[6] 7666[3] 7891[4]

**Perche** *Charlie Appleby* a66 66
2 ch c New Approach(IRE) Persian Filly (IRE) (Persian Bold)
7498[4] 7811[4]

**Perci French** *David O'Meara* a23 35
4 b g Tiger Hill(IRE) Annabelle Ja (FR) (Singspiel (IRE))
2913[5] 3308[11]

**Percy Alleline** *Ralph Beckett* a80 90
2 b g Sir Percy Dominica (Alhaarth (IRE))
(2487) 2845[4] 3751[3] 4670[4] 6229[5] 6684[5] 7131[2] 8241[2]

**Percybelle** *William Knight* a61 55
3 ch f Sir Percy Chelsea (USA) (Miswaki (USA))
7804[7]

**Percy's Dream** *William Jarvis* a33 23
2 b f Sir Percy Monaco Dream (IRE) (Hawk Wing (USA))
5644[9] 6268[9]

**Percy's Gal** *Karen Tutty* 79
3 ch f Sir Percy Galette (Caerleon (USA))
2130[7] 2737[2] 3343[3] 4019[3] 5055[4] 5641[2] (5997) 6692[9] 7178[2] 7505[3]

**Percy's Lass** *Brian Ellison* 58
2 gr f Sir Percy Brave Mave (Daylami (IRE))
3975[3] 4751[6]

**Percys Princess** *Michael Appleby* a79 26
3 b f Sir Percy Enford Princess (Pivotal)
1107[5] 5504[13] 6015[8] 6946[8] 7977[4] 8138[2] (8261)

**Percy Veer** *Sylvester Kirk* 65
2 ch g Sir Percy Fandangerina (Hernando (FR))
3748[7] (5072) 6250[3] 7328[11]

**Perdu** *Marcus Tregoning* a58
4 b g Sir Percy Misplace (IRE) (Green Desert (USA))
6485[7]

**Perdurable** *Charlie Fellowes* a14
2 br f Sakhee's Secret Pain Perdu (IRE) (Waajib (IRE))
6032[12]

**Perennial** *Philip Kirby* a91 84
5 ch g Motivator Arum Lily (USA) (Woodman (USA))
1935[6] 3192[3] 5017[8] 6099[7] 7422[11] 7702[12] 7822[9] 7990[3]

**Perestroika** *Henry Candy* 51
2 b f Sir Percy Lekka Ding (IRE) (Raise A Grand (IRE))
7377[10]

**Perfect Alchemy (IRE)** *Ralph Beckett* a81 88
3 b f Clodovil(IRE) Desert Alchemy (IRE) (Green Desert (USA))
(1409) 1952[8] 2745[9] (5211) 6607[6]

**Perfect Blessings (IRE)** *Clive Cox* 92
3 b f Kheleyf(USA) Yxenery (IRE) (Sillery (USA))
1422[3] (1713) 2564[3] 3245[5] 4171[8] 6922[12]

**Perfect Blossom** *Alan Berry* a58 80
7 b m One Cool Cat(USA) Perfect Peach (Lycius (USA))
1500[5] 1759[5] 3239[15] 3462[4] (3659) 3921[5] 4016[5] 4391[9] 4521[4] 5817[6] 6109[3] 6512[20] 6763[13] 7103[10]

**Perfect Bounty** *Clive Cox* a47
2 ch f Bahamian Bounty Perfect Cover (IRE) (Royal Applause)
6032[7] 7062[11] 7741[8] 8069[3]

**Perfect Concord** *Michael Blanshard* a22 21
2 b f Kheleyf(USA) Perfect Flight (Hawk Wing (USA))
2644[5] 4103[3] 4909[5]

**Perfect Cracker** *Clive Cox* a79 85
6 ch g Dubai Destination(USA) Perfect Story (IRE) (Desert Story (IRE))
79[6] 849[4] ◆ 1022[2] 2382[3] (3065) (3802) 4349[7] 5487[7] 6357[4]

**Perfect Fit (IRE)** *David Wachman* a65 80
2 ch f Teofilo(IRE) Queen Of Lyons (USA) (Dubai Destination (USA))
3763a[9]

**Perfect Girl (IRE)** *Tim Easterby* 54
2 b f Iffraaj Chatline (IRE) (One Cool Cat (USA))
3570[5] 3975[6] 4286[7] 6427[5] 6643[11] 7003[8]

**Perfect Glance (USA)** *Sir Michael Stoute* a71
2 bb f Rock Hard Ten(USA) Brief Look (Sadler's Wells (USA))
7756[3]

**Perfect Haven** *Clive Cox* a73 77
4 gr f Singspiel(IRE) Night Haven (Night Shift (USA))
84[6]

**Perfect Heart** *Roger Varian* a77 100
5 gr g Dalakhani(IRE) Maid To Perfection (Sadler's Wells (USA))
(1692) 3321[5]

**Perfect Legend** *Andrew Balding* a55
3 b g Norse Dancer(IRE) Flamjica (USA) (Real Quiet (USA))
5186[7] 5822[7] 6634[8]

**Perfect Light (IRE)** *William Haggas* 93
3 ch f Galileo(IRE) Beauty Bright (IRE) (Danehill (USA))
1701[6] 2310[5] (3434) (5713) 6464[8] 7105[16]

**Perfect Mission** *Andrew Balding* a70 78
6 b g Bertolini(USA) Sharp Secret (IRE) (College Chapel)
52[8] 161[5] 451[11] 3177[5] (3589) 4154[5] 4907[4] 5523[8] 5979[4] 6617[5]

**Perfect Muse** *Clive Cox* a54 95
4 b f Oasis Dream Perfect Echo (Lycius (USA))
1787[2] 2994[2] (3561) (4553) 6130[11] (6296) 7330[2]

**Perfect Orange** *Marcus Tregoning* a72 42
2 ch f Sir Percy La Peinture (GER) (Peintre Celebre (USA))
4825[9] 7398[3] 7756[2] 8016[5]

**Perfect Outcome** *Patrick Chamings* a59 26
3 b f Echo Of Light Cautiously (USA) (Distant View (USA))
3276[7] 4265[5] 5010[5] 5829[5] 6682[5] 8011[8] 8189[7]

**Perfect Pastime** *Jim Boyle* a62 75
6 ch g Pastoral Pursuits Puritanical (IRE) (Desert King (IRE))
*288[3] 428[11] 846[5] 1110[6] 1408[5]* 1668[5] (2723) 3328[7] *3528[DSQ] 4578[5]* (5518) 5951[3] 6266[11] 7215[2] (7342)

**Perfect Pasture** *Michael Easterby* a105 97
4 b g Pastoral Pursuits Word Perfect (Diktat)
*(55) 534[4] 8101[6]*

**Perfect Peak** *Michael Easterby*
2 ch f Distant Peak(IRE) Word Perfect (Diktat)
6453[14]

**Perfect Persuasion** *William Haggas* a90 87
3 b f Myboycharlie(IRE) Just Dreams (Salse (USA))
*3117[3]* ◆ 4367[2] 4668[7] 5656[4] ◆ 6459[3] *7196[2]*

**Perfect Print (IRE)** *Maurice Barnes*
5 b g Kodiac Naughtiness (Singspiel (IRE))
3601[8]

**Perfect Pursuit** *Clive Cox* a68 73
3 b f Pastoral Pursuits Perfect Cover (IRE) (Royal Applause)
*82[2]* 2278[9] *2929[4]* 3145[11] (3821)

**Perfect Rhythm** *Patrick Chamings* a68
3 b f Halling(USA) Bassinet (USA) (Stravinsky (USA))
*5007[7] 6033[7] 7032[5] 7744[3] 8029[4] 8202[6] 8313[5]*

**Perfect Romance** *Patrick Chamings* 48
5 ch m Singspiel(IRE) Flamjica (USA) (Real Quiet (USA))
2279[10] 2925[8]

**Perfect Slipper** *Noel Quinlan* a38 52
2 ch f Footstepsinthesand Perfect Peach (Lycius (USA))
*5509[7]* 6435[7] 7245[10]

**Perfect Son** *C Zeitz* a90 74
7 ch g Sabiango(GER) Pacific Blue (GER) (Bluebird (USA))
4776a[4]

**Perfect Summer (IRE)** *Lady Cecil* a85 85
4 b f High Chaparral(IRE) Power Of Future (GER) (Definite Article)
2139[2] (2327) 2782[9] 4423[3] *5825[4]* 7235[5] 7565[3]

**Perfect Ten (IRE)** *Anthony Mulholland* a56 47
3 b f Thousand Words La Galeisa (IRE) (Warning)
*7962a[9]*

**Perfect Timber (CAN)** *Roger L Attfield* 105
5 bb h Perfect Soul(IRE) Timber Ice (USA) (Woodman (USA))
6390a[7]

**Perfect Words (IRE)** *Marjorie Fife* a62 75
4 ch g Thousand Words Zilayah (USA) (Zilzal (USA))
1376[6] 1596[12] 2658[3] 2955[7] (4994) (5375) 5635[2] 6406[4] 6763[8] 6938[10]

**Peri (GER)** *A Wohler* 74
2 ch f Lord Of England(GER) Peace Time (GER) (Surumu (GER))
6950a[3]

**Peril** *Lady Cecil* a72 76
3 ch g Pivotal Portodora (USA) (Kingmambo (USA))
5347[4] 6634[2] 7210[3]

**Perivale (USA)** *Mark Johnston* a54 47
4 b f Street Cry(IRE) Windsharp (USA) (Lear Fan (USA))
*1[5] 154[7] 349[8]*

**Perle Express** *Michael Appleby*
2 b f Rail Link Perle D'Or (IRE) (Entrepreneur)
*8220[6]*

**Permitted** *Lee Carter* a44 41
3 b f Authorized(IRE) Discerning (Darshaan)
*847[6] 1233[10]* 1654[5] *8315[10]*

**Permsiri (IRE)** *Malcolm Saunders* a18 26
3 b f Ad Valorem(USA) Swiss Roll (IRE) (Entrepreneur)
*1287[5]* 3178[7] 3754[8] 4340[7]

**Pernica** *Lucy Wadham* a90 78
4 b f Sir Percy Nicola Bella (IRE) (Sadler's Wells (USA))
1934[4] 2628[2] *7922[9]*

**Perrault (IRE)** *Ralph Beckett* 73
2 b c Rip Van Winkle(IRE) La Persiana (Daylami (IRE))
7414[2] ◆

**Perrecalla (FR)** *D De Waele* a71 64
4 ch f Anabaa Blue Pomposa (IRE) (Barathea (IRE))
*805a[10]*

**Perrydot (IRE)** *Jo Crowley* a51
3 b f Footstepsinthesand Titoli Di Coda (IRE) (Bertolini (USA))
*756[5] 1298[4]* 2946[10] 5907[8]

**Persepolis (IRE)** *Lee Carter* a91 78
4 gr g Dansili La Persiana (Daylami (IRE))
*5411 840[10]* 1351[9] 3065[8] 3878[8] *6035[11] 7205[7] (7757) 8042[3] 8194[5]*

**Persevere (FR)** *Y Durepaire* a53
2 ch c Sevres Rose(IRE) Pretty Soon (FR) (Zafonic (USA))
*3871a[2]*

**Perseverent Pete (USA)** *Christine Dunnett* a51 41
4 bb g Johannesburg(USA) Indian Halloween (USA) (Sunday Break (JPN))
1877[6] *2399[7]* 2875[6] *4658[2]* 5109[7] *7291[4] 7785[11] 7868[10]*

**Pershing** *Marco Botti* a66 75
3 gr g Mount Nelson La Gandilie (FR) (Highest Honor (FR))
*1208[5]* 1635[2] 2273[5] 3643[5] ◆ 4026[2]

**Persian Bolt (USA)** *Eve Johnson Houghton* a66 74
3 b f US Ranger(USA) Silent Cat (USA) (Rahy (USA))
2031[4] 2639[3] 3067[6] 3280[6] 3970[2] *4612[5]* 5352[2] 5775[3] 6247[2] 6617[2] 6988[3] 7220[4]

**Persian Caliph (IRE)** *Mrs John Harrington* a89 57
3 ch g Intikhab(USA) Persian Memories (IRE) (Indian Ridge)
3686a[8]

**Persian Patriot** *William Jarvis* a73 68
4 ch f Bahamian Bounty Persian Lass (IRE) (Grand Lodge (USA))
*(97) 358[2]*

**Persian Peril** *Alan Swinbank* a71 75
10 br g Erhaab(USA) Brush Away (Ahonoora)
*253[8]* 2674[8]

**Persona Grata** *Ed Walker* a86
3 b f Sir Percy Kaldounya (Kaldoun (FR))
*(7074) (7998) (8122) 8290[2]*

**Personal Opinion** *Charlie Appleby* a99 96
3 ch g New Approach(IRE) Sentimental Value (USA) (Diesis)
*(1856)* 2303[2] 3379[10] 5179[9] 5720[10] *(7974) 8062[2]* (Dead)

**Personal Touch** *Richard Fahey* 87
5 ch g Pivotal Validate (Alhaarth (IRE))
2202[2] 3202[10] 5199[6] 7085[6] (7601) 7719[9]

**Perspicace** *Roger Charlton* a82 77
3 b g Sir Percy Cassique Lady (IRE) (Langfuhr (CAN))
*2081[2]* 3631[2] *4325[7] 6239[2] 7067[2]*

**Perspicacity** *J R Jenkins* 45
3 ch f Sir Percy Sakhacity (Sakhee (USA))
2877[8] *7764[8]*

**Persun** *Mick Channon* 83
2 ch f Sir Percy Sunley Shines (Komaite (USA))
2302[2] 2641[2] 3107[5] 5147[2] 5436[2] 5626[2] 6253[7]

**Pertemps Networks** *Michael Easterby* a80 67
10 b g Golden Snake(USA) Society Girl (Shavian)
*514[6] 641[7]* 2980[3] 3205[13] 3546[4] 4115[7] 4319[10]

**Pertuis (IRE)** *Micky Hammond* a78 77
8 gr g Verglas(IRE) Lady Killeen (IRE) (Marju (IRE))
(1362) 1885[4] 2168[6] 2872[2] (3371) 3785[5] 4351[8] 5371[9] 5678[9] 6062[6] 6696[4]

**Petale Noir** *Jonathan Portman* a44 28
3 b f Mount Nelson Apple Blossom (IRE) (Danehill Dancer (IRE))
*1143[7]* 2028[9] *7360[13]*

**Petaluma** *Mick Channon* a41 71
5 b m Teofilo(IRE) Poppo's Song (CAN) (Polish Navy (USA))
2011[5] 2801[3]

**Petara Bay (IRE)** *Sophie Leech*
10 b g Peintre Celebre(USA) Magnificient Style (USA) (Silver Hawk (USA))
3453[P] *4080[7]*

**Petella** *George Moore* 65
8 b m Tamure(IRE) Miss Petronella (Petoski)
1605[11] 2139[5] 2620[2] 2980[4] 4296[7]

**Petergate** *Brian Rothwell* a51 61
3 b g Alhaarth(IRE) Shamayel (Pivotal)
1346[5] 1906[3] 2204[3] 2828[2] 3362[6] 3946[13] 5269[8] 5761[8] *7368[7]*

**Peterhof** *Sir Michael Stoute* a80
2 b c Dansili Spinning Queen (Spinning World (USA))
*(7199)* ◆

**Peterhouse (USA)** *John Gosden* a61
2 ch c Elusive Quality(USA) Dynaire (USA) (Dynaformer (USA))
*7730[8] 7926[7] 8192[7]*

**Peterkin (IRE)** *Mark Johnston* a87 97
3 ch c Invincible Spirit(IRE) Alizes (NZ) (Rory's Jester (AUS))
*2083[2]* 2344[4] 2778[9] (3219) 3478[5] (4158) 4700[3] 4898[3] 5575[13] 6745[11] 7441[11]

**Petersboden** *Michael Blanshard* a58 53
5 b g Iceman Bowden Rose (Dashing Blade)
*116[5] 459[5] 571[2] 821[3] 1016[4]* 2066[8] 2863[3] 3208[4] 3552[3] 4105[5] *4738[8]*

**Peter's Friend** *Michael Herrington* a77 60
5 b g Gentleman's Deal(IRE) Giffoine (Timeless Times (USA))
*29[3] (96) 388[5]*

**Pether's Moon (IRE)** *Richard Hannon* a112 117
4 b c Dylan Thomas(IRE) Softly Tread (IRE) (Tirol)
1950[2] 2143[2] 3450[3] 4124[3] (4849) 5432[9] (6184a) (6919) 7275[7]

**Petit Chevalier (FR)** *W Mongil* a103 111
6 bb g High Chaparral(IRE) Pivoline (FR) (Pivotal)
4006a[7]

**Petite Fille** *Jeremy Gask* a46 38
3 ch f Sleeping Indian Ravenna (Compton Place)
2489[10] 2846[8] *5548[9]* 5907[3]

**Petite Madame (IRE)** *David Thompson* 55
3 b f Champs Elysees Seeking The Fun (USA) (Alhaarth (IRE))
1600[4] 3498[7] 5200[9] 5682[8] *6768[13]* 7176[8]

**Petits Potins (IRE)** *Rod Collet* a94 94
3 b f Verglas(IRE) Babacora (IRE) (Indian Ridge)
7319a[7] 7720a[6]

**Petrify** *Bernard Llewellyn* a51 61
4 b g Rock Of Gibraltar(IRE) Frigid (Indian Ridge)
*1815[4]* 2672[7] 2834[5] 3147[4] 3778[5] 4149[4] 4942[8] 5338[7]

**Petticoat Lane** *Luca Cumani* 79
3 b f High Chaparral(IRE) Barter (Daylami (IRE))
1701[13] 3652[4] 4089[2] 4802[4] (5313) (Dead)

**Pettochside** *Chris Gordon* a78 80
5 b g Refuse To Bend(IRE) Clear Impression (IRE) (Danehill (USA))
*1144[8]* 1789[3] (2250) 2718[5] 3422[2] 4146[4] 4401[5] 5817[2] 7159[9] *7403[12]*

**Petty Officer (IRE)** *A bin Harmash* a68 52
6 b g Dubawi(IRE) Miss Particular (IRE) (Sadler's Wells (USA))
*239a[11]*

**Peut Etre (IRE)** *P Sogorb* a87 105
3 b f Whipper(USA) Zut Alors (IRE) (Pivotal)
*391a[6]* 7736a[2]

**Phaenomena (IRE)** *Lady Cecil* a89 95
4 ch f Galileo(IRE) Caumshinaun (IRE) (Indian Ridge)
3204[13] 4204[4] 5723[4]

**Phantasmagoric (IRE)** *Sir Michael Stoute* 60
2 b f Dansili Sacred Song (USA) (Diesis)
6208[6]

**Phantasmo (IRE)** *John Quinn* 50
2 b c Dark Angel(IRE) Monsusu (IRE) (Montjeu (IRE))
4570[11] 4993[5] 5493[10] 6669[8] 7208[7]

**Phantom Spirit** *George Baker* a20 21
3 b f Invincible Spirit(IRE) Jackie's Opera (FR) (Indian Ridge)
2489[13] 3469[8] 3916[12] *4733[12]* 6023[9] 6297[9] *7197[12]*

**Pharoh Jake** *John Bridger* a72 72
6 ch g Piccolo Rose Amber (Double Trigger (IRE))
*114[3] 339[2] 424[3] 714[4] 845[2] 921[4] 1109[4]* 2029[4] *2459[5]* 2865[5] *3392[6]* (5860) 6266[3] (6983) (7215) 7342[3] 7989[8] 8039[3] 8245[4] (8322)

**Phase Shift** *Brian Ellison* a63 58
6 b m Iceman Silent Waters (Polish Precedent (USA))
2216[8] 3269[8]

**Philba** *Michael Appleby* 67
2 b c Cockney Rebel(IRE) Hisaronu (IRE) (Stravinsky (USA))
4633[9] 5922[4] 6456[4] 6869[3] 7595[7]

**Philosofy** *David O'Meara* 41
4 ch f Barathea(IRE) Idealistic (IRE) (Unfuwain (USA))
*871[6] 1088[5]* 6762[4] 7007[P]

**Phoenix Flight (IRE)** *James Evans* a73 73
9 b g Hawk Wing(USA) Firecrest (IRE) (Darshaan)
*72[3] 292[5] 818[8] 7065[7]*

**Phoenix Phil** *Shaun Harris* 6
2 ch g Phoenix Reach(IRE) Pearl's Girl (King's Best (USA))
1712[7]

**Phoenix Storm (IRE)** *Richard Fahey* 29
2 b c Zebedee Dabtiyra (IRE) (Dr Devious (IRE))
4684[9] 5807[9]

**Phoibe** *P Schiergen* 80
2 b f Royal Applause Polish Belle (Polish Precedent (USA))
6555[4]

**Phosphorescence (IRE)** *Lady Cecil* a65 83
4 b g Sakhee(USA) Eccentricity (USA) (Kingmambo (USA))
1934[3] 2700[4]

**Phyllis Maud (IRE)** *Mark Johnston* 65
2 ch f Halling(USA) Debonnaire (Anabaa (USA))
(6812) 7328[12]

**Pianota (USA)** *J S Bolger* 53
3 ch f Birdstone(USA) Paiota Falls (USA) (Kris S (USA))
2042a[10]

**Piazon** *Michael Bell* 93
3 br g Striking Ambition Colonel's Daughter (Colonel Collins (USA))
1396[2] (1615) 2317[10] (2626) 3219[5] 3478[8] 4158[3] 4700[4] 5204[2] 5438[7] 7080[9]

**Picanight** *Eve Johnson Houghton* a41 36
3 b f Piccolo Midnight Fling (Groom Dancer (USA))
*1384[4]* 1683[7] *1890[4]* 2249[5]

**Picansort** *Peter Crate* a93 68
7 b g Piccolo Running Glimpse (IRE) (Runnett)
*55[5] 532[4] 802[5] 1041[3] (1145)* 2070[2] 2865[3] 3707[8] 4675[5] *8019[4] 8171[8]*

**Picatchu (FR)** *H-A Pantall* a40
3 b f King's Best(USA) Trazando (Forzando)
*599a[10]*

**Piccadillo** *Daniel Kubler* a58 60
2 b f Piccolo Dahshah (Mujtahid (USA))
3975[8] 4499[4] 4781[6] 5525[4] *5798[10] 7014[4] 7257[11] 7529[5]*

**Piccadilly Jim (IRE)** *Richard Fahey* a67 73
3 gr g Royal Applause Silver Dip (Gulch (USA))
2217[4] 2789[3] 3370[2] 5497[3] 7513[4] *7812[5] 8224[5]*

**Picc Of Burgau** *Geoffrey Deacon* a59 70
4 b f Piccolo Rosein (Komaite (USA))
*605[4] 756[4]* 1573[4] 2488[3] 3231[5] (3520) 3848[12] 4675[2] 4981[5] 5860[8] 7213[4] 7670[8]

**Piccolo Express** *Brian Baugh* a64 49
8 b g Piccolo Ashfield (Zilzal (USA))
*562[6] 740[13] 963[5] 1081[3] 8063[7]* ◆ *8291[3]*

**Piceno (IRE)** *Scott Dixon* a83 89
6 b g Camacho Ascoli (Skyliner)
*11[2] 75[7] 1113[7]* (1376) *1630[7]* 1903[3] 2054[2] 2351[9] 2549[7] *2905[2]* 3221[2] 4938[11] 5031[2] 5346[5] 7507[9] 7988[10] 8209[9] 8281[6]

**Pick A Little** *Michael Blake* a81 69
6 b g Piccolo Little Caroline (IRE) (Great Commotion (USA))
*(34) 1115[5]* 1689[5] 2012[2] *2400[3]* 2721[3] 3327[3] 3562[6] *4073[6]*

**Picket Line** *Geoffrey Deacon* 59
2 b c Multiplex Dockside Strike (Docksider (USA))
*4054[12]* 4740[10] 7491[4]

**Pickle Lilly Pearl** *David C Griffiths* a38 58
2 b f Captain Gerrard(IRE) Branston Jewel (IRE) (Prince Sabo)
*1259[9]* 2134[3] 2313[13] 4018[4] 4857[6] 5384[2] 5637[5] 5985[9] 6791[7] *7649[5]*

**Picks Pinta** *Jo Hughes* a76 78
3 b g Piccolo Past 'N' Present (Cadeaux Genereux)
*1315[4]* (3566) 3662[2] 4161[2] ◆ 4342[2] 6316[5] *7352[4] 7729[5] 8071[7]*

**Pick Your Choice** *William Haggas* 70
2 b c Elusive Quality(USA) Enticement (Montjeu (IRE))
7380[6]

**Picnic In The Glen** *Sylvester Kirk* a29 43
3 b f Piccolo True Magic (Magic Ring (IRE))
5181[7] 5775[9] 6356[5] *7036[9] 7548[7] 7864[10]*

**Picture Dealer** *Lydia Pearce* a99 96
5 b g Royal Applause Tychy (Suave Dancer (USA))
2254[10] 2778[7] 3271[8] 4146[9] 4305[4] ◆ 4683[13]

**Picture Postcard** *William Haggas* a52 55
2 ch f Kyllachy My Girl Jode (Haafhd)
5524[4] 5982[10] *6563[4]* 7488[2]

**Piddie's Power** *Kevin Frost* a83 73
7 ch m Starcraft(NZ) Telori (Muhtarram (USA))
3256[14] 3384[5] 4108[3] 5079[5] *7905[6]*

**Pied A Terre (AUS)** *Saeed bin Suroor* a86 105
6 b g Ad Valorem(USA) Masonette (AUS) (Grand Lodge (USA))
*240a[6]*

**Pieman's Girl** *Anthony Carson* a49 65
3 b f Henrythenavigator(USA) Aromatherapy (Oasis Dream)
*311[13]* 4306[6] (5061) 5860[5] *6488[9]* 7213[11]

**Pierre D'Or (IRE)** *J T Gorman* a65 70
5 ch g Rock Of Gibraltar(IRE) Gilded Edge (Cadeaux Genereux)
*790a[11]*

**Pierre Precieuse (FR)** *E Caroux* a51 76
2 b f Vertigineux(FR) Poca De Gracia (IRE) (Royal Applause)
3027a[6] 3170a[2] 4603a[4] 5405a[8] 6591a[8]

**Pigeon Pie** *Mark Johnston* a59 73
3 b f Bahamian Bounty Pixie Ring (Pivotal)
*667[7]* 2676[3] 3608[3] 5787[3] 6515[5] (6795) 6980[6] 7098[9] *7225[5] 7459[8]*

**Pilgrim** *Eve Johnson Houghton* 44
2 ch f Bahamian Bounty Deep Bleu (Kyllachy)
5774[7] 6361[7]

**Pilgrims Rest (IRE)** *George Baker* a88 94
5 ch g Rock Of Gibraltar(IRE) Holly Blue (Bluebird (USA))
2091[2] 2259[2] 2760[7] 3217[9] 6061[8]

**Pillar Box (IRE)** *William Haggas* 85
2 ch g Sakhee's Secret Red Red Rose (Piccolo)
2541[7] (3210) 4439[7] 4686[5] 7079[9] 7415[6]

**Pilote (IRE)** *A Fabre* 115
4 ch c Pivotal Legerete (USA) (Rahy (USA))
1371a[5] 1908a[8] 3291a[6] 4008a[2] 5461a[3] 6957a[6]

**Pim Street (USA)** *David O'Meara* a71 66
4 b f Street Sense(USA) Crown Of Jewels (USA) (Half A Year (USA))
*1053[2] 2937[7] 3798[7]* 4014[6] (4468) 4665[5] 5495[10] *(6267)* 6706[4] *7288[5] 7522[2] 7569[4] 7829[4]* 8261[2]

**Pindar (GER)** *Joanne Foster* a17 51
10 b g Tertullian(USA) Pierette (GER) (Local Suitor (USA))
3785[6] 4962[12]

**Pindora (GER)** *Noel Quinlan* a38 52
3 ch f Sholokhov(IRE) Poule D'Essai (GER) (Dashing Blade)
2511[6] 2850[10] 3432[9] *4085[8]* 4497[P] 5200[4] 5850[4]

**Pink (FR)** *S Kobayashi* a73 70
2 b f Elusive City(USA) Unbaka (Red Ransom (USA))
5590a[8] 6958a[3]

**Pink And Black (IRE)** *William Muir* a67 59
3 b f Yeats(IRE) Raysiza (IRE) (Alzao (USA))
1423[9] 2418[7] 3803[11] 4563[4] *8114[2] 8246[7]*

**Pink Cadillac (IRE)** *Ben Haslam* a36 43
4 b f Clodovil(IRE) Green Life (Green Desert (USA))
*76[4]* 4796[8] *7909[8]*

**Pink Chalice** *F Doumen* a69 80
3 b f Authorized(IRE) Flamingo Flower (USA) (Diesis)
3372a[6] 7722a[15]

**Pink Courageous (FR)** *J-P Gauvin* 76
3 gr f Kouroun(FR) Pink Cloud (FR) (Octagonal (NZ))
5368a[8]

**Pink Diamond** *Eve Johnson Houghton* 69
3 b f Champs Elysees Fairy Dance (IRE) (Zafonic (USA))
2109[9] 2850[5] 3423[7] (4210) 4540[2] 5277[3]

**Pink Lips** *J R Jenkins* a22 67
6 b m Noverre(USA) Primrose Queen (Lear Fan (USA))
2843[2] 3308[3] 3682[4] 4617[5] 5291[6] 5731[2] 7302[6] 7514[7]

**Pink Mirage (IRE)** *Jonathan Portman* a54 58
3 gr f Verglas(IRE) Deira (USA) (Green Desert (USA))
*1794[5]* 2224[7] 6087[6]

**Pink Mischief** *Andrew Crook* a53 16
4 gr f Holy Roman Emperor(IRE) Feather (USA) (Unbridled's Song (USA))
*6410[8]*

**Pink Ribbon (IRE)** *Sylvester Kirk* a60 54
2 b c Dark Angel(IRE) My Funny Valentine (IRE) (Mukaddamah (USA))
2298[11] 2964[11] 4207[7] 5875[4] 6294[4] 7156[4] 7338[3] *7740[4]*

**Pink Rose** *A Fabre* 96
2 b f Shirocco(GER) La Nuit Rose (FR) (Rainbow Quest (USA))
6967a[9]

**Pinotage** *Peter Niven* a66 63
6 br g Danbird(AUS) Keen Melody (USA) (Sharpen Up)
*513[2] 695[2] 872[3] (1426)*

**Pinter** *Charlie Appleby* a75 65
2 b g Exceed And Excel(AUS) Pickle (Piccolo)
2480[7] 2859[7] 4044[5] *(5554)* 6064[8]

**Pintrada** *James Bethell* a88 86
6 b g Tiger Hill(IRE) Ballymore Celebre (IRE) (Peintre Celebre (USA))
(6152) 6433[7] 7125[5] *7702[2] 7838[4] 8243[5]*

**Pintura** *Kevin Ryan* a97 110
7 ch g Efisio Picolette (Piccolo)
1443[5] 2113[9] 2784[8] 4771a[10]

**Pinturicchio (IRE)** *E Lellouche* a109 114
6 b g Holy Roman Emperor(IRE) Precious Pearl (IRE) (Peintre Celebre (USA))
1908a[4] (3291a) 5223a[14] 6955a[13] 7559a[2]

**Pin Up (IRE)** *Richard Fahey* a75
2 b f Lookin At Lucky(USA) All My Loving (IRE) (Sadler's Wells (USA))
*7367[2] 7778[2]* ◆ *8220[2]*

**Pinzolo** *Charlie Appleby* 109
3 b g Monsun(GER) Pongee (Barathea (IRE))
1953[3] ◆ (2345) 2990[14] 4007a[15] 5688[2] 6321[3]

**Pipe Bomb** *Kevin Ryan* a50 72
2 b g Acclamation Dorelia (IRE) (Efisio)
3255[6] 3827[5] 5684[10] *6104[10]* 6538[2] 6925[13] 7378[5]

**Pipe Dream** *Brian Meehan* a59 66
3 ch g Piccolo Bold Love (Bold Edge)
1680[4] 2163[4] *2647[8]*

**Piper Bill** *Jim Goldie* 26
3 b g Halling(USA) Murielle (Diktat)
7176[6]

**Pipers Note** *Richard Whitaker* a103 101
4 ch g Piccolo Madam Valentine (Primo Valentino (IRE))
3714[8] 4347[5] (4976) 5445[5] 7408[15] *7543[2]* ◆ *7700[2] 7923[8]*

**Pipers Piping (IRE)** *Mandy Rowland* a55 46
8 b g Noverre(USA) Monarchy (IRE) (Common Grounds)
290[7] 516[2] (676) (918) 1036[6] 4073[14] 5899[10] 6267[12] 6715[7] 7187[8] 8063[9] 8258[3]

**Piping Dream (IRE)** *Richard Hannon* a43 58
2 b f Approve(IRE) French Fern (IRE) (Royal Applause)
3583[4] 4396[11] 4784[10] 5517[U] 5828[4] (6040) 6248[8]

**Pipita (GER)** *Daniel Paulick* 49
4 b f Shrek(GER) Pashmina (GER) (Lomitas)
6589a[9]

**Pippa Greene** *Nicky Henderson* a51 69
10 b g Galileo(IRE) Funny Girl (IRE) (Darshaan)
1941[8]

**Pique Sous (FR)** *W P Mullins* a75 101
7 gr g Martaline Six Fois Sept (FR) (Epervier Bleu)
(3453)

**Pira Palace (IRE)** *Jim Boyle* a50 47
4 b f Acclamation Takrice (Cadeaux Genereux)
1266[4] 1921[8]

**Pirate Cove (IRE)** *Mark Johnston* a71 71
4 b f Lawman(FR) Uncharted Haven (Turtle Island (IRE))
8313[2]

**Piri Wango (IRE)** *G M Lyons* a104 109
5 ch g Choisir(AUS) Zoldan (Deploy)
4771a[2] 6354a[4] 7276[25]

**Piscean (USA)** *Tom Keddy* a95 93
9 bb g Stravinsky(USA) Navasha (USA) (Woodman (USA))
534[8] 991[7] 1172[11] 1301[5] 1576[7] 2995[6]

**Pisces** *David Elsworth* a33 56
2 b f Halling(USA) Optimistic (Reprimand)
4444[13] 4914[10] 5416[11] 7832[11] 7994[13]

**Pisco Sour (USA)** *S Seemar* a93 93
6 br g Lemon Drop Kid(USA) Lynnwood Chase (USA) (Horse Chestnut (SAF))
205a[10] 593a[8]

**Pise (IRE)** *J-P Gallorini* 75
3 b f King's Best(USA) Pavlovna (FR) (Singspiel (IRE))
7722a[11]

**Pissarro (GER)** *R Rohne* a55 78
3 ch c Tertullian(USA) Palmeira (GER) (Lomitas)
7269a[5] 7630a[8]

**Pitch (FR)** *F Rossi* 101
3 ch g Manduro(GER) Wedge (USA) (Storm Cat (USA))
4775a[2]

**Piton** *Mark Johnston* a76 87
3 b g Archipenko(USA) Scandalette (Niniski (USA))
(1032) (1124) ◆ 2761[9] 4361[2]

**Pitrella (GER)** *U Stech* 90
3 b f War Blade(GER) Pashmina (GER) (Lomitas)
3046a[7]

**Pit Stop (IRE)** *M Halford* a80 97
3 b c Iffraaj Journey's End (IRE) (In The Wings)
5656[6] 6354a[11]

**Pitt Rivers** *Linda Perratt* 58
5 br g Vital Equine(IRE) Silca Boo (Efisio)
6114[11] 6475[16] 6595[4] (6833) 7061[5]

**Pivoina (IRE)** *D Prod'Homme* a69 85
7 b m Marchand De Sable(USA) Golden Wings (USA) (Devil's Bag (USA))
5225a[4]

**Pivotal Prospect** *Tracy Waggott* 56
6 b m Nayef(USA) Buon Amici (Pivotal)
1838[12]

**Pivotal Rio (IRE)** *Manila Illuminati* 92
2 ch g Captain Rio Luvmedo (IRE) (One Cool Cat (USA))
7655a[4]

**Pivot Bridge** *Adrian McGuinness* a73 79
6 ch g Pivotal Specifically (USA) (Sky Classic (CAN))
4951a[2] 6349a[9]

**Pivotman** *Michael Easterby* a84 70
6 ch g Pivotal Grandalea (Grand Lodge (USA))
1362[P] 2823[4] 3254[12] 7334[9] 7411[14] (7626) 7871[2] ◆ (8161) ◆

**Pivot Point (IRE)** *Brian Meehan* 75
2 b g Excellent Art Lily Of Laguna (IRE) (Zafeen (FR))
3081[7] 3626[4] 4109[2] 4884[2] 5408[5] 6393[2] 6783[7] 7379[10]

**Pixeleen** *Malcolm Saunders* a57 66
2 b f Pastoral Pursuits Ballyalla (Mind Games)
3279[7] 3728[7] (4499) 5779[4] 6312[4] 6679[4]

**Pixey Punk** *Tim Easterby* 47
2 gr f Mount Nelson Mosquera (GER) (Acatenango (GER))
3267[9] 4018[9] 4626[9] 6449[7]

**Pixie** *Ian Williams* 12
2 b f Piccolo Spinning Coin (Mujahid (USA))
2644[6] 3267[13]

**Pixie Cut (IRE)** *Alistair Whillans* a76 74
4 b f Chineur(FR) Fantastic Cee (IRE) (Noverre (USA))
1377[3] 1971[4] 2327[5] 2678[4] 7509[11]

**Place Des Anges (FR)** *J-L Pelletan* a68 65
4 ro g Desert Style(IRE) My Vanessa (FR) (Medaaly)
5225a[8]

**Placidia (IRE)** *David Lanigan* a92 90
3 b f Sea The Stars(IRE) Palmeraie (USA) (Lear Fan (USA))
2133[2] (2650) 3183[8] 5730[5] 6044[4] (6500) 7105[9] 7717[10]

**Plaine Monceau (FR)** *Braem Horse Racing Sprl* a65 67
4 gr f One Cool Cat(USA) Luroya (FR) (Daylami (IRE))
7620a[6]

**Plain Striking** *Dr Jeremy Naylor*
5 b m Striking Ambition Daphne's Doll (IRE) (Polish Patriot (USA))
8008[9]

**Plaisanciere (FR)** *F Rohaut* a101 78
3 ch f Astronomer Royal(USA) Princesse Jasmine (FR) (Gold Away (IRE))
7619a[2] 8300a[3]

**Plaisir (IRE)** *Marco Botti* a69
2 b f Elusive City(USA) Sea Sex Sun (Desert Prince (IRE))
7944[3] 8201[2] 8318[2]

**Planetaire** *C Laffon-Parias* a83 110
3 b c Galileo(IRE) Occupandiste (IRE) (Kaldoun (FR))
(5591a) 6592a[3] 6957a[4]

**Planetoid (IRE)** *Jim Best* a82 84
6 b g Galileo(IRE) Palmeraie (USA) (Lear Fan (USA))
79[12] 146[9] 582[10] 801[12] 990[6] 7359[12] (7932) (8037) (8193) 8296[2]

**Planet Rock** *Keiran Burke*
3 b g Shirocco(GER) Demand (Red Ransom (USA))
2917[11] 3517[6] 4432[7] 5135[7]

**Plantagenet (SPA)** *Niels Petersen* a100 96
7 ch h Trade Fair Crafty Buzz (USA) (Crafty Prospector (USA))
307a[4] 593a[11] 681a[3] 807a[3] 2245a[5] 5744a[10]

**Platelet (AUS)** *Darren Weir* 113
6 b m Strategic(AUS) Bloodline (AUS) (Dracula (AUS))
7724a[9]

**Platinum Pearl** *Peter Chapple-Hyam* a72 67
3 b f Shamardal(USA) Gimasha (Cadeaux Genereux)
(275) 1381[5] 2274[7] 3300[9]

**Plauseabella** *Stuart Kittow* a32 52
3 b f Royal Applause Ellablue (Bahamian Bounty)
3801[5] 4539[2] 5905[6] 6356[6] 7197[7] 7632[12]

**Playboy Bay** *Mick Channon* 69
2 b g Indesatchel(IRE) Dim Ofan (Petong)
2298[13] 3194[12] 3945[2] 4330[6] 4659[10] 5335[2] 5718[7] 7230[3] 7404[6]

**Play Nicely** *James Given* a56 30
2 ch c Naaqoos Aalya (IRE) (Peintre Celebre (USA))
6147[8] 6668[12] 7228[6] 7994[12]

**Play Street** *Jonathan Portman* a57 81
5 ch m Tobougg(IRE) Zoena (Emarati (USA))
1568[3] 1910[3] 3085[9] 4116[4] (4799) 5503[4] 5721[8] 6365[3] 6787[5]

**Play The Blues (IRE)** *Dominic Ffrench Davis* a48 67
7 gr m Refuse To Bend(IRE) Paldouna (IRE) (Kaldoun (FR))
100[4] 448[5] 556[4] 5972[7] 7519[5] 7883[10]

**Play Tiger (FR)** *Peter Hiatt* a43 43
5 b g Tiger Hill(IRE) Shagadellic (USA) (Devil's Bag (USA))
5030[8]

**Playtothewhistle** *Bryan Smart* a62 62
3 b g Sakhee's Secret Prima Ballerina (Pivotal)
254[2] 564[4] 861[5] 4791[11] 5497[6] 5891[10]

**Pleasant Flight (FR)** *D Windrif* a83 75
3 ch g Redback Silent Flight (FR) (Sicyos (USA))
5368a[10]

**Pleasant Valley (IRE)** *Luca Cumani* 94
3 b f Shamardal(USA) Poughkeepsie (IRE) (Sadler's Wells (USA))
2129[7] 3141[3] 3891[3] (4886) (5420) 6464[5]

**Pleascach (IRE)** *J S Bolger* 90
2 b f Teofilo(IRE) Toirneach (USA) (Thunder Gulch (USA))
3763a[4]

**Please Don't Tease (IRE)** *Bill Turner* 32
2 b g Strategic Prince Moon Crest (IRE) (Singspiel (IRE))
1663[5] 3157[5] 3312[11]

**Please Let Me Go** *Julie Camacho* 60
3 ch f Sleeping Indian Elhida (IRE) (Mujtahid (USA))
2205[4] 2828[7]

**Pleasure Bent** *Luca Cumani* a87 86
4 b c Dansili Nitya (FR) (Indian Ridge)
1724[16] 2462[3] 3314[7] 5727[2] 6466[3]

**Pleasure Gains** *K L Man* 112
5 b g Cape Cross(IRE) Viola Da Braccio (IRE) (Vettori (IRE))
8154a[10]

**Pleiades** *Sir Michael Stoute* 83
2 b c Galileo(IRE) Angara (Alzao (USA))
5201[7] 6190[3] (6621)

**Plinth (IRE)** *A P O'Brien* 97
4 b g Montjeu(IRE) Crazy Volume (IRE) (Machiavellian (USA))
3321[10]

**Plough Boy (IRE)** *Willie Musson* a74 35
3 b c Dandy Man(IRE) Ribald (Alhaarth (IRE))
157[6] 378[3] (577) 1124[5] 1401[11] 2224[11] 3389[5] 4266[2] (4970) 6337[3] 7000[6] (7288)

**Plovdiv (FR)** *E Leenders* a56 84
4 b g Hurricane Cat(USA) Septieme Face (USA) (Lit De Justice (USA))
805a[14]

**Plover** *Michael Attwater* a64 77
4 b f Oasis Dream Short Dance (USA) (Hennessy (USA))
2462[10] 3425[6] 4053[9] 6890[11] 7356[8] 7775[10] 7842[6] 8013[11] 8185[7]

**Plucky Dip** *John Ryan* a90 64
3 b g Nayef(USA) Plucky (Kyllachy)
1403[13] 1683[8] (2078) 2416[2] 2878[2] 3158[3] 3670[4] 4074[2] 5006[3] 5557[7] 6034[4] 6243[2] (6568) (6767) 6902[3] 7183[2] 7600[11] 7851[2] 7947[3] 8101[4]

**Plume D'Outarde** *F Doumen* a11 69
2 b f Equiano(FR) Azlaa (Dubawi (IRE))
5544a[8] 6591a[2]

**Plumetot (FR)** *J-C Rouget* 75
2 ch c Le Havre(IRE) Polysheba (FR) (Poliglote)
(7344a)

**Plunder** *Alan Berry* a76 29
4 ch g Zamindar(USA) Reaching Ahead (USA) (Mizzen Mast (USA))
407[6] 464[3] 565[4] 2653[7] 3056[8] 3908[12] 5996[5]

**Plusquemavie (IRE)** *V Fazio* 71
3 b c Kheleyf(USA) Kathy Pekan (IRE) (Sri Pekan (USA))
7322a[8]

**Plutocracy (IRE)** *David Lanigan* a95 99
4 b g Dansili Private Life (FR) (Bering)
2779[6] 7289[7] 7718[19]

**Plymouth Sound** *Eve Johnson Houghton* 85
2 b g Fastnet Rock(AUS) Shardette (IRE) (Darshaan)
(4676) 5906[2] 6256[19]

**Poco Piccolo** *Deborah Sanderson* a4 37
3 b g Piccolo Angel Maid (Forzando)
1285[7] 1801[5] 3951[10]

**Poetic Belle** *Shaun Harris* a57 48
4 b f Byron Sahariri (IRE) (Red Ransom (USA))
18[10]

**Poetic Choice** *Nick Littmoden* a76 81
3 b f Byron Ennobling (Mark Of Esteem (IRE))
501[4] 892[6] 1769[4] 2470[8] (3588) 4862[2] 5501[3] 6189[2] 6468[5] 7286[5]

**Poetic License (IRE)** *Sir Mark Prescott Bt* a42
2 b g Dylan Thomas(IRE) Bright Bank (IRE) (Sadler's Wells (USA))
7039[9] 7425[8]

**Poetic Verse** *John Quinn* a76 85
4 gr f Byron Nina Fontenail (FR) (Kaldounevees (FR))
2728[5] 3226[3] (3699) 5049[4] (6541)

**Poet Mark (IRE)** *Tim Easterby* 43
2 b g Vale Of York(IRE) Attanagh (IRE) (Darnay)
4467[11] 4885[8] 5494[10]

**Poetree In Motion** *Keith Dalgleish* 58
3 b f Milk It Mick Suka Ramai (Nashwan (USA))
1757[3] 2217[6] 2910[5]

**Point Blank (GER)** *Mario Hofer* a90 105
6 b g Royal Dragon(USA) Princess Li (GER) (Monsun (GER))
2715a[6] 6384a[5]

**Point North (IRE)** *John Balding* a80 59
7 b g Danehill Dancer(IRE) Briolette (IRE) (Sadler's Wells (USA))
60[6] 432[2] 1031[2] 2159[6] 6562[9] 6898[10] (8142)

**Point The Toes (IRE)** *Mark Fahey* 75
9 b m Atraf Fern Fields (IRE) (Be My Native (USA))
(4962) ◆ 5146[5]

**Poitin** *Harry Dunlop* a92 78
4 b f Kheleyf(USA) Port Providence (Red Ransom (USA))
79[4] 293[2] 369[3] (758) 1383[5] 1941[5] 2430[5] 3078[6] 4076[3] 4552[3] 5551[5] 5878[7]

**Poker Gold (FR)** *Heather Main* a70 70
3 b g Gold Away(IRE) Becquarette (FR) (Nombre Premier)
955[6] 1494[5] 2494[5] 3183[10]

**Poker Hospital** *John Stimpson* a52 40
5 b m Rock Of Gibraltar(IRE) Empress Anna (IRE) (Imperial Ballet (IRE))
351[8] 676[7] 844[9]

**Polar Express** *Jonathan Portman* a47 55
3 ch g Sakhee's Secret Polar Dawn (Polar Falcon (USA))
738[3] 1257[5]

**Polar Eyes** *Tom Dascombe* a64 87
3 b f Dubawi(IRE) Everlasting Love (Pursuit Of Love)
1280[2] 1645[2] 2118[3] (2740) 3357[20] 4397[4] 5448[3] 6945[7] (7416) 7641[9]

**Polar Forest** *Richard Guest* a71 78
4 br g Kyllachy Woodbeck (Terimon)
105[6] 497[3] 736[4] 964[4] 1012[3] (1428) 1675[2] 2164[2] (2427) 2730[3] 4613[10] 4904[4] 5537[2] 5899[11] (6341) 6578[4] (7044) (7249) 7672[3]

**Polarisation** *Mark Johnston* a65 82
2 b g Echo Of Light Concordia (Pivotal)
3794[2] 4216[3] (4723) 5580[14] 6550[6]

**Polarix** *H-A Pantall* a81 92
8 gr h Linamix(FR) Freezing (USA) (Bering)
3373a[7]

**Polar Kite (IRE)** *Roger Ingram* a79 43
6 b g Marju(IRE) Irina (IRE) (Polar Falcon (USA))
113[5] 677[2] 806a[3] 1025[2] 1217[5] 4907[8] 6890[7] 7636[7] 8251[6]

**Polar Vortex (IRE)** *Clive Cox* 76
2 ch f Pastoral Pursuits Valandraud (IRE) (College Chapel)
1488[2] (2128) 3353[17] 4345[3] 5129[2] 7038[4]

**Polish Vulcano (GER)** *H-J Groschel* 105
6 ch h Lomitas Polska Infa (GER) (Trempolino (USA))
2815a[4] 4720a[5] 5938a[4] 6914a[6] 7316a[5] 7727a[7]

**Politibureau** *Michael Easterby* a43 56
7 b g Red Ransom(USA) Tereshkova (USA) (Mr Prospector (USA))
1891[3] 2396[9] 2738[3] 3398[4] 3912[8]

**Political Policy (IRE)** *M Halford* a80 73
3 b g Bushranger(IRE) Alexander Express (IRE) (Sri Pekan (USA))
416a[2]

**Politico** *John Gosden* a49 49
2 ch f Medicean Tafawut (Nayef (USA))
6605[12] 6976[5] 7667[8] 7816[3] 7996[6]

**Pollination (IRE)** *Charlie Appleby* a73
3 b g Bushranger(IRE) Lilium (Nashwan (USA))
(7063)

**Pollyana (IRE)** *J E Hammond* 112
5 b m Whipper(USA) Shamah (Unfuwain (USA))
2587a[3] 5742a[11] 7273[4]

**Polly Jackson** *Karen Tutty* 67
2 b f Sir Percy Fly In Style (Hernando (FR))
6935[5] 7174[4] 7498[5]

**Polly's Rose** *Ian Semple* a75 45
5 b m Bahamian Bounty Tiana (Diktat)
7501[5] (7818) 7993[8]

**Polo Dream (FR)** *L A Urbano-Grajales* 73
2 b c Naaqoos Chaussette (FR) (High Chaparral (IRE))
5292a[4]

**Polski Max** *Brian Ellison* a71 102
4 b g Kyllachy Quadrophenia (College Chapel)
1172[10] 2352[7] 2562[10] 3342[6] 4471[7] 5170[5] 5444[4] 7159[6] (7505)

**Polstar (FR)** *Harry Whittington* 76
5 b g Poliglote Star Dancing (Danehill Dancer (IRE))
4678[6]

**Polvere D'Oro** *Michael Mullineaux* a27 28
4 b g Revoque(IRE) Dusty Anne (IRE) (Dushyantor (USA))
460[8] 640[12]

**Polybius** *David Lanigan* a106 99
3 b g Oasis Dream Freedonia (Selkirk (USA))
2339[5] (2846) ◆ 3539[5] (4502) 4697[5] (6607) 7802[3] ◆

**Polydamos** *Tony Carroll* a57 57
5 b g Nayef(USA) Spotlight (Dr Fong (USA))
116[3] ◆ 377[2] 484[2] 570[2] 754[3] 838[5] 1100[6] 2770[3] 3115[2] 3576[7] 4738[5] 4798[3] 5033[4] 6028[3] 6407[6] 6883[5]

**Polydus** *Ed Dunlop* 41
2 b c Rock Of Gibraltar(IRE) Missy Wassie Gal (USA) (High Chaparral (IRE))
5646[15] 5947[7] 6261[11] 6643[P]

**Polyphemus (USA)** *S Deeb* a27
7 ch h Giant's Causeway(USA) Aqaarid (USA) (Nashwan (USA))
238a[15]

**Pomme De Guerre (IRE)** *Eve Johnson Houghton* a65
2 b g Kodiac Lucky Apple (IRE) (Key Of Luck (USA))
6675[5]

**Pomme De Terre (IRE)** *Michael Dods* 60
2 ch g Sakhee's Secret Suzie Quw (Bahamian Bounty)
1505[4] 2386[15]

**Pomology (USA)** *John Gosden* a91 113
4 bb f Arch(USA) Sharp Apple (USA) (Diesis)
(3961) 6380a[2]

**Pomone (IRE)** *D De Watrigant* a60 68
2 b f Orpen(USA) Lapistanera (IRE) (Cape Cross (IRE))
1402a[4]

**Pompilius (FR)** *C Lotoux* a91 94
3 b c Holy Roman Emperor(IRE) Rumored (USA) (Royal Academy (USA))
(6913a) 7619a[4]

**Ponfeigh (IRE)** *John M Oxx* 104
3 gr c Teofilo(IRE) Water Fountain (Mark Of Esteem (IRE))
3739a[4] 4477a[3]

**Poniel** *Ian Semple* 34
2 b g Bahri(USA) Rafta (IRE) (Atraf)
7097[8] 7498[12]

**Pontchatrain (USA)** *Thomas F Proctor* a88 108
4 bb f War Front(USA) Dominica (USA) (Housebuster (USA))
7615a[7]

**Ponte Di Rosa** *Simon Hodgson* a23 45
6 b m Avonbridge Ridgewood Ruby (IRE) (Indian Ridge)
1916[5]

**Pont Marie (FR)** *F Chappet* a99 99
4 b c Great Journey(JPN) Cite Fleurie (IRE) (Mark Of Esteem (IRE))
3373a[3]

**Pont Neuilly (FR)** *Yves de Nicolay* a100 100
4 ch c Medecis Panzella (FR) (Kahyasi)
7916a[10] 8150a[11]

**Ponty Grigio (IRE)** *Tim Easterby* 58
2 b c Acclamation Inishtearaght (IRE) (Verglas (IRE))
4884[10] 6058[8] 6449[5] 7084[14]

**Poole Harbour (IRE)** *David Nicholls* a54 104
5 b g Elusive City(USA) Free Lance (IRE) (Grand Lodge (USA))
5918[10] 6290[10] 7233[14] 7507[14]

**Pool House** *Andrew Balding* a98 78
3 b g Sakhee's Secret Gitane (FR) (Grand Lodge (USA))
(371) (487) (850) 1067[6] 1555[3] 2544[4] 3694[6]

**Poolstock** *Les Eyre* 64
2 b c Equiano(FR) Pure Speculation (Salse (USA))
2450[5] 3461[5] 4011[4] 4493[3] 5714[5] 6401[2] ◆ 6820[5] 7497[8]

**Poor Duke (IRE)** *Michael Mullineaux* a69 64
4 b g Bachelor Duke(USA) Graze On Too (IRE) (Rainbow Quest (USA))
49[11] (1450) 3299[9] 3616[4] 3696[5] 3880[5] 4156[8] 4293[10] 4959[5] 5512[6] 6076[12] 6267[6] 6771[9] 6856[4] 7115[4] (7188) 7292[9] 7813[4] ◆ 7868[5] 8265[9]

**Pop Art (IRE)** *Charles O'Brien* 98
4 b f Excellent Art Doctrine (Barathea (IRE))
1076a[4] 1252a[2] 1473a[5] 2185a[4] 2572a[8]

**Popeswood (IRE)** *Mick Channon* 86
2 b g Haatef(USA) Binfield (IRE) (Officer (USA))
2007[5] 2276[4] 2756[3] 3324[5] 4157[3] 4944[2] 5250[2] 5645[4] (5929) 6165[9] 6436[4] (7131) 7443[3]

**Poppet Rocket (IRE)** *Brian Meehan* a60 54
2 b f Myboycharlie(IRE) Zacchera (Zamindar (USA))
6517[10] 7228[2]

**Popping Candy** *Roger Varian* a62 57
3 br f Oasis Dream Blessing (Dubai Millennium)
1534[17] 1767[9] 3588[3] 4428[10] 5105[7] 5522[9]

**Poppy Bond** *Alan Bailey* a70 63
4 b f Misu Bond(IRE) Matilda Peace (Namaqualand (USA))
8265[5]

**Poppy In The Wind** *Alan Brown* a47 54
2 b f Piccolo Vintage Steps (IRE) (Bahamian Bounty)
3841[9] 4751[4] 5140[4] 5569[4] 5896[4] 6412[10] 6643[3] 7003[5] 7329[5] 7487[10]

**Pornichet (FR)** *Gai Waterhouse* a97 113
3 b c Vespone(IRE) Porza (FR) (Septieme Ciel (USA))
2196a[3] 3994a[9]

**Porsenna (IRE)** *Stefano Botti* 105
4 b c Dylan Thomas(IRE) Miss Mariduff (USA) (Hussonet (USA))
2589a[5] 3776a[5] (7616a)

**Port** *Richard Hannon* 51
2 b c Hurricane Run(IRE) Captain's Paradise (IRE) (Rock Of Gibraltar (IRE))
6456[7]

**Port Alfred** *Charlie Appleby* a88 87
4 b g Oasis Dream Cape Merino (Clantime)
1922[3] 2275[10] 4027[3] 4594[5]

**Portamento (IRE)** *Charlie Appleby* a93 104
2 gr c Shamardal(USA) Octave (USA) (Unbridled's Song (USA))
1512[5] (2480) 3318[14] 4670[2] (5134) (7232) 7439[2] (8059)

**Portenio (FR)** *C Lerner* a69 76
2 b c Zafeen(FR) Pomposa (IRE) (Barathea (IRE))
(3691a) 4932a[9] 5544a[5] 6244a[5] 6958a[5]

**Porthos Du Vallon** *Keith Dalgleish* 74
3 b g Jeremy(USA) Princess Caraboo (IRE) (Alzao (USA))
2827[4] 3187[4] (3360) 3662[4] 3911[7] (4490) 6111[6] 6217[11] 6478[10] 6836[4] 7489[4]

**Port Lairge** *John Gallagher* a63 60
4 b g Pastoral Pursuits Stylish Clare (IRE) (Desert Style (IRE))
1771[10] 4306[9] 5532[4] 6409[12] 6995[6] (7222) 7813[12] 7986[11]

**Porto Stephano (IRE)** *T Castanheira* 37
2 gr c Verglas(IRE) Heaven's Command (Priolo (USA))
5544a[11]

**Portulan (FR)** *Y Fertillet* a50
3 b c King's Best(USA) Titree (Highest Honor (FR))
482a[10]

**Posh Bounty** *Joseph Tuite* a46 63
3 ch f Bahamian Bounty Fission (Efisio)
2946[11] 5034[2] 6090[2] 6567[5] 6988[2] 7221[2]

**Posh Boy (IRE)** *Chris Wall* a71 73
4 b g Duke Of Marmalade(IRE) Sauvage (FR) (Sri Pekan (USA))
1209[3] 1798[8] 3080[6] 3761[2]

**Postbag** *Henry Candy* a60
2 b f Three Valleys(USA) Postage Stampe (Singspiel (IRE))
7739[3]

**Poste Restante** *David Simcock* a52 57
4 b f Halling(USA) Postage Stampe (Singspiel (IRE))
116[6] 246[6] 455[5] 580[4] 959[3] 997[3] 3115[7] (3682) 4343[3] 5001[8] 6339[6]

**Postillion (IRE)** *Richard Ford* a56 42
6 b h Sleeping Indian Princess Of Eden (GER) (Eden Rock (GER))
4805a[9] 8259[8]

**Postponed (IRE)** *Luca Cumani* 121
3 b c Dubawi(IRE) Ever Rigg (Dubai Destination (USA))
1532[3] 1953[4] 3375[3] (4385) (5577)

**Postscript (IRE)** *David Simcock* a91 91
6 ch g Pivotal Persian Secret (FR) (Persian Heights)
887[8] 1164[22] 1721[13] 3221[8] 3463[2] 4154[4] 4938[4] 5528[2] (5895) 6770[4]

**Potentate (IRE)** *Richard Hannon* a78 87
3 b c Acclamation Wish List (IRE) (Mujadil (USA))
1681[3] (3517) 4169[5] (4810) 5311[2] 6284[2] 6737[7]

**Potent Embrace (USA)** *Mark Johnston* a72 90
3 b f Street Cry(IRE) Karen's Caper (USA) (War Chant (USA))
2422[3] 2650[5] 3434[3] 3925[2] 4290[7] 4513[2] 4922[5] 5196[4] 5634[3] 6011[2] (6323) (6490) 6737[4] 6978[6] 7641[5]

**Poudlard Express (FR)** *D De Watrigant* a83 71
3 b c Panis(USA) Rizierella (FR) (Bering)
194a[4] 390a[3] 1620a[2]

**Pouncing Tiger** *Stuart Williams* a50 44
3 b f Tiger Hill(IRE) Ipsa Loquitur (Unfuwain (USA))
422[7] 1008[5] 1680[8] 3326[10]

**Pour La Victoire (IRE)** *Tony Carroll* a76 71
4 b g Antonius Pius(USA) Lady Lucia (IRE) (Royal Applause)
184[10] 575[2] 755[3] 851[2] 1105[3] (1666) 1877[2] 6086[3] (6397) 6657[10] 7078[2] 7368[2] (7556) 7758[7] 8017[7] 8186[2]

**Poursuite (FR)** *R Martens* a23
2 b f Spirit One(FR) Persephassa (FR) (Tiger Hill (IRE))
3872a[12]

**Powerful Pierre** *Noel Quinlan* a85 65
7 ch g Compton Place Alzianah (Alzao (USA))
(20) 153[7] (432) 540[5] 909[7] 1368[2] 4406[7] 4866[10] 5392[5] 5777[5] 7494[8] 7687[U] 7928[8]

**Powerful Presence (IRE)** *David O'Meara* a62 97
8 ch g Refuse To Bend(IRE) Miss A Note (USA) (Miswaki (USA))
1537[3] 1928[5] 2549[2] 2953[2] 3221[7] 3646[7] 4013[3] 4258[2] 5143[7] 6094[4] 6639[7]

**Powerfulstorm** *Ronald Harris* a52 59
2 b f Bertolini(USA) Frisson (Slip Anchor)
1169[9] 3550[7] 3813[6] 5746[5] 6246[4] 7832[12]

**Powerful Wind (IRE)** *Ronald Harris* a90 86
5 ch g Titus Livius(FR) Queen Of Fools (IRE) (Xaar)
4[5] 175[4] 444[7] 719[9] 863[8] (3551) 4284[5] 4762[20] 5677[9] 6313[10] 6650[10]

**Power Game** *Saeed bin Suroor* a78
2 ch c Shamardal(USA) Counterclaim (Pivotal)
5488[2] ◆ 6138[4]

**Power Of The Moon (IRE)** *M Nigge* 95
2 b f Acclamation Amenixa (FR) (Linamix (FR))
4931a[6] 5405a[2] 5741a[5] 6619a[3]

**Power Play (IRE)** *Richard Hannon* a77 90
2 b c Zebedee Elizabelle (IRE) (Westerner)
1936[5] 2172[2] (3387) 4203[3] (4944) (6529) 7331[6]

**Power Up** *Jane Chapple-Hyam* a73 62
3 b f Rail Link Melpomene (Peintre Celebre (USA))
99[3] 492[3] 1135[3] 2018[3] 2523[6] 2998[13] 3545[9] 4793[5] 5300[3] 5786[4] 6410[3] 6564[6] 6981[4] 7458[6] 7846[8] 8161[8]

**Poyle Jessica** *Ralph Beckett* a47 67
2 b f Royal Applause Poyle Caitlin (IRE) (Bachir (IRE))
5344[4] 6032[6] 6700[6] 7379[2]

**Poyle Thomas** *Ralph Beckett* a99 95
5 b g Rail Link Lost In Lucca (Inchinor)
(2782) 3859[2]

**Poyle Toby (IRE)** *Ralph Beckett* a71
4 b g Bahamian Bounty Lost In Lucca (Inchinor)
7733[5]

**Poyle Vinnie** *Michael Appleby* a103 92
4 b g Piccolo Poyle Dee Dee (Oasis Dream)
2233[10] (3222) 3887[3] 4833[3] (5053) (5470) 6095[2] ◆ 6692[3] 7365[2] (7767) ◆ 8136[2] ◆

**Prairie City (IRE)** *G-J Raveneau* a55
4 b f Elusive City(USA) Canouan (IRE) (Sadler's Wells (USA))
752a[8]

**Prairie Rose (GER)** *Olly Stevens* a37 79
3 b f Exceed And Excel(AUS) Prairie Lilli (GER) (Acatenango (GER))
1587[6] 2109[7] 2280[3] 2967[3] 4543[8] 5274[4] 7161[6]

**Praise N Glory** *Linda Jewell* 20
3 ch f Resplendent Glory(IRE) Tapsalteerie (Tipsy Creek (USA))
4029[10] 4587[8] 5249[6] 8198[10]

**Prato Mariante (ITY)** *M Corradini* 98
5 b g Munir Papete (Slip Anchor)
1603a[6] 3776a[6]

**Pravda Street** *Christopher Kellett* a76 61
9 ch g Soviet Star(USA) Sari (Faustus (USA))
172[7] 359[8] 733[7] 928[4] 1085[6] 1450[7]

**Prayer For Relief (USA)** *Dale Romans* a113
6 bb h Jump Start(USA) Sparklin Lil (USA) (Mr Sparkles (USA))
7614a[12]

**Prayer Time** *Mark H Tompkins* 51
2 ch g Pastoral Pursuits Nice Time (IRE) (Tagula (IRE))
5646[14] 6203[6] 6462[8]

**Precariously Good** *Paul Cole* a59 20
3 b f Oasis Dream Danceabout (Shareef Dancer (USA))
94[2] 298[2] 1039[9]

**Precast** *David Simcock* a64 57
2 ch f Halling(USA) Preceder (Polish Precedent (USA))
6333[4] 7184[6]

**Precedence (NZ)** *Bart & James Cummings* 108
9 b g Zabeel(NZ) Kowtow (USA) (Shadeed (USA))
7653a[6]

**Precinct** *James Eustace* a56 65
4 b f Refuse To Bend(IRE) Preceder (Polish Precedent (USA))
5007[8] 5831[10]

**Preciously (FR)** *D Guillemin* 93
3 ch f Lord Of England(GER) Prema (GER) (Big Shuffle (USA))
3027a[3] 3806a[5]

**Precision Five** *Jeremy Gask* a73 76
5 b m Proclamation(IRE) Sashay (Bishop Of Cashel)
2415[4] 2947[11] 3585[9] 4433[4] 5139[3] 5560[2]

**Precision Strike** *Richard Guest* a71 83
4 b g Multiplex Dockside Strike (Docksider (USA))
(1132) (1740) 2620[8] (2980) 3101[3] 3699[6] (4423) (5083) 5466[2] 5890[6] 6864[8] (7235) 7566[7]

**Premier Jack's** *Nikki Evans* a40
3 b g Tobougg(IRE) Arabellas Homer (Mark Of Esteem (IRE))
291[8] 675[7] 941[9] 4041a[8] 5339[5]

**Premio Loco (USA)** *Chris Wall* a107 113
10 ch g Prized(USA) Crazee Mental (Magic Ring (IRE))
749[3] 1068[12] 7066[3] 7836[10]

**Premium Pressure (USA)** *David Barron* a69 74
3 bb c War Front(USA) Judy's Magic (USA) (Wavering Monarch (USA))
626[3] 1962[3]

**Presburg (IRE)** *Joseph Tuite* a90 95
5 b g Balmont(USA) Eschasse (USA) (Zilzal (USA))
54[5] ◆ 386[4] 623[8] 956[6] 1171[7] 1556[9] (2033) 2627[5] (3931) 4608[3] 5162[5] 5687[4] 6479[6] 6878[7]

**Presidente** *Ed Walker* a51 66
3 b c Myboycharlie(IRE) Madam President (Royal Applause)
3914[6] 4544[6] 5892[8] 6240[10] 6865[8]

**Pres Rapide (IRE)** *John Quinn* 86
2 ch c Fast Company(IRE) Titian Saga (IRE) (Titus Livius (FR))
2214[2] ◆ (3199) 4172[2]

**Pressure** *Clive Cox* a59 68
2 ch c Equiano(FR) Classical Dancer (Dr Fong (USA))
4695[5] 7155[3] 7742[4]

**Pressure Point** *Keith Dalgleish* 77
4 b g Oasis Dream Arrive (Kahyasi)
3103[7] 4705[4] 5562[6] (6113) 6536[6] 7100[4]

**Prestige Vendome (FR)** *N Clement* 116
3 gr c Orpen(USA) Place Vendome (FR) (Dr Fong (USA))
1481a[4] 2196a[2] 2818a[10] 4278a[7]

**Presto Boy** *James Fanshawe* a68 39
2 b g Compton Place Presto Levanter (Rock Of Gibraltar (IRE))
3626[7] 4409[8] 5488[4] 6016[4] 6679[5]

**Presto Volante (IRE)** *Amanda Perrett* a95 88
6 b g Oratorio(IRE) Very Racy (USA) (Sri Pekan (USA))
(1770) 2482[4] 3034[5] (3859) 4777[6]

**Presumido (IRE)** *Simon Dow* a79 62
4 b g Iffraaj Miss Megs (IRE) (Croco Rouge (IRE))
53[6] 340[4] 496[3] 817[2] (1017) (1297) 1796[7] 2341[11] 2691[5] 4024[11] 6890[9] 7356[7] 7776[4] 8017[2] (8248)

**Pretend (IRE)** *Charlie Appleby* a107 91
3 b g Invincible Spirit(IRE) Fafinta (IRE) (Indian Ridge)
505a[7] 7455[4] (8228) (8263)

**Pretty Angel (IRE)** *M Halford* a76 76
3 gr f Dark Angel(IRE) Colleville (Pharly (FR))
7435a[4]

**Pretty Blonde (AUS)** *Kym Healy* 93
6 ch m High Rolling(AUS) Elladior (AUS) (Kingston Seattle (USA))
7395a[7]

**Pretty Bubbles** *J R Jenkins* a88 82
5 b m Sleeping Indian Willmar (IRE) (Zafonic (USA))
155[2] 491[3] 853[3] 952[5] (1245) 1857[3] (2775) 3890[4] 5058[6] 5320[2] (5573) 6302[3] 6891[7] 7160[6] 7885[8] (7988) 8209[3]

**Pretty Luna (GER)** *Henk Grewe* a45 88
3 ch f Bahamian Bounty Pleasant Night (IRE) (Law Society (USA))
5661a[5] 6221a[11]

**Pretty Mobile (FR)** *Paul Webber* a32
3 bl f Al Namix(FR) Gobeline (FR) (Robin Des Champs (FR))
6901[6]

**Pretty Panther (FR)** *F Rohaut* a91 99
4 ch f Hurricane Run(IRE) Princesse Jasmine (FR) (Gold Away (IRE))
836a[5] 7026a[5]

**Pretty Pearl (FR)** *N Caullery* a60 60
3 b f Kingsalsa(USA) Perle Rare (IRE) (Dansili)
391a[9] 629a[7]

**Pretty Picture** *Gay Kelleway* 79
2 gr f Zebedee Sophie'Jo (Agnes World (USA))
4839a[8] 5119a[5] 5617a[4] 5946[2] 6386a[3]

**Pretzel (IRE)** *John Gosden* 108
3 ch c New Approach(IRE) Foodbroker Fancy (IRE) (Halling (USA))
2781[2] (3455) 4127[2]

**Previous Acclaim (IRE)** *Julia Feilden* a51 41
3 b f Acclamation Erstwhile (FR) (Desert Prince (IRE))
98[5] 480[4] 653[6] 738[2] 960[7] 1257[4] 1918[5] 3121[4] 3627[8] 4048[7] 5106[5] 6194[5] 6394[3] 8259[9]

**Pride And Joy (IRE)** *Riccardo Santini* a82 99
5 b h Dark Angel(IRE) Fey Rouge (IRE) (Fayruz)
2375a[3] 7725a[7]

**Priestley's Reward (IRE)** *Alan Phillips* 25
5 b g Whipper(USA) Prima Figlia (IRE) (Inchinor)
2672[11] 3155[13]

**Prigsnov Dancer (IRE)** *Deborah Sanderson* a62 67
9 ch g Namid Brave Dance (IRE) (Kris)
996[5] 1148[6] 1282[4] (2127) 2955[4] 3150[6] 4571[6] 4994[5] 5287[12] 6272[9] 6720[5] 7025[11] 7423[9] (7783) 7972[12] 8285[9]

**Primacy (IRE)** *Neil Mulholland* a57 53
5 br m Primary(USA) Seaborne (Slip Anchor)
(68) 185[13]

**Prim And Proper** *Brendan Powell* a58 64
3 b f Sleeping Indian Quite Fantastic (IRE) (Fantastic Light (USA))
1101[6] (1384) 1683[5] 2078[4] 2416[3] 2695[7] (3281) 3559[8] 5122[2] 7347[6] 7556[6]

**Prima Pagina** *Dr Jon Scargill* a42 47
2 ch f Showcasing La Gazzetta (IRE) (Rossini (USA))
3387[7] 4784[8] 5315[5] 6294[10]

**Primary Route (IRE)** *Jason Ward* a26 59
4 ch f Primary(USA) Ashtaroute (USA) (Holy Bull (USA))
31[3] 671[11] 1929[9] 3052[6] 3363[8] 5374[4] 5773[5] 6119[8]

**Prime Exhibit** *Daniel Mark Loughnane* a79 76
9 b g Selkirk(USA) First Exhibit (Machiavellian (USA))
66[2] (152) (320) 421[4] 677[4] 782[7] 940[4] 1083[5] 2381[4] 3382[3] 3908[3] 4156[3] ◆ 4805a[3] 4950a[2] 5957a[18] 6285[9] 7871[8] 7954[10] 8044[8] 8168[7] (8316)

**Primo Uomo (IRE)** *Gerard O'Leary* 84
2 b c Strategic Prince Mooching Along (IRE) (Mujahid (USA))
2569a[3]

**Primrose Valley** *Ed Vaughan* a82 88
2 b f Pastoral Pursuits Cosmic Destiny (IRE) (Soviet Star (USA))
2151[3] ◆ 4320[2] 4784[2] (5253) (5637) 6067[8] 6513[9] 6933[16]

**Prince Alzain (USA)** *Robert Cowell* a114 80
5 b h Street Sense(USA) Monaassabaat (USA) (Zilzal (USA))
508a[13] 8018[4]

**Prince Ballygowen** *Clifford Lines* a36 17
3 b g Prince Arch(USA) Ball Gown (Jalmood (USA))
2346[9] 2883[U] 6634[9]

**Prince Bishop (IRE)** *Saeed bin Suroor* a121 118
7 ch g Dubawi(IRE) North East Bay (USA) (Prospect Bay (CAN))
(508a) (901a) 1183a[9] (6139)

**Prince Bonnaire** *David Brown* 90
2 b c Kheleyf(USA) Sparkling Clear (Efisio)
2328[4] (2610) 3001[4] 3322[21] 4439[10] 5447[2] 5770[4] 6230[4] 6933[21]

**Prince D'Aumone (FR)** *S Jesus* a55 51
2 b c Miesque's Son(USA) Arthurs Princess (IRE) (Monashee Mountain (USA))
3029a[8] 5900a[5]

**Prince Du Goyen (FR)** *A Bonin* 67
2 ch c Vatori(FR) Xiberua (FR) (Kingsalsa (USA))
7344a[3]

**Prince Gagarin (IRE)** *Ed Dunlop* 99
2 b c Dubawi(IRE) Cara Fantasy (IRE) (Sadler's Wells (USA))
4395[3] (4865) 5576[10] 6684[2] (7331)

**Prince Gibraltar (FR)** *J-C Rouget* 119
3 ch c Rock Of Gibraltar(IRE) Princess Sofia (UAE) (Pennekamp (USA))
(1965a) 2818a[3] ◆ 4251a[2] 5406a[3] 6970a[7]

**Prince Jean D'o** *F Head* a75 71
3 b c Soldier Of Fortune(IRE) Chic Retreat (USA) (Elusive Quality (USA))
5227a[8]

**Prince Jock (USA)** *John Patrick Shanahan* a81 78
7 b g Repent(USA) My Special K'S (USA) (Tabasco Cat (USA))
5849[8] (6082a)

**Princely Hero (IRE)** *Chris Gordon* a56 51
10 b g Royal Applause Dalu (IRE) (Dancing Brave (USA))
471[5] 656[11]

**Prince Nomad (FR)** *X Thomas-Demeaulte* 98
3 b c Galileo(IRE) En Public (FR) (Rainbow Quest (USA))
4251a[8]

**Prince Of All** *P D Deegan* a111 113
3 ch c Iffraaj Ya Hajar (Lycius (USA))
3320[7] 6350a[4] 6909a[2]

**Prince Of Burma (IRE)** *David Evans* a82 81
6 b h Mujadil(USA) Spinning Ruby (Pivotal)
211[3] 310[5] 399[5] 1718[2] 1876[4] 2529[3] 2947[10] (3526) 3971[3] 4080[3]

**Prince Of Cardamom (IRE)** *Andrew Balding* 62
2 b g Nayef(USA) Tiger Spice (Royal Applause)
6545[8] 7134[4]

**Prince Of Clowns (IRE)** *John Quinn* 34
2 b c Vale Of York(IRE) Queen Of Fools (IRE) (Xaar)
3394[6] 4286[13] 5194[9]

**Prince Of Islay (IRE)** *Robert Mills* a55 36
3 ch g Nayef(USA) Feolin (Dr Fong (USA))
2221[14] 2924[7] 3856[7] 5102[4] 5556[6]

**Prince Of Johanne (IRE)** *Tom Tate* a38 110
8 gr g Johannesburg(USA) Paiute Princess (FR) (Darshaan)
2286[3] 3356[24] 3982[5] 5609[9] 6332[6] 6748[2]

**Prince Of Paris** *Roger Ingram* a79 61
2 b c Champs Elysees Cool Kitten (IRE) (One Cool Cat (USA))
3578[6] 4809[8] 5881[8] 6663[2] 6884[12] (7396) 7798[4] 8009[2] (8241)

**Prince Of Passion (CAN)** *Derek Shaw* a61 56
6 ch g Roman Ruler(USA) Rare Passion (CAN) (Out Of Place (USA))
(59) 297[2] 489[4] 651[7] 766[9] 993[6] 1127[4] 1369[3] 1487[12] 1892[8] 6843[13] 6983[6] 7111[3] 7423[10] 7782[10] 7972[11] 8133[7] 8223[5]

**Prince Of Stars** *John Gosden* 97
3 b c Sea The Stars(IRE) Queen's Logic (IRE) (Grand Lodge (USA))
1529[5] ◆ (2075) (5094)

**Princeofthedesert** *Garry Woodward* a56 56
8 b g Nayef(USA) Twilight Sonnet (Exit To Nowhere (USA))
3269[10] 4062[7] 5101[5]

**Prince Of Time** *Mark Johnston* 68
2 ch g Bahamian Bounty Touching (IRE) (Kheleyf (USA))
4486[4] 4829[5] 5296[4] 6556[5]

**Prince Regal** *Timothy Jarvis* a74 83
4 ch g Cockney Rebel(IRE) Wachiwi (IRE) (Namid)
1731[3] 2147[16] 2350[7] 2732[9] 4401[8] 5784[5] 5951[5] 7356[2] 7759[12]

**Prince Rofan (IRE)** *Derek Shaw* a39 14
2 gr g Strategic Prince Rofan (USA) (Cozzene (USA))
2288[8] 4577[3] 5253[7] 5798[11]

**Princess Alba (GER)** *Mario Hofer* 55
2 b f Lando(GER) Praia (GER) (Big Shuffle (USA))
6950a[6]

**Princess Bavaroise (FR)** *H-A Pantall* a86 85
3 b f Desert Prince(IRE) Sascilaria (Fasliyev (USA))
2006a[7] 3030a[8]

**Princess Bounty** *Phil McEntee* a48 34
4 b f Bahamian Bounty Regal Magic (IRE) (Sadler's Wells (USA))
215[7] 1860[9]

**Princess Caetani (IRE)** *David Dennis* a75 93
5 b m Dylan Thomas(IRE) Caladira (IRE) (Darshaan)
6559[9]

**Princess Cammie (IRE)** *John Bridger* a44 58
4 b f Camacho Hawattef (IRE) (Mujtahid (USA))
2045[4] 2689[12] 2994[7] 3329[4] 3549[9]

**Princess Charm (IRE)** *C Lerner* 78
2 b f Rip Van Winkle(IRE) Gold Charm (GER) (Key Of Luck (USA))
(8276a)

**Princesse Fleur** *Michael Scudamore* 58
6 b m Grape Tree Road Princesse Grec (FR) (Grand Tresor (FR))
2252[4]

**Princesse Rebelle (FR)** *M Nigge* 71
2 b f Sageburg(IRE) Daykerisks (FR) (Take Risks (FR))
1271a[8] 2976a[4] 4882a[13] 5662a[2] 6591a[6]

**Princesse Savoie** *J Bertran De Balanda* 63
2 b f Tamayuz Savoie (FR) (Anabaa (USA))
2755a[4]

**Princess Icicle** *Jo Crowley* a72 68
6 b m Iceman Sarabah (IRE) (Ela-Mana-Mou)
491[2] 853[8] 5848[2] 7302[8]

**Princess Kheleyf** *Geoffrey Oldroyd*
5 b m Kheleyf(USA) Jugendliebe (IRE) (Persian Bold)
1722[11]

**Princess Kiara (FR)** *N Caullery* a70 72
3 b f Spirit One(FR) Lizzy's Cat (FR) (Sir Cat (USA))
7722a[14]

**Princess Loulou (IRE)** *Roger Varian* 110
4 ch f Pivotal Aiming (Highest Honor (FR))
1945[2] 2572a[3] 3355[11] 5742a[2] 7070a[4] 7717[2]

**Princess Myla (IRE)** *Paul Midgley* 56
3 b f Intense Focus(USA) Romany Princess (IRE) (Viking Ruler (AUS))
1642[5] 3440[9] 3600[7] 3913[11] 4059[5] 4318[4] 4974[6] 5375[10]

**Princess Noor (IRE)** *Roger Varian* a72 110
3 b f Holy Roman Emperor(IRE) Gentle Night (Zafonic (USA))
1976[12]

**Princess Ombu (IRE)** *Charles Hills* 57
3 gr f High Chaparral(IRE) Cause Celebre (IRE) (Peintre Celebre (USA))
1353[10]

**Princess P** *Alan McCabe*
2 b f Stimulation(IRE) Baby Princess (BRZ) (Crimson Tide (IRE))
6718[8]

**Princess Rose** *John Weymes* a66 51
3 b f Royal Applause Mystical Spirit (IRE) (Xaar)
1361[3] 2516[6] 2870[7] 3564[6] 4071[4] 4512[6] 5853[8] 6116[6] 6543[4] 6834[4] 7420[7] 7940[6] 8111[12] 8256[7]

**Princess Spirit** *Edward Creighton* a71 45
5 b m Invincible Spirit(IRE) Habariya (IRE) (Perugino (USA))
1230[3] 1392[5] 1554[8] 2463[11] 2646[2] 3390[5] 3890[9] 4073[7] 5041[2] 6242[3] 6857[2]

**Princess Vati (FR)** *P Monfort* a69 69
5 ch m Vatori(FR) Reine De Vati (FR) (Take Risks (FR))
*57a[3] 806a[7]*

**Princess Willow** *John E Long* a63 46
6 b m Phoenix Reach(IRE) Highland Hannah (IRE) (Persian Heights)
*277[8] 590[11]*

**Prince's Trust** *William Haggas* a111 105
4 b g Invincible Spirit(IRE) Lost In Wonder (USA) (Galileo (IRE))
(5728) ◆ 6921[13] *(7555)* ◆ *7836[7]*

**Principe Uromonte (IRE)** *J-M Capitte* a57 71
8 ch g Talkin Man(CAN) Pichola Lake (USA) (Quest For Fame)
*392a[9]*

**Principiante** *Marco Gasparini* 94
4 ch c Sir Percy Ekagra (Barathea (IRE))
2374a[5]

**Principle Equation (IRE)** *Ralph Beckett* a86 90
3 b f Oasis Dream Dame Alicia (IRE) (Sadler's Wells (USA))
1808[2] ◆ 2690[2] (3755) 4782[12] 5448[2] 6258[2] 7043[2] *7773[4]*

**Prinsessen** *Bent Olsen* 88
3 ch f Dutch Art Sallysaysso (IRE) (Danehill Dancer (IRE))
6388a[14]

**Printmaker (IRE)** *Tim Easterby* a49 56
6 b g Shamardal(USA) Marie Laurencin (Peintre Celebre (USA))
2169[17] 2607[7] 3436[3] 3623[7]

**Priore Philip (ITY)** *Stefano Botti* 118
3 ch c Dane Friendly Lan Force (ITY) (Blu Air Force (IRE))
1779a[2] (2589a) (6808a) (7617a)

**Priors Brook** *Andrew Balding* a73
3 b g Champs Elysees Dyanita (Singspiel (IRE))
*6482[4] 7841[5] (8098)*

**Priors Gate (IRE)** *Marcus Tregoning* 47
2 b g Acclamation Key Rose (IRE) (Key Of Luck (USA))
6517[16]

**Prisca** *Jamie Osborne* a44 40
3 b f Holy Roman Emperor(IRE) Ainia (Alhaarth (IRE))
*298[6] 573[8] 823[3]*

**Prisenflag (FR)** *G Nicot* a68 77
3 gr f Pyrus(USA) Proud Douna (FR) (Kaldoun (FR))
6913a[9]

**Private Dancer** *Alan Swinbank* 65
3 b g Halling(USA) Anamilina (IRE) (Anabaa (USA))
2292[5] 2655[6]

**Private Prospect (USA)** *Michael B Campbell* a104
2 b c Discreet Cat(USA) Private Deputy (USA) (Private Terms (USA))
*7610a[9]*

**Private Zone (CAN)** *Alfredo Velazquez* a122 103
5 b g Macho Uno(USA) Auburn Beauty (USA) (Siphon (BRZ))
*7612a[3]*

**Privet Hedge (USA)** *D Smaga* a101 92
3 b f First Defence(USA) Privity (USA) (Private Account (USA))
1782a[6]

**Prize** *Sylvester Kirk* a54 55
3 b f Exceed And Excel(AUS) Holamo (IRE) (Montjeu (IRE))
3564[5] *3855[5]* 4155[6] 7221[10]

**Prize Exhibit** *Jamie Osborne* a89 100
2 b f Showcasing Roodeye (Inchinor)
3076[4] ◆ 3583[2] *(4610)* 4913[4] (5286) 6067[6] 6530[7] 6926[3] 7592a[4]

**Probably (IRE)** *Rune Haugen* 87
4 b c Danehill Dancer(IRE) Wedding Morn (IRE) (Sadler's Wells (USA))
3090a[11] 5744a[15] 6389a[10]

**Proclamationofwar** *Kevin Ryan* a73 74
3 b g Proclamation(IRE) Rockburst (Xaar)
*765[2] (1137)* 1396[6] 2015[7] 2517[3] 3137[2] 3625[4] 3957[3]

**Procurement** *Simon Dow* a75 68
3 b f Zamindar(USA) Acquisition (Dansili)
*8310[6]*

**Procurer (FR)** *Scott Dixon* a26 54
3 b g Milk It Mick Veils Of Salome (Arkadian Hero (USA))
*2093[5]* 2619[2] 4295[4] *5574[8]*

**Producer** *Richard Hannon* a107 116
5 ch h Dutch Art River Saint (USA) (Irish River (FR))
3317[5] 4180[4] 4682[4] 5354[2] 5434[6] 5666[4] 6458[2] 6710[5]

**Professor** *Richard Hannon* 114
4 ch c Byron Jubilee (Selkirk (USA))
1728[4] 2848[3] 3278[2] 3452[2] 4200[12] (4425) 5434[4] 5722[3] 6134[13] 6328[5] 6710[10] 7242[13]

**Profile Star (IRE)** *Violet M Jordan* a79 59
5 b g Kodiac Fingal Nights (IRE) (Night Shift (USA))
*35[5] 175[10] 444[6] 777[2] 909[9] (1019) 1283[8]* 1843[10] *1922[4]* 2233[6] 2637[4] 6236[8] 6764[6] 7623[7] 8255[U] 8322[5]

**Profitable (IRE)** *Clive Cox* 100
2 b c Invincible Spirit(IRE) Dani Ridge (IRE) (Indian Ridge)
3889[2] (4583) 5173[2] 6128[2] 6703[2] 7238[5]

**Prohibit** *Robert Cowell* a92 102
9 b g Oasis Dream Well Warned (Warning)
*4[6] 271[9]*

**Prohibition (IRE)** *Mandy Rowland* a62 65
8 b g Danehill Dancer(IRE) Crumpetsfortea (IRE) (Henbit (USA))
*1795 2014* ◆ *(290) 592[2] (673) 916[5] 1288[8]*

**Promesse D'Ecouves (FR)** *K Borgel* 35
4 b f Kentucky Dynamite(USA) Shawnee (IRE) (Sadler's Wells (USA))
2192a[10]

**Prometheus (IRE)** *A De Royer-Dupre* a77 77
3 b c Montjeu(IRE) Ahdaab (USA) (Rahy (USA))
*5027a[2] 5705a[2]*

**Prominna** *Tony Carroll* a51
4 ch g Proclamation(IRE) Minnina (IRE) (In The Wings)
*7370[5] 7682[10] 7865[6]*

**Promised Wings (GER)** *Chris Gordon* a53 40
7 ch g Monsun(GER) Panagia (USA) (Diesis)
7419[10]

**Proper Charlie** *Lee Carter* a65 46
6 b g Cadeaux Genereux Ring Of Love (Magic Ring (IRE))
*192[7] 662[7] 4049[2] 4732[5] 5136[4] 6720[9]*

**Proper Job** *Polly Gundry*
6 b g Rainbow High Merlin Cider (Un Desperado (FR))
*468[12]*

**Properus (IRE)** *Kevin Ryan* 79
2 b c Lord Shanakill(USA) Amistad (GER) (Winged Love (IRE))
5050[4] 6509[4] (7246)

**Prophesize** *Noel Quinlan* 80
2 b g Captain Rio Rapid Revalation (USA) (Bianconi (USA))
(2386)

**Prophesy (IRE)** *Tim Easterby* 83
5 ch g Excellent Art Race The Wild Wind (USA) (Sunny's Halo (CAN))
1483[11] 2016[7] 2520[4] 3205[7] 4349[6] 4793[4] 5421[5] 6227[6] 7044[4] 7281[2]

**Prophets Pride** *F Vermeulen* a90 56
4 b c Sakhee(USA) Winner's Call (Indian Ridge)
6569a[10]

**Proposal (FR)** *Mme J Bidgood* a73 66
4 b g Orpen(USA) Note To Cathy (USA) (Notebook (USA))
*722a[16]*

**Proposed** *Richard Hannon* 59
2 b c Invincible Spirit(IRE) On A Soapbox (USA) (Mi Cielo (USA))
5377[7] ◆ 6259[11]

**Prostate Awareness (IRE)** *Patrick Holmes* a32 60
3 b g Camacho Genuinely (IRE) (Entrepreneur)
2355[12] 3439[7] 3662[3] 4473[12] 4998[13] *6771[8]* 6823[2] *7426[10]*

**Protected** *James Tate* 75
3 b c Exceed And Excel(AUS) Pink Stone (FR) (Bigstone (IRE))
2516[2] 3465[3] 3814[6]

**Protectionist (GER)** *A Wohler* 122
4 b c Monsun(GER) Patineuse (IRE) (Peintre Celebre (USA))
2815a[2] (3770a) (5743a) 7126a[4] (7653a)

**Proud Chieftain** *Clifford Lines* a103 103
6 b g Sleeping Indian Skimra (Hernando (FR))
1948[19] 3726[3] 4667[5] 5162[2] 5651[12] *6106[9]* 6685[8] 7440[6] 7598[5]

**Proud Of You (IRE)** *Nigel Tinkler* 71
2 b g Fast Company(IRE) Shambodia (IRE) (Petardia)
2866[5] 4416[10]

**Proud Possibility (USA)** *Niels Petersen* a98 82
4 ch g Tale Of The Cat(USA) Mysterious Lina (FR) (Linamix (FR))
*109a[12] 304a[7] 3996a[4]* 4957a[9]

**Proud Times (USA)** *Ali Stronge* a70 54
8 bb g Proud Citizen(USA) Laura's Pistolette (USA) (Big Pistol (USA))
*8037[9] 8134[9]*

**Proved You Wrong (IRE)** *Jo Hughes* 33
2 b c Approve(IRE) Island Destiny (Kris)
4449[5] 4528[8]

**Provenance** *Sir Michael Stoute* a88 104
3 b f Galileo(IRE) Echelon (Danehill (USA))
*(2061)* 2495[3] (4551) (5177) ◆ 6707[3] 7105[5]

**Provident Spirit** *John Gosden* 91
3 b c Invincible Spirit(IRE) Port Providence (Red Ransom (USA))
1192[2] (1511) 2257[8] 3243[5] 5177[4] 5649[6]

**Prudhoe Bay (USA)** *Edward Plesa Jr* a100
3 bb c Songandaprayer(USA) Cameron Crazies (USA) (Lion Heart (USA))
*813a[4]*

**Pryers Princess** *Michael Herrington* 47
2 ch f Medicean Opening Ceremony (USA) (Quest For Fame)
2615[5]

**Prying** *Charlie Appleby* a45
2 ch f Dubawi(IRE) Pryka (ARG) (Southern Halo (USA))
*7659[7] 7756[8]*

**Psichedelic (IRE)** *M Manili* 93
4 b g Excellent Art Pack Ice (USA) (Wekiva Springs (USA))
7604a[6]

**Psychometry (FR)** *Sir Michael Stoute* a80 92
3 b f Danehill Dancer(IRE) Seven Magicians (USA) (Silver Hawk (USA))
2072[4] 2484[3] 3357[8] 5176[5] 5627[7]

**Ptit Beaumont (FR)** *P Bourgoin* a30
3 b c Ski Chief(USA) La Bernardina (IRE) (Mtoto)
*5959a[9]*

**P'Tit Milord (FR)** *M Ortholan* a24
3 b g Al Namix(FR) Arum D'Or (FR) (Kendor (FR))
2003a[P]

**Ptolemy** *David Barron* a26 66
5 b g Royal Applause Rydal Mount (IRE) (Cape Cross (IRE))
*126[11]* 2844[7]

**Ptolomeos** *Sean Regan* a45 53
11 b g Kayf Tara Lucy Tufty (Vin St Benet)
2476[2] 2806[2] 6644[12] 7540[6]

**Publilia** *Mark Johnston* 92
2 b f Makfi Terentia (Diktat)
3613[2] 4117[3] (4382) 5664[5] ◆ 6778a[5]

**Puca (USA)** *William Mott* a101 87
2 b f Big Brown(USA) Boat's Ghost (USA) (Silver Ghost (USA))
*7606a[6]*

**Pucker Up** *David Brown* a62 49
4 b f Royal Applause Smooch (Inchinor)
*84[8]*

**Pucon** *Roger Teal* a78 78
5 b m Kyllachy The Fugative (Nicholas (USA))
*1896[2] (2645)* 3246[3] 4121[8] 5880[5] 6296[2] 6658[3] *7357[3] 7886[8]*

**Pudding (IRE)** *Lady Cecil* a27 43
3 b f Bushranger(IRE) Kahyasi Moll (IRE) (Brief Truce (USA))
*4610[8]* 5344[10] 5725[8]

**Puissant (IRE)** *Marco Botti* 90
2 b c Galileo(IRE) Elletelle (IRE) (Elnadim (USA))
6551[8] 6859[2] (7244) ◆

**Pulcinella (IRE)** *Charlie Appleby* 91
2 b f Dubawi(IRE) Petrushka (IRE) (Unfuwain (USA))
3223[5] (6333) ◆ 7237[2]

**Pullmen** *Paul Henderson* a59
6 gr g Silver Patriarch(IRE) Moon Spinner (Elmaamul (USA))
*657[10]*

**Pull The Pin (IRE)** *Ann Stokell* a76 60
5 b g Kheleyf(USA) Inscribed (IRE) (Fasliyev (USA))
*87[5] 257[2] 572[3] 654[8] 834[5] 1019[8] 1127[6] 1224[2] 1244[3]* 1448[9] 1739[4] 1892[3] 2459[6] 3093[4] 3609[6] 4362[3] 4960[3] 5207[3] 5486[2] 5858[2] 5907[2] 7009[4] 7644[9] 7826[4]

**Pull The Plug (IRE)** *Declan Carroll* a66 76
3 b f Sleeping Indian Babylonian (Shamardal (USA))
2745[7] 3484[8] 3957[4] 6235[15] *7286[9]*

**Pulpitarian (USA)** *Lucinda Russell* 81
6 b g Pulpit(USA) Bedanken (USA) (Geri (USA))
3055[4]

**Pumaflor (IRE)** *Richard Guest* a3 66
2 br g Aussie Rules(USA) Krasotka (IRE) (Soviet Star (USA))
4424[10] 4684[6] 5128[5] (5790) 6165[11] 6643[4] 7005[4] *7258[12]*

**Pumpkin Rumble (USA)** *Danny Gargan* 100
3 ch g English Channel(USA) Clarins (USA) (Storm Cat (USA))
6949a[4]

**Pump Pump Boy (FR)** *J-P Gauvin* a99 105
6 b h Kingsalsa(USA) Pump Pump Girl (FR) (Kendor (FR))
*(177a) 669a[4]* 4644a[4]

**Punk** *George Peckham* a74 76
3 b g Bahamian Bounty Maysarah (IRE) (Green Desert (USA))
*4263[4]* 5320[3] *6034[11] 6414[3] 6680[8] 7071[6] 7352[6]*

**Punk Rocker (IRE)** *Michael Dods* 70
2 b f Fastnet Rock(AUS) Cape Vintage (IRE) (Cape Cross (IRE))
(4109) 4625[5]

**Pupil (IRE)** *Richard Hannon* 96
3 b c Mastercraftsman(IRE) Blue Iris (Petong)
1953[6] 3378[18] 4147[2] 4821[7] 5720[6] 6785[2] 6892[3]

**Puppet Theatre (IRE)** *David O'Meara* a44 38
4 ch f Pivotal Eilean Ban (USA) (Silver Hawk (USA))
*914[7] 1069[8] 1888[3]* 2389[5] *2937[5] 3798[5]* ◆ *5570[4]* 5997[5]

**Purana** *Tony Carroll* a53 45
3 ch f Pastoral Pursuits Arruhan (IRE) (Mujtahid (USA))
*660[6] 1024[6]* 1680[7] 2025[11] *3389[10]*

**Purcell (IRE)** *Andrew Balding* a104 91
4 b g Acclamation Lyca Ballerina (Marju (IRE))
*(1042) (1301)* 2145[16] 2758[9] 6124[17]

**Pure Amber (IRE)** *Ismail Mohammed* a79 70
3 b g Shamardal(USA) Ile Rousse (Danehill (USA))
*1897[2]* 2510[8] 3670[6] 4120[8]

**Pure Line** *Ralph Beckett* a70
2 b f Zamindar(USA) Pure Grain (Polish Precedent (USA))
*7808[2]* ◆ *8036[4]*

**Purford Green** *Michael Attwater* a58 19
5 ch m Kyllachy Mo Stopher (Sharpo)
*666[4] 845[7] 1018[4] 1238[6] 7887[10] 8024[6] 8319[7]*

**Purley Queen (IRE)** *Mrs C Gilbert* a51 58
5 b m Piccolo Queenie (Indian Ridge)
(2591a) 3496a[3] 4038a[2] 4715a[6] (5228a) 6186a[4]

**Purple Lane (IRE)** *David Simcock* a71 72
3 ch g Danehill Dancer(IRE) Big Heart (Mr Greeley (USA))
4446[3] 5004[5] *6154[3]*

**Purple 'n Gold (IRE)** *David Pipe* a66 83
5 b g Strategic Prince Golden Dew (IRE) (Montjeu (IRE))
4331[6] 4799[5]

**Purple Rock (IRE)** *Charles Hills* 80
2 b c Fastnet Rock(AUS) Amethyst (IRE) (Sadler's Wells (USA))
6551[4] (6935)

**Purple Sage (IRE)** *Brendan Powell* a87 98
8 b m Danehill Dancer(IRE) Kylemore (IRE) (Sadler's Wells (USA))
*8243[9]*

**Purple Spectrum** *J R Jenkins* a93 90
3 gr g Verglas(IRE) Rainbow's Edge (Rainbow Quest (USA))
(2221) 2761[7] 3892[6] (4584) 5193[2] 6137[8] *7838[11] 8096[2]*

**Purple Spot** *Rod Millman* a45 60
3 br f Kyllachy Regal Gallery (IRE) (Royal Academy (USA))
*2682[13]* 3277[9] 4029[5] 4742[5] 5846[6] *6682[10] 7369[14]*

**Purple Surprise** *Andrew Reid* a50 23
2 b f Teofilio(IRE) Manic (Polar Falcon (USA))
*5488[11]* 6435[11] *7011[9] 7684[3] 7824[2] 7991[5] 8179[9]*

**Purr Along** *J P Murtagh* a80 111
4 b f Mount Nelson Purring (USA) (Mountain Cat (USA))
(2572a) 3355[3] 4165[4] 5869a[6] 6351a[7]

**Pusey Street Vale** *John Gallagher* a29 29
3 b f Moss Vale(IRE) Pusey Street Girl (Gildoran)
*1243[4]*

**Pushkin Museum (IRE)** *Richard Fahey* a85 83
3 gr g Soviet Star(USA) Chaste (Groom Dancer (USA))
1700[10] 2090[11] 3219[10] (3669) 4186[2] 4977[3] 5923[7] 6324[9] 6736[14]

**Push Me (IRE)** *Iain Jardine* a69 84
7 gr m Verglas(IRE) Gilda Lilly (USA) (War Chant (USA))
*1[4]* 1638[2] 2199[8] (2676) 3005[5] 3301[3] 3439[2] 4472[2] (4729)

**Putin (IRE)** *Phil McEntee* a76 73
6 b g Fasliyev(USA) Consignia (IRE) (Definite Article)
*(339) (2901)* 3160[8] 3707[2] 4024[3] *4262[3]* 4406[9] 4768[4] *5281[4] 5486[4] 6240[11] 6843[8] 7647[8] 7765[4]* 7829[2] 8282[4]

**Putra Eton (IRE)** *Roger Varian* a65 86
4 b g Danehill Dancer(IRE) Anna Pallida (Sadler's Wells (USA))
1612[3] 2162[6] *4736[9]*

**Putting Green** *Richard Hannon* a73 61
2 ch c Selkirk(USA) Ryella (USA) (Cozzene (USA))
6985[6] *7892[2] 8067[2]*

**Puzzle Time** *Giles Bravery* a80 91
4 b f Araafa(IRE) Puzzling (Peintre Celebre (USA))
*463[2] 649[2] (871) (1099)* (5448) 6292[6] 6713[20] 6987[3] *7554[12] 7850[7] 8211[6]*

**Pyla (IRE)** *Ed Dunlop* a41 57
2 b f Footstepsinthesand Beautiful Hill (IRE) (Danehill (USA))
6333[5] *7354[11]*

**Pyrite Mountain (CAN)** *Todd Pletcher* a105 106
4 b c Silent Name(JPN) Gold Lined (CAN) (Numerous (USA))
7324a[8]

**Pyroclastic (IRE)** *Jim Boyle* a62
2 b c Tagula(IRE) Gypsy Royal (IRE) (Desert Prince (IRE))
*7840[8] 8112[3] 8318[6]*

**Pyrocumulus (IRE)** *Alan McCabe* a61 49
2 b g Kodiac Dry Lightning (Shareef Dancer (USA))
3467[6] 3934[8] 4429[9] *5009[11]* 6205[6] 6428[3] ◆ *(7648) 8087[3]*

**Pyromaniac (IRE)** *A J Martin* a69 81
4 b g Invincible Spirit(IRE) Silly Goose (IRE) (Sadler's Wells (USA))
(4951a)

**Qanan** *Chris Wall* a90 95
5 b g Green Desert(USA) Strings (Unfuwain (USA))
1636[9] *(2882) 3582[2]* 4586[2] *5487[3]* (6465) 7110[3]

**Qasser (IRE)** *Harry Whittington* a70 69
5 b g Intikhab(USA) Surrender To Me (USA) (Royal Anthem (USA))
*1899[8]* 2300[5]

**Qatar Breeze** *G E Mikhalides* 49
2 b c Hellvelyn Tropical Breeze (IRE) (Kris)
5706a[9]

**Qatar Falcon (IRE)** *Kevin Ryan* a46
2 ch c Mastercraftsman(IRE) Nouveau Riche (IRE) (Entrepreneur)
*8093[10]*

**Qatar Princess (IRE)** *J R Jenkins* a57 71
3 b f Marju(IRE) Bridal Dance (IRE) (Danehill Dancer (IRE))
*6765[4] 7285[6] 7652[8] 7929[4] 8229[3] 8322[6]*

**Qatar Road (FR)** *Marco Botti* a89 76
2 ch c Footstepsinthesand Amarinda (GER) (Tiger Hill (IRE))
5439[5] (6039) 6977[4] *(7374) 7882[3]*

**Qatar Rock (IRE)** *Kevin Ryan* a59
2 gr g Zebedee Spinning Gold (Spinning World (USA))
*8092[6]*

**Qatar Success** *Olly Stevens* a37
2 b f Kyllachy Cherokee Stream (IRE) (Indian Ridge)
7037[14] *7920[6] 8027[5]*

**Qatoomah (KSA)** *N Bachalard* a101
5 b m El Corredor(USA) Kiss A Miss (USA) (Kissin Kris (USA))
*679a[7] 808a[4]*

**Qawaasem (IRE)** *Charles Hills* 100
3 b f Shamardal(USA) Misdaqeya (Red Ransom (USA))
2316[9]

**Qewy (IRE)** *John M Oxx* 104
4 b g Street Cry(IRE) Princess Nada (Barathea (IRE))
(1252a) 2185a[7] 5361a[6] 6350a[5] 7144a[10]

**Qibtee (FR)** *Les Eyre* a62 61
4 b g Antonius Pius(USA) Embers Of Fame (IRE) (Sadler's Wells (USA))
*1132[6]* 1356[3] 1660[10] 4473[7] 4709[2] 5077[2] 5301[4] *7846[2] 7990[11] 8261[6]*

**Qoosine (FR)** *Rod Collet* a66 66
2 b f Naaqoos Adamantina (FR) (Muhtathir)
3029a[7] *3872a[4]* 4882a[6] *5619a[7]*

**Q Twenty Girl (IRE)** *Mark Usher* 53
2 b f Fast Company(IRE) Extravagance (IRE) (King's Best (USA))
4740[6] 5210[7] 5684[8] 6040[4] 7515[7]

**Quadriga (IRE)** *Robert Eddery* a69 49
4 b g Acclamation Turning Light (GER) (Fantastic Light (USA))
*171[3] 317[7] 366[5]*

**Quadriller (FR)** *Philip Hobbs* a74 70
7 b g Lando(GER) Tabachines (FR) (Art Francais (USA))
2942[5] 3818[5] (4843)

**Quadrivium (USA)** *David Wachman* a93 91
3 b c Henrythenavigator(USA) Sea Of Showers (USA) (Seattle Slew (USA))
1200a[9]

**Quaduna** *A Wohler* 108
4 b f Duke Of Marmalade(IRE) Quelle Amore (GER) (Monsun (GER))
1974[4] 3873a[7] (7146a)

**Quae Supra** *Richard Hannon* a35 57
2 b g Exceed And Excel(AUS) Noodle Soup (USA) (Alphabet Soup (USA))
3748[10] 4330[9] 6652[7] *7014[11]* 7165[3] 7487[7] *7740[12]*

**Quaintrelle (IRE)** *Ed Vaughan* a57 60
3 b f Dandy Man(IRE) Extravagance (IRE) (King's Best (USA))
4446[6] 6042[2] *6661[3] 8002[2] 8280[4]*

**Qualify (IRE)** *A P O'Brien* a93 105
2 b f Fastnet Rock(AUS) Perihelion (IRE) (Galileo (IRE))
4598a[3] 5734a[5] 6372a[6] (6798a) ◆ 7592a[8]

**Quality Art (USA)** *Simon Hodgson* a70 49
6 b g Elusive Quality(USA) Katherine Seymour (Green Desert (USA))
*93[4] 272[8] 478[9] 694[2] 889[6] 921[2] 1238[4]* 1787[7] 1912[8] *2459[8]* 6631[7] 6983[5] 7520[3] 7781[3] 8023[5] 8230[3]

**Quality Rocks (USA)** *William Mott* a97 97
2 bb f Rock Hard Ten(USA) Elusive Virgin (USA) (Elusive Quality (USA))
7592a[10]

**Quality Song (USA)** *Roger Varian* 57
2 b c Elusive Quality(USA) Run In (USA) (Dynaformer (USA))
6457[4]

**Quantum Dot (IRE)** *Ed de Giles* a72 41
3 ch g Exceed And Excel(AUS) Jeed (IRE) (Mujtahid (USA))
*1260[5] 2208[6]* 4186[7] 4535[7] 5183[7] *5795[9] 7783[6]* ◆ *7940[7] 8111[6] 8200[5]*

**Quart De Rhum (FR)** *Yannick Fouin* 81
5 b g Anabaa(USA) Wells Vision (GER) (Monsun (GER))
3172a[4]

**Quasqazah** *Ruth Carr* 65
3 ch g Bahamian Bounty Rock Lily (Rock Of Gibraltar (IRE))
2442[12] 2789[4] 3925[6] 4871[7] 5415[8] 5892[7]

**Queen Aggie (IRE)** *Tony Carroll* a77 59
4 b f Elnadim(USA) Catfoot Lane (Batshoof)
*233[7] 376[8] 461[3] (697) 952[3] 1393[5]* 1665[6] 5290[6] 5776[6] *6562[4] 6857[10]* 7213[8] (7704) 7906[3] 7959a[4] 8268[2]

**Queen Anne (IRE)** *W McCreery* 79
2 ch f Iffraaj Queen Of Poland (Halling (USA))
6798a[6]

**Queen Bee (FR)** *E Lellouche* 105
2 b f Le Havre(IRE) Pan Tadeus (Kyllachy)
1402a[5] (3170a) 3806a[9] 4931a[4] (5707a) 6967a[5] 7655a[2]

**Queen Catrine (IRE)** *Charles Hills* 108
3 b f Acclamation Kahira (IRE) (King's Best (USA))
1515[5] 2195a[11] 3357[2] 3983[5] 4854[6] 6922[9]

**Queen Cee** *Simon Hodgson* a47 26
3 b f Royal Applause Tee Cee (Lion Cavern (USA))
4677[9] *8008[7]*

**Queen Grace (IRE)** *Michael J Browne* a87 78
7 b m Choisir(AUS) Petitesse (Petong)
*788a[2]*

**Queen Hermione (IRE)** *Derek Shaw* a52 58
6 b m Camacho Almeida (IRE) (Sadler's Wells (USA))
2890[8] 3150[9] *4611[8]* 5287[8] *5797[9] 6720[4] 7253[8] 7547[6]*

**Queenie's Home** *James Given* a74 64
3 gr f Shamardal(USA) Nolas Lolly (IRE) (Lomitas)
*62[2] 217[3] 1409[2]* 1611[14] 2020[5] 2643[8] *2906[3]*

**Queen Of Arts** *Richard Fahey* 29
3 ch f Dutch Art Grande Terre (IRE) (Grand Lodge (USA))
4017[6]

**Queen Of Ice** *William Haggas* a92 108
3 ch f Selkirk(USA) Ice Palace (Polar Falcon (USA))
*(1579)* 2255[5] 3143[3] 4443[4] (5611) (6708)

**Queen Of Power (IRE)** *M D O'Callaghan* 98
3 gr f Medicean Danamight (IRE) (Danetime (IRE))
1201a[5] 2581a[7] 3357[13]

**Queen Of Skies (IRE)** *Michael Appleby* a71 41
5 b m Shamardal(USA) Attractive Crown (USA) (Chief's Crown (USA))
*7[2] (171) 366[2] 647[2] 767[4] (8177)*

**Queen Of The Scots** *Keith Dalgleish* a27 34
2 b f Royal Applause Katina (USA) (Danzig (USA))
*2206[6]* 3296[10] 3658[4] 4065[7]

**Queensberry Rules (IRE)** *William Haggas* a88 105
4 b g Teofilo(IRE) Fantastic Spring (USA) (Fantastic Light (USA))
3356[20] 4214[7] 5174[7] (5695) ◆ 6752[30]

**Queen's Dream (IRE)** *Roger Varian* 56
3 b f Oasis Dream Queen Of Pentacles (IRE) (Selkirk (USA))
2804[7] 3653[8]

**Queen's Estate (GER)** *Miss Joey Ellis* a38 57
5 b g Hurricane Run(IRE) Questabelle (Rainbow Quest (USA))
2701[6]

**Queen's Hussar (GER)** *Frau C Brandstatter* a49
3 b g Oratorio(IRE) Queen Of Dance (IRE) (Sadler's Wells (USA))
*8005a[11]*

**Queens Park (FR)** *John Davies* 82
3 b f King's Best(USA) Anna Deesse (FR) (Anabaa (USA))
1303[5] 2737[6] (3302) 3950[2] ◆ (6822)

**Queen's Pearl (IRE)** *Roger Varian* 78
2 b f Exceed And Excel(AUS) Gimasha (Cadeaux Genereux)
4828[5] 5973[2] (6435)

**Queen's Princess** *John Wainwright* a43 43
6 b m Danbird(AUS) Queen's Lodge (IRE) (Grand Lodge (USA))
*40[10]*

**Queen's Prize** *Sir Michael Stoute* a78 59
3 b f Dansili Daring Aim (Daylami (IRE))
2152[10]

**Queen Zain (IRE)** *Robert Cowell* a52
2 b f Lawman(FR) Tropical Lady (IRE) (Sri Pekan (USA))
*7192[8]*

**Quelamour (FR)** *Robert Collet*
3 b f Laveron Baraka Du Berlais (FR) (Bonnet Rouge (FR))
7681a[11]

**Quenelle** *Ed Dunlop* a83 72
3 b f Nayef(USA) Cruinn A Bhord (Inchinor)
2109[8] 2613[2] 3106[5] 7304[6] *7734[2] 7866[4] (8202)*

**Querido (GER)** *Paddy Butler* a57 52
10 b g Acatenango(GER) Quest Of Fire (FR) (Rainbow Quest (USA))
*377[13] 1016[7] 1236[6] 1386[8]*

**Quest For More (IRE)** *Roger Charlton* a85 95
4 b g Teofilo(IRE) No Quest (IRE) (Rainbow Quest (USA))
1493[3] ◆ (4113) 4819[2] 5579[2] 6133[12] (6896)

**Quest For Peace (IRE)** *Luca Cumani* 110
6 b h Galileo(IRE) Play Misty For Me (IRE) (Danehill Dancer (IRE))
4849[5] 5688[5] 6546[5]

**Quest For Wonder** *James Tate* a72
2 b f Makfi Sindiya (IRE) (Pharly (FR))
*7625[2] 7941[2] (8187)*

**Quest Of Colour (IRE)** *Richard Fahey* a49 70
3 b f Iffraaj With Colour (Rainbow Quest (USA))
*2095[4]* (4793) (6010)

**Quevedo (SPA)** *Ana Imaz Ceca* 99
2 b c Diktat Tiviski (IRE) (Desert Style (IRE))
5741a[9]

**Quiaa Nominoor (FR)** *Remy Nerbonne* a63 63
3 b c Naaqoos Mamounia (GER) (Platini (GER))
3810a[8] 5226a[6]

**Quickaswecan** *Mark Johnston* a79 77
3 b g Shamardal(USA) Arctic Air (Polar Falcon (USA))
1358[4] 1513[8] 2090[12] *7774[8] 7955[13] 8071[3] 8182[5]*

**Quick Defence (USA)** *Sir Michael Stoute* 82
2 b c First Defence(USA) Quickfire (Dubai Millennium)
6204[5] 6652[2]

**Quick Jack (IRE)** *A J Martin* a67 103
5 ch g Footstepsinthesand Miss Polaris (Polar Falcon (USA))
(4746a) 7107[3]

**Quick Succession (USA)** *Keith Dalgleish* a54 63
3 b g Successful Appeal(USA) Chaffinch (USA) (Lear Fan (USA))
4387[4] 4904[5] 5268[6]

**Quick Touch** *Robert Cowell* a48 70
3 b g Kyllachy Fondled (Selkirk (USA))
*4735[3] 5568[4]* 5916[2] 6356[2] *7285[7]*

**Quick Wit** *Saeed bin Suroor* a108 112
7 b g Oasis Dream Roo (Rudimentary (USA))
683a[7] 902a[9] 2554[7] 6752[8]

**Quidamo** *Frau J Mayer* 110
7 b g Monsun(GER) Qelle Amie (CAN) (Beau Genius (CAN))
723a[10] 7769a[12]

**Quiet Beauty** *Robert Cowell* a40
2 b f Acclamation Upperville (IRE) (Selkirk (USA))
*3858[9]*

**Quiet Warrior (IRE)** *Marco Botti* a82 89
3 b g Kodiac Pretty Woman (IRE) (Night Shift (USA))
1518[6] *2083[5]* 2333[6] (3225)

**Quill Art** *Richard Fahey* a64
2 b g Excellent Art Featherweight (IRE) (Fantastic Light (USA))
*8166[6]*

**Quincel** *Tom Dascombe* a66 66
3 b g Exceed And Excel(AUS) Quinzey's Best (IRE) (King's Best (USA))
*1315[3]* 1723[9] 2429[15]

**Quint (IRE)** *Martyn Meade* a69
2 b f Footstepsinthesand Chica Whopa (IRE) (Oasis Dream)
*2395[2]* ◆

**Quinta Verde (IRE)** *Edward Lynam* 98
2 b f Tamayuz Tatbeeq (IRE) (Invincible Spirit (IRE))
3763a[3]

**Quintus Cerialis (IRE)** *Clive Cox* 73
2 b c Vale Of York(IRE) Red Fox (IRE) (Spectrum (IRE))
2480[6] 3728[3] 6363[4] 7082[3] 7491[2]

**Quinzieme Monarque (USA)** *P Schiergen* a92 106
4 bb c Rock Hard Ten(USA) Quintela (Giant's Causeway (USA))
2229a[7] 2815a[7] 4006a[6] 5938a[6] 7603a[11]

**Quirinus** *S Smrczek* a96 94
7 b g Okawango(USA) Habidancer (IRE) (Groom Dancer (USA))
3030a[3] 7856a[10]

**Quite Smart (IRE)** *Robert Cowell* 66
2 b f Arcano(IRE) Lyca Ballerina (Marju (IRE))
5104[2] 5774[3] 6753[4]

**Quite Sparky** *Geoffrey Harker* a47 90
7 b g Lucky Story(USA) Imperialistic (IRE) (Imperial Ballet (IRE))
2540[7] 3544[3] 3912[5] 4498[6] 4755[5] 5331[7] *8137[6]*

**Quixote** *Clive Brittain* a79 64
5 ch g Singspiel(IRE) Rainbow Queen (FR) (Spectrum (IRE))
*891[7] 1071[9]* 7641[11] *7702[9]*

**Quixote (GER)** *P Schiergen* a76 102
4 b c Pivotal Quebrada (IRE) (Devil's Bag (USA))
4247a[8]

**Quiz Mistress** *Hughie Morrison* a79 106
6 ch m Doyen(IRE) Seren Quest (Rainbow Quest (USA))
1434[7] 2284[7] 2764[4] 3962[5] 4945[5] 5611[7] (6218a) 6917a[4] 7447[4]

**Qwhipper (FR)** *C Boutin* a46
2 b f Whipper(USA) Mermaids Quay (IRE) (Key Of Luck (USA))
*5619a[12] 5901a[8]*

**Raajis (IRE)** *Richard Hannon* 78
3 gr f Dark Angel(IRE) Rumline (Royal Applause)
2968[10]

**Raamz (IRE)** *Kevin Morgan* a61 68
7 ch m Haafhd Tarbiyah (Singspiel (IRE))
*345[8] 571[9] 1097[4]* 2674[2] (3363) 4942[7] 6578[2] 7302[5]

**Race And Status (IRE)** *Andrew Balding* 77
4 b g Raven's Pass(USA) Love Excelling (FR) (Polish Precedent (USA))
1870[10]

**Race For Fame (IRE)** *M Boutin* a64 86
3 b c Meshaheer(USA) Rocky Mixa (FR) (Rock Of Gibraltar (IRE))
*5482a[10]* 7269a[8]

**Raceness (FR)** *S Wattel* a65 77
3 b f Zamindar(USA) Relight's Best (Grand Lodge (USA))
7857a[15]

**Race To Glory (FR)** *Roger Charlton* a74 81
3 b g Montjeu(IRE) Cawett (IRE) (Danehill Dancer (IRE))
1730[6] 2075[6] 2696[3] *3857[6]* 4672[2] 5851[3] 6432[2]

**Racing Angel (IRE)** *John Quinn* 38
2 b f Dark Angel(IRE) Roclette (USA) (Rock Of Gibraltar (IRE))
7712[6]

**Racing History (IRE)** *Saeed bin Suroor* 50
2 b c Pivotal Gonbarda (GER) (Lando (GER))
7382[11]

**Racing Knight (IRE)** *John Quinn* 61
2 b g Sir Percy Salydora (FR) (Peintre Celebre (USA))
4790[4] 5493[9] 6319[6]

**Racing's Dream** *Brian Meehan* a65 67
3 b g Iffraaj There's Two (IRE) (Ashkalani (IRE))
3925[5]

**Racing Spirit** *John Quinn* 44
2 ch g Sir Percy Suertuda (Domedriver (IRE))
7244[7] 7498[13] 7637[7]

**Racy** *Brian Ellison* a105 105
7 b g Medicean Soar (Danzero (AUS))
107a[8] *304a[6]* 393a[5] 680a[7] *769a[2]* 1531[8] 2786[9] 2989[15] 3241[5] 3452[10] 4179[8] 4648[27] (4700) 5160[8] 5575[12] *6159[8]* 6533[13] 6745[8] 7122[19]

**Racy Rules (IRE)** *Mario Hofer* a59 59
2 b f Aussie Rules(USA) Greta Road (FR) (Grape Tree Road)
6244a[6] *8149a[7]*

**Raddeh** *Sir Michael Stoute* 55
2 gr f Shamardal(USA) Hathrah (IRE) (Linamix (FR))
7594[9]

**Radebe (USA)** *Kevin Ryan* a30 37
3 b g Distorted Humor(USA) Sweet Hope (USA) (Lemon Drop Kid (USA))
*423[6] 748[10]* 1608[6] 2028[8]

**Radhaadh (IRE)** *Sir Michael Stoute* a61
2 b f Nayef(USA) Safwa (IRE) (Green Desert (USA))
*7184[7]*

**Radiator** *Sir Michael Stoute* 104
3 b f Dubawi(IRE) Heat Haze (Green Desert (USA))
2316[2] 3418[8] 3983[6]

**Rafaadah** *J-C Rouget* 96
2 br f Oasis Dream Joanna (IRE) (High Chaparral (IRE))
(4839a) 5543a[2]

**Rafaaf (IRE)** *Richard Phillips* a66 84
6 b g Royal Applause Sciunfona (IRE) (Danehill (USA))
*503[7] 841[10] 1125[5] 3854[10] 5303[11] 8085[9]*

**Rafeej** *M Al Muhairi* a110 92
5 b h Iffraaj Muffled (USA) (Mizaaya)
107a[7] *206a[3] 597a[9]*

**Raffinee (FR)** *D Smaga* a69 78
3 b f Air Eminem(IRE) Gioconda Umbra (ITY) (Sicyos (USA))
7722a[13]

**Ragazzo (FR)** *Mario Hofer* a71 97
3 b c Footstepsinthesand Rosa Di Brema (ITY) (Lomitas)
*4838a[2]*

**Ragazzo (NOR)** *Annike Bye Hansen* a105 102
5 b g Academy Award(IRE) Private Property (IRE) (Pips Pride)
*3996a[3]* (4957a) (6387a)

**Ragdollianna** *Mark Hoad* a52 84
10 b m Kayf Tara Jupiters Princess (Jupiter Island)
*7204[7]*

**Ragged Robbin (FR)** *David Lanigan* a90 49
3 ch g Speightstown(USA) Ikat (IRE) (Pivotal)
*2998[11] (5011) (5139) (5898) (6019) 6665[4] 7289[3]*

**Raging Bear (USA)** *James Evans* a76 76
4 b g Leroidesanimaux(BRZ) Gliding Light (USA) (Always A Classic (CAN))
*29[6] 457[10] 647[3] 859[3] 928[3]* 1167[5] 1845[4] 2251[8]

**Raging Bob (IRE)** *Ralph Beckett* a64
3 br g Big Bad Bob(IRE) Lanasara (Generous (IRE))
*468[8]*

**Ragtime Dancer** *Jonathan Portman* a66 43
2 ch f Medicean Honky Tonk Sally (Dansili)
3557[9] *(4541)* 7488[5] *7753[9] 8069[8]*

**Rahlah** *J E Hammond* 73
3 b f Dansili Tanfidh (Marju (IRE))
5227a[6]

**Rahmah (IRE)** *Robert Cowell* a75 75
2 b c Vale Of York(IRE) Sweet Home Alabama (IRE) (Desert Prince (IRE))
4790[3] 5671[3] 6496[4] 7277[3] *7973[2] 8184[3] 8262[2]*

**Rainbow Beauty** *Richard Ford* a79 82
4 ch f Manduro(GER) Just Like A Woman (Observatory (USA))
3918[5] 5503[2]

**Rainbow Chic (IRE)** *C Fownes* 111
5 ch g Peintre Celebre(USA) Doohulla (USA) (Stravinsky (USA))
7898a[5] 8151a[11]

**Rainbow Knight** *J-M Capitte* a76
6 b g Rainbow Quest(USA) Poli Knight (Polish Precedent (USA))
*584a[9]*

**Rainbow Orse** *Robert Cowell* a47 61
2 b c Zebedee Khafayif (USA) (Swain (IRE))
*5488[7]* 6059[5] 6690[9]

**Rainbow Pride (IRE)** *Sir Mark Prescott Bt* a58 29
2 gr g Clodovil(IRE) Rahila (IRE) (Kalanisi (IRE))
*6719[7]* 6997[5] *7199[6]*

**Rainbow Rock (IRE)** *Mark Johnston* a79 90
3 b g Rock Of Gibraltar(IRE) Celtic Fling (Lion Cavern (USA))
2433[3] *2936[2]* 3187[3] (4498) 4821[2] 6127[17] 6656[6] 7410[9]

**Rainford Glory (IRE)** *Tim Fitzgerald* a62 65
4 ch g Rock Of Gibraltar(IRE) My Dolly Madison (In The Wings)
*106[5] 123[5] 497[8] 643[9]* 2738[5] 3209[7] (3912) 4259[3] 4749[3] *8044[4] 8162[8] 8277[8]*

**Rain God (USA)** *Gary Moore* a70 88
4 b g Henrythenavigator(USA) Lotta Dancing (USA) (Alydar (USA))
*8203[6] 8295[7]*

**Rainha Da Bateria (USA)** *H Graham Motion* 100
2 ch f Broken Vow(USA) Amelia (USA) (Dixieland Band (USA))
7592a[9]

**Raiponce (FR)** *C Lerner* 29
2 b f Orpen(USA) Patagonian Dream (USA) (Mr Greeley (USA))
6958a[15]

**Raise A Billion** *Alan Berry* 56
3 b c Major Cadeaux Romantic Destiny (Dubai Destination (USA))
2388[2] (2675) 3100[3] 3487[8] 4071[3] 4512[5] 5631[5] 5853[7] 6601[9] 6833[10]

**Raise Your Gaze** *Clive Cox* 95
3 gr g Mastercraftsman(IRE) Regal Magic (IRE) (Sadler's Wells (USA))
1586[6] 2481[4] 3197[3] (3986) 4698[3] 5164[5] 5720[7] (6460) 6870[10]

**Raison D'Etre (FR)** *F Vermeulen* a72 92
2 gr f Elusive City(USA) Restless Rixa (FR) (Linamix (FR))
*3640a[3]* 4931a[5]

**Rajang (FR)** *F Chappet* a72 76
3 b g Yeats(IRE) Rockabout (IRE) (Rock Of Gibraltar (IRE))
*545a[7]*

**Rajeh (IRE)** *Peter Grayson* a52 43
11 b g Key Of Luck(USA) Saramacca (IRE) (Kahyasi)
4744[6] *5283[2] 5558[2] 5864[2] 6157[8] 6410[7] 6682[7] 8208[10] 8277[4]*

**Rakaan (IRE)** *Brendan Powell* a89 73
7 ch g Bahamian Bounty Petite Spectre (Spectrum (IRE))
*89[5] 200[6] 407[3] 602[3] 689[4] 2922[11]* 3314[9] 4028[7] 4761[11] 6263[11] 7042[12] *7533[11]* 7871[10] (8102)

**Rakmanova (IRE)** *C Martinon* a59 56
3 b f Kheleyf(USA) Riabouchinska (Fantastic Light (USA))
2978a[5]

**Ralph McTell** *Alan Coogan* a26
2 ch g Tobougg(IRE) Alashaan (Darshaan)
1512[8] 1859[7] 4618[10] *5278[5]*

**Ralphy Boy (IRE)** *Alistair Whillans* a52 84
5 b g Acclamation Silcasue (Selkirk (USA))
1610[8] (2215) 2603[9] 3361[3] (3646) 4161[6] 4451[5] 4661[3] 5143[2] 5632[7] 6111[3] 6285[3] 6511[7]

**Ralphy Lad (IRE)** *Alan Swinbank* 71
3 b g Iffraaj Hawattef (IRE) (Mujtahid (USA))
1346[7] 2133[3] 3268[7] 3789[7]

**Ralston Road (IRE)** *John Patrick Shanahan* a92 110
4 b c Dylan Thomas(IRE) Advertising Space (IRE) (Galileo (IRE))
*202a[7]* 507a[4] 900a[11] 1177a[5] (2785) 3377[12]

**Rambo Will** *J R Jenkins* a80 71
6 b g Danbird(AUS) Opera Belle (Dr Fong (USA))
*(299) 1244[2]* 1490[7] 2147[14] 2637[5] 4151[8] 7342[6] (7670) *8180[5]*

**Ramone (IRE)** *W T Farrell* 92
4 b f Marju(IRE) Hayworth (IRE) (Night Shift (USA))
5958a[10]

**Ramshackle** *Sir Michael Stoute* a75 77
3 b f Dansili Purissima (USA) (Fusaichi Pegasus (USA))
1534[5] ◆ 5622[3] *(6073)* 6459[4]

**Rancho Montoya (IRE)** *Andrew Balding* a72 48
4 b f High Chaparral(IRE) Congress (IRE) (Dancing Brave (USA))
*33[2] 176[2] 303[3]*

**Random** *Daniel Mark Loughnane* a73 55
3 b f Shamardal(USA) Paracel (USA) (Gone West (USA))
6215[4] *(7111) 7906[7] 8319[6]*

**Random Success (IRE)** *Roger Charlton* a79 89
4 b f Shamardal(USA) Foreplay (IRE) (Lujain (USA))
*(114)* ◆ *(340)* ◆ *714[2]* 3920[2] ◆ 4412[7] (4946) 5350[6] 6314[3]

**Randwick (IRE)** *Charles Hills* 87
3 b c High Chaparral(IRE) Subito (Darshaan)
1529[8] 2114[6] 2485[3] 3434[5]

**Rangali** *H-A Pantall* 118
3 ch c Namid Tejaara (USA) (Kingmambo (USA))
(2226a) (2820a) 5654[7] 6378a[DSQ] 6966a[2]

**Rangi Chase (IRE)** *Richard Fahey* 79
3 b g Lawman(FR) Tirunesh (USA) (More Than Ready (USA))
2075[10] 2871[4] 3647[4] 4161[4] ◆ 4426[3] 4941[5] (5891) 6625[4] (6980) 7514[4]

**Ranjaan (FR)** *Paul Nicholls* a96 96
6 b g Dubai Destination(USA) Ridafa (IRE) (Darshaan)
*803[6] 1213[4] 1770[5]*

**Ranyan (SPA)** *E Buzon Bobillo* 81
5 ch g Gold Away(IRE) Triple Two (Pivotal)
1828a[7]

**Raphinae** *H-A Pantall* a86 107
3 b f Dubawi(IRE) Dodo (IRE) (Alzao (USA))
2817a[8] *5843a[6]* 7268a[4] 7629a[3] 7916a[6]

**Rapid Advance** *Sir Michael Stoute* a77 87
3 b g Medicean Snow Gretel (IRE) (Green Desert (USA))
1582[4] (2968) 4332[8] 5031[12] 5669[3] 6431[4]

**Rapid Applause** *M D O'Callaghan* 107
2 b c Royal Applause Madam Ninette (Mark Of Esteem (IRE))
3738a$^{4}$ 4460a$^{3}$ ◆ 5954a$^{2}$

**Rapid Heat Lad (IRE)** *Andrew Hollinshead* a81 68
5 b g Aussie Rules(USA) Alwiyda (USA) (Trempolino (USA))
16$^{6}$ 868$^{6}$

**Rapido (GER)** *Andreas Lowe* 104
3 b c Rock Of Gibraltar(IRE) Rondinay (FR) (Cadeaux Genereux)
3293a$^{2}$

**Rapid Water** *Pat Eddery* a47 32
8 b g Anabaa(USA) Lochsong (Song)
14$^{7}$ 575$^{10}$

**Rapprochement (IRE)** *Charlie Appleby* 96
3 b g New Approach(IRE) Firth Of Lorne (IRE) (Danehill (USA))
(4407) 4850$^{6}$

**Rapunzal** *Henry Candy* 61
3 b f Mount Nelson Cinnas Ransom (Red Ransom (USA))
1808$^{6}$ 2221$^{13}$ 5005$^{7}$ (5183) 5522$^{7}$ 6070$^{12}$

**Rare Coincidence** *Alan Berry* a40 42
13 ch g Atraf Green Seed (IRE) (Lead On Time (USA))
2512$^{5}$

**Rare Rhythm** *Charlie Appleby* 80
2 b c Dubawi(IRE) Demisemiquaver (Singspiel (IRE))
6928$^{8}$ (7382)

**Rasaman (IRE)** *Jim Goldie* a82 86
10 b g Namid Rasana (Royal Academy (USA))
1967$^{2}$ 2332$^{11}$ 2456$^{2}$ 3239$^{14}$ 3458$^{5}$ 4700$^{8}$ 5081$^{10}$ 5632$^{3}$ 6094$^{5}$ 6511$^{14}$ 6824$^{10}$ 7820$^{3}$ 8257$^{12}$

**Rasameel (USA)** *B W Hills* a86 84
3 ch c Jazil(USA) Positioning (USA) (Boundary (USA))
(2211) 3182$^{5}$ 5345$^{6}$ 6044$^{11}$ 6357$^{2}$

**Raseel** *Peter Chapple-Hyam* 42
2 b f Aqlaam Waafiah (Anabaa (USA))
7594$^{15}$

**Rasha (IRE)** *Roger Varian* a43
2 b f Zebedee Sonny Sunshine (Royal Applause)
2057$^{6}$ 2402$^{9}$

**Rashash (IRE)** *Roger Varian* a56
2 b c Kyllachy Labisa (IRE) (High Chaparral (IRE))
3524$^{7}$

**Rasheed** *Lucy Wadham* a86 75
6 b g Oasis Dream Alexandrine (IRE) (Nashwan (USA))
591$^{4}$ 856$^{3}$

**Rasheeda** *Marco Botti* 88
3 ro f Mastercraftsman(IRE) Violette (Observatory (USA))
1868$^{4}$ 2144$^{6}$

**Raskova (USA)** *William Jarvis* 100
4 b f Henrythenavigator(USA) Diamond Necklace (USA) (Unbridled's Song (USA))
1636$^{4}$ 2162$^{3}$ 2783$^{7}$ (3335) 4184$^{2}$ 4634$^{2}$ 6464$^{9}$ 7717$^{4}$

**Rasmy** *M Al Muhairi* a70 98
7 b g Red Ransom(USA) Shadow Dancing (Unfuwain (USA))
110a$^{8}$

**Raspberry Ripple** *Richard Hannon* 73
2 b f Camacho Cinnamon Tree (IRE) (Barathea (IRE))
3140$^{10}$ 5429$^{5}$ 6066$^{3}$ 7192$^{12}$

**Rasselas (IRE)** *Michael Appleby* a57 64
7 b g Danehill Dancer(IRE) Regal Darcey (IRE) (Darshaan)
2477$^{7}$ 3096$^{6}$ 3485$^{6}$ (3604) 3908$^{6}$ 4387$^{6}$ 4498$^{10}$ (4959) 5267$^{6}$ 5711$^{7}$ 6402$^{3}$ 7036$^{5}$ 7115$^{6}$

**Rastanora (USA)** *John Gosden* a70 72
2 b f Dynaformer(USA) So Long Sonoma (USA) (American Chance (USA))
4403$^{4}$ 4914$^{7}$ 6606$^{5}$ 7943$^{2}$

**Rasuan (FR)** *Yannick Fouin* a84 84
3 gr c Elusive City(USA) Tassara (FR) (Sendawar (IRE))
169a$^{10}$

**Rat Catcher (IRE)** *Lisa Williamson* a54 72
4 b g One Cool Cat(USA) Molly Marie (IRE) (Fasliyev (USA))
2435$^{11}$ 3338$^{15}$ 5399$^{7}$ 6023$^{7}$ 6561$^{3}$ 7010$^{5}$ 7520$^{5}$ 7781$^{2}$ 8230$^{4}$ 8284$^{2}$

**Rathaath (IRE)** *Brian Meehan* a52 76
2 b f Oasis Dream Jamaayel (Shamardal (USA))
2918$^{7}$ (3563)

**Ratmansky (ITY)** *F Camici* 89
3 gr c Mastercraftsman(IRE) Sharafanya (IRE) (Zafonic (USA))
2376a$^{15}$

**Rattling Jewel** *Andrew Balding* a81
2 b c Royal Applause Mutoon (IRE) (Erhaab (USA))
7031$^{7}$ (7551) 7882$^{6}$

**Rave Dancer** *Stuart Kittow* 21
2 b f Alhaarth(IRE) Kahalah (IRE) (Darshaan)
3558$^{11}$

**Ravenous** *Ralph Beckett* 83
3 b g Raven's Pass(USA) Supereva (IRE) (Sadler's Wells (USA))
1192$^{5}$ (1654) 3538$^{2}$

**Raven Ridge (IRE)** *Michael Bell* 92
3 b g High Chaparral(IRE) Green Castle (IRE) (Indian Ridge)
1535$^{4}$ 2303$^{4}$ 5345$^{2}$ 5757$^{4}$ 7410$^{6}$

**Raven's Tower (USA)** *Ben Pauling* a38 40
4 b g Raven's Pass(USA) Tizdubai (USA) (Cee's Tizzy (USA))
7411$^{12}$

**Ravisseur** *F Head* a101 101
3 ch c Green Tune(USA) Russiana (IRE) (Red Ransom (USA))
(795a)

**Rawaki (IRE)** *Andrew Balding* a100 112
6 b g Phoenix Reach(IRE) Averami (Averti (IRE))
1434$^{3}$ 1736$^{5}$ 2294$^{2}$ 2785$^{4}$ 3722$^{4}$ 5432$^{6}$ (6069) 7447$^{8}$ 7922$^{5}$

**Rawnaq (IRE)** *Matthew J Smith* a87 90
7 b g Azamour(IRE) Sharemata (IRE) (Doyoun)
7142a$^{16}$

**Rawoof (IRE)** *Rae Guest* a65 90
3 b f Nayef(USA) Tanaghum (Darshaan)
3673$^{7}$ (5534) 6218a$^{6}$ 7554$^{13}$

**Raw Sugar (IRE)** *Francisco Castro* 60
4 ch g Iffraaj Livius Lady (IRE) (Titus Livius (FR))
6387a$^{11}$

**Rayadour (IRE)** *Micky Hammond* a70 70
5 b g Azamour(IRE) Rayyana (IRE) (Rainbow Quest (USA))
(2900) 4662$^{8}$ 5171$^{8}$

**Rayak (IRE)** *Jonjo O'Neill* 84
4 b g Invincible Spirit(IRE) Rayyana (IRE) (Rainbow Quest (USA))
1682$^{6}$

**Raydara (IRE)** *M Halford* 109
2 bb f Rock Of Gibraltar(IRE) Raydiya (IRE) (Marju (IRE))
4598a$^{4}$ (5734a)

**Ray Of Joy** *J R Jenkins* a76 76
8 b m Tobougg(IRE) Once Removed (Distant Relative)
248$^{2}$ 453$^{4}$ (819) 1266$^{3}$ 1405$^{2}$ 1500$^{2}$ 2096$^{2}$ 3854$^{4}$ 4024$^{2}$ ◆ 4401$^{6}$ 5059$^{2}$ 5247$^{4}$ 5861$^{7}$ 6463$^{4}$ 6758$^{10}$

**Rayoumti (IRE)** *George Margarson* a75 81
3 b f Lawman(FR) Sveva (IRE) (Danehill Dancer (IRE))
1711$^{6}$ (3760) 4271$^{4}$ 4767$^{3}$ 5685$^{2}$ 7196$^{11}$

**Ray Ward (IRE)** *David Simcock* a74 99
4 b g Galileo(IRE) Kentucky Warbler (IRE) (Spinning World (USA))
1973$^{11}$ 2779$^{9}$ 3321$^{6}$ 4777$^{2}$ 6557$^{3}$ 7107$^{12}$

**Razaan** *Mick Channon* 30
2 b f Royal Applause Rolexa (Pursuit Of Love)
5667$^{11}$ 5973$^{10}$

**Razin' Hell** *Alan McCabe* a80 66
3 b g Byron Loose Caboose (IRE) (Tagula (IRE))
(302) (1005) 1130$^{3}$ 1585$^{6}$ 2204$^{11}$ 3124$^{9}$ 3380$^{10}$ (4820) 6297$^{5}$ (8182)

**Razor Wind (IRE)** *Charlie Appleby* a95 88
3 b c Dubawi(IRE) Tender Is Thenight (IRE) (Barathea (IRE))
3315$^{3}$ ◆ 4168$^{2}$ 7733$^{2}$ (7901) 8080$^{2}$ (8194)

**Reach Out** *Mrs A Malzard* a56 40
6 ch g Phoenix Reach(IRE) Cocorica (IRE) (Croco Rouge (IRE))
2595a$^{5}$

**Reach The Beach** *Brendan Powell* a67 65
5 ch m Phoenix Reach(IRE) Comtesse Noire (CAN) (Woodman (USA))
247$^{8}$ 475$^{2}$ 831$^{3}$ 912$^{4}$ 1129$^{5}$ 1622a$^{3}$ 5277$^{2}$ (5850) 6252$^{2}$ 6817$^{2}$ 7129$^{11}$ 7532$^{5}$ (7760) 7914$^{4}$

**Ready (IRE)** *Garry Moss* a87 91
4 ch g Elnadim(USA) Fusili (IRE) (Silvano (GER))
917$^{7}$ 1103$^{4}$ 5196$^{2}$ 5915$^{9}$ 6214$^{10}$ 7282$^{2}$ 7507$^{11}$ 7719$^{17}$ 7821$^{8}$ 8209$^{8}$ 8320$^{5}$

**Reaffirmed (IRE)** *Ed Vaughan* a74 61
3 ch g Pivotal Quiet Protest (USA) (Kingmambo (USA))
3124$^{4}$ 3627$^{6}$ 5061$^{4}$ (6272) (6889) 7356$^{3}$

**Reality Show (IRE)** *Shaun Harris* a68 68
7 b g Cape Cross(IRE) Really (IRE) (Entrepreneur)
(106) (246) 382$^{7}$ 7744$^{12}$ 7932$^{9}$ 8074$^{2}$ 8261$^{10}$

**Realize** *Kevin Ryan* a88 79
4 b g Zafeen(FR) Relkida (Bertolini (USA))
(1499) 1803$^{5}$ 4181$^{12}$ 5031$^{8}$ 5629$^{3}$ 6334$^{4}$ (7071) 7365$^{7}$ (7687) 8141$^{9}$

**Real Jazz (IRE)** *Sir Mark Prescott Bt* a84 76
3 b f Marju(IRE) Sedna (IRE) (Priolo (USA))
4152$^{2}$ 4490$^{2}$ (5917) 6091$^{2}$ 7359$^{4}$ (7459) ◆ 7662$^{6}$

**Really Tonic (FR)** *F Doumen* a69 53
2 b f Country Reel(USA) Hertzienne (FR) (Hernando (FR))
5619a$^{3}$ 6244a$^{8}$ 8149a$^{5}$

**Really Wild** *X Thomas-Demeaulte* a49
3 b f Lawman(FR) Haven's Wave (IRE) (Whipper (USA))
795a$^{14}$

**Real Solution (USA)** *Chad C Brown* 116
5 b h Kitten's Joy(USA) Reachfortheheavens (USA) (Pulpit (USA))
2228a$^{2}$ (3025a) 5460a$^{7}$

**Real Specialist (NZ)** *J Size* 116
7 b g Storming Home There's No Doubt (NZ) (Pompeii Court (USA))
2004a$^{12}$

**Real Tigress (IRE)** *Les Eyre* a73 77
5 b m Tiger Hill(IRE) Truly Genuine (IRE) (Hernando (FR))
1245$^{4}$ 1446$^{5}$ (1510) (2019) ◆ 2169$^{6}$ 3220$^{3}$ 3533$^{5}$ 4291$^{3}$ 5079$^{3}$ 5638$^{4}$ 5915$^{7}$ 6626$^{9}$ 7397$^{5}$

**Realtra (IRE)** *Richard Fahey* 96
2 gr f Dark Angel(IRE) Devious Diva (IRE) (Dr Devious (IRE))
1504$^{2}$ ◆ 1732$^{2}$ ◆ (2269) 2856a$^{2}$ 4439$^{5}$ 5608$^{4}$ 6375a$^{3}$ 6933$^{9}$

**Realyfrajj (FR)** *Mlle S-V Tarrou* a34 12
3 ch f Iffraaj Reallymissgreeley (USA) (Mr Greeley (USA))
3809a$^{12}$

**Reassert** *Tim Easterby* 52
2 b g Assertive Zonta Zitkala (Daylami (IRE))
1536$^{5}$ 1732$^{6}$ 2214$^{5}$ 6222$^{3}$ 7055$^{9}$

**Rebecca Romero** *Denis Coakley* a66 83
7 b m Exceed And Excel(AUS) Cloud Dancer (Bishop Of Cashel)
1489$^{7}$ 2275$^{5}$ 2945$^{4}$ 3275$^{7}$ 3817$^{2}$ 4146$^{7}$ 4946$^{7}$ 5830$^{6}$ 7357$^{9}$

**Rebel Code (USA)** *James Given* a52 46
3 b g City Zip(USA) Confederate Lady (USA) (Dixie Union (USA))
15$^{3}$ 261$^{8}$ 481$^{8}$ 933$^{4}$ 1137$^{5}$

**Rebel Dane (AUS)** *Gary Portelli* 116
5 bb h California Dane(AUS) Texarcana (AUS) (More Than Ready (USA))
1468a$^{2}$ 7724a$^{7}$

**Rebellious Guest** *George Margarson* a104 96
5 b g Cockney Rebel(IRE) Marisa (GER) (Desert Sun)
256$^{3}$ (342) ◆ (426) ◆ 625$^{4}$ (840) 1068$^{7}$ ◆ 1171$^{3}$ 1559$^{7}$ 3356$^{23}$ 3416$^{9}$ 4608$^{7}$ 7801$^{4}$ ◆ 8095$^{8}$ 8266$^{6}$ 8312$^{3}$

**Rebel Song (IRE)** *A bin Harmash* a97 98
5 b h Refuse To Bend(IRE) Dubai Opera (USA) (Dubai Millennium)
394a$^{8}$ 683a$^{9}$ 810a$^{3}$

**Rebel Woman** *Mrs A Corson* a33 27
8 b m Royal Applause Wild Woman (Polar Falcon (USA))
1625a$^{3}$ 2594a$^{F}$ 4040a$^{3}$ 4717a$^{7}$ 5229a$^{3}$ 5970a$^{5}$

**Recently Acquired** *Lady Cecil* 69
2 b g Beat Hollow Acquisition (Dansili)
5646$^{6}$ ◆ 6293$^{9}$

**Recepta (USA)** *James J Toner* a77 102
3 bb f Speightstown(USA) Honor Bestowed (USA) (Honor Grades (USA))
3995a$^{10}$

**Recession Proof (FR)** *John Quinn* a73 67
8 ch g Rock Of Gibraltar(IRE) Elevate (Ela-Mana-Mou)
1091$^{4}$ 1366$^{3}$ 2259$^{13}$

**Recite (NZ)** *John Bary* 103
4 b f Darci Brahma(NZ) Chant (NZ) (Traditionally (USA))
7128a$^{12}$

**Reckless Abandon** *Charlie Appleby* 116
4 b c Exchange Rate(USA) Sant Elena (Efisio)
5674$^{3}$ 6231$^{2}$ 6920$^{13}$

**Reckless Blue** *Michael Easterby* 31
2 ch f Bahamian Bounty Frambroise (Diesis)
4286$^{11}$ 6453$^{9}$ 7329$^{7}$

**Reckless Lad (IRE)** *Patrick Martin* a75 75
4 b g Chevalier(IRE) Zingeeyah (Singspiel (IRE))
(790a)

**Recover (USA)** *Brian Meehan* a56 54
2 ch f Eskendereya(USA) Rebuke (USA) (Carson City (USA))
3671$^{11}$ 3933$^{12}$ 4320$^{5}$ 4857$^{5}$ 7529$^{9}$ 7848$^{7}$

**Rectitude** *John Gosden* 59
3 b f Virtual Evasive Quality (FR) (Highest Honor (FR))
4867$^{4}$ ◆ 5504$^{9}$ 6042$^{6}$

**Red Aggressor (IRE)** *Clive Brittain* a70 85
5 b g Red Clubs(IRE) Snap Crackle Pop (IRE) (Statoblest)
4866$^{9}$ 5281$^{6}$ (5726) 6467$^{4}$ 6880$^{4}$

**Redalani (IRE)** *Alan Brown* a57 58
4 b f Redback Zafaraya (IRE) (Ashkalani (IRE))
3530$^{6}$ 3832$^{3}$ 5683$^{12}$ 6638$^{6}$ 7420$^{2}$ 7783$^{9}$ 8133$^{12}$

**Red All Star (IRE)** *Patrick Martin* a56 75
4 b g Haatef(USA) Star Of Russia (IRE) (Soviet Star (USA))
5958a$^{8}$

**Red Art (IRE)** *Tony Newcombe* a84 84
5 b h Excellent Art All Began (IRE) (Fasliyev (USA))
96$^{6}$ 245$^{9}$ 1017$^{F}$

**Red Avenger (USA)** *Ed Dunlop* 105
4 bb g War Front(USA) Emotional Rescue (USA) (Smart Strike (CAN))
1653$^{12}$ 2959$^{3}$ 3356$^{18}$ 4214$^{11}$ (4851) 5609$^{6}$ 6124$^{16}$

**Red Baron (IRE)** *Eric Alston* a79 92
5 b g Moss Vale(IRE) Twinberry (IRE) (Tagula (IRE))
1283$^{5}$ 1565$^{2}$ (1695) 1961$^{15}$ 2074$^{6}$ 3006$^{7}$ 3239$^{2}$ 3666$^{12}$ 4531$^{5}$ 6096$^{9}$ 6235$^{10}$ 6512$^{3}$ 7212$^{14}$

**Red Biba (IRE)** *Alan McCabe* a48 48
3 ch f Intense Focus(USA) Vital Laser (USA) (Seeking The Gold (USA))
547$^{4}$ 651$^{6}$

**Redbrook (IRE)** *A De Royer-Dupre* 107
3 b c Raven's Pass(USA) Nawal (FR) (Homme De Loi (IRE))
3352$^{8}$ 4930a$^{4}$ 5960a$^{4}$

**Red Cadeaux** *Ed Dunlop* a109 119
8 ch g Cadeaux Genereux Artisia (IRE) (Peintre Celebre (USA))
1183a$^{6}$ 2002a$^{14}$ 5432$^{4}$ 6139$^{7}$ 7653a$^{2}$ 8151a$^{6}$

**Red Cape (FR)** *Ruth Carr* a74 60
11 b g Cape Cross(IRE) Muirfield (FR) (Crystal Glitters (USA))
913$^{6}$ 1311$^{2}$ (1431) 1814$^{3}$ 2297$^{7}$ 2552$^{8}$ 3150$^{12}$ 3530$^{18}$ 4287$^{6}$ 4532$^{2}$ 4795$^{3}$ 4997$^{3}$ 5817$^{4}$ 6077$^{3}$ 6346$^{11}$ 6674$^{12}$ 6843$^{2}$ 7252$^{6}$ 7622$^{5}$

**Red Catkin** *George Margarson* a50 66
4 b f Notnowcato Red Salvia (Selkirk (USA))
2443$^{4}$ 2874$^{4}$

**Red Caviar (SWE)** *Patrick Wahl* 88
2 ch f Eishin Dunkirk(USA) Lady Alize (USA) (Indian Charlie (USA))
(6386a)

**Red Charmer (IRE)** *Ann Duffield* 82
4 b g Red Clubs(IRE) Golden Charm (IRE) (Common Grounds)
1598$^{4}$ 1885$^{2}$ 2293$^{8}$ 4359$^{3}$ 4635$^{6}$ ◆ 5446$^{11}$ 5810$^{5}$ 6214$^{9}$ 6626$^{7}$ ◆

**Red Cobra (IRE)** *Tim Easterby* a58 64
4 b g Redback Queen Cobra (IRE) (Indian Rocket)
2606$^{6}$ ◆ 3298$^{10}$ 4487$^{7}$ 5082$^{3}$ 5399$^{8}$ 5574$^{4}$

**Red Connect** *Alan McCabe* a46 71
2 b g Aqlaam Close Knit (USA) (Hennessy (USA))
1161$^{6}$ 1504$^{3}$ 1879$^{3}$ 2200$^{2}$ 2395$^{7}$ 2873$^{4}$ 5286$^{4}$

**Red Cossack (CAN)** *Paul Webber* a60 62
3 ch g Rebellion Locata (USA) (Stravinsky (USA))
1725$^{10}$ 3114$^{6}$ 3503$^{4}$ 5532$^{6}$

**Red Current** *Michael Scudamore* a43 46
10 b m Soviet Star(USA) Fleet Amour (USA) (Afleet (CAN))
5904$^{RR}$ 6343$^{7}$ 7657$^{9}$ 7990$^{6}$

**Red Dragon (IRE)** *Michael Blanshard* a79 71
4 b g Acclamation Delphie Queen (IRE) (Desert Sun)
79$^{3}$ 250$^{4}$ 450$^{7}$ 1439$^{9}$ 1791$^{6}$ 2471$^{5}$ 3080$^{4}$ 3585$^{6}$ 4030$^{5}$ 4656$^{5}$ 6007$^{2}$ 6699$^{4}$ 7133$^{3}$ 7343$^{9}$ 7744$^{6}$ 7932$^{13}$

**Red Dubawi (IRE)** *Frau Erika Mader* a98 116
6 ch h Dubawi(IRE) Maredsous (FR) (Homme De Loi (IRE))
107a$^{13}$ 304a$^{12}$ 593a$^{13}$ (2715a) 3511a$^{3}$ (4247a) 5480a$^{5}$ 6054a$^{6}$ 7559a$^{5}$

**Red Duke (USA)** *M F De Kock* a88 98
5 ch g Hard Spun(USA) Saudia (USA) (Gone West (USA))
240a$^{9}$

**Red Explorer (USA)** *Ann Stokell* a52 88
4 b c Henrythenavigator(USA) Remote (USA) (Seattle Slew (USA))
20$^{9}$ 2602$^{14}$ 2933$^{9}$ 3246$^{9}$ 3611$^{7}$ 3795$^{8}$ 4494$^{11}$ 5125$^{4}$ 6023$^{3}$

**Red Flute** *Alan McCabe* a41 55
2 ch g Piccolo Fee Faw Fum (IRE) (Great Commotion (USA))
2507$^{7}$ 3330$^{9}$ 5488$^{8}$ 5759$^{6}$

**Red Forever** *Alan Berry* a54 66
3 ch g Major Cadeaux Spindara (IRE) (Spinning World (USA))
2023$^{2}$ 2759$^{4}$ 2985$^{2}$ (3440) 3600$^{5}$ 3959$^{5}$ 4186$^{8}$ 4315$^{4}$ 4977$^{5}$ 5169$^{2}$ 5389$^{6}$ 5923$^{3}$ 7058$^{4}$ 7457$^{5}$

**Red Four** *George Baker* a57 77
4 ch f Singspiel(IRE) Protectorate (Hector Protector (USA))
1915$^{4}$ (7343) 8015$^{7}$

**Red Galileo** *Ed Dunlop* a82 110
3 b c Dubawi(IRE) Ivory Gala (FR) (Galileo (IRE))
1699$^{4}$ 2153$^{6}$ 2990$^{5}$ 4778$^{7}$ 5577$^{8}$ 6233$^{2}$ 6711$^{2}$ 7447$^{6}$

**Red Glory (SWE)** *Henrik Engblom* 60
2 ch f Philomatheia(USA) Raise The Rhythm (IRE) (Raise A Grand (IRE))
6386a$^{10}$

**Red Harry (IRE)** *Tom Tate* 76
2 ch c Manduro(GER) Iktidar (Green Desert (USA))
4416$^{5}$ 5397$^{4}$ 6059$^{2}$

**Red House** *David C Griffiths* a56 53
3 b g Auction House(USA) Highest Dream (IRE) (Highest Honor (FR))
315$^{10}$

**Red House Rebel (IRE)** *Stuart Williams* a47 37
2 b c Cockney Rebel(IRE) Avril Rose (IRE) (Xaar)
6852$^{8}$ 7380$^{9}$

**Red Icon (IRE)** *Tom Dascombe* a83 88
2 b c Acclamation Society Gal (IRE) (Galileo (IRE))
2089$^{4}$ (2698) 2987$^{3}$ 3786$^{3}$ 4853$^{8}$ 7116$^{4}$ 7374$^{3}$

**Red Inca** *Brian Ellison* a59 78
6 ch g Pivotal Magicalmysterykate (USA) (Woodman (USA))
4922$^{U}$ 5238$^{4}$ 6696$^{6}$ 6937$^{6}$ 7249$^{8}$

**Red Inferno (IRE)** *Miss Joey Ellis* 17
3 b g Tiger Hill(IRE) Red Yellow Blue (USA) (Sky Classic (CAN))
2925$^{7}$ 3822$^{5}$

**Reding (FR)** *C Laffon-Parias* a92 89
3 b g Pivotal Alfaguara (USA) (Red Ransom (USA))
(3372a)

**Redinha** *Clive Cox* a71 71
3 b f Dansili So Squally (GER) (Monsun (GER))
3755$^{9}$ 4367$^{6}$ 5256$^{4}$ 6034$^{7}$

**Red Invader (IRE)** *Paul D'Arcy* a45 64
4 b g Red Clubs(IRE) Tifariti (USA) (Elusive Quality (USA))
963$^{4}$ ◆ 1105$^{7}$ (1365) ◆ 1668$^{10}$ 2435$^{4}$ 3231$^{6}$ 5499$^{14}$ 5873$^{8}$ 6014$^{6}$ (7010) 7909$^{5}$

**Red Ivy (IRE)** *P D Deegan* a70 85
2 b f Clodovil(IRE) Hedera (USA) (Woodman (USA))
2856a$^{6}$

**Red Joker (IRE)** *Andrew Crook* 38
4 br g Red Clubs(IRE) Lady Singspiel (IRE) (Singspiel (IRE))
1649$^{12}$

**Redkirk** *William Haggas* 101
3 ch g Notnowcato Flag (Selkirk (USA))
(3631) (4698)

**Red Lady (IRE)** *Brian Meehan* a73 86
3 ch f Dutch Art Felucca (Green Desert (USA))
1952$^{11}$ 2340$^{12}$ 2768$^{3}$ 3384$^{3}$ (3817) 4328$^{6}$ 4859$^{3}$ (6355) 6814$^{2}$

**Redlake (FR)** *D Guillemin* 74
2 b c Orpen(USA) Blueprint (USA) (Shadeed (USA))
2755a$^{2}$

**Red Legacy** *Sean Regan* 16
6 ch m Distant Music(USA) Emma May (Nicholas Bill)
3652$^{11}$ 4299$^{8}$ 6118$^{8}$

**Red Lips (GER)** *Andreas Lowe* 112
4 b f Areion(GER) Rosarium (GER) (Zinaad)
5742a$^{6}$ 6380a$^{8}$

**Redlorryellowlorry (IRE)** *George Baker* a15 51
3 b g Bushranger(IRE) Bronze Baby (USA) (Silver Charm (USA))
865$^{8}$ 1235$^{11}$ 2694$^{8}$ (3326) 3819$^{6}$ 4085$^{10}$

**Red Majesty** *Kevin Ryan* 55
2 b c Acclamation Red Shareef (Marju (IRE))
4787$^{10}$ 5886$^{5}$

**Red Oasis** *Robert Eddery* a45 22
3 b g Captain Gerrard(IRE) Sahara Silk (IRE) (Desert Style (IRE))
15$^{6}$

**Red Paladin (IRE)** *Kevin Ryan* a71 78
4 b g Red Clubs(IRE) Alexander Goldmine (Dansili)
1689$^{4}$ 2169$^{15}$ 3272$^{10}$ 3485$^{3}$ (4108) 4537$^{2}$ 5536$^{4}$ 5986$^{2}$ 6639$^{10}$ 7403$^{8}$

**Red Passiflora** *Sir Mark Prescott Bt* a77 75
3 b f Danehill Dancer(IRE) Red Peony (Montjeu (IRE))
(3711) 3823$^{2}$ 4547$^{4}$

**Red Perdita (IRE)** *George Baker* a66 71
2 b f Approve(IRE) Bakewell Tart (IRE) (Tagula (IRE))
1788$^{5}$ 3210$^{3}$ 3858$^{3}$ 4589$^{2}$ 6361$^{2}$ 7254$^{3}$ 7631$^{2}$ (7999) 8317$^{8}$

**Red Pike (IRE)** *Bryan Smart* 100
3 ch g Kheleyf(USA) Fancy Feathers (IRE) (Redback)
(1441) 2295$^{2}$ (2508) 3480$^{3}$ 5143$^{5}$ (5632) 6893$^{2}$ 7408$^{2}$ (7564)

**Red Pilgrim (IRE)** *James Toller* a65 78
4 b g Authorized(IRE) Plenty Of Action (USA) (Hennessy (USA))
1810[7] 2774[9] 4051[6] 5101[9] 6564[3] 6942[5] 7524[7]

**Red Primo (IRE)** *Tony Coyle* a82 50
3 b g Iffraaj Testa Unica (ITY) (Nordance (USA))
(1223) ◆ (1801) 2429[9] (3405) 5603[8] 7035[8] 8209[6]

**Red Rebel** *Clive Cox* a69 73
2 b c Cockney Rebel(IRE) Smart Red (Bachelor Duke (USA))
3181[5] 4330[3] (4906) 5310[6] 6769[5]

**Red Refraction (IRE)** *Richard Hannon* a90 101
4 b c Red Clubs(IRE) Dreamalot (Falbrav (IRE))
1275[3] 1538[2] 2110[2] ◆ (2500) (2984) 4146[6] 4650[6] 5178[5] 5444[2] (6498) 6755[12] 7227[10] 7555[11] 8101[12] 8263[4]

**Red Renee** *Mark Gillard* 21
2 ch f Piccolo Bint Baddi (FR) (Shareef Dancer (USA))
3583[8] 4676[9] 6024[9]

**Red Rubles (IRE)** *Andrew Balding* 79
2 b g Soviet Star(USA) Shantalla Peak (IRE) (Darshaan)
3194[3] 3474[3] 4353[4] 7084[2]

**Red Runaway** *Ed Dunlop* a91 85
4 ch g Medicean Gretna (Groom Dancer (USA))
(1241) 1651[4] 2782[5] 3139[7] 3696[3] (4736) 5442[5] (6141) ◆ 7110[5] 7289[4]

**Red Seventy** *Sarah Humphrey* a51 56
5 b g Sakhee(USA) Dimakya (USA) (Dayjur (USA))
2091[5] 2991[13] 7205[12]

**Red Shadow** *Alan Brown* a54 57
5 b m Royal Applause Just A Glimmer (Bishop Of Cashel)
34[7] 77[4] 502[3] 2653[6] 3092[3] 3833[7] 4532[4] 4795[2] 5390[2] 6120[6] 6409[3] 7036[3] 8085[6]

**Red Shuttle** *Andi Brown* a85 78
7 b g Starcraft(NZ) Red Azalea (Shirley Heights)
146[4] (498) 698[2] 1636[11] 3544[7]

**Red Skipper (IRE)** *John O'Shea* a49 66
9 ch g Captain Rio Speed To Lead (IRE) (Darshaan)
490[3] 639[6]

**Red Springer (IRE)** *Alan McCabe* a35 24
2 b g Zebedee Solo Symphony (IRE) (Fayruz)
3119[9] 5488[10]

**Red Stargazer (IRE)** *David Barron* 101
3 b g Intikhab(USA) Autumn Star (IRE) (Mujadil (USA))
1658[4] (2148) 2565[12]

**Red Star Lady (IRE)** *Shaun Harris* a46 42
4 b f Redback Vigorous (IRE) (Danetime (IRE))
100[2] 215[3] 353[11] 502[7] 973[9]

**Redstart** *Ralph Beckett* a79 78
2 b f Cockney Rebel(IRE) Ecstasy (Pursuit Of Love)
7018[2] ◆ (7944)

**Red Stripes (USA)** *Brian Meehan* a67 49
2 b c Leroidesanimaux(BRZ) Kaleidoscopic (USA) (Fortunate Prospect (USA))
2698[6] 5078[9] 6603[9] 6903[6] 7487[2] 7816[2] 7902[3] 8267[4]

**Red Tide (IRE)** *Marjorie Fife* a77 68
3 gr g Tamayuz Rectify (IRE) (Mujadil (USA))
2433[7] 4627[7] 5244[4] (5853) 7502[3] (7825)

**Red Tiger Lily** *Nigel Tinkler* a48 32
3 ch f Piccolo Juncea (Elnadim (USA))
15[8] 302[5]

**Red Tornado (FR)** *Harry Dunlop* 97
2 ch g Dr Fong(USA) Encircle (USA) (Spinning World (USA))
2298[12] 2829[3] 4312a[2] (5588a) (6618a) 7317a[4]

**Red Touch (USA)** *Alan McCabe* a69
2 bb g Bluegrass Cat(USA) Touchnow (CAN) (Pleasant Tap (USA))
2680[2] 6719[4] 7031[11]

**Red Tracer (AUS)** *Chris Waller* 112
7 b m Dane Shadow(AUS) Kisma (AUS) (Snippets (AUS))
1186a[10]

**Red Turtle (FR)** *Mme Pia Brandt* a96 96
3 ch c Turtle Bowl(IRE) Morlane (IRE) (Entrepreneur)
5481a[8]

**Red Tycoon (IRE)** *Ed Dunlop* a54 70
2 b g Acclamation Rugged Up (IRE) (Marju (IRE))
3063[8] 4864[4] 5248[5] 6104[9]

**Red Unico (IRE)** *Alan McCabe* a17 51
2 b g Vale Of York(IRE) Testa Unica (ITY) (Nordance (USA))
4787[5] 6667[11] 7030[11]

**Red Velour** *Jeremy Noseda* a80 81
3 ch f Pivotal Regal Velvet (Halling (USA))
1534[7] 1831[2] 2346[5] 2847[4] 4434[2] 5150[2] 5831[3] 6634[4]

**Redvers (IRE)** *Ed Vaughan* a86 105
6 br g Ishiguru(USA) Cradle Brief (IRE) (Brief Truce (USA))
1679[4] 2145[15] 4648[16] 5665[6] ◆ 6124[2] 6531[11] 6921[11]

**Red Warrior (IRE)** *Ismail Mohammed* a83 91
4 ch c Iffraaj Wiolante (GER) (Lagunas)
(1636) 3065[2] 3802[2] 4175[9] 5203[8] 5487[12] 7774[7]

**Red Wifey (IRE)** *Alan McCabe* a61 17
3 b f High Chaparral(IRE) Raspberry Beret (IRE) (Danehill Dancer (IRE))
456[7] 734[6] 1083[2] 1588[15] 1852[6]

**Red Willow** *John E Long* a51 38
8 ch m Noverre(USA) Chelsea Blue (ITY) (Barathea (IRE))
116[9] 1923[4] 3710[3] 4264[9]

**Red Words (IRE)** *George Margarson* 62
2 b f Intikhab(USA) Literacy (USA) (Diesis)
4784[13] 6435[6] 7594[6]

**Redy To Rumble** *Michael Attwater* a27
3 ch g Three Valleys(USA) Sorara (Aragon)
142[8] 378[9] 577[6]

**Reedcutter** *James Toller* a83 87
3 b g Passing Glance Violet's Walk (Dr Fong (USA))
(1894) ◆ (2495) 3243[6] 3980[5] 4580[7] 6885[3] 7438[5]

**Reeflex** *Eric Alston*
3 b g Multiplex Reem Two (Mtoto)
1962[8] 4360[6]

**Reelside (FR)** *Y Fertillet* a68 72
5 b m Country Reel(USA) Jamouna (FR) (Trempolino (USA))
178a[5]

**Reesha** *Roger Varian* a72 92
3 b f Teofilo(IRE) Sana Abel (IRE) (Alhaarth (IRE))
1233[4] (1730) 3197[2] 3918[2] 5003[2] ◆ 6137[6]

**Ree's Rascal (IRE)** *Jim Boyle* a87 96
6 gr g Verglas(IRE) Night Scent (IRE) (Scenic (IRE))
1241[4] (2772) 5213[2] 6713[9] 6892[9]

**Reetaj** *Peter Chapple-Hyam* a84
2 b c Medicean Bakhoor (IRE) (Royal Applause)
7827[2] 8083[2]

**Reet Petite (IRE)** *James Evans* a43 46
2 b f Fast Company(IRE) Damjanich (IRE) (Mull Of Kintyre (USA))
1342[5] 1656[9] 2360[4] 3435[4] 4302[3] 4528[2] 5194[8] 5372[5] 6072[4] 6663[8] 7912[4] 8165[4]

**Reet Thicknstrong** *Bryan Smart* a15 60
3 b f Captain Gerrard(IRE) Dazzling Quintet (Superlative)
1671[5] 2388[3] 2932[6] 4890[11]

**Referendum (IRE)** *Sir Michael Stoute* 72
2 b g Cape Cross(IRE) Mary Stuart (IRE) (Nashwan (USA))
4800[7] 5315[4] 5886[3] 6648[4] 7207[7]

**Reflation** *Richard Hannon* a63 49
2 b c Stimulation(IRE) Miss Poppy (Averti (IRE))
5500[10] 6293[10] 7082[6] 7529[2] 7753[3]

**Reflect (IRE)** *Derek Shaw* a76 83
6 b g Hurricane Run(IRE) Raphimix (FR) (Linamix (FR))
250[5] 641[5] 856[4] 990[2] 1231[3] 1729[8] 2301[4] 2806[10] 3699[10]

**Reflecting (USA)** *Claude McGaughey III* a75 104
5 bb h Elusive Quality(USA) Daydreaming (USA) (A.P. Indy (USA))
4231a[5]

**Reflection** *Brian Baugh* a34 45
3 ch f Major Cadeaux River Song (USA) (Siphon (BRZ))
1683[10] 2416[14] 3303[10] 3849[7] 5321[4] 6088[9] 7187[12]

**Refreshestheparts (USA)** *George Baker* a70 34
5 ch m Proud Citizen(USA) St Francis Wood (USA) (Irish River (FR))
6890[12] 7397[11] 7831[12] 7998[6] 8190[3]

**Refuse Colette (IRE)** *Mick Quinn* a50 86
5 ch m Refuse To Bend(IRE) Roclette (USA) (Rock Of Gibraltar (IRE))
321[3] 435[6] 672[6] 916[6] 1086[4] 2092[4] 2901[2] (3123) 3678[2] (4306) (4595) (5059) 5398[4] 5726[3] (6463) 6689[7] 6891[16]

**Refuse To Bobbin (IRE)** *A Giorgi* 105
4 ch c Refuse To Bend(IRE) Super Bobbina (IRE) (Daggers Drawn (USA))
(2191a) 6808a[10] 7323a[5] 7617a[4]

**Regal Accolade** *David O'Meara* a34 34
2 b g Royal Applause Sindarbella (Sinndar (IRE))
3403[5] 3945[12] 4528[7] 5372[7]

**Regal Dan (IRE)** *David O'Meara* a78 94
4 b g Dark Angel(IRE) Charlene Lacy (IRE) (Pips Pride)
689[3] 917[4] 1191[9] 5346[8] 5650[3] 7085[9]

**Regal Hawk** *James Tate* a83 93
4 br f Singspiel(IRE) Elegant Hawk (Generous (IRE))
3665[2] 4634[5] 6389a[3] 6708[12] 7554[10]

**Regal Missile (IRE)** *Mark Walford* 71
2 b c Royal Applause Leenane (IRE) (Grand Lodge (USA))
6690[7] 7329[2] 7712[7]

**Regal Parade** *Milton Bradley* a94 94
10 ch g Pivotal Model Queen (USA) (Kingmambo (USA))
890[5] 1114[6] 1719[11] 2254[7] 2778[10] 2992[3] 4892[15] (5392) 6740[7] 6898[4]

**Regal Park (IRE)** *Miss Imogen Pickard* a46 61
7 b g Montjeu(IRE) Classic Park (Robellino (USA))
5193[5] 6721[9] 7129[6] 7333[8] 7508[2] 7643[7] 8146[7] 8208[11]

**Regal Power** *J P Murtagh* a70 78
5 b g Royal Applause Be My Charm (Polish Precedent (USA))
4556a[8]

**Regal Selection** *James Tate* a41
3 b f Royal Applause Choosey Girl (IRE) (Choisir (AUS))
1287[4]

**Regal Warrior (IRE)** *J J Lambe* a70 76
11 b g King's Theatre(IRE) Cheyenne Spirit (Indian Ridge)
7435a[11] 7962a[8]

**Regal Ways (IRE)** *Mark Johnston* a63 71
2 bb f Royal Applause Step This Way (USA) (Giant's Causeway (USA))
6474[5] 7019[3] 7234[3] 7549[7] 7809[4] 7891[8]

**Regarde Moi** *Stefano Botti* 106
6 b g King's Best(USA) Life At Night (IRE) (Night Shift (USA))
7604a[3]

**Regardez** *Ralph Beckett* 104
3 b f Champs Elysees Look So (Efisio)
2255[3] 2960[12] (3665) 4634[3] 6585a[2] 7558a[4]

**Reggie Bond** *Geoffrey Oldroyd* a70 72
4 ch g Monsieur Bond(IRE) Triple Tricks (IRE) (Royal Academy (USA))
(263) 736[2] (1718) 3439[8] 5415[3] 7569[5] 8168[5]

**Reggie Perrin** *Pat Phelan* a65 59
6 ch g Storming Home Tecktal (FR) (Pivotal)
4076[4] 4656[3]

**Regiment** *Richard Fahey* 88
3 ch g Major Cadeaux My First Romance (Danehill (USA))
1601[3] (2176) 2734[2] (3137) 3651[5] 4551[5] 5410[9] 5656[7] 6170[8] 7060[P] (Dead)

**Reginald Claude** *Mark Usher* a67 42
6 b g Monsieur Bond(IRE) Miller's Melody (Chief Singer)
(192) 511[6] 2174[7] 2648[9] 3150[15] 3393[8] 4049[6] 4733[3] 5136[2] 6409[11] 6720[2] 7364[8] 7783[2] 7887[9] 8014[10] (8319)

**Regulation (IRE)** *Neil King* a99 101
5 br g Danehill Dancer(IRE) Source Of Life (IRE) (Fasliyev (USA))
207a[9] 394a[9] 595a[12] 678a[4] 812a[4] 1078a[12] 3356[10] ◆ 3726[5] 6548[12]

**Rehanaat (USA)** *Ed Dunlop* a57 27
3 b f Daaher(CAN) Sultana (USA) (Storm Cat (USA))
1794[9] 3333[9]

**Reigning** *Michael Blanshard* 13
2 b f Sakhee's Secret Raindrop (Primo Dominie)
6333[8]

**Reillys Daughter** *Richard Mitchell* a47 44
6 b m Diktat Compose (Anabaa (USA))
382[11] 657[5]

**Reimpose (USA)** *Pat Eddery* a63 46
3 b f First Defence(USA) Rougeur (USA) (Blushing Groom (FR))
1846[9] 4152[6] 4658[11] 7664[2]

**Reine Marie (FR)** *F Chappet* a78 55
4 b f Librettist(USA) Starlaire (FR) (Beaudelaire (USA))
796a[4]

**Reinor (FR)** *Mlle A Voraz*
2 gr c Sageburg(IRE) Vanezia (FR) (Kouroun (FR))
7027a[11]

**Rekdhat (IRE)** *Roger Varian* a84 96
3 bb f Shamardal(USA) Taarkod (IRE) (Singspiel (IRE))
(1768) 2333[7] 3117[2] (4271) 5627[4] (6793)

**Related** *David Simcock* a100 94
4 b g Kheleyf(USA) Balladonia (Primo Dominie)
2500[3] 3180[2] 3969[3] 4355[5] (4783) 5665[11] (8117)

**Related To Ewe (IRE)** *Tim Easterby* 16
2 b g Vale Of York(IRE) Near Relation (Distant Relative)
1955[10] 4750[9]

**Relation Alexander (IRE)** *Paul D'Arcy* a73 79
3 ch f Dandy Man(IRE) Elshamms (Zafonic (USA))
955[5] 1769[2] (2447) 3724[10] 4367[3] 5467[9] 5826[8] 6414[6]

**Relight My Fire** *Tim Easterby* a81 80
4 ch g Firebreak Making Music (Makbul)
1609[8] 1957[12] 2522[5] 2825[2] 3256[7] 3533[6] (3910) 4291[6] 4923[6] 5915[11] 6213[9] 6478[6]

**Rembrandt** *Richard Hannon* 60
2 b c Dutch Art Authoritative (Diktat)
6875[5]

**Rembrandt Van Rijn (IRE)** *David Lanigan* a87 77
3 b g Peintre Celebre(USA) Private Life (FR) (Bering)
2334[8] 5831[2] 6485[2] 6901[U] 7195[2]

**Remember** *Richard Hannon* 102
3 b f Selkirk(USA) Forgotten Dreams (IRE) (Olden Times)
2781[7] (3674) 4166[2] 4668[4] 5165[3] 6068[4] 6689[2] 6929[2]

**Rememberance Day** *Les Eyre* a72 65
3 ch f Major Cadeaux Today's The Day (Alhaarth (IRE))
5469[7] 6215[2] 6638[5] 7078[4] (8090)

**Remember Babi (FR)** *F Vermeulen* 23
3 bb f High Chaparral(IRE) Simay (TUR) (Down The Flag (USA))
5227a[9]

**Remember Rocky** *Lucy Normile* a47 68
5 ch g Haafhd Flower Market (Cadeaux Genereux)
(2457) (2674) 3364[3] 5084[3] (5811) (6223) 6578[6]

**Remember You (IRE)** *David Wachman* 95
3 b f Invincible Spirit(IRE) Miss Dela (IRE) (King's Best (USA))
1201a[7] 1333a[3]

**Reminem Basc (FR)** *Mlle J Legatte* a14
3 b g Air Eminem(IRE) Olga Luck (Inchinor)
5959a[10]

**Remix (IRE)** *Ian Williams* a63 68
5 b m Oratorio(IRE) Miss Lopez (IRE) (Key Of Luck (USA))
358[3] 612[6] 1099[6] 2609[6] 3540[7] 4958[8] 5689[8] 6635[10]

**Remus De La Tour (FR)** *K Borgel* a80 112
5 b h Stormy River(FR) Calithea (IRE) (Marju (IRE))
4250a[8]

**Remy** *Nick Littmoden* 41
3 b f Oratorio(IRE) Kristina (Kris)
2780[13] 3477[6]

**Renaissance Art (USA)** *J S Bolger* 94
3 br c More Than Ready(USA) Lady Siphonica (USA) (Siphon (BRZ))
2579a[4]

**Renaissant** *Richard Hannon* a72 74
2 ch f Dutch Art Sofonisba (Rock Of Gibraltar (IRE))
4269[5] ◆ 4583[3] 5042[2] 5436[6] (5973) 6610[7]

**Reneesgotzip (USA)** *Peter Miller* a110 110
5 ch m City Zip(USA) No Dress Code (USA) (Distorted Humor (USA))
7609a[9]

**Renegotiate** *Peter Niven* a70 63
5 ch g Trade Fair L'Extra Honor (USA) (Hero's Honor (USA))
4662[6]

**Rene Mathis (GER)** *Richard Fahey* a84 105
4 ch g Monsieur Bond(IRE) Remina (GER) (Erminius (GER))
(2778) 3420[23] 4683[3] (5189) 5665[2] 6354a[13] 6533[19] 7122[4] 7444[4]

**Renew (IRE)** *Archie Alexander* 108
4 b g Dansili Hold Me Love Me (IRE) (Sadler's Wells (USA))
811a[8] 1950[4] 2785[7] 5688[6] 6069[3] 7126a[12] 7301a[16]

**Renewing** *Roy Brotherton* a58 16
3 b g Halling(USA) Electric Society (IRE) (Law Society (USA))
7304[10] 7627[4]

**Rennie Mackintosh (IRE)** *Mark Johnston* a65 36
2 b c Excellent Art Mac Melody (IRE) (Entrepreneur)
7495[11] 7685[2] 7741[9] 7867[8]

**Rennsenas (FR)** *C Lotoux* a73 73
3 gr g Montmartre(FR) Cable Beach (USA) (Langfuhr (CAN))
(5370a)

**Renoir's Lady** *Joseph Tuite* a61 42
6 b m Peintre Celebre(USA) Marie De Blois (IRE) (Barathea (IRE))
244[9] 448[6] 798[6] 973[8] 1009[8]

**Repeater** *David O'Meara* a62 112
5 b g Montjeu(IRE) Time Over (Mark Of Esteem (IRE))
1398[5] 2315[10] 2785[6] 3717[3] 3985[2] 4759[11] 5693[11] 6288[10] 6557[9] 6979[3]

**Repetition** *Kristin Stubbs* a88 91
4 b g Royal Applause Uno (Efisio)
75[4] (300) 388[3] 552[2] 767[5] 862[5] (1689) 2169[4] (2400) 2905[3] (3533) (4161) 4661[5] 4923[9] 6531[14] 7085[7] 7375[12] 7820[5] 8135[4]

**Reporting Star (USA)** *Pat Parente* a98 109
4 bb g Circular Quay(USA) Classic Beauty (USA) (Sword Dance)
6390a[3] 7324a[6]

**Reposer (IRE)** *Keith Dalgleish* a83 81
6 br g Kheleyf(USA) Tragic Point (IRE) (Tragic Role (USA))
5385[5] 5887[11] 6639[9] 6824[5] 7178[3] ◆ 7403[2] 7530[5]

**Representation (USA)** *A bin Huzaim* a88 73
5 ch h Street Cry(IRE) Portrayal (USA) (Saint Ballado (CAN))
243a[2]

**Reprint (IRE)** *C Laffon-Parias* 66
2 b f Nayef(USA) Desertiste (Green Desert (USA))
4839a[4]

**Reroute (IRE)** *Ed Walker* 98
3 b f Acclamation Divert (IRE) (Averti (IRE))
1572[2] 3459[3] 4215[5] 4852[12]

**Rerouted (USA)** *M F De Kock* a102 113
6 ch h Stormy Atlantic(USA) Rouwaki (USA) (Miswaki (USA))
111a[7] 4425[3] 5354[3] 5653[11] 6522[10]

**Resist** *James Given* a56 59
3 b f Rock Of Gibraltar(IRE) Cecily (Oasis Dream)
4295[3] 4873[3] 6116[4] 7285[10]

**Resolute** *Ed de Giles* a86 79
3 b g Pivotal Coy (IRE) (Danehill (USA))
307[3] 1563[11] 1983[4]

**Resolve** *David Simcock* a37 39
2 ch f Dutch Art Crooked Wood (USA) (Woodman (USA))
6333[7] 6754[10] 7625[9]

**Resonant (IRE)** *Mark Johnston* 71
2 b c Cape Cross(IRE) Last Rhapsody (IRE) (Kris)
6362[3] 6621[4] 6998[3]

**Resonare** *Stuart Williams* a62 64
5 b g Echo Of Light Pretty Kool (Inchinor)
288[2] 425[6] 740[8]

**Resonated (USA)** *Brian Ellison* a69
3 bb g Pleasant Tap(USA) Third Times Better (USA) (Carson City (USA))
5796[11] 6073[4] (6717)

**Response** *Steve Gollings* 66
4 ch g New Approach(IRE) Spotlight (Dr Fong (USA))
4786[4]

**Restorer** *William Muir* a81 103
2 gr c Mastercraftsman(IRE) Moon Empress (FR) (Rainbow Quest (USA))
(5847) 6241[3] 7104[2] 7442[6]

**Restraint Of Trade (IRE)** *Charlie Appleby* 86
4 br g Authorized(IRE) Zivania (IRE) (Shernazar)
305a[10] 2142[8]

**Resurge (IRE)** *Stuart Kittow* a65 95
9 b g Danehill Dancer(IRE) Resurgence (Polar Falcon (USA))
1653[10] 2957[8] 3730[10] 4175[8] 4736[10]

**Retirement Plan** *Lady Cecil* 107
4 bb c Monsun(GER) Passage Of Time (Dansili)
1444[9] 4696[4] (5161) 5693[5] ◆ 6287[2]

**Retouched (IRE)** *V Luka Jr* a30 52
2 gr f Verglas(IRE) Lady Pitrizza (IRE) (Night Shift (USA))
5844a[15]

**Retrofit** *William Muir* 48
3 b g Exceed And Excel(AUS) Passe Passe (USA) (Lear Fan (USA))
4816[4] 6540[6]

**Retro Valley (IRE)** *David Dennis* a54 44
2 b g Vale Of York(IRE) Retrato (USA) (Fusaichi Pegasus (USA))
3881[9] 4965[5] 5500[11] 6250[9]

**Returntobrecongill** *James Given* a89 75
4 ch g Pastoral Pursuits Turn Back (Pivotal)
3[3] 285[9] 514[4] 764[5] 1091[6] 1128[4]

**Revedargent (FR)** *H-A Pantall* 95
3 ch f Kendargent(FR) Matwan (FR) (Indian Rocket)
7856a[3]

**Reve De Gosse (FR)** *Mrs A Malzard* a58 21
4 b c Green Desert(USA) The Best Girl (FR) (Bigstone (IRE))
2593a[6]

**Reve De Nuit (USA)** *K R Burke* a96 75
8 ch g Giant's Causeway(USA) My Dream Castles (USA) (Woodman (USA))
(2) (1743) 7279[4] (7651) (8178)

**Reveries D'Avril (FR)** *D Sepulchre* a37 62
3 b f Creachadoir(IRE) Black Voodoo (FR) (Tel Quel (FR))
5592a[7]

**Revise (IRE)** *David Elsworth* a74 74
4 b g Dansili Niner's Home (USA) (Forty Niner (USA))
115[5]

**Revision (FR)** *John Best* a46 50
2 bb g Vision D'Etat(FR) Karmibola (FR) (Persian Bold)
6545[9] 6903[7] 7631[10]

**Revolutionist (IRE)** *Mark Johnston* 64
2 b c Pivotal Mysterial (USA) (Alleged (USA))
2507$^{5}$

**Rewaaya (IRE)** *John Gosden* 107
3 b f Authorized(IRE) Sulaalah (IRE) (Darshaan)
2109$^{4}$ (2613) ◆ (6559) 7106$^{8}$ (7492) 7768a$^{7}$

**Rewarding Hero** *J Moore* 109
5 b g Exceed And Excel(AUS) Caldy Dancer (IRE) (Soviet Star (USA))
7898a$^{6}$

**Rewritten** *Charlie Appleby* a52 60
2 b g Dubawi(IRE) Portrayal (USA) (Saint Ballado (CAN))
6497$^{4}$ 7040$^{6}$ 7811$^{7}$

**Rex Imperator** *William Haggas* 116
5 b g Royal Applause Elidore (Danetime (IRE))
2848$^{2}$ 3319$^{15}$ 4201$^{13}$ 4895$^{24}$ 5778$^{3}$ 6440$^{5}$ 7122$^{18}$

**Rex Romanorum (IRE)** *Patrick Holmes* a49 60
6 b g Holy Roman Emperor(IRE) Willowbridge (IRE) (Entrepreneur)
2654$^{5}$ 3958$^{8}$ 6267$^{11}$

**Rex Whistler (IRE)** *Julie Camacho* a81 77
4 b g Tamayuz Dangle (IRE) (Desert Style (IRE))
2423$^{10}$ 3095$^{5}$ 3919$^{5}$ 4427$^{2}$ 5077$^{5}$ 5716$^{4}$ 6699$^{2}$ (7366)

**Reynaldothewizard (USA)** *S Seemar* a112
8 b g Speightstown(USA) Holiday Runner (USA) (Meadowlake (USA))
206a$^{7}$ 898a$^{2}$ 1180a$^{4}$

**Rezwaan** *Murty McGrath* a62 54
7 b g Alhaarth(IRE) Nasij (USA) (Elusive Quality (USA))
345$^{9}$ 1021$^{10}$ 1664$^{3}$ 3473$^{7}$ 5428$^{6}$ 6028$^{10}$ 6883$^{7}$ 7635$^{4}$ 8028$^{6}$ 8198$^{5}$ 8315$^{4}$

**Rhagori** *Simon Callaghan* a92 93
5 bb m Exceed And Excel(AUS) Cresta Gold (Halling (USA))
7615a$^{6}$

**Rhinestone Rebel (IRE)** *Peter Hiatt* a49 46
8 ch g Rashar(USA) Flute Opera (IRE) (Sharifabad (IRE))
246$^{4}$ 455$^{8}$ 2885$^{10}$ 3336$^{3}$ 3976$^{6}$ 6542$^{14}$

**Rhombus (IRE)** *Ismail Mohammed* 103
4 b g Authorized(IRE) Mathool (IRE) (Alhaarth (IRE))
2142$^{3}$ 3034$^{3}$ 4217$^{4}$ (5193) (6518) 7107$^{19}$ 7718$^{8}$

**Rhythm To Spare (NZ)** *Michael Moroney* 103
5 b g Pins(AUS) Stanica (NZ) (Zabeel (NZ))
7128a$^{5}$

**Ria Antonia (USA)** *Thomas Amoss* a110
3 b f Rockport Harbor(USA) Beer Baroness (USA) (Mr Greeley (USA))
2357a$^{10}$ 6973a$^{2}$ 7593a$^{4}$

**Rialto Magic** *Jamie Osborne* a60
2 b f Monsieur Bond(IRE) Discover Roma (IRE) (Rock Of Gibraltar (IRE))
7228$^{8}$ 7573$^{5}$ 7631$^{3}$ 7848$^{3}$

**Riba Roja** *John Gallagher*
2 b f Refuse To Bend(IRE) Satin Braid (Diktat)
6246$^{12}$ 6630$^{9}$

**Ribblehead (USA)** *Tim Easterby* 86
3 bb c Arch(USA) Moolakaya (FR) (Alzao (USA))
(4791) 5420$^{3}$ 6166$^{3}$ ◆ 7125$^{3}$ ◆

**Ribbleton** *David Barron* a45 75
3 b g Bushranger(IRE) Bayleaf (Efisio)
1136$^{6}$

**Ribbons** *James Fanshawe* a98 114
4 ch f Manduro(GER) Sister Act (Marju (IRE))
(1577) 2144$^{2}$ (5742a) 6969a$^{2}$

**Rib Reserve (IRE)** *Sir Michael Stoute* 31
2 b g Azamour(IRE) Fringe Success (IRE) (Selkirk (USA))
7382$^{14}$

**Rich Again (IRE)** *James Bethell* a80 72
5 b g Amadeus Wolf Fully Fashioned (IRE) (Brief Truce (USA))
2825$^{3}$ 3298$^{7}$ 3882$^{4}$ (4391) 4752$^{6}$ 5265$^{7}$ 5912$^{5}$ 6213$^{7}$ 6674$^{5}$ (7077) 7636$^{3}$ 7905$^{3}$ (8124) (8257)

**Richard Pankhurst** *John Gosden* 111
2 ch c Raven's Pass(USA) Mainstay (Elmaamul (USA))
2776$^{4}$ (3448)

**Rich Harvest (USA)** *Ray Peacock*
9 bb g High Yield(USA) Mangano (USA) (Quiet American (USA))
8219$^{9}$

**Richo** *Shaun Harris* a45 46
8 ch g Bertolini(USA) Noble Water (FR) (Noblequest (FR))
4737$^{4}$ 5283$^{6}$ 5850$^{5}$ 6426$^{6}$

**Rich Tapestry (IRE)** *C W Chang* a119 108
6 b g Holy Roman Emperor(IRE) Genuine Charm (IRE) (Sadler's Wells (USA))
(898a) 1180a$^{2}$ 7612a$^{14}$

**Rictrude (FR)** *Tom Dascombe* a68 61
2 b f Zamindar(USA) Park Acclaim (IRE) (Clodovil (IRE))
4999$^{5}$ (5509) 6679$^{7}$ 6941$^{2}$

**Ride Like The Wind (IRE)** *F Head* 101
2 b c Lope De Vega(IRE) Biswa (USA) (Kafwain (USA))
4953a$^{4}$ 5741a$^{6}$ 6245a$^{2}$

**Rideonastar (IRE)** *Ralph Beckett* a42 82
3 b g Manduro(GER) Capestar (IRE) (Cape Cross (IRE))
2334$^{12}$ 2746$^{8}$ 4325$^{10}$ (7162)

**Ride On Curlin (USA)** *William Gowan* a121
3 b c Curlin(USA) Magical Ride (USA) (Storm Cat (USA))
1964a$^{7}$ 2357a$^{2}$ 3026a$^{11}$

**Ridge Racer (ITY)** *A Peraino* 51
3 b c Giovane Imperatore Kathy Ridge (IRE) (Indian Ridge)
2375a$^{15}$

**Ridge Ranger (IRE)** *Eric Alston* 80
3 b f Bushranger Dani Ridge (IRE) (Indian Ridge)
(4900) 5526$^{2}$ 5923$^{9}$ 6598$^{4}$ 7159$^{5}$

**Ridgeway Hawk** *Mark Usher* a59 29
6 ch g Monsieur Bond(IRE) Barefooted Flyer (USA) (Fly So Free (USA))
34$^{U}$ 273$^{9}$

**Ridgeway Storm (IRE)** *Alan King* a88 76
4 b g Hurricane Run(IRE) Hesperia (Slip Anchor)
1088$^{2}$ 1491$^{3}$ 1981$^{8}$ 3860$^{2}$ 5924$^{10}$ (7401) 7702$^{3}$ (8096)

**Rightcar** *Peter Grayson* a51 40
7 b g Bertolini(USA) Loblolly Bay (Halling (USA))
100$^{7}$ 164$^{4}$ 290$^{3}$ 448$^{4}$ 556$^{3}$ 8230$^{5}$

**Right Madam (IRE)** *Andrew Hollinshead* 58
2 b f Jeremy(USA) Mawaared (Machiavellian (USA))
3613$^{8}$ 4129$^{6}$ 4784$^{7}$ 6623$^{10}$

**Right Of Appeal** *Mark Johnston* a79 77
3 b g Dubawi(IRE) Easy To Love (USA) (Diesis)
(198) ◆ 1367$^{3}$ (1898) ◆ 2222$^{5}$ 2728$^{7}$ 3696$^{2}$ 3823$^{3}$ 4189$^{7}$ 4704$^{6}$ 5259$^{7}$ 5716$^{5}$ 6403$^{3}$ (6579) 6787$^{3}$ 7008$^{5}$ 7100$^{12}$ 7366$^{2}$

**Right Touch** *Richard Fahey* 94
4 b g Royal Applause Amira (Efisio)
1537$^{2}$ (1938)

**Rightway (IRE)** *Tony Carroll* a75 78
3 b g Cockney Rebel(IRE) Caeribland (IRE) (Namaqualand (USA))
7921$^{2}$ (8003)

**Rigid** *Tony Carroll* a50 48
7 ch g Refuse To Bend(IRE) Supersonic (Shirley Heights)
88$^{7}$ 661$^{6}$ 844$^{11}$ 869$^{3}$ 939$^{4}$

**Rigid Rock (IRE)** *J T Gorman* a55 41
7 b g Refuse To Bend(IRE) Delia (IRE) (Darshaan)
790a$^{9}$

**Rigolleto (IRE)** *Anabel K Murphy* a76 77
6 b g Ad Valorem(USA) Jallaissine (IRE) (College Chapel)
91$^{3}$ (248) 746$^{4}$ 1144$^{2}$ 1678$^{7}$ 2890$^{3}$ 3422$^{6}$ 3935$^{2}$ 4581$^{7}$ 5750$^{7}$ 6249$^{9}$ 8186$^{6}$

**Rimbaud (GER)** *Alfredino Sauli* 94
6 br h Law Society(USA) Rosomachia (GER) (Machiavellian (USA))
7616a$^{7}$

**Rinaldo (FR)** *I Endaltsev* a68 79
3 ch c Le Havre(IRE) New Style (GER) (Tertullian (USA))
795a$^{12}$

**Ri Na Si** *Michael Appleby* a33 46
4 b g Green Horizon Luisa Miller (IRE) (Entrepreneur)
7907$^{11}$ 8280$^{5}$

**Ring Eye (IRE)** *John O'Shea* a65
6 b g Definite Article Erins Lass (IRE) (Erins Isle (IRE))
686$^{5}$

**Ring Of Fire (GER)** *Brian Ellison* a52 53
5 ch g Tertullian(USA) Rowina (GER) (Hamond (GER))
7524$^{5}$

**Ring Weekend (USA)** *H Graham Motion* a103 108
3 ch g Tapit(USA) Free The Magic (USA) (Cryptoclearance (USA))
2357a$^{5}$ (6949a)

**Rio Cobolo (IRE)** *Keith Reveley* a68 52
8 b g Captain Rio Sofistication (IRE) (Dayjur (USA))
1125$^{2}$ 1649$^{7}$ 2169$^{11}$ 2763$^{8}$ 3299$^{7}$ 3547$^{10}$ 4905$^{6}$ 5854$^{5}$ 5895$^{11}$ 8282$^{8}$

**Rioja Day (IRE)** *Jim Goldie* a40 69
4 b g Red Clubs(IRE) Dai E Dai (USA) (Seattle Dancer (USA))
1970$^{8}$ 2477$^{6}$ 2914$^{6}$ 3054$^{6}$ 4254$^{7}$ 4523$^{8}$ 6009$^{7}$ 6601$^{4}$ 6833$^{3}$ 7061$^{4}$ 7644$^{20}$

**Rio Ranger (IRE)** *Bryan Smart* a26
3 b f Bushranger(IRE) Desert D'Argent (IRE) (Desert Story (IRE))
167$^{7}$

**Rio Ronaldo (IRE)** *Mike Murphy* a76 79
2 b g Footstepsinthesand Flanders (IRE) (Common Grounds)
4025$^{5}$ 4787$^{3}$ (6270) 7665$^{3}$

**Rio Sands** *Richard Whitaker* 46
9 b g Captain Rio Sally Traffic (River Falls)
2166$^{10}$ 6595$^{13}$

**Rio's Rosanna (IRE)** *Richard Whitaker* a91 93
7 b m Captain Rio Ling Lane (Slip Anchor)
2787$^{10}$ 4940$^{4}$ 5465$^{3}$ 6761$^{7}$

**Rio Tigre (IRE)** *A Fabre* a84 106
3 b c Teofilo(IRE) Braziliz (USA) (Kingmambo (USA))
5224a$^{2}$ 5962a$^{4}$ 6954a$^{4}$

**Rio Yuma (ITY)** *Kristin Stubbs* a60 38
3 b f Gold Sphinx(USA) Selsey (Selkirk (USA))
1024$^{3}$ 1303$^{8}$ 1794$^{8}$ 4563$^{6}$ 6454$^{12}$ 8123$^{7}$

**Ripinto (IRE)** *Jim Boyle* a74
2 ch c Rip Van Winkle(IRE) For Evva Silca (Piccolo)
7542$^{8}$ (7833)

**Riponian** *Susan Corbett* 46
4 ch g Trade Fair Dispol Katie (Komaite (USA))
7176$^{7}$ 7499$^{6}$ 7642$^{3}$

**Ripon Rose** *Paul Midgley* 57
2 br f Ferrule(IRE) Dispol Isle (IRE) (Trans Island)
2358$^{9}$ 2725$^{5}$ 2949$^{4}$ 5014$^{7}$ 5384$^{6}$ 5767$^{2}$

**Riptide** *Michael Scudamore* 87
8 b g Val Royal(FR) Glittering Image (IRE) (Sadler's Wells (USA))
1981$^{6}$ 2482$^{9}$ 3501$^{7}$ 4441$^{9}$ (4818) 6169$^{5}$

**Riquet Enfin (FR)** *E Lellouche* a73 68
3 b c Brave Mansonnien(FR) Brave Ville (FR) (Villez (USA))
360a$^{5}$ 585a$^{6}$

**Risby (IRE)** *J-M Osorio* a97 98
6 br g Big Shuffle(USA) Lonicera (GER) (Charmer)
207a$^{7}$ 396a$^{7}$ 679a$^{10}$

**Risen Sun** *Mark Johnston* 89
2 b f Shamardal(USA) Bright Morning (Dubai Millennium)
(5852) 6291$^{5}$ 6876$^{2}$

**Rise To Glory (IRE)** *Shaun Harris* a74 72
6 b h King's Best(USA) Lady At War (Warning)
141$^{10}$ 510$^{3}$ 663$^{2}$ 777$^{4}$ 845$^{5}$ 1148$^{9}$ 1312$^{8}$ 4655$^{11}$ 5236$^{10}$ 5683$^{14}$ (5801) (6014) (6090) 6272$^{3}$ 6475$^{4}$ 6835$^{10}$ 7535$^{13}$

**Rise To Power** *Kevin Ryan* 43
2 b g Exceed And Excel(AUS) Capistrano Day (USA) (Diesis)
6058$^{10}$ 6621$^{6}$ 7407$^{11}$

**Rise Up Lotus (IRE)** *Charles Hills* 78
2 gr f Zebedee Face The Storm (IRE) (Barathea (IRE))
1528$^{6}$ (2022) (4422) 4869$^{4}$ 5790$^{5}$ 7038$^{7}$

**Rising Breeze (FR)** *K R Burke* a79 81
3 b g Shirocco(GER) Moon Tree (FR) (Groom Dancer (USA))
1195$^{6}$ 2148$^{7}$ 3466$^{7}$ (3974) 4388$^{4}$ 4651$^{7}$ 5818$^{5}$ 6722$^{5}$ 7350$^{6}$

**Rising Rainbow** *Garry Woodward*
3 b g Rainbow High Lord Conyers (IRE) (Inzar (USA))
7332$^{9}$

**Rising Romance (NZ)** *Donna Logan* 109
4 b f Ekraar(USA) Post Romance (NZ) (Postponed (USA))
7301a$^{2}$ 7602a$^{6}$

**Riskit Fora Biskit (IRE)** *Michael Bell* a80 105
4 b f Kodiac Miss Brief (IRE) (Brief Truce (USA))
1572$^{9}$ 2197a$^{9}$ 3459$^{6}$ 4179$^{10}$ 5419$^{16}$ 6130$^{7}$

**Risk 'N' Reward (IRE)** *Martin Smith* a51 57
3 ch g Dandy Man(IRE) Sharp Diversion (USA) (Diesis)
4324$^{5}$ 4733$^{9}$ 4969$^{3}$ 5321$^{2}$

**Risquillo (FR)** *M Boutin* a85 71
8 b h Ballingarry(IRE) Alexia Fedorovna (USA) (Steinlen)
584a$^{11}$ 3907a$^{10}$

**Rita's Boy (IRE)** *K R Burke* a79 70
2 b c Captain Rio The Oldladysays No (IRE) (Perugino (USA))
1889$^{2}$ ◆ 2291$^{3}$ 3148$^{6}$ 3937$^{5}$ (5569) 7038$^{6}$ 7231$^{4}$ 8222$^{2}$ (8278)

**Rite To Reign** *Philip McBride* a74 91
3 b g Tiger Hill(IRE) Magical Cliche (USA) (Affirmed (USA))
1028$^{3}$ 1727$^{3}$ 2319$^{4}$ 3110$^{2}$ 3673$^{4}$ 6741$^{2}$ 7235$^{2}$ (7566)

**Rive Gauche** *William Haggas* 65
2 b f Fastnet Rock(AUS) Raysiza (IRE) (Alzao (USA))
7594$^{4}$

**Rivellino** *K R Burke* a110 108
4 b g Invincible Spirit(IRE) Brazilian Bride (IRE) (Pivotal)
55$^{2}$ (534) 713$^{2}$ 1557$^{3}$ 3452$^{3}$ 4438$^{8}$

**Riverboat Springs (IRE)** *Mick Channon* 94
3 b g Bushranger(IRE) Mashie (Selkirk (USA))
2148$^{5}$ 2565$^{10}$ 3108$^{7}$

**River Dart (IRE)** *Marcus Tregoning* 73
2 ch c Dutch Art Sky Galaxy (USA) (Sky Classic (CAN))
5377$^{12}$ 5947$^{2}$ 6517$^{19}$

**River Dreamer (IRE)** *Robert Stephens* a47
3 ch f Intense Focus(USA) Guard Hill (USA) (Rahy (USA))
298$^{5}$ 500$^{3}$ 786$^{5}$ 1235$^{10}$ (1855) 8200$^{8}$

**River Du Nord (FR)** *Sue Gardner* a42 40
7 b m Voix Du Nord(FR) Palala River (Colmore Row)
1622a$^{4}$ 2593a$^{2}$ 3048a$^{3}$ 4041a$^{3}$ 4718a$^{6}$ 5969a$^{3}$ (6188a) 6817$^{6}$

**River Glass (IRE)** *Charles Hills* 35
3 gr g Verglas(IRE) Spartan Girl (IRE) (Ela-Mana-Mou)
5191$^{4}$

**River Goddess (IRE)** *Charles Hills* a68 63
3 b f Marju(IRE) Talwin (IRE) (Alhaarth (IRE))
275$^{4}$ 645$^{2}$ 1403$^{12}$ 1832$^{2}$

**Riverlynx (IRE)** *Ben Haslam* 37
2 b f Holy Roman Emperor(IRE) Banba (IRE) (Docksider (USA))
4018$^{8}$ 7495$^{8}$

**River Of Dreams (IRE)** *Kevin Ryan* a67 64
2 br g Big Bad Bob(IRE) Toberanthawn (IRE) (Danehill Dancer (IRE))
3701$^{5}$ 4129$^{9}$ 6268$^{7}$

**River Prince (FR)** *P Adda* a71 71
4 b g Stormy River(FR) Princess Liu (IRE) (Desert Style (IRE))
2192a$^{9}$ 5225a$^{10}$

**River Seven (CAN)** *Nicholas Gonzalez* a115 110
4 b g Johannesburg(USA) Sans Souci Island (CAN) (Chester House (USA))
6391a$^{4}$

**Riversou (FR)** *J-M Lefebvre* a34
3 ch c Stormy River(FR) A La Plage (IRE) (Galileo (IRE))
169a$^{13}$ 600a$^{10}$

**River Spirit** *Mick Channon* a65 63
2 ch f Avonbridge Pooka's Daughter (IRE) (Eagle Eyed (USA))
1788$^{6}$ 2206$^{2}$ 2692$^{5}$ (2993) 3211$^{4}$ 3937$^{3}$ 4283$^{3}$ 4702$^{2}$ 5028$^{4}$ 5985$^{10}$ 6447$^{4}$ 6888$^{5}$ 7190$^{8}$ 7421$^{5}$ 7529$^{3}$

**Rivolochop (FR)** *C Boutin* a68 68
2 ch c American Post Bouboulina (Grand Lodge (USA))
1271a$^{4}$ 4881a$^{4}$ 5618a$^{6}$ 5900a$^{3}$ 8212a$^{3}$

**Rizal Park (IRE)** *Andrew Balding* a80 71
3 b g Amadeus Wolf Imelda (USA) (Manila (USA))
1390$^{P}$ 5308$^{7}$ 5903$^{5}$ 6262$^{4}$ 7013$^{3}$ (8041) (8188)

**Rizeena (IRE)** *Clive Brittain* 113
3 b f Iffraaj Serena's Storm (IRE) (Statue Of Liberty (USA))
1976$^{7}$ (3418) 4165$^{2}$ 5480a$^{4}$ 6351a$^{2}$

**Roachdale House (IRE)** *Richard Fahey* a77 95
3 b g Mastercraftsman(IRE) Golden Legacy (IRE) (Rossini (USA))
1563$^{7}$ 1937$^{6}$ 3369$^{5}$ (3694) 4198$^{12}$ 5410$^{7}$ 7715$^{5}$ 7851$^{7}$

**Road Map (IRE)** *Daniel Mark Loughnane* a61 36
3 b g Saville Road Lauren Eria (Singspiel (IRE))
6421$^{7}$ 7063$^{5}$ 7528$^{11}$ 7830$^{13}$ 8050$^{6}$

**Road To Damascus (FR)** *F Sanchez* 66
2 b f Desert Style(IRE) Winding Road (FR) (Barathea (IRE))
4839a$^{7}$ 5617a$^{8}$

**Road Warrior (ITY)** *G Botti* 57
2 b c Blu Air Force(IRE) Desert Harmony (Green Desert (USA))
5662a$^{3}$

**Robben** *John Mackie* a56 57
2 b g Dutch Art Little Greenbird (Ardkinglass)
2291$^{5}$ 2601$^{5}$ 3924$^{7}$ 5141$^{4}$ 5489$^{4}$ 6413$^{6}$ 6669$^{11}$ 7208$^{2}$ ◆ 7379$^{6}$ 8087$^{7}$

**Robbian** *Charles Smith* 54
3 b c Bertolini(USA) Crathes (Zilzal (USA))
477$^{11}$ 765$^{9}$ 1277$^{6}$ (2230) 3228$^{8}$ 3679$^{5}$ 5574$^{9}$ 6454$^{14}$ 7167$^{8}$

**Robert Le Diable (FR)** *D Prod'Homme* a67 104
5 ch g Dutch Art Red Begonia (Pivotal)
5963a$^{3}$ 6994a$^{2}$ 7656a$^{4}$ 7856a$^{8}$

**Robertson (IRE)** *James Fanshawe* a77
4 b g Duke Of Marmalade(IRE) Mythologie (FR) (Bering)
3857$^{5}$ 4325$^{3}$

**Robert The Painter (IRE)** *David O'Meara* a86 104
6 b g Whipper(USA) Lidanna (Nicholas (USA))
207a$^{12}$ 394a$^{11}$ 683a$^{12}$ 1165$^{3}$ (1399) 1721$^{8}$ 1958$^{7}$ 2758$^{6}$

**Robin Hill** *William Muir* a62 71
2 b f Misu Bond(IRE) Enchanting Eve (Risk Me (FR))
3312$^{3}$ ◆ 3799$^{2}$ 4269$^{4}$ 4913$^{13}$ 5506$^{3}$ 5859$^{3}$ 7948$^{8}$ 8118$^{9}$

**Robin Hood (IRE)** *Philip Mitchell* a61 71
6 b g Galileo(IRE) Banquise (IRE) (Last Tycoon)
4030$^{4}$ 4586$^{5}$ 5395$^{7}$ 7346$^{4}$ 7494$^{7}$ 7813$^{9}$ 8010$^{11}$

**Robin Hoods Bay** *Ed Vaughan* a112 112
6 b g Motivator Bijou A Moi (Rainbow Quest (USA))
144$^{6}$ (344) 716$^{4}$ (1068) 1559$^{3}$ 6139$^{6}$

**Robin Park** *Clive Cox* 62
2 b f Invincible Spirit(IRE) Haigh Hall (Kyllachy)
4814$^{2}$ 5464$^{3}$ 5774$^{2}$

**Robins Pearl (FR)** *Olly Stevens* a58
2 ch f Linngari(IRE) Fire Sale (ARG) (Not For Sale (ARG))
7631$^{5}$ 7835$^{5}$

**Robot Boy (IRE)** *David Barron* 110
4 ch g Shamardal(USA) Pivotal's Princess (IRE) (Pivotal)
1492$^{4}$ 2352$^{2}$ (3239) (3666) ◆ 4179$^{3}$ 4700$^{5}$ ◆ 5575$^{4}$ 6371a$^{4}$

**Robyn** *Scott Dixon* a53 46
4 b f Byron Discoed (Distinctly North (USA))
164$^{7}$

**Robynelle** *Alan Jarvis* a50 69
3 b f Royal Applause Chicita Banana (Danehill Dancer (IRE))
1146$^{7}$ 1277$^{7}$

**Rocco Breeze (IRE)** *Mark Brisbourne*
5 b g Shirocco(GER) Crossbreeze (USA) (Red Ransom (USA))
639$^{11}$

**Rocco's Delight** *John Wainwright* a52 43
2 b g Multiplex No Page (IRE) (Statue Of Liberty (USA))
1955$^{8}$ 2231$^{8}$ 2903$^{3}$ 6623$^{9}$ 7649$^{9}$

**Roc De Prince** *James Ewart* a58 75
5 b g Shirocco(GER) Louella (USA) (El Gran Senor (USA))
6012$^{7}$ 7059$^{7}$

**Roc Fort** *James Moffatt* 50
5 b g Rock Of Gibraltar(IRE) Frangy (Sadler's Wells (USA))
2170$^{7}$ 2427$^{11}$ 2724$^{12}$ 3301$^{11}$ 4492$^{8}$

**Rochambeau (IRE)** *Ruth Carr* a70 70
3 b g Sir Percy Tableau Vivant (IRE) (Pivotal)
2334$^{10}$ 2850$^{6}$ 3391$^{4}$ 4921$^{3}$

**Rochdale** *R Bouresly* a81 87
11 ch g Bertolini(USA) Owdbetts (IRE) (High Estate)
109a$^{13}$

**Rochefort (FR)** *Mme C Head-Maarek* a59
3 b g Mr. Sidney(USA) Roanne (FR) (Saumarez)
3869a$^{9}$ 5027a$^{6}$

**Rochelle (IRE)** *William Muir* a67 64
3 b f Duke Of Marmalade(IRE) Emilion (Fantastic Light (USA))
6033$^{6}$ (6481) 6986$^{4}$ 7225$^{3}$

**Rockabilly Riot (IRE)** *Martin Todhunter* a62 70
4 br g Footstepsinthesand Zawariq (IRE) (Marju (IRE))
2509$^{6}$ 2915$^{3}$ 3482$^{6}$ 3843$^{3}$ 4319$^{3}$

**Rock Academy (GER)** *Christian Sprengel* 93
2 bb c Areion(GER) Rocket Light (GER) (Lando (GER))
7145a$^{4}$ 7726a$^{8}$

**Rock A Doodle Doo (IRE)** *Sally Hall* a73 74
7 b g Oratorio(IRE) Nousaiyra (IRE) (Be My Guest (USA))
2700$^{5}$ 3205$^{9}$ 4726$^{7}$

**Rockaroundtheclock (IRE)** *Paul Cole* a74 71
2 ch c Starspangledbanner(AUS) Lulawin (Kyllachy)
2499$^{5}$ 4087$^{3}$ 4965$^{3}$ 5118a$^{3}$ 5981$^{7}$ 6678$^{7}$ 6887$^{4}$ (7631) 7902$^{4}$ 8293$^{3}$

**Rockawango (FR)** *James Ewart* 73
8 b g Okawango(USA) Janou La Belle (FR) (Shining Steel)
1485$^{6}$ 6012$^{DSQ}$ (7175) 7508$^{3}$

**Rock Band** *Emmet Michael Butterly* a57 57
5 b g Rock Of Gibraltar(IRE) Decision Maid (USA) (Diesis)
4264$^{7}$ 4327$^{3}$ 4730$^{3}$ 5854$^{2}$ 6407$^{9}$ 6481$^{3}$

**Rock Canyon (IRE)** *Linda Perratt* a40 57
5 b g Rock Of Gibraltar(IRE) Tuesday Morning (Sadler's Wells (USA))
1972$^{11}$ 2451$^{2}$ 2473$^{3}$ 2675$^{4}$ 2909$^{2}$ 3099$^{3}$ 3609$^{5}$ (3833) 4195$^{5}$ 4362$^{5}$ 4960$^{9}$ 5237$^{2}$ 5635$^{4}$ 5858$^{5}$ 6014$^{10}$ 6595$^{9}$ 6819$^{5}$ 6834$^{3}$ 7057$^{2}$

**Rock Charm** *Stuart Williams* a58 41
3 b g Araafa(IRE) Evening Charm (IRE) (Bering)
4984$^{8}$ 7360$^{4}$ 7976$^{2}$ 8315$^{3}$

**Rock Choir** *William Haggas* 101
4 b f Pivotal Choir Mistress (Chief Singer)
1948$^{11}$ 3307$^{5}$ 4443$^{14}$

**Rock Critic (IRE)** *D K Weld* a88 89
9 b g Pivotal Diamond Trim (IRE) (Highest Honor (FR))
6350a$^{8}$

**Rocked The Boat** *David O'Meara* a63 9
3 b g Mizzen Mast(USA) Jazz Jam (Pivotal)
5101$^{6}$ 5495$^{15}$ 5788$^{7}$

**Rocket Bob (FR)** *C Boutin* 66
2 b c Whipper(USA) Raise In Aspen (FR) (Iron Mask (USA))
5544a$^{2}$

**Rocket Dive (JPN)** *S Kobayashi* 55
7 b h Kingmambo(USA) Bejoyfulandrejoyce (USA) (Dynaformer (USA))
5330a$^{7}$

**Rocket Rob (IRE)** *Willie Musson* a83 77
8 b g Danetime(IRE) Queen Of Fibres (IRE) (Scenic (IRE))
3854$^{7}$ 4406$^{6}$ 5392$^{4}$ 6006$^{7}$ 6455$^{3}$ 6872$^{3}$ 7886$^{9}$ 7989$^{11}$ 8297$^{9}$

**Rocket Ronnie (IRE)** *David Nicholls* 88
4 b g Antonius Pius(USA) Ctesiphon (USA) (Arch (USA))
1190$^{16}$ 1483$^{9}$ 1903$^{7}$ 2351$^{12}$ 3791$^{8}$ 4753$^{2}$ 5496$^{9}$ 6626$^{5}$ 6937$^{4}$ 7538$^{7}$

**Rocket Ship** *Sir Michael Stoute* a86 92
3 b g Sinndar(IRE) Bimini (Sadler's Wells (USA))
1809$^{7}$ 2354$^{4}$ 2696$^{2}$ 3183$^{2}$ ◆ 3857$^{2}$ (4066) (5052) 5691$^{11}$

**Rockfast** *Gary Moore* a69
2 b g Fastnet Rock(AUS) Empress Anna (IRE) (Imperial Ballet (IRE))
8192$^{2}$

**Rockfella** *Denis Coakley* a57 84
8 ch g Rock Of Gibraltar(IRE) Afreeta (USA) (Afleet (CAN))
1981$^{2}$ 4144$^{6}$ 7305$^{7}$

**Rock Follies** *Lady Cecil* 64
2 b f Rock Of Gibraltar(IRE) Ashraakat (USA) (Danzig (USA))
4652$^{2}$ 5297$^{3}$ 5946$^{3}$

**Rock Heroine** *Hughie Morrison* a52
2 br f Rock Of Gibraltar(IRE) Kinetix (Linamix (FR))
7549$^{10}$ 7833$^{7}$

**Rockie Road (IRE)** *Mick Quinn* a57 60
3 b g Footstepsinthesand Roclette (USA) (Rock Of Gibraltar (IRE))
2165$^{5}$ 2729$^{2}$ 3333$^{3}$ 3880$^{7}$ 4998$^{9}$ 6647$^{4}$ (7218) 7517$^{13}$ 7645$^{4}$ 8246$^{2}$

**Rocking The Boat (IRE)** *Charles Hills* a40 75
2 b f Zebedee Rocking (Oasis Dream)
2220$^{3}$ 2612$^{6}$ (4450) 5409$^{6}$ 6104$^{11}$

**Rockinit (IRE)** *Peter Bowen* 35
8 b m Rock Of Gibraltar(IRE) Tidal Reach (USA) (Kris S (USA))
3781$^{10}$ 5005$^{12}$ 6367$^{5}$

**Rock Kristal (IRE)** *John Gosden* a79
2 b f Fastnet Rock(AUS) Pellinore (USA) (Giant's Causeway (USA))
5037$^{3}$ 5549$^{2}$ 7194$^{9}$ (8027)

**Rock Lobster** *Ed Dunlop* a69
2 ch g Bahamian Bounty Reeling N' Rocking (IRE) (Mr Greeley (USA))
6603$^{6}$ 6903$^{2}$

**Rockmount** *Ed McMahon* a45
2 b c Major Cadeaux Fisher Island (IRE) (Sri Pekan (USA))
6702$^{11}$ 7223$^{7}$

**Rock 'N' Roll Star** *Peter Chapple-Hyam* a74 74
3 b g Cockney Rebel(IRE) Sweet Afton (IRE) (Mujadil (USA))
(409) 1516$^{8}$ 2347$^{6}$ 7110$^{11}$

**Rock N Rouge (IRE)** *Olly Stevens* a65 76
3 ch f Rock Of Gibraltar(IRE) Samorra (IRE) (In The Wings)
(1018)

**Rock Of Ages** *Neil King* a65 37
5 ch g Pivotal Magic Peak (IRE) (Danehill (USA))
14$^{3}$ 2904$^{6}$ 3404$^{8}$ 6632$^{11}$ 8208$^{2}$

**Rock Of Cashel (GER)** *Frau Erika Mader* 72
3 b c Areion(GER) Rocket Light (GER) (Lando (GER))
1781a$^{9}$ 2377a$^{9}$

**Rock Of Dreams (IRE)** *Charles Hills* a69 76
3 b g Rock Of Gibraltar(IRE) Manhattan Dream (USA) (Statue Of Liberty (USA))
1507$^{4}$ 1913$^{8}$

**Rock Of Leon** *Michael Bell* a63 54
3 b g Rock Of Gibraltar(IRE) Leonica (Lion Cavern (USA))
1395$^{8}$ 2078$^{6}$ 2927$^{7}$ 3120$^{2}$ 4261$^{2}$ 4834$^{3}$ 5558$^{4}$ 7118$^{2}$ (7287) 7458$^{3}$

**Rock Of Nassau (FR)** *X Nakkachdji* a101 75
8 ch g Rock Of Gibraltar(IRE) Solosole (USA) (Gulch (USA))
177a$^{8}$

**Rock Of Ridd (IRE)** *Lennart Reuterskiold Jr* a36 93
4 b f Antonius Pius(USA) Wewantitall (Pivotal)
5965a$^{6}$ 6388a$^{5}$

**Rock Of Romance (IRE)** *A Wohler* 110
4 br c Rock Of Gibraltar(IRE) Romantic Venture (IRE) (Indian Ridge)
2229a$^{2}$ 6589a$^{3}$ (7469a)

**Rock On Bollinski** *Tim Fitzgerald* 72
4 b g Bollin Eric Bred For Pleasure (Niniski (USA))
5374$^{9}$ 6092$^{13}$ 6432$^{4}$ 7124$^{11}$

**Rock On Candy** *John Spearing* a49 70
5 b m Excellent Art Rock Candy (IRE) (Rock Of Gibraltar (IRE))
2056$^{5}$ 2727$^{5}$ 7534$^{14}$ 8180$^{13}$

**Rock Relief (IRE)** *Chris Grant* a48 73
8 gr g Daylami(IRE) Sheer Bliss (IRE) (Sadler's Wells (USA))
1485$^{4}$ 7177$^{11}$

**Rocksee (IRE)** *Tom Dascombe* a67 70
3 ch f Rock Of Gibraltar(IRE) Sightseer (USA) (Distant View (USA))
1280$^{6}$ 1832$^{3}$ 2274$^{10}$ 2805$^{5}$ 3733$^{2}$ 4426$^{4}$ 5079$^{4}$ 5573$^{7}$ 6904$^{7}$ 7225$^{6}$

**Rocksilla** *Chris Wall* a68 69
4 b f Rock Of Gibraltar(IRE) Hope Island (IRE) (Titus Livius (FR))
1576$^{9}$ 3203$^{8}$ 4061$^{7}$ 5888$^{13}$ 6558$^{7}$ 7159$^{11}$ 7729$^{8}$

**Rock The Legend (IRE)** *Wido Neuroth* 90
4 b f Rock Of Gibraltar(IRE) Funny Legend (NOR) (Funambule (USA))
6388a$^{11}$

**Rockview Emperor (IRE)** *John C McConnell* a58 52
4 b g Holy Roman Emperor(IRE) River Fairy (USA) (Irish River (FR))
6014$^{7}$

**Rockweiller** *Shaun Harris* a53 65
7 b g Rock Of Gibraltar(IRE) Ballerina Suprema (IRE) (Sadler's Wells (USA))
781$^{4}$ 831$^{11}$ 1050$^{3}$ 1197$^{3}$ 1428$^{4}$ 1644$^{8}$ (2476) 2894$^{4}$ 3052$^{3}$ 3556$^{4}$ 3699$^{13}$ (7059) 7284$^{6}$ 7846$^{11}$

**Rocky Desert (IRE)** *Marco Botti* 61
2 b c Rock Of Gibraltar(IRE) Souter's Sister (IRE) (Desert Style (IRE))
3701$^{6}$ 4809$^{4}$ 5922$^{7}$ 6643$^{6}$

**Rocky Elsom (USA)** *Sophie Leech* a72 76
7 b g Rock Of Gibraltar(IRE) Bowstring (IRE) (Sadler's Wells (USA))
343$^{3}$ 747$^{2}$ (990) 1628$^{3}$ (2835)

**Rocky Ground (IRE)** *Roger Varian* 114
4 b c Acclamation Keriyka (IRE) (Indian Ridge)
1949$^{9}$ (2848) 3452$^{6}$ 4438$^{6}$ 5219a$^{7}$ 5911$^{6}$ (Dead)

**Rocky Hill Ridge** *Alan McCabe* a50 18
3 b g Auction House(USA) Amwell Star (USA) (Silver Buck (USA))
515$^{4}$ 649$^{6}$ 1452$^{6}$ 7256$^{6}$

**Rocky Rebel** *Michael Blake* a66 66
6 b g Norse Dancer(IRE) Gulchina (USA) (Gulch (USA))
277$^{5}$ 349$^{3}$ 657$^{2}$ 872$^{5}$ 3579$^{8}$

**Rocky Rider** *Andrew Balding* 79
2 b c Galileo(IRE) Blue Symphony (Darshaan)
6056$^{4}$ (6984)

**Rocky's Pride (IRE)** *Richard Whitaker* a58 57
8 b g Rock Of Gibraltar(IRE) L'Animee (Green Tune (USA))
3547$^{9}$ 3908$^{8}$ 4381$^{2}$ 5512$^{7}$ (6122) 6600$^{4}$ 7423$^{5}$ 7547$^{2}$ 7853$^{3}$ 7884$^{3}$ 8311$^{9}$

**Rocky Two (IRE)** *Philip Kirby* a35 61
4 ch g Rock Of Gibraltar(IRE) Toorah Laura La (USA) (Black Minnaloushe (USA))
1674$^{4}$ (2512) 2915$^{4}$ 3657$^{2}$ 4319$^{9}$ 5145$^{3}$ 5567$^{7}$ 6216$^{4}$ 6542$^{8}$ 7007$^{4}$

**Rocquaine (IRE)** *Mrs A Malzard* 17
5 b m Oratorio(IRE) Watch The Clock (Mtoto)
1625a$^{4}$ 2599a$^{4}$ 2594a$^{6}$ 4718a$^{5}$ 5229a$^{4}$

**Rodrigo De Torres** *Frederick Watson* a76 53
7 ch g Bahamian Bounty Leonica (Lion Cavern (USA))
5444$^{19}$ 5888$^{18}$ 6824$^{14}$ 7507$^{10}$ 7888$^{5}$ 8124$^{6}$

**Roero (FR)** *F Rohaut* a88 111
5 b g Acclamation Ricine (IRE) (Titus Livius (FR))
(4644a) 5960a$^{5}$ (7095a)

**Roger Thorpe** *Deborah Sanderson* a69 67
5 b g Firebreak Nunthorpe (Mystiko (USA))
(31) 388$^{8}$ 1168$^{10}$ 1800$^{3}$ (2092) 2546$^{4}$ 2894$^{2}$ 7068$^{4}$ 8122$^{10}$ 8282$^{3}$

**Rogue Wave (IRE)** *Timothy Jarvis* a84 82
3 b c Iffraaj Lady Naomi (USA) (Distant View (USA))
(1962) 2257$^{15}$ 3108$^{6}$ 3667$^{2}$ 4355$^{7}$ 5311$^{7}$ 6144$^{2}$ 6891$^{12}$ 7375$^{11}$

**Roheryn (IRE)** *G M Lyons* a72 103
3 b f Galileo(IRE) La Chunga (USA) (More Than Ready (USA))
5115a$^{2}$ 6370a$^{3}$

**Rohesia** *Sir Mark Prescott Bt* a69
3 b f High Chaparral(IRE) Common Knowledge (Rainbow Quest (USA))
323$^{3}$ 434$^{2}$ 7772$^{6}$

**Roicead (USA)** *D Selvaratnam* a107 107
7 b g Giant's Causeway(USA) Coachella (Danehill (USA))
107a$^{4}$ (240a) 393a$^{10}$ 809a$^{3}$

**Roi d'Aragon (IRE)** *F Rossi* 84
4 b g Zamindar(USA) Jarhes (IRE) (Green Desert (USA))
5546a$^{4}$

**Roi De Vitesse (IRE)** *Ali Jan* a101 100
7 ch h Chineur(FR) Face The Storm (IRE) (Barathea (IRE))
112a$^{4}$ 308a$^{11}$ 597a$^{8}$ 769a$^{6}$ 897a$^{8}$

**Rokbaan** *Roger Varian* a31
2 b g Camacho Salinia (IRE) (Rainbow Quest (USA))
6603$^{13}$

**Rokeby** *George Moore* a26 53
3 b g Byron Scarlet Royal (Red Ransom (USA))
2053$^{3}$ 2729$^{4}$ 3105$^{5}$ 4058$^{8}$ 5239$^{3}$ 5495$^{5}$ 5794$^{3}$ 7500$^{7}$ 8134$^{10}$

**Role Player** *Michael Bell* a90 71
4 ch c Exceed And Excel(AUS) Dresden Doll (USA) (Elusive Quality (USA))
2442$^{6}$ (2681) 3122$^{6}$ (4078) 4983$^{8}$

**Role Reversal** *James Tate* a62
3 ch f Shamardal(USA) Miss Hepburn (USA) (Gone West (USA))
495$^{3}$ 824$^{3}$ 994$^{3}$ 1430$^{4}$ 2209$^{6}$

**Rolling Dice** *Dominic Ffrench Davis* a33 78
3 b g Rail Link Breathing Space (USA) (Expelled (USA))
2163$^{3}$ 5557$^{10}$ (5903) 7514$^{3}$

**Rollin 'n Tumblin** *Michael Attwater* a51
10 ch g Zaha(CAN) Steppin Out (First Trump)
580$^{5}$ 842$^{7}$ 1895$^{8}$ 2207$^{5}$ 4615$^{8}$ 6339$^{4}$ 6632$^{P}$

**Roly Tricks** *Natalie Lloyd-Beavis* a59 70
3 b f Pastoral Pursuits Freya Tricks (Noverre (USA))
2780$^{7}$ 2996$^{5}$ 4086$^{2}$ 7023$^{11}$ 7355$^{6}$ 7799$^{5}$ 7942$^{8}$ 8063$^{12}$

**Romance Story (IRE)** *Saeed bin Suroor* a74 64
2 b f New Approach(IRE) Perfect Note (Shamardal (USA))
3858$^{4}$ ◆ 4626$^{5}$ 5500$^{5}$ 6250$^{2}$ 6648$^{7}$ 7075$^{2}$ (7525)

**Roman De Brut (IRE)** *Ian Williams* a54 53
2 ch g Rock Of Gibraltar(IRE) Nesmeh (USA) (More Than Ready (USA))
2698$^{5}$ 3701$^{7}$ 4787$^{7}$ 6842$^{4}$ 7075$^{7}$

**Roman Flight (IRE)** *David Dennis* a83 93
6 b g Antonius Pius(USA) Flight Sequence (Polar Falcon (USA))
427$^{5}$ ◆

**Roman Riches** *Gary Moore* a62 64
3 b g Holy Roman Emperor(IRE) Dyna Bowl (USA) (Dynaformer (USA))
847$^{7}$ 954$^{7}$ 1107$^{6}$ 1793$^{3}$ 2080$^{6}$ (2926) 4106$^{7}$ 5829$^{3}$ 5949$^{4}$ 7343$^{13}$

**Romantic Bliss (IRE)** *K R Burke* a58 47
3 b f Holy Roman Emperor(IRE) Thea Di Bisanzio (IRE) (Dr Fong (USA))
541$^{2}$ 653$^{4}$ 919$^{3}$ 1101$^{2}$ 1235$^{2}$ 1647$^{2}$ (1854) 4067$^{5}$ 4464a$^{11}$ 4785$^{4}$ 6121$^{9}$ 6716$^{9}$

**Romantic Link** *Luke Dace*
3 b f Rail Link Romantic Retreat (Rainbow Quest (USA))
2649$^{10}$

**Romantic Settings** *Richard Fahey* 99
4 ch f Mount Nelson Lacework (Pivotal)
1194$^{4}$ 1360$^{6}$

**Rome** *Gary Moore* a85 77
4 b g Holy Roman Emperor(IRE) Magical Cliche (USA) (Affirmed (USA))
1237$^{3}$ 1796$^{2}$ 2079$^{2}$ 2684$^{2}$ 3118$^{7}$ 5040$^{3}$ 5504$^{3}$ 6042$^{3}$ 6877$^{5}$ 7158$^{3}$ 7552$^{9}$

**Romeo Lima (USA)** *J-C Rouget* 103
2 b c Medaglia d'Oro(USA) Storybook (UAE) (Halling (USA))
6181a$^{4}$

**Romeo Montague** *Ed Dunlop* a85 91
6 b g Montjeu(IRE) Issa (Pursuit Of Love)
1770$^{7}$ 2779$^{14}$ 3453$^{8}$ 4441$^{2}$

**Romina (FR)** *Y Barberot* a59 79
3 b f Slickly(FR) Aznavour (GER) (Lagunas)
5370a$^{8}$

**Romsdal** *John Gosden* a96 118
3 ch c Halling(USA) Pure Song (Singspiel (IRE))
1166$^{3}$ ◆ (1380) ◆ 2087$^{2}$ 2990$^{3}$ 4649$^{7}$ 6329$^{2}$

**Ronald Gee (IRE)** *Jim Goldie* 69
7 ch g Garuda(IRE) Panache Lady (IRE) (Cyrano De Bergerac)
1691$^{5}$ 2354$^{7}$ 2696$^{5}$ 3238$^{2}$ 4015$^{5}$ 5171$^{6}$ 5765$^{2}$ 6012$^{5}$ 6597$^{6}$ 7059$^{5}$

**Ronaldinho (IRE)** *Alan King* a68 85
4 b g Jeremy(USA) Spring Glory (Dr Fong (USA))
2851$^{2}$ 4144$^{7}$

**Roncalli (IRE)** *Klaudia Freitag* 92
5 b h Hawk Wing(USA) Raiska (IRE) (Grand Lodge (USA))
7469a$^{7}$

**Ronnie Rockcake** *Ben Pauling* 73
4 b g Tiger Hill(IRE) Vitesse (IRE) (Royal Academy (USA))
3517$^{4}$ 4500$^{2}$ 5339$^{3}$

**Ron The Greek (USA)** *N Bachalard* a126
7 b h Full Mandate(USA) Flambe' (USA) (Fortunate Prospect (USA))
1183a$^{12}$

**Ronya (IRE)** *K R Burke* a43 64
3 b f Bushranger(IRE) Beenablaw (IRE) (Alzao (USA))
157$^{9}$ 378$^{6}$ 1588$^{4}$ 2135$^{3}$ 2393$^{4}$ 3224$^{2}$

**Rookery (IRE)** *Roger Ingram* a70 48
3 b g Raven's Pass(USA) Zacheta (Polish Precedent (USA))
1044$^{5}$ 1153$^{3}$ 1635$^{10}$ 2018$^{2}$ 2319$^{14}$ 3829$^{7}$ 3986$^{6}$ 4910$^{3}$ 5628$^{8}$ 6899$^{6}$ 8253$^{10}$

**Rookie Sensation (USA)** *John Shirreffs* a88 107
4 rg c Unbridled's Song(USA) My Marchesa (USA) (Stately Don (USA))
3025a$^{8}$

**Roomie** *Barry Leavy* a51 48
3 b f Pastoral Pursuits Pomponette (USA) (Rahy (USA))
1243$^{2}$ 1441$^{8}$ 1925$^{3}$ 2388$^{8}$ 3792$^{4}$ 4495$^{13}$ 7252$^{11}$ 7698$^{9}$

**Room Key** *Eve Johnson Houghton* 102
2 ch c Mount Nelson Saturday Girl (Peintre Celebre (USA))
(3081) 3751$^{2}$ 4780$^{3}$ ◆ 6326$^{5}$

**Room Service (USA)** *Wayne Catalano* a111 104
3 b f More Than Ready(USA) Dream Lady (USA) (Old Trieste (USA))
3995a$^{7}$

**Roossey (IRE)** *William Haggas* 88
2 b c Acclamation Tatiana Romanova (USA) (Mr Greeley (USA))
1712$^{6}$ 2358$^{2}$ (3394) 5580$^{4}$ 6135$^{3}$ (6510)

**Roring Samson (IRE)** *George Baker* a56 63
3 b g Art Connoisseur(IRE) Marju Guest (IRE) (Marju (IRE))
3083$^{7}$ 4048$^{3}$ 4306$^{3}$ 5138$^{5}$ 6297$^{12}$

**Rosaceous** *Daniel Kubler* a80 88
4 ch f Duke Of Marmalade(IRE) Briery (IRE) (Salse (USA))
1716$^{7}$ 2501$^{5}$ 3226$^{9}$

**Rosairlie (IRE)** *Micky Hammond* a69 85
6 ch m Halling(USA) Mrs Mason (IRE) (Turtle Island (IRE))
1374$^{6}$ (2139) 2739$^{3}$ 3501$^{2}$ 4289$^{6}$ 5017$^{6}$ 5890$^{13}$

**Rosalie Bonheur** *Clive Cox* 82
2 ch f Siyouni(FR) Crozon (Peintre Celebre (USA))
(4018) (6064) (6749)

**Rosalind (USA)** *Kenneth McPeek* a111 87
3 ch f Broken Vow(USA) Critics Acclaim (USA) (Theatrical (IRE))
3418$^{U}$ 3995a$^{9}$

**Rosarina** *Jo Crowley* a53 74
3 ch f Rock Of Gibraltar(IRE) Spring Fashion (IRE) (Galileo (IRE))
5382$^{5}$ 6002$^{P}$

**Rosa Rot (GER)** *Mario Hofer* 88
3 bb f Lord Of England(GER) Red Love (GER) (Surako (GER))
7483a$^{11}$

**Rose Abella** *Andrew Hollinshead* 65
2 b f Royal Applause Lady Lindsay (IRE) (Danehill Dancer (IRE))
6093$^{8}$ 6700$^{5}$

**Rose Above** *Andrew Balding* 61
2 b f Yeats(IRE) Sabah (Nashwan (USA))
5187$^{4}$

**Rose Acclaim (IRE)** *David O'Meara* 53
2 b f Acclamation Carmona (Rainbow Quest (USA))
4790$^{9}$ 5910$^{8}$ 6641$^{7}$

**Roseal Des Bois (FR)** *R Chotard* a63 74
7 b m Bonbon Rose(FR) Equatoriale (FR) (Saint Estephe (FR))
(4776a)

**Rosebay (GER)** *Markus Klug* a85 83
3 b f It's Gino(GER) Royal Fong (GER) (Dr Fong (USA))
7619a$^{7}$

**Roseberry Hill (FR)** *J-M Capitte* a54
3 gr f Creachadoir(IRE) Lila Rose (IRE) (Kendor (FR))
391a$^{10}$

**Rose Buck** *Giles Bravery* a68 66
3 b f Acclamation Housekeeper (IRE) (Common Grounds)
187$^{4}$ 311$^{3}$ (495) 867$^{2}$ 1006$^{3}$ 1425$^{5}$ 5307$^{7}$ 5897$^{10}$ 6266$^{2}$ 6617$^{8}$

**Roseburg (IRE)** *Luca Cumani* 104
3 ch c Tamayuz Raydaniya (IRE) (In The Wings)
1395$^{3}$ (1880) (2982) (3965) ◆ 4821$^{6}$ 6548$^{8}$

**Rose Doloise (FR)** *A Bonin* a69 79
2 gr f Silver Frost(IRE) Rose Du Roi (IRE) (Royal Academy (USA))
2755a$^{3}$ 5617a$^{5}$

**Rose Et Or (IRE)** *A Fabre* 76
2 b f Iffraaj Cracovie (Caerleon (USA))
4839a$^{2}$

**Rose Garnet (IRE)** *Tony Carroll* a65 54
6 b m Invincible Spirit(IRE) Chanterelle (IRE) (Indian Ridge)
83$^{7}$ 353$^{6}$ 556$^{2}$ 798$^{2}$ 973$^{4}$ 1030$^{2}$

**Rosehill Artist (IRE)** *Charles Hills* a91 93
3 b f Excellent Art Conference (IRE) (Montjeu (IRE))
1535$^{7}$ 2277$^{3}$ (3085) 3725$^{4}$ 4211$^{3}$ 4397$^{3}$ 6746$^{7}$ 7565$^{4}$ 7773$^{3}$

**Rose Kazan (IRE)** *Marco Botti* a77 70
3 ch f Teofilo(IRE) Zahour Al Yasmeen (Cadeaux Genereux)
323$^{5}$ 542$^{2}$ 734$^{2}$ 1348$^{2}$ 1765$^{3}$

**Rosenbaum** *Charlie Appleby* 65
2 b g Dubawi(IRE) Rave Reviews (IRE) (Sadler's Wells (USA))
6056$^{5}$ 6456$^{5}$ 7134$^{6}$

**Rosendhal (IRE)** *G Botti* 107
7 ch h Indian Ridge Kathy College (IRE) (College Chapel)
2375a$^{2}$ 7725a$^{3}$

**Rose Of Kiev (IRE)** *Mark Johnston* a59 70
2 b f Archipenko(USA) Roses From Ridey (IRE) (Petorius)
1259$^{7}$ 1583$^{4}$ 1889$^{3}$ 2306$^{3}$ 3497$^{7}$ 4018$^{5}$ 4659$^{7}$ (Dead)

**Rose Of Marron (IRE)** *John Upson*
7 b g Dilshaan Sunset Park (IRE) (Red Sunset)
4080$^{8}$

**Rose Rized (GER)** *P Schiergen* 96
2 b f Authorized(IRE) Rosenreihe (IRE) (Catcher In The Rye (IRE))
6778a$^{2}$ 7315a$^{10}$

**Roserrow** *Andrew Balding* a93 102
5 ch g Beat Hollow Sabah (Nashwan (USA))
1399$^{2}$ 1948$^{17}$ 3251$^{3}$ 3731$^{6}$

**Rose Vista (FR)** *J-L Guillochon* a92 102
5 ch m Vatori(FR) Rose Ciel (FR) (Septieme Ciel (USA))
984a$^{3}$ 5462a$^{9}$

**Rosie Cheeks** *Chris Dwyer*
2 b f Lucarno(USA) Split Briefs (IRE) (Mull Of Kintyre (USA))
3157$^{7}$

**Rosie Crowe (IRE)** *David C Griffiths* a49 50
2 b f Approve(IRE) Tolzey (USA) (Rahy (USA))
2200$^{7}$ 4110$^{6}$ 4828$^{6}$ 5569$^{3}$ 5985$^{12}$

**Rosie Hall (IRE)** *Les Eyre* a23 52
4 ch f Lion Heart(USA) Baltic Dip (IRE) (Benny The Dip (USA))
2729$^{9}$ 2937$^{9}$ 4530$^{6}$ 4875$^{5}$ 5636$^{7}$ 7009$^{9}$

**Rosie Probert** *Tony Carroll* a17 80
5 b m Dylan Thomas(IRE) Corsican Sunset (USA) (Thunder Gulch (USA))
6855$^{8}$

**Rosie Prospects** *Roger Ingram* a59 19
3 b f Byron Sea Jade (IRE) (Mujadil (USA))
82$^{4}$ 447$^{3}$ 622$^{5}$ 1106$^{3}$ 1389$^{11}$ 3679$^{7}$ 4614$^{4}$ 5034$^{6}$ 6030$^{7}$ 7845$^{8}$ 8097$^{6}$ 8314$^{3}$

**Rosie Rebel** *Rae Guest* a80 81
4 ch f Cockney Rebel(IRE) Meandering Rose (USA) (Irish River (FR))
1307$^{2}$ 1909$^{3}$ 2490$^{3}$ 3859$^{4}$ 5047$^{5}$

**Rosie Royale (IRE)** *Roger Teal* a67 59
2 gr f Verglas(IRE) Fearn Royal (IRE) (Ali-Royal (IRE))
3557$^{5}$ 4075$^{4}$ 4604$^{9}$ 5626$^{6}$ 6678$^{9}$

**Rosie's Premiere (IRE)** *Dean Ivory* 94
2 b f Showcasing Golden Rosie (IRE) (Exceed And Excel (AUS))
3232$^{4}$ (3799) 4159$^{2}$ 4646$^{5}$ 5380$^{5}$ 5694$^{6}$ (6703) 7238$^{6}$ 7439$^{3}$

**Rosina Jay (IRE)** *Simon Dow* a47
3 b f Art Connoisseur(IRE) Noora (IRE) (Bahhare (USA))
1794$^{13}$

**Roskilly (IRE)** *Andrew Balding* a79 88
3 ch g Hurricane Run(IRE) Party Feet (IRE) (Noverre (USA))
827$^{3}$ 1044$^{3}$ 1530$^{11}$ (4941) 5302$^{6}$ 6284$^{5}$ 6737$^{10}$ 7161$^{2}$

**Rossetti** *Mrs A Malzard* a75 81
6 gr g Dansili Snowdrops (Gulch (USA))
1439$^{11}$ 1651$^{7}$ 2991$^{11}$ 3495a$^{2}$ 4040a$^{5}$ (4716a) 5230a$^{4}$

**Rosslare (IRE)** *Charles Hills* 33
2 b f Fastnet Rock(AUS) Waterways (IRE) (Alhaarth (IRE))
6545[13]

**Rosslyn Castle** *Philip McBride* a80 86
5 ch g Selkirk(USA) Margarula (IRE) (Doyoun)
2461[10] 3574[11] 4204[2] 4736[5] (5317) 5442[3] 5924[7] 6439[P] (Dead)

**Rostrum Farewell** *David Brown* a47 61
3 b g Royal Applause Acicula (IRE) (Night Shift (USA))
1006[4] 1315[5] 2388[9] 3124[7] 3548[3] 3896[2]

**Rosy Blush** *A Wohler* 81
2 b f Youmzain(IRE) Sweet Lilly (Tobougg (IRE))
7481a[4]

**Rosy Ryan (IRE)** *Tina Jackson* a27 52
4 b f Tagula(IRE) Khaydariya (IRE) (Akarad (FR))
2937[8] 4420[10] 4958[5] 5337[5] 5773[2]

**Rotherwick (IRE)** *Paul Cole* a83 88
2 ch c Starspangledbanner(AUS) Pivotalia (IRE) (Pivotal)
3889[5] 4142[3] 4896[2] 5306[4] (5712) 6331[3] (6436) 7226[4] (7595)

**Rothesay Chancer** *Jim Goldie* a67 86
6 ch g Monsieur Bond(IRE) Rhinefield Beauty (IRE) (Shalford (IRE))
1759[2] 2167[4] 2456[4] (3006) 3239[9] (3571) 4016[4] 4700[13] 5170[7] 5888[12] 6511[8] 7669[5]

**Roudee** *Tom Dascombe* 90
2 b g Kodiac Eau Rouge (Grand Lodge (USA))
(1536) 2071[2] 2703[3] 3322[7] 4439[11] 4936[4] 5607[10] 6933[7]

**Rouge Desir (FR)** *Mlle Y Vollmer* 35
2 b c Croco Rouge(IRE) Desir Desir (FR) (Star Maite (FR))
6385a[9]

**Rouge Nuage (IRE)** *Conrad Allen* a83 76
4 ch g Indian Haven Nom Francais (First Trump)
2687[2] 2882[5] 3162[5] 3629[4] 4181[8] 4613[8] 5006[5] 5394[4] (5537) 5899[2] 5950[3] 6341[10] 6625[2] 8124[2] 8204[9] (8268)

**Rough Courte (IRE)** *Mick Channon* a62 85
3 b f Clodovil(IRE) Straight Sets (IRE) (Pivotal)
1344[2] 1616[2] 1844[3] (2433) 3195[10] 3625[5] 4191[3] 4674[3] (5198) (5427) 6877[4] 6980[4]

**Rousayan (IRE)** *David O'Meara* 78
3 b g Invincible Spirit(IRE) Rose Quartz (Lammtarra (USA))
7085[15]

**Rowan Ridge** *William Knight* a76 68
6 ch g Compton Place Lemon Tree (USA) (Zilzal (USA))
120[4] ◆ 458[2] (801) 1065[6] 8196[4]

**Rowe Park** *Linda Jewell* a80 85
11 b g Dancing Spree(USA) Magic Legs (Reprimand)
299[2] 834[7]

**Rowlestone Express** *Tony Carroll* 37
3 b f Rail Link Charmante Femme (Bin Ajwaad (IRE))
2667[S]

**Rowlestone Lass** *Richard Price* a81 60
4 b f Hernando(FR) Charmante Femme (Bin Ajwaad (IRE))
246[3] 380[6] 2942[6] 3309[2] 3852[2] 4492[2] 5001[2] 5689[2] 6027[2] 6651[4] 7290[2] (7524) 7817[3] (8001) 8164[3]

**Roxie Lot** *Pam Sly* 69
2 b f Exceed And Excel(AUS) Orlena (USA) (Gone West (USA))
4346[8] 5201[4] 5910[4] 6610[4]

**Roxy De Vindecy (FR)** *J Phelippon* a87 83
9 b g Spadoun(FR) High Light (FR) (Zino)
1828a[5]

**Roxy Hart** *Robert Cowell* a66 68
3 ch f Halling(USA) Possessive Artiste (Shareef Dancer (USA))
3631[5] 5010[4] 5831[12] 6500[5] 7068[10] 8207[4]

**Roxy Lane** *Peter Hiatt* a36 60
5 b m Byron Comme Ca (Cyrano De Bergerac)
81[13] 563[8] 755[9] 833[10] (3427) ◆ 3678[6] 4548[9] 5383[5] 5811[6] 6454[9]

**Roxy Madam** *Mandy Rowland* a43
5 br m Generous(IRE) Masouri Sana (IRE) (Broken Hearted)
7901[8] 8167[4]

**Roxy Star (IRE)** *William Haggas* a75
2 b f Fastnet Rock(AUS) Sweet Dreams Baby (IRE) (Montjeu (IRE))
(7398)

**Royal Acquisition** *Robert Cowell* a79 55
4 b g Royal Applause Flavian (Catrail (USA))
1431[7] 1922[2] 2645[10] 3470[7] 4768[5] 5830[9] 7073[5] (7357) 7886[4] 8025[9]

**Royal Albert Hall** *Olly Stevens* a71
2 b g Royal Applause Victoria Sponge (IRE) (Marju (IRE))
7030[6] 7731[2] 7926[2] 8288[3]

**Royal Alcor (IRE)** *Gay Kelleway* a87 78
7 b g Chevalier(IRE) Arundhati (IRE) (Royal Academy (USA))
(21) 125[4] 212[3] 427[8] (891) 999[4] 1091[3] 2272[10] 2701[10] 3632[DSQ] 3976[5] 4575[7] 5073[7] 6171[8] 7350[9] 7822[3]

**Royal Altitude** *Chris Wall* a81 72
2 b c Zamindar(USA) Royal Assent (Royal Applause)
6056[14] 6497[2] (7523)

**Royal Bajan (USA)** *James Given* a92 73
6 rg g Speightstown(USA) Crown You (USA) (Two Punch (USA))
4[4] 719[2] (863) 1172[12] 1566[8] 1742[6] 1961[17] 3697[6] 4114[10] 4833[10] 6475[15] 6671[5] (6873) 6938[7] 7761[8] 8025[8] (8136)

**Royal Battalion** *Stuart Williams* a72 42
3 b c Sea The Stars(IRE) Yummy Mummy (Montjeu (IRE))
4407[10] 7951[2] 8064[3]

**Royal Birth** *Stuart Williams* a84 83
3 b c Exceed And Excel(AUS) Princess Georgina (Royal Applause)
3068[5] 3331[7] (6814)

**Royal Blessing** *George Peckham* a60
2 b g Royal Applause Zuleika Dobson (Cadeaux Genereux)
7113[5] 7973[8]

**Royal Brave (IRE)** *William Muir* a74 85
3 b g Acclamation Daqtora (Dr Devious (IRE))
2044[3] (3124) 3426[3] 4043[2] (4328) 4898[5] 6109[2] 6355[2] 6880[3] 7521[10]

**Royal Bushida** *Derek Shaw* a49
3 b g Royal Applause Moonmaiden (Selkirk (USA))
28[2] (280) 653[5] 774[6] 1235[4] 4969[8] 5257[7]

**Royal Caper** *Miss Joey Ellis* a63 64
4 b g Royal Applause Ukraine (IRE) (Cape Cross (IRE))
(3230) 3820[3] (4341) 5773[8] 6396[6]

**Royal College** *Gary Moore* a62 64
4 b g Pastoral Pursuits Stroppi Poppi (Mtoto)
2126[11] 2625[6] 3229[5] 4073[9] 4578[12]

**Royal Connection** *Richard Hannon* a70 75
3 b f Bahamian Bounty Fisadara (Nayef (USA))
2383[6] 2775[2] 3280[2] 3733[4] (4047) 4503[2] 4813[2] 5785[6] 6191[7] 7397[8]

**Royal Connoisseur (IRE)** *Richard Fahey* a59 83
3 b g Art Connoisseur(IRE) Valferno (IRE) (Val Royal (FR))
1441[2] 1802[2] 2329[6] 3700[2] 3951[3] (5246) 5923[2] 6575[2] (7178) 7505[6]

**Royal Defence (IRE)** *Richard Ford* a60 47
8 b g Refuse To Bend(IRE) Alessia (GER) (Warning)
214[9] (1150) 1284[2] 2213[8] 3051[6] 3579[9] 5508[8]

**Royal Descent (AUS)** *Chris Waller* 113
5 br m Redoute's Choice(AUS) Mulan Princess (NZ) (Kaapstad (NZ))
7467a[12]

**Royal Diamond (IRE)** *J P Murtagh* a101 115
8 b g King's Best(USA) Irresistible Jewel (IRE) (Danehill (USA))
2370a[2] 3377[11] 5736a[2] 6374a[6] 7653a[20]

**Royal Dolois (FR)** *J-M Lefebvre* 82
2 gr c Silver Frost(IRE) Mixture (Linamix (FR))
1094a[7] 5118a[4] 6245a[3]

**Royal Duchess** *Lucy Normile* 64
4 b f Dutch Art Royal Citadel (IRE) (City On A Hill (USA))
4489[2] 5089[8] 5233[2] (7061)

**Royal Encounter** *Ed Vaughan* a70 68
3 b c Royal Applause Alhufoof (USA) (Dayjur (USA))
218[2] 477[3] 2847[7] 4411[6] 5530[2] 6647[3] 7180[12]

**Royal Etiquette (IRE)** *Lawney Hill* a60 66
7 b g Royal Applause Alpine Gold (IRE) (Montjeu (IRE))
116[8] 459[3] 821[5] 3147[3] 4985[4] (5208) 5567[5]

**Royale Way (FR)** *E Caroux* a51 66
4 b f Way Of Light(USA) John Quatz (FR) (Johann Quatz (FR))
722a[17]

**Royal Flag** *Saeed bin Suroor* a86 91
4 b g New Approach(IRE) Gonbarda (GER) (Lando (GER))
5039[2] 5648[2]

**Royal Flush** *Simon Waugh*
3 b c Multiplex Mystical Feelings (BEL) (Feelings (FR))
5772[7]

**Royal Fox** *P Schiergen* 96
4 ch g Manduro(GER) Rahada (GER) (Peintre Celebre (USA))
7618a[4]

**Royal Fury (USA)** *Brian A Lynch* a91 104
5 b m Langfuhr(CAN) Miss Chapin (USA) (Royal Academy (USA))
7326a[7]

**Royal Holiday (IRE)** *Marjorie Fife* a78 77
7 ch g Captain Rio Sunny Slope (Mujtahid (USA))
96[2] 408[4] 1191[4] 1499[2] 1839[3] 1886[3] 2169[5] 2905[7] 4023[8] 5269[4] 5571[2] 6009[2] (7765) 7829[7] 8281[4]

**Royal Intruder** *Ann Stokell* a36 42
9 b g Royal Applause Surprise Visitor (IRE) (Be My Guest (USA))
1015[11]

**Royal Irish Hussar (IRE)** *Nicky Henderson* 94
4 b g Galileo(IRE) Adjalisa (IRE) (Darshaan)
3453[10]

**Royalmania** *F Head* 105
3 ch f Elusive Quality(USA) Safari Queen (ARG) (Lode (USA))
3808a[7] 4840a[3]

**Royal Marskell** *Alison Hutchinson* a88 76
5 b g Multiplex Socialise (Groom Dancer (USA))
1[2] 405[2] 848[3] 1197[6] 1806[3] (2097) 2468[5] 2801[8] (3617) 4093[3] (4369) 4754[3] 5572[2] 5984[5] 6264[6] 7008[6] 7760[2] 7914[5] (8089) (8211)

**Royal Mezyan (IRE)** *William Haggas* a93 93
3 b g Royal Applause Rice Mother (IRE) (Indian Ridge)
3253[7] 5696[10] 6170[10] 6607[2]

**Royal Mizar (SPA)** *Ralph J Smith* a53 67
4 b g What A Caper(IRE) Zahaadid (FR) (Limpid)
1771[9] 2301[6] 3233[8] 3521[10] 5030[4] 5596[2] 6028[2] 6394[4] 7869[4] 7976[8] 8315[6]

**Royal Navy Ship (USA)** *A P O'Brien* 101
2 b c War Front(USA) Indy Punch (USA) (Pulling Punches (USA))
7462a[2]

**Royal Normandy** *Andrew Balding*
2 b g Royal Applause Border Minstral (IRE) (Sri Pekan (USA))
7561[9]

**Royal Party** *William Knight* 46
2 b f Royal Applause Foxtrot Alpha (IRE) (Desert Prince (IRE))
4604[7]

**Royal Preserve** *Andrew Balding* a83 73
3 ch g Duke Of Marmalade(IRE) Castaway Queen (IRE) (Selkirk (USA))
1381[4] ◆ 2063[2] 2510[4] 6609[6] 7205[2]

**Royal Prize** *Mme M Bollack-Badel* a95 93
4 ch g Nayef(USA) Spot Prize (USA) (Seattle Dancer (USA))
426[5] 625[8] 1341a[7]

**Royal Rascal** *Tim Easterby* 100
4 b f Lucky Story(USA) Royal Punch (Royal Applause)
1484[6] 2254[5] 2757[2] 3203[6] 3716[2] 4212[17] 4681[8] 5612[15] 6740[11] 7168[10]

**Royal Razalma (IRE)** *Jonathan Portman* 105
2 ch f Lope De Vega(IRE) Twiggy's Sister (IRE) (Flying Spur (AUS))
2771[12] 3934[2] (4781) 6067[5] 6530[4] (7238)

**Royal Regent** *Lucy Normile* 75
2 b g Urgent Request(IRE) Royal Citadel (IRE) (City On A Hill (USA))
6831[7] (7054)

**Royal Rettie** *Amy Weaver* 59
2 b f Royal Applause Bended Knee (Refuse To Bend (IRE))
5500[4]

**Royal Ridge (SAF)** *M F De Kock* a109 108
6 ch g Tiger Ridge(USA) Princess Faberge (SAF) (Jallad (USA))
112a[5]

**Royal Rock** *Chris Wall* a81 107
10 b g Sakhee(USA) Vanishing Point (USA) (Caller I.D. (USA))
1679[3] 2254[11] 4889[2] (6440) 6920[11]

**Royal Roman** *Mel Brittain* 15
2 b f Holy Roman Emperor(IRE) Noble Penny (Pennekamp (USA))
1504[10]

**Royal Roslea** *Marcus Tregoning* a51
2 b f Royal Applause Roslea Lady (IRE) (Alhaarth (IRE))
8112[4] 8247[5]

**Royal Seal** *Sir Michael Stoute* 96
3 b f Dansili Queen's Best (King's Best (USA))
1280[4] 1722[7] (2442) 3478[6] (3980) 4166[9] 4826[9] 6068[3]

**Royal Silk** *Roger Charlton* a76 39
2 b f Royal Applause Silky Dawn (IRE) (Night Shift (USA))
6517[17] 7192[6] (7741)

**Royal Spring (FR)** *N Clement* a81 99
2 ch c Tamayuz Main Spring (Pivotal)
7094a[3]

**Royal Straight** *Linda Perratt* a48 73
9 ch g Halling(USA) High Straits (Bering)
3242[7] 3829[3] 4255[4] 4387[7] 4517[3] 4858[6] 5145[4] 5639[8] 5855[4] 6012[3] 6223[6] 6597[9] 6795[7] 7098[11]

**Royal Street** *Seamus Durack*
2 b c Street Cry(IRE) Touch My Soul (FR) (Tiger Hill (IRE))
1417[13] 2623[8] 3194[14]

**Royal Style (FR)** *Matthieu Palussiere* a85 89
2 ch c Astronomer Royal(USA) Fast Style (FR) (Fasliyev (USA))
5329a[5]

**Royal Sun (FR)** *F Rohaut* a95 105
3 gr c Astronomer Royal(USA) Princess Love (FR) (Verglas (IRE))
721a[7]

**Royal Talisman** *Jo Hughes* a75 83
6 b g Val Royal(FR) Talismatic (IRE) (Tagula (IRE))
3373a[17] 4776a[3] 5225a[2] (5546a) 5964a[3] (6569a)

**Royal Temptress (IRE)** *Alan Swinbank* 76
3 br f Strategic Prince Love Thirty (Mister Baileys)
(1959)

**Royal Trooper (IRE)** *Mark Brisbourne* a69 83
8 b g Hawk Wing(USA) Strawberry Roan (IRE) (Sadler's Wells (USA))
361[7] 609[11] 3398[8] 4533[5] 5030[5] 6157[2] 6267[3] ◆ 6410[2] (7628) 8061[6] 8231[RR] 8261[RR]

**Royal Warranty** *Andrew Balding* a81 86
3 ch f Sir Percy Royal Patron (Royal Academy (USA))
1830[2] (2418) 6239[3] (6608) 7306[3]

**Royal Warrior** *Alan McCabe* a63 81
3 b g Royal Applause Tiana (Diktat)
1225[4] 1368[4] 2015[5] 2508[4] (2717) 3185[5] 3331[3] 3704[5] 4186[3] 4697[6]

**Roy Rocket (FR)** *John Berry* a48 43
4 gr g Layman(USA) Minnie's Mystery (FR) (Highest Honor (FR))
821[8] 1263[6] 2084[10] 3209[5] 4769[6] 7754[4] 7924[5] 8175[7]

**Roy's Legacy** *Shaun Harris* a78 71
5 b h Phoenix Reach(IRE) Chocolada (Namid)
114[2] (313) (470) 628[2] 654[3] 1019[6] (1109) 1311[6] 1602[2] 1972[3] (2514) 3191[8] 3561[2] 4114[11] 7886[10] 8040[10] 8071[11]

**Rozene (IRE)** *David Barron* 78
3 b f Sleeping Indian Few Words (Fraam)
1851[2] 2889[6] 3669[4] (4307) 5087[2]

**Ruban (IRE)** *Stuart Williams* a74 62
5 ch g Dubawi(IRE) Piece Unique (Barathea (IRE))
8042[8]

**Rubheira** *Hugo Froud* a29 32
2 ch f Arkadian Hero(USA) Devon Ruby (Zilzal (USA))
5042[6] 5789[11] 7308[8] 7648[12]

**Ruby Looker** *J R Jenkins* a65
3 b c Bertolini(USA) Ellcon (IRE) (Royal Applause)
(5)

**Ruby Rose (IRE)** *Kevin Ryan* a60 19
2 b f Vale Of York(IRE) High Society Girl (IRE) (Key Of Luck (USA))
4751[10] 5253[6] (5896) 6412[6] 7112[10]

**Ruby's Day** *David Brown* a69 83
5 ch m Vital Equine(IRE) Isabella's Best (IRE) (King's Best (USA))
(1541) 2050[4] 3676[5] 4132[4] 4712[4] 4976[7] 6213[13] 6492[8]

**Ruby's Teddy Bear (IRE)** *S Wattel* 65
2 gr c Verglas(IRE) Torosay Spring (First Trump)
7344a[6] 8212a[P]

**Ruby Wedding (FR)** *G Nicot* a72 83
4 ch f Panis(USA) Loda (FR) (Zieten (USA))
805a[7]

**Rudi Five One (FR)** *Robert Eddery* a71 86
3 b c American Post Dansia (GER) (Lavirco (GER))
(600a) (1195) 1535[3] 2347[5]

**Rue Du Temple (IRE)** *F Vermeulen* 50
2 b f Bahamian Bounty Roseska (USA) (Include (USA))
4882a[9]

**Ruffled** *Rae Guest* a65 77
4 b f Harlan's Holiday(USA) Mirabilis (USA) (Lear Fan (USA))
(264)

**Rufford (IRE)** *Lee Carter* a73 58
3 b g Invincible Spirit(IRE) Speedy Sonata (USA) (Stravinsky (USA))
1867[3] 2304[7] 3253[14] 5165[10] 7168[9] 8117[11]

**Ruggero** *Roy Brotherton* a28 101
4 b g Tiger Hill(IRE) Bergamask (USA) (Kingmambo (USA))
5379[9] 5931[9] 6425[4] 7975[8] 8258[8]

**Rugosa** *Charles Hills* a83 42
5 b m Oasis Dream Zathonia (Zafonic (USA))
491[6]

**Ruler Of The World (IRE)** *A P O'Brien* a92 125
4 ch c Galileo(IRE) Love Me True (USA) (Kingmambo (USA))
1183a[13] (6381a) 6970a[9] 7275[9]

**Rumble Of Thunder (IRE)** *Philip Kirby* a72 75
8 b g Fath(USA) Honey Storm (IRE) (Mujadil (USA))
2900[2] 3622[3]

**Rummaging (IRE)** *M Halford* a103 71
6 ch g Chineur(FR) Roundabout Girl (IRE) (Doubletour (USA))
249[2] 713[5] 6354a[18]

**Rum Swizzle** *Harry Dunlop* a59
2 b f Mawatheeq(USA) Port Providence (Red Ransom (USA))
7198[10] 7625[5] 7835[4] ◆ 8009[6]

**Runaiocht (IRE)** *Paul Burgoyne* a55 55
4 ch g Teofilo(IRE) Julie Girl (USA) (Jules (USA))
7347[9] 7632[4] 7982[4]

**Run By Faith** *Roger Charlton* 71
2 b f Sixties Icon Sweet Pilgrim (Talkin Man (CAN))
4784[9] 7377[4]

**Run Fat Lass Run** *Conor Dore* a65 73
4 b f Sakhee(USA) Feolin (Dr Fong (USA))
928[5] 1131[4] 1446[10] 1857[4] (2426) (2823) 3254[15] 4254[5] 5206[2] 5678[2] 6615[3] 7302[7] 7651[6] 7842[10] 7907[9] 8028[7]

**Run It Twice (IRE)** *David Evans* a77 62
4 b g Dark Angel(IRE) Alinda (IRE) (Revoque (IRE))
141[3] 359[3] 496[4] 627[4] 940[3] 1021[4] 1388[3] (2471) 2930[3] 3235[2]

**Runner Runner (IRE)** *George Baker* a76 89
2 gr f Dark Angel(IRE) Distant Piper (IRE) (Distant Music (USA))
3082[8] 4054[2] 4825[3] (5604) 6749[5] 7481a[2]

**Running Deer (IRE)** *Eve Johnson Houghton* a77 97
5 b m Hurricane Run(IRE) Sweet Sioux (Halling (USA))
(1811) 2119[2] 2501[3] (3217) 4211[5] 4782[4] 5928[5] 6548[13] 7598[6]

**Running Reef (IRE)** *Tracy Waggott* 73
5 b g Hurricane Run(IRE) Half-Hitch (USA) (Diesis)
1376[5] ◆ 1609[10] 2605[3] 3242[4] 3952[3] 4070[2] 4523[5] 5269[6] 5793[5] 6227[7] (6405) ◆ 6544[4]

**Running Water** *John David Riches* a5 56
6 ch m Blue Dakota(IRE) Floral Spark (Forzando)
3104[8]

**Running Wolf (IRE)** *Michael Dods* 71
3 b g Amadeus Wolf Monet's Lady (IRE) (Daylami (IRE))
1508[5] 2132[5] 3303[5] 3789[11] 4292[8] 4536[3]

**Run The Red Light (IRE)** *A Oliver* 89
2 b f Alfred Nobel(IRE) Lilakiya (IRE) (Dr Fong (USA))
5734a[9]

**Run With Pride (IRE)** *Derek Shaw* 90
4 b g Invincible Spirit(IRE) Zibilene (Rainbow Quest (USA))
(1939) 2562[6] 3152[2] 5199[7] 6260[3] 6744[6]

**Rural Celebration** *David O'Meara* a73 92
3 b f Pastoral Pursuits Queens Jubilee (Cayman Kai (IRE))
2015[2] ◆ (2727) (2897) 3253[16] 5696[7] 6130[4]

**Rush** *Paul Cole* a62 51
3 ch f Compton Place Dorelia (IRE) (Efisio)
311[12]

**Russian Bolero (GER)** *A Wohler* 92
3 ch g Tertullian(USA) Russian Samba (IRE) (Laroche (GER))
4007a[13]

**Russian Heroine** *Sir Michael Stoute* a70 74
2 b f Invincible Spirit(IRE) Russian Rhythm (USA) (Kingmambo (USA))
2220[2] 2493[2] 5725[4] 6977[2] 7201[3]

**Russian Ice** *Dean Ivory* a64 42
6 ch m Iceman Dark Eyed Lady (IRE) (Exhibitioner)
84[3] 451[2] ◆ 817[8] 924[5] 1799[7] 6857[12] 7368[9] 7704[6] 7853[7] 7986[6] 8175[6] 8259[7]

**Russian Khan (GER)** *Yasmin Almenrader* a78 70
6 ch g Sholokhov(IRE) Russian Samba (IRE) (Laroche (GER))
3907a[3] 5964a[11]

**Russian Punch** *James Given* 98
2 b f Archipenko(USA) Punch Drunk (Beat Hollow)
(2652) 3649[2] 4585[4] (5680) 6126[4] 6926[6] (7448)

**Russian Realm** *Sir Michael Stoute* 102
4 b g Dansili Russian Rhythm (USA) (Kingmambo (USA))
1871[2] (2483) 3420[DSQ] 3982[4] 5609[7] 5919[6] 7276[8]

**Russian Remarque** *Jonathan Portman* a72 72
3 b g Archipenko(USA) Accede (Acclamation)
988[2] ◆ 1808[4] 2221[8] 2749[4] 7340[5]

**Russian Reward (IRE)** *Paul Cole* a78 64
2 b c Iffraaj Forever Times (So Factual (USA))
5684[3] 6138[3]

**Russian Rock (IRE)** *M Al Muhairi* a112 107
7 b h Rock Of Gibraltar(IRE) Mala Mala (IRE) (Brief Truce (USA))
*504a$^{12}$*

**Russian Roulette (IRE)** *Charles O'Brien* 59
3 b g Peintre Celebre(USA) Rejuvenation (IRE) (Singspiel (IRE))
4556a$^{13}$

**Russian Royale** *Stuart Kittow* a73 76
4 b f Royal Applause Russian Ruby (FR) (Vettori (IRE))
3585$^{3}$ 4617$^{3}$ 5948$^{3}$ 6318$^{2}$ (6881) *7422$^{7}$*

**Russian Soul (IRE)** *M Halford* a112 112
6 b g Invincible Spirit(IRE) Russian Hill (Indian Ridge)
*206a$^{2}$ (597a) 898a$^{6}$ 1180a$^{7}$* 5154a$^{3}$ 5699a$^{6}$ 6371a$^{3}$ 7140a$^{4}$ *7433a$^{3}$*

**Rust (IRE)** *Ann Duffield* a62 68
4 b g Elnadim(USA) Reddening (Blushing Flame (USA))
3535$^{11}$ (4318) 4727$^{7}$ 5088$^{8}$ 6600$^{3}$ 6833$^{5}$

**Rustique** *Ed Walker* a52
2 ch f Pastoral Pursuits Nihal (IRE) (Singspiel (IRE))
*7944$^{5}$ 8173$^{12}$*

**Rusty Rocket (IRE)** *Paul Green* a83 93
5 ch h Majestic Missile(IRE) Sweet Compliance (Safawan)
*4$^{10}$* 1305$^{2}$ *1742$^{4}$* 2074$^{9}$ 2732$^{8}$ 3948$^{12}$ 4391$^{11}$

**Rusty Slipper (USA)** *H Graham Motion* 102
4 bb f Lemon Drop Kid(USA) Classic Approval (USA) (With Approval (CAN))
7607a$^{10}$

**Rutherglen** *John Quinn* a86 82
4 b g Tiger Hill(IRE) Hanella (IRE) (Galileo (IRE))
*(591) 7903$^{2}$*

**Rutland Boy** *Michael Bell* a109 59
6 ch g Bertolini(USA) Israar (Machiavellian (USA))
*768a$^{7}$ 899a$^{14}$*

**Rutland Panther** *Declan Carroll* 49
2 b g Alhaarth(IRE) Desert Lynx (IRE) (Green Desert (USA))
1955$^{9}$ 2360$^{5}$ 3945$^{7}$ 4528$^{3}$ 4870$^{3}$

**Rutterkin (USA)** *James Moffatt* a53 50
6 gr g Maria's Mon(USA) Chilukki Cat (USA) (Storm Cat (USA))
*83$^{6}$ 274$^{6}$ 290$^{5}$ 563$^{5}$ 740$^{5}$ 1228$^{3}$* 3562$^{7}$ 4960$^{14}$ 5082$^{6}$ 6580$^{6}$

**Ruwaiyan (USA)** *James Tate* a90 108
5 bb h Cape Cross(IRE) Maskunah (IRE) (Sadler's Wells (USA))
*153$^{6}$ 552$^{9}$* (1957) 2145$^{10}$ 3036$^{2}$ 3715$^{2}$ 4895$^{4}$ 5674$^{10}$ 6387a$^{7}$ 6533$^{6}$ 7140a$^{6}$

**Ruwasi** *James Tate* a57 92
3 b c Authorized(IRE) Circle Of Love (Sakhee (USA))
2354$^{2}$ (2952) 3787$^{3}$ (6433) ◆ 6930$^{3}$ 7440$^{P}$

**Ruzeiz (USA)** *Peter Hedger* a75 73
5 b g Muhtathir Saraama (USA) (Bahri (USA))
*270$^{5}$ 744$^{9}$ 1014$^{7}$* 2627$^{9}$ 7411$^{4}$ *7672$^{7}$ 7918$^{3}$ 8196$^{3}$*

**R Woody** *George Baker* a77 66
7 ch g Ishiguru(USA) Yarrita (Tragic Role (USA))
*35$^{2}$ 93$^{3}$ (318) 555a$^{5}$ 728a$^{6}$ 826$^{6}$ 889$^{7}$*

**Ryan Style (IRE)** *Lisa Williamson* a53 67
8 b g Desert Style(IRE) Westlife (IRE) (Mind Games)
*184$^{6}$ 351$^{7}$* 3520$^{4}$ 3784$^{2}$

**Rydan (IRE)** *Robert Mills* a104 92
3 ch c Intense Focus(USA) Lough Mewin (IRE) (Woodman (USA))
1353$^{4}$ 1809$^{4}$ 3031$^{4}$ (3197) ◆ 3931$^{3}$ 4855$^{4}$ 5928$^{11}$ *(6665) 7662$^{3}$ 8095$^{5}$*

**Ryedale Lass** *Geoffrey Deacon* a45 46
6 b m Val Royal(FR) First Dawn (Dr Fong (USA))
*179$^{8}$ 290$^{2}$ 370$^{5}$ 586$^{7}$* 1986$^{8}$ 2723$^{3}$

**Ryedale Mist** *Tim Easterby* 44
2 b f Equiano(FR) Alhufoof (USA) (Dayjur (USA))
3648$^{11}$ 4450$^{6}$ 4751$^{9}$ ◆ 6212$^{11}$

**Ryedale Valley** *Mlle M Henry* a55 54
4 ch g Three Valleys(USA) Phi Phi (IRE) (Fasliyev (USA))
*266a$^{9}$*

**Rye House (IRE)** *Sir Michael Stoute* 101
5 b g Dansili Threefold (USA) (Gulch (USA))
2253$^{5}$ 2779$^{11}$ 5174$^{5}$

**Ryeolliean** *David O'Meara* 81
3 ch g Haafhd Brave Mave (Daylami (IRE))
3719$^{5}$ 4419$^{4}$ 5015$^{3}$ 5387$^{5}$ (6637)

**Rylee Mooch** *Richard Guest* a83 71
6 gr g Choisir(AUS) Negligee (Night Shift (USA))
*1283$^{9}$* 2159$^{8}$ 2364$^{11}$ 3222$^{8}$ 3707$^{3}$ 3887$^{5}$ *5045$^{4}$* 5437$^{6}$ 6580$^{2}$ 6819$^{4}$ 7213$^{2}$ 7510$^{3}$ 7535$^{2}$ 7671$^{2}$

**Ryton Runner (IRE)** *Lucinda Russell* a68 65
6 b g Sadler's Wells(USA) Love For Ever (IRE) (Darshaan)
7177$^{8}$

**Saab Almanal** *James Fanshawe* 104
3 b c Dubawi(IRE) Caribbean Pearl (USA) (Silver Hawk (USA))
1587$^{2}$ 2285$^{6}$ 2746$^{5}$ (4435) 5676$^{3}$ 6518$^{2}$ 7106$^{21}$

**Saakhen (IRE)** *Richard Fahey* a79 84
3 b g Invincible Spirit(IRE) Upperville (IRE) (Selkirk (USA))
1671$^{3}$ *(2093)* 3331$^{4}$ ◆ 3565$^{3}$ 3936$^{2}$ ◆

**Saalib (USA)** *Brian Meehan* a63 53
3 b c War Front(USA) Dixie Quest (USA) (Coronado's Quest (USA))
1582$^{13}$ 2025$^{4}$ 2346$^{6}$ *2998$^{12}$* 3430$^{5}$

**Saane (FR)** *J-C Rouget* a98 104
3 b g Le Havre(IRE) Salamon (Montjeu (IRE))
*(5027a)*

**Saarrem (USA)** *John Gosden* a83 84
3 b c Dynaformer(USA) Effectual (USA) (Carson City (USA))
*1391$^{3}$* ◆ 1691$^{8}$ *2917$^{3}$ 4543$^{3}$ 5135$^{2}$* (6092) 6756$^{6}$

**Saas Fee (FR)** *Mme Pia Brandt* a90 41
3 b f Holy Roman Emperor(IRE) Suissesse (USA) (Malibu Moon (USA))
6882a$^{12}$

**Saayerr** *William Haggas* a96 103
3 b g Acclamation Adorn (Kyllachy)
1514$^{4}$ 3715$^{3}$

**Sabbra Cadabra** *Philip Kirby* 12
2 b c Multiplex Mighty Aphrodite (Observatory (USA))
4253$^{8}$ 4723$^{6}$ 5372$^{8}$

**Sabha (IRE)** *Timothy Jarvis* a50
2 b f Thewayyouare(USA) Genipabu (IRE) (Danetime (IRE))
*7659$^{5}$*

**Sabi Sand (FR)** *S Wattel* a66 72
3 b g Irish Wells(FR) Mala Mala (FR) (Balleroy (USA))
*169a$^{3}$*

**Saborido (USA)** *Amanda Perrett* a90 89
8 gr g Dixie Union(USA) Alexine (ARG) (Runaway Groom (CAN))
2490$^{6}$ *2920$^{5}$* 3249$^{9}$ 4441$^{10}$ *5137$^{2}$ (5863) (6107)* 7306$^{7}$

**Sabre Rock** *Julia Feilden* a66 66
4 b g Dubawi(IRE) Retainage (USA) (Polish Numbers (USA))
*1209$^{7}$* 5727$^{8}$ 6303$^{12}$ *6635$^{12}$ 7426$^{4}$ 7526$^{3}$ (7805) (8315)*

**Sacha Park (IRE)** *Richard Hannon* a85 95
3 ch c Iffraaj Silicon Star (FR) (Starborough)
*(1237)* 1700$^{9}$ 2090$^{8}$ 2962$^{11}$ 4502$^{7}$ 4983$^{3}$ *5553$^{3}$* 5945$^{8}$ 6249$^{4}$ *(6562) 6898$^{5}$ 7375$^{8}$*

**Sacred Act** *John Gosden* 96
3 b c Oasis Dream Stage Presence (IRE) (Selkirk (USA))
(1394) ◆ 1696$^{5}$

**Sacred Bond** *Richard Fahey* a59 59
2 ch f Exceed And Excel(AUS) Gay Romance (Singspiel (IRE))
7712$^{4}$ ◆ *7970$^{4}$*

**Sacred Falls (NZ)** *Chris Waller* 120
5 b h O'Reilly(NZ) Iguazu's Girl (NZ) (Redoute's Choice (AUS))
1186a$^{4}$ 7127a$^{4}$ 7467a$^{11}$

**Sacred Square (GER)** *Donald McCain* 80
4 ch g Peintre Celebre(USA) Square The Circle (Second Empire (IRE))
(5121) 5403$^{3}$

**Sacrilege** *Daniel O'Brien*
9 ch g Sakhee(USA) Idolize (Polish Precedent (USA))
3310$^{U}$

**Sacrosanctus** *Scott Dixon* a58 72
6 ch g Sakhee(USA) Catalonia (IRE) (Catrail (USA))
*1742$^{10}$* 1938$^{11}$ 4121$^{7}$ 5888$^{17}$ 6235$^{20}$ 6398$^{7}$

**Saddlers Mot** *Karen Tutty* a40 64
10 b m Saddlers' Hall(IRE) Be My Mot (IRE) (Be My Native (USA))
1960$^{8}$ 2354$^{5}$ *2904$^{4}$* 3482$^{7}$ 4259$^{7}$ 4749$^{8}$

**Saddler's Rock (IRE)** *Jonjo O'Neill* 112
6 b h Sadler's Wells(USA) Grecian Bride (IRE) (Groom Dancer (USA))
811a$^{11}$ 1177a$^{13}$ 2370a$^{6}$ 3377$^{10}$ 7107$^{25}$

**Sadeek's Song (USA)** *Charlie Appleby* a72 98
6 ch h Kingmambo(USA) New Morning (IRE) (Sadler's Wells (USA))
*202a$^{8}$*

**Sadiigah** *Julia Feilden* a51 31
4 b f Medicean Regal Riband (Fantastic Light (USA))
*6767$^{5}$ 7252$^{7}$* 7670$^{11}$ *7825$^{9}$*

**Safe Home (IRE)** *John Quinn* 94
4 ch g Danehill Dancer(IRE) In Safe Hands (IRE) (Intikhab (USA))
1360$^{4}$ 1715$^{9}$ 2052$^{4}$

**Safe Investment (USA)** *Lawney Hill* a48 49
10 b g Gone West(USA) Fully Invested (USA) (Irish River (FR))
5030$^{3}$ 5502$^{5}$ 5909$^{5}$

**Safety Check (IRE)** *Charlie Appleby* a100 108
3 ch c Dubawi(IRE) Doors To Manual (USA) (Royal Academy (USA))
*204a$^{2}$ 594a$^{4}$ 1178a$^{10}$* 4198$^{10}$ ◆ (4826) 5665$^{4}$ ◆ (6124) 6522$^{6}$

**Saffire Song** *Alan Bailey* a73 63
3 ch f Firebreak Saffwah (IRE) (King's Best (USA))
*315$^{2}$ 373$^{2}$ (608)* ◆ *(762) 936$^{4}$* 3433$^{8}$ 3959$^{9}$ 4128$^{10}$ 4531$^{4}$ 4862$^{6}$ *5281$^{11}$ 5826$^{9}$* 8040$^{12}$ 8210$^{5}$

**Safwaan** *Michael Squance* a67 66
7 b g Selkirk(USA) Kawn (Cadeaux Genereux)
*83$^{4}$ 289$^{4}$ 451$^{4}$ 750$^{9}$ 1085$^{7}$ 1288$^{P}$*

**Safzebos (FR)** *C Ferland* a82 73
2 b c Aussie Rules(USA) Elusive Queen (FR) (Elusive City (USA))
3691a$^{2}$ 5544a$^{4}$

**Sagaciously (IRE)** *Ed Dunlop* 89
2 b f Lawman(FR) Saga Celebre (FR) (Peintre Celebre (USA))
(6208) 7596$^{4}$

**Sagal Nel Vento (SER)** *B Vidovic* 68
3 b c Depth(USA) Seron Sek (SER) (Gilgames)
1907a$^{8}$

**Saga Lout** *Andrew Hollinshead* a72 18
4 b g Assertive Intellibet One (Compton Place)
*938$^{7}$* 2691$^{10}$ 3222$^{12}$ *4049$^{12}$ 6272$^{12}$ 6409$^{13}$ 6561$^{10}$ 6720$^{P}$*

**Saga Man (FR)** *F Lemercier* a45
3 b c Sandwaki(USA) Saga (FR) (Nombre Premier)
*600a$^{8}$*

**Sage Riquet (FR)** *E Lellouche* a47 82
7 b g Dallapour(IRE) Dear Shrimp (FR) (Pistolet Bleu (IRE))
*584a$^{15}$*

**Sagesse** *Sir Mark Prescott Bt* a84 82
4 ch f Smart Strike(CAN) Summer Night (Nashwan (USA))
*(276) 514$^{2}$ 623$^{5}$ 891$^{3}$* 3681$^{3}$ 4045$^{2}$ 4351$^{9}$ *8001$^{3}$ 8096$^{7}$*

**Sagua La Grande (IRE)** *Lady Cecil* a65 78
4 b g Teofilo(IRE) Water Fountain (Mark Of Esteem (IRE))
*4325$^{6}$ 5831$^{8}$*

**Sahaafy (USA)** *B W Hills* 72
2 b c Kitten's Joy(USA) Queen's Causeway (USA) (Giant's Causeway (USA))
4666$^{5}$ ◆

**Sahand (IRE)** *J Hirschberger* 93
3 b c Shamardal(USA) Shraayef (Nayef (USA))
2377a$^{7}$ (7269a)

**Sahara (IRE)** *Chris Wall* 53
2 b f Clodovil(IRE) Celtic Lynn (IRE) (Celtic Swing)
7406$^{5}$

**Sahara Desert (IRE)** *Sir Michael Stoute* a59 67
3 b g Montjeu(IRE) Festoso (IRE) (Diesis)
1401$^{7}$ 2447$^{6}$

**Saharia (IRE)** *Daniel Mark Loughnane* a86 80
7 b g Oratorio(IRE) Inchiri (Sadler's Wells (USA))
*(66) (262) 775$^{2}$*

**Sahawar (FR)** *C Ferland* a103 113
4 bl c Dark Angel(IRE) Saaryeh (Royal Academy (USA))
205a$^{9}$ *394a$^{6}$* 5263a$^{9}$

**Sahra Al Khadra** *Charles Hills* a71 84
3 b c Green Desert(USA) Maimoona (IRE) (Pivotal)
*1389$^{3}$* ◆ (2027) 3273$^{2}$ 3670$^{2}$ 4280$^{2}$ (4868)

**Sahrawi (GER)** *M Delzangles* 103
3 b f Pivotal Sand River (IRE) (High Chaparral (IRE))
6419a$^{3}$ 7720a$^{2}$

**Saigon City** *Luca Cumani* 89
4 b g Mount Nelson Hoh Chi Min (Efisio)
1351$^{2}$ 2162$^{2}$ 2627$^{3}$

**Sail Home** *John E Long* a57 57
7 b m Mizzen Mast(USA) Bristol Channel (Generous (IRE))
*7358$^{10}$ 7805$^{11}$*

**Sailing Club (USA)** *D Smaga* a88 88
3 b c Mizzen Mast(USA) Storm Dove (USA) (Storm Bird (CAN))
1551a$^{2}$ *(5294a)*

**Sailor (FR)** *J Heloury* a68 97
3 b c Soldier Of Fortune(IRE) Tiptonia (USA) (Kendor (FR))
*360a$^{7}$* 3290a$^{8}$ 5481a$^{6}$

**Sailors Warn (IRE)** *E J O'Grady* a60 85
7 b g Redback Coral Dawn (IRE) (Trempolino (USA))
7476a$^{10}$

**Sail With Sultana** *Mark Rimell* a53 39
3 ch f Black Sam Bellamy(IRE) Strathtay (Pivotal)
6247$^{5}$ 7210$^{5}$ *7627$^{3}$ 8134$^{13}$*

**Saint Bernard** *D Camuffo* a71 105
5 b h Three Valleys(USA) Savignano (Polish Precedent (USA))
2191a$^{8}$ 2589a$^{9}$

**Sainte Amarante (FR)** *Yves de Nicolay* a60
2 ch f Le Havre(IRE) Loyal Lass (USA) (Cadeaux Genereux)
*8132a$^{7}$*

**Sainte Croix (FR)** *M Boutin* 83
3 b f Le Havre(IRE) Sainte Adresse (Elusive City (USA))
(5661a) 6913a$^{8}$

**Sainte Glace (IRE)** *Robert Collet*
3 gr f Verglas(IRE) Lorientaise (IRE) (Xaar)
*194a$^{13}$*

**Saint Gervais (IRE)** *John E Kiely* 80
9 b g Revoque(IRE) Just Precious (Ela-Mana-Mou)
4746a$^{16}$ 7142a$^{10}$

**Saint Hilary** *W Walton* 93
5 b m Authorized(IRE) Bright Halo (IRE) (Bigstone (IRE))
723a$^{8}$

**Saint Honore** *Pat Phelan* a62 59
2 b f Champs Elysees Gwyneth (Zafonic (USA))
*5821$^{6}$ 6675$^{11}$* 6984$^{5}$ *7396$^{8}$*

**Saint Jerome (IRE)** *Jamie Osborne* a71 86
4 b g Jeremy(USA) Eminence Gift (Cadeaux Genereux)
*744$^{13}$*

**Saint Lucy** *John Gosden* a71 65
3 b f Selkirk(USA) Sister Maria (USA) (Kingmambo (USA))
3142$^{3}$ *3856$^{4}$*

**Saint Pois (FR)** *Tony Carroll* a97 74
3 b g Le Havre(IRE) Our Dream Queen (Oasis Dream)
*194a$^{2}$ (390a) (5482a) 8228$^{7}$ 8279$^{7}$*

**Saint Thomas (IRE)** *John Mackie* a65 72
7 b g Alhaarth(IRE) Aguilas Perla (IRE) (Indian Ridge)
1660$^{9}$ 2540$^{6}$ 3616$^{5}$ 4369$^{2}$ 5301$^{2}$ (6000) 6696$^{2}$ *7182$^{7}$ 7866$^{9}$*

**Sairaam (IRE)** *Charles Smith* a40 51
8 b m Marju(IRE) Sayedati Eljamilah (USA) (Mr Prospector (USA))
*1365$^{11}$* 1639$^{5}$ 3160$^{11}$ 3384$^{7}$ 4534$^{6}$ 5057$^{4}$ 5110$^{2}$ *8084$^{9}$ 8291$^{7}$*

**Sakal** *Matthieu Palussiere* a44 52
3 b f Exceed And Excel(AUS) Sentimental (IRE) (Galileo (IRE))
2290a$^{7}$ *5482a$^{12}$*

**Sakash** *J R Jenkins* a79 76
4 b c Sakhee(USA) Ashwell Rose (Anabaa (USA))
*245$^{14}$ 1082$^{3}$* ◆ *(1286) 1630$^{2}$ 2400$^{2}$* 3628$^{4}$ 4148$^{5}$ 4907$^{7}$ (5729) *6414$^{4}$ 7183$^{9}$*

**Sakhalin Star (IRE)** *Richard Guest* a64 77
3 ch g Footstepsinthesand Quela (GER) (Acatenango (GER))
1725$^{12}$ (2204) 2391$^{4}$ 2805$^{3}$ 3273$^{7}$ 3618$^{4}$ 4108$^{2}$ 4387$^{5}$ 5385$^{14}$ 5441$^{4}$ 5915$^{10}$ 6232$^{14}$ *6766$^{5}$* 7248$^{7}$

**Sakhee's Alround** *K F Clutterbuck* a52 54
4 ch f Sakhee's Secret Regal Run (USA) (Deputy Minister (CAN))
*1015$^{RR}$*

**Sakhee's Return** *Tim Easterby* 75
2 b g Sakhee's Secret Sofia Royale (Royal Applause)
2358$^{8}$ (3297) 4057$^{4}$ 5085$^{4}$ 6331$^{6}$

**Sakhee's Rose** *Ed McMahon* a69 68
4 b f Sakhee's Secret Isobel Rose (IRE) (Royal Applause)
*993$^{4}$* 3668$^{8}$ ◆ 4629$^{5}$ *5303$^{2}$* 6266$^{6}$ 6674$^{16}$ 6863$^{5}$

**Sakhee'Ssquirrel** *Sean Curran* a47 57
3 ch f Sakhee's Secret China Cherub (Inchinor)
*37$^{6}$ 608$^{9}$ 745$^{6}$ 1107$^{7}$* 1666$^{5}$ 2045$^{6}$

**Sakhra** *Mark Brisbourne* a64 57
3 b g Nayef(USA) Noble Desert (FR) (Green Desert (USA))
*5898$^{8}$ 6343$^{10}$ 6899$^{4}$ 7118$^{3}$ 7458$^{4}$ 7628$^{4}$* ◆ *7895$^{3}$ 8047$^{6}$ 8277$^{7}$*

**Saktoon (USA)** *Derek Shaw* a27
6 b m El Prado(IRE) Galore (USA) (Gulch (USA))
*353$^{13}$ 477$^{10}$*

**Sakuramachi** *Nikki Evans* 3
3 b f Sixties Icon Queen Of Narnia (Hunting Lion (IRE))
*378$^{11}$* 5747$^{5}$ 6087$^{9}$ *7547$^{10}$*

**Salai (FR)** *J-C Rouget* 110
3 b c Myboycharlie(IRE) Mabadi (USA) (Sahm (USA))
2196a$^{8}$ 3028a$^{2}$

**Salam Alaykum (IRE)** *Gary Moore* a76 91
6 b g Galileo(IRE) Alicia (IRE) (Darshaan)
6655$^{6}$

**Salateen** *Kevin Ryan* 99
2 ch c Dutch Art Amanda Carter (Tobougg (IRE))
3454$^{3}$ 4424$^{2}$ (4935) ◆ 5576$^{5}$ (6229) ◆ 6750$^{3}$

**Salford Dream** *Pauline Robson* 49
5 ch g Halling(USA) Spitting Image (IRE) (Spectrum (IRE))
6644$^{11}$ 7283$^{4}$

**Salford Prince (IRE)** *David Elsworth* a48
6 b g Invincible Spirit(IRE) Bring Plenty (USA) (Southern Halo (USA))
*251$^{3}$ 290$^{6}$ 370$^{4}$*

**Salford Secret (IRE)** *Riccardo Santini* a81 105
3 b c Sakhee's Secret Dhuyoof (IRE) (Sinndar (IRE))
(1779a) 2376a$^{7}$ 6808a$^{6}$ 7322a$^{7}$ 7616a$^{11}$

**Salient** *Michael Attwater* a64 64
10 b g Fasliyev(USA) Savannah Belle (Green Desert (USA))
*117$^{9}$ 210$^{9}$ 490$^{4}$ 1263$^{3}$ 1835$^{2}$* 2046$^{2}$ 2720$^{8}$ *3473$^{9}$ 4326$^{8}$ 6636$^{7}$* (7002) 7219$^{2}$ 7518$^{2}$ (7846) 8037$^{4}$ 8196$^{5}$

**Salinas Road (FR)** *M Figge* a59 84
4 b c Elusive City(USA) Mamounia (GER) (Platini (GER))
*392a$^{15}$ 722a$^{15}$*

**Sallabeh** *George Margarson* 73
2 b f Showcasing Clincher Club (Polish Patriot (USA))
2873$^{5}$ 4499$^{5}$ (4980) 5626$^{4}$ 6064$^{12}$ 7515$^{4}$

**Sally Bruce** *Edward Creighton* a49 55
4 b f Byron Show Trial (IRE) (Jade Robbery (USA))
*179$^{12}$*

**Salma Gondis (IRE)** *David O'Meara* a66
2 b f Kodiac Rainbowskia (FR) (Rainbow Quest (USA))
*7809$^{3}$ 8060$^{2}$ 8288$^{5}$*

**Salmon Sushi** *David Lanigan* a81 66
3 ch g Dalakhani(IRE) Salsa Steps (USA) (Giant's Causeway (USA))
*7841$^{4}$ 8064$^{2}$ (8310)*

**Saltarello (IRE)** *John Quinn* a67 74
2 b c Fast Company(IRE) Step Dancing (Distant Music (USA))
4110$^{4}$ 4750$^{5}$ 5078$^{5}$ 5630$^{2}$ 6008$^{2}$ 6211$^{8}$ *7116$^{5}$*

**Saltire (IRE)** *John Patrick Shanahan* 38
3 gr f Dalakhani(IRE) My Special K'S (USA) (Tabasco Cat (USA))
2737$^{8}$

**Salt Island** *Charles Hills* 88
2 b c Exceed And Excel(AUS) Tiana (Diktat)
(5684) 7439$^{5}$

**Saltwater Creek (IRE)** *Michael Bell* a77 80
3 b f Marju(IRE) Crossing (Cape Cross (IRE))
*(1427)* 1882$^{2}$ 2769$^{7}$ 4182$^{3}$ 4782$^{13}$ 5505$^{6}$ *6633$^{8}$ 7459$^{5}$*

**Salut (GER)** *P Schiergen* 107
6 b h Lomitas Saldentigerin (GER) (Tiger Hill (IRE))
7469a$^{2}$ 7769a$^{2}$

**Salutation (IRE)** *Mark Johnston* a102 108
4 b g Iffraaj Totally Yours (IRE) (Desert Sun)
*(1171)* 1653$^{14}$ 1973$^{4}$ 2957$^{11}$ 3449$^{2}$ 4756$^{3}$ 5174$^{12}$ 5651$^{2}$

**Salut Lilly (FR)** *S Jesus* a52 63
2 b f Doctor Dino(FR) Salut Lisa (FR) (Sagacity (FR))
4882a$^{10}$ *5901a$^{7}$*

**Salutos Amigos (USA)** *David Jacobson* a112
4 b g Salute The Sarge(USA) Sarasota (ARG) (Luhuk (USA))
*7612a$^{7}$*

**Salvado (IRE)** *Tony Carroll* a74 71
4 b g Invincible Spirit(IRE) Easter Fairy (USA) (Fusaichi Pegasus (USA))
*2648$^{8}$* 3313$^{7}$ 4401$^{9}$ 5777$^{8}$ *6889$^{8}$ 7347$^{7}$ 7864$^{12}$ 8229$^{2}$ 8285$^{4}$*

**Salvadori (IRE)** *A bin Harmash* a60 89
3 b c Teofilo(IRE) Rachelle (IRE) (Mark Of Esteem (IRE))
505a$^{9}$ ◆

**Salvatore Fury (IRE)** *Keith Dalgleish* a86 76
4 b g Strategic Prince Nocturnal (FR) (Night Shift (USA))
1759$^{3}$ 2606$^{13}$ 2677$^{13}$ 3298$^{2}$ 3611$^{3}$ (3954) 4194$^{2}$ 4521$^{3}$ 4762$^{3}$ 6013$^{13}$ 6313$^{2}$ 6512$^{7}$ *(7351) 8025$^{2}$ 8171$^{4}$ 8297$^{2}$*

**Salve Hibernia (IRE)** *D Henderson* 99
5 ch m Hurricane Run(IRE) Salve Regina (GER) (Monsun (GER))
723a$^{2}$

**Same World** *J Moore* 112
6 b g Hawk Wing(USA) Spinamix (Spinning World (USA))
7898a$^{8}$ 8154a$^{9}$

**Samhain** *David Brown* a75 45
3 b g Compton Place Athboy Nights (IRE) (Night Shift (USA))
*(933)*

**Sammy's Choice** *Paul Burgoyne* a54
2 ch g Pastoral Pursuits Diane's Choice (Komaite (USA))
*7919$^{6}$*

**Sammy's Warrior** *Marco Botti* a67
2 b c Myboycharlie(IRE) Tahfeez (IRE) (Alhaarth (IRE))
6268[6]

**Samoan (IRE)** *Alan Berry* 69
5 b g Danehill Dancer(IRE) Rain Flower (IRE) (Indian Ridge)
1112[6] 1969[5] 2738[9] 2950[4] 3364[9]

**Samoset** *Pam Sly* a56 61
4 b g Sir Percy Great Quest (IRE) (Montjeu (IRE))
(475) 648[6] 1496[7] 2607[4] ◆ 6027[5]

**Sampera (IRE)** *Michael Bell* 71
2 b f Iffraaj Al Cobra (IRE) (Sadler's Wells (USA))
6066[7] 6742[2] 7174[5]

**Sample (FR)** *Roger Charlton* a48
2 b f Zamindar(USA) Sanabyra (FR) (Kahyasi)
7919[7] 8201[6]

**Samraat (USA)** *Richard Violette Jr* a113
3 bb c Noble Causeway(USA) Little Indian Girl (USA) (Indian Charlie (USA))
1964a[5] 3026a[6]

**Samsamsam** *Robert Cowell* a47 29
2 b c Sakhee's Secret Greenfly (Green Desert (USA))
7412[8] 7840[7]

**Sam Spade (IRE)** *Derek Shaw* a74 48
4 gr g Clodovil(IRE) Red Empress (Nashwan (USA))
75[8] 366[11] 815[7] 922[7] 1081[5] (1228) 1365[3] (1800) 2164[8] (2399) 2841[6] 7830[12] 8086[12] 8282[10]

**Samtu (IRE)** *Clive Brittain* a71 74
3 b c Teofilo(IRE) Samdaniya (Machiavellian (USA))
190[2] 316[4] 828[3] 2769[5] 3146[2] 3986[2] 4584[6] 5878[6] 7305[5]

**Samurai Sword** *A bin Harmash* a106 65
6 b h Motivator Japanese Whisper (UAE) (Machiavellian (USA))
111a[5] 508a[7] 681a[16] (807a) 902a[13]

**Samuraj (FR)** *M Munch* a61 77
4 b g Zamindar(USA) Samando (FR) (Hernando (FR))
(935a) 4776a[10]

**Samyntha (FR)** *M Maillard* a79 78
5 b m Cape Town(USA) Cobblestone Road (USA) (Grindstone (USA))
806a[13]

**Sanaija** *A De Royer-Dupre* 98
3 ch f Pivotal Sanjida (IRE) (Polish Precedent (USA))
7768a[5]

**San Benedetto (USA)** *Gianluca Bietolini* a70
3 b c Two Step Salsa(USA) Northern Trip (USA) (Trippi (USA))
6221a[10]

**San Cassiano (IRE)** *Ruth Carr* a66 95
7 b g Bertolini(USA) Celtic Silhouette (FR) (Celtic Swing)
1196[8] 1539[4] 1724[8] 1926[2] 2137[2] 2423[6] (2790) (3055) 3457[8] (3718) 4667[6] 4888[5] 5238[6] 5792[3] 6098[13] 6479[8] 6943[11] 7211[8]

**Sanctioned** *Robert Stephens* a48 30
5 b g Authorized(IRE) Kazeem (Darshaan)
742[7]

**Sandaura (IRE)** *Clive Cox* a72 46
4 b f Footstepsinthesand Stratospheric (Slip Anchor)
1768[3] 2404[11] 3708[4]

**Sand Dancer (IRE)** *Richard Hannon* 13
3 b f Footstepsinthesand Annacloy Pearl (IRE) (Mull Of Kintyre (USA))
1422[16]

**Sandfield (IRE)** *Paul Midgley* 52
3 b g Kodiac Red Rabbit (Suave Dancer (USA))
6[6]

**Sandfrankskipsgo** *Peter Crate* a89 94
5 ch g Piccolo Alhufoof (USA) (Dayjur (USA))
80[7] (572) 719[5] (1922) (3676) 4179[16] 4762[6] 6467[7] 6923[10]

**Sandgate** *Richard Fahey* 57
2 ch g Compton Place Jump Ship (Night Shift (USA))
2736[6] 3454[5] 4701[6]

**Sandiva (IRE)** *Richard Fahey* 108
3 ch f Footstepsinthesand Miss Corinne (Mark Of Esteem (IRE))
(1515) 1976[9] 3418[5]

**Sandra's Diamond (IRE)** *Keith Dalgleish* 83
3 b f Footstepsinthesand Lucky Us (IRE) (Fayruz)
1968[5] 2295[4] 3460[5] (3956) 4067[2] 4761[19] 5496[10] 6112[7] 6512[13] 6792[7] 7179[6]

**Sands Chorus** *James Given* a64 72
2 b g Footstepsinthesand Wood Chorus (Singspiel (IRE))
3701[3] 6146[3] 6667[8] 7810[5]

**Sandsman's Girl (IRE)** *James Given* a57 49
3 b f Kodiac Inter Madera (IRE) (Toca Madera)
6[5] 232[4] 401[8] 2657[11] 2838[3] 3487[10] 3972[11] 4627[5] 5257[6] 5801[7]

**Sand Stormer (IRE)** *William Muir* a60 5
3 b g Footstepsinthesand Claustra (FR) (Green Desert (USA))
188[5] 422[U] 614[6] 1277[9] 1829[4] 2638[5]

**Sandwith** *Ian Semple* 33
11 ch g Perryston View Bodfari Times (Clantime)
7103[11] 7510[14]

**Sandy Cay (USA)** *Sir Michael Stoute* a83 73
2 gr f Mizzen Mast(USA) Camanoe (USA) (Gone West (USA))
4914[6] (5305) 6749[12]

**Sandy Cove** *James Eustace* a63 69
3 br g Oasis Dream Maganda (IRE) (Sadler's Wells (USA))
665[4] 774[3] 1235[3] (2066) 3326[8] 3683[3] 4085[2] 4911[3] 5123[3] 5520[2] 6037[5] 6787[7]

**Sandy De Luz (FR)** *L Edon* 46
2 b f Namid Absolutely (FR) (Footstepsinthesand)
3170a[5]

**Sandy Duke (FR)** *E Lellouche* 63
2 b c Duke Of Marmalade(IRE) Sandy Light (IRE) (Footstepsinthesand)
5588a[10]

**Sandy Smile (IRE)** *M Halford* a68 64
3 b f Footstepsinthesand Shy Smile (IRE) (Peintre Celebre (USA))
7959a[6]

**Sangster (NZ)** *Trent Busuttin & Natalie Young* 109
6 b g Savabeel(AUS) Quinta Special (IRE) (Spectrum (IRE))
7126a[11]

**Sanjii Danon (GER)** *Gerald Geisler* a89 89
8 b h Big Shuffle(USA) Serpina (IRE) (Grand Lodge (USA))
7618a[6]

**Sannibel** *David Bridgwater* a48 39
6 ch m Needwood Blade Socialise (Groom Dancer (USA))
7025[13] 7376[5] 7737[5] 7864[8]

**San Quentin (IRE)** *Tony Carroll* a59 48
3 gr g Lawman(FR) In The Soup (USA) (Alphabet Soup (USA))
2028[3] ◆ 2247[4] 2694[7] (7664) 7977[2] 8049[3] 8145[9]

**San Remo Rose (IRE)** *Tony Coyle* 44
3 b f Tagula(IRE) Satin Rose (Lujain (USA))
1611[16] 3485[9]

**Sanshaawes (SAF)** *M F De Kock* a113 109
5 b g Ashaawes(USA) Vicario (SAF) (Northern Guest (USA))
309a[4] (593a) (812a) 901a[2] 1183a[7]

**Santadelacruze** *Mark Hoad* a67 64
5 b g Pastoral Pursuits Jupiters Princess (Jupiter Island)
154[9] 7358[14] 7925[2] 8102[3]

**Santa Helena (FR)** *Ana Imaz Ceca* 72
2 ch f Bannaby(FR) Lady Nour (FR) (Valanour (IRE))
5707a[6]

**Sant'Alberto (ITY)** *F Chappet* 103
6 b h Colossus(IRE) Adya (FR) (Sillery (USA))
723a[3]

**Santa Teresa (IRE)** *William Haggas* a85 71
3 b f Cape Cross(IRE) Avila (Ajdal (USA))
5796[5] (6482) 6904[2] 7417[3] 7885[7]

**Santefisio** *Keith Dalgleish* a105 105
8 b g Efisio Impulsive Decision (IRE) (Nomination)
396a[11] 504a[10] 678a[9] 886[4] 1578[3] ◆ 3356[15] 3420[6] 4212[9] 4648[22] 5609[19] 6140[4] 6531[9] 7227[5] 7545[11] 7663[7] 8295[8]

**Santillana (GER)** *Markus Klug* a79 93
5 b m Konigstiger(GER) Sinaada (GER) (Zinaad)
5961a[11]

**Santo Thomas (FR)** *Venetia Williams* 30
8 gr g Chichicastenango(FR) European Style (FR) (Ezzoud (IRE))
1810[8]

**Sanzatu (TUR)** *H Harmanbasi* 99
5 b h Bin Ajwaad(IRE) Red Fact (TUR) (Asakir)
6184a[6]

**Saoi (USA)** *William Knight* a93 94
7 ch g Wiseman's Ferry(USA) Careyes (IRE) (Sadler's Wells (USA))
4184[7] 4832[3] (6366) 6761[2]

**Saon Risk (FR)** *T Castanheira* a67 73
3 b c My Risk(FR) Secret Formula (So Factual (USA))
7269a[7]

**Saphira Silver (IRE)** *James Evans* a44
2 gr f Verglas(IRE) Mean Lae (IRE) (Johannesburg (USA))
2071[0] 2413[8] 3210[8] 3563[9] 5254[4] 6412[9] 6842[12] 7824[7]

**Saptapadi (IRE)** *Brian Ellison* a87 98
8 ch g Indian Ridge Olympienne (IRE) (Sadler's Wells (USA))
1735[6] 2314[5] 2991[6] 3250[2] 4759[10] 5579[10] 6133[11]

**Saraaba (IRE)** *F Head* a80 101
3 ch f New Approach(IRE) Thamarat (Anabaa (USA))
4249a[2] 5479a[9]

**Sarafina** *John Best* a33
2 b f Mullionmileanhour(IRE) Nala (USA) (Lion Heart (USA))
8075[9]

**Saraha** *William Haggas* 64
2 b f Dansili Kareemah (IRE) (Peintre Celebre (USA))
7594[5]

**Sarah Berry** *Chris Dwyer* a64 64
5 b m First Trump Dolly Coughdrop (IRE) (Titus Livius (FR))
313[8] 797[3] 1010[5]

**Sarah Catherine** *Mark Usher* a20 41
2 ch f Monsieur Bond(IRE) Dazzling Daisy (Shareef Dancer (USA))
1571[12] 1788[7] 3467[8] 3967[8] 4302[4] 5823[14]

**Sarah Joyce (IRE)** *John Patrick Shanahan* 77
2 b f The Carbon Unit(USA) The Real Thing (IRE) (Traditionally (USA))
5232[3]

**S Arancha (USA)** *J Hirschberger* 91
5 bb m Arch(USA) Sweet Temper (USA) (Stormy Atlantic (USA))
5938a[12]

**Sarangoo** *Malcolm Saunders* a72 83
6 b m Piccolo Craic Sa Ceili (IRE) (Danehill Dancer (IRE))
1985[6] 2559[4] 3468[6] (4024) 4154[6] 4502[6] 5211[3] 6089[5] 6249[8] 7307[13]

**Saranta** *Richard Fahey* a54 51
3 b f Mount Nelson Oh Hebe (IRE) (Night Shift (USA))
2737[10] 3486[6] 4728[5] 5336[5] 6074[6] 6596[5] 7291[10]

**Saratoga Baby (IRE)** *Peter Fahey* a82 82
6 b m High Chaparral(IRE) Miss Moses (USA) (Gulch (USA))
1078a[11]

**Sardinia (IRE)** *Paul Nolan* 85
4 b g Galileo(IRE) Shouk (Shirley Heights)
3321[17]

**Sarina (GER)** *J Hirschberger* 96
3 b f Lord Of England(GER) Sovereign Baby (IRE) (Cadeaux Genereux)
6183a[5]

**Sarinda** *H-A Pantall* a70 98
3 ch f Dubawi(IRE) Viola Da Braccio (IRE) (Vettori (IRE))
5407a[8]

**Sarista (IRE)** *David Barron* 86
2 b f Kodiac Suffer Her (IRE) (Whipper (USA))
1342[2] ◆ (1732) ◆ 2313[6] 3322[4]

**Sarlat** *Mark Brisbourne* a60 50
3 b f Champs Elysees Midnight Sky (Desert Prince (IRE))
71[6] 198[7] 3326[11] 3950[11] 5075[8] 5846[2] 6647[11] 6946[2] 7188[7] 7292[7] (7868) 7976[5] 8050[7] (8123) 8259[2]

**Sarpech (IRE)** *Sir Mark Prescott Bt* a72 50
3 b g Sea The Stars(IRE) Sadima (IRE) (Sadler's Wells (USA))
3857[7] 4325[8]

**Sarsted** *Hughie Morrison* a74 72
2 b c Paco Boy(IRE) Red Blooded Woman (USA) (Red Ransom (USA))
6551[3] (7198)

**Sartori** *Marjorie Fife* 71
3 b c Elnadim(USA) Little Caroline (IRE) (Great Commotion (USA))
1543[7] 2205[6] (4019) 5055[7] 7640[9]

**Sash Of Honour (IRE)** *Tim Vaughan* a64 63
5 ch g Galileo(IRE) Adoration (USA) (Honor Grades (USA))
581[8]

**Saskia's Dream** *Jane Chapple-Hyam* a68 62
6 b m Oasis Dream Swynford Pleasure (Reprimand)
3125[8] 3895[2] 4431[3] 6995[9] 7364[11] 7887[4] 8195[4]

**Sassaway (IRE)** *Eamonn O'Connell* a90 89
7 ch m Bertolini(USA) Sassari (IRE) (Darshaan)
4557a[9]

**Satanic Beat (IRE)** *Jedd O'Keeffe* a53 87
5 br g Dark Angel(IRE) Slow Jazz (USA) (Chief's Crown (USA))
1377[6] 3574[8] 4454[2] 5633[2]

**Satanicjim (IRE)** *Alain Couetil* a93 95
5 ch h Pivotal Infinity (FR) (Bering)
4561a[6] 5961a[4] 7486a[12]

**Satanic Mills (IRE)** *Nigel Tinkler* 16
2 rg g Dark Angel(IRE) Few Are Chosen (IRE) (Sulamani (IRE))
7123[11] 7407[18]

**Satchville Flyer** *Brett Johnson* a55 49
3 ch g Compton Place Palinisa (FR) (Night Shift (USA))
5862[8] 6483[7] 6788[4] 7197[11] 7376[2] 7548[4]

**Satellite (IRE)** *William Haggas* 102
3 b g Danehill Dancer(IRE) Perihelion (IRE) (Galileo (IRE))
(1738) ◆ 2337[4] 2982[2] 5179[7] 5651[10] 6127[16]

**Satellite Express (IRE)** *David Evans* a57 49
3 ch f Observatory(USA) Composition (Wolfhound (USA))
4539[3] 6765[5] 6988[7] 7704[9] 8090[5] (8181)

**Satin Waters** *Peter Charalambous* a47 50
3 b f Halling(USA) Velvet Waters (Unfuwain (USA))
1382[8] 1793[5] 2694[9] 2997[4] 4617[9] 5106[2]

**Satono Noblesse (JPN)** *Yasutoshi Ikee* 117
4 bb c Deep Impact(JPN) Cry With Joy (JPN) (Tony Bin)
2002a[8]

**Satono Shuren (JPN)** *Akira Murayama* 96
6 bb h Stay Gold(JPN) Red Diamond (JPN) (Erhaab (USA))
7981a[17]

**Saturation Point** *James Toller* a71 50
3 b f Beat Hollow Query (USA) (Distant View (USA))
3712[10] 4435[9] 5186[5] 5865[2] 6338[6] 6856[13] (7292) 7804[3] 8232[6]

**Satwa Laird** *Ann Stokell* a65 80
8 b g Johannesburg(USA) Policy Setter (USA) (Deputy Minister (CAN))
12[5] 201[5] 351[5]

**Saucy Minx (IRE)** *Amanda Perrett* a87 94
4 b f Dylan Thomas(IRE) Market Day (Tobougg (IRE))
1020[5] 1985[3] 2121[2] 2528[2] (2861) 3425[3] 3727[3] 4827[8] (5627) 6068[2] (6302) 7553[8]

**Saumur** *Denis Coakley* a58 56
2 b f Mawatheeq(USA) Sparkling Montjeu (IRE) (Montjeu (IRE))
3467[4] 4541[3]

**Saute** *Mlle K Hoste* a60 70
8 br g Hawk Wing(USA) Lifting (IRE) (Nordance (USA))
3089a[6]

**Savannah Beau** *Marjorie Fife* a53 61
2 b f Major Cadeaux Mancunian Way (Green Desert (USA))
2731[6] 3841[7] (4790) 7362[6]

**Savanna Spring (IRE)** *Timothy Jarvis* a39 49
3 b f Bushranger(IRE) Brogan's Well (IRE) (Caerleon (USA))
3755[8] 5892[6] 7187[9]

**Savanne (IRE)** *A Fabre* a95 108
3 b f Rock Of Gibraltar(IRE) Sevenna (FR) (Galileo (IRE))
(2816a) 3773a[2] 5462a[3] 6956a[9]

**Savant (IRE)** *Sir Michael Stoute* a80 71
3 gr c Oasis Dream Shreyas (IRE) (Dalakhani (IRE))
2497[4] 3315[5] 5039[5] 5884[12]

**Saved By The Bell (IRE)** *David O'Meara* a81 96
4 b g Teofilo(IRE) Eyrecourt (IRE) (Efisio)
1970[9] 2327[2] (2678) (2872) (3205) ◆ 4173[7] 5144[5] 7083[6] 7409[5] 7703[7]

**Saved My Bacon (IRE)** *Chris Dwyer* a53
3 b f Camacho Sally Green (IRE) (Common Grounds)
5531[4] 7652[3] 7865[4] 8133[3] ◆

**Save The Bees** *Declan Carroll* a83 84
6 b g Royal Applause Rock Concert (Bishop Of Cashel)
1345[12] 2131[2] 2351[5] 3139[5] 4113[3] 4921[6] 6672[4] 7008[3] 7366[9]

**Save The Date** *Charles Hills* 18
2 b c Zamindar(USA) Daring Miss (Sadler's Wells (USA))
6928[10]

**Saving Grace (GER)** *Waldemar Hickst* 51
2 b f Manduro(GER) Servenya (GER) (Dashing Blade)
6950a[7]

**Saving Kenny (IRE)** *Roy Arne Kvisla* 84
4 b c Footstepsinthesand Cycle Of Life (USA) (Spinning World (USA))
6387a[10]

**Savoy Showgirl (IRE)** *Michael Bell* 87
2 ch f Kyllachy The Strand (Gone West (USA))
2306[5] (2697) (4178) 5190[7]

**Sawaahel** *Richard Hannon* 74
2 b c Pastoral Pursuits Sheer Indulgence (FR) (Pivotal)
(4864) 5607[11]

**Sawwala** *J R Jenkins* a60 55
4 b f Sakhee(USA) Jawwala (USA) (Green Dancer (USA))
1011[5] 1797[7] 2613[6] 3899[3] 4737[8] 5731[4] 6486[4] 6768[7] 7823[3] 8134[5] 8172[2]

**Saxo Jack (FR)** *Saeed bin Suroor* a91 107
4 b g King's Best(USA) Gamma (FR) (Sadler's Wells (USA))
202a[6] (398a) 812a[3] 3416[13] 4214[10] 6257[9]

**Saxonette** *Linda Perratt* a51 60
6 b m Piccolo Solmorin (Fraam)
1602[11] 1758[10] 2452[6] 4005[3] 4257[3] 4725[3] 5237[5] (5565) 6114[7] 6475[14] 6595[7] 6796[2] 6835[6] 7056[3]

**Saxon Princess (IRE)** *Roger Charlton* a42 55
3 b f Dalakhani(IRE) Rhadegunda (Pivotal)
1582[10] 2026[6] 2416[5] 6635[8]

**Saxony** *Paul Morgan* 32
3 b f Bertolini(USA) Just Down The Road (IRE) (Night Shift (USA))
4564[9] 5005[13]

**Sayaad (USA)** *Kiaran McLaughlin* 111
4 b c Street Sense(USA) Time For A Crown (USA) (Time For A Change (USA))
7613a[14]

**Sayed Youmzain** *Marco Botti* 84
3 b c Dalakhani(IRE) Silver Touch (IRE) (Dansili)
1438[4] (1841) 2496[7] 3675[3]

**Say Something** *Ann Duffield* 34
3 b f Major Cadeaux Eloquent Isle (IRE) (Mull Of Kintyre (USA))
4318[5] 4900[5] 5814[4]

**Saythatagain (IRE)** *Tim Easterby* 60
3 b f Echo Of Light The Oldladysays No (IRE) (Perugino (USA))
4022[9] 4754[5] 5269[9]

**Sbraase** *James Tate* a83 79
3 ch c Sir Percy Hermanita (Hernando (FR))
1509[10] 3159[3] 3464[5] 3667[5] 4593[3] 5320[6] (6722) 7186[3] 7784[2]

**Scafell Pike** *Dr Jon Scargill* a27 22
3 b g Bertolini(USA) Torver (Lake Coniston (IRE))
2525[5] 3074[8] 7921[6]

**Scalambra** *F Rohaut* a67 78
3 ch f Nayef(USA) Seal Bay (IRE) (Hernando (FR))
5368a[6]

**Scallop** *Sir Michael Stoute* a89 91
3 b f Oasis Dream Quiff (Sadler's Wells (USA))
2650[2] ◆ (3602) (5401) 5914[4] 7203[5]

**Scalzo** *Martyn Meade* a71
2 ch c Paco Boy(IRE) Cruinn A Bhord (Inchinor)
7181[2]

**Scamperdale** *Brian Baugh* a69 56
12 br g Compton Place Miss Up N Go (Gorytus (USA))
67[8] 737[3] 1016[9] 1249[5] 1836[6]

**Scarborough (IRE)** *Michael Appleby* a83 88
3 ch f Dandy Man(IRE) Alchimie (IRE) (Sri Pekan (USA))
(1130) (1246) ◆ 1396[5] (1851) 2317[4] 3219[2] 5696[5] 5923[6] 7212[6] 8136[3]

**Scariff Hornet (IRE)** *Sylvester Kirk* a57 42
3 b f Tagula(IRE) Housa Dancer (FR) (Fabulous Dancer (USA))
1422[14] 1768[8] 2061[12] 2688[11] 3389[11] 6946[6] 7292[6] 7517[12] 7844[8]

**Scarlet Bounty (IRE)** *Richard Fahey* 70
2 b f Bahamian Bounty Red Kyte (Hawk Wing (USA))
3330[3] 4129[4] 4723[3] 5637[3] (6610) 6977[6]

**Scarlet Minstrel** *Andrew Balding* 66
2 bb g Sir Percy Sweet Mandolin (Soviet Star (USA))
6653[5] 7230[4]

**Scarlet Plum** *Roger Charlton* a60 57
3 b f Pivotal Scarlet Runner (Night Shift (USA))
1422[12] 2025[5] 2432[9] 6022[3] 6484[7]

**Scarlet Sash** *Henry Candy* a71 65
3 b f Sir Percy Scarlet Buttons (IRE) (Marju (IRE))
4029[3] 7528[7] 7686[4]

**Scatty Cat (IRE)** *Daniel Mark Loughnane* a64 83
4 b f One Cool Cat(USA) Shinko Dancer (IRE) (Shinko Forest (IRE))
6078a[10] 7622[7] 7826[9] 7997[3]

**Scent Of Power** *Anthony Carson* a55 53
2 b f Authorized(IRE) Aromatherapy (Oasis Dream)
3813[3] 4589[5] 5133[7] 6040[5] ◆ 6663[3] 7014[2] 7740[10]

**Scent Of Summer (USA)** *William Haggas* a69
2 bb f Rock Hard Ten(USA) Wild Forest (USA) (Forest Wildcat (USA))
7062[2] ◆ 7254[4]

**Schelm (GER)** *John Quinn* a24 60
12 b g Alwuhush(USA) Shoba (GER) (Local Suitor (USA))
4319[11]

**Schimea (IRE)** *S Smrczek* a71 84
4 b c Footstepsinthesand Subtle Shimmer (Danehill Dancer (IRE))
4776a$^{8}$

**Schmooze (IRE)** *Linda Perratt* a51 71
5 b m One Cool Cat(USA) If Dubai (USA) (Stephen Got Even (USA))
1929$^{8}$ 5172$^{7}$ 6480$^{11}$ 6597$^{5}$ 6825$^{3}$

**School Fees** *Olly Stevens* a64 88
5 b m Royal Applause Cankara (IRE) (Daggers Drawn (USA))
4121$^{4}$ 4892$^{10}$

**Schoolmaster** *Giles Bravery* a35 25
6 b g Motivator Londonnetdotcom (IRE) (Night Shift (USA))
3917$^{10}$

**Schoolofhardrocks (USA)** *David Hofmans* a88 94
3 bb c Rock Hard Ten(USA) Miss Chapin (USA) (Royal Academy (USA))
4230a$^{4}$

**Schottische** *Derek Haydn Jones* a65 62
4 ch f Pastoral Pursuits Calligraphy (Kris)
154$^{5}$ 388$^{2}$ 750$^{8}$ 1085$^{3}$ 1813$^{2}$ 3230$^{3}$ 5273$^{2}$ 6074$^{5}$ 6342$^{12}$ 7288$^{8}$ 7983$^{3}$

**Schulz (GER)** *Markus Klug* 99
4 b c Rail Link Simply Red (GER) (Dashing Blade)
3770a$^{8}$

**Scighera** *Stefano Botti* 98
3 ch f New Approach(IRE) Zina La Belle (Mark Of Esteem (IRE))
2590a$^{2}$

**Scillonian Sunset (IRE)** *Charles Hills* a58 58
3 ch f Teofilo(IRE) Hundred Year Flood (USA) (Giant's Causeway (USA))
1422$^{10}$ 2118$^{5}$ 3315$^{11}$ 7349$^{4}$

**Scimitarra** *Paul Cole* a49
2 gr f Motivator Scrupulous (Dansili)
7399$^{8}$ 7658$^{8}$

**Sciustree** *Marco Botti* a60
2 b c Royal Applause Tia Mia (Dr Fong (USA))
8060$^{6}$ ◆

**Scommettitrice (IRE)** *Nigel Twiston-Davies* a47 53
6 b m Le Vie Dei Colori Hard To Lay (IRE) (Dolphin Street (FR))
100$^{3}$ 201$^{10}$ 274$^{10}$ 7221$^{5}$ 7546$^{7}$

**Scooner (USA)** *Roger Charlton* a48 78
2 ch c Mizzen Mast(USA) Palisade (USA) (Gone West (USA))
6604$^{6}$ 7413$^{3}$

**Scoppio Del Carro** *Andrew Balding* a64 80
3 b g Medicean Sadie Thompson (IRE) (King's Best (USA))
2850$^{4}$ 3421$^{5}$ 4540$^{3}$ 5002$^{2}$ ◆ 5689$^{4}$ (5980) 6323$^{4}$ 7172$^{3}$

**Scoreline** *David O'Meara* a77 73
3 b g Captain Gerrard(IRE) Waterline Twenty (IRE) (Indian Danehill (IRE))
2387$^{2}$ 2675$^{2}$ (2932) 3100$^{5}$ 3972$^{8}$ (4860) 5169$^{4}$ 5389$^{2}$ 6109$^{6}$ 6452$^{8}$ 6843$^{4}$ 7058$^{3}$ 7534$^{7}$ 8082$^{4}$ 8180$^{4}$ (8255)

**Scotland (GER)** *Andrew Balding* 109
3 b g Monsun(GER) Sqillo (IRE) (Bachelor Duke (USA))
1419$^{4}$ 2087$^{3}$ 3417$^{3}$ 4778$^{5}$ 6329$^{12}$

**Scotland Forever (IRE)** *S Seemar* a84 94
4 b g Rock Of Gibraltar(IRE) Wee Mad Snout (IRE) (Soviet Star (USA))
241a$^{10}$

**Scotsbrook Cloud** *David Evans* a18 49
9 gr g Cloudings(IRE) Angie Marinie (Sabrehill (USA))
1740$^{7}$ 5342$^{3}$

**Scots Fern** *Andrew Balding* 64
2 b f Selkirk(USA) Ushindi (IRE) (Montjeu (IRE))
6554$^{6}$ 6868$^{8}$

**Scots Gaelic (IRE)** *John Quinn* a60 85
7 ch g Tomba Harmonic I (USA) (Shadeed (USA))
1935$^{9}$

**Scots Law (IRE)** *Keith Dalgleish* 70
3 b f Lawman(FR) Misaayef (USA) (Swain (IRE))
3300$^{10}$ 4300$^{7}$ 4490$^{7}$

**Scottish (IRE)** *Andrew Balding* 45
2 b g Teofilo(IRE) Zeiting (IRE) (Zieten (USA))
7666$^{13}$

**Scottish Boogie (IRE)** *Seamus Durack* a91 87
7 b g Tobougg(IRE) Scottish Spice (Selkirk (USA))
16$^{2}$ 270$^{4}$

**Scottish Glen** *Patrick Chamings* a87 84
8 ch g Kyllachy Dance For Fun (Anabaa (USA))
56$^{3}$ 2012$^{3}$ 3180$^{4}$ 3861$^{4}$ (4181) 5031$^{3}$ 6334$^{2}$ 6891$^{4}$ 7601$^{6}$

**Scottish Isles** *Michael Easterby* 38
2 ch g Distant Peak(IRE) Choral Singer (Daylami (IRE))
6447$^{10}$ 7245$^{9}$

**Scottish Star** *James Eustace* a89 83
6 gr g Kirkwall Child Star (FR) (Bellypha)
160$^{3}$ (494) (623) 1071$^{2}$ 1553$^{9}$

**Scottish Strand** *James Tate* 80
3 b g Selkirk(USA) Starlit Sands (Oasis Dream)
(5272) 5855$^{9}$

**Scouting (IRE)** *J Hirschberger* a65 83
4 ch f New Approach(IRE) Scatina (IRE) (Samum (GER))
2229a$^{8}$

**Scrafton** *James Bethell* 73
3 b g Leporello(IRE) Some Diva (Dr Fong (USA))
5388$^{7}$ (6117) (6539) 6832$^{2}$ 7247$^{2}$

**Scream Blue Murder (IRE)** *T Stack* 106
4 b f Oratorio(IRE) Holly Blue (Bluebird (USA))
1333a$^{2}$ 1824a$^{5}$ 3284a$^{6}$ 3736a$^{6}$ (5219a) 6549$^{5}$

**Scribe (IRE)** *Andy Turnell* a67 68
6 b g Montjeu(IRE) Crafty Example (USA) (Crafty Prospector (USA))
197$^{2}$ 260$^{2}$ 513$^{5}$ 1485$^{9}$ 2595a$^{3}$ (4107) 4962$^{7}$

**Scripturist** *Bernard Llewellyn*
5 b g Oratorio(IRE) Lambroza (IRE) (Grand Lodge (USA))
1916$^{8}$ 2252$^{12}$

**Scruffy Tramp (IRE)** *John Butler* a89 65
3 br g Kheleyf(USA) Reem One (IRE) (Rainbow Quest (USA))
183$^{3}$ 375$^{4}$ 624$^{6}$ 1278$^{6}$ 1700$^{7}$ 2317$^{19}$ 2401$^{4}$ 2879$^{7}$ 5045$^{5}$ ◆ 5492$^{4}$ ◆ 6154$^{RR}$ 7013$^{RR}$

**Scrutinise** *Ed Dunlop* 68
2 b g Intense Focus(USA) Tetravella (IRE) (Groom Dancer (USA))
7169$^{4}$ 7512$^{5}$

**Scrutiny** *David O'Meara* 88
3 b g Aqlaam Aunty Mary (Common Grounds)
1513$^{13}$ 1937$^{7}$ 3651$^{6}$ 4530$^{5}$ 5198$^{5}$ 5295$^{4}$ 5717$^{7}$ 6932$^{3}$ ◆

**Sculptured (FR)** *Jo Hughes* a51 70
2 b f Archipenko(USA) Kelang (Kris)
2128$^{8}$ 2413$^{7}$ 3550$^{2}$ 4054$^{4}$ 4178$^{4}$ 5293a$^{3}$ 5590a$^{2}$ 5941a$^{4}$ 6244a$^{2}$ 6529$^{7}$

**Scurr Mist (IRE)** *Keith Dalgleish* 67
3 gr g Aussie Rules(USA) Stratospheric (Slip Anchor)
7411$^{10}$

**Scutum (IRE)** *Brian Meehan* 75
2 b g Kodiac Bronze Baby (USA) (Silver Charm (USA))
2777$^{8}$ (3875) 4619$^{4}$ 4944$^{5}$ 5645$^{6}$

**Seachantach (USA)** *S Seemar* a75 103
8 b g Elusive Quality(USA) Subtle Breeze (USA) (Storm Cat (USA))
107a$^{10}$ 393a$^{13}$ 809a$^{7}$

**Sea Cliff (IRE)** *Andrew Crook* a41 33
10 b g Golan(IRE) Prosaic Star (IRE) (Common Grounds)
4533$^{7}$

**Sea Coast (IRE)** *M Halford* a101 92
3 b f Rock Of Gibraltar(IRE) Varna (Efisio)
7579a$^{2}$

**Sea Defence (USA)** *Roger Charlton* a72 97
3 rg g Mizzen Mast(USA) Palisade (USA) (Gone West (USA))
2176$^{3}$ (4147)

**Sea Fantasy** *Jo Crowley* a29
2 b f Paco Boy(IRE) Takarna (IRE) (Mark Of Esteem (IRE))
6032$^{11}$

**Sea Flower (FR)** *J-M Beguigne* 68
3 ch f My Risk(FR) Sea Well (FR) (Pistolet Bleu (IRE))
7722a$^{4}$

**Seaforth (IRE)** *John Joseph Murphy* 80
2 b c Acclamation Hendrina (IRE) (Daylami (IRE))
6053a$^{9}$

**Sea Front (FR)** *E Libaud* a76 98
3 b f Le Havre(IRE) Freedom Herself (FR) (Freedom Cry)
4009a$^{6}$ 7268a$^{6}$

**Seagull (IRE)** *John Gosden* 93
3 b f Sea The Stars(IRE) Caumshinaun (IRE) (Indian Ridge)
1587$^{10}$ (2310) 3085$^{2}$ ◆ 3725$^{2}$

**Seagull Star** *William Haggas* 96
3 b g Sea The Stars(IRE) Dash To The Top (Montjeu (IRE))
1530$^{3}$ ◆ 2087$^{4}$ 3417$^{9}$

**Seaham** *Rod Millman* a75 72
3 b g Myboycharlie(IRE) Be Decisive (Diesis)
564$^{6}$ 1381$^{2}$ 2063$^{6}$ 2638$^{2}$

**Sea Here** *Ralph Beckett* a74 70
3 ch c Sea The Stars(IRE) Look Here (Hernando (FR))
1069$^{3}$ 3197$^{9}$ 3655$^{6}$

**Sealed (USA)** *Gay Kelleway* a83
3 b g Speightstown(USA) Sinister Sister (USA) (Formal Dinner (USA))
194a$^{5}$ 360a$^{3}$ 585a$^{2}$ 720a$^{6}$ 5705a$^{4}$ 6901$^{2}$ 7349$^{5}$ 8005a$^{9}$

**Sealed With A Kiss** *James Fanshawe* a41 71
3 b f Authorized(IRE) Always On My Mind (Distant Relative)
3653$^{6}$ 4500$^{3}$ 5340$^{3}$

**Seal Of Approval** *James Fanshawe* a102 118
5 b m Authorized(IRE) Hannda (IRE) (Dr Devious (IRE))
2315$^{4}$ 3961$^{8}$ 5432$^{3}$ 6255$^{4}$ 7273$^{5}$

**Sealord (GER)** *Christian Sprengel* 63
2 ch c Lord Of England(GER) Sudsee (GER) (Local Suitor (USA))
7145a$^{9}$

**Seal Rock** *John Quinn* a71 87
6 b g Ishiguru(USA) Satin Doll (Diktat)
(5265) 6089$^{8}$ 6346$^{5}$ 7337$^{8}$

**Sea Meets Sky (FR)** *Lady Cecil* 100
4 b f Dansili Sacred Song (USA) (Diesis)
2331$^{2}$ 3111$^{4}$

**Sea Moon** *Robert Hickmott* 120
6 b h Beat Hollow Eva Luna (USA) (Alleged (USA))
7301a$^{18}$

**Seamoor Secret** *Alex Hales* a48 57
2 b f Sakhee's Secret Labaqa (USA) (Rahy (USA))
1314$^{8}$ 1571$^{9}$ 2128$^{5}$ 2436$^{4}$ 3223$^{10}$ 4529$^{6}$ 6888$^{6}$ 7075$^{10}$

**Seamour (IRE)** *Jo Crowley* a86
3 b g Azamour(IRE) Chifney Rush (IRE) (Grand Lodge (USA))
5822$^{2}$ (6677)

**Seamster** *Richard Ford* a82 52
7 ch g Pivotal Needles And Pins (IRE) (Fasliyev (USA))
81$^{4}$ 274$^{2}$ (402) (688) 987$^{3}$ ◆ 2233$^{7}$ 2606$^{12}$ (3392) ◆ (4050) 5601$^{5}$ (6078a) 7357$^{6}$ 7776$^{10}$

**Seanie (IRE)** *David Marnane* a92 103
5 b g Kodiac Cakestown Lady (IRE) (Petorius)
3737a$^{20}$ 4771a$^{17}$

**Sea Of Heaven (IRE)** *Sir Mark Prescott Bt* a58 58
2 b g Sea The Stars(IRE) Maid Of Killeen (IRE) (Darshaan)
6565$^{6}$ 7040$^{5}$

**Sea Of Red** *J S Moore* a62
2 b g Duke Of Marmalade(IRE) Abandon (USA) (Rahy (USA))
6838$^{4}$ 7198$^{3}$

**Sea Queen (USA)** *Christophe Clement* 106
3 bb f Lemon Drop Kid(USA) Dowry (USA) (Belong To Me (USA))
3995a$^{2}$

**Searching (IRE)** *Roger Varian* 74
2 b c Mastercraftsman(IRE) Miracolia (IRE) (Montjeu (IRE))
6300$^{7}$ 7170$^{2}$ 7512$^{4}$

**Searchlight** *Kevin Ryan* a90 90
3 b g Kyllachy Baralinka (IRE) (Barathea (IRE))
62$^{3}$ (213) 1585$^{4}$ 2406$^{3}$ 3067$^{7}$ 3790$^{5}$ (4565) (4847) 5696$^{12}$ 6511$^{12}$ 7101$^{5}$ 7687$^{2}$ (7886) 8025$^{5}$ 8136$^{5}$

**Sea Rebelle** *Jo Crowley* a58
5 b m Cockney Rebel(IRE) Bianca Sforza (Anabaa (USA))
7195$^{7}$ 7349$^{7}$ 7841$^{10}$

**Sea Shanty (USA)** *Richard Hannon* a98 103
4 b g Elusive Quality(USA) Medley (Danehill Dancer (IRE))
(1578) (3244) 3356$^{4}$ 4756$^{14}$ 6257$^{13}$

**Seaside Rock (IRE)** *Keith Dalgleish* a65 65
4 b g Oratorio(IRE) Miss Sacha (IRE) (Last Tycoon)
582$^{5}$ 1168$^{4}$ 1675$^{11}$ 2219$^{10}$ 7805$^{3}$

**Seaside Sizzler** *Ralph Beckett* a94 93
7 ch g Rahy(USA) Via Borghese (USA) (Seattle Dancer (USA))
(1581)

**Seas Of Wells (IRE)** *John M Oxx* 92
3 b f Dansili Kiyra Wells (IRE) (Sadler's Wells (USA))
3167a$^{4}$ 3864a$^{7}$ 4557a$^{7}$

**Sea Soldier (IRE)** *Andrew Balding* a61 64
6 b g Red Ransom(USA) Placement (Kris)
155$^{7}$ 428$^{3}$ ◆ 496$^{8}$ 740$^{7}$ 1215$^{2}$ 1986$^{2}$ 2282$^{2}$ 8103$^{7}$ 8298$^{5}$

**Sea Spear** *David Barron* a63
3 ch g Virtual Fred's Dream (Cadeaux Genereux)
861$^{4}$

**Sea The Bloom** *Sir Michael Stoute* 77
3 b f Sea The Stars(IRE) Red Bloom (Selkirk (USA))
1491$^{2}$ 3174$^{3}$ (3953) 4397$^{5}$

**Sea The Moon (GER)** *Markus Klug* 122
3 bb c Sea The Stars(IRE) Sanwa (GER) (Monsun (GER))
(3293a) (4007a) ◆ 6180a$^{2}$

**Sea Tiger** *Chris Gordon* a57 57
4 b g Tiger Hill(IRE) Possessive Artiste (Shareef Dancer (USA))
988$^{6}$ 6661$^{9}$ 7158$^{4}$ 7785$^{8}$ 8011$^{9}$ 8198$^{6}$

**Sea Vision (IRE)** *Jo Crowley* a77
4 b g Haatef(USA) Fantastic Account (Fantastic Light (USA))
5831$^{9}$ 6677$^{4}$ 7015$^{2}$ 7734$^{5}$ 8099$^{5}$

**Sea Whisper** *Ann Stokell* a46 25
3 ch f Compton Place Starfleet (Inchinor)
3083$^{10}$ 6033$^{8}$ 6494$^{5}$ 6982$^{6}$ 7910$^{6}$ 8085$^{2}$ 8280$^{3}$

**Sea Wolf (IRE)** *Michael Dods* 91
2 b g Amadeus Wolf Rose De France (IRE) (Diktat)
(1712) 2543$^{3}$ 3619$^{3}$ 4218$^{4}$ (5131) 6291$^{7}$ 6933$^{15}$

**Sebastian Beach (IRE)** *Richard Hannon* 88
3 b g Yeats(IRE) Night Club (Mozart (IRE))
1844$^{2}$ (2273) 3183$^{3}$ 3892$^{5}$ (4803) 5356$^{3}$ 5691$^{7}$

**Sebs Sensei (IRE)** *Mark Hoad* a73 47
3 ch g Art Connoisseur(IRE) Capetown Girl (Danzero (AUS))
188$^{4}$ 422$^{6}$ 741$^{2}$ 1008$^{6}$ 3229$^{8}$ 4342$^{7}$ 5427$^{5}$ 6037$^{10}$ 6636$^{11}$ 7347$^{4}$ 7854$^{5}$ 7987$^{7}$

**Secateur** *John Gosden* 79
2 b g Danehill Dancer(IRE) Rose Cut (IRE) (Montjeu (IRE))
6259$^{8}$ 6683$^{4}$ 7134$^{2}$

**Seche (FR)** *L A Urbano-Grajales* a96 90
4 b c Speightstown(USA) Soignee (GER) (Dashing Blade)
5222a$^{5}$

**Secondo (FR)** *Robert Stephens* a99 93
4 b g Sakhee's Secret Royal Jade (Last Tycoon)
1975$^{12}$ 3271$^{7}$ 4892$^{11}$ 5623$^{3}$ 7543$^{3}$ (8045) ◆ 8228$^{3}$

**Second Step (IRE)** *Luca Cumani* 103
3 b g Dalakhani(IRE) My Dark Rosaleen (Sadler's Wells (USA))
(2773) (3892) 4893$^{3}$ 6127$^{7}$ (7144a) ◆

**Second Wave (IRE)** *Charlie Appleby* 73
2 b c New Approach(IRE) Tessa Reef (IRE) (Mark Of Esteem (IRE))
(6668)

**Secret Applause** *Michael Dods* a47 62
3 b f Sakhee's Secret Royal Pardon (Royal Applause)
1611$^{15}$ 3487$^{5}$ 3669$^{6}$ 4019$^{6}$ 4512$^{2}$ 4796$^{9}$ 5631$^{4}$ 6122$^{8}$ 7058$^{5}$ 7420$^{5}$

**Secret Archive (USA)** *Ralph Beckett* a80 82
3 rg g Arch(USA) Mystic Miracle (Dalakhani (IRE))
1586$^{2}$ 2112$^{10}$ 3247$^{10}$ 6886$^{7}$ 7185$^{4}$

**Secret Art (IRE)** *William Knight* a102 94
4 ch g Excellent Art Ivy Queen (IRE) (Green Desert (USA))
1437$^{17}$ (2062) 2707$^{6}$ 3420$^{11}$ 3982$^{6}$ 4761$^{4}$ 5824$^{10}$ 6140$^{2}$ 6892$^{4}$

**Secret Asset (IRE)** *Jane Chapple-Hyam* a87 89
9 gr g Clodovil(IRE) Skerray (Soviet Star (USA))
2778$^{12}$ 3452$^{16}$ 4412$^{6}$ 4765$^{5}$ 7080$^{11}$ 7700$^{9}$ 7889$^{8}$ 8045$^{7}$ 8252$^{3}$

**Secret Beau** *John Spearing* a86 56
4 gr g Sakhee's Secret Belle Reine (King Of Kings (IRE))
294$^{9}$ 2251$^{7}$ 2669$^{5}$

**Secret Brief (IRE)** *Mark Johnston* 101
2 b c Shamardal(USA) Discreet Brief (IRE) (Darshaan)
2359$^{3}$ 4896$^{6}$ ◆ 5655$^{2}$ (6146) (6556) (6925) 7241$^{6}$

**Secret Circle (USA)** *Bob Baffert* a119
5 b h Eddington(USA) Ragtime Hope (USA) (Dixieland Band (USA))
7612a$^{2}$

**Secret City (IRE)** *Robin Bastiman* 77
8 b g City On A Hill(USA) Secret Combe (IRE) (Mujadil (USA))
1309$^{3}$ 1649$^{8}$ 2171$^{6}$ 2451$^{5}$ 3149$^{8}$ 3530$^{13}$ 4070$^{3}$ (4728) 5376$^{10}$ 6122$^{4}$ (6834) 7061$^{8}$ 7249$^{10}$

**Secret Fantasies** *Paul Cole* a23
2 b f Fastnet Rock(AUS) Trinkila (USA) (Cat Thief (USA))
7985$^{7}$

**Secret Friend (IRE)** *Tim Easterby* 62
2 b f Royal Applause Oasis Fire (IRE) (Oasis Dream)
1924$^{4}$ 2349$^{5}$ 4450$^{8}$ (6008) 6253$^{17}$ 7003$^{7}$

**Secret Gesture** *Ralph Beckett* 111
4 b f Galileo(IRE) Shastye (IRE) (Danehill (USA))
2284$^{2}$ (3307) 4682$^{2}$ 5742a$^{3}$ 7607a$^{5}$

**Secret Glance** *Ed McMahon* a75 75
2 b c Sakhee's Secret Look Here's Dee (Dansili)
6489$^{4}$ 7361$^{2}$ 7741$^{2}$ 7920$^{2}$ 8140$^{3}$ 8262$^{3}$

**Secret Hint** *Andrew Balding* a69 92
3 b f Oasis Dream Teeky (Daylami (IRE))
(4111) 4826$^{12}$ 6006$^{4}$ (6689)

**Secret House** *Michael Easterby* 23
2 b f Monsieur Bond(IRE) Villa Del Sol (Tagula (IRE))
3201$^{10}$ 3529$^{11}$ 4449$^{7}$

**Secretinthepark** *Ed McMahon* a84 100
4 ch g Sakhee's Secret Lark In The Park (IRE) (Grand Lodge (USA))
1975$^{6}$ 4188$^{8}$ 4683$^{9}$ 5418$^{3}$ 6207$^{2}$ 6755$^{7}$

**Secret Journey (IRE)** *Hughie Morrison* 64
2 ch g Sakhee's Secret Hinokia (IRE) (Forestry (USA))
2480$^{4}$ 2944$^{3}$

**Secret Kode (IRE)** *Simon Waugh* a13 74
3 b f Kodiac Finty (IRE) (Entrepreneur)
1543$^{9}$ 3833$^{11}$ 4066$^{6}$ 4473$^{10}$ 5084$^{11}$ 6117$^{12}$

**Secret Liaison (IRE)** *James Tate* a78 92
2 b f Dandy Man(IRE) Kiss And Don'Tell (USA) (Rahy (USA))
(2349) 3415$^{12}$ 4083$^{2}$ 4686$^{10}$ 6513$^{4}$ 7238$^{12}$

**Secret Lightning (FR)** *Michael Appleby* a68 63
2 ch f Sakhee's Secret Dimelight (Fantastic Light (USA))
2928$^{2}$ ◆ 3415$^{15}$ 3888$^{6}$ 4967$^{6}$ 5875$^{10}$ (6205) 7075$^{6}$ 7328$^{7}$

**Secret Look** *Ed McMahon* a77 96
4 ch g Sakhee's Secret Look Here's Carol (IRE) (Safawan)
3271$^{9}$ 4061$^{2}$ 4976$^{6}$ 6097$^{5}$ 6740$^{10}$ 7233$^{13}$

**Secret Millionaire (IRE)** *Luke Dace* a73 83
7 b g Kyllachy Mithl Al Hawa (Salse (USA))
87$^{7}$ 296$^{5}$ 470$^{2}$ 576$^{9}$ (845) (987) 1431$^{6}$ 1878$^{2}$ 3033$^{3}$ 3551$^{2}$ (3749) 4284$^{3}$ 4762$^{12}$ 5124$^{5}$ 5945$^{2}$ 6130$^{5}$ 6441$^{2}$ 8171$^{7}$ 8252$^{7}$ 8320$^{7}$

**Secret Missile** *William Muir* a84 92
4 b g Sakhee's Secret Malelane (IRE) (Prince Sabo)
1261$^{3}$ ◆ 1490$^{9}$ 2050$^{3}$ 2645$^{3}$ ◆ 3275$^{6}$ 3551$^{3}$ 4078$^{5}$ 4609$^{2}$ 4946$^{2}$ (5350) (5945) 6923$^{7}$

**Secret Number** *Saeed bin Suroor* a111 115
4 b c Raven's Pass(USA) Mysterial (USA) (Alleged (USA))
6139$^{2}$

**Secret Oasis** *Bryan Smart* 61
3 b f Captain Gerrard(IRE) Annellis (UAE) (Diesis)
1902$^{2}$ 2619$^{P}$

**Secret Of Dubai** *Brian Ellison* 49
2 ch f Sakhee's Secret Dubai Legend (Cadeaux Genereux)
2348$^{7}$ 2895$^{6}$ 3620$^{7}$ 4313$^{5}$ 5335$^{7}$ 6211$^{7}$ 6643$^{10}$

**Secret Pattern** *Ollie Pears*
2 b g Sakhee's Secret Saddlers Bend (IRE) (Refuse To Bend (IRE))
5050$^{P}$

**Secret Pursuit (IRE)** *Marcus Tregoning* a74 106
3 b f Lawman(FR) Secret Melody (FR) (Inchinor)
119$^{2}$ (341) (1400) ◆ 2072$^{2}$ 2484$^{5}$ 3357$^{23}$ (7720a)

**Secret Recipe** *David Nicholls* 77
4 ch g Sakhee's Secret Fudge (Polar Falcon (USA))
3202$^{15}$ 4491$^{9}$ 5178$^{6}$ 5446$^{10}$ 7060$^{10}$

**Secret Sham (AUS)** *J Moore* 111
5 ch g Shamardal(USA) Confidential Miss (AUS) (Rivotious (USA))
7898a$^{4}$ 8153a$^{9}$

**Secret Song** *Sir Mark Prescott Bt* a66
4 b g Singspiel(IRE) Confidante (USA) (Dayjur (USA))
90$^{2}$ 210$^{5}$ 349$^{5}$

**Secret Spirit** *Clive Cox* 76
2 b f Sakhee's Secret Naayla (IRE) (Invincible Spirit (IRE))
2771$^{3}$ 3557$^{2}$ 4439$^{21}$ 5285$^{3}$ 6253$^{8}$ 7378$^{7}$

**Secrets Safe (IRE)** *David Brown* 45
2 b c Arcano(IRE) Keritana (FR) (One Cool Cat (USA))
5760$^{9}$ 6056$^{11}$ 6462$^{7}$

**Secret Success** *Paul Cole* a83 75
4 b g Exceed And Excel(AUS) Magic Music (IRE) (Magic Ring (IRE))
(1385) 1771$^{3}$ 2282$^{10}$ 2646$^{4}$ (2930) 3427$^{11}$ (4072) 4866$^{2}$ 5308$^{13}$ (5834) 7035$^{9}$

**Secret Suspect** *James Tate* a73 69
3 b f Invincible Spirit(IRE) Madura (GER) (Dashing Blade)
(70) 561$^{4}$ 1315$^{2}$ 1507$^{5}$ 3663$^{5}$ 6902$^{8}$

**Secret Talent** *Hughie Morrison* a78 81
4 b g Sakhee's Secret Aqaba (Lake Coniston (IRE))
7227$^{11}$

**Secret Witness** *Ronald Harris* a76 92
8 ch g Pivotal It's A Secret (Polish Precedent (USA))
1193$^{8}$ 2110$^{5}$ 2254$^{8}$ 2283$^{5}$ 2786$^{3}$ 3271$^{11}$ 3732$^{10}$ 4889$^{3}$ 5152$^{3}$ 5419$^{15}$ 5575$^{8}$ 6130$^{10}$ 6260$^{9}$ 6744$^{14}$ 7624$^{8}$ 7947$^{8}$ 8141$^{7}$

**Secular Society** *George Baker* a76 79
4 b g Royal Applause Fantastic Santanyi (Fantastic Light (USA))
(265) 942$^{4}$ 1871$^{11}$ 2876$^{6}$ 3681$^{6}$ (4340) 5031$^{9}$ 6303$^{11}$

**Secure Cloud (IRE)** *Charles Hills* a82 66
3 b g High Chaparral(IRE) Cabo (FR) (Sagamix (FR))
2271[12] 3248[8] 4106[2] (4910) 5185[2] 5670[7]

**See And Be Seen** *Sylvester Kirk* a76 85
4 b g Sakhee's Secret Anthea (Tobougg (IRE))
590[10] 1027[5] 1263[5] (1574) 1895[6] 2774[4] (3234) (3579) 3932[4] (4441) 4685[2] 5825[7] 6360[2] (6557) 7306[4]

**Seebeedee** *Harry Dunlop* a65 62
2 b f Multiplex Border Ballet (IRE) (Noverre (USA))
3933[11] 4499[9] 4999[3] (5489) 5875[5] 6884[9]

**See Clearly** *Tim Easterby* a65 64
5 b m Bertolini(USA) True Vision (IRE) (Pulpit (USA))
1487[6] 1694[2] 2296[7] 2955[10] 3530[10] 3956[6] 4294[7] (5103) 5573[3] 6121[2] 6217[8] 6543[3] 6716[2]

**Seek Again (USA)** *William Mott* a104 115
4 ch c Speightstown(USA) Light Jig (Danehill (USA))
3025a[3] 7613a[9]

**Seek A Star (USA)** *Luca Cumani* a54 70
3 ch f Smart Strike(CAN) Queen Of The Night (Sadler's Wells (USA))
1722[6] 2492[6]

**Seeking Approval (IRE)** *Kevin Ryan* 60
2 b f Approve(IRE) Causeway Charm (USA) (Giant's Causeway (USA))
2386[4] 3358[7]

**Seeking Magic** *Clive Cox* a92 107
6 b g Haafhd Atnab (USA) (Riverman (USA))
1975[9] 2989[2] 3452[11] 4895[10] 6327[8] ◆ 6760[4] 7122[6] 7802[8]

**Seeking The Sherif (USA)** *Ronald W Ellis* a110
5 b g Officer(USA) Seeking Adel (USA) (Seeking The Gold (USA))
7612a[11]

**Seek The Fair Land** *Lee Carter* a79 67
8 b g Noverre(USA) Duchcov (Caerleon (USA))
91[2] 233[5] 287[5] 312[3] 399[3] (602) 757[2] 825[2] (1025) 1261[7] 1796[6] 1921[2] 2157[5] (2469) 2995[4] 3422[8] 3854[3] 4581[3] 5308[12] 5559[6]

**See No Ships** *Mark Usher* a51 48
3 b f Compton Place Queen Of Havana (USA) (King Of Kings (IRE))
2625[4] 2946[8] 3966[7] 4611[4] 5138[8] 5751[7] ◆ 6194[8]

**See The Rock (IRE)** *Mario Hofer* 97
4 b g Shirocco(GER) Samara (IRE) (Polish Patriot (USA))
4006a[8]

**See The Storm** *Ian Williams* a63 85
6 bb g Statue Of Liberty(USA) Khafayif (USA) (Swain (IRE))
646[9] 677[5] 1082[8] 1487[4] (3519) 3848[6] (4471) (4650) 5433[8]

**See The Sun** *Tim Easterby* 100
3 ch g Assertive Cocabana (Captain Rio)
1358[2] 2116[4] (3253) 4166[6] 4683[6] 5575[10] 6327[13] 6745[3] 7080[3]

**See The World (AUS)** *Joseph Pride* 109
8 b g Danzero(AUS) Global Dance (AUS) (Spinning World (USA))
1468a[5]

**See Vermont** *Robin Bastiman* a31 52
6 b g Kyllachy Orange Lily (Royal Applause)
2514[3] 3440[5] 3913[6] 4306[2] 4337[2] (6030) 6120[3] 6595[10]

**See You Soon (FR)** *H-A Pantall* a92 102
3 b c Zafeen(FR) Summer Dance (FR) (Machiavellian (USA))
194a[3] 1272a[6]

**Sefri (USA)** *E Charpy* a94 99
4 b g Jazil(USA) Taseel (USA) (Danzig (USA))
205a[11] 398a[8]

**Seismic (IRE)** *Gordon Elliott* a49 60
4 b g Papal Bull Alifandango (IRE) (Alzao (USA))
221[6] (Dead)

**Seismos (IRE)** *Marco Botti* a112 114
6 ch g Dalakhani(IRE) Sasuela (GER) (Dashing Blade)
1177a[10] 2704[6] 4250a[4] (5432) 7301a[15] 7653a[9]

**Sejel (IRE)** *John Gosden* a70 71
3 b f Cape Cross(IRE) Wajaha (IRE) (Haafhd)
1920[6] ◆ 2682[3] 3277[5] 3916[3]

**Sekuras Girl (IRE)** *Michael Dods* 52
2 b f Approve(IRE) Alinda (IRE) (Revoque (IRE))
3481[3] 6147[4] 6931[5]

**Seldom (IRE)** *Mel Brittain* a61 63
8 b g Sesaro(USA) Daisy Dancer (IRE) (Distinctly North (USA))
1673[8] 2426[4] 2546[9] 3155[7] 3949[8]

**Seldom Seen** *Sir Michael Stoute* a82 74
3 b f Observatory(USA) Rare Virtue (USA) (Empire Maker (USA))
5382[4] (5894) 6681[4] 7136[9]

**Self Employed** *Garry Woodward* a77 83
7 b g Sakhee(USA) Twilight Sonnet (Exit To Nowhere (USA))
647[5] (750) 2131[3] 2462[4] (3272) 3703[8] 3917[2] 4414[2]

**Self Indulgence (FR)** *C Ferland* a73 84
3 bl f Elnadim(USA) In The Woods (You And I (USA))
7026a[9]

**Selfrespect** *Henry Candy* a10
2 b f Thewayyouare(USA) Self Esteem (Suave Dancer (USA))
7752[12] 8036[10]

**Sellingallthetime (IRE)** *Michael Appleby* a77 72
3 ch g Tamayuz Anthyllis (GER) (Lycius (USA))
1588[5] 1661[3] 2319[9] (2934) 3268[8] 3797[4] 4631[5] 5980[4] 6491[3]

**Selma Louise (FR)** *W Mongil* a41 58
3 gr f Stormy River(FR) Starks (FR) (Daylami (IRE))
5589a[4] 7270a[9]

**Semaral (IRE)** *Chris Wall* a90 71
3 b f High Chaparral(IRE) Semaphore (Zamindar (USA))
1233[9] 1612[8] 2025[3] 3268[3] 4303[4] (7012) 7397[3] 7732[2] (7885) 8080[3]

**Semblance** *John Gosden* a65 65
3 b f Pivotal Illusion (Anabaa (USA))
5883[2] 7024[5] 7528[6]

**Semeen** *Luca Cumani* a72 97
5 b g Dubawi(IRE) Zeeba (IRE) (Barathea (IRE))
2142[4] 3341[7] (5162) 5651[14] (6501)

**Semilla (FR)** *A Schaerer* 97
3 b f Dunkerque(FR) Rose Rose (USA) (Cozzene (USA))
3512a[6]

**Senafe** *Marco Botti* a94 98
4 b f Byron Kiruna (Northern Park (USA))
1577[4] 2155[10] 2984[5]

**Senator Bong** *Peter Grayson* a77 64
4 ch g Dutch Art Sunley Gift (Cadeaux Genereux)
91[7] 208[6] 451[9] 4614[3] 5045[6] 8142[8]

**Senator Matt** *John Berry* a46
4 b c Joe Bear(IRE) Anytime Anywhere (Daring March)
8249[5]

**Sendiym (FR)** *Dianne Sayer* 56
7 b g Rainbow Quest(USA) Seraya (FR) (Danehill (USA))
3051[4] 4962[6]

**Sendmylovetorose** *M Halford* 70
4 b f Bahamian Bounty Windy Gulch (USA) (Gulch (USA))
1333a[9]

**Sennockian Star** *Mark Johnston* a99 110
4 ch g Rock Of Gibraltar(IRE) Chorist (Pivotal)
716[7] 1360[3] (1653) 2085[2] 2618[10] 2957[12] 3416[4] 3962[10] 4214[6] (4756) 5688[4] 6321[5] (6532) 7120[9]

**Senora Lobo (IRE)** *Lisa Williamson* a39 48
4 b f Amadeus Wolf Valencia (FR) (Croco Rouge (IRE))
592[8] 799[6] 963[7] 2452[3] 2831[3] 3630[8] 5499[7] 7221[6] 7510[11] 8142[10]

**Senor Firecracker (IRE)** *Brett Johnson* a47 49
2 b g Acclamation Miss Eze (Danehill Dancer (IRE))
4330[11] 4864[7] 5555[7] 6237[9] 6888[8]

**Senor George (IRE)** *Brian Ellison* a68 73
7 b g Traditionally(USA) Mrs St George (IRE) (Orpen (USA))
(3299) 5142[3] 5811[4] 7180[4] 7765[3] ◆

**Sensible Way (USA)** *Richard Hannon* a79 82
3 b f Street Sense(USA) Nasheej (USA) (Swain (IRE))
2780[9] (2967) 3476[7] 8188[4] 8312[5]

**Sentence (SPA)** *G Arizkorreta Elosegui* 70
5 b m Federal Trial(USA) Alameda (FR) (Kabool)
6392a[5]

**Seperate Opinion** *C Zala* 98
5 b m Osorio(GER) Diamond White (Robellino (USA))
7482a[7]

**Sequester** *David Lanigan* a76 66
3 ch f Selkirk(USA) Al Theraab (USA) (Roberto (USA))
2210[4] 3545[4] 4763[4] (5284) 6341[2] 7359[2]

**Sequined (USA)** *Charlie Appleby* a84 89
3 bb f Street Cry(IRE) Sunspangled (IRE) (Caerleon (USA))
(1240) 3476[3] 5074[2] 6681[10]

**Seradora (FR)** *S Smrczek* 73
2 b f Deportivo Serfalya (FR) (Fasliyev (USA))
1402a[6] 3029a[2] 5119a[4] 6619a[4]

**Seraffimo** *Sharon Watt* 41
2 ch g Monsieur Bond(IRE) Hula Ballew (Weldnaas (USA))
4109[11] 4528[6] 5386[11] 6428[8] 7328[5] 7488[3]

**Serans (FR)** *E Lellouche* 99
3 b c Le Havre(IRE) Miss Maybe (IRE) (Hawk Wing (USA))
1481a[7] 6379a[8]

**Seraphima** *Lisa Williamson* a45 60
4 b f Fusaichi Pegasus(USA) Millestan (IRE) (Invincible Spirit (IRE))
3966[10] 5079[11] 5510[4] 6121[13] 7074[10] 8285[7]

**Serata Di Gala (FR)** *Marco Botti* a69 69
3 b f Footstepsinthesand Sea Sex Sun (Desert Prince (IRE))
1853[2] 2329[5] 2525[2] 2686[2] 3855[7]

**Serena (FR)** *N Minner* a79 52
3 ch f King's Best(USA) Sonate Jem (FR) (Fasliyev (USA))
4464a[8]

**Serenade** *Kevin Ryan*
2 b f Oratorio(IRE) After You (Pursuit Of Love)
8220[U]

**Serena Grae** *Marcus Tregoning* a80 92
3 gr f Arakan(USA) Success Story (Sharrood (USA))
1237[4] 3516[2] (4152) (4845) 5123[5] 6315[2] (6654) (7020) 7203[9]

**Serene Abella** *Rod Collet* a75
3 ch f Manduro(GER) Lady Lindsay (IRE) (Danehill Dancer (IRE))
4838a[8]

**Serenity Spa** *Tony Carroll* a89 85
4 gr f Excellent Art Molly Mello (GER) (Big Shuffle (USA))
118[4] 369[5] (952) 1392[2] 2024[2] 2121[4] 2448[3] (3384) 3920[6] 4741[3] 5437[7] (5776) 6929[7] 7802[6] (7873a)

**Sergeant Pink (IRE)** *Dianne Sayer* a63 66
8 b g Fasliyev(USA) Ring Pink (USA) (Bering)
609[9] 1763[4] 2139[8] 2424[7] 3365[3] (4964) (5090) 5270[3] 6480[12]

**Serpentin (FR)** *D Prod'Homme* 63
2 b c Orpen(USA) Serandine (IRE) (Hernando (FR))
5616a[4]

**Serrella (FR)** *J Van Handenhove* 41
3 b f Dr Fong(USA) Belle D'Argent (USA) (Silver Hawk (USA))
2978a[13]

**Sertorius (AUS)** *Jamie Edwards & Bruce Elkingto* 114
7 b g Galileo(IRE) Pretty Penny (AUS) (Encosta De Lago (AUS))
7127a[9] 7395a[8]

**Servery** *Richard Hannon* 79
2 b g Sir Percy Heat Of The Night (Lear Fan (USA))
4207[6] 4884[3] 5393[5] 6331[7]

**Sessions (AUS)** *Peter Snowden* 114
5 br h Lonhro(AUS) Seances (AUS) (Canny Lad (AUS))
1468a[10]

**Setai** *Brian Meehan* a59 35
3 b f Dubawi(IRE) Zietory (Zieten (USA))
1832[12]

**Set The Trend** *David Dennis* a85 87
8 br g Reset(AUS) Masrora (USA) (Woodman (USA))
1174[4] 1719[14] 2336[9] 2758[12] 3244[9] 3969[7] 4982[2] 5274[3] 5686[7] 6057[9] 6466[7] 6498[7] 6990[8] (7373) 7533[2] 7568[5] 7732[10]

**Settle For Red (IRE)** *Jeremy Gask* a67 51
4 ch g Redback Balmy Choice (IRE) (Balla Cove)
2646[10] 3112[7] 5899[7] 6243[7] 6857[3] 7252[3] 7644[8]

**Seve** *Tom Dascombe* 81
2 ch c Exceed And Excel(AUS) Flamenco Dancer (Mark Of Esteem (IRE))
(3215) ◆

**Seven Lucky Seven** *Michael Herrington* a70 71
3 b g Avonbridge Moon Bird (Primo Dominie)
665[3] ◆ 816[3] 1669[6] 2447[4] (3087) 3380[6] 3946[4] 6568[7] 6902[11] 7621[3] ◆ 7950[2] 8090[2] 8143[5]

**Severiano (USA)** *Alan McCabe* a72 62
4 b g Danehill Dancer(IRE) Time Control (Sadler's Wells (USA))
319[3] 589[8] 1440[7] 1873[3] 2400[5] 3123[7] 4473[5] 5421[10] 5797[10]

**Severn Crossing** *William Muir* a67
3 br g Authorized(IRE) Croeso Cariad (Most Welcome)
2081[6] 2883[10] 4658[7] 5006[10] 6883[12] 7292[10]

**Sewn Up** *Keith Dalgleish* a75 59
4 ch c Compton Place Broughton Bounty (Bahamian Bounty)
20[4] 102[6] 319[7] 347[3] 432[3] 766[8] 835[7] 938[3] 1148[4] (1282) 1312[4] 1448[5] 1813[3] 2127[14] 2435[5] 3393[3] 4049[3] 4101[3] 4314[6] 4728[4] 5265[5] 5635[3] 6014[9] 6405[8] 6475[2] 6819[6] 7364[3] (7424) (7621) 7905[2] 6835[8] 7056[5] 8142[2]

**Sexy Legs** *David Wachman* 83
2 b f Dutch Art Classic Lass (Dr Fong (USA))
3415[9]

**Sexy Secret** *Lydia Pearce* a69 52
3 b g Sakhee's Secret Orange Walk (IRE) (Alzao (USA))
1855[3] 2078[9] 2526[3] 2878[5] 3380[7] 3971[7] 4304[6] 5030[2] 5865[7] (6015) 6635[3] 7001[4] 7527[3] 7799[2] 8103[10] 8232[4]

**Seychelloise** *Sir Mark Prescott Bt* a63 57
2 b f Pivotal Starlit Sands (Oasis Dream)
7114[5] 7491[3] 7649[3] 7840[2] 8222[3]

**Seyfeddine (IRE)** *R Le Gal* a82 95
4 ch c Tot Ou Tard(IRE) Safayeli (TUR) (Down The Flag (USA))
5546a[9]

**Sgomma (IRE)** *Pamela Demuro* 50
4 b f Windsor Knot(IRE) Liberty Grace (IRE) (Statue Of Liberty (USA))
1477a[8]

**Shaakis (IRE)** *Marcus Tregoning* 76
2 bg g Dark Angel(IRE) Curious Lashes (IRE) (Footstepsinthesand)
2776[7] (4044) 4897[5] 5645[3] ◆ 6331[5]

**Shabra Emperor (IRE)** *Patrick O Brady* a73 59
5 b g Holy Roman Emperor(IRE) Fearn Royal (IRE) (Ali-Royal (IRE))
6078a[5]

**Shackled N Drawn (USA)** *Olly Stevens* a75 73
2 b c Candy Ride(ARG) Cajun Flash (USA) (Bertrando (USA))
1977[5] 3889[4] 7454[2] 7771[3] (7881) 8059[3] (8170)

**Shadarpour (IRE)** *Alan King* a70 71
5 b g Dr Fong(USA) Shamadara (IRE) (Kahyasi)
214[2] 7946[3]

**Shades Of Grey** *Clive Cox* a56 79
7 gr m Dr Fong(USA) Twosixtythreewest (FR) (Kris)
2693[2] 3086[7] 4948[5] 5878[8] 7452[2]

**Shades Of Silk** *James Given* a77 71
3 b f Bahamian Bounty Terentia (Diktat)
355[10] 930[7] 1962[5] (2397) ◆ (2931) 3406[4] 4411[2] 5080[2] 5389[8] (5994) 6872[8] 7697[3] 7906[9] 8182[2]

**Shades Of Silver** *Michael Scudamore* a74 66
4 b g Dansili Silver Pivotal (IRE) (Pivotal)
1355[10] 1909[8] 2801[7] 4420[6] (5291) (5529) 6091[3] (6682)

**Shadow Of The Day** *Lee James* 9
7 b g Sugarfoot She Who Dares Wins (Atraf)
1608[11] 2902[6] 4022[12]

**Shadow Rock (IRE)** *Richard Hannon* 80
2 gr c Verglas(IRE) Ice Rock (IRE) (Rock Of Gibraltar (IRE))
4666[11] 5646[2] ◆ 6293[4] 6653[2] (7134) 7595[6]

**Shadows Ofthenight (IRE)** *Mick Channon* 73
3 b f Fastnet Rock(AUS) Madaen (USA) (Nureyev (USA))
2280[5] ◆ 2613[4] 3877[3] 4392[6] 5670[3] 6461[3] 6832[6]

**Shadowtime** *Tracy Waggott* a73 88
9 b g Singspiel(IRE) Massomah (USA) (Seeking The Gold (USA))
1881[7] 2017[2] 2603[5] 3190[6] 3572[10] (3791) 4290[8] (4753) 5054[2] 5915[12]

**Shady McCoy (USA)** *Ian Williams* a33 59
4 b g English Channel(USA) Raw Gold (USA) (Rahy (USA))
1967[10] 7212[11] 7505[11] 7729[10] 8122[12]

**Shaf (IRE)** *Ed Dunlop* a65 40
3 b c Medaglia d'Oro(USA) Jaish (USA) (Seeking The Gold (USA))
4130[10] 4978[6] 5606[5]

**Shafrah (IRE)** *Richard Hannon* a85 90
3 b c Acclamation Rosy Dudley (IRE) (Grand Lodge (USA))
(1069) 3243[3] 5430[7] 6688[9]

**Shaft Of Light** *Derek Shaw* a64 57
3 b g Exceed And Excel(AUS) Injaaz (Sheikh Albadou)
3677[4] 4263[9] 5492[8] 5820[4] (8230)

**Shagah (IRE)** *Richard Hannon* a63 103
2 b f Invincible Spirit(IRE) Propaganda (IRE) (Sadler's Wells (USA))
2918[4] 4202[2] (4825) 6126[3] 6289[3] 6926[4] 7448[2]

**Shahah** *A Fabre* 105
2 b f Motivator Elegant Beauty (Olden Times)
3648[2] 4781[3] 5746[3] (6219a) 6967a[12]

**Shahdaroba (IRE)** *Micky Hammond* a97 91
4 b g Haatef(USA) Gold Script (FR) (Script Ohio (USA))
1442[13] 1957[3] 2869[5] 3251[12] 3573[13] 3703[3] (4414) 4635[8] 4681[10] 6226[7] 6639[8] 7784[9]

**Shahralasal (IRE)** *Roger Varian* a63 74
2 b f Oasis Dream Khulood (USA) (Storm Cat (USA))
3223[2] 3648[4] 4403[12] 6104[7]

**Shahrazad (IRE)** *Patrick Gilligan* a72 61
5 b m Cape Cross(IRE) Khulasah (IRE) (Darshaan)
1385[11] (1857) 3310[8] 3577[6] 4073[5] 5041[9] 5256[7]

**Shake Baby Shake** *Bill Turner*
5 b m Reel Buddy(USA) Sheik'n Swing (Celtic Swing)
5907[7]

**Shakespeare Dancer** *James Evans*
5 b m Norse Dancer(IRE) Sharbasia (IRE) (King's Best (USA))
6027[6]

**Shakopee** *Luca Cumani* 80
2 b c High Chaparral(IRE) Tentpole (USA) (Rainbow Quest (USA))
6190[2] ◆ (7170)

**Shalabina** *Richard Fahey* 73
2 b f Nayef(USA) Shibina (IRE) (Kalanisi (IRE))
5416[2] ◆

**Shalaman (IRE)** *Denis Gerard Hogan* a89 89
5 b g Oratorio(IRE) Shalama (IRE) (Kahyasi)
2314[11]

**Shalambar (IRE)** *Tony Carroll* a71 83
8 gr g Dalakhani(IRE) Shalama (IRE) (Kahyasi)
293[7] 430[2] 590[3] (656) 818[2] 992[8] 1262[3] 6019[4] 7129[13] (7532) 7962a[4] 8070[3]

**Shalianzi (IRE)** *Gary Moore* a71 76
4 b g Azamour(IRE) Shalama (IRE) (Kahyasi)
115[3] (581) 7129[14]

**Shalimah (IRE)** *Clive Cox* 82
2 br c Dark Angel(IRE) Jemima's Art (Fantastic Light (USA))
5351[4] ◆ (5718) 7041[4]

**Shama (IRE)** *Sir Michael Stoute* a83 86
3 b f Danehill Dancer(IRE) Shamadara (IRE) (Kahyasi)
(1258) 2255[8] 6746[4] 7110[10]

**Shamahan** *Luke Dace* a77 78
5 b g Shamardal(USA) Hanella (IRE) (Galileo (IRE))
4983[6] 5595[4] 6006[3] 6313[5] 6657[9] 7357[4] 7776[5]

**Shamaheart (IRE)** *Geoffrey Harker* a74 78
4 b g Shamardal(USA) Encouragement (Royal Applause)
1306[6] 1881[3] 2054[10] 2519[7] 3400[4] 4023[4] (4523) 5562[4] 6217[3] 6625[5] 7183[5] 7624[6] 7906[4] 8168[6]

**Shamal (FR)** *Y-M Porzier* 98
2 b c Siyouni(FR) Sagalix (FR) (Linamix (FR))
7655a[9]

**Shamal** *John Gosden* a47
4 b g Exceed And Excel(AUS) Miss Meltemi (IRE) (Miswaki Tern (USA))
6634[7]

**Shamar (FR)** *W P Mullins* 94
6 br g Dr Fong(USA) Shamalana (IRE) (Sinndar (IRE))
4771a[13]

**Shamardyh (IRE)** *David Evans* a65 59
3 b f Shamardal(USA) State Secret (Green Desert (USA))
86[2] 149[3] 315[4] 531[2] (614)

**Shama's Crown (IRE)** *Jeremy Noseda* 85
3 ch f New Approach(IRE) Classic Park (Robellino (USA))
4886[2] (5504) 6460[3] 6990[11]

**Shama's Song (IRE)** *Sir Michael Stoute* a66 78
3 b f Teofilo(IRE) Green Dollar (IRE) (Kingmambo (USA))
1841[2] 2279[4] 3154[2] 4504[5] 6282[2]

**Shamazing** *Kevin Ryan* a42 27
2 b f Makfi Rababah (USA) (Woodman (USA))
4570[10] 7944[8] 8220[5]

**Shamdarley (IRE)** *Marco Botti* a93 89
6 b g Shamardal(USA) Siphon Melody (USA) (Siphon (BRZ))
426[7] 559[6]

**Shamexpress (NZ)** *Danny O'Brien* 118
5 b h O'Reilly(NZ) Volkrose (NZ) (Volksraad)
1468a[7]

**Shamiana** *Daniel Kubler* a55 63
4 bb f Manduro(GER) Camp Riverside (USA) (Forest Camp (USA))
671[3] 833[3] 1138[3] 1865[6] 2092[11] 7376[7] 7785[5] 8123[10]

**Shamiya (IRE)** *J S Moore* a30 30
2 b f Acclamation Fully Fashioned (IRE) (Brief Truce (USA))
5248[7] 5725[9] 6032[10]

**Shamkala (FR)** *A De Royer-Dupre* 111
3 b f Pivotal Shamakiya (IRE) (Intikhab (USA))
(2267a) 3289a[4] 5462a[8] 6969a[7]

**Shamkhani** *Alan Berry* 46
2 b c Mullionmileanhour(IRE) Matilda Peace (Namaqualand (USA))
2214[7] 2736[8] 3337[4] 3713[7] 5384[7] 5922[8] 6211[13] 7497[14]

**Shamkiyr (FR)** *A De Royer-Dupre* 113
3 b c Sea The Stars(IRE) Shemaya (IRE) (Darshaan)
2818a[2] 4483a[4]

**Shamouti (IRE)** *Ollie Pears* a30 50
3 ch f Duke Of Marmalade(IRE) Pitrizza (IRE) (Machiavellian (USA))
2165[11] 2679[5] 3098[7] 3545[3] 4014[9]

**Shamrock Sheila (IRE)** *J S Moore* a63 72
2 ch f Fast Company(IRE) Green Vision (IRE) (Green Desert (USA))
*1314[7]* 3312[2] 3744a[8] (4449) *(4542)* 4920[2] 5770[7] 6513[13] *7255[5]* *7363[8]*

**Shamshon (IRE)** *Richard Hannon* 109
3 b c Invincible Spirit(IRE) Greenisland (IRE) (Fasliyev (USA))
(2287) 2767[4]

**Shanawest (FR)** *C Scandella* a74 64
2 b f Kingsalsa(USA) Anawest (IRE) (Anabaa (USA))
5941a[5]

**Shanghai Sunrise** *Keiran Burke* a35 20
3 b f Royal Applause Duchcov (Caerleon (USA))
3276[8] *7686[9]* *8020[8]*

**Shankly** *Clive Cox* 81
3 br g Monsun(GER) Miracle Seeker (Rainbow Quest (USA))
1419[7] 3466[4]

**Shannon Haven (IRE)** *Daniel Mark Loughnane* a61 29
3 b g Oratorio(IRE) Red Shoe (Selkirk (USA))
*70[8]* *355[6]* *(577)* *743[2]* *1029[2]* *1098[4]* 3326[12] *4084[10]*

**Shanooan (USA)** *George Kent* a87 93
3 ch f English Channel(USA) Bright Generation (IRE) (Rainbow Quest (USA))
4276a[10] 5955a[9] *7579a[8]*

**Shanti** *Michael Bell* a71 25
4 b g Dansili Maycocks Bay (Muhtarram (USA))
1691[6] 2270[16]

**Shaolin (IRE)** *Seamus Durack* a89 84
4 b g Footstepsinthesand Baboosh (IRE) (Marju (IRE))
*52[3]* ◆ *(245)* *493[2]* *587[9]* *(1217)* 1796[3] 2341[2] *(2919)* 4146[13] 4892[17]

**Shared Account** *P Bary* 106
4 br f Dansili Imbabala (Zafonic (USA))
5462a[4] 6218a[3] 6956a[4]

**Shared Belief (USA)** *Jerry Hollendorfer* a128
3 bb g Candy Ride(ARG) Common Hope (USA) (Storm Cat (USA))
*(5781a)* *7614a[4]*

**Shared Equity** *Jedd O'Keeffe* 98
3 b g Elnadim(USA) Pelican Key (IRE) (Mujadil (USA))
(1304) (1884) ◆ (5385) ◆ 7233[2]

**Sharestan (IRE)** *Saeed bin Suroor* 113
6 b g Shamardal(USA) Sharesha (IRE) (Ashkalani (IRE))
(2705) 3450[5]

**Share The Dosh** *J R Jenkins* a42
6 ch m Doyen(IRE) Lady Starlight (IRE) (Almutawakel)
*13[P]*

**Sharin (GER)** *Markus Klug* 82
3 b f Areion(GER) Sisika (IRE) (King's Theatre (IRE))
5965a[10]

**Sharissima** *Lady Cecil* a62
2 ch f Shamardal(USA) Purissima (USA) (Fusaichi Pegasus (USA))
*6852[3]* *7345[7]*

**Sharjah (IRE)** *Andrew Slattery* a78 68
4 b g Shamardal(USA) Lunar Lustre (IRE) (Desert Prince (IRE))
*7435a[2]* *7962a[2]*

**Sharp Lookout** *Roger Charlton* a74 55
3 b g Shamardal(USA) Tempting Prospect (Shirley Heights)
3814[7] *7401[5]*

**Sharp Sailor (USA)** *Marco Botti* a90 85
2 b c Henrythenavigator(USA) Lady Ilsley (USA) (Trempolino (USA))
3474[5] *(5184)* *6241[2]* *6853[2]* 7331[5]

**Sharp Shoes** *Christopher Wilson* a28 30
7 br g Needwood Blade Mary Jane (Tina's Pet)
4288[12]

**Sharp Volley (IRE)** *Stuart Williams* 78
3 b c Shamardal(USA) Policalle (FR) (Poliglote)
(2025) ◆

**Sharqeyih** *William Haggas* a68 78
2 br f Shamardal(USA) Shabiba (USA) (Seeking The Gold (USA))
7108[2] *7550[2]*

**Shar Shar (IRE)** *Brian Ellison* a66 57
2 ch f Majestic Missile(IRE) Miss Amadeus (IRE) (Mozart (IRE))
3312[4] *5799[6]* *6271[2]*

**Shasag (IRE)** *Roger Varian* 15
2 b f Arcano(IRE) Popolo (IRE) (Fasliyev (USA))
6754[11]

**Shasta Daisy** *Lady Cecil* a75 62
3 ch f Champs Elysees Bouvardia (Oasis Dream)
1280[10] *1768[2]* *2929[5]* 3895[3]

**Shatin Secret** *Noel Wilson* a53 43
4 b g Sakhee's Secret Al Corniche (IRE) (Bluebird (USA))
3908[16]

**Shaunas Spirit (IRE)** *Dean Ivory* a79 50
6 b m Antonius Pius(USA) Shaunas Vision (IRE) (Dolphin Street (FR))
*118[6]* *376[10]* *587[8]* *746[5]* *(924)* *1217[7]* *6414[8]* *6890[10]* 7222[3] *7530[9]* 8185[10]

**Shavansky** *Rod Millman* a96 90
10 b g Rock Of Gibraltar(IRE) Limelighting (USA) (Alleged (USA))
*54[6]* *344[4]* *533[2]* *840[7]* *(956)* *1171[4]* *3860[5]* 4819[3] 5379[4] ◆

**Shawkantango** *Derek Shaw* a79 42
7 b g Piccolo Kitty Kitty Cancan (Warrshan (USA))
*(93)* *318[3]* *549[2]* *730[4]* *1127[8]* 7534[15] *7949[8]* *8180[3]*

**Shawnee Saga (FR)** *W Mongil* a65 95
9 b g Sagacity(FR) Shawnee (GER) (Dashing Blade)
920a[10]

**Shaw Ting** *Tom Dascombe* a73 75
2 b f Winker Watson Shawhill (Dr Fong (USA))
5774[4] 6208[4] ◆ *6840[2]* 7156[5]

**Shayboob (IRE)** *N Clement* 77
3 ch c Rock Of Gibraltar(IRE) Perfidie (IRE) (Monsun (GER))
2290a[4]

**Shearian** *Tracy Waggott* a48 68
4 b g Royal Applause Regal Asset (USA) (Regal Classic (CAN))
1610[6] 2019[10] ◆ 2427[2] 3439[5] 3791[5] 4468[5] 5142[7] 5640[8] 6121[8] 6670[5]

**Shea Shea (SAF)** *M F De Kock* 123
7 b g National Emblem(SAF) Yankee Clipper (SAF) (Jallad (USA))
(897a) 1179a[3] 3319[11] 5654[12]

**She Bang (FR)** *Jean-Pierre Carvalho* 71
3 b f Monsun(GER) Servenya (GER) (Dashing Blade)
1619a[10]

**Sheer Poetry (IRE)** *Mike Murphy* a57 56
3 b f Yeats(IRE) Sassari (IRE) (Darshaan)
2850[7] 3652[6] 4617[4] 5529[6] *6015[2]*

**Sheikh The Reins (IRE)** *John Best* a76 72
5 b g Iffraaj Wychwood Wanderer (IRE) (Barathea (IRE))
*245[8]* *555a[6]* *638a[8]* *728a[5]* *817[3]* *925[5]* *1026[7]* 1613[3] 2341[3] *(2884)* 3646[8] 4408[3] 4650[11] 5729[8] 6240[13] 7530[10] 7759[14] 8251[8]

**Sheikhzayedroad** *David Simcock* 115
5 b g Dubawi(IRE) Royal Secrets (IRE) (Highest Honor (FR))
(205a) 598a[3] 900a[6] 1177a[9] 2705[2] (3722) (4682) (6390a) 7275[6]

**Sheila Belle (IRE)** *J S Moore* a40 41
2 b f Alfred Nobel(IRE) Fantastic Belle (IRE) (Night Shift (USA))
5212[4] *6602[10]* *7816[7]* *7992[8]*

**Sheila's Buddy** *J S Moore* a85 84
5 ch g Reel Buddy(USA) Loreto Rose (Lahib (USA))
1439[5] 1871[10] 2248[4] 2627[2] 3196[6] (3815) 4761[17] 5669[5] 6523[3] 6713[22] *8042[2]* *8194[4]*

**Sheila's Castle** *Sean Regan* a55 59
10 b m Karinga Bay Candarela (Damister (USA))
3546[7] 4319[U]

**Sheila's Heart** *John E Long* a69 32
4 ch g Dubai Destination(USA) Sefemm (Alhaarth (IRE))
*97[2]* *1088[3]* *6899[3]* *7204[8]* *7760[3]* *8208[5]*

**She Is No Lady** *Ralph Beckett* 81
2 b f Lope De Vega(IRE) Capestar (IRE) (Cape Cross (IRE))
7206[2] 7596[7]

**Sheldon (USA)** *James J Toner* 103
3 ch c Purim(USA) Golden Disk (USA) (Diesis)
3994a[5] 5458a[3] 6949a[7]

**Shelford (IRE)** *Michael Appleby* a95 91
5 b g Galileo(IRE) Lyrical (Shirley Heights)
*(16)* *462[4]*

**Shell Bay (USA)** *Richard Hannon* a70 63
2 b c Hard Spun(USA) Rebel Account (USA) (Dixieland Band (USA))
7413[5] *7752 [4]*

**Shell House (IRE)** *A P O'Brien* 99
3 b f Galileo(IRE) Bonnie Byerly (USA) (Dayjur (USA))
5024a[3] 6370a[6] 7144a[13]

**She Loves You** *A De Royer-Dupre* a68 84
3 b f Lawman(FR) On Fair Stage (IRE) (Sadler's Wells (USA))
5589a[2]

**Shepherd's Purse** *Joseph G Murphy* 105
2 b c Pastoral Pursuits Neyraan (Lujain (USA))
5954a[4] 7655a[7]

**Sheriff Of Nawton (IRE)** *David O'Meara* a77 76
3 b g Lawman(FR) Pivotal Role (Pivotal)
*614[7]* *696[4]* *930[8]* (1647) (1906) 2391[2] 5245[6] 6166[8] 7172[10] *8122[6]* ◆ *(8260)*

**Sherjawy (IRE)** *Zoe Davison* a58 45
10 b g Diktat Arruhan (IRE) (Mujtahid (USA))
*114[8]* *274[5]* *402[4]* *586[9]* *798[7]*

**Sherlock (GER)** *M Rulec* 104
2 b c Areion(GER) Sun Valley (GER) (Lando (GER))
7145a[2] 7557a[3]

**Sherman McCoy** *Marjorie Fife* a65 83
8 ch g Reset(AUS) Naomi Wildman (USA) (Kingmambo (USA))
*16[7]* 1377[9] 2052[2] 2259[7] (2950) 3250[6] 4015[6] 6541[3]

**Sherry For Nanny (IRE)** *Marjorie Fife* 50
3 b f Amadeus Wolf Sugars For Nanny (USA) (Brocco (USA))
*3792[10]* 4314[4] 4627[11] 5858[6] 6819[9]

**Sherston** *Mark Johnston* a68 75
3 b g Shamardal(USA) Shersha (IRE) (Priolo (USA))
*847[3]* *1149[4]* *1389[6]* 1947[3] 3135[8] 3603[3] 3814[2] 3979[5]

**She's A Honey** *Kevin Morgan* a42 46
4 ch f Firebreak Manuka Too (IRE) (First Trump)
*581[7]* *1012[9]*

**She's A Lucky Lady** *Bill Turner* a26 2
3 ch f Avonbridge Lady Killer (IRE) (Daggers Drawn (USA))
*140[6]* *373[7]*

**She's A Pistol (IRE)** *P J Prendergast* a53 82
2 b f Danehill Dancer(IRE) Foofaraw (USA) (Cherokee Run (USA))
2856a[7]

**Shesastar** *David Barron* 90
6 b m Bahamian Bounty Celestial Welcome (Most Welcome)
1191[12] 3573[9] 3917[9]

**She's A Worldie (IRE)** *Bryan Smart* 92
2 b f Kodiac Petite Boulangere (IRE) (Namid)
3656[3] (3909) 4920[3] 5608[7] 6286[8] 6739[4] 7099[3]

**She's Gorgeous (IRE)** *James Fanshawe* a75 76
3 b f Acclamation Acquiesced (IRE) (Refuse To Bend (IRE))
1394[7] 2129[4] 2749[3] 3974[6] 5150[4] *(6033)* *6681[3]*

**She's Not Simple (IRE)** *Patrick Martin* a68 71
4 b f Holy Roman Emperor(IRE) Sheer Elegance (IRE) (Pivotal)
5958a[RR]

**She's Some Girl (IRE)** *Ian Semple*
4 ch f Camacho Tea Service (IRE) (Roi Danzig (USA))
1761[11]

**Shiftin Bobbins** *Michael Dods* a48 54
3 b f Selkirk(USA) Rhythm Queen (IRE) (Danehill Dancer (IRE))
4363[4] 5234[2] 6010[4] *7188[10]*

**Shifting Moon** *Hughie Morrison* a49 26
2 b f Kheleyf(USA) Fleeting Moon (Fleetwood (IRE))
*7367[11]* 7450[14] *7833[9]*

**Shifting Power** *Richard Hannon* 117
3 ch c Compton Place Profit Alert (IRE) (Alzao (USA))
(1514) 1951[4] 2571a[2] 4278a[2] 4850[5]

**Shifting Star (IRE)** *John Bridger* a69 75
9 ch g Night Shift(USA) Ahshado (Bin Ajwaad (IRE))
*52[9]* *451[10]* *496[2]* *628[4]* *1017[5]* *1217[4]* *1385[3]* *1771[4]* 2124[5] *(2463)* 2884[3] 3328[2] (3805) 4355[2] 4907[6] 5308[9] 5686[8] 6191[3] 6657[8] 6999[2] 7340[3] 7633[6] 7842[5] 8298[8]

**Shikari** *Robin Bastiman* 57
3 ch g Sakhee's Secret Hickleton Lady (IRE) (Kala Shikari)
2387[10] 2870[6] 4019[7] 4532[6] 5683[10]

**Shilla (IRE)** *Henry Candy* 75
3 b f Kodiac Shimla (IRE) (Rudimentary (USA))
1585[3] 3817[4] 4411[5] 4787[7] 5355[2] 5724[2] 6314[6] 6814[7]

**Shillito** *Tony Coyle* a40 67
4 b g Kyllachy Kiss Me Kate (Aragon)
(1487) 2364[4] 2606[10] 3298[4] 3846[4] 4069[2] ◆ 4571[4] 4795[6] 4875[2] 5806[5] 6014[12] 6544[8] 6674[17]

**Shimba Hills** *Mick Channon* a76 77
3 b g Sixties Icon Search Party (Rainbow Quest (USA))
*1135[2]* 1400[3] 1635[3] 2120[4] 2769[6] 4671[6] (5004) 5336[4]

**Shimmering Silver (IRE)** *Daniel Mark Loughnane* a56 34
2 b f Clodovil(IRE) Sara Mana Mou (Medicean)
4764[5] *5509[5]* *6270[8]* *6838[7]* *7529[11]*

**Shingle** *Ed de Giles* a81 77
3 b c Oasis Dream Orford Ness (Selkirk (USA))
(4816) ◆ 5526[4] 6249[11] *6680[2]* *6902[9]*

**Shining Emerald** *P D Deegan* 107
3 b g Clodovil(IRE) Janayen (USA) (Zafonic (USA))
1200a[2] 3352[11] 4459a[7]

**Shining Glitter (IRE)** *James Fanshawe* a76 66
3 b f Shamardal(USA) Lune Rose (High Chaparral (IRE))
2271[7] 3106[7] *4434[4]* *5036[2]* *6238[2]* *(7015)*

**Shining Life** *M Planard* a53
4 b f American Post Ask For Rain (Green Desert (USA))
*722a[13]*

**Shining Sun (FR)** *J Bertran De Balanda* a58 79
7 b g Bernebeau(FR) Shining Light (FR) (Shining Steel)
(920a)

**Ship Canal** *Michael Easterby* 41
2 ch g Major Cadeaux Smooth As Silk (IRE) (Danehill Dancer (IRE))
4510[8] 5194[5] 5372[6]

**Ship Rock (IRE)** *Robert Collet* a93 93
4 b c Whipper(USA) Cashel Queen (USA) (Kingmambo (USA))
*6992a[7]*

**Shipwright (IRE)** *Mark Johnston* a55 75
2 b c Shamardal(USA) Shinko Hermes (IRE) (Sadler's Wells (USA))
*5488[5]* 6059[4] 6496[5] 6996[3]

**Shipyard (USA)** *A Oliver* a90 91
5 ch g Pivotal Nadia (Nashwan (USA))
1078a[18] 3737a[10] 4480a[6] 6369a[8]

**Shirataki (IRE)** *Peter Hiatt* a73 73
6 b g Cape Cross(IRE) Noodle Soup (USA) (Alphabet Soup (USA))
*146[8]* *293[11]* *1231[5]* *1798[12]* *2916[9]* 3209[3] 3682[2]

**Shirazz** *Seamus Durack* a64 49
5 b m Shirocco(GER) Streccia (Old Vic)
*67[2]* *303[2]* *1132[4]* *1740[5]* 2301[7] 2720[10]

**Shirley's Pride** *Michael Appleby* a73 58
4 b f Byron Feeling Blue (Missed Flight)
*1019[2]* 1604[7] 2486[8] 6455[10] 6872[17] 7213[15] 7510[8] *7900[5]* *(7997)* *8142[9]*

**Shirley Vanessa (IRE)** *Luke Dace* a47 48
3 b f Camacho Mas A Fuera (IRE) (Alzao (USA))
*373[5]* *531[4]*

**Shirls Son Sam** *Chris Fairhurst* a52 57
6 b g Rambling Bear Shirl (Shirley Heights)
*73[6]* *7823[5]* *8208[3]*

**Shirocco Passion** *Tony Coyle* 74
3 b f Shirocco(GER) Pete's Passion (Rock Of Gibraltar (IRE))
1346[11] 2319[11] *5101[8]* 5387[6] 7672[8]

**Shock** *Daniel Kubler* 29
3 b g Kheleyf(USA) Montcalm (IRE) (Montjeu (IRE))
3224[6]

**Sholaan (IRE)** *D Selvaratnam* a114 106
5 b g Invincible Spirit(IRE) Jazz Up (Cadeaux Genereux)
1179a[10]

**Shomberg** *Dai Burchell* a48 53
5 b g Bahamian Bounty Qilin (IRE) (Second Set (IRE))
*538[7]* *910[9]*

**Shootingsta (IRE)** *Bryan Smart* 75
2 b c Fast Company(IRE) Kiva (Indian Ridge)
3148[4] 3881[5] 5807[2] 6594[2] 6931[3]

**Shorana (IRE)** *C F Swan* a76 76
3 b f Holy Roman Emperor(IRE) Sharesha (IRE) (Ashkalani (IRE))
*8310[2]*

**Shoreham (AUS)** *Saab Hasan* 104
5 b g Reset(AUS) Teneales Pearl (AUS) (Redoute's Choice (AUS))
7395a[6]

**Shore Step (IRE)** *Mick Channon* 99
4 br g Footstepsinthesand Chatham Islands (USA) (Elusive Quality (USA))
2110[8] 2562[2] 3479[3] (4146) (6260)

**Shortmile Lady (IRE)** *Michael Dods* 57
2 br f Arcano(IRE) Jinsiyah (USA) (Housebuster (USA))
2824[6] 4382[5] 4973[11] 5637[7] 6791[4]

**Short N Sweet** *Tim Easterby* 71
2 b f Showcasing Tilly's Dream (Arkadian Hero (USA))
3199[2] ◆ 3713[6] 4011[2]

**Short Shrift (IRE)** *Richard Fahey* a70 65
4 ch f Nayef(USA) Dusty Answer (Zafonic (USA))
*(1)* *253[5]*

**Short Squeeze (IRE)** *Hugo Palmer* a78 112
4 b g Cape Cross(IRE) Sunsetter (USA) (Diesis)
3356[26] 3731[5] 4681[4] (5609) 6132[6]

**Short Takes (USA)** *Donald McCain* a30 39
6 ch g Lemon Drop Kid(USA) Gabriellina Giof (Ashkalani (IRE))
5240[9]

**Shotgun Start** *Michael Wigham* a77 66
4 b g Kyllachy Fly In Style (Hernando (FR))
*(7950)* *8043[3]*

**Shot In The Dark (IRE)** *Jonathan Geake* a42 55
5 ch g Dr Fong(USA) Highland Shot (Selkirk (USA))
4744[2] 5689[5]

**Shot In The Sun (IRE)** *Richard Fahey* 90
3 b f Kodiac Summer Sunshine (Dubai Destination (USA))
1540[2] 2257[2] 2565[11] 2962[4] 4176[6] 4826[10] 6476[7] 6793[3] 7119[9] 7445[7]

**Shouranour (IRE)** *David O'Meara* 94
4 b g Lawman(FR) Sharesha (IRE) (Ashkalani (IRE))
2423[3] 2912[6] 3368[3] 4175[5] 4451[2] 4710[9] (5496) 7085[4] 7719[2]

**Show Boat** *Ann Duffield* a56 52
2 b c Showcasing Bluegrass Gal (USA) (Cape Canaveral (USA))
5679[7] *7454[8]*

**Showboating (IRE)** *Alan McCabe* a89 86
6 b g Shamardal(USA) Sadinga (IRE) (Sadler's Wells (USA))
*832[3]* 1164[5] 1442[3] ◆ 1646[5] ◆ 1958[8] 2548[9] 3431[5] 3703[7] 3969[4] 4181[7] 4661[12] 6430[10] 6713[16] 7085[10] 7282[5] 7600[2] *7953[6]*

**Showcard** *Gary Moore* a55 74
2 b f Showcasing Dimakya (USA) (Dayjur (USA))
2107[5] ◆ (2557) 3415[17] 4853[12] 5626[8] *6769[7]*

**Showing Character** *Tom Dascombe* 97
2 b c Showcasing Lalectra (King Charlemagne (USA))
(3692) ◆ (4159) ◆ 5694[10] 6703[6] 7099[4] 7415[3]

**Show Me Baileys (FR)** *James Given* 23
2 b g Naaqoos Exhibitor (USA) (Royal Academy (USA))
7407[17]

**Show Me The Bar** *Jo Hughes* a41
2 b g Showcasing Barboukh (Night Shift (USA))
*7779[8]*

**Showmethemoney (FR)** *P Sogorb* 59
2 b f Diamond Green(FR) Winterliebe (GER) (Big Shuffle (USA))
1094a[5]

**Showpiece** *Richard Hannon* a80 86
3 b g Kyllachy Striving (IRE) (Danehill Dancer (IRE))
1420[4] ◆ 1714[2] 2148[4] 3480[4] 4414[3] 4761[12] 5177[7] 6704[3] *7634[4]*

**Show Spirit** *Kevin Ryan* 50
2 br f Showcasing Sahariri (IRE) (Red Ransom (USA))
2014[3] 2436[9] 4357[7] 4899[7] 5194[11]

**Showstoppa** *Mark Johnston* 77
2 ch f Showcasing Harryana (Efisio)
3232[5] (3656) 3909[3] (5266) 6053a[7] 6322[4] 6739[3] 7079[4]

**Showtime Blues** *Amanda Perrett* a82
2 b g Showcasing Night Symphonie (Cloudings (IRE))
*7920[5]* *(8201)*

**Showtime Star** *Gay Kelleway* a84 71
4 b g Byron Piddies Pride (IRE) (Indian Lodge (IRE))
2170[5] 3601[5] 4318[2] 4796[4] 4997[2] 5375[7] (5857) *(8082)* *8223[2]*

**Shrewd** *Keith Dalgleish* 98
4 b g Street Sense(USA) Cala (FR) (Desert Prince (IRE))
6133[8] 6514[4] ◆ 6536[8] 7235[10]

**Shrewd Bob (IRE)** *Robert Eddery* a69 48
3 b c Whipper(USA) Cheyenne Spirit (Indian Ridge)
*855[2]* *1379[3]* 3037[13]

**Shropshire (IRE)** *Charles Hills* a96 107
6 gr g Shamardal(USA) Shawanni (Shareef Dancer (USA))
5445[15] 6290[7]

**Shu Lewis (IRE)** *Ms M Dowdall Blake* a95 104
8 b m Pyrus(USA) Poppy Lewis (IRE) (Paris House)
3764a[5] 5736a[3] 6374a[8]

**Shuriken (IRE)** *Peter Chapple-Hyam* a64 72
3 b f Hurricane Run(IRE) Wurfklinge (GER) (Acatenango (GER))
5191[2] *6045[2]* 7332[3]

**Shuruq (USA)** *Saeed bin Suroor* a115 113
4 b f Elusive Quality(USA) Miss Lucifer (FR) (Noverre (USA))
*(111a)* 395a[6] *(899a)* 1176a[8] (6164a) *6973a[6]*

**Shushu Sugartown (IRE)** *Ian Williams* a64 67
3 b f Invincible Spirit(IRE) Landela (Alhaarth (IRE))
1645[3] *2470[10]* 4502[5] 5314[6] 6463[7] 7248[6] *7704[5]*

**Shwaiman (IRE)** *James Fanshawe* a102 108
4 br g Authorized(IRE) Blue Lightning (Machiavellian (USA))
1581[3] 2073[6] 2785[3] 3377[8] 4213[7] 4759[13] 6687[4] 7492[4]

**Shyron** *George Margarson* a95 84
3 b g Byron Coconut Shy (Bahamian Bounty)
(1614) 1861[6] (7820) 8257[2] (8320)

**Sian Gwalia** *David Simcock* a76 60
4 b f Echo Of Light House Maiden (IRE) (Rudimentary (USA))
41[2] 1154[1] (612) 872[2] (978) 1065[5] 1628[2] 1815[2] 2628[7] 3325[5] 3705[4]

**Sibling Honour** *Charlie Appleby* a70
3 b f Bernardini(USA) Porto Roca (AUS) (Barathea (IRE))
2649[9]

**Sicilian Bay (IRE)** *Paul Midgley* a17 57
3 b f Jeremy(USA) Taormina (IRE) (Ela-Mana-Mou)
551[6] 651[8] 1303[4] 1906[4] 2393[8] 2742[3] 4063[2] 4473[2] 5198[6] 5892[3]

**Side Glance** *Andrew Balding* a110 116
7 br g Passing Glance Averami (Averti (IRE))
901a[7] 1183a[4] 2379a[5] 3317[9] 4010a[3] 5460a[3] 7127a[3] 7467a[4]

**Sidestep (AUS)** *J O'Shea* 112
4 b c Exceed And Excel(AUS) Dextrous (AUS) (Quest For Fame)
7724a[8]

**Sierra Leona (FR)** *C Lerner* 83
2 b f Elusive City(USA) Coco (USA) (Storm Bird (CAN))
5293a[7]

**Sighora (IRE)** *Ismail Mohammed* a81 81
3 b f Royal Applause Singitta (Singspiel (IRE))
1192[4] 1534[3] 2118[4] (8094)

**Significant Move** *Stuart Kittow* a57 81
7 b g Motivator Strike Lightly (Rainbow Quest (USA))
1354[9] 1811[7] 3851[7] 4678[2] 5597[3] 5878[13]

**Signoff (IRE)** *Darren Weir* 106
4 b g Authorized(IRE) Miss Hepburn (USA) (Gone West (USA))
7126a[2] 7653a[4]

**Sign Of Lucky (USA)** *Doug Watson* a83
3 br f Sharp Humor(USA) Chelsea Green (USA) (Key To The Mint (USA))
506a[11] 771a[6]

**Signore Piccolo** *Eric Alston* 87
3 b g Piccolo Piccolo Cativo (Komaite (USA))
(1396) ◆ 1737[4] 2317[12] 3460[2] 3959[4] 4390[5] 7212[9]

**Signoret (IRE)** *Richard Fahey* 69
2 ch f Naaqoos Katelyns Kiss (USA) (Rahy (USA))
4510[3] 5807[5] 6489[5] 7130[4]

**Signorina Roseina** *Eric Alston* a55 26
2 b f Captain Gerrard(IRE) Rosein (Komaite (USA))
6093[13] 6408[7] 6701[9]

**Signposted (IRE)** *Andrew Balding* 103
3 b c Rock Of Gibraltar(IRE) Portentous (Selkirk (USA))
1652[4] 2153[5] 2502[3]

**Signs And Signals (IRE)** *Ed Vaughan* a7
2 b f Kodiac Larrocha (IRE) (Sadler's Wells (USA))
5187[9] 7867[11] 8027[6]

**Signs Of Blessing (IRE)** *F Rohaut* 112
3 b c Invincible Spirit(IRE) Sun Bittern (USA) (Seeking The Gold (USA))
2197a[2] 3746a[3] (5966a) 6920[9]

**Sign Your Name (GER)** *Mario Hofer* 86
2 b f Areion(GER) Salzgitter (Salse (USA))
4524a[2] 6778a[7]

**Silas Marner (FR)** *J-C Rouget* a113 113
7 b h Muhtathir Street Kendra (FR) (Kendor (FR))
1371a[3] 3291a[3] 6620a[10] 7095a[5]

**Silence In Court (IRE)** *Eve Johnson Houghton* 34
2 b c Invincible Spirit(IRE) Hammrah (Danehill (USA))
6556[9] 7412[12]

**Silent Achiever (NZ)** *Roger James* 115
6 br m O'Reilly(NZ) Winning Spree (NZ) (Zabeel (NZ))
7467a[3]

**Silent Bullet (IRE)** *Saeed bin Suroor* 104
3 b g Exceed And Excel(AUS) Veil Of Silence (IRE) (Elusive Quality (USA))
3247[2] 3753[5] 4681[3] 5665[16]

**Silentio (USA)** *Gary Mandella* a103 118
5 bb h Silent Name(JPN) Listen A P (USA) (A.P. Indy (USA))
7609a[14]

**Silent Melody (JPN)** *Sakae Kunieda* a90 108
7 b h Symboli Kris S(USA) Silent Happiness (JPN) (Sunday Silence (USA))
2002a[10]

**Silent Pursuit** *Philip Hide* a58 21
3 br f Pastoral Pursuits Lay A Whisper (Night Shift (USA))
188[3] 1844[11] 8119[2]

**Silent Sam** *Michael Appleby*
6 b g Elusive City(USA) Luisa Miller (IRE) (Entrepreneur)
94[8]

**Silent Thunder (IRE)** *William Haggas* a65
2 b c Sea The Stars(IRE) Speed Song (Fasliyev (USA))
8060[5] ◆ 8292[3]

**Siljan's Saga (FR)** *J-P Gauvin* 115
4 b f Sagamix(FR) Humoriste (FR) (Saint Cyrien (FR))
1827a[3] (2631a) 3774a[2] 6380a[7] 6970a[12] 7486a[5]

**Silken Express (IRE)** *Robert Cowell* a102 84
5 ch m Speightstown(USA) Laureldean Express (Inchinor)
4[2] (271) 431[3] 644[2] 802[6] 1066[7]

**Silken Ocean** *Ralph Beckett* a43
2 b f Dynaformer(USA) Mambo Jambo (USA) (Kingmambo (USA))
7927[9]

**Silken Poppy** *Patrick Chamings* a50 61
3 b f Assertive Ela Paparouna (Vettori (IRE))
2489[6] 2946[7] 3729[4] 4675[6] 5307[6] 6090[5] 6851[6]

**Silken Waters** *Eve Johnson Houghton* a56 55
3 ch f Halling(USA) Faraway Waters (Pharly (FR))
3141[8] 3750[7] 4543[10] 5402[4] 5865[3] 6946[5] 7369[6] 7570[7]

**Silk Route** *Giles Bravery* a66 69
4 ch f Dubai Destination(USA) Crinolette (IRE) (Sadler's Wells (USA))
747[9] 1000[6]

**Silk Sari** *Luca Cumani* a67 112
4 b f Dalakhani(IRE) So Silk (Rainbow Quest (USA))
(1934) 2764[3] 3961[5] (4945) (6255) 7273[2]

**Silk Train** *Alexandra Dunn* a76 78
4 b f Rail Link Monsoon Wedding (Monsun (GER))
2467[2] 3079[2] 3681[5] 7734[13]

**Silly Billy (IRE)** *John Balding* a76 60
6 b g Noverre(USA) Rock Dove (IRE) (Danehill (USA))
(10) 255[2] (388) 647[6] 767[3] 928[2] 1113[4] 1689[6] 2019[7] 3439[13] 8086[11] 8224[7]

**Silsol (GER)** *Paul Nicholls* a79 64
5 b g Soldier Hollow Silveria (GER) (Groom Dancer (USA))
85[2]

**Si Luna (GER)** *W Mongil* a87 99
5 ch m Kallisto(GER) Signorita (GER) (Generous (IRE))
6914a[10] 7483a[6] 7629a[13] 8150a[13] 8300a[11]

**Silvala Dance** *Chris Wall* a54 63
4 b f Kyllachy Bride Of The Sea (Cape Cross (IRE))
2399[10] 3527[3] 4056[6] 4732[6] (5105) 6077[4]

**Silvanus (IRE)** *Paul Midgley* a69 99
9 b g Danehill Dancer(IRE) Mala Mala (IRE) (Brief Truce (USA))
1019[5] (1565) 1961[11] 2275[2] 3239[8] 3571[8] 4174[2] (4531) (5016) 5754 6209[4] 6614[5] 7080[14]

**Silvas Romana (IRE)** *Mark Brisbourne* a69 77
5 b m Holy Roman Emperor(IRE) Triple Wood (USA) (Woodman (USA))
2399[12] 3176[4]

**Silvee** *John Bridger* a50 56
7 gr m Avonbridge Silver Louie (IRE) (Titus Livius (FR))
1896[7] 1986[4] 2486[5] 2689[7] 2864[2] 3230[9] 3528[5] 3824[9] 4433[7] 4911[11] 5313[4] 5425[9] 7339[8] 7546[2] 7804[8] 7845[11]

**Silver Alliance** *Julia Feilden* a74 82
6 gr g Proclamation(IRE) Aimee Vibert (Zilzal (USA))
1134[2] 1636[8] (2444) 3162[6] 4116[3] (5049) 5730[6] 6465[8]

**Silver Craftsman (IRE)** *Alan Swinbank* 56
3 gr c Mastercraftsman(IRE) Shining Hour (USA) (Red Ransom (USA))
1608[4] 1969[7] 2354[10]

**Silver Dixie (USA)** *Peter Hedger* a87 80
4 br g Dixie Union(USA) More Silver (USA) (Silver Hawk (USA))
2462[8] 2882[6] 3802[4] 4148[4] 4786[2] 5487[4] 6141[7] 7205[6] 7552[4] 7918[10]

**Silver Duke (IRE)** *Jim Goldie* 76
3 gr g Papal Bull Dumaani's Dream (USA) (Dumaani (USA))
1433[7] 1844[7] 2201[6] 2737[12] 4903[6] 5420[2] 6110[6] 7098[2]

**Silver Fawn (IRE)** *John Weymes* a54 44
4 gr g Clodovil(IRE) Tinareena (IRE) (Barathea (IRE))
435[5] 484[6] 783[5] 916[4] 1087[7] 1228[7]

**Silver Freak (USA)** *Brian A Lynch* 73
5 ch g Badge Of Silver(USA) Sweet Gold (USA) (Gilded Time (USA))
6391a[10]

**Silverheels (IRE)** *Paul Cole* a93 87
5 gr g Verglas(IRE) Vasilia (Dansili)
287[6] 457[4] (806a) (1014) 1558[12] 2062[6] 2462[5] 2922[2] 5222a[4] 5824[5] 6140[9] 6885[2] (6992a) 7545[7] 8295[3]

**Silver Lightening (IRE)** *Eric Alston* a25 78
4 gr g Verglas(IRE) Church Road (IRE) (Danehill Dancer (IRE))
4796[10] 6011[8] 6161[8]

**Silver March (FR)** *P Sogorb* a78 70
3 b c Early March Quatz Melody (FR) (Johann Quatz (FR))
390a[5]

**Silver Marizah (IRE)** *Roger Ingram* a53 21
5 b m Manduro(GER) Maharani (USA) (Red Ransom (USA))
13[7]

**Silver Mirage** *Michael Bell* a69 74
3 b f Oasis Dream Phantom Gold (Machiavellian (USA))
2129[3] 3154[7] 3979[11] 5079[7] 5729[5] 7253[3] 7699[3] 7865[2] (8008)

**Silver Mountain** *J R Jenkins* a73
3 gr g Sir Percy Pearl Bright (FR) (Kaldoun (FR))
(8114)

**Silver Ocean (USA)** *Niels Petersen* a98 87
6 br g Silver Train(USA) Endless Sea (CAN) (Mt. Livermore (USA))
306a[15] 504a[9] 809a[8] 2245a[9] 4957a[10]

**Silver Quay (IRE)** *Richard Hannon* 80
2 gr c Dark Angel(IRE) She Runs (FR) (Sheyrann (IRE))
2298[16] 3929[4] 4896[7] ◆ 5625[7] (5875) ◆ 6331[4] 6550[5]

**Silver Rainbow (IRE)** *Charles Hills* a74 13
2 gr f Starspangledbanner(AUS) Enchanting Way (Linamix (FR))
5037[5] (7228) 7448[7]

**Silver Ranger** *Richard Hannon* a56 81
2 gr c Dutch Art Jillolini (Bertolini (USA))
2288[3] 2642[6] 3279[2] 4353[2] 4809[2] 5625[3] 7226[8]

**Silverrica (IRE)** *Malcolm Saunders* 79
4 gr f Ad Valorem(USA) Allegorica (IRE) (Alzao (USA))
2030[8] 3470[2] 3817[3] 4027[7] 4981[2] (5595) 6025[9] 6314[5]

**Silver Rime (FR)** *Linda Perratt* a60 94
9 gr g Verglas(IRE) Severina (Darshaan)
1564[8] 1928[6] 2453[3] 2478[4] 3189[3] 3573[12] 4002[4] (4013) 4258[3] 4661[9] (4963) 5695[13] 6226[8] 6535[6] 7060[7]

**Silver Secret** *Miss Joey Ellis* a58
3 gr g Moss Vale(IRE) Alphilda (Ezzoud (IRE))
8249[3]

**Silver Shuffle (IRE)** *Malcolm Jefferson* a21 69
7 ch g Big Shuffle(USA) Silvetta (Lando (GER))
6699[12]

**Silver Songstress** *John Weymes*
4 b f Singspiel(IRE) Composing (IRE) (Noverre (USA))
7951[6]

**Silver Tigress** *Iain Jardine* 67
6 gr m Tiger Hill(IRE) Cinnamon Tree (IRE) (Barathea (IRE))
1567[7] 3605[3] 3912[10] 4319[8] (4665) 5084[6] 5773[11] 6119[5] 6628[12]

**Silver Treasure (FR)** *Amy Weaver* 94
3 gr g Clodovil(IRE) Ardesia Si (FR) (Treasure Kay)
1551a[3] (2290a) 2961[5] 3810a[2] 4252a[8] 6913a[3] 7327a[4] 7600[5] 7856a[14]

**Silver Tycoon (IRE)** *John Quinn* 50
2 bg c Arcano(IRE) Sallanches (USA) (Gone West (USA))
5759[8] 6279[8]

**Silverware (USA)** *Kristin Stubbs* a93 83
6 bb g Eurosilver(USA) Playing Footsie (USA) (Valiant Nature (USA))
163[2] 674[3] (917) 1316[4] 2017[10] 3272[13] 7455[11] 7955[10] 8257[5]

**Silvery Blue** *Hugo Palmer* a67 70
2 b f Paco Boy(IRE) Blue Echo (Kyllachy)
6660[2] 7062[5] (7496)

**Silvery Moon (IRE)** *Tim Easterby* 94
7 gr g Verglas(IRE) Starry Night (Sheikh Albadou)
1164[7] 2253[6] 2618[3] 6098[14] 7236[6] 7449[2]

**Silwana (IRE)** *D K Weld* 98
3 b f Peintre Celebre(USA) Simawa (IRE) (Anabaa (USA))
6349a[3]

**Simba (FR)** *C Lerner* a104 104
6 gr h Anabaa Blue Saiga (FR) (Baryshnikov (AUS))
8006a[7]

**Simba** *A Wohler* 106
3 ch c Teofilo(IRE) Sarabia (GER) (One Cool Cat (USA))
3511a[2] 5484a[2]

**Simenon (IRE)** *W P Mullins* 116
7 b g Marju(IRE) Epistoliere (IRE) (Alzao (USA))
811a[5] 1177a[15] 1869[6] 3377[4]

**Simma (IRE)** *Sylvester Kirk* a61 64
3 gr f Dark Angel(IRE) Staylily (IRE) (Grand Lodge (USA))
3729[6] 4029[7] 4677[7] 5257[2] 5908[3]

**Simone Angel (FR)** *C Scandella* 65
2 b f American Post Berceuse (Mtoto)
5590a[3]

**Simone On Time (IRE)** *Sylvester Kirk* a65 61
2 b f Lord Shanakill(USA) Kathy Sun (IRE) (Intikhab (USA))
5429[10] 6024[8] 6646[2] 6838[2] 7207[3] 7544[6] 7839[3] 7994[9] 8009[8]

**Simple Elegance (USA)** *Charlie Appleby* a71 65
2 bb f Street Cry(IRE) Rutherienne (USA) (Pulpit (USA))
3648[5] 4075[2] 6606[3] 7062[9]

**Simple Magic (IRE)** *John Gosden* a91 80
3 b f Invincible Spirit(IRE) Cephalonie (USA) (Kris S (USA))
2304[8] 3245[6] 4405[4]

**Simplified** *Michael Chapman*
11 b m Lend A Hand Houston Heiress (USA) (Houston (USA))
7651[7]

**Simply A Star (IRE)** *A P O'Brien* 94
2 ch f Giant's Causeway(USA) Cherry Hinton (Green Desert (USA))
6372a[10]

**Simply Black (IRE)** *David O'Meara* a72 61
3 br f Kheleyf(USA) Tashyra (IRE) (Tagula (IRE))
4890[9] 5375[11] (6116) 6340[2] 6819[3] (7457) 7806[4] ◆ 7949[5]

**Simply Magic (IRE)** *Richard Hannon* a72 74
2 b f Zebedee Penny Rouge (IRE) (Pennekamp (USA))
1571[4] 2022[3] 2859[3] 4410[4] 4967[2] 5554[2] 6359[3]

**Simply Shining (IRE)** *Richard Fahey* a73 82
4 ch f Rock Of Gibraltar(IRE) Bright Smile (IRE) (Caerleon (USA))
1510[2] 1842[3] 2604[3] 3272[8] 3979[2] 4635[7] (5763) 6129[10] 7575[8]

**Sinaadi (IRE)** *Brian Meehan* a84 85
4 b f Kyllachy Quantum (IRE) (Alhaarth (IRE))
1568[2] 3307[9] 4112[9]

**Sinbad The Sailor** *George Baker* a69 64
9 b g Cape Cross(IRE) Sinead (USA) (Irish River (FR))
606[5]

**Sindymarch (FR)** *J Heloury* a76 76
3 b g Early March Arborea (IRE) (Fantastic Light (USA))
751a[2]

**Singapore Spur (FR)** *D De Waele* a84 70
3 b g Sandwaki(USA) Singapore Treat (FR) (Sagacity (FR))
237a[8] 629a[5] 720a[5]

**Singapore West (FR)** *G Pannier* 30
3 b g Sagacity(FR) L'Etrangere (IRE) (Desert Prince (IRE))
5592a[8]

**Singeur (IRE)** *Robin Bastiman* a85 94
7 b g Chineur(FR) Singitta (Singspiel (IRE))
1305[8] 1506[4] 1938[4] 2390[3] 2786[5] 3239[6] 3666[7] 4418[5] 4925[9] 5563[4] 6235[3] 6763[4] 7330[3] 7669[3]

**Singing (FR)** *A Wohler* a84 114
4 b c Singspiel(IRE) Ring Beaune (USA) (Bering)
984a[2] 1341a[5] 2106a[3] 3770a[2]

**Singing Star (IRE)** *Mel Brittain* a44 50
3 b f Iffraaj Seven Sing (USA) (Machiavellian (USA))
1441[6] 2388[6] 3093[3] 4288[7] 4796[U] 5389[5]

**Singoalla** *Sir Mark Prescott Bt* a61
2 b f Arch(USA) Songerie (Hernando (FR))
6840[5] 7011[8] 7367[6]

**Sings Poet** *Peter Hiatt* a40
4 ch g Singspiel(IRE) Royale Rose (FR) (Bering)
400[7] 652[7]

**Singular Quest** *Ralph Beckett* a71
2 ch c Dalakhani(IRE) Singuliere (IRE) (Singspiel (IRE))
7926[5] ◆

**Singzak** *Michael Easterby* a82 80
6 ch g Singspiel(IRE) Zakuska (Zafonic (USA))
(513) 758[3] 1151[2] 1692[6] 3204[14] 3699[11] 4575[8]

**Sinnamary (IRE)** *M Delzangles* 101
3 b f Galileo(IRE) Prudenzia (IRE) (Dansili)
2267a[5]

**Sioux Chieftain (IRE)** *Michael Appleby* a84 83
4 b g Mount Nelson Lady Gin (USA) (Saint Ballado (CAN))
2520[7] 3205[15] 5288[6] 5572[5] (7008) 7281[3] 7504[2] 7822[2] 8001[5]

**Sioux Dakota (FR)** *L Baudron* 41
2 bl c Alex The Winner(USA) Petite Elite (USA) (Fusaichi Pegasus (USA))
2755a[10]

**Siouxperhero (IRE)** *William Muir* a77 79
5 b g Sleeping Indian Tintern (Diktat)
1665[4] 2721[4] 3314[8] 3427[8] 3805[3] (4342) (4767) (4831) 5528[8] 6191[5] 6616[9] 7186[2] 7757[9]

**Siouxsie Gee** *Jim Goldie*
4 ch f Sleeping Indian Annie Gee (Primo Valentino (IRE))
1303[13]

**Sir Acclam (IRE)** *Keith Dalgleish* 56
2 br g Acclamation Cradle Brief (IRE) (Brief Truce (USA))
3454[9] 4382[6] 5995[7]

**Sir Billy Wright (IRE)** *David Evans* a70 59
3 b g High Chaparral(IRE) Lure Of The Moon (USA) (Lure (USA))
6988[6] 7285[5] 7699[2] 8147[2] 8256[2]

**Sir Charlie Kunz** *Mark Johnston* a81 85
3 gr c Dalakhani(IRE) Darrfonah (IRE) (Singspiel (IRE))
231[2] ◆ (357) 5299[3] ◆ 5818[6] 6141[6] 6450[2] 6541[7] 7335[9]

**Sir Chauvelin** *Jim Goldie* 69
2 b g Authorized(IRE) Jabbara (IRE) (Kingmambo (USA))
4253[6] 5167[4] 5759[2] 6529[2] 7054[2]

**Sirdaab (USA)** *B W Hills* 65
2 b c City Zip(USA) Stormy Union (USA) (Dixie Union (USA))
4760[9]

**Sirdal** *David O'Meara* 53
3 b g War Front(USA) Siyadah (USA) (Mr Prospector (USA))
6429[5] 6673[4]

**Sir Domino (FR)** *Kevin Ryan* 79
2 b c Evasive Domino Queen I (IRE) (Primo Dominie)
7246[2] (7491)

**Sir Ector (USA)** *J J Lambe* 107
7 br g Dynaformer(USA) Beyond The Waves (USA) (Ocean Crest (USA))
1750a[4] 2370a[4] 3717[11] 7476a[17]

**Siren's Cove** *James Tate* a65 64
2 b f Sir Percy Siren Sound (Singspiel (IRE))
3119[3] 3626[3] 5973[3] 6944[4] 7257[4]

**Sir Frank Morgan (IRE)** *Mark Johnston* a90 89
4 b g Montjeu(IRE) Woodland Orchid (IRE) (Woodman (USA))
(915) (997) 1092[5] (1284) 1426[3] 1599[4] 2011[3] 2108[2] 2430[2] 2739[11] (3078) 3501[10] (4068) 4606[9] 5017[2] 5161[10] 5579[5] 5825[2] 6228[3] 6557[5] 6896[5] 7107[26]

**Sir Freddie (USA)** *Fredrik Reuterskiold* a78 84
5 gr g Unbridled's Song(USA) Judy Soda (USA) (Personal Flag (USA))
2244a[3] 3996a[8]

**Sir Geoffrey (IRE)** *Scott Dixon* a78 73
8 b g Captain Rio Disarm (IRE) (Bahamian Bounty)
(9) 299[7] (383) 510[4] 654[4] (834) 1049[6] 1244[4] 1541[7] 2434[7] (2951) 3092[5] 5290[5] 5498[8] 7213[6] 7510[10] 7761[6] 8180[6]

**Sir Graham Wade (IRE)** *Mark Johnston* a95 109
5 gr g Dalakhani(IRE) Needwood Epic (Midyan (USA))
1213[5] 1581[7] 3321[P]

**Sir Guy Porteous (IRE)** *Mark Johnston* a76 99
3 ch g Shamardal(USA) Ermine And Velvet (Nayef (USA))
1260[4] 1601[2] 1897[6] (2218) 2827[2] (3361) 3455[3] (3957) 4118[2] 4647[10] 4938[13] 5656[13] 6895[12] 7455[6]

**Sirheed (IRE)** *Richard Hannon* a70 53
2 ch c Rip Van Winkle(IRE) Rozella (IRE) (Anabaa (USA))
6928[9] 7382[12] 7731[4]

**Sir Henry Raeburn (IRE)** *Paul Cole* a51 70
2 b c Henrythenavigator(USA) La Traviata (USA) (Johannesburg (USA))
4270[15] 7560[3] 7741[6]

**Sirius (GER)** *Andreas Lowe* 109
3 ch c Dashing Blade Saratina (IRE) (Monsun (GER))
3770a[3] (5231a) 6180a[5] 6806a[9]

**Sirius Prospect (USA)** *Dean Ivory* a113 110
6 bb g Gone West(USA) Stella Blue (FR) (Anabaa (USA))
1558[7] 1870[6] 2784[2] 3452[8] 6522[4] 6921[4] 7276[22] 7715[10] (7851)

**Sir Jack Layden** *David Brown* a91 105
3 b g Sir Percy Barawin (IRE) (Hawk Wing (USA))
1178a[8] 1953[7] 4127[6] 4366[3] 5720[11]

**Sir John Hawkins (USA)** *A P O'Brien* a12 104
3 b c Henrythenavigator(USA) Peeping Fawn (USA) (Danehill (USA))
1178a[12]

**Sir Keltic Blue** *Brian Ellison* a69
2 b g Sir Percy Bougainvilia (IRE) (Bahamian Bounty)
*7970$^5$ 8227$^4$*

**Sir Lancelott** *Keith Dalgleish* 57
2 b g Piccolo Selkirk Rose (IRE) (Pips Pride)
5167$^8$ 6225$^4$ 6474$^4$

**Sir Lando** *Wido Neuroth* 103
7 b h Lando(GER) Burqa (Nashwan (USA))
2001a$^6$

**Sir Lexington (IRE)** *Brian Forsey* a8 6
5 b g Desert Style(IRE) Shulammite Woman (IRE) (Desert Sun)
*263$^{11}$ 321$^9$ 446$^{12}$ 781$^9$*

**Sir Maximilian (IRE)** *Ian Williams* a109 109
5 b g Royal Applause Nebraska Lady (IRE) (Lujain (USA))
(2074) 3715$^6$ 3830$^3$ (4480a) 4895$^7$ (5154a) 6371a$^2$ 6966a$^7$ *(7433a)*

**Sir Medbury** *M Nigge* a81 85
3 ch g Sir Percy Bombazine (IRE) (Generous (IRE))
*8005a$^3$*

**Sir Mike** *Luca Cumani* a92 95
5 ch g Haafhd Tara Moon (Pivotal)
(1637) 2311$^5$ 3431$^4$ 6498$^6$

**Sirnita** *Richard Guest* 24
5 br m Striking Ambition Zenita (IRE) (Zieten (USA))
1713$^9$ 2053$^7$ 2170$^8$

**Sirocco De Pame (FR)** *R Le Gal* a59 71
8 b g Enrique Royal Pame (FR) (Garde Royale)
3089a$^2$

**Sir Oscar (GER)** *T Potters* 108
7 b g Mark Of Esteem(IRE) Sintenis (GER) (Polish Precedent (USA))
6182a$^5$

**Sir Pedro** *Robert Cowell* a81 85
5 b g Acclamation Milly-M (Cadeaux Genereux)
*532$^5$* 1490$^{10}$ 2050$^2$ 2275$^8$ 2838$^4$ (3077) 3470$^4$ 3676$^4$

**Sir Percy Blakeney** *Marcus Tregoning* a38 44
3 b g Sir Percy Sulitelma (USA) (The Minstrel (CAN))
*4084$^7$* 4562$^7$ 5273$^5$ *6488$^8$*

**Sirpertan** *Marjorie Fife* a53 58
3 b g Sir Percy Tanwir (Unfuwain (USA))
1372$^P$ 1508$^7$ (1840) 2237$^2$ 2735$^8$ 5495$^8$ 6644$^7$ 7643$^5$ *8134$^6$*

**Sirrah Star (IRE)** *Neil Mulholland* a4 28
6 gr m Great Palm(USA) Simply Deep (IRE) (Simply Great (FR))
*3857$^9$* 5382$^8$

**Sir Reginald** *Richard Fahey* a90 99
6 b g Compton Place Clincher Club (Polish Patriot (USA))
*38$^3$* 1193$^4$ 1719$^8$ 2336$^7$ 2984$^2$ 3420$^{16}$ 4384$^4$ 4681$^5$ 6290$^9$ 6531$^{17}$

**Sir Robert Cheval** *Marco Botti* a95 99
3 b g Green Desert(USA) Aunt Ruby (USA) (Rubiano (USA))
*1067$^4$* ◆ *1555$^5$* 2111$^7$ 5165$^5$ 6234$^2$ ◆ 6895$^2$ *7663$^6$*

**Sir Rosco** *Sir Michael Stoute* a75 63
3 b g Sir Percy Rosacara (Green Desert (USA))
2221$^7$ *2917$^5$* 3804$^7$ *5010$^3$ 6075$^5$*

**Sir Tyto (IRE)** *Peter Makin* a57 61
6 b g Fruits Of Love(USA) Sophie May (Glint Of Gold)
2693$^7$ *3115$^{12}$* 3824$^5$ 4279$^4$ 4343$^2$ (5033) 5904$^3$ (6395)

**Sir Veillance** *John Butler*
2 b c Authorized(IRE) Caught You Looking (Observatory (USA))
5397$^7$ *6268$^{12}$ 8192$^9$*

**Sirvino** *David Barron* a94 100
9 b g Vettori(IRE) Zenita (IRE) (Zieten (USA))
1444$^5$ 1562$^2$ (1971) 2294$^3$ 2785$^9$ 5673$^7$ 6061$^{10}$ 6747$^U$

**Sir Walter Scott (IRE)** *Luca Cumani* a89 101
4 b g Galileo(IRE) Flamingo Sea (USA) (Woodman (USA))
4437$^6$ 5693$^7$ ◆ 6287$^9$ 6747$^6$ 7718$^P$

**Sir Woodgate** *Edward Creighton* a45 47
3 ch g Tobougg(IRE) Brogue Lanterns (IRE) (Dr Devious (IRE))
*2997$^5$* 3315$^{14}$ 3891$^8$

**Si Sage (FR)** *Darrell Vienna* a102 108
4 b c Sageburg(IRE) Sans Rien (FR) (Poliglote)
2379a$^6$

**Si Senor (IRE)** *Ed Vaughan* a91 95
3 b g Dansili Kotsi (IRE) (Nayef (USA))
*(1214) 2058$^3$ (5008) (5550)* 6140$^5$ 6704$^4$ ◆

**Si Seulement (IRE)** *T G McCourt* 14
3 br f Iffraaj Ellanova (Kyllachy)
4556a$^{14}$

**Sissi Pompon (IRE)** *M Boutin* a60 75
3 b f Whipper(USA) Ziride (FR) (Valanour (IRE))
*545a$^8$* 4464a$^7$

**Sistanbul (FR)** *E Leenders* a51
3 b g Turtle Bowl(IRE) Sybilia (GER) (Spectrum (IRE))
*600a$^6$*

**Sister Guru** *Peter Hedger* a63 52
5 b m Ishiguru(USA) Ulysses Daughter (IRE) (College Chapel)
*141$^8$* 5228a$^4$

**Sister Love (FR)** *L Baudron* a48 45
2 b f Sageburg(IRE) Kayza (GER) (Acatenango (GER))
*3872a$^9$* 4882a$^8$

**Sister Of Mercy (IRE)** *Roger Charlton* 81
2 b f Azamour(IRE) Green Tambourine (Green Desert (USA))
3888$^{16}$ 4604$^3$ (5351) 5929$^8$ 6521$^5$

**Sister Slew (IRE)** *Gordon Elliott* a65 64
4 br f Kheleyf(USA) Capote West (USA) (Capote (USA))
4805a$^{14}$

**Sitting Pretty (IRE)** *Tom Dascombe* a40 73
3 b f Compton Place Queen Bodicea (IRE) (Revoque (IRE))
*1045$^3$* 2118$^2$ (2553) 3137$^7$ 4161$^5$

**Sivoliere (IRE)** *Chad C Brown* 100
2 b f Sea The Stars(IRE) Sefroua (USA) (Kingmambo (USA))
5707a$^3$ 7592a$^5$

**Sixcentdixneuf (FR)** *M Boutin* a82 82
3 ch c Kentucky Dynamite(USA) Raflebery (Hernando (FR))
*360a$^{11}$*

**Six Of Hearts** *Cecil Ross* a81 87
10 b g Pivotal Additive (USA) (Devil's Bag (USA))
*6082a$^5$*

**Six Silver Lane** *John James Feane* a70 74
6 gr g Aussie Rules(USA) Aurelia (Rainbow Quest (USA))
*370$^2$ 6082a$^6$*

**Sixties Love** *Simon Dow* a71 69
3 b f Sixties Icon Love Always (Piccolo)
*1830$^4$* 2466$^5$ 3423$^5$ 6262$^3$ 7303$^5$ *8068$^3$ 8309$^3$*

**Sixties Queen** *Alan Bailey* a65 63
4 b f Sixties Icon Lily Of Tagula (IRE) (Tagula (IRE))
*406$^9$ 497$^7$ 671$^4$* 1617$^3$ 1638$^3$ *(1745)* 2199$^7$ 2457$^{DSQ}$ 2475$^5$ 2875$^4$ *3115$^9$* 5283$^5$ 5551$^7$

**Sixty (IRE)** *Richard Hannon* 96
2 b c Iffraaj Follow My Lead (Night Shift (USA))
2964$^2$ (3279) 4822$^6$

**Six Wives** *Scott Dixon* a81 74
7 b m Kingsalsa(USA) Regina (Green Desert (USA))
1695$^6$ 1850$^3$ *(2096)* 2350$^{13}$ 2542$^3$ 3033$^6$ 3920$^8$ 5333$^8$ *7767$^9$ 8025$^7$ 8180$^{10}$*

**Sizing Stars** *J Bertran De Balanda* 99
3 ch c Sea The Stars(IRE) Straight Lass (IRE) (Machiavellian (USA))
3290a$^7$

**Sizzler** *Ralph Beckett* a85 105
4 ch g Hernando(FR) Gino's Spirits (Perugino (USA))
1735$^4$ 3321$^3$

**Skate** *Roger Charlton* 77
2 gr g Verglas(IRE) Strut (Danehill Dancer (IRE))
4270$^4$ 4787$^2$ 5500$^2$ (6059)

**Skaters Waltz (IRE)** *Paul Cole* a92 102
3 gr g Verglas(IRE) Xarzee (IRE) (Xaar)
1946$^3$ (2339) *2921$^9$* 3480$^{10}$ 4447$^4$ *(4838a)* 5661a$^2$ *(6221a)*

**Sketch Map (IRE)** *Jedd O'Keeffe* 61
3 b g Excellent Art Atlas Silk (Dansili)
1346$^6$ 1904$^5$ 2355$^{11}$ 5084$^9$ 5631$^2$ 5853$^9$

**Skiddy Mill (IRE)** *Laura Mongan* a66 52
4 b f Ramonti(FR) Glasnas Giant (Giant's Causeway (USA))
*92$^{10}$ (155) 467$^2$ 775$^4$ 952$^2$ 1040$^3$ 1392$^4$* 1876$^5$ *2469$^4$ 7368$^{10}$* 7845$^4$ 7884$^5$ 7986$^{10}$ 8311$^4$

**Ski Lift** *John Gosden* 90
3 ch f Pivotal Morzine (Miswaki (USA))
1422$^4$ 1722$^8$ 2804$^4$ (5319) (5884) ◆ 6559$^7$

**Skilled** *Roger Charlton* 76
3 b g Mastercraftsman(IRE) Treacle (USA) (Seeking The Gold (USA))
2485$^4$ 4435$^6$ 6092$^5$ ◆

**Skimp** *John Gosden* a47
2 b c Exceed And Excel(AUS) Scorn (USA) (Seeking The Gold (USA))
*7551$^{10}$*

**Skinny Latte** *Micky Hammond* 49
3 ch c Piccolo Coffee Ice (Primo Dominie)
1648$^{10}$ 2742$^7$ 3333$^7$ 3828$^9$ 4069$^9$ 4627$^4$ 4998$^4$ 5853$^3$ 7009$^8$

**Skinny Love** *Zoe Davison* a67 66
3 b f Holy Roman Emperor(IRE) Lady Mickataine (USA) (Speightstown (USA))
*(232)* 2049$^3$ 2994$^4$ *3523$^3$*

**Skip And Jump (USA)** *Roger Varian* a65 61
2 b f Elusive Quality(USA) Skip A Dare (USA) (Skip Away (USA))
6753$^5$ *7367$^4$ 7811$^5$*

**Skiperia (FR)** *Y Barberot* a80 86
3 ch f Gold Away(IRE) Lerina (FR) (Priolo (USA))
*193a$^6$* 5661a$^3$

**Ski Slope** *Richard Hannon* a83 69
2 b f Three Valleys(USA) Danehurst (Danehill (USA))
2306$^4$ *(2928)* ◆

**Sky Blazer (USA)** *Barclay Tagg* 111
6 b g Sky Mesa(USA) Highland Hope (USA) (Unaccounted For (USA))
4231a$^3$

**Sky Crossing** *Tom Tate* a51 58
5 b g Cape Cross(IRE) Sky Wonder (Observatory (USA))
*29$^{10}$ 171$^8$ 366$^{12}$* (4797) 5640$^3$ 6122$^5$

**Skye's The Limit** *Richard Fahey* a70 82
3 ch g Pastoral Pursuits Sound Of Sleat (Primo Dominie)
1396$^4$ (1585) 2317$^5$ 2768$^7$ 3669$^5$ 4133$^5$ (5243) 5696$^{13}$ 6512$^{10}$ 7212$^3$

**Skyfire** *Nick Kent* a34 72
7 ch g Storm Cat(USA) Sunray Superstar (Nashwan (USA))
2894$^5$ 4831$^3$ 5206$^8$ 5773$^{10}$

**Skygazer (IRE)** *Charlie Appleby* 64
2 b c Echo Of Light Calando (USA) (Storm Cat (USA))
2428$^6$ 2777$^7$

**Sky Hunter** *Saeed bin Suroor* 117
4 b g Motivator Pearl Kite (USA) (Silver Hawk (USA))
1697$^4$ 2335$^6$ 6532$^{DSQ}$ (7447)

**Sky Khan** *John Wainwright* a90 89
5 b g Cape Cross(IRE) Starlit Sky (Galileo (IRE))
*560$^4$ (674) 887$^7$* 2253$^{14}$ 2618$^8$ 3718$^3$ 4710$^2$ 5756$^2$ 6433$^5$

**Sky Lantern (IRE)** *Richard Hannon* 120
4 rg f Red Clubs(IRE) Shawanni (Shareef Dancer (USA))
3355$^5$ 4165$^5$ 6927$^6$

**Skylight (IRE)** *Mick Channon* a59 56
2 b f Acclamation Swingsky (IRE) (Indian Ridge)
6246$^9$ *6605$^9$* 7019$^8$ *7396$^5$ 7740$^7$ (7880)*

**Skyline Du Casse (FR)** *F Plouganou* 99
8 b g East Of Heaven(IRE) Ordalie Du Casse (FR) (Seurat)
5330a$^2$

**Sky Ranger (IRE)** *James Tate* a60
3 b f Bushranger(IRE) Cassava (IRE) (Vettori (IRE))
*568$^9$ 1007$^2$ 1632$^8$*

**Sky Rose** *William Knight* 64
2 b f Sakhee(USA) Intersky High (USA) (Royal Anthem (USA))
7209$^3$

**Sky Steps (IRE)** *Philip McBride* a51 4
2 ch g Strategic Prince Best Dancing (GER) (Keos (USA))
1977$^{14}$ 3429$^{11}$ 4589$^7$ *6072$^3$ 6413$^2$ 6663$^6$ 7453$^3$ 7683$^2$ 7904$^6$ 8069$^7$*

**Skytrain** *Mark Johnston* a92 89
4 ch g Exceed And Excel(AUS) Viola Da Braccio (IRE) (Vettori (IRE))
*715$^{13}$ 1113$^3$ 1267$^2$ (1451)* 1646$^7$ 1721$^{16}$ 2117$^9$ 2425$^5$ 2762$^3$ 3050$^8$ 3463$^5$ 3718$^8$ 4190$^5$ 4514$^4$ 4761$^3$ 5031$^{10}$ 5446$^{13}$ 5895$^{10}$ 6424$^7$ 7183$^{10}$ 7456$^2$

**Slade Power (IRE)** *Edward Lynam* a107 123
5 b h Dutch Art Girl Power (IRE) (Key Of Luck (USA))
(2570a) (3451) (4201) 7724a$^{11}$

**Slanderous** *Scott Dixon* a4 48
3 b f Sleeping Indian Honesty Pays (Dr Fong (USA))
*6720$^{11}$*

**Slava (USA)** *Gennadi Dorochenko* a63 52
2 ch f Sharp Humor(USA) Splendorella (USA) (Deputy Minister (CAN))
*6915a$^{12}$*

**Sleekfonteine (FR)** *F Doumen* a71 77
2 gr f Slickly(FR) Turfontein (FR) (Kahyasi)
7163a$^3$ *8132a$^8$ 8276a$^8$*

**Sleep Easy** *Hughie Morrison* a55 64
2 b c Rip Van Winkle(IRE) Strictly Lambada (Red Ransom (USA))
6300$^5$ ◆ 6875$^8$ *7731$^9$*

**Sleeper** *Ralph Beckett* a88 81
3 b f Rail Link Guermantes (Distant Relative)
1433$^{11}$ 2031$^6$ 4029$^8$ (4504) *(5036)* (5353) *6036$^2$* 6559$^6$ *7402$^3$*

**Sleeper Class** *Jim Goldie* 70
3 b f Sleeping Indian Class Wan (Safawan)
1304$^6$ 1925$^4$ (2474) 3460$^4$ 4724$^3$ 5169$^5$ 5631$^8$ 7058$^6$

**Sleeper King (IRE)** *Luca Cumani* a94 82
3 b c Holy Roman Emperor(IRE) Catherine Palace (Grand Lodge (USA))
2344$^{12}$ 3253$^{11}$ 4669$^{13}$ 5696$^{15}$ 7408$^{14}$ *8078$^3$*

**Sleeping Angel** *David Evans* a32
3 ch f Sleeping Indian Ellopassoff (Librate)
*468$^{11}$*

**Sleeping Apache (IRE)** *Michael Dods* 74
4 ch g Sleeping Indian Remedy (Pivotal)
1486$^5$ 2392$^3$ (3486) ◆ 4108$^8$ 5197$^{14}$ 7178$^6$ 7534$^4$ ◆

**Sleeping Rough** *Stuart Kittow*
2 b c Sleeping Indian Our Piccadilly (IRE) (Piccolo)
5210$^{11}$

**Sleeping Star** *Mel Brittain* a47 49
3 ch f Sleeping Indian Silver Purse (Interrex (CAN))
1959$^7$ 2204$^{10}$ 2657$^6$ 5497$^7$ 7644$^{18}$ *7782$^6$ 8084$^4$*

**Sleeping Venus (IRE)** *George Baker* a57 57
3 ch f Excellent Art Sun Moon And Stars (IRE) (Galileo (IRE))
*2210$^9$ 4084$^5$*

**Sleep Walk** *Roger Charlton* a78 90
3 gr f Oasis Dream Scuffle (Daylami (IRE))
(1790) (4788) *5012$^4$* (6025) *7624$^7$*

**Sleepy Blue Ocean** *John Balding* a88 80
8 b g Oasis Dream Esteemed Lady (IRE) (Mark Of Esteem (IRE))
*(175) 863$^4$* 1695$^4$ 1961$^{12}$ 3138$^8$ 3948$^5$ 4391$^7$ 4833$^2$ 5535$^4$ 6096$^7$ 6235$^5$ 6873$^8$ *7073$^8$ 7767$^5$ (8180)*

**Sleepy Dust (IRE)** *Sylvester Kirk* 79
2 b f Rip Van Winkle(IRE) Knockatotaun (Spectrum (IRE))
(2771) 5436$^9$ 6555$^7$

**Sleepy Sioux** *David Elsworth* a100 96
3 b f Sleeping Indian Bella Chica (IRE) (Bigstone (IRE))
1518$^8$ *2083$^7$* (2406) 3245$^{14}$ 5419$^{14}$ 6131$^7$ (6441) 7441$^{17}$ *(7738) 7889$^7$ 8019$^3$*

**Sleet (IRE)** *Michael Appleby* a58 13
3 b g Amadeus Wolf Secret Justice (USA) (Lit De Justice (USA))
1542$^{12}$ *1890$^2$ 2095$^3$ 2397$^4$ 2906$^4$ 3407$^3$ 8139$^2$* ◆

**Sleipnir** *Philip Hide* a68 72
3 ch g Medicean Resistance Heroine (Dr Fong (USA))
*291$^2$* ◆ *579$^5$ 1008$^3$* 2545$^6$ 3555$^4$ 3970$^3$ 5523$^3$

**Slemy (IRE)** *Richard Hannon* a83 85
3 b g Raven's Pass(USA) Wolf Cleugh (IRE) (Last Tycoon)
1394$^4$ *(1831)* 2257$^{17}$

**Slew Of Lode (ARG)** *Patrick Shaw* 94
5 ch g Lode(USA) Slew Of Reality (ARG) (Political Ambition (USA))
2378a$^7$

**Slick Indian** *Michael Easterby* 58
3 b g Sleeping Indian Jesting (Muhtarram (USA))
4295$^5$ 4873$^4$ 5417$^6$ 5715$^5$ 5994$^3$ 6405$^{10}$ 6515$^8$ 7025$^8$

**Slim Chance (IRE)** *Simon West* a77 82
5 b m Clodovil(IRE) Valluga (IRE) (Ashkalani (IRE))
3533$^{10}$ 3844$^8$ (4511) 4714$^5$ 4901$^3$ 4961$^3$ 5265$^6$ 5333$^4$ 5806$^2$ 6014$^3$ 6266$^7$ (6580) (6595) *7365$^8$*

**Slingsby** *Michael Easterby* a65 58
3 b g Dutch Art Ballet Fame (USA) (Quest For Fame)
2355$^{15}$ 3618$^2$ 4063$^6$ 4468$^{12}$ 5198$^2$ 5376$^2$ *6154$^2$ 6567$^2$ 7077$^2$*

**Slinky McVelvet** *Garry Moss* a75 54
3 ch f Refuse To Bend(IRE) Rania (GER) (Paolini (GER))
*(74) 301$^4$* 2638$^7$ *2936$^5$* 3382$^5$ 4468$^{11}$ *5571$^6$*

**Slip Of A Girl (IRE)** *Patrick Holmes* a41 47
4 b f Strategic Prince Fig Leaf (FR) (Distant Relative)
*81$^8$* 2738$^{11}$ 3238$^6$ 4066$^8$ 6210$^9$

**Slip Of The Tongue** *Derek Haydn Jones* a85 84
4 ch g Zamindar(USA) Kiswahili (Selkirk (USA))
*160$^5$ 494$^5$*

**Slipper Orchid (IRE)** *M Halford* a102 102
5 ro m Verglas(IRE) Lahiba (IRE) (Lahib (USA))
6963a$^7$ *7579a$^3$*

**Slipper Satin (IRE)** *Noel Quinlan* a66 67
4 b f Excellent Art In The Ribbons (In The Wings)
1916$^9$

**Slippers Best** *J E Hammond* a93 97
4 b f Mount Nelson Last Slipper (Tobougg (IRE))
*8300a$^7$*

**Slip Sliding Away (IRE)** *Peter Hedger* a87 93
7 b g Whipper(USA) Sandy Lady (IRE) (Desert King (IRE))
1492$^8$ 2147$^5$ (2559) 3033$^2$ 4146$^{10}$ 4762$^{11}$ 4892$^4$ 6130$^9$ 6880$^2$ 7233$^5$

**Sloane Avenue (USA)** *Jeremy Noseda* a109 88
3 ch c Candy Ride(ARG) Apt (USA) (A.P. Indy (USA))
*(536)* ◆ 2345$^5$ *(5824)* ◆ 6949a$^8$ *(7836)*

**Slovak (IRE)** *James Tate* a67
2 ch f Iffraaj Bratislava (Dr Fong (USA))
*6270$^4$ 7192$^3$*

**Slowpoke (IRE)** *L Riccardi* 96
3 b c High Chaparral(IRE) Clefairy (IRE) (Sri Pekan (USA))
2376a$^{14}$ 7617a$^6$

**Slunovrat (FR)** *David Menuisier* a39 66
3 b g Astronomer Royal(USA) Slewmamba (FR) (Kingsalsa (USA))
1844$^8$ *2211$^7$ 2883$^U$ 4265$^7$* 4948$^2$ (5765) 6699$^{14}$ 7500$^5$

**Smageta** *Marco Botti* a60 67
3 b f Shirocco(GER) Sensibility (Halling (USA))
*2081$^7$* 3141$^7$ 3652$^{10}$

**Smaih (GER)** *Richard Hannon* 102
2 b c Paco Boy(IRE) Solola (GER) (Black Sam Bellamy (IRE))
2845$^2$ (3173) 4199$^8$ 4670$^3$ (5543a) 6136$^3$ (7446)

**Smalljohn** *Bryan Smart* a76 43
8 ch g Needwood Blade My Bonus (Cyrano De Bergerac)
*11$^7$ 319$^2$ (359)* 3533$^8$ 4291$^{10}$ *6767$^7$ 7953$^4$*

**Smart (GER)** *Richard Hannon* 27
2 ch c Siyouni(FR) Samerous (FR) (Generous (IRE))
7414$^8$

**Smart Alec (IRE)** *Alan Swinbank* a44 68
3 br g Dandy Man(IRE) Art Critic (USA) (Fusaichi Pegasus (USA))
*1498$^5$* 2657$^5$ 3360$^9$ 4861$^2$ (5376) 5816$^3$ 7249$^5$

**Smart Daisy K** *Andrew Hollinshead* a96 95
4 b f Pastoral Pursuits Katy-Q (IRE) (Taufan (USA))
5419$^7$ 6096$^3$ (6314) 6614$^6$ *7889$^2$* ◆ *8045$^9$*

**Smart Dj** *Andrew Hollinshead* a43 35
3 ch g Major Cadeaux Katy-Q (IRE) (Taufan (USA))
3700$^5$ 4111$^{10}$ 4873$^7$ *5801$^5$*

**Smart Life** *Robert Eddery* 23
3 b g Multiplex Vita Mia (Central Park (IRE))
*254$^P$* 2525$^4$ 2838$^8$

**Smart Ruler (IRE)** *James Moffatt* a60 65
8 ch g Viking Ruler(AUS) Celebrated Smile (IRE) (Cadeaux Genereux)
4964$^9$

**Smart Salute** *Ed Walker* a81 79
3 b g Royal Applause Naizak (Medicean)
*2083$^6$ 2921$^6$* 3225$^{10}$ 4206$^2$ 4697$^2$ 5197$^5$ *7729$^2$ 8100$^6$*

**Smart Sayaah (FR)** *E Large* 28
3 b f Country Reel(USA) Saayebah (USA) (Smarty Jones (USA))
5226a$^7$

**Smart Stepper (IRE)** *Michael Dods* a41 60
2 b g Acclamation Miss Smilla (Red Ransom (USA))
4110$^9$ 4708$^5$ (5194) 5630$^8$ 6645$^3$ *7421$^8$*

**Smart Volatility (AUS)** *K W Lui* 116
6 gr g Danewin(AUS) Something Funny (AUS) (Baryshnikov (AUS))
7897a$^2$ 8152a$^7$

**Smarty Socks (IRE)** *David O'Meara* a65 104
10 ch g Elnadim(USA) Unicamp (Royal Academy (USA))
2869$^8$ 3202$^9$ 3716$^6$ 4347$^6$ 6097$^{10}$ 6430$^7$ 6891$^{15}$

**Smaug (FR)** *X Nakkachdji* 84
2 bl c Zafeen(FR) La Meralaise (FR) (Rajpoute (FR))
5616a$^3$ 6619a$^2$

**Smidgen (IRE)** *Ed de Giles* a62 77
3 b c Bahamian Bounty Brazilian Style (Exit To Nowhere (USA))
*1379$^5$* ◆ 1884$^2$

**Smile For Me (IRE)** *Alan Berry* a47 52
3 b f Elnadim(USA) Pershaan (IRE) (Darshaan)
2489$^8$ 3938$^5$ 4653$^2$ *6015$^4$* 6837$^6$ *7699$^8$*

**Smile That Smile** *Mark H Tompkins* 65
2 b f Champs Elysees Tenpence (Bob Back (USA))
(6998)

**Smiling Stranger (IRE)** *Andrew Balding* a76 91
3 b g Nayef(USA) Carraigoona (IRE) (Rock Of Gibraltar (IRE))
*1797$^3$* 2334$^2$ 3498$^2$ 4435$^2$ 4893$^7$

**Smirfys Blackcat (IRE)** *Michael Mullineaux*
5 b m One Cool Cat(USA) Smirfys Dance Hall (IRE) (Halling (USA))
1722$^{12}$ 5814$^6$ 6597$^{13}$ *7256$^{13}$*

**Smirfy's Silver** *Michael Mullineaux* a30 45
10 b g Desert Prince(IRE) Goodwood Blizzard (Inchinor)
6028$^{12}$ 6601$^8$ *7187$^{10}$*

**Smoker** *P J Prendergast* a78 83
4 b g Motivator Request (Rainbow Quest (USA))
1078a$^{8}$

**Smoke Ring (USA)** *Donald McCain*
2 rg c Smoke Glacken(USA) With This Ring (USA) (Green Dancer (USA))
6489$^{8}$

**Smoke Signals (IRE)** *Matthieu Palussiere* 78
2 b c Elusive City(USA) Silent Sunday (IRE) (Testa Rossa (AUS))
5405a$^{11}$

**Smokethatthunders (IRE)** *James Unett* a86 80
4 gr g Elusive City(USA) Zinstar (IRE) (Sinndar (IRE))
91$^{5}$ 287$^{2}$ 372$^{3}$ 1022$^{9}$ 1286$^{2}$ 1451$^{5}$ 2341$^{10}$ 3216$^{6}$ 3939$^{8}$ 5411$^{2}$ 5987$^{2}$ 6346$^{2}$ (7023) 7521$^{5}$ 7888$^{3}$ 7953$^{2}$ (8058) 8257$^{7}$ 8263$^{2}$

**Smoking Sun (USA)** *P Bary* a104 116
5 bb h Smart Strike(CAN) Burning Sunset (Caerleon (USA))
(1341a) 1783a$^{4}$ 2379a$^{2}$ 5460a$^{6}$ 6592a$^{2}$

**Smooth Daddy (USA)** *Thomas Albertrani* 102
3 b c Scat Daddy(USA) Prairie Maiden (USA) (Badger Land (USA))
6949a$^{3}$

**Smooth Operator (GER)** *Mario Hofer* a90 110
8 b g Big Shuffle(USA) Salzgitter (Salse (USA))
2006a$^{6}$ 3373a$^{2}$

**Smoothtalkinrascal (IRE)** *David O'Meara* a89 88
4 b g Kodiac Cool Tarifa (IRE) (One Cool Cat (USA))
1333a$^{8}$ (1561) 2197a$^{10}$ 2563$^{9}$ 2989$^{11}$ 6327$^{17}$ 6745$^{12}$

**Smuggler's Cove (IRE)** *A P O'Brien* a106 108
2 b c Fastnet Rock(AUS) Chenchikova (IRE) (Sadler's Wells (USA))
7241$^{3}$

**Smugglers Lane (IRE)** *David Evans* a49 47
2 b g Bushranger(IRE) Finty (IRE) (Entrepreneur)
1363$^{7}$ 2642$^{5}$ 2837$^{6}$ 3847$^{6}$ 5489$^{6}$ 6250$^{10}$ 6811$^{7}$ 7815$^{4}$ 7994$^{8}$

**Snappy Guest** *George Margarson* 58
2 b g Kodiac Golden Shadow (IRE) (Selkirk (USA))
4270$^{12}$ 6462$^{9}$ 6694$^{6}$

**Snappy Mann** *Willie Musson* a10
2 ch g Sleeping Indian Laminka (Intikhab (USA))
4260$^{8}$ 7999$^{5}$

**Snap Shots (IRE)** *Tom Dascombe* 94
2 b g Kodiac Refuse To Give Up (IRE) (Refuse To Bend (IRE))
(2731) 3374$^{4}$ 3928$^{3}$ (4566) 5791$^{2}$ 6933$^{11}$

**Sneaking Budge** *David Lanigan* a32
2 b c Nayef(USA) Ikat (IRE) (Pivotal)
7778$^{9}$

**Snitzerland (AUS)** *Gerald Ryan* 116
5 b m Snitzel(AUS) Monte Rosa (AUS) (Fraar (USA))
1468a$^{12}$

**Snoano** *John Gosden* 98
2 b c Nayef(USA) White Dress (IRE) (Pivotal)
4167$^{7}$ (5093) (6520) 7442$^{5}$

**Snooker (GER)** *Rose Dobbin* 57
8 ch g Acambaro(GER) Sheraton (IRE) (Brief Truce (USA))
1761$^{5}$ 2476$^{4}$ 3623$^{9}$

**Snow And Ice (FR)** *T Castanheira* a75 88
2 b c Panis(USA) Xcape To Victory (IRE) (Cape Cross (IRE))
5616a$^{2}$

**Snoway** *Tony Coyle* 48
2 b f Sakhee's Secret Snow Moccasin (IRE) (Oasis Dream)
2358$^{4}$ 3842$^{4}$ 4216$^{10}$ 5384$^{5}$ 5885$^{5}$ 6428$^{2}$ 6669$^{10}$ 7245$^{6}$ 7487$^{9}$

**Snow Bay** *Paul Midgley* a41 92
8 ch g Bahamian Bounty Goodwood Blizzard (Inchinor)
1020$^{11}$ 1345$^{8}$ 2054$^{8}$ 2549$^{10}$ 3533$^{2}$ 4861$^{7}$ 5197$^{11}$ 5629$^{6}$ 5887$^{3}$ 6263$^{10}$

**Snowboarder (USA)** *Charlie Appleby* a99 111
4 ch g Raven's Pass(USA) Gaudete (USA) (Distorted Humor (USA))
596a$^{8}$ 3252$^{7}$ 3982$^{11}$

**Snow Cloud (IRE)** *David O'Meara* a75 74
2 b f Kodiac Thistlestar (USA) (Lion Heart (USA))
2134$^{4}$ (6212) 7038$^{2}$ 7231$^{2}$ 7665$^{2}$ 7807$^{2}$

**Snow Conditions** *Philip Hide* a63 64
3 b f Aussie Rules(USA) Snow Gonal (FR) (Octagonal (NZ))
1793$^{2}$ 2225$^{4}$ 2926$^{8}$ 4210$^{5}$ (6193) 6395$^{4}$ 7001$^{9}$ 7526$^{4}$ 7846$^{16}$

**Snow Cover** *Roger Varian*
2 gr f Verglas(IRE) Cover Look (SAF) (Fort Wood (USA))
4444$^{17}$

**Snow Dancer (IRE)** *John David Riches* a55 60
10 b m Desert Style(IRE) Bella Vie (IRE) (Sadler's Wells (USA))
2701$^{9}$ 3705$^{3}$ 4293$^{3}$ 4665$^{4}$ 5077$^{7}$ 5600$^{4}$ 6157$^{4}$ 6410$^{4}$ 6597$^{7}$ 7868$^{3}$ 7977$^{5}$

**Snow Dragon (JPN)** *Noboru Takagi* a111 117
6 gr h Admire Cozzene(JPN) Meine Caprice (JPN) (Tayasu Tsuyoshi (JPN))
8152a$^{8}$

**Snow Guest (FR)** *Y Barberot* a64 63
2 b f On Est Bien(IRE) Convent Guest (IRE) (Be My Guest (USA))
4882a$^{2}$ 5544a$^{12}$ 5901a$^{4}$ 7027a$^{5}$ 8149a$^{10}$

**Snow King (USA)** *Ted Powell* a85 57
4 ch g Elusive Quality(USA) Cloudspin (USA) (Storm Cat (USA))
426$^{11}$ 2157$^{8}$ 3931$^{8}$ 4968$^{12}$ 7633$^{10}$ 7925$^{10}$ 8037$^{5}$ ◆ 8313$^{4}$

**Snowmane (IRE)** *James Given* a100 90
3 b g Galileo(IRE) Tree Tops (Grand Lodge (USA))
7803$^{9}$ 7922$^{8}$ 8146$^{5}$

**Snow Sky** *Sir Michael Stoute* 117
3 b c Nayef(USA) Winter Silence (Dansili)
1419$^{2}$ (2153) 3417$^{4}$ (4778) 5577$^{2}$ 6329$^{3}$ 8151a$^{7}$

**Snow Squall** *Mark Johnston* a78 93
3 b g Dansili Snow Ballerina (Sadler's Wells (USA))
1540$^{6}$ 3200$^{5}$ 3587$^{6}$ 4160$^{4}$ (4361) 4584$^{4}$ 5164$^{3}$

**Snow Trouble (USA)** *Marcus Tregoning* a91 84
3 gr c Tapit(USA) Smara (USA) (Storm Cat (USA))
1580$^{2}$ 1979$^{6}$ 2502$^{5}$ 4323$^{3}$

**Snowy Dawn** *Ben Case* a79 82
4 gr g Notnowcato Tereyna (Terimon)
1935$^{7}$ 3249$^{4}$ 4144$^{4}$ 4575$^{6}$ (6283) 6896$^{6}$ 7566$^{3}$ 8096$^{6}$

**Snowy Valley** *Paul Burgoyne* a53
5 ch g Three Valleys(USA) Rasseem (IRE) (Fasliyev (USA))
1263$^{7}$ 1406$^{8}$

**Snugfit Sam** *John Quinn* 53
3 b g Acclamation Swanky Lady (Cape Cross (IRE))
1611$^{13}$ 2020$^{14}$

**Soaring Spirits (IRE)** *Dean Ivory* a85 80
4 ch g Tamayuz Follow My Lead (Night Shift (USA))
56$^{10}$ 2833$^{3}$ 3577$^{9}$ 4028$^{6}$ 6990$^{13}$ 7403$^{9}$ (7776) 8072$^{9}$ (8297)

**So Beautiful (FR)** *Doug Watson* a93 109
5 ch g Zamindar(USA) Silver Tulip (USA) (Silver Hawk (USA))
205a$^{12}$ 595a$^{9}$ 812a$^{8}$

**So Beloved** *Ruth Carr* a98 96
4 b g Dansili Valencia (Kenmare (FR))
1437$^{23}$ (1834) ◆ 2483$^{3}$ 3431$^{7}$ 4976$^{5}$ 5445$^{14}$

**Social Inclusion (USA)** *Manuel J Azpurua* a111
3 b c Pioneerof The Nile(USA) Saint Bernadette (USA) (Saint Ballado (CAN))
2357a$^{3}$

**Social Riser (IRE)** *Charles Hills* a70 68
3 b f High Chaparral(IRE) Parvenue (FR) (Ezzoud (IRE))
3385$^{4}$ 3877$^{4}$ 5490$^{3}$ 6338$^{5}$

**Society Diva (IRE)** *George Baker* a15 54
3 b f Kheleyf(USA) Mistle Thrush (USA) (Storm Bird (CAN))
4048$^{9}$

**Society Pearl (IRE)** *David Evans* 76
4 b f Kheleyf(USA) Mamonta (Fantastic Light (USA))
5340$^{5}$ 5621$^{4}$ 5848$^{4}$ 6426$^{9}$

**Sociopath (IRE)** *Peter Chapple-Hyam* 49
2 b c Fastnet Rock(AUS) Nancy Spain (IRE) (Sadler's Wells (USA))
6259$^{13}$

**Sofias Number One (USA)** *Roy Bowring* a76 46
6 bb g Silver Deputy(CAN) Storidawn (USA) (Hennessy (USA))
10$^{4}$ 172$^{5}$ 364$^{4}$ 862$^{2}$ 929$^{2}$ 2400$^{4}$ 3155$^{12}$ 5100$^{3}$ 5529$^{8}$ 6341$^{6}$ 7651$^{4}$ 8178$^{2}$

**Soft Drink (USA)** *A Fabre* 93
2 ch f Lemon Drop Kid(USA) Toppisme (USA) (Saint Ballado (CAN))
6967a$^{10}$

**Soft Falling Rain (SAF)** *M F De Kock* a115 123
5 b h National Assembly(CAN) Gardener's Delight (USA) (Giant's Causeway (USA))
898a$^{9}$ 1176a$^{2}$ 3317$^{6}$

**Soft Love (IRE)** *Kevin Ryan* a62
2 b f Kodiac Appley Bridge (IRE) (One Cool Cat (USA))
2472$^{4}$ 7970$^{3}$ 8140$^{4}$

**Softly She Treads (IRE)** *Pat Phelan* a69 55
3 b f Azamour(IRE) Lady Lucre (IRE) (Last Tycoon)
951$^{6}$ 1812$^{5}$ 2491$^{8}$ 2927$^{5}$ 4812$^{5}$ 7517$^{5}$ (8028) (8250) ◆

**Softsong (FR)** *James Evans* a91 98
6 b g Singspiel(IRE) Soft Gold (USA) (Gulch (USA))
591$^{3}$ 2920$^{7}$ 3249$^{6}$

**Sohar** *James Toller* a81 97
6 b m Iceman Desert Joy (Daylami (IRE))
2108$^{3}$ 2782$^{2}$ 3321$^{4}$ 6255$^{7}$ 7107$^{11}$ 7566$^{2}$

**Sohcahtoa (IRE)** *Andrew Crook* a74 70
8 b g Val Royal(FR) Stroke Of Six (IRE) (Woodborough (USA))
546$^{6}$ 1763$^{7}$ 3845$^{6}$

**Soie D'Leau** *Kristin Stubbs* 63
2 b g Monsieur Bond(IRE) Silky Silence (High Chaparral (IRE))
2014$^{4}$ 2386$^{8}$ 2824$^{5}$ 3461$^{4}$

**So In Love** *A Fabre* 102
3 b f Smart Strike(CAN) Soft Morning (Pivotal)
4721a$^{3}$ 6882a$^{11}$ 7629a$^{6}$

**Soiree D'Ete** *Sir Mark Prescott Bt* a54 47
3 b f Selkirk(USA) Souvenance (Hernando (FR))
4105$^{8}$ 4563$^{3}$ 5122$^{4}$ 5682$^{7}$ 7002$^{9}$

**So It's War (FR)** *Keith Dalgleish* a62 60
3 b g Orpen(USA) Impulsive Decision (IRE) (Nomination)
6011$^{6}$ 6599$^{5}$ 7074$^{6}$

**Solaras Exhibition (IRE)** *Tim Vaughan* a81 83
6 b g Great Exhibition(USA) Solara (GER) (Danehill (USA))
4819$^{4}$ 5317$^{5}$ (6367)

**Solar Deity (IRE)** *Marco Botti* a113 87
5 b h Exceed And Excel(AUS) Dawn Raid (IRE) (Docksider (USA))
306a$^{5}$ 681a$^{6}$ 810a$^{4}$ 1559$^{4}$ 7688$^{5}$ 8144$^{3}$ 8266$^{2}$

**Solar Flair** *William Knight* a72
2 b c Equiano(FR) Air Biscuit (IRE) (Galileo (IRE))
8093$^{6}$ (8292)

**Solar Focus (IRE)** *J S Bolger* 76
3 b c Intense Focus(USA) Saor Sinn (IRE) (Galileo (IRE))
4951a$^{5}$

**Solar Magic** *John Gosden* 93
3 ch f Pivotal Moon Goddess (Rainbow Quest (USA))
1534$^{4}$ ◆ 1868$^{3}$ (4699) 5176$^{6}$

**Solarmaite** *Roy Bowring* a69 46
5 b m Needwood Blade Marinaite (Komaite (USA))
273$^{5}$ 367$^{2}$ 835$^{4}$ 1087$^{4}$ 1496$^{3}$ (1891) 2092$^{3}$ 2935$^{4}$ 3971$^{9}$ 5097$^{4}$

**Solar Moon** *Charlie Appleby* a50 44
3 b f Pivotal Dubai Sunrise (USA) (Seeking The Gold (USA))
1534$^{12}$ 2125$^{7}$ 2780$^{15}$

**Solar Spirit (IRE)** *Tracy Waggott* a80 81
9 b g Invincible Spirit(IRE) Misaayef (USA) (Swain (IRE))
1375$^{2}$ 1646$^{8}$ 2054$^{3}$ 2522$^{4}$ 2549$^{5}$ 2953$^{3}$ 3844$^{2}$ 4317$^{4}$ 4421$^{6}$ (4997) 5470$^{8}$ 6150$^{3}$ 7282$^{6}$ 7624$^{3}$

**Solar View (IRE)** *Sir Mark Prescott Bt* a62 85
5 ch g Galileo(IRE) Ellen (IRE) (Machiavellian (USA))
(3680) ◆ 3851$^{4}$ 4777$^{5}$ (Dead)

**Soldat Bleu (FR)** *D Prod'Homme* a70 63
3 bl g Soldier Of Fortune(IRE) Wedding Night (FR) (Valanour (IRE))
390a$^{8}$ 630a$^{4}$

**Soldier Sam (IRE)** *Brian Ellison* a26 47
2 gr g Zebedee Fey Rouge (IRE) (Fayruz)
3728$^{10}$ 4142$^{8}$ 5377$^{9}$ 6642$^{11}$ 7421$^{10}$ 7536$^{4}$

**Sole Danser (IRE)** *Milton Bradley* a73 76
6 b g Dansili Plymsole (USA) (Diesis)
746$^{7}$

**Solemn** *Milton Bradley* a76 74
9 b g Pivotal Pious (Bishop Of Cashel)
259$^{6}$ 866$^{6}$ 1787$^{4}$ 1912$^{2}$ 2250$^{6}$ 2691$^{8}$ 3222$^{3}$ 3561$^{8}$ 3939$^{7}$ 5207$^{5}$

**Solent Lad (USA)** *Robert Eddery* a46 49
3 ch c English Channel(USA) Ting A Folie (ARG) (Careafolie (IRE))
173$^{7}$ 480$^{7}$ 2694$^{2}$

**Soleon (GER)** *F-X De Chevigny* 17
3 b g Areion(GER) Sooleen (GER) (Acatenango (GER))
630a$^{8}$

**Sole Power** *Edward Lynam* a101 120
7 b g Kyllachy Demerger (USA) (Distant View (USA))
897a$^{4}$ 1179a$^{7}$ (1949) (3319) (5654) 6134$^{4}$ 6966a$^{8}$ 8152a$^{9}$

**Solicit (AUS)** *Mathew Ellerton & Simon Zahra* 107
4 bb f Street Cry(IRE) Princesa (AUS) (Danehill (USA))
7128a$^{8}$

**Solidarity** *Charlie Appleby* a103 93
3 b g Dubawi(IRE) Assabiyya (IRE) (Cape Cross (IRE))
1509$^{2}$ (2009) 2530$^{2}$ 2839$^{4}$ 3923$^{2}$ (4272) 6106$^{6}$ 6366$^{3}$ 7289$^{5}$ (7784) (7850) 8095$^{13}$

**Solid Justice (IRE)** *Jason Ward* a55 74
3 b g Rock Of Gibraltar(IRE) Burnin' Memories (USA) (Lit De Justice (USA))
1542$^{10}$ 2902$^{3}$ 3362$^{2}$ 4420$^{9}$ 6516$^{4}$ 6980$^{2}$ (7251) 7626$^{7}$ 7760$^{9}$

**Solis (GER)** *Dianne Sayer* a7 24
11 ch g In The Wings Seringa (GER) (Acatenango (GER))
1248$^{5}$

**Solmen (FR)** *K Demme* a89 88
6 b g Solon(GER) Amen (GER) (Dashing Blade)
5961a$^{5}$

**Solo Hunter** *Martyn Meade* a78 78
3 b g Sleeping Indian Night Owl (Night Shift (USA))
976$^{3}$ 1353$^{8}$ (1786) 2363$^{5}$ (2481) 2761$^{6}$ 3643$^{7}$ 4208$^{2}$ 4679$^{7}$ 5213$^{7}$ 5378$^{6}$ 5795$^{2}$ 6423$^{2}$ 7513$^{6}$

**Solojorie (FR)** *J Parize* 77
3 b f Solon(GER) Sandra Lawyer (FR) (Sky Lawyer (FR))
7270a$^{5}$

**Solomon Northup (USA)** *Charles O'Brien* a86 94
2 b c Scat Daddy(USA) Fashion Fur (USA) (Mr Greeley (USA))
6800a$^{6}$

**So Long Malpic (FR)** *T Lemer* a94 109
7 b m Fairly Ransom(USA) Poussiere D'Or (FR) (Marchand De Sable (USA))
3030a$^{6}$ 3997a$^{3}$ 5223a$^{8}$ 6182a$^{10}$

**Solow** *F Head* 119
4 gr g Singspiel(IRE) High Maintenance (FR) (Highest Honor (FR))
2588a$^{6}$ (5263a) (5960a) (6955a)

**Solstalla** *William Jarvis* a65 61
2 b f Halling(USA) Solstice (Dubawi (IRE))
4784$^{5}$ 5799$^{5}$

**Solveig's Song** *Steve Woodman* a37
2 b f Norse Dancer(IRE) Ivory Lace (Atraf)
7550$^{10}$ 7756$^{10}$ 8191$^{9}$

**Solyway (FR)** *H-A Pantall* a57
4 b f Way Of Light(USA) Lasso Calypso (FR) (Anabaa Blue)
4776a$^{11}$

**Somalian (IRE)** *Ismail Mohammed* a83 93
5 b h Tiger Hill(IRE) Somoushe (IRE) (Black Minnaloushe (USA))
243a$^{11}$

**Somali Lemonade (USA)** *Michael Matz* 108
5 b m Lemon Drop Kid(USA) Chic Corine (USA) (Nureyev (USA))
5459a$^{5}$

**So Many Shots (IRE)** *Stefano Botti* 100
3 b f Duke Of Marmalade(IRE) Cland Di San Jore (IRE) (Lando (GER))
2590a$^{3}$ (3513a) 7146a$^{2}$ 7480a$^{5}$

**Sombre Heros (FR)** *Mlle H Mennessier* 74
2 b c Kingsalsa(USA) Tanarock (FR) (Rock Of Gibraltar (IRE))
4932a$^{8}$ 5616a$^{7}$

**Some Boy Lukey** *David Thompson* 37
3 b g Archipenko(USA) Cuyamaca (IRE) (Desert King (IRE))
1962$^{6}$ 2392$^{6}$ 2952$^{6}$ 3438$^{6}$ 3846$^{8}$ 3914$^{12}$ 5761$^{12}$

**Somedaysrdiamonds** *J S Moore* a65 61
2 b f Equiano(FR) Good Health (Magic Ring (IRE))
3311$^{9}$ 3934$^{6}$ 4087$^{2}$ (4576) 4920$^{4}$ 6016$^{3}$ 6401$^{3}$ 7362$^{4}$ 7571$^{4}$ (7780) 8059$^{5}$

**Someone's Darling** *Lydia Pearce* a54 77
4 b f Jeremy(USA) Green Sensazione (Green Desert (USA))
3479$^{7}$ 4024$^{10}$ 4766$^{6}$ 5602$^{9}$

**Somerton Star** *Pat Eddery* a42
4 b c Avonbridge Leaping Flame (USA) (Trempolino (USA))
484$^{9}$ 974$^{6}$ 1088$^{6}$ 4327$^{8}$

**Some Show** *Henry Candy* a67 74
2 ch f Showcasing Dancing Nelly (Shareef Dancer (USA))
4269$^{12}$ 4784$^{3}$ (5210) 5983$^{2}$ 6678$^{4}$

**Some Site (IRE)** *David Simcock* 82
3 b f Nayef(USA) Horatia (IRE) (Machiavellian (USA))
2279$^{3}$ (3103) 4417$^{4}$

**Some Spirit (IRE)** *G M Lyons* a99 100
3 b f Invincible Spirit(IRE) Recite (JPN) (Forty Niner (USA))
5869a$^{2}$ 6963a$^{4}$ 7579a$^{4}$

**Something Extra (USA)** *Gail Cox* a104 110
6 bb g Indian Charlie(USA) Our Mariah (USA) (Mt. Livermore (USA))
7609a$^{10}$

**Something Lucky (IRE)** *Kristin Stubbs* a82 92
2 gr c Clodovil(IRE) Lucky Leigh (Piccolo)
2755a$^{11}$ 3170a$^{3}$ 3744a$^{4}$ 4883a$^{3}$ 5405a$^{5}$ 6591a$^{5}$ (6991a) 7485a$^{2}$ 7855a$^{6}$

**Somewhat (USA)** *Mark Johnston* 114
3 b g Dynaformer(USA) Sometime (IRE) (Royal Academy (USA))
1516$^{5}$ 2114$^{3}$ 3375$^{7}$ 3984$^{3}$ 4778$^{3}$ 5432$^{5}$ 6329$^{10}$

**Sommerabend** *M Rulec* a110 116
7 b h Shamardal(USA) Sommernacht (GER) (Monsun (GER))
306a$^{16}$ 678a$^{2}$ (1371a) (1908a) 2799a$^{2}$ (3997a) 5223a$^{7}$ 6382a$^{6}$ 6955a$^{3}$

**Sommersturm (GER)** *David Evans* a70 69
10 b g Tiger Hill(IRE) Sommernacht (GER) (Monsun (GER))
123$^{2}$ 214$^{8}$ 349$^{6}$ 400$^{4}$

**Sona** *John Gosden* a84 60
3 b f Dansili Neartica (FR) (Sadler's Wells (USA))
4413$^{5}$ (4966)

**Sonar (IRE)** *Michael Bell* 56
2 b c Thewayyouare(USA) Ecco Mi (IRE) (Priolo (USA))
4884$^{8}$ 5718$^{8}$ 5981$^{9}$ 7165$^{7}$

**Son Cesio (FR)** *H-A Pantall* 110
3 b c Zafeen(FR) Slitana (FR) (Dansili)
2226a$^{2}$ (3030a) 4841a$^{2}$ 5966a$^{2}$

**Song And Dance Man** *Gary Moore* a69 78
4 b g Danehill Dancer(IRE) Song (IRE) (Sadler's Wells (USA))
686$^{4}$ 827$^{4}$ 7516$^{11}$

**Songcraft (IRE)** *Saeed bin Suroor* 113
6 b g Singspiel(IRE) Baya (USA) (Nureyev (USA))
(598a) 900a$^{2}$ 1177a$^{7}$ 4849$^{6}$ 5668$^{4}$ ◆

**Song Light** *David Elsworth* a75 76
4 b g Echo Of Light Blue Lullaby (IRE) (Fasliyev (USA))
79$^{13}$ 293$^{3}$ 450$^{4}$

**Song Of Norway** *Peter Makin* a75 71
3 b f Halling(USA) Amarullah (FR) (Daylami (IRE))
1722$^{3}$ 2431$^{6}$ 4802$^{5}$ 5352$^{4}$ 6042$^{4}$ 7682$^{4}$ 7818$^{5}$

**Song Of Parkes** *Peter Grayson* a78 74
7 b m Fantastic Light(USA) My Melody Parkes (Teenoso (USA))
(191) 532$^{6}$ 1038$^{3}$

**Song Of Rowland (IRE)** *John Spearing* a49 56
3 b g Holy Roman Emperor(IRE) Makarova (IRE) (Sadler's Wells (USA))
149$^{7}$ 608$^{10}$ 936$^{9}$ 3150$^{7}$ 3549$^{7}$ 4820$^{8}$ 5820$^{12}$

**Songye** *Kevin Ryan* 82
2 b c Makfi Liberty Chery (Statue Of Liberty (USA))
3136$^{4}$ ◆ 3569$^{2}$ 4740$^{P}$

**Sonic Rainbow (GR)** *Amanda Perrett* a52
2 ch f Harmonic Way Rainbow Way (High Chaparral (IRE))
7011$^{7}$ 7193$^{9}$

**Sonnetation (IRE)** *Jim Boyle* a70 75
4 b f Dylan Thomas(IRE) Southern Migration (USA) (Kingmambo (USA))
2721$^{5}$ 2930$^{2}$ (3390) 3971$^{2}$ (4280) 4842$^{2}$ 6337$^{5}$

**Sonnolento (IRE)** *Andrew Balding* a74 65
2 b c Rip Van Winkle(IRE) Dreams Come True (FR) (Zafonic (USA))
6551$^{7}$ 7030$^{U}$ 7833$^{2}$ 8067$^{5}$

**So Noble** *William Muir* 80
3 ch g Pivotal Noble One (Primo Dominie)
5775$^{4}$ (6421) (7339) ◆ 7514$^{5}$

**Son Of Africa** *Henry Candy* a50 87
2 b g Equiano(FR) Generously Gifted (Sakhee (USA))
(3063) 3786$^{6}$ (4853) ◆ 6510$^{10}$ 7807$^{6}$

**Son Of Feyan (IRE)** *Roger Teal* a66 66
3 ch g Nayef(USA) Miss Penton (Primo Dominie)
827$^{5}$ 1218$^{4}$ 1494$^{7}$ 1898$^{6}$

**Sooqaan** *Mel Brittain* a71 64
3 bl g Naaqoos Dream Day (FR) (Spectrum (IRE))
1962$^{4}$ (2165) 2545$^{3}$ 3946$^{7}$ 5891$^{7}$ 7570$^{3}$ 8049$^{5}$ (8218)

**Sooth Al Ssalam (USA)** *S Seemar* a73 73
4 br c Henrythenavigator(USA) Rosemark (USA) (Deputy Minister (CAN))
238a$^{5}$

**Sophie's Beau (USA)** *Michael Chapman* a42 57
7 b g Stormy Atlantic(USA) Lady Buttercup (USA) (Meadowlake (USA))
1089$^{8}$ 1584$^{10}$ 2637$^{7}$ 3149$^{14}$ 3548$^{11}$ 4293$^{6}$ (4534) 4797$^{9}$ 5530$^{5}$

**Sophie's World (IRE)** *Kevin F O'Donnell* a59 89
3 b f Captain Rio Nirvavita (FR) (Highest Honor (FR))
5957a$^{10}$

**Sophisticated Heir (IRE)** *David O'Meara* a56 86
4 b g New Approach(IRE) My Girl Sophie (USA) (Danzig (USA))
(2841) ◆ 4290$^{2}$ (5299) 6491$^{5}$ 7125$^{13}$ 7719$^{10}$

**Sopran Nicolo (IRE)** *B Grizzetti* 87
3 bb c Sea The Stars(IRE) Sopran Londa (IRE) (Danehill (USA))
2376a$^{12}$ 7323a$^{4}$

**Soqotra** *Peter Chapple-Hyam* a33
2 b f King's Best(USA) Yemen Desert (IRE) (Sadler's Wells (USA))
8241$^{5}$

**Sorcier (FR)** *Iain Jardine* 23
8 b g Shaanmer(IRE) Donitille (FR) (Italic (FR))
3602$^{6}$

**Sorry Saeed** *James Tate* a50 6
3 b f Raven's Pass(USA) Clear Impression (IRE) (Danehill (USA))
*731$^3$* 3951$^7$

**Sorry Woman (FR)** *H-A Pantall* 104
4 b f Ivan Denisovich(IRE) Oppamattox (FR) (Munir)
1207a$^4$

**Sors (IRE)** *Andrew Slattery* a89 89
2 b c Acclamation Maid Of Ailsa (USA) (Pivotal)
2569a$^2$ 2855a$^8$ 6933$^{19}$

**Sosia (GER)** *C Laffon-Parias* a95 100
3 b f Shamardal(USA) Sahel (GER) (Monsun (GER))
7629a$^{10}$ *8300a$^5$*

**Sotise (IRE)** *Marco Botti* a69 37
3 br f Shamardal(USA) Tropical Glamour (IRE) (Rock Of Gibraltar (IRE))
1534$^{16}$ *1832$^{10}$*

**Soubrette** *Geoffrey Deacon* a42 37
4 ch f Zafeen(FR) Nihal (IRE) (Singspiel (IRE))
*755$^6$* 1666$^7$

**Souk Al Tahab (IRE)** *Ed Dunlop* a72
2 b c Arcano(IRE) Quiet Dream (USA) (Seattle Slew (USA))
*7840$^6$ 8092$^4$ 8227$^5$ 8317$^3$*

**Soul (AUS)** *Saeed bin Suroor* a53 105
7 b g Commands(AUS) Marvilha (AUS) (Night Shift (USA))
3960$^5$

**Soul Artist (IRE)** *Tim Easterby* a33 50
3 b f Bushranger(IRE) Itsanothergirl (Reprimand)
*1112$^4$* 1648$^4$ 2020$^{13}$

**Soul Brother (IRE)** *Tim Easterby* 90
3 b g Captain Rio Goodwood March (Foxhound (USA))
1304$^2$ 1671$^2$ 2138$^2$ (2420) 3478$^{10}$ 5444$^{17}$ 6170$^{12}$

**Soulef (FR)** *J Heloury* a69
3 ch c Vatori(FR) Saryshnikova (FR) (Baryshnikov (AUS))
*751a$^5$*

**Soul Instinct** *Simon Dow* a60 67
3 b g Myboycharlie(IRE) However (IRE) (Hector Protector (USA))
*401$^6$ 650$^6$ 867$^4$ 1047$^3$* 1343$^3$ 4974$^9$ 5631$^9$ 5994$^5$ *7928$^9$ 8311$^3$*

**Soul Intent (IRE)** *Charles Hills* a86 83
4 b c Galileo(IRE) Flamingo Guitar (USA) (Storm Cat (USA))
1724$^9$ 2272$^2$ 3335$^4$ 3874$^{DSQ}$ *(6664)* 6930$^{11}$

**Soul Of Motion** *Gay Kelleway* a70 77
3 b g Phoenix Reach(IRE) Chocolada (Namid)
630a$^3$ *795a$^{15}$ (1002)* 4742$^7$ *5304$^8$* 6673$^P$

**Sound Advice** *Keith Dalgleish* a94 98
5 b g Echo Of Light Flylowflylong (IRE) (Danetime (IRE))
*145$^4$ 550$^2$ 1014$^3$ (1113) 1234$^2$* 1721$^7$ 2145$^{11}$ 2478$^6$ 3437$^2$ 3573$^2$ (4002) 4491$^5$ *6140$^{13}$* 6752$^{29}$ 6936$^3$ 7545$^{13}$ 7688$^8$

**Sound Amigo (IRE)** *Ollie Pears* a42 67
6 b g Iceman Holly Hayes (IRE) (Alzao (USA))
2602$^{10}$

**Soundbyte** *John Gallagher* a59 59
9 b g Beat All(USA) Gloaming (Celtic Swing)
2067$^4$ 2801$^5$ *3579$^2$* 4082$^3$ (5403) *5863$^6$*

**Sound Of Guns** *Ed Walker* 88
4 b f Acclamation Eastern Lily (USA) (Eastern Echo (USA))
4445$^9$

**Sound Of Life (IRE)** *Rae Guest* a48 49
3 b f Cape Cross(IRE) Stylist (IRE) (Sadler's Wells (USA))
*660$^{12}$* 1395$^{10}$ 2025$^{10}$ 2926$^4$ *4321$^3$* 7284$^5$

**Sound Of Summer (IRE)** *Charles Hills* a61 76
3 b f Excellent Art Ibtikar (USA) (Private Account (USA))
2655$^7$ 3818$^2$

**Sound Reflection (USA)** *Charlie Appleby* a92 100
3 b f Street Cry(IRE) Echoes In Eternity (IRE) (Spinning World (USA))
1978$^3$ 2299$^6$

**Soundtrack (IRE)** *William Knight* a72 58
3 br g Excellent Art Umthoulah (IRE) (Unfuwain (USA))
2690$^{10}$ *3712$^4$* ◆ *4543$^7$ 5557$^3$*

**Souper Colossal (USA)** *Edward Plesa Jr* a100
2 b c War Front(USA) Soaring Emotions (USA) (Kingmambo (USA))
*7610a$^7$*

**Source D'Honneur (FR)** *D De Watrigant* 87
3 b f Baroud D'Honneur(FR) Belle Lagune (Barathea (IRE))
7857a$^6$

**Sourdeval** *C Lerner* a58 55
2 b f Paco Boy(IRE) Starfleet (Inchinor)
4883a$^4$ *8149a$^6$*

**Souriyan (FR)** *J-C Rouget* a74 97
3 b g Alhaarth(IRE) Serasana (Red Ransom (USA))
*(751a)*

**Southampton (GER)** *S Smrczek* a76 46
3 ch c Tertullian(USA) Sayada (GER) (Dr Fong (USA))
*7630a$^{11}$*

**South Bank (USA)** *Mme C Head-Maarek* 97
2 gr f Tapit(USA) Special Duty (Hennessy (USA))
4482a$^5$ 5617a$^3$

**South Cape** *Gary Moore* a69 70
11 b g Cape Cross(IRE) Aunt Ruby (USA) (Rubiano (USA))
*211$^6$ 690$^9$ 1097$^2$*

**Southern Cross** *Andy Turnell* a60 60
3 ch f Mount Nelson Bread Of Heaven (Machiavellian (USA))
1422$^{13}$ *1767$^3$ 2126$^5$* 6070$^9$ *6564$^{10}$ 6883$^{11}$* 7021$^2$ 7517$^{DSQ}$ *8050$^5$ 8315$^{11}$*

**Southern Honey (USA)** *George R Arnold II* a104
3 b f Colonel John(USA) Mama Tia (USA) (Carson City (USA))
*7608a$^6$*

**Southview Lady** *Mark Walford* a34
2 b f Misu Bond(IRE) Salalah (Lion Cavern (USA))
*6408$^{10}$*

**Souvenir Delondres (FR)** *J E Pease* 105
2 b f Siyouni(FR) Dilag (IRE) (Almutawakel)
(5405a) 6220a$^3$ (7094a) 7655a$^5$

**Souville** *Chris Wall* a92 87
3 b f Dalakhani(IRE) Royale Danehill (IRE) (Danehill (USA))
2429$^2$ (3185) 4445$^6$ *5553$^2$* 6260$^{10}$ *6607$^5$*

**Sov (IRE)** *Alan McCabe* 71
3 rg c Duke Of Marmalade(IRE) Exotic Mix (FR) (Linamix (FR))
(6494)

**Sovalla** *P Schiergen* 97
3 ch f Pomellato(GER) Soiree De Vienne (IRE) (Marju (IRE))
7483a$^{13}$

**Sovento (GER)** *Thomas McLaughlin* a55 41
10 ch g Kornado Second Game (GER) (Second Set (IRE))
*459$^{10}$ 530$^6$*

**Sovereign Bounty** *Jedd O'Keeffe* 65
2 ch g Bahamian Bounty Sovereign Abbey (IRE) (Royal Academy (USA))
3569$^7$ 4467$^4$ 4790$^2$

**Soviet Courage (IRE)** *William Haggas* a74 93
3 ch g Dutch Art Place De Moscou (IRE) (Rock Of Gibraltar (IRE))
4407$^4$ 5347$^2$ (6002) 7135$^3$

**Soviet Rock (IRE)** *Andrew Balding* 103
4 b g Rock Of Gibraltar(IRE) Anna Karenina (USA) (Atticus (USA))
1653$^3$ (2154) ◆ 2957$^{10}$ 6878$^2$ 7120$^7$

**Soviet Union (IRE)** *Mark Walford* 35
3 b f Soviet Star(USA) Miznapp (Pennekamp (USA))
4791$^8$ 5195$^7$ 5469$^6$ 6454$^{13}$ 6932$^7$

**Space Age (IRE)** *Charlie Appleby* 84
2 ch c New Approach(IRE) Historian (IRE) (Pennekamp (USA))
4167$^8$ 4666$^3$ (5296)

**Space Artist (IRE)** *Bryan Smart* a82 86
4 b g Captain Marvelous(IRE) Dame Laura (IRE) (Royal Academy (USA))
1566$^5$ 1961$^6$ 2352$^{10}$ (4521) 5563$^9$ 6096$^{13}$ 6650$^9$

**Spacelab** *Amanda Perrett* a89 91
3 b f Champs Elysees Shuttle Mission (Sadler's Wells (USA))
*(5831)* ◆ 6654$^2$ ◆ *7554$^8$*

**Space Sheriff (IRE)** *Jamie Osborne* a55
2 b g Lawman(FR) Launch Time (USA) (Relaunch (USA))
*7353$^9$ 7625$^7$ 7763$^2$ 7904$^{10}$*

**Space Walker (IRE)** *Harry Dunlop* a71 82
3 b g Astronomer Royal(USA) Hot Property (USA) (Thunder Gulch (USA))
*1404$^3$* 2027$^2$ (2624) *3861$^{12}$* 5274$^7$ *6633$^9$* 7341$^2$ 7516$^4$

**Space War** *Michael Easterby* a65 75
7 b g Elusive City(USA) Princess Luna (GER) (Grand Lodge (USA))
1446$^6$ 2169$^7$ 2546$^5$ (3344) 3547$^6$ 4451$^7$ 5142$^9$ 5793$^6$ *6161$^4$* 6625$^3$ 7502$^9$

**Spacious Sky (USA)** *A J Martin* a85 90
5 b g North Light(IRE) Ratings (USA) (Caveat (USA))
4746a$^4$ 5579$^3$ 6349a$^6$ 7476a$^2$

**Spalato (NZ)** *John F O'Hara* 110
5 b g Elusive City(USA) Ellington (NZ) (Express Duke (AUS))
7897a$^{13}$ 8152a$^{12}$

**Spaliburg Rosetgri (FR)** *M Boutin* a64 72
3 b g Sageburg(IRE) Spalitas (FR) (Medaaly)
*482a$^8$ 585a$^8$*

**Spanish Bounty** *Mrs A Malzard* a49 60
9 b g Bahamian Bounty Spanish Gold (Vettori (IRE))
1623a$^6$ 2592a$^3$ 4715a$^3$ 5228a$^5$ (6186a)

**Spanish Danser (IRE)** *George Baker* 29
2 ch f Lord Shanakill(USA) Highwater Dancer (IRE) (Sadler's Wells (USA))
7412$^7$

**Spanish Fork (IRE)** *Sheena West* a30 68
5 br g Trans Island Wings Awarded (Shareef Dancer (USA))
*6486$^{13}$*

**Spanish Pipedream (USA)** *Wesley A Ward* a90 96
2 b f Scat Daddy(USA) Doc's Leading Lady (USA) (Doc's Leader (USA))
3353$^4$

**Spanish Plume** *Andrew Hollinshead* a75 81
6 b g Ishiguru(USA) Miss Up N Go (Gorytus (USA))
*151$^2$ 514$^{10}$ 733$^5$ (1000) 1034$^5$ 1628$^5$ (1815)* 3546$^2$ (4190) 4710$^{11}$ 4940$^3$ *6274$^5$*

**Spanish Squeeze (IRE)** *Hugo Palmer* a83 77
2 ch c Lope De Vega(IRE) Appetina (Perugino (USA))
6712$^3$ *(7372)* ◆

**Spanish Whipper (IRE)** *M Delcher Sanchez* a67 81
3 b g Whipper(USA) Janistra (USA) (Grand Slam (USA))
3809a$^{10}$

**Sparbrook (IRE)** *Simon Dow* a62 36
2 b f Kodiac Summer Sunshine (Dubai Destination (USA))
*1314$^3$* 1488$^{10}$ *2206$^7$* 3312$^8$ 5180$^{10}$ *5279$^8$ 6017$^2$ (6888) (7190) 7453$^8$ 7683$^7$* 7848$^8$ 8069$^{12}$ 8240$^5$

**Sparkel D'Hermeray (FR)** *Mme C De La Soudiere-Niault* a65 59
3 b f Tomorrows Cat(USA) Illumination (Saddlers' Hall (IRE))
2978a$^{14}$

**Sparkle Factor (IRE)** *D K Weld* 95
3 b f Arch(USA) Thoughtless Moment (IRE) (Pivotal)
4276a$^5$ 5612$^{14}$

**Sparkle Girl** *Tim Easterby* 48
2 ch f Stimulation(IRE) Seren Teg (Timeless Times (USA))
1505$^{10}$ 2386$^{13}$ 3542$^5$ 6148$^6$ 6428$^5$

**Sparkling Beam (IRE)** *J E Pease* 114
4 b f Nayef(USA) Pearl Dance (USA) (Nureyev (USA))
1827a$^6$ 3291a$^9$ 5459a$^8$ (7070a) 7558a$^3$

**Sparkling Frost (FR)** *S Wattel* a55 55
2 gr f Silver Frost(IRE) Grosgrain (USA) (Diesis)
5544a$^6$ *8149a$^8$*

**Sparkling Ice (IRE)** *Zoe Davison* a68 51
3 gr f Verglas(IRE) Sand Crystal (IRE) (Singspiel (IRE))
*800$^4$ 1024$^2$ 1233$^6$* 1947$^9$ 2688$^7$ 3898$^4$ *4910$^4$ 5491$^4$* (5719) *(6043) 8099$^8$*

**Sparkling Sapphire** *Richard Whitaker* a38 37
2 ro f Monsieur Bond(IRE) Velvet Band (Verglas (IRE))
2349$^7$ 2895$^8$ 3909$^6$ 4973$^8$ 6642$^3$ *7648$^3$ 7824$^3$*

**Spark Plug (IRE)** *Brian Meehan* 104
3 b g Dylan Thomas(IRE) Kournikova (SAF) (Sportsworld (USA))
(2330) 3375$^6$ 4366$^2$ 5755$^5$

**Sparring (IRE)** *Charlie Appleby* a67
2 b c Teofilio(IRE) Henties Bay (IRE) (Cape Cross (IRE))
*7892$^5$*

**Sparrow (IRE)** *A P O'Brien* 94
3 b f Oasis Dream All Too Beautiful (IRE) (Sadler's Wells (USA))
1201a$^8$ 3167a$^3$ 3864a$^5$

**Spa's Dancer (IRE)** *James Eustace* a97 107
7 b g Danehill Dancer(IRE) Spa (Sadler's Wells (USA))
*625$^3$ 840$^8$* 1165$^9$ 1437$^2$ 2286$^7$ 2618$^2$ 3251$^8$ 5928$^4$ 6458$^7$ 7022$^6$ 7449$^8$

**Spavento (IRE)** *Eric Alston* a42 58
8 gr m Verglas(IRE) Lanasara (Generous (IRE))
1345$^6$ 1607$^{11}$ 2454$^2$ 2676$^5$ 2826$^4$ 3005$^6$ 3608$^5$ 3885$^7$ 4255$^5$ 6009$^6$ 6601$^5$ 6836$^7$ *7115$^{12}$*

**Special Code (IRE)** *John Gosden* a68
2 b c Iffraaj Najmati (Green Desert (USA))
*7833$^6$* ◆ *8067$^9$ 8292$^8$*

**Special Dream (FR)** *H-A Namur* a62 65
4 b f Slickly(FR) Apostrophe (IRE) (Barathea (IRE))
*266a$^{11}$ 722a$^{11}$*

**Special Fighter (IRE)** *Mark Johnston* 91
3 ch c Teofilo(IRE) Susu (Machiavellian (USA))
2075$^7$ 2365$^8$ 3568$^2$ 4120$^6$ (4754) (4995) 5132$^5$ 5633$^{12}$ 6005$^7$ 6366$^4$

**Special Meaning** *Mark Johnston* a63 100
4 b f Mount Nelson Specifically (USA) (Sky Classic (CAN))
1562$^3$ (1942) 2294$^5$ 2764$^5$ 4443$^9$ 5673$^3$ 5920$^4$ 6589a$^4$ 7482a$^2$

**Special Miss** *Ali Stronge* a68 78
3 b f Authorized(IRE) Whatamiss (USA) (Miswaki (USA))
*167$^4$* 2867$^7$ 3803$^3$ (4802) 5095$^4$ (5930) 6459$^6$ 7567$^7$

**Special Mix** *Martin Smith* a72 75
6 b g Proclamation(IRE) Flaming Spirt (Blushing Flame (USA))
*120$^5$ 940$^5$* 1196$^{10}$ 2270$^{11}$

**Special Report (IRE)** *Neil Mulholland* a22 52
4 b g Mujadil(USA) Ellistown Lady (IRE) (Red Sunset)
4040a$^4$

**Special Request (FR)** *N Caulley* a93 79
7 gr g Kaldounevees(FR) Radio Mesnil (FR) (Nashamaa)
*584a$^2$ (5961a)*

**Specialty (IRE)** *Pam Sly* a40 79
4 b f Oasis Dream Speciosa (IRE) (Danehill Dancer (IRE))
1613$^2$ 2021$^4$ 2529$^2$ 3123$^2$ (3678) (4620) 5727$^3$ 6303$^{10}$

**Special Venture (IRE)** *Tim Easterby* 77
2 b c Azamour(IRE) La Reine Mambo (USA) (High Yield (USA))
2288$^6$ 2895$^4$ (3542) 4897$^2$ 6151$^4$ 6529$^8$ 7005$^2$ 7443$^{10}$

**Specific Gravity (FR)** *Adrian McGuinness* a96 97
6 b g Dansili Colza (USA) (Alleged (USA))
*108a$^8$* 242a$^7$ *593a$^7$ 681a$^9$* 4771a$^{16}$

**Speckled (USA)** *Charlie Appleby* a96 78
4 b f Street Cry(IRE) Painted Lady (USA) (Broad Brush (USA))
4443$^8$ *7554$^5$*

**Spectacle Attendu (FR)** *Y Gourraud* a61
2 ch c Panis(USA) Spectacular Groove (USA) (Trempolino (USA))
*8148a$^5$*

**Spectator** *Andrew Balding* a62 91
3 br g Passing Glance Averami (Averti (IRE))
1786$^3$ 2417$^4$ (2671) 2839$^3$ (4189) 4803$^5$ 6137$^3$ 6705$^3$ (7409)

**Speculative Bid (IRE)** *David Elsworth* a80 86
3 b g Excellent Art Barzah (IRE) (Darshaan)
1511$^7$ *1795$^2$* (2201) 2781$^5$

**Speculator** *David Menuisier* a48 15
2 gr c Bahamian Bounty Swift Dispersal (Shareef Dancer (USA))
4025$^{15}$ *7542$^6$*

**Speechday (IRE)** *Marco Botti* a68 46
3 b f Kodiac Privileged Speech (USA) (General Assembly (USA))
*189$^2$ 456$^2$ 660$^2$* 2492$^7$ 3683$^5$

**Speedbird One** *James Given* a56 67
3 ch f Mount Nelson Good Girl (IRE) (College Chapel)
*962$^3$ 1888$^4$* 2643$^6$ 3545$^6$ 3950$^{13}$

**Speed Dream (IRE)** *James M Barrett* a82 80
10 ch g Pivotal Copper Creek (Habitat (USA))
3686a$^5$

**Speedfiend** *Noel Quinlan* a95 104
3 b g Bahamian Bounty Vive Les Rouges (Acclamation)
*(1229)* 1867$^7$ 3245$^7$ 4669$^{15}$

**Speedfit Rules (IRE)** *George Margarson* 57
2 gr c Aussie Rules(USA) Jusoor (USA) (El Prado (IRE))
7037$^{13}$ 7383$^5$ 7536$^5$

**Speed Hawk (USA)** *Robert Cowell* a97 105
3 bb c Henny Hughes(USA) Cosmic Wing (USA) (Halo (USA))
2317$^2$ 3219$^6$ 3478$^2$ 4179$^7$ (4281) 5696$^8$ *6159$^3$* (6467)

**Speediness (AUS)** *Colin Scott* 118
7 b g Testa Rossa(AUS) Fine Glass (AUS) (Flying Spur (AUS))
1186a$^2$ 7128a$^2$

**Speed Machine (IRE)** *Paul Cole* a82 83
2 b c Naaqoos Copernica (IRE) (Galileo (IRE))
2800$^5$ *3113$^4$ (3640a)* 4932a$^5$ 5478a$^5$ *8149a$^4$*

**Speedrider (IRE)** *Mme Pia Brandt* a86 86
4 gr g Dansili Dariena (FR) (Highest Honor (FR))
6971a$^{14}$

**Speed Society** *Jim Boyle* a63 55
3 b g Bertolini(USA) Tamara (Marju (IRE))
*(1285)* 1683$^4$ *2209$^7$* 3087$^9$ *4055$^{10}$* 4352$^6$ *5257$^5$*

**Speed Steed (IRE)** *Tim Vaughan* a68 65
7 b g One Cool Cat(USA) Dhakhirah (IRE) (Sadler's Wells (USA))
*2885$^2$* 4843$^4$

**Speedy Approach** *A Wohler* 101
3 ch c New Approach(IRE) Height Of Vanity (IRE) (Erhaab (USA))
1781a$^8$ 3073a$^2$ 4007a$^6$

**Speedy Boarding** *James Fanshawe* 65
2 b f Shamardal(USA) Dash To The Front (Diktat)
7405$^3$ ◆

**Speedy Crown (FR)** *M Nigge* a74 71
8 gr g True Brave(USA) Queen's Crown (FR) (Adieu Au Roi (IRE))
920a$^2$

**Speedyfix** *Christine Dunnett* a63 68
7 b g Chineur(FR) Zonnebeke (Orpen (USA))
*53$^{11}$ 164$^5$ 313$^4$ 937$^5$*

**Speedy Glaz (FR)** *A Clement* a68 65
3 b c Literato(FR) South Island (IRE) (Sadler's Wells (USA))
*600a$^7$*

**Speedy Move (IRE)** *Ismail Mohammed* a84 84
2 b c Iffraaj Beautiful Filly (Oasis Dream)
2777$^4$ 3255$^7$ 3881$^3$ (4787) *(5306) 6142$^{10}$*

**Speedy Rio (IRE)** *Luke Dace* a42
3 ch g Captain Rio Love Sonnet (Singspiel (IRE))
*4432$^6$ 4735$^4$ 5044$^9$ 6161$^9$ 6243$^9$ 6851$^9$* 6983$^7$

**Speedy Star (IRE)** *Tina Jackson* 38
5 b g Authorized(IRE) North Sea (IRE) (Selkirk (USA))
3482$^8$ 4293$^{13}$

**Speedy Writer** *Henry Candy* a72 73
4 b g Byron Merch Rhyd-Y-Grug (Sabrehill (USA))
2012$^9$ *3112$^8$* 3562$^4$ 4030$^6$ 4548$^8$ 5383$^6$ 6617$^4$ *(6883)*

**Speightowns Kid (USA)** *Ann Stokell* a71 59
6 rg g Speightstown(USA) Seize The Wind (USA) (Maria's Mon (USA))
*1814$^2$* 2232$^8$ *2933$^7$ 6898$^{11}$ 7698$^8$ 7915$^2$ 8082$^2$ 8182$^4$*

**Spellbind** *Charlie Appleby* a66 79
3 b f Shamardal(USA) Bedazzle (USA) (Dixieland Band (USA))
2780$^3$ 4867$^3$ *5548$^7$ 6033$^5$*

**Spellmaker** *Tony Newcombe* a79 76
5 b g Kheleyf(USA) Midnight Spell (Night Shift (USA))
*53$^{10}$ (244) (449) (628) 714$^3$ (925) 1921$^3$* (3213) *4078$^6$ 5281$^{10}$* 6263$^{13}$ 7307$^3$ 8072$^8$

**Spencers Lad** *Michael Easterby* a11
4 b g Sixties Icon Black Opal (Machiavellian (USA))
*76$^5$*

**Spend A Penny (IRE)** *John Quinn* 64
2 b g Acclamation Coachhouse Lady (USA) (Rahy (USA))
2291$^4$ 3215$^5$ 4170$^5$ 6401$^7$

**Sperrin (IRE)** *Charlie Appleby* a59
2 b c Dubawi(IRE) Speciosa (IRE) (Danehill Dancer (IRE))
*7985$^4$ 8288$^6$*

**Sperry (IRE)** *John Gosden* a82 70
2 b f Shamardal(USA) Badee'A (IRE) (Marju (IRE))
6554$^8$ 7174$^3$ *(7809)* ◆

**Spes Nostra** *David Barron* a96 78
6 b g Ad Valorem(USA) Millagros (IRE) (Pennekamp (USA))
*29$^5$ (782) (942) (1133)* 2091$^8$ *7955$^7$ 8144$^2$ 8266$^4$*

**Spessartine (IRE)** *Robert Eddery* a31
4 b g Duke Of Marmalade(IRE) Lasting Chance (USA) (American Chance (USA))
*17$^{13}$*

**Spice Fair** *Mark Usher* a87 91
7 ch g Trade Fair Focosa (ITY) (In The Wings)
*1383$^4$* 1981$^4$ *(2920)* (3249) *3859$^5$* 4606$^5$ (5334) 6005$^5$ 7107$^{33}$

**Spiceupyourlife (IRE)** *Richard Fahey* 81
3 b f Sakhee's Secret Tiger Spice (Royal Applause)
2090$^9$ (2545) 3187$^6$ 4013$^5$ 4631$^3$ 5713$^4$ 6626$^8$ 7172$^8$

**Spic 'n Span** *Ronald Harris* a58 51
9 b g Piccolo Sally Slade (Dowsing (USA))
*272$^6$ 478$^8$ 694$^9$ 797$^8$ 908$^5$ (1089) 1270$^8$ 1887$^4$* 2008$^{10}$ 2830$^3$ 3520$^7$ 3784$^3$ 4337$^4$ 4567$^8$ 5126$^5$ 5594$^4$ 5907$^5$ 6090$^6$ 6368$^2$ 6897$^5$ 7191$^6$ 7781$^{10}$ 8039$^5$

**Spider Bay** *Lydia Richards* a43 21
5 gr m Almaty(IRE) Severance (USA) (Dispersal (USA))
2044$^6$ 2846$^9$ *4735$^5$* 5518$^7$ *8008$^6$ 8311$^8$*

**Spider Lily** *Peter Makin* a50 66
3 b f Sleeping Indian Scarlett Ribbon (Most Welcome)
*2931$^8$* 3214$^{10}$ 4567$^5$ (5126) (5399) (6368) *6631$^6$ 7252$^{10}$ 8014$^8$*

**Spiekeroog** *Alan Brown* a36 71
8 ch g Lomitas Special (Polar Falcon (USA))
2900$^5$ 3482$^5$ 3912$^9$

**Spielberg (JPN)** *Kazuo Fujisawa* 119
5 b h Deep Impact(JPN) Princess Olivia (USA) (Lycius (USA))
7981a$^3$

**Spieta (IRE)** *John Quinn* a50 72
4 gr f Shirocco(GER) Zarawa (IRE) (Kahyasi)
2678[6]

**Spifer (IRE)** *Marco Botti* a100 94
6 gr g Motivator Zarawa (IRE) (Kahyasi)
1948[15] *2461[7]*

**Spillway** *David A Hayes & Tom Dabernig* a88 111
4 b c Rail Link Flower Market (Cadeaux Genereux)
7602a[4]

**Spinaminnie (IRE)** *Mark Johnston* a68 62
2 b f Moss Vale(IRE) Spinamix (Spinning World (USA))
7277[5] 7493[3] 7637[4] *7742[2]* *7919[3]* *8000[3]* *(8222)*

**Spin Artist (USA)** *Mark Johnston* a86 92
4 b g Hard Spun(USA) Miss Cap (USA) (Capote (USA))
*779[3]* *917[8]* *1102[7]* 1598[8] *2059[8]* 2603[10] *3080[5]* 3334[2] ◆ 3572[4] 3999[3]

**Spinatrix** *Michael Dods* 114
6 b m Diktat Shrink (Mind Games)
2161[2] 2564[6] 5445[2] 5467[2] (6760) (7122) 7716[3] 7856a[6]

**Spin Cast** *Brian Ellison* a48 52
6 b g Marju(IRE) Some Diva (Dr Fong (USA))
2169[13] 2540[8] 4964[12] *5600[9]*

**Spindle (IRE)** *Mark Usher* a69 69
2 b f Dubai Destination(USA) Phantom Turtle (IRE) (Turtle Island (IRE))
*1363[2]* *3403[3]* *(3794)* 5306[6] 6944[5] 7156[3] 7338[2] *7911[3]* *(8165)*

**Spin For A Harp (IRE)** *David Dennis* a55
3 b g Bushranger(IRE) Shining Desert (IRE) (Green Desert (USA))
*423[9]* *741[10]* *1107[4]* *1384[9]* 2416[15]

**Spinner Lane** *Richard Whitaker* 42
3 ch f Three Valleys(USA) Petra Nova (First Trump)
1361[5] 1671[9] 2619[4] 3440[8] 4294[P] 4795[15] 5715[8] 6215[7] 6670[8]

**Spinning Cobblers** *Stuart Williams* a67 55
3 b g Royal Applause Tychy (Suave Dancer (USA))
*423[5]* *741[5]* *1018[5]* 2049[4] 3198[6] 4813[6] 5321[13] *6946[13]* *(7547)* *(7697)* *(7884)* 8090[3]

**Spiraea** *Mark Rimell* 79
4 ch f Bahamian Bounty Salvia (Pivotal)
2065[3] (2488) 3305[4] (3935) 4741[DSQ] (5355) 6006[5] 6492[7]

**Spirited Acclaim (IRE)** *David Elsworth* a68 68
2 b f Acclamation Lafleur (IRE) (Grand Lodge (USA))
6125[10] 6553[3] *7399[4]*

**Spirited Silver** *John Bridger* a14 38
3 gr f Proclamation(IRE) Real Emotion (USA) (El Prado (IRE))
1980[8] 2505[6] 3426[8] 3754[8] *4084[8]* *4911[12]*

**Spiriting (IRE)** *Luca Cumani* 83
2 b c Invincible Spirit(IRE) Gold Bubbles (USA) (Street Cry (IRE))
5149[7] 6462[2] 7037[6]

**Spirit In Time (IRE)** *Malcolm Saunders* 51
2 b f Vale Of York(IRE) Star Port (Observatory (USA))
3557[14] 3813[4] 4338[7] 5517[3] 6024[6] 6248[5]

**Spiritjim (FR)** *P Bary* 119
4 b c Galileo(IRE) Hidden Silver (Anabaa (USA))
(2106a) (2819a) 3774a[DSQ] 6381a[3] 6970a[16]

**Spirit Of Alsace (IRE)** *Jim Goldie* a50 68
3 b f Invincible Spirit(IRE) Alsace (King's Best (USA))
1758[15] 2217[5] 2474[3] 3191[6] (3460) 3575[2] 4017[5] 4256[3] 4724[5] 5080[5] 5816[5] 6515[7] 6863[4] 7056[11]

**Spirit Of Battle (USA)** *A bin Huzaim* a104 98
6 b h Elusive Quality(USA) Victoria Star (IRE) (Danehill (USA))
*304a[5]* *504a[7]*

**Spirit Of Gondree (IRE)** *Milton Bradley* a70 67
6 b g Invincible Spirit(IRE) Kristal's Paradise (IRE) (Bluebird (USA))
*155[6]* *289[5]* *750[2]* *(815)* *1454[10]* *2884[10]* 3562[9] *4073[11]* *5041[10]* *6160[3]* 6342[2] 7068[5] 7427[4] 7942[6] 8265[4]

**Spirit Of Rosanna** *Steph Hollinshead* a29
2 gr f Hellvelyn Tharwa (IRE) (Last Tycoon)
*7685[8]* *7917[6]* *8060[12]* *8225[5]*

**Spirit Of Sound (FR)** *Hugo Palmer* 39
2 b f Invincible Spirit(IRE) Sound Of Summer (USA) (Fusaichi Pegasus (USA))
6700[8]

**Spirit Of The Law (IRE)** *Richard Fahey* a93 97
5 b g Lawman(FR) Passion Bleue (In The Wings)
1715[7] 2253[8] 2959[11] (3251) 4379a[4] 4888[2] 5695[2] 6548[6] 6752[19] 7081[2]

**Spirit Of The Sea (IRE)** *Jim Goldie* 58
2 b f Invincible Spirit(IRE) Cedar Sea (IRE) (Persian Bold)
3454[6] 4486[3] 4973[7] 5630[4]

**Spiritoftheunion** *Michael Bell* a43 83
3 b f Authorized(IRE) Kahlua Kiss (Mister Baileys)
2899[2] (4978) 5723[6] 6559[10] 7565[13]

**Spiritoftomintoul** *Tony Carroll* a93 88
5 gr g Authorized(IRE) Diamond Line (FR) (Linamix (FR))
7235[3] ◆ *8096[3]*

**Spirit Of Wedza (IRE)** *David Wachman* 80
2 b c Footstepsinthesand Sampers (IRE) (Exceed And Excel (AUS))
6375a[21]

**Spirit Of Winning** *John Gosden* a55 76
3 b f Invincible Spirit(IRE) Crossmolina (IRE) (Halling (USA))
2804[3]

**Spirit Of Xian (IRE)** *Richard Hannon* 93
2 b f Kodiac Gold Again (USA) (Touch Gold (USA))
(1528) 2302[3] 2856a[4] 3806a[6] 4757[6] 5380[7] (5921) 6530[11]

**Spirit Of Zeb (IRE)** *Richard Fahey* a74 77
2 ch g Zebedee Miss Glitters (IRE) (Chevalier (IRE))
1536[6] 4129[2] 4439[18] 6474[3] 7277[2] *(7649)*

**Spirit O Goodchild** *Alan McCabe* a16 19
3 b g Sleeping Indian Well Of Echoes (Diktat)
*355[11]*

**Spiritorio (IRE)** *Mark Johnston* 49
3 b g Oratorio(IRE) The Spirit Of Pace (IRE) (In The Wings)
2170[6]

**Spirit Or Soul (FR)** *Marco Botti* a69 68
3 bb c Soldier Of Fortune(IRE) Far Across (Common Grounds)
1395[4] 1904[4] *3116[2]* *4547[7]*

**Spirit Quartz (IRE)** *X Nakkachdji* a98 113
6 b g Invincible Spirit(IRE) Crystal Gaze (IRE) (Rainbow Quest (USA))
4841a[4] 6966a[4]

**Spirit Raiser (IRE)** *James Fanshawe* a61 83
3 b f Invincible Spirit(IRE) Macadamia (IRE) (Classic Cliche (IRE))
1722[4] 2201[4] ◆ 3144[2] (3670)

**Spirit Rapping (IRE)** *Andrew Hollinshead* 49
2 b g Azamour(IRE) Snowpalm (Halling (USA))
7170[6] 7537[8]

**Spirit Rider (USA)** *Giles Bravery* a78 75
4 b g Candy Ride(ARG) Teenage Queen (USA) (Regal Classic (CAN))
*757[10]* *929[8]* *1234[9]* 1638[7] *2399[6]*

**Spirit's Revench (FR)** *P Demercastel* a81 104
4 ch c Spirit One(FR) European Style (FR) (Ezzoud (IRE))
984a[8] 2106a[5] 2821a[3] 5263a[8]

**Spiritual Acclaim (IRE)** *John Weymes* 21
2 b f Acclamation Sister Clement (IRE) (Oasis Dream)
5807[10]

**Spiritual Journey (IRE)** *Ann Duffield* 51
2 b f Zebedee Daneville (IRE) (Danetime (IRE))
6623[5] 7246[5]

**Spiritual Star (IRE)** *Anthony Carson* a97 86
5 b g Soviet Star(USA) Million Spirits (IRE) (Invincible Spirit (IRE))
*804[5]* ◆ *1070[3]* 2145[17] 2747[6] 3036[12] 3759[5] 4866[4] 5346[10] *(6100)* *6566[3]* *6943[7]* *7545[8]* 7774[2] ◆

**Spitfire** *J R Jenkins* a70 66
9 b g Mujahid(USA) Fresh Fruit Daily (Reprimand)
*297[3]* *387[2]* *1368[3]* *(1497)* *1892[2]* *4050[5]* 7337[3] *7647[12]* *8082[5]*

**Spithead** *Mike Sowersby* a44 48
4 b g Tiger Hill(IRE) Cyclone Connie (Dr Devious (IRE))
1503[6] 2019[13] 4069[12] 6644[9] 7007[5]

**Splash Of Verve (IRE)** *Philip Kirby* a63 61
2 b g Fast Company(IRE) Ellistown Lady (IRE) (Red Sunset)
5443[12] 5995[5] 6319[8] 6642[8] *7257[8]* *7810[3]* ◆ *(7994)*

**Split Step** *H-A Pantall* a69 67
3 b c Bahamian Bounty Nellie Gwyn (King's Best (USA))
1551a[9]

**Split The Atom (IRE)** *John Patrick Shanahan* a81 74
2 ch c The Carbon Unit(USA) The Mighty Atom (USA) (Sky Mesa (USA))
2736[2] 3358[4] 4382[3] 5167[2] 5847[3]

**Spoil The Fun (FR)** *C Ferland* a104 112
5 ch h Rock Of Gibraltar(IRE) Avezia (FR) (Night Shift (USA))
*306a[7]* 509a[12] 3291a[2] 4644a[3] 5960a[2] (7322a)

**Spoken Words** *John David Riches* a53 55
5 b m Fruits Of Love(USA) Jerre Jo Glanville (USA) (Skywalker (USA))
3099[4] 3548[2] 3833[5] 4287[8] 4532[5] 4795[8] *5510[8]* *5605[10]* *6076[6]* 7057[11] *(8291)*

**Spokesperson (USA)** *Frederick Watson* a58 72
6 b g Henny Hughes(USA) Verbal (USA) (Kingmambo (USA))
2426[5] 3364[4] 4000[4] 4958[7] 5337[11] 5854[4] 6223[10] 6670[4] *8004[3]* *(8258)*

**Sporting Bob** *Robert Eddery* a44
2 b c Mawatheeq(USA) Tanwir (Unfuwain (USA))
7560[9] *7835[10]* *8187[6]*

**Sporting Gold (IRE)** *Roger Varian* a83 84
5 b g Shirocco(GER) Pink Stone (FR) (Bigstone (IRE))
*856[2]* *1219[4]* 1659[2] 2272[12] 2851[3] 3699[2]

**Sporting Prince** *Ed Dunlop* 54
2 b g Pastoral Pursuits Queen Of Iceni (Erhaab (USA))
6204[7]

**Sportlobster (IRE)** *Tom Dascombe* a65 62
2 b c Strategic Prince First Bank (FR) (Anabaa (USA))
1349[3] 1504[8] *3524[4]* 4057[6] 4157[4] 4939[6] *5828[3]* *6678[6]*

**Spot (USA)** *Nicholas Zito* a108
3 rg g Pulpit(USA) Quiet Summernight (USA) (Quiet American (USA))
*(813a)*

**Spot The Pro (IRE)** *Rebecca Menzies* 62
5 b g Barathea(IRE) Truly Precious (IRE) (Pennekamp (USA))
3302[4] 4062[4] 4705[3] 5270[7]

**Spowarticus** *Scott Dixon* a64 50
5 ch g Shamardal(USA) Helen Bradley (IRE) (Indian Ridge)
*477[4]* *918[7]* 2658[6] 4795[5] 5499[5] *(7864)* *8014[5]* *8143[2]*

**Spray Tan** *Tony Carroll* a66 63
4 b f Assertive Even Hotter (Desert Style (IRE))
*196[3]* *295[11]* *694[6]* *819[7]* 2435[12] 3520[3] 4102[5] (4285) 4567[7] 6815[8] *7364[9]* *7781[4]* *(8229)*

**Spreadable (IRE)** *Nick Littmoden* a82 72
3 br g Duke Of Marmalade(IRE) Spring View (Fantastic Light (USA))
*(165)* ◆ *(261)* ◆ *311[4]* *(429)* *501[2]* *573[2]* *667[4]* 1700[11] *1818[3]* 2717[3] 3480[11] 4043[4] *4612[3]* 5603[4] 6262[5] (6633) 6902[4]

**Spring Bird** *David Nicholls* a57 71
5 b m Danbird(AUS) Dolphin Dancer (Dolphin Street (FR))
1378[5] 1602[5] *(1887)* 1972[5] 2514[2] 3338[17] 3913[10] (4664) 5375[4] 5565[2] 5819[7] (6406) 6938[4]

**Spring Carnival (USA)** *H-A Pantall* 73
3 b f Bernardini(USA) Shesabullwinkle (USA) (Hesabull (USA))
5226a[4]

**Spring Dixie (IRE)** *Rae Guest* a48 69
2 gr f Zebedee Dixie Jazz (Mtoto)
5056[3] 5718[3] 6317[2] 6691[4] *7544[7]*

**Spring Fling** *Henry Candy* a86 83
3 b f Assertive Twilight Mistress (Bin Ajwaad (IRE))
1534[11] 1980[2] ◆ (3067) *7947[2]*

**Springinmystep (IRE)** *Ed de Giles* a70 91
5 b g Footstepsinthesand Joyful (IRE) (Green Desert (USA))
1731[12] 2522[8] (3216)

**Spring Lady** *Alan Jarvis* a43 43
3 b f Refuse To Bend(IRE) Spring Goddess (IRE) (Daggers Drawn (USA))
*1384[6]* 1647[10] 2045[7]

**Springlike (IRE)** *Amy Weaver* a72 62
3 b f Acclamation Spring Wave (IRE) (Dr Fong (USA))
6423[5] *7071[12]*

**Spring Loaded (IRE)** *Paul D'Arcy* a80 68
2 rg g Zebedee Nisriyna (IRE) (Intikhab (USA))
4087[4] *(4965)* 5672[7] *6104[3]* *(6679)* *7755[2]*

**Spring Offensive (IRE)** *Richard Fahey* 82
2 b g Iffraaj Night Sphere (IRE) (Night Shift (USA))
3827[3] (4467) 6165[2] ◆

**Spring Seraph (IRE)** *Olly Stevens* a48
2 gr g Dark Angel(IRE) Saffron Crocus (Shareef Dancer (USA))
*8026[12]*

**Spring Tonic** *Simon Dow* a77 72
5 b g Fantastic View(USA) Nukhbah (USA) (Bahri (USA))
*1798[11]*

**Spring Willow (IRE)** *Eric Alston* 28
3 b g Camacho Twinberry (IRE) (Tagula (IRE))
1347[6]

**Spruzzo** *Chris Fairhurst* 13
8 b g Emperor Fountain Ryewater Dream (Touching Wood (USA))
1197[13] 1485[7] 3661[8]

**Spykes Bay (USA)** *Vanja Sandrup* a82 82
5 ch g Speightstown(USA) She's A Rich Girl (USA) (Affirmed (USA))
*2244a[7]*

**Square Lamartine (FR)** *M Boutin* a82 70
3 b c Great Journey(JPN) Cite Fleurie (IRE) (Mark Of Esteem (IRE))
*795a[6]*

**Squats (IRE)** *William Haggas* 102
2 b g Dandy Man(IRE) Light Sea (IRE) (King's Best (USA))
3193[4] (3454) 4143[3] (5173) (6128) 6513[3] 7238[4]

**Squaw King** *Eve Johnson Houghton* a50 53
3 b g Sleeping Indian Change Partners (IRE) (Hernando (FR))
1792[8] 2694[11]

**Squire** *Michael Attwater* a70 42
3 b g Teofilo(IRE) Most Charming (FR) (Darshaan)
*7841[6]* *8094[2]*

**Squire Osbaldeston (IRE)** *Martyn Meade* a104 100
4 b c Mr Greeley(USA) Kushnarenkovo (Sadler's Wells (USA))
*(744)* *1170[3]* 2085[4] 3449[18]

**Squirrel Wood (IRE)** *Mary Hambro* a64 53
6 b m Sadler's Wells(USA) Didbrook (Alzao (USA))
2689[9] *3528[6]* *4266[4]* *5797[4]* 6028[4] *6481[8]* *7115[13]*

**Sretaw (IRE)** *Gavin Cromwell* a63 89
5 b m Kalanisi(IRE) Thats The Lot (IRE) (Flemensfirth (USA))
(5957a) 6354a[10]

**Sr Swing** *Philip Kirby* 52
3 b f Passing Glance Wigman Lady (IRE) (Tenby)
4022[7] 6282[4] 6762[3]

**Srucahan (IRE)** *P D Deegan* a80 101
5 b g Kheleyf(USA) Giveupyeraulsins (IRE) (Mark Of Esteem (IRE))
1824a[7] 3737a[14] (Dead)

**Sruthan (IRE)** *P D Deegan* a83 114
4 b g Arakan(USA) Giveupyeraulsins (IRE) (Mark Of Esteem (IRE))
(1473a) 2338[7] 5361a[3] 6963a[3]

**Ssafa** *Paul Cole* a81 79
6 b m Motivator Orange Sunset (IRE) (Roanoke (USA))
*655[10]* *857[2]* *1099[4]* (2067) *2651[3]* 2774[5] *(5551)* 6171[4] *7402[7]* *7620a[4]*

**Staffhoss** *Mark Johnston* a81 69
4 b g Lucky Story(USA) Jerre Jo Glanville (USA) (Skywalker (USA))
1345[13] 1607[12] 1970[10] 2341[7] 2607[9] 3005[3] 3094[3] 3436[6] 3604[7] 4014[3] (4517) 5166[8] 5267[3] 6227[4] 6600[2] 6837[3] 6936[15] 7098[4]

**Stafford Charlie** *John O'Shea* a18 17
8 ch g Silver Patriarch(IRE) Miss Roberto (IRE) (Don Roberto (USA))
4149[5]

**Staff Sergeant** *Michael Appleby* a86 57
7 b g Dubawi(IRE) Miss Particular (IRE) (Sadler's Wells (USA))
*39[3]* *(253)* *385[3]* *763[3]* *830[3]*

**Stage Girl** *Mark Hoad* a52
3 b f Tiger Hill(IRE) Primavera (Anshan)
*8020[6]* *8294[5]*

**Stag Hill (IRE)** *Bernard Llewellyn* a62 65
5 ch g Redback Counting Blessings (Compton Place)
*278[3]* *490[7]* 6628[11]

**Stags Leap (IRE)** *Philip Kirby* a58 57
7 b g Refuse To Bend(IRE) Swingsky (IRE) (Indian Ridge)
6542[4]

**Staines Massive** *Jane Chapple-Hyam* 46
4 b g Delta Dancer Russian Silk (Fasliyev (USA))
2044[4] 2442[11] 3123[8] 3800[4]

**Stake Acclaim (IRE)** *Dean Ivory* 80
2 b c Acclamation Golden Legacy (IRE) (Rossini (USA))
5646[7] 6702[2] ◆ (7712)

**Stamp Duty (IRE)** *Suzzanne France* a55 49
6 b g Ad Valorem(USA) Lothian Lass (IRE) (Daylami (IRE))
*40[9]* *317[10]* *538[5]* 1674[3] 2614[9] 3535[10] 5765[5] 6119[7] *(8265)*

**Stampede (IRE)** *Sir Michael Stoute* a74 83
3 b g High Chaparral(IRE) Summerhill Parkes (Zafonic (USA))
1395[6] *1795[4]* (2222) 2617[4] 4448[6]

**Stamp Of Approval (IRE)** *Chris Wall* a43 32
2 b f Approve(IRE) Wassendale (Erhaab (USA))
*3387[6]* 4444[12]

**Stamp Of Authority (IRE)** *James Tate* a69
2 b c Invincible Spirit(IRE) Silver Bracelet (Machiavellian (USA))
*7114[6]* *7833[5]* *8026[3]*

**Stanarley Pic** *Alan Swinbank* 84
3 b g Piccolo Harlestone Lady (Shaamit (IRE))
1344[4] 2235[3] 5015[2] 5387[2] 5818[4] (6596) (6825) 7102[6]

**Stand Beside Me (IRE)** *Tony Newcombe* a58 23
7 b g Footstepsinthesand Aleganza (IRE) (Lake Coniston (IRE))
1573[13] 2282[9]

**Stand Guard** *John Butler* a90 58
10 b g Danehill(USA) Protectress (Hector Protector (USA))
*2[2]* *(124)* *(363)* *601[2]* *(830)* *(860)* *1495[2]* *2904[5]* *3710[4]*

**Standing Strong (IRE)** *Zoe Davison* a67 68
6 b g Green Desert(USA) Alexander Three D (IRE) (Pennekamp (USA))
*117[5]* *229[4]* *490[2]* *(737)* *801[4]* *1100[3]* *1302[3]* *1919[2]* 2862[7] *3080[11]*

**Stand My Ground (IRE)** *David O'Meara* a86 102
7 b g Cape Cross(IRE) Perfect Hedge (Unfuwain (USA))
1164[2] 1948[18] 3109[5] (6402) 7490[9]

**Standpoint** *Conor Dore* a84 83
8 b g Oasis Dream Waki Music (USA) (Miswaki (USA))
*49[10]*

**Stand To Reason (IRE)** *Tony Carroll* a70 65
6 ch g Danehill Dancer(IRE) Ho Hi The Moon (IRE) (Be My Guest (USA))
6518[5] 7211[6] *7850[9]* *8012[5]* *8281[7]*

**Stand Up In Paris (FR)** *H Fortineau* 81
2 gr f Rip Van Winkle(IRE) Mixfeeling (IRE) (Red Ransom (USA))
7468a[4]

**Stanghow** *Mel Brittain* 68
2 b c Monsieur Bond(IRE) Melandre (Lujain (USA))
1955[5] 2134[2] 2328[6] 3367[2] 4172[3] 4686[8] 6212[5] 7038[13]

**Stanlow** *Daniel Mark Loughnane* a63 58
4 b g Invincible Spirit(IRE) Ghazal (USA) (Gone West (USA))
*17[9]* *40[2]* *(117)* *(435)* *737[5]* 2863[4] 3824[3] 4268[7] 5596[4] *6076[5]* *6407[7]* 6771[4] 7115[2] 7292[4] 7868[4] 8063[8] 8265[3]

**Stan Nineteen (IRE)** *Simon Hodgson* a66 31
3 b g Kodiac Redwood Forest (IRE) (Barathea (IRE))
1786[8] 2278[14] 2695[10] 3087[10] *8198[8]*

**Stanwyck (USA)** *John Shirreffs* a110
5 b m Empire Maker(USA) Set Them Free (USA) (Stop The Music (USA))
*7593a[7]*

**Stapleford Lad** *Stuart Williams* a62 47
3 b g Shirocco(GER) World Spirit (Agnes World (USA))
*2681[8]* 3709[8] 4329[13] 5034[4] *5820[3]* *6488[3]* *6666[2]* *7036[2]* (Dead)

**Star Anise (FR)** *Harry Dunlop* a74 48
3 b f Astronomer Royal(USA) Sasicha (IRE) (Montjeu (IRE))
3805[7] *5284[4]* *5865[8]* *(7118)* *(7290)* *8164[6]*

**Star Ascending (IRE)** *Brian Ellison* 60
2 ch g Thousand Words Sakaka (Tobougg (IRE))
2359[4] 3186[4] 3529[5] 6449[4] 7165[2]

**Starboard** *David Simcock* a98 104
5 b g Zamindar(USA) Summer Shower (Sadler's Wells (USA))
309a[8] 595a[11] *773a[6]* 2554[6] 3356[21] 4214[14] 5749[2] 7081[13]

**Starbotton** *James Bethell* a61 46
4 b f Kyllachy Bonne Etoile (Diesis)
*18[4]* *(370)* *516[3]* *846[7]*

**Starchaser (USA)** *Philip Hobbs* 53
4 bb g Pleasant Tap(USA) Salon Prive (USA) (Private Account (USA))
3106[8]

**Star Citizen** *Charlie Appleby* 88
2 b c New Approach(IRE) Faslen (USA) (Fasliyev (USA))
2428[3] (2837) ◆

**Star Cloud** *James Bennett* a13
3 b g Nayef(USA) Space Quest (Rainbow Quest (USA))
*8094[7]*

**Star Code (IRE)** *Richard Hannon* a82 75
3 b c Kodiac Mira (IRE) (Turtle Island (IRE))
1350[6] 1913[7]

**Star Cracker (IRE)** *Michael Dods* 75
2 ch g Starspangledbanner(AUS) Champagne Cracker (Up And At 'Em)
4624[7] ◆ (5297) ◆ 6427[8]

**Stardanse (IRE)** *John Bridger* a30
3 b f High Chaparral(IRE) Danse Spectre (IRE) (Spectrum (IRE))
*8294[7]*

**Star Date (IRE)** *Oliver Sherwood* a71 63
5 b g Galileo(IRE) Play Misty For Me (IRE) (Danehill Dancer (IRE))
*829[5]*

**Star De La Barre (FR)** *C Plisson* 38
3 b c Loup Solitaire(USA) Haute Et Claire (FR) (Smadoun (FR))
2003a[14]

**Star Dolois (FR)** *A Bonin* a87 74
3 ch c Naaqoos Bee Bee (FR) (Barathea (IRE))
3372a[4] *4952a[2]*

**Stardrifter** *Richard Fahey* 75
2 b g Rock Of Gibraltar(IRE) Alchemilla (Dubai Destination (USA))
3136$^{10}$ 3924$^{6}$ (4528) 5762$^{5}$ 6229$^{6}$ 7005$^{6}$

**Star Empire (SAF)** *M F De Kock* a99 111
8 b g Second Empire(IRE) Lady Maroof (NZ) (Maroof (USA))
205a$^{3}$ ◆ 507a$^{2}$ 811a$^{2}$ 1177a$^{3}$

**Starfield** *Michael Appleby* a96 87
5 b g Marju(IRE) Sister Moonshine (FR) (Piccolo)
2851$^{6}$ *6904$^{3}$ 7373$^{6}$ 7552$^{6}$ (7829) 7998$^{7}$ (8281)* ◆

**Star Fire** *Roger Charlton* a61 30
2 b f Dark Angel(IRE) Bunditten (IRE) (Soviet Star (USA))
4269$^{8}$ *6659$^{4}$* 7037$^{10}$ *7454$^{3}$ 7780$^{4}$*

**Starflower** *D Smaga* 91
3 b f Champs Elysees Posteritas (USA) (Lear Fan (USA))
4721a$^{9}$

**Starki (FR)** *C Boutin* a77 68
4 b g Meshaheer(USA) Starks (FR) (Daylami (IRE))
*266a$^{10}$*

**Star Lahib (IRE)** *A Wohler* 109
5 b m Cape Cross(IRE) Cannikin (IRE) (Lahib (USA))
2631a$^{7}$ (5462a)

**Starlet (IRE)** *D K Weld* 83
3 b f Sea The Stars(IRE) Treasure The Lady (IRE) (Indian Ridge)
5611$^{10}$

**Starlight June** *Jonathan Portman* 59
2 gr f Hellvelyn Pelican Key (IRE) (Mujadil (USA))
3558$^{9}$ 4270$^{9}$ 6517$^{15}$

**Starlight Princess (IRE)** *J S Moore* a71 53
3 b f Mastercraftsman(IRE) Definitely Royal (IRE) (Desert Prince (IRE))
*(157) 404$^{3}$ (473) 659$^{5}$ 3745a$^{9}$ 4952a$^{12}$*

**Starlight Serenade** *Ralph Beckett* a59 78
3 ch f Three Valleys(USA) Melody Maker (Diktat)
1711$^{4}$ 2355$^{2}$ (2504) 3727$^{4}$ 4112$^{3}$ 4426$^{2}$ 5394$^{2}$ 6057$^{4}$ *6681$^{8}$*

**Starlight Symphony (IRE)** *Eve Johnson Houghton* a81 76
4 b f Oratorio(IRE) Phillippa (IRE) (Galileo (IRE))
*1392$^{3}$ 1796$^{5}$* 2415$^{2}$ *7885$^{4}$ 8079$^{4}$ 8248$^{11}$*

**Star Links (USA)** *S Donohoe* a97 89
8 b g Bernstein(USA) Startarette (USA) (Dixieland Band (USA))
*(163) 465$^{2}$ (559) 887$^{10}$ 977$^{5}$ 8144$^{8}$*

**Starlit Cantata** *Eve Johnson Houghton* a76 74
3 b f Oratorio(IRE) Starlit Sky (Galileo (IRE))
*1403$^{4}$ 1794$^{3}$ 2210$^{2}$ (2998)* 3897$^{3}$ *4434$^{8}$* 4947$^{3}$ *5557$^{2}$* 6654$^{4}$ *7552$^{7}$*

**Starlite Jewel** *Stuart Coltherd* a19 52
3 b f Virtual Celestial Empire (USA) (Empire Maker (USA))
1634$^{4}$ 1860$^{8}$ 2526$^{4}$ *3389$^{12}$* 4728$^{3}$ 5233$^{8}$ 5631$^{10}$ 5853$^{0}$

**Starluck (IRE)** *David Arbuthnot* a73 61
9 gr g Key Of Luck(USA) Sarifa (IRE) (Kahyasi)
*7033$^{8}$*

**Star Of Mayfair (USA)** *Timothy Jarvis* a49 50
4 ch g Tale Of The Cat(USA) Kinsale Lass (USA) (Royal Academy (USA))
5403$^{7}$ *7360$^{8}$ 7524$^{8}$*

**Star Of Namibia (IRE)** *Michael Mullineaux* a66 64
4 b g Cape Cross(IRE) Sparkle Of Stones (FR) (Sadler's Wells (USA))
*85$^{7}$ 463$^{3}$ 567$^{5}$ 978$^{2}$ 1000$^{3}$* 2327$^{6}$ *5600$^{8}$*

**Star Of Seville** *John Gosden* 81
2 b f Duke Of Marmalade(IRE) Stage Presence (IRE) (Selkirk (USA))
7018$^{3}$ (7405) ◆

**Star Of Spring (IRE)** *Charles Hills* a64 69
2 b f Iffraaj Gift Of Spring (USA) (Gilded Time (USA))
3558$^{5}$ ◆ 4403$^{6}$ *5305$^{5}$* 5875$^{8}$ 6312$^{5}$ 6555$^{5}$ 6924$^{5}$

**Star Of The Stage** *Richard Fahey* a73
2 b g Invincible Spirit(IRE) Enact (Kyllachy)
*7361$^{4}$ 7742$^{3}$ 8026$^{7}$ (8317)*

**Star Pursuits** *Noel Quinlan* a16 57
2 b f Pastoral Pursuits Garter Star (Mark Of Esteem (IRE))
2692$^{7}$ 5885$^{4}$ 6393$^{3}$ *7112$^{8}$* 7497$^{12}$

**Star Request** *Ollie Pears* a50 45
4 b f Urgent Request(IRE) Carahill (AUS) (Danehill (USA))
*435$^{4}$ 783$^{6}$* 1503$^{9}$

**Starring Guest (IRE)** *Mick Channon* a43 62
2 b f Teofilo(IRE) Queen Of Stars (USA) (Green Desert (USA))
5644$^{5}$ 6001$^{4}$ 6246$^{7}$ *6663$^{7}$* 6869$^{7}$

**Star Rolling (AUS)** *Peter Morgan & Craig Widdison* 111
5 b g Casino Prince(AUS) Uneasy (NZ) (Zabeel (NZ))
7602a$^{10}$

**Stars Above Me** *Roger Charlton* 97
3 b f Exceed And Excel(AUS) Kalinova (IRE) (Red Ransom (USA))
1952$^{2}$ 2344$^{10}$ ◆ 3478$^{3}$

**Stars Aligned (IRE)** *Richard Hannon* a22 24
3 b f Sea The Stars(IRE) Senora Galilei (IRE) (Galileo (IRE))
2109$^{11}$

**Stars And Stripes** *Luca Cumani* 83
2 ch c Selkirk(USA) Capannina (Grand Lodge (USA))
7206$^{6}$ 7561$^{2}$

**Star Seed (FR)** *R Chotard* a76 55
5 b m Layman(USA) Nefouda (FR) (Neverneyev (USA))
*392a$^{7}$*

**Starsic (FR)** *Yves de Nicolay* 83
2 b f Sageburg(IRE) L'Hommee (FR) (Voix Du Nord (FR))
(6698a)

**Stars Over The Sea (USA)** *Mark Johnston* 99
3 b g Sea The Stars(IRE) Exciting Times (FR) (Jeune Homme (USA))
1652$^{3}$ 2087$^{5}$ 2986$^{6}$ ◆ 3379$^{13}$

**Starspangled Heat (USA)** *Barry Abrams* a87 102
6 ch g Unusual Heat(USA) Bel Air Belle (USA) (Runaway Groom (CAN))
7611a$^{12}$

**Stars So Bright (IRE)** *John M Oxx* a80 88
3 b f Sea The Stars(IRE) Night Fairy (IRE) (Danehill (USA))
2186a$^{7}$ *7579a$^{14}$*

**Star System (IRE)** *Frau R Weissmeier* a82 83
4 b c Danehill Dancer(IRE) Silver Rain (FR) (Rainbow Quest (USA))
*729a$^{P}$* 2821a$^{6}$

**Start Right** *S Seemar* a101 106
7 b g Footstepsinthesand Time Crystal (IRE) (Sadler's Wells (USA))
*207a$^{10}$ 394a$^{3}$ 593a$^{4}$ 681a$^{2}$* 812a$^{2}$ 900a$^{9}$

**Startup Nation (USA)** *Chad C Brown* 105
2 bb c Temple City(USA) Pennyrile (USA) (Wagon Limit (USA))
7590a$^{11}$

**Star Up In The Sky (USA)** *Kevin Ryan* a81 62
4 rg f Speightstown(USA) Prenuptial Plans (USA) (Runaway Groom (CAN))
*170$^{5}$ (384) 448$^{9}$ (766) 909$^{4}$ (1080) (1266)* 1672$^{6}$

**Starwatch** *John Bridger* a83 94
7 b g Observatory(USA) Trinity Reef (Bustino)
1351$^{3}$ 1810$^{2}$ 2033$^{3}$ (2627) 3065$^{6}$ *3582$^{3}$* 4354$^{4}$ (5213) (5758) (6523) 6786$^{7}$ 7449$^{5}$ *8012$^{4}$ 8095$^{12}$*

**Starwood (GER)** *P Schiergen* 90
2 bb c Motivator Starla Dancer (GER) (Danehill Dancer (IRE))
6123a$^{5}$ 7145a$^{6}$

**Stasio (USA)** *David Simcock* a93 81
4 b g Street Boss(USA) Believe (USA) (Chimes Band (USA))
*163$^{3}$* ◆ *559$^{2}$ 1070$^{5}$*

**State Of The Union (IRE)** *Richard Hannon* a75 53
2 ch c Approve(IRE) First Lady (IRE) (Indian Ridge)
4618$^{3}$ *4965$^{2}$* 5684$^{9}$ *(6104)*

**Statsminister** *Luke Dace* a37 83
3 b f Champs Elysees Sailing Days (Kris)
2404$^{10}$ *2881$^{9}$* 3568$^{3}$ (4106) (4863) 5356$^{2}$ ◆ 6318$^{4}$ 6894$^{5}$

**Statutory (IRE)** *Saeed bin Suroor* 107
4 b g Authorized(IRE) Mialuna (Zafonic (USA))
507a$^{10}$ 811a$^{12}$ 2785$^{5}$ 3453$^{9}$ 4213$^{6}$ 5579$^{4}$ 6005$^{4}$ (6979)

**Stay De Night (IRE)** *D K Weld* 102
3 b g Shamardal(USA) Where We Left Off (Dr Devious (IRE))
6354a$^{6}$

**Stay Silent (IRE)** *Saeed bin Suroor* a77 75
2 b f Cape Cross(IRE) Veil Of Silence (IRE) (Elusive Quality (USA))
4914$^{4}$ 5643$^{3}$ *(7184)*

**Stay Strong (GER)** *Saeed bin Suroor* a67
2 b g Monsun(GER) Sasuela (GER) (Dashing Blade)
*7892$^{4}$ 8093$^{5}$*

**St Brelades Bay (IRE)** *Richard Hannon* 84
2 b c Camacho Tides (Bahamian Bounty)
2146$^{4}$ 3140$^{4}$ (3728) 4143$^{4}$ 7415$^{8}$

**Steady Major (IRE)** *David Simcock* 74
2 b g Invincible Spirit(IRE) Combust (USA) (Aptitude (USA))
2776$^{6}$ 3324$^{2}$ 4666$^{7}$ 5373$^{5}$

**Stealing Thunder (IRE)** *Eve Johnson Houghton* a57 51
2 b c Makfi Brazilian Bride (IRE) (Pivotal)
4440$^{3}$ 5745$^{5}$ 6038$^{7}$ *6662$^{7}$ 6842$^{3}$* 7488$^{4}$

**Steal The Scene (IRE)** *Richard Hannon* a72 74
2 b c Lord Shanakill(USA) Namoos (USA) (Sahm (USA))
4864$^{3}$ (5248) *6678$^{5}$* ◆ 6977$^{7}$ 7379$^{4}$

**Stealth Missile (IRE)** *Clive Brittain* a93 86
3 b f Invincible Spirit(IRE) Wing Stealth (IRE) (Hawk Wing (USA))
3357$^{19}$ *(4053)* 4668$^{11}$ 5396$^{3}$

**Steaming Kitten (USA)** *Gianluca Bietolini* 104
3 ch c Kitten's Joy(USA) Steaming Home (USA) (Salt Lake (USA))
2376a$^{4}$ 3047a$^{4}$ (3776a) 5406a$^{5}$

**Stec (IRE)** *Tom Dascombe* 90
2 b c Bushranger(IRE) Start The Music (IRE) (King's Best (USA))
3613$^{9}$ (3924) (4440) 4897$^{9}$ (7404)

**Steel Blaze** *Nikki Evans* 2
2 b f Striking Ambition Ocean Blaze (Polar Prince (IRE))
2436$^{8}$ 3779$^{5}$

**Steel City Boy (IRE)** *Ann Stokell* a53 44
11 b g Bold Fact(USA) Balgren (IRE) (Ballad Rock)
*586$^{8}$ 692$^{6}$ 937$^{10}$ 973$^{5}$* 1679$^{5}$ *6843$^{10}$ 8133$^{5}$*

**Steelcut** *Mark Buckley* a70 48
10 b g Iron Mask(USA) Apple Sauce (Prince Sabo)
*35$^{3}$*

**Steeler (IRE)** *Charlie Appleby* a105 113
4 ch g Raven's Pass(USA) Discreet Brief (IRE) (Darshaan)
*111a$^{4}$* 397a$^{5}$ *681a$^{12}$* 3356$^{3}$ 4851$^{4}$ 5722$^{6}$ 6358$^{2}$

**Steele Ranger** *Peter Chapple-Hyam* a70 68
3 b g Bushranger(IRE) Tatora (Selkirk (USA))
*1243$^{3}$* 1513$^{11}$ 1884$^{7}$ 3618$^{5}$

**Steel Rain** *Nikki Evans* a58 81
6 b g Striking Ambition Concentration (IRE) (Mind Games)
*122$^{7}$* 1789$^{11}$ 2803$^{9}$ 4946$^{6}$ 5275$^{RR}$ 5750$^{6}$ 7215$^{6}$ 7307$^{16}$ 7534$^{10}$ 7669$^{11}$

**Steelriver (IRE)** *Michael Herrington* a102 73
4 b g Iffraaj Numerus Clausus (FR) (Numerous (USA))
*369$^{2}$ 849$^{10}$ 1103$^{3}$* 1607$^{14}$ *2079$^{7}$* 3254$^{9}$ 3880$^{3}$ *6766$^{2}$* ◆ *(7183) (7543) 7923$^{5}$* 8101$^{10}$ 8117$^{2}$

**Steel Stockholder** *Mel Brittain* a67 72
8 b g Mark Of Esteem(IRE) Pompey Blue (Abou Zouz (USA))
1446$^{3}$ 1609$^{3}$ 2169$^{8}$ 3096$^{10}$ 4023$^{10}$ 7180$^{5}$ *7568$^{9}$ (8063)*

**Steel Train (FR)** *H-A Pantall* a82 88
3 b c Zafeen(FR) Silent Sunday (IRE) (Testa Rossa (AUS))
(1620a)

**Steely** *K Kukk* a20 66
6 b g Librettist(USA) No Comebacks (Last Tycoon)
1624a$^{3}$ 2593a$^{4}$

**Steevo (IRE)** *Gary Moore* a53 47
2 b c Dark Angel(IRE) Moriches (IRE) (Alhaarth (IRE))
5091$^{11}$ 5752$^{5}$ 6039$^{8}$ *(7014)*

**Steip Amach (IRE)** *J S Bolger* 100
2 b f Vocalised(USA) Ceist Eile (IRE) (Noverre (USA))
(7462a)

**Stella Bellissima (IRE)** *John Gosden* 90
3 b f Sea The Stars(IRE) Dolores (Danehill (USA))
(3891) ◆ 4824$^{6}$ 5611$^{8}$

**Stella D'Oro (FR)** *Mlle S-V Tarrou* 40
3 ch f Bernebeau(FR) Time Bere (FR) (Russian Blue (IRE))
4464a$^{10}$

**Stella D'Oroux (FR)** *S Smrczek* a72 85
3 ch f Monos(GER) Stella Di Quattro (Best Of The Bests (IRE))
7270a$^{3}$

**Stella Etoile (IRE)** *Richard Fahey* 74
2 b f Duke Of Marmalade(IRE) Sangita (Royal Academy (USA))
7174$^{2}$

**Stellar Express (IRE)** *Michael Appleby* a72 95
5 b m Royal Applause Aitch (IRE) (Alhaarth (IRE))
1483$^{2}$ (2091) 3217$^{11}$ 4060$^{9}$

**Stellar Glow (IRE)** *J S Bolger* 97
2 b f Sea The Stars(IRE) Glinting Desert (IRE) (Desert Prince (IRE))
6798a$^{3}$

**Stellar Jet (IRE)** *Roger Varian* a26 33
2 ch f Intense Focus(USA) Raise Your Spirits (IRE) (Generous (IRE))
4784$^{12}$ *6605$^{10}$ 7808$^{9}$*

**Stellar Path (FR)** *X Thomas-Demeaulte* 107
3 gr f Astronomer Royal(USA) America Nova (FR) (Verglas (IRE))
1096a$^{2}$ 2195a$^{5}$ 2817a$^{5}$ 6808a$^{8}$

**Stellarta** *Michael Blanshard* a80 70
3 b f Sakhee's Secret Torgau (IRE) (Zieten (USA))
4553$^{4}$ 4946$^{4}$ 7342$^{4}$ 7535$^{4}$ *(7989) 8072$^{6}$*

**Stellato** *Waldemar Hickst* a66 83
4 ch g Dalakhani(IRE) Sky Dancing (IRE) (Exit To Nowhere (USA))
2229a$^{6}$

**Stenid** *Kevin Ryan* a57
2 ch g Exceed And Excel(AUS) Indian Mystery (IRE) (Indian Ridge)
*8026$^{10}$*

**Stentorian (IRE)** *Gary Moore* a49 58
6 ch g Street Cry(IRE) Nomistakeaboutit (CAN) (Affirmed (USA))
*6721$^{10}$*

**Stephanie's Kitten (USA)** *Chad C Brown* a109 114
5 b m Kitten's Joy(USA) Unfold The Rose (USA) (Catienus (USA))
5459a$^{2}$ 7607a$^{2}$

**Stephen Hero (IRE)** *Dan Skelton* 71
4 br g Celtic Swing Albaiyda (IRE) (Brief Truce (USA))
6264$^{5}$

**Step Into The Tide (IRE)** *Joseph Tuite* a59
2 ch c Footstepsinthesand Pivka (Pivotal)
*7919$^{8}$ 8026$^{9}$ 8092$^{8}$*

**Step On It (IRE)** *Eve Johnson Houghton* a61 65
2 b c Footstepsinthesand Woodyousmileforme (USA) (Woodman (USA))
6293$^{8}$ 6984$^{4}$ *7354$^{8}$*

**Steppe Daughter (IRE)** *Denis Coakley* a78 76
3 b f Steppe Dancer(IRE) Carmencita (Rock Of Gibraltar (IRE))
*2211$^{3}$* 4500$^{6}$ 5976$^{2}$ *6634$^{2}$ 7032$^{3}$ 7841$^{2}$*

**Stepper Point** *William Muir* a116 117
5 b g Kyllachy Sacre Coeur (Compton Place)
*(1066) 1557$^{5}$* ◆ 1949$^{4}$ 2197a$^{3}$ 2820a$^{4}$ 3319$^{2}$ 3981$^{6}$ 4852$^{4}$ 5654$^{2}$ (6371a) 6966a$^{9}$

**Stepping Ahead (FR)** *K R Burke* a101 103
4 ch g Footstepsinthesand Zghorta (USA) (Gone West (USA))
*344$^{6}$ 764$^{3}$* ◆ *956$^{8}$* 1360$^{2}$ 2618$^{4}$ 5330a$^{5}$ 5440$^{4}$ 6098$^{8}$ 6548$^{15}$

**Stepping Out (IRE)** *Tom Dascombe* 96
3 b f Tagula(IRE) Teodora (IRE) (Fairy King (USA))
2340$^{7}$ (2965) (3788) 4892$^{14}$

**Steps (IRE)** *Roger Varian* a84 115
6 br g Verglas(IRE) Killinallan (Vettori (IRE))
1421$^{3}$ ◆ (2766) 2989$^{4}$ 3319$^{6}$ 3981$^{5}$ 5654$^{13}$ 6231$^{3}$ 6918$^{7}$ 7441$^{7}$

**Steps In Time (AUS)** *Joseph Pride* 112
7 b m Danehill Dancer(IRE) Rare Insight (NZ) (O'Reilly (NZ))
1468a$^{13}$

**Step To The Shears** *Richard Hannon* 91
2 ch c Footstepsinthesand Rockie Bright (Rock Of Gibraltar (IRE))
2499$^{3}$ (3181) (3751) 4398$^{4}$ 6004$^{4}$

**Stereo Love (FR)** *Clive Cox* a93 88
3 b f Champs Elysees My Heart's Deelite (USA) (Afternoon Deelites (USA))
1280$^{3}$ (2130) 2504$^{2}$ 3560$^{7}$ 4211$^{4}$ 5627$^{3}$ (6316) ◆ *(6681) 7579a$^{6}$ 7836$^{8}$ 8300a$^{8}$*

**Sterling City (AUS)** *J Moore* a121 119
6 br g Nadeem(AUS) So Gorgeous (AUS) (Brief Truce (USA))
*(1180a)* 2378a$^{5}$ 7897a$^{12}$ 8152a$^{10}$

**Sterling Cooper (IRE)** *P J Rothwell* a68 61
6 ch g Selkirk(USA) Ooh Aah Camara (IRE) (Danehill Dancer (IRE))
*7961a$^{11}$*

**Sterling Kate** *Roger Ingram* a40 43
3 b f Byron Sunny Times (IRE) (Raise A Grand (IRE))
2489$^{11}$ 3469$^{7}$ 3801$^{10}$ *4611$^{10}$ 5548$^{11}$*

**Sternrubin (GER)** *Peter Chapple-Hyam* 78
3 b g Authorized(IRE) Sworn Mum (GER) (Samum (GER))
1438$^{6}$ 1960$^{2}$

**Stetchworth (IRE)** *Mark Johnston* 87
3 ch c New Approach(IRE) Hallowed Park (IRE) (Barathea (IRE))
(6599) (6937) 7106$^{13}$ ◆

**Steuben (GER)** *J P Murtagh* a79 47
8 ch g Monsun(GER) Schwarzach (GER) (Grand Lodge (USA))
*(5101)*

**Stevalseba (FR)** *P Monfort* 76
2 b f Elusive City(USA) Maddie G (USA) (Blush Rambler (USA))
6591a$^{7}$

**Steventon Star** *Michael Scudamore* a99 76
3 b g Pastoral Pursuits Premiere Dance (IRE) (Loup Solitaire (USA))
*778$^{4}$ 850$^{3}$ 1067$^{12}$ 1555$^{14}$* 6755$^{13}$ *7227$^{12}$ 7543$^{12}$ (7799) 7971$^{7}$ 8188$^{6}$*

**Steve Prescott** *Richard Fahey* 86
2 rg g Dutch Art Toy Top (USA) (Tactical Cat (USA))
(3461) 3692$^{2}$ 4159$^{3}$ 4936$^{5}$ 6135$^{5}$ 6322$^{2}$ 6739$^{8}$

**Steve Rogers (IRE)** *Roger Varian* a60 52
3 b g Montjeu(IRE) Three Owls (IRE) (Warning)
4587$^{7}$

**Stevie Marvelous (IRE)** *C Boutin*
2 b c Captain Marvelous(IRE) Ceol Loch Aoidh (IRE) (Medecis)
2976a$^{10}$

**Stevie Thunder** *Ian Williams* a86 87
9 ch g Storming Home Social Storm (USA) (Future Storm (USA))
*344$^{9}$ 427$^{6}$ 744$^{5}$*

**St Georges Rock (IRE)** *Clive Cox* 69
2 b c Camacho Radio Wave (Dalakhani (IRE))
5377$^{11}$ 6985$^{5}$ 7512$^{3}$

**Stickleback** *Micky Hammond* a44 63
5 ch m Manduro(GER) The Stick (Singspiel (IRE))
1359$^{10}$

**St Ignatius** *Alan Bailey* a83 68
7 b g Ishiguru(USA) Branston Berry (IRE) (Mukaddamah (USA))
*3$^{4}$ 350$^{3}$ 623$^{12}$ 870$^{7}$ 1219$^{5}$* 2272$^{11}$ *2920$^{12}$* 3475$^{5}$ 4119$^{7}$ *5600$^{6}$* 6818$^{6}$

**Stilla Afton** *Marcus Tregoning* a53 55
3 bb f Nayef(USA) Sourire (Domedriver (IRE))
4587$^{5}$ 5313$^{6}$ 6194$^{6}$ *7118$^{5}$ 7777$^{5}$*

**Stillman (FR)** *P Khozian* a90 97
3 b c Vespone(IRE) Kikinda (FR) (Daliapour (IRE))
1781a$^{6}$ 2377a$^{3}$ 2818a$^{16}$ *8150a$^{7}$*

**Stinky Socks (IRE)** *Charles Hills* a67 72
2 b f Footstepsinthesand City Of Cities (IRE) (In The Wings)
1571$^{2}$ 2107$^{11}$ *4965$^{4}$* 5789$^{4}$ *6629$^{4}$* 6989$^{3}$ *(7255)*

**Stipulate** *David A Hayes & Tom Dabernig* 114
5 b g Dansili Indication (Sadler's Wells (USA))
7301a$^{12}$

**Stirabout (USA)** *J S Bolger* a47 78
3 b g Leroidesanimaux(BRZ) Fardus (IRE) (Danehill (USA))
1200a$^{10}$ 1458a$^{8}$

**St James Gate (IRE)** *John Joseph Murphy* 63
3 b g Papal Bull Summercove (IRE) (Cape Cross (IRE))
7494$^{14}$

**St Lawrence Gap (IRE)** *Robert Mills* a57
2 ch c Tagula(IRE) Kannon (Kyllachy)
5625$^{10}$ *6241$^{4}$*

**St Moritz (IRE)** *David O'Meara* a81 98
8 b g Medicean Statua (IRE) (Statoblest)
1724$^{7}$ 2137$^{5}$ (2654) (2868) 3244$^{3}$ 3982$^{7}$ 5178$^{10}$ 6479$^{11}$

**Stockhill Diva** *Brendan Powell* a61 77
4 ch f Haafhd April Stock (Beveled (USA))
(1729) 2248$^{3}$ (2947) 3540$^{3}$ 4354$^{6}$ 5503$^{6}$ *7831$^{8}$ 8068$^{6}$*

**Stock Hill Fair** *Brendan Powell* a82 89
6 b g Sakhee(USA) April Stock (Beveled (USA))
6518$^{4}$ 6987$^{5}$ 7235$^{8}$ *7838$^{5}$ 8073$^{5}$*

**Stocking** *Roger Varian* a71 71
2 gr f Acclamation Red Boots (IRE) (Verglas (IRE))
3671$^{10}$ 4973$^{2}$ 5429$^{6}$ 6253$^{9}$ 6555$^{6}$ *7728$^{2}$*

**Stocksandshares (IRE)** *Matthieu Palussiere* a47 54
2 ch c Approve(IRE) Dalal (Cadeaux Genereux)
*3640a$^{7}$* 5118a$^{5}$ 5662a$^{8}$

**Stoked (IRE)** *Ed Walker* 81
2 b c Fast Company(IRE) Es Que (Inchinor)
5646$^{4}$ ◆ 6545$^{2}$ (7039)

**Stolen Story (IRE)** *George Margarson* 73
2 b c Kodiac Mirwara (IRE) (Darshaan)
4025$^{4}$ ◆ 4416$^{7}$ 5212$^{2}$ 5875$^{11}$ 6648$^{8}$

**Stomachion (IRE)** *Sir Michael Stoute* a61 103
4 b g Duke Of Marmalade(IRE) Insight (FR) (Sadler's Wells (USA))
1444$^{4}$ (2783) 2991$^{2}$ 4756$^{8}$ 5651$^{5}$ (6287) 7476a$^{11}$

**Stomp** *Roger Charlton* a75 95
3 b g Nayef(USA) Strut (Danehill Dancer (IRE))
(1350) (2122) ◆ 2344$^{3}$ ◆

**Stoneacre Hull (IRE)** *Peter Grayson* a53 42
5 b m Bachelor Duke(USA) Amount (Salse (USA))
*731$^{4}$ 994$^{4}$ 1137$^{4}$ 1430$^{6}$*

**Stoneacre Oskar** *Peter Grayson* a52 44
5 b m Echo Of Light Keidas (FR) (Lomitas)
4362$^{4}$ 5390$^{7}$ 6595$^{12}$ 6834$^{6}$

**Stoneacre Thirsk (IRE)** *Peter Grayson* a34
5 br m Red Clubs(IRE) Alexander Eliott (IRE) (Night Shift (USA))
*1137$^{6}$*

**Stoneboat Bill** *Declan Carroll* 54
2 ch g Virtual Applauding (IRE) (Royal Applause)
6668$^{7}$ 6860$^{5}$ 7244$^{10}$

**Stonecrabstomorrow (IRE)** *Michael Attwater* a21 51
11 b g Fasliyev(USA) Tordasia (IRE) (Dr Devious (IRE))
3555[5] 5071[6] 5518[6] 5972[5] 6195[5] 6397[5]

**Stonecutter (IRE)** *Marco Botti* a84 77
3 gr c Mastercraftsman(IRE) Sparkle Of Stones (FR) (Sadler's Wells (USA))
2422[4] *7841[9]* *(8138)* ◆

**Stonefield Flyer** *Keith Dalgleish* a92 86
5 b g Kheleyf(USA) Majestic Diva (IRE) (Royal Applause)
*249[4]* *348[4]* *(574)* *1301[6]* 1564[7] 1928[3] 3456[8] 4384[7] 4783[15] 6511[22] 6535[8] *7521[4]* *(7636)* 7988[8] 8045[3]

**Stoneham** *Mick Channon* a60 52
3 b f Sixties Icon Cibenze (Owington)
*735[3]* *941[5]* *1084[2]* 1494[6] 1847[10] *2210[7]* 2695[2] 2878[3] 3281[6] 3821[6] 4210[4] 4562[4] 5005[8] *(6946)* 7256[9]

**Stone Of Folca** *John Best* a67 79
6 b g Kodiac Soyalang (FR) (Alydeed (CAN))
2390[11] 4174[7] 4762[9] *5830[7]*

**Stone Roses (IRE)** *Michael Bell* 69
2 ch f Zebedee Blanche Dubois (Nashwan (USA))
2744[7] 3119[8] 5344[5] 5973[4] 6989[6]

**Stonetastic (USA)** *Kelly Breen* a112 89
3 rg f Mizzen Mast(USA) Special Me (USA) (Unbridled's Song (USA))
*7608a[4]*

**Stoney Quine (IRE)** *Keith Dalgleish* a65 61
3 b f Royal Applause Shauna's Honey (IRE) (Danehill (USA))
*464[6]*

**Stopped Out** *Philip Kirby* 88
9 gr g Montjoy(USA) Kiomi (Niniski (USA))
3204[12] (4289) 4777[9] 5564[5] 7235[7]

**Storey Hill (USA)** *Richard Guest* a60 32
9 bb g Richter Scale(USA) Crafty Nan (USA) (Crafty Prospector (USA))
*17[10]* *269[3]* *672[P]*

**Storm (GER)** *Frau C Barsig* 94
3 b g Liquido(GER) Seefluh (GER) (Orpen (USA))
7769a[4]

**Storm (IRE)** *Charles Hills* a77 69
4 b f Excellent Art Bali Breeze (IRE) (Common Grounds)
2033[6] 2305[5] 2628[9] *3582[5]* *4081[6]*

**Stormardal (IRE)** *Ismail Mohammed* 96
3 b c Shamardal(USA) Dievotchkina (IRE) (Bluebird (USA))
1516[10] 2148[3] 2748[3] 4125[6] 4855[9] (5792) 6786[5]

**Storm Away (IRE)** *Patrick J Flynn* 78
5 b m Kalanisi(IRE) Dance Up A Storm (USA) (Storm Bird (CAN))
1750a[7] 4746a[17]

**Storm Belt (USA)** *Doug Watson* a103 93
5 b h More Than Ready(USA) Man's Thunder (USA) (Thunder Gulch (USA))
*593a[2]*

**Stormbound (IRE)** *Paul Cole* a78 71
5 b g Galileo(IRE) A Footstep Away (USA) (Giant's Causeway (USA))
*3112[2]* (3562) *6100[2]* *7205[4]* *7373[7]* *7633[3]* *8321[5]*

**Stormfly (IRE)** *D K Weld* 92
2 gr f Dark Angel(IRE) Intaglia (GER) (Lomitas)
2856a[3] 3763a[10] 6798a[4]

**Storm Force Ten** *Andrew Balding* a81 86
3 b g Shirocco(GER) Stravinsky Dance (Stravinsky (USA))
*(1220)* (2077) 2761[4]

**Storm Hawk (IRE)** *Pat Eddery* a77 59
7 b g Hawk Wing(USA) Stormy Larissa (IRE) (Royal Applause)
*1091[8]* *1770[3]* *2920[10]* *3859[9]* *4322[5]*

**Storming Harry** *Robin Dickin* a15 32
2 ch g Assertive Miss Pebbles (IRE) (Lake Coniston (IRE))
1807[4] 2172[8] *3578[10]*

**Storming Loose** *B Grizzetti* 103
7 bb g Storming Home Dan Loose (IRE) (Danehill (USA))
1603a[4] 2374a[7]

**Stormin Tom (IRE)** *Tim Easterby* 49
2 b g Dylan Thomas(IRE) She Storm (IRE) (Rainbow Quest (USA))
3481[5] 5296[7] 6056[12]

**Storm King** *David C Griffiths* a91 104
5 b h Shamardal(USA) Tarandot (IRE) (Singspiel (IRE))
1715[3] 2253[17] 3886[5] 4888[7] 5418[6] (5915) 6320[4] 7081[9]

**Storm Lightning** *Mark Brisbourne* a79 78
5 b g Exceed And Excel(AUS) All For Laura (Cadeaux Genereux)
*1431[3]* 1878[3] 2232[7] (2865) 3612[5] 3697[5] 4339[3] 5070[3] 5124[3] *5601[2]* 5945[4] 6398[6] *7071[8]*

**Storm Of Choice** *Michael Attwater* a38 22
3 b g Shirocco(GER) New Choice (IRE) (Barathea (IRE))
*717[6]* *951[9]* *1382[7]* 2850[11] *4615[9]*

**Storm Rider (IRE)** *Richard Hannon* 77
3 b c Fastnet Rock(AUS) On The Nile (IRE) (Sadler's Wells (USA))
1808[5] 2026[9] (2927) ◆ 3146[15] 5395[3] (5689) 5984[7]

**Storm River (FR)** *J Phelippon* 101
5 gr g Stormy River(FR) Embattle (FR) (Dernier Empereur (USA))
3172a[3] (5330a)

**Storm Rock** *Harry Dunlop* 81
2 b c Rock Of Gibraltar(IRE) Seasonal Cross (Cape Cross (IRE))
6085[2] ◆ (7084)

**Storm Runner (IRE)** *George Margarson* a70 51
6 b g Rakti Saibhreas (IRE) (Last Tycoon)
*286[9]* *589[5]* *780[6]* *7805[9]* *8030[7]*

**Storm The Stars (USA)** *William Haggas* 83
2 b c Sea The Stars(IRE) Love Me Only (IRE) (Sadler's Wells (USA))
6928[2] 7537[2] ◆

**Storm Trooper (IRE)** *Richard Hannon* a47 59
3 b c Acclamation Maid To Order (IRE) (Zafonic (USA))
3927[14] 5441[6] 6249[10] *7017[12]*

**Storm Ultralight (ARG)** *S Seemar* a63 82
8 b g Bernstein(USA) Ultrasexy (ARG) (Equalize (USA))
*207a[16]*

**Stormy Morning** *Philip Kirby* a68 54
8 ch g Nayef(USA) Sokoa (USA) (Peintre Celebre (USA))
*123[3]* *513[7]* *868[4]* 1567[5] 2055[12] 2620[11] 4259[11] *4656[4]* *5508[2]* *6343[6]* 6644[5] 7007[3]

**Stormy Ocean (FR)** *C Lotoux* a76 86
6 gr h Verglas(IRE) Miss Bio (FR) (River Mist (USA))
*3907a[8]*

**Stormy Paradise (IRE)** *Brian Meehan* 96
3 br g Excellent Art Stormy Larissa (IRE) (Royal Applause)
6560[8]

**Stormyra (FR)** *J-P Gallorini* 108
3 gr f Stormy River(FR) One Day (FR) (Act One)
(1096a) 1502a[3] 2586a[4] 2817a[4] 4009a[4] 4721a[8] 5960a[8]

**Stormy Weather (FR)** *Brian Ellison* a27 80
8 gr g Highest Honor(FR) Stormy Moud (USA) (Storm Bird (CAN))
*1743[5]*

**Storyline (IRE)** *Tim Easterby* 71
3 b f Kodiac Petite Histoire (IRE) (Desert Story (IRE))
1441[3] 1671[4] (2387) 3487[4] 4059[7] 4469[6] 6109[5] 6671[2] 6938[3]

**Storytale** *Michael Bell* 51
2 ch c Rip Van Winkle(IRE) Night Haven (Night Shift (USA))
6059[7]

**Story Writer** *William Knight* a86 85
5 b g Sakhee(USA) Celestial Princess (Observatory (USA))
1418[5] ◆ 1941[2] (2482) 3034[7] *3859[3]* 4441[5] *(5047)*

**Stosur (IRE)** *Gay Kelleway* a94 90
3 b f Mount Nelson Jules (IRE) (Danehill (USA))
*(391a)* *629a[3]* *721a[12]* 1868[6] 2639[6] (4842) *5843a[3]* 6388a[4] 7451[8] *7952[4]* *8300a[10]*

**Stout Cortez** *Mark Johnston* a43 71
3 b g Hernando(FR) Zooming (IRE) (Indian Ridge)
2319[8] 2893[3] 3120[4] 3498[5] 4316[4] 4386[5]

**St Paul De Vence (IRE)** *Paul Cole* a76 76
4 b g Oratorio(IRE) Ring The Relatives (Bering)
1881[5] 2270[4] *2687[3]* *2882[3]* 3515[3] 4028[2] 4743[4] *4968[11]* *6035[2]* 6523[9] *7522[4]*

**St Paul'S (IRE)** *David C Griffiths* a54 35
3 b g Bushranger(IRE) Regina Ballerina (IRE) (High Chaparral (IRE))
*316[11]* *564[5]* 2657[8] 3846[11] *4085[9]*

**St Paul's Square (IRE)** *Jamie Osborne* a21 19
2 b g Amadeus Wolf Swynford Lady (IRE) (Invincible Spirit (IRE))
*2928[10]* 3467[11] 3613[U] *4054[11]*

**Straight Gin** *Alan Berry* a29 46
3 b g Major Cadeaux Nee Lemon Left (Puissance)
1373[2] 1925[5] 2910[4] 3609[3] 4193[6] 7510[7] *7781[7]* *8229[9]*

**Straight Girl (JPN)** *Hideaki Fujiwara* 113
5 b m Fuji Kiseki(JPN) Never Period (JPN) (Taiki Shuttle (USA))
8152a[3]

**Straightothepoint** *Bryan Smart* a17 75
2 b g Kyllachy Choisette (Choisir (AUS))
2231[10] 2731[5] 3236[2] 3570[3] 5297[6] 5561[4] 6008[5] 6574[2] (6820) *7224[9]* 7714[5]

**Straight Thinking (USA)** *A Fabre* 105
3 gr f Mizzen Mast(USA) Hachita (USA) (Gone West (USA))
1480a[2] 2195a[14] 7319a[8]

**Strait Of Magellan (IRE)** *Michael Bell* a47
2 ch g Captain Rio Golden (FR) (Sanglamore (USA))
*7834[8]* *8000[10]* *8318[8]*

**Strait Of Zanzibar (USA)** *K J Condon* a93 89
5 b g Arch(USA) Royal Opportunity (USA) (Kingmambo (USA))
5957a[14] 6369a[14]

**Strait Run (IRE)** *Richard Hannon* 75
3 ch g Rock Of Gibraltar(IRE) Gentlemen's Guest (USA) (Gentlemen (ARG))
2968[6] 3182[4] 4147[8] 4574[7] 6654[5] 7309[2]

**Straits Of Malacca** *Kevin Ryan* a53 78
3 ch g Compton Place Cultural Role (Night Shift (USA))
*1818[6]* 2429[7] 3338[11] (4059) (4193)

**Strandfield Bay (IRE)** *Sharon Watt* a44 42
8 b m Wizard King Stylish Chic (IRE) (Arazi (USA))
*13[2]* *150[3]* *695[7]* *998[4]* *1249[6]* 1761[9] *2092[9]*

**Strandfield Lady (IRE)** *H Rogers* a62 83
9 ch m Pairumani Star(IRE) Stylish Chic (IRE) (Arazi (USA))
1078a[16]

**Strategic Action (IRE)** *Linda Jewell* a58 53
5 ch g Strategic Prince Ruby Cairo (IRE) (Nashwan (USA))
*184[8]* *370[7]* *586[2]* *760[4]* *858[4]* 1387[6] 7002[8] *7844[12]* *8175[4]*

**Strategical (USA)** *Charlie Appleby* a70 103
3 b g More Than Ready(USA) Mary Ellise (USA) (In Excess)
3245[8] 4405[3] 5289[5]

**Strategic Force (IRE)** *Clive Cox* a92 85
3 b g Strategic Prince Mooching Along (IRE) (Mujahid (USA))
*(1404)* 1952[3] 3185[4] 3539[7] 4697[8] *8071[2]* *(8252)* ◆

**Strategic Heights (IRE)** *John James Feane* a85 72
5 b g Strategic Prince Shot Of Redemption (Shirley Heights)
*128a[2]* *(788a)* 6324[6] *7873a[4]*

**Strategic Order (IRE)** *Paul Midgley* 66
2 b g Strategic Prince Glencoagh Order (IRE) (Danehill (USA))
1901[2] 3201[4] 3786[4] 4870[5] 5447[5] 5885[3]

**Strategise (IRE)** *Daniel Mark Loughnane* a52 42
2 ch f Strategic Prince Fikrah (Medicean)
2888[5] 3799[9] 4527[6] 5384[8] *5896[3]* *6563[3]* 6645[6] *8118[11]*

**Strath Burn** *Charles Hills* 108
2 b c Equiano(FR) Irish Light (USA) (Irish River (FR))
3889[DSQ] ◆ 4482a[2] 6547[4] 7238[2]

**Strathnaver** *H Graham Motion* a96 105
5 b m Oasis Dream River Belle (Lahib (USA))
7615a[2]

**Stravagante (IRE)** *Sir Michael Stoute* 77
2 b c Rip Van Winkle(IRE) Star Ruby (IRE) (Rock Of Gibraltar (IRE))
5881[10] (6859)

**Strawberriesncream (IRE)** *Rae Guest* 67
3 b f Teofilo(IRE) Jellett (IRE) (Green Desert (USA))
(2832)

**Strawberry Martini** *William Muir* a84 82
3 ch f Mount Nelson Strawberry Lolly (Lomitas)
1701[10] 2613[3] 3498[4] ◆ 4504[4] *6274[6]* 6651[2] *(7067)* *(7946)*

**Streama (AUS)** *Guy Walter* 115
6 b m Stratum(AUS) Pensiamo (AUS) (Sovereign Red (NZ))
1186a[6]

**Stream Of Light** *John Mackie* 42
3 b f Multiplex Flawspar (Montjoy (USA))
3097[9] 3650[12] *3792[7]* 4785[6] 5244[3]

**Street Artist (IRE)** *David Nicholls* a98 81
4 ch g Street Cry(IRE) Portrayal (USA) (Saint Ballado (CAN))
2952[7] 7279[8] *(7822)* *(7914)* *8062[6]*

**Street Boss (IRE)** *Jedd O'Keeffe* a53 62
3 gr g Verglas(IRE) Gladstone Street (IRE) (Waajib (IRE))
1657[8] 2204[8] *3406[3]* 3625[3] 3911[2] 4363[8] (4627) 4998[7] 5376[11] 6121[3] 6495[6] 7078[7] *7423[4]*

**Streetcar To Stars** *John M Oxx* 107
3 b c Sea The Stars(IRE) Approach (Darshaan)
5115a[3] 5736a[4]

**Street Entertainer (IRE)** *David Pipe* a78 75
7 br g Danehill Dancer(IRE) Opera Ridge (FR) (Indian Ridge)
6881[5]

**Street Force (USA)** *Clive Brittain* 91
3 b c Street Cry(IRE) Maskunah (IRE) (Sadler's Wells (USA))
1696[8] 3159[8]

**Streethowlingmama (USA)** *Olly Stevens* a48 39
3 bb f Street Cry(IRE) Mama Nadine (USA) (A.P. Indy (USA))
*480[5]* *653[2]* *786[10]* *1007[7]*

**Street Lair (USA)** *L Baudron* a98 71
7 ch g Street Cry(IRE) Hideaway Heroine (IRE) (Hernando (FR))
*178a[2]* *437a[5]*

**Street Of Gold (USA)** *Eric R Reed* a77 103
4 b f Street Sense(USA) Harriett Lane (USA) (Giant's Causeway (USA))
5459a[7]

**Street Party (IRE)** *Mrs Julie Cashin* a76 74
4 b g Rock Of Gibraltar(IRE) Lady Lafitte (USA) (Stravinsky (USA))
7476a[18]

**Street Power (USA)** *Jeremy Gask* a78 79
9 bb g Street Cry(IRE) Javana (USA) (Sandpit (BRZ))
*(296)*

**Street Runner** *Karl Thornton* a59 63
8 b g Rainbow Quest(USA) Dansara (Dancing Brave (USA))
*695[4]*

**Streets Of Newyork** *Brian Ellison* a77 86
7 b g Dalakhani(IRE) Minute Waltz (Sadler's Wells (USA))
*564[2]* ◆ *930[3]* ◆ *1171[8]* 1377[5] (2259) 2787[7] 3574[2] 4746a[7] 5579[14] 6171[5] *8144[7]*

**Strelkita (FR)** *D Smaga* 77
2 ch f Dr Fong(USA) Olonella (Selkirk (USA))
5941a[2] 7163a[2]

**Strictly Glitz (IRE)** *John Quinn* 73
3 b f Kodiac Dancing Steps (Zafonic (USA))
3946[6] 4495[2] (5245) (5336) ◆ 5566[5] 6980[5]

**Strictly Silver (IRE)** *Alan Bailey* a104 107
5 gr g Dalakhani(IRE) Miss Chaussini (IRE) (Rossini (USA))
*235[10]* *344[5]* *559[5]* *887[12]* 1948[9] 2085[5] 2618[11] 3217[3] (3457) 3962[14]

**Strictly The One (IRE)** *Neil Mulholland* a57
4 b g Robin Des Pres(FR) Rita's Charm (IRE) (Arctic Lord)
*8048[6]* *8172[3]* *8249[7]*

**Striding Out (IRE)** *David Simcock* 70
2 b f Cape Cross(IRE) Honours Stride (IRE) (Red Ransom (USA))
7406[2] ◆

**Strike A Light** *Rae Guest* 79
3 gr f Dutch Art Bridal Path (Groom Dancer (USA))
1681[5] (2526) 2878[4] 4428[7] (5057) (5320) 5861[5] 7248[3] 7640[4]

**Strikemaster (IRE)** *Lee James* a1 60
8 b g Xaar Mas A Fuera (IRE) (Alzao (USA))
5567[9]

**Striking Echo** *Andrew Hollinshead* a69 22
4 b g Striking Ambition Sunderland Echo (IRE) (Tagula (IRE))
*105[8]*

**Striking Stone** *Jo Hughes* a39 33
2 ch g Archipenko(USA) Lady Le Quesne (IRE) (Alhaarth (IRE))
1726[12] 3063[9] 4429[8] *7762[5]* *7912[3]* *8179[10]*

**String Theory (IRE)** *Marco Botti* a106 88
4 b c Medicean Shebelia (GER) (Black Sam Bellamy (IRE))
*394a[2]* *679a[13]*

**Strobe** *Lucy Normile* a44 49
10 ch g Fantastic Light(USA) Sadaka (USA) (Kingmambo (USA))
3365[4] 3661[4] 4522[5]

**Stroll On (IRE)** *Rae Guest* 65
3 ch f Exceed And Excel(AUS) Violet (IRE) (Mukaddamah (USA))
1677[7] 3156[6] 3566[2] 3970[6] 4795[12] 5532[5] 6437[2] 6862[5]

**Stroll Patrol** *Philip McBride* 100
2 b f Mount Nelson Maid For Winning (USA) (Gone West (USA))
4202[3] ◆ (4784) 5190[6] 6067[3] 6709[5]

**Strong Chemistry** *Charlie Appleby* a95 98
2 b c Oasis Dream Mambo Light (USA) (Kingmambo (USA))
*6138[2]* ◆ *(6603)* 7104[4]

**Strong Conviction** *Simon Hodgson* a71 41
4 ch g Piccolo Keeping The Faith (IRE) (Ajraas (USA))
*1022[6]* *1209[6]* *1454[7]* 1717[8] 6086[13] 6396[8] *6636[10]* *7115[10]*

**Strong Flame** *David Brown* a46 58
2 ch f Makfi Nadeszhda (Nashwan (USA))
3267[7] 5416[9] 6641[10] 7328[8] *7810[6]*

**Strong Man** *Michael Easterby* a81 81
6 b g Gentleman's Deal(IRE) Strong Hand (First Trump)
*75[2]* *245[5]* *646[3]* *(757)* *1026[2]* *1286[3]* (4861) 7282[12]

**Structured Note (IRE)** *Jedd O'Keeffe* 69
2 b c Acclamation Saik (USA) (Riverman (USA))
6935[2] 7234[5]

**St Saviour** *Andrew Balding* 22
2 b c Danehill Dancer(IRE) Titivation (Montjeu (IRE))
7667[14]

**Stubbins** *John Gosden* 52
2 b f Rip Van Winkle(IRE) Skimmia (Mark Of Esteem (IRE))
7594[12]

**Stubbs (IRE)** *Bettina Andersen* 93
3 b c Danehill Dancer(IRE) Moonstone (Dalakhani (IRE))
3772a[5]

**Stuccodor (IRE)** *D K Weld* 111
5 b g Modigliani(USA) Armilina (FR) (Linamix (FR))
(1078a)

**Studfarmer** *Polly Gundry* a49 50
4 b g Multiplex Samadilla (IRE) (Mujadil (USA))
*289[13]* 1915[6] 2672[8] 3035[7] 3939[4] 5247[9] 5594[5] 5907[6] *7864[6]* *8024[3]* *8285[6]*

**Studio Star** *Ollie Pears* 64
2 ch g Showcasing Forrest Star (Fraam)
2541[3] 3201[9] 4493[4] (5384) 5767[3] 6447[5] 7003[10]

**Stun Gun** *Derek Shaw* a66 47
4 b g Medicean Tapas En Bal (FR) (Mille Balles (FR))
*367[3]* *750[6]* 1168[8] 6210[8] *7632[7]* *7766[7]* *7972[8]* *8111[14]*

**Sturmwind (GER)** *J S Moore* 73
3 b g Samum(GER) Suave (IRE) (Sadler's Wells (USA))
*1269[6]*

**Stybba** *Andrew Balding* a67 68
3 b f Medicean Time Saved (Green Desert (USA))
*2078[2]* 3281[3] 3603[6] *5006[4]* *6242[5]* 6999[3] 7218[3] (7672)

**Style And Panache (IRE)** *R Storp* a47 55
6 b m Trans Island El Corazon (IRE) (Mujadil (USA))
(2598a)

**Style Boreale (FR)** *M Planard* a57 83
4 b f Desert Style(IRE) Fleur Boreale (FR) (Sicyos (USA))
*722a[10]*

**Style D'Ouilly (FR)** *H De Nicolay* a65 62
2 b f Desert Style(IRE) Eubea (FR) (Anabaa (USA))
*5901a[2]* *8149a[16]*

**Stylish Sky (FR)** *Y Gourraud* 13
2 ch c Naaqoos Bright Style (FR) (Fasliyev (USA))
5616a[9]

**Stynes (IRE)** *John C McConnell* a67 65
4 b g Aussie Rules(USA) Magic Princess (Bahhare (USA))
6012[4] *7961a[6]*

**Subcontinent (IRE)** *Charlie Appleby* 73
2 b c Dubawi(IRE) Saree (Barathea (IRE))
6362[4] 6875[2] 7244[3]

**Sublimation (IRE)** *Ian Williams* a17 64
4 ch g Manduro(GER) Meon Mix (Kayf Tara)
7211[9] 7538[15] *7831[14]*

**Submariner (USA)** *A bin Huzaim* a92 85
8 ch g Singspiel(IRE) Neptune's Bride (USA) (Bering)
*108a[9]* 305a[14]

**Substantivo (IRE)** *Timothy Jarvis* a66 61
4 b g Duke Of Marmalade(IRE) Damson (IRE) (Entrepreneur)
*1408[2]* 1689[12] *2463[3]* 3589[4] *5041[5]* *5303[4]* *6858[6]*

**Subtle Knife** *Giles Bravery* a84 85
5 ch m Needwood Blade Northern Bows (Bertolini (USA))
*779[5]* *1014[5]* *1234[8]* 2318[2] 2861[4] *3402[6]* 5092[4] *5826[7]* 6129[6] 6466[4] 6990[4] 7416[7] *7918[12]* 8122[8]

**Subversive (IRE)** *Mark Johnston* a74 75
2 b c Invincible Spirit(IRE) Persian Secret (FR) (Persian Heights)
2736[5] 5439[4] 6058[2] *(6271)* *6854[3]* *7224[5]*

**Succeed And Excel** *John Butler* a65 53
3 b g Exceed And Excel(AUS) Woodbeck (Terimon)
*(7197)*

**Such Fun (IRE)** *F-H Graffard* a74 74
3 b f Whipper(USA) Balamiyda (IRE) (Ashkalani (IRE))
*795a[7]* 5368a[14] *5959a[8]*

**Sudden Wish (IRE)** *Gary Moore* a61 60
5 b m Jeremy(USA) Fun Time (Fraam)
*459[6]* *(838)*

**Sudden Wonder (IRE)** *Charlie Appleby* 111
3 ch c New Approach(IRE) Dubai Surprise (IRE) (King's Best (USA))
(1530) 2153[3] 2990[15] 4385[5] (7120) 7598[2]

**Suddyan (IRE)** *Sir Michael Stoute* 84
2 b c Holy Roman Emperor(IRE) Raydaniya (IRE) (In The Wings)
(7561)

**Sudest (IRE)** *Kevin Ryan* 73
2 b g Tagula(IRE) Bold Bunny (Piccolo)
1536[7] 2673[4] (3201)

**Sudirman (USA)** *David Wachman* 115
3 b c Henrythenavigator(USA) Shermeen (IRE) (Desert Style (IRE))
3352[20]

**Suegioo (FR)** *Marco Botti* a89 107
5 ch g Manduro(GER) Mantesera (IRE) (In The Wings)
1736[3] (2073) 3717[2] 5693[9] 6287[3] 7107[32]

**Suehail** *Robert Cowell* a88 88
5 b g Cadeaux Genereux Why Dubai (USA) (Kris S (USA))
(2922) 3577[5] 6140[16]

**Suerte Al Salto (IRE)** *Chris Gordon* a60
7 b g Old Vic The Great O'Malley (IRE) (Mandalus)
1208[6]

**Suffolk Sky** *Ed Vaughan* a46
2 b f Pastoral Pursuits Charlevoix (IRE) (King Charlemagne (USA))
8247[7]

**Suffused** *Roger Charlton* 75
2 ch f Champs Elysees Scuffle (Daylami (IRE))
(7594)

**Sufranel (IRE)** *Marco Botti* a74 64
3 b c Galileo(IRE) Noelani (IRE) (Indian Ridge)
1357[4]

**Sugar Boy (GER)** *John Gosden* a64 65
2 bb c Areion(GER) Sugar Baby Love (GER) (Second Empire (IRE))
6125[9] 6630[4]

**Sugarformyhoney (IRE)** *Brendan Powell* a79 70
5 ch m Dutch Art Sweetsformysweet (USA) (Forest Wildcat (USA))
57a[7] 924[4]

**Sugar Hiccup (IRE)** *Jim Best* a37 80
6 b m Refuse To Bend(IRE) Raysiza (IRE) (Alzao (USA))
250[12]

**Sugar Love (GER)** *P Schiergen* 85
3 b f Elusive City(USA) Sugar Baby Love (GER) (Second Empire (IRE))
5965a[7] 7483a[9]

**Sugar Lump** *Richard Hannon* 76
2 b c Sakhee's Secret Icing (Polar Falcon (USA))
3148[2] (3584)

**Sugarpie (SWE)** *Madeleine Smith* 40
2 b f Astronomer Royal(USA) Calling Card (SWE) (Eagle Day (USA))
6386a[13]

**Sugar Town** *Peter Niven* a56 60
4 b f Elusive City(USA) Sweetsformysweet (USA) (Forest Wildcat (USA))
3096[13] (4294) 4515[2] 5142[6] 6121[10] 6495[5]

**Suhali (FR)** *J Heloury* a53 57
3 b f Air Eminem(IRE) Sharsala (IRE) (Shahrastani (USA))
3372a[8]

**Suits Me** *David Barron* a107 98
11 ch g Bertolini(USA) Fancier Bit (Lion Cavern (USA))
2869[6] 3397[5]

**Suitsus** *Peter Makin* a74 73
3 b g Virtual Point Perfect (Dansili)
2278[2] ◆ 3145[10] 3709[4] 4677[3] 5080[9] 6070[8]
7117[2] (7800) 8040[3]

**Sulaalaat** *Brian Meehan* 95
2 b f New Approach(IRE) Danehill Dreamer (USA) (Danehill (USA))
3076[2] ◆ (4828) 5608[5] 6295[2]

**Sula Two** *Jo Hughes* a70 90
7 b m Sulamani(IRE) There's Two (IRE) (Ashkalani (IRE))
2501[2] 3034[13] 6747[11] 7107[14]

**Sulis Minerva (IRE)** *Jeremy Gask* a92 78
7 b m Arakan(USA) Lacinia (Groom Dancer (USA))
80[8] 658[7] 825[8]

**Sulphur (FR)** *Mario Hofer* a34 55
2 b f Vespone(IRE) Sweet Smile (GER) (Distinctly North (USA))
3744a[10] 4882a[3] 5619a[13]

**Sultanina** *John Gosden* 116
4 ch f New Approach(IRE) Soft Centre (Zafonic (USA))
(2280) ◆ (2764) ◆ 3961[2] (4894) 6380a[5]
6969a[10]

**Sumatra Tiger (GER)** *W Mongil* a77 74
9 b g Tiger Hill(IRE) Sohaila (GER) (Owington)
4776a[7]

**Sumeida (USA)** *Jeremy Noseda* a53
2 bb c Street Sense(USA) Camargue (USA) (Mineshaft (USA))
8067[10]

**Summer Dancer (IRE)** *Eugene Stanford* a61 70
10 br g Fasliyev(USA) Summer Style (IRE) (Indian Ridge)
5415[5] 6074[7] 6397[6] 6625[8]

**Summer Fall (USA)** *B Grizzetti* 94
5 rg m Mizzen Mast(USA) Momix (Selkirk (USA))
2589a[7] 6807a[6] 7146a[7]

**Summerfree (USA)** *Mark Johnston* a82 59
4 bb g Medaglia d'Oro(USA) Summer Flash (USA) (Belong To Me (USA))
72[2] 158[2] 260[4] 385[2]

**Summer Front (USA)** *Christophe Clement* a97 116
5 b h War Front(USA) Rose Of Summer (USA) (El Prado (IRE))
7613a[4]

**Summerinthecity (IRE)** *Richard Fahey* a68 73
7 ch g Indian Ridge Miss Assertive (Zafonic (USA))
2254[19] 7775[8] 7953[7]

**Summerlea (IRE)** *Micky Hammond* a46 59
8 ch g Alhaarth(IRE) Verbania (IRE) (In The Wings)
639[7] 1605[6] 2424[2] 2550[3]

**Summerling (IRE)** *Phil McEntee* a63 13
3 br f Excellent Art Sun Seasons (IRE) (Salse (USA))
1233[11] 4543[5] 5600[7] 7777[11] 8028[8]

**Summer Moon (FR)** *J-C Rouget* a90 102
3 b f Elusive City(USA) Kalatuna (FR) (Green Tune (USA))
(5843a)

**Summersault (IRE)** *Jamie Osborne* a73
3 b g Footstepsinthesand Sumingasefa (Danehill (USA))
7921[4] 8119[4] (8256)

**Summer Solo (USA)** *Christophe Clement* 102
3 b f Arch(USA) Summer Solstice (IRE) (Caerleon (USA))
3995a[3]

**Summer Stroll (IRE)** *David O'Meara* 66
2 br f Hurricane Run(IRE) Precautionary (Green Desert (USA))
3312[5] 3648[8] 4416[3] 4750[3] (4870) 5335[6] 6211[3]
6759[3] 7245[2]

**Summer Surprice (FR)** *F-H Graffard* 105
3 ch f Le Havre(IRE) Summer Exhibition (Royal Academy (USA))
5545a[5] 6882a[2] 7480a[7]

**Summer Times** *Mark Johnston* 81
2 b g Bahri(USA) Young Sue (Local Suitor (USA))
3842[2] ◆ 4527[3] 5013[2] 5386[5] 5807[8] 7097[4]

**Sunblazer (IRE)** *Kim Bailey* a86 83
4 gr g Dark Angel(IRE) Damask Rose (IRE) (Dr Devious (IRE))
(6721) 7422[6] 7838[3]

**Sunday Royal (FR)** *Harry Dunlop* 69
2 b g Sunday Break(JPN) Princess D'Orange (FR) (Anabaa (USA))
6293[3]

**Sunfyre (IRE)** *James Evans*
2 ch g Virtual Dimensional (Dansili)
7827[7] 8166[11]

**Sunhill Lodge Lady** *Ann Duffield* a44 41
2 ch f Avonbridge Sareb (FR) (Indian Ridge)
1900[7] 3297[6] 3827[6] 4065[5] 4528[5] 4899[4] 5194[7]
5767[4] 6447[8] 6941[5]

**Suni Dancer** *Paul Green* a46 61
3 b f Captain Gerrard(IRE) Sunisa (IRE) (Daggers Drawn (USA))
960[4] 1308[2] 1588[9] 2805[2] (3135) 3603[7] 3885[8]
4706[2] 5077[11] (5809) 6227[5] 7570[10]

**Sun My Dance (FR)** *C Schiff*
2 gr f Centennial(IRE) Valse Des Coeurs (FR) (Enrique)
6385a[F]

**Sunndale** *M Weiss*
5 gr h Clodovil(IRE) Sunningdale (IRE) (Indian Ridge)
638a[7]

**Sunningdale Rose (IRE)** *Gay Kelleway* a57 59
3 b f Art Connoisseur(IRE) Eloquent Rose (IRE) (Elnadim (USA))
19[4] 216[7] 480[8]

**Sunny (FR)** *J-C Rouget* a108 102
5 ch g Muhtathir Vol Sauvage (FR) (Always Fair (USA))
(836a) 2799a[8]

**Sunny Again** *Amanda Perrett* a53
3 ch f Shirocco(GER) Spotlight (Dr Fong (USA))
6661[5]

**Sunny Future (IRE)** *Malcolm Saunders* a76 84
8 b g Masterful(USA) Be Magic (Persian Bold)
1909[9] (3086) (3752) 4209[4] 4777[8] 5414[6] (6318)

**Sunny Side Up (IRE)** *Karen Tutty* a50 80
5 b m Refuse To Bend(IRE) Feeling Wonderful (IRE) (Fruits Of Love (USA))
1440[12] 2167[14] 2552[7] 3611[5] 3954[3] 4256[5]
4795[7] 4960[6] 5053[8] 6451[2] 6695[9]

**Sunny Ying** *J Moore* a77 107
5 ch g Haafhd Antigua (Selkirk (USA))
7899a[10]

**Sunny York (IRE)** *James Tate* 71
2 b f Vale Of York(IRE) Alexander Ridge (IRE) (Indian Ridge)
(3232) 4150[4] 5974[8]

**Sun Odyssey** *William Haggas* 61
2 b f Mastercraftsman(IRE) Penolva (IRE) (Galileo (IRE))
7084[7] 7450[7]

**Sunraider (IRE)** *Paul Midgley* a37 91
7 b g Namid Doctrine (Barathea (IRE))
1375[4] 1967[4] 2332[9] 2602[3] ◆ (2825) 3599[3]
4061[4] 4632[6] 4712[3] 5199[12] 5632[4] 6369a[18]
(6692)

**Sunrise Dance** *Robert Johnson* a50 83
5 ch m Monsieur Bond(IRE) Wachiwi (IRE) (Namid)
1440[15] 1604[9] 1839[7] 2421[8] 2743[5] 3338[9]
3668[13] 4664[4] 5089[11] 5636[8] 6866[8] 7510[5]

**Sunrise Star** *Lady Cecil* 88
3 b f Shamardal(USA) Tudor Court (IRE) (Cape Cross (IRE))
(2946) 4133[3] 5392[3]

**Sunsational Girl** *Dai Burchell*
5 ch m Byron Sun Bonnet (Grand Lodge (USA))
2667[10] 3174[9]

**Sunset Glow (USA)** *Wesley A Ward* a109 107
2 rg f Exchange Rate(USA) Perfectforthepart (USA) (Dynaformer (USA))
3415[2] 7592a[2]

**Sunset Sail (IRE)** *Richard Hannon* a88 89
2 b c Arcano(IRE) Mythologie (FR) (Bering)
2146[5] 2487[2] (3311) 4853[3] ◆ 5134[2] 5672[4]
6003[3] 6128[4]

**Sunstream (FR)** *P Bary* a78 85
3 b f Falco(USA) Suenna (GER) (Lando (GER))
(4464a) 5482a[7]

**Suntracer (USA)** *Chris Block* a100 106
6 ch h Kitten's Joy(USA) Taxable Deduction (USA) (Prized (USA))
5457a[9] 7324a[5]

**Supachap** *Hughie Morrison* a65 70
3 br g High Chaparral(IRE) Supamova (USA) (Seattle Slew (USA))
1401[8] 1898[5] 4657[5]

**Supa Seeker (USA)** *Tony Carroll* a47 52
8 bb g Petionville(USA) Supamova (USA) (Seattle Slew (USA))
17[6] 179[2] 352[3] 661[4] 759[6] 869[2] (939) 1819[4]
2770[6] 4798[10] 5033[3] 6407[8] 7908[6] 8123[4]

**Supa U** *Tim Easterby* a62 66
3 b f Authorized(IRE) Supa Sal (King's Best (USA))
3135[9]

**Super Ale (FR)** *G Botti* 88
2 b c Elusive City(USA) Troiecat (FR) (One Cool Cat (USA))
3806a[8]

**Superciliary** *Chris Gordon* a66 55
5 b g Dansili Supereva (IRE) (Sadler's Wells (USA))
380[7] 2252[8] 6107[6] 6486[9] 8070[8]

**Super City (FR)** *J-L Mace* 65
3 b f Elusive City(USA) Super Anna (FR) (Anabaa (USA))
3810a[7]

**Super Cookie** *Anthony Carson* a42 70
4 b f Dylan Thomas(IRE) Dance Lesson (In The Wings)
1617[8] 1864[5] 2750[6] 5109[5] 5832[7] 6627[10]

**Super Duplex** *Roger Teal* a66 42
7 b g Footstepsinthesand Penelope Tree (IRE) (Desert Prince (IRE))
538[2] 822[2] 989[8] 1302[5] 4327[4] 4351[7] 5076[5]
5428[8] 7115[9]

**Super Eria (FR)** *C Boutin* 94
2 ch f Hold That Tiger(USA) Dark Mile (USA) (Woodman (USA))
1402a[2] (5119a) 5405a[3]

**Superior Duchess** *Michael Blanshard*
9 b m Superior Premium Downclose Duchess (King's Signet (USA))
7546[12]

**Super Jockey (NZ)** *A T Millard* 108
6 b g Sandtrap(USA) Pennies In Heaven (NZ) (Pompeii Court (USA))
7897a[6]

**Super Kid** *Saeed bin Suroor* a90 77
2 b c Exceed And Excel(AUS) Crimson Year (USA) (Dubai Millennium)
3148[3] (4117) 7882[2]

**Superlative (IRE)** *James Tate* 55
2 ch f Iffraaj Slieve Mish (IRE) (Cape Cross (IRE))
3076[8]

**Super Moment (IRE)** *Saeed bin Suroor* a75 63
3 b f Oasis Dream Philae (USA) (Seeking The Gold (USA))
3653[5] 4434[3] 5284[5] 6341[7] 6904[4]

**Super Nothing (IRE)** *G Botti* a80 63
2 ch g Siyouni(FR) Back To My Roots (USA) (Fusaichi Pegasus (USA))
5616a[5] 8148a[3]

**Supernoverre (IRE)** *Alan Jones* a30 32
8 b g Noverre(USA) Caviare (Cadeaux Genereux)
5558[9]

**Superplex (FR)** *Waldemar Hickst* a84 104
4 b c Multiplex Salute The Sun (FR) (Fly To The Stars)
984a[10] 1341a[6] 8006a[15]

**Super Quick (IRE)** *Richard Fahey* 70
2 b f Rip Van Winkle(IRE) Public Ransom (IRE) (Red Ransom (USA))
3255[5] 3642[5] 5416[12]

**Super Say (IRE)** *Michael Appleby* a95 86
8 ch g Intikhab(USA) Again Royale (IRE) (Royal Academy (USA))
125[5]

**Supersta** *Ronald Harris* 76
3 ch g Pivotal Resort (Oasis Dream)
1192[13] 1940[2] 3145[5] (3729) 5081[6] 5629[9] 6657[7]

**Superstition** *Michael Madgwick* a45
5 b m Red Ransom(USA) Go Supersonic (Zafonic (USA))
277[6] 455[6] 1895[9]

**Supplicant** *Richard Fahey* 109
3 b c Kyllachy Pious (Bishop Of Cashel)
1436[10] 2556[6] ◆ 3253[12] 4166[7] 5445[9] 6533[15]
6760[2] 7122[14]

**Supreme Belle (IRE)** *Derek Shaw* 38
2 b f Tamayuz Final Opinion (IRE) (King's Theatre (IRE))
2888[9] 3107[8] 4202[9] 5180[6]

**Supreme Occasion (IRE)** *David O'Meara* 100
2 b f Teofilo(IRE) Pirie (USA) (Green Dancer (USA))
(4626) ◆ (5085) 6165[4] ◆ 6289[4] 6555[3]

**Suprise Vendor (IRE)** *Stuart Coltherd* a64 66
8 ch g Fath(USA) Dispol Jazz (Alhijaz)
(1359)

**Suracon (GER)** *A Wohler* 73
3 b c Monsun(GER) Sasuela (GER) (Dashing Blade)
3293a[6]

**Suraj** *Nicky Henderson* 96
5 ch g Galileo(IRE) Maid Of Killeen (IRE) (Darshaan)
2289[6] 3321[8]

**Surcingle (USA)** *Sir Michael Stoute* 80
3 b f Empire Maker(USA) Promising Lead (Danehill (USA))
1978[6] 2277[8]

**Sure Fire (GER)** *David Evans* a48 24
9 b g Monsun(GER) Suivez (FR) (Fioravanti (USA))
3579[6] (Dead)

**Surelookit (IRE)** *John Butler* a32
2 b f Equiano(FR) Rosa Midnight (USA) (Lemon Drop Kid (USA))
8247[9]

**Sur Empire** *Mark Johnston* a67
2 b f Equiano(FR) Shersha (IRE) (Priolo (USA))
7550[3]

**Sureness (IRE)** *Charlie Mann* a65 65
4 ch f Hurricane Run(IRE) Silk Dress (IRE) (Gulch (USA))
1099[7]

**Surety (IRE)** *Clive Brittain* a78 79
3 b c Cape Cross(IRE) Guarantia (Selkirk (USA))
1612[6] 2544[3] 2879[3] 4671[2] 5008[5] 6484[3] 6736[10]
7600[8]

**Surewecan** *Mark Johnston* a89 96
2 b c Royal Applause Edge Of Light (Xaar)
3454[2] (3827) 4348[2] 4822[5] 5447[4] 6142[7] 6612[2]

**Surfer (USA)** *S Seemar* a111 83
5 ch g Distorted Humor(USA) Surf Club (USA) (Ocean Crest (USA))
508a[8] 901a[3] 1183a[15]

**Surprise Us** *Mark Gillard* a56 48
7 b g Indian Ridge Pingus (Polish Precedent (USA))
3852[5] 4149[2] 5001[9] 5596[9]

**Surrey Dream (IRE)** *John Bridger* a47 47
5 b g Oasis Dream Trois Graces (USA) (Alysheba (USA))
81[3] 184[5] 251[6] 370[8]

**Surrey Pink (FR)** *William Muir* a48 48
2 ch f Kyllachy Idle Tears (Selkirk (USA))
2402[8] 2644[3] 3706[4] 4083[4] 4283[4] 4857[4] 5517[4]
6040[10] 6791[2] 7190[9]

**Surround Sound** *Tim Easterby* a30 66
4 b g Multiplex Tintera (IRE) (King's Theatre (IRE))
1356[5] 1607[7] 2162[13] 3237[4] 3547[7] 3949[3] 4489[4]
4903[3] 5415[9] 6627[7] 8282[9]

**Surspenders (FR)** *S Wattel* a82 82
3 b c Whipper(USA) Lanciana (IRE) (Acatenango (GER))
7630a[5]

**Survived** *William Haggas* 92
3 b f Kyllachy Regina (Green Desert (USA))
3459[4] 4171[6] 4669[14] 5467[7]

**Suspiron (IRE)** *G Arizkorreta Elosegui* 82
5 b g Diamond Green(FR) Daftiyna (IRE) (Darshaan)
6392a[4]

**Sussudio (FR)** *N Sauer* a83 87
4 ch c Nayef(USA) Soudaine (GER) (Monsun (GER))
6992a[5]

**Sutton Sid** *Paddy Butler* a71 62
4 ch g Dutch Art Drastic Measure (Pivotal)
(88) 229[3] 379[4] 1454[8] 1675[9] 2399[5] 2806[6]
3155[2] 3576[9] 4264[8] 4473[4] 4592[4] 4797[3] 5208[5]
7846[14] 8316[6]

**Sutton Sioux** *Jeremy Gask* a38 35
3 b f Sleeping Indian Once Removed (Distant Relative)
1039[7] 1430[7] 1833[5] 4055[11] 4820[7]

**Suzi Gold (TUR)** *C Turan* 97
3 b f Banknote Golden Leaf (TUR) (West By West (USA))
6164a[4]

**Suzi's Connoisseur** *Hugo Palmer* 107
3 b g Art Connoisseur(IRE) Suzi Spends (IRE) (Royal Applause)
2962[3] 3378[20] 4166[5] 4669[3] 5438[5] 6234[8] 6755[3]
(7168)

**Svatantra** *L Riccardi* 88
3 b c Sir Percy Sopran Middlen (IRE) (Entrepreneur)
2376a[11]

**Svoul (FR)** *F-H Graffard* 95
2 b c Siyouni(FR) Dansia (GER) (Lavirco (GER))
5478a[4] 7855a[5]

**Swacadelic (GER)** *Jean-Pierre Carvalho* 106
3 ch c Adlerflug(GER) Swish (GER) (Monsun (GER))
3293a[3] 4007a[10] 5224a[5]

**Swaheen** *Sir Michael Stoute* a53 68
2 b g Lawman(FR) Whole Grain (Polish Precedent (USA))
4429[3] 5760[5] 6630[6]

**Swakopmund (USA)** *Michael Hushion* 78
5 b m Any Given Saturday(USA) African Sunrise (USA) (Tale Of The Cat (USA))
2227a[4]

**Swale Star** *Seamus Mullins* a44
3 b f Three Valleys(USA) Salim Toto (Mtoto)
316[13] 577[5]

**Swampfire (IRE)** *Gary Moore* a63 68
6 b g Anabaa(USA) Moonfire (Sadler's Wells (USA))
450[11] 801[10] 1027[6] 1919[4]

**Swan Lakes (IRE)** *David Simcock* a80 85
3 gr f Dalakhani(IRE) Rock Salt (Selkirk (USA))
2310[2] (3174) 4145[3] 5003[6] 6365[2]

**Swansirized (IRE)** *Alain Couetil* 101
3 b c Authorized(IRE) Sister Swank (USA) (Skip Away (USA))
3290a[6]

**Swan Song** *Andrew Balding* 105
5 br m Green Desert(USA) Lochsong (Song)
1572[4] (2076) 2766[9] 2989[5] 5160[5] 6231[5]

**Swanwick Shore (IRE)** *Richard Hannon* 81
3 b c Tagula(IRE) Cinzia Vegas (IRE) (Dr Fong (USA))
2031[7] 2418[2] 3428[2]

**Sweeping Rock (IRE)** *Marcus Tregoning* a63 67
4 b g Rock Of Gibraltar(IRE) Sweeping Story (USA) (End Sweep (USA))
1874[5] 2252[10] (4279) 5001[3] 5597[4] 6027[3] 6395[3]
6856[3] 7182[6]

**Sweeping Up** *Hughie Morrison* a79 73
3 b f Sea The Stars(IRE) Farfala (FR) (Linamix (FR))
2082[2] 2925[4] (6238) 7033[7]

**Sweet Alibi (IRE)** *J S Moore* a71 66
3 b f Lawman(FR) Zingari (Groom Dancer (USA))
1577[7] 190[3] 1400[8] (2695) 3760[6] 4152[7] 4536[5]
5370a[10] 5592a[4] 5959a[6]

**Sweet Angelica** *James Given* a60 65
3 ch f Pastoral Pursuits Glencal (Compton Place)
(94)

**Sweet Charlie** *Mike Murphy* a49
3 b f Myboycharlie(IRE) Play Around (IRE) (Niniski (USA))
5606[9] 6483[6] 7458[8]

**Sweet Cherry (IRE)** *Peter Makin* a40 76
3 b f Mastercraftsman(IRE) Dear Gracie (IRE) (In The Wings)
1173[8] 1854[3] 2688[4] 3407[7] 3781[4]

**Sweet Dream** *Ralph Beckett* 89
2 b f Oasis Dream Sweet Stream (ITY) (Shantou (USA))
5881[2] 6553[7] (7174) 7448[3]

**Sweet Fede** *Stefano Botti* 67
3 ch f Shirocco(GER) Touch Of Light (IRE) (Xaar)
1780a[15] 6807a[8]

**Sweetheart Abbey** *William Knight* a85 81
3 b f Dancing Spree(USA) Hinton Pearl (Loch Pearl)
1793[4] 2417[5] 2927[8] 3711[2] 4303[2] 4616[2] (5426) (5600) 6325[7] 7033[4] 7422[8]

**Sweet Idea (AUS)** *Gai Waterhouse* 112
4 ch f Snitzel(AUS) Flidais (AUS) (Timber Country (USA))
1468a[9]

**Sweet Liberta (IRE)** *T Le Brocq* a72 65
5 b m Cape Cross(IRE) Hendrina (IRE) (Daylami (IRE))
2593a[5] (3495a) 4041a[7] 4716a[6] 5230a[5] 6188a[6]

**Sweet Lightning** *David O'Meara* a96 112
9 b g Fantastic Light(USA) Sweetness Herself (Unfuwain (USA))
108a[10] 307a[7] 681a[7] 1165[4] 1437[5] 1721[14] 2286[8] 3251[13] 3645[7]

**Sweet Lily Pea (USA)** *Mrs Ilka Gansera-Leveque* a54 54
3 ch f Hard Spun(USA) Tree Pipit (USA) (Woodman (USA))
4056[7] 4791[6] 5183[2] 6022[9] 6647[5] 7424[8]

**Sweetly Does It** *Stuart Williams* 17
2 ch f Shirocco(GER) Sweetness Herself (Unfuwain (USA))
7377[15]

**Sweet Martoni** *William Knight* a61 82
4 b f Dubawi(IRE) Sweetness Herself (Unfuwain (USA))
1846[5] (2251) 2930[6] (3733) 5206[4] 5849[6] 6704[2] 7160[2] 7567[12]

**Sweet Marwell (IRE)** *Jo Crowley* a61
4 b f Excellent Art Bee Eater (IRE) (Green Desert (USA))
155[8] 582[8] 3526[3] 4579[6]

**Sweet Midnight** *John Holt* a26
2 b f Mawatheeq(USA) Sweet Reply (Opening Verse (USA))
7828[4] 8083[8]

**Sweet Missi (IRE)** *Brian Ellison* 55
2 b f Thousand Words Touch And Love (IRE) (Green Desert (USA))
4751[3] 5086[6] 5332[7] 6222[4]

**Sweetness Lady** *Olly Stevens* a64
3 ch f Sleeping Indian Eforetta (GER) (Dr Fong (USA))
157[3] 401[10] ◆

**Sweet P** *Marcus Tregoning* a73 66
3 b f Sir Percy Desert Run (IRE) (Desert Prince (IRE))
5004[7] 5598[4] (6636) 7359[8]

**Sweet Piccolo** *Paddy Butler* a41 49
4 ch g Piccolo Quality Street (Fraam)
495[5] 575[11] 798[9] 1877[5] 2045[2] 2723[8] 8111[9]

**Sweet Reason (USA)** *Leah Gyarmati* a112
3 b f Street Sense(USA) Livermore Leslie (USA) (Mt. Livermore (USA))
7608a[8]

**Sweet Selection** *Hughie Morrison* a68 59
2 b f Stimulation(IRE) Sweet Coincidence (Mujahid (USA))
7450[6] 7835[3] 8166[5]

**Sweet Summer** *John Holt* a5 34
3 ch f Sakhee(USA) Sweet Reply (Opening Verse (USA))
1587[11] 1984[10] 2621[7] 5717[11] 7913[5]

**Sweet Swap (USA)** *John W Sadler* a96 111
5 ch h Candy Ride(ARG) Fair Exchange (USA) (Storm Cat (USA))
7609a[5]

**Sweet Talker** *Tim Easterby* a34 52
2 b f Sir Percy Herminoe (Rainbow Quest (USA))
3481[4] ◆ 5296[6] 5886[8] 7648[9]

**Sweet Talking Guy (IRE)** *Lydia Pearce* a77 64
4 b g Oratorio(IRE) Sweet Namibia (IRE) (Namid)
244[8] (448) 576[4] 841[2] (1221) 2147[18] 3630[4] 4078[7] 5059[6] 5281[2] 6020[2] 6680[7] 7352[9] 7931[7] 7989[12]

**Sweet Vintage (IRE)** *Mark Brisbourne* a62 49
4 b f Singspiel(IRE) Sauterne (Rainbow Quest (USA))
126[2] 562[5] 852[8]

**Swehan (IRE)** *Kevin Ryan* a84 73
4 b g Diamond Green(FR) Golden (FR) (Sanglamore (USA))
(79) 1598[11] 2423[8] 3361[10]

**Sweltering (FR)** *P Monfort* a80 76
3 b f Zambezi Sun Pragmatica (Inchinor)
5482a[3]

**Swendab (IRE)** *John O'Shea* a54 83
6 b g Trans Island Lavish Spirit (USA) (Southern Halo (USA))
2074[10] 3033[11] 3395[4] 3783[6] 4284[6] 4399[2] 4594[7] 5060[6] 6296[5] 6313[7] 6650[6] 7735[8] 8014[11] 8286[4]

**Sweynesse (AUS)** *J O'Shea* 107
3 bb c Lonhro(AUS) Swansea (IRE) (Singspiel (IRE))
7467a[8]

**Swift Act** *Nikki Evans* a34 45
5 b m Act One Lasting Image (Zilzal (USA))
3176[5] 3778[7] 5339[4]

**Swift Approval (IRE)** *Kevin Ryan* a83 81
2 ch g Approve(IRE) Tiltili (IRE) (Spectrum (IRE))
4633[4] ◆ 5167[6] (6108) 6473[2] 7116[3]

**Swift Blade (IRE)** *Lady Herries* a81 73
6 ch g Exceed And Excel(AUS) Gold Strike (IRE) (Rainbow Quest (USA))
(405) (856) 1219[6] 2851[5]

**Swift Campaign (IRE)** *John Gosden* 95
3 b f Intikhab(USA) Indolente (IRE) (Diesis)
(2780) 3724[3]

**Swift Cedar (IRE)** *David Evans* a78 76
4 ch g Excellent Art Ravish (Efisio)
286[7] 627[2] 690[5] 1234[7] (2381) 3221[4] 3646[2] ◆ 4190[8] 5274[5] 5849[5] 6251[4] (7489) 8044[3] 8260[2]

**Swift Emperor (IRE)** *David Barron* 78
2 b g Holy Roman Emperor(IRE) Big Swifty (IRE) (Intikhab (USA))
(6667)

**Swiftly Done (IRE)** *Declan Carroll* a74 95
7 b g Whipper(USA) Ziffany (Taufan (USA))
1733[4]

**Swift Susie** *Stuart Williams* 25
2 b f Kheleyf(USA) Overwing (IRE) (Fasliyev (USA))
2022[9] 5091[10] 5859[6]

**Swilken** *Mark H Tompkins* a76 68
3 ch g Halling(USA) Azure Mist (Bahamian Bounty)
1880[4] 2883[5] 3631[6] 6437[3] 6717[6] 7000[5]

**Swing Alone (IRE)** *Gay Kelleway* a102 96
5 b g Celtic Swing Groupetime (USA) (Gilded Time (USA))
54[3] (145) 427[2] 723a[9] 1071[3] 1299[5] 1556[6] 2142[5] 2461[8] 3424[2] (8078) 8243[6]

**Swingdream (GER)** *M Figge* 88
3 b f Soldier Hollow Smaranda (GER) (Kornado)
7618a[8]

**Swinging Hawk (GER)** *Ian Williams* a82 85
8 ch g Hawk Wing(USA) Saldenschwinge (GER) (In The Wings)
2108[8] 2760[3]

**Swingking (FR)** *M Figge* a79 70
2 bb c Myboycharlie(IRE) Salute The Sun (FR) (Fly To The Stars)
7723a[5]

**Swiss Cross** *Phil McEntee* a103 94
7 b g Cape Cross(IRE) Swiss Lake (USA) (Indian Ridge)
(431) 644[8] 802[7] 1066[8] 1862[5] 1975[15] 2992[2] (3876) 4405[2] 4762[19] 5754 6159[5] 7555[10] 7851[10]

**Swiss Kiss** *John Gosden* a79 75
3 br f Dansili Swiss Lake (USA) (Indian Ridge)
1920[4] ◆ 2442[3] 3195[4] 4029[2] 4434[10] (5046) 5685[6] 6269[4]

**Swiss Lait** *David Elsworth* a57 64
3 b f Milk It Mick Matilda Peace (Namaqualand (USA))
1422[15] 1767[7] 2780[11] 3588[4] 4306[4] 4970[6] 5972[3] 6613[2] 7025[4] 7424[6] 7489[2]

**Switched Off** *Kevin Frost* a16 68
9 b g Catcher In The Rye(IRE) Button Hole Flower (IRE) (Fairy King (USA))
1362[6] 1729[10] 2097[7]

**Switcher (IRE)** *M Halford* a71 96
5 b m Whipper(USA) Bahamamia (Vettori (IRE))
2042a[5] 2572a[9]

**Swivel** *Mark Johnston* a91 102
3 ch c Shirocco(GER) Pivotal Drive (IRE) (Pivotal)
51[7] (142) (301) (404) 659[3] (785) 1563[12] 2077[3] 3003[11] 3379[14] 4183[4] 4696[6] 5164[4] (5633) 6127[10] 6287[10] 6501[4] (6747) 7102[4]

**Swnymor (IRE)** *John Quinn* 99
5 b g Dylan Thomas(IRE) Propaganda (IRE) (Sadler's Wells (USA))
(2760) 4746a[5] 7107[23]

**Swordbearer** *James Fanshawe* a76 60
3 ch g Selkirk(USA) Isis (USA) (Royal Academy (USA))
2883[3] 4130[6] 5008[2] 6018[2] 6714[7] 7373[5]

**Sword Of The Lord** *George Margarson* a58 85
4 b g Kheleyf(USA) Blue Echo (Kyllachy)
1281[2] 1871[9] 2603[8] 3791[4] 4342[6] 5031[7] 7042[5]

**Swords** *Ray Peacock* a20 22
12 b g Vettori(IRE) Pomorie (IRE) (Be My Guest (USA))
2396[10] 4327[5] 5208[7]

**Swordshire (GER)** *Werner Glanz* 95
3 b c Shirocco(GER) Sword Roche (GER) (Laroche (GER))
6917a[5] 7769a[3]

**Sworn Mammy (GER)** *R Storp* a18 48
7 ch m Mamool(IRE) Sweet Tern (GER) (Arctic Tern (USA))
(3048a) 4041a[5] 4716a[4] 5969a[5]

**Swot** *John Gosden* a65 74
2 b c Exceed And Excel(AUS) House Point (Pivotal)
4864[2] 5655[12] 6925[12] 7551[6]

**Sybilicious** *Stuart Williams* 41
3 b f Royal Applause Tora Bora (Grand Lodge (USA))
4446[9] 4590[6] 5532[9]

**Sycophantic (IRE)** *Jamie Osborne* a51
4 b g Cape Cross(IRE) Amarice (Suave Dancer (USA))
686[9] 941[8] 1035[4] 4082[10]

**Sydney Darnoult (FR)** *B Recher* a21
3 b c Sirzane(FR) Tanis Darnoult (FR) (Isfandiyar)
8005a[14]

**Sydney James (IRE)** *Dai Burchell* a62 14
3 b g Thousand Words Blue Bamboo (Green Desert (USA))
1765[7] 2013[7] (Dead)

**Sydney Ruffdiamond** *Richard Hannon* a73 65
2 b g Equiano(FR) Pirouetting (Pivotal)
5646[9] 6039[3] 7400[4]

**Sylvan Mist (IRE)** *Edward Lynam* a83 83
4 bb f Footstepsinthesand Silview (USA) (Saint Ballado (CAN))
788a[7] 7433a[6]

**Sylvan Spirit (IRE)** *Roger Teal* a46
3 gr f Camacho Spree (IRE) (Dansili)
213[4] 622[4] 2931[4] 6631[3] 7191[9]

**Sylvette** *Roger Varian* a65 58
2 ch f Selkirk(USA) Souvenance (Hernando (FR))
6554[7] 7406[4] 7809[2] 8220[3]

**Symbolic Star (IRE)** *Charlie Appleby* 81
2 b c New Approach(IRE) Epitome (IRE) (Nashwan (USA))
1977[3]

**Sympathy (USA)** *Sir Michael Stoute* 87
2 b f Henrythenavigator(USA) Sweet Temper (USA) (Stormy Atlantic (USA))
6295[3] (7019) ◆

**Synaesthesia (FR)** *Lady Cecil* a66
3 bb f High Chaparral(IRE) I'm Sensational (Selkirk (USA))
7686[5] 8020[5] 8310[4]

**Syncopate** *Pam Sly* a80 82
5 b g Oratorio(IRE) Millistar (Galileo (IRE))
89[9] 1022[3] 1241[3] 1724[2] 2162[11] 3335[5] 5984[4] 6487[9] 7831[13] 8122[9]

**Syndic (FR)** *A Schaerer* a87
5 b g Sinndar(IRE) Kalatuna (FR) (Green Tune (USA))
729a[4]

**Synergise** *Roger Varian* 89
3 ch g Danehill Dancer(IRE) Splashdown (Falbrav (IRE))
(4569)

**Synodic (USA)** *David Lanigan* 14
2 br c Henrythenavigator(USA) Seven Moons (JPN) (Sunday Silence (USA))
3194[13]

**Synonym (ITY)** *Michael Appleby* a56 22
3 ch f Haatef(USA) Shatarah (Gulch (USA))
645[4] 923[4] 1211[9] 1829[3] 2416[12] 6454[11] 7376[3] (7737) 7864[5] 8133[8]

**Synthese (IRE)** *J Boisnard* 31
2 ch f Notnowcato World's Heroine (IRE) (Spinning World (USA))
7468a[7]

**Syrian** *Richard Ford* a62 68
7 b g Hawk Wing(USA) Lady Lahar (Fraam)
8063[11] 8162[2] ◆ 8265[8]

**Syrian Pearl** *Chris Wall* a77 85
3 gr f Clodovil(IRE) Syrian Queen (Slip Anchor)
1379[4] (1832) (2647) (3966) ◆ 4572[2] 5437[11] 6468[6] 7035[5]

**Syros (IRE)** *Michael Easterby* a79 73
3 ch g Kheleyf(USA) Starring (FR) (Ashkalani (IRE))
2333[10] 2897[7] 3464[9] 3911[6] 4300[4] (4871) 5387[7] 7438[6]

**Szoff (GER)** *A Kleinkorres* a97 102
4 b c Shirocco(GER) Slawomira (GER) (Dashing Blade)
3511a[5] 6914a[9] 7727a[6] 8006a[6]

**Taajub (IRE)** *Peter Crate* a95 101
7 b g Exceed And Excel(AUS) Purple Tiger (IRE) (Rainbow Quest (USA))
234[6] 534[7] (719) 802[8] 1650[9] 2989[8] 3927[12] 4700[15] 5677[3] 6130[3] 6614[2] 6923[4]

**Taanif** *Michael Easterby* a49 49
3 b g Aqlaam Firebelly (Nicolotte)
1346[13] 1507[9] 1847[6] 7118[6]

**Taaqah (USA)** *James Tate* 91
2 bb f Arch(USA) Classic West (USA) (Gone West (USA))
3223[3] (4396) 6295[4] 6926[5]

**Taaresh (IRE)** *Kevin Morgan* a77 70
9 b g Sakhee(USA) Tanaghum (Darshaan)
(8029)

**Tabjeel** *Saeed bin Suroor* a88 74
3 b g Sakhee(USA) Intishaar (IRE) (Dubai Millennium)
3332[3] 4265[2] 5186[3] 5894[2] (6634) 7531[2]

**Tableforten** *J S Moore* a70 56
3 ch g Pastoral Pursuits Twitch Hill (Piccolo)
1350[8] 1570[10] 6029[8] 6568[4] 7570[9] 7972[4] 8139[5] 8219[2] 8319[8]

**Table Rock (IRE)** *A P O'Brien* 109
3 b g Fastnet Rock(AUS) Small Sacrifice (IRE) (Sadler's Wells (USA))
3378[14] (4127)

**Tabreek (USA)** *Richard Hannon* 86
3 ch g Distorted Humor(USA) Blushing (USA) (Maria's Mon (USA))
1529[6] (2271) 3200[7] 5676[6]

**Tac De Boistron (FR)** *Marco Botti* 119
7 gr g Take Risks(FR) Pondiki (FR) (Sicyos (USA))
(1869) 2315[2] (7486a)

**Tachophobia** *Richard Fahey* 80
2 br c Showcasing Mille Feuille (IRE) (Choisir (AUS))
2541[6] 3199[3] (3842) 4439[17] 5607[16] 6499[6] (7005) (7443)

**Tactical Strike** *Shaun Harris* a39 40
3 ch g Pivotal Alvee (IRE) (Key Of Luck (USA))
1391[4] 1691[9] 2132[4] 2893[6] 6637[5] 8289[8]

**Tacticus (USA)** *Lady Cecil* a81 68
3 b c A.P. Indy(USA) Visions Of Clarity (IRE) (Sadler's Wells (USA))
1960[5] 2334[14] 4077[3]

**Tadalavil** *Linda Perratt* a50 61
9 gr g Clodovil(IRE) Blandish (USA) (Wild Again (USA))
1602[10] 1972[8] 2219[12] 2296[13] 2514[4] 2909[6] 3099[11] 3833[9] (4257) 4664[7] 4860[2] 4960[2] 5236[7] 5636[2] 5858[3] 6114[6] 6406[6] 6475[12] 7057[4]

**Tadpole** *William Haggas* 74
2 b f Sir Percy Frog (Akarad (FR))
5391[3] (6148) 6691[7]

**Tadqeeq** *William Haggas* a74 72
2 b g Makfi Perfect Spirit (IRE) (Invincible Spirit (IRE))
5104[5] 6147[2] (6718)

**Tafahom (IRE)** *B W Hills* 67
2 b c Acclamation Dance Set (Selkirk (USA))
7234[6] 7560[5]

**Tafawuk (USA)** *Roger Varian* a75 79
5 b g Nayef(USA) Yaqeen (Green Desert (USA))
1899[6] 2445[2] 2966[3] 3544[9]

**Taffetta** *Tony Coyle* 52
2 ch f Paco Boy(IRE) Tarneem (USA) (Zilzal (USA))
5332[6] 6867[8]

**Tagar Bere (FR)** *Y Barberot* a79 95
7 ch h High Yield(USA) Arrondie (FR) (Inchinor)
3172a[2]

**Taghreeb** *Brian Meehan* 76
3 b c Dubawi(IRE) Ghaneema (USA) (Forestry (USA))
(5352)

**Taghrooda** *John Gosden* 126
3 b f Sea The Stars(IRE) Ezima (IRE) (Sadler's Wells (USA))
(1978) (2960) (4649) 5610[2] 6970a[3]

**Taglietelle** *Gordon Elliott* a79 90
5 b g Tagula(IRE) Averami (Averti (IRE))
4746a[12]

**Tagtale (IRE)** *Richard Fahey* 63
2 b f Tagula(IRE) Story (Observatory (USA))
1342[11] (1901) 2360[6] 3091[4] 3894[4] 4449[6] (4899) 6749[11] 7379[11]

**Tagula Nation (IRE)** *Paul Midgley*
2 b f Tagula(IRE) Rainbow Nation (Rainbow Quest (USA))
4624[10] 5194[10]

**Tagula Night (IRE)** *Dean Ivory* a86 89
8 ch g Tagula(IRE) Carpet Lady (IRE) (Night Shift (USA))
233[4] 2890[2] (3246) 3927[8] 4502[4] 5925[14] 6260[16] (6736) 7233[7] 7624[5]

**Tahaany (IRE)** *D K Weld* 94
3 b f Raven's Pass(USA) Photophore (IRE) (Clodovil (IRE))
2042a[4] 2263a[5]

**Tahadee (IRE)** *M F De Kock* a58 78
3 b g Teofilo(IRE) Queen Of Lyons (USA) (Dubai Destination (USA))
239a[10]

**Tahaf (IRE)** *Mark Brisbourne* a61 69
4 b g Authorized(IRE) Lady Zonda (Lion Cavern (USA))
4805a[2] 7042[13] 7568[8]

**Tahchee** *James Fanshawe* a79 73
3 ch g Sleeping Indian Neyraan (Lujain (USA))
2886[4] 3406[5] (4972) (5307) 7023[4] 7351[2] ◆

**Tahira (GER)** *John Quinn* 105
4 ch f Doyen(IRE) Tennessee Queen (GER) (Big Shuffle (USA))
2253[7] ◆ 3217[2] 4214[12] 4634[7]

**Tahiti Way (FR)** *L A Urbano-Grajales* a76 44
3 b f Soldier Of Fortune(IRE) Happy Way (FR) (Kingsalsa (USA))
5404a[2]

**Tailoring (IRE)** *E Charpy* a53
5 br g Dansili Subtle Charm (Machiavellian (USA))
238a[7]

**Tajathub** *Ed Dunlop* a77
2 rg c Bahamian Bounty Galapagar (USA) (Miswaki (USA))
7199[4] ◆

**Tajneed (IRE)** *David Nicholls* a64 81
11 b g Alhaarth(IRE) Indian Express (Indian Ridge)
1375[6] 1537[6] 1905[5]

**Takaatuf (IRE)** *Tina Jackson* 48
8 b g Dubai Destination(USA) Karlaka (IRE) (Barathea (IRE))
4470[9] 5371[12] 6216[8] 6864[14]

**Takafol (IRE)** *Charles Hills* 63
2 b g Fast Company(IRE) Jamary (IRE) (Grand Reward (USA))
6517[9] 7308[4] ◆

**Takahiro** *Richard Hannon* a46
2 b c Kyllachy Marliana (IRE) (Mtoto)
7891[9]

**Takara Girl (FR)** *P Sogorb* 72
2 b f Kodiac Choirgirl (Unfuwain (USA))
(6591a)

**Take A Guess (FR)** *Matthieu Palussiere* 72
2 b c Palace Episode(USA) Somewhere (FR) (Noverre (USA))
5544a[7] 6244a[9]

**Take A Note** *Patrick Chamings* a85 96
5 b g Singspiel(IRE) Ela Paparouna (Vettori (IRE))
2068[4] 3314[10] (4154) (5092) (6207) 6755[8]

**Take Charge Brandi (USA)** *D Wayne Lukas* a108
2 ch f Giant's Causeway(USA) Charming (USA) (Seeking The Gold (USA))
6915a[8] (7606a)

**Take Cover** *David C Griffiths* a107 116
7 b g Singspiel(IRE) Enchanted (Magic Ring (IRE))
3319[8] (4215) (4852) ◆ 5654[8] 6549[4] 6966a[6]

**Takeitfromalady (IRE)** *Lee Carter* a88 66
5 b g Intikhab(USA) Pinheiros (IRE) (Rock Of Gibraltar (IRE))
2882[8] 6881[6] 8037[11] 8250[4]

**Take It To The Max** *George Moore* 41
7 b g Bahamian Bounty Up And About (Barathea (IRE))
2763[9] 4451[8] 5385[12]

**Take Note (IRE)** *James Toller* a66 50
2 b f Azamour(IRE) Lolla's Spirit (IRE) (Montjeu (IRE))
7594[13] 7798[3]

**Take Ten** *S Seemar* a101 99
7 b g Bahamian Bounty See You Later (Emarati (USA))
107a[5] 393a[9] 809a[4]

**Take The Crown (FR)** *J-C Rouget* a84 78
3 ch c Creachadoir(IRE) Taking Haven (FR) (Septieme Ciel (USA))
360a[4] 4952a[8]

**Take The Lead** *John Weymes* a70 73
4 ch f Assertive My Dancer (IRE) (Alhaarth (IRE))
93[5] (362) 432[8] 651[12] 1500[6] (2552) 2951[7] 4487[6] 5097[5] 8082[13]

**Take Two** *Alex Hales* a77 88
5 b g Act One Lac Marmot (FR) (Marju (IRE))
7341[8] 7702[10] 8260[6]

**Takitwo** *Geoffrey Deacon* a55 63
11 b g Delta Dancer Tiama (IRE) (Last Tycoon)
3589[9] 5873[3]

**Takreym (IRE)** *Roger Varian* 83
3 b g Clodovil(IRE) Somoushe (IRE) (Black Minnaloushe (USA))
(2031) 2567[3]

**Talent** *Ralph Beckett* a81 115
4 ch f New Approach(IRE) Prowess (IRE) (Peintre Celebre (USA))
2988$^{5}$ 3961$^{3}$ 4824$^{4}$ 5610$^{5}$

**Talented Kid** *Mark Johnston* a92 88
5 b g Teofilo(IRE) See You Later (Emarati (USA))
625$^{9}$ 1301$^{7}$ 1442$^{10}$ 1721$^{9}$ 2156$^{3}$ 2453$^{7}$ 3306$^{4}$ 3759$^{3}$ 4148$^{9}$ 4753$^{4}$

**Talent Scout (IRE)** *Karen Tutty* a62 90
8 b g Exceed And Excel(AUS) Taalluf (USA) (Hansel (USA))
1483$^{5}$ 1957$^{7}$ 3221$^{11}$ 3573$^{8}$ (3955) 4963$^{2}$ 5385$^{8}$ 5810$^{7}$ 6430$^{8}$ 7085$^{13}$

**Tales Of Grimm (USA)** *Richard Fahey* a101 113
5 b g Distorted Humor(USA) Stupendous Miss (USA) (Dynaformer (USA))
110a$^{4}$ 397a$^{7}$ 679a$^{15}$ 1162$^{5}$ 2286$^{4}$ ◆ 3356$^{6}$

**Taleteller (USA)** *H-A Pantall* a66 72
3 b f Bernardini(USA) Taletobetold (USA) (Tale Of The Cat (USA))
795a$^{9}$

**Talitha Kum (IRE)** *P D Deegan* 94
4 b f Chineur(FR) Belle Of The Blues (IRE) (Blues Traveller (IRE))
4276a$^{12}$

**Talksalot (IRE)** *J S Moore* a86 60
3 b g Thousand Words Lady Piste (IRE) (Ali-Royal (IRE))
5824$^{12}$ 7375$^{13}$ 7636$^{10}$

**Tall Ship (IRE)** *Gary Moore* a76 100
3 b g Sea The Stars(IRE) Magical Romance (IRE) (Barathea (IRE))
1216$^{4}$ 3758$^{5}$ 4120$^{2}$ (4855) (5670) ◆

**Tallulah Mai** *Alastair Lidderdale* a56 55
7 b m Kayf Tara Al Awaalah (Mukaddamah (USA))
997$^{2}$

**Talmada (USA)** *Roger Varian* a55 106
3 b f Cape Cross(IRE) Aryaamm (IRE) (Galileo (IRE))
1423$^{3}$ (1720) 2347$^{3}$ 3376$^{7}$ 7105$^{2}$

**Tamaathul** *A Al Raihe* a109 94
7 gr g Tiger Hill(IRE) Tahrir (IRE) (Linamix (FR))
308a$^{9}$ 597a$^{6}$ 768a$^{3}$ 898a$^{14}$

**Tamakh (FR)** *M Rulec* 83
2 bb c Makfi Time Pressure (Montjeu (IRE))
6123a$^{7}$

**Tamamo Best Play (JPN)** *Katsumi Minai* 112
4 ch c Fuji Kiseki(JPN) Hot Play (JPN) (Northern Taste (CAN))
7981a$^{10}$

**Tamarin** *David Evans* a64 62
2 ch f Paco Boy(IRE) Les Hurlants (IRE) (Barathea (IRE))
3671$^{7}$ 4980$^{6}$ 6719$^{3}$ 7363$^{2}$ 7973$^{11}$ 8140$^{7}$

**Tamarkuz (USA)** *M Al Muhairi* a107 80
4 ch c Speightstown(USA) Without You Babe (USA) (Lemon Drop Kid (USA))
396a$^{5}$ 808a$^{U}$

**Tamasha** *Ralph Beckett* a92 87
3 ch f Sea The Stars(IRE) Tamarind (IRE) (Sadler's Wells (USA))
(6298) ◆ 7554$^{6}$

**Tamayuz Magic (IRE)** *Michael Easterby* a53 68
3 b g Tamayuz Anne Tudor (IRE) (Anabaa (USA))
1285$^{4}$ 1648$^{2}$ 2020$^{4}$ 2355$^{3}$ (2896) 4496$^{4}$ 5088$^{13}$ 5892$^{5}$ (6627) 7251$^{11}$

**Tamayuz Star (IRE)** *George Margarson* 102
4 ch g Tamayuz Magical Peace (IRE) (Magical Wonder (USA))
1975$^{18}$ 2747$^{7}$ 3420$^{14}$ 3969$^{6}$ 4650$^{9}$ 6094$^{3}$ ◆ 6441$^{4}$ 6880$^{8}$

**Taming The Tweet** *J R Jenkins* a55
4 b f Act One Pants (Pivotal)
97$^{4}$

**Tammis** *Ron Hodges* a37 50
4 b f Whipper(USA) Tamise (USA) (Time For A Change (USA))
115$^{6}$ 368$^{10}$ 546$^{9}$

**Tammuz (IRE)** *Tony Carroll* a66 56
4 ch f Tamayuz Favourita (Diktat)
84$^{7}$ 289$^{11}$

**Tammy The Torpedo (USA)** *Chad C Brown* 97
2 bb f More Than Ready(USA) Search And Seizure (USA) (War Chant (USA))
7592a$^{7}$

**Tamujin (IRE)** *Ken Cunningham-Brown* a46 50
6 b g Elusive City(USA) Arabian Princess (Taufan (USA))
1986$^{9}$ 2722$^{4}$ 4733$^{5}$ 5529$^{3}$ 5873$^{6}$ 7002$^{5}$ 7924$^{12}$

**Tanamia (GER)** *A Wohler* 98
3 bb f Nayef(USA) Tanami (Green Desert (USA))
4955a$^{7}$

**Tanawar (IRE)** *Ruth Carr* a72 69
4 b g Elusive City(USA) Parakopi (IRE) (Green Desert (USA))
1673$^{6}$ 2215$^{9}$ (3439) 4001$^{5}$ 4620$^{6}$ 5337$^{3}$ 5640$^{7}$ 6217$^{5}$ (6544) 6865$^{7}$

**Tancred (IRE)** *Michael Wigham* a40 58
3 b g Oratorio(IRE) Mythologie (FR) (Bering)
1346$^{12}$ 2218$^{6}$ 2737$^{11}$ 5795$^{7}$

**Tanfeeth** *M Al Muhairi* a102 103
6 ch h Singspiel(IRE) Nasij (USA) (Elusive Quality (USA))
305a$^{3}$ 507a$^{13}$ 598a$^{11}$ 807a$^{2}$ 902a$^{8}$

**Tanforan** *Brian Baugh* a57 66
12 b g Mujahid(USA) Florentynna Bay (Aragon)
3299$^{12}$

**Tangatchek (IRE)** *H-A Pantall* a88 82
5 ch h Mr Greeley(USA) Tivadare (FR) (Distant View (USA))
6992a$^{4}$

**Tangerine Trees** *Bryan Smart* a103 104
9 b g Mind Games Easy To Imagine (USA) (Cozzene (USA))
1561$^{4}$ 2989$^{12}$ 3241$^{9}$ 3830$^{2}$ 6624$^{4}$ 7101$^{6}$

**Tango Sky (IRE)** *James Unett* a64 75
5 b g Namid Sky Galaxy (USA) (Sky Classic (CAN))
2727$^{2}$ 2953$^{8}$ 3216$^{3}$ 3697$^{3}$ ◆ 4256$^{8}$ 5236$^{8}$ 6013$^{8}$ 6512$^{15}$ 6821$^{2}$ 7253$^{6}$ 7621$^{6}$

**Tango Turner (IRE)** *Jamie Poulton* a53
2 ch c Excellent Art Kassyderia (IRE) (Docksider (USA))
8292$^{11}$

**Tangramm** *Simon Dow* a53
2 bb g Sakhee's Secret Tripti (IRE) (Sesaro (USA))
4965$^{6}$ 6103$^{8}$ 6659$^{9}$

**Tanguero (FR)** *Mlle A Bretel*
3 gr g Al Namix(FR) Sweet Magic (FR) (Goldneyev (USA))
7681a$^{10}$

**Tanino Epaulette (JPN)** *Akira Murayama* 113
7 b h Dance In The Dark(JPN) Tanino Charis (JPN) (Generous (IRE))
2002a$^{5}$

**Tannaaf (IRE)** *M F De Kock* 85
2 b c High Chaparral(IRE) Wanna (IRE) (Danehill Dancer (IRE))
(5646) ◆ 6925$^{7}$

**Tannery (IRE)** *Alan E Goldberg* a90 110
5 b m Dylan Thomas(IRE) Danse Grecque (IRE) (Sadler's Wells (USA))
5459a$^{10}$

**Tanojin (IRE)** *Mick Channon* a61 61
3 ch f Thousand Words Indiannie Moon (Fraam)
311$^{7}$ 492$^{4}$

**Tanqeya (IRE)** *Richard Hannon* a78 86
3 b g Intense Focus(USA) Spinning Well (IRE) (Pivotal)
2510$^{2}$ 3977$^{7}$

**Tanseeb** *Mark Johnston* a43 92
3 b g Royal Applause Perfect Story (IRE) (Desert Story (IRE))
1952$^{9}$ 2778$^{13}$ 3244$^{2}$ 4442$^{9}$ 4915$^{2}$

**Tansfeeq** *B W Hills* 75
2 b g Aqlaam Qelaan (USA) (Dynaformer (USA))
2480$^{3}$ 3136$^{8}$ 5309$^{3}$ 5845$^{3}$

**Tantalising (IRE)** *Martyn Meade* a56 90
6 b m Sadler's Wells(USA) Bluffing (IRE) (Darshaan)
2501$^{4}$ 2782$^{4}$

**Tantric Lady** *Alan McCabe* a31 52
2 b f Stimulation(IRE) Immortelle (Arazi (USA))
3297$^{4}$ 3542$^{8}$ 3933$^{7}$ 6669$^{16}$ 6842$^{11}$ 7421$^{9}$

**Tanzeel (IRE)** *Charles Hills* 101
3 b g Elusive City(USA) Royal Fizz (IRE) (Royal Academy (USA))
3479$^{2}$ ◆ (4305) ◆

**Taper Tantrum (IRE)** *Michael Bell* 82
2 b c Azamour(IRE) Maramba (USA) (Hussonet (USA))
3467$^{2}$ ◆ (4330) (5250)

**Tapestry (IRE)** *A P O'Brien* 121
3 b f Galileo(IRE) Rumplestiltskin (IRE) (Danehill (USA))
1976$^{17}$ 3418$^{6}$ 4461a$^{2}$ (5610) 6351a$^{9}$ 6970a$^{13}$

**Tapis Libre** *Michael Easterby* a66 69
6 b g Librettist(USA) Stella Manuela (FR) (Galileo (IRE))
1710$^{8}$ 3192$^{5}$ 4351$^{4}$ 4964$^{7}$ 5600$^{3}$ 6564$^{5}$

**Tapiture (USA)** *Steven Asmussen* a119
3 ch c Tapit(USA) Free Spin (USA) (Olympio (USA))
1964a$^{15}$ 7591a$^{2}$

**Tappanappa (IRE)** *Michael Appleby* a81 89
7 b g High Chaparral(IRE) Itsibitsi (IRE) (Brief Truce (USA))
803$^{10}$ 1140$^{6}$ 4217$^{10}$ 4995$^{6}$ 5825$^{3}$ 5924$^{9}$ 6721$^{7}$

**Tap Your Toes (IRE)** *Luca Cumani* 74
3 b c Danehill Dancer(IRE) Sharplaw Star (Xaar)
2842$^{6}$ 3914$^{7}$ 4677$^{2}$ 5417$^{2}$ 6215$^{5}$

**Taqneen (IRE)** *Ed Dunlop* 82
3 b g Cape Cross(IRE) Badee'A (IRE) (Marju (IRE))
1841$^{4}$ 2877$^{2}$ 3465$^{2}$ 4393$^{2}$ (4924) 5849$^{10}$

**Taqneyya (IRE)** *Charles Hills* 81
2 b f Raven's Pass(USA) Misdaqeya (Red Ransom (USA))
4126$^{9}$ 6246$^{2}$ ◆ (6753)

**Taquka (IRE)** *Ralph Beckett* a85 82
3 b g Kodiac Dubai Princess (IRE) (Dubai Destination (USA))
371$^{2}$ (531) 926$^{2}$ 1737$^{2}$ 2626$^{5}$ 4133$^{8}$ 4636$^{10}$ (5012) 5553$^{4}$ 6021$^{5}$ 7017$^{2}$ 7365$^{4}$

**Taqweem (USA)** *Saeed bin Suroor* 49
2 bb f Medaglia d'Oro(USA) Hatheer (USA) (Storm Cat (USA))
6041$^{9}$

**Taraakum (FR)** *Andrew Crook*
4 gr g Clodovil(IRE) Lockup (IRE) (Inchinor)
41$^{5}$

**Tarana (IRE)** *John M Oxx* 106
4 b f Cape Cross(IRE) Tarakala (IRE) (Dr Fong (USA))
(1750a) ◆ 3764a$^{3}$ 5024a$^{4}$ 7144a$^{6}$

**Tarando** *Michael Bell* a37 65
2 b f Equiano(FR) Christmas Tart (IRE) (Danetime (IRE))
1528$^{9}$ 2022$^{4}$ 2349$^{3}$ 4345$^{5}$ 5879$^{3}$ 7112$^{6}$

**Tarap (IRE)** *Richard Hannon* a53 39
3 b f Myboycharlie(IRE) Tanzania (IRE) (Alzao (USA))
2061$^{11}$ 2690$^{11}$

**Tarara** *Michael Blanshard* a56 77
4 b f Royal Applause Anneliina (Cadeaux Genereux)
605$^{6}$ 1144$^{7}$ 1405$^{6}$

**Tara River (FR)** *F Rossi* 105
5 b g Stormy River(FR) Tarabela (FR) (Johann Quatz (FR))
5330a$^{3}$

**Tara's Treasure (IRE)** *Gary Moore* a49 48
3 b g Amadeus Wolf Bean Island (USA) (Afleet (CAN))
4536$^{6}$

**Taraz** *Richard Hannon* 61
2 b c Oasis Dream Tamarind (IRE) (Sadler's Wells (USA))
6056$^{6}$ 6362$^{5}$

**Tarbawi (IRE)** *A bin Harmash* a77 105
4 b g Anabaa(USA) Born Something (IRE) (Caerleon (USA))
110a$^{5}$ 309a$^{3}$ 595a$^{5}$ 812a$^{12}$

**Tarfasha (IRE)** *D K Weld* 112
3 ch f Teofilo(IRE) Grecian Bride (IRE) (Groom Dancer (USA))
(2263a) 2960$^{2}$ 4461a$^{5}$ (6370a) 6969a$^{4}$

**Targaryen (IRE)** *G Marras* 98
4 b g Red Clubs(IRE) Beenablaw (IRE) (Alzao (USA))
1603a$^{3}$ 7469a$^{5}$

**Tarikhi (USA)** *Saeed bin Suroor* 101
4 b g Bernardini(USA) Caffe Latte (IRE) (Seattle Dancer (USA))
3251$^{5}$ 4214$^{15}$ (Dead)

**Tariq Too** *Amy Weaver* a63 106
7 ch g Kyllachy Tatora (Selkirk (USA))
1443$^{3}$

**Tarnag (FR)** *E Lellouche* a91 88
3 ch f Muhaymin(USA) Kenz (FR) (Indian Rocket)
(4952a) 5843a$^{9}$

**Tarooq (USA)** *David Barron* a111 80
8 b g War Chant(USA) Rose Of Zollern (IRE) (Seattle Dancer (USA))
(713) 1557$^{9}$ 2898$^{5}$ 3714$^{7}$ 8101$^{3}$ 8228$^{8}$

**Taro Tywod (IRE)** *Mark Brisbourne* a75 81
5 br m Footstepsinthesand Run To Jane (IRE) (Doyoun)
1454$^{4}$ (1864) 2509$^{4}$ 2947$^{2}$ 3218$^{4}$ (3325) 3644$^{7}$ 4045$^{5}$ 4799$^{3}$ 5074$^{3}$ 5284$^{2}$ 5948$^{8}$ 6323$^{8}$ 6904$^{5}$

**Taroum (IRE)** *John Flint* a48 75
7 b g Refuse To Bend(IRE) Taraza (IRE) (Darshaan)
8261$^{7}$

**Tarquin (IRE)** *Kristin Stubbs* a66 56
5 b g Excellent Art Umlani (IRE) (Great Commotion (USA))
245$^{13}$ 5105$^{12}$ 6342$^{8}$ 7259$^{8}$

**Tarrafal (IRE)** *Mark Johnston* a81 63
3 b c Shamardal(USA) Cape Verdi (IRE) (Caerleon (USA))
696$^{3}$ 888$^{2}$ 1090$^{4}$ 1352$^{9}$ 1662$^{3}$ 1969$^{6}$ 2545$^{5}$ 3672$^{7}$ 4023$^{2}$

**Tarragon** *Jeremy Gask* a65
2 b c Compton Place Hennalaine (IRE) (Lujain (USA))
7114$^{4}$ 7752$^{8}$ 7919$^{4}$

**Tarrsille (IRE)** *Paul Midgley* a36 84
8 b g Dansili Tara Gold (IRE) (Royal Academy (USA))
297$^{6}$ 766$^{12}$ 1838$^{10}$ 2166$^{9}$

**Tartan Gigha (IRE)** *Geoffrey Harker* a73 79
9 b g Green Desert(USA) High Standard (Kris)
379$^{5}$

**Tartan Jura** *Mark Johnston* a84 80
6 b g Green Desert(USA) On A Soapbox (USA) (Mi Cielo (USA))
(1366) 1485$^{10}$

**Tartan Trip** *Michael Appleby* a79 49
7 b g Selkirk(USA) Marajuana (Robellino (USA))
101$^{3}$ 268$^{2}$ (389) 552$^{6}$ 832$^{5}$ 929$^{3}$ 1609$^{7}$ 2400$^{6}$ 8124$^{4}$

**Taryn** *M Delcher Sanchez* a77
2 ch c Kheleyf(USA) Fabulous Speed (USA) (Silver Hawk (USA))
8148a$^{2}$

**Tarziyna (IRE)** *John M Oxx* 97
3 ch f Raven's Pass(USA) Taraza (IRE) (Darshaan)
5024a$^{9}$

**Tasaaboq** *Phil McEntee* a61 61
3 b g Aqlaam Seldemosa (Selkirk (USA))
3432$^{8}$ 4407$^{7}$ 4785$^{3}$ 7764$^{7}$ 7799$^{3}$

**Tasaday (USA)** *Saeed bin Suroor* 116
4 rg f Nayef(USA) Tashelka (FR) (Mujahid (USA))
397a$^{9}$ (683a) 1181a$^{9}$ (4634) 5610$^{3}$ 6546$^{2}$ 7273$^{10}$

**Tashbeeh (IRE)** *Dianne Sayer* a65 45
3 b g Iffraaj Kayak (Singspiel (IRE))
614$^{4}$ 787$^{6}$ 871$^{4}$ 2729$^{6}$ 3135$^{7}$

**Tasmanian** *Mark Johnston* a53 76
3 b c Invincible Spirit(IRE) Devil's Imp (IRE) (Cadeaux Genereux)
5469$^{4}$ 5772$^{4}$ (6118) 6625$^{6}$ 6886$^{9}$

**Tasrih (USA)** *Alan McCabe* a91
5 b g Hard Spun(USA) Rare Gift (USA) (Unbridled's Song (USA))
3728$^{8}$ 550$^{7}$ (1803) 2202$^{8}$ 2922$^{8}$ 4580$^{5}$ 6145$^{8}$ 6692$^{10}$

**Taste The Wine (IRE)** *Bernard Llewellyn* a63 72
8 gr g Verglas(IRE) Azia (IRE) (Desert Story (IRE))
292$^{7}$ 460$^{4}$ (2252) 3179$^{2}$ 3698$^{4}$ 4818$^{5}$ 5208$^{2}$ 5403$^{2}$ 5756$^{4}$

**Tatawu (IRE)** *Brian Meehan* a71 51
2 b c Mawatheeq(USA) Mooteeah (IRE) (Sakhee (USA))
6875$^{7}$ 7354$^{2}$

**Tatiani** *Jose Santos* a26 47
2 ch f Refuse To Bend(IRE) Tech Zinne (Zinaad)
4604$^{6}$ 5549$^{7}$ 6066$^{12}$ 6412$^{8}$

**Tatlisu (IRE)** *Richard Fahey* 99
4 b g Red Clubs(IRE) Zwadi (IRE) (Docksider (USA))
2453$^{5}$ 3152$^{3}$ (3714) 4384$^{2}$ 4892$^{3}$ 5445$^{3}$ 6369a$^{10}$ 6531$^{8}$

**Tatting** *Chris Dwyer* a88 84
5 ch g Street Cry(IRE) Needlecraft (IRE) (Mark Of Esteem (IRE))
(29) 172$^{3}$ 256$^{4}$ (698) 832$^{8}$ 977$^{6}$ 1871$^{4}$ 2311$^{6}$ 2762$^{5}$ 3272$^{2}$ 3703$^{9}$ 4028$^{3}$ 5258$^{7}$ 5758$^{7}$ 6100$^{6}$

**Taurus Twins** *Richard Price* a50 91
8 b g Deportivo Intellibet One (Compton Place)
1221$^{10}$ (1912) (2159) (2456) 2786$^{16}$ 3386$^{3}$ 4027$^{4}$ (4412) 4488$^{4}$ 5754 6130$^{17}$

**Tautira (IRE)** *Michael Bell* a70 66
3 b f Kheleyf(USA) Ballantrae (IRE) (Diktat)
(338)

**Tavener** *William Jarvis* a58
2 b c Exceed And Excel(AUS) Sea Chorus (Singspiel (IRE))
8262$^{4}$

**Tawaasheeh (IRE)** *Roger Varian* 78
2 b c New Approach(IRE) Sana Abel (IRE) (Alhaarth (IRE))
6683$^{3}$ 7244$^{4}$

**Tawan** *Brian Rothwell* 52
3 b g Tiger Hill(IRE) Lady Netbetsports (IRE) (In The Wings)
1166$^{7}$ 1840$^{7}$ 2616$^{11}$ 2867$^{8}$ 3543$^{3}$ 5336$^{6}$

**Tawdeea** *Richard Hannon* 62
2 b c Intikhab(USA) Sharedah (IRE) (Pivotal)
7561$^{6}$

**Taweel (FR)** *Mlle B Renk* 66
4 b g Orpen(USA) Tazilia (SWI) (Zilzal Zamaan (USA))
3373a$^{18}$ 4776a$^{9}$

**Taweyla (IRE)** *Roger Varian* a68 70
3 b f Teofilo(IRE) Qasirah (IRE) (Machiavellian (USA))
5382$^{6}$ 6092$^{9}$ 6901$^{3}$

**Tawhid** *Saeed bin Suroor* 114
4 gr g Invincible Spirit(IRE) Snowdrops (Gulch (USA))
2765$^{7}$ 3723$^{5}$ 6934$^{2}$ 7242$^{4}$

**Taws** *Rod Millman* 86
3 b f Hernando(FR) Reaf (In The Wings)
1911$^{4}$ 2280$^{8}$ (2893) 3183$^{7}$ 4134$^{2}$ 4803$^{3}$ (5356) ◆ 5878$^{2}$ 6325$^{4}$ 6705$^{2}$ (7306)

**Tawteen (USA)** *John Gosden* a81
3 b f Street Sense(USA) Wid (USA) (Elusive Quality (USA))
(6940) 7196$^{5}$

**Tax Free (IRE)** *David Nicholls* a92 98
12 b g Tagula(IRE) Grandel (Owington)
41$^{1}$ 148$^{5}$ 444$^{5}$ 658$^{8}$ 1212$^{8}$ 1565$^{4}$ 1695$^{2}$ 1961$^{2}$ 2350$^{4}$ 2656$^{7}$ 2953$^{7}$ 3571$^{9}$ 4471$^{17}$ 5498$^{9}$

**Taxiformissbyron** *Iain Jardine* a66 52
4 b f Byron Miss Respect (Mark Of Esteem (IRE))
67$^{7}$ 289$^{10}$ 1596$^{4}$ 2427$^{9}$ 3364$^{5}$ 3657$^{5}$ 4000$^{8}$ 4381$^{9}$ 4665$^{2}$ 4730$^{6}$ 6000$^{7}$ 6564$^{6}$ 6823$^{4}$ 7115$^{5}$ 7292$^{8}$

**Tax Reform (IRE)** *Gary Moore* a67 68
4 b g Namid Happy Flight (IRE) (Titus Livius (FR))
291$^{4}$ 684$^{2}$ 927$^{4}$ 1876$^{6}$ 2646$^{5}$ 3526$^{6}$ 4579$^{11}$ 6195$^{2}$ 6636$^{13}$ 7000$^{8}$

**Taylor S (USA)** *Dale Romans* a62
2 bb f Medaglia d'Oro(USA) Miss Macy Sue (USA) (Trippi (USA))
6915a$^{10}$

**Taylor Said (CAN)** *Charlie Appleby* a74
6 br g Stephanotis(CAN) Fleet Amyanne (CAN) (Western Fame (USA))
679a$^{14}$

**Tayma (IRE)** *Saeed bin Suroor* a75 69
3 ch f Exceed And Excel(AUS) Bergamask (USA) (Kingmambo (USA))
5548$^{4}$ 6018$^{11}$ 6982$^{2}$ 7459$^{2}$ (7568) 7626$^{6}$

**Taysh (USA)** *John Gosden* a79 66
2 bb c Bernstein(USA) Normandy's Nell (USA) (Mt. Livermore (USA))
6861$^{2}$ (7354)

**Tazffin (IRE)** *Roger Varian* 77
2 b f Iffraaj Tarfshi (Mtoto)
7108$^{3}$

**Tea Gown (IRE)** *A Fabre* a77 77
3 ch f Iffraaj Dignify (IRE) (Rainbow Quest (USA))
7722a$^{12}$

**Tea In Transvaal (IRE)** *John O'Shea* a69 71
3 b f Teofilo(IRE) Mpumalanga (Observatory (USA))
2510$^{5}$ 2892$^{6}$ 3670$^{5}$ 3979$^{6}$ 5304$^{4}$ 6459$^{7}$ 7302$^{4}$ 7633$^{7}$

**Teajaybe (USA)** *Chris Dwyer* a80 66
6 bb g Street Cry(IRE) Wild Heaven (IRE) (Darshaan)
1004$^{2}$ (1092) 1366$^{2}$ 2097$^{6}$ 2394$^{4}$ 2774$^{7}$

**Teak (IRE)** *Ian Williams* a80 88
7 b g Barathea(IRE) Szabo (IRE) (Anabaa (USA))
1692$^{4}$ 3034$^{6}$ 3234$^{2}$ (3501) 3752$^{3}$ 4217$^{9}$ (4777) (6360) 7107$^{7}$

**Tea Leaf (IRE)** *Ralph Beckett* a87 86
3 b f Bushranger(IRE) Boston Ivy (USA) (Mark Of Esteem (IRE))
1543$^{2}$ (1985) 2257$^{16}$ 3117$^{5}$

**Tearless** *Charlie Appleby* a102 100
4 b f Street Cry(IRE) Playful Act (IRE) (Sadler's Wells (USA))
(3423) (4211) 5312$^{7}$ (7553)

**Tears And Rain (IRE)** *Tim Easterby* 54
3 b f Iffraaj Massalia (IRE) (Montjeu (IRE))
1347$^{4}$ 1647$^{12}$ 2235$^{6}$

**Tears Of The Sun** *Roger Varian* a87 86
3 b f Mastercraftsman(IRE) Perfect Star (Act One)
(2719) 3644$^{5}$ ◆ 4272$^{3}$ 6746$^{12}$ 7689$^{2}$

**Technokrat (IRE)** *S Smrczek* a79 111
6 b h Oratorio(IRE) Tech Engine (GER) (Enrique)
2229a$^{3}$ 4722a$^{11}$

**Tectonic (IRE)** *Keith Dalgleish* a67 74
5 b g Dylan Thomas(IRE) Pine Chip (USA) (Nureyev (USA))
1970$^{12}$ 2607$^{8}$ 2823$^{6}$ 3301$^{2}$ 3572$^{2}$ 3958$^{2}$ 4001$^{3}$ 4197$^{3}$ 4387$^{8}$ 4729$^{3}$ 4903$^{7}$ 5235$^{6}$ 6009$^{3}$ (6227) 6578$^{3}$ 6795$^{2}$ 6822$^{3}$ 7533$^{6}$ 7626$^{8}$

**Tecumseh (IRE)** *K R Burke* 70
2 br g Danehill Dancer(IRE) Absolute Music (USA) (Consolidator (USA))
3454$^{8}$ 4382$^{7}$ 4739$^{3}$ (6401) 6989$^{7}$

**Ted Dolly (IRE)** *Tom Symonds* a68 76
10 bb g Bob's Return(IRE) Little Pearl (IRE) (Bigstone (IRE))
8164$^{7}$ 8231$^{2}$

**Ted Larkin (IRE)** *Richard Guest* 26
2 b g Dandy Man(IRE) Shewillifshewants (IRE) (Alzao (USA))
4286$^{14}$ 5242$^{8}$ 5886$^{12}$ 6147$^{9}$

**Ted's Brother (IRE)** *Richard Guest* a58 82
6 b g Fath(USA) Estertide (IRE) (Tagula (IRE))
1286$^{5}$ 1446$^{4}$ 1610$^{7}$ (1970) 2234$^{5}$ 3094$^{4}$ 3361$^{4}$ (3979) 4196$^{6}$ 4903$^{5}$ 5320$^{8}$ 5638$^{2}$ 5855$^{6}$ 6836$^{12}$ 7060$^{11}$ 7282$^{9}$ 7538$^{13}$ 7601$^{5}$

**Ted Spread** *Suzy Smith* a98 98
7 b g Beat Hollow Highbrook (USA) (Alphabatim (USA))
285$^{3}$ 803$^{7}$ (2558) 7107$^{13}$ 8146$^{2}$ 8296$^{4}$

**Ted Veale (IRE)** *A J Martin* 102
7 b g Revoque(IRE) Rose Tanner (IRE) (Roselier (FR))
5693$^{14}$ 7142a$^{12}$

**Tee It Up Tommo (IRE)** *Michael Wigham* a85 59
5 gr g Clodovil(IRE) Lamh Eile (IRE) (Lend A Hand)
(154) ◆ (211) 627$^{5}$ (927) (995) 1103$^{7}$ (4432) 7456$^{5}$ 7894$^{4}$ 8194$^{8}$

**Teenage Dream (IRE)** *Derek Shaw* a61
6 b g Antonius Pius(USA) Lucayan Star (IRE) (First Trump)
150$^{2}$ 276$^{4}$ 463$^{5}$ 818$^{6}$ 932$^{3}$ 1605$^{15}$

**Teen Ager (FR)** *Paul Burgoyne* a65 51
10 b g Invincible Spirit(IRE) Tarwiya (IRE) (Dominion)
155$^{5}$ 663$^{4}$ 817$^{9}$ 993$^{2}$ 1110$^{2}$ 1408$^{3}$ 1799$^{5}$ 2282$^{7}$ 8299$^{9}$

**Teetotal (IRE)** *Nigel Tinkler* 82
4 ch g Footstepsinthesand Tea Service (USA) (Atticus (USA))
1190$^{8}$ 1440$^{3}$ 2136$^{6}$ (2522) 3256$^{4}$ 3599$^{6}$ 4632$^{12}$ 5053$^{7}$ 5470$^{7}$ 6150$^{2}$ 6692$^{6}$ 7179$^{13}$

**Teide Mistress (USA)** *Alistair Whillans*
4 bb f Medaglia d'Oro(USA) Chandelle No. Five (USA) (Yes It's True (USA))
5388$^{10}$

**Teide Peak (IRE)** *Grace Harris* a66 61
5 b g Cape Cross(IRE) Teide Lady (Nashwan (USA))
405$^{5}$ 538$^{4}$ (998) 1406$^{6}$ 3308$^{7}$ 3971$^{8}$ 5529$^{11}$ 7068$^{8}$ 7188$^{4}$ 7369$^{12}$ 7932$^{12}$

**Teixidor (ITY)** *Ottavio Di Paolo* 97
5 ch h St Paul House Rosetta Stone (ITY) (Tisserand (ITY))
3776a$^{8}$

**Tekneas (GR)** *F Sanchez* 98
3 b c Kavafi(IRE) Tritonia (GR) (Saddlers' Hall (IRE))
6620a$^{9}$

**Telamon (IRE)** *Milton Bradley* a21
4 b g Rock Of Gibraltar(IRE) Laureldean Express (Inchinor)
377$^{14}$

**Telefono** *Amanda Perrett* a83 83
3 b c Three Valleys(USA) Dialing Tone (USA) (Distant View (USA))
2339$^{2}$ 2883$^{2}$ (3525) 5931$^{4}$ 6460$^{6}$

**Telegraph (IRE)** *David Evans* a62 67
3 b g Bushranger(IRE) Vampire Queen (IRE) (General Monash (USA))
1570$^{5}$ 1769$^{7}$ 2278$^{12}$ 2667$^{9}$ 4820$^{6}$ (6995) 7502$^{4}$ 7765$^{9}$ 8043$^{8}$ 8284$^{4}$

**Telegraphy (USA)** *Ed Dunlop* a55 63
3 gr f Giant's Causeway(USA) Cable (USA) (Dynaformer (USA))
1517$^{10}$ 1701$^{8}$ 2621$^{5}$ 3098$^{4}$ 4261$^{6}$ 4497$^{5}$ 5343$^{4}$

**Telescope (IRE)** *Sir Michael Stoute* 125
4 b c Galileo(IRE) Velouette (Darshaan)
1697$^{2}$ 2086$^{2}$ (3450) ◆ 4649$^{2}$ 5578$^{3}$ 7611a$^{4}$

**Teletext (USA)** *P Bary* 116
3 b c Empire Maker(USA) Conference Call (Anabaa (USA))
3290a$^{2}$ 4251a$^{3}$ 6379a$^{2}$

**Tellatail** *Chris Dwyer*
4 ch g Zafeen(FR) Bithnah (Halling (USA))
1612$^{13}$ 2093$^{7}$

**Tell Me When** *Brian Rothwell* 51
3 b f Monsieur Bond(IRE) Giffoine (Timeless Times (USA))
1611$^{2}$ 2657$^{9}$ 3440$^{4}$ 3650$^{6}$ 4796$^{6}$ 5683$^{11}$ 6116$^{8}$ 8084$^{11}$ 8207$^{6}$

**Tellovoi (IRE)** *Ann Stokell* a99 90
6 b h Indian Haven Kloonlara (IRE) (Green Desert (USA))
(11) (162) (364) 550$^{4}$ 625$^{2}$ 887$^{2}$ 1164$^{8}$ 1316$^{6}$ 1721$^{4}$ 1862$^{2}$ 2336$^{8}$ 2758$^{8}$ 3753$^{8}$ 4323$^{8}$ 4712$^{7}$ 6097$^{12}$ 6320$^{12}$ 6558$^{2}$ 6824$^{7}$ 7375$^{14}$

**Telmeyd** *William Haggas* 109
3 b g Dutch Art Blithe (Pivotal)
2339$^{6}$ (2759) (4021) ◆ 5165$^{4}$ (6893)

**Temperance Society (IRE)** *Richard Fahey* 75
2 b g Dark Angel(IRE) Cover Girl (IRE) (Common Grounds)
6496$^{2}$

**Templar Boy** *J R Jenkins* a48 38
3 br g Myboycharlie(IRE) Zagala (Polar Falcon (USA))
2093$^{3}$ 2932$^{4}$ 3792$^{6}$ 5321$^{3}$ 6073$^{6}$ 7370$^{7}$ 7652$^{5}$ 8139$^{9}$

**Template (IRE)** *Amanda Perrett* a48 69
3 ch g Iffraaj Sagaing (Machiavellian (USA))
1983$^{2}$ 2225$^{2}$ 2494$^{8}$ 3421$^{8}$ 4547$^{6}$ 5313$^{3}$ ◆ 5621$^{7}$ 7309$^{14}$

**Temple Of Boom (AUS)** *Tony Gollan* 116
8 b g Piccolo Temple Spirit (AUS) (Special Dane (AUS))
7724a$^{12}$

**Temple Road (IRE)** *Milton Bradley* a79 64
6 b g Street Cry(IRE) Sugarhoneybaby (IRE) (Docksider (USA))
2331$^{2}$ 412$^{3}$ 628$^{3}$ (826) 1041$^{9}$ 1144$^{4}$ 1678$^{11}$ 1921$^{4}$ 2414$^{12}$ 7073$^{9}$ 7351$^{4}$ 7931$^{4}$ 8040$^{4}$ 8186$^{4}$ 8297$^{4}$

**Tempo Royale (FR)** *S Wattel* a87 87
3 b f Boris De Deauville(IRE) Macho Tempo (USA) (Macho Uno (USA))
4252a$^{6}$

**Temptress (IRE)** *Roger Charlton* 94
3 ch f Shirocco(GER) Femme Fatale (Fairy King (USA))
1422$^{11}$ (1946) 3425$^{2}$ (4182) 7384$^{6}$

**Tempuran** *David Bridgwater* a68 70
5 rg g Unbridled's Song(USA) Tenderly (IRE) (Danehill (USA))
49$^{6}$ 382$^{10}$

**Tempus Temporis (USA)** *John Gosden* a86 67
2 b c Dynaformer(USA) Tempus Fugit (USA) (Alphabet Soup (USA))
6683$^{7}$ 7382$^{5}$ 7927$^{6}$ (8174)

**Tenango (USA)** *David Jacobson* a96
4 bb g Lion Heart(USA) Ochi Chernye (USA) (Mr Greeley (USA))
2005a$^{2}$

**Tenbridge** *Derek Haydn Jones* a65 71
5 b m Avonbridge Tenebrae (IRE) (In The Wings)
1846$^{7}$ 2251$^{4}$ 2669$^{12}$ 2775$^{5}$ (3176) 3850$^{3}$ 4153$^{3}$ 5274$^{6}$ 5751$^{4}$ 6086$^{9}$

**Tender Emotion** *H-A Pantall* a64 87
3 ch f Pivotal Silca's Sister (Inchinor)
1882$^{5}$ 7483a$^{16}$ 7857a$^{12}$

**Tendu** *John Gosden* a93 106
2 b f Oasis Dream Arabesque (Zafonic (USA))
5429$^{7}$ (6032) 6751$^{5}$

**Tenenbaum** *Charlie Appleby* 107
5 b g Authorized(IRE) Al Hasnaa (Zafonic (USA))
507a$^{6}$

**Tenhoo** *Eric Alston* a28 76
8 b g Reset(AUS) Bella Bambina (Turtle Island (IRE))
3880$^{8}$ 4792$^{8}$

**Tennessee Wildcat (IRE)** *G M Lyons* a97 85
4 b g Kheleyf(USA) Windbeneathmywings (IRE) (In The Wings)
109a$^{9}$ 304a$^{14}$ 396a$^{10}$ 1172$^{9}$ 1421$^{7}$ 1650$^{8}$ 1944$^{9}$ 2390$^{7}$ 7873a$^{9}$

**Tenor (IRE)** *John Ryan* a106 115
4 b g Oratorio(IRE) Cedar Sea (IRE) (Persian Bold)
(1142) 1317$^{4}$ 1682$^{2}$ 1926$^{3}$ (2311) 3050$^{6}$ 3577$^{4}$ (3861) (4323) 4711$^{2}$ 5163$^{2}$ 6140$^{10}$ (6358) (6458) 6752$^{5}$ 7836$^{11}$ 8018$^{2}$

**Teochrios (IRE)** *J S Bolger* a59 66
4 b f Teofilo(IRE) Tamra Delight (USA) (Diesis)
7435a$^{12}$

**Teofilo's Princess (IRE)** *Clive Brittain* 89
2 b f Teofilo(IRE) Very Nice (Daylami (IRE))
6554$^{3}$ 7331$^{2}$

**Teolagi (IRE)** *J S Moore* a90 74
4 ch g Teofilo(IRE) Satulagi (USA) (Officer (USA))
54$^{8}$ 8078$^{5}$

**Teosroyal (IRE)** *Clive Brittain* 72
2 br f Teofilo(IRE) Fille De Joie (IRE) (Royal Academy (USA))
3888$^{4}$ 4585$^{6}$

**Tepeleni** *Clive Brittain* a39 54
2 b f Teofilo(IRE) Bronwen (IRE) (King's Best (USA))
5827$^{5}$ 6246$^{6}$

**Tepmokea (IRE)** *Conor Dore* a99 86
8 ch g Noverre(USA) Eroica (GER) (Highest Honor (FR))
177a$^{7}$ 437a$^{7}$ 584a$^{8}$ 669a$^{7}$ (752a) 977$^{2}$ 1268$^{2}$ 1444$^{13}$ 2091$^{3}$ 2627$^{7}$ 2981$^{2}$ 3341$^{2}$ 3696$^{4}$ 4538$^{4}$ 6156$^{9}$

**Tercel (IRE)** *Sir Michael Stoute* 84
3 b g Monsun(GER) Kitty Hawk (Danehill Dancer (IRE))
1529$^{9}$ (4587) 5311$^{8}$ 5930$^{3}$ 6523$^{2}$ 7043$^{6}$

**Terhaab (USA)** *John Gosden* a74 73
3 b f Elusive Quality(USA) Star Of Paris (USA) (Dayjur (USA))
1409$^{4}$ 2745$^{5}$

**Terhaal (IRE)** *William Haggas* 80
2 b g Raven's Pass(USA) Silk Trail (Dubai Destination (USA))
(7234)

**Terntheothercheek** *Jennie Candlish*
5 b m Multiplex My Tern (IRE) (Glacial Storm (USA))
197$^{5}$

**Terra Fina** *H-A Pantall* 60
2 b f American Post Pink Topaz (USA) (Tiznow (USA))
5590a$^{10}$

**Terravista (AUS)** *Joseph Pride* 126
5 ch g Captain Rio Parfore (NZ) (Gold Brose (AUS))
1186a$^{11}$ (7724a)

**Terrific (IRE)** *A P O'Brien* 96
3 b f Galileo(IRE) Shadow Song (IRE) (Pennekamp (USA))
2072$^{5}$ 3376$^{10}$ 4276a$^{8}$

**Territories (IRE)** *A Fabre* 112
2 b c Invincible Spirit(IRE) Taranto (Machiavellian (USA))
6181a$^{3}$ 6968a$^{2}$

**Terror (IRE)** *David Simcock* 107
2 b f Kodiac Baltic Belle (IRE) (Redback)
(5774) ◆ 6751$^{4}$ (7563)

**Terrubi (IRE)** *A Wohler* 116
4 gr c Dalakhani(IRE) Altruiste (USA) (Diesis)
1784a$^{2}$ 2588a$^{3}$ (4250a) 6180a$^{11}$

**Terse** *David Lanigan* 64
2 b f Dansili Cut Short (USA) (Diesis)
3076$^{6}$ 3497$^{8}$

**Teruntum Star (FR)** *Kevin Ryan* 97
2 ch c Dutch Art Seralia (Royal Academy (USA))
4170$^{2}$ (4510) 5140$^{2}$ 5692$^{8}$ (6135) 7121$^{7}$

**Tesslam** *D Selvaratnam* a89 91
7 ch g Singspiel(IRE) Rowaasi (Green Desert (USA))
242a$^{8}$

**Testa Rossa (IRE)** *Jim Goldie* a68 66
4 b g Oratorio(IRE) Red Rita (IRE) (Kefaah (USA))
2457$^{3}$ 3056$^{6}$ (4000) 4517$^{4}$ 5172$^{2}$ 5639$^{3}$ 6113$^{2}$ 6480$^{7}$ 7100$^{11}$

**Tested** *D K Weld* 109
3 b f Selkirk(USA) Prove (Danehill (USA))
2581a$^{6}$ (5869a)

**Testing (FR)** *Mark Johnston* a54 69
3 gr f New Approach(IRE) Testama (FR) (Testa Rossa (AUS))
1452$^{3}$ 2506$^{6}$

**Tete Orange** *Stuart Williams* a31 67
3 ch f Pastoral Pursuits Imperialistic (IRE) (Imperial Ballet (IRE))
1860$^{3}$ 3037$^{12}$ 3567$^{7}$ 4092$^{2}$ (4304) 5395$^{5}$ 6262$^{6}$ 7998$^{8}$

**Teutonic Knight (IRE)** *Tony Newcombe* a21 46
7 ch g Daggers Drawn(USA) Azyaa (Kris)
1923$^{7}$ 2942$^{13}$

**Tevez** *Des Donovan* a72 74
9 b g Sakhee(USA) Sosumi (Be My Chief (USA))
1317$^{5}$ 2471$^{10}$ 2884$^{9}$ 4544$^{8}$ 5041$^{7}$ 7288$^{11}$ 7942$^{2}$ 8030$^{5}$

**Texalila (FR)** *Mme A-M Poirier* 70
2 b f Sunday Break(JPN) Texalina (FR) (Kaldoun (FR))
7468a$^{5}$

**Texas Red (USA)** *J Keith Desormeaux* a120
2 b c Afleet Alex(USA) Ramatuelle (CHI) (Jeune Homme (USA))
(7610a)

**Texas Rock (IRE)** *M C Grassick* 88
3 b g Rock Of Gibraltar(IRE) Vestavia (IRE) (Alhaarth (IRE))
7140a$^{7}$

**Thackeray** *Chris Fairhurst* a45 65
7 b g Fasliyev(USA) Chinon (IRE) (Entrepreneur)
3052$^{2}$ 4964$^{2}$ ◆ 5270$^{5}$ 6644$^{6}$ 7175$^{12}$ 7643$^{12}$

**Thahab (IRE)** *Richard Hannon* 73
2 ch c Dubawi(IRE) Mise (IRE) (Indian Ridge)
7407$^{3}$ 7713$^{3}$

**Tha'ir (IRE)** *Saeed bin Suroor* a108 109
4 b c New Approach(IRE) Flashing Green (Green Desert (USA))
205a$^{4}$ 593a$^{5}$ (773a) 3930$^{3}$ 4756$^{7}$ 6330$^{5}$

**Thalie De La Vis (FR)** *Mme C Barande-Barbe* a64 67
3 b f Sandwaki(USA) Milady De La Vis (FR) (Lost World (IRE))
720a$^{7}$

**Thames Knight** *Marcus Tregoning* a64
2 b c Sir Percy Bermondsey Girl (Bertolini (USA))
7660$^{11}$ 7840$^{3}$ 8026$^{6}$

**Thanaaya (IRE)** *Ed Dunlop* 65
2 b f Haatef(USA) Mejala (IRE) (Red Ransom (USA))
7377$^{6}$

**Thane Of Cawdor (IRE)** *Joseph Tuite* a68 57
5 b g Danehill Dancer(IRE) Holy Nola (USA) (Silver Deputy (CAN))
246$^{2}$ 382$^{6}$ 571$^{8}$ ◆ (821) (989) 1406$^{2}$ 1798$^{4}$ 2248$^{5}$ 2672$^{5}$ 3473$^{10}$ (6031) 6706$^{13}$ 7744$^{9}$ 7975$^{3}$ 8029$^{2}$ 8250$^{7}$

**Thanksgiving Day (IRE)** *Jamie Osborne* a76 35
2 b c Thewayyouare(USA) Cozzene's Pride (USA) (Cozzene (USA))
5519$^{7}$ 6102$^{4}$ 6268$^{3}$ 6769$^{2}$ 7226$^{9}$ 7810$^{2}$ (8009) 8267$^{3}$

**Thanks Harry** *Andrew Balding* a76 67
3 br g Lucky Story(USA) Africa's Star (IRE) (Johannesburg (USA))
1216$^{6}$ (1498) 2112$^{4}$ 2624$^{5}$ 4263$^{7}$ 7831$^{5}$ 8073$^{10}$

**Thankstomonty** *David O'Meara* 66
2 b g Dylan Thomas(IRE) Beldarian (IRE) (Last Tycoon)
6935$^{4}$ 7097$^{3}$ 7496$^{4}$

**Thank You Bye Bye (FR)** *J-P Gauvin* 100
2 b f Zanzibari(USA) Puritanical (IRE) (Desert King (IRE))
6219a$^{3}$ 6967a$^{11}$

**Thank You Marylou (USA)** *Michael J Maker* a109
3 ch f Birdstone(USA) Menifeeque (USA) (Menifee (USA))
7608a$^{3}$

**Thankyou Very Much** *James Bethell* a70 72
4 b f Lucky Story(USA) Maid Of Perth (Mark Of Esteem (IRE))
1857$^{5}$ 2540$^{2}$ 3095$^{6}$ (4023) 4271$^{6}$ 5079$^{6}$ 5793$^{3}$ 6865$^{5}$

**Thataboy (IRE)** *Tom Dascombe* a81 65
3 b g Green Desert(USA) Hawas (Mujtahid (USA))
(149) ◆ 429$^{6}$ 2090$^{5}$ 2945$^{9}$ 3522$^{3}$ 4262$^{4}$ 4581$^{5}$ 5553$^{6}$ 6346$^{8}$ (6843) 7521$^{3}$ 7888$^{7}$ 8040$^{2}$ 8255$^{7}$

**That Be Grand** *Shaun Harris* a32 63
3 b f Firebreak Manila Selection (USA) (Manila (USA))
2198$^{3}$ (2621) 3655$^{10}$ 4657$^{7}$ 6216$^{5}$ 6480$^{14}$ 7643$^{13}$

**Thatchereen (IRE)** *Michael Bell* 81
3 ro f Mastercraftsman(IRE) Roof Fiddle (USA) (Cat Thief (USA))
1711$^{7}$ 2274$^{3}$ 2740$^{4}$ 3614$^{2}$ 4617$^{2}$ (4947) 5401$^{4}$ 5948$^{5}$ 7416$^{3}$

**Thatcherite (IRE)** *Tony Coyle* a78 79
6 gr g Verglas(IRE) Damiana (IRE) (Thatching)
1440$^{5}$ 1643$^{6}$ 2056$^{6}$ ◆ 2364$^{5}$ 2606$^{2}$ 3298$^{9}$ 3668$^{4}$ (3948) 4317$^{6}$ 4712$^{6}$ 5470$^{11}$ 5912$^{9}$ 6452$^{5}$ 6695$^{3}$

**Thatchmaster (USA)** *Mark Johnston* a90 57
4 br g Street Cry(IRE) Michita (USA) (Dynaformer (USA))
(365) 550$^{5}$ (977) 1128$^{3}$ 1483$^{17}$ 1926$^{5}$ 2540$^{10}$ 3582$^{6}$

**That Is The Spirit** *David O'Meara* 105
3 b g Invincible Spirit(IRE) Fraulein (Acatenango (GER))
(1192) (2257) ◆ (2961) 3352$^{9}$ 4438$^{5}$ 5653$^{6}$ 6971a$^{10}$

**That Man Of Mine (IRE)** *Jamie Osborne* a24 27
2 ch g Thewayyouare(USA) Do The Deal (IRE) (Halling (USA))
4207$^{11}$ 4740$^{11}$ 4965$^{9}$ 8121$^{10}$ ◆

**That's Ours (USA)** *James M Barcoe* a52 47
6 b g Giant's Causeway(USA) Magnificent Honour (USA) (A.P. Indy (USA))
7962a$^{7}$

**That's Plenty (IRE)** *John Patrick Shanahan* a88 105
5 b g Dr Fong(USA) Tyranny (Machiavellian (USA))
1078a$^{2}$ (1564) 2085$^{3}$

**Thawaany (IRE)** *F Head* 113
4 ch f Tamayuz Chelsea Rose (IRE) (Desert King (IRE))
2799a$^{5}$ (3746a) 5223a$^{2}$

**Thawraat** *Saeed bin Suroor* a67 57
2 b f Cape Cross(IRE) Raaya (USA) (Giant's Causeway (USA))
5416$^{8}$ 6630$^{2}$

**The Absent Mare** *Robin Dickin* a74 28
6 gr m Fair Mix(IRE) Precious Lucy (FR) (Kadrou (FR))
818$^{10}$ 992$^{6}$ 2885$^{8}$ 3579$^{4}$

**The Alamo (IRE)** *Richard Hannon* 81
3 b g High Chaparral(IRE) Inner Strength (FR) (Take Risks (FR))
1983$^{3}$ 2347$^{7}$ 6523$^{4}$ 7161$^{9}$ 7305$^{3}$

**The Artista (FR)** *J Phelippon* a75 79
3 b c Art Connoisseur(IRE) Passion Bleue (In The Wings)
7269a$^{9}$

**The Art Of Racing (IRE)** *C Von Der Recke* a76 89
4 b g Acclamation Divert (IRE) (Averti (IRE))
80$^{9}$ 175$^{6}$ 318$^{4}$ 555a$^{3}$ 728a$^{7}$

**The Bay Bandit** *Neil Mulholland* a53 56
7 b g Highest Honor(FR) Pescara (IRE) (Common Grounds)
(869) 1050$^{2}$ 2596a$^{2}$ (5970a)

**The Bay Tigress** *Jo Hughes* a39 20
4 b f Tiger Hill(IRE) Singasongosixpence (Singspiel (IRE))
31$^{5}$ 546$^{8}$

**The Best Doctor (IRE)** *Jeremy Noseda* a80 73
4 ch c Pivotal Strawberry Fledge (USA) (Kingmambo (USA))
1142$^{2}$

**The Black Devil (IRE)** *Gerard Keane* a73 68
5 br g Kheleyf(USA) Patteness (FR) (General Holme (USA))
4805a$^{11}$

**The Blue Banana (IRE)** *Edwin Tuer* a46 66
5 b g Red Clubs(IRE) Rinneen (IRE) (Bien Bien (USA))
2519$^{10}$ 3094$^{7}$ 3949$^{5}$ 4797$^{10}$ 5376$^{8}$ 5761$^{7}$ (6543) 7248$^{8}$ 7639$^{6}$

**The Blue Dog (IRE)** *Phil McEntee* a80 67
7 b m High Chaparral(IRE) Jules (IRE) (Danehill (USA))
(120) ◆ (158) (221) 358$^{4}$ 494$^{3}$ 641$^{4}$ 891$^{4}$ 1046$^{3}$ 2750$^{7}$ 8029$^{9}$ 8202$^{8}$ 8313$^{9}$

**The Blue Eye** *C Ferland* 88
2 b c Dubawi(IRE) Soneva (USA) (Cherokee Run (USA))
6618a$^{2}$

**The Boss Of Me** *Sean Curran* a49 38
3 ch g Bahamian Bounty Orange Pip (Bold Edge)
481$^{6}$ 7451$^{10}$ 4056$^{9}$ 4732$^{9}$ 8200$^{6}$

**The Brockster** *Richard Ford*
3 ch g Proclamation(IRE) Synergie (IRE) (Exit To Nowhere (USA))
906$^{7}$ 2236$^{9}$

**The Bunny Catcher** *Sharon Watt* 2
3 b f Jeremy(USA) Passionforfashion (IRE) (Fasliyev (USA))
6010$^{7}$ 7645$^{10}$ 8231$^{9}$

**The Card Players (IRE)** *Brian Ellison* 71
2 b c Excellent Art Sonic Night (IRE) (Night Shift (USA))
1670$^{8}$ 1900$^{2}$ 3620$^{8}$

**The Cashel Man (IRE)** *David Simcock* 62
2 b g High Chaparral(IRE) Hadarama (IRE) (Sinndar (IRE))
6984$^{6}$ 7230$^{6}$ 7667$^{11}$

**The Cash Generator (IRE)** *Ralph J Smith* a66 71
6 b g Peintre Celebre(USA) Majestic Launch (Lear Fan (USA))
1017$^{7}$ 1923$^{P}$ 7291$^{2}$

**The Cat** *Nigel Twiston-Davies* a45 21
3 gr f Josr Algarhoud(IRE) Animal Cracker (Primo Dominie)
275$^{7}$

**The Character (IRE)** *Tom Dascombe* 85
3 b g Bushranger(IRE) Operissimo (Singspiel (IRE))
2075$^{5}$ 3925$^{3}$ 4393$^{3}$ 5413$^{3}$ 5884$^{7}$ 6491$^{2}$ (6738) 7043$^{6}$

**The Cleaner (AUS)** *Mick Burles* 116
7 b g Savoire Vivre Dash Of Scotch (AUS) (Blessington (AUS))
7467a$^{9}$

**The Confessor** *Henry Candy* a77 97
7 b g Piccolo Twilight Mistress (Bin Ajwaad (IRE))
1943$^{5}$ 3036$^{9}$ 4783$^{11}$ 6498$^{3}$ 7375$^{7}$ 7821$^{5}$

**Thecornishassassin** *Robert Eddery* a81 72
2 b c Vale Of York(IRE) Harmonist (USA) (Hennessy (USA))
3613$^{6}$ (4054) 4731$^{2}$ 5580$^{10}$

**Thecornishcockney** *John Ryan* a103 92
5 bl g Cockney Rebel(IRE) Glittering Image (IRE) (Sadler's Wells (USA))
305a$^{13}$ 507a$^{11}$ 1213$^{P}$ 2342$^{9}$

**Thecornishcowboy** *John Ryan* a77 92
5 b g Haafhd Oriental Dance (Fantastic Light (USA))
623$^{10}$ 801$^{8}$ 990$^{5}$ 1065$^{2}$ 1168$^{6}$ 1355$^{3}$ 1636$^{6}$ 1798$^{6}$ 2272$^{7}$ 2445$^{3}$ (2894) (3052) (3310) (3546) (3761) 3977$^{2}$ 4077$^{8}$ 4204$^{7}$ 4622$^{6}$ 5035$^{5}$ 5487$^{10}$ 6036$^{8}$ 7562$^{5}$ 8029$^{3}$ 8099$^{4}$

**The Corsican (IRE)** *David Simcock* a83 105
3 b c Galileo(IRE) Walklikeanegyptian (IRE) (Danehill (USA))
1984$^{3}$ (2917) 4122$^{5}$ (5720) (6257)

**The Dancing Lord** *Brett Johnson* a77 64
5 br g Imperial Dancer Miss Brookie (The West (USA))
52$^{10}$ 425$^{4}$ 576$^{11}$ 663$^{5}$ 826$^{4}$

**The Dandy Yank (IRE)** *Jamie Osborne* a80 77
3 b g Dandy Man(IRE) Bronze Queen (IRE) (Invincible Spirit (IRE))
5$^{2}$ 195$^{3}$ (315) (485) 650$^{4}$ 2505$^{3}$ 2889$^{4}$ 3084$^{3}$ 3561$^{10}$ 3707$^{5}$ (3972) 4267$^{5}$ 4565$^{4}$ 4847$^{2}$ 5601$^{3}$ 6025$^{2}$ (6236) 6562$^{8}$ 6814$^{5}$

**The Dapper Tapper (IRE)** *Eve Johnson Houghton* a68 72
2 b g Dandy Man(IRE) Sound Tap (IRE) (Warning)
2859$^{2}$ 3181$^{6}$ 3934$^{4}$ (4260) 4939$^{5}$ 5554$^{5}$ 5974$^{4}$ 7728$^{7}$ 7948$^{2}$ 8113$^{2}$

**The Doyle Machine (IRE)** *Noel Quinlan* 65
3 b g Camacho Berenica (IRE) (College Chapel)
298$^{4}$ 346$^{4}$ 547$^{7}$

**The Dream Fast** *Rae Guest* a78
2 b c Sleeping Indian Past 'N' Present (Cadeaux Genereux)
8000$^{2}$

**The Drunken Dr (IRE)** *Niall Moran* a37 35
6 ch g Dr Fong(USA) Evening Promise (Aragon)
7877a$^{14}$

**The Ducking Stool** *Julia Feilden* a64 76
7 ch m Where Or When(IRE) Dance Sequel (Selkirk (USA))
1617$^4$ 2199$^5$ 2445$^4$ 3161$^3$ 3556$^3$ (4093) 4591$^3$ 5062$^3$ 5317$^2$ 6062$^2$ 6500$^3$ 7672$^2$ 7846$^6$

**The Dukkerer (IRE)** *James Given* a68 69
3 bb f Footstepsinthesand Saffron Crocus (Shareef Dancer (USA))
1101$^3$ 1403$^8$ 2020$^2$ (3380) 3846$^2$ ◆ (4727) 5415$^{11}$ 6217$^6$ 7494$^6$ 7575$^4$ 7906$^5$ 8044$^5$ 8177$^6$

**The Fairy (IRE)** *John Gosden* a69 67
2 b f Invincible Spirit(IRE) Cinnamon Rose (USA) (Trempolino (USA))
6093$^5$ ◆ 6701$^6$ 7062$^6$ (7684) 7890$^4$

**The Fenland Man** *James Unett* a18
3 b g Rob Roy(USA) Spark Up (Lahib (USA))
8002$^6$ 8147$^6$

**The Firm (IRE)** *Daniel Mark Loughnane* a71 73
5 b g Acclamation Aspen Falls (IRE) (Elnadim (USA))
1040$^4$ 1302$^4$ 1729$^3$ 2301$^3$ 2610$^5$ 3235$^4$ 4190$^3$ 4793$^2$ 5421$^6$ 5898$^4$ 6341$^4$ 7427$^8$ 8102$^5$

**The French Grey (FR)** *Ron Hodges* a56 4
3 gr f Stormy River(FR) Khaliyna (IRE) (Danehill (USA))
2489$^{12}$ 7686$^8$ 7818$^9$

**The Frog Prince (IRE)** *Sabrina J Harty* a49 54
10 b g Princely Heir(IRE) Morning Georgie (IRE) (Thatching)
794a$^{14}$

**The Fugue** *John Gosden* 126
5 bb m Dansili Twyla Tharp (IRE) (Sadler's Wells (USA))
1181a$^{11}$ (3354) 3984$^6$

**The Fulwell End** *Noel Wilson* 36
2 b g Amadeus Wolf Green Silk (IRE) (Namid)
4919$^9$ 5443$^{10}$ 6146$^8$

**The Gay Cavalier** *John Ryan* a74 65
3 b g Henrythenavigator(USA) Dear Daughter (Polish Precedent (USA))
5976$^7$ 6540$^4$ 6634$^5$ 7402$^8$ 7901$^5$ 8098$^2$

**The Ginger Berry** *Dr Jon Scargill* a71 48
4 ch g First Trump Dolly Coughdrop (IRE) (Titus Livius (FR))
(247) (382) 3226$^{12}$ 4402$^8$ 5011$^2$ 6019$^5$

**The Gold Cheongsam (IRE)** *Jeremy Noseda* a91 105
4 b f Red Clubs(IRE) Fuerta Ventura (IRE) (Desert Sun)
112a$^{11}$ 396a$^8$ 3203$^5$ 4668$^2$ 4854$^8$ 5612$^{13}$

**The Great Gabrial** *Michael Appleby* a94 83
5 b g Oasis Dream Quiff (Sadler's Wells (USA))
56$^4$ 287$^9$ (552) 1103$^6$ 1190$^8$ 1607$^{16}$ 2922$^{12}$ (3402) 5895$^2$ 6430$^3$ 6943$^3$ 7455$^5$

**The Great War (USA)** *A P O'Brien* a102 102
2 b c War Front(USA) Guide (USA) (Pulpit (USA))
3374$^5$ 4123$^6$ 6256$^{11}$ 7610a$^4$

**The Grey Gatsby (IRE)** *Kevin Ryan* 126
3 gr c Mastercraftsman(IRE) Marie Vison (IRE) (Entrepreneur)
1532$^2$ 1951$^{10}$ (2285) (2818a) 4251a$^6$ 5578$^2$ (6353a)

**The Grumpy Gnome (IRE)** *Richard Fahey* a66 66
3 b g Dandy Man(IRE) Certain Charm (USA) (Thunder Gulch (USA))
3002$^7$

**The Hamptons (IRE)** *Niall Madden* a42 44
9 b g Statue Of Liberty(USA) Fleur (GER) (Perugino (USA))
128a$^8$

**The Happy Hammer (IRE)** *Eugene Stanford* a71 51
8 b g Acclamation Emma's Star (ITY) (Darshaan)
245$^6$ (496) 825$^6$ 2059$^6$ 2646$^3$ 3075$^5$ 3589$^7$ 4428$^5$ 6337$^8$ 7759$^5$ 8298$^9$

**The Holyman (IRE)** *Jo Crowley* a79 80
6 ch g Footstepsinthesand Sunset (IRE) (Polish Precedent (USA))
158$^6$ 1108$^4$ (3472) 4051$^3$ 5073$^{12}$

**The Hooded Claw (IRE)** *Tim Easterby* 91
3 ch g Dandy Man(IRE) Changari (USA) (Gulch (USA))
1445$^4$ 1693$^6$ (2090) 3369$^4$ 4166$^4$ 4669$^{12}$ 5410$^{11}$ 6170$^5$ 6744$^4$

**The Ice Meister (IRE)** *G M Lyons* 86
2 gr g Dark Angel(IRE) Cape Cod (IRE) (Unfuwain (USA))
6375a$^{12}$

**The Iron Man (FR)** *H-F Devin* a42 56
2 b c Orpen(USA) Kocooning (IRE) (King's Best (USA))
4883a$^7$ 5739a$^5$

**The Kernigal (IRE)** *Bernard Llewellyn* a49 8
5 b g Red Clubs(IRE) Ellens Princess (IRE) (Desert Prince (IRE))
1138$^{12}$

**The Kid** *Tom Dascombe* 81
3 b g High Chaparral(IRE) Shine Like A Star (Fantastic Light (USA))
1166$^5$ 1588$^7$ 2385$^2$ 2893$^2$ (3818) 4392$^5$

**The Kurator (IRE)** *Ann Duffield* a43 45
2 ch g Art Connoisseur(IRE) A L'Aube (IRE) (Selkirk (USA))
6667$^5$ 7173$^5$ 7523$^4$

**The Lampo Genie** *K R Burke* 76
2 b g Champs Elysees Samar Qand (Selkirk (USA))
5078$^3$ ◆ 5718$^2$ 6743$^3$

**The Lark** *Michael Bell* 108
4 ch f Pivotal Gull Wing (IRE) (In The Wings)
2284$^5$

**The Lock Master (IRE)** *Michael Appleby* a97 63
7 b g Key Of Luck(USA) Pitrizza (IRE) (Machiavellian (USA))
61$^2$ 256$^2$ 559$^4$ (764) (999) (1128) 1553$^{10}$ 2142$^7$ 2700$^8$ 7688$^{10}$ 7974$^6$ 8062$^7$

**The Madding Crowd** *Hughie Morrison* a33 50
2 b f Dansili Night Frolic (Night Shift (USA))
6868$^{11}$ 7184$^{11}$ 7450$^{10}$

**Them And Us (IRE)** *Michael Bell* a78 76
2 ch c Rock Of Gibraltar(IRE) Sagrada (GER) (Primo Dominie)
(6757) 7443$^6$ 7945$^2$

**Theme Astral (FR)** *P Bary* 104
3 b c Cape Cross(IRE) Lumiere Astrale (FR) (Trempolino (USA))
6183a$^3$ 6954a$^8$

**The Moat Field (IRE)** *Michael J Browne* a35 47
3 b g Diamond Green(FR) Our Juliette (IRE) (Namid)
261$^5$ 480$^{12}$

**The Mongoose** *David Evans* a69 75
6 b g Montjeu(IRE) Angara (Alzao (USA))
52$^{13}$ 399$^8$ 918$^5$ 1236$^5$ 1649$^5$ 2597a$^2$

**The Name Is Frank** *Mark Gillard* a42 61
9 b g Lujain(USA) Zaragossa (Paris House)
2669$^9$ 3422$^9$ 3589$^6$ 4046$^5$ 5005$^9$

**The Name's Bond** *Keith Reveley* 30
2 ch g Monsieur Bond(IRE) Fairlie (Halling (USA))
6667$^9$ 6935$^8$ 7246$^{10}$

**The New Pharaoh (IRE)** *Chris Wall* 62
3 b c Montjeu(IRE) Out West (USA) (Gone West (USA))
6092$^{11}$ 7332$^5$

**The Nifty Fox** *Tim Easterby* a54 85
10 b g Foxhound(USA) Nifty Alice (First Trump)
1966$^6$ 2606$^{11}$ 3006$^9$ 3191$^{11}$ 4005$^9$ 4511$^5$ 5237$^5$ 5565$^3$ 6114$^8$ 6406$^{11}$ 6674$^8$ 6835$^7$ 7057$^{15}$

**The Nutcracker (IRE)** *Thomas Gibney* a51 45
4 b f Antonius Pius(USA) Katies Crown (IRE) (Royal Abjar (USA))
7961a$^7$

**Theo Danon (GER)** *Mario Hofer* a98 94
6 ch g Lord Of England(GER) Ticinella (GER) (Hernando (FR))
177a$^9$ 4776a$^2$

**The Offer (IRE)** *Gai Waterhouse* 115
5 b g Montjeu(IRE) Valdara (Darshaan)
7301a$^{11}$

**Theology** *Steve Gollings* a99 92
7 b g Galileo(IRE) Biographie (Mtoto)
285$^6$ 803$^{11}$ 2561$^{11}$

**The Olympus Man** *Olly Stevens* a65 56
2 b g Paco Boy(IRE) Blandish (USA) (Wild Again (USA))
6203$^8$ 6496$^7$ 7155$^5$ 7487$^4$ 7753$^{11}$ 7832$^2$ 8087$^4$ 8192$^6$

**The Osteopath (IRE)** *John Davies* 83
11 ch g Danehill Dancer(IRE) Miss Margate (IRE) (Don't Forget Me)
1483$^{12}$ 1842$^4$ 2169$^2$ 2477$^4$ 4058$^9$ (5267) (5761) 6670$^2$ 7042$^8$

**The Other Lady** *Alan McCabe*
2 b f Peintre Celebre(USA) Tamalain (USA) (Royal Academy (USA))
4626$^{11}$ 4784$^{14}$

**The Paco Kid** *Olly Stevens* a36 75
2 b g Paco Boy(IRE) Linea (King's Best (USA))
1417$^4$ 2146$^6$ 3194$^5$ 4430$^5$ 6268$^{10}$

**The Pizza Man (USA)** *Roger Brueggemann* 111
5 b g English Channel(USA) I Can Fan Fan (USA) (Lear Fan (USA))
(5457a) 6390a$^5$ 7324a$^4$

**The Pocket Dot** *Mick Channon* a24 30
3 ch f Lucky Story(USA) Daisy Do (IRE) (Danehill (USA))
1918$^8$ 2281$^9$ 6613$^9$

**The Quarterjack** *Ron Hodges* a73 77
5 b g Haafhd Caressed (Medicean)
1791$^2$ (2011) (2490) 3034$^{11}$ 7452$^8$ 7817$^5$

**The Racer (FR)** *K Borgel* 36
3 b c Meshaheer(USA) Hijaziyah (Testa Rossa (AUS))
630a$^6$

**The Rebel (FR)** *Matthieu Palussiere* a18 37
2 b c Elusive City(USA) Juvenil Delinquent (USA) (Dynaformer (USA))
5618a$^{11}$

**The Rectifier (USA)** *Seamus Durack* a107 111
7 bb g Langfuhr(CAN) Western Vision (USA) (Gone West (USA))
(749) 1721$^3$ (3753) 4180$^7$ 4711$^3$ 6358$^3$ 6752$^{24}$

**The Reel Way (GR)** *Patrick Chamings* a45 50
3 br f Reel Buddy(USA) Nephetriti Way (IRE) (Dockside (USA))
3074$^6$ 4029$^9$ 6247$^3$ 7036$^7$

**The Right Time** *Tony Carroll* a27 37
6 b m Val Royal(FR) Esligier (IRE) (Sabrehill (USA))
570$^9$ 781$^8$

**Thermal Column (IRE)** *Richard Fahey* a64
2 b c Vale Of York(IRE) Swiss Roll (IRE) (Entrepreneur)
7867$^7$ 8000$^7$ 8184$^5$

**The Silver Kebaya (FR)** *Jeremy Noseda* a70 72
3 b f Rock Of Gibraltar(IRE) Music House (IRE) (Singspiel (IRE))
660$^{DSQ}$ 1690$^9$ 2274$^5$ 3268$^6$ 3885$^4$

**The Steward (USA)** *Sir Mark Prescott Bt* a84
3 b g Street Cry(IRE) Candlelight (USA) (Kingmambo (USA))
6018$^7$ (6483) ◆ 6886$^2$

**The Strig** *Nigel Tinkler* a49 81
7 b g Mujahid(USA) Pretty Kool (Inchinor)
1447$^{15}$ 1695$^{13}$ 2167$^{12}$ 2606$^{14}$ 3399$^{12}$ 4114$^{12}$ 4314$^8$ 4875$^4$ 5287$^7$ 5390$^{11}$ 5499$^9$ 5806$^4$ 6030$^4$ 6495$^7$

**The Third Man** *John Gosden* a77 79
3 gr g Dalakhani(IRE) Spinning Queen (Spinning World (USA))
3144$^4$ 3760$^3$

**The Tichborne (IRE)** *Roger Teal* a85 76
6 b g Shinko Forest(IRE) Brunswick (Warning)
342$^8$ 1871$^5$

**The Troyster** *Brian Ellison* a22 21
4 b g Indesatchel(IRE) Spindara (IRE) (Spinning World (USA))
78$^7$ 176$^8$

**The Twisler** *Charles Hills* a59 61
2 b g Motivator Panna (Polish Precedent (USA))
4395$^8$ 6102$^5$ 6874$^6$

**The Wallace Line (IRE)** *Tim Vaughan* a59
3 b g Mastercraftsman(IRE) Surval (IRE) (Sadler's Wells (USA))
4616$^7$

**The Warrior (IRE)** *A P O'Brien* 107
2 b c Exceed And Excel(AUS) Aymara (Darshaan)
6925$^9$ 7239$^6$

**Thewaythewindblows (IRE)** *Daniel Kubler* a68 54
2 gr c Thewayyouare(USA) Bali Breeze (IRE) (Common Grounds)
3929$^{10}$ 4633$^8$ (5098) 6944$^3$ 7208$^5$

**The Way You Dance (IRE)** *Ismail Mohammed* 48
2 b g Thewayyouare(USA) Beautiful Dancer (IRE) (Danehill Dancer (IRE))
3929$^9$

**The Wee Barra (IRE)** *Kevin Ryan* a63 60
2 b f Rock Of Gibraltar(IRE) Gamra (IRE) (Green Desert (USA))
4973$^{12}$ 5910$^6$ 6448$^3$ 7075$^3$

**The Wee Chief (IRE)** *Jimmy Fox* a60 68
8 ch g King Charlemagne(USA) La Belle Clare (IRE) (Paris House)
3088$^{12}$ 3820$^4$

**Thewestwalian (USA)** *Peter Hiatt* a44 59
6 bb g Stormy Atlantic(USA) Skies Of Blue (USA) (Ogygian (USA))
1138$^6$ 1365$^5$ 1668$^6$ 2069$^6$ 2720$^6$ 4153$^9$ 4960$^{10}$ 5499$^{11}$ (5806) 6495$^3$ 7010$^2$ 7420$^9$

**The Wispe** *Robert Cowell* a63 70
2 ch f Kyllachy Twitch Hill (Piccolo)
3563$^5$ 4583$^4$ 5042$^4$ 5845$^2$ (6791) 7079$^{10}$

**The Wonga Coup (IRE)** *Pat Phelan* a67 54
7 b g Northern Afleet(USA) Quichesterbahn (USA) (Broad Brush (USA))
88$^8$ 281$^6$ 484$^5$ 661$^7$ 844$^6$

**The Wow Signal (IRE)** *John Quinn* 118
2 b c Starspangledbanner(AUS) Muravka (IRE) (High Chaparral (IRE))
(2450) ◆ (3318) ◆ (5741a) 6968a$^9$

**The Yank** *Tony Carroll* a54 47
5 b g Trade Fair Silver Gyre (IRE) (Silver Hawk (USA))
68$^3$ 8011$^2$

**Theydon Bois** *Peter Charalambous* a64 64
2 b f Three Valleys(USA) Velvet Waters (Unfuwain (USA))
4444$^9$ 5344$^6$ 6085$^7$ 6840$^4$

**Theydon Thunder** *Peter Charalambous* a47
2 b g Virtual Lady Agnes (Singspiel (IRE))
3403$^6$ 3794$^3$ 4965$^8$ 8221$^4$

**The Young Master** *Neil Mulholland* a59
5 b g Echo Of Light Fine Frenzy (IRE) (Great Commotion (USA))
(455) 656$^{10}$

**Thimaar (USA)** *Donald McCain* 67
6 bb g Dynaformer(USA) Jinaan (USA) (Mr Prospector (USA))
5144$^{10}$

**Think** *Clive Mulhall* a50 51
7 ch g Sulamani(IRE) Natalie Jay (Ballacashtal (CAN))
33$^3$ 639$^4$ 3155$^{10}$ (5337) 6627$^8$ 7284$^9$

**Think Snow (USA)** *Mark Johnston* 76
2 ch f Giant's Causeway(USA) Snow Forest (USA) (Woodman (USA))
3107$^2$ ◆

**Third Dimension** *G M Lyons* a56 93
3 b g Dubawi(IRE) Round The Cape (Cape Cross (IRE))
3378$^{13}$

**Third Strike** *Gary Moore* a64 27
3 b g Tertullian(USA) Shaabra (IRE) (Rainbow Quest (USA))
51$^5$ 230$^7$ 371$^7$ 4340$^6$ 4969$^9$ 8084$^{10}$ 8314$^5$

**Third Time Lucky (IRE)** *Richard Fahey* 78
2 gr g Clodovil(IRE) Speckled Hen (IRE) (Titus Livius (FR))
3620$^3$ 4684$^5$ 5493$^2$ 6108$^2$

**This Charming Man (IRE)** *Keith Dalgleish* a40 33
3 b g Diamond Green(FR) Incendio (Siberian Express (USA))
37$^5$ 254$^5$ 557$^3$ 1211$^5$ 1373$^9$ 1657$^7$ 1906$^{13}$

**This Is The Day** *Charlie Fellowes* a72 96
3 b f Footstepsinthesand Miss Pinkerton (Danehill (USA))
3159$^7$ 4356$^2$ 5521$^3$ (6192) (6746) 7105$^7$

**This Is Too (IRE)** *Alan Bailey* 26
2 b f Fast Company(IRE) Suzi's A Smartlady (IRE) (Rakti)
2269$^9$ 2615$^9$ 7377$^{11}$

**This Time (FR)** *H-A Pantall* 105
3 b f Zafeen(FR) Scalotta (GER) (Winged Love (IRE))
1273a$^4$ 2195a$^6$ 4009a$^2$ 4854$^5$ 6182a$^7$ 7268a$^5$

**Thistleandtworoses (USA)** *David O'Meara* a73 69
4 ch g Lion Heart(USA) Country Again (USA) (Awesome Again (CAN))
1376$^{13}$ 1717$^7$ 2509$^8$

**Thistle Bird** *Roger Charlton* a56 115
6 b m Selkirk(USA) Dolma (FR) (Marchand De Sable (USA))
2284$^6$ (2956) (3766a)

**Thomaraz (FR)** *P Sogorb* a87 75
7 ch h Nombre Premier Niraz (FR) (Nikos)
(437a)

**Thomas Blossom (IRE)** *Patrick Chamings* a59 51
4 b g Dylan Thomas(IRE) Woman Secret (IRE) (Sadler's Wells (USA))
17$^{11}$ 5977$^7$ (6195) 6715$^5$ 7291$^3$ 7932$^3$ (8010)

**Thorkhill Star (IRE)** *Richard Fahey* 76
2 b g Equiano(FR) Reine De Romance (IRE) (Vettori (IRE))
4286$^8$ 4919$^2$ ◆ 5443$^5$ 5981$^2$ 6261$^2$ 6621$^3$

**Thornaby Princess** *Marjorie Fife* 69
3 b f Camacho Ingleby Princess (Bold Edge)
(2870) 3600$^3$ 4297$^4$ 4890$^6$ 5333$^2$ 5641$^7$ 6671$^{15}$

**Thorntoun Care** *Jim Goldie* 82
3 b g Rail Link Thorntoun Piccolo (Groom Dancer (USA))
2516$^4$ 4255$^2$ (4726) ◆ 6099$^8$ 6536$^2$ 7102$^3$

**Thorntoun Lady (USA)** *Jim Goldie* 73
4 b f Henrythenavigator(USA) Valery Lady (ARG) (Roy (USA))
1760$^2$ 2454$^7$ 3272$^{11}$ 3667$^4$ 4004$^2$ 4256$^7$ 4487$^8$ 5763$^7$

**Thorpe Bay** *Michael Appleby* a81 64
5 b g Piccolo My Valentina (Royal Academy (USA))
95$^6$ 257$^5$ 834$^2$ 866$^3$ 1487$^3$ 1843$^8$ 2250$^{11}$ 2552$^9$ 7623$^2$ 7888$^4$ 7949$^2$ 8182$^3$

**Thowar (USA)** *Kevin Ryan* a66 51
2 rg g Exchange Rate(USA) Elusive Fancy (USA) (Elusive Quality (USA))
5886$^{11}$ 6577$^4$ 8093$^4$

**Thrasos (IRE)** *Jo Crowley* a40 27
5 b g Invincible Spirit(IRE) Plymsole (USA) (Diesis)
244$^{11}$ 858$^7$ 3230$^{10}$

**Threatorapromise (IRE)** *Tony Coyle* 57
2 b f Zebedee Honey For Money (IRE) (Alzao (USA))
3841$^8$ 5297$^5$ 7082$^8$ 7497$^{11}$

**Threave** *Jo Crowley* a26 80
6 b m Diktat Bianca Sforza (Anabaa (USA))
5275$^2$ 7307$^{14}$

**Three Choirs (IRE)** *William Stone* a49 65
4 br f Rock Of Gibraltar(IRE) Three Owls (IRE) (Warning)
838$^{11}$ 3075$^9$ 4081$^8$

**Three Cliffs** *Roger Varian* a76 77
3 b g Exceed And Excel(AUS) Gower Song (Singspiel (IRE))
696$^2$ 954$^3$ 2717$^2$ 3936$^7$

**Three D Alexander (IRE)** *David Evans* a74 88
3 ch f Aqlaam Pivotal's Princess (IRE) (Pivotal)
140$^2$ 213$^2$ (500) 624$^5$ 1572$^{15}$

**Three Gracez** *Noel Quinlan* a63 48
2 b f Kyllachy Three Ducks (Diktat)
5982$^6$ 6646$^5$ 6903$^3$ (7258)

**Three Heart's** *Hugo Palmer* a50 58
3 b f Three Valleys(USA) Heart's Harmony (Blushing Groom (FR))
236$^9$

**Three Merry Lads** *Mark Johnston* 74
2 b c Danehill Dancer(IRE) Obsessive (USA) (Seeking The Gold (USA))
3186$^2$

**Three Peaks** *Charles Hills* a79 79
3 ch c Three Valleys(USA) Coming Back (Fantastic Light (USA))
1237$^2$ 1587$^4$ 2170$^2$ 2733$^4$ 3891$^5$ 4651$^8$

**Three Pips** *Ed McMahon* a69 51
3 b g Captain Gerrard(IRE) Samadilla (IRE) (Mujadil (USA))
149$^4$ 338$^2$ 573$^{10}$ 5526$^5$ 5987$^5$ 6695$^{13}$ 7111$^{11}$

**Three Robins** *Richard Hannon* a54 63
2 b f Cape Cross(IRE) Three Wrens (IRE) (Second Empire (IRE))
2888$^3$ 3584$^3$ 4346$^7$ 4913$^{16}$ 5554$^6$ 7064$^5$

**Threes Grand** *Scott Dixon* a82 90
4 b f Milk It Mick Ginger Cookie (Bold Edge)
2275$^7$ 3256$^{11}$ 3920$^7$ 4762$^{13}$ 5880$^4$

**Threetimesalady** *Sir Mark Prescott Bt* a67 77
3 b f Royal Applause Triple Joy (Most Welcome)
3615$^6$ 3957$^5$ 4367$^7$ 6089$^9$ 6814$^3$ 7351$^6$

**Throwing Roses** *John Weymes* a7 55
4 b f Clodovil(IRE) Mizooka (Tobougg (IRE))
2937$^{10}$ 4195$^{10}$ 5244$^8$

**Thrtypointstothree (IRE)** *Nikki Evans* a21 49
3 b g Kodiac Miss Taken (IRE) (Dubai Destination (USA))
2598a$^8$ 2591a$^3$ 5862$^5$ 7074$^{11}$

**Thrust Control (IRE)** *Tracy Waggott* a56 64
7 ch g Fath(USA) Anazah (USA) (Diesis)
1125$^3$ 1503$^4$ 1649$^6$ 2019$^5$ 3344$^5$ 3547$^3$ 3908$^7$ 4069$^4$ 4314$^9$ 4797$^8$ 5103$^2$ 5376$^6$ 5711$^6$ 6402$^5$ 6543$^8$

**Thumper (FR)** *Robert Cowell* a61 71
2 gr c Namid Pearl Argyle (FR) (Oasis Dream)
2007$^7$ 2458$^5$ 2837$^2$ 3170a$^6$ 5285$^{10}$

**Thundering Cloud (IRE)** *Brendan Powell* a63 41
3 b f Clodovil(IRE) Porky Pie (IRE) (Grand Lodge (USA))
2296$^{15}$ 4472$^9$ 5090$^5$ 6119$^{RR}$ 8090$^{RR}$

**Thundering Home** *Richard Mitchell* a70 59
7 gr g Storming Home Citrine Spirit (IRE) (Soviet Star (USA))
2942$^8$ 3552$^4$

**Thunder In Myheart (IRE)** *Michael Bell* 77
2 gr f Mastercraftsman(IRE) Happy Land (IRE) (Refuse To Bend (IRE))
4444$^2$ 4825$^6$ 6924$^4$ 7237$^{15}$

**Thunder Pass (IRE)** *Hughie Morrison* a73 76
3 b g High Chaparral(IRE) Hadarama (IRE) (Sinndar (IRE))
6682$^2$ (6981) 7366$^4$

**Thurayaat** *Roger Varian* a74 88
3 b f Tamayuz Ghaidaa (IRE) (Cape Cross (IRE))
(914) 1240$^4$ (1635) (2431) 3502$^3$ 5723$^7$ 6460$^5$

**Thyan (FR)** *P Capelle* a69 50
7 b h Indian Rocket Slyders (IRE) (Hector Protector (USA))
57a$^9$

**Tianjin City (FR)** *A Bonin* a82 87
4 gr g Holy Roman Emperor(IRE) Tenepia (FR) (Keltos (FR))
4776a$^6$ (5225a) 6569a$^4$

**Tianshan City** *C Ferland* a81 90
3 b f American Post Tenepia (FR) (Keltos (FR))
5368a$^3$

**Ticking Katie (IRE)** *K R Burke* a62 99
3 b f Baltic King Danccalli (IRE) (Traditionally (USA))
183$^6$ 1563$^8$ 3247$^3$ (4176) 4912$^2$ 5612$^3$ 6149$^4$ (6534)

**Ticks The Boxes (IRE)** *Clive Cox* a90 84
2 ch c Fast Company(IRE) Swan Sea (USA) (Sea Hero (USA))
3311$^4$ (4025) 4936$^3$ 5607$^{17}$ (7807)

**Tidal Beauty** *Lee Carter* a40 59
3 gr f Verglas(IRE) Tidal (Bin Ajwaad (IRE))
753$^{11}$ 1047$^4$ 1285$^5$ 6194$^9$ 7009$^3$ ◆ (7221)

**Tidal's Baby** *Lee Carter* a72 79
5 b g Dutch Art Tidal (Bin Ajwaad (IRE))
2030[7] 2645[9] 3246[7] 4267[3] 4762[18] 5986[5] 6890[8] 7205[8] 7757[10] 7931[6] 8041[6]

**Tidentime (USA)** *Mick Channon* a84 90
5 bb g Speightstown(USA) Casting Call (USA) (Dynaformer (USA))
2995[2] 3313[2] 3646[6] 4594[6] 6313[6] 6880[12]

**Tide Runner** *Liam Corcoran* a36 9
8 b g Selkirk(USA) Robellino Miss (USA) (Robellino (USA))
639[9] 822[9]

**Tides Reach (IRE)** *Roger Charlton* a82 81
3 ch f Mastercraftsman(IRE) Oystermouth (Averti (IRE))
2340[10] 3733[3] ◆ (4503) 5096[5] 5849[9] 6609[7] (7397) 7885[5] 8080[7]

**Tiffany Bay (IRE)** *John Patrick Shanahan* a65 73
3 b f The Carbon Unit(USA) Crackling Rosie (IRE) (Dr Fong (USA))
1601[4] 2740[8] 4001[6] 5168[4] (Dead)

**Tiger Cliff (FR)** *J-L Bertin* a50 55
9 b m Tiger Hill(IRE) Vertige (USA) (Gulch (USA))
57a[10]

**Tiger Cliff (IRE)** *Alan King* a86 114
5 b g Tiger Hill(IRE) Verbania (IRE) (In The Wings)
2315[3] 2704[5] 3453[4] (Dead)

**Tiger Heights** *Jim Goldie* 30
3 b g Tiger Hill(IRE) Primo Heights (Primo Valentino (IRE))
4111[9] 4569[10] 5388[9]

**Tiger Jim** *Jim Goldie* a63 82
4 b g Tiger Hill(IRE) Quintrell (Royal Applause)
4111[4] 5088[4] (5415) 5766[4] 6232[4] (6639) 7601[4]

**Tiger Lilly (IRE)** *Richard Fahey* 87
3 b f Galileo(IRE) Banquise (IRE) (Last Tycoon)
(1960) 3250[4] 3884[4] (5288) 6137[7]

**Tiger Reigns** *John Butler* a77 80
8 b g Tiger Hill(IRE) Showery (Rainbow Quest (USA))
(105) 210[3] 498[4] 1317[2] 1628[7]

**Tiger's Home** *Julia Feilden* a59 59
4 b f Tiger Hill(IRE) Homeward (IRE) (Kris)
1863[4] 2127[10] 2723[6] 3231[9] 4042[2] 4337[3] 5110[6]

**Tigers In Red (USA)** *David Simcock* a84 71
3 ch g Speightstown(USA) Gaudete (USA) (Distorted Humor (USA))
(551) 1122[6] 4208[7]

**Tigers Tale (IRE)** *Roger Teal* a103 95
5 b g Tiger Hill(IRE) Vayenga (FR) (Highest Honor (FR))
(1103) 1578[2] 2309[2] 2959[13] 4331[3] 4827[4] (6140) 6752[6] 7276[19] 7545[2] 8116[6] 8295[2]

**Tiger Stone** *Michael Blanshard* a50
3 b f Tiger Hill(IRE) Lacandona (USA) (Septieme Ciel (USA))
6045[5] 6485[9] 8249[4]

**Tiger Tees (NZ)** *Joseph Pride* 116
7 ch g Dubawi(IRE) Parfore (NZ) (Gold Brose (AUS))
1468a[4]

**Tiger Twenty Two** *Richard Fahey* 87
3 b g Authorized(IRE) Collette's Choice (Royal Applause)
2257[4] 3200[9] 3694[3] 4635[11] 5656[14] 7060[9] 7438[7]

**Tiggy Wiggy (IRE)** *Richard Hannon* a90 117
2 b f Kodiac Kheleyf's Silver (IRE) (Kheleyf (USA))
(1169) ◆ (1982) 2313[2] (2703) 3353[2] (4439) (5608) (6751)

**Tightend Touchdown (USA)** *Jason Servis* a67 116
5 ch g Pure Precision(USA) Starry Mark (USA) (Marquetry (USA))
7609a[6]

**Tight Fit** *Henry Candy* a64 94
4 ch f Assertive Bikini (Trans Island)
1731[2] 2318[10] 3788[6] 4573[2] 6068[8]

**Tight Knit (USA)** *John Weymes* a67
4 b g Hard Spun(USA) Tamdiid (USA) (Horse Chestnut (SAF))
601[4] 1245[6] 1503[11] 2394[5] 2455[8] 3623[10] 7785[9] 8134[11]

**Tight Lipped (IRE)** *Julia Feilden* a75 73
5 gr g Dark Angel(IRE) Kayoko (IRE) (Shalford (IRE))
744[8] 1196[9] 1810[6] 2270[2] ◆ 2876[3] 5931[7] 6303[7] 7044[6] 8162[4]

**Tight Times (IRE)** *B R Hamilton* a57 69
5 b g Helissio(FR) Secret Conquest (Secret Appeal)
7877a[5]

**Tigrilla (IRE)** *Roger Varian* 103
2 gr f Clodovil(IRE) Lisieux Orchid (IRE) (Sadler's Wells (USA))
2612[2] (3107) 3721[3] (4931a) 5734a[8] 6709[4] 7393a[3]

**Tijan (IRE)** *Saeed bin Suroor* a79 28
3 b g Shamardal(USA) Cherry Orchard (IRE) (King's Best (USA))
7250[5] 7528[2]

**Tijuca (IRE)** *Ed de Giles* a68 52
5 b m Captain Rio Some Forest (IRE) (Charnwood Forest (IRE))
78[8] 184[2] 290[13] 446[7] 575[3] 754[2] (851) 1123[3] 1385[2] (1923) 2523[5] 3080[7] 3540[6] 4073[13] 7907[12]

**Tilly Range (IRE)** *David Evans* a45 43
2 b f Bushranger(IRE) Tiber Tilly (King Charlemagne (USA))
2928[11] 3173[6] 5133[4] 6205[8]

**Tilstarr (IRE)** *Roger Teal* a79 78
4 b f Shamardal(USA) Vampire Queen (IRE) (General Monash (USA))
(1393) 1899[3] 2498[3] 2750[3] 3325[4] 3874[3] 4434[5] 4799[6] 5551[4] 6007[6] 6338[2] 8161[6]

**Tilsworth Annalisa** *J R Jenkins* a11 38
3 br f Observatory(USA) Tilsworth Charlie (Dansili)
5531[5] 6042[8] 6437[5] 7800[7] 8003[4]

**Timba** *John Gosden* 87
2 b f Oasis Dream Teeky (Daylami (IRE))
(6001) ◆ 6521[2]

**Time And Place** *Richard Fahey* a88 83
4 ch g Compton Place Forthefirstime (Dr Fong (USA))
1672[7] 2332[3] 3256[P] 8252[2]

**Time Check (USA)** *Saeed bin Suroor* a77
2 ch f Shamardal(USA) Alizes (NZ) (Rory's Jester (AUS))
8007[2]

**Time Continuum** *Eric Alston* 39
2 b f Monsieur Bond(IRE) Primum Tempus (Primo Dominie)
4450[7]

**Time Dream (IRE)** *L Baudron* a79 77
3 b f Bushranger(IRE) Softlanding (IRE) (Nashwan (USA))
599a[5]

**Time Flies** *John Gosden* a63
2 b c Exceed And Excel(AUS) Simply Times (USA) (Dodge (USA))
7779[3] ◆

**Time For Crabbies (IRE)** *Lisa Williamson* a57 30
4 b g Moss Vale(IRE) Westlife (IRE) (Mind Games)
5207[7] 5897[12] 6121[15]

**Time For Lambrini (IRE)** *Lisa Williamson* a52
4 b f Amadeus Wolf Princess Madaen (IRE) (Elusive Quality (USA))
453[6] 687[8] 1030[6]

**Timeless Call (IRE)** *Reginald Roberts* a98 104
6 b m Sakhee(USA) Pourquoi Pas (IRE) (Nordico (USA))
1824a[4] (3284a) 3736a[5]

**Timeless War (USA)** *William Haggas* a47
3 b g Bernardini(USA) The Best Day Ever (USA) (Brahms (USA))
50[7] 231[3]

**Time Medicean** *Tony Carroll* a63 69
8 gr g Medicean Ribbons And Bows (IRE) (Dr Devious (IRE))
663[8] (1010) 1221[5] 1678[9] 2691[9] 3313[8] 6025[11] 7023[8] 7670[9] 7735[2] 8014[12]

**Time Of My Life (IRE)** *Patrick Holmes* a40 55
5 b g Galileo(IRE) In My Life (IRE) (Rainbow Quest (USA))
1885[5] 2327[14] 3301[9] 4000[10] 4474[5] 6644[4] 7643[3] 7893[10]

**Time Signal** *Sir Michael Stoute* 77
3 b f Champs Elysees Sandglass (Zafonic (USA))
1701[7] 2280[10]

**Times In Anatefka (IRE)** *Adrian Brendan Joyce* a66 51
4 b f Pyrus(USA) Brooklands Time (IRE) (Danetime (IRE))
128a[3] 2452[8]

**Time Square (FR)** *Tony Carroll* a67 59
7 b g Westerner Sainte Parfaite (FR) (Septieme Ciel (USA))
67[5] 278[5] 571[7] 821[6] 1012[2] 1168[3] (1406) 1909[7] 2300[6] 2464[8] 7540[4] 7846[5] (7982) 8169[8]

**Times Up** *Ed Dunlop* 115
8 b g Olden Times Princess Genista (Ile De Bourbon (USA))
1950[7] 2588a[7] 5652[3] 6288[8] 6687[5]

**Time Test** *Roger Charlton* 90
2 b c Dubawi(IRE) Passage Of Time (Dansili)
4440[2] (5881) 6457[2]

**Time To Work (IRE)** *Gordon Elliott* 79
6 b g Hurricane Run(IRE) Viscoumtess Brave (IRE) (Law Society (USA))
4951a[8] (Dead)

**Timjoe (IRE)** *Thomas Cleary* a69 44
7 b g Arakan(USA) Lucky Coin (Hadeer)
7962a[3]

**Timothy T** *Philip Hide* a68 50
6 bl g Pastoral Pursuits Point Perfect (Dansili)
154[2] 583[7] 815[11] 1025[3]

**Tinchy Ryder** *Bryan Smart* a42 40
3 b g Dylan Thomas(IRE) Keyaki (IRE) (Shinko Forest (IRE))
173[10] 547[5] 765[6] 5853[10] 7652[6] 8085[12]

**Tindaro (FR)** *Paul Webber* a80 87
7 gr g Kingsalsa(USA) Star's Mixa (FR) (Linamix (FR))
4575[4] 4917[2] (6392a)

**Tinga (IRE)** *Ralph Beckett* a65 79
3 ch f Galileo(IRE) Tingling (USA) (Storm Cat (USA))
1424[8] 4435[8] 4845[3] 5606[3] 6238[8]

**Tinghir (IRE)** *David Lanigan* a106 101
4 b c Dansili Palmeraie (USA) (Lear Fan (USA))
1437[20] 2707[5] 5188[3] 5928[10] (6566) (6943) 7243[13]

**Tingleo** *Sir Michael Stoute* a65 61
2 ch f Galileo(IRE) Tingling (USA) (Storm Cat (USA))
6208[5] 7184[4]

**Tingle Tangle (USA)** *Tony Carroll* a53 74
4 bb g Mizzen Mast(USA) Tinge (USA) (Kingmambo (USA))
83[9] 295[12] 575[9] 783[11] 2689[14] 3224[7]

**Tingo In The Tale (IRE)** *David Arbuthnot* a69 60
5 b g Oratorio(IRE) Sunlit Skies (Selkirk (USA))
1798[3] 2464[5] 3761[7] 5786[3] 6942[8] 7359[13]

**Tinkers Kiss (IRE)** *Philip McBride* a62 47
2 b f Intikhab(USA) Edmondstown Lass (IRE) (Imperial Ballet (IRE))
4444[10] 5443[3] (6017) 6662[8] 7029[5] 7529[4] 7753[5] 8076[3] 8240[4]

**Tin Pan Alley** *David C Griffiths* a70 65
6 b g Singspiel(IRE) Tazmeen (Darshaan)
3123[5] 3473[2] 4433[3] 4964[14] 7830[5] 8103[3]

**Tinseltown** *Brian Rothwell* a38 72
8 b g Sadler's Wells(USA) Peony (Lion Cavern (USA))
1197[10] 1644[3] 2728[6] 3095[3] 3398[3] 4058[10] 4293[8] (4533) 4995[7] 5371[6] 6541[6] 7008[11]

**Tinshu (IRE)** *Derek Haydn Jones* a100 83
8 ch m Fantastic Light(USA) Ring Of Esteem (Mark Of Esteem (IRE))
145[2] 344[3] 716[6] 1068[13] 1170[4] 1559[9] 2627[10] 3802[3] 4184[10] 5095[2] 6303[6] 7803[11] 8078[4] 8244[4]

**Tinsill** *Nigel Tinkler* a9 77
3 ch g Firebreak Concentration (IRE) (Mind Games)
1396[9] 1676[4] 2015[12] (2388) 2802[4] (3100) 3600[8] 4059[3] 4636[9] 4890[7] (5087) 5389[3] 5912[3] 6452[6]

**Tioga Pass** *Paul Cole* a80 96
3 b f High Chaparral(IRE) Seren Devious (Dr Devious (IRE))
1809[3] (2082) (2501) 4145[6] 5723[2] 7135[6] 7554[14]

**Tiolache (FR)** *J-M Capitte* a64 63
4 b f Layman(USA) Wivenhoe (UAE) (Timber Country (USA))
266a[5] 722a[5]

**Tipsy Star** *Jonathan Geake* a62 58
3 b f Tobougg(IRE) Extremely Rare (IRE) (Mark Of Esteem (IRE))
3712[5] 4540[5] 5622[5] 5908[6] 6026[6]

**Tiptree Lace** *William Knight* a68 73
3 b f Duke Of Marmalade(IRE) Crinolette (IRE) (Sadler's Wells (USA))
2560[4] 2967[11] 3712[3] 4427[7] 5284[7] 6337[11] 6981[12]

**Tiramisu (FR)** *G Botti* 69
2 b c Siyouni(FR) Panna Cotta (IRE) (Intikhab (USA))
4881a[8]

**Tirghra (IRE)** *J S Bolger* a70 72
3 b f Teofilo(IRE) National Swagger (IRE) (Giant's Causeway (USA))
1201a[9]

**Tirion (USA)** *M Boutin* a83 94
6 b h Royal Academy(USA) Domenica's Dream (USA) (Woodman (USA))
(392a)

**Tirol Livit (IRE)** *Mark Hoad* a44 50
11 ch g Titus Livius(FR) Orange Royale (IRE) (Exit To Nowhere (USA))
186[4]

**Titan Goddess** *Mike Murphy* a57
2 b f Equiano(FR) Phoebe Woodstock (IRE) (Grand Lodge (USA))
7228[9] 7631[9] 7943[7]

**Titan Triumph** *Michael Attwater* a72 50
10 b g Zamindar(USA) Triple Green (Green Desert (USA))
690[10] 1040[5] 1302[10] 1917[9]

**Titian Lord (IRE)** *Charles Hills* 47
2 b c Lord Shanakill(USA) Titian Queen (Tobougg (IRE))
4395[11] 4906[8] 5377[8]

**Titled Lady** *David Elsworth* 79
2 ch f Sir Percy May West (Act One)
4444[7] ◆ 4914[2] 5416[7]

**Titus Bolt (IRE)** *Jim Goldie* a55 72
5 b g Titus Livius(FR) Megan's Bay (Muhtarram (USA))
2475[10] (5145) 5567[6] 6113[3] (7100)

**Tizcano (USA)** *Peter Miller* a94
2 b c Tiznow(USA) Westerly Breeze (USA) (Gone West (USA))
7605a[3]

**Tiziana (FR)** *Mario Hofer* a65 66
2 b f Touch Down(GER) Tizia (IRE) (Linamix (FR))
5119a[12]

**Tizlove Regardless (USA)** *Mark Johnston* a83 60
3 b c Tiznow(USA) Dianehill (IRE) (Danehill (USA))
(774) ◆ (828) (1028) 1727[7] 7350[7] 7689[4] 8015[8]

**Tiz Midnight (USA)** *Bob Baffert* a111
4 b f Midnight Lute(USA) Tough Tiz's Sis (USA) (Tiznow (USA))
7593a[6]

**T Kers (FR)** *H Hesse* a77 72
3 b c Sinndar(IRE) Tempola (FR) (Anabaa (USA))
5959a[2]

**Toast Of Newbury (IRE)** *Jamie Osborne* a65 55
2 ch c Captain Rio Pearl Of The Sea (IRE) (Fusaichi Pegasus (USA))
4025[10] 4338[6] 4541[4] 4967[7] 8069[5] 8317[10]

**Toast Of New York (USA)** *Jamie Osborne* a123 101
3 b c Thewayyouare(USA) Claire Soleil (USA) (Syncline (USA))
(1178a) 3994a[6] 5781a[2] 7614a[2]

**Toast Of The Town (IRE)** *John Gosden* a81 97
4 b f Duke Of Marmalade(IRE) Boast (Most Welcome)
2109[2] 2649[2] 3307[4] 3877[2] (5606) 7105[12] 7717[9]

**Tobacco Road (IRE)** *Richard Hannon* a80 96
4 b g Westerner Virginias Best (King's Best (USA))
(1351) 2062[8] 2707[7] 3196[4] 4184[9] 4756[17] 6877[2] 6987[2]

**Tobago Cays** *Bill Turner*
3 b f Tobougg(IRE) Cove Mountain (IRE) (Indian Danehill (IRE))
3801[11] 5400[8]

**Tobann (IRE)** *J S Bolger* a88 105
4 b f Teofilo(IRE) Precipitous (IRE) (Indian Ridge)
1473a[7] 2572a[11] (3864a) 4557a[2] 5869a[4] 6351a[3]

**To Be Determined (USA)** *Wesley A Ward* a55 89
2 b f Elusive Quality(USA) Katori (USA) (Dixie Union (USA))
3374[9]

**To Begin** *Tim Easterby* 41
3 b g Tobougg(IRE) Sagina (Shernazar)
1192[12] 1542[8] 1962[7] 2621[4] 3789[10] 4497[8] 5200[11]

**Toboggan's Gift** *Ann Duffield* 54
2 b f Major Cadeaux Toboggan Lady (Tobougg (IRE))
7174[6] 7498[6] 7637[8]

**Toboggan Star** *Ann Duffield* a59 68
3 b g Lucky Story(USA) Toboggan Lady (Tobougg (IRE))
1346[10] 1940[9] 4489[10] 5853[4] 6758[8] 7061[9]

**Tobouggan Run** *Michael Appleby* a27 25
2 b g Tobougg(IRE) Justbetweenfriends (USA) (Diesis)
1726[10] 3620[10] 5098[5]

**Tobougg Happy** *Andrew Balding* 84
3 b f Tobougg(IRE) Happy Lady (FR) (Cadeaux Genereux)
3759[6] 6922[13]

**Tobrata** *Mel Brittain* a63 60
8 ch g Tobougg(IRE) Sabrata (IRE) (Zino)
1674[5] 2620[10]

**Tocantins (IRE)** *M Boutin* a76 73
3 b c Elusive City(USA) Totem (USA) (Mizzen Mast (USA))
545a[4] 7269a[11]

**Tocororo (IRE)** *Ed Dunlop* a54 60
2 b f Teofilo(IRE) Firecrest (IRE) (Darshaan)
6553[9] 7108[14] 7367[9] 7994[7]

**Todegica** *Ralph Beckett* a72 5
2 b f Giant's Causeway(USA) Totally Devoted (USA) (Seeking The Gold (USA))
4403[13] (6268) 7116[7] 7544[3]

**Toe The Line (IRE)** *John E Kiely* 101
5 b m Shantou(USA) Bluebell Line (IRE) (Charnwood Forest (IRE))
(6349a)

**Toga Tiger (IRE)** *Kevin Frost* a83 81
7 b g Antonius Pius(USA) Minerwa (GER) (Protektor (GER))
287[10] 574[3] 1014[4] ◆ 1439[7] 2519[5] 3254[3] ◆ 3861[11] (7186) 7732[4] 7870[8] 8251[12]

**Together Forever (IRE)** *A P O'Brien* 111
2 b f Galileo(IRE) Green Room (USA) (Theatrical (IRE))
(7240)

**Togoville (IRE)** *Patrick Martin* a80 76
4 gr g Verglas(IRE) Road Harbour (USA) (Rodrigo De Triano (USA))
4950a[9]

**Tohaveandtohold** *William Haggas* a57 53
3 ch f Pivotal Wedding Party (Groom Dancer (USA))
2118[6] 2442[9] 2780[12] 3281[7] 7570[5] 8050[3] 8246[6] 8309[5]

**Tohfa (IRE)** *Richard Hannon* 78
2 ch f Dutch Art The Fairies Did It (USA) (Elusive Quality (USA))
3107[4] 4170[4] 4914[3]

**Tokei Halo (JPN)** *Hisashi Shimizu* 121
5 b h Gold Halo(JPN) Dance Queen (JPN) (Mill George (USA))
1181a[7] 2379a[4]

**Token Of Love** *William Haggas* 108
3 b f Cape Cross(IRE) Nyarhini (Fantastic Light (USA))
2340[2] 3195[3] (3476) ◆ 4436[2] (5176) 6254[11]

**Tokomaro (IRE)** *Richard Hannon* a49
2 ch c Sakhee's Secret Corton Charlemagne (IRE) (King Charlemagne (USA))
7835[7] 7880[4]

**Tokyo Brown (USA)** *Heather Main* a65 58
5 b g Marquetry(USA) Miasma (USA) (Lear Fan (USA))
(609) (848) 974[3] 1574[9]

**Tokyo Time (USA)** *Claude McGaughey III* 96
4 b f Medaglia d'Oro(USA) Flying Passage (USA) (A.P. Indy (USA))
2227a[2]

**Tolka (IRE)** *S Wattel* a90 96
5 b g Danehill Dancer(IRE) Russian Hill (Indian Ridge)
5961a[10]

**Tolly McGuiness** *Julia Feilden* a51 31
3 ch c Araafa(IRE) Golden Flyer (FR) (Machiavellian (USA))
3525[5] 4089[6] 4972[5] 6765[7] 7800[4] 8119[3]

**Tolmias (GR)** *Luca Cumani* 66
3 br g Ialysos(GR) Shikasta (IRE) (Kris)
2442[4] 2996[8] 3566[4]

**Tombelaine (USA)** *D K Weld* 105
2 b c First Defence(USA) Kithira (Danehill (USA))
4599a[2] 6348a[2] 6800a[5]

**Tom Dooley (IRE)** *Michael Mulvany* a64 72
3 b g Dylan Thomas(IRE) Shizao (IRE) (Alzao (USA))
4950a[11]

**Tom Hall** *David Menuisier* a61
4 b g Pastoral Pursuits Villarosi (IRE) (Rossini (USA))
8195[8]

**Tom Hark (FR)** *Richard Hannon* a66 88
2 ch c Makfi Raisonable (USA) (El Prado (IRE))
3578[4] 3929[3] 4800[2] 5645[2] ◆ (6063)

**Tom Mann (IRE)** *David Barron* a63 71
3 ch g Sir Percy Fantasy Princess (USA) (Johannesburg (USA))
675[5] 3362[7] 6429[3] 7251[2] ◆

**Tommy Docc (IRE)** *Keith Dalgleish* 41
2 b c Thewayyouare(USA) Liturgy (IRE) (Catcher In The Rye (IRE))
5852[4]

**Tommys Geal** *Michael Madgwick* a52 37
2 b f Halling(USA) Steel Free (IRE) (Danehill Dancer (IRE))
1349[6] 1663[4] 2460[6] 4576[8] 5489[8] 6237[3] 6662[3] 6888[3] 7848[5]

**Tommy's Secret** *Jane Chapple-Hyam* a80 81
4 gr g Sakhee's Secret La Gessa (Largesse)
2919[9] 3468[7] 3861[7] 4181[4] (4766) 5058[5] 6035[5] 6466[6] 8041[3] 8248[10]

**Tom Paine** *Garry Moss* a62
2 ch g Three Valleys(USA) Lee Miller (IRE) (Danehill Dancer (IRE))
8166[8]

**Tom Sawyer** *Julie Camacho* a80 82
6 b g Dansili Cayman Sunset (IRE) (Night Shift (USA))
2656[9] 3831[2] 4553[7] 5060[7] 5563[3] (5913) 6441[5]

**Tom's Tribute (USA)** *James Cassidy* 114
4 ch c Lion Heart(USA) Halloween Fun (USA) (El Prado (IRE))
7613a[7]

**Tonalist (USA)** *Christophe Clement* a121
3 b c Tapit(USA) Settling Mist (USA) (Pleasant Colony (USA))
(3026a) 7614a[5]

**Tongue Twista** *Nick Littmoden* a71 87
2 b f Stimulation(IRE) Lady-Love (Pursuit Of Love)
3757$^{2}$ 4164$^{3}$ 4646$^{6}$ 5509$^{2}$ (5946) 6286$^{10}$ 6751$^{7}$ 7563$^{6}$

**Tonica (FR)** *J-J Chiozzi* a38 45
3 b f Enrique Tonic Stream (FR) (Bering)
7164a$^{8}$

**Toni Fortebracci (FR)** *G Botti* a83 83
4 b c Muhtathir Fosool (IRE) (Pivotal)
805a$^{6}$ 5964a$^{5}$

**Toni's A Star** *Paul Green* a50 42
2 b f Avonbridge Canina (Foxhound (USA))
1936$^{7}$ 2089$^{9}$ 2601$^{9}$ 3215$^{11}$ (7453) 7948$^{10}$ 8118$^{10}$

**Tonto's Spirit** *Michael Dods* 42
2 b g Authorized(IRE) Desert Royalty (IRE) (Alhaarth (IRE))
5760$^{8}$ 6860$^{7}$ 7495$^{9}$

**Tony Hollis** *Michael Appleby* a54 57
6 b g Antonius Pius(USA) Seasons Parks (Desert Prince (IRE))
18$^{6}$ 2901$^{5}$ 3242$^{6}$ 4415$^{9}$ 4473$^{15}$

**Too Bend** *Patrick Chamings* a42 21
3 b g Tobougg(IRE) Benjarong (Sharpo)
3525$^{6}$ 5976$^{6}$

**Toocoolforschool (IRE)** *K R Burke* 116
2 b g Showcasing Spring Surprise (Hector Protector (USA))
4409$^{3}$ (5013) 5576$^{2}$ 6291$^{2}$ (6547)

**Too Elusive** *Kristin Stubbs* a59 66
3 b g Major Cadeaux Elusive Kitty (USA) (Elusive Quality (USA))
1344$^{7}$

**Toofeeg (IRE)** *William Haggas* a68 70
2 ch g Approve(IRE) Zabadani (Zafonic (USA))
3381$^{5}$ 6621$^{5}$ 6998$^{2}$ 7827$^{3}$ 8075$^{2}$

**Toofi (FR)** *Roger Varian* 104
3 b c Henrythenavigator(USA) Silver Bark (Royal Applause)
1513$^{2}$ 2343$^{2}$ 3352$^{10}$ 4669$^{11}$

**Toogoodtobetrue (IRE)** *A P O'Brien* 103
2 b f Oasis Dream All For Glory (USA) (Giant's Causeway (USA))
5734a$^{3}$

**Toolain (IRE)** *S Seemar* a89 71
6 br g Diktat Qasirah (IRE) (Machiavellian (USA))
241a$^{5}$

**Too Many Diamonds (IRE)** *Damian Joseph English* a47 42
3 b g Diamond Green(FR) Too Much Color (USA) (Spectrum (IRE))
416a$^{6}$ 4556a$^{9}$

**Toormore (IRE)** *Richard Hannon* 122
3 b c Arakan(USA) Danetime Out (IRE) (Danetime (IRE))
(1532) 1951$^{7}$ 3320$^{6}$ 4758$^{2}$ 6185a$^{3}$ 7274$^{3}$ ◆

**Too The Stars (IRE)** *John Gosden* 76
3 ch f Sea The Stars(IRE) Finsceal Beo (IRE) (Mr Greeley (USA))
2279$^{8}$ 5382$^{3}$ 6002$^{2}$ (6788)

**Toot Your Flute (IRE)** *William Haggas* a63 45
2 b c Invincible Spirit(IRE) Navajo Moon (IRE) (Danehill (USA))
6038$^{8}$ 6630$^{3}$ 7200$^{6}$

**Topaling** *Mark H Tompkins* a72 47
3 ch f Halling(USA) Topatori (IRE) (Topanoora)
1894$^{6}$ 2310$^{8}$ 2649$^{8}$ 4085$^{7}$ (5048) 5318$^{3}$ (7360) (7866) (8164) ◆

**Topamichi** *Mark H Tompkins* a75 85
4 b g Beat Hollow Topatori (IRE) (Topanoora)
1483$^{10}$ 5299$^{8}$ 5931$^{5}$ 6855$^{4}$ 7172$^{5}$ (7341)

**Top Billing** *Nicky Richards* 62
5 br g Monsun(GER) La Gandilie (FR) (Highest Honor (FR))
4492$^{7}$ 5146$^{4}$

**Top Boy** *Derek Shaw* a92 96
4 b g Exceed And Excel(AUS) Injaaz (Sheikh Albadou)
1049$^{3}$ (1283) 1506$^{3}$ 1742$^{2}$ 2074$^{4}$ 2283$^{3}$ (2786) 4179$^{11}$ 5918$^{9}$ 6614$^{7}$ 7080$^{15}$

**Topclas (FR)** *A bin Harmash* a103 104
8 b g Kutub(IRE) Noble Presence (FR) (Fasliyev (USA))
305a$^{2}$ 598a$^{5}$

**Top Cop** *Ronald Harris* a78 92
5 b g Acclamation Speed Cop (Cadeaux Genereux)
294$^{6}$ 535$^{4}$ 730$^{2}$ 925$^{6}$ 1031$^{4}$ (1311) 1739$^{2}$ 2065$^{2}$ 2414$^{11}$ 2691$^{6}$ 3088$^{10}$ 3519$^{2}$ 4581$^{4}$ 5595$^{8}$ 6249$^{6}$ 6658$^{8}$

**Top Decile (USA)** *Albert M Stall Jr* a107
2 ch f Congrats(USA) Sequoia Queen (USA) (Forestry (USA))
6915a$^{2}$ 7606a$^{2}$

**Top Diktat** *Gary Moore* a83 94
6 b g Diktat Top Romance (IRE) (Entrepreneur)
250$^{7}$ (379) (655) (1439) (1810) 2783$^{5}$ 7545$^{14}$ 7850$^{10}$ 8012$^{6}$ 8188$^{8}$

**Top Dollar** *James Tate* a81 66
3 ch f Elusive Quality(USA) Elrehaan (Sadler's Wells (USA))
2604$^{5}$

**Top Line Banker** *Tim Pitt* 47
4 b g Top Line Dancer(IRE) Ice Pack (Mukaddamah (USA))
695$^{8}$

**Top Notch Tonto (IRE)** *Brian Ellison* 120
4 ch g Thousand Words Elite Hope (USA) (Moment Of Hope (USA))
1698$^{4}$ 2338$^{6}$ 2705$^{3}$ 3723$^{6}$ 5609$^{2}$ 6352a$^{4}$ 7274$^{10}$ 7444$^{2}$

**Top Offer** *Peter Crate* a77 73
5 b g Dansili Zante (Zafonic (USA))
52$^{4}$ 245$^{4}$ 496$^{6}$ 3118$^{8}$ 3589$^{5}$ (4431) 5987$^{3}$ 6398$^{5}$ (7356) 7775$^{2}$ 8072$^{3}$

**Top Of The Glas (IRE)** *Brian Ellison* a61 94
3 gr g Verglas(IRE) Fury Dance (USA) (Cryptoclearance (USA))
1690$^{10}$ 2481$^{8}$ (3663) 4631$^{2}$ ◆ (5410) 6534$^{10}$ 6978$^{2}$ 7410$^{4}$

**Topolski (IRE)** *David Arbuthnot* a81 70
8 b g Peintre Celebre(USA) Witching Hour (IRE) (Alzao (USA))
856$^{6}$ 992$^{10}$

**Top Pocket** *Michael Madgwick* a49
2 b g Royal Applause Movie Mogul (Sakhee (USA))
6293$^{12}$ 7372$^{8}$ 7926$^{8}$

**Top Set (IRE)** *Simon Dow* a74 58
4 ch g Tamayuz Pray (IRE) (Priolo (USA))
1810$^{5}$ 2687$^{6}$ 3112$^{9}$ 6019$^{9}$ 6616$^{10}$ 7001$^{8}$ 7527$^{9}$ 7844$^{3}$ 7924$^{7}$ 8314$^{2}$

**Topsy Turvy (IRE)** *Jeremy Noseda* 50
2 b g Pivotal Helter Helter (USA) (Seeking The Gold (USA))
6984$^{9}$ 7382$^{9}$

**Toptempo** *Mark H Tompkins* a67 79
5 ch m Halling(USA) Topatoo (Bahamian Bounty)
1942$^{5}$ 2782$^{8}$ 6685$^{7}$ 7281$^{11}$ 7565$^{5}$ 7817$^{7}$ 7903$^{4}$

**Top Tug (IRE)** *Sir Michael Stoute* a87 96
3 ch g Halling(USA) Top Romance (IRE) (Entrepreneur)
1535$^{6}$ (2748) 7106$^{7}$ ◆

**Topza (FR)** *F-H Graffard* 40
4 b f Zamindar(USA) Topka (FR) (Kahyasi)
935a$^{10}$

**Torchlighter (IRE)** *Mark Johnston* 105
3 ch g Shamardal(USA) Ever Love (BRZ) (Nedawi)
1420$^{8}$ 1903$^{8}$ 2257$^{5}$ 2962$^{7}$ 3243$^{2}$ (3758) (4125)

**Toretto (IRE)** *Bernard Llewellyn* a65 55
6 ch g Peintre Celebre(USA) Petite-D-Argent (Noalto)
7990$^{5}$ 8289$^{4}$

**Torino (ITY)** *L Riccardi* 55
2 ch f Mastercraftsman(IRE) Time Of Gold (USA) (Banker's Gold (USA))
7321a$^{7}$

**Tornesel** *Brian Rothwell* 77
3 b c Teofilo(IRE) Bezant (IRE) (Zamindar (USA))
4500$^{4}$ 6982$^{4}$

**Toronado (IRE)** *Richard Hannon* 129
4 b c High Chaparral(IRE) Wana Doo (USA) (Grand Slam (USA))
(3317) 4779$^{2}$ 6382a$^{2}$ 7613a$^{8}$

**Torres Del Paine** *Roger Ingram* a58
7 b g Compton Place Noble Story (Last Tycoon)
184$^{9}$ (586) 1009$^{4}$ 7036$^{13}$

**Torrid** *Amanda Perrett* 92
3 ch c Three Valleys(USA) Western Appeal (USA) (Gone West (USA))
5882$^{4}$ 6301$^{5}$

**Torridon** *Mark Johnston* a54 50
3 b g Bahamian Bounty Intellibet One (Compton Place)
994$^{5}$ 1137$^{3}$ 1430$^{5}$ 1648$^{11}$ 2517$^{9}$ 3105$^{8}$ 4363$^{2}$ 4728$^{7}$ 5257$^{3}$ 5854$^{6}$ 6267$^{8}$ 6833$^{6}$

**Torridonian** *James Tate* a52 55
2 b f Kodiac Scottish Heights (IRE) (Selkirk (USA))
4583$^{5}$ 5774$^{5}$ 6408$^{9}$ 8118$^{8}$ ◆

**Tortilla Jackson** *Tom Dascombe* 69
2 b c Kodiac Somersault (Pivotal)
6319$^{5}$ 6757$^{9}$ 7170$^{3}$

**Tortoise** *Richard Guest* a54 60
3 b f Multiplex Wonderful Island (GER) (Turtle Island (IRE))
28$^{3}$ 280$^{2}$ 480$^{11}$ 2237$^{8}$ 2393$^{11}$ (2741) 3053$^{2}$ 3105$^{4}$ 3545$^{10}$ 4611$^{7}$ 5084$^{2}$ 5239$^{4}$ 5892$^{4}$ 6010$^{6}$ 6407$^{12}$ 6837$^{4}$

**Toscanelli (IRE)** *A P O'Brien* 97
2 b c Galileo(IRE) Massarra (Danehill (USA))
6373a$^{5}$

**Toscanini (IRE)** *M Halford* a94 111
2 b c Shamardal(USA) Tuzla (FR) (Panoramic)
2855a$^{2}$ 3448$^{2}$ 4460a$^{2}$ 6373a$^{2}$

**Tosen Jordan (JPN)** *Yasutoshi Ikee* 116
8 b h Jungle Pocket(JPN) Every Whisper (JPN) (Northern Taste (CAN))
7981a$^{14}$

**Tostaky Blue (FR)** *Y Gourraud* a84 71
5 b g Anabaa Blue Jane Eria (IRE) (King's Best (USA))
6992a$^{2}$

**Total Demolition (IRE)** *Olly Stevens* a50 43
2 ch g Thewayyouare(USA) Margaux Dancer (IRE) (Danehill Dancer (IRE))
3728$^{8}$ 4025$^{12}$ 4787$^{9}$ 7992$^{6}$

**Totalize** *Brian Ellison* a84 98
5 b g Authorized(IRE) You Too (Monsun (GER))
2558$^{3}$ (3204) 3717$^{7}$ 5579$^{12}$

**Total Obsession** *Mark Hoad* a58 42
7 b m Mujahid(USA) Buon Amici (Pivotal)
156$^{7}$ 368$^{6}$ 484$^{7}$

**To The Sky (IRE)** *John O'Shea* a34 53
6 b g Saffron Walden(FR) Tara Tara (IRE) (Fayruz)
2830$^{7}$ 3035$^{3}$ 3208$^{9}$

**To The Victor (IRE)** *Jim Boyle*
2 b g Approve(IRE) Wonders Gift (Dr Devious (IRE))
7353$^{10}$

**Toto Skyllachy** *David O'Meara* a80 93
9 b g Kyllachy Little Tramp (Trempolino (USA))
1564$^{3}$ 2017$^{6}$ 2234$^{4}$ 3573$^{15}$ 3955$^{4}$ 4514$^{5}$ 5054$^{8}$ (6670) 7568$^{6}$ (7647) 7765$^{2}$ 7894$^{5}$ 8209$^{5}$ 8281$^{2}$

**Totxo (IRE)** *R Avial Lopez* a99 104
6 b h Diktat Mehany (FR) (Danehill (USA))
7327a$^{6}$ 7437a$^{6}$

**Touche De Rouge (IRE)** *Peter Makin* a50 28
3 b f Sholokhov(IRE) Chaguaramas (IRE) (Mujadil (USA))
378$^{8}$

**Touch Gold (IRE)** *Ernst Oertel* a98 92
5 b g Oasis Dream Seek Easy (USA) (Seeking The Gold (USA))
(239a)

**Touching Kings (FR)** *C Boutin* a48 44
9 gr g Kutub(IRE) Touchee D'Amour (GER) (Neshad (USA))
920a$^{12}$

**Touchline** *Michael Bell* 82
2 b f Exceed And Excel(AUS) Trianon (Nayef (USA))
4781$^{7}$ (5725) 6067$^{9}$

**Touch Of Honour (FR)** *J-M Capitte* a70
3 bl f Goodricke Texas Melody (GER) (Lavirco (GER))
720a$^{15}$

**Touch Of Honour (GER)** *Yasmin Almenrader* a70 76
5 bl m Sholokhov(IRE) Torbay (IRE) (Surumu (GER))
3907a$^{2}$ 5225a$^{11}$

**Touch Of Luck (FR)** *Laura Grizzetti* a32 77
5 b g Orpen(USA) Touch Of Light (IRE) (Xaar)
392a$^{6}$

**Touch The Clouds** *William Stone* a74 76
3 b g Sleeping Indian Aptina (USA) (Aptitude (USA))
1396$^{8}$ 1893$^{6}$ 2406$^{8}$ 2889$^{2}$ 3433$^{3}$ 4328$^{9}$ 4862$^{7}$ 5350$^{2}$ 5677$^{5}$ 6153$^{6}$ 6873$^{5}$ 7806$^{5}$

**Touig** *Stuart Howe*
3 ch f Tobougg(IRE) Uig (Bien Bien (USA))
5007$^{14}$ 5622$^{7}$

**Toujours L'Amour** *William Haggas* 88
2 b f Authorized(IRE) High Heel Sneakers (Dansili)
(6553) 7596$^{5}$

**Tourist (USA)** *William Mott* 111
3 bb c Tiznow(USA) Unbridled Melody (USA) (Unbridled's Song (USA))
5458a$^{2}$ 7613a$^{13}$

**Tournament** *Seamus Durack* a93 73
3 b c Oasis Dream Concentric (Sadler's Wells (USA))
(8312)

**Tout En Cardoun (FR)** *Mme P Butel* a71 53
3 b f Layman(USA) Bairgaine (FR) (Cardoun (FR))
237a$^{12}$ 545a$^{6}$

**Tout En Style (FR)** *T Lemer* a91 85
3 gr c Desert Style(IRE) Tengeline (FR) (Cardoun (FR))
5482a$^{2}$

**Tout Va Bien (IRE)** *Yves de Nicolay* a73 79
3 gr f Verglas(IRE) Gold Again (USA) (Touch Gold (USA))
7270a$^{2}$

**Touzr** *Richard Hannon* a71 64
3 b c Invincible Spirit(IRE) Carrig Girl (Nayef (USA))
605$^{2}$ 1677$^{6}$ 2278$^{10}$

**Towbee** *Michael Easterby* a78 85
5 b g Doyen(IRE) Bow Bridge (Bertolini (USA))
1538$^{9}$ 1961$^{7}$ 2332$^{17}$ 2637$^{2}$

**Tower Power** *Ismail Mohammed* a63 84
3 b c Nayef(USA) Voile (IRE) (Barathea (IRE))
50$^{3}$ 2433$^{2}$ (2867) 4058$^{14}$ (4574) 5420$^{7}$ 6166$^{13}$

**Town Council (IRE)** *Richard Fahey* 63
2 gr g Mastercraftsman(IRE) Catch The Blues (IRE) (Bluebird (USA))
5881$^{7}$ 6743$^{4}$

**Town Crier (IRE)** *William Haggas* 78
2 b c Acclamation Miss Dela (IRE) (King's Best (USA))
2151$^{5}$ 2380$^{2}$ 3324$^{4}$ 3847$^{7}$

**Toxic (SPA)** *C Boutin* a40
3 ch c Sakhee(USA) Fear To Tread (USA) (Peintre Celebre (USA))
751a$^{9}$

**Toydini (AUS)** *Guy Walter* 112
5 b g Bernardini(USA) Johan's Toy (AUS) (Johan Cruyff)
1186a$^{5}$

**Toymaker** *Phil McEntee* a82 62
7 b g Starcraft(NZ) Eurolink Raindance (IRE) (Alzao (USA))
286$^{10}$ (539) 674$^{6}$ 820$^{8}$ 917$^{9}$ 1152$^{5}$ 1665$^{8}$ 2079$^{5}$ 5729$^{4}$ 6240$^{9}$ 7012$^{8}$ 7765$^{6}$ 7925$^{7}$

**Toytown (IRE)** *Derek Shaw* a53 54
2 b g Excellent Art Teddy Bears Picnic (Oasis Dream)
1161$^{12}$ 1363$^{4}$ 2328$^{5}$ 3201$^{6}$ 3937$^{7}$ 4576$^{7}$ 6413$^{11}$ 6645$^{7}$

**Tracks Of My Tears** *Giles Bravery* a67 65
4 b f Rail Link Policy Setter (USA) (Deputy Minister (CAN))
1265$^{2}$ 1426$^{4}$ 2628$^{3}$ 3803$^{8}$ 4582$^{5}$

**Trader Jack** *David Flood* a83 89
5 b g Trade Fair Azeema (IRE) (Averti (IRE))
80$^{5}$ 1672$^{10}$ 2030$^{3}$ 2110$^{7}$ 2147$^{2}$ 2336$^{6}$ 2562$^{5}$ 3244$^{12}$ 3697$^{7}$ 3927$^{4}$ 3981$^{10}$ 4146$^{2}$ 4438$^{11}$ 5433$^{9}$ 6313$^{9}$ 8251$^{13}$ 8320$^{8}$

**Trade Secret** *Mel Brittain* a69 86
7 b g Trade Fair Kastaway (Distant Relative)
1190$^{3}$ (1447) 1672$^{4}$ 1957$^{5}$ 2332$^{12}$ 3256$^{13}$ 4632$^{14}$ 5197$^{P}$

**Trade Storm** *David Simcock* a98 118
6 bb h Trade Fair Frisson (Slip Anchor)
397a$^{10}$ 772a$^{2}$ 902a$^{4}$ 1181a$^{12}$ 4425$^{2}$ 5690$^{2}$ (6391a) 7613a$^{3}$ 8153a$^{7}$

**Trading Leather (IRE)** *J S Bolger* 116
4 b c Teofilo(IRE) Night Visit (Sinndar (IRE))
1950$^{3}$ 3984$^{2}$ 4649$^{5}$ 6353a$^{3}$ 7981a$^{P}$ (Dead)

**Traditional Chic (IRE)** *L Riccardi* 95
6 ch h Ad Valorem(USA) Minimal Chic (IRE) (King's Best (USA))
7725a$^{5}$

**Traditionelle** *Tim Easterby* a73 63
3 b f Indesatchel(IRE) Mookhlesa (Marju (IRE))
1441$^{4}$ ◆ 2397$^{5}$ 2802$^{5}$ 3650$^{2}$ 4019$^{2}$ 4891$^{5}$ 5087$^{4}$ 5641$^{5}$ (6340) 6671$^{17}$ 7286$^{12}$

**Trafalgar Rock** *Mark Johnston* a69 69
3 b g Mount Nelson Helter Helter (USA) (Seeking The Gold (USA))
607$^{6}$ 734$^{4}$ 871$^{2}$ 1011$^{3}$ 1391$^{6}$ 2132$^{2}$

**Trail Blaze (IRE)** *Kevin Ryan* 102
5 b g Tagula(IRE) Kingpin Delight (Emarati (USA))
1078a$^{14}$ (1733) 1958$^{14}$ 2362$^{7}$ 2959$^{9}$ 3456$^{3}$ 4212$^{14}$ 4922$^{13}$ 5174$^{11}$ 6097$^{8}$ 6476$^{6}$ 7236$^{11}$

**Tram Express (FR)** *Shaun Lycett* a36 23
10 ch g Trempolino(USA) Molly Dance (FR) (Groom Dancer (USA))
6900$^{9}$ 7990$^{12}$

**Tranquil Glen** *Michael Appleby* a46
2 b f Moss Vale(IRE) Glen Molly (IRE) (Danetime (IRE))
7741$^{10}$ 7970$^{8}$

**Transfer** *Richard Price* a69 56
9 br g Trans Island Sankaty Light (USA) (Summer Squall (USA))
1605$^{12}$

**Transluscent (IRE)** *Sue Gardner*
4 b g Trans Island Little Miss Diva (IRE) (Diktat)
4718a$^{8}$

**Transparent (USA)** *Saeed bin Suroor* a102 102
4 bb r Bernardini(USA) Habiboo (USA) (Unbridled's Song (USA))
108a$^{4}$

**Travel (USA)** *Mark Johnston* a83 60
4 ch f Street Cry(IRE) Away (USA) (Dixieland Band (USA))
648$^{3}$ 822$^{8}$ (1046) 1150$^{2}$ (1265) (1501) (1629) 1692$^{9}$ 2139$^{9}$ 2515$^{7}$ 2920$^{4}$

**Travel Brand** *C H Yip* 94
6 b g Beat Hollow Jumeela (Rainbow Quest (USA))
7899a$^{12}$

**Travelling** *Tony Carroll* a81 57
5 b m Dubai Destination(USA) Attune (Singspiel (IRE))
79$^{2}$ ◆ 250$^{6}$ 655$^{4}$

**Travis Bickle (IRE)** *John Flint* a54 62
3 b g Sky Mesa(USA) Out Of Woods (USA) (Woodman (USA))
731$^{6}$ 2492$^{4}$ 2948$^{2}$ 3224$^{3}$ 7162$^{8}$ 7754$^{3}$ 7982$^{9}$

**Travis County (IRE)** *Brian Ellison* a42 48
5 b g Jeremy(USA) Manchaca (FR) (Highest Honor (FR))
2327$^{18}$ 2790$^{11}$ 3365$^{6}$ 3623$^{12}$

**Treadwell (IRE)** *Jamie Osborne* a73 84
7 b h Footstepsinthesand Lady Wells (IRE) (Sadler's Wells (USA))
451$^{8}$ 757$^{5}$

**Treasure Cay (IRE)** *Paul Cole* a75 31
3 ch g Bahamian Bounty Expedience (USA) (With Approval (CAN))
169a$^{4}$ 579$^{2}$

**Treasure The Ridge (IRE)** *Andrew Reid* a85 96
5 b g Galileo(IRE) Treasure The Lady (IRE) (Indian Ridge)
655$^{11}$ 856$^{5}$ 1355$^{8}$ 1941$^{7}$ 4273$^{7}$ (4433) (4616) (5035) (5928) 6532$^{5}$ 6930$^{4}$ 7718$^{18}$

**Treasury Bond** *Oliver Sherwood* 41
7 ch g Monsieur Bond(IRE) Rainbow Treasure (IRE) (Rainbow Quest (USA))
3155$^{6}$ 4107$^{10}$

**Treaty Of York (IRE)** *Henry Candy* a64 57
2 b g Haatef(USA) Pretty Woman (IRE) (Night Shift (USA))
5684$^{7}$ 6038$^{6}$ 6702$^{8}$ 7112$^{3}$ 7683$^{3}$

**Tree Of Grace (FR)** *Richard Hannon* a83 67
3 ch g Gold Away(IRE) Three Times (SWE) (Domynsky)
1122$^{3}$ 1352$^{7}$ 3137$^{6}$

**Trefnant (IRE)** *Chris Dwyer* a46 24
3 ch f Bahamian Bounty Miss Trish (IRE) (Danetime (IRE))
477$^{7}$ 745$^{7}$ 933$^{7}$ 1277$^{5}$ 1626$^{5}$ 1855$^{2}$

**Tregereth (IRE)** *Jonathan Portman* a60 65
4 b f Footstepsinthesand Ringmoor Down (Pivotal)
2775$^{11}$ 3734$^{6}$ 3966$^{6}$ 4431$^{7}$ 5355$^{5}$ 6023$^{2}$

**Trending (IRE)** *Jeremy Gask* a72 40
5 gr g Dark Angel(IRE) Call Later (USA) (Gone West (USA))
1238$^{8}$ 1787$^{9}$ 2648$^{6}$ 3150$^{11}$ 4151$^{6}$ 4567$^{11}$ 8023$^{7}$ 8285$^{2}$

**Trendsetter (IRE)** *John Butler* 80
3 b g Mastercraftsman(IRE) Fashion Trade (Dansili)
6092$^{8}$ 6738$^{7}$ 6981$^{2}$ ◆ (7500)

**Tres Blue (IRE)** *Gai Waterhouse* a72 117
4 b c Anabaa Blue Tres Ravi (GER) (Monsun (GER))
1186a$^{13}$

**Tres Coronas (IRE)** *David Barron* a95 108
7 b g Key Of Luck(USA) Almansa (IRE) (Dr Devious (IRE))
887$^{9}$ 1165$^{8}$ 1653$^{5}$ (2085) 2253$^{2}$ 2957$^{9}$ 5174$^{10}$ 5928$^{9}$

**Tres Forte (FR)** *M Delzangles* a78 94
2 b f Whipper(USA) Trissa (FR) (Anabaa (USA))
7654a$^{5}$

**Tres Rock Danon (FR)** *Gerald Geisler* 99
8 b h Rock Of Gibraltar(IRE) Tres Ravi (GER) (Monsun (GER))
2229a$^{4}$ 4722a$^{7}$ 6917a$^{6}$

**Tres Solid (FR)** *N Caullery* a72 84
3 b c Honours List(IRE) Tres Passing (FR) (Medaaly)
5368a$^{5}$

**Treve (FR)** *Mme C Head-Maarek* 131
4 b f Motivator Trevise (FR) (Anabaa (USA))
1783a$^{2}$ 3354$^{3}$ 6380a$^{4}$ (6970a)

**Tribal Diamond** *Edward Creighton* a28 20
2 b f Kheleyf(USA) Black Tribal (IRE) (Mukaddamah (USA))
3232$^{10}$ 3889$^{8}$ 4542$^{7}$

**Tribulina** *Marco Botti* a60 42
3 b f Dansili Wickwing (In The Wings)
2279$^{11}$ 3857$^{8}$ 4966$^{6}$ 6037$^{11}$

**Trigger Flash (FR)** *N Caullery* a52 72
3 b f Librettist(USA) Trigger Shot (IRE) (High Chaparral (IRE))
5368a$^{12}$ 7270a$^{8}$

**Trigger Park (IRE)** *Ronald Harris* a50 61
3 ch g Tagula(IRE) Raazi (My Generation)
173$^{9}$ 2668$^{3}$ 3178$^{4}$ 3849$^{4}$ 4733$^{8}$ 5530$^{8}$ 6088$^{5}$ 6995$^{5}$

**Triggers Broom (IRE)** *Richard Fahey* 36
2 ch f Arcano(IRE) Great Joy (IRE) (Grand Lodge (USA))
2231$^{9}$ 2895$^{5}$ 3569$^{5}$ 4899$^{3}$ 6830$^{9}$

**Trikala (IRE)** *Marco Botti* a63 77
3 b f High Chaparral(IRE) Thiella (USA) (Kingmambo (USA))
2929$^{8}$ 3614$^{4}$ 4092$^{7}$

**Trikasana** *Clive Cox* a59
2 ch f Leporello(IRE) Baileys Honour (Mark Of Esteem (IRE))
8247$^{3}$

**Trillian Astra (IRE)** *Clive Cox* a65 63
3 b f Bahamian Bounty Ms Sophie Eleanor (USA) (Grand Slam (USA))
2470$^{4}$ 2886$^{3}$ 3178$^{3}$ 3588$^{5}$

**Trimoulet** *Daniel Kubler* 68
5 b g Teofilo(IRE) Riberac (Efisio)
3925[8] 4393[5]

**Tri Nations (UAE)** *Brian Ellison* a22 42
9 ch g Halling(USA) Six Nations (USA) (Danzig (USA))
4293[11]

**Trinityelitedotcom (IRE)** *Tom Dascombe* a109 99
4 b g Elusive City(USA) Beal Ban (IRE) (Daggers Drawn (USA))
148[2] (234) 348[2] (1172) 1557[2] ◆ 2076[3] 3452[24]

**Trinity Lorraine (IRE)** *Alan Bailey* a48 45
3 b f Dark Angel(IRE) Known Class (USA) (Known Fact (USA))
6[4] 261[3] 411[5] 960[6] 2209[3] 2695[9] 2878[10] 4304[12]

**Trinity Star (IRE)** *Michael Dods* 82
3 gr g Kheleyf(USA) Zamiyla (IRE) (Daylami (IRE))
1648[5] 1906[2] (2393) 3135[6] 3303[3] 4292[2] ◆ 5387[4] 5717[4] (6516) (6647)

**Triple Aitch (USA)** *Conrad Allen* a67 58
4 b g Harlan's Holiday(USA) Hadley (USA) (Kingmambo (USA))
384[7] 963[3] 1282[3] 1766[9]

**Triple Chief (IRE)** *Rod Millman* a74 79
3 bb g High Chaparral(IRE) Trebles (IRE) (Kenmare (FR))
1433[13] 1681[2] 2681[10] 3243[8] 4208[5] 4743[3] 5302[5] 5884[8]

**Triple Chocolate** *Roger Ingram* a77 91
4 b g Danehill Dancer(IRE) Enticing (IRE) (Pivotal)
655[8] 843[6] 2147[4] 2629[4] 2849[8] (4983) (5650) (6095) ◆ 6872[4]

**Triple Dip (IRE)** *Mark Johnston* 70
2 ch f Three Valleys(USA) Melpomene (Peintre Celebre (USA))
6224[4] 6735[7] 7209[2] 7595[2]

**Triple Dream** *Milton Bradley* a88 72
9 ch g Vision Of Night Triple Joy (Most Welcome)
(444) 719[6] 1145[5] 1490[8] 3470[8] 4267[8] 7886[6] 8025[6] 8171[5]

**Triple Eight (IRE)** *Philip Kirby* a75 73
6 b g Royal Applause Hidden Charm (IRE) (Big Shuffle (USA))
1167[8] 2872[7] 3301[4] 3958[5] 5371[4] 5856[U] 6542[2] 6597[8] 7822[7]

**Triple O Seven (IRE)** *John Best* a39 19
3 b g Kodiac Triple Zero (IRE) (Raise A Grand (IRE))
1634[10] 3228[9] 6242[10]

**Triple Star** *Hughie Morrison* a63 58
3 b f Royal Applause Triple Sharp (Selkirk (USA))
1920[8] 2690[8] 3184[5] 3890[8] 5136[6] 6022[10] 7115[3] 7517[9] (7869) 8049[2] 8246[9]

**Triple Threat (FR)** *A Fabre* 115
4 b c Monsun(GER) Drei (USA) (Lyphard (USA))
1341a[3] 1783a[7] 4437[7]

**Trip To Paris (IRE)** *Ed Dunlop* a76 94
3 b g Champs Elysees La Grande Zoa (IRE) (Fantastic Light (USA))
1652[7] 3003[10] 3379[6] (4651) ◆ 5164[10] 6127[14] 6438[4]

**Trip To Rhodos (FR)** *Pavel Tuma* 108
5 b g Rail Link Tropical Mark (Mark Of Esteem (IRE))
4722a[2] 6383a[5] 6972a[6]

**Triptyka (IRE)** *J-M Beguigne* 88
3 bb f Mastercraftsman(IRE) Acatama (USA) (Efisio)
(7164a)

**Tristram's Sun (NZ)** *Robbie Laing* 93
6 b g Yamanin Vital(NZ) Second Edition (AUS) (Desert Sun)
7128a[13]

**Triumphant (IRE)** *Gary Moore* 103
5 b g Danehill Dancer(IRE) Meek Appeal (USA) (Woodman (USA))
5432[11] 6005[3]

**Trixie Malone** *K R Burke* 82
4 b f Ishiguru(USA) Lady-Love (Pursuit Of Love)
(1310) (1716) (2032) 2608[2] 7060[5] 7489[5]

**Trixy** *Jo Hughes* 4
2 b f Indesatchel(IRE) Emmone (First Trump)
2944[13] 3933[13] 7412[10]

**Trojan Rocket (IRE)** *Michael Wigham* a97 76
6 b g Elusive City(USA) Tagula Bay (IRE) (Tagula (IRE))
153[4] 257[3] (381) (658) 890[2] 991[4] 6159[11] 6531[20] 7600[6] (7847) (8141)

**Tropaios** *M Freedman* a80 99
5 ch g Excellent Art Light Quest (USA) (Quest For Fame)
2379a[11]

**Tropenfeuer (FR)** *Dianne Sayer* a68 53
7 b m Banyumanik(IRE) Tropensonne (GER) (Konigsstuhl (GER))
3051[2] 3101[4]

**Tropical Bachelor (IRE)** *Brian Baugh* a53 63
8 b g Bachelor Duke(USA) Tropical Coral (IRE) (Pennekamp (USA))
2872[5] (3398) 5371[5]

**Tropical Beat** *David O'Meara* a95 103
6 b g Beat Hollow Tropical Heights (FR) (Shirley Heights)
2342[3] 3717[14]

**Tropicana Bay** *Roger Varian* a67 77
2 b f Oasis Dream Ballet Ballon (USA) (Rahy (USA))
5305[4] 6093[2] 6735[3]

**Tropics (USA)** *Dean Ivory* a88 117
6 ch g Speightstown(USA) Taj Aire (USA) (Taj Alriyadh (USA))
1163[7] 1531[5] 2256[13] 3451[9] 4201[2] (5674) 6134[14] 6920[4] 7272[2] 7716[5]

**Troy Boy** *Robin Bastiman* a51 53
4 b g Choisir(AUS) Love Thing (Phountzi (USA))
321[7] 672[4] 783[2] 869[7] 1050[5] 1891[6] 2475[2] 2875[5] 4000[3] 5084[5] 5765[8]

**Truancy (IRE)** *K R Burke* a72 93
3 b g Intense Focus(USA) Date Mate (USA) (Thorn Dance (USA))
143[3] 375[2] 604[3] 2391[3] 2867[4] (3268) (4120) (5015) (5914)

**Trucanini** *Chris Wall* a92 84
4 b f Mount Nelson Jalissa (Mister Baileys)
1492[16] 3122[10] 4053[5] 5826[5] 6144[10]

**True Course** *Charlie Appleby* a69 57
2 b f Dubawi(IRE) Sugar Free (IRE) (Oasis Dream)
2306[7] 2979[7] 3583[6] 5985[4] 7190[2] 7728[5] (7948) (8118)

**True Pleasure (IRE)** *James Bethell* a72 86
7 b m Choisir(AUS) Absolute Pleasure (Polar Falcon (USA))
697[2] 853[2] (2454) (2954) 3202[13] 4514[2] 5054[6] 5887[7] 6836[5] 7282[11] 7634[7]

**True Respect (IRE)** *Saeed bin Suroor* 69
2 b c Shamardal(USA) Deveron (USA) (Cozzene (USA))
7407[4]

**True Spirit** *Paul D'Arcy* a62 51
4 b g Shamardal(USA) Petonellajill (Petong)
(219) 467[9] 2844[4] 4732[2] 5103[5] 5729[7] 7036[8] 7548[5] 8111[7]

**True Story** *Saeed bin Suroor* 114
3 bb g Manduro(GER) Tanzania (USA) (Darshaan)
(1516) ◆ 2285[3] 2990[7] 3984[5] 5175[3] 5687[2]

**True That (IRE)** *Brian Ellison* a34 29
4 b g Captain Marvelous(IRE) Bratislava (Dr Fong (USA))
353[9] 502[9]

**True To Form (IRE)** *Alan McCabe* a103 83
7 b g Rock Of Gibraltar(IRE) Truly Yours (IRE) (Barathea (IRE))
145[6] 235[4] 426[8] (804) 1070[P]

**Trulee Scrumptious** *Peter Charalambous* a53 75
5 b m Strategic Prince Morning Rise (GER) (Acatenango (GER))
(2750) 3325[2] 3675[4] 3878[5] (5394) 5503[7] 6616[8]

**Truly Delightful (IRE)** *Thomas Cleary* a53 73
4 b f Kalanisi(IRE) Almost Twilight (USA) (Silver Hawk (USA))
4805a[4]

**Trumpet Major (IRE)** *Richard Hannon* a95 117
5 b h Arakan(USA) Ashford Cross (Cape Cross (IRE))
1170[5] 1948[4] 3356[28] 4180[8]

**Trust In A Gust (AUS)** *Darren Weir* 113
4 ch c Keep The Faith(AUS) Subtle Breeze (USA) (Storm Cat (USA))
(7128a)

**Trust Me Boy** *John E Long* a54 46
6 gr g Avonbridge Eastern Lyric (Petong)
3230[5] 5425[10] 7221[4] 7645[3] 8084[2]

**Trust The Captain (FR)** *Robert Collet* a68 62
2 b f Great Journey(JPN) Loralas (FR) (Kahyasi)
5619a[10] 5901a[3] 6698a[6] 7027a[6]

**Trust The Wind** *John Gosden* a73
3 b f Dansili Hypnology (USA) (Gone West (USA))
645[3] (800)

**Truth Or Dare** *Richard Hannon* 104
3 b g Invincible Spirit(IRE) Unreachable Star (Halling (USA))
1516[3] 1699[6] 2345[3] 3379[11] 3930[5] 6257[11] 7110[2]

**Tryster (IRE)** *Charlie Appleby* 92
3 b g Shamardal(USA) Min Alhawa (USA) (Riverman (USA))
3432[3] (3822) ◆ 4667[4]

**Try With Me (IRE)** *Mario Hofer* 63
2 ch f Nayef(USA) Three French Hens (IRE) (Elnadim (USA))
5293a[11]

**Tsarglas** *Stuart Williams* a56 39
3 gr g Verglas(IRE) Russian Empress (IRE) (Trans Island)
5044[8] 5504[12] 5862[7] 6939[3] 7546[8] (8199)

**Tubeanie (IRE)** *Amy Weaver* 64
3 ch f Intense Focus(USA) Ryalahna (IRE) (High Chaparral (IRE))
1725[5] 2224[8] 2860[2] 3087[4] 3518[6] 5105[5] 5729[2] 6397[9] 7025[12]

**Tucano (IRE)** *N Clement* a71 67
3 b c Monsun(GER) Tenderly (IRE) (Danehill (USA))
2290a[2] 8005a[4]

**Tucci (ITY)** *M Guarnieri* 85
3 b f Azamour(IRE) Terynka (GER) (Exit To Nowhere (USA))
1780a[13]

**Tuco (IRE)** *Jamie Osborne* a66
2 ch g Exceed And Excel(AUS) Life Rely (USA) (Maria's Mon (USA))
6603[3]

**Tucson Arizona** *Anthony Carson* a77 79
3 b g High Chaparral(IRE) Kasakiya (IRE) (Zafonic (USA))
2685[6] 4402[3] 5884[4] ◆ 6608[6] 7172[4] 7531[5]

**Tuddenham (USA)** *Anthony Carson* a38 56
3 bb g Latent Heat(USA) Storming On (USA) (Storm Cat (USA))
3477[3]

**Tuebrook** *Michael Easterby* a41 46
2 b g Misu Bond(IRE) Waterpark (Namaqualand (USA))
1889[5] 4389[10] 5194[4] 5507[3] 7245[11]

**Tuibama (IRE)** *Tracy Waggott* a45 66
5 ch g Bertolini(USA) Supportive (IRE) (Nashamaa)
1378[8] 1643[11] 2743[4] 3338[7] 3913[13] 4314[2] 4664[5] 5683[9]

**Tukitinyasok (IRE)** *Clive Mulhall* a58 63
7 b g Fath(USA) Mevlana (IRE) (Red Sunset)
263[4] 671[2] 1718[6] 3095[2] 3949[2] 4468[8] 5300[5] 7868[9] 8258[6]

**Tullia (IRE)** *William Knight* a77 84
3 b f Footstepsinthesand Whipped Queen (USA) (Kingmambo (USA))
1913[2] 2504[3] 3476[6] 4271[12] 5004[2] 5394[5] 6722[7] (7160) 7417[2] ◆

**Tullius (IRE)** *Andrew Balding* a90 121
6 ch g Le Vie Dei Colori Whipped Queen (USA) (Kingmambo (USA))
1165[2] (1698) 2338[2] 3317[4] 6710[4] 7274[4]

**Tumbledown (USA)** *Ed Walker* a63 30
4 b f Bernardini(USA) Freeroll (USA) (Touch Gold (USA))
359[5]

**Tumblewind** *Richard Whitaker* 95
4 ch f Captain Rio African Breeze (Atraf)
1506[8] 1961[5] (2350) 2786[11] 3239[11] 3788[4] 5888[15] 6692[5]

**Tumut (IRE)** *Mick Channon* a61 63
2 b c Acclamation Pampas (USA) (Distant View (USA))
3748[6] 4044[6] 4353[5] 6250[11] 6662[9] 6676[2] 6996[4] 7257[9] 7421[2]

**Tundridge** *John Spearing*
5 b g Authorized(IRE) Salanka (IRE) (Persian Heights)
8167[5]

**Tunkwa (FR)** *D Sepulchre* 106
4 b f Gold Away(IRE) Tigresse Africaine (FR) (Tiger Hill (IRE))
2106a[7]

**Tunnel Creek** *Henry Candy* 61
2 b g Tobougg(IRE) Free Offer (Generous (IRE))
6702[5] ◆

**Tunnel Tiger (IRE)** *William Knight* a61 66
3 b f Dylan Thomas(IRE) Nakiska (Darshaan)
1684[2] 2210[6] 2416[6] 3037[5] 3814[5] 4340[3] 4592[2] 5529[5] 5949[3] 6193[3] 6395[2] 6817[5] 7290[7]

**Tupi (IRE)** *Richard Hannon* 102
2 b c Tamayuz Carioca (IRE) (Rakti)
(3194) 4780[2] 5478a[2] 5876[5] 7442[7]

**Turbulent Priest** *Zoe Davison* a49 52
6 b g Storming Home Hymn Book (IRE) (Darshaan)
1874[2] 2396[11] 2836[11] 2923[6] 3309[6] 3552[5]

**Turfmaid (GER)** *J Hirschberger* a83 95
3 ch f Call Me Big(GER) Turfblume (GER) (Lando (GER))
1619a[4] 2584a[8]

**Turjuman (USA)** *Simon West* a28 51
9 ch g Swain(IRE) Hachiyah (IRE) (Generous (IRE))
2424[9] 3482[12] 3843[9]

**Turmalina (GER)** *J Hirschberger* 93
3 b f Doyen(IRE) Trinidad (GER) (Big Shuffle (USA))
3046a[6] 4064a[6]

**Turnbuckle** *Mark Johnston* a86
4 ch c Teofilo(IRE) Forest Pearl (USA) (Woodman (USA))
(649) (Dead)

**Turnbury** *Robert Mills* a68 66
3 b g Azamour(IRE) Scottish Heights (IRE) (Selkirk (USA))
607[3] 761[3] 828[5] 1947[6] 6002[3] 6337[9] 7012[6] 7218[2] 7517[2] 7805[2] 7907[7] 8309[6]

**Turning Times (IRE)** *Charlie Appleby* a76 73
2 ro f Pivotal Antiquities (Kaldounevees (FR))
2979[2] 5037[2] (5827)

**Turtle Beach (FR)** *M Pimbonnet* 39
2 b f Turtle Bowl(IRE) La Minardiere (FR) (Verglas (IRE))
6698a[9]

**Turtle Boson (IRE)** *G Martin* a47
3 b c Turtle Bowl(IRE) Nobilissime (Halling (USA))
360a[13] 545a[9]

**Tuscany (GER)** *P Schiergen* 87
2 gr f Kandahar Run Tuiga (IRE) (Rakti)
6778a[6] 7481a[6]

**Tutti Frutti** *John Gosden* 70
2 b f Teofilo(IRE) Soft Centre (Zafonic (USA))
7019[2]

**Tuxedo** *Peter Hiatt* a36
9 ch g Cadeaux Genereux Serengeti Bride (USA) (Lion Cavern (USA))
116[10] 759[P]

**Tweedswood (IRE)** *Roger Varian* a46
3 ch g New Approach(IRE) Rafting (IRE) (Darshaan)
6611[5] 7195[8]

**Tweety Pie (IRE)** *Declan Carroll* a40 74
3 ch f Rock Of Gibraltar(IRE) Princesse Sonia (FR) (Ashkalani (IRE))
2015[9] 2657[7] 3487[3] 4019[9] 4469[4] 4636[2] 4891[8] 6452[2] 6873[10] 7575[12]

**Twelve Strings (IRE)** *Brian Ellison* a61 88
5 b g Iffraaj Favoritely (USA) (Favorite Trick (USA))
1599[9] 1935[5]

**Twenty One Choice (IRE)** *Ed de Giles* a90 83
5 ch g Choisir(AUS) Midnight Lace (Tomba)
2462[7] 3036[7] 3737a[15] 4712[5] 6144[6] 7035[6]

**Twenty Roses (IRE)** *Ed Walker* a59 49
3 b f Mastercraftsman(IRE) Stunning Rose (IRE) (Sadler's Wells (USA))
1847[7] 3054[10]

**Twice Certain (IRE)** *Ed Walker* a71 53
2 b f Lawman(FR) Leopard Hunt (USA) (Diesis)
6641[6] 7018[11] 7198[2] (7625)

**Twilight Angel** *Pat Eddery* a52 50
6 ch m Compton Place Leaping Flame (USA) (Trempolino (USA))
94[5] 2946[4] 4733[11] 8200[9]

**Twilight Eclipse (USA)** *Thomas Albertrani* a110 117
5 b g Purim(USA) My Twilight Dancer (USA) (Twilight Agenda (USA))
1182a[12] 4010a[2] 7611a[3]

**Twilight Son** *Henry Candy* 86
2 b c Kyllachy Twilight Mistress (Bin Ajwaad (IRE))
(5309) ◆ (6427) ◆

**Twin Appeal (IRE)** *David Barron* a56 89
3 b g Oratorio(IRE) Velvet Appeal (IRE) (Petorius)
1542[5] 2204[2] (2517) 3002[3] (3625) (5441)

**Twinkle Twinkle** *Julie Camacho* a47 27
2 b f Exceed And Excel(AUS) Kalinova (IRE) (Red Ransom (USA))
6115[12] 7361[7]

**Twin Mix (FR)** *Y Gourraud* 43
2 gr c Al Namix(FR) Mahfadha (Erhaab (USA))
1271a[10]

**Twin Point** *John Gosden* a79 83
3 br g Invincible Spirit(IRE) Gemini Joan (Montjeu (IRE))
1296[2] 1612[4] (3198) ◆ 3672[4]

**Twin Turbo (IRE)** *Mark Johnston* 72
2 b g Dark Angel(IRE) Scarlet O'Hara (IRE) (Sadler's Wells (USA))
2601[8] 3181[3] 3569[3] 5335[5] 5762[6]

**Twist And Twirl** *Derek Shaw* a52
4 b f Cockney Rebel(IRE) Silent Miracle (IRE) (Night Shift (USA))
274[7]

**Twitch (IRE)** *Hugo Palmer* 66
2 b f Azamour(IRE) Blinking (Marju (IRE))
6754[4] 7108[9]

**Two B'S** *Tim Easterby* 62
3 b g Bollin Eric Bollin Nellie (Rock Hopper)
1608[7] 1959[8] 2170[4] 4979[7] 5682[4] 6117[8]

**Two Days In Paris (FR)** *Stuart Williams* a79 96
5 b m Authorized(IRE) Isalou (FR) (Unfuwain (USA))
285[4] 716[10]

**Two For Two (IRE)** *David O'Meara* 106
6 b g Danehill Dancer(IRE) D'Articleshore (IRE) (Definite Article)
1948[13] 2362[4] 2891[3] (3456) 4214[16] 4851[9] 5163[8] 5609[16] 6534[3]

**Two In The Pink (IRE)** *Ralph J Smith* a68 51
4 b f Clodovil(IRE) Secret Circle (Magic Ring (IRE))
53[8] 219[2] 367[5] 718[3] 819[3] 952[4] 1123[2] 2775[8] 3390[2] 4072[3] 5006[2] 5284[3] 5560[3] 6242[9] 6636[2]

**Two Jabs** *Mark Brisbourne* a81 71
4 b g Teofilo(IRE) Red Bravo (USA) (Red Ransom (USA))
5606[4] 6092[6] 6344[3] (6901) 7422[5]

**Twombly (SPA)** *C Boutin* a79 44
3 b c Pyrus(USA) Topita (IRE) (Daggers Drawn (USA))
193a[4] 3372a[13]

**Two Moons** *Brian Ellison* a84 73
4 b g Echo Of Light Forever Loved (Deploy)
861[2] (930) 1483[7] (2905) 3402[5] 7821[6]

**Two No Bids (IRE)** *Phil McEntee* a85 64
4 bb g Footstepsinthesand Milwaukee (FR) (Desert King (IRE))
11[9] 1864[6] 2527[4] 3160[9] 3427[14]

**Two Pancakes** *Declan Carroll* 55
4 b g Compton Place Fancy Rose (USA) (Joyeux Danseur (USA))
4111[7] 4925[11] 6766[7] 7078[12]

**Two Shades Of Grey (IRE)** *Richard Fahey* a73 60
3 gr g Oratorio(IRE) Elitista (FR) (Linamix (FR))
(1543) 1940[6] 2429[6] 3405[3] 3625[7] 5205[3] 5437[8] 7502[8] 7906[6] 8086[2] 8218[2]

**Two Smart (IRE)** *Daniel Kubler* a68 79
3 b f Cape Cross(IRE) Smartest (IRE) (Exceed And Excel (AUS))
1361[2] 2257[14] 2768[8] 5055[2] 5814[2] 5997[3] 6492[5] 6638[4] 7818[3] 7929[2] 8008[3]

**Two Sugars** *Edward Creighton* a40 12
6 b g Val Royal(FR) Princess Galadriel (Magic Ring (IRE))
1874[11] 3526[8]

**Two Turns** *Lydia Pearce* a41
3 bl f Lucky Story(USA) Scisciabubu (IRE) (Danehill (USA))
7699[5] 7800[P]

**Two Turtle Doves (IRE)** *Michael Mullineaux* a53 67
8 b m Night Shift(USA) Purple Rain (IRE) (Celtic Swing)
258[12] 466[10] 1001[8] 1378[4] 1972[9] 2831[7] 3612[4] 4005[4] 4288[4] 4567[4] 4960[5] ◆ (5130) (5290) 5499[10] (5724) 6455[8] 6819[8] 7671[9] 8229[5] 8284[7]

**Tychaios** *Stuart Williams* a73 71
4 b g Green Desert(USA) Tychy (Suave Dancer (USA))
(3323) 3887[7] 4406[4] 4768[2] 5880[3] (6266) 7758[3] 7989[2] 8040[6]

**Ty Cobb (IRE)** *John Quinn* 55
3 b g Dandy Man(IRE) Mrs Moonlight (Ajdal (USA))
2619[3] 3600[4] 4019[10] 4455[3] 4998[6]

**Tyfos** *Brian Baugh* a80 86
9 b g Bertolini(USA) Warminghamsharpish (Nalchik (USA))
479[6] 820[6] 909[13] 1431[2] 1643[3] 2434[3] (3612) 3887[2] 4391[5] 5498[5] 6096[15] (6324) 6650[3]

**Ty Gwr** *Brian Ellison* a92 94
5 b g Echo Of Light House Maiden (IRE) (Rudimentary (USA))
5895[8] 6523[8] 6713[5] 7211[2] (7335) 7641[3] 7971[5]

**Tylery Wonder (IRE)** *W McCreery* a75 92
4 ch g Choisir(AUS) Over The Tylery (IRE) (Swallow Flight (IRE))
3686a[3] 6369a[11] 7140a[9]

**Typhoon Season** *Richard Hannon* a68 77
2 b c Kyllachy Alovera (IRE) (King's Best (USA))
4167[5] (4740) 6853[4]

**Tyrsal (IRE)** *Robert Eddery* a67 71
3 b g Jeremy(USA) Blanchelande (IRE) (Subotica (FR))
1400[4] 1794[2] 2163[6] (3627) 4263[6] 4766[5] 6337[10]

**Ty Ty** *Michael Easterby* 60
2 ch g Monsieur Bond(IRE) Royal Distant (USA) (Distant View (USA))
4510[7] 5493[5] 7245[8]

**Tzharr (IRE)** *Marco Botti* 59
3 gr c Teofilo(IRE) Netrebko (IRE) (Linamix (FR))
1394[8]

**Tzora** *Martin Hill* a92 50
9 b g Sakhee(USA) Lucky Arrow (Indian Ridge)
1213[8]

**Ubedizzy (IRE)** *Noel Wilson* 3
2 b c Captain Rio Karenka (IRE) (Arakan (USA))
2615[10] 3570[9] 4624[9]

**Ubetterbegood (ARG)** *Robert Cowell* a94 94
6 b g Distorted Humor(USA) Movie Star (BRZ) (Royal Academy (USA))
644[4] 802[2] 1489[11] 1742[9] 2446[4] 3246[4] 3749[7] 4833[4] 5535[3] 6650[4]

**Ucandri (IRE)** *C Ferland* a68 89
7 ch g Refuse To Bend(IRE) Original (Caerleon (USA))
5961a[14]

**Uchenna (IRE)** *David Simcock* a61 93
3 b f Fastnet Rock(AUS) Uriah (GER) (Acatenango (GER))
1978[4] 2484[6] 3143[6] 4443[12] 4782[14]

**Udododontu (IRE)** *Richard Guest* 64
2 b g Lope De Vega(IRE) Fifer (IRE) (Soviet Star (USA))
7407[12] 7638[2]

**Uele River** *Henry Candy* a70 49
2 b f Refuse To Bend(IRE) Baddi Heights (FR) (Shirley Heights)
6066[8] 6606[4]

**Uganda Glory (USA)** *George Baker* a62 67
4 br f Hat Trick(JPN) Febrile (USA) (Trempolino (USA))
2067[3] 2628[5] 3803[10] 4296[5] 6899[7] 7219[10] 7532[2] 7657[7] 8011[6] (8145) 8261[9]

**Ujagar (IRE)** *Tom Dascombe* a79 79
3 gr g Dalakhani(IRE) No Secrets (USA) (El Corredor (USA))
951[5] (1367) 1508[3] 2077[5] 3884[3] 4803[7] 5572[4]

**Ultima Ora (IRE)** *Mark Johnston* a28 23
2 b f Thewayyouare(USA) Prima Volta (Primo Dominie)
7638[8] 7835[9] 7926[11]

**Ultimate** *Brian Ellison* a52 82
8 b g Anabaa(USA) Nirvana (Marju (IRE))
2119[7] 3004[8] 3250[10] 3622[5]

**Ultimate Act** *Seamus Mullins* a73 78
3 ro g Act One Ruffie (IRE) (Medicean)
1401[2] ◆ 2685[7] 2925[2] 3797[3] 6881[9] 7125[7] 7539[4]

**Ultimate Warrior (IRE)** *Richard Ford* a72 68
3 ch g Winker Watson Sakaka (Tobougg (IRE))
404[6] 664[2] 738[4]

**Ultradargent (FR)** *Yannick Fouin* a91 89
3 b f Kendargent(FR) Dulce De Leche (FR) (Victory Note (USA))
1480a[5]

**Umneyati** *James Tate* a74 96
3 b f Iffraaj Honky Tonk Sally (Dansili)
4281[3] 5165[9] 6387a[9]

**Umniyah (IRE)** *Saeed bin Suroor* 66
2 b f Shamardal(USA) Desert Frolic (IRE) (Persian Bold)
4126[4]

**Una Bella Cosa** *Alan McCabe* a54 27
4 b f Dubai Destination(USA) Blinding Mission (IRE) (Marju (IRE))
73[7] 263[5] 352[4] 537[6] 673[5]

**Unanimite (FR)** *David Pipe* a98
3 ch g Kentucky Dynamite(USA) Dame Blanche (USA) (Cherokee Run (USA))
721a[4] 8062[3]

**Unbreak My Heart (IRE)** *Ann Stokell* a28 42
9 ch g Bahamian Bounty Golden Heart (Salse (USA))
939[6] 1016[11]

**Unbridled Forever (USA)** *Dallas Stewart* a106
3 b f Unbridled's Song(USA) Lemons Forever (USA) (Lemon Drop Kid (USA))
7593a[5]

**Unbridled Joy (IRE)** *Clive Cox* a62 59
3 b f Acclamation Unlock (IRE) (Key Of Luck (USA))
3729[5] 4677[8] 5548[3] 6022[6] 7077[7] 7347[5] ◆ 8049[4] 8232[7]

**Unchain My Heart (AUS)** *David A Hayes & Tom Dabernig* 99
8 b m Al Maher(AUS) Fly By Night (AUS) (Prince Of Birds (USA))
7126a[9] 7301a[17] 7653a[16]

**Uncle Bernie (IRE)** *Andrew Hollinshead* a79 59
4 gr g Aussie Rules(USA) Alwiyda (USA) (Trempolino (USA))
221[5] 349[2] (430) 609[3] 695[3] 1740[6] 2885[4] 3404[12] (5508) (6343) 7182[8] (7903) 7995[5]

**Uncle Brit** *Rebecca Menzies* a68 61
8 b g Efisio Tarneem (USA) (Zilzal (USA))
1307[7] 2476[6] 3105[6] 5244[7] 7061[2] (7909) 8086[13]

**Uncle Bunge (IRE)** *Liam Corcoran* a26 24
8 b g Rock Of Gibraltar(IRE) Ouija's Sister (Groom Dancer (USA))
3115[13] 4082[9]

**Uncle Dermot (IRE)** *Brendan Powell* a70 92
6 b g Arakan(USA) Cappadoce (IRE) (General Monash (USA))
1281[3] (1665) 1845[3] 2177[2] (2453) (2478) 2772[7] 3759[4] 6943[12] 7597[9] 7719[13]

**Uncle Fred** *Patrick Chamings* a71 49
9 b g Royal Applause Karla June (Unfuwain (USA))
1023[11]

**Uncle Muf (USA)** *Ali Stronge* a62 36
4 b g Curlin(USA) Peak Maria's Way (USA) (Pyramid Peak (USA))
2917[7] 3385[9] 3856[8] 6632[7] 7287[8]

**Uncle Sigh (USA)** *Gary Contessa* a107
3 b c Indian Charlie(USA) Cradlesong (USA) (Pine Bluff (USA))
1964a[14]

**Uncoiled (FR)** *Yoshito Yahagi* a76 113
5 b h Giant's Causeway(USA) Tanzania (IRE) (Alzao (USA))
7981a[13]

**Under Approval** *Karen Tutty* a65 32
3 b g Captain Gerrard(IRE) Dockside Strike (Docksider (USA))
429[3] 650[7] 867[3] 936[2] 1246[2] 1642[9] 1801[2] 2230[5] 3792[5] ◆ 4998[11] 5715[7] 8088[3]

**Under Review (IRE)** *Bernard Llewellyn* a44 41
8 b g Danetime(IRE) Coloma (JPN) (Forty Niner (USA))
4038a[4] 4564[8] 5499[13] 5897[11] 6666[12] 7009[7] 7520[7] 7782[8] 7940[9]

**Understory (USA)** *Tim McCarthy* a75 67
7 b g Forestry(USA) Sha Tha (USA) (Mr Prospector (USA))
79[10] 345[6] 582[9] 922[3] 1302[6] 1919[5] 3080[9] 6635[4] 7527[6] 7982[2]

**Underwritten** *Shaun Harris* a72 75
5 b g Authorized(IRE) Grain Of Gold (Mr Prospector (USA))
3661[3] (4082) 4474[2] (4615) 5047[2] 5171[3] (5764) 5800[3] 5924[5] 6404[2] 7129[5] 7903[6]

**Undrafted (USA)** *Wesley A Ward* a97 116
4 ch g Purim(USA) French Jeannette (USA) (French Deputy (USA))
4201[4] 7609a[3]

**Undress (IRE)** *William Haggas* 60
3 ch f Dalakhani(IRE) Dress Uniform (USA) (Red Ransom (USA))
3653[7] 4621[4]

**Undulate** *Peter Niven* a67
3 b f Three Valleys(USA) Singleton (Singspiel (IRE))
7686[6] 7818[7] (8147)

**Unex Michelangelo (IRE)** *Michael Easterby* a70 76
5 b g Dansili Chenchikova (IRE) (Sadler's Wells (USA))
11[6] 155[4] 3095[7] 3544[5] 3958[3] (4755) 5371[8] 6166[10] 7042[4] 7411[11]

**Unfinishedbusiness** *Richard Fahey* 61
3 b g Selkirk(USA) Alizadora (Zilzal (USA))
1347[5] 2133[5] 3135[5] 3789[8] 4386[6]

**Unforgettable You (IRE)** *Declan Carroll* 36
2 br f Captain Rio The Gibson Girl (IRE) (Norwich)
4286[9] 6453[11] 6861[8]

**Unforgiving Minute** *Clive Cox* a113 81
3 b c Cape Cross(IRE) Ada River (Dansili)
(5039) 6060[5] 6871[7] (7375) (7852) (8203)

**Unfuwan (IRE)** *A De Mieulle* 73
4 b g Teofilo(IRE) Menesteem (IRE) (Mark Of Esteem (IRE))
3373a[13]

**Unidexter (IRE)** *Sheena West* a45 51
4 br g Footstepsinthesand Run To Jane (IRE) (Doyoun)
2465[9] (5030)

**Union Rose** *Ronald Harris* 96
2 b c Stimulation(IRE) Dot Hill (Refuse To Bend (IRE))
1571[8] 1936[3] 2200[3] (2692) 3173[3] 3322[2] 3928[4] 4757[5] 5607[19] 6128[3] 6703[5]

**Union Sacree (FR)** *H-A Pantall* 50
2 b f Naaqoos Queen's Conquer (King's Best (USA))
7163a[5]

**Unison (IRE)** *Peter Makin* a67 83
4 b g Jeremy(USA) Easter Song (USA) (Rubiano (USA))
2947[8] (3314) 4148[2] (5274) 5849[7] 6713[18] 6990[5] (7562)

**United Color (USA)** *D Selvaratnam* a112 102
5 b h Ghostzapper(USA) Silk Candy (CAN) (Langfuhr (CAN))
(206a) 597a[10] 898a[10] 1180a[3]

**Universal Star (GER)** *R Dzubasz* 66
2 b f Areion(GER) Universe (GER) (Refuse To Bend (IRE))
7481a[7]

**Universo Star (IRE)** *A Marcialis* 102
4 br f Excellent Art Shinkoh Rose (FR) (Warning)
1477a[2] 2375a[13] 7320a[4] 7604a[5]

**Unknown Villain (IRE)** *A Schennach* a65 76
4 gr g Verglas(IRE) Ragtime Blues (IRE) (Grand Lodge (USA))
638a[5]

**Unmoothaj** *Pam Sly* a74 70
4 b g Green Desert(USA) Sundus (USA) (Sadler's Wells (USA))
146[6] 345[5] 458[10]

**Unnoticed** *Ollie Pears* a72 67
2 b g Observatory(USA) Celestial Empire (USA) (Empire Maker (USA))
6668[5] 7076[2] 7573[2]

**Unscripted (IRE)** *Richard Hannon* a91
3 b c Oratorio(IRE) Fancy Intense (Peintre Celebre (USA))
(37)

**Unsinkable (IRE)** *Ian Semple* a88 98
4 gr g Verglas(IRE) Heart's Desire (IRE) (Royal Applause)
804[11] 1165[14] 4002[5] 4938[12] 5238[8] 5632[9] 5766[10]

**Untapable (USA)** *Steven Asmussen* a122
3 b f Tapit(USA) Fun House (USA) (Prized (USA))
(7593a)

**Until Midnight (IRE)** *Eugene Stanford* a76 70
4 b g Moss Vale(IRE) Emma's Star (ITY) (Darshaan)
740[9] (1105) (1408) (1799) 2341[4] 7758[3] 8041[2] 8248[2]

**Until The Man (IRE)** *Natalie Lloyd-Beavis* a50 52
7 b g Tillerman Canoe Cove (IRE) (Grand Lodge (USA))
(759) 1012[10] 4264[10]

**Upavon** *David Elsworth* a94 74
4 b g Avonbridge Blaina (Compton Place)
235[11] (991) 1576[8] 2157[4] 2562[12] 7923[6] 8117[6]

**Updated (FR)** *Ismail Mohammed* a37 44
3 ch f New Approach(IRE) Dance Treat (USA) (Nureyev (USA))
1216[9] 1793[12]

**Upgrade (USA)** *Chad C Brown* a90 104
7 b g Saint Liam(USA) Emily Ring (USA) (Fit To Fight (USA))
7325a[10]

**Up Hill Battle's** *Daniel Mark Loughnane* a45 42
3 b f Tiger Hill(IRE) Nasij (USA) (Elusive Quality (USA))
70[9] 355[8] 2066[8] 2694[4] 5033[6] 5558[7] 6087[8]

**Uphold** *Gay Kelleway* a89 84
7 b g Oasis Dream Allegro Viva (USA) (Distant View (USA))
178a[4] 437a[4] 584a[3] 870[8] 1071[6] 1636[2] 2034[5] 2700[9] 8073[6]

**Upholland** *Richard Fahey* a78 71
3 b g Dutch Art Never Away (Royal Applause)
355[3] 492[2] (670) 975[3] 1352[5] 1658[3]

**Up In Flames (IRE)** *Mrs A Malzard* a54 54
5 b g Red Clubs(IRE) Flames (Blushing Flame (USA))
2594a[4] 4041a[4] 4718a[4] 5970a[4]

**Uplifted (IRE)** *Kevin Ryan* a58 63
3 b g Jeremy(USA) Misty Peak (IRE) (Sri Pekan (USA))
865[7] 960[3] (1308) 1657[12] 2355[6] 2674[9] 4490[6] 5245[5]

**Upper Lambourn (IRE)** *Christopher Kellett* a62 33
6 b g Exceed And Excel(AUS) In The Fashion (IRE) (In The Wings)
58[3] 258[5] 384[4] 502[8] 563[7] 692[10] 864[8] 1001[7] 1228[6] 1887[3] 2907[5] 3366[7] 4534[7] 5574[6]

**Upper Street (IRE)** *Sir Michael Stoute* a71 46
3 b f Dansili Islington (IRE) (Sadler's Wells (USA))
3385[10] 4325[4] ◆ 4543[6] 5036[7] 6026[7] (7358)

**Up Pompeii** *George Peckham* 47
3 ch g Kyllachy Anneliina (Cadeaux Genereux)
3914[10]

**Uprise** *George Margarson* a67 73
5 b g Pivotal Soar (Danzero (AUS))
2463[8] (3630) 4571[9] 4766[3] 5059[4] 5861[8] 6397[4]

**Upstaging** *Paul Cole* a78
2 b c Mount Nelson Corndavon (USA) (Sheikh Albadou)
7031[8] (7542)

**Upstart (USA)** *Richard Violette Jr* a114
2 bb r Flatter(USA) Party Silks (USA) (Touch Gold (USA))
7610a[3]

**Uptight (FR)** *Kevin Ryan* 79
2 b c Zamindar(USA) Terre D'Espoir (FR) (Oasis Dream)
(4829) 5580[9] (7665)

**Up Tipp** *Mike Murphy* a62 22
4 ch g Medicean Jetbeeah (IRE) (Lomond (USA))
90[4] 1023[6] 1771[11]

**Upward Trend (IRE)** *Tim Easterby* 61
2 b g Dark Angel(IRE) Camassina (IRE) (Taufan (USA))
1504[6] ◆ 2788[4] 3529[5] ◆ 6165[10] 6669[2]

**Up With The Birds (CAN)** *Malcolm Pierce* a111 114
4 b c Stormy Atlantic(USA) Song Of The Lark (CAN) (Seeking The Gold (USA))
5460a[4] 7981a[16]

**Uradel (GER)** *W P Mullins* a79 86
3 b g Kallisto(GER) Unavita (GER) (Vettori (IRE))
5691[5]

**Uramazin (IRE)** *Philip Hide* a102 68
8 ch g Danehill Dancer(IRE) Uriah (GER) (Acatenango (GER))
54[10] 716[9] 840[2] 1171[9] 1559[12] 2154[8] 2405[7] 7688[9] 7974[3] 8243[4] (8296)

**Urban Castle (USA)** *James Tate* a81
3 b f Street Cry(IRE) Cloud Castle (In The Wings)
7901[4] (8064) 8264[2]

**Urban Dance (IRE)** *Charlie Appleby* a85 106
4 b g Street Cry(IRE) Melikah (IRE) (Lammtarra (USA))
1973[7] 3726[4]

**Urban Moon (IRE)** *J P Murtagh* a66 90
3 b c Galileo(IRE) Velouette (Darshaan)
3491a[6] 5691[13]

**Urban Sanctuary** *Ed Walker* a12 48
3 ch c Mount Nelson White Dress (IRE) (Pivotal)
3333[6] 4738[11] 5033[8] 5978[4]

**Urban Space** *John Flint* a65 71
8 ch g Sulamani(IRE) Rasmalai (Sadler's Wells (USA))
2672[2] 2947[7] 3761[5] 4985[5] 5214[2] 5338[2] 5621[5] (6426) (7309) 7516[7]

**Uriah Heep (FR)** *Alan King* a81 79
5 b g Danehill Dancer(IRE) Canasita (Zafonic (USA))
2920[9]

**Usbeke (GER)** *R Houthoofd* a59 74
8 b g Big Shuffle(USA) Ustimona (GER) (Mondrian (GER))
5546a[5]

**Use Your Filbert (IRE)** *Robert Cowell* 76
2 b c Acclamation Wishing Chair (USA) (Giant's Causeway (USA))
(6058)

**Ustinov** *Brian Meehan* 79
2 b c Exceed And Excel(AUS) Tamzin (Hernando (FR))
2507[3] (3148) 4123[12] 4645[6]

**Uta (FR)** *J Parize* a82 65
3 b f Shirocco(GER) Joyce (GER) (Chato (USA))
436a[5]

**U Think Ur Funny (IRE)** *Tony Coyle* 51
2 b f Zebedee Northern Tara (IRE) (Fayruz)
5789[8] ◆ 6212[6]

**Vaargas (IRE)** *Mme Pia Brandt* 76
2 b g Manduro(GER) Fever Fever (USA) (Elusive Quality (USA))
8276a[6]

**Va Benny** *J R Jenkins* a61 22
3 b g Byron Apple Of My Eye (Fraam)
1364[2] 2095[5] 2877[10] 3380[9] 3756[4] 4304[13] 5321[9]

**Vacationer** *H-A Pantall* a80 92
3 ch f Dubawi(IRE) Tropical Breeze (IRE) (Kris)
3810a[4]

**Vadamos (FR)** *F Rohaut* 108
3 b c Monsun(GER) Celebre Vadala (FR) (Peintre Celebre (USA))
6379a[7]

**Vado Di Siella (ITY)** *Stefano Botti* 96
3 b g Dane Friendly Candok (IRE) (Celtic Swing)
7469a[3]

**Vaguely Spanish** *Tony Carroll* a63 58
3 b g Oratorio(IRE) Spanish Quest (Rainbow Quest (USA))
6342[11] 6939[7] 7218[4] (7517) (7785) 8028[2]

**Vague Nouvelle (IRE)** *R Biondi* 100
3 ch f Mastercraftsman(IRE) Zona (ITY) (Mr Greeley (USA))
(1780a) 2590a[8] 6807a[4] 7480a[6]

**Vainglory (USA)** *David Simcock* a76 95
10 ch g Swain(IRE) Infinite Spirit (USA) (Maria's Mon (USA))
1862[6] 2156[7] 2959[15] 3244[10] 4868[3] 5319[3] 5533[3] 6616[4] 6930[9]

**Valais Girl** *Marcus Tregoning* a82 96
4 b f Holy Roman Emperor(IRE) Ellen (IRE) (Machiavellian (USA))
2155[9] 3753[7] 4783[9]

**Valantino Oyster (IRE)** *Tracy Waggott* a62 79
7 b g Pearl Of Love(IRE) Mishor (Slip Anchor)
1674[10] (2607) 3546[5] (4293) (4520) 4904[3] 4979[3] 6402[2] 6672[2] 7008[12]

**Valbchek (IRE)** *Jane Chapple-Hyam* a108 91
5 b g Acclamation Spectacular Show (IRE) (Spectrum (IRE))
1557[10] 2254[12] 2848[13] 3732[7] 6131[10] 6440[4] 6755[10] 7034[4] 7437a[12] 8117[4] 8203[5]

**Valbucca (IRE)** *Amy Weaver* a56 96
7 b m Val Royal(FR) Nambucca (Shirley Heights)
1750a[8] 2294[7] 3089a[7]

**Valdaw** *Mike Murphy* a80 68
6 b g Val Royal(FR) Delight Of Dawn (Never So Bold)
52[12] 296[7] 511[10] 1766[5] ◆

**Val De Majorque (FR)** *D Sepulchre* a75 79
6 b g Poliglote Valdemossa (FR) (Highest Honor (FR))
1828a[2]

**Valdiyana (FR)** *A De Royer-Dupre* a82 104
3 b f Sinndar(IRE) Vadasouna (IRE) (Monsun (GER))
6218a[2]

**Vale Mentor (IRE)** *Denis Quinn* a35 57
3 b c Moss Vale(IRE) Sinamay (USA) (Saint Ballado (CAN))
3465[5] 4017[3] 4495[4] 5084[8] 5891[5] 6862[4] 7250[3] 7845[9] 8088[12] 8219[7]

**Valen (IRE)** *Michael Bell* a74 85
3 gr f Acclamation Ardea Brave (IRE) (Chester House (USA))
1614[7] 1985[7] 2745[6] 4367[4] 5320[5] 6269[3] 6902[10] 7494[17]

**Valencia (SPA)** *T Martins* a38
4 b f Caradak(IRE) Moody Affair (USA) (Colonial Affair (USA))
805a[13]

**Valencin (FR)** *P Decouz* a86 62
5 ch g Limnos(JPN) Vallee Fertile (FR) (Turgeon (USA))
584a[12]

**Valentine Belle** *Paul Midgley* 18
2 b f Monsieur Bond(IRE) Sheka (Ishiguru (USA))
4751[11] 4919[11]

**Valentine's Gift** *Neville Bycroft* 67
6 b g Presidium Efipetite (Efisio)
1885[6] 2327[13] 2872[9] 3546[8] 3912[7] 4293[7] 5678[10] 6628[8] 7540[7]

**Vale Of Clara (IRE)** *Peter Niven* a51 57
6 b m Iffraaj Luggala (IRE) (Kahyasi)
18[3] 201[7] 351[2] 516[4] 692[2] 864[6] 1649[2] 1838[5]

**Vale Of Iron (IRE)** *John Best* a65
2 b c Vale Of York(IRE) Lady Van Gogh (Dubai Destination (USA))
6603[10] 8318[5]

**Vale Of Paris (IRE)** *Rae Guest* 31
2 b f Vale Of York(IRE) Paris Glory (USA) (Honour And Glory (USA))
7037[9]

**Valiant Emilia (PER)** *Gary Mandella* a103
5 br m Pegasus Wind(USA) Valiant Saint (USA) (Aljabr (USA))
7593a[8]

**Valid Reason** *Dean Ivory* a41 72
7 b g Observatory(USA) Real Trust (USA) (Danzig (USA))
292[9] 7129[3]

**Validus** *Saeed bin Suroor* a107 107
5 b g Zamindar(USA) Victoire Finale (Peintre Celebre (USA))
207a[13]

**Vallarta (IRE)** *Mick Channon* 81
4 b g Footstepsinthesand Mexican Miss (IRE) (Tagula (IRE))
1538[5] 1731[7] 2147[6] 2945[6] 3213[4] 3628[2] 3783[4] (4206) 4632[15] 4983[2] 5650[9] 6006[8] 6880[9]

**Vallecupa (ITY)** *D Zarroli* 93
3 b f Mujahid(USA) My Meltemi (IRE) (Hawk Wing (USA))
2590a[6]

**Vallemi (IRE)** *Sir Michael Stoute* a60
2 b f Invincible Spirit(IRE) Vologda (IRE) (Red Ransom (USA))
6605[6]

**Valley Of Fire** *William Haggas* 93
2 b c Firebreak Charlie Girl (Puissance)
(4684) 5607[3] 6686[8]

**Vallicola (IRE)** *F Vermeulen* a85 97
3 b f Zambezi Sun Valley Orchard (FR) (Zilzal (USA))
1096a[5]

**Vally Jem (FR)** *D Sepulchre* a83 107
5 b m Dylan Thomas(IRE) Ballymena Lassie (Giant's Causeway (USA))
984a[7] 1827a[9] 2631a[2] 4561a[F] 6592a[7] 7558a[6]

**Valmina** *Tony Carroll* a85 80
7 b g Val Royal(FR) Minnina (IRE) (In The Wings)
(91) (233) 714[7] 820[4] 1041[6] 1261[6] 1489[6] 4267[6] 4762[21] 5624[7] 6025[6] 6658[5]

**Valonia** *Henry Candy* 107
3 ch f Three Valleys(USA) Descriptive (IRE) (Desert King (IRE))
1435[8] 3278[3] 3459[5] 4854[4] (5467) 6254[4]

**Value (IRE)** *Gay Kelleway* a66 73
3 gr f Clodovil(IRE) Shalev (GER) (Java Gold (USA))
1006[5] 2470[3] 2768[5] 3462[7]

**Vancouverite** *Charlie Appleby* a102 118
4 b g Dansili Villarrica (USA) (Selkirk (USA))
902a[2] 1183a[8] 4437[2] ◆ 5175[7]

**Vanishing** *Ed Walker* a69
2 b f Sir Percy Valoria (Hernando (FR))
7550[5] 7891[3] 8173[4]

**Vanishing Cupid (SWI)** *H-A Pantall* 107
4 b c Galileo(IRE) Vanishing Prairie (USA) (Alysheba (USA))
984a[5] 4006a[2] 5938a[9] 7727a[3]
**Vanity Rules** *Ed Vaughan* a85 101
4 b f New Approach(IRE) Miss Pinkerton (Danehill (USA))
1945[5] 4060[3] 5312[6] 6708[3] 7105[10]
**Van Mildert (IRE)** *Dianne Sayer* 39
5 b m Observatory(USA) Vanilla Delight (IRE) (Orpen (USA))
6429[7] 6638[7]
**Van Rooney (USA)** *Ali Jan* a101 104
5 ch h Van Nistelrooy(USA) Royal Shyness (Royal Academy (USA))
*207a[6]* 397a[8] *679a[2]* *808a[3]* *899a[7]*
**Vanvidd (FR)** *C Boutin* a60 59
3 gr c Verglas(IRE) Magic Spin (USA) (Lord Avie (USA))
*720a[14]*
**Vanvitelli** *Pat Murphy* a10 73
4 b g Shamardal(USA) Treble Seven (USA) (Fusaichi Pegasus (USA))
*376[11]*
**Varadero (IRE)** *L Baudron* a100 86
6 b g Dalakhani(IRE) Miss Wind (FR) (Sri Pekan (USA))
*177a[10]* *437a[6]* *5961a[7]* *(7620a)*
**Vardaris (IRE)** *P Adda* a79 73
4 b g Beat Hollow Drosia (IRE) (King's Best (USA))
*7620a[3]*
**Variety Club (SAF)** *M F De Kock* a119 124
6 ch h Var(USA) La Massine (SAF) (Secret Prospector (USA))
*(596a)* *899a[2]* *(1176a)* (2004a)
**Varsovian** *Dean Ivory* a78 58
4 ch g Refuse To Bend(IRE) Queen Of Poland (Halling (USA))
*2883[8]* 3153[7] 4130[7] *4579[9]* *5303[7]* *(6666)* *6889[2]* *(7775)* *(7931)* *8204[2]*
**Vasias (FR)** *C Lotoux* a85 100
6 b g Motivator Vivacity (Trempolino (USA))
*7620a[5]*
**Vasily** *M F De Kock* a63 105
6 b h Sadler's Wells(USA) Red Bloom (Selkirk (USA))
309a[5] 598a[8] *773a[10]*
**Vastly (USA)** *Julia Feilden* a74 69
5 rg g Mizzen Mast(USA) Valentine Band (USA) (Dixieland Band (USA))
*365[3]* *(642)*
**Vastonea (IRE)** *Kevin Prendergast* a94 100
6 gr g Verglas(IRE) Roystonea (Polish Precedent (USA))
4379a[5] (4771a) 5957a[2]
**Vaudemont (IRE)** *A Fabre* a64 80
3 b g Cape Cross(IRE) Cicerole (FR) (Barathea (IRE))
6913a[6]
**Vazira (FR)** *A De Royer-Dupre* a84 108
3 b f Sea The Stars(IRE) Vadaza (FR) (Zafonic (USA))
(1782a) (2586a) 3376[4] ◆ 5545a[4] 6954a[9]
**Vecheka (IRE)** *Andrew Balding* 71
3 b g Lawman(FR) Lidanski (IRE) (Soviet Star (USA))
2525[3] 3469[5]
**Veda (FR)** *A De Royer-Dupre* 115
3 b f Dansili Vadapolina (FR) (Trempolino (USA))
2195a[2] 2817a[6] 6955a[2] 7613a[12]
**Vedani (IRE)** *Tony Carroll* a37 62
5 b g Dalakhani(IRE) Velandia (IRE) (Sadler's Wells (USA))
*462[6]* *758[8]* 3932[7] 4948[8]
**V. E. Day (USA)** *James Jerkens* a119
3 ch c English Channel(USA) California Sunset (USA) (Deputy Minister (CAN))
*7614a[11]*
**Vedelago (IRE)** *Stefano Botti* 108
5 b h Red Clubs(IRE) Queen Shy (Marju (IRE))
2191a[5] 2589a[6]
**Vedeux (IRE)** *C Lerner* a90 70
3 b c Elusive City(USA) Qahatika (FR) (Polish Precedent (USA))
2226a[10] *7619a[9]*
**Veeraya** *Julia Feilden* a97 91
4 b g Rail Link Follow Flanders (Pursuit Of Love)
*342[4]* *804[3]* *1241[6]* *1559[8]* 1948[16] 3196[8]
**Vegas Rebel (IRE)** *Peter Chapple-Hyam* a79 79
2 b c Alfred Nobel(IRE) Van De Cappelle (IRE) (Pivotal)
*2680[6]* 3082[2] ◆ 3330[2] 4203[2] *5799[4]* 6279[4] 6667[2] (6997) 7415[2] *7849[2]* *7945[4]*
**Vehemence D'Amour (FR)** *H-A Pantall* a82 87
3 ch f Linngari(IRE) Fire Sale (ARG) (Not For Sale (ARG))
*6221a[8]*
**Veiled Intrigue** *Henry Candy* 98
3 b f Pastoral Pursuits Verbal Intrigue (USA) (Dahar (USA))
2155[2] ◆ 3983[4] 4607[5] 5312[4] 6464[11]
**Vejovis** *Sir Mark Prescott Bt* a48
2 b g Fastnet Rock(AUS) Violet (IRE) (Mukaddamah (USA))
*6852[11]* *7030[8]* *7223[6]* *8179[11]*
**Veligandu (GER)** *R Dzubasz* 88
3 ch f Hurricane Run(IRE) Venia Legendi (GER) (Zinaad)
3046a[8]
**Velociter (IRE)** *Richard Hannon* a68 56
2 ch g Zebedee Polly Jones (USA) (Lear Fan (USA))
6702[7] *7030[3]* *7354[3]*
**Velox** *Luca Cumani* 104
4 b g Zamindar(USA) Victoire Finale (Peintre Celebre (USA))
2309[4] 2959[7] (3982) 4851[11] 6332[3] 6752[2] 7276[24]
**Velum** *Marco Gasparini* 90
4 br f Singspiel(IRE) Clouds Of Magellan (USA) (Dynaformer (USA))
7146a[5]

**Venezia (IRE)** *Martyn Meade* a73 95
3 gr g Galileo(IRE) St Roch (IRE) (Danehill (USA))
1517[2] 2271[2] 3379[4] 3891[6]
**Vent De Force** *Hughie Morrison* a66 108
3 b c Hurricane Run(IRE) Capriolla (In The Wings)
*1797[5]* (2494) (3110) 4122[6] (5691) ◆ 6954a[2] 7486a[11]
**Ventriloquist** *Charlie Appleby* a84 72
2 ch g New Approach(IRE) Illusion (Anabaa (USA))
3136[5] ◆ *3578[2]* 5093[3] *6101[3]* *6718[3]*
**Ventura Canyon (IRE)** *Keith Dalgleish* a41 58
2 ch c Approve(IRE) Tarrara (UAE) (Lammtarra (USA))
4790[11] 5264[5] *7181[7]* 7497[9]
**Ventura Castle** *Richard Hannon* 67
2 b g Paco Boy(IRE) Bisaat (USA) (Bahri (USA))
5718[5] 6646[3] 6976[6]
**Ventura Ice (IRE)** *Richard Hannon* a60 49
3 gr f Oratorio(IRE) Tipperary Honor (FR) (Highest Honor (FR))
3087[6]
**Ventura Mist** *Tim Easterby* 99
3 ch f Pastoral Pursuits Kerry's Dream (Tobougg (IRE))
1518[9] 2116[3] 3253[6] 4171[10] 4669[16] 5438[2] 6170[6] 6598[2] 6893[10]
**Ventura Quest (USA)** *Richard Fahey* 90
3 b g Henrythenavigator(USA) Ing Ing (FR) (Bering)
1563[6] 1927[2] 3572[5] 4125[2] 4821[13] 5914[5] 6548[3] 6737[3] 7106[18] 7562[4]
**Ventura Reef (IRE)** *Richard Fahey* a54
3 b c Excellent Art Run To Jane (IRE) (Doyoun)
*477[6]* *743[4]*
**Ventura Shadow** *Richard Fahey* 73
2 ch f Equiano(FR) Stavinsky's Gal (USA) (Stravinsky (USA))
2348[8] 2866[6] 3199[5] 3658[2] (4172) 4686[4] 5790[6] 6375a[16] 6783[5] (7245)
**Venturous Spirit (FR)** *M Delzangles* a90 103
4 b f Arch(USA) Vatrouchka (USA) (Kingmambo (USA))
1827a[7]
**Venturous Spirit (IRE)** *John Gosden* a77 71
3 b f Invincible Spirit(IRE) Venturi (Danehill Dancer (IRE))
2780[6] 3755[3] 4446[4] *5008[3]* *(5796)*
**Venus De Milo (IRE)** *A P O'Brien* 115
4 br f Duke Of Marmalade(IRE) Inchmahome (Galileo (IRE))
(3285a) 3766a[2] 4894[3] 5610[7] 6255[10]
**Venus Grace** *Ralph Beckett* a68 80
3 b f Royal Applause Basque Beauty (Nayef (USA))
1534[10] 2340[3] ◆ *2929[6]* 3586[5] 7042[7]
**Venus Marina** *Chris Wall* a48 60
3 b f Tiger Hill(IRE) Danvers (Cape Cross (IRE))
1844[10] *2681[11]* *3389[8]* 4304[5] *4970[4]* (5321) *6022[7]*
**Venutius** *Ed McMahon* a51 75
7 b g Doyen(IRE) Boadicea's Chariot (Commanche Run)
6227[2] 6865[11] *7569[7]* *8168[11]*
**Vera Lou (IRE)** *Pat Eddery* a47 38
3 ch f Manduro(GER) Baltica (IRE) (Sadler's Wells (USA))
*1029[6]* 2926[12] 3333[8] 7518[9] *8021[7]*
**Verchild Lad (IRE)** *David Evans* a41 47
2 gr g Verglas(IRE) Confidentiality (IRE) (Desert Style (IRE))
1276[11] 2413[5] 2756[7] 4410[5] *4967[9]* *6412[11]* *7064[9]*
**Vercingetorix (IRE)** *A Fabre* a76 97
3 b c Dylan Thomas(IRE) Great Artist (FR) (Desert Prince (IRE))
5591a[6]
**Vercingetorix (SAF)** *M F De Kock* 118
5 b h Silvano(GER) National Vixen (SAF) (National Assembly (CAN))
(595a) (902a) 1181a[2]
**Verdetto Finale** *R Biondi* 109
4 b g Nayef(USA) Love Roi (ITY) (Roi Danzig (USA))
2589a[2] 3776a[4] 6808a[2] 7616a[6]
**Verdura (USA)** *J-C Rouget* a63 88
3 ch f Smart Strike(CAN) Wonder Woman (USA) (Storm Cat (USA))
*(194a)* *(629a)*
**Vereri Senes** *Ed Dunlop* a63
2 b f Nayef(USA) Whazzat (Daylami (IRE))
*8173[7]*
**Vergality Ridge (IRE)** *Ronald Harris* a64 48
4 gr g Verglas(IRE) Phoenix Factor (IRE) (Indian Ridge)
*368[5]* *484[P]*
**Verismo** *Ed Dunlop* 69
2 b g Hurricane Run(IRE) Cross Current (Sakhee (USA))
7039[5] 7382[3]
**Vermeer (SAF)** *Doug Watson* a44
6 b g Daylami(IRE) Perfect Guest (SAF) (Northern Guest (USA))
*238a[16]*
**Vermuyden** *Pam Sly* a54 28
5 b g Oasis Dream Speciosa (IRE) (Danehill Dancer (IRE))
*1594* *468[7]* *740[12]* 3160[10]
**Veronica's Pursuit** *Peter Hedger* a45
4 b f Pastoral Pursuits Veronica Franco (Darshaan)
*454[10]*
**Verrazano (USA)** *A P O'Brien* a124 122
4 b c More Than Ready(USA) Enchanted Rock (USA) (Giant's Causeway (USA))
2338[3] 3317[2] 3984[9]
**Verse Of Love** *David Evans* a95 93
5 b g Byron Lovellian (Machiavellian (USA))
*314[3]* *426[6]* *566[4]* *715[12]* *804[4]* *917[5]* 1564[4] 1646[4] (2117) 2483[6] 3753[3] 4188[11] 4938[5] 5749[5] 6207[3] (6424) 7227[6] 7555[12]
**Vert De Grece (IRE)** *Roger Varian* 116
2 gr c Verglas(IRE) Tiny Petal (IRE) (Grand Lodge (USA))
5735a[2] (7557a)

**Vertiformer (USA)** *Christophe Clement* a98 107
7 b h Dynaformer(USA) Tempo West (USA) (Rahy (USA))
2228a[5]
**Vertueux (FR)** *Tony Carroll* a59 44
9 gr g Verglas(IRE) Shahrazad (FR) (Bering)
*974[4]* *1150[3]* 5904[7] *6768[12]* *7572[8]*
**Verus Delicia (IRE)** *Daniel Mark Loughnane* a53 78
5 b m Chineur(FR) Ribbon Glade (UAE) (Zafonic (USA))
1447[11] 1758[11] 2250[9] 3150[5] (3549) 3848[3] (4282) 4629[2] 4891[4] 5958a[4] 6736[8] 7178[11]
**Very Bad Trip (FR)** *T Castanheira* a84 78
5 ch g Muhtathir Red Valentine (IRE) (Bad As I Wanna Be (IRE))
3373a[9]
**Very First Blade** *Michael Mullineaux* a56 57
5 b g Needwood Blade Dispol Verity (Averti (IRE))
*215[5]* *502[6]* *563[4]* *676[3]* *833[2]* *973[3]* *1081[4]* *1282[6]* *1365[2]* 1631[5] 4055[7] 5287[2] 5510[2] 5797[8] 6595[5] 7025[6] 7644[6] 7766[2] 7783[10] 7909[3] (8133) 8285[10]
**Very Good Day (FR)** *Richard Fahey* a83 83
7 b g Sinndar(IRE) Picture Princess (Sadler's Wells (USA))
6288[12] 7107[17] 7409[13] *7702[8]* *7870[10]* *8001[2]*
**Very Special (IRE)** *Saeed bin Suroor* 89
2 ch f Lope De Vega(IRE) Danielli (IRE) (Danehill (USA))
(6496) 6924[3]
**Vesly (FR)** *Y Barberot* a64 68
3 gr f Le Havre(IRE) Velsheda (FR) (Hawk Wing (USA))
4252a[7] *4952a[9]*
**Vesnina** *Richard Hannon* a55 90
2 b f Sea The Stars(IRE) Safina (Pivotal)
4403[3] *5037[6]* (5429) 6067[4] 6253[14]
**Vespero (ITY)** *Stefano Botti*
4 b g Stroll(USA) Love Secret (USA) (Secreto (USA))
*178a[0]*
**Vexillum (IRE)** *Simon Hodgson* a54 51
5 br g Mujadil(USA) Common Cause (Polish Patriot (USA))
*609[10]* *747[7]* *6486[10]* 6817[7] *8010[10]*
**Vhujon (IRE)** *Peter Grayson* a51 49
9 b g Mujadil(USA) Livius Lady (IRE) (Titus Livius (FR))
*100[6]* *251[8]* *290[4]* *449[3]* *483[2]* *586[3]* *760[3]* *937[7]* *1081[6]*
**Via Manzoni (IRE)** *A Fabre* 99
2 b f Monsun(GER) Via Milano (FR) (Singspiel (IRE))
7393a[8]
**Vianella (FR)** *S Wattel* a67 75
2 gr f Le Havre(IRE) Viane (FR) (Cardoun (FR))
*3640a[4]* 6245a[5]
**Via Via (IRE)** *Clive Brittain* 82
2 b c Lope De Vega(IRE) Atalina (FR) (Linamix (FR))
(2358) 2703[5] 3448[11]
**Vicar's In Trouble (USA)** *Michael J Maker* a115
3 bb c Into Mischief(USA) Vibrant (CAN) (Vicar (USA))
*1964a[19]* *7591a[9]*
**Viceroyalty** *Charlie Appleby* a76 81
3 b c Sea The Stars(IRE) Argentina (IRE) (Sadler's Wells (USA))
5976[3] 6265[2] 6611[2] *7195[4]*
**Vicky Valentine** *Alistair Whillans* 69
4 b f Rock Of Gibraltar(IRE) Silcasue (Selkirk (USA))
1763[2] 2213[7] 2701[2] 3218[3] 3698[5] 4417[2] 4663[4] 5270[4] 6000[5] 6403[4] 6706[11]
**Vicosoprano (IRE)** *M Nigge* a82 69
3 b g Selkirk(USA) Rue La Fayette (SWE) (Flying Spur (AUS))
4465a[11] *4838a[6]*
**Vicquemare (FR)** *Alex Fracas* a87
3 b g Le Havre(IRE) Saldenarie (GER) (Areion (GER))
*(8005a)*
**Victis Hill (FR)** *A Marcialis* 96
3 b c Tiger Hill(IRE) A Ma Guise (USA) (Silver Hawk (USA))
6590a[6]
**Victoire De Lyphar (IRE)** *Ruth Carr* a16 99
7 b g Bertolini(USA) Victory Peak (Shirley Heights)
1191[7] (1609) (1839) (1903) 2747[4] 3716[10] 4384[11] 4661[8] 5189[2] 5418[8] 6207[12] 6704[11] 7060[6] 7507[6] 7719[6]
**Victordina (FR)** *R Rohne* a71 88
3 ch f Doctor Dino(FR) Victory Road (FR) (Grape Tree Road)
3372a[5] 4252a[4]
**Victorian Number (FR)** *Geoffrey Deacon* a74 82
6 ch g Numerous(USA) Malaisia (FR) (Anabaa (USA))
*170[2]* *366[3]* *2463[9]* *2901[3]* *3393[2]* *4050[7]*
**Victoria Prada (FR)** *Niels Petersen* 80
2 b f Siyouni(FR) Fair West (USA) (Gone West (USA))
6386a[2]
**Victoria Regina (IRE)** *J Heloury* a92 105
3 ch f Mastercraftsman(IRE) For Joy (Singspiel (IRE))
1096a[3]
**Victorina** *Stuart Kittow* a54 26
2 ch f Kyllachy Enrapture (USA) (Lear Fan (USA))
3888[13] *7367[8]* *7659[10]*
**Victorious Champ (FR)** *D Smaga* a97 98
3 b c New Approach(IRE) Sasanuma (USA) (Kingmambo (USA))
6446a[3]
**Victoriously** *Brian Meehan* 70
2 b c Azamour(IRE) Ambria (GER) (Monsun (GER))
4395[14] 4906[3]
**Victor's Beach (IRE)** *M Halford* a76 62
4 b g Footstepsinthesand Your Village (IRE) (Be My Guest (USA))
*790a[7]* 4805a[0]

**Victor's Bet (SPA)** *Ralph J Smith* a67 84
5 b g Leadership Marmaria (SPA) (Limpid)
2124[4] *2471[8]* (4942) (5721)
**Victor Springs** *H Fortineau*
3 b c Rail Link Victoria Page (FR) (Anabaa (USA))
5370a[14]
**Victory Danz (IRE)** *David O'Meara* 64
3 b g Bushranger(IRE) Victoria Lodge (IRE) (Grand Lodge (USA))
3333[5] 3545[2] 3912[11] 4292[5] 4706[5]
**Victory Laurel (IRE)** *Robert Cowell* 98
4 b g Holy Roman Emperor(IRE) Special Cause (IRE) (Fasliyev (USA))
3030a[7] 3830[4]
**Victory Megastar** *Clive Cox* a80 66
2 b c Medicean Bourbon Ball (USA) (Peintre Celebre (USA))
6545[7] *(7660)* *8226[2]*
**Victory Rich (IRE)** *Henry Tett* 68
3 b g Kheleyf(USA) Imperial Graf (USA) (Blushing John (USA))
5313[9] 6262[7]
**Victory Song (IRE)** *W Figge* a91 93
4 b c Dansili All Too Beautiful (IRE) (Sadler's Wells (USA))
7469a[4]
**Vied (USA)** *David O'Meara* a56 51
3 b f Elusive Quality(USA) Unacloud (USA) (Unaccounted For (USA))
3158[6] 4623[7] *5257[4]* *5833[3]* *6160[6]* *7570[4]* *7646[6]*
**Viewpoint (IRE)** *Richard Hannon* a103 98
5 b g Exceed And Excel(AUS) Lady's View (USA) (Distant View (USA))
*1071[5]* *1299[2]* *(1553)* ◆ 1973[13] 3449[16] 3730[6] 4756[DSQ] 5162[6] 5928[15] 6930[12] *7930[5]* *8243[7]*
**Vif Monsieur (GER)** *S Smrczek* 110
4 bb c Doyen(IRE) Vive Madame (GER) (Big Shuffle (USA))
2815a[6] 3770a[6] 4561a[3] 6184a[3] 6806a[8] (7727a)
**Vigor (IRE)** *Ernst Oertel* a89 89
3 b c Iffraaj Miss Gibraltar (Rock Of Gibraltar (IRE))
*204a[7]*
**Viking Warrior (IRE)** *Shaun Harris* a42 63
7 ch g Halling(USA) Powder Paint (Mark Of Esteem (IRE))
*12[8]* *77[5]* 1375[8] 1649[4] 2219[5] 3054[2] 4070[5] 4489[6] 5071[4] 5376[5] 5978[7]
**Vilaz** *Brian Meehan* a46 58
3 ch g Byron Flamenco Dancer (Mark Of Esteem (IRE))
2690[9] *7901[9]*
**Village Wind (TUR)** *R Tasdemir* 113
4 b c Sri Pekan(USA) Steel Girl (TUR) (Shining Steel)
6184a[2]
**Villainous (IRE)** *John Gosden* 51
3 b c Pivotal Infamous Angel (Exceed And Excel (AUS))
1433[11] 1808[9]
**Villandry (USA)** *Charles LoPresti* a101 112
5 ch g Mr Greeley(USA) Al Beedaa (USA) (Swain (IRE))
6390a[4]
**Villanueva (IRE)** *C Laffon-Parias* a78 77
3 b f Whipper(USA) Mabalane (IRE) (Danehill (USA))
*4952a[7]*
**Villa Royale** *Michael Appleby* a94 98
5 b m Val Royal(FR) Villa Carlotta (Rainbow Quest (USA))
*(870)* *(961)* *1071[4]* *1556[5]* (2289) 3321[12] 7107[8]
**Villa Verde (AUS)** *Anthony Cummings* 109
4 gr f Not A Single Doubt(AUS) Young And Free (AUS) (Kenmare (FR))
1468a[8]
**Villoresi (IRE)** *John Quinn* a88 89
5 b g Clodovil(IRE) Villafranca (IRE) (In The Wings)
*784[5]*
**Vim (FR)** *C Boutin* a78 64
3 ch c Zafeen(FR) Version Originale I (FR) (Poliglote)
*4838a[3]*
**Vimy Ridge** *Alan Bailey* a81 91
2 ch c American Post Fairy Shoes (Kyllachy)
1726[5] (2214) 2543[2] 3001[3] 3619[4] (4625) ◆ 4853[9] 5607[7] 6256[12] 6933[12] *7661[5]* *7882[5]* *8046[4]*
**Vinamar (IRE)** *Roger Teal* a42 50
2 b f Approve(IRE) Shalev (GER) (Java Gold (USA))
3799[7] 4117[5] 5973[5] *6662[10]* 6997[6] *7839[6]*
**Vincentti (IRE)** *Ronald Harris* a83 84
4 b g Invincible Spirit(IRE) Bint Al Balad (IRE) (Ahonoora)
*1041[5]* *1212[2]* *1429[3]* 1789[2] 2629[6] 2945[7] *4078[2]* 4406[3] 4632[9] 5677[8] 6006[10] *8297[12]*
**Vinceremos (USA)** *Todd Pletcher* a100
3 bb c Pioneerof The Nile(USA) Kettle's Sister (USA) (More Than Ready (USA))
*1964a[17]*
**Violent Velocity (IRE)** *John Quinn* a61 69
11 b g Namid Lear's Crown (USA) (Lear Fan (USA))
*152[4]* 1310[4] 1673[3] 3096[3] 4023[7] 4517[5] 5337[10] 6600[5]
**Violet Plum** *Laura Mongan* 47
4 br f Araafa(IRE) Raphaela (FR) (Octagonal (NZ))
2381[8]
**Violet Symphony (FR)** *M Delzangles* a85 95
3 b f Invincible Spirit(IRE) Celebre Fragance (FR) (Peintre Celebre (USA))
*5843a[7]*
**Vip (GER)** *B Recher*
3 b c Liquido(GER) Verbatim (Vettori (IRE))
*751a[0]*
**Virginia Sun (GER)** *J Hirschberger* 107
3 b f Doyen(IRE) Valdina (GER) (Lomitas)
6162a[3] 6589a[2] 7603a[9]
**Virile (IRE)** *Richard Hannon* 67
3 ch c Exceed And Excel(AUS) Winding (USA) (Irish River (FR))
5181[4] 5862[4]

**Virtualise** *John Gallagher* 19
2 ch g Virtual Snake Skin (Golden Snake (USA))
3381[8] 4550[9]
**Virtual Money (FR)** *G Botti* a56 52
3 b c Lawman(FR) Art Fair (FR) (Fairy King (USA))
*482a[9]*
**Virtual Reality** *Philip McBride* a65
2 b g Virtual Regal Riband (Fantastic Light (USA))
*8225[3]*
**Virtual Symphony** *John Best* a16
3 b f Virtual Hucking Harmony (IRE) (Spartacus (IRE))
*756[6] 1018[6] 1106[5]*
**Visioner (FR)** *C Boutin* a68 68
3 b c Racinger(FR) Famous Celt (USA) (Quest For Fame)
*(720a)* 3372a[10]
**Visoriyna (FR)** *J-C Rouget* 108
3 b f Dansili Visorama (IRE) (Linamix (FR))
5407a[3] 7559a[3]
**Vital Evidence (USA)** *Sir Michael Stoute* a90 95
4 b g Empire Maker(USA) Promising Lead (Danehill (USA))
*1171[5]* 1651[9] 3196[2] 3931[2]
**Vita Mina** *David Evans* a48 64
2 b f Multiplex Vita Mia (Central Park (IRE))
3173[4] 3642[6] 4207[8] 5250[5] (6250) 6359[7] 7156[9] *7810[7]*
**Vite Princesse (FR)** *Frau M Weber*
3 ch f Intendant(GER) Chavala (GER) (Protektor (GER))
*7630a[12]*
**Vito Volterra (IRE)** *Michael Smith* a29 47
7 b g Antonius Pius(USA) River Abouali (Bluebird (USA))
2423[11] 3667[P]
**Vittachi** *Alistair Whillans* a56 65
7 b g Bertolini(USA) Miss Lorilaw (FR) (Homme De Loi (IRE))
1970[11] 2515[6] 4259[8] 4520[6] 6825[7] 7100[7] 7283[7]
**Vitznau (IRE)** *K F Clutterbuck* a66 50
10 b g Val Royal(FR) Neat Dish (CAN) (Stalwart (USA))
*858[2] 1009[5] 1387[3]*
**Viva Colonia (IRE)** *Brian Ellison* 50
9 ch g Traditionally(USA) Ansariya (USA) (Shahrastani (USA))
6864[11]
**Viva Cuba (FR)** *C Scandella* 71
2 b c On Est Bien(IRE) Petite Flotilla (FR) (Crillon (FR))
5588a[8]
**Viva Madiba (IRE)** *Daniel Kubler* a41
2 b f Kodiac Degree Of Honor (FR) (Highest Honor (FR))
*6675[10] 7113[9]*
**Vivat Rex (IRE)** *Alan Bailey* a86 85
3 b c Fastnet Rock(AUS) Strawberry Roan (IRE) (Sadler's Wells (USA))
7144a[15] *7662[7] 7974[8] 8290[3]*
**Viva Verglas (IRE)** *David Barron* a97 94
3 gr g Verglas(IRE) Yellow Trumpet (Petong)
1968[6] 2116[2] 7101[8] 7280[8] 7441[18] *7738[7] 7889[9] 8136[6] 8279[2]* ◆
**Viva Vettori** *Brian Forsey* a59 60
10 ch g Vettori(IRE) Cruinn A Bhord (Inchinor)
*1025[4]* 1845[5] 2251[11]
**Vivere (IRE)** *David O'Meara* 85
3 b f Montjeu(IRE) Valdara (Darshaan)
1303[7]
**Vivi's Charis (IRE)** *Sir Michael Stoute* a50 57
2 ch f Rock Of Gibraltar(IRE) Amathusia (Selkirk (USA))
*5821[10]* 6868[7] *7372[5]*
**Vivo Per Lei (IRE)** *Marco Botti* a49 57
2 b f Mastercraftsman(IRE) Sabancaya (Nayef (USA))
4444[15] *5549[5]* 6333[3]
**Vivre La Reve** *James Unett* a66
2 b f Assertive Noor El Houdah (IRE) (Fayruz)
*6408[8] 7181[4] 7573[3] 7763[3] 8000[5] 8254[3]*
**Vixen Hill** *Charles Hills* a63 42
2 b f Acclamation Heckle (In The Wings)
5774[8] *7062[8] 7549[6]*
**Vizadora (FR)** *G Doleuze* 66
2 gr f Deportivo Viziyya (FR) (Sinndar (IRE))
5293a[10]
**Viztoria (IRE)** *Edward Lynam* 114
4 b f Oratorio(IRE) Viz (IRE) (Darshaan)
2570a[4] 5223a[12] (7140a) 7272[9]
**Vlatori (FR)** *J Van Handenhove* a67 79
6 ch g Vatori(FR) Dame De Bosnie (FR) (Linamix (FR))
920a[7]
**Vocaliser (IRE)** *J S Bolger* 90
2 b c Vocalised(USA) Bring Back Matron (IRE) (Rock Of Gibraltar (IRE))
6348a[5]
**Vocal Nation (IRE)** *J S Bolger* 72
2 b f Vocalised(USA) Six Nations (USA) (Danzig (USA))
6375a[26]
**Vocational (USA)** *A Al Raihe* a80 77
5 b m Exceed And Excel(AUS) Carry On Katie (USA) (Fasliyev (USA))
240a[8]
**Vodka Chaser (IRE)** *Alison Hutchinson* a54 78
3 b f Baltic King Suffer Her (IRE) (Whipper (USA))
*86[6]* 1860[2] 2943[2] 3487[7] (3679) 3972[2] 4565[2] 4890[4] 5060[3] (5535) 5945[9] 6355[3] 6441[3]
**Vodka Time (IRE)** *Shaun Harris* a20 82
3 b c Indian Haven Cappuccino (IRE) (Mujadil (USA))
*501[5] 624[9] 892[7]* 2281[5] 4365[3] 4536[2] 4674[4] 6213[5] ◆ 6674[20] 6873[12] 7167[7]
**Vodkato (FR)** *S Wattel* a104 99
6 b g Russian Blue(IRE) Perfidie (IRE) (Monsun (GER))
*1068[11] (8006a)*
**Vodka Wells (FR)** *Brian Ellison* a41 68
4 b g Irish Wells(FR) Kahipiroska (FR) (Mansonnien (FR))
3302[3] *3401[3]* 4066[2] 4548[4] 5270[6]
**Vogarth** *Michael Chapman* a41 44
10 ch g Arkadian Hero(USA) Skara Brae (Inchinor)
*93[8]* 5240[11]
**Voice Control (IRE)** *Sir Michael Stoute* a75 70
2 gr g Dalakhani(IRE) Scottish Stage (IRE) (Selkirk (USA))
5149[6] *6101[2]* 6875[4]
**Voice From Above (IRE)** *Patrick Holmes* a52 67
5 b m Strategic Prince Basin Street Blues (IRE) (Dolphin Street (FR))
*1012[6]* 1348[7] 1674[6] 2055[6] 2620[7] (2915) 3661[5] 4522[6] 6644[2] 7100[10] 7284[8] 7643[16]
**Voice Of A Leader (IRE)** *Peter Chapple-Hyam* 93
3 b g Danehill Dancer(IRE) Thewaytosanjose (IRE) (Fasliyev (USA))
7715[13]
**Voila Baileys (FR)** *F-H Graffard* 63
2 b f Slickly(FR) Jolie Et Belle (FR) (Oratorio (IRE))
1094a[10] (2976a) 3691a[8]
**Voix De La Baie (FR)** *Mlle I Gallorini* 78
3 b g Voix Du Nord(FR) Kool Girl (FR) (True Brave (USA))
5370a[9]
**Vola E Va** *B Grizzetti* 103
5 b g Oratorio(IRE) Veronica Franco (ITY) (Lomitas)
2589a[4] 3776a[10]
**Volatile (SWE)** *Jessica Long* a99 102
2 b g Strategic Prince Look That Chick (USA) (Souvenir Copy (USA))
7238[3]
**Volcanic Dust (IRE)** *Milton Bradley* a59 61
6 b m Ivan Denisovich(IRE) Top Of The Form (IRE) (Masterclass (USA))
*(164) 466[11] 797[4] 1270[4]* 2008[8] *3392[4]* 3520[2] 4151[7] 4285[6] *6561[8] 6851[4] 7737[9]*
**Volcanic Jack (IRE)** *Michael Chapman* a27 56
6 b g Kodiac Rosaria Panatta (IRE) (Mujtahid (USA))
3785[7] 4620[9] 5150[6] 5403[4] *7572[6]*
**Volito** *Anabel K Murphy* a69 55
8 ch g Bertolini(USA) Vax Rapide (Sharpo)
*192[3] 295[6] 353[2] 449[2] (663) (687) 826[3] 1144[6] 1221[6]* 3329[5] 3551[5] 4206[7] 7622[13] 7950[13] 8195[7]
**Volodina (IRE)** *Alan McCabe* a57
3 ch f Soviet Star(USA) Why Now (Dansili)
*173[6] 543[P]* 1503[10] *1890[6]*
**Volume** *Luca Cumani* 111
3 b f Mount Nelson Victoire Finale (Peintre Celebre (USA))
1535[3] (2299) 2960[3] 4461a[3] 5610[6]
**Volunteer Point (IRE)** *Mick Channon* a72
2 b f Footstepsinthesand Piffling (Pivotal)
*(8184)*
**Vorda (FR)** *P Sogorb* 113
3 b f Orpen(USA) Velda (Observatory (USA))
1273a[2] 1976[8] 3997a[4] 5223a[5] 6971a[4]
**Vortex Star** *Michael Chapman*
5 gr g Dalakhani(IRE) Spinning The Yarn (Barathea (IRE))
*930[10] 1004[5]*
**Vosne Romanee** *Keith Dalgleish* a54 69
3 ch g Arakan(USA) Vento Del Oreno (FR) (Lando (GER))
*(1632)* 1840[2] *2098[4]* 2393[6] 2741[2] 3053[5] 3105[2] (3364) 3603[2]
**Votary (IRE)** *John Gosden* a77 68
3 b c Authorized(IRE) So Admirable (Suave Dancer (USA))
*(1118)* 1690[8] 2319[15]
**Vote Often** *D K Weld* 104
3 b f Beat Hollow Minority (Generous (IRE))
(1076a) 2581a[3]
**Voyageofdiscovery (USA)** *Clive Cox* a84 86
3 bb g Henrythenavigator(USA) Look Out Lorie (USA) (Orientate (USA))
*140[4] 423[2]* ◆ 1680[2] 3464[2] (3538) 4147[5] 4647[8] 5092[6] *5550[3]*
**Waabel** *Ann Stokell* a58 52
7 bb g Green Desert(USA) Najah (IRE) (Nashwan (USA))
*766[11] 921[6] 1127[5] 1369[4]* 1838[13] *5574[5] (7940)*
**Waady (IRE)** *John Gosden* 80
2 b c Approve(IRE) Anne Bonney (Jade Robbery (USA))
5671[5] (6299) ◆
**Waahej** *Peter Hiatt* a62 59
8 b g Haafhd Madam Ninette (Mark Of Esteem (IRE))
3310[6] 3761[8] 4964[8]
**Waaleef** *Marco Botti* a68 53
2 ch c Nayef(USA) Ulfah (USA) (Danzig (USA))
7206[5] *7739[4] 7973[5] 8091[3]*
**Wachau (FR)** *K Demme* a76 67
3 bb f Dashing Blade Windsbraut (GER) (All Pride (GER))
2290a[10]
**Wadi Al Hattawi (IRE)** *Saeed bin Suroor* a77 105
4 b g Dalakhani(IRE) Carisolo (Dubai Millennium)
(2787) 3449[7] 5693[15]
**Wadirum (IRE)** *C Lotoux* a84 78
3 b c Dashing Blade Dubai (IRE) (Galileo (IRE))
*5404a[6] 5959a[3]*
**Waffle (IRE)** *David Barron* a37 85
8 ch g Kheleyf(USA) Saphire (College Chapel)
2353[7] 2849[7] 4358[2] 4976[8] 5444[11] 5996[3]
**Wag'n Tail (SPA)** *C Delcher-Sanchez* 103
2 ch c Dyhim Diamond(IRE) All Woman (Groom Dancer (USA))
7557a[6]
**Wahaab (IRE)** *Richard Hannon* 86
3 ch g Tamayuz Indian Ink (IRE) (Indian Ridge)
2556[9] 4918[7] 6260[15]
**Wahgah (USA)** *Saeed bin Suroor* a103 98
3 b f Distorted Humor(USA) Basaata (USA) (Dixieland Band (USA))
2129[5] *(2649)* 3560[3] 4710[13] *(5487)* ◆ *6566[2]* 7105[3] *7553[3]*
**Wahib (FR)** *M Delzangles* a70 92
4 b g Invincible Spirit(IRE) Wardat Allayl (IRE) (Mtoto)
*7437a[13]*
**Waikika (FR)** *Y Barberot* a84 98
3 b f Whipper(USA) Fruhling Feuer (FR) (Green Tune (USA))
*5843a[8]*
**Waila** *Sir Michael Stoute* 106
4 ch f Notnowcato Crystal Cavern (USA) (Be My Guest (USA))
1942[4] 3500[2] 4213[2] 4824[3] 5611[6]
**Wakea (USA)** *Jeremy Noseda* a88 92
3 bb c Cape Cross(IRE) Imiloa (USA) (Kingmambo (USA))
3315[4] ◆ *(3856)* 4887[2]
**Wake Forest (GER)** *A Wohler* 112
4 b c Sir Percy Wurfspiel (GER) (Lomitas)
(6914a) 7316a[6]
**Wakeup Little Suzy (IRE)** *Marco Botti* a78 76
4 ch f Peintre Celebre(USA) Maramba (USA) (Hussonet (USA))
*180[4] 461[4] 1099[3]*
**Waldfest** *A De Royer-Dupre* a68 54
3 ch f Hurricane Run(IRE) Gifted Icon (IRE) (Peintre Celebre (USA))
7164a[5]
**Waldnah** *John Gosden* a74 69
2 ch f New Approach(IRE) Waldmark (GER) (Mark Of Esteem (IRE))
6868[2] *7184[2] 7658[2] 8173[10]*
**Walk Like A Giant** *Michael Appleby* a71 63
3 b g Sir Percy Temple Of Thebes (IRE) (Bahri (USA))
2365[5] 3332[4] *8282[2]* ◆
**Walk Right Back (IRE)** *Micky Hammond* a58 64
3 b c Dandy Man(IRE) Certainlei (IRE) (Definite Article)
6625[10] 7178[13]
**Walk With An Angel** *Amy Weaver* a70 90
3 b f Myboycharlie(IRE) Broughtons Revival (Pivotal)
*579[4] (756) 957[5]* 2227a[3]
**Wall Of Sound** *Tom Dascombe* 103
4 b f Singspiel(IRE) Veiled Beauty (USA) (Royal Academy (USA))
(1539) 1942[7] 3307[2] 4634[4] 6464[3] 7326a[4] 7615a[3]
**Wall Street Boss (USA)** *James Fanshawe* a77 77
4 b g Street Boss(USA) Pad The Wallet (USA) (Skip Away (USA))
*1798[10]* 3226[2] 3699[4] 4369[3] 5062[4] *5863[3] 6721[3]*
**Wally's Wisdom** *Lee Carter* a73 69
2 b c Dutch Art Faldal (Falbrav (IRE))
6125[7] *7660[4] 7927[7] 8174[5]*
**Walta (IRE)** *Roy Bowring* a65 40
3 b g Tagula(IRE) Hi Katriona (IRE) (Second Empire (IRE))
*(1243)* 1585[8] 2163[8] 3222[11] *3406[6]* 3650[10] 4411[10] *7825[8] 7997[9] 8088[11]*
**Walter De La Mare (IRE)** *Anabel K Murphy* a33 55
7 b g Barathea(IRE) Banutan (IRE) (Charnwood Forest (IRE))
2942[2] 3309[8] 4279[5] 6252[3] 6542[10]
**Waltz Darling (IRE)** *Keith Reveley* 69
6 b g Iffraaj Aljafliyah (Halling (USA))
1374[2] 2055[10] 2213[2] 6216[9] 6542[9] (7007) 7509[7]
**Waltzing Matilda (IRE)** *T Stack* 104
3 b f Danehill Dancer(IRE) Simadartha (USA) (Gone West (USA))
2186a[4] 3352[5] 4459a[5] 5955a[4]
**Waltzing To Win (AUS)** *David Huxtable* 95
5 b m Benicio(AUS) Empress Waltz (AUS) (Rubiton (AUS))
7126a[8] 7395a[9]
**Wandjina (AUS)** *Gai Waterhouse* 109
3 b c Snitzel(AUS) La Bamba (AUS) (Last Tycoon)
7467a[10]
**Wandsworth (IRE)** *Roger Varian* a85 82
4 br g Authorized(IRE) Henties Bay (IRE) (Cape Cross (IRE))
3212[3] *6100[7] 8080[5]*
**Wannabe Better (IRE)** *T Stack* a67 109
4 b f Duke Of Marmalade(IRE) Wannabe (Shirley Heights)
1076a[6] 1473a[3] 2042a[3] 2572a[12] (3412a) 3864a[4] 4478a[6] 5869a[3] 6351a[5]
**Wannabe King** *Geoffrey Harker* a67 86
8 b g King's Best(USA) Wannabe Grand (IRE) (Danehill (USA))
1646[3] 1958[13] 2548[11] 3483[9] 3915[2] 4451[4] 5196[8] 5496[12] 6490[6] *7871[6]*
**Wannabe Magic** *Geoffrey Deacon* a26 50
3 b f Authorized(IRE) Wannabe Free (Red Ransom (USA))
2432[8] 5596[10] 5846[10] *7197[10]*
**Wannabe Your Man** *George Baker* a75 82
4 b g Halling(USA) Wannabe Posh (IRE) (Grand Lodge (USA))
*1118[4]* (1849) 2774[2] 3680[2] 6439[3] 7129[10] *7402[9]*
**Wannabe Yours (IRE)** *John Gosden* 114
3 b c Dubawi(IRE) Wannabe Posh (IRE) (Grand Lodge (USA))
(2432) (2983) ◆ (4850) 6710[11]
**War Alert (USA)** *David Brown* a48 86
2 b f War Front(USA) Pastel Gal (USA) (Lemon Drop Kid (USA))
3063[3] (4269) 5983[4] (6312) 6530[5] *7605a[6]*
**Warapito** *Richard Guest* 30
2 b g Stimulation(IRE) Shining Oasis (IRE) (Mujtahid (USA))
3358[8] 3934[11] 5886[10]
**Warbird** *M Halford* a88 95
3 b c Royal Applause Air Biscuit (IRE) (Galileo (IRE))
5957a[9]
**Warbond** *Michael Madgwick* a62 47
6 ch g Monsieur Bond(IRE) Pick A Nice Name (Polar Falcon (USA))
*211[7] 467[3] 740[2] 815[4] 1141[4] 1917[3] 2930[5] 3576[5] 4266[7]* 6242[6] 6481[6] 6883[10] 7369[9] 8111[2] 8198[2]
**Warbrook (IRE)** *John Gosden* a69 74
3 ch c Tamayuz Squander (Dr Fong (USA))
*157[8] 355[2] 468[3]*
**War Command (USA)** *A P O'Brien* 118
3 b c War Front(USA) Wandering Star (USA) (Red Ransom (USA))
1951[9] 3320[4] 3984[7]
**War Dancer (USA)** *Kenneth McPeek* a75 108
4 bb c War Front(USA) Deed I Do (USA) (Alydeed (CAN))
7324a[7]
**Wardat Dubai** *B W Hills* 76
2 b f Mawatheeq(USA) Efisio's Star (Efisio)
6928[5] 7377[3]
**Warden Bond** *William Stone* a69 44
6 ch g Monsieur Bond(IRE) Warden Rose (Compton Place)
*7526[8] 7813[6] 8004[7] 8199[4]*
**War Dispatch (USA)** *J-C Rouget* a88
2 rg c War Front(USA) Photograph (USA) (Unbridled's Song (USA))
*(7723a)*
**War Envoy (USA)** *A P O'Brien* 111
2 b c War Front(USA) La Conseillante (USA) (Elusive Quality (USA))
2855a[3] 3318[9] 3738a[3] 5954a[3] 6326[2] 6968a[5] 7590a[12]
**Warfare** *Tim Fitzgerald* a79 71
5 b g Soviet Star(USA) Fluffy (Efisio)
*172[4]* ◆ *300[5] 832[7]* 1356[9] 1842[5] *2399[3] 3795[2] 4968[3]* (5269) *8161[4]*
**War Lord (IRE)** *Philip Kirby* 72
4 b g Aussie Rules(USA) Carn Lady (IRE) (Woodman (USA))
2913[6] 4468[9]
**Warlu Way** *Michael Easterby* 79
7 b g Sakhee(USA) Conspiracy (Rudimentary (USA))
1934[6] 2259[12] 2787[11] 3250[9] 4175[4] 4498[5] 4921[9] 5150[5] 6171[6]
**War Monger (USA)** *Doug Watson* a65 96
10 b h War Chant(USA) Carnival Delight (USA) (Half A Year (USA))
309a[9]
**Warm Order** *Tony Carroll* a55 49
3 b f Assertive Even Hotter (Desert Style (IRE))
3214[4] 3564[10] *7285[4] 7737[7] 8023[2] (8119) 8230[6]*
**War Of Art (IRE)** *Tom Dascombe* a88
3 b c Tamayuz Lucky Clio (IRE) (Key Of Luck (USA))
*(230) (604)*
**War Paint (IRE)** *Tom Dascombe* 66
2 br f Excellent Art Stairway To Glory (IRE) (Kalanisi (IRE))
1482[3] 2022[2] 2313[12] 5129[4] 6610[12]
**War Poet** *Clive Mulhall* a86 89
7 b g Singspiel(IRE) Summer Sonnet (Baillamont (USA))
1196[12] *1816[2]* (2052) 2790[3] 7125[19] 7279[2] 7504[7]
**Warrigal (IRE)** *Jeremy Noseda* a86 75
4 ch g Mount Nelson Waldblume (GER) (Halling (USA))
*1798[2]* 2640[3] *3472[2]* 3761[3] *(5259)*
**Warrior Of Light (IRE)** *David Lanigan* a91 103
3 b g High Chaparral(IRE) Strawberry Fledge (USA) (Kingmambo (USA))
*2060[2]* ◆ 2496[5] 3182[2] (4819) ◆ 5673[8] 6061[13]
**Warsaw (IRE)** *S Seemar* a83 81
9 ch h Danehill Dancer(IRE) For Evva Silca (Piccolo)
240a[10]
**War Singer (USA)** *Johnny Farrelly* a72 89
7 b g War Chant(USA) Sister Marilyn (USA) (Saint Ballado (CAN))
*3860[7]* 4441[13] (5931) 6303[5] 6878[5] (7136) 7597[7]
**War Spirit** *Richard Hannon* a68 89
3 ro g Exceed And Excel(AUS) Alybgood (CAN) (Alydeed (CAN))
*1173[4]* 2278[3] (2985) (3433) (3959) 4898[8] 7212[12]
**Wasabi (IRE)** *John Berry* a48 55
5 b m Tiger Hill(IRE) Quinzey (JPN) (Carnegie (IRE))
1865[4] 3780[6] *4615[6]* 5342[4] 6542[13]
**Waseem Faris (IRE)** *Mick Channon* a75 84
5 b g Exceed And Excel(AUS) Kissing Time (Lugana Beach)
1489[5] 1541[4] 1944[2] 2503[10] 3275[5] 3697[9] 4027[6] 4391[6] 4762[7] 5275[5] 5880[8] 6191[2] 6296[3] 6658[4] 6873[3]
**Waspy** *Dr Jeremy Naylor* a57 28
5 ch m King's Best(USA) Gib (IRE) (Rock Of Gibraltar (IRE))
*687[10]*
**Watchable** *David O'Meara* 107
4 ch g Pivotal Irresistible (Cadeaux Genereux)
(1757) ◆ 2503[3] ◆ 2898[4] 3420[3] 4648[3] (6369a) 6533[12] 7122[13]
**Waterclock (IRE)** *Jedd O'Keeffe* a70 96
5 ch g Notnowcato Waterfall One (Nashwan (USA))
2073[15] 3321[16] 3717[19] 5334[8] 6640[4] 7107[27]
**Water For Life** *Dave Morris* a50 43
3 ch f Mount Nelson Echo River (USA) (Irish River (FR))
*28[4] 198[6]* 1684[5] 2526[9] 2878[7] 4304[11] 5321[7] 6194[U] *7546[11] 7645[8]*
**Water Hole (IRE)** *John Gosden* a79 103
3 b f Oasis Dream Arosa (IRE) (Sadler's Wells (USA))
(4112) (5151) 5927[3] 6464[10] 7319a[4] *7553[11]*
**Waterloo Dock** *Emma Baker* a58
9 b g Hunting Lion(IRE) Scenic Air (Hadeer)
*192[10] 340[2] 424[6] 688[7] 799[8] 851[5] 996[8] 1104[4] 1236[7]* 2312[9] 8111[13]
**Waterloo Sunrise (IRE)** *S M Duffy* a67 64
9 b g Craigsteel Waterloo Sunset (Deep Run)
*7435a[10]*
**Water Queen** *William Haggas* a80 73
3 b f Shamardal(USA) Central Force (Pivotal)
2780[5] 3277[4] 5622[2] (6247) *6945[2]*

**Watersmeet** *Mark Johnston* a72 80
3 gr g Dansili Under The Rainbow (Fantastic Light (USA))
*626[2] 816[2] 1035[2]* 2867[9] 3466[3] (3880) 4388[3] 4786[3] 5647[4]

**Water Thief (USA)** *Mark Johnston* a80 75
2 b c Bellamy Road(USA) Sometime (IRE) (Royal Academy (USA))
4353[3] 4633[5] 5712[3] 6108[4] 6364[2] *(6769) 7226[7]*

**Watheeq (USA)** *A Al Raihe* a81 51
5 b g Street Cry(IRE) Mehthaaf (USA) (Nureyev (USA))
*243a[15]*

**Wattaboutsteve** *Ralph J Smith* a38
3 b g Araafa(IRE) Angel Kate (IRE) (Invincible Spirit (IRE))
*7370[8] 7699[7] 7865[8]*

**Watt Broderick (IRE)** *Ian Williams* a81 70
5 ch g Hawk Wing(USA) Kingsridge (IRE) (King's Theatre (IRE))
*(747) 848[5] 7866[2]*

**Watts Up Son** *Richard Price* a35 80
6 b g Diktat Local Fancy (Bahamian Bounty)
5750[3] 7042[10] 7516[9]

**Waveguide (IRE)** *David Simcock* a74 82
5 b m Dubawi(IRE) Million Waves (IRE) (Mull Of Kintyre (USA))
*365[2] (491) (691) 857[4]* 2032[3] (2528) (3066) 3476[2] 3727[2] 4182[5] *6945[6]*

**Waverunner** *Mark Johnston* a77 80
4 ch f Raven's Pass(USA) Danuta (USA) (Sunday Silence (USA))
*96[4]*

**Waving** *Tony Carroll* a77 63
5 b g High Chaparral(IRE) Pretty Davis (USA) (Trempolino (USA))
*277[3] 368[3] (460) (530) (606) (695) (794a) 868[2]*

**Waydownsouth (IRE)** *Patrick J Flynn* a82 82
7 b g Chevalier(IRE) Ruffit (IRE) (Revoque (IRE))
7476a[6]

**Weald** *Hans-Inge Larsen* a75 75
9 b g Bering New Abbey (Sadler's Wells (USA))
5744a[11]

**Weald Of Kent (USA)** *John Gosden* a67
2 bb c Successful Appeal(USA) Apple Of Kent (USA) (Kris S (USA))
*8075[6]*

**Wealth (IRE)** *Richard Fahey* a66 69
3 b g Invincible Spirit(IRE) Whisp (GER) (Rainbow Quest (USA))
*99[5]* 3978[10]

**Weapon Of Choice (IRE)** *Stuart Kittow* a85 90
6 b g Iffraaj Tullawadgeen (IRE) (Sinndar (IRE))
1164[18] 1653[13] 4184[5] 4827[10] 6523[11] 6786[8] 7136[8]

**Weardiditallgorong** *Des Donovan* a46 50
2 b f Fast Company(IRE) Little Oz (IRE) (Red Ransom (USA))
3311[6] 3671[13] *4075[8]* 6333[6] (7536)

**We Are (IRE)** *F Head* 114
3 b f Dansili In Clover (Inchinor)
2586a[DSQ] (6969a)

**Wedding Ring (IRE)** *Charlie Appleby* a94 99
3 b f Oasis Dream Cast In Gold (USA) (Elusive Quality (USA))
*(203a) 506a[4]* 1513[6] 3724[4] 4163[3] 4668[3] ◆ 5612[F] (Dead)

**Weddings Off** *Bernard Llewellyn*
3 ch f Dreams End Wax Lyrical (Safawan)
2118[7]

**Wedding Speech (IRE)** *James Fanshawe* a58 60
4 b f Acclamation Wedding Cake (IRE) (Groom Dancer (USA))
1874[8]

**Wedding Wish (IRE)** *George Margarson* 85
3 b f Acclamation Have Faith (IRE) (Machiavellian (USA))
1534[19] 4816[3] 6638[8]

**Wedgewood Estates** *Tony Carroll* a62 59
3 ch f Assertive Heaven (Reel Buddy (USA))
*315[5] 745[3]* 2943[3] 3564[8] 4155[5] *4972[11] 6488[2]* 6816[2] *(7420)* 7547[7] *8142[5]*

**Wedlock** *Sir Mark Prescott Bt* a69
2 ch f Pivotal Wedding Party (Groom Dancer (USA))
*7400[5] (7771)* ◆

**Wednaan** *M F De Kock* a99 85
3 b c Dubawi(IRE) Marine Bleue (IRE) (Desert Prince (IRE))
*594a[3]* 770a[10]

**Wee Frankie (IRE)** *Keith Dalgleish* 91
3 ch g Heliostatic(IRE) Kimono (IRE) (Machiavellian (USA))
(2292) (3923) 5633[5] 6479[7]

**Wee Jean** *Mick Channon* a94 103
3 b f Captain Gerrard(IRE) Reeli Silli (Dansili)
*1067[10]* 1278[2] 1614[3] 2111[2] (2556) 3357[3] 3983[2] 4854[7] 5176[7] 6351a[5]

**Weeken (FR)** *Y Gourraud* a62 69
3 gr c Kendargent(FR) Miss Breezy (FR) (Sicyos (USA))
7269a[6]

**Weekendatbernies (IRE)** *Ed de Giles* a72 87
3 b g War Chant(USA) Morena Park (Pivotal)
3537[3] 3804[3] (4813) ◆ *5550[6]* 5930[2] 6263[3] 6552[5] 6871[2] 7136[5]

**Weekend Getaway (IRE)** *Clive Brittain* a69 68
3 b f Acclamation Week End (Selkirk (USA))
*1427[4]* 2433[9]

**Wefeen (FR)** *F Chappet* a37 81
3 bl g Zafeen(FR) Nexia (FR) (Linamix (FR))
1620a[3] 2290a[5]

**We Have A Dream** *Ann Stokell* a81 74
9 bb g Oasis Dream Final Shot (Dalsaan)
*9[10] 694[11] 845[8] 1010[9]*

**Weichsel (GER)** *Markus Klug* 96
2 bb f Soldier Hollow Well Known (GER) (Konigsstuhl (GER))
(6778a) 7315a[11]

**Weisse Girl** *Nick Kent* a36 54
3 b f Halling(USA) White Turf (GER) (Tiger Hill (IRE))
1847[9] 2355[9] *3792[9]* 4070[10]

**Welcome Sir (FR)** *E Lellouche* a56 87
4 b g Zamindar(USA) Chandi Dasa (IRE) (Sadler's Wells (USA))
5225a[6] *5964a[12]*

**Welcometothejungle** *Keiran Burke* 25
6 b m Lucky Story(USA) Kasamba (Salse (USA))
2925[5]

**Weld Al Emarat** *Kevin Ryan* a87
2 b c Dubawi(IRE) Spirit Of Dubai (IRE) (Cape Cross (IRE))
*(8083)* ◆

**Weld Arab (IRE)** *D K Weld* 60
3 b g Shamardal(USA) Itqaan (USA) (Danzig (USA))
4951a[6]

**Welease Bwian (IRE)** *Stuart Williams* a76 74
5 b g Kheleyf(USA) Urbanize (USA) (Chester House (USA))
*141[2] 233[3]* ◆ *714[9] 777[3] 987[5]* 1878[6] 2312[3] 2865[2] 3246[5] 3470[3] (3826) 4553[8] 5070[4] 5861[6] 6266[12] 7775[5] (8186)

**Well Acquainted (IRE)** *Charlie Appleby* a90 97
4 b c Orientate(USA) Stunning Rose (IRE) (Sadler's Wells (USA))
*808a[10]*

**We'll Deal Again** *Michael Easterby* a83 81
7 b g Gentleman's Deal(IRE) Emma Amour (Emarati (USA))
*719[4] 1049[4] 1283[7]* 1566[3] 3256[10] 3599[8] (4925) 5470[2] 6150[4] 6478[2] 7282[7]

**Well Finished** *Ralph Beckett* a55 31
3 rg f Mastercraftsman(IRE) Grain Of Gold (Mr Prospector (USA))
5347[5] *6238[9]*

**Well Fleeced** *D Prod'Homme* a74 75
2 b g Excellent Art Diksie Dancer (Diktat)
1161[8] 1504[7] 2623[2] 3081[4] 3691a[3] *(3871a) 5618a[2]*

**We'll Go Walking (IRE)** *J P Murtagh* 105
4 b f Authorized(IRE) Senora Galilei (IRE) (Galileo (IRE))
1078a[13] 2263a[2] 3307[3] 3996[4] 7273[8]

**Welliesinthewater (IRE)** *Derek Shaw* a64 57
4 b g Footstepsinthesand Shadow Ash (IRE) (Ashkalani (IRE))
*489[10] (1125) 3402[8]* ◆ *4613[9] 5605[4] 7427[3]*

**Well Owd Mon** *Andrew Hollinshead* a61 55
4 b g Vitus Farina (IRE) (Golan (IRE))
*460[3] 639[5] 781[2] 915[7] 1132[3] (1453) 1815[5]* 2942[9] 3617[3] 3973[7] 5127[4] 5508[5] 5904[2] 6410[5] 6900[4] (7895) 8145[4] 8289[2]

**Well Painted (IRE)** *Andy Turnell* a93 54
5 ch g Excellent Art Aoife (IRE) (Thatching)
*1453[3] 408[5] 559[7]* 3718[7] *(4080)* 4959[4] *5487[11] 7757[12] 7998[10] 8190[5]*

**We'll Shake Hands (FR)** *K R Burke* 75
3 b g Excellent Art Amou Daria (FR) (Kendor (FR))
1723[6] 2205[5] (2828) 4465a[4] 5497[2] 6057[12] 7269a[10]

**Welsh Dancer** *John Butler*
6 b g Dubawi(IRE) Rosie's Posy (IRE) (Suave Dancer (USA))
*7376[11]*

**Welsh Inlet (IRE)** *John Bridger* a60 67
6 br m Kheleyf(USA) Ervedya (IRE) (Doyoun)
*184[4] 244[7] 425[2] 592[5] 687[3] 798[3] 987[7] 1110[7] 1408[6]* 1631[2] (1877) (2282) 2775[6] 3390[6] 4047[3] 4342[2] 4811[4] 5125[3] 5252[4] 5685[7] 5979[5] 6481[11]

**Welsh Rebel** *Nikki Evans* 47
2 ch g Cockney Rebel(IRE) Lasting Image (Zilzal (USA))
7667[9]

**Welsh Sunrise** *Stuart Williams* a82 70
4 b f Vita Rosa(JPN) Chapel Corner (IRE) (Alhaarth (IRE))
*(84) (453) 779[2] 1217[6] 1554[9]* 4918[8] 5726[6] 6463[3] 6657[5] *7196[7] 7993[4] 8185[8]*

**Weltmacht** *Markus Klug* 97
3 b f Mount Nelson Wild Side (GER) (Sternkoenig (IRE))
3046a[2] 4007a[12]

**We Miss Artie (CAN)** *Todd Pletcher* a112 102
3 bb c Artie Schiller(USA) Athena's Gift (USA) (Fusaichi Pegasus (USA))
*1964a[10]*

**Wentworth (IRE)** *Bettina Andersen* 69
4 b c Acclamation Miss Corinne (Mark Of Esteem (IRE))
5744a[12]

**Wentworth Falls** *Charlie Appleby* a99 79
2 gr g Dansili Strawberry Morn (CAN) (Travelling Victor (CAN))
*5278[U]* 5646[3] *6268[2] 7371[5] (7920) (8113)*

**Wesie's Dream** *Mark Usher* a54 45
2 b f Stimulation(IRE) Morning Queen (IRE) (Night Shift (USA))
4740[8] *5509[4]* 6024[7] *8076[5] 8287[5]*

**West Coast Dream** *Roy Brotherton* a72 70
7 b g Oasis Dream Californie (IRE) (Rainbow Quest (USA))
*191[6] 412[5] 694[5] 841[4] (1030) 1431[4]* 1912[7] 2434[6] 3222[4] 3561[3] 4981[7] *(5486)* 7342[8] 7806[7] 7949[7] 8255[6]

**West End Lad** *Roy Bowring* a71 76
11 b g Tomba Cliburnel News (IRE) (Horage)
*176[4] (546)*

**Westerly** *Luke Dace* a71 71
3 b f Rail Link Humility (Polar Falcon (USA))
*2650[6]* (3498) 4020[7] 4948[11] *5557[4]* 6110[2] *7689[6] 8015[6]*

**Western Bella** *Clive Cox* 65
3 b f High Chaparral(IRE) Sindarbella (Sinndar (IRE))
6298[4] 7304[4]

**Western Hymn** *John Gosden* a87 114
3 b g High Chaparral(IRE) Blue Rhapsody (Cape Cross (IRE))
(1419) (1699) 2990[6] (4483a) 5406a[4] 7275[4]

**Western Playboy (IRE)** *Sylvester Kirk* a65 63
2 b g Kodiac Dreamalot (Falbrav (IRE))
2298[15] 2859[6] 3140[9] *5043[2] 5306[3] 5798[6]*

**Western Sands (IRE)** *Richard Fahey* 68
3 ch f Footstepsinthesand West One (Gone West (USA))
2203[5] 2827[6]

**Westhoughton** *David O'Meara* 73
2 b c Equiano(FR) Khyber Knight (IRE) (Night Shift (USA))
2472[3] 4110[8] 4357[4] 4857[2] 5266[3] 5885[2] 6401[4] 6453[3] 6831[2] 7055[5]

**West Leake (IRE)** *Paul Burgoyne* a64 45
8 b g Acclamation Kilshanny (Groom Dancer (USA))
*295[2] 576[8] 688[4] 1017[3] 1110[3] 1408[4] 1766[3]* 2282[6] *2648[4] 8298[2]*

**West Leake Diman (IRE)** *Mrs Ilka Gansera-Leveque* a27 85
5 b g Namid Roselyn (Efisio)
4620[10] 5470[12]

**West Leake Hare (IRE)** *David Nicholls* a66 83
5 b g Choisir(AUS) March Hare (Groom Dancer (USA))
1376[9]

**Westminster (IRE)** *Michael Appleby* a89 56
3 b g Exceed And Excel(AUS) Pivka (Pivotal)
1352[10] 1614[9] 2495[5] *2921[4]* 4572[8] *5603[5] 7732[8] 7955[5] 8209[2]*

**West Of Venus (USA)** *J E Pease* a79 94
4 b f Street Cry(IRE) Wild Planet (USA) (Nureyev (USA))
4722a[6] 6218a[8]

**Westwood Hoe** *John Gosden* a81
3 b c Oasis Dream Disco Volante (Sadler's Wells (USA))
*7901[2] 8048[2] (8294)*

**Wet Sail (USA)** *Charlie Fellowes* 102
2 b g Henrythenavigator(USA) Aljawza (USA) (Riverman (USA))
1977[7] 5248[3] (5874) 6933[3] 7590a[14]

**Wevanella (FR)** *Alain Couetil* a79 102
5 gr m Gentlewave(IRE) Pimpinella (FR) (Highest Honor (FR))
6917a[10]

**Wexford Town (IRE)** *J S Bolger* 105
3 b c Teofilo(IRE) Night Visit (Sinndar (IRE))
(3491a) 6349a[13]

**Weybridge Light** *David Thompson* a51 44
9 b g Fantastic Light(USA) Nuryana (Nureyev (USA))
3843[6] 4319[7] 6117[5] *7572[3] 7893[8]*

**Whaileyy (IRE)** *M Halford* a91 81
6 b g Holy Roman Emperor(IRE) Alshoowg (USA) (Riverman (USA))
*5510[10] 271[7]* 5958a[14] *7873a[8]*

**Whaleweigh Station** *J R Jenkins* a90 89
3 b g Zamindar(USA) Looby Loo (Kyllachy)
*2682[5]* 3229[3] 3980[6] 5531[2] (6042) 6895[10] *7852[9] 8252[5] 8279[4]*

**What About Carlo (FR)** *Eve Johnson Houghton* 103
3 b g Creachadoir(IRE) Boccatenera (GER) (Artan (IRE))
(1696) 2565[9] (2986) 4125[4] 5666[8] 5928[12]

**What A Dandy (IRE)** *Jim Boyle* a72 63
3 b g Dandy Man(IRE) Ibtihal (IRE) (Hamas (IRE))
*291[3]* 2624[7] 3559[3] 4329[12] *4545[7]* 5247[8] 5532[3] 6297[7] *6857[9] 7759[8] 7805[4] (7942) (8169)* 8321[4]

**What A Party (IRE)** *Gay Kelleway* a75 75
2 ch f Windsor Knot(IRE) Tarziyma (IRE) (Kalanisi (IRE))
3893[5] 4444[3] (4764) *(5279)* 5664[7] 6436[5] *8174[3] 8276a[4]*

**What A Scorcher** *Clive Cox* 73
3 b f Authorized(IRE) Street Fire (IRE) (Street Cry (IRE))
1701[3] 2280[6] 3892[7] 7304[2]

**What Asham** *Ralph Beckett* a62
2 b c Pivotal Coy (IRE) (Danehill (USA))
*7973[7] 8292[9]*

**What A Squirtle** *Dave Roberts*
2 b c What A Caper(IRE) Squirtle (IRE) (In The Wings)
4103[6]

**What A Story (FR)** *C Boutin* 74
2 ch c Gold Away(IRE) Jackanory (FR) (Marchand De Sable (USA))
7344a[2]

**What Could She Be (IRE)** *Bryan Smart* a64 60
2 b f Dark Angel(IRE) Halliwell House (Selkirk (USA))
7712[3] *8007[6] 8205[2]*

**What Lies Ahead (IRE)** *W McCreery* 85
4 ch f Saffron Walden(FR) Millennium Lilly (IRE) (Mujadil (USA))
4951a[3] 7144a[12]

**What Say You (IRE)** *K R Burke* 91
2 b f Galileo(IRE) Alta Anna (FR) (Anabaa (USA))
4604[4] (5644) ◆ 6709[6]

**What's Up Doc (IRE)** *Lawney Hill* a35 79
13 b g Dr Massini(IRE) Surprise Treat (IRE) (Shalford (IRE))
*881[0]*

**What Usain** *Geoffrey Oldroyd* a51 44
2 b g Misu Bond(IRE) Bond Shakira (Daggers Drawn (USA))
3255[10] 4790[10] 6449[9] 6931[9] *(7992)*

**Wheat Sheaf** *Roger Charlton* 80
2 b c Iffraaj Harvest Queen (IRE) (Spinning World (USA))
7382[2]

**When Will It End (IRE)** *Richard Hannon* a66 85
2 b c Kodiac Alexander Duchess (IRE) (Desert Prince (IRE))
*2458[3]* (2859) (4203) 4897[4] 5310[2] 6229[3] 7443[7]

**Where's Reiley (USA)** *Michael Attwater* a75 71
8 bb g Doneraile Court(USA) Plateau (USA) (Seeking The Gold (USA))
*93[6] 312[6] 424[2] (557) 662[5] 826[5] 889[3] 1017[6] 1312[2]* 1573[7] 2723[10] 4042[7] 4544[2]

**Where's Sue (IRE)** *Charles Hills* 26
2 br f Dark Angel(IRE) The Hermitage (IRE) (Kheleyf (USA))
4396[15] 4973[13]

**Where's Susie** *Michael Madgwick* a77 66
9 ch m Where Or When(IRE) Linda's Schoolgirl (IRE) (Grand Lodge (USA))
*214[6] 292[8] 742[5]*

**Where's Tiger** *Jedd O'Keeffe* 69
3 b g Tiger Hill(IRE) Where's Broughton (Cadeaux Genereux)
1308[3] 1906[8] 2393[2] 3098[6] 3789[5] 5077[3] (5300) 5717[2] 6981[8]

**Where The Boys Are (IRE)** *Ed McMahon* a51 71
3 b f Dylan Thomas(IRE) Promise Of Love (Royal Applause)
(2023) 2943[4] 3462[6] (4890) 6455[6]

**While You Wait (IRE)** *Gary Moore* a81 66
5 b g Whipper(USA) Azra (IRE) (Danehill (USA))
*186[2] 471[3] 758[4]*

**Whim** *F Head* 98
3 br f Nayef(USA) Whazzis (Desert Prince (IRE))
1502a[6] 2816a[5] 6419a[4]

**Whimsical (IRE)** *P D Deegan* a83 89
5 b m Strategic Prince Sweet Namibia (IRE) (Namid)
3864a[6] 4276a[6]

**Whinging Willie (IRE)** *Gary Moore* a71 83
5 b g Cape Cross(IRE) Pacific Grove (Persian Bold)
*4057* 3147[7] (3556) 4119[6] 5073[6] (5521) 6264[2] 6787[2]

**Whiplash Willie** *Andrew Balding* a82 113
6 ch g Phoenix Reach(IRE) Santa Isobel (Nashwan (USA))
(1981) 2704[3] 5920[2] 6288[2] 6972a[4] 7271[4]

**Whip My Heart (IRE)** *M Delcher Sanchez* a83 76
5 b g Whipper(USA) Capetown Girl (Danzero (AUS))
*806a[14]*

**Whipper Snapper (FR)** *J-V Toux* a72 77
4 b g Whipper(USA) Margot Mine (IRE) (Choisir (AUS))
*796a[10]*

**Whipper Snapper (IRE)** *William Knight* a88 86
4 b g Whipper(USA) Topiary (IRE) (Selkirk (USA))
*(1796)* 2156[2] *2922[6]* 3180[8] 4148[8] 5213[3] *6100[3] 6609[3]* 7136[11]

**Whipphound** *Mark Brisbourne* a67 78
6 b g Whipper(USA) Golden Symbol (Wolfhound (USA))
*1148[2] 1448[7]* (1787) 2174[2] 2606[4] 2945[2] 3939[3] *6346[9]* 6695[7] 7023[15] 7307[9] *7621[8] 7950[12]*

**Whiskey N Stout (IRE)** *Sean Curran* a51 39
4 b g Amadeus Wolf Yasmin Satine (IRE) (Key Of Luck (USA))
*570[3] 640[5] 759[3]*

**Whisky Bravo** *David C Griffiths* a72 72
5 b g Byron Dress Design (IRE) (Brief Truce (USA))
*147[7]*

**Whisky Marmalade (IRE)** *David O'Meara* a58 59
2 b f Duke Of Marmalade(IRE) Nashatara (USA) (Nashwan (USA))
6935[3] 7174[11] *7816[8] 7996[4] 8165[3] 8206[5]*

**Whispered Times (USA)** *Tracy Waggott* a25 69
7 bb g More Than Ready(USA) Lightning Show (USA) (Storm Cat (USA))
1606[3] 3485[4] 3660[4] 3908[2] 4291[5] 4707[2] 5142[4] 5638[5] 5761[6]

**Whispering Star (USA)** *David Simcock* a71
3 b f War Front(USA) Eclisse (FR) (Ski Chief (USA))
*174[6] 774[2] 1098[2] 1632[2] 4321[2] 7910[2]*

**Whispering Warrior (IRE)** *David Simcock* a100 101
5 b g Oasis Dream Varenka (IRE) (Fasliyev (USA))
*804[8] (887)* 1165[11] 2618[6] 3251[6] ◆ 4173[3] (4888) 5695[14] 6321[6] 6878[3] *7803[8]*

**Whitby High Light** *Andrew Hollinshead* a79 68
3 b g Halling(USA) Ballroom Dancer (IRE) (Danehill Dancer (IRE))
*237a[7] 360a[2] 545a[3] 721a[11]* 2077[11] 2655[3] 3243[11] 4496[6] 4941[6] *5259[4]*

**Whitby Jet (IRE)** *Ed Vaughan* a76 77
6 b g Mujadil(USA) Anazah (USA) (Diesis)
*(210) (582) 849[7]* 1354[8] 1665[3] *2687[7]* 3314[5] 3825[3] 4340[5] 5758[2] 5975[2] 6192[8]

**Whitchurch** *Andrew Balding* a68
2 b g Mawatheeq(USA) Silvereine (FR) (Bering)
*7631[7] 7941[3] 8166[3]*

**White City (USA)** *S Seemar* a54
5 br g Medaglia d'Oro(USA) Bubbling Heights (FR) (Darshaan)
*238a[6]*

**Whitecrest** *John Spearing* a58 85
6 ch m Ishiguru(USA) Risky Valentine (Risk Me (FR))
1850[4] 2050[5] 2637[6] (2994) 3470[5] 3920[4] 4267[2] 4399[3] 5070[2] 5275[6] 5677[7] 5945[3] 6296[6] 6650[7] 6873[7] 7215[9] 7535[9]

**White Diamond** *Nigel Twiston-Davies* a66 66
7 b m Bertolini(USA) Diamond White (Robellino (USA))
*117[7] 278[8]*

**White Dog (IRE)** *Eugene Stanford* a69
2 b c Le Cadre Noir(IRE) Little Annie (Compton Place)
*7833[4] 8092[5] 8292[10]*

**White Flag** *Tim Easterby* a32 62
3 b f Sakhee's Secret Rainbow Spectrum (FR) (Spectrum (IRE))
2230[3] 3100[2] 3548[6] 4469[5] (4974) 5853[2] *6409[10]* 7502[5] 7644[14]

**White Lake** *Luca Cumani* 99
2 b c Pivotal White Palace (Shirley Heights)
(5655) 6291[4]

**White Nile (IRE)** *Ed Dunlop* a98 91
5 b h Galileo(IRE) Super Gift (IRE) (Darshaan)
*(1383)* ◆ *1581[6]* 2073[12] 3034[10] 4759[5]

**White Rose Runner** *Mel Brittain* a59 62
3 b f Virtual Entrap (USA) (Phone Trick (USA))
1344[3] 1441[5] 2020[12] 5336[3] 5717[8] 7640[7] *8050[4]*

**White Russian** *Henry Candy* a74 75
3 ch f Sir Percy Danse Russe (Pivotal)
1809[9] 2224[4] 3154[9] 4329[2] (4907) 5441[3] 6302[6] *7397[4]*

**White Vin Jan** *Michael Bell* a45 70
2 b f Hellvelyn Startori (Vettori (IRE))
2771[8] *4260[6]* *4610[4]* (5180) (5525) (5630) 5983[3] 6610[2] 6820[2] 7109[2]

**Who Dares Wins (IRE)** *Richard Hannon* 72
2 b c Jeremy(USA) Savignano (Polish Precedent (USA))
6551[13] 7084[4]

**Who Knows (IRE)** *C Lerner* a61 51
2 b f Captain Rio Festivite (IRE) (Fasliyev (USA))
*3872a[3]* 4882a[7] *5026a[3]* *5619a[4]*

**Whole Lotta Love (FR)** *Y Barberot* a68 67
2 b f Vespone(IRE) Fantastic Fire (GER) (Platini (GER))
*3872a[2]* *5026a[4]* *5619a[9]* 6958a[7]

**Wholelottashakin (USA)** *Thomas Bush* 95
5 b m Scat Daddy(USA) Carr Shaker (USA) (Carr De Naskra (USA))
(2227a)

**Whoopie Do** *John Gallagher* 38
2 ch f Piccolo Endear (Pivotal)
1726[11] 3223[9] 3933[10]

**Whoopsy Daisy** *William Haggas* a57
2 b f Champs Elysees Humility (Polar Falcon (USA))
*7354[7]*

**Who Shot Thebarman (NZ)** *Chris Waller* 113
6 b g Yamanin Vital(NZ) Ears Carol (NZ) (Carolingian (AUS))
7301a[13] 7653a[3]

**Who Splashed Me** *J R Jenkins* a37 31
3 ch f Medicean Cavallo Da Corsa (Galileo (IRE))
*933[6]* *1802[4]*

**Who's Shirl** *Chris Fairhurst* a70 81
8 b m Shinko Forest(IRE) Shirl (Shirley Heights)
*995[2]* 1609[2] 1881[4] 2604[2] 3572[14] 5681[8] 6936[12]

**Who's That Chick (IRE)** *Ralph J Smith* a58 86
5 ch m Footstepsinthesand Poule De Luxe (IRE) (Cadeaux Genereux)
1664[6] (1986) 2069[2] 2963[3] 3327[2] (3825) 4548[2] (4798) (5074) 6129[3] 6793[2] 6922[11]

**Who'Sthedaddy** *Daniel Kubler* a42 38
2 br g Avonbridge Lisathedaddy (Darnay)
4207[12] 5212[6] *6602[9]*

**Who'Sthedude (IRE)** *Ralph Beckett* a80 79
2 b g Duke Of Marmalade(IRE) Island Dreams (USA) (Giant's Causeway (USA))
4429[6] 5351[2] *(6102)*

**Whozthecat (IRE)** *Declan Carroll* a71 101
7 b g One Cool Cat(USA) Intaglia (GER) (Lomitas)
2254[17] 4215[7] 4480a[11] 4683[17] 6290[8] 6744[12] 7085[2] 7233[9] *7455[10]*

**Why No Rein (IRE)** *Richard Fahey* 54
2 ch c Tagula(IRE) Chehalis Sunset (Danehill Dancer (IRE))
3606[5] 4110[10]

**Why Not Now** *Roger Charlton* a61 61
3 ch f Notnowcato Perfect Night (Danzig Connection (USA))
*371[3]* *1769[8]* 2429[8] 3426[4] 4048[6] 4655[6] (5522) 5846[4] 6396[5] *7256[4]*

**Why Whipping (FR)** *Robert Collet* a67 63
2 b f Whipper(USA) Sometimes Perhaps (FR) (Munir)
5590a[9] *5901a[5]* 6698a[7]

**Wiccalina (FR)** *E Leenders* a57
3 ro f Martaline Wicca Eria (FR) (Turgeon (USA))
*599a[7]*

**Wicked Strong (USA)** *James Jerkens* a120
3 b c Hard Spun(USA) Moyne Abbey (USA) (Charismatic (USA))
*1964a[4]* *3026a[4]*

**Wicked Tara** *Natalie Lloyd-Beavis* a16 25
4 b f Assertive Tara King (Deploy)
(4039a) *5428[9]* 5977[10]

**Wicked Wilma (IRE)** *Alan Berry* a13 56
10 b m Tagula(IRE) Wicked (Common Grounds)
*693[8]* 3104[7] 4005[11] 4362[8] 4519[6] 4725[8] 4960[15] 5237[3] 5635[9]

**Wickhambrook (IRE)** *Ismail Mohammed* a77 80
3 ch c Dubawi(IRE) Beautiful Filly (Oasis Dream)
*1897[8]* 2734[3] 3325[9] 3979[9] *5308[11]*

**Wiener Valkyrie** *Ed Walker* 73
2 b f Shamardal(USA) Wiener Wald (USA) (Woodman (USA))
6065[3] 6554[2] ◆ (7637)

**Wiggle** *Tim Pitt* a19 44
2 ch f Dutch Art Mookhlesa (Marju (IRE))
*1314[9]* 2089[11] *5255[6]* 6645[5]

**Wight Is Wight (IRE)** *P Nicot* a92 97
4 b g Peintre Celebre(USA) Alenteja (IRE) (Danehill (USA))
*805a[5]*

**Wigmore Hall (IRE)** *Michael Bell* a89 114
7 b g High Chaparral(IRE) Love And Laughter (IRE) (Theatrical (IRE))
2085[6] 3416[10] 3962[13] 4756[13] 5440[2] 5651[9] 6330[F]

**Wikita (FR)** *F Chappet* a77 75
3 b f Desert Style(IRE) Vagabonde (FR) (Valanour (IRE))
1907a[3]

**Wiki Tiki** *Stuart Williams* a68 66
3 br f Dixie Union(USA) Witten (USA) (Fusaichi Pegasus (USA))
*86[7]* *374[3]* *(481)* *608[2]* ◆

**Wilberfoss (IRE)** *Mel Brittain* a29 56
3 b g Amadeus Wolf Pietra Dura (Cadeaux Genereux)
1308[7] 1906[12]

**Wild Affaire (IRE)** *Charles Hills* 28
3 b f High Chaparral(IRE) En Garde (USA) (Irish River (FR))
1529[15]

**Wildcat Lass (USA)** *David O'Meara* a73 52
3 bb f Street Cry(IRE) Lexington Girl (USA) (Storm Cat (USA))
*323[7]* *542[7]* *930[5]* *1126[2]* *(1802)* 2205[7] *2936[3]* *3405[6]*

**Wildcat Red (USA)** *Jose Garoffalo* a116
3 b c D'Wildcat(USA) Racene (USA) (Miner's Mark (USA))
*1964a[18]*

**Wild Chief (GER)** *J Hirschberger* 112
3 ch c Doyen(IRE) Wild Angel (IRE) (Acatenango (GER))
2818a[4] 4007a[5] 6806a[5] 7603a[5]

**Wild Desert (FR)** *Tony Carroll* a63 54
9 bb g Desert Prince(IRE) Sallivera (IRE) (Sillery (USA))
*197[3]* *450[9]* *641[8]* *818[7]* *992[9]* *1231[4]* 2693[6] 3309[7] 6818[5] *7893[12]*

**Wilde Inspiration (IRE)** *Julie Camacho* a51 91
3 ch g Dandy Man(IRE) Wishing Chair (USA) (Giant's Causeway (USA))
2333[2] ◆ (2737) ◆ 4191[2] (4923) 5410[3] ◆ 6234[5] 6704[5]

**Wildes (IRE)** *Tim Pitt* a78
3 b g Manduro(GER) Balloura (USA) (Swain (IRE))
*167[5]* *(717)*

**Wild Geese** *S Burridge* a78 103
5 b g Exceed And Excel(AUS) Court Lane (USA) (Machiavellian (USA))
2379a[12]

**Wild Hill Boy** *David C Griffiths* a55 38
4 b g Tiger Hill(IRE) Kalamansi (IRE) (Sadler's Wells (USA))
2392[5] 4130[14] 4791[10] *5570[3]* *6074[11]*

**Wildomar** *Peter Hiatt* a66 48
5 b g Kyllachy Murrieta (Docksider (USA))
*197[4]* *407[5]* *1133[5]* *1317[3]* *4077[11]* *5011[12]*

**Wild Step (GER)** *Markus Klug* 93
3 b f Footstepsinthesand Zaynaat (Unfuwain (USA))
1619a[6] 2584a[9]

**Wild Storm** *Saeed bin Suroor* a75
2 b f Dubawi(IRE) The World (Dubai Destination (USA))
*7193[2]*

**Wild Tobacco** *Richard Hannon* 78
2 br c More Than Ready(USA) Princess Janie (USA) (Elusive Quality (USA))
(2151) ◆

**Wild Wild West (FR)** *Yannick Fouin* a63 77
2 b f Whipper(USA) Elle S'Voyait Deja (USA) (Carson City (USA))
*(5901a)* 6698a[5] (7027a) *8276a[7]*

**Wild Wolf (IRE)** *Stefano Botti* 107
5 b g Rail Link Mary Rose (ITY) (Royal Academy (USA))
2374a[3] 3047a[7] 7323a[7]

**Wilfred Pickles (IRE)** *Jo Crowley* a77 75
8 ch g Cadeaux Genereux Living Daylights (IRE) (Night Shift (USA))
*(286)* *843[5]* *1142[6]* *2687[4]* 3562[3]

**Wilful Minx (FR)** *James Given* a14 49
3 b f Le Havre(IRE) Miskina (Mark Of Esteem (IRE))
2804[9] 3652[9] 4299[5] *8085[10]*

**Wilhana (IRE)** *Pam Sly* a83 89
4 b f Singspiel(IRE) Jathaabeh (Nashwan (USA))
*282[2]* *(463)* *612[2]* 1811[2] 2520[8] (3218) 4160[7] (4663) 5723[5]

**Will** *Nick Littmoden* a71 69
3 ch c Kyllachy Stormy Monday (Cadeaux Genereux)
*741[3]* ◆ *5490[2]* 6092[7] *7015[5]* *7349[6]*

**Willbeme** *Neville Bycroft* 99
6 b m Kyllachy Befriend (USA) (Allied Forces (USA))
1541[2] 2332[5] (2542) (3203) 4171[4] 5911[5]

**William Hogarth** *Brian Ellison* a53 50
9 b g High Chaparral(IRE) Mountain Holly (Shirley Heights)
*1284[3]* 5337[2] ◆ 5850[3] 6117[3] *6768[5]* 7006[8]

**William Of Orange** *Sir Mark Prescott Bt* a44 91
3 b g Duke Of Marmalade(IRE) Critical Acclaim (Peintre Celebre (USA))
4130[11] 4830[7] *5039[11]* 5339[2] (6099) ◆ (6705) ◆

**Willibr (IRE)** *P Monfort* a63 1
5 b h Layman(USA) Kate Winslet (USA) (Signal Tap (USA))
5225a[13]

**Willie Cazals (IRE)** *A S Cruz* 114
6 gr g Aussie Rules(USA) Secrete Marina (IRE) (Mujadil (USA))
7899a[7] 8151a[2]

**Willie Wag Tail (USA)** *Ed Walker* a87 91
5 b g Theatrical(IRE) Night Risk (USA) (Wild Again (USA))
*7838[9]* *8073[3]*

**Willing Foe (USA)** *Saeed bin Suroor* a59 113
7 bb g Dynaformer(USA) Thunder Kitten (USA) (Storm Cat (USA))
5432[2] ◆ 6374a[4] 7653a[5]

**Willow Creek** *William Haggas* a72 78
2 ch f Iffraaj Camp Riverside (USA) (Forest Camp (USA))
*4260[4]* *6071[4]* 6448[2]

**Willow Island (IRE)** *David Evans* a50 49
5 b g Dark Angel(IRE) Cidaris (IRE) (Persian Bold)
*413[8]* *88[9]* *569[5]* *652[5]* *842[3]* *1895[4]* 2531[5] *2885[6]* 3780[2]

**Willow Jubilee** *John E Long* a19 19
2 b f Champs Elysees Opera Belle (Dr Fong (USA))
*5184[5]* *7031[13]* 7512[11] *7834[9]*

**Willshebetrying** *Robert Mills* a46
3 b f Act One Precedence (IRE) (Polish Precedent (USA))
*5186[9]* *6238[10]*

**Willy Brennan (IRE)** *Andrew Balding* a89 82
3 br g Bushranger(IRE) Miss Assertive (Zafonic (USA))
*824[2]* *(1126)* 1937[4] 2556[5] *5012[7]* *6144[8]*

**Wilona (IRE)** *J Heloury* a64
3 ch f Mastercraftsman(IRE) Street Romance (USA) (Street Cry (IRE))
*391a[7]*

**Wilshire Boulevard (IRE)** *Bettina Andersen* 110
3 b c Holy Roman Emperor(IRE) Tyranny (Machiavellian (USA))
2377a[8]

**Wimboldsley** *Scott Dixon* a58 56
3 ch g Milk It Mick Chrystal Venture (IRE) (Barathea (IRE))
3153[11] 3700[3] 3914[11] (4796) 5683[8] 6297[10] *7547[5]* *8081[7]* *(8219)*

**Windfast (IRE)** *Brian Meehan* 108
3 b g Exceed And Excel(AUS) Fair Sailing (IRE) (Docksider (USA))
1436[7] 2343[3] 3352[4] 4850[4]

**Wind Fire (USA)** *David Brown* a76 105
3 b f Distorted Humor(USA) A P Dream (USA) (A.P. Indy (USA))
1515[7] 2304[4] (3245) 3981[4] 4852[7] 6378a[4] *7612a[13]*

**Windforpower (IRE)** *Tracy Waggott* a69 70
4 b g Red Clubs(IRE) Dubai Princess (IRE) (Dubai Destination (USA))
1487[13] 1643[2] 2056[4] 2232[3] 2552[5] 2743[2] 2951[3] 3338[5] 3954[7] 4287[4] (4519) 4901[6] 5053[6] 5375[2] 5819[5] 5912[4] 6406[8] 6938[6] 7510[6]

**Windhoek** *Saeed bin Suroor* a111 114
4 b c Cape Cross(IRE) Kahlua Kiss (Mister Baileys)
*(307a)* *1068[2]* 2554[2] 2958[3] (3930) 4682[3] *(6163a)*

**Wind Inher Sleeves (USA)** *M Halford* a72 87
3 ch f Speightstown(USA) Deputy Rose (USA) (Silver Deputy (CAN))
4480a[13] 5958a[18]

**Wind In My Sails** *Ed de Giles* a69
2 b c Footstepsinthesand Dylanesque (Royal Applause)
*6604[4]* *7030[7]* *7551[3]*

**Windlass (IRE)** *John Gosden* a67
3 b f Teofilo(IRE) Emerald Peace (IRE) (Green Desert (USA))
*189[3]* *486[6]* *774[7]*

**Windpfeil (IRE)** *Dominic Ffrench Davis* a43 50
8 bl g Indian Ridge Flying Kiss (IRE) (Sadler's Wells (USA))
*640[8]*

**Wind Place And Sho** *James Eustace* 65
2 b g Shirocco(GER) Coh Sho No (Old Vic)
5881[12] 6293[6]

**Windsea (IRE)** *Y Barberot* a76 78
4 ch g King's Best(USA) Spring Sea (FR) (Kutub (IRE))
*805a[3]*

**Windshear** *Richard Hannon* 113
3 b c Hurricane Run(IRE) Portal (Hernando (FR))
1535[2] (1702) 2337[2] 3379[2] 4122[2] 4778[2] 6329[4] 6711[4]

**Windshield** *Sir Mark Prescott Bt* a72 73
3 b f Montjeu(IRE) Westerly Air (USA) (Gone West (USA))
*189[7]* *456[10]* 3819[5] *(4261)* *4615[2]* (4844) 5200[3] *5572[3]*

**Windsor Secret** *Keith Dalgleish* a53 38
4 ch f Sakhee's Secret Lady Of Windsor (IRE) (Woods Of Windsor (USA))
*40[4]*

**Windy Citi** *Chris Wall* a83 64
3 ch f Zamindar(USA) Windy Britain (Mark Of Esteem (IRE))
1612[7] 2026[4] 2805[6] *(4969)* ◆ *(5304)* *6034[3]*

**Windy King** *J Bertran De Balanda* a66 99
5 b g Hurricane Run(IRE) Vanishing Prairie (USA) (Alysheba (USA))
920a[3] (7769a)

**Windy Mandy (USA)** *Fredrik Reuterskiold* a32 83
4 b f Dynaformer(USA) Must Be A Lady (USA) (Lord At War (ARG))
6388a[8]

**Windy Miller** *Robin Dickin* a46
3 ch g Sakhee's Secret Oatcake (Selkirk (USA))
5249[7] *5570[6]* *6765[3]*

**Wingate** *J-V Toux* a50 101
4 b g Zamindar(USA) Sirene Doloise (FR) (Marchand De Sable (USA))
7026a[11]

**Wings Of Fire (IRE)** *Denis Quinn* a63
4 b g Verglas(IRE) Allspice (Alzao (USA))
*684[4]* *787[7]* *988[8]* *1302[13]* *4327[9]* *4911[9]* *5283[11]*

**Winitall** *S Cerulis* a80 81
3 b g Invincible Spirit(IRE) Rapid Ransom (USA) (Red Ransom (USA))
3372a[3]

**Wink Oliver** *Kristin Stubbs* a62 59
2 b g Winker Watson Nadinska (Doyen (IRE))
2666[6] 2859[8] 3157[2] 4012[2] 4449[2] *5489[3]* *6413[3]* *6663[9]* *(7257)* *7684[4]*

**Winnemark (GER)** *P Schiergen* 96
3 bb f Lando(GER) Winterthur (GER) (Alkalde (GER))
7315a[3]

**Winning Cause (USA)** *Todd Pletcher* a106 111
4 ch c Giant's Causeway(USA) Raffishing Look (USA) (Kingmambo (USA))
4010a[4]

**Winning Express (IRE)** *Ed McMahon* 108
4 gr f Camacho Lady Fabiola (USA) (Open Forum (USA))
2155[8]

**Winning Hunter** *Philip Hide* a70 72
2 b c Iffraaj Miss Lacey (IRE) (Diktat)
6039[4] *6603[4]* 7155[2] *7755[3]* *7970[7]*

**Winshine (FR)** *S Smrczek* a80 98
3 b f Chineur(FR) Fusee Francaise (FR) (Anabaa (USA))
*5482a[5]* 7857a[3] *8300a[16]*

**Winslow (USA)** *Charlie Appleby* 89
2 b g Distorted Humor(USA) Justwhistledixie (USA) (Dixie Union (USA))
2146[3] (2507) 5424[4]

**Winstanley (IRE)** *Richard Fahey* a74 76
2 b c Dandy Man(IRE) Lucayan Beauty (IRE) (Marju (IRE))
1924[3] 2258[3] 3255[2] 3786[2] 4760[7] 5607[15] *6158[4]* 6594[3] *7114[3]*

**Winter Lion (IRE)** *Denis Gerard Hogan* a56 82
4 ch g Galileo(IRE) Hill Of Snow (Reference Point)
6349a[5] 7142a[11]

**Winterlude (IRE)** *Charlie Appleby* a108 100
4 b g Street Cry(IRE) New Morning (IRE) (Sadler's Wells (USA))
*593a[6]* *773a[7]*

**Winter Magic (FR)** *T Castanheira*
2 b f Soldier Of Fortune(IRE) Massana (FR) (Red Ransom (USA))
*8276a[5]*

**Winter Picnic (IRE)** *Tim Easterby* a25 33
3 b f Oratorio(IRE) Salpiglossis (GER) (Monsun (GER))
2741[8] 3650[9]

**Winter Queen** *Charlie Appleby* a71 47
2 ch f Dubawi(IRE) Straight Lass (IRE) (Machiavellian (USA))
*2644[4]* 3267[10] *5037[9]* *5489[2]* *(5823)* *(7810)*

**Winters Moon (IRE)** *Saeed bin Suroor* 110
2 ch f New Approach(IRE) Summertime Legacy (Darshaan)
(4202) 5190[3] 5876[4] 7240[3]

**Winter Spice (IRE)** *Clive Cox* 83
3 gr g Verglas(IRE) Summer Spice (IRE) (Key Of Luck (USA))
1588[3] 2133[4] 3146[4] 3541[2] 4134[3] 6318[3] (6651)

**Winter Springs (FR)** *J Reynier* 95
2 ch c Stormy River(FR) Hallen (FR) (Midyan (USA))
7317a[5]

**Winter Thunder** *Saeed bin Suroor* a66 114
3 gr c New Approach(IRE) Summer Sonnet (Baillamont (USA))
*2126[4]* ◆ (3432) ◆ (4448) 5440[5] (6930)

**Winterval** *Luca Cumani* 71
2 b c Dubawi(IRE) Festivale (IRE) (Invincible Spirit (IRE))
6551[6] 7039[2]

**Winterwell (USA)** *David O'Meara* a79 58
4 b f First Defence(USA) Kinetic Force (USA) (Holy Bull (USA))
*195[2]* *503[6]*

**Winterwind (IRE)** *Carmen Bocskai* a64 65
9 b g Orpen(USA) Brickey Beech (IRE) (Precocious)
*729a[2]*

**Wintour Leap** *Robert Stephens* a68 65
3 b f Nayef(USA) Mountain Leap (IRE) (Sadler's Wells (USA))
4279[2] *5048[2]* *5556[2]* *6343[3]* *7204[2]* *7817[4]* *8193[8]*

**Win Variation (JPN)** *Masahiro Matsunaga* 117
6 b h Heart's Cry(JPN) Super Ballerina (CAN) (Storm Bird (CAN))
2002a[2]

**Wise Boy (GER)** *J-P Perruchot* a79 54
7 b g Banyumanik(IRE) Wahieda (GER) (Sternkoenig (IRE))
*392a[16]*

**Wiseton (IRE)** *David Barron* a46 60
2 b g Majestic Missile(IRE) Laylati (IRE) (Green Desert (USA))
3947[9] 4624[2] 5813[4] *7701[4]*

**Wisewit** *James Toller* a49 57
2 b g Royal Applause Loveleaves (Polar Falcon (USA))
4618[11] 6712[11] *7551[9]*

**Wish Come True (IRE)** *Peter G Moody* 105
4 b g Aussie Rules(USA) Tibouchina (IRE) (Daylami (IRE))
7395a[5]

**Wishformore (IRE)** *Ian Williams* a66 60
7 b m Chevalier(IRE) Terra Nova (Polar Falcon (USA))
*81[5]* *377[3]* *(446)* *(575)* *672[3]* *1021[3]* *1141[5]* 1568[5] 1638[4]

**Wish Me Luck (FR)** *A Al Raihe* a69
3 b f Lucky Story(USA) Nadira (FR) (Green Desert (USA))
*203a[9]*

**Wiskee Lil** *Edwin Tuer*
3 b f Rob Roy(USA) Bula Rose (IRE) (Alphabatim (USA))
6982[7] 7332[8]

**Wistar** *Luca Cumani* 81
3 b c Dubawi(IRE) Vallota (Polish Precedent (USA))
(2877) ◆

**Wisteria** *David C Griffiths* a41 41
2 br f Winker Watson Begonia (IRE) (Selkirk (USA))
7712[5] *8225[4]*

**Witches Brew (IRE)** *Edward Lynam* 100
3 b f Duke Of Marmalade(IRE) Macheera (IRE) (Machiavellian (USA))
5869a[5] 7857a[7]

**Witch From Rome** *John Holt* a60 27
3 b g Holy Roman Emperor(IRE) Spangle (Galileo (IRE))
*231[5]* *536[4]* *1382[6]* 1812[6] *3471[4]*

**Witch Way Went** *Brian Ellison* a40 58
4 b f Royal Applause Celestial Princess (Observatory (USA))
*358[5]* *497[9]*

**Witchy Woman** *Geoffrey Deacon* a63 56
3 b f Intikhab(USA) Lady McBeth (IRE) (Avonbridge)
*173[2]* *411[2]* *665[7]* *1101[4]*

**With Approval (IRE)** *Charles Hills* a65 64
2 b c Approve(IRE) Kelsey Rose (Most Welcome)
*7223[4]* 7412[3] *7742[5]*

**With A Twist** *Andrew Balding* a29 31
3 b f Excellent Art Bint Zamayem (IRE) (Rainbow Quest (USA))
3849[9] *8119[7]*

**With Charm (USA)** *Charlie Appleby* a47 43
2 b f Dubawi(IRE) Secret Charm (IRE) (Green Desert (USA))
*4320[7]* 4914[12] 5725[10]

**Wither Hills (IRE)** *B R Hamilton* a83 80
8 b g Karinga Bay Bonnie Article (IRE) (Definite Article)
4746a[14]

**Withernsea (IRE)** *Richard Fahey* 93
3 b g Dark Angel(IRE) Charlene Lacy (IRE) (Pips Pride)
2897[3] 3693[3] 4390[6] 5381[2] ◆ 6736[6] 7159[3] (7438) 7715[8]

**With Hindsight (IRE)** *John Spearing* a60 57
6 ch g Ad Valorem(USA) Lady From Limerick (IRE) (Rainbows For Life (CAN))
*1408[7] 2396[4] (3473) 4738[2] 5428[7]* 7219[5] *7868[11]*

**Without Fear (FR)** *Niels Petersen* a89 105
6 b g Refuse To Bend(IRE) Kansas (Kahyasi)
309a[12] 507a[9] 683a[10] 811a[10] 3090a[6] (3772a) (4956a) 5744a[2] 6389a[5] 6914a[5]

**Wojha (IRE)** *William Haggas* a70 75
3 ch f Pivotal Hureyа (USA) (Woodman (USA))
1422[5] *2061[6]* (2842) 4397[6] 5448[8]

**Wolcharo (IRE)** *Matthieu Palussiere* 88
2 b c Amadeus Wolf Love And Devotion (Shamardal (USA))
3806a[10]

**Wolf Albarari** *Marco Botti* a73
2 ch c Medicean Pure Song (Singspiel (IRE))
7498[14] *(7811)*

**Wolf Heart (IRE)** *Lucy Normile* a76 53
6 b g Dalakhani(IRE) Lisieux Orchid (IRE) (Sadler's Wells (USA))
2475[6] 3101[5]

**Wolfofwallstreet (IRE)** *Ed Walker* 77
2 br c Bushranger(IRE) Rafelite (Fraam)
1859[3] 3082[5] 7082[4] 7336[2] (7497)

**Wolf Of Windlesham (IRE)** *Charles Hills* a62 45
2 ch g Mastercraftsman(IRE) Al Amlah (USA) (Riverman (USA))
*3578[8]* 4207[9] *5278[3]* 5875[7] *7740[8] (8115)*

**Wolfwood** *John Davies* a30 46
3 b g Ferrule(IRE) Wedgewood Star (Bishop Of Cashel)
2387[8] 2896[4] 3547[12] 4795[14]

**Wonderfully (IRE)** *A P O'Brien* 101
3 b f Galileo(IRE) Massarra (Danehill (USA))
2195a[9] 2581a[9] 3995a[5]

**Wonder Gal (USA)** *Leah Gyarmati* a106
2 bb f Tiz Wonderful(USA) Passe (USA) (Dixie Union (USA))
*7606a[3]*

**Wonder Laish** *William Haggas* 71
2 b c Halling(USA) Wonder Why (GER) (Tiger Hill (IRE))
6985[3]

**Wonder Of Qatar (IRE)** *Richard Hannon* 78
2 b c Exceed And Excel(AUS) Imperial Quest (Rainbow Quest (USA))
3847[3] 5201[2] ◆ 5671[4] (6363)

**Wonderstruck (IRE)** *William Haggas* 101
3 b f Sea The Stars(IRE) Bordighera (USA) (Alysheba (USA))
2109[3] (2746) ◆ 3376[6] 4945[4]

**Wonder Weapon (GER)** *Andrew Balding* a80
3 b c Konigstiger(GER) Wurfspiel (GER) (Lomitas)
*(988) 1407[2]* (Dead)

**Won Diamond** *M Halford* a90 95
4 b g Mount Nelson Read Federica (Fusaichi Pegasus (USA))
5957a[15]

**Woodacre** *Richard Whitaker* 90
7 b g Pyrus(USA) Fairy Ring (IRE) (Fairy King (USA))
2016[4] (4058) (4975) 5299[2] ◆ 5792[2] 6693[2]

**Wood Breizh (FR)** *W P Mullins* 74
4 gr g Stormy River(FR) Polynevees (FR) (Poliglote)
5456a[2]

**Woodbridge** *Richard Fahey* a74 69
3 ch g Exceed And Excel(AUS) Kristal Bridge (Kris)
*8474* 1192[11] 2163[5] (3037) 3559[10] *7954[2] 8248[5]*

**Wooden King (IRE)** *Malcolm Saunders* a63 78
9 b g Danetime(IRE) Olympic Rock (IRE) (Ballad Rock)
2414[15]

**Woodland Aria** *John Gosden* a86 104
4 b f Singspiel(IRE) Magic Tree (UAE) (Timber Country (USA))
3355[6] 4607[7]

**Woodland Girl** *Richard Fahey* 70
3 ch f Kyllachy Locharia (Wolfhound (USA))
4471[12] 5265[8] 6863[6] 7249[12]

**Woodstock (IRE)** *Alistair Whillans* a68 71
4 b g High Chaparral(IRE) Woodwin (IRE) (Woodman (USA))
3624[5] 4015[4] 4255[3] 4533[6]

**Woody Bay** *Mark Walford* a75 83
4 b g New Approach(IRE) Dublino (USA) (Lear Fan (USA))
1399[4] 2017[8] 2654[8] 3400[7] 3979[7] 6057[3] 6865[2] 7538[3]

**Woofie (IRE)** *Richard Fahey* a65 50
2 b g Duke Of Marmalade(IRE) Violet Ballerina (IRE) (Namid)
7054[5] *7779[6] 8192[5]*

**Woolfall Sovereign (IRE)** *George Margarson* a102 71
8 b g Noverre(USA) Mandragore (USA) (Slew O'Gold (USA))
*271[3] 5341[1] 802[9] 8136[4] 8263[5]*

**Woolston Ferry (IRE)** *Henry Candy* a76 74
8 b g Fath(USA) Cathy Garcia (IRE) (Be My Guest (USA))
1729[12] *2079[9]* 3327[6] *4073[4]* 4415[13] *5041[11]*

**Woomera** *H-J Groschel* 50
2 ch f Strategic Prince Wigan Lane (Kheleyf (USA))
6778a[8]

**Worcharlie'slass** *Michael Herrington* a40 8
3 b f Myboycharlie(IRE) Angry Bark (USA) (Woodman (USA))
*7541[4] 8178[5]*

**Wordismybond** *Peter Makin* a69 78
5 b g Monsieur Bond(IRE) La Gessa (Largesse)
4588[2] (4905) (5383) 5629[2] 6990[10] *7205[9]* 7567[11]

**Work All Week (USA)** *Roger Brueggemann* a121
5 ch g City Zip(USA) Danzig Matilda (USA) (Repriced (USA))
*(7612a)*

**Wor Lass** *Iain Jardine* 62
6 br m And Beyond(IRE) Patience Please (King Of Spain)
2952[3] 3302[6] 3602[4] 4259[2] (4492) 5171[4] 5765[4] 6117[2] 6644[3] 6864[5] 7177[4] 7508[6]

**World Ace (JPN)** *Yasutoshi Ikee* 117
5 b h Deep Impact(JPN) Mandela (GER) (Acatenango (GER))
8153a[4]

**World Fair (IRE)** *Charlie Appleby* a45 46
2 b f Shamardal(USA) Nashama (IRE) (Pivotal)
4825[8] *5305[7]* 5973[9]

**World Record (IRE)** *Mick Quinn* a68 75
4 b g Choisir(AUS) Dancing Debut (Polar Falcon (USA))
3339[2] (3949) 4197[5] 5269[2] 6615[4] 7567[4] *7829[10] 8068[5]*

**World's Dream (GER)** *Markus Klug* 92
3 ch f Doyen(IRE) World's Vision (GER) (Platini (GER))
4955a[10]

**Wotalad** *Richard Whitaker* a63 58
4 b g Bertolini(USA) Cosmic Song (Cosmonaut)
2232[10] 3339[9] *3798[4] 4578[4] 5103[7] (5510) 6074[3] 6481[2] 7424[4] 7883[2]* 8176[7]

**Wowee** *Tony Carroll* a69 31
3 b g Archipenko(USA) Katya Kabanova (Sadler's Wells (USA))
*6483[4]* ◆ 7418[7]

**Wrangler** *William Haggas* 96
3 b g High Chaparral(IRE) Tipsy Me (Selkirk (USA))
1517[8] (1984) ◆ (2566) 5164[9]

**Wrecking Ball (IRE)** *Amy Weaver* a58 63
4 b g Royal Applause Shatarah (Gulch (USA))
*2521[0] 6719*

**Wreningham** *Pat Eddery* a58 54
9 br g Diktat Slave To The Rythm (IRE) (Hamas (IRE))
*7781[9] 8088[2] 8230[8]*

**Wrood (USA)** *James Fanshawe* a93
3 bb f Invasor(ARG) Ras Shaikh (USA) (Sheikh Albadou)
*2211[2] 3525[2]* ◆ *(5186) 6044[3]* ◆ *(7773)* ◆

**Wulfthryth** *Tobias B P Coles* a56 36
3 b f Champs Elysees Bolsena (USA) (Red Ransom (USA))
*488[9]*

**Wunder (GER)** *Markus Klug* 107
3 ch f Adlerflug(GER) Wonderful World (GER) (Dashing Blade)
(3808a) 4955a[5]

**Wunderkind (USA)** *Sir Mark Prescott Bt* a38 42
3 b f Langfuhr(CAN) Traum (USA) (Elusive Quality (USA))
5977[6] 6628[9] *6946[9] 7360[9]*

**Wu Zetian** *Pam Sly* a72 67
3 b f Invincible Spirit(IRE) China (Royal Academy (USA))
6421[2] 7024[4] *7528[3] 7818[2] (7910) 8177[4]*

**Wyldfire (IRE)** *Ruth Carr* a47 74
4 ch g Raven's Pass(USA) Miss Sally (IRE) (Danetime (IRE))
*1245[5]* 1660[11] 2654[9] 3052[7] 4000[6] 4473[9] 5077[8]

**Wylye** *Andrew Balding* 80
3 gr f Dalakhani(IRE) Tavy (Pivotal)
1494[4]

**Wyndham Wave** *Rod Millman* a63 50
5 gr g Dr Fong(USA) Atlantic Light (Linamix (FR))
*7546 1023[7] 1232[4] 1406[4]*

**Wyoyo (IRE)** *Tim Vaughan* a63 73
4 b g Moss Vale(IRE) Jersey Lillie (IRE) (Hector Protector (USA))
*7822[11]*

**Xander (IRE)** *Tim Easterby* 16
2 ch c Shamardal(USA) English Ballet (IRE) (Danehill Dancer (IRE))
5494[12] 5995[8] *6719[8]*

**Xanthos** *Ed Walker* a68 80
3 ch g Medicean My Girl Jode (Haafhd)
1540[7] 2333[5] 2734[6] 3428[9] 4631[4] 5092[7] *7373[9]*

**Xcellence (FR)** *F Doumen* 111
3 b f Champs Elysees Xanadu Bliss (FR) (Xaar)
(1273a) 2195a[3] 3289a[3] 3995a[4]

**Xclusive** *Ronald Harris* a65 68
4 b g Pivotal Dance A Daydream (Daylami (IRE))
*(76) 171[11] 458[6] 571[3] 815[5] 1087[5]* 2672[10] 4153[10]

**Xellent (FR)** *J Heloury* 36
2 b f Naaqoos Boaka (FR) (Kahyasi)
5590a[13]

**Xilerator (IRE)** *David Nicholls* a30 94
7 b g Arakan(USA) Grandel (Owington)
1646[11] 1903[9]

**Xinbama (IRE)** *Charles Hills* a91 90
5 b h Baltic King Persian Empress (IRE) (Persian Bold)
*(1899)* 2882[2] (3274) 4160[2] 4622[2] 5651[6] 6061[6] *7289[6] 7838[2]*

**Xotic (FR)** *D Prod'Homme* a83 105
5 b g Holy Roman Emperor(IRE) Xstase (SWE) (Trempolino (USA))
7026a[13]

**Xpres Maite** *Roy Bowring* a69 48
11 b g Komaite(USA) Antonias Melody (Rambo Dancer (CAN))
*171[5] 269[4] 546[4]*

**X Raise (IRE)** *David Brown* 66
2 gr f Aussie Rules(USA) Raise (USA) (Seattle Slew (USA))
(5264)

**Yaakooum (IRE)** *Richard Hannon* 95
3 br c Cape Cross(IRE) Anna's Rock (IRE) (Rock Of Gibraltar (IRE))
2773[7] 3974[4] (5276) (5527) 6137[5] 6518[3] (6786) (7135)

**Yaa Wayl (IRE)** *D Selvaratnam* a108 102
7 b g Whipper(USA) Lidanna (Nicholas (USA))
*808a[8]*

**Yagheer (IRE)** *Roger Varian* a78 74
3 b g Lawman(FR) Dawn Raid (IRE) (Docksider (USA))
1347[3] 1614[8] *(2902)* 3694[7]

**Yagulin (IRE)** *W Hefter* 37
2 ch c Manduro(GER) Yacht Club (USA) (Sea Hero (USA))
6385a[8]

**Ya Hade Ye Delil** *Richard Hannon* 75
2 b c Raven's Pass(USA) Palatial (Green Desert (USA))
6653[3] ◆

**Ya Hafed** *Sheena West* a53 55
6 ch g Haafhd Rule Britannia (Night Shift (USA))
7129[8]

**Ya Halla (IRE)** *David Evans* a56 52
2 gr f Dark Angel(IRE) Stormy View (USA) (Cozzene (USA))
3626[6] 4919[7] 5789[6] 6248[4] 6642[5] *7991[3]*

**Yair Hill (IRE)** *Geoffrey Deacon* a74 72
6 b g Selkirk(USA) Conspiracy (Rudimentary (USA))
4866[7] 5378[7]

**Ya Latif (IRE)** *Roger Varian* 73
2 b f Iffraaj Albahja (Sinndar (IRE))
3558[4] ◆ 5416[4] 6246[3]

**Yamllik** *Saeed bin Suroor* 76
2 b g King's Best(USA) Anaamil (IRE) (Darshaan)
6712[7] 7498[2]

**Yankee Red** *John Best* a46 61
3 b g Pastoral Pursuits Miriam (Forzando)
1634[2] 2249[4] *2886[9]* 4431[10] 5105[9] 5532[8] 6120[4] *6561[12] 7355[10]*

**Yard Of Ale** *Kristin Stubbs* a70 60
3 ch g Compton Place Highly Liquid (Entrepreneur)
1939[8] 2737[5] *7063[2] 7682[8] 7764[2] (8002) 8268[6]*

**Yarrow (IRE)** *Sir Michael Stoute* a74 61
2 b f Sea The Stars(IRE) Highland Gift (IRE) (Generous (IRE))
*7011[2]* 7405[5]

**Yasir (USA)** *Conor Dore* a76 71
6 b g Dynaformer(USA) Khazayin (USA) (Bahri (USA))
*64[2] 168[3] 253[4] 567[2] 829[4] 1046[4] 1629[2]* 2327[7] 2620[3] *2885[5]* 3269[6] 5101[3] 7760[6] 8134[4] 8208[9]

**Yat Ding Yau (FR)** *William Jarvis* a49 72
2 b f Air Chief Marshal(IRE) The Jostler (Dansili)
4973[6] (6385a)

**Yawail** *Brian Rothwell* a62 52
3 bb f Medicean Al Tamooh (IRE) (Dalakhani (IRE))
2365[6] 3434[7] 3916[8] 4472[8] *6715[2] 7188[3] 8049[8] 8137[5]*

**Yazan (IRE)** *Tom Dascombe* 75
2 gr c Zebedee Idle Fancy (Mujtahid (USA))
6059[3] 6702[3]

**Yazdi (IRE)** *Henry Oliver* a58 92
5 b g Galileo(IRE) Lucky Spin (Pivotal)
*932[4]*

**Yeager (USA)** *Jeremy Noseda* a100 97
4 bb g Medaglia d'Oro(USA) Lucky Flyer (USA) (Fusaichi Pegasus (USA))
*1834[2]* ◆ 2362[11] 4648[20] 6752[21]

**Yeah Baby (IRE)** *Charles Hills* a75 76
3 b f Danehill Dancer(IRE) Street Shaana (FR) (Darshaan)
*74[2] 403[3] 649[3]* 1812[2] 2225[5] (3803) 4504[6] *5185[6] 6239[4]*

**Yeah Cool** *Peter Chapple-Hyam* 45
2 br g Kheleyf(USA) Piverina (IRE) (Pivotal)
4829[8]

**Yeats Magic (IRE)** *John Gosden* a82
2 b c Yeats(IRE) Orinoco (IRE) (Darshaan)
*(7778)*

**Yeenaan (FR)** *Marco Botti* 87
2 b c Rip Van Winkle(IRE) Japan (GER) (Key Royal (GER))
5759[4] (6545) ◆ (7338)

**Yeeoow (IRE)** *K R Burke* a90 99
5 b g Holy Roman Emperor(IRE) Taraya (IRE) (Doyoun)
*715[10] 991[8]* 1484[3] 1975[2] 2254[13] 3271[3] 3737a[7] 4384[6] 4681[9] 6290[6] 6531[22]

**Yenhaab (IRE)** *William Haggas* 100
3 b c Cape Cross(IRE) Skiphall (Halling (USA))
(1542) 1954[4] 2986[4] 3758[2] (4162) ◆ 4888[3] 5914[3] 6930[10]

**Yes Chef** *Chris Gordon* a64 81
7 ch g Best Of The Bests(IRE) Lady Chef (Double Trigger (IRE))
*247[7]*

**Yodelling (USA)** *Charlie Appleby* a90
2 b f Medaglia d'Oro(USA) Echoes In Eternity (IRE) (Spinning World (USA))
*(6105) (7348)* ◆

**Yojojo (IRE)** *Gay Kelleway* a91 91
5 ch m Windsor Knot(IRE) Belle Of The Blues (IRE) (Blues Traveller (IRE))
*163[5] 1020[6]* 2047[2] 2783[9] 4680[4] 5074[4] 5948[2] 6258[6] 6559[4] *7531[6] 7838[7] 8042[5]*

**Yoninaelle (FR)** *Ecurie Saint Simeon* a53 48
4 ch f Dream Well(FR) La Blondinette (FR) (Vert Amande (FR))
935a[8]

**Yonna (FR)** *E Lellouche* 99
3 bb f Le Havre(IRE) Folie Danse (FR) (Petit Loup (USA))
6882a[4] 7319a[10]

**York Express** *Ismail Mohammed* a71 73
2 b f Vale Of York(IRE) Star Express (Sadler's Wells (USA))
2269[7] 2697[3] 3415[16] *4079[2]* 4589[4] *5604[5] 6158[5]*

**York Glory (USA)** *Kevin Ryan* a78 114
6 rg h Five Star Day(USA) Minicolony (USA) (Pleasant Colony (USA))
2766[7] 3452[28] 4215[9] 4895[19] 5575[11] 6327[20] 6533[25]

**Yorkidding** *Mark Johnston* 76
2 b f Dalakhani(IRE) Claxon (Caerleon (USA))
6148[4] (6577) 6924[6] 7595[5]

**Yorkie Talkie (IRE)** *Mark Johnston* a17 65
2 b c Paco Boy(IRE) Ultra Finesse (USA) (Rahy (USA))
2541[10] 5759[3] 6556[7] 6925[14] *7201[10]*

**Yorkindred Spirit** *Mark Johnston* a63 69
2 b f Sea The Stars(IRE) Paracel (USA) (Gone West (USA))
6448[4] 6860[3] 7278[5] *7808[4]*

**Yorkshire (IRE)** *Shaun Harris* a41 57
2 b g Tagula(IRE) Bun Penny (Bertolini (USA))
4618[9] 5086[3] 5464[7] 7378[6] *7994[11] 8179[8]*

**Yorkshire Dales (IRE)** *David Elsworth* 61
2 b c Vale Of York(IRE) Rock Exhibition (Rock Of Gibraltar (IRE))
3148[7] 4110[5]

**Yorkshireman (IRE)** *Lynn Siddall* a69 53
4 b g Red Clubs(IRE) Ossiana (IRE) (Polish Precedent (USA))
2738[13] 3301[10] 3843[7] 5765[9] 6119[6] 6644[8] 7006[3] *7287[3] 7572[2] (7893) 8061[3]*

**Yorkshire Monarch (IRE)** *Tim Easterby* 54
3 b c Montjeu(IRE) Inkling (USA) (Seeking The Gold (USA))
1608[10] 1960[10] 2354[12]

**Yorkshire Nanny (IRE)** *David Brown* 53
2 b f Tagula(IRE) Sweet Surprise (IRE) (Danetime (IRE))
7004[7] 7308[5]

**Yorksters Prince (IRE)** *Marjorie Fife* a58 53
7 b g Beat Hollow Odalisque (IRE) (Machiavellian (USA))
2654[4] 3438[4] 3623[8] 4468[2] 4792[6] 5331[5] *6076[3]* 6627[4] *7813[5] 7977[10]*

**Yosra (FR)** *J Heloury* 76
3 b f Desert Style(IRE) Miss Balines (FR) (Grape Tree Road)
3809a[2]

**You Be Lucky (IRE)** *Jo Crowley* a62
2 b f Thewayyouare(USA) Lovely Dream (IRE) (Elnadim (USA))
*5821[9] 6605[8] 7752[5] 7992[2] 8069[6]*

**Youcouldntmakeitup (IRE)** *Tim Easterby* 75
2 b f Captain Rio Miss Donovan (Royal Applause)
(5332) 5790[7] 6401[6] 7038[3]

**You Know I Know (USA)** *John W Sadler* a109
5 bb g Simon Pure(USA) Magic Show (USA) (Notebook (USA))
*5781a[8]*

**Youm Jamil (USA)** *Tony Carroll* a52 51
7 gr g Mizzen Mast(USA) Millie's Choice (IRE) (Taufan (USA))
2942[12] 3308[4] 3853[7] *4738[6] 6267[9] 8175[2]*

**Young Dottie** *Pat Phelan* a74 65
8 b m Desert Sun Auntie Dot Com (Tagula (IRE))
2770[5] 4118[5] 4808[5] *7397[14] 7734[10] (7925) 8169[3]*

**Young Jackie** *George Margarson* a55 42
6 b m Doyen(IRE) Just Warning (Warning)
*7909[6] 8314[8]*

**Young Jay** *Andrew Crook* 65
4 b g Josr Algarhoud(IRE) Young Sue (Local Suitor (USA))
2055[14]

**Young Lou** *Robin Dickin* a18 58
5 b m Kadastrof(FR) Wanna Shout (Missed Flight)
*992[11]*

**Youonlyliveonce (IRE)** *John Quinn* a45 56
2 b g Lawman(FR) Caerlonore (IRE) (Traditionally (USA))
3481[9] 4416[8] 4885[9] 7207[2] 7328[4] *7815[8] 8087[6]*

**Yourartisonfire** *K R Burke* 94
4 ch g Dutch Art Queens Jubilee (Cayman Kai (IRE))
1164[3] (1721) 2156[6] 3437[7] 5178[3] 6097[3] 6704[13]

**You're Cool** *James Given* a60 64
2 b g Exceed And Excel(AUS) Ja One (IRE) (Acclamation)
6168[8] *6659[5]* 6867[3] *7683[5] 7728[6]*

**You're Fired (IRE)** *K R Burke* a75 94
3 b c Firebreak My Sweet Georgia (IRE) (Royal Applause)
1693[3] (2734) ◆ 4198[2] 4647[5] 6892[7]

**You're My Cracker** *Donald McCain* a60 75
2 ch f Captain Gerrard(IRE) Dalmunzie (IRE) (Choisir (AUS))
3107[3] ◆ 3642[3] 4382[2] 4701[2] *5253[2]* (5813) 6322[8]

**Your Game (FR)** *A Fabre* 89
3 b f Montjeu(IRE) Polygreen (FR) (Green Tune (USA))
6956a[8]

**Your Gifted (IRE)** *Lisa Williamson* a67 57
7 b m Trans Island Dame Laura (IRE) (Royal Academy (USA))
*259[4] 313[3] 425[5] 466[2] 654[7] 730[3] 797[6] 866[2] 1030[5]* 4344[4] 4860[5] 5130[3] 5399[6] 5801[3] 6273[5] 6561[4] 7519[3] (7781) 7900[4] 7997[2] 8088[14] (8284)

**Yourholidayisover (IRE)** *Patrick Holmes* 53
7 ch g Sulamani(IRE) Whitehaven (Top Ville)
3365[5]

**Yourinthewill (USA)** *Daniel Mark Loughnane* a68 52
6 ch g Aragorn(IRE) Lenarue (USA) (Gone West (USA))
*105[2] 229[2] 406[5] 578[3] 643[3] 958[3] 1034[2] 1051[2] 1454[5]* 1761[8] 6342[6] 7068[7] 7426[7] 7869[6] 8265[6]

**Your Pal Tal** *J F Levins* a79 77
4 b g Dark Angel(IRE) Good Health (Magic Ring (IRE))
*7959a[2]*

**You've Got It** *M Halford* a61 62
3 b f Sea The Stars(IRE) Song (IRE) (Sadler's Wells (USA))
*7435a[7]*

**Ypres** *Jason Ward* a63 79
5 b g Byron Esligier (IRE) (Sabrehill (USA))
1609[11] 2056[8] 2602[6] 3399[7] 3611[2] 4131[4] 4632[5] 5053[4] 5298[6] 6406[5] 6695[12] 7179[9] *7621[7]*

**Ysper (FR)** *David O'Meara* a69 73
4 b f Orpen(USA) Velda (Observatory (USA))
(298) 383$^{9}$

**Ythan Waters** *Bryan Smart* 79
2 b g Hellvelyn Primrose Queen (Lear Fan (USA))
1505$^{5}$ 2386$^{3}$ 3481$^{2}$ 4253$^{2}$ 4659$^{2}$ 5760$^{6}$ 7097$^{2}$ (7495)

**Yucatan (ITY)** *Stefano Botti* 98
2 ch c Muhtathir Youthopia (IRE) (Titus Livius (FR))
7479a$^{3}$

**Yuften** *William Haggas* 116
3 b c Invincible Spirit(IRE) Majestic Sakeena (IRE) (King's Best (USA))
(2346) ◆ 3320$^{5}$ 4278a$^{4}$ 5354$^{4}$

**Yuki (IRE)** *B Goudot* 78
3 b f Lawman(FR) High Limits (IRE) (High Chaparral (IRE))
3809a$^{7}$

**Yukon Gold** *Charlie Appleby* 63
2 b c Dubawi(IRE) Cresta Gold (Halling (USA))
4389$^{8}$ 4809$^{7}$ 5201$^{5}$

**Yukos Flyer (IRE)** *Richard Fahey* a20 43
2 b f Thewayyouare(USA) Wattrey (Royal Academy (USA))
3542$^{7}$ 3945$^{6}$ ◆ 4510$^{6}$ 5335$^{11}$ 6413$^{10}$

**Yul Finegold (IRE)** *George Baker* a68 80
4 b g Invincible Spirit(IRE) Mascara (Mtoto)
1355$^{2}$ 1791$^{4}$ 2835$^{4}$ 3032$^{5}$ (5747) ◆ 7133$^{2}$ 7516$^{2}$ 7914$^{6}$

**Yulong Baoju (IRE)** *Edward Lynam* a101 96
4 gr f Acclamation Masaader (USA) (Wild Again (USA))
3737a$^{11}$ 4480a$^{5}$ 4557a$^{4}$ 6172a$^{4}$

**Zaadig (FR)** *Y Barberot* a63
4 b c Librettist(USA) Zamilia (IRE) (Zamindar (USA))
805a$^{8}$

**Zaawia (IRE)** *Ed Dunlop* 63
3 ch f Elnadim(USA) Nidhaal (IRE) (Observatory (USA))
1422$^{6}$ ◆ 1902$^{3}$ 2780$^{8}$

**Zabeel Star (IRE)** *Luca Cumani* 48
2 ch c Arcano(IRE) Deep Winter (Pivotal)
6712$^{12}$

**Zabrov (IRE)** *J Phelippon* a72 72
3 b g Mastercraftsman(IRE) Fine And Mellow (FR) (Lando (GER))
5227a$^{2}$

**Zac Brown (IRE)** *David Barron* a98 70
3 b g Kodiac Mildmay (USA) (Elusive Quality (USA))
(3531) 4418$^{7}$ 4898$^{10}$ 5243$^{5}$ 7073$^{3}$ (7624) ◆ 8045$^{4}$ ◆

**Zack Hall (FR)** *F Rohaut* a100 109
7 b g Muhtathir Halawa (IRE) (Dancing Brave (USA))
669a$^{3}$

**Zack Hope** *N Caullery* a102 104
6 b g Araafa(IRE) Afaf (FR) (Spectrum (IRE))
177a$^{3}$ 723a$^{7}$ 4722a$^{8}$

**Zac Spirit (AUS)** *Cliff Brown* 106
5 b g Flying Spur(AUS) Kidman (AUS) (Quest For Fame)
2378a$^{3}$

**Zac Truth (USA)** *Gay Kelleway* a62
2 ch c Lookin At Lucky(USA) Rose Of Zollern (IRE) (Seattle Dancer (USA))
7811$^{6}$ ◆

**Zacynthus (IRE)** *Shaun Harris* a82 96
6 ch g Iffraaj Ziria (IRE) (Danehill Dancer (IRE))
1301$^{9}$ 1637$^{4}$ 2425$^{2}$ 3431$^{8}$ 5433$^{6}$ 5728$^{4}$ 6334$^{3}$ 6639$^{5}$ (7085) 7719$^{3}$

**Zadrak (FR)** *C Boutin* a72 72
3 bb c Dragon Dancer Zanatiya (FR) (Sinndar (IRE))
751a$^{6}$

**Zaeem** *Dean Ivory* a75 42
5 b g Echo Of Light Across (ARG) (Roy (USA))
181$^{6}$ 345$^{4}$ 582$^{4}$ 801$^{11}$ 5011$^{11}$ 5521$^{7}$ 6635$^{7}$ 6999$^{4}$ (7187) 7568$^{4}$ 7907$^{6}$ 8103$^{5}$

**Zaeemah (IRE)** *Saeed bin Suroor* 83
3 ch f Shamardal(USA) Shane (GER) (Kornado)
(1587) 2982$^{5}$ 4211$^{7}$

**Zafaraban (IRE)** *Aytach Sadik* a57 53
7 gr g Dalakhani(IRE) Zafaraniya (IRE) (Doyoun)
352$^{6}$

**Zafayan (IRE)** *D K Weld* 93
3 b g Acclamation Zafayra (IRE) (Nayef (USA))
3491a$^{5}$

**Zafraaj** *Ronald Harris* a30 58
3 b g Iffraaj Woodbury (Woodborough (USA))
1569$^{6}$ 1914$^{5}$ 2249$^{3}$ 2668$^{7}$ 4102$^{6}$ 5518$^{5}$ 5820$^{11}$

**Zafranagar (IRE)** *Ian Williams* a63 75
9 b g Cape Cross(IRE) Zafaraniya (IRE) (Doyoun)
1168$^{2}$ 1729$^{13}$ 2610$^{3}$ 2702$^{4}$ 2834$^{2}$ 6649$^{7}$ 7279$^{6}$

**Zagalo (FR)** *Guy Denuault*
3 b g Echo Of Light Beringhina (FR) (Bering)
600a$^{11}$

**Zagros (FR)** *J Heloury* a98 106
5 b g Slickly(FR) Jalapegnas (FR) (Hamas (IRE))
177a$^{5}$ 669a$^{2}$ 984a$^{6}$

**Zahee (NZ)** *M F De Kock* a112 112
5 b h Dylan Thomas(IRE) Zaheeya (AUS) (Encosta De Lago (AUS))
(396a) 508a$^{5}$ 678a$^{3}$ 899a$^{16}$

**Zahenda** *Ismail Mohammed* a31
2 b f Exceed And Excel(AUS) Impetious (Inchinor)
8083$^{6}$

**Zaidan (USA)** *A S Cruz* 114
6 bb g Street Cry(IRE) Element Of Truth (USA) (Atticus (USA))
2004a$^{14}$

**Zaidiyn (FR)** *Brian Ellison* 104
4 b g Zamindar(USA) Zainta (IRE) (Kahyasi)
4437$^{10}$ 5651$^{11}$ 7142a$^{21}$

**Zainda (IRE)** *Paul Midgley* a49 52
4 b f Dr Fong(USA) Zafayra (IRE) (Nayef (USA))
14$^{8}$ 97$^{3}$ 3097$^{5}$ 4534$^{4}$ 5103$^{9}$ 5337$^{6}$ 5773$^{4}$ 6628$^{3}$ 7187$^{11}$ 7672$^{6}$ 7846$^{12}$

**Zain Dream (IRE)** *Robert Cowell* a71
3 br c Mastercraftsman(IRE) Timeless Dream (Oasis Dream)
1008$^{2}$ 1287$^{3}$

**Zain Eagle** *Robert Cowell* a101 101
4 b c Dylan Thomas(IRE) Pearl City (USA) (Carson City (USA))
2461$^{4}$ 4214$^{2}$ 4608$^{5}$

**Zain Empire** *Robert Cowell* a78 83
3 b c Dubawi(IRE) Just Like A Woman (Observatory (USA))
(3601) 4551$^{3}$ 5349$^{2}$ 5930$^{4}$ 6885$^{5}$ 7417$^{9}$

**Zain Shamardal (IRE)** *A Al Raihe* a105 104
6 b h Shamardal(USA) Novelina (IRE) (Fusaichi Pegasus (USA))
(207a) 508a$^{9}$ 681a$^{14}$ 810a$^{6}$

**Zain Zone (IRE)** *Ruth Carr* a78 80
3 ch g Pastoral Pursuits Right After Moyne (IRE) (Imperial Ballet (IRE))
279$^{6}$ 1884$^{3}$ 2218$^{2}$ ◆ 3957$^{2}$ 4628$^{6}$ 5197$^{13}$ 5497$^{5}$ 6009$^{5}$ 6414$^{5}$ 6613$^{3}$ (7167) 7489$^{3}$

**Zaitsev (IRE)** *Ollie Pears* a52 80
4 ch g Refuse To Bend(IRE) Zuniga's Date (USA) (Diesis)
29$^{8}$ 1598$^{5}$ 2017$^{5}$ 2341$^{8}$ (3096) 3910$^{3}$ 4291$^{8}$ 5295$^{5}$ 5788$^{3}$ 6490$^{9}$ 6821$^{5}$

**Zakatal** *Simon Earle* a2 9
8 gr g Kalanisi(IRE) Zankara (FR) (Linamix (FR))
4441$^{12}$

**Zakhar Star (USA)** *A Savujev* 99
3 b c Henrythenavigator(USA) Brilliance (FR) (Priolo (USA))
2196a$^{11}$

**Zakiyyah (FR)** *N Clement* 77
3 b f Monsun(GER) Shemissa (IRE) (Fairy King (USA))
7857a$^{16}$

**Zakopane (FR)** *C Martinon* a68 64
4 b g Desert Style(IRE) Parmelie (FR) (Pivotal)
722a$^{14}$

**Zalty (FR)** *David Marnane* a92 101
4 b g Elusive City(USA) Dubai's Gazal (Fraam)
3737a$^{2}$ 4683$^{4}$ 6369a$^{2}$

**Zamaam** *F Rohaut* a96 100
4 bb c Muhtathir Nasheed (USA) (Riverman (USA))
669a$^{6}$

**Zamarrila** *C Laffon-Parias* 44
3 b f High Chaparral(IRE) Highphar (FR) (Highest Honor (FR))
7270a$^{12}$

**Zambeasy** *Philip Hide* a79 74
3 b g Zamindar(USA) Hanella (IRE) (Galileo (IRE))
1216$^{10}$ (1794) 2968$^{8}$ 3516$^{5}$ 4074$^{12}$ (5908) 6813$^{4}$ 7309$^{3}$ (8313)

**Zambucca (SAF)** *Gay Kelleway* a107 105
6 ch h Lundy's Liability(BRZ) Jazz Champion (SAF) (Dancing Champ (USA))
397a$^{11}$ 508a$^{3}$ 901a$^{10}$ 3354$^{7}$ 3722$^{7}$ 4180$^{5}$ 4682$^{5}$ 5687$^{6}$

**Zammy** *Michael Wigham* a53 19
5 ch g Zamindar(USA) Barbs Pink Diamond (USA) (Johannesburg (USA))
1110$^{12}$ 1387$^{2}$ 1917$^{10}$ 3123$^{9}$

**Zamorano (IRE)** *Ismail Mohammed* a15
2 b f Teofilo(IRE) Petit Calva (FR) (Desert King (IRE))
6605$^{11}$

**Zamoura** *John Gosden* a82
2 b f Azamour(IRE) Move (Observatory (USA))
8036$^{2}$ ◆

**Zampa Manos (USA)** *Andrew Balding* a92 94
3 b g Arch(USA) Doryphar (USA) (Gone West (USA))
1122$^{2}$ (1580) 2114$^{5}$ 2986$^{10}$ 3378$^{25}$ 5824$^{4}$ 6566$^{9}$

**Zamperini (IRE)** *Mike Murphy* a61 61
2 ch c Fast Company(IRE) Lucky Date (IRE) (Halling (USA))
4618$^{6}$ 5671$^{6}$ 7031$^{5}$ 7525$^{8}$

**Zamra (IRE)** *Brian Ellison* a66 75
3 b f Azamour(IRE) Deauville Vision (IRE) (Danehill Dancer (IRE))
127$^{5}$ 341$^{4}$ 422$^{2}$ (684) 828$^{2}$ 1033$^{2}$ 1135$^{4}$ (1508) 1661$^{5}$ 2319$^{13}$ 3110$^{9}$ 7177$^{9}$ 7500$^{6}$ 7565$^{11}$

**Zamuja** *G Botti* a78 85
3 b c Mujahid(USA) Mazaya (IRE) (Sadler's Wells (USA))
6221a$^{3}$ 7269a$^{2}$

**Zamzama (IRE)** *Saeed bin Suroor* a68
2 b f Shamardal(USA) Zahrat Dubai (Unfuwain (USA))
8173$^{3}$

**Zanbagh (AUS)** *Patrick Payne* 107
4 b f Bernardini(USA) Wild Iris (AUS) (Spectrum (IRE))
7395a$^{11}$

**Zand (IRE)** *Carmen Bocskai* 105
4 b g Zamindar(USA) Zanara (IRE) (Kahyasi)
7189a$^{5}$

**Zand Man** *Milton Bradley*
4 b g Zahran(IRE) Shellatana (Mister Baileys)
3517$^{7}$ 6421$^{11}$ 7349$^{10}$ 7853$^{11}$ 8199$^{8}$

**Zanetto** *Andrew Balding* a78 96
4 b g Medicean Play Bouzouki (Halling (USA))
1975$^{16}$ 2778$^{8}$ 3420$^{13}$ 4765$^{2}$ 5152$^{4}$

**Zanouska (USA)** *Mark Johnston* a70 70
3 b f Bernardini(USA) Zanoubia (USA) (Our Emblem (USA))
(1143) 1348$^{9}$ 2080$^{3}$ (2679) 2934$^{2}$ 4196$^{4}$ 4704$^{4}$ 5302$^{2}$ 6596$^{4}$

**Zantenor (FR)** *Yves de Nicolay* a83 83
3 b c Della Francesca(USA) Zitana (FR) (Zieten (USA))
795a$^{3}$ 5294a$^{5}$

**Zaraee (IRE)** *William Haggas* a72 98
3 b g Dubawi(IRE) Camaret (IRE) (Danehill (USA))
3253$^{15}$ 4176$^{4}$ (4660) ◆

**Zarazalay (FR)** *J-M Capitte* a54 52
3 ch f Layman(USA) Zarazienne (FR) (Zieten (USA))
391a$^{8}$

**Zari** *Roger Varian* a78
3 b f Azamour(IRE) Epiphany (Zafonic (USA))
6606$^{2}$ (7194)

**Zaria** *Richard Price* a52
3 b f Tomba Princess Zara (Reprimand)
7682$^{11}$ 7818$^{6}$ 8085$^{11}$ 8256$^{4}$

**Zariyano (FR)** *H-A Pantall* 74
2 ch c Linngari(IRE) Zariyana (IRE) (Desert Prince (IRE))
5940a$^{4}$

**Zarliman (IRE)** *Martyn Meade* a78 56
4 ch g Zamindar(USA) Zarlana (IRE) (Darshaan)
3861$^{9}$ 4262$^{9}$ 5831$^{7}$ 7044$^{11}$ 7427$^{7}$

**Zarnia (FR)** *Henk Grewe* a71 43
3 b f Soldier Of Fortune(IRE) Zarnitza (USA) (Quiet American (USA))
7270a$^{11}$

**Zarosa (IRE)** *John Berry* a33 68
5 b m Barathea(IRE) Shantalla Peak (IRE) (Darshaan)
1916$^{4}$ 2424$^{6}$ 4962$^{2}$ 5748$^{2}$ 7177$^{15}$ 7419$^{5}$ 7509$^{8}$

**Zarras (GER)** *P Schaerer* a92 92
5 b g Big Shuffle(USA) Zanana (Zafonic (USA))
555a$^{2}$ (638a) 728a$^{3}$

**Zarshana (IRE)** *A De Royer-Dupre* 111
3 b f Sea The Stars(IRE) Zarkasha (IRE) (Kahyasi)
2816a$^{3}$ (4249a) (5479a) 6956a$^{3}$ 7486a$^{7}$

**Zarwaan** *Ed Dunlop* 105
3 b g Dutch Art Develyn (Pivotal)
1420$^{2}$ ◆ 2565$^{2}$ 3378$^{5}$ ◆ 4127$^{4}$

**Zashka (FR)** *J-V Toux* 78
3 b f Manduro(GER) Maid Marion (UAE) (Jade Robbery (USA))
2978a$^{4}$ 3372a$^{2}$ 5370a$^{2}$ 5592a$^{2}$

**Zat Be Zat** *Violet M Jordan* a39
7 b g Sampower Star Blakeshall Girl (Piccolo)
8002$^{5}$ 8147$^{3}$ 8256$^{6}$

**Zavallya (FR)** *A De Royer-Dupre* a82 99
3 b f Elusive City(USA) Zewara (IRE) (Alhaarth (IRE))
2817a$^{7}$

**Zawatar (FR)** *W Delalande* a75 60
4 b c Great Journey(JPN) Zannkiya (Sendawar (IRE))
935a$^{11}$

**Zayade (FR)** *J Boisnard* a97 96
5 b m Country Reel(USA) Hallen (FR) (Midyan (USA))
4644a$^{6}$ 6620a$^{6}$ 7327a$^{5}$

**Zaza Zest (IRE)** *Richard Fahey* a71 69
2 ch f Approve(IRE) Happy Talk (IRE) (Hamas (IRE))
4751$^{7}$ 5297$^{11}$ 6212$^{3}$ 7003$^{3}$ 7362$^{2}$ (7763) 7945$^{5}$

**Zazou (GER)** *Waldemar Hickst* a109 112
7 b h Shamardal(USA) Zaza Top (GER) (Lomitas)
1478a$^{5}$ 4720a$^{8}$ 5938a$^{3}$ 6965a$^{5}$

**Zazoulino (GER)** *P Vovcenko* 56
2 b c Tiger Hill(IRE) Zarah Top (GER) (Big Shuffle (USA))
6377a$^{5}$

**Zealand (IRE)** *John Best* a38
3 b c Baltic King Zafaraya (IRE) (Ashkalani (IRE))
51$^{9}$ 316$^{14}$ 5491$^{9}$

**Zebead (IRE)** *William Jarvis* a58
2 gr c Zebedee Sinead (USA) (Irish River (FR))
8092$^{9}$

**Zebed (IRE)** *John M Oxx* a63 71
2 gr g Zebedee Tea Service (USA) (Atticus (USA))
6375a$^{22}$

**Zebedeedoodah (IRE)** *Matthieu Palussiere* 52
2 b f Zebedee Presently Blessed (IRE) (Inchinor)
1271a$^{6}$

**Zebelini (IRE)** *Mrs Ilka Gansera-Leveque* a60 68
2 rg f Zebedee Ma Nikitia (IRE) (Camacho)
(5789) 6401$^{5}$ 7038$^{11}$ 7363$^{4}$

**Zebella** *Rod Millman* a56
2 b f Paco Boy(IRE) Delitme (IRE) (Val Royal (FR))
6551$^{15}$ 7011$^{6}$ 7550$^{9}$

**Zebs Lad (IRE)** *Ronald Harris* a65 75
2 ro c Zebedee Dubai Princess (IRE) (Dubai Destination (USA))
1349$^{10}$ 2458$^{4}$ 2944$^{7}$ (3937) 4430$^{6}$ 4815$^{6}$ 5779$^{6}$ 7029$^{9}$ 7762$^{3}$ 8278$^{2}$

**Zeb Un Nisa** *Roger Charlton* 85
2 b f Iffraaj Tullynally (Dansili)
2402$^{5}$ ◆ (2944) 3721$^{4}$ 4566$^{2}$ 5791$^{3}$

**Zed Candy Girl** *John Stimpson* a70 58
4 ch f Sakhee's Secret Musical Twist (USA) (Woodman (USA))
40$^{8}$ (352) 661$^{2}$ 851$^{3}$ 1015$^{6}$ (2689) (3576) 4153$^{8}$ 4968$^{5}$ 5041$^{4}$ (5605) 6074$^{4}$ 6155$^{4}$ 7077$^{9}$ 7368$^{5}$ 7942$^{9}$

**Zee Bros (USA)** *Seth Benzel* a108 93
4 b c Brother Derek(USA) Nyanza (USA) (Montbrook (USA))
769a$^{4}$ 897a$^{11}$ 1180a$^{6}$

**Zeela (IRE)** *Tim Easterby* 71
2 b f Zebedee Vintage Allure (IRE) (Barathea (IRE))
1879$^{2}$ ◆ 2348$^{2}$

**Zee Zeely** *William Haggas* a75 89
3 ch c Champs Elysees Zee Zee Gee (Galileo (IRE))
1357$^{6}$ (1979) 3379$^{15}$ 4448$^{5}$

**Zeftan (IRE)** *Adrian Paul Keatley* a75 78
5 ch g Bachelor Duke(USA) Zarafsha (IRE) (Alzao (USA))
3463$^{4}$

**Zejel** *C Ferland* a87 109
4 b f Gold Away(IRE) Dinaha (FR) (Octagonal (NZ))
3746a$^{2}$ 5223a$^{4}$ 5963a$^{8}$

**Ze King** *Chris Wall* a74 60
5 b g Manduro(GER) Top Flight Queen (Mark Of Esteem (IRE))
1362$^{8}$ 6019$^{2}$ 6699$^{8}$ 7358$^{2}$ 7626$^{2}$ 7918$^{9}$

**Zelos Diktator** *Sean Curran* a49 54
8 br g Diktat Chanterelle (IRE) (Indian Ridge)
185$^{5}$ 455$^{4}$ 759$^{8}$

**Zelos Dream (IRE)** *Seamus G O'Donnell* a45 56
7 ch m Redback Endless Peace (IRE) (Russian Revival (USA))
4468$^{3}$

**Zeminenza (FR)** *J-M Capitte* a37
3 b f Air Eminem(IRE) Zannkiya (Sendawar (IRE))
482a$^{11}$

**Zenarinda** *Mark H Tompkins* a73 71
7 b m Zamindar(USA) Tenpence (Bob Back (USA))
49$^{9}$

**Zenobios (USA)** *A Fabre* a87 104
3 b c Smart Strike(CAN) Zinziberine (USA) (Zieten (USA))
7619a$^{8}$

**Zen Zansai Zaid (SWE)** *Tommy Gustafsson* a66 94
5 ch g Dubai Destination(USA) La Petite Chinoise (Dr Fong (USA))
6389a$^{7}$

**Zephir (FR)** *D Prod'Homme* a62 66
2 b c Lawman(FR) Mensa Sonne (FR) (Monsun (GER))
8149a$^{9}$

**Zephuros (IRE)** *Charlie Appleby* 91
2 b g Invincible Spirit(IRE) West Wind (Machiavellian (USA))
(3720) 4865$^{2}$ 5424$^{3}$ 6063$^{3}$

**Zephyr** *Jamie Snowden* a64 61
3 ch g Shirocco(GER) Pelagia (IRE) (Lycius (USA))
1090$^{3}$ ◆ 1635$^{11}$ 2098$^{6}$ 2616$^{6}$ 2679$^{3}$ 4333$^{9}$

**Zeppelin (FR)** *H-F Devin* 93
2 ch c Zanzibari(USA) Belle Gabrielle (FR) (Kaldounevees (FR))
4932a$^{3}$ 5740a$^{4}$

**Zerfaal** *John Gosden* a76 89
3 b c Dubawi(IRE) Dhelaal (Green Desert (USA))
1173$^{2}$ (1582) (2112) 2781$^{10}$ 4147$^{7}$ 4801$^{6}$

**Zermintrudee (IRE)** *David Evans* a55 56
2 b f Zebedee River Style (IRE) (Desert Style (IRE))
1314$^{2}$ 1488$^{4}$

**Zero Money (IRE)** *Hugo Palmer* a67 90
8 ch g Bachelor Duke(USA) Dawn Chorus (IRE) (Mukaddamah (USA))
1975$^{20}$ 3452$^{26}$ 4179$^{18}$ 4895$^{22}$ 6130$^{6}$ 7543$^{10}$ 7843$^{12}$

**Zeshov (IRE)** *Jeremy Noseda* 70
3 b g Acclamation Fathoming (USA) (Gulch (USA))
4169$^{6}$ 5349$^{6}$

**Zeteah** *David Lanigan* a45 47
4 b f Passing Glance Ajeebah (IRE) (Mujtahid (USA))
2066$^{5}$ 6028$^{9}$ 6940$^{6}$

**Zeus Magic** *Brian Ellison* a82 87
4 b g Zamindar(USA) Milly Of The Vally (Caerleon (USA))
1196$^{13}$ 1539$^{5}$ 2728$^{8}$ (5716) (6171) 6541$^{5}$ 7142a$^{15}$ 7409$^{18}$

**Zeyran (IRE)** *Hugo Palmer* a55 88
5 ch m Galileo(IRE) Chervil (Dansili)
1483$^{4}$ 1956$^{5}$ 2528$^{3}$

**Zhayrem (FR)** *J Heloury* a72 89
3 b f Montmartre(FR) Cortiguera (Oasis Dream)
193a$^{8}$

**Zhiggy's Stardust** *Henry Candy* a92 44
5 b g Zafeen(FR) Lady Natilda (First Trump)
7543$^{11}$

**Zhiyi (USA)** *P Bary* 114
4 b g Henrythenavigator(USA) Burning Sunset (Caerleon (USA))
6955a$^{11}$ 7559a$^{10}$

**Zibelina (IRE)** *Charlie Appleby* 109
4 b f Dansili Zaeema (Zafonic (USA))
1945$^{3}$ 5927$^{7}$ 6707$^{5}$

**Zifena** *Eve Johnson Houghton* 96
2 b f Zamindar(USA) Luminous Gold (Fantastic Light (USA))
2888$^{6}$ 3583$^{3}$ 4396$^{2}$ (4913) 5664$^{3}$ ◆ 6067$^{10}$

**Zigayani (IRE)** *Sir Michael Stoute* a73 72
2 b c Clodovil(IRE) March Star (IRE) (Mac's Imp (USA))
4618$^{8}$ 5050$^{3}$ 5752$^{2}$ 7116$^{6}$

**Ziggy Lee** *Peter Hedger* a86 90
8 b g Lujain(USA) Mary O'Grady (USA) (Swain (IRE))
2353$^{11}$ 2803$^{3}$ 3033$^{9}$ 4027$^{2}$ 4946$^{3}$ 5925$^{12}$

**Ziggy's Secret** *Lucy Wadham* 86
4 b f Sakhee's Secret Ziggy Zaggy (Diktat)
3125$^{3}$ 4907$^{2}$ (5536) 6492$^{9}$

**Zigzag (FR)** *J E Hammond* a91 84
4 ch f Dylan Thomas(IRE) Gabare (FR) (Galileo (IRE))
8006a$^{12}$

**Zigzag Hill** *Bill Turner* a20
3 b f Compton Place Ziggy Zaggy (Diktat)
1918$^{10}$

**Zilber (GER)** *Ed Dunlop* 80
3 b c High Chaparral(IRE) Zephyrine (IRE) (Highest Honor (FR))
1511$^{3}$ 2877$^{3}$

**Zinger (IRE)** *E J O'Neill* a62 82
2 gr f Zebedee Lucy Liu (IRE) (Grand Lodge (USA))
5844a$^{4}$ 6244a$^{7}$

**Zingiber** *Noel Quinlan* 10
2 ch g Manduro(GER) Titoli Di Coda (IRE) (Bertolini (USA))
7561$^{8}$

**Zinnobar** *Jonathan Portman* a69 52
4 gr f Ishiguru(USA) Demolition Jo (Petong)
1865$^{3}$ 2465$^{4}$ 2836$^{14}$ 3540$^{5}$ 4734$^{3}$ (5283) (5864) 6339$^{2}$ 7290$^{3}$ 7777$^{2}$ 8037$^{3}$ 8313$^{7}$

**Zipedeedodah (IRE)** *Joseph Tuite* a74 69
2 b c Zebedee Beverley Macca (Piccolo)
4025$^{9}$ 4286$^{6}$ 4909$^{2}$ (5985) 6422$^{5}$ 6629$^{2}$ 7362$^{9}$

**Zipp (IRE)** *Ralph Beckett* a82 93
4 b f Excellent Art Subito (Darshaan)
2160$^{5}$ 5288$^{2}$ 6708$^{8}$ 7409$^{14}$ 7838$^{6}$

**Zip Top (IRE)** *Charlie Appleby* a91 93
5 b g Smart Strike(CAN) Zofzig (USA) (Danzig (USA))
307a$^{8}$ 598a$^{13}$

**Zip Wire (IRE)** *Donald McCain* a73 86
5 b g Oratorio(IRE) Jaya (USA) (Ela-Mana-Mou)
1360$^{10}$

**Ziriyan (FR)** *M Delzangles* 97
3 b c Zamindar(USA) Zerkeriya (IRE) (Soviet Star (USA))
5591a$^{8}$

**Zivo (USA)** *Chad C Brown* a115
5 b h True Direction(CAN) American Skipper (USA) (Quiet American (USA))
*7614a*$^{8}$

**Zlatan In Paris (FR)** *J-C Rouget* a92 95
3 gr c Slickly(FR) Tossup (USA) (Gone West (USA))
4930a$^{5}$

**Zman Awal (IRE)** *James Fanshawe* a84 6
3 ch f Dubawi(IRE) Pivotal Lady (Pivotal)
1422$^{18}$ *(2126) 3117*$^{6}$ *4074*$^{9}$ *6902*$^{5}$ *7575*$^{2}$ *8071*$^{6}$ *8320*$^{3}$

**Zoom In** *Lee James* 42
6 b g Indesatchel(IRE) Korolieva (IRE) (Xaar)
*7*$^{12}$

**Zora Seas (IRE)** *Brian Meehan* 79
3 bb f Marju(IRE) Urgele (FR) (Zafonic (USA))
4699$^{3}$ 5272$^{2}$ (5622)

**Zubaidah** *George Baker* a63 68
2 b f Exceed And Excel(AUS) Bedouin Bride (USA) (Chester House (USA))
3558$^{6}$ 4444$^{6}$ 6066$^{9}$ *7258*$^{3}$ *7753*$^{12}$

**Zugzwang (IRE)** *Ed de Giles* a87 89
3 b c Kodiac Kris's Bank (Inchinor)
*1381*$^{8}$ 1723$^{5}$ *(5557)* *6044*$^{2}$ 6323$^{2}$ 6737$^{14}$ *6943*$^{8}$

**Zuhoor Baynoona (IRE)** *Richard Fahey* 93
2 b f Elnadim(USA) Spasha (Shamardal (USA))
(1859) 2313$^{3}$ 6751$^{9}$ (7099)

**Zumurudah (FR)** *Mark Johnston* a19 81
3 b f Dubawi(IRE) Brianza (USA) (Thunder Gulch (USA))
5757$^{7}$

**Zuri Chop (FR)** *A De Watrigant* 102
3 ch g Muhaymin(USA) Zaliana (FR) (Daliapour (IRE))
3807a$^{4}$

**Zurigha (IRE)** *Richard Hannon* a104 109
4 b f Cape Cross(IRE) Noyelles (IRE) (Docksider (USA))
*1577*$^{DSQ}$ 1974$^{7}$ 2956$^{7}$ 4607$^{3}$ 5927$^{4}$ 7243$^{6}$

**Zuzinia (IRE)** *Mick Channon* 71
2 b f Mujadil(USA) Sinegronto (IRE) (Kheleyf (USA))
2022$^{6}$ 2493$^{4}$ 3119$^{2}$ 3454$^{4}$ 3706$^{2}$ 4185$^{5}$ 5091$^{7}$ 5789$^{2}$ 6168$^{6}$ 6453$^{2}$ 6610$^{8}$ 7004$^{2}$ 7082$^{7}$ 7308$^{9}$

**Zvarov (IRE)** *J-C Rouget* a101 101
3 b g Elusive City(USA) Marie Rossa (Testa Rossa (AUS))
*(237a) 553a*$^{2}$

**Zygmunt (FR)** *Mme M Bollack-Badel* a88 95
3 ch g Vespone(IRE) Zython (FR) (Kabool)
1272a$^{7}$ 2226a$^{8}$

**Zylpha (IRE)** *H-A Pantall* a46 89
3 b f Elusive City(USA) Zaltana (USA) (Cherokee Run (USA))
7857a$^{14}$

**Zynah (IRE)** *Saeed bin Suroor* a64 71
3 b f Oasis Dream Vincennes (King's Best (USA))
*1768*$^{7}$ 2432$^{7}$ 6788$^{3}$ *7185*$^{10}$ *7575*$^{7}$

# Index to meetings Flat 2014


Amiens 935a,
Angers 6913a,
Arlington 4230a, 5457a-5460a,
Ascot 1866, 2107, 2142, 3317, 3352, 3374, 3415, 3448, 4142, 4178, 4604, 4645, 4695, 5160, 6124, 6891, 6918, 7271,
Ayr 1757, 2450, 2472, 3049, 3454, 3998, 4011, 4253, 4486, 4723, 5166, 5232, 6473, 6509, 6529, 6830, 7054,
Baden-Baden 2715a, 2815a, 5938a, 5965a-5966a, 6053a-6054a, 6123a, 6162a, 6180a, 7314a-7315a,
Bath 1568, 1786, 2007, 2413, 2688, 2942, 3208, 3562, 3813, 4101, 4279, 4562, 4842, 5593, 5903, 6023, 6312, 6355, 6811, 7302,
Belmont Park 2005a, 2227a-2228a, 3025a-3026a, 3994a-3995a, 4231a, 6949a,
Beverley 1503, 1656, 2014, 2230, 2540, 2660†, 3091, 3542, 3908, 3945, 4286, 4493, 4749, 5295, 5331, 5711, 5910, 6447, 6621,
Brighton 1663, 1872, 2044, 2064, 2716, 2859, 3323, 3549, 3820, 4042, 4337, 5028, 5070, 5120, 5517, 5945, 5972, 6189, 6393, 6995, 7215,
Cagnes-Sur-Mer 177a-178a, 193a-194a, 237a, 266a, 360a, 390a-392a, 436a-437a, 482a, 545a, 553a, 584a-585a, 629a-630a, 669a, 720a-723a,
Capannelle 1477a, 1779a-1780a, 2191a, 2374a-2376a, 7479a-7480a, 7616a-7617a, 7725a,
Carlisle 2601, 2823, 3296, 3569, 3599, 3952, 4510, 4701, 4958, 5264, 5806, 5994, 6222,
Catterick 1372, 1642, 2051, 2547, 2724, 2949, 3841, 4065, 4313, 4527, 4993, 5371, 5813, 6537, 7003, 7277, 7503,
Caulfield 7126a-7128a, 7301a,
Chantilly 795a-796a, 836a, 1402a, 1827a, 2242a, 2816a-2821a, 3027a-3030a, 3289a-3291a, 3806a-3809a, 4278a, 4775a-4776a, 6218a-6221a, 6618a-6619a, 6882a, 6991a-6992a, 6994a, 7094a-7095a, 7619a-7620a, 7629a-7630a, 7723a, 7916a,
Chepstow 1909, 2246, 2666, 2829, 3173, 3514, 3847, 4149, 5338, 5745, 6085, 6246, 6420,
Chester 2071, 2085, 2113, 2756, 3215, 3642, 3692, 4156, 4185, 4935, 5408, 5918, 6279, 6319, 6735,
Cholet 7327a,
Churchill Downs 1964a,
Clairefontaine 3691a, 4881a-4882a, 5263a, 5368a-5370a, 5588a-5592a, 5661a, 7344a,
Cologne 1619a, 2001a, 2377a, 3293a, 4524a, 6778a, 6806a, 7145a,
Compiegne 1139a, 2976a, 2978a, 3372a-3373a, 4312a, 7163a-7164a,
Cork 1333a, 3284-3285a, 5024a,
Craon 6620a,
Curragh 1076a, 1078a, 1473a, 2040a, 2042a, 2569a-2572a, 2579a-2581a, 3686a, 3736a-3739a, 3763a-3766a, 4459a-4461a, 4477a-4478a, 4480a, 5218a-5219a, 5699a, 5733a-5736a, 5954a-5955a, 5957a-5958a, 6369a-6375a, 6798a, 6800a, 7140a, 7142a, 7144a,
Deauville 57a*, 169a*, 805a*-806a*, 3640a, 3744a-3746a, 3869a, 3871a-3872a, 3907a, 4838a-4841a, 4930a-4932a, 4952a-4954a, 5026a-5027a, 5118a-5119a, 5222a-5225a, 5292a-5294a, 5404a-5407a, 5461a-5462a, 5478a-5482a, 5543a-5546a, 5516a-5519a, 5705a-5707a, 5739a-5743a, 5843a-5844a, 5900a-5901a, 5940a-5941a, 5959a-5964a, 7393a, 7437a, 8005a-8006a, 8132*, 8148a-8150a*, 8212a*, 8276a*, 8300a*,
Del Mar 5781a,
Dieppe 4464a-4465a,
Doncaster 1161, 1190, 1689, 1710, 1934, 2198, 2327, 2979, 3267, 3648, 3699, 4884, 3914, 4108, 4344, 4569, 5415, 6229, 6253, 6286, 6326, 7404, 7438, 7712,
Dortmund 3511a, 6589a,
Down Royal 3491a,
Dundalk 128a*, 615a*, 788a*, 790a*, 794a*, 6172a*, 6909a*, 7433a*, 7435a*, 7579a*, 7873a*, 7877a*, 7959a*, 7961a-7962a*,
Dusseldorf 1478a, 2584a, 4955a, 6377a, 6965a,
Epsom 1650, 2956, 2986, 3874, 4116, 4351, 4808, 5752, 5782, 6261, 6783,
Fairyhouse 3864a,
Ffos Las 3778, 4814, 4999, 5271, 5620, 5845, 6362,
Flemington 7602a, 7653a, 7724a,
Fontainebleau 1207a, 7855a-7857a,
Frankfurt 6950a, 7618a,
Frauenfeld 3512a,
Galway 4746a, 4771a, 4805a, 4949a-4951a,
Geelong 7395a,
Goodwood 1941, 2480, 2499, 2554, 2963, 3031, 3180, 3421, 4756, 4777, 4821, 4849, 4892, 5624, 5664, 5718, 6001, 6652, 7129,
Gowran Park 6585a,
Gulfstream Park 813a,
Hamburg 3770a, 3873a, 4006a-4007a, 4064a,
Hamilton 1966, 2291, 2673, 2909, 3099, 3358, 3605, 3827, 4192, 4357, 4381, 4899, 5630, 5852, 6008, 6574, 6594, 6819,
Hanover 4247a, 7481a-7483a,
Haydock 1717, 2148, 2506, 2561, 2696, 2730, 2763, 3106, 3134, 3461, 3880, 3921, 3959, 4388, 4422, 5077, 5127, 5173, 6056, 6092, 6131, 6699, 6742, 7230,
Hoppegarten 2229a, 3046a, 5231a, 6914a,
Jagersro 2244a-2245a, 3996a,
Keeneland 6915a, 6973a,
Kempton 79*, 179*, 244*, 274*, 289*, 368*, 376*, 444*, 452*, 483*, 570*, 586*, 654*, 744*, 753*, 815*, 838*, 852*, 921*, 987*, 1008*, 1023*, 1097*, 1118*, 1169*, 1208*, 1215*, 1229*, 1379*, 1403*, 1575*, 1764*, 1793*, 2057*, 2078*, 2458*, 2680*, 2881*, 2916*, 3112*, 3576*, 3854*, 4072*, 4965*, 5006*, 5035*, 5302*, 5486*, 5547*, 5820*, 6015*, 6031*, 6100*, 6138*, 6236*, 6481*, 6602*, 6659*, 6675*, 6851*, 6883*, 7011*, 7029*, 7190*, 7345*, 7369*, 7396*, 7526*, 7541*, 7631*, 7657*, 7728*, 7737*, 7752*, 7831*, 7847*, 7917*, 7940*, 7982*, 8007*, 8023*, 8067*, 8090*, 8111*, 8169*, 8183*, 8197*, 8247*,
Killarney 4276a,
Klampenborg 3772a,
Kranji 2378a-2379a,
Krefeld 1781a, 5484a, 7726a-7727a,
Kyoto 2002a,
L'Ancresse 2595a-2599a,
Laytown 6078a*, 6082a*,
Le Croise-Laroche 2290a, 3089a, 7681a,
Le Lion-d'Angers 1620a, 5226a,
Le Touquet 5227a,
Leicester 1275, 2380, 2608, 2637, 2837, 3222, 3380, 3612, 3966, 4364, 4534, 4784, 5201, 5524, 5980, 6203, 6610, 7018, 7165, 7487,
Leopardstown 1200a-1201a, 1252a, 2185a-2187a, 3167a, 3412a, 4379a, 4598a-4599a, 5115a, 5361a, 6348a-6354a, 7462a, 7476a,
Les Landes 1622a-1625a, 2591a-2594a, 3048a, 3495a-3496a, 4038a-4041a, 4715a-4718a, 5228a-5230a, 5969a-5971a, 6186a-6188a,
Limerick 1750a,
Lingfield 49*, 86*, 113*, 140*, 154*, 186*, 208*, 229*, 282*, 310*, 338*, 399*, 421*, 467*, 490*, 530*, 577*, 601*, 622*, 662*, 684*, 713*, 737*, 774*, 797*, 822*, 845*, 951*, 1016*, 1038*, 1065*, 1104*, 1140*, 1236*, 1257*, 1296*, 1386*, 1553*, 1829*, 1893*, 1917*, 2120(M), 2151*, 2206*, 2465(M), 2644*, 2923(M), 2993(M), 3074(M), 3229(M), 3387*, 3467(M), 3521*, 3706 (M), 4049*, 4079*, 4260*, 4320*, 4428(M), 4541*, 4576*, 4610*, 4652(M), 4731*, 4905 (M), 5042*, 5133*, 5180(M), 5278*, 5422(M), 5554*, 5827*, 5859(M), 6038(M), 6333(M), 6629*, 7198*, 7353*, 7549*, 7770*, 7798*, 7839*, 7880a*, 7925*, 8015*, 8036*, 8075*, 8097*, 8190*, 8240*, 8292*, 8308*, 8316*,
Longchamp 1340a-1341a, 1480a-1481a, 1551a, 1621a, 1782a-1784a, 2106a, 2192a, 2194a-2197a, 2586a-2588a, 2799a, 3170a-3172a, 3997a, 4249a-4251a, 6181a-6183a, 6244a-6245a, 6378a-6383a, 6569a-6571a, 6954a-6958a, 6966a-6972a, 7317a-7319a, 7485a-7486a,
Lyon-La Soie 751a-752a,
Lyon Parilly 7189a, 7896a,
Maisons-Laffitte 1271a-1273a, 1828a, 2226a, 2755a, 4008a-4009a, 4482a-4483a, 4721a-4722a, 6446a, 6591a-6592a, 6698a, 7026a-7027a, 7268a, 7654a-7656a,
Meydan 107a-112a, 202a-207a, 238a-243a, 304a-309a, 393a-398a, 504a-509a, 593a-598a, 678a-683a, 768a-773a, 807a-812a, 896a-902a, 1176a-1183a,
Monmouth 4010a,
Moonee Valley 7467a,
Munich 2006a, 3073a, 4720a, 6384a, 7603a,
Musselburgh 1560, 1596, 1924, 2213, 2512, 3000, 3186, 3236, 3656, 4517, 4856, 5140, 5561, 6108, 6400, 6790, 7097,
Naas 1824a, 2263a, 2855a-2856a, 4556a-4557a,
Nantes 3810a, 7478a,
Navan 1458a, 2370a,
Newbury 1417, 1433, 2298, 2334, 2770, 3140, 3556, 3887, 4395, 4435, 4942, 5377, 5429, 6517, 6545, 7412, 7446,
Newcastle 1303, 1670, 1837, 2420, 2736, 3007†, 3619, 3663, 3713, 4659, 5084, 5384, 5636, 5759, 6115, 6637, 6859, 7173,
Newmarket 1511, 1528, 1948, 1973, 2269, 2306, 2341, 2744, 2776, 3427, 3474, 3670, 3720, 4122, 4163, 4198, 4402, 4442, 4617, 4666, 4862, 4912, 5147, 5187, 5391, 5436, 5643, 5671, 6553, 6683, 6707, 6749, 6924, 7104, 7237, 7377, 7560, 7594,
Nottingham 1394, 1582, 1844, 2127, 2158, 2428, 2800, 2888, 3148, 3304, 3330, 3973, 4129, 4409, 4828, 5285, 5344, 5397, 6645, 6867, 7037, 7206, 7534, 7665,
Ovrevoll 4956a-4957a, 5744a,
Pimlico 2357a,
Pontefract 1356, 1482, 1879, 2519, 3057†, 3497, 3785, 4057, 4416, 4708, 5049, 5464, 6489, 6690, 6976, 7328,
Pornichet-La-Baule 599a-600a,
Randwick 1468a,
Redcar 1342, 1604, 1900, 2386, 2615, 2652, 3434, 3481, 4467, 4790, 5194, 5678, 6211, 6667, 6931, 7244, 7495, 7637,
Ripon 1536, 1732, 2134, 2358, 2866, 2895, 3366, 3394, 4019, 4449, 4973, 5013, 5443, 5767, 5788, 6757,
Rosehill 1186a,
Saint-Cloud 920a, 984a, 1094a, 1096a, 1371a, 1502a, 1907a-1908a, 1965a, 2267a, 2411a, 2630a-2631a, 3773a-3774a, 6419a, 6916a-6917a, 7069a-7070a, 7269a-7270a, 7557a-7559a, 7768a-7769a,
Saint-Malo 4252a, 4883a, 5662a, 7720a-7722a,
Salisbury 1980, 2276, 2487, 3081, 3274, 3583, 3748, 4205, 4673, 5309, 5351, 5873, 6063, 6293, 6874, 7149†,
San Sebastian 6392a,
San Siro 1603a, 2589a-2590a, 3047a, 3513a, 3775a-3776a, 6590a, 6807a-6808a, 7146a-7147a, 7320a-7323a, 7469a, 7604a,
Sandown 1696, 2493, 2702, 3193, 3243, 3927, 3980, 4328, 4548, 4583, 4798, 5091, 5879, 5925, 6299, 6455,
Santa Anita 7590a-7593a, 7605a-7613a, 7614a-7615a,
Senonnes-Pouance 2003a,
Sha Tin 2004a, 7897a-7899a, 8151a-8154a,
Southwell 1*, 8*, 28*, 58*, 72*, 93*, 170*, 252*, 267*, 297*, 361*, 383*, 474*, 546*, 563*, 647*, 761*, 829*, 859*, 906*, 928*, 1001*, 1087*, 1111*, 1125*, 1222*, 1243*, 1363*, 1495*, 1800*, 1886*, 2092*, 2394*, 2901*, 2931*, 3401*, 3792*, 5097*, 5568*, 7645*, 7760*, 7823*, 7908*, 8082*, 8133*, 8176*, 8205*, 8218*, 8277*, 8301*†,
St Moritz 555a, 638a, 728a-729a,
Strasbourg 6385a,
Taby 3090a, 6386a-6389a,
Thirsk 1440, 1955, 2165, 2348, 3337, 3529, 4294, 4624, 4869, 4919, 5240, 5493, 5885, 6146, 6427,
Tipperary 5154a, 5869a, 6963a,
Tokyo 7981a,
Toulouse 7736a,
Tramore 5456a,
Veliefendi 6163a-6164a, 6184a-6185a,
Vichy 4561a, 4603a, 4644a, 5329a-5330a,
Warwick 1677, 2021, 2172, 2435, 3933, 5774,
Windsor 1349, 1488, 1807, 2029, 2220, 2401, 2622, 2845, 3063, 3310, 3536, 3728, 3755, 3799, 4024, 4267, 4499, 4739, 4980, 5208, 5247, 5500, 5684, 6983, 7155, 7336, 7511,
Wolverhampton 15*, 35*, 65*, 100*, 121*, 147*, 162*, 195*, 215*, 259*, 317*, 346*, 353*, 406*, 429*, 460*, 497*, 510*, 537*, 556*, 608*, 639*, 670*, 692*, 730*, 781*, 866*, 886*, 913*, 936*, 958*, 972*, 994*, 1030*, 1045*, 1080*, 1132*, 1147*, 1264*, 1282*, 1311*, 1425*, 1448*, 1626*, 1739*, 1813*, 1852*, 5253*, 5506*, 5600*, 5795*, 5893*, 6071*, 6154*, 6267*, 6340*, 6407*, 6561*, 6715*, 6764*, 6838*, 6897*, 6939*, 7062*, 7071*, 7111*, 7181*, 7223*, 7252*, 7285*, 7361*, 7420*, 7453*, 7519*, 7568*, 7621a*, 7682*, 7697*, 7778*, 7806*, 7815*, 7864*, 7888*, 7900*, 7948*, 7970*, 7990*, 7998*, 8043*, 8058*, 8118*, 8140*, 8161*, 8225*, 8254*, 8262*, 8284*,
Woodbine 6390a-6391a, 7324a-7326a,
Yarmouth 1612, 1633, 1859, 2442, 2525, 2873, 3119, 3156, 3626, 3677, 3893, 4087, 4301, 4589, 4763, 5056, 5104, 5315, 5531, 5725, 6434, 6462, 6496,
York 2253, 2283, 2313, 2784, 3199, 3250, 4170, 4212, 4631, 4680, 5575, 5607, 5651, 5690, 6165, 7079, 7119,


† Abandoned
* All-Weather
(M) Mixed meeting

# Season Statistics Trainers - British Flat Turf 2014

| NAME | WINS–RUNS | % | 2ND | 3RD | 4TH | WIN PRIZE | TOTAL PRIZE | £1 STAKE |
|---|---|---|---|---|---|---|---|---|
| Richard Hannon | 165–1129 | 15% | 162 | 161 | 129 | £2,535,180 | £4,462,370 | -273.64 |
| John Gosden | 86–423 | 20% | 66 | 55 | 51 | £2,704,927 | £3,979,665 | +22.33 |
| A P O'Brien | 11–81 | 14% | 8 | 9 | 5 | £2,025,979 | £2,882,212 | -29.82 |
| Richard Fahey | 168–1283 | 13% | 177 | 153 | 137 | £1,707,242 | £2,645,329 | -125.09 |
| Mark Johnston | 137–1001 | 14% | 124 | 138 | 108 | £1,689,965 | £2,580,079 | -207.74 |
| Roger Varian | 61–366 | 17% | 61 | 59 | 35 | £1,314,905 | £2,155,996 | -40.50 |
| Sir Michael Stoute | 62–363 | 17% | 61 | 35 | 44 | £1,229,227 | £2,123,316 | -121.12 |
| William Haggas | 92–419 | 22% | 55 | 53 | 39 | £1,255,332 | £2,017,703 | +40.55 |
| Andrew Balding | 72–433 | 17% | 50 | 53 | 58 | £1,104,181 | £1,677,681 | -22.58 |
| David O'Meara | 94–673 | 14% | 68 | 92 | 63 | £1,155,769 | £1,619,183 | -73.51 |
| Saeed bin Suroor | 57–285 | 20% | 43 | 30 | 33 | £731,458 | £1,260,173 | -61.53 |
| Edward Lynam | 7–15 | 47% | 3 | 1 | 1 | £1,083,161 | £1,219,176 | +12.25 |
| Marco Botti | 43–324 | 13% | 41 | 36 | 45 | £613,018 | £1,141,728 | -66.10 |
| Charlie Appleby | 52–373 | 14% | 51 | 56 | 32 | £626,174 | £1,130,308 | -127.81 |
| Kevin Ryan | 57–494 | 12% | 55 | 57 | 59 | £541,224 | £1,112,904 | -130.77 |
| Luca Cumani | 48–264 | 18% | 44 | 38 | 23 | £580,123 | £1,052,555 | -68.70 |
| Lady Cecil | 11–95 | 12% | 15 | 17 | 11 | £937,437 | £1,027,172 | -46.68 |
| David Simcock | 40–290 | 14% | 35 | 40 | 30 | £768,700 | £1,023,955 | -69.35 |
| Mick Channon | 67–612 | 11% | 94 | 89 | 72 | £494,576 | £904,473 | -77.12 |
| Roger Charlton | 38–218 | 17% | 32 | 31 | 21 | £371,127 | £874,171 | -13.40 |
| Charles Hills | 48–410 | 12% | 45 | 47 | 36 | £507,337 | £823,368 | -132.21 |
| Tim Easterby | 47–728 | 6% | 80 | 77 | 84 | £319,181 | £700,984 | -316.98 |
| F Head | 1–3 | 33% | 0 | 1 | 0 | £632,345 | £688,062 | +3.00 |
| Ralph Beckett | 48–312 | 15% | 54 | 32 | 41 | £395,956 | £687,190 | -62.90 |
| Clive Cox | 44–301 | 15% | 47 | 40 | 32 | £303,659 | £631,948 | -75.19 |
| Brian Ellison | 47–469 | 10% | 47 | 45 | 51 | £377,878 | £599,623 | -146.22 |
| K R Burke | 48–334 | 14% | 42 | 59 | 37 | £327,342 | £591,304 | -9.24 |
| D K Weld | 3–8 | 38% | 1 | 1 | 0 | £306,234 | £565,311 | +4.50 |
| A Fabre | 3–11 | 27% | 3 | 2 | 1 | £320,341 | £518,098 | +2.75 |
| Henry Candy | 31–214 | 14% | 17 | 26 | 24 | £357,274 | £508,740 | -34.27 |
| Tom Dascombe | 39–320 | 12% | 30 | 43 | 41 | £304,653 | £505,218 | -105.83 |
| David Barron | 40–306 | 13% | 34 | 20 | 34 | £297,177 | £461,880 | -47.02 |
| Michael Dods | 37–280 | 13% | 43 | 32 | 35 | £293,059 | £440,448 | -63.14 |
| Ed Dunlop | 17–235 | 7% | 28 | 24 | 29 | £209,892 | £429,156 | -90.02 |
| Robert Cowell | 22–176 | 13% | 33 | 20 | 25 | £238,434 | £410,781 | +6.48 |
| Michael Appleby | 36–259 | 14% | 25 | 24 | 30 | £286,138 | £399,768 | +9.83 |
| Peter Chapple-Hyam | 16–147 | 11% | 18 | 17 | 17 | £133,720 | £399,491 | -46.06 |
| Marcus Tregoning | 18–128 | 14% | 18 | 18 | 17 | £333,025 | £394,244 | +1.01 |
| Brian Meehan | 31–250 | 12% | 32 | 26 | 30 | £225,402 | £380,800 | -14.66 |
| Clive Brittain | 10–127 | 8% | 11 | 11 | 18 | £261,180 | £371,638 | -30.00 |
| Jim Goldie | 45–450 | 10% | 49 | 40 | 65 | £205,452 | £364,160 | -52.69 |
| Hugo Palmer | 18–115 | 16% | 20 | 13 | 8 | £199,308 | £360,678 | -4.52 |
| John Quinn | 31–268 | 12% | 29 | 34 | 28 | £227,964 | £349,601 | -67.11 |
| William Muir | 28–200 | 14% | 30 | 24 | 30 | £122,664 | £346,589 | -14.06 |
| Dean Ivory | 10–101 | 10% | 12 | 6 | 10 | £67,320 | £313,136 | -31.75 |
| Hughie Morrison | 21–171 | 12% | 17 | 15 | 26 | £180,579 | £309,776 | -48.04 |
| Ruth Carr | 35–366 | 10% | 34 | 46 | 44 | £176,397 | £294,239 | -77.08 |
| James Fanshawe | 16–177 | 9% | 19 | 22 | 27 | £108,616 | £288,811 | -66.87 |
| David Elsworth | 17–121 | 14% | 12 | 9 | 19 | £161,695 | £271,519 | -2.92 |
| Keith Dalgleish | 42–411 | 10% | 44 | 44 | 43 | £164,115 | £271,109 | -158.46 |

# Season Statistics Jockeys - British Flat Turf 2014

| JOCKEY | WINS–RUNS | % | 2ND | 3RD | 4TH | WIN PRIZE | TOTAL PRIZE | £1 STAKE |
|---|---|---|---|---|---|---|---|---|
| Richard Hughes | 132–744 | 18% | 119 | 89 | 88 | £1,901,956 | £3,596,698 | -177.86 |
| Ryan Moore | 128–649 | 20% | 99 | 73 | 75 | £2,447,269 | £4,004,637 | -132.55 |
| Graham Lee | 126–816 | 15% | 96 | 79 | 102 | £972,166 | £1,385,234 | -45.72 |
| Joe Fanning | 98–699 | 14% | 94 | 83 | 62 | £1,257,544 | £1,736,145 | -40.95 |
| Paul Mulrennan | 93–621 | 15% | 65 | 69 | 71 | £493,302 | £737,835 | -10.24 |
| Andrea Atzeni | 93–539 | 17% | 72 | 78 | 63 | £2,036,997 | £3,282,770 | +45.73 |
| Paul Hanagan | 93–497 | 19% | 69 | 47 | 61 | £2,063,680 | £2,853,329 | -39.05 |
| William Buick | 90–539 | 17% | 76 | 72 | 62 | £1,536,785 | £2,731,031 | -56.89 |
| Daniel Tudhope | 84–547 | 15% | 52 | 84 | 59 | £862,155 | £1,225,922 | -110.87 |
| Adam Kirby | 78–514 | 15% | 62 | 59 | 52 | £859,290 | £1,261,011 | -78.01 |
| James Doyle | 77–483 | 16% | 84 | 53 | 54 | £2,077,853 | £2,954,709 | -35.26 |
| Silvestre De Sousa | 70–490 | 14% | 59 | 56 | 46 | £787,294 | £1,268,715 | -17.99 |
| Luke Morris | 68–579 | 12% | 71 | 60 | 60 | £435,985 | £692,429 | -166.18 |
| George Baker | 67–360 | 19% | 39 | 47 | 38 | £514,745 | £1,111,678 | +34.08 |
| Graham Gibbons | 61–466 | 13% | 52 | 32 | 48 | £399,632 | £552,390 | -74.59 |
| Jim Crowley | 61–447 | 14% | 48 | 44 | 39 | £971,607 | £1,431,356 | +43.33 |
| David Probert | 59–492 | 12% | 35 | 54 | 62 | £483,286 | £790,625 | -141.44 |
| Oisin Murphy | 56–452 | 12% | 67 | 49 | 56 | £614,019 | £914,491 | -74.72 |
| Tony Hamilton | 52–445 | 12% | 65 | 56 | 47 | £297,580 | £495,975 | -161.13 |
| Kieren Fallon | 52–404 | 13% | 30 | 50 | 40 | £758,132 | £1,182,171 | -96.76 |
| David Allan | 51–474 | 11% | 56 | 59 | 50 | £311,176 | £542,598 | -39.73 |
| Phillip Makin | 49–414 | 12% | 45 | 60 | 40 | £244,811 | £402,502 | -131.31 |
| P J McDonald | 48–559 | 9% | 61 | 72 | 70 | £234,061 | £414,833 | -203.47 |
| Dane O'Neill | 48–401 | 12% | 46 | 64 | 49 | £295,101 | £652,477 | -97.55 |
| Richard Kingscote | 48–358 | 13% | 38 | 45 | 55 | £459,475 | £722,096 | -55.06 |
| Robert Winston | 46–377 | 12% | 54 | 44 | 40 | £225,825 | £600,172 | -86.57 |
| Jamie Spencer | 45–408 | 11% | 59 | 47 | 49 | £438,877 | £1,276,543 | -178.24 |
| Frederik Tylicki | 44–306 | 14% | 45 | 40 | 29 | £270,611 | £485,370 | -18.36 |
| Jason Hart | 43–421 | 10% | 42 | 34 | 44 | £180,889 | £276,030 | -66.54 |
| George Chaloner | 42–318 | 13% | 44 | 28 | 27 | £383,497 | £530,845 | -52.79 |
| Martin Harley | 42–284 | 15% | 42 | 29 | 43 | £340,736 | £601,117 | -72.68 |
| Franny Norton | 41–395 | 10% | 53 | 65 | 50 | £267,481 | £568,502 | -116.50 |
| Martin Dwyer | 41–300 | 14% | 33 | 30 | 38 | £180,110 | £468,976 | +9.16 |
| Tom Eaves | 40–578 | 7% | 51 | 38 | 65 | £180,351 | £353,807 | -300.88 |
| Cam Hardie | 40–384 | 10% | 55 | 44 | 47 | £303,926 | £487,271 | -153.47 |
| Connor Beasley | 37–378 | 10% | 47 | 52 | 48 | £219,324 | £375,679 | -154.93 |
| Pat Dobbs | 36–286 | 13% | 33 | 37 | 44 | £270,341 | £471,153 | -48.31 |
| Ben Curtis | 35–318 | 11% | 39 | 37 | 31 | £178,747 | £322,590 | -94.18 |
| Fergus Sweeney | 34–281 | 12% | 26 | 31 | 23 | £240,330 | £345,482 | -84.06 |
| Sean Levey | 33–313 | 11% | 44 | 31 | 28 | £195,562 | £380,901 | -116.72 |
| Joey Haynes | 32–272 | 12% | 34 | 29 | 31 | £162,799 | £280,070 | -2.36 |
| Jack Garritty | 30–279 | 11% | 25 | 35 | 20 | £209,539 | £295,874 | -43.94 |
| David Nolan | 30–227 | 13% | 36 | 33 | 22 | £246,784 | £421,143 | +32.58 |
| Ryan Tate | 30–172 | 17% | 24 | 19 | 15 | £158,877 | £263,117 | +21.60 |
| Charles Bishop | 29–179 | 16% | 22 | 17 | 19 | £192,177 | £243,290 | +38.15 |
| James Sullivan | 28–422 | 7% | 38 | 49 | 49 | £196,368 | £328,646 | -161.08 |
| William Twiston-Davies | 28–351 | 8% | 48 | 51 | 35 | £134,354 | £305,198 | -128.94 |
| Jimmy Fortune | 28–307 | 9% | 33 | 33 | 41 | £387,770 | £677,046 | -83.13 |
| Tom Queally | 27–374 | 7% | 35 | 30 | 50 | £334,973 | £537,104 | -122.56 |
| Andrew Mullen | 27–285 | 9% | 25 | 24 | 28 | £199,346 | £286,407 | -47.88 |

# Season Statistics Owners - British Flat Turf 2014

| NAME | WINS–RUNS | % | 2ND | 3RD | 4TH | WIN PRIZE | TOTAL PRIZE |
|---|---|---|---|---|---|---|---|
| Hamdan Al Maktoum | 116–579 | 20% | 102 | 62 | 51 | £2,342,284 | £3,453,976 |
| Godolphin | 110–664 | 17% | 96 | 87 | 65 | £1,419,446 | £2,607,676 |
| K Abdullah | 43–230 | 19% | 36 | 19 | 25 | £1,638,808 | £2,133,908 |
| Sheikh Hamdan bin Mohammed Al Maktoum | 68–457 | 15% | 56 | 58 | 50 | £1,072,930 | £1,493,438 |
| D Smith/Mrs J Magnier/M Tabor/T Ah Khing | 2–3 | 67% | 0 | 1 | 0 | £1,236,278 | £1,284,698 |
| Al Shaqab Racing | 23–107 | 21% | 16 | 21 | 9 | £860,250 | £1,091,100 |
| Cheveley Park Stud | 32–241 | 13% | 34 | 32 | 30 | £716,451 | £1,029,613 |
| Mrs S Power | 5–8 | 63% | 1 | 0 | 1 | £986,754 | £1,011,492 |
| Qatar Racing Limited | 31–221 | 14% | 21 | 25 | 27 | £380,439 | £894,420 |
| Saeed Manana | 13–205 | 6% | 28 | 27 | 20 | £324,413 | £805,658 |
| Dr Marwan Koukash | 37–297 | 12% | 44 | 40 | 28 | £465,988 | £762,128 |
| Paul Smith | 1–4 | 25% | 1 | 0 | 1 | £368,615 | £689,435 |
| HRH Princess Haya Of Jordan | 8–77 | 10% | 11 | 10 | 9 | £139,941 | £681,425 |
| H H Sheikh Abdulla Bin Khalifa Al Thani | 1–2 | 50% | 0 | 0 | 0 | £632,345 | £644,450 |
| D Smith & Mrs J Magnier & MTabor | 5–21 | 24% | 2 | 3 | 0 | £339,764 | £599,401 |
| F Gillespie | 6–22 | 27% | 3 | 1 | 0 | £285,772 | £492,170 |
| Miss K Rausing | 9–54 | 17% | 3 | 5 | 10 | £446,469 | £471,457 |
| Highclere Thoroughbred Racing -Wavertree | 1–5 | 20% | 3 | 1 | 0 | £120,962 | £462,355 |
| Sheikh Mohammed Obaid Al Maktoum | 23–92 | 25% | 16 | 12 | 4 | £305,310 | £431,526 |
| Sheikh Rashid Dalmook Al Maktoum | 12–66 | 18% | 10 | 11 | 9 | £288,350 | £407,494 |
| MTabor & D Smith & Mrs J Magnier | 2–19 | 11% | 2 | 1 | 0 | £121,019 | £385,603 |
| Prince A A Faisal | 9–30 | 30% | 2 | 3 | 5 | £349,575 | £376,309 |
| D J Deer | 5–40 | 13% | 5 | 6 | 3 | £64,958 | £370,501 |
| Potensis Ltd C Giles Merriebelle Stables | 3–4 | 75% | 1 | 0 | 0 | £325,663 | £347,163 |
| Mrs J Magnier & M Tabor & D Smith | 2–20 | 10% | 2 | 2 | 3 | £175,801 | £340,340 |
| Moyglare Stud Farm | 1–4 | 25% | 0 | 1 | 0 | £178,637 | £324,838 |
| Crown Select | 3–6 | 50% | 1 | 0 | 1 | £288,090 | £312,515 |
| The Queen | 17–92 | 18% | 16 | 13 | 7 | £183,125 | £304,863 |
| Lord Lloyd-Webber | 1–4 | 25% | 0 | 0 | 0 | £297,728 | £303,803 |
| Ballymore Thoroughbred Ltd | 1–5 | 20% | 1 | 0 | 0 | £246,618 | £289,618 |
| Lady Tennant | 3–12 | 25% | 1 | 1 | 2 | £271,398 | £289,278 |
| J C Smith | 15–110 | 14% | 13 | 8 | 16 | £103,460 | £284,418 |
| Normandie Stud Ltd | 10–37 | 27% | 11 | 6 | 0 | £231,243 | £282,096 |
| H R H Sultan Ahmad Shah | 10–49 | 20% | 8 | 9 | 3 | £226,401 | £276,318 |
| Mrs Fitri Hay | 12–101 | 12% | 8 | 16 | 9 | £151,997 | £266,716 |
| Dr Cyrus Poonawalla & Morgan J Cahalan | 1–3 | 33% | 1 | 0 | 0 | £207,856 | £266,551 |
| N A Jackson | 4–13 | 31% | 3 | 2 | 0 | £206,120 | £259,992 |
| Saleh Al Homaizi & Imad Al Sagar | 15–110 | 14% | 20 | 15 | 17 | £87,415 | £257,969 |
| George Strawbridge | 10–56 | 18% | 14 | 6 | 7 | £169,428 | £256,694 |
| Sheikh Ahmed Al Maktoum | 14–67 | 21% | 7 | 13 | 12 | £208,628 | £255,495 |
| Jean-Claude-Alain Dupouy | 1–2 | 50% | 0 | 0 | 0 | £218,901 | £255,451 |
| Lady Bamford | 7–32 | 22% | 1 | 6 | 4 | £158,467 | £243,562 |
| Kingsclere Racing Club | 12–36 | 33% | 2 | 7 | 4 | £205,923 | £235,067 |
| Seasons Holidays | 5–25 | 20% | 4 | 3 | 1 | £108,221 | £221,039 |
| Dean Ivory | 1–10 | 10% | 2 | 0 | 1 | £22,684 | £216,637 |
| Andrew Tinkler | 3–32 | 9% | 6 | 3 | 6 | £183,659 | £209,360 |
| Kennet Valley Thoroughbreds VI | 1–6 | 17% | 2 | 0 | 3 | £53,875 | £205,858 |
| Middleham Park Racing IX & James Pak | 1–5 | 20% | 1 | 1 | 0 | £36,862 | £194,153 |
| Lady Rothschild | 13–68 | 19% | 14 | 7 | 12 | £124,981 | £193,849 |
| Mrs Magnier/Tabor/Smith/Flaxman Stables | 1–3 | 33% | 0 | 0 | 0 | £187,143 | £192,206 |

# Raceform Ratings - Top Rated 2014

## 4yo+ Worldwide

|  |  |
|---|---|
| Just A Way | 130 |
| Able Friend | 127 |
| Treve | 127 |
| Cirrus Des Aigles | 126 |
| Epiphaneia | 126 |
| Terravista | 126 |
| Chautauqua | 125 |
| Flintshire | 125 |
| Gold Ship | 125 |
| Lankan Rupee | 125 |
| Magician | 125 |
| Olympic Glory | 125 |
| Telescope | 125 |
| Toronado | 124 |
| Variety Club | 124 |
| Designs On Rome | 123 |
| Military Attack | 123 |
| Mukhadram | 123 |
| Noble Mission | 123 |
| Slade Power | 123 |

## 2yo European

|  |  |
|---|---|
| Belardo | 119 |
| Elm Park | 118 |
| The Wow Signal | 118 |
| Charming Thought | 117 |
| Ivawood | 117 |
| Tiggy Wiggy | 117 |
| Estidhkaar | 116 |
| Gleneagles | 116 |
| Hootenanny | 116 |
| Limato | 116 |
| Toocoolforschool | 116 |
| Vert De Grece | 116 |
| Anthem Alexander | 115 |
| Found | 115 |
| Dick Whittington | 114 |
| Kodi Bear | 114 |
| Ol' Man River | 114 |

## 3yo Worldwide

|  |  |
|---|---|
| Australia | 129 |
| Kingman | 128 |
| Taghrooda | 126 |
| The Grey Gatsby | 126 |
| Charm Spirit | 124 |
| Night Of Thunder | 124 |
| Harp Star | 123 |
| Kingston Hill | 123 |
| Sea The Moon | 122 |
| Toormore | 122 |
| G Force | 121 |
| Mustajeeb | 121 |
| Postponed | 121 |
| Tapestry | 121 |
| To The World | 121 |
| Eagle Top | 120 |
| Free Eagle | 120 |
| Karakontie | 120 |

## Dirt & Synthetics

|  |  |
|---|---|
| Shared Belief | 128 |
| Palace Malice | 126 |
| California Chrome | 125 |
| Game On Dude | 125 |
| African Story | 124 |
| Bayern | 124 |
| Goldencents | 123 |
| Mucho Macho Man | 123 |
| Toast Of New York | 123 |
| Will Take Charge | 123 |
| Private Zone | 122 |
| Untapable | 122 |
| Close Hatches | 121 |
| Prince Bishop | 121 |
| Ride On Curlin | 121 |
| Sterling City | 121 |
| Tonalist | 121 |
| Work All Week | 121 |

# Raceform Flat Median Times 2014

Some distances have been omitted where insufficient data exists to establish a reliable median time

## ASCOT

- 5f ........ 1m 0.5s
- 6f ........ 1m 14.5s
- 7f ........ 1m 27.6s
- 1m (Str) ........ 1m 40.8s
- 1m (Rnd) ........ 1m 40.7s
- 1m 2f ........ 2m 7.4s
- 1m 4f ........ 2m 32.5s
- 1m 6f ........ 3m 1.0s
- 2m ........ 3m 29.0s
- 2m 4f ........ 4m 24.8s
- 2m 5f 159y ........ 4m 49.4s

## AYR

- 5f ........ 59.4s
- 6f ........ 1m 12.4s
- 7f 50y ........ 1m 33.4s
- 1m ........ 1m 43.8s
- 1m 1f 20y ........ 1m 57.5s
- 1m 2f ........ 2m 12.0s
- 1m 5f 13y ........ 2m 54.0s
- 1m 7f ........ 3m 20.4s
- 2m 1f 105y ........ 3m 55.0s

## BATH

- 5f 11y ........ 1m 2.5s
- 5f 161y ........ 1m 11.2s
- 1m 5y ........ 1m 40.8s
- 1m 2f 46y ........ 2m 11.0s
- 1m 3f 144y ........ 2m 30.6s
- 1m 5f 22y ........ 2m 52.0s
- 2m 1f 34y ........ 3m 51.9s

## BEVERLEY

- 5f ........ 1m 3.5s
- 7f 100y ........ 1m 33.8s
- 1m 100y ........ 1m 47.6s
- 1m 1f 207y ........ 2m 7.0s
- 1m 4f 16y ........ 2m 39.8s
- 2m 35y ........ 3m 39.8s

## BRIGHTON

- 5f 59y ........ 1m 2.3s
- 5f 213y ........ 1m 10.2s
- 6f 209y ........ 1m 23.1s
- 7f 214y ........ 1m 36.0s
- 1m 1f 209y ........ 2m 3.6s
- 1m 3f 196y ........ 2m 32.7s

## CARLISLE

- 5f ........ 1m 0.8s
- 5f 193y ........ 1m 13.7s
- 6f 192y ........ 1m 27.1s
- 7f 200y ........ 1m 40.0s
- 1m 1f 61y ........ 1m 57.6s
- 1m 3f 107y ........ 2m 23.1s
- 1m 6f 32y ........ 3m 7.5s
- 2m 1f 52y ........ 3m 53.0s

## CATTERICK

- 5f ........ 59.8s
- 5f 212y ........ 1m 13.6s
- 7f ........ 1m 27.0s
- 1m 3f 214y ........ 2m 38.9s
- 1m 5f 175y ........ 3m 3.6s
- 1m 7f 177y ........ 3m 32.0s

## CHEPSTOW

- 5f 16y ........ 59.3s
- 6f 16y ........ 1m 12.0s
- 7f 16y ........ 1m 23.2s
- 1m 14y ........ 1m 36.2s
- 1m 2f 36y ........ 2m 10.6s
- 1m 4f 23y ........ 2m 39.0s
- 2m 49y ........ 3m 38.9s
- 2m 2f ........ 4m 3.6s

## CHESTER

- 5f 16y ........ 1m 1.0s
- 5f 110y ........ 1m 6.2s
- 6f 18y ........ 1m 13.8s
- 7f 2y ........ 1m 26.5s
- 7f 122y ........ 1m 33.8s
- 1m 2f 75y ........ 2m 11.2s
- 1m 3f 79y ........ 2m 24.8s
- 1m 4f 66y ........ 2m 38.5s
- 1m 5f 89y ........ 2m 52.7s
- 1m 6f 91y ........ 3m 7.0s
- 1m 7f 195y ........ 3m 28.0s
- 2m 2f 147y ........ 4m 4.8s

## DONCASTER

- 5f ........ 1m 0.5s
- 5f 140y ........ 1m 8.8s
- 6f ........ 1m 13.6s
- 6f 110y ........ 1m 19.9s
- 7f ........ 1m 26.3s
- 1m (Str) ........ 1m 39.3s
- 1m (Rnd) ........ 1m 39.7s
- 1m 2f 60y ........ 2m 9.4s
- 1m 4f ........ 2m 34.9s
- 1m 6f 132y ........ 3m 7.4s
- 2m 110y ........ 3m 40.4s
- 2m 2f ........ 3m 55.0s

## EPSOM

- 5f ........ 55.7s
- 6f ........ 1m 9.4s
- 7f ........ 1m 23.3s
- 1m 114y ........ 1m 46.1s
- 1m 2f 18y ........ 2m 9.7s
- 1m 4f 10y ........ 2m 38.9s

## FFOS LAS

- 5f ........ 58.3s
- 6f ........ 1m 10.0s
- 1m ........ 1m 41.0s
- 1m 2f ........ 2m 9.4s
- 1m 4f ........ 2m 37.4s
- 1m 6f ........ 3m 3.8s
- 2m ........ 3m 30.0s

## GOODWOOD

- 5f ........ 1m 0.2s
- 6f ........ 1m 12.2s
- 7f ........ 1m 27.0s
- 1m ........ 1m 39.9s
- 1m 1f ........ 1m 56.3s
- 1m 1f 192y ........ 2m 8.1s
- 1m 3f ........ 2m 26.5s
- 1m 4f ........ 2m 38.4s
- 1m 6f ........ 3m 3.6s
- 2m ........ 3m 29.0s
- 2m 5f ........ 4m 31.0s

## HAMILTON

- 5f 4y ........ 1m
- 6f 5y ........ 1m 12.2s
- 1m 65y ........ 1m 48.4s
- 1m 1f 36y ........ 1m 59.7s
- 1m 3f 16y ........ 2m 25.6s
- 1m 4f 17y ........ 2m 38.6s
- 1m 5f 9y ........ 2m 53.9s

## HAYDOCK

- 5f (Inner) ........ 1m 0.8s
- 5f ........ 1m 0.8s
- 6f (Inner) ........ 1m 13.8s
- 6f ........ 1m 13.8s
- 7f ........ 1m 30.7s
- 1m ........ 1m 43.7s
- 1m 2f 95y ........ 2m 15.5s
- 1m 3f 200y ........ 2m 33.8s
- 1m 6f ........ 3m 2.0s
- 2m 45y ........ 3m 34.3s

## KEMPTON (AW)

- 5f ........ 1m 0.5s
- 6f ........ 1m 13.1s
- 7f ........ 1m 26.0s
- 1m ........ 1m 39.8s
- 1m 2f ........ 2m 8.0s
- 1m 3f ........ 2m 21.9s
- 1m 4f ........ 2m 34.5s
- 2m ........ 3m 30.1s

## LEICESTER

- 5f 2y ........ 1m
- 5f 218y ........ 1m 13.0s
- 7f 9y ........ 1m 26.2s
- 1m 60y ........ 1m 45.1s
- 1m 1f 218y ........ 2m 7.9s
- 1m 3f 183y ........ 2m 33.9s

## LINGFIELD

- 5f ........ 58.2s
- 6f ........ 1m 11.2s
- 7f ........ 1m 23.3s
- 7f 140y ........ 1m 32.3s
- 1m 1f ........ 1m 56.6s
- 1m 2f ........ 2m 10.5s
- 1m 3f 106y ........ 2m 31.5s
- 1m 6f ........ 3m 10.0s

## LINGFIELD (AW)

- 5f 6y ........ 58.8s
- 6f 1y ........ 1m 11.9s
- 7f 1y ........ 1m 24.8s
- 1m 1y ........ 1m 38.2s
- 1m 2f ........ 2m 6.6s
- 1m 4f ........ 2m 33.0s
- 1m 5f ........ 2m 46.0s
- 1m 7f 169y ........ 3m 25.7s

## MUSSELBURGH

- 5f ........ 1m 0.4s
- 7f 30y ........ 1m 29.0s
- 1m ........ 1m 41.2s
- 1m 1f ........ 1m 53.9s
- 1m 4f 100y ........ 2m 42.0s
- 1m 5f ........ 2m 52.0s
- 1m 6f ........ 3m 5.3s
- 2m ........ 3m 33.5s

## NEWBURY

- 5f 34y ........ 1m 1.4s
- 6f 8y ........ 1m 13.0s
- 6f 110y ........ 1m 19.3s
- 7f (Str) ........ 1m 25.7s
- 1m (Str) ........ 1m 39.7s
- 1m 7y (Rnd) ........ 1m 38.7s
- 1m 1f ........ 1m 55.5s
- 1m 2f 6y ........ 2m 8.8s
- 1m 3f 5y ........ 2m 21.2s
- 1m 4f 5y ........ 2m 35.5s
- 1m 5f 61y ........ 2m 52.0s
- 2m ........ 3m 32.0s

## NEWCASTLE

- 5f ........ 1m 1.1s
- 6f ........ 1m 14.6s
- 7f ........ 1m 27.8s
- 1m (Rnd) ........ 1m 45.3s
- 1m 3y (Str) ........ 1m 43.4s
- 1m 2f 32y ........ 2m 11.9s
- 1m 4f 93y ........ 2m 45.6s
- 1m 6f 97y ........ 3m 11.3s
- 2m 19y ........ 3m 39.4s

## NEWMARKET

- 5f (Row) ........ 59.1s
- 6f (Row) ........ 1m 12.2s
- 7f (Row) ........ 1m 25.4s
- 1m (Row) ........ 1m 38.6s
- 1m 1f (Row) ........ 1m 51.7s
- 1m 2f (Row) ........ 2m 5.8s
- 1m 4f (Row) ........ 2m 32.0s
- 1m 6f (Row) ........ 2m 57.0s
- 2m (Row) ........ 3m 30.5s
- 2m 2f (Row) ........ 3m 52.0s

## NEWMARKET (JULY)

- 5f (July) ........ 59.1s
- 6f (July) ........ 1m 12.5s
- 7f (July) ........ 1m 25.7s
- 1m (July) ........ 1m 40.0s
- 1m 2f (July) ........ 2m 5.5s
- 1m 4f (July) ........ 2m 32.9s
- 1m 5f (July) ........ 2m 44.0s
- 1m 6f 175y (July) ........ 3m 8.4s
- 2m 24y (July) ........ 3m 27.0s

## NOTTINGHAM

- 5f 13y (Inner) ........ 1m 1.5s
- 5f 13y ........ 1m 1.5s
- 6f 15y ........ 1m 14.7s
- 1m 75y (Inner) ........ 1m 49.0s
- 1m 75y ........ 1m 49.0s
- 1m 1f ........ 1m 57.6s
- 1m 2f 50y (Inner) ........ 2m 14.3s
- 1m 2f 50y ........ 2m 14.3s
- 1m 6f 15y (Inner) ........ 3m 7.0s
- 1m 6f 15y ........ 3m 7.0s
- 2m 9y ........ 3m 34.5s

## PONTEFRACT

- 5f ........ 1m 3.3s
- 6f ........ 1m 16.9s
- 1m 4y ........ 1m 45.9s
- 1m 2f 6y ........ 2m 13.7s
- 1m 4f 8y ........ 2m 40.8s
- 2m 1f 22y ........ 3m 44.6s
- 2m 1f 216y ........ 3m 56.2s
- 2m 5f 122y ........ 4m 51.0s

## REDCAR

- 5f ........ 58.6s
- 6f ........ 1m 11.8s
- 7f ........ 1m 24.5s
- 1m ........ 1m 36.6s
- 1m 1f ........ 1m 53.0s
- 1m 2f ........ 2m 7.1s
- 1m 6f 19y ........ 3m 4.7s
- 2m 4y ........ 3m 31.4s

## RIPON

- 5f ........ 1m
- 6f ........ 1m 13.0s
- 1m ........ 1m 41.4s
- 1m 1f ........ 1m 54.7s
- 1m 1f 170y ........ 2m 5.4s
- 1m 4f 10y ........ 2m 36.7s
- 2m ........ 3m 31.8s

## SALISBURY

- 5f ........ 1m 1.0s
- 6f ........ 1m 14.8s
- 6f 212y ........ 1m 28.6s
- 1m ........ 1m 43.5s
- 1m 1f 198y ........ 2m 9.9s
- 1m 4f ........ 2m 38.0s
- 1m 6f 21y ........ 3m 7.4s

## SANDOWN

- 5f 6y ........ 1m 1.6s
- 7f 16y ........ 1m 29.5s
- 1m 14y ........ 1m 43.3s
- 1m 1f ........ 1m 55.7s
- 1m 2f 7y ........ 2m 10.5s
- 1m 6f ........ 3m 4.5s
- 2m 78y ........ 3m 38.7s

## SOUTHWELL (AW)

- 5f ........ 59.7s
- 6f ........ 1m 16.5s
- 7f ........ 1m 30.3s
- 1m ........ 1m 43.7s
- 1m 3f ........ 2m 28.0s
- 1m 4f ........ 2m 41.0s
- 1m 6f ........ 3m 8.3s
- 2m ........ 3m 45.5s

## THIRSK

- 5f ........ 59.6s
- 6f ........ 1m 12.7s
- 7f ........ 1m 27.2s
- 1m ........ 1m 40.1s
- 1m 4f ........ 2m 36.2s
- 2m ........ 3m 28.3s

## WARWICK

- 5f ........ 59.6s
- 5f 110y ........ 1m 5.9s
- 6f ........ 1m 11.8s
- 7f ........ 1m 23.2s
- 7f 26y ........ 1m 24.6s
- 1m 20y ........ 1m 41.0s
- 1m 20y ........ 1m 41.0s
- 1m 2f 202y ........ 2m 21.1s
- 1m 7f 9y ........ 3m 19.0s

## WINDSOR

- 5f 10y ........ 1m 0.3s
- 6f ........ 1m 13.0s
- 1m 67y ........ 1m 44.7s
- 1m 2f 7y ........ 2m 8.7s
- 1m 3f 135y ........ 2m 29.5s

## WOLVERHAMPTON (AW)

- 5f 20y ........ 1m 1.9s
- 5f 216y ........ 1m 14.5s
- 7f 32y ........ 1m 28.8s
- 1m 141y ........ 1m 50.1s
- 1m 1f 103y ........ 2m 0.8s
- 1m 4f 50y ........ 2m 40.8s
- 1m 5f 194y ........ 3m 4.8s
- 2m 119y ........ 3m 43.7s

## YARMOUTH

- 5f 43y ........ 1m 2.7s
- 6f 3y ........ 1m 14.4s
- 7f 3y ........ 1m 26.6s
- 1m 3y ........ 1m 40.6s
- 1m 1f ........ 1m 55.8s
- 1m 2f 21y ........ 2m 10.5s
- 1m 3f 101y ........ 2m 28.7s
- 1m 6f 17y ........ 3m 7.6s
- 2m ........ 3m 32.4s

## YORK

- 5f ........ 59.3s
- 5f 89y ........ 1m 4.1s
- 6f ........ 1m 11.9s
- 7f ........ 1m 25.3s
- 1m ........ 1m 39.0s
- 1m 110y ........ 1m 45.9s
- 1m 208y ........ 1m 52.0s
- 1m 2f 88y ........ 2m 12.5s
- 1m 4f ........ 2m 33.2s
- 1m 6f ........ 3m 0.2s
- 2m 88y ........ 3m 34.5s
- 2m 2f ........ 3m 55.4s

# Raceform Flat Record Times 2014

## ASCOT

| Distance | Time | Age | Weight | Going | Horse | Date |
|---|---|---|---|---|---|---|
| 5f | 58.80 | 2 | 9-1 | Good To Firm | No Nay Never | Jun 20 2013 |
| 5f | 57.44 | 6 | 9-1 | Good To Firm | Miss Andretti (AUS) | Jun 19 2007 |
| 6f | 1m 12.46 | 2 | 9-1 | Good To Firm | Henrythenavigator (USA) | Jun 19 2007 |
| 6f | 1m 11.50 | 3 | 9-10 | Good To Firm | Mince | Aug 11 2012 |
| 7f | 1m 26.55 | 2 | 9-0 | Good To Firm | Malabar | Jly 25 2014 |
| 7f | 1m 24.28 | 4 | 8-11 | Good To Firm | Galician | Jly 27 2013 |
| 1m | 1m 39.55 | 2 | 8-12 | Good | Joshua Tree (IRE) | Sep 26 2009 |
| 1m | 1m 38.32 | 3 | 9-0 | Good To Firm | Ghanaati (USA) | Jun 19 2009 |
| 1m | 1m 37.09 | 4 | 9-0 | Good To Firm | Integral | Jun 18 2014 |
| 1m 2f | 2m 1.90 | 5 | 8-11 | Good To Firm | The Fugue | Jun 18 2014 |
| 1m 4f | 2m 24.60 | 4 | 9-7 | Good To Firm | Novellist | Jly 27 2013 |
| 2m | 3m 24.13 | 3 | 9-1 | Good To Firm | Holberg (UAE) | Jun 19 2009 |
| 2m 4f | 4m 16.92 | 6 | 9-2 | Good To Firm | Rite of Passage | Jun 17 2010 |
| 2m 5f 159y | 4m 47.79 | 7 | 9-2 | Good To Firm | Bergo (GER) | Jun 19 2010 |

## AYR

| Distance | Time | Age | Weight | Going | Horse | Date |
|---|---|---|---|---|---|---|
| 5f | 56.98 | 2 | 8-11 | Good | Boogie Street | Sep 18 2003 |
| 5f | 55.68 | 3 | 8-11 | Good To Firm | Look Busy (IRE) | Jun 21 2008 |
| 6f | 1m 9.73 | 2 | 7-10 | Firm | Sir Bert | Sep 17 1969 |
| 6f | 1m 8.37 | 5 | 8-6 | Good To Firm | Maison Dieu | Jun 21 2008 |
| 7f 50y | 1m 28.99 | 2 | 9-0 | Good | Tafaahum (USA) | Sep 19 2003 |
| 7f 50y | 1m 28.07 | 5 | 9-0 | Good To Firm | Ginger Jack | May 30 2012 |
| 1m | 1m 39.18 | 2 | 9-7 | Good | Moonlightnavigator | Sep 18 2014 |
| 1m | 1m 36.00 | 4 | 7-13 | Firm | Sufi | Sep 16 1959 |
| 1m 1f 20y | 1m 50.30 | 4 | 9-3 | Good | Retirement | Sep 19 2003 |
| 1m 2f | 2m 4.02 | 4 | 9-9 | Good To Firm | Endless Hall | Jly 17 2000 |
| 1m 5f 13y | 2m 45.81 | 4 | 9-7 | Good To Firm | Eden's Close | Sep 18 1993 |
| 1m 7f | 3m 13.16 | 3 | 9-4 | Good | Romany Rye | Sep 19 1991 |
| 2m 1f 105y | 3m 45.20 | 4 | 6-13 | Firm | Curry | Sep 16 1955 |

## BATH

| Distance | Time | Age | Weight | Going | Horse | Date |
|---|---|---|---|---|---|---|
| 5f 11y | 59.50 | 2 | 9-2 | Firm | Amour Propre | Jly 24 2008 |
| 5f 11y | 58.75 | 3 | 8-12 | Firm | Enticing (IRE) | May 1 2007 |
| 5f 161y | 1m 8.70 | 2 | 8-12 | Firm | Qalahari (IRE) | Jly 24 2008 |
| 5f 161y | 1m 8.10 | 6 | 9-0 | Firm | Madraco | May 22 1989 |
| 1m 5y | 1m 39.51 | 2 | 9-2 | Firm | Natural Charm (IRE) | Sep 14 2014 |
| 1m 5y | 1m 37.20 | 5 | 8-12 | Good To Firm | Adobe | Jun 17 2000 |
| 1m 5y | 1m 37.20 | 3 | 8-7 | Firm | Alasha (IRE) | Aug 18 2002 |
| 1m 2f 46y | 2m 5.80 | 3 | 9-0 | Good To Firm | Connoisseur Bay (USA) | May 29 1998 |
| 1m 3f 144y | 2m 25.74 | 3 | 9-0 | Hard | Top The Charts | Sep 8 2005 |
| 1m 5f 22y | 2m 47.20 | 4 | 10-0 | Firm | Flown | Aug 13 1991 |
| 2m 1f 34y | 3m 43.41 | 6 | 7-9 | Firm | Yaheska (IRE) | Jun 14 2003 |

## BEVERLEY

| Distance | Time | Age | Weight | Going | Horse | Date |
|---|---|---|---|---|---|---|
| 5f | 1m 0.89 | 2 | 8-12 | Good To Firm | Langavat | Jun 8 2013 |
| 5f | 1m 0.12 | 4 | 9-5 | Firm | Pic Up Sticks | Apr 16 2003 |
| 7f 100y | 1m 31.10 | 2 | 9-7 | Good To Firm | Champagne Prince | Aug 10 1995 |
| 7f 100y | 1m 31.10 | 2 | 9-0 | Firm | Majal (IRE) | Jly 30 1991 |
| 7f 100y | 1m 29.50 | 3 | 7-8 | Firm | Who's Tef | Jly 30 1991 |
| 1m 100y | 1m 43.30 | 2 | 9-0 | Firm | Arden | Sep 24 1986 |
| 1m 100y | 1m 42.20 | 3 | 8-4 | Firm | Legal Case | Jun 14 1989 |
| 1m 1f 207y | 2m 1.00 | 3 | 9-7 | Good To Firm | Eastern Aria | Aug 29 2009 |
| 1m 4f 16y | 2m 34.75 | 3 | 8-13 | Good To Firm | Leaderene | Sep 17 2014 |
| 2m 35y | 3m 29.50 | 4 | 9-2 | Good To Firm | Rushen Raider | Aug 14 1996 |

## BRIGHTON

| Distance | Time | Age | Weight | Going | Horse | Date |
|---|---|---|---|---|---|---|
| 5f 59y | 1m 0.10 | 2 | 9-0 | Firm | Bid for Blue | May 6 1993 |
| 5f 59y | 59.30 | 3 | 8-9 | Firm | Play Hever Golf | May 26 1993 |
| 5f 213y | 1m 8.10 | 2 | 8-9 | Firm | Song Mist (IRE) | Jly 16 1996 |
| 5f 213y | 1m 7.30 | 3 | 8-9 | Firm | Third Party | Jun 3 1997 |
| 5f 213y | 1m 7.30 | 5 | 9-1 | Good To Firm | Blundell Lane | May 4 2000 |
| 6f 209y | 1m 19.90 | 2 | 8-11 | Hard | Rain Burst | Sep 15 1988 |
| 6f 209y | 1m 19.40 | 4 | 9-3 | Good To Firm | Sawaki | Sep 3 1991 |
| 7f 214y | 1m 32.80 | 2 | 9-7 | Firm | Asian Pete | Oct 3 1989 |
| 7f 214y | 1m 30.50 | 5 | 8-11 | Firm | Mystic Ridge | May 27 1999 |
| 1m 1f 209y | 2m 4.70 | 2 | 9-0 | Good To Soft | Esteemed Master | Nov 2 2001 |
| 1m 1f 209y | 1m 57.20 | 3 | 9-0 | Firm | Get The Message | Apr 30 1984 |
| 1m 3f 196y | 2m 25.80 | 4 | 8-2 | Firm | New Zealand | Jly 4 1985 |

## CARLISLE

| Distance | Time | Age | Weight | Going | Horse | Date |
|---|---|---|---|---|---|---|
| 5f | 1m 0.10 | 2 | 8-5 | Firm | La Tortuga | Aug 2 1999 |
| 5f | 58.80 | 3 | 9-8 | Good To Firm | Esatto | Aug 21 2002 |
| 5f 193y | 1m 12.45 | 2 | 9-6 | Good To Firm | Musical Guest (IRE) | Sep 11 2005 |
| 5f 193y | 1m 10.83 | 4 | 9-0 | Good To Firm | Bo McGinty (IRE) | Sep 11 2005 |
| 6f 192y | 1m 24.30 | 3 | 8-9 | Good To Firm | Marjurita (IRE) | Aug 21 2002 |
| 7f 200y | 1m 37.34 | 5 | 9-7 | Good To Firm | Hula Ballew | Aug 17 2005 |
| 1m 1f 61y | 1m 53.84 | 3 | 9-0 | Firm | Little Jimbob | Jun 14 2004 |
| 1m 3f 107y | 2m 22.00 | 7 | 9-5 | Good To Firm | Tartan Gigha | Jun 4 2012 |
| 1m 6f 32y | 3m 2.20 | 6 | 8-10 | Firm | Explosive Speed | May 26 1994 |
| 2m 1f 52y | 3m 46.20 | 3 | 7-10 | Good To Firm | Warring Kingdom | Aug 25 1999 |

## CATTERICK

| Distance | Time | Age | Weight | Going | Horse | Date |
|---|---|---|---|---|---|---|
| 5f | 57.60 | 2 | 9-0 | Firm | H Harrison | Oct 8 2002 |
| 5f | 57.10 | 4 | 8-7 | Firm | Kabcast | Jly 6 1989 |
| 5f 212y | 1m 11.40 | 2 | 9-4 | Firm | Captain Nick | Jly 11 1978 |
| 5f 212y | 1m 9.86 | 9 | 8-13 | Good To Firm | Sharp Hat | May 30 2003 |
| 7f | 1m 24.10 | 2 | 8-11 | Firm | Linda's Fantasy | Sep 18 1982 |
| 7f | 1m 22.56 | 6 | 8-7 | Firm | Differential (USA) | May 31 2003 |
| 1m 3f 214y | 2m 30.50 | 3 | 8-8 | Good To Firm | Rahaf | May 30 2003 |
| 1m 5f 175y | 2m 54.80 | 3 | 8-5 | Firm | Geryon | May 31 1984 |
| 1m 7f 177y | 3m 20.80 | 4 | 7-11 | Firm | Bean Boy I | Jly 8 1982 |

## CHEPSTOW

| Distance | Time | Age | Weight | Going | Horse | Date |
|---|---|---|---|---|---|---|
| 5f 16y | 57.60 | 2 | 8-11 | Firm | Micro Love | Jly 8 1986 |
| 5f 16y | 56.80 | 3 | 8-4 | Firm | Torbay Express | Sep 15 1979 |
| 6f 16y | 1m 8.50 | 2 | 9-2 | Firm | Ninjago | Jly 27 2012 |
| 6f 16y | 1m 8.10 | 3 | 9-7 | Firm | America Calling (USA) | Sep 18 2001 |
| 7f 16y | 1m 20.80 | 2 | 9-0 | Good To Firm | Royal Amaretto (IRE) | Sep 12 1996 |
| 7f 16y | 1m 19.30 | 3 | 9-0 | Firm | Taranaki | Sep 18 2001 |
| 1m 14y | 1m 33.10 | 2 | 8-11 | Good To Firm | Ski Academy (IRE) | Aug 28 1995 |
| 1m 14y | 1m 31.60 | 3 | 8-13 | Firm | Stoli (IRE) | Sep 18 2001 |
| 1m 2f 36y | 2m 4.10 | 5 | 8-9 | Hard | Leonidas | Jly 5 1983 |
| 1m 2f 36y | 2m 4.10 | 5 | 7-8 | Good To Firm | It's Varadan | Sep 9 1989 |
| 1m 2f 36y | 2m 4.10 | 3 | 8-5 | Good To Firm | Ela Athena | Jly 23 1999 |
| 1m 4f 23y | 2m 31.00 | 3 | 8-9 | Good To Firm | Spritsail | Jly 13 1989 |
| 1m 4f 23y | 2m 31.00 | 5 | 8-11 | Hard | The Friend | Aug 29 1983 |
| 2m 49y | 3m 27.70 | 4 | 9-0 | Good To Firm | Wizzard Artist | Jly 1 1989 |
| 2m 2f | 3m 56.40 | 5 | 8-7 | Good To Firm | Laffah | Jly 8 2000 |

## CHESTER

| Distance | Time | Age | Weight | Going | Horse | Date |
|---|---|---|---|---|---|---|
| 5f 16y | 59.94 | 2 | 9-2 | Good To Firm | Leiba Leiba | Jun 26 2010 |
| 5f 16y | 58.88 | 3 | 8-7 | Good To Firm | Peterkin | Jly 11 2014 |
| 5f 110y | 1m 6.39 | 2 | 8-7 | Good To Soft | Kinematic | Sep 27 2014 |
| 5f 110y | 1m 5.28 | 3 | 9-1 | Good To Firm | Mappin Time (IRE) | Aug 20 2011 |
| 6f 18y | 1m 12.85 | 2 | 8-10 | Good To Firm | Flying Express | Aug 31 2002 |
| 6f 18y | 1m 12.78 | 3 | 8-3 | Good To Firm | Play Hever Golf | May 4 1993 |
| 6f 18y | 1m 12.78 | 6 | 9-2 | Good | Stack Rock | Jun 23 1993 |
| 7f 2y | 1m 25.29 | 2 | 9-0 | Good To Firm | Due Respect (IRE) | Sep 25 2002 |
| 7f 2y | 1m 23.75 | 5 | 8-13 | Good To Firm | Three Graces (GER) | Jly 9 2005 |
| 7f 122y | 1m 32.29 | 2 | 9-0 | Good To Firm | Big Bad Bob (IRE) | Sep 25 2002 |
| 7f 122y | 1m 30.91 | 3 | 8-12 | Good To Firm | Cupid's Glory | Aug 18 2005 |
| 1m 2f 75y | 2m 7.15 | 3 | 8-8 | Good To Firm | Stotsfold | Sep 23 2006 |
| 1m 3f 79y | 2m 22.17 | 3 | 8-12 | Good To Firm | Perfect Truth (IRE) | May 6 2009 |
| 1m 4f 66y | 2m 33.70 | 3 | 8-10 | Good To Firm | Fight Your Corner | May 7 2002 |
| 1m 5f 89y | 2m 45.43 | 5 | 8-11 | Firm | Rakaposhi King | May 7 1987 |
| 1m 7f 195y | 3m 20.33 | 4 | 9-0 | Good To Firm | Grand Fromage (IRE) | Jly 13 2002 |
| 2m 2f 147y | 3m 58.89 | 7 | 9-2 | Good To Firm | Greenwich Meantime | May 9 2007 |

## DONCASTER

| Distance | Time | Age | Weight | Going | Horse | Date |
|---|---|---|---|---|---|---|
| 5f | 58.10 | 2 | 8-11 | Good To Firm | Sand Vixen | Sep 11 2009 |
| 5f | 57.31 | 7 | 9-10 | Good | Tabaret | Aug 14 2010 |
| 5f 140y | 1m 5.38 | 4 | 9-7 | Good | Muthmir | Sep 13 2014 |
| 6f | 1m 10.87 | 2 | 9-5 | Firm | Andhesontherun (IRE) | Jly 18 2013 |
| 6f | 1m 9.56 | 3 | 8-10 | Good To Firm | Proclaim | May 30 2009 |
| 6f 110y | 1m 17.22 | 2 | 8-3 | Good To Firm | Swilly Ferry (USA) | Sep 10 2009 |
| 7f | 1m 22.78 | 2 | 9-5 | Good | Basateen | Jly 24 2014 |
| 7f | 1m 21.81 | 6 | 8-7 | Good To Firm | Signor Peltro | May 30 2009 |
| 1m | 1m 36.72 | 2 | 8-12 | Good | Dance Of Fire | Sep 13 2014 |
| 1m | 1m 38.37 | 2 | 8-6 | Good To Soft | Antoniola (IRE) | Oct 23 2009 |

| Distance | Time | Age | Weight | Going | Horse | Date |
|---|---|---|---|---|---|---|
| 1m | 1m 34.46 | 4 | 8-12 | Good To Firm | Staying On | Apr 18 2009 |
| 1m | 1m 34.95 | 6 | 8-9 | Firm | Quick Wit | Jly 18 2013 |
| 1m 2f 60y | 2m 4.81 | 4 | 8-13 | Good To Firm | Red Gala | Sep 12 2007 |
| 1m 4f | 2m 27.48 | 3 | 8-4 | Good To Firm | Swift Alhaarth | Sep 10 2011 |
| 1m 6f 132y | 3m 0.44 | 3 | 9-0 | Good To Firm | Masked Marvel | Sep 10 2011 |
| 2m 110y | 3m 34.52 | 7 | 9-0 | Good To Firm | Inchnadamph | Nov 10 2007 |
| 2m 2f | 3m 48.41 | 4 | 9-4 | Good To Firm | Septimus (IRE) | Sep 14 2007 |

## EPSOM

| Distance | Time | Age | Weight | Going | Horse | Date |
|---|---|---|---|---|---|---|
| 5f | 55.02 | 2 | 8-9 | Good To Firm | Prince Aslia | Jun 9 1995 |
| 5f | 53.60 | 4 | 9-5 | Firm | Indigenous | Jun 2 1960 |
| 6f | 1m 7.85 | 2 | 8-11 | Good To Firm | Showbrook | Jun 5 1991 |
| 6f | 1m 7.21 | 5 | 9-13 | Good To Firm | Mac Gille Eoin | Jly 2 2009 |
| 7f | 1m 21.30 | 2 | 8-9 | Good To Firm | Red Peony | Jly 29 2004 |
| 7f | 1m 20.15 | 4 | 8-7 | Firm | Capistrano I | Jun 7 1972 |
| 1m 114y | 1m 42.80 | 2 | 8-5 | Good To Firm | Nightstalker | Aug 30 1988 |
| 1m 114y | 1m 40.75 | 3 | 8-6 | Good To Firm | Sylva Honda | Jun 5 1991 |
| 1m 2f 18y | 2m 3.50 | 5 | 7-11 | Firm | Crossbow | Jun 7 1967 |
| 1m 4f 10y | 2m 31.33 | 3 | 9-0 | Good To Firm | Workforce | Jun 5 2010 |

## FFOS LAS

| Distance | Time | Age | Weight | Going | Horse | Date |
|---|---|---|---|---|---|---|
| 5f | 57.06 | 2 | 9-3 | Good To Firm | Mr Majeika (IRE) | May 5 2011 |
| 5f | 56.35 | 5 | 8-8 | Good | Haajes | Sep 12 2009 |
| 6f | 1m 9.00 | 2 | 9-5 | Good To Firm | Wonder Of Qatar | Sep 14 2014 |
| 6f | 1m 7.80 | 8 | 8-4 | Good To Firm | The Jailer | May 5 2011 |
| 1m | 1m 39.36 | 2 | 9-2 | Good To Firm | Hala Hala | Sep 2 2013 |
| 1m | 1m 37.12 | 5 | 9-0 | Good To Firm | Zebrano | May 5 2011 |
| 1m 2f | 2m 4.85 | 8 | 8-12 | Good To Firm | Pelham Crescent (IRE) | May 5 2011 |
| 1m 4f | 2m 31.58 | 4 | 8-9 | Good To Firm | Men Don't Cry | Jly 23 2013 |
| 1m 6f | 2m 58.61 | 4 | 9-7 | Good To Firm | Lady Eclair | Jly 12 2010 |
| 2m | 3m 29.58 | 4 | 8-9 | Good To Firm | Annaluna | Jly 1 2013 |

## GOODWOOD

| Distance | Time | Age | Weight | Going | Horse | Date |
|---|---|---|---|---|---|---|
| 5f | 57.30 | 2 | 9-1 | Good To Firm | Cotai Glory | Jly 29 2014 |
| 5f | 56.01 | 5 | 9-0 | Good To Firm | Rudi's Pet | Jly 27 1999 |
| 6f | 1m 9.81 | 2 | 8-11 | Good To Firm | Bachir (IRE) | Jly 28 1999 |
| 6f | 1m 9.10 | 6 | 9-0 | Good To Firm | Tamagin | Sep 12 2009 |
| 7f | 1m 24.99 | 2 | 8-11 | Good To Firm | Ekraar | Jly 29 1999 |
| 7f | 1m 23.88 | 3 | 8-7 | Firm | Brief Glimpse (IRE) | Jly 25 1995 |
| 1m | 1m 37.21 | 2 | 9-0 | Good | Caldra (IRE) | Sep 9 2006 |
| 1m | 1m 35.61 | 4 | 8-9 | Good To Firm | Spectait | Aug 4 2006 |
| 1m 1f | 1m 56.27 | 2 | 9-3 | Good To Firm | Dordogne (IRE) | Sep 22 2010 |
| 1m 1f | 1m 52.81 | 3 | 9-6 | Good | Vena (IRE) | Jly 27 1995 |
| 1m 1f 192y | 2m 2.81 | 3 | 9-3 | Good To Firm | Road To Love (IRE) | Aug 3 2006 |
| 1m 3f | 2m 23.00 | 3 | 8-8 | Good To Firm | Asian Heights | May 22 2001 |
| 1m 4f | 2m 31.57 | 3 | 8-10 | Firm | Presenting | Jly 25 1995 |
| 1m 6f | 2m 57.61 | 4 | 9-6 | Good To Firm | Meeznah (USA) | Jly 28 2011 |
| 2m | 3m 21.55 | 5 | 9-10 | Good To Firm | Yeats (IRE) | Aug 3 2006 |

## HAMILTON

| Distance | Time | Age | Weight | Going | Horse | Date |
|---|---|---|---|---|---|---|
| 5f 4y | 57.95 | 2 | 8-8 | Good To Firm | Rose Blossom | May 29 2009 |
| 5f 4y | 57.95 | 2 | 8-8 | Good To Firm | Rose Blossom | May 29 2009 |
| 6f 5y | 1m 10.00 | 2 | 8-12 | Good To Firm | Break The Code | Aug 24 1999 |
| 6f 5y | 1m 9.30 | 4 | 8-7 | Firm | Marcus Game | Jly 11 1974 |
| 1m 65y | 1m 45.80 | 2 | 8-11 | Firm | Hopeful Subject | Sep 24 1973 |
| 1m 65y | 1m 42.70 | 6 | 7-7 | Firm | Cranley | Sep 25 1972 |
| 1m 1f 36y | 1m 53.60 | 5 | 9-6 | Good To Firm | Regent's Secret (USA) | Aug 10 2005 |
| 1m 3f 16y | 2m 18.66 | 3 | 9-3 | Good To Firm | Postponed (IRE) | Jly 18 2014 |
| 1m 4f 17y | 2m 30.52 | 5 | 9-10 | Good To Firm | Record Breaker | Jun 10 2009 |
| 1m 5f 9y | 2m 45.10 | 6 | 9-6 | Firm | Mentalasanythin | Jun 14 1995 |

## HAYDOCK

| Distance | Time | Age | Weight | Going | Horse | Date |
|---|---|---|---|---|---|---|
| 5f | 58.56 | 2 | 8-2 | Good To Firm | Barracuda Boy | Aug 11 2012 |
| 5f | 59.66 | 2 | 8-12 | Good | Deeds Not Words (IRE) | Sep 27 2013 |
| 5f | 57.67 | 4 | 9-4 | Good To Firm | Sole Power | May 21 2011 |
| 5f | 56.39 | 5 | 9-4 | Firm | Bated Breath | May 26 2012 |
| 6f | 1m 10.98 | 4 | 9-9 | Good To Firm | Wolfhound (USA) | Sep 4 1993 |
| 6f | 1m 10.72 | 2 | 9-2 | Good To Firm | Easy Ticket (IRE) | Sep 4 2010 |
| 6f | 1m 9.40 | 7 | 9-3 | Good To Firm | Markab | Sep 4 2010 |
| 6f | 1m 9.92 | 4 | 9-0 | Good To Firm | Iktamal (USA) | Sep 7 1996 |
| 7f | 1m 27.62 | 2 | 9-4 | Good | Tickle Time (IRE) | Aug 10 2012 |
| 7f | 1m 25.95 | 7 | 9-9 | Good To Firm | Set The Trend | Jly 20 2013 |
| 1m | 1m 39.02 | 3 | 8-11 | Good | Lady Macduff | Aug 10 2012 |
| 1m 2f 95y | 2m 8.25 | 3 | 9-0 | Good To Firm | Prussian | Sep 7 2012 |
| 1m 3f 200y | 2m 25.53 | 4 | 8-12 | Good To Firm | Number Theory | May 24 2012 |
| 1m 6f | 2m 55.20 | 5 | 9-9 | Good To Firm | Huff And Puff | Sep 7 2012 |
| 2m 45y | 3m 26.98 | 5 | 8-13 | Good To Firm | De Rigueur | Jun 8 2013 |

## KEMPTON (A.W)

| Distance | Time | Age | Weight | Going | Horse | Date |
|---|---|---|---|---|---|---|
| 5f | 58.96 | 2 | 8-6 | Standard | Glamorous Spirit (IRE) | Nov 28 2008 |
| 5f | 58.33 | 3 | 9-1 | Standard | Exceedance | May 7 2012 |
| 6f | 1m 11.36 | 2 | 9-0 | Standard | Tendu | Sep 3 2014 |
| 6f | 1m 9.79 | 4 | 8-11 | Standard | Trinityelitedotcom | Mar 29 2014 |
| 7f | 1m 23.95 | 2 | 8-10 | Standard | Tamarkuz | Oct 10 2012 |
| 7f | 1m 23.10 | 6 | 9-9 | Standard | Sirius Prospect | Nov 20 2014 |
| 1m | 1m 37.50 | 2 | 9-4 | Standard | I'm Back (IRE) | Oct 3 2012 |
| 1m | 1m 35.73 | 3 | 8-9 | Standard | Western Aristocrat | Sep 15 2011 |
| 1m 2f | 2m 2.97 | 5 | 9-0 | Standard | Rebellious Guest | Mar 5 2014 |
| 1m 3f | 2m 16.09 | 4 | 8-7 | Standard | Salutation | Mar 29 2014 |
| 1m 4f | 2m 28.99 | 6 | 9-3 | Standard | Spring Of Fame (USA) | Nov 7 2012 |
| 2m | 3m 21.50 | 4 | 8-12 | Standard | Colour Vision (FR) | May 2 2012 |

## LEICESTER

| Distance | Time | Age | Weight | Going | Horse | Date |
|---|---|---|---|---|---|---|
| 5f 2y | 58.40 | 2 | 9-0 | Firm | Cutting Blade | Jun 9 1986 |
| 5f 2y | 57.85 | 5 | 9-5 | Good To Firm | The Jobber (IRE) | Sep 18 2006 |
| 5f 218y | 1m 9.99 | 2 | 9-0 | Good | El Manati (IRE) | Aug 1 2012 |
| 5f 218y | 1m 9.12 | 6 | 8-12 | Good To Firm | Peter Island | Apr 25 2009 |
| 7f 9y | 1m 22.60 | 2 | 9-0 | Good To Firm | Marie De Medici | Oct 6 2009 |
| 7f 9y | 1m 20.80 | 3 | 8-7 | Firm | Flower Bowl | Jun 9 1986 |
| 1m 60y | 1m 44.05 | 2 | 8-11 | Good To Firm | Congressional (IRE) | Sep 6 2005 |
| 1m 60y | 1m 41.89 | 5 | 9-7 | Good To Firm | Vainglory | Jun 18 2009 |
| 1m 1f 218y | 2m 5.30 | 2 | 9-1 | Good To Firm | Windsor Castle | Oct 14 1996 |
| 1m 1f 218y | 2m 2.40 | 3 | 8-11 | Firm | Effigy I | Nov 4 1985 |
| 1m 1f 218y | 2m 2.40 | 4 | 9-6 | Good To Firm | Lady Angharad (IRE) | Jun 18 2000 |
| 1m 3f 183y | 2m 27.10 | 5 | 8-12 | Good To Firm | Murghem (IRE) | Jun 18 2000 |

## LINGFIELD

| Distance | Time | Age | Weight | Going | Horse | Date |
|---|---|---|---|---|---|---|
| 5f | 57.07 | 2 | 9-0 | Good To Firm | Quite A Thing | Jun 11 2011 |
| 5f | 56.09 | 3 | 9-4 | Good To Firm | Whitecrest | Sep 16 2011 |
| 6f | 1m 8.36 | 2 | 8-12 | Good To Firm | Folly Bridge | Sep 8 2009 |
| 6f | 1m 8.13 | 6 | 9-8 | Firm | Clear Praise | Aug 10 2013 |
| 7f | 1m 20.55 | 2 | 8-11 | Good To Firm | Hiking | Aug 17 2013 |
| 7f | 1m 20.05 | 3 | 8-5 | Good To Firm | Perfect Tribute | May 7 2011 |
| 7f 140y | 1m 29.32 | 2 | 9-3 | Good To Firm | Dundonnell (USA) | Aug 4 2012 |
| 7f 140y | 1m 26.73 | 3 | 8-6 | Good To Firm | Hiaam | Jly 11 1987 |
| 1m 1f | 1m 52.40 | 4 | 9-2 | Good To Firm | Quandary (USA) | Jly 15 1995 |
| 1m 2f | 2m 4.61 | 3 | 9-3 | Firm | Usran | Jly 15 1989 |
| 1m 3f 106y | 2m 23.95 | 3 | 8-5 | Firm | Night-Shirt | Jly 14 1990 |
| 1m 6f | 2m 59.10 | 5 | 9-5 | Firm | Ibn Bey | Jly 1 1989 |
| 2m | 3m 23.71 | 3 | 9-5 | Good To Firm | Lauries Crusador | Aug 13 1988 |

## LINGFIELD (A.W)

| Distance | Time | Age | Weight | Going | Horse | Date |
|---|---|---|---|---|---|---|
| 5f 6y | 58.11 | 2 | 9-5 | Standard | Ivors Rebel | Sep 23 2014 |
| 5f 6y | 56.67 | 5 | 8-12 | Standard | Ladies Are Forever | Mar 16 2013 |
| 6f 1y | 1m 9.99 | 2 | 8-12 | Standard | Swiss Diva | Nov 19 2008 |
| 6f 1y | 1m 8.75 | 7 | 9-2 | Standard | Tarooq | Dec 18 2013 |
| 7f 1y | 1m 22.67 | 2 | 9-3 | Standard | Complicit | Nov 23 2013 |
| 7f 1y | 1m 21.92 | 5 | 9-6 | Standard | Grey Mirage | Feb 22 2014 |
| 1m 1y | 1m 36.33 | 2 | 9-7 | Standard | Yarroom | Dec 5 2012 |
| 1m 1y | 1m 34.51 | 5 | 9-5 | Standard | Captain Cat (IRE) | Apr 18 2014 |
| 1m 2f | 2m 0.99 | 4 | 9-0 | Standard | Farraaj (IRE) | Mar 16 2013 |
| 1m 4f | 2m 27.97 | 4 | 9-3 | Standard | Midsummer Sun | Apr 14 2012 |
| 1m 5f | 2m 39.70 | 3 | 8-10 | Standard | Hidden Gold | Oct 30 2014 |
| 1m 7f 169y | 3m 16.73 | 5 | 9-2 | Standard | Arch Villain | Jan 22 2014 |

## MUSSELBURGH

| Distance | Time | Age | Weight | Going | Horse | Date |
|---|---|---|---|---|---|---|
| 5f | 57.70 | 2 | 8-2 | Firm | Arasong | May 16 1994 |
| 5f | 57.30 | 3 | 8-12 | Firm | Corunna | Jun 3 2000 |
| 7f 30y | 1m 27.46 | 2 | 8-8 | Good | Durham Reflection (IRE) | Sep 14 2009 |
| 7f 30y | 1m 26.30 | 3 | 9-5 | Firm | Waltzing Wizard | Aug 22 2002 |
| 1m | 1m 40.34 | 2 | 8-12 | Good To Firm | Succession | Sep 26 2004 |
| 1m | 1m 36.83 | 3 | 9-5 | Good To Firm | Ginger Jack | Jly 13 2010 |
| 1m 1f | 1m 50.42 | 8 | 8-11 | Good To Firm | Dhaular Dhar | Sep 3 2010 |
| 1m 4f 100y | 2m 36.80 | 3 | 8-3 | Good To Firm | Harris Tweed | Jun 5 2010 |
| 1m 5f | 2m 46.41 | 3 | 9-5 | Good To Firm | Alcaeus | Sep 29 2013 |
| 1m 6f | 2m 57.98 | 7 | 8-5 | Good To Firm | Jonny Delta | Apr 18 2014 |
| 2m | 3m 26.23 | 9 | 9-7 | Good To Firm | La Bacouetteuse | Jly 22 2014 |

## NEWBURY

| Distance | Time | Age | Weight | Going | Horse | Date |
|---|---|---|---|---|---|---|
| 5f 34y | 59.19 | 2 | 8-6 | Good To Firm | Superstar Leo | Jly 22 2000 |
| 5f 34y | 59.24 | 3 | 9-5 | Good To Firm | The Trader (IRE) | Aug 18 2001 |
| 6f 8y | 1m 11.07 | 2 | 8-4 | Good To Firm | Bahati (IRE) | May 30 2009 |
| 6f 8y | 1m 9.42 | 3 | 8-11 | Good To Firm | Nota Bene | May 13 2005 |
| 7f | 1m 23.04 | 2 | 8-11 | Good To Firm | Haafhd | Aug 15 2003 |
| 7f | 1m 21.50 | 3 | 8-4 | Good To Firm | Three Points | Jly 21 2000 |
| 1m | 1m 37.50 | 2 | 9-1 | Good To Firm | Winged Cupid (IRE) | Sep 16 2005 |
| 1m | 1m 33.59 | 6 | 9-0 | Firm | Rakti | May 14 2005 |
| 1m 7y | 1m 37.29 | 2 | 9-0 | Good | Master Willie | Oct 1 1979 |
| 1m 7y | 1m 34.90 | 3 | 8-9 | Good To Firm | Philidor | May 16 1992 |
| 1m 1f | 1m 49.65 | 3 | 8-0 | Good To Firm | Holtye | May 21 1995 |
| 1m 2f 6y | 2m 1.29 | 3 | 8-7 | Good To Firm | Wall Street (USA) | Jly 20 1996 |
| 1m 3f 5y | 2m 16.54 | 3 | 8-9 | Good To Firm | Grandera (IRE) | Sep 22 2001 |
| 1m 4f 5y | 2m 28.26 | 4 | 9-7 | Good To Firm | Azamour (IRE) | Jly 23 2005 |
| 1m 5f 61y | 2m 44.90 | 5 | 10-0 | Good To Firm | Mystic Hill | Jly 20 1996 |
| 2m | 3m 25.42 | 8 | 9-12 | Good To Firm | Moonlight Quest | Jly 19 1996 |

## NEWCASTLE

| Distance | Time | Age | Weight | Going | Horse | Date |
|---|---|---|---|---|---|---|
| 5f | 58.83 | 2 | 9-0 | Firm | Atlantic Viking (IRE) | Jun 4 1997 |
| 5f | 57.81 | 3 | 9-3 | Good | G Force | Apr 24 2014 |
| 6f | 1m 11.98 | 2 | 9-3 | Good | Pearl Arch (IRE) | Sep 6 2010 |
| 6f | 1m 10.58 | 4 | 9-9 | Good To Firm | Jonny Mudball | Jun 26 2010 |
| 7f | 1m 24.26 | 2 | 9-0 | Good To Firm | Iscan (IRE) | Aug 31 1998 |
| 7f | 1m 23.34 | 4 | 9-2 | Good To Firm | Quiet Venture | Aug 31 1998 |
| 1m | 1m 38.90 | 2 | 9-0 | Good To Firm | Stowaway | Oct 2 1996 |
| 1m | 1m 38.96 | 3 | 8-12 | Firm | Jacamar I | Jly 22 1989 |
| 1m 3y | 1m 37.10 | 2 | 8-3 | Good To Firm | Hoh Steamer (IRE) | Aug 31 1998 |
| 1m 3y | 1m 37.30 | 3 | 8-8 | Good To Firm | It's Magic | May 27 1999 |
| 1m 2f 32y | 2m 6.59 | 3 | 8-11 | Good To Firm | Missionary Ridge | Jun 29 1990 |
| 1m 4f 93y | 2m 36.90 | 4 | 9-3 | Good To Firm | Livia's Dream | Jly 27 2013 |
| 1m 6f 97y | 3m 6.46 | 3 | 9-6 | Good To Firm | One Off | Aug 6 2003 |
| 2m 19y | 3m 24.32 | 4 | 8-10 | Good | Far Cry (IRE) | Jun 26 1999 |

## NEWMARKET

| Distance | Time | Age | Weight | Going | Horse | Date |
|---|---|---|---|---|---|---|
| 5f | 58.76 | 2 | 8-5 | Good To Firm | Valiant Romeo | Oct 3 2002 |
| 5f | 56.81 | 6 | 9-2 | Good To Firm | Lochsong | Apr 30 1994 |
| 6f | 1m 9.56 | 2 | 8-12 | Good To Firm | Bushranger | Oct 3 2008 |
| 6f | 1m 9.56 | 2 | 8-12 | Good To Firm | Bushranger | Oct 3 2008 |
| 7f | 1m 22.39 | 2 | 8-12 | Good To Firm | Ashram | Oct 2 2008 |
| 7f | 1m 22.18 | 3 | 9-0 | Good To Firm | New Deerfield | May 14 2011 |
| 1m | 1m 35.67 | 2 | 8-12 | Good | Steeler (IRE) | Sep 29 2012 |
| 1m | 1m 34.07 | 4 | 9-0 | Good To Firm | Eagle Mountain | Oct 3 2008 |
| 1m 1f | 1m 47.26 | 5 | 8-12 | Good To Firm | Manduro (GER) | Apr 19 2007 |
| 1m 2f | 2m 4.65 | 2 | 9-4 | Good | Highland Chieftain | Nov 2 1985 |
| 1m 2f | 2m 0.13 | 3 | 8-12 | Good | New Approach (IRE) | Oct 18 2008 |
| 1m 4f | 2m 26.07 | 3 | 8-9 | Good To Firm | Mohedian Lady (IRE) | Sep 22 2011 |
| 1m 6f | 2m 51.59 | 3 | 8-7 | Good | Art Eyes (USA) | Sep 29 2005 |
| 2m | 3m 18.64 | 5 | 9-6 | Good To Firm | Times Up | Sep 22 2011 |
| 2m 2f | 3m 47.50 | 3 | 7-12 | Hard | Whiteway | Oct 15 1947 |

## NEWMARKET (JULY)

| Distance | Time | Age | Weight | Going | Horse | Date |
|---|---|---|---|---|---|---|
| 5f | 58.52 | 2 | 8-10 | Good | Seductress | Jly 10 1990 |
| 5f | 56.09 | 6 | 9-11 | Good | Borderlescott | Aug 22 2008 |
| 6f | 1m 10.35 | 2 | 8-11 | Good | Elnawin | Aug 22 2008 |
| 6f | 1m 9.11 | 4 | 9-5 | Good To Firm | Lethal Force | Jly 13 2013 |
| 7f | 1m 23.57 | 2 | 9-5 | Good To Firm | Light Up My Life | Aug 18 2012 |
| 7f | 1m 22.59 | 3 | 9-7 | Firm | Ho Leng (IRE) | Jly 9 1998 |
| 1m | 1m 37.47 | 2 | 8-13 | Good | Whippers Love | Aug 28 2009 |
| 1m | 1m 35.53 | 3 | 8-6 | Good To Firm | Lovers Knot | Jly 8 1998 |
| 1m 2f | 2m 0.91 | 3 | 9-5 | Good To Firm | Maputo | Jly 11 2013 |
| 1m 4f | 2m 25.11 | 3 | 8-11 | Good | Lush Lashes | Aug 22 2008 |
| 1m 5f | 2m 42.01 | 3 | 9-0 | Good | Kite Wood | Jly 9 2009 |
| 1m 6f 175y | 3m 4.27 | 3 | 8-5 | Good | Arrive | Jly 11 2001 |
| 2m 24y | 3m 20.28 | 7 | 9-10 | Good | Yorkshire I | Jly 11 2001 |

## NOTTINGHAM

| Distance | Time | Age | Weight | Going | Horse | Date |
|---|---|---|---|---|---|---|
| 5f 13y | 57.90 | 2 | 8-9 | Firm | Hoh Magic | May 13 1994 |
| 5f 13y | 59.43 | 2 | 9-5 | Good To Firm | Burtonwood | Apr 19 2014 |
| 5f 13y | 57.71 | 4 | 8-11 | Good To Firm | Dinkum Diamond (IRE) | Aug 14 2012 |
| 5f 13y | 58.49 | 4 | 9-2 | Good To Soft | It Must Be Faith | Oct 29 2014 |
| 6f 15y | 1m 11.40 | 2 | 8-11 | Firm | Jameelapi | Aug 8 1983 |
| 6f 15y | 1m 10.00 | 4 | 9-2 | Firm | Ajanac | Aug 8 1988 |
| 1m 75y | 1m 45.23 | 2 | 9-0 | Good To Firm | Tactfully | Sep 28 2011 |
| 1m 75y | 1m 46.69 | 2 | 9-0 | Good To Soft | Golden Horn | Oct 29 2014 |
| 1m 75y | 1m 42.25 | 5 | 9-1 | Good To Firm | Rio De La Plata | Jun 2 2010 |
| 1m 75y | 1m 43.41 | 3 | 9-2 | Good | Al Mukhdam | Apr 20 2013 |
| 1m 2f 50y | 2m 16.66 | 2 | 9-3 | Soft | Lethal Glaze (IRE) | Oct 1 2008 |
| 1m 2f 50y | 2m 7.13 | 5 | 9-8 | Good To Firm | Vasily | Jly 19 2013 |
| 1m 2f 50y | 2m 9.40 | 3 | 9-5 | Good | Centurius | Apr 20 2013 |
| 1m 6f 15y | 2m 57.80 | 3 | 8-10 | Firm | Buster Jo | Oct 1 1985 |
| 2m 9y | 3m 25.25 | 3 | 9-5 | Good | Bulwark (IRE) | Sep 27 2005 |
| 2m 9y | 3m 34.39 | 3 | 8-0 | Good | Benozzo Gozzoli | Oct 28 2009 |

## PONTEFRACT

| Distance | Time | Age | Weight | Going | Horse | Date |
|---|---|---|---|---|---|---|
| 5f | 1m 1.10 | 2 | 9-0 | Firm | Golden Bounty | Sep 20 2001 |
| 5f | 1m 0.84 | 4 | 8-9 | Firm | Blue Maeve | Sep 23 2004 |
| 6f | 1m 14.00 | 2 | 9-3 | Firm | Fawzi | Sep 6 1983 |
| 6f | 1m 12.60 | 3 | 7-13 | Firm | Merry One | Aug 29 1970 |
| 1m 4y | 1m 42.80 | 2 | 9-13 | Firm | Star Spray | Sep 6 1983 |
| 1m 4y | 1m 42.80 | 2 | 9-0 | Firm | Alasil (USA) | Sep 26 2002 |
| 1m 4y | 1m 40.60 | 4 | 9-10 | Good To Firm | Island Light | Apr 13 2002 |
| 1m 2f 6y | 2m 10.10 | 2 | 9-0 | Firm | Shanty Star (IRE) | Oct 7 2002 |
| 1m 2f 6y | 2m 8.20 | 4 | 7-8 | Hard | Happy Hector | Jly 9 1979 |
| 1m 2f 6y | 2m 8.20 | 3 | 7-13 | Hard | Tom Noddy | Aug 21 1972 |
| 1m 4f 8y | 2m 33.72 | 3 | 8-7 | Firm | Ajaan | Aug 8 2007 |
| 2m 1f 22y | 3m 40.67 | 4 | 8-7 | Good To Firm | Paradise Flight | Jun 6 2005 |
| 2m 1f 216y | 3m 51.10 | 3 | 8-8 | Good To Firm | Kudz | Sep 9 1986 |
| 2m 5f 122y | 4m 47.80 | 4 | 8-4 | Firm | Physical | May 14 1984 |

## REDCAR

| Distance | Time | Age | Weight | Going | Horse | Date |
|---|---|---|---|---|---|---|
| 5f | 56.88 | 2 | 9-7 | Good To Soft | Wolfofwallstreet | Oct 27 2014 |
| 5f | 56.01 | 10 | 9-3 | Firm | Henry Hall | Sep 20 2006 |
| 6f | 1m 8.84 | 2 | 8-3 | Good To Firm | Obe Gold | Oct 2 2004 |
| 6f | 1m 8.60 | 3 | 9-2 | Good To Firm | Sizzling Saga | Jun 21 1991 |
| 7f | 1m 21.28 | 2 | 9-3 | Firm | Karoo Blue | Sep 20 2006 |
| 7f | 1m 21.00 | 3 | 9-1 | Firm | Empty Quarter | Oct 3 1995 |
| 1m | 1m 34.37 | 2 | 9-0 | Firm | Mastership | Sep 20 2006 |
| 1m | 1m 32.42 | 4 | 10-0 | Firm | Nanton | Sep 20 2006 |
| 1m 1f | 1m 52.44 | 2 | 9-0 | Firm | Spear (IRE) | Sep 13 2004 |
| 1m 1f | 1m 48.50 | 5 | 8-12 | Firm | Mellottie | Jly 25 1990 |
| 1m 2f | 2m 10.10 | 2 | 8-11 | Good | Adding | Nov 10 1989 |
| 1m 2f | 2m 1.40 | 5 | 9-2 | Firm | Eradicate | May 28 1990 |
| 1m 6f 19y | 2m 59.81 | 4 | 9-1 | Good To Firm | Esprit de Corps | Sep 11 2006 |
| 2m 4y | 3m 24.90 | 3 | 9-3 | Good To Firm | Subsonic | Oct 8 1991 |

## RIPON

| Distance | Time | Age | Weight | Going | Horse | Date |
|---|---|---|---|---|---|---|
| 5f | 57.80 | 2 | 8-8 | Firm | Super Rocky | Aug 5 1991 |
| 5f | 57.60 | 5 | 8-5 | Good | Broadstairs Beauty | May 21 1995 |
| 6f | 1m 10.40 | 2 | 9-2 | Good | Cumbrian Venture | Aug 17 2002 |
| 6f | 1m 9.72 | 4 | 8-9 | Good | Baccarat (IRE) | Aug 17 2013 |
| 1m | 1m 38.77 | 2 | 9-4 | Good | Greed Is Good | Sep 28 2013 |
| 1m | 1m 36.62 | 4 | 8-11 | Good To Firm | Granston (IRE) | Aug 29 2005 |
| 1m 1f | 1m 49.97 | 6 | 9-3 | Good To Firm | Ginger Jack | Jun 20 2013 |
| 1m 1f 170y | 1m 59.12 | 5 | 8-9 | Good To Firm | Wahoo Sam (USA) | Aug 30 2005 |
| 1m 4f 10y | 2m 31.40 | 4 | 8-8 | Good To Firm | Dandino | Apr 16 2011 |
| 2m | 3m 27.07 | 5 | 9-12 | Good To Firm | Greenwich Meantime | Aug 30 2005 |

## SALISBURY

| Distance | Time | Age | Weight | Going | Horse | Date |
|---|---|---|---|---|---|---|
| 5f | 59.30 | 2 | 9-0 | Good To Firm | Ajigolo | May 12 2005 |
| 5f | 59.30 | 2 | 9-0 | Good To Firm | Ajigolo (when 2yo) | May 12 2005 |
| 6f | 1m 12.10 | 2 | 8-0 | Good To Firm | Parisian Lady (IRE) | Jun 10 1997 |
| 6f | 1m 11.09 | 3 | 9-0 | Firm | L'Ami Louis | May 1 2011 |
| 6f 212y | 1m 25.97 | 2 | 9-0 | Firm | More Royal (USA) | Jun 29 1995 |
| 6f 212y | 1m 24.91 | 3 | 9-4 | Firm | Chilworth Lad | May 1 2011 |
| 1m | 1m 40.48 | 2 | 8-13 | Firm | Choir Master (USA) | Sep 17 2002 |
| 1m | 1m 38.29 | 3 | 8-7 | Good To Firm | Layman (USA) | Aug 11 2005 |
| 1m 1f 198y | 2m 4.81 | 3 | 8-5 | Good To Firm | Primevere | Aug 10 2011 |
| 1m 4f | 2m 31.69 | 3 | 9-5 | Good To Firm | Arrive | Jun 27 2001 |
| 1m 6f 21y | 3m 0.84 | 8 | 8-12 | Firm | Kangaroo Court | May 24 2012 |

## SANDOWN

| Distance | Time | Age | Weight | Going | Horse | Date |
|---|---|---|---|---|---|---|
| 5f 6y | 59.48 | 2 | 9-3 | Firm | Times Time | Jly 22 1982 |
| 5f 6y | 58.82 | 6 | 8-9 | Good To Firm | Palacegate Touch | Sep 17 1996 |
| 7f 16y | 1m 26.56 | 2 | 9-0 | Good To Firm | Raven's Pass (USA) | Sep 1 2007 |
| 7f 16y | 1m 26.36 | 3 | 9-0 | Firm | Mawsuff | Jun 14 1986 |
| 1m 14y | 1m 41.14 | 2 | 8-11 | Good To Firm | Reference Point | Sep 23 1986 |
| 1m 14y | 1m 38.87 | 7 | 9-10 | Good To Firm | Prince Of Johanne | Jly 6 2013 |
| 1m 1f | 1m 54.63 | 2 | 8-8 | Good To Firm | French Pretender | Sep 20 1988 |

| | | | | | | |
|---|---|---|---|---|---|---|
| 1m 1f | 1m 52.40 | 7 | 9-3 | Good To Firm | Bourgainville | Aug 11 2005 |
| 1m 2f 7y | 2m 2.14 | 4 | 8-11 | Good | Kalaglow | May 31 1982 |
| 1m 6f | 2m 56.90 | 4 | 8-7 | Good To Firm | Lady Rosanna | Jly 19 1989 |
| 2m 78y | 3m 29.38 | 6 | 9-0 | Good To Firm | Caucus | Jly 6 2013 |

## SOUTHWELL (A.W)

| Distance | Time | Age | Weight | Going | Horse | Date |
|---|---|---|---|---|---|---|
| 5f | 57.85 | 2 | 9-3 | Standard | Arctic Feeling | Mar 31 2010 |
| 5f | 56.80 | 5 | 9-7 | Standard | Ghostwing | Jan 3 2012 |
| 6f | 1m 14.00 | 2 | 8-5 | Standard | Panalo | Nov 8 1989 |
| 6f | 1m 13.50 | 4 | 10-0 | Standard | Saladan Knight | Dec 30 1989 |
| 7f | 1m 26.82 | 2 | 8-12 | Standard | Winged Icarus | Aug 28 2012 |
| 7f | 1m 26.80 | 5 | 8-4 | Standard | Amenable | Dec 13 1990 |
| 1m | 1m 38.00 | 2 | 8-9 | Standard | Alpha Rascal | Nov 13 1990 |
| 1m | 1m 38.00 | 2 | 8-10 | Standard | Andrew's First | Dec 30 1989 |
| 1m | 1m 37.25 | 3 | 8-6 | Standard | Valira | Nov 3 1990 |
| 1m 3f | 2m 21.50 | 4 | 9-7 | Standard | Tempering | Dec 5 1990 |
| 1m 4f | 2m 33.90 | 4 | 9-12 | Standard | Fast Chick | Nov 8 1989 |
| 1m 6f | 3m 1.60 | 3 | 7-8 | Standard | Erevnon | Dec 29 1990 |
| 2m | 3m 37.60 | 9 | 8-12 | Standard | Old Hubert | Dec 5 1990 |

## THIRSK

| Distance | Time | Age | Weight | Going | Horse | Date |
|---|---|---|---|---|---|---|
| 5f | 57.20 | 2 | 9-7 | Good To Firm | Proud Boast | Aug 5 2000 |
| 5f | 56.92 | 5 | 9-6 | Firm | Charlie Parkes | Apr 11 2003 |
| 6f | 1m 9.20 | 2 | 9-6 | Good To Firm | Westcourt Magic | Aug 25 1995 |
| 6f | 1m 8.80 | 6 | 9-4 | Firm | Johayro | Jly 23 1999 |
| 7f | 1m 23.70 | 2 | 8-9 | Firm | Courting | Jly 23 1999 |
| 7f | 1m 22.80 | 4 | 8-5 | Firm | Silver Haze I | May 21 1988 |
| 1m | 1m 37.97 | 2 | 9-0 | Firm | Sunday Symphony | Sep 4 2004 |
| 1m | 1m 34.80 | 4 | 8-13 | Firm | Yearsley | May 5 1990 |
| 1m 4f | 2m 29.90 | 5 | 9-12 | Firm | Gallery God | Jun 4 2001 |
| 2m | 3m 22.30 | 3 | 9-0 | Firm | Tomaschek | Jly 17 1981 |

## WARWICK

| Distance | Time | Age | Weight | Going | Horse | Date |
|---|---|---|---|---|---|---|
| 5f | 57.95 | 2 | 8-9 | Good To Firm | Amour Propre | Jun 26 2008 |
| 5f | 57.70 | 4 | 9-6 | Good To Firm | Little Edward | Jly 7 2002 |
| 5f 110y | 1m 3.60 | 5 | 8-6 | Good To Firm | Dizzy In The Head | Jun 27 2004 |
| 6f | 1m 10.70 | 2 | 9-5 | Good To Firm | Greeb | Aug 21 2013 |
| 6f | 1m 9.36 | 8 | 9-5 | Good To Firm | Fathsta | Aug 21 2013 |
| 7f | 1m 24.80 | 2 | 8-9 | Good To Firm | Nocino | Jly 28 1979 |
| 7f | 1m 23.60 | 4 | 9-2 | Good To Firm | Russian Music | Mar 31 1997 |
| 7f 26y | 1m 22.74 | 2 | 9-0 | Good To Firm | Chriselliam | Jly 11 2013 |
| 7f 26y | 1m 21.26 | 3 | 8-11 | Good To Firm | Lucky Spin | Jun 19 2004 |
| 1m 20y | 1m 37.10 | 3 | 8-11 | Firm | Orinocovsky (IRE) | Jun 26 2002 |
| 1m 2f 202y | 2m 14.98 | 4 | 8-12 | Good To Firm | Ronaldsay | Jun 16 2008 |
| 1m 7f 9y | 3m 13.80 | 3 | 8-10 | Good To Firm | Darn Good | Jly 2 2004 |

## WINDSOR

| Distance | Time | Age | Weight | Going | Horse | Date |
|---|---|---|---|---|---|---|
| 5f 10y | 58.69 | 2 | 9-0 | Good To Firm | Charles The Great | May 23 2011 |
| 5f 10y | 58.08 | 5 | 8-13 | Good To Firm | Taurus Twins | Apr 4 2011 |
| 6f | 1m 10.50 | 2 | 9-5 | Good To Firm | Cubism (USA) | Aug 17 1998 |
| 6f | 1m 9.89 | 4 | 9-0 | Good To Firm | Bated Breath | May 23 2011 |
| 1m 67y | 1m 42.46 | 2 | 8-9 | Good To Firm | Tiger Cub | Oct 10 2011 |
| 1m 67y | 1m 39.81 | 5 | 9-7 | Good | French Navy | Jun 29 2013 |
| 1m 2f 7y | 2m 1.62 | 6 | 9-1 | Good | Al Kazeem | Aug 23 2014 |
| 1m 3f 135y | 2m 21.50 | 3 | 9-2 | Firm | Double Florin | May 19 1980 |

## WOLVERHAMPTON (A.W)

| Distance | Time | Age | Weight | Going | Horse | Date |
|---|---|---|---|---|---|---|
| 5f 20y | 1m 0.50 | 2 | 9-0 | Standard | Portamento (IRE) | Dec 6 2014 |
| 5f 20y | 1m 0.25 | 3 | 8-12 | Standard | Boom The Groom | Nov 22 2014 |
| 5f 216y | 1m 13.24 | 2 | 9-5 | Standard | Encore d'Or | Oct 11 2014 |
| 5f 216y | 1m 11.84 | 3 | 8-6 | Standard | Pretend | Dec 19 2014 |
| 7f 32y | 1m 27.79 | 2 | 9-0 | Standard | Sperry | Nov 15 2014 |
| 7f 32y | 1m 26.44 | 4 | 9-6 | Standard | Capo Rosso (IRE) | Oct 25 2014 |
| 1m 141y | 1m 47.38 | 2 | 9-5 | Standard | Jack Hobbs | Dec 27 2014 |
| 1m 141y | 1m 47.37 | 5 | 8-6 | Standard | Brocklebank | Nov 28 2014 |
| 1m 1f 103y | 1m 57.15 | 5 | 8-5 | Standard | Docs Legacy | Nov 6 2014 |
| 1m 4f 50y | 2m 37.01 | 5 | 9-10 | Standard | Gabrial's Star | Nov 7 2014 |
| 1m 5f 194y | 2m 57.55 | 6 | 9-7 | Standard | Entihaa | Dec 6 2014 |
| 2m 119y | 3m 34.76 | 4 | 9-7 | Standard | Purple Spectrum | Jan 2 2015 |

## YARMOUTH

| Distance | Time | Age | Weight | Going | Horse | Date |
|---|---|---|---|---|---|---|
| 5f 43y | 1m 0.40 | 2 | 8-6 | Good To Firm | Ebba | Jly 26 1999 |
| 5f 43y | 59.80 | 4 | 8-13 | Good To Firm | Roxanne Mill | Aug 25 2002 |
| 6f 3y | 1m 10.40 | 2 | 9-0 | Firm | Lanchester (USA) | Sep 15 1988 |
| 6f 3y | 1m 9.90 | 4 | 8-9 | Firm | Malhub (USA) | Jun 13 2002 |
| 7f 3y | 1m 22.20 | 2 | 9-0 | Good To Firm | Warrshan | Sep 14 1988 |
| 7f 3y | 1m 22.12 | 4 | 9-4 | Good To Firm | Glenbuck (IRE) | Apr 26 2007 |
| 1m 3y | 1m 36.30 | 2 | 8-2 | Firm | Out Run | Sep 15 1988 |
| 1m 3y | 1m 33.90 | 3 | 8-8 | Firm | Bonne Etoile | Jun 27 1995 |
| 1m 1f | 1m 52.00 | 3 | 9-5 | Good To Firm | Touch Gold | Jly 5 2012 |
| 1m 2f 21y | 2m 2.83 | 3 | 8-8 | Firm | Reunite | Jly 18 2006 |
| 1m 3f 101y | 2m 23.10 | 3 | 8-9 | Firm | Rahil | Jly 1 1993 |
| 1m 6f 17y | 2m 57.80 | 3 | 8-2 | Good To Firm | Barakat | Jly 24 1990 |
| 2m | 3m 26.70 | 4 | 8-2 | Good To Firm | Alhesn (USA) | Jly 26 1999 |

## YORK

| Distance | Time | Age | Weight | Going | Horse | Date |
|---|---|---|---|---|---|---|
| 5f | 57.33 | 2 | 9-0 | Good To Firm | Star Rover (IRE) | Aug 19 2009 |
| 5f | 56.16 | 3 | 9-3 | Good To Firm | Dayjur | Aug 23 1990 |
| 5f 89y | 1m 3.20 | 2 | 9-3 | Good To Firm | The Art Of Racing | Sep 9 2012 |
| 5f 89y | 1m 1.72 | 4 | 9-7 | Good To Firm | Bogart | Aug 21 2013 |
| 6f | 1m 8.90 | 2 | 9-0 | Good | Tiggy Wiggy | Aug 21 2014 |
| 6f | 1m 8.23 | 3 | 8-11 | Good To Firm | Mince | Sep 9 2012 |
| 7f | 1m 22.32 | 2 | 9-1 | Good To Firm | Dutch Connection | Aug 20 2014 |
| 7f | 1m 21.83 | 4 | 9-8 | Good To Firm | Dimension | Jly 28 2012 |
| 1m | 1m 39.20 | 2 | 8-1 | Good To Firm | Missoula (IRE) | Aug 31 2005 |
| 1m | 1m 35.14 | 6 | 9-11 | Good To Firm | The Rectifier | Jly 13 2013 |
| 1m 208y | 1m 46.76 | 5 | 9-8 | Good To Firm | Echo Of Light | Sep 5 2007 |
| 1m 2f 88y | 2m 5.29 | 3 | 8-11 | Good To Firm | Sea The Stars (IRE) | Aug 18 2009 |
| 1m 4f | 2m 26.28 | 6 | 8-9 | Firm | Bandari (IRE) | Jun 18 2005 |
| 1m 6f | 2m 54.96 | 4 | 9-0 | Good To Firm | Tactic | May 22 2010 |
| 2m 88y | 3m 28.97 | 5 | 9-5 | Good To Firm | Gabrial's King | Jly 12 2014 |

# SPLIT SECOND SPEED RATINGS

The following lists the fastest performances of 3yo+ and 2yo horses which have recorded a speed figure of 105 or over during the 2014 season. Additional information in the parentheses following the speed figure shows the distance of the race in furlongs, course, state of going and the date on which the figure was achieved.

## Turf

**A Star In My Eye 105** *(12½f,Ncs,GF,Aug 22)*
**Above The Rest 108** *(8½f,Not,GF,Aug 15)*
**Abseil 110** *(8½f,Eps,G,Jun 6)*
**Absolutely So 113** *(7f,Yor,G,Aug 22)*
**Abys 106** *(12½f,Lon,G,Oct 4)*
**Accession 108** *(7f,Nby,GS,Aug 16)*
**Achnaha 106** *(8f,Cur,SH,Mar 23)*
**Adam's Ale 107** *(5f,Rip,G,Aug 5)*
**Addictive Dream 110** *(5f,Eps,G,Jun 7)*
**Adelaide 114** *(12f,Asc,GF,Jun 20)*
**Adventure Seeker 113** *(14f,Yor,G,Aug 23)*
**Aeolus 108** *(6f,Hay,GS,May 31)*
**Aertex 108** *(7f,Nby,GF,May 17)*
**Aetna 114** *(6f,Don,HY,Nov 8)*
**Affaire Solitaire 107** *(8f,Lon,G,Oct 4)*
**Afonso De Sousa 109** *(10f,Leo,YS,Oct 25)*
**Afternoon Sunlight 106** *(8f,Leo,YS,May 11)*
**Agena 105** *(10f,Cur,GF,Jun 29)*
**Agent Murphy 107** *(12f,Asc,GF,Sep 6)*
**Ahtoug 107** *(5f,Asc,G,Jun 17)*
**Air Pilot 113** *(10f,Eps,G,Jun 6)*
**Ajig 106** *(8f,San,G,Sep 17)*
**Ajjaadd 109** *(5f,Don,S,Oct 25)*
**Ajman Bridge 109** *(10f,Goo,G,Jly 29)*
**Ajmany 109** *(10f,Sal,G,Oct 1)*
**Akemi 110** *(8f,Cha,G,Jun 15)*
**Al Busayyir 106** *(10½f,Hay,GS,Jly 5)*
**Al Furat 107** *(12f,Cat,G,Apr 23)*
**Al Kazeem 117** *(10f,Wdr,G,Aug 23)*
**Al Khan 105** *(6f,Crl,GF,Jun 26)*
**Al Muheer 105** *(8f,Rip,G,Jun 19)*
**Al Mukhdam 105** *(8f,Rip,G,Jun 19)*
**Al Saham 108** *(12f,Asc,GS,May 10)*
**Al Thakhira 108** *(7f,Nmk,S,Oct 17)*
**Alaskan Bullet 107** *(5f,Ayr,GF,Jun 21)*
**Albasharah 117** *(10f,Nmk,G,Oct 11)*
**Alben Star 110** *(6f,Nmk,GF,Aug 23)*
**Albert Bridge 109** *(15f,Leo,Y,Oct 26)*
**Albonny 105** *(16f,Asc,GS,May 9)*
**Alejandro 111** *(7f,Hay,GS,Jly 5)*
**Aleksandar 105** *(12f,Ham,G,Jly 1)*
**Alex My Boy 108** *(14f,Mus,G,Aug 8)*
**Alex Vino 107** *(10f,Sal,G,Oct 1)*
**Alexandrakollontai 105** *(6f,Ham,G,Sep 22)*
**Alfred Hutchinson 107** *(8f,Yor,GS,May 15)*
**Algar Lad 107** *(5f,Asc,GF,Sep 6)*
**Alive Alive Oh 106** *(10f,Cur,Y,Apr 13)*
**Aljamaaheer 114** *(7f,Don,G,Sep 13)*
**All At Sea 107** *(12½f,Lon,G,Oct 4)*
**All Talk N No Do 105** *(10f,San,G,Sep 17)*
**Allnecessaryforce 105** *(12f,Yor,GS,May 31)*
**Alluring Star 105** *(7f,Cat,G,Apr 23)*
**Almargo 110** *(7f,Ncs,GF,Jun 28)*
**Almuheet 105** *(8f,Ayr,G,Sep 18)*
**Alnoomaas 105** *(6f,Bri,G,Sep 15)*
**Along Came Casey 106** *(8f,Leo,G,Jun 12)*
**Alpine Storm 105** *(8f,Asc,GF,Sep 6)*
**Altano 112** *(15½f,Lon,VS,Oct 26)*
**Altesse 110** *(16f,Cur,GF,Sep 28)*
**Altruism 107** *(10f,Lin,G,May 10)*
**Alwilda 106** *(12f,Nby,G,Aug 3)*
**Amadeus Wolfe Tone 106** *(6f,Wdr,G,Jun 16)*
**American Devil 112** *(7f,Lon,G,Sep 7)*
**American Hope 106** *(8f,Asc,G,Jly 26)*
**Amour A Papa 112** *(10½f,Cha,G,Jun 15)*
**Amralah 110** *(10f,Nby,G,Jly 19)*
**Amulet 107** *(8f,San,G,Sep 17)*
**Amy Eria 108** *(7f,Lon,G,Sep 7)*
**An Cat Dubh 105** *(9f,Mus,G,Oct 11)*
**An Saighdiur 108** *(6f,Cur,SH,May 24)*
**Anaconda 105** *(7½f,Chs,GS,Jun 27)*
**Anderiego 108** *(8f,Ayr,G,Sep 18)*
**Andry Brusselles 106** *(15½f,Lon,VS,Oct 26)*
**Angel Gabrial 113** *(16½f,Yor,G,Aug 22)*
**Angelic Upstart 107** *(9f,Goo,GF,Jly 31)*
**Angus Og 106** *(6f,Rip,GS,May 9)*
**Anipa 109** *(11½f,Chs,G,May 7)*
**Anjaal 106** *(8f,Nmk,G,Sep 26)*
**Annaluna 105** *(16f,Chp,GF,Jly 2)*
**Annecdote 109** *(7f,Lin,G,May 10)*
**Annunciation 109** *(6f,Hay,S,May 10)*
**Anodin 115** *(9f,Lon,S,May 25)*
**Another Cocktail 107** *(20f,Asc,G,Jun 17)*
**Another For Joe 105** *(8f,Ham,GS,May 4)*
**Another Party 113** *(6½f,Dea,HY,Aug 10)*
**Another Wise Kid 108** *(6f,Rip,G,Aug 16)*
**Ansaab 107** *(8f,Pon,G,Apr 14)*
**Ansgar 115** *(7f,Don,G,Sep 13)*
**Answered 114** *(10f,Leo,YS,Oct 25)*
**Antiquus 105** *(5f,Cur,GF,Sep 28)*
**Apostle 108** *(7½f,Chs,GS,Aug 3)*
**Appyjack 107** *(8f,Ffo,GS,Aug 5)*
**Apricot Sky 106** *(5f,Hay,G,Sep 5)*
**Aqua Ardens 105** *(7f,Bri,GS,Apr 24)*
**Arab Dawn 107** *(10f,Don,GS,Sep 11)*
**Arab Spring 110** *(12f,Asc,GF,Jun 21)*
**Arabian Comet 110** *(10½f,Yor,G,Jun 13)*
**Aramist 105** *(14f,Hay,G,Sep 6)*
**Arctic Feeling 108** *(5f,Yor,S,Oct 10)*
**Arctic Lynx 105** *(5f,Lin,G,May 9)*
**Ardlui 106** *(16f,Ncs,GF,Jun 28)*
**Ardmay 105** *(10f,Rip,GS,May 9)*
**Arnold Lane 106** *(6f,Wdr,GS,Jun 28)*
**Arod 117** *(10½f,Yor,GS,May 15)*
**Art Scholar 105** *(10f,Not,S,Oct 15)*
**Artful Artist 107** *(15f,Leo,Y,Oct 26)*
**Artful Prince 107** *(9f,Yor,G,Jun 14)*
**Artful Rogue 105** *(12f,Goo,G,Aug 23)*
**Artigiano 111** *(9f,Mey,GS,Jan 9)*
**Artistic Jewel 105** *(6f,Yor,GF,Sep 7)*
**Arty Campbell 105** *(14f,Goo,G,Jun 20)*
**Aryal 105** *(10f,Bev,GF,Jun 24)*
**Asbury Boss 108** *(16f,Cur,Y,Oct 12)*
**Ashpan Sam 108** *(6f,Eps,G,Jun 7)*
**Asian Trader 107** *(5f,Not,GS,Jun 1)*
**Askaud 107** *(7f,Thi,GS,Apr 12)*
**Astaire 112** *(5f,Yor,G,Aug 22)*
**Astonishing 109** *(12f,Nby,G,Apr 12)*
**Astronereus 108** *(10f,Nmk,S,Jly 11)*
**Asyad 105** *(10f,Nby,G,Jun 24)*
**Athletic 108** *(7f,Chs,G,Sep 12)*
**Au Revoir 106** *(12f,Lon,G,Sep 14)*
**Auction 107** *(8f,Asc,GF,Sep 6)*
**Audacia 106** *(8f,Pon,S,Jly 8)*
**Aussie Reigns 107** *(14f,Yor,G,Aug 23)*
**Australia 117** *(10½f,Yor,GF,Aug 20)*
**Auvray 115** *(15f,Lon,G,Oct 4)*
**Avenir Certain 115** *(12f,Lon,G,Oct 5)*
**Aventador 108** *(10½f,Cha,G,Jun 1)*
**Avenue Gabriel 107** *(10f,Cur,GF,Jun 29)*
**Avon Breeze 106** *(5f,Red,GF,May 19)*
**Awake My Soul 108** *(10f,Ayr,S,Aug 11)*
**Ayaar 107** *(8f,Asc,GF,Sep 6)*
**Ayrad 109** *(10f,Asc,HY,Oct 18)*
**Azurite 107** *(10f,Cur,GF,May 5)*

**B Fifty Two 109** *(5½f,Chs,GS,Aug 30)*
**Baccarat 111** *(6f,Asc,GF,Jun 21)*
**Bachotheque 105** *(6f,Crl,G,May 26)*
**Badr Al Badoor 110** *(6½f,Don,G,Sep 12)*
**Bahamian C 105** *(10f,Not,GF,Sep 23)*
**Bahamian Heights 105** *(6f,Don,G,Sep 11)*
**Baino Hope 114** *(15f,Lon,G,Oct 4)*
**Balducci 110** *(8f,Yor,G,Aug 21)*
**Ball Dancing 112** *(11f,Lon,GS,May 11)*
**Ballyadam Brook 105** *(15f,Leo,Y,Oct 26)*
**Ballybacka Queen 105** *(8f,Leo,YS,May 11)*
**Balmoral Castle 107** *(9f,Goo,G,Aug 23)*
**Baltic Baroness 108** *(10½f,Lon,VS,Apr 27)*
**Baltic Knight 112** *(7f,Hay,GS,Sep 4)*
**Balty Boys 110** *(8½f,Not,S,Jun 4)*
**Bamiyan 113** *(7f,Lon,G,Sep 7)*
**Bancnuanaheireann 108** *(8f,Nmk,GS,Nov 1)*
**Barack 105** *(8f,Leo,YS,Oct 25)*
**Baraweez 110** *(7f,Leo,GF,Sep 13)*
**Barkston Ash 109** *(6f,Rip,GS,Apr 26)*
**Barley Mow 107** *(10f,Nmk,GF,May 3)*
**Barnet Fair 110** *(6f,Goo,GF,Aug 2)*
**Baron Run 106** *(6f,Ham,GS,Sep 2)*
**Barracuda Boy 106** *(6f,Hay,G,Sep 27)*
**Barren Brook 107** *(9f,Yor,G,Jun 14)*
**Bartack 109** *(8f,Rip,G,Aug 25)*
**Barwick 105** *(12f,Bri,GF,Aug 7)*
**Basem 106** *(10f,Sal,G,Oct 1)*
**Basil Berry 105** *(7f,Chs,GS,Jun 28)*
**Bathyrhon 116** *(20f,Lon,G,Oct 5)*
**Batrana 113** *(8f,Nmk,G,Aug 22)*
**Battalion 106** *(12f,Nby,S,Oct 25)*
**Battersea 111** *(12f,Asc,GF,Jly 12)*
**Bawina 111** *(10½f,Cha,G,Jun 15)*
**Bayan 106** *(14f,Leo,GF,Sep 13)*
**Bayrir 108** *(10f,Wdr,G,Aug 23)*
**Be My Gal 107** *(10f,Nby,GS,Apr 11)*
**Be Perfect 105** *(16f,Bev,G,Aug 14)*
**Beach Bar 105** *(8f,Hay,S,Jun 11)*
**Beakers N Num Nums 106** *(10f,San,G,Sep 17)*
**Bear Behind 109** *(6f,Thi,S,May 10)*
**Beau Nash 110** *(7½f,Chs,GS,Aug 30)*
**Beau Satchel 106** *(8f,Cur,GF,Aug 23)*
**Belgian Bill 109** *(8f,Goo,GF,Aug 1)*
**Belle D'Or 112** *(8f,Nmk,G,Sep 26)*
**Beltor 111** *(10f,Red,G,Sep 24)*
**Ben Hall 105** *(7f,Lei,GF,Jly 5)*
**Bereni Ka 106** *(10f,Lon,S,May 25)*
**Berkshire 111** *(9f,Nmk,S,Oct 17)*
**Berlusca 105** *(8f,Yor,GF,Jly 25)*
**Bertiewhittle 106** *(7f,Hay,G,Apr 26)*
**Best Of Order 106** *(7f,Yor,GS,May 31)*
**Best Trip 106** *(6f,Rip,GS,Apr 26)*
**Between Wickets 105** *(8½f,Eps,G,Sep 28)*
**Beyond Brilliance 107** *(12f,Cur,GF,Jly 19)*
**Big Bad Lily 105** *(6f,Cur,YS,Jun 8)*
**Big Baz 107** *(8f,Hay,S,Oct 17)*
**Big Break 110** *(7f,Leo,GF,Jun 19)*
**Big Easy 107** *(18f,Nmk,G,Oct 11)*
**Big Johnny D 111** *(9f,Nmk,GF,Sep 27)*
**Big Orange 111** *(14f,Asc,G,Oct 3)*
**Bilimbi 106** *(8f,Mus,GF,Apr 18)*
**Billingsgate 107** *(8f,San,GF,Jly 16)*
**Billyford 105** *(8f,Cur,G,Aug 31)*
**Biographer 113** *(16f,Asc,HY,Oct 18)*
**Birzali 105** *(12f,Cur,GF,Jun 29)*
**Bishop's Castle 106** *(9f,Yor,G,Jun 14)*
**Bispham Green 105** *(5f,Hay,GS,Jun 12)*
**Black Shadow 105** *(10f,Eps,G,Jun 7)*
**Blackstone 105** *(10f,Leo,Y,Oct 26)*
**Blaine 109** *(6f,Ham,GF,Jly 18)*
**Blessington 108** *(6f,Asc,G,May 9)*
**Blithe Spirit 110** *(5f,Chs,S,May 9)*
**Blue Hussar 105** *(14f,Leo,GF,Sep 13)*
**Blue Rambler 105** *(12f,Lei,S,Oct 27)*
**Blue Soave 110** *(7f,Lon,G,Sep 7)*
**Blue Surf 108** *(10f,Lin,G,May 10)*
**Blue Waltz 107** *(10f,Don,GS,Sep 11)*
**Blurred Vision 109** *(6f,Yor,GS,May 31)*
**Bocaiuva 111** *(10½f,Cha,G,Jun 15)*
**Body And Soul 109** *(6f,Yor,GS,May 31)*
**Body Beautiful 105** *(5f,Cur,GF,Sep 28)*
**Body Language 106** *(12f,Ham,GS,May 16)*
**Bogart 112** *(6f,Don,G,Sep 13)*
**Bold Lass 109** *(8f,Asc,GF,Sep 6)*
**Bold Prediction 108** *(8f,Thi,G,May 3)*
**Bold Sniper 110** *(10f,Asc,GF,Jun 20)*
**Bold Spirit 107** *(6f,Lei,S,Aug 10)*
**Bold Thady Quill 109** *(8f,Cur,SH,May 24)*
**Bond Club 106** *(6f,Thi,S,May 10)*
**Bondesire 108** *(5f,Bev,G,Apr 16)*
**Bookrunner 107** *(7f,Msn,G,Apr 3)*
**Boom And Bust 107** *(7f,Chs,GF,Jly 12)*
**Boomerang Bob 106** *(6f,Asc,GF,Jun 21)*
**Boomshackerlacker 106** *(10f,Asc,GF,Jun 20)*
**Boots And Spurs 107** *(7f,Don,S,Jun 7)*
**Border Bandit 106** *(8f,Rip,G,Jun 19)*
**Border Legend 108** *(10f,Lin,G,May 10)*
**Borderlescott 107** *(5f,Mus,GF,Apr 18)*
**Born In Bombay 106** *(8f,Asc,GF,Jun 19)*
**Bow Creek 113** *(8f,Goo,GF,Aug 1)*
**Bowie Boy 105** *(8f,San,GF,Jly 30)*
**Boy In The Bar 106** *(6f,Pon,GF,Jly 27)*
**Bracelet 111** *(12f,Cur,GF,Jly 19)*
**Brae Hill 108** *(8f,Don,S,Mar 29)*
**Bragging 109** *(7f,Nmk,GF,Jly 26)*
**Braidley 108** *(10f,Goo,GF,Jly 31)*
**Brass Ring 106** *(18f,Nmk,G,Oct 11)*
**Brazos 114** *(7f,Nby,GS,Aug 16)*
**Breathe Easy 107** *(10f,Cur,GF,May 5)*
**Brendan Brackan 112** *(7f,Leo,GF,Jun 19)*
**Bretherton 106** *(7f,Hay,S,May 24)*
**Breton Rock 116** *(7f,Nby,GS,Aug 16)*
**Bright Approach 109** *(10f,Nby,GS,Apr 11)*
**Bright Cecily 105** *(10f,Ffo,GF,Sep 14)*
**Broadway Duchess 107** *(7f,Lin,G,May 10)*
**Brockwell 106** *(16f,Hay,G,May 24)*
**Bronze Angel 115** *(9f,Nmk,GF,Sep 27)*
**Brown Panther 121** *(14f,Cur,GF,Sep 14)*
**Brown Sugar 105** *(6f,Nmk,GF,Aug 23)*
**Brownsea Brink 105** *(8f,Nby,G,Apr 12)*
**Bubbly Bellini 108** *(7f,Cur,Y,Apr 13)*
**Buckstay 112** *(9f,Nmk,GF,Sep 27)*
**Bunce 106** *(5f,Ayr,G,Jly 21)*
**Bunker 115** *(10½f,Yor,GS,May 15)*
**Burano 110** *(10f,Nby,S,Oct 25)*
**Bureau 106** *(12f,Nmk,G,Oct 4)*
**Buredyma 105** *(8f,Nmk,S,Oct 22)*
**Burn The Boats 107** *(8f,Cur,G,Aug 31)*
**Burning Thread 108** *(5f,Ayr,GF,Jun 21)*
**Busatto 109** *(9f,Yor,G,Jun 14)*
**Buthelezi 108** *(13f,Nmk,GF,Aug 23)*
**Byron's Dream 105** *(8f,Ncs,G,May 20)*

**Cable Bay 110** *(7f,Nmk,S,Oct 17)*
**Cafe Society 109** *(10f,Asc,GF,Jun 20)*
**Caffeine 106** *(6f,Yor,GF,Sep 7)*
**Cailini Alainn 105** *(12f,Leo,YS,Oct 25)*
**Caledonia 105** *(16f,Mus,S,Jun 14)*
**Caledonia Lady 110** *(5f,Bat,F,Apr 19)*
**Calm Attitude 109** *(10f,San,GS,Aug 30)*
**Calyxa 113** *(10f,Dea,VS,Aug 24)*
**Can't Change It 106** *(7f,Chp,S,Jun 2)*
**Canary Row 109** *(8f,Cur,SH,Mar 23)*
**Cannock Chase 107** *(10f,Asc,GF,Jun 19)*
**Canova 106** *(8f,Chp,GF,Jun 23)*
**Cape Caster 108** *(10f,Don,S,Mar 29)*
**Cape Of Hope 105** *(7f,Cat,GF,Jly 23)*
**Caprella 105** *(7f,Cur,GF,Jun 29)*
**Captain Bob 109** *(7f,San,G,Jun 14)*
**Captain Cat 111** *(8f,Sal,GF,Aug 14)*
**Captain Cullen 107** *(6f,Cur,GY,Aug 31)*
**Captain Dunne 106** *(5f,Rip,G,Sep 27)*
**Captain Joy 107** *(8f,Cur,GF,Jun 28)*
**Captain Morley 107** *(14f,Yor,G,Aug 23)*
**Captain Ramius 111** *(6f,Don,S,Mar 29)*
**Cascading 108** *(12f,Nby,G,Aug 3)*
**Cashpoint 110** *(10f,Red,GS,May 26)*
**Caspar Netscher 111** *(6f,Asc,S,Oct 4)*
**Caspian Prince 111** *(5f,Eps,G,Jun 7)*
**Cassells Rock 108** *(14f,Leo,GF,Sep 13)*
**Castle Bar Sling 106** *(10f,Leo,G,Jun 6)*
**Castorienta 108** *(6f,Lei,S,Aug 10)*
**Catcall 113** *(5f,Lon,GS,May 11)*
**Categorical 105** *(13f,Ham,GS,May 4)*
**Cavalieri 109** *(12f,Cat,G,Apr 23)*
**Cavalryman 113** *(16½f,Yor,G,Aug 22)*
**Cay Dancer 105** *(7f,Nby,GF,May 17)*
**Ceisteach 108** *(10f,Leo,SH,Mar 30)*
**Century 111** *(16f,Asc,GF,Jun 20)*
**Certerach 111** *(14f,Cur,GF,Jun 29)*
**Chalnetta 105** *(12f,Cha,G,Jun 1)*
**Championship 109** *(8f,Don,G,Sep 13)*
**Chance To Dance 110** *(10f,Leo,GF,Jly 17)*
**Chancery 106** *(9f,Nmk,GF,Sep 27)*
**Charles Camoin 106** *(10f,Goo,G,Jly 29)*
**Charlie Wells 108** *(8f,Chp,GF,Jun 23)*
**Charm Spirit 111** *(8f,Lon,G,Sep 14)*
**Charter 105** *(6f,Nmk,GS,Sep 20)*
**Chesil Beach 105** *(14f,Mus,G,Oct 11)*
**Cheworee 105** *(5f,Goo,GF,Jly 29)*
**Chicago 109** *(14f,Cur,GF,Jun 29)*
**Chicago Girl 107** *(7f,Cur,G,May 5)*
**Chicquita 113** *(12f,Lon,G,Oct 5)*
**Chil The Kite 110** *(7f,Nby,GF,May 17)*
**Chillie Billie 105** *(7f,Cur,G,Aug 23)*
**Chilworth Icon 110** *(6f,Don,G,Sep 13)*
**Chinese Jade 105** *(8f,Mus,G,Sep 5)*
**Chocala 107** *(16f,Asc,GS,May 9)*
**Chocolatier 111** *(9f,Lon,VS,Apr 27)*
**Chooseday 107** *(5f,Bev,G,Apr 16)*
**Chopin 114** *(8f,Nby,GF,May 17)*
**Choral Festival 105** *(10f,Wdr,GS,Aug 10)*
**Chosen Character 108** *(8f,Hay,S,Jun 11)*
**Christopher Wren 106** *(11½f,Wdr,G,Apr 14)*
**Cinnilla 109** *(14f,Sal,G,Aug 29)*
**Circumvent 106** *(8f,Lei,GF,Jun 19)*
**Cirrus Des Aigles 117** *(10½f,Lon,VS,Apr 27)*
**Classical Art 107** *(10½f,Hay,GS,May 31)*
**Classy Anne 108** *(5f,Not,GS,Nov 5)*
**Clayton 109** *(10f,Pon,S,Apr 8)*
**Clear Spell 106** *(10½f,Hay,GS,May 31)*
**Clear Spring 108** *(6f,Rip,GS,Apr 26)*
**Clever Cookie 111** *(14f,Yor,G,Aug 23)*
**Cliff House 108** *(15f,Leo,Y,Oct 26)*
**Clockmaker 107** *(7f,Goo,G,Jun 8)*
**Clon Brulee 108** *(10f,San,GS,Aug 30)*
**Clondaw Warrior 110** *(15f,Leo,Y,Oct 26)*
**Cloudscape 115** *(12f,Goo,GF,Jly 30)*
**Cocktail Queen 108** *(12f,Nby,G,Apr 12)*
**Coincidently 106** *(8f,Ayr,G,Sep 18)*
**Colonel Mak 108** *(6f,Rip,HY,Jun 4)*
**Colour Blue 108** *(7f,Cur,GF,Jun 28)*
**Come On Dave 106** *(5f,Wdr,GF,Aug 4)*
**Comino 106** *(7f,Thi,G,Sep 16)*
**Communicator 107** *(14f,Hay,G,Sep 6)*
**Complicate 110** *(6f,War,S,Aug 25)*
**Complicit 111** *(10f,Wdr,G,Aug 23)*
**Compton 110** *(7f,Lei,GF,Jly 5)*
**Compton Bird 108** *(10f,Eps,GF,Jly 17)*
**Compton Park 107** *(6f,Pon,GF,Jly 27)*
**Confessional 108** *(6f,Rip,G,Aug 16)*
**Connecticut 113** *(14f,Yor,G,Aug 23)*
**Cono Zur 107** *(8f,Ayr,GF,Jly 7)*
**Conry 107** *(7f,Cat,S,May 24)*
**Continuum 105** *(12f,Asc,GF,Jun 21)*
**Contributer 111** *(10f,Asc,GF,Jun 20)*
**Cool Sky 106** *(16f,Nmk,GS,Oct 31)*
**Coolfighter 107** *(15f,Leo,Y,Oct 26)*
**Cordial 105** *(6f,Yar,G,Sep 17)*
**Cornborough 107** *(7f,Red,GS,Apr 7)*
**Cornrow 108** *(9f,Nmk,GF,Sep 27)*
**Corporal Maddox 106** *(7f,Bri,GS,Apr 24)*
**Correggio 106** *(9f,Yor,G,Jun 14)*
**Cosette 106** *(12f,Sal,GF,Jly 12)*
**Cosmic Chatter 105** *(6f,Rip,GS,Apr 26)*
**Cosmic Halo 106** *(10½f,Yor,GF,Sep 7)*
**Cosseted 107** *(10½f,Chs,G,Jun 27)*
**Cougar Mountain 113** *(5f,Yor,G,Aug 22)*
**Coulsty 106** *(6f,Chs,GS,Aug 3)*
**Counter Ridge 106** *(6f,Don,G,Sep 11)*
**Craggaknock 116** *(12f,Pon,G,Jun 30)*
**Crisolles 112** *(9f,Lon,VS,Apr 27)*
**Cristoforo Colombo 108** *(7f,Cur,Y,Apr 13)*
**Criteria 109** *(14½f,Don,GS,Sep 11)*
**Crowdmania 105** *(8f,Yar,GF,Apr 29)*
**Crowley's Law 107** *(10f,Sal,GF,Aug 13)*
**Cruise Tothelimit 105** *(6f,Hay,GS,May 30)*
**Crystal Lake 109** *(8f,Nmk,S,Jly 12)*
**Cubanita 112** *(12f,Nby,G,Apr 12)*
**Cullentry Royal 108** *(14f,Leo,SH,Mar 30)*
**Custom Cut 115** *(8f,Pon,GF,Jly 27)*

**Da'Quonde 106** *(5f,Hay,GS,May 31)*
**Dabadiyan 110** *(14f,Cur,GF,Jun 29)*
**Daisy Boy 111** *(10f,Not,GF,Sep 23)*

**Dalayna 106** *(7f,Lin,G,May 10)*
**Dalgig 105** *(10f,Eps,GF,Jly 17)*
**Dame Lucy 106** *(10f,Not,S,Oct 8)*
**Danadana 110** *(10f,Goo,G,Sep 24)*
**Dance And Dance 108** *(8f,Ncs,GF,Jun 26)*
**Dance King 106** *(10f,Pon,GF,Jly 27)*
**Dank 110** *(10f,Asc,GF,Jun 18)*
**Dansili Dutch 105** *(8f,Ncs,G,May 20)*
**Danzeno 115** *(6f,Asc,S,Oct 4)*
**Dare To Achieve 110** *(12f,Ham,GS,May 16)*
**Dark Crystal 106** *(8f,Ayr,GS,Jly 14)*
**Dark Emerald 111** *(7f,Hay,GS,Jly 5)*
**Dark Ocean 105** *(8f,Pon,GS,Apr 8)*
**Dark Ruler 106** *(12f,Hay,GS,Sep 4)*
**Darwin 109** *(7f,Cur,GF,Jly 19)*
**Dashing Star 106** *(12f,Asc,GF,Jun 21)*
**Dashwood 108** *(6f,Cur,HY,May 25)*
**Daylight 105** *(6f,Bri,G,May 30)*
**De Rigueur 108** *(12f,Hay,GS,Jly 5)*
**Deauville Prince 106** *(7f,Hay,G,Sep 5)*
**Debdebdeb 107** *(12f,Bat,G,May 5)*
**Decathlete 105** *(8f,Lon,G,Oct 4)*
**Decent Fella 106** *(6f,Yar,GF,Jly 24)*
**Deeds Not Words 116** *(6f,Nmk,S,Jly 11)*
**Defining Year 106** *(10f,Leo,GF,Jly 17)*
**Democretes 105** *(7f,Hay,G,Sep 5)*
**Demora 111** *(5f,Mus,S,Jun 14)*
**Denny Crane 105** *(10f,Leo,G,Jun 6)*
**Der Meister 106** *(12f,Nmk,G,Sep 25)*
**Derbaas 107** *(9f,Mey,GS,Jan 9)*
**Desert Ace 106** *(5f,Not,GF,Jun 17)*
**Desert Blanc 109** *(7f,Lon,G,Sep 7)*
**Desert Law 105** *(6f,Wdr,GS,Jun 28)*
**Desert Snow 106** *(10f,Sal,GS,May 15)*
**Despot 109** *(7f,Sal,GF,Jly 26)*
**Devilment 105** *(14f,San,GF,Jly 24)*
**Dhaular Dhar 105** *(8f,Ayr,GS,Jly 14)*
**Diamond Lady 105** *(6f,Lin,GF,Sep 13)*
**Dibajj 108** *(5f,Lon,GS,May 11)*
**Dick Doughtywylie 106** *(10f,Asc,GF,Jun 20)*
**Digeanta 105** *(14f,Leo,GF,Sep 13)*
**Diletta Tommasa 108** *(10f,Red,G,Sep 24)*
**Dinkum Diamond 113** *(6f,Don,S,Mar 29)*
**Discussiontofollow 112** *(5f,Asc,GF,Jly 12)*
**Dishy Guru 118** *(5f,Goo,G,Sep 24)*
**Do It All 108** *(9f,Mey,GS,Jan 9)*
**Doc Hay 106** *(5f,Pon,S,Oct 20)*
**Doc Holliday 109** *(7f,Cur,G,Aug 23)*
**Docs Legacy 105** *(10½f,Hay,G,Sep 5)*
**Doctor Parkes 106** *(5f,Goo,G,Jun 8)*
**Dolce N Karama 107** *(10f,Leo,Y,Oct 26)*
**Dolniya 117** *(12f,Lon,G,Oct 5)*
**Domeside 109** *(15½f,Lon,VS,Oct 26)*
**Dominate 105** *(6f,Chp,GS,Sep 5)*
**Domination 108** *(20f,Asc,G,Jun 17)*
**Don't Call Me 108** *(7f,Asc,G,Jly 26)*
**Don't Stare 106** *(10f,Don,GS,Sep 12)*
**Donncha 105** *(8f,Wdr,S,Oct 6)*
**Donny Rover 110** *(10½f,Yor,G,Jun 13)*
**Dont Bother Me 109** *(7f,Asc,G,Jly 26)*
**Doonard Prince 105** *(7f,Cur,GF,Jun 29)*
**Double Bluff 111** *(12f,Goo,GF,Aug 2)*
**Double Discount 105** *(10f,Nmk,GF,May 16)*
**Doumaran 113** *(15f,Lon,G,Oct 4)*
**Dr Irv 108** *(16f,Ncs,G,Sep 23)*
**Dream Spirit 110** *(8f,Nmk,S,Aug 9)*
**Dream Walker 109** *(8f,Nmk,GS,Nov 1)*
**Dreams Of Glory 106** *(5f,Goo,G,Sep 24)*
**Dubai Dynamo 107** *(7½f,Chs,G,Jun 14)*
**Dubai Hills 106** *(8f,Ayr,G,Jly 21)*
**Duchess Andorra 105** *(8f,Cur,GF,Sep 28)*
**Due Diligence 107** *(6f,Asc,GF,Jun 21)*
**Duke Cosimo 106** *(6f,Rip,G,Aug 16)*
**Duke Of Firenze 108** *(5f,Cat,S,Oct 18)*
**Duke Of Yorkshire 105** *(10½f,Yor,GF,Sep 7)*
**Dungannon 111** *(5f,Don,S,Oct 25)*
**Dusky Queen 107** *(7f,Nby,S,Oct 25)*
**Dutch Breeze 106** *(6f,Yor,GS,May 31)*
**Dutch Courage 106** *(8f,Asc,GF,Jun 18)*
**Dutch Rose 110** *(7f,Yor,GS,May 31)*
**Dutch S 105** *(7f,Nby,GF,May 17)*
**Dux Scholar 108** *(9f,Mey,GS,Jan 9)*
**Dylar 108** *(8f,Cha,G,Jun 15)*
**Dynamite Dixie 106** *(8f,Cur,GF,Sep 28)*

**Eagle Rock 105** *(14f,Yor,G,Jun 13)*
**Eagle Top 119** *(12f,Asc,G,Jly 26)*
**Early Morning 107** *(10½f,Hay,GS,May 31)*
**Earth Amber 110** *(16f,Asc,S,Apr 30)*
**Earth Drummer 107** *(7f,Ayr,GF,Sep 20)*
**Eastern Belle 111** *(10f,Goo,S,May 22)*
**Eastern Impact 109** *(6f,Nmk,GF,Jly 26)*
**Eastern Rules 112** *(7f,Leo,GF,Jun 19)*
**Ebanoran 109** *(10f,Cur,GF,Jun 29)*
**Ebasani 110** *(10f,Leo,YS,Oct 25)*
**Ebony Express 107** *(14f,Crl,GF,Sep 10)*
**Ectot 113** *(12f,Lon,G,Oct 5)*
**Ederan 110** *(15½f,Lon,G,Sep 14)*
**Edge Of Sanity 107** *(16f,Cur,GF,Jun 28)*
**Edu Querido 106** *(8½f,Eps,G,Jun 6)*
**Educate 110** *(9f,Nmk,GF,Sep 27)*
**Eeny Mac 105** *(8½f,Bev,GS,Jun 11)*
**Egyptian Warrior 107** *(12f,Cur,GF,Jun 29)*
**Eighteen Summers 106** *(10f,Leo,GF,Jly 17)*
**Eilean Mor 107** *(11f,Ham,G,Sep 22)*
**Einsteins Folly 107** *(8f,Cur,GF,Jun 28)*
**Ejadah 106** *(8f,Hay,GS,Jly 3)*
**El Salvador 110** *(16f,Cur,Y,Oct 12)*
**El Viento 107** *(5f,Yor,GS,May 31)*
**Eland Ally 105** *(6f,Don,GF,Jun 28)*
**Elegant Peace 107** *(7f,Leo,Y,Oct 26)*
**Elhaame 108** *(10½f,Hay,G,Aug 9)*
**Elidor 112** *(14f,Yor,G,Aug 23)*
**Elite Army 105** *(12f,Asc,GF,Jun 19)*
**Elleval 109** *(10f,Cur,GF,Jun 29)*
**Elliptique 110** *(12f,Lon,G,Sep 14)*
**Elusive Time 108** *(8f,Cur,GF,Sep 28)*
**Elusivity 107** *(5f,Yor,GS,May 15)*
**Emell 108** *(8f,Goo,G,Aug 23)*
**Emerald Star 111** *(7f,Lin,G,May 10)*
**Emjayem 105** *(5f,Don,G,Jly 10)*
**Empire Storm 112** *(8f,Nby,GF,May 17)*
**Empress Ali 108** *(10½f,Chs,GS,Sep 27)*
**Encke 117** *(14f,Cur,GF,Sep 14)*
**Endless Credit 105** *(10f,Not,GF,Jly 31)*
**Energia Davos 110** *(10½f,Hay,G,Aug 9)*
**Energia Fox 107** *(11½f,Wdr,G,Aug 23)*
**Energia Fribby 108** *(12f,Chs,G,Sep 13)*
**Energizer 107** *(10f,Asc,GF,Jun 20)*
**English Summer 106** *(14f,San,G,Jun 14)*
**Englishman 107** *(6f,Hay,S,Oct 17)*
**Ennistown 109** *(10f,Pon,GF,Sep 25)*
**Enobled 107** *(10½f,Hay,G,Sep 5)*
**Entihaa 107** *(16f,Hay,G,May 24)*
**Epsom Hill 108** *(14f,Hay,G,Sep 6)*
**Ernest Hemingway 113** *(14f,Cur,GF,Jun 29)*
**Ertijaal 107** *(7f,Nmk,GS,Jly 12)*
**Es Que Love 112** *(6f,Nmk,G,Apr 17)*
**Escape To Glory 110** *(7f,Ayr,GS,Jly 14)*
**Esoterique 109** *(8f,Lon,G,Sep 14)*
**Esteaming 107** *(13f,Nmk,GF,Aug 23)*
**Estimate 114** *(16½f,Yor,G,Aug 22)*
**Etaab 113** *(8f,Nmk,G,Sep 26)*
**Ethics Girl 105** *(11½f,Yar,GF,Jun 12)*
**Eton Forever 111** *(6f,Asc,HY,Oct 18)*
**Eton Rifles 109** *(5f,Hay,GS,May 31)*
**Euphrasia 115** *(10½f,Cur,S,May 25)*
**Euro Charline 110** *(8f,Asc,G,Jly 25)*
**Eurystheus 108** *(9f,Yor,G,Jun 14)*
**Eutropius 105** *(9f,Mus,GF,Apr 20)*
**Evanescent 106** *(7f,Ayr,G,Sep 18)*
**Evita Peron 106** *(7f,Nmk,S,Jun 28)*
**Ex Oriente 108** *(14f,Yar,G,Sep 18)*
**Exactement 107** *(8f,Leo,G,Jun 12)*
**Examiner 110** *(8f,Nmk,S,Jly 12)*
**Excellent Puck 105** *(10½f,Chs,G,Sep 13)*
**Exclusive Waters 109** *(10f,Red,G,Sep 24)*
**Expose 106** *(5f,Don,G,Sep 10)*
**Express Himself 108** *(8½f,Not,GF,Oct 1)*
**Extortionist 116** *(5f,Yor,G,Aug 22)*
**Extrasolar 108** *(5f,Bat,F,Jly 15)*
**Extremity 109** *(8f,Goo,GF,Jly 29)*
**Eye Of The Storm 111** *(12f,Leo,Y,Aug 7)*
**Eye Of The Tiger 105** *(16f,Cur,Y,Oct 12)*

**Fairway To Heaven 110** *(6f,Wdr,GS,Jun 28)*
**Farlow 108** *(7f,Thi,GS,Apr 12)*
**Farquhar 111** *(10½f,Hay,GS,May 31)*
**Farraaj 115** *(10f,Eps,G,Jun 6)*
**Fascinating Rock 105** *(12f,Eps,G,Jun 7)*
**Fast Shot 110** *(6f,Rip,GS,Apr 26)*
**Fast Track 110** *(6f,Nmk,GF,Jly 26)*
**Fathom Five 105** *(5f,Chp,S,Jun 2)*
**Fattsota 110** *(12f,Nmk,GS,Aug 16)*
**Faure Island 106** *(6f,Lei,GF,Jly 23)*
**Fazza 106** *(9f,Yor,G,Jun 14)*
**Feedyah 109** *(8f,Asc,GF,Jun 18)*
**Feel The Heat 105** *(6f,Ham,G,Sep 29)*
**Felician 111** *(8f,Cha,G,Jun 15)*
**Felwah 105** *(7f,Asc,S,Oct 4)*
**Fencing 110** *(9f,Nmk,G,Apr 17)*
**Feodora 110** *(10f,Lon,G,Oct 5)*
**Fervent Prince 105** *(9f,Mey,GS,Jan 9)*
**Field Of Dream 111** *(8f,Asc,GF,Jun 18)*
**Fiery Sunset 105** *(12f,Chp,G,Jun 13)*
**Fiesolana 115** *(6½f,Dea,HY,Aug 10)*
**Fintry 116** *(8f,Cha,G,Jun 1)*
**Fire Fighting 109** *(12f,Nmk,G,Oct 4)*
**Fire Ship 110** *(8f,Cha,G,Jun 15)*
**First Experience 108** *(6f,Lei,GF,Jly 23)*
**First Flight 109** *(10f,Nby,S,Sep 20)*
**First Mohican 105** *(9f,Nmk,G,Apr 17)*
**First Post 107** *(10f,Nby,G,Apr 12)*
**Flash City 107** *(5f,Don,G,Jly 10)*
**Flemish School 106** *(11½f,Wdr,GS,May 5)*
**Flight Risk 107** *(6f,Cur,S,Aug 10)*
**Flintshire 118** *(12f,Lon,G,Oct 5)*
**Flipping 106** *(8f,Ffo,GS,Aug 5)*
**Flow 108** *(9f,Yor,G,Jun 14)*
**Fly To The Moon 109** *(7f,Cur,SH,Mar 23)*
**Fly With Me 114** *(20f,Lon,G,Oct 5)*
**Flying Jib 112** *(7f,Cur,G,May 5)*
**Flying Officer 110** *(16f,Nmk,G,Sep 25)*
**Flying The Flag 107** *(9f,Yor,G,Aug 23)*
**Flyman 109** *(6f,Don,S,Mar 30)*
**Focussed 105** *(7f,Cur,GF,Jun 29)*
**Forest Edge 111** *(7f,Lei,GF,Jly 5)*
**Forgotten Hero 108** *(12f,Don,G,Sep 13)*
**Forgotten Rules 114** *(16f,Asc,HY,Oct 18)*
**Forgotten Voice 113** *(16½f,Yor,G,Aug 22)*
**Fort Bastion 110** *(7f,Nmk,GS,Jly 12)*
**Fort Knox 107** *(7f,Nby,GF,May 17)*
**Fountain Of Youth 115** *(5f,Cur,GF,Jun 28)*
**Foxtrot Romeo 107** *(7f,Ncs,GF,Jun 28)*
**Fractal 106** *(12f,Chp,G,Sep 16)*
**Francis Of Assisi 109** *(7f,Leo,Y,Oct 26)*
**Free Eagle 116** *(10f,Asc,HY,Oct 18)*
**Free Port Lux 111** *(12f,Lon,G,Oct 5)*
**Free Wheeling 110** *(7f,Thi,GF,Aug 1)*
**Free Zone 106** *(5f,Yor,S,Oct 10)*
**Freedom's Light 111** *(12f,Pon,G,Jun 22)*
**French Navy 113** *(8½f,Eps,G,Jun 6)*
**Frine 114** *(15½f,Lon,VS,Oct 26)*
**Fruit Pastille 107** *(8f,Nmk,S,Oct 22)*
**Full Moon Fever 106** *(12f,Bat,GS,Oct 19)*
**Fun Mac 106** *(12f,Goo,GF,Aug 2)*
**Fury 108** *(8½f,Eps,G,Jun 6)*

**G Force 114** *(5f,Yor,G,Aug 22)*
**Gabrial 111** *(9f,Mey,GS,Jan 9)*
**Gabrial's Hope 106** *(10f,Red,G,Sep 24)*
**Gabrial's Kaka 109** *(8f,San,GF,Jly 5)*
**Gabrial's Star 108** *(12f,Chs,S,May 9)*
**Gabriel's Lad 110** *(7f,Asc,GS,May 10)*
**Gaelic Silver 105** *(10f,Wdr,S,Oct 28)*
**Gaga A 111** *(10f,Dea,VS,Aug 24)*
**Galilee Chapel 105** *(8f,Ayr,GF,Jly 7)*
**Galiway 106** *(10½f,Cha,G,Jun 1)*
**Galizzi 105** *(12f,Asc,GF,Jly 12)*
**Gallante 106** *(12f,Lon,G,Sep 14)*
**Gamesome 108** *(6f,Wdr,GS,Jun 28)*
**Gammarth 109** *(7f,Lon,G,Oct 5)*
**Ganymede 107** *(7f,Goo,G,Sep 24)*
**Garswood 117** *(6½f,Dea,HY,Aug 10)*
**Gatepost 107** *(7f,Ayr,GS,Jly 14)*
**Gatewood 113** *(12½f,Dea,HY,Aug 10)*
**Gathering Power 111** *(6f,Asc,HY,Oct 18)*
**General Brook 106** *(10f,Leo,G,Jun 12)*
**Genius Boy 107** *(8f,Red,GF,Jun 20)*
**George Cinq 106** *(8f,San,GF,Jly 16)*
**George Guru 105** *(7f,Goo,S,May 22)*
**George Rooke 105** *(6f,Ham,S,Jun 11)*
**Georgian Bay 107** *(7f,Nmk,GS,Jly 12)*
**Giant's Quest 107** *(16f,Cur,GF,Aug 24)*
**Giantstepsahead 105** *(10f,Yar,GF,May 20)*
**Gifted Girl 111** *(10f,Sal,GF,Aug 13)*
**Ginger Jack 108** *(8f,Nmk,GS,Nov 1)*
**Giovanni Boldini 110** *(7f,Asc,G,Jun 18)*
**Glam Gerry 106** *(14f,Leo,SH,Mar 30)*
**Glaring 112** *(15f,Lon,G,Oct 4)*
**Gleese The Devil 107** *(8f,Ncs,GF,Sep 5)*
**Glen Moss 110** *(7f,Hay,G,Apr 26)*
**Glenard 107** *(14f,Hay,G,Sep 6)*
**Global Village 105** *(10f,Don,S,Apr 26)*
**Glorious Empire 106** *(8f,Nmk,S,Jly 11)*
**Glorious Protector 110** *(11½f,Wdr,G,Aug 23)*
**Glory Awaits 111** *(7f,Yor,G,Aug 22)*
**Gm Hopkins 107** *(9f,Nmk,G,Sep 26)*
**Go Far 110** *(6f,Don,G,Sep 13)*
**Go For Broke 107** *(8f,Chp,GF,Jun 23)*
**Go For Goal 107** *(7f,Cur,SH,Mar 23)*
**Go Go Green 106** *(6f,Hay,GS,May 30)*
**Go Nani Go 105** *(5f,Mus,GF,Apr 18)*
**Go Sakhee 106** *(10f,Rip,G,Aug 25)*
**God Willing 105** *(9f,Yor,GS,Oct 11)*
**Going Somewhere 115** *(20f,Lon,G,Oct 5)*
**Gold Ship 114** *(12f,Lon,G,Oct 5)*
**Golden Jubilee 105** *(10f,Ffo,G,Aug 22)*
**Golden Steps 112** *(6f,Nmk,S,Jly 11)*
**Golden Town 113** *(8f,Nmk,S,Jly 12)*
**Goldream 111** *(6f,Don,G,Sep 13)*
**Goldtara 106** *(15½f,Lon,G,Sep 14)*
**Gone Dutch 107** *(10f,Nby,G,Apr 12)*
**Gone Viral 105** *(8f,Cur,S,Aug 10)*
**Gonna Run 110** *(10½f,Cha,G,Jun 1)*
**Good Authority 105** *(7f,Chp,G,Sep 16)*
**Good Luck Charm 108** *(7f,Goo,G,Sep 24)*
**Good Speech 105** *(10f,Red,G,Sep 24)*
**Good Value 107** *(12f,Asc,GF,Jly 12)*
**Gordon Lord Byron 115** *(6f,Asc,HY,Oct 18)*
**Gospel Choir 109** *(9f,Nmk,G,Apr 17)*
**Gothic 106** *(10f,Lei,S,Aug 10)*
**Gowanharry 105** *(5f,Mus,S,Jun 7)*
**Graceful Grit 110** *(8f,Asc,GF,Jun 18)*
**Gramercy 108** *(7f,Don,S,Jun 7)*
**Gran Canaria Queen 105** *(6f,Red,G,Jly 20)*
**Gran Maestro 106** *(12f,Cat,G,Apr 23)*
**Granddukeoftuscany 107** *(12f,Yor,GF,Aug 20)*
**Grandeur 112** *(10f,Goo,G,Sep 24)*
**Graphic 111** *(8½f,Eps,G,Jun 6)*
**Gratzie 109** *(8½f,Eps,G,Sep 11)*
**Grayswood 106** *(12f,Cat,G,Apr 23)*
**Great Fighter 105** *(14f,Goo,G,Jun 20)*
**Great Minds 109** *(6f,Cur,SH,Mar 23)*
**Grecian Tiger 107** *(16f,Cur,Y,Oct 12)*
**Greeb 106** *(6f,Don,GF,Jun 28)*
**Greek Canyon 106** *(6f,Cur,GF,Aug 24)*
**Green Door 108** *(5f,Chs,GF,Jly 11)*
**Green Howard 106** *(8f,Mus,G,Sep 5)*
**Green Light 108** *(10f,Red,S,Nov 4)*
**Gregorian 115** *(7f,Nby,GS,Aug 16)*
**Grevillea 106** *(8½f,Not,GF,Oct 1)*
**Greyemkay 107** *(8f,Ffo,GS,Aug 12)*
**Grissom 106** *(6f,Hay,GS,May 24)*
**Groovejet 110** *(14½f,Don,GS,Sep 11)*
**Groundbreaking 111** *(10f,Nmk,GF,May 16)*
**Guardini 106** *(12f,Lon,G,Sep 14)*
**Guerre 108** *(5f,Lon,G,Oct 5)*
**Guest Of Honour 106** *(8f,Asc,GF,Jly 12)*
**Gwafa 108** *(12f,Asc,GF,Sep 6)*
**Gworn 106** *(10f,Eps,G,Jun 6)*

**Hadaatha 111** *(10f,Lon,G,Oct 5)*
**Hadaj 108** *(6f,Nmk,GF,May 4)*
**Halation 106** *(8f,San,GF,Jly 30)*
**Half A Billion 105** *(6f,Thi,HY,Aug 2)*
**Hall Of Mirrors 108** *(10f,Cur,GF,May 5)*
**Hallbeck 107** *(12f,Pon,G,Jun 30)*
**Hallingham 106** *(10f,San,GF,Jly 23)*
**Hamelin 107** *(12f,Asc,GS,May 10)*
**Hamza 113** *(6f,Nmk,G,Apr 17)*
**Handheld 105** *(10f,Nmk,GS,Oct 31)*
**Hannah's Magic 106** *(10f,Cur,S,May 24)*
**Happy Families 105** *(13f,Bat,F,May 20)*
**Harasiya 110** *(8f,Leo,S,Aug 14)*
**Harley's Harley 106** *(7f,Leo,YS,May 11)*
**Harp Star 116** *(12f,Lon,G,Oct 5)*
**Harris Tweed 109** *(12f,Lei,S,Oct 27)*
**Hartnell 112** *(16f,Asc,GF,Jun 20)*
**Hasanour 109** *(8f,Cur,GF,Aug 23)*
**Hassle 107** *(14f,Hay,G,Sep 6)*
**Havana Cooler 107** *(12f,Asc,GF,Jun 21)*
**Have A Nice Day 106** *(7f,Cur,GF,Jun 29)*
**Hawkeyethenoo 108** *(6f,Hay,S,May 10)*
**Hay Chewed 109** *(5f,San,G,Jun 14)*
**He'llberemembered 107** *(16f,Cur,Y,Oct 12)*
**Head Space 109** *(5f,Don,G,Jly 10)*
**Head Waiter 105** *(16f,Cur,GF,Aug 24)*
**Headline News 107** *(12f,Hay,GS,Sep 4)*
**Heaven's Guest 113** *(7f,Nmk,GS,Jly 12)*
**Heavy Metal 112** *(7f,Hay,GS,Jly 5)*
**Hedge End 106** *(9f,Goo,GF,Jly 30)*
**Henry Higgins 106** *(14f,Leo,G,Jun 6)*
**Here Comes When 112** *(7f,Nmk,S,Oct 17)*
**Hesbaan 110** *(10f,Not,GF,Sep 25)*
**Hi Emperor 105** *(7f,Cur,GF,Jly 19)*
**Hi There 108** *(10f,Nby,S,Oct 25)*
**Hidden Cove 111** *(15½f,Lon,G,Sep 14)*
**Hidden Universe 109** *(16f,Cur,Y,Oct 12)*
**High Church 106** *(12f,Lei,G,Sep 9)*
**High Jinx 117** *(20f,Lon,G,Oct 5)*
**High Office 106** *(12f,Yor,GS,May 31)*
**High On Life 109** *(5f,Hay,G,Sep 27)*
**High Spirit 105** *(8f,Lon,G,Oct 4)*
**Highland Acclaim 109** *(6f,Asc,G,Aug 9)*
**Highland Castle 106** *(12f,Hay,GS,Sep 4)*
**Highland Colori 108** *(7f,Yor,G,Aug 22)*
**Highland Knight 109** *(8½f,Eps,G,Jun 6)*
**Hillbilly Boy 108** *(6f,Rip,GS,Apr 26)*
**Hillstar 109** *(12f,Asc,GF,Jun 21)*
**Hippy 111** *(10f,Dea,VS,Aug 24)*
**Hisaabaat 109** *(15f,Leo,Y,Oct 26)*
**Hit The Jackpot 107** *(10f,Bev,GF,Apr 24)*
**Hitchens 105** *(6f,Nmk,G,Apr 17)*
**Homage 109** *(9f,Nmk,GF,Sep 27)*
**Hoodna 111** *(7f,Nmk,GS,Jly 12)*
**Hopes N Dreams 109** *(5f,Ham,G,Jly 1)*
**Hors De Combat 116** *(8f,Goo,GF,Aug 1)*
**Horsted Keynes 105** *(7f,Asc,GF,Jun 20)*
**Hot Spice 107** *(12f,Cat,G,Apr 23)*
**Hot Streak 114** *(5f,Hay,S,May 24)*
**Howyadoingnotsobad 108** *(5f,Goo,G,Sep 24)*
**Huff And Puff 105** *(16f,Hay,G,May 24)*
**Hulcolt 107** *(7½f,Bev,GF,Sep 23)*
**Humidor 112** *(6f,Don,G,Sep 13)*
**Hunters Creek 105** *(8f,Hay,GS,Jly 3)*
**Huntsmans Close 107** *(6f,Wdr,G,Apr 14)*
**Hurricane Ridge 105** *(14f,Leo,SH,Mar 30)*
**Hymenaios 109** *(10f,Don,S,Mar 29)*

**I'll Be Your Clown 105** *(10f,Leo,Y,Oct 26)*
**I'm Fraam Govan 107** *(10½f,Yor,G,Aug 23)*
**Ice Slice 106** *(8f,Nby,S,Oct 24)*
**Iceblast 105** *(7f,Cat,GF,Jly 9)*
**Iffranesia 106** *(5f,Asc,GS,Jly 25)*
**Ifwecan 111** *(8f,San,GF,Jly 5)*
**Ihtimal 108** *(8f,Nmk,GF,May 4)*
**Imperiator 107** *(7f,Msn,G,Apr 3)*
**Imshivalla 108** *(9f,Yor,GS,Oct 11)*
**In Salutem 105** *(6f,Cur,GF,Aug 24)*
**Inciting Incident 105** *(6f,Goo,GS,Sep 2)*
**Indignant 111** *(6f,Sal,GF,Jun 15)*
**Indira 105** *(12f,Nmk,GF,Aug 1)*
**Indy 106** *(10f,Don,S,Oct 24)*
**Inevitable 114** *(12f,Pon,G,Jun 30)*
**Ingleby Angel 109** *(9f,Nmk,GF,Sep 27)*
**Ingleby Symphony 105** *(8f,Ayr,GF,Apr 27)*
**Inis Meain 113** *(10f,Cur,Y,Apr 13)*
**Insaany 107** *(10f,Goo,GF,Jly 31)*
**Inspector Norse 108** *(8½f,Eps,G,Sep 11)*
**Instant Attraction 105** *(8f,Nmk,G,May 31)*
**Integral 115** *(8f,Asc,GF,Jun 18)*
**Intense Tango 106** *(12f,Hay,G,Aug 8)*
**Intensical 108** *(7f,Cur,GF,Jly 19)*
**Interception 106** *(6f,Lin,GF,Sep 13)*

**Interconnection 108** *(12f,Pon,G,Jun 30)*
**Intibaah 112** *(6f,Asc,HY,Oct 18)*
**Intransigent 109** *(6f,Chs,GS,Aug 3)*
**Intrinsic 111** *(6f,Goo,GF,Aug 2)*
**Investissement 106** *(12f,Nmk,G,Oct 4)*
**Invincible Fresh 105** *(7f,Lin,G,Jun 7)*
**Inxile 107** *(5f,Goo,GF,Jly 29)*
**Inyordreams 114** *(6f,Nmk,G,Oct 4)*
**Ipswich 111** *(10f,Dea,VS,Aug 24)*
**Iron Major 105** *(8f,Cur,GF,Jun 27)*
**Ishikawa 108** *(8f,San,S,May 29)*
**Island Remede 107** *(12f,Nby,S,Oct 25)*
**It Must Be Faith 111** *(5f,Not,GS,Nov 5)*
**Itlaaq 105** *(14f,Mus,GF,Apr 18)*
**Ivanhowe 113** *(12f,Lon,G,Oct 5)*
**Ixelles Diamond 106** *(7f,Nmk,F,Aug 2)*

**J Wonder 108** *(7f,Goo,GF,Aug 1)*
**Jack Daddy 105** *(16f,Cur,GF,Aug 24)*
**Jack Dexter 112** *(6f,Asc,HY,Oct 18)*
**Jack Luey 107** *(5f,Mus,S,Jun 14)*
**Jack's Revenge 106** *(7f,Nmk,GF,Sep 27)*
**Jacob Black 105** *(8f,Crl,GF,Jly 22)*
**Jailawi 106** *(8f,Wdr,G,Aug 23)*
**Jakey 105** *(10f,Eps,GF,Jly 3)*
**Jaladee 105** *(8f,Lin,GF,Jun 21)*
**Jalingo 105** *(9f,Ham,GS,Aug 28)*
**Jallota 105** *(7f,Don,S,Oct 25)*
**Jamaican Bolt 109** *(6f,Don,GS,Oct 24)*
**Jamesbo's Girl 107** *(6f,Pon,GF,Jly 18)*
**Jamesie 112** *(5f,Cur,GF,Jun 28)*
**Janaab 105** *(8f,Rip,GF,Aug 26)*
**Jazz 109** *(7f,Ayr,GF,Jly 7)*
**Jazz Girl 105** *(10f,Cur,GF,May 5)*
**Jazz Master 106** *(10f,Don,S,Apr 26)*
**Jelly Fish 107** *(12f,Sal,GF,Jly 12)*
**Jersey Brown 107** *(8½f,Not,GF,Sep 23)*
**Jillnextdoor 105** *(5f,Bat,F,Apr 19)*
**Jimmy Styles 108** *(6f,Don,S,Mar 29)*
**Jodies Jem 106** *(9f,Goo,GF,Jly 31)*
**Joe Eile 107** *(8f,Thi,G,May 3)*
**Joey's Destiny 108** *(6f,Don,S,Mar 30)*
**John Constable 106** *(10f,Cur,S,May 24)*
**Johnno 107** *(8f,Crl,GF,Jun 25)*
**Johnny Cavagin 106** *(7f,Cat,S,May 24)*
**Jonny Delta 107** *(14f,Mus,GF,Apr 18)*
**Jordan Princess 111** *(12f,Nmk,G,Sep 26)*
**Joshua Tree 111** *(10½f,Lon,VS,Apr 27)*
**Joyeuse 110** *(6½f,Dea,HY,Aug 10)*
**Joys Of Spring 108** *(8f,Asc,GF,Sep 6)*
**Judge 'n Jury 110** *(5f,Not,G,Aug 12)*
**Jungle Bay 105** *(6f,Yar,GF,Jly 24)*
**Jupiter Storm 105** *(11½f,Wdr,G,Jun 2)*
**Just A Way 116** *(12f,Lon,G,Oct 5)*
**Just The Judge 111** *(10f,Cur,GF,Jun 29)*
**Justice Day 111** *(5f,Asc,GS,Oct 4)*
**Justineo 107** *(6f,Don,GF,Aug 2)*

**Kafeel 106** *(7f,Eps,G,Jun 6)*
**Kakatosi 105** *(8f,Nmk,GF,May 16)*
**Kalann 109** *(16f,Cur,GF,Sep 28)*
**Kaldera 112** *(15f,Lon,G,Oct 4)*
**Kaleefa 107** *(10f,Leo,SH,Mar 30)*
**Kalk Bay 106** *(8f,Pon,G,Apr 14)*
**Kanes Pass 111** *(7f,Leo,Y,Oct 26)*
**Karakontie 108** *(10½f,Cha,G,Jun 1)*
**Karam Albaari 107** *(10f,Not,GF,Sep 23)*
**Karezak 105** *(12f,Cur,GF,Jun 27)*
**Kashgar 105** *(16f,Goo,S,May 22)*
**Kashmiri Sunset 111** *(14f,Yor,G,Aug 23)*
**Katie T 106** *(12f,Leo,YS,Oct 25)*
**Keep It Dark 106** *(5f,Red,GS,May 27)*
**Kelinni 107** *(10f,Don,GS,Sep 11)*
**Kenhope 108** *(8f,Lon,G,Oct 4)*
**Kenzadargent 114** *(9f,Lon,VS,Apr 27)*
**Kernoff 107** *(5f,Cur,GF,Jun 27)*
**Khee Society 105** *(8f,Ffo,GS,Aug 12)*
**Khelman 106** *(7f,Mus,G,Aug 8)*
**Khione 109** *(12f,Nby,G,Apr 12)*
**Khubala 107** *(6f,Don,GS,Oct 24)*
**Kickboxer 109** *(5f,Asc,GS,Oct 4)*
**Kicky Blue 115** *(20f,Lon,G,Oct 5)*
**Kikonga 106** *(12f,Hay,GS,Sep 4)*
**Kimberella 109** *(6f,Rip,G,Sep 27)*
**King Of Macedon 105** *(7f,Mus,G,Aug 8)*
**King Of The Danes 105** *(9f,Ham,GS,Jun 5)*
**King Torus 108** *(8f,Rip,G,Jun 3)*
**King's Warrior 105** *(10f,Eps,GS,Apr 23)*
**Kingfisher 107** *(10½f,Yor,GF,Aug 20)*
**Kinglami 105** *(6f,Goo,GF,Aug 2)*
**Kingman 113** *(7f,Nby,G,Apr 12)*
**Kings Bayonet 106** *(12f,Hay,GS,Sep 4)*
**Kings Fete 109** *(12f,Goo,GF,Aug 2)*
**Kingsbarns 106** *(12f,Lon,G,Sep 14)*
**Kingscroft 106** *(8f,Hay,GF,Jun 21)*
**Kingsgate Choice 107** *(5f,Lon,GS,May 11)*
**Kingsgate Native 108** *(5f,Hay,S,May 24)*
**Kingston Hill 117** *(12f,Lon,G,Oct 5)*
**Kinshasa 105** *(12f,Asc,GF,Jly 12)*
**Kiram 107** *(7f,Msn,G,Apr 3)*
**Kiss Of Spring 107** *(8f,Ncs,GF,Sep 5)*
**Kiwi Bay 106** *(8f,Red,GS,Apr 7)*
**Kiyoshi 108** *(8f,Asc,G,Jly 25)*

**Kleitomachos 106** *(16f,Nmk,GS,Oct 31)*
**Kleo 109** *(10f,Don,S,Oct 24)*
**Knife Point 105** *(12f,Nmk,G,Sep 25)*
**Knight Owl 105** *(8½f,Not,GS,May 9)*
**Knight's Parade 106** *(14f,Leo,GF,Jly 24)*
**Knightly Escapade 105** *(16f,Ncs,GF,Jun 26)*
**Kosika 108** *(8f,Nby,G,Jly 19)*
**Krypton Factor 108** *(6f,Ham,G,Sep 21)*
**Kune Kune 106** *(5f,Bat,F,Apr 19)*

**L'Amour De Ma Vie 113** *(8f,Asc,GF,Jun 18)*
**La Bacouetteuse 109** *(16f,Mus,GF,Jly 22)*
**La Banderilla 110** *(10f,Nmk,G,Oct 11)*
**La Hoguette 114** *(8f,Cha,G,Jun 1)*
**Ladies Are Forever 113** *(5f,Bat,F,Apr 19)*
**Lady Frances 106** *(6f,Cat,GF,Jly 16)*
**Lady Kashaan 108** *(14f,Yar,G,Sep 18)*
**Lady Lara 109** *(8f,Asc,GF,Jun 18)*
**Lady Mega 106** *(5f,Cur,GF,May 5)*
**Lady Penko 105** *(10f,Lon,S,May 25)*
**Lady Phill 116** *(5f,Goo,G,Sep 24)*
**Lady Pimpernel 113** *(10f,Sal,GF,Aug 13)*
**Lady Sylvia 107** *(8f,Nmk,GF,Jun 20)*
**Lady Tiana 108** *(10f,Not,S,Oct 15)*
**Lady Tyne 106** *(12f,Nby,G,Aug 3)*
**Laffan 109** *(7f,Hay,GS,Jly 5)*
**Laftah 107** *(7f,Lei,GF,Jly 17)*
**Lahaag 105** *(12f,Asc,GF,Jun 21)*
**Lahinch Classics 106** *(10f,Nby,G,May 16)*
**Lake George 106** *(7f,Cur,G,Aug 23)*
**Lamar 108** *(8f,Asc,GF,Jun 18)*
**Lancelot Du Lac 110** *(6f,Don,HY,Nov 8)*
**Las Verglas Star 105** *(10f,Ayr,S,Aug 11)*
**Lastchancelucas 105** *(5f,Thi,G,May 3)*
**Late Shipment 105** *(14f,Crl,GF,Aug 27)*
**Latenightrequest 109** *(12f,Don,S,Oct 25)*
**Latin Charm 105** *(12f,Hay,G,Aug 8)*
**Laughing Jack 106** *(14f,Crl,GF,Aug 27)*
**Lavender Lane 111** *(10½f,Cha,G,Jun 15)*
**Laviniad 108** *(12f,Cur,GF,Jun 29)*
**Lawyer 105** *(8f,Wdr,GS,Jly 7)*
**Layla's Hero 105** *(6f,Ham,GS,Sep 2)*
**Le Chat D'Or 106** *(8f,Ayr,GS,May 22)*
**Leaderene 105** *(12f,Bev,GF,Sep 17)*
**Leading Light 117** *(14f,Cur,GF,Sep 14)*
**Legal Waves 106** *(10f,Pon,GF,Sep 18)*
**Leitir Mor 109** *(8f,Leo,G,Jun 12)*
**Lesha 109** *(8f,Nmk,S,Jly 12)*
**Levitate 110** *(7f,Don,HY,Nov 8)*
**Lexington Abbey 105** *(5f,Yor,G,Aug 23)*
**Lexington Place 105** *(5f,Mus,S,Jun 7)*
**Liberty Jack 108** *(6f,Ffo,G,Aug 22)*
**Lightning Moon 116** *(6f,Asc,S,Oct 4)*
**Lightning Spear 106** *(8½f,Not,GS,Oct 29)*
**Lightning Thunder 108** *(8f,Nmk,GF,May 4)*
**Lilac Lace 108** *(7f,Nby,S,Oct 25)*
**Limario 105** *(8f,Lon,G,Oct 4)*
**Lincoln 110** *(7f,Chs,GS,Sep 27)*
**Line Of Reason 110** *(6f,Cur,GF,Jun 28)*
**Linguine 108** *(12f,Don,S,Jun 7)*
**Links Drive Lady 105** *(6f,Nmk,S,Aug 8)*
**Lion Beacon 107** *(14f,Goo,G,Jun 20)*
**Little Rocky 106** *(12f,Cur,Y,Apr 13)*
**Little Shambles 105** *(7f,Yor,G,Aug 21)*
**Livia's Dream 107** *(12f,Chs,G,Sep 13)*
**Living Leader 107** *(8f,Nmk,GF,Jun 20)*
**Llanarmon Lad 109** *(8½f,Eps,G,Jun 6)*
**Local Flier 107** *(6f,Cur,GF,Aug 24)*
**Lockhart 105** *(8f,Yar,G,Sep 17)*
**Long Awaited 106** *(5f,Don,G,Aug 16)*
**Long John 106** *(10½f,Yor,GF,Jly 26)*
**Long Journey Home 105** *(10f,Leo,G,Jun 12)*
**Longshadow 105** *(21f,Goo,GF,Jly 30)*
**Lord Aeryn 106** *(8½f,Not,S,Apr 9)*
**Lord Franklin 105** *(8½f,Not,S,Oct 8)*
**Lord Van Percy 113** *(14f,Yor,G,Aug 23)*
**Louis The Pious 112** *(6f,Asc,S,Oct 4)*
**Love Island 106** *(6f,Yor,G,Jun 13)*
**Love Marmalade 105** *(14f,Mus,GF,Apr 18)*
**Lucky Beggar 106** *(5f,Nby,GS,Apr 11)*
**Lulu The Zulu 111** *(7f,Don,S,Oct 25)*
**Lungarno Palace 106** *(10f,Eps,G,Sep 28)*
**Lustrous 107** *(12f,Yor,G,Aug 21)*
**Lyn Valley 110** *(10f,Goo,GF,Jly 31)*

**Maarek 112** *(6f,Asc,HY,Oct 18)*
**Macbeth 105** *(12f,Nmk,GS,Aug 16)*
**Madame Chiang 113** *(12f,Asc,HY,Oct 18)*
**Madame Defarge 107** *(10f,Not,GF,Jun 16)*
**Madame Rouge 109** *(12f,Chp,S,Aug 14)*
**Madeed 109** *(10f,Goo,GF,Jly 31)*
**Maggie Dalton 108** *(8f,Cur,G,Aug 31)*
**Maggie Pink 105** *(7f,Nmk,G,Nov 1)*
**Magic City 109** *(8f,Goo,GF,Aug 1)*
**Magic Hurricane 107** *(12f,Hay,GS,Jly 5)*
**Magic Of Reality 106** *(8f,Hay,S,Jun 11)*
**Magician 117** *(10f,Asc,GF,Jun 18)*
**Magique 108** *(9f,Goo,GF,Jly 30)*
**Magnolia Beach 109** *(10f,Leo,GF,Jly 17)*
**Magnus Maximus 107** *(6f,Nmk,G,Apr 16)*
**Maid In Rio 109** *(12f,Asc,GF,Jly 12)*
**Maid Of The Glens 106** *(12f,Cur,GF,Jly 19)*
**Majestic Moon 109** *(7f,Mus,GS,Jun 13)*

**Majestic Myles 105** *(6f,Pon,G,Apr 14)*
**Majestic Queen 106** *(6f,Leo,G,Jun 12)*
**Major Crispies 105** *(6f,Nby,G,May 16)*
**Major Jack 106** *(6f,Nmk,GF,Jly 26)*
**Majorities 105** *(8f,Mus,GS,Jun 13)*
**Manalapan 105** *(8f,Cur,GF,Jun 28)*
**Manderley 107** *(8f,Nmk,GF,May 4)*
**Mange All 109** *(10f,Don,GS,Sep 11)*
**Mango Diva 109** *(10½f,Yor,GS,May 15)*
**Manomine 105** *(12f,Nmk,G,Oct 4)*
**Maoi Chinn Tire 107** *(16f,Mus,GF,Jly 22)*
**Mar Mar 108** *(6f,War,G,Apr 24)*
**Maracuja 105** *(10½f,Chs,G,Jun 27)*
**March 105** *(5f,Bat,F,Apr 19)*
**Marchese Marconi 108** *(16f,Cur,Y,Oct 12)*
**Marcret 107** *(7½f,Chs,G,Sep 13)*
**Maremmadiavola 108** *(7f,Leo,GF,Sep 13)*
**Market Share 110** *(8f,Cha,G,Jun 15)*
**Marmalady 106** *(5f,Asc,GF,Sep 6)*
**Marmoom 105** *(7f,Nmk,GF,Jly 19)*
**Marsh Daisy 113** *(10f,Goo,S,May 22)*
**Marvellous 110** *(8f,Cur,S,May 25)*
**Marzocco 110** *(16f,Asc,GF,Jun 20)*
**Masai 105** *(6f,Cur,GF,Aug 24)*
**Masamah 109** *(5f,Mus,S,Jun 14)*
**Masarah 106** *(8½f,Eps,G,Jun 6)*
**Maskoon 107** *(8f,Cur,GF,Jun 27)*
**Mass Rally 107** *(6f,Hay,S,May 10)*
**Massini's Trap 107** *(16f,Cur,Y,Oct 12)*
**Master Bond 105** *(5f,Ayr,GS,Aug 9)*
**Master Of Finance 107** *(10½f,Chs,GS,Sep 27)*
**Master Speaker 106** *(5f,Cur,GF,Sep 14)*
**Master The World 106** *(8f,Nmk,S,Jly 12)*
**Matorio 113** *(9f,Lon,S,May 25)*
**Matravers 106** *(7f,Lei,GF,Jly 5)*
**Maureen 106** *(6f,Don,S,Mar 29)*
**Maven 109** *(10f,Red,S,Nov 4)*
**Maverick Wave 109** *(8f,Nmk,S,Aug 9)*
**Maverik 105** *(7½f,Chs,G,Sep 13)*
**Maybeme 108** *(10f,Rip,G,Jun 18)*
**Mayhem 109** *(12½f,Lon,G,Oct 4)*
**Mayumi 106** *(11f,Lon,GS,May 11)*
**Meadway 108** *(5f,Rip,G,Sep 27)*
**Mecca's Angel 114** *(5f,Thi,GS,Aug 1)*
**Medicean Man 108** *(5f,Asc,G,Jun 17)*
**Meet Me Halfway 106** *(7f,Yar,GF,May 20)*
**Meeting Waters 106** *(7f,Asc,S,Oct 4)*
**Meetings Man 105** *(14f,San,GF,Jly 23)*
**Megaleka 107** *(5f,Not,GF,Jly 18)*
**Mehdi 105** *(6f,Ayr,GF,Sep 20)*
**Mekong River 112** *(10f,Cur,GF,Jun 29)*
**Meleagros 110** *(12½f,Dea,HY,Aug 10)*
**Melody Of Love 106** *(7f,Lin,G,May 10)*
**Melvin The Grate 108** *(8f,Hay,S,Oct 17)*
**Merry Me 105** *(8f,Ffo,S,Aug 28)*
**Mezzotint 110** *(7½f,Chs,GS,Aug 30)*
**Mia San Triple 105** *(6f,Wdr,GS,Jly 28)*
**Michaelmas 107** *(7f,Cur,GF,Jly 19)*
**Mick's Yer Man 106** *(6f,Asc,S,Apr 30)*
**Micras 105** *(10f,Nmk,G,Sep 26)*
**Midnite Angel 107** *(8f,Nmk,S,Jun 28)*
**Mighty Yar 107** *(14f,Yor,G,Aug 23)*
**Milly's Gift 111** *(5f,Asc,GF,Jly 12)*
**Mime Dance 105** *(8f,Bri,G,Aug 6)*
**Min Alemarat 108** *(12f,Sal,S,May 4)*
**Minalisa 108** *(6f,Sal,GF,Jun 15)*
**Mindurownbusiness 110** *(8½f,Eps,GF,Jly 10)*
**Mindy 107** *(12f,Cur,S,May 25)*
**Miner's Lamp 109** *(12f,Asc,GF,Jun 20)*
**Miracle Of Medinah 109** *(7f,Chs,GF,Jly 12)*
**Mirza 110** *(5f,Lon,G,Oct 5)*
**Mishaal 110** *(8f,Crl,G,Jly 27)*
**Mishko 105** *(12f,Nmk,GF,Aug 1)*
**Miss France 111** *(10½f,Cha,G,Jun 15)*
**Miss Marjurie 109** *(12f,Eps,G,Jun 7)*
**Miss Tree 105** *(12f,Cat,S,Jun 6)*
**Mission Approved 109** *(6f,Goo,GF,Aug 2)*
**Missunited 108** *(16f,Asc,S,Apr 30)*
**Mister Fizz 105** *(13f,Nby,S,Aug 15)*
**Mister Manannan 106** *(5f,Don,G,Jly 10)*
**Mister Musicmaster 108** *(8f,Chp,GF,Jly 11)*
**Mistiroc 108** *(10½f,Hay,G,Sep 5)*
**Mizzava 108** *(10f,Leo,YS,Oct 25)*
**Mizzou 110** *(14f,Asc,G,Oct 3)*
**Mogadishio 106** *(8f,Lon,G,Sep 14)*
**Moidore 106** *(16f,Ncs,S,May 30)*
**Moment In Time 108** *(12f,Nby,G,Aug 3)*
**Momo No Sekku 109** *(9f,Lon,VS,Apr 27)*
**Mon Brav 106** *(6f,Cat,S,Jun 6)*
**Monarch Maid 105** *(5f,Lin,G,Jun 7)*
**Monsieur Chevalier 106** *(7f,Nby,GF,May 17)*
**Monsieur Joe 113** *(5f,Cur,GF,Jun 28)*
**Montaly 107** *(16f,Asc,GF,Jun 20)*
**Montiridge 108** *(8f,San,S,Apr 25)*
**Montviron 105** *(12f,Lon,G,Oct 5)*
**Monumental Man 106** *(5f,Bat,F,Jly 15)*
**Moonday Sun 105** *(9f,Goo,G,Aug 23)*
**Morache Music 109** *(7f,Hay,GS,Sep 4)*
**Morning Frost 105** *(7f,Cur,G,May 5)*
**Moscato 110** *(16f,Ncs,G,Sep 23)*
**Moshe 108** *(12f,Lei,GF,Sep 22)*
**Mount Athos 106** *(13f,Nby,GF,May 17)*
**Mount Logan 110** *(12f,Don,G,Sep 13)*
**Move In Time 113** *(5f,Lon,G,Oct 5)*
**Move To Strike 105** *(8f,Cur,G,Aug 31)*

**Moviesta 115** *(5f,Yor,G,Aug 22)*
**Mr Gatsby 106** *(8f,Ncs,GF,Sep 5)*
**Mr Good Guy 106** *(5f,Cur,GF,Sep 28)*
**Mr Pommeroy 108** *(10½f,Cha,G,Jun 1)*
**Mr Win 107** *(7f,Lin,G,Jun 28)*
**Mu'Ajiza 109** *(6f,Pon,G,Aug 17)*
**Mubaraza 109** *(16f,Rip,GS,Apr 26)*
**Muffin McLeay 107** *(10f,Rip,G,Jun 18)*
**Muharrer 108** *(8f,Ayr,G,Jly 21)*
**Muhawalah 106** *(10f,Bri,GF,Aug 8)*
**Mujazif 107** *(7f,Don,HY,Nov 8)*
**Mukhadram 120** *(12f,Asc,G,Jly 26)*
**Mull Of Killough 112** *(9f,Nmk,G,Apr 17)*
**Multi Bene 107** *(8f,Hay,S,Jun 11)*
**Munfallet 105** *(6f,Ham,G,Sep 21)*
**Mushir 111** *(7f,Thi,GF,Aug 1)*
**Mushreq 113** *(9f,Mey,GS,Jan 9)*
**Music In The Rain 107** *(7f,Cat,G,Apr 23)*
**Music Master 111** *(6f,War,G,Apr 24)*
**Musical Comedy 107** *(6f,Nby,G,May 16)*
**Mustadaam 105** *(10f,Lei,GF,Jly 17)*
**Mustajeeb 114** *(7f,Asc,G,Jun 18)*
**Mustamir 107** *(16f,Ncs,G,Sep 23)*
**Mutafaakir 106** *(6f,Lei,G,Apr 26)*
**Mutakayyef 110** *(9f,Nmk,S,Oct 17)*
**Mutatis Mutandis 108** *(10f,Nmk,G,Oct 11)*
**Muteela 111** *(8f,Asc,GF,Jun 18)*
**Muthmir 115** *(6f,Don,G,Sep 13)*
**Mutual Regard 114** *(14f,Yor,G,Aug 23)*
**Muwaary 112** *(7f,Asc,G,Jun 18)*
**My Ambivalent 113** *(10½f,Yor,GS,May 15)*
**My Good Brother 105** *(5f,Cur,G,Jly 20)*
**My Name Is Rio 106** *(6f,Ncs,G,Apr 24)*
**My Single Malt 106** *(7½f,Chs,GS,Aug 3)*
**My Spirit 109** *(10f,Sal,GF,Aug 13)*
**Myboyalfie 106** *(8f,War,G,Apr 24)*

**Naadirr 109** *(6f,Nmk,GF,Aug 23)*
**Nabatean 111** *(11½f,Lin,G,Jun 5)*
**Nabucco 108** *(10f,Nby,G,Jly 19)*
**Nakuti 105** *(7f,Eps,G,Jun 6)*
**Nameitwhatyoulike 105** *(7f,Thi,G,Sep 16)*
**Nancy From Nairobi 106** *(10f,Goo,G,Sep 24)*
**Narniyn 113** *(10f,Dea,VS,Aug 24)*
**Narrow Hill 116** *(15½f,Lon,VS,Oct 26)*
**Nashville 107** *(17½f,Ayr,G,Sep 19)*
**Native Heart 108** *(7f,Lei,HY,May 27)*
**Nautilus 109** *(13f,Nmk,GF,Aug 23)*
**Navajo Chief 110** *(8f,Yor,GS,May 15)*
**Nearly Caught 110** *(14f,Yor,G,Aug 23)*
**Neatico 113** *(9f,Lon,S,May 25)*
**Ned's Indian 109** *(10f,Leo,GF,Jly 17)*
**New Bidder 105** *(6f,Pon,S,Apr 8)*
**New Fforest 105** *(5f,Eps,G,Jun 7)*
**New Street 106** *(10½f,Hay,GF,Jun 21)*
**News At Six 106** *(12f,Cur,GF,Jun 27)*
**Newsroom 108** *(11f,Lon,GS,May 11)*
**Newstead Abbey 108** *(7f,Hay,G,Apr 26)*
**Niceofyoutotellme 113** *(9f,Nmk,GF,Sep 27)*
**Nicholascopernicus 107** *(10f,Wdr,S,Aug 11)*
**Night Of Thunder 113** *(8f,Nmk,GF,May 3)*
**Ninjago 109** *(6f,Goo,GF,Aug 2)*
**No Dominion 107** *(8f,Cur,S,Aug 10)*
**No Leaf Clover 108** *(6f,Nmk,S,Jly 11)*
**No Poppy 107** *(8½f,Yor,S,Oct 10)*
**No Win No Fee 107** *(10f,Not,GF,Jly 5)*
**Noble Gift 105** *(10f,Lei,S,Aug 10)*
**Noble Mission 118** *(10f,Asc,HY,Oct 18)*
**Noble Protector 110** *(12f,Nmk,GF,Jly 19)*
**Noble Raven 105** *(15f,Dea,S,Aug 17)*
**Noble Silk 109** *(16f,Hay,G,May 24)*
**Noble Storm 109** *(5f,Thi,G,May 17)*
**Noozhoh Canarias 114** *(7f,Lon,G,Oct 5)*
**Normal Equilibrium 108** *(5f,Lin,G,May 9)*
**Norse Blues 105** *(8f,Ayr,G,Sep 18)*
**Norse King 113** *(10½f,Lon,VS,Apr 27)*
**Norville 106** *(6f,Cur,YS,Apr 13)*
**Notarised 105** *(11½f,Yar,G,Sep 16)*
**Novirak 107** *(14f,Hay,G,Sep 6)*
**Now We Can 106** *(12f,Cha,G,Jun 1)*
**Nullarbor Sky 106** *(11½f,Yar,GF,May 20)*
**Number One London 106** *(14f,Crl,GF,Sep 10)*
**Nymphea 108** *(10f,Lon,G,Oct 5)*

**O Ma Lad 106** *(13f,Ham,GS,May 4)*
**O'Gorman 105** *(6f,Wdr,G,Jun 16)*
**Oasis Fantasy 109** *(12f,Asc,GF,Jly 12)*
**Obliterator 107** *(9f,Nmk,G,Apr 16)*
**Observational 112** *(12f,Goo,GF,Jly 30)*
**Ocean Applause 105** *(10f,Not,GF,Oct 1)*
**Ocean Tempest 111** *(8f,Asc,S,Apr 30)*
**Ode To Psyche 107** *(10f,Leo,SH,Mar 30)*
**Odeliz 110** *(10½f,Yor,GS,May 15)*
**Odeon 115** *(10½f,Yor,GS,May 15)*
**Odisseia 106** *(8f,Asc,GF,Jun 18)*
**Oetzi 105** *(10f,Nby,G,Apr 12)*
**Off Art 105** *(8f,Don,S,Mar 29)*
**Off The Pulse 107** *(8f,Hay,S,May 29)*
**Olympic Glory 119** *(8f,Nby,GF,May 17)*
**One Chance 106** *(5f,San,G,Jun 14)*
**One Pekan 105** *(10f,Ayr,GF,Jun 21)*
**One Pursuit 106** *(12f,Don,S,Jun 7)*
**One Spirit 106** *(8f,Leo,YS,May 11)*

**Onenightidreamed 108** *(8f,Cur,SH,May 24)*
**Online Alexander 107** *(5f,Yor,G,Aug 23)*
**Oor Jock 105** *(6f,Leo,S,Aug 14)*
**Open Eagle 111** *(10f,Red,S,Nov 4)*
**Orbit The Moon 105** *(6f,Ncs,G,Apr 24)*
**Orchestra 108** *(12f,Chs,S,May 8)*
**Oriental Fox 110** *(16f,Asc,S,Apr 30)*
**Osteopathic Remedy 107** *(8f,Thi,G,May 3)*
**Our Boy Jack 108** *(7f,Ayr,S,Oct 9)*
**Our Channel 107** *(8f,Goo,GF,Aug 1)*
**Our Folly 109** *(16f,Nmk,GS,Oct 31)*
**Our Gabrial 108** *(14f,Yor,G,Aug 23)*
**Our Queenie 108** *(6f,Nmk,GF,Jly 26)*
**Out Do 110** *(6f,Rip,G,Aug 16)*
**Out Of Bounds 106** *(10f,Nby,G,Jly 19)*
**Outback Traveller 110** *(7f,Nmk,F,Aug 2)*
**Outstrip 106** *(8f,Nmk,G,Sep 26)*

**Pacific Heights 109** *(7f,Chs,GS,May 31)*
**Paddy The Celeb 105** *(16f,Cur,GF,Aug 24)*
**Paene Magnus 108** *(8f,Cur,GF,Jun 28)*
**Pal Of The Cat 105** *(5f,Wdr,G,Apr 14)*
**Palace 111** *(8f,Leo,S,Aug 14)*
**Pale Mimosa 116** *(20f,Lon,G,Oct 5)*
**Palerma 105** *(8f,Sal,GF,Jun 15)*
**Pallasator 113** *(14f,Cur,GF,Sep 14)*
**Panama Hat 107** *(10f,Leo,G,Jun 12)*
**Pandar 108** *(5f,Goo,GS,May 3)*
**Pandorica 105** *(10f,Chp,S,Jun 2)*
**Papa's Way 107** *(14f,Leo,GF,Jly 24)*
**Parbold 106** *(8f,Nmk,GS,Jly 10)*
**Parish Hall 111** *(10f,Cur,GF,Jun 29)*
**Pasaka Boy 109** *(10f,Nmk,G,Oct 11)*
**Pashan Garh 105** *(7f,Chp,S,Jun 2)*
**Pass Muster 105** *(16f,Mus,GF,Apr 20)*
**Past Forgetting 106** *(10f,Red,G,Sep 24)*
**Pastoral Player 105** *(8f,Nmk,GS,Nov 1)*
**Patentar 109** *(7f,Lin,GF,Sep 13)*
**Patterned 106** *(9f,Goo,GF,Jly 30)*
**Pavlosk 108** *(7f,Lin,G,May 10)*
**Pea Shooter 105** *(5f,Don,G,Sep 10)*
**Peace Burg 111** *(7f,Cur,G,May 5)*
**Peace Seeker 106** *(5f,Yar,GF,May 20)*
**Pearl Blue 105** *(5f,Nmk,GS,Jly 10)*
**Pearl Nation 107** *(7f,Hay,G,Sep 5)*
**Pearl Of Africa 111** *(8f,Leo,G,Jun 12)*
**Pearl Secret 113** *(5f,Hay,S,May 24)*
**Pelerin 110** *(8f,Nmk,G,Sep 26)*
**Pencil Hill 106** *(5f,Cur,GF,Sep 28)*
**Penhill 109** *(14f,Yor,G,Aug 23)*
**Penitent 108** *(7f,Chs,GF,Jly 12)*
**Penny Drops 110** *(6f,Nmk,G,Oct 4)*
**Penny's Boy 105** *(10f,Sal,G,Oct 1)*
**Perfect Alchemy 106** *(6f,Wdr,GS,Aug 10)*
**Perfect Blessings 110** *(6f,Don,S,Apr 26)*
**Perfect Cracker 106** *(10f,Wdr,GF,Jun 9)*
**Perfect Heart 106** *(16½f,Don,S,Apr 25)*
**Perfect Muse 106** *(5f,Sal,G,Sep 12)*
**Perfect Persuasion 106** *(7f,Lei,GF,Jly 17)*
**Persian Bolt 105** *(7f,Lei,GF,Jly 5)*
**Peterkin 109** *(5f,Chs,GF,Jly 11)*
**Pether's Moon 109** *(12f,Asc,GF,Jun 21)*
**Photo Call 106** *(8f,Cur,GF,Jly 19)*
**Piazon 107** *(5f,Asc,GF,Jly 27)*
**Piceno 105** *(7½f,Chs,G,Jun 14)*
**Picks Pinta 106** *(8f,Bri,GF,Jly 17)*
**Pilgrims Rest 105** *(12f,Hay,GS,Sep 4)*
**Pilote 110** *(8f,Cha,G,Jun 15)*
**Pinturicchio 113** *(8f,Cha,G,Jun 15)*
**Pinzolo 108** *(11½f,Wdr,G,Aug 23)*
**Pipers Note 108** *(6f,Rip,G,Aug 4)*
**Piri Wango 108** *(7f,Leo,GF,Sep 13)*
**Pit Stop 105** *(8f,Cur,GF,Sep 28)*
**Pixie Cut 105** *(13f,Ham,GS,May 4)*
**Poetic Verse 106** *(12f,Cat,G,Sep 20)*
**Point The Toes 107** *(17f,Crl,G,Aug 4)*
**Polar Eyes 106** *(10f,Nby,S,Oct 24)*
**Polished Rock 106** *(12f,Cur,Y,Apr 13)*
**Pollyana 114** *(9f,Lon,S,May 25)*
**Polski Max 105** *(6f,Rip,G,Aug 16)*
**Polybius 106** *(6f,Wdr,GF,Jly 21)*
**Pomology 111** *(12f,Hay,GS,Jly 5)*
**Pop Art 108** *(7f,Cur,Y,Apr 13)*
**Port Merrion 107** *(7f,Cur,S,Aug 10)*
**Postponed 116** *(12f,Yor,GF,Aug 20)*
**Postscript 105** *(8f,Hay,GF,Jun 21)*
**Potent Embrace 106** *(10½f,Chs,G,Sep 13)*
**Potentate 105** *(8½f,Eps,GF,Jly 31)*
**Powerful Presence 108** *(7f,Ayr,GS,Jly 14)*
**Powerful Wind 105** *(5f,Bri,GF,Jun 24)*
**Poyle Thomas 106** *(15f,Nmk,G,May 31)*
**Precision Strike 105** *(14f,Hay,GS,Jly 19)*
**Presburg 108** *(10f,Wdr,G,Aug 23)*
**Prestige Vendome 105** *(10½f,Cha,G,Jun 1)*
**Pretzel 109** *(8f,Nmk,G,May 31)*
**Primogeniture 106** *(16f,Cur,GF,Aug 24)*
**Prince Connoisseur 109** *(5f,Cur,GF,Sep 28)*
**Prince Gibraltar 116** *(12f,Lon,G,Oct 5)*
**Prince Of All 105** *(10f,Leo,GF,Sep 13)*
**Prince Of Johanne 109** *(8f,San,GF,Jly 5)*
**Princess Loulou 115** *(10f,Dea,VS,Aug 24)*
**Privet Hedge 105** *(9f,Lon,VS,Apr 27)*
**Producer 110** *(8f,Asc,G,Jun 17)*
**Professor 111** *(7f,Nby,GS,Aug 16)*
**Progenitor 105** *(12f,Cur,GF,Jun 29)*
**Provenance 111** *(8f,Nmk,G,Sep 26)*
**Psychometry 107** *(8f,Asc,GF,Jun 18)*
**Pucon 112** *(5f,Goo,G,Sep 24)*
**Pupil 106** *(8½f,Eps,G,Sep 28)*
**Purple Spectrum 107** *(14f,San,GF,Jly 24)*
**Purr Along 111** *(8f,Asc,GF,Jun 18)*
**Pyromaniac 109** *(10f,Leo,G,Jun 6)*

**Qanan 106** *(10f,Yar,G,Sep 17)*
**Qewy 108** *(8f,Leo,S,Aug 14)*
**Queen Catrine 110** *(8f,Asc,GF,Jun 18)*
**Queen Of Alba 109** *(10f,Leo,YS,Oct 25)*
**Queen Of Ice 112** *(12f,Nmk,G,Sep 26)*
**Queensberry Rules 109** *(10½f,Yor,G,Aug 23)*
**Quest For Peace 105** *(11½f,Wdr,G,Aug 23)*
**Quick Jack 106** *(18f,Nmk,G,Oct 11)*
**Quick Wit 110** *(9f,Nmk,GF,Sep 27)*
**Quiz Mistress 108** *(12f,Hay,GS,May 31)*

**Racy 110** *(5f,Asc,GF,Jly 27)*
**Rainbow Rock 109** *(10f,Goo,GF,Jly 31)*
**Raise Your Gaze 109** *(10f,San,GF,Jly 5)*
**Ralphy Boy 105** *(7f,Mus,G,Aug 8)*
**Ramone 107** *(8f,Cur,GF,Sep 28)*
**Random Success 106** *(5f,Nby,G,Aug 3)*
**Rangali 113** *(5f,Yor,G,Aug 22)*
**Rangi Chase 106** *(8f,Pon,S,Oct 6)*
**Rapid Advance 106** *(9f,Goo,G,Aug 23)*
**Rapprochement 108** *(8f,Nmk,GF,Jly 18)*
**Rasaman 105** *(5f,Ayr,GS,May 21)*
**Raskova 108** *(10½f,Yor,GF,Jly 25)*
**Rasmy 107** *(9f,Mey,GS,Jan 9)*
**Rasselas 107** *(9f,Crl,G,Aug 4)*
**Rawaki 110** *(12f,Nby,G,Apr 12)*
**Rawnaq 106** *(16f,Cur,GF,Jun 28)*
**Rawoof 106** *(11½f,Yar,GF,Aug 19)*
**Ray Ward 107** *(21f,Goo,GF,Jly 30)*
**Razor Wind 106** *(10f,Nmk,S,Jly 11)*
**Reckless Abandon 110** *(6f,Nmk,GF,Aug 23)*
**Red Avenger 110** *(8f,Goo,GF,Aug 1)*
**Red Baron 108** *(5f,Mus,S,Jun 14)*
**Red Galileo 107** *(12f,Nmk,G,Sep 26)*
**Red Lips 113** *(10f,Dea,VS,Aug 24)*
**Red Pike 108** *(6f,Don,GS,Oct 24)*
**Red Refraction 109** *(7f,Don,S,Jun 7)*
**Red Warrior 105** *(10f,Yar,G,Apr 22)*
**Redbrook 105** *(7f,Asc,G,Jun 18)*
**Redkirk 107** *(10f,Yar,GF,Jun 26)*
**Redvers 107** *(7f,Asc,GF,Sep 6)*
**Ree's Rascal 107** *(8f,Nby,GS,May 31)*
**Refractor 105** *(10f,Leo,G,Jun 6)*
**Refuse Colette 107** *(6f,Yar,GF,Jly 24)*
**Regal Parade 105** *(6f,Eps,G,Jun 7)*
**Regardez 108** *(10½f,Yor,GF,Jly 25)*
**Regulation 105** *(8f,Asc,GF,Jun 18)*
**Rekdhat 107** *(8f,Mus,GF,Sep 28)*
**Related 109** *(7f,Lei,GF,Jly 5)*
**Relation Alexander 105** *(7f,Lei,GF,Jly 17)*
**Relight My Fire 105** *(7½f,Bev,GF,Jly 4)*
**Remember 114** *(6f,Nmk,S,Jly 11)*
**Rene Mathis 109** *(6f,Nmk,G,May 31)*
**Renew 105** *(11½f,Wdr,G,Aug 23)*
**Repeater 108** *(14f,Yor,G,Aug 23)*
**Repetition 105** *(7f,Chs,GF,Jly 11)*
**Reroute 111** *(5f,Bat,F,Apr 19)*
**Rerouted 106** *(8f,Sal,GF,Aug 14)*
**Resurge 105** *(10f,Eps,G,Jun 6)*
**Retirement Plan 111** *(14f,Yor,G,Aug 23)*
**Rewaaya 110** *(12f,Lei,S,Oct 27)*
**Rex Imperator 109** *(6f,Wdr,G,Jun 2)*
**Ribbons 117** *(10f,Dea,VS,Aug 24)*
**Right Touch 107** *(6f,Don,GS,May 3)*
**Rio Tigre 113** *(15f,Lon,G,Oct 4)*
**Rising Breeze 105** *(10f,Not,GF,Jly 5)*
**Rite To Reign 112** *(16f,Nmk,GS,Oct 31)*
**Rivellino 108** *(6f,Asc,GF,Jun 21)*
**Rizal Park 105** *(8½f,Eps,G,Sep 11)*
**Rizeena 109** *(8f,Nmk,S,Jly 11)*
**Roachdale House 108** *(7f,Chs,GS,Jun 28)*
**Robert The Painter 108** *(8½f,Not,S,Apr 9)*
**Robot Boy 111** *(5f,Cur,GF,Sep 14)*
**Rock Choir 110** *(10f,Not,GF,Jun 16)*
**Rocket Ronnie 105** *(8½f,Bev,GF,Jly 29)*
**Rocket Ship 106** *(12f,Pon,GF,Aug 6)*
**Rockfella 107** *(14f,Sal,S,May 4)*
**Rocky Ground 112** *(6f,Wdr,G,Jun 2)*
**Roheryn 110** *(12f,Leo,Y,Aug 7)*
**Romeo Montague 105** *(16f,Nby,G,Jly 19)*
**Romsdal 110** *(12f,Eps,G,Jun 7)*
**Rosairlie 105** *(16f,Ncs,S,May 30)*
**Roseburg 108** *(10½f,Hay,GS,Jly 5)*
**Rosehill Artist 106** *(10f,Sal,GF,Jun 10)*
**Roserrow 109** *(9f,Yor,G,Jun 14)*
**Rothesay Chancer 106** *(5f,Mus,S,Jun 7)*
**Rouge Nuage 106** *(7½f,Bev,GF,Sep 23)*
**Rough Courte 105** *(7f,Red,GS,Apr 7)*
**Roxy Lane 108** *(8f,Nmk,GF,Jun 20)*
**Royal Birth 105** *(5f,Bat,F,Sep 29)*
**Royal Diamond 115** *(14f,Cur,GF,Aug 24)*
**Royal Encounter 106** *(8½f,Not,GF,Sep 23)*
**Royal Flag 109** *(8f,Nmk,G,Aug 22)*
**Royal Rascal 108** *(7f,Ncs,GF,Jun 28)*
**Royal Rock 109** *(6f,Yar,G,Sep 16)*
**Royal Seal 108** *(7f,Yar,GF,May 20)*
**Ruby Tuesday 106** *(10f,Leo,SH,Mar 30)*
**Ruler Of The World 116** *(12f,Lon,G,Oct 5)*
**Run Fat Lass Run 106** *(8f,Ncs,G,May 20)*
**Run With Pride 106** *(6f,Don,G,Sep 11)*
**Running Deer 109** *(10½f,Chs,G,Jun 14)*
**Rural Celebration 106** *(5f,Cat,S,May 30)*
**Russian Realm 109** *(8f,San,GF,Jly 5)*
**Russian Soul 111** *(5f,Cur,GF,Sep 14)*
**Rusty Rocket 105** *(5f,Ncs,S,Apr 5)*
**Ruwaiyan 108** *(6f,Goo,GF,Aug 2)*
**Ruwasi 107** *(12f,Nmk,G,Oct 4)*
**Rydan 105** *(10f,San,GF,Jly 4)*
**Rye House 105** *(10½f,Yor,S,May 14)*

**Saab Almanal 114** *(10½f,Yor,GS,May 15)*
**Safety Check 108** *(7f,Asc,GF,Sep 6)*
**Sahrawi 108** *(11f,Lon,GS,May 11)*
**Sailors Warn 106** *(15f,Leo,Y,Oct 26)*
**Saint Gervais 106** *(16f,Cur,Y,Oct 12)*
**Saltwater Creek 105** *(10f,Pon,G,Apr 30)*
**Salutation 109** *(10f,Goo,G,Jly 29)*
**Salvatore Fury 105** *(5f,Goo,GF,Jly 29)*
**Samtu 106** *(10½f,Hay,GS,May 31)*
**San Cassiano 106** *(10f,Rip,G,Apr 17)*
**Sandiva 105** *(7f,Nmk,G,Apr 16)*
**Saoi 105** *(10f,Not,GF,Jly 31)*
**Sarangoo 105** *(6f,Wdr,GS,Jly 7)*
**Satanic Beat 106** *(12f,Ham,GS,Aug 22)*
**Satanicjim 109** *(15½f,Lon,VS,Oct 26)*
**Saucy Minx 106** *(7f,San,G,Sep 12)*
**Save The Bees 108** *(10f,Red,G,Sep 24)*
**Schottische 106** *(8f,Ffo,GS,Aug 12)*
**Scooping 108** *(10f,Leo,G,Jun 12)*
**Scotland 114** *(12f,Goo,GF,Jly 30)*
**Scottish Glen 106** *(7f,Asc,GF,Jly 12)*
**Scream Blue Murder 110** *(6f,Cur,S,Aug 10)*
**Sea Shanty 108** *(8f,San,G,Jun 14)*
**Sea The Bloom 105** *(12f,Chp,G,Jun 13)*
**Seagull 105** *(10f,Sal,GF,Jun 10)*
**Seal Of Approval 110** *(12f,Asc,HY,Oct 18)*
**Seanie 108** *(7f,Leo,Y,Oct 26)*
**Sebastian Beach 108** *(14f,Yor,G,Aug 23)*
**Second Step 108** *(12f,Goo,GF,Aug 2)*
**Secondo 106** *(6f,Ffo,G,Aug 22)*
**Secret Art 108** *(8f,San,GF,Jly 5)*
**Secret Gesture 114** *(10f,Dea,VS,Aug 24)*
**Secret Hint 106** *(6f,Don,G,Jly 10)*
**Secret Millionaire 106** *(5f,Bat,F,Jly 15)*
**Secret Missile 106** *(5f,Nmk,S,Aug 14)*
**Secret Pursuit 108** *(11½f,Chs,G,May 7)*
**Secret Witness 109** *(5f,Yor,GS,May 31)*
**Secretinthepark 107** *(6f,Nmk,GF,May 4)*
**Security Breach 105** *(12f,Cur,GF,Jun 29)*
**See And Be Seen 106** *(16f,Nby,G,Jly 19)*
**See The Storm 106** *(6f,Red,G,Jly 20)*
**See The Sun 110** *(6f,Nmk,S,Jly 11)*
**Seeking Magic 110** *(5f,Eps,G,Jun 7)*
**Self Employed 105** *(8f,Don,G,Jun 15)*
**Semeen 109** *(14f,Yar,G,Sep 18)*
**Senafe 105** *(7f,Don,S,Jun 7)*
**Sennockian Star 110** *(10f,Eps,GS,Apr 23)*
**Serena Grae 107** *(8f,Chp,GF,Jun 23)*
**Serenity Spa 105** *(6f,War,S,Aug 25)*
**Shadowtime 106** *(8½f,Bev,GF,Jly 29)*
**Shama's Crown 106** *(10f,San,G,Sep 17)*
**Shamkala 112** *(10½f,Cha,G,Jun 15)*
**Shamkiyr 110** *(10½f,Cha,G,Jun 1)*
**Shanooan 109** *(8f,Cur,GF,Jly 19)*
**Shared Account 108** *(12½f,Lon,G,Oct 4)*
**Shared Equity 106** *(7f,Ncs,GS,Aug 15)*
**Sharestan 107** *(12f,Asc,GF,Jun 21)*
**She's Mine 105** *(10f,Leo,SH,Mar 30)*
**Shea Shea 109** *(5f,Yor,G,Aug 22)*
**Sheikhzayedroad 113** *(10½f,Yor,GF,Jly 26)*
**Sheila's Buddy 105** *(10f,Nby,G,Apr 12)*
**Shifting Power 110** *(8f,Nmk,GF,May 4)*
**Shining Emerald 105** *(8f,Leo,SH,Mar 30)*
**Shipyard 107** *(5f,Cur,GF,Sep 28)*
**Shore Step 107** *(6f,Don,G,Jun 15)*
**Short Squeeze 111** *(8f,Yor,G,Aug 21)*
**Shot In The Sun 105** *(7f,Eps,G,Jun 6)*
**Shouranour 106** *(10f,Rip,G,Jun 18)*
**Show Court 106** *(10f,Leo,Y,Oct 26)*
**Showboating 107** *(7f,Thi,GS,Apr 12)*
**Shrewd 105** *(14f,Hay,G,Sep 6)*
**Shu Lewis 115** *(14f,Cur,GF,Aug 24)*
**Shukhov 106** *(10f,Leo,Y,Oct 26)*
**Side Glance 106** *(8f,Asc,G,Jun 17)*
**Signs Of Blessing 110** *(5f,Lon,GS,May 11)*
**Silas Marner 112** *(8f,Cha,G,Jun 15)*
**Silent Bullet 108** *(7f,San,G,Jun 14)*
**Siljan's Saga 115** *(12f,Lon,G,Oct 5)*
**Silk Hall 107** *(14f,Leo,SH,Mar 30)*
**Silk Sari 113** *(14½f,Don,GS,Sep 11)*
**Silvanus 108** *(5f,Mus,GF,Apr 18)*
**Silver Chief 105** *(14f,Leo,G,Jun 6)*
**Silver Rime 110** *(7f,Ayr,GF,Jly 7)*
**Silvery Moon 109** *(10f,Nby,S,Oct 25)*
**Silwana 108** *(14f,Leo,GF,Sep 13)*
**Simply Shining 105** *(8½f,Not,GF,Jly 5)*
**Sinaadi 105** *(10f,Not,GF,Jun 16)*
**Singeur 108** *(5f,Yor,GS,May 31)*
**Sinkal 106** *(10f,Cur,Y,Apr 13)*
**Siouxperhero 108** *(8f,Bri,GF,Jly 17)*
**Sir Frank Morgan 106** *(16f,Asc,GS,May 9)*
**Sir Guy Porteous 109** *(8½f,Eps,GF,Jly 10)*
**Sir Maximilian 111** *(5f,Cur,GF,Sep 14)*
**Sir Mike 106** *(8f,Yar,G,Apr 22)*
**Sir Oscar 110** *(7f,Lon,G,Sep 7)*
**Sir Reginald 108** *(7f,Don,S,Jun 7)*
**Sir Walter Scott 110** *(14f,Yor,G,Aug 23)*
**Sirius Prospect 109** *(7f,Yor,GS,May 31)*
**Sirvino 108** *(13f,Ham,GS,May 4)*
**Sixties Love 105** *(8½f,Eps,G,Sep 11)*
**Sizzler 106** *(20f,Asc,G,Jun 17)*
**Sky Hunter 113** *(12f,Nby,S,Oct 25)*
**Sky Lantern 109** *(8f,Asc,GF,Jun 18)*
**Skye's The Limit 106** *(5f,Thi,S,Aug 11)*
**Skytrain 105** *(8f,Goo,GF,Jly 29)*
**Slade Power 113** *(6f,Cur,SH,May 24)*
**Sli Na Fiarana 106** *(10f,Leo,Y,Oct 26)*
**Slip Sliding Away 107** *(6f,Goo,GF,Aug 2)*
**Smart Daisy K 106** *(5f,Bat,F,Sep 13)*
**Smiling Stranger 106** *(10f,Nby,G,Jly 19)*
**Smoking Sun 112** *(10½f,Lon,VS,Apr 27)*
**Smoothtalkinrascal 108** *(5f,Mus,GF,Apr 18)*
**Snow Scene 105** *(10f,Leo,G,Jun 6)*
**Snow Sky 116** *(12f,Goo,GF,Jly 30)*
**Snow Squall 105** *(10½f,Yor,G,Jun 13)*
**Snowmane 106** *(14f,Leo,GF,Jly 24)*
**Snowy Dawn 111** *(16f,Nmk,GS,Oct 31)*
**So Long Malpic 111** *(6½f,Dea,HY,Aug 10)*
**Soft Falling Rain 110** *(8f,Asc,G,Jun 17)*
**Sohar 111** *(16f,Nmk,GS,Oct 31)*
**Sole Power 117** *(5f,Yor,G,Aug 22)*
**Solow 111** *(8f,Lon,G,Oct 4)*
**Somewhat 116** *(10f,San,GF,Jly 5)*
**Sommerabend 113** *(6½f,Dea,HY,Aug 10)*
**Sophie's World 106** *(8f,Cur,G,Aug 31)*
**Soul Brother 107** *(5f,Ncs,G,May 20)*
**Sound Advice 106** *(8f,Red,GF,Jun 20)*
**Soviet Rock 109** *(10f,Lin,G,May 10)*
**Spa's Dancer 109** *(10f,Red,GS,May 26)*
**Space Artist 105** *(5f,Mus,GF,Jly 22)*
**Space Walker 105** *(10f,Wdr,HY,Oct 20)*
**Spacious Sky 109** *(15f,Leo,Y,Oct 26)*
**Sparkle Factor 109** *(7f,Cur,GF,Jun 28)*
**Sparkling Beam 110** *(8f,Cha,G,Jun 15)*
**Special Fighter 106** *(14f,Cat,GF,Aug 5)*
**Special Meaning 108** *(12f,Goo,GS,May 3)*
**Specific Gravity 106** *(10f,Leo,Y,Oct 26)*
**Spectator 107** *(14½f,Don,S,Oct 24)*
**Speed Hawk 106** *(5f,Asc,GF,Jly 12)*
**Spice Fair 107** *(14f,San,G,Jun 14)*
**Spinatrix 110** *(6f,Pon,G,Aug 17)*
**Spirit Of The Law 110** *(9f,Yor,G,Jun 14)*
**Spirit Quartz 112** *(5f,Lon,G,Oct 5)*
**Spiritjim 113** *(12f,Lon,G,Oct 5)*
**Spiritoftheunion 107** *(12f,Rip,G,Aug 4)*
**Spoil The Fun 112** *(8f,Cha,G,Jun 15)*
**Spring Fling 105** *(6f,Sal,S,May 4)*
**Squire Osbaldeston 106** *(10½f,Chs,S,May 8)*
**Sretaw 110** *(8f,Cur,G,Aug 31)*
**Srucahan 107** *(6f,Cur,YS,Apr 13)*
**Sruthan 113** *(7f,Cur,Y,Apr 13)*
**St Moritz 107** *(8f,San,G,Jun 14)*
**Stand My Ground 107** *(8f,Don,S,Mar 29)*
**Starwatch 107** *(8f,Wdr,GS,Aug 10)*
**Statsminister 107** *(14f,Sal,GF,Aug 14)*
**Stay De Night 107** *(7f,Leo,GF,Sep 13)*
**Steeler 109** *(8f,Goo,GF,Aug 1)*
**Stella Bellissima 105** *(12f,Nby,G,Jly 3)*
**Stellar Express 106** *(8f,Pon,G,Apr 14)*
**Stellar Path 111** *(8f,Cha,G,Jun 1)*
**Stepper Point 116** *(5f,Yor,G,Aug 22)*
**Stepping Ahead 108** *(10f,Pon,S,Apr 8)*
**Steps 110** *(5f,Hay,GS,May 31)*
**Stetchworth 105** *(10f,Red,G,Oct 4)*
**Stomachion 107** *(12f,Eps,G,Jun 7)*
**Storm King 106** *(7½f,Bev,GF,Aug 30)*
**Stormardal 107** *(10f,Rip,GF,Aug 26)*
**Stormyra 112** *(8f,Cha,G,Jun 1)*
**Story Writer 106** *(16f,Goo,S,May 22)*
**Storyline 105** *(5f,Red,GF,May 19)*
**Strait Of Zanzibar 105** *(8f,Cur,G,Aug 31)*
**Strandfield Lady 108** *(14f,Leo,GF,Jly 24)*
**Streetcar To Stars 115** *(14f,Cur,GF,Aug 24)*
**Strictly Silver 106** *(10f,Ayr,GF,Jun 21)*
**Stronger Than Me 108** *(10f,Leo,Y,Oct 26)*
**Stuccodor 111** *(8f,Cur,SH,Mar 23)*
**Sudden Wonder 111** *(10½f,Yor,GS,Oct 11)*
**Suegioo 110** *(14f,Yor,G,Aug 23)*
**Sultanina 109** *(12f,Hay,GS,May 31)*
**Sundara 106** *(12f,Leo,YS,May 11)*
**Sunny Future 107** *(14f,Sal,GF,Jun 29)*
**Sunraider 107** *(6f,Pon,GF,Sep 25)*
**Supplicant 109** *(6f,Nmk,S,Jly 11)*
**Supposing 105** *(7f,Leo,S,Aug 14)*
**Suzi's Connoisseur 110** *(6f,Nmk,S,Jly 11)*
**Swacadelic 110** *(12½f,Dea,HY,Aug 10)*
**Swan Lakes 106** *(12f,Chp,G,Jun 13)*
**Swan Song 109** *(5f,Chs,G,May 7)*
**Sweet Lightning 106** *(8f,Yor,GS,May 15)*
**Swift Cedar 105** *(7f,Lei,S,Oct 27)*
**Swing Alone 106** *(14f,Goo,G,Jun 20)*
**Swiss Cross 106** *(6f,Eps,G,Jun 7)*
**Switcher 107** *(7f,Cur,G,May 5)*

**Swivel 108** *(12f,Asc,GF,Jly 12)*
**Sylvan Mist 106** *(5f,Cur,GF,Sep 28)*
**System Overload 107** *(10f,Cur,Y,Jun 8)*

**Taajub 106** *(5f,Eps,G,Jun 7)*
**Table Rock 109** *(8f,Cur,GF,Jun 27)*
**Tac De Boistron 117** *(15½f,Lon,VS,Oct 26)*
**Taghrooda 123** *(12f,Asc,G,Jly 26)*
**Taglietelle 106** *(12f,Cur,Y,Apr 13)*
**Tagula Night 105** *(5f,San,G,Jun 14)*
**Tahaany 107** *(7f,Cur,G,May 5)*
**Tahira 107** *(10½f,Chs,G,Jun 14)*
**Take A Note 108** *(7f,Lei,G,Sep 9)*
**Take Cover 115** *(5f,Goo,GF,Aug 1)*
**Talent 107** *(12f,Hay,GS,Jly 5)*
**Talent Scout 107** *(8f,Crl,GF,Jly 5)*
**Talented Kid 105** *(8f,Lin,G,May 10)*
**Tales Of Grimm 110** *(9f,Mey,GS,Jan 9)*
**Tall Ship 110** *(12f,Goo,G,Aug 23)*
**Talmada 114** *(10f,Nmk,G,Oct 11)*
**Tamayuz Star 105** *(7f,Lei,GF,Jly 5)*
**Tangerine Trees 108** *(5f,Ham,G,Jly 1)*
**Tanseeb 107** *(8f,San,G,Jun 14)*
**Tanzeel 106** *(6f,Yar,GF,Jly 15)*
**Tapestry 115** *(12f,Lon,G,Oct 5)*
**Tarana 111** *(10f,Cur,Y,Apr 13)*
**Tarbawi 109** *(9f,Mey,GS,Jan 9)*
**Tarfasha 111** *(10f,Lon,G,Oct 5)*
**Tarikhi 108** *(9f,Yor,G,Jun 14)*
**Tariq Too 109** *(7f,Thi,GS,Apr 12)*
**Tasaday 109** *(10½f,Yor,GF,Jly 25)*
**Tasmanian 109** *(8f,Ncs,GF,Sep 5)*
**Tatlisu 110** *(6f,Ncs,GF,Jun 28)*
**Taurus Twins 108** *(5f,Not,GF,Jly 18)*
**Tawhid 110** *(7f,Nmk,S,Oct 17)*
**Taws 108** *(14f,Sal,GF,Aug 14)*
**Teak 108** *(21f,Goo,GF,Jly 30)*
**Tearless 107** *(10f,Sal,GF,Aug 13)*
**Ted Veale 107** *(14f,Yor,G,Aug 23)*
**Ted's Brother 107** *(8f,Ham,GS,May 4)*
**Teetotal 106** *(6f,Pon,S,May 23)*
**Telescope 121** *(12f,Asc,G,Jly 26)*
**Teletext 111** *(12f,Lon,G,Sep 14)*
**Telmeyd 109** *(6f,Asc,G,Oct 3)*
**Temptress 107** *(8f,Asc,GF,Jly 12)*
**Tenor 113** *(8f,Pon,GF,Jly 27)*
**Tepmokea 106** *(12f,Don,S,Jun 7)*
**Tercel 105** *(10f,Nby,GS,Sep 19)*
**Tha'ir 106** *(10f,San,GF,Jly 4)*
**That Is The Spirit 109** *(7f,Lon,G,Oct 5)*
**That's Plenty 110** *(8f,Cur,SH,Mar 23)*
**Thawaany 116** *(6½f,Dea,HY,Aug 10)*
**The Character 105** *(10f,Pon,GF,Sep 18)*
**The Corsican 110** *(10f,Don,GS,Sep 11)*
**The Dancing Lord 107** *(7f,Cur,G,Aug 23)*
**The Fugue 119** *(10f,Asc,GF,Jun 18)*
**The Grey Gatsby 118** *(10½f,Yor,GS,May 15)*
**The Hooded Claw 111** *(6f,Nmk,S,Jly 11)*
**The Lark 109** *(10½f,Yor,GS,May 15)*
**The Osteopath 105** *(8f,Ncs,G,Aug 25)*
**The Rectifier 110** *(8f,Pon,GF,Jly 27)*
**Theme Astral 111** *(15f,Lon,G,Oct 4)*
**Theophilus 107** *(10f,Leo,YS,Oct 25)*
**Third Dimension 106** *(10f,Leo,Y,Oct 26)*
**This Is The Day 108** *(10f,Nmk,G,Oct 11)*
**This Time 109** *(7f,Lon,G,Sep 7)*
**Thistle Bird 114** *(10f,Cur,GF,Jun 29)*
**Thomas Edison 108** *(12f,Cur,S,May 25)*
**Ticking Katie 109** *(8f,Ayr,GF,Sep 20)*
**Tidentime 105** *(6f,Wdr,G,Jun 16)*
**Tiger Jim 105** *(7f,Ncs,G,Sep 23)*
**Tigers Tale 111** *(9f,Nmk,GF,Sep 27)*
**Tight Fit 105** *(6f,Lei,G,Apr 26)*
**Timeless Call 109** *(5f,Cur,GF,Jun 28)*
**Times Up 113** *(16½f,Yor,G,Aug 22)*
**Tinseltown 107** *(12f,Cat,G,Apr 23)*
**Toast Of The Town 110** *(10f,Not,GF,Jun 16)*
**Tobacco Road 106** *(8f,Wdr,S,Apr 7)*
**Tobann 108** *(7f,Cur,GF,Jun 28)*
**Toe The Line 111** *(16f,Cur,GF,Sep 28)*
**Toga Tiger 107** *(9f,Yor,G,Jun 14)*
**Token Of Love 107** *(7f,Nby,GF,May 17)*
**Tonton Macoute 107** *(10f,Cur,S,May 24)*
**Toofi 106** *(6f,Nmk,G,Apr 16)*
**Tooreen Legend 108** *(12f,Cur,GF,Jun 29)*
**Toormore 113** *(8f,Nmk,G,Apr 17)*
**Top Boy 110** *(5f,Yor,GS,May 31)*
**Top Diktat 108** *(10f,Nby,G,Apr 12)*
**Top Notch Tonto 111** *(8f,Nby,GF,May 17)*
**Top Of The Glas 106** *(7½f,Chs,GS,Aug 16)*
**Topamichi 106** *(10f,Wdr,HY,Oct 20)*
**Torchlighter 107** *(10f,Nmk,G,Jly 10)*
**Toronado 114** *(8f,Asc,G,Jun 17)*
**Totalize 107** *(14f,Yor,G,Jun 13)*
**Trade Storm 108** *(9f,Yor,G,Aug 23)*
**Trader Jack 106** *(6f,Asc,GS,May 10)*
**Trading Leather 117** *(10f,San,GF,Jly 5)*
**Trail Blaze 105** *(8½f,Eps,G,Jun 6)*
**Treasure The Ridge 110** *(10f,San,GS,Aug 30)*
**Tres Coronas 110** *(10½f,Chs,S,May 8)*
**Treve 120** *(12f,Lon,G,Oct 5)*
**Trinity Star 108** *(8½f,Not,GF,Sep 23)*
**Trinityelitedotcom 105** *(5f,Chs,G,May 7)*
**Trip To Rhodos 115** *(20f,Lon,G,Oct 5)*
**Triple Chocolate 106** *(6f,Wdr,GF,Aug 4)*
**Tropics 113** *(6f,Asc,HY,Oct 18)*
**Truancy 108** *(10f,Bev,GF,Aug 30)*
**True Pleasure 105** *(7f,Cat,S,Jun 6)*
**True Story 116** *(10½f,Yor,GS,May 15)*
**Truth Or Dare 105** *(10f,Nmk,G,Oct 11)*
**Truthwillsetufree 107** *(14f,Leo,SH,Mar 30)*
**Tukitinyasok 106** *(8½f,Bev,G,Jly 5)*
**Tullia 105** *(8f,Wdr,HY,Oct 13)*
**Tullius 116** *(8f,Nby,GF,May 17)*
**Tumblewind 106** *(5f,Thi,G,May 17)*
**Two For Two 109** *(8f,Ayr,GF,Jun 21)*
**Ty Gwr 109** *(10f,Red,S,Nov 4)*
**Tylery Wonder 108** *(6f,Cur,GF,Aug 24)*

**Ultimate Act 108** *(11½f,Lin,G,Jun 5)*
**Uncle Dermot 108** *(8f,Ayr,GS,May 22)*
**Undrafted 110** *(6f,Nmk,GS,Jly 12)*
**Unison 106** *(8f,Ffo,GS,Aug 12)*
**Unsinkable 108** *(8f,Leo,YS,Oct 25)*
**Uradel 109** *(14f,Yor,G,Aug 23)*

**Valantino Oyster 110** *(10f,Red,G,Sep 24)*
**Valmina 110** *(5f,Goo,G,Sep 24)*
**Valonia 111** *(6f,Pon,G,Aug 17)*
**Vancouverite 109** *(10f,Nby,G,Jly 19)*
**Vanity Rules 110** *(12f,Nmk,G,Sep 26)*
**Vastonea 109** *(8f,Cur,G,Aug 31)*
**Vazira 115** *(9f,Lon,VS,Apr 27)*
**Veda 111** *(8f,Cha,G,Jun 1)*
**Veiled Intrigue 109** *(7f,Lin,G,May 10)*
**Velox 114** *(8f,San,GF,Jly 5)*
**Vent De Force 114** *(14f,Yor,G,Aug 23)*
**Ventura Quest 107** *(10½f,Chs,GS,Sep 27)*
**Venus De Milo 111** *(10f,Cur,GF,Jun 29)*
**Venus Grace 106** *(7f,Nby,GF,May 17)*
**Verdura 105** *(11f,Lon,GS,May 11)*
**Verrazano 115** *(8f,Nby,GF,May 17)*
**Verse Of Love 107** *(7f,Lei,G,Sep 9)*
**Victoire De Lyphar 106** *(7f,Red,S,May 1)*
**Victory Laurel 106** *(5f,Ham,G,Jly 1)*
**Vital Evidence 105** *(10f,San,GF,Jly 4)*
**Viva Verglas 105** *(5f,Chs,S,May 9)*
**Viztoria 111** *(6f,Cur,Y,Oct 12)*
**Volume 110** *(12f,Cur,GF,Jly 19)*
**Vorda 114** *(6½f,Dea,HY,Aug 10)*
**Vote Often 113** *(10f,Leo,YS,Oct 25)*

**Wadi Al Hattawi 107** *(12f,Yor,GS,May 31)*
**Wahgah 110** *(10f,Nmk,G,Oct 11)*
**Waila 110** *(12f,Pon,G,Jun 22)*
**Wall Of Sound 111** *(10f,Not,GF,Jun 16)*
**Waltzing Matilda 109** *(7f,Asc,G,Jun 18)*
**Wannabe Better 113** *(7f,Leo,GF,Jun 19)*
**Wannabe Yours 117** *(8f,Goo,GF,Aug 1)*
**War Command 113** *(10f,San,GF,Jly 5)*
**War Singer 107** *(8f,Goo,S,Oct 12)*
**Warbird 106** *(8f,Cur,G,Aug 31)*
**Waseem Faris 112** *(5f,Goo,G,Sep 24)*
**Watchable 110** *(6f,Cur,GF,Sep 14)*
**Water Hole 105** *(8f,Don,G,Jly 10)*
**Waterclock 105** *(16f,Ncs,G,Sep 23)*
**Waydownsouth 108** *(15f,Leo,Y,Oct 26)*
**We Are 112** *(10f,Lon,G,Oct 5)*
**We'll Deal Again 106** *(6f,Thi,HY,Aug 2)*
**We'll Go Walking 111** *(10f,Not,GF,Jun 16)*
**Wee Jean 110** *(8f,Asc,GF,Jun 18)*
**Weekendatbernies 107** *(8½f,Not,GF,Oct 1)*
**Welsh Inlet 106** *(8f,Bri,GF,Jly 17)*
**Western Hymn 113** *(10f,Asc,HY,Oct 18)*
**What About Carlo 107** *(10f,Eps,G,Jun 7)*
**Whim 108** *(11f,Lon,GS,May 11)*
**Whimsical 105** *(7f,Cur,GF,Jun 28)*
**Whiplash Willie 115** *(20f,Lon,G,Oct 5)*
**Whipper Snapper 105** *(8f,Lin,G,May 10)*
**Whipphound 105** *(5f,Bat,S,Apr 28)*
**Whispering Warrior 107** *(9f,Yor,G,Jun 14)*
**Whitecrest 106** *(5f,Lin,G,Jun 7)*
**Who's That Chick 107** *(8f,Asc,GF,Sep 6)*
**Whozthecat 105** *(7f,Yor,GS,Oct 10)*
**Why Not Now 105** *(8f,Bri,G,Aug 19)*
**Wigmore Hall 109** *(12f,Nmk,GS,Aug 16)*
**Wild Chief 110** *(10½f,Cha,G,Jun 1)*
**Wilde Inspiration 105** *(7f,Thi,S,Aug 2)*
**Wilhana 105** *(12½f,Ncs,GF,Jly 26)*
**Willbeme 112** *(6f,Yor,G,Jun 13)*
**William Of Orange 108** *(12f,Chp,S,Aug 14)*
**Willing Foe 116** *(14f,Cur,GF,Sep 14)*
**Willowing 105** *(12f,Cur,GF,Jun 29)*
**Wind Fire 110** *(5f,San,G,Jun 14)*
**Windfast 111** *(8f,Goo,GF,Aug 1)*
**Windhoek 112** *(10½f,Yor,GF,Jly 26)*
**Windshear 115** *(12f,Goo,GF,Jly 30)*
**Winter Lion 106** *(14f,Leo,GF,Sep 13)*
**Winter Thunder 110** *(12f,Nmk,G,Oct 4)*
**Witches Brew 109** *(7f,Leo,Y,Oct 26)*
**Won Diamond 105** *(8f,Cur,G,Aug 31)*
**Wonderstruck 107** *(12f,Nby,G,Aug 3)*
**Woodacre 108** *(10f,Pon,GF,Sep 25)*
**Woodland Aria 108** *(8f,Asc,GF,Jun 18)*
**Woodsophiesmile 106** *(8f,Cur,GF,May 5)*
**World Record 107** *(8½f,Bev,G,Jly 5)*
**Wrangler 111** *(12f,Sal,S,May 4)*

**Xcellence 112** *(10½f,Cha,G,Jun 15)*
**Xinbama 106** *(12f,Hay,GS,Sep 4)*

**Yaakooum 107** *(10f,Eps,G,Sep 28)*
**Yava 106** *(7f,Cur,S,Aug 10)*
**Yeeoow 109** *(6f,Nmk,GF,May 4)*
**Yenhaab 106** *(10f,Bev,GF,Aug 30)*
**You're Fired 112** *(8f,Nmk,S,Jly 12)*
**Yourartisonfire 106** *(7f,Hay,G,Sep 5)*
**Yuften 105** *(8f,Sal,GF,Aug 14)*

**Zacynthus 106** *(7f,Ncs,G,May 20)*
**Zain Eagle 107** *(10½f,Yor,GF,Jly 12)*
**Zain Zone 107** *(7f,Lei,HY,Oct 14)*
**Zalty 109** *(6f,Cur,GF,Jun 28)*
**Zambucca 108** *(10½f,Yor,GF,Jly 26)*
**Zarshana 113** *(15½f,Lon,VS,Oct 26)*
**Zarwaan 105** *(7f,Nby,GS,Apr 11)*
**Zeftan 109** *(12f,Cur,GF,Jun 29)*
**Zejel 114** *(6½f,Dea,HY,Aug 10)*
**Zeus Magic 105** *(10f,Rip,G,Apr 17)*
**Zeyran 105** *(8f,Pon,G,Apr 14)*
**Zibelina 108** *(8f,Nmk,G,Sep 26)*
**Zugzwang 105** *(10½f,Chs,G,Sep 13)*
**Zurigha 106** *(8f,Asc,G,Jly 25)*

## THREE YEAR-OLDS AND UPWARDS - Sand

**A Little Bit Dusty 108** *(12f,Wol,SD,Feb 17)*
**Abi Scarlet 108** *(6f,Sth,SD,Feb 4)*
**Absolutely So 116** *(6f,Kem,SD,Mar 29)*
**Addictive Dream 113** *(5f,Lin,SD,Mar 1)*
**Addikt 105** *(10f,Kem,SD,Feb 5)*
**Adiynara 106** *(11f,Kem,SD,Mar 6)*
**Admirable Duque 105** *(14f,Wol,SD,Sep 26)*
**Aertex 106** *(6f,Lin,SD,Nov 15)*
**Afkar 107** *(7f,Lin,SD,Jan 24)*
**Ain't No Surprise 105** *(7f,Wol,SD,Feb 3)*
**Al Destoor 106** *(12f,Lin,SD,Nov 14)*
**Al Mukhdam 105** *(9f,Wol,SD,Sep 30)*
**Al's Memory 106** *(7f,Lin,SD,Feb 21)*
**Alba Verde 105** *(16½f,Wol,SD,Sep 27)*
**Alben Star 112** *(6f,Wol,SD,Jan 26)*
**Alejandro 107** *(7f,Lin,SD,Oct 30)*
**Alex Vino 106** *(10f,Lin,SD,Sep 3)*
**Alexandra Palace 109** *(8f,Mey,SD,Jan 23)*
**Alfred Hutchinson 112** *(7f,Lin,SD,Jan 24)*
**Alfresco 106** *(7f,Lin,SD,Mar 5)*
**Almanack 105** *(9f,Wol,SD,Oct 14)*
**Almerzem 109** *(11f,Kem,SD,Sep 18)*
**Almuheet 105** *(7f,Wol,SD,Oct 16)*
**Alnashmy 109** *(8f,Mey,SD,Jan 16)*
**Alnoomaas 106** *(6f,Kem,SD,Oct 7)*
**Alumina 109** *(7f,Wol,SD,Feb 14)*
**Alutiq 115** *(6f,Kem,SD,Jan 15)*
**Alwilda 111** *(13f,Lin,SD,Oct 30)*
**Amadeus Wolfe Tone 108** *(6f,Wol,SD,Oct 21)*
**American Hope 106** *(7f,Lin,SD,Mar 22)*
**Amood 105** *(7f,Kem,SD,Oct 29)*
**Amygdala 106** *(6f,Kem,SD,Oct 7)*
**Ana Shababiya 107** *(10f,Lin,SD,Jun 10)*
**Anaconda 113** *(10f,Lin,SD,Feb 22)*
**Angel Gabrial 109** *(12f,Lin,SD,Mar 14)*
**Angel's Pursuit 105** *(6f,Kem,SD,Jan 23)*
**Angelic Upstart 107** *(9f,Wol,SD,Apr 3)*
**Anglo Irish 108** *(11f,Kem,SD,Aug 20)*
**Anglophile 116** *(11f,Kem,SD,Dec 10)*
**Angus Glens 105** *(12f,Wol,SD,Dec 19)*
**Annunciation 113** *(6f,Kem,SD,Mar 29)*
**Another Wise Kid 108** *(6f,Kem,SD,Mar 17)*
**Ansaab 107** *(10f,Kem,SD,Mar 5)*
**Anya 107** *(8f,Kem,SD,Sep 25)*
**Apostle 110** *(7f,Wol,SD,Jan 3)*
**Appease 110** *(10f,Lin,SD,Apr 2)*
**Aqua Ardens 106** *(8f,Sth,SD,Jan 14)*
**Arab Dawn 113** *(11f,Kem,SD,May 28)*
**Arabian Flight 106** *(7f,Sth,SD,Apr 2)*
**Arabian Heights 110** *(10f,Kem,SD,Mar 12)*
**Arashi 105** *(16½f,Wol,SD,Nov 17)*
**Arch Villain 116** *(16f,Lin,SD,Jan 22)*
**Archie's Advice 105** *(10f,Kem,SD,Oct 29)*
**Archipeligo 106** *(9½f,Wol,SD,Dec 19)*
**Arr' Kid 109** *(16f,Sth,SD,Feb 11)*
**Art Scholar 108** *(9½f,Wol,SD,Nov 14)*
**Artful Rogue 106** *(12f,Lin,SD,Oct 15)*
**Artistical 108** *(11f,Kem,SD,Jan 19)*
**Aryal 108** *(11f,Kem,SD,Mar 29)*
**Ashkari 108** *(6f,Kem,SD,Oct 21)*
**Atalanta Bay 105** *(12f,Lin,SD,May 2)*
**Athletic 105** *(7f,Lin,SD,Oct 30)*
**Atlantis Crossing 110** *(8f,Lin,SD,Mar 1)*
**Auction 106** *(8f,Lin,SD,Oct 30)*
**Aussie Reigns 114** *(10f,Lin,SD,Mar 22)*
**Automotive 106** *(10f,Lin,SD,Nov 15)*
**Avondream 105** *(6f,Lin,SD,Feb 21)*
**Ayaar 108** *(7f,Kem,SD,Apr 19)*

**Back Burner 105** *(9f,Wol,SD,Feb 20)*
**Baddilini 110** *(6f,Kem,SD,Mar 17)*
**Badr Al Badoor 110** *(6f,Wol,SD,Dec 19)*
**Ballista 108** *(5f,Lin,SD,Mar 1)*
**Baltic Knight 110** *(8f,Kem,SD,Nov 19)*
**Baltic Prince 105** *(7f,Wol,SD,Mar 11)*
**Bancnuanaheireann 115** *(10f,Kem,SD,Mar 5)*
**Banoffee 109** *(10f,Mey,SD,Jan 23)*
**Bapak Bangsawan 107** *(5f,Kem,SD,Jan 8)*
**Barley Mow 107** *(8f,Lin,SD,Apr 5)*
**Barracuda Boy 106** *(6f,Lin,SD,Nov 19)*
**Barwick 107** *(12f,Lin,SD,Jly 28)*
**Basingstoke 110** *(7f,Sth,SD,Jan 14)*
**Battalion 107** *(12f,Kem,SD,Sep 6)*
**Bennelong 105** *(11f,Kem,SD,Apr 2)*
**Benoordenhout 106** *(10f,Lin,SD,Jly 9)*
**Berlusca 108** *(9½f,Wol,SD,Nov 14)*
**Bertie Blu Boy 105** *(7f,Lin,SD,Mar 5)*
**Bertiewhittle 108** *(7f,Mey,SD,Jan 9)*
**Big Baz 113** *(8f,Lin,SD,Nov 15)*
**Billingsgate 112** *(8f,Kem,SD,Aug 27)*
**Biotic 105** *(8f,Kem,SD,Oct 7)*
**Birdie Queen 105** *(5f,Lin,SS,Dec 20)*
**Birdman 112** *(8f,Lin,SD,Jan 18)*
**Bishop's Castle 106** *(11f,Kem,SD,Mar 29)*
**Black Iceman 107** *(16½f,Wol,SD,Dec 6)*
**Blazeofenchantment 105** *(8f,Sth,SD,Aug 7)*
**Blessington 106** *(5f,Kem,SD,Jan 8)*
**Blue Wave 112** *(12f,Wol,SD,Feb 28)*
**Bluegrass Blues 107** *(7f,Kem,SD,Apr 19)*
**Bognor 106** *(8f,Sth,SD,Dec 9)*
**Bogsnog 108** *(7f,Wol,SD,Mar 28)*
**Bold Prediction 106** *(8f,Kem,SD,Mar 26)*
**Bon Port 105** *(8f,Lin,SD,Jly 25)*
**Boogangoo 105** *(7f,Wol,SD,Dec 1)*
**Boom The Groom 113** *(6f,Wol,SD,Dec 19)*
**Born To Surprise 111** *(10f,Kem,SD,Mar 5)*
**Bow Creek 108** *(8f,Lin,SD,Apr 5)*
**Bowstar 108** *(7f,Kem,SD,Jan 29)*
**Bravo Echo 108** *(7f,Lin,SD,Mar 21)*
**Brendan Brackan 110** *(8f,Mey,SD,Jan 9)*
**Bretherton 106** *(6f,Sth,SD,Feb 4)*
**Bridge That Gap 106** *(10f,Lin,SD,Oct 21)*
**Brocklebank 110** *(7f,Lin,SD,Jan 24)*
**Broughtons Charm 112** *(7f,Sth,SD,Apr 2)*
**Brown Eyed Honey 111** *(8f,Kem,SD,Jly 9)*
**Brownsea Brink 109** *(7f,Lin,SD,Mar 21)*
**Buckland 105** *(16f,Kem,SD,Nov 19)*
**Buckstay 107** *(8f,Kem,SD,Sep 6)*
**Bureau 106** *(12f,Wol,SD,Nov 7)*
**Burning Blaze 107** *(7f,Lin,SD,Jan 24)*
**Burren View Lady 105** *(6f,Wol,SD,Jan 26)*
**Bustopher 106** *(8f,Lin,SD,Apr 29)*
**Bute Hall 109** *(12f,Wol,SD,Feb 28)*
**Button Down 108** *(8f,Lin,SD,Jly 23)*
**By Jupiter 105** *(12f,Lin,SD,Nov 14)*

**Cai Shen 110** *(9½f,Wol,SD,Apr 3)*
**Call Me Pj 105** *(16½f,Wol,SD,Nov 24)*
**Callisto Light 108** *(8f,Kem,SD,Jan 22)*
**Cameo Tiara 105** *(8f,Kem,SD,Apr 2)*
**Canadian Run 108** *(10f,Kem,SD,Mar 5)*
**Canon Law 105** *(9f,Wol,SD,Feb 8)*
**Canyari 107** *(6f,Sth,SD,Dec 27)*
**Cape Of Hope 109** *(7f,Wol,SD,Mar 11)*
**Cape Summit 105** *(8f,Kem,SD,Sep 3)*
**Capital Attraction 108** *(8f,Mey,SD,Jan 23)*
**Capo Rosso 110** *(9f,Wol,SD,Apr 5)*
**Captain Cat 113** *(10f,Lin,SD,Jan 25)*
**Captain George 105** *(10f,Lin,SD,Aug 20)*
**Captain Joy 107** *(8f,Mey,SD,Jan 23)*
**Captain Myles 107** *(6f,Kem,SD,Jan 15)*
**Captain Secret 109** *(6f,Wol,SD,Mar 27)*
**Caramack 107** *(7f,Wol,SD,Feb 8)*
**Carnevale 108** *(11f,Kem,SD,Sep 24)*
**Cascading 106** *(13f,Lin,SD,Oct 30)*
**Caspian Prince 109** *(5f,Kem,SD,Jan 8)*
**Castilo Del Diablo 112** *(16f,Lin,SD,Apr 18)*
**Castle Combe 106** *(11f,Kem,SD,Sep 18)*
**Cat O'Mountain 110** *(11f,Mey,SD,Jan 16)*
**Cathedral 110** *(10f,Kem,SD,Mar 31)*
**Cayuga 109** *(10f,Lin,SD,Jan 8)*
**Celestial Bay 105** *(12f,Lin,SS,Dec 17)*
**Celestial Ray 107** *(8f,Lin,SD,Jly 24)*
**Centurius 112** *(9½f,Wol,SD,Mar 15)*
**Chantecler 106** *(12f,Wol,SD,Sep 15)*
**Chapter And Verse 109** *(11f,Kem,SD,Dec 10)*
**Cherry Street 107** *(10f,Lin,SD,Oct 21)*
**Chil The Kite 110** *(10f,Lin,SD,Mar 22)*
**Chilworth Icon 108** *(7f,Lin,SD,Mar 21)*
**Chookie Royale 116** *(9f,Wol,SD,Feb 3)*
**Chunghua 106** *(6f,Lin,SD,Feb 25)*
**Cincinnati Girl 108** *(10f,Lin,SD,Oct 21)*
**Circumvent 112** *(10f,Lin,SD,Mar 22)*
**Cladocera 111** *(8f,Kem,SD,Nov 19)*
**Clapperboard 105** *(7f,Lin,SD,May 21)*
**Clear Mind 107** *(12f,Lin,SD,Jly 16)*
**Clear Praise 108** *(6f,Kem,SD,Mar 17)*
**Clearing 105** *(5f,Lin,SD,Nov 22)*
**Club House 111** *(8f,Lin,SD,Feb 12)*
**Coillte Cailin 107** *(9½f,Wol,SD,Oct 28)*
**Collodi 105** *(8f,Kem,SD,Jan 30)*

**Colourbearer 108** *(6f,Wol,SD,Jan 26)*
**Come On Blue Chip 105** *(9½f,Wol,SD,Jan 17)*
**Come On Dave 106** *(5f,Wol,SD,Mar 8)*
**Commissar 111** *(9½f,Wol,SD,Mar 15)*
**Communicator 115** *(16f,Lin,SD,Jan 22)*
**Complicit 108** *(10f,Lin,SD,Dec 3)*
**Compton 106** *(7f,Lin,SD,Jan 22)*
**Comrade Bond 106** *(9f,Wol,SD,Dec 15)*
**Confessional 106** *(6f,Wol,SD,Nov 7)*
**Conry 105** *(9f,Wol,SD,Apr 3)*
**Cool Bahamian 107** *(7f,Wol,SD,Nov 17)*
**Cool Sky 114** *(14f,Wol,SD,Dec 6)*
**Corporal Maddox 109** *(6f,Kem,SD,Mar 17)*
**Corton Lad 107** *(12f,Wol,SD,Nov 7)*
**Counter Ridge 105** *(6f,Kem,SD,Oct 30)*
**Counterglow 105** *(8f,Mey,SD,Jan 16)*
**Courageous Rock 105** *(12f,Lin,SD,Jly 16)*
**Cousin Khee 111** *(12f,Wol,SD,Sep 6)*
**Cricklewood Green 113** *(8f,Lin,SD,Dec 8)*
**Crisis Averted 106** *(5f,Wol,SD,Mar 13)*
**Crowdmania 107** *(8f,Lin,SD,Mar 14)*
**Crystal Pearl 108** *(10f,Lin,SD,Oct 21)*

**Daaree 108** *(11f,Kem,SD,Oct 1)*
**Daddy Long Legs 107** *(8f,Mey,SD,Jan 9)*
**Daghash 105** *(14f,Wol,SD,Dec 2)*
**Dame Lucy 107** *(16½f,Wol,SD,Dec 1)*
**Dance And Dance 110** *(8f,Lin,SD,Jan 18)*
**Dandino 105** *(12f,Kem,SD,Sep 6)*
**Dangerous Age 109** *(5f,Wol,SD,Feb 17)*
**Daring Indian 109** *(12f,Wol,SD,Apr 26)*
**Dark Days 107** *(16½f,Wol,SD,Oct 31)*
**Derbaas 108** *(8f,Mey,SD,Jan 16)*
**Desert Snow 110** *(12f,Wol,SD,Oct 18)*
**Desert Strike 106** *(5f,Wol,SD,Mar 7)*
**Devilment 111** *(12f,Wol,SD,Sep 6)*
**Dialogue 105** *(9½f,Wol,SD,Dec 22)*
**Diamond Charlie 109** *(6f,Lin,SD,Dec 10)*
**Dick Doughtywylie 113** *(10f,Lin,SD,Mar 22)*
**Diletta Tommasa 106** *(10f,Lin,SD,Jun 10)*
**Dimitar 106** *(7f,Wol,SD,Feb 17)*
**Dire Straits 106** *(12f,Wol,SD,Dec 5)*
**Disa Leader 108** *(8f,Mey,SD,Jan 23)*
**Discussiontofollow 112** *(6f,Kem,SD,Jan 23)*
**Dissent 109** *(6f,Lin,SD,Aug 12)*
**Divine Rule 105** *(8f,Kem,SD,Jan 23)*
**Dixie's Dream 108** *(9f,Wol,SD,Jan 13)*
**Doc Hay 106** *(6f,Kem,SD,Nov 20)*
**Docs Legacy 115** *(9½f,Wol,SD,Nov 6)*
**Doctor Parkes 107** *(5f,Kem,SD,Dec 16)*
**Dolce N Karama 105** *(7f,Mey,SD,Jan 16)*
**Doldrums 107** *(12f,Wol,SD,Feb 17)*
**Dominandros 108** *(10f,Lin,SD,Nov 20)*
**Dominate 105** *(6f,Kem,SD,Nov 27)*
**Don't Be 105** *(7f,Wol,SD,Nov 24)*
**Don't Call Me 106** *(8f,Kem,SD,Feb 26)*
**Don't Stare 106** *(8f,Kem,SD,Jun 5)*
**Dont Have It Then 106** *(6f,Kem,SD,Dec 8)*
**Double Discount 111** *(11f,Kem,SD,Dec 10)*
**Dozy Joe 107** *(8f,Lin,SD,Feb 12)*
**Dr Red Eye 106** *(7f,Lin,SD,Feb 22)*
**Dream Child 107** *(9½f,Wol,SD,Sep 30)*
**Dreams Of Glory 106** *(5f,Lin,SS,Dec 20)*
**Dreams Of Reality 105** *(5f,Wol,SD,Apr 11)*
**Drive On 111** *(6f,Kem,SD,Jan 22)*
**Dubai Celebration 108** *(9½f,Wol,SD,Feb 24)*
**Duchess Of Gazeley 110** *(12f,Lin,SD,Mar 14)*
**Dukes Delight 106** *(12f,Wol,SD,Oct 4)*
**Dukes Den 117** *(16½f,Wol,SD,Dec 6)*
**Dullingham 106** *(8f,Lin,SD,Jly 24)*
**Dungannon 105** *(6f,Kem,SD,Nov 26)*
**Dutch Art Dealer 107** *(7f,Kem,SD,Sep 6)*
**Dutch Interior 105** *(6f,Kem,SD,Oct 7)*

**Earth Drummer 113** *(9½f,Wol,SD,Nov 6)*
**Echo Brava 110** *(13f,Lin,SD,Feb 5)*
**Echua 105** *(14f,Wol,SD,Jan 20)*
**Economy 105** *(11f,Kem,SD,May 21)*
**Edu Querido 110** *(8f,Lin,SS,Dec 20)*
**Elbereth 109** *(11f,Kem,SD,Nov 20)*
**Elegant Ophelia 108** *(12f,Kem,SD,Jan 22)*
**Ellaal 105** *(9½f,Wol,SD,Apr 12)*
**Elpida 107** *(12f,Lin,SD,Nov 14)*
**Elusivity 107** *(6f,Wol,SD,Jan 26)*
**Emell 105** *(8f,Kem,SD,Feb 26)*
**Emerald Wilderness 114** *(10f,Kem,SD,Mar 5)*
**Emirates Flyer 111** *(7f,Mey,SD,Jan 16)*
**Emjayem 105** *(5f,Wol,SD,Aug 21)*
**Emkanaat 105** *(7f,Kem,SD,Jan 29)*
**Emman Bee 106** *(8f,Kem,SD,Jan 30)*
**Empire Storm 110** *(8f,Mey,SD,Jan 9)*
**Emulating 105** *(11f,Kem,SD,Jly 9)*
**Energia Davos 108** *(11f,Mey,SD,Jan 16)*
**Energia Flavio 112** *(9½f,Wol,SD,Nov 6)*
**Energia Fox 107** *(10f,Lin,SD,Nov 26)*
**Enriching 106** *(8f,Lin,SD,Feb 12)*
**Entihaa 117** *(14f,Wol,SD,Dec 6)*
**Epic Battle 109** *(10f,Kem,SD,Mar 5)*
**Ertijaal 107** *(7f,Lin,SD,Mar 22)*
**Ertikaan 106** *(8f,Kem,SD,Nov 4)*
**Estibdaad 106** *(10f,Lin,SD,Jly 28)*
**Eton Forever 108** *(8f,Kem,SD,Nov 19)*
**Euro Charline 105** *(7f,Wol,SD,Mar 8)*
**Even Stevens 111** *(5f,Sth,SD,Jan 1)*
**Evening Attire 105** *(7f,Lin,SD,Dec 31)*
**Ex Ex 106** *(6f,Kem,SD,Feb 5)*
**Exceedexpectations 106** *(7f,Lin,SD,Nov 26)*
**Exceeding Power 110** *(6f,Kem,SD,Jan 22)*
**Excellent Puck 109** *(9½f,Wol,SD,Jan 17)*
**Expose 113** *(5f,Wol,SD,Jan 31)*
**Eye Of The Tiger 108** *(13f,Lin,SD,Jan 22)*

**Fair Value 108** *(5f,Kem,SD,Dec 16)*
**Fairway To Heaven 108** *(6f,Lin,SD,Dec 10)*
**Famous Kid 108** *(11f,Kem,SD,Sep 5)*
**Fanoos 107** *(7f,Kem,SD,Mar 20)*
**Farraaj 113** *(10f,Lin,SD,Mar 22)*
**Fashion Line 109** *(9f,Wol,SD,Feb 20)*
**Fat Gary 108** *(5f,Wol,SD,Feb 1)*
**Faure Island 107** *(8f,Lin,SD,Sep 13)*
**Favorite Girl 105** *(12f,Wol,SD,Oct 4)*
**Favourite Treat 107** *(7f,Lin,SD,Feb 21)*
**Fearless Lad 106** *(11f,Kem,SD,Feb 3)*
**Fiery Sunset 109** *(12f,Lin,SD,Jly 23)*
**Fiftyshadesfreed 106** *(9f,Wol,SD,Sep 27)*
**Fiftyshadesofgrey 106** *(8f,Kem,SD,Oct 22)*
**Figure Of Speech 107** *(7f,Mey,SD,Jan 16)*
**Filament Of Gold 106** *(12f,Lin,SD,Jly 8)*
**Fire Fighting 107** *(11f,Kem,SD,Aug 20)*
**Firmdecisions 108** *(7f,Lin,SD,Mar 19)*
**Fitzgerald 106** *(9f,Wol,SD,Mar 15)*
**Flemish School 105** *(11f,Kem,SD,Nov 20)*
**Flow 107** *(9½f,Wol,SD,Dec 13)*
**Flying Power 107** *(12f,Wol,SD,Feb 14)*
**Footstepsintherain 107** *(8f,Kem,SD,Nov 13)*
**Forceful Appeal 115** *(7f,Lin,SD,Feb 21)*
**Forest Edge 111** *(6f,Kem,SD,Jan 19)*
**Fort Berkeley 107** *(12f,Lin,SD,Jly 23)*
**Foxtrot Romeo 111** *(6f,Wol,SD,Sep 6)*
**Foxy Forever 105** *(6f,Wol,SD,Oct 21)*
**Frederic 107** *(11f,Kem,SD,Oct 21)*
**Free Wheeling 108** *(8f,Mey,SD,Jan 23)*
**Fresles 110** *(6f,Lin,SD,Nov 15)*
**From Frost 108** *(12f,Sth,SD,Jun 30)*
**Frontier Fighter 114** *(7f,Sth,SD,Mar 26)*
**Fruit Pastille 109** *(8f,Lin,SD,Sep 13)*
**Fulbright 110** *(7f,Mey,SD,Jan 9)*
**Full Combat 107** *(7f,Mey,SD,Jan 16)*

**Gabrial's King 113** *(14f,Wol,SD,Nov 7)*
**Gabrial's Star 114** *(14f,Wol,SD,Dec 6)*
**Gaelic Silver 107** *(10f,Kem,SD,Nov 19)*
**Galizzi 110** *(12f,Wol,SD,Apr 29)*
**Gannicus 105** *(8f,Kem,SD,Nov 4)*
**Gavlar 108** *(12f,Lin,SD,Jly 23)*
**Geordan Murphy 106** *(8f,Kem,SD,Dec 18)*
**George Benjamin 105** *(7f,Sth,SD,Jan 14)*
**George Cinq 107** *(8f,Kem,SD,Sep 6)*
**George Fenton 105** *(6f,Wol,SD,Jan 2)*
**George Guru 109** *(8f,Lin,SD,Jan 18)*
**Georgian Bay 112** *(7f,Kem,SD,Apr 19)*
**Ghany 107** *(10f,Lin,SD,Nov 19)*
**Ghazi 106** *(9½f,Wol,SD,Nov 21)*
**Ghost Train 107** *(6f,Lin,SD,Feb 21)*
**Giant Sequoia 106** *(12f,Lin,SD,Aug 20)*
**Gilbey's Mate 106** *(8f,Kem,SD,Jly 9)*
**Ginger Jack 107** *(9½f,Wol,SD,Nov 6)*
**Glen Moss 109** *(7f,Kem,SD,Apr 19)*
**Glorious Empire 105** *(7f,Lin,SD,Apr 9)*
**Go Far 112** *(6f,Wol,SD,Sep 6)*
**Go For Broke 106** *(8f,Kem,SD,Oct 7)*
**God Willing 111** *(8f,Lin,SD,Nov 15)*
**God's Speed 105** *(11f,Kem,SD,Sep 5)*
**Gogeo 109** *(12f,Sth,SD,Feb 27)*
**Golden Amber 110** *(6f,Kem,SD,Jan 15)*
**Golden Journey 106** *(11f,Kem,SD,Aug 20)*
**Golden Jubilee 106** *(12f,Wol,SD,Feb 17)*
**Golden Steps 109** *(6f,Lin,SD,Nov 15)*
**Goldmadchen 106** *(12f,Wol,SD,Mar 14)*
**Gone Dutch 107** *(12f,Wol,SD,Oct 18)*
**Gone With The Wind 106** *(6f,Kem,SD,Mar 12)*
**Good Luck Charm 111** *(8f,Lin,SD,Dec 8)*
**Good Value 112** *(11f,Kem,SD,May 28)*
**Gracious George 105** *(8f,Kem,SD,Jan 30)*
**Grand Meister 110** *(11f,Kem,SD,May 28)*
**Grandeur 115** *(10f,Lin,SD,Feb 22)*
**Graphic 111** *(8f,Kem,SD,Nov 19)*
**Grasped 105** *(10f,Kem,SD,Aug 18)*
**Greeleys Love 107** *(10f,Lin,SD,Oct 21)*
**Gregori 105** *(5f,Lin,SD,Feb 8)*
**Grendisar 115** *(11f,Kem,SD,Dec 10)*
**Grey Mirage 110** *(7f,Lin,SD,Feb 22)*
**Greyfriarschorista 111** *(7f,Sth,SD,Mar 26)*
**Guishan 108** *(6f,Sth,SD,Dec 27)*
**Guising 105** *(11f,Kem,SD,Sep 18)*
**Gworn 105** *(9f,Wol,SD,Apr 5)*

**Haadeeth 107** *(6f,Wol,SD,Jan 26)*
**Haaf A Sixpence 107** *(8f,Lin,SD,Dec 28)*
**Haafaguinea 108** *(11f,Mey,SD,Jan 16)*
**Hagree 107** *(7f,Wol,SD,Apr 4)*
**Hail Promenader 106** *(8f,Sth,SD,Mar 25)*
**Hajras 111** *(10f,Lin,SD,Feb 22)*
**Halfsin 105** *(10f,Lin,SD,Jan 25)*
**Hallelujah 110** *(6f,Kem,SD,Nov 26)*
**Handsome Stranger 107** *(10f,Kem,SD,Mar 12)*
**Hannahs Turn 110** *(7f,Sth,SD,Apr 2)*
**Harris Tweed 111** *(16½f,Wol,SD,Dec 13)*
**Harrogate Fair 106** *(5f,Kem,SD,Dec 16)*
**Harvest Mist 106** *(6f,Kem,SD,Feb 3)*
**Harwoods Volante 113** *(6f,Kem,SD,Jan 22)*
**Hasopop 108** *(7f,Wol,SD,Mar 8)*
**Havelovewilltravel 105** *(10f,Lin,SD,Apr 9)*
**Hawkeyethenoo 110** *(7f,Lin,SD,Jan 24)*
**Head Space 110** *(6f,Kem,SD,Oct 21)*
**Hedge End 109** *(11f,Kem,SD,Dec 8)*
**Heisman 107** *(8f,Kem,SD,Oct 30)*
**Hell Hath No Fury 112** *(16½f,Wol,SD,Nov 17)*
**Hernando Torres 105** *(9½f,Wol,SD,Oct 28)*
**Heska 105** *(12f,Wol,SD,Nov 29)*
**Hidden Gold 113** *(13f,Lin,SD,Oct 30)*
**Hidden Justice 105** *(16½f,Wol,SD,Dec 1)*
**Hierarch 107** *(8f,Lin,SD,Feb 12)*
**High Time Too 110** *(8f,Kem,SD,Apr 2)*
**Highland Knight 110** *(8f,Lin,SD,Apr 18)*
**Hill Of Dreams 106** *(8f,Kem,SD,Mar 27)*
**Hillbilly Boy 106** *(7f,Wol,SD,Feb 8)*
**History Book 107** *(8f,Lin,SD,Nov 22)*
**Hoist The Colours 109** *(13f,Lin,SD,Aug 8)*
**Homage 106** *(8f,Kem,SD,Aug 27)*
**Honey Of A Kitten 106** *(9½f,Wol,SD,Feb 24)*
**Honoured 110** *(11f,Sth,SD,Jan 3)*
**Hoof It 113** *(6f,Kem,SD,Mar 29)*
**Hot Right Now 109** *(8f,Sth,SD,Jan 28)*
**Hunting Ground 112** *(12f,Wol,SD,Sep 6)*

**I'm Back 106** *(9½f,Wol,SD,Oct 4)*
**I'm Fraam Govan 114** *(11f,Kem,SD,Dec 10)*
**I'm Super Too 105** *(8f,Sth,SD,Apr 2)*
**Ice Slice 106** *(8f,Kem,SD,Jly 9)*
**Ice Tres 105** *(12f,Wol,SD,Mar 14)*
**Icy Blue 106** *(8f,Kem,SD,Jan 23)*
**If I Were A Boy 108** *(10f,Lin,SD,Jun 10)*
**Ifan 106** *(9½f,Wol,SD,Apr 12)*
**Iffranesia 107** *(5f,Kem,SD,Feb 19)*
**Ifwecan 110** *(8f,Lin,SD,Nov 15)*
**Imaginary World 105** *(7f,Sth,SD,Mar 6)*
**Incendo 105** *(11f,Kem,SD,Jan 19)*
**Indastar 105** *(6f,Wol,SD,Sep 15)*
**India's Song 107** *(9½f,Wol,SD,Feb 24)*
**Indian Jack 112** *(10f,Kem,SD,Mar 5)*
**Indus Valley 109** *(6f,Kem,SD,Jan 22)*
**Ingleby Angel 111** *(8f,Lin,SD,Nov 15)*
**Instant Attraction 105** *(7f,Wol,SD,Sep 13)*
**Intransigent 111** *(10f,Lin,SD,Nov 15)*
**Intrigo 109** *(8f,Mey,SD,Jan 16)*
**Invasor Luck 105** *(12f,Lin,SD,Jly 8)*
**Investissement 107** *(14f,Wol,SD,Sep 26)*
**Invigilator 108** *(6f,Kem,SD,Mar 5)*
**Invincible Ridge 105** *(6f,Kem,SD,Dec 8)*
**Invincible Strike 105** *(6f,Wol,SD,Sep 6)*
**Iptisam 110** *(6f,Lin,SD,Feb 22)*
**Ishikawa 106** *(9½f,Wol,SD,Mar 13)*
**Island Legend 105** *(5f,Kem,SD,Mar 17)*
**Itsnowcato 106** *(11f,Kem,SD,Sep 18)*

**Jaahiez 105** *(9f,Wol,SD,Mar 15)*
**Jack Of Diamonds 116** *(8f,Lin,SD,Dec 8)*
**Jacobs Son 108** *(11f,Sth,SD,Jun 5)*
**Jakkalberry 112** *(9½f,Wol,SD,Jan 17)*
**Jalingo 107** *(12f,Lin,SD,Oct 15)*
**Jamesie 108** *(6f,Mey,SD,Jan 23)*
**Jan Smuts 106** *(16½f,Wol,SD,Nov 17)*
**Jarlath 106** *(11f,Kem,SD,Aug 20)*
**Jay Bee Blue 106** *(7f,Kem,SD,Feb 12)*
**Jazz Master 107** *(11f,Kem,SD,Oct 8)*
**Jewelled 105** *(11f,Kem,SD,Mar 6)*
**Jiroft 107** *(5f,Wol,SD,Feb 1)*
**Jodies Jem 105** *(8f,Kem,SD,Oct 30)*
**Johara 105** *(6f,Kem,SD,Aug 4)*
**John Reel 106** *(14f,Wol,SD,Nov 28)*
**Johnny Splash 105** *(5f,Lin,SD,Dec 8)*
**Joohaina 107** *(7f,Wol,SD,Feb 14)*
**Jubilee Brig 107** *(7f,Lin,SD,Jan 31)*
**Jungle Bay 106** *(7f,Kem,SD,Dec 18)*
**Just One Kiss 109** *(8f,Kem,SD,Jan 30)*

**Karam Albaari 105** *(12f,Lin,SD,Jly 28)*
**Kashmir Peak 108** *(12f,Lin,SD,Jan 4)*
**Kastini 105** *(11f,Kem,SD,Sep 18)*
**Katmai River 105** *(9f,Wol,SD,Jan 2)*
**Keene 106** *(10f,Lin,SD,Jan 25)*
**Kelinni 109** *(12f,Wol,SD,Oct 18)*
**Khajaaly 109** *(7f,Sth,SD,Mar 6)*
**Khatiba 108** *(7f,Kem,SD,Nov 5)*
**Kiama Bay 105** *(12f,Lin,SD,Jan 4)*
**Killing Time 105** *(8f,Kem,SD,Sep 22)*
**Kindlelight Storm 106** *(9½f,Wol,SD,Feb 17)*
**Kinema 111** *(10f,Lin,SD,Oct 21)*
**King Bertie 107** *(6f,Sth,SD,Mar 11)*
**King Calypso 105** *(11f,Kem,SD,Sep 3)*
**King Olav 105** *(11f,Kem,SD,Mar 27)*
**King's Request 105** *(16f,Lin,SD,Feb 25)*
**Kings Bayonet 105** *(11f,Kem,SD,Dec 3)*
**Kingscombe 105** *(16f,Sth,SD,Nov 4)*
**Kleo 108** *(10f,Lin,SD,Jly 8)*
**Klynch 105** *(6f,Sth,SD,Apr 1)*
**Knavery 107** *(8f,Lin,SD,Jly 16)*
**Knight Owl 106** *(8f,Kem,SD,Oct 30)*
**Knockgraffon Lad 106** *(12f,Lin,SD,Mar 14)*
**Krypton Factor 105** *(6f,Kem,SD,Oct 8)*
**Kuanyao 106** *(5f,Lin,SD,Feb 19)*
**Kung Hei Fat Choy 109** *(7f,Wol,SD,Apr 22)*

**L'Avenue 105** *(9½f,Wol,SD,Mar 28)*
**L'Inganno Felice 105** *(9½f,Wol,SD,Dec 22)*
**Lacan 110** *(8f,Kem,SD,Dec 11)*
**Lacey 116** *(16½f,Wol,SD,Dec 6)*
**Ladies Are Forever 108** *(6f,Lin,SD,Feb 22)*
**Lady Lunchalot 105** *(10f,Lin,SD,Jan 25)*
**Lamar 107** *(8f,Lin,SD,Oct 30)*
**Lancelot Du Lac 113** *(6f,Lin,SD,Dec 10)*
**Langley Vale 105** *(6f,Lin,SD,Jly 24)*
**Larghetto 107** *(6f,Kem,SD,Nov 10)*
**Last Minute Lisa 108** *(13f,Lin,SD,Oct 30)*
**Late Shipment 106** *(12f,Lin,SD,Apr 2)*
**Latin Charm 109** *(12f,Kem,SD,Nov 19)*
**Lawmans Thunder 108** *(7f,Kem,SD,Nov 5)*
**Layali Al Andalus 110** *(10f,Mey,SD,Jan 23)*
**Layl 109** *(11f,Sth,SD,Jan 1)*
**Layline 107** *(13f,Lin,SD,Feb 5)*
**Leaderene 105** *(10f,Lin,SD,Jly 9)*
**Lean On Pete 107** *(11f,Sth,SD,Mar 18)*
**Legendary 108** *(9½f,Wol,SD,Jan 16)*
**Lehaaf 108** *(8f,Mey,SD,Jan 16)*
**Leitrim Pass 105** *(11f,Kem,SD,Jan 19)*
**Leonard Thomas 107** *(9f,Wol,SD,Dec 15)*
**Lexi's Hero 111** *(6f,Lin,SD,Jan 24)*
**Libeccio 111** *(11f,Kem,SD,Mar 20)*
**Liberty Jack 108** *(8f,Kem,SD,Mar 26)*
**Life And Times 109** *(9½f,Wol,SD,Apr 5)*
**Light From Mars 107** *(7f,Kem,SD,Mar 26)*
**Likelihood 109** *(11f,Kem,SD,May 28)*
**Lily Edge 109** *(10f,Lin,SD,Jun 10)*
**Lincoln 108** *(6f,Wol,SD,Mar 27)*
**Lindart 106** *(7f,Lin,SD,Dec 10)*
**Litigant 115** *(16f,Lin,SD,Apr 18)*
**Little Buxted 108** *(12f,Lin,SD,Jly 28)*
**Livia's Dream 111** *(13f,Lin,SD,Oct 30)*
**Living Leader 107** *(7f,Lin,SD,Nov 26)*
**Living The Life 114** *(7f,Lin,SD,Feb 21)*
**Lord Ofthe Shadows 106** *(8f,Kem,SD,Jun 5)*
**Lord Van Percy 108** *(12f,Lin,SD,Mar 22)*
**Loud 107** *(7f,Sth,SD,Mar 12)*
**Love Excel 106** *(7f,Wol,SD,Apr 22)*
**Loving Spirit 107** *(8f,Kem,SD,Sep 6)*
**Low Key 110** *(12f,Kem,SD,Jan 22)*
**Lowther 111** *(10f,Lin,SD,Jan 25)*
**Loyalty 113** *(8f,Lin,SD,Dec 8)*
**Luhaif 111** *(8f,Lin,SD,Jan 18)*
**Lunasea 110** *(10f,Lin,SD,Nov 19)*
**Luv U Whatever 111** *(11f,Sth,SD,Jan 3)*
**Lyn Valley 109** *(10f,Lin,SD,Nov 26)*

**Maggie Pink 112** *(7f,Wol,SD,Mar 11)*
**Magic Art 106** *(12f,Wol,SD,Sep 6)*
**Magic City 107** *(7f,Kem,SD,Nov 12)*
**Magic Hurricane 107** *(11f,Kem,SD,May 21)*
**Magic Of Reality 105** *(8f,Kem,SD,Apr 19)*
**Magika 110** *(12f,Wol,SD,Jan 10)*
**Mahadee 105** *(12f,Lin,SD,Feb 14)*
**Maison Brillet 106** *(11f,Kem,SD,Apr 2)*
**Majeyda 107** *(7f,Wol,SD,Nov 28)*
**Major Crispies 105** *(7f,Lin,SD,Mar 22)*
**Major Jack 109** *(6f,Kem,SD,Nov 26)*
**Malaysian Boleh 112** *(8f,Lin,SD,Dec 8)*
**Manalapan 109** *(10f,Mey,SD,Jan 23)*
**Manomine 106** *(11f,Kem,SD,Sep 18)*
**Mappin Time 112** *(5f,Wol,SD,Apr 26)*
**Maraheb 106** *(7f,Mey,SD,Jan 9)*
**Marjong 106** *(6f,Lin,SD,Aug 12)*
**Masamah 106** *(6f,Mey,SD,Jan 23)*
**Master Dan 105** *(12f,Sth,SD,Aug 7)*
**Master Dancer 105** *(10f,Lin,SD,Oct 21)*
**Master Of Finance 105** *(9½f,Wol,SD,Nov 6)*
**Masterful Act 110** *(11f,Sth,SD,Jan 1)*
**Masterpaver 114** *(14f,Wol,SD,Nov 7)*
**Matravers 106** *(8f,Kem,SD,Sep 3)*
**Maverick Wave 113** *(9½f,Wol,SD,Nov 6)*
**Maymyo 105** *(6f,Kem,SD,Aug 27)*
**Mazaaher 105** *(9f,Wol,SD,Aug 11)*
**Medicean Man 109** *(6f,Lin,SD,Nov 15)*
**Megaleka 105** *(5f,Wol,SD,Feb 3)*
**Melvin The Grate 115** *(8f,Lin,SD,Dec 28)*
**Men Don't Cry 106** *(12f,Wol,SD,Sep 11)*
**Merhee 106** *(6f,Mey,SD,Jan 23)*
**Mia's Boy 108** *(8f,Lin,SD,Jan 18)*
**Mica Mika 106** *(12f,Lin,SD,Apr 18)*
**Mick Duggan 105** *(16f,Lin,SD,Aug 8)*
**Midaz 105** *(8f,Sth,SD,Apr 2)*
**Midnight Feast 109** *(8f,Lin,SD,Feb 12)*
**Midnight Rider 105** *(6f,Kem,SD,Nov 20)*
**Midnite Angel 108** *(8f,Kem,SD,Apr 19)*
**Miguel Grau 108** *(10f,Lin,SD,Jan 8)*
**Minstrels Gallery 105** *(10f,Kem,SD,Mar 31)*
**Mishaal 115** *(6f,Kem,SD,Nov 27)*
**Mishrif 105** *(8f,Sth,SD,Apr 30)*
**Miss Buckshot 107** *(8f,Lin,SD,Nov 22)*
**Miss Lillie 108** *(9f,Wol,SD,Dec 15)*
**Miss Marjurie 111** *(13f,Lin,SD,Oct 30)*

**Missed Call 111** *(11f,Kem,SD,Dec 10)*
**Mister Bob 111** *(16½f,Wol,SD,Nov 17)*
**Mister Musicmaster 107** *(8f,Lin,SD,Jly 24)*
**Modern History 109** *(7f,Mey,SD,Jan 9)*
**Modern Tutor 105** *(7f,Kem,SD,Nov 20)*
**Modernism 109** *(9½f,Wol,SD,Jan 16)*
**Modernstone 114** *(10f,Lin,SD,Feb 22)*
**Momayyaz 105** *(9f,Wol,SD,Sep 15)*
**Mondlicht 108** *(8f,Sth,SD,Mar 4)*
**Monsieur Chevalier 107** *(8f,Lin,SD,Jly 16)*
**Mont Ras 106** *(7f,Mey,SD,Jan 9)*
**Moonday Sun 115** *(10f,Kem,SD,Mar 5)*
**Moonspring 105** *(6f,Kem,SD,May 28)*
**Moonvoy 107** *(10f,Lin,SS,Dec 17)*
**Morache Music 105** *(7f,Kem,SD,Nov 20)*
**Moshe 105** *(10f,Lin,SD,Aug 20)*
**Mr Burbidge 109** *(12f,Sth,SD,Jan 7)*
**Mr David 109** *(7f,Lin,SD,Jan 31)*
**Mr Lando 105** *(10f,Kem,SD,Mar 12)*
**Mr Red Clubs 107** *(9½f,Wol,SD,Feb 24)*
**Mubtadi 108** *(9½f,Wol,SD,Mar 13)*
**Mufarrh 105** *(8f,Mey,SD,Jan 9)*
**Muhawalah 105** *(10f,Lin,SD,Jly 8)*
**Muhdiq 111** *(5f,Wol,SD,Mar 21)*
**Muir Lodge 105** *(6f,Wol,SD,Mar 27)*
**Multitask 105** *(8f,Kem,SD,Jan 23)*
**Munsarim 107** *(10f,Lin,SD,Jan 8)*
**Musaddas 111** *(8f,Kem,SD,Aug 27)*
**Music Theory 108** *(7f,Lin,SD,Oct 30)*
**Mutajare 110** *(10f,Mey,SD,Jan 23)*
**My Catch 110** *(7f,Mey,SD,Jan 16)*
**My Freedom 105** *(7f,Mey,SD,Jan 9)*
**My Single Malt 107** *(9f,Wol,SD,Feb 8)*
**My Son Max 105** *(8f,Sth,SD,Mar 26)*
**My Target 108** *(8f,Lin,SD,Jly 24)*
**Myboyalfie 105** *(8f,Kem,SD,Mar 19)*
**Mymatechris 107** *(12f,Lin,SD,Dec 3)*
**Mystery Drama 107** *(12f,Lin,SD,Jly 28)*
**Mystical Sapphire 106** *(8f,Kem,SD,Aug 27)*

**Naabegha 106** *(7f,Lin,SD,Jan 24)*
**Naaz 108** *(8f,Lin,SD,Jan 4)*
**Najm Suhail 107** *(7f,Mey,SD,Jan 16)*
**Nakuti 107** *(8f,Lin,SD,Oct 30)*
**Nassau Storm 108** *(7f,Lin,SD,Feb 22)*
**Nautilus 111** *(12f,Wol,SD,Feb 28)*
**New Year's Night 106** *(8f,Kem,SD,Sep 18)*
**Nigel's Destiny 108** *(8f,Kem,SD,Nov 10)*
**Nixyba 105** *(7f,Wol,SD,Feb 14)*
**No Win No Fee 111** *(8f,Sth,SD,Jan 3)*
**Noble Citizen 112** *(7f,Sth,SD,Mar 26)*
**Noble Deed 105** *(6f,Lin,SD,Feb 8)*
**Noble Gift 113** *(11f,Kem,SD,Dec 10)*
**Noble Silk 112** *(14f,Wol,SD,Nov 7)*
**Nocturn 105** *(6f,Lin,SD,Feb 22)*
**Norab 112** *(14f,Wol,SD,Nov 7)*
**Nova Princesse 108** *(6f,Kem,SD,Jan 22)*
**Novabridge 105** *(5f,Kem,SD,Feb 19)*
**Numrood 106** *(10f,Lin,SD,Oct 21)*

**Ocean Applause 108** *(8f,Kem,SD,Dec 11)*
**Ocean Boulevard 105** *(12f,Lin,SD,Nov 14)*
**Ocean Legend 105** *(7f,Kem,SD,Mar 20)*
**Ocean Tempest 107** *(8f,Kem,SD,Nov 19)*
**Ogbourne Downs 106** *(8f,Kem,SD,Oct 2)*
**Oh So Sassy 105** *(6f,Kem,SD,Jun 25)*
**Olivers Mount 107** *(8f,Kem,SD,Jan 22)*
**On Demand 105** *(7f,Sth,SD,Mar 12)*
**Only Ten Per Cent 105** *(6f,Sth,SD,Mar 26)*
**Opera Box 106** *(11f,Kem,SD,Sep 5)*
**Oratorio's Joy 106** *(12f,Wol,SD,Dec 26)*
**Order Of Service 108** *(7f,Wol,SD,Nov 17)*
**Oriental Relation 114** *(6f,Kem,SD,Jan 15)*
**Orpen'Arry 105** *(11f,Kem,SD,Apr 2)*
**Osaruveetil 109** *(11f,Kem,SD,Oct 21)*
**Our Gabrial 109** *(14f,Wol,SD,Nov 7)*
**Our Golden Girl 109** *(12f,Kem,SD,Jan 22)*
**Out Do 111** *(6f,Kem,SD,Nov 26)*
**Outbacker 108** *(6f,Wol,SD,Mar 27)*
**Outer Space 108** *(7f,Kem,SD,Nov 5)*
**Outlaw Torn 108** *(9½f,Wol,SD,Jan 6)*
**Oyster 105** *(12f,Lin,SD,Jly 23)*

**Palace Moon 109** *(6f,Kem,SD,Jan 23)*
**Panatella 108** *(11f,Kem,SD,Oct 21)*
**Panther Patrol 107** *(6f,Kem,SD,Nov 27)*
**Party Royal 106** *(9f,Wol,SD,Mar 8)*
**Past Forgetting 110** *(11f,Kem,SD,Dec 8)*
**Patriotic 107** *(7f,Sth,SD,Dec 18)*
**Peace Accord 105** *(7f,Kem,SD,Sep 10)*
**Peace Seeker 108** *(6f,Kem,SD,Oct 7)*
**Pearl Ice 107** *(6f,Kem,SD,Mar 29)*
**Pearl Nation 112** *(7f,Sth,SD,Dec 13)*
**Pelmanism 106** *(8f,Sth,SD,Jan 28)*
**Percys Princess 107** *(12f,Wol,SD,Dec 22)*
**Perfect Pasture 108** *(6f,Lin,SD,Dec 10)*
**Persepolis 111** *(10f,Kem,SD,Mar 5)*
**Persona Grata 105** *(9½f,Wol,SD,Dec 2)*
**Personal Opinion 116** *(14f,Wol,SD,Dec 6)*
**Peter's Friend 109** *(8f,Sth,SD,Jan 3)*
**Picansort 107** *(5f,Lin,SD,Mar 1)*
**Pim Street 106** *(9½f,Wol,SD,Oct 28)*
**Pinotage 107** *(14f,Wol,SD,Feb 7)*
**Pintrada 107** *(12f,Wol,SD,Nov 7)*
**Pipers Note 109** *(6f,Kem,SD,Oct 30)*
**Pipers Piping 106** *(7f,Wol,SD,Feb 20)*
**Piscean 107** *(6f,Kem,SD,Mar 17)*
**Pivotman 105** *(9½f,Wol,SD,Nov 3)*
**Placidia 105** *(10f,Lin,SD,Sep 3)*
**Planetoid 105** *(16f,Lin,SD,Dec 28)*
**Plantagenet 110** *(10f,Mey,SD,Jan 23)*
**Plough Boy 105** *(8f,Lin,SD,Sep 13)*
**Plucky Dip 111** *(6f,Kem,SD,Nov 27)*
**Plutocracy 107** *(12f,Wol,SD,Oct 18)*
**Polybius 109** *(6f,Lin,SD,Nov 15)*
**Pool House 107** *(7f,Lin,SD,Mar 5)*
**Posh Boy 107** *(10f,Lin,SD,Jun 10)*
**Postscript 106** *(9f,Wol,SD,Aug 29)*
**Powerful Pierre 106** *(6f,Wol,SD,Jan 2)*
**Poyle Thomas 107** *(16f,Kem,SD,Jly 2)*
**Poyle Vinnie 111** *(5f,Sth,SD,Dec 13)*
**Premio Loco 107** *(10f,Lin,SD,Mar 22)*
**Presburg 109** *(12f,Lin,SD,Jan 4)*
**Presto Volante 108** *(16f,Kem,SD,Jly 2)*
**Presumido 106** *(8f,Kem,SD,Dec 22)*
**Pretend 114** *(6f,Wol,SD,Dec 19)*
**Pretty Bubbles 107** *(7f,Kem,SD,Dec 1)*
**Prince Bishop 110** *(12f,Kem,SD,Sep 6)*
**Prince Of Burma 105** *(8f,Lin,SD,Jun 23)*
**Prince's Trust 109** *(7f,Lin,SD,Oct 30)*
**Priors Brook 106** *(10f,Lin,SD,Nov 19)*
**Profile Star 107** *(5f,Lin,SD,Mar 19)*
**Pull The Pin 106** *(6f,Sth,SD,Jan 20)*
**Purcell 110** *(7f,Lin,SD,Mar 21)*

**Qanan 107** *(10f,Kem,SD,Jun 4)*
**Queen Of Ice 110** *(8f,Kem,SD,Apr 19)*
**Queen Of Skies 107** *(8f,Sth,SD,Jan 28)*

**Ragged Robbin 108** *(12f,Wol,SD,Oct 18)*
**Rakaan 109** *(7f,Lin,SD,Feb 21)*
**Rambo Will 106** *(5f,Sth,SD,Jan 23)*
**Ramshackle 105** *(7f,Wol,SD,Sep 4)*
**Ranjaan 106** *(16f,Lin,SD,Mar 1)*
**Rasameel 106** *(8f,Lin,SD,May 12)*
**Razor Wind 115** *(8f,Lin,SD,Dec 8)*
**Reach The Beach 107** *(12f,Sth,SD,Nov 13)*
**Ready 107** *(7f,Wol,SD,Mar 11)*
**Real Jazz 108** *(10f,Lin,SD,Oct 21)*
**Realize 110** *(6f,Wol,SD,Nov 6)*
**Rebellious Guest 118** *(10f,Kem,SD,Mar 5)*
**Red Dragon 107** *(10f,Lin,SD,Jun 10)*
**Red Runaway 112** *(10f,Lin,SD,Apr 2)*
**Red Shuttle 106** *(9½f,Wol,SD,Feb 21)*
**Red Velour 108** *(10f,Lin,SD,Aug 27)*
**Ree's Rascal 109** *(10f,Lin,SD,Apr 2)*
**Regal Dan 111** *(7f,Lin,SD,Feb 21)*
**Reggie Bond 105** *(9f,Wol,SD,Dec 15)*
**Regulation 106** *(8f,Mey,SD,Jan 16)*
**Related 110** *(7f,Kem,SD,Dec 11)*
**Rembrandt Van Rijn 109** *(10f,Lin,SD,Aug 27)*
**Repetition 108** *(7f,Sth,SD,May 19)*
**Rerouted 107** *(8f,Mey,SD,Jan 9)*
**Returntobrecongill 108** *(11f,Sth,SD,Jan 1)*
**Reve De Nuit 111** *(12f,Wol,SD,Apr 26)*
**Rex Whistler 105** *(12f,Wol,SD,Oct 21)*
**Ribbons 105** *(8f,Kem,SD,Apr 19)*
**Ridgeway Storm 107** *(12f,Wol,SD,Nov 7)*
**Rigolleto 106** *(6f,Kem,SD,Jan 19)*
**Risby 108** *(8f,Mey,SD,Jan 16)*
**Rite To Reign 107** *(11f,Kem,SD,Mar 20)*
**Rivellino 112** *(6f,Lin,SD,Feb 22)*
**Rizal Park 106** *(8f,Kem,SD,Dec 17)*
**Robin Hoods Bay 116** *(10f,Lin,SD,Mar 22)*
**Rock Of Leon 106** *(16½f,Wol,SD,Oct 18)*
**Role Player 105** *(6f,Kem,SD,Jly 9)*
**Rosie Rebel 106** *(16f,Kem,SD,Jly 2)*
**Rosslyn Castle 107** *(12f,Lin,SD,Jly 28)*
**Rowan Ridge 105** *(11f,Kem,SD,Feb 3)*
**Rowe Park 105** *(5f,Sth,SD,Jan 23)*
**Rowlestone Lass 110** *(16½f,Wol,SD,Nov 17)*
**Roy's Legacy 106** *(5f,Lin,SD,Feb 4)*
**Royal Alcor 106** *(14f,Wol,SD,Mar 8)*
**Royal Bajan 112** *(5f,Sth,SD,Dec 13)*
**Royal Defence 111** *(14f,Wol,SD,Mar 28)*
**Royal Marskell 107** *(12f,Sth,SD,Dec 18)*
**Royal Trooper 105** *(12f,Wol,SD,Sep 15)*
**Rummaging 109** *(6f,Lin,SD,Feb 22)*
**Russian Soul 106** *(6f,Mey,SD,Jan 16)*
**Rusty Rocket 107** *(5f,Wol,SD,Apr 26)*
**Rutherglen 107** *(16½f,Wol,SD,Nov 24)*
**Ruzeiz 106** *(8f,Kem,SD,Mar 19)*
**Rydan 113** *(11f,Kem,SD,Sep 24)*

**Saarrem 106** *(13f,Lin,SD,Aug 8)*
**Saborido 105** *(16f,Lin,SD,Aug 28)*
**Safety Check 110** *(7f,Mey,SD,Jan 16)*
**Sagesse 105** *(14f,Wol,SD,Mar 8)*
**Sakash 107** *(7f,Wol,SD,Apr 22)*
**Salmon Sushi 106** *(10f,Lin,SD,Nov 19)*
**Salutation 116** *(11f,Kem,SD,Mar 29)*
**Salvatore Fury 105** *(5f,Kem,SD,Dec 4)*
**Samurai Sword 107** *(8f,Mey,SD,Jan 9)*
**Santa Teresa 107** *(8f,Kem,SD,Sep 18)*
**Santefisio 107** *(8f,Kem,SD,Apr 19)*
**Saturation Point 105** *(10f,Lin,SD,Nov 15)*
**Saved By The Bell 108** *(14f,Wol,SD,Nov 7)*
**Sbraase 108** *(9½f,Wol,SD,Nov 14)*
**Scallop 106** *(12f,Lin,SD,Oct 15)*
**Scarborough 107** *(5f,Sth,SD,Dec 13)*
**Scottish Star 111** *(13f,Lin,SD,Feb 5)*
**Scruffy Tramp 111** *(6f,Kem,SD,Jan 15)*
**Sea Shanty 108** *(8f,Kem,SD,Apr 19)*
**Seamster 108** *(6f,Kem,SD,Jan 22)*
**Searchlight 108** *(5f,Lin,SD,Nov 22)*
**Secondo 111** *(6f,Wol,SD,Dec 19)*
**Secret Art 110** *(8f,Kem,SD,Sep 6)*
**Secret Asset 107** *(6f,Kem,SD,Dec 22)*
**Secret Millionaire 107** *(5f,Kem,SD,Mar 17)*
**Secret Number 108** *(12f,Kem,SD,Sep 6)*
**Seek The Fair Land 106** *(7f,Lin,SD,May 21)*
**Seeking Magic 106** *(6f,Lin,SD,Nov 15)*
**Semaral 114** *(8f,Lin,SD,Dec 8)*
**Sennockian Star 109** *(10f,Lin,SD,Feb 22)*
**Sequester 110** *(10f,Lin,SD,Oct 21)*
**Serenity Spa 107** *(6f,Lin,SD,Nov 15)*
**Set The Trend 107** *(8f,Kem,SD,Oct 22)*
**Shalambar 106** *(16f,Kem,SD,Feb 19)*
**Shama 106** *(10f,Lin,SD,Apr 3)*
**Shamaheart 105** *(9f,Wol,SD,Dec 15)*
**Shamardyh 107** *(7f,Wol,SD,Feb 14)*
**Shamdarley 107** *(9½f,Wol,SD,Feb 10)*
**Shaolin 107** *(8f,Lin,SD,Feb 5)*
**Shavansky 112** *(10f,Lin,SD,Jan 25)*
**Shawkantango 106** *(5f,Sth,SD,Jan 9)*
**Sheila's Buddy 106** *(10f,Lin,SS,Dec 17)*
**Sheriff Of Nawton 106** *(9½f,Wol,SD,Dec 22)*
**Shirazz 106** *(9½f,Wol,SD,Jan 6)*
**Shirley's Pride 105** *(5f,Lin,SD,Mar 19)*
**Showboating 105** *(8f,Sth,SD,Mar 4)*
**Showtime Star 108** *(6f,Sth,SD,Dec 9)*
**Shuruq 111** *(8f,Mey,SD,Jan 9)*
**Shyron 106** *(7f,Lin,SD,Dec 31)*
**Si Senor 107** *(8f,Kem,SD,Sep 6)*
**Sighora 106** *(8f,Kem,SD,Dec 10)*
**Silken Express 110** *(5f,Wol,SD,Feb 17)*
**Silverheels 112** *(8f,Kem,SD,Mar 19)*
**Silverware 113** *(7f,Wol,SD,Mar 11)*
**Singzak 108** *(14f,Wol,SD,Feb 7)*
**Sir Frank Morgan 105** *(16½f,Wol,SD,Mar 17)*
**Sir Robert Cheval 106** *(7f,Kem,SD,Nov 5)*
**Sirius Prospect 112** *(7f,Kem,SD,Nov 20)*
**Six Wives 106** *(5f,Sth,SD,May 8)*
**Sky Khan 109** *(9f,Wol,SD,Feb 20)*
**Skytrain 106** *(9f,Wol,SD,Apr 3)*
**Sleepy Blue Ocean 105** *(5f,Sth,SD,Jan 14)*
**Sleepy Sioux 106** *(5f,Kem,SD,Nov 12)*
**Sloane Avenue 113** *(8f,Kem,SD,Aug 27)*
**Smalljohn 105** *(7f,Wol,SD,Jan 27)*
**Smokethatthunders 106** *(7f,Lin,SD,Jan 22)*
**Snow Trouble 107** *(8f,Lin,SD,Jly 16)*
**Snowmane 105** *(16½f,Wol,SD,Dec 13)*
**So Beloved 108** *(8f,Lin,SD,Apr 29)*
**Sofias Number One 106** *(7f,Sth,SD,Mar 6)*
**Softly She Treads 105** *(11f,Kem,SD,Dec 22)*
**Solar Deity 111** *(9½f,Wol,SD,Nov 6)*
**Solarmaite 108** *(11f,Sth,SD,Apr 30)*
**Solidarity 112** *(9½f,Wol,SD,Nov 14)*
**Song Of Parkes 105** *(5f,Lin,SD,Jan 15)*
**Sound Advice 111** *(8f,Sth,SD,Mar 26)*
**Soundtrack 105** *(10f,Lin,SD,Aug 20)*
**Spa's Dancer 112** *(10f,Kem,SD,Mar 5)*
**Spacelab 110** *(10f,Lin,SD,Aug 27)*
**Spanish Plume 105** *(12f,Wol,SD,Mar 17)*
**Speckled 109** *(13f,Lin,SD,Oct 30)*
**Speed Hawk 106** *(6f,Wol,SD,Sep 6)*
**Speightowns Kid 107** *(6f,Sth,SD,Dec 9)*
**Spellmaker 107** *(6f,Kem,SD,Mar 12)*
**Spes Nostra 110** *(9½f,Wol,SD,Mar 13)*
**Spice Fair 105** *(16f,Kem,SD,Jly 2)*
**Spin Artist 107** *(10f,Lin,SD,Jun 10)*
**Spirit Of Gondree 106** *(8f,Kem,SD,Mar 3)*
**Spiritual Star 109** *(8f,Lin,SD,Mar 1)*
**Spoil The Fun 106** *(8f,Mey,SD,Jan 23)*
**Spring Fling 112** *(6f,Kem,SD,Nov 27)*
**Squire Osbaldeston 105** *(10f,Kem,SD,Feb 26)*
**Ssafa 105** *(11f,Kem,SD,Mar 6)*
**St Paul De Vence 105** *(9½f,Wol,SD,Oct 28)*
**Stag Hill 108** *(12f,Kem,SD,Jan 22)*
**Stand Guard 105** *(11f,Sth,SD,Mar 4)*
**Star Links 114** *(9½f,Wol,SD,Feb 10)*
**Star Up In The Sky 106** *(6f,Wol,SD,Mar 24)*
**Starfield 111** *(8f,Sth,SD,Dec 27)*
**Starlight Symphony 106** *(8f,Lin,SD,Nov 22)*
**Starlit Cantata 106** *(10f,Lin,SD,Aug 20)*
**Start Right 106** *(8f,Mey,SD,Jan 16)*
**Starwatch 105** *(11f,Kem,SD,Dec 10)*
**Stasio 112** *(9½f,Wol,SD,Feb 10)*
**Steeler 108** *(8f,Mey,SD,Jan 9)*
**Steelriver 110** *(7f,Wol,SD,Oct 14)*
**Stellarta 108** *(6f,Kem,SD,Dec 1)*
**Steppe Daughter 109** *(10f,Lin,SD,Nov 19)*
**Stepper Point 109** *(5f,Lin,SD,Mar 22)*
**Stepping Ahead 111** *(10f,Lin,SD,Jan 25)*
**Stereo Love 108** *(8f,Kem,SD,Sep 25)*
**Steuben 106** *(12f,Sth,SD,Aug 7)*
**Steventon Star 105** *(7f,Lin,SD,Mar 5)*
**Stevie Thunder 107** *(10f,Lin,SD,Jan 25)*
**Stock Hill Fair 106** *(12f,Kem,SD,Nov 19)*
**Stonecutter 107** *(12f,Sth,SD,Dec 13)*
**Stonefield Flyer 107** *(7f,Kem,SD,Feb 12)*
**Storm Force Ten 105** *(11f,Kem,SD,Apr 1)*
**Story Writer 107** *(16f,Kem,SD,Jly 2)*
**Stosur 106** *(7f,Wol,SD,Nov 28)*
**Strategic Force 109** *(6f,Kem,SD,Dec 22)*
**Street Artist 109** *(12f,Sth,SD,Nov 25)*
**Streets Of Newyork 107** *(11f,Kem,SD,Mar 29)*
**Strictly Silver 112** *(10f,Lin,SD,Jan 25)*
**Strong Man 105** *(7f,Sth,SD,Jan 7)*
**Subtle Knife 108** *(8f,Kem,SD,Mar 19)*
**Suehail 110** *(8f,Kem,SD,Jun 5)*
**Summerfree 108** *(12f,Sth,SD,Jan 7)*
**Sunblazer 108** *(14f,Wol,SD,Sep 26)*
**Sutton Sid 106** *(10f,Lin,SD,Jan 8)*
**Sweet Lightning 106** *(10f,Mey,SD,Jan 23)*
**Sweet P 106** *(10f,Lin,SD,Oct 21)*
**Sweet Talking Guy 107** *(6f,Kem,SD,Mar 5)*
**Sweetheart Abbey 105** *(12f,Lin,SD,Jly 25)*
**Swift Cedar 105** *(9½f,Wol,SD,Dec 22)*
**Swing Alone 110** *(12f,Lin,SD,Jan 4)*
**Swiss Cross 112** *(5f,Wol,SD,Feb 1)*
**Syncopate 109** *(10f,Lin,SD,Apr 2)*

**Taajub 105** *(6f,Lin,SD,Feb 8)*
**Tamasha 109** *(13f,Lin,SD,Oct 30)*
**Taquka 107** *(6f,Kem,SD,Oct 7)*
**Tarooq 113** *(6f,Lin,SD,Feb 22)*
**Tartan Jura 108** *(16f,Sth,SD,Apr 8)*
**Tasrih 110** *(7f,Sth,SD,Apr 28)*
**Tatting 112** *(8f,Sth,SD,Jan 3)*
**Teajaybe 107** *(16f,Sth,SD,Apr 8)*
**Tearless 109** *(8f,Lin,SD,Oct 30)*
**Ted Spread 115** *(16f,Lin,SD,Jan 22)*
**Tee It Up Tommo 105** *(8f,Kem,SD,Mar 26)*
**Telefono 107** *(8f,Lin,SD,Jun 23)*
**Tellovoi 113** *(8f,Sth,SD,Jan 28)*
**Temple Road 105** *(5f,Wol,SD,Jan 31)*
**Tenor 109** *(8f,Lin,SD,Jly 16)*
**Teolagi 107** *(12f,Lin,SD,Jan 4)*
**Tepmokea 113** *(9½f,Wol,SD,Mar 15)*
**Thataboy 105** *(6f,Lin,SD,Dec 5)*
**Thatchmaster 114** *(9½f,Wol,SD,Mar 15)*
**The Blue Dog 109** *(12f,Lin,SD,Jan 10)*
**The Great Gabrial 107** *(7f,Sth,SD,Jun 19)*
**The Holyman 106** *(12f,Lin,SD,Jun 21)*
**The Lock Master 110** *(9½f,Wol,SD,Feb 10)*
**The Quarterjack 108** *(16½f,Wol,SD,Nov 17)*
**The Rectifier 109** *(8f,Kem,SD,Feb 26)*
**The Steward 105** *(8f,Kem,SD,Oct 2)*
**Theology 107** *(16f,Lin,SD,Jan 22)*
**Tides Reach 113** *(8f,Lin,SD,Dec 8)*
**Tiger Reigns 107** *(9½f,Wol,SD,Jan 9)*
**Tigers Tale 113** *(8f,Lin,SD,Dec 28)*
**Tijuca 107** *(10f,Lin,SD,Jun 10)*
**Tilstarr 106** *(10f,Lin,SD,Apr 9)*
**Time And Place 108** *(6f,Kem,SD,Dec 22)*
**Time Square 107** *(12f,Kem,SD,Jan 22)*
**Timothy T 106** *(8f,Lin,SD,Feb 12)*
**Tinghir 107** *(9½f,Wol,SD,Oct 4)*
**Tinshu 113** *(10f,Lin,SD,Jan 25)*
**Tizlove Regardless 113** *(11f,Kem,SD,Mar 20)*
**Toga Tiger 108** *(8f,Kem,SD,Mar 19)*
**Tokyo Brown 105** *(13f,Lin,SD,Mar 5)*
**Top Boy 111** *(5f,Wol,SD,Apr 26)*
**Top Diktat 105** *(10f,Kem,SD,Feb 19)*
**Topaling 106** *(14f,Wol,SD,Dec 15)*
**Toptempo 107** *(16½f,Wol,SD,Nov 17)*
**Toto Skyllachy 107** *(7f,Sth,SD,Nov 4)*
**Toymaker 109** *(9f,Wol,SD,Feb 8)*
**Travel 108** *(14f,Wol,SD,Mar 28)*
**Treasure The Ridge 106** *(12f,Lin,SD,Jly 25)*
**Trinityelitedotcom 117** *(6f,Kem,SD,Mar 29)*
**Triple Dream 105** *(5f,Kem,SD,Dec 16)*
**Trojan Rocket 109** *(6f,Kem,SD,Mar 17)*
**True To Form 111** *(8f,Lin,SD,Mar 1)*
**Tucson Arizona 107** *(11f,Kem,SD,May 28)*
**Two Days In Paris 109** *(16f,Lin,SD,Jan 22)*
**Two Moons 106** *(7f,Sth,SD,Mar 12)*
**Two Shades Of Grey 105** *(8f,Sth,SD,Dec 9)*
**Ty Gwr 106** *(9f,Wol,SD,Nov 29)*
**Tychaios 105** *(6f,Kem,SD,Dec 1)*

**Ubetterbegood 108** *(5f,Wol,SD,Feb 17)*
**Ultimate Act 107** *(11f,Kem,SD,May 28)*
**Unanimite 114** *(14f,Wol,SD,Dec 6)*
**Uncle Bernie 109** *(16½f,Wol,SD,Nov 24)*
**Under Approval 105** *(5f,Wol,SD,Mar 13)*
**Understory 105** *(10f,Kem,SD,Mar 12)*
**Unforgiving Minute 109** *(7f,Kem,SD,Dec 18)*
**United Color 107** *(6f,Mey,SD,Jan 16)*
**Until Midnight 105** *(8f,Kem,SD,Dec 22)*
**Upavon 111** *(6f,Kem,SD,Mar 17)*
**Uphold 105** *(12f,Lin,SD,Mar 22)*
**Uramazin 116** *(10f,Kem,SD,Mar 5)*
**Urban Castle 105** *(12f,Wol,SD,Dec 26)*

**Valbchek 108** *(7f,Kem,SD,Dec 11)*
**Van Rooney 108** *(8f,Mey,SD,Jan 16)*
**Varsovian 105** *(6f,Lin,SD,Nov 26)*
**Veeraya 109** *(8f,Lin,SD,Mar 1)*
**Verse Of Love 110** *(7f,Lin,SD,Jan 24)*

**Vertueux 106** *(14f,Wol,SD,Mar 28)*
**Very Good Day 105** *(12f,Wol,SD,Nov 7)*
**Victorian Number 107** *(7f,Sth,SD,Jan 14)*
**Viewpoint 109** *(12f,Lin,SD,Apr 18)*
**Vigor 106** *(7f,Mey,SD,Jan 16)*
**Villa Royale 112** *(16f,Lin,SD,Apr 18)*
**Villoresi 108** *(12f,Wol,SD,Feb 28)*
**Vital Evidence 109** *(11f,Kem,SD,Mar 29)*
**Viva Verglas 107** *(6f,Sth,SD,Dec 27)*
**Vodkato 108** *(10f,Lin,SD,Mar 22)*
**Volito 105** *(6f,Lin,SD,Feb 21)*

**Wahgah 110** *(10f,Kem,SD,Aug 18)*
**Wakea 105** *(12f,Kem,SD,Jly 2)*
**Wall Street Boss 106** *(14f,Wol,SD,Sep 26)*
**Wandsworth 113** *(8f,Lin,SD,Dec 8)*
**Warbond 106** *(7f,Lin,SD,Feb 25)*
**Warrigal 105** *(12f,Lin,SD,Jun 21)*
**Warrior Of Light 107** *(11f,Kem,SD,May 6)*
**We'll Deal Again 106** *(5f,Wol,SD,Mar 21)*
**Wedding Ring 105** *(7f,Mey,SD,Jan 16)*
**Welease Bwian 105** *(6f,Kem,SD,Dec 17)*
**Well Painted 108** *(10f,Lin,SD,Jly 9)*
**Welsh Sunrise 107** *(6f,Kem,SD,Feb 3)*
**Westerly 105** *(10f,Lin,SD,Aug 20)*
**Westminster 106** *(7f,Sth,SD,Dec 18)*
**Whaleweigh Station 107** *(6f,Sth,SD,Dec 27)*
**Whispering Warrior 107** *(8f,Lin,SD,Mar 1)*
**White Nile 105** *(16f,Kem,SD,Apr 9)*
**Willie Wag Tail 108** *(11f,Kem,SD,Dec 8)*
**Willy Brennan 106** *(6f,Sth,SD,Mar 27)*
**Windhoek 115** *(10f,Lin,SD,Mar 22)*
**Wintour Leap 108** *(16½f,Wol,SD,Nov 17)*
**With Hindsight 105** *(10f,Lin,SD,Jly 28)*
**Woolfall Sovereign 105** *(5f,Sth,SD,Dec 13)*
**Wrood 106** *(8f,Lin,SD,Jun 23)*
**Wu Zetian 105** *(8f,Sth,SD,Nov 25)*
**Wyndham Wave 105** *(11f,Kem,SD,Apr 2)*

**Xinbama 108** *(12f,Kem,SD,Nov 19)*

**Yeager 107** *(8f,Lin,SD,Apr 29)*
**Yeeoow 105** *(7f,Lin,SD,Feb 22)*
**Yojojo 107** *(9f,Wol,SD,Jan 13)*
**Yorkshireman 111** *(16½f,Wol,SD,Dec 6)*

**Zac Brown 105** *(6f,Wol,SD,Nov 3)*
**Zain Shamardal 110** *(8f,Mey,SD,Jan 16)*
**Zampa Manos 108** *(8f,Kem,SD,Aug 27)*
**Zipp 105** *(12f,Kem,SD,Nov 19)*
**Zugzwang 107** *(10f,Lin,SD,Aug 20)*
**Zurigha 107** *(8f,Kem,SD,Apr 19)*

## TWO YEAR-OLDS - Sand

**Apache Storm 105** *(5f,Wol,SD,Dec 6)*

**Dreamlike 108** *(8f,Lin,SD,Dec 5)*
**Dutch Uncle 106** *(9f,Wol,SD,Dec 27)*

**Four Seasons 109** *(7f,Lin,SD,Nov 22)*

**Ghost Cat 105** *(6f,Sth,SD,Aug 7)*
**Greatest Journey 107** *(9f,Wol,SD,Dec 26)*

**Jack Hobbs 109** *(9f,Wol,SD,Dec 27)*

**La Cuesta 105** *(5f,Wol,SD,Sep 15)*
**Lyfka 105** *(6f,Wol,SD,Oct 21)*

**Never Change 107** *(8f,Lin,SD,Dec 5)*

**Oregon Gift 106** *(8f,Lin,SD,Nov 26)*

**Portamento 108** *(5f,Wol,SD,Dec 6)*
**Primrose Valley 105** *(5f,Wol,SD,Aug 11)*

**Qatar Road 107** *(7f,Lin,SD,Nov 22)*

**Royal Albert Hall 106** *(9f,Wol,SD,Dec 27)*

**Super Kid 107** *(7f,Lin,SD,Nov 22)*

**Tendu 108** *(6f,Kem,SD,Sep 3)*

**Weld Al Emarat 105** *(8f,Sth,SD,Dec 9)*
**Wentworth Falls 106** *(6f,Kem,SD,Dec 11)*

**Zamoura 107** *(8f,Lin,SD,Dec 5)*

## TWO YEAR-OLDS - Turf

**Accepted 107** *(5f,Don,G,Sep 12)*
**Agnes Stewart 105** *(8f,Nmk,S,Oct 17)*
**Ahlan Emarati 105** *(6f,Yor,G,Aug 23)*
**Ainippe 105** *(5f,Don,G,Sep 12)*
**Albecq 106** *(7f,Goo,S,Oct 12)*
**Angelic Lord 109** *(6f,Nmk,GF,Jly 10)*
**Anthem Alexander 109** *(6f,Yor,G,Aug 21)*
**Assault On Rome 107** *(7f,Goo,S,Oct 12)*
**Astrophysics 108** *(5f,Don,G,Sep 12)*

**Basateen 108** *(7f,Yor,GF,Aug 20)*
**Bazzana 107** *(6f,Wdr,S,May 26)*
**Be Bold 113** *(7f,Goo,S,Oct 12)*
**Beacon 109** *(5f,Don,G,Sep 12)*
**Belardo 109** *(6f,Nmk,GF,Jly 10)*
**Burma Bridge 105** *(7f,Bri,S,Oct 7)*
**Burtonwood 106** *(7f,Goo,S,Oct 12)*

**Calypso Beat 105** *(7f,Nmk,S,Aug 9)*
**Cappella Sansevero 110** *(6f,Nmk,S,Oct 17)*
**Charming Thought 113** *(6f,Nmk,S,Oct 17)*
**Christophermarlowe 107** *(8½f,Eps,G,Sep 28)*
**Code Red 105** *(6f,Don,S,Oct 25)*
**Cotai Glory 106** *(6f,Nby,GF,Jly 18)*
**Cursory Glance 110** *(6f,Yor,G,Aug 21)*

**Dance Of Fire 105** *(8f,Don,G,Sep 13)*
**Dancetrack 105** *(7f,Lei,G,Sep 9)*
**Dr No 105** *(6f,Asc,G,Jun 17)*
**Dutch Connection 110** *(7f,Yor,GF,Aug 20)*

**Elite Gardens 105** *(7f,Sal,G,Sep 12)*
**Elm Park 109** *(8f,Nmk,GF,Sep 27)*
**Elysian Flyer 107** *(6f,Bat,GS,Aug 30)*
**Ervedya 108** *(6f,Dea,VS,Aug 24)*
**Estidhkaar 107** *(7f,Nmk,GS,Jly 12)*
**Evening Rain 105** *(6f,Nby,GS,Aug 16)*

**Fadhayyil 110** *(7f,Nmk,G,Sep 26)*
**Fast Act 106** *(5f,Don,G,Sep 12)*
**Faydhan 108** *(6f,Hay,GS,Jly 3)*
**Finial 111** *(7f,Goo,S,Oct 12)*
**Found 110** *(8f,Lon,G,Oct 5)*

**Game Pie 105** *(8f,Ncs,GS,Oct 14)*
**George Dryden 105** *(5f,Don,G,Sep 12)*
**Giovanni Canaletto 106** *(8f,Leo,YS,Oct 25)*
**Gleneagles 107** *(7f,Cur,GF,Sep 14)*
**Goken 108** *(5f,Lon,G,Oct 5)*
**Good Contact 106** *(8½f,Eps,G,Sep 28)*

**Henrytheaeroplane 105** *(7f,Mus,G,Oct 11)*
**Hootenanny 110** *(5f,Asc,G,Jun 17)*

**Iceberg 106** *(7f,Dea,S,Aug 17)*
**Its Gonna Be Me 114** *(7f,Goo,S,Oct 12)*
**Ivawood 114** *(6f,Nmk,GF,Jly 10)*
**Izzthatright 107** *(6f,Cat,G,Aug 15)*

**Jack Naylor 110** *(8f,Cur,G,Aug 31)*
**Jamaica 107** *(7f,Yor,GF,Aug 20)*
**John F Kennedy 105** *(8f,Leo,GF,Sep 13)*
**Juncart 109** *(5f,Hay,S,Oct 17)*
**Jungle Cat 110** *(6f,Nmk,GF,Jly 10)*
**Justice Good 106** *(6f,Asc,G,Jun 17)*

**Kodi Bear 105** *(6f,Asc,G,Jun 17)*
**Kool Kompany 109** *(6f,Nmk,S,Oct 17)*

**Laidback Romeo 106** *(8f,Rip,G,Sep 27)*
**Lear's Rock 105** *(8f,Rip,G,Sep 27)*
**Legatissimo 109** *(8f,Cur,G,Aug 31)*
**Limato 110** *(6f,Red,G,Oct 4)*
**Little Lady Katie 109** *(7f,Nmk,S,Oct 17)*
**Lola Beaux 108** *(7f,Cur,GF,Sep 28)*
**Louie De Palma 105** *(6f,Asc,GF,Jly 11)*
**Lucida 112** *(7f,Nmk,G,Sep 26)*

**Maftool 110** *(7f,Nmk,G,Sep 25)*
**Malabar 108** *(7f,Cur,GF,Sep 14)*
**Markaz 107** *(7f,Nmk,G,Sep 25)*
**Marsh Hawk 110** *(7f,Nmk,S,Aug 9)*
**Mattmu 108** *(6f,Red,G,Oct 4)*
**Muhaarar 111** *(6f,Nmk,S,Oct 17)*
**Mukhmal 107** *(5f,Chs,G,May 7)*
**Muqtaser 108** *(8f,Ncs,GS,Oct 14)*
**Muraaqaba 107** *(7f,Nmk,S,Aug 9)*

**Nafaqa 108** *(7f,Don,G,Sep 12)*
**New Providence 108** *(6f,Sal,G,Sep 4)*
**Newsletter 105** *(5f,Asc,GF,Jun 18)*
**No One Knows 108** *(7f,Goo,S,Oct 12)*
**Nucifera 109** *(7f,Dea,S,Aug 17)*

**Ol' Man River 105** *(8f,Cur,G,Aug 31)*
**Order Of St George 107** *(8f,Leo,S,Aug 14)*
**Osaila 108** *(7f,Cur,GF,Sep 14)*

**Pamona 106** *(7f,Nmk,S,Oct 22)*
**Peacock 107** *(7f,Don,G,Sep 12)*
**Percy Alleline 115** *(7f,Goo,S,Oct 12)*
**Popeswood 116** *(7f,Goo,S,Oct 12)*
**Profitable 107** *(5f,Hay,G,Sep 26)*
**Publilia 105** *(6f,Ham,GF,Jly 18)*
**Puck Fair 105** *(6f,Leo,S,Aug 14)*
**Pulcinella 108** *(7f,Nmk,S,Oct 17)*

**Qualify 112** *(7f,Cur,GF,Sep 28)*
**Queen Nefertiti 106** *(7f,Leo,G,Jun 12)*

**Raydara 106** *(7f,Cur,GF,Aug 24)*
**Rosie's Premiere 108** *(5f,Hay,G,Sep 26)*
**Roudee 105** *(5f,Chs,G,May 7)*
**Royal Razalma 107** *(5f,Nmk,S,Oct 17)*

**Salateen 105** *(7f,Yor,GF,Aug 20)*
**Snoano 105** *(8f,Nby,GS,Sep 19)*
**Snow Cloud 106** *(5f,Hay,S,Oct 17)*
**Stellar Glow 108** *(7f,Cur,GF,Sep 28)*
**Stroll Patrol 107** *(7f,Nmk,G,Sep 26)*

**Terror 107** *(6f,War,GS,Aug 25)*
**The Great War 107** *(6f,Nmk,GF,Jly 10)*
**The Warrior 108** *(6f,Nmk,S,Oct 17)*
**The Wow Signal 110** *(6f,Dea,VS,Aug 24)*
**Tiggy Wiggy 112** *(6f,Yor,G,Aug 21)*
**Tigrilla 108** *(7f,Nmk,G,Sep 26)*
**Together Forever 108** *(8f,Cur,G,Aug 31)*
**Toocoolforschool 109** *(7f,Yor,GF,Aug 20)*
**Toscanini 105** *(7f,Cur,GF,Sep 14)*
**Tupi 106** *(7f,Dea,S,Aug 17)*

**Vegas Rebel 109** *(7f,Bri,S,Oct 7)*
**Very Special 109** *(6f,Yar,G,Sep 18)*
**Vesnina 106** *(6f,Nby,GS,Aug 16)*

**Wet Sail 106** *(6f,Red,G,Oct 4)*
**What Say You 107** *(7f,Nmk,G,Aug 22)*
**White Lake 106** *(7f,Don,G,Sep 12)*
**Winters Moon 105** *(8f,Nmk,S,Oct 17)*

**Zifena 105** *(6f,Nmk,F,Aug 2)*
**Zuhoor Baynoona 109** *(5f,Mus,G,Oct 11)*